The Video Source Book

⏴ⓣⓗⓔ Video Source Book

54th Edition

A Guide to Programs Currently Available on Video in the Areas of:

Movies / Entertainment

General Interest / Educaton

Sports / Recreation

Fine Arts

Health / Science

Business / Industry

Children / Juvenile

How-To / Instruction

GALE
CENGAGE Learning·

Farmington Hills, Mich • San Francisco • New York • Waterville, Maine
Meriden, Conn • Mason, Ohio • Chicago

The Video Source Book, 54th Edition

Project Editor: James Craddock

Editorial: Michael J. Tyrkus

Editorial Support Services: Wayne Fong

Manufacturing: Rita Wimberley

Composition and Prepress: Gary Leach

For product information and technology assistance, contact us at
Gale Customer Support, 1-800-877-4253.
For permission to use material from this text or product,
submit all requests online at **www.cengage.com/permissions.**
Further permissions questions can be emailed to
permissionrequest@cengage.com

Gale
27500 Drake Rd.
Farmington Hills, MI, 48331-3535

ISBN-13: ISBN 978-1-57302-471-6 (set)
ISBN-13: ISBN 978-1-57302-472-3 (v.1)
ISBN-13: ISBN 978-1-57302-473-0 (v.2)
ISBN-13: ISBN 978-1-57302-474-7 (v.3)
ISBN-13: ISBN 978-1-57302-475-4 (v.4)
ISBN-13: ISBN 978-1-57302-476-1 (v.5)
ISBN-13: ISBN 978-1-57302-477-8 (v.6)
ISBN-13: ISBN 978-1-57302-478-5 (v.7)
ISBN-13: ISBN 978-1-57302-479-2 (v.8)
ISBN-13: ISBN 978-1-57302-480-8 (v.9)

ISSN 0748-0881

Printed in the United States of America
1 2 3 4 5   18 17 16 15 14

Contents

Highlights

From classroom aids to corporate training programs, technical resources to self-help guides, children's features to documentaries, theatrical releases to straight-to-video movies, the *Video Source Book (VSB)* continues its comprehensive coverage of the wide universe of video offerings with listings for more than 117,000 videos. *VSB* covers all subject areas, including:

- Business/Industry
- Children/Juvenile
- Fine Arts
- General Interest/Education
- Health/Science
- How-To/Instruction
- Movies/Entertainment
- Sports/Recreation

Whether you're looking for a video to complement a history lesson, guide you through a home improvement project, teach your children bicycle safety, improve the techniques of your sales staff, demonstrate surgical techniques, or round out your collection of movies starring a favorite actress, *VSB* offers unparalleled access to the videos that meet your needs.

Arrangement

VSB consists of video program listings arranged alphabetically by title; alternative title, subject, credits, and special formats indexes; and the program distributors section, which includes complete contact information.

Video Source Book: A VideoHound® Reference

The *Video Source Book* is now part of the VideoHound family of movie and entertainment reference products. Data from the *VSB* database is available in a variety of alternate formats:

- Listings for some 29,000 movies and selected entertainment videos drawn from the VSB database make up *VideoHound's Golden Movie Retriever* the guide USA Today rated ★★★★. *VideoHound* provides additional indexing—ten indexes in all for pinpoint searching.

- *Magill's Cinema Annual*, the most recent addition to the VideoHound series, is an important resource for serious film researchers and movie lovers alike. Over 250 essay reviews provide critical analysis of significant domestic and foreign films released each year and are accompanied by complete cast and character listings, production credits, award information, photos, and a cumulative index covering the entire Magill's line.

- The entire *VSB* database is available for licensing on magnetic tape or diskette. Customized mailing lists and labels are offered from the program distributor database. Call Customer Services at 800-877-GALE for more information on these products.

Introduction

The *Video Source Book (VSB)* is the single "most comprehensive listing of available video programs" (*Reference Books Bulletin*). *VSB* is the largest member of the VideoHound family of reference products. With more than 1117,000 listings representing some 165,000 programs, *VSB* continues to provide complete coverage of the ever-expanding universe of video programs of all types, including:

- Movies and home entertainment
- Fine arts
- Children's programs
- Education
- Sports and recreation
- Health and science
- How-to
- Business and industry

VSB covers programs designed for in-home viewing as well as specialized programs for educational, instructional, or vocational/professional use in organizational settings. It lists programs that are available for rent, lease, loan, purchase, duplication, off-air recording, or by subscription or trade-in for use on a variety of equipment including:

- VHS
- 8mm
- CD-I
- 3/4″ U-matic
- DVD
- UMD
- Blu-Ray Disc
- HD-DVD

VSB also provides information on the status of videos that are on moratorium or no longer offered for distribution.

Content and Arrangement

VSB consists of seven sections:

Video Program Listings. Entries are arranged alphabetically by program title. Each entry provides a description of the program and information on obtaining the title.

Alternate Title Index. Lists variant titles of movies and other video programs and refers users to the titles by which they are found in the main body.

Subject Index. Classifies the listed video programs by

one to three of 500 specific subject headings. A triangle denotes a movie rated three stars or higher.

Credits Index. Cites directors and cast members with at least two citations in the Movie/Entertainment video program listings.

Awards Index. Lists over 6300 films honored by 12 national and international award bodies, representing some 90 competitive categories.

Special Formats Index. Identifies programs that are closed captioned, available on digital, high-definition, or laser disc, or offered in 8mm videocassette format.

Program Distributors. Provides complete contact information for all distributors cited in the program listings.

For additional details on the content, arrangement, and indexing of *VSB*, consult the "User's Guide" following this introduction.

Compilation Methods

The Video Source Book is compiled from video catalogs, press releases, and other information provided by the program distributors, as well as from standard reference sources. When necessary, follow-up telephone calls and letters are used to obtain additional information.

Alternate Formats

Information from the VSB database is offered in several alternate formats:

VideoHound's Golden Movie Retriever (VGMR), given a 4-star rating by *USA Today*, is available in paperback. Larger than other video guides, *VGMR* includes complete listings for more than 34,000 movies, including price and ordering information. Ten indexes help users find that elusive video.

Videos for Business and Training (VBT) is accessible online through the Human Resources Information Network.

VSB and VBT information is available for licensing on magnetic tape or diskette.

Customized mailing lists and labels are offered from the *VSB* distributor database.

For information on these products, contact Gale Customer Support at 1-800-877-4253.

Magill's Cinema Annual

The esteemed *Magill's Cinema Annual*, a compilation of extensive commentary on feature films, is part of the Video-Hound family of entertainment reference products. *Magill's Cinema Annual* offers reviews of over 250 films, accompanied by complete credit and character name listings, boxoffice statistics, award information, quotes, tag lines, and trivia. Nine indexes, including a cumulative title index encompassing the entire Magill's series, provide unparalled access to film information for both the film researcher and the casual movie buff.

Comments and Suggestions Welcome

Users are invited to submit information on titles not currently covered as well as additional information on titles listed in VSB. Comments and suggestions concerning the format and usefulness of this title are also welcome. Please direct all questions and comments to:

Video Source Book

Gale, Cengage Learning

27500 Drake Rd.

Farmington Hills, MI 48331-3535

Phone: (248)699-4253

Toll-free: 1-800-877-4253

Fax: (248)699-8067

James M. Craddock

jim.craddock@cengage.com

User's Guide

The *Video Source Book* is organized into seven sections:

- Video Program Listings
- Alternate Title Index
- Subject Index
- Credits Index
- Awards Index
- Special Formats Index
- Program Distributors

Each section is described below.

Video Program Listings

Video program listings are presented alphabetically by title. The following abbreviations are used in the video program listings to identify specific pieces of information:

A:	Audience
Acq:	Acquisition
Awds.	Awards
C:	Credits
Dist:	Distributor
Indiv. Titles	Individual Titles (in a series)
L:	Languages
Pr:	Producer
P:	Purpose
TV Std:	Television Standards
U:	Use

The fictional sample entry appearing on the following page illustrates the information typically provided in a program listing. The number preceding each portion of the entry designates an item of information that is explained in the following paragraph of the same number.

❚1❚ The Inside Story ❚2❚ 1990 ❚3❚ (G)   ❚4❚ (★)

❚5❚ In this series, Slim Goodbody uses song, dance and huge working models of the human heart, lungs, and digestive system to help viewers understand how their bodies function. He also gives basic health education lessons. Programs are available individually. ❚6❚ 15m; ❚7❚ B/W; ❚8❚ Silent; ❚9❚ VHS, 3/4U; ❚10❚ Closed Captioned. ❚11❚ C: John Burstein; Directed by Michael Ganz. ❚12❚ TV Std: NTSC, PAL. ❚13❚ University of Wisconsin. ❚14❚ A: Primary-Jr. High. ❚15❚ P: Education. ❚16❚ U: Institution, BCTV. ❚17❚ L: English, Spanish. ❚18❚ Hea-Sci: Anatomy and physiology. ❚19❚ Awds: Educational Media Awards '88. ❚20❚ Acq: Purchase, Duplication License. ❚21❚ Dist: Agencyfor Instructional Technology (AIT)

❚22❚ $49.95. ❚23❚ Indiv. Titles: 1. Lubba Dubba: The Inside Story of Your Heart and Blood 2. The Breath of Life: The Inside Story of Respiration 3. The Sensational Five: The Inside Story of Your Senses.

Description of Numbered Elements

❚1❚ **Program Title.** The title of the video as supplied by its distributor. Series titles are reconciled to eliminate variations. All music videos begin with the artist's name, and are alphabetized by the first name, so, for example, Eric Clapton will appear under "E."

❚2❚ **Year of Release.** The release date refers to the year in which the program was initially created, not the year it was first released on video. When the decade in which the program was produced is known, but not the precise year, the date is listed with a question mark for the last digit, as in "198?" for the decade of the 1980s. When neither the decade nor the year can be determined, the notation is "19??."

❚3❚ **MPAA Rating.** For movies, the standard Motion Picture Association of America ratings are listed according to the MPAA Classification and Rating Program and code system, as outlined below:

G	GENERAL AUDIENCES. All ages admitted.
PG	PARENTAL GUIDANCE SUGGESTED. Some material may not be suitable for children.
PG-13	PARENTS STRONGLY CAUTIONED. Some material may be inappropriate for children under 13.
R	RESTRICTED. Under 17 requires accompanying parent or adult guardian.
NC-17	NO ONE UNDER 17 ADMITTED. (Age limit may vary in certain areas.)

A listed MPAA rating denotes the rating given by the MPAA for theatrical release. The ratings listed are the latest from the distributor and the MPAA.

❚4❚ **Critical Rating.** Movies have been assigned evaluatory ratings to provide the user with an idea of the critical opinion about these entries. Ratings are expressed by one to four stars (★), where one star reflects a critical evaluation of poor, two stars—good, three stars—very good, and four stars—excellent. If the notation "Bomb!" appears, the movie is considered a critical disappointment. *VSB* editors have scanned a variety of film review media and drawn on their own knowledge to determine a consensus.

❙5❙ Description. A short synopsis details the major subject, theme, plot, or special features of the program. It also identifies films with subtitles, films with dubbed or different language soundtracks, films that are tinted, colorized, or in partial color. If ancillary materials such as study guides, brochures, or other printed or audio materials are provided with the video, they are described here.

❙6❙ Running Time. The running time is given in number of minutes (m). When edited or different versions of a program are available, they are listed as separate entries with approximate running times. "?m" will appear when the running time is unknown and also for interactive videodisc programs, since the viewer controls the pace and length of the program with interactive technology. In a series entry, the running time given is the average running time of each program in the series.

❙7❙ Black and White Programs. All programs are available in color unless a "B/W" (black and white) notation appears. Programs that are tinted, colorized, or in partial color are identified as such in the description.

❙8❙ Silent. All programs contain dialogue unless a "Silent" notation appears.

❙9❙ Format Options. Each entry includes the video formats available for that particular program. Format options and the codes used in *VSB* entries (when applicable) are shown below:

Videotape

1/4" compact videocassette VHS	(CV)
Super-VHS	(SVS)
8 millimeter videocassette	(8mm)
1/2" open reel, also known as EIAJ	(EJ)
3/4" U-matic cassette	(3/4U)
1" broadcast type "C"	(1C)
2" quadraplex open reel	(Q)

Videodisc

Blu-Ray Disc	
CD-I	
Digital versatile disc	(DVD)
HD DVD	
Universal Media Disc	(UMD)

Other

Formats other than those listed are available from the distributor by special arrangement	(Special order formats)

❙10❙ Hearing Impaired. When a program has been captioned or signed for hearing impaired viewers, the entry includes the notation "Open Captioned," "Closed Captioned," or "Signed." Closed captioned tapes may require a special video hookup in order to view the captions.

❙11❙ Credits. The major stars, selected cast members, and the director, screenwriter, and other selected credits of

entertainment television programs or movies are listed. For instructional programs, talk shows, and documentaries, the host, narrator, director, or instructor is given when known.

❙12❙ Television Standards. Television standards refer to the technical transmission system by which programs are broadcast or taped in different countries. All tapes and discs listed in this directory conform to the NTSC (United States) television standard. This is not specifically indicated in the entry unless the program is also available in a foreign standard. In such cases, the notation "NTSC, PAL" or "NTSC, SECAM" will appear. The following standards may be listed:

NTSC	North America, Japan, most of South America
PAL	United Kingdom, Asia, most of Western Europe, and the Middle East
PAL-M	Brazil
SECAM	France, Eastern Europe, most of Africa

Only tapes made in NTSC will play on U.S. video systems. Other standards require a multi-standard video machine for use in the United States.

❙13❙ Producer. The original producer (studio, company, and/or individual person) is listed in each entry. When the actual producer cannot be determined, but the country of origin (other than the U.S.) is known, this information will be supplied instead.

❙14❙ Audience. To assist the user in identifying the intended audience level for the program, one of the following levels is specified for each entry:

- Preschool
- Primary
- Jr. High
- Sr. High
- College
- Adult
- Family

If two levels are listed, a program is suitable for the broader range of audience indicated by those two levels.

❙15❙ Purpose. The intended use of the program is listed as selected from these options:

- Teacher Education
- Professional
- Special Education
- Entertainment
- Religious
- Education
- Vocational
- Instruction

❙16❙ Use. The programs listed in this book may be used in many different ways, ranging from in-home viewing to broadcast. The codes for these uses and their definitions are:

BCTV	Broadcast television
CATV	Cable television
CCTV	Closed circuit television
Home	In-home viewing
Institution	For classroom, institutional, business, or other organized group viewing

SURA (Special Use Restrictions Apply.) In addition to those uses specifically listed in the entry, the distributor may make the Program available for other purposes,

usually for an additional fee. Contact the distributor for further information.

▮17▮ Languages. Virtually all the videos included in this publication are available in English. Programs that offer foreign-language versions in addition to English are noted within the individual entry. If a program has no English-language counterpart, this is mentioned in the description.

▮18▮ Subject Categories. Each program has been assigned to one of eight broad subject category headings corresponding to general areas of interest. Abbreviations for these main categories are used in *VSB* entries, as shown below:

Bus-Ind	Business/Industry
Chl-Juv	Children/Juvenile
Fin-Art	Fine Arts
Gen-Edu	General Interest/Education
Hea-Sci	Health/Science
How-Ins	How-To/Instruction
Mov-Ent	Movies/Entertainment
Spo-Rec	Sports/Recreation

In addition, each program has been assigned to one or more of over 480 specific subject categories describing the topics covered. By consulting the Subject Index at the end of Volume 3, the user can locate programs in a given subject category. The three most relevant categories will print within an entry, although it may appear in more than three categories in the index.

▮19▮ Awards. Major awards and award year are listed where applicable. Unless there is an obvious abbreviation for a well-known award, names are spelled out. Major award nominations are included if known. Award names are followed by a colon and specific category when applicable.

▮20▮ Acquisition. Video programs may be acquired in a number of ways. The following terms are used to indicate the means by which the viewer can obtain the program from the distributor listed:

Rent/Lease User may rent or lease the program for a specific period of time

Loan User may borrow the program for a small fee and keep it for an extended period

Purchase User may purchase the program

Duplication User may supply distributor with a blank tape to duplicate program for a small fee

Subscription User may obtain the program as part of a membership for an annual fee or through a club

Trade-in User may exchange a purchased program for a credit on another program

Free Loan User may borrow the program for a postage and handling charge

Free Duplication User may duplicate the program at no additional charge

Off-Air Record User may obtain permission to record the program off the air

Duplication License User may purchase a license to duplicate the program

▮21▮ Distributor. Programs in this directory are available from the distributors or wholesalers mentioned here. More than one source is listed when the program is legitimately available from multiple distributors. When multiple sources are listed, the formats and availabilities given in the entry apply to the first source.

If the notation "On Moratorium" appears, the program is not currently being distributed, but the distributor may still hold distribution rights. The program may also be available from other sources such as a retailer or a library. This generally applies to movies that are distributed only for a specified period of time, although they may be redistributed at a later date. The last known distributor is listed for reference.

Videos that are not available from any distributor will show the notation "No longer distributed." This generally applies to videos that the distributor does not intend to release again or to defunct distributors that did not transfer the video rights to another distributor or wholesaler.

Foreign distributors are included only if their video titles conform to the United States television standard (NTSC) and are not available from any U.S. source.

The "Program Distributors" section provides the full distributor name; address; telephone, toll-free, and fax numbers; and email and website (when applicable), to facilitate ordering.

▮22▮ Price. Prices are given for most entertainment-oriented programs and newer non-entertainment titles. Listed prices are the video retail price, as provided by the distributor's most recent catalog or press release. Since prices, especially those of home consumer-oriented programs, are subject to constant change, current prices may vary. For programs that are available from multiple distributors, the price given is that of the first listed distributor. For program series, the price given is for the entire series, unless specified in the individual entry.

▮23▮ Individual Titles. The titles of each program in a video series are listed separately in the sequence provided by the distributor, if available. In many cases, these titles will be available either as a series or on an individual basis. Contact the distributor for details.

Five Indexes Serve Special Needs

Alternate Title Index. Lists variant titles of movies and other video programs and refers users to the titles by which they are found in the main body.

Subject Index. Each video program has been assigned to one or more of 480 specific subject headings. The Subject Index then provides hundreds of "videographies," citing every program assigned to each term. By consulting the Subject

Index, a user can locate a how-to tape on a home improvement project, a video on the destination of a planned vacation, training material on personnel management, programs on holidays for classroom use, or any genre of entertainment from musicals to westerns. A triangle denotes a movie rated three stars or higher.

Credits Index. Fans of a given performer or director can easily find which of his or her works are available on video through this complete listing of every cast and director name with at least two movies cited in Movie/Entertainment entries in *VSB*. For those individuals indexed, an effort is made to cite every video appearance, including cameos, soundtrack narrations, and other peripheral involvements.

Awards Index. Lists over 6300 films honored by 20 national and international award bodies, representing some 90 competitive categories.

Special Formats Index. Includes all listed programs available in the following formats:

Blu-Ray Disc. One of two new High Definition DVD formats.

Closed Captioned. Identifies cassettes and discs with captioning for hearing impaired viewers provided by either the National Captioning Institute (Falls Church, Virginia) or the Caption Center (Los Angeles, California).

CD-I. A list of all programs available in CD format.

DVD. Identifies title available on digital versatile disc.

8mm. Includes all listed titles currently available in the 8mm videocassette format.

HD DVD. One of two High Definition DVD formats.

UMD. Universal Media Disc-format for movies available for the Sony Playstation Personal (PSP).

Program Distributors

The Program Distributors section provides an alphabetical listing of the distributors or wholesalers of videos listed in VSB, including non-U.S. distributors. Entries include the full distributor name, address, and telephone number, as well as fax and toll-free numbers and email and website, if available. Some entries also include information on format options and availability of the programs handled by each distributor, and additional ordering information if applicable. Further details can be obtained directly from the distributors.

Alphabetizing Rules

Video titles, both within the program listings and the indexes, are presented alphabetically by title on a word-by-word basis. The following sort conventions are observed:

The leading articles "A," "An," and "The" are ignored in English-language titles. However, foreign-language articles are included in the sort. For example, *The Kiss of the Spider Woman* appears under "K" while *Los Santeros* appears under "L."

Abbreviated words are sorted as if spelled out in order to fall in place alphabetically, so Dr. and Mr. can be located within the sort as Doctor and Mister. The film *St. Elmo's Fire* will sort as the spelled-out "Saint Elmo's Fire."

Acronyms are treated as regular words, so *NFL's Greatest Games* comes after *Next Time You Go Camping* and before *Nightmare on the 13th Floor.*

Numbers file initially in alphabetical order in the appropriate letter section; but a series of numbers will appear in numerical order. For example, *1900* files after *Night of the Demon*, followed by *1970* and *1980*, but before *Ninja Turf.*

Proper names are sorted on the individual's first name, hence *Martin Luther King, Jr.: From Montgomery to Memphis* under "M."

List of Abbreviations

The Video Source Book uses the following abbreviations. See the "User's Guide" for further details.

A

A:	Audience
Acq:	Acquisition

B

BCTV:	Broadcast television
Blu-Ray:	Blu-Ray Disc format
Bus-Ind:	Business/Industry

C

C:	Credits
CATV:	Cable television
CCTV:	Closed circuit television
CDV:	CD-Video
Chl-Juv:	Children/Juvenile
CV:	1/4″ compact videocassette

D

DVD:	Digital Versatile Disc
Dist:	Distributor

E

8mm:	8 millimeter videocassette
EJ:	1/2″ open reel

F

Fin-Art:	Fine Arts
Fmt:	Format(s)

G

G:	General Audiences
Gen-Edu:	General Interest/Education

H

HD DVD:	High Definition DVD
Hea-Sci:	Health/Science
How-Ins:	How-To/Instruction

L

L:	Languages
LV:	Laser optical videodisc

M

Mov-Ent:	Movies/Entertainment

N

NC-17	No One Under 17 Admitted
NTSC:	A television transmission standard

O

1C:	1″ broadcast type "C"

P

P:	Purpose
PAL:	A television transmission standard
PAL-M:	A television transmission standard
PG:	Parental Guidance Suggested
PG-13:	Parents Strongly Cautioned
Pr:	Producer

Q

Q:	2″ quadraplex open reel

R

R:	Restricted

S

SECAM:	A television transmission standard
Spo-Rec:	Sports/Recreation
SURA:	Special Use Restrictions Apply
SVS:	Super-VHS

T

3/4U:	3/4″ U-matic cassette
TV Std:	Television Standards

U

U:	Use
UMD:	Universal Media Disc

A

A 1998
Filmmaker Tatsuya Mori began investigating the activities of the Aum Shinrikyo religious cult in 1996—a year after some cult members released sarin gas into the Tokyo subway. He looks at their daily life as well as the media frenzy that surrounded them. Followed by "A2." Japanese with subtitles. 136m; DVD. **A:** Sr. High-Adult. **P:** Entertainment. **U:** Home. **L:** Japanese. **Gen-Edu**: Documentary Films. **Acq:** Purchase. **Dist:** Facets Multimedia Inc.

The A B C's and D's of Portable Fire Extinguishers 1995
Details the construction and use of different types of extinguishers that should be used on various types of fires. 23m; VHS. **A:** Adult. **P:** Professional. **U:** Institution. **Bus-Ind**: Safety Education, Occupational Training, Fires. **Acq:** Rent/Lease. **Dist:** National Safety Council, California Chapter, Film Library.

A Coeur Joie 1967 (Unrated) — ★★
Beautiful 30-something Cecile is married to a much older Englishman. She's content with her peaceful life until she meets a young man who rekindles her passions. Will Cecile run off with her new lover or stay with the man who makes her secure? French with subtitles. 96m; VHS, DVD. **C:** Brigitte Bardot; Laurent Terzieff; Jean Rochefort; James Robertson Justice; Michael Sarne; Murray Head; Directed by Serge Bourguignon; Written by Serge Bourguignon; Pascal Jardin. **A:** Sr. High-Adult. **P:** Entertainment. **U:** Home. **L:** French. **Mov-Ent**: Drama. **Acq:** Purchase. **Dist:** Lions Gate Entertainment Inc. $19.95.

A/D and D/A Converters 1992
Reviews how to use power source converters. Intended for training of technicians in an industrial setting. Comes with study guide. 73m; VHS. **A:** Adult. **P:** Professional. **U:** Institution. **Bus-Ind**: Industry & Industrialists, Job Training, Electricity. **Acq:** Purchase. **Dist:** Bergwall Productions, Inc. $299.00.
Indiv. Titles: 1. The Theory Behind the Hardware 2. Simultaneous or Flash A/D Circuits 3. Binary-Weighted and R-2R D/A Circuits 4. Stairstep, Tracking and Successive Approximation A/D.

A. Einstein: How I See the World 1991
PBS program detailing how the greatest scientific genius of this century became its greatest advocate for peace. Much of the script follows Einstein's own words, taken from diaries, personal letters and writings. The man in public and at home is revealed through news film and photos, home movies and collected family photos. 60m; VHS. **C:** Narrated by William Hurt. **Pr:** PBS. **A:** Family. **P:** Education. **U:** Home. **Gen-Edu**: Documentary Films, Scientists. **Acq:** Purchase. **Dist:** PBS Home Video. $19.95.

A. I.: Artificial Intelligence 2001 (PG-13) — ★★
The uneasy melding of an homage directed by Spielberg of a long-cherished idea by late director Stanley Kubrick. Global warming submerges the world's coastal cities but advanced humanoid robots, or "mechas," keep things going. Professor Hobby (Hurt) made a child mecha, David (Osment), designed to be loving and extremely loyal—in this case to his human mother Monica (O'Connor) who eventually abandons him to the cruel world. Having heard the Pinocchio story, David searches for the Blue Fairy who can make David a "real" boy. En route, David meets mecha Gigolo Joe (Law), who advises David about human beings' perfidy. An acquired taste--it's long, dark, confusing, sometimes boring, and sometimes touching. Law's role is small but Osment carries the picture. Based on Brian Aldiss' 1969 short story "Supertoys Last All Summer Long." 145m; VHS, DVD, Wide. **C:** Haley Joel Osment; Jude Law; Frances O'Connor; Sam Robards; Brendan Gleeson; William Hurt; Jake Thomas; Clara Bellar; Enrico Colantoni; Adrian Grenier; Emmanuelle Chriqui; Voice(s) by Robin Williams; Chris Rock; Meryl Streep; Jack Angel; Narrated by Ben Kingsley; Directed by Steven Spielberg; Written by Steven Spielberg; Cinematography by Janusz Kaminski; Music by John Williams. **Pr:** Steven Spielberg; Kathleen Kennedy; Steven Spielberg; Amblin Entertainment; Warner Bros; DreamWorks SKG. **A:** Jr. High-Adult. **P:** Entertainment. **U:** Home. **Mov-Ent**: Science Fiction, Family. **Acq:** Purchase. **Dist:** DreamWorks Home Entertainment.

A Is for AIDS 1990
For pre-teens, an explanation of the hows and whys of AIDS presented in an easy to understand, non-threatening manner. 15m; VHS, 3/4 U. **Pr:** Altschul Group. **A:** Primary-Jr. High. **P:** Education. **U:** Institution. **Hea-Sci**: AIDS, Health Education, Children. **Acq:** Purchase, Rent/Lease. **Dist:** United Learning Inc. $275.00.

A Is for Alligator, B Is for Bear 19??
Preschoolers learn and grow both mentally and spiritually with this educational program. 30m; VHS. **Pr:** Bridgestone Production Group. **A:** Preschool-Primary. **P:** Education. **U:** Home. **Chl-Juv**: Family Viewing, Children, Education. **Acq:** Purchase. **Dist:** School-Tech Inc. $17.95.

A la Guerra 1979
Author Bimbo Rivas reads a poem on the cultural and racial discrimination against Puerto Ricans. English subtitles. 10m; VHS, 3/4 U. **TV Std:** NTSC, PAL, SECAM. **Pr:** Thomas Sigel. **A:** Sr. High-Adult. **P:** Education. **U:** Institution, SURA. **L:** English, Spanish. **Gen-Edu**: Caribbean, Minorities. **Acq:** Purchase, Rent/Lease. **Dist:** The Cinema Guild.

A la Mode 1994 (R) — ★★1/2
It's Paris in the '60s as shy 17-year-old orphan Fausto (Higelin) is apprenticed to fatherly Jewish tailor Mietek (Yanne). But Fausto is transfixed by lovely mechanic Tonie (Darel) and decides what he really wants (besides the girl) is to design women's fashions. Very frothy coming-of-age tale, anchored by Yanne's veteran charm. Based on the novel "Fausto" by Richard Morgieve. French with subtitles. 89m; VHS, DVD. **C:** Ken Higelin; Jean Yanne; Florence Darel; Francois Hautesserre; Directed by Remy Duchemin; Written by Remy Duchemin; Richard Morgieve; Music by Denis Barbier. **Pr:** Joel Foulon; Daniel Daujon; Miramax Film Corp. **A:** Sr. High-Adult. **P:** Entertainment. **U:** Home. **L:** French. **Mov-Ent**: Clothing & Dress, France, Adoption. **Acq:** Purchase. **Dist:** Miramax Film Corp.

A-Lone-Some I Make All the Noise 1975
Situations in the artist's life, poetically interpreted using imagery, documentary and scripted material. Part of the "A Family Album of Moving Polaroids" series. 8m/B/W; VHS, 3/4 U. **Pr:** Maxi Cohen. **A:** Family. **P:** Entertainment. **U:** Institution, SURA. **Gen-Edu**: Family. **Acq:** Purchase, Rent/Lease. **Dist:** Maxi Cohen Film & Video Productions.

A Lot Like Love 2005 (PG-13) — ★
More like "A Lot Like a Million Other Disposable Romantic Comedies." On a plane from New York to L.A., shy Oliver (Kutcher) meets aggressive Emily (Peet), who goads Oliver into joining the Mile High Club and unceremoniously dumps him once they land, claiming he's not her type. Apparently the universe and the writers disagree. Over the next seven years, their paths keep crossing, and they wonder if perhaps it's true love. Kutcher and Peet do their best to fake on-screen chemistry, but come off as the poor man's Tom Hanks and Meg Ryan. 95m; DVD. **C:** Ashton Kutcher; Amanda Peet; Kathryn Hahn; Kal Penn; Taryn Manning; James Read; Molly Cheek; Gabriel Mann; Ty(rone) Giordano; Aimee Garcia; Ali Larter; Amy Aquino; Jeremy Sisto; Holmes Osborne; Lee Garlington; Linda Hunt; Melissa van der Schyff; Directed by Nigel Cole; Written by Colin Patrick Lynch; Cinematography by John de Borman; Music by Alex Wurman. **Pr:** Armyan Bernstein; Kevin J. Messick; Beacon Production; Buena Vista. **A:** Jr. High-Adult. **P:** Entertainment. **U:** Home. **L:** English. **Mov-Ent**: Comedy--Romantic. **Acq:** Purchase. **Dist:** Buena Vista Home Entertainment. $29.99.

A-M-E-R-I-C-A-N-S 1977
In interviews, a number of children of all colors speak about how they feel about being Americans, about their own origins, about racial bias, and about intercultural friendships. 12m; VHS, 3/4 U, Special order formats. **Pr:** Churchill. **A:** Primary. **P:** Education. **U:** Institution, Home, SURA. **Chl-Juv**: Documentary Films, Human Relations, Children. **Acq:** Purchase, Duplication License. **Dist:** Clear Vue Inc.

A Nos Amours 1984 (R) — ★★★
Craving the attention she is denied at home, a young French girl searches for love and affection from numerous boyfriends in hopes of eradicating her unhappy home. Occasional lapses in quality and slow pacing hamper an otherwise excellent effort. The characterization of the girl Suzanne is especially memorable. In French with English subtitles. 99m; VHS, DVD. **C:** Sandrine Bonnaire; Dominique Besnehard; Maurice Pialat; Evelyne Ker; Directed by Maurice Pialat; Written by Maurice Pialat; Arlette Langmann; Cinematography by Jacques Loiseleux; Music by Henry Purcell. **Pr:** Triumph Films. **A:** Sr. High-Adult. **P:** Entertainment. **U:** Home. **L:** French. **Mov-Ent**. **Acq:** Purchase. **Dist:** Sony Pictures Home Entertainment Inc. $59.95.

A Nous la Liberte 1931 (Unrated) — ★★★★
Two tramps encounter industrialization and automation, making one into a wealthy leader, the other into a nature-loving iconoclast. A poignant, fantastical masterpiece by Clair, made before he migrated to Hollywood. Though the view of automation may be dated, it influenced such films as Chaplin's "Modern Times." In French with English subtitles. 87m/B/W; VHS, DVD, 8 mm. **C:** Henri Marchand; Raymond Cordy; Rolla France; Paul Olivier; Jacques Shelly; Andre Michaud; Directed by Rene Clair; Written by Rene Clair; Cinematography by Georges Perinal; Music by Georges Auric. **Pr:** Societe des Films Sonores Tobis. **A:** Family. **P:** Entertainment. **U:** Home. **L:** English, French. **Mov-Ent**: Fantasy, Classic Films, Technology. **Acq:** Purchase. **Dist:** Glenn Video Vistas Ltd.; Hen's Tooth Video; Baker and Taylor. $49.95.

A. Philip Randolph 1996
A documentary on the civil rights leader who believed the key to civil rights were economic rights. 86m; VHS, DVD. **A:** Sr. High-Adult. **P:** Education. **U:** Home, Institution. **Gen-Edu**: Documentary Films, Biography. **Acq:** Purchase. **Dist:** California Newsreel. $26.95.

A. Phillip Randolph: For Jobs and Freedom 1996
Chronicles the life of labor leader and civil rights activist A. Phillip Randolph. 86m; VHS. **A:** Sr. High-Adult. **P:** Education. **U:** Home, Institution. **Gen-Edu**: Sociology, Biography, Civil Rights. **Acq:** Purchase. **Dist:** California Newsreel. $195.00.

A Propos de Nice 1929 — ★★★
First film by French director Vigo, the silent film parodies French travelogues in a manner that indicates the director's later brilliance. 25m/B/W; Silent; VHS, DVD. **C:** Directed by Jean Vigo; Written by Jean Vigo; Cinematography by Boris Kaufman. **A:** Family. **P:** Entertainment. **U:** Institution, Home. **Mov-Ent**: Satire & Parody, Silent Films. **Acq:** Purchase. **Dist:** Criterion Collection Inc.

A-rab Summer 19??
The dying art of street huckstering in Baltimore is noted in this look at the Allen family business. 30m; VHS, 3/4 U. **A:** Sr. High-Adult. **P:** Education. **U:** Institution, CCTV. **Gen-Edu**: Documentary Films, Family. **Acq:** Purchase, Rent/Lease. **Dist:** Maryland Public Television. $29.95.

A-scan Biometry 1988
This program provides the viewer with the information necessary to perform accurate axial eye length measurements. 30m; VHS, 3/4 U. **Pr:** American Academy of Ophthalmology. **A:** College-Family. **P:** Professional. **U:** Home, SURA. **Hea-Sci**: Medical Education, Eye, Surgery. **Acq:** Purchase, Rent/Lease. **Dist:** American Academy of Ophthalmology.

The A-Team 2010 (PG-13) — ★★★
The 1983-87 TV series successfully takes to the big screen, and its four members are now Iraq War vets trying to clear their names after being framed for a heist of some American currency engraving plates. Perfectly cast, with just the right tone for summer blockbuster season, Carnahan delivers exactly what the show did: Mindless, loud, and fun entertainment. You don't necessarily have to be a fan of the show to enjoy it, but it might help. Stephen J. Cannell, who created and produced the TV show, is a producer of the film version. 117m; Blu-Ray, Wide. **C:** Liam Neeson; Bradley Cooper; Sharlto Copley; Quinton 'Rampage' Jackson; Jessica Biel; Patrick Wilson; Brian Bloom; Gerald McRaney; Henry Czerny; Omari Hardwick; Jon Hamm; Yul Vazquez; Maury Sterling; Cameo(s) Dirk Benedict; Dwight Schultz; Directed by Joe Carnahan; Written by Skip Woods; Michael Brandt; Derek Haas; Cinematography by Mauro Fiore; Music by Alan Silvestri. **Pr:** Stephen J. Cannell; Jules Daly; Ridley Scott; Tony Scott; Iain Smith; Dune Entertainment; Scott Free; 20th Century-Fox. **P:** Entertainment. **U:** Home. **L:** English. **Mov-Ent**: Veterans, Mexico, Intelligence Service. **Acq:** Purchase. **Dist:** Movies Unlimited; Fox Home Entertainment.

The A-Team: Season Five, the Final Season 1986
Presents the fifth and final season of the 1983-1987 action-drama-comedy television series with a group of four falsely-accused Vietnam War veterans living in L.A. as they try to elude the government while serving as do-gooders fighting criminals. Includes: the A-Team are roped into saving hostages on a plane in Spain only to later be court-martialed and scheduled for execution (three-part season opener), and the men must locate a former partner who's been corrupted or else face the possibility of never being cleared of the charges against them. 13 episodes. 622m; DVD. **C:** George Peppard; Dwight Schultz; Mr. T; Dirk Benedict; John Ashley. **A:** Jr. High-Adult. **P:** Entertainment. **U:** Home. **Mov-Ent**: Television Series, Action-Adventure, Comedy-Drama. **Acq:** Purchase. **Dist:** Universal Studios Home Video. $49.98.

The A-Team: Season Four 1985
Presents the fourth season of the 1983-1987 action-drama-comedy television series with a group of four Vietnam War veterans living in L.A. as they try to elude the government while serving as do-gooders fighting criminals. Includes: in a two-part episode, the guys go to Italy to go against the mob to save a judge's daughter but can't shake them as they travel with her on an oceanliner; singer Rick James makes a special appearance and hires the A-Team to help an imprisoned friend; and a mix-up causes Face (Benedict) to book makeup-wearing pop star Boy George into a rough, country music dance hall. 22 episodes. 1111m; DVD. **C:** George Peppard; Dwight Schultz; Mr. T; Dirk Benedict; John Ashley. **A:** Jr. High-Adult. **P:** Entertainment. **U:** Home. **Mov-Ent**: Television Series, Action-Adventure, Comedy-Drama. **Acq:** Purchase. **Dist:** Universal Studios Home Video. $49.98.

The A-Team: Season One 1983
Presents the debut season of the 1983-1987 action-drama-comedy television series with a group of four Vietnam War veterans living in L.A. as they try to elude the government while serving as do-gooders fighting criminals. Includes: the team is hired by a newspaper reporter to find her missing colleague; they rescue a kidnapped college professor but the kidnapper and casino owner winds up dead, leaving the A-Team looking guilty; and the guys confront a murderous gang who are responsible for their friend's death. 14 episodes. 677m; DVD. **C:** George Peppard; Dwight Schultz; Mr. T; Dirk Benedict; John Ashley. **A:** Jr. High-Adult. **P:** Entertainment. **U:** Home. **Mov-Ent**: Television Series, Action-Adventure, Comedy-Drama. **Acq:** Purchase. **Dist:** Universal Studios Home Video. $49.98.

The A-Team: Season Three 1984
Presents the third season of the 1983-1987 action-drama-comedy television series with a group of four Vietnam War veterans living in L.A. as they try to elude the government while serving as do-gooders fighting criminals. Includes: the men come to the aid of two women to save their Miami hotel from gangsters; the team's time off in the mountains is interrupted by a union dispute; and they go to Kenya to intervene when game poachers threaten a local game warden and his preserve. 25 episodes. 1196m; DVD. **C:** George Peppard; Dwight Schultz; Mr. T; Dirk Benedict; John Ashley. **A:** Jr. High-Adult. **P:** Entertainment. **U:** Home. **Mov-Ent**: Television Series, Action-Adventure, Comedy-Drama. **Acq:** Purchase. **Dist:** Universal Studios Home Video. $49.98.

The A-Team: Season Two 1983
Features the 23-episode second season of the 1980s action-adventure television series comprised of four Vietnam vets on the lamb from the military after being set up. 1108m; DVD, CC. **A:** Jr. High-Adult. **P:** Entertainment. **U:** Home. **Mov-Ent**: Television, Action-Adventure, Television Series. **Acq:** Purchase. **Dist:** Universal Studios Home Video. $49.98.

A-10 Down and Dirty 1991
Come aboard the A-10 fighter plane and see what it is like to actually man one of these powerful weapons with a view from the cockpit. 30m; VHS. **Pr:** Fusion Video. **A:** Sr. High-Adult. **P:** Entertainment. **U:** Home. **Gen-Edu**: Documentary Films, Aeronautics, Armed Forces--U.S. **Acq:** Purchase. **Dist:** Fusion Video. $19.98.

A2 2001
Tatsuya Mori's sequel to "A" continues to look at the Aum Shinrikyo sect after a law is passed to mandate continuous surveillance of its members and operations. Japanese with subtitles. 131m; DVD. **A:** Sr. High-Adult. **P:** Entertainment. **U:** Home. **L:** Japanese. **Gen-Edu**: Documentary Films. **Acq:** Purchase. **Dist:** Facets Multimedia Inc.

The A-V History of American Literature 1987
Presents a two part program that starts with Early American literature, and ends with literature in the 1980s. 174m; VHS. **A:** Primary-Adult. **P:** Education. **U:** Institution. **Gen-Edu**: Literature, Literature--American. **Acq:** Purchase. **Dist:** Knowledge Unlimited, Inc. $350.00.

AA Coaching Girls Volleyball: High Energy, High Rep Practice Drills 2013 (Unrated)
Coach Bond Shymansky demonstrates warm-up, situational, and competitive drills for volleyball practice sessions. 101m; DVD. **A:** Family. **P:** Education. **U:** Home. **L:** English. **Spo-Rec**: Athletic Instruction/Coaching, Volleyball, How-To. **Acq:** Purchase. **Dist:** Championship Productions. $29.99.

A.A.:Rap with Us 19??
Fast-paced and involving, this video features four young A.A. members talking about what they were like drinking, what happened to them, and what it is like in A.A. 17m; VHS. **A:** Jr. High. **P:** Education. **U:** Institution. **L:** English. **Hea-Sci**: Alcoholism. **Acq:** Purchase. **Dist:** Hazelden Publishing. $29.95.

AAO Code of Ethics and You 1987
Clarifies the AAO Code of Ethics, with particular emphasis on those aspects that are most often misinterpreted. 40m; VHS, 3/4 U. **Pr:** American Academy of Ophthalmology. **A:** College-Family. **P:** Professional. **U:** Home, SURA. **Hea-Sci**: Eye, Surgery, Medical Education. **Acq:** Purchase, Rent/Lease. **Dist:** American Academy of Ophthalmology.

Aardman Animations: The Lip Sync Series 1991 (Unrated)
Always visually enticing, England's Aardman Animations present this spectacular series created around recorded conversation. Included is the 1991 Academy Award-winning "Creature Comforts." Also featured are "War Story," "Going Equipped," "Ident," and "Next" which, amazingly enough, depicts the complete works of Shakespeare in under five minutes. 60m; VHS. **Pr:** Expanded Entertainment. **A:** Family. **P:** Entertainment. **U:** Home. **Mov-Ent**: Family Viewing, Animation & Cartoons. **Acq:** Purchase. **Dist:** Tapeworm Video Distributors Inc. $39.95.

Aaron Carter: Aaron's Party—Come Get It 2000
Contains Aaron Carter music videos, performance and behind-the-scenes footage, photo gallery, trivia game and web links. ?m; DVD. **A:** Jr. High. **P:** Entertainment. **U:** Home. **Mov-Ent**: Music Video, Music--Pop/Rock. **Acq:** Purchase. **Dist:** BMG Entertainment. $14.98.

Aaron Copland 1977
Once a kid from Brooklyn who liked music, Aaron Copland has become a celebrated composer/conductor. He discusses the process of finding his musical voice and his resulting work. 30m; 3/4 U, EJ. **Pr:** NETCHE. **A:** College-Adult. **P:** Education. **U:** Institution, CCTV, BCTV, SURA. **Fin-Art**. **Acq:** Purchase, Rent/Lease, Subscription. **Dist:** NETCHE.

Aaron Copland: A Self-Portrait 1989
Composer Aaron Copland discusses his musical career starting with piano lessons in Brooklyn, New York and studying with Nadia Boulanger. The program features ballet sequences with Agnes de Mille daning in "Rodeo" and Martha Graham in "Appalachian Spring," scenes of Copland conducting, and interviews with Leonard Bernstein and Ned Rorem. 58m; VHS, 3/4 U. **Pr:** Films for the Humanities and Sciences. **A:** College. **P:** Education. **U:** Institution, CCTV, CATV, BCTV. **Fin-Art**: Biography. **Acq:** Purchase, Rent/Lease, Duplication License. **Dist:** Films for the Humanities & Sciences.

Aaron Loves Angela 1975 (R) — ★★
Puerto Rican girl falls in love with a black teen amidst the harsh realities of the Harlem ghetto. "Romeo and Juliet" meets "West Side Story" in a cliched comedy drama. 99m; VHS, DVD. **C:** Kevin Hooks; Irene Cara; Moses Gunn; Robert Hooks; Cameo(s) Jose Feliciano; Directed by Gordon Parks, Jr.; Cinematography by Richard Kratina; Music by Jose Feliciano. **Pr:** Columbia Pictures. **A:** Sr. High-Adult. **P:** Entertainment. **U:** Home. **Mov-Ent**: Black Culture, Drama, Prejudice. **Acq:** Purchase. **Dist:** Sony Pictures Home Entertainment Inc. $59.95.

Aaron Siskind 1981
A documentary on Siskind, the pioneer who extended the limits of photography and began making personal abstract pictures in the early '40s. 17m; VHS, 3/4 U, Special order formats. **C:** Directed by Theodore R. Haimes. **Pr:** Edgar B. Howard; Checkerboard Productions, Inc. **A:** Sr. High-Adult. **P:** Education. **U:** Institution, SURA. **Fin-Art**: Documentary Films, Art & Artists, Photography. **Acq:** Purchase, Rent/Lease. **Dist:** Museum of Modern Art. $39.95.

AAU Coaching Girls Volleyball: Winning Defensive Systems 2013 (Unrated)
Coach Anne Kordes demonstrates three successful defensive systems used by volleyball teams from middle school to the national level. 68m; DVD. **A:** Family. **P:** Education. **U:** Home. **L:** English. **Spo-Rec**: Athletic Instruction/Coaching, Volleyball, How-To. **Acq:** Purchase. **Dist:** Championship Productions. $29.99.

AAU Coaching Girls Volleyball: Winning Offensive Systems 2013 (Unrated)
Coach Anne Kordes presents this companion video on offensive volleyball play to her other one on defensive play. 46m; DVD. **A:** Family. **P:** Education. **U:** Home. **L:** English. **Spo-Rec**: Athletic Instruction/Coaching, Volleyball, How-To. **Acq:** Purchase. **Dist:** Championship Productions. $29.99.

AAU Coaching Wrestling Series: Practice Drills for Developing Wrestlers 2013 (Unrated)
Coach Greg Strobel demonstrates training drills and methods for younger wrestlers. 70m; DVD. **A:** Family. **P:** Education. **U:** Home. **L:** English. **Spo-Rec**: Athletic Instruction/Coaching, Sports--General, How-To. **Acq:** Purchase. **Dist:** Championship Productions. $29.99.

AAU Coaching Wrestling Series: Practice Planning for Developing Wrestlers 2013 (Unrated)
Coach Greg Strobel follows up his video of practice training drills for wrestlers with this on planning out the practice session itself. 67m; DVD. **A:** Family. **P:** Education. **U:** Home. **L:** English. **Spo-Rec**: Athletic Instruction/Coaching, Sports--General, How-To. **Acq:** Purchase. **Dist:** Championship Productions. $29.99.

AAU Coaching Wrestling Series: Strength Training for Developing Wrestlers 2013 (Unrated)
Coach Thomas Koch presents various strength and conditioning drills for wrestler training. 75m; DVD. **A:** Family. **P:** Education. **U:** Home. **L:** English. **Spo-Rec**: Athletic Instruction/Coaching, Sports--General, How-To. **Acq:** Purchase. **Dist:** Championship Productions. $29.99.

AAU Wrestling Skills Series: Counter Offense 2013 (Unrated)
Coach Eric Guerrero demonstrates various defensive wrestling techniques when wrestling from a standing position. 41m; DVD. **A:** Family. **P:** Education. **U:** Home. **L:** English. **Spo-Rec**: Athletic Instruction/Coaching, Sports--General, How-To. **Acq:** Purchase. **Dist:** Championship Productions. $29.99.

AAU Wrestling Skills Series: Scoring from the Bottom Position 2013 (Unrated)
Coach Eric Guerrero discusses escaping from the bottom position and getting into a scoring position. 39m; DVD. **A:** Family. **P:** Education. **U:** Home. **L:** English. **Spo-Rec**: Athletic Instruction/Coaching, Sports--General, How-To. **Acq:** Purchase. **Dist:** Championship Productions. $29.99.

AAU Wrestling Skills Series: Scoring from the Top Position 2013 (Unrated)
Coach Eric Guerrero demonstrates controlling opponents from the top position while going for a pin or breakdown. 36m; DVD. **A:** Family. **P:** Education. **U:** Home. **L:** English. **Spo-Rec**: Athletic Instruction/Coaching, Sports--General, How-To. **Acq:** Purchase. **Dist:** Championship Productions. $29.99.

AAU Wrestling Skills Series: Set Ups, Takedowns and Finishes 2013 (Unrated)
Coach Eric Guerrero demonstrates which set-ups to use with which takedowns, along with finishes for each one. 68m; DVD. **A:** Family. **P:** Education. **U:** Home. **L:** English. **Spo-Rec**: Athletic Instruction/Coaching, Sports--General, How-To. **Acq:** Purchase. **Dist:** Championship Productions. $29.99.

AAUU Basketball Skills Series: Increasing Your Vertical Jump 2012
University of Florida Strength Coach Preston Greene discusses techniques for increasing a basketball team's jumping power. 40m; DVD. **A:** Jr. High-Adult. **P:** Education. **U:** Home, Institution. **L:** English. **Gen-Edu**: Athletic Instruction/Coaching, Basketball, Education. **Acq:** Purchase. **Dist:** Championship Productions. $29.99.

AB Attack 2000
An intense abdominal workout designed by fitness expert Trish Muse. Includes 30 minutes of abs and another 30 minutes focusing on stabilization, lower back and upper back strengthening. 68m; VHS. **A:** Adult. **P:** Instruction. **U:** Home. **Hea-Sci**: Fitness/Exercise, How-To. **Acq:** Purchase. **Dist:** Body Productions, Inc. $19.95.

Ab-Normal Beauty 2005 (R) — ★★
Photographer Jiney (Race Wong) is impatient with her own work despite its winning many awards. But after filming the dead bodies at a car accident, she gains an obsession with photographing death. She is followed by fellow classmate and videographer Anson, who has his own obsession with filming her, despite her constant rejections of him. As she is about to leave her obsessions with death behind her, Jiney receives a tape of a woman being murdered. When the second snuff tape arrives, things start to get creepy. 98m; DVD. **C:** Race Wong; Rosanne Wong; Anson Leung; Directed by Oxide Pang Chun; Written by Oxide Pang Chun; Thomas Pang; Cinematography by Decha Srimantra; Music by Payont Permsith. **A:** Sr. High-Adult. **P:** Entertainment. **U:** Home. **L:** English, Cantonese, Spanish. **Mov-Ent**: Horror, Mystery & Suspense, Sexual Abuse. **Acq:** Purchase. **Dist:** Palisades Tartan Video. $14.95.

The ABA Commission on Minorities and Judicial Administration Division 1988
Issues of prejudice in the courtroom. 15m; VHS, 3/4 U. **Pr:** ABA. **A:** Adult. **P:** Professional. **U:** Institution, CCTV, Home, SURA. **Bus-Ind**: Documentary Films, Law, Minorities. **Acq:** Purchase, Rent/Lease. **Dist:** American Bar Association.

ABA Section of Law Practice Management 1984
This series serves as a "how to" guide on managing the business side of a law firm. 55m; VHS, 3/4 U. **Pr:** ABA. **A:** Adult. **P:** Professional. **U:** Institution, CCTV, Home, SURA. **How-Ins**: Law, Management, How-To. **Acq:** Purchase. **Dist:** American Bar Association. $69.00.
Indiv. Titles: 1. Ten Rules for Developing Your Practice 2. Attracting and Keeping Good People for Your Support Staff 3. Managing Your Time 4. Keeping Tabs on Your Firm's Financial Performance 5. How to Determine a Partner's Interest in a Firm 6. Putting Your Small Firm on the Path to Profits 7. Protecting the Most Important Property in Your Office 8. Getting Your Name Out in Your Community 9. Getting and Keeping the Clients You Want 10. How to Set a Fair Fee 11. Five Computer Applications for the Busy Lawyer 12. Organizing Your Law Library.

The Abacos: Video Cruising Little Bahamas Bank 19??
Comprehensive tour of every cay in this part of the islands. 60m; VHS. **A:** Adult. **P:** Entertainment. **U:** Home. **Spo-Rec**: Boating, Travel, Caribbean. **Acq:** Purchase. **Dist:** Bennett Marine Video. $39.95.

Abandon 2002 (PG-13) — ★★½
"Traffic" screenwriter Stephen Gaghan makes his directorial debut in this psychological thriller that centers on bookworm college student Katie (Holmes) and her mysteriously missing boyfriend Embry (Hunnam). When police detective Wade (Bratt) arrives to question Katie two years after the disappearance of the eccentric Embry, she begins to see glimpses of him all over campus. The "twist" ending is fairly predictable, but the cast, particularly Union, Mann and Deschanel as Katie's classmates, get the most out of the script. Based on the book "Adam's Fall" by Sean Desmond. 99m; VHS, DVD, CC. **C:** Katie Holmes; Benjamin Bratt; Charlie Hunnam; Zooey Deschanel; Gabrielle Beauvais; Gabriel Mann; Mark Feuerstein; Melanie Lynskey; Will McCormack; Philip Bosco; Tony Goldwyn; Fred Ward; Directed by Stephen Gaghan; Written by Stephen Gaghan; Cinematography by Matthew Libatique; Music by Clint Mansell. **Pr:** Lynda Obst; Gary Barber; Edward Zwick; Roger Birnbaum; Spyglass Entertainment; Paramount Pictures. **A:** Jr. High-Adult. **P:** Entertainment. **U:** Home. **Mov-Ent**: Alcoholism. **Acq:** Purchase. **Dist:** Paramount Pictures Corp.

Abandon Ship 1943
A U.S. Navy training film demonstrating emergency escape techniques, as well as water safety and survival methods. 30m/B/W; VHS. **TV Std:** NTSC, PAL. **C:** Narrated by Mike Wallace. **Pr:** U.S. Navy. **A:** Jr. High-Adult. **P:** Education. **U:** Home. **Gen-Edu**: Boating, Armed Forces--U.S. **Acq:** Purchase. **Dist:** International Historic Films Inc. $24.95.

Abandon Ship 1957 (Unrated) — ★★½
A luxury liner hits a derelict mine and sinks within minutes, leaving 27 survivors clinging to one tiny lifeboat. Ship's officer Alex Holmes (Power) knows that the amount of food and water they have is limited, the waters are shark-infested, and the injured stand little chance, so he must decide who will survive. 97m/B/W; VHS. **C:** Tyrone Power; Mai Zetterling; Lloyd Nolan; Stephen Boyd; Moira Lister; James Hayter; Marie Lohr; Gordon Jackson; Laurence Naismith; John Stratton; Victor Maddern; Eddie Byrne; Noel Willman; Ralph Michael; David Langton; Ferdinand "Ferdy" Mayne; Austin Trevor; Finlay Currie; Jill Melford; Directed by Richard Sale; Written by Richard Sale; Cinematography by Wilkie Cooper; Music by Arthur Bliss. **Pr:** Columbia Pictures. **A:** Jr. High-Adult. **P:** Entertainment. **U:** Home. **Mov-Ent**: Action-Adventure, Boating. **Acq:** Purchase. **Dist:** Sony Pictures Home Entertainment Inc.

Abandon Ship: Preparing to Survive 1988
A how-to video which explains emergency procedures for boating disasters. 30m; VHS. **Pr:** Avon. **A:** Jr. High-Adult. **P:** Instruction. **U:** Home. **How-Ins**: How-To, Emergencies, Boating. **Acq:** Purchase. **Dist:** Bennett Marine Video. $24.95.

Abandoned 1947 (Unrated) — ★½
A young woman goes missing in Los Angeles, and her sister starts searching. Turns out the missing girl had a baby—but the baby is nowhere to be found. The police are disinterested until a local crime reporter gets involved and winds up finding a shady detective and black market baby ring. 78m/B/W; DVD. **C:** Dennis O'Keefe; Gale Storm; Marjorie Rambeau; Raymond Burr; Will Kuluva; Jeff Chandler; Meg Randall; Jeannette Nolan; Directed by Joseph M. Newman; Written by Irwin Gielgud; William Bowers. **A:** Jr. High-Adult. **P:** Entertainment. **U:** Home. **Mov-Ent**: Crime Drama, Journalism. **Acq:** Purchase. **Dist:** Nostalgia Collectibles.

The Abandoned 2006 (R) — ★★
Euro-horror. Marie and her twin brother Nicolai were abandoned as babies and only meet again when they must deal with their parents' abandoned farmhouse, located in a creepy Russian forest. The haunted house is the site of the 40-year-old murder of their mother, and the siblings soon find themselves trapped by ghostly images that want to re-create the past and make sure that this time they die. 99m; DVD. **C:** Anastasia Hille; Karel Roden; Valentin Ganev; Carlos Reig-Plaza; Directed by Nacho Cerda; Written by Richard Stanley; Nacho Cerda; Karim Hussani; Cinematography by Xavi Gimenez; Music by Alfons Conde. **A:** Sr. High-Adult. **P:** Entertainment. **U:** Home. **Mov-Ent**: Horror, USSR. **Acq:** Purchase. **Dist:** Lions Gate Entertainment Inc.

Abandoned 2010 (PG-13) — Bomb!
Distressingly bad, low-budget medical thriller that was the last completed film feature for Murphy, who looks much worse than even her unstable character warrants. Mary takes new boyfriend Kevin to an L.A. hospital for some minor surgery but he vanishes and there's no record he was ever a patient. Because of her own mental issues, Mary is suspected of being a nutcase but, because she works as a bank manager, there's more involved that just delusions. 93m; DVD, Blu-Ray. **C:** Brittany

Murphy; Dean Cain; Peter Bogdanovich; Mimi Rogers; Jay Pickett; Tim Thomerson; Directed by Michael Feifer; Written by Peter Sullivan; Cinematography by Denis Maloney; Music by Andres Boulton. **A:** Jr. High-Adult. **P:** Entertainment. **U:** Home. **Mov-Ent:** Hospitals, Psychiatry. **Acq:** Purchase. **Dist:** Anchor Bay Entertainment.

Abandoned and Deceived 1995 (Unrated) — ★★
ABC TV movie based on a true story. Gerri's (Loughlin) ex-husband Doug (Kerwin) doesn't pay his child support and even though she works two jobs the bills pile up. Not getting any help from social services, Gerri and her two sons move in with her parents and she decides to place a newspaper ad asking for moms in similar situations to contact her, leading to the founding of the Association for Enforcement of Child Support. 90m; DVD. **C:** Lori Loughlin; Brian Kerwin; Farrah Forke; Anthony Tyler Quinn; Eric Lloyd; Gordon Clapp; Bibi Besch; Linden Chiles; Directed by Joseph Dougherty; Written by Joseph Dougherty; Cinematography by Thomas Del Ruth; Music by Laura Karpman. **A:** Jr. High-Adult. **P:** Entertainment. **U:** Home. **Mov-Ent:** TV Movies, Divorce. **Acq:** Purchase. **Dist:** Movies Unlimited.

Abandoned: Season One 2012
Carpenter and collector Jay Chaikin and his friends travel across the country to find forgotten relics in abandoned buildings such as banks, churches, factories, and barns. 13 episodes. 270m; DVD. **A:** Jr. High-Adult. **P:** Entertainment. **U:** Home. **Gen-Edu:** Antiques, Television Series. **Acq:** Purchase. **Dist:** National Geographic. $29.95.

ABBA 1983
The internationally famous group performs "Knowing Me, Knowing You," "Take a Chance on Me," "The Name of the Game," "Dancing Queen," "Gimme, Gimme, Gimme," "Voulez-vous" and lots more. 60m; VHS. **C:** Abba. **Pr:** Polar Music International. **A:** Jr. High-Adult. **P:** Entertainment. **U:** Home. **Mov-Ent:** Music--Performance. **Acq:** Purchase. **Dist:** Music Video Distributors; Monterey Home Video. $39.95.

ABBA: Again 1983
The popular rock group performs such hits as "Supertrooper" and "When All Is Said And Done," "I Know There's Something Going On," "The Heat is On," and more. 35m; VHS. **C:** Abba. **Pr:** Polar Music International. **A:** Family. **P:** Entertainment. **U:** Home. **Mov-Ent:** Music--Performance. **Acq:** Purchase. **Dist:** Music Video Distributors; Monterey Home Video. $19.95.

ABBA Gold: Greatest Hits 199?
The clean vocals of this Swedish band are combined with an assemblage of clips from various performances and music videos from 20 years of performances. Tracks include "Dancing Queen," "Knowing Me, Knowing You," "Take a Chance on Me," "Mamma Mia," "Lay All Your Love on Me," "Voulez Vous," "Waterloo," and more. 78m; VHS. **A:** College-Adult. **P:** Entertainment. **U:** Home. **Mov-Ent:** Music Video. **Acq:** Purchase. **Dist:** Music Video Distributors. $19.95.

ABBA: In Concert 1979
This concert combines sequences from an American tour and London's Wembley Arena in 1979. Features songs such as "I Have a Dream," "Gimme! Gimme! Gimme!," "Summer Night," and "Dancing Queen." In stereo. 60m. **C:** Abba. **Pr:** Curt Edman. **A:** Family. **P:** Entertainment. **U:** Home. **Mov-Ent:** Music--Performance. **Acq:** Purchase. **Dist:** Music Video Distributors. $50.95.

ABBA: Story 1974-1982 1982
This Japanese import chronicles the glory years of this Swedish group. Live material accompanies "Waterloo," "Fernando," "Super Trouper," and much more. 56m; VHS. **C:** Abba. **A:** Family. **P:** Entertainment. **U:** Home. **Mov-Ent:** Music Video. **Acq:** Purchase. **Dist:** Music Video Distributors. $64.95.

Abbey Lincoln: You Gotta Pay the Band 1992
Jazz singer Lincoln is featured in live and studio versions of her hit songs, as well as in her movie clips from the '50s and '60s. Also features interviews with Stan Getz, Ruth Brown, and Spike Lee. ?m; VHS. **A:** Jr. High-Adult. **P:** Entertainment. **U:** Home. **Mov-Ent:** Music Video, Music--Jazz, Interviews. **Acq:** Purchase. **Dist:** Music Video Distributors. $19.95.

Abbott and Costello Go to Mars 1953 — ★½
Poor parody of sci-fi films finds the frantic duo aboard a rocket ship and accidentally heading off into outer space. They don't land on Mars, but Venus, which is populated by lots of pretty women and no men. Even this duo looks good to the ladies. Cheapie production and uninspired buffoonery. 77m/B/W; VHS, DVD, CC. **C:** Bud Abbott; Lou Costello; Mari Blanchard; Robert Paige; Martha Hyer; Horace McMahon; Jack Kruschen; Anita Ekberg; Jean Willes; Joe (Joseph) Kirk; Jackie Loughery; James Flavin; Directed by Charles Lamont; Written by John Grant; D.D. Beauchamp; Cinematography by Clifford Stine; Music by Joseph Gershenson. **Pr:** Howard Christie; Universal Pictures. **A:** Family. **P:** Entertainment. **U:** Home. **Mov-Ent:** Comedy--Slapstick, Science Fiction, Satire & Parody. **Acq:** Purchase. **Dist:** Universal Music and Video Distribution. $14.98.

Abbott and Costello in Hollywood 1945 (Unrated) — ★★
Bud and Lou appear as a barber and porter of a high-class tonsorial parlor in Hollywood. A rather sarcastic look at backstage Hollywood, Abbott & Costello style. Ball makes a guest appearance. 111m/B/W; VHS, DVD. **C:** Bud Abbott; Lou Costello; Frances Rafferty; Warner Anderson; Jean Porter; Robert Stanton; Mike Mazurki; Directed by S. Sylvan Simon; Music by George Bassman. **Pr:** MGM. **A:** Family. **P:** Entertainment. **U:** Home. **Mov-Ent:** Comedy--Slapstick. **Acq:** Purchase. **Dist:** MGM Home Entertainment; Critics' Choice Video & DVD. $19.98.

Abbott and Costello in the Foreign Legion 1950 — ★★½
Fight promoters Jonesy and Max trail their runaway fighter to Algiers where they're tricked into joining the French Foreign Legion. They have to cope with a sadistic sergeant, a sexy spy, and still find their man. Most amusement comes from Lou's wild desert mirages. 80m/B/W; VHS, DVD, CC. **C:** Bud Abbott; Lou Costello; Walter Slezak; Patricia Medina; Douglass Dumbrille; Leon Belasco; Marc Lawrence; Tor Johnson; Directed by Charles Lamont; Written by John Grant; Martin Ragaway; Leonard Stern; Cinematography by George Robinson. **Pr:** Robert Arthur; Universal Pictures. **A:** Family. **P:** Entertainment. **U:** Home. **Mov-Ent:** Comedy--Slapstick. **Acq:** Purchase. **Dist:** Universal Music and Video Distribution. $14.98.

Abbott and Costello Meet Captain Kidd 1952 (Unrated) — ★★
With pirates led by Captain Kidd on their trail, Abbott and Costello follow a treasure map. Bland A&C swashbuckler spoof with a disinterested Laughton impersonating the Kidd. One of the duo's few color films. 70m; VHS, DVD. **C:** Bud Abbott; Lou Costello; Charles Laughton; Hillary Brooke; Fran Warren; Bill (William) Shirley; Leif Erickson; Directed by Charles Lamont. **Pr:** Warner Bros. **A:** Family. **P:** Entertainment. **U:** Home. **Mov-Ent:** Comedy--Slapstick. **Acq:** Purchase. **Dist:** Movies Unlimited; Warner Home Video, Inc. $14.99.

Abbott and Costello Meet Dr. Jekyll and Mr. Hyde 1952 (Unrated) — ★★
Slim (Abbott) and Tubby (Costello) are a couple of cops sent to London, who become involved with crazy Dr. Jekyll (Karloff), who has transformed himself into Mr. Hyde via an experimental serum, and is terrorizing London. Naturally, he goes after the boys. A lame attempt at recapturing the success of "Abbott and Costello Meet Frankenstein" but Karloff is top-notch as always. 77m/B/W; VHS, DVD. **C:** Bud Abbott; Lou Costello; Boris Karloff; Craig Stevens; Helen Westcott; Reginald Denny; John Dierkes; Marjorie Bennett; Lucille Lamarr; Patti McKay; Directed by Charles Lamont; Written by John Grant; Leo Loeb; Howard Dimsdale; Cinematography by George Robinson. **Pr:** Mark Huffam. **A:** Family. **P:** Entertainment. **U:** Home. **Mov-Ent:** Comedy--Slapstick. **Acq:** Purchase. **Dist:** Movies Unlimited; Alpha Video; Universal Studios Home Video. $14.95.

Abbott and Costello Meet Frankenstein 1948 (Unrated) — ★★★
Big-budget A&C classic is one of their best efforts and was rewarded handsomely at the boxoffice. Unsuspecting baggage clerks Chick (Abbott) and Wilbur (Costello) deliver a crate containing the last but not quite dead remains of Dracula (Lugosi) and Dr. Frankenstein's monster (Strange) to a wax museum. When Drac revives, he replaces the monster's brain with Wilbur's so he'll be easier to control. Chaney Jr. makes a special wolfish appearance to warn the boys that trouble looms. Last film to use the Universal creature pioneered by Karloff in 1931. 83m/B/W; VHS, DVD, Blu-Ray. **C:** Bud Abbott; Lou Costello; Lon Chaney, Jr.; Bela Lugosi; Glenn Strange; Lenore Aubert; Jane Randolph; Frank Ferguson; Charles Bradstreet; Howard Negley; Clarence Straight; Voice(s) by Vincent Price; Directed by Charles T. Barton; Written by John Grant; Robert Lees; Frederic Rinaldo; Cinematography by Charles Van Enger; Music by Frank Skinner. **Pr:** Mark Huffam. **A:** Family. **P:** Entertainment. **U:** Home. **Mov-Ent:** Comedy--Slapstick. **Awds:** Natl. Film Reg. '01. **Acq:** Purchase. **Dist:** Universal Studios Home Video; Movies Unlimited; Alpha Video. $14.95.

Abbott and Costello Meet Jerry Seinfeld 1994
Seinfeld hosts this retrospective on the legendary comedy team from their days in burlesque to Broadway, radio, movies, and television. Shown are classic routines from some of their most popular films as well as home movies, interviews with their children, and behind-the-scenes footage. 46m; DVD, CC. **A:** Family. **P:** Entertainment. **U:** Home. **Mov-Ent.** **Acq:** Purchase. **Dist:** Universal Studios Home Video. $14.98.

Abbott and Costello Meet the Creature From the Black Lagoon 1954
The comedy duo perform on an extended segment of the Colgate Comedy Hour. The boys meet not only the Creature, but the Frankenstein monster as well. ?m/B/W; VHS. **C:** Bud Abbott; Lou Costello. **Pr:** National Broadcasting Company. **A:** Family. **P:** Entertainment. **U:** Home. **Mov-Ent:** Television Series. **Acq:** Purchase. **Dist:** Sinister Cinema. $16.95.

Abbott and Costello Meet the Invisible Man 1951 (Unrated) — ★★★
Abbott and Costello play newly graduated detectives who take on the murder case of a boxer (Franz) accused of killing his manager. Using a serum that makes people invisible, the boxer helps Costello in a prizefight that will frame the real killers, who killed the manager because the boxer refused to throw a fight. Great special effects and hilarious gags make this one of the best from the crazy duo. 82m/B/W; VHS, DVD. **C:** Bud Abbott; Lou Costello; Nancy Guild; Adele Jergens; Sheldon Leonard; William Frawley; Gavin Muir; Arthur Franz; Syd Saylor; Bobby Barber; Directed by Charles Lamont; Written by Frederic Rinaldo; John Grant; Robert Lees; Cinematography by George Robinson; Music by Hans J. Salter. **Pr:** Mark Huffam; Howard Christie. **A:** Family. **P:** Entertainment. **U:** Home. **Mov-Ent:** Comedy--Slapstick, Boxing. **Acq:** Purchase. **Dist:** Movies Unlimited; Alpha Video; Universal Studios Home Video. $14.98.

Abbott and Costello Meet the Keystone Kops 1954 — ★★½
It's 1912 and the boys are bilked into buying a fake movie studio by a clever con man. When they find out they've been tricked, the duo head to Hollywood to track him down and find out the crook is trying to cheat Sennett's film company. Sennett himself trained A&C and the new Keystone Kops in their recreations of his silent screen routines. Good final chase sequence but the earlier work is tired. 79m/B/W; VHS, DVD, CC. **C:** Bud Abbott; Lou Costello; Fred Clark; Lynn Bari; Mack Sennett; Maxie "Slapsie" Rosenbloom; Frank Wilcox; Harold Goodwin; Directed by Charles Lamont; Written by John Grant; Cinematography by Reggie Lanning; Music by Joseph Gershenson. **Pr:** Howard Christie; Universal Pictures. **A:** Family. **P:** Entertainment. **U:** Home. **Mov-Ent:** Comedy--Slapstick, Filmmaking. **Acq:** Purchase. **Dist:** Universal Music and Video Distribution. $14.98.

Abbott and Costello Meet the Killer, Boris Karloff 1949 (Unrated) — ★★
Unremarkable Abbott and Costello murder mystery. Karloff plays a psychic who tries to frame Lou for murder. Pleasant enough but not one of their best. 84m/B/W; VHS, DVD, CC. **C:** Bud Abbott; Lou Costello; Boris Karloff; Lenore Aubert; Gar Moore; Donna Martell; Alan Mowbray; James Flavin; Roland Winters; Nicholas Joy; Mikel Conrad; Morgan Farley; Victoria Horne; Directed by Charles T. Barton; Written by John Grant; Hugh Wedlock, Jr.; Howard Snyder; Cinematography by Charles Van Enger; Music by Milton Schwarzwald. **Pr:** Mark Huffam. **A:** Family. **P:** Entertainment. **U:** Home. **Mov-Ent:** Comedy--Slapstick. **Acq:** Purchase. **Dist:** Movies Unlimited; Alpha Video. $14.98.

Abbott and Costello Meet the Mummy 1955 — ★★½
Okay comedy from the duo has them stranded in Egypt with a valuable medallion which will lead to secret treasure and the mummy who guards the tomb. The last of the films the twosome made for Universal. 90m/B/W; VHS, DVD. **C:** Bud Abbott; Lou Costello; Marie Windsor; Michael Ansara; Dan Seymour; Kurt Katch; Richard Deacon; Mel Welles; Edwin Parker; Richard Karlan; George Khoury; Directed by Charles Lamont; Written by John Grant; Cinematography by George Robinson; Music by Joseph Gershenson; Hans J. Salter. **Pr:** Howard Christie; Mark Huffam. **A:** Family. **P:** Entertainment. **U:** Home. **Mov-Ent:** Comedy--Slapstick, Middle East. **Acq:** Purchase. **Dist:** Facets Multimedia Inc. $14.98.

The Abbott and Costello Outtakes Series 1951
A collection of bloopers from the comedy team's best films. 45m; VHS. **A:** Family. **P:** Entertainment. **U:** Home. **Mov-Ent:** Outtakes & Bloopers. **Acq:** Purchase. **Dist:** Video Resources.

The Abbott and Costello Show - Season 1: 100th Anniversary Collection 1953 (Unrated)
Features the entire first season's TV episodes in honor of what would have been Lou Costello's 100th birthday. Bonus footage includes Costello's home videos and family interviews. 26 episodes. 885m/B/W; DVD. **C:** Bud Abbott; Lou Costello; Sid Fields. **A:** Family. **P:** Entertainment. **U:** Home. **Mov-Ent:** Television Series. **Acq:** Purchase. **Dist:** Entertainment One US LP. $39.98.

The Abbott and Costello Show - Season 2: 100th Anniversary Collection 1953 (Unrated)
Features the entire second season's TV episodes in honor of what would have been Lou Costello's 100th birthday. Bonus footage includes Costello's home videos and family interviews. 26 episodes. 800m/B/W; DVD. **C:** Bud Abbott; Lou Costello; Sid Fields. **A:** Family. **P:** Entertainment. **U:** Home. **Mov-Ent:** Television Series. **Acq:** Purchase. **Dist:** Entertainment One US LP. $39.98.

The Abbott and Costello Show: Vol. 1 1952
The popular comedy team made the move to television with a series of half-hour shows featuring some of their best burlesque routines. Four shows per tape. 110m/B/W; VHS, DVD. **C:** Bud Abbott; Lou Costello. **A:** Family. **P:** Entertainment. **U:** Home. **Mov-Ent:** Television Series. **Acq:** Purchase. **Dist:** Shanachie Entertainment.
Indiv. Titles: 1. Duck Dinner 2. Hillary's Birthday 3. Million Dollar Refund 4. Actor's Home.

The Abbott and Costello Show: Vol. 2 1952
The duo in four more of their television shows which featured an ensemble cast for their comedy sketches. 110m/B/W; VHS, DVD. **C:** Bud Abbott; Lou Costello. **A:** Family. **P:** Entertainment. **U:** Home. **Mov-Ent:** Television Series. **Acq:** Purchase. **Dist:** Shanachie Entertainment.
Indiv. Titles: 1. Lou's Birthday 2. Getting a Job 3. Uncle Bozzo 4. Stolen Skates.

The Abbott and Costello Show: Vol. 3 1952
Four episodes of the comedy show which featured the misadventures of Abbott & Costello as boarders in a rooming house. 110m/B/W; VHS. **C:** Bud Abbott; Lou Costello. **A:** Family. **P:** Entertainment. **U:** Home. **Mov-Ent:** Television Series. **Acq:** Purchase. **Dist:** Shanachie Entertainment.
Indiv. Titles: 1. Lou Falls for Ruby 2. Hillary's Father 3. Uncle Ruppert 4. Bingo's Troubles.

The Abbott and Costello Show: Vol. 4 1953 (Unrated)
Features the classic television burlesque comedy duo of Bud Abbott and Lou Costello in "The Drugstore," "Square Meal," "$1000 Prize," and "Wife Wanted." 4 episodes. 110m/B/W; DVD. **C:** Bud Abbott; Lou Costello; Sid Fields. **A:** Family. **P:** Entertainment. **U:** Home. **Mov-Ent:** Television Series. **Acq:** Purchase. **Dist:** Entertainment One US LP. $24.98.

The Abbott and Costello Show: Vol. 5 1953 (Unrated)
Features the classic television burlesque comedy duo of Bud Abbott and Lou Costello in "Police Academy," "Charity Bazaar," "Killer's Wife," and "Well Oiled." 4 episodes. 110m/B/W; DVD. **C:** Bud Abbott; Lou Costello; Sid Fields. **A:** Family. **P:** Enter-

tainment. **U:** Home. **Mov-Ent:** Television Series. **Acq:** Purchase. **Dist:** Entertainment One US LP. $24.98.

The Abbott and Costello Show: Vol.
6 1953 (Unrated)
Features the classic television burlesque comedy duo of Bud Abbott and Lou Costello in "Wrestling Match," "In Society," "Lou's Marriage," and "Beauty Contest." 4 episodes. 110m/B/W; DVD. **C:** Bud Abbott; Lou Costello; Sid Fields. **A:** Family. **P:** Entertainment. **U:** Home. **Mov-Ent:** Television Series. **Acq:** Purchase. **Dist:** Entertainment One US LP. $24.98.

The Abbott and Costello Show: Vol.
7 1953 (Unrated)
Features the classic television burlesque comedy duo of Bud Abbott and Lou Costello in "Jail," "Private Eye," "Vacuum Cleaner Salesman," and "Fall Guy." 4 episodes. 110m/B/W; DVD. **C:** Bud Abbott; Lou Costello; Sid Fields. **A:** Family. **P:** Entertainment. **U:** Home. **Mov-Ent:** Television Series. **Acq:** Purchase. **Dist:** Entertainment One US LP. $24.98.

The Abbott and Costello Show: Vol.
8 1953 (Unrated)
Features the classic television burlesque comedy duo of Bud Abbott and Lou Costello in "Little Old Lady," "Bank Holdup," "Dentist Office," and "Fencing Master." 4 episodes. 110m/B/W; DVD. **C:** Bud Abbott; Lou Costello; Sid Fields. **A:** Family. **P:** Entertainment. **U:** Home. **Mov-Ent:** Television Series. **Acq:** Purchase. **Dist:** Entertainment One US LP. $24.98.

The Abbott and Costello Show: Vol.
9 1953 (Unrated)
Features the classic television burlesque comedy duo of Bud Abbott and Lou Costello in "Politician," "Public Enemies," "From Bed and Worst," and "Car Trouble." 4 episodes. 110m/B/W; DVD. **C:** Bud Abbott; Lou Costello; Sid Fields. **A:** Family. **P:** Entertainment. **U:** Home. **Mov-Ent:** Television Series. **Acq:** Purchase. **Dist:** Entertainment One US LP. $24.98.

The Abbott and Costello Show: Vol.
10 1953 (Unrated)
Features the classic television burlesque comedy duo of Bud Abbott and Lou Costello in "The Army Story," "Efficiency Experts," "Peace and Quiet," and "Honeymoon House." 4 episodes. 110m/B/W; DVD. **C:** Bud Abbott; Lou Costello; Sid Fields. **A:** Family. **P:** Entertainment. **U:** Home. **Mov-Ent:** Television Series. **Acq:** Purchase. **Dist:** Entertainment One US LP. $24.98.

The Abbott and Costello Show: Vol.
11 1953 (Unrated)
Features the classic television burlesque comedy duo of Bud Abbott and Lou Costello in "The Western Story," "Barber Lou," "Las Vegas," and "Pest Exterminators." 4 episodes. 110m/B/W; DVD. **C:** Bud Abbott; Lou Costello; Sid Fields. **A:** Family. **P:** Entertainment. **U:** Home. **Mov-Ent:** Television Series. **Acq:** Purchase. **Dist:** Entertainment One US LP. $24.98.

The Abbott and Costello Show: Vol.
12 1953 (Unrated)
Features the classic television burlesque comedy duo of Bud Abbott and Lou Costello in "Television," "The Haunted House," "The Vacation," and "South of Dixie." 4 episodes. 110m/B/W; DVD. **C:** Bud Abbott; Lou Costello; Sid Fields. **A:** Family. **P:** Entertainment. **U:** Home. **Mov-Ent:** Television Series. **Acq:** Purchase. **Dist:** Entertainment One US LP. $24.98.

The Abbott and Costello Show: Vol.
13 1953 (Unrated)
Features the classic television burlesque comedy duo of Bud Abbott and Lou Costello in "Safari," "The Paperhangers," "Life Insurance," and "Alaska." 4 episodes. 110m/B/W; DVD. **C:** Bud Abbott; Lou Costello; Sid Fields. **A:** Family. **P:** Entertainment. **U:** Home. **Mov-Ent:** Television Series. **Acq:** Purchase. **Dist:** Entertainment One US LP. $24.98.

ABC 1989
A unique, animated look at how our alphabet evolved from Egyptian picture symbols to Roman letters and the English alphabet in use today. 32m/B/W; VHS, 3/4 U, Special order formats. **Pr:** Doug Miller. **A:** Jr. High-Adult. **P:** Education. **U:** Institution, Home, SURA. **Gen-Edu:** Documentary Films, Language Arts, Animation & Cartoons. **Acq:** Purchase, Rent/Lease, Duplication License. **Dist:** Pyramid Media. $175.00.

ABC/ABM: Understanding Manufacturing Costs 1995
Learn how Activity Based Costing and Activity Based Management can help you zero in on true product costs so you can use the data to optimize the competitive advantage. You'll see many advantages ABC and ABM has over traditional systems, and how to identify cost drivers. 34m; VHS. **A:** Adult. **P:** Professional. **U:** Institution. **L:** English. **Bus-Ind:** Industry & Industrialists. **Acq:** Purchase. **Dist:** Society of Manufacturing Engineers. $228.

ABC: Absolutely ABC 1990
A collection of greatest hits from Martin Fry and the gang. Songs include, "Poison Arrow," "Look of Love," "Vanity Kills," "King without a Crown," "How to be a Millionaire," "Be Near Me," "All of my Heart" and seven others. 60m; VHS. **Pr:** Polygram Music Video. **A:** Jr. High-Adult. **P:** Entertainment. **U:** Home. **Mov-Ent:** Music Video. **Acq:** Purchase. **Dist:** Music Video Distributors. $19.95.

ABC: Ants and Plants 19??
Examines the relationship shared between ants and plants, as plants provide food and nesting sites while ants provide pest protection. 25m; VHS. **A:** Jr. High-Adult. **P:** Education. **U:** Institution. **Gen-Edu:** Insects. **Acq:** Purchase. **Dist:** Ark Media Group Ltd.

ABC: Beautiful Killers 19??
A look at the killer whales in their native British Columbian habitat. 50m; VHS. **A:** Jr. High-Adult. **P:** Education. **U:** Institution. **Gen-Edu:** Animals. **Acq:** Purchase. **Dist:** Ark Media Group Ltd.

ABC: Chasing India's Monsoon 19??
Celebrates India's legendary Monsoon. 50m; VHS. **A:** Jr. High-Adult. **P:** Education. **U:** Institution. **Gen-Edu.** **Acq:** Purchase. **Dist:** Ark Media Group Ltd.

ABC: Cougar—Ghost of the Rockies 19??
Documents a two year study of the cougar conducted by mountain lion expert Dr. Hornocker. 50m; VHS. **A:** Jr. High-Adult. **P:** Education. **U:** Institution. **Gen-Edu:** Animals. **Acq:** Purchase. **Dist:** Ark Media Group Ltd.

ABC: Earthquakes—The Terrifying Truth 19??
Looks at 20th century earthquakes and their damaging effects. 50m; VHS. **A:** Jr. High-Adult. **P:** Education. **U:** Institution. **Gen-Edu:** Earthquakes. **Acq:** Purchase. **Dist:** Ark Media Group Ltd.

ABC: Family of Wolves 19??
Visits a Nova Scotia wolf preserve to study a pack of nine wolves. 25m; VHS. **A:** Jr. High-Adult. **P:** Education. **U:** Institution. **Gen-Edu:** Animals, Canada. **Acq:** Purchase. **Dist:** Ark Media Group Ltd.

ABC: Hummingbirds—Jewels of the Forest 19??
Visits the hummingbirds of Belize to discover how they survive, bathe, fight, and more. 25m; VHS. **A:** Jr. High-Adult. **P:** Education. **U:** Institution. **Gen-Edu:** Birds. **Acq:** Purchase. **Dist:** Ark Media Group Ltd.

ABC: Hunt for Hammerhead Sharks 19??
Visits the Sea of Cortez for an in-depth look at hammerhead sharks in their natural environment. 25m; VHS. **A:** Jr. High-Adult. **P:** Education. **U:** Institution. **Gen-Edu:** Fish. **Acq:** Purchase. **Dist:** Ark Media Group Ltd.

ABC: Lion—Africa's King of the Beasts 19??
A one year study of lions in the Ngorongoro Crater in Northern Tanzania. 50m; VHS. **A:** Jr. High-Adult. **P:** Education. **U:** Institution. **Gen-Edu:** Animals, Africa. **Acq:** Purchase **Dist:** Ark Media Group Ltd.

The ABC Man 1969
Treats such topics as personal growth in a technological age, career development, and individual versus organizational responsibilities. 22m; VHS, 3/4 U. **A:** College-Adult. **P:** Professional. **U:** Institution, SURA. **L:** English, Dutch, French, German, Portuguese, Spanish, Swedish. **Bus-Ind:** Management, Self-Help. **Acq:** Purchase, Rent/Lease. **Dist:** Learning Communications L.L.C.

ABC: Mantrap 1983
A music video that follows "Mantrap" on a path that leads from obscurity to international stardom. Includes many of their top hits: "Look of Love," "All of My Heart," and "Poison Arrow," and "Tears Are Not Enough," plus more. 54m; VHS. **Pr:** Michael Hamlyn. **A:** Family. **P:** Entertainment. **U:** Home. **Mov-Ent:** Music--Performance, Music--Pop/Rock. **Acq:** Purchase. **Dist:** Music Video Distributors; Sony Pictures Home Entertainment Inc. $16.95.

ABC News: A Line in the Sand—What Did America Win? 199?
Examines the prospects for peace in the Middle East and, in the wake of Operation Desert Storm, the effects of the war on weapons build-ups and political leadership in the region. 50m; VHS. **C:** Hosted by Peter Jennings. **Pr:** ABC News. **A:** Sr. High-Adult. **P:** Education. **U:** Home. **Gen-Edu:** Documentary Films, Middle East, Persian Gulf War. **Acq:** Purchase. **Dist:** MPI Media Group. $19.98.

ABC News: America Held Hostage—The Iran Crisis 1981
Relive the Iran Hostage Crisis through a compilation of original reports by ABC News' Ted Koppel and Sam Donaldson. This presentation chronicles the entire 444-day saga of Iran's kidnapping and detention of Americans after the U.S. granted refuge to the deposed Shah of Iran. 60m; VHS. **C:** Hosted by Ted Koppel; Sam Donaldson. **Pr:** ABC News. **A:** Jr. High-Adult. **P:** Education. **U:** Institution, Home. **Gen-Edu:** Documentary Films, Terrorism, Politics & Government. **Acq:** Purchase. **Dist:** MPI Media Group. $24.98.

ABC News: Behind Kremlin Walls 1989
The first American news team allowed to film inside the Kremlin, Sam Donaldson and Diane Sawyer host this look at the startling treasures that are housed within the Russian landmark. View the Grand Kremlin Palace which includes the Red Staircase (built by Czar Nicholas I), the Terem Palace (home to Russia's first Czar, Ivan the Terrible), the Armory Palace Museum, and more. 60m; VHS. **C:** Diane Sawyer; Sam Donaldson. **Pr:** ABC News. **A:** Jr. High-Adult. **P:** Education. **U:** Institution, Home. **Gen-Edu:** Documentary Films, USSR, International Relations. **Acq:** Purchase. **Dist:** MPI Media Group. $19.98.

ABC News: Capitol to Capitol 1989
A look at the discussions between world leaders and journalists, which were broadcast simultaneously to the Soviet Union and the United States. Also provided is an analysis of the goals and lifestyles of both countries when the Cold War ends. 55m; VHS. **C:** Hosted by Peter Jennings. **Pr:** ABC News. **A:** Sr. High-Adult. **P:** Education. **U:** Home. **Gen-Edu:** Documentary Films, World Affairs. **Acq:** Purchase. **Dist:** MPI Media Group. $19.98.

The ABC News Collection 1996
Features ABC News resources to give a retrospective of the political, social, and cultural events of the past 30 years. 1680m;

VHS. **A:** Jr. High-Adult. **P:** Education. **U:** Home, Institution. **Gen-Edu:** Politics & Government, History--U.S. **Acq:** Purchase. **Dist:** Knowledge Unlimited, Inc. $598.50.
Indiv. Titles: 1. The Fabulous '60s: The Decade that Changed Us All 2. The Sensational '70s 3. History of the '80s.

ABC News: Dark Days at the White House—The Watergate Scandal and the Resignation of President Richard M. Nixon 197?
A chronicle of ABC News' original coverage of the Watergate crisis, from the break-in at the office of Daniel Ellsberg's psychiatrist, to Nixon's unprecedented withdrawal from office. 60m; VHS. **Pr:** ABC News. **A:** Jr. High-Adult. **P:** Education. **U:** Institution, Home. **Gen-Edu:** Documentary Films, Politics & Government, History--U.S. **Acq:** Purchase. **Dist:** MPI Media Group. $24.98.

ABC News: Death on the Nile—The Struggle for Peace and the Assassination of Anwar Sadat 198?
The attempts of Egypt's Anwar Sadat to stop the bloodshed in the Middle East are chronicled via actual ABC News footage. Follow Sadat from his ambitious summit with Israel's Menachem Begin and Jimmy Carter in the U.S., to his vicious and senseless murder at the hands of Arab zealots. 60m; VHS. **C:** Hosted by Barbara Walters; Howard K. Smith; Frank Reynolds; Harry Reasoner. **Pr:** ABC News. **A:** Jr. High-Adult. **P:** Education. **U:** Institution, Home. **Gen-Edu:** Documentary Films, Middle East, Biography. **Acq:** Purchase. **Dist:** MPI Media Group. $24.98.

ABC News: Drugs—A Plague Upon the Land 198?
Hard investigative reporting on the out-of-control, gang-run drug scene in America. Use of cocaine, crack, heroin, PCP, and other drugs is literally destroying large segments of our society. 60m; VHS. **C:** Hosted by Peter Jennings. **Pr:** ABC News. **A:** Jr. High-Adult. **P:** Education. **U:** Home. **Gen-Edu:** Documentary Films, Drugs. **Acq:** Purchase. **Dist:** MPI Media Group. $19.98.

ABC News: Emergency! Health Care in America—A National Town Meeting 199?
Ted Koppel travels to the University of Chicago to discuss the lack of a comprehensive health care plan in the United States. A panel of experts, including congressmen, doctors, and representatives of several health care companies, answer audience questions. 120m; VHS. **C:** Hosted by Ted Koppel. **Pr:** ABC News. **A:** Sr. High-Adult. **P:** Education. **U:** Home. **Gen-Edu:** Documentary Films, Health Education. **Acq:** Purchase. **Dist:** MPI Media Group. $19.98.

ABC News: Events that Shaped Our World 1986
Includes key newscasts of 14 major events over the past 30 years that shaped world history such as assassinations, disasters, terrorism, the Vietnam war, and the Iran crisis. 30m; VHS. **Pr:** ABC News. **A:** Sr. High-Adult. **P:** Education. **U:** Home. **Gen-Edu:** Documentary Films, World Affairs, Politics & Government. **Acq:** Purchase. **Dist:** MPI Media Group. $9.98.

ABC News: Fall of Communism 1990
An examination of events surrounding the fall of the Berlin Wall, and the subsequent crumbling of communist regimes in Eastern Europe. 80m; VHS. **Pr:** ABC News. **A:** Sr. High-Adult. **P:** Education. **U:** Home. **Gen-Edu:** Documentary Films, World Affairs. **Acq:** Purchase. **Dist:** MPI Media Group. $19.98.

ABC News: First Ladies 1989
If you've ever wondered what kind of duties the Presidents' wives have, this ABC News special will show you. The presentation profiles the activities of Dolly Madison, Abigail Adams, Mary Todd Lincoln, Eleanor Roosevelt, Jacqueline Kennedy Onassis, Betty Ford, and, the queen of expensive clothing, Nancy Reagan. See what really goes on behind the doors of the White House. In color with black and white footage. 60m; VHS. **Pr:** ABC News. **A:** Jr. High-Adult. **P:** Education. **U:** Institution, Home. **Gen-Edu:** Documentary Films, Presidency, Politics & Government. **Acq:** Purchase. **Dist:** MPI Media Group. $19.98.

ABC News: From Disaster to Discovery—The Challenger Explosion and the Rebirth of America's Space Shuttle 1987
A collection of ABC News stories which chronicle the events surrounding the Challenger's last tragic mission, including a profile of and interviews with Crista McAuliffe, the first teacher in space. This presentation also examines the space shuttle program's recovery from the catastrophe. 60m; VHS. **Pr:** ABC News. **A:** Primary-Adult. **P:** Education. **U:** Institution, Home. **Gen-Edu:** Documentary Films, Space Exploration, History--Modern. **Acq:** Purchase. **Dist:** MPI Media Group. $24.98.

ABC News: Growing Up in the Age of AIDS 1992
Focuses on AIDS, the HIV virus, and what children, teenagers, and parents should know about the disease. Features some of the leading experts in health, medicine, and research with the latest available information. 75m; VHS. **C:** Hosted by Peter Jennings. **Pr:** ABC News. **A:** Jr. High-Adult. **P:** Education. **U:** Home. **Gen-Edu:** Documentary Films, AIDS. **Acq:** Purchase. **Dist:** MPI Media Group. $19.98.

ABC News: Guns 1990
Following a 1990 California killing spree with an AK-47 assault rifle, the question of restricting the sale of these weapons was heavily debated throughout the country. ABC News produced this examination of the gun control question including heated discussions between politicians and activists on both sides of the issue. 120m; VHS. **C:** Hosted by Peter Jennings. **Pr:** ABC News. **A:** Jr. High-Adult. **P:** Education. **U:** Institution, Home. **Gen-Edu:** Documentary Films, Gun control. **Acq:** Purchase. **Dist:** MPI Media Group. $19.98.

ABC News: Images of the '80s 198?
A retrospective of the biggest news stories of the 1980s. 52m; VHS. **C:** Hosted by Peter Jennings. **Pr:** ABC News. **A:** Jr. High-Adult. **P:** Education. **U:** Institution, Home. **Gen-Edu:** Documentary Films, Politics & Government. **Acq:** Purchase. **Dist:** MPI Media Group. $19.98.

ABC News: Inauguration 1993 1993
Coverage of President Bill Clinton's 1993 inauguration, from the bus trip to Washington, D.C., to the President's inaugural speech (in its entirety), and all the gala celebrations. 90m; VHS. **C:** Hosted by Peter Jennings; David Brinkley. **Pr:** ABC News. **A:** Sr. High-Adult. **P:** Entertainment. **U:** Home. **Gen-Edu:** Documentary Films, Presidency. **Acq:** Purchase. **Dist:** MPI Media Group. $19.98.

ABC News: Inside the White House 1989
Take a guided journey through the White House with the actual occupants, George and Barbara Bush. Discover the rooms where historical events took place. Marvel at the invaluable antiquities displayed throughout the mansion. Sam Donaldson and Dianne Sawyer originally hosted this presentation for ABC News. 50m; VHS. **C:** Hosted by Diane Sawyer; George Bush; Sam Donaldson; Barbara Bush. **Pr:** ABC News. **A:** Family. **P:** Education. **U:** Institution, Home. **Gen-Edu:** Documentary Films, Presidency. **Acq:** Purchase. **Dist:** MPI Media Group. $19.98.

ABC News: Israel vs. the PLO--Invasion of Lebanon 1982
In attempt to root out terrorists aligned with the Palestine Liberation Organization, Israel attacked Lebanon in 1982. This collection of ABC News reports chronicles the ensuing violence and examines the lingering hatred. 60m; VHS. **C:** Hosted by Peter Jennings; Sam Donaldson; Geraldo Rivera; Pierre Salinger; Frank Reynolds. **Pr:** ABC News. **A:** Jr. High-Adult. **P:** Education. **U:** Institution, Home. **Gen-Edu:** Documentary Films, War--General, Middle East. **Acq:** Purchase. **Dist:** MPI Media Group. $24.98.

ABC News: Mandela—The Man and His Country 1990
Following his release from prison in 1990, ABC News prepared this comprehensive biography of Nelson Mandela, from his place of birth to the celebration that accompanied his freedom. 50m; VHS. **C:** Narrated by Morton Dean. **Pr:** ABC. **A:** Jr. High-Family. **P:** Education. **U:** Institution, Home. **Gen-Edu:** Documentary Films, Biography, Africa. **Acq:** Purchase. **Dist:** MPI Media Group. $19.98.

ABC News: Muammar Qaddafi, Libya's Radical Ruler 1986
A collection of ABC News reports on the "Mad Dog of Libya" which recounts his rise to infamy in world affairs through dealmaking, terrorism, and his quest for nuclear technology. Includes clips of America's anti-terrorism, retaliatory air strikes in Tripoli. 60m; VHS. **Pr:** ABC News. **A:** Jr. High-Adult. **P:** Education. **U:** Institution, Home. **Gen-Edu:** Documentary Films, Biography, History--Modern. **Acq:** Purchase. **Dist:** MPI Media Group. $24.98.

ABC News: Nature's Fury—A Decade of Disasters 1989
Nature bats last and hits a grand slam in this collection of ABC News reports on catastrophes around the globe. The disasters include earthquakes, floods, tornados, hurricanes, and the eruption of Mt. St. Helens. 60m; VHS. **C:** Hosted by Peter Jennings; Hugh Downs; Max Robinson; Frank Reynolds. **Pr:** ABC News. **A:** Jr. High-Adult. **P:** Education. **U:** Institution, Home. **Gen-Edu:** Documentary Films, History--Modern. **Acq:** Purchase. **Dist:** MPI Media Group. $24.98.

ABC News: Nightline & Town Meeting—Pearl Harbor Plus 50 199?
Japanese commentators join Ted Koppel in Tokyo and Americans in five U.S. cities to discuss U.S.-Japanese relations, the trade deficit, and future relations between both countries. 90m; VHS. **C:** Hosted by Ted Koppel. **Pr:** ABC News. **A:** College-Adult. **P:** Education. **U:** Home. **Gen-Edu:** Documentary Films, Japan, U.S. States. **Acq:** Purchase. **Dist:** MPI Media Group. $19.98.

ABC News: On Trial—The William Kennedy Smith Case 1991
Chronicles the ABC News coverage of the rape trial of the accused, William Kennedy Smith, in Palm Beach, Florida. Includes courtroom coverage, reaction to the "not guilty" verdict, and Diane Sawyer's interview with Patricia Bowman, the alleged victim. 50m; VHS. **Pr:** ABC News. **A:** Sr. High-Adult. **P:** Education. **U:** Home. **Gen-Edu:** Documentary Films, Law, Rape. **Acq:** Purchase. **Dist:** MPI Media Group. $19.98.

ABC News: Pearl Harbor—Two Hours that Changed the World 199?
ABC News and NHK, the Japanese television network, combined to produced a program about the attack on Pearl Harbor 50 years ago. Includes archival stills and footage and a collection of interviews from more than 20 Pearl Harbor survivors, both Japanese and American. Also includes personal memories of the day from President George Bush, Hawaii's Senator Daniel Inouye, Japanese Prime Minister Kiichi Miyazawa, and former reporter Eric Sevareid. 100m; VHS. **C:** Hosted by David Brinkley. **Pr:** ABC News. **A:** Sr. High-Adult. **P:** Education. **U:** Home. **Gen-Edu:** Documentary Films, History--Modern, History--U.S. **Acq:** Purchase. **Dist:** MPI Media Group. $19.98.

ABC News: Peter Jennings from the Killing Fields 1986
An in-depth report of the continuing conflict in Southeast Asia since U.S. troops departed in 1975. The news team visited the killing fields; interviewed government and ex-government leaders, military commanders, and U.S politicians about the explosive situation in Cambodia. 160m; VHS. **C:** Hosted by Peter Jennings. **Pr:** ABC News. **A:** Sr. High-Adult. **P:** Education. **U:** Home. **Gen-Edu:** Documentary Films, War--General, Asia. **Acq:** Purchase. **Dist:** MPI Media Group. $19.98.

ABC News: Peter Jennings Reporting—Men, Sex and Rape 199?
ABC News traveled to Palm Beach, Florida, the site of the highly publicized William Kennedy Smith rape trial, to talk to rapists about what motives them; to victims about how the act has changed them; and to sexual assault experts about the link between sex and aggression. 75m; VHS. **C:** Hosted by Peter Jennings. **Pr:** ABC News. **A:** Sr. High-Adult. **P:** Education. **U:** Home. **Gen-Edu:** Documentary Films, Rape. **Acq:** Purchase. **Dist:** MPI Media Group. $19.98.

ABC News: Prejudice—Answering Children's Questions 199?
Peter Jennings leads an audience of culturally diverse children in an exploration of prejudice for a greater understanding of ourselves and to help appreciate our differences. 75m; VHS. **C:** Hosted by Peter Jennings. **Pr:** ABC News. **A:** Family. **P:** Education. **U:** Home. **Gen-Edu:** Documentary Films, Prejudice. **Acq:** Purchase. **Dist:** MPI Media Group. $19.98.

ABC News Presents: Jesus, Mary and Da Vinci 2004
Elizabeth Vargas uses Dan Brown's book, "The Da Vinci Code," to explore the idea that Jesus was married to Mary Magdalene and they had children. 55m; DVD. **A:** Jr. High-Adult. **P:** Entertainment. **U:** Home. **Gen-Edu:** Documentary Films. **Acq:** Purchase. **Dist:** Entertainment One US LP.

ABC News Presents: 25 on 20/20 2005
Newscaster Barbara Walters presents 25 years of her interviews, from presidents to celebrities. 88m; DVD. **A:** Jr. High-Adult. **P:** Entertainment. **U:** Home. **Gen-Edu:** Documentary Films. **Acq:** Purchase. **Dist:** Entertainment One US LP.

ABC News: Presidents 1990
Fascinating, comprehensive overview of the American presidency from Washington to Bush. Contains color and black and white footage. 60m; VHS. **Pr:** ABC News. **A:** Jr. High-Adult. **P:** Education. **U:** Institution, Home. **Gen-Edu:** Documentary Films, Presidency, History--U.S. **Acq:** Purchase. **Dist:** MPI Media Group. $19.95.

ABC News: Pushed to the Edge 199?
A special edition of the television newsmagazine "20/20" focusing on the growing number of women fighting back against abusive partners and rapists, including fighting through the judicial system. 50m; VHS. **Pr:** ABC News. **A:** Sr. High-Adult. **P:** Education. **U:** Home. **Gen-Edu:** Documentary Films, Women. **Acq:** Purchase. **Dist:** MPI Media Group. $19.98.

ABC News: Racing for the Moon—America's Glory Days in Space 1987
A review of America's blast-off into space, from the desperate Cold War race with the Russians to the triumphant lunar landing. 60m; VHS. **Pr:** ABC News. **A:** Jr. High-Adult. **P:** Entertainment. **U:** Home. **Gen-Edu:** Documentary Films, Space Exploration, History--U.S. **Acq:** Purchase. **Dist:** MPI Media Group. $24.98.

ABC News: Red Star Rising—The Dawn of the Gorbachev Era 1987
When Gorbachev took power after the death of Yuri Andropov, the world knew very little about this young and vital Soviet leader. This video examines his background, personal life, and professional ambitions. 60m; VHS. **Pr:** ABC News. **A:** Jr. High-Adult. **P:** Entertainment. **U:** Home. **Gen-Edu:** Documentary Films, Politics & Government, USSR. **Acq:** Purchase. **Dist:** MPI Media Group. $24.98.

ABC News: 17 Days of Terror—Hijack of TWA 847 198?
Recounts coverage by ABC News of the commandeering of a jetliner in the skies over Europe and its harrowing journey to the Middle East. Television veterans Peter Jennings, Sam Donaldson, Pierre Salinger, and Peter Glass are shown in fine form through actual news footage. 60m; VHS. **C:** Hosted by Peter Jennings; Sam Donaldson; Pierre Salinger; Peter Glass. **Pr:** ABC News. **A:** Jr. High-Adult. **P:** Education. **U:** Institution, Home. **Gen-Edu:** Documentary Films, Terrorism, History--Modern. **Acq:** Purchase. **Dist:** MPI Media Group. $24.98.

ABC News: 72 Hours to Victory: Behind the Scenes with Bill Clinton 1992
This ABC News Special highlights the days of November 2, 3, and 4th with a look at Bill Clinton, from presidential candidate to President-Elect. 60m; VHS. **C:** Hosted by Ted Koppel. **Pr:** ABC News. **A:** Sr. High-Adult. **P:** Entertainment. **U:** Home. **Gen-Edu:** Documentary Films, Presidency. **Acq:** Purchase. **Dist:** MPI Media Group. $19.98.

ABC News: Terrorism, the New World War 198?
A compilation of on-the-spot coverage by ABC News of terrorist acts around the world, from the murder of Israeli athletes in Munich to non-stop violence in Beirut. Discusses how terrorism has become an ever-increasing tool of protest by religious and political extremists. 60m; VHS. **C:** Hosted by Peter Jennings; Jim McKay; Sam Donaldson; Hugh Downs. **Pr:** ABC News. **A:** Jr. High-Adult. **P:** Education. **U:** Institution, Home. **Gen-Edu:** Documentary Films, Terrorism, History--Modern. **Acq:** Purchase. **Dist:** MPI Media Group. $24.98.

ABC News: The Great Debates—John F. Kennedy vs. Richard M. Nixon 1960
See the debates that changed the shape of American history as they actually happened in 1960. Moderated by Howard K.

Smith. 60m; VHS. **Pr:** ABC News. **A:** Jr. High-Adult. **P:** Entertainment. **U:** Home. **Gen-Edu:** Documentary Films, Politics & Government, Presidency. **Acq:** Purchase. **Dist:** MPI Media Group. $24.98.

ABC News: The Perfect Baby 1988
Discusses the problems and ethical choices that future parents may have to face regarding genetic engineering. 59m; VHS. **C:** Hosted by Barbara Walters. **Pr:** ABC News. **A:** Jr. High-Adult. **P:** Education. **U:** Home. **Gen-Edu:** Documentary Films, Genetics, Ethics & Morals. **Acq:** Purchase. **Dist:** MPI Media Group. $14.98.

ABC News: The San Francisco Earthquake, October 17, 1989 1990
An account of what happened on the day when the Earth shook at 7.1 on the Richter scale. Many people were on the Nimitz Highway on their way to the World Series and were killed when portions of the road collapsed. This video examines the loss in terms of lives and dollars, and looks at the many accounts of heroics that took place. 60m; VHS. **Pr:** ABC News. **A:** Jr. High-Adult. **P:** Education. **U:** Institution, Home. **Gen-Edu:** Documentary Films, Earthquakes, U.S. States. **Acq:** Purchase. **Dist:** MPI Media Group. $19.98.

ABC News: The Turbulent End to a Tragic War—America's Final Hours in Vietnam 1975
A collection of ABC News stories on the end of the United States' involvement in the Vietnam War. This presentation chronicles the tragic abandonment of the U.S. embassy in Saigon and the general havoc in a country about to be overrun by the Khmer Rouge. 60m; VHS. **C:** Hosted by Ted Koppel; Frank Reynolds; Harry Reasoner; Tom Jerrell. **Pr:** ABC News. **A:** Jr. High-Adult. **P:** Education. **U:** Institution, Home. **Gen-Edu:** Documentary Films, Vietnam War, History--U.S. **Acq:** Purchase. **Dist:** MPI Media Group. $24.98.

ABC News: The Week that Shook the World—The Soviet Coup 1991
A chronicle of ABC News coverage of the attempted coup in the Soviet Union from August 19-25, 1991. Includes Diane Sawyer's interview with Boris Yeltsin while he was under siege in the Russian Parliament building and Ted Koppel's "Nightline" broadcast from Moscow. 65m; VHS. **C:** Hosted by Peter Jennings; Ted Koppel; Diane Sawyer. **Pr:** ABC News. **A:** Sr. High-Adult. **P:** Education. **U:** Home. **Gen-Edu:** Documentary Films, History--Modern, USSR. **Acq:** Purchase. **Dist:** MPI Media Group. $19.98.

ABC News: Town Meeting—A Process Run Amok—Thomas/Hill Hearings 1991
Ted Koppel leads a discussion focusing on the Supreme Court nomination hearings of Clarence Thomas and the controversial testimony of Anita Hill. He is joined by Senators Alan Simpson, Arlen Specter, Paul Simon, and Bill Bradley as well as a number of journalists and government officials. 90m; VHS. **C:** Hosted by Ted Koppel. **Pr:** ABC News. **A:** Sr. High-Adult. **P:** Education. **U:** Home. **Gen-Edu:** Documentary Films, Law. **Acq:** Purchase. **Dist:** MPI Media Group. $19.98.

ABC News: Volcano! The Eruption of Mt. St. Helens 1983
The eruption of Mount St. Helens brought incredible destruction to the Northwest, and the cameras were there to record it. 60m; VHS. **Pr:** ABC News. **A:** Jr. High-Adult. **P:** Entertainment. **U:** Home. **Gen-Edu:** Documentary Films, Volcanos, History--Modern. **Acq:** Purchase. **Dist:** MPI Media Group. $24.98.

ABC News: We Interrupt this Program 1990
The viewer is taken back in time to three major interrupting broadcasts of recent history: The Martin Luther King assassination of April 4, 1968; the hijack of TWA Flight #847 and the San Francisco earthquake of October 17, 1989. Using the original news footage from special bulletins, this program makes you feel that you were actually there when the story broke. 55m; VHS. **Pr:** ABC News. **A:** Jr. High-Adult. **P:** Entertainment. **U:** Home. **Gen-Edu:** Documentary Films, Mass Media. **Acq:** Purchase. **Dist:** MPI Media Group. $19.98.

ABC News: What's a Parent to Do? 199?
The trials and tribulations of raising children are explored with host John Stossel. 50m; VHS. **C:** Hosted by John Stossel. **Pr:** ABC News. **A:** College-Adult. **P:** Education. **U:** Home. **Gen-Edu:** Documentary Films, Parenting. **Acq:** Purchase. **Dist:** MPI Media Group. $19.98.

ABC Notebook: Learn to Read 1987
Ted Koppel hosts this look at three formerly illiterate adults, including the programs and friends that helped them learn to read. Discusses the many ways illiterate adults can learn to read. 23m; VHS, 8 mm, 3/4 U. **TV Std:** NTSC, PAL, SECAM. **Pr:** ABC Community Relations. **A:** Family. **P:** Education. **U:** Institution, CCTV, SURA. **Gen-Edu:** Documentary Films, Learning Disabilities. **Acq:** Purchase, Rent/Lease, Duplication License. **Dist:** Phoenix Learning Group. $250.00.

ABC Notebook: Making the News 1986
Provides an informative behind-the-scenes look at television news. 24m; VHS, 3/4 U. **Pr:** ABC Community Relations. **A:** Sr. High-Adult. **P:** Education. **U:** Institution, CCTV, SURA. **Gen-Edu:** Documentary Films, Mass Media. **Acq:** Purchase, Rent/Lease. **Dist:** Phoenix Learning Group.

ABC: Puffins 19??
Looks at Scotland's Shetland Isles' mysterious puffins. 25m; VHS. **A:** Jr. High-Adult. **P:** Education. **U:** Institution. **Gen-Edu:** Scotland, Animals. **Acq:** Purchase. **Dist:** Ark Media Group Ltd.

ABC: Realm of the Serpent 19??
Takes a look at snakes, from Burmese cobras to Texas rattlesnakes. 50m; VHS. **A:** Jr. High-Adult. **P:** Education. **U:** Institution. **Gen-Edu**: Animals. **Acq:** Purchase. **Dist:** Ark Media Group Ltd.

ABC: Secrets of the Golden River 19??
Documentary look at the Amiga River Basin, its people, and surrounding life. 50m; VHS. **A:** Jr. High-Adult. **P:** Education. **U:** Institution. **Gen-Edu. Acq:** Purchase. **Dist:** Ark Media Group Ltd.

ABC: Shark Chronicles 19??
Travels the depths of the ocean capturing the beauty and grace of sharks. 50m; VHS. **A:** Jr. High-Adult. **P:** Education. **U:** Institution. **Gen-Edu**: Animals. **Acq:** Purchase. **Dist:** Ark Media Group Ltd.

ABC: Sharks—Perfect Predators 19??
Spotlights the amazing predatory abilities of sharks as they continue to dominate the underwater realm. 25m; VHS. **A:** Jr. High-Adult. **P:** Education. **U:** Institution. **Gen-Edu**: Fish. **Acq:** Purchase. **Dist:** Ark Media Group Ltd.

ABC: Spiders—Web of Steel 19??
Investigates spiders and their web-building techniques. 25m; VHS. **A:** Jr. High-Adult. **P:** Education. **U:** Institution. **Gen-Edu**: Insects. **Acq:** Purchase. **Dist:** Ark Media Group Ltd.

ABC Stage 67: Truman Capote's A Christmas Memory 1966 — ★★½
Capote narrates his remembered childhood experience of baking dozens of fruitcakes for friends at Christmas with his elderly distant cousin, Miss Sook Faulk (Page). She is quiet, lovely, and true in this sensitive portrait of why we give and what we have to be thankful for. Adapted from a short story by Capote and Eleanor Perry. 51m/B/W; VHS, DVD, 8 mm. **C:** Geraldine Page; Donnie Melvin; Narrated by Truman Capote; Directed by Frank Perry; Written by Truman Capote. **Pr:** ABC. **A:** Family. **P:** Entertainment. **U:** Home. **Mov-Ent**: Christmas, TV Movies. **Acq:** Purchase. **Dist:** Movies Unlimited; Amazon.com Inc. $24.99.

ABC: The Legend of the Bison 19??
Visits Yellowstone National Park to take a look at the bison. 25m; VHS. **A:** Jr. High-Adult. **P:** Education. **U:** Institution. **Gen-Edu**: Animals. **Acq:** Purchase. **Dist:** Ark Media Group Ltd.

ABC: Whale Rescue 19??
Examines whale rescues from fishing nets. 25m; VHS. **A:** Jr. High-Adult. **P:** Education. **U:** Institution. **Gen-Edu**: Animals. **Acq:** Purchase. **Dist:** Ark Media Group Ltd.

ABC: Wild Dogs 19??
Visits Africa's Serengeti Plain to study a pack of wild dogs. Investigates their hunting, battle and socializing skills. 25m; VHS. **A:** Jr. High-Adult. **P:** Education. **U:** Institution. **Gen-Edu**: Animals. **Acq:** Purchase. **Dist:** Ark Media Group Ltd.

ABC: Wildebeest—Race for Life 19??
Looks at the struggle of the wildebeests during their migration across African plains. 50m; VHS. **A:** Jr. High-Adult. **P:** Education. **U:** Institution. **Gen-Edu**: Animals, Africa. **Acq:** Purchase. **Dist:** Ark Media Group Ltd.

ABC World of Discovery 199?
Six-part nature education series featuring live-action footage of different animals in their natural habitats. 300m; VHS. **A:** Primary-College. **P:** Education. **U:** Institution. **Hea-Sci**: Wildlife, Animals, Documentary Films. **Acq:** Purchase. **Dist:** Cambridge Educational. $119.88.
Indiv. Titles: 1. Cougar: Ghost of the Rockies 2. Beautiful Killers 3. Wildebeest: Race for Life 4. The Secret Life of 118 Green Street 5. Crocodile's Revenge 6. Wolf: Return of a Legend.

ABC World of Discovery: Crocodile's Revenge 1990
Part of the "ABC World of Discovery" series. Enters the world of the crocodile, illustrating some of the creature's daily activities. 50m; VHS. **Pr:** ABC. **A:** Jr. High-Adult. **P:** Education. **U:** Institution. **Hea-Sci**: Science, Wildlife, Documentary Films. **Acq:** Purchase. **Dist:** Cambridge Educational. $24.98.

ABC World of Discovery: The Secret Life of 118 Green Street 1993
Part of the "ABC World of Discovery" series. Examines the amazing unseen world, illustrating the beauty of the things which we take for granted. 50m; VHS. **Pr:** ABC. **A:** Jr. High-Adult. **P:** Education. **U:** Institution. **Hea-Sci**: Science, Wildlife, Documentary Films. **Acq:** Purchase. **Dist:** Cambridge Educational. $24.98.

ABCD 1999 (Unrated) — ★★½
Touching story of an Asian Indian-American family living in New York. Siblings Raj and Nina have grown up in America, and have struggled with the competing pressures of their peers and their parent's old-world expectations. Their widowed mother wants them to settle down with suitable Indian spouse. Patel shows humor, and largely avoids stereotypes (although the mother ventures dangerously close), and the kids manage to be fully-realized characters. 102m; VHS, DVD. **C:** Madhur Jaffrey; Faran Tahir; Sheetal Sheth; Aasif Mandvi; Adriane Forlana Erdos; Rex Young; Directed by Krutin Patel; Written by Krutin Patel; James McManus; Cinematography by Milton Kam; Music by Deirdre Broderick. **Pr:** Krutin Patel; Krutin Patel; Naju Patel; Laxmi Pictures; Eros Films. **A:** Sr. High-Adult. **P:** Entertainment. **U:** Home. **Mov-Ent**: Marriage. **Acq:** Purchase. **Dist:** Wellspring Media.

The ABC's of AIDS 1991
Two-part video that provides skill-building techniques and information on HIV/AIDS. Part One demonstrates ways to avoid negative peer pressure. Part Two uses a MTV-style presentation to introduce HIV and AIDS transmission and risk behaviors. 15m; VHS, 3/4 U, Special order formats. **Pr:** O.D.N. Productions. **A:** Primary. **P:** Education. **U:** Institution. **Chl-Juv**: Health Education, AIDS. **Acq:** Purchase, Rent/Lease. **Dist:** Select Media, Inc. $295.00.

The ABC's of Canadian Family Life 1978
A series that covers several aspects of Canadian parents and children, including child and wife abuse, divorce, and single parents. Available separately. 8m; VHS, 3/4 U. **Pr:** University of Toronto. **A:** College-Adult. **P:** Education. **U:** Institution, CCTV. **Gen-Edu**: Family Viewing, Family. **Acq:** Purchase, Rent/Lease. **Dist:** University of Toronto.
Indiv. Titles: 1. C Is for Child Abuse 2. D Is for Divorce 3. F Is for Female Labour Force 4. J Is for Joy of Family 5. O Is for Old People 6. S Is for Single Parent Families 7. V Is for Voluntary Childlessness 8. W Is for Wife Abuse.

The ABCs of Death 2012 (Unrated) — ★★½
Twenty-six vignettes offer death-by-alphabet. Some fun, some repulsive, and some head-scratchers, 26 directors are set loose in each of their segments, making for some fairly twisted storytelling. No filmmaker was limited in style, direction or subject; thus, there are multiple languages and formats, keeping things interesting. And, fortunately none are very long, as 26 letters are represented in the anthology's two-plus hours of runtime, so if D is for Dogfight is bringing you down, hang on because F is for Fart isn't far behind. 123m; DVD, Blu-Ray. **C:** Ivan Gonzalez; Kyra Zagorsky; Voice(s) by Ingrid Bolso Berdal; Directed by Kaare Andrews; Angela Bettis; Helene Cattet; Ernesto Diaz Espinoza; Jason Eisener; Bruno Forzani; Andria Bogliano; Xavier Gens; Lee Hardcastle; Noboru Iguchi; Thomas Cappelen Maaling; Jorge Grau; Anders Morgenthaler; Yoshihiro Nishimura; Banjong Pisanthanakun; Marcel Samiento; Jon Schnepp; Srdjan Spasojevic; Timo Tjahjanto; Andrew Traucki; Nacho Vigalondo; Jake West; Ti West; Ben Wheatley; Adam Wingard; Yudai Yamaguchi; Written by Kaare Andrews; Helene Cattet; Bruno Forzani; Andria Bogliano; Lee Hardcastle; Noboru Iguchi; Yoshihiro Nishimura; Simon Rumley; Srdjan Spasojevic; Nacho Vigalondo; Ti West; Yudai Yamaguchi; Simon Barrett; Dimitrie Vojnov; Cinematography by Harris Charalambous; Manuel Dacosse; Magnus Flato; Ernesto Herrera; Karim Hussain; Nicolas Ibieta; Nemanja Jovanov; Antoine Marteau; Shu G. Momose; Yasutaka Nagano; Laurie Rose; Music by Phillip Blackford; Simon Boswell; Yasuhiko Fukuda; Nobuhiko Morino; Kou Nakagawa; Julio Pillado; Johannes Ringen. **Pr:** Nahikari Ipina; Claire Jones; Julie Lind-holm; Petter Lindblad; Douglas Nabors; Andrea Quiroz; Chris Sergi; Andrew Starke; Lino P. Stavole; Christopher White; Yoshihiro Nishimura; Simon Boswell; Drafthouse Films; Magnet Releasing. **A:** Sr. High-Adult. **P:** Entertainment. **U:** Home. **L:** English. **Mov-Ent. Acq:** Purchase. **Dist:** Not Yet Released.

The ABC's of Decision Making 1984
Enables supervisors to identify the three keys to a good decision. 90m; 3/4 U. **Pr:** Creative Media. **A:** College-Adult. **P:** Education. **U:** Institution. **Bus-Ind**: How-To, Business, Management. **Acq:** Purchase, Rent/Lease. **Dist:** SkillSoft.

ABCs of Eligibility for College-Bound Student Athletes 1994
Program for students, parents, counselors, and coaches which explains everything that student athletes need to know when they are deciding about their academic and sports goals. Includes information on 1995 and 1996 NCAA regulations, academic requirements, recruitment rules, recruiting pressures, and the pros and cons of aiming for a career in sports. 33m; VHS. **A:** Sr. High-Adult. **P:** Education. **U:** Institution, Home. **Gen-Edu**: Education, Sports--General. **Acq:** Purchase. **Dist:** The College Board. $49.95.

ABC's of Family Life Series 1978
Eight-part series which focuses on different aspects of family life in Canada. 61m; VHS. **A:** Family. **P:** Education. **U:** Institution, Home. **Gen-Edu**: Family, Sociology, Canada. **Acq:** Purchase. **Dist:** University of Toronto. $139.00.
Indiv. Titles: 1. C is for Child Abuse 2. D is for Divorce 3. F is for Female Labour Force 4. J is for Joy of Family 5. O is for Old People 6. S is for Single Parent 7. V is for Voluntary Childlessness 8. W is for Wife Abuse.

The ABC's of Landscape Pruning 1989
Two short tapes designed for landscape maintenance professionals with an emphasis on large trees and public landscapes and an explantaion of Shigo's principles. Photographed in Arizona; includes reference guides. 20m; VHS. **A:** Adult. **P:** Instruction. **U:** Institution. **How-Ins**: Landscaping. **Acq:** Purchase. **Dist:** American Nurseryman Publishing Co. $189.00.

The ABC's of Learning the ABC's 1995
Teaches a child his/her ABC's. 15m; VHS. **A:** Preschool. **P:** Instruction. **U:** Home. **Chl-Juv**: How-To, Children. **Acq:** Purchase. **Dist:** Paragon Home Video. $14.95.

The ABC's of Pediatric Trauma Nursing 1989
Airway, Breathing, and Circulation are given as the three things to look for first in a pediatric emergency. 28m; VHS, 3/4 U. **Pr:** Hospital Satellite Network. **A:** Adult. **P:** Professional. **U:** Institution, CCTV, SURA. **Hea-Sci**: How-To, Nursing, Pediatrics. **Acq:** Purchase, Rent/Lease. **Dist:** AJN Video Library/Lippincott Williams & Wilkins. $275.00.

The ABC's of Personal Finance: An Essential Management ????
Identifies for young buyers the advantages of being an education consumer and financial enemies such as inflation and taxes. 24m; VHS. **A:** Sr. High. **P:** Education. **U:** Institution. **Gen-Edu**: Economics, Consumer Education. **Acq:** Purchase. **Dist:** Zenger Media. $39.95.

The ABC's of Sewing 1993
Lina Ingraham, a home economist, clearly demonstrates how to sew a pair of shorts, a tank top, and a straight skirt. Includes step-by-step instructions on stitching, seam finishing, final pressing, and applying a zipper. 120m; VHS. **A:** Jr. High-Adult. **P:** Education. **U:** Home. **How-Ins**: How-To, Sewing, Hobbies. **Acq:** Purchase. **Dist:** Cambridge Educational. $49.00.

The ABC's of STD's 1989
Outlines the risks of sexually transmitted diseases, and encourages greater partner communication. 20m; VHS, 3/4 U. **Pr:** Polymorph Films. **A:** Jr. High-Adult. **P:** Education. **U:** Institution, Home. **Hea-Sci**: Health Education, Sexually Transmitted Diseases. **Acq:** Purchase, Rent/Lease. **Dist:** Polymorph Films, Inc.

The ABC's of STD's Straight Talk 2000
Overviews many types of sexually transmitted diseases and their effects. 24m; VHS. **A:** Adult. **P:** Professional. **U:** Institution. **Hea-Sci**: Sexually Transmitted Diseases, Health Education. **Acq:** Purchase. **Dist:** Aquarius Health Care Media. $99.00.

The Abdication 1974 (Unrated) — ★½
Unconvincing historical bio of Sweden's Queen Christina (Ullmann) who relinquishes her 17th-century throne after converting to Catholicism. She heads to Rome but rather than finding herself dedicated to God, Christina becomes more interested in Cardinal Azzolino (Finch). Wolff adapted from her play. Garbo did it much better in 1933's "Queen Christina." 102m; DVD. **C:** Peter Finch; Cyril Cusack; Graham Crowden; Michael Dunn; Liv Ullman; Kathleen Byron; Directed by Anthony Harvey; Written by Ruth Wolff; Cinematography by Geoffrey Unsworth; Music by Nino Rota. **A:** Jr. High-Adult. **P:** Entertainment. **U:** Home. **Mov-Ent**: Drama, Biography: Royalty, Religion. **Acq:** Purchase. **Dist:** WarnerArchive.com.

The Abdominal Cavity 1984
A medical definition of the body cavity and its visceral organs. 28m; 3/4 U. **Pr:** McMaster University. **A:** Adult. **P:** Professional. **U:** Institution, SURA. **Hea-Sci**: Anatomy & Physiology, Medical Education. **Acq:** Purchase, Rent/Lease. **Dist:** McMaster University.

Abdominal Contents 1984
A medical survey of abdominal organs, provided on two tapes. 43m; 3/4 U. **Pr:** McMaster University. **A:** Adult. **P:** Professional. **U:** Institution, SURA. **Hea-Sci**: Anatomy & Physiology, Medical Education. **Acq:** Purchase, Rent/Lease. **Dist:** McMaster University.

Abdominal Hysterectomy 1991
Follows a hysterectomy patient from her hospital admission through her complete recovery weeks later. Animation shows the anatomy and physiology of the procedure. 15m; VHS, 3/4 U. **Pr:** Milner-Fenwick. **A:** Adult. **P:** Education. **U:** Institution, CCTV. **L:** English, French, Spanish. **Hea-Sci**: Gynecology. **Acq:** Purchase. **Dist:** Milner-Fenwick, Inc.

The Abdominal Wall 1984
Abdominal muscles are examined medically. 26m; 3/4 U. **Pr:** McMaster University. **A:** Adult. **P:** Professional. **U:** Institution, SURA. **Hea-Sci**: Anatomy & Physiology, Medical Education. **Acq:** Purchase, Rent/Lease. **Dist:** McMaster University.

Abducted 1986 (PG) — ★½
A woman jogger is abducted by a crazed mountain man in the Canadian Rockies. Weird and unbelievably tedious film is nevertheless highlighted by some spectacular wilderness footage of the Vancouver area, a travelogue bonus for those in the mood. 87m; VHS. **C:** Dan Haggerty; Roberta Weiss; Lawrence King Phillips; Directed by Boon Collins. **Pr:** Modern Cinema Marketing. **A:** Jr. High-Adult. **P:** Entertainment. **U:** Home. **Mov-Ent**: Wilderness Areas, Canada. **Acq:** Purchase. **Dist:** Unknown Distributor.

Abducted 2: The Reunion 1994 (R) — ★½
Three girlfriends decide to go camping for their reunion trip. Oops—psycho mountain man alert! 91m; VHS. **C:** Dan Haggerty; Jan-Michael Vincent; Donna Jason; Raquel Bianca; Debbie Rochon; Lawrence King; Directed by Boon Collins; Written by Boon Collins; Cinematography by Danny Nowak. **A:** Sr. High-Adult. **P:** Entertainment. **U:** Home. **Mov-Ent**: Horror. **Acq:** Purchase.

Abducted: The Carlina White Story 2012 (Unrated) — ★★½
True crime from the Lifetime Channel. In 1987, new mom Joy White has her infant daughter kidnapped from a Harlem hospital by a woman posing as a nurse. Some years later, pregnant teen Netty Pettway (Parker) needs her birth certificate and social security info, which her mom Ann (Ellis) doesn't have. A long investigation ensues but it's not entirely a happy ending. 90m; DVD. **C:** Keke Palmer; Aunjanue Ellis; Sherri Shepherd; Roger R. Cross; Directed by Vondie Curtis-Hall; Written by Elizabeth Hunter; Cinematography by Thomas M. (Tom) Harting; Music by Terence Blanchard. **A:** Jr. High-Adult. **P:** Entertainment. **U:** Home. **L:** English. **Mov-Ent**: TV Movies, Family. **Acq:** Purchase. **Dist:** A&E Television Networks L.L.C.

Abduction 1975 (R) — ★½
Exploitative account of the Patty Hearst kidnapping, loosely adapted from the Harrison James novel written before the kidnapping. A young woman from a wealthy capitalist family is kidnapped by black radicals and held for an unusual ransom.

Oh, and she tangles with lesbians, too. 100m; VHS. **C:** Judith-Marie Bergan; David Pendleton; Gregory Rozakis; Leif Erickson; Dorothy Malone; Lawrence Tierney; Directed by Joseph Zito. **Pr:** Kent E. Carroll. **A:** Sr. High-Adult. **P:** Entertainment. **U:** Home. **Mov-Ent:** Satire & Parody, Exploitation. **Acq:** Purchase. **Dist:** Movies Unlimited. $18.99.

The Abduction 1996 (Unrated) — ★★½
Fact-based melodrama about Kate Olavsky (Principal) and her abusive marriage to cop Paul (Hays). Afraid to press charges, she finally manages to leave him and get on with her life. But Paul refuses to let Kate go, constantly hounding her, until he takes Kate hostage at gunpoint. 91m; VHS, DVD. **C:** Victoria Principal; Robert Hays; Christopher Lawford; William Greenblatt; Directed by Larry Peerce; Written by Marshall Goldberg; Cinematography by Tony Imi; Music by Fred Mollin. **A:** Sr. High-Adult. **P:** Entertainment. **U:** Home. **Mov-Ent:** Domestic Abuse. **Acq:** Purchase. **Dist:** Alpha Video.

Abduction 2007 (R) — ★
Low budget crapfest about a New Jersey town that kidnaps tourists so they can sell women and babies to the wealthy and cut up everyone else to harvest their organs. 106m; DVD. **C:** John Orrichio; Tony Rugnetta; Roberto Lombardi; Directed by John Orrichio; Written by John Orrichio; Cinematography by John Orrichio; Music by John Orrichio. **A:** Sr. High-Adult. **P:** Entertainment. **U:** Home. **L:** English. **Mov-Ent. Acq:** Purchase. **Dist:** R2 Films Llc. $14.99.

Abduction 2011 (PG-13) — **Bomb!**
A young man (Lautner) discovers his secret past and must go on the run when his whereabouts are revealed to people seeking him for over a decade. Lautner is unbelievable as the strong leading man type and the film completely flies off the rails in a rushed and senseless final act. And what was the accomplished Weaver thinking when she signed on? Filled with plot holes more interesting to think about than the actual plot. 106m; DVD, Blu-Ray. **C:** Taylor Lautner; Lily Collins; Alfred Molina; Jason Isaacs; Maria Bello; Michael Nyqvist; Sigourney Weaver; Directed by John Singleton; Written by Shawn Christensen; Cinematography by Peter Menzies, Jr.; Music by Edward Shearmur. **Pr:** Doug Davison; Dan Lautner; Lee Stollman; Ellen Goldsmith-Vein; Roy Lee; Gotham Group; Vertigo Entertainment; Quick Six Entertainment; Mango Farms; Lionsgate. **A:** Jr. High-Adult. **P:** Entertainment. **U:** Home. **L:** English. **Mov-Ent. Acq:** Purchase. **Dist:** Lions Gate Home Entertainment.

Abduction from the Seraglio 1980
The delightfully playful opera about human love, ideas, and faith written by young Mozart features the comic figure Osmin. Performed by The Dresden State Opera in its original German arrangement. Conducted by Harry Kupfer. 129m; VHS. **A:** Adult. **P:** Entertainment. **U:** Home. **Fin-Art:** Opera. **Acq:** Purchase. **Dist:** V.I.E.W. Inc./Arkadia Entertainment Corp.; Music Video Distributors; German Language Video Center. $29.98.

Abduction from the Seraglio 1986
A performance of the Mozart opera performed at the Royal Opera House in Convent Garden. In German with English subtitles. In hi-fi Stereo. 146m; VHS. **C:** Deon van der Walt; Oliver Tobias; Inge Nielsen; Directed by George Solti. **Pr:** NVC Arts International; British Broadcasting Corporation; Royal Opera House. **A:** Family. **P:** Entertainment. **U:** Home. **L:** German. **Fin-Art:** Opera. **Acq:** Purchase. **Dist:** Home Vision Cinema; Facets Multimedia Inc.; Music Video Distributors. $99.95.

The Abduction of Allison Tate 1992 (R) — ★½
Rich developer takes land belonging to a group of Native Americans. Three young tribe members retaliate by kidnapping the developer's daughter. But when their plans go awry and one of the trio is killed, Allison finds herself sympathizing more with them than with her father's ambitions. 95m; VHS. **C:** Leslie Hope; Bernie (Bernard) White; Directed by Paul Leder. **A:** Sr. High-Adult. **P:** Entertainment. **U:** Home. **Mov-Ent:** Crime Drama, Native Americans. **Acq:** Purchase. **Dist:** No Longer Available.

The Abduction of Kari Swenson 1987 — ★½
An account of the true-life (it really happened) kidnapping of Olympic biathalon hopeful Swensen by a pair of mischievous Montana mountain men with matrimony in mind. The movie details the abduction of Swenson by the scruffy father and son duo and the massive manhunt. As the put-upon Kari, Pollan exceeds script expectations in this exercise in stress avoidance. 100m; VHS. **C:** Joe Don Baker; M. Emmet Walsh; Ronny Cox; Michael Bowen; Geoffrey Blake; Dorothy Fielding; Tracy Pollan; Directed by Stephen Gyllenhaal. **A:** Jr. High-Adult. **P:** Entertainment. **U:** Home. **Mov-Ent:** Crime Drama, TV Movies. **Acq:** Purchase. **Dist:** CinemaNow Inc. $79.95.

Abduction of St. Anne 1975 (Unrated) — ★★
An almost interesting mystical thriller about a detective and a bishop trying to track down a gangster's daughter, who may have nifty supernatural healing powers the Church would be very interested in having documented. 78m; VHS. **C:** Robert Wagner; E.G. Marshall; William Windom; Lloyd Nolan; Directed by Harry Falk; Music by George Duning. **Pr:** Quinn Martin Productions. **A:** Jr. High-Adult. **P:** Entertainment. **U:** Home. **Mov-Ent:** Mystery & Suspense, TV Movies, Religion. **Acq:** Purchase. **Dist:** $49.95.

The Abductors 1972 (R) — ★
Caffaro's super-agent takes on international white slavery, a worthy target for any exploitation effort. While the novelty is a tough and intelligent on-screen heroine, sufficient sleaze and violence bring it all down to the proper level of swampland video. Sequel to the never-to-be-forgotten "Ginger." 90m; VHS, DVD. **C:** Cheri Caffaro; William Grannel; Richard Smedley; Patrick Wright; Laurie Rose; Jeramie Rain; Directed by Don Schain; Written by Don Schain; Cinematography by R. Kent Evans; Music by Robert G. Orpin. **A:** College-Adult. **P:** Entertainment. **U:** Home. **Mov-Ent:** Slavery. **Acq:** Purchase. **Dist:** Monterey Home Video. $39.95.

Abdulaziz 1999
Documents the fifty year reign of King Abdulaziz ibn Saud, a soldier, statesman and religious leader committed to strengthening and developing peace in Saudi Arabia. 90m; VHS. **A:** Adult. **P:** Education. **U:** Home. **Gen-Edu:** Middle East, Biography, Documentary Films. **Acq:** Purchase. **Dist:** Arab Film Distribution. $49.99.

Abdulla the Great 1956 (Unrated) — ★★
A dissolute Middle Eastern monarch falls for a model, who spurns him for an army officer. While distracted by these royal shenanigans, the king is blissfully unaware of his subjects' disaffection—until they revolt. Dares to lampoon Egypt's dead King Farouk, going against conventional Hollywood wisdom ("Farouk in film is boxoffice poison"). 89m; VHS, DVD. **TV Std:** NTSC, PAL. **C:** Gregory Ratoff; Kay Kendall; Syd Chaplin; Alexander D'Arcy; Directed by Gregory Ratoff; Cinematography by Lee Garmes; Music by Georges Auric. **Pr:** Gregory Ratoff; Gregory Ratoff. **A:** Sr. High-Adult. **P:** Entertainment. **U:** Home. **Mov-Ent:** Comedy--Romantic, Africa. **Acq:** Purchase. **Dist:** Movies Unlimited. $24.95.

Abdullah Ibrahim: A Brother with Perfect Timing 1987
An unusual biography of the innovative jazz musician. Abdullah Ibrahim (Dollar Brand) who left South Africa in the 1960s and integrated many different cultures into his music: African, Arabic, Oriental, European and American. The musician talks about his childhood, the spiritual implications behind his music and demonstrates parts of his music that he doesn't show in concert. 90m; VHS. **C:** Directed by Ekaya. **A:** Jr. High-Adult. **P:** Entertainment. **U:** Home. **Mov-Ent:** Documentary Films, Music--Jazz, Biography. **Acq:** Purchase. **Dist:** Rhapsody Films, Inc. $29.95.

Abe Ajay: Dimension x 3 1990
Artist Abe Ajay talks about his childhood, his student days in New York City, the Federal Arts Project, and the philosophy behind his meticulous art. 29m; VHS. **A:** Jr. High-Adult. **P:** Education. **U:** Institution. **Fin-Art:** Biography, Art & Artists. **Acq:** Purchase. **Dist:** Green Mountain Post Films. $29.95.

Abe Lincoln in Illinois 1940 (Unrated) — ★★★★
Massey considered this not only his finest film but a part he was "born to play." Correct on both counts, this Hollywood biography follows Lincoln from his log cabin days to his departure for the White House. The Lincoln-Douglass debate scene and Massey's post-presidential election farewell to the citizens of Illinois are nothing short of brilliant. Written by Sherwood from his Pulitzer-Prize winning play. Contrasted with the well-known "Young Mr. Lincoln" (Henry Fonda), its relative anonymity is perplexing. 110m/B/W; VHS, DVD. **C:** Raymond Massey; Gene Lockhart; Ruth Gordon; Mary Howard; Dorothy Tree; Harvey Stephens; Minor Watson; Alan Baxter; Howard da Silva; Maurice Murphy; Clem Bevans; Herbert Rudley; Directed by John Cromwell; Written by Robert Sherwood; Cinematography by James Wong Howe; Music by Roy Webb. **Pr:** Max Gordon; RKO. **A:** Family. **P:** Entertainment. **U:** Institution, Home. **Mov-Ent:** Drama, Biography: Politics, Presidency. **Acq:** Purchase. **Dist:** WarnerArchive.com. $19.95.

The Abe Lincoln of Ninth Avenue 1939 — ★★½
All-American tale of a poor young man making good in New York. His role model is Abraham Lincoln. Cooper is exceptional, supported by effective performances by the rest of the cast. 68m/B/W; VHS, DVD, 8 mm. **C:** Jackie Cooper; Martin Spelling; Marjorie Reynolds; Dick Purcell; George Cleveland; George Irving; Directed by William Nigh. **Pr:** Monogram. **A:** Family. **P:** Entertainment. **U:** Home. **Mov-Ent. Acq:** Purchase. **Dist:** Movies Unlimited; Alpha Video. $24.95.

Abel Gance at Work 19??
Vintage footage of Abel Gance at work on "Napoleon" and "La Roue." 43m/B/W; VHS. **A:** Jr. High-Adult. **P:** Education. **U:** Home. **Gen-Edu:** Documentary Films, Filmmaking. **Acq:** Purchase. **Dist:** Facets Multimedia Inc. $19.95.

Abel Gance: Yesterday and Tomorrow 1961
Film director Abel Gance, from his early silent masterpieces to his re-emergence as a cinematic legend as the director of "Napoleon." 28m; VHS, 3/4 U, Special order formats. **C:** Abel Gance. **Pr:** Nelly Kaplan; Janus Films. **A:** Sr. High-Adult. **P:** Education. **U:** Institution. **Gen-Edu:** Documentary Films, Filmmaking, Biography. **Acq:** Purchase. **Dist:** Glenn Video Vistas Ltd.

Abel Sanchez 1989
A Spanish version of Cain and Abel as seen through the eyes of a philosopher for whom good and evil are neither absolutes nor opposites. 180m/B/W; VHS, 3/4 U. **Pr:** Films for the Humanities and Sciences. **A:** College. **P:** Education. **U:** Institution, CCTV, CATV, BCTV. **L:** Spanish. **Fin-Art:** Performing Arts, Literature. **Acq:** Purchase, Rent/Lease, Duplication License. **Dist:** Films for the Humanities & Sciences.

Abel's Field 2012 (PG) — ★★½
Solid, if predictable, faith-based drama. High school senior Seth McArdle (Davis) is caring for his younger sisters after his mother's death and his father's abandonment. Seth gets into trouble and is assigned to after-school work, supervised by groundskeeper Abel (Sorbo), who may be the only one to help Seth before he makes some seriously bad decisions. 104m; DVD; Closed Captioned. **C:** Samuel Davis; Kevin Sorbo; Richard Dillard; Directed by Gordie Haakstad; Written by Aron Flasher; Cinematography by Ian Ellis; Music by Jeff Toyne. **A:** Family. **P:** Entertainment. **U:** Home. **L:** English. **Mov-Ent:** Adolescence. **Acq:** Purchase. **Dist:** Sony Pictures Home Entertainment Inc.

Abel's Island 1988
William Steig's story about a mouse who is carried off to a deserted island by a storm is brought to life. 28m; VHS, CC, 3/4 U. **C:** Voice(s) by Tim Curry; Lionel Jeffries; Directed by Michael Sporn. **Pr:** Michael Sporn. **A:** Family. **P:** Entertainment. **U:** Institution, SURA. **Chl-Juv:** Animation & Cartoons. **Acq:** Purchase. **Dist:** Lucerne Media; Random House of Canada Ltd. $14.95.

The Abercrombie/Erskine/Mintzer/Patitucci Band: Live in New York City 199?
Live group performances of original compositions interspersed with discussions of playing techniques. 105m; VHS. **A:** Sr. High-Adult. **P:** Instruction. **U:** Home. **How-Ins:** Music--Instruction, Music--Performance. **Acq:** Purchase. **Dist:** Hal Leonard Corp. $24.95.

Aberdeen 2000 (Unrated) — ★★
Ambitious London attorney Kaisa (Headey) gets a call from her terminally ill mother Helen (Rampling), who lives in Aberdeen, Scotland. Helen wants Kaisa to travel to Oslo and retrieve Tomas (Skargard), her alcoholic and estranged father, so Helen and he can have a deathbed reconciliation. Assertive Kaisa tracks the drunk down and makes him come with her on a nightmare trip back. Lead performances are utterly unsentimental. 103m; VHS, DVD. **C:** Stellan Skarsgard; Lena Headey; Ian Hart; Charlotte Rampling; Directed by Hans Petter Moland; Written by Hans Petter Moland; Kristin Amundsen; Cinematography by Philip Ogaard; Music by Zbigniew Preisner. **A:** College-Adult. **P:** Entertainment. **U:** Home. **Mov-Ent:** Alcoholism, Scandinavia, Scotland. **Acq:** Purchase. **Dist:** First Run Features.

Aberdeen 2003
A young Scottish woman, at the request of her mother, sets out on a hilarious yet heartbreaking journey to find her estranged father. 103m; VHS. **A:** Adult. **P:** Entertainment. **U:** Home. **Mov-Ent:** Drama, Film--Avant-Garde. **Acq:** Purchase. **Dist:** First Run Features. $24.95.

Aberration 1997 (R) — ★
Amy (Gidley) has traveled to her parents remote cabin and notices a lizard infestation. So she heads to the store for some exterminating equipment and meets biologist Marshall (Bossell), who studies eco-abnormalities. Seems the lizards are vicious mutants who eat Amy's cat and are working their way up the food chain. Doesn't offer many scares. 93m; VHS, Streaming, CC. **C:** Pamela Gidley; Simon Bossell; Valery (Valeri Nikolayev) Nikolaev; Directed by Tim Boxell; Written by Darrin Oura; Scott Lew; Cinematography by Allen Guilford. **A:** Sr. High-Adult. **P:** Entertainment. **U:** Home. **Mov-Ent:** Horror. **Acq:** Purchase. **Dist:** Lions Gate Television Corp.

Abigail's Party 1977 (Unrated) — ★★
Steadman plays the hostess for a very ill-fated dinner party, especially when she realizes her husband has just died on her new carpet. 105m; VHS, DVD. **C:** Alison Steadman; Directed by Mike Leigh. **A:** Jr. High-Adult. **P:** Entertainment. **U:** Home. **Mov-Ent:** Comedy--Black, TV Movies. **Acq:** Purchase. **Dist:** Water Bearer Films Inc.; Baker and Taylor. $79.95.

The Abilene Paradox 1985
The Paradox is described as a decision no one agrees with but no one wants to speak against. This tape shows how to eliminate The Paradox. 21m; VHS, 3/4 U, Special order formats. **Pr:** McGraw-Hill Training Systems. **A:** Sr. High-Adult. **P:** Professional. **U:** Institution, CATV, SURA. **Bus-Ind:** Business, Management, Organizations. **Acq:** Purchase, Rent/Lease. **Dist:** Jossey-Bass; Excellence in Training Corp. $745.00.

Abilene Town 1946 (Unrated) — ★★★
In a post-Civil War Kansas town far from the freeway, Scott is the tough marshal trying to calm the conflict between cattlemen and homesteaders. He also finds time to participate in a romantic triangle with dance hall vixen Dvorak and heart-of-gold Fleming. Snappy pace keeps it interesting. Based on a novel by Ernest Haycox. 90m/B/W; VHS, DVD, 3/4 U, Special order formats. **C:** Randolph Scott; Ann Dvorak; Edgar Buchanan; Rhonda Fleming; Lloyd Bridges; Directed by Edwin L. Marin; Written by Harold Shumate; Cinematography by Archie Stout. **Pr:** United Artists. **A:** Family. **P:** Entertainment. **U:** Home. **Mov-Ent:** Western. **Acq:** Purchase. **Dist:** Karol Media; Amazon.com Inc. $9.95.

Abilities and Assets of the Laity 19??
Details the unique opportunities of the laity to spread the Catholic faith. ?m; VHS. **A:** Jr. High-Adult. **P:** Religious. **U:** Institution. **Gen-Edu:** Religion. **Acq:** Purchase. **Dist:** Keep the Faith Inc. $20.00.

Ability Issues in the U.S.A. 1992
Discusses discrimination against individuals with disabilities. 60m; VHS. **A:** Adult. **P:** Education. **U:** Institution. **Gen-Edu:** Prejudice. **Acq:** Purchase. **Dist:** RMI Media. $99.00.

Ablaze 2000 (R) — ★½
Greedy developer Wendell Mays (Arnold) arranges for his industrial refinery to be torched and the ensuing fire and explosion taxes both the fire fighters and the hospital that has to deal with the casualties. Wynorski directs under the pseudonym Jay Andrews. 97m; VHS, DVD. **C:** John Bradley; Tom Arnold; Michael Dudikoff; Ice-T; Amanda Pays; Cathy Lee Crosby; Pat Harrington; Edward Albert; Mary Jo Catlett; Richard Biggs; Directed by Jim Wynorski; Written by Steve Latshaw; Cinematography by Andrea V. Rossotto; Music by Neal Acree. **A:** Sr. High-Adult. **P:** Entertainment. **U:** Home. **Mov-Ent:** Fires. **Acq:** Purchase. **Dist:** Fox Home Entertainment.

Able to Laugh 1993
San Francisco's Access to Comedy troupe, a group of disabled comedians, performs before a live audience, using their own handicaps as material to reveal their frustrations and increase sensitivity among the able-bodied. 27m; VHS, CC. **A:** Adult. **P:** Entertainment. **U:** Institution. **Gen-Edu:** Comedy--Performance, Handicapped. **Acq:** Purchase, Rent/Lease. **Dist:** Fanlight Productions. $195.00.

The Abnaki: Native People of Maine 1984
Follows the Abnaki Indians in their efforts to accomplish their legal victory. Furthermore, we explore the historical, cultural and spiritual factors that have contributed to the survival of their Native American heritage. 29m; VHS, 3/4 U. **Pr:** Centre Productions, Inc. **A:** Jr. High-Adult. **P:** Education. **U:** Institution, SURA. **Gen-Edu:** Documentary Films, Native Americans. **Acq:** Purchase. **Dist:** Clear Vue Inc.

Abnormal Auscultatory Findings Related to First and Second Heart Sounds 1973
Features Ravin's Heart Sound Simulator in the discussion and demonstration of normal and abnormal heart sounds, differentiating between normal and abnormal splitting of the first and second heart sounds. 30m; 3/4 U. **Pr:** American College of Cardiology. **A:** College-Adult. **P:** Professional. **U:** Institution, CCTV. **Hea-Sci:** Heart, Medical Education. **Acq:** Purchase. **Dist:** American College of Cardiology.

Abnormal Heart and Breath Sounds 197?
Each program in this series highlights a specific area of sounds, and provides the learner with a clear, concise, and comprehensive understanding of this assessment tool. Programs are available individually. 15m; VHS, 3/4 U. **Pr:** Trainex. **A:** College-Adult. **P:** Professional. **U:** Institution. **Hea-Sci:** Nursing, Heart. **Acq:** Purchase. **Dist:** Medcom Inc.
Indiv. Titles: 1. Abnormal Breath Sounds 2. Adventitious Breath Sounds 3. Abnormalities of the First and Second Heart Sounds 4. Abnormalities of the Third and Fourth Heart Sounds 5. An Introduction to Heart Murmurs 6. Systolic Murmurs 7. Innocent Systolic Murmurs and Diastolic Murmurs.

Abnormal Vaginal Bleeding 1988
A discussion of the many irregular bleeding problems encountered by women of all ages, from menarche through menopause. 15m; VHS, 3/4 U. **Pr:** Milner-Fenwick. **A:** Jr. High-Adult. **P:** Education. **U:** Institution, CCTV. **L:** English, French, Spanish. **Hea-Sci:** Gynecology, Medical Education. **Acq:** Purchase. **Dist:** Milner-Fenwick, Inc.

Abnormalities of the Mitral Valve 1982
Illustrates cardiac problems and valve replacement therapy. 52m; VHS, 3/4 U. **Pr:** Emory University. **A:** College-Adult. **P:** Professional. **U:** Institution, CCTV, Home, SURA. **Hea-Sci:** Heart, Medical Education. **Acq:** Purchase, Rent/Lease, Subscription. **Dist:** Emory Medical Television Network.

Abo Canyon & the Burlington Northern Santa Fe Railroad 19?? (Unrated)
Classic railroading footage captures BNSF trains from unique and hard-to-reach locations along at the rugged yet scenic Abo Canyon on the east-west mainline between Chicago and Los Angeles. 58m; DVD. **A:** Family. **P:** Education. **U:** Home. **Gen-Edu:** Trains, U.S. States. **Acq:** Purchase. **Dist:** The Civil War Standard. $24.95.

Abode of Illusion: The Life and Art of Chang Dai-Chien 1993
Profiles the acclaimed Chinese artist who achieved international recognition through his original works as well as for his skill at emulating and forging past masterpieces. 60m; VHS. **A:** Sr. High-Adult. **P:** Education. **U:** Home. **Gen-Edu:** Documentary Films, Art & Artists, China. **Acq:** Purchase. **Dist:** Direct Cinema Ltd. $34.95.

Abolition 2011 (Unrated) — ★½
A handyman is taken in by a fallen priest before suffering from blackouts that result in him always waking up near someone in trouble. His compulsions to hlep them out only seem to cause suffering for someone else. 82m; DVD, Blu-Ray, Streaming. **C:** Caroline Williams; Reggie Bannister; Emily Alatalo; Elissa Dowling; Andrew Roth; Directed by Mike Klassen; Written by Mike Klassen; Chris Lawson; Chantelle Kadyschuk; Cinematography by Nick Matthews; Music by Colin Parrish. **A:** Sr. High-Adult. **P:** Entertainment. **U:** Home. **L:** English. **Mov-Ent**. **Acq:** Purchase, Rent/Lease. **Dist:** R Squared Inc. $19.99 12.95 1.99.

Abolition: Broken Promises ????
Examines the lives of slaves in post-Civil War America. Addresses the shortcomings of the Reconstruction, the start of the Ku Klux Klan, failure of post-war land-distribution act, and the preconceived image of black males as criminals. 51m; VHS. **A:** Sr. High-Adult. **P:** Education. **U:** Institution. **Gen-Edu:** Slavery, History--U.S., Black Culture. **Acq:** Purchase, Rent/Lease. **Dist:** Films for the Humanities & Sciences. $129.00.

The Abolitionist Movement 19??
An examination of the abolitionist movement, the Underground Railroad, and Harriet Beecher Stowe's novel, Uncle Tom's Cabin. 12m; VHS. **A:** Jr. High-Sr. High. **P:** Education. **U:** Institution. **Gen-Edu:** History--U.S., History. **Acq:** Purchase. **Dist:** Thomas S. Klise Co. $58.00.

Abominable 2006 (R) — ★★
A man wheelchair bound after a mountain climbing incident watched Bigfoot devour a cabin of co-eds next door but no one believes him. 94m; DVD. **C:** Matt McCoy; Jeffrey Combs; Michael Deak; Paul Gleason; Hayley Joel; Lance Henriksen; Tiffany Shepis; Directed by Ryan Schifrin; Written by Ryan Schifrin; James Morrison; Cinematography by Neal Fredericks; Music by Lalo Schifrin. **A:** Sr. High-Adult. **P:** Entertainment. **U:** Home. **L:** English. **Mov-Ent**. **Acq:** Purchase. **Dist:** Anchor Bay Entertainment Inc. $19.98.

The Abominable Dr. Phibes 1971 (PG) — ★★★
After being disfigured in a freak car accident that killed his wife, an evil genius decides that the members of a surgical team let his wife die and shall each perish by a different biblical plague. High camp with the veteran cast in top form. 90m; VHS, DVD, Blu-Ray, Wide. **C:** Vincent Price; Joseph Cotten; Hugh Griffith; Terry-Thomas; Virginia North; Susan Travers; Alex Scott; Caroline Munro; Peter Jeffrey; Peter Gilmore; Edward Burnham; Sean Bury; David Hutcheson; Maurice Kaufmann; Charles Farrell; Directed by Robert Fuest; Written by William Goldstein; James Whiton; Cinematography by Norman Warwick; Music by Basil Kirchin; Jack Nathan. **Pr:** American International Pictures. **A:** Primary-Adult. **P:** Entertainment. **U:** Home. **Mov-Ent:** Horror. **Acq:** Purchase. **Dist:** MGM Studios Inc. $14.98.

The Abominable Snowman 1957 — ★★
Corny Hammer horror about adventurer Tom Friend (Tucker), Dr. John Rollason (Cushing), and guide Ed Shelley (Brown) searching for the legandary Yeti. The harsh conditions cause the explorers to lose their grip and, after Shelley shoots a Yeti, Rollason begins to suspect that the creatures practice mind control. 91m/B/W; VHS, DVD, Wide. **C:** Peter Cushing; Forrest Tucker; Robert Brown; Richard Wattis; Maureen Connell; Directed by Val Guest; Written by Nigel Kneale; Cinematography by Arthur Grant; Music by Humphrey Searle. **Pr:** Hammer Film Productions; Clarion Pictures. **A:** Jr. High-Adult. **P:** Entertainment. **U:** Home. **Mov-Ent:** Arctic Regions, Mountaineering. **Acq:** Purchase. **Dist:** Anchor Bay Entertainment.

The Abomination 1988 (R) — ★
After a 5,000-year-old creature possesses him during a nightmare, a boy goes on an eye-gouging frenzy. Only the audience gets hurt. 100m; VHS, DVD. **C:** Van Connery; Victoria Chaney; Suzy Meyer; Jude Johnson; Blue Thompson; Scott Davis; Directed by Max Raven. **Pr:** Donna Michelle Productions. **A:** Adult. **P:** Entertainment. **U:** Home. **Mov-Ent:** Horror. **Acq:** Purchase. **Dist:** Navarre Corp.

Aboo 1987
A philosophical dramatization about the evils of money. 43m; VHS, 3/4 U. **Pr:** Video Out. **A:** Jr. High-Adult. **P:** Education. **U:** Institution, SURA. **Gen-Edu:** Philosophy & Ideology, Documentary Films. **Acq:** Rent/Lease. **Dist:** Video Out Distribution.

Aboriginal Art: Past, Present, and Future 19??
Explores the art, prehistoric through contemporary, of Australia's Aboriginal people. 13m; VHS. **A:** Jr. High-College. **P:** Education. **U:** Institution. **Gen-Edu:** Art & Artists. **Acq:** Purchase. **Dist:** Crystal Productions. $29.95.

Aboriginal Rights: I Can Get It For You Wholesale 1976
Debates the pro side of Native American aboriginal rights, claiming precedence and respect for nature as its major arguments. 60m; VHS, 1C, 3/4 U, Q. **Pr:** TV Ontario. **A:** Jr. High-Adult. **P:** Education. **U:** Institution, BCTV, SURA. **Gen-Edu:** Documentary Films, Native Americans. **Acq:** Purchase, Rent/Lease. **Dist:** Vision Maker Media.

Abortion Clinic 1984
Looks at abortion clinics and women making decisions about abortions. 58m; VHS, 3/4 U. **Pr:** PBS Video. **A:** Sr. High-Adult. **P:** Education. **U:** Institution, CCTV, CATV. **Gen-Edu:** Documentary Films, Abortion. **Acq:** Purchase, Rent/Lease, Off-Air Record. **Dist:** PBS Home Video.

Abortion: Desperate Choices 1992
Originally broadcast on HBO, an inside look at an abortion clinic including actual footage of abortions. Includes personal interviews with the subjects, women who have aborted previously, and foes of abortion. 60m; VHS, CC. **Pr:** Maysles Films; HBO. **A:** Sr. High-Adult. **P:** Education. **U:** Home, Institution, BCTV. **Hea-Sci:** Abortion. **Acq:** Purchase. **Dist:** Ambrose Video Publishing, Inc. $34.95.

Abortion for Survival 1989
Examines issues relating to abortion, including the lack of access to birth control worldwide and women's desire to limit their family size. Documentary opens with the performance of an abortion at six weeks into pregnancy. ?m; VHS. **A:** Sr. High-Adult. **P:** Education. **U:** Home. **Gen-Edu:** Abortion, Women, Documentary Films. **Acq:** Purchase. **Dist:** The Feminist Majority. $19.95.

Abortion in Adolescence 1983
A discussion of the Center for Disease Control's statistics on teenage pregnancies and abortions in the United States. 58m; VHS, 3/4 U. **Pr:** Emory University. **A:** College-Adult. **P:** Education. **U:** Institution, CCTV, Home, SURA. **Hea-Sci:** Documentary Films, Abortion, Adolescence. **Acq:** Purchase, Rent/Lease, Subscription. **Dist:** Emory Medical Television Network.

The Abortion Providers 19??
Doctors Anthony Levatino and Joseph Randall host a conference where medical doctors are asked to give their opinions on abortion...and deliver surprising answers. ?m; VHS. **A:** Sr. High-Adult. **P:** Education. **U:** Institution. **Gen-Edu:** Abortion. **Acq:** Purchase. **Dist:** Keep the Faith Inc. $60.00.

Abortion: Stories From North and South 1989
An examination into the worldwide practice of abortion and the degree it has crossed religious, social, racial, and cultural boundaries. 55m; VHS, 3/4 U. **TV Std:** NTSC, PAL, SECAM. **Pr:** Gail Singer. **A:** Sr. High-Adult. **P:** Education. **U:** Institution, SURA. **Gen-Edu:** Documentary Films, Abortion. **Acq:** Purchase, Rent/Lease. **Dist:** National Film Board of Canada.

About a Boy 2002 (PG-13) — ★★★
After "Bridget Jones's Diary," Grant continues the role of charming cad. This time, he's Will, a 38-year-old bachelor who doesn't work thanks to his father's legacy and eschews lasting emotional commitments. Will's latest dating scheme is that of a single parent who joins support groups to hit on the single mums. Here he meets Marcus (Hoult), the 12-year-old misfit son of seriously depressed Fiona (Collette). Will likes Marcus despite himself and becomes his confidante. He finds romance with single mum Rachel (Weitz) but that's almost beside the point. Adapted from Nick Hornby's novel. 100m; VHS, DVD, Blu-Ray. **C:** Hugh Grant; Rachel Weisz; Toni Collette; Nicholas Hoult; Isabel Brook; Victoria Smurfit; Directed by Chris Weitz; Paul Weitz; Written by Chris Weitz; Paul Weitz; Peter Hedges; Cinematography by Remi Adefarasin; Music by Badly Drawn Boy. **Pr:** Jane Rosenthal; Robert De Niro; Tim Bevan; Eric Fellner; Jennifer Chaiken; Tribeca Productions; Working Title Productions; Jour de Fete Films; Universal Pictures. **A:** Jr. High-Adult. **P:** Entertainment. **U:** Home. **Mov-Ent**. **Acq:** Purchase. **Dist:** Movies Unlimited; Alpha Video.

About Adam 2000 (R) — ★★
Adam (Townsend) is a duplicitous Dublin charmer who worms his way into the Owens family. Waitress Lucy (Hudson) falls in love with Adam and takes him to meet her family and before anyone realizes what's happening, Adam seduces both her sisters, telling each woman exactly what she needs to hear. And no one holds a grudge! 98m; VHS, DVD, Wide. **C:** Stuart Townsend; Kate Hudson; Frances O'Connor; Charlotte Bradley; Rosaleen Linehan; Brendan F. Dempsey; Alan Maher; Tommy Tiernan; Cathleen Bradley; Directed by Gerard Stembridge; Written by Gerard Stembridge; Cinematography by Bruno de Keyzer; Music by Adrian Johnston. **Pr:** Anna Devlin; Marina Hughes; BBC Films; Venus Productions; Miramax Film Corp. **A:** Sr. High-Adult. **P:** Entertainment. **U:** Home. **Mov-Ent:** Comedy--Romantic, Sex & Sexuality. **Acq:** Purchase. **Dist:** Buena Vista Home Entertainment.

About AIDS 1989
Takes a candid look at Acquired Immune Deficiency Syndrome; what AIDS is, how it spreads, and what we can do to protect ourselves. 15m; VHS, 3/4 U. **Pr:** Rosenthal/Kightley. **A:** Jr. High-Adult. **P:** Education. **U:** Institution, Home, SURA. **Hea-Sci:** Documentary Films, Health Education, AIDS. **Acq:** Purchase, Rent/Lease, Duplication License. **Dist:** Pyramid Media. $125.00.

About Baghdad 2004
Documentary about the effects of years of oppression, war, sanctions, and occupation have had on Baghdad. With English subtitles. 90m; DVD. **A:** Sr. High-Adult. **P:** Education. **U:** Home, Institution. **L:** Arabic. **Gen-Edu:** Documentary Films, Middle East. **Acq:** Purchase, Rent/Lease. **Dist:** Arab Film Distribution. $29.99.

About Cherry 2012 (R) — ★½
Traditional coming of age story about an abused young woman moving to the big city to procure fame in the adult entertainment industry and a powerful boyfriend with a massive drug addiction. 102m; DVD, Blu-Ray, Streaming. **C:** Ashley Hinshaw; Lili Taylor; Dev Patel; Diane Farr; Johnny Weston; Directed by Stephen Elliott; Written by Stephen Elliott; Lorelei Lee; Cinematography by Darren Genet; Music by Jeff Russo. **A:** Sr. High-Adult. **P:** Entertainment. **U:** Home. **L:** English. **Mov-Ent**. **Acq:** Purchase, Rent/Lease. **Dist:** MPI Media Group. $29.98 24.98 14.99.

About Conception and Contraception 1972
This non-narrative program uses animated drawings to illustrate how conception occurs and how various birth control devices, surgical methods and the pill function in preventing conception. 11m; 3/4 U, Special order formats. **Pr:** National Film Board of Canada. **A:** Jr. High-Adult. **P:** Education. **U:** Institution, Home, SURA. **L:** Spanish. **How-Ins:** How-To, Birth Control, Pregnancy. **Acq:** Purchase, Rent/Lease, Trade-in, Duplication License. **Dist:** United Learning Inc.

About Fifty 2011 (R) — ★★
Amusing midlife comedy. Miserable, heading towards divorce Adam is talked into a golf weekend in Palm Springs by his single pal Jon as they both unwillingly negotiate the facts of middle age. Jon still thinks he can bed half-his-age Alix, who's too smart to fall for his shtick, but she does introduce Adam to her divorced mom Kate. 80m; DVD. **C:** Martin Grey; Drew Pillsbury; Wendie Malick; Michaela McManus; Anne-Marie Johnson; Jessalyn Gilsig; Directed by Thomas Johnston; Written by Martin Grey; Drew Pillsbury; Thomas Johnston; Cinematography by Keith J. Duggan. **A:** Sr. High-Adult. **P:** Entertainment. **U:** Home. **Mov-Ent:** Golf. **Acq:** Purchase. **Dist:** Screen Media Ventures, LLC.

About Flowers 1989
Provides answers to some common questions that children ask about flowers such as: why do flowers attract bees? how does fertilization occur? and how are seeds formed? 7m; VHS, 3/4 U. **Pr:** Frank Spiller. **A:** Primary. **P:** Education. **U:** Institution, SURA. **Hea-Sci:** Flowers, Education. **Acq:** Rent/Lease. **Dist:** National Film Board of Canada.

About Last Night. . . 1986 (R) — ★★★
Semi-realistic comedy-drama which explores the ups and downs of one couple's (Lowe, Moore) relationship. Mostly quality performances, especially Perkins and Belushi as friends of the young lovers. Based on David Mamet's play "Sexual Perversity in Chicago," but considerably softened so that more people would buy tickets at the boxoffice, the film acts as a historical view of contemporary mating rituals before the onset of the AIDS crisis. 113m; VHS, DVD, Blu-Ray. **C:** Rob Lowe; Demi Moore; Elizabeth Perkins; James Belushi; George

DiCenzo; Robin Thomas; Michael Alldredge; Directed by Edward Zwick; Written by Tim Kazurinsky; Denise DeClue; Cinematography by Andrew Dintenfass; Music by Miles Goodman. **Pr:** Tri-Star Pictures. **A:** Sr. High-Adult. **P:** Entertainment. **U:** Home. **Mov-Ent**: Comedy--Romantic. **Acq:** Purchase. **Dist:** Sony Pictures Home Entertainment Inc. $14.95.

About Last Night 2014 (R) — ★★½
A modern take on a 1974 David Mamet play, previously brought to the big screen in 1986 with Rob Lowe and Demi Moore in the leads. This time around Kevin Hart cranks the raunch-factor to the max as Bernie, a hard-partying player who meets his match in Joan (Hall). The new couple fight over all things sexual, and one-up each other in every phase of life. On paper, it shouldn't have worked, but the razor sharp banter and dynamite chemistry between Hall and Hart overcome all mediocre in story, even as the credits roll. 100m; DVD, Blu-Ray. **C:** Kevin Hart; Michael Ealy; Joy Bryant; Regina Hall; Christopher McDonald; Paula Patton; Adam Rodriguez; Directed by Steve Pink; Written by Leslye Headland; Cinematography by Michael Barrett; Music by Marcus Miller. **Pr:** Sony Pictures Entertainment Inc. **A:** Sr. High-Adult. **P:** Entertainment. **U:** Home. **L:** English. **Mov-Ent**: Comedy--Romantic, Black Culture, Sex & Sexuality. **Acq:** Purchase. **Dist:** Sony Pictures Home Entertainment Inc.

About Puberty and Reproduction 1974
Meant for special audiences who need tailor-made explanations, in simple language, sign language, a foreign language or carefully selected terminology. Consisting of silent, animated, stylized illustrations of puberty changes, an instructor is required to explain the screen action to his specific audience. 12m; VHS, 3/4 U. **Pr:** National Film Board of Canada. **A:** Primary-Jr. High. **P:** Education. **U:** Institution, SURA. **Hea-Sci**: Documentary Films, Adolescence, Reproduction. **Acq:** Purchase, Rent/Lease. **Dist:** National Film Board of Canada.

About Schmidt 2002 (R) — ★★★½
Jack's back and playing against type as Warren Schmidt, a man left with virtually no identity once he retires from his ho-hum insurance job. Left only with time to reflect on a meaningless life, he questions everything he once took for granted, including Helen (Squibb), his wife of 42 years. The day after his retirement, the couple shares breakfast before Helen suddenly dies. With nothing left to lose, Schmidt hits the road in a Winnebago to visit his daughter and try to find some meaning in his poorly thought-out life. In Denver, he meets and immediately hates his daughter's cheesy salesman fiance Randall (Mulroney), while Randall's flowsy mother Roberta (Bates) tries to seduce the lonely introvert in a hot tub. Combines humor, pathos, and hope with a first rate performance by Nicholson, who quashes any of his characteristic animation. Davis, Mulroney, and especially Bates are also excellent. 124m; VHS, DVD. **C:** Jack Nicholson; Hope Davis; Dermot Mulroney; Kathy Bates; Len Cariou; Howard Hesseman; June Squibb; Directed by Alexander Payne; Written by Alexander Payne; Jim Taylor; Cinematography by James Glennon; Music by Rolfe Kent. **Pr:** Harry Gittes; Michael Besman; New Line Cinema. **A:** Sr. High-Adult. **P:** Entertainment. **U:** Home. **Mov-Ent**: Aging, Insurance. **Awds:** Golden Globes '03: Actor--Drama (Nicholson), Screenplay; L.A. Film Critics '02: Actor (Nicholson), Film, Screenplay; Natl. Bd. of Review '02: Support. Actress (Bates). **Acq:** Purchase. **Dist:** Warner Home Video, Inc.

About Self-Esteem 1990
Defines self-esteem and its importance to good mental health. 17m; VHS. **A:** Adult. **P:** Education. **U:** Institution. **Hea-Sci**: Mental Health. **Acq:** Purchase. **Dist:** Channing Bete Company Inc. $129.00.

About Sex 1972
Facts and fallacies about sex are discussed for teenagers. Includes body growth, sexual fantasies, birth control, abortion, venereal disease, and mutuality between the sexes. 23m; VHS, 3/4 U. **A:** Sr. High. **P:** Education. **U:** Institution, CCTV. **L:** English, Spanish. **Hea-Sci**: Sex & Sexuality, Adolescence, Education. **Acq:** Purchase, Rent/Lease. **Dist:** Discovery Education.

About Sharks 1981
Children are taught that sharks are some of the largest, most beautiful, and most dangerous inhabitants of the ocean. 25m; 3/4 U, Special order formats. **Pr:** National Geographic Society. **A:** Primary. **P:** Education. **U:** Institution, Home, SURA. **Chl-Juv**: Documentary Films, Fish. **Acq:** Purchase, Trade-in, Duplication License. **Dist:** National Geographic Society.

About Stress 1990
Discusses the causes and effects of stress and how to seek professional help. 17m; VHS. **A:** Adult. **P:** Education. **U:** Institution. **Hea-Sci**: Stress. **Acq:** Purchase. **Dist:** Channing Bete Company Inc. $129.00.

About Sunny 2012 (Unrated) — ★★★
Star Ambrose propels this recession-themed examination of a single mother trying to keep her head above water and hold on to her daughter as best she can. Writer/director Wizemann doesn't hold back from presenting his conflicted protagonist in a three-dimensional way that's heartbreaking. The fact is that Angela may not be able to give her daughter Sunny (Scott) what she needs and that the girl could conceivably be better off without her economically- and responsibility-deprived mother. Ambrose gives a fantastic performance by making a possibly clichéd character feel devastatingly real. 104m; Streaming. **C:** Lauren Ambrose; Audrey P. Scott; Dylan Baker; David Conrad; Penelope Ann Miller; Directed by Bryan Wizemann; Written by Bryan Wizemann; Cinematography by Mark Schwartzbard; Music by Jeff Grace. **Pr:** Blythe Robertson; Mike Ryan; Oscilloscope Films. **A:** Sr. High-Adult. **P:** Entertainment. **U:** Home. **L:** English. **Mov-Ent**: Parenting, Children. **Acq:** Purchase. **Dist:** Amazon.com Inc.

About Tap 1985
An examination of the art of tap dancing, its history and various styles. 28m; VHS, 3/4 U, Special order formats. **Pr:** George T. Nierenberg. **A:** Jr. High-Adult. **P:** Education. **U:** Institution, SURA. **Gen-Edu**: Documentary Films, Dance--History. **Acq:** Purchase, Rent/Lease. **Dist:** Direct Cinema Ltd.

About the Holocaust 1983
Features interviews with Holocaust survivors and the children of survivors. 30m; VHS, 3/4 U. **Pr:** Anti-Defamation League of B'nai B'rith. **A:** Primary-Adult. **P:** Education. **U:** Institution, CCTV, CATV, BCTV, Home. **Gen-Edu**: World War Two, Judaism, Interviews. **Acq:** Purchase. **Dist:** Anti-Defamation League of B'nai B'rith.

About the Jews of India: Cochin 1976
Learn the story of a small group of Jews that still live in India. 30m; VHS. **Pr:** Johanna Spector. **A:** Family. **P:** Education. **U:** Institution, Home. **Gen-Edu**: Documentary Films, Judaism, India. **Acq:** Purchase, Rent/Lease. **Dist:** Alden Films. $600.00.

About the Jews of India: Shanwar Telis or Bene Israel 1978
The story of how a group of Jews fled persecution and came to settle in India. 40m; VHS. **Pr:** Johanna Spector. **A:** Family. **P:** Education. **U:** Institution, Home. **Gen-Edu**: Documentary Films, Judaism, History. **Acq:** Purchase, Rent/Lease. **Dist:** Alden Films. $700.00.

About the Jews of Yemen: A Vanishing Culture 1986
A history of Jewish people in Yemen. 77m; VHS. **Pr:** Johanna Spector. **A:** Family. **P:** Education. **U:** Institution, Home. **Gen-Edu**: Documentary Films, Judaism, History. **Acq:** Purchase, Rent/Lease. **Dist:** Alden Films. $1000.00.

About the United Nations: Africa Recovery 1990
In this edition of the educational series produced for grades 5-12, a Zambian reporter comments on the major problems threatening Africa today and what might be done to solve them. Includes a 48 page guide book for teachers. 15m; VHS. **Pr:** United Nations. **A:** Primary-Sr. High. **P:** Teacher Education. **U:** Home. **Gen-Edu**: Documentary Films, World Affairs, Africa. **Acq:** Purchase. **Dist:** The Cinema Guild.

About the United Nations: Apartheid 1990
This volume of the series produced for students in grades 5-12 is hosted by a young South African girl who describes the various injustices of the apartheid system. Included is a 48 page teacher's guide. 10m; VHS. **Pr:** United Nations. **A:** Primary-Sr. High. **P:** Education. **U:** Home. **Gen-Edu**: Documentary Films, History--Modern, Apartheid. **Acq:** Rent/Lease. **Dist:** The Cinema Guild. $17.95.

About the United Nations: Decolonization 1990
This edition of the series designed for grades 5-12 looks at the process of independence that has taken place over the last 30 years in nations that were once colonized. Interviews, maps and aarchival footage are used. Included is a 48-page guide book for teachers. 20m; VHS. **Pr:** United Nations. **A:** Primary-Sr. High. **P:** Teacher Education. **U:** Institution. **Gen-Edu**: Documentary Films, World Affairs, History--Modern. **Acq:** Purchase, Rent/Lease. **Dist:** The Cinema Guild. $150.00.

About the United Nations: Environment and Development 1992
Discusses what the United Nations is doing to improve people's lives without destroying natural resources. Also looks at the UN Environment Program and its efforts to clean up the environment. 20m; VHS. **C:** Narrated by Olivia Newton-John. **Pr:** United Nations Department of Public Info. **A:** Primary-Sr. High. **P:** Education. **U:** Institution. **Gen-Edu**: Documentary Films, United Nations, Ecology & Environment. **Acq:** Purchase, Rent/Lease. **Dist:** The Cinema Guild. $150.00.

About the United Nations: Literacy 1990
Produced for grades 5-12, this volume describes the world's illiteracy problem and what the UN and other organizations are doing about it. Includes a 48-page guide book for teachers. 18m; VHS. **Pr:** United Nations. **A:** Primary-Sr. High. **P:** Teacher Education. **U:** Institution. **Gen-Edu**: World Affairs, Education, United Nations. **Acq:** Purchase, Rent/Lease. **Dist:** The Cinema Guild. $175.00.

About the United Nations: Palestine 1990
This volume of the series intended for students in grades 5-12 and looks at the background of the Palestinian problem and the Intifada. The video comes with a 45-page guide book. 19m; VHS. **Pr:** United Nations. **A:** Sr. High-Adult. **P:** Education. **U:** Home. **Gen-Edu**: Documentary Films, World Affairs, History--Modern. **Acq:** Purchase. **Dist:** The Cinema Guild. $17.95.

About the United Nations: Peacekeeping 1990
This volume of the series produced for students in grades 5-12 examines the role of the UN in encouraging disgruntled international neighbors to find peaceful solutions. Included are interviews with the women and men who make up the UN Peacekeeping Force. Comes with a 48 page teacher's guide. 19m; VHS. **Pr:** United Nations. **A:** Primary-Adult. **P:** Education. **U:** Home. **Gen-Edu**: Documentary Films, World Affairs, United Nations. **Acq:** Rent/Lease. **Dist:** The Cinema Guild. $17.95.

About the United Nations: Rights of the Child 1992
The United Nations has established standards that guarantee children the right to life, liberty, a name, a nationality, an education, and good health. This video examines what the UN is doing to meet those standards, and shows the plight of many children around the world. 16m; VHS. **Pr:** United Nations Department of Public Info; Nucleus Productions Ltd. **A:** Primary-Sr. High. **P:** Education. **U:** Institution. **Gen-Edu**: Documentary Films, United Nations, Children. **Acq:** Purchase, Rent/Lease. **Dist:** The Cinema Guild. $150.00.

About Time 2013 (R) — ★★½
A rom com about a young man, Tim (Gleeson), who can time travel may sound like a recipe for drivel, but writer/director Curtis ends up with a wistful, sentimental gem. Though he time travels, he can't drastically alter history but he can fine-tune his life, starting with Mary (a luminous McAdams) with whom he has fallen in love. Tim has the glorious gift of being able to hit restart to come up with the perfect date, romantic proposal, etc. Curtis' comedy is gentle and sweet, anchored by characters you truly hope finally get it right. 123m; DVD, Blu-Ray. **C:** Domhnall Gleeson; Rachel McAdams; Bill Nighy; Tom Hollander; Margot Robbie; Directed by Richard Curtis; Written by Richard Curtis; Cinematography by John Guleserian; Music by Nick Laird-Clowes. **Pr:** Tim Bevan; Eric Fellner; Working Title Films; Universal Pictures Inc. **A:** Sr. High-Adult. **P:** Entertainment. **U:** Home. **L:** English. **Mov-Ent**: Comedy--Romantic. **Acq:** Purchase. **Dist:** Universal Studios Home Video.

About VD 1974
Designed for special audiences, this program is a silent, animated, stylized depiction of facts on VD. An instructor is required to explain the film to his specific audience. 14m; VHS, 3/4 U. **Pr:** National Film Board of Canada. **A:** Jr. High-Sr. High. **P:** Education. **U:** Institution, SURA. **Hea-Sci**: Sexually Transmitted Diseases, Health Education. **Acq:** Purchase, Rent/Lease. **Dist:** National Film Board of Canada.

About Women 19??
Five programs explore the implications of women's evolving position in the domestic and economic spheres. Discussion guide available separately. 29m; VHS. **A:** Sr. High-Adult. **P:** Education. **U:** Institution. **Gen-Edu**: Women. **Acq:** Purchase. **Dist:** Access The Education Station. $399.00.
Indiv. Titles: 1. The Eternal Other 2. Home Fires 3. 10% of the Pie 4. Fit For Life 5. Organizing For Change.

About Words 1979
Steffens demonstrates ways in which some contemporary poets use language: the quality of spareness, the creation of surprise, the expression of passion and pathos. Part of the "Poetry for People Who Hate Poetry" series. 16m; VHS, 3/4 U, Special order formats. **C:** Roger Steffens. **Pr:** Steffens Shedd Poetry Films. **A:** Jr. High-Adult. **P:** Education. **U:** Institution, Home, SURA. **Gen-Edu**: Literature, Education. **Acq:** Purchase, Duplication License. **Dist:** Clear Vue Inc.

About Your Body 1976
Presented in two parts, a physical examination at the doctor's office is the occasion for a discussion of (Part I) the skeletal, muscular, and nervous systems; (Part II) the respiratory, digestive, and circulatory systems. 25m; VHS, 3/4 U, Special order formats. **Pr:** Churchill. **A:** Primary-Jr. High. **P:** Education. **U:** Institution, Home, SURA. **Hea-Sci**: Health Education, Anatomy & Physiology, Education. **Acq:** Purchase, Duplication License. **Dist:** Clear Vue Inc. $99.95.

Above 3751 to San Diego 2008 (Unrated)
Aerial photography plus trackside and onboard cameras captured the AT&SF 3751 as it made the trip from Los Angeles to San Diego on June 1, 2008, for the first time in 55 years. Pulled nearly entirely by steam it went along the west side of the Los Angeles River, past Amtrak's Redondo Yard, and east to Fullerton then San Juan Capistrano, up the grades of Miramar Hill and into the Mission Revival style station of San Diego. 90m; DVD. **A:** Family. **P:** Education. **U:** Home. **Gen-Edu**: Trains, U.S. States. **Acq:** Purchase. **Dist:** Pentrex Media Group L.L.C. $29.95.

Above All. . .Keep Your Head 1988
Shows workers how to protect their head. The techniques and equipment for preventing injury to eyes, ears, nose, mouth, neck, throat, brain, and skin are demonstrated in typical workplaces. 9m; VHS, 3/4 U. **C:** Johnny Osbourne; Mikey Jarratt. **Pr:** National Safety Council. **A:** Adult. **P:** Education. **U:** Institution, SURA. **Bus-Ind**: Safety Education. **Acq:** Purchase, Rent/Lease. **Dist:** National Safety Council, California Chapter, Film Library.

Above and Beyond 1953 — ★★★
Good performance by Taylor as Col. Paul Tibbets, the man who piloted the Enola Gay, which dropped the atomic bomb on Hiroshima. Focuses on the secrecy of the mission and the strain this puts on Tibbets marriage. Exciting action sequences of the mission itself. 122m/B/W; VHS, DVD. **C:** Robert Taylor; Eleanor Parker; James Whitmore; Larry Keating; Larry Gates; Robert Burton; Jim Backus; Marilyn Erskine; Steve (Stephen) Dunne; John Pickard; Hayden Rorke; Lawrence (Larry) Dobkin; Jack Raine; Jeff Richards; Barbara Ruick; Harlan Warde; John Close; Frank Gerstle; Dabbs Greer; Ewing Mitchell; Gregory Walcott; John Baer; Jonathon Cott; Dick Simmons; John McKee; G. Pat Collins; John Hedloe; Mack Williams; Dorothy Kennedy; Directed by Melvin Frank; Norman Panama; Written by Melvin Frank; Norman Panama; Beirne Lay, Jr.; Cinematography by Ray June; Music by Hugo Friedhofer. **Pr:** Melvin Frank; Norman Panama; Melvin Frank; Norman Panama; MGM. **A:** Jr. High-Adult. **P:** Entertainment. **U:** Home. **Mov-Ent**: World War Two, Aeronautics, Skateboarding. **Acq:** Purchase. **Dist:** WarnerArchive.com. $19.98.

Above and Beyond 1987
Documentary about five veterans who reveal their experiences as POWs in Vietnam. 58m; VHS, 3/4 U. **Pr:** Centre Productions,

Inc. **A:** Sr. High-Adult. **P:** Education. **U:** Institution, SURA. **Mov-Ent:** Documentary Films, Vietnam War, Veterans. **Acq:** Purchase. **Dist:** Clear Vue Inc.

Above and Beyond 2006 (Unrated) — ★★
In 1940, German U-boats prevent American ships from transporting plane parts to England so the Atlantic Ferry Command is set up. The RAF will fly the planes from Gander, Newfoundland to England instead. Capt. Don Bennett is commissioned to start the operation at the airfield run by Nathan Burgess, who isn't happy about the increased military presence. Nathan also isn't happy when ex-girlfriend Shelagh returns as a liaison since she's now interested in pilot Bill Jacobson. Has a number of inaccuracies (particularly regarding the planes) that will bother those in the know but otherwise is a decent Canadian TV miniseries. 179m; DVD. **C:** Richard E. Grant; Liane Balaban; Jonathan Scarfe; Allan Hawco; Kenneth Welsh; Jason Priestley; Joss Ackland; Peter MacNeill; Robert Wisden; Directed by Sturla Gunnarsson; Written by John W. Doyle; Lisa Porter; Cinematography by Rene Ohashi; Music by Jonathan Goldsmith. **A:** Jr. High-Adult. **P:** Entertainment. **U:** Home. **Mov-Ent:** Aeronautics, Canada, World War Two. **Acq:** Purchase. **Dist:** Timeless Media Group.

Above and Beyond: Managing for Productivity 1993
Presents Domaine Chandon, a wine producer, and the Ford Motor Company as examples of how to implement Deming's management principles. 30m; VHS. **A:** Adult. **P:** Professional. **U:** Institution. **Bus-Ind:** Business, Management. **Acq:** Purchase. **Dist:** RMI Media. $99.00.

Above Suspicion 1943 (Unrated) — ★★★
MacMurray and Crawford are American honeymooners (poor Fred!) asked to assist an international intelligence organization. They engage the Nazis in a tense battle of wits. Well-made and engaging. 91m/B/W; VHS, DVD. **C:** Joan Crawford; Fred MacMurray; Conrad Veidt; Basil Rathbone; Reginald Owen; Richard Ainley; Cecil Cunningham; Directed by Richard Thorpe; Written by Patricia Coleman; Cinematography by Robert Planck; Music by Bronislau Kaper. **Pr:** MGM. **A:** Jr. High-Adult. **P:** Entertainment. **U:** Home. **Mov-Ent:** Mystery & Suspense, World War Two, International Relations. **Acq:** Purchase. **Dist:** WarnerArchive.com. $19.98.

Above Suspicion 1995 (R) — ★★
Dempsey Cain (Reeve) seems to be the perfect cop, as well as a loving husband and father and a mentor to his younger brother. But when Cain is paralyzed by a drug dealer's bullet, he begins to notice just how close his wife (Cattrall) and brother (Kerr) are. There's adultery, there's murder, and there's the cop who just may be a cold-blooded killer. Unnervingly, Reeve plays a paraplegic in the last movie he made before his own paralyzing riding accident. 92m; VHS, DVD. **C:** Christopher Reeve; Kim Cattrall; Joe Mantegna; Edward Kerr; Directed by Steven Schachter. **A:** Sr. High-Adult. **P:** Entertainment. **U:** Home. **Mov-Ent:** Mystery & Suspense, TV Movies. **Acq:** Purchase. **Dist:** Home Box Office Inc.

Above Suspicion 2000 (R) — ★★
James Stockton (Bakula) seems like the perfect family man but his wife Lisa (Sciorra) starts becoming suspicious of his past—fearing that he's a killer on the lam. 99m; VHS, DVD, CC. **C:** Scott Bakula; Annabella Sciorra; George Dzundza; Ed Asner; Jack Blessing; Directed by Steven La Rocque. **A:** Sr. High-Adult. **P:** Entertainment. **U:** Home. **Mov-Ent:** Marriage. **Acq:** Purchase.

Above Suspicion: Set 1 2009
ITV crime drama 2009-2012; based on the novels by Lynda La Plante. "Above Suspicion": Young DC Anna Travis joins a murder squad headed by middle-aged DCI James Langton. Despite her inexperience, Anna's sent undercover to draw out the main suspect in a series of brutal killings--popular actor Alan Daniels (Jason Durr). Corresponds to the 1st UK TV series. "The Red Dahlia": The body of model Louise Pennell is found mutilated and reporter Richard Reynolds (Edward Machiam) realizes the killer's copying the unsolved L.A. 'Black Dahlia' murder. Corresponds to the 2nd UK TV series (2010). 5 episodes total. 254m; DVD. **C:** Kelly Reilly; Ciaran Hinds. **A:** Sr. High-Adult. **P:** Entertainment. **U:** Home. **Mov-Ent:** Crime Drama, Great Britain, Television Series. **Acq:** Purchase. **Dist:** Acorn Media Group Inc. $39.99.

Above Suspicion: Set 2 2011
ITV crime drama 2009-2012. "Deadly Intent": Anna Travis is now a Detective Inspector who's once again teamed with also-promoted Detective Superintendent James Langton. This time it's the murder of a retired police officer, a friend of Langton's, who was found in a London crack house. They go after a drug dealer who's putting the powerful narcotic Fentanyl out on the street. Corresponds to the 3rd UK TV series; 3 episodes. 138m; DVD. **C:** Kelly Reilly; Ciaran Hinds. **A:** Sr. High-Adult. **P:** Entertainment. **U:** Home. **Mov-Ent:** Crime Drama, Great Britain, Television Series. **Acq:** Purchase. **Dist:** Acorn Media Group Inc. $29.99.

Above the Law 1988 (R) — ★★
In his debut, Seagal does his wooden best to portray a tough Chicago police detective planning an enormous drug bust of one of the biggest felons in the state. Unfortunately, the FBI has ordered him to back off and find another bust. The reasons are almost as complex as Seagal's character, and like most details of the flick, stupid. However, people don't watch these movies for the acting or the plot, but for the fight scenes, which are well-choreographed and violent. Watch it with someone you love. 99m; VHS, DVD, Blu-Ray, 8 mm, CC. **C:** Steven Seagal; Pam Grier; Henry Silva; Sharon Stone; Ron Dean; Daniel Faraldo; Chelcie Ross; Thalmus Rasulala; Michael Rooker; Directed by Andrew Davis; Written by Andrew Davis; Steven Pressfield; Cinematography by Robert Steadman; Music by David Michael Frank. **A:** College-Adult. **P:** Entertainment. **U:** Home. **Mov-Ent:** Martial Arts, Drugs. **Acq:** Purchase. **Dist:** Warner Home Video, Inc.; Time-Life Video and Television. $19.95.

Above the Rim 1994 (R) — ★★½
Vulgar, violent hoopster drama about a fiercely competitive inner-city playground game. Kyle-Lee Watson (Martin), a self-involved high school star raised by a saintly single mom (Pinkins), is torn between the lure of the streets and his college recruiting chances. His odds aren't made any easier by homeboy hustler Birdie (Shakur), who wants to improve his chances of making money on the local games by making sure Watson plays for his team. Energetic b-ball sequences, strong performances lose impact amid formulaic melodrama and the usual obscenities. Debut for director Pollack. 97m; VHS, DVD, CC. **C:** Duane Martin; Tupac Shakur; Leon; Marlon Wayans; Tonya Pinkins; Bernie Mac; Directed by Jeff Pollack; Written by Jeff Pollack; Barry Michael Cooper; Music by Marcus Miller. **Pr:** Jeff Pollack; Benny Medina; James D. Brubaker; Jeff Pollack; New Line Cinema. **A:** Sr. High-Adult. **P:** Entertainment. **U:** Home. **Mov-Ent:** Basketball, Black Culture, Security Officer Training. **Acq:** Purchase. **Dist:** New Line Home Video. $19.98.

Above Us the Waves 1955 (Unrated) — ★★★
During WWII, the British navy immobilizes a huge German battleship off the coast of Norway. Effectively dramatizes the British naval preparations for what seemed a suicidal mission: using midget submarines to plant underwater explosives on the hull of the German vessel and detonating them before the Germans could detect the danger. 92m; VHS, DVD. **C:** John Mills; John Gregson; Donald Sinden; James Robertson Justice; Michael Medwin; James Kenney; O.E. Hasse; Theodore Bikel; Thomas Heathcote; Lee Patterson; Lyndon Brook; Anthony Newley; Directed by Ralph Thomas. **Pr:** Rank; Republic. **A:** Jr. High-Adult. **P:** Entertainment. **U:** Home. **Mov-Ent:** World War Two, Documentary Films. **Acq:** Purchase. **Dist:** Lions Gate Entertainment Inc.

Abraham 1994 (Unrated) — ★★½
Biblical epic chronicling the Old Testament story of humble shepherd Abraham (Harris), who's commanded by God to lead his family into the promised land of Canaan. Among his family's many trials will be God's command that Abraham sacrifice his son Isaac as a test of faith and obedience. Filmed on location in Morocco with a commanding performance by Harris that somewhat redeems the film's dullness. 175m; VHS, DVD. **C:** Richard Harris; Barbara Hershey; Maximilian Schell; Vittorio Gassman; Carolina Rosi; Gottfried John; Kevin McNally; Directed by Joseph Sargent; Written by Robert McKee; Cinematography by Raffaele Mertes; Music by Ennio Morricone; Marco Frisina. **Pr:** Turner Network Television. **A:** Family. **P:** Entertainment. **U:** Home. **Mov-Ent:** TV Movies, Family. **Acq:** Purchase. **Dist:** Turner Broadcasting System Inc. $59.98.

Abraham Lincoln 1930 (Unrated) — ★★½
Griffith's first talking movie takes Abraham Lincoln from his birth through his assassination. This restored version includes the original slavery sequences which were believed to be lost, but obviously were not. Musical score included. 97m/B/W; VHS, DVD, Blu-Ray, 3/4 U, Special order formats. **C:** Walter Huston; Una Merkel; Kay Hammond; E. Alyn (Fred) Warren; Hobart Bosworth; Henry B. Walthall; Russell Simpson; Ian Keith; Frank Campeau; Directed by D.W. Griffith; Cinematography by Karl Struss. **Pr:** United Artists. **A:** Jr. High-Adult. **P:** Entertainment. **U:** Home. **Mov-Ent:** Biography: Politics, Civil War. **Acq:** Purchase. **Dist:** Grapevine Video; Critics' Choice Video & DVD; Glenn Video Vistas Ltd. $19.95.

Abraham Lincoln 1990
Award-winning author James McPherson narrated this engaging epic examination of the most renowned American president. Experience Lincoln's journey from the poverty of an Illinois farm to his assassination during an evening of theatre. 35m; VHS. **C:** Narrated by James McPherson. **A:** Family. **P:** Entertainment. **U:** Home. **Gen-Edu:** Documentary Films, Biography, Presidency. **Acq:** Purchase. **Dist:** Cambridge Educational; Acorn Media Group Inc.; Facets Multimedia Inc. $19.95.

Abraham Lincoln: A New Birth of Freedom 1992
Provides background information on the self-educated lawyer but focuses on Lincoln's involvement with the Civil War. Interviews with historians and public figures, still photos, and modern footage document the accomplishments and impact of the 16th President. 60m; VHS. **C:** Voice(s) by Peter Coyote; Louis Gossett, Jr.; Narrated by Andrew Young. **Pr:** Judith Leonard Productions; Quest Productions. **A:** Jr. High-College. **P:** Education. **U:** Institution. **Gen-Edu:** Biography, History, Civil War. **Acq:** Purchase. **Dist:** PBS Home Video. $69.95.

Abraham Lincoln and the Emancipation Proclamation 1973
An examination of the dilemma confronting Lincoln over the troubling issue of Negro slavery. 25m; VHS, 3/4 U. **Pr:** American Educational Films. **A:** Jr. High-Sr. High. **P:** Education. **U:** Institution, SURA. **Gen-Edu:** Documentary Films, Presidency, Slavery. **Acq:** Purchase. **Dist:** Capital Communications.

Abraham Lincoln: Vampire Hunter 2012 (R) — ★½
Working from Seth Grahame-Smith's 2010 bestselling novel (who adapted the script), producer Tim Burton and director Bekmambetov drain the life out of this unique concept by presenting something remarkably lacking in personality. The basis of the 3D action extravaganza is simple enough--the legendary President is re-imagined as a killer of the undead after seeing his mom die at the fangs of a vampire as a child. But, save for two clever action scenes, the result is bloody (literally) boring. It doesn't help that the leading man has all the charisma of a robot at Disney's Hall of Presidents. 105m; DVD, Blu-Ray, Streaming. **C:** Benjamin Walker; Dominic Cooper; Anthony Mackie; Mary Elizabeth Winstead; Rufus Sewell; Directed by Timur Bekmambetov; Written by Seth Graham-Smith; Cinematography by Caleb Deschanel; Music by Henry Jackman. **Pr:** Tim Burton; Jim Lemley; Timur Bekmambetov; Tim Burton Productions; Blazelevs Production. **A:** Sr. High-Adult. **P:** Entertainment. **U:** Home. **L:** English, French, Spanish. **Mov-Ent:** Horror, Presidency, Civil War. **Acq:** Purchase, Rent/Lease. **Dist:** Fox Home Entertainment. $39.99 29.98 12.99.

Abraham Lincoln vs. Zombies 2012 (R) — **Bomb!**
Another attempt by Asylum to cash in on making a film with a name similar to a much bigger studio release. President Lincoln has to rehearse the Gettysburg Address while sneaking into Georgia with the Secret Service to quell a zombie uprising. 90m; DVD, Blu-Ray, Streaming. **C:** Bill Oberst, Jr.; Jason Vail; Don McGraw; Richard Schenkman; Baby Norman; Directed by Richard Schenkman; Written by Richard Schenkman; Karl T. Hirsch; J. Lauren Proctor; Cinematography by Tim Gill; Music by Chris Ridenhour. **A:** Sr. High-Adult. **P:** Entertainment. **U:** Home. **L:** English. **Mov-Ent. Acq:** Purchase, Rent/Lease. **Dist:** The Asylum. $24.95 14.95 14.95.

Abraham's People 1983
Traces the history of the Jews in the Middle East. 53m; VHS, 3/4 U. **Pr:** Anti-Defamation League of B'nai B'rith. **A:** Primary-Adult. **P:** Education. **U:** Institution, CCTV, CATV, BCTV, Home. **Gen-Edu:** Documentary Films, Judaism, Middle East. **Acq:** Purchase. **Dist:** Anti-Defamation League of B'nai B'rith.

Abraham's Valley 1993 (Unrated) — ★★
Beautiful Ema (Silveira) is forced into a wealthy marriage to a friend of her father's and they move to the vineyards of Abraham's Valley where the bride knows no one. Unhappy, Ema refuses to submit to her husband and decides to take a lover of her own. Based on the novel by Augustina Bessa-Luis. Portuguese with subtitles. 180m; VHS, DVD. **C:** Leonor Silveira; Luis Miguel Cintra; Diogo Doria; Ruy de Carvalho; Luis Lima Barreto; Directed by Manoel de Oliveira; Written by Manoel de Oliveira; Cinematography by Mario Barroso. **A:** College-Adult. **P:** Entertainment. **U:** Home. **L:** Portuguese. **Mov-Ent:** Marriage. **Acq:** Purchase. **Dist:** Vanguard International Cinema, Inc.

Abrasive Wheels 19??
This chart topping band from the U.K. plays their best alternative numbers. ?m; VHS. **A:** Jr. High-Adult. **P:** Entertainment. **U:** Home. **Mov-Ent:** Music Video. **Acq:** Purchase. **Dist:** Music Video Distributors. $29.95.

Abraxas: Guardian of the Universe 1990 (R) — ★½
Good space cop versus bad space cop with an ecological twist. Good-guy Abraxas (Ventura) has the task of stopping planets from destroying their environments and fighting senseless wars. His ex-partner Secundas (Ole-Thorsen) has his own mission, seeking an anti-life power which could destroy the universe. They decide to fight it out, using Earth as the battleground. Also available in an edited PG-13 version. 90m; VHS, DVD. **C:** Jesse Ventura; Sven-Ole Thorsen; Damian Lee; Marjorie Bransfield; Ken Quinn; Marilyn Lightstone; Moses Znaimer; Layne Coleman; Sonja Belliveau; James Belushi; Directed by Damian Lee; Written by Damian Lee; Cinematography by Curtis Petersen. **Pr:** Damian Lee. **A:** Sr. High-Adult. **P:** Entertainment. **U:** Home. **Mov-Ent:** Science Fiction. **Acq:** Purchase. **Dist:** BFS Video.

Abrazos: Tango in Buenos Aires 2003
Director Daniel Rivas documents the 5th Buenos Aires Tango Festival, including rehearsals, performances, and interviews. Spanish with subtitles. 85m; DVD. **A:** Sr. High-Adult. **P:** Entertainment. **U:** Home. **L:** Spanish. **Gen-Edu:** Documentary Films. **Acq:** Purchase. **Dist:** Facets Multimedia Inc.

Abroad with Two Yanks 1944 (Unrated) — ★★
Two Marine buddies on furlough exhibit slapstick tendencies while competing for the same girl. Along the way a big chase ensues with the two soldiers in drag. Typical wartime shenanigans likely to incite only weak chuckling or inspired snoozing. 81m/B/W; VHS. **C:** William Bendix; Dennis O'Keefe; Helen Walker; John Loder; George Cleveland; Janet Lambert; James Flavin; Arthur Hunnicutt; Directed by Allan Dwan. **Pr:** Edward Small; United Artists. **A:** Family. **P:** Entertainment. **U:** Home. **Mov-Ent:** Comedy--Slapstick, World War Two. **Acq:** Purchase. **Dist:** Lions Gate Television Corp. $12.95.

Abs of Steel: Intense Abdominal Workouts 19??
Olympic trainer Kurt Brungardt illustrates two complete workouts which center on the abdominal area. He provides a basic 10-minute workout and a 15-minute intermediate workout. 40m; VHS. **A:** Adult. **P:** Instruction. **U:** Home. **How-Ins:** Fitness/Exercise. **Acq:** Purchase. **Dist:** Calibre Press Inc. $19.95.

Absence 1986
An experimental video which uses the recurring image of a pair of lips unable to speak to express a young woman's loss of self. 5m; VHS, 3/4 U. **Pr:** Women in Focus. **A:** Sr. High-Adult. **P:** Entertainment. **U:** Institution, SURA. **Gen-Edu:** Video, Women. **Acq:** Purchase, Rent/Lease. **Dist:** Video Out Distribution.

The Absence of Light 2006 (Unrated) — ★
Lame micro budget flick about a scientist discovering the secret of life who immediately becomes pursued by agents of the two mega corporations secretly controlling America. 77m; DVD. **C:** Tom Savini; Caroline Munro; Directed by Patrick Desmond; Written by Patrick Desmond; Cinematography by Patrick Desmond; Music by Andy L. Halter; Todd Skeie. **A:** Sr. High-Adult. **P:** Entertainment. **U:** Home. **L:** English. **Mov-Ent. Acq:** Purchase. **Dist:** York Pictures Inc. $24.99.

Absence of Malice 1981 (PG) — ★★½
High-minded story about the harm that the news media can inflict. Field is the earnest reporter who, after being fed some facts by an unscrupulous federal investigator, writes a story implicating Newman in a murder he didn't commit. Field hides behind journalistic confidentiality privilege to put off the outraged Newman, who loses a friend to suicide during the debacle. Interesting performances by Field and Newman. 116m; VHS, DVD. **C:** Paul Newman; Sally Field; Bob Balaban; Melinda Dillon; Luther Adler; Barry Primus; Josef Sommer; John Harkins; Don Hood; Wilford Brimley; Directed by Sydney Pollack; Written by Kurt Luedtke; Cinematography by Owen Roizman; Music by Dave Grusin. **Pr:** Columbia Pictures. **A:** Jr. High-Adult. **P:** Entertainment. **U:** Home. **Mov-Ent:** Journalism, Suicide. **Acq:** Purchase. **Dist:** Sony Pictures Home Entertainment Inc. $14.95.

Absence of the Good 1999 (R) — ★★
Homicide detective Caleb Barnes (Baldwin) is mourning the accidental death of his only child while investigating a series of murders in Salt Lake City. He's under pressure to solve the case, even as his home life is disintegrating, and Caleb's investigation leads to a family's malignant history. 99m; VHS, DVD. **C:** Stephen Baldwin; Tyne Daly; Allen Garfield; Robert Knepper; Directed by John Flynn; Written by James Reid. **A:** Sr. High-Adult. **P:** Entertainment. **U:** Home. **Mov-Ent. Acq:** Purchase. **Dist:** Sony Pictures Home Entertainment Inc.

The Absent 2011 (Unrated) — ★
Twin brothers part ways when one of them poisons their parents after he finds out they plan to murder him for insurance money. Fast forward 25 years and he's released and free to interfere with his brother's life again. 80m; DVD, Streaming. **C:** Jesse Gullion; Lucas Dick; Bryan Kirkwood; Denny Kirkwood; Matthew Josten; Sam Ball; Kelly B. Eviston; Jamielyn Kane; Moniqua Plante; Vanessa Zima; Yvonne Zima; Jennifer Blanc; Directed by Sage Bannick; Written by Sage Bannick; Damon Abdallah; Ari Bernstein; Cinematography by Eric Curtis. **A:** Sr. High-Adult. **P:** Entertainment. **U:** Home. **L:** English. **Mov-Ent. Acq:** Purchase, Rent/Lease. **Dist:** Last Night LLC. $14.95 9.95.

Absent 2011 (Unrated) — ★½
Unsettling, if frustrating, drama finds teenage student Martin deliberately trying to seduce his obtuse swimming coach Sebastian. He lies to get to stay the night at Sebastian's apartment and uses that questionable choice to try to push the man into an illicit liaison. Spanish with subtitles. 85m; DVD. **C:** Javier De Pietro; Carlos Echevarria; Alejandro Barbero; Antonella Costa; Directed by Marco Berger; Written by Marco Berger; Cinematography by Tomas Perez Silva. **A:** Sr. High-Adult. **P:** Entertainment. **U:** Home. **L:** Spanish. **Mov-Ent:** Adolescence, South America, Homosexuality. **Acq:** Purchase. **Dist:** TLA Releasing.

The Absent-Minded Professor 1961 (Unrated) — ★★★½
Classic dumb Disney fantasy of the era. A professor accidentally invents an anti-gravity substance called flubber, causing inanimate objects and people to become airborne. Great sequence of the losing school basketball team taking advantage of flubber during a game. MacMurray is convincing as the absent-minded genius in this newly colored version. Followed by "Son of Flubber." 97m; VHS, DVD. **C:** Fred MacMurray; Nancy Olson; Keenan Wynn; Tommy Kirk; Leon Ames; Ed Wynn; Edward Andrews; Wally Brown; Wendell Holmes; Directed by Robert Stevenson; Written by Bill Walsh; Cinematography by Edward Colman; Music by George Bruns. **Pr:** Walt Disney Studios. **A:** Family. **P:** Entertainment. **U:** Home. **Mov-Ent:** Family Viewing, Basketball, Scientists. **Acq:** Purchase. **Dist:** Walt Disney Studios Home Entertainment; Baker and Taylor. $19.99.

Absent Without Leave 1995 (Unrated) — ★★½
Ed (McLachlan) marries his pregnant girlfriend Daisy (Hobbs) in 1942 before joining the army. When Daisy miscarries, Ed pledges to take her home even though it means leaving the army wihout permission. As the newleyweds travel across the New Zealand countryside, they struggle with the new demands of their relationship. 104m; VHS. **C:** Craig McLachlan; Katrina Hobbs; Directed by John Laing. **A:** Sr. High-Adult. **P:** Entertainment. **U:** Home. **Mov-Ent:** Drama, New Zealand, World War Two. **Acq:** Purchase. **Dist:** Leo Films.

Absenteeism 1979
The causes and cures of absenteeism on the job are explored in this program, which follows a typical worker who has trouble getting started in the morning. 12m; VHS, 3/4 U. **Pr:** Xerox Films. **A:** Adult. **P:** Professional. **U:** Institution, SURA. **Bus-Ind:** Documentary Films, Personnel Management. **Acq:** Purchase. **Dist:** Center for Humanities, Inc./Guidance Associates.

Absentia 2011 (R) — ★★
Callie (Katie Parker) moves in with her sister, to help her get her life back together after her husband's disappearance. She quickly discovers many local disappearances all connected to a nearby tunnel. 91m; DVD, Streaming. **C:** Katie Parker; Courtney Bell; Dave Levine; Morgan Peter Brown; Justin Gordon; Directed by Mike Flanagan; Written by Mike Flanagan; Cinematography by Rustin Cerveny; Music by Ryan David Leack. **A:** Sr. High-Adult. **P:** Entertainment. **U:** Home. **L:** English, French. **Mov-Ent. Acq:** Purchase, Rent/Lease. **Dist:** Phase 4. $29.99 12.99.

Absolute Beginners 1986 (PG) — ★★
Fervently stylish camp musical exploring the lives of British teenagers in the 1950s never quite gets untracked, although MTV video moments fill out a spare plotline. Based on a novel by Colin MacInnes. 107m; VHS, DVD. **C:** David Bowie; Ray Davies; Mandy Rice-Davies; James Fox; Eddie O'Connell; Patsy Kensit; Anita Morris; Sade Adu; Sandie Shaw; Directed by Julien Temple; Written by Richard Burridge; Don MacPherson; Cinematography by Oliver Stapleton. **Pr:** Orion Pictures. **A:** Jr. High-Adult. **P:** Entertainment. **U:** Home. **Mov-Ent:** Musical. **Acq:** Purchase. **Dist:** Movies Unlimited. $12.74.
Songs: Absolute Beginners; That's Motivation; Volare; Killer Blow; Have You Ever Been Blue?; Quiet Life; Having It All; Selling Out; Va Va Voom; The Naked and the Dead; Better Git It In Your Soul (The Hot and the Cool); Boogie Stop Shuffle (The Rough and the Smooth); Rodrigo Bay; Riot City; Ted Ain't Dead; Napoli; Cool Napoli; Little Cat; Landlords and Tenants; Santa Lucia; So What?; Hey Little Schoolgirl; Rock Baby Rock; Scorpio; Switching It Off; Hancock's Half Hour; Here Comes the Bride; My Mammy; Sleep Lagoon; Teddy Bears Picnic; Rocking at the 21's; Bongo Rock; Great Balls of Fire; Heat Doesn't Bother Me.

Absolute Deception 2013 (R) — ★½
Generic action-thriller. Magazine reporter Rebecca Scott (Vaugier) is informed by FBI agent John Nelson (Gooding Jr.) that her long-presumed dead husband Miles has, in fact, just been murdered. Miles was an informant and Rebecca and John travel to Australia's Gold Coast for amswers from people who want to stop their investigation in the same deadly manner. 92m; DVD. **C:** Cuba Gooding, Jr.; Emmanuelle Vaugier; Evert McQueen; Ty Hungerford; Directed by Brian Trenchard-Smith; Written by Kraig Wenman; Cinematography by Dan Macarthur; Music by Michael Richard Plowman. **A:** Sr. High-Adult. **P:** Entertainment. **U:** Home. **L:** English. **Mov-Ent:** Action-Adventure, Australia, Federal Bureau of Investigation (FBI). **Acq:** Purchase. **Dist:** Sony Pictures Home Entertainment Inc.

Absolute Evel: The Evel Knievel Story 2005
Presents the History Channel's special on daredevil Evel Knievel as he relives some of his most dangerous tricks and explores the adverse effects these had on his health (Knievel died in late 2007). 100m; DVD. **A:** Jr. High-Adult. **P:** Entertainment. **U:** Home, CATV. **Mov-Ent:** Television Series, Documentary Films, Biography: Show Business. **Acq:** Purchase. **Dist:** A&E Television Networks L.L.C. $29.95.

Absolute Power 1997 (R) — ★★½
Eastwood is "In the Line of Fire," (against the very agents he previously glorified) as an expert thief being pursued by rogue Secret Service men in this fast-paced thriller. While looting a Washington official's place, Luther (Eastwood) inadvertently witnesses a murder committed by none other than U.S. President Richmond (Hackman) and his goons. Immediately, a cover-up is organized by his unbalanced chief-of-staff (Davis) and Luther becomes the prime suspect. Harris gives his usual solid performance as the homicide detective. Eastwood's simple directorial style keeps up the suspense and propels the film steadily forward, alongside a generally solid plot that gets a bit improbable near the end. Based on the novel by David Baldacci. 120m; VHS, DVD, Blu-Ray, CC. **C:** Clint Eastwood; Gene Hackman; Ed Harris; Laura Linney; Judy Davis; Scott Glenn; Dennis Haysbert; E.G. Marshall; Melora Hardin; Directed by Clint Eastwood; Written by William Goldman; Cinematography by Jack N. Green; Music by Lennie Niehaus. **Pr:** Clint Eastwood; Karen Spiegel; Tom Rooker; Clint Eastwood; Malpaso Productions; Castle Rock Entertainment; Columbia Pictures; Sony Pictures Home Entertainment Inc. **A:** Sr. High-Adult. **P:** Entertainment. **U:** Home. **Mov-Ent:** Mystery & Suspense, Presidency, Politics & Government. **Acq:** Purchase. **Dist:** Warner Home Video, Inc.

Absolute Trash: A Recycling Story 1989
Two escaped convicts learn about recycling while trying to retrieve hidden money. Humorous look at the importance of recycling and keeping the environment clean. 25m; VHS, 3/4 U. **A:** Primary-Sr. High. **P:** Education. **U:** Institution. **Gen-Edu:** Ecology & Environment. **Acq:** Rent/Lease. **Dist:** New Dimension Media. $45.00.

Absolute Zero 2005 (Unrated) — ★
Climatologist David Koch (Fahey) warns that a shift in the earth's polarity (thanks to global warming) could quickly cause a second ice age. When his predictions start coming true, scientist have to find a way to prevent the temps from reaching absolute zero and destroying life as we know it. 86m; DVD. **C:** Jeff Fahey; Erika Eleniak; Bill Dow; Jessica Amlee; Michael Ryan; Fred Ewanuick; Brittney Irvin; Directed by Robert Lee; Written by Sarah Watson; Cinematography by Adam Sliwinski; Music by Annette Ducharme; John Webster. **A:** Jr. High-Adult. **P:** Entertainment. **U:** Home. **Mov-Ent:** TV Movies, Action-Adventure, Arctic Regions. **Acq:** Purchase. **Dist:** Echo Bridge Home Entertainment.

Absolutely Fabulous 1994
(Mis)adventures of drunken, drug-taking, sexual promiscuous, shallow, self-involved, ill-tempered, and absolutely fabulous life-long friends Edina Monsoon (Saunders) and Patsy Stone (Lumley). 87m; VHS, DVD, CC. **C:** Jennifer Saunders; Joanna Lumley; Julia Sawalha; Written by Jennifer Saunders. **A:** Sr. High-Adult. **P:** Entertainment. **U:** Home. **Mov-Ent. Acq:** Purchase. **Dist:** Fox Home Entertainment. $19.98.

Absolutely Fabulous, Absolutely Special 2003 (Unrated)
The lady lushes go to New York where Edina (Saunders) is reunited with long-lost son who's gay but not enough so for Edina's standards. Saffy (Sawalha) gets engaged to a handsome and wealthy man and guest-star Whoopi Goldberg is a gay relationship counselor who tries to fix Edina and Patsy (Lumley) up. 2 episodes. 150m; DVD. **C:** Jennifer Saunders; Joanna Lumley; Julia Sawalha; June Whitfield; Jane Horrocks. **A:** Sr. High-Adult. **P:** Entertainment. **U:** Home. **Mov-Ent:** Television Series. **Acq:** Purchase. **Dist:** Warner Home Video, Inc. $24.98.

Absolutely Fabulous, Complete DVD Collection 2005 (Unrated)
Features all episodes from the TV series run and includes bonus features such as Edina (Saunders) chronicling her life in a documentary titled "Absolutely Fabulous Moments," a how-to on being absolutely fabulous, celebrity guest star guide, and a map to the maniacal boozy world of Edina and Patsy (Lumley). 18 episodes. 720m; DVD. **C:** Jennifer Saunders; Joanna Lumley; Julia Sawalha; June Whitfield; Jane Horrocks. **A:** Sr. High-Adult. **P:** Entertainment. **U:** Home. **Mov-Ent:** Television Series. **Acq:** Purchase. **Dist:** Warner Home Video, Inc. $19.98.

Absolutely Fabulous, Series 1 2005 (Unrated)
Egotistical British best friends Edina (Saunders) and Patsy (Lumley) booze it up as they face life's misadventures in this BBC TV series. In season one, the ladies hold a fashion show, Edina tries to get in shape to confront an old rival, they go to France for the sake of wine, Edina's daughter Saffy (Sawalha) puts up with the pair at her school, Edina faces her 40th birthday, and Patsy actually goes to her job at a fashion magazine publisher. 6 episodes. 180m; DVD. **C:** Jennifer Saunders; Joanna Lumley; Julia Sawalha; June Whitfield; Jane Horrocks. **A:** Sr. High-Adult. **P:** Entertainment. **U:** Home. **Mov-Ent:** Television Series. **Acq:** Purchase. **Dist:** Warner Home Video, Inc. $19.98.

Absolutely Fabulous, Series 2 2005 (Unrated)
The sassy, drunken duo of Edina (Saunders) and Patsy (Lumley) are back; in season two, Patsy needs to look younger for a fashion shoot so heads to the hospital for some work, Edina's father dies, the gals head to Morocco for some illicit fun but Soffy (Sawalha) cramps their style, Edina is not fond of her friends' baby's barf, Edina stresses out after losing her ex-husbands' financial support, and Edina must deal with Saffy's new beau. 6 episodes. 180m; DVD. **C:** Jennifer Saunders; Joanna Lumley; Julia Sawalha; June Whitfield; Jane Horrocks. **A:** Sr. High-Adult. **P:** Entertainment. **U:** Home. **Mov-Ent:** Television Series. **Acq:** Purchase. **Dist:** Warner Home Video, Inc. $19.98.

Absolutely Fabulous, Series 3 2005 (Unrated)
Best pals Edina (Saunders) and Patsy's (Lumley) inebriated adventures continue as Edina goes to New York via Concorde for the sole purpose of purchasing a doorknob, the gals celebrate New Year's Eve, an orgy is in the works, Edina has esteem issues at work, Patsy considers moving to New York after Saffy (Sawalha) moveds out, and Edina first looks for inner peace but then looks for Patsy in New York. 6 episodes. 180m; DVD. **A:** Sr. High-Adult. **P:** Entertainment. **U:** Home. **Mov-Ent:** Television Series. **Acq:** Purchase. **Dist:** Warner Home Video, Inc. $29.98.

Absolutely Fabulous, Series 4 2002
Best pals Edina (Saunders) and Patsy's (Lumley) inebriated adventures continue. Patsy injects Eddy with a wrinkle-reducing treatment in "Parallox," Eddy tries to seduce a millionaire in "Fish Farm," and the friends visit Paris for a fashion shoot in "Paris." 6 episodes. 240m; DVD. **A:** Jr. High-Adult. **P:** Entertainment. **U:** Home. **Mov-Ent:** Television Series. **Acq:** Purchase. **Dist:** BBC Worldwide Ltd. $34.98.

Absolutely Fabulous, Series 5 2005 (Unrated)
Boozy best pals face more adventures: Edina is (Saunders) shocked by Saffy's (Sawalha) pregnancy, Edina falls in love, Patsy (Lumley) has old sex tapes distributed by a company in Japan, and Patsy passes out while arguing with Edina and doctors tell her she's dying. Minnie Driver guest stars. 8 episodes. 240m; DVD. **C:** Jennifer Saunders; Joanna Lumley; Julia Sawalha; June Whitfield; Jane Horrocks. **A:** Sr. High-Adult. **P:** Entertainment. **U:** Home. **Mov-Ent:** Television Series. **Acq:** Purchase. **Dist:** Warner Home Video, Inc. $34.98.

Absolutely Fabulous: The Last Shout 1996 — ★★½
The first TV movie from the British comedy series finds Edina (Saunders) selling her fashion PR business after a near-death experience and doing some soul-searching—AbFab style, which involves shopping, travel, and champagne. Naturally, Patsy (Lumley) goes along for the ride. The duo's favorite designer Christian LaCroix even has a cameo. 90m; VHS, DVD. **C:** Jennifer Saunders; Joanna Lumley; Cameo(s) Marianne Faithfull. **A:** Sr. High-Adult. **P:** Entertainment. **U:** Home. **Mov-Ent:** TV Movies, Women. **Acq:** Purchase. **Dist:** BBC Worldwide Publishing Ltd.

Absolutely Positive 1990
Director Peter Adair, who is gay and HIV+, profiles an "eclectic roll call" of people testing HIV+ because of a tainted blood transfusion, drug use or heterosexual transmission, revealing their initial reactions and changes in their lifestyles. 87m; VHS, DVD. **A:** Sr. High-Adult. **P:** Education. **U:** Institution. **Hea-Sci:** Documentary Films, AIDS, Sexually Transmitted Diseases. **Acq:** Purchase, Rent/Lease. **Dist:** Frameline; Select Media, Inc. $295.00.

Absolutely the Best of the Soupy Sales Show 19??
Two episodes featuring comedian Soupy Sales. 50m; VHS. **A:** Family. **P:** Entertainment. **U:** Home. **Mov-Ent:** Comedy--Performance. **Acq:** Purchase. **Dist:** Rhino Entertainment Co.

Absolutely Tofu 1 19??
Explains and demonstrates how to make seven vegetarian dishes. 60m; VHS. **A:** Adult. **P:** Instruction. **U:** Home. **How-Ins:** Cooking. **Acq:** Purchase. **Dist:** Tapeworm Video Distributors Inc. $24.95.

Absolutely Tofu 2 19??
Explains and demonstrates how to make six vegetarian dishes. 60m; VHS. **A:** Adult. **P:** Instruction. **U:** Home. **How-Ins:** Cooking. **Acq:** Purchase. **Dist:** Tapeworm Video Distributors Inc. $24.95.

Absolution 1981 (R) — ★★
Two English boys trapped in a Catholic boarding school conspire to drive a tyrannical priest over the edge of sanity. As a result, bad things (including murder) occur. Burton is interesting in sadistic character study. Not released in the U.S. until 1988 following Burton's death, maybe due to something written in the will. 105m; VHS, DVD. **C:** Richard Burton; Dominic Guard; Dai Bradley; Andrew Keir; Billy Connolly; Willoughby Gray; Preston Lockwood; James Ottaway; Brook Williams; Jon Plowman; Robin Soans; Trevor Martin; Directed by Anthony Page; Written by Anthony Shaffer; Cinematography by John Coquillon; Music by Stanley Myers. **Pr:** Danny O'Donovan; Elliot Kastner; Enterprise Pictures Ltd. **A:** Sr. High-Adult. **P:** Entertainment. **U:** Home. **Mov-Ent:** Mystery & Suspense, Education, Religion. **Acq:** Purchase. **Dist:** Facets Multimedia Inc. $9.95.

Absolution 1997 (Unrated) — **Bomb!**
Bad acting, bad dialogue, cretinous plot even by low-budget sci fi standards. A meteor causes severe planetary destruction and one set of survivors lives in an Arctic military colony. Ryan Murphy is sent to investigate the disappearance of a soldier and sees that the colony's tyrannical leader has the inhabitants involved in some weird outer space conspiracy. 100m; DVD. **C:** Mario Lopez; Jaime Pressly; Richard Grieco; Greg Serano; Justin Walker; Directed by David DeCoteau; Written by Chris Chaffin; Cinematography by Howard Wexler; Music by Marco Marinangeli. **A:** Sr. High-Adult. **P:** Entertainment. **U:** Home. **Mov-Ent:** Conspiracies or Conspiracy Theories, Science Fiction, Arctic Regions. **Acq:** Purchase. **Dist:** Echo Bridge Home Entertainment.

Absolution 2003 (Unrated) — ★
An angel who wants to know what being human is like becomes involved in a deal to turn chemicals used in nuclear weapons into vhs tape shells and ships them overseas disguised as porn. 99m/B/W, DVD. **C:** John Specht; Jonas Moses; Paul Wendell; Terry Hopper; Eric Whitman; Daniel Byington; Bryan Lane; Eric Peniston; Leah Schumacher; Emily Haack; Halley Moore; Anna Knobeloch; Directed by John Specht; Written by John Specht; Jonas Moses; Stacy Key. **A:** Sr. High-Adult. **P:** Entertainment. **U:** Home. **L:** English. **Mov-Ent. Acq:** Purchase. **Dist:** Sub Rosa Studios. $14.99.

Absolution 2005 (Unrated) — ★★
New York journalist Bettina hasn't been back to her Ohio hometown in years but gets an assignment to investigate a man who's allegedly performing hands-on miracles. She's shocked to find out it's her high school boyfriend Paolo, who's now comatose but whose mother Maria lays his hands on the sick. Flashbacks show why Bettina had to get away from her own dysfunctional family. 90m; DVD. **C:** Samantha Mathis; Stephen McHattie; Nicky Guadagni; Dan Petronijevic; Peter Mooney; Maria Ricossa; Stefano DiMatteo; Directed by Holly Dale; Written by Bethany Rooney; Cinematography by Malcolm Cross; Music by Zack Ryan. **A:** Sr. High-Adult. **P:** Entertainment. **U:** Home. **Mov-Ent:** Journalism. **Acq:** Purchase. **Dist:** A&E Television Networks L.L.C.

Abstinence: It's the Right Choice 2001
Peer counselors teach curious teens refusal techniques and alternatives to engaging in sexual activity. 23m; VHS, DVD; Closed Captioned. **A:** Jr. High-Sr. High. **P:** Education. **U:** Institution. **Gen-Edu:** Adolescence, Sex & Sexuality. **Acq:** Purchase. **Dist:** Zenger Media. $99.95.

Abstract Expressionism 1990
A look at the artistic movement of the '40s and '50s, including works by Pollock, de Kooning, Hofmann and others. 40m; VHS. **Pr:** Crystal Productions. **A:** Jr. High-Adult. **P:** Education. **U:** Institution, Home. **Gen-Edu:** Documentary Films, Art & Artists, Museums. **Acq:** Purchase. **Dist:** Crystal Productions. $84.00.

Abstract Impressionism 2012 (Unrated)
This episode of the acclaimed television series about art focuses on the works of the great abstract expressionist painters, including Asger Jorn ("In the Wing-Beat of the Swans"), Willem de Kooning ("Morning. The Springs."), Arshile Gorky ("On Year the Milkweed"), Franz Kline ("C & O"), Helen Frankenthaler ("Mountains and Sea"), and many more. Includes commentary from the authors of five art surveys to provide insight into this painting movement, which drew inspiration from European Modernism and gained popularity in the decades following World War II. 50m; DVD. **A:** Family. **P:** Entertainment. **U:** Home. **L:** German, French, English. **Gen-Edu:** Art & Artists. **Acq:** Purchase. **Dist:** Arthaus Musik. $19.99.

Abstract Oil: Bob Tapia 19??
Tapia demonstrates the knife and brush technique of creating abstract still life paintings. 60m; VHS. **A:** Sr. High-Adult. **P:** Instruction. **U:** Institution. **How-Ins:** Painting, Art & Artists. **Acq:** Purchase. **Dist:** Educational Video Network. $59.95.

Abstraction 1971
Abstract means of visual communication play an important part in our lives. Numbers, colors, signs, and diagrams all serve in this capacity. An artist can choose his own abstract tools among color, structure, and dark and light. 10m; VHS, 3/4 U. **Pr:** American Federation of Arts. **A:** Primary-Jr. High. **P:** Education. **U:** Institution, SURA. **Gen-Edu:** How-To, Art & Artists. **Acq:** Purchase. **Dist:** Home Vision Cinema.

Abuse ????
Explains to care givers situations and interactions that nursing-home residents might view as abusive treatment. 20m; VHS. **A:** Adult. **P:** Vocational. **U:** Institution. **Hea-Sci:** Mental Health, Occupational Training, Medical Education. **Acq:** Purchase. **Dist:** University of Maryland. $150.00.

Abuse 1982 — ★★
Fourteen-year-old Tommy (Sbarge) is the victim of child abuse. After a beating causes convulsions, his parents rush him to a New York hospital where the intern on duty phones his student filmmaker friend Larry (Ryder), who's doing a documentary on child abuse as his master thesis. When Tommy learns that Larry is also gay, he agrees to discuss his problems but their continuing contact leads the duo to fall in love and Larry to worry about exploiting Tommy's affections. Interspersed with their story are interviews and photos of child abuse victims and their abusers. Not necessarily for the squeamish. 93m/B/W; VHS. **C:** Richard Ryder; Raphael Sbarge; Directed by Arthur J. Bressan, Jr.; Written by Arthur J. Bressan, Jr.; Cinematography by Douglas Dickinson; Music by Shawn Phillips. **A:** College-Adult. **P:** Entertainment. **U:** Home. **Mov-Ent:** Child Abuse, Adolescence. **Acq:** Purchase.

Abuse 1989
The four kinds of abuse (physical, sexual, emotional and neglect) are explained, their consequences are seen and the benefits of professional help are extolled. 20m; VHS. **Pr:** United Learning Inc. **A:** Sr. High-Adult. **P:** Education. **U:** Institution, CCTV, CATV, Home, SURA. **Gen-Edu:** Documentary Films, Sexual Abuse, Child Abuse. **Acq:** Purchase, Duplication. **Dist:** United Learning Inc. $99.95.

Abuse and the Dementia Patient ????
Presents the challenges a nursing staff faces when dealing with dementia patients. 20m; VHS. **A:** Adult. **P:** Vocational. **U:** Institution. **Hea-Sci:** Mental Health, Occupational Training, Medical Education. **Acq:** Purchase. **Dist:** University of Maryland. $150.00.

The Abuse of Memory 1994
The life of a Multiple Personality Disorder (MPD) patient is recounted to study the disorder and its impact on patients, family members, and friends. 84m; VHS. **A:** Sr. High-Adult. **P:** Education. **U:** Home. **Gen-Edu:** Documentary Films, Mental Health. **Acq:** Rent/Lease. **Dist:** The Cinema Guild. $395.00.

Abuse Triggers ????
Dr. Rabins and experienced nursing assistants explain positive ways of handling nursing-home residents' behaviors that can trigger abuse. 100m; VHS. **A:** Adult. **P:** Vocational. **U:** Institution. **Hea-Sci:** Mental Health, Occupational Training, Medical Education. **Acq:** Purchase. **Dist:** University of Maryland. $800.00.
Indiv. Titles: 1. Trigger: Physical Violence 2. Trigger: Verbal Violence 3. Trigger: Resistive Behavior 4. Trigger: Repetitive Behavior 5. Trigger: Incontinence and Other Physical Problems 6. Trigger: Non-responsive/Needy Patient.

Abused Children and the Law 1988
The emotional and legal horrors that parents go through when their children have been abused are documented here. 35m; VHS, 3/4 U. **C:** Narrated by Valerie Harper. **Pr:** Churchill Films. **A:** Sr. High-Adult. **P:** Education. **U:** Institution, Home, SURA. **Gen-Edu:** Documentary Films, Child Abuse. **Acq:** Purchase, Rent/Lease, Duplication License. **Dist:** Clear Vue Inc. $285.00.

Abused Men 1990
Presents stories about male victims suffering from abuse. Addresses the need for sexual assault support programs for men and warns about the cycle of the abused becoming the abuser. 14m; VHS, 3/4 U. **Pr:** Canadian Broadcasting Corp. **A:** Adult. **P:** Education. **U:** Institution. **Gen-Edu:** Sexual Abuse, Human Relations. **Acq:** Rent/Lease. **Dist:** New Dimension Media. $45.00.

Abusive Parents 1977
Presents a discussion among a group of women each convicted of child abuse and each belonging to a prison chapter of Parents Anonymous. 30m; VHS, 3/4 U, Special order formats. **Pr:** National Center on Child Abuse. **A:** College-Adult. **P:** Education. **U:** Institution, SURA. **Gen-Edu:** Documentary Films, Child Abuse. **Acq:** Purchase. **Dist:** National Audiovisual Center.

Abusive Relationships 1994
Uses interviews with two women who were abused and a former abuser to demonstrate how to recognize and avoid abusive relationships. Defines abuse as behavior used to control. Details the four types of abuse: physical, emotional/mental, verbal, and sexual. 30m; VHS. **Pr:** Schlessinger Video Productions. **A:** Jr. High-Sr. High. **P:** Education. **U:** Institution. **Gen-Edu:** Violence, Psychiatry. **Acq:** Purchase. **Dist:** Library Video Inc. $39.95.

Abyss 1974
A documentary on R. Sorgato's climb of the West Peak of Lavaredo in the Dolomites, during which he fell 140 feet from a sheer overhang of rock. 17m; VHS, 3/4 U. **A:** Jr. High-Adult. **P:** Entertainment. **U:** Institution, SURA. **Spo-Rec:** Documentary Films, Mountaineering. **Acq:** Purchase. **Dist:** Phoenix Learning Group.

The Abyss 1989 (PG-13) — ★★★
Underwater sci-fi adventure about a team of oil-drilling divers pressed into service by the navy to locate and disarm an inoperative nuclear submarine. A high-tech thriller with fab footage underwater and pulsating score. 140m; VHS, DVD, Wide, CC. **C:** Ed Harris; Mary Elizabeth Mastrantonio; Todd Graff; Michael Biehn; John Bedford Lloyd; J.C. Quinn; Leo Burmester; Kidd Brewer, Jr.; Kimberly Scott; Adam Nelson; George Robert Kirk; Chris Elliott; Jimmie Ray Weeks; Directed by James Cameron; Written by James Cameron; Cinematography by Mikael Salomon; Music by Alan Silvestri. **Pr:** 20th Century-Fox. **A:** Jr. High-Adult. **P:** Entertainment. **U:** Home. **Mov-Ent:** Science Fiction, Scuba, Oil Industry. **Awds:** Oscars '89: Visual FX. **Acq:** Purchase. **Dist:** Fox Home Entertainment. $14.98.

AC and the Sine Wave 1981
Discusses amplitude descriptions of a sinusoidal waveform; reviews time and frequency measurements; and introduces trigonometric function. 29m; VHS. **A:** Adult. **P:** Education. **U:** Institution. **Gen-Edu:** Electricity. **Acq:** Purchase. **Dist:** RMI Media. $89.95.

AC/DC: Clipped 1991
The Australian rock band shows off its newest tunes. Includes "Thunderstruck," "Moneytalks," "Are You Ready" and more. 25m; VHS. **Pr:** Warner Reprise Video. **A:** Sr. High-Adult. **P:** Entertainment. **U:** Home. **Mov-Ent:** Music Video, Music--Pop/Rock. **Acq:** Purchase. **Dist:** WarnerVision; Fast Forward. $16.98.

AC/DC: Fly on the Wall 1985
Those hard rock headbangers show pretenders how it's done as they thrash out the songs "Stand Up," "Danger," "Shake Your Foundations," "Sink The Pink," and the title track in this promotional video. 27m; VHS. **A:** Jr. High-Adult. **P:** Entertainment. **U:** Home. **Mov-Ent:** Music Video, Music--Pop/Rock. **Acq:** Purchase. **Dist:** Music Video Distributors; WarnerVision; Fast Forward. $14.95.

AC/DC: Let There Be Rock 1982 (PG)
Australian hard rockers AC/DC perform such headbangers as "Live Wire," "Shot Down in Flames," "The Jacks," "Highway to Hell" and give interviews in this classic from a 1980 Paris show. 97m; VHS. **Pr:** Warner Bros; High Speed Productions. **A:** Sr. High-Adult. **P:** Entertainment. **U:** Home. **Mov-Ent:** Music--Performance, Music--Pop/Rock. **Acq:** Purchase. **Dist:** Music Video Distributors; Warner Home Video, Inc. $19.95.

AC/DC: Live at Donington 1992
AC/DC performs live August 17, 1991 at the international Castle Donington Festival. All AC/DC material is covered including "Back in Black," "You Shook Me (All Night Long)," "Dirty Deeds," and more. 120m; VHS, Blu-Ray. **A:** Jr. High-Adult. **P:** Entertainment. **U:** Home. **Mov-Ent:** Music--Performance, Music--Pop/Rock. **Acq:** Purchase. **Dist:** Music Video Distributors; WarnerVision; Fast Forward. $19.98.

AC/DC: The Interview Sessions 1990
This British import captures Angus, Brian and the boys in rare and private footage from all over the world. 60m; VHS. **A:** Jr. High-Adult. **P:** Entertainment. **U:** Home. **Mov-Ent:** Music Video, Music--Pop/Rock, Interviews. **Acq:** Purchase. **Dist:** Music Video Distributors. $19.95.

AC/DC: Who Made Who 1986
The veteran hard rock warriors in promotional videos of their past hits. This presentation includes the relentless anthem, "Who Made Who," which appeared in the opening of "Maximum Overdrive," a fantasy/ horror flick directed by Stephen King. Other tracks presented are "Hell's Bells," "You Shook Me All Night Long," "Shake Your Foundation," and a 1983 concert rendition of "For Those About to Rock (We Salute You)." 24m; VHS. **Pr:** Warner Bros. **A:** Jr. High-Adult. **P:** Entertainment. **U:** Home. **Mov-Ent:** Music Video, Music--Pop/Rock. **Acq:** Purchase. **Dist:** Music Video Distributors; WarnerVision; Fast Forward. $14.95.

A.C. Jobim/Gal Costa: Rio Revisited 198?
The duo perform top Bossa Nova live. 59m; VHS. **A:** Adult. **P:** Entertainment. **U:** Home. **Mov-Ent:** Music--Performance. **Acq:** Purchase. **Dist:** Music Video Distributors. $19.98.

AC Motor Options and Variations 1986
Part of a series offering instruction on selection procedures of common power transmission products for various applications. 15m; VHS. **A:** Adult. **P:** Vocational. **U:** Institution. **Gen-Edu:** Industrial Arts, Technology. **Acq:** Purchase. **Dist:** RMI Media. $132.50.

AC Variable Speed Drive Controllers 1987
Part of a series offering instruction on power transmission products, including nomenclature, applications, classification, numbering systems, and other information on components and equipment. 20m; VHS. **A:** Adult. **P:** Vocational. **U:** Institution. **Gen-Edu:** Industrial Arts, Technology. **Acq:** Purchase. **Dist:** RMI Media. $112.50.

AC Variable Speed Drive Controllers 1995
Explains how the speed of an AC motor is determined. Also discusses a six step sine wave and PWM simulated AC power, ramping, motor running characteristics when control is used, and considerations when selecting a controller. 20m; VHS. **A:** Adult. **P:** Professional. **U:** Institution. **Bus-Ind:** Job Training, Management. **Acq:** Rent/Lease. **Dist:** National Safety Council, California Chapter, Film Library.

Academy Award Winners Animated Short Films 1984
A collection of six short films that includes Jimmy Picker's "Sundae in New York," "The Hole," "Munro" and "Closed Mondays." 60m; VHS. **Pr:** Videoline Inc. **A:** Family. **P:** Entertainment. **U:** Home. **Mov-Ent:** Animation & Cartoons, Film History. **Acq:** Purchase. **Dist:** Lions Gate Television Corp. $59.98.

Academy Awards: Oscar's Best 1987
A package of trailers for Academy Award-winning Best Pictures, from 1927's "Wings" to 1959's "Ben Hur," also including "The Bridge on the River Kwai," "On the Waterfront," "The Greatest Show on Earth," "The Lost Weekend," and others. Some are in black and white. 60m; VHS. **C:** Alec Guinness; Charlton Heston; Marlon Brando; Clara Bow; Gary Cooper; Lee J. Cobb; Karl Malden; Jane Wyman; Ray Milland; James Stewart; Dor-

othy Lamour. **Pr:** SF Rush Video. **A:** Jr. High-Adult. **P:** Entertainment. **U:** Home. **Mov-Ent**. **Acq:** Purchase. **Dist:** Passport International Entertainment L.L.C.

Acadia 1995
Features beautiful photograpy of headlands and harbors, quiet ponds, ocean waves, and wildlife. 30m; VHS. **A:** Primary-Adult. **P:** Education. **U:** Home. **Gen-Edu**: Photography, Art & Artists. **Acq:** Purchase. **Dist:** Paragon Home Video. $19.95.

Acapulco 1985
An overview of all that Acapulco has to offer, from cliff diving to casinos. 60m; VHS. **Pr:** Travelview International. **A:** Jr. High-Adult. **P:** Education. **U:** Home. **Gen-Edu**: Travel, Mexico. **Acq:** Purchase. **Dist:** Travelview International Inc. $29.95.

Acapulco Gold 1978 (PG) — ★1/2
Mockumentary follows Gortner as he's framed for drug smuggling and becomes entangled in a Hawaiian drug deal. Not worth the time it'll take to track down a copy. 105m; DVD. **C:** Marjoe Gortner; Robert Lansing; Ed Nelson; John Harkins; Lawrence Casey; Phil Hoover; Directed by Burt Brinckerhoff; Written by Don Enright; Cinematography by Robert Steadman; Music by Craig Safan. **A:** Jr. High-Adult. **P:** Entertainment. **U:** Home. **Mov-Ent**: Drug Trafficking/Dealing. **Acq:** Purchase. **Dist:** Movies Unlimited. $17.99.

Acapulco H.E.A.T. 2006 (Unrated)
Ashley (Oxenberg) and Mike (Kelly) head up the H.E.A.T. (Hemisphere Emergency Action Team) that operates out of a Mexican beach fashion boutique to fight international terrorism in this TV series that ran from 1993-1994. The good-looking group travels to exotic locales in the region with assignments including: protecting an ambassador from possible murder, a white-slavery ring that kidnaps Ashley, a scientist who's possibly creating biological weapons, and a black-market baby ring run by a doctor; also, the group gets stranded on a deserted island and the season ends with Mike getting shot. 22 episodes. 973m; DVD. **C:** Catherine Oxenberg; Brendan Kelly; Spencer Rochfort; Holly Floria; Alison Armitage. **A:** Sr. High-Adult. **P:** Entertainment. **U:** Home. **Mov-Ent**: Television Series, Drama, Action-Adventure. **Acq:** Purchase. **Dist:** Mill Creek Entertainment L.L.C. $29.98.

Accabonac Harbor 2002
Documentary about a small harbor in East Hampton, New York. 9m; VHS, DVD. **A:** Sr. High-Adult. **P:** Education. **U:** Home, Institution. **Gen-Edu**: Ecology & Environment, Documentary Films. **Acq:** Purchase. **Dist:** The Cinema Guild. $19.95.

Accademia Museum of Venice 19??
Teaching aid for art appreciation provides a tour of Venice's leading museum. 60m; VHS. **A:** Jr. High-College. **P:** Education. **U:** Institution. **Gen-Edu**: Art & Artists, Museums. **Acq:** Purchase. **Dist:** Crystal Productions. $39.95.

Accatone! 1961 — ★★★
Accatone (Citti), a failure as a pimp, tries his luck as a thief. Hailed as a return to Italian neo-realism, this is a gritty, despairing, and dark look at the lives of the street people of Rome. Pasolini's first outing, adapted by the director from his novel, "A Violent Life." Pasolini served as mentor to Bernardo Bertolucci, listed in the credits as an assistant director. 116m/B/W; VHS, DVD. **C:** Franco Citti; Franca Pasut; Roberto Scaringelli; Silvana Corsini; Paolo Guidi; Adriana Asti; Directed by Pier Paolo Pasolini; Written by Pier Paolo Pasolini; Cinematography by Tonino Delli Colli. **Pr:** Cino del Duca. **A:** College-Adult. **P:** Entertainment. **U:** Home. **L:** English, Italian. **Mov-Ent**: Italy, Prostitution, Homeless. **Acq:** Purchase. **Dist:** Water Bearer Films Inc. $29.95.

Accelerated Learning 199?
Uses video hypnosis and subliminal messages to improve your ability to learn faster and remember what you learn better. 30m; VHS. **A:** Adult. **P:** Instruction. **U:** Home. **Hea-Sci**: Self-Help, Education. **Dist:** Valley of the Sun Publishing. $19.95.

Accelerated Learning: A Guide for Parents and Teachers 1987
Dr. Ron Hering, Director of Wisconsin's Peak Performance Center, discusses ten specific techniques to improve students' academic achievement. 28m; VHS. **Pr:** RMI Media Productions. **A:** Adult. **P:** Education. **U:** Institution. **Gen-Edu**: How-To, Education. **Acq:** Purchase. **Dist:** RMI Media. $19.95.

Accelerated Life Testing and Reliability Determination 1989
Models present the advantages of accelerated testing in a reduced time. 50m; VHS, 3/4 U, EJ. **C:** Dimitri Kececioglu. **Pr:** University of Arizona. **A:** College-Adult. **P:** Education. **U:** Institution, CCTV, Home. **How-Ins**: How-To, Education. **Acq:** Purchase, Rent/Lease. **Dist:** University of Arizona.

Accent on Architecture—1990 1990
Contains highlights from the four-day Honor Awards celebration of design excellence. Peter Jennings was master of ceremonies and the Prince of Wales delivered the keynote speech. Also shows the 10 Honor Award projects with remarks given by Fay Jones, the 1990 AIA Gold Medalist. 76m; VHS. **A:** Adult. **P:** Education. **U:** Institution, Home. **Gen-Edu**: Architecture, Education. **Acq:** Purchase, Rent/Lease. **Dist:** American Institute of Architects.

Accent on Architecture—1991 1991
Contains highlights from the 1991 Honor Awards celebration, centering on the 19 award-winning projects, comments from 1991 Gold Medalist Charles W. Moore, and interviews with fellow participants. Also exhibits the works of the 1991 Firm Award-winner, Zimmer Gunsul Frasca Partnership, and the Twenty-Five Year Award for the Condominium at Sea Ranch project. 25m; VHS. **A:** Adult. **P:** Professional. **U:** Institution, Home. **Gen-Edu**: Architecture, Education. **Acq:** Rent/Lease. **Dist:** American Institute of Architects.

Accent on Architecture—1992 1992
Centers on the 10 projects that received 1992 Honor Awards. Provides comments from their owners and contains comments from 1992 Gold Medalist Benjamin Thompson and his partners on his work and philosophy of architecture. 40m; VHS. **A:** Adult. **P:** Professional. **U:** Institution, Home. **Gen-Edu**: Architecture, Education. **Acq:** Rent/Lease. **Dist:** American Institute of Architects.

Accent on Architecture—1993 1993
Highlights the 1993 AIA Honor Awards, centering on the 18 projects that won these awards. Features an address from 1993 Gold Medalist Kevin Roche and the presentation of the 1993 Twenty-Five Year Award. 50m; VHS. **A:** Adult. **P:** Professional. **U:** Institution, Home. **Gen-Edu**: Architecture, Education. **Acq:** Purchase, Rent/Lease. **Dist:** American Institute of Architects. $29.95.

Accent on Love 1941 (Unrated) — ★1/2
Sentimental sludge. John (Montgomery) dumps his diva wife Linda (Wright) and his executive job to work as a ditch-digger (honest labor you know) in a New York slum, which is also where he now lives. After making some new friends, John confronts his tenement's absentee landlord about the terrible living conditions. Of course, the man is John's greedy father-in-law (Hall). 62m/B/W; DVD. **C:** George Montgomery; Cobina Wright, Jr.; Thurston Hall; Osa Massen; J. Carrol Naish; Directed by Ray McCarey; Written by John Larkin; Cinematography by Charles G. Clarke. **A:** Sr. High-Adult. **P:** Entertainment. **U:** Home. **L:** English. **Mov-Ent**: Poverty. **Acq:** Purchase. **Dist:** Twentieth Century Fox Film Corp.

Accent on the Offbeat 1994
Follows the New York City Ballet as they put together a dance and musical piece. Features original choreography by Peter Martins. 56m; VHS. **C:** Directed by Albert Maysles; Music by Wynton Marsalis. **A:** Jr. High-Adult. **P:** Entertainment. **U:** Home. **Fin-Art**: Performing Arts, Dance--Ballet, Documentary Films. **Acq:** Purchase. **Dist:** Maysles Films, Inc.

Acceptable Risk 1987
This documentary explores the town of Canonsburg, PA where 500,000 tons of radioactive waste was buried in the town center. Today, many of Canonsburg's residents are dying of cancer. 54m; VHS, 3/4 U. **Pr:** Channel 4. **A:** Jr. High-Adult. **P:** Education. **U:** Institution, Home, SURA. **Gen-Edu**: Documentary Films, Ecology & Environment, Cancer. **Acq:** Purchase, Rent/Lease, Duplication. **Dist:** Filmakers Library Inc.

Acceptable Risk 2001 — ★★
Pharmaceutical scientist Edward Wells (Lowe) discovers a strange fungus in a walled-in part of his basement. He takes it into the lab, finds unusual healing properties in the substance, and immediately begins to test it on himself. At first, he feels superhuman, but monstrous side effects quickly surface. There is some suspense in this TV movie, but the inconsistent story and poor performances are hard to get past. 92m; DVD. **C:** Chad Lowe; Kelly Rutherford; Sean Patrick Flanery; Patty McCormack; Danielle von Zerneck; Directed by William A. Graham; Written by Michael J. Murray; Cinematography by Eyal Grodin. **A:** Sr. High-Adult. **P:** Entertainment. **U:** Home. **Mov-Ent**: Science Fiction. **Acq:** Purchase. **Dist:** Movies Unlimited; Lions Gate Television Corp.

Acceptable Risk? 1980
An exploration of the nuclear fuel chain which links nuclear weapons and nuclear power. 60m; VHS, 3/4 U. **Pr:** NARMIC; American Friends Service Committee. **A:** Sr. High-Adult. **P:** Education. **U:** Institution, Home, SURA. **Gen-Edu**: Documentary Films, Nuclear Energy, Nuclear Warfare. **Acq:** Purchase, Duplication License. **Dist:** Bullfrog Films, Inc.

Acceptable Risks 1986 (R) — ★1/2
Toxic disaster strikes when a plant manager is ordered to cut costs and sacrifice safety at the Citichem plant. Predictable plot stars Dennehy as the plant manager who risks all and fights politicians to reinstate the safety standards. Meanwhile, Tyson is the city manager who tries to warn the town of a possible chemical accident that could have devastating effects on the community. TV drama that shamelessly preys on audience fears. 97m; VHS, CC. **C:** Brian Dennehy; Cicely Tyson; Kenneth McMillan; Christine Ebersole; Beah Richards; Richard Gilliland; Directed by Rick Wallace. **Pr:** ABC Circle Films. **A:** Sr. High-Adult. **P:** Entertainment. **U:** Home. **Mov-Ent**: TV Movies. **Acq:** Purchase. **Dist:** Unknown Distributor.

Acceptance 2009 (Unrated) — ★1/2
Disjointed and sentimental Lifetime comedy about high school seniors and the stress-ridden process of college applications. Taylor's (Whitman) parents have separated, Maya's (Daryanani) immigrant parents expect her to pursue science studies while she prefers the arts, and Harry (Keltz) is only (and obsessively) interested in going to Harvard. There are some minor subplots featuring the adults but they don't add up to much. Adaptation of the Susan Coll novel. 90m; DVD. **C:** Mae Whitman; Deepti Daryanani; Jonathan Keltz; Joan Cusack; Mark Moses; Kiersten Warren; Brigid Brannagh; Rob Mayes; Directed by Sanaa Hamri; Written by Suzette Couture; Cinematography by Anthony B. Richmond; Music by Richard (Rick) Marvin; Alan Derian. **A:** Jr. High-Adult. **P:** Entertainment. **U:** Home. **Mov-Ent**. **Acq:** Purchase. **Dist:** Vivendi Visual Entertainment.

Accepted 2006 (PG-13) — ★1/2
Flunky campus farce about what to do after getting one too many thin envelopes from college admissions offices: create your own university. Bartleby (Long) and his buds pretend to matriculate at the fictitious South Harmon Institute of Technology. So-so jokes about beer and babes and that oh-so-hilarious acronym abound, until the tale attempts to take an unexpectedly touching turn. Ultimately lands on the failing side of the campus-movie bell curve (with "Animal House" and "Back to School" at the top of the class). 92m; DVD, Wide. **C:** Justin Long; Blake Lively; Mark Derwin; Anthony Heald; Adam Herschman; Jonah Hill; Columbus Short; Maria Thayer; Lewis Black; Ann Cusack; Travis Van Winkle; Hannah Marks; Diora Baird; Directed by Steve Pink; Written by Mark Perez; Adam Cooper; Bill Collage; Cinematography by Matthew F. Leonetti; Music by David Schommer. **Pr:** Tom Shadyac; Michael Bostick; Shady Acres; Universal Pictures. **A:** Jr. High-Adult. **P:** Entertainment. **U:** Home. **L:** English. **Mov-Ent**. **Acq:** Purchase. **Dist:** Movies Unlimited; Alpha Video.

Access Challenge 2002
Six teams with captains in wheelchairs face wilderness and physical challenges as they trek British Columbia's Manning Park. 50m; VHS. **A:** Adult. **P:** Professional. **U:** Institution. **Hea-Sci**: Handicapped, Medical Education. **Acq:** Purchase. **Dist:** Aquarius Health Care Media. $195.00.

Access Code 1984 (Unrated) — ★
Government agents attempt to uncover a private organization that has gained control of nuclear weapons for the purpose of world domination. A ragged patchwork of disconnected scenes meant to test the virtue of patience. 90m; VHS. **C:** Martin Landau; Michael Ansara; MacDonald Carey; Directed by Mark Sobel. **Pr:** Michael Applefield; Sandy Cobe; Lawrence Rotunno. **A:** Sr. High-Adult. **P:** Entertainment. **U:** Home. **Mov-Ent**: Science Fiction, Nuclear Warfare. **Acq:** Purchase. **Dist:** No Longer Available.

Access Denied 19??
Deals with the issue of computer security in the corporate environment. Maintains that access issues are fundamental to computer crime. Provides tips on how to reduce chance of system infiltration. 23m; VHS. **A:** College-Adult. **P:** Professional. **U:** Institution. **Bus-Ind**: Computers, Safety Education, Business. **Acq:** Purchase, Rent/Lease. **Dist:** Commonwealth Films Inc. $525.00.

Access Denied 1991
Addresses cutbacks in women's reproductive freedom and civil rights against the backdrop of Operation Rescue's religious anti-abortion fervor. Documents growing community activism around AIDS, reproductive rights, and racism. 28m; VHS. **A:** College-Adult. **P:** Education. **U:** Institution. **Gen-Edu**: Women, Reproduction, Abortion. **Acq:** Purchase, Rent/Lease. **Dist:** Women Make Movies. $175.00.

Accessories 1990
Describes all sorts of accessories and how they can be used to stretch any wardrobe. Also details the differences between fad pieces and the timeless classics which can be used over and over again. ?m; VHS. **A:** Jr. High-Sr. High. **P:** Education. **U:** Institution. **Gen-Edu**: Clothing & Dress, Home Economics. **Acq:** Purchase. **Dist:** Meridian Education Corp. $45.00.

ACCESSories: Adapted Physical Education Equipment Designed with Activity in Mind 2004 (Unrated)
Physical Education teacher Ann Griffin showcases low-tech and hi-tech PE equipment designed with disabled children in mind. 41m; VHS, DVD. **A:** Family. **P:** Education. **U:** Home, Institution. **Spo-Rec**: Physical Education, Handicapped. **Acq:** Purchase. **Dist:** Championship Productions. $34.99.

Accessory Advantage: Tacky to Terrific in 10 Easy Steps! 1992
Reid gives helpful hints on dressing for the nineties, including how to working with what's already in the closet. 30m; VHS. **C:** Hosted by T.J. Reid. **A:** Jr. High-Adult. **P:** Education. **U:** Institution. **Gen-Edu**: Clothing & Dress, Home Economics. **Acq:** Purchase. **Dist:** Cambridge Educational. $29.95.

Accessory Allure 1987
This video shows viewers how to make the most of their wardrobe by using scarves, earrings, hats, and other accessories. 30m; VHS. **Pr:** Cambridge Career Productions. **A:** Jr. High-Adult. **P:** Education. **U:** Institution, Home. **How-Ins**: How-To, Clothing & Dress. **Acq:** Purchase. **Dist:** Cambridge Educational. $29.95.

Accessory Transit Company 1980
This experimental video explores the tensions between men and women. 12m; VHS, 3/4 U. **Pr:** Jorge Lozano. **A:** College-Adult. **P:** Education. **U:** Institution. **Gen-Edu**: Video. **Acq:** Rent/Lease. **Dist:** Video Out Distribution.

The Accident 19??
A young, pregnant housewife faces overwhelming responsibilities after her husband is seriously injured. She threatens to leave him and a widowed nurse shares the intimate details of her own life and points to Christ as her savior. 28m; VHS, 3/4 U. **A:** Jr. High-Adult. **P:** Religious. **U:** Institution, SURA. **Gen-Edu**: Religion. **Acq:** Purchase, Rent/Lease. **Dist:** Faith for Today.

Accident 1967 — ★★1/2
A tangled web of guilt, remorse, humor and thwarted sexuality is unravelled against the background of the English countryside in this complex story of an Oxford love triangle. An inside view of English repression at the university level adapted for the screen by Pinter from the novel by Nicholas Mosley. Long-winded but occasionally engrossing character study with interesting performances. 100m; VHS, DVD, Wide. **C:** Dirk Bogarde; Michael York; Stanley Baker; Jacqueline Sassard; Delphine Seyrig; Alexander Knox; Vivien Merchant; Freddie Jones; Harold Pinter; Directed by Joseph Losey; Written by Harold Pinter;

Cinematography by Gerry Fisher; Music by John Dankworth. **Pr:** Lippert Productions. **A:** Sr. High-Adult. **P:** Entertainment. **U:** Home. **Mov-Ent:** Sex & Sexuality, Education. **Awds:** Cannes '67: Grand Jury Prize. **Acq:** Purchase. **Dist:** Movies Unlimited. $33.99.

The Accident 1979
A film documenting the hypothesis of Dr. Zhores Medvedev that a nuclear catastrophe occurred in the Soviet Union in 1957, and both the US and USSR have endeavored to cover it up since. 33m; VHS, 3/4 U. **Pr:** Granada Television International Ltd. **A:** Sr. High-Adult. **P:** Education. **U:** Institution, CATV, BCTV, SURA. **Gen-Edu:** Documentary Films, Nuclear Energy. **Acq:** Purchase, Rent/Lease. **Dist:** Green Mountain Post Films.

Accident 1983 — ★½
Skate for your life. A hockey game turns into a nightmare when the roof over the arena collapses under the weight of too much ice and snow. One of the few hockey disaster films. 104m; VHS. **C:** Terence Kelly; Fiona Reid; Frank Perry. **Pr:** Independent. **A:** Sr. High-Adult. **P:** Entertainment. **U:** Home. **Mov-Ent:** Action-Adventure, Hockey. **Acq:** Purchase. **Dist:** No Longer Available.

Accident 1989
The body is shown healing itself when bones are broken or flesh is cut. 26m; VHS, 3/4 U. **Pr:** Films for the Humanities. **A:** Jr. High-Adult. **P:** Education. **U:** Institution, SURA. **Hea-Sci:** Documentary Films, Bones, Medical Education. **Acq:** Purchase, Rent/Lease. **Dist:** Films for the Humanities & Sciences. $149.00.

Accident Causes and Prevention: Safety on the Job 1984
In this production, both staff and supervisors are shown how to look for lack of attention, irritability, tenseness, conflict with fellow workers, and health problems and to recognize them as potential safety hazards. 16m; VHS, 3/4 U. **Pr:** AIMS Video. **A:** Adult. **P:** Instruction. **U:** Institution, CCTV. **Bus-Ind:** How-To, Employee Counseling, Safety Education. **Acq:** Purchase, Rent/Lease. **Dist:** CEV Multimedia. $79.95.

Accident Evaluation 1984
Covers evaluation forms, investigative procedures, and techniques for interviewing. 16m; VHS. **A:** Adult. **P:** Professional. **U:** Institution. **Bus-Ind:** Safety Education, Job Training, Management. **Acq:** Purchase. **Dist:** $110.00.

The Accident Hazards of Nuclear Power 1981
A talk by a nuclear reactor physicist who criticizes the current approach to studying accident potentials of nuclear reactor systems. 29m; VHS, 3/4 U, EJ. **Pr:** Media Bus. **A:** Sr. High-Adult. **P:** Education. **U:** Institution, SURA. **Hea-Sci:** Documentary Films, Nuclear Energy. **Acq:** Purchase. **Dist:** Media Bus, Inc.

Accident Investigation 1987
The importance of and means of conducting an accident report are emphasized. 11m; VHS, 3/4 U. **Pr:** Educational Resources Foundation. **A:** Adult. **P:** Instruction. **U:** Institution, SURA. **Bus-Ind:** How-To, Safety Education, Management. **Acq:** Rent/Lease. **Dist:** ERI Safety Videos. $425.00.

Accident Investigation 1995
Explains why accident investigation is important, and what causes accidents. Also gives tips to supervisors on how to implement accident prevention in the workplace. 10m; VHS. **A:** Adult. **P:** Professional. **U:** Institution. **Bus-Ind:** Job Training, Safety Education. **Acq:** Purchase. **Dist:** National Safety Council, California Chapter, Film Library. $175.00.

Accident Investigation: A Tool for Effective Prevention 1992
Provides accident investigation techniques for supervisors and managers. Includes Leader's Guide. 13m; VHS, 3/4 U. **A:** College-Adult. **P:** Professional. **U:** Institution. **Bus-Ind:** Safety Education. **Acq:** Rent/Lease, Duplication License. **Dist:** Learning Communications L.L.C.

Accident Investigation in the Workplace 1995
Details how to follow an accident investigation. Includes taking action; gathering evidence; interviewing witnesses; analyzing information; determining the causes; and suggests corrective actions. 22m; VHS. **A:** Adult. **P:** Professional. **U:** Institution. **Bus-Ind:** Job Training, Safety Education. **Acq:** Purchase. **Dist:** National Safety Council, California Chapter, Film Library.

Accident Investigation: What to Do 1995
Features steps in investigating an accident in the workplace including how to put together an accident kit, interviewing witnesses and gathering evidence. 14m; VHS. **A:** Adult. **P:** Professional. **U:** Institution. **Bus-Ind:** Job Training, Safety Education. **Acq:** Purchase. **Dist:** National Safety Council, California Chapter, Film Library.

Accident Investigations for Municipal Employees 19??
Details how to conduct a thorough accident investigation. Instructs in how to write complete reports. 18m; VHS. **A:** Adult. **P:** Professional. **U:** Institution. **Bus-Ind:** Cities & Towns, Insurance. **Acq:** Purchase. **Dist:** National Safety Council. $95.00.

Accident Prevention and Causes 1995
Features unsafe acts and behavior, and how employees must take responsibility for their own actions. 10m; VHS. **A:** Adult. **P:** Professional. **U:** Institution. **L:** Spanish. **Bus-Ind:** Safety Education, Management, Occupational Training. **Acq:** Purchase, Rent/Lease. **Dist:** National Safety Council, California Chapter, Film Library. $175.00.

Accident Prevention Through Equipment Guarding 198?
The safety rules and regulations involving mining machinery guards are demonstrated in this program. 15m; VHS, 3/4 U. **A:** College-Adult. **P:** Education. **U:** Institution. **Bus-Ind:** How-To, Safety Education, Miners & Mining. **Acq:** Rent/Lease. **Dist:** National Safety Council, California Chapter, Film Library.

Accident-Proof Kids 1992
O.J. Anderson's characters, Cowboy Careful, Sergeant Stop-N-Go, and Louie the Lifeguard, teach safety lessons to kids in a fun way. 28m; VHS. **A:** Preschool-Primary. **P:** Entertainment. **U:** Home. **Chl-Juv:** Children, Safety Education, Music--Children. **Acq:** Purchase. **Dist:** Move Communications; WGTE-TV Home Video. $14.95.

Accident Report 198?
A film designed to make workers aware of the consequences of unsafe behavior and of the need to take responsibility for their own safety. 15m; VHS, 3/4 U. **A:** College-Adult. **P:** Education. **U:** Institution. **Bus-Ind:** How-To, Safety Education. **Acq:** Rent/Lease. **Dist:** National Safety Council, California Chapter, Film Library.

The Accidental Hero: Oskar Schindler 19??
Documentary of Oskar Schindler, who rescued some 1200 Jews during World War II. Presents details of his deeply flawed personal life contrasted to his heroic actions. Features interviews with Holocaust survivors, researchers and author Tomas Keneally. 30m; VHS. **A:** Adult. **P:** Education. **U:** Home. **Gen-Edu:** Documentary Films, Judaism, Holocaust. **Acq:** Purchase, Rent/Lease. **Dist:** Filmakers Library Inc. $195.

The Accidental Husband 2008 (PG-13) — ★½
In this feeble romcom, New York firefighter Patrick Sullivan (Morgan) is incensed when his fiancee dumps him, thanks to the advice of frigid radio therapist Emma Lloyd (Thurman). In an unlikely chain of events, Patrick forges a marriage license between himself and the doc that throws a wrench into Emma's plans with her own stuffy fiance Richard (Firth). Morgan is hunky but Thurman is boring. 91m; DVD. **C:** Uma Thurman; Jeffrey Dean Morgan; Colin Firth; Justina Machado; Sam Shepard; Lindsay Sloane; Ajay Naidu; Keir Dullea; Directed by Griffin Dunne; Written by Mimi Hare; Clare Naylor; Bonnie Sikowitz; Cinematography by William Rexer; Music by Andrea Guerra. **A:** Jr. High-Adult. **P:** Entertainment. **U:** Home. **Mov-Ent:** Comedy--Romantic, Psychiatry. **Acq:** Purchase. **Dist:** Sony Pictures Home Entertainment Inc.

Accidental Meeting 1993 (R) — ★★½
A female version of "Strangers on a Train." Two women meet because of an auto accident and wind up talking about their lives. The main topic is man trouble and both "jokingly" plot to murder each other's man. Only, one woman does the deed and the other soon finds herself on the murderess' hit list. 91m; VHS, CC. **C:** Linda Gray; Linda Purl; Leigh McCloskey; David Hayward; Ernie Lively; Kent McCord; Directed by Michael Zinberg; Written by Pete Best; Christopher Horner. **Pr:** Walter Klenhard; Ed Milkovich; Fast Track Films, Inc; Wilshire Court Productions. **A:** Sr. High-Adult. **P:** Entertainment. **U:** Home. **Mov-Ent:** Mystery & Suspense, Women. **Acq:** Purchase. **Dist:** Paramount Pictures Corp.

The Accidental Spy 2001 (R) — ★★½
Salesman Bei (Chan) longs for some excitement in his life but gets more than anticipated when he foils the plans of two bank robbers. The resulting publicity leads Bei to discover that he's the long-lost son of a wealthy Korean businessman who also turns out to be a spy and Bei decides to join the family profession. 87m; VHS, DVD. **C:** Jackie Chan; Eric Tsang; Vivian Hsu; Alfred Cheung; Min-jeong Kim; Hsing-kuo Wu; Directed by Teddy Chen; Written by Ivy Ho; Cinematography by Wing-Hung Wong; Music by Peter Kam. **Pr:** Dimension Films. **A:** Jr. High-Adult. **P:** Entertainment. **U:** Home. **Mov-Ent:** Action-Comedy. **Acq:** Purchase. **Dist:** Buena Vista Home Entertainment.

The Accidental Tourist 1988 (PG) — ★★★½
A bittersweet and subtle story, adapted faithfully from Anne Tyler's novel, of an introverted, grieving man who learns to love again after meeting an unconventional woman. After his son's death and subsequent separation from wife Turner, Macon Leary (Hurt) avoids emotional confrontation, burying himself in routines with the aid of his obsessive-compulsive siblings. Kooky dog-trainer Muriel Pritchett (an exuberant Davis) wins his attention, but not without struggle. Hurt effectively uses small gestures to describe Macon's emotional journey, while Davis grabs hearts with her open performance. Outstanding supporting cast. 121m; VHS, DVD, 8 mm, Wide, CC. **C:** William Hurt; Geena Davis; Kathleen Turner; Ed Begley, Jr.; David Ogden Stiers; Bill Pullman; Amy Wright; Directed by Lawrence Kasdan; Written by Lawrence Kasdan; Cinematography by John Bailey; Music by John Williams. **A:** Jr. High-Adult. **P:** Entertainment. **U:** Home. **Mov-Ent:** Drama, Travel, Pets. **Awds:** Oscars '88: Support. Actress (Davis); N.Y. Film Critics '88: Film. **Acq:** Purchase. **Dist:** Warner Home Video, Inc.; Baker and Taylor. $19.98.

Accidentally Yours 198?
Stresses consumer product safety as a husband and wife become involved in household accidents with glass doors and power mowers. 14m; VHS, 3/4 U. **Pr:** National Safety Council. **A:** College-Adult. **P:** Education. **U:** Institution. **Gen-Edu:** Safety Education. **Acq:** Rent/Lease. **Dist:** National Safety Council, California Chapter, Film Library.

Accidents 1989 (R) — ★½
A scientist discovers that his invention has been stolen and is going to be used to cause worldwide havoc. He becomes concerned and spends the remainder of the movie trying to relieve himself of anxiety. 90m; VHS, Streaming. **C:** Edward Albert; Leigh Taylor-Young; Jon Cypher; Directed by Gideon Amir. **Pr:** Elmo De Witt. **A:** College-Adult. **P:** Entertainment. **U:** Home. **Mov-Ent:** Mystery & Suspense. **Acq:** Purchase. **Dist:** No Longer Available.

Accidents: Causes and Prevention 1995
Trains workers in the number one cause of accidents in the workplace, unsafe acts. Reveals how lifting, carrying, forklifts, personal protective equipment cause accidents. 10m; VHS. **A:** Adult. **P:** Professional. **U:** Institution. **L:** Spanish. **Bus-Ind:** Job Training, Management, Health Education. **Acq:** Purchase. **Dist:** National Safety Council, California Chapter, Film Library. $175.00.

Accidents Don't Have to Happen 1986
This newly revised tape demonstrates the importance of being habitually safety-concious from the home to the car. Easy-to-follow, effective guidelines for "child-proofing" the home are given. 14m; VHS, 3/4 U. **Pr:** Professional Research. **A:** Adult. **P:** Education. **U:** Institution, CCTV, SURA. **L:** English, Spanish. **Hea-Sci:** How-To, Safety Education. **Acq:** Purchase, Rent/Lease. **Dist:** Discovery Education. $295.00.

Accidents Happen 2009 (R) — ★½
Meandering melodrama finds a tragedy pulling apart the dysfunctional Conway family. Since he can't connect with his bitter, grief-stricken mom (Davis), 15-year-old Billy (Gilbertson) copes by shunning responsibility and getting involved in pranks that usually backfire. 92m; DVD. **C:** Geena Davis; Harrison Gilbertson; Harry Cook; Joel Tobeck; Anthony (Tony) Vorno; Sarah Woods; Directed by Andrew Lancaster; Written by Brian Carbee; Cinematography by Ben Nott; Music by Antony Partos. **A:** Sr. High-Adult. **P:** Entertainment. **U:** Home. **Mov-Ent:** Adolescence. **Acq:** Purchase. **Dist:** Image Entertainment Inc.

Accidents: Infant & Toddler Emergency First Aid 1995
Teaches actions that could save your child's life in case of emergency. Includes preparedness for bites, heat stroke, burns and frostbite. 36m; VHS. **A:** Adult. **P:** Instruction. **U:** Home. **Hea-Sci:** Safety Education, First Aid, How-To. **Acq:** Purchase. **Dist:** Cambridge Educational. $29.95.

Accidents: It Can't Happen to Me 1995
Advises that accidents don't happen, they are caused. Reiterates the need for a pro-active approach to accident prevention. 10m; VHS. **A:** Adult. **P:** Professional. **U:** Institution. **L:** Spanish. **Bus-Ind:** Job Training, Management, Health Education. **Acq:** Purchase. **Dist:** National Safety Council, California Chapter, Film Library. $175.00.

Accidents Made Easy 198?
A group of supervisors find out about their employees' attitudes toward safety after reviewing a series of accidents that could have been avoided. 15m; VHS, 3/4 U. **A:** College-Adult. **P:** Education. **U:** Institution. **Bus-Ind:** How-To, Safety Education. **Acq:** Rent/Lease. **Dist:** National Safety Council, California Chapter, Film Library.

Accidents: The Gory Story 1995
Features gruesome pictures of persons injured in the workplace. 10m; VHS. **A:** Adult. **P:** Professional. **U:** Institution. **Bus-Ind:** Job Training, Safety Education. **Acq:** Purchase. **Dist:** National Safety Council, California Chapter, Film Library. $10.

Accion Sobre Ruedas 1987 (Unrated) — ★★
Two friends buy and share a car with zany consequences. In Spanish. 90m; VHS. **C:** Pancho Cordova; Leonorilda Ochoa. **A:** Adult. **P:** Entertainment. **U:** Home. **L:** Spanish. **Mov-Ent:** Comedy-Drama. **Acq:** Purchase. **Dist:** CinemaNow Inc. $59.50.

The Accompanist 1993 (PG) — ★★½
Centers around a Parisian diva Irene's (Safonova) relationship with her talented pianist Sophie (Romane Bohringer), amidst the clamor of WWII Europe. Sophie impresses Irene with her musical abilities, and takes on additional work as her housekeeper. Meanwhile, Charles (Richard Bohringer), Irene's husband, schmoozes with the Nazis to line his own pockets while she helps the war effort by having an affair with a member of the resistance (Labarthe). Unfortunately, Sophie starts to resent living in Irene's shadow. Adapted from the novel by Nina Berberouva. The Bohringers are father and daughter. French with subtitles. 111m; VHS. **C:** Elena Safonova; Romane Bohringer; Richard Bohringer; Samuel Labarthe; Nelly Borgeaud; Julien Rassam; Directed by Claude Miller; Written by Claude Miller; Luc Beraud; Claude Rich; Cinematography by Yves Angelo; Music by Alain Jomy. **Pr:** Jean-Louis Livi; Sony Pictures Classics. **A:** College-Adult. **P:** Entertainment. **U:** Home. **L:** French. **Mov-Ent:** Drama, World War Two, France. **Acq:** Purchase. **Dist:** Sony Pictures Home Entertainment Inc. $19.95.

Accomplice 1946 — ★½
Plodding whodunit with Arlen as a shy, bookish private eye hired by his old flame to locate her missing husband. His investigations uncover several murders and long after the viewers have put 2 + 2 together, the P.I. smells a rat. The missing husband was a ruse to divert him from the real scam-a bank heist. Painfully low-level excitement. 66m/B/W; VHS. **C:** Richard Arlen; Veda Ann Borg; Tom Dugan; Francis Ford; Directed by Walter Colmes. **Pr:** PRC. **A:** Jr. High-Adult. **P:** Entertainment. **U:** Home. **Mov-Ent:** Mystery & Suspense. **Acq:** Purchase. **Dist:** Movies Unlimited. $14.99.

Accomplish Your Goals 199?
Uses hypnosis and subliminal messages to promote success through achievement of goals. 30m; VHS. **A:** Adult. **P:** Instruction. **U:** Home. **Hea-Sci:** Self-Help. **Dist:** Valley of the Sun Publishing. $19.95.

Accomplished Women 1974
A story which cites how, despite innumerable barriers put in the way of women, people such as Katherine Graham, Virginia Apgar, Shirley Chisholm, and Helen Reddy have "made it." They talk about the new attitude and image women have of themselves. 26m; VHS, 3/4 U. **Pr:** Charles Braverman. **A:** Jr. High-College. **P:** Education. **U:** Institution, SURA. **Gen-Edu:** Documentary Films, Women. **Acq:** Purchase. **Dist:** Home Vision Cinema.

According to Greta 2008 (PG-13) — ★★
Duff acquits herself quite well as a suicidal teen who's fobbed off on her grandparents for the summer by her preoccupied mother. Greta gets a job as a waitress and starts an interracial romance with the unfortunately-named Julie (Ross), the cook. But her grandparents really freak when they find out the boy has a criminal past. 91m; DVD. **C:** Hilary Duff; Evan Ross; Ellen Burstyn; Michael Murphy; Melissa Leo; Directed by Nancy Bardawil; Written by Michael Gilvary; Cinematography by Michael Lohmann; Music by Joseph E. Nordstrom. **A:** Jr. High-Adult. **P:** Entertainment. **U:** Home. **Mov-Ent:** Suicide. **Acq:** Purchase. **Dist:** Anchor Bay Entertainment.

According to Hoyle 1980
An entire business deal is enacted, from the purchasing of goods to the sales. 30m; VHS, 3/4 U. **Pr:** Commonwealth Films. **A:** Adult. **P:** Education. **U:** Institution, Home. **Bus-Ind:** Customer Service, Business, Documentary Films. **Acq:** Purchase, Rent/Lease. **Dist:** Commonwealth Films Inc. $395.00.

According to Jim: Season 1 2001 (Unrated)
Television comedy series on ABC (2001-). Yin and Yang spouses Jim (Belushi) and Cheryl (Thorne-Smith) raise three precocious kids, run a construction business, and feed their inner passions with humor and zest. Along for the laughs are Cheryl's brother, Andy and sister, Dana with their own quirky takes on life. Cheryl finds out her sister Dana buys all Jim's "Anniversary" gifts, and plans a surprise party for Jim in "No Surprises" but he'd rather go bowling. 22 episodes. 500m; DVD. **A:** Family. **P:** Entertainment. **U:** Home. **Mov-Ent:** Family, Television Series. **Acq:** Purchase. **Dist:** Lions Gate Entertainment Inc.

According to Jim: Season 2 2002 (Unrated)
ABC 2001-9 family comedy. Macho "everyman" Jim exasperates his feisty wife Cheryl as well as their three precocious kids. Cheryl is not a fan of Jim's latest invention in "Smell of Success," Jim becomes the host of Ruby's "Slumber Party," Cheryl helps Dana buy a new car in "Chicks and Cars," and the couple becomes addicted to eavesdropping in "The Baby Monitor." 28 episodes. 595m; DVD. **C:** James Belushi; Larry Joe Campbell; Kimberly Williams; Courtney Thorne-Smith. **A:** Family. **P:** Entertainment. **U:** Home. **Mov-Ent:** Family, Television Series. **Acq:** Purchase. **Dist:** Lions Gate Entertainment Inc. $29.99.

Accordion Styles and Techniques 1990
Joey Miskulin demonstrates his techniques for getting supreme sounds out of the accordion as he follows several songs and instrumentals. 80m; VHS. **Pr:** Homespun Video. **A:** Sr. High-Adult. **P:** Instruction. **U:** Home. **How-Ins:** How-To, Music--Instruction. **Acq:** Purchase. **Dist:** Homespun Tapes Ltd. $49.95.

Accountability and Liability in Nursing Practice 1988
As the role of nurses expands, they become more liable to lawsuits. This video shows them how to cover themselves. 28m; VHS, 3/4 U. **Pr:** Hospital Satellite Network. **A:** Adult. **P:** Professional. **U:** Institution, CCTV, SURA. **Hea-Sci:** How-To, Nursing, Law. **Acq:** Purchase, Rent/Lease. **Dist:** AJN Video Library/Lippincott Williams & Wilkins. $275.00.

Accountability: The Secret Weapon of a Successful Hospital 1982
The program suggests reasons why the true legacy of quality assurance programs and risk management programs should be a hospital-wide accountability system that has importance. 17m; VHS, 3/4 U. **Pr:** Health Communications Network. **A:** Adult. **P:** Professional. **U:** Institution, SURA. **Hea-Sci:** How-To, Medical Education. **Acq:** Purchase, Rent/Lease, Subscription.

The Accountant as a Business Advisor 1988
Independent public accountancy can also include management and financial consulting, this video claims, and then provides information to help accountants lay claim to this new field of endeavor. 60m; VHS. **Pr:** William K. Grollman. **A:** Adult. **P:** Professional. **U:** Institution. **Bus-Ind:** Finance, Management. **Acq:** Purchase. **Dist:** SmartPros Ltd. $449.00.

Accountant's Professional Liability 1982
For the staff accountant, this is a course on duties and liable professionalism. 45m; VHS, 3/4 U. **Pr:** Center for Video Education Inc. **A:** Adult. **P:** Professional. **U:** Institution. **Bus-Ind:** How-To, Business, Finance. **Acq:** Purchase, Rent/Lease. **Dist:** SmartPros Ltd.

Accounting & Auditing Update: Implementation of Recent Developments 19??
Details techniques for implementing the latest changes in accounting principles and auditing. Provides information on post-retirement benefits, market value, income taxes, and GAAP. Includes workbook and quizzer. 120m; VHS. **A:** College-Adult. **P:** Education. **U:** Institution, Home. **Gen-Edu:** Economics, Finance. **Acq:** Purchase. **Dist:** Bisk Education. $179.00.

Accounting and Finance for Non-Financial Managers 1986
This tape shows non-financial executives how to handle and process business finances. 180m; VHS, 3/4 U. **Pr:** Center for Video Education Inc. **A:** Adult. **P:** Education. **U:** Institution. **Bus-Ind:** How-To, Finance. **Acq:** Purchase. **Dist:** SmartPros Ltd.

Accounting for Lawyers 1988 1988
Lawyers are taught the basics of accounting in this program. 250m; VHS. **Pr:** Practicing Law Institute. **A:** Adult. **P:** Professional. **U:** Institution, Home. **How-Ins:** How-To, Finance. **Acq:** Purchase. **Dist:** Practising Law Institute. $95.00.

Accounting Library 1992
Covers accounting software Quicken, Peachtree, DacEasy Accounting, and DacEasy Payroll for IBM and IBM-compatible computers. Each of the seven tapes is available individually. ?m; VHS. **A:** Jr. High-Adult. **P:** Instruction. **U:** Institution. **Gen-Edu:** Computers. **Acq:** Purchase. **Dist:** Moonbeam Publications Inc. $229.65.

Accoustic Tumors: 1984 Update 1984
Dr. William House talks about the difficulties of acoustic tumor surgery. 30m; VHS, 3/4 U. **Pr:** House Ear Institute. **A:** Adult. **P:** Professional. **U:** Institution, CCTV. **Hea-Sci:** How-To, Ear, Surgery. **Acq:** Purchase. **Dist:** House Research Institute. $30.00.

Accreditation for Elementary Schools 19??
Discusses the process of elementary accreditation. Includes the processes of using self-study as a period of reflection, assessment, collaboration, and renewal, visitation and evaluation by the accreditation committee, and planning and follow-up. 25m; VHS. **A:** Adult. **P:** Education. **U:** Institution. **Gen-Edu:** Education. **Acq:** Purchase. **Dist:** Instructivision Inc. $54.95.

Accuracy in Measurement 1968
This animated film uses a box and a ruler to demonstrate that all measurement is approximate. 10m; VHS, 3/4 U. **Pr:** William Boundey. **A:** Primary. **P:** Education. **U:** Institution, SURA. **Gen-Edu:** How-To, Mathematics. **Acq:** Purchase. **Dist:** Phoenix Learning Group.

The Accursed 1957 — ★½
A 'dark old house' mystery. A group of former WWII resistance fighters meet each year at the home of Col. Charles Price (Wolfit) to commemorate the murder of their leader by the Nazis. Price gets a phone call saying they were betrayed and the traitor is now killing off the rest of the group, but the caller is killed before he reveals the name. Now, everyone is a suspect when they meet. 74m/B/W; DVD. **C:** Donald Wolfit; Robert Bray; Jane Griffiths; Anton Diffring; Christopher Lee; Karel Stepanek; Carl Jaffe; Directed by Michael McCarthy; Written by Michael McCarthy; Cinematography by Bert Mason; Music by Jackie Brown. **A:** Adult. **P:** Entertainment. **U:** Home. **L:** English. **Mov-Ent:** Mystery & Suspense. **Acq:** Purchase. **Dist:** WarnerArchive.com.

Accused 1936 (Unrated) — ★★½
Married dancers Fairbanks and Del Rio are working in a Parisian revue when the show's sultry leading lady (Desmond) makes a pass at Fairbanks. Though he's turned her down, through a series of misunderstandings Del Rio believes the worst and the two women get into a vicious argument. When the star is found dead guess who gets the blame? Del Rio is lovely, Desmond is spiteful, and Fairbanks serves as a fine object of two women's affections. 83m/B/W; VHS, DVD. **C:** Douglas Fairbanks, Jr.; Dolores Del Rio; Florence Desmond; Basil Sydney; Athole Stewart; Esme Percy; Googie Withers; Cecil Humphreys; Directed by Thornton Freeland. **Pr:** Marcel Hellman; United Artists. **A:** Jr. High-Adult. **P:** Entertainment. **U:** Home. **Mov-Ent:** Mystery & Suspense, Marriage. **Acq:** Purchase. **Dist:** Movies Unlimited.

The Accused 1948 — ★★½
Young is cast against character in this story of a college professor who is assaulted by one of her students and kills him in self-defense. A courtroom drama ensues, where Young is defended by the dead man's guardian. Film noir with nice ensemble performance. 101m/B/W; VHS. **C:** Loretta Young; Robert Cummings; Wendell Corey; Sam Jaffe; Douglas Dick; Sara Allgood; Ann Doran; Directed by William Dieterle; Cinematography by Milton Krasner. **Pr:** Hal B. Wallis; Paramount Pictures. **A:** Jr. High-Adult. **P:** Entertainment. **U:** Home. **Mov-Ent.** **Acq:** Purchase. **Dist:** Paramount Pictures Corp. $89.95.

The Accused 1988 (R) — ★★★
Provocative treatment of a true story involving a young woman gang raped in a bar while onlookers cheer. McGillis is the assistant district attorney who takes on the case and must contend with the victim's questionable past and a powerful lawyer hired by a wealthy defendant's parents. As the victim with a past, Foster gives an Oscar-winning performance that won raves for its strength and complexity. 110m; VHS, DVD, 8 mm, Wide, CC. **C:** Jodie Foster; Kelly McGillis; Bernie Coulson; Leo Rossi; Ann Hearn; Carmen Argenziano; Steve Antin; Tom O'Brien; Peter Van Norden; Woody Brown; Directed by Jonathan Kaplan; Written by Tom Topor; Cinematography by Ralf Bode; Music by Brad Fiedel. **Pr:** Paramount Pictures. **A:** Sr. High-Adult. **P:** Entertainment. **U:** Home. **Mov-Ent:** Rape, Sexual Abuse. **Awds:** Oscars '88: Actress (Foster); Golden Globes '89: Actress--Drama (Foster); Natl. Bd. of Review '88: Actress (Foster). **Acq:** Purchase. **Dist:** Facets Multimedia Inc.; Baker and Taylor; Paramount Pictures Corp. $14.95.

Accused at 17 2009 (Unrated) — ★★
Lifetime drama. High schooler Bianca complains to her best friends Fallyn and Sarah that her boyfriend Chad has cheated with slut Dory. A revenge plot goes awry when Fallyn loses her temper and kills Dory. When the cops start investigating, she pins the blame on Bianca and tries bullying Sarah into keeping quiet while Bianca's mom Jacqui works to prove her daughter's innocence. 90m; DVD. **C:** Nicole Gale Anderson; Janet Montgomery; Stella Maeve; Cynthia Gibb; Jason Brooks; Lindsay Taylor; Reiley McClendon; Linden Ashby; William R. Moses; Barbara Niven; Directed by Doug Campbell; Written by Christine Conradt; Cinematography by Robert Ballo; Music by Steve Gurevitch. **A:** Jr. High-Adult. **P:** Entertainment. **U:** Home. **Mov-Ent.** **Acq:** Purchase. **Dist:** Bedford Entertainment Inc.

Accutane and the Vitamin A Analogs 1983
The benefits and side effects of the drug Accutane, which is used for patients with severe cystic acne, are discussed. 37m; VHS, 3/4 U. **Pr:** Emory University. **A:** Adult. **P:** Professional. **U:** Institution, CCTV, CATV, BCTV, Home, SURA. **Hea-Sci:** Documentary Films, Drugs, Skin. **Acq:** Purchase, Rent/Lease, Subscription. **Dist:** Emory Medical Television Network.

Ace Crawford, Private Eye 19?? (Unrated) — ★★
Bumbling private eye struggles with confusing murder and somehow manages to solve the case. 71m; VHS. **C:** Tim Conway; Billy Barty; Bill Henderson. **A:** Adult. **P:** Entertainment. **U:** Home. **Mov-Ent:** Comedy--Slapstick, Mystery & Suspense. **Acq:** Purchase. **Dist:** Management Company Entertainment Group (MCEG), Inc.

Ace Drummond 1936 — ★★
The complete 13-chapter serial about a murder organization that tries to stop several countries from forming a worldwide clipper ship air service and government troubleshooter Ace Drummond who's out to stop them. 260m/B/W; VHS, DVD. **C:** John "Dusty" King; Jean Rogers; Noah Beery, Jr.; Directed by Ford Beebe. **A:** Family. **P:** Entertainment. **U:** Home. **Mov-Ent:** Mystery & Suspense, Serials, Aeronautics. **Acq:** Purchase. **Dist:** Grapevine Video; Facets Multimedia Inc.; Sinister Cinema. $24.95.

Ace High 1968 — ★½
Spaghetti western about a ruthless outlaw named Cat Stevens trying to save himself from the noose. Patterned after the famous Sergio Leone-Clint Eastwood westerns, with less of a budget and more camp tendencies. 120m; VHS, DVD. **C:** Eli Wallach; Terence Hill; Bud Spencer; Brock Peters; Kevin McCarthy; Directed by Giuseppe Colizzi. **Pr:** Paramount Pictures. **A:** Jr. High-Adult. **P:** Entertainment. **U:** Home. **Mov-Ent.** **Acq:** Purchase. **Dist:** Facets Multimedia Inc.; Paramount Pictures Corp. $14.95.

Ace Hits the Big Time 1995
A musical of a shy teen who is inadvertantly recruited into a gang and must concoct a whimsical scheme to win his girlfriend back from rival gang, the Piranhas. Based on the novel by Barbara Beasley Murphy and Judie Wolkoff. ?m; VHS. **Pr:** Martin Tahse. **A:** Jr. High-Sr. High. **P:** Entertainment. **U:** Home. **Mov-Ent:** Adolescence, Musical. **Acq:** Purchase. **Dist:** New Kid Home Video. $39.95.

Ace in the Hole 1951 (Unrated) — ★★★
Moralist Wilder brilliantly captures a cynical media circus. Alcoholic SOB reporter Chuck Tatum (Douglas) is bored crazy working a podunk paper in New Mexico when he gets a big scoop. Unhappy Lorraine (Sterling) tells Tatum her husband Leo (Benedict) was searching for Indian artifacts and is now trapped in a cave-in. Tatum teams up with corrupt local sheriff Gus Kretzer (Teal) to delay rescue operations to milk the story for maximum exposure while poor Leo suffers and the public come to gawk. Based on the Floyd Collins mining disaster of the 1920s. 111m/B/W; DVD, Blu-Ray. **C:** Kirk Douglas; Richard Benedict; Ray Teal; Jan Sterling; Robert Arthur; Porter Hall; Frank Cady; Gene Evans; Lewis Martin; Harry Harvey; Richard Gaines; Directed by Billy Wilder; Written by Billy Wilder; Lesser Samuels; Walter Newman; Cinematography by Charles B(ryant) Lang, Jr.; Music by Hugo Friedhofer. **A:** Sr. High-Adult. **P:** Entertainment. **U:** Home. **Mov-Ent:** Alcoholism, Journalism, Miners & Mining. **Acq:** Purchase. **Dist:** Criterion Collection Inc.

Ace in the Hole 2005
Documentary follows American soldiers and investigators as they search for Iraqi President Saddam Hussein for about eight months during the American-led invasion in 2003. 50m; DVD. **A:** Sr. High-Adult. **P:** Entertainment. **U:** Home. **Gen-Edu:** Documentary Films, War--General. **Acq:** Purchase. **Dist:** Sony Pictures Home Entertainment Inc. $19.94.

Ace of Aces 1933 — ★★
An American sculptor is reviled, particularly by his girlfriend, when he does not join fellows in enlisting in what becomes WWI. Out to prove he's not lacking testosterone, he becomes a pilot in France, but is embittered by his experiences. Dated but well-acted war melodrama. 77m/B/W; DVD. **C:** Richard Dix; Elizabeth Allan; Theodore Newton; Ralph Bellamy; William Cagney; Frank Conroy; Directed by J. Walter Ruben; Written by John Monk Saunders; Cinematography by Henry Cronjager; Music by Max Steiner. **Pr:** RKO. **A:** Adult. **P:** Entertainment. **U:** Home. **Mov-Ent:** Action-Adventure, World War One, Aeronautics. **Acq:** Purchase. **Dist:** WarnerArchive.com. $19.98.

The Ace of Hearts 1921 (Unrated) — ★★
Betray your ideals or your friends? Farallone (Chaney Sr.) and Forrest (Bowers) belong to a secret socialist society of vigilantes who target greedy, capitalist tycoons for death. The assassin is chosen by a random drawing of the ace of hearts but Forrest has fallen in love with Lilith (Joy) and can't kill. He's become the target after Farallone draws the deadly card. Silent drama is a subtle, sympathetic role for Chaney. 74m/B/W; Silent; DVD. **C:** Lon Chaney, Sr.; John Bowers; Leatrice Joy; Hardee Kirkland; Raymond Hatton; Directed by Wallace Worsley, II; Written by Ruth Wightman; Cinematography by Don Short. **A:** College-Adult. **P:** Entertainment. **U:** Home. **Mov-Ent:** Silent Films. **Acq:** Purchase. **Dist:** Warner Home Video, Inc.

Ace of Hearts 1985 (Unrated) — ★
A seedy story about a rich guy in the South Pacific who pays heavily to have himself killed. 90m; VHS. **C:** Mickey Rooney;

Chris Robinson; Pilar Velasquez. **A:** Jr. High-Adult. **P:** Entertainment. **U:** Home. **Mov-Ent**: Mystery & Suspense. **Acq:** Purchase. **Dist:** $39.95.

Ace of Hearts 2008 (PG) — ★★½
Officer Daniel Harding (Cain) is a member of the K-9 unit with his German Shepherd police partner, Ace. When Ace is unjustly accused of mauling a suspect, an over-zealous DA wants the dog euthanized. But Dan and his family are determined to clear Ace's name and save his furry life. 99m; DVD. **C:** Dean Cain; Mike Dopud; Anne Marie Deluise; Matthew Harrison; Britt Mckillip; David Patrick Green; Directed by David McKay; Written by Frederick Ayeroff; Cinematography by Gordon Verheul; Music by Michael Richard Plowman. **A:** Family. **P:** Entertainment. **U:** Home. **Mov-Ent**: Pets. **Acq:** Purchase. **Dist:** Fox Home Entertainment.

Ace the SAT 1990
Anyone looking for that extra edge to help them through one of the most influential aspects of getting into college, the SAT, will be interested in this video created by Suzee Vik. Vik's innovative look at the SAT has proven to raise scores by an average of 100 points. Includes a workbook. 80m; VHS. **Pr:** SyberVision Systems. **A:** Sr. High. **P:** Instruction. **U:** Home. **How-Ins**: How-To, Education. **Acq:** Purchase. **Dist:** Meridian Education Corp. $39.95.

Ace Ventura Jr.: Pet Detective 2008 (PG) — ★★
Eccentric 12-year-old Ace Jr. (Flitter) is following in his dad's footsteps when his mom (Cusack) is falsely accused of stealing a zoo's baby panda. He teams up with girl-next-door Laura (Lockhart) and gizmo-crazy pal A-Plus (Rogers) to clear the family name. Alrighty then! 93m; DVD. **C:** Josh Flitter; Emma Lockhart; Austin Rogers; Ann Cusack; Ralph Waite; Brian Patrick Clarke; Art LaFleur; Reed Alexander; Cullen Douglas; Directed by David Mickey Evans; Written by David Mickey Evans; Jeffrey Sank; Jason Heimberg; Justin Heimberg; Cinematography by Mark Irwin; Music by Laura Karpman. **A:** Family. **P:** Entertainment. **U:** Home. **Mov-Ent**. **Acq:** Purchase. **Dist:** Warner Home Video, Inc.

Ace Ventura: Pet Detective 1993 (PG-13) — ★★
Shamelessly silly comedy casts human cartoon Carrey, he of the rubber limbs and spasmodic facial muscles, as Ace, the guy who'll find missing pets, big or small. When the Miami Dolphins' mascot Snowflake is kidnapped, he abandons his search for an albino pigeon to save the lost dolphin just in time for the Super Bowl. This is brain candy, running full throttle with juvenile humor, some charm, and the hyper-energetic Carrey, not to mention Young as the police chief with a secret. Critically trashed boxoffice smash catapulted Carrey into nearly instant stardom after seven seasons as the geeky white guy on "In Living Color." 87m; VHS, DVD, Blu-Ray, 8 mm, CC. **C:** Jim Carrey; Courteney Cox; Sean Young; Tone Loc; Noble Willingham; Troy Evans; Udo Kier; Cameo(s) Dan Marino; Directed by Tom Shadyac; Written by Jim Carrey; Tom Shadyac; Jack Bernstein; Cinematography by Julio Macat; Music by Ira Newborn. **Pr:** James G. Robinson; Gary Barber; Morgan Creek Productions; Warner Bros. **A:** Jr. High-Adult. **P:** Entertainment. **U:** Home. **Mov-Ent**: Comedy--Slapstick, Pets, Football. **Awds:** Blockbuster '95: Comedy Actor, V. (Carrey), Male Newcomer, V. (Carrey). **Acq:** Purchase. **Dist:** Warner Home Video, Inc. $24.96.

Ace Ventura: When Nature Calls 1995 (PG-13) — ★★
Ace is back on the case as the pet dick (Carrey) ventures to Africa to restore peace among rival tribes by finding an albino bat that's M.I.A. Plot is secondary, however, to multi-million dollar man Carrey's outrageous brand of physical comedy combined with his unique ability to deliver junior high level lines with pseudo-suave savoir-faire. Contains only a handful of outstanding gags, the best with Ace and a mechanical rhino. Mainly for Carrey aficionados (of which there are many) and original "Ace" fans—the low-brow humor runs a bit thin by the end. 94m; VHS, DVD, Blu-Ray, CC. **C:** Jim Carrey; Ian McNeice; Simon Callow; Maynard Eziashi; Bob Gunton; Sophie Okonedo; Tommy Davidson; Directed by Steve Oedekerk; Written by Steve Oedekerk; Cinematography by Donald E. Thorin; Music by Robert Folk. **Pr:** James G. Robinson; Gary Barber; Morgan Creek Productions; Warner Bros. **A:** Jr. High-Adult. **P:** Entertainment. **U:** Home. **Mov-Ent**: Comedy--Slapstick, Animals, Africa. **Awds:** MTV Movie Awards '96: Comedic Perf. (Carrey), Male Perf. (Carrey); Blockbuster '96: Comedy Actor, T. (Carrey). **Acq:** Purchase. **Dist:** Warner Home Video, Inc. $22.98.

Aces 1990
The evolution of the fighter pilot through the years from WWI through the Vietnamese war. With B&W footage. 60m; VHS. **Pr:** MPI Media Group. **A:** Jr. High-Adult. **P:** Education. **U:** Home. **Gen-Edu**: Documentary Films, Aeronautics, War--General. **Acq:** Purchase. **Dist:** MPI Media Group. $19.98.

Aces: A Story of the First Air War 1995
Documentary look at a WWI airman, from his 1914 commissioning to his battles as fighter pilot. 93m; VHS. **A:** Jr. High-Adult. **P:** Education. **U:** Institution. **Gen-Edu**: War--General, Documentary Films. **Acq:** Purchase, Rent/Lease. **Dist:** National Film Board of Canada. $300.

Aces and Eights 1936 — ★★½
Gambler McCoy catches a fellow cardsharp cheating and the marshal runs the varmint out of town. When the cheater is murdered, the lawman suspects McCoy, who sets out to prove his innocence. Title refers to the "death hand" held by Wild Bill Hickok, killed while playing poker. Film opens with a shot of Hickok and a speech about gambler's luck. 62m/B/W; VHS, DVD. **C:** Tim McCoy; Jimmy Aubrey; Luana Walters; Wheeler Oakman; Earle Hodgins; Frank Glennon; Rex Lease; Joseph Girard; John Merton; Directed by Sam Newfield. **Pr:** Leslie Simmonds; Puritan. **A:** Jr. High-Adult. **P:** Entertainment. **U:** Home. **Mov-Ent**: Western. **Acq:** Purchase. **Dist:** Rex Miller Artisan Studio. $19.95.

Aces Go Places 1982 (Unrated)
A notorious burglar and the Hong Kong police join hands to fight crime in this slapstick, James Bond-type suspense film. In Cantonese with English subtitles. 94m; VHS. **C:** Sam Hui; Directed by Eric Tsang. **A:** Sr. High-Adult. **P:** Entertainment. **U:** Home. **Mov-Ent**: Comedy--Slapstick. **Acq:** Purchase. **Dist:** Facets Multimedia Inc. $39.95.

Aces Go Places 2 1983
Hong Kong's master jewel thief is back in a sequel, leaving a trail of slapstick and James Bond heroics in his wake. In Cantonese with English subtitles. 100m; VHS. **C:** Sam Hui; Sylvia Chang; Carl Mak; Directed by Eric Tsang. **A:** Sr. High-Adult. **P:** Entertainment. **U:** Home. **L:** English, Chinese. **Mov-Ent**: Comedy--Slapstick. **Acq:** Purchase. **Dist:** Facets Multimedia Inc. $39.95.

Aces Go Places 3 198? (Unrated) — ★
The third in the slapstick series featuring a master thief played by Hui. In Cantonese with English subtitles. ?m; VHS. **C:** Sam Hui; Directed by Eric Tsang. **A:** Sr. High-Adult. **P:** Entertainment. **U:** Home. **L:** English, Chinese. **Mov-Ent**: Comedy--Slapstick. **Acq:** Purchase. **Dist:** Facets Multimedia Inc. $49.95.

Aces: Iron Eagle 3 1992 (R) — ★★
Colonel "Chappy" Sinclair returns once again in this air adventure. He's been keeping busy flying in air shows when he stumbles across the nefarious activities of a Peruvian drug baron working out of a remote village. Sinclair recruits a team of maverick air circus pilots and they "borrow" a fleet of WWII vintage aircraft to raid the village, coming up against a fellow Air Force officer who turns out to be another villain. Lots of action and a stalwart cast. 98m; VHS, DVD, CC. **C:** Louis Gossett, Jr.; Rachel McLish; Paul Freeman; Horst Buchholz; Christopher Cazenove; Sonny Chiba; Fred Dalton Thompson; Mitchell Ryan; Robert Estes; J.E. Freeman; Directed by John Glen. **Pr:** Seven Arts Pictures. **A:** Sr. High-Adult. **P:** Entertainment. **U:** Home. **Mov-Ent**: Aeronautics, Drugs. **Acq:** Purchase. **Dist:** Sony Pictures Home Entertainment Inc. $19.95.

Aces 'n Eights 2008 (Unrated) — ★★
Luke Rivers (Van Dien) has retired as a gunslinger and is now working on an Arizona ranch owned by crusty Thurmond Prescott (Borgnine). The local land owners band together to fight ruthless railroad mogul Howard (Atherton), who uses intimidation and murder to seize their land. Looks like Rivers is going to have to strap on his six-guns and go up against some of his old saddle-mates in order to defend his new life. Title refers to poker's so-called "dead man's hand," held by Wild Bill Hickok when he was killed. 87m; DVD. **C:** Casper Van Dien; Bruce Boxleitner; Ernest Borgnine; William Atherton; Jeff Kober; Jack Noseworthy; Jake Thomas; Rodney Scott; Deirdre Quinn; Directed by Craig R. Baxley; Written by Ronald M. Cohen; Dennis Shryack; Cinematography by Yaron Levy. **A:** Jr. High-Adult. **P:** Entertainment. **U:** Home. **Mov-Ent**: Western. **Acq:** Purchase. **Dist:** Genius.com Incorporated.

Aces of the I.A.F. 19??
Aviation footage of modern Israeli fighter jets in action and action footage of the Yom Kipper War. 46m; VHS. **A:** Jr. High-Adult. **P:** Education. **U:** Home. **Gen-Edu**: Documentary Films, Aeronautics, War--General. **Acq:** Purchase. **Dist:** Bennett Marine Video; Military/Combat Stock Footage Library. $24.95.

Aces Wild 1937 — ★½
Another poker title. Outlaws menace an honest newspaper until the lawmen show up and send them on their way. 62m/B/W; VHS. **C:** Harry Carey, Sr.; Gertrude Messinger; Edward Cassidy; Roger Williams; Directed by Harry Fraser. **Pr:** Commodore. **A:** Family. **P:** Entertainment. **U:** Home. **Mov-Ent**: Western. **Acq:** Purchase. **Dist:** Movies Unlimited. $14.99.

Acetaminophen and Tricyclic Antidepressant Overdoses 1981
Presents a case study of a fatal acetaminophen overdose, followed by a discussion of the pathophysiology, diagnosis, and management of acetaminophen and tricyclic antidepressant overdoses. 52m; VHS, 3/4 U. **Pr:** Emory University. **A:** College-Adult. **P:** Professional. **U:** Institution, CCTV, Home, SURA. **Hea-Sci**: Documentary Films, Drugs. **Acq:** Purchase, Rent/Lease, Subscription. **Dist:** Emory Medical Television Network.

Acetylene Cylinder Safety 19??
Demonstrates procedures to use for the detection of leaks in acetylene cylinders and welding equipment. Discusses the use of reverse flow check valve, checking valves, and general safety. 22m; VHS. **A:** Sr. High-Adult. **P:** Vocational. **U:** Institution. **Bus-Ind**: Industrial Arts, Metal Work, Safety Education. **Acq:** Purchase. **Dist:** CEV Multimedia. $89.95.

ACF Best Sellers: Advanced Stunts & Pyramids Volume 2 1998 (Unrated)
The American Cheerleading Federation demonstrates over 15 new stunts for cheerleaders at the advanced level. 40m; VHS. **A:** Family. **P:** Education. **U:** Home, Institution. **Spo-Rec**: Cheerleaders, Athletic Instruction/Coaching. **Acq:** Purchase. **Dist:** Championship Productions. $39.99.

ACF Best Sellers: Advanced Stunts & Pyramids Volume 3 1999 (Unrated)
The American Cheerleading Federation demonstrates 15 new stunts for cheerleaders at the advanced level. 32m; VHS. **A:** Family. **P:** Education. **U:** Home, Institution. **Spo-Rec**: Cheerleaders, Athletic Instruction/Coaching. **Acq:** Purchase. **Dist:** Championship Productions. $39.99.

ACF Best Sellers: Advanced Stunts & Pyramids Volume 4 2000 (Unrated)
The American Cheerleading Federation demonstrates 16 new stunts for cheerleaders at the advanced level. 34m; VHS. **A:** Family. **P:** Education. **U:** Home, Institution. **Spo-Rec**: Cheerleaders, Athletic Instruction/Coaching. **Acq:** Purchase. **Dist:** Championship Productions. $39.99.

ACF Best Sellers: Beginning Stunts & Pyramids Volume 6 2002 (Unrated)
The American Cheerleading Federation demonstrates 12 new stunts for cheerleaders at the beginning level. 28m; VHS. **A:** Family. **P:** Education. **U:** Home, Institution. **Spo-Rec**: Cheerleaders, Athletic Instruction/Coaching. **Acq:** Purchase. **Dist:** Championship Productions. $29.99.

The Aches and Pains Test 1988
The entire story of aches—their causes, their severity, and their cures. 22m; VHS, 3/4 U, Special order formats. **Pr:** Perennial Education Inc. **A:** Sr. High-Adult. **P:** Education. **U:** Institution, Home, SURA. **Hea-Sci**: Health Education. **Acq:** Purchase, Rent/Lease, Trade-in. **Dist:** United Learning Inc.; Discovery Education. $295.00.

Achieve Success by Prospecting with Phillip Wexler 19??
Phillip Wexler offers prospecting training program for sales people. Only available in the U.S. 25m; VHS. **A:** College-Adult. **P:** Professional. **U:** Institution. **Bus-Ind**: Sales Training, How-To. **Acq:** Purchase. **Dist:** Instructional Video. $95.00.

The Achievement Challenge 1988
A series of programs that explain things to be done and attitudes to be taken to do better in business. 60m; VHS. **Pr:** Beveridge Business Systems, Inc. **A:** Adult. **P:** Instruction. **U:** Institution. **Bus-Ind**: Business, How-To. **Acq:** Purchase. **Dist:** 4th Generation Systems. $995.00.
Indiv. Titles: 1. If It Is To Be, It Is Up to Me 2. A Mandatory Goals Attitude 3. A Crisis to Perform 4. Identify and Satisfy Customer Needs...Profitably 5. Why Successful Businesses and Successful People Don't Stay Successful 6. Quick...Stop Compromising!.

Achievement Skills: Reaching Your Potential 1981
This program wonders why people with a lot of skills, talents, and intelligence still fall short of their goals. 30m; VHS. **Pr:** HRM. **A:** Jr. High-Sr. High. **P:** Education. **U:** Institution. **Gen-Edu**: Documentary Films, Personality, Self-Help. **Acq:** Purchase. **Dist:** HRM Video. $145.00.

The Achievers 1988
Five-part series that outlines five outstanding Black Americans, outlining their lives, goals, and achievements. Summarizes the lives of Bill Parrot, Cheryl Glass, Pete Tzomes, Willie Brown, and Katherine Dunham. 60m; VHS, SVS, 3/4 U. **Pr:** Turner Broadcasting. **A:** Jr. High-Adult. **P:** Education. **U:** Institution. **Gen-Edu**: Black Culture. **Acq:** Purchase. **Dist:** Encyclopedia Britannica. $265.00.

Achieving High Quality Child Care 1993
Discusses how to run a child care facility as a business. Covers safe food handling practices, ways to insure a safe environment, positive guidance and discipline, how to communicate with children and families and national requirements to be aware of. 120m; VHS. **A:** Adult. **P:** Vocational. **U:** Institution. **Bus-Ind**: Child Care, Occupational Training. **Acq:** Purchase. **Dist:** University of Idaho. $25.00.

Achieving in the Futuristic Workplace 1994
Part of the "Habits of Wealth" series. One of today's most successful entrepreneurs, Bill Byrne, discusses and offers advice on what it will take to be successful in the future. Includes insight on the personal mission statement and core principals. 29m; VHS. **A:** Sr. High-Adult. **P:** Education. **U:** Institution, Home. **Bus-Ind**: Business, How-To, Job Training. **Acq:** Purchase. **Dist:** Cambridge Educational. $89.95.

Acholic Stools and Abdominal Mass in an Infant 1987
The case of a one-month-old boy with jaundice and abdominal pain. 58m; VHS, 3/4 U. **C:** W. Dean Wilcox; Michael Finch. **A:** Adult. **P:** Professional. **U:** Institution, CCTV, Home, SURA. **Hea-Sci**: Documentary Films, Pediatrics, Infants. **Acq:** Purchase, Rent/Lease, Subscription. **Dist:** Emory Medical Television Network.

Acid-Base Balance 1984
This series reviews the concepts of acid, base, hydrogen ion concentration, and ph; shows how the respiratory system and the kidneys attempt to compensate for excess acids and bases in body fluids; defines respiratory acidosis and alkalosis; and discusses metabolic acidosis and alkalosis. 25m; VHS, 3/4 U. **Pr:** Trainex. **A:** College. **P:** Professional. **U:** Institution. **Hea-Sci**: Medical Education. **Acq:** Purchase, Rent/Lease. **Dist:** Medcom Inc.
Indiv. Titles: 1. The Body's Regulation of pH 2. Compensation of Imbalances 3. Respiratory Acidosis and Alkalosis.

Acid Battery Safety and Jump Starting 1995
Discusses how batteries are constructed, types of batteries and how to jump start batteries safely. 12m; VHS. **A:** Adult. **P:** Instruction. **U:** Institution. **Bus-Ind**: Safety Education, Occupational Training. **Acq:** Purchase, Rent/Lease. **Dist:** National Safety Council, California Chapter, Film Library. $175.00.

The Acid Eaters 1967 — ★
Straight-laced desk jockeys spend their weekends exploring the realm of the senses. Includes nudity. 62m; VHS, DVD. **C:** Buck

Kartalian; Pat Barrington; Directed by B. Ron Elliott; Written by B. Ron Elliott; Carl Monson; Music by William Allen Castleman. **A:** College-Adult. **P:** Entertainment. **U:** Home. **Mov-Ent:** Fantasy, Drug Abuse, Motorcycles. **Acq:** Purchase. **Dist:** Something Weird Video; Tapeworm Video Distributors Inc. $23.00.

Acid from Heaven 1983
Looks at a person whose income was cut off as a direct result of acid rain. 31m; VHS, 3/4 U. **Pr:** National Film Board of Canada. **A:** Jr. High-Adult. **P:** Education. **U:** Institution, SURA. **Gen-Edu:** Documentary Films, Ecology & Environment. **Acq:** Purchase, Rent/Lease. **Dist:** National Film Board of Canada.

The Acid House 1998 (Unrated) — ★★½
Trilogy of tales written by Irving Welsh, author of "Trainspotting," similarly centers on down-on-their-luck Scottish hooligans ravaged by drugs and drink. Its tone, however, makes its predecessor look like a light-hearted romp in the countryside. In "The Granton Star Cause," freeloading loser Boab (McCole) gets turned into a fly by God during a trip to the pub. He proceeds to exact some disgusting revenge on those he feels have wronged him. "A Soft Touch" depicts the twisted relationship between brow-beaten Johnny (McKidd) and kinky wife Catriona (Gomez), who is sleeping with psycho neighbor Larry (McCormack). In the last chapter, "The Acid House," tripped-out rave party boy Coco (Bremner) exchanges personalities with the newborn baby of suburban couple Rory (Clunes) and Jenny (Redgrave). First-time director McGuigan does a good job of translating the material to the screen, but sometimes goes over the top in showing these skanky Scots. Also, be warned that the Scottish accents are so thick that the movie ran with subtitles during its limited U.S. theatre run. If you liked "Trainspotting," however, you'll probably like this similar entry in the "if it's Scottish, it's crap!" genre. 118m; VHS, DVD, Wide. **C:** Stephen McCole; Maurice Roeves; Garry Sweeney; Kevin McKidd; Ewen Bremner; Martin Clunes; Jemma Redgrave; Arlene Cockburn; Jenny McCrindle; Michelle Gomez; Tam Dean Burn; Gary McCormack; Jane Stabler; Directed by Paul McGuigan; Written by Irvine Welsh; Cinematography by Alasdair Walker. **A:** College-Adult. **P:** Entertainment. **U:** Home. **Mov-Ent:** Comedy--Black, Scotland. **Acq:** Purchase. **Dist:** Zeitgeist Films Ltd.

Acid Rain 199?
CBS series "60 Minutes" reports on the effects of acid rain. 12m; VHS. **A:** Sr. High-Adult. **P:** Entertainment. **U:** Institution. **Gen-Edu:** Public Health. **Acq:** Purchase. **Dist:** Ambrose Video Publishing, Inc. $69.95.

Acid Rain 1984
An in-depth look at this phenomenal environmental problem, first aired as an episode of NOVA. 57m; VHS, 3/4 U, Special order formats. **Pr:** PBS. **A:** Family. **P:** Education. **U:** Institution, SURA. **Gen-Edu:** Documentary Films, Ecology & Environment. **Acq:** Purchase, Rent/Lease. **Dist:** Time-Life Video and Television.

Acid Rain 1986
This animated film can serve as an introduction to the subject of acid rain to young children, even though it is not fact-based. 4m; VHS, 3/4 U. **Pr:** Wolf Koenig. **A:** Primary-Adult. **P:** Education. **U:** Institution, SURA. **Chl-Juv:** Family Viewing, Animation & Cartoons, Children. **Acq:** Purchase, Rent/Lease. **Dist:** National Film Board of Canada. $150.00.

Acid Rain 1989
History and explanation of acid rain, including chemical definitions, geological and meteorological interactions, and traces the sources of acid precipitation. Ecological concepts and possible solutions are demonstrated. 20m; VHS, 3/4 U. **Pr:** Films for the Humanities and Sciences. **A:** College. **P:** Education. **U:** Institution, CCTV, CATV, BCTV. **Hea-Sci:** Documentary Films, Ecology & Environment. **Acq:** Purchase, Rent/Lease, Duplication License. **Dist:** Films for the Humanities & Sciences.

Acid Rain: A North American Challenge 1988
This, a shortened version of the film "Trouble in the Forest," summarizes what we know about the scourge of acid rain. 16m; VHS, 3/4 U. **Pr:** Gary Toole; Craig Graham. **A:** Sr. High-Adult. **P:** Education. **U:** Institution, SURA. **Gen-Edu:** Documentary Films, Ecology & Environment, Propaganda. **Acq:** Purchase, Rent/Lease. **Dist:** National Film Board of Canada. $250.00.

Acid Rain and Our Forests 19??
Explains the ecological effects that acid rain is having on the earth's environment. Includes teacher's manual. 20m; VHS. **A:** Jr. High-Adult. **P:** Education. **U:** Institution. **Hea-Sci:** Geography, Science, Ecology & Environment. **Acq:** Purchase. **Dist:** Educational Video Network. $49.95.

Acid Rain: Requiem or Recovery 1983
Examines the origins and impact of acid rain on the environment and wildlife. 27m; VHS, 3/4 U. **Pr:** National Film Board of Canada. **A:** Jr. High-Adult. **P:** Education. **U:** Institution, SURA. **Gen-Edu:** Documentary Films, Ecology & Environment. **Acq:** Purchase, Rent/Lease. **Dist:** National Film Board of Canada.

Acid Rain: The Invisible Threat 1992
Explains how acid rain affects forests, lakes, and the human environment. Teacher's Guide and glossary included. 20m; VHS. **A:** Jr. High-Sr. High. **P:** Education. **U:** Institution. **Hea-Sci:** Ecology & Environment. **Acq:** Purchase. **Dist:** American Educational Products LLC; Crystal Productions; United Learning Inc. $64.95.

Acid Rainbows 1988
Acid rain and its effects are just beginning to poison the once-pristine air of the Rockies and the Southwest. 30m; VHS, 3/4 U. **Pr:** Pacific Mountain Network; KRMA Denver. **A:** Jr. High-Adult. **P:** Education. **U:** Institution, SURA. **Gen-Edu:** Documentary Films, Ecology & Environment. **Acq:** Purchase, Rent/Lease. **Dist:** PBS Home Video. $39.95.

Acid Reign 1983
Put the problem of acid rain into perspective as another part of man's ongoing battle to save the environment. 10m; 3/4 U. **C:** Narrated by Ralph Nader. **Pr:** Helen Henshaw. **A:** Sr. High-Adult. **P:** Education. **U:** Institution, SURA. **Hea-Sci:** Ecology & Environment. **Acq:** Purchase, Rent/Lease. **Dist:** Kinetic Film Enterprises Ltd.

Acidburn Flashback Tabu 1991
These 11 psychedelic animated shorts are designed to create an altered state of mind in the viewer. Includes "Life is Flashing Before Your Eyes" by Vincent Collins, "Ace of Light" by Dennis Pies, and "Delivery Man" by Emily Hubley. 60m; VHS. **A:** Sr. High-Adult. **P:** Entertainment. **U:** Home. **Mov-Ent:** Animation & Cartoons. **Acq:** Purchase. **Dist:** Next Gen Video. $24.95.

Acidizing: Freedom to Flow 1981
This program covers basic factors involved in acidizing oil and gas wells. 18m; VHS, 3/4 U. **Pr:** University of Texas Austin. **A:** College-Adult. **P:** Instruction. **U:** Institution, CCTV. **Bus-Ind:** Oil Industry. **Acq:** Purchase.

Acids and Bases 1993
Profiles the chemical compounds known as acids and bases and illustrates that when they react together they produce entirely new products, some of which are vital to life processes and invaluable to industry. 15m; VHS, SVS, 3/4 U. **A:** Jr. High-Sr. High. **P:** Education. **U:** Institution. **Hea-Sci:** Chemistry. **Acq:** Purchase. **Dist:** Encyclopedia Britannica. $99.00.

ACL Injury Prevention for Female Athletes 2009 (Unrated)
Strength Coach Alan Stein presents techniques for female athletes to use to avoid ACL injuries while playing basketball, which women athletes are four-eight times more likely to do than men. 70m; DVD. **A:** Family. **P:** Education. **U:** Home, Institution. **Spo-Rec:** Basketball, Athletic Instruction/Coaching. **Acq:** Purchase. **Dist:** Championship Productions. $39.99.

Acla's Descent into Floristella 1987 — ★★
Twelve-year-old Acla (Cusimano) is sold by his father to work underground in the sulfur mines for eight years. Repeatedly beaten by his owner, Acla runs away, but there are dire consequences for him and his family. Set in 1930s Sicily. Italian with subtitles. 86m; VHS, DVD. **C:** Francesco Cusimano; Tony Sperandeo; Directed by Aurelio Grimaldi; Written by Aurelio Grimaldi; Cinematography by Maurizio Calvesi; Music by Dario Lucantoni. **A:** College-Adult. **P:** Entertainment. **U:** Home. **L:** Italian. **Mov-Ent:** Children, Italy, Slavery. **Acq:** Purchase. **Dist:** Amazon.com Inc.; Facets Multimedia Inc. $69.95.

ACLS Skills Review Video Series 19??
Eight-part series outlining techniques in ACLS care. Includes Instructor's Guide. ?m; VHS. **A:** College-Adult. **P:** Instruction. **U:** Institution. **How-Ins:** Job Training, First Aid. **Acq:** Purchase. **Dist:** Fire Engineering Books & Videos. $995.00.
Indiv. Titles: 1. Airway Management 2. IV Procedures 3. ECG Recognition 4. Arrhythmia Interpretation 5. Conversion Techniques 6. Pharmacology, Part I 7. Pharmacology, Part II 8. Mega Code.

The ACLU Freedom Files 2006
A 10-part series from Robert Greenwald that shows how people have fought against threats to civil liberties from free speech to religious freedom. 358m; DVD. **A:** Sr. High-Adult. **P:** Entertainment. **U:** Home. **Gen-Edu:** Documentary Films. **Acq:** Purchase. **Dist:** Rykodisc Corp.

Acne 1979
New treatments which can control acne and prevent scarring are presented. Myths about the causes of acne are discussed. 30m; VHS, 3/4 U. **Pr:** NET. **A:** Jr. High-Adult. **P:** Education. **U:** Institution, CCTV, Home. **Hea-Sci:** Skin. **Acq:** Purchase, Rent/Lease. **Dist:** WNET/Thirteen Non-Broadcast.

Acne: Why Me? I Don't Eat Chocolates 1976
Young people discuss the abuse and pain they suffer from comments by friends, relatives, and even strangers about their acne problem. Three dermatologists dispel the myths about the causes and care of acne, and suggest some practical ways of controlling it. 26m; 3/4 U, Special order formats. **Pr:** Hobel Leiterman Productions. **A:** Jr. High-Adult. **P:** Education. **U:** Institution. **Hea-Sci:** Skin. **Acq:** Purchase. **Dist:** The Cinema Guild.

A.C.O.D. 2013 (R) — ★★
As it has so many times, divorce becomes the basis for comedy in this tale of a grown man named Carter (Scott) who discovers that his childhood of divorce was used as the basis of a hit book. Years later, when his brother is about to get married, Carter is forced to play peacekeeper again between his antagonistic parents (scene-stealing O'Hara & Jenkins). The ensemble cast is uniformly great but the film goes off on too many tangents (a brief affair with Alba, as another "child of divorce" is totally superfluous) and it kind of just ends. 88m; DVD, Blu-Ray. **C:** Adam Scott; Richard Jenkins; Catherine O'Hara; Mary Elizabeth Winstead; Jessica Alba; Directed by Stuart Zicherman; Written by Stuart Zicherman; Ben Karlin; Cinematography by John Bailey; Music by Nick Urata. **Pr:** Tim Perell; Teddy Schwarzman; Ben Karlin; Film Arcade; Black Bear. **A:** Sr. High-Adult. **P:** Entertainment. **U:** Home. **L:** English. **Mov-Ent:** Divorce, Family, Marriage. **Acq:** Purchase. **Dist:** Paramount Pictures Corp.

Acolytes 2008 (Unrated) — ★★
A couple of high school kids have a serious bully problem and decide to blackmail a local serial killer into fixing it when they find one of his victims. 91m; DVD. **C:** Joel Edgerton; Michael Dorman; Sebastian Gregory; Joshua Payne; Hanna Mangan Lawrence; Belinda McClory; Directed by Jon Hewitt; Written by Jon Hewitt; Shane Krause; Shayne Armstrong; Cinematography by Mark Pugh; Music by David Franzke. **A:** Sr. High-Adult. **P:** Entertainment. **U:** Home. **L:** English. **Mov-Ent. Acq:** Purchase. **Dist:** Anchor Bay Entertainment Inc.; Starz Entertainment. $9.98.

Acolytes, Greeters, Ushers 19??
Practical tips on serving as acolytes, greeters or ushers in Protestant services, to ensure a smooth flow of responsibilities. 23m; VHS. **A:** Jr. High-Adult. **P:** Religious. **U:** Institution. **Gen-Edu:** Religion, Job Training. **Acq:** Purchase, Rent/Lease. **Dist:** EcuFilm. $29.95.

Acompaname 1966 — ★½
A musical love story about a rich Mexican student who goes to Spain and falls in love with a Spanish girl. 100m; VHS. **C:** Enrique Guzman; Rocio Durcal; Directed by Luis Cesar Amadori. **Pr:** KNBC. **A:** Jr. High-Adult. **P:** Entertainment. **U:** Home. **L:** Spanish. **Mov-Ent:** Musical, Romance, Spain. **Acq:** Purchase. **Dist:** Spanishmultimedia. $69.95.

Acorn Entrepeneurs 1998
Features interviews with eight children ages nine to seventeen who have started their own businesses. Covers such subjects as money management, working long hours, overcoming obstacles, knowing their customers and balancing school, friends and business. ?m; VHS. **A:** Family. **P:** Education. **U:** Home. **Gen-Edu:** Children, Business. **Acq:** Purchase. **Dist:** Tapeworm Video Distributors Inc. $14.95.

Acorn People 1982 (Unrated) — ★★
An unemployed teacher takes a summer job at a camp for handicapped children and learns sensitivity. Weeper adapted by Tewkesbury from the book by Ron Jones. 97m; VHS. **C:** Ted Bessell; Cloris Leachman; LeVar Burton; Dolph Sweet; Cheryl Anderson; Directed by Joan Tewkesbury. **Pr:** National Broadcasting Company. **A:** Primary-Adult. **P:** Entertainment. **U:** Institution, SURA. **Mov-Ent:** Melodrama, Handicapped, TV Movies. **Acq:** Purchase. **Dist:** Time-Life Video and Television.

The Acoustic Bass 199?
Jazz bassist Gary Peacock imparts his philosophy of musical ideas and improvisational approaches to viewers. Includes written material. 75m; VHS. **A:** Family. **P:** Instruction. **U:** Home. **How-Ins:** Music--Instruction. **Acq:** Purchase. **Dist:** Hal Leonard Corp. $29.95.

Acoustic Blues Guitar 199?
Presents key blues techniques for players familiar with basic chords and have some guitar experience. Includes musical examples. 75m; VHS. **A:** Sr. High-Adult. **P:** Education. **U:** Home. **How-Ins:** Music--Instruction. **Acq:** Purchase. **Dist:** Hal Leonard Corp. $19.95.

Acoustic Finger Picking 199?
Jamie Findlay, from the Musicians Institute, provides in-depth instruction on acoustic finger picking and demonstrates technique building exercises. 30m; VHS. **A:** Sr. High-Adult. **P:** Instruction. **U:** Home. **How-Ins:** Music--Instruction. **Acq:** Purchase. **Dist:** Hal Leonard Corp. $9.95.

Acoustic Guitar Instrumentals, Vol. 1: Arrangements in Alternate Tunings 1993
Features British guitarist Martin Simpson as he teaches dropped-D and altered-G tunings that help you bring the widest harmonic range on the guitar. Includes tab and music. 75m; VHS. **A:** Jr. High-Adult. **P:** Instruction. **U:** Home. **How-Ins:** Music--Instruction. **Acq:** Purchase. **Dist:** Homespun Tapes Ltd. $49.95.

Acoustic Guitar Instrumentals, Vol. 2: Creating Your Arrangements 1995
Martin Simpson provides extensive analysis of his guitar arragements. 60m; VHS. **A:** Jr. High-Adult. **P:** Instruction. **U:** Home. **How-Ins:** How-To, Music--Instruction. **Acq:** Purchase. **Dist:** Homespun Tapes Ltd. $49.95.

Acoustic Guitar Instrumentals, Vol. 3: Developing Style and Repertoire 1995
Martin Simpson teaches several complex arrangements. 60m; VHS. **A:** Jr. High-Adult. **P:** Instruction. **U:** Home. **How-Ins:** How-To, Music--Instruction. **Acq:** Purchase. **Dist:** Homespun Tapes Ltd. $49.95.

The Acoustic Guitar of Jorma Kaukonen: Blues, Rags and Originals 199?
Three-volume set teaches blues style fingerpicking using traditional and original tunes. 270m; VHS. **A:** Sr. High-Adult. **P:** Education. **U:** Home. **How-Ins:** Music--Instruction. **Acq:** Purchase. **Dist:** Hal Leonard Corp. $99.95.

The Acoustic Guitar of Jorma Kaukonen: Video One 199?
Teaches fingerpicking blues style using traditional and original tunes. 100m; VHS. **A:** Sr. High-Adult. **P:** Education. **U:** Home. **How-Ins:** Music--Instruction. **Acq:** Purchase. **Dist:** Hal Leonard Corp. $39.95.

The Acoustic Guitar of Jorma Kaukonen: Video Three 199?
Final installment teaches intermediate-level blues fingerpicking style using traditional and original tunes. 80m; VHS. **A:** Sr. High-Adult. **P:** Education. **U:** Home. **How-Ins:** Music--Instruction. **Acq:** Purchase. **Dist:** Hal Leonard Corp. $39.95.

The Acoustic Guitar of Jorma Kaukonen: Video Two 199?
A continued examination of blues-based fingerpicking using traditional and original tunes. 90m; VHS. **A:** Sr. High-Adult. **P:** Education. **U:** Home. **How-Ins:** Music--Instruction. **Acq:** Purchase. **Dist:** Hal Leonard Corp. $39.95.

Acoustic Guitar of Jorma Kaukonen, Vol. 1 1991
Kaukonen is joined by band-mate Jack Casady to demonstrate some of the finer aspects of fingerpicking, right-hand picking, slide techniques and open tunings. They also give special pointers on how to develop a song together. 100m; VHS. **Pr:** Homespun Video. **A:** Sr. High-Adult. **P:** Instruction. **U:** Home. **How-Ins:** How-To, Music--Instruction. **Acq:** Purchase. **Dist:** Homespun Tapes Ltd. $49.95.

Acoustic Guitar of Jorma Kaukonen, Vol. 2 1993
Kaukonen covers runs, chord shapes, bass runs, right-hand picking, rhythmic figures, back picking, double-time patterns, vibrato, harmonized scales, string bends, and other techniques. 90m; VHS. **A:** Jr. High-Adult. **P:** Instruction. **U:** Home. **How-Ins:** How-To, Music--Instruction. **Acq:** Purchase. **Dist:** Homespun Tapes Ltd. $49.95.

Acoustic Neuroma Series 1971
A lecture given by Theodore Kurze, M.D., Chief of Neurosurgery, Los Angeles County Hospital. 30m; VHS, 3/4 U, Special order formats. **Pr:** Ohio State University Health Sciences AV Center. **A:** College-Adult. **P:** Professional. **U:** Institution, SURA. **Hea-Sci:** Neurology. **Acq:** Purchase, Rent/Lease. **Dist:** Ohio State University.
Indiv. Titles: 1. Acoustic Neuroma Part I 2. Acoustic Neuroma Part II 3. Acoustic Neuroma Part III.

Acoustic Neuroma Surgery 1972
The complete work-up and surgery for the removal of a 2.5 centimeter acoustic neuroma are presented in a condensed format. 55m; VHS, 3/4 U. **Pr:** House Ear Institute. **A:** Adult. **P:** Professional. **U:** Institution, CCTV. **Hea-Sci:** Ear. **Acq:** Purchase, Rent/Lease. **Dist:** House Research Institute.

Acoustic Rock Guitar Soloing 199?
Jamie Findlay, from the Musicians Institute, teaches various techniques used for soloing in blues, country, Latin, Brazilian, jazz, and pop styles. ?m; VHS. **A:** Sr. High-Adult. **P:** Instruction. **U:** Home. **How-Ins:** Music--Instruction. **Acq:** Purchase. **Dist:** Hal Leonard Corp. $14.95.

Acoustic Tumor Surgery—1982 1983
This program demonstrates the translabyrinthine removal of a three-centimeter acoustic tumor. 45m; VHS, 3/4 U. **Pr:** House Ear Institute. **A:** Adult. **P:** Education. **U:** Institution, CCTV. **Hea-Sci:** Medical Education, Ear. **Acq:** Purchase, Rent/Lease. **Dist:** House Research Institute.

Acqua e Sapone 1983 (PG) — ★½
A young innocent model goes to Rome under the watchful eyes of an appointed priest-chaperon, but finds love, fun and other sinful things. Sudsy/romantic comedy. 100m; VHS. **C:** Carlo Verdone; Natasha Hovey; Florinda Bolkan; Elena Bolkan; Directed by Carlo Verdone. **Pr:** Mario Cecchi Gori. **A:** Jr. High-Adult. **P:** Entertainment. **U:** Home. **L:** Italian. **Mov-Ent:** Comedy--Romantic, Italy. **Acq:** Purchase. **Dist:** Unknown Distributor.

Acquaintance Rape Series 1979
Four-program series dramatizes situations that lead to date rape, including poor communication skills, sex role stereotypes, and peer pressure. Also illustrates how assertive communication can help avoid date rape. Accompanying film guide and study materials facilitate group discussion. 8m; VHS, 3/4 U, Special order formats. **A:** Jr. High-College. **P:** Education. **U:** Institution. **Gen-Edu:** Adolescence, Rape. **Acq:** Purchase, Rent/Lease. **Dist:** Select Media, Inc. $475.00.
Indiv. Titles: 1. The Party Game 2. The Date 3. Just One of the Boys 4. End of the Road.

Acquired Heart Disease as Seen on Chest X-Ray 1982
This program examines atrial and ventricular enlargement and other findings that can be seen on ordinary chest films. 54m; VHS, 3/4 U. **Pr:** Emory University. **A:** College-Adult. **P:** Professional. **U:** Institution, CCTV, Home, SURA. **Hea-Sci:** Heart, Radiography. **Acq:** Purchase, Rent/Lease, Subscription. **Dist:** Emory Medical Television Network.

An Acquired Taste 1983
This tape looks at the memories of a man who has reached the age of 40. 26m; VHS, 3/4 U. **Pr:** Ralph Arlyck. **A:** Adult. **P:** Education. **U:** Institution, SURA. **Gen-Edu:** Aging. **Acq:** Purchase, Rent/Lease. **Dist:** New Day Films Library.

Acquisitions, Spin-Offs, and Split-Ups of Closely Held Corporations 1989
Reviews the inter-relation between corporate law and tax, securities, and accounting principles applicable to business acquisitions. Includes study materials. 210m; VHS. **A:** Adult. **P:** Professional. **U:** Institution. **Bus-Ind:** Law, Finance, Business. **Dist:** American Law Institute - Committee on Continuing Professional Education. $200.

Acrobatics of Dance 1974
The Sierra Leone National Dance Troupe perform native dances from their country in this program. 30m; VHS, 3/4 U, EJ, Q. **Pr:** WCBS Television; Camera Three Productions. **A:** Sr. High-Adult. **P:** Entertainment. **U:** Institution, SURA. **Fin-Art:** Dance, Native Americans. **Acq:** Duplication, Free Duplication. **Dist:** Camera Three Productions, Inc.

Acrobats of God 1970
This is Miss Graham's personal celebration of the trials and tribulations, glories, and delights of being a dancer. 22m; VHS, 3/4 U. **Pr:** John Houseman. **A:** Family. **P:** Entertainment. **U:** Institution, Home, SURA. **Fin-Art:** Dance. **Acq:** Purchase, Rent/Lease, Duplication License. **Dist:** Pyramid Media.

Across Cultures 1983
This series was designed to introduce students to the concept of culture and help them appreciate cultures that are vastly different from their own. Programs in this series are also available individually. 15m; VHS, 3/4 U, Q. **Pr:** Positive Image Productions. **A:** Jr. High. **P:** Education. **U:** Institution, CCTV, CATV, BCTV. **Gen-Edu:** Sociology. **Acq:** Purchase, Rent/Lease, Duplication License. **Dist:** Agency for Instructional Technology.
Indiv. Titles: 1. The Japanese 2. The Tarahomara 3. The Baoole 4. Providing for Family Needs 5. The Environment 6. Religion 7. Passing on Tradition 8. Education 9. Sports, Society and Self 10. Communication 11. Cultural Exchange 12. Cultural Change 13. Choices for the Future.

Across Donner Summit 1992
Steep hills, sharp curves and inclement weather are just a few obstacles waiting for trains as they rumble through Donner Pass. Freight and passenger trains regularly make this trek to the top of the historical pass in the Sierra Nevada Mountains. 120m; VHS. **C:** Hosted by Richard Steinheimer. **Pr:** Pentrex Media Group L.L.C. **A:** Sr. High-Adult. **P:** Entertainment. **U:** Home. **Gen-Edu:** Trains. **Acq:** Purchase. **Dist:** Pentrex Media Group L.L.C. $39.95.

Across Five Aprils 1989
The Civil War deeply affects Jethro Creighton and his family. Based on a book by Irene Hunt. The two part series includes "A Time To Choose" and "War and Hope." 33m; VHS, Special order formats. **Pr:** Learning Corporation of America. **A:** Primary-Sr. High. **P:** Entertainment. **U:** Institution. **Chl-Juv:** Family, Civil War, Literature. **Acq:** Purchase, Rent/Lease. **Dist:** Phoenix Learning Group. $250.00.

Across Marias Pass 1991
The scenic splendor of the Rockies is the backdrop as long freight, grain and passenger trains wind across Marias Pass on Burlington Northern's transcontinental mainline railway. Forests of aspen decked out in fall colors, desolate countryside and the banks of the middle fork of the Flathead River are just a few of the striking scenes. 90m; VHS. **A:** Jr. High-Adult. **P:** Entertainment. **U:** Home. **Gen-Edu:** Trains. **Acq:** Purchase. **Dist:** Pentrex Media Group L.L.C. $39.95.

Across 110th Street 1972 (R) — ★★
Gritty, violent cop thriller in the blaxploitation genre. Both the Mafia and the cops hunt down three black hoods who, in a display of extremely bad judgment, knocked over a mob-controlled bank while disguised as police. Lots of bullets create buckets of blood. Filmed on location in Harlem. 102m; VHS, DVD, Wide. **C:** Anthony Quinn; Yaphet Kotto; Anthony (Tony) Franciosa; Paul Benjamin; Ed Bernard; Antonio Fargas; Tim O'Connor; Lewis Gilbert; Richard Ward; Directed by Barry Shear; Written by Luther Davis; Cinematography by Jack Priestley. **Pr:** United Artists. **A:** College-Adult. **P:** Entertainment. **U:** Home. **Mov-Ent. Acq:** Purchase. **Dist:** MGM Home Entertainment. $14.95.

Across Siberia on Fiery Dragon ????
Travels via steam train from Berlin through Siberia to Vladivostok, Russia with many stops along the route to explore the area's culture. 60m; VHS. **A:** College-Adult. **P:** Education. **U:** Home. **Gen-Edu:** Trains. **Acq:** Purchase. **Dist:** The Civil War Standard. $19.95.

Across the Bridge 1957 — ★★½
A man on the run from Scotland Yard for stealing a fortune flees to Mexico, in the process killing a man and assuming his identity. An ironic twist and his love for a dog seal his final destiny. Steiger's psychological study as the fugitive is compelling. Based on a novel by Graham Greene. 103m/B/W; DVD. **C:** Rod Steiger; David Knight; Marla Landi; Noel Willman; Bernard Lee; Directed by Ken Annakin; Written by Guy Elmes; Denis Freeman; Cinematography by Reginald Wyer; Music by James Bernard. **Pr:** Rank. **A:** Jr. High-Adult. **P:** Entertainment. **U:** Home. **Mov-Ent:** Mystery & Suspense, Mexico, Trains. **Acq:** Purchase. **Dist:** VCI Entertainment.

Across the Great Divide 1976 (G) — ★★½
Two orphans must cross the rugged snow-covered Rocky Mountains in 1876 in order to claim their inheritance—a 400-acre plot of land in Salem, Oregon. Pleasant coming-of-age tale with majestic scenery. 102m; VHS, DVD. **C:** Robert F. Logan; George "Buck" Flower; Heather Rattray; Mark Hall; Directed by Stewart Raffill; Written by Stewart Raffill; Music by Angelo Badalamenti. **Pr:** Pacific International Enterprises. **A:** Family. **P:** Entertainment. **U:** Home. **Mov-Ent:** Wilderness Areas, Adoption. **Acq:** Purchase. **Dist:** Anchor Bay Entertainment. $9.98.

Across the Hall 2009 (R) — ★½
Somewhat slow-paced and non-linear modern noir, with plot twists you may see coming. June (Murphy) has checked into a seedy hotel, followed by fiance Terry (Pino) who's sure she's meeting some other guy. Distraught, Terry rents a room and calls his best friend Julian (Vogel), threatening to use the gun he's waving around although he agrees to wait until Julian shows up. Based on Merkin's 2005 short film. 93m; DVD. **C:** Danny Pino; Brittany Murphy; Mike Vogel; Brad Greenquist; Arie Verveen; Natalia Smyka; Guillermo Diaz; Dov Davidoff; Directed by Alex Merkin; Written by Julian Schwab; Jesse Mittletadt; Cinematography by Andrew Carranza; Music by Bobby Tahouri. **A:** Sr. High-Adult. **P:** Entertainment. **U:** Home. **Mov-Ent:** Hotels & Hotel Staff Training. **Acq:** Purchase. **Dist:** Image Entertainment Inc.

Across the Line 2000 (R) — ★★½
Miranda (Erez) crosses the border from Mexico into the U.S. and immediately witnesses the murder of a tourist and her husband by corrupt Border Patrol officers. A sheriff (Johnson) tries to protect his witness even as he falls in love with her. 97m; VHS, DVD. **C:** Brad Johnson; Sigal Erez; Brian Bloom; Marshall Teague; Adrienne Barbeau; Directed by Martin Spottl; Written by Sigal Erez. **A:** Sr. High-Adult. **P:** Entertainment. **U:** Home. **Mov-Ent:** Western. **Acq:** Purchase. **Dist:** Alpha Video; Movies Unlimited.

Across the Line: The Exodus of Charlie Wright 2010 (Unrated) — ★★
Las Vegas financier Charlie Wright ripped off his investors for two billion in a ponzi scheme and fled to Tijuana, Mexico. The head of a Mexican crime family, Russian mobsters, and the FBI all want Charlie—and more importantly—his money. 95m; DVD. **C:** Aidan Quinn; Mario Van Peebles; Luke Goss; Andy Garcia; Danny Pino; Corbin Bernsen; Jordan Belfi; Bokeem Woodbine; Raymond J. Barry; Gina Gershon; Claudia Ferri; Gary Daniels; Directed by R. Ellis Frazier; Written by R. Ellis Frazier; Cinematography by Anthony J. Rickert-Epstein; Music by Kim Carroll. **A:** Sr. High-Adult. **P:** Entertainment. **U:** Home. **Mov-Ent:** Crime Drama, Federal Bureau of Investigation (FBI), Mexico. **Acq:** Purchase. **Dist:** Maya Entertainment.

Across the Moon 1994 (R) — ★★
A road trip to the desert takes Carmen and Kathy away from their incarcerated boyfriends but into troubles with cowboys and prospectors. 88m; VHS, DVD. **C:** Elizabeth Pena; Christina Applegate; Tony Fields; Peter Berg; James Remar; Michael McKean; Burgess Meredith; Jack Nance; Jack Kehler; Directed by Lisa Gottlieb; Written by Stephen Schneck; Cinematography by Andrzej Sekula; Music by Christopher Tyng; Exene Cervenka. **Pr:** Robert Mickelson; Hemdale Communications, Inc. **A:** Sr. High-Adult. **P:** Entertainment. **U:** Home. **Mov-Ent. Acq:** Purchase. **Dist:** Movies Unlimited. $12.74.

Across the Pacific 1942 (Unrated) — ★★★½
Classic Bogie/Huston vehicle made on the heels of "The Maltese Falcon." Bogie is an American Army officer booted out of the service on false charges of treason. When no other military will accept him, he sails to China (via the Panama Canal) to offer his services to Chiang Kai-Shek. On board, he meets a variety of seedy characters who plan to blow up the canal. Huston again capitalizes on the counterpoint between the rotundly acerbic Greenstreet, who plays a spy, and stiff-lipped Bogart, who's wooing Astor. Great Bogie moments and fine direction make this an adventure classic. When he departed for the service just prior to filming the final scenes, Huston turned over direction to Vincent Sherman. Also available colorized. 97m/B/W; VHS, DVD. **C:** Humphrey Bogart; Mary Astor; Sydney Greenstreet; Charles Halton; Victor Sen Yung; Roland Got; Keye Luke; Richard Loo; Frank Wilcox; Paul Stanton; Lester Matthews; Tom Stevenson; Roland Drew; Monte Blue; Rudy Robles; Lee Tung Foo; Chester Gan; Kam Tong; Spencer Chan; Philip Ahn; Frank Faylen; Frank Mayo; Directed by John Huston; Written by Richard Macaulay; Cinematography by Arthur Edeson; Music by Adolph Deutsch. **Pr:** Jerry Wald; Jack Saper; Warner Bros. **A:** Jr. High-Adult. **P:** Entertainment. **U:** Home. **Mov-Ent:** Mystery & Suspense, Classic Films. **Acq:** Purchase. **Dist:** MGM Home Entertainment; Facets Multimedia Inc. $19.98.

Across the Plains 1928 (Unrated) — ★½
A cowtown filled with an assortment of gamblers, drunks, and dance-hall girls is just the place for a rough ranch foreman. But when he falls for a pretty newcomer, Bill decides to mend his manners—if he survives a crooked gambler's gun battle. Bill previously acted in westerns under the name Ted Wells. 51m/B/W; Silent; On Demand. **C:** Pawnee Bill, Jr.; Ione Reed; Jack (H.) Richardson; Martha Barclay; Directed by Robert J. Horner. **A:** Family. **P:** Entertainment. **U:** Home. **Mov-Ent:** Western, Silent Films. **Acq:** Purchase. **Dist:** Amazon.com Inc. $19.95.

Across the Plains 1939 — ★½
Predictable oater about two brothers who are raised separately after their parents are murdered by outlaws. One is brought up by Indians, the other by the outlaws responsible for wiping out the folks, who tell the boy that Indians did in his ma and pa. Eventually the brothers meet and fight. Odds favor the good one winning, aided by Indian pals. 59m/B/W; VHS, DVD. **C:** Addison "Jack" Randall; Frank Yaconelli; Joyce Bryant; Hal Price; Dennis Moore; Glenn Strange; Bud Osborne; Directed by Spencer Gordon Bennet. **Pr:** Monogram. **A:** Family. **P:** Entertainment. **U:** Home. **Mov-Ent:** Western. **Acq:** Purchase, Rent/Lease. **Dist:** Alpha Video; Mill Creek Entertainment L.L.C.; Sinister Cinema. $19.95.

Across the Sea of Time 1998 (G)
Filmed in the "larger-than-life" IMAX system, portrays an 11-year-old Russian boy's journey through New York City in search of his ancestry. 51m; VHS. **A:** Family. **P:** Entertainment. **U:** Home. **Mov-Ent:** Cities & Towns. **Acq:** Purchase. **Dist:** Sony Pictures Home Entertainment Inc. $19.95.

Across the Tracks 1989 (PG-13) — ★★
Two brothers, Billy (Schroder), a juvie-home rebel, and Joe (Pitt), a straight-A jock, are at odds when the black sheep is pressured into selling drugs. In an attempt to save his brother from a life of crime, saintly Joe convinces Billy to join him on the school track team, and the brothers are forced to face off in a big meet. Fairly realistic good guy/bad guy who's really a good guy teen drama. 101m; VHS, DVD. **C:** Rick Schroder; Brad Pitt; Carrie Snodgress; Directed by Sandy Tung; Written by Sandy Tung; Cinematography by Michael Delahoussaye; Music by Joel Goldsmith. **Pr:** Dale Rosenbloom; Desert Production. **A:** Sr. High-Adult. **P:** Entertainment. **U:** Home. **Mov-Ent:** Adolescence, Drug Abuse, Sports--Track & Field. **Acq:** Purchase. **Dist:** MPI Media Group. $19.95.

Across the Universe 2007 (PG-13) — ★★
Director Julie Taymor has certainly crafted a mystical tour, from middle America to bohemian Greenwich Village to Vietnam. Whether this portrayal of the Vietnam era, using gorgeous visuals, a stylized 60s aesthetic, a nice chunk of the Beatles

songbook, and surprisingly little spoken dialogue, is also magical is debatable. Lucy Even (Wood) moves from a small town to New York City, where she and her brother Max (Anderson) meet and befriend a number of predictable characters including Jude (Sturgess), a Brit from—where else??Liverpool. The music has been tasked with propelling the plot along via a vision of this revolutionary time from hippie idealism through the duty of military service to the anti-war counter culture, which is where the message of the film finally lands. See it for the stunning visuals and the fresh interpretation of Beatles classics. 133m; DVD, Blu-Ray. **C:** Evan Rachel Wood; Joe Anderson; Jim Sturgess; Dana Fuchs; Martin Luther McCoy; T.V. Carpio; Cameo(s) Bono; Directed by Julie Taymor; Written by Dick Clement; Ian La Frenais; Cinematography by Bruno Delbonnel; Music by Elliot Goldenthal. **Pr:** Suzanne Todd; Jennifer Todd; Matthew Gross; Revolution Studios; Columbia Pictures; Sony Pictures Home Entertainment Inc. **A:** Jr. High-Adult. **P:** Entertainment. **U:** Home. **L:** English. **Mov-Ent:** Musical--Drama. **Acq:** Purchase. **Dist:** Sony Pictures Home Entertainment Inc.

Across the Wide Missouri 1951 (Unrated) — ★★½
Pioneer epic stars Gable as a rugged fur trapper who marries an Indian woman (Marques) so he can trap beaver pelts on her people's rich land. On the journey to the Indian territory however, the trapper truly falls in love with his bride. Superior historical drama is marred slightly by the use of narration (provided by Howard Keel). Look for lively performances from Menjou as a French tippler and Naish as the quirky Indian Chief. Beautiful scenery filmed in the spectacular Rocky Mountains. 78m; VHS, DVD, Streaming. **C:** Clark Gable; Ricardo Montalban; John Hodiak; Adolphe Menjou; Maria Elena Marques; J. Carrol Naish; Jack Holt; Alan Napier; Narrated by Howard Keel; Directed by William A. Wellman; Cinematography by William Mellor. **Pr:** MGM. **A:** Jr. High-Adult. **P:** Entertainment. **U:** Home. **Mov-Ent:** Drama, Native Americans, Marriage. **Acq:** Purchase, Rent/Lease. **Dist:** WarnerArchive.com; MGM Home Entertainment; Critics' Choice Video & DVD. $26.99 14.99.

Across to Singapore 1928 (Unrated) — ★★
Convoluted family/romantic drama based on the Ben Ames Williams novel "All the Brothers Were Valiant." Childhood friends Joel Shore (Novarro) and Priscilla Crowninshield (Crawford) have grown up in seafaring New England. When Joel's older brother Mark (Torrence) returns home from a long voyage, he's immediately smitten by Priscilla and both fathers agree to their marriage (without consulting Priscilla). Joel refuses to hear Priscilla's pleas that she loves only him and agrees to join his brothers on a voyage to Singapore where multiple tragedies strike. 85m/B/W; Silent; DVD. **C:** Ramon Novarro; Joan Crawford; Ernest Torrence; Jim Mason; Frank Currier; Louis Wolheim; Duke Martin; Edward Connelly; Anna May Wong; Directed by William Nigh; Written by Joe Farnham; Cinematography by John Seitz. **A:** Sr. High-Adult. **P:** Entertainment. **U:** Home. **Mov-Ent:** Silent Films, Drama, Boating. **Acq:** Purchase. **Dist:** WarnerArchive.com.

Acrylic 1990
Two programs designed to teach the techniques of painting with acrylic. 36m; VHS. **Pr:** Crystal Productions. **A:** Jr. High-Adult. **P:** Instruction. **U:** Institution. **How-Ins:** How-To, Art & Artists, Painting. **Acq:** Purchase. **Dist:** Crystal Productions. $59.95.
Indiv. Titles: 1. Acrylic: The Medium 2. Acrylic: Special Techniques.

Acrylic As Water Media 19??
Artist Stephen Quiller introduces acrylic painting through seven demonstrations in this teaching aid for art education. 55m; VHS. **A:** Jr. High-College. **P:** Education. **U:** Institution. **Gen-Edu:** Art & Artists, Painting. **Acq:** Purchase. **Dist:** Crystal Productions. $39.95.

Acrylic Heads and Hands 19??
Demonstrates techniques for making sophisticated acrylic heads and hands for feature film special effects sequences or whenever a realistic "dummy" must be substituted for an actor. 12m; VHS. **Pr:** Australian Film, Radio and Television School. **A:** College-Adult. **P:** Education. **U:** Home, Institution. **Gen-Edu:** Filmmaking. **Acq:** Purchase, Rent/Lease. **Dist:** TMW Media Group. $99.

Acrylic Painting #1: Mountain and Valley Landscape with Linda Flannery 19??
Features instruction from Linda Flannery on how to use acrylic painting techniques to paint mountain and valley landscape scenes, including the proper use of color and composition to create depth and dimension. 60m; VHS. **A:** Primary-Adult. **P:** Instruction. **U:** Institution. **How-Ins:** Art & Artists, Education, How-To. **Acq:** Purchase. **Dist:** Instructional Video. $29.95.

Acrylic Painting #2: Red Rock & Still Lifes with Linda Flannery 19??
Linda Flannery teaches acrylic painting techniques for painting red rock scenery and still lifes. She demonstrates the building of texture and the effects of holding a piece of tissue paper on a bowl of holiday eggs. 60m; VHS. **A:** Jr. High-Adult. **P:** Instruction. **U:** Institution. **How-Ins:** Art & Artists, Education, How-To. **Acq:** Purchase. **Dist:** Instructional Video. $29.95.

Acrylic Painting #3: Flowers with Steve Lawrence Peterson 19??
Steve Lawrence Peterson offers acrylic painting techniques for recreating flowers on the canvas. 60m; VHS. **A:** Jr. High-Adult. **P:** Instruction. **U:** Institution. **How-Ins:** Art & Artists, Education, How-To. **Acq:** Purchase. **Dist:** Instructional Video. $29.95.

Acrylic Painting #4: Line Drawing with Steve Lawrence Peterson 19??
Steve Lawrence Peterson demonstrates how to transfer an acrylic still life into a unique original painting with the use of marking pencils. 60m; VHS. **A:** Primary-Adult. **P:** Instruction. **U:** Institution. **How-Ins:** Art & Artists, Education, How-To. **Acq:** Purchase. **Dist:** Instructional Video. $29.95.

Acrylic Painting #5: Abstract with Linda Flannery 19??
Linda Flannery demonstrates how to transfer a three dimensional object to a flat, two-dimensional painting. Contains an example using an egg beater to produce a colorful abstract. 60m; VHS. **A:** Jr. High-Adult. **P:** Instruction. **U:** Institution. **How-Ins:** Art & Artists, Education, How-To. **Acq:** Purchase. **Dist:** Instructional Video. $29.95.

Acrylic Painting #6: Portraits with Stuart Heimdal 19??
Stuart Heimdal shows how anyone can create portrait paintings. 60m; VHS. **A:** Jr. High-Adult. **P:** Instruction. **U:** Institution. **How-Ins:** Art & Artists, Education, How-To. **Acq:** Purchase. **Dist:** Instructional Video. $29.95.

Acrylic Painting Basics with Linda Flannery 19??
Linda Flannery illustrates the basics of acrylic painting, including supplies, composition, perspective, sketching, and color. 60m; VHS. **A:** Jr. High-Adult. **P:** Instruction. **U:** Institution. **How-Ins:** Art & Artists, Education, How-To. **Acq:** Purchase. **Dist:** Instructional Video. $29.95.

Acrylic Painting: Getting a Start 19??
Artist Stephen Quiller explains the basic techniques of acrylic painting in this teaching aid for art education. 28m; VHS. **A:** Jr. High-College. **P:** Education. **U:** Institution. **Gen-Edu:** Art & Artists, Painting. **Acq:** Purchase. **Dist:** Crystal Productions. $24.95.

Acrylic Techniques 19??
Artist Stephen Quiller explores different types of acrylic painting through seven demonstrations in this teaching aid for art education. 55m; VHS. **A:** Jr. High-College. **P:** Education. **U:** Institution. **Gen-Edu:** Art & Artists, Painting. **Acq:** Purchase. **Dist:** Crystal Productions. $39.95.

Acrylics 19??
Artist Gail Price demonstrates techniques for painting with acrylics, including opaque, transparency, underpainting, glazing, drybrush, scumbling, impasto, and non-brush techniques. 37m; VHS. **A:** Jr. High-Adult. **P:** Instruction. **U:** Institution, Home. **How-Ins:** How-To, Painting. **Acq:** Purchase. **Dist:** Cambridge Educational. $69.95.

The Act 1982 (R) — ★★
A muddled satire about political double dealing and union corruption further muddled by a twangy musical score manufactured by folksy Sebastian. 90m; VHS. **C:** Jill St. John; Eddie Albert; Pat Hingle; Robert Ginty; Sarah Langenfeld; Nicolas Surovy; Directed by Sig Shore; Music by John Sebastian. **Pr:** Film Ventures International. **A:** Adult. **P:** Entertainment. **U:** Home. **Mov-Ent:** Satire & Parody, Politics & Government. **Acq:** Purchase. **Dist:** $69.95.

ACT Math Review 1990
Brush up on the math skills necessary for the ACT college admission test. Includes information on algebra, geometry, and trigonometry. A study guide is included. 120m; VHS. **Pr:** Video Aided Instruction. **A:** Sr. High-College. **P:** Education. **U:** Home, Institution. **Gen-Edu:** Study Skills, Mathematics. **Acq:** Purchase. **Dist:** Video Aided Instruction Inc. $39.95.

Act of Aggression 1973 (R) — ★★
When a Parisian man finds his wife and daughter murdered at a summer resort, he takes the law into his own hands, with predictable results. 100m; VHS. **C:** Jean-Louis Trintignant; Catherine Deneuve; Claude Brasseur; Milena Vukotic; Jacques Rispal; Philippe Brigaud; Michele Grellier; Robert Charlebois; Franco Fabrizi; Directed by Gerard Pires; Cinematography by Silvano Ippoliti. **Pr:** Joseph Green Pictures. **A:** Sr. High-Adult. **P:** Entertainment. **U:** Home. **Mov-Ent. Acq:** Purchase. **Dist:** Facets Multimedia Inc. $59.95.

An Act of Congress 1979
Documentary that records legislative powers in action by showing how a law is made in Congress. 58m; VHS, 3/4 U. **Pr:** Jerry Colbert. **A:** Jr. High-Adult. **P:** Education. **U:** Institution, SURA. **Gen-Edu:** Politics & Government. **Acq:** Purchase, Rent/Lease. **Dist:** Phoenix Learning Group.

An Act of Conscience ?
Follows the struggles of a young couple who are fighting the seizure of their house by the government after they refused to pay taxes in protest of military build-up. Includes a brief history of war tax resistance in America from the colonial era to the Vietnam war. Special pricing available to high schools, libraries, and community organizations. 90m; VHS. **A:** Sr. High-Adult. **P:** Education. **U:** Institution. **Gen-Edu:** Politics & Government, Documentary Films. **Acq:** Purchase, Rent/Lease. **Dist:** Turning Tide Productions. $289.00.

An Act of Faith 1961
A film about how the Danish people rescued their countrymen from invading Nazis in WWII. 28m/B/W; VHS, 3/4 U. **Pr:** CBS. **A:** Jr. High-Adult. **P:** Education. **U:** Institution, SURA. **Gen-Edu:** World War Two. **Acq:** Purchase. **Dist:** Anti-Defamation League of B'nai B'rith.

The Act of Killing 2013 (Unrated) — ★★★
A rare documentary that sheds light on a horrific period of history in a way that glorifies it into a surreal nightmare. Director Oppenheimer not only sits down with a pair of gangsters considered heroes in their native Indonesia for executing an untold number of so-called communists following the 1965 government overthrow, but the director somehow gets the killers to reenact their brutality in elaborately staged send ups and musical interpretations of the slaughters. 115m; DVD, Blu-Ray. **C:** Directed by Christine Cynn; Joshua Oppenheimer; Cinematography by Lars Skree; Carlos Arango De Montis; Music by Simon Thamdrup Jensen. **Pr:** Anne Kohncke; Michael Uwemedimo; Signe Byrge Sorensen; Final Cut for Real; Drafthouse Films. **P:** Entertainment. **U:** Home. **Mov-Ent:** Documentary Films, Politics & Government, Asia. **Awds:** British Acad. '13: Feature Doc. **Acq:** Purchase.

Act of Passion: The Lost Honor of Kathryn Beck 1983 — ★★½
A woman meets a man at a party and has the proverbial one-night stand. Her privacy is shattered when she discovers that he's a terrorist under surveillance by the police and press. Strong performances by Thomas and Kristofferson help turn this into an interesting American TV remake of the German "Lost Honor of Katharina Blum," based loosely on a novel by Heinrich Boll. 100m; VHS. **C:** Marlo Thomas; Kris Kristofferson; George Dzundza; Jon (John) DeVries; Directed by Simon Langton. **Pr:** Open Road/ComWorld. **A:** Family. **P:** Entertainment. **U:** Home. **Mov-Ent:** Terrorism, Journalism, TV Movies. **Acq:** Purchase. **Dist:** CinemaNow Inc. $69.95.

Act of Piracy 1989 (R) — ★½
A bankrupt contractor reunites with his estranged wife to track down the brutal terrorists who have kidnapped their son. 105m; VHS; Open Captioned. **C:** Gary Busey; Belinda Bauer; Ray Sharkey; Nancy Mulford; Dennis Casey Park; Arnold Vosloo; Ken Gampu; Directed by John Cardos; Written by Hal Reed; Cinematography by Vincent Cox; Music by Morton Stevens. **Pr:** Edgar Bold; Hal Reed. **A:** Sr. High-Adult. **P:** Entertainment. **U:** Home. **Mov-Ent:** Action-Adventure, Terrorism. **Acq:** Purchase. **Dist:** Warner Home Video, Inc. $89.98.

Act of Valor 2012 (R) — ★★
Combination of combat footage featuring active duty Navy SEALs and a plot involving a kidnapped CIA operative that reveals a coordinated terrorist plot leading Bandito Platoon to the U.S.-Mexico border. 110m; DVD, Blu-Ray. **C:** Alex Veadov; Roselyn Sanchez; Jason Cottle; Nestor Serrano; Emilio Rivera; Gonzalo Menendez; Ailsa Marshall; Directed by Scott Waugh; Mike McCoy; Written by Kurt Johnstad; Cinematography by Shane Hurlbut; Music by Nathan Furst. **Pr:** Scott Waugh; Mike McCoy; Bandito Brothers; Relativity Media. **P:** Entertainment. **U:** Home. **L:** English. **Mov-Ent:** Mexico, Terrorism, Intelligence Service. **Acq:** Purchase. **Dist:** Relativity Media.

Act of Vengeance 1974 (R) — ★★
A group of women band together to hunt down and exact revenge on the man who raped them. Exploitative action-filled thriller. 90m; VHS. **C:** Jo Ann Harris; Peter Brown; Jennifer Lee; Lisa Moore; Connie Strickland; Pat Estrin; Directed by Bob Kelljan. **Pr:** Buzz Feitshans; American International Pictures. **A:** Sr. High-Adult. **P:** Entertainment. **U:** Home. **Mov-Ent:** Rape. **Acq:** Purchase. **Dist:** No Longer Available.

Act of Vengeance 1986 (Unrated) — ★★½
Drama about Jock Yablonski, a United Mine Workers official who challenged the president, Tony Boyle. Based on fact, showing the events that led up to the murder of Yablonski and his family. Intriguing story lacking cinematic drive. 97m; VHS, CC. **C:** Charles Bronson; Ellen Burstyn; Wilford Brimley; Hoyt Axton; Robert Schenkkan; Ellen Barkin; Keanu Reeves; Directed by John MacKenzie; Written by Scott Spencer. **A:** Adult. **P:** Entertainment. **U:** Home. **L:** English, Spanish. **Mov-Ent:** Labor & Unions, Miners & Mining, TV Movies. **Acq:** Purchase. **Dist:** Amazon.com Inc.

Act of Violence 1948 (Unrated) — ★★½
Postwar melodrama. Small-town businessman and war hero Frank Enley (Heflin) has a pretty wife (Leigh), a young son, and a good life that gets him recognition. But this brings Frank to the attention of embittered, crippled vet Joe Parkson (Ryan), who's got a beef. Seems both were POWs in a German camp and Enley informed on the men's escape plans, which got everyone but Parkson killed. As Parkson pursues Enley through the seedier sides of L.A., Astor enters the picture as a down-heels dame at a dive bar who offers Enley some assistance that results in a lot more trouble. 82m/B/W; DVD. **C:** Van Heflin; Robert Ryan; Janet Leigh; Mary Astor; Phyllis Thaxter; Berry Kroeger; Taylor Holmes; Directed by Fred Zinnemann; Written by Robert L. Richards; Cinematography by Robert L. Surtees; Music by Bronislau Kaper. **A:** Jr. High-Adult. **P:** Entertainment. **U:** Home. **Mov-Ent:** Veterans, Handicapped. **Acq:** Purchase. **Dist:** Warner Home Video, Inc.

Act of War 1996 (Unrated) — ★★
Disgraced diplomat/spy Jack Gracey (Scalia) has to stop renegade communists who've taken over a remote nuclear missile site from pressing the button on a missle aimed directly at the White House. Lots of action should hold viewers' interest. 100m; VHS, DVD. **C:** Jack Scalia; Ingrid Torrance; Douglas Arthurs; Directed by Robert Lee; Written by Michael Bafaro; Cinematography by David Pelletier; Music by Peter Allen. **A:** Sr. High-Adult. **P:** Entertainment. **U:** Home. **Mov-Ent:** Terrorism. **Acq:** Purchase. **Dist:** York Entertainment.

Act of War: The Overthrow of the Hawaiian Nation 1993
Examines events leading up to the U.S. invasion and annexation of the Hawaiian Islands in the 1890s. Intersperses commentary with readings, reenactments, still photographs, and vintage film footage. 58m; VHS. **A:** Sr. High-Adult. **P:** Education. **U:** Institution. **Gen-Edu:** History--U.S. **Acq:** Purchase. **Dist:** Na Maka o ka Aina. $165.00.

Act Up: The Story of a Performance 1990
Documents the learning experience of 14 children from rural West Virginia as they train for a theatre piece called "Broken Bough," the story of child laborers in the early 1900s and how

they were helped by Mother Jones. Five 15-minute programs and one 30-minute program are available individually or as a set. 15m; VHS. **A:** Primary. **P:** Education. **U:** Institution. **Gen-Edu:** Education, Children, Theater. **Acq:** Purchase. **Dist:** GPN Educational Media. $139.95.

ACT Verbal Review 1989
Learn test taking techniques for the verbal section of the ACT college entrance exam, with information on reading, English, and science reasoning. Includes a study guide. 120m; VHS. **Pr:** Video Aided Instruction. **A:** Sr. High-College. **P:** Education. **U:** Home, Institution. **Gen-Edu:** Study Skills, Language Arts. **Acq:** Purchase. **Dist:** Video Aided Instruction Inc. $39.95.

Acting Class 1980
A close-up look at students and instructors sweating through a typical work day at the National Theater School, Canada's foremost training ground for young performers. 28m; VHS, 3/4 U. **Pr:** National Film Board of Canada. **A:** Sr. High-Adult. **P:** Education. **U:** Institution, SURA. **Fin-Art:** Performing Arts. **Acq:** Purchase, Rent/Lease. **Dist:** National Film Board of Canada.

Acting for Film: Wilder's "The Long Christmas Dinner" 1976
A discussion of the differences between acting for a stage presentation and acting for a film production. 14m; VHS, 3/4 U. **Pr:** Encyclopedia Britannica Educational Corporation. **A:** Sr. High-College. **P:** Education. **U:** Institution, SURA. **Fin-Art:** Filmmaking, Performing Arts. **Acq:** Purchase, Rent/Lease, Trade-in. **Dist:** Encyclopedia Britannica.

Acting in Film 19??
Caine provides acting lessons from this BBC Master Class series. 60m; VHS. **A:** Sr. High-Adult. **P:** Instruction. **U:** Home. **How-Ins:** Performing Arts. **Acq:** Purchase. **Dist:** Stagestep. $39.95.

Acting in High Comedy 19??
Actress Aitkens presents this BBC Master Class with scenes from Coward, Wilde, Sheridan, and Congreve, and her own reading from "Private Lives." 60m; VHS. **A:** Sr. High-Adult. **P:** Instruction. **U:** Home. **How-Ins:** Theater. **Acq:** Purchase. **Dist:** Stagestep. $79.95.

Acting in Restoration Comedy 19??
Actor/director Callow directs this BBC Master Class using scenes from "The Relapse" by Sir John Vanbrugh. 60m; VHS. **A:** Sr. High-Adult. **P:** Instruction. **U:** Home. **How-Ins:** Theater. **Acq:** Purchase. **Dist:** Stagestep. $79.95.

Acting in Shakespearean Comedy 19??
A BBC Master Class with Suzman who uses excerpts from "Twelfth Night," "As You Like It," and "Much Ado About Nothing" to demonstrate the difference between playing comedy and tragedy. 60m; VHS. **A:** Sr. High-Adult. **P:** Instruction. **U:** Home. **How-Ins:** Theater. **Acq:** Purchase. **Dist:** Stagestep. $79.95.

Acting in Tragedy 19??
A BBC Master Class with Cox uses scenes from Shakespeare to demonstrate the nature of playing tragedy. 60m; VHS. **A:** Sr. High-Adult. **P:** Instruction. **U:** Home. **How-Ins:** Theater. **Acq:** Purchase. **Dist:** Stagestep. $79.95.

Acting on Impulse 1993 (R) — ★★
Impulsive, troublemaking movie star (Fiorentino) becomes a murder suspect when her producer is killed. This doesn't slow her down. She checks into a hotel with a major party attitude and manages to seduce a conservative businessman (Howell) and his junior exec (Allen) into helping her forget her troubles. And then the businessman's fiancee turns up dead. Any connection? 94m; VHS. **C:** Linda Fiorentino; C. Thomas Howell; Nancy Allen; Adam Ant; Judith Hoag; Patrick Bauchau; Isaac Hayes; Paul Bartel; Donny Most; Miles O'Keeffe; Dick Sargent; Charles Lane; Mary Woronov; Zelda Rubinstein; Nicholas Sadler; Peter Lupus; Kim McGuire; Cassandra Peterson; Brinke Stevens; Michel Talbot; Robert Alan Golub; Cliff Dorfman; Craig Shoemaker; Scott Thompson Stevens; Directed by Sam Irvin; Written by Mark Pittman; Alan Moskowitz; Cinematography by Dean Lent; Music by Daniel Licht. **A:** Sr. High-Adult. **P:** Entertainment. **U:** Home. **Mov-Ent:** Mystery & Suspense, TV Movies, Sex & Sexuality. **Acq:** Purchase. **Dist:** Unknown Distributor.

Acting on Your Values 1988
Discusses how values systems help us in the choices we make. 30m; VHS. **A:** Adult. **P:** Education. **U:** Institution. **Gen-Edu:** Human Relations. **Acq:** Purchase. **Dist:** RMI Media. $64.95.

Acting One, Day One 19??
Unscripted and unrehearsed videotaped class in which Robert Cohen illustrates his four principles of acting: goal, other people, tactics, and expectation. 35m; VHS. **A:** Adult. **P:** Instruction. **U:** Institution. **How-Ins:** How-To, Performing Arts. **Acq:** Purchase. **Dist:** Stagestep. $79.00.

Acting Our Age 1987
Elderly women talk candidly about such subjects as sexuality, loneliness, financial difficulties, dealing with death and growing old in America. 58m; VHS, 3/4 U. **Pr:** Michael Aviad. **A:** Sr. High-Adult. **P:** Education. **U:** Institution, SURA. **Gen-Edu:** Aging, Women. **Acq:** Purchase, Rent/Lease. **Dist:** Direct Cinema Ltd. $350.00.

Acting Our Age: A Film about Women Growing Old 1987
Profiles six ordinary women in their 60s and 70s as they share their lives and offer empowering insights about women and aging for all generations. Topics include self-image, sexuality, financial concerns, dying, and changing family relationships. 58m; VHS. **A:** College-Adult. **P:** Education. **U:** Institution.

Gen-Edu: Women, Aging. **Acq:** Purchase, Rent/Lease. **Dist:** Women Make Movies. $275.00.

Acting Techniques of Kutiyattam 1980
Examines the use of gesture as language, and illustrates basic body postures for portraying male and female characters in Sanskrit drama. 55m; VHS. **A:** Adult. **P:** Education. **U:** Institution. **Fin-Art:** Theater. **Acq:** Purchase. **Dist:** Insight Media. $199.00.

Acting Techniques of the Noh Theater of Japan 1980
Demonstrates hand gestures, fan movements, and different patterns of walking and turning for portraying characters of different age, gender, personality and temperament. 30m; VHS. **A:** Adult. **P:** Education. **U:** Institution. **Fin-Art:** Theater. **Acq:** Purchase. **Dist:** Insight Media. $179.00.

Acting Up and Speaking Out 19??
Psychology and social work film from the University of Calgary Learning Commons. ?m; VHS. **A:** Adult. **P:** Professional. **U:** Institution. **Gen-Edu:** Psychology, Social Service. **Acq:** Purchase. **Dist:** University of Calgary Library, Visual Resources Centre.

Acting Up for Prisoners 1992
Depicts ACT-UP's successful campaign to bring health care services to women prisoners with HIV at Frontera, the California Institution for Women. 27m; VHS. **A:** College-Adult. **P:** Education. **U:** Institution. **Hea-Sci:** Medical Care, AIDS. **Acq:** Purchase, Rent/Lease. **Dist:** Frameline. $200.00.

Action 1985
This is a behind-the-scenes look at how special effects for "The Terminator," "Life Force" and "Missing in Action" were done by the Hollywood masters of the art. 60m; VHS. **C:** Arnold Schwarzenegger. **Pr:** Drew Cummings. **A:** Family. **P:** Entertainment. **U:** Home. **Mov-Ent:** Film History. **Acq:** Purchase. **Dist:** MGM Studios Inc. $39.98.

Action and Reaction 1967
Newton's Third Law is developed in a logical series of demonstrations. 15m; VHS, 3/4 U. **Pr:** Iwanami Films. **A:** Jr. High-Sr. High. **P:** Education. **U:** Institution, SURA. **Hea-Sci:** Physics. **Acq:** Purchase. **Dist:** Phoenix Learning Group.

Action Down-Under 1988
A couple of programs about fishing in New Zealand. 99m; VHS. **Pr:** Bennett Marine Video. **A:** Family. **P:** Entertainment. **U:** Home. **Spo-Rec:** Sports--General, Fishing. **Acq:** Purchase. **Dist:** Bennett Marine Video. $79.94.
Indiv. Titles: 1. In Zane Gray's Footsteps 2. Mako on Fly 3. Trophy Trout Lakes 4. Mountain Rainbows and Southern Browns 5. Masters Meet the Challenger.

Action Energy Circuit with Mindy Mylrea: Energetic, Athletic, Effective ????
A beginner to advanced workout using dynamic and fun cardio/strength intervals. 60m; VHS. **A:** Adult. **P:** Instruction. **U:** Home. **Hea-Sci:** Fitness/Exercise, How-To. **Acq:** Purchase. **Dist:** Body Bar Systems. $19.95.

Action for Slander 1938 (Unrated) — ★★½
A British army officer sporting the typical stiff upper lip is accused of cheating during a card game, and the slander mars his reputation until the case is taken to court. Dryly earnest and honest in its depiction of class differences in pre-war England. Based on a novel by Mary Borden. 84m/B/W; VHS, 8 mm. **C:** Clive Brook; Ann Todd; Margaretta Scott; Ronald Squire; Francis L. Sullivan; Felix Aylmer; Googie Withers; Directed by Tim Whelan; **Pr:** Victor Saville; London Films Productions; United Artists. **A:** Family. **P:** Entertainment. **U:** Home. **Mov-Ent:** Gambling. **Acq:** Purchase. **Dist:** $24.95.

Action Force: The Movie 1987 (Unrated) — ★
Terrorist group COBRA awakens an ancient race of snake people after immobilizing most of G.I. Joe, forcing some new recruits to try saving the world. 93m; DVD, Blu-Ray. **C:** Voice(s) by Don Johnson; Burgess Meredith; Robert Remus; Richard Gautier; Chris Latta; Directed by Don Jurwich; Written by Ron Friedman; Music by Johnny Douglas; Robert J. Walsh. **A:** Primary-Adult. **P:** Entertainment. **U:** Home. **L:** English. **Mov-Ent:** Acq:** Purchase. **Dist:** Shout! Factory. $26.97 14.97.

Action Game Series: Indoor Games 1997
Presents a group of rainy day games that promote good behavior. 30m; VHS. **A:** Family. **P:** Entertainment. **U:** Home. **Gen-Edu:** Games. **Acq:** Purchase. **Dist:** 411 Video Information. $14.95.

Action Game Series: Party Games 1997
Presents a new twist to old fashion party games. 30m; VHS. **A:** Family. **P:** Entertainment. **U:** Home. **Gen-Edu:** Games. **Acq:** Purchase. **Dist:** 411 Video Information. $14.95.

Action in an Emergency 198?
This film demonstrates the first aid procedures to administer to an unconscious person who has stopped breathing. 8m; VHS, 3/4 U. **Pr:** National Safety Council. **A:** College-Adult. **P:** Education. **U:** Institution. **Hea-Sci:** First Aid. **Acq:** Rent/Lease. **Dist:** National Safety Council, California Chapter, Film Library.

Action in Arabia 1944 (Unrated) — ★★
A newsman uncovers a Nazi plot to turn the Arabs against the Allies while investigating a colleague's murder in Damascus. The desert teems with spies, double agents, and sheiks as suave Sanders goes about his investigative business. Quintessential wartime B-movie. 75m/B/W; VHS, Streaming. **C:** George Sanders; Virginia Bruce; Lenore Aubert; Gene Lockhart; Robert Armstrong; H.B. Warner; Alan Napier; Michael Ansara; Directed by Leonide Moguy; **Pr:** RKO. **A:** Family. **P:** Entertainment. **U:**

Home. **Mov-Ent:** Middle East, Journalism. **Acq:** Purchase. **Dist:** Warner Brothers; Turner Broadcasting System Inc. $19.98.

Action in the North Atlantic 1943 — ★★
Massey and Bogart are the captain and first mate of a Merchant Marine vessel running the lone supply route to the Soviet Union. Eventually they wind up locking horns with a Nazi U-boat. Plenty of action and strenuous flag waving in this propagandorama. Gordon fans won't want to miss her as Massey's wife. Also available colorized. 126m/B/W; VHS, DVD. **C:** Humphrey Bogart; Raymond Massey; Alan Hale; Julie Bishop; Ruth Gordon; Sam Levene; Dane Clark; Peter Whitney; Minor Watson; J.M. Kerrigan; Dick Hogan; Kane Richmond; Chick Chandler; Donald "Don" Douglas; Creighton Hale; Iris Adrian; Elliott Sullivan; Glenn Strange; Directed by Lloyd Bacon; Written by A(lbert) I(saac) Bezzerides; W.R. Burnett; John Howard Lawson; Cinematography by Ted D. McCord; Music by Adolph Deutsch. **Pr:** Jerry Wald; Warner Bros; First National Pictures. **A:** Jr. High-Adult. **P:** Entertainment. **U:** Home. **Mov-Ent:** Action-Adventure, World War Two. **Acq:** Purchase. **Dist:** MGM Home Entertainment; Facets Multimedia Inc. $19.98.

Action Jackson 1988 (R) — ★★
Power-hungry auto tycoon Nelson tries to frame rebellious black police sergeant Weathers for murder. Being a graduate of Harvard and a tough guy, the cop doesn't go for it. Nelson eats up the screen as the heavy with no redeeming qualities, while Weathers is tongue-in-cheek as the resourceful good guy who keeps running afoul of the law in spite of his best efforts. Lots of action, violence, and a few sexy women help cover the plot's lack of common sense. 96m; VHS, DVD, Blu-Ray, CC. **C:** Carl Weathers; Vanity; Craig T. Nelson; Sharon Stone; Thomas F. Wilson; Mary Ellen Trainor; Directed by Craig R. Baxley; Written by Robert Reneau; Cinematography by Matthew F. Leonetti; Music by Herbie Hancock; Michael Kamen; **Pr:** Lorimar Productions. **A:** Sr. High-Adult. **P:** Entertainment. **U:** Home. **Mov-Ent:** Automobiles. **Acq:** Purchase. **Dist:** MGM Studios Inc. ; Warner Home Video, Inc. $19.98.

Action Man 1967 (Unrated) — ★★
Ferrand (Gabin) has reformed his criminal ways to run a restaurant but he's bored and ready to get involved in one last caper with crooked pal Beckley (Stack). The bank job goes fine but drug dealers kidnap Ferrand's wife and want the loot in exchange for her life. French with subtitles. 95m; DVD. **C:** Jean Gabin; Robert Stack; Suzanne Flon; Georges Aminel; Walter Giller; Jean Topart; Margaret Lee; Directed by Jean Delannoy; Written by Jean Delannoy; Alphonse Boudard; Cinematography by Walter Wottitz; Music by Francis Lai. **A:** Sr. High-Adult. **P:** Entertainment. **U:** Home. **L:** French. **Mov-Ent:** Acq:** Purchase. **Dist:** VCI Entertainment.

Action on the Long Island Railroad ????
Travel to the Long Island rail yards for morning rush hour, then ride the rail to Mineola to see express trains zip by. DVD includes an additional 20 minutes of footage. 30m; VHS, DVD. **A:** College-Adult. **P:** Education. **U:** Home. **Gen-Edu:** Trains. **Acq:** Purchase. **Dist:** The Civil War Standard. $27.95.

Action Options: Alcohol, Drugs and You 19??
Explores options for adolescents and adults involved in substance abuse. First three programs look at human behaviors associated with alcohol and drugs. Last four programs focus more specifically on methods of recovery from substance abuse. 30m; VHS. **Pr:** Alberta Alcohol and Drug Abuse Commission. **A:** Sr. High-Adult. **P:** Education. **U:** Institution. **Hea-Sci:** Alcoholism, Drug Abuse. **Acq:** Purchase. **Dist:** Access The Education Station. $299.00.
Indiv. Titles: 1. Why We Do What We Do 2. Freedom From, Freedom To 3. Living is Learning 4. Mood-Altering Drugs: No Need To Get Mad 5. Drug Abuse: When It's A Family Affair 6. Treatment and Recovery: Making Changes 7. Relapse: An Ounce of Prevention.

ACTION Series 1980
This series of three programs discusses the philosophy behind ACTION and its methods of operation. Programs are available individually. 20m; VHS, 3/4 U. **C:** Andy Anderson. **Pr:** Broadman. **A:** Family. **P:** Religious. **U:** Institution, CCTV. **Gen-Edu:** Religion. **Acq:** Purchase. **Dist:** Broadman & Holman Publishers.
Indiv. Titles: 1. Action 2. Get Set for Action 3. Swing into Action.

Action: The Complete Series 2006 (Unrated)
Features the complete series of the 1999-2000 comedy-drama TV show. Movie producer Peter Dragon (Mohr) is a morally-bankrupt guy whose last flick bombed and he's trying to bounce back with a no-holds-barred action movie with help from Wendy (Douglas), a child star who took up prostitution as an adult and has a pimp to also answer to. 13 episodes. 299m; DVD. **C:** Jay Mohr; Illeana Douglas; Lee Arenberg. **A:** Sr. High-Adult. **P:** Entertainment. **U:** Home. **Mov-Ent:** Television Series, Comedy-Drama, Satire & Parody. **Acq:** Purchase. **Dist:** Sony Pictures Home Entertainment Inc. $24.96.

Action: The October Crisis of 1970 1989
An historical retrospective on the tense days in October, 1970 when Montreal awaited the outcome of FLQ terrorist acts. 87m; VHS, 3/4 U. **Pr:** Normand Clout. **A:** Jr. High-Adult. **P:** Education. **U:** Institution, SURA. **Gen-Edu:** Canada, History--Modern. **Acq:** Purchase, Rent/Lease. **Dist:** National Film Board of Canada.

Action Under the Wires ????
Features footage of vintage Pennsylvania Railroad electric locomotives on rail lines between Long Island and Baltimore. 60m; VHS, DVD. **A:** College-Adult. **P:** Education. **U:** Home. **Gen-Edu:** Trains. **Acq:** Purchase. **Dist:** The Civil War Standard. $29.95.

Action U.S.A. 1989 (Unrated) — ★½
A young woman witnesses the murder of her boyfriend by gangsters, who then pursue her to make sure she will never tell what she saw. Throughout Texas she rambles with the mob sniffing at her heels, grateful for the opportunity to participate in numerous stunts and car crashes. 90m; VHS. **C:** Barri Murphy; Gregory Scott Cummins; William Knight; William (Bill) Smith; Cameron Mitchell; Directed by John Stewart; Written by David Reskin; Cinematography by Thomas Callaway. **A:** Adult. **P:** Entertainment. **U:** Home. **Mov-Ent. Acq:** Purchase. **Dist:** Imperial Entertainment Corp. $79.95.

Actions Speak Louder than Words 1992
Six deaf performers—three men and three women—offer staged pieces based on their experience in both the deaf and gay cultures. British sign language, with subtitles. 22m; VHS. **A:** College-Adult. **P:** Education. **U:** Institution. **Hea-Sci:** Deafness. **Acq:** Purchase, Rent/Lease. **Dist:** Frameline. $200.00.

Actium Maximus: War of the Alien Dinosaurs 2005 (Unrated) — ★
A ship captain is ordered to find sock puppets (sorry we meant dinosaurs) to compete in a gladiatorial arena for the amusement of a dictator modeled on old Rome. Meant for the fans of films so indescribably bad they're beyond belief. 78m; DVD, Streaming. **C:** Jonathan Daniel McCuin; Mark Hicks; Jennifer Hamil; David Matt Duncan; Selwyn Findley; Directed by Mark Hicks; Written by Mark Hicks; Cinematography by Mark Hicks; Music by Mark Hicks. **A:** Sr. High-Adult. **P:** Entertainment. **U:** Home. **L:** English. **Mov-Ent. Acq:** Purchase, Rent/Lease. **Dist:** Troma Entertainment. $14.98 9.99.

Active Listening 1988
A nursing home resident can't seem to get the staff to listen to her. 18m; VHS, 3/4 U. **A:** Adult. **P:** Education. **U:** Institution. **Gen-Edu:** Patient Care, Communication. **Acq:** Purchase. **Dist:** Victoria International Corp. $199.00.

Active Parenting 1988
Six programs provide the viewers with important information in the preparation for parenthood. Explores parent-child relationships and examines common parenting problems. 30m; VHS, 3/4 U. **Pr:** Guidance Associates. **A:** Family. **P:** Education. **U:** Institution, SURA. **Gen-Edu:** Parenting, Family. **Acq:** Purchase. **Dist:** EcuFilm. $325.00.
Indiv. Titles: 1. The Active Parent 2. Developing Responsibility 3. Winning Cooperation: Communication 4. Instilling Courage: Encouragement 5. Understanding Children 6. The Democratic Family in Action.

Active Parenting Today 1993
Takes parents of two- to twelve-year-olds through six sessions discussing common family behavior and communication problems and their solutions. Covers self-esteem and -confidence enrichment, understanding children, responsibility through consequences, cooperation through family activities and council meetings, and how to put an end to power struggles. Two videocassettes complete with leader's, parent, family, and program guides. 180m; VHS. **A:** Jr. High-Adult. **P:** Education. **U:** Institution. **Gen-Edu:** Parenting, Family. **Acq:** Purchase. **Dist:** Cambridge Educational. $345.00.

Active Stealth 1999 (R) — ★★
The Army's most secret weapon, an undetectable fighter jet, is hijacked by terrorists during a training mission. Now, it's up to Jefferson Pike (Baldwin) to lead a team into the Central American jungles to retrieve the military's property. 99m; VHS, DVD, CC. **C:** Daniel Baldwin; Fred Williamson; Hannes Jaenicke; Chick Vennera; Lisa Vidal; Directed by Fred Olen Ray. **A:** Sr. High-Adult. **P:** Entertainment. **U:** Home. **Mov-Ent:** Aeronautics, Terrorism. **Acq:** Purchase. **Dist:** Paramount Pictures Corp.

Activities of Daily Living 19??
Part of the Functional Assessment of the Elderly nursing training series. Teaches methods on assessing an elderly client's functions as changed by age and pathophysiology and how to use assessment data to plan appropriate nursing interventions. Contains information on activities of daily life, including eating, ambulating, toileting, grooming, climbing stairs, shopping, keeping house, interacting with others, and traveling. Also discusses how the cardiovascular, respiratory, neuromuscular, gastrointestinal, and genitourinary systems affect daily functions. Includes study guide. Approved for CE credit. 28m; VHS. **A:** College-Adult. **P:** Education. **U:** Institution. **Hea-Sci:** Nursing, Medical Education, Aging. **Acq:** Purchase, Rent/Lease. **Dist:** AJN Video Library/Lippincott Williams & Wilkins. $285.00.

Activities of Daily Living 19??
Part of the Restorative Care Series. Details the activities of daily living in the nursing home environment. Covers bed activities, wheelchair abilities, ambulation, elevation activities, and self-care. 26m; VHS. **A:** Adult. **P:** Education. **U:** Institution. **Hea-Sci:** Aging, Medical Care, Patient Care. **Acq:** Purchase, Rent/ Lease. **Dist:** University of Maryland. $200.00.

Activity-Based Mathematics: Algebra 19??
Program 3 of the five-part Activity-Based Mathematics teacher educational series. Profiles algebra using various demonstrations and examples. 28m; VHS. **A:** College-Adult. **P:** Teacher Education. **U:** Institution. **Gen-Edu:** Mathematics, Education. **Acq:** Purchase. **Dist:** Coastal Training Technologies Corp. $99.00.

Activity-Based Mathematics: Data Analysis 19??
Program 5 of the five-part Activity-Based Mathematics series. Contains examples and demonstrations that help teach a better understanding of statistics and how to organize and interpret information. 28m; VHS. **A:** College-Adult. **P:** Teacher Education. **U:** Institution. **Gen-Edu:** Mathematics, Education. **Acq:** Purchase. **Dist:** Coastal Training Technologies Corp. $99.00.

Activity-Based Mathematics: Geometry 19??
Program 4 of the five-part Activity-Based Mathematics educational series. Uses demonstrations, illustrations, and examples to teach the principles of geometry. 28m; VHS. **A:** College-Adult. **P:** Teacher Education. **U:** Institution. **Gen-Edu:** Mathematics, Education. **Acq:** Purchase. **Dist:** Coastal Training Technologies Corp. $99.00.

The Actor 1993
When his wife in unable to have a baby she forces her actor husband to take on a mute Gypsy girl as a second wife in order to provide them with a baby and comedy ensues. 88m; VHS. **A:** Adult. **P:** Entertainment. **U:** Home. **Mov-Ent:** Middle East, Comedy-Drama. **Acq:** Purchase. **Dist:** Arab Film Distribution. $29.99.

Actor: The Paul Muni Story 1978 — ★★
Musical biography of Paul Muni, from his beginnings as a traveling actor in Hungary to his New York theatre and movie career. 105m; VHS. **C:** Herschel Bernardi; Georgia Brown; Harold Gould. **A:** Family. **P:** Entertainment. **U:** Home. **Mov-Ent:** Musical--Drama, Biography: Show Business. **Acq:** Purchase. **Dist:** Lions Gate Television Corp. $39.95.

Actor Training and Kalarippayatt Martial Art of India 1971
Demonstrates how in integrate Kalarippayatt into an actor's training. 46m; VHS. **A:** Adult. **P:** Education. **U:** Institution. **Fin-Art:** Theater. **Acq:** Purchase. **Dist:** Insight Media. $189.00.

An Actor Works 1978
Actress Viveca Lindfors is seen in her home and at dress rehearsal. She gives her philosophies on acting, and performs a scene from the Greek drama, "The Trojan Women." 20m; VHS, 3/4 U. **C:** Viveca Lindfors. **Pr:** Bert Rashby. **A:** Jr. High-Adult. **P:** Education. **U:** Institution, SURA. **Fin-Art:** Theater. **Acq:** Purchase. **Dist:** Phoenix Learning Group.

Actors and Sin 1952 (Unrated) — ★★½
Two-part film casting a critical eye toward actors and Hollywood. "Actor's Blood" is the melodramatic story of Shakespearean actor Robinson and his unhappy actress daughter. She commits suicide and he sets out to prove it was murder. Heavy going. Lighter and more entertaining is "Woman of Sin," which relates a Hollywood satire involving a theatrical agent and his newest client, a precocious nine-year-old. 82m/ B/W; VHS, DVD. **C:** Edward G. Robinson; Marsha Hunt; Eddie Albert; Alan Reed; Dan O'Herlihy; Tracey Roberts; Rudolph Anders; Paul Guilfoyle; Alice Key; Douglas Evans; Rick Roman; Jenny Hecht; Jody Gilbert; John Crawford; Directed by Lee Garmes; Ben Hecht; Written by Ben Hecht; Cinematography by Lee Garmes; Music by George Antheil. **Pr:** United Artists. **A:** Jr. High-Adult. **P:** Entertainment. **U:** Home. **Mov-Ent. Acq:** Purchase. **Dist:** VCI Entertainment. $19.95.

Actor's Face as a Canvas 1973
This tape details various techniques from emphasizing facial contours to the creation of fantasy in this three part special. 30m; 3/4 U, EJ. **Pr:** NETCHE. **A:** College-Adult. **P:** Education. **U:** Institution, CCTV, BCTV, SURA. **Fin-Art:** Theater. **Acq:** Purchase, Rent/Lease, Subscription. **Dist:** NETCHE.
Indiv. Titles: 1. Modeling with Light and Shadow 2. Stylized Realism 3. Stylization and Fantasy.

An Actor's Revenge 1963 — ★★
In the early 19th century, a female impersonator in a Kabuki troupe takes revenge on the three men who killed his parents. Fascinating study of opposites—male/female, stage/life, love/ hate. In Japanese with English subtitles. 110m; VHS, DVD. **C:** Kazuo Hasegawa; Fujiko Yamamoto; Ayako Wakao; Ganjiro Nakamura; Directed by Kon Ichikawa; Written by Teinosuke Kinugasa; Daisuke Ito; Natto Wada; Cinematography by Setsuo Kobayashi; Music by Yashushi Akutagawa. **Pr:** Daiei. **A:** College-Adult. **P:** Entertainment. **U:** Home. **L:** Japanese. **Mov-Ent:** Theater. **Acq:** Purchase. **Dist:** AnimEigo Inc.; Ingram Entertainment Inc. $79.95.

The Actor's Video Library: Building a Character 1989
Acting professor R. Scott Lank explains how actors develop a character. He covers character analysis, using the body and voice, creating emotions, and guides to rehearsing. 86m; VHS. **A:** College-Adult. **P:** Instruction. **U:** Institution. **How-Ins:** Performing Arts, How-To. **Acq:** Purchase. **Dist:** Design Video Communications (DVC), Inc.; Baker and Taylor. $59.95.

The Actor's Video Library: Combat for the Stage 1989
Raoul Johnson teaches the techniques of fighting on stage without getting hurt. Covers the selection and use of guns and swords, how to take stage falls, and choreographing a fight scene. 96m; VHS. **A:** College-Adult. **P:** Instruction. **U:** Institution. **How-Ins:** Performing Arts, How-To. **Acq:** Purchase. **Dist:** Design Video Communications (DVC), Inc.; Baker and Taylor. $59.95.

The Actor's Video Library: Creative Drama and Improvisation 1990
Rives Collins provides a series of practical exercises designed to develop improvisational skills for character analysis. 110m; VHS. **A:** College-Adult. **P:** Instruction. **U:** Institution. **How-Ins:** Performing Arts, How-To. **Acq:** Purchase. **Dist:** Design Video Communications (DVC), Inc.; Baker and Taylor. $59.95.

The Actor's Video Library: Mime Over Matter 1987
Jodi Rae Lynn demonstrates basic mime illusions and exercises such as the lean, the sit, the wall, the robot, exaggerated actions, and how to create a mime piece. 101m; VHS. **A:** College-Adult. **P:** Instruction. **U:** Institution. **How-Ins:** Performing Arts, How-To. **Acq:** Purchase. **Dist:** Design Video Communications (DVC), Inc.; Baker and Taylor. $59.95.

The Actor's Video Library: The Directing Process 1990
Dale McFadden guides viewers through each step of the directorial process, including play selection, script analysis, organizing auditions, working with designers, blocking, and rehearsing. 90m; VHS. **A:** College-Adult. **P:** Instruction. **U:** Institution. **How-Ins:** Performing Arts, How-To. **Acq:** Purchase. **Dist:** Design Video Communications (DVC), Inc.; Baker and Taylor. $59.95.

The Actor's Video Library: The Make-up Workshop 1988
Majorie Duehmig demonstrates make-up design and application, including supplies and tools, facial anatomy, choosing the right make-up, corrective make-up, and special effects. 90m; VHS. **A:** College-Adult. **P:** Instruction. **U:** Institution. **How-Ins:** Performing Arts, How-To. **Acq:** Purchase. **Dist:** Design Video Communications (DVC), Inc.; Baker and Taylor. $59.95.

The Actress 1953 (Unrated) — ★★½
Solid performances from Tracy and Wright as the concerned parents although Simmons seems out of her depth (although it befits the character). Working-class Clinton Jones is dismayed that his daughter Ruth is stagestruck and tries to persuade her to a more conventional life. When she is rejected for theater roles in Boston, dad finally realizes how much being an actress means to his little girl and he gives Ruth his only valuable possession to sell so she can move to New York. Film debut of Perkins as the suitor. Based on Gordon's autobiographical play "Years Ago." 90m/B/W; DVD. **C:** Spencer Tracy; Jean Simmons; Teresa Wright; Anthony Perkins; Ian Wolfe; Mary Wickes; Directed by George Cukor; Written by Ruth Gordon; Cinematography by Harold Rosson. **A:** Family. **P:** Entertainment. **U:** Home. **Mov-Ent. Acq:** Purchase. **Dist:** WarnerArchive.com.

Actresses Advise Young Aspirants 1975
Four top Broadway actresses answer students' questions about the theatre and acting in this program. 30m/B/W; VHS, 3/4 U, EJ, Q. **C:** Ruby Dee; Elaine Stritch; Inga Swenson. **Pr:** WCBS New York; Camera Three Productions. **A:** Sr. High-Adult. **P:** Entertainment. **U:** Institution, SURA. **Fin-Art:** Theater. **Acq:** Duplication, Free Duplication. **Dist:** Camera Three Productions, Inc.

Acts of Betrayal 1998 — ★★
Alonso is about to divulge wise guy secrets and for her protection, she's paired with FBI agent McColm to make certain the bad guys don't silence her first. 112m; VHS, CC. **C:** Maria Conchita Alonso; Matt McColm; Muse Watson; David Groh; Gregory Alan Williams; Susan Lee Hoffman; Joe Estevez; Directed by Joakim (Jack) Ersgard; Written by Patrick Highsmith; Cinematography by Jerry Sidell; Music by Roger Neill. **A:** Sr. High-Adult. **P:** Entertainment. **U:** Home. **Mov-Ent:** Intelligence Service, Federal Bureau of Investigation (FBI). **Acq:** Purchase. **Dist:** Lions Gate Television Corp.

Acts of Caring 19??
Features three different nurses, one in labor and delivery, one in cardiac surgery, and one in the oncology unit, as they go through their daily routines. They speak of their satisfaction and frustrations as they care for patients and their families. Emphasis is placed on their warmth and compassion as they perform their duties. 50m; VHS. **A:** College-Adult. **P:** Education. **U:** Institution. **Hea-Sci:** Nursing. **Acq:** Purchase, Rent/Lease. **Dist:** AJN Video Library/Lippincott Williams & Wilkins. $285.00.

Acts of Contrition 1995 (Unrated) — ★★½
Boston radio talk-show host Jonathan Franye (Harmon) has his listeners call in and confess their deepest secrets. Then one caller confesses to a murder and Jonathan decides to investigate and see if the claim is true. But bringing a murderer to justice could be hazardous to his own health. 89m; DVD. **C:** Mark Harmon; Julianne Phillips; Sarah Trigger; Ron Perlman; David Clennon; Gustave Johnson; Betty Miller; Directed by Jan Egleson; Written by John Pielmeier; Cinematography by Andrzej Sekula; Music by Gary Chang. **A:** Jr. High-Adult. **P:** Entertainment. **U:** Home. **Mov-Ent:** TV Movies, Crime Drama. **Acq:** Purchase. **Dist:** Echo Bridge Home Entertainment.

Acts of Death 2007 (R) — ★
Re-imagining of 'I Know What You Did Last Summer' set in a locked college theater with various fraternity types paying for an accident they covered up from the day before. 103m; DVD. **C:** Bill Vincent; Reggie Bannister; Jason Carter; Derek J. Dubuque; Nathaniel Nose; James Ohngren; Glenn Shadix; Finn Wrisely; Niki Huey; Monica Percich; Erin Scheiner; Directed by Jeff Burton; Written by Bill Vincent; Jeff Burton; Erik F. Hill; Cinematography by Jeff Burton; Music by John Roome. **A:** Sr. High-Adult. **P:** Entertainment. **U:** Home. **L:** English, Spanish. **Mov-Ent. Acq:** Purchase. **Dist:** Lions Gate Entertainment Inc. $14.98.

Acts of Faith 1992
Historical outline of the 1492 expulsion of the Jews from Spain. Includes documentary footage of American Catholics speaking about the Spanish Jewish rites that they practice. 52m; VHS. **Pr:** IFS. **A:** Jr. High-Adult. **P:** Religious. **U:** Institution. **Gen-Edu:** History, Judaism, Religion. **Acq:** Purchase. **Dist:** Alden Films; Films for the Humanities & Sciences.

The Acts of Venice Beach 1997
A collection of the 12 greatest street performers from Venice Beach Boardwalk, the second most visited tourist attraction in California. Includes a man who jumps into a pile of broken glass, a chainsaw juggler, and a man who puts a torch on his

head. 56m; VHS. **A:** Jr. High-Adult. **P:** Entertainment. **U:** Home. **Mov-Ent:** Variety. **Acq:** Purchase. **Dist:** Tapeworm Video Distributors Inc. $19.95.

Acts of Violence 1987
The demented motives of murderers are exposed in this fictional film. 72m; VHS. **Pr:** Vestron Video. **A:** Sr. High-Adult. **P:** Entertainment. **U:** Home. **Gen-Edu:** Violence. **Acq:** Purchase. **Dist:** Lions Gate Television Corp. $59.98.

Acts of Worship 2001 (R) — ★★½
Kicked out by her boyfriend, junkie Alix finds a safe haven with Digna, a former addict. But her attempt to straighten Alix out leads Digna back to her old, bad habits. 94m; VHS, DVD. **C:** Ana Reeder; Michael Hyatt; Nestor Rodriguez; Christopher Kadish; Directed by Rosemary Rodriguez; Written by Rosemary Rodriguez; Cinematography by Luke Geissbuhler; Music by Jim Coleman. **A:** Sr. High-Adult. **P:** Entertainment. **U:** Home. **Mov-Ent:** Drug Abuse, Women. **Acq:** Purchase. **Dist:** Virgil Films & Entertainment. $24.99.

The Actualization Group 1967
A series showing authentic, unrehearsed psychological group therapy through seven sequential sessions dealing with aggression, actualization, manipulation, and independence. Seven untitled programs. 315m/B/W; VHS, 3/4 U, Special order formats. **Pr:** Psychological Films. **A:** College-Adult. **P:** Education. **U:** Institution, SURA. **Hea-Sci:** Psychology. **Acq:** Purchase. **Dist:** Psychological & Educational Films.

Actualization Therapy: An Integration of Rogers, Perls and Ellis 197?
The styles of Carl Rogers, Frederick Perls, and Albert Ellis in psychotherapy are described and contrasted. 27m; VHS, 3/4 U, Special order formats. **C:** Everett Shostrom; Dr. Carl Rogers; Dr. Frederick Perls; Dr. Albert Ellis. **Pr:** Psychological Films. **A:** College-Adult. **P:** Education. **U:** Institution, SURA. **Hea-Sci:** Psychology. **Acq:** Purchase. **Dist:** Psychological & Educational Films.

Actualization Through Assertion 1976
Assertive training techniques that improve the client-counselor relationship. 26m; VHS, 3/4 U. **Pr:** University of California at Los Angeles. **A:** Adult. **P:** Education. **U:** Institution. **Bus-Ind:** Business, Human Relations. **Acq:** Purchase. **Dist:** University of California at Los Angeles Neuropsychiatric Institute. $225.00.

Actuators and Positioners 199?
An instrument technology training program on positioners. Includes a workbook and guide. 60m; VHS. **A:** Adult. **P:** Instruction. **U:** Institution. **Bus-Ind:** Technology, Job Training. **Acq:** Purchase. **Dist:** ISA -The International Society of Automation. $95.00.

Acu-Yoga for Flexibility 19??
Demonstrates stretches for the lower, middle and upper back, pelvis and legs. 45m; VHS. **A:** Adult. **P:** Instruction. **U:** Home. **Hea-Sci:** Yoga. **Acq:** Purchase. **Dist:** Acupressure Institute. $29.95.

Acu-Yoga for the Meridians 19??
Shows vital points and postures that stimulate the 12 meridians. 45m; VHS. **A:** Adult. **P:** Instruction. **U:** Home. **Hea-Sci:** Yoga. **Acq:** Purchase. **Dist:** Acupressure Institute. $29.95.

Acu-Yoga Stress Relief 19??
Presents two sets of relaxing postures. 45m; VHS. **A:** Adult. **P:** Instruction. **U:** Home. **Hea-Sci:** Yoga, Stress. **Acq:** Purchase. **Dist:** Acupressure Institute. $29.95.

The Acupressure Facelift 1986
An interactive video designed to restore youth and relive tensions, using an Asian method demonstrated by Lindsay Wagner. 60m; VHS, CC. **C:** Hosted by Lindsay Wagner. **A:** Jr. High-Adult. **P:** Instruction. **U:** Home. **Hea-Sci:** How-To, Health Education, Fitness/Exercise. **Acq:** Purchase. **Dist:** Warner Home Video, Inc. $19.95.

Acupuncture Anesthesia 1973
Acupuncture anesthesia techniques are demonstrated as the basic anesthetic for surgical procedures including pulmonary lobectomy, ligation of patent ductas arteriosus, dental extractions, and gastrectomy. Narrated in Chinese and English. 60m; 3/4 U. **Pr:** Peking Acupuncture Anesthesia. **A:** College-Adult. **P:** Professional. **U:** Institution, CCTV. **L:** English, Chinese. **Hea-Sci:** Cults, Pain. **Acq:** Purchase. **Dist:** American College of Cardiology.

Acute Abdomen 1986
A doctor's review of the causes of serious abdominal pain in children and adults. 45m; VHS, 3/4 U. **A:** Adult. **P:** Professional. **U:** Institution, CCTV, Home, SURA. **Hea-Sci:** Urology. **Acq:** Purchase, Rent/Lease, Subscription. **Dist:** Emory Medical Television Network.

Acute Abdominal Pain and Appendicitis in Children 1983
A surgeon classifies the causes of abdominal pain and appendicitis in children. 48m; VHS, 3/4 U. **Pr:** Emory University. **A:** College-Adult. **P:** Education. **U:** Institution, CCTV, Home, SURA. **Hea-Sci:** Pediatrics. **Acq:** Purchase, Rent/Lease, Subscription. **Dist:** Emory Medical Television Network.

Acute Asthma 1986
A review of current treatments and findings regarding this condition. For doctors. 58m; VHS, 3/4 U. **A:** Adult. **P:** Professional. **U:** Institution, CCTV, Home, SURA. **Hea-Sci:** Respiratory System. **Acq:** Purchase, Rent/Lease, Subscription. **Dist:** Emory Medical Television Network.

Acute Digitalis Toxicity 1982
Diagnosis and management of acute digitalis toxicity are discussed. 32m; VHS, 3/4 U. **Pr:** Emory University. **A:** College-Adult. **P:** Professional. **U:** Institution, CCTV, Home, SURA. **Hea-Sci:** Heart, Drugs. **Acq:** Purchase, Rent/Lease, Subscription. **Dist:** Emory Medical Television Network.

Acute Intermittent Porphyria 1971
A patient interview and description of the symptoms of porphyria. 11m; VHS, 3/4 U, Special order formats. **Pr:** Ohio State University Health Sciences AV Center. **A:** College-Adult. **P:** Professional. **U:** Institution, SURA. **Hea-Sci:** Blood. **Acq:** Purchase, Rent/Lease. **Dist:** Ohio State University.

Acute Ophthalmologic Emergencies in Children 1982
This program discusses and illustrates eye problems seen in newborns and young children. 50m; VHS, 3/4 U. **Pr:** Emory University. **A:** College-Adult. **P:** Professional. **U:** Institution, CCTV, Home, SURA. **Hea-Sci:** Eye, Emergencies. **Acq:** Purchase, Rent/Lease, Subscription. **Dist:** Emory Medical Television Network.

Acute Pain Management in Children: Operative or Medical Procedures 1996
Focuses on identifying degrees of pain in children in order to prevent or control it. 13m; VHS. **A:** Adult. **P:** Education. **U:** Institution. **Hea-Sci:** Medical Education, Pediatrics, Patient Care. **Acq:** Purchase, Rent/Lease. **Dist:** AJN Video Library/ Lippincott Williams & Wilkins. $199.00.

Acute Pain Management: Operative or Medical Procedures and Trauma 1996
Looks at methods of pain assessment as well as pain management options. Features the needs of the elderly. 27m; VHS. **A:** Adult. **P:** Education. **U:** Institution. **Hea-Sci:** Health Education, Medical Education, Pain. **Acq:** Purchase, Rent/Lease. **Dist:** AJN Video Library/Lippincott Williams & Wilkins. $199.00.

Acute Renal Failure in Children 1983
A pediatrician gives a lecture on the causes, pathophysiology, and treatment of acute renal failure in children. 48m; VHS, 3/4 U. **Pr:** Emory University. **A:** College-Adult. **P:** Education. **U:** Institution, CCTV, Home, SURA. **Hea-Sci:** Pediatrics, Kidneys. **Acq:** Purchase, Rent/Lease, Subscription. **Dist:** Emory Medical Television Network.

Acute Respiratory Failure 1974
A live broadcast on the topic of acute respiratory failure. 60m; VHS, 3/4 U, Special order formats. **Pr:** Ohio State University Health Sciences AV Center. **A:** College-Adult. **P:** Professional. **U:** Institution, SURA. **Hea-Sci:** Respiratory System. **Acq:** Purchase, Rent/Lease. **Dist:** Ohio State University.

Acute Respiratory Failure 1991
Looks at respiratory pathophysiology, assessment of acute respiratory failure, including danger signs and symptoms, and much more. Includes a booklet. 30m; VHS. **A:** Adult. **P:** Education. **U:** Institution. **Hea-Sci:** Medical Care, Medical Education, Nursing. **Acq:** Purchase. **Dist:** Nursing Center. $36.95.

Acute Respiratory Failure—Hypoxemia 1974
A prepared segment on the subject of hypoxemia from a one-hour broadcast on acute respiratory failure. 15m; VHS, 3/4 U, Special order formats. **Pr:** Ohio State University Health Sciences AV Center. **A:** College-Adult. **P:** Professional. **U:** Institution, SURA. **Hea-Sci:** Respiratory System. **Acq:** Purchase, Rent/Lease. **Dist:** Ohio State University.

Acute Surgical Abdomen in Children 1986
For medical pros, a survey of findings and tests effective on children with abdominal pain. 46m; VHS, 3/4 U. **A:** Adult. **P:** Professional. **U:** Institution, CCTV, Home, SURA. **Hea-Sci:** Surgery. **Acq:** Purchase, Rent/Lease, Subscription. **Dist:** Emory Medical Television Network.

Acutely Decompensated Diabetes Mellitus 1981
Prevention and management of acutely decompensated diabetes mellitus are discussed. 46m; VHS, 3/4 U. **Pr:** Emory University. **A:** College-Adult. **P:** Professional. **U:** Institution, CCTV, Home, SURA. **Hea-Sci:** Diabetes. **Acq:** Purchase, Rent/ Lease, Subscription. **Dist:** Emory Medical Television Network.

A.D. 1985 — ★★½
Set shortly after Jesus' death, this rather low-budget miniseries chronicles the life and adventures of Christ's disciples (especially Peter and Paul) and the growing conflicts between Jewish zealots, early Christians, and the power of the Roman empire. Based on the Acts of the Apostles. 540m; VHS, DVD. **C:** Denis Quilley; Philip Sayer; Anthony Andrews; Colleen Dewhurst; Ava Gardner; Richard Kiley; James Mason; David Hedison; John Houseman; John McEnery; Ian McShane; Jennifer O'Neill; Fernando Rey; Richard Roundtree; Ben Vereen; Susan Sarandon; Diane Venora; Anthony Zerbe; Jack Warden; Amanda Pays; Millie Perkins; Michael Wilding, Jr.; Directed by Stuart Cooper; Written by Anthony Burgess; Cinematography by Ennio Guarnieri; Music by Lalo Schifrin. **A:** Jr. High-Adult. **P:** Entertainment. **U:** Home. **Mov-Ent:** Middle East, Drama. **Acq:** Purchase. **Dist:** Alpha Omega Publications Inc.

A.D. 1990
Set in the years following Christ's death and resurrection, this is the story of the Roman persecution of the early Christian church. 360m; VHS. **Pr:** Ignatius Press. **A:** Jr. High-Adult. **P:** Entertainment. **U:** Institution, Home. **Gen-Edu:** Religion, History--Ancient. **Acq:** Purchase. **Dist:** Ignatius Press. $129.95.

The Ad and Ego 1996
Depicts how commericalism and advertising have invaded the lives of the average American, and the creation of a psychology of need by aggressive marketing. 57m; VHS. **A:** Sr. High-Adult.

P: Education. **U:** Home, Institution. **Gen-Edu:** Sociology, Marketing. **Acq:** Purchase. **Dist:** California Newsreel. $195.00.

Ad Campaigns That Work 19??
Three successful ad agency executives furnish information on successful ad campaigns and why they were successful. Covers principles of successful advertising. 30m; VHS. **A:** College-Adult. **P:** Professional. **U:** Home. **Bus-Ind:** Advertising. **Acq:** Purchase. **Dist:** Instructional Video. $89.95.

Ad Libbing It 1991
Helps kids understand that advertisements for liquor and cigarettes can be deceitful. Interviews opponents of this type of advertising. 17m; VHS. **Pr:** Snoqualmie Films. **A:** Jr. High. **P:** Education. **U:** Institution. **Gen-Edu:** Alcoholism, Advertising. **Acq:** Purchase. **Dist:** United Learning Inc. $200.00.

AD Police Files, File. 1: The Phantom Woman 1990 — ★★
In Mega Tokyo of 2027, the AD Police keep the androids known as Boomers from wrecking the city when they occasionally go haywire. After a rookie is killed on a routine call, detectives Jeena and Leon do a little investigating so his family can collect on his insurance policy. They're led to a chop shop where Boomers are rebuilt and their parts are recycled Meanwhile, Leon is being stalked by a rebuilt female Boomer. The story of the female Boomer is bizarre and disturbing, but reasonably interesting. Provides some good background information on the nature of the Boomers. This three-volume series is the prequel to the popular "Bubblegum Crisis" series. Includes the Mega Tokyo Mix music vidoes "Heartbreaker," "What a Fool I Am" and "Rockin' the Beat." 40m; VHS. **A:** College-Adult. **P:** Entertainment. **U:** Home. **L:** Japanese, English. **Mov-Ent:** Anime, Animation & Cartoons. **Acq:** Purchase. **Dist:** AnimEigo Inc. $34.95.

AD Police Files, File 2: The Ripper 1990 — ★★★
Prostitutes are being disemboweled on Paradise Loop. There are a lot of things that point to the perp being a Boomer which means the AD Police are about to take over the case. An intriguing story that provides a very personal look at the effect of technology on humanity The serial killer is suitably unnerving and the climax action-packed. But it's the final scene that makes this anime truly haunting. Includes bonus music videos "Love Me Tonight" and "I Need Your Love." 40m; VHS. **A:** College-Adult. **P:** Entertainment. **U:** Home. **L:** Japanese, English. **Mov-Ent:** Anime, Animation & Cartoons, Music Video. **Acq:** Purchase. **Dist:** AnimEigo Inc. $34.95.

AD Police Files, File 3: The Man Who Bites His Tongue 1990 — ★★½
After being critically injured, police officer Billy Fanwood is reconstructed into a cyber cop and used as the AD Police's newest weapon against the Boomers. Combat for him is emotionless and without sensation. The only way Billy can feel anything is when he bites his tongue. Jeena, his ex-girlfriend, is distressed by Billy's condition and by the fact he seems unable to remember her. Once again, scientists who would go to these extremes are portrayed as glory seekers who view humanity as so many lab rats. 40m; VHS. **A:** College-Adult. **P:** Entertainment. **U:** Home. **L:** Japanese, English. **Mov-Ent:** Anime. **Acq:** Purchase. **Dist:** AnimEigo Inc. $39.95.

A.D. Police To Protect and Serve: Complete Series 2002 (Unrated)
Anime prequel to the "Bubblegum Crisis" TV series. Violent robots take over Tokyo after an enormous earthquake pummels the city. When his partner receives a serious injury from one of the robots a loner cop, Kenji Sasaki, takes on a new partner, Hans Klief, to fight them and the bigwigs that control them. 12 episodes. 300m; DVD. **C:** C. Markham Anderson; Christine M. Auten; Victor Carsrud; Emily Carter; Juliet Cesario. **A:** Sr. High-Adult. **P:** Entertainment. **U:** Home. **Mov-Ent:** Television Series, Animation & Cartoons, Science Fiction. **Acq:** Purchase. **Dist:** Amazon.com Inc. $34.98.

Ada 1961 (Unrated) — ★½
Southern-fried, Depression-era setting adds to the melodrama, which is based on Wirt Williams' novel, "Ada Dallas." Crooked party boss Sylvester Marin (Hyde-White) picks pliable country boy sheriff Bo Gillis (Martin) and pushes through his election to governor. Bo's ambitious wife Ada (Hayward) wants Bo to be his own man so Marin uses her ex-prostitute past to create a scandal and more dirty tactics to keep political power. 108m; DVD. **C:** Susan Hayward; Dean Martin; Wilfrid Hyde-White; Ralph Meeker; Martin Balsam; Frank Maxwell; Directed by Daniel Mann; Written by Arthur Sheekman; Cinematography by Joseph Ruttenberg; Music by Bronislau Kaper. **A:** Sr. High-Adult. **P:** Entertainment. **U:** Home. **L:** English. **Mov-Ent:** Marriage, Politics & Government, Political Campaigns. **Acq:** Purchase. **Dist:** WarnerArchive.com.

ADA: A Team Approach 1993
Offers suggestions on how managers can follow the Americans with Disabilities Act to avoid costly lawsuits. Stresses the role human resource departments play in insuring compliance with the regulation. 16m; VHS. **A:** College-Adult. **P:** Professional. **U:** Institution. **Bus-Ind:** Safety Education, Business, Handicapped. **Acq:** Purchase, Rent/Lease. **Dist:** Core Media Training Solutions. $425.00.

ADA and You: Compliance Guidelines 1993
Shows how agricultural institutions can make their facilities more accessible to the differently abled. 9m; VHS. **A:** College-Adult. **P:** Education. **U:** Institution. **Gen-Edu:** Agriculture, Politics & Government. **Acq:** Purchase. **Dist:** Purdue University. $15.00.

ADA: Commonsense Compliance 19??
Illustrates the legal issues of the ADA through well-acted vignettes. Designed to be viewed in conjunction with "ADA: Understanding the Law." 24m; VHS. **A:** Sr. High-Adult. **P:** Professional. **U:** Institution. **Bus-Ind:** Business, Law, Handicapped. **Acq:** Purchase. **Dist:** Audio Graphics Training Systems. $695.00.

ADA: Communication and Service Skills 199?
Outlines ways hotels and motels can provide hospitality service to guests with disabilities. Includes guides and resource list. 21m; VHS, CC. **A:** Adult. **P:** Instruction. **U:** Institution. **Bus-Ind:** Job Training, Human Relations. **Acq:** Rent/Lease. **Dist:** American Hotel & Lodging Educational Institute. $199.95.

ADA: Customer Courtesies 1991
Presents methods for bank employees on how to follow American Disabilities Act guidelines when interacting with differently abled customers. Includes four-minute leader guide (on tape) summarizing content. 23m; VHS. **A:** College-Adult. **P:** Instruction. **U:** Institution. **Bus-Ind:** Law, Handicapped, Customer Service. **Acq:** Purchase. **Dist:** 1st Financial Training Services. $495.00.

The ADA Maze: What You Can Do 1991
Defines the legal aspects of hiring according to the ADA through a combination of interviews and graphics. Aimed at managers, topics include the intent of the ADA, writing job descriptions, interviewing guidelines and more. 16m; VHS. **A:** Sr. High-Adult. **P:** Professional. **U:** Institution. **Bus-Ind:** Business, Law, Handicapped. **Acq:** Purchase. **Dist:** Commonwealth Films Inc.; ERI Safety Videos; American Media, Inc. $425.00.

ADA-Talk 1992
A different approach to describing the ADA utilizes a question-and-answer format in a radio-talk show context to address issues. Self-limiting in that the information is not reinforced through graphics or acted vignettes. 28m; VHS. **A:** Sr. High-Adult. **P:** Professional. **U:** Institution. **Bus-Ind:** Business, Law, Handicapped. **Acq:** Purchase. **Dist:** Learning Communications L.L.C. $495.00.

ADA: The Hiring Process 199?
Highlights the process of hiring people with disabilities. Includes guides and resources list. 48m; VHS. **A:** Adult. **P:** Instruction. **U:** Institution. **Bus-Ind:** Job Training, Human Relations. **Acq:** Rent/Lease. **Dist:** American Hotel & Lodging Educational Institute. $199.95.

ADA: Understanding the Law 19??
Discusses the new ADA laws in a conference room setting. Confronts typical objections from management and gives clear information on legal requirements and ramifications. Designed to be viewed in conjunction with "ADA: Commonsense Compliance." 47m; VHS. **A:** Sr. High-Adult. **P:** Professional. **U:** Institution. **Bus-Ind:** Business, Law, Handicapped. **Acq:** Purchase. **Dist:** Audio Graphics Training Systems. $695.00.

Adam 1983 — ★★★½
Docu-drama based on a tragic, true story. John and Reve Williams (Travanti and Williams) desperately search for their six-year-old son abducted during an outing. During their long search and struggle, they lobby Congress for use of the FBI's crime computer. Eventually their efforts led to the creation of the Missing Children's Bureau. Sensitive, compelling performances by Travanti and Williams as the agonized, courageous parents. 100m; VHS, DVD, CC. **C:** Daniel J. Travanti; JoBeth Williams; Martha Scott; Richard Masur; Paul Regina; Mason Adams; Directed by Michael Tuchner. **Pr:** Alan Landsburg Productions. **A:** Jr. High-Adult. **P:** Entertainment. **U:** Home. **Mov-Ent:** TV Movies, Parenting, Documentary Films. **Acq:** Purchase. **Dist:** Hen's Tooth Video.

Adam 2009 (PG-13) — ★★½
New York-set romantic drama with a twist. Having just moved into her apartment building, teacher Beth (Byrne) becomes intrigued by good-looking neighbor Adam (Dancy) although he's ill at ease socially. After gaining his trust, Adam explains to Rose that he has Asperger's syndrome (a form of autism) and doesn't understand empathy or what people are thinking. Still recovering from a painful breakup, Rose is uncertain if she wants to get involved or how much Adam can participate in a romantic relationship, especially when her parents' reservations and problems begin interfering. Dancy never overdoes his role and Byrne is sympathetic without being cloying. 97m; Blu-Ray, On Demand, Wide. **C:** Hugh Dancy; Rose Byrne; Frankie Faison; Amy Irving; Peter Gallagher; Mark Linn-Baker; Directed by Max Mayer; Written by Max Mayer; Cinematography by Seamus Tierney; Music by Christopher Lennertz. **Pr:** Dean Vanech; Leslie Urdang; Miranda De Pencier; Serenade Films; Deer Path Films; VOX3 Films; Olympus Pictures; Fox Searchlight. **A:** Sr. High-Adult. **P:** Entertainment. **U:** Home. **L:** English. **Mov-Ent:** Drama, Autism. **Acq:** Purchase. **Dist:** Fox Home Entertainment; Amazon.com Inc.; Movies Unlimited.

Adam Abdul Hakeem: One Who Survived 19??
Tells the story of Hakeem, who tried to extricate himself from a police-run drug ring in which he had participated for six years. It examines the relationships between law enforcement agencies, the criminal justice system, and the African-American community. 40m; VHS. **A:** Sr. High. **P:** Education. **U:** Institution. **Gen-Edu:** Drugs. **Acq:** Purchase. **Dist:** Filmakers Library Inc. $250.

Adam & Steve 2005 (Unrated) — ★★
Contrived but generally amusing gay romance begins in 1987 when shy goth boy Adam (writer/director Chester) meets glittery party boy Steve (Gets) and their trick turns into disaster. They meet cute 17 years later, don't recognize each other, and start a romance fraught with individual neuroses that stem from that

fateful night. Each man also comes complete with the prerequisite straight best friend: for Adam, it's former-fatty turned skinny comic Rhonda (Posey) and for Steve it's caustic roommate Michael (Kattan). A couple of musical fantasy sequences provide some unexpected distraction. 99m; DVD. **C:** Craig Chester; Malcolm Gets; Parker Posey; Chris Kattan; Sally Kirkland; Noah Segan; Directed by Craig Chester; Written by Craig Chester; Cinematography by Carl F. Bartels; Music by Roddy Bottum. **Pr:** Kirkland Tibbels; George Bendele; Funnyboy Production. **A:** Sr. High-Adult. **P:** Entertainment. **U:** Home. **L:** English. **Mov-Ent:** Comedy--Romantic. **Dist:** TLA Releasing.

Adam Ant: Antics in the Forbidden Zone 1990
Perennial punk Adam (sans Ants) sings his hits, including "King of the Wild Frontier," "Antmusic," "Ant Rap," "Prince Charming," "Vive le Rock" and more. 42m; VHS. **C:** Adam Ant. **Pr:** CBS/Fox Music Video. **A:** Jr. High-Adult. **P:** Entertainment. **U:** Home. **Mov-Ent:** Music Video, Music--Performance. **Acq:** Purchase. **Dist:** Music Video Distributors; Sony Music Entertainment Inc. $17.98.

Adam at 6 a.m. 1970 (PG) — ★★
Douglas is a young college professor who decides to spend a summer laboring in Missouri, where life, he thinks, is simpler. Of course, he learns that life in the boonies has its own set of problems, but unfortunately it takes him the entire movie before he catches the drift. 100m; VHS, DVD; Open Captioned. **C:** Michael Douglas; Lee Purcell; Joe Don Baker; Charles Aidman; Marge Redmond; Louise Latham; Grayson Hall; Dana Elcar; Meg Foster; Richard Derr; Anne Gwynne; Directed by Robert Scheerer. **Pr:** Solar Productions; CBS. **A:** Jr. High-Adult. **P:** Entertainment. **U:** Home. **Mov-Ent.** **Acq:** Purchase. **Dist:** $59.98.

Adam Clayton Powell 19??
Biography of the rise and fall of African American leader Adam Clayton Powell and modern black politics in the U.S. Features interviews from politicians, scholars, and family members. 54m; VHS. **A:** Adult. **P:** Education. **U:** Home. **Gen-Edu:** Documentary Films, Black Culture, Politics & Government. **Acq:** Purchase, Rent/Lease. **Dist:** Filmakers Library Inc. $150.

Adam Clayton Powell 1977
The story of the controversial black congressman and his struggle against oppression and injustice to blacks in America. The program contains an interview with Powell, conducted shortly before his death by WABC-TV's Gil Noble. 58m; VHS, 3/4 U. **Pr:** Gil Noble. **A:** Sr. High-Adult. **P:** Education. **U:** Institution, SURA. **Gen-Edu:** Civil Rights. **Acq:** Purchase. **Dist:** Phoenix Learning Group.

Adam Had Four Sons 1941 (Unrated) — ★★½
Satisfying character study involving the typical turn-of-the-century family nearly consumed by love, jealousy, and hatred. In the early part of the century, a goodly governess (Bergman in her second U.S. film) watches sympathetically over four sons of an American businessman after their mother dies. Economic necessity separates Bergman from the family for several years. Upon her return, she tangles with scheming bride-to-be Hayward, a bad girl intent on dividing and conquering the family before walking down the aisle with one of the sons. Based on a novel by Charles Bonner. 81m/B/W; VHS, DVD. **C:** Ingrid Bergman; Warner Baxter; Susan Hayward; Fay Wray; Richard Denning; June Lockhart; Robert Shaw; Johnny Downs; Directed by Gregory Ratoff. **Pr:** Robert Sherwood; Columbia Pictures. **A:** Family. **P:** Entertainment. **U:** Home. **Mov-Ent.** **Acq:** Purchase. **Dist:** Sony Pictures Home Entertainment Inc. $59.95.

Adam Resurrected 2008 (R) — ★½
An unsettling story, with a brilliant lead performance by Goldblum, but Schrader's tone veers uncertainly. Adam Stein (Goldblum) was a successful Jewish cabaret performer in Berlin until the Nazis came to power. Sent to a concentration camp, Adam survives because the camp's Commandant (Defoe) is an admirer. But he also treats Adam (literally) like a dog so it's no wonder that Adam eventually winds up in an Israeli mental hospital for Holocaust survivors. He's still using humor as a coping mechanism but circumstances and survivors' guilt undermine an already shaky foundation. Based on the novel by Yoram Kaniuk. 106m; Blu-Ray, Wide. **C:** Jeff Goldblum; Willem Dafoe; Derek Jacobi; Ayelet Zurer; Moritz Bleibtreu; Hana Laszlo; Tudor Rapiteanu; Directed by Paul Schrader; Written by Noah Stollman; Cinematography by Sebastian Edscmid; Music by Gabriel Yared. **Pr:** Ehud Bleiberg; Werner Wirsing; ThreeL Filmproduktion; Bleiberg Entertainment. **A:** Sr. High-Adult. **P:** Entertainment. **U:** Home. **L:** English. **Mov-Ent:** Holocaust, Israel. **Acq:** Purchase. **Dist:** Image Entertainment Inc.; Movies Unlimited; Alpha Video.

Adam Sandler's 8 Crazy Nights 2002 (PG-13) — ★★
Parents should be warned that Adam Sandler's foray into animated holiday fare is more for the big kids than the tiny tots. When eyes are aglow, it's usually the bloodshot peepers of party animal Davey Stone (voiced by Sandler), who harbors a grudge against the holiday season. After he goes on a spree of booze-soaked vandalism, the judge is about to throw the book at Davey until Whitey, the ref of a youth basketball league, intercedes for him. Davey proceeds to torment Whitey and his sister Eleanor (both also voiced by Sandler) until the last act less-than-believably transforms him into a good guy. At turns offensive and interesting, this foul-mouthed cartoon does manage to set a record for animated product placement. 71m; VHS, DVD, CC. **C:** Voice(s) by Adam Sandler; Kevin Nealon; Rob Schneider; Norm Crosby; Jackie Titone; Austin Stout; Jon Lovitz; Directed by Seth Kearsley; Written by Adam Sandler; Allen Covert; Brooks Arthur; Brad Isaacs; Music by Marc Ellis; Ray Ellis; Teddy Castellucci. **Pr:** Jack Giarraputo; Adam

Sandler; Allen Covert; Adam Sandler; Allen Covert; Happy Madison Productions; Columbia Pictures. **A:** Jr. High-Adult. **P:** Entertainment. **U:** Home. **Mov-Ent:** Animation & Cartoons, Judaism, Holidays. **Acq:** Purchase. **Dist:** Sony Pictures Home Entertainment Inc.

Adam 12: Season 2 1969 (Unrated)
Television drama series on NBC (1968-1975). Officers Malloy (Milner) and Reed (McCord) patrol the streets of Los Angeles harassed by freelance reporters doing a story on police brutality in "Log 52: Good Cop-Handle with Care," go in to ward off a riot after a shooting in "Log 23: Pig Is a Three-Letter Word," get accused of improper search and seizure in "Log 123: Courtroom," and question a young man not wanting attention for his good deeds in "Log 114: The Hero." 26 episodes. 660m; DVD. **A:** Family. **P:** Entertainment. **U:** Home. **Mov-Ent:** Drama, Television Series. **Acq:** Purchase. **Dist:** Shout! Factory.

Adam-12: Season 3 1970 (Unrated)
NBC 1968-75 cop drama. Pete Malloy (Milner) and Jim Reed (McCord) are two Los Angeles cops that patrol the streets for arsonists, con artists, nude drunk drivers, loan sharks, drug lords, gang violence and bombings, all in a days work. The partners pull over an Army truck in "Post Time," deliver a baby in "Poachers," find a "Missing Child," search for a bar fly that can clear a cop of blackmail in "I.A.D." and arrest Santa Claus in "The Pilgrimage." 26 episodes. 600m; DVD. **C:** Martin Milner; Kent McCord; William Boyett. **A:** Jr. High-Adult. **P:** Entertainment. **U:** Home. **Mov-Ent:** Drama, Television Series. **Acq:** Purchase. **Dist:** Shout! Factory. $34.99.

Adam-12: Season 4 1971 (Unrated)
NBC 1968-75 crime drama. Officers Pete Malloy (Milner) and Jim Reed (McCord) are confronted with anti-Semitic criminals, assassins, hallucinating drunks, and more on the gritty streets of L.A. Mallory goes missing during a pursuit in Griffith Park in "The Search," a clergyman helps catch a dope dealer in "The Grandmothers," Reed is faced with an "Ambush" while transporting a witness, an actor abducts a stewardess in "Sub-Station," and "Truant" youths are responsible for a serious of thefts. 24 episodes. 540m; DVD. **C:** Martin Milner; Jim Reed; William Boyette; Fred Stromsoe. **A:** Jr. High-Adult. **P:** Entertainment. **U:** Home. **Mov-Ent:** Drama, Television Series. **Acq:** Purchase. **Dist:** Shout! Factory. $34.99.

Adam-12: Season 1 2005 (Unrated)
Features the debut season of the 1968-1975 L.A. TV police drama by creator Jack Webb. When veteran officer Pete Malloy's (Milner) young partner is killed while on duty he considers resigning but ends up getting a new partner, rookie Jim Reed (McCord) to join him in police cruiser dubbed "Adam-12." Known for giving a realistic portrayal of a tamer L.A.P.D. in that era, it included topics such as drug abuse, high-speed chases, murder cases, robbery, student riots, and domestic violence along with lighter subjects including an overwhelmed babysitter and assisting an older man who they find trying to walk to his South Dakota home. 26 episodes. 647m; DVD. **C:** Martin Milner; Kent McCord. **A:** Family. **P:** Entertainment. **U:** Home. **Mov-Ent:** Television Series, Action-Adventure. **Acq:** Purchase. **Dist:** Universal Studios Home Video. $39.98.

Adam's Apples 2005 (R) — ★★
Danish black comedy about a Neo-Nazi forced to finish a prison sentence doing community service at a church. Adam (Thomsen) is EVIL and meets his opposite in the positive-to-a-fault priest Ivan (Mikkelsen). Adam promises Ivan that he'll make a pie from the apples that grow in the churchyard, but as crows and disease peck away at the apples, Adam decides to break Ivan down, mentally and physically. Alternately bleak and ludicrous, the movie is mostly style over substance and rarely digs deeper than the basic absurdity of its premise. 93m; DVD. **C:** Ulrich Thomsen; Mads Mikkelsen; Paprika Steen; Nikolaj Lie Kaas; Nicolas Bro; Ali Kazim; Ole Thestrup; Directed by Anders Thomas Jensen; Written by Anders Thomas Jensen; Cinematography by Sebastian Blenkov; Music by Jeppe Kaas. **Pr:** Tivi Magnusson; Mie Andeasen; M&M Film Productions, Ltd; Nordisk; Outsider Pictures. **A:** College-Adult. **P:** Entertainment. **U:** Home. **L:** Danish. **Mov-Ent:** Comedy--Black, Religion, Forests & Trees. **Acq:** Purchase. **Dist:** Film Movement.

The Adams Chronicles 1976
The drama and proud history of the Adams family which covered the pre-Revolutionary War period through the Industrial Revolution. The six years of research and six million dollars that went into the series is well evidenced in its superb authenticity and detail. 60m; VHS, 3/4 U. **Pr:** WNET New York. **A:** Family. **P:** Education. **U:** Institution, SURA. **Gen-Edu:** History--U.S. **Acq:** Purchase. **Dist:** Home Vision Cinema.
Indiv. Titles: 1. John Adams: Lawyer (1758-1770) 2. John Adams: Revolutionary (1770-1776) 3. John Adams: Diplomat (1776-1783) 4. John Adams: Minister to Great Britain (1784-1787) 5. John Adams: Vice President (1788-1796) 6. John Adams: President (1797-1801) 7. John Quincy Adams: Diplomat (1809-1815) 8. John Quincy Adams: Secretary of State (1817-1825) 9. John Quincy Adams: President (1825-1829) 10. John Quincy Adams: Congressman (1830-1848) 11. Charles Francis Adams: Minister to Great Britain (1861-1863) 12. Henry Adams: Historian (1870-1885) 13. Charles Francis Adams II: Industrialist (1886-1893).

Adam's Mark 1994
Five male college students discuss issues of relationships, violence, sexuality, male bonding, rape, parents, fear of failure, and what it means to be a man. 45m; VHS. **A:** Adult. **P:** Education. **U:** Institution. **Gen-Edu:** Sociology. **Acq:** Purchase. **Dist:** RMI Media. $89.95.

Adam's Rib 1950 (Unrated) — ★★★★
Classic war between the sexes cast Tracy and Hepburn as married attorneys on opposite sides of the courtroom in the trial of blonde bombshell Holliday, charged with attempted murder of the lover of her philandering husband. The battle in the courtroom soon takes its toll at home as the couple is increasingly unable to leave their work at the office. Sharp, snappy dialogue by Gordon and Kanin with superb direction by Cukor. Perhaps the best of the nine movies pairing Tracy and Hepburn. Also available colorized. 101m/B/W; VHS, DVD. **C:** Spencer Tracy; Katharine Hepburn; Judy Holliday; Tom Ewell; David Wayne; Jean Hagen; Hope Emerson; Polly Moran; Marvin Kaplan; Paula Raymond; Tommy Noonan; Directed by George Cukor; Written by Garson Kanin; Ruth Gordon; Cinematography by George J. Folsey; Music by Miklos Rozsa. **Pr:** MGM. **A:** Family. **P:** Entertainment. **U:** Home. **Mov-Ent:** Comedy--Romantic, Classic Films, Law. **Awds:** Natl. Film Reg. '92. **Acq:** Purchase. **Dist:** MGM Home Entertainment; Home Vision Cinema. $19.95.

Adam's Rib 1992 (Unrated) — ★★★
Set in the waning days of Communism, three generations of Soviet women share a drab big-city apartment in a comedy of love and family. A twice-divorced museum guide cares for her bedridden mother and her two daughters while embarking on an affair with a shy suitor. Meanwhile, her older daughter is having an affair with her married boss and her cynical 15-year-old is pregnant by an ex-boyfriend. All the men, past and present, show up to celebrate the grandmother's birthday bringing the film to its poignant conclusion. Based on the novel "House of Young Women" by Anatole Kourtchatkine. In Russian with English subtitles. 77m; VHS. **C:** Inna Churikova; Svetlana Ryabova; Maria Golubkina; Directed by Vyacheslav Krishtofovich. **Pr:** October Productions. **A:** College-Adult. **P:** Entertainment. **U:** Home. **L:** Russian. **Mov-Ent:** Comedy-Drama, Family, Women. **Acq:** Purchase. **Dist:** Wellspring Media. $89.98.

Adam's Woman 1970 (Unrated) — ★★½
In the 1840s, American sailor Adam (Bridges) is falsely convicted of a crime while on shore leave in Liverpool and is transported to an outback Australian penal colony. He's recaptured after escaping with brutal inmate Dyson (Booth) and offered a chance by reform-minded governor Sir Philip (Mills) to marry fellow prisoner Bess (Merrow) and start a new settlement. However, Dyson and his band of marauders comes calling. 116m; DVD. **C:** Beau Bridges; Jane Merrow; James Booth; John Mills; Andrew Keir; Peter O'Shaughnessy; Tracy Reed; Directed by Philip Leacock; Written by Richard Fielder; Cinematography by Wilmer C. Butler; Music by Bob Young. **A:** Sr. High-Adult. **P:** Entertainment. **U:** Home. **Mov-Ent:** Australia, Agriculture. **Acq:** Purchase. **Dist:** WarnerArchive.com.

Adam's World 19??
Feminist theologian Elizabeth Dodson offers information on the global environmental threats in terms of the patriarchal system built by our society. 19m; VHS. **A:** Jr. High-Adult. **P:** Education. **U:** Institution. **Gen-Edu:** Ecology & Environment. **Acq:** Purchase, Rent/Lease. **Dist:** National Film Board of Canada. $195.

Adaptation 2002 (R) — ★★★½
Quirky but highly entertaining comedy about blocked L.A. screenwriter Charlie Kaufman (Cage), hired to adapt author Susan Orlean's (Streep) book "The Orchid Thief." The book recounts the story of John Laroche (Cooper), one of a breed of orchid-obsessed con men who schemes to steal the desirable plants from the Florida Everglades. At a loss as to how to treat the story, the neurotic Charlie becomes obsessed with Orlean, gazing at her picture while his lesser twin brother Donald (also Cage), breezily announces the sales of his own million dollar screenplay, which he wrote after one seminar. Meanwhile, Orlean travels to Florida to interview the gap-toothed Laroche and begins her own minor obsession. Plot twists keep you on your toes right down to the surprise ending. Cage is at his best as the twin writers, while Streep shows off her comic chops and Cooper turns in a career-making performance. Deftly directed by Jonze. 114m; VHS, DVD, CC. **C:** Nicolas Cage; Meryl Streep; Chris Cooper; Tilda Swinton; Cara Seymour; Brian Cox; Judy Greer; Maggie Gyllenhaal; Ron Livingston; Stephen Tobolowsky; Jay Tavare; Litefoot; Gary Farmer; Peter Jason; Curtis Hanson; Directed by Spike Jonze; Written by Charlie Kaufman; Cinematography by Lance Acord; Music by Carter Burwell. **Pr:** Edward Saxon; Jonathan Demme; Vincent Landay; Intermedia Films; Clinica Estetico; Magnet; Columbia Pictures. **A:** Sr. High-Adult. **P:** Entertainment. **U:** Home. **Mov-Ent:** Flowers. **Awds:** Oscars '02: Support. Actor (Cooper); British Acad. '02: Adapt. Screenplay; Golden Globes '03: Support. Actor (Cooper), Support. Actress (Streep); L.A. Film Critics '02: Support. Actor (Cooper); Natl. Bd. of Review '02: Screenplay, Support. Actor (Cooper); N.Y. Film Critics '02: Screenplay. **Acq:** Purchase. **Dist:** Sony Pictures Home Entertainment Inc.

Adaptations of Animals: Second Edition 1989
The relationship between an animal's body structure and habits and its environment is explained to younger children. 14m; VHS, 8 mm, 3/4 U. **TV Std:** NTSC, PAL, SECAM. **Pr:** Mike Carlson; Coronet Films. **A:** Primary-Jr. High. **P:** Education. **U:** Institution, CCTV, SURA. **Gen-Edu:** Animals. **Acq:** Purchase, Rent/Lease, Duplication License. **Dist:** Phoenix Learning Group. $250.00.

Adaptations of Plants and Animals 1988
Examples illustrate the adaptations of living things to environment for food getting and for protection, in this video. 13m; VHS, 3/4 U. **Pr:** Coronet Films. **A:** Jr. High-Adult. **P:** Education. **U:** Institution, SURA. **Hea-Sci:** Science, Ecology & Environment. **Acq:** Purchase, Rent/Lease. **Dist:** Phoenix Learning Group. $220.00.

Adaptations of Plants: Second Edition 1989
All plants are different, and their differences are related to the environment each must live in. This video explains this differentiation to younger viewers. 14m; VHS, 8 mm, 3/4 U. **TV Std:** NTSC, PAL, SECAM. **Pr:** Mike Carlson; Coronet Films. **A:** Primary-Jr. High. **P:** Education. **U:** Institution, CCTV, SURA. **Gen-Edu:** Plants. **Acq:** Purchase, Rent/Lease, Duplication License. **Dist:** Phoenix Learning Group. $250.00.

Adaptations to Ocean Environments 1970
This show explores the adaptations that are found in animals that live in the open ocean, on the sandy ocean floor, and on the rocky reefs. 11m; VHS, 3/4 U; Open Captioned. **Pr:** Michael DeLeau and Associates. **A:** Sr. High-College. **P:** Education. **U:** Institution, SURA. **Hea-Sci:** Oceanography. **Acq:** Purchase. **Dist:** Phoenix Learning Group.

Adapting Successfully to Parkinson's Disease 1982
Parkinson's patients and their families are given information and encouragement to adapt to the effects of the disease. 30m; VHS, 3/4 U. **Pr:** Good Samaritan Hospital. **A:** Family. **P:** Education. **U:** Institution, CCTV, Home. **Hea-Sci:** Diseases. **Acq:** Purchase, Rent/Lease. **Dist:** Good Samaritan Hospital & Medical Center.

Adapting to Parenthood 1976
The program follows a young couple as they adjust to the arrival of their baby. As the viewer observes early morning feedings, rushed breakfast conversations, frayed nerves and tension, along with the exhilaration, he gets a sense of what parenting really is. 16m; VHS, 3/4 U. **Pr:** Alvin Fiering; Altschul Group. **A:** Sr. High-Adult. **P:** Education. **U:** Institution. **Gen-Edu:** Parenting, Infants. **Acq:** Purchase, Rent/Lease. **Dist:** Polymorph Films, Inc.; Discovery Education. $99.00.

Adapting Topeng: The Masked Theater of Bali 1980
Producer/director John Emigh explains his methods of mask training and improvisation in his work. 46m; VHS. **A:** Adult. **P:** Education. **U:** Institution. **Fin-Art:** Theater. **Acq:** Purchase. **Dist:** Insight Media. $160.00.

Adaptive Radiation: The Mollusks 1961
Illustrates the principle of adaptive radiation and shows how the typical molluscan characteristics are modified in each of the six classes. 18m; VHS, 3/4 U. **Pr:** Encyclopedia Britannica Educational Corporation. **A:** Sr. High-College. **P:** Education. **U:** Institution, SURA. **L:** English, Spanish. **Hea-Sci:** Animals. **Acq:** Purchase, Rent/Lease, Trade-in. **Dist:** Encyclopedia Britannica.

Add and Mabel's Punkin Center 1986
A look at an elderly couple in Punkin Center, a Midwestern community of Indiana, who talk of their recollections of American life during the early part of the 20th century. 16m; 3/4 U. **Pr:** Richard Kane; Dillon Bustin. **A:** Family. **P:** Entertainment. **U:** Institution, SURA. **Gen-Edu:** Documentary Films, History--U.S. **Acq:** Purchase. **Dist:** Documentary Educational Resources.

The Addams Family 1964
The positively ooky family, based on the characters created by cartoonist Charles Addams, appear in the original, uncut television episodes. Two episodes per tape. This volume includes "The Addams Family Goes to School" and "Morticia and the Psychiatrist." 50m/B/W; VHS. **C:** John Astin; Carolyn Jones; Jackie Coogan; Ted Cassidy; Blossom Rock; Ken Weatherwax; Lisa Loring; Felix Silla. **Pr:** Filmways Pictures. **A:** Family. **P:** Entertainment. **U:** Home. **Mov-Ent:** Television Series. **Acq:** Purchase. **Dist:** Movies Unlimited. $9.95.

The Addams Family 1991 (PG-13) — ★★½
Everybody's favorite family of ghouls hits the big screen, but something is lost in the translation. An imposter claiming to be long-lost Uncle Fester (Lloyd), who says he was in the Bermuda Triangle for 25 years, shows up at the Addams' home to complete a dastardly deed—raid the family's immense fortune. Although Fester's plan is foiled, a series of plot twists highlight the ghoulish family's eccentricities. Darkly humorous but eventually disappointing: Julia, Huston, and Ricci (as Gomez, Morticia, and Wednesday, respectively) are great in their roles and the sets look good, but the plot is thin. Much closer to the original comic strip by Charles Addams than the popular TV show ever was. 102m; VHS, DVD, Blu-Ray, Wide, CC. **C:** Anjelica Huston; Raul Julia; Christopher Lloyd; Dan Hedaya; Elizabeth Wilson; Judith Malina; Carel Struycken; Dana Ivey; Paul Benedict; Christina Ricci; Jimmy Workman; Christopher Hart; John Franklin; Cameo(s) Marc Shaiman; Directed by Barry Sonnenfeld; Written by Caroline Thompson; Larry Thompson; Cinematography by Owen Roizman; Music by Marc Shaiman. **Pr:** Scott Rudin; Graham Place. **A:** Jr. High-Adult. **P:** Entertainment. **U:** Home. **Mov-Ent:** Comedy--Black. **Awds:** Golden Raspberries '91: Worst Song ("Addams Groove"). **Acq:** Purchase. **Dist:** Paramount Pictures Corp. $14.95.

The Addams Family: At Sea 1973
Their fellow sailors aren't very fond of our strange family—until they help capture some crooks. 30m; VHS. **Pr:** Hanna-Barbera Productions. **A:** Family. **P:** Entertainment. **U:** Home. **Chl-Juv:** Animation & Cartoons. **Acq:** Purchase. **Dist:** Turner Broadcasting System Inc. $9.98.

The Addams Family: Circus Story 1974
The Addams' become involved in a high-flying circus adventure in this episode from the animated TV series. 30m; VHS. **C:** Voice(s) by Ted Cassidy; Jackie Coogan; Jodie Foster; Janet Waldo; Lennie Weinrib. **Pr:** Hanna-Barbera Productions. **A:** Family. **P:** Entertainment. **U:** Home. **Chl-Juv:** Animation & Cartoons. **Acq:** Purchase. **Dist:** Turner Broadcasting System Inc. $9.95.

The Addams Family: Complete Series 1964
The creepy, kooky Addams family look to fit into regular American suburban life despite their altogether ooky ways. 64 shows on 9 discs plus loads of bonus material. 1758m; DVD. **C:** Carolyn Jones; John Astin; Ted Cassidy; Jackie Coogan; Ken Weatherwax; Lisa Loring; Marie Blake. **A:** Family. **P:** Entertainment. **U:** Home. **Mov-Ent:** Horror. **Acq:** Purchase. **Dist:** Fox Home Entertainment.

The Addams Family: Ghost Town 1974
In these animated adventures with Charles Addams' ghoulish but lovable family, Gomez, Morticia, and the gang travel around the country in their creepy camper, a castle-like construction complete with bats, moat, and a thundercloud. Ted Cassidy and Jackie Coogan were the only cast members from the live-action series to recreate their character's voices (Lurch and Uncle Fester respectively) while the voice of Pugsley is provided by none other than pre-"Taxi Driver" Jodie Foster! Episodes here are "Ghost Town," "Addams Go West," "Follow that Loaf of Bread," and "The Fastest Creepy Camper in the West." 90m; VHS. **C:** Voice(s) by Ted Cassidy; Jackie Coogan; Jodie Foster; Janet Waldo; Lennie Weinrib. **Pr:** Hanna-Barbera Productions. **A:** Family. **P:** Entertainment. **U:** Home. **Chl-Juv:** Animation & Cartoons. **Acq:** Purchase. **Dist:** Turner Broadcasting System Inc. $29.95.

The Addams Family: Kentucky Derby 1973
Pugsley's birthday present is a worn-out old horse but with Grandma's help they enter him in the Kentucky Derby. 30m; VHS. **Pr:** Hanna-Barbera Productions. **A:** Family. **P:** Entertainment. **U:** Home. **Chl-Juv:** Animation & Cartoons. **Acq:** Purchase. **Dist:** Turner Broadcasting System Inc. $9.98.

The Addams Family: Left in the Lurch 1974
More episodes from the '70s cartoon version of the hit series. Episodes are "Left in the Lurch," "The Mardi Gras Story," "The Voodoo Story" and "Aloha Hoolamagoola." 90m; VHS. **C:** Voice(s) by Ted Cassidy; Jackie Coogan; Jodie Foster; Janet Waldo; Lennie Weinrib. **Pr:** Hanna-Barbera Productions. **A:** Family. **P:** Entertainment. **U:** Home. **Chl-Juv:** Animation & Cartoons, Comedy--Black, Family Viewing. **Acq:** Purchase. **Dist:** Turner Broadcasting System Inc. $29.95.

Addams Family Reunion 1998 (PG) — Bomb!
The Addams family decides to hold a reunion in order to cure Grandma and Grandpa Addams of turning 'normal.' Of course, there's a mix-up and they must interact with mainstream society. Hilarity does not ensue. Worse than "Addams Family Values" and led to a bad syndicated revival series. 90m; VHS. **C:** Daryl Hannah; Tim Curry; Ed Begley, Jr.; Ray Walston; Kevin McCarthy; Estelle Harris; Alice Ghostley; Carel Struycken; Patrick Thomas; Directed by Dave Payne; Cinematography by Christian Sebaldt; Music by Amotz Plessner. **Pr:** Saban Entertainment. **A:** Primary-Adult. **P:** Entertainment. **U:** Home. **Mov-Ent:** Acq: Purchase. **Dist:** Warner Home Video, Inc.

The Addams Family: The Addams Family in New York 1974
In this episode from the cartoon series, Gomez sets out to prove to the NYPD that he is the actual owner of Central Park. 30m; VHS. **C:** Voice(s) by Ted Cassidy; Jackie Coogan; Jodie Foster; Janet Waldo; Lennie Weinrib. **Pr:** Hanna-Barbera Productions. **A:** Family. **P:** Entertainment. **U:** Home. **Chl-Juv:** Animation & Cartoons. **Acq:** Purchase. **Dist:** Turner Broadcasting System Inc. $9.95.

The Addams Family: The Animated Series 1973
Hanna-Barbera animated series, shown on NBC, that was based on the Charles Addams' characters. The spooky Addams family takes off in their customized RV for a series of cross-country misadventures. 16 episodes. 480m; DVD. **A:** Family. **P:** Entertainment. **U:** Home. **L:** English. **Chl-Juv:** Animation & Cartoons, Television Series. **Acq:** Purchase. **Dist:** WarnerArchive.com. $35.99.

The Addams Family: The Reluctant Astronauts 1973
When eccentric Uncle Fester wins some land on the moon he insists the family launch their own rocketship in order to visit their new property. 30m; VHS. **Pr:** Hanna-Barbera Productions. **A:** Family. **P:** Entertainment. **U:** Home. **Chl-Juv:** Animation & Cartoons. **Acq:** Purchase. **Dist:** Turner Broadcasting System Inc. $9.98.

The Addams Family: The Roller Derby Story 1973
Wednesday's birthday party is interrupted by the family's competing in a roller derby battle. 30m; VHS. **Pr:** Hanna-Barbera Productions. **A:** Family. **P:** Entertainment. **U:** Home. **Chl-Juv:** Animation & Cartoons. **Acq:** Purchase. **Dist:** Turner Broadcasting System Inc. $9.98.

Addams Family Values 1993 (PG-13) — ★★½
The creepy Addams' are back, but this time they leave the dark confines of the mansion to meet the "real" world. New baby Pubert causes homicidal jealousy in sibs Wednesday and Pugsley, causing Mom and Dad to hire a gold-digging, serial-killing nanny (Cusack) with designs on Uncle Fester to watch over the tot. A step above its predecessor, chock full of black humor, sub-plots, and one-liners. Cusack fits right in with an outrageously over the top performance and Ricci nearly steals the show again as the deadpan Wednesday. 93m; VHS, DVD, Wide, CC. **C:** Anjelica Huston; Raul Julia; Christopher Lloyd; Joan Cusack; Carol Kane; Christina Ricci; Jimmy Workman; Kaitlyn Hooper; Kristen Hooper; Carel Struycken; David Krumholtz; Christopher Hart; Dana Ivey; Peter MacNichol; Christine Baranski; Mercedes McNab; Directed by Barry Sonnenfeld; Written by Paul Rudnick; Music by Marc Shaiman. **Pr:** Scott Rudin; David Nicksay; Paramount Pictures. **A:** Jr. High-Adult. **P:** Entertainment. **U:** Home. **Mov-Ent:** Comedy--Black, Camps & Camping, Parenting. **Awds:** Golden Raspberries '93:

Worst Song ("WHOOMP! There It Is"). **Acq:** Purchase. **Dist:** Paramount Pictures Corp. $19.95.

The Addams Family: Volume 1 2006 (Unrated)
Features the first season of the 1964-1966 TV comedy on the darkly "creepy and kooky" Addams family headed up by patriarch Gomez (Astin) and tight-dress-wearing wife Morticia (Jones) with their two children Pugsley (Weatherwax) and Wednesday (Loring) as well as Uncle Fester (Coogan), Grandmama Addams (Blake), their freakishly tall butler Lurch (Cassidy), a very hairy Cousin Itt and the hand-in-a-box Thing. The peculiar and wealthy clan doesn't realize that their neighbors see them as oddballs. This season includes: the family worries when Pugsley wants to join the Boy Scouts so they take him to a therapist, robbers hide out at their home on Halloween and try to steal from them, Wednesday pretends to run away then really does, the family teaches Lurch how to dance, Uncle Fester gets sick and loses his electrical powers, Gomez gets amnesia and thinks the family wants to kill him for his life insurance, and the city commissioner tries to evict them. Based on the cartoons of Charles Addams. 34 episodes. 572m/B/W; DVD. **C:** John Astin; Carolyn Jones; Ted Cassidy; Jackie Coogan; Ken Weatherwax; Lisa Loring; Marie Blake. **A:** Family. **P:** Entertainment. **U:** Home. **Mov-Ent**: Television Series, Family. **Acq:** Purchase. **Dist:** Fox Home Entertainment. $29.98.

The Addams Family: Volume 2 2006 (Unrated)
Features the second season of the 1964-1966 TV comedy on the "creepy and kooky" Addams family. This season includes: Cousin Itt changes his voice for a play then thinks he's too good for it, Morticia (Jones) and Gomez (Astin) celebrate their thirtieth wedding anniversary by recounting the story of how they met when Gomez was to marry Morticia's sister Ophelia (also Jones), Gomez runs for mayor, Cousin Itt's hair falls out, Morticia tries her hand at writing children's books ("Cinderella, the Teenage Delinquent") leaving Gomez to worry about her possibly rising to fame and leaving him, Gomez goes on a sleepwalking Robin Hood-like stealing binge, the children are bored when Morticia forbids them from going outside on a "dreadfully" sunny day, the children face getting kicked out of school, and Lurch falls in love with an old friend of Morticia's. Based on the cartoons of Charles Addams. 29 episodes. 572m/B/W; DVD. **C:** John Astin; Carolyn Jones; Ted Cassidy; Jackie Coogan; Ken Weatherwax; Lisa Loring; Marie Blake. **A:** Family. **P:** Entertainment. **U:** Home. **Mov-Ent**: Television Series, Family. **Acq:** Purchase. **Dist:** Fox Home Entertainment. $29.98.

The Addict/Stop the Madness 19??
Features comments from Whitney Houston, Kareem Abdul Jabbar, and Arnold Schwarzenegger on the causes and dangers of heroin addiction. Includes statistics and information on peer pressure and parental influence. Filmed on location in Los Angeles and on the Hollywood sound stage where "Stop the Madness" was filmed. ?m; VHS. **C:** Whitney Houston; Kareem Abdul-Jabbar; Arnold Schwarzenegger; Narrated by Tim Reid. **A:** Jr. High-Adult. **P:** Education. **U:** Institution. **Hea-Sci**: Adolescence, Drugs, Drug Abuse. **Acq:** Purchase. **Dist:** CEV Multimedia. $85.00.

Addicted 2002 (Unrated) — ★★
Ho-jin (Eol Lee) and Dae-jin (Byung-hun Lee) are brothers so close that even after Dae-jin marries Eun-su (Mi-yeon Lee), his brother continues to live with them. At least until they both have tragic car accidents on the same day and end up in comas. After a year only Dae-jin awakens, but he goes home to keep the same routine his brother always had. Even weirder he has his brother's skills as a cook, and knows things only Ho-jin would know. 112m; DVD. **C:** Byung-hun Lee; Mi-yeon Lee; Eol Lee; Seon-Yeong Park; Directed by Young-hoon Park; Written by Won-mi Byun; Cinematography by Byeong-il Kim; Music by Jae-hyeong Jeong. **A:** Sr. High-Adult. **P:** Entertainment. **U:** Home. **L:** English, Cantonese, Korean, Mandarin Dialects. **Mov-Ent**: Drama. **Acq:** Purchase. **Dist:** Tai Seng Video Marketing. $14.95.

The Addicted Brain 1989
The changing behavioral patterns of a cocaine-addicted rat are examined. 26m; VHS, 3/4 U. **Pr:** Films for the Humanities. **A:** Jr. High-Adult. **P:** Education. **U:** Institution, SURA. **Hea-Sci**: Drug Abuse, Psychology. **Acq:** Purchase, Rent/Lease. **Dist:** Films for the Humanities & Sciences. $149.00.

Addicted to Black: The Rich Brew of Israeli Society 19??
Looks at the diversity of Israeli society by examining the habits of its coffee drinkers at various establishments. Hebrew with subtitles. 53m; VHS. **A:** College-Adult. **P:** Entertainment. **U:** Home, Institution. **L:** Hebrew. **Gen-Edu**: Food Industry. **Acq:** Purchase. **Dist:** SISU Home Entertainment, Inc.

Addicted to Her Love 2006 (R) — ★½
Boilerplate troubled-teen drama about a working class student obsessed with a rich girl at his private high school where everyone seems to drink, drug, and have casual sex. Jonah (Amedori) works at a pharmacy, which gets him an in with Sara (Caplan) and her spiteful crowd. He becomes a pill supplier but, not surprisingly, the partying gets out of control and there's a tragedy. 98m; DVD. **C:** John Patrick Amedori; Lizzy Caplan; D.J. Cotrona; Jonathan Trent; Jenny Wade; Daryl Hannah; Bruce A. Young; Directed by Elliott Lester; Written by Wesley Strick; Steve Allison; Cinematography by Florian Stadler. **A:** Sr. High-Adult. **P:** Entertainment. **U:** Home. **Mov-Ent**: Adolescence, Drug Trafficking/Dealing. **Acq:** Purchase. **Dist:** Entertainment One US LP.

Addicted to Love 1996 (R) — ★★½
Warning: Do not rent this movie with your significant other if you're thinking about breaking up with them. After they're both dumped, mild-mannered Sam (Broderick) and wild woman Maggie (Ryan) discover they have a lot in common. First of all, their exes Linda (Preston) and Anton (Karyo) are dating each other. Secondly, they're both stalkers! Yep! A romantic comedy about stalking. Sam wants nothing more than to reclaim Linda as his own. Maggie wants nothing less than Anton's head on a plate. Interesting comedy wavers between dark and light moments, aided by the rather murky sets and lighting. Directorial debut for Dunne, who makes his father eat a bug in one scene. 100m; VHS, DVD. **C:** Meg Ryan; Matthew Broderick; Kelly Preston; Tcheky Karyo; Maureen Stapleton; Remak Ramsay; Nesbitt Blaisdell; Dominick Dunne; Directed by Griffin Dunne; Written by Robert Gordon; Cinematography by Andrew Dunn; Music by Rachel Portman. **Pr:** Jeffrey Silver; Robert Newmyer; Bob Weinstein; Harvey Weinstein; Miramax Film Corp; Outlaw Productions; Warner Bros. **A:** Sr. High-Adult. **P:** Entertainment. **U:** Home. **Mov-Ent**: Comedy--Romantic, Photography. **Acq:** Purchase. **Dist:** Warner Home Video, Inc.

Addicted to Murder 1995 — ★★
Joel Winter (McCleery) was abused as a child and now takes his anger out on women by killing them. Then he meets vampire Angie (Graham), who decides to transform him since he's already a predator. But Joel develops a conscience and tries to reform, which ticks Angie off and she frames him for a murder he didn't commit. Which ticks Joel off so he becomes a vampire (and a vampire hunter) to get even. 90m; VHS, DVD. **C:** Michael (Mick) McCleery; Sasha Graham; Laura McLaughlin; Directed by Kevin J. Lindenmuth; Written by Kevin J. Lindenmuth; Cinematography by Kevin J. Lindenmuth. **A:** Sr. High-Adult. **P:** Entertainment. **U:** Home. **Mov-Ent**. **Acq:** Purchase. **Dist:** Brimstone Media Productions.

Addicted to Murder 2: Tainted Blood 1997 (Unrated) — ★½
It's a case of diminishing returns as is usual with sequels in this plotwise mishmash. New York City is the happy hunting grounds for a rogue vamp who's turning others whom Angie (Graham) doesn't considered worthy of getting "The Gift." So she intends to put a stop to it. And just around for more laughs is Joel (McCleery)?the serial killer turned vampire turned vampire hunter. 80m; VHS, DVD. **C:** Sasha Graham; Michael (Mick) McCleery; Sarah K. Lippmann; Robbi Firestone; Ted Grayson; Joe Moretti; Joel D. Wynkoop; Tom NonDorf; Cameo(s) Ted V. Mikels; Directed by Kevin J. Lindenmuth; Written by Kevin J. Lindenmuth. **A:** Sr. High-Adult. **P:** Entertainment. **U:** Home. **Mov-Ent**. **Acq:** Purchase. **Dist:** Brimstone Media Productions.

Addicted to Murder 3: Bloodlust 1999 (Unrated) — ★½
Serial killer Joel Winter (McCleery) continues his quest to eliminate vampires in revenge for his own transformation. One master vamp thinks he has a secure haven but he's very wrong. 85m; VHS, DVD. **C:** Michael (Mick) McCleery; Sarah K. Lippmann; Nick Kostopoulos; Cloud Michaels; Grant Cramer; Frank Lopez; Joe Zaso; Jon Sanborne; Reid Ostrowski; Directed by Kevin J. Lindenmuth; Tom Vollmann; Written by Kevin J. Lindenmuth; Tom Vollmann. **A:** Sr. High-Adult. **P:** Entertainment. **U:** Home. **Mov-Ent**. **Acq:** Purchase. **Dist:** Brimstone Media Productions.

The Addiction 1995 (R) — ★★½
Ph.D. candidate Kathleen Conklin (Taylor, in a haunting performance) gets bitten by more than the philosophy bug while attending university in Manhattan. When attacked by a female vampire (Sciorra), Kathleen quickly becomes driven by a ferocious blood need, beginning with an attack that parallels drug addiction when she stabs a derelict with a hypodermic needle and injects his blood into her own veins. Bitingly pretentious, themes experiment with the philosophy of Kirkegaard, Nietzsche, and Sartre, and exploitative glimpses of the Holocaust and the My Lai massacre attempt to connect Kathleen's struggle to resist evil to historical atrocities. 82m/B/W; VHS. **C:** Lili Taylor; Christopher Walken; Annabella Sciorra; Edie Falco; Paul Calderon; Fredro Starr; Kathryn Erbe; Michael Imperioli; Directed by Abel Ferrara; Written by Nicholas St. John; Cinematography by Ken Kelsch; Music by Joe Delia. **Pr:** Denis Hann; Fernando Sulichin; Preston Holmes; Russell Simmons. **A:** Sr. High-Adult. **P:** Entertainment. **U:** Home. **Mov-Ent**: Horror, Philosophy & Ideology, Religion. **Acq:** Purchase.

Addiction 2007
Brings together experts on drug and alcohol addiction to discuss causes and the latest treatments. 86m; DVD. **A:** Adult. **P:** Education. **U:** Home. **Hea-Sci**: Alcoholism, Drug Abuse, Documentary Films. **Acq:** Purchase. **Dist:** Home Box Office Inc. $19.98.

Addiction and Mental Illness 1994
Discusses the problems and treatments involved with persons battling both substance abuse and mental illness. 27m; VHS, DVD. **A:** Sr. High-Adult. **P:** Education. **U:** Institution. **Hea-Sci**: Health Education, Psychology, Alcoholism. **Acq:** Purchase. **Dist:** Aquarius Health Care Media. $149.00.

Addiction and Responsibility 199?
Francis Seeburger compares the addict and the saint, pointing out that both sacrifice everything to meet their longings and further notes the process of spiritual redemption addicts reach while battling to recover. 90m; DVD. **A:** Adult. **P:** Education. **U:** Home, Institution. **Gen-Edu**: Psychology, Philosophy & Ideology. **Acq:** Purchase. **Dist:** Thinking Allowed Productions. $49.95.

Addiction, Attachment and Spiritual Crisis 199?
Christina Grof testifies about her battle with alcoholism and healing from addictive behavior through spiritual renewal. When we lack spiritual union, it is comparable to a type of psychosis, she explains. 90m; DVD. **A:** Adult. **P:** Education. **U:** Home, Institution. **Gen-Edu**: Psychology, Psychiatry, Religion. **Acq:** Purchase. **Dist:** Thinking Allowed Productions. $49.95.

Addiction: The Problems, the Solutions 1991
Introductory overview of addictive behaviors. Includes interviews with five individuals in their late teens and early twenties who are in recovery. Discusses the genetic aspects and the traits common to all addicts. Geared toward social studies and health students. 30m; VHS. **A:** Sr. High. **P:** Education. **U:** Institution. **Gen-Edu**: Health Education, Adolescence, Drug Abuse. **Acq:** Purchase. **Dist:** Sunburst Digital Inc. $189.00.

Addictive Behavior: It Could Happen to You 1992
Interview format features a number of teens from different backgrounds sharing personal experiences with a variety of addictions, such as chemical, food, sex, physical, etc. Includes guides. 15m; VHS. **A:** Jr. High-Sr. High. **P:** Education. **U:** Institution. **Gen-Edu**: Drug Abuse, Alcoholism, Eating Disorders. **Acq:** Purchase. **Dist:** United Learning Inc. $89.95.

Addictive Personality: Who Uses Drugs and Why? 1979
The emotions and behaviors common to people who become addicts of some sort are studied. 30m; VHS. **Pr:** HRM. **A:** Jr. High-Sr. High. **P:** Education. **U:** Institution. **Hea-Sci**: Drug Abuse, Personality. **Acq:** Purchase. **Dist:** HRM Video. $145.00.

Adding and Subtracting Algebraic Expressions 1991
Defines "like terms" and "polynomials," and provides instruction for and examples of adding and subtracting algebraic expression. 28m; VHS. **A:** Jr. High-Adult. **P:** Education. **U:** Institution. **Gen-Edu**: Mathematics, How-To. **Acq:** Purchase. **Dist:** Film Ideas, Inc. $190.00.

Adding and Subtracting Decimal Fractions 1973
Part of a series that offers instruction in pre-algebra math, covering whole numbers, fractions, decimals, percentages, and signed numbers. 19m; VHS. **A:** Sr. High-Adult. **P:** Education. **U:** Institution. **Gen-Edu**: Mathematics. **Acq:** Purchase. **Dist:** RMI Media. $89.95.

Adding Fractions with Different Denominators 1973
Part of a series that offers instruction in pre-algebra math, covering whole numbers, fractions, decimals, percentages, and signed numbers. 26m; VHS. **A:** Sr. High-Adult. **P:** Education. **U:** Institution. **Gen-Edu**: Mathematics. **Acq:** Purchase. **Dist:** RMI Media. $89.95.

Adding Fractions with Same Denominators 1973
Part of a series that offers instruction in pre-algebra math, covering whole numbers, fractions, decimals, percentages, and signed numbers. 20m; VHS. **A:** Sr. High-Adult. **P:** Education. **U:** Institution. **Gen-Edu**: Mathematics. **Acq:** Purchase. **Dist:** RMI Media. $89.95.

Adding Signed Numbers 1973
Part of a series that offers instruction in pre-algebra math, covering whole numbers, fractions, decimals, percentages, and signed numbers. 25m; VHS. **A:** Sr. High-Adult. **P:** Education. **U:** Institution. **Gen-Edu**: Mathematics. **Acq:** Purchase. **Dist:** RMI Media. $89.95.

Adding to Make Seven 1967
Brilliant colors and lively animation help a young child understand sets and the commutative principle of addition. 10m; VHS, 3/4 U. **Pr:** William Boundey. **A:** Primary. **P:** Education. **U:** Institution, SURA. **L:** English, Spanish. **Chl-Juv**: Mathematics. **Acq:** Purchase. **Dist:** Phoenix Learning Group.

Adding Whole Numbers, Part 1 1973
Part of a series that offers instruction in pre-algebra math, covering whole numbers, fractions, decimals, percentages, and signed numbers. 16m; VHS. **A:** Sr. High-Adult. **P:** Education. **U:** Institution. **Gen-Edu**: Mathematics. **Acq:** Purchase. **Dist:** RMI Media. $89.95.

Adding Whole Numbers, Part 2 1973
Part of a series that offers instruction in pre-algebra math, covering whole numbers, fractions, decimals, percentages, and signed numbers. 17m; VHS. **A:** Sr. High-Adult. **P:** Education. **U:** Institution. **Gen-Edu**: Mathematics. **Acq:** Purchase. **Dist:** RMI Media. $89.95.

Addition and Subtraction Work Together 1991
Demonstrates the correlation between addition and subtraction using an example of two boys shopping and coming up with the correct change for their purchases and learning how to take inventory. Stresses that there is more than one way to solve a math problem. Part of the Math Sense Series. 13m; VHS, SVS, 3/4 U. **A:** Preschool-Primary. **P:** Education. **U:** Institution. **Gen-Edu**: Mathematics. **Acq:** Purchase. **Dist:** Encyclopedia Britannica. $99.00.

Additional Vegetable Techniques 199?
Teaches food industry and kitchen workers the fundamentals of prepping tomatoes, mushrooms, peppers, chiles, asparagus, snow peas and snap peas. Part of the Kitchen Preparation Series. 17m; VHS. **A:** Sr. High-Adult. **P:** Instruction. **U:** Home. **How-Ins**: Cooking, Food Industry, How-To. **Acq:** Purchase. **Dist:** Culinary Institute of America. $75.00.

Address Unknown 1944 (Unrated) — ★★
Martin Schulz (Lukas) and Max Eisenstein (Carnovsky) are German immigrants working as art dealers in San Francisco. Their long friendship tears apart when Martin returns to Germany and is swayed by Nazi propaganda, which causes a series of family tragedies. The title isn't explained until the end of the movie. 75m/B/W; DVD. **C:** Paul Lukas; Morris Carnovsky; K.T. Stevens; Mady Christians; Peter Van Eyck; Carl Esmond; Directed by William Cameron Menzies; Written by Herbert

Dalmas; Kressman Taylor; Cinematography by Rudolph Mate; Music by Ernst Toch. **A:** Sr. High-Adult. **P:** Entertainment. **U:** Home. **Mov-Ent**: Judaism, Germany. **Acq:** Purchase. **Dist:** Sony Pictures Home Entertainment Inc.

Address Unknown 1996 (PG) — ★★½
A ten-year-old letter and a priceless stamp provide a teenager with clues to dad's mysterious death. 92m; VHS, DVD. **C:** Kyle Howard; Johna Stewart; Patrick Renna; Corbin Allred; Michael Flynn; Directed by Shawn Levy. **Pr:** Leucadia Film Corporation. **A:** Jr. High-Adult. **P:** Entertainment. **U:** Home. **Mov-Ent**: Mystery & Suspense, Adolescence. **Acq:** Purchase. **Dist:** Feature Films for Family.

Addressing Economic Inequality in Marriage 1995
Counseling sessions address financial issues married people face. 29m; VHS. **A:** Adult. **P:** Professional. **U:** Institution. **Hea-Sci**: Psychology, Marriage. **Acq:** Purchase. **Dist:** Guilford Publications, Inc. $29.95.

Adelaide Village 1974
A tribute to the people and life of Adelaide Village in the Bahamas, depicted by the pastel sketches of Montreal artist Pierre L'Amare. 15m; VHS, 3/4 U. **Pr:** National Film Board of Canada. **A:** Jr. High-Adult. **P:** Education. **U:** Institution, SURA. **Fin-Art**: Drawing. **Acq:** Purchase. **Dist:** Phoenix Learning Group.

Adelante Mujeres! The History of Mexican-American/Chicana Women 1992
A look at Mexican-American/Chicana women from the Spanish Conquest through the 1990s. Comes with teacher's guide. 25m; VHS. **A:** Jr. High-Adult. **P:** Education. **U:** Institution. **Gen-Edu**: Women, History. **Acq:** Purchase, Rent/Lease. **Dist:** National Women's History Project; Women Make Movies. $69.50.

Adelheid 1969 (Unrated) — ★★
Viktor, a Czech soldier, returns home after WWII and is told to inventory the contents of a mansion that was owned by a wealthy German family. Adelheid, the daughter of the previous owner, is now a servant there and though Viktor falls in love, the lingering bitterness of the war ruins the romance. Czech with subtitles. 99m; DVD. **C:** Petr Cepek; Emma Cerna; Directed by Frantisek Vlacil; Written by Frantisek Vlacil; Vladmir Korner; Cinematography by Frantisek Uldrich; Music by Zdenek Liska. **A:** College-Adult. **P:** Entertainment. **U:** Home. **L:** Czech. **Mov-Ent**: Drama. **Acq:** Purchase. **Dist:** Facets Multimedia Inc.

Adenauer: Germany Reborn 1980
In 1917, Konrad Adenauer become Mayor of Koeln (Cologne). In 1949, he was elected Chancellor of the Federal Republic and presided over difficult rebuilding years in Germany. Part of the "Portraits of Power" series. 24m/B/W; VHS, 3/4 U. **A:** Sr. High-Adult. **P:** Education. **U:** Institution, SURA. **Gen-Edu**: History--Modern, Germany. **Acq:** Purchase, Rent/Lease. **Dist:** Phoenix Learning Group.

ADHD in the Classroom 1994
Aides teachers on how to deal with children suffering with Attention Deficit Hyperactivity Disorder in their classroom. Encourages and shows teachers how they can create a positive learning atmosphere for all students. 40m; VHS. **Pr:** Guilford Publication, Inc. **A:** College-Adult. **P:** Professional. **U:** Institution. **Gen-Edu**: Children, Education. **Acq:** Purchase. **Dist:** Guilford Publications, Inc. $95.00.

ADHD: What Can We Do? 1993
Demonstrates parent-training methods and effective strategies for managing ADHD. Includes interviews with parents and teachers. Companion to "ADHD-What Do We Know?" 36m; VHS. **A:** Adult. **P:** Education. **U:** Institution, Home. **Hea-Sci**: Health Education, Mental Health, Handicapped. **Acq:** Purchase, Rent/Lease. **Dist:** Fanlight Productions; Childswork/Childsplay L.L.C.; Guilford Publications, Inc. $75.00.

ADHD: What Do We Know? 1993
Russell A. Barkley, Professor of Psychiatry and Neurolgy and founder of the Center for ADHD at the University of Massachusetts Medical Center, combines scientific information with the true stories of those struggling with ADHD. Outlines the consequences of ADHD on the families, schools, and young people it affects. Companion to "ADHD—What Can We Do?" 37m; VHS. **A:** Adult. **P:** Education. **U:** Home, Institution. **Hea-Sci**: Health Education, Mental Health, Handicapped. **Acq:** Purchase, Rent/Lease. **Dist:** Fanlight Productions; Childswork/Childsplay L.L.C.; Guilford Publications, Inc. $75.00.

Adio Kerida 2002
Anthropologist Ruth Behar returns to her roots in Cuba and chronicles her family's journey to the United States as Cuban-Jewish exiles. Discusses interfaith marriages, the country's Jewish community, and the embargo on contemporary Cuban-Sephardic cultural identity. Subtitled. 82m; VHS. **A:** Adult. **P:** Education. **U:** Institution. **Gen-Edu**: South America, Judaism, Women. **Acq:** Purchase, Rent/Lease. **Dist:** Women Make Movies. $295.00.

Adios Amigo 1975 (PG) — ★★
Offbeat western comedy has ad-libbing Pryor hustling as a perennially inept con man. Script and direction (both provided by Williamson) are not up to Pryor's level, although excessive violence and vulgarity are avoided in a boring attempt to provide good clean family fare. 87m; VHS, DVD. **C:** Fred Williamson; Richard Pryor; Thalmus Rasulala; James Brown; Robert Phillips; Mike Henry; Directed by Fred Williamson; Written by Fred Williamson. **Pr:** Fred Williamson; Fred Williamson; Atlas International. **A:** Jr. High-Adult. **P:** Entertainment. **U:** Home. **Mov-Ent**. **Acq:** Purchase. **Dist:** CinemaNow Inc. $9.95.

Adios Gringo 1965 — ★½
Routine oater in which a young rancher is swindled in a cattle deal and forced to kill in self defense. 98m; VHS, Blu-Ray. **C:** Giuliano Gemma; Evelyn Stewart; Directed by Giorgio Stegani. **A:** Jr. High-Adult. **P:** Entertainment. **U:** Home. **Mov-Ent**. **Acq:** Purchase. **Dist:** Sinister Cinema. $16.95.

Adios, Hombre 1968 (Unrated) — ★
An innocent man who was imprisoned for murder escapes from prison and seeks revenge. You'll be saying adios as well. 90m; VHS. **C:** Craig Hill; Giulia Rubini; Directed by Mario Caiano. **A:** Jr. High-Adult. **P:** Entertainment. **U:** Home. **Mov-Ent**. **Acq:** Purchase. **Dist:** $49.95.

Adios, Sabata 1971 (PG-13) — ★½
Brynner took over the role for one sequel. In 1873, Sabata comes to the aid of a band of Mexican revolutionaries who want to steal a wagonload of gold from sadistic Austrian interloper, Colonel Von Skimmel. 102m; DVD. **C:** Yul Brynner; Pedro Sanchez; Gerard Herter; Dean Reed; Sal Borgese; Franco Fantasia; Directed by Gianfranco Parolini; Written by Gianfranco Parolini; Renato Izzo; Cinematography by Sandro Moncori; Music by Bruno Nicolai. **A:** Jr. High-Adult. **P:** Entertainment. **U:** Home. **Mov-Ent**: Mexico. **Acq:** Purchase. **Dist:** MGM Home Entertainment.

The Adirondacks 1987
A visually striking portrait of the Adirondack Park of New York State, the largest wilderness area in the Eastern United States. 30m; VHS, 3/4 U. **Pr:** Lawrence Hott and Diane Garey. **A:** Jr. High-Adult. **P:** Education. **U:** Institution, SURA. **Gen-Edu**: National Parks & Reserves. **Acq:** Purchase, Rent/Lease. **Dist:** Direct Cinema Ltd. $195.00.

Adjectives and Adverbs: Trim and Decoration 1991
Part of a series that offers instruction on specific aspects of basic English grammar skills. 18m; VHS. **A:** Adult. **P:** Education. **U:** Institution. **Gen-Edu**: Communication, Language Arts. **Acq:** Purchase. **Dist:** RMI Media. $50.00.

Adjust Your Set: The Static Is Real 19??
Addresses the issues that exist between men and women on the subject of sexual harassment. Contains vignettes on emotional manipulation, subtle threats of violence, heterosexism, feminist backlash in the classroom, harassment of disabled women, and battering in heterosexual relationships. Written and presented by students. ?m; VHS. **Pr:** University of Toronto. **A:** Sr. High-Adult. **P:** Education. **U:** Institution. **Bus-Ind**: Sexual Abuse, Violence, Education. **Acq:** Purchase. **Dist:** University of Toronto. $79.95.

The Adjuster 1991 (R) — ★★½
Critics either loved or hated this strange film. Insurance adjuster Noah Render's clients look to him for all sorts of comfort, so much so that his own identity becomes a blurred reflection of their tragedies. Wife Hera is a film censor who secretly tapes the pornographic videos she watches at work. Their carefully organized lives are invaded by Bubba and Mimi, a wealthy couple who pass themselves off as filmmakers who want to use the Render house as a movie set. They are instead looking to involve the Renders in their latest and most elaborate erotic fantasy. Lots of symbolism, but little substance. 102m; VHS, DVD, Wide. **C:** Elias Koteas; Arsinee Khanjian; Maury Chaykin; Gabrielle Rose; David Hemblen; Jennifer Dale; Don McKellar; Raoul Trujillo; Directed by Atom Egoyan; Written by Atom Egoyan; Cinematography by Paul Sarossy; Music by Mychael Danna. **Pr:** Orion Pictures. **A:** College-Adult. **P:** Entertainment. **U:** Home. **Mov-Ent**: Insurance, Marriage, Filmmaking. **Awds:** Toronto-City '91: Canadian Feature Film. **Acq:** Purchase. **Dist:** MGM Studios Inc. $79.98.

Adjusting Caster: Hunter 57 1988
Offers instruction on specific aspects of automotive maintenance and repair. 3m; VHS. **A:** Adult. **P:** Instruction. **U:** Institution. **How-Ins**: Automobiles. **Acq:** Purchase. **Dist:** RMI Media. $29.95.

Adjusting to Aging 1981
This series discusses specific physical, emotional, mental and financial changes that occur with aging. 50m; 3/4 U. **Pr:** Good Samaritan Hospital. **A:** Adult. **P:** Education. **U:** Institution, CCTV. **Hea-Sci**: Aging. **Acq:** Purchase, Rent/Lease. **Dist:** Good Samaritan Hospital & Medical Center.
Indiv. Titles: 1. Aging: Easing the Transition 2. Preventing and Managing Medical Aspects of Aging 3. Cognitive and Mental Adjustments to Aging 4. Vocational and Financial Aspects of Aging 5. Adjusting to Aging Profile.

Adjusting Your Multiple Defensive System to Win! 2004 (Unrated)
Coach Bill Tierney discusses defensive theory for the game of lacrosse, and how to adjust your defense to newer offensive systems. 41m; DVD. **A:** Family. **P:** Education. **U:** Home, Institution. **Spo-Rec**: Lacrosse, Athletic Instruction/Coaching. **Acq:** Purchase. **Dist:** Championship Productions. $39.99.

Adjustment & Work 1986
Documentary takes a look at the E. H. Gentry Technical Facility, which provides evaluation and personal adjustment services to impaired individuals and also functions as a vocational training center. Also examined is the Alabama Industries for the Blind, the second largest employer of blind people in the U.S. 120m; VHS. **A:** Sr. High-Adult. **P:** Entertainment. **U:** Home, Institution. **Gen-Edu**: Documentary Films, Handicapped, Education. **Acq:** Purchase, Rent/Lease. **Dist:** Zipporah Films. $350.00.

The Adjustment Bureau 2011 (PG-13) — ★★½
Big Brother IS watching. The movie, loosely based on a 1954 story by Philip K. Dick, who didn't include the love story that's really the heart of Nolfi's sci-fi/romance/thriller. David Norris (Damon) has just lost his senatorial bid when he meets ballet dancer Elise (Blunt) and they discover an instant rapport. Then fate, literally in the form of guys wearing suits and fedoras, strives to keep them apart so they won't alter the future. However, David believes he should control his own destiny and he and Elise refuse to give each other up despite increasing pressures (and multiple chase scenes). 106m; Blu-Ray, On Demand, Wide. **C:** Matt Damon; Emily Blunt; Anthony Mackie; Anthony Michael Ruivivar; Michael Kelly; Terence Stamp; Directed by George Nolfi; Written by George Nolfi; Cinematography by John Toll; Music by Thomas Newman. **Pr:** George Nolfi; Michael Hackett; Chris Moore; Bill Carraro; Electric Shepherd Productions; Gambit Pictures; Universal Pictures. **A:** Jr. High-Adult. **P:** Entertainment. **U:** Home. **L:** English. **Mov-Ent**: Science Fiction, Romance, Political Campaigns. **Acq:** Purchase. **Dist:** Universal Studios Home Video; Amazon.com Inc.; Movies Unlimited.

Administer Emergency Medical Care for a Blister Agent Casualty 1983
Describes the initial medical care necessary to treat effects of a blister agent. 7m; VHS, 3/4 U. **Pr:** USAAHS. **A:** Adult. **P:** Instruction. **U:** Institution, SURA. **How-Ins**: First Aid, Poisons. **Acq:** Purchase. **Dist:** National Audiovisual Center. $80.00.

Administer Emergency Medical Care for a Nerve Agent Casualty 1983
This video demonstrates the initial medical attention necessary for a nerve agent casualty. 15m; VHS, 3/4 U. **Pr:** USAAHS. **A:** Adult. **P:** Instruction. **U:** Institution, SURA. **How-Ins**: First Aid, Poisons. **Acq:** Purchase. **Dist:** National Audiovisual Center. $95.00.

Administration of IV Medications 1988
For nursing students or practicing nurses, this program shows how to administer intravenous medications. 30m; VHS, 3/4 U. **Pr:** Intercollegiate Center for Nursing. **A:** College-Adult. **P:** Professional. **U:** Institution, CCTV, SURA. **Hea-Sci**: Nursing. **Acq:** Purchase, Rent/Lease. **Dist:** AJN Video Library/Lippincott Williams & Wilkins. $250.00.

Administrative Controls 1995
Includes ergonomic principles, cost/benefit analysis, and discusses a three-phase ergonomic action plan. 8m; VHS. **A:** Adult. **P:** Professional. **U:** Institution. **Bus-Ind**: Job Training, Safety Education. **Acq:** Rent/Lease. **Dist:** National Safety Council, California Chapter, Film Library.

Administrative Series 19??
Two-part program which provides training on different aspects of administrative management training. Includes discussion on temps, freelancers, and receptionist training. 46m; VHS. **A:** Sr. High-Adult. **P:** Special Education. **U:** Institution, Home. **Bus-Ind**: Business, How-To, Management. **Acq:** Purchase. **Dist:** Cambridge Educational. $259.95.
Indiv. Titles: 1. When and How to Hire Temps and Freelancers 2. Complete Training for the Complete Receptionist.

The Administrative Woman 1984
This program helps guide administrative personnel to manage their individual careers. 30m; VHS, 3/4 U. **Pr:** Gulf Publishing Co. **A:** College-Adult. **P:** Education. **U:** Institution. **Bus-Ind**: Occupations. **Acq:** Purchase. **Dist:** Gulf Publishing Co.
Indiv. Titles: 1. Career Planning and Goal Setting 2. Managing Stress and Anger.

The Admirable Crichton 1957 — ★★½
Social satire about an aristocratic family and their butler who are marooned on a tropical island. Crichton (More), the butler, has a good deal more practical experience and sense than his employers so he's soon in charge of their survival. Filmed in Bermuda and based on the play by James M. Barrie. 93m; VHS, DVD. **C:** Kenneth More; Cecil Parker; Sally Ann Howes; Diane Cilento; Martita Hunt; Jack Watling; Peter Graves; Gerald Harper; Directed by Lewis Gilbert; Written by Vernon Harris; Cinematography by Wilkie Cooper; Music by Douglas Gamley. **A:** Jr. High-Adult. **P:** Entertainment. **U:** Home. **Mov-Ent**: Action-Adventure. **Acq:** Purchase. **Dist:** Sony Pictures Home Entertainment Inc.; Critics' Choice Video & DVD. $20.95.

The Admiral Was a Lady 1950 (Unrated) — ★★
Four ex-GIs try to get by in life without going to work. Hendrix walks into their lives as a winning ex-Wave gifted with a knack for repartee who is disgusted by their collective lack of ambition. Nevertheless, she is pursued by the zany quartet with predictable results. 87m/B/W; VHS, DVD. **TV Std**: NTSC, PAL. **C:** Edmond O'Brien; Wanda Hendrix; Rudy Vallee; Steve Brodie; Directed by Albert Rogell. **Pr:** United Artists. **A:** Family. **P:** Entertainment. **U:** Home. **Mov-Ent**: Comedy--Romantic. **Acq:** Purchase. **Dist:** VCX Ltd. $14.98.

The Admiral's Cup 1985 1986
In near-gale force winds, these small boats dared the elements in the 1985 Admiral's Cup race. It was a battle of man against a very angry nature. 45m; VHS. **A:** Family. **P:** Entertainment. **U:** Home. **Spo-Rec**: Boating. **Acq:** Purchase. **Dist:** Video Collectibles. $29.95.

The Admiral's Cup 1987 1988
Highlights of the 1987 sailing tournament. 55m; VHS. **Pr:** Bennett Marine Video. **A:** Adult. **P:** Entertainment. **U:** Home. **Spo-Rec**: Boating, Sports--Water. **Acq:** Purchase. **Dist:** Bennett Marine Video. $39.95.

Admission 2013 (PG-13) — ★★½
Portia Nathan (Fey) is an admissions officer at Princeton University and follows a structured routine. While on a recruiting visit to an alternative high school run by old friend John Pressman (Rudd), she's stunned to come face-to-face with a

young man who may be the son she gave up years ago. Questioning the decisions she's made and facing new romance, Fey does her best with material that isn't nearly as smart as it should be. The apt and charming cast can't quite get this comedy applicant into the school of success. 107m; DVD, Blu-Ray. **C:** Tina Fey; Paul Rudd; Nat Wolff; Michael Sheen; Wallace Shawn; Gloria Reuben; Lily Tomlin; Sarita Choudhury; Directed by Paul Weitz; Written by Karen Croner; Cinematography by Declan Quinn; Music by Stephen Trask. **Pr:** Andrew Miano; Kerry Kohansky; Paul Weitz; Focus Features L.L.C; Depth of Field. **A:** Jr. High-Adult. **P:** Entertainment. **U:** Home. **L:** English. **Mov-Ent:** Adoption, Education, Comedy-Drama. **Acq:** Purchase. **Dist:** Universal Studios Home Video.

Admission and Discharge 1985
A step-by-step demonstration of procedures to be followed by a nursing assistant during admission and discharge of a patient. 25m; VHS, 3/4 U. **Pr:** Trainex. **A:** College-Adult. **P:** Instruction. **U:** Institution. **L:** English, Spanish. **Hea-Sci:** Hospitals, Patient Care. **Acq:** Purchase, Rent/Lease. **Dist:** Medcom Inc.

Admission Impossible: The "White Australian Policy" 1995
Explains how Australia evolved from a white Anglo Saxon nation to a multicultural society. In the beginning, Australia chose to have a "White Australia Policy," until, in 1972 the Policy was officially scrapped after 70 years. 56m; VHS. **A:** College-Adult. **P:** Education. **U:** Institution. **Gen-Edu:** Documentary Films, Australia, Prejudice. **Acq:** Purchase, Rent/Lease. **Dist:** Filmakers Library Inc. $295.00.

Adobe 1988
Designer/builder Larry Wier and do-it-yourselfer John Joyce demonstrate all of the intricacies of building a structure made out of adobe. Step-by-step instructions show how to make brick forms, weatherproof, avoid cracking, and lay adobe bricks. 60m; VHS, 3/4 U. **Pr:** Joyce Media. **A:** College-Adult. **P:** Education. **U:** Institution, Home. **How-Ins:** How-To, Construction, Architecture. **Acq:** Purchase. **Dist:** Joyce Media Inc. $69.00.

Adolescence 19??
Guide for parents to help their children adapt to the developmental changes that occur during adolescence. Discusses methods of balancing freedom while teaching responsibilty and strengthening family relationships. 20m; VHS. **A:** Adult. **P:** Education. **U:** Home, Institution. **Gen-Edu:** Parenting, Adolescence. **Acq:** Purchase. **Dist:** Alliance for Children and Families. $95.00.

Adolescence 1990
Teens talk about the problems they face today and solutions they have used. Issues include physical and emotional changes, family and friends, and the future. ?m; VHS. **A:** Jr. High-Sr. High. **P:** Education. **U:** Institution. **Gen-Edu:** Adolescence. **Acq:** Purchase. **Dist:** Meridian Education Corp. $45.00.

Adolescence: Crisis or Change? 1991
Focuses on the developmental challenges of adolescence such as autonomy, peer relationships, and personal identity. 60m; VHS. **A:** Adult. **P:** Teacher Education. **U:** Institution. **Gen-Edu:** Child Care, Children. **Acq:** Purchase. **Dist:** RMI Media. $89.95.

Adolescent Depression 1987
Through case studies, this program teaches students to recognize the differences between normal adolescent mood swings and serious depression. A video transfer of filmstrip material. 30m; VHS, 3/4 U. **Pr:** Guidance Associates. **A:** Primary-Sr. High. **P:** Education. **U:** Institution, SURA. **Gen-Edu:** Adolescence. **Acq:** Purchase. **Dist:** Center for Humanities, Inc./Guidance Associates.

Adolescent Depression and Suicide 1988
Signs of lengthy depression may indicate that a teenager is contemplating suicide. 10m; VHS, 3/4 U. **Pr:** Professional Research. **A:** Sr. High-Adult. **P:** Education. **U:** Institution, CCTV. **Hea-Sci:** Adolescence, Suicide. **Acq:** Purchase, Rent/Lease. **Dist:** Discovery Education. $295.00.

Adolescent Depression Curriculum 1990
Explains the symptoms, causes, and treatments for clinical depression, using original music, graphics, and dramatic sequences. Intended to fill up four classroom sessions. Individual programs can be used separately or together. Comes with manual. 48m; VHS. **A:** Jr. High-Sr. High. **P:** Education. **U:** Institution. **Gen-Edu:** Mental Health, Health Education. **Acq:** Purchase. **Dist:** Intervision. $295.00.
Indiv. Titles: 1. Chasing the Blues 2. Reversing the Spiral of the Blues.

Adolescent Development 1990
Part of a series offering instruction on the study of human behavior. 30m; VHS. **A:** Adult. **P:** Education. **U:** Institution. **Gen-Edu:** Psychology. **Acq:** Purchase. **Dist:** RMI Media. $89.95.

Adolescent Growth, Development and Puberty Delay 1982
The important subject of delayed adolescent development is discussed. 48m; VHS, 3/4 U. **Pr:** Emory University. **A:** College-Adult. **P:** Professional. **U:** Institution, CCTV, Home, SURA. **Hea-Sci:** Adolescence. **Acq:** Purchase, Rent/Lease, Subscription. **Dist:** Emory Medical Television Network.

Adolescent Interview—Female 1973
An adolescent female and her mother are interviewed for the purpose of obtaining the medical history of both. 25m; VHS, 3/4 U, Special order formats. **Pr:** Health Sciences Learning Resources. **A:** College-Adult. **P:** Professional. **U:** Institution, CCTV. **Hea-Sci:** Medical Education. **Acq:** Purchase. **Dist:** Health Sciences Center for Educational Resources.

Adolescent Transitions 1989
Five short programs are a key part of a comprehensive curriculum aimed at preventing a broad range of problem behaviors which commonly surface during the teen years. Intended to be used in conjunction with classroom discussion over a 12-session period. Addresses the issues of making friends, setting goals, changing one's own behavior, and more. Comes with manual. Separate packages are available for parents and teenagers. ?m; VHS. **A:** Jr. High. **P:** Education. **U:** Institution. **Gen-Edu:** Adolescence, Mental Health, Self-Help. **Acq:** Purchase. **Dist:** Intervision. $179.00.

Adolf Hitler 19??
Through newsreel footage and home movies, Hitler's rise and fall is examined. 101m/B/W; VHS. **A:** Family. **P:** Education. **U:** Home. **Gen-Edu:** Documentary Films, Biography, World War Two. **Acq:** Purchase. **Dist:** VCI Entertainment; German Language Video Center. $59.95.

Adolf Hitler 1983
This program details the rise and fall of one of the world's most powerful leaders, Adolf Hitler. 14m/B/W; VHS, 3/4 U. **Pr:** WGBH Boston. **A:** Jr. High-Adult. **P:** Education. **U:** Institution, SURA. **Gen-Edu:** Germany, World War Two. **Acq:** Purchase, Rent/Lease. **Dist:** Hearst Entertainment/King Features.

Adolf Hitler: My Part in His Downfall 1974 (Unrated) — ★½
Mild war comedy based on Spike Milligan's memoirs. Young jazz drummer Spike (Dale) is forced into duty when WWII begins and there are various absurd mishaps with Spike and his fellow recruits during basic training with the Royal Artillery. Milligan himself plays his father Leo. 103m; DVD. **C:** Jim Dale; Arthur Lowe; Bill Maynard; Tony Selby; Spike Milligan; Directed by Norman Cohen; Written by Norman Cohen; Johnny Byrne; Cinematography by Terry Maher; Music by Wilfred Burns. **A:** Sr. High-Adult. **P:** Entertainment. **U:** Home. **L:** English. **Mov-Ent:** Great Britain, World War Two. **Acq:** Purchase. **Dist:** MGM Home Entertainment.

Adomas Nori Buti Zmogumi 1959 (Unrated) — ★★
Soviet Lithuanian feature in its original form, with dialogue in Lithuanian. A young worker scrapes together money for a ticket to Buenos Aires, but the money is stolen by the manager of the travel office. 90m/B/W; VHS, DVD. **C:** Donatas Banionis; Juozas Miltinis; Directed by V. Zhalakyavichus; Written by V. Zhalakyavichus; Cinematography by Algimantas Mockus. **A:** Family. **P:** Entertainment. **U:** Institution, Home. **L:** Russian, Lithuanian. **Mov-Ent. Acq:** Purchase. **Dist:** International Historic Films Inc.

Adopt a Sailor 2008 (Unrated) — ★★
Character drama based on writer/director Evered's own experiences. A nameless, naive young Arkansas sailor (Peck) is visiting New York during Fleet Week and is spending the evening with Patricia (Neuwirth) and Richard (Coyote) who have agreed to look after him. Only wealthy passive-aggressive Patricia and her dilettante filmmaker hubby have a now-loveless marriage and more-than-embarrassing issues that are revealed during a very uncomfortable dinner. 85m; DVD. **C:** Ethan Peck; Bebe Neuwirth; Peter Coyote; Directed by Charles Evered; Written by Charles Evered; Cinematography by Ulf Soderqvist; Music by Joshua Fardon. **A:** Sr. High-Adult. **P:** Entertainment. **U:** Home. **Mov-Ent. Acq:** Purchase. **Dist:** Echo Bridge Home Entertainment.

Adopted 2009 (R) — **Bomb!**
The movie is supposed to be intentionally stupid and offensive but Shore's flick just goes beyond that into unwatchable. Shore plays himself as a burned-out party guy who decides to go respectable by adopting an African orphan like some other better-known celebrities. But his American ignorance and arrogance makes the entire process trickier. It's a really looong 80 minutes and you really have to like Shore to endure even more than a few of those. 80m; DVD. **C:** Pauly Shore; Directed by Pauly Shore; Written by Pauly Shore; Cinematography by Bruce Cunningham; Grant Nelson; Music by The Newton Brothers. **A:** Sr. High-Adult. **P:** Entertainment. **U:** Home. **Mov-Ent:** Adoption, Africa. **Acq:** Purchase. **Dist:** Phase 4/kaBOOM Entertainment.

Adoption 1975 (Unrated) — ★★★
The third of Meszaros's trilogy, involving a middle-aged Hungarian woman who longs for a child and instead forms a deep friendship with a 19-year-old orphan. In Hungarian with English subtitles. 89m/B/W; VHS, DVD. **C:** Kati Berek; Laszlo Szabo; Gyongyver Vigh; Dr. Arpad Perlaky; Directed by Marta Meszaros; Written by Marta Meszaros; Gyula Hernadi; Cinematography by Lajos Koltai; Music by Gyorgy Kovacs. **Pr:** Marta Meszaros; Marta Meszaros. **A:** Sr. High-Adult. **P:** Entertainment. **U:** Home. **L:** Hungarian. **Mov-Ent:** Adoption. **Awds:** Berlin Intl. Film Fest. '75: Golden Berlin Bear. **Acq:** Purchase. **Dist:** Kino on Video. $69.95.

Adoption: A Lifelong Process 1987
Describes post-placement therapeutic approaches to working with older adoptees and their families. 30m; VHS. **A:** Adult. **P:** Education. **U:** Institution. **Gen-Edu:** Adoption. **Dist:** Edmund S. Muskie Institute National Child Welfare Resource Center. $40.

Adoption: Children Are Waiting 1989
Professionals in the child welfare field as well as couples who have adopted, relate their experiences. 28m; VHS, 3/4 U. **Pr:** National Film Board of Canada. **A:** Jr. High-Adult. **P:** Education. **U:** Institution, SURA. **Gen-Edu:** Adolescence. **Acq:** Purchase, Rent/Lease. **Dist:** National Film Board of Canada.

Adoption: It's an Option 19??
"Adoption" explores the adoption option in a factual manner, and includes interviews with mothers who have given up their babies for adoption. A straightforward presentation, this program does not advocate adoption over any other problem pregnancy solution. 24m; VHS. **A:** Sr. High. **P:** Education. **U:** Institution. **L:** English. **Gen-Edu:** Child Care. **Acq:** Purchase. **Dist:** Meridian Education Corp. $95.

The Adoption Series 1977
Four programs that deal with the joys and the difficulties of adoption. Programs are available individually. 20m; 3/4 U. **Pr:** Los Angeles County. **A:** Adult. **P:** Education. **U:** Institution, SURA. **Gen-Edu:** Children. **Acq:** Purchase, Rent/Lease. **Dist:** Kinetic Film Enterprises Ltd.
Indiv. Titles: 1. One of the Family 2. The Parents' Group-Working with the Adoptive Family 3. The Scrapbook Experience-Building a Child's Identity 4. The Children's Group-Preparing a Child for Adoption.

The Adorable Cheat 1928 — ★★
A low-budget, late-silent melodrama about a young woman who tries to get involved in the family business, despite her father's refusal of her help. Once in the business, she finds love. 76m/B/W; Silent; DVD. **C:** Lila Lee; Cornelius Keefe; Burr McIntosh; Directed by Burton King. **Pr:** Chesterfield Productions. **A:** Family. **P:** Entertainment. **U:** Home. **Mov-Ent:** Drama, Silent Films. **Acq:** Purchase. **Dist:** Alpha Video. $16.95.

Adorable Julia 1962 (Unrated) — ★★
When an actress takes on a lover many years younger than herself, the laughs begin to fly in this sex comedy based on W. Somerset Maugham's novel. 97m; VHS. **C:** Lilli Palmer; Charles Boyer; Directed by Alfred Weidenmann. **A:** Sr. High-Adult. **P:** Entertainment. **U:** Home. **L:** English, French. **Mov-Ent:** Comedy--Romantic. **Acq:** Purchase. **Dist:** Facets Multimedia Inc. $29.95.

Adorables Criminales 1987 (Unrated) — ★★½
A rich detective looks into the affairs of four female criminals. 96m; VHS. **C:** Roberto "Flaco" Guzman; Zoila Flor; Luz Maria Jerez; Lorenzo de Monteclaro. **Pr:** Madera. **A:** Adult. **P:** Entertainment. **U:** Home. **L:** Spanish. **Mov-Ent. Acq:** Purchase. **Dist:** Spanishmultimedia. $77.95.

Adoration 2008 (R) — ★★
High-school French teacher Sabine (Khanjian) gives her class a translation exercise based on a news story about a terrorist and his pregnant girlfriend. Student Simon (Bostick) has a lot of unresolved feelings about his parents' death in a car crash, especially since his bigoted grandfather (Welsh) has led Simon to believe that his Lebanese father deliberately caused the accident. Simon uses the article to imagine himself as the terrorist's now-grown son but presents his work as fact not fiction when he uses a webcam to take the story to internet chat rooms, which has the deception spiraling out of control. English and French with subtitles. 101m; Blu-Ray, On Demand, Wide. **C:** Arsinee Khanjian; Scott Speedman; Rachel Blanchard; Noam Jenkins; Kenneth Welsh; Devon Bostick; Directed by Atom Egoyan; Written by Atom Egoyan; Cinematography by Paul Sarossy; Music by Mychael Danna. **Pr:** Simone Urdl; Jennifer Weiss; Atom Egoyan; Serendipity Point Films; ARP Selection; Ego Film Arts; Sony Pictures Classics. **A:** Sr. High-Adult. **P:** Entertainment. **U:** Home. **L:** English, French. **Mov-Ent:** Adolescence, Adoption. **Acq:** Purchase. **Dist:** Amazon.com Inc.; Movies Unlimited; Alpha Video.

Adore 2013 (R) — ★½
Solemn yet sudsy melodrama of two blonde, 40-something lifelong best friends who each have a sexual relationship with the other's son. Widow Lil (Watts) and married Roz (Wright) live next door to each other along the Australian coast. Though they have jobs, the women seem to spend most of their time sunbathing and watching their sons, Tom (Frechville) and Ian (Samuel), also best friends, surf. After Tom witnesses an encounter between his mother Roz and Ian, he seduces Lil. There are some momentary pangs of conscience but that doesn't stop them from carrying on. Adapted from Doris Lessing's novel, "The Grandmothers." 100m; DVD, Blu-Ray. **C:** Robin Wright; Naomi Watts; James Frecheville; Xavier Samuel; Ben Mendelsohn; Sophie Lowe; Jessica Tovey; Gary Sweet; Directed by Anne Fontaine; Written by Christopher Hampton; Cinematography by Christophe Beaucarne; Music by Christopher Gordon. **Pr:** Philippe Carcassonne; Michel Feller; Barbara Gibbs; Andrew Mason; Screen Australia; Exclusive Media Group. **A:** Sr. High-Adult. **P:** Entertainment. **U:** Home. **L:** English. **Mov-Ent:** Australia, Sex & Sexuality, Family. **Acq:** Purchase. **Dist:** Paramount Pictures Corp.

The Adrenal Safari 1995
Features snowboarding, surfing, cliff diving, and bungee jumping. Reveals a great way to get pumped before an outing of your own. 40m; VHS. **A:** Jr. High-Adult. **P:** Entertainment. **U:** Home. **Gen-Edu:** Sports--General. **Acq:** Purchase. **Dist:** Paragon Home Video. $19.95.

Adrenalin: Fear the Rush 1996 (R) — ★
Dull future thriller in the deadly virus category. In 2007, a plague in Eastern Europe causes those that survive to turn into cannabalistic killers. The U.S. has started quarantine camps, one of which is in Boston, and two cops (Henstridge and Lambert) must track down an infected killer who's escaped. Not worth your time. 77m; VHS, DVD, CC. **C:** Christopher Lambert; Natasha Henstridge; Norbert Weisser; Craig Davis, MD; Elizabeth Barondes; Xavier DeClie; Directed by Albert Pyun; Written by Albert Pyun; Cinematography by George Mooradian; Music by Tony Riparetti. **Pr:** Gary Schmoeller; Tom Karnwoski; Largo Entertainment; Miramax Film Corp. **A:** Sr. High-Adult. **P:** Enter-

tainment. **U:** Home. **Mov-Ent:** Science Fiction. **Acq:** Purchase. **Dist:** Buena Vista Home Entertainment.

Adrenaline Drive 1999 (Unrated) — ★★
Sad sack Suzuki (Ando), who's working for a car rental company, accidentally plows a car into the Jaguar of yakuza big guy Kuroiwa (Matushige). Before punishment can be exacted, there's an explosion that lands them in the hospital. There shy nurse Shizuko (Ishida) latches on both to Suzuki and to a yakuza suitcase full of money and drags both on a road trip to freedom. Silly, good-natured comedy. Japanese with subtitles. 111m; VHS, DVD, Wide. **C:** Hikari Ishida; Mansanobu Ando; Yataka Matushige; Kazue Tsunogae; Directed by Shinobu Yaguchi; Written by Shinobu Yaguchi; Cinematography by Takashi Hamada; Music by Seiichi Yamamoto. **A:** College-Adult. **P:** Entertainment. **U:** Home. **L:** Japanese. **Mov-Ent:** Comedy--Romantic. **Acq:** Purchase. **Dist:** Image Entertainment Inc.

Adrian Belew: Electronic Guitar 1985
The great journeyman guitarist instructs in tuning, fretless guitars, electronic effects and two-handed fingerboards. Musical illustrations include selections from his solo albums and work with King Crimson. 60m; VHS. **TV Std:** NTSC, PAL. **Pr:** DCI Music Video. **A:** Sr. High-Adult. **P:** Instruction. **U:** Home. **Fin-Art. Acq:** Purchase. **Dist:** Music Video Distributors. $39.95.

Adriana Lecouvreur 1985
The Elizabethan Sydney Opera performs the classic Francesco Cilea opera, in French with English subtitles. 135m; VHS. **C:** Joan Sutherland; Conducted by Richard Bonynge. **Pr:** The Australian Opera. **A:** Family. **P:** Entertainment. **U:** Home. **L:** French. **Fin-Art:** Opera. **Acq:** Purchase. **Dist:** Music Video Distributors.

Adriana Lecouvreur 1990
Francesco Cilea opera about the 18th-century French actress, Adriana Lecouvreur. The Count of Saxony's love was the object of a fierce rivalry between Adriana and the Princess of Bouillon. Performed at La Scala and conducted by Gianandrea Gavazzeni. Italian with English subtitles. 157m; VHS, CC. **C:** Mirella Freni; Peter Dvorsky; Fiorenza Cossotto; Ivo Vinco; Directed by Lamberto Puggelli; Conducted by Gianandrea Gavazzeni. **Pr:** Home Vision. **A:** Jr. High-Adult. **P:** Entertainment. **U:** Home. **L:** English, Italian. **Fin-Art:** Opera. **Acq:** Purchase. **Dist:** Home Vision Cinema; Facets Multimedia Inc. $39.95.

Adrift 1993 — ★★½
Yet another couple-in-terror-from-psychos-on-the-high-seas flick. Katie and Guy Nast (Jackson and Welsh) are on an anniversary sailing adventure intended to shore up their shaky marriage. They discover a boat adrift with two survivors (Greenwood and Rowan) who have a suspicious story but they help them nonetheless. Big mistake. 92m; VHS, CC. **C:** Kate Jackson; Kenneth Welsh; Bruce Greenwood; Kelly Rowan; Directed by Christian Duguay. **A:** Jr. High-Adult. **P:** Entertainment. **U:** Home. **Mov-Ent:** Mystery & Suspense, Boating, TV Movies. **Acq:** Purchase. **Dist:** Lions Gate Entertainment Inc. $89.95.

Adrift 2009 (Unrated) — ★½
Unoriginal but well-played family drama finds Mathias taking his wife Claire and their 14-year-old daughter Filipa to spend the summer at their beach house. Claire drinks while Mathias has an affair, which compels their pouty teen into the bed of a local hunk. Portuguese with subtitles. 97m; DVD. **C:** Laura Neiva; Vincent Cassel; Debora Bloch; Camilla Belle; Caua Reymond; Directed by Heitor Dhalia; Written by Heitor Dhalia; Cinematography by Ricardo Della Rosa; Music by Antonio Pinto. **A:** College-Adult. **P:** Entertainment. **U:** Home. **L:** Portuguese. **Mov-Ent. Acq:** Purchase. **Dist:** Universal Studios Home Video.

Adrift in Manhattan 2007 (R) — ★★
Chance encounters change the lives of three lonely New Yorkers. Simon (Rasuk) is a young man with a passion for photography. Snapping street pics, he finds his muse in depressed optometrist Rose (Graham), who's estranged from her husband (Baldwin) after their young child's death. Rose's patient Tommaso (Chianese), a painter, is going blind and she encourages him to find comfort with someone, deciding to take her own advice after Simon gets the courage to introduce himself. 91m; DVD, Wide. **C:** Heather Graham; William Baldwin; Victor Rasuk; Dominic Chianese; Elizabeth Pena; Marta Colon; Erika Michels; Directed by Alfredo de Villa; Written by Alfredo de Villa; Nat Moss; Cinematography by John Foster; Music by Michael A. Levine. **A:** Sr. High-Adult. **P:** Entertainment. **U:** Home. **Mov-Ent:** Photography. **Acq:** Purchase. **Dist:** Alpha Video; Movies Unlimited.

Adrift on the Nile 1971
A reporter visits a houseboat where a group of hedonistic middle-aged friends party and tell tales of alienation from society. With English or French subtitles. 115m; DVD. **A:** Sr. High-Adult. **P:** Entertainment. **U:** Home, Institution. **L:** Arabic. **Mov-Ent:** Drama, Middle East. **Acq:** Purchase, Rent/Lease. **Dist:** Arab Film Distribution. $29.99.

The ADS Epidemic 1987
Musical look at the media-induced paranoia about AIDS. Parody story of Aschenbach, who succumbs to an attack of ADS (Acquired Dread of Sex), and Tadzio, who learns that safe sex is fun. These and other characters warn the viewer that ADS can happen to anyone. 4m; VHS, 3/4 U. **A:** Adult. **P:** Education. **U:** Institution. **Hea-Sci:** Sex & Sexuality, Health Education, AIDS. **Acq:** Rent/Lease. **Dist:** Video Out Distribution.

AdSmarts 19??
Part of the "AdSmarts" multi-media program that discusses techniques used in advertising and shows how to see through these techniques and not get trapped by the advertising. ?m; VHS. **A:** Jr. High. **P:** Education. **U:** Home, Institution. **Gen-Edu:** Advertising. **Acq:** Purchase. **Dist:** Center for Media Literacy.

Adua and Her Friends 1960 (Unrated) — ★★
When Rome's legalized brothels are shut down, four prostitutes use their savings to buy a rundown restaurant but they need a front man to get the property and licenses. Ercoli agrees for a hefty commission and only if they will continue to offer their services in the upstairs rooms. The restaurant is a success but the women become increasingly frustrated when they can't shake their pasts. Italian with subtitles. 98m/B/W; DVD. **C:** Simone Signoret; Sandra Milo; Emmanuelle Riva; Gina Rovere; Claudio Gora; Marcello Mastroianni; Gianrico Tedeschi; Directed by Antonio Pietrangeli; Written by Antonio Pietrangeli; Ruggero Maccari; Ettore Scola; Cinematography by Armando Nannuzzi; Music by Piero Piccioni. **A:** College-Adult. **P:** Entertainment. **U:** Home. **L:** Italian. **Mov-Ent:** Prostitution, Food Industry. **Acq:** Purchase. **Dist:** Entertainment One US LP.

Adult Animation 1991
Kinky, sexy, gruesome, nightmarish, hilarious, and they're cartoons. A collection of eight animated shorts by independent filmmakers. 60m; VHS. **A:** Adult. **P:** Entertainment. **U:** Home. **Mov-Ent:** Animation & Cartoons, Sex & Sexuality. **Acq:** Purchase. **Dist:** Facets Multimedia Inc.; Next Gen Video; Tapeworm Video Distributors Inc. $29.95.

Adult Development 1990
Part of a series offering instruction on the study of human behavior. 30m; VHS. **A:** Adult. **P:** Education. **U:** Institution. **Gen-Edu:** Psychology. **Acq:** Purchase. **Dist:** RMI Media. $89.95.

The Adult Learner Videotape Workshop 1991
Adult education expert Malcolm Knowles discusses how to understand the adult student, including the differences between adults and youths and modern learning theory. A facilitator's guide and participants' materials are included, along with a copy of "The Adult Learner: An Endangered Species" by Knowles. 76m; VHS, 3/4 U. **TV Std:** NTSC, PAL, SECAM. **Pr:** Gulf Publishing Co. **A:** Adult. **P:** Vocational. **U:** Institution, SURA. **Bus-Ind:** Education. **Acq:** Purchase. **Dist:** Gulf Publishing Co. $495.00.

Adult Learning Video? You've Got to Be Kidding! 1989
A look at the seven steps to becoming an all-star trainer in business and industry. Describes how to use the principles of learning theory to improve training sessions. Focuses on the issues of the adult learner, including fear of failure, new technology vs. past experience, and bureaucractic systems. 60m; VHS, 3/4 U. **Pr:** American Society for Training and Development. **A:** College-Adult. **P:** Professional. **U:** Institution. **Bus-Ind:** Business, Job Training, Occupational Training. **Acq:** Purchase, Rent/Lease. **Dist:** ASTD.

Adult Literacy 1985
Reading specialists Drs. Ken and Yetta Goodman, codirectors of the Program for Language and Literacy in Tucson, Arizona, discuss literacy training. Features conversations with teenagers and adults who have overcome their illiteracy. 30m; VHS, 3/4 U. **Pr:** RMI Media Productions. **A:** Adult. **P:** Education. **U:** Institution. **Gen-Edu:** Language Arts. **Acq:** Purchase. **Dist:** RMI Media.
Indiv. Titles: 1. Out of the Shadows 2. Once More With Meaning With Ken Goodman 3. Choosing Directions.

Adult Literacy Project: It Works Both Ways 19??
An insightful look at the life of an adult literacy tutor over the course of a year. 30m; VHS. **A:** Adult. **P:** Education. **U:** Institution. **Gen-Edu:** Education, Language Arts. **Acq:** Purchase. **Dist:** Access The Education Station. $49.00.

Adult Literacy Project: Safer than a Sock 19??
An illiterate man named Frank avoids the consequences of his condition at every turn. An often humorous yet poignant story. Supported by a handbook on banking for new readers (available separately). 28m; VHS. **A:** Adult. **P:** Education. **U:** Institution. **Gen-Edu:** Education, Language Arts. **Acq:** Purchase. **Dist:** Access The Education Station. $49.00.

Adult Living 1993
Two-part documentary-style program addresses the skills needed for independent adult living, including employment, housing, finances, and interpersonal relationships. Young people living independently and experts in relevant fields comment. ?m; VHS. **A:** Sr. High-Adult. **P:** Education. **U:** Institution. **Gen-Edu:** Personal Finance, Housing. **Acq:** Purchase. **Dist:** Meridian Education Corp. $45.00.

Adult Physical Assessment 1983
This tape is designed to help nurses refine and integrate their basic physical assessment skills. 55m; 3/4 U, Special order formats. **A:** Adult. **P:** Professional. **U:** Institution, CCTV, SURA. **Hea-Sci:** Nursing. **Acq:** Purchase, Rent/Lease. **Dist:** AJN Video Library/Lippincott Williams & Wilkins.

Adult Respiratory Distress Syndrome 1985
Presents the use of positive and expiratory pressure as well as other means of adult respiratory distress management. 50m; VHS, 3/4 U. **TV Std:** NTSC, PAL, SECAM. **Pr:** HSC. **A:** College-Adult. **P:** Professional. **U:** Institution, CCTV, SURA. **Hea-Sci:** Respiratory System, Medical Education. **Acq:** Purchase, Rent/Lease, Subscription.

Adult World 2013 (R) — ★★½
When not stuck working in a dinky porn shop, hopeful writer Amy (Roberts) spends most of her time stalking her idol, the once-famous poet Rat Billings (Cusack). Yes, his name is Rat. Set in a wintry Syracuse, the back-and-forth resistance from the petulant has-been, pushing away his diehard fan, is loaded with biting dark humor. An original coming-of-age story that never dives into sentimentality or melodrama, with a sharp performance from Cusack at his most wry and witty. 97m; On Demand. **C:** Emma Roberts; John Cusack; Evan Peters; John Cullum; Cloris Leachman; Directed by Scott Coffey; Written by Andy Cochran; Cinematography by James Laxton; Music by B.C. Smith. **Pr:** IFC Films. **A:** Sr. High-Adult. **P:** Entertainment. **U:** Home. **L:** English. **Mov-Ent:** Comedy--Black. **Acq:** Purchase, Rent/Lease. **Dist:** Amazon.com Inc.

The Adult Years: Continuity and Change 1985
A series of films dealing with the emotional traumas and adjustments that accompany adulthood and parenthood. 30m; VHS, 3/4 U. **Pr:** Maryland Center for Public Broadcasting; Ohio University Telecommunications Center. **A:** Sr. High-Adult. **P:** Education. **U:** Institution, CCTV, SURA. **Gen-Edu:** Family. **Acq:** Purchase, Rent/Lease. **Dist:** WOUB Public Media.
Indiv. Titles: 1. Rites of Renewal 2. The Refracted Image 3. The Fountain of Youth 4. Love and Marriage 5. My Mother, My Daughter, Myself 6. Lifework 7. The Moving Experience.

Adulthood's End: A Look at Adolescent Suicide 1982
Offers portraits of three suicidal young people, and stresses how important it is to use all resources to help troubled youngsters. American Psychiatric Association, 1984; National Council on Family Relations, 1982. 28m; VHS. **A:** Sr. High-Adult. **P:** Education. **U:** Institution. **Gen-Edu:** Adolescence, Suicide, Documentary Films. **Acq:** Purchase, Rent/Lease. **Dist:** Filmakers Library Inc. $295.00.

The Adultress 1977 (R) — ★
When a husband and wife cannot satisfy their desire to have a family, they hire a young man to help them in this dumb melodrama. 85m; VHS. **C:** Tyne Daly; Eric Braeden; Gregory Morton; Directed by Norbert Meisel. **Pr:** Cinema Overseas Ltd. **A:** Sr. High-Adult. **P:** Entertainment. **U:** Home. **Mov-Ent:** Sex & Sexuality, TV Movies, Marriage. **Acq:** Purchase. **Dist:** No Longer Available.

Adults with Attention Deficit Disorder 1994
Attention Deficit Disorder (ADD) expert Dr. Thomas W. Phelan describes the symptoms of ADD in adults and discusses the effects of the disorder on work, home marriage, parenting, and social interaction; its impact on mood and self-esteem; and diagnosis and treatment. A panel of six adults share their experiences with ADD. 86m; VHS. **A:** College-Adult. **P:** Education. **U:** Home, Institution. **Hea-Sci:** Mental Health. **Acq:** Purchase. **Dist:** Parent Magic, Inc. $39.95.

Advance Directives and the Elderly: Making Decisions about Treatment Limitations 19??
Discusses with three nursing home residents their wishes to limit treatment. Covers artificial feeding, CPR, and use of antibiotics. 20m; VHS. **Pr:** John Hopkins. **A:** Adult. **P:** Education. **U:** Institution. **Hea-Sci:** Aging, Medical Care, Patient Care. **Acq:** Purchase, Rent/Lease. **Dist:** University of Maryland. $150.00.

Advance Directives: CPR in Nursing Homes 19??
Explains the use of CPR in the nursing home. Includes discussions with a physician, a nursing home patient, and the resident's daughter as they address emotional concerns and need for information. 19m; VHS. **Pr:** John Hopkins. **A:** Adult. **P:** Education. **U:** Institution. **Hea-Sci:** Aging, Medical Care, Patient Care. **Acq:** Purchase, Rent/Lease. **Dist:** University of Maryland. $300.00.

Advance Directives: Guidelines for Health-Care Providers 1992
Offers suggestions for communicating with patients and overviews advanced directives. Program approved for 1 hour of CEU credit. 15m; VHS. **A:** Adult. **P:** Education. **U:** Institution. **Hea-Sci:** Ethics & Morals, Health Education. **Acq:** Purchase. **Dist:** Channing Bete Company Inc. $75.00.

Advance Level Lacrosse Skills Made Easy 2002 (Unrated)
Coach Kim Simons demonstrates building advanced skills for lacrosse coaches. 43m; DVD. **A:** Family. **P:** Education. **U:** Home, Institution. **Spo-Rec:** Lacrosse, Athletic Instruction/Coaching. **Acq:** Purchase. **Dist:** Championship Productions. $39.99.

Advance to the Rear 1964 (Unrated) — ★★½
Light-hearted military comedy. A misfit band of Union Army soldiers are sent westward to do as little damage as possible while they frustrate their by-the-book captain, Jared Heath (Ford). Instead, they manage to get involved in protecting a gold shipment from southern sympathizer Zattig (Griffith) and get vamped by some beautiful Confederate spies, including Martha Lou (Stevens) who's very interested in Jared. 97m/B/W; DVD. **C:** Glenn Ford; Stella Stevens; Melvyn Douglas; Joan Blondell; James J. Griffith; Jim Backus; Andrew Prine; Alan Hale, Jr.; Whit Bissell; Britt Ekland; Directed by George Marshall; Written by Samuel A. Peeples; William Bowers; Cinematography by Milton Krasner; Music by Randy Sparks. **A:** Jr. High-Adult. **P:** Entertainment. **U:** Home. **Mov-Ent:** Civil War. **Acq:** Purchase. **Dist:** WarnerArchive.com.

Advanced AC Circuits 1993
Presents concepts of circuitry with attention to capacitors, resistors, voltage, impedance-frequency relationships, and more on five programs. ?m; VHS. **A:** Adult. **P:** Professional. **U:** Institution. **Bus-Ind:** Business, Electricity. **Acq:** Purchase. **Dist:** Bergwall Productions, Inc. $439.00.
Indiv. Titles: 1. Time Constants 2. Phasors and AC Phase Relationships 3. The RC Circuit 4. The RL Circuit 5. The RLC Circuit.

Advanced Arc Welding 1984
On six tapes, trainees learn how to safely arc weld. 105m; VHS, 3/4 U. **Pr:** Bergwall Productions. **A:** Sr. High-Adult. **P:** Vocational. **U:** Institution. **Bus-Ind:** Welding. **Acq:** Purchase. **Dist:** Bergwall Productions, Inc.

Advanced Attacking 2000 (Unrated)
Coach Mary Wise discusses various offensive techniques for volleyball players at the intermediate and advanced levels. 33m; DVD. **A:** Family. **P:** Education. **U:** Home, Institution. **Spo-Rec:** Volleyball, Athletic Instruction/Coaching. **Acq:** Purchase. **Dist:** Championship Productions. $39.99.

Advanced Basketball Drills for Women: Point Guard 2011 (Unrated)
Former basketball trainer Steph Wood and professional player Ticha Penicheiro demonstrate drills for players wishing to expand their abilities in the point guard position. 69m; DVD. **A:** Family. **P:** Education. **U:** Home, Institution. **Spo-Rec:** Basketball, Athletic Instruction/Coaching. **Acq:** Purchase. **Dist:** Championship Productions. $39.99.

Advanced Basketball Drills for Women: Post 2011 (Unrated)
Trainer Steph Wood and pro basketball trainer Khadijah Whittington discuss standards every post players should aspire to, as well as the offensive and defensive drills necessary to develop them. 48m; DVD. **A:** Family. **P:** Education. **U:** Home, Institution. **Spo-Rec:** Basketball, Athletic Instruction/Coaching. **Acq:** Purchase. **Dist:** Championship Productions. $39.99.

Advanced Basketball Drills for Women: Wing 2011 (Unrated)
Trainer Steph Wood and former player Lori Drake present drills for developing your basketball team's wing guard players. 43m; DVD. **A:** Family. **P:** Education. **U:** Home, Institution. **Spo-Rec:** Basketball, Athletic Instruction/Coaching. **Acq:** Purchase. **Dist:** Championship Productions. $39.99.

Advanced Bass Grooves 199?
Bassist Tony Smith provides an in-depth study of bass grooves. 30m; VHS. **A:** Sr. High-Adult. **P:** Instruction. **U:** Home. **How-Ins:** Music--Instruction. **Acq:** Purchase. **Dist:** Hal Leonard Corp. $9.95.

Advanced Bassin' Today 19??
Explains the strengths and weaknesses of modern bass lures and the best conditions to use them under. 75m; VHS. **A:** Adult. **P:** Instruction. **U:** Home. **Spo-Rec:** Fishing. **Acq:** Purchase. **Dist:** In-Fisherman.

Advanced Blackjack 1989
A video for gamblers who have already mastered basic blackjack. 60m; VHS. **A:** College-Adult. **P:** Instruction. **U:** Home. **Gen-Edu:** Gambling. **Acq:** Purchase. **Dist:** John Patrick Entertainment, Inc. $39.95.

Advanced Car Care: Cooling System Service 1984
This program tells how to repair your car's cooling system in a step by step manner. 60m; VHS, 3/4 U. **Pr:** RMI Media Productions. **A:** Sr. High-Adult. **P:** Instruction. **U:** Institution, CCTV, Home. **How-Ins:** Automobiles. **Acq:** Purchase. **Dist:** RMI Media.

Advanced Car Care: Tune-Up and Shocks 1984
This program tells how to tune up your car in a step-by-step manner. 60m; VHS, 3/4 U. **Pr:** RMI Media Productions. **A:** Sr. High-Adult. **P:** Instruction. **U:** Institution, CCTV, Home. **How-Ins:** Automobiles. **Acq:** Purchase. **Dist:** RMI Media.

Advanced Centerpieces, One-Sided and Layered "Mass" Designs 1984
This program contains the various ways you can make a layered-looking floral centerpiece. 60m; VHS, 3/4 U. **Pr:** RMI Media Productions. **A:** Sr. High-Adult. **P:** Instruction. **U:** Institution, CCTV, Home. **How-Ins:** Flowers, Hobbies. **Acq:** Purchase. **Dist:** RMI Media.

Advanced Chocolate Decoration Techniques 199?
Ewald Notter of the International School of Confectionary Arts instructs viewers on the art of using chocolate to create decorative showpieces in this two part series. In this volume, he teaches the viewer how to make chocolate shavings, piping and more complicated pieces. 24m; VHS. **A:** Sr. High-Adult. **P:** Instruction. **U:** Home. **How-Ins:** Cooking, Food Industry, How-To. **Acq:** Purchase. **Dist:** Culinary Institute of America. $75.00.

Advanced Chords and Rhythms 199?
Tom Kolb demonstrates a variety of rock, funk, and blues riffs used by many contemporary artists. 30m; VHS. **A:** Sr. High-Adult. **P:** Instruction. **U:** Home. **How-Ins:** Music--Instruction. **Acq:** Purchase. **Dist:** Hal Leonard Corp. $9.95.

Advanced Co-Ed Stunts 1997 (Unrated)
Coach Mark Bagon and the ACF staffs first video of stunts for co-ed cheerleading squads who have moved beyond the basic level. 33m; VHS. **A:** Family. **P:** Education. **U:** Home, Institution. **Spo-Rec:** Cheerleaders, Athletic Instruction/Coaching. **Acq:** Purchase. **Dist:** Championship Productions. $39.99.

Advanced Co-Ed Stunts Volume 2 2001 (Unrated)
Coach Mark Bagon and the ACF staff demonstrate 15 stunts for co-ed cheerleading squads who have moved beyond the basic level. 25m; DVD. **A:** Family. **P:** Education. **U:** Home, Institution. **Spo-Rec:** Cheerleaders, Athletic Instruction/Coaching. **Acq:** Purchase. **Dist:** Championship Productions. $39.99.

Advanced Conga with Rolando Soto ????
Explains and demonstrates variations of basic rhythm patterns, bolero rhythms, and their musical applications. Plus traditional Afro-Cuban rhythms such as yambu, guaguanco, columbia and more. 63m; VHS. **A:** Adult. **P:** Instruction. **U:** Home. **How-Ins:**

How-To, Music--Instruction. **Acq:** Purchase. **Dist:** Calprod Pro Film/Video Production, Inc. $19.95.

Advanced Copper Foil Panel Techniques 19??
Centers on how to expand current foiling skills with professional tips and techniques. Includes two full-size patterns of a seagull and an iris. 60m; VHS. **A:** Adult. **P:** Instruction. **U:** Home. **How-Ins:** Crafts, Hobbies, How-To. **Acq:** Purchase. **Dist:** Cutters Productions. $24.95.

Advanced Craps 1 1989
This video provides tips from professional gamblers for the advanced craps player. 60m; VHS. **Pr:** John Patrick Productions. **A:** College-Adult. **P:** Instruction. **U:** Home. **Gen-Edu:** Gambling. **Acq:** Purchase. **Dist:** John Patrick Entertainment, Inc. $39.95.

Advanced Craps 2: Super Craps 1989
Professional John Patrick explains the "Super Patrick System" for the expert craps player. 60m; VHS. **Pr:** John Patrick Productions. **A:** College-Adult. **P:** Instruction. **U:** Home. **Spo-Rec:** Gambling. **Acq:** Purchase. **Dist:** John Patrick Entertainment, Inc.

Advanced Digital Systems 199?
An instrument technology training program on advanced digital systems. Includes a manual. 60m; VHS. **A:** Adult. **P:** Instruction. **U:** Institution. **Bus-Ind:** Technology, Job Training. **Acq:** Purchase. **Dist:** ISA -The International Society of Automation. $95.00.

Advanced DOS 19??
Teaches some of the more advanced functions of DOS, such as hard disk management, DOS Shell usage, and DOS productivity features. Comes with diskette, textbook, and quizzer. 60m; VHS. **A:** Sr. High-Adult. **P:** Instruction. **U:** Institution, Home. **How-Ins:** Computers, How-To. **Acq:** Purchase. **Dist:** Bisk Education. $179.00.

Advanced Dressage 19??
Provides advanced tips that help the rider compete successfully at the international level of dressage. ?m; VHS. **A:** Sr. High-Adult. **P:** Instruction. **U:** Institution. **How-Ins:** Horses, How-To. **Acq:** Purchase. **Dist:** CEV Multimedia. $39.95.

Advanced Dribble-Drive Offense: Zone & Transition Game 2010 (Unrated)
Coach Vance Walberg gives a quick review of what he covers in his first DVD before moving on to more advanced variations of the dribble drive offense. 408m; DVD. **A:** Family. **P:** Education. **U:** Home. **Spo-Rec:** Basketball, Athletic Instruction/Coaching. **Acq:** Purchase. **Dist:** Championship Productions. $119.99.

Advanced Drum Grooves 199?
Jamie Bordern explains five essential rudiments and demonstrates several popular grooves including Latin, funk, and boogie shuffles. 30m; VHS. **A:** Sr. High-Adult. **P:** Instruction. **U:** Home. **How-Ins:** Music--Instruction. **Acq:** Purchase. **Dist:** Hal Leonard Corp. $9.95.

Advanced EKG Interpretation: Axis Deviation 19??
Demonstrates methods for determining axis based on electro-cardiographic readings and for choosing appropriate nursing actions for patients with left and right axis deviation. Provides information on the underlying anatomy and physiology, three different types of normal axis, causes of right and left axis deviation, nursing diagnosis for these conditions, and hexaxial reference. Includes study guide. Approved for CE credit. Winner of the American Film and Video Festival Award. 28m; VHS. **A:** College-Adult. **P:** Education. **U:** Institution. **Hea-Sci:** Nursing, Medical Education, Heart. **Acq:** Purchase, Rent/Lease. **Dist:** AJN Video Library/Lippincott Williams & Wilkins. $285.00.

Advanced Electronic Ignition Tune-Up 1984
On three tapes, ignition repair and tune-up are demonstrated. 40m; VHS, 3/4 U. **Pr:** Bergwall Productions. **A:** Sr. High-Adult. **P:** Vocational. **U:** Institution. **Bus-Ind:** Automobiles. **Acq:** Purchase. **Dist:** Bergwall Productions, Inc.

Advanced Excel for Windows 19??
Explores the more advanced features and functions of the Excel for Windows software package. Covers formulas, charts, graphics, reporting, database structure and usage, and customization. Comes with diskette, textbook, and quizzer. 60m; VHS. **A:** Sr. High-Adult. **P:** Instruction. **U:** Institution, Home. **How-Ins:** Computers, How-To. **Acq:** Purchase. **Dist:** Bisk Education. $179.00.

Advanced Flag Fundamentals 19??
Illustrates advanced flag fundamental techniques. Contains information on a variety of spins and tosses and includes a complete stretch out routine for daily warm-up exercises. 90m; DVD. **A:** Jr. High-Adult. **P:** Instruction. **U:** Institution, Home. **How-Ins:** Dance--Instruction. **Acq:** Purchase. **Dist:** Alfred Music Publishing Company Inc. $39.95.

Advanced Game Acceleration Tactics for Field Hockey 2009 (Unrated)
Coach Tjerk Van Herwaarden techniques for field hockey teams to accelerate the speed of play during the game. ??m; DVD. **A:** Family. **P:** Education. **U:** Home, Institution. **Spo-Rec:** Hockey, Athletic Instruction/Coaching. **Acq:** Purchase. **Dist:** Championship Productions. $39.99.

Advanced Glide Waxing and Tuning Techniques 1991
Ski maintenance and speed techniques for cross country skis include base preparation; glide waxing, scraping and brushing; and fluorocarbon waxing. 30m; VHS. **A:** Jr. High-Adult. **P:** Instruction. **U:** Home. **How-Ins:** Sports--Winter, Skiing, How-To. **Acq:** Purchase. **Dist:** NordicTrack Inc. $16.95.

Advanced Handling and Extension Diving for Goalkeepers 2014 (Unrated)
Soccer coach Jason Hamilton presents various training drills for improving goalie skills. 86m; DVD. **A:** Family. **P:** Education. **U:** Home. **L:** English. **Spo-Rec:** Athletic Instruction/Coaching, Soccer. **Acq:** Purchase. **Dist:** Championship Productions. $29.99.

Advanced Heavyweight Technique: Taking Away the Power Position 2002 (Unrated)
Coach Kerry McCoy demonstrates takedowns and finishers for heavyweight wrestlers to use when they are lighter than their opponents. 60m; DVD. **A:** Family. **P:** Education. **U:** Home, Institution. **Spo-Rec:** Athletic Instruction/Coaching. **Acq:** Purchase. **Dist:** Championship Productions. $39.99.

Advanced Hitting Techniques 2013 (Unrated)
Coach Gordon Eakin demonstrates drills for improving a softball player's hitting percentages, as well as discusses the mental side of being a batter. 52m; DVD. **A:** Family. **P:** Education. **U:** Home. **L:** English. **Spo-Rec:** Athletic Instruction/Coaching, Softball, How-To. **Acq:** Purchase. **Dist:** Championship Productions. $39.99.

Advanced Intelligent Network 199?
An in-depth overview of the Advanced Intelligent Network. 120m; VHS. **A:** Adult. **P:** Vocational. **U:** Institution. **Bus-Ind:** Technology. **Acq:** Purchase. **Dist:** Telcordia Technologies Inc. $495.00.

Advanced Jumps & Tumbling Combinations 2005 (Unrated)
Coach Mark Bagon and the ACF staff demonstrate four basic and eight advanced jumps, seven tumbling combinations, and five jump exercises for cheerleading squads. 34m; DVD. **A:** Family. **P:** Education. **U:** Home, Institution. **Spo-Rec:** Cheerleaders, Athletic Instruction/Coaching. **Acq:** Purchase. **Dist:** Championship Productions. $29.99.

Advanced Koi Keeping 1997
Provides instruction on koi keeping. 48m; VHS. **A:** Adult. **P:** Instruction. **U:** Home. **Gen-Edu:** Fish. **Acq:** Purchase. **Dist:** Karol Media. $14.95.

Advanced-Level Lacrosse Skills Made Easy! 2002
Presents advanced stick skills, shooting techniques, passing and catching, grips, and moves in comprehensive detail with demonstrations. 43m; VHS. **A:** Adult. **P:** Instruction. **U:** Institution, Home. **Spo-Rec:** Sports--General, How-To. **Acq:** Purchase. **Dist:** Championship Productions. $29.98.

Advanced Lifts and Partner Work ????
Traveling lifts, wrap-around lifts, drop lifts, and one-handed overhead lifts for ballroom competitions and pas de deux are demonstrated. 60m; VHS. **A:** Adult. **P:** Instruction. **U:** Institution, Home. **How-Ins:** Dance, Dance--Instruction. **Acq:** Purchase. **Dist:** Stagestep. $36.95.

Advanced Listening Comprehension 1983
This series of 10 untitled programs, is designed to improve listening comprehension for those students taking English as a second language. 20m; VHS, 3/4 U, EJ. **Pr:** University of Arizona. **A:** Jr. High-Adult. **P:** Education. **U:** Institution, CCTV, Home. **Gen-Edu:** Language Arts. **Acq:** Purchase, Rent/Lease. **Dist:** University of Arizona.

Advanced Lotus for Windows 19??
Covers some of the more advanced features of the Lotus 1-2-3 for Windows software, including spreadsheet applications, database applications, and graphics. Comes with diskette, textbook, and quizzer. 60m; VHS. **A:** Sr. High-Adult. **P:** Instruction. **U:** Institution, Home. **How-Ins:** Computers, How-To. **Acq:** Purchase. **Dist:** Bisk Education. $179.00.

Advanced Manufacturing 1994
Provides a look at technological manufacturing facilities and various processes used to produce final products. 22m; VHS. **A:** Adult. **P:** Vocational. **U:** Institution. **Gen-Edu:** Industrial Arts, Technology. **Acq:** Purchase. **Dist:** RMI Media. $95.00.

Advanced Mega Memory 19??
Kevin Trudeau offers memory applications training, placing emphasis on increased memory abilities and mind power. 54m; VHS. **A:** Sr. High-Adult. **P:** Instruction. **U:** Home. **Bus-Ind:** Self-Help. **Acq:** Purchase. **Dist:** Instructional Video. $79.95.

Advanced Methods of DC Circuit Analysis 1976
Introduces superposition theorem and its use in multiple-source DC circuit analysis. 28m; VHS. **A:** Adult. **P:** Education. **U:** Institution. **Gen-Edu:** Electricity. **Acq:** Purchase. **Dist:** RMI Media. $89.95.

Advanced Microskills 19??
This video presents three critical skills of the microtraining program with introductory lectures followed by counseling demonstrations which enable trainers to see subtle dimensions of skill usage. Three skills examined are Focusing, Reflection of Meaning, and Confrontation and Assertion. 60m; VHS. **A:** Adult. **P:** Professional. **U:** Institution. **L:** English. **Hea-Sci:** Psychology. **Acq:** Purchase. **Dist:** Microtraining Associates, Inc. $125.

Advanced Microskills: Focusing, Meaning, Confrontation ????
Demonstrates appropriate and inappropriate counseling methods, how to assess client conceptual frameworks in-depth, and eight steps for constructive confrontation. 60m; VHS. **A:** Adult. **P:** Professional. **U:** Institution. **Hea-Sci:** Psychology, Mental Health. **Acq:** Purchase. **Dist:** Microtraining Associates, Inc. $129.00.

Advanced Oxyacetylene Flame Cutting 1985
On seven tapes, expert oxyacetylene cutting is demonstrated. 110m; VHS, 3/4 U. **Pr:** Bergwall Productions. **A:** Sr.

High-Adult. **P:** Vocational. **U:** Institution. **Bus-Ind:** Welding. **Acq:** Purchase. **Dist:** Bergwall Productions, Inc.

Advanced Oxyacetylene Welding & Brazing 1985
On six tapes, welding and brazing for experts is demonstrated. 76m; VHS, 3/4 U. **Pr:** Bergwall Productions. **A:** Sr. High-Adult. **P:** Vocational. **U:** Institution. **Bus-Ind:** Welding. **Acq:** Purchase. **Dist:** Bergwall Productions, Inc.

Advanced Power Development Through Complex Training 2002
Provides detailed explanations and demonstrations for dynamic mobility exercises, "standard" exercises for the lower and upper body, and sports specific core exercises. 35m; VHS, DVD. **A:** Adult. **P:** Instruction. **U:** Institution. **How-Ins:** Fitness/Exercise, Sports--General, How-To. **Acq:** Purchase. **Dist:** Championship Productions. $39.95.

Advanced Power Principles—Heat Rate Improvement 19??
Industrial training program aimed at teaching operators the principles of efficient power plant operation by increasing the operator's understanding and awareness of how operating actions affect the efficiency of a plant and what can be done to operate a plant more efficiently. Comes with textbook and instructor guide. 35m; VHS. **Pr:** NUS Training Corporation. **A:** College-Adult. **P:** Vocational. **U:** Institution, CCTV. **Bus-Ind:** Industrial Arts, Occupational Training. **Acq:** Purchase, Rent/Lease. **Dist:** Williams Learning Network.
Indiv. Titles: 1. Introduction to Heat Rate Improvement 2. Principles of Heat Transfer 3. Power Plant Thermodynamics 4. Cycle Efficiency 5. Analysis of Boiler Efficiency 6. Boiler Efficiency 1 - Air Heaters and Preheaters 7. Boiler Efficiency 2 - (Windboxes, Burners, and the Furnace) or (Oil- and Gas-Fired Furnaces) 8. Boiler Efficiency 3 - (Superheaters, Reheaters, and the Economizer) or (Efficient Operations of Oil- and Gas-Fired Boilers) 9. Efficient Boiler Operation 10. Boiler Instruments and Controls 11. Analysis of Turbine Efficiency 12. Turbine Efficiency 1 13. Turbine Efficiency 2 14. Turbine Efficiency 3 15. Condenser Efficiency 16. Efficient Condenser Operation 17. Feedwater Heater Efficiency 18. Efficent Pump Operation 19. Efficient Power Plant Operation 20. Power Plant Efficency - Problems and Analyses.

Advanced Process Control 199?
An instrument technology training program on advanced process control. Includes a manual. 30m; VHS. **A:** Adult. **P:** Instruction. **U:** Institution. **Bus-Ind:** Technology, Job Training. **Acq:** Purchase. **Dist:** ISA -The International Society of Automation. $95.00.

Advanced Progressions for Across the Floor 19??
Cathy Roe demonstrates a number of dance progressions, including time steps, jumps, and kicks. 60m; VHS. **A:** Adult. **P:** Instruction. **U:** Institution. **How-Ins:** Dance--Instruction. **Acq:** Purchase. **Dist:** Stagestep. $39.95.

Advanced Pruning 19??
Offers advanced pruning techniques, as well as information on the influence of the apical bud, how cuts influence plant growth, two basic tree forms, and tips on establishing young trees and rejuvenating old ones. Also illustrates methods of pruning conifers, hedges, and deciduous fruit trees. Comes with teaching guide. 23m; VHS. **A:** Sr. High-Adult. **P:** Instruction. **U:** Institution. **How-Ins:** Landscaping, Horticulture, How-To. **Acq:** Purchase. **Dist:** CEV Multimedia; San Luis Video Publishing. $95.00.

Advanced Quattro Pro for DOS 19??
Explains the more advanced features and functions of the Quattro Pro for DOS software. Includes information on multipage technology, graphical user interface, new SpeedBar buttons, enhanced data analysis, and file transaction capabilities. Comes with diskette, textbook, and quizzer. 60m; VHS. **A:** Sr. High-Adult. **P:** Instruction. **U:** Institution, Home. **How-Ins:** Computers, How-To. **Acq:** Purchase. **Dist:** Bisk Education. $179.00.

Advanced Quattro Pro for Windows 19??
Teaches the new features of Quattro Pro for Windows, including sharing data with other applications, multi-tasking, performing commands with the SpeedBar, and sharing notebook data with other users. Comes with diskette, textbook, and quizzer. 60m; VHS. **A:** Sr. High-Adult. **P:** Instruction. **U:** Institution, Home. **How-Ins:** Computers, How-To. **Acq:** Purchase. **Dist:** Bisk Education. $179.00.

Advanced Riffs & Tricks 19??
John McCarthy and Scott Boland illustrate some of the more advanced techniques for playing rock and metal guitar. They cover strength and coordination exercises, arpeggios, bi-dextral hammer-ons, pivoting, lead patterns, and bi-dextral arpeggios. Includes tab booklet. 60m; VHS. **A:** Jr. High-Adult. **P:** Instruction. **U:** Home. **How-Ins:** Music--Instruction, How-To. **Acq:** Purchase. **Dist:** Hal Leonard Corp. $39.95.

Advanced Rock & Roll Bass Playing 19??
Designed for the player with basic skills, this video teaches popular bass styles heard in music today. ?m; VHS. **A:** Jr. High-Adult. **P:** Entertainment. **U:** Home. **How-Ins:** How-To, Music--Instruction. **Acq:** Purchase. **Dist:** Texas Music and Video. $29.95.

Advanced Rock Lead Guitar 199?
Dave Celentano teaches the viewer advanced rock lead guitar techniques. Includes booklet. 60m; VHS. **A:** Family. **P:** Instruction. **U:** Home. **How-Ins:** Music--Instruction. **Acq:** Purchase. **Dist:** Hal Leonard Corp. $19.95.

Advanced Rock Rhythm Guitar 199?
Dave Celentano teaches the viewer advanced rock rhythm guitar techniques. Includes booklet. 60m; VHS. **A:** Family. **P:** Instruction. **U:** Home. **How-Ins:** Music--Instruction. **Acq:** Purchase. **Dist:** Hal Leonard Corp. $19.95.

Advanced Roulette 1989
This video expands on the "action number" system and introduces other roulette techniques. 60m; VHS. **Pr:** John Patrick Productions. **A:** College-Adult. **P:** Instruction. **U:** Home. **Gen-Edu:** Gambling. **Acq:** Purchase. **Dist:** John Patrick Entertainment, Inc. $39.95.

Advanced S Corporation Taxation 19??
Shows how to do tax planning for S Corporations. Tax experts analyze, simplify, and explain recent developments affecting S Corporations and also discuss tax planning strategies. Comes with textbook and quizzer. Can be used for Tax CPE credit hours. 120m; VHS. **A:** College-Adult. **P:** Professional. **U:** Institution, Home. **Bus-Ind:** Business, Economics. **Acq:** Purchase. **Dist:** Bisk Education. $249.00.

Advanced Shiatsu Massage 1991
Understand the techniques of fine Oriental massage after viewing this video. 115m; VHS. **C:** Hosted by Jerry Luglio. **A:** Adult. **P:** Instruction. **U:** Home. **How-Ins:** How-To, Massage. **Acq:** Purchase. **Dist:** Artistic Video. $39.95.

Advanced Shooting ????
Covers how to use shot sheets, storyboards, logs and slates to map shots and boost production quality; use of filters; Charge Coupled Devices; use of dollys, trucks, arcs and cranes; handheld techniques; converging lines, depth of frame, and much much more. 30m; VHS. **A:** Adult. **P:** Instruction. **U:** Institution. **How-Ins:** Video, Filmmaking. **Acq:** Purchase. **Dist:** Stagestep. $19.95.

Advanced Shot Put Technique 2006 (Unrated)
Coach Larry Judge demonstrates advanced training techniques and drills for both the Glide and Rotational Shot Put events. 62m; DVD. **A:** Family. **P:** Education. **U:** Home, Institution. **Spo-Rec:** Sports--Track & Field, Athletic Instruction/Coaching. **Acq:** Purchase. **Dist:** Championship Productions. $39.99.

Advanced Skill Development for Post Players 2014 (Unrated)
Coach Danny Manning presents a workout for developing a basketball team's post players. 45m; DVD. **A:** Family. **P:** Education. **U:** Home. **L:** English. **Spo-Rec:** Athletic Instruction/Coaching, Basketball. **Acq:** Purchase. **Dist:** Championship Productions. $39.99.

Advanced Skills for the EMT 1988
A video series desinged to supplement the teachings of an EMT Intermediate course. 30m; VHS. **Pr:** Emergency Training Institute. **A:** Adult. **P:** Professional. **U:** Institution, Home. **Hea-Sci:** Medical Education, Emergencies. **Acq:** Purchase. **Dist:** Emergency Training. $620.00.
Indiv. Titles: 1. Circulation, Fluids, and Shock 2. Respiration and Ventilation 3. Patient Assessment 4. Using Anti-Shock Trousers 5. Basic Intravenous Infusion 6. Airway Management 7. Esophageal Intubation 8. Endotracheal Intubation.

Advanced Sliderobics 1995
Advanced exercise program combines basic slide aerobics patterns with a variety of proven aerobics/toning routines for a very challenging workout. 43m; VHS. **A:** Jr. High-Adult. **P:** Instruction. **U:** Home. **Hea-Sci:** Fitness/Exercise. **Acq:** Purchase. **Dist:** Collage Video Specialties, Inc. $19.95.

Advanced Smallmouth Tactics for Lakes and Reservoirs 19??
Presents Al Lindner, Dan Sura, and Tony Bean as they freshwater fish. 62m; VHS. **A:** Adult. **P:** Instruction. **U:** Home. **Spo-Rec:** Fishing. **Acq:** Purchase. **Dist:** In-Fisherman.

Advanced Step and Sculpt 1993
Jeff Vandiver from ESPN's Fitness Pros leads an aerobic workout. 65m; VHS. **C:** Hosted by Jeff Vandiver. **A:** Sr. High-Adult. **P:** Instruction. **U:** Home. **Hea-Sci:** Fitness/Exercise. **Acq:** Purchase. **Dist:** WarnerVision. $19.95.

Advanced Stunts Volume 10 2008 (Unrated)
Coach Mark Bagon and the Iowa All-Stars demonstrate 11 new stunts for cheerleaders at the advanced level. 24m; DVD. **A:** Family. **P:** Education. **U:** Home, Institution. **Spo-Rec:** Cheerleaders, Athletic Instruction/Coaching. **Acq:** Purchase. **Dist:** Championship Productions. $29.99.

Advanced Sugar Decoration 199?
Ewald Notter of the International School of Confectionary Arts instructs viewers on the art of using sugar works to create decorative showpieces in this two part series. In this volume, he demonstrates how to blow sugar, add color, and store and transport finished works. 39m; VHS. **A:** Sr. High-Adult. **P:** Instruction. **U:** Home. **How-Ins:** Cooking, Food Industry, How-To. **Acq:** Purchase. **Dist:** Culinary Institute of America. $75.00.

Advanced Tactics & Techniques for Goalkeeping 2011 (Unrated)
Coach Marybeth Freeman uses live demonstrations to presents tips and drills for improving the skills of goalies. 48m; DVD. **A:** Family. **P:** Education. **U:** Home, Institution. **Spo-Rec:** Hockey, Athletic Instruction/Coaching. **Acq:** Purchase. **Dist:** Championship Productions. $39.99.

Advanced Tax Issues in Estate Planning 1991
Series offers an overview of Internal Revenue Code Chapter 14 special evalution rules, and Chapter 13. Includes study guide. 210m; VHS. **A:** Adult. **P:** Professional. **U:** Institution. **Bus-Ind:** Law, Finance. **Dist:** American Law Institute - Committee on Continuing Professional Education. $200.

Advanced Tax Issues in Estate Planning: New Proposed Generation-Skipping Tax Regulations and Other Recently Issued Transfer Tax Regulations 1993
In-depth look at generation-skipping transfer (GST) regulations and the proposed Qualified Domestic Trust (QDOT) marital deduction regulations of 1992. Covers GST regulations, terms, exemption, inclusion, lifetime transfers, separate share rules, and much more. Includes study guide. 210m; VHS. **A:** Adult. **P:** Professional. **U:** Institution. **Bus-Ind:** Law. **Dist:** American Law Institute - Committee on Continuing Professional Education. $200.

Advanced Team Defense Drills for Softball 2010 (Unrated)
Softball coach Patty Gasso demonstrates 24 drills for warming up as well as infield and outfield play. 91m; DVD. **A:** Family. **P:** Education. **U:** Home, Institution. **Spo-Rec:** Softball, Athletic Instruction/Coaching. **Acq:** Purchase. **Dist:** Championship Productions. $39.99.

Advanced Technique Training: Hitting, Serving, & Blocking 2004 (Unrated)
Coach Bond Shymansky breaks down the mechanics of arm swing techniques for volleyball and shows how they apply to various aspects of the game. 70m; DVD. **A:** Family. **P:** Education. **U:** Home, Institution. **Spo-Rec:** Volleyball, Athletic Instruction/Coaching. **Acq:** Purchase. **Dist:** Championship Productions. $49.99.

Advanced Technique Training: Setting, Passing, & Defense 2004 (Unrated)
Coach Bond Shymansky provides a demonstrative lecture on defensive and ball control techniques for volleyball. 90m; DVD. **A:** Family. **P:** Education. **U:** Home, Institution. **Spo-Rec:** Volleyball, Athletic Instruction/Coaching. **Acq:** Purchase. **Dist:** Championship Productions. $49.99.

Advanced Techniques for the Hammer and Weight Throw 2006 (Unrated)
Coach Larry Judge demonstrates drills designed to increase an athlete's abilities at the Hammer and Weight Throwing Events. 41m; DVD. **A:** Family. **P:** Education. **U:** Home, Institution. **Spo-Rec:** Sports--Track & Field, Athletic Instruction/Coaching. **Acq:** Purchase. **Dist:** Championship Productions. $39.99.

Advanced Television Lighting, Vol. 1: Introduction to Drama 19??
BBC wizard Bill Millar discusses a complex series of lighting problems through use of diagrams, slides, and excerpts from his work. 35m; VHS. **Pr:** Australian Film, Radio and Television School. **A:** College-Adult. **P:** Education. **U:** Home, Institution. **Gen-Edu:** Television. **Acq:** Purchase, Rent/Lease. **Dist:** TMW Media Group. $149.

Advanced Television Lighting, Vol. 2: A Question of Quality 19??
Examines the sophisticated lighting techniques used by Bill Millar in several BBC productions, including "The Cherry Orchard" and "All's Well That Ends Well." 45m; VHS. **Pr:** Australian Film, Radio and Television School. **A:** College-Adult. **P:** Education. **U:** Home, Institution. **Gen-Edu:** Television. **Acq:** Purchase, Rent/Lease. **Dist:** TMW Media Group. $149.

Advanced Television Lighting, Vol. 3: Introduction to Light Entertain-ment 19??
Lighting expert Bill Millar describes the BBC approach to preparing and lighting music programs and entertainment specials through utilization of lighting plot plans and excerpts from finished programs. 38m; VHS. **Pr:** Australian Film, Radio and Television School. **A:** College-Adult. **P:** Education. **U:** Home, Institution. **Gen-Edu:** Television. **Acq:** Purchase, Rent/Lease. **Dist:** TMW Media Group. $149.

Advanced Television Lighting, Vol. 4: High Technology 19??
BBC master Bill Millar examines a variety of special effects lighting systems. He also discusses working with neons, lasers, and other specialized systems. 33m; VHS. **Pr:** Australian Film, Radio and Television School. **A:** College-Adult. **P:** Education. **U:** Home, Institution. **Gen-Edu:** Television. **Acq:** Purchase, Rent/Lease. **Dist:** TMW Media Group. $149.

Advanced Throwing: Projects and Techniques 19??
Demonstrates wheel throwing ceramics, including bottles and closed forms, covered jars, tips on lid fitting, facetting and cutting, throwing off the hump, donuts, and more. ?m; VHS. **A:** Jr. High-Adult. **P:** Instruction. **U:** Institution. **How-Ins:** How-To, Art & Artists. **Acq:** Purchase. **Dist:** Cambridge Educational. $49.95.

Advanced Training for Your Retriever 1993
Professional dog trainer and hunting guide Mike Mathiot provides continued training for retrievers. In this installment he covers steadying, decoys, blind retrieves, pattern work, cover, and distance. Contains actual hunting footage. 55m; VHS. **A:** Adult. **P:** Instruction. **U:** Home. **How-Ins:** Hunting, Pets. **Acq:** Purchase. **Dist:** Stoney-Wolf Productions, Inc. $19.95.

Advanced Training of Oxen 1988
A video training guide that takes the viewer beyond what he learned in Conroy's "Basic Training of Oxen." 44m; VHS. **C:** Drew Conroy. **Pr:** Doug Butler. **A:** Adult. **P:** Instruction. **U:** Institution, Home. **How-Ins:** Animals, Agriculture. **Acq:** Purchase. **Dist:** Doug Butler Enterprises Inc. $69.95.

Advanced Transportation and Solar Energy 1993
Contains news of automotive and transportation industries. Refers to joint agreement of auto manufacturers and the federal government in 1993. Visits a solar-powered energy plant in desert capable of generating enough power for the entire U.S. Comes in two versions, one geared for grades 4-8, and the the other for grades 9 and up. Includes study guide. 18m; VHS, SVS, 3/4 U. **A:** Primary-Adult. **P:** Education. **U:** Institution, CCTV. **Gen-Edu:** Energy, Automobiles. **Acq:** Purchase, Rent/Lease. **Dist:** Lucerne Media. $195.00.

Advanced Trolling for Saltwater Fish 199?
Informative program of advanced techniques including slow trolling, setting reel drags, how to follow bottom contours and more. 60m; VHS. **A:** Adult. **P:** Instruction. **U:** Home. **Spo-Rec:** Fishing. **Acq:** Purchase. **Dist:** Bennett Marine Video. $29.95.

Advanced Two-Step Dancin', Vol. 1 19??
Covers Whip Transitions, Throw Outs, Reverse Pass, Fake Belt Loop, and more. ?m; VHS. **A:** Sr. High-Adult. **P:** Instruction. **U:** Home. **Spo-Rec:** Dance. **Acq:** Purchase. **Dist:** SI Video Sales Group. $29.95.

Advanced Two-Step Dancin', Vol. 2 19??
Learn the Lariat, Whip to Lariat, Duck Outs, Ladies' Pretzel, and more. ?m; VHS. **A:** Sr. High-Adult. **P:** Instruction. **U:** Home. **Spo-Rec:** Dance. **Acq:** Purchase. **Dist:** SI Video Sales Group. $29.95.

Advanced Two-Step Dancin', Vol. 3 19??
Features Advanced Whip Leads, Neck Wraps, Double Ducks, Tunnels, and Body Wrap. ?m; VHS. **A:** Sr. High-Adult. **P:** Instruction. **U:** Home. **Spo-Rec:** Dance. **Acq:** Purchase. **Dist:** SI Video Sales Group. $29.95.

Advanced Voice Workout for the Actor 19??
Demonstrates the mechanics of breathing and vocal projection for the theatre. Can be used by the beginning actor to develop breath and projection skills, or by the experienced actor as a new approach to solving old problems. 85m; VHS. **A:** College-Adult. **P:** Education. **U:** Home. **Gen-Edu:** Theater. **Acq:** Purchase, Rent/Lease. **Dist:** TMW Media Group; Stagestep. $99.

Advanced Walk Aerobics 1990
The advantages of walking, but with the comfort of indoors. Shape the body while burning up fat and calories. 30m; VHS. **C:** Hosted by Leslie Tommelleo. **A:** Family. **P:** Instruction. **U:** Home. **Hea-Sci:** Fitness/Exercise. **Acq:** Purchase. **Dist:** Inspired Corp. $19.95.

Advanced Walleye Systems I 19??
Covers rigging techniques, hot locations in rivers, beating the postspawn slowdown, and more. 58m; VHS. **A:** Adult. **P:** Instruction. **U:** Home. **Spo-Rec:** Fishing. **Acq:** Purchase. **Dist:** In-Fisherman.

Advanced Walleye Systems II 19??
Provides step-by-step instructions for locating and successfully catching walleye. 53m; VHS. **A:** Adult. **P:** Instruction. **U:** Home. **Spo-Rec:** Fishing. **Acq:** Purchase. **Dist:** In-Fisherman.

Advanced Walleye Systems III 19??
Presents veteran anglers as they combine fishing techniques and boat control maneuvers to catch more fish. 58m; VHS. **A:** Adult. **P:** Instruction. **U:** Home. **Spo-Rec:** Fishing. **Acq:** Purchase. **Dist:** In-Fisherman.

Advanced Walleye Trolling Tactics 19??
Covers boat rigging, bait selection, leadcore line fishing, and more. 45m; VHS. **A:** Adult. **P:** Instruction. **U:** Home. **Spo-Rec:** Fishing. **Acq:** Purchase. **Dist:** In-Fisherman.

Advanced Waltz Dancin' Texas Style 19??
Covers advanced steps such as Twinkles, Grapevine Skaters, Windmills, Spiral with Turns, and more. ?m; VHS. **A:** Sr. High-Adult. **P:** Instruction. **U:** Home. **Spo-Rec:** Dance. **Acq:** Purchase. **Dist:** SI Video Sales Group. $29.95.

Advanced Windows 19??
Covers some of the more advanced operating procedures for the Windows software including directory usage and network set-up and operations. Comes with diskette, textbook, and quizzer. 60m; VHS. **A:** Sr. High-Adult. **P:** Instruction. **U:** Institution, Home. **How-Ins:** Computers, How-To. **Acq:** Purchase. **Dist:** Bisk Education. $179.00.

Advanced Word for Windows 19??
Provides a complete understanding on how to use some of the more advanced features of Word for Windows, including style concepts, templates, glossaries, macros, tables, print merge, sorting, and specialized desktop tools. Comes with diskette, textbook, and quizzer. 60m; VHS. **A:** Sr. High-Adult. **P:** Instruction. **U:** Institution, Home. **How-Ins:** Computers, How-To. **Acq:** Purchase. **Dist:** Bisk Education. $179.00.

Advanced Wordperfect 19??
Master Wordperfect with this video. Demonstrates how to save time, build columns, and design and publish a newsletter. 40m; VHS. **A:** College-Adult. **P:** Instruction. **U:** Home, Institution. **How-Ins:** Computers. **Acq:** Purchase. **Dist:** Silver Mine Video Inc. $29.95.

Advanced WordPerfect for DOS 19??
Teaches the more advanced features of WordPerfect including macros, columns, tables, math, merging, tables of contents, outlines, footnotes, and sorting. Comes with diskette, textbook, and quizzer. 60m; VHS. **A:** Sr. High-Adult. **P:** Instruction. **U:** Institution, Home. **How-Ins:** Computers, How-To. **Acq:** Purchase. **Dist:** Bisk Education. $179.00.

Advanced WordPerfect for Windows 19??
Teaches the more advanced functions of WordPerfect for Windows, by covering macros, columns, tables, math, merging, tables of contents, outlines, footnotes, and sorting. Comes with diskette, textbook, and quizzers. 60m; VHS. **A:** Sr. High-Adult. **P:** Instruction. **U:** Institution, Home. **How-Ins:** Computers, How-To. **Acq:** Purchase. **Dist:** Bisk Education. $179.00.

Advanced Wrestling Techniques 1992
Designed as a training aide for intermediate to advanced wrestlers. Different moves are demonstrated by Olympic gold medalist Bobby Weaver. 110m; VHS. **A:** Jr. High-College. **P:** Instruction. **U:** Institution, Home. **Spo-Rec:** Sports--General. **Acq:** Purchase. **Dist:** Cambridge Educational. $39.95.

Advanced Youth Wrestling Escapes 2010 (Unrated)
Coaches Joe MacFarland and Dave Mills discuss scoring bonus points on escapes and demonstrate various escape and takedown maneuvers. 43m; DVD. **A:** Family. **P:** Education. **U:** Home, Institution. **Spo-Rec:** Athletic Instruction/Coaching. **Acq:** Purchase. **Dist:** Championship Productions. $29.95.

Advanced Youth Wrestling Pinning 2010 (Unrated)
Coaches Joe MacFarland and Dave Mills discuss transitioning from breakdown moves to pinfalls as well as demonstrating various wrestling maneuvers. 45m; DVD. **A:** Family. **P:** Education. **U:** Home, Institution. **Spo-Rec:** Athletic Instruction/Coaching. **Acq:** Purchase. **Dist:** Championship Productions. $29.95.

Advanced Youth Wrestling Strength & Flexibility 2010 (Unrated)
Coach (and former pro baseball player) Chad Curtis and cheerleading champion Stacy Steensma demonstrate various strength and flexibility training exercises for young wrestlers. 68m; DVD. **A:** Family. **P:** Education. **U:** Home, Institution. **Spo-Rec:** Fitness/Exercise. **Acq:** Purchase. **Dist:** Championship Productions. $24.95.

Advanced Youth Wrestling Takedowns 2010 (Unrated)
Coaches Joe MacFarland and Dave Mills demonstrate over thirty different takedowns for teaching young wrestlers. 36m; DVD. **A:** Family. **P:** Education. **U:** Home, Institution. **Spo-Rec:** Athletic Instruction/Coaching. **Acq:** Purchase. **Dist:** Championship Productions. $29.95.

Advancement of Cattlemen for Tomorrow 1991
Documents a University of Idaho College of Agriculture and University of Idaho Caine Veterinary Teaching and Research Center pilot program designed to encourage high school students familiar with ranching to begin careers in the beef cattle industry. 10m; VHS. **A:** Sr. High-Adult. **P:** Education. **U:** Institution. **Gen-Edu:** Agriculture, Animals, Occupational Training. **Acq:** Purchase. **Dist:** University of Idaho. $25.00.

Advances in Cardiac Surgery 1998
Examines the introduction of minimally invasive cardiac surgery techniques and the resultant impact on the body and recuperation times. Experienced cardiac surgeons from Deborah Heart and Lung Center in New Jersey describe these new techniques and the patients who qualify for them. 28m; VHS. **A:** Sr. High-Adult. **P:** Education. **U:** Institution. **Hea-Sci:** Health Education, Medical Education, Medical Care. **Acq:** Purchase. **Dist:** Aquarius Health Care Media. $150.00.

Advances in Computer Numerical Control 1990
Visit Electro labs where computers play an active role in forming operations and real-time floor shop floor scheduling. Additionally, visit other companies that have brought CNC into the mainstream for their production techniques. 27m; VHS. **A:** Adult. **P:** Professional. **U:** Institution. **L:** English. **Bus-Ind:** Industry & Industrialists. **Acq:** Purchase. **Dist:** Society of Manufacturing Engineers. $228.

Advances in Leukemia 1981
A close study of the disease, including common diseases that are usually suspected at the beginning of the disease. 55m; VHS, 3/4 U. **A:** College-Adult. **P:** Professional. **U:** Institution, CCTV, Home, SURA. **Hea-Sci:** Diseases, Cancer. **Acq:** Purchase, Rent/Lease, Subscription. **Dist:** Emory Medical Television Network.

Advances in Metalworking Fluids 1991
See how Therm, Incorporated overcame coolant problems, and how McDonnel Douglas changed coolant, increasing coolant life from one to over 13 weeks. 30m; VHS. **A:** Adult. **P:** Professional. **U:** Institution. **L:** English. **Bus-Ind:** Industry & Industrialists. **Acq:** Purchase. **Dist:** Society of Manufacturing Engineers. $228.

Advancing Television by Satellite 1980
Examines two-way television and the role satellites, especially the Communications Technology Satellite, may play in this new technology. 28m; 3/4 U, Q. **Pr:** National Aeronautics and Space Administration. **A:** Jr. High-Adult. **P:** Education. **U:** BCTV, SURA. **Hea-Sci:** Communication, Technology, Television. **Acq:** Free Loan. **Dist:** NASA Lyndon B. Johnson Space Center.

Advantage/Disadvantage Drills and Motion Offense Drills & Skills 2013 (Unrated)
The third in a series of basketball clinics, coaches Geno Auriemma and Bob Knight offer further instruction on practice structure as well as team and individual skill building. 89m; DVD. **A:** Family. **P:** Education. **U:** Home. **L:** English. **Spo-Rec:** Athletic Instruction/Coaching, Basketball. **Acq:** Purchase. **Dist:** Championship Productions. $39.99.

Advantage Hornet 1990
Exciting footage of the Hornet in action. 62m; VHS. **A:** Jr. High-Adult. **P:** Entertainment. **U:** Home. **Gen-Edu:** Documentary Films, Aeronautics. **Acq:** Purchase. **Dist:** Bennett Marine Video. $24.95.

Advantages of the 1-3-4-3 and the 1-4-3-2-1 Systems 2013 (Unrated)
Coach Anson Dorrance gives a breakdown and on-field presentation of the two soccer systems he teaches at UNC. 89m; DVD. **A:** Family. **P:** Education. **U:** Home. **L:** English. **Spo-Rec:** Athletic Instruction/Coaching, Soccer. **Acq:** Purchase. **Dist:** Championship Productions. $39.99.

The Advent of Fashion 198?
The effect that music written for dance halls and other public forums had on the composer is shown. Popular styles forced the composers to be aware of public tastes, and this is illustrated by the work of Handel. 60m; VHS, 3/4 U. **A:** Jr. High-Adult. **P:** Education. **U:** Institution, SURA. **Fin-Art. Acq:** Purchase. **Dist:** Films for the Humanities & Sciences.

Advent: The Journey of Christ 1983
This series considers four varying aspects of the liturgical season of Advent. 30m; VHS, 3/4 U. **Pr:** Diocese of Rockville Centre. **A:** Family. **P:** Religious. **U:** Institution, SURA. **Gen-Edu:** Religion. **Acq:** Purchase. **Dist:** St. Anthony Messenger Press. **Indiv. Titles:** 1. Awakening 2. Conversion 3. Growth 4. Re-Birth.

Adventure 1945 — ★★
Gable's first postwar film has him as a roughneck sailor romancing a shy and reserved librarian (Garson). Dull and disappointing—both stars deserve better. However, there is a touching scene of Gable with newborn child that might be of interest to some. Based on the novel by Clyde Brion Davis. 130m/B/W; VHS. **C:** Clark Gable; Greer Garson; Joan Blondell; Thomas Mitchell; Tom Tully; John Qualen; Richard Haydn; Lina Romay; Directed by Victor Fleming; Written by Vincent Lawrence; Frederick Hazlitt Brennan; Cinematography by Joseph Ruttenberg. **Pr:** Sam Zimbalist; MGM. **A:** Sr. High-Adult. **P:** Entertainment. **U:** Home. **Mov-Ent:** Comedy-Drama, Romance. **Acq:** Purchase. **Dist:** MGM Home Entertainment. $19.98.

Adventure at the Center of the Earth 1963 — ★
Mexican horror film featuring dinosaurs, cyclops, bat-creatures, and a rat-faced monster. In Spanish without subtitles. ?m; VHS. **A:** Sr. High-Adult. **P:** Entertainment. **U:** Home. **L:** Spanish. **Mov-Ent:** Horror, Dinosaurs. **Acq:** Purchase. **Dist:** Something Weird Video. $20.

The Adventure Called Menudo 1982 (Unrated) — ★½
Xavier, Miguel, Johnny, Ricky and Charlie (the members of Menudo) sing 14 songs in this story of their misadventures, which begin with a flight in a balloon. In Spanish. 90m; VHS. **Pr:** Embassy Communications. **A:** Family. **P:** Entertainment. **U:** Home. **L:** Spanish. **Mov-Ent:** Musical--Drama. **Acq:** Purchase. **Dist:** New Line Home Video. $19.95.

Adventure Coral Reef 3D: Under the Sea of Egypt 2013 (PG)
Documentary filming the local sea life in Egypt's Red Sea. 52m; Blu-Ray. **A:** Primary-Adult. **P:** Entertainment. **U:** Home. **L:** English, German. **Gen-Edu:** Documentary Films, Nature, Africa. **Acq:** Purchase. **Dist:** 3D Media International. $12.99.

Adventure Enough 1985
A boy's trip to the supermarket stimulates his imagination. Designed to promote language skills. 12m; VHS, 3/4 U. **Pr:** John Walsh. **A:** Primary-Jr. High. **P:** Education. **U:** Institution, SURA. **Gen-Edu:** Language Arts. **Acq:** Purchase. **Dist:** Phoenix Learning Group. $175.00.

Adventure in Manhattan 1936 (Unrated) — ★★½
Smug crime reporter/criminologist George Melville (McCrea) is investigating a series of art thefts when he falls for Claire (Arthur), who's actually an actress hired to puncture his ego. Claire's starring in a WWI-set play (complete with loud explosions) that's a front for a jewel heist masterminded by the very man George has been pursuing. 73m/B/W; DVD. **C:** Joel McCrea; Jean Arthur; Reginald Owen; Thomas Mitchell; Victor Kilian; Directed by Edward Ludwig; Written by Sidney Buchman; Harry Sauber; Jack Kirkland; Cinematography by Henry Freulich; Music by William Grant Still. **A:** Sr. High-Adult. **P:** Entertainment. **U:** Home. **Mov-Ent:** Journalism. **Acq:** Purchase. **Dist:** Sony Pictures Home Entertainment Inc.

Adventure in Sahara 1938 (Unrated) — ★½
Typical desert soldier saga. Savatt (Gordon) is the cruel commander of a detachment of Foreign Legionnaires. Most of his brutalized men eventually mutiny and send him and a few loyalists off into the desert. They survive, and Savatt vows revenge, but when they arrive back at their outpost it is under siege. 60m/B/W; DVD. **C:** Paul Kelly; C. Henry Gordon; Adrian Booth; Robert (Fisk) Fiske; Marc Lawrence; Dick Curtis; Directed by David Ross Lederman; Written by Maxwell Shane; Cinematography by Franz Planer. **A:** Jr. High-Adult. **P:** Entertainment. **U:** Home. **Mov-Ent. Acq:** Purchase. **Dist:** Sony Pictures Home Entertainment Inc.

Adventure in Venice 1974
The adventures of a little boy at play in Venice. Shows many Venetian landmarks. 25m; VHS, 3/4 U. **Pr:** Encyclopedia Britannica Educational Corporation. **A:** Primary. **P:** Education. **U:** Institution, SURA. **Chl-Juv:** Italy. **Acq:** Purchase, Rent/Lease, Trade-in. **Dist:** Encyclopedia Britannica.

Adventure in Washington 1941 (Unrated) — ★
Unbelievable political drama has DC gossip maven Jane Scott (Bruce), the girlfriend of Senator John Coleridge (Marshall), revealing that someone is selling government info. Coleridge discovers it's Senate page Marty Driscoll (Reynolds), a troubled youth Coleridge tried to help by getting him the job. How the plot plays out next is ridiculous. 82m/B/W; DVD. **C:** Herbert Marshall; Virginia Bruce; Gene Reynolds; Samuel S. Hinds; Ralph Morgan; Vaughan Glaser; Directed by Alfred E. Green;

Written by Arthur Caesar; Lewis R. Foster; Cinematography by Henry Sharp; Music by W. Franke Harling. **A:** Sr. High-Adult. **P:** Entertainment. **U:** Home. **L:** English. **Mov-Ent**: Politics & Government. **Acq:** Purchase. **Dist:** Sony Pictures Home Entertainment Inc.

Adventure Island 1947 — ★½
En route to Australia, a small ship stops at a remote island for supplies. The crew is greeted by a crazed, tyrannical leader who makes their lives difficult. Dull low-budget remake of 1937's "Ebb Tide." 66m; VHS, DVD. **C:** Rory Calhoun; Rhonda Fleming; Paul Kelly; John Abbott; Alan Napier; Directed by Sam Newfield. **Pr:** Paramount Pictures. **A:** Jr. High-Adult. **P:** Entertainment. **U:** Home. **Mov-Ent**: Boating. **Acq:** Purchase. **Dist:** Sinister Cinema; Mill Creek Entertainment L.L.C. $16.95.

The Adventure of English 2002
British author Melvyn Bragg and other linguistic experts look at how the English language began, evolved, and became the premier language worldwide. 405m; DVD. **A:** Adult. **P:** Education. **U:** Home. **Gen-Edu**: Language Arts. **Acq:** Purchase. **Dist:** Acorn Media Group Inc. $79.99.

The Adventure of Photography: 150 Years of the Photographic Image 2003
A collection of 1700 pictures from the surreal to the sublime capture the history of an amazing art form including the first daguerreotypes, glossy fashion spreads, and war photojournalism. 260m; VHS, DVD. **A:** Adult. **P:** Education. **U:** Home. **Gen-Edu**: Photography, Art & Artists, History. **Acq:** Purchase. **Dist:** Kultur International Films Ltd., Inc. $39.95.

Adventure of the Action Hunters 1987 (PG) — ★
A dying sailor leaves a tourist couple a message leading to a treasure, and they vie for it along with gangsters, mercenaries and other unsavory types. 81m; VHS. **C:** Ronald Hunter; Sean Murphy; Joe Cimino; Directed by Lee Bonner. **Pr:** Troma Team. **A:** Jr. High-Adult. **P:** Entertainment. **U:** Home. **Mov-Ent**. **Acq:** Purchase. **Dist:** Unknown Distributor.

Adventure 1: Trailers on Tape 1984
Nearly 40 trailers for adventure movies are compiled on this tape, including "Rebel Without a Cause," "Lost Horizon," "Torn Curtain," "From Russia With Love," "Wild in the Street," "The Wild One" and "Sunset Boulevard." Some black and white segments. 61m; VHS. **C:** Paul Newman; Julie Andrews; Shelley Winters; James Dean; Sam Jaffe; Jane Wyatt; Edward Everett Horton; Sean Connery. **A:** Family. **P:** Entertainment. **U:** Home. **Mov-Ent**. **Acq:** Purchase. **Dist:** Passport International Entertainment L.L.C. $34.95.

Adventure: The Logan Challenge 1993
Two mountain climbers attempt to climb Mt. Logan, the highest mountain in Canada, by dogsled. 58m; VHS. **A:** Sr. High-Adult. **P:** Entertainment. **U:** Home. **Spo-Rec**: Mountaineering. **Acq:** Purchase. **Dist:** Mystic Fire Video. $24.95.

Adventure Theatre 1953
A collection of clips featuring various "adventure" scenes, including London under attack by giant dinosaurs, a crazy cartoon, and scenes from "Phantom of the Opera." 60m; VHS. **A:** Family. **P:** Entertainment. **U:** Home. **Mov-Ent**: Action-Adventure. **Acq:** Purchase. **Dist:** Video Resources.

Adventure Travel in Israel 1990
If you are looking for something new from Israel, this is the video for you. Explore hiking, rappelling, snorkeling, diving, horseback riding, and archaeology, all activities available across the country. 40m; VHS. **Pr:** Ergo Media. **A:** Family. **P:** Entertainment. **U:** Home. **Gen-Edu**: Travel, Israel. **Acq:** Purchase. **Dist:** Ergo Media Inc. $39.95.

Adventureland 2009 (R) — ★★★
With his post-college dreams of a European trip squashed by his dad's financial problems, James (Eisenberg) instead must move back home to Pennsylvania in the summer of 1987 and with his limited degree can only find work at the "Adventureland," the ragged local amusement park. Still a virgin, James encounters Em (Stewart), a sexually-experienced though troubled young woman who can't stand her stepmother and is having an affair with the park's married handyman (Reynolds). The pair genuinely connect, in large part to the actors, particularly Stewart. Yes, it's a coming-of-age comedy and has the usual sophomoric jokes, vulgarity, and drug use but they are just background to a charming love story. Based in part on writer-director Mottola's own life, also features a great '80s soundtrack and a fun pairing of SNLers Wiig and Hader as the park's married owners. 107m; Blu-Ray, Wide. **C:** Jesse Eisenberg; Kristen Stewart; Martin Starr; Bill Hader; Kristen Wiig; Ryan Reynolds; Directed by Greg Mottola; Written by Greg Mottola; Cinematography by Terry Stacey. **Pr:** Miramax Film Corp. **A:** Sr. High-Adult. **P:** Entertainment. **U:** Home. **L:** English. **Mov-Ent**. **Acq:** Purchase. **Dist:** Miramax Film Corp.; Movies Unlimited; Alpha Video.

The Adventurer 1917 — ★★½
An escaped convict saves two wealthy women from death. They mistake him for a gallant sportsman and bring him home. Early Chaplin silent with music track. 20m/B/W; Silent; VHS, DVD, 3/4 U, Special order formats. **TV Std:** NTSC, PAL, SECAM. **C:** Charlie Chaplin; Charles Halton; Directed by Charlie Chaplin. **Pr:** Mutual Film Corporation. **A:** Family. **P:** Entertainment. **U:** Institution, CCTV, CATV, BCTV, Home. **Mov-Ent**: Comedy--Slapstick, Silent Films. **Acq:** Purchase. **Dist:** Cable Films/i2bs Online World.

The Adventurer: The Curse of the Midas Box 2013 (PG) — ★★½
When his parents go missing and his younger brother is kidnapped, 17-year-old Mariah Mundi follows clues that lead him to the mysterious Prince Regent Hotel. There he learns about an artifact with supernatural powers that can grant limitless wealth and that there are monsters who steal children. Brit fantasy based on the young adult novel by G.P. Taylor. 98m; DVD, Blu-Ray. **C:** Aneurin Barnard; Michael Sheen; Sam Neill; Ioan Gruffudd; Keeley Hawes; Lena Headey; Tristan Gemmill; Directed by Jonathan Newman; Written by Christian Taylor; Matthew Huffman; Cinematography by Unax Mendia; Music by Fernando Velazquez. **A:** Jr. High-Adult. **P:** Entertainment. **U:** Home. **L:** English. **Mov-Ent**: Adolescence, Fantasy. **Acq:** Purchase. **Dist:** Acorn Media Group Inc.

The Adventurers 1951 (Unrated) — ★★
At the turn of the century, two Boers and an English officer set out to recover stolen jewels hidden in the jungles of South Africa. On the way, greed and anger take their toll a la "The Treasure of Sierra Madre," only on a less convincing scale. 82m/B/W; VHS. **C:** Dennis Price; Jack Hawkins; Siobhan McKenna; Peter Hammond; Bernard Lee; Directed by David MacDonald. **Pr:** J. Arthur Rank. **A:** Family. **P:** Entertainment. **U:** Home. **Mov-Ent**: Africa. **Acq:** Purchase. **Dist:** Movies Unlimited. $18.99.

The Adventurers 1970 (R) — **Bomb!**
Sleazy Harold Robbins novel retains its trashy aura on film. Unfortunately, this turkey is also long and boring. Set in South America, it tells the tale of a rich playboy who uses and destroys everyone who crosses his path. His vileness results from having seen his mother murdered by outlaws, but his obsession is to avenge his father's murder. Blood, gore, revolutions, and exploitive sex follow him everywhere. Watch and be amazed at the big-name stars who signed on for this one. 171m; DVD, CC. **C:** Candice Bergen; Olivia de Havilland; Bekim Fehmiu; Charles Aznavour; Alan Badel; Ernest Borgnine; Leigh Taylor-Young; Fernando Rey; Thommy Berggren; John Ireland; Sydney Tafler; Rossano Brazzi; Anna Moffo; Christian Roberts; Yorgo Voyagis; Angela Scoular; Yolande Donlan; Ferdinand "Ferdy" Mayne; Jaclyn Smith; Peter Graves; Roberta Haynes; Directed by Lewis Gilbert. **Pr:** Paramount Pictures. **A:** College-Adult. **P:** Entertainment. **U:** Home. **Mov-Ent**: Rape. **Acq:** Purchase. **Dist:** WarnerArchive.com. $29.95.

The Adventurers 1998
Follows the stories and lives of five of the world's greatest explorers through historical footage, first-hand accounts and re-enactments. Featured in the series are astronaut Neil Armstrong, scholar Thor Heyderdahl, the stratospheric pioneering Piccards, mountain climbers Hillary and Tenzing and polar explorer Richard Byrd. Five hours on five videocassettes. 60m; VHS; Closed Captioned. **A:** Jr. High-Adult. **P:** Education. **U:** Home. **Gen-Edu**: History, Documentary Films. **Acq:** Purchase. **Dist:** PBS Home Video. $59.98.

Adventures 1967
The adventures of a little raccoon who strays from home to explore the world. 11m; VHS, 3/4 U. **Pr:** National Film Board of Canada. **A:** Preschool-Primary. **P:** Education. **U:** Institution, SURA. **Chl-Juv**: Wildlife. **Acq:** Purchase, Rent/Lease. **Dist:** National Film Board of Canada.

Adventures Beyond Belief 1987 (Unrated) — ★
An irreverent motorcyclist is chased across Europe for a murder he didn't commit. Firmly within the boundaries of belief. 95m; VHS. **C:** Elke Sommer; Jill Whitlow; Graham Stark; Stella Stevens; Larry Storch; Thick Wilson; Skyler Cole; Edie Adams; John Astin; Directed by Marcus Thompson. **Pr:** Lightyear Entertainment. **A:** Jr. High-Adult. **P:** Entertainment. **U:** Home. **Mov-Ent**: Action-Adventure, Motorcycles. **Acq:** Purchase. **Dist:** No Longer Available.

Adventures in Art 1981
A tour through the National Gallery, and a look at the various paintings and the different ways of seeing. 28m; 3/4 U, Special order formats. **C:** Hosted by Julie Harris. **Pr:** National Gallery of Art. **A:** Jr. High-Adult. **P:** Education. **U:** Institution, SURA. **Fin-Art**: Documentary Films, Painting, Museums. **Acq:** Free Loan. **Dist:** National Gallery of Art.

Adventures in Asia 1994
Spin, National Geographic's animated globe-on-the-go, explores the vast regions and wildlife associated with Asia. 40m; VHS, CC. **Pr:** National Geographic Society. **A:** Family. **P:** Education. **U:** Institution, Home. **Gen-Edu**: Documentary Films, Asia, Wildlife. **Acq:** Purchase. **Dist:** Sony Pictures Home Entertainment Inc. $14.95.

Adventures in Assimilation 1992
A dance performance by Moss examines self discovery and identity. 8m; VHS, 3/4 U. **A:** College-Adult. **P:** Education. **U:** Institution. **Gen-Edu**: Dance--Performance. **Acq:** Purchase, Rent/Lease. **Dist:** Third World Newsreel. $125.00.

Adventures in Awareness 19??
Harvey Cohen discusses techniques for awakening the subconscious to achieve success. Includes six audio cassettes, a workbook and a kazoo(!?). ?m; VHS. **A:** Sr. High-Adult. **P:** Education. **U:** Institution, Home. **How-Ins**: How-To, Self-Help, Psychology. **Acq:** Purchase. **Dist:** Nightingale-Conant Corp. $195.00.

Adventures in Babysitting 1987 (PG-13) — ★★½
Pleasant comedy has its moments when a babysitter and her charges leave peaceful suburbia for downtown Chicago to rescue a friend in trouble. After a flat tire strands them on the freeway, trouble takes on a new meaning. Shue is charming as the hapless sitter, unexpectedly dateless, who finds herself doing a lot more than just watching the kids. Ludicrous at times, but still fun to watch. 102m; VHS, DVD, Blu-Ray, 8 mm, CC. **C:** Elisabeth Shue; Keith Coogan; Maia Brewton; Anthony Rapp; Calvin Levels; Vincent D'Onofrio; Penelope Ann Miller; George Newbern; John Ford Noonan; Lolita Davidovich; Albert Collins; Directed by Chris Columbus; Written by David Simkins; Cinematography by Ric Waite; Music by Michael Kamen. **Pr:** Touchstone Pictures. **A:** Jr. High-Adult. **P:** Entertainment. **U:** Home. **Mov-Ent**: Action-Adventure. **Acq:** Purchase. **Dist:** Buena Vista Home Entertainment. $89.95.

Adventures in Baja: Cabo to La Paz 19??
Forge beyond the border and sample some of the eloquent, stark beauty that is Baja. Includes information on customs and procedures. 60m; VHS. **A:** College-Adult. **P:** Entertainment. **U:** Home. **Spo-Rec**: Boating, Travel. **Acq:** Purchase. **Dist:** Bennett Marine Video. $29.95.

Adventures in Baja California: My "Rio Rita" 198?
Join the Rio Rita on her daily run around the most popular diving sites at La Paz. Includes a diving trip with the Sea Lions of Los Isoltes. 30m; VHS. **Pr:** Bennett Marine Video. **A:** Family. **P:** Entertainment. **U:** Home. **Spo-Rec**: Travel, Oceanography, Scuba. **Acq:** Purchase. **Dist:** Bennett Marine Video. $19.95.

Adventures in Biggleland: Billy's Birthday 1998
The Kidsongs Kids are whisked away to the make-believe world of their fantasy friends Billy and Ruby Biggle, where they help Billy celebrate his birthday and sing songs. 30m; VHS. **A:** Family. **P:** Entertainment. **U:** Home. **Chl-Juv**: Family Viewing. **Acq:** Purchase. **Dist:** SONY Wonder. $12.98.

Adventures in Biggleland: Meet the Biggles 1998
The Kidsongs Kids are whisked away to the make-believe world of their fantasy friends Billy and Ruby Biggle, where they tour Biggleland, meet people and sing songs. 30m; VHS. **A:** Family. **P:** Entertainment. **U:** Home. **Chl-Juv**: Family Viewing. **Acq:** Purchase. **Dist:** SONY Wonder. $12.98.

Adventures in Birdwatching 1998
Professor Ken Dial hosts this three volume set that looks at the world of birds across the globe. Titles include: Florida Wading Birds and Massachusetts Songbirds, Washington Predators and Arizona Hummingbirds, and Rare Birds of Costa Rica and Prime Tropical Real Estate. 60m; VHS. **A:** Family. **P:** Education. **U:** Home. **Gen-Edu**: Birds. **Acq:** Purchase. **Dist:** Janson Media. $49.95.

Adventures in Customer Courtesy 2000
Telephone customer service methods are taught through the use of dramatic recreations and demonstrations by Kirby the Leprechaun, who is summoned by harried employees in time of need. ?m; VHS. **A:** Sr. High-Adult. **P:** Education. **U:** Home. **Bus-Ind**: Business. **Acq:** Purchase. **Dist:** Advantage Media.

Adventures in Dinosaur City 1992 (PG) — ★★
Expect to see lots of movies riding on the coattails of the dino mania sweeping the land. Some will be good, others will not. "Adventures" falls into the latter category. Modern-day pre-teen siblings are transported back in time to the stone age. There they meet their favorite TV characters (they're dinosaurs) and help them solve prehistoric crimes. Family film may amuse kids, but adults should stick to "Jurassic Park." 88m; VHS, CC. **C:** Omri Katz; Shawn Hoffman; Tiffanie Poston; Pete Koch; Megan Hughes; Tony Doyle; Mimi Maynard; Directed by Brett Thompson; Written by Willie Baronet; Lisa Morton; Music by Fredric Teetsel. **Pr:** Luigi Cingolani; Smart Egg Pictures. **A:** Primary-Adult. **P:** Entertainment. **U:** Home. **Mov-Ent**: Fantasy, Dinosaurs, Adolescence. **Acq:** Purchase. **Dist:** Lions Gate Entertainment Inc. $89.98.

Adventures in Fingerstyle Guitar, Altered Tunings 199?
Laurence Juber provides detailed instructions and techniques for playing some of his better-known repertoire. 60m; VHS. **A:** Sr. High-Adult. **P:** Education. **U:** Home. **How-Ins**: Music--Instruction. **Acq:** Purchase. **Dist:** Hal Leonard Corp. $29.95.

Adventures in Fingerstyle Guitar, Standard Tunings 199?
Laurence Juber provides detailed instructions and techniques for playing some of his better-known repertoire. 70m; VHS. **A:** Sr. High-Adult. **P:** Education. **U:** Home. **How-Ins**: Music--Instruction. **Acq:** Purchase. **Dist:** Hal Leonard Corp. $29.95.

Adventures in Fingerstyle Guitar: The Guitar of Peppino D'Agostino 199?
Popular Italian guitarist provides detailed instructions and techniques for playing some of his better-known repertoire. 80m; VHS. **A:** Sr. High-Adult. **P:** Education. **U:** Home. **How-Ins**: Music--Instruction. **Acq:** Purchase. **Dist:** Hal Leonard Corp. $39.95.

Adventures in Fingerstyle Guitar: The Techniques and Arrangements of Alex de Grassi 199?
Guitarist/composer provides detailed instructions and techniques for playing some of his better-known repertoire. 90m; VHS. **A:** Sr. High-Adult. **P:** Education. **U:** Home. **How-Ins**: Music--Instruction. **Acq:** Purchase. **Dist:** Hal Leonard Corp. $39.95.

Adventures in Fingerstyle Guitar: The Techniques and Arrangements of Laurence Juber 199?
Two-tape set provides detailed instructions and techniques for playing some of Juber's better-known repertoire. 130m; VHS. **A:** Sr. High-Adult. **P:** Education. **U:** Home. **How-Ins**: Music--Instruction. **Acq:** Purchase. **Dist:** Hal Leonard Corp. $49.95. **Indiv. Titles:** 1. Standard Tunings 2. Altered Tunings.

Adventures in Fingerstyle Guitar: The Techniques and Arrangements of Muriel Anderson 199?
Classical, jazz, and folk-based guitarist provides detailed instructions and techniques for playing some of her better-known repertoire. 85m; VHS. **A:** Sr. High-Adult. **P:** Education. **U:** Home. **How-Ins:** Music--Instruction. **Acq:** Purchase. **Dist:** Hal Leonard Corp. $29.95.

Adventures in Perception 1973
Examines both the views and works of the famous artist. 22m; VHS, 3/4 U. **Pr:** Hans Van Gelder. **A:** Sr. High-College. **P:** Education. **U:** Institution, SURA. **Fin-Art:** Art & Artists. **Acq:** Purchase. **Dist:** Phoenix Learning Group.

Adventures in Spying 1992 (PG-13) — ★★
Brian McNichols is just trying to enjoy his summer vacation when he discovers that a notorious drug lord is living in his neighborhood. After realizing there is a $50,000 reward for his capture, he enlists the help of his friend (Schoelen) to get the man's picture for the police. Action-packed film is geared towards the junior high set, but relies too heavily on coincidence and other plot connivances to compete with espionage flicks directed at an older market. 92m; VHS, CC. **C:** Jill Schoelen; Bernie Coulson; Seymour Cassel; G. Gordon Liddy; Michael Emil; Directed by Hil Covington; Written by Hil Covington; Music by James Stemple. **Pr:** New Line Cinema. **A:** Jr. High-Adult. **P:** Entertainment. **U:** Home. **Mov-Ent:** Action-Adventure, Family Viewing, Drugs. **Acq:** Purchase. **Dist:** New Line Home Video. $89.95.

Adventures in the Gender Trade: A Case for Diversity 1994
Centers around Kate Bornstein, writer and performer, born a man. We take a trip with her from an unhappy boy child into a liberated transsexual lesbian. Provokes discussion. Shown at the Association for Women in Psychology, 1994; Margaret Mead Film Festival, 1993; Directors Citation, Black Maria Film Festival, 1993. 40m; VHS. **A:** College-Adult. **P:** Education. **U:** Institution. **Gen-Edu:** Documentary Films, Sociology, Prejudice. **Acq:** Purchase, Rent/Lease. **Dist:** Filmakers Library Inc. $295.00.

Adventures in Wonderland: Hare-Raising Magic 1993
Live action rendition of the Adventures of Alice in Wonderland based on the stories by Lewis Carroll. 45m; VHS. **A:** Primary. **P:** Entertainment. **U:** Home. **Chl-Juv:** Fantasy, Literature--Children. **Acq:** Purchase. **Dist:** Buena Vista Home Entertainment. $12.99.

Adventures in Zambezia 2012 (G) — ★½
A young falcon leaves for the big city to make his mark on the world. 83m; DVD, Blu-Ray. **C:** Leonard Nimoy; Jeremy Suarez; Abigail Breslin; Jeff Goldblum; Samuel L. Jackson; Directed by Wayne Thornley; Written by Wayne Thornley; Andrew Cook; Raffaella Delle Donne; Anthony Silverston; Music by Bruce Retief. **A:** Family. **P:** Entertainment. **U:** Home. **L:** English, French, Spanish. **Mov-Ent. Acq:** Purchase. **Dist:** Sony Pictures Home Entertainment Inc. $26.99 19.99.

Adventures of a Baby Fox 1987
A young fox searches the forest for food and adventure. 13m; VHS, 3/4 U. **A:** Primary. **P:** Entertainment. **U:** Institution, SURA. **Chl-Juv:** Fairy Tales. **Acq:** Purchase, Trade-in. **Dist:** Encyclopedia Britannica. $109.00.

Adventures of a Chipmunk Family 1959
Shows how baby chipmunks are trained and how a family prepares for winter by digging a burrow and storing food. 11m; VHS, 3/4 U. **Pr:** Encyclopedia Britannica Educational Corporation. **A:** Primary. **P:** Education. **U:** Institution, SURA. **Chl-Juv:** Animals. **Acq:** Purchase, Rent/Lease, Trade-in. **Dist:** Encyclopedia Britannica.

The Adventures of a Gnome Named Gnorm 1993 (PG) — ★★½
Silly cop caper finds LAPD detective Casey (Hall) stuck with a very strange new partner—a bark-wearing gnome named Gnorm. The two team up to go after a diamond smuggling ring. The special-effects creature may hold the kiddies interest. 86m; VHS. **C:** Anthony Michael Hall; Jerry Orbach; Claudia Christian; Directed by Stan Winston. **Pr:** Robert W. Cort; Scott Kroopf; Pen Densham; Richard B. Lewis; Interscope Comm; Gramercy Pictures. **A:** Primary-Adult. **P:** Entertainment. **U:** Home. **Mov-Ent:** Puppets, Fantasy. **Acq:** Purchase. **Dist:** $94.99.

Adventures of a Plumber's Helper 1978 (Unrated) — ★
Seems this stud-muffin plumber's helper is no Maytag man when it comes to house calls: when he stumbles on some stolen moolah whilst romping in the boudoir, he finds his chosen profession to be even more lucrative than the trade school brochures promised. 72m; VHS. **C:** Christopher Neil; Anna Quayle; Arthur Mullard; Richard Caldicot; William Rushton; Lyndie Benson; Directed by Stanley Long; Written by Aubrey Cash; Stephen D. Frances; Cinematography by Peter Sinclair; Music by Christopher Neil. **Pr:** Academy. **A:** Adult. **P:** Entertainment. **U:** Home. **Mov-Ent:** Comedy--Slapstick, Sex & Sexuality. **Acq:** Purchase. **Dist:** Movies Unlimited. $19.95.

Adventures of a Private Eye 1977 (Unrated) — ★
A self-mocking British detective farce about an inept private eye who takes his time tracking down a beautiful girl's blackmailer, bedding down with all the women he meets along the way. 96m; VHS. **C:** Christopher Neil; Suzy Kendall; Irene Handl; Directed by Stanley Long; Written by Stanley Long; Michael Armstrong; Cinematography by Peter Sinclair. **Pr:** Academy Entertainment. **A:** Sr. High-Adult. **P:** Entertainment. **U:** Home. **Mov-Ent:** Mystery & Suspense, Action-Adventure, Sex & Sexuality. **Acq:** Purchase. **Dist:** Unknown Distributor.

Adventures of a Taxi Driver 1976 (Unrated) — **Bomb!**
Cabbie finds sex, crime, sex, adventure and sex on the road in this off-duty comedy. 89m; VHS. **C:** Barry Evans; Judy Geeson; Adrienne Posta; Diana Dors; Liz Fraser; Directed by Stanley Long. **A:** Adult. **P:** Entertainment. **U:** Home. **Mov-Ent:** Action-Adventure, Sex & Sexuality. **Acq:** Purchase. **Dist:** Amazon.com Inc. $29.95.

Adventures of a Teenage Dragonslayer 2010 (PG) — ★★½
Fantasy adventure flick that hits its young target audience. Junior high dweeb Arthur is being bullied at school when he's rescued by Bart the troll, who tells Arthur he's the only one who can stop a dragon's destruction. After convincing his divorced mom Laura that what's happening is real, she, videogamer Shane, Bart, and Arthur team up to save the world. 88m; DVD. **C:** Hunter Allan; Lea Thompson; Richard Sellers; Eric Lutes; Wendie Malick; Jordan Reynolds; Amy Pietz; Directed by Andrew Lauer; Written by Jamie Nash; Cinematography by Luis M. Robinson; Music by Mark Oates. **A:** Family. **P:** Entertainment. **U:** Home. **Mov-Ent:** Fantasy. **Acq:** Purchase. **Dist:** Screen Media Ventures, LLC.

The Adventures of a Two-Minute Werewolf 1991
When a teenage boy watches a scary horror movie, he turns into a werewolf! Based on the book by Gene DeWeese; originally aired as an ABC Weekend Special. 60m; VHS. **C:** Lainie Kazan; Melba Moore; Barrie Youngfellow. **Pr:** ABC. **A:** Family. **P:** Entertainment. **U:** Home. **Chl-Juv:** Family Viewing, TV Movies. **Acq:** Purchase. **Dist:** Anchor Bay Entertainment. $12.98.

Adventures of a Young Eagle 1968
Follows a young eagle as he learns to fly, from his first attempt when he falls out of the nest to his success. 18m; VHS, 3/4 U. **Pr:** Hungarofilm. **A:** Primary. **P:** Education. **U:** Institution, SURA. **Chl-Juv:** Birds. **Acq:** Purchase, Rent/Lease, Trade-in. **Dist:** Encyclopedia Britannica.

The Adventures of Annie Oakley 1953
Two episodes of the vintage TV show based on the famous woman sharpshooter; "Annie and the Twisted Trail" and "Annie's Desert Adventure." 60m/B/W; VHS. **C:** Gail Davis; Brad Johnson; Jimmy Hawkins. **A:** Family. **P:** Entertainment. **U:** Home. **Mov-Ent:** Western, Television Series. **Acq:** Purchase. **Dist:** Moviecraft Home Video. $19.95.

The Adventures of Baron Munchausen 1989 (PG) — ★★★½
From the director of "Time Bandits," "Brazil," and "The Fisher King" comes an ambitious, imaginative, chaotic, and under-appreciated marvel based on the tall (and often confused) tales of the Baron. Munchausen encounters the King of the Moon, Venus, and other odd and fascinating characters during what might be described as a circular narrative in which flashbacks dovetail into the present and place and time are never quite what they seem. Wonderful special effects and visually stunning sets occasionally dwarf the actors and prove what Gilliam can do with a big budget. 126m; VHS, DVD, 8 mm, CC. **C:** John Neville; Eric Idle; Sarah Polley; Valentina Cortese; Oliver Reed; Uma Thurman; Sting; Jonathan Pryce; Bill Paterson; Peter Jeffrey; Alison Steadman; Charles McKeown; Winston Dennis; Jack Purvis; Don Henderson; Andrew MacLachlan; Cameo(s) Robin Williams; Directed by Terry Gilliam; Written by Terry Gilliam; Charles McKeown; Cinematography by Giuseppe Rotunno; Music by Michael Kamen. **A:** Jr. High-Adult. **P:** Entertainment. **U:** Home. **Mov-Ent:** Fantasy, History, Whales. **Acq:** Purchase. **Dist:** Sony Pictures Home Entertainment Inc. $19.95.

The Adventures of Batman & Robin: Robin 1995
"Robin's Reckoning, Parts I & II" finds the boy wonder discovering the man who killed his parents and deciding to take revenge—against Batman's wishes. 46m; VHS, CC. **A:** Family. **P:** Entertainment. **U:** Home. **Mov-Ent:** Animation & Cartoons. **Acq:** Purchase. **Dist:** Warner Home Video, Inc. $9.95.

The Adventures of Batman & Robin: The Joker 1995
The Joker breaks out of the asylum in "Christmas with The Joker," bent on destroying Batman's holiday cheer, and a lethal chemical compound will be turned upon Gotham's populace unless The Joker gets his way in "The Laughing Fish." 46m; VHS, CC. **A:** Family. **P:** Entertainment. **U:** Home. **Mov-Ent:** Animation & Cartoons. **Acq:** Purchase. **Dist:** Warner Home Video, Inc. $9.95.

The Adventures of Batman & Robin: The Riddler 1995
"If You're So Smart, Why Aren't You Rich" finds games-whiz Edward Nygma transformed into The Riddler to get revenge on the man who betrayed him and it's up to Batman and Robin to come to the rescue. "Riddler's Reform" finds the Dynamic Duo's nemesis up to his old tricks, using Wacko Toys as a front. 45m; VHS, CC. **A:** Family. **P:** Entertainment. **U:** Home. **Mov-Ent:** Animation & Cartoons. **Acq:** Purchase. **Dist:** Warner Home Video, Inc. $9.95.

The Adventures of Batman & Robin: Two-Face 1995
"Shadow of the Bat, Parts I & II" finds Batman and Robin trying to clear the name of Police Commissioner Gordon, who's been arrested for corruption. Batman goes undercover to find criminal mastermind Two-Face and Gordon's daughter turns up as Batgirl to help out Robin. 46m; VHS, CC. **A:** Family. **P:** Entertainment. **U:** Home. **Mov-Ent:** Animation & Cartoons. **Acq:** Purchase. **Dist:** Warner Home Video, Inc. $9.95.

The Adventures of Batman & Robin—Poison Ivy and the Penguin 199?
Presents episodes from the 1992-1995 animated television series about the Caped Crusader and sidekick Robin as they battle crime and injustice at night while in the day living as the normal-yet-wealthy Bruce Wayne. Includes villains Poison Ivy and the Penguin. 4 episodes. 89m; DVD. **C:** Voice(s) by Kevin Conroy; Efrem Zimbalist, Jr; Bob Hastings; Loren Lester. **A:** Family. **P:** Entertainment. **U:** Home. **Chl-Juv:** Television Series, Animation & Cartoons, Action-Adventure. **Acq:** Purchase. **Dist:** Warner Home Video, Inc. $12.98.

The Adventures of Batman & Robin—the Joker and Batman, Fire and Ice 199?
Presents episodes from the 1992-1995 animated television series about the Caped Crusader and sidekick Robin as they battle crime and injustice at night while in the day living as the normal-yet-wealthy Bruce Wayne. Includes villains the Joker, Maxie Zeus, and Mr. Freeze. 4 episodes. 89m; DVD. **C:** Voice(s) by Kevin Conroy; Efrem Zimbalist, Jr; Bob Hastings; Loren Lester. **A:** Family. **P:** Entertainment. **U:** Home. **Chl-Juv:** Television Series, Animation & Cartoons, Action-Adventure. **Acq:** Purchase. **Dist:** Warner Home Video, Inc. $12.98.

The Adventures of Black Beauty 1972
The endearing children's story of the brave and beautiful horse is told once again in this series. Programs are available individually. 50m; VHS. **C:** Judi Bowker; William Lucas. **Pr:** LWI Productions; Tablot Television. **A:** Family. **P:** Entertainment. **U:** Home. **Mov-Ent:** Family Viewing, Children, Horses. **Acq:** Purchase. **Dist:** Karol Media. $19.95.
Indiv. Titles: 1. The Fugitive/The Pet Pony 2. Lost, Parts 1 & 2 3. A Member of the Family, Parts 1 & 2 4. Out of the Night/Good Neighbors 5. The Quarry/The Challenge 6. A Ribbon for Beauty/A Mission of Mercy 7. The Fugitive (25 min.) 8. Game of Chance (25 min.) 9. A Long Hard Run (25 min.).

The Adventures of Black Beauty: Series 1 1972 (Unrated)
Drama series adapted from the literary classic. Vicky and Kevin Gordon live with their widowed doctor father and no-nonsense housekeeper Charlotte. One day their lives are changed forever when the children happen upon a majestic ebony horse and nurse him back to health and welcome it as a beloved family member. 26 episodes. 780m; DVD. **C:** William Lucas; Judi Bowker; Stacy Dorning; Michael Culver; Charlotte Mitchell. **A:** Family. **P:** Entertainment. **U:** Home. **Mov-Ent:** Drama, Horses. **Acq:** Purchase. **Dist:** Image Entertainment Inc. $24.99.

The Adventures of Black Beauty: Series 2 1973 (Unrated)
1972-74 family drama. The endearing aventures of Dr. Gordon, his two children and an extraordinary ebony horse. 26 episodes. 588m; DVD. **C:** William Lucas; Judi Bowker; Stacy Dorning; Michael Culver; Charlotte Mitchell. **A:** Family. **P:** Entertainment. **U:** Home. **Mov-Ent:** Drama, Family, Television Series. **Acq:** Purchase. **Dist:** Image Entertainment Inc. $24.99.

The Adventures of Blinky Bill 1994
Animated Australian TV series about a cute koala bear and his pals who are environmentally conscious. Two episodes per tape. 50m; VHS. **A:** Preschool. **P:** Entertainment. **U:** Home. **Chl-Juv:** Animation & Cartoons, Ecology & Environment. **Acq:** Purchase. **Dist:** CinemaNow Inc. $12.99.
Indiv. Titles: 1. Blinky Bill's Zoo/Blinky and the Magician 2. Blinky Bill's Fire Brigade/Blinky Bill's Fund Run.

The Adventures of Brisco County, Jr.: The Complete Series 1993
Western fantasy/comedy, set in 1893, follows the adventures of a Harvard-educated lawyer turned bounty hunter, Brisco County, Jr. (Campbell). Brisco is after the murderer of his father—dastardly criminal John Bly (Drago). A mystical golden orb that can bring the dead back to life also figures into the action. 27 episodes. 1260m; DVD. **C:** Bruce Campbell; Billy Drago; John Astin; Julius J. Carry, III; Christian Clemenson. **A:** Jr. High-Adult. **P:** Entertainment. **U:** Home. **Mov-Ent:** Television Series. **Acq:** Purchase. **Dist:** Warner Home Video, Inc.

The Adventures of Buckaroo Banzai Across the Eighth Dimension 1984 (PG) — ★★★
A man of many talents, Buckaroo Banzai (Weller) travels through the eighth dimension in a jet-propelled Ford Fiesta to battle Planet 10 aliens led by the evil Lithgow. Buckaroo incorporates his vast knowledge of medicine, science, music, racing, and foreign relations to his advantage. Offbeat and often humorous cult sci-fi trip. 100m; VHS, DVD, Wide, CC. **C:** Peter Weller; Ellen Barkin; Jeff Goldblum; Christopher Lloyd; John Lithgow; Lewis Smith; Rosalind Cash; Robert Ito; Pepe Serna; Vincent Schiavelli; Dan Hedaya; Yakov Smirnoff; Jamie Lee Curtis; Ronald Lacey; Matt Clark; Clancy Brown; Carl Lumbly; Boyd 'Red' Morgan; Damon Hines; Billy Vera; Bill Henderson; Jonathan Banks; John Ashton; James Saito; Directed by W.D. Richter; Written by Earl MacRauch; Cinematography by Fred W. Koenekamp; Music by Michael Boddicker. **Pr:** 20th Century-Fox. **A:** Family. **P:** Entertainment. **U:** Home. **Mov-Ent:** Comedy--Slapstick, Cult Films, Music--Pop/Rock. **Acq:** Purchase. **Dist:** Lions Gate Television Corp. $9.99.

The Adventures of Bullwhip Griffin 1966 — ★★½
A rowdy, family-oriented comedy-adventure set during the California Gold Rush. Light Disney farce catches Russell at the tail end of his teenage star days. Pleshette and McDowall embark upon an ocean trip from Boston to San Francisco to find her brother, Russell, who's out west digging for gold. Assorted comedic adventures take place. 110m; VHS, DVD. **C:** Roddy McDowall; Suzanne Pleshette; Karl Malden; Harry Guardino; Bryan Russell; Directed by James Neilson; Cinematography by Edward Colman; Music by George Bruns. **Pr:** Walt Disney

Studios. **A:** Family. **P:** Entertainment. **U:** Home. **Mov-Ent:** Action-Adventure, Miners & Mining, Family Viewing. **Acq:** Purchase. **Dist:** Walt Disney Studios Home Entertainment. $69.95.

Adventures of Bunny Rabbit 1937
A baby rabbit encounters an angry farmer and a hungry fox when his food hunt takes him from the woodlands to a nearby lettuce patch. Britnnica also offers a second edition of the film; produced in color by Wolfgang Bayer Productions in 1984, it runs 11 minutes. 10m/B/W; VHS, 3/4 U. **Pr:** Encyclopedia Britannica Educational Corporation. **A:** Preschool-Primary. **P:** Education. **U:** Institution, SURA. **Chl-Juv:** Animals. **Acq:** Purchase, Rent/Lease, Trade-in. **Dist:** Encyclopedia Britannica.

Adventures of Captain Fabian 1951 — ★½
When the captain of the "China Sea" learns that a beautiful woman has been falsely imprisoned, he comes to her rescue. Not one of Flynn's better swashbucklers, with typically low-quality Republic production. 100m/B/W; VHS. **C:** Errol Flynn; Vincent Price; Agnes Moorehead; Micheline Presle; Directed by William Marshall. **Pr:** Republic Pictures. **A:** Family. **P:** Entertainment. **U:** Home. **Mov-Ent:** Romance. **Acq:** Purchase. **Dist:** Unknown Distributor.

The Adventures of Captain Marvel 1941 — ★★½
A 12-episode cliff-hanging serial based on the comic book character. Details the adventures of klutzy Billy Batson, who transforms into superhero Captain Marvel by speaking the magic word, "Shazam!" 240m/B/W; VHS, DVD. **C:** Tom Tyler; Frank "Junior" Coghlan; Louise Currie; Directed by William Witney. **Pr:** Republic. **A:** Family. **P:** Entertainment. **U:** Institution, Home. **Mov-Ent:** Serials. **Acq:** Purchase. **Dist:** Lions Gate Entertainment Inc.; Anchor Bay Entertainment. $29.98.

The Adventures of Champion: The Best of Season 1 1955 (Unrated)
Vintage television inspired by the 1940s Gene Autry radio show. Stories center on Ricky North (Curtis), a boy with a gift for troublesome adventures, his Uncle Sandy (Bannon), and German Shepherd, Rebel. Ricky captures a gang of rustlers in "The Saddle Tramp," saves a general store owner from being conned into buying a salt mine in "Salted Ground," and gets caught up in "The Medicine Man Mystery" when stolen gems are hidden in a ventriloquist dummy. 10 episodes. 300m; DVD. **C:** Champion; Barry Curtis; Jim Bannon; Blaze. **A:** Family. **P:** Entertainment. **U:** Home. **Mov-Ent:** Drama, Western, Television Series. **Acq:** Purchase. **Dist:** Timeless Media Group. $9.98.

The Adventures of Chico and Guapo: The Complete First Season 2006 (Unrated)
Features the first season of MTV2's animated comedy about two janitors who become music recording studio interns who spend their days getting into trouble then chatting about TV shows they flip through (ala Beavis & Butthead style). 8 episodes. 160m; DVD. **C:** P.J. Pesce; Paul deArchi. **A:** Jr. High-Adult. **P:** Entertainment. **U:** Home. **Mov-Ent:** Television Series, Animation & Cartoons. **Acq:** Purchase. **Dist:** Paramount Pictures Corp. $26.99.

The Adventures of China Smith 1953
Features two episodes of an adventure series, "Yellow Jade" and "Night the Dragon Walked," in which an American gets involved in intrigue in the Orient by selling his services to the highest bidder. 60m/B/W; VHS. **C:** Dan Duryea; Douglass Dumbrille; Myrna Dell. **A:** Family. **P:** Entertainment. **U:** Home. **Mov-Ent:** Television Series. **Acq:** Purchase. **Dist:** Moviecraft Home Video. $19.95.

Adventures of Chip 'n' Dale 19??
Animated tales of the two lovable chipmunks. Includes: "Two Chips and a Miss," "Chicken in the Rough Chips," "Ahoy The Lone Chipmunks." 47m; VHS. **Pr:** Walt Disney Studios. **A:** Family. **P:** Entertainment. **U:** Home. **Chl-Juv:** Animation & Cartoons, Animals. **Acq:** Purchase. **Dist:** Sony Pictures Home Entertainment Inc. $24.95.

Adventures of Cubby Bear 1933
Collection of seven black and white Van Beuren animated shorts featuring Cubby Bear (a.k.a. Brownie Bear). 137m/B/W; DVD. **A:** Family. **P:** Entertainment. **U:** Home. **Mov-Ent:** Animation & Cartoons. **Acq:** Purchase. **Dist:** Mackinac Media Inc. $15.95.

The Adventures of Curious George 1993
Includes two animated episodes based on the series by Margaret and H.A. Rey. In "Curious George," the Man in the Yellow Hat captures George in Africa and brings him home where George tries to learn a new lifestyle. When George eats a puzzle piece in "Curious George Goes to the Hospital," he gets a tummyache and goes to the hospital for help. 30m; VHS. **A:** Preschool-Primary. **P:** Entertainment. **U:** Home. **Chl-Juv:** Animation & Cartoons, Hospitals. **Acq:** Purchase. **Dist:** Golden Book Video. $9.95.

Adventures of Don Juan 1949 — ★★★½
Flynn's last spectacular epic features elegant costuming and loads of action. Don Juan saves Queen Margaret from her evil first minister. He then swashbuckles his way across Spain and England in an effort to win her heart. Grand, large-scale fun and adventure with Flynn at his self-mocking best. 111m; VHS, DVD. **C:** Errol Flynn; Viveca Lindfors; Robert Douglas; Romney Brent; Alan Hale; Raymond Burr; Aubrey Mather; Ann Rutherford; Directed by Vincent Sherman; Music by Max Steiner. **Pr:** Warner Bros. **A:** Jr. High-Adult. **P:** Entertainment. **U:** Home. **Mov-Ent:** Romance. **Awds:** Oscars '49: Costume Des. (C). **Acq:** Purchase. **Dist:** MGM Home Entertainment. $19.98.

Adventures of Droopy 1955
A collection of seven classic cartoons featuring that sad-eyed bloodhound Droopy including: "Dumb-Hounded," "Wags to Riches," "Champ Champ" and "Deputy Droopy." 53m; VHS. **C:** Directed by Tex Avery. **Pr:** MGM. **A:** Family. **P:** Entertainment. **U:** Home. **Chl-Juv:** Animation & Cartoons. **Acq:** Purchase. **Dist:** MGM Home Entertainment. $14.95.

Adventures of Eliza Fraser 1976 — ★½
A young shipwrecked couple move from bawdy pleasures to cannibalism after being captured by aborigines. 114m; VHS. **C:** Susannah York; Trevor Howard; Leon Lissek; Abigail; Noel Ferrier; Carole Skinner; Directed by Tim Burstall. **Pr:** Hexagon Productions. **A:** Sr. High-Adult. **P:** Entertainment. **U:** Home. **Mov-Ent. Acq:** Purchase. **Dist:** Unknown Distributor.

The Adventures of Elmer and Friends: Freedom Rocks 1998
Live action musical program for children stars Elmer the tree and a variety of friends. Stresses the importance of nature and equality. 30m; VHS. **A:** Primary. **P:** Entertainment. **U:** Home. **Chl-Juv:** Children, Musical. **Acq:** Purchase. **Dist:** 411 Video Information. $14.95.

The Adventures of Elmer and Friends: Pirate Island 1998
Live action musical program for children stars Elmer the tree and a variety of friends. Stresses the importance of friendship. 30m; VHS. **A:** Primary. **P:** Entertainment. **U:** Home. **Chl-Juv:** Children, Musical. **Acq:** Purchase. **Dist:** 411 Video Information. $14.95.

The Adventures of Elmer and Friends: The Magic Map 1998
Live action musical program for children stars Elmer the tree and a variety of friends. Stresses the importance of reading. 30m; VHS. **A:** Primary. **P:** Entertainment. **U:** Home. **Chl-Juv:** Children, Musical. **Acq:** Purchase. **Dist:** 411 Video Information. $14.95.

The Adventures of Elmer and Friends: Treasure Beyond Measure 1998
Live action musical program for children stars Elmer the tree and a variety of friends. Stresses the importance of self-esteem. 30m; VHS. **A:** Primary. **P:** Entertainment. **U:** Home. **Chl-Juv:** Children, Musical. **Acq:** Purchase. **Dist:** 411 Video Information. $14.95.

The Adventures of Elmo in Grouchland 1999 (G)
Sweet-voiced Elmo loses his security blanket when it's accidentally tossed into the garbage can of Oscar the Grouch. So Elmo must leave the safety of Sesame Street and brave the unknown Grouchland, where he meets selfish bad guy Huxley (Patinkin), who takes Elmo's blankie for himself. Naturally, everything turns out okay. (Bert and Ernie tell us so!) 77m; VHS, DVD. **C:** Mandy Patinkin; Vanessa L(ynne) Williams; Ruth Buzzi; Voice(s) by Kevin Clash; Carroll Spinney; Frank Oz; Steve Whitmire; Joseph Mazzarino; Directed by Gary Halvorson; Written by Joseph Mazzarino; Mitchell Kriegman; Cinematography by Alan Caso; Music by John Debney. **Pr:** Brian Henson; Columbia Pictures; Jim Henson Productions; Children's Television Workshop; Sony Pictures Home Entertainment Inc. **A:** Family. **P:** Entertainment. **U:** Home. **Chl-Juv:** Puppets. **Acq:** Purchase. **Dist:** Sony Pictures Home Entertainment Inc.

The Adventures of Felix 1999 (Unrated) — ★★
Felix (Bouajila) is a gay, HIV-positive Frenchman of Arab descent who decides to go on a road trip to Marseilles after finding some old letters from the father he never knew. Felix has a number of adventures while hitchhiking and makes an impromptu family of those he meets along the way, which leads him to wonder if he really needs to meet his biological dad after all. French with subtitles. 95m; VHS, DVD. **C:** Sami Bouajila; Patachou; Ariane Ascaride; Pierre-Loup Rajot; Charly Sergue; Clement Reverend; Maurice Benichou; Directed by Olivier Ducastel; Jacques Martineau; Written by Olivier Ducastel; Jacques Martineau; Cinematography by Mathieu Poirot-Delpech. **Pr:** Philippe Martin; Arte France; Les Films Pelleas; Pyramide Productions; Winstar Cinema. **A:** College-Adult. **P:** Entertainment. **U:** Home. **L:** French. **Mov-Ent:** France, Immigration, Family. **Acq:** Purchase. **Dist:** Wellspring Media.

The Adventures of Ford Fairlane 1990 (R) — **Bomb!**
The Diceman plays an unusual detective specializing in rock 'n' roll cases. When a heavy metal singer dies on stage, he takes the case in his own inimitable fashion, pursuing buxom gals, sleazy record executives, and even his ex-wife. Not surprisingly, many of his stand-up bits are worked into the movie. Clay, the ever-so-controversial comic in his first (and likely last) starring role haplessly sneers his way through this rock 'n' roll dud of a comedy thriller. A quick effort to cash in on Clay's fading star. Forget about it. 101m; VHS, DVD, Wide, CC. **C:** Andrew Silverstein; Wayne Newton; Priscilla Presley; Morris Day; Lauren Holly; Maddie Corman; Gilbert Gottfried; David Patrick Kelly; Brandon Call; Robert Englund; Ed O'Neill; Sheila E; Kari Wuhrer; Tone Loc; Directed by Renny Harlin; Written by David Arnott; Daniel Waters; James Cappe. **Pr:** Joel Silver; 20th Century-Fox. **A:** College-Adult. **P:** Entertainment. **U:** Home. **Mov-Ent:** Automobiles, Animals. **Awds:** Golden Raspberries '90: Worst Actor (Silverstein), Worst Picture, Worst Screenplay. **Acq:** Purchase. **Dist:** Wellspring Media. $19.98.

The Adventures of Frank and Jesse James 1948 — ★★
The bad brothers of the Wild West are trying to make good for rip-offs committed in their names, so they're hoping to hit pay-dirt with a silver mine. A 13-episode serial on two cassettes. 180m/B/W; VHS. **C:** Steve Darrell; Clayton Moore; Noel Neill; Stanley Andrews; Directed by Yakima Canutt. **A:** Family. **P:** Entertainment. **U:** Home. **Mov-Ent:** Serials. **Acq:** Purchase. **Dist:** Lions Gate Entertainment Inc.; Movies Unlimited. $29.98.

The Adventures of Frontier Fremont 1975 (Unrated) — ★★
A rough and tumble story of a man who leaves the city, grows a beard, and makes the wilderness his home (and the animals his friends). Mountain life, that's the life for me. Almost indistinguishable from Haggerty's "Grizzly Adams," with the usual redeeming panoramic shots of majestic mountains. 95m; VHS. **C:** Dan Haggerty; Denver Pyle; Directed by Richard Friedenberg. **Pr:** Sunn Classic Pictures. **A:** Family. **P:** Entertainment. **U:** Home. **Mov-Ent:** Action-Adventure, Wilderness Areas. **Acq:** Purchase. **Dist:** No Longer Available.

The Adventures of Fu Manchu 1956
Two episodes of the campy television program. 60m/B/W; VHS. **C:** Glenn Gordon. **A:** Family. **P:** Entertainment. **U:** Home. **Mov-Ent:** Mystery & Suspense, Television Series. **Acq:** Purchase, Rent/Lease. **Dist:** Moviecraft Home Video. $24.95.

The Adventures of Gallant Bess 1948 (Unrated) — ★★
The time-honored story of a rodeo man torn between his girl and his talented horse (the Bess of the title). 73m; VHS, DVD. **C:** Cameron Mitchell; Audrey Long; Fuzzy Knight; James Millican; Directed by Lew Landers. **Pr:** Eagle Lion. **A:** Family. **P:** Entertainment. **U:** Home. **Mov-Ent:** Western, Romance, Horses. **Acq:** Purchase. **Dist:** Movies Unlimited; Alpha Video.

The Adventures of Hairbreadth Harry 192?
Three short spoofs of the early melodramas cranked out by the movie industry. Includes "Sawdust Baby," "Fearless Harry," and "Rudolph's Revenge." 65m/B/W; Silent; VHS. **C:** Billy West. **A:** Family. **P:** Entertainment. **U:** Home. **Mov-Ent:** Satire & Parody, Silent Films. **Acq:** Purchase. **Dist:** Grapevine Video.

The Adventures of Hiram Holiday: Lapidary Wheel/Romantic Pigeon 1956
Two episodes of this vintage television show feature Hiram getting mixed up with jewel thieves and falling in love thanks to a carrier pigeon. Contains original Sanka and Jello commercials. ?m; VHS. **C:** Wally Cox; Ainslie Pryor. **A:** Family. **P:** Entertainment. **U:** Home. **Mov-Ent:** Television Series. **Acq:** Purchase. **Dist:** Grapevine Video. $12.95.

The Adventures of Hiram Holiday: Sea Cucumber/Hawaiian Humza 195?
These two episodes of the rare 1950s television show take Hiram to Hong Kong and Hawaii. Contains the original Sanka and Jello commercials that aired with the shows. ?m; VHS. **C:** Wally Cox; Ainslie Pryor. **A:** Family. **P:** Entertainment. **U:** Home. **Mov-Ent:** Television Series. **Acq:** Purchase. **Dist:** Grapevine Video. $12.95.

The Adventures of Hiram Holiday/The Hank McCune Show 1956
Contains two vintage TV comedy shows. Hiram Holiday encounters a comical situation in "Morroco," one of the foreign country he visits as a reward for finding a major error as a newspaper proofreader, and avoiding a lawsuit against his employer. Hank McCune plays the host of a TV show who finds himself in another comic predicament in "The Prize." 60m/B/W; VHS. **C:** Wally Cox; Hank McCune. **Pr:** National Broadcasting Company. **A:** Family. **P:** Entertainment. **U:** Home. **Mov-Ent:** Comedy-Drama, Television Series. **Acq:** Purchase. **Dist:** Moviecraft Home Video. $19.95.

The Adventures of Huck Finn 1993 (PG) — ★★★
Decent Disney attempt at adapting an American favorite by Mark Twain. Mischievious Huck and runaway slave Jim travel down the muddy Mississippi, working on life and friendship and getting into all sorts of adventures in the pre-Civil War era. Fast-paced and amusing with good performances by Wood (in the title role) and Broadway trained Vance (as Jim). Racial epithets and minstrel show dialect have been eliminated in this version. Some material, including Jim's close call with a lynch mob and Huck's drunken, brutal father may be too strong for immature children. 108m; VHS, DVD, Wide, CC. **C:** Elijah Wood; Courtney B. Vance; Robbie Coltrane; Jason Robards, Jr.; Ron Perlman; Dana Ivey; Anne Heche; James Gammon; Paxton Whitehead; Tom Aldredge; Curtis Armstrong; Mary Louise Wilson; Frances Conroy; Directed by Stephen Sommers; Written by Stephen Sommers; Cinematography by Janusz Kaminski; Music by Bill Conti. **Pr:** Laurence Mark; John Baldecchi; Barry Bernardi; Steve White; Buena Vista. **A:** Jr. High-Adult. **P:** Entertainment. **U:** Home. **Mov-Ent:** Action-Adventure, Rivers & Streams. **Acq:** Purchase. **Dist:** Walt Disney Studios Home Entertainment; Baker and Taylor. $39.99.

The Adventures of Huckleberry Finn 1939 (Unrated) — ★★★
Mark Twain's classic story about a boy who runs away and travels down the Mississippi on a raft, accompanied by a runaway slave, is done over in MGM-style. Rooney is understated as Huck (quite a feat), while the production occasionally floats aimlessly down the Mississippi. An entertaining follow-up to "The Adventures of Tom Sawyer." 89m/B/W; VHS, DVD, Streaming. **C:** Mickey Rooney; Lynne Carver; Rex Ingram; William Frawley; Walter Connolly; Directed by Richard Thorpe. **Pr:** MGM. **A:** Family. **P:** Entertainment. **U:** Home. **Mov-Ent:** Action-Adventure, Boating, Rivers & Streams. **Acq:** Purchase. **Dist:** WarnerArchive.com; Home Vision Cinema. $19.98.

The Adventures of Huckleberry Finn 1960 — ★★½
A lively adaptation of the Twain saga in which Huck and runaway slave Jim raft down the Mississipi in search of freedom and adventure. Miscasting of Hodges as Huck hampers the proceedings, but Randall shines as the treacherous King. Strong supporting cast includes Keaton as a lion-tamer and boxing champ Moore as Jim. 107m; VHS, DVD. **C:** Tony Randall; Eddie Hodges; Archie Moore; Patty McCormack;

Neville Brand; Mickey Shaughnessy; Judy Canova; Andy Devine; Sherry Jackson; Buster Keaton; Finlay Currie; Josephine Hutchinson; Parley Baer; John Carradine; Royal Dano; Sterling Holloway; Harry Dean Stanton; Directed by Michael Curtiz. **Pr:** Samuel Goldwyn; MGM. **A:** Family. **P:** Entertainment. **U:** Home. **Mov-Ent:** Family Viewing, Rivers & Streams, Literature--American. **Acq:** Purchase. **Dist:** MGM Home Entertainment; Facets Multimedia Inc. $19.98.

The Adventures of Huckleberry Finn 1978 — ★★
The classic adventure by Mark Twain of an orphan boy and a runaway slave done again as a TV movie and starring "F-Troop" regulars Tucker and Storch. Lacks the production values of earlier versions. 100m; VHS. **C:** Forrest Tucker; Larry Storch; Kurt Ida; Mike Mazurki; Brock Peters; Directed by Jack B. Hively. **Pr:** Sunn Classic Pictures. **A:** Family. **P:** Entertainment. **U:** Home. **Mov-Ent:** Action-Adventure, Children, TV Movies. **Acq:** Purchase. **Dist:** No Longer Available.

The Adventures of Huckleberry Finn 1985 — ★★½
An adaptation of the Mark Twain story about the adventures encountered by Huckleberry Finn and a runaway slave as they travel down the Mississippi River. Top-notch cast makes this an entertaining version. Originally made in a much longer version for PBS's "American Playhouse." 121m; VHS, DVD. **C:** Sada Thompson; Lillian Gish; Richard Kiley; Jim Dale; Barnard Hughes; Patrick Day; Frederic Forrest; Geraldine Page; Butterfly McQueen; Samm-Art Williams; Directed by Peter H. Hunt. **Pr:** Great Amwell Company. **A:** Family. **P:** Entertainment. **U:** Home. **Mov-Ent:** TV Movies, Slavery, Rivers & Streams. **Acq:** Purchase. **Dist:** Monterey Home Video. $19.95.

The Adventures of Huckleberry Finn 1993
Two-part adaptation of Mark Twain's story of Huckleberry Finn. 240m; VHS. **Pr:** Film Ideas, Inc. **A:** Family. **P:** Education. **U:** Home. **Gen-Edu:** Literature--American, Rivers & Streams. **Acq:** Purchase. **Dist:** Film Ideas, Inc. $69.96.

Adventures of Hunting Trophy Caribou 1991
A record-book bull caribou is taken by Bill Krenz in this dramatic and beautifully filmed hunting video filmed in Quebec. 70m; VHS. **Pr:** Stoney Wolf Video Productions. **A:** Sr. High-Adult. **P:** Entertainment. **U:** Home. **Spo-Rec:** Sports--General, Hunting. **Acq:** Purchase. **Dist:** Stoney-Wolf Productions, Inc. $29.95.

The Adventures of Ichabod and Mr. Toad 1949 — ★★★½
Disney's wonderfully animated versions of Kenneth Grahame's "The Wind in the Willows" and "The Legend of Sleepy Hollow" by Washington Irving. Rathbone narrates the story of Mr. Toad, who suffers from arrogance and eventually must defend himself in court after being charged with driving a stolen vehicle (Disney did take liberties with the story). Crosby provides all the voices for "Ichabod," which features one of the all-time great animated sequences—Ichabod riding in a frenzy through the forest while being pursued by the headless horseman. A treat for all ages. 68m; VHS, DVD. **C:** Voice(s) by Jack Kinney; Bing Crosby; Eric Blore; Pat O'Malley; Narrated by Basil Rathbone; Directed by Clyde Geronimi; James Nelson Algar; Written by Winston Hibler; Erdman Penner; Joe Rinaldi; Ted Sears; Homer Brightman; Harry Reeves; Music by Oliver Wallace. **Pr:** Walt Disney Studios; RKO. **A:** Family. **P:** Entertainment. **U:** Home. **Mov-Ent:** Animation & Cartoons. **Acq:** Purchase. **Dist:** Walt Disney Studios Home Entertainment.

The Adventures of Jim Bowie 1956
Includes two episodes that follow the adventures of Jim Bowie, the inventor of the Bowie knife. The shows, "Birth of the Blade" and "Trapline," are set in 1830s New Orleans. 55m/B/W; VHS. **TV Std:** NTSC, PAL. **C:** Scott Forbes. **A:** Family. **P:** Entertainment. **U:** Home. **Mov-Ent:** Television Series. **Acq:** Purchase. **Dist:** Moviecraft Home Video. $19.95.

The Adventures of Jim Bowie: TV Collection 2003 (Unrated)
Offers fictionalized episodes about real-life frontiersman Jim Bowie (creator of the Bowie Knife) from the 1956-1958 TV western series such as "The Squatter," "Jim Bowie Comes Home," "Outlaw Kingdom," and "Gone to Texas." 13 episodes. 300m/B/W; DVD. **C:** Scott Forbes. **A:** Sr. High-Adult. **P:** Entertainment. **U:** Home. **Mov-Ent:** Television Series, Western, Action-Adventure. **Acq:** Purchase. **Dist:** VCI Entertainment. $14.99.

The Adventures of Jim Bowie, Vol. 1 1956
Contains two episodes, "The Squatter" and "The Gambler," from the classic television series. 104m/B/W; DVD. **C:** Scott Forbes. **A:** Family. **P:** Entertainment. **U:** Home. **Mov-Ent:** Television Series, Western. **Acq:** Purchase. **Dist:** Critics' Choice Video & DVD; Infinity Entertainment Group.

The Adventures of Jim Bowie, Vol. 2 1956
Includes two episodes, "The Pearl" and "The Crown & Apache Silver," from the classic television series. 104m/B/W; DVD. **C:** Scott Forbes. **A:** Family. **P:** Entertainment. **U:** Home. **Mov-Ent:** Television Series, Western. **Acq:** Purchase. **Dist:** Critics' Choice Video & DVD; Infinity Entertainment Group.

The Adventures of J.J. Dubois/Things that Go Bump in the Night 19??
A diving double feature from Jack McKenney filled with side-splitting humor. 20m; VHS. **A:** Jr. High-Adult. **P:** Entertainment. **U:** Home. **Gen-Edu:** Scuba. **Acq:** Purchase. **Dist:** Bennett Marine Video. $19.95.

Adventures of Justine 2000 (Unrated) — ★★
Compilation of a late-night cable series is a soft-core "Perils of Pauline" with a bit of light bondage. Justine (Boone) is a student who accompanies Professor Robson (DiPri) on a series of escapades involving Egyptian tombs, satanists, Nazis, etc. Given the levels of explicitness that have become common in the genre, this is tepid stuff. The cast is thespianically challenged, but attractive and comfortable with nudity. Image is moderately grainy with flatteringly soft focus, but it improves—and the grain is radically lessened—in the sex scenes which occur about every 30 minutes. 638m; DVD. **C:** Daneen Boone; Kimberly Rowe; Timothy DiPri; Jennifer Behr; Bo Zena; Alex Veadov; Directed by L.L. Shapira; Kevin Alber; David Cove; Written by T. C. McKelvey; Noel Harrison; Edward Laraby; Thomas Roberdeau; Cinematography by Amit Bhattacharya; Nick Hutak; Brad Rushing; Music by Nigel Holton; Kevin Kiner; Tim Wynn. **A:** College-Adult. **P:** Entertainment. **U:** Home. **Mov-Ent. Acq:** Purchase. **Dist:** New Horizons Picture Corp.

Adventures of Kit Carson 1951
Television western, which ran from 1951-55, set in the 1880s about the famed frontiersman who kept the peace with the help of Mexican sidekick El Toro. Two episodes per tape. 50m; VHS. **C:** Bill Williams; John Hamilton; Don Diamond. **A:** Family. **P:** Entertainment. **U:** Home. **Mov-Ent:** Television Series, Western. **Acq:** Purchase. **Dist:** Movies Unlimited; Moviecraft Home Video. $19.99.

The Adventures of Kit Carson and the Hawk 1951
An episode of the weekly '50s TV show. Includes the original commercials. 60m/B/W; VHS. **C:** Bill Williams; Kit Carson; Don Diamond. **A:** Family. **P:** Entertainment. **U:** Home. **Mov-Ent:** Television Series. **Acq:** Purchase. **Dist:** Video Resources.

The Adventures of Marco Polo 1938 — ★★½
Lavish Hollywood production based on the exploits of 13th-century Venetian explorer Marco Polo (Cooper). He becomes the first white man to record his visit to the Eastern court of Kublai Khan, where he falls for a beautiful princess also desired by the evil Rathbone. Lots of action, though its hard to picture the laconic Cooper in the title role. 100m/B/W; VHS, DVD. **C:** Gary Cooper; Sigrid Gurie; Basil Rathbone; Ernest Truex; George Barbier; Binnie Barnes; Alan Hale; H.B. Warner; Directed by Archie Mayo; Written by Robert Sherwood; Music by Hugo Friedhofer. **Pr:** Samuel Goldwyn; United Artists. **A:** Family. **P:** Entertainment. **U:** Home. **Mov-Ent:** Romance, Explorers. **Acq:** Purchase. **Dist:** Facets Multimedia Inc. $19.98.

The Adventures of Mark Twain 1944 — ★★★
March stars as Mark Twain, the nom de plume of Samuel Clemens, the beloved humorist and writer. His travels and adventures along the Mississippi and on to the California gold rush would later result in the books and stories which would make him so well-known. March attains a quiet nobility as he goes from young man to old sage, along with Smith, who plays Olivia, Twain's beloved wife. 130m/B/W; VHS, DVD. **C:** Fredric March; Alexis Smith; Donald Crisp; Alan Hale; Sir C. Aubrey Smith; John Carradine; William Henry; Robert Barrat; Walter Hampden; Percy Kilbride; Directed by Irving Rapper; Written by Alan LeMay; Harry Chandlee; Music by Max Steiner. **Pr:** Jesse L. Lasky; Warner Bros. **A:** Jr. High-Adult. **P:** Entertainment. **U:** Home. **Mov-Ent:** Literature--American, Marriage. **Acq:** Purchase. **Dist:** WarnerArchive.com; Facets Multimedia Inc.; Baker and Taylor. $19.98.

The Adventures of Mark Twain 1985 (G) — ★★★
A clay-animated fantasy based on, and radically departing from, the life and work of Mark Twain. Story begins with Twain flying into outer space in a blimp with stowaways Huck Finn, Tom Sawyer and Becky Thatcher and takes off from there. Above average entertainment for kids and their folks. 86m; VHS, DVD, Blu-Ray. **C:** Voice(s) by James Whitmore; Chris Ritchie; Gary Krug; Michele Mariana; Directed by Will Vinton; Written by Susan Shadburne. **Pr:** Will Vinton; Clubhouse Pictures. **A:** Family. **P:** Entertainment. **U:** Home. **Mov-Ent:** Animation & Cartoons, Fantasy, Family Viewing. **Acq:** Purchase.

The Adventures of Mary-Kate & Ashley: The Case of the Fun House Mystery 1996
The Olsen twins must solve a at an amusement park involving an unusual funhouse. 30m; VHS. **A:** Primary. **P:** Entertainment. **U:** Home. **Chl-Juv:** Music--Children. **Acq:** Purchase. **Dist:** WarnerVision.

The Adventures of Mary-Kate & Ashley: The Case of the Logical Ranch 1996
Olsen twins Mary-Kate and Ashley investigate strange goings-on at a ranch. 30m; VHS. **A:** Primary. **P:** Entertainment. **U:** Home. **Chl-Juv:** Music--Children. **Acq:** Purchase. **Dist:** WarnerVision.

The Adventures of Mary-Kate & Ashley: The Case of the Mystery Cruise 1996
A cruise ship is the setting for this musical, mystery adventure for Olsen twins, Mary-Kate and Ashley. 30m; VHS. **A:** Primary. **P:** Entertainment. **U:** Home. **Chl-Juv:** Music--Children. **Acq:** Purchase. **Dist:** WarnerVision.

The Adventures of Mary-Kate & Ashley: The Case of the Sea World Adventure 1996
Olsen twins, Mary-Kate and Ashley, head to Sea World for fun but end up solving a mystery. 30m; VHS. **A:** Primary. **P:** Entertainment. **U:** Home. **Chl-Juv:** Music--Children. **Acq:** Purchase. **Dist:** WarnerVision.

The Adventures of Mary-Kate & Ashley: The Case of the Shark Encounter 1996
Mary-Kate and Ashley are on the case involving a great white shark. Filmed at Sea World. 30m; VHS. **A:** Primary. **P:** Entertainment. **U:** Home. **Chl-Juv:** Music--Children. **Acq:** Purchase. **Dist:** WarnerVision.

The Adventures of Mary-Kate & Ashley: The Case of the U.S. Space Camp Mission 1996
Mary-Kate and Ashley must solve a space mystery before it destroys the next rocket launch. 30m; VHS. **A:** Primary. **P:** Entertainment. **U:** Home. **Chl-Juv:** Music--Children. **Acq:** Purchase. **Dist:** WarnerVision.

The Adventures of Mary-Kate & Ashley: The Case of Thorn Mansion 1996
Olsen twins, Mary-Kate and Ashley take their investivgative skills to a local mansion. 30m; VHS. **A:** Primary. **P:** Entertainment. **U:** Home. **Chl-Juv:** Music--Children. **Acq:** Purchase. **Dist:** WarnerVision.

The Adventures of Mary-Kate & Ashley: The Christmas Caper 1996
The Olsen twins have to solve a mystery that will may destroy their Christmas. 30m; VHS. **A:** Primary. **P:** Entertainment. **U:** Home. **Chl-Juv:** Music--Children, Christmas. **Acq:** Purchase. **Dist:** WarnerVision.

The Adventures of Milo & Otis 1989 (G) — ★★★
Delightful Japanese children's film about a farm-dwelling dog and cat and their odyssey after the cat is accidentally swept away on a river. Notable since no humans appear in the film. A record-breaking success in its homeland. Well received by U.S. children. Narrated by Dudley Moore. 76m; VHS, DVD, Blu-Ray, CC. **C:** Narrated by Dudley Moore; Directed by Masanori Hata; Written by Mark Saltzman; Cinematography by Hideo Fujii; Shinji Tomita; Music by Michael Boddicker. **Pr:** Fujisankei Comm. **A:** Family. **P:** Entertainment. **U:** Home. **Mov-Ent:** Action-Adventure, Pets, Pets. **Acq:** Purchase. **Dist:** Sony Pictures Home Entertainment Inc.; Reader's Digest Home Video; Home Vision Cinema. $19.95.

The Adventures of Monty the Moose: Amazing Alaska Animals 1995
Animated character Monty the Moose heads north to Alaska to visit the many animals who live on the Last Frontier. Includes footage of caribou, brown bears, humpback whales, shorebirds, moose, walrus, and more. Also contains five original music videos. 40m; VHS. **TV Std:** NTSC, PAL. **A:** Family. **P:** Education. **U:** Institution, Home. **Gen-Edu:** Animals, Wildlife, Wilderness Areas. **Acq:** Purchase. **Dist:** Alaska Video Postcards Inc. $19.95.

Adventures of Mowgli 1997
Russian-American animated co-production of Rudyard Kipling's tale of young Mowgli, who is adopted by the Seeone Wolf Pack in an Indian jungle and is befriended by Baloo bear, panther Bagheera and python Kaa. 92m; VHS. **A:** Primary. **P:** Entertainment. **U:** Home. **Chl-Juv:** Animation & Cartoons. **Acq:** Purchase. **Dist:** Monarch Home Video.

The Adventures of Nellie Bly 1981 — ★
"Classics Illustrated" story of Nellie Bly, a strong-willed female reporter doing her best to expose wrongdoings in the late 19th century. A decent performance by Purl is overshadowed by the general lack of direction. 100m; VHS. **C:** Linda Purl; Gene Barry; John Randolph; Raymond Buktenica; J.D. Cannon; Elayne Heilveil; Cliff Osmond; Directed by Henning Schellerup. **Pr:** James L. Conway; Charles E. Sellier, Jr.; Schick Sunn Classic; Taft International Pictures. **A:** Jr. High-Adult. **P:** Entertainment. **U:** Home. **Mov-Ent:** Journalism, Mental Health, TV Movies. **Acq:** Purchase. **Dist:** No Longer Available.

The Adventures of Oliver Twist 1993
Animated version of Dickens' masterpiece about an impoverished orphan eking out a living on the streets. 91m; VHS. **A:** Primary. **P:** Entertainment. **U:** Home. **Chl-Juv:** Animation & Cartoons, Adoption. **Acq:** Purchase. **Dist:** Anchor Bay Entertainment. $14.99.

The Adventures of Ozzie & Harriet 195?
Each volume in this 12-set series contains four episodes of the Nelsons' hit TV show from 1953-64. Vol. 1 features 17-year-old Mary Tyler Moore doing the commercials. Vol. 2 features Mamie Van Doren as the housemother of Ricky's fraternity (some housemother!). The program was the prototype of family sitcoms. Original commercials included. Tapes are available for purchase individually. 56m/B/W; VHS. **C:** Ozzie Nelson; Harriet Hilliard Nelson; Ricky Nelson; David Nelson; Directed by Ozzie Nelson. **A:** Family. **P:** Entertainment. **U:** Home. **Mov-Ent:** Television Series. **Acq:** Purchase. **Dist:** Movies Unlimited. $19.99.

The Adventures of Ozzie & Harriet 1956
"A Day in Bed" and "Art Studies," two Ozzie and Harriet television shows from 1956 are offered on this tape which also features a young Mary Tyler Moore selling Hotpoint refrigerators. 60m/B/W; VHS, 3/4 U. **TV Std:** NTSC, PAL. **C:** Ozzie Nelson; Harriet Hilliard Nelson; Ricky Nelson. **Pr:** ABC. **A:** Jr. High-Adult. **P:** Entertainment. **U:** Institution, Home. **Mov-Ent:** Television, Television Series. **Acq:** Purchase. **Dist:** International Historic Films Inc. $7.99.

The Adventures of Ozzie & Harriet 1964
Two complete episodes of the long-running situation comedy: "Ricky's Horse," where Ricky finds himself the proud owner of a horse after a financial "discussion" between Ozzie and Harriet, and "Ozzie the Babysitter," where Ozzie's in big trouble after damaging a slot car set belonging to the nine-year-old he's babysitting. Black and white commercials included. 55m; VHS. **TV Std:** NTSC, PAL. **C:** Ozzie Nelson; Harriet Hilliard Nelson; Ricky Nelson; David Nelson. **Pr:** ABC. **A:** Family. **P:** Entertainment. **U:** Home. **Mov-Ent:** Television. **Acq:** Purchase. **Dist:** Shout! Factory. $24.95.

The Adventures of Ozzie and Harriet 2003
Includes 14 episodes of the classic family sitcom about the Nelson family. 420m; DVD. **A:** Family. **P:** Entertainment. **U:** Home. **Mov-Ent:** Television Series, Drama. **Acq:** Purchase. **Dist:** Navarre Corp. $11.99.

The Adventures of Ozzie & Harriet: Best of 1959
Stars the entire Nelson family (bandleader Ozzie, his wife Harriet, dutiful son David, and mischievous son Ricky) portraying themselves with the majority of episodes directed, produced, and co-written by its patriarch. In "Rick's Riding Lessons" he becomes smitten with a beautiful riding instructors and makes a deal to teach her how to play the guitar if she'll teach him out to ride. "David, the Law Clerk" has the young overachiever almost not getting a job because of his family's helpfulness. Ozzie's scheme to skip out on bridge night and go fishing instead backfires in "The Prowler." 24 classic episodes. 570m; DVD. **C:** Ozzie Nelson; Harriet Hilliard Nelson; Ricky Nelson; David Nelson. **A:** Family. **P:** Entertainment. **U:** Home. **Mov-Ent:** Television Series. **Acq:** Purchase. **Dist:** Shout! Factory.

The Adventures of Ozzie & Harriet: Christmas with the Nelsons 2007 (Unrated)
Collection of holiday classics from the 1952-1966 family series: The Boys' Christmas Money from Season 1, Late Christmas Gift from Season 2, The Fruitcake from Season 3, The Day After Christmas-Season 4, The Christmas Tree Lot-Season 5 and Ricky singing "Baby I'm Sorry" as a bonus. 90m; DVD. **C:** Ricky Nelson; Ozzie Nelson; Harriet Hilliard Nelson; David Nelson. **A:** Family. **P:** Entertainment. **U:** Home. **Mov-Ent:** Family, Holidays, Television Series. **Acq:** Purchase. **Dist:** Shout! Factory.

The Adventures of Ozzie and Harriet, Vol. 1 19??
Ricky and David want their own rooms in "Separate Rooms." In "Orchids and Violets," see what happens when Harriet receives flowers. 56m; DVD. **C:** Ozzie Nelson; Harriet Hilliard Nelson; David Nelson; Ricky Nelson. **Pr:** ABC. **A:** Family. **P:** Entertainment. **U:** Home. **Mov-Ent:** Television Series, Family. **Acq:** Purchase. **Dist:** Alpha Video.

The Adventures of Ozzie and Harriet, Vol. 2 19??
Ozzie and Thorny are in a weight loss contest in "Pills," and which son will Ozzie choose for the "Father and Son Tournament." 56m/B/W; DVD. **C:** Ozzie Nelson; Harriet Hilliard Nelson; David Nelson; Ricky Nelson. **Pr:** ABC. **A:** Family. **P:** Entertainment. **U:** Home. **Mov-Ent:** Television Series, Family. **Acq:** Purchase. **Dist:** Alpha Video.

The Adventures of Ozzie and Harriet, Vol. 3 19??
See how the Nelsons handle Shakespeare in "An Evening with Hamlet," and Jerry Mathers (the Beaver) knocks at their door in "Halloween." 56m/B/W; DVD. **C:** Ozzie Nelson; Harriet Hilliard Nelson; David Nelson; Ricky Nelson; John Carradine; Jerry Mathers. **Pr:** ABC. **A:** Family. **P:** Entertainment. **U:** Home. **Mov-Ent:** Television Series, Family. **Acq:** Purchase. **Dist:** Alpha Video.

The Adventures of Ozzie and Harriet, Vol. 4 19??
A new "Hair Style for Harriet" sends Ozzie into a tizzy, and Ozzie the "Jet Pilot" breaks the sound barrier. 56m/B/W; DVD. **C:** Ozzie Nelson; Harriet Hilliard Nelson; David Nelson; Ricky Nelson. **A:** Family. **P:** Entertainment. **U:** Home. **Mov-Ent:** Television Series, Family. **Acq:** Purchase. **Dist:** Alpha Video.

The Adventures of Ozzie and Harriet, Vol. 5 19??
In "Ricky the Drummer," Ricky becomes the singing star at the local teen dance, and in "The 14-Mile Hike," Ozzie volunteers to lead some kids on a hike. 56m/B/W; DVD. **C:** Ozzie Nelson; Harriet Hilliard Nelson; David Nelson; Ricky Nelson. **Pr:** ABC. **A:** Family. **P:** Entertainment. **U:** Home. **Mov-Ent:** Television Series, Family. **Acq:** Purchase. **Dist:** Alpha Video.

The Adventures of Ozzie and Harriet, Vol. 6 19??
Ozzie plans to take Harriet on a cruise in "A Cruise for Harriet," and in "Rick's Dinner Guests," Ozzie's poker game is interrupted by Ricky's friends. 56m/B/W; DVD. **C:** Ozzie Nelson; Harriet Hilliard Nelson; David Nelson; Ricky Nelson. **Pr:** ABC. **A:** Family. **P:** Entertainment. **U:** Home. **Mov-Ent:** Television Series, Family. **Acq:** Purchase. **Dist:** Alpha Video.

The Adventures of Ozzie and Harriet, Vol. 7 19??
"David Goofs Off" to the chagrin of boss Joe Flynn, and a "Little House Guest" visits the Nelsons. 56m/B/W; DVD. **C:** Ozzie Nelson; Harriet Hilliard Nelson; David Nelson; Ricky Nelson. **A:** Family. **P:** Entertainment. **U:** Home. **Mov-Ent:** Television Series, Family. **Acq:** Purchase. **Dist:** Alpha Video.

The Adventures of Ozzie and Harriet, Vol. 8 19??
David does not get the right person for the job in "David Hires a Secretary," and Ricky and his girlfind all kinds of trouble in "Girl Who Loses Things." 56m/B/W; DVD. **C:** Ozzie Nelson; Harriet Hilliard Nelson; David Nelson; Ricky Nelson. **Pr:** ABC. **A:** Family. **P:** Entertainment. **U:** Home. **Mov-Ent:** Television Series, Family. **Acq:** Purchase. **Dist:** Alpha Video.

The Adventures of Ozzie and Harriet, Vol. 9 19??
Prof. Wally Cox rents a room putting a damper on the partying in "The Fraternity Rents Out a Room," and Wally is made to study by Ricky in "Making Wally Study." 56m/B/W; DVD. **C:** Ozzie Nelson; Harriet Hilliard Nelson; David Nelson; Ricky Nelson. **Pr:** ABC. **A:** Family. **P:** Entertainment. **U:** Home. **Mov-Ent:** Television Series, Family. **Acq:** Purchase. **Dist:** Alpha Video.

The Adventures of Ozzie and Harriet, Vol. 10 19??
There's trouble for David in "An Old Friend of June's," and Wally and Ginger find all kinds of problems in "Kris Plays Cupid." 56m/B/W; DVD. **C:** Ozzie Nelson; Harriet Hilliard Nelson; David Nelson; Ricky Nelson. **Pr:** ABC. **A:** Family. **P:** Entertainment. **U:** Home. **Mov-Ent:** Television Series, Family. **Acq:** Purchase. **Dist:** Alpha Video.

The Adventures of Ozzie and Harriet, Vol. 11 19??
In "Rick's Raise," Ozzie and Harriet find themselves in the middle as David ends up with the goods, and in "Breakfast for Harriet," Ozzie cooks for Harriet. 56m/B/W; DVD. **C:** Ozzie Nelson; Harriet Hilliard Nelson; David Nelson; Ricky Nelson. **Pr:** ABC. **A:** Family. **P:** Entertainment. **U:** Home. **Mov-Ent:** Television Series, Family. **Acq:** Purchase. **Dist:** Alpha Video.

The Adventures of Ozzie and Harriet, Vol. 12 19??
In "The Trip Trap," David and June have it out over a Hawaiian vacation, and in "Flying Down to Lunch in...Mexico?," Ozzie has lunch in an unexpected place. 56m/B/W; DVD. **C:** Ozzie Nelson; Harriet Hilliard Nelson; David Nelson; Ricky Nelson. **Pr:** ABC. **A:** Family. **P:** Entertainment. **U:** Home. **Mov-Ent:** Television Series, Family. **Acq:** Purchase. **Dist:** Alpha Video.

Adventures of Paddington Bear: The Complete Paddington Bear Collection 2002 (Unrated)
Features episodes from the animated children's show about the adventures of the classic English bear named Paddington including "Paddington Turns Detective," "Paddington's Birthday Dinner," and "Paddington's Magical Birthday." 14 episodes. 420m; DVD. **C:** Voice(s) by Frank Lenart; Pete Musaus; Margit Weinert; Fritz von Hardenberg; Simone Brahmann. **A:** Family. **P:** Entertainment. **U:** Home. **Chl-Juv:** Television Series, Animation & Cartoons, Children's Shows. **Acq:** Purchase. **Dist:** Ventura Distribution Inc. $19.98.

The Adventures of Peer Gynt 1992
Peer Gynt, witches, and trolls are brought to life by marionettes and the music of Edward Grieg, performed by the Budapest Philharmonic Orchestra and Debreccen Philharmonic Orchestra. Based on the story by Henrik Ibsen. 30m; VHS. **C:** Directed by David Touster. **Pr:** Jonathan Bogner. **A:** Preschool-Primary. **P:** Entertainment. **U:** Home. **Chl-Juv:** Puppets, Music--Classical. **Acq:** Purchase. **Dist:** Bogner Entertainment Inc. $14.95.

The Adventures of Pete & Pete: Farewell, My Little Viking 1994
Two episodes from the series about the two brothers with the same name. 45m; DVD. **A:** Family. **P:** Entertainment. **U:** Home. **Chl-Juv:** Serials, Children. **Acq:** Purchase. **Dist:** Viacom International Inc.

The Adventures of Pete & Pete: School Dazed 1994
Two school-themed episodes from the series about the two brothers with the same name. 45m; DVD. **A:** Family. **P:** Entertainment. **U:** Home. **Chl-Juv:** Serials, Children. **Acq:** Purchase. **Dist:** Viacom International Inc.

The Adventures of Pete & Pete: Season One 2005 (Unrated)
Presents the 1993-1994 debut season of the Nickelodeon channel's family-oriented show about two adolescent brothers both named Pete who have many unusual experiences in their not-so-ordinary suburban neighborhood such as Pete and his friends boycott sleeping to beat the world record, the brothers argue over who gets a special bowling ball, and young Pete gets a band together just to remember another local band's song. 8 episodes. 292m; DVD. **C:** Michael Maronna; Danny Tamberelli. **A:** Family. **P:** Entertainment. **U:** Home. **Chl-Juv:** Television Series, Family, Children's Shows. **Acq:** Purchase. **Dist:** Paramount Pictures Corp. $26.98.

The Adventures of Pete & Pete: Season Two 2005 (Unrated)
Presents the second season of the Nickelodeon channel's family-oriented show about two adolescent brothers both named Pete who have many unusual experiences in their not-so-ordinary suburban neighborhood such as young Pete digging his way out of a grounding on the Fourth of July, a mysterious phone call, young Pete's lizard dies and big Pete goes on a long trip with dad to get another, and big Pete tries to keep a big bass from being caught. 10 episodes. 286m; DVD. **C:** Michael Maronna; Danny Tamberelli. **A:** Family. **P:** Entertainment. **U:** Home. **Chl-Juv:** Television Series, Family, Children's Shows. **Acq:** Purchase. **Dist:** Paramount Pictures Corp. $26.99.

The Adventures of Picasso 1980 (Unrated) — ★★
A Swedish satire on the life of Picasso, dubbed in English. Don't look for art or facts here, or, for that matter, many laughs. 88m; VHS. **C:** Gosta Ekman, Jr.; Lena Nyman; Hans Alfredson; Margareta Krook; Bernard Cribbins; Wilfrid Brambell; Directed by Tage Danielsson. **Pr:** ABSF. **A:** College-Adult. **P:** Entertainment. **U:** Home. **L:** Swedish, English. **Mov-Ent:** Satire & Parody, Art & Artists. **Acq:** Purchase. **Dist:** No Longer Available.

The Adventures of Pinocchio 198?
The children's classic of the wooden puppet whose one wish is to become a real boy. 90m; VHS. **A:** Family. **P:** Entertainment. **U:** Home. **Chl-Juv:** Animation & Cartoons, Fairy Tales. **Acq:** Purchase. **Dist:** Anchor Bay Entertainment. $19.95.

The Adventures of Pinocchio 1996 (G) — ★★½
Live-action version of Carlo Collodi's story about woodcarver Gepetto (Landau) who carves himself a puppet son (Thomas) who longs to be a real boy. Story differs from the Disney cartoon version in that it's a little darker and the cat, the fox, and the cricket have larger roles. Jim Henson's Creature Shop provided the animatronic magic to bring Pinocchio to life. His head alone was jammed with wiring and 18 tiny motors to give the "boy" a full range of facial expressions. It took as many as five puppeteers at a time to animate the character. So lifelike was the puppet that some of the crew actually spoke to it as they did the human actors. 88m; VHS, DVD, CC. **C:** Martin Landau; Jonathan Taylor Thomas; Rob Schneider; Bebe Neuwirth; Udo Kier; Directed by Steven Barron; Written by Steven Barron; Tom Benedek; Sherry Mills; Cinematography by Juan Ruiz-Anchia; Music by Rachel Portman. **Pr:** Jeffrey M. Sneller; Raju Patel; Savoy Pictures; New Line Cinema. **A:** Family. **P:** Entertainment. **U:** Home. **Mov-Ent:** Fantasy, Puppets, Fairy Tales. **Acq:** Purchase. **Dist:** New Line Home Video.

The Adventures of Pluto Nash 2002 (PG-13) — **Bomb!**
Pluto Nash (Murphy) owns a nightclub on the moon in the year 2087, and some gangsters want it. Murphy should save us all a lot of time, trouble, and wasted effort and hand it over. On the shelf for two years (and some good reasons), this steaming pile of "action-comedy" has nothing going for it. The performances are "collecting-a-paycheck" quality, the script and direction are a mess, and it's howlingly unfunny. If you avoid seeing one movie this year, make it this one. 97m; VHS, DVD. **C:** Eddie Murphy; Rosario Dawson; Randy Quaid; Joe Pantoliano; Jay Mohr; John Cleese; Pam Grier; Peter Boyle; Luis Guzman; James Rebhorn; Burt Young; Miguel A. Nunez, Jr.; Illeana Douglas; Victor Varnado; Directed by Ron Underwood; Written by Neil Cuthbert; Cinematography by Oliver Wood; Music by John Powell. **Pr:** Martin Bregman; Michael S. Bregman; Louis Stroller; Village Roadshow Pictures; Castle Rock Entertainment; NPV Entertainment; Warner Bros. **A:** Jr. High-Adult. **P:** Entertainment. **U:** Home. **Mov-Ent:** Nightclubs, The Moon. **Acq:** Purchase. **Dist:** Warner Home Video, Inc.

Adventures of Power 2008 (PG-13) — ★½
Underdog satire (that's not very adventurous) about an aging misfit with a fixation on air-drumming. After getting fired, Power (Gold) finally makes his way from New Mexico to New Jersey where he finds some soulmates in Newark and faces off in a New York competition to be the best darn air drummer anywhere. Comedy is inconsistent and triple-duty Gold is more irksome than weirdo appealing. 96m; DVD, Streaming, Wide, CC. **C:** Ari Gold; Michael McKean; Jane Lynch; Soshannah Stern; Adrian Grenier; Steven Williams; Jimmy Jean-Louis; Chi Ling Chiu; Richard Fancy; Directed by Ari Gold; Written by Ari Gold; Cinematography by Lisa Weigand; Music by Ethan Gold. **Pr:** Andrea Sperling; Grack Films; Group Entertainment; SpaceTime Films; Variance Films. **A:** Jr. High-Adult. **P:** Entertainment. **U:** Home. **L:** English. **Mov-Ent:** Musical, Satire & Parody. **Acq:** Purchase. **Dist:** Phase 4; Alpha Video; Amazon.com Inc. $14.99 12.99.

Adventures of Prince Achmed 1927
Three years in the making using the cutout/silhouette animation method. Based on the Arabian Nights stories. 50m; VHS. **C:** Directed by Lotte Reiniger. **Pr:** Lotte Reiniger. **A:** Family. **P:** Entertainment. **U:** Home. **Mov-Ent:** Animation & Cartoons, Fairy Tales. **Acq:** Purchase. **Dist:** Glenn Video Vistas Ltd.

The Adventures of Priscilla, Queen of the Desert 1994 (R) — ★★★
Quirky down-under musical-comedy follows two drag queens and a transsexual across the Australian Outback on their way to a gig in a small resort town. They make the drive in a pink bus nicknamed Priscilla. Along the way they encounter, and perform for, the usual unusual assortment of local characters. Scenes depicting homophobic natives play out as expected. Finest moments occur on the bus or onstage (all hail ABBA). Strong performances, especially by usually macho Stamp as the widowed Bernadette, rise above the cliches in what is basically a bitchy, cross-dressing road movie, celebrating drag as art and the nonconformity of its heroes. Costumes (by Lizzy Gardner and Tim Chappel) are a lark, the photography's surreal, and the soundtrack fittingly campy. 102m; VHS, DVD, Wide. **C:** Terence Stamp; Hugo Weaving; Guy Pearce; Bill Hunter; Sarah Chadwick; Mark Holmes; Julia Cortez; Rebel Russell; June Marie Bennett; Alan Dargin; Margaret Pomeranz; Directed by Stephan Elliott; Written by Stephan Elliott; Cinematography by Brian J. Breheny; Music by Guy Gross. **Pr:** Michael Hamlyn; Al Clark; Rebel Penfold-Russell; Polygram; Australian Film Finance Corp; Latent Image; Gramercy Pictures. **A:** College-Adult. **P:** Entertainment. **U:** Home. **Mov-Ent:** Musical, Australia. **Awds:** Oscars '94: Costume Des.; Australian Film Inst. '94: Costume Des. **Acq:** Purchase. **Dist:** MGM Home Entertainment. $19.95.

The Adventures of Raggedy Ann & Andy: The Ransom of Sunny Bunny Adventure 1993
Vivid animation will appeal in this tale of Raggedy Ann trying to rescue Sunny Bunny from bumbling doll-napper Cracklen. Our rag-doll heroine is aided by her pals Andy, Camel, and Raggedy Dog. 30m; DVD. **A:** Preschool-Primary. **P:** Entertainment. **U:** Home. **Chl-Juv:** Animation & Cartoons. **Acq:** Purchase. **Dist:** New Video Group. $9.98.

Adventures of Red Ryder 1940 — ★★
The thrills of the rugged West are presented in this 12-episode serial. Based on the then-famous comic strip character. 240m/B/W; VHS, DVD. **C:** Donald (Don "Red") Barry; Noah Beery, Sr.; Tommy Cook; Harry Worth; Wally Wales; William Farnum; Carleton Young; Directed by William Witney; John English; Written by Frank (Franklyn) Adreon; Norman S. Hall; Barney A. Sarecky; Cinematography by William Nobles; Music by Cy Feuer. **Pr:** Republic. **A:** Family. **P:** Entertainment. **U:** Institution, Home. **Mov-Ent:** Western, Serials. **Acq:** Purchase. **Dist:** Alpha Video; VCI Entertainment. $80.00.

The Adventures of Rex & Rinty 1935 — ★★
An adventure serial in 12 chapters, featuring Rin-Tin-Tin Jr. 156m/B/W; VHS. **C:** Kane Richmond; Harry Woods; Smiley Burnette; Directed by Ford Beebe; B. Reeves Eason; Written by

Barney A. Sarecky. **Pr:** Mark Huffam. **A:** Family. **P:** Entertainment. **U:** Home. **Mov-Ent:** Serials, Pets. **Acq:** Purchase. **Dist:** Alpha Video. $49.95.

The Adventures of Rin Tin Tin 1947 — ★★½
Chronicles the adventures of that crime-fighting dog, Rin-Tin-Tin. 65m/B/W; VHS. **C:** Robert (Bobby) Blake. **A:** Family. **P:** Entertainment. **U:** Home. **Mov-Ent:** Pets. **Acq:** Purchase. **Dist:** Critics' Choice Video & DVD. $9.99.

The Adventures of Robin Hood 1938 (Unrated) — ★★★★
Rollicking technicolor tale of the legendary outlaw, regarded as the swashbuckler standard-bearer. The justice-minded Saxon knight battles the Normans, outwits evil Prince John, and gallantly romances Maid Marian. Grand Castle sets and lush forest photography display ample evidence of the huge (for 1938) budget of $2 million plus. Just entering his prime, Flynn enthusiastically performed most of his own stunts, including intricate swordplay and advanced tree and wall climbing. His Robin brims with charm and bravura. THe rest of the cast likewise attacks with zest: de Havilland, a cold, but ultimately sympathetic Marian; Rains's dastardly Prince John; and Rathbone's convincing Sir Guy to Robin's band of very merry men. Based on the many Robin Hood legends, as well as Sir Walter Scott's "Ivanhoe" and the opera "Robin Hood" by De Koven-Smith. 102m; VHS, DVD, HD-DVD. **C:** Errol Flynn; Olivia de Havilland; Claude Rains; Basil Rathbone; Alan Hale; Una O'Connor; Patric Knowles; Eugene Pallette; Herbert Mundin; Melville Cooper; Ian Hunter; Montagu Love; Directed by Michael Curtiz; Written by Seton I. Miller; Norman Reilly Raine; Cinematography by Gaetano Antonio "Tony" Gaudio; Sol Polito; Music by Erich Wolfgang Korngold. **A:** Family. **P:** Entertainment. **U:** Home. **Mov-Ent:** Classic Films, Forests & Trees. **Awds:** Oscars '38: Film Editing, Orig. Score; Natl. Film Reg. '95. **Acq:** Purchase. **Dist:** Warner Home Video, Inc.; MGM Home Entertainment. $19.98.

The Adventures of Robin Hood 1955
Filmed on location in England and starring Greene as the legendary outlaw/hero, with Pleasance as the evil Prince John. Two episodes per tape. Volume 1 features "The Highlander" and "Tables Turned." Additional episodes are available. 60m; VHS. **C:** Richard Greene; Donald Pleasence. **A:** Family. **P:** Entertainment. **U:** Home. **Mov-Ent:** Television Series. **Acq:** Purchase. **Dist:** Moviecraft Home Video; Movies Unlimited. $19.95.

The Adventures of Robin Hood: The Complete 1st Series 1955
Richard Greene plays the leader of Merry Men that live in Sherwood Forest and seek justice for the common people and loyal subjects of King Richard, who is gone fighting the crusades, leaving the evil Prince John and Sheriff of Nottingham to rule in his absence. 39 episodes. 983m; DVD. **C:** Richard Greene; Donald Pleasence; Rufus Cruickshank; Alan Wheatley; Alexander Gauge. **A:** Family. **P:** Entertainment. **U:** Home. **Mov-Ent:** Drama, Television Series, Comedy-Drama. **Acq:** Purchase. **Dist:** Mill Creek Entertainment L.L.C.

The Adventures of Robin Hood, Vol. 2 1956
Four adventures from the television series including "Queen Eleanor," "The Thorkil Ghost," "Ladies of Sherwood," and "Secret Mission." Contains the originally broadcast commercials. 120m/B/W; VHS. **C:** Richard Greene; Bernadette O'Farrell; Patricia Driscoll; Ian Hunter; Alexander Guage; Archie Duncan; Rufus Cruickshank; Alan Wheatley; Donald Pleasence. **Pr:** CBS. **A:** Family. **P:** Entertainment. **U:** Home. **Mov-Ent:** Television Series. **Acq:** Purchase. **Dist:** Shokus Video; Moviecraft Home Video. $24.95.

The Adventures of Rocky & Bullwinkle 2000 (PG) — ★★½
Flying squirrel and his moose pal--living on residuals since their TV show was cancelled--discover their old enemies, Russian spies Boris Badenov (Alexander), Natasha Fatale (Russo), and their Fearless Leader (De Niro), have escaped from their two-dimensional existence. The troublemaking trio heads for Hollywood and plots to--what else?—take over the world. Someone seriously miscalculated in targeting the Pokemon set (the show was 35 years old, and the majority of the jokes were aimed at adults), but it's more effective on the small screen, providing a few good laughs. 88m; VHS, DVD, Wide, CC. **C:** Robert De Niro; Jason Alexander; Rene Russo; Janeane Garofalo; Randy Quaid; Piper Perabo; Carl Reiner; Jonathan Winters; John Goodman; Kenan Thompson; Kel Mitchell; James Rebhorn; David Alan Grier; Norman Lloyd; Jon Polito; Whoopi Goldberg; Billy Crystal; Don Novello; Harrison Young; Dian Bachar; Paget Brewster; Voice(s) by June Foray; Keith Scott; Directed by Des McAnuff; Written by Kenneth Lonergan; Cinematography by Thomas Ackerman; Music by Mark Mothersbaugh. **Pr:** Universal Pictures. **A:** Jr. High-Adult. **P:** Entertainment. **U:** Home. **Mov-Ent.** **Acq:** Purchase. **Dist:** Movies Unlimited; Alpha Video.

The Adventures of Rocky & Bullwinkle: Banana Formula 1992
Bullwinkle swallows the secret formula for the "hush-a-boom" silent explosive. Mr. Peabody and his boy Sherman visit Bonnie Prince Charlie. Aesop & Son present another catastrophic fable. Fractured Fairy Tales features a 24-karat goose, and Dudley Do-Right is once again on the trail of Snidely Whiplash. 45m; VHS, CC. **C:** Voice(s) by June Foray; William Conrad; Bill Scott. **Pr:** Jay Ward. **A:** Family. **P:** Entertainment. **U:** Home. **Mov-Ent:** Animation & Cartoons, Family Viewing, Television Series. **Acq:** Purchase. **Dist:** Buena Vista Home Entertainment. $12.99.

The Adventures of Rocky & Bullwinkle: Blue Moose 1991
Boris Badenov and Natasha Fatale try to stop Bullwinkle from inheriting a fortune in "Rue Brittania." Mr. Peabody rescues Cleopatra, Fractured Fairy Tales features the Ugly Duckling, and Snidely Whiplash goes on a crime spree. 41m; VHS, CC. **C:** Voice(s) by June Foray; Bill Scott; William Conrad. **Pr:** Jay Ward. **A:** Family. **P:** Entertainment. **U:** Home. **Mov-Ent:** Animation & Cartoons, Family Viewing, Television Series. **Acq:** Purchase. **Dist:** Buena Vista Home Entertainment; Facets Multimedia Inc. $12.99.

The Adventures of Rocky & Bullwinkle: Canadian Gothic 1991
Four episodes of that hopeless Mountie, Dudley Do-Right, along with his true love Nell Fenwick, and his nemesis, the evil Snidely Whiplash. Also Fractured Fairy Tales features Prince Charming, Mr. Peabody and Sherman visit Toronto, and Bullwinkle becomes a stunt moose. 39m; VHS, CC. **C:** Voice(s) by June Foray; Bill Scott; William Conrad. **Pr:** Jay Ward. **A:** Family. **P:** Entertainment. **U:** Home. **Mov-Ent:** Animation & Cartoons, Family Viewing, Television Series. **Acq:** Purchase. **Dist:** Buena Vista Home Entertainment; Facets Multimedia Inc. $12.99.

The Adventures of Rocky & Bullwinkle: La Grande Moose 1991
Boris Badenov and Natasha Fatale pull off "The Box Top Robbery." Snidely Whiplash tries to prevent Dudley Do-Right from marrying Little Nell, Aesop and Son features a well-learned lesson, and Fractured Fairy Tales has the story of the unfortunate Frog Prince. 46m; VHS, CC. **C:** Voice(s) by June Foray; Bill Scott; William Conrad. **Pr:** Jay Ward. **A:** Family. **P:** Entertainment. **U:** Home. **Mov-Ent:** Animation & Cartoons, Family Viewing, Television Series. **Acq:** Purchase. **Dist:** Buena Vista Home Entertainment; Facets Multimedia Inc. $12.99.

The Adventures of Rocky & Bullwinkle: Mona Moose 1991
Rocky the Squirrel and Bullwinkle the Moose outwit Boris and Natasha for the "Treasure of Monte Zoom." Fractured Fairy Tales features Little Red Riding Hood, Mr. Peabody and his boy Sherman visit Robinson Crusoe, and Dudley Do-Right manages to overcome Snidely Whiplash. 46m; VHS, CC. **C:** Voice(s) by June Foray; Bill Scott; William Conrad. **Pr:** Jay Ward. **A:** Family. **P:** Entertainment. **U:** Home. **Mov-Ent:** Animation & Cartoons, Family Viewing, Television Series. **Acq:** Purchase. **Dist:** Buena Vista Home Entertainment; Facets Multimedia Inc. $12.99.

The Adventures of Rocky & Bullwinkle: Norman Moosewell 1991
Bullwinkle becomes the big moose on campus in "Wossamatta U." Mr. Peabody and Sherman visit Shakespeare, Fractured Fairy Tales has the son of Rumpelstiltskin, and Snidely Whiplash discovers Dudley Do-Right is his brother! 45m; VHS, CC. **Pr:** Jay Ward. **A:** Family. **P:** Entertainment. **U:** Home. **Mov-Ent:** Animation & Cartoons, Family Viewing, Television Series. **Acq:** Purchase. **Dist:** Buena Vista Home Entertainment. $12.99.

The Adventures of Rocky & Bullwinkle: Painting Theft 1992
Boris and Natasha try to steal Bullwinkle's unique artwork. Fractured Fairy Tales finds a melon-nosed Prince searching for romance. Dudley Do-Right goes bad with the aid of Snidely's evil cloak and Mr. Peabody and Sherman spy on Mata Hari. 45m; VHS, CC. **C:** Voice(s) by June Foray; William Conrad; Bill Scott. **Pr:** Jay Ward. **A:** Family. **P:** Entertainment. **U:** Home. **Mov-Ent:** Animation & Cartoons, Family Viewing, Television Series. **Acq:** Purchase. **Dist:** Buena Vista Home Entertainment. $12.99.

The Adventures of Rocky & Bullwinkle: Pottsylvania Creeper 1992
Rocky and Bullwinkle try to keep the people-munching Pottsylvania Creeper from taking over the world. Mr. Peabody and Sherman meet Lawrence of Arabia. Dudley Do-Right tries to recruit a new Mountie. Fractured Fairy Tales investigates the tale of a red-haired Duke and Aesop & Son find out two heads are sillier than one. 45m; VHS, CC. **C:** Voice(s) by June Foray; William Conrad; Bill Scott. **Pr:** Jay Ward. **A:** Family. **P:** Entertainment. **U:** Home. **Mov-Ent:** Animation & Cartoons, Family Viewing, Television Series. **Acq:** Purchase. **Dist:** Buena Vista Home Entertainment. $12.99.

The Adventures of Rocky & Bullwinkle: The Birth of Bullwinkle 1991
Bullwinkle the Moose discovers "The Ruby Yacht of Omar Khayyam." Fractured Fairy Tales features Sleeping Beautyland. Mr. Peabody and his boy Sherman visit Robin Hood and Snidely Whiplash tries to get the better of Dudley Do-Right. 38m; VHS, CC. **C:** Voice(s) by June Foray; William Conrad; Bill Scott. **Pr:** Jay Ward. **A:** Family. **P:** Entertainment. **U:** Home. **Mov-Ent:** Animation & Cartoons, Family Viewing, Television Series. **Acq:** Purchase. **Dist:** Buena Vista Home Entertainment; Facets Multimedia Inc. $12.99.

The Adventures of Rocky & Bullwinkle: The Weather Lady 1992
Nogoodnik Boris Badenov plots to kidnap the Weather Lady. Mr. Peabody and Sherman visit with William Tell. Snidely Whiplash tries to foreclose on the Mountie Camp (unless Dudley can stop him), and Hansel and Gretel are the subject of Fractured Fairy Tales. 45m; VHS, CC. **C:** Voice(s) by June Foray; William Conrad; Bill Scott. **Pr:** Jay Ward. **A:** Family. **P:** Entertainment. **U:** Home. **Mov-Ent:** Animation & Cartoons, Family Viewing, Television Series. **Acq:** Purchase. **Dist:** Buena Vista Home Entertainment. $12.99.

The Adventures of Rocky & Bullwinkle: Vincent Van Moose 1991
Only Bullwinkle J. Moose is stupid enough to stop Boris Badenov from sucking the smarts from America's brains in "Goof Gas Attack." Fractured Fairy Tales has Rapunzel letting her hair down, Dudley Do-Right tries to win Little Nell's heart, and Aesop and Son try to come up with a proper moral tale. 44m; VHS, CC. **C:** Voice(s) by June Foray; Bill Scott; William Conrad. **Pr:** Jay Ward. **A:** Family. **P:** Entertainment. **U:** Home. **Mov-Ent:** Animation & Cartoons, Family Viewing, Television Series. **Acq:** Purchase. **Dist:** Buena Vista Home Entertainment; Facets Multimedia Inc. $12.99.

The Adventures of Rocky & Bullwinkle: Whistler's Moose 1991
The campaign for statehood is begun in "Moosylvania" and the swampy spot is "Moosylvania Saved" from the nefarious Boris and Natasha. Mr. Peabody and Sherman see Mrs. Whistler's son, and everyone, including Dudley Do-Right, tries dressing like Little Nell for a day. 45m; VHS, CC. **Pr:** Jay Ward. **A:** Family. **P:** Entertainment. **U:** Home. **Mov-Ent:** Animation & Cartoons, Family Viewing, Television Series. **Acq:** Purchase. **Dist:** Buena Vista Home Entertainment. $12.99.

The Adventures of Rusty 1945 — ★★½
Forties family film series begins with this classic boy-meets-dog story. Danny's dog dies in an accident and his widowed father has just remarried so the kid's feeling pretty bad. Then he meets neglected German Shepherd Rusty, a former police dog with an undeservedly bad rep. Naturally, boy and dog bond and even capture a couple of escaped convicts (and Danny learns to love his stepmom too). 67m/B/W; VHS. **C:** Ted Donaldson; Margaret Lindsay; Conrad Nagel; Gloria Holden; Directed by Paul Burnford; Written by Aubrey Wisberg. **Pr:** Rudolph C. Flothow. **A:** Family. **P:** Entertainment. **U:** Home. **Mov-Ent:** Pets, Children, Parenting. **Acq:** Purchase. **Dist:** Sony Pictures Home Entertainment Inc.

The Adventures of Sadie 1955 (Unrated) — ★★½
Collins is stranded on a desert island with three men, two of whom continuously chase her around. Naturally, she falls for the guy who ignores her. Obvious sex comedy which plays on Collins' scantily clad physical assets. Based on the novel "The Cautious Amorist" by Norman Lindsay. 87m; VHS, DVD. **C:** Joan Collins; George Cole; Kenneth More; Robertson Hare; Hermione Gingold; Walter Fitzgerald; Directed by Noel Langley; Written by Noel Langley. **Pr:** Fox; Renown Pictures. **A:** Jr. High-Adult. **P:** Entertainment. **U:** Home. **Mov-Ent:** Comedy--Romantic, Sex & Sexuality. **Acq:** Purchase. **Dist:** VCI Entertainment. $14.24.

The Adventures of Sebastian Cole 1999 (R) — ★★½
Sebastian (Grenier) is a misfit highschooler in upstate New York in 1983. Not only does he have to deal with the usual trials of adolescence but there's his unusual family problems. His mother, Joan (Colin), returns to her native England upon learning that Sebastian's stepdad, Hank (Gregg), has decided to become a woman. Sebastian eventually winds up living with Hank, who is now known as Henrietta, and who's still the most stable adult in the teen's fractured world. 99m; DVD. **C:** Adrian Grenier; Clark Gregg; Aleksa Palladino; Margaret Colin; John Shea; Joan Copeland; Marni Lustig; Tom Lacy; Directed by Tod Harrison Williams; Written by Tod Harrison Williams; Cinematography by John Foster; Music by Lynne Geller. **Pr:** Paramount Classics. **A:** Sr. High-Adult. **P:** Entertainment. **U:** Home. **Mov-Ent:** Adolescence, Education, Parenting. **Acq:** Purchase. **Dist:** WarnerArchive.com.

The Adventures of Sharkboy and Lavagirl in 3-D 2005 (PG) — ★★½
Multi-hyphenate Rodriguez uses a story from son Racer as the basis for this kid-friendly adventure. Ten year-old misfit Max (Boyd) dreams up a couple of young superheroes and finds them coming to life. Sharkboy (Lautner) and Lavagirl (Dooley) need Max's help to save their home world, Planet Drool, from the evil Mr. Electric (Lopez). The cartoonish gee-wizardry will no doubt appeal to its target audience, but might struggle to hold the attention of older kids. 94m; DVD, Blu-Ray, UMD. **C:** Kristin Davis; David Arquette; George Lopez; Taylor Lautner; Taylor Dooley; Cayden Boyd; Jacob Davich; Sasha Pieterse; Rico Torres; Rebel Rodriquez; Racer Rodriguez; Rocket Rodriguez; Directed by Robert Rodriguez; Written by Robert Rodriguez; Cinematography by Robert Rodriguez; Music by John Debney; Graeme Revell. **Pr:** Elizabeth Avellan; Robert Rodriguez; Robert Rodriguez; Troublemaker Studios; Dimension Films. **A:** Family. **P:** Entertainment. **U:** Home. **L:** English. **Mov-Ent:** Fantasy. **Acq:** Purchase. **Dist:** Sony Pictures Home Entertainment Inc. $29.99.

The Adventures of Sherlock Holmes 1939 (Unrated) — ★★½
The immortal Sherlock Holmes and his assistant Dr. Watson conflict with Scotland Yard as they both race to stop arch-criminal Professor Moriarty. The Yard is put to shame as Holmes, a mere amateur sleuth, uses his brilliant deductive reasoning to save the damsel in distress and to stop Moriarty from stealing the Crown Jewels. Second in the series. 83m/B/W; VHS, DVD, CC. **C:** Basil Rathbone; Nigel Bruce; Ida Lupino; George Zucco; E.E. Clive; Mary Gordon; Directed by Alfred Werker; Written by Edwin Blum; Cinematography by Leon Shamroy. **Pr:** Darryl F. Zanuck; 20th Century-Fox. **A:** Family. **P:** Entertainment. **U:** Home. **Mov-Ent:** Mystery & Suspense. **Acq:** Purchase. **Dist:** Movies Unlimited; Alpha Video; MPI Media Group. $14.95.

The Adventures of Sherlock Holmes: A Scandal in Bohemia 1985

A mysterious masked gentleman visits Holmes and reveals himself to be the King of Bohemia. He's about to be married to a Scandinavian princess but a past indiscretion is about to come to light unless Holmes can recover the incriminating photograph. 52m; VHS, DVD. **C:** Jeremy Brett; David Burke. **A:** Jr. High-Adult. **P:** Entertainment. **U:** Home. **Mov-Ent:** Mystery & Suspense. **Acq:** Purchase. **Dist:** MPI Media Group; Phoenix Learning Group. $19.98.

The Adventures of Sherlock Holmes: Abbey Grange 1985

Holmes and Watson travel to the Abbey Grange when the old meeting hall is the site of a crime. 55m; VHS. **C:** Jeremy Brett; David Burke. **A:** Jr. High-Adult. **P:** Entertainment. **U:** Home. **Mov-Ent:** Mystery & Suspense. **Acq:** Purchase. **Dist:** Home Vision Cinema; MPI Media Group. $24.98.

The Adventures of Sherlock Holmes: Blue Carbuncle 1985

The Blue Carbuncle is a precious stone with a sinister past. Now it's been stolen from the Countess of Morcar and Holmes is called in to investigate. Based on the story by Arthur Conan Doyle; made for British TV. 52m; VHS. **C:** Jeremy Brett; David Burke. **A:** Jr. High-Adult. **P:** Entertainment. **U:** Home. **Mov-Ent:** Mystery & Suspense. **Acq:** Purchase. **Dist:** MPI Media Group; Phoenix Learning Group. $19.98.

The Adventures of Sherlock Holmes: Bruce Partington Plans 1985

Based on Arthur Conan Doyle's famous detective, this British television production is a fine dramatic series. 55m; VHS. **C:** Jeremy Brett; David Burke. **A:** Family. **P:** Entertainment. **U:** Home. **Mov-Ent:** Mystery & Suspense, TV Movies. **Acq:** Purchase. **Dist:** MPI Media Group. $24.98.

The Adventures of Sherlock Holmes: Copper Beaches 1985

The famous detective is called by a panicky woman, whose new employer insists she cut her hair. Why? Fine dramatic production for British television. 55m; VHS. **C:** Jeremy Brett; David Burke. **A:** Jr. High-Adult. **P:** Entertainment. **U:** Home. **Mov-Ent:** Mystery & Suspense, Television Series. **Acq:** Purchase. **Dist:** MPI Media Group; Home Vision Cinema. $19.98.

The Adventures of Sherlock Holmes: Crooked Man 1985

When the servants of Colonel Barclay and his wife are suspicious of wrongdoing in the household, Sherlock Holmes is called upon to investigate. 55m; VHS. **C:** Jeremy Brett; David Burke. **A:** Jr. High-Adult. **P:** Entertainment. **U:** Home. **Mov-Ent:** Mystery & Suspense, Television Series. **Acq:** Purchase. **Dist:** MPI Media Group. $24.95.

The Adventures of Sherlock Holmes: Dancing Men 1985

While working in her garden, Elsie Cubitt finds some seemingly harmless chalk drawings of matchstick men dancing in a line. But Elsie and husband Hilton are both perturbed and send for Holmes to crack the puzzling code. 52m; VHS. **C:** Jeremy Brett; David Burke; Directed by Paul Annett; John Bruce; David Carson. **A:** Jr. High-Adult. **P:** Entertainment. **U:** Home. **Mov-Ent:** Mystery & Suspense, TV Movies. **Acq:** Purchase. **Dist:** MPI Media Group; Phoenix Learning Group. $19.98.

The Adventures of Sherlock Holmes: Devil's Foot 1985

This British television series features Conan Doyle's famous detective in a fine dramatic production. 55m; VHS. **C:** Jeremy Brett; David Burke. **A:** Family. **P:** Entertainment. **U:** Home. **Mov-Ent:** Mystery & Suspense, Television Series. **Acq:** Purchase. **Dist:** MPI Media Group. $24.98.

The Adventures of Sherlock Holmes: Empty House 1985

Has Sherlock Holmes met his match when he and Professor Moriarty go at each other's throats? Find out when you watch this companion tape to "The Adventures of Sherlock Holmes: The Final Problem." 55m; VHS. **C:** Jeremy Brett; David Burke. **A:** Family. **P:** Entertainment. **U:** Home. **Mov-Ent:** Mystery & Suspense, Television Series. **Acq:** Purchase. **Dist:** MPI Media Group; Home Vision Cinema. $24.98.

The Adventures of Sherlock Holmes: Final Problem 1985

More adventures with the world's most famous detective. From British TV. 55m; VHS. **C:** Jeremy Brett; David Burke; Directed by Paul Annett; John Bruce; David Carson; Ken Grieve. **A:** Family. **P:** Entertainment. **U:** Home. **Mov-Ent:** Mystery & Suspense, Television Series. **Acq:** Purchase. **Dist:** MPI Media Group; Home Vision Cinema. $24.98.

The Adventures of Sherlock Holmes: Greek Interpreter 1985

Mycroft, Sherlock's brother, calls the famous detective in to help him unravel a baffling mystery about a Greek interpreter and a late night visitor. A fine dramatic production from British television. 55m; VHS. **C:** Jeremy Brett; David Burke. **A:** Family. **P:** Entertainment. **U:** Home. **Mov-Ent:** Mystery & Suspense, Television Series. **Acq:** Purchase. **Dist:** MPI Media Group. $24.95.

The Adventures of Sherlock Holmes: Hound of the Baskervilles 1989

Holmes tackles the mysterious and long-lived curse of the Baskervilles. Made for British television. Fine acting, detailed production. A pleasure. 120m; VHS. **C:** Jeremy Brett; Edward Hardwicke. **A:** Jr. High-Adult. **P:** Entertainment. **U:** Home. **Mov-Ent:** Mystery & Suspense, Television Series. **Acq:** Purchase. **Dist:** MPI Media Group. $39.95.

The Adventures of Sherlock Holmes: Man with the Twisted Lip 1985

A fine British television production has the famous detective solving baffling mysteries. 55m; VHS. **C:** Jeremy Brett; David Burke. **A:** Family. **P:** Entertainment. **U:** Home. **Mov-Ent:** Mystery & Suspense, Television Series. **Acq:** Purchase. **Dist:** MPI Media Group. $24.98.

The Adventures of Sherlock Holmes: Musgrave Ritual 1985

Made for British television production of the famous Arthur Conan Doyle detective and his partner's escapades. 55m; VHS. **C:** Jeremy Brett; David Burke. **A:** Family. **P:** Entertainment. **U:** Home. **Mov-Ent:** Mystery & Suspense, Television Series. **Acq:** Purchase. **Dist:** MPI Media Group. $24.98.

The Adventures of Sherlock Holmes: Naval Treaty 1985

Percy Phelps is an old school chum of Dr. Watson and calls on him for help when the secret new treaty between England and Italy that he has been copying is stolen. Naturally, Holmes gets involved as well. 52m; VHS. **C:** Jeremy Brett; David Burke. **A:** Jr. High-Adult. **P:** Entertainment. **U:** Home. **Mov-Ent:** Mystery & Suspense. **Acq:** Purchase. **Dist:** MPI Media Group; PBS Home Video. $24.98.

The Adventures of Sherlock Holmes: Norwood Builder 1985

Another in the fine dramatic British television series, based on Conan Doyle's famous detective. Holmes is called in to investigate the innocence of the young solicitor (attorney) John McFarlane, who is accused of murdering "the Norwood builder." 55m; VHS. **C:** Jeremy Brett; David Burke. **A:** Family. **P:** Entertainment. **U:** Home. **Mov-Ent:** Mystery & Suspense, Television Series. **Acq:** Purchase. **Dist:** MPI Media Group. $24.95.

The Adventures of Sherlock Holmes: Red-Headed League 1989

Holmes investigates the mysterious goings-on of an organization whose members all have red hair. Made for British television. Witty, with fine acting and attention to detail. 50m; VHS. **C:** Jeremy Brett; Edward Hardwicke; Leo McKern. **A:** Family. **P:** Entertainment. **U:** Home. **Mov-Ent:** Mystery & Suspense, Television Series. **Acq:** Purchase. **Dist:** MPI Media Group. $29.95.

The Adventures of Sherlock Holmes: Resident Patient 1985

This fine dramatic British television series features Conan Doyle's famous detective in another baffling mystery: a Russian father and son disappear during a consultation with a doctor. Now the doctor's benefactor is terrified—why? 55m; VHS. **C:** Jeremy Brett; David Burke. **A:** Family. **P:** Entertainment. **U:** Home. **Mov-Ent:** Mystery & Suspense, Television Series. **Acq:** Purchase. **Dist:** MPI Media Group; Home Vision Cinema. $24.95.

The Adventures of Sherlock Holmes: Second Stain 1985

The Secretary of European Affairs discovers that an important document has been stolen and sets Sherlock Holmes off to find the thief. 55m; VHS. **C:** Jeremy Brett; David Burke. **A:** Jr. High-Adult. **P:** Entertainment. **U:** Home. **Mov-Ent:** Mystery & Suspense, Television Series. **Acq:** Purchase. **Dist:** MPI Media Group. $24.98.

The Adventures of Sherlock Holmes Set 2 1985

Classic Holmes mysteries including the case of a murdered colonel and the theft of the Mona Lisa. 110m; DVD. **A:** Adult. **P:** Entertainment. **U:** Home. **Mov-Ent:** Classic Films, Drama, Mystery & Suspense. **Acq:** Purchase. **Dist:** MPI Media Group. $119.98.

The Adventures of Sherlock Holmes Set I 1984

Six classic Holmes mysteries including the case of a sinister gem and a young music teacher stalked by a mysterious cyclist. 210m; DVD. **A:** Adult. **P:** Entertainment. **U:** Home. **Mov-Ent:** Classic Films, Drama, Mystery & Suspense. **Acq:** Purchase. **Dist:** MPI Media Group. $99.98.

The Adventures of Sherlock Holmes: Sign of Four 1985

The beautiful Miss Morstan begins receiving one pearl a year, beginning with the disappearance of her father. She calls in Sherlock Holmes to solve this baffling mystery. A fine dramatic production from British television. Based on the character introduced by Sir Arthur Conan Doyle. 120m; VHS. **C:** Jeremy Brett; David Burke. **A:** Family. **P:** Entertainment. **U:** Home. **Mov-Ent:** Mystery & Suspense, Television Series. **Acq:** Purchase. **Dist:** MPI Media Group. $39.95.

The Adventures of Sherlock Holmes: Silver Blaze 1985

Holmes and Watson battle another degenerete criminal. 55m; VHS. **C:** Jeremy Brett; David Burke. **A:** Jr. High-Adult. **P:** Entertainment. **U:** Home. **Mov-Ent:** Mystery & Suspense, Television Series, Horses. **Acq:** Purchase. **Dist:** MPI Media Group; Home Vision Cinema. $24.98.

The Adventures of Sherlock Holmes: Six Napoleons 1985

A fine dramatic production from British television, based on the famous detective of Sir Arthur Conan Doyle. 55m; VHS. **C:** Jeremy Brett; David Burke. **A:** Family. **P:** Entertainment. **U:** Home. **Mov-Ent:** Mystery & Suspense. **Acq:** Purchase. **Dist:** MPI Media Group. $24.98.

The Adventures of Sherlock Holmes' Smarter Brother 1978 (PG) — ★★★

The unknown brother of the famous Sherlock Holmes takes on some of his brother's more disposable excess cases and makes some hilarious moves. Moments of engaging farce borrowed from the Mel Brooks school of parody (and parts of the Brooks ensemble as well). 91m; VHS, DVD. **C:** Gene Wilder; Madeline Kahn; Marty Feldman; Dom DeLuise; Leo McKern; Roy Kinnear; John Le Mesurier; Douglas Wilmer; Thorley Walters; Directed by Gene Wilder; Written by Gene Wilder. **Pr:** 20th Century-Fox. **A:** Jr. High-Adult. **P:** Entertainment. **U:** Home. **Mov-Ent:** Satire & Parody. **Acq:** Purchase. **Dist:** Alpha Video; Fox Home Entertainment.

The Adventures of Sherlock Holmes: Solitary Cyclist 1985

Music teacher Violet Smith takes a position with a friend of her late uncle, traveling to London on the weekends to spend time with her family. When she notices a man on a bicycle following her to and from the train station, she calls on Sherlock Holmes to find out who the man is and why she's been shadowed. 52m; VHS. **C:** Jeremy Brett; David Burke. **A:** Jr. High-Adult. **P:** Entertainment. **U:** Home. **Mov-Ent:** Mystery & Suspense, Television Series. **Acq:** Purchase. **Dist:** MPI Media Group. $24.98.

The Adventures of Sherlock Holmes: Speckled Band 1985

Holmes and Watson come to the aid of Helen Stoner, whose dying sister left her a mysterious message. Excellent production; made-for-British-television. 52m; VHS. **C:** Jeremy Brett; David Burke. **A:** Jr. High-Adult. **P:** Entertainment. **U:** Home. **Mov-Ent:** Mystery & Suspense. **Acq:** Purchase. **Dist:** MPI Media Group. $24.98.

The Adventures of Sherlock Holmes: The Eligible Bachelor 2003 (Unrated)

Features Arthur Conan Doyle's sleuth Sherlock Holmes and his sidekick Dr. Watson from the 1984-1985 TV series solving a mystery of a missing rich American bride who disappears after her wedding to a London man. 1 episode. 105m; DVD. **C:** Jeremy Brett; David Burke. **A:** Jr. High-Adult. **P:** Entertainment. **U:** Home. **Mov-Ent:** Television Series, Action-Adventure, Mystery & Suspense. **Acq:** Purchase. **Dist:** MPI Media Group. $14.98.

The Adventures of Sherlock Holmes: The Last Vampyre 2003 (Unrated)

Features Arthur Conan Doyle's sleuth Sherlock Holmes and his sidekick Dr. Watson from the 1984-1985 TV series solving a mystery of a man whose community suspects is a vampire committing horrific acts including a young child's murder. 1 episode. 105m; DVD. **C:** Jeremy Brett; David Burke. **A:** Jr. High-Adult. **P:** Entertainment. **U:** Home. **Mov-Ent:** Television Series, Action-Adventure, Mystery & Suspense. **Acq:** Purchase. **Dist:** MPI Media Group. $14.98.

The Adventures of Sherlock Holmes: Volume 1 2000 (Unrated)

Features tales of Arthur Conan Doyle's sleuth Sherlock Holmes and his sidekick Dr. Watson from the 1984-1985 TV series solving various mysteries; includes "A Scandal in Bohemia," "The Dancing Men," "The Naval Treaty," and "The Solitary Cyclist." 4 episodes. 210m; DVD. **C:** Jeremy Brett; David Burke. **A:** Jr. High-Adult. **P:** Entertainment. **U:** Home. **Mov-Ent:** Television Series, Action-Adventure, Mystery & Suspense. **Acq:** Purchase. **Dist:** MPI Media Group. $19.98.

The Adventures of Sherlock Holmes: Volume 2 2001 (Unrated)

Features tales of Arthur Conan Doyle's sleuth Sherlock Holmes and his sidekick Dr. Watson from the 1984-1985 TV series solving various mysteries; includes "The Crooked Man," and "The Speckled Band." 2 episodes. 100m; DVD. **C:** Jeremy Brett; David Burke. **A:** Jr. High-Adult. **P:** Entertainment. **U:** Home. **Mov-Ent:** Television Series, Action-Adventure, Mystery & Suspense. **Acq:** Purchase. **Dist:** MPI Media Group. $14.98.

The Adventures of Sherlock Holmes: Volume 3 2001 (Unrated)

Features tales of Arthur Conan Doyle's sleuth Sherlock Holmes and his sidekick Dr. Watson from the 1984-1985 TV series solving various mysteries; includes "The Blue Carbuncle," and "The Copper Beeches." 2 episodes. 100m; DVD. **C:** Jeremy Brett; David Burke. **A:** Jr. High-Adult. **P:** Entertainment. **U:** Home. **Mov-Ent:** Television Series, Action-Adventure, Mystery & Suspense. **Acq:** Purchase. **Dist:** MPI Media Group. $14.98.

The Adventures of Sherlock Holmes: Volume 4 2002 (Unrated)

Features tales of Arthur Conan Doyle's sleuth Sherlock Holmes and his sidekick Dr. Watson from the 1984-1985 TV series solving various mysteries; includes "The Greek Interpreter," and "The Norwood Builder." 2 episodes. 100m; DVD. **C:** Jeremy Brett; David Burke. **A:** Jr. High-Adult. **P:** Entertainment. **U:** Home. **Mov-Ent:** Television Series, Action-Adventure, Mystery & Suspense. **Acq:** Purchase. **Dist:** MPI Media Group. $14.98.

The Adventures of Sherlock Holmes: Volume 5 2002 (Unrated)

Features tales of Arthur Conan Doyle's sleuth Sherlock Holmes and his sidekick Dr. Watson from the 1984-1985 TV series solving various mysteries; includes "The Resident Patient," "The Red Headed League" and "The Final Problem." 3 episodes. 150m; DVD. **C:** Jeremy Brett; David Burke. **A:** Jr. High-Adult. **P:** Entertainment. **U:** Home. **Mov-Ent:** Television Series, Action-Adventure, Mystery & Suspense. **Acq:** Purchase. **Dist:** MPI Media Group. $14.98.

The Adventures of Sherlock Holmes: Wisteria Lodge 1985

Another fine dramatic production from the British television series. Based on the famous detective of Sir Arthur Conan Doyle. 55m; VHS. **C:** Jeremy Brett; David Burke. **A:** Family. **P:**

Entertainment. **U:** Home. **Mov-Ent:** Mystery & Suspense. **Acq:** Purchase. **Dist:** MPI Media Group. $24.98.

The Adventures of Sinbad 1962
Fully animated version of the adventures of Sinbad the sailor. ?m; VHS. **A:** Preschool-Primary. **P:** Entertainment. **U:** Home. **Chl-Juv:** Animation & Cartoons. **Acq:** Purchase. **Dist:** Sinister Cinema. $16.95.

The Adventures of Sinbad 1979
The adventures of the Arabian mythic hero in an animated film version. 47m; VHS. **Pr:** API Television Productions. **A:** Family. **P:** Entertainment. **U:** Home. **Mov-Ent:** Fantasy, Animation & Cartoons. **Acq:** Purchase. **Dist:** MGM Home Entertainment; Lions Gate Television Corp. $29.98.

The Adventures of Sinbad: The Complete First Season 2004 (Unrated)
Features the debut season of the 1996-1998 live-action fantasy television series on a ship's captain and his crew who fend off trouble in the form of sea monsters, evil sorcerers, and genies with their magical powers. 22 episodes. 990m; DVD. **C:** Zen Gesner; George Buza; Tim Progosh; Mariah Shirley; Oris Erhuero. **A:** Family. **P:** Entertainment. **U:** Home. **Mov-Ent:** Television Series, Action-Adventure, Fantasy. **Acq:** Purchase. **Dist:** Entertainment One US LP. $44.96.

The Adventures of Sinbad the Sailor 1973 (Unrated)
Sinbad receives a map to a treasure island where fabulous stores of jewels are hidden, and, in his search, falls in love with the King's daughter. Animated adventure. 88m; VHS. **Pr:** International Film Exchange. **A:** Preschool-Primary. **P:** Entertainment. **U:** Home. **Mov-Ent:** Animation & Cartoons, Fantasy. **Acq:** Purchase. **Dist:** Lions Gate Television Corp. $59.98.

The Adventures of Sir Lancelot, Vol. 1 1956
Contains two episodes from the Sir Lancelot television series of the 1950s: "The Theft of Excalibur" and "Lady Lilith." 60m; DVD. **C:** William Russell; Jane Hylton. **A:** Family. **P:** Entertainment. **U:** Home. **Mov-Ent:** Television Series. **Acq:** Purchase. **Dist:** Alpha Video; Timeless Media Group.

The Adventures of Sir Lancelot, Vol. 2 1956
Features two episodes from the 1950s Sir Lancelot television series: "The Ferocious Fathers" and "Montaise Fair." 60m; DVD. **C:** William Russell; Jane Hylton. **A:** Family. **P:** Entertainment. **U:** Home. **Mov-Ent:** Television Series. **Acq:** Purchase. **Dist:** Alpha Video; Timeless Media Group.

The Adventures of Sir Lancelot, Vol. 3 1957
Provides two episodes from the 1950s Sir Lancelot television series: "The Ugly Duckling" and "Knight with the Red Plume." 60m; DVD. **C:** William Russell; Jane Hylton. **A:** Family. **P:** Entertainment. **U:** Home. **Mov-Ent:** Television Series. **Acq:** Purchase. **Dist:** Alpha Video; Timeless Media Group.

The Adventures of Sir Lancelot, Vol. 4 1957
Features two episodes from the 1950s Sir Lancelot television series: "The Lesser Breed" and "Ruby od Radnor." 60m; DVD. **C:** William Russell; Jane Hylton. **A:** Family. **P:** Entertainment. **U:** Home. **Mov-Ent:** Television Series. **Acq:** Purchase. **Dist:** Alpha Video; Timeless Media Group.

The Adventures of Sir Lancelot, Vol. 5 1957
Contains two episodes from the 1950s Sir Lancelot television series: "The Prince of Limerick" and "Witches Brew." 60m; DVD. **C:** William Russell; Jane Hylton. **A:** Family. **P:** Entertainment. **U:** Home. **Mov-Ent:** Television Series. **Acq:** Purchase. **Dist:** Alpha Video; Timeless Media Group.

Adventures of Smilin' Jack 1943 (Unrated) — ★★
WWII flying ace Smilin' Jack Martin comes to life in this action-packed serial. Character from the Zack Mosley comic strip about air force fighting over China. 90m/B/W; VHS, DVD. **C:** Tom Brown; Sidney Toler; Directed by Ray Taylor. **Pr:** Mark Huffam. **A:** Family. **P:** Entertainment. **U:** Home. **Mov-Ent:** World War Two, China, Aeronautics. **Acq:** Purchase. **Dist:** Sinister Cinema. $26.95.

The Adventures of Sonic the Hedgehog: Volume 1 1993
Classic slapstick escapades have Sonic and Tails repeatedly saving planet Mobius from Dr. Robotnik and his no-good robots. 22 episodes. 480m; DVD. **C:** Voice(s) by Jaleel White; Long John Baldry. **A:** Adult. **P:** Entertainment. **U:** Home. **Chl-Juv:** Animation & Cartoons. **Acq:** Purchase. **Dist:** Shout! Factory.

The Adventures of Sonic the Hedgehog: Volume 2 1994 (Unrated)
Fox Kids Network 1993-96 animated action adventure. Sonic and Tails continue the fight to protect their home world Mobius from the evil Dr. Robotnik and his mindless henchmen Scratch, Grounder, and Coconuts. 22 episodes. 300m; DVD. **C:** Voice(s) by Jaleel White; Long John Baldry; Garry Chalk; Phil Hayes. **A:** Preschool-Primary. **P:** Entertainment. **U:** Home. **Chl-Juv:** Animation & Cartoons, Action-Adventure, Television Series. **Acq:** Purchase. **Dist:** Shout! Factory. $29.99.

The Adventures of Sport Billy 19??
Evil Queen Vanda wants to wipe out fair play and sportsmanship on Earth. 75m; VHS. **Pr:** Sony Pictures Home Entertainment Inc. **A:** Family. **P:** Entertainment. **U:** Home. **Chl-Juv:** Animation & Cartoons, Sports--General. **Acq:** Purchase. **Dist:** New Line Home Video. $29.95.

Adventures of Superman: The Complete Fifth and Sixth Seasons 2006 (Unrated)
Features the fifth and sixth seasons of the 1952-1958 sci-fi television series with superhero Superman (Reeves). Episodes include: Perry (Hamilton) is suspected of stealing from the Planet and setting fire to its warehouse, Jimmy (Larson) and Lois (Neill) are threatened by gangsters, and Superman marries

a gorgeous police sergeant, which crushes Lois. 26 episodes. 677m; DVD. **C:** George Reeves; John Hamilton; Noel Neill; Jack Larson; Bill Kennedy. **A:** Family. **P:** Entertainment. **U:** Home. **Mov-Ent:** Television Series, Action-Adventure, Science Fiction. **Acq:** Purchase. **Dist:** Warner Home Video, Inc. $39.98.

Adventures of Superman: The Complete First Season 2005 (Unrated)
Features the premiere season of the 1952-1958 sci-fi television series with superhero Superman (Reeves)?the last survivor of the planet Krypton who uses his powers to protect the citizens of Metropolis. Meanwhile during the day he poses as clumsy news reporter Clark Kent at the Daily Planet with his boss Perry White (Hamilton), fellow reporter and love interest Lois Lane (Neill), and photographer Jimmy Olsen (Larson). Episodes include: Lois investigates art theft and is kidnapped, an atomic bomb secret is stolen, Lois gets trapped in a coal mine, and a museum robber attempts to subdue Superman. 26 episodes. 662m; DVD. **C:** George Reeves; John Hamilton; Noel Neill; Jack Larson; Bill Kennedy. **A:** Family. **P:** Entertainment. **U:** Home. **Mov-Ent:** Television Series, Action-Adventure, Science Fiction. **Acq:** Purchase. **Dist:** Warner Home Video, Inc. $39.98.

Adventures of Superman: The Complete Second Season 2006 (Unrated)
Features the second season of the 1952-1958 sci-fi television series with superhero Superman (Reeves). Episodes include: Lois (Neill) and Jimmy (Larson) are kidnapped while on assignment, a bad guy uncovers Superman's only weakness Kryptonite, and Superman leaves Metropolis to the criminals' delight after a nuclear incident makes him radioactive. 26 episodes. 683m; DVD. **C:** George Reeves; John Hamilton; Noel Neill; Jack Larson; Bill Kennedy. **A:** Family. **P:** Entertainment. **U:** Home. **Mov-Ent:** Television Series, Action-Adventure, Science Fiction. **Acq:** Purchase. **Dist:** Warner Home Video, Inc. $39.98.

Adventures of Superman: The Complete Third and Fourth Seasons 2006 (Unrated)
Features the third and fourth seasons of the 1952-1958 sci-fi television series with superhero Superman (Reeves). Episodes include: Jimmy (Larson), Lois (Neill), and Clark are transported in a time machine with a criminal, Lois is kidnapped by a gangster when she writes about a relic, and Lois fantasizes about marrying Superman. 26 episodes. 706m; DVD. **C:** George Reeves; John Hamilton; Noel Neill; Jack Larson; Bill Kennedy. **A:** Family. **P:** Entertainment. **U:** Home. **Mov-Ent:** Television Series, Action-Adventure, Science Fiction. **Acq:** Purchase. **Dist:** Warner Home Video, Inc. $39.98.

The Adventures of Superted 1990
Four animated adventures for children starring the flying, inter-galactic super bear. ?m; VHS. **Pr:** Hanna-Barbera Productions. **A:** Family. **P:** Entertainment. **U:** Home. **Chl-Juv:** Animation & Cartoons, Children. **Acq:** Purchase. **Dist:** Turner Broadcasting System Inc. $29.95.

The Adventures of Tartu 1943 — ★★½
A British secret agent, sent to blow up a Nazi poison gas factory in Czechoslovakia, poses as a Romanian. One of Donat's lesser films, in the style of "The 39 Steps." 103m; VHS, DVD. **C:** Robert Donat; Valerie Hobson; Glynis Johns; Directed by Harold Bucquet. **Pr:** MGM. **A:** Family. **P:** Entertainment. **U:** Home. **Mov-Ent:** Acq: Purchase. **Dist:** Movies Unlimited; Alpha Video. $19.95.

The Adventures of Tarzan 1921 — ★★
The screen's first Tarzan in an exciting jungle thriller. Silent. 153m/B/W; Silent; VHS, DVD. **TV Std:** NTSC, PAL. **C:** Elmo Lincoln; Louise Lorraine; Lilian Worth; Frank Whitson; Frank Merrill; Directed by Robert F. "Bob" Hill; Written by Robert F. "Bob" Hill. **Pr:** Artclass. **A:** Family. **P:** Entertainment. **U:** Home. **Mov-Ent:** Serials, Classic Films, Silent Films. **Acq:** Purchase. **Dist:** Glenn Video Vistas Ltd. $27.95.

The Adventures of Taxi Dog 1990
There's never a dull moment for Maxi the dog and his taxi-driver owner Jim as they drive the city streets picking up every kind of passenger imaginable. Adapted from the book by Debra and Sal Barracca, and illustrated by Mark Buehner. Teacher's guide available. 30m; VHS. **A:** Preschool-Primary. **P:** Entertainment. **U:** Home, Institution. **Chl-Juv:** Animation & Cartoons, Pets. **Acq:** Purchase. **Dist:** GPN Educational Media. $35.95.

The Adventures of Teddy Ruxpin 1986
Teddy Ruxpin and his friend Grubby the Octopede set out on a search for a fabulous treasure, but are captured by the grime-encrusted Mudblups. 44m; VHS. **Pr:** Vestron Video. **A:** Preschool. **P:** Entertainment. **U:** Home. **Chl-Juv:** Animation & Cartoons, Family Viewing, Ethics & Morals. **Acq:** Purchase. **Dist:** Lions Gate Television Corp. $14.98.

The Adventures of Teddy Ruxpin: Come Dream with Me: The Complete Series 1987 (Unrated)
Teddy Ruxpin and his friend Grubby leave their homeland in Rillonia on a quest for the Treasure of Grundo, along the way they meet Dr. Newton Gimmick who aids the search until they find six power-filled crystals that many others seek, some to use for good and others for evil. 1339m; DVD. **A:** Preschool-Primary. **P:** Entertainment. **U:** Home. **Chl-Juv:** Animation & Cartoons, Fantasy. **Acq:** Purchase. **Dist:** Mill Creek Entertainment L.L.C. $24.98.

The Adventures of the Flying Cadets 1944 — ★½
Early aerial war adventure serial in 13 complete chapters. 169m/B/W; VHS. **C:** Johnny Downs; Regis Toomey; Directed by Ray Taylor; Lewis D. Collins. **Pr:** Mark Huffam. **A:** Family. **P:** Entertainment. **U:** Home. **Mov-Ent:** War--General, Serials, Aeronautics. **Acq:** Purchase. **Dist:** Sinister Cinema. $39.95.

Adventures of the Galaxy Rangers, Vol. 3 1987
Three animated adventures of space-age crime fighters. Includes "Phoenix," "New Frontier" and "Torture." 70m; VHS. **Pr:** Gaylord. **A:** Family. **P:** Entertainment. **U:** Home. **Chl-Juv:** Animation & Cartoons. **Acq:** Purchase. **Dist:** Magic Window Productions, Inc. $29.95.

Adventures of the Galaxy Rangers, Vol. 4 1987
Three animated episodes of the space-age crimebusters. Includes "Chained," "Supertrooper" and "Galaxy Stranger." 70m; VHS. **Pr:** Gaylord Productions. **A:** Family. **P:** Entertainment. **U:** Home. **Chl-Juv:** Animation & Cartoons. **Acq:** Purchase. **Dist:** Magic Window Productions, Inc. $29.95.

Adventures of the Galaxy Rangers, Vol. 5 1987
Five further adventures of the animated crimefighters. Includes "Mindnet," "Smuggler's Gauntlet," "Scarecrow," "One Million Emotions" and "The Power Within." 110m; VHS. **Pr:** Gaylord Productions. **A:** Family. **P:** Entertainment. **U:** Home. **Chl-Juv:** Animation & Cartoons. **Acq:** Purchase. **Dist:** Magic Window Productions, Inc. $59.95.

Adventures of the Galaxy Rangers, Vol. 6 1987
5 more animated stories of the space-age crimefighters including "Birds of a Feather," "Space Moby," "Mothmooses," "Progress" and "Traash." 110m; VHS. **Pr:** Gaylord Productions. **A:** Family. **P:** Entertainment. **U:** Home. **Chl-Juv:** Animation & Cartoons, Science Fiction. **Acq:** Purchase. **Dist:** Magic Window Productions, Inc.

Adventures of the Galaxy Rangers, Vol. 7 1987
5 animated stories of crimebusters in the future. Includes "The Gift of Life," "Sundancer," "Shoot Out," "Marshmallow Trees" and "Tune Up." 110m; VHS. **A:** Family. **P:** Entertainment. **U:** Home. **Chl-Juv:** Animation & Cartoons. **Acq:** Purchase. **Dist:** Magic Window Productions, Inc. $59.95.

Adventures of the Galaxy Rangers, Vol. 8 1988
5 more cartoons featuring those intrepid foes of all evil in the future. Episodes include "Westridge," "Boomtown," "Fire & Iron," "Renegade Rangers" and "In Sheep's Clothing." 110m; VHS. **Pr:** Gaylord Productions. **A:** Family. **P:** Entertainment. **U:** Home. **Chl-Juv:** Animation & Cartoons. **Acq:** Purchase. **Dist:** Magic Window Productions, Inc. $59.95.

Adventures of the Galaxy Rangers, Vol. 9 1988
5 more cartoons of space crimebusters. Includes "Games," "Heart of Tarkon," "Scarecrow's Revenge," "Heartbeat" and "Aces & Apes." 110m; VHS. **A:** Family. **P:** Entertainment. **U:** Home. **Chl-Juv:** Animation & Cartoons. **Acq:** Purchase. **Dist:** Magic Window Productions, Inc. $59.95.

Adventures of the Galaxy Rangers, Vol. 10 1988
Five more animated tales of futuristic crimebusting. Episodes include "Mistwalker," "Natural Balance," "Murder on the Andorian Express," "Bronto Bear," and "Rainmaker." 110m; VHS. **A:** Family. **P:** Entertainment. **U:** Home. **Chl-Juv:** Animation & Cartoons. **Acq:** Purchase. **Dist:** Magic Window Productions, Inc. $59.95.

Adventures of the Galaxy Rangers, Vol. 11 1989
Yet five more cartoons of future cops. Includes "Battle of the Bandits," "Tortuna Rocks," "Ax," "Shaky," and "The Magnificent Kiwi." 110m; VHS. **A:** Family. **P:** Entertainment. **U:** Home. **Chl-Juv:** Animation & Cartoons. **Acq:** Purchase. **Dist:** Magic Window Productions, Inc. $59.95.

Adventures of the Galaxy Rangers, Vol. 12 1989
The final volume of five cartoons about fighting crime in the future. This volume contains "Tower of Combat," "Changeling," "Lord of the Sands," "Trouble at Texton," and "Rogue Arm." 110m; VHS. **A:** Family. **P:** Entertainment. **U:** Home. **Chl-Juv:** Animation & Cartoons. **Acq:** Purchase. **Dist:** Magic Window Productions, Inc.

Adventures of the Little Prince: Higher Than Eagles Fly 2005
Early 1980s animated television series based on the classic stories of Antoine de Saint-Exupery that follow a young prince as he flies himself to the Andes Mountains, Australia, and Newfoundland while learning life lessons from friends he meets; includes "Higher Than Eagles Fly," and "Shipwreck!". 2 episodes. 72m; DVD. **C:** Voice(s) by Christa Haussler; Katheryn Leigh; Jillian McWhirter; Hal Smith. **A:** Family. **P:** Entertainment. **U:** Home. **L:** English, Spanish. **Chl-Juv:** Television Series, Children's Shows, Animation & Cartoons. **Acq:** Purchase. **Dist:** Entertainment One US LP. $9.98.

Adventures of the Little Prince: Somewhere in Space 2005 (Unrated)
Early 1980s animated television series based on the classic stories of Antoine de Saint-Exupery that follows a young prince as he flies himself around the world and beyond while learning life lessons from friends he meets; includes "Rob the Rainbow," "A Small Alien," and "Somewhere in Space." 3 episodes. 72m; DVD. **C:** Voice(s) by Christa Haussler; Katheryn Leigh; Hal Smith; Jillian McWhirter. **A:** Family. **P:** Entertainment. **U:** Home. **Chl-Juv:** Television Series, Children's Shows, Animation & Cartoons. **Acq:** Purchase. **Dist:** Entertainment One US LP. $9.98.

Adventures of the Little Prince: The Complete Animated Series 2005 (Unrated)
Early 1980s animated television series based on the classic stories of Antoine de Saint-Exupery that follow a young prince as he flies himself around the world and beyond while learning life lessons from friends he meets. 26 episodes. 600m; DVD. **C:** Voice(s) by Katheryn Leigh; Jillian McWhirter; Hal Smith; Christa Haussler. **A:** Family. **P:** Entertainment. **U:** Home. **Chl-Juv:** Television Series, Children's Shows, Animation & Cartoons. **Acq:** Purchase. **Dist:** Entertainment One US LP. $49.98.

Adventures of the Little Prince: The Greatest Gift 2006 (Unrated)
Early 1980s animated television series based on the classic stories of Antoine de Saint-Exupery that follows a young prince as he flies himself around the world and beyond while learning life lessons from friends he meets; includes "The Greatest Gift," "Too Big for This World," and "The Winning Ride." 3 episodes. 72m; DVD. **C:** Voice(s) by Christa Haussler; Katheryn Leigh; Jillian McWhirter; Hal Smith. **A:** Family. **P:** Entertainment. **U:** Home. **Chl-Juv:** Television Series, Children's Shows, Animation & Cartoons. **Acq:** Purchase. **Dist:** Entertainment One US LP. $9.98.

Adventures of the Little Prince: The Magic Case 2006 (Unrated)
Early 1980s animated television series based on the classic stories of Antoine de Saint-Exupery that follows a young prince as he flies himself around the world and beyond while learning life lessons from friends he meets; includes "To Be a Man," "The Magic Case," and "Always Listen to a Fox." 3 episodes. 72m; DVD. **C:** Voice(s) by Simone Brahmann; Katheryn Leigh; Jillian McWhirter; Hal Smith. **A:** Family. **P:** Entertainment. **U:** Home. **Chl-Juv:** Television Series, Children's Shows, Animation & Cartoons. **Acq:** Purchase. **Dist:** Entertainment One US LP. $9.98.

Adventures of the Little Prince: The Perfect Planet 2006 (Unrated)
Early 1980s animated television series based on the classic stories of Antoine de Saint-Exupery that follows a young prince as he flies himself around the world and beyond while learning life lessons from friends he meets; includes "Visit to Another Planet," "The Perfect Planet," and "The Wolf Pack." 3 episodes. 72m; DVD. **C:** Voice(s) by Christa Haussler; Katheryn Leigh; Jillian McWhirter; Hal Smith. **A:** Family. **P:** Entertainment. **U:** Home. **Chl-Juv:** Television Series, Children's Shows, Animation & Cartoons. **Acq:** Purchase. **Dist:** Entertainment One US LP. $9.98.

Adventures of the Little Prince: The Star Gazer 2006 (Unrated)
Early 1980s animated television series based on the classic stories of Antoine de Saint-Exupery that follows a young prince as he flies himself around the world and beyond while learning life lessons from friends he meets; includes "The Star Gazer," "Last Voyage of the Rose," and "The Chimney Sweep." 3 episodes. 72m; DVD. **C:** Voice(s) by Christa Haussler; Katheryn Leigh; Jillian McWhirter; Hal Smith. **A:** Family. **P:** Entertainment. **U:** Home. **Chl-Juv:** Television Series, Children's Shows, Animation & Cartoons. **Acq:** Purchase. **Dist:** Entertainment One US LP. $9.98.

The Adventures of the Little Rascals 193?
Six classic "Our Gang" comedies featuring the Little Rascals. Each short is presented in its original form. 100m/B/W; VHS. **Pr:** MGM. **A:** Family. **P:** Entertainment. **U:** Home. **Mov-Ent:** Comedy--Slapstick, Children. **Acq:** Purchase. **Dist:** Lions Gate Entertainment Inc.
Indiv. Titles: 1. When the Wind Blows 2. For Pete's Sake 3. Glove Tapes 4. Love Business 5. Hi Neighbor! 6. Came the Brawn.

The Adventures of the Lone Ranger: Count the Clues 1957
Three episodes from the classic television series, involving the masked man's investigation and apprehension of a corrupt cattle baron. 72m; VHS. **C:** Clayton Moore; Jay Silverheels. **Pr:** Wrather Corporation. **A:** Family. **P:** Entertainment. **U:** Home. **Mov-Ent:** Western, Television Series. **Acq:** Purchase. **Dist:** MGM Home Entertainment. $29.95.

The Adventures of the Masked Phantom 1938 — ★½
The adventures of the Masked Phantom. 56m/B/W; VHS. **C:** Monte Rawlins; Betty Burgess; Larry Mason; Sonny Lamont; Jack Ingram; Directed by Charles Abbott. **Pr:** Monogram. **A:** Family. **P:** Entertainment. **U:** Home. **Mov-Ent:** Serials. **Acq:** Purchase. **Dist:** Rex Miller Artisan Studio. $19.95.

The Adventures of the Swiss Family Robinson 1998
Oft-told Johann Wyss novel gets yet another re-telling in this series, which consists of 10, 75-minute installments. David Robinson (Thomas) embarks on a sailing voyage with his wife and children and the family winds up shipwrecked on a deserted tropical island. 750m; DVD. **C:** Richard Thomas. **A:** Family. **P:** Entertainment. **U:** Home. **Chl-Juv:** Family. **Acq:** Purchase. **Dist:** Questar Inc.

The Adventures of the Wilderness Family 1976 (G) — ★★
The story of a modern-day pioneer family who becomes bored with the troubles of city life and heads for life in the wilderness. There, they find trouble in paradise. Family-oriented adventure offering pleasant scenery. Followed by "The Wilderness Family, Part 2." 100m; VHS, DVD. **C:** Robert F. Logan; Susan Damante-Shaw; Directed by Stewart Raffill; Written by Stewart Raffill. **Pr:** Arthur R. Dubs. **A:** Family. **P:** Entertainment. **U:** Home. **Mov-Ent:** Action-Adventure, Family, Wilderness Areas. **Acq:** Purchase. **Dist:** Anchor Bay Entertainment. $9.98.

The Adventures of Tintin 2011 (PG) — ★★½
Spielberg explores both motion-capture animation and the world of 3D with his adaptation of the hit Belgian comic book series by Herge. With mo-cap work by Bell, Serkis, and Craig, Spielberg works straight from one of the original stories, "The Secret of the Unicorn." In the tale, reporter Tintin (Bell) and his fox terrier Snowy team up with an alcoholic sea captain to get to the bottom of the mystery behind a secret scroll found in a model ship. Some of the 3D sequences—which could only be accomplished in the motion-capture form—are undeniably tasty eye candy, but the whole experience feels remarkably hollow. 107m; DVD, Blu-Ray. **C:** Voice(s) by Jamie Bell; Daniel Craig; Andy Serkis; Simon Pegg; Toby Jones; Sebastien Roche; Mackenzie Crook; Gad Elmaleh; Directed by Steven Spielberg; Written by Edgar Wright; Steven Moffatt; Joe Cornish; Music by John Williams. **Pr:** Steven Spielberg; Peter Jackson; Kathleen Kennedy; Steven Spielberg; Hemisphere Productions; Amblin Entertainment; Wignut Films; Columbia Pictures; Paramount Pictures. **A:** Primary-Adult. **P:** Entertainment. **U:** Home. **L:** English. **Mov-Ent:** Animation & Cartoons, Journalism. **Awds:** Golden Globes '12: Animated Film. **Acq:** Purchase. **Dist:** Paramount Pictures Corp.

The Adventures of Tintin: Cigars Of The Pharaoh 1991
Boy reporter, TinTin, travels to Egypt and India to crack a mysterious smuggling ring. Animated. 45m; DVD. **A:** Preschool. **P:** Entertainment. **U:** Home. **Chl-Juv:** Animation & Cartoons, Children, Mystery & Suspense. **Acq:** Purchase. **Dist:** Shout! Factory.

The Adventures of Tintin: The Secret Of The Unicorn 1991
TinTin searches for sunken pirate treasures. Animated. 45m; DVD. **A:** Preschool. **P:** Entertainment. **U:** Home. **Chl-Juv:** Animation & Cartoons, Children, Mystery & Suspense. **Acq:** Purchase. **Dist:** Shout! Factory.

The Adventures of Tom Sawyer 1938 (Unrated) — ★★★
The vintage Hollywood adaptation of the Mark Twain classic, with art direction by William Cameron Menzies. Not a major effort from the Selznick studio, but quite detailed and the best Tom so far. 91m; VHS, DVD; Open Captioned. **C:** Tommy Kelly; Walter Brennan; Victor Jory; May Robson; Victor Kilian; Jackie Moran; Donald Meek; Ann Gillis; Marcia Mae Jones; David Holt; Margaret Hamilton; Directed by Norman Taurog; Cinematography by James Wong Howe; Music by Max Steiner. **Pr:** David O. Selznick. **A:** Family. **P:** Entertainment. **U:** Home. **Mov-Ent:** Action-Adventure, Literature--American, Classic Films. **Acq:** Purchase. **Dist:** Amazon.com Inc.; Facets Multimedia Inc.; Home Vision Cinema. $14.98.

The Adventures of Tom Sawyer 1973 (Unrated) — ★★½
Tom Sawyer is a mischievous Missouri boy who gets into all kinds of trouble in this white-washed, made for TV adaptation of the Mark Twain classic. 76m; VHS. **C:** Jane Wyatt; Buddy Ebsen; Vic Morrow; John McGiver; Josh Albee; Jeff Tyler; Directed by James Neilson. **Pr:** Universal Television. **A:** Family. **P:** Entertainment. **U:** Home. **Mov-Ent:** Children, Drama, TV Movies. **Acq:** Purchase. **Dist:** $39.95.

The Adventures of Trogmoffy: Rescue on a Strange Planet 198?
Trogmoffy demonstrates a number of techniques to develop decoding skills through the use of phonics and sight vocabulary. 14m; VHS, 3/4 U. **A:** Primary. **P:** Education. **U:** Institution, SURA. **Gen-Edu:** Language Arts. **Acq:** Purchase. **Dist:** Phoenix Learning Group.

The Adventures of Trogmoffy: Timmy and Margaret Meet the Orange Creature 198?
Trogmoffy demonstrates a number of techniques to develop decoding skills through the use of phonics and sight vocabulary. 14m; VHS, 3/4 U. **A:** Primary. **P:** Education. **U:** Institution, SURA. **Gen-Edu:** Language Arts. **Acq:** Purchase. **Dist:** Phoenix Learning Group.

Adventures of Ulysses 19??
Follows the adventures of Ulysses as he invents the Trojan Horse, struggles to return home, and defeats his wife's suitors. 56m; VHS. **A:** Sr. High-Adult. **P:** Education. **U:** Institution. **Gen-Edu:** Literature, Folklore & Legends. **Acq:** Purchase. **Dist:** Educational Video Network. $89.95.

The Adventures of Walt Disney's Alice 1925
Three early Disney shorts featuring Lewis Carroll's cast of characters: "Alice's Egg Plant," "Alice's Orphan," and "Alice the Toreador." Silent. 35m/B/W; Silent; VHS. **Pr:** Walt Disney Studios. **A:** Family. **P:** Entertainment. **U:** Home. **Mov-Ent:** Animation & Cartoons, Silent Films. **Acq:** Purchase. **Dist:** JEF Films, Inc. $29.95.

The Adventures of Wayan and the Three R's 1996
Centers on Reduce, Reuse and Recycle Garbage, the three R's. Reveals how one little boy leads an effort to clean up his village. 15m; VHS. **A:** Primary. **P:** Education. **U:** Home, Institution. **Gen-Edu:** Ecology & Environment, Children. **Acq:** Purchase, Rent/Lease. **Dist:** The Video Project. $59.95.

The Adventures of Werner Holt 1965 — ★★
Two teenagers, Werner Holt and Gilbert Wolzow, are taken out of school and conscripted into Hitler's army. Gilbert is a fanatical soldier, while the horrors of the front call Werner's loyalties into question. But when Gilbert is executed by the SS, Werner turns his gun on his own side. Based on the novel by Dieter Noll. German with subtitles. 163m/B/W; VHS, DVD. **C:** Klaus-Peter Thiele; Manfred Karge; Arno Wyzniewski; Gunter Junghans; Peter Reusse; Wolfgang Langhoff; Directed by Joachim Kunert. **Pr:** Deutsche Film-Aktiengesellschaft. **A:** College-Adult. **P:** Entertainment. **U:** Home. **L:** German. **Mov-Ent:** World War Two, Adolescence. **Acq:** Purchase. **Dist:** First Run Features.

Adventures: Past, Present & Future Featurettes 1985
This is a rousing collection of trailers from such films as "Doc Savage," "Alien," "Futureworld" and "Airport 77." 58m; VHS. **C:** Sigourney Weaver; Ron Ely; Harry Dean Stanton; Veronica Cartwright; Yaphet Kotto; Tom Skerritt; James Stewart; Jack Lemmon. **Pr:** 20th Century-Fox. **A:** Family. **P:** Entertainment. **U:** Home. **Mov-Ent.** **Acq:** Purchase. **Dist:** Passport International Entertainment L.L.C. $29.95.

Adventuresome Max: Discovering the World 1990
Eight wordless, animated programs teach children about the world around them using sound effects and original music. Includes 24 Skill Sheets and teacher's guide with activity projects. 20m; VHS, 3/4 U. **Pr:** SVE. **A:** Primary. **P:** Education. **U:** Institution, BCTV, SURA. **Chl-Juv:** Animation & Cartoons, Children, Education. **Acq:** Purchase, Duplication License. **Dist:** Clear Vue Inc. $79.00.

The Adventurous Blonde 1937 (Unrated) — ★½
The third entry in the series has Torchy and Steve's wedding interrupted by a prank that turns deadly. Torchy's fellow newshounds hire stage actor Harvey Hammond to pretend to be a murder victim—only he does wind up dead. Hammond had a long-suffering wife, a mistress, and some disgruntled fellow thespians, so the list of suspects is varied. 60m/B/W; DVD. **C:** Glenda Farrell; Barton MacLane; Anne Nagel; Anderson Lawler; Tom Kennedy; Virginia Brissac; Leyland Hodgson; Raymond Hatton; Natalie Moorhead; Directed by Frank McDonald; Written by Robertson White; David Diamond; Cinematography by Arthur L. Todd. **A:** Jr. High-Adult. **P:** Entertainment. **U:** Home. **Mov-Ent:** Journalism. **Acq:** Purchase. **Dist:** WarnerArchive.com.

The Adventurous Knights 1935 — **Bomb!**
An athlete learns he is the heir to a Transylvanian throne. 60m/B/W; VHS. **C:** David Sharpe; Mary Kornman; Mickey Daniels; Gertrude Messinger; Directed by Edward Roberts. **Pr:** Ajax. **A:** Family. **P:** Entertainment. **U:** Home. **Mov-Ent.** **Acq:** Purchase. **Dist:** No Longer Available.

The Adversary 1971 (Unrated) — ★★½
A young man must quit college because of his father's death. He struggles to find employment in Calcutta but his hardships are magnified by the impersonal society. In Bengali with English subtitles. 110m; VHS. **C:** Dhritiman Chatterjee; Jayshree Roy; Debraj Roy; Krishna Bose; Directed by Satyajit Ray; Written by Satyajit Ray; Cinematography by Soumendu Roy; Purnendu Bose; Music by Satyajit Ray. **A:** College-Adult. **P:** Entertainment. **U:** Home. **Mov-Ent:** India. **Acq:** Purchase. **Dist:** Facets Multimedia Inc. $39.95.

Advertising Alcohol: Calling the Shots 1991
Examines the images used by advertisers to sell alcohol; based on lectures, slide presentations, and research by Jean Kilbourne. Second edition to "Calling the Shots." 30m; VHS. **A:** College-Adult. **P:** Education. **U:** Institution. **Gen-Edu:** Documentary Films, Advertising, Alcoholic Beverages. **Acq:** Purchase, Rent/Lease. **Dist:** Cambridge Documentary Films, Inc. $350.00.

Advertising and the End of the World 19??
Asks questions about the cultural messages ads project and evaluates the physical and material costs to the consumer society. 50m; VHS. **A:** Adult. **P:** Education. **U:** Institution. **Gen-Edu:** Advertising. **Acq:** Purchase. **Dist:** Media Education Foundation. $195.00.

Advertising and the Public Interest 197?
An expert panel argues whether advertising serves the public interest and whether consumers need more protection in the form of government regulation. 60m; 3/4 U. **Pr:** American Enterprise Institute. **A:** College-Adult. **P:** Education. **U:** Institution, BCTV. **Gen-Edu:** Public Affairs, Advertising. **Acq:** Purchase, Rent/Lease. **Dist:** American Enterprise Institute for Public Policy Research.

Advertising Missionaries 1996
A theatre company brings the consumer revolution to the people in Papua New Guinea, a population unreachable by the advertising mediums of TV, radio, or print. Also discusses the impact of the touted products of these remote villages. 52m; VHS. **A:** Adult. **P:** Education. **U:** BCTV, Institution. **Gen-Edu:** Pacific Islands, Advertising. **Acq:** Purchase, Rent/Lease. **Dist:** First Run/Icarus Films. $390.00.

Advertising Rules! 2001 (R) — ★★
Graphic artist Viktor Vogel actually lands a job after sneaking into an ad agency board meeting. And his luck continues when he meets sexy artist Rosa and helps her with an idea for her debut art exhibition. Then Viktor inadvertantly pitches the same idea for the ad campaign and has to find a way to satisfy both work and Rosa. German with subtitles. 109m; VHS, DVD, Wide. **C:** Alexander Scheer; Goetz George; Chulpan Khamatova; Maria Schrader; Vadim Glowna; Gudrun Landgrebe; Directed by Lars Kraume; Written by Lars Kraume; Tom Schlessinger; Cinematography by Andreas Daub; Music by Robert Jan Meyer. **A:** Sr. High-Adult. **P:** Entertainment. **U:** Home. **L:** German. **Mov-Ent:** Advertising, Comedy--Romantic, Art & Artists. **Acq:** Purchase. **Dist:** Sony Pictures Home Entertainment Inc.

Advertising: The Fastest Game in Town 1984
Presents advertising firm Chiat-Day, Inc. to explain the objectives of advertising and how copy strategy and media selection affect those objectives. 30m; VHS. **A:** Adult. **P:** Professional. **U:** Institution. **Bus-Ind:** Business, Marketing. **Acq:** Purchase. **Dist:** RMI Media. $89.95.

Advertising: The Hidden Language 19??
Features Dr. Phillip Bell as he demostrates how successful ads grab the consumer and make them want to purchase the product. 50m; VHS. **A:** Adult. **P:** Professional. **U:** Institution. **Gen-Edu:** Advertising. **Acq:** Purchase. **Dist:** TMW Media Group.

Advertising the Small Business 1981
These two tapes, provide a step-by-step instructional course on how to best publicize a small business, from research/planning to managing/implementation. 60m; VHS, 3/4 U. **C:** Narrated by Pat Smythe. **Pr:** NETCHE. **A:** Adult. **P:** Education. **U:** Institution, CCTV, BCTV, SURA. **Bus-Ind**: Business, Advertising. **Acq:** Purchase, Rent/Lease, Off-Air Record. **Dist:** NETCHE; GPN Educational Media. $100.00.
Indiv. Titles: 1. Research and Planning 2. Managing and Implementing.

Advertising Tricks Without the Gimmicks 19??
Offers an overview and practical hints on the basics of advertising. 15m; VHS. **A:** Sr. High-Adult. **P:** Education. **U:** Home. **Bus-Ind**: Advertising. **Acq:** Purchase. **Dist:** Instructional Video. $79.00.

Advice from a Survivor: Gerda Klein at Columbine High School 2000
A Holocaust survivor talks with students from Columbine High School about coping with trauma and loss, "survivor guilt," and questions of "Why did this happen to me?" and "What should I do with my life?" 21m; VHS. **A:** Sr. High. **P:** Education. **U:** Institution. **Gen-Edu**: History--U.S., Stress. **Acq:** Purchase. **Dist:** Zenger Media. $29.95.

Advice on Lice 1987
Rapunzel learns from the school nurse about symptoms, transmission, treatment and prevention of head lice. 13m; VHS, 3/4 U, EJ, Special order formats. **TV Std:** NTSC, PAL, SECAM. **Pr:** Disney Educational Productions. **A:** Primary-Jr. High. **P:** Education. **U:** Institution, CCTV, SURA. **Hea-Sci**: Health Education. **Acq:** Purchase, Rent/Lease. **Dist:** Phoenix Learning Group. $265.00.

Advice Without Consent 1975
Through the example of a motorist with car trouble, emphasizes the fact that when we need help with a problem in interpersonal relations, we ought to go to people who specialize in such help. 5m; VHS, 3/4 U, Special order formats. **Pr:** Hungarofilm. **A:** College-Adult. **P:** Education. **U:** Institution, Home, SURA. **Bus-Ind**: Human Relations, Meeting Openers. **Acq:** Purchase, Duplication License. **Dist:** Clear Vue Inc.

Advise and Consent 1962 — ★★★
An interesting political melodrama with a fascinating cast, based upon Allen Drury's novel. The President chooses a candidate for the Secretary of State position which divides the Senate and causes the suicide of a senator. Controversial in its time, though somewhat turgid today. Laughton's last film. 139m/B/W; VHS, DVD. **C:** Don Murray; Charles Laughton; Henry Fonda; Walter Pidgeon; Lew Ayres; Burgess Meredith; Gene Tierney; Franchot Tone; Paul Ford; George Grizzard; Betty White; Peter Lawford; Edward Andrews; Directed by Otto Preminger; Written by Wendell Mayes; Cinematography by Sam Leavitt. **Pr:** Columbia Pictures; Alpha-Alpina. **A:** Jr. High-Adult. **P:** Entertainment. **U:** Home. **Mov-Ent**: Presidency. **Awds:** Natl. Bd. of Review '62: Support. Actor (Meredith). **Acq:** Purchase. **Dist:** Warner Home Video, Inc.; Karol Media; Anchor Bay Entertainment. $19.98.

Advising Business Clients on Trade Secrets 1992
Discusses topics on identifying and protecting business trade secrets, including interplay of patent copyright protections, requisite level of secrecy and business advantage, ways to prevent litigations, and much more. Complete with study guide. 50m; VHS. **A:** Adult. **P:** Professional. **U:** Institution. **Bus-Ind**: Law. **Dist:** American Law Institute - Committee on Continuing Professional Education. $95.

Advising Clients About the U.S.-Canada Free Trade Bill 1988
Discusses legal issues revolving around the U.S.-Canada Free Trade Agreement of 1989. Topics include elimination and reduction of trade barriers and tariffs, treatment of subsidies, increased opportunities for bilateral trade and services, and more. Includes study guide. 45m; VHS. **A:** Adult. **P:** Professional. **U:** Institution. **Bus-Ind**: Law, Business. **Dist:** American Law Institute - Committee on Continuing Professional Education. $95.

Advising Clients with Expanding Businesses: New Problems, New Challenges 1992
Offers advice to expanding businesses looking to do more than subsist. Covers issues on S corportaions, taxes, the effect of the Revenue Reconciliation Act of 1993, family and estate planning, acquisitions, investors, and more. Includes study guide. 95m; VHS. **A:** Adult. **P:** Professional. **U:** Institution. **Bus-Ind**: Law. **Dist:** American Law Institute - Committee on Continuing Professional Education. $95.

Advising Corporate Clients on the New Federal Sentencing Guidelines 1991
Summarizes the first set of guidelines for sentencing corporations, partnerships, associations, labor unions, non-profit groups, and others convicted of federal crimes. Includes study guide. 50m; VHS. **A:** Adult. **P:** Professional. **U:** Institution. **Bus-Ind**: Law. **Dist:** American Law Institute - Committee on Continuing Professional Education. $95.

Advocacy and the Art of Storytelling 1990
Instructs budding lawyers in the importance of telling a good story. Discussion led by John D. Mooy. Comes with course booklet. 47m; VHS. **A:** College-Adult. **P:** Education. **U:** Institution. **Gen-Edu**: Law. **Acq:** Purchase. **Dist:** National Institute for Trial Advocacy. $79.95.

Advocacy Lectures 1987
A series of lectures for law students outlining trial technique. 45m; VHS, 3/4 U. **Pr:** National Institute for Trial Advocacy. **A:** Adult. **P:** Professional. **U:** Institution. **Gen-Edu**: Law. **Acq:** Purchase, Rent/Lease. **Dist:** National Institute for Trial Advocacy.
Indiv. Titles: 1. Discovery Deposition 2. Principles of Direct Examination 3. Principles of Cross Examination 4. Liturgy of Foundation 5. Trial Notebook 6. Experts I 7. Experts II 8. Jury Selection 9. Closing Arguments 10. Demonstrative Evidence.

The Advocate 1993 (R) — ★★★
Bizarre black comedy about 15th-century Paris lawyer Richard Courtois (Firth) who decides to ply his trade in the country, only to find things stranger than he can imagine. His first case turns out to be defending a pig that's accused of murdering a child. And the pig is owned by beautiful gypsy Samira (Annabi), so the idealistic lawyer can fall in love (or lust). There's religion and superstition, there's power struggles, there's ignorance versus knowledge—things sound very modern indeed. 102m; VHS, DVD, CC. **C:** Colin Firth; Amina Annabi; Nicol Williamson; Ian Holm; Lysette Anthony; Donald Pleasence; Michael Gough; Harriet Walter; Jim Carter; Dave Atkins; Directed by Leslie Megahey; Written by Leslie Megahey. **Pr:** David H. Thompson; BBC Films; CIBY 2000; Miramax. **A:** College-Adult. **P:** Entertainment. **U:** Home. **Mov-Ent**: Comedy--Black, Sex & Sexuality, Law. **Acq:** Purchase. **Dist:** Miramax Film Corp.; Buena Vista Home Entertainment.

Adynata 1983
Allegorical investigation of the fantasies spawned in the West about the East, particularly that which associates femininity with the mysterious Orient. 30m; VHS. **A:** College-Adult. **P:** Education. **U:** Institution. **Gen-Edu**: Women, Filmmaking, Asia. **Acq:** Purchase, Rent/Lease. **Dist:** Women Make Movies. $295.00.

AE: Apocalypse Earth 2013 (Unrated) — ★
The film follows a small group of survivors shipwrecked on a foreign world full of monsters after aliens invade Earth. 87m; DVD, Blu-Ray. **C:** Adrian Paul; Richard Grieco; Bali Rodriguez; Gray Hawks; Directed by Thunder Levin; Written by Thunder Levin; Cinematography by Richard J. Vialet; Music by Chris Ridenhour. **A:** Sr. High-Adult. **P:** Entertainment. **U:** Home. **L:** English. **Mov-Ent. Acq:** Purchase. **Dist:** The Asylum. $14.95 14.95.

A.E. Wood Fish Hatchery 19??
Tours the A.E. Wood Fish Hatchery, explaining the various processes involved in the day-to-day operations of the hatchery. Includes discussion on egg hatching, raceway fry management, spawning, reservoir collection, fish tagging, and sexing, collecting, and spawning of Koi. 34m; VHS. **A:** Jr. High-Adult. **P:** Education. **U:** Institution. **Bus-Ind**: Fish, Food Industry, Agriculture. **Acq:** Purchase. **Dist:** CEV Multimedia. $79.95.

Aelita: Queen of Mars 1924 — ★★
Though the title has blockbuster potential, "Aelita" is a little-known silent Soviet sci-fi flick destined to remain little known. After building a rocket to fly to Mars, a Russian engineer finds it's no Martian holiday on the fourth planet from the sun, with the Martians in the midst of a revolution. Silent, with a piano score. 113m/B/W; Silent; VHS, DVD. **C:** Yulia Solntseva; Nikolai Batalov; Nikolai Tseretelli; Vera Orlova; Pavel Poi; Konstantin Eggert; Yuri Zavadski; Valentina Kuindzi; N. Tretyakova; Directed by Yakov Protazanov; Written by Fedor Ozep; Aleksey Fajko; Cinematography by Yuri Zhelyabuzhsky; Emil Schunemann. **A:** Jr. High-Adult. **P:** Entertainment. **U:** Home. **Mov-Ent**: Science Fiction, Silent Films. **Acq:** Purchase. **Dist:** Kino on Video; Facets Multimedia Inc.; Sinister Cinema. $29.95.

The Aeneid 19??
Adapted from Homer's story of the same name that follows the journeys of the Trojan prince Aeneas and the founding of Rome. 34m; VHS. **A:** Sr. High-Adult. **P:** Education. **U:** Institution. **Gen-Edu**: Folklore & Legends, Literature. **Acq:** Purchase. **Dist:** Educational Video Network. $89.95.

Aeneid: Lessons 7, 8, and 9 1994
Discusses Virgil's purpose in writing the epic and the ambivalence of his epic as he celebrates the greatness of Rome. 174m; VHS. **A:** Adult. **P:** Education. **U:** Institution. **Gen-Edu**: Literature. **Acq:** Purchase. **Dist:** RMI Media. $169.95.

Aeon Flux 2005 (PG-13) — ★★½
It's hard to fault a movie ostensibly about Charlize Theron in spandex shooting people. Based on the MTV cartoon, Kusama's sci fi/actioner is a goofy guilty pleasure that succeeds largely due to Theron's on-screen charisma. Set 400 years in the future, a plague wipes out most of humanity and survivors live in Bregna, a walled city ruled by Trevor Goodchild's (Csokas) fascist government. A resistance movement sends their top assassin, Aeon Flux (Theron), to dispatch Goodchild but Aeon realizes some disturbing truths might lie behind her brave new world. Things get cheesy, but Kusama has fun with her wonky futuristic designs. 95m; DVD, Blu-Ray, HD-DVD. **C:** Charlize Theron; Marton Csokas; Jonny Lee Miller; Sophie Okonedo; Frances McDormand; Pete Postlethwaite; Amelia Warner; Nikolai Kinski; Caroline Chikezie; Directed by Karyn Kusama; Written by Phil Hay; Matt Manfredi; Cinematography by Stuart Dryburgh; Music by Graeme Revell. **Pr:** Martha Griffin; Gale Anne Hurd; David Gale; Gary Lucchesi; Gregory Goodman; Lakeshore Entertainment; Valhalla Motion Pictures; MTV Films; Paramount. **A:** Jr. High-Adult. **P:** Entertainment. **U:** Home. **L:** English. **Mov-Ent**: Science Fiction, Television Series, Martial Arts. **Dist:** Paramount Pictures Corp.

Aeon Flux: The Complete Animated Collection 2005 (Unrated)
Presents the 1995 MTV animated science fiction series about the futuristic adventures of Aeon Flux, a provocative secret agent battling villains in a society mired in mayhem. 10 episodes. 221m; DVD. **C:** Voice(s) by John Rafter Lee; Denise Poirier. **A:** Sr. High-Adult. **P:** Entertainment. **U:** Home. **Mov-Ent**: Television Series, Animation & Cartoons, Action-Adventure. **Acq:** Purchase. **Dist:** Paramount Pictures Corp. $39.98.

Aerial Lift Safety 1995
Looks at manlift safety in many industries such as refining, chemical, manufacturing, and municipalities. Complies with the latest OSHA regulation (1910.67). 13m; VHS. **A:** Adult. **P:** Professional. **U:** Institution. **Bus-Ind**: Job Training, Safety Education. **Acq:** Rent/Lease. **Dist:** National Safety Council, California Chapter, Film Library.

Aerial Lifts, Cranes and Swing Stages: Safety on the Job 1995
Features how to safely operate cranes, slings and rigging equipment. Includes wearing safety gear and the safest ways to enter and exit aerial equipment. 15m; VHS. **A:** Adult. **P:** Professional. **U:** Institution. **Bus-Ind**: Job Training, Safety Education. **Acq:** Purchase, Rent/Lease. **Dist:** National Safety Council, California Chapter, Film Library. $195.00.

Aerial Photo Interpretation of Forestry 1990
A look at how an area's forest resources can be surveyed and evaluated by using aerial photography. 39m; VHS. **Pr:** Crystal Productions. **A:** Jr. High-Sr. High. **P:** Education. **U:** Institution. **Hea-Sci**: Forests & Trees, Technology, Photography. **Acq:** Purchase. **Dist:** Crystal Productions. $39.95.

Aerial Photo Interpretation of Geologic Resources 1990
The discovery and evaluation of natural resources through the interpretation of aerial photographs is explained. 34m; VHS. **Pr:** Crystal Productions. **A:** Jr. High-Sr. High. **P:** Education. **U:** Institution. **Hea-Sci**: Geology, Technology, Photography. **Acq:** Purchase. **Dist:** Crystal Productions. $39.95.

Aerobic Curriculum Videos 1988
Different aerobic workouts that are suited to different people are included in this package. 60m; VHS, 3/4 U. **Pr:** Champions on Film. **A:** Sr. High-Adult. **P:** Instruction. **U:** Institution, CCTV, Home. **Hea-Sci**: Fitness/Exercise. **Acq:** Purchase. **Dist:** School-Tech Inc. $59.95.
Indiv. Titles: 1. Low-Impact Aerobics 2. Fitkids Aerobics 3. Free-Style Aerobics 4. Jazz-Dancercise.

Aerobic Dance 1984
A combination of easy-to-learn dance steps with aerobic exercise techniques. 60m; VHS, 3/4 U. **Pr:** Champions on Film. **A:** Family. **P:** Instruction. **U:** Institution, CCTV, Home. **Hea-Sci**: Fitness/Exercise, Dance. **Acq:** Purchase, Rent/Lease. **Dist:** School-Tech Inc.

Aerobic Dancing 1984
This videocassette shows you the physical aspects of aerobic dancing along with how to lessen your chances of hurting yourself while exercising. 30m; VHS. **Pr:** Star Merchants. **A:** Sr. High-Adult. **P:** Instruction. **U:** Institution, Home. **Hea-Sci**: Fitness/Exercise, Dance. **Acq:** Purchase. **Dist:** Silver Mine Video Inc. $29.95.

Aerobic Dancing, Medicine, Health, Exercise 1989
This program shows people how to dance or exercise with a lesser chance of injury. 30m; VHS. **Pr:** Increase. **A:** Jr. High-Adult. **P:** Instruction. **U:** Institution, Home. **Hea-Sci**: Safety Education, Fitness/Exercise. **Acq:** Purchase. **Dist:** Silver Mine Video Inc. $29.95.

Aerobic Exercising 1981
This is an introduction and explanation of what aerobic exercising is and how it affects the body. 14m; VHS, 3/4 U. **Pr:** National Safety Council. **A:** Sr. High-Adult. **P:** Instruction. **U:** Institution. **Hea-Sci**: Fitness/Exercise. **Acq:** Rent/Lease. **Dist:** National Safety Council, California Chapter, Film Library.

Aerobic Power Test 1982
A normal 20-year-old male athlete completes a maximum oxygen consumption test on a treadmill. 19m; 3/4 U. **Pr:** IMS. **A:** College-Adult. **P:** Professional. **U:** Institution. **Hea-Sci**: Fitness/Exercise. **Acq:** Purchase, Rent/Lease. **Dist:** Instructional Media Services.

Aerobic Sitting: Aerobic Exercise Designed to Be Effective without Ever Leaving Your Chair 1991
Program shows the many ways available to stretch with a minimal amount of lower body movement. Comes with guide. 38m; VHS. **A:** Adult. **P:** Instruction. **U:** Home. **Hea-Sci**: Fitness/Exercise. **Acq:** Purchase. **Dist:** United Learning Inc. $39.00.

Aerobicise: The Beautiful Workout 1981
Aerobic dancing to original music, produced by Ron Harris, fashion photographer. An erotic exercise program. 113m; VHS. **Pr:** Ron Harris. **A:** Sr. High-Adult. **P:** Instruction. **U:** Home. **Hea-Sci**: Fitness/Exercise. **Acq:** Purchase. **Dist:** Paramount Pictures Corp.

Aerobicise: The Beginning Workout 1982
This is a basic, simple exercise regimen for the uninitiated aerobiciser. 96m; VHS. **Pr:** Ron Harris. **A:** Sr. High-Adult. **P:** Instruction. **U:** Home. **Hea-Sci**: Fitness/Exercise. **Acq:** Purchase. **Dist:** Paramount Pictures Corp.

Aerobicise: The Ultimate Workout 1982
The last installment of Paramount's Aerobicise trilogy is the most advanced, designed for those in excellent shape. In stereo. 105m; VHS. **Pr:** Ron Harris. **A:** Family. **P:** Entertainment. **U:** Home. **Hea-Sci**: Fitness/Exercise. **Acq:** Purchase. **Dist:** Paramount Pictures Corp.

Aerobics 1992
Develop a personal fitness program that will leave you feeling fit and trim. Teaches the importance of stretching prior to exercise.

The instructor, Dr. Kenneth Cooper, is the director of the Aerobics Center in Dallas, Texas. 25m; VHS. **A:** Jr. High-Sr. High. **P:** Instruction. **U:** Institution, Home. **Hea-Sci:** Fitness/Exercise. **Acq:** Purchase. **Dist:** Cambridge Educational. $19.95.

Aerobics for All Ages 1991
Dr. Kenneth Cooper demonstrates the proper running form to avoid injuries and offers suggestions on developing a practical exercise program. 25m; VHS. **Pr:** Champions on Film. **A:** Family. **P:** Instruction. **U:** Home. **Hea-Sci:** Fitness/Exercise. **Acq:** Purchase. **Dist:** School-Tech Inc. $12.95.

Aerobics: Medicine, Health & Exercise 1984
A comparison of aerobic and anaerobic exercise and the connection between diet and exercise. 30m; VHS, 8 mm. **Pr:** Star Merchants. **A:** Sr. High-Adult. **P:** Instruction. **U:** Home. **Hea-Sci:** Fitness/Exercise. **Acq:** Purchase. **Dist:** Silver Mine Video Inc. $29.95.

Aerobics with Soul—Kilimanjaro 1996
Teaches a workout featuring tribal dances and African music. Features traditional dance steps done at an aerobic pace. 75m; VHS. **A:** Adult. **P:** Instruction. **U:** Home. **Hea-Sci:** Dance, Fitness/Exercise, How-To. **Acq:** Purchase. **Dist:** Collage Video Specialties, Inc. $24.95.

Aerodynamic Generation of Sound 1969
Describes the mechanism of sound generation by turbulence resulting from an instability of steady flow. Part of EBE's "Fluid Mechanics Program." 44m/B/W; VHS, 3/4 U. **Pr:** NCFMF. **A:** College-Adult. **P:** Education. **U:** Institution, SURA. **Hea-Sci:** Physics. **Acq:** Purchase, Rent/Lease, Trade-in. **Dist:** Encyclopedia Britannica.

Aerojump 19??
Former boxer Michael Olajide Jr. takes the viewer step-by-step through an athletic jump rope workout for beginner, intermediate, and advanced exercisers. ?m; VHS. **A:** Sr. High-Adult. **P:** Instruction. **U:** Home. **Spo-Rec:** Fitness/Exercise. **Acq:** Purchase. **Dist:** Tapeworm Video Distributors Inc. $19.95.

Aeronautics and Space Report 185: Sun Up Close 1980
Describes the Solar Maximum Satellite and its ability to relay pictures and data on the Sun. 30m; 3/4 U. **Pr:** National Aeronautics and Space Administration. **A:** Jr. High-Adult. **P:** Education. **U:** BCTV, SURA. **Hea-Sci:** Science. **Acq:** Free Loan. **Dist:** NASA Lyndon B. Johnson Space Center. $59.95.

Aeronautics and Space Report 186: Space Shuttle Practice Landing/Makani Wind Generator 1980
This two part program describes ground based practice landings in NASA's shuttle simulator and the 200,000 watt wind turbine generator on Oahu, Hawaii. 30m; 3/4 U. **Pr:** National Aeronautics and Space Administration. **A:** Jr. High-Adult. **P:** Education. **U:** BCTV, SURA. **Hea-Sci:** Space Exploration. **Acq:** Free Loan. **Dist:** NASA Lyndon B. Johnson Space Center.

Aeronautics and Space Report 188/189: Saturn Press Conference/Manned Maneuvering Unit 1980
The first program contains the press briefing given before Voyager's flyby of Saturn. The second program examines the Manned Maneuvering Unit which allows astronauts to move without a tether in space. 30m; 3/4 U. **Pr:** National Aeronautics and Space Administration. **A:** Jr. High-Adult. **P:** Education. **U:** BCTV, SURA. **Hea-Sci:** Space Exploration, Technology. **Acq:** Free Loan. **Dist:** NASA Lyndon B. Johnson Space Center. **Indiv. Titles:** 1. Voyager/Saturn Encounter 2. Astronaut Backpack.

Aeronautics and Space Report 190: Aeronautics and Space Highlights 1981
A tape of video highlights of stories from the 1980 Aeronautics and Space Reports. 14m; 3/4 U. **Pr:** National Aeronautics and Space Administration. **A:** Jr. High-Adult. **P:** Education. **U:** BCTV, SURA. **Hea-Sci:** Aeronautics, Space Exploration. **Acq:** Free Loan. **Dist:** NASA Lyndon B. Johnson Space Center.

Aeronautics and Space Report 193: Space Shuttle/The First Flight 1981
The preparation of the Space Shuttle Columbia's maiden flight into space is described. 30m; 3/4 U. **Pr:** National Aeronautics and Space Administration. **A:** Jr. High-Adult. **P:** Education. **U:** BCTV, SURA. **Hea-Sci:** Space Exploration. **Acq:** Free Loan. **Dist:** NASA Lyndon B. Johnson Space Center.

Aeronautics and Space Report 197: Voyager 2/Saturn 1981
Examines the Voyager 2 flyby of Saturn and its mission of following-up on the discoveries made by Voyager 1. 30m; 3/4 U. **Pr:** National Aeronautics and Space Administration. **A:** Jr. High-Adult. **P:** Education. **U:** BCTV, SURA. **Hea-Sci:** Space Exploration. **Acq:** Free Loan. **Dist:** NASA Lyndon B. Johnson Space Center.

Aeronautics and Space Report 201: XV-15 Tiltroter 1981
An examination of the XV-15 Tiltroter, an experimental vertical-takeoff-landing aircraft. 30m; 3/4 U. **Pr:** National Aeronautics and Space Administration. **A:** Jr. High-Adult. **P:** Education. **U:** BCTV, SURA. **Hea-Sci:** Aeronautics. **Acq:** Free Loan. **Dist:** NASA Lyndon B. Johnson Space Center.

Aeronautics and Space Report: Suiting Up for Shuttle 1980
Describes the space suit worn by the Space Shuttle astronauts. 30m; 3/4 U. **Pr:** National Aeronautics and Space Administration. **A:** Jr. High-Adult. **P:** Education. **U:** BCTV, SURA.

Hea-Sci: Clothing & Dress, Space Exploration, Aeronautics. **Acq:** Free Loan. **Dist:** NASA Lyndon B. Johnson Space Center.

Aeroplane Dance 1994
Relates the story of the U.S. bomber Little Eva and her crew, who crashed in northern Australia in December, 1942. The events were recorded in the journal of a survivor and in a "corroboree," or story-telling dance, by the aboriginal people who helped search for the bomber and her crew. 58m; VHS. **A:** Sr. High-Adult. **P:** Education. **U:** Home, Institution. **Gen-Edu:** Documentary Films, Sociology, Australia. **Acq:** Purchase, Rent/Lease. **Dist:** First Run/Icarus Films. $390.00.

Aerosmith: Big Ones You Can Look At 1994
Twelve video clips, plus performance coverage, primarily from the albums "Get a Grip," "Pump," and "Permanent Vacation." 100m; VHS. **A:** Jr. High-Adult. **P:** Entertainment. **U:** Home. **Mov-Ent:** Music Video, Music--Pop/Rock. **Acq:** Purchase. **Dist:** Universal Music and Video Distribution; Music Video Distributors. $19.95.
Songs: Cryin'; Love in an Elevator; Janie's Got a Gun; Rag Doll; Angel; Dude (Looks Like a Lady); Blind Man; Walk on Water; Deuces are Wild.

Aerosmith Live: Texas Jam '78 1978
The hard rocking band was the main attraction at the Texas World Music Festival in Dallas in 1978. Some of the songs they performed were "Walk This Way," "Sweet Emotion," and "Same Old Song and Dance." 60m; VHS. **Pr:** CBS. **A:** Jr. High-Adult. **P:** Entertainment. **U:** Home. **Mov-Ent:** Music--Pop/Rock. **Acq:** Purchase. **Dist:** Music Video Distributors; Sony Music Entertainment Inc. $14.95.

Aerosmith: Rock for the Rising Sun 2013 (Unrated)
A concert film featuring Aerosmith dates in Japan in 2011. 94m; DVD, Blu-Ray. **A:** Sr. High-Adult. **P:** Entertainment. **U:** Home. **Mov-Ent:** Music--Performance, Documentary Films, Japan. **Acq:** Purchase. **Dist:** Eagle Rock Entertainment Inc. $14.98 19.98.

Aerosmith: The Making of "Pump" 1990
Heavy metal demigods, Aerosmith, take you behind the scenes during the making of their most popular album to date, "Pump." 60m; VHS, DVD. **A:** Sr. High-Adult. **P:** Entertainment. **U:** Home. **Mov-Ent:** Documentary Films, Music--Performance, Music--Pop/Rock. **Acq:** Purchase. **Dist:** Music Video Distributors; Sony Music Entertainment Inc.; Image Entertainment Inc. $29.95.

Aerosmith: Things That Go Pump in the Night 1990
A history of the band Aerosmith, plus a variety of concert and recording sessions including "What It Takes," "F.I.N.E." "Janie's Got A Gun," "Love in an Elevator," and "Young Lust," plus behind the scenes footage. 45m; VHS. **Pr:** Warner Reprise Video. **A:** Sr. High-Adult. **P:** Entertainment. **U:** Home. **Mov-Ent:** Music Video, Interviews. **Acq:** Purchase. **Dist:** Music Video Distributors. $16.98.

Aerosmith: 3 x 5 1988
This presentation offers three conceptual videos based on songs from the hard rock group's 1987 comeback album entitled "Permanent Vacation," and provides behind-the-scenes glimpses of the band, plus interviews. The tunes featured on the video are "Dude Looks Like a Lady," "Rag Doll," and "Angel." 26m; VHS. **A:** Jr. High-Adult. **P:** Entertainment. **U:** Home. **Mov-Ent:** Music Video, Music--Pop/Rock, Interviews. **Acq:** Purchase. **Dist:** Music Video Distributors. $14.95.

Aerosmith: Video Scrapbook 1987
A collection of videos and performance clips from the classic heavy metal group, emphasizing its 1980s resurgence. Clips include "Dream On," "Toys in the Attic," "Walk This Way," "Sweet Emotion," "Lightning Strikes," "Chip Away the Stone," and more. 60m; VHS. **Pr:** CBS/Fox. **A:** Jr. High-Adult. **P:** Entertainment. **U:** Home. **Mov-Ent:** Music--Performance, Music Video, Music--Pop/Rock. **Acq:** Purchase. **Dist:** Music Video Distributors. $14.95.

Aesop's Fables ????
Animated fables: The Grasshopper and the Ants, The Tortoise and the Hare, The Boy Who Cried Wolf, and The Horse's Mistake. ?m; VHS. **A:** Primary. **P:** Education. **U:** Institution. **Chl-Juv:** Fairy Tales, Literature--Children. **Acq:** Purchase. **Dist:** Educational Activities Inc. $79.95.

Aesop's Fables 1985 — ★★
The young shepherd Aesop discovers what happens when you yell "wolf" once too often and picks up some pointers from an industrious ant along the way. 60m; VHS. **Pr:** Turner Program Services, Inc. **A:** Family. **P:** Entertainment. **U:** Home. **Mov-Ent:** Animation & Cartoons, Fairy Tales. **Acq:** Purchase. **Dist:** Sony Pictures Home Entertainment Inc. $9.95.

Aesop's Fables 1988
These stories with morals are perfect for teaching kids what's right and wrong. 30m; VHS, 3/4 U. **C:** Bill Cosby; Voice(s) by Larry Storch; John Byner; Roger C. Carmel. **Pr:** SVE. **A:** Preschool-Primary. **P:** Education. **U:** Institution, CCTV, Home. **Chl-Juv:** Fairy Tales, Storytelling. **Acq:** Purchase, Duplication. **Dist:** Clear Vue Inc.; Warner Home Video, Inc. $14.95.

Aesop's Fables 1991
Five three-minute fables with introductions are presented: "The Grasshopper and the Ant," "The Sun and the Wind," "The Fox and the Grapes," "The Animals and the Children," and "The Donkey Trip." Can be used for both entertainment as well as the introduction of values to youngsters. Comes with catalog kit. 15m; VHS. **A:** Primary. **P:** Education. **U:** Institution. **Chl-Juv:** Fairy Tales. **Acq:** Purchase, Rent/Lease. **Dist:** Clear Vue Inc. $175.00.

Aesop's Fables & Associates, Vol. 1 192?
Collection of Aesop's favorite fables. 60m; VHS. **A:** Preschool-Primary. **P:** Entertainment. **U:** Home. **Chl-Juv:** Animation & Cartoons. **Acq:** Purchase. **Dist:** Video Resources. $24.95.
Indiv. Titles: 1. Circus Capers 2. The Last Dance 3. College Capers 4. Jail Breakers 5. The Office Boy 6. Minnie's Yoo Hoo 7. Down In Dixie 8. Dizzy Days.

Aesop's Fables: The Boy Who Cried Wolf/The Wolf and the Lamb 19??
Two stories from the famous Greek noted for his use of animals to convey messages are presented. Children will be thrilled by the charming stories that always leave a lasting impression on the young mind. ?m; VHS. **A:** Preschool-Primary. **P:** Entertainment. **U:** Home. **Chl-Juv:** Children, Animation & Cartoons, Fairy Tales. **Acq:** Purchase. **Dist:** Golden Book Video.

Aesop's Fables, Vol. 1: The Hen with the Golden Egg 1987
Nine fables are retold in this delightful collection, including "The Lion in Love," "The Dog and His Image," and "The Crow and the Fox." Animated. 50m; VHS. **Pr:** Children's Video Library. **A:** Family. **P:** Entertainment. **U:** Home. **Chl-Juv:** Animation & Cartoons, Fairy Tales. **Acq:** Purchase. **Dist:** Lions Gate Television Corp. $29.98.

Aesop's Fables, Vol. 2: The Lion and the Stag 1987
A collection of nine animated fables including, "The Lion and the Stag," "The Camel and the Countryman," and "The Elephant Who Was Chosen The New King Of Beasts." Plus many more. 50m; VHS. **Pr:** Children's Video Library. **A:** Family. **P:** Entertainment. **U:** Home. **Chl-Juv:** Animation & Cartoons, Children, Fairy Tales. **Acq:** Purchase. **Dist:** Lions Gate Television Corp. $29.98.

Aesop's Fables, Vol. 3: The Tortoise & the Hare 1987
Nine of Aesop's most popular fables, including "The Tortoise and the Hare," "The Frog and the Bull," and "The Two Dogs and the Meaty Bone." Plus many more! Animated. 50m; VHS. **Pr:** Children's Video Library. **A:** Family. **P:** Entertainment. **U:** Home. **Chl-Juv:** Children, Animation & Cartoons, Fairy Tales. **Acq:** Purchase. **Dist:** Lions Gate Television Corp. $29.98.

An Aesthetic Indulgence 1989
The story of an absent-minded professor who finds beauty in the abstract. 15m; VHS, 3/4 U. **Pr:** Michael Scott. **A:** Jr. High-Adult. **P:** Education. **U:** Institution, SURA. **Gen-Edu:** Philosophy & Ideology. **Acq:** Purchase, Rent/Lease. **Dist:** National Film Board of Canada.

The Affair 1973 (Unrated) — ★★★
Songwriter/polio victim Wood falls in love for the first time with attorney Wagner. Delicate situation handled well by a fine cast. 74m; VHS, DVD. **C:** Natalie Wood; Robert Wagner; Bruce Davison; Kent Smith; Frances Reid; Pat Harrington; Directed by Gilbert Cates. **A:** Sr. High-Adult. **P:** Entertainment. **U:** Home. **Mov-Ent:** Drama, TV Movies, Diseases. **Acq:** Purchase. **Dist:** Movies Unlimited. $12.47.

The Affair 1995 (R) — ★★½
It's 1944 in a small English town, where a troop of black American soldiers are billeted prior to the D-Day invasion. Travis (Vance) falls for the married Maggie (Fox)?whose husband, Edward (Hinds), is supposed to be away at sea—and they begin an affair. Unfortunately, Edward arrives home unexpectedly and accuses Travis of raping his wife. If Maggie denies the accusation, she'll lose her home and family but if she confirms it, Travis, according to Army law, will be condemned to death. 105m; VHS, DVD. **C:** Courtney B. Vance; Kerry Fox; Ciaran Hinds; Beatie Edney; Leland Gantt; Bill Nunn; Ned Beatty; Directed by Paul Seed; Written by Pablo F. Fenjves; Bryan Goluboff; Cinematography by Ivan Strasburg; Music by Christopher Gunning. **Pr:** John Smithson; David H. Thompson; Harry Belafonte; HBO; British Broadcasting Corporation. **A:** Sr. High-Adult. **P:** Entertainment. **U:** Home. **Mov-Ent:** Drama, Great Britain, World War Two. **Acq:** Purchase. **Dist:** Universal Music and Video Distribution.

An Affair in Mind 1989 (Unrated) — ★★
A professional writer falls in love with a beautiful woman who tries to convince him to assist her in murdering her husband. 88m; VHS, CC. **C:** Amanda Donohoe; Stephen (Dillon) Dillane; Matthew Marsh; Jean-Laurent Cochot; Directed by Michael Baker. **Pr:** British Broadcasting Corporation. **A:** Sr. High-Adult. **P:** Entertainment. **U:** Home. **Mov-Ent:** Mystery & Suspense, TV Movies, Marriage. **Acq:** Purchase. **Dist:** $19.98.

Affair in Trinidad 1952 — ★★
Fun in the tropics as nightclub singer Hayworth enlists the help of brother-in-law Ford to find her husband's murderer. The trail leads to international thieves and espionage in a romantic thriller that reunites the stars of "Gilda." Hayworth sings (with Jo Ann Greer's voice) "I've Been Kissed Before." 98m/B/W; DVD. **C:** Rita Hayworth; Glenn Ford; Alexander Scourby; Torin Thatcher; Valerie Bettis; Steven Geray; Directed by Vincent Sherman. **A:** Family. **P:** Entertainment. **U:** Home. **Mov-Ent:** Acq:** Purchase. **Dist:** Sony Pictures Home Entertainment Inc.; Critics' Choice Video & DVD. $19.95.

An Affair of Love 1999 (R) — ★★½
French love story sounds like "Last Tango in Paris" but really owes more to "sex, lies and videotape." Elle (Baye) places an ad in a sex magazine and arranges to meet a respondent, Lui (Lopez), for afternoon sexual encounters in a hotel. Virtually all of the physical action takes place behind a closed door. The point is emotional and so, in after-the-fact monologues, they both discuss (separately) what's happened. French with subtitles. 80m; VHS, DVD, Wide, CC. **C:** Nathalie Baye; Sergi

Lopez; Paul Pavel; Directed by Frederic Fonteyne; Written by Philippe Blasband; Cinematography by Virginie Saint-Martin; Music by Andre Dziezuk; Marc Mergen; Jeannot Sanavia. **A:** College-Adult. **P:** Entertainment. **U:** Home. **L:** French. **Mov-Ent:** Drama, Sex & Sexuality, Hotels & Hotel Staff Training. **Acq:** Purchase. **Dist:** New Line Home Video.

Affair of the Heart 1987
An instructional program for patients in how to cope with recuperative activity after heart surgery or illness. 60m; VHS. **C:** Phyllis Denny. **Pr:** Active Entertainment. **A:** Adult. **P:** Instruction. **U:** Home. **Hea-Sci:** Heart. **Acq:** Purchase. **Dist:** Karol Media. $29.95.

The Affair of the Necklace 2001 (R) — ★½
Louis XVI-era history is given a tabloid treatment in this costume drama concerning the vengeful efforts of orphaned Jeanne de la Motte-Valois to restore nobility to her family name. She conspires with a court rogue to hatch a sophisticated scam involving the cardinal of France, Marie Antoinette, German Illuminati, and the fabulous necklace of the title, paving the way for the French Revolution. Excessive narration and flashbacks bog the plot; film offers little other than eye candy in the form of intricate set pieces and fancy dress. Intriguing story potential is mishandled, and Swank is terribly miscast but looks nice in a corset. The remaining actors are underused, except Walken in a scene-chewing role as a Svengali-like mesmerist. 120m; VHS, DVD. **C:** Hilary Swank; Jonathan Pryce; Simon Baker; Adrien Brody; Brian Cox; Joely Richardson; Christopher Walken; Paul Brooke; Peter Eyre; Simon Kunz; Hayden Panettiere; Directed by Charles Shyer; Written by John Sweet; Cinematography by Ashley Rowe; Music by David Newman. **Pr:** Charles Shyer; Redmond Morris; Andrew A. Kosove; Broderick Johnson; Charles Shyer; Alcon Entertainment; Warner Bros. **A:** Sr. High-Adult. **P:** Entertainment. **U:** Home. **Mov-Ent:** France, Adoption, Drama. **Acq:** Purchase. **Dist:** Warner Home Video, Inc.

The Affair of the Pink Pearl 1984
The husband-and-wife private investigation team of Tommy and Tuppence must find within 24 hours the culprit who stole a valuable pink pearl. Based on the Agatha Christie series of short stories. Made for British television. 60m; VHS. **C:** James Warwick; Francesca Annis. **Pr:** London Weekend Television. **A:** Jr. High-Adult. **P:** Entertainment. **U:** Home. **Mov-Ent:** Mystery & Suspense. **Acq:** Purchase. **Dist:** Tapeworm Video Distributors Inc. $14.95.

An Affair to Remember 1957 (Unrated) — ★★½
McCarey remakes his own "Love Affair," with less success. Nightclub singer Kerr and wealthy bachelor Grant discover love on an ocean liner and agree to meet six months later on top of the Empire State Building to see if their feelings are the same. Not as good as the original, but a winner of a fairy tale just the same. Notable for causing many viewers to sob uncontrollably. "Affair" was gathering dust on store shelves until "Sleepless in Seattle" used it as a plot device and rentals skyrocketed. In 1994 real life couple Warren Beatty and Annette Bening attempted a third "Love Affair" remake. 115m; VHS, DVD, Blu-Ray, Wide, CC. **C:** Cary Grant; Deborah Kerr; Richard Denning; Cathleen Nesbitt; Neva Patterson; Robert Q. Lewis; Fortunio Bonanova; Matt Moore; Nora Marlowe; Sarah Selby; Directed by Leo McCarey; Written by Leo McCarey; Delmer Daves; Donald Ogden Stewart; Cinematography by Milton Krasner; Music by Hugo Friedhofer. **Pr:** 20th Century-Fox. **A:** Family. **P:** Entertainment. **U:** Home. **Mov-Ent:** Drama, Melodrama, Boating. **Acq:** Purchase. **Dist:** Movies Unlimited; Alpha Video; Fox Home Entertainment. $9.98.

Affairs 1992
Part of a series that examines various aspects of contemporary psychology and human interactions. 30m; VHS. **A:** Adult. **P:** Education. **U:** Institution. **Gen-Edu:** Psychology. **Acq:** Purchase. **Dist:** RMI Media. $89.95.

Affairs and Repairs 1992
Part of a series that examines various aspects of contemporary psychology and human interactions. 30m; VHS. **A:** Adult. **P:** Education. **U:** Institution. **Gen-Edu:** Psychology. **Acq:** Purchase. **Dist:** RMI Media. $89.95.

Affairs of Anatol 1921 — ★★
Philandering playboy Anatol Spencer (Reid) finds no luck with women. He's robbed by one (Ayres), two-timed by another (Hawley), and even madam Satan Synne (Daniels) isn't what she seems. Then Anatol decides to return to his wife, Vivian (Swanson), only to discover that she's being amusing herself with another. Based on a play by Arthur Schnitzler. 117m/B/W; Silent; VHS, DVD. **C:** Wallace Reid; Gloria Swanson; Bebe Daniels; Wanda (Petit) Hawley; Agnes Ayres; Monte Blue; Theodore Roberts; Elliott Dexter; Directed by Cecil B. DeMille; Written by Beulah Marie Dix; Cinematography by Karl Struss; Alvin Wyckoff. **A:** College-Adult. **P:** Entertainment. **U:** Home. **Mov-Ent:** Marriage, Sex & Sexuality. **Acq:** Purchase. **Dist:** Kino on Video.

The Affairs of Annabel 1938 — ★★½
The first of the popular series of Annabel pictures Lucy made in the late 1930s. Appealing adolescent is zoomed to movie stardom by her press agent's stunts. A behind-the-scenes satire on Hollywood, stars, and agents. 68m/B/W; VHS. **C:** Lucille Ball; Jack Oakie; Ruth Donnelly; Fritz Feld; Bradley Page; Directed by Ben Stoloff. **Pr:** Lou Lusty Republic; RKO. **A:** Family. **P:** Entertainment. **U:** Home. **Mov-Ent:** Satire & Parody. **Acq:** Purchase. **Dist:** Image Entertainment Inc.; Turner Broadcasting System Inc. $29.95.

The Affairs of Dobie Gillis 1953 — ★★½
Light musical-comedy about a group of college kids and their carefree antics. Complete with big-band tunes, dance numbers,

and plenty of collegiate shenanigans, this '50s classic inspired a hit TV series, "The Many Loves of Dobie Gillis." 72m/B/W; VHS, DVD. **C:** Debbie Reynolds; Bobby Van; Barbara Ruick; Bob Fosse; Lurene Tuttle; Hans Conried; Charles Lane; Directed by Don Weis; Written by Max Shulman; Cinematography by William Mellor. **Pr:** MGM; MGM/UA Entertainment Company. **A:** Jr. High-Adult. **P:** Entertainment. **U:** Home. **Mov-Ent:** Musical, Romance. **Acq:** Purchase. **Dist:** WarnerArchive.com; MGM Home Entertainment. $19.98.
Songs: I'm Through with Love; All I Do Is Dream of You; You Can't Do Wrong Doing Right; Those Endearing Young Charms.

Affairs of the Heart 1993 (R) — ★½
Josie Hart is a psychologist, who is also a supermodel with an advice column but she's too busy to get her own romantic life in gear. Then she meets a handsome baseball player. Lots of bodies on display and sexual interludes based on Dr. Hart's advice to her readers. 90m; VHS. **C:** Amy Lynn Baxter; Michael Montana; Danny Berger; Cody Carmacy; Directed by Ernest G. Sauer. **A:** College-Adult. **P:** Entertainment. **U:** Home. **Mov-Ent:** Sex & Sexuality. **Acq:** Purchase. **Dist:** York Entertainment.

Affairs of the Heart: Series 1 1974 (Unrated)
Vintage adaptations of Henry James stories filled with scoundrels, schemers, and love affairs, including Washington Square, The Aspern Papers, and The Wings of the Dove. 7 episodes. 411m; DVD. **C:** Georgina Hale; Anton Rodgers. **A:** Adult. **P:** Entertainment. **U:** Home. **Mov-Ent:** Drama, Literature. **Acq:** Purchase. **Dist:** Acorn Media Group Inc. $46.99.

Affairs of the Heart: Series 2 1974 (Unrated)
London Weekend Television presents dramatic adaptations of 19th century romances written by Henry James. 302m; DVD. **C:** Georgina Hale; Anton Rodgers. **A:** Sr. High-Adult. **P:** Entertainment. **U:** Home. **Mov-Ent:** Comedy--Romantic. **Acq:** Purchase. **Dist:** Acorn Media Group Inc. $39.99.

Affected Community Decisions... 1995
Centers on community notification, evacuation and shelters, shutting off utilities, determining risk, outside assistance. 15m; VHS. **A:** Adult. **P:** Professional. **U:** Institution. **Bus-Ind:** Waste Products, Safety Education, Management. **Acq:** Rent/Lease. **Dist:** National Safety Council, California Chapter, Film Library.

Affected Employees 1995
Explains why there is a lockout/tagout program, and how to prevent accidents on the job. 10m; VHS. **A:** Adult. **P:** Professional. **U:** Institution. **Bus-Ind:** Job Training, Safety Education. **Acq:** Rent/Lease. **Dist:** National Safety Council, California Chapter, Film Library.

Affengeil 1991
Introduces Lotte Huber, 79-year-old cabaret star who has performed on stages from Nazi Germany to Palestine to Cyprus, and has been a focal point in von Praunheim's life. 87m; VHS, Special order formats. **A:** Jr. High-Adult. **P:** Education. **U:** Institution. **Gen-Edu:** Singing, Dance. **Acq:** Purchase, Rent/Lease. **Dist:** First Run/Icarus Films. $490.00.

Affinity 2008 (Unrated) — ★★
In 1870s Victorian England, a woman of Margaret Prior's (Madeley) upper social class and age should be married. Instead, she lives with her mother and is suffering a deep depression after the recent death of her father and the marriage of her best friend (and secret lover) Helen (Young) to her brother. Encouraged to do good works, Margaret mentors the female inmates of Milbank prison and becomes curious about Selina Dawes (Tapper), a so-called spirit medium incarcerated for murder after a seance gone wrong. At first skeptical of Selina's alleged gifts, Margaret becomes fascinated by the allure of the unknown. Based on the novel by Sarah Waters. 94m; DVD. **C:** Anna Madeley; Zoe Tapper; Domini Blythe; Anne Reid; Amanda Plummer; Anna Massey; Ferelith Young; Vincent Leclerc; Directed by Tim Fywell; Written by Andrew Davies; Cinematography by Bernard Couture; Music by Frederic Weber. **A:** Sr. High-Adult. **P:** Entertainment. **U:** Home. **Mov-Ent.** **Acq:** Purchase. **Dist:** Wolfe Video.

Affirmations 1990
Riggs' continued exploration of the African-American gay identity. 10m; VHS. **C:** Directed by Marlon Riggs. **A:** College-Adult. **P:** Education. **U:** Institution. **Hea-Sci:** Black Culture. **Acq:** Purchase, Rent/Lease. **Dist:** Frameline. $150.00.

Affirmative Action: Is It the Answer to Discrimination? 197?
A panel of lawyers, academicians, and journalists meet to discuss the legality of granting preference to people on the basis of sex, race, and national origin. 60m; 3/4 U. **C:** Owen Fiss; Richard Posner; William Raspberry; Vera Glaser; Paul Seabury; Ralph K. Winter. **Pr:** American Enterprise Institute. **A:** College-Adult. **P:** Education. **U:** Institution, BCTV. **Gen-Edu:** Public Affairs, Civil Rights. **Acq:** Purchase, Rent/Lease. **Dist:** American Enterprise Institute for Public Policy Research.

Affirmative Action: The History of an Idea ????
Explores the historical roots and current debate over the usefulness of affirmative action. 58m; VHS. **A:** Adult. **P:** Education. **U:** Institution. **Gen-Edu:** Education, Ethnicity, Prejudice. **Acq:** Purchase, Rent/Lease. **Dist:** Films for the Humanities & Sciences. $129.00.

Affirmative Action Under Fire: When Is It Reverse Discrimination? ????
Reports on a reverse discrimination case brought against a New Jersey high school in 1989. Cokie Roberts also moderates a debate with the President of the NAACP and the Director of Litigation from the Institute for Justice on the issues of affirmative action. 22m; VHS. **A:** Adult. **P:** Education. **U:** Institution.

Gen-Edu: Education, Prejudice. **Acq:** Purchase. **Dist:** Films for the Humanities & Sciences. $89.95.

Afflicted 1982
Short used as the basis for Guttman's debut feature "Nagu'a (Afflicted)" depicts a visit to a drag bar by a young, closeted Israeli man. Hebrew with subtitles. 25m/B/W; VHS. **C:** Directed by Amos Guttman. **A:** College-Adult. **P:** Entertainment. **U:** Institution. **L:** Hebrew. **Fin-Art.** **Acq:** Purchase, Rent/Lease. **Dist:** Frameline. $200.00.

Afflicted 2014 (R) — ★★½
Found-footage horror movies might be the most overdone genre du jour, but directors Prowse and Lee breathe some life into shaky-cam cinema with this tense first-person account of a young man's transformation into something else. Resembling "American Werewolf in London" more than "Paranormal Activity," the story follows two friends, Clif and Derek (played by the writer-directors), documenting their trip around the world. But, after Derek gets bit by a strange woman in Paris, his body starts changing and he develops a taste for blood. Prowse and Lee do a fantastic job of making their characters feel like real people, which only makes Derek's transformation that much creepier. 85m; DVD. **C:** Clif Prowse; Derek Lee; Baya Rehaz; Benjamin Zeitoun; Edo Van Breemen; Directed by Clif Prowse; Derek Lee; Written by Clif Prowse; Derek Lee; Cinematography by Norm Li; Music by Edo Van Breemen. **Pr:** Chris Ferguson; CBS Films. **A:** Sr. High-Adult. **P:** Entertainment. **U:** Home. **L:** English, French, Italian. **Mov-Ent:** Horror, Men, Italy. **Acq:** Purchase.

Affliction 1997 (R) — ★★★½
Nolte, Schrader, and Coburn turn in the finest work of their careers in this bleak tale of one man's battle with the demons of his past and the failures of the present. Nolte is small-town, small-time sheriff Wade Whitehouse, who wants to do the right things, but never does. Damaged beyond repair by his abusive alcoholic father (Coburn), he alienates or scares away anyone who might care for him, including his daughter (Tierney) and his girlfriend (Spacek). When a local businessman dies under mysterious circumstances, Wade sees a chance at redemption, but the investigation turns out to be the catalyst for his final degradation. Schrader has studied the beaten-down male psyche before, but never with this much discipline or implicit knowledge. He adapted the screenplay from Russell Banks' 1989 novel. 113m; VHS, DVD, CC. **C:** Nick Nolte; James Coburn; Sissy Spacek; Willem Dafoe; Mary Beth Hurt; Jim True-Frost; Marian Seldes; Brigid Tierney; Sean McCann; Wayne Robson; Holmes Osborne; Directed by Paul Schrader; Written by Paul Schrader; Cinematography by Paul Sarossy; Music by Michael Brook. **Pr:** Largo Entertainment. **A:** College-Adult. **P:** Entertainment. **U:** Home. **Mov-Ent:** Alcoholism. **Awds:** Oscars '98: Support. Actor (Coburn); N.Y. Film Critics '98: Actor (Nolte); Natl. Soc. Film Critics '98: Actor (Nolte). **Acq:** Purchase. **Dist:** Lions Gate Entertainment Inc.

Afghan Knights 2007 (R) — ★½
An ex-Navy SEAL recruits some former comrades to go back to Afghanistan as mercenaries in order to sneak a warlord out of the country. They meet some opposition and are forced to hide out in a cave where they find some weapons that contain the spirit of Genghis Khan and his Mongol warriors. Said ghostly hordes are looking for some new recruits. Surprisingly, not as ridiculous as it sounds. 90m; DVD. **C:** Francesco Quinn; Steve Bacic; Gary Stretch; Michael Madsen; Chris Kramer; Directed by Allan Harmon; Written by Christine Stringer; Cinematography by Randal Platt; Music by Jon Lee; Stu Goldberg. **A:** Sr. High-Adult. **P:** Entertainment. **U:** Home. **Mov-Ent:** Horror, Middle East. **Acq:** Purchase. **Dist:** Bedford Entertainment Inc.

Afghan Luke 2011 (R) — ★½
Journalist Luke Benning (Stahl) quits his job after his story about a Canadian sniper mutilating corpses in Afghanistan is rejected. He returns to the war, accompanied by pal Tom (Wright), to get more evidence but they get caught up in various surreal situations. Maybe the onscreen hash haze spilled over because the film is rambling and incoherent. 97m; DVD, Blu-Ray. **C:** Nick Stahl; Nicholas Wright; Ali Liebert; Stephen Lobo; Pascale Hutton; Directed by Mike Clattenberg; Written by Mike Clattenberg; Cinematography by Jeremy Benning; Music by Blaine Morris. **A:** Sr. High-Adult. **P:** Entertainment. **U:** Home. **L:** English. **Mov-Ent:** Afghanistan, Drug Abuse, Journalism. **Acq:** Purchase. **Dist:** Screen Media Ventures, LLC.

Afghan Nomads: The Maldar 1974
Introduces the Maldar nomads, and portrays their lifestyle as they travel, camp, buy, and sell. 21m; VHS. **A:** Sr. High-Adult. **P:** Education. **U:** Institution. **Gen-Edu:** Documentary Films, Middle East. **Acq:** Purchase. **Dist:** University of Washington Educational Media Collection. $17.00.

The Afghan Solution 2011 (Unrated)
Documentary covering the country of Afghanistan and the efforts of its central government to impose order on various local tribes, ethnic groups, and warlords--all of which have differing beliefs and needs. 55m; DVD. **A:** Sr. High-Adult. **P:** Entertainment. **U:** Home. **L:** English. **Mov-Ent:** Documentary Films, War--General, Afghanistan. **Acq:** Purchase. **Dist:** Janson Media. $24.95.

Afghan Star 2009 (Unrated)
Documentary following the participants of Afghan Star, Afghanistan's version of 'American Idol'. In English, Dari, and Pashto with subtitles. 88m; DVD. **A:** Sr. High-Adult. **P:** Entertainment. **U:** Home. **Gen-Edu:** Documentary Films, Afghanistan. **Acq:** Purchase. **Dist:** Arab Film Distribution. $29.99.

Afghan Women: A History of Struggle 2007
Documentary on Afghan women and their struggle for equality. 69m; VHS, DVD. **A:** Sr. High-Adult. **P:** Education. **U:**

Institution. **Gen-Edu**: Documentary Films, Afghanistan, Women. **Acq:** Purchase, Rent/Lease. **Dist:** The Cinema Guild. $295.00.

Afghanistan: Exporting the Taliban Revolution ????
Examines firsthand the results and implications of the escalating tensions between Afghanistan's Taliban militant Sunni fundamentalists and other militant groups from neighboring countries. 23m; VHS. **A:** Sr. High-Adult. **P:** Education. **U:** Institution. **Gen-Edu**: Middle East. **Acq:** Purchase, Rent/Lease. **Dist:** Films for the Humanities & Sciences. $129.00.

Afghanistan 1982—The Struggle for Freedom Continues 1982
Documentary on the war in Afghanistan, including interviews with Afghan rebels and journalists working in the country. 47m; VHS, 3/4 U. **Pr:** USIA. **A:** Sr. High-Adult. **P:** Education. **U:** Institution, SURA. **Gen-Edu**: Asia, International Relations. **Acq:** Purchase. **Dist:** National Audiovisual Center. $140.00.

Afghanistan: The Hidden War 1986
This video documents the war in Afghanistan, including footage of news coverage of the war from several countries around the world. 58m; VHS, 3/4 U. **Pr:** USIA. **A:** Sr. High-Adult. **P:** Education. **U:** Institution, SURA. **Gen-Edu**: Asia, International Relations. **Acq:** Purchase. **Dist:** National Audiovisual Center. $155.00.

Afghanistan: The Lost Truth 2003 (Unrated)
Iranian filmmaker Yassamin Maleknasr travels across Afghanistan from Herat to Balkh after the fall of the Taliban, speaking with families, a medical student, female judge, filmmaker Siddig Barnak and others about their hopes and dreams for the future and remorse over the senseless destruction in their country. 64m; DVD. **A:** Adult. **P:** Education. **U:** Institution. **Gen-Edu**: Middle East, Documentary Films, War--General. **Acq:** Purchase. **Dist:** Women Make Movies. $295.00.

Afghanistan: Threads of Life 1982
The culture, lifestyles, and physical features of Afghanistan and its people are highlighted. 29m; VHS, 3/4 U. **Pr:** Encyclopedia Britannica Educational Corporation. **A:** Jr. High-Adult. **P:** Education. **U:** Institution, SURA. **Gen-Edu**: Middle East. **Acq:** Purchase, Rent/Lease, Trade-in. **Dist:** Encyclopedia Britannica.

Afghanistan Unveiled 2003 (Unrated)
Fourteen video journalist trainees from Afghanistan leave the Taliban-controlled Kabul for the first time ever and head for more rural regions of the country to capture on tape the plight of Hazara women who now live in caves with little food and water, fending for themselves, virtually abandoned after the U.S. invasion. 52m; DVD. **A:** Adult. **P:** Education. **U:** Institution. **L:** French. **Gen-Edu**: Women, Middle East, Documentary Films. **Acq:** Purchase. **Dist:** Women Make Movies. $295.00.

AFI's 100 Years, 100 Stars 1999
This CBS special is a pleasant little stroll down memory lane, though the title is somewhat misleading. It's really about 50 favorite older stars (25 men and 25 women) from the "classic era" (as narrator Shirley Temple Black puts it) who are ranked according to their "popularity and historical context." Ava Gardner and William Holden come in at #25; Humphrey Bogart and Katherine Hepburn share #1. Clips of the 50 "classic" stars are introduced by 50 relative whippersnappers. 135m; DVD. **C:** Narrated by Shirley Temple; Directed by Gary Smith; Written by Richard Schickel; Marty Farrell. **A:** Jr. High-Adult. **P:** Entertainment. **U:** Home. **Gen-Edu**: Film History, Filmmaking. **Acq:** Purchase. **Dist:** Image Entertainment Inc. $24.99.

AFP: American Fighter Pilot 2005 (Unrated)
Follows the real-life training of three pilots striving to become F-15 fighter pilots at Florida's Tyndale Air Force Base with a focus on aerial videos. 435m; DVD. **C:** Mike Love; Christopher Penn; Todd Giggy; Marcus Gregory; Regina Pope. **A:** Jr. High-Adult. **P:** Entertainment. **U:** Home. **Mov-Ent**: Television Series, Military History. **Acq:** Purchase. **Dist:** Hannover House. $24.95.

Afraid of the Dark 1992 (R) — ★★
Convoluted psycho-thriller from a child's point of view. Young Lucas is fearful for his blind mother. It seems a vicious slasher has been attacking blind women and Lucas' father, a policeman, has yet to apprehend the criminal. But...Lucas it seems has a problem with reality. With his fantasies and realities mixed, all the people in his life also play entirely different roles. Characters are so detached and unreal that a viewer is prevented from a clear understanding of anything that may, or may not, be going on. Directorial debut of Peploe. 91m; VHS, DVD, CC. **C:** Ben Keyworth; James Fox; Fanny Ardant; Paul McGann; Clare Holman; Robert Stephens; Directed by Mark Peploe; Written by Mark Peploe; Cinematography by Bruno de Keyzer. **Pr:** Fine Line Features. **A:** Sr. High-Adult. **P:** Entertainment. **U:** Home. **Mov-Ent**: Mystery & Suspense, Parenting, Blindness. **Acq:** Purchase. **Dist:** Sony Pictures Home Entertainment Inc.; New Line Home Video. $89.95.

Afraid to Live 1988
Kids talk to kids about drug and alcohol abuse prevention, how to avoid peer pressure, and how to find a rehabilitation program. 16m; VHS. **A:** Jr. High-Sr. High. **P:** Education. **U:** Institution. **Gen-Edu**: Drug Abuse, Alcoholism, Education. **Acq:** Purchase. **Dist:** GPN Educational Media. $189.00.

Africa 1984
Contains an overview of African history, geography, and culture from ancient times to the present. 456m; VHS. **A:** Primary-Adult. **P:** Education. **U:** Institution. **Gen-Edu**: History--U.S., Africa, Black Culture. **Acq:** Purchase. **Dist:** Knowledge Unlimited, Inc. $119.80.

Africa 1986
An eight-part documentary about the continent, its people and terrain. Two programs per tape. 106m; VHS. **Pr:** RM Arts. **A:** Jr. High-Adult. **P:** Education. **U:** Home. **Gen-Edu**: Documentary Films, Africa, Anthropology. **Acq:** Purchase. **Dist:** Home Vision Cinema; Facets Multimedia Inc.; Knowledge Unlimited, Inc. $54.95.
Indiv. Titles: 1. Different but Equal/Mastering a Continent 2. Caravans of Gold/Kings and Cities 3. The Bible and the Gun/The Magnificent African Cake 4. The Rise of Nationalism/ The Legacy.

Africa 1991
Teaches how the landscapes and climates interact as the viewer visits Africa's regions: tropical rain forests, savannas, semi-deserts, deserts, and mountains. Part of a seven part series. 27m; VHS, 3/4 U. **A:** Primary-Jr. High. **P:** Education. **U:** Institution. **Gen-Edu**: Geography, Africa. **Acq:** Purchase. **Dist:** National Geographic Society. $99.00.

Africa 1993
Four programs present the striking beauty of Africa and explore the themes of human interaction with the environment. 22m; VHS. **A:** Primary-Sr. High. **P:** Education. **U:** Institution. **Gen-Edu**: Africa, Travel, Geography. **Acq:** Purchase. **Dist:** Encyclopedia Britannica. $99.00.
Indiv. Titles: 1. Central and Eastern Regions 2. Northern Region 3. Southern Region 4. Western Region.

Africa 2001
Five-volume series presents African natives telling their personal stories revealing the history, culture, religions, and art of the different regions in Africa. 480m; VHS, DVD. **A:** Sr. High. **P:** Education. **U:** Institution. **Gen-Edu**: Africa, Geography. **Acq:** Purchase. **Dist:** Zenger Media. $74.98.

Africa 2013 (Unrated)
A six-part nature documentary on the continent of Africa from the BBC. 360m; DVD, Blu-Ray, Streaming. **A:** Family. **P:** Education. **U:** Home. **L:** English, French, Spanish. **Gen-Edu**: Documentary Films, Nature. **Acq:** Purchase, Rent/Lease. **Dist:** BBC Worldwide Ltd. $34.98 29.98 14.99.

Africa: A Continent of Many Nations 1990
The culture, history and geography of the African continent. ?m; VHS. **Pr:** United Learning Inc. **A:** Jr. High-Sr. High. **P:** Education. **U:** Institution, CCTV, CATV, Home, SURA. **Gen-Edu**: Documentary Films, Africa, History. **Acq:** Purchase, Duplication. **Dist:** United Learning Inc. $180.00.
Indiv. Titles: 1. The Land 2. The People 3. Civilizations in Conflict 4. The Explosion of Freedom 5. Toward the Year 2000.

Africa: A New Look 1981
This program shows how urbanized Africa has become by focusing on the people who live and work on the continent today. 27m; 3/4 U, Special order formats. **Pr:** International Film Foundation. **A:** Primary-Adult. **P:** Education. **U:** Institution, SURA. **Gen-Edu**: Africa. **Acq:** Purchase, Rent/Lease. **Dist:** International Film Foundation.

Africa: A Voyage of Discovery with Basil Davidson 1984
Four-volume series provides an introduction to African history, geography, and culture from ancient times to the present. Topics discussed include Bronze Age African kingdoms, European prejudice of Africans, and many other issues detailed in interviews with scholars, researchers, and political leaders. 114m; VHS. **A:** Jr. High-Sr. High. **P:** Education. **U:** Institution. **Gen-Edu**: Africa, History. **Acq:** Purchase. **Dist:** Zenger Media. $83.95.
Indiv. Titles: 1. Different But Equal and Mastering a Continent 2. Caravans of Gold and Kings and Cities 3. The Bible and the Gun and The Magnificent African Cake 4. The Rise of Nationalism and The Legacy.

Africa, Africas 2001
Collection of three films explores the social and cultural realities of skin bleaching in Cameroon; the upheaval of Ethiopian women and children forced into refugee camps; and the causes of unemployment and poverty in Burkina Faso. 60m; VHS. **A:** Adult. **P:** Education. **U:** Institution. **Gen-Edu**: Africa, Poverty, Women. **Acq:** Purchase, Rent/Lease. **Dist:** Women Make Movies. $295.00.
Indiv. Titles: 1. Fantacoca 2. The River Between Us 3. Laafi Bala.

Africa: An Introduction—Revised 1981
This show is an overview of Africa and the many different people who make up the population. 22m; VHS, 3/4 U. **Pr:** Wayne Mitchell. **A:** Primary-Adult. **P:** Education. **U:** Institution, SURA. **Gen-Edu**: Africa. **Acq:** Purchase. **Dist:** Phoenix Learning Group.

Africa and the Indian Ocean 19??
An island in the Indian Ocean that is not revealed is the diving destination on this program. 30m; VHS. **A:** Sr. High-Adult. **P:** Entertainment. **U:** Home. **Spo-Rec**: Scuba, Travel. **Acq:** Purchase. **Dist:** Bennett Marine Video. $19.95.

Africa Between Myth and Reality: The Paintings and Etchings of Betty LaDuke 1996
Documentary examines the work of artist Betty LaDuke, inspired by her ten years of travel throughout Africa. 28m; VHS. **A:** College. **P:** Education. **U:** Institution. **Fin-Art**: Documentary Films, Africa, Art & Artists. **Acq:** Purchase. **Dist:** The Cinema Guild; Crystal Productions. $39.95.

Africa, Blood & Guts 1967
A documentary that captures the racial, ethnic, political and social upheavals that rocked Africa during the 1960s. 83m; VHS. **C:** Directed by Gualtiero Jacopetti; Franco Prosperi; Written by Gualtiero Jacopetti; Franco Prosperi. **Pr:** Rizzoli Films. **A:** College-Adult. **P:** Entertainment. **U:** Home. **Gen-Edu**: Documentary Films, Africa. **Acq:** Purchase. **Dist:** Vidcrest.

Africa Changes: A Young Leader in a Young Nation 1970
The aspirations, projects, and problems of the people of emerging African nations are examined in this show which documents a young African commissioner's tour of his district. 14m; VHS, 3/4 U. **Pr:** Frank Gardonyi; Clifford Janoff. **A:** Jr. High-Sr. High. **P:** Education. **U:** Institution, SURA. **Gen-Edu**: Africa. **Acq:** Purchase. **Dist:** Phoenix Learning Group.

Africa: Continent of Contrasts 19??
Describes the geography, cultural diversity, history, and traditions of the many regions of the African continent. Includes information on the various wildlife of the different regions. Comes with teacher's manual. 34m; VHS. **A:** Jr. High-Adult. **P:** Education. **U:** Institution. **Gen-Edu**: Africa, Geography, History. **Acq:** Purchase. **Dist:** Educational Video Network. $69.95.

Africa Dreaming 1997
Contains four dramatic short films based on the theme "love in Africa" and taken from different parts of the continent. 104m; VHS. **A:** Sr. High-Adult. **P:** Entertainment. **U:** Home, Institution. **Gen-Edu**: Africa, Fiction, Romance. **Acq:** Purchase. **Dist:** California Newsreel. $195.00.

Africa I Remember 1996
Documentary follows Tunde Jegede, a black musician and composer whose music combines West African and classical European traditions. 30m; VHS. **A:** Adult. **P:** Education. **U:** Home. **Gen-Edu**: Documentary Films, Africa, Music. **Acq:** Purchase, Rent/Lease. **Dist:** Filmakers Library Inc. $295.

Africa in Transition 2000
Provides an historical overview of Africa and examines issues of poverty, disease, war, social and cultural affairs, U.S. foreign policy, and the concept of an African Renaissance. 119m; VHS. **A:** Sr. High. **P:** Education. **U:** Institution. **Gen-Edu**: Africa, Geography. **Acq:** Purchase. **Dist:** Zenger Media; Social Studies School Service. $150.00.

Africa: Lake Malawi 19??
In an area that has been called the cradle of civilization, come watch as divers explore a lake that is three million years old. 30m; VHS. **A:** Sr. High-Adult. **P:** Entertainment. **U:** Home. **Spo-Rec**: Scuba, Travel. **Acq:** Purchase. **Dist:** Bennett Marine Video. $19.95.

Africa: Living in Two Worlds 1970
Vivid pictorial scenes illustrate the contrasts between centuries-old tribal communities and customs and the new African nations. Part of "The African Scene" series. 17m; VHS, 3/4 U. **Pr:** Encyclopedia Britannica Educational Corporation. **A:** Primary-Sr. High. **P:** Education. **U:** Institution, SURA. **Gen-Edu**: Africa. **Acq:** Purchase, Rent/Lease, Trade-in. **Dist:** Encyclopedia Britannica.

Africa on the Move 1992
Documentary study of Africa's Uganda region explores the efforts being made by hardworking citizens to improve health care, crops, transportation, and drinking water. Shares interviews with Ugandan families at town meetings, marketplaces, fields, and schools. Complete with guide. 55m; VHS. **Pr:** Hunger Project; Soyuztelefilm Gosteleradio. **A:** Jr. High-Adult. **P:** Education. **U:** Institution. **Gen-Edu**: Documentary Films, Africa, Agriculture. **Acq:** Purchase, Rent/Lease. **Dist:** Bullfrog Films, Inc. $275.00.

Africa: People and Places 1997
The diversity of Africa is portrayed in four journeys, to tribes in Kenya and Gabon, along the Nile in Egypt, and in a den of leopard cubs. Recommended for use with grades 3 to 8. 34m; VHS. **A:** Primary-Jr. High. **P:** Education. **U:** Institution. **Gen-Edu**: Africa, Geography. **Acq:** Purchase. **Dist:** Zenger Media. $49.95.

Africa Recovery 1990
Potential solutions to Africa's problems of drought, famine, war, and debt are discussed. 15m; VHS. **A:** Sr. High-Adult. **P:** Education. **U:** Home. **Gen-Edu**: Documentary Films, Africa. **Acq:** Rent/Lease. **Dist:** The Cinema Guild. $150.00.

Africa Screams 1949 (Unrated) — ★★1/2
Abbott and Costello go on an African safari in possession of a secret map. Unheralded independent A&C film is actually quite good in the stupid vein, with lots of jungle slapstick, generally good production values, and a supporting cast of familiar comedy faces. 79m/B/W; VHS, DVD, 3/4 U, Special order formats. **C:** Lou Costello; Bud Abbott; Shemp Howard; Hillary Brooke; Joe Besser; Clyde Beatty; Max Baer, Sr.; Directed by Charles T. Barton; Written by Earl Baldwin; Music by Walter Schumann. **Pr:** United Artists. **A:** Family. **P:** Entertainment. **U:** Home. **Mov-Ent**: Comedy--Slapstick, Africa. **Acq:** Purchase. **Dist:** Karol Media; VCX Ltd.; Legend Films. $9.95.

Africa Series 1993
Examines four regions of Africa, and discusses the environmental and cultural changes by modern times, economic activities, lifestyles, vegetation, climate and more. 80m; VHS. **A:** Jr. High-Sr. High. **P:** Education. **U:** Institution. **Gen-Edu**: Africa. **Acq:** Purchase. **Dist:** Zenger Media. $212.00.
Indiv. Titles: 1. Western Region 2. Southern Region 3. Central and Eastern Regions 4. Northern Region.

Africa Speaks! 1930
An early wildlife documentary that takes the viewer across Equatorial Africa, viewing animals in their unspoiled habitats. 58m/B/W; VHS. **C:** Directed by Paul L. Hoefler. **Pr:** Paul L.

Hoefler. **A:** Family. **P:** Entertainment. **U:** Home. **Gen-Edu:** Documentary Films, Africa, Wildlife. **Acq:** Purchase. **Dist:** Sinister Cinema. $16.95.

Africa Texas Style 1967 — ★★
An East African rancher hires an American cowboy and his Navajo sidekick to help run his wild game ranch. Decent family adventure which served as the pilot for the short-lived TV series "Cowboy in Africa." Features lots of wildlife footage and a cameo appearance by Hayley Mills. 109m; VHS, Streaming. **C:** Hugh O'Brian; John Mills; Nigel Green; Tom Nardini; Adrienne Corri; Cameo(s) Hayley Mills; Directed by Andrew Marton; Music by Malcolm Arnold. **Pr:** Paramount Pictures; Ivan Tors Productions. **A:** Family. **P:** Entertainment. **U:** Home. **Mov-Ent:** Animals. **Acq:** Purchase. **Dist:** Lions Gate Entertainment Inc. $19.98.

Africa the Serengeti 2005
Filmed on location in Kenya and Tanzania as more than two million wildebeests, zebras, and antelopes begin their annual 500-mile migration. 40m; DVD, Blu-Ray. **A:** Jr. High-Adult. **P:** Entertainment. **U:** Home. **Gen-Edu:** Documentary Films. **Acq:** Purchase. **Dist:** Razor Digital.

Africa to America to Paris: The Migration of Black Writers ????
Traces the path of African-American literature through the lives of writers James Baldwin, Richard Wright, and others. Includes readings from the writers' diaries and literary works. 52m; VHS. **A:** Sr. High-Adult. **P:** Education. **U:** Institution. **Gen-Edu:** Black Culture, Literature--American. **Acq:** Purchase, Rent/Lease. **Dist:** Films for the Humanities & Sciences. $149.00.

Africa Today 1983
This program studies all of the changes and conflicts that affect African nations right now. 14m/B/W; VHS, 3/4 U. **Pr:** WGBH Boston. **A:** Jr. High-Adult. **P:** Education. **U:** Institution, SURA. **Gen-Edu:** Africa. **Acq:** Purchase, Rent/Lease. **Dist:** Hearst Entertainment/King Features.

Africa Tomorrow 1987
Using clips from the Live Aid concert, the devastating effects of the African drought are displayed. 29m; VHS, 3/4 U. **C:** Narrated by Bob Geldof; Ben Kingsley. **Pr:** Video Arts. **A:** Jr. High-Adult. **P:** Education. **U:** Institution. **Gen-Edu:** Documentary Films, Africa, Poverty. **Acq:** Purchase, Rent/Lease. **Dist:** New Dimension Media. $280.00.

L'Africaine: Meyerbeer 1988
Placido Domingo, Shirley Verrett, Ruth Ann Swenson, and Justino Diaz perform. Maurizio Arena conducts. Italian with subtitles. ?m; VHS. **A:** Adult. **P:** Entertainment. **U:** Home. **L:** Italian. **Fin-Art:** Music--Classical, Music--Performance. **Acq:** Purchase. **Dist:** Video Artists International. $29.95.

African-American Art: Past and Present 1992
A three-volume comprehensive survey of African-American art with more than 400 visuals gathered from private collections. Covers decorative arts to 20th-century artists, including Malvin Gray Johnson, Selma Burke, David Hammons, and Archibald Motey Jr. 90m; VHS. **A:** College-Adult. **P:** Education. **U:** Institution. **Fin-Art:** Art & Artists, Black Culture. **Acq:** Purchase. **Dist:** Baker and Taylor; Knowledge Unlimited, Inc. $199.00.

African-American Artists: Affirmation Today 1994
Contains five contemporary black artists speaking about their works. 28m; VHS. **A:** Jr. High-Adult. **P:** Education. **U:** Institution, Home. **Fin-Art:** Black Culture, Art & Artists. **Acq:** Purchase. **Dist:** Crystal Productions.

African American Counseling & Psychotherapy ????
Discusses Afrocentric theory and its implication for practice, and specifics needed for treatment planning. Two-tape set. 101m; VHS. **A:** Adult. **P:** Professional. **U:** Institution. **Hea-Sci:** Psychology, Mental Health. **Acq:** Purchase. **Dist:** Microtraining Associates, Inc. $149.00.
Indiv. Titles: 1. Issues in Counseling African-American Clients 2. Managing Therapeutic Issues With African-American Clients.

African American Cultures in the U.S.A.: Part One 1992
Reviews statistical and demographic data of African Americans. 60m; VHS. **A:** Adult. **P:** Education. **U:** Institution. **Gen-Edu:** Prejudice. **Acq:** Purchase. **Dist:** RMI Media. $99.00.

African American Cultures in the U.S.A.: Part Two 1992
Examines concepts of African history and religion, such as poor academic performance and how schools perpetuate stereotypes. 60m; VHS. **A:** Adult. **P:** Education. **U:** Institution. **Gen-Edu:** Prejudice. **Acq:** Purchase. **Dist:** RMI Media. $99.00.

The African American Impact on American Life and Culture 1995
Looks at the damage prejudice can cause and how it has harmed millions of people. 20m; VHS. **A:** Jr. High-Adult. **P:** Education. **U:** Home, Institution. **Gen-Edu:** Prejudice. **Acq:** Purchase. **Dist:** Knowledge Unlimited, Inc. $59.95.

African-American Inventors 19??
Looks at minority inventors who have contributed to the fields of science, technology, and medicine. 28m; VHS. **C:** Narrated by Ossie Davis. **A:** Jr. High-Adult. **P:** Education. **U:** Institution. **Gen-Edu:** Black Culture, Inventors & Inventions, Science. **Acq:** Purchase. **Dist:** Educational Video Network. $49.95.

African American Lives 2006
Host Henry Louis Gates Jr. profiles prominent African Americans while researchers, genealogists, and DNA forensic scientists investigate their family histories and ties to Africa. 240m; DVD. **A:** Jr. High-Adult. **P:** Entertainment. **U:** Home. **Gen-Edu:** Documentary Films. **Acq:** Purchase. **Dist:** Paramount Pictures Corp.

African-American Perspectives: Conducting a Life Review Interview ????
Demonstrates a life review interview with Onawumi, who tells her stories of growing up with racism. Provides a unique understanding of racism and sexism. 80m; VHS. **A:** Adult. **P:** Professional. **U:** Institution. **Hea-Sci:** Psychology, Mental Health. **Acq:** Purchase. **Dist:** Microtraining Associates, Inc. $129.00.

African American Quilting: The Cloth Sings to Me 1995
Documentary of women quilters in the African American folk tradition. Features issues of cultural heritage and the storytelling tradition. 16m; VHS. **A:** Adult. **P:** Education. **U:** Home. **Gen-Edu:** Documentary Films, Black Culture, Women. **Acq:** Purchase, Rent/Lease. **Dist:** Filmakers Library Inc. $125.

African American Quilting: The Spirit of the Individual 199?
Documentary of fiber artists of the African American folk tradition, Michael Cummings and Peggy Hartwell. Features issues of cultural heritage and the storytelling tradition. 22m; VHS. **A:** Adult. **P:** Education. **U:** Home. **Gen-Edu:** Documentary Films, Black Culture, Crafts. **Acq:** Purchase, Rent/Lease. **Dist:** Filmakers Library Inc. $150.

The African-American Show 19??
Centers on young African-American musicians who are planning on careers as classical concert performers. Includes teacher's guide. 30m; VHS. **A:** Primary-Jr. High. **P:** Education. **U:** Institution. **Chl-Juv:** Education, Black Culture. **Acq:** Purchase. **Dist:** GPN Educational Media. $29.95.

African-American Stories Series 19??
Dr. Jackie Torrence uses her hands, face, body movements, and speech to share many favorite African-American stories from her personal collection. 90m; VHS. **A:** Preschool-Primary. **P:** Education. **U:** Institution, Home. **Chl-Juv:** Black Culture, Storytelling. **Acq:** Purchase. **Dist:** Curriculum Associates. $69.95.
Indiv. Titles: 1. Pre-K?-K 2. Primary 3. Intermediate.

African Americans in WWII: A Legacy of Patriotism and Valor 2000
African American war veterans from all branches of the military describe their personal experiences in World War II. Includes a tributes by General Colin Powell and President Bill Clinton. 60m; VHS. **A:** Family. **P:** Education. **U:** Home. **Gen-Edu:** Black Culture, History--U.S., World War Two. **Acq:** Purchase. **Dist:** OnDeck Home Entertainment. $19.95.

African-Americans: Marching to Freedom ????
ABC News anchor Peter Jennings chronicles America's journey through the civil rights movement. Topics addressed include segregation, denial of voting rights, public lynching, KKK rallies, lunch counter sit-ins, police brutality, Black Panther militancy, urban riots, and forced busing. 54m; VHS. **A:** Sr. High-Adult. **P:** Education. **U:** Institution. **Gen-Edu:** Civil Rights, Black Culture, History--U.S. **Acq:** Purchase. **Dist:** Films for the Humanities & Sciences. $89.95.

African Americans Tell Their Story 19??
Traces the history of leading black figures in America and discusses the impact that the black experience has had on the country's culture, history, and society. Includes teacher information and skill sheets. 15m; VHS. **A:** Primary-Jr. High. **P:** Education. **U:** Institution, Home. **Gen-Edu:** Black Culture, History--U.S. **Acq:** Purchase. **Dist:** Clear Vue Inc. $89.00.

African and African-American Folktales 1993
Author Donna Washington narrates three tales offering insight to African and African-American culture. One explanatory tale, a West African story, and a "Br'er Rabbit" selection. Teacher's guide included. 20m; VHS. **A:** Primary. **P:** Education. **U:** Institution. **Gen-Edu:** Animation & Cartoons, Language Arts, Black Culture. **Acq:** Purchase. **Dist:** United Learning Inc.; Rainbow Educational Media, Inc. $89.95.

African Art 19??
Teaching aid for art appreciation examines the art of the Bambana, Dogon, and Djenne people of Mali. 47m; VHS. **A:** Jr. High-College. **P:** Education. **U:** Institution. **Gen-Edu:** Art & Artists. **Acq:** Purchase. **Dist:** Crystal Productions. $29.95.

African Art & Culture 19??
Explores African art, including painting, sculpture, and crafts, to illustrate African developments and migrations. Also outlines African influences in European art. Complete with teacher's guide. 51m; VHS. **A:** Jr. High-Sr. High. **P:** Education. **U:** Institution. **Gen-Edu:** Black Culture, Art & Artists. **Acq:** Purchase. **Dist:** Cambridge Educational. $89.00.

African Art: Legacy of Oppression ????
Journalists Paul Solman and Adam Hochschild and art historian Ramona Austin discuss the collection of Central African art found at Belgium's Tervuren Museum. Topics include cultural background, stylistic comparisons, and stories as to how the treasures were obtained. 14m; VHS. **A:** Sr. High-Adult. **P:** Education. **U:** Institution. **Gen-Edu:** Africa, Art & Artists. **Acq:** Purchase. **Dist:** Films for the Humanities & Sciences. $89.95.

African Art, Women, History: The Luba People of Central Africa ????
Documents the mystery of Luba art and the relationship between women, art, and history. 28m; VHS. **A:** Sr. High-Adult. **P:** Education. **U:** Home, Institution. **Gen-Edu:** Art & Artists, Africa, Women. **Acq:** Purchase. **Dist:** Crystal Productions. $39.95.

African Carving: A Dogon Kanaga Mask 1975
The story of the Kanaga mask, used by the Dogon people of West Africa in deeply sacred rituals. Shows how the mask is carved and explains the function of the mask in Dogon society. 19m; VHS, 3/4 U. **Pr:** Film Study Center of Harvard University. **A:** Primary-Adult. **P:** Education. **U:** Institution, SURA. **Fin-Art:** Africa. **Acq:** Purchase. **Dist:** Phoenix Learning Group.

An African City: Contrasting Cultures 1970
This show portrays the dichotomies in Abidjan by two distinct areas. 11m; VHS, 3/4 U. **Pr:** Frank Gardonyi; Clifford Janoff. **A:** Jr. High-Sr. High. **P:** Education. **U:** Institution, SURA. **Gen-Edu:** Africa. **Acq:** Purchase. **Dist:** Phoenix Learning Group.

An African Community: The Masai 1969
This show illustrates the Masai's dependence on the land, their adaptation to the environment, and their family and tribal interdependence. 17m; VHS, 3/4 U. **Pr:** Frank Gardonyi; Clifford Janoff. **A:** Jr. High-Sr. High. **P:** Education. **U:** Institution, SURA. **Gen-Edu:** Anthropology. **Acq:** Purchase. **Dist:** Phoenix Learning Group.

African Craftsmen: The Ashanti 1970
The Ashanti tribesmen of West Africa are skilled in various arts. 11m; VHS, 3/4 U. **Pr:** Frank Gardonyi; Clifford Janoff. **A:** Jr. High-Sr. High. **P:** Education. **U:** Institution, SURA. **Gen-Edu:** Africa. **Acq:** Purchase. **Dist:** Phoenix Learning Group.

African Dance Workout 2003
Intermediate to advanced fitness program using African style dance moves. 56m; VHS, DVD. **A:** Adult. **P:** Instruction. **U:** Home. **Hea-Sci:** Fitness/Exercise, Dance--Instruction, How-To. **Acq:** Purchase. **Dist:** Body Be Good. $19.95.

An African Dream 1990 (PG) — ★½
A period tale about a black man and a white woman fighting against repression in South Africa. 94m; VHS. **C:** Kitty Aldridge; John Kani; Dominic Jephcott; John Carson; Richard Haines; Joy Stewart Spence; Directed by John Smallcombe. **Pr:** Hemdale Films. **A:** Preschool. **P:** Entertainment. **U:** Home. **Mov-Ent:** Africa, Civil Rights, Apartheid. **Acq:** Purchase. **Dist:** Image Entertainment Inc.; Facets Multimedia Inc. $14.95.

An African Election 2011 (Unrated) — ★★
Rather generic documentary has the Merz brothers looking at the sub-Saharan country of Ghana, which is preparing for the 2008 presidential elections. Although the country achieved independence in 1957, it's been subjected to five military regimes as well as three republics since then. The two main presidential candidates may represent leftist and right-wing parties but don't differ much politically. The most dramatic part of the film is the millions of citizens who show up at the polls on election day determined to exercise their democratic rights. English and various Ghanaian languages with subtitles. 89m; DVD. **C:** Directed by Jarreth Merz; Kevin Merz; Written by Erika Tasini; Shjun Yantara Marcacci; Cinematography by Kevin Merz; Topher Osborn; Music by Patrick Kirst. **Pr:** Jareth Merz; Cell Film Prod; Urban Republic. **A:** College-Adult. **P:** Entertainment. **U:** Home. **L:** English. **Mov-Ent:** Documentary Films, Africa, Political Campaigns. **Acq:** Purchase. **Dist:** Not Yet Released.

African Healing Dance ????
Present a high energy African dance class taught by Wyoma, lead dancer of the Damballa dance troupe. 77m; VHS. **A:** Adult. **P:** Teacher Education. **U:** Institution. **How-Ins:** Dance, Dance--Instruction. **Acq:** Purchase. **Dist:** Stagestep. $29.95.

African Horse Sickness 1960
This program discusses the causes, symptoms and treatment of African Horse Sickness. 28m; VHS. **Pr:** U.S. Government. **A:** College-Adult. **P:** Education. **U:** Home. **Hea-Sci:** Veterinary Medicine. **Acq:** Purchase. **Dist:** , On Moratorium.

African Journey 1989 — ★★★
A moving, cross-cultural drama of friendship. A young black American goes to Africa for the summer to be with his divorced father who is working in the diamond mines. There he meets a young black African like himself; they overcome cultural clashes and learn respect for one another. Beautiful scenery, filmed in Africa. Part of the "Wonderworks" series. 174m; VHS, CC. **C:** Jason Blicker; Pedzisai Sithole. **Pr:** PMV. **A:** Family. **P:** Entertainment. **U:** Home. **Mov-Ent:** Africa, Family Viewing, TV Movies. **Acq:** Purchase. **Dist:** Baker and Taylor; Home Vision Cinema; Facets Multimedia Inc. $79.95.

The African Lion Series 1990
The wilds of Africa set the backdrop for this exploration into the natural habitats of the king of beasts, elephants, birds, baboons, hippos and many more jungle dwellers. 19m; VHS, 3/4 U, EJ, Special order formats. **TV Std:** NTSC, PAL, SECAM. **Pr:** Disney Educational Productions. **A:** Primary-College. **P:** Education. **U:** Institution, CCTV, SURA. **Gen-Edu:** Wildlife, Africa. **Acq:** Purchase, Rent/Lease. **Dist:** Phoenix Learning Group. $250.00.
Indiv. Titles: 1. The African Lion and His Realm 2. Birds, Baboons and Other Animals: Their Struggle for Survival 3. Elephants and Hippos in Africa.

African Market Women Series: Fair Trade 19??
Introduces some women in Tanzania who have gone against the norm of the country and ventured into the world of business and the marketplace. 27m; VHS. **Pr:** National Film Board of Canada. **A:** Jr. High-Adult. **P:** Education. **U:** Institution. **Gen-Edu:** Black Culture, Africa, Women. **Acq:** Purchase. **Dist:** Indiana University; National Film Board of Canada.

African Market Women Series: From the Shore 19??
Tells the story of how a small group of women in the Muslim village of Shimoni, Kenya entered into the mostly male fishing

industry. 16m; VHS. **Pr:** National Film Board of Canada. **A:** Jr. High-Adult. **P:** Education. **U:** Institution. **Gen-Edu:** Black Culture, Africa, Women. **Acq:** Purchase. **Dist:** Indiana University; National Film Board of Canada.

African Market Women Series: Where Credit Is Due 19??
Explains the problems African women in East Africa have in obtaining credit and tells the story of a group of Kenyan market women who were able to obtain loans through a special credit program introduced by Women's World Banking. 28m; VHS. **Pr:** National Film Board of Canada. **A:** Jr. High-Adult. **P:** Education. **U:** Institution. **Gen-Edu:** Black Culture, Africa, Women. **Acq:** Purchase. **Dist:** Indiana University; National Film Board of Canada.

African Odyssey 1988
Scientific study of lions and brown hyenas in Botswana's Central Kalahari Game Reserve. 59m; VHS. **A:** Primary-Adult. **P:** Education. **U:** Institution. **Gen-Edu:** Animals, Documentary Films. **Acq:** Purchase. **Dist:** National Geographic Society. $50.

The African Odyssey: Red Bicycle 1971
Following the adventures of a bicycle in East Africa, this cleverly conceived program becomes an introduction to the realities of life in an underdeveloped nation, as the bicycle passes from owner to owner. 13m; VHS, 3/4 U. **Pr:** Albert Waller; Learning Corporation of America. **A:** Primary-Jr. High. **P:** Education. **U:** Institution, SURA. **Gen-Edu:** Africa. **Acq:** Purchase, Rent/Lease. **Dist:** Phoenix Learning Group.

The African Odyssey: Two Worlds of Musembe 1971
Shows the two worlds of 20th-century Africa: the modern city and the primitive village. 15m; VHS, 3/4 U. **Pr:** Albert Waller; Learning Corporation of America. **A:** Primary-Jr. High. **P:** Education. **U:** Institution, SURA. **L:** English, Spanish. **Gen-Edu:** Africa. **Acq:** Purchase, Rent/Lease. **Dist:** Phoenix Learning Group.

African Origins 19??
A look at African history from the time of the Egyptians on. 60m; VHS. **A:** Jr. High-Adult. **P:** Education. **U:** Institution, Home, SURA. **Gen-Edu:** Documentary Films, Africa, History. **Acq:** Purchase. **Dist:** African-American Images. $40.00.

African Patrol 1959
John Bentley stars as Inspector Paul Derek in two episodes of the adventure series filmed on location in Kenya. 60m; VHS. **C:** John Bentley. **A:** Jr. High-Adult. **P:** Entertainment. **U:** Home. **Mov-Ent:** Television Series, Africa. **Acq:** Purchase. **Dist:** Rex Miller Artisan Studio. $28.

The African Queen 1951 (Unrated) — ★★★★
After Bible-thumping spinster Hepburn's missionary brother is killed in WWI Africa, hard-drinking, dissolute steamer captain Bogart offers her safe passage. Not satisfied with sanctuary, she persuades him to destroy a German gunboat blocking the British advance. The two spend most of their time battling aquatic obstacles and each other, rather than the Germans. Time alone on a African river turns mistrust and aversion to love, a transition effectively counterpointed by the continuing suspense of their daring mission. Classic war of the sexes script adapted from C.S. Forester's novel makes wonderful use of natural dialogue and humor. Shot on location in Africa. 105m; VHS, DVD, Blu-Ray. **C:** Humphrey Bogart; Katharine Hepburn; Robert Morley; Theodore Bikel; Peter Bull; Walter Gotell; Peter Swanwick; Richard Marner; Directed by John Huston; Written by John Huston; James Agee; Cinematography by Jack Cardiff. **Pr:** United Artists; Horizon Romulus Productions. **A:** Family. **P:** Entertainment. **U:** Home. **L:** English, Spanish. **Mov-Ent:** Drama, World War One, Classic Films. **Awds:** Oscars '51: Actor (Bogart); AFI '98: Top 100; Natl. Film Reg. '94. **Acq:** Purchase. **Dist:** Facets Multimedia Inc.; Time-Life Video and Television; Baker and Taylor. $59.98.

African Rage 1978 — ★★
Little known release about an aging male nurse (yes, Quinn) who discovers he's dying of an incurable disease. With nothing left to lose, he plans the kidnapping of an African leader, hoping that the ransom will support his family. Meanwhile, another man is plotting the same leader's death. Decent performances help move along the improbable plot. 90m; VHS, DVD. **C:** Anthony Quinn; John Phillip Law; Simon Sabela; Ken Gampu; Marius Weyers; Sandra Prinsloo; Directed by Peter Collinson. **Pr:** Alan Girney; Heyns Films. **A:** Sr. High-Adult. **P:** Entertainment. **U:** Home. **Mov-Ent:** Mystery & Suspense, Africa. **Acq:** Purchase. **Dist:** MPI Media Group. $9.95.

An African Recovery 1988
Examines the causes of the devastating droughts and famines during the early '80s in the Niger River Valley in Africa and shows the various recovery projects that are in effect now to stop them from recurring. Lou Rawls narrates. 28m; 3/4 U. **C:** Narrated by Lou Rawls. **Pr:** Sandra Nichols; United Nations. **A:** Sr. High-Adult. **P:** Education. **U:** Institution, SURA. **Gen-Edu:** Agriculture, Africa, Ecology & Environment. **Acq:** Purchase, Rent/Lease. **Dist:** First Run/Icarus Films. $190.00.

African Religions: Zulu Zions 1978
Explores the black African response to Christianity, taking us to the Zulu Independent Churches in South Africa. From "Long Search" series. 52m; VHS, 3/4 U, Special order formats. **Pr:** British Broadcasting Corporation. **A:** Sr. High-College. **P:** Education. **U:** Institution, SURA. **Gen-Edu:** Religion. **Acq:** Purchase, Rent/Lease. **Dist:** Time-Life Video and Television.

African Shark Safari 19??
An up-close look at great white sharks. 60m; VHS. **A:** Family. **P:** Education. **U:** Home. **Gen-Edu:** Animals. **Acq:** Purchase. **Dist:** Discovery Home Entertainment. $19.95.

African Story Journey 1992
Diane Ferlatte dramatically recounts classic African folktales set in Africa and the Caribbean, and more modern stories set in the American South and urban ghettos. Delightful blend of lush scenery and spirited music combine for a fine performance. 20m; VHS. **A:** Primary-Adult. **P:** Entertainment. **U:** Institution. **Mov-Ent:** Folklore & Legends, Africa, Black Culture. **Acq:** Purchase. **Dist:** Clear Vue Inc. $275.00.
Indiv. Titles: 1. Across Time and Place 2. The American South.

African Story Magic 1992
A young boy finds the roots of African folklore on a magical journey that takes him from his inner-city streets. 27m; VHS. **C:** Narrated by Brock Peters. **A:** Primary. **P:** Entertainment. **U:** Home. **Chl-Juv:** Children, Black Culture, Folklore & Legends. **Acq:** Purchase. **Dist:** Lions Gate Television Corp.; Fast Forward. $12.98.

African Story Telling 1988
This program shows teachers of elementary age students how to use story telling as an educational tool. 60m; VHS, 3/4 U. **Pr:** Michigan State University. **A:** Adult. **P:** Teacher Education. **U:** Institution, CCTV. **Gen-Edu:** Education, Storytelling. **Acq:** Purchase, Rent/Lease. **Dist:** Michigan State University.

African Treasure 1952 — ★½
Bomba is summoned by jungle drum telegraph when two geologists turn out to actually be diamond smugglers. They're forcing the local tribe to get the gems for them and Bomba must defeat the villains in the 7th film in the Monogram series. 70m/B/W; DVD. **C:** John(ny) Sheffield; Laurette Luez; Lyle Talbot; Lane Bradford; Arthur Space; Leonard Mudie; Directed by Ford Beebe; Written by Ford Beebe; Cinematography by Harry Neumann; Music by Raoul Kraushaar. **A:** Family. **P:** Entertainment. **U:** Home. **L:** English. **Mov-Ent:** Action-Adventure, Africa. **Acq:** Purchase. **Dist:** WarnerArchive.com.

The African Village Life Series 1968
This series of programs focuses on specific regions and records objectively the lives of African people. Each part is available individually. Non-narrative. 12m; 3/4 U, Special order formats. **Pr:** International Film Foundation. **A:** Primary-Adult. **P:** Education. **U:** Institution, SURA. **Gen-Edu:** Anthropology, Africa. **Acq:** Purchase, Rent/Lease. **Dist:** International Film Foundation.
Indiv. Titles: 1. Bozo Daily Life 2. Building a Boat 3. Building a House 4. Fishing on the Niger 5. Masked Dances 6. Onion Farming 7. Annual Festival of the Dead 8. Cotton Growing and Spinning 9. Divination by Animal Tracks 10. Divination by Chicken 11. Herding Cattle 12. Hunting Wild Doves.

African Wildlife 19??
Looks at the wondrous variety of wild animals that make the African continent their home. 59m; VHS, 3/4 U; Closed Captioned. **A:** Primary-Adult. **P:** Education. **U:** Institution. **Gen-Edu:** Africa, Wildlife. **Acq:** Purchase. **Dist:** National Geographic Society. $39.95.

The Africans 1986
Examines the history and culture of Africa, from the time of the pharaohs to the modern struggle against apartheid in South Africa. 60m; VHS, 3/4 U. **C:** Dr. Ali Mazrui. **Pr:** WETA; British Broadcasting Corporation. **A:** College. **P:** Education. **U:** Institution, CCTV, CATV, SURA. **Gen-Edu:** Africa, Black Culture. **Acq:** Purchase, Rent/Lease, Free Loan, Duplication. **Dist:** Annenberg Media. $250.00.
Indiv. Titles: 1. The Nature of the Continent 2. A Legacy of Lifestyles 3. New Gods 4. Tools of Exploitation 5. New Conflicts 6. In Search of Stability 7. A Garden of Eden in Decay? 8. A Clash of Cultures 9. Global Africa.

Africans in America: America's Journey Through Slavery 1998
Music, imagery, and narratives tell of slavery's growth from 1450 to 1750, the days of being born half-free, abolition in the South and white racism in the North. Four-volume set recommended for Grades 7 and up. 90m; VHS, DVD; Closed Captioned. **A:** Jr. High-Sr. High. **P:** Education. **U:** Institution. **Gen-Edu:** History--U.S., Civil War, Slavery. **Acq:** Purchase. **Dist:** Social Studies School Service; Zenger Media. $59.95.
Indiv. Titles: 1. The Terrible Transformation 2. Revolution 3. Brotherly Love 4. Judgment Day.

Africa's Cats: Fight for Life 1992
The beauty and power of these great predatory animals is revealed in a trip to the Masai Mara Game Reserve. 48m; VHS. **C:** Hosted by Bryan Brown. **Pr:** ESPN. **A:** Family. **P:** Entertainment. **U:** Home. **Gen-Edu:** Animals, Africa. **Acq:** Purchase. **Dist:** Fast Forward.

Africa's Lost Eden 2010 (Unrated)
A area of Mozambique just 1,500 square miles in size that forms the Gorongosa National Park was once one of the most fertile animal habitats in the world, but years of violent civil war have all but wiped out many of the species that live there. Today, scientists are attempting to return the area to its former state by relocating large numbers of animals there. 50m; DVD, Blu-Ray. **A:** Family. **P:** Education. **U:** Institution, Home. **Mov-Ent:** Documentary Films, Africa, Wildlife. **Acq:** Purchase. **Dist:** National Geographic Society. $32.95.

Africa's Poaching Wars 1991
Although the elephant and the rhinocerous rapidly approach extinction, they are still ruthlessly hunted by poachers for their ivory, skin, and meat. Witness the struggle to save the elephants in Kenya and Zimbabwe with hosts Peggy Fleming and Jim Fowler. Part of the "Mutual of Omaha's Spirit of Adventure" series. 60m; VHS. **C:** Hosted by Jim Fowler. **A:** Family. **P:** Education. **U:** Home. **Gen-Edu:** Documentary Films, Africa, Wildlife. **Acq:** Purchase. **Dist:** MPI Media Group. $19.98.

Africa's Stolen River 19??
Tells the complex story surrounding Africa's stolen river. 59m; VHS, 3/4 U; Closed Captioned. **A:** Primary-Adult. **P:** Education. **U:** Institution. **Gen-Edu:** Africa, Wilderness Areas. **Acq:** Purchase. **Dist:** National Geographic Society. $39.95.

Africa's Wildlife: Elephants 2007 (Unrated)
Two episodes examining the lives and habits of Africa's elephants. "Survivors of the Skeleton Coast" focuses on the elephants of the Namib Desert and how they have acclimated to life in this merciless environment. "Elephant" offers an informative look at the lives of these amazingly intelligent animals and the difficulties they face for future survival. 111m; DVD. **A:** Family. **P:** Education. **U:** Institution, Home. **Mov-Ent:** Documentary Films, Africa, Animals. **Acq:** Purchase. **Dist:** National Geographic Society. $24.95.

Africa's Wildlife: Endangered Species 2007 (Unrated)
Two episodes featuring more of Africa's amazing wildlife. In "Wildlife Warriors," join soldiers as they track poachers who kill and mutilate animals for ivory, while "African Wildlife" provides rare footage of everyday animal life. 111m; DVD. **A:** Family. **P:** Education. **U:** Institution, Home. **Mov-Ent:** Documentary Films, Animals, Africa. **Acq:** Purchase. **Dist:** National Geographic Society. $24.95.

Africa's Wildlife: Gorillas & Great Apes 2007 (Unrated)
Two informative films showcasing Africa's primates. "Gorilla" takes an in-depth look at central Africa's rare mountain gorilla. Portrayed incorrectly as aggressive and violent in Hollywood films, the huge animals are actually gentle, timid, and very clever. "Search for the Great Apes" examines the work of scientists Dian Fossey and Birute Galdikas-Brindamour as they study the gorilla and orangutan and their unique connection to humans. 109m; DVD. **A:** Family. **P:** Education. **U:** Institution, Home. **Mov-Ent:** Documentary Films, Africa, Wildlife. **Acq:** Purchase. **Dist:** National Geographic Society. $24.95.

Africa's Wildlife: Lions 2007 (Unrated)
Travel to Africa with National Geographic to once again study the wildlife unique to this continent. In "Lions of Darkness," filmmakers document a pride of lions in Botswana as its leader is violently removed, while "Walking with Lions" takes viewers to Zimbabwe for a look at the lives of lions during the African dry season as thousands gather at a single watering-hole. 123m; DVD. **A:** Family. **P:** Education. **U:** Institution, Home. **Mov-Ent:** Documentary Films, Africa, Animals. **Acq:** Purchase. **Dist:** National Geographic Society. $24.95.

Africa's Wildlife: Predators & Hunters 2007 (Unrated)
Two unique films involving different aspects of Africa's circle of life. "Beauty and the Beasts: A Leopard's Story" offers detailed footage of the life and death battle between the leopard and its prey, the warthog. "Wings Over the Serengeti" explains the purpose of vultures and other scavengers as they clean up the waste left lying across the desert. 114m; DVD. **A:** Family. **P:** Education. **U:** Institution, Home. **Mov-Ent:** Documentary Films, Africa, Animals. **Acq:** Purchase. **Dist:** National Geographic Society. $24.95.

Africa's Wildlife: Zebras and Rhinos 2007 (Unrated)
A visually spectacular look at two of Africa's most recognized native animals. "Zebra's: Patterns in the Grass" examines the life and habits of the zebra, from its first newborn moments to its annual migration in Botswana. "The Rhino War" investigates the black rhino's near extinction due to poachers' hunt for rhino horns during the 1970s and 1980s, as well as the efforts being made to save them now. 100m; DVD. **A:** Family. **P:** Education. **U:** Institution, Home. **Mov-Ent:** Documentary Films, Animals, Wildlife. **Acq:** Purchase. **Dist:** National Geographic Society. $24.95.

Afrika Bambaataa & Family: Electric Dance Hop 1991
Afrika Bambaataa and Grandmaster Flash explore the music that inspired the rap music of today. Songs include, "Planet Rock," "Street Happiness," "Free South Africa" and many more. 45m; VHS. **Pr:** MPI Media Group. **A:** Jr. High-Adult. **P:** Entertainment. **U:** Home. **Mov-Ent:** Music--Performance, Music--Rap. **Acq:** Purchase. **Dist:** Music Video Distributors; MPI Media Group. $9.95.

The Afrika Korps 1942
This taped collection of Nazi newsreels filmed from February through November 1942 shows the German Army attacking North Africa. In German with English subtitles. 81m/B/W; VHS, 3/4 U. **TV Std:** NTSC, PAL. **Pr:** International Historic Films Inc. **A:** Jr. High-Adult. **P:** Education. **U:** Home. **L:** German. **Gen-Edu:** Documentary Films, World War Two, Germany. **Acq:** Purchase. **Dist:** International Historic Films Inc.; German Language Video Center. $39.95.

The Afrikaner Experience: Politics of Exclusion 1978
This documentary traces the history of the Afrikaners from the early days when they fought off attacks from behind their covered wagons (laagers) to today's apartheid legislation. Edited from "South Africa: The White Laager." 35m; VHS, 3/4 U. **Pr:** United Nations Television. **A:** Jr. High-College. **P:** Education. **U:** Institution, SURA. **Gen-Edu:** Africa. **Acq:** Purchase, Rent/Lease. **Dist:** Phoenix Learning Group.

Afrique, Je Te Plumerai 1992
Documentary essay moving from present to past traces 100 years of cultural genocide in Africa as three European powers colonize the indigenous culture of Cameroon. Once a Sho-mon speaking people, 30 years into its independence Cameroon

must work toward reclaiming its intellectual and artistic culture, suppressed by the European influences still evident today. In French with English subtitles. 88m; VHS, 3/4 U. **C:** Directed by Jean-Marie Teno. **Pr:** Jean-Marie Teno. **A:** College-Adult. **P:** Education. **U:** Institution. **L:** French, English. **Gen-Edu:** Documentary Films, Africa, History--Modern. **Acq:** Purchase, Rent/Lease. **Dist:** California Newsreel. $195.00.

Afrita Hanem 1950
A poor singer/actor gets three wishes from a genie and uses them to woo his girlfriend away from a rich suitor. With English or French subtitles. 111m; DVD. **A:** Sr. High-Adult. **P:** Entertainment. **U:** Home, Institution. **L:** Arabic. **Mov-Ent:** Fantasy, Musical. **Acq:** Purchase, Rent/Lease. **Dist:** Arab Film Distribution. $29.99.

Afrita Hanen 1947 (Unrated)
A rare Egyptian fantasy starring the famous Mid-Eastern actor, Farrid El Atrache. In Arabic with titles. 97m/B/W; VHS. **C:** Farrid El Atrache. **Pr:** Egyptian. **A:** Family. **P:** Entertainment. **U:** Home. **L:** Arabic. **Mov-Ent:** Fantasy. **Acq:** Purchase. **Dist:** Facets Multimedia Inc. $39.95.

Afro-American History Series 1972
Black Americans' struggle for identity and equality are explored. 10m; VHS, 3/4 U. **Pr:** Encyclopedia Britannica Educational Corporation. **A:** Jr. High-Sr. High. **P:** Education. **U:** Institution, SURA. **Gen-Edu:** History--U.S. **Acq:** Purchase, Rent/Lease, Trade-in. **Dist:** Encyclopedia Britannica.
Indiv. Titles: 1. Africa: Historical Heritage 2. Benjamin Benneker: Man of Science 3. Black People in the Slave South, 1850 4. Fredrick Douglas.

Afro-American Music, Its Heritage 1972
Represents 250 years of Black music, from the talking drums of West Africa to contemporary rhythm and blues, and gospel. 16m; VHS, 3/4 U, EJ. **C:** Duke Ellington; George Gershwin; Louis Armstrong; Stephen Foster; W.C. Handy. **Pr:** Communications Group West. **A:** Primary-College. **P:** Education. **U:** Institution, CCTV, SURA. **Gen-Edu:** Music--Jazz. **Acq:** Purchase, Rent/Lease. **Dist:** Communications West.

Afro-American Perspectives 1979
"Afro-American Perspectives" presents a college credit course combining televised lessons, on-campus seminars, and related work assignments. Focuses on the black American: the heritage and the struggles as one component in a complex society. 30m; VHS, 3/4 U. **Pr:** Maryland State Department of Education. **A:** College-Adult. **P:** Education. **U:** Institution, CCTV, CATV, BCTV. **Gen-Edu:** Minorities. **Acq:** Purchase, Rent/Lease. **Dist:** Maryland Public Television.
Indiv. Titles: 1. Why African Heritage 2. African Historiography 3. Africans in Antiquity 4. Facets of West African History 5. Facets of West African Culture 6. Color and Race 7. Racism, How Pervasive Is It? 8. Early Protest 9. Middle Protest 10. Modern Protest 11. Black Role Models 12. The Black Family 13. Black Organizations 14. Black Urban Community 15. The Black Church 16. The Black Press 17. Black Colleges and Universities 18. Music and Dance 19. Art, Architecture and Style 20. Literature 21. Language 22. Theatre, Opera, The Concert Stage 23. Light Stage, Cinema, Radio, TV 24. The Economics of Being Black 25. Health 26. Education 27. Black Society 28. Politics 29. Awareness, Feeling and Behavior 30. The Future.

Afro-Caribbean Festival 1983
Dance troupes from Africa, Puerto Rico, Haiti, and the Dominican Republic perform in this dance extravaganza. 90m; VHS, 3/4 U. **Pr:** Luis Alonso. **A:** Sr. High-Adult. **P:** Entertainment. **U:** Institution. **Fin-Art:** Caribbean, Dance. **Acq:** Purchase, Rent/Lease. **Dist:** New Jersey Network.

Afro-Caribbean Step: Not the Same Old Step ????
Workout program that combines African dance with traditional step choreography. 56m; VHS. **A:** Adult. **P:** Instruction. **U:** Home. **Hea-Sci:** Fitness/Exercise. **Acq:** Purchase. **Dist:** Body Be Good. $19.95.

Afro-punk 2003 (Unrated)
Investigates relations between races in the punk scene, a primarily white community, through the lives of four individuals dedicated to the punk rock lifestyle. Features performances by Bad Brains, Tamar Kali, Cipher, and Ten Grand plus interviews with players from Fishbone, 247-spyz, Dead Kennedys, Candiria, Orange 9mm, and TV on the Radio. 66m; DVD. **A:** Adult. **P:** Education. **U:** Institution. **Gen-Edu:** Black Culture, Music--Pop/Rock. **Acq:** Purchase. **Dist:** Third World Newsreel. $275.

Afro Samurai 2006
Afro Samurai (voiced by Samuel L. Jackson) spends his life working to avenge the death of his father, who was beheaded by the number-one fighter in the world, known as Justice. During his quest to earn the rank of number-two fighter, worthy to challenge the top contender, he battles bounty hunters, bar thugs, and fanatical monks. Director's Cut edition has 15 minutes of extra action and is more graphic than the edited version. 87m; DVD. **C:** Voice(s) by Samuel L. Jackson; Ron Perlman; Kelly Hu; Jeff Glenn Bennett; Steven Jay Blum. **A:** Adult. **P:** Entertainment. **U:** Home. **Mov-Ent:** Action-Adventure, Animation & Cartoons, Fantasy. **Acq:** Purchase. **Dist:** FUNimation Entertainment.

Afro Samurai: Resurrection 2004 (Unrated)
Spike TV adult animated drama. The legendary Afro Samurai if forced out of his life of solitude by an alluring and deadly woman from his past. Sio seeks vengence for her brother Jinno almost being killed, so she has Professor Dharman recreate Afro's father from a jawbone they stole from his grave. 95m; DVD. **A:** Adult. **P:** Entertainment. **U:** Home. **Mov-Ent:** Animation & Cartoons, Drama. **Acq:** Purchase. **Dist:** FUNimation Entertainment. $29.98.

Afro@digital 2003
Documentary exploring the impact of digital technologies on modern African life. In English, French, Jula, and Yoruba with English subtitles. 52m; VHS, DVD. **A:** Sr. High-Adult. **P:** Education. **U:** Home, Institution. **L:** English, French. **Gen-Edu:** Documentary Films, Africa, Computers. **Acq:** Purchase. **Dist:** California Newsreel. $26.95.

After 9.11: New Politics & the Left 2002
Discussions at the 20th Socialist Scholars Conference in New York regarding the state of the Left following 9.11 such as reparations to the war on terror and the need for continued resistance. 35m; VHS. **A:** Adult. **P:** Education. **U:** Institution. **Gen-Edu:** Politics & Government, World Affairs. **Acq:** Purchase. **Dist:** Third World Newsreel. $65.00.

After a Suicide 1996
Filmmaker chronicles the reasons for her mother's suicide and for her own failed attmept. Provides support and identification for survivors of suicide. Also encourages one to communicate feelings in order to avoid such harmful actions. 12m; VHS. **A:** Sr. High-Adult. **P:** Education. **U:** Institution. **Gen-Edu:** Documentary Films, Suicide, Mental Health. **Acq:** Purchase, Rent/Lease. **Dist:** Filmakers Library Inc. $150.00.

After All, You're the Supervisor! 1979
A look at the duties and responsibilities of a supervisor, and what it takes to be effective in that position. A leader's guide is included. 18m; VHS, 3/4 U. **Pr:** Roundtable Films. **A:** College-Adult. **P:** Professional. **U:** Institution. **Bus-Ind:** Business, Management, Organizations. **Acq:** Purchase, Rent/Lease. **Dist:** Excellence in Training Corp. $700.00.

After Auschwitz: Battle for the Holocaust 2001
Controversial documentary about the Holocaust, and how it has shaped contemporary politics in the Middle East. 50m; VHS, DVD. **A:** Sr. High-Adult. **P:** Education. **U:** Institution. **Gen-Edu:** Holocaust, Middle East, Documentary Films. **Acq:** Purchase, Rent/Lease. **Dist:** The Cinema Guild. $275.00.

After Childbirth 1979
This program explores many important questions new mothers might have regarding the first weeks following childbirth, including mental and physical adjustment. 14m; VHS, 3/4 U, CV. **Pr:** Professional Research. **A:** Sr. High-Adult. **P:** Education. **U:** Institution, CCTV. **Hea-Sci:** Childbirth. **Acq:** Purchase, Rent/Lease. **Dist:** Discovery Education.

After Childbirth: The Post-Partum Experience 1987
A look at the physical and emotional adjustments mothers must make immediately after birth. 14m; VHS, 3/4 U. **Pr:** Professional Research. **A:** Adult. **P:** Education. **U:** Institution, CCTV, SURA. **L:** English, Spanish. **Hea-Sci:** Childbirth. **Acq:** Purchase, Rent/Lease. **Dist:** Discovery Education. $295.00.

After Dark 1976
Displays the meaning of courage in a child's life. Theme: courage is not the denial of fear, it is the strength to face one's fears and proceed to live fully. 12m; VHS, 3/4 U, Special order formats. **Pr:** Paulist Productions. **A:** Primary. **P:** Religious. **U:** Institution, CCTV, SURA. **Chl-Juv:** Psychology. **Acq:** Purchase, Rent/Lease. **Dist:** Paulist Productions.

After Dark, My Sweet 1990 (R) — ★★★
A troubled young man in search of a little truth ends up entangled in a kidnapping scheme. Muddled direction is overcome by above average performances and gritty realism. Based on the novel by Jim Thompson. 114m; VHS, DVD, Wide, CC. **C:** Jason Patric; Rachel Ward; Bruce Dern; George Dickerson; James Cotton; Corey Carrier; Directed by James Foley; Written by Robert Redlin; James Foley; Cinematography by Mark Plummer; Music by Maurice Jarre. **Pr:** Avenue Pictures. **A:** Adult. **P:** Entertainment. **U:** Home. **Mov-Ent:** Mystery & Suspense, Romance. **Acq:** Purchase. **Dist:** Lions Gate Television Corp. $89.95.

After Darkness 1985 — ★
Slow-moving psycho-suspenser about a man obsessed with trying to remedy his twin brother's schizophrenia. 104m; VHS. **C:** John Hurt; Julian Sands; Victoria Abril; Pamela Salem; Directed by Dominique Othenin-Girard. **Pr:** T&C Film Ltd. **A:** Sr. High-Adult. **P:** Entertainment. **U:** Home. **Mov-Ent:** Mystery & Suspense. **Acq:** Purchase. **Dist:** $19.95.

After Death 2000
Doctors share stories and persona experiences of after life communications. 10m; VHS, DVD. **A:** Adult. **P:** Professional. **U:** Institution. **Hea-Sci:** Death, Patient Care. **Acq:** Purchase. **Dist:** Aquarius Health Care Media. $99.00.

After Death Communication 1998
Host John J. Edward reveals his philosophy of communicating with departed loved ones. He shares excerpts from some of his readings and offers evidence that those that have passed away are happy and bring us inner peace and hope ?m; VHS. **A:** Sr. High-Adult. **P:** Education. **U:** Home. **Gen-Edu:** New Age, Occult Sciences. **Acq:** Purchase. **Dist:** Tapeworm Video Distributors Inc. $24.95.

After Discharge Services 1988
Ways of caring for a patient in his home are demonstrated. 11m; VHS, 3/4 U. **Pr:** Professional Research. **A:** Sr. High-Adult. **P:** Professional. **U:** Institution, CCTV, SURA. **Hea-Sci:** Patient Care. **Acq:** Purchase, Rent/Lease. **Dist:** Discovery Education. $295.00.

After Earth 2013 (PG-13) — ★
In this sci-fi blockbuster, Kitai Raige (Jaden Smith) and his legendary Ranger father Cypher (Will Smith) crash-land on a futuristic Earth that has been unable to sustain human life for centuries. With both of his legs broken, the elder Raige can only monitor and advise his adolescent son as he treks across the inhospitable planet in search of the other half of their ship, the one with the homing beacon...and the deadly alien creature. With more silly motivational nuggets ("Fear is a choice") than a midnight infomercial, the script for the pic is depressingly slight and the performances are stunningly ineffective. 100m; DVD, Blu-Ray. **C:** Jaden Smith; Will Smith; Sophie Okonedo; Zoe Kravitz; Glenn Morshower; David Denham; Directed by M. Night Shyamalan; Written by M. Night Shyamalan; Gary Whitta; Cinematography by Peter Suschitzky; Music by James Newton Howard. **Pr:** Will Smith; Sony Pictures Entertainment Inc. **A:** Jr. High-Adult. **P:** Entertainment. **U:** Home. **L:** English. **Mov-Ent:** Science Fiction, Family. **Awds:** Golden Raspberries '13: Worst Actor (Smith), Worst Ensemble Cast, Worst Support. Actor (Smith). **Acq:** Purchase. **Dist:** Sony Pictures Home Entertainment Inc.

After Fall, Winter 2011 (Unrated) — **Bomb!**
And after yawning, boredom. Schaeffer's broke, self-pitying writer Michael Shiver moves to Paris and meets younger beauty, Sophie (Brochere), who inexplicably gets involved with him. She works as both a hospice nurse and a dominatrix while keeping the latter info from Michael. Too bad, since he's a closet masochist. Eventually, this all results in a cringe-inducing ending (if you've made it that far). The second part of Schaefer's projected film quartet, following 1997's "Fall." English and French with subtitles. 131m; DVD. **C:** Eric Schaeffer; Lizzie Brochere; Directed by Eric Schaeffer; Written by Eric Schaeffer; Cinematography by Zoran Veljkovic; Music by Matthew Puckett. **A:** Adult. **P:** Entertainment. **U:** Home. **L:** English, French. **Mov-Ent:** Sex & Sexuality. **Acq:** Purchase. **Dist:** Kino on Video.

After Goodbye: An AIDS Story 19??
Tells a compelling story of love and loss, grief and healing, and the resilience of the human heart while exploring the world of AIDS. 60m; VHS. **C:** Narrated by Ruby Dee. **Pr:** KERA Dallas. **A:** Jr. High-Adult. **P:** Education. **U:** Home. **Gen-Edu:** Documentary Films, AIDS. **Acq:** Purchase. **Dist:** KERA. $19.95.

After Hours 1984
A docu-drama on sexual harassment in the work place. Award-winning director Jane Campion's short piece raises important questions about discrimination, sexual harassment, gender relations, and the interpretation of events. 26m; VHS, 3/4 U. **C:** Directed by Jane Campion. **Pr:** Women in Focus. **A:** Sr. High-Adult. **P:** Education. **U:** Institution, SURA. **Gen-Edu:** Women. **Acq:** Purchase, Rent/Lease. **Dist:** Women Make Movies.

After Hours 1985 (R) — ★★★½
An absurd, edgy black comedy that's filled with novel twists and turns and often more disturbing than funny. An isolated uptown New York yuppie (Dunne) takes a late night stroll downtown and meets a sexy woman in an all-night coffee shop. From there he wanders through a series of threatening and surreal misadventures, leading to his pursuit by a vigilante mob stirred by ice cream dealer O'Hara. Something like "Blue Velvet" with more Catholicism and farce. Or similar to "Something Wild" without the high school reunion. Great cameos from the large supporting cast, including Cheech and Chong as burglars. A dark view of a small hell-hole in the Big Apple. 97m; VHS, DVD, Wide, CC. **C:** Griffin Dunne; Rosanna Arquette; John Heard; Teri Garr; Catherine O'Hara; Verna Bloom; Linda Fiorentino; Dick Miller; Bronson Pinchot; Will Patton; Rockets Redglare; Rocco Sisto; Larry Block; Victor Argo; Cameo(s) Richard "Cheech" Marin; Thomas Chong; Martin Scorsese; Directed by Martin Scorsese; Written by Joe Minion; Cinematography by Michael Ballhaus; Music by Howard Shore. **Pr:** Geffen Film Company. **A:** Sr. High-Adult. **P:** Entertainment. **U:** Home. **Mov-Ent:** Comedy--Black. **Awds:** Cannes '86: Director (Scorsese); Ind. Spirit '86: Director (Scorsese), Film. **Acq:** Purchase. **Dist:** Warner Home Video, Inc. $19.98.

After Hours: Coleman Hawkins & Roy Eldridge 198?
Roy Eldridge, Coleman Hawkins, and other jazz stars perform "Lover Man," "Taking a Chance on Love," "Sunday," and "Just You, Just Me." 27m/B/W; VHS. **C:** Directed by Shepherd Traube. **A:** Sr. High-Adult. **P:** Entertainment. **U:** Home. **Fin-Art:** Performing Arts, Music--Jazz, Black Culture. **Acq:** Purchase. **Dist:** Music Video Distributors; Rhapsody Films, Inc.; Facets Multimedia Inc. $24.95.

After Innocence 2005 (Unrated) — ★★★
Sanders exposes the cracks in the criminal justice system by examining the cases of seven men—four white and three black—who were convicted on murder and rape charges. Eventually, after spending many years in prison, each was exonerated because of DNA evidence. Also examined are the roadblocks thrown up by authorities who don't want to admit to mistakes, the question of compensation after wrongful imprisonment, and life after release. Documentary was made in collaboration with the nonprofit legal clinic, the Innocence Project, now expanded into the Innocence Network. Since its founding in 1992 more than 160 people have been exonerated through DNA testing. 95m; DVD. **C:** Directed by Jessica Sanders; Written by Jessica Sanders; Marc H. Simon; Cinematography by Buddy Squires; Shana Hagan; Music by Charles Bernstein. **A:** Sr. High-Adult. **P:** Entertainment. **U:** Home. **L:** English. **Mov-Ent:** Documentary Films, Law, Science. **Acq:** Purchase. **Dist:** New Yorker Video.

After Julius 1978 (Unrated) — ★★
Twenty years after Julius Grace's death, his memory still hovers over his wife's and daughters' lives. British soap opera moves with glacier-like speed. Adapted from the book by Elizabeth Jane Howard. 150m; VHS. **C:** Faith Brook; John Carson; Cyd Hayman; Directed by John Glenister. **A:** Adult. **P:** Entertainment. **U:** Home. **Mov-Ent:** Drama, Family. **Acq:** Purchase. **Dist:** No Longer Available.

After Kony: Staging Hope 2011 (Unrated)
Chronicles an effort to assist teenagers who were child soldiers or sex slaves used by Joseph Kony and his Lord's Resistance Army in Uganda by telling their stories through theater. 99m; DVD. **A:** Sr. High-Adult. **P:** Entertainment. **U:** Home. **Mov-Ent:** Theater, Documentary Films, Africa. **Acq:** Purchase. **Dist:** First Run Features. $24.95.

After Life 1998 (Unrated) — ★★
A drab office building turns out to be a metaphysical doorway and those who pass through are the recently deceased. Each person is assigned a caseworker and told that they have three days to decide on one particular memory to take with them into the after life. If they cannot chose, they will be forced to remain in the limbo of the processing center until they can do so. Japanese with subtitles. 118m; VHS, DVD. **C:** Taketoshi Naito; Susumu Terajima; Arata; Erika Oda; Takashi Naito; Hisako Hara; Directed by Hirokazu Kore-eda; Written by Hirokazu Kore-eda; Cinematography by Yutaka Yamazaki; Masayoshi Sukita; Music by Yasuhiro Kasamatsu. **A:** College-Adult. **P:** Entertainment. **U:** Home. **L:** Japanese. **Mov-Ent:** Death. **Acq:** Purchase. **Dist:** New Yorker Video.

After Matisse 1979
Eight American artists exhibit their own works at the Museum of Modern Art and explain the influence that the master Matisse has on their efforts. 30m; VHS, 3/4 U. **Pr:** WNET New York. **A:** Sr. High-Adult. **P:** Education. **U:** Institution, CCTV, Home. **Fin-Art:** Art & Artists. **Acq:** Purchase, Rent/Lease. **Dist:** WNET/ Thirteen Non-Broadcast.

After Mein Kampf: The Story of Adolf Hitler 1942
This combination of newsreel footage and re-creations presents the life story of Hitler, made by the British as a propaganda movie during the early months of WWII. 43m/B/W; VHS, 3/4 U. **TV Std:** NTSC, PAL. **Pr:** British Lion. **A:** Sr. High-Adult. **P:** Education. **U:** Home. **Gen-Edu:** Propaganda, World War Two, Germany. **Acq:** Purchase. **Dist:** International Historic Films Inc.; German Language Video Center. $24.95.

After Midnight 1933 — ★
An aspiring playwright tries to get his work produced, only to meet with dead ends. Eventually, he hooks up with a talented young actress with whom he finds romance and success. 69m/ B/W; VHS, CC. **C:** Alan Dinehart; Anita Page; Allen Vincent; Gertrude Astor; Directed by Richard Thorpe. **Pr:** Chesterfield Motion Picture Corporation; First Division. **A:** Jr. High-Adult. **P:** Entertainment. **U:** Home. **Mov-Ent:** Drama, Theater. **Acq:** Purchase. **Dist:** Sinister Cinema. $16.95.

After Midnight 1989 (R) — ★★
Suspended in a central story about an unorthodox professor who preys upon the deepest fears of his students, a trio of terror tales come to life. From the writers of "The Fly II" and "Nightmare on Elm Street 4." Some chills, few thrills. 90m; VHS, DVD, CC. **C:** Marg Helgenberger; Marc McClure; Alan Rosenberg; Pamela Segall; Nadine Van Der Velde; Ramy Zada; Jillian McWhirter; Billy Ray Sharkey; Judie Aronson; Tracy Wells; Ed Monaghan; Monique Salcido; Penelope Sudrow; Directed by Jim Wheat; Ken Wheat; Written by Jim Wheat; Ken Wheat; Music by Marc Donahue. **Pr:** High Bar Pictures. **A:** College-Adult. **P:** Entertainment. **U:** Home. **Mov-Ent:** Horror, Mystery & Suspense. **Acq:** Purchase. **Dist:** MGM Home Entertainment. $89.98.

After Midnight 2004 (Unrated) — ★★
Quiet Martino lives a simple life as the night watchman for the National Museum of Cinema at the Mole Antonelliana in Turin, Italy, with the film aficionado spending his spare time dabbling on a pieced-together project of the city's history on film. But the entrance of eye-catching Amanda—on the lam from the police for scalding her boss with hot cooking fat—changes all that, especially once she's cleared of the charges and free to return to her car-thief boyfriend. The romantic triangle, in the end, doesn't offer much sizzle. In Italian, with English subtitles. 99m. **C:** Giorgio Pasotti; Silvio Orlando; Francesca Inaudi; Fabio Troiano; Francesca Picozza; Directed by Davide Ferrario; Written by Davide Ferrario; Music by Banda Ionica; Daniele Sepe; Fabio Barovero. **Pr:** Davide Ferrario; Davide Ferrario; Rossofuoco. **P:** Entertainment. **U:** Home. **L:** Italian. **Mov-Ent:** Comedy--Romantic, Italy.

After Mr. Sam 1974
A record of a major corporation's top level conference held to select a successor to the company's retiring president. From the "Corporation" series. 78m/B/W; VHS, 3/4 U. **Pr:** National Film Board of Canada. **A:** Sr. High-Adult. **P:** Education. **U:** Institution, SURA. **Gen-Edu:** Business. **Acq:** Purchase, Rent/Lease. **Dist:** National Film Board of Canada.

After Modernism: The Dilemma of Influence 1992
Explores the dismantling of the modernist myth as the central issue in the world of contemporary art and art criticism. 58m; VHS. **Pr:** Michael Blackwood Productions. **A:** College-Adult. **P:** Education. **U:** Home, Institution. **Gen-Edu:** Art & Artists. **Acq:** Purchase, Rent/Lease. **Dist:** Michael Blackwood Productions.

After Office Hours 1935 — ★
The title's provocative but this rom com is standard 30s fare enlivened by the beautiful Bennett. New York newspaper editor Jim (Gable) sneers at society gal Sharon (Bennett) until he realizes she has the in to stories on the rich and scandalous. They bicker their way to romance until they wind up on opposites sides of a murder involving a society wife. 72m/B/W; DVD. **C:** Clark Gable; Constance Bennett; Stuart Erwin; Billie Burke; Harvey Stephens; Katherine Alexander; Hale Hamilton; Directed by Robert Z. Leonard; Written by Herman J. Mankiewicz; Cinematography by Charles Rosher. **A:** Adult. **P:** Entertainment. **U:** Home. **L:** English. **Mov-Ent:** Comedy--Romantic, Journalism. **Acq:** Purchase. **Dist:** WarnerArchive.com.

After Our Baby Died 1975
This program discusses how health professionals can contribute to allaying the parents' fears, guilt and despair from the loss of their child to Sudden Infant Death Syndrome. 20m; VHS, 3/4 U, Special order formats. **Pr:** Bureau of Community Health Services. **A:** College-Adult. **P:** Education. **U:** Institution, SURA. **Hea-Sci:** Death, Infants. **Acq:** Purchase. **Dist:** National Audiovisual Center.

After Pilkington 1988 — ★★
Thriller about an uptight Oxford professor who runs into his bewitching childhood sweetheart after many years. She persuades him to help search for a missing archaeologist. 100m; VHS, CC. **C:** Bob Peck; Miranda Richardson; Barry Foster; Directed by Christopher Morahan. **Pr:** British Broadcasting Corporation. **A:** Sr. High-Adult. **P:** Entertainment. **U:** Home. **Mov-Ent:** Mystery & Suspense, Anthropology, TV Movies. **Acq:** Purchase. **Dist:** $19.98.

After Romeo ????
Story of two teens who elope and find that married life isn't easy. 100m; VHS. **A:** College-Adult. **P:** Entertainment. **U:** Home. **Mov-Ent:** Marriage. **Acq:** Purchase. **Dist:** Moose School Productions. $24.00.

After Sex 1997 (Unrated) — ★★
Passion and madness—French style. Confident, middleaged Diane (Rouan) has a successful career and a complacent marriage. Then she meets twentysomething hunk Emilio (Terral) and all bets are off. The twosome have a delirious affair but Diane's passion teeters towards obsession, with reckless disregard for her family. Then the affair ends and Diane falls apart. French with subtitles. 97m; VHS, DVD. **C:** Brigitte Rouan; Boris Terral; Patrick Chesnais; Nils (Niels) Tavernier; Jean-Louis Richard; Francoise Arnoul; Directed by Brigitte Rouan; Written by Brigitte Rouan; Jean-Louis Richard; Santiago Amigorena; Guy Zilberstein; Cinematography by Pierre Dupouey; Music by Michel Musseau; Umberto Tozzi. **Pr:** Humbert Balsan; New Yorker Films. **A:** College-Adult. **P:** Entertainment. **U:** Home. **L:** French. **Mov-Ent:** Drama, Marriage. **Acq:** Purchase. **Dist:** Amazon.com Inc.; New Yorker Video.

After Solidarity: Three Polish Families in America 1988
Chronicles the lives of three Solidarity activists who were forced to leave Poland and immigrate to the United States. Filmed over a two year period, the video examines many of the emotions experienced by the immigrants as they adjust to American life. 58m; VHS, 3/4 U. **Pr:** Gaylen Ross. **A:** Jr. High-Adult. **P:** Education. **U:** Institution, Home, SURA. **Gen-Edu:** Sociology, Immigration. **Acq:** Purchase, Rent/Lease, Duplication. **Dist:** Filmakers Library Inc.

After Stonewall 1998
Sequel to "Before Stonewall" covers gay and lesbian life from the 1969 Stonewall riots in Greenwich Village to the present. 88m; VHS. **A:** Sr. High-Adult. **P:** Education. **U:** Institution, Home. **Gen-Edu:** Documentary Films, Homosexuality. **Acq:** Purchase. **Dist:** First Run Features.

After Sundown 2006 (R) — ★
A vampire from the Old West is searching for his daughter and creating a small army of zombies in his wake. 90m; DVD. **C:** Christopher Abram; Reece Rios; Natalie Jones; Susanna Gibb; Directed by Christopher Abram; Michael W. Brown; Written by Christopher Abram; Cinematography by David Pinkston; Music by Steven Barnett; Timothy Edward Smith. **A:** Sr. High-Adult. **P:** Entertainment. **U:** Home. **L:** English, Spanish. **Mov-Ent. Acq:** Purchase. **Dist:** Lions Gate Entertainment Inc. $14.98.

After Sunset: The Life and Times of the Drive-In Theater 19??
Filmmaker Jon Bokenkamp documents the cultural history of drive-in theatres in the American West. 45m; VHS, DVD. **A:** Adult. **P:** Entertainment. **U:** Home. **Gen-Edu:** Documentary Films, Film History. **Acq:** Purchase. **Dist:** Janson Media. $24.95.

After the Axe 1981
A dramatized production which follows the firing of an executive in a big corporation and the aftermath of his job loss. 57m; VHS, 3/4 U. **Pr:** National Film Board of Canada. **A:** College-Adult. **P:** Education. **U:** Institution, SURA. **Bus-Ind:** Business. **Acq:** Purchase, Rent/Lease. **Dist:** National Film Board of Canada. $450.00.

After the Battle 1990
An overview of the results of the war for Angolan independence which was supported by Cuban troops and opposed by South Africa. Included are interviews with the commanders of the armies of Cuba, Angola and South Africa. 58m; VHS. **Pr:** The Cinema Guild. **A:** Jr. High-Adult. **P:** Education. **U:** Home. **Gen-Edu:** Documentary Films, War--General, Africa. **Acq:** Purchase. **Dist:** The Cinema Guild. $95.00.

After the Big One: Nuclear War on the Prairies 1983
This tape looks at the effects of a large-scale, limited nuclear war on the farm lands of Canada. 23m; VHS, 3/4 U. **Pr:** National Film Board of Canada. **A:** Jr. High-Adult. **P:** Education. **U:** Institution, SURA. **Gen-Edu:** Nuclear Warfare. **Acq:** Purchase, Rent/Lease. **Dist:** National Film Board of Canada.

After the Black Book 2005
Documentary on Alejandra Matus, who wrote an expose of the Chilean justice system in 1999, and was promptly forced to flee the country. 55m; DVD. **A:** Sr. High-Adult. **P:** Education. **U:** Institution. **Gen-Edu:** Documentary Films, Biography. **Acq:** Purchase, Rent/Lease. **Dist:** The Cinema Guild. $295.00.

After the Break 1992
Lesbian therapy group concentrates its attention on abusive partners and co-dependency. 13m/B/W; VHS, Special order formats. **A:** College-Adult. **P:** Education. **U:** Institution. **Hea-Sci:** Mental Health. **Acq:** Purchase, Rent/Lease. **Dist:** Frameline. $200.00.

After the Deluge 2003 (Unrated) — ★★★
Dogged with their own problems, three brothers must deal with their distant father's decline from Alzheimer's while he is pained by flashbacks of his WWII tour of duty. 103m; VHS, DVD. **C:** David Wenham; Hugo Weaving; Samuel Johnson; Aden Young; Catherine McClements; Ray Barrett; Rachel Griffiths; Essie Davis; Kate Beahan; Vince Colosimo; Marta Dusseldorp; Bob Franklin; Marco Chiappi; Simon Burke; Directed by Brendan Maher; Written by Deb Cox; Andrew Knight; Cinematography by Geoff Burton; Music by Cezary Skubiszewski. **A:** Sr. High-Adult. **P:** Entertainment. **U:** Home. **Mov-Ent:** Family, World War Two. **Acq:** Purchase. **Dist:** BFS Video. $19.99.

After the Earthquake 1979
A young immmigrant Nicaraguan woman faces the challenges of life in the U.S. and re-evaluates her relationships with her boyfriend and family. 23m; VHS, 3/4 U. **Pr:** Lourdes Portillo. **A:** Jr. High-Adult. **P:** Education. **U:** Institution, SURA. **Gen-Edu:** Immigration, Women, Human Relations. **Acq:** Purchase, Rent/Lease. **Dist:** Women Make Movies.

After the Fall of New York 1985 (R) — Bomb!
Dim-witted post-apocalyptic tale set in New York after the fall of the "Big Bomb." A man, driven to search for the last normal woman, has reason to believe she is frozen alive and kept in the heart of the city. His mission: locate her, thaw her, engage in extremely limited foreplay with her, and repopulate the planet. A poorly dubbed dating allegory. 95m; VHS, DVD. **C:** Michael Sopkiw; Valentine Monnier; Anna Kanakis; Roman Geer; Edmund Purdom; George Eastman; Directed by Sergio Martino. **Pr:** Almi Pictures. **A:** Sr. High-Adult. **P:** Entertainment. **U:** Home. **Mov-Ent:** Science Fiction. **Acq:** Purchase. **Dist:** Lions Gate Television Corp. $79.98.

After the First 1971
A boy receives a rifle as a birthday present, and is taken by his father on his first hunting trip. 14m; VHS, 3/4 U. **A:** Jr. High-Sr. High. **P:** Religious. **U:** Institution, SURA. **Gen-Edu:** Ethics & Morals. **Acq:** Purchase. **Dist:** St. Anthony Messenger Press.

After the Fox 1966 — ★★
Sellers is a con artist posing as a film director to carry out a bizarre plan to steal gold from Rome. Features occasional backhand slaps at Hollywood, with Mature turning in a memorable performance as the has-been actor starring in Sellers' movie. Though the screenplay was co-written by Neil Simon, the laughs are marginal. 103m; VHS, DVD, Wide. **C:** Peter Sellers; Victor Mature; Martin Balsam; Britt Ekland; Directed by Vittorio De Sica; Written by Neil Simon; Cesare Zavattini; Cinematography by Leonida Barboni; Music by Burt Bacharach. **Pr:** Delegate Productions. **A:** Sr. High-Adult. **P:** Entertainment. **U:** Home. **Mov-Ent:** Comedy--Slapstick. **Acq:** Purchase. **Dist:** MGM Home Entertainment. $14.95.

After the Heart Attack—The First Three Months 1988
A look at a heart attack victim's post-operative programs and treatment alternatives. 10m; VHS, 3/4 U. **Pr:** Professional Research. **A:** Adult. **P:** Education. **U:** Institution, CCTV. **Hea-Sci:** Heart, Patient Care. **Acq:** Purchase, Rent/Lease. **Dist:** Discovery Education. $295.00.

After the Heart Attack—The Longer Term 1988
A guide for the heart attack victim's long-term requirements, including a redress of diet and exercise habits. 10m; VHS, 3/4 U. **Pr:** Professional Research. **A:** Adult. **P:** Education. **U:** Institution, CCTV. **Hea-Sci:** Heart, Patient Care. **Acq:** Purchase, Rent/Lease. **Dist:** Discovery Education. $295.00.

After the Hospital: What's Next? 1992
Educates patients and their families about caring for an older person after being in the hospital. Discusses the options of long-term nursing home care or going home and using in-home services. 15m; VHS, 3/4 U, Special order formats. **Pr:** Jane Matlaw; Nicolas Kaufman. **A:** Adult. **P:** Education. **U:** Institution. **Hea-Sci:** Health Education, Hospitals, Aging. **Acq:** Purchase, Rent/Lease. **Dist:** Terra Nova Films. $195.00.

After the Montreal Massacre 1990
Documents a gunman who entered the engineering building at the University of Montreal and killed 14 women in 1989. Studies the impact, and links the massacre with cases of rape, sexual harassment, and torture worldwide. 27m; VHS. **A:** College-Adult. **P:** Education. **U:** Institution. **Gen-Edu:** Women, Human Rights, Violence. **Acq:** Purchase, Rent/Lease. **Dist:** Women Make Movies. $250.00.

After the Ouch 1978
After a series of small accidents, children learn how to apply first aid. Animation shows the healing process. 15m; VHS, 3/4 U, Special order formats. **Pr:** Churchill Films. **A:** Primary. **P:** Education. **U:** Institution, Home, SURA. **Hea-Sci:** First Aid. **Acq:** Purchase, Duplication License. **Dist:** Clear Vue Inc.

After the Promise 1987 — ★★
During the Depression, a poor carpenter tries to regain custody of his four sons following the death of his wife. Maudlin melodrama based on a true story. 100m; VHS. **C:** Mark Harmon; Diana Scarwid; Rosemary Dunsmore; Donnelly Rhodes; Mark Hildreth; Trey Ames; Richard Billingsley; Directed by David Greene; Music by Ralph Burns. **Pr:** New World Pictures. **A:** Jr. High-Adult. **P:** Entertainment. **U:** Home. **L:** Spanish. **Mov-Ent**: Melodrama, TV Movies. **Acq:** Purchase. **Dist:** Anchor Bay Entertainment. $19.95.

After the Rain 1999 (R) — ★★
Hard-hitting apartheid story that unfortunately descends into melodrama. In 1970s South Africa, Steph (Bettany) is a conflicted soldier in love with dancer Emma (Lombard). After his brigade is posted, lonely Emma befriends a black co-worker, Joseph (Bakare). Upon learning that he is living on the streets, Emma invites Joseph to stay with her. Of course that just happens to be when Steph, who's deserted, returns and assumes the worst. Writer/director Kettle adapted the film from his play "Soweto's Burning." 110m; DVD. **C:** Paul Bettany; Louise Lombard; Ariyon Bakare; Directed by Ross Kettle; Written by Ross Kettle; Cinematography by Koos Roets; Music by Hummie Mann. **A:** Sr. High-Adult. **P:** Entertainment. **U:** Home. **Mov-Ent**: Apartheid. **Acq:** Purchase. **Dist:** Alpha Video; Movies Unlimited.

After the Rehearsal 1984 (R) — ★★★
Two actresses, one young, the other at the end of her career, challenge their director with love and abuse. Each questions his right to use them on stage and off. A thoughtful discussion of the meaning and reason for art originally made for Swedish TV. Swedish with English subtitles. 72m; VHS. **C:** Erland Josephson; Ingrid Thulin; Lena Olin; Directed by Ingmar Bergman; Written by Ingmar Bergman; Cinematography by Sven Nykvist. **Pr:** Triumph Films. **A:** Sr. High-Adult. **P:** Entertainment. **U:** Home. **L:** Swedish. **Mov-Ent**: Aging, TV Movies. **Acq:** Purchase. **Dist:** Sony Pictures Home Entertainment Inc. $59.95.

After the Revolution 1990 — ★★
A struggling novelist decides to write his next book from the viewpoint of his cat. In Hungarian with English subtitles. 82m; VHS, DVD. **C:** Io Tillett Wright; Directed by Andras Szirtes. **A:** College-Adult. **P:** Entertainment. **U:** Home. **L:** Hungarian, English. **Mov-Ent**: Literature, Pets. **Acq:** Purchase. **Dist:** Facets Multimedia Inc. $59.95.

After the Shock 1990 (PG) — ★★
Documentary-like dramatization of the San Francisco-Oakland earthquake of October 1989 and, of course, its aftermath. Incorporates actual footage of the disaster. 92m; VHS, CC. **C:** Yaphet Kotto; Rue McClanahan; Jack Scalia; Scott Valentine; Directed by Gary Sherman; Written by Gary Sherman. **Pr:** Wilshire Court Productions. **A:** Jr. High-Adult. **P:** Entertainment. **U:** Home. **Mov-Ent**: Action-Adventure, Earthquakes, Documentary Films. **Acq:** Purchase. **Dist:** Paramount Pictures Corp. $79.95.

After the Spill: The Last Catch 2010 (Unrated)
National Geographic visited Venice, Louisiana, after the devastating April 2010 British Petroleum oil spill to chronicle the attempts of local fisherman to salvage their livelihoods and deal with the economic ruin and joblessness that followed the environmental disaster. 45m; DVD. **A:** Family. **P:** Education. **U:** Institution, Home. **Mov-Ent**: Documentary Films, Ecology & Environment, Fishing. **Acq:** Purchase. **Dist:** National Geographic Society. $19.95.

After the Storm 2001 (R) — ★★½
Beachcomber Arno (Bratt) discovers a sunken yacht but can't salvage the loot, even with the help of girlfriend Coquina (Avital). So he hooks up with Jean-Pierre (Assante) and his wife Janine (Girard), but greed gets the best of everyone. Based on a story by Ernest Hemingway; filmed in Belize. 103m; VHS, DVD, Wide. **C:** Benjamin Bratt; Armand Assante; Mili Avital; Simone-Elise Girard; Stephen Lang; Directed by Guy Ferland; Written by A.E. Hotchner; Cinematography by Gregory Middleton; Music by Bill Wandel. **A:** Sr. High-Adult. **P:** Entertainment. **U:** Home. **Mov-Ent**. **Acq:** Purchase. **Dist:** CinemaNow Inc.

After the Storm: American Exile of Bela Bartok 1991
This documentary chronicles the twilight of the life and career of a gifted creator of classical music. Banished from his native Hungary to the U.S. during WWII, Bartok died a broken and destitute man in 1945. This presentation combines footage from interviews with Bartok, his family and friends with performances of the beautiful music he created while eking out his final days in America. 75m; VHS. **C:** Conducted by George Solti; Ervin Lukacs. **Pr:** RM Arts. **A:** College-Adult. **P:** Entertainment. **U:** Home. **Fin-Art**: Documentary Films, Biography, Art & Artists. **Acq:** Purchase. **Dist:** Home Vision Cinema; Facets Multimedia Inc. $39.95.

After the Storm: Power and Peace in the Middle East 1992
Discusses geographic, economic, political, and religious factors that have contributed to the permanent importance of the Middle East in world affairs. 29m; VHS. **A:** Sr. High. **P:** Education. **U:** Institution. **Gen-Edu**: History, Middle East. **Acq:** Purchase. **Dist:** National Training Center for Resource Center Directors. $19.95.

After the Sunset 2004 (PG-13) — ★★
Lightweight crime caper is as memorable as a soap bubble, although the scenery (Hayek in a variety of skimpy attire and the sun-drenched island setting) is appealing. Max (Brosnan) is a suave thief who, with partner Lola (Hayek), has pulled off a successful diamond heist that ruins the career of FBI agent Stan (Harrelson). The thieves then retire to the Bahamas where Max is soon bored, bored, bored, and ready for some action when an ocean liner docks in port with a priceless jewel exhibit onboard. Stan, of course, shows up, determined to finally outwit Max. Hayek plays another firecracker while Brosnan slums charmingly; Cheadle is wasted in a throwaway role as a gangster. 93m; VHS, DVD. **C:** Pierce Brosnan; Salma Hayek; Woody Harrelson; Don Cheadle; Naomie Harris; Christopher Penn; Mykelti Williamson; Obba Babatunde; Russell Hornsby; Rex Linn; Kate Walsh; Troy Garity; Directed by Brett Ratner; Written by Craig Rosenberg; Paul Zbyszewski; Cinematography by Dante Spinotti; Music by Lalo Schifrin. **Pr:** Jay Stern; Beau Flynn; Tripp Vinson; Firm Films; Contrafilm; New Line Cinema. **A:** Jr. High-Adult. **P:** Entertainment. **U:** Home. **Mov-Ent**: Action-Comedy, Federal Bureau of Investigation (FBI). **Acq:** Purchase. **Dist:** New Line Home Video. $27.95.

After the Sunset Again 1974
Through poems and songs, Ric and Billie Barbara Masten explore the confusion today's couples go through. They offer personal insight into their struggles with questions like women's changing role and what it means to be male and female. 74m; 3/4 U, EJ. **Pr:** NETCHE. **A:** College-Adult. **P:** Education. **U:** Institution, CCTV, BCTV, SURA. **Gen-Edu**: Marriage. **Acq:** Purchase, Rent/Lease, Subscription. **Dist:** NETCHE.

After the Tears: Teens Talk About Mental Illness in Their Families 1987
Teens talk about the anger, guilt, fear, resentment, and confusion they feel around a relative who is mentally ill. 21m; VHS. **A:** Jr. High-Adult. **P:** Education. **U:** Institution. **Hea-Sci**: Mental Health, Family. **Acq:** Purchase. **Dist:** HRM Video. $179.00.

After the Thin Man 1936 — ★★★
Second in a series of six "Thin Man" films, this one finds Nick, Nora and Asta, the lovable terrier, seeking out a murderer from Nora's own blue-blooded relatives. Fast-paced mystery with a witty script and the popular Powell/Loy charm. Sequel to "The Thin Man," followed by "Another Thin Man." 113m/B/W; VHS, DVD. **C:** William Powell; Myrna Loy; James Stewart; Elissa Landi; Joseph Calleia; Jessie Ralph; Alan Marshal; Directed by W.S. Van Dyke. **Pr:** MGM. **A:** Family. **P:** Entertainment. **U:** Home. **Mov-Ent**: Mystery & Suspense, Pets. **Acq:** Purchase. **Dist:** MGM Home Entertainment. $19.98.

After the Velvet Revolution 1993
Three-year documentary study of Czechoslovakian families and individuals after the peaceful fall of communism. 58m; VHS. **Pr:** Moira Productions. **A:** Sr. High-College. **P:** Education. **U:** Institution. **Gen-Edu**: USSR. **Acq:** Purchase, Rent/Lease. **Dist:** The Video Project. $150.00.

After the War 1989 (Unrated) — ★★½
Masterpiece Theatre mini-series follows two young Jewish men—Joe Hirsh (Reynolds) and Michael Jordan (Lukis)?from their meeting at an English private school in 1942 through their careers in the entertainment business. As is so often the case with these imports, the action is talky and supremely well acted. Production values are good. 518m; DVD. **C:** Susannah York; Denis Quilley; Adrian Lukis; Robert Reynolds; Caroline Goodall; Serena Gordon; Patrick Malahide; Art Malik; Directed by John Madden; John Glenister; Nicholas Renton; Written by Frederic Raphael. **A:** Sr. High-Adult. **P:** Entertainment. **U:** Home. **Mov-Ent**. **Acq:** Purchase. **Dist:** BFS Video.

After the War: American Literature from 1945 to the Present 19??
The literature of post-World War II authors such as Bellow, Ellison, Heller, Kerouac, Mailer, Roth, Salinger, and Updike. 16m; VHS. **A:** Jr. High-Adult. **P:** Education. **U:** Institution. **Gen-Edu**: Literature, Documentary Films. **Acq:** Purchase. **Dist:** Thomas S. Klise Co. $58.00.

After the Warming 1991
A new analysis of the theories concerning global warming using computerized models. Watch the greenhouse effect and how man can influence the changes of the earth. On two cassettes. 110m; VHS. **C:** Hosted by James Burke. **A:** Sr. High-Adult. **P:** Education. **U:** Institution, Home. **Gen-Edu**: Ecology & Environment, Meteorology. **Acq:** Purchase. **Dist:** PBS Home Video; Ambrose Video Publishing, Inc.; Reader's Digest Home Video. $49.96.

After the Wedding 2006 (R) — ★★★
Jacob (Mikkelsen), director of a struggling Indian orphanage, is given the opportunity to solve all his problems via a rich benefactor back in Denmark. Once he returns home, however, he finds things much more complicated than he expected, and he must choose between the world he knows in India and the obligations towards an ex-girlfriend and illegitimate daughter in Denmark. Oscar-nominated, poignant film teeters on the fine line between melodrama and soap opera. 120m; DVD. **C:** Mads Mikkelsen; Rolf Lassgard; Sidse Babett Knudsen; Stine Fischer Christensen; Christian Tafdrup; Directed by Suzanne (Susanne) Bier; Written by Anders Thomas Jensen; Cinematography by Morten Soborg; Music by Johan Soderqvist. **Pr:** Sisse Graum Jorgensen; Zentropa Entertainment; Sigma Film; Nordisk; IFC Films. **A:** College-Adult. **P:** Entertainment. **U:** Home. **L:** Danish, Swedish, Hindi. **Mov-Ent**: Adoption. **Acq:** Purchase. **Dist:** IFC Films.

After the Whale 1971
Studies the behavior of the whale, a marvelous creature on the verge of extinction. From the "Life Around Us" series. 30m; VHS, 3/4 U, Special order formats. **Pr:** Time-Life Films. **A:** Jr. High-Sr. High. **P:** Education. **U:** Institution, SURA. **L:** English, Spanish. **Gen-Edu**: Animals. **Acq:** Purchase, Rent/Lease. **Dist:** Time-Life Video and Television.

After Tiller 2013 (PG-13) — ★★★
George Tiller was assassinated in 2009, leaving only four working doctors who perform late-term abortions, terminations of pregnancies in the final trimester, most often because of horrendous illnesses that would leave the child with no quality of life were they to be taken to term. This incredibly important film takes these four people who have been turned into demons by those who believe them wrong and heroes by those who believe them right and makes them human again. It's an incredibly hard film to watch at times but it perfectly captures the complexity of an issue that has divided us for decades and will likely continue to do so. 85m; DVD. **C:** Directed by Martha Shane; Lana Wilson; Written by Martha Shane; Lana Wilson; Greg O'Toole; Cinematography by Hilary Spera; Emily Topper; Music by Andy Cabic; Eric D. Johnson. **Pr:** Martha Shane; Lana Wilson; Oscilloscope Films. **A:** Sr. High-Adult. **P:** Entertainment. **U:** Home. **L:** English. **Mov-Ent**: Abortion, Documentary Films, Hospitals. **Acq:** Purchase.

After Tomorrow 1932 (Unrated) — ★★
In this Depression-era film, Peter (Farrell) and Sidney (Nixon) struggle to work and save their money to get married but are frequently separated by hardship. Fearing she's losing her beau, Sidney suggests they go away together (there's a sex talk) while Peter nobly insists they wait until marriage. 70m/B/W; DVD. **C:** Charles Farrell; Marion (Marian) Nixon; Minna Gombell; Josephine Hull; William Collier, Sr.; William Pawley; Directed by Frank Borzage; Written by Sonya Levien; Cinematography by James Wong Howe. **A:** Sr. High-Adult. **P:** Entertainment. **U:** Home. **Mov-Ent**: Poverty, Sex & Sexuality. **Acq:** Purchase. **Dist:** Fox Home Entertainment.

After Twenty Years 1989
O. Henry's short story comes to life in this film about two friends torn apart by emotions and the law. Includes a teachers guide. 14m; VHS, Special order formats. **Pr:** Learning Corporation of America. **A:** Jr. High-Sr. High. **P:** Education. **U:** Institution. **Gen-Edu**: Literature--American. **Acq:** Purchase, Rent/Lease. **Dist:** Phoenix Learning Group. $250.00.

After Your Mastectomy 1989
A look at the emotional traumas women who have had a mastectomy are apt to go through. 9m; VHS, 3/4 U. **Pr:** Professional Research. **A:** Adult. **P:** Education. **U:** Institution, CCTV, SURA. **Hea-Sci**: Women, Cancer. **Acq:** Purchase, Rent/Lease. **Dist:** Discovery Education. $295.00.

Afterburn 1992 (R) — ★★★
When Ted, her Air Force pilot husband, is killed in a crash of his F-16 fighter, Janet Harduvel learns the official explanation is pilot error. Convinced that something was wrong with his plane, Janet sets out to investigate, and eventually sue, military contractor General Dynamics. Dern turns in a great performance as the tough widow determined to clear her husband's name. Based on a true story. 103m; VHS, DVD, CC. **C:** Laura Dern; Robert Loggia; Vincent Spano; Michael Rooker; Andy Romano; Directed by Robert Markowitz; Written by Elizabeth Chandler. **A:** Sr. High-Adult. **P:** Entertainment. **U:** Home. **Mov-Ent**: Law, Aeronautics, TV Movies. **Acq:** Purchase. **Dist:** Facets Multimedia Inc. $89.99.

Afterglow 1997 (R) — ★★
Romantic quadrangle skates by on the performances of its two veterans. Lucky Mann (Nolte) is experiencing marital boredom with his longtime wife Phyllis (the ever-beautiful Christie), a former B-movie actress. Meanwhile twentysomething Marianne Byron (Boyle), who is desperate to have a baby, is sexually frustrated by her workaholic hubby, Jeffrey (Miller). Repairman Lucky happens to come along to work on the Bryon's apartment and Marianne decides to throw herself at him. Then Jeffrey meets the sophisticated Phyllis and soon both couples have uncoupled and re-formed. 113m; VHS, DVD, CC. **C:** Nick Nolte; Julie Christie; Lara Flynn Boyle; Jonny Lee Miller; Jay Underwood; Domini Blythe; Directed by Alan Rudolph; Written by Alan Rudolph; Cinematography by Toyomichi Kurita; Music by Mark Isham. **Pr:** Robert Altman; Sandcastle 5 Productions; Moonstone Entertainment; Sony Pictures Classics. **A:** Sr. High-Adult. **P:** Entertainment. **U:** Home. **Mov-Ent**: Drama, Marriage, Sex & Sexuality. **Awds:** Ind. Spirit '98: Actress (Christie); N.Y. Film Critics '97: Actress (Christie); Natl. Soc. Film Critics '97: Actress (Christie). **Acq:** Purchase. **Dist:** Sony Pictures Home Entertainment Inc.

The Afterglow: A Tribute to Robert Frost 1989
The poetry of Robert Frost is brought to life with recreations from events in his life. 35m; VHS, 3/4 U, Special order formats. **C:** Burgess Meredith. **Pr:** Burgess Meredith; Burgess Meredith. **A:** Jr. High-Adult. **P:** Education. **U:** Institution, Home, SURA. **Gen-Edu**: Biography, Literature. **Acq:** Purchase, Rent/Lease. **Dist:** Pyramid Media. $325.00.

Afterimage 1979
This program answers the question, "Are those who lose their sight restricted to a world of darkness, fear and dependence?" A look at people whose creative spirits have not been deterred by their visual handicaps. 18m; VHS, 3/4 U, Special order formats. **Pr:** Thomas Ott; Jan Krawitz. **A:** Jr. High-Adult. **P:** Education. **U:** Institution, Home, SURA. **Gen-Edu**: Blindness. **Acq:** Purchase, Rent/Lease. **Dist:** Direct Cinema Ltd.

Afterlife 197?
Ancient myths and transcultural beliefs of afterlife experiences are expressed and analyzed by Ishu Patel. 7m; VHS, 3/4 U. **Pr:** National Film Board of Canada. **A:** Sr. High-Adult. **P:** Education. **U:** Institution, SURA. **Gen-Edu**: Death. **Acq:** Purchase, Rent/Lease. **Dist:** National Film Board of Canada.

Afterlife 2005
Independent Television 2005-2006 psychological drama. Bristol psychology lecturer Robert Bridge confronts medium Allison

Mundy about her abilities and then discovers her psychic gifts are real as they try to help those whose lives are literally haunted by tragedy. 6 episodes. 282m; DVD. **C:** Lesley Sharp; Andrew Lincoln. **A:** Sr. High-Adult. **P:** Entertainment. **U:** Home. **L:** English. **Mov-Ent**: Great Britain, Occult Sciences, Television Series. **Acq:** Purchase. **Dist:** BBC Worldwide Ltd. $24.98.

After.life 2010 (R) — ★½
After a car crash, Anna (Ricci) wakes up on the mortuary table of sorta creepy undertaker Eliot Deacon (Neeson). She is quite certain she is still alive; he is equally certain she is dead. He can see and speak to the recently deceased while they are trying to adjust to the fact that they are, indeed, dead. Anna thinks he is some kind of serial killer keeping her prisoner since Deacon locks the door anytime he leaves the room. She gets hysterical and tries to escape, he is calm. Though Ricci is unselfconscious about her frequent nudity and the picture looks stylish (nice use of red), it's also boring and doesn't actually make much sense. 97m; Blu-Ray, On Demand, Wide. **C:** Christina Ricci; Liam Neeson; Justin Long; Chandler Canterbury; Celia Weston; Josh Charles; Directed by Agnieszka Wojtowicz-Vosloo; Written by Agnieszka Wojtowicz-Vosloo; Paul Vosloo; Jakub Korolczuk; Cinematography by Anastas Michos; Music by Paul Haslinger. **Pr:** Brad M. Gilbert; Celine Rattray; William (Bill) O. Perkins, III; Plum Pictures; Lleju Prods; Harbor Light Entertainment; Anchor Bay Entertainment Inc. **A:** Sr. High-Adult. **P:** Entertainment. **U:** Home. **L:** English. **Mov-Ent**: Death, Horror. **Acq:** Purchase. **Dist:** Anchor Bay Entertainment; Amazon.com Inc.; Movies Unlimited.

The Aftermath 1976
From the "Europe" series, depicts an era in recent European history best characterized by Churchill's observation that "an iron curtain" had descended across the continent. 52m; VHS, 3/4 U, Special order formats. **C:** Winston Churchill; Narrated by Peter Ustinov. **Pr:** British Broadcasting Corporation; Time-Life Films. **A:** Sr. High-College. **P:** Education. **U:** Institution, SURA. **Gen-Edu**: History--Modern. **Acq:** Purchase, Rent/Lease. **Dist:** Time-Life Video and Television.

Aftermath 1985 (Unrated) — ★½
Three astronauts return to Earth and are shocked to discover that the planet has been ravaged by a nuclear war. Quickly they make new plans. 96m; VHS, DVD. **C:** Steve Barkett; Larry Latham; Lynne Margulies; Sid Haig; Forrest J Ackerman; Directed by Ted V. Mikels. **Pr:** Independent. **A:** Sr. High-Adult. **P:** Entertainment. **U:** Home. **Mov-Ent**: Science Fiction. **Acq:** Purchase. **Dist:** Timeless Media Group. $18.99.

The Aftermath of the War with Iraq 1991
A look at unresolved political, economic and environmental issues left over from the Persian Gulf War. 29m; VHS, 3/4 U, Special order formats. **Pr:** Center for Defense Information. **A:** College-Adult. **P:** Education. **U:** Institution, CCTV, CATV, BCTV, Home, SURA. **Gen-Edu**: Persian Gulf War, Middle East, Journalism. **Acq:** Purchase. **Dist:** The Video Project. $25.00.

Aftermath: Unanswered Questions from 9/11 2005
Documentary by director Stephen Marshall who debates the actions of the Bush administration surrounding the terrorist attacks on 9/11; also features various political experts discussing, in particular, potential connections among the hijackers, Pakistani intelligence, and the Central Intelligence Agency (CIA) along with the tightening of civil liberties on American citizens. 35m; DVD. **A:** Sr. High-Adult. **P:** Entertainment. **U:** Home. **Mov-Ent**: Documentary Films, Terrorism, Politics & Government. **Acq:** Purchase. **Dist:** Alternative Distribution Alliance. $14.95.

Afternoon Delight 2013 (R) — ★½
Debuting feature director Soloway tries for a female raunch comedy but her characters are generally self-absorbed and unlikeable with the exception of Temple's confident young exotic dancer McKenna. Bored wife/mother Rachel (Hahn) wants to spice up her sex life with husband Jeff (Radnor) so they go to a strip club, which is where Rachel encounters McKenna. Intrigued, Rachel's soon offering her a temporary place to live although McKenna definitely isn't interested in being reformed. Drinking and fantasies (men's and women's) are prominently featured but it never adds up to anything sexy, fun, or believable. 99m; DVD, Blu-Ray. **C:** Kathryn Hahn; Juno Temple; Josh Radnor; Jane Lynch; Michaela Watkins; Josh Stamberg; John Kapelos; Keegan Michael Key; Directed by Jill Soloway; Written by Jill Soloway; Cinematography by Jim Frohna; Music by Craig (Shudder to Think) Wedren. **Pr:** Sebastian Dungan; 72 Productions; Rincon Entertainment; Film Arcade. **A:** Sr. High-Adult. **P:** Entertainment. **U:** Home. **L:** English. **Mov-Ent**: Marriage, Sex & Sexuality. **Acq:** Purchase. **Dist:** New Video Group Inc.

An Afternoon with Father Flye 1995
The age-old friend of writer James Agee is interviewed several times between his 90th and 100th birthdays, about his life as a priest, his friendship with Agee and general philosophy about life and love. 28m; 3/4 U. **Pr:** Ross Spears. **A:** Jr. High-Adult. **P:** Education. **U:** Institution, SURA. **Gen-Edu**: Interviews. **Acq:** Purchase. **Dist:** James Agee Film Project.

An Afternoon with Gregory Piatigorsky 1978
One of the greatest cellists ever is followed through a typical day of playing the cello, strolling through his garden, talking with his wife and students, and playing more cello. 15m; VHS, 3/4 U. **Pr:** Steve Grumette. **A:** Jr. High-Adult. **P:** Education. **U:** Institution, SURA. **Fin-Art**. **Acq:** Purchase. **Dist:** Phoenix Learning Group.

Afternoon with Music 1983
The program develops concepts into the nature of the three basic types of musical instruments and discusses the evolution of the modern orchestra. Part of the "Inventive Child" series. 10m; VHS, 3/4 U. **Pr:** Film Polski. **A:** Primary-Jr. High. **P:** Education. **U:** Institution, SURA. **Chl-Juv**. **Acq:** Purchase, Rent/Lease. **Dist:** Encyclopedia Britannica.

Afternoons and Alice McClure 1974
A sensitive portrayal of the bittersweet world of a fatherless adolescent girl who must learn to cope with reality. Alice spends her afternoons in an abandoned house, until she meets a vagrant and tragedy results. Also available in a fantasy version without the tragic ending. 28m; VHS, 3/4 U. **Pr:** David Gulick; William Schwartz. **A:** Primary-Adult. **P:** Education. **U:** Institution, SURA. **Gen-Edu**: Film--Avant-Garde. **Acq:** Purchase. **Dist:** Phoenix Learning Group.

Afterschool 2008 (Unrated) — ★★
Feature film debut for writer/director Campos who was 24 at the time of filming. Socially awkward, self-absorbed teen Robert (Miller) is boarding at a New England prep school where he's generally ignored and his roommate deals drugs. Repressed, Robert finds his sexual outlet in violent Internet porn. During an afterschool student film project, Robert accidentally films the drug overdose deaths of twin sisters who die in his arms. The school tries to cover up the scandal and Robert is asked to supply a tasteful memorial film, which turns out to be truthful and wildly inappropriate—much like the movie. 121m; On Demand, Wide. **C:** Ezra Miller; Jeremy White; Emory Cohen; Christopher McCann; Michael Stuhlbarg; Addison Timlin; Lee Wilkof; Directed by Antonio Campos; Written by Antonio Campos; Cinematography by Jody Lee Lipes; Music by Rakotondrabe Gael. **Pr:** Josh Mond; Sean Durkin; Hidden St. Productions; Borderline Films; IFC Films. **A:** Sr. High-Adult. **P:** Entertainment. **U:** Home. **L:** English. **Mov-Ent**: Drug Abuse, Drug Trafficking/Dealing, Adolescence. **Acq:** Purchase. **Dist:** Amazon.com Inc.; Movies Unlimited; MPI Media Group.

Aftershock 1988 (R) — ★½
A beautiful alien and a mysterious stranger battle the Earth's repressive, evil government. 90m; VHS, DVD. **C:** Jay Roberts, Jr.; Elizabeth Kaitan; Chris Mitchum; Richard Lynch; John Saxon; Russ Tamblyn; Michael Berryman; Chris De Rose; Chuck Jeffreys; Directed by Frank Harris; Written by Michael Standing; Music by Kevin Klinger; Bob Mamet. **Pr:** Spectrum Entertainment Group. **A:** Preschool. **P:** Entertainment. **U:** Home. **Mov-Ent**: Science Fiction, Satire & Parody. **Acq:** Purchase. **Dist:** Movies Unlimited. $9.99.

Aftershock 2012 (R) — ★½
Part ho-hum horror/part disaster flick, it's the English-language debut of Chilean director Lopez. A vacationing American nicknamed Gringo (horror helmer Roth) heads to an underground club in Valparaiso with some friends when they get caught in an earthquake. Eventually making their way out, they emerge into chaos, a lot of disturbing violence thanks to a prison collapse and a group of escaped cons, and a lot more gore. English and Spanish with subtitles. 90m; DVD, Blu-Ray, Streaming. **C:** Eli Roth; Ariel Levy; Nicolas Martinez; Lorenza Izzo; Andrea Osvart; Natasha Yarovenko; Directed by Nicolas Lopez; Written by Eli Roth; Nicolas Lopez; Guillermo Amoedo; Cinematography by Antonio Quercia; Music by Manuel Riveiro. **Pr:** Dimension Films. **A:** Sr. High-Adult. **P:** Entertainment. **U:** Home. **L:** English, Spanish. **Mov-Ent**: Earthquakes, Horror, South America. **Acq:** Purchase, Rent/Lease. **Dist:** Anchor Bay Entertainment Inc.; Amazon.com Inc.

Aftershock: Earthquake in New York 1999 — ★½
Typical TV disaster movie based on the novel by Chuck Scarborough. You're introduced to a bunch of nice people (there's quite a good cast), disaster strikes, death and destruction are everywhere and all it brings out (rather than hysteria, looting, violence and assorted evilness) is good deeds and rescues. Nifty special effects though. 139m; VHS, DVD, CC. **C:** Tom Skerritt; Sharon Lawrence; Charles S. Dutton; Lisa Nicole Carson; Cicely Tyson; Jennifer Garner; Rachel Ticotin; Frederick Weller; Erika Eleniak; Mitchell Ryan; Directed by Mikael Salomon; Written by David Stevens; Paul Eric Meyers; Loren Boothby; Cinematography by Jon Joffin; Music by Irwin Fisch. **A:** Jr. High-Adult. **P:** Entertainment. **U:** Home. **Mov-Ent**: Action-Adventure, Earthquakes. **Acq:** Purchase.

Afterwards 2008 (Unrated) — ★½
Sentimental and slow-paced (and a little creepy). Successful New York lawyer Nathan Del Amico (Duris) encounters mysterious hospice physician, Dr. Kay (Malkovich), who claims to have supernatural abilities to see a white aura around people who will soon die. Thinking he's next, Nathan decide to make peace with his past, including his ex-wife Claire (Lilly), while trying to thwart what he thinks is supposed to be his destiny. 107m; DVD. **C:** Romain Duris; John Malkovich; Evangeline Lilly; Pascale Bussieres; Reece Thompson; Sara Waisglass; Directed by Gilles Bourdos; Written by Gilles Bourdos; Michel Spinosa; Cinematography by Mark Ping Bin Lee; Music by Alexandre Desplat. **A:** Sr. High-Adult. **P:** Entertainment. **U:** Home. **Mov-Ent**: Death, Law. **Acq:** Purchase. **Dist:** Weinstein Company L.L.C.

Ag Education: A Degree With Options 1992
Agri-business, marketing, finance and public relations professionals explain the benefits gained from having a degree in Agricultural Education. ?m; VHS. **A:** Adult. **P:** Education. **U:** Institution. **Gen-Edu**: Agriculture, Education. **Acq:** Purchase. **Dist:** University of Idaho. $25.00.

Ag in the Classroom 1986
This is an overview of a project designed to help teachers include agriculture in their elementary school curriculum. 16m; VHS, 3/4 U. **Pr:** USDA. **A:** Adult. **P:** Teacher Education. **U:** Institution, SURA. **Gen-Edu**: Agriculture. **Acq:** Purchase. **Dist:** National Audiovisual Center. $95.00.

Again, the Ringer 1964 (Unrated) — ★★
Well-done German adaptation of the Edgar Wallace novel "The Ringer" (also known as "The Squeaker"). The sister of a famous criminal, who's a master of disguise, is murdered in London and her brother seeks revenge. Meanwhile, Scotland Yard detectives think they finally have a chance of catching him. German with subtitles. 85m/B/W; DVD. **C:** Joachim Fuchsberger; Heinz Drache; Siegfried Lowitz; Margot Trooger; Rene Deltgen; Siegfried Schurenberg; Sophie Hardy; Carl Lange; Directed by Alfred Vohrer; Written by Herbert Reinecker; Cinematography by Karl Lob; Music by Peter Thomas. **A:** College-Adult. **P:** Entertainment. **U:** Home. **L:** German. **Mov-Ent**: Crime Drama. **Acq:** Purchase. **Dist:** Sinister Cinema.

Again . . . the Second Time 1991
Documents "Operation Solomon," the modern day exodus of 14,200 Ethiopian Jews to Israel. Follows one family in particular to examine the average refugee's experience. 19m; VHS. **A:** Jr. High-Adult. **P:** Education. **U:** Home, Institution. **Gen-Edu**: Judaism, Africa, Israel. **Acq:** Purchase. **Dist:** Ergo Media Inc. $29.95.

Again—From Measure 55 1991
Discussion with Principle Conductor and Musical Director of the Seattle Symphony, Gerard Schwartz, on his work, his music, and his vision. 28m; VHS. **A:** Sr. High-Adult. **P:** Education. **U:** Institution. **Gen-Edu**: Biography, Art & Artists. **Acq:** Purchase. **Dist:** University of Washington Educational Media Collection. $15.00.

Against a Crooked Sky 1975 (G) — ★★
A young boy sets out with an elderly trapper to find his sister, who was captured by the Indians. Similiar story to "The Searchers," but no masterpiece. 89m; VHS, DVD. **C:** Richard Boone; Stewart Petersen; Jewel Blanch; Geoffrey Land; Henry Wilcoxon; Directed by Earl Bellamy. **Pr:** Cinema Shares International. **A:** Family. **P:** Entertainment. **U:** Home. **Mov-Ent**: Western. **Acq:** Purchase. **Dist:** Lions Gate Television Corp. $14.98.

Against All Flags 1952 (Unrated) — ★★★
An enjoyable Flynn swashbuckler about a British soldier slashing his way through the Spanish fleet at the turn of the 18th century. Though the story has been told before, tight direction and good performances win out. O'Hara is a tarty eyeful as a hot-tempered pirate moll. 81m; VHS, DVD. **C:** Errol Flynn; Maureen O'Hara; Anthony Quinn; Mildred Natwick; Directed by George Sherman. **Pr:** U-I. **A:** Family. **P:** Entertainment. **U:** Home. **Mov-Ent**. **Acq:** Purchase. **Dist:** Movies Unlimited; Alpha Video; Universal Studios Home Video. $14.95.

Against All Odds 19??
Cliff Chadderton examines the Battle for the Scheldt Estuary in Holland and Belgium during World War II, which resulted 6500 Canadian casualties. 120m; VHS. **A:** Jr. High-Adult. **P:** Education. **U:** Home. **Gen-Edu**: War--General, World War Two. **Acq:** Purchase. **Dist:** The War Amps. $14.00.

Against All Odds 1984 (R) — ★★½
An interesting love triangle evolves when recently cut quarterback Terry Brogan (Bridges) is asked by his nightclub owning/bookie buddy, Jack (Woods), to travel to Mexico and bring back Jack's sultry girlfriend, Jessie (Ward). Then Terry discovers that Jessie is the daughter of Mrs. Wyler, the football team owner. Contains complicated plot, numerous double crosses, sensual love scenes, and a chase scene along Sunset Boulevard. As the good friend sans conscience, Woods stars. A remake of 1947's "Out of the Past." 122m; VHS, DVD, 8 mm, Wide, CC. **C:** Jeff Bridges; Rachel Ward; James Woods; Alex Karras; Jane Greer; Richard Widmark; Dorian Harewood; Swoosie Kurtz; Bill McKinney; Saul Rubinek; Directed by Taylor Hackford; Written by Eric Hughes; Cinematography by Donald E. Thorin; Music by Michel Colombier; Larry Carlton. **A:** Sr. High-Adult. **P:** Entertainment. **U:** Home. **Mov-Ent**: Drama, Mexico. **Acq:** Purchase. **Dist:** Sony Pictures Home Entertainment Inc. $12.95.

Against All Odds 1985
Underdog Gaston Rayler's spectacular victory in the 1985 Paris Dakar rally is a highlight in this documentary of the race. 107m; VHS. **A:** Family. **P:** Entertainment. **U:** Home. **Spo-Rec**: Documentary Films, Automobiles--Racing. **Acq:** Purchase. **Dist:** Powersports - Powerdocs. $39.99.

Against All Odds: Inside Statistics 1989
These programs feature mathematical formulas and living examples that inspire and motivate learning in math. 30m; VHS, 3/4 U. **Pr:** Jean-Jacques Annaud. **A:** Sr. High-Adult. **P:** Education. **U:** Institution, CCTV, SURA. **Gen-Edu**: Mathematics. **Acq:** Purchase, Rent/Lease, Duplication. **Dist:** Annenberg Media. $350.00.
Indiv. Titles: 1. What is Statistics? 2. Picturing Distributors 3. Describing Distributions 4. Normal Distributions 5. Normal Calculations 6. Time Series 7. Models for Growth 8. Describing Relationships 9. Correlation 10. Multidimensional Data Analysis 11. The Question of Causation 12. Experimental Design 13. Blocking and Sampling 14. Samples and Surveys 15. What is Probability 16. Random Variables 17. Binomial Distributions 18. The Sample Mean and Control Charts 19. Confidence Intervals 20. Significance Tests 21. Inference for One Mean 22. Comparing Two Means 23. Inference for Proportions 24. Inference for Two-Way Tables 25. Inference for Relationships 26. Case Study.

Against the Current 1988
Portrays the residents of Kirishi and their fight against a major synthetic protein plant. 27m; VHS; Closed Captioned. **A:** Sr. High-Adult. **P:** Education. **U:** Institution, Home. **Gen-Edu**: USSR, Ecology & Environment. **Acq:** Purchase, Rent/Lease. **Dist:** The Video Project; Tapeworm Video Distributors Inc. $59.95.

Against the Current 2009 (Unrated) — ★½
Maudlin and slow-paced drama. Paul (Fiennes) persuades his friend Jeff (Kirk) that it's time to carry through with his long-held wish to swim the 150 miles down the Hudson River from Troy, New York to Manhattan. Jeff and acquaintance Liz (Reaser) will provide assistance but Jeff soon realizes that it's the fifth anniversary of the death of Paul's pregnant wife and he has another purpose beyond swimming in mind. 98m; DVD. **C:** Joseph Fiennes; Justin Kirk; Elizabeth Reaser; Pell James; Mary Tyler Moore; Michelle Trachtenberg; Amy Hargreaves; Directed by Peter Callahan; Written by Peter Callahan; Cinematography by Sean Kirby; Music by Anton Sanko. **A:** Sr. High-Adult. **P:** Entertainment. **U:** Home. **Mov-Ent**: Swimming, Suicide. **Acq:** Purchase. **Dist:** MPI Media Group.

Against the Dark 2008 (R) — ★
Seagal vs. the vampires. In a post-apocalyptic world the few human survivors are being sucked dry by vampires. Trapped in a hospital, Commander Tao and his group of ex-military vigilantes are about to make their last stand. 94m; DVD. **C:** Skye Bennett; Emma Catherwood; Keith David; Jenna Harrison; Linden Ashby; Steven Seagal; Tanoai Reed; Directed by Richard Crudo; Written by Matthew Klickstein; Cinematography by William Trautvetter; Music by Philip White. **A:** Sr. High-Adult. **P:** Entertainment. **U:** Home. **Mov-Ent**: Hospitals. **Acq:** Purchase. **Dist:** Sony Pictures Home Entertainment Inc.

Against the Law 1998 (Unrated) — ★½
Criminal Rex (Grieco) prides himself on his abilities with a gun—leaving a trail of dead cops in his wake. His wants notoriety and, after spotting detective John Shepard (Mancuso) on a news show, decides that TV is the perfect medium to get his 15 minutes of infamy. 85m; VHS, DVD. **C:** Richard Grieco; Nick Mancuso; Nancy Allen; Steven Ford; Directed by Jim Wynorski; Written by Steve Mitchell; Bob Sheridan; Cinematography by Andrea V. Rossotto; Music by Kevin Kiner. **A:** Sr. High-Adult. **P:** Entertainment. **U:** Home. **Mov-Ent**: Crime Drama, Mass Media. **Acq:** Purchase. **Dist:** Echo Bridge Home Entertainment.

Against the Odds: The Artists of the Harlem Renaissance ????
Archival footage and rarely seen paintings, prints, photographs, and sculptures depict the story of black artists during the 1920s and '30s. 60m; VHS. **A:** Sr. High-Adult. **P:** Education. **U:** Home, Institution. **Gen-Edu**: Art & Artists, History. **Acq:** Purchase. **Dist:** Crystal Productions. $19.98.

Against the Ropes 2004 (PG-13) — ★★
"Erin Brockovich" meets "Rocky" in this biopic loosely based on the life of Detroit boxing manager Jackie Kallen (although for some reason, they set it in Cleveland). Jackie (Ryan) is a tough, harried secretary for the Cleveland Coliseum who's smarter than her skimpy outfits would indicate. She sees her chance to go somewhere in the boxing world when she buys crackhead/boxer Luther's (Epps) contract from mobbed-up manager Sam (Shalhoub) for a dollar. Ryan plays Jackie as a walking cliche spouting lousy dialogue. Shalhoub injects the movie with a bit of fun doing his best Snidley Whiplash. Dutton does better playing Luther's trainer, Felix, than he does directing fight scenes that don't show the action with much clarity. There's no clear winner here, but the audience is definitely the loser. Paramount shelved the movie for a year and a half. 111m; VHS, DVD. **C:** Meg Ryan; Omar Epps; Tony Shalhoub; Timothy Daly; Charles S. Dutton; Kerry Washington; Joe Cortese; Directed by Charles S. Dutton; Written by Cheryl Edwards; Cinematography by Jack N. Green; Music by Michael Kamen. **Pr:** Robert W. Cort; David Madden; Paramount Pictures. **A:** Jr. High-Adult. **P:** Entertainment. **U:** Home. **Mov-Ent**: Boxing, Journalism. **Acq:** Purchase. **Dist:** Paramount Pictures Corp. $29.95.

Against the Tide: Debating the Constitution 1992
Recreates the debate in the colonies over the merits of the Constitution, as it might have happened in one county in North Carolina in 1789. 16m; VHS, 3/4 U. **Pr:** Video Dialog. **A:** Primary-Sr. High. **P:** Education. **U:** Institution. **Gen-Edu**: Politics & Government, History--U.S. **Acq:** Purchase, Rent/Lease. **Dist:** New Dimension Media. $280.00.

Against the Wall 1994 (Unrated) — ★★★
Compelling and tense dramatization of the 1971 Attica, New York prison uprising in which 10 guards were held hostage and state troopers and the National Guard killed 29 prisoners before regaining control. Partially fictionalized version of the story told from the viewpoints of a young prison guard (MacLachlan) and a politicized prisoner (Jackson). Filmed at a prison in Clarksville, Tennessee. 115m; VHS, DVD. **C:** Kyle MacLachlan; Samuel L. Jackson; Clarence Williams, III; Frederic Forrest; Harry Dean Stanton; Tom Bower; Philip Bosco; Anne Heche; David Ackroyd; Directed by John Frankenheimer; Written by Ron Hutchinson; Music by Gary Chang. **Pr:** Steve McGlothen; Irwin Meyer; Jonathan Axelrod; Harvey Bibicoff; Producers Entertainment Group Ltd. **A:** Sr. High-Adult. **P:** Entertainment. **U:** Home. **Mov-Ent**: TV Movies. **Acq:** Purchase. **Dist:** Home Box Office Inc.

Against the Wall 2004 (R) — ★★
Mikey (Garrison) and Curtis (Burnam) make their claim to fame as graffiti artists in San Francisco's hard-luck Mission District. But when their illegal activity gets them arrested, Mikey starts thinking about the future and going legit while Curtis violates his probation and his self-destructive behavior shatters their friendship. Debut for Morgan. 84m; DVD. **C:** MacKenzie Firgens; Luis Saguar; Lane Garrison; Brian Burnam; Directed by Benjamin Morgan; Written by Benjamin Morgan; Cinematography by Kev Robertson. **A:** Sr. High-Adult. **P:** Entertainment. **U:** Home. **Mov-Ent**. **Acq:** Purchase. **Dist:** Screen Media Ventures, LLC.

Against the Wind 1948 (Unrated) — ★★½
A motley crew is trained for a mission into Nazi Germany to blow up records and rescue a prisoner. The first half of the film focuses on the group's training, but despite its intensity they win only a pyrrhic victory. A well-done production with solid performances from the cast. 96m/B/W; VHS, DVD. **C:** Robert Beatty; Jack Warner; Simone Signoret; Gordon Jackson; Paul Dupuis; Peter Illing; Directed by Charles Crichton. **Pr:** Ealing Studios; GFD. **A:** Jr. High-Adult. **P:** Entertainment. **U:** Home. **Mov-Ent**. **Acq:** Purchase. **Dist:** Synergy Entertainment, Inc. $19.95.

Against the Wind 1990 — ★★
Juan (Banderas) takes refuge in a remote area of Andalusia in an effort to get away from a mutally obsessive love. But his exile is in vain when his lover appears—his sister (Suarez). Spanish with subtitles. 117m; VHS, DVD. **C:** Antonio Banderas; Emma Suarez; Directed by Paco Perinan. **A:** College-Adult. **P:** Entertainment. **U:** Home. **L:** Spanish. **Mov-Ent**: Drama, Spain. **Acq:** Purchase. **Dist:** Facets Multimedia Inc. $19.95.

Against Violence 1991
Six women featured at the conference "Women in a Violent Society" speak out about violence against women. Andrea Dworkin, Sandra Butler, Carla McKague, Shirley Turcotte, Kate Millet and Rosemary Brown explore women's issues such as: pornography and serial killers, pollution and breast cancer, the sexual abuse of children, ritual abuse, women and the mental health system and violence against women from an international perspective. Each speaker's presentation is approximately eight to ten minutes long with the times logged on the tape for easy access. A discussion guide is included. 54m; VHS. **A:** Sr. High-Adult. **P:** Education. **U:** Home, Institution. **Gen-Edu**: Women, Rape. **Acq:** Purchase. **Dist:** Moving Images Distribution.

Against Wind and Tide: A Cuban Odyssey 1981
Focusing on the Cuban refugees who came during the Mariel boatlift in 1980, this program looks at the often arbitrary and unclear American immigration policy and shows an American public that is divided in its attitudes towards newcomers. 55m; VHS, 3/4 U. **Pr:** Suzanne Bauman; Jim Burroughs; Paul Neshamkin. **A:** Sr. High-Adult. **P:** Education. **U:** Institution. **Gen-Edu**: Immigration. **Acq:** Purchase. **Dist:** Filmakers Library Inc.

Agamemnon 1991
Presents a modernized production of Aeschylus' play performed by the London Small Theater Company. 120m; VHS. **A:** Adult. **P:** Education. **U:** Institution. **Fin-Art**: Theater. **Acq:** Purchase. **Dist:** Insight Media. $195.00.

Agapeland 1988
Presents religious entertainment for children. 30m; VHS. **Pr:** Bridgestone Production Group. **A:** Preschool-Primary. **P:** Religious. **U:** Home. **Gen-Edu**. **Acq:** Purchase. **Dist:** Alpha Omega Publications Inc. $14.95.
Indiv. Titles: 1. Doog's Garage #1 2. Doog's Garage #2 3. Peter and Magic Seeds 4. Nathaniel 5. Humpty 6. Red Nose Express.

Agata and the Storm 2004 (Unrated) — ★★
Determinedly cheerful, middle-aged Genoa bookstore owner Agata is surprised when she is suddenly wooed by young customer Nico, who turns out to be married. But her pleasure at the unexpected romance literally causes electrical sparks. Meanwhile, Agata's brother Gustavo learns he was adopted, so he leaves his troubled marriage to meet his newly-discovered brother Romeo, a traveling salesman whose dream is to start a trout farm. Italian with subtitles. 118m; DVD. **C:** Licia Maglietta; Emilio Solfrizzi; Guiseppe Battiston; Claudio Santamaria; Marina Massironi; Giselda Volodi; Directed by Silvio Soldini; Written by Silvio Soldini; Doriana Leondeff; Francesco Piccolo; Cinematography by Arnaldo Catinari; Music by Giovanni Venosta. **A:** College-Adult. **P:** Entertainment. **U:** Home. **L:** Italian. **Mov-Ent**: Adoption. **Acq:** Purchase. **Dist:** Film Movement.

Agatha 1979 (PG) — ★★½
A speculative period drama about Agatha Christie's still unexplained disappearance in 1926, and a fictional American reporter's efforts to find her. Beautiful but lackluster mystery. Unfortunately, Hoffman and Redgrave generate few sparks. 98m; VHS, DVD. **C:** Dustin Hoffman; Vanessa Redgrave; Timothy Dalton; Helen Morse; Tony Britton; Timothy West; Celia Gregory; Pam(ela) Austin; Directed by Michael Apted. **A:** Primary-Adult. **P:** Entertainment. **U:** Home. **Mov-Ent**: Mystery & Suspense, Romance. **Acq:** Purchase. **Dist:** WarnerArchive.com. $64.95.

Agatha Christie: A Life in Pictures 2004 (Unrated) — ★★½
In 1926, famed mystery writer Agatha Christie (Williams) went missing for 11 days. She was found at a hotel and couldn't remember what had happened to her, although hypnosis revealed that Christie knew her husband Archie (Coulthard) was an unfaithful wastrel. But Christie also left clues in her writings and, in 1962, the aged Agatha (Massey) speaks of her disappearance to a journalist. 90m; DVD. **C:** Olivia Williams; Anna Massey; Raymond Coulthard; Stephen Boxer; Anthony O'Donnell; Directed by Richard Curson Smith; Written by Richard Curson Smith; Cinematography by Jeff Baynes; Music by Andrew Phillips. **A:** Jr. High-Adult. **P:** Entertainment. **U:** Home. **Mov-Ent**. **Acq:** Purchase. **Dist:** Acorn Media Group Inc.

Agatha Christie: How Did She Do It? 1986
This survey of the career of Agatha Christie includes excerpts from her books, plays and films, which include 87 crime novels, as well as film footage of the author, and interviews. 45m; VHS. **C:** Directed by Toby Wallace. **Pr:** London Weekend Television. **A:** Jr. High-Adult. **P:** Entertainment. **U:** Home. **Gen-Edu**: Literature--English. **Acq:** Purchase. **Dist:** Home Vision Cinema. $39.95.

Agatha Christie's A Caribbean Mystery 1983 — ★★½
Miss Marple's vacation turns into another sluething adventure when she must solve the murder of a retired British Army officer. Faithful adaptation updates the action form the 1950s to the '80s in fine fashion. 96m; VHS, DVD. **C:** Helen Hayes; Barnard Hughes; Jameson Parker; Season Hubley; Swoosie Kurtz; Cassie Yates; Zakes Mokae; Stephen Macht; Maurice Evans; Lynne Moody; George Innes; Brock Peters; Directed by Robert Lewis; Written by Sue Grafton; Steve Humphrey; Cinematography by Ted Voightlander; Music by Lee Holdridge. **A:** Jr. High-Adult. **P:** Entertainment. **U:** Home. **Mov-Ent**: Mystery & Suspense, Caribbean. **Acq:** Purchase. **Dist:** Movies Unlimited. $13.49.

Agatha Christie's Garden: Murder and Mystery in Devon 20?? (Unrated)
A guided tour of Greenway, the 30-acre garden owned by author Agatha Christie, and used by her as a retreat to escape public life. 66m; DVD. **A:** Sr. High-Adult. **P:** Entertainment. **U:** Home. **Gen-Edu**: Documentary Films. **Acq:** Purchase. **Dist:** Acorn Media Group Inc. $14.99.

Agatha Christie's Miss Marple 198?
Elderly, proper Jane Marple hardly seems the sort to get involved in murder and mayhem but her prim exterior hides a razor-sharp mind and intuitive understanding of criminal behavior. Two boxed collections. 65m; VHS. **C:** Joan Hickson. **Pr:** British Broadcasting Corporation. **A:** Jr. High-Adult. **P:** Entertainment. **U:** Home. **Mov-Ent**: Mystery & Suspense. **Acq:** Purchase. **Dist:** Video Collectibles; A&E Television Networks L.L.C.; New Video Group.
Indiv. Titles: 1. A Caribbean Mystery 2. The Mirror Cracked from Side to Side 3. Sleeping Murder 4. 4:50 from Paddington 5. Murder at the Vicarage 6. The Moving Finger 7. They Do It with Mirrors 8. Nemesis 9. At Bertram's Hotel.

Agatha Christie's Miss Marple: At Bertram's Hotel 1986
London's Betram Hotel is a properly quiet retreat—until Miss Marple arrives. First society beauty Bess Sedgwick and her daughter are romantic rivals and then the Irish doorman turns up dead. 100m; VHS, DVD. **C:** Joan Hickson; Caroline Blakiston; Helena Michell; George Baker; James Cossins; Directed by Mary McMurray; Written by Jill Hyem; Cinematography by John Walker. **Pr:** George Gallaccio; British Broadcasting Corporation. **A:** Jr. High-Adult. **P:** Entertainment. **U:** Home. **Mov-Ent**: Mystery & Suspense. **Acq:** Purchase. **Dist:** A&E Television Networks L.L.C. $19.95.

Agatha Christie's Miss Marple: Murder at the Vicarage 1986
Colonel Lucius Protheroe may be the most unpopular man in St. Mary Mead, unpopular enough to get himself murdered. There's no shortage of suspects and it's up to Miss Marple to find the killer. 100m; VHS, DVD. **C:** Joan Hickson; Paul Eddington; Cheryl Campbell; Robert Lang; Polly Adams; Directed by Julian Amyes; Written by T.R. Bowen; Cinematography by John Walker. **Pr:** George Gallaccio; British Broadcasting Corporation. **A:** Jr. High-Adult. **P:** Entertainment. **U:** Home. **Mov-Ent**: Mystery & Suspense. **Acq:** Purchase. **Dist:** A&E Television Networks L.L.C. $19.95.

Agatha Christie's Miss Marple: Nemesis 1986
A cryptic letter from a recently deceased friend sends Jane Marple on a bus tour of historic homes, with a group of passengers who have not gathered by chance. 100m; VHS, DVD. **C:** Joan Hickson; Margaret Tyzack; Anna Cropper; Valerie Lush; Directed by David Tucker; Written by T.R. Bowen; Cinematography by John Walker. **Pr:** George Gallaccio; British Broadcasting Corporation. **A:** Jr. High-Adult. **P:** Entertainment. **U:** Home. **Mov-Ent**: Mystery & Suspense. **Acq:** Purchase. **Dist:** A&E Television Networks L.L.C. $19.95.

Agatha Christie's Miss Marple Set I 1983
Collection of four mysteries with Miss Jane Marple investigating a murder at a posh resort, hunting for a corpse on a train, and poking around a haunting house. 480m; VHS, DVD. **A:** Adult. **P:** Entertainment. **U:** Home. **Mov-Ent**: Mystery & Suspense, Drama. **Acq:** Purchase. **Dist:** A&E Television Networks L.L.C. $39.95.
Indiv. Titles: 1. Murder at the Vicarthge 2. Nemesis 3. The Do It With Mirrors 4. The Moving Finger.

Agatha Christie's Miss Marple Set II 1986
Collection of four mysteries with Miss Jane Marple cracking a chain of deadly letter and puzzling over a poisoning. 480m; VHS, DVD. **A:** Adult. **P:** Entertainment. **U:** Home. **Mov-Ent**: Mystery & Suspense, Drama. **Acq:** Purchase. **Dist:** A&E Television Networks L.L.C. $49.95.
Indiv. Titles: 1. Sleeping Mirror 2. The Mirror Cracked from Side to Side 3. 50 From Paddington.

Agatha Christie's Miss Marple: The Moving Finger 1985
Lymston village has been besieged by poion-pen letters and Maud Calthrop, the vicar's wife, calls in her old friend Jane Marple to see who's causing all the mischief. Then two murders occur and still the letters keep coming. 100m; VHS, DVD. **C:** Joan Hickson; Michael Culver; Richard Pearson; Andrew Bicknell; Sandra Payne; Directed by Roy Boulting; Written by Julia Jones; Cinematography by Ian Hilton. **Pr:** Guy Slater; British Broadcasting Corporation. **A:** Jr. High-Adult. **P:** Entertainment. **U:** Home. **Mov-Ent**: Mystery & Suspense. **Acq:** Purchase. **Dist:** A&E Television Networks L.L.C. $19.95.

Agatha Christie's Miss Marple: They Do It with Mirrors 1991
Miss Marple travels to the country mansion of her friend Carrie-Louise Serrocold to discover who's poisoning her. It could be anyone in her extended family and then there's that nearby reformatory for young criminals... 100m; VHS, DVD. **C:** Joan Hickson; Joss Ackland; Jean Simmons; Faith Brook; Gillian Barge; Directed by Norman Stone; Written by T.R. Bowen; Cinematography by John Walker. **Pr:** George Gallaccio; British Broadcasting Corporation. **A:** Jr. High-Adult. **P:** Entertainment. **U:** Home. **Mov-Ent:** Mystery & Suspense. **Acq:** Purchase. **Dist:** A&E Television Networks L.L.C. $19.95.

Agatha Christie's Murder is Easy 1982 — ★★
Luke Williams (Bixby), an American computer expert, is on a train to London when he meets an old woman (Hayes) who confides that she is going to Scotland Yard to report some mysterious deaths in her village. When she is killd by a hit-and-run driver after leaving the train, he decides to investigate. When he reaches the village, he is aided by a local girl who also suspects foul play. So-so mystery suffers from attempts to update the mystery with computer technology. Adapted from the Agatha Christie novel "Easy to Kill." 95m; VHS, DVD. **C:** Bill Bixby; Lesley-Anne Down; Olivia de Havilland; Helen Hayes; Patrick Allen; Freddie Jones; Shane Briant; Leigh Lawson; Jonathan Pryce; Carol MacReady; Directed by Claude Whatham; Written by Carmen Culver; Cinematography by Brian Tufano; Music by Gerald Fried. **A:** Jr. High-Adult. **P:** Entertainment. **U:** Home. **Mov-Ent:** Mystery & Suspense, Computers, Trains. **Acq:** Purchase. **Dist:** Movies Unlimited. $11.99.

Agatha Christie's Murder with Mirrors 1985 — ★★
Lightweight TV mystery has Miss Marple (Hayes) once again sleuthing about to help an old friend (Davis) who thinks she's going to be killed for her estate. Hayes is once again delightful, but things begin to fade about half way through. Look for Tim Roth spicing things up in an early role. 96m; VHS, DVD. **C:** Helen Hayes; Bette Davis; Leo McKern; John Mills; John Laughlin; Dorothy Tutin; Anton Rodgers; John Woodvine; James Coombes; Tim Roth; Directed by Dick Lowry; Written by George Eckstein; Cinematography by Brian West; Music by Richard Rodney Bennett. **A:** Jr. High-Adult. **P:** Entertainment. **U:** Home. **Mov-Ent:** Mystery & Suspense. **Acq:** Purchase. **Dist:** Movies Unlimited. $13.49.

Agatha Christie's Partners in Crime Set 1 2003
Features Christie's rarely seen but always loved newlyweds, Tommy and Prudence "Tuppence" Beresford, who take over a London detective agency and find missing jewels, a poltergeist, poison chocolates, and many more mysteries. 330m; DVD. **C:** James Warwick; Francesca Annis. **A:** Sr. High-Adult. **P:** Entertainment. **U:** Home. **Mov-Ent:** Mystery & Suspense, Drama. **Acq:** Purchase. **Dist:** Acorn Media Group Inc.

Agatha Christie's Partners in Crime Set 2 2004
Tommy and Prudence "Tuppence" Beresford continue their London detective agency duties solving high-society crimes involving a nightclub forgery, a missing fiancee, and other delightful debauchery. 324m; DVD. **C:** James Warwick; Francesca Annis. **A:** Adult. **P:** Entertainment. **U:** Home. **Mov-Ent:** Mystery & Suspense, Drama. **Acq:** Purchase. **Dist:** Acorn Media Group Inc.

Agatha Christie's Poirot 2000 — ★★★
This set includes two stylized films based on the writings of Agatha Christie and the adventures of her famous detective, Hercule Poirot (Suchet). In the first feature, "Lord Edgware Dies," Poirot finds himself smitten with the actress Jane Wilkinson. When her estranged husband is murdered, Poirot must find the killer. In the second film, "The Murder of Roger Ackroyd," Poirot again finds himself forced to solve a murder. This time out, the killing of a wealthy industrialist exposes a web of blackmail, envy, and murder. 200m; DVD. **A:** Jr. High-Adult. **P:** Entertainment. **U:** Home. **Mov-Ent:** Mystery & Suspense. **Acq:** Purchase. **Dist:** A&E Television Networks L.L.C. $39.95.

Agatha Christie's Poirot: Death in the Clouds 2000
A blackmailer is found dead aboard a plane that is none too short of suspects. Enter unconventional but always cordial Belgian Hercule Poirot to solve the case, with a poison dart gun and an illegitimate daughter who unexpectedly appears and disappears as his only clues. Aerial shots of England and art deco interiors make this one of the most lavishly filmed in the whodunit series. 103m; DVD. **C:** David Suchet; Philip Jackson. **A:** Adult. **P:** Entertainment. **U:** Home. **Mov-Ent:** Mystery & Suspense, Drama. **Acq:** Purchase. **Dist:** Acorn Media Group Inc.

Agatha Christie's Poirot: Evil Under the Sun 2002
Poirot is ordered to take some time off at "Burgh Island," a seaside health farm, after collapsing in front of Inspector Japp, his rival. But as we would expect, mysteries follow him, and the savvy detective is on the case of the strangled heiress. Suspects include the victim's husband and 17-year old stepson, and the jealous wife of a journalist who had been seen fraternizing with the lovely heiress. 100m; DVD. **C:** David Suchet; Philip Jackson. **A:** Adult. **P:** Entertainment. **U:** Home. **Mov-Ent:** Mystery & Suspense, Drama. **Acq:** Purchase. **Dist:** A&E Television Networks L.L.C.

Agatha Christie's Poirot: Hickory Dickory Dock 2002
Miss Lemon asks Poirot to look into some shady goings-on at her sister's boarding house business, where it seems there has been a rash of thefts lately. As the investigation proceeds theft turns to murder and only a house mouse knows who is responsible. 103m; DVD. **C:** David Suchet; Philip Jackson. **A:** Adult. **P:** Entertainment. **U:** Home. **Mov-Ent:** Mystery & Suspense, Drama. **Acq:** Purchase. **Dist:** Acorn Media Group Inc.

Agatha Christie's Poirot: Murder in Mesopotamia 2001
Hercule Poirot (Suchet) is vacationing near Baghdad and he travels to an archeological dig with his friend Hastings (Fraser). The wife (Barnes) of archeologist Dr. Leidner (Berglas) tells the sleuth that she has been receiving threatening letters from her first husband, who was presumed dead. Then she's killed and Poirot helps the police expose the killer. 100m; VHS, DVD. **C:** David Suchet; Hugh Fraser; Ron Berglas; Dinah Stabb; Barbara Barnes. **A:** Jr. High-Adult. **P:** Entertainment. **U:** Home. **Mov-Ent:** Middle East, Archaeology. **Acq:** Purchase. **Dist:** A&E Television Networks L.L.C.

Agatha Christie's Poirot: Murder on the Links 2002
While Hastings enjoys some golf and Poirot some French cuisine at a seaside resort, their holiday turns to a case of abduction and murder. To spice up matters Hastings becomes smitten with the beautiful prime suspect and Poirot's sleuthing skills are challenged by an egotistical French detective. 103m; DVD. **C:** David Suchet; Philip Jackson; Hugh Fraser. **A:** Adult. **P:** Entertainment. **U:** Home. **Mov-Ent:** Mystery & Suspense, Drama. **Acq:** Purchase. **Dist:** Acorn Media Group Inc.

Agatha Christie's Poirot: Mysterious Affair at Styles 2001
Toward the end of World War I, Hastings brings his friend Poirot to the Styles St. Mary estate, where the Cavendish family is facing troubles that turn deadly after the suspicious marriage of the matriarch to a younger man. A broken coffee cup, spilled candle grease, disheveled mantel ornaments, a false beard, and an all too eager suspect are the puzzle pieces the sleuthing duo has to work with to find the killer. 103m; DVD. **C:** David Suchet; Philip Jackson; Hugh Fraser. **A:** Adult. **P:** Entertainment. **U:** Home. **Mov-Ent:** Mystery & Suspense, Drama. **Acq:** Purchase. **Dist:** Acorn Media Group Inc.

Agatha Christie's Poirot: One Two Buckle My Shoe 2001
After an uneventful but dreaded trip to the dentist, Poirot is called back to the office when the dentist and two of his patients of the day are found murdered. As expected, Poirot maneuvers the twists and turns of the case before Inspector Japp is any the wiser and the killer is climactically revealed. 103m; DVD. **C:** David Suchet; Philip Jackson; Hugh Fraser. **A:** Adult. **P:** Entertainment. **U:** Home. **Mov-Ent:** Mystery & Suspense, Drama. **Acq:** Purchase. **Dist:** Acorn Media Group Inc.

Agatha Christie's Poirot, Vol. 1: The Adventure of the Clapham Cook 199? (Unrated)
Christie's fussy Belgian detective with the little gray cells is asked to find a vanished cook who may be involved in a bank robbery. Made for British television. 50m; VHS. **C:** David Suchet; Hugh Fraser. **A:** Jr. High-Adult. **P:** Entertainment. **U:** Home. **Mov-Ent:** Mystery & Suspense, TV Movies. **Acq:** Purchase. **Dist:** Signals Video; Movies Unlimited; Home Vision Cinema. $19.99.

Agatha Christie's Poirot, Vol. 2: Murder in the Mews 199?
A young woman commits suicide during a fireworks celebration but when Poirot is asked to investigate he suspects foul play. Made for British television. 50m; VHS. **C:** David Suchet; Hugh Fraser. **A:** Jr. High-Adult. **P:** Entertainment. **U:** Home. **Mov-Ent:** Mystery & Suspense, TV Movies. **Acq:** Purchase. **Dist:** Signals Video; Movies Unlimited; Home Vision Cinema. $19.99.

Agatha Christie's Poirot, Vol. 3: The Adventure of Johnnie Waverly 199?
Police ignore the kidnapping threats to a three-year-old boy but Poirot believes them and tries to foil the criminals. Made for British television. 50m; VHS. **C:** David Suchet; Hugh Fraser. **A:** Jr. High-Adult. **P:** Entertainment. **U:** Home. **Mov-Ent:** Mystery & Suspense, TV Movies. **Acq:** Purchase. **Dist:** Signals Video; Movies Unlimited; Home Vision Cinema. $19.99.

Agatha Christie's Poirot, Vol. 4: Four and Twenty Blackbirds 199?
Poirot's visit to the dentist ties in with murder. Made for British television. 50m; VHS. **C:** David Suchet; Hugh Fraser. **A:** Jr. High-Adult. **P:** Entertainment. **U:** Home. **Mov-Ent:** Mystery & Suspense, TV Movies. **Acq:** Purchase. **Dist:** Signals Video; Movies Unlimited; Home Vision Cinema. $19.99.

Agatha Christie's Poirot, Vol. 5: The Third Floor Flat 199?
A shooting occurs in the flat two floors below him and Poirot decides to put his little gray cells to work. Made for British television. 50m; VHS. **C:** David Suchet; Hugh Fraser. **A:** Jr. High-Adult. **P:** Entertainment. **U:** Home. **Mov-Ent:** Mystery & Suspense, TV Movies. **Acq:** Purchase. **Dist:** Signals Video; Movies Unlimited; Home Vision Cinema. $19.99.

Agatha Christie's Poirot, Vol. 6: Triangle at Rhodes 199?
While on vacation in Greece Poirot offers advice to a happily married couple. Unfortunately, they happen to be married to other people. Made for British television. 50m; VHS. **C:** David Suchet; Hugh Fraser. **A:** Jr. High-Adult. **P:** Entertainment. **U:** Home. **Mov-Ent:** Mystery & Suspense, TV Movies. **Acq:** Purchase. **Dist:** Signals Video; Movies Unlimited; Home Vision Cinema. $19.99.

Agatha Christie's Poirot, Vol. 7: Problem at Sea 199?
Poirot and Captain Hastings sail to the Egyptian city of Alexandria but murder disrupts their holiday. Made for British television. 50m; VHS. **C:** David Suchet; Hugh Fraser. **A:** Jr. High-Adult. **P:** Entertainment. **U:** Home. **Mov-Ent:** Mystery & Suspense, TV Movies. **Acq:** Purchase. **Dist:** Signals Video; Movies Unlimited; Home Vision Cinema. $19.99.

Agatha Christie's Poirot, Vol. 8: The Incredible Theft 199?
Poirot investigates the theft of wartime plans but the case may have more significance than he first suspected. Made for British television. 50m; VHS. **C:** David Suchet; Hugh Fraser. **A:** Jr. High-Adult. **P:** Entertainment. **U:** Home. **Mov-Ent:** Mystery & Suspense, TV Movies. **Acq:** Purchase. **Dist:** Signals Video; Movies Unlimited; Home Vision Cinema. $19.99.

Agatha Christie's Poirot, Vol. 9: The King of Clubs 199?
Poirot meets a group of eccentric movie stars and discovers a murder—but is it a stage murder or real? Made for British television. 50m; VHS. **C:** David Suchet; Hugh Fraser. **A:** Jr. High-Adult. **P:** Entertainment. **U:** Home. **Mov-Ent:** Mystery & Suspense, TV Movies. **Acq:** Purchase. **Dist:** Signals Video; Movies Unlimited; Home Vision Cinema. $19.99.

Agatha Christie's Poirot, Vol. 10: The Dream 199?
A tyrannical tycoon is frightened by strange dreams and calls on Poirot for assistance. But when the detective gets to close to the truth, trouble occurs. Made for British television. 50m; VHS. **C:** David Suchet; Hugh Fraser. **A:** Jr. High-Adult. **P:** Entertainment. **U:** Home. **Mov-Ent:** Mystery & Suspense, TV Movies. **Acq:** Purchase. **Dist:** Signals Video; Movies Unlimited; Home Vision Cinema. $19.99.

Agatha Christie's Romantic Detectives 2005
A collection of Agatha Christie's romantic crime solving duos. Includes "Tommy and Tuppence: Partners in Crime", "Why Didn't They Ask Evans?", "Seven Dials Mystery", and the documentary "Agatha Christie: A Life in Pictures". 1020m; DVD. **A:** Family. **P:** Entertainment. **U:** Home. **Mov-Ent:** Drama, Mystery & Suspense. **Acq:** Purchase. **Dist:** Acorn Media Group Inc. $99.99.

Agatha Christie's Sparkling Cyanide 1983 — ★★
Somebody spiked the champagne—with cyanide! This really brings down a socialite couple's anniversary party as they have to set aside the hor's douvres to solve the whodunit. Cheesy but enjoyable, the twist ending adds to the fun. 96m; VHS, DVD. **C:** Anthony Andrews; Deborah Raffin; Pamela Bellwood; Nancy Marchand; Josef Sommer; David Huffman; Christine Belford; June Chadwick; Harry (Henry) Morgan; Michael Woods; Directed by Robert Lewis; Written by Robert M. Young; Sue Grafton; Steve Humphrey; Cinematography by Ted Voightlander. **A:** Jr. High-Adult. **P:** Entertainment. **U:** Home. **Mov-Ent:** Mystery & Suspense, Poisons. **Acq:** Purchase. **Dist:** Warner Home Video, Inc. $13.49.

Agatha Christie's The Pale Horse 1996 (Unrated) — ★★½
When writer Mark Easterbrook is accused of murdering a priest, the only clue to clearing himself is a mysterious list of names. Now he has to figure out the connection between the names if he expects to clear himself. 100m; VHS, DVD. **C:** Michael Byrne; Ruth Madoc; Leslie Phillips; Jean Marsh; Directed by Charles Beeson. **A:** Jr. High-Adult. **P:** Entertainment. **U:** Home. **Mov-Ent:** Mystery & Suspense, TV Movies. **Acq:** Purchase. **Dist:** A&E Television Networks L.L.C.

Agatha Christie's Thirteen at Dinner 1985 — ★★
Hercule Poirot must solve the case when an actress's ex-husband dies shortly after granting her a divorce. Lack of character development hurt this otherwise solid outing. Fine cast is highlighted by Ustinov and Dunaway. 91m; VHS, DVD. **C:** Peter Ustinov; Faye Dunaway; David Suchet; Jonathan Cecil; Bill Nighy; Lee Horsley; Diane Keen; Allan Cuthbertson; John Barron; Amanda Pays; Lesley Dunlop; Cameo(s) David Frost; Directed by Lou Antonio; Written by Rod Browning; Cinematography by Curtis Clark; Music by John Addison. **A:** Jr. High-Adult. **P:** Entertainment. **U:** Home. **Mov-Ent:** Mystery & Suspense. **Acq:** Purchase. **Dist:** Movies Unlimited. $13.49.

Agatha Christie's Tommy & Tuppence: Partners in Crime 1983
Married crime-solving duo Tommy and Tuppence Beresford tackle mysteries in the glittering 1920s. 330m; VHS, DVD. **A:** Adult. **P:** Entertainment. **U:** Home. **Mov-Ent:** Drama, Mystery & Suspense. **Acq:** Purchase. **Dist:** Acorn Media Group Inc. $49.95.

Agatha Christie's Tommy and Tuppence: Partners in Crime, Set 2 2004
The second season featuring Agatha Christie's crime solving duo Tommy and Tuppence Beresford. 320m; DVD. **A:** Sr. High-Adult. **P:** Entertainment. **U:** Home. **Mov-Ent:** Drama, Mystery & Suspense. **Acq:** Purchase. **Dist:** Acorn Media Group Inc. $39.99.

Agatha Christie's Why Didn't They Ask Evans? 1981
When Bobby Jones discovers a man lying injured on the rocks during a round of golf on a cliff-top course, a mystery ensues. 180m; VHS, DVD. **A:** Adult. **P:** Entertainment. **U:** Home. **Mov-Ent:** Drama, Mystery & Suspense. **Acq:** Purchase. **Dist:** Acorn Media Group Inc. $29.95.

Age Discrimination: No Gray Areas 1989
This video helps employers understand the impact of the recent Age Discrimination Act, and how to avoid discrimination suits and best utilize older workers. 26m; VHS, 8 mm, 3/4 U. **TV Std:** NTSC, PAL, SECAM. **Pr:** CTF. **A:** College-Adult. **P:** Education.

U: Institution, CCTV, SURA. **Gen-Edu**: Management, Aging. **Acq:** Purchase, Rent/Lease, Duplication License. **Dist:** Phoenix Learning Group. $600.00.

Age Discrimination Problems in the Contest of a Reduction in Work Force 1983
This program examines age discrimination under the Age Discrimination Employment Act and other laws that guard against age discrimination. 300m; VHS, 3/4 U. **Pr:** Practicing Law Institute. **A:** Sr. High-Adult. **P:** Education. **U:** Institution, Home. **Bus-Ind**: Law. **Acq:** Purchase, Rent/Lease. **Dist:** Practising Law Institute.

Age Happens 2000
Explains psychological and physiological aspects of aging, and ways older people can maintain their health and functional independence. 28m; VHS. **A:** Adult. **P:** Professional. **U:** Institution. **Hea-Sci**: Aging, Patient Care, Health Education. **Acq:** Purchase. **Dist:** Aquarius Health Care Media. $99.00.

Age Is No Barrier 19??
Encourages the aging adult population of Canada to work towards optimal health through physical fitness and centers on the story of a group of seniors who call themselves "U of Agers." This group is involved heavily in the use of gymnastics as a form of staying fit. 24m; VHS. **Pr:** National Film Board of Canada. **A:** Jr. High-Adult. **P:** Education. **U:** Institution. **Gen-Edu**: Aging, Fitness/Exercise, Canada. **Acq:** Purchase. **Dist:** National Film Board of Canada; Filmakers Library Inc. $295.00.

Age Isn't Everything 1991 (R) — ★
An appalling clumsy comedy about a recent college graduate who abruptly becomes an old man while retaining his youthful exterior. He looks the same, but walks slowly and talks with a thick Yiddish accent, get it? The cast just marks time until an inexplicable ending. 91m; VHS. **C:** Jonathan Silverman; Robert Prosky; Rita Moreno; Paul Sorvino; Rita Karin; Robert Cicchini; Brian Williams; Dee Hoty; Dr. Joyce Brothers; Bella Abzug; Directed by Douglas Katz; Written by Douglas Katz; Cinematography by Michael Spiller. **Pr:** Joan Fishman. **A:** Sr. High-Adult. **P:** Entertainment. **U:** Home. **Mov-Ent**: Comedy--Black, Aging, Adolescence. **Acq:** Purchase. **Dist:** $89.99.

Age Issues in the U.S.A.: Senior Citizens 1992
Discusses issues such as healthcare, income distribution, housing, and quality of life. 60m; VHS. **A:** Adult. **P:** Education. **U:** Institution. **Gen-Edu**: Prejudice. **Acq:** Purchase. **Dist:** RMI Media. $99.00.

Age Issues in the U.S.A.: Youth Culture 1992
Focuses on gang culture through the eyes of a police detective at an Illinois high school. 60m; VHS. **A:** Adult. **P:** Education. **U:** Institution. **Gen-Edu**: Prejudice. **Acq:** Purchase. **Dist:** RMI Media. $99.00.

An Age of Conformity 1991
Examines domestic life in the late 1940s and 1950s. 30m; VHS. **A:** Adult. **P:** Education. **U:** Institution. **Gen-Edu**: History--U.S. **Acq:** Purchase. **Dist:** RMI Media. $99.00.

The Age of Consent 1932 (Unrated) — ★1/2
College student Michael (Cromwell) and his girlfriend Betty (Wilson) plan to be virtuous until they can get married after Michael graduates. However, Michael is lured by the charms of young waitress Dora (Judge) whose father thinks a shotgun wedding is in order. Michael's facing a marriage to a girl he doesn't love and losing forever the girl he does. 62m/B/W; DVD. **C:** Richard Cromwell; Dorothy Wilson; Arline Judge; Eric Linden; John Halliday; Aileen Pringle; Reginald Barlow; Directed by Gregory La Cava; Written by Sarah Y. Mason; Francis Cockrell; Cinematography by J. Roy Hunt. **A:** Sr. High-Adult. **P:** Entertainment. **U:** Home. **L:** English. **Mov-Ent**: Romance. **Acq:** Purchase. **Dist:** WarnerArchive.com.

Age of Consent 1969 (Unrated) — ★★
Disillusioned painter Bradley Morahan (Mason) leaves his successful career in New York to return to his Australian homeland. He rents a house on a sparsely populated Great Barrier Reef island and promptly notices the fleshy beauty of teenager Cora (Mirren), who agrees to pose nude for him, which reinvigorates Morahan in more than one way. Morahan's paradise is invaded by a mooching old friend (MacGowran) who steals from him, and Cora's alcoholic granny (Carr-Glynn) makes trouble. 103m; DVD. **C:** James Mason; Helen Mirren; Jack MacGowran; Andonia Katsaros; Neva Carr-Glynn; Michael Bodde; Directed by Michael Powell; Written by Peter Yeldham; Cinematography by Hannes Staudinger; Music by Peter Sculthorpe. **A:** Sr. High-Adult. **P:** Entertainment. **U:** Home. **Mov-Ent**: Art & Artists, Australia. **Acq:** Purchase. **Dist:** Sony Pictures Home Entertainment Inc.

Age of Dinosaurs 2013 (Unrated) — ★
Reminiscent of 'Jurassic Park,' a fireman must work to save his daughter after cloned dinosaurs escape from a museum exhibit. 89m; DVD, Blu-Ray, Streaming. **C:** Treat Williams; Ronny Cox; Jillian Rose Reed; Joshua Michael Allen; Andray Johnson; Directed by Joseph J. Lawson; Written by Hank Woon, Jr.; Cinematography by Richard J. Vialet; Music by Chris Ridenhour. **A:** Sr. High-Adult. **P:** Entertainment. **U:** Home. **L:** English. **Mov-Ent. Acq:** Purchase, Rent/Lease. **Dist:** The Asylum. $14.95 14.95 9.99.

The Age of Discovery 1998
Presents facts and interpretations of events from 1400 to 1550. 30m; VHS, DVD; Closed Captioned. **A:** Jr. High. **P:** Education. **U:** Institution. **Gen-Edu**: History--Renaissance, Explorers. **Acq:** Purchase. **Dist:** Zenger Media. $95.00.

The Age of Enlightenment 19??
Overviews the period of Enlightenment and profiles the achievements of such greats as Newton, Locke, and Rousseau, discussing the connection between natural laws and human existence. Complete with teacher's guide. 30m; VHS. **A:** Sr. High-College. **P:** Education. **U:** Institution. **Gen-Edu**: History--Enlightenment, Philosophy & Ideology. **Acq:** Purchase. **Dist:** Cambridge Educational. $49.95.

The Age of Exploration ????
Five-volume set examines how people thought about the European discovery of America, early attempts at discovering a Northwest Passage to the Indies, voyages of the Spanish to Central and South America, and cultural interactions between the Old and New World. 115m; VHS. **A:** Jr. High. **P:** Education. **U:** Institution. **Gen-Edu**: History--Renaissance, Explorers. **Acq:** Purchase. **Dist:** Zenger Media. $265.00.
Indiv. Titles: 1. The Beginnings of Exploration 2. Christopher Columbus 3. Europe Explores the Americas: Southern Voyages & Settlements 4. Europe Explores the America: Northern Voyages & Settlements 5. The Age of Exploration.

Age of Exploration 1998
Three video set covers native people of America; voyages of Cabot, Columbus, Cortes, and Pizarro; Ponce de Leon, the Vikings; explorations of Cartier, Coronado, De Soto, Drake, Hudson, and Champlain; the Huguenots; St. Augustine; and the Roanoke, Jamestown and Plymouth colonies. 26m; VHS. **A:** Jr. High. **P:** Education. **U:** Institution. **Gen-Edu**: History--Renaissance, Explorers. **Acq:** Purchase. **Dist:** Zenger Media. $171.00.

The Age of Exploration: How Did It Change the World? 1990
Part of the Age of Exploration Series. Details the exchange of ideas, materials, and foods that took place between the early European explorers and the Native Americans. 16m; VHS, SVS, 3/4 U. **A:** Primary-Sr. High. **P:** Education. **U:** Institution. **Gen-Edu**: History, Explorers. **Acq:** Purchase, Rent/Lease. **Dist:** Encyclopedia Britannica. $99.00.

Age of Flight Series 19??
Educational series discusses the history of flight, from Kitty Hawk through present-day jet fighters. Contains aerial footage of profiled flying machines. 780m; VHS. **A:** Family. **P:** Education. **U:** Institution. **Gen-Edu**: Aeronautics, History. **Acq:** Purchase. **Dist:** Instructional Video.
Indiv. Titles: 1. Kitty Hawk 2. Choppers 3. Bombers 4. Modern Warplanes 5. Dawn of the Jet Age: The First 25 Years 6. Jets: The New Generation 7. MIG Alley 8. X-Planes (experimental) 9. Story of Naval Air Power 10. Rolling Thunder 11. Lift Off to Space 12. Aces 13. Those Magnificent Men in their Flying Machines.

Age of Flight: X-Planes 2008
Chronicles the development of experimental supersonic aircraft and the test pilots who flew them, including Chuck Yeager. 60m; DVD. **A:** Jr. High-Adult. **P:** Entertainment. **U:** Home. **Gen-Edu**: Documentary Films, Aeronautics. **Acq:** Purchase. **Dist:** MPI Media Group. $14.98.

The Age of Innocence 1934 (Unrated) — ★★1/2
Best seen for the radiant Dunne's performance since Boles isn't quite up to the task as her romantic partner. In 1875 New York, lawyer Newland Archer (Boles) has just become engaged to oh-so-proper May Welland (Haydon). May's cousin Ellen, the Countess Olenska (Dunne), returns to the city seeking a divorce and asks Archer's advice. They become deeply attracted to one another but a scandal would cause social ruin. Based on the Edith Wharton novel; remade in 1993. 71m/B/W; DVD. **C:** Irene Dunne; John Boles; Julie Haydon; Lionel Atwill; Helen Westley; Laura Hope Crews; Herbert Yost; Directed by Philip Moeller; Written by Victor Heerman; Sarah Y. Mason; Cinematography by James Van Trees. **A:** Sr. High-Adult. **P:** Entertainment. **U:** Home. **Mov-Ent**: Drama. **Acq:** Purchase. **Dist:** WarnerArchive.com.

The Age of Innocence 1993 (PG) — ★★★
Magnificently lavish adaptation of Edith Wharton's novel of passion thwarted by convention is visually stunning, but don't expect action since these people kill with a word or gesture. In 1870s New York, proper lawyer Newland Archer (Day-Lewis) is engaged to the equally proper May Welland (Ryder). He discovers unexpected romance when May's cousin, the rather scandalous Ellen Olenska (Pfeiffer), returns to the city from Europe but his hesitancy costs them dearly. Woodward's narration of Wharton's observations helps sort out what goes on behind the facades. Although slow, see this one for the beautiful period authenticity, thanks to Scorsese, who obviously labored over the small details. He shows up as a photographer; his parents appear in a scene on a train. 138m; VHS, DVD, 8 mm, Wide, CC. **C:** Daniel Day-Lewis; Michelle Pfeiffer; Winona Ryder; Martin Scorsese; Richard E. Grant; Alec McCowen; Miriam Margolyes; Mary Beth Hurt; Geraldine Chaplin; Stuart Wilson; Michael Gough; Alexis Smith; Jonathan Pryce; Robert Sean Leonard; Narrated by Joanne Woodward; Directed by Martin Scorsese; Written by Martin Scorsese; Jay Cocks; Cinematography by Michael Ballhaus; Music by Elmer Bernstein. **Pr:** Barbara De Fina; Cappa Films. **A:** Jr. High-Adult. **P:** Entertainment. **U:** Home. **Mov-Ent**: Drama, Marriage, Food Industry. **Awds:** Oscars '93: Costume Des.; British Acad. '93: Support. Actress (Margolyes); Golden Globes '94: Support. Actress (Ryder); Natl. Bd. of Review '93: Director (Scorsese), Support. Actress (Ryder). **Acq:** Purchase. **Dist:** Sony Pictures Home Entertainment Inc. $19.95.

The Age of Intelligent Machines 1987
A program outlining current advances in practical robotics, including machines designed to aid the handicapped. 29m; VHS, 3/4 U. **Pr:** Martin L. Schneider; Robert Richter. **A:** Family. **P:** Education. **U:** Institution, Home, SURA. **Hea-Sci**: Technology. **Acq:** Purchase. **Dist:** Martin L. Schneider Associates.

The Age of Invention 1989
A filmed narrative about the coming of age on the eve of WWI. 11m; VHS, 3/4 U. **Pr:** Albert Kish. **A:** Jr. High-Adult. **P:** Education. **U:** Institution, SURA. **Gen-Edu**: World War One. **Acq:** Purchase, Rent/Lease. **Dist:** National Film Board of Canada.

The Age of Reason 19??
A survey of 18th century English authors, including Addison and Steele, James Boswell, Daniel Defore, Samuel Johnson, Alexander Pope, and Jonathan Swift. 17m; VHS. **A:** Jr. High-Adult. **P:** Education. **U:** Institution. **Gen-Edu**: Literature--English. **Acq:** Purchase. **Dist:** Thomas S. Klise Co. $58.00.

The Age of Reason: Europe After the Renaissance—1642-1800 1995
Explains the effect that English philosopher John Locke and scientist Isaac Newton had on the history of Europe and the world after the Renaissance period. Combines live-action footage with historical artwork. Comes with teacher's guide and blackline masters. 20m; VHS. **A:** Jr. High-Sr. High. **P:** Education. **U:** Institution. **Gen-Edu**: History. **Acq:** Purchase. **Dist:** United Learning Inc. $95.00.

An Age of Renaissance: American Literature from 1820 to 1865 19??
The works of writers that include Emerson, Hawthorne, Melville, Poe, and Thoreau. 16m; VHS. **A:** Jr. High-Adult. **P:** Education. **U:** Institution. **Gen-Edu**: Literature--American, Biography. **Acq:** Purchase. **Dist:** Thomas S. Klise Co. $58.00.

The Age of Sophocles I 1959
A historical perspective on the ancient Greeks. Includes the opening scene of "Oedipus Rex." 30m; VHS, 3/4 U. **Pr:** Encyclopedia Britannica Educational Corporation. **A:** Sr. High-College. **P:** Education. **U:** Institution, SURA. **L:** English, Spanish. **Gen-Edu**: Literature. **Acq:** Purchase, Rent/Lease, Trade-in. **Dist:** Encyclopedia Britannica.

The Age of Space Transportation 1976
Examines advances in health care, education, communications, manufacturing, and other industries that are a result of the space program. 20m; 3/4 U, Q. **Pr:** National Aeronautics and Space Administration. **A:** Jr. High-Adult. **P:** Education. **U:** BCTV, SURA. **Hea-Sci**: Science, Technology. **Acq:** Free Loan. **Dist:** NASA Lyndon B. Johnson Space Center.

The Age of Steel: Diego Rivera 19??
North America's great muralist Diego Rivera is profiled in this Emmy Award-winning documentary. The artist's own writings provide the background for the narration, and vintage film from 1932 shows Rivera at work. 28m; VHS. **A:** Family. **P:** Education. **U:** Home. **Gen-Edu**: Documentary Films, Art & Artists. **Acq:** Purchase. **Dist:** WNET/Thirteen Non-Broadcast. $39.95.

The Age of the Absolute Monarchs in Europe: Western World History ????
Focuses on the rule of King Louis XIV of France to explain the power, luxuries, and aggressions of an absolute monarch. 13m; VHS. **A:** Sr. High. **P:** Education. **U:** Institution. **Gen-Edu**: History--Renaissance, History. **Acq:** Purchase. **Dist:** Zenger Media. $59.00.

The Age of the Composer 1980
The great composers of the Baroque and Classical eras-Vivaldi, Bach, Mozart, Hadyn, Beethoven, and Schubert-are examined for their contributions to Western music. Part of the "Music of Man" series. 57m; VHS, 3/4 U, Special order formats. **C:** Hosted by Yehudi Menuhin. **Pr:** Canadian Broadcasting Corp. **A:** Sr. High-Adult. **P:** Education. **U:** Institution, SURA. **Fin-Art. Acq:** Purchase, Rent/Lease. **Dist:** Time-Life Video and Television.

Age of the Dragons 2011 (PG-13) — ★1/2
In this reworking of Herman Melville's "Moby Dick" into a medieval fantasy, Ahab (Glover) was scarred by the white dragon that killed his sister. He and his crew rumble through the land in a boat-shaped contraption in a search for dragon's vitriol, the liquid that allows the beasties to breathe fire and serves as a power source for the local villages. It's a goof but the CGI's not bad for a low-budget indie. 92m; DVD, Blu-Ray. **C:** Danny Glover; Corey Sevier; Kepa Kruse; Vinnie Jones; Sofia Pernas; David Morgan; Larry Bagby; McKay Daines; Directed by Ryan Little; Written by McKay Daines; Cinematography by Ryan Little; Music by J Bateman. **A:** Jr. High-Adult. **P:** Entertainment. **U:** Home. **L:** English. **Mov-Ent**: Fantasy. **Acq:** Purchase. **Dist:** ARC Entertainment, LLC.

The Age of the Enlightenment 1984
This college credit course examines the literature, music, and art of the 18th century. 30m; VHS, 3/4 U. **Pr:** International University Consortium. **A:** College-Adult. **P:** Education. **U:** Institution, Home. **Gen-Edu**: History, Literature. **Acq:** Purchase. **Dist:** International University Consortium.
Indiv. Titles: 1. Freedom and Plenty: England Through Foreign Eyes 2. Innocents: Images in Hogarthis Painting 3. Bath-A theatre for Pleasure or Intrigue 4. The Chateau and the Cottage 5. Frederick and Voltaire: The Story of a Visit 6. The Noble Savage 7. The Marriage of Figaro 8. Chardin and the Female Image.

Age of the Hobbits 2012 (Unrated) — ★
A tribe of little people in ancient Thailand appeal to their neighbors to help them rescue their peers from dragon riding cavemen cannibals. 87m; DVD, Blu-Ray, Streaming. **C:** Bai Ling; Sun Korng; Srogn; Khom Lyly; Christopher Judge; Directed by Joseph J. Lawson; Written by Eric Forsberg; Cinematography by Richard J. Vialet; Music by Chris Ridenhour. **A:** Jr. High-Adult. **P:** Entertainment. **U:** Home. **L:** English. **Mov-Ent. Acq:** Purchase, Rent/Lease. **Dist:** The Asylum; Gaiam Inc. $14.95 6.66 14.99.

The Age of the Individual 1980
A look at the changes in Western music during the Romantic era, from the modern grand piano and the huge orchestra, to the use of folk idioms and the increasing chromaticism. Music by Paganini, Chopin, Liszt, Verdi, Brahms, Wagner, Tchaikovsky, and Strauss. Part of the "Music of Man" series. 57m; VHS, 3/4 U, Special order formats. **C:** Hosted by Yehudi Menuhin. **Pr:** Canadian Broadcasting Corp. **A:** Sr. High-Adult. **P:** Education. **U:** Institution, SURA. **Fin-Art. Acq:** Purchase, Rent/Lease. **Dist:** Time-Life Video and Television.

The Age of Uncertainty 1977
John Kenneth Galbraith-economist, diplomat, political scientist, lecturer, author-takes viewers on a vivid and personal tour through two hundred years of social thought and political economics in this insightful series. 57m; VHS, 3/4 U. **C:** John Kenneth Galbraith. **Pr:** British Broadcasting Corporation. **A:** Sr. High-College. **P:** Education. **U:** Institution, SURA. **Gen-Edu:** Economics. **Acq:** Purchase. **Dist:** Home Vision Cinema.
Indiv. Titles: 1. The Prophets and Promise of Classical Capitalism 2. The Manners and Morals of High Capitalism 3. Karl Marx-The Massive Dissent 4. The Colonial Idea 5. Lenin and the Great Ungluing 6. The Rise and Fall of Money 7. The Mandarin Revolution 8. The Fatal Competition 9. The Big Corporation 10. Land and the People 11. The Metropolis 12. Democracy, Leadership and Commitment 13. Weekend in Vermont.

Age Old Friends 1989 (Unrated) — ★★★½
Crusty octogenarian Cronyn must choose. His daughter (played by real-life offspring Tandy) wants him to move out of a retirement home and into her house. But he's struggling to keep neighbor and increasingly senile friend Gardenia from slipping into "zombieland." An emotional treat with two fine actors deploying dignity and wit in the battle against old age. Originally adapted for HBO from the Broadway play, "A Month of Sundays" by Bob Larbey. 89m; VHS, DVD, CC. **C:** Vincent Gardenia; Hume Cronyn; Tandy Cronyn; Esther Rolle; Michelle Scarabelli; Directed by Allen Kroeker. **Pr:** HBO. **A:** Family. **P:** Entertainment. **U:** Home. **Mov-Ent:** Aging. **Acq:** Purchase. **Dist:** Movies Unlimited; Alpha Video. $79.99.

Age Seven Around the World: 7 Up in South Africa 1993
Seven-year-olds of various status in South Africa are interviewed and asked questions about family, friends, societal roles, weapons, and fighting. 83m; VHS. **A:** Jr. High-College. **P:** Education. **U:** Institution. **Gen-Edu:** Documentary Films, Africa, Children. **Acq:** Purchase. **Dist:** Shanachie Entertainment. $19.95.

Age 7 in the USSR 1993
Children from three republics, as well as Russia, give us a glimpse of childhood and family life in a time of political unrest. 64m; VHS. **A:** College-Adult. **P:** Education. **U:** Institution. **Gen-Edu:** USSR, Documentary Films, Politics & Government. **Acq:** Purchase, Rent/Lease. **Dist:** Filmakers Library Inc. $150.00.

The Age to Be 1999
Documentary following active seniors challenging perceptions of retirement and old age. 60m; VHS, DVD. **A:** Sr. High-Adult. **P:** Education. **U:** Home, Institution. **Gen-Edu:** Documentary Films, Aging. **Acq:** Purchase, Rent/Lease. **Dist:** The Cinema Guild. $295.00.

Age 12: Love with a Little L 1990
Forbidden desire, transgression, piercing self-recognition and issues of lesbian identity are contemplated. 22m; VHS. **A:** Adult. **P:** Education. **U:** Institution. **Gen-Edu:** Sex & Sexuality, Women. **Acq:** Purchase, Rent/Lease. **Dist:** Women Make Movies. $275.00.

Agee 1979
A feature documentary about the life and work of Pulitzer Prize-winning author James Agee, a legend in his own time, as a superb writer and a unique individual. 88m; 3/4 U. **C:** John Huston; Dwight MacDonald; Jimmy Carter. **Pr:** Ross Spears. **A:** Jr. High-Adult. **P:** Education. **U:** Institution, SURA. **Gen-Edu:** Literature--Modern, Biography. **Acq:** Purchase. **Dist:** James Agee Film Project.

Ageless Fitness: Fresh Start 19??
Features Dian Nissen-Ramirez, a certified instructor and fitness expert, as she demonstrates a low-intensity yet energizing exercise routine with simple moves that are easy to follow. Includes warm-up, lower body toning, upper body strengthening, and a seated coll down. 45m; VHS. **A:** Family. **P:** Instruction. **U:** Institution, Home. **Hea-Sci:** Fitness/Exercise, Health Education. **Acq:** Purchase. **Dist:** Tapeworm Video Distributors Inc. $19.95.

Ageless Fitness: Fresh Start 2 19??
Certified instructor and fitness expert Dian Nissen-Ramirez demonstrates a safe and smooth fitness workout aimed at imroving cardiovascular health, strengthening bones and joints, and minimizing fat gain. She includes a thorough, whole body warm-up, light and easy low-impact aerobics, floor exercises centering on abdominal, upper body, and lower back strengthening, stretching, cool-down, and safety tips. 47m; VHS. **A:** Family. **P:** Instruction. **U:** Institution, Home. **Hea-Sci:** Fitness/Exercise, Health Education. **Acq:** Purchase. **Dist:** Tapeworm Video Distributors Inc. $19.95.

The Agency 1981 (R) — ★★
An advertising agency attempts to manipulate public behavior and opinion through the use of subliminal advertising. A good premise is bogged down by a dull script and plodding performances by all concerned. Based on a Paul Gottlieb novel. 94m; VHS, DVD. **C:** Robert Mitchum; Lee Majors; Valerie Perrine; Saul Rubinek; Alexandra Stewart; Directed by George Kaczender; Music by Lewis Furey. **Pr:** Jensen Farley Pictures. **A:** Sr. High-Adult. **P:** Entertainment. **U:** Home. **Mov-Ent:** Advertising, Canada. **Acq:** Purchase. **Dist:** MNTEX Entertainment, Inc.; Anchor Bay Entertainment. $69.95.

Agenda For a Small Planet Series 1988
This film focuses on efforts being undertaken to promote world peace, offering viewers some rare insights into other cultures and countries. ?m; VHS, 3/4 U. **Pr:** Centre Productions, Inc. **A:** Jr. High-Adult. **P:** Education. **U:** Institution, SURA. **Gen-Edu:** International Relations. **Acq:** Purchase. **Dist:** Clear Vue Inc.

Agent Cody Banks 2003 (PG) — ★★½
Muniz is Cody Banks, a seemingly normal 15-year-old kid who lives a secret life as a CIA spy. After training for a few years at a "junior spy" summer camp, he's given his first mission: talk to a girl! He must befriend and protect classmate Natalie (Duff), the daughter of a scientist (Donovan) who's created a nanotechnology that could help villains McShane and Vosloo CONTROL THE WORLD!!! Much junior 007 action ensues, mixed with some quirky comedy and innocent teen romance. "Spy Kids" had more charm, but the target audience probably won't mind the difference. Harmon keeps things interesting for the older set with her vavoom-ish wardrobe and surprising knack for comedy. If the characters aren't exactly fleshed out, at least the actors playing them seem to be enjoying themselves. 95m; VHS, DVD, CC. **C:** Frankie Muniz; Hilary Duff; Angie Harmon; Keith David; Cynthia Stevenson; Arnold Vosloo; Martin Donovan; Daniel Roebuck; Ian McShane; Darrell Hammond; Directed by Harald Zwart; Written by Scott M. Alexander; Ashley Edward Miller; Zack Stentz; Larry Karaszewski; Cinematography by Denis Crossan; Music by John Powell. **Pr:** David Nicksay; Guy Oseary; James Wong; David C. Glasser; Dylan Sellers; Maverick Films; Splendid Pictures; MGM. **A:** Family. **P:** Entertainment. **U:** Home. **Mov-Ent:** Action-Adventure, Science, Intelligence Service. **Acq:** Purchase. **Dist:** MGM Home Entertainment.

Agent Cody Banks 2: Destination London 2004 (PG) — ★★
Banks is back to take on more evildoers who want to RULE THE WORLD!!! AGAIN!!! Now it's British industrialist Lord Kenworth (Faulkner) and Diaz (Allen), Banks's CIA camp commandor turned traitor, who have a device that allows them to control what people do and say. Off to London for the big showdown. Cody goes undercover in a youth symphony where he meets his handler (the funny Anderson, who's not given much to work with) and Hilary Duff fill-in Spearritt as Emily, the prerequisite pretty girl (albeit a drab one here). While the first effort thrived on the normal-teenager-becomes-secret-agent concept the second surprisingly ignores the first part and focuses on the at-times hard-to-follow action scenes. Muniz puts in another fine performance and the kids will probably still find it a fun ride, but a trilogy is probably not needed. 99m; VHS, DVD. **C:** Frankie Muniz; Anthony Anderson; Cynthia Stevenson; Daniel Roebuck; Hannah Spearritt; Anna Chancellor; Keith Allen; James Faulkner; David Kelly; Santiago Segura; Connor Widdows; Keith David; Directed by Kevin Allen; Written by Don Rhymer; Harald Zwart; Cinematography by Denis Crossan; Music by Mark Thomas. **Pr:** Guy Oseary; David C. Glasser; David Nicksay; Dylan Sellers; Bob Yari; Maverick Films; MGM. **A:** Primary-Adult. **P:** Entertainment. **U:** Home. **L:** English. **Mov-Ent:** Action-Comedy, Family. **Acq:** Purchase. **Dist:** MGM Home Entertainment.

Agent of Death 1999 (R) — ★★
Philandering President Beck is not Mr. Popularity and there's an election coming up. So his PR head arranges for a fake kidnapping to garner sympathy. But the plans goes wrong and he winds up in the hands of a psycho Secret Service agent (Genesse). And the one man (Roberts) who might be able to rescue the Prez doesn't want the job. 105m; VHS, DVD, CC. **C:** Ice-T; Eric Roberts; Michael Madsen; Bryan Genesse; John Beck; Directed by Sam Firstenberg; Written by Bryan Genesse. **A:** Sr. High-Adult. **P:** Entertainment. **U:** Home. **Mov-Ent:** Presidency, Hotels & Hotel Staff Training, Secret Service. **Acq:** Purchase. **Dist:** CinemaNow Inc.

Agent on Ice 1986 (R) — ★★
Hockey team is stalked by lawyers. No, wait. An ex-CIA agent is stalked for cover-up purposes by the agency and the mob. One slippery fellow. 96m; VHS. **C:** Tom Ormeny; Clifford David; Louis Pastore; Matt Craven; Directed by Clark Worswick. **Pr:** Clark Worswick. **A:** Sr. High-Adult. **P:** Entertainment. **U:** Home. **Mov-Ent:** Intelligence Service. **Acq:** Purchase. **Dist:** Anchor Bay Entertainment. $19.95.

Agent Orange: A Story of Dignity and Doubt 1981
Vietnam veterans and their wives talk openly about the effects of Agent Orange (a toxic herbicide used in Vietnam between 1961 and 1975) on their health and their everyday lives. 28m; VHS, 3/4 U. **C:** Narrated by Martin Sheen. **Pr:** Jim Gambone; Film in the Cities. **A:** Sr. High-Adult. **P:** Education. **U:** Institution, SURA. **Gen-Edu:** Vietnam War. **Acq:** Purchase, Rent/Lease. **Dist:** New Day Films Library.

The Agent Orange Registry Program for MAS Employees 1986
This is an training program for Mas workers to show them how to deal with veterans, their questions about Agent Orange, and the registry program. 23m; VHS, 3/4 U. **Pr:** USVAST. **A:** Adult. **P:** Instruction. **U:** Institution, SURA. **Gen-Edu:** Public Health. **Acq:** Purchase. **Dist:** National Audiovisual Center. $110.00.

Agent Red 2000 (R) — ★½
Oh so typical story done in a less-than-enthralling manner. Naval Specials Ops Commander Matt Hendricks (Lundgren) is aboard a U.S. sub, escorting a deadly chemical weapon to a safe storage facility. Then the sub is boarded by Russian terrorists who want to unleash the virus on New York City. Naturally, Hendricks must prevent that. 95m; VHS, DVD, Wide, CC. **C:** Dolph Lundgren; Randolph Mantooth; Meilani Paul; Alexander Kuznitsov; Natalie Radford; Steve Eastin; Tony Becker; Directed by Damian Lee; Written by Damian Lee; Cinematography by Ken Blakey; Music by David Wurst; Eric Wurst. **A:** Sr. High-Adult. **P:** Entertainment. **U:** Home. **Mov-Ent:** Terrorism. **Acq:** Purchase. **Dist:** Sony Pictures Home Entertainment Inc.

Agent Steel: Mad Locust Rising 1987 (Unrated)
British thrash metal specialists play the Hammersmith Palais, including songs "Nothing Left," "The Unexpected," "The Day at Guyana" and six others. ?m; VHS. **A:** Jr. High-Adult. **P:** Entertainment. **U:** Home. **Mov-Ent:** Music--Performance, Music--Pop/Rock. **Acq:** Purchase. **Dist:** Music Video Distributors. $29.95.

Agents "Tell It Like It Is"?Actors at Work Series 19??
Joel Asher, award-winning director and distinguished acting coach, interviews top commercial, film, and TV agents to find out exactly what they look for in new talent. 50m; VHS. **A:** Adult. **P:** Instruction. **U:** Home. **How-Ins:** Filmmaking, Performing Arts, How-To. **Acq:** Purchase. **Dist:** Victory Multimedia. $29.95.

Ages 4 and 5 1970
Through a one-way mirror the viewer observes children at play in the Ruth Staples Child Development laboratory at the University of Nebraska. Explores what makes a good nursery school. 30m; 3/4 U, EJ. **Pr:** NETCHE. **A:** College-Adult. **P:** Education. **U:** Institution, CCTV, BCTV, SURA. **Gen-Edu:** Children. **Acq:** Purchase, Rent/Lease, Subscription. **Dist:** NETCHE.

Ages of Humankind 1986 — ★★★
This tape compiles several jazzy short subjects from the famed independent filmmakers Faith and John Hubley. These productions look at people and relationships. Included are: "The Tender Game," "Dig," "WOW," "People, People, People," and "Cockaboody." 53m; VHS. **C:** Emily Hubley; John Hubley. **Pr:** Walt Disney Studios. **A:** Family. **P:** Entertainment. **U:** Home. **Mov-Ent:** Animation & Cartoons, Film--Avant-Garde. **Acq:** Purchase. **Dist:** Walt Disney Studios Home Entertainment. $49.95.

Ages of Infancy: Caring for Young, Mobile, and Older Infants 1990
Identifies the three stages of infant development, as well as each stage's accompanying development issue. Provides guidelines and suggestions for caregiving in each stage. A 10-page video magazine is included. 22m; VHS. **A:** College-Adult. **P:** Education. **U:** Institution. **Gen-Edu:** Child Care, Children, Infants. **Acq:** Purchase. **Dist:** CDE Press. $65.00.

The Ages of Rocks: Earth's Proof of Evolution 19??
Documents ten case studies on the age of the earth, which geologists estimate to be nearly five billion years old. ?m; VHS. **A:** Jr. High-College. **P:** Education. **U:** Institution. **Gen-Edu:** Geology. **Acq:** Purchase. **Dist:** Educational Images Ltd. $135.00.

Agganis the Man/The Jackie Jensen Story 19?? (Unrated)
The biographies of two famous Boston Red Sox players are included. —Agganis the Man? is a made-for-television documentary that covers the life of Harry Agganis, who grew up in Boston and later starred for the Sox before dying of a blood clot when just 25 years old. —The Jackie Jensen Story? is a Hollywood film biography detailing how Jensen overcame a tough childhood to become a star with the Red Sox. 51m/B/W; DVD. **A:** Family. **P:** Entertainment. **U:** Home. **Mov-Ent:** Baseball, Sports Documentary, Death. **Acq:** Purchase. **Dist:** Rare Sportsfilms, Inc. $29.95.

Aggie Appleby, Maker of Men 1933 (Unrated) — ★½
A wimpy society boy transforms himself into a tough guy, all for the love of a dame. Based on a play by Joseph O. Kesselring. Very slight comedy. 73m/B/W; VHS. **C:** Charles Farrell; Wynne Gibson; William Gargan; Zasu Pitts; Betty Furness; Directed by Mark Sandrich; Music by Max Steiner. **A:** Family. **P:** Entertainment. **U:** Home. **Mov-Ent:** Comedy--Romantic. **Acq:** Purchase. **Dist:** Facets Multimedia Inc. $19.98.

Aggression, Bullying, and Intimidation 2001
Explains personality traits of bullies and victims, discusses methods for motivating bullies to change, and addresses how bystanders can help combat abusive scenarios. 18m; VHS. **A:** Jr. High-Sr. High. **P:** Education. **U:** Institution. **Gen-Edu:** Psychology, Adolescence. **Acq:** Purchase. **Dist:** Zenger Media. $79.95.

The Aggression Scale 2012 (R) — ★★
Humor and gore are successfully combined in this sicko thriller. Mobster Reg's (Wise) getaway money is missing, and he sends henchman Lloyd (Ashbook) and his crew after the likely suspects. They descend on the Rutledge family and kill off the parents. It turns out that young weirdo Owen (Hartwig) and his older stepsister Lauren (Therese) are more ruthless than the hit men can imagine. 85m; DVD, Blu-Ray. **C:** Ryan Hartwig; Fabianne Therese; Dana Ashbrook; Ray Wise; Derek Mears; Jacob Reynolds; Joseph McKelheer; Directed by Steven C. Miller; Written by Ben Powell; Cinematography by Jeff Dolen; Music by Kevin Riepl. **A:** Sr. High-Adult. **P:** Entertainment. **U:** Home. **L:** English. **Mov-Ent:** Crime Drama. **Acq:** Purchase. **Dist:** Anchor Bay Entertainment Inc.

Aggression Training Drills to Bring Out the Warrior Within 2002
Presents a series of boxing, martial arts, and judo drills to help athletes gain a competitive advantage. 51m; VHS. **A:** Adult. **P:** Instruction. **U:** Institution. **How-Ins:** Fitness/Exercise, Sports--General, How-To. **Acq:** Purchase. **Dist:** Championship Productions. $39.95.

Aggressive Base Running Tactics and Drills 2013 (Unrated)
Coach Andy Lopez demonstrates base-running drills and strategies along with the philosophy he teaches his own baseball team. 69m; DVD. **A:** Family. **P:** Education. **U:** Home. **L:** English. **Spo-Rec:** Athletic Instruction/Coaching, Baseball, How-To. **Acq:** Purchase. **Dist:** Championship Productions. $39.99.

Aggressive Baserunning 1999
University of Tennessee baseball coach demonstrates how to teach aggressive baserunning skills. Includes sections on dug-out, stealing signs, going from home to first, from first to second, from second to third, reading pitchers, fly balls, andcreating speed. 30m; VHS. **A:** Jr. High-Adult. **P:** Instruction. **U:** Home, Institution. **Spo-Rec:** Baseball. **Acq:** Purchase. **Dist:** Baseball Direct. $29.95.

Aggressive Baserunning 2009 (Unrated)
Coach Gary Gilmore lectures on increasing the willingness of your baseball team's runners to steal bases. 83m; DVD. **A:** Family. **P:** Education. **U:** Home, Institution. **Spo-Rec:** Baseball, Athletic Instruction/Coaching. **Acq:** Purchase. **Dist:** Championship Productions. $39.99.

Aggressive Behavior in Mature Male American Bison 1975
Straight-on threat, broadside threat, nod, bellowing and wallowing types of aggression are illustrated. Submission patterns are shown, with special attention to the mounting inention movement in sexual and aggressive interactions. 12m; 3/4 U, Special order formats. **Pr:** Pennsylvania State University. **A:** College-Adult. **P:** Education. **U:** Institution, SURA. **Hea-Sci:** Animals. **Acq:** Purchase. **Dist:** International Science Film Collection.

Aggressive Defensive Strategies 2013 (Unrated)
Coach Patty Gasso discusses softball relays and how to best defend against bunts, slaps and steals. 54m; DVD. **A:** Family. **P:** Education. **U:** Home. **L:** English. **Spo-Rec:** Athletic Instruction/Coaching, Softball. **Acq:** Purchase. **Dist:** Championship Productions. $39.99.

Aggressive Drills for Defensive Linemen 2010 (Unrated)
Coach Brick Haley presents for drills each for both the passing and running game to help defensive lines. 48m; DVD. **A:** Family. **P:** Education. **U:** Home, Institution. **Spo-Rec:** Football, Athletic Instruction/Coaching. **Acq:** Purchase. **Dist:** Championship Productions. $39.99.

Aggressive Face-Offs: How to Win Every Draw 2014 (Unrated)
Coaches Tim McDermott and Dominic Starsia presents intermediate and aggressive face-off techniques for lacrosse. 114m; DVD. **A:** Family. **P:** Education. **U:** Home. **L:** English. **Spo-Rec:** Athletic Instruction/Coaching, Lacrosse. **Acq:** Purchase. **Dist:** Championship Productions. $119.99.

Aggressive 4-3 Defense: Setting up the System 2011 (Unrated)
Defensive football coach Chris Ash gives an overview of the 4-3 defense, and uses practice footage to demonstrate drills. 80m; DVD. **A:** Family. **P:** Education. **U:** Home, Institution. **Spo-Rec:** Football, Athletic Instruction/Coaching. **Acq:** Purchase. **Dist:** Championship Productions. $39.99.

Aggressive 4-3 Defense: Shutting Down the Passing Game 2011 (Unrated)
Defensive football coach Chris Ash discusses using the 4-3 defense to derail the opposing team's passing game; also includes a .pdf of the player responsibilities and diagrams. 72m; DVD. **A:** Family. **P:** Education. **U:** Home, Institution. **Spo-Rec:** Football, Athletic Instruction/Coaching. **Acq:** Purchase. **Dist:** Championship Productions. $39.99.

Aggressive 4-3 Defense: Stuffing the Run 2011 (Unrated)
Football defensive coach Chris Ash discusses using the 4-3 defense to shut down the opposing team's running game; also includes a .pdf of the player responsibilities and diagrams. 75m; DVD. **A:** Family. **P:** Education. **U:** Home, Institution. **Spo-Rec:** Football, Athletic Instruction/Coaching. **Acq:** Purchase. **Dist:** Championship Productions. $39.99.

Aggressive Ground Ball Play 2011 (Unrated)
Lacrosse coach John Danowski lectures about aggressively pursuing ground balls. 55m; DVD. **A:** Family. **P:** Education. **U:** Home, Institution. **Spo-Rec:** Lacrosse, Athletic Instruction/Coaching. **Acq:** Purchase. **Dist:** Championship Productions. $39.99.

Aggressive Job Hunting Techniques 1989
Discusses how to get your resume noticed, what a company wants from an employee, where to find jobs that aren't listed in the newspaper, and how to feel comfortable in an interview situation. 30m; VHS. **A:** Adult. **P:** Professional. **U:** Institution. **Bus-Ind:** Business. **Acq:** Purchase. **Dist:** RMI Media. $89.95.

Aggressive Offense: Baserunning & the Short Game 2010 (Unrated)
Coach George Wares demonstrates and discusses offensive techniques for softball. 119m; DVD. **A:** Family. **P:** Education. **U:** Home, Institution. **Spo-Rec:** Softball, Athletic Instruction/Coaching. **Acq:** Purchase. **Dist:** Championship Productions. $49.99.

Aggressive Offense: Baserunning and the Short Game 2010
Coach George Wares shares strategies for playing the short game in softball. 119m; DVD. **A:** Family. **P:** Education. **U:** Home, Institution. **Spo-Rec:** Softball, Athletic Instruction/Coaching. **Acq:** Purchase. **Dist:** Championship Productions. $49.99.

Aggressive Offensive Strategies 2014 (Unrated)
Softball coach Patty Gasso discusses, bunts, slappers, rundowns, and first and third situations. 54m; DVD. **A:** Family. **P:** Education. **U:** Home. **L:** English. **Spo-Rec:** Athletic Instruction/Coaching, Softball. **Acq:** Purchase. **Dist:** Championship Productions. $39.99.

Aggressive Rides and Pins 2001 (Unrated)
Olympian Ben Peterson demonstrates aggressive riding tactics for wrestling, and how to use different moves from them to score points or a fall. 61m; DVD. **A:** Family. **P:** Education. **U:** Home, Institution. **Spo-Rec:** Athletic Instruction/Coaching. **Acq:** Purchase. **Dist:** Championship Productions. $39.99.

Aggressive Team Forechecking Systems 1999 (Unrated)
Coach Jack Parker demonstrates four checking systems he teaches his hockey teams. 40m; DVD. **A:** Family. **P:** Education. **U:** Home, Institution. **Spo-Rec:** Hockey, Athletic Instruction/Coaching. **Acq:** Purchase. **Dist:** Championship Productions. $29.99.

The Aggressives 2005
Documentary exploring the lives of six New York lesbians who define themselves as "aggressives" through masculine behavior and dress. 72m; VHS, DVD. **A:** Sr. High-Adult. **P:** Education. **U:** Home, Institution. **Gen-Edu:** Documentary Films, Homosexuality. **Acq:** Purchase, Rent/Lease. **Dist:** The Cinema Guild. $295.00.

Agile Manufacturing: Moving to the Next Level 1994
Examine how agile manufacturing combines virtual manufacturing relationships, closed-loop processing, planning and control, product design and enterprise concurrency. 32m; VHS. **A:** Adult. **P:** Professional. **U:** Institution. **L:** English. **Bus-Ind:** Industry & Industrialists. **Acq:** Purchase. **Dist:** Society of Manufacturing Engineers. $228.

Agility and Core Strength 2001 (Unrated)
Coach John Cook demonstrates jump rope routines and drills for bettering your volleyball team's balance, coordination, and power. 35m; DVD. **A:** Family. **P:** Education. **U:** Home, Institution. **Spo-Rec:** Volleyball, Athletic Instruction/Coaching, Fitness/Exercise. **Acq:** Purchase. **Dist:** Championship Productions. $39.99.

Agility Training and Conditioning for Women's Lacrosse 2011 (Unrated)
Veronica Dyer explains and demonstrates various conditioning exercises for female lacrosse players. 54m; DVD. **A:** Family. **P:** Education. **U:** Home, Institution. **Spo-Rec:** Lacrosse, Fitness/Exercise. **Acq:** Purchase. **Dist:** Championship Productions. $39.99.

Aging 1984
Describes the aging process and discusses why some people age faster than others. 27m; VHS. **A:** Sr. High-Adult. **P:** Education. **U:** Institution. **Hea-Sci:** Aging, Health Education. **Acq:** Purchase. **Dist:** University of Washington Educational Media Collection. $20.00.

Aging 1989
Examines the relationship between the elderly individual and society, interviewing several older people concerning their lifestyles. 26m; VHS, 3/4 U. **A:** College-Adult. **P:** Education. **U:** Institution, SURA. **Hea-Sci:** Health Education, Aging. **Acq:** Purchase, Rent/Lease. **Dist:** Films for the Humanities & Sciences. $149.00.

The Aging: Aging of North America 1990
Describes the changing demographics of the U.S. and its closest neighbors, and the ways these changes will be reflected in our lifestyles. 25m; VHS, 3/4 U. **Pr:** Altschul Group. **A:** College-Adult. **P:** Education. **U:** Institution. **Hea-Sci:** Aging, Family, Health Education. **Acq:** Purchase, Rent/Lease. **Dist:** United Learning Inc. $400.00.

Aging and Vision: Declarations of Independence 1985
A look at how sightless senior citizens have overcome their handicaps. 18m; VHS, 3/4 U. **Pr:** BFA Educational Media; Phoenix Films. **A:** Jr. High-Adult. **P:** Education. **U:** Institution, SURA. **Gen-Edu:** Aging, Blindness. **Acq:** Purchase. **Dist:** Phoenix Learning Group.

Aging: Beyond Retirement 1990
Discusses the need to continue activity after retirement. 25m; VHS, 3/4 U. **Pr:** Altschul Group. **A:** College-Adult. **P:** Education. **U:** Institution. **Hea-Sci:** Aging, Health Education, Fitness/Exercise. **Acq:** Purchase, Rent/Lease. **Dist:** United Learning Inc. $400.00.

The Aging: Body Ages 1990
Discussion of the natural process of aging, and continued enjoyment of an active lifestyle despite aging. 25m; VHS, 3/4 U. **Pr:** Altschul Group. **A:** College-Adult. **P:** Education. **U:** Institution. **Hea-Sci:** Aging, Health Education. **Acq:** Purchase, Rent/Lease. **Dist:** United Learning Inc. $400.00.

The Aging Game 2003
Medical students become patients so they can better understand how to administer healthcare to the aged. Part of the Caregiver Resource Library series covering caregiving issues appropriate for use in courses for nursing, psychology, and gerontology. 25m; VHS. **A:** Adult. **P:** Vocational. **U:** Institution. **Hea-Sci:** Health Education, Medical Care, Occupational Training. **Acq:** Purchase. **Dist:** Aquarius Health Care Media. $125.00.

The Aging: Gold Medal Years 1990
Four athletes discuss and exhibit their training and competition methods. 25m; VHS, 3/4 U. **Pr:** Altschul Group. **A:** College-Adult. **P:** Education. **U:** Institution. **Hea-Sci:** Aging, Health Education, Fitness/Exercise. **Acq:** Purchase, Rent/Lease. **Dist:** United Learning Inc. $400.00.

Aging Grace 1981
The needs and experiences of the aging are explored. 5m; VHS, 3/4 U. **Pr:** Franciscan Communications. **A:** Jr. High-Adult. **P:** Education. **U:** Institution, SURA. **Gen-Edu:** Aging. **Acq:** Purchase, Rent/Lease. **Dist:** St. Anthony Messenger Press.
Indiv. Titles: 1. Knock at the Door 2. Love Waits 3. The Visit 4. The Wedding 5. The Bus 6. The Wheelchair 7. What?.

The Aging Heart 1982
Common heart findings in older patients are covered in this program. 30m; VHS, 3/4 U. **Pr:** Emory University. **A:** College-Adult. **P:** Professional. **U:** Institution, CCTV, Home, SURA. **Hea-Sci:** Heart, Aging. **Acq:** Purchase, Rent/Lease, Subscription. **Dist:** Emory Medical Television Network.

Aging in Rural America 1981
A positive look at growing older in a rural environment with interviews with senior citizens discussing the way they have aged. 25m; 3/4 U. **Pr:** Ohio University Telecommunications Center. **A:** Jr. High-Adult. **P:** Education. **U:** Institution, CCTV, SURA. **Gen-Edu:** Aging, Sociology. **Acq:** Purchase, Rent/Lease. **Dist:** WOUB Public Media.

Aging in Soviet Georgia: A Toast to Old Age 1987
The remarkable longevity of persons from Soviet Georgia and the respect accorded to these people are examined. Also examines the social aspects of aging and ends with a panel discussion with Maggie Kuhn, founder of the Gray Panthers, and Richard Ham, M.D., president of the American Geriatric Association. 54m; VHS, 3/4 U. **Pr:** Richard Breyer. **A:** Jr. High-Adult. **P:** Education. **U:** Institution, Home, SURA. **Gen-Edu:** Sociology, Aging, USSR. **Acq:** Purchase, Rent/Lease, Duplication. **Dist:** Filmakers Library Inc.

Aging: Life's Hidden Agenda Series 1988
A series that covers many aspects of aging in our society, which has seen a dramatic rise in senior citizens. 25m; VHS, 3/4 U. **Pr:** Altschul Group. **A:** Adult. **P:** Education. **U:** Institution, SURA. **Hea-Sci:** Aging. **Acq:** Purchase, Rent/Lease. **Dist:** United Learning Inc. $400.00.
Indiv. Titles: 1. The Aging of North America 2. Beyond Retirement 3. The Body Ages 4. The Gold Medal Years 5. The Search for Intimacy: Love, Sex, and Relationships in the Later Years.

The Aging Mind 1998
Explains the difference between normal and pathological symptoms of aging in order to assert that poor health does not necessarily come with age. 28m; VHS, DVD. **A:** Sr. High-Adult. **P:** Education. **U:** Institution. **Hea-Sci:** Health Education, Aging, Patient Education. **Acq:** Purchase. **Dist:** Aquarius Health Care Media. $150.00.

The Aging of Lakes 1971
Introduces geological and ecological factors of normal aging of lakes and shows how man is speeding up this natural process by indiscriminate disposal of sewage, fertilizers, and industrial waste. 14m; VHS, 3/4 U. **Pr:** Encyclopedia Britannica Educational Corporation. **A:** Jr. High-Sr. High. **P:** Education. **U:** Institution, SURA. **L:** English, Spanish. **Hea-Sci:** Ecology & Environment. **Acq:** Purchase, Rent/Lease, Trade-in. **Dist:** Encyclopedia Britannica.

Aging Out 2006
Filmmakers Robert Weisberg and Vanessa Roth follow three foster children as they age out of the system and try to make it on their own for the first time. 90m; DVD. **A:** Jr. High-Adult. **P:** Entertainment. **U:** Home. **Gen-Edu:** Documentary Films. **Acq:** Purchase. **Dist:** New Video Group.

Aging Patients: Are We Doing Them Any Favors? 1982
Theories of the aging process are listed, and results of the aging process-altered physiology-are discussed. 51m; VHS, 3/4 U. **Pr:** Emory University. **A:** College-Adult. **P:** Professional. **U:** Institution, CCTV, Home, SURA. **Hea-Sci:** Aging. **Acq:** Purchase, Rent/Lease, Subscription. **Dist:** Emory Medical Television Network.

An Aging Process—Osteoporosis 1986
A look at medical pros at care and causes of osteoporosis in the aged. 20m; VHS, 3/4 U. **Pr:** Fairview Audio-Visuals. **A:** Sr. High-Adult. **P:** Professional. **U:** Institution, CCTV. **Hea-Sci:** Aging, Bones. **Acq:** Purchase, Rent/Lease. **Dist:** Kinetic Film Enterprises Ltd.; Medcom Inc. $295.00.

Aging Skin 1986
A demonstration of skin degeneration due to sun damage, dermatitis, tumors, and other aging factors. 34m; VHS, 3/4 U. **A:** Adult. **P:** Professional. **U:** Institution, CCTV, Home, SURA. **Hea-Sci:** Skin. **Acq:** Purchase, Rent/Lease, Subscription. **Dist:** Emory Medical Television Network.

Aging: Staying Active—Wellness After Sixty 1990
Lead an active, happy life for as long as you want with proper diet and exercise. This tape provides guidelines. 28m; VHS, 3/4 U. **Pr:** Altschul Group. **A:** College-Adult. **P:** Education. **U:** Institution. **Hea-Sci:** Aging, Fitness/Exercise, Health Education. **Acq:** Purchase, Rent/Lease. **Dist:** United Learning Inc. $415.00.

Aging: The Methuselah Syndrome 1982
An important report on research which is making giant strides toward pinpointing the body controls that cause aging. Part of the "Nova" series. 57m; VHS, 3/4 U, Special order formats. **Pr:** WGBH Boston. **A:** College-Adult. **P:** Education. **U:** Institution, SURA. **Hea-Sci:** Science, Anatomy & Physiology. **Acq:** Purchase, Rent/Lease. **Dist:** Time-Life Video and Television.

Aging: The Search for Eternal Youth 198?
Dr. Robert Butler, a specialist on aging, discusses the way our society catagorizes people into groups based on age and doesn't keep people intellectually stimulated as they grow old. Butler speculates on a new militance that will surface as old people demand to be accounted. 20m; 3/4 U, Special order formats. **Pr:** Hobel Leiterman Productions. **A:** College-Adult. **P:** Education. **U:** Institution. **Gen-Edu:** Biology, Aging. **Acq:** Purchase. **Dist:** The Cinema Guild.

Aging: The Search for Intimacy—Love, Sex & Relationships in Later Years 1990
A forthright discussion of the needs of the aging for relationships, sexual activity and love. 25m; VHS, 3/4 U. **Pr:** Altschul Group. **A:** College-Adult. **P:** Education. **U:** Institution. **Hea-Sci:** Aging, Romance, Health Education. **Acq:** Purchase, Rent/Lease. **Dist:** United Learning Inc. $400.00.

Aging Well: Memory and Movement 2000
Dr. Dharma Singh Kalsa, M.D. tells how to remain active, healthy, and engaged with life as one grows older. Discusses using Tai Chi as a means to stay flexible. 27m; VHS, DVD. **A:** Adult. **P:** Professional. **U:** Institution. **Hea-Sci:** Aging, Health Education, Martial Arts. **Acq:** Purchase. **Dist:** Aquarius Health Care Media. $99.00.

Aging With Grace 2000
Senior citizens share their experiences and advice on growing old with grace. 22m; VHS. **A:** Adult. **P:** Professional. **U:** Institution. **Hea-Sci:** Patient Care, Aging. **Acq:** Purchase. **Dist:** Aquarius Health Care Media. $140.00.

Agitation, Aggression and Violence 19??
Part of the Nursing Home Mental Health Series. Details verbal and physical aggression in the nursing home, outlining an approach that stresses proper assessment, early recognition, specific interventions, and avoidance of future episodes. 20m; VHS. **A:** Adult. **P:** Education. **U:** Institution. **Hea-Sci:** Aging, Medical Care, Mental Health. **Acq:** Purchase, Rent/Lease. **Dist:** University of Maryland. $150.00.

Agnes and His Brothers 2004 (Unrated) — ★
Transsexual Agnes has little in common with her two brothers, Hans-Jorg and Werner, except for their loathing of their weirdo recluse father, Gunther. Agnes has man trouble (she's always a victim) and Hans-Jorg and Werner are sexually desperate, albeit for different reasons. These are strange, unlikable people and you will be very glad they're not part of your family. German with subtitles. 115m; DVD. **C:** Moritz Bleibtreu; Herbert Knaup; Vadim Glowna; Katja Riemann; Martin Weiss; Tom Schilling; Directed by Oskar Roehler; Written by Oskar Roehler; Cinematography by Carl F. Koschnick; Music by Martin Todsharow. **A:** College-Adult. **P:** Entertainment. **U:** Home. **L:** German. **Mov-Ent. Acq:** Purchase. **Dist:** First Run Features.

Agnes Browne 1999 (R) — ★★½
Sentimental, old-fashioned saga concerning recent widow Agnes Browne (Huston), who's trying to cope with her seven children under difficult circumstances in Dublin in 1967. Agnes, who works a market stall, has one personal dream—she wants to see Tom Jones in an upcoming concert. Guess what happens. Director Huston does try to keep the bathos under control. Based on the novel "The Mammy" of Brendan O'Carroll. 91m; VHS, DVD, Wide. **C:** Anjelica Huston; Ray Winstone; Arno Chevrier; Marion O'Dwyer; Ciaran Owens; Tom Jones; Directed by Anjelica Huston; Written by John Goldsmith; Brendan O'Carroll; Cinematography by Anthony B. Richmond; Music by Paddy Moloney. **Pr:** October Films. **A:** Sr. High-Adult. **P:** Entertainment. **U:** Home. **Mov-Ent:** Poverty. **Acq:** Purchase.

Agnes Escapes from the Nursing Home 1989
This animated movie, inspired by the filmmaker's relationship with an elderly woman who was continually trying to escape from the nursing home where she lived, represents the emotions and thoughts of its central character, the fleeing Agnes. 4m; VHS, 3/4 U. **Pr:** Eileen O'Meara. **A:** Sr. High-Adult. **P:** Education. **U:** Institution, SURA. **Gen-Edu:** Animation & Cartoons, Aging. **Acq:** Purchase, Rent/Lease. **Dist:** National Film Board of Canada. $125.00.

Agnes of God 1985 (PG-13) — ★★
Stage to screen translation of John Pielmeier's play loses something in the translation. Coarse chain-smoking psychiatrist Fonda is sent to a convent to investigate whether young nun Tilly is fit to stand trial. Seems that the nun may have given birth to and then strangled her baby, although she denies ever having sexual relations and knows nothing about an infant. Naive Tilly is frightened by probing Fonda, while worldly mother-superior Bancroft is distrusting. Melodramatic stew of Catholicism, religious fervor, and science features generally good performances, although Fonda often seems to be acting (maybe it's the cigarettes). 98m; VHS, DVD, Wide, CC. **C:** Jane Fonda; Anne Bancroft; Meg Tilly; Anne Pitoniak; Winston Rekert; Gratien Gelinas; Directed by Norman Jewison; Written by John Pielmeier; Cinematography by Sven Nykvist; Music by Georges Delerue. **Pr:** Columbia Pictures. **A:** Sr. High-Adult. **P:** Entertainment. **U:** Home. **Mov-Ent:** Psychiatry. **Awds:** Golden Globes '86: Support. Actress (Tilly). **Acq:** Purchase. **Dist:** Sony Pictures Home Entertainment Inc. $12.95.

Agnes Varda 1969
The Belgian filmmaker talks with Susan Sontag and critic Jack Kroll about women in films. 28m/B/W; VHS, 3/4 U. **A:** Sr. High-Adult. **P:** Education. **U:** Home. **Gen-Edu:** Filmmaking. **Acq:** Purchase. **Dist:** Camera Three Productions, Inc.

Agnus Berenato: Man-to-Man Defensive Breakdown Drills 2012 (Unrated)
Coach Agnus Berenato presents training drills for basketball coaches using the man-to-man defensive scheme. ??m; DVD. **A:** Family. **P:** Education. **U:** Home, Institution. **Spo-Rec:** Basketball, Athletic Instruction/Coaching. **Acq:** Purchase. **Dist:** Championship Productions. $39.99.

Agonies of Nationalism, 1800-1927 1972
The Chinese false sense of security collapsed in their faces in the early 20th century. Sun Yat-sen and Chiang Kai-Shek battled the penetrating chaos, but, unforeseen, communism had grown in their very midst. A segment in the series, "China: A Century of Revolution." 23m/B/W; VHS, 3/4 U. **C:** Theodore White. **Pr:** Metromedia Producers Corporation. **A:** Sr. High-College. **P:** Education. **U:** Institution, SURA. **Gen-Edu:** China. **Acq:** Purchase. **Dist:** Home Vision Cinema.

Agony 198?
Reggae bands include Peter Metro, Tonto Metro, Dillinger, Junior Cat, Papa San, Beany Man, General Trees, Lady G and more. ?m; VHS. **A:** Sr. High-Adult. **P:** Entertainment. **U:** Home. **Mov-Ent:** Music Video. **Acq:** Purchase. **Dist:** Music Video Distributors. $19.95.

The Agony and the Ecstasy 1965 — ★★½
Big-budget (for 1965 anyway at $12 million) adaptation of the Irving Stone book recounts the conflict between Michelangelo and Pope Julius II after His Holiness directs the artist to paint the Sistine Chapel. Follow the tortured artist through his unpredictable creative process and the hours (it seems literal due to movie length) of painting flat on his back. Heston exudes quiet strength in his sincere interpretation of the genius artist, while Harrison has a fling as the Pope. Slow script is not up to the generally good performances. Disappointing at the boxoffice, but worth a look on the small screen for the sets alone. 136m; VHS, DVD, Blu-Ray, Wide. **C:** Charlton Heston; Rex Harrison; Harry Andrews; Diane Cilento; Alberto Lupo; Adolfo Celi; Directed by Carol Reed; Written by Philip Dunne; Cinematography by Leon Shamroy; Music by Jerry Goldsmith; Alex North. **Pr:** 20th Century-Fox. **A:** Jr. High-Adult. **P:** Entertainment. **U:** Home. **Mov-Ent:** Drama, Art & Artists. **Awds:** Natl. Bd. of Review '65: Support. Actor (Andrews). **Acq:** Purchase. **Dist:** Ignatius Press. $19.98.

The Agony and the Ecstasy 1976
This experimental video examines how hard it is to penetrate good literature. 10m; VHS, 3/4 U. **Pr:** John Mitchel. **A:** College-Adult. **P:** Education. **U:** Institution. **Gen-Edu:** Video, Literature. **Acq:** Rent/Lease. **Dist:** Video Out Distribution.

The Agony and the Ecstasy—The Special Problems of Running a Closely-Held or Family Business 1989
About 90% of American businesses are family-owned. Find out their disadvantages and advantages and what makes them so special. 40m; VHS, 3/4 U. **C:** Ted Cohn. **Pr:** RMI Media Productions. **A:** Adult. **P:** Education. **U:** Institution, CCTV, Home. **Bus-Ind:** Business. **Acq:** Purchase. **Dist:** RMI Media. $149.00.

The Agony of Decision: The Media and the Military 1991
Roundtable discussion on the role of the media in covering a war. Includes insight from former Ambassador Jeanne Kirkpatrick and former Secretary of Defense and Energy James Schlesinger. ?m; VHS, 3/4 U. **A:** College-Adult. **P:** Education. **U:** Institution. **Gen-Edu:** Journalism, Armed Forces--U.S., War--General. **Acq:** Purchase. **Dist:** PBS Home Video.

Agony of Love 1966 — ★
An unhappy homemaker rents a nearby apartment to live out her wildest fantasies and bring some excitment into her otherwise dull life. ?m; VHS, DVD. **C:** Pat Barrington; William Rotsler; Directed by William Rotsler; Written by William Rotsler. **A:** Adult. **P:** Entertainment. **U:** Home. **Mov-Ent:** Exploitation. **Acq:** Purchase. **Dist:** Something Weird Video; Tapeworm Video Distributors Inc. $20.

Agora 2009 (Unrated) — ★★
Despite being a woman living in 4th-century Alexandria, philosopher, mathematician, and astronomer Hypatia (Weisz, who gives a dominating performance) teaches and spends her time in the city's fabled library. But the ancient pagan world is giving way to a firebrand cult of Christians who begin to dominate their Roman rulers to the detriment of such knowledge. Could use some editing with too much exposition and too many monologues slowing down the too-timely story of religious fundamentalist intolerance vs. personal freedom and reason. 141m; Blu-Ray, On Demand, Wide, CC. **C:** Rachel Weisz; Max Minghella; Oscar Isaac; Ashraf Barhoum; Rupert Evans; Michael (Michel) Lonsdale; Sami Samir; Directed by Alejandro Amenabar; Written by Alejandro Amenabar; Mateo Gil; Cinematography by Xavi Gimenez; Music by Dario Marianelli. **Pr:** Fernando Bovaira; Alvaro Augustin; Himenoptero; Mod Producciones; Telecinco Cinema; Newmarket Films. **A:** College-Adult. **P:** Entertainment. **U:** Home. **L:** English. **Mov-Ent:** Drama, Women, Religion. **Acq:** Purchase. **Dist:** Amazon.com Inc.; Movies Unlimited; Lions Gate Entertainment Inc.

Agricultural Cluster 1984
People who work in agriculture describe their daily work routines for students interested in entering this occupation. 20m; VHS, 3/4 U. **Pr:** Minnesota State Private Industry Company. **A:** Sr. High-Adult. **P:** Education. **U:** Institution, SURA. **Gen-Edu:** Occupations, Agriculture. **Acq:** Purchase. **Dist:** Center for Humanities, Inc./Guidance Associates.

Agricultural Field Equipment 19??
Provides an in-depth look at the most recent innovations in agricultural field equipment. Covers equipment used for tillage, planting, harvesting, and chemical applications. Explains how they are used and what they are used for. 30m; VHS. **A:** Jr. High-Adult. **P:** Education. **U:** Institution, SURA. **Bus-Ind:** Agriculture. **Acq:** Purchase. **Dist:** San Luis Video Publishing. $90.00.

Agricultural Innovations in Israel 1988
A discussion of how Israel became one of the most efficient agricultural nations in the world. 25m; VHS. **Pr:** Alden Films. **A:** Jr. High-Adult. **P:** Education. **U:** Institution, Home. **Gen-Edu:** Agriculture, Judaism, Middle East. **Acq:** Purchase, Rent/Lease. **Dist:** Alden Films. $50.00.

Agricultural Laboratory Safety 19??
Stresses the importance of following proper safety precautions when working in the agricultural laboratory. Includes coverage of personal protective equipment, precaution and prevention, hazards, first aid, and more. Comes with study guide. 27m; VHS. **A:** Sr. High-Adult. **P:** Instruction. **U:** Institution. **How-Ins:** Agriculture, Safety Education, First Aid. **Acq:** Purchase. **Dist:** CEV Multimedia. $79.95.

Agricultural Wetlands 1994
Describes the benefits of preserving wetlands, such as livestock watering, crop irrigation and fish and wildlife habitat. Also shows farm management practices that protect wetlands and outlines assistance programs available to help conserve or restore wetlands areas. Two programs on one tape: a ten minute short and a 28 minute feature. 38m; VHS. **A:** Family. **P:** Education. **U:** Home. **Gen-Edu:** Ecology & Environment, Agriculture. **Acq:** Purchase. **Dist:** Cornell University. $25.00.

Agriculture: America's Most Crucial Industry 19??
Discusses the role of agriculture as it effects the overall growth of the United States and the contribution it makes to the national and international economies. Comes with teacher's manual. 15m; VHS. **A:** Jr. High-Adult. **P:** Education. **U:** Institution. **Gen-Edu:** Agriculture, Economics. **Acq:** Purchase. **Dist:** Educational Video Network. $49.95.

Agriculture and Groundwater Contamination: Exploring the Issues ????
Overviews groundwater contamination concerns in Michigan. 19m; VHS. **A:** Adult. **P:** Education. **U:** Home. **Gen-Edu:** Agriculture, Science, Natural Resources. **Acq:** Purchase. **Dist:** Michigan State University. $25.00.

Agriculture/Horticulture 1992
Part of a series offering instruction on applied vocational mathematics. 30m; VHS. **A:** Adult. **P:** Education. **U:** Institution. **Gen-Edu:** Mathematics. **Acq:** Purchase. **Dist:** RMI Media. $149.00.

Agriculture in the San Joaquin Valley of California 19??
Reveals many of the agricultural products being produced in the San Joaquin Valley area of California. Covers frit, nut, vegetable, grain, meat, and fiber production. 45m; VHS. **A:** Jr. High-Adult. **P:** Education. **U:** Institution, Home. **Gen-Edu:** Agriculture, Food Industry. **Acq:** Purchase. **Dist:** CEV Multimedia. $79.95.

Agriculture Laboratory Safety 19??
Stresses the importance of following proper safety procedures in the agricultural laboratory. Covers personal protective clothing, hazards, chemicals, emergency guidelines, and first aid. 27m; VHS. **A:** Adult. **P:** Vocational. **U:** Institution, SURA. **Bus-Ind:** Safety Education, Agriculture, Occupational Training. **Acq:** Purchase. **Dist:** San Luis Video Publishing. $49.95.

Agrippina 1984
A performance of the rare Handel opera about the Roman empress, with the Koelner Opera and the London Baroque Players. In Italian with subtitles. 159m; VHS. **C:** Barbara Daniels; David Kuebler; Gunter von Kannen; Conducted by Michael Hampe. **Pr:** Cologne Opera. **A:** Family. **P:** Entertainment. **U:** Home. **L:** Italian. **Fin-Art:** Opera. **Acq:** Purchase. **Dist:** Music Video Distributors; Home Vision Cinema; Facets Multimedia Inc. $49.95.

The Agronomist 2004
Director Jonathan Demme follows the career of Haitian journalist and civil rights activist Jean Dominique from the 1991 overthrow of President Aristide to Dominique's assassination in 2000. 90m; DVD. **A:** Sr. High-Adult. **P:** Entertainment. **U:** Home. **Gen-Edu:** Documentary Films. **Acq:** Purchase. **Dist:** Warner Home Video, Inc.

Aguirre, the Wrath of God 1972 (Unrated) — ★★★½
Herzog at his best, combining brilliant poetic images and an intense narrative dealing with power, irony, and death. Spanish conquistadors in 1590 search for the mythical city of gold in Peru. Instead, they descend into the hell of the jungle. Kinski is fabulous as Aquirre, succumbing to insanity while leading a continually diminishing crew in this compelling, extraordinary drama shot in the jungles of South America. Both English- and German-language versions available. 94m; VHS, DVD. **C:** Klaus Kinski; Ruy Guerra; Del Negro; Helena Rojo; Cecilia

Rivera; Peter Berling; Danny Ades; Directed by Werner Herzog; Written by Werner Herzog; Cinematography by Thomas Mauch; Music by Popul Vuh. **Pr:** Werner Herzog; Werner Herzog. **A:** Sr. High-Adult. **P:** Entertainment. **U:** Home. **L:** English, German. **Mov-Ent**: Classic Films, South America. **Awds:** Natl. Soc. Film Critics '77: Cinematog. **Acq:** Purchase. **Dist:** Anchor Bay Entertainment; New Yorker Video.

Ah, We Humans 1979
This nonnarrative program, designed to stimulate discussion about respect for the ways of others, shows the threatening behavior of two primitive tribal groups toward each other over differences in custom, color, worship, and establishing territorial rights. 11m; VHS, 3/4 U. **Pr:** Benchmark Films. **A:** Primary. **P:** Education. **U:** Institution, CCTV. **Chl-Juv**: Ethics & Morals. **Acq:** Purchase. **Dist:** Benchmark Media.

Ah, Wilderness! 1935 (Unrated) — ★★★1/2
Delightful tale of a teen boy coming of age in small town America. Watch for the hilarious high school graduation scene. Based on the play by Eugene O'Neill. Remade in 1948 as "Summer Holiday," a musical with Mickey Rooney in the lead. 101m/B/W; VHS, DVD. **C:** Wallace Beery; Lionel Barrymore; Aline MacMahon; Eric Linden; Cecilia Parker; Spring Byington; Mickey Rooney; Charley Grapewin; Frank Albertson; Directed by Clarence Brown; Cinematography by Clyde De Vinna. **Pr:** Hunt Stromberg; MGM. **A:** Jr. High-Adult. **P:** Entertainment. **U:** Home. **Mov-Ent**: Adolescence. **Acq:** Purchase. **Dist:** WarnerArchive.com; Baker and Taylor. $19.98.

Ah Ying 1983 (Unrated) — ★★1/2
A movie director is trying to start a project in Hong Kong while also giving lectures on film. He becomes obsessed with Ah Ying, an aspiring actress who works as a fishmarket vendor. In Cantonese with English subtitles. 110m; VHS. **C:** Peter Wang; Directed by Allen Fong. **A:** Sr. High-Adult. **P:** Entertainment. **U:** Home. **L:** Chinese. **Mov-Ent. Acq:** Purchase. **Dist:** Facets Multimedia Inc. $49.95.

A-Ha: The Hits 19??
Compilation of 17 clips, featuring their hit "Take on Me," and several others. ?m; VHS. **A:** Jr. High-Adult. **P:** Entertainment. **U:** Home. **Mov-Ent**: Music Video, Music--Performance, Music--Pop/Rock. **Acq:** Purchase. **Dist:** Music Video Distributors. $79.95.

Ahi Madre 197? (Unrated) — ★1/2
A Mexican mother gets into all kinds of scrapes and misunderstandings. 90m; VHS. **C:** Eduardo Manzano; Cristina Blum. **Pr:** KNBC. **A:** Jr. High-Adult. **P:** Entertainment. **U:** Home. **L:** Spanish. **Mov-Ent**: Family. **Acq:** Purchase. **Dist:** Spanishmultimedia. $69.95.

Ahimsa: Non-Violence 1987
An inside look at the customs of these non-violent people. 58m; VHS, 3/4 U. **Pr:** Michael Tobias. **A:** Sr. High-Adult. **P:** Education. **U:** Institution, SURA. **Gen-Edu**: Religion. **Acq:** Purchase, Rent/Lease. **Dist:** Direct Cinema Ltd. $250.00.

Ai City 1986 — ★1/2
Kei is an unwilling participant in an experiment to increase telekinetic abilities in humans. He and the young Ai escape from the omnipotent Fraud Corporation. Soon, they are part of a terrible power struggle that will determine the fate of the Earth because it seems there is something special about Ai. The straining plot barely holds together many action-packed chase scenes. Strange and interesting things happen in a sometimes confusing sort of way. There is a reason so many people are in pursuit of Ai that's revealed in a dialogue-heavy confrontation near the end of the movie. 86m; VHS, Wide. **A:** Sr. High-College. **P:** Entertainment. **U:** Home. **L:** Japanese. **Mov-Ent**: Anime, Animation & Cartoons. **Acq:** Purchase. **Dist:** The Right Stuf Inc. $24.95.

Ai Weiwei: Never Sorry 2012 (R) — ★★★
The title of Alison Klayman's brassy documentary refers to its subject matter, a Chinese artist who has become internationally renowned not just for his creative abilities but his activism. The filmmaker was granted access to the acclaimed public figure from 2008 to 2010 and watched as Ai went through small moments with his family to international ones with the Chinese government. As with several great documentaries about artistic figures who transcend their art form to become something greater, "Never Sorry" paints a fully-rounded picture of both the personal and the political side of its subject matter. 91m; DVD, Blu-Ray. **C:** Directed by Alison Klayman; Written by Alison Klayman; Cinematography by Alison Klayman; Music by Ilan Isakov. **Pr:** Adam Schlesinger; Alison Klayman; Sundance Selects; United Expression Media. **A:** Sr. High-Adult. **P:** Entertainment. **U:** Home. **L:** English, Mandarin Chinese. **Mov-Ent**: Documentary Films, China, Art & Artists. **Acq:** Purchase. **Dist:** MPI Media Group.

AIA Legal Hard Hat 1991
Explains the fundamentals associated with antitrust laws and fulfills the requirement of the AIA's 1990 consent decree. 13m; VHS. **A:** Adult. **P:** Professional. **U:** Institution, Home. **Bus-Ind**: Architecture, Education. **Acq:** Rent/Lease. **Dist:** American Institute of Architects.

AIA: Prince Charles Visit 1985
Contains highlights from Prince Charles's visit to the AIA in November 1985. Includes scenes of the Prince's arrival and departure, his Octagon Museum visit, and the R/UDAT press conference with R/UDAT participants and representatives from revitalized neighborhoods in Savannah and Baltimore. 20m; VHS. **A:** Adult. **P:** Education. **U:** Institution, Home. **Gen-Edu**: Architecture, Education. **Acq:** Rent/Lease. **Dist:** American Institute of Architects.

Aida 1981
Verdi's tragic opera conducted by Toscanini with the NBC Symphony Orchestra, chorus and soloists. 210m; VHS. **Pr:** Covent Garden Video Productions Ltd. **A:** Family. **P:** Entertainment. **U:** Home. **Fin-Art**: Opera. **Acq:** Purchase. **Dist:** Music Video Distributors. $29.95.

Aida 1984
A performance of Giuseppe Verdi's opera taped at the Arena di Verona in Italy. An Ethopian slave girl is trapped between love for an Egyptian warrior, her patriotism for Ethiopia, and the jealousy of a noblewoman. Stunning production values enhance Verdi's glorious melodies. Originally composed to celebrate the opening of the Suez Canal. 150m; VHS. **C:** Maria Chiara; Nicola Martinucci; Fiorenza Cossotto. **Pr:** Radiotelevisione Italiana. **A:** College-Adult. **P:** Entertainment. **U:** Home. **L:** Italian. **Fin-Art**: Music--Performance, Opera, Middle East. **Acq:** Purchase. **Dist:** Home Vision Cinema. $39.99.

Aida 1988
A performance of the classic opera, taped at La Scala, Italy; Lorin Maazel conducts. In hi-fi Stereo. 161m; VHS. **Pr:** RM Arts. **A:** Family. **P:** Entertainment. **U:** Home. **Fin-Art**: Opera. **Acq:** Purchase. **Dist:** Home Vision Cinema; Music Video Distributors; Stagestep. $39.95.

Aida 1990
The Metropolitan Opera Chorus and Orchestra, featuring soloists Zajick, Milnes, Burchuladze, and Kavrakos, performs Verdi's opera as conducted by James Levine. 158m; VHS. **Pr:** Polygram. **A:** Jr. High-Adult. **P:** Entertainment. **U:** Home. **Fin-Art**: Music--Classical. **Acq:** Purchase. **Dist:** Music Video Distributors. $34.95.

The Aida File 1990
Luciano Pavarotti takes a look at the success of Verdi's famous opera. Features a tour of Verdi's home in Parma, comparisons of "Aida" productions, and interviews with performers. 77m; VHS. **C:** Luciano Pavarotti. **Pr:** RM Arts. **A:** Jr. High-Adult. **P:** Education. **U:** Home. **Gen-Edu**: Documentary Films, Opera. **Acq:** Purchase. **Dist:** Home Vision Cinema. $39.95.

AIDS 1987
This documentary, hosted by Jack Palance, examines the myths about AIDS, its history, and its symptoms. Also addresses common questions about AIDS and describes how to offer support to AIDS patients. 30m; VHS, 3/4 U. **Pr:** RMI Media Productions. **A:** Jr. High-Adult. **P:** Education. **U:** Institution. **Hea-Sci**: AIDS, Health Education. **Acq:** Purchase. **Dist:** RMI Media. $49.95.

AIDS 1988
The deadly disease is broken down into terms that kids can understand. 12m; VHS, 3/4 U. **Pr:** SVE. **A:** Primary-Jr. High. **P:** Education. **U:** Institution, CCTV, Home. **L:** Spanish. **Hea-Sci**: AIDS, Health Education. **Acq:** Purchase, Duplication. **Dist:** Clear Vue Inc. $39.00.

AIDS: A Christian Perspective 1988
A Christian fundamentalist perspective on AIDS is provided. 43m; VHS. **Pr:** Bridgestone Production Group. **A:** Family. **P:** Religious. **U:** Home. **Gen-Edu**: AIDS. **Acq:** Purchase. **Dist:** Alpha Omega Publications Inc.

AIDS: A Deck of Cards 1985
This tape follows the management of an AIDS patient through diagnosis and treatment. 58m; VHS, 3/4 U. **A:** Adult. **P:** Professional. **U:** Institution, CCTV, Home, SURA. **Hea-Sci**: Immunology. **Acq:** Purchase, Rent/Lease, Subscription. **Dist:** Emory Medical Television Network.

AIDS: A Different Kind of Germ 1990
Tracy and her cartoon friend, Microscopic Mike, help teach young children about HIV, showing why it is different from other kinds of infections. They offer precautions that children can take to limit their chances of contracting the disease. Winner of many awards including the CINE Golden Eagle. 15m; VHS, 3/4 U, Special order formats. **Pr:** MTI. **A:** Primary. **P:** Education. **U:** Institution, CCTV, SURA. **Chl-Juv**: AIDS, Children. **Acq:** Purchase, Rent/Lease, Duplication License. **Dist:** Phoenix Learning Group. $350.00.

AIDS: A Family Experience 1988
This program is a personal account of a young man dying of AIDS and his family's reaction and support. Family members openly discuss their often contradictory feelings to the knowledge that their son and brother is dying because of AIDS. The film was made in partnership with Don, who wanted to leave a legacy to his family and other families living with the disease. 33m; VHS, 3/4 U. **Pr:** Weatherstone Productions. **A:** Jr. High-Adult. **P:** Education. **U:** Institution, SURA. **Hea-Sci**: Diseases, AIDS, Death. **Acq:** Purchase, Rent/Lease. **Dist:** Leo Media, Inc. $395.00.

AIDS: A Global Approach 1989
A discussion group of doctors suggest a world-wide approach to deal with the AIDS crisis. 30m; VHS, 3/4 U. **Pr:** Centre Productions, Inc. **A:** Sr. High-Adult. **P:** Education. **U:** Institution, SURA. **Hea-Sci**: AIDS. **Acq:** Purchase, Rent/Lease. **Dist:** Clear Vue Inc. $395.00.

AIDS: A Matter of Corporate Policy 1988
The formulation and implementation of AIDS policy in the workplace is examined in panel discussions covering: AIDS in the workplace, the CEO's perspective; managing social, legal, and medical implications; health care costs; employee education; public relations and solutions. 150m; VHS, 3/4 U. **Pr:** KPBS San Diego; PBS National Narrowcast Service. **A:** College-Adult. **P:** Education. **U:** Institution, CCTV, Home, SURA. **Bus-Ind**: Business, AIDS. **Acq:** Purchase, Rent/Lease, Duplication License, Off-Air Record. **Dist:** PBS Home Video.

AIDS: A Topic for Life 1989
Within the moral guidelines of the Church, AIDS is discussed as openly as possible. 35m; VHS. **Pr:** Awakening Productions. **A:** Sr. High-Adult. **P:** Religious. **U:** Institution, SURA. **Gen-Edu**: Religion, AIDS. **Acq:** Purchase. **Dist:** Harcourt Religion Publishers.

AIDS: A Working Definition 1996
Focuses on the factual information which will serve as a foundation for professional people to better care for AIDS patients. 17m; VHS. **A:** Adult. **P:** Education. **U:** Institution. **Hea-Sci**: Nursing, Diseases, Infection. **Acq:** Purchase, Rent/Lease. **Dist:** University of Maryland. $300.00.

AIDS: A Worldwide Dilemma 19??
Contains group discussion on AIDS with a diverse group of students and two doctors as they provide educational information aimed at preventing the contraction of the disease. 23m; VHS. **A:** Jr. High-Adult. **P:** Education. **U:** Institution. **Hea-Sci**: Health Education, AIDS. **Acq:** Purchase. **Dist:** Educational Video Network. $49.95.

AIDS: Acquired Immune Deficiency Syndrome 1988
Using computer animated graphics, this film explains how the AIDS virus attacks the immune system, and what precautions can be taken to avoid getting and spreading the disease. 19m; VHS, 3/4 U, EJ, Special order formats. **TV Std:** NTSC, PAL, SECAM. **C:** Hosted by Ally Sheedy. **Pr:** Disney Educational Productions. **A:** Jr. High-Sr. High. **P:** Education. **U:** Institution, CCTV, SURA. **Hea-Sci**: AIDS. **Acq:** Purchase, Rent/Lease. **Dist:** Phoenix Learning Group. $345.00.

AIDS, Alcohol, and Drugs: Perception vs. Reality 19??
Dr. Larry Siegel, co-chairman of the American Society of Addiction Medicine, discusses the connection between the high-risk behaviors of addiction and HIV exposure. Also covers the important role recovery can play in those diagnosed with AIDS. 30m; VHS. **A:** Adult. **P:** Education. **U:** Institution. **Hea-Sci**: Drug Abuse, AIDS. **Acq:** Purchase. **Dist:** Hazelden Publishing. $195.00.

AIDS Alert 1987
For the youngster, a look at the deadly disease, and the steps to take to avoid catching it. Updated every six months. Includes one leader's guide. 20m; VHS, 3/4 U. **Pr:** Cambridge Career Productions. **A:** Jr. High-Sr. High. **P:** Education. **U:** Institution, CCTV, CATV, Home, SURA. **Hea-Sci**: AIDS, Sex & Sexuality, Sexually Transmitted Diseases. **Acq:** Purchase. **Dist:** United Learning Inc.

AIDS Alert for Youth 1990
Geared towards kids and teens, this video was designed to help clarify the facts about AIDS, and ways to protect yourself from the fatal disease. Includes one comprehensive leader's guide. 20m; VHS, 3/4 U. **Pr:** International Film Bureau. **A:** Jr. High-Adult. **P:** Education. **U:** Institution, CCTV, CATV, Home, SURA. **Hea-Sci**: AIDS, Health Education, Adolescence. **Acq:** Purchase, Rent/Lease. **Dist:** Film Ideas, Inc.; United Learning Inc. $95.00.

AIDS: An ABC News Special Assignment 1988
This comprehensive documentary was designed to demystify the fatal disease. Health professionals, medical experts and AIDS patients speak candidly and encourage a more compassionate attitude towards those suffering from the disease. 12m; VHS, 3/4 U. **Pr:** ABC World News Tonight. **A:** Jr. High-Adult. **P:** Education. **U:** Institution, SURA. **Hea-Sci**: Documentary Films, AIDS. **Acq:** Purchase, Rent/Lease. **Dist:** Aspen Publishers, Inc.; Phoenix Learning Group. $350.00.

AIDS: An Enemy Among Us 1988
A small town is forced to deal with reality when one of its members contracts the AIDS virus. 45m; VHS, 3/4 U. **C:** Gladys Knight; Dee Wallace. **Pr:** Helios Productions. **A:** Jr. High-Adult. **P:** Education. **U:** Institution, Home, SURA. **Hea-Sci**: AIDS. **Acq:** Purchase, Rent/Lease, Duplication License. **Dist:** Clear Vue Inc. $295.00.

AIDS: An Olde or New Acquaintance? 1985
How long has AIDS been around? Where did it come from? Is it a mutation of a different virus? Dr. Krause gives his opinions on these subjects. 42m; VHS, 3/4 U. **A:** Adult. **P:** Professional. **U:** Institution, CCTV, Home, SURA. **Hea-Sci**: AIDS. **Acq:** Purchase, Rent/Lease, Subscription. **Dist:** Emory Medical Television Network.

AIDS and Attitudes 1992
Host Collin Seidor looks at people living with AIDS and discusses society's feelings towards the disease. Also provides facts on medical opinions and recent medical trends relating to HIV and AIDS. 32m; VHS. **Pr:** Dystar Television; MTI. **A:** Sr. High-Adult. **P:** Education. **U:** Institution, CCTV, SURA. **Hea-Sci**: Health Education, AIDS. **Acq:** Purchase, Rent/Lease, Duplication License. **Dist:** Phoenix Learning Group. $495.00.

AIDS and Chemical Dependency 19??
Dr. David Smith, the founder of the Haight-Ashbury Free Medical Clinics, lectures on the relationship between AIDS and chemical dependency. In addition, he emphasizes the specifics of a recovery program for those living with HIV/AIDS. 29m; VHS. **A:** Jr. High. **P:** Education. **U:** Institution. **L:** English. **Hea-Sci**: AIDS. **Acq:** Purchase. **Dist:** Hazelden Publishing. $49.95.

AIDS and Love: An Interview with Dr. Elisabeth Kubler-Ross 1992
Elisabeth Kubler-Ross discusses the rewards of caring for infants with AIDS, and her work of placing AIDS babies in adoptive homes. Others involved in the field also share their

stories of compassion for these tiny victims. 39m; VHS. **A:** Sr. High-Adult. **P:** Education. **U:** Institution. **Hea-Sci**: AIDS, Infants, Adoption. **Acq:** Purchase. **Dist:** Filmakers Library Inc. $99.00.

AIDS and Sexually Transmitted Diseases 1993
Provides information concerning STDs such as causative organisms, symptoms, potential risks, and treatment. 30m; VHS. **A:** Adult. **P:** Education. **U:** Institution. **Gen-Edu**: Health Education. **Acq:** Purchase. **Dist:** RMI Media. $99.00.

AIDS and the Health Care Worker 1988
The physical risks as well as the emotional traumas that the AIDS worker must deal with are compassionately explored in this film. 26m; VHS. **Pr:** AMI Television. **A:** College-Adult. **P:** Professional. **U:** Institution, SURA. **Hea-Sci**: AIDS, Health Education. **Acq:** Purchase, Rent/Lease. **Dist:** Phoenix Learning Group. $425.00.

AIDS and the Immune System 1988
What the immune system does and how the AIDS virus causes damage up are explained. 12m; VHS, 3/4 U. **Pr:** Churchill Films. **A:** Primary-Jr. High. **P:** Education. **U:** Institution, Home, SURA. **Hea-Sci**: Immunology, AIDS. **Acq:** Purchase, Rent/Lease, Duplication License. **Dist:** Clear Vue Inc. $225.00.

AIDS and the Native American Family 1996
Addresses the need for family and cultural support of Native Americans with the AIDS virus. 11m; VHS. **A:** Sr. High. **P:** Education. **U:** Home. **Gen-Edu**: Native Americans, AIDS. **Acq:** Purchase. **Dist:** Upstream Productions. $55.00.

AIDS and Women: The Greatest Gamble 1993
Two teenagers interview five women with HIV. Comes with guide. 26m; VHS. **Pr:** Peregrine Productions. **A:** Sr. High-Adult. **P:** Education. **U:** Institution. **Gen-Edu**: AIDS, Women, Interviews. **Acq:** Purchase, Rent/Lease. **Dist:** United Learning Inc. $205.00.

AIDS and Your World 1996
Features a group of young adults who speak candidly about their contact with the AIDS virus and how it has changed their outlook on life. 25m; VHS. **A:** Adult. **U:** Institution. **Gen-Edu**: AIDS, Interviews. **Acq:** Rent/Lease. **Dist:** Fanlight Productions. $50.

AIDS: Answers for Everyone 1990
A comprehensive presentation on the causes, effects, and possible prevention of AIDS, featuring interviews with doctors and AIDS patients. A separate guide is available. 55m; VHS, 3/4 U. **Pr:** Bridgestone Production Group. **A:** Jr. High-Adult. **P:** Education. **U:** Institution, Home. **Hea-Sci**: Documentary Films, Diseases, AIDS. **Acq:** Purchase, Rent/Lease. **Dist:** Karol Media. $24.95.

AIDS: Answers for Young People 1988
The latest information about AIDS is explained in a way that will make it easy for junior high kids to understand. 19m; VHS, 3/4 U. **Pr:** University of California at Los Angeles AIDS Center. **A:** Jr. High. **P:** Education. **U:** Institution, Home, SURA. **Hea-Sci**: AIDS. **Acq:** Purchase, Rent/Lease, Duplication License. **Dist:** Clear Vue Inc. $275.00.

AIDS at Issue: Coping with an Epidemic 1991
Numerous issues related to the AIDS crisis are covered in this program, including how AIDS is transmitted, how to prevent AIDS, discrimination against people who have AIDS, and more. Program features interviews with a diverse group of subjects. 22m; VHS. **A:** Sr. High. **P:** Education. **U:** Institution. **Chl-Juv**: AIDS. **Acq:** Purchase, Rent/Lease. **Dist:** Filmakers Library Inc. $55.00.

AIDS Babies 1990
A look at the treatment of children with AIDS, focusing on the drug users whose behavior affects their partners and puts children at risk. Compares the attempts of various world governments to curb the spread of AIDS and includes interviews with noted caregivers. 58m; VHS. **C:** Hosted by Leeza Gibbons; Monique Oomen. **Pr:** The Cinema Guild. **A:** Sr. High-Adult. **P:** Education. **U:** Institution, Home. **Gen-Edu**: AIDS, Infants, Medical Education. **Acq:** Purchase, Rent/Lease. **Dist:** The Cinema Guild. $350.00.

AIDS, Blood & Politics 1993
Covers the early effects of AIDS on the United States' blood supply. Originally shown on PBS's Frontline. 57m; VHS. **A:** Sr. High. **P:** Education. **U:** Home. **Gen-Edu**: AIDS. **Acq:** Purchase. **Dist:** PBS Home Video. $69.95.

AIDS: Can I Get It? 1987
Interviews with medical personnel and AIDS patients explore various topics including what AIDS is, how it is contracted, the safety of dental procedures and donating blood, and exactly what constitutes safe sex. 48m; VHS. **A:** Jr. High-College. **P:** Education. **U:** Institution, Home. **Hea-Sci**: AIDS, Health Education. **Acq:** Purchase. **Dist:** Educational Images Ltd.; Cambridge Educational. $19.95.

AIDS: Caring for the Caregiver 19??
Explains the psychosocial stressors which affect caregivers of AIDS patients, including fear of contagion, feelings and attitudes about homosexuality and/or drug abuse, intense physical and emotional care demands, identification with the patient, and helplessness and repetitive grief related to the disease's high mortality rate. Offers methods of coping that promote growth and ensure the best patient care. Contains insight from caregivers. Includes study guide. Approved for CE credit. 28m; VHS. **A:** College-Adult. **P:** Education. **U:** Institution. **Hea-Sci**: Nursing, AIDS, Stress. **Acq:** Purchase, Rent/Lease. **Dist:** AJN Video Library/Lippincott Williams & Wilkins. $285.00.

AIDS: Changing the Rules 1987
This acclaimed prevention film stands out for its directness in explaining the urgent necessity for safe sex in the fight against AIDS. Sexually active adolescents and adult heterosexuals are the target group for the documentary. A memorable as well as practical segment features singer Ruben Blades using a banana to demonstrate the proper techniques for using a condom. Also available in Spanish language version. 26m; VHS, CC. **C:** Ruben Blades; Beverly Johnson; Ron Reagan. **Pr:** AIDSFILMS. **A:** Primary-Adult. **P:** Education. **U:** Institution. **L:** English, Spanish. **Gen-Edu**: Documentary Films, AIDS, Health Education. **Acq:** Purchase. **Dist:** PBS Home Video.

AIDS: Chapter One 1985
This is an episode from the "Nova" series about the doctors and laboratory technicians who are trying to find a cure for AIDS. 57m; VHS, 3/4 U, Special order formats. **Pr:** WGBH Boston. **A:** Sr. High-Adult. **P:** Education. **U:** Institution, SURA. **Gen-Edu**: Diseases. **Acq:** Purchase, Rent/Lease. **Dist:** Time-Life Video and Television.

AIDS: Emotional Needs of the Patient and Family 19??
Details the psychological problems of AIDS patients and their families. Furnishes information on establishing therapeutic rapport, understanding the unique needs of the patient, and handling the patient's emotional state with death approaching. 32m; VHS. **A:** Adult. **P:** Education. **U:** Institution. **Hea-Sci**: AIDS, Patient Care, Family. **Acq:** Purchase, Rent/Lease. **Dist:** University of Maryland. $300.00.

The AIDS Epidemic: Is Anyone Safe? 1988
Interviews with medical experts and researchers present up to date information to dispel AIDS myths. The film examines the risks drug users and sexually active individuals face and offers information on protection against AIDS. 50m; VHS, 3/4 U. **Pr:** Guidance Associates. **A:** Jr. High-College. **P:** Education. **U:** Institution, SURA. **Hea-Sci**: AIDS, Safety Education. **Acq:** Purchase. **Dist:** Center for Humanities, Inc./Guidance Associates.

AIDS: Everything You and Your Family Need to Know. . .But Were Afraid to Ask 1988
Former U.S. Surgeon General C. Everett Koop hosts this documentary discussing commonly asked questions about Acquired Immune Deficiency Syndrome (AIDS). 30m; VHS, CC. **C:** Hosted by C. Everett Koop. **Pr:** HBO. **A:** Family. **P:** Education. **U:** Institution, CCTV, CATV, BCTV, Home, SURA. **Hea-Sci**: Health Education, Diseases, AIDS. **Acq:** Purchase, Duplication. **Dist:** Ambrose Video Publishing, Inc. $99.95.

AIDS: Facts and Fears, Crisis and Controversy 1987
National health experts present up-to-date medical facts about this dread disease, separating fact from myth, to help increase understanding of AIDS and its' victims. 30m; VHS, 3/4 U. **Pr:** Guidance Associates. **A:** Jr. High-Adult. **P:** Education. **U:** Institution, SURA. **Gen-Edu**: Diseases, Diseases. **Acq:** Purchase. **Dist:** Center for Humanities, Inc./Guidance Associates. $9.95.

AIDS: Facts for Kids ????
Candid advice for students about HIV and how to stay safe and healthy. Geared toward grades 4-6. 9m; VHS; Closed Captioned. **A:** Primary. **P:** Education. **U:** Institution. **Chl-Juv**: Hygiene, Health Education, AIDS. **Acq:** Purchase. **Dist:** Marshmedia. $69.95.

AIDS: Facts Over Fear 1995
Describes how behavior, not casual contact, can puts teens at risk to AIDS. Encourages abstinence, or the use of condoms to those who are sexually active. Teacher's guide included. Silver Apple, National Educational Film and Video Festival; Two Stars Award, Canadian Inte4rnational Annual Filom Festival. 20m; VHS. **A:** Sr. High. **P:** Education. **U:** Institution. **Gen-Edu**: AIDS, Education. **Acq:** Purchase. **Dist:** Sunburst Digital Inc. $149.00.

AIDS: Facts Over Fears 1988
Barbara Walters hosts this program which looks beyond the hysteria surrounding the disease and explains the actual medical facts. Many questions are answered: Can you get AIDS from kissing and hugging? Is it safe to swim in public pools? and what is the possibility of contracting AIDS from public facilities? 10m; VHS, 3/4 U. **Pr:** MTI. **A:** Primary-Adult. **P:** Education. **U:** Institution, SURA. **Hea-Sci**: AIDS. **Acq:** Purchase, Rent/Lease. **Dist:** Phoenix Learning Group. $160.00.

AIDS, Hepatitis and the Emergency Responder 1988
The tape shows how an emergency worker can better help victims and reduce his own risk of getting a disease. 25m; VHS, 3/4 U, Special order formats. **Pr:** Commonwealth Films. **A:** Adult. **P:** Professional. **U:** Institution, Home. **Hea-Sci**: Emergencies, AIDS, Diseases. **Acq:** Purchase, Rent/Lease. **Dist:** Commonwealth Films Inc.; Emergency Film Group. $250.00.

AIDS: Hitting Home 1994
Discusses the causes and treatment of AIDS and the HIV virus. 19m; VHS. **A:** Adult. **P:** Education. **U:** Institution. **Gen-Edu**: Health Education, Sociology. **Acq:** Purchase. **Dist:** RMI Media. $95.00.

AIDS in Africa ????
Reports on the grim future of Zimbabwe, a nation plagued with AIDS and HIV. 66m; VHS. **A:** Sr. High-Adult. **P:** Education. **U:** Institution. **Gen-Edu**: Africa, AIDS. **Acq:** Purchase, Rent/Lease. **Dist:** Films for the Humanities & Sciences. $129.00.

AIDS in Africa 1990
Examines the impact of the AIDS epidemic on Africa, where several million people have been infected. 52m; VHS. **A:** Sr. High-Adult. **P:** Education. **U:** Institution. **Hea-Sci**: Documentary Films, AIDS, Sexually Transmitted Diseases. **Acq:** Purchase. **Dist:** University of Washington Educational Media Collection. $30.00.

AIDS in Africa 1991
Documentary reporting on AIDS in Uganda, Zaire, the Ivory Coast, Burundi, Rwanda, South Africa, and other African countries. 52m; VHS. **A:** College-Adult. **P:** Education. **U:** Institution. **Gen-Edu**: AIDS, Africa. **Acq:** Purchase, Rent/Lease. **Dist:** Filmakers Library Inc. $295.00.

AIDS in Rural America 1989
While many people think that the AIDS epidemic is an urban problem, this documentary shows that its effects reach into small town America. 28m; VHS. **A:** Sr. High. **P:** Education. **U:** Institution. **Gen-Edu**: AIDS. **Acq:** Purchase. **Dist:** Filmakers Library Inc. $295.

AIDS in the Barrio: Eso No Me Pasa a Mi 1990
A comprehensive examination of cultural, social and religious obstacles encountered when dealing with AIDS in a Hispanic community. 28m; VHS, Special order formats. **Pr:** The Cinema Guild. **A:** Sr. High-Adult. **P:** Education. **U:** Institution, Home. **Gen-Edu**: Hispanic Culture, AIDS, Human Relations. **Acq:** Purchase, Rent/Lease. **Dist:** The Cinema Guild. $250.00.

AIDS in the Pediatric Age Group 1986
A look at children and AIDS, and how their care differs from that of the infected adult. 4m; VHS, 3/4 U. **A:** Adult. **P:** Professional. **U:** Institution, CCTV, Home, SURA. **Hea-Sci**: Immunology, Children. **Acq:** Purchase, Rent/Lease, Subscription. **Dist:** Emory Medical Television Network.

AIDS in Your School 1987
A straightforward look at the transmission, maintenance and basic prevention of AIDS inside the school environment. 20m; VHS, 3/4 U, Special order formats. **Pr:** Altschul Group. **A:** Jr. High-Sr. High. **P:** Education. **U:** Institution, Home, SURA. **L:** English, Spanish. **Gen-Edu**: Health Education, Sexually Transmitted Diseases. **Acq:** Purchase, Rent/Lease, Trade-in. **Dist:** United Learning Inc. $320.00.

AIDS: Infection Control 1995
Features the hazards this disease creates, and how several other, less sensational diseases are far more virulent. 20m; VHS. **A:** Adult. **P:** Professional. **U:** Institution. **Hea-Sci**: AIDS, Health Education, Safety Education. **Acq:** Rent/Lease. **Dist:** National Safety Council, California Chapter, Film Library.

AIDS: Learn for Your Life 1987
This tape and teacher's guide offer guidelines on informing high school students about AIDS. 24m; VHS, 3/4 U. **Pr:** New Dimension Films. **A:** Adult. **P:** Teacher Education. **U:** Institution. **Hea-Sci**: How-To, Education, AIDS. **Acq:** Purchase, Rent/Lease. **Dist:** New Dimension Media. $350.00.

AIDS: Let's Talk 1989
This educational program is aimed at children in grades 2-5, and stresses that AIDS does not spread easily and that children with AIDS often say the worst part is that other children are not friendly to them. 15m; VHS. **Pr:** NDM. **A:** Primary. **P:** Education. **U:** Institution. **Chl-Juv**: AIDS, Children, Health Education. **Acq:** Purchase, Rent/Lease. **Dist:** New Dimension Media. $295.00.

AIDS Mass 1986
A tape of the Eucharist for victims of AIDS at St. Augustine's-by-the-Sea, in Santa Monica, California. Included are interviews with AIDS patients and ministers. 28m; VHS, 3/4 U. **Pr:** Episcopal Radio-TV Foundation. **A:** Jr. High-Adult. **P:** Religious. **U:** Institution, CCTV, CATV, BCTV, Home. **Gen-Edu**: Religion, AIDS. **Acq:** Purchase, Rent/Lease. **Dist:** Alliance for Christian Media.

AIDS: Me & My Baby 19??
Outlines how HIV and AIDS affect pregnancy. Features interviews of women discussing these issues. 22m; VHS, 3/4 U. **A:** Sr. High-Adult. **P:** Education. **U:** Institution, SURA. **Hea-Sci**: AIDS, Women, Pregnancy. **Acq:** Purchase. **Dist:** HIV Center for Women & Children. $75.00.

The AIDS Movie 1986
Features three people with the AIDS virus as they discuss what it's like to live with it and how to protect yourself against it. Includes teacher's discussion guide. 26m; VHS, 3/4 U. **A:** Jr. High-Adult. **P:** Education. **U:** Institution. **Gen-Edu**: Documentary Films, AIDS. **Acq:** Purchase, Rent/Lease. **Dist:** Durrin Productions Inc. $200.00.

AIDS: No Sad Song 1985
The emotional and psychological trauma experienced by AIDS patients, families, and friends is examined in this film. The program follows Jim Black, a 37-year-old AIDS patient who recounts his family's rejection, and Catherine Hunt, sister of a man with AIDS who supported her brother throughout the course of the disease. 61m; VHS, 3/4 U. **Pr:** Nick Sheehan. **A:** Jr. High-Adult. **P:** Education. **U:** Institution, Home, SURA. **Gen-Edu**: AIDS, Sex & Sexuality. **Acq:** Purchase, Rent/Lease, Duplication. **Dist:** Filmakers Library Inc.

AIDS, Not Us 1990
This video, aimed at high school students, chronicles the lives of five youths coping with AIDS in New York housing projects. Skyman is a crack dealer trying to deal with his brother's AIDS contraction, Miguel must come to grips with his best friend's homosexuality, Andy learns to accept the risks involved in unsafe sex, an abused Jose deals with his first experience with an STD, and Chris encounters homophobia in the locker room. 36m; VHS, 3/4 U. **Pr:** New York State Psychiatric Institute. **A:** Primary-Sr. High. **P:** Education. **U:** Institution. **Hea-Sci**: Documentary Films, AIDS, Health Education. **Acq:** Purchase. **Dist:** HIV Center for Women & Children. $125.00.

AIDS: One Teenager's Story 1996
Features the story of Tracy, a college-bound high school senior, who learns through a blood test that she is HIV-positive. Reveals the dangers of un-protected sex. Includes teacher's guide. 33m; VHS. **A:** Jr. High-Sr. High. **P:** Education. **U:** Institution. **Gen-Edu:** AIDS, Adolescence. **Acq:** Purchase. **Dist:** Sunburst Digital Inc. $199.00.

AIDS: Our Worst Fears 1989
What scientists do and don't know about AIDS is talked about. 57m; VHS, 3/4 U. **Pr:** Films for the Humanities. **A:** Jr. High-Adult. **P:** Education. **U:** Institution, SURA. **Hea-Sci:** AIDS. **Acq:** Purchase, Rent/Lease. **Dist:** Films for the Humanities & Sciences. $179.00.

AIDS: Preventing Infection 19??
Outlines procedures to avoid exposure to HIV. Includes examples of accidental exposures. Winner of the Red Ribbon Award at the American Film Festival. 17m; VHS. **A:** Adult. **P:** Education. **U:** Institution. **Hea-Sci:** AIDS. **Acq:** Purchase, Rent/Lease. **Dist:** University of Maryland. $300.00.

AIDS Prevention: Choice not Chance 1987
AIDS and how not to get it are explained to pre-teens in an effort to destroy some of the mysteries surrounding the disease. 20m; VHS. **Pr:** Educational Activities, Inc. **A:** Primary-Jr. High. **P:** Education. **U:** Institution, Home. **Hea-Sci:** AIDS, Health Education. **Acq:** Purchase. **Dist:** Educational Activities Inc. $69.00.

AIDS: Profile of an Epidemic—Update 1986
An examination of this insidious disease shows how it transfers, how it attacks the body's immune system and the prognosis. 60m; VHS, 3/4 U, EJ. **C:** Narrated by Ed Asner. **Pr:** WNET. **A:** Jr. High-Adult. **P:** Education. **U:** Institution, CCTV, BCTV, Home, SURA. **Hea-Sci:** Health Education, Sexually Transmitted Diseases, AIDS. **Acq:** Purchase, Rent/Lease, Duplication License. **Dist:** Cambridge Educational. $39.95.

The AIDS Quarterly 1990
A series of quarterly news updates on the AIDS epidemic and its effects on society. 60m; VHS, CC, 3/4 U. **Pr:** WGBH Boston. **A:** Sr. High-Adult. **P:** Education. **U:** Institution, CCTV, CATV, SURA. **Hea-Sci:** AIDS, Health Education, Diseases. **Acq:** Purchase, Duplication License, Off-Air Record. **Dist:** PBS Home Video. $39.95.

AIDS: Questions with Answers 1990
A dramatization focusing on the issues surrounding AIDS. ?m; VHS, 3/4 U. **A:** Sr. High-Adult. **P:** Education. **U:** Institution, Home. **Hea-Sci:** Health Education, AIDS, Homosexuality. **Acq:** Purchase. **Dist:** Meridian Education Corp. $89.00.

The AIDS Show: Artists Involved with Death and Survival 1986
Performance and documentary footage are interwoven in this film about the effects of the AIDS crisis. 58m; VHS, 3/4 U. **Pr:** Peter Adair. **A:** Jr. High-Adult. **P:** Education. **U:** Institution, SURA. **Gen-Edu:** AIDS, Art & Artists. **Acq:** Purchase, Rent/Lease. **Dist:** Direct Cinema Ltd. $250.00.

AIDS: Taking Action—Revised Edition 1992
Emphasizes abstinence as the safest way for teens to avoid AIDS, but discusses other options for teens who are sexually active. Stresses pro-active stance in the battle against the disease. Contains updated information. 22m; VHS, 3/4 U. **Pr:** NDM; All Media Productions. **A:** Jr. High-Sr. High. **P:** Education. **U:** Institution. **Hea-Sci:** Education, AIDS, Health Education. **Acq:** Purchase, Rent/Lease. **Dist:** New Dimension Media. $275.00.

AIDS: The Classroom Conflict 1991
Youngsters are taught about AIDS in an informative and comprehensive manner, addressing safe sex, abstinence and the confrontation of sexual situations. 28m; VHS. **Pr:** Films for the Humanities. **A:** Primary-Sr. High. **P:** Education. **U:** Institution. **Hea-Sci:** AIDS, Health Education, Sexually Transmitted Diseases. **Acq:** Purchase. **Dist:** Films for the Humanities & Sciences. $149.00.

AIDS: The Heart of the Matter 1996
Profiles one man's five-year battle with AIDS, from his HIV diagnosis to his memorial service. The patient candidly discusses his physical and emotional traumas through the latter stages of the disease. 31m; VHS. **A:** Sr. High-Adult. **P:** Education. **U:** Institution. **Hea-Sci:** Health Education, AIDS, Documentary Films. **Acq:** Purchase. **Dist:** Aquarius Health Care Media. $195.00.

AIDS: The Surgeon General's Update 1987
Former Surgeon General Koop talks about AIDS and the concerns surrounding it. 32m; VHS. **C:** Hosted by C. Everett Koop. **Pr:** Future Vision Production. **A:** Jr. High-Adult. **P:** Education. **U:** Institution, Home. **Gen-Edu:** AIDS, Health Education. **Acq:** Purchase. **Dist:** Pyramid Media. $125.00.

AIDS: The Workplace and the Law 1988
Dionne Warwick, in her official capacity as U.S. Ambassador of Health, hosts this look at the deadly disease and what ordinary people can do to stop its destructive spread. 35m; VHS, 8 mm, 3/4 U. **TV Std:** NTSC, PAL, SECAM. **Pr:** CTF. **A:** College-Adult. **P:** Education. **U:** Institution, CCTV, SURA. **Hea-Sci:** AIDS. **Acq:** Purchase, Rent/Lease, Duplication License. **Dist:** Phoenix Learning Group. $600.00.

Aids to Navigation 19??
Guide on how to read different types of boating navigational aids including buoys, daybeacons, lights, light platforms, radio beacons, and foghorns. 50m; VHS. **Pr:** Bennett Marine Video. **A:** Jr. High-Adult. **P:** Instruction. **U:** Home. **Spo-Rec:** Boating, How-To. **Acq:** Purchase. **Dist:** Bennett Marine Video. $24.95.

AIDS: Truth or Consequences 19??
Provides a candid, informative look at the HIV virus and the reulting acquisition of AIDS. Explains how the virus is transmitted, who's at risk, the ramifications of infection, and methods of prevention. Comes in two versions, one with a condom demonstration and one without the condom demonstration. Comes with study guide. 30m; VHS. **A:** Sr. High-Adult. **P:** Education. **U:** Institution. **Hea-Sci:** AIDS, Health Education. **Acq:** Purchase. **Dist:** CEV Multimedia. $49.95.

AIDS: What Are the Risks? 1991
The methods of AIDS transmission are explained, in order to calm unreasonable fears about the disease. Updated in 1991. 30m; VHS. **Pr:** HRM. **A:** Jr. High-College. **P:** Education. **U:** Institution. **Hea-Sci:** AIDS. **Acq:** Purchase. **Dist:** HRM Video. $145.00.

AIDS: What Do We Tell Our Children? 1988
Designed to help adults teach children about AIDS and how it relates to sex, this film provides important facts about the transmission of the disease and how children can protect themselves and each other. 20m; VHS, 3/4 U, EJ, Special order formats. **TV Std:** NTSC, PAL, SECAM. **A:** Adult. **P:** Education. **U:** Institution, CCTV, SURA. **Hea-Sci:** AIDS. **Acq:** Purchase, Rent/Lease. **Dist:** Phoenix Learning Group. $345.00.

AIDS: What Every Teacher Must Know 1988
Teachers must not only know how to deal with a person with AIDS but how to educate their students about the disease. 90m; VHS. **Pr:** Cambridge Career Productions. **A:** Adult. **P:** Teacher Education. **U:** Institution, Home. **Hea-Sci:** AIDS, Education. **Acq:** Purchase. **Dist:** Cambridge Educational. $259.00.

AIDS: What Everyone Needs to Know 1986
A film for general audiences about the basic facts of AIDS and how they affect everyday life for the layman. 18m; VHS, 3/4 U, Special order formats. **Pr:** Churchill Films; University of California at Los Angeles AIDS Center. **A:** Jr. High-Adult. **P:** Education. **U:** Institution, Home, SURA. **Hea-Sci:** Diseases. **Acq:** Purchase, Duplication License. **Dist:** Clear Vue Inc.

AIDS: What Everyone Should Know 1992
Answers specific questions about the AIDS virus. Targeted to a professional health care audience. 45m; VHS. **A:** College-Adult. **P:** Education. **U:** Institution. **Hea-Sci:** AIDS, Medical Education. **Acq:** Purchase. **Dist:** Geographical Studies and Research Center, Department of Geography and Planning.

AIDS: What You Haven't Been Told 1989
Fundamentalist Christians give their views on "the AIDS plague," who is to blame, and how to protect yourself. 60m; VHS. **Pr:** Jeremiah Films. **A:** Jr. High-Adult. **P:** Religious. **U:** Home. **Gen-Edu:** Documentary Films, AIDS, Public Health. **Acq:** Purchase. **Dist:** Jeremiah Films. $39.95.

AIDS . . . What You Need to Know 1988
The factual information about the deadly virus on this tape should dispel any rumors about the disease. 45m; VHS. **C:** Hosted by C. Everett Koop. **Pr:** Cambridge Career Productions. **A:** Jr. High-Adult. **P:** Education. **U:** Institution, Home. **Hea-Sci:** AIDS, Health Education, Drug Abuse. **Acq:** Purchase. **Dist:** Alpha Omega Publications Inc.; Cambridge Educational; Karol Media. $19.99.

AIDS-Wise, No Lies 1989
A moving portrait of ten kids whose lives are each directly affected by AIDS. They reveal their thoughts, feelings and experiences on the subject. The video, which is aimed at adolescents, leaves viewers feeling empowered, knowing they have choice and control over contracting AIDS. 22m; VHS, 3/4 U. **Pr:** David Current; Anne Rutledge. **A:** Jr. High-Adult. **P:** Education. **U:** Institution, SURA. **Gen-Edu:** AIDS, Adolescence. **Acq:** Purchase. **Dist:** New Day Films Library.

AIDS Work 1996
Features six healthcare professionals who reflect on their decades of combined experience in caring for patients with HIV/AIDS. 23m; VHS. **A:** Adult. **P:** Education. **U:** Institution. **Gen-Edu:** AIDS, Occupational Training. **Acq:** Rent/Lease. **Dist:** Fanlight Productions. $50.

AIDS: You've Got to Do Something 1992
Music-video style peer group discussion featuring TV star Mayim Bialik and the peer education group P.E.P.L.A. that offers up-to-the-minute facts on HIV and AIDS. Covers such topics as condoms, peer pressure, risky sexual behavior, HIV testing, the role of drugs and alcohol, and transmission of the disease. 19m; VHS. **Pr:** Disney Educational Productions. **A:** Jr. High-Sr. High. **P:** Education. **U:** Institution, CCTV, SURA. **Hea-Sci:** Health Education, AIDS, Sex & Sexuality. **Acq:** Purchase, Rent/Lease, Duplication License. **Dist:** Phoenix Learning Group. $325.00.

AIDS—Changing Lifestyles 1988
Discusses the fact that there is currently no cure for AIDS and what one should do to protect themselves from this disease. Part of the Young People and AIDS Series. 15m; VHS, SVS, 3/4 U. **A:** Jr. High-College. **P:** Education. **U:** Institution. **Hea-Sci:** AIDS, Drug Abuse, Sex & Sexuality. **Acq:** Purchase. **Dist:** Encyclopedia Britannica. $99.00.

AIDS—Issues for Health Care Workers 1995
Centers on how to guard against infection from AIDS, treating the AIDS patient with courtesy, compassion and respect, and how workers can protect themselves from AIDS. 23m; VHS. **A:** Adult. **P:** Professional. **U:** Institution. **Bus-Ind:** Safety Education, Occupational Training, Health Education. **Acq:** Rent/Lease. **Dist:** National Safety Council, California Chapter, Film Library.

AIDS—Nobody Is Immune 1988
Discusses how the AIDS virus can attack anyone and demonstrates how the AIDS virus attacks the immune system. Part of the Young People and AIDS Series. 15m; VHS, SVS, 3/4 U. **A:** Jr. High-College. **P:** Education. **U:** Institution. **Hea-Sci:** AIDS, Sexually Transmitted Diseases. **Acq:** Purchase. **Dist:** Encyclopedia Britannica. $99.00.

AIDS—The Global Impact 1988
Demonstrates the kinds of behavior that spread AIDS. Includes examples of the sex market in Bangkok, the availability of drugs in the Bronx, and the male prostitutes in Rio de Janeiro. Part of the Young People and AIDS Series. 15m; VHS, SVS, 3/4 U. **A:** Jr. High-College. **P:** Education. **U:** Institution. **Hea-Sci:** AIDS, Drug Abuse, Prostitution. **Acq:** Purchase. **Dist:** Encyclopedia Britannica. $99.00.

Aileen: Life and Death of a Serial Killer 2003 (Unrated) — ★★★
Documentary studies the life and crimes of serial killer Aileen Wuornos. In-depth work recounts her horrible childhood and the psychoses that led to her murderous spree. Chilling. 89m; VHS, DVD. **C:** Directed by Joan Churchill; Nick Broomfield; Cinematography by Joan Churchill; Music by Robert (Rob) Lane. **Pr:** Jo Human; Lafayette Films. **A:** Sr. High-Adult. **P:** Entertainment. **U:** Home. **L:** English. **Mov-Ent:** Documentary Films, Biography: Law Enforcement. **Acq:** Purchase. **Dist:** Sony Pictures Home Entertainment Inc. $19.99.

Aileen Wuornos: The Selling of a Serial Killer 1994
Media frenzy surrounding America's first female serial killer. Prostitute Wuornos admitted to the murder of seven men in Florida between 1989 and 1990, pleaded no contest, and was sentenced to death. Director Broomfield not only interviews Wuornos but her lawyer, her lesbian lover who elicited Wuornos' confession, and the woman who adopted Wuornos after her sentencing. 87m; VHS. **C:** Directed by Nick Broomfield; Cinematography by Barry Ackroyd; Music by David Bergeaud. **A:** Adult. **P:** Entertainment. **U:** Home. **Gen-Edu:** Documentary Films, Women, Mass Media. **Acq:** Purchase. **Dist:** Wellspring Media; MGM Studios Inc. $89.98.

Ailey Dances 19??
Features "Cry," "The Lark Ascending," "Revelations," and "Night Creatures." Recorded live at New York City's Center Theatre with dancer Judith Jamison. 85m; VHS. **A:** Jr. High-Adult. **P:** Entertainment. **U:** Home. **Fin-Art:** Dance--Performance, Black Culture. **Acq:** Purchase. **Dist:** Stagestep; Facets Multimedia Inc. $39.95.

Aime Cesaire 2003
Documentary interviewing Aime Cesaire, a French Caribbean poet and statesman. 52m; VHS, DVD. **A:** Sr. High-Adult. **P:** Education. **U:** Institution. **L:** English, French. **Gen-Edu:** Documentary Films, Biography. **Acq:** Purchase, Rent/Lease. **Dist:** The Cinema Guild. $250.00.

Aime Cesaire: Une Voix Pour l'Histoire 1994
Explores the life of celebrated Martinican author Aime Cesaire and his work. 150m; VHS. **A:** Sr. High-Adult. **P:** Education. **U:** Home, Institution. **Gen-Edu:** Literature--Modern, Biography. **Acq:** Purchase. **Dist:** California Newsreel. $195.00.

Aimee & Jaguar 1998 (Unrated) — ★★
In 1943 Berlin, Jewish Felice (Schrader) is hiding her identity and working for a Nazi newspaper where she can gather information to leak to the resistance. She leads a hedonistic night life with a group of lesbian friends and, one night, encounters Lilly (Koehler), the unfaithful wife of an SS soldier who's away at the Russian front. The odd couple begin a risky affair (the title refers to the nicknames the women gave each other) until the inevitable discovery. Based on a true story from the 1994 book by Erica Fischer. German with subtitles. 125m; VHS, DVD, Wide. **C:** Maria Schrader; Juliane Kohler; Johanna Wokalek; Heike Makatsch; Elisabeth Degen; Detlev Buck; Directed by Max Farberbock; Written by Rona Munro; Max Farberbock; Cinematography by Tony Imi; Music by Jan A.P. Kaczmarek. **A:** College-Adult. **P:** Entertainment. **U:** Home. **L:** German. **Mov-Ent:** Drama, Judaism. **Acq:** Purchase. **Dist:** Wolfe Video; Zeitgeist Films Ltd.

Ainsi Murent Les Anges 2001
Avant garde drama about a troubled Senegalese poet living outside Paris. In French and Wolof with English subtitles. 56m/B/W; VHS, DVD. **A:** Sr. High-Adult. **P:** Entertainment. **U:** Home, Institution. **L:** French. **Mov-Ent:** Drama, Film--Avant-Garde. **Acq:** Purchase. **Dist:** California Newsreel. $26.95.

Ain't In It For My Health: A Film About Levon Helm 2010 (Unrated) — ★★★
Compelling rock documentary by Hatley was filmed over more than two years at the Woodstock, New York home of multiple-Grammy winning singer/musician Levon Helm. It details the recording of his first studio album in 25 years, 2007's "Dirt Farmer," while also covering Helm's battle with throat cancer, which would leave him with a ravaged voice, as well as his, sometimes bitter, memories of his time with The Band. Includes archival footage and interviews. 83m; DVD, Blu-Ray. **C:** Directed by Jacob Hatley; Cinematography by Emily Topper. **A:** Adult. **P:** Entertainment. **U:** Home. **L:** English. **Mov-Ent:** Biography: Music, Documentary Films, Cancer. **Acq:** Purchase. **Dist:** Kino on Video.

Ain't No Way Back 1989 (Unrated) — ★
Two hunters stumble upon a feudin' bunch of moonshiners and must leave their city ways behind if they plan to survive. 90m; VHS, DVD. **C:** Campbell Scott; Virginia Lantry; Bernie (Bernard) White; John Durbin; Len Lesser; Joe Mays; Directed by Michael

Borden. **Pr:** Jim Hanson. **A:** Adult. **P:** Entertainment. **U:** Home. **Mov-Ent. Acq:** Purchase. **Dist:** Amazon.com Inc.

Ain't Nobody's Business 19??
Battered women express the agony of sharing life with men who constantly beat them. 21m/B/W; VHS, SVS, 3/4 U, EJ, Special order formats. **Pr:** New Orleans Video Access Center. **A:** College-Adult. **P:** Education. **U:** Institution, CCTV, CATV, SURA. **Gen-Edu:** Domestic Abuse. **Acq:** Purchase, Rent/Lease. **Dist:** New Orleans Video Access Center.

Ain't Them Bodies Saints 2013 (R) — ★★★
Affleck & Mara star as lovers split by crime as the former goes to prison just as the latter is about to give birth. Years later, he escapes and works his way back to his true love, just as a cop involved with putting him away (Foster) gets closer to his family. Sometimes too sluggish for its own good, the stunning cinematography (set in Texas) and score mesmerize enough to overcome any storytelling flaws. Young writer/director Lowery's Sundance hit borrows liberally from the filmmaking school of Terrence Malick, but he's assembled a cast and crew who pulled off copying one of film's masters. 96m; Blu-Ray, Streaming. **C:** Rooney Mara; Casey Affleck; Ben Foster; Keith Carradine; Nate Parker; Directed by David Lowery; Written by David Lowery; Cinematography by Bradford Young; Music by Daniel Hart. **Pr:** Cassian Elwes; Toby Halbrooks; James M. Johnston; Amy Kaufman; Lars Knudsen; Jay Van Hoy; Sailor Bear; Parts&Labor; Primary Productions; Evolution Independent; Paradox Entertainment; Lagniappe Films; IFC Films. **A:** Sr. High-Adult. **P:** Entertainment. **U:** Home. **L:** English. **Mov-Ent:** Drama. **Acq:** Purchase. **Dist:** Amazon.com Inc.

A.I.P.: Fast & Furious: Trailers on Tape 1979
A collection of coming attractions from the studios of American International Pictures including such favorites as "Beach Blanket Bingo," "The Raven" and "I Was a Teenage Werewolf." Some segments in black and white. 59m; VHS. **Pr:** American International Pictures. **A:** Family. **P:** Entertainment. **U:** Home. **Mov-Ent. Acq:** Purchase. **Dist:** Passport International Entertainment L.L.C. $34.95.

Air: A First Film 1989
The many uses of air and the reasons why it's important are explained. 12m; VHS, 3/4 U. **Pr:** Norman Bean. **A:** Primary-Jr. High. **P:** Education. **U:** Institution, SURA. **Hea-Sci:** Science. **Acq:** Purchase. **Dist:** Phoenix Learning Group.

Air America 1990 (R) — ★★
It's the Vietnam War and the CIA is operating a secret drug smuggling operation in Southeast Asia to finance the effort. Flyboys Gibson and Downey drop opium and glib lines all over Laos. Big-budget Gibson vehicle with sufficient action but lacking much of a story, which was adapted from a book by Christopher Robbins. 113m; VHS, DVD, CC. **C:** Mel Gibson; Robert Downey, Jr.; Marshall Bell; Nancy Travis; David Marshall Grant; Tim Thomerson; Lane Smith; Directed by Roger Spottiswoode; Written by Richard Rush; Cinematography by Roger Deakins; Music by Charles Gross. **Pr:** Daniel Melnick; Carolco Pictures. **A:** Adult. **P:** Entertainment. **U:** Home. **Mov-Ent:** Action-Adventure, Vietnam War, Aeronautics. **Acq:** Purchase. **Dist:** Image Entertainment Inc.; Lions Gate Television Corp. $19.95.

Air America: Operation Jaguar 2003 (Unrated)
Taken from the 1998-1999 television series about undercover pilots who use their Latin American air transport company as a front for missions on behalf of the U.S. State Department. 2 episodes. 82m; DVD. **C:** Lorenzo Lamas; Scott Plank; Diana Barton. **A:** Jr. High-Adult. **P:** Entertainment. **U:** Home. **Mov-Ent:** Television Series, Action-Adventure. **Acq:** Purchase. **Dist:** Bedford Entertainment Inc. $24.95.

Air America: The Complete Series 1998
Rio and his buddy Wiley are undercover agents working for the State Department, investigating international crime under the guise of pilots at Air America, a Latin American air transport company. Uses the title and basic premise of the 1990 Mel Gibson movie. 22 episodes of the syndicated series. 1170m; DVD. **C:** Lorenzo Lamas; Scott Plank; Diana Barton; Gary Wood. **A:** Jr. High-Adult. **P:** Entertainment. **U:** Home. **Mov-Ent:** Television Series, Action-Adventure. **Acq:** Purchase. **Dist:** Sony Pictures Home Entertainment Inc.

Air and Water: Concerns for Planet Earth 1990
The many harms that we are doing to the earth are explored in this series, and proposals for correcting the situation are offered. ?m; VHS. **Pr:** United Learning Inc. **A:** Primary-Sr. High. **P:** Education. **U:** Institution, CCTV, CATV, Home, SURA. **Gen-Edu:** Documentary Films, Ecology & Environment. **Acq:** Purchase, Duplication. **Dist:** United Learning Inc. $150.00. **Indiv. Titles:** 1. Our Restless Atmosphere 2. Ozone: Friend or Foe 3. Acid Rain: The Rain that Kills 4. A Warming World: The Greenhouse Effect.

Air Austral Boeing 737-800, 777-200LR, & 777-300ER 2012 (G)
Documentary covering 10 flights in Air Austral's modernized fleet, 2 of them in cabin. 30.00m; DVD, Blu-Ray. **A:** Family. **P:** Entertainment. **U:** Home. **L:** English. **Gen-Edu:** Aeronautics, Documentary Films, Travel. **Acq:** Purchase. **Dist:** Justplanes.com. $30.00 30.00.

Air Bag Operation and Service 1993
Overviews the construction, operation, and service of typical air bag systems. 25m; VHS. **A:** Adult. **P:** Instruction. **U:** Institution. **How-Ins:** Automobiles. **Acq:** Purchase. **Dist:** RMI Media. $95.00.

Air Brakes—Principles of Operation 1968
This video shows in detail what happens when the brakes on large military vehicles are depressed and released. 25m; VHS,

3/4 U. **Pr:** U.S.A. **A:** Adult. **P:** Education. **U:** Institution, SURA. **Gen-Edu:** Engineering. **Acq:** Purchase. **Dist:** National Audiovisual Center. $110.00.

Air Brush Techniques: Cakes, Arts, and Crafts 1988
A video lesson in how to use an airbrush in decorating cakes, as well as various other crafts and hobbies. 55m; VHS. **C:** Frances Kuyper. **Pr:** Cine-Video West. **A:** Family. **P:** Instruction. **U:** Home. **How-Ins:** Cooking, Crafts. **Acq:** Purchase. **Dist:** Cine-Video West.

Air Bud 1997 (PG) — ★★½
Buddy's a basketball-playing golden retriever (no relation) who befriends lonely misfit Josh (Zegers) and teaches him the nuances of the layup, fade-away J, and pick-and-roll. It's good to see dog athletes getting to stretch beyond the usual frisbee and stick-fetching roles. Teaming animals (especially canines) with kids usually adds up to success. This one's no exception, especially for the grade school crowd. 92m; VHS, DVD, CC. **C:** Kevin Zegers; Michael Jeter; Bill Cobbs; Wendy Makkena; Eric Christmas; Brendan Fletcher; Jay Brazeau; Stephen E. Miller; Nicola Cavendish; Directed by Charles Martin Smith; Written by Paul Tamasy; Aaron Mendelsohn; Cinematography by Mike Southon; Music by Brahm Wenger. **Pr:** Robert Vince; William Vince; Michael Strange; Bob Weinstein; Harvey Weinstein; Anne Vince; Keystone Pictures; Walt Disney Productions; Buena Vista. **A:** Primary-Adult. **P:** Entertainment. **U:** Home. **Mov-Ent:** Pets, Basketball, Sports--Fiction: Comedy. **Acq:** Purchase. **Dist:** Walt Disney Studios Home Entertainment.

Air Bud 2: Golden Receiver 1998 (G) — ★★
Buddy, the canine Michael Jordan of last year's "Air Bud," is back for more organized team sports with small children. His owner, Josh (Zegers) is still mourning the death of his father and isn't ready to deal with his mother's budding romance with the new veterinarian in town (Harrison). Meanwhile, Josh joins the school's football team and finds himself thrust into the spotlight as the team's quarterback when the starter is injured (big surprise!), only to be bailed out by his multi-sport pooch. Actually, Buddy is played by four different Golden Retrievers, as the original died shortly after completing the original. This rehash tries to take itself seriously, with lessons about overcoming tragedy and adjusting to change, but isn't much more than sappy melodrama and cute dog tricks. 90m; VHS, DVD, CC. **C:** Kevin Zegers; Cynthia Stevenson; Gregory Harrison; Nora Dunn; Robert Costanzo; Tim Conway; Dick Martin; Perry Anzilotti; Suzanne Ristic; Jay Brazeau; Directed by Richard Martin; Written by Paul Tamasy; Aaron Mendelsohn; Cinematography by Mike Southon; Music by Brahm Wenger. **Pr:** Robert Vince; Anne Vince; William Vince; Michael Strange; Keystone Pictures; Dimension Films; Miramax Film Corp. **A:** Family. **P:** Entertainment. **U:** Home. **Mov-Ent:** Sports--Fiction: Comedy, Football, Family Viewing. **Acq:** Purchase. **Dist:** Buena Vista Home Entertainment.

Air Bud 3: World Pup 2000 (G) — ★★½
Buddy went from basketball to football and now to soccer in this third installment. This time he teams up with the U.S. Women's Soccer Team and also becomes a dad. And wouldn't you know—just before the championship game, dad Buddy must rescue one of his pups from a gang of dog-nappers. 83m; VHS, DVD, CC. **C:** Kevin Zegers; Dale Midkiff; Caitlin Wachs; Martin Ferrero; Duncan Regehr; Brittany Paige Bouck; Briana Scurry; Brandi Chastain; Tisha Venturini; Directed by Bill Bannerman. **A:** Family. **P:** Entertainment. **U:** Home. **Mov-Ent:** Pets, Soccer, Sports--Fiction: Comedy. **Acq:** Purchase. **Dist:** Buena Vista Home Entertainment.

Air Bud 4: Seventh Inning Fetch 2002 (G) — ★★½
Since Josh is off at college, it's his little sis Andrea who needs Buddy's help on her baseball team. But Buddy's got other problems—Rocky the Raccoon has kidnapped Buddy's puppies! 93m; VHS, DVD, CC. **C:** Richard Karn; Cynthia Stevenson; Kevin Zegers; Caitlin Wachs; Directed by Robert Vince. **A:** Family. **P:** Entertainment. **U:** Home. **Mov-Ent:** Sports--Fiction: Comedy, Baseball, Pets. **Acq:** Purchase. **Dist:** Buena Vista Home Entertainment.

Air Bud 5: Buddy Spikes Back 2003 (G) — ★★
After her best friend moves to California, Andrea (Wachs) takes up volleyball so she can win a chance to visit. Naturally, all-around sports dog Buddy can do a little spiking of his own. 87m; VHS, DVD. **C:** Caitlin Wachs; Katija Pevec; Jake D. Smith; Tyler Boissonnault; Edie McClurg; Patrick Cranshaw; Cynthia Stevenson; Rob Tinkler; Directed by Mike Southon; Cinematography by Adam Sliwinski. **A:** Family. **P:** Entertainment. **U:** Home. **Mov-Ent:** Pets, Sports--Fiction: Comedy, Volleyball. **Acq:** Purchase. **Dist:** Buena Vista Home Entertainment.

Air Bud 6: Air Buddies 2006 (PG) — ★★
When doggie parents Buddy and Molly are abducted, their five talking puppies—B-Dawg, RoseBud, Bud-dha, Mudbud, and Budderball—must come to the rescue. Yeah, it's cute—you expected more? 80m; DVD. **C:** Slade Pearce; Trevor Wright; Voice(s) by Abigail Breslin; Spencer Breslin; Josh Flitter; Spencer Fox; Michael Clarke Duncan; Don Knotts; Mike Southon; Directed by Robert Vince; Written by Robert Vince; Anna McRoberts; Music by Brahm Wenger. **A:** Family. **P:** Entertainment. **U:** Home. **Mov-Ent. Acq:** Purchase. **Dist:** Buena Vista Home Entertainment.

Air Canada Airbus A319 & A321 2011 (G)
Documentary detailing several Airbus flights from pre-flight prep to landing and departure. 223m; DVD. **A:** Family. **P:** Entertainment. **U:** Home. **L:** English. **Gen-Edu:** Aeronautics, Documentary Films, Canada. **Acq:** Purchase. **Dist:** Justplanes.com. $30.00.

Air Canada B777-200LR Polar Route 2013 (G)
Justplanes celebrates their 20 year anniversary with their first Blu-ray release, focusing on an Air Canada flight from Toronto to Hong Kong. 279m; DVD, Blu-Ray. **A:** Family. **P:** Education. **U:** Home. **L:** English. **Gen-Edu:** Aeronautics, Documentary Films, Canada. **Acq:** Purchase. **Dist:** Naxos of America Inc. $30.00 30.00.

Air Canada Boeing 767-300 St. Maarten & Hawaii 2013 (G)
Justplanes 11th cockpit flight in one of Air Canada's Boeing 767s filmed on flights to Hawaii and St. Maarten. 262m; Blu-Ray. **A:** Family. **P:** Education. **U:** Home. **L:** English. **Gen-Edu:** Aeronautics, Documentary Films, Canada. **Acq:** Purchase. **Dist:** Naxos of America Inc. $30.00.

Air Canada Boeing 777-200LR 2010 (G)
Documentary following flight crews at the Air Canada airline as they prepare for long range flights. 270m; DVD. **A:** Family. **P:** Entertainment. **U:** Home. **L:** English. **Gen-Edu:** Aeronautics, Documentary Films, Canada. **Acq:** Purchase. **Dist:** Justplanes.com. $30.00.

Air Canada EMB-175 USA 2013 (G)
Justplanes 10th Air Canada documentary, this time covering airports within the United States. 270m; Blu-Ray. **A:** Family. **P:** Entertainment. **U:** Home. **L:** English. **Gen-Edu:** Documentary Films, Aeronautics, Travel. **Acq:** Purchase. **Dist:** Justplanes.com. $30.00.

Air Canada Express by Jazz (West Coast) CRJ-200 & Dash 8 2014 (G)
Documentary follows Air Canada's west coast operations, including cockpit operations and in flight scenery. 278m; Blu-Ray. **A:** Family. **P:** Entertainment. **U:** Home. **L:** English. **Gen-Edu:** Aeronautics, Documentary Films, Canada. **Acq:** Purchase. **Dist:** Justplanes.com. $30.00.

Air Canada Express-Jazz CRJ-200, CRJ-705 & Q-400 2012 (G)
Aircraft documentary following Air Canada Express' Jazz airlines on several flights. 268m; Blu-Ray. **A:** Family. **P:** Entertainment. **U:** Home. **L:** English. **Gen-Edu:** Aeronautics, Documentary Films, Canada. **Acq:** Purchase. **Dist:** Janson Media. $30.00 30.00.

Air Combat II 1998
Thirteen-part series details the history and exploits of war in the air through the use of film footage and personal interviews. Nine hours and 47 minutes on 13 videocassettes. 45m. **A:** Family. **P:** Education. **U:** Home. **Gen-Edu:** History, Military History. **Acq:** Purchase. **Dist:** PBS Home Video. $179.98.

Air Compressor Repair Training 1987
For industrial training, the basics in air compressor disassembly, repair and re-assembly. 30m; VHS. **Pr:** Industrial Training Corporation. **A:** Adult. **P:** Vocational. **U:** Institution. **Bus-Ind:** Engineering, Industrial Arts. **Acq:** Purchase, Rent/Lease. **Dist:** ITC Learning L.L.C.

Air Conditioned Comfort 1977
An insensitive family drives through the national parks of the western U.S. in a comfortable trailer, oblivious to the natural surroundings and beauty. They only care about real estate prospects and rest stops. 6m; VHS, 3/4 U. **Pr:** John Strawbridge. **A:** Sr. High-Adult. **P:** Education. **U:** Institution, SURA. **Gen-Edu:** Ethics & Morals. **Acq:** Purchase. **Dist:** Phoenix Learning Group.

Air Conditioning and Refrigeration 1983
A series of eight one-hour programs designed to train operation and repair personnel for the above-titled systems. 60m; VHS, 3/4 U. **Pr:** Industrial Training Corporation. **A:** Adult. **P:** Vocational. **U:** Institution. **Bus-Ind:** Industrial Arts. **Acq:** Purchase, Rent/Lease. **Dist:** ITC Learning L.L.C.

Air Conditioning Discharge and Evacuation 1982
Offers instruction on specific aspects of automotive maintenance and repair. 20m; VHS. **A:** Adult. **P:** Instruction. **U:** Institution. **How-Ins:** Automobiles. **Acq:** Purchase. **Dist:** RMI Media. $59.95.

Air Conditioning: Recharge System 1982
Offers instruction on specific aspects of automotive maintenance and repair. 38m; VHS. **A:** Adult. **P:** Instruction. **U:** Institution. **How-Ins:** Automobiles. **Acq:** Purchase. **Dist:** RMI Media. $89.95.

Air Directional Valve 1992
Discusses operation and construction of a typical five-ported air valve. 29m; VHS. **A:** Adult. **P:** Education. **U:** Institution. **Gen-Edu:** Electronics. **Acq:** Purchase. **Dist:** RMI Media. $108.00.

Air Eagles 1931 (Unrated) — ★½
Former WWI flying ace Bill Ramsey and his German counterpart Otto Schuman have teamed up for an aerial carnival act. Otto's engaged to circus star Eve but she discovers he plans to shoot down a mining company's plane to steal the payroll. Bill's kid brother Eddie is the pilot and Bill loads his Sopwith Camel's machine guns with live rounds and prepares for a final dogfight. 72m/B/W; DVD. **C:** Lloyd Hughes; Norman Kerry; Shirley Grey; Matty Kemp; Berton Churchill; Directed by Philip H. (Phil, P.H.) Whitman; Written by Hampton Del Ruth. **A:** Sr. High-Adult. **P:** Entertainment. **U:** Home. **Mov-Ent:** Aeronautics, Circuses. **Acq:** Purchase. **Dist:** Alpha Video.

The Air Experience 1997
Richard Sturdevant shows airbrush painting techniques for the beginner, including preparing the work surface, special effects and the products and materials that are available. 40m; VHS. **A:**

Sr. High-Adult. **P:** Instruction. **U:** Home. **How-Ins:** Art & Artists, How-To. **Acq:** Purchase. **Dist:** Tapeworm Video Distributors Inc. $39.95.

Air for the G String ????
Documentary of dancer/choreographer Doris Humphrey provides behind-the-scenes analysis of each movement and phrase, coaching and commentary by Ernestine Stodelle of the Humphry-Weidman Company, and a compete performance of Air for the G String. 90m; VHS. **A:** Adult. **P:** Entertainment. **U:** Institution. **Fin-Art:** Dance--Ballet, Dance--Performance, Documentary Films. **Acq:** Purchase. **Dist:** Stagestep. $79.95.

Air Force 1943 — ★★★½
One of the finest of the WWII movies, Hawks' exciting classic has worn well through the years, in spite of the Japanese propaganda. It follows the hazardous exploits of a Boeing B-17 bomber crew who fight over Pearl Harbor, Manila, and the Coral Sea. Extremely realistic dogfight sequences and powerful, introspective real guy interfacing by the ensemble cast are masterfully combined by Hawks. 124m/B/W; DVD. **C:** John Garfield; John Ridgely; Gig Young; Arthur Kennedy; Charles Drake; Harry Carey, Sr.; George Tobias; Ray Montgomery; James Brown; Stanley Ridges; Willard Robertson; Moroni Olsen; Edward Brophy; Richard Lane; Faye Emerson; Addison Richards; James Flavin; Ann Doran; Dorothy Peterson; William Forrest; Ward Wood; Directed by Howard Hawks; Written by Dudley Nichols; William Faulkner; Cinematography by James Wong Howe; Elmer Dyer; Charles A. Marshall; Music by Franz Waxman. **Pr:** Hal B. Wallis; Warner Bros. **A:** Jr. High-Adult. **P:** Entertainment. **U:** Home. **Mov-Ent:** Action-Adventure, World War Two, Propaganda. **Awds:** Oscars '43: Film Editing. **Acq:** Purchase. **Dist:** WarnerArchive.com; Movies Unlimited.

Air Force One 1997 (R) — ★★★
Ford stars as U.S. President James Marshall, who is not only tough on crime but tough, period. His policy is to not negotiate with terrorists. Then Air Force One, with him, the First Lady and their daughter aboard is hijacked by Russian nationalists, led by ice cold Ivan (Oldman). Close is first woman Veep, Kathryn Bennett, stuck in D.C. coping with the situation. Ford is in fine form as the President who's forced to kick some Commie butt to save the day. Director Petersen ("In The Line of Fire") is becoming a master of building tension in confined places and puts his strong cast to good use. Nail-biting suspense and breath-taking action sequences cap off tour-de-force adventure. 124m; VHS, DVD, UMD, Wide, CC. **C:** Harrison Ford; Gary Oldman; Glenn Close; Dean Stockwell; William H. Macy; Wendy Crewson; Xander Berkeley; Paul Guilfoyle; Liesl Matthews; Bill Smitrovich; Elya Baskin; David Vadim; Tom Everett; Philip Baker Hall; Spencer Garrett; Donna Bullock; Cameo(s) Jurgen Prochnow; Directed by Wolfgang Petersen; Written by Andrew Marlowe; Cinematography by Michael Ballhaus; Music by Jerry Goldsmith. **Pr:** Wolfgang Petersen; Armyan Bernstein; Gail Katz; Jonathan Shestack; Thomas A. Bliss; Marc Abraham; David Lester; Wolfgang Petersen; Beacon Films; Radiant; Columbia Pictures. **A:** Sr. High-Adult. **P:** Entertainment. **U:** Home. **Mov-Ent:** Action-Adventure, Presidency, Terrorism. **Acq:** Purchase. **Dist:** Sony Pictures Home Entertainment Inc.

Air Force One: The Planes and the Presidents 1991
A documentary look at the President's personal planes, and how they have changed over the years. 60m; VHS. **C:** Narrated by James Stewart. **Pr:** Elliot Sluhan. **A:** Family. **P:** Education. **U:** Home. **Gen-Edu:** Aeronautics, Presidency. **Acq:** Purchase. **Dist:** ESPN Inc. $59.95.

Air Force One: The Planes and the Presidents—Flight II 1997
Charlton Heston hosts on in-depth look at the history and evolution of the flying "White House." 90m; VHS, DVD. **A:** Adult. **P:** Education. **U:** Home. **Gen-Edu:** Presidency, Aeronautics. **Acq:** Purchase. **Dist:** MPI Media Group. $14.98.

The Air Force Story 1941
A vintage documentary showing the development of the U.S. Air Force from its inception in 1930 through the attack on Pearl Harbor. 55m/B/W; VHS. **TV Std:** NTSC, PAL. **Pr:** U.S. Air Force. **A:** Jr. High-Adult. **P:** Education. **U:** Institution, Home. **Gen-Edu:** Documentary Films, War--General, Military History. **Acq:** Purchase. **Dist:** International Historic Films Inc. $24.95.

Air Force Training Film, Vol. 1 1962
Rare Air Force short training films made in the '60s focusing on loading nuclear weapons, aircraft ejection seats, and fuel contamination. 60m; VHS. **A:** Adult. **P:** Entertainment. **U:** Home. **Gen-Edu:** Documentary Films, Military History. **Acq:** Purchase. **Dist:** Video Resources.

Air France Airbus A380 2014 (G)
Documentary following flights from Air France, which was the first European Airline to introduce the Airbus A380. 277m; Blu-Ray. **A:** Family. **P:** Education. **U:** Home. **L:** English. **Gen-Edu:** Aeronautics, Documentary Films, France. **Acq:** Purchase. **Dist:** Justplanes.com. $30.00.

Air France Boeing 777-200ER (New York JFK) 2013 (G)
Documentary filmed in the cockpit of a Boeing 777 flying from Paris CDG to New York's JFK airport. 180m; Blu-Ray. **A:** Family. **P:** Education. **U:** Home. **L:** English. **Gen-Edu:** Aeronautics, Documentary Films, France. **Acq:** Purchase. **Dist:** Justplanes.com. $30.00.

Air Guitar Nation 2006 (R) — ★★★
Suit up, grab your guitars...wait, you don't need them. First time director (and reality TV vet) Lipsitz follows rivals David "C. Diddy" Jung and Dan "Bjorn Turoque" Crane as they air guitar-battle their way from American competitions to the World Championships in Finland. Lipsitz doesn't push many boundaries with her direction or narrative, but still manages to create a film that's often hilarious without making its subjects the butt of the joke. 81m; DVD. **C:** Directed by Alexandra Lipsitz; Cinematography by Anthony Sacco; Music by Dan Crane. **Pr:** Jane Lipsitz; Anna Barber; Dan Cutforth; Magical Elves Productions; Shadow Distribution. **A:** Sr. High-Adult. **P:** Entertainment. **U:** Home. **L:** English. **Gen-Edu:** Documentary Films, Music--Performance. **Acq:** Purchase. **Dist:** Docurama.

Air Hawk 1984 (Unrated) — ★
Australian made for TV release details the adventures of an outback pilot involved with stolen diamonds. 90m; VHS. **C:** Eric Oldfield; Louise Howitt; Ellie MacLure; David Robson; David Baker; Directed by David Baker. **Pr:** Ron McLean Productions. **A:** Jr. High-Adult. **P:** Entertainment. **U:** Home. **Mov-Ent:** Aeronautics, TV Movies. **Acq:** Purchase. **Dist:** $59.95.

Air Hawks 1935 (Unrated) — ★★
Barry Eldon (Bellamy) owns a small air courier company and is after a big government contract. He refuses to be bought out by a larger firm that's also after the contract, they use a ray machine developed by one of their scientists that can cause a plane's engines to shut down and cause a crash. Famed aviator Wiley Post briefly appears as himself. 70m/B/W; DVD. **C:** Ralph Bellamy; Robert "Tex" Allen; Douglass Dumbrille; Edward Van Sloan; Tala Birell; Billie Seward; Directed by Albert Rogell; Written by Griffin Jay; Cinematography by Henry Freulich. **A:** Adult. **P:** Entertainment. **U:** Home. **L:** English. **Mov-Ent:** Action-Adventure, Scientists, Aeronautics. **Acq:** Purchase. **Dist:** Sony Pictures Entertainment Inc.

The Air I Breathe 2007 (R) — ★
Four interlocking stories are delivered in the form of an allegorical gangster movie that ends up an overwrought mess. Characters Happiness (Whitaker), Pleasure (Fraser), Sorrow (Gellar), and Love (Bacon), named for the key emotions of a Chinese proverb, muddle through individual challenges while the menacing gangster Fingers (Garcia) casts a shadow over all their lives. Standout cast fails to overcome the challenges presented by such a poorly executed, pretentious movie. 97m; DVD, Blu-Ray. **C:** Forest Whitaker; Brendan Fraser; Sarah Michelle Gellar; Kevin Bacon; Andy Garcia; Emile Hirsch; Julie Delpy; Directed by Jieho Lee; Written by Jieho Lee; Bob DeRosa; Cinematography by Walt Lloyd; Music by Marcelo Zarvos. **Pr:** Paul Schiff; Darlene Caamano Loquet; Emilio Diez Barroso; Nala Films; ThinkFilm. **A:** Sr. High-Adult. **P:** Entertainment. **U:** Home. **L:** English. **Mov-Ent:** Crime Drama, Philosophy & Ideology. **Acq:** Purchase. **Dist:** ThinkFilm Company Inc.; Velocity Home Entertainment.

Air Is Matter: Air Is There 19??
Details how air actually has matter, using its weight to hold objects up or down. Uses parachute-drop exercises to show students how this actually happens. Includes teacher's guide. ?m; VHS. **Pr:** Children's Television Workshop. **A:** Primary-Jr. High. **P:** Education. **U:** Institution. **Chl-Juv:** Science, Physics. **Acq:** Purchase. **Dist:** GPN Educational Media. $15.00.

Air Line Filters 1992
Discusses purpose, operation, construction, and maintenance of basic air line filters. 23m; VHS. **A:** Adult. **P:** Education. **U:** Institution. **Gen-Edu:** Electronics. **Acq:** Purchase. **Dist:** RMI Media. $93.00.

The Air Mail Story 1992
An informative look at the development of air mail in America. Features early aviation pioneers, including Wilbur and Orville Wright, Charles Lindbergh, Amelia Earhart, Earl Ovington, and Max Miller. Includes footage of early mail flights and archival photography. 45m; VHS. **A:** Family. **P:** Entertainment. **U:** Home. **Gen-Edu:** Documentary Films, Aeronautics, Postal Service. **Acq:** Purchase. **Dist:** Acorn Media Group Inc. $19.95.

Air Monitoring 1991
Teaches how to read even the most modern sophisticated air monitoring equipment. Instructs in the basics of air quality testing when associated with incident management. Comes with manual. 46m; VHS. **A:** Adult. **P:** Professional. **U:** Institution. **Bus-Ind:** Emergencies, Occupational Training. **Acq:** Purchase, Rent/Lease. **Dist:** Emergency Film Group. $545.00.

Air Monitoring: Direct Reading Instruments 1991
Renders complex instructions simple for a variety of air monitoring instruments. Especially crafted for those in emergency response situations. Allows viewers to see and hear how others operate the equipment without wading through a morass of material. Comes with manual. 27m; VHS. **A:** Adult. **P:** Professional. **U:** Institution. **Bus-Ind:** Job Training, Emergencies, Ecology & Environment. **Acq:** Purchase, Rent/Lease. **Dist:** Emergency Film Group. $545.00.

Air Monitoring Series: Contamination Assessment 1991
Covers the essential techniques for those who must measure air quality. A must for career-minded rescue professionals. Includes manual. Additional literature available separately. 46m; VHS. **A:** Adult. **P:** Professional. **U:** Institution. **Bus-Ind:** Job Training, Emergencies, Ecology & Environment. **Acq:** Purchase, Rent/Lease. **Dist:** Emergency Film Group. $545.00.

Air Police 1931 — ★½
Two pilot buddies joing the airplane border patrol and are sent to Mexico to break up a gang of smugglers. 64m/B/W; VHS. **C:** Kenneth Harlan; Charles Delaney; Josephine Dunn; Richard Cramer; Tom London; George Chesebro; Directed by Stuart Paton. **A:** Family. **P:** Entertainment. **U:** Home. **Mov-Ent:** Aeronautics. **Acq:** Purchase. **Dist:** Grapevine Video. $14.95.

Air Pollution: A First Film—Revised 1985
This revised program updates the subject of air pollution, and offers suggestions on how to keep this problem under control. 12m; VHS, 3/4 U. **Pr:** Norman Bean. **A:** Primary-Jr. High. **P:** Education. **U:** Institution, SURA. **L:** English, French, Norwegian. **Hea-Sci:** Ecology & Environment. **Acq:** Purchase. **Dist:** Phoenix Learning Group.

Air Pollution: Indoor 1989
This tape explores indoor air pollution, particularly pollutants introduced in homes from painting, thermal insulation and other energy saving improvements, and water-proofing devices. 26m; VHS, 3/4 U. **Pr:** Films for the Humanities and Sciences. **A:** College. **P:** Education. **U:** Institution, CCTV, CATV, BCTV. **Hea-Sci:** Ecology & Environment. **Acq:** Purchase, Rent/Lease, Duplication License. **Dist:** Films for the Humanities & Sciences.

Air Pollution: Outdoor 1989
A tape that explores the burning of fuels, methods to burn fuel more efficiently with less hazardous by-products, the filtering out of pollutants, safe recycling and disposal of by-products, and the state of research on new and cleaner fuels and combustion methods. 26m; VHS, 3/4 U. **Pr:** Films for the Humanities and Sciences. **A:** College. **P:** Education. **U:** Institution, CCTV, CATV, BCTV. **Hea-Sci:** Ecology & Environment. **Acq:** Purchase, Rent/Lease, Duplication License. **Dist:** Films for the Humanities & Sciences.

Air Pollution: Sweetening the Air 198?
This film explains the laws of entropy and demonstrates that through effort and invention, desire and legislative action, even the harmful pollutants of modern man can be changed into useful forms. 20m; 3/4 U, Special order formats. **Pr:** Hobel Leiterman Productions. **A:** Jr. High-Adult. **P:** Education. **U:** Institution. **Gen-Edu:** Ecology & Environment. **Acq:** Purchase. **Dist:** The Cinema Guild.

Air Power 19??
Two WWII stock-footage films: "Air Power & Armies," about American air strategy, and "Target Germany-8th AF," about American air force flights over Germany. 68m/B/W; VHS. **A:** Jr. High-Adult. **P:** Education. **U:** Home. **Gen-Edu:** Aeronautics, World War Two. **Acq:** Purchase. **Dist:** Bennett Marine Video; Military/Combat Stock Footage Library. $24.95.

Air Power and Missiles 19??
See exciting footage of military aircraft in action, and follow air-to-air missiles in flight. 37m; VHS. **A:** Sr. High-Adult. **P:** Entertainment. **U:** Home. **Gen-Edu:** Documentary Films, Military History, Aeronautics. **Acq:** Purchase. **Dist:** Anchor Bay Entertainment. $9.99.

Air-Purifying Respirators 19??
Profiles selection and use of various types of cartridge and escape respirators with emphasis on selecting the proper equipment for the proper hazards involved. Also demonstrates how to check respirators for positive and negative pressure checks. Includes Leader's Guide and 25 Program Guides. 12m; VHS, 3/4 U. **A:** Adult. **P:** Education. **U:** Institution. **Bus-Ind:** Safety Education. **Acq:** Purchase. **Dist:** Williams Learning Network.

Air Race 1984
A lyrical look at the Reno Air Races. 22m; 3/4 U. **Pr:** Davidson Films. **A:** Jr. High-Adult. **P:** Entertainment. **U:** Institution, CCTV. **Spo-Rec:** Aeronautics. **Acq:** Purchase. **Dist:** Davidson Films, Inc.

Air Rage 2001 (R) — ★★
General Prescott (Cord) screwed over five Marines, setting them up and sending them to prison in order to advance his career. Now they're out and have just hijacked a 747 with the general on board—they not only want revenge but $100 million as well. Captain Marshall (Ice-T) and his team are sent on a rescue mission but things go wrong and Marshall is left to tackle the bad guys on his own. Familiar but fast-paced. 99m; VHS, DVD, Wide, CC. **C:** Ice-T; Cyril O'Reilly; Steve Hytner; Gil Gerard; Alex Cord; Kim Oja; Directed by Fred Olen Ray; Written by Sean O'Bannon; Cinematography by Mac Ahlberg. **A:** Sr. High-Adult. **P:** Entertainment. **U:** Home. **Mov-Ent:** Aeronautics. **Acq:** Purchase. **Dist:** Paramount Pictures Corp.

Air Raid 19??
Exciting aerial feats in motorcross, snowboarding, surfing, skateboarding, wakeboarding, and BMX racing. 35m; VHS. **A:** Family. **P:** Entertainment. **U:** Home. **Spo-Rec:** Bicycling, Skateboarding, Motorcycles. **Acq:** Purchase. **Dist:** Tapeworm Video Distributors Inc. $19.95.

Air Raid Offense Football Clinic 2011 (Unrated)
Football coaches Mike Leach, Hal Mumme, Tom Horne, and Pat Poore each give a presentation on different aspects of the air raid offense. ??m; DVD. **A:** Family. **P:** Education. **U:** Home, Institution. **Spo-Rec:** Football, Athletic Instruction/Coaching. **Acq:** Purchase. **Dist:** Championship Productions. $79.99.

Air Raid Offense I 2004 (Unrated)
Coach Chris Hatcher discusses the routes and coverages that make up the Air Raid Offense he teaches his football team. 44m; DVD. **A:** Family. **P:** Education. **U:** Home, Institution. **Spo-Rec:** Football, Athletic Instruction/Coaching. **Acq:** Purchase. **Dist:** Championship Productions. $39.99.

Air Raid Offense II 2004 (Unrated)
Coach Chris Hatcher shares plays and strategies for football teams in his follow up to his first video on the Air Raid Offense. 50m; DVD. **A:** Family. **P:** Education. **U:** Home, Institution. **Spo-Rec:** Football, Athletic Instruction/Coaching. **Acq:** Purchase. **Dist:** Championship Productions. $39.99.

Air Raid Wardens 1943 (Unrated) — ★★½
Laurel & Hardy play a couple of small-town failures who become the local air raid wardens during WWII. They even manage to make a mess of this but redeem themselves when they overhear a spy plot and save the town's munitions factory from a German spy ring. A so-so effort from the comic duo. 67m/B/W; VHS, DVD. **C:** Stan Laurel; Oliver Hardy; Edgar Kennedy; Jacqueline White; Stephen McNally; Russell Hicks; Howard Freeman; Donald Meek; Henry O'Neill; Directed by Edward Sedgwick. **Pr:** Metro-Goldwyn-Mayer Pictures. **A:** Family. **P:** Entertainment. **U:** Home. **Mov-Ent:** Comedy--Slapstick. **Acq:** Purchase. **Dist:** MGM Home Entertainment. $19.98.

Air Sampling 1995
Features how to identify and sample airborne hazards, and to select the proper method of controlling these hazards. 13m; VHS. **A:** Adult. **P:** Professional. **U:** Institution. **Bus-Ind:** Job Training, Safety Education, Management. **Acq:** Purchase, Rent/Lease. **Dist:** National Safety Council, California Chapter, Film Library.

Air Strike! 1944
Four mini-documentaries featuring WWII aerial combat footage, including secret declassified material from the AAF. 71m/B/W; VHS. **Pr:** U.S. Army Air Forces. **A:** Family. **P:** Education. **U:** Institution, Home. **Gen-Edu:** Aeronautics, World War Two. **Acq:** Purchase. **Dist:** Bennett Marine Video; Military/Combat Stock Footage Library. $29.95.

Air Superiority: U.S./Soviet Fighter Match Up 1990
A look at the lethal air weapons of the United States and the Soviet Union. Includes never-before-seen Soviet footage. 60m; VHS, SVS. **Pr:** McGraw Hill Films. **A:** Jr. High-Adult. **P:** Entertainment. **U:** Home. **Gen-Edu:** Aeronautics, Military History, USSR. **Acq:** Purchase. **Dist:** Time-Life Video and Television. $49.95.

Air-Supplied Respirators 1995
Reveals the different types of respirators and demonstrates rules that must be followed when using one. 15m; VHS. **A:** Adult. **P:** Professional. **U:** Institution. **L:** Spanish. **Bus-Ind:** Job Training, Safety Education. **Acq:** Purchase. **Dist:** National Safety Council, California Chapter, Film Library. $295.00.

Air Supply: Live in Hawaii 1982 (Unrated)
This concert features Air Supply's biggest hits, including "Lost in Love," "The One That You Love" and "Even the Nights Are Better." 75m; VHS. **Pr:** Danny O'Donovan. **A:** Family. **P:** Entertainment. **U:** Home. **Mov-Ent:** Music--Performance. **Acq:** Purchase. **Dist:** Music Video Distributors. $14.95.

Air-Supplying Respirators 1995
Describes what situations this type of respirator is suited for. Also offers safety tips. 11m; VHS. **A:** Adult. **P:** Professional. **U:** Institution. **Bus-Ind:** Job Training, Safety Education. **Acq:** Rent/Lease. **Dist:** National Safety Council, California Chapter, Film Library.

Air to Breathe 198?
The effects of toxic gas on the human body, and the speed in which it can overpower a person are demonstrated. 21m; VHS, 3/4 U. **A:** College-Adult. **P:** Education. **U:** Institution. **Bus-Ind:** Safety Education. **Acq:** Rent/Lease. **Dist:** National Safety Council, California Chapter, Film Library.

Air Traffic Control VFR Tower Simulator: A New Approach 1979
A realistic environment for training basic students in visual flight control tower operation is provided. This program shows air traffic control students using the simulator during training exercises. 13m; VHS, 3/4 U, Special order formats. **Pr:** Department of the Air Force. **A:** College-Adult. **P:** Education. **U:** Institution, SURA. **Gen-Edu:** Aeronautics, Occupations. **Acq:** Purchase. **Dist:** National Audiovisual Center.

The Air Up There 1994 (PG) — ★★
Assistant basketball coach Jimmy Dolan (Bacon) heads to the African village of Winabi to recruit talented (and tall) Saleh (Maina) to play b-ball in the U.S. But Saleh is next in line to be the tribe's king and doesn't want to leave. Stupid American in foreign country learning from the natives story is lighthearted, but relies heavily on formula—and borders on the stereotypical, though climatic game is a lot of fun. 108m; VHS, DVD, CC. **C:** Kevin Bacon; Charles Gitona Maina; Sean McCann; Dennis Patrick; Directed by Paul Michael Glaser; Written by Max Apple; Cinematography by Elliot Davis; Music by David Newman. **Pr:** Ted Field; Robert W. Cort; Lance Hool; Scott Kroopf; Interscope Comm; Polygram; Hollywood Pictures. **A:** Jr. High-Adult. **P:** Entertainment. **U:** Home. **Mov-Ent:** Basketball, Africa, Sports--Fiction: Comedy. **Acq:** Purchase. **Dist:** Walt Disney Studios Home Entertainment.

Air War in the Pacific: WWII 1946
This blow-by-blow account of the war against the Japanese makes use of vintage combat film. 56m/B/W; VHS. **Pr:** USAF. **A:** Family. **P:** Education. **U:** Home. **Gen-Edu:** Documentary Films, World War Two, Pacific Islands. **Acq:** Purchase. **Dist:** Finley Holiday Film Corp.; Karol Media. $24.95.

Air War in Vietnam 1991
The aerial fire power unleashed in the Vietnam conflict is exhibited here in combat footage and interviews with U.S. Advisors and other various officials. 60m; VHS. **Pr:** Fusion Video. **A:** Sr. High-Adult. **P:** Education. **U:** Home. **Gen-Edu:** Documentary Films, Vietnam War, Armed Forces--U.S. **Acq:** Purchase. **Dist:** Fusion Video. $29.98.

Air War over Europe: WWII 1946
A vintage combat film depicting the Allies' battle against the Luftwaffe. 56m/B/W; VHS. **Pr:** USAF. **A:** Family. **P:** Education. **U:** Home. **Gen-Edu:** Documentary Films, World War Two, Aeronautics. **Acq:** Purchase. **Dist:** Finley Holiday Film Corp.; Karol Media. $24.95.

Air Wars: Fighter Aircraft of World War II 2003 (Unrated)
Looks at World War II fighter pilots and their aircraft. 229m; DVD. **A:** Sr. High-Adult. **P:** Entertainment. **U:** Home. **Mov-Ent:** World War Two, Documentary Films, Aeronautics. **Acq:** Purchase. **Dist:** Eagle Rock Entertainment Inc. $9.99.

Air We Breathe in Industrial Environments 198?
This tape looks at the composition of air in various working environments and how to protect workers through protective equipment and proper ventilation. 16m; VHS, 3/4 U. **A:** College-Adult. **P:** Education. **U:** Institution. **Bus-Ind:** Safety Education. **Acq:** Rent/Lease. **Dist:** National Safety Council, California Chapter, Film Library.

Airborne 1993 (PG) — ★½
Cool California rollerblade dude gets transplanted to Cincinnati for a school year, and has to prove himself when those good ol' midwestern boys come after him. Nothing short of a skate vehicle appealing largely, if not solely, to the high school contingent. 91m; VHS, DVD, CC. **C:** Shane McDermott; Seth Green; Brittney Powell; Edie McClurg; Jack Black; Alanna Ubach; Jacob Vargas; Directed by Rob Bowman; Written by Bill Apablasa; Music by Stewart Copeland. **Pr:** Bruce Davey; Icon Productions; Warner Bros. **A:** Jr. High-Adult. **P:** Entertainment. **U:** Home. **Mov-Ent:** Sports--Fiction: Drama, Skating, Adolescence. **Acq:** Purchase. **Dist:** WarnerArchive.com.

Airborne 1998 (R) — ★★
Members of a covert Special Forces team are targeted for assassination after recovering a biochemical weapon from terrorists. But their leader (Guttenberg) decides to use the virus as bait to find out who wants them dead. Guttenberg tries but can't convince as a tough guy but there's lots of action to make up for this casting quirk. 94m; VHS, DVD, CC. **C:** Steve Guttenberg; Sean Bean; Colm Feore; Directed by Julian Grant. **A:** Sr. High-Adult. **P:** Entertainment. **U:** Home. **Mov-Ent:** Aeronautics, Terrorism. **Acq:** Purchase. **Dist:** Bedford Entertainment Inc.

Airborne: A Sentimental Journey 1988
A video adaptation of William Buckley's book about the sailing journey he took with his son and friends across the Atlantic Ocean. 145m; VHS. **C:** William F. Buckley. **Pr:** Avant Communications. **A:** Family. **P:** Entertainment. **U:** Home. **Spo-Rec:** Documentary Films, Boating, Travel. **Acq:** Purchase. **Dist:** Bennett Marine Video. $49.95.

Airboss 1997 (R) — ★½
A special forces team of FBI agents and the military must track down a hijacked shipment of plutonium before it falls into terrorist hands. When a team member is killed, fighter pilot Frank White (Zagarino) is called in. Lots of machinery, guns, and explosions make up for the lack of believable story. 90m; VHS, DVD. **C:** Frank Zagarino; John Christian; Kayle Watson; Caroline Strong; Jerry Kokich; Directed by J. Christian Ingvordsen. **A:** Sr. High-Adult. **P:** Entertainment. **U:** Home. **Mov-Ent:** Terrorism, Aeronautics, Federal Bureau of Investigation (FBI). **Acq:** Purchase. **Dist:** Bedford Entertainment Inc.

Airheads 1994 (PG-13) — ★★½
"Wayne's World" meets "Dog Day Afternoon." Silly farce has three metal heads (Buscemi, Fraser, Sandler) holding a radio station hostage in order to get their demo tape played. Events snowball and they receive instant fame. Cast and crew rich with subversive comedic talents, including Sandler and Farley from "Saturday Night Live." Soundtrack authenticity supplied by White Zombie and The Galatic Cowboys. 81m; VHS, DVD, Blu-Ray, Wide, CC. **C:** Brendan Fraser; Steve Buscemi; Adam Sandler; Chris Farley; Michael McKean; Judd Nelson; Joe Mantegna; Michael Richards; Ernie Hudson; Amy Locane; Nina Siemaszko; John Melendez; Harold Ramis; Marshall Bell; David Arquette; Reg E. Cathey; Allen Covert; Sam Whipple; China Kantner; Directed by Michael Lehmann; Written by Rich Wilkes; Cinematography by John Schwartzman; Music by Carter Burwell. **Pr:** Mark Burg; Robert Simonds; Todd Baker; Fox; Island World Productions. **A:** Jr. High-Adult. **P:** Entertainment. **U:** Home. **Mov-Ent.** **Acq:** Purchase. **Dist:** Fox Home Entertainment.

Airline Disaster 2010 (Unrated) — ★
It's a disaster alright. President Franklin (Baxter) learns that her brother Joseph (Valentine) is flying a super-techno new passenger jet that has been hijacked by neo-Nazi terrorists. Now she must decide between saving the plane's crew and passengers or protecting the safety of those below. This time it's the Washington Monument that takes one for the team. 90m; DVD. **C:** Meredith Baxter; Scott Valentine; Lindsey McKeon; Geoff Meed; Jude Gerard Prest; Matt Lagan; Directed by John Willis, III; Written by Paul Shor; Victoria Dadi; Cinematography by Alexander Yellen; Music by Chris Ridenhour. **A:** Jr. High-Adult. **P:** Entertainment. **U:** Home. **Mov-Ent:** Terrorism, Presidency. **Acq:** Purchase. **Dist:** The Asylum.

Airline: The Complete Season 1 2005
A&E reality series captures obscure human behavior in-flight. 396m; DVD. **A:** Adult. **P:** Entertainment. **U:** Home. **Mov-Ent:** Television, Travel. **Acq:** Purchase. **Dist:** A&E Television Networks L.L.C. $29.95.

AirObics Healthy Bouncing & Toning 1992
Holly Anderson instructs this beginning-to-intermediate level aerobics program developed for use with a mini-trampoline. 50m; VHS. **A:** Jr. High-Adult. **P:** Instruction. **U:** Home. **Hea-Sci:** Fitness/Exercise. **Acq:** Purchase. **Dist:** Collage Video Specialties, Inc. $19.95.

Airplane! 1980 (PG) — ★★★½
Classic lampoon of disaster flicks is stupid but funny and launched a bevy of wanna-be spoofs. Former pilot Ted Striker (Hays), who's lost both his stewardess girlfriend Elaine (Hagerty) and his nerve, takes over the controls of a jet when the crew is hit with food poisoning. The passengers become increasingly crazed and ground support more surreal as our hero struggles to land the plane. Clever, fast-paced, and very funny parody mangles every Hollywood cliche within reach. The gags are so furiously paced that when one bombs it's hardly noticeable. Launched Nielsen's second career as a comic actor. And it ain't over till it's over: don't miss the amusing final credits. Followed by "Airplane 2: The Sequel." 88m; VHS, DVD, Blu-Ray, 8 mm, Wide. **C:** Robert Hays; Julie Hagerty; Lloyd Bridges; Peter Graves; Robert Stack; Kareem Abdul-Jabbar; Leslie Nielsen; Stephen Stucker; Ethel Merman; Jerry Zucker; Barbara Billingsley; Jim Abrahams; Lorna Patterson; Joyce Bulifant; David Zucker; James Hong; Maureen McGovern; Jimmie Walker; Rossie (Ross) Harris; Directed by Jerry Zucker; Jim Abrahams; David Zucker; Written by Jerry Zucker; Jim Abrahams; David Zucker; Cinematography by Joseph Biroc; Music by Elmer Bernstein. **Pr:** Howard W. Koch, Jr. **A:** Family. **P:** Entertainment. **U:** Home. **Mov-Ent:** Satire & Parody, Aeronautics, Classic Films. **Awds:** Natl. Film Reg. '10; Writers Guild '80: Adapt. Screenplay. **Acq:** Purchase. **Dist:** Paramount Pictures Corp. $14.95.

Airplane 2: The Sequel 1982 (PG) — ★★
Not a Zucker, Abrahams and Zucker effort, and sorely missing their slapstick and script finesse. The first passenger space shuttle has taken off for the moon and there's a mad bomber on board. Given the number of stars mugging, it's more of a loveboat in space than a fitting sequel to "Airplane." Nonetheless, some funny laughs and gags. 84m; VHS, DVD, Blu-Ray, Wide. **C:** Robert Hays; Julie Hagerty; Lloyd Bridges; Raymond Burr; Peter Graves; William Shatner; Sonny Bono; Chuck Connors; Chad Everett; Stephen Stucker; Rip Torn; Kent McCord; Sandahl Bergman; Jack Jones; John Dehner; Richard Jaeckel; Cameo(s) Ken Finkleman; Directed by Ken Finkleman; Written by Ken Finkleman; Cinematography by Joseph Biroc; Music by Elmer Bernstein. **Pr:** Paramount Pictures. **A:** Jr. High-Adult. **P:** Entertainment. **U:** Home. **Mov-Ent:** Satire & Parody, Aeronautics. **Acq:** Purchase. **Dist:** Paramount Pictures Corp. $14.95.

The Airplane and NASA 5: Quieter, Faster, and Safer Aircraft 1985
An examination of NASA's role in developing quieter, faster, and safer aircraft. ?m; 1C, 3/4 U. **Pr:** National Aeronautics and Space Administration. **A:** Jr. High-Adult. **P:** Education. **U:** BCTV, SURA. **Hea-Sci:** Aeronautics, Technology. **Acq:** Free Loan. **Dist:** NASA Lyndon B. Johnson Space Center.

Airplane Trip—4th Edition 1973
Shows the many activities involved in jet travel; filmed on location at airports and on board an actual flight. 15m; VHS, 3/4 U. **Pr:** Janice Laine; Encyclopedia Britannica Educational Corporation. **A:** Primary. **P:** Education. **U:** Institution, SURA. **Chl-Juv:** Aeronautics. **Acq:** Purchase, Rent/Lease, Trade-in. **Dist:** Encyclopedia Britannica.

Airport 1970 (G) — ★★★
Old-fashioned disaster thriller built around an all-star cast, fairly moronic script, and an unavoidable accident during the flight of a passenger airliner. A boxoffice hit that paved the way for many lesser disaster flicks (including its many sequels) detailing the reactions of the passengers and crew as they cope with impending doom. Considered to be the best of the "Airport" series; adapted from the Arthur Hailey novel. 137m; VHS, DVD, Blu-Ray. **C:** Dean Martin; Burt Lancaster; Jean Seberg; Jacqueline Bisset; George Kennedy; Helen Hayes; Van Heflin; Maureen Stapleton; Barry Nelson; Lloyd Nolan; Dana Wynter; Barbara Hale; Gary Collins; Jessie Royce Landis; Directed by George Seaton; Written by George Seaton; Cinematography by Ernest Laszlo; Music by Alfred Newman. **Pr:** Mark Huffam; Ross Hunter. **A:** Family. **P:** Entertainment. **U:** Home. **Mov-Ent:** Action-Adventure, Aeronautics. **Awds:** Oscars '70: Support. Actress (Hayes); Golden Globes '71: Support. Actress (Stapleton). **Acq:** Purchase. **Dist:** Baker and Taylor. $14.98.

Airport '75 1975 (PG) — ★★
After a mid-air collision, a jumbo 747 is left pilotless. Airline attendant Black must fly da plane. She does her cross-eyed best in this absurd sequel to "Airport" built around a lesser "all-star cast." Safe on the ground, Heston tries to talk the airline hostess/pilot into landing, while the impatient Kennedy continues to grouse as leader of the foam-ready ground crew. A slick, insincere attempt to find box office magic again (which unfortunately worked, leading to two more sequels). 107m; VHS, DVD. **C:** Charlton Heston; Karen Black; George Kennedy; Gloria Swanson; Helen Reddy; Sid Caesar; Efrem Zimbalist, Jr.; Susan Clark; Dana Andrews; Linda Blair; Nancy Olson; Roy Thinnes; Myrna Loy; Ed Nelson; Larry Storch; Directed by Jack Smight; Written by Don Ingalls; Cinematography by Philip H. Lathrop; Music by John Cacavas. **Pr:** William Frye; Mark Huffam. **A:** Jr. High-Adult. **P:** Entertainment. **U:** Home. **Mov-Ent:** Action-Adventure, Aeronautics. **Acq:** Purchase. **Dist:** Movies Unlimited; Alpha Video. $59.95.

Airport '77 1977 (PG) — ★★
Billionaire Stewart fills his converted passenger jet with priceless art and sets off to Palm Beach for a museum opening, joined by an uninvited gang of hijackers. Twist to this in-flight disaster is that the bad time in the air occurs underwater, a novel (and some might say, desperate) twist to the old panic in the plane we're all gonna die formula. With a cast of familiar faces, some of them stars and some of them just familiar faces, this is yet another sequel to "Airport" and another boxoffice

success, leading to the last of the tired series in 1979. 114m; VHS, DVD. **C:** Jack Lemmon; James Stewart; Lee Grant; Brenda Vaccaro; Joseph Cotten; Olivia de Havilland; Darren McGavin; Christopher Lee; George Kennedy; Kathleen Quinlan; Monte Markham; Directed by Jack Smight. **Pr:** William Frye; Mark Huffam. **A:** Jr. High-Adult. **P:** Entertainment. **U:** Home. **Mov-Ent:** Action-Adventure, Aeronautics, The Bermuda Triangle. **Acq:** Purchase. **Dist:** Movies Unlimited; Alpha Video. $14.98.

Airto and Flora Purim: Latin Jazz 1988
A live set performance by percussionist Airto and Brazilian singer Flora Purim with feed player Joe Farrell. 60m; VHS. **A:** Jr. High-Adult. **P:** Education. **U:** Home. **Fin-Art:** Music--Jazz. **Acq:** Purchase. **Dist:** V.I.E.W. Inc./Arkadia Entertainment Corp. $29.98.

Airto & Flora Purim—The Latin Jazz All-Stars 199?
Live performance footage from the Queen Mary Jazz Festival. 60m; VHS. **A:** Sr. High-Adult. **P:** Entertainment. **U:** Home. **Gen-Edu:** Music--Performance, Music--Jazz. **Acq:** Purchase. **Dist:** Hal Leonard Corp. $29.95.

Airway Management 1985
A review of emergency procedures to establish airways. 35m; VHS, 3/4 U. **C:** Dr. Leila Martin. **A:** Adult. **P:** Special Education. **U:** Institution, CCTV, SURA. **Hea-Sci:** Respiratory System, Emergencies. **Acq:** Purchase. **Dist:** Emory Medical Television Network.

Airway Management and Artificial Respiration 1973
This program shows airway management and artificial resuscitation including mouth-to-mouth resuscitation, bag-mask resuscitation and endotracheal intubation. 24m; VHS, 3/4 U, Special order formats. **Pr:** Ohio State University Health Sciences AV Center. **A:** College-Adult. **P:** Professional. **U:** Institution, SURA. **Hea-Sci:** Respiratory System. **Acq:** Purchase, Rent/Lease. **Dist:** Ohio State University.

Airwolf: Season 1 1984
Jan-Michael Vincent and his posse of helicopter aces get up and running in the debut season of CBS's popular series. Gen-Xers looking for a guilty pleasure, look no further. 592m; DVD. **A:** Family. **P:** Entertainment. **U:** Home. **Gen-Edu:** Television. **Acq:** Purchase. **Dist:** Universal Studios Home Video. $39.98.

Airwolf: Season Three 2007 (Unrated)
Presents the third season of the 1984-1986 CBS action-adventure television series with Hawke (Vincent) piloting the souped-up helicopter and tackling dangerous missions while looking for his missing brother in Vietnam. Includes: Hawke is hypnotized by a madman trying to take control of a small country, an old girlfriend of Hawke's escapes her criminal husband in hopes of testifying against him, someone tries to steal the Airwolf, and Hawke must help find his nephew's missing aunt. Marked the departure of creator Donald P. Bellisario and cast member Deborah Pratt (Caitlin O'Shannessy)?who had married during season two. 22 episodes. 1056m; DVD. **C:** Jan-Michael Vincent; Alex Cord; Ernest Borgnine; Jean Bruce Scott; Deborah Pratt. **A:** Jr. High-Adult. **P:** Entertainment. **U:** Home. **Mov-Ent:** Television Series, Action-Adventure. **Acq:** Purchase. **Dist:** Universal Studios Home Video. $39.98.

Airwolf: Season Two 2006 (Unrated)
Presents the second season of the 1984-1986 CBS action-adventure television series with Stringfellow Hawke (Vincent) piloting the souped-up helicopter and tackling dangerous missions while looking for his missing brother in Vietnam. Includes: the Airwolf contracts a virus giving it the potential to become a killing machine, Dominic (Borgnine) is distraught over his sister's death and then shocked to find he's being charged with her murder, Caitlin's (Pratt) plane is hijacked, and Hawke is taken hostage by Latin American revolutionaries. First season for cast member Deborah Pratt as Caitlin O'Shannessy. 22 episodes. 1062m; DVD. **C:** Jan-Michael Vincent; Alex Cord; Ernest Borgnine; Deborah Pratt; Jean Bruce Scott. **A:** Jr. High-Adult. **P:** Entertainment. **U:** Home. **Mov-Ent:** Television Series, Action-Adventure. **Acq:** Purchase. **Dist:** Universal Studios Home Video. $39.98.

Aisha Tyler is Lit 2009 (Unrated)
Live comedy performance by Aisha Tyler filmed at the Fillmore in San Francisco. 85m; DVD. **A:** Sr. High-Adult. **P:** Entertainment. **U:** Home. **Mov-Ent:** Comedy--Performance, Television. **Acq:** Purchase. **Dist:** Comedy Central; Image Entertainment Inc. $14.98.

Ajami 2009 (Unrated) — ★★★½
A non-professional cast, many from Jaffa's multi-ethnic Ajami neighborhood, are featured in Copti and Shani's intense story of culture clash in Israel. A revenge killing has many repercussions that involve Palestinians and Israelis, Christians, Muslims, and Jews—all of whom are hostile to the differing communities. Moving, powerful portrait of a society where violence permeates even the most insignificant aspects of daily life. Arabic and Hebrew with subtitles. 120m; Blu-Ray, On Demand, Wide. **C:** Shahir Kabaha; Fouad Habash; Ibrahim Frege; Youseff Sahwani; Ramin Karim; Eran Naim; Scandar Copti; Directed by Scandar Copti; Yaron Shani; Written by Scandar Copti; Yaron Shani; Cinematography by Boaz Yehonatan Yaacov; Music by Rabiah Buchari. **Pr:** Mosh Danon; Thanassis Karathanos; Talia Kleinhendler; arte; Kino International Corporation; Inosan Prods; Twenty Twenty Filmproduktion; Vertigo Films; Das Kleine Fernsehspiel. **A:** College-Adult. **P:** Entertainment. **U:** Home. **L:** Arabic, Hebrew. **Mov-Ent:** Crime Drama, Israel, Middle East. **Acq:** Purchase. **Dist:** Kino on Video; Amazon.com Inc.; Movies Unlimited.

Ajax 1991
Presents the London Small Theater Company's modernized production of Sophocles's play. 71m; VHS. **A:** Adult. **P:** Education. **U:** Institution. **Fin-Art:** Theater. **Acq:** Purchase. **Dist:** Insight Media. $195.00.

Ajit 1996
Documentary of Ajit, an eight year old child working as a domestic in Calcutta. Illustrates childhood in impoverished and underdeveloped countries. 28m; VHS. **A:** Adult. **P:** Education. **U:** Home. **Gen-Edu:** Documentary Films, Asia, Children. **Acq:** Purchase, Rent/Lease. **Dist:** Filmakers Library Inc. $225.

Ajith Fernando: Exposition of the Book of Jonah 1987
Ajith Fernando, the national director of Youth for Christ in Sri Lanka, reads from the book of Jonah at the Urbana conference of 1987. Includes four 40-minute tapes. 40m; VHS. **Pr:** TwentyOneHundred Productions. **A:** College-Adult. **P:** Religious. **U:** Institution, Home. **Gen-Edu:** Bible. **Acq:** Purchase. **Dist:** InterVarsity Video. $14.95.
Indiv. Titles: 1. Running Away From God 2. Praise for Deliverance 3. Revival in Nineveh 4. God's Concern for Nineveh.

A.K. 1985
Essay on Japanese director Akira Kurosawa, examining his artistic and working processes during the filming of "Ran." 71m; VHS. **C:** Directed by Chris Marker. **A:** College-Adult. **P:** Entertainment. **U:** Home. **Fin-Art:** Filmmaking. **Acq:** Purchase. **Dist:** Facets Multimedia Inc. $59.95.

AKA 2002 (R) — ★★
Unhappy with his family life, young man Dean leeches off of rich socialite Lady Gryffoyn until her son, Alex, smells a rat and Dean scampers away to Paris. Unable to forgo his taste for the good life, he opts to pass himself off as Alex—causing him to face his sexuality. British writer-director Roy uses offbeat three-screen device to tell his own real-life tale. 107m; VHS, DVD. **C:** Diana Quick; Blake Ritson; Bill Nighy; Geoff Bell; Matthew Leitch; George Asprey; Lindsey Coulson; Directed by Duncan Roy; Written by Duncan Roy. **A:** Sr. High-Adult. **P:** Entertainment. **U:** Home. **Mov-Ent. Acq:** Purchase. **Dist:** Ventura Distribution Inc. $26.99.

A.K.A. Cassius Clay 2002
Looks at the life and achievements of boxing legend Muhammad Ali, who was born Cassius Clay. Features fight clips and interviews. ?m; DVD. **A:** Jr. High-Adult. **P:** Entertainment. **U:** Home. **Gen-Edu:** Documentary Films. **Acq:** Purchase. **Dist:** Fox Home Entertainment.

Akeelah and the Bee 2006 (PG) — ★★½
Inspirational story focuses on 11-year-old Akeelah (Palmer), a vocabulary whiz (thanks to her late father's Scrabble prowess) who doesn't want to be humiliated as a brainiac at her tough South Central L.A. school. But after a couple of spelling bee wins, and the coaching of no-nonsense UCLA English professor Larabee (Fishburne), Akeelah is encouraged to dream big and head for the National Spelling Bee. Bassett plays her overworked widow mom, who has too many other worries to help her daughter (at least at first). Palmer's character is both sweet and determined although the film may seem overly familiar. 107m; DVD. **C:** Laurence Fishburne; Angela Bassett; Keke Palmer; Curtis Armstrong; Tzi Ma; Lee Thompson Young; Sahara Garey; J.R. Villarreal; Sean Michael Afable; Directed by Doug Atchison; Written by Doug Atchison; Cinematography by M. David Mullen; Music by Aaron Zigman. **Pr:** Sid Ganis; Laurence Fishburne; Nancy Hult Ganis; Michael Romersa; Danny Llewelyn; Laurence Fishburne; Lionsgate; 2929 Productions; Out of the Blue Entertainment; Reactor Films Production; Cinema Gypsy Prods; Starbucks Entertainment. **A:** Primary-Adult. **P:** Entertainment. **U:** Home. **L:** English. **Mov-Ent:** Black Culture. **Acq:** Purchase. **Dist:** CinemaNow Inc.; Lions Gate Entertainment Inc.

Akihabara Geeks 2007
Explores the subculture of Tokyo's Akihabara neighborhood, known for its discount computer and electronics stores, and its various enthusiasts. 45m; DVD. **A:** Jr. High-Adult. **P:** Entertainment. **U:** Home. **Gen-Edu:** Documentary Films. **Acq:** Purchase. **Dist:** Amazon.com Inc.

Akira 1989 — ★★
Secret government experiments on children with ESP go awry, resulting in an cataclysmic explosion on Tokyo. The city in turn builds itself up into a Megalopolis and the experiments continue. Animated; in Japanese with English subtitles or dubbed. 124m; VHS, DVD, UMD. **C:** Voice(s) by Mitsuo Iwata; Nozomu Sasaki; Mami Koyama; Directed by Katsuhiro Otomo; Sheldon Renan; Written by Katsuhiro Otomo; Izo Hashimoto; Cinematography by Katsuji Misawa; Music by Shoji Yamashiro. **Pr:** Akira Committee. **A:** College-Adult. **P:** Entertainment. **U:** Home. **L:** English, Japanese. **Mov-Ent:** Animation & Cartoons, Science Fiction, Japan. **Acq:** Purchase. **Dist:** FUNimation Entertainment; Streamline Pictures. $29.95.

Akira Kurosawa's Dreams 1990 (PG) — ★★½
An anthological lesson regarding the simultaneous loss of humanity and nature that threatens us all from the renowned Japanese director. Although the startling and memorable imagery is still present, Kurosawa's lessons are strangely trite and consequently lack the power that is normally associated with his work. Watch for Scorsese as Van Gogh. With English subtitles. 120m; VHS, DVD, Wide. **C:** Akira Terao; Mitsuko Baisho; Meiko Harada; Chishu Ryu; Hisashi Igawa; Mitsunori Isaki; Toshihiko Nakano; Yoshitaka Zushi; Toshie Negishi; Martin Scorsese; Directed by Akira Kurosawa; Written by Akira Kurosawa; Cinematography by Kazutami Hara; Takao Saito; Masaharu Ueda; Music by Shinichiro Ikebe. **Pr:** Akira Kurosawa; Akira Kurosawa; Warner Bros. **A:** Jr. High-Adult. **P:** Entertainment. **U:** Home. **L:** Japanese. **Mov-Ent. Acq:** Purchase. **Dist:** Warner Home Video, Inc.; Facets Multimedia Inc. $89.95.

Akira Production Report 1990
Otomo, artist and creator of "Akira," the popular Japanese graphic novel and animated feature, is the focus of this documentary by Streamline Pictures. Noted for his technical adroitness, he explains the production techniques that complement the well-storied plot of "Akira." Taking place in 2019, after the world has suffered and survived a nuclear war, and the governmental powers that be are attempting to re-engender a primal power known as Akira. Rather than utilize rotoscoping, where the artist traces over live-action figures, Otomo employs a more precise and technically advanced manner of creating movement and perspective. In English. 52m; VHS. **C:** Katsuhiro Otomo. **Pr:** Akira Committee. **A:** Jr. High-Adult. **P:** Entertainment. **U:** Home. **Mov-Ent:** Documentary Films, Animation & Cartoons, Filmmaking. **Acq:** Purchase. **Dist:** Streamline Pictures. $24.95.

Akropolis 1968
Presents a production by Jerzy Grotowski's Polish Laboratory Theater and commentary by director Peter Brook. 60m; VHS. **A:** Adult. **P:** Education. **U:** Institution. **Fin-Art:** Theater. **Acq:** Purchase. **Dist:** Insight Media. $139.00.

AKS Assault Rifle 1991
Complete information on AK assault weapon field maintenance. 30m; VHS. **A:** College-Adult. **P:** Instruction. **U:** Home. **How-Ins:** How-To, Firearms. **Acq:** Purchase. **Dist:** Gun Video. $39.95.

Akwesasne: Another Point of View 1981
This program explores some of the social, political, and legal obstacles faced by traditional Mowhawks in recent years in their struggle to retain traditional rights. 28m; 3/4 U. **Pr:** Robert Stiles; John Akin. **A:** Sr. High-Adult. **P:** Education. **U:** Institution, SURA. **Gen-Edu:** Native Americans. **Acq:** Purchase. **Dist:** First Run/Icarus Films.

Al-Anon Habia Por Si Mismo 19??
Spanish version of "Al-Anon Speaks for Itself" features spouses, siblings, children, and friends explaining how the Twelve Step Al-Anon and Alateen programs helped them deal with the addictions of their family members. 15m; VHS. **A:** Family. **P:** Education. **U:** Institution. **L:** Spanish. **Hea-Sci:** Alcoholism, Family. **Acq:** Purchase. **Dist:** Hazelden Publishing. $39.95.

Al-Anon Speaks for Itself 19??
Spouses, siblings, children, and friends explain how the Twelve Step Al-Anon and Alateen programs helped them deal with the addictions of their family members. 15m; VHS. **A:** Family. **P:** Education. **U:** Institution. **Hea-Sci:** Alcoholism, Drug Abuse, Family. **Acq:** Purchase. **Dist:** Hazelden Publishing. $39.95.

Al Capone 1959 — ★★★
Film noir character study of one of the most colorful gangsters of the Roaring '20s. Sort of an underworld "How to Succeed in Business." Steiger chews scenes and bullets as they fly by, providing the performance of his career. Plenty of gangland violence and mayhem and splendid cinematography keep the fast-paced period piece sailing. 104m; VHS, DVD. **C:** Rod Steiger; Fay Spain; Murvyn Vye; Nehemiah Persoff; Martin Balsam; Al Ruscio; Joe De Santis; Directed by Richard Wilson. **Pr:** Allied Artists International. **A:** Primary-Adult. **P:** Entertainment. **U:** Home. **Mov-Ent:** Crime Drama, Biography: Law Enforcement, Documentary Films. **Acq:** Purchase. **Dist:** Facets Multimedia Inc. $14.98.

Al Capone & Eliot Ness 19??
The story behind the legendary rivalry of Prohibition-era Chicago mobster Capone and lawman Ness, who worked to bring him to justice. 50m; VHS. **Pr:** A&E (Arts & Entertainment) Network. **A:** Sr. High-Adult. **P:** Entertainment. **U:** Home. **Gen-Edu:** Biography. **Acq:** Purchase. **Dist:** A&E Television Networks L.L.C.; New Video Group. $19.95.

Al Capone: Chicago's Scarface 1986
A documentary using vintage footage about the mob king of the 1920s and his eventual demise. 60m; VHS, 3/4 U. **TV Std:** NTSC, PAL. **C:** Narrated by Geraldo Rivera. **A:** Jr. High-Adult. **P:** Education. **U:** Home. **Gen-Edu:** Documentary Films. **Acq:** Purchase. **Dist:** MPI Media Group. $39.95.

Al Capone: The Untouchable Legend 1998
Uses historical film footage, movie scenes and dramatic recreations to examine the life of Al Capone, America's most notorious and legendary gangster. 52m; VHS. **A:** Sr. High-Adult. **P:** Education. **U:** Home. **Gen-Edu:** Biography, History--Modern. **Acq:** Purchase. **Dist:** Janson Media. $19.95.

Al Di Meola 19??
Di Meola demonstrates his scale choices for soloing. Several of his melodic lines, licks, rhythm patterns and solos are documented in an accompanying booklet. 60m; VHS. **A:** Jr. High-Adult. **P:** Instruction. **U:** Home. **How-Ins:** How-To, Music--Instruction. **Acq:** Purchase. **Dist:** Music Video Distributors. $49.95.

Al Fin a Solas 197? (Unrated) — ★
A pair of newlyweds are beset by mobs of unhappy in-laws in this Spanish semi-musical. 99m; VHS. **C:** Cesar Costa; Rosa Maria Vasquez; Alicia Bonet; Carlos East. **A:** Jr. High-Adult. **P:** Entertainment. **U:** Home. **L:** Spanish. **Mov-Ent:** Musical. **Acq:** Purchase. **Dist:** Spanishmultimedia. $75.95.

Al Fracassa's Complete Quarterback Technique Teaching System 2007 (Unrated)
Coach Al Fracassa lectures on teaching a quarterback the skills he needs, as well as demonstrating a few drills and techniques. 46m; DVD. **A:** Family. **P:** Education. **U:** Home, Institution. **Spo-Rec**: Football, Athletic Instruction/Coaching. **Acq:** Purchase. **Dist:** Championship Productions. $39.99.

Al Franken: God Spoke 2007 (Unrated)
Documentary following comedian Al Franken's career after his two-decade stint on "Saturday Night Live" to his decision to enter politics. 84m; DVD. **A:** Sr. High-Adult. **P:** Entertainment. **U:** Home. **Gen-Edu**: Politics & Government. **Acq:** Purchase. **Dist:** Docurama. $26.95.

Al Golden: Play Action Pass Coverages 2013 (Unrated)
Football coach Al Golden discusses using the run game to set up the play-action pass. 65m; DVD. **A:** Family. **P:** Education. **U:** Home. **L:** English. **Spo-Rec**: Athletic Instruction/Coaching, Football. **Acq:** Purchase. **Dist:** Championship Productions. $29.99.

Al Green: Gospel According to Al Green 1988 (Unrated)
A live, inspirational extravaganza from Gospel's greatest name. 94m; VHS. **C:** Al Green. **A:** Family. **P:** Entertainment. **U:** Home. **Mov-Ent**: Music--Performance, Singing, Religion. **Acq:** Purchase. **Dist:** Music Video Distributors; Image Entertainment Inc.; Facets Multimedia Inc.

Al Green: On Fire in Tokyo 1988
The great gospel singer sings "Jesus Will Fix It," "You Brought the Sunshine Into My Life" and other gospel songs in concert in Tokyo. 60m; VHS. **C:** Al Green. **Pr:** Xenon Video. **A:** Family. **P:** Entertainment. **U:** Home. **Mov-Ent**: Music--Performance, Religion. **Acq:** Purchase. **Dist:** Music Video Distributors; Xenon Pictures Inc. ; Facets Multimedia Inc. $29.95.

Al Jarreau in London 1985
Jarreau performs in concert at the Wembley Arena. Includes songs "Raging Waters," "Trouble In Paradise," "We're In This Love Together," "Let's Pretend," "Our Love," "Take Five," "High Crimo," "Boogie Down," and "Roof Garden." 54m; VHS. **Pr:** Warner Reprise Video. **A:** Family. **P:** Entertainment. **U:** Home. **Mov-Ent**: Music--Performance, Music--Jazz, Black Culture. **Acq:** Purchase. **Dist:** Music Video Distributors; Facets Multimedia Inc. $19.98.

Al Jarreau: Tenderness 1994
Recorded live before an invited audience, Jarreau covers his classic songs, pop standards, and music from his new album. 60m; VHS. **A:** College-Adult. **P:** Entertainment. **U:** Home. **Mov-Ent**: Music--Jazz, Music--Performance, Singing. **Acq:** Purchase. **Dist:** Warner Reprise Video. $19.98.
Songs: We Got By; You Don't See Me; Your Song; Summertime; She's Leaving Home.

The Al Jolson Collection 1992 (Unrated)
The famous star of early sound film is honored through seven volumes of his works. Films featured are "The Jazz Singer," "The Singing Fool," "Say It with Songs," "Mammy," "Big Boy," "Wonder Bar," "Go Into Your Dance" and "The Singing Kid." 100m/B/W; Silent. **C:** Al Jolson. **Pr:** MGM/UA Entertainment Company. **A:** College-Adult. **P:** Entertainment. **U:** Home. **Mov-Ent**: Documentary Films, Silent Films. **Acq:** Purchase. **Dist:** MGM Home Entertainment. $149.98.

Al McKay: Rhythm Guitar Instruction 1990
The famed guitarist demonstrates the tricks of the trade. ?m; VHS. **A:** Jr. High-Adult. **P:** Instruction. **U:** Home. **How-Ins**: Music--Instruction. **Acq:** Purchase. **Dist:** Music Video Distributors. $44.95.

Al Nakba: The Palestinian Catastrophe, 1948 1998
Pursues in-depth why and how at the end of the first Arab-Israeli war of 1948 750,000 Palestinian Arabs became refugees. 56m; VHS. **A:** Adult. **P:** Education. **U:** Institution, BCTV. **Gen-Edu**: Documentary Films, Middle East. **Acq:** Purchase, Rent/Lease. **Dist:** Arab Film Distribution. $225.00.

Al Neuharth, Malcolm Forbes and Thomas Monaghan 1989
Business tycoons Forbes, USA Today founder Neuharth and Domino's Pizza founder Monaghan offer advice on achieving success in business and attaining the power it takes to be number one. Specially adapted from the Phil Donahue Show. 28m; VHS. **Pr:** Films for the Humanities. **A:** College-Adult. **P:** Education. **U:** Institution. **Gen-Edu**: Industry & Industrialists, Economics, Business. **Acq:** Purchase. **Dist:** Films for the Humanities & Sciences. $149.00.

Al-Sabbar 2000
Documentary of young Arabs with Israeli passports searching for ruins of Arab villages destroyed in 1948 by the Israeli army. With English subtitles. 97m; VHS. **A:** Sr. High-Adult. **P:** Education. **U:** Institution. **L:** Arabic, Hebrew. **Gen-Edu**: Documentary Films, Middle East. **Acq:** Purchase, Rent/Lease. **Dist:** Arab Film Distribution. $195.00.

Al Sabbar Cactus 2000
Portrays the work of a youth group in Nazareth peacefully resisting Israeli attempts to remove all traces of when the land was Palestinian. Subtitled in English. 97m; VHS. **A:** Adult. **P:** Education. **U:** Institution, BCTV. **L:** Arabic, Hebrew. **Gen-Edu**: Documentary Films, Middle East. **Acq:** Purchase, Rent/Lease. **Dist:** Arab Film Distribution. $195.00.

Al-Tasmim 1995
Documents the Edmonton Muslim community's efforts to relocate and restore the Al-Rashid Mosque, the first mosque to be built in Canada. The 50th anniversary of the mosque marked the year that it was slated for demolition. Features interviews with individuals who were involved with the project, its history and its role in the community. 21m; VHS. **A:** Sr. High-Adult. **P:** Entertainment. **U:** Home, Institution. **Gen-Edu**: Canada, Islam. **Acq:** Purchase. **Dist:** Moving Images Distribution.

Alabama Departure 1980
This visual poem evokes a sense of the South through recurring images of land, water, and an old man who speaks of his attitude towards life. 9m; VHS, 3/4 U. **Pr:** Center for Southern Folklore. **A:** Sr. High-Adult. **P:** Education. **U:** Institution, Home, SURA. **Gen-Edu**: U.S. States. **Acq:** Purchase. **Dist:** Center for Southern Folklore.

Alabama: Greatest Hits Video 1986
The famed country group performs nine of their hits. 37m; VHS. **Pr:** RCA Video Productions. **A:** Family. **P:** Entertainment. **U:** Home. **Mov-Ent**: Music Video, Music--Country/Western. **Acq:** Purchase. **Dist:** Music Video Distributors; Sony Pictures Home Entertainment Inc.; Lightyear Entertainment. $14.95.

Alabama: Pass It on Down 1990
The country group goes to the studio to record "Pass It On" and five other songs. 32m; VHS. **A:** Preschool-Jr. High. **P:** Entertainment. **U:** Home. **Mov-Ent**: Music Video. **Acq:** Purchase. **Dist:** Music Video Distributors; BMG Entertainment. $9.98.

Alabama's Ghost 1972 (PG) — ★1/2
Musician steals a dead master magician's secrets, incurring the wrath of the paranormal underworld. Far from the best of the "blaxploitation" films of the '70s. 96m; VHS. **C:** Christopher Brooks; E. Kerrigan Prescott; Directed by Fredric Hobbs. **Pr:** Vistar Int'l Productions. **A:** Jr. High-Adult. **P:** Entertainment. **U:** Home. **Mov-Ent**: Horror, Magic, Occult Sciences. **Acq:** Purchase. **Dist:** Lions Gate Television Corp. $29.95.

Aladdin 1980
A children's version of Aladdin's suspenseful and humorous encounters with a wicked magician, the mysterious lamp, and a beautiful princess. 19m; VHS, 3/4 U. **A:** Primary. **P:** Education. **U:** Institution, SURA. **Chl-Juv**: Language Arts. **Acq:** Purchase. **Dist:** Home Vision Cinema.

Aladdin 1986 (PG) — ★
A comedic Italian modernization of the Aladdin fable. 97m; VHS, DVD, CC. **C:** Bud Spencer; Luca Venantini; Janet Agren; Julian Voloshin; Umberto Raho; Directed by Bruno Corbucci. **Pr:** Golan-Globus Productions. **A:** Jr. High-Adult. **P:** Entertainment. **U:** Home. **Mov-Ent**: Fantasy, Fairy Tales. **Acq:** Purchase. **Dist:** Movies Unlimited. $13.49.

Aladdin 1992 (G) — ★★★1/2
Boy meets princess, loses her, finds her, wins her from evil vizier and nasty parrot, while being aided by big blue genie. Superb animation triumphs over average songs and storyline by capitalizing on Williams' talent for ad-lib with lightning speed genie changes, lots of celebrity spoofs, and even a few pokes at Disney itself. Adults will enjoy the 1,001 impersonations while kids will get a kick out of the big blue genie and the songs, three of which are the late Ashman's legacy. Kane and Salonga are responsible for the singing voices of Aladdin and Jasmine; Gottfried is a riot as the obnoxious parrot sidekick. Be forewarned: small children may be frightened by some of the scarier sequences. 90m; VHS, DVD, CC. **C:** Voice(s) by Robin Williams; Scott Weinger; Linda Larkin; Jonathan Freeman; Frank Welker; Gilbert Gottfried; Douglas Seale; Brad Caleb Kane; Lea Salonga; Directed by Ron Clements; John Musker; Written by Ron Clements; John Musker; Ted Elliott; Terry Rossio; Music by Alan Menken; Lyrics by Howard Ashman; Tim Rice. **Pr:** John Musker; Ron Clements; Ron Clements; John Musker; Walt Disney Pictures. **A:** Family. **P:** Entertainment. **U:** Home. **Mov-Ent**: Animation & Cartoons, Family Viewing, Fairy Tales. **Awds:** Oscars '92: Orig. Score, Song ("A Whole New World"); Golden Globes '93: Score, Song ("A Whole New World"); MTV Movie Awards '93: Comedic Perf. (Williams). **Acq:** Purchase. **Dist:** Baker and Taylor; Walt Disney Studios Home Entertainment. $24.99.
Songs: A Whole New World; Prince Ali; Friend Like Me; One Jump Ahead; Arabian Nights.

Aladdin and His Magic Lamp 1969
Jean Image brings this classic tale of greed to life via animation. 72m; VHS. **C:** Directed by Jean Image. **A:** Family. **P:** Entertainment. **U:** Home. **Chl-Juv**: Animation & Cartoons, Magic. **Acq:** Purchase. **Dist:** Rhino Entertainment Co. $59.95.

Aladdin and His Magic Lamp 1976
Aladdin visits the palace of Scheherezade and falls in love with its beautiful princess. Animated. 72m; VHS. **Pr:** Children's Treasures. **A:** Family. **P:** Entertainment. **U:** Home. **Chl-Juv**: Children, Animation & Cartoons, Fairy Tales. **Acq:** Purchase. **Dist:** Lions Gate Television Corp. $59.98.

Aladdin and His Magic Lamp 1976
Aladdin is a young boy who owns a magic lamp. Unfortunately, he must contend with the merchant who will stop at nothing to gain control of the lamp. 90m; VHS. **Pr:** Majestic International Pictures. **A:** Family. **P:** Entertainment. **U:** Home. **Chl-Juv**: Fairy Tales. **Acq:** Purchase. **Dist:** VCI Entertainment. $39.95.

Aladdin and His Wonderful Lamp 1977
This tale, from the Arabian Nights, is the story of a lazy boy who whiles away his days in the market place. Through a series of adventures, learns that it is better to be self-reliant and work to earn things. 9m; VHS, 3/4 U. **Pr:** Greatest Tales, Inc. **A:** Primary. **P:** Entertainment. **U:** Institution, SURA. **Chl-Juv**: Fairy Tales. **Acq:** Purchase. **Dist:** Phoenix Learning Group.

Aladdin and His Wonderful Lamp 1984 — ★★1/2
The story of Aladdin, a young man who finds a magical oil lamp when he is trapped in a tiny cave. From the "Faerie Tale Theatre" series and director of "Beetlejuice" and "Batman" Tim Burton. 60m; VHS, DVD, CC. **C:** Valerie Bertinelli; Robert Carradine; Leonard Nimoy; James Earl Jones; Directed by Tim Burton. **Pr:** Platypus Productions; Lions Gate Films. **A:** Family. **P:** Entertainment. **U:** Home. **Mov-Ent**: Fantasy, Fairy Tales, Children. **Acq:** Purchase. **Dist:** Knowledge Unlimited, Inc.; Facets Multimedia Inc. $14.98.

Aladdin & Jasmine's Moonlight Magic 19??
Contains two animated tales featuring the characters from the animated classic Aladdin. In the first, "Moonlight Madness," Aladdin enchants Jasmine with the promise of a romantic date and then bows out as he hears of an enchanted treasure which will disappear that same night. In the second, "Some Enchanted Genie," Genie falls in love with Eden, another genie. 45m; VHS. **Pr:** Walt Disney Productions. **A:** Family. **P:** Entertainment. **U:** Home. **Chl-Juv**: Animation & Cartoons, Family Viewing. **Acq:** Purchase. **Dist:** Walt Disney Studios Home Entertainment. $12.99.

Aladdin and the Adventure of All Time 1999 (G)
Aladdin and his new friend Paige take a magic carpet ride in order to retrieve a stolen magic lamp. Along the way they meet kings, queens, dinosaurs, and pirates. 81m; VHS, DVD. **C:** Voice(s) by Elizabeth Daily; Directed by Cirio H. Santiago. **A:** Family. **P:** Entertainment. **U:** Home. **Chl-Juv**: Animation & Cartoons. **Acq:** Purchase. **Dist:** Buena Vista Home Entertainment.

Aladdin and the King of Thieves 1996 — ★★
Second-direct-to-video saga (following "The Return of Jafar") once again features Williams as the voice of the genie (after settling a dispute with Disney). On the eve of Aladdin's marriage to Jasmine, theives try to steal a magic talisman, sending Aladdin on a mission to find the thieves—and his father. Disney had such terrific success with "Return" that it was inevitable they would try again. 82m; VHS, DVD, CC. **C:** Voice(s) by Robin Williams; Scott Weinger; Jerry Orbach; John Rhys-Davies; Gilbert Gottfried; Linda Larkin; CCH Pounder; Frank Welker; Directed by Ted Stones; Written by Mark McCorkle; Robert Schooley; Music by Mark Watters. **A:** Family. **P:** Entertainment. **U:** Home. **Mov-Ent**: Animation & Cartoons. **Acq:** Purchase. **Dist:** Walt Disney Studios Home Entertainment.

Aladdin and the Magic Lamp 1990
The genie and Aladdin set out to become way-cool dudes in this modern animated version. 25m; VHS. **A:** Preschool-Primary. **P:** Entertainment. **U:** Home. **Chl-Juv**: Animation & Cartoons, Fairy Tales. **Acq:** Purchase. **Dist:** Anchor Bay Entertainment. $9.99.

Alambrista! 1977 (Unrated) — ★★
Spare, affecting, unsentimental drama marks the directorial debut of Young. Mexican Roberto (Ambiz) becomes an illegal immigrant in California, doing backbreaking farm work to send money back to his destitute family. English and Spanish with subtitles. 110m; DVD, Blu-Ray. **C:** Domingo Ambiz; Trinidad Silva; Linda Gillin; Paul Berrones; Directed by Robert M. Young; Written by Robert M. Young; Cinematography by Robert M. Young; Tom Hurwitz; Music by Michael Martin Murphey. **A:** College-Adult. **P:** Entertainment. **U:** Home. **L:** English, Spanish. **Mov-Ent**: Illegal Immigration, Poverty. **Acq:** Purchase. **Dist:** Criterion Collection Inc.

The Alamo ????
Depicts the siege in San Antonio, 1836, using archival materials, eyewitness battle accounts, historian analysis, and brief reenactments. Appropriate for Grades 7 and up. 110m; VHS. **A:** Jr. High-Sr. High. **P:** Education. **U:** Institution, Home. **Gen-Edu**: History--U.S., U.S. States. **Acq:** Purchase. **Dist:** Zenger Media; Social Studies School Service. $29.95.

The Alamo 1960 — ★★★
Old-fashioned patriotic battle epic recounts the real events of the 1836 fight for independence in Texas. The usual band of diverse and contentious personalities, including Wayne as a coonskin-capped Davy Crockett, defend a small fort against a very big Mexican raiding party outside of San Antonio. Before meeting mythic death, they fight with each other, learn the meaning of life, and ultimately come to respect each other. Just to make it more entertaining, Avalon sings. Big-budget production features an impeccable musical score by Tiomkin and an impressive 7,000 extras for the Mexican army alone. Wayne reportedly received directorial assistance from John Ford, particularly during the big massacre finale. 161m; VHS, DVD, Wide, CC. **C:** John Wayne; Richard Widmark; Laurence Harvey; Frankie Avalon; Richard Boone; Carlos Arruza; Chill Wills; Veda Ann Borg; Linda Cristal; Patrick Wayne; Joan O'Brien; Joseph Calleia; Ken Curtis; Jester Hairston; Denver Pyle; John Dierkes; Guinn "Big Boy" Williams; Olive Carey; William Henry; Hank Worden; Ruben Padilla; Jack Pennick; Directed by John Wayne; Written by James Edward Grant; Cinematography by William Clothier; Music by Dimitri Tiomkin; Paul Francis Webster. **Pr:** John Wayne; John Edward Grant; John Wayne; United Artists. **A:** Family. **P:** Entertainment. **U:** Home. **L:** English, Spanish. **Mov-Ent**: Western, Drama, War--General. **Awds:** Oscars '60: Sound; Golden Globes '61: Score. **Acq:** Purchase. **Dist:** MGM Home Entertainment; Time-Life Video and Television. $19.98.

The Alamo 2004 (PG-13) — ★★1/2
Dry as a tumbleweed epic is the latest and not so greatest in a dozen odd big-screen tries of dubious success at depicting the historic Texas battle. Thornton stars as Davy Crockett along with Wilson, Patric, and Quaid as William Travis, Jim Bowie, and Sam Houston who, along with 189 others, form the "Texican" holdouts who, after nearly two weeks of anxious

waiting, battle the Mexican army of nearly 2,500 and their General, Santa Anna (Echevarria). Mostly tedious waiting, while the actual battle is surprisingly sterile. Thornton (if not his character) emerges unscathed with an excellent performance, especially in the winning rooftop fiddle serenade scene. Supporting work is more uneven. Big-budgeter looks great and is exacting in historical accuracy but ultimately lacks dramatic punch and a cohesive plot. 137m; DVD. **C:** Dennis Quaid; Billy Bob Thornton; Jason Patric; Patrick Wilson; Emilio Echeverria; Jordi Molla; Leon Rippy; Marc Blucas; Tom Davidson; Robert Prentiss; Ken Page; Joe Stevens; Steven Prince; Tom Everett; Brandon Smith; Rance Howard; Stephen Bruton; Emily Deschanel; Laura Clifton; Edward "Blue" Deckert; Directed by John Lee Hancock; Written by John Lee Hancock; Leslie Bohem; Stephen Gaghan; Cinematography by Dean Semler; John O'Connor; Music by Carter Burwell. **Pr:** Mark Johnson; Ron Howard; Imagine Entertainment; Touchstone Pictures; Buena Vista. **A:** Jr. High-Adult. **P:** Entertainment. **U:** Home. **L:** English. **Mov-Ent:** Drama, Mexico, Western. **Acq:** Purchase. **Dist:** Buena Vista Home Entertainment. $29.95.

Alamo Bay 1985 (Unrated) — ★★½
A slow-moving but sincere tale of contemporary racism. An angry Vietnam veteran and his red-neck buddies feel threatened by Vietnamese refugees who want to go into the fishing business. Set in Texas, filled with Texas-sized characters, and based on a true Texas story, as interpreted by the French Malle. 99m; VHS, Blu-Ray, Streaming, CC. **C:** Ed Harris; Ho Nguyen; Amy Madigan; Donald Moffat; Cynthia Carle; Truyen V. Tran; Rudy Young; Directed by Louis Malle; Written by Alice Arlen; Music by Ry Cooder. **Pr:** Tri-Star Pictures. **A:** Sr. High-Adult. **P:** Entertainment. **U:** Home. **Mov-Ent:** Fishing, Veterans. **Acq:** Purchase. **Dist:** Sony Pictures Home Entertainment Inc. $79.95.

The Alamo: Thirteen Days to Glory 1987 — ★★
The legendary Davy Crockett (Keith), Colonel William Travis (Baldwin), and Jim Bowie (Arness) overcome personal differences to unite against the Mexican Army, vowing to hold down the fort or die. It takes a true Texan to fully appreciate the merits of this rather pedestrian retelling of a familiar story, but the battle scenes are pretty heady (although they lose some of their froth on the small screen). If nothing else, the ever-versatile Julia is worth seeing as Santa Anna in this made-for-TV rendering of J. Lon Tinkle's "Thirteen Days to Glory." You may not want to remember the Alamo this way. 180m; VHS, Streaming, CC. **C:** James Arness; Lorne Greene; Alec Baldwin; Brian Keith; Raul Julia; Laura Elena Harring; Directed by Peter Werner; Music by Peter Bernstein. **A:** Family. **P:** Entertainment. **U:** Home. **Mov-Ent:** Drama, History--U.S., TV Movies. **Acq:** Purchase. **Dist:** Unknown Distributor.

Alamut Ambush 1986 (Unrated) — ★
A federal agent is stalked by assassins, and decides to hunt them in return. Sequel to "Cold War Killer." 94m; VHS, DVD. **C:** Terence Stamp; Michael Culver; Directed by Ken Grieve. **A:** Sr. High-Adult. **P:** Entertainment. **U:** Home. **Mov-Ent.** **Acq:** Purchase. **Dist:** Movies Unlimited. $13.49.

Alan & Naomi 1992 (PG) — ★★½
In 1944, 14-year-old Alan Silverman is more concerned with his Brooklyn stickball team than the war raging across Europe. This changes when his upstairs neighbor offers refuge to a French-Jewish mother and her young daughter and he is asked to befriend the girl. Naomi witnessed the brutal death of her father by the Nazis and retreated into a world of her own. Together the two build a sweet, if unlikely, friendship. Fine performances save this average coming of age tale. Based on the novel by Myron Levoy. 95m; VHS. **C:** Lukas Haas; Vanessa Zaoui; Michael Gross; Amy Aquino; Kevin Connolly; Zohra Lampert; Directed by Sterling Van Wagenen; Written by Jordan Horowitz; Music by Dick Hyman. **Pr:** Leucadia Film Corporation; Maltese Companies, Inc. **A:** Jr. High-Adult. **P:** Entertainment. **U:** Home. **Mov-Ent:** World War Two, Holocaust. **Acq:** Purchase. **Dist:** Sony Pictures Home Entertainment Inc. $89.95.

Alan Bean: Art Off This Planet 1991
Alan Bean, one of the Apollo astronauts who set foot on the moon, returned to earth with a yearning to paint and share the things he saw in space. He is now a celebrated painter, termed a modern day frontier artist, in the Frederic Remmington and Charles Russell vein. This video profiles his work and style. 26m; VHS. **C:** Directed by Murray Battle. **A:** Family. **P:** Education. **U:** Institution, Home. **Gen-Edu:** Art & Artists. **Acq:** Purchase. **Dist:** The Cinema Guild. $250.00.

Alan Holdsworth 19??
Holdworth demonstrates the fusion guitar technique. 60m; VHS. **A:** Jr. High-Adult. **P:** Instruction. **U:** Home. **How-Ins:** How-To, Music--Instruction. **Acq:** Purchase. **Dist:** Music Video Distributors. $49.95.

Alan Holdsworth 199?
Features Alan Holdsworth and his band performing live in the studio, with forcus on Holdsworth's improvisation technique. Music and tab booklet included. 75m; DVD. **A:** Jr. High-Adult. **P:** Instruction. **U:** Home. **How-Ins:** Music--Instruction. **Acq:** Purchase. **Dist:** Warner Home Video, Inc. $49.95.

Alan Holdsworth: Tokyo Dream 198? (Unrated)
This extraordinary guitarist performs live "Road Games," "White Line," "Material Real," "Metal Fatigue" and more. 83m; VHS. **A:** Jr. High-College. **P:** Entertainment. **U:** Home. **Mov-Ent:** Music--Performance. **Acq:** Purchase. **Dist:** Music Video Distributors. $139.95.

Alan in Action 1980
In this first episode of "The Backstreet Six," Alan must pass a series of tests (such as recovering a trophy stolen by a rival gang) to join the Backstreet gang. 26m; VHS, 3/4 U. **Pr:** Les Productions Prisma. **A:** Primary-Jr. High. **P:** Entertainment. **U:** Institution, SURA. **Chl-Juv.** **Acq:** Purchase. **Dist:** Phoenix Learning Group.

Alan Jackson: Here in the Reel World 1990
The popular country singer is seen in clips including "Wanted," "Blue Blooded Woman," "Chasin' That Neon Rainbow," "Here in the Reel World" and two live cuts. 25m; VHS. **A:** Sr. High-Adult. **P:** Entertainment. **U:** Home. **Mov-Ent:** Music--Country/Western. **Acq:** Purchase. **Dist:** Music Video Distributors. $9.95.

Alan Jackson: Livin', Lovin' and Rockin' That Jukebox 1993
Videos from country star Jackson's platinum album "A Lot About Livin' (And A Little 'Bout Love)." Includes behind-the-scenes tour footage. 28m; VHS. **A:** Sr. High-Adult. **P:** Entertainment. **U:** Home. **Mov-Ent:** Music--Country/Western, Music Video. **Acq:** Purchase. **Dist:** Music Video Distributors. $14.98.
Songs: She's Got the Rhythm (And I Got the Blues); Chattahoochee; Mercury Blues; Don't Roc the Jukebox; Midnight in Montgomery.

Alan Munde Banjo Workshop, Vol. 1 19??
Alan Munde teaches his banjo secrets to the intermediate to advanced banjo player. ?m; VHS. **C:** Alan Munde. **A:** Jr. High-Adult. **P:** Entertainment. **U:** Home. **How-Ins:** Music--Instruction. **Acq:** Purchase. **Dist:** Music Video Distributors; Texas Music and Video. $39.95.

Alan Munde's Basic Bluegrass Banjo 19??
Teaches easy chord forms for the banjo beginner. ?m; VHS. **C:** Alan Munde. **A:** Jr. High-Adult. **P:** Entertainment. **U:** Home. **How-Ins:** Music--Instruction. **Acq:** Purchase. **Dist:** Music Video Distributors; Texas Music and Video. $29.95.

Alan Munde's Bluegrass Banjo Favorites 19??
Alan Munde teaches the banjo player everything they need to know to play in a bluegrass band. ?m; VHS. **C:** Alan Munde. **A:** Jr. High-Adult. **P:** Entertainment. **U:** Home. **How-Ins:** Music--Instruction. **Acq:** Purchase. **Dist:** Music Video Distributors; Texas Music and Video. $29.95.

Alan Munde's Bluegrass Banjo Models 19??
Alan Munde teaches the beginning to intermediate banjo player everything they need to know to play in a bluegrass band. ?m; VHS. **C:** Alan Munde. **A:** Jr. High-Adult. **P:** Entertainment. **U:** Home. **How-Ins:** Music--Instruction. **Acq:** Purchase. **Dist:** Music Video Distributors; Texas Music and Video. $29.95.

Alan Munde's Easy Gospel Guitar 19??
Alan Munde teaches the beginning to intermediate guitarist to play some timeless gospel favorites. ?m; VHS. **C:** Alan Munde. **A:** Jr. High-Adult. **P:** Entertainment. **U:** Home. **How-Ins:** Music--Instruction. **Acq:** Purchase. **Dist:** Music Video Distributors; Texas Music and Video. $29.95.

Alan Partridge 2013 (R) — ★★★
If you know who comedian Steve Coogan is, you've got Alan Partridge to thank for it. Partridge, Coogan's self-obsessed talk-show-host character--Britain's Ron Burgundy--made the comedian a UK fixture in the 1990s, inspiring various radio series, TV shows, and an autobiography. But this is Partridge's first movie and it succeeds largely thanks to an incredibly clever script by Coogan and Iannucci. Partridge is now a local DJ swept up in the media circus when disgruntled ex-co-worker Pat (Meaney) takes his radio station hostage. It's all very droll, very witty, and very, very English. (Titled "Alan Partridge: Alpha Papa" in the UK.) 90m; Blu-Ray, On Demand. **C:** Steve Coogan; Colm Meaney; Felicity Montagu; Nigel Lindsay; Simon Greenall; Monica Dolan; Directed by Declan Lowney; Written by Steve Coogan; Neil Gibbons; Armando Iannucci; Cinematography by Ben Smithard; Music by Ilan Eshkeri. **Pr:** Magnolia Pictures. **A:** Sr. High-Adult. **P:** Entertainment. **U:** Home. **L:** English. **Mov-Ent:** Great Britain, Mass Media. **Acq:** Purchase. **Dist:** Amazon.com Inc.

An Alan Smithee Film: Burn, Hollywood, Burn 1997 (R) — ★½
Follows a British director (Idle), whose given name is Alan Smithee, as he kidnaps the reels of his own picture when he realizes he hates the movie but can't remove his name from it since the Directors Guild of America's official pseudonym for disputed films is "Alan Smithee." O'Neal stars as the boorish producer who drives Smithee to the desperate act. This extended in-joke ran into its own problem when director Arthur Hiller, in what seemed like a publicity stunt, repudiated the version producer/writer Eszterhas recut and had his own name removed from the film, thus making "An Alan Smithee Film" one of the more than 30 Alan Smithee films in as many years. The tedious mockumentary style is relentless in narrating the story to the audience, who is never allowed to just watch what happens. Only interest is the parade of star cameos, including Stallone, Goldberg, and Chan (as themselves), along with writer Eszterhas in a scene with the director who declined credit for the film, Hiller. 86m; VHS, DVD, CC. **C:** Eric Idle; Ryan O'Neal; Coolio; Richard Jeni; Sandra Bernhard; Cherie Lunghi; Harvey Weinstein; M.C. Lyte; Stephen Tobolowsky; Chuck D; Leslie Stefanson; Gavin Polone; Marcello Thedford; Nicole Nagel; Dina Spybey; Cameo(s) Joe Eszterhas; Sylvester Stallone; Whoopi Goldberg; Jackie Chan; Larry King; Billy Bob Thornton; Dominick Dunne; Robert Evans; Shane Black; Directed by Arthur Hiller; Written by Joe Eszterhas; Cinematography by Reynaldo Villalobos; Music by Gary G-Wiz. **Pr:** Joe Eszterhas; Joe Eszterhas; Cinergi Productions; Hollywood Pictures. **A:** Sr. High-Adult. **P:** Entertainment. **U:** Home. **Mov-Ent:** Satire & Parody, Filmmaking. **Awds:** Golden Raspberries '98: Worst New Star (Eszterhas), Worst Picture, Worst Screenplay, Worst Song ("I Wanna Be Mike Ovitz!"), Worst Support. Actor (Eszterhas). **Acq:** Purchase. **Dist:** Buena Vista Home Entertainment.

Alan Stein: In-Season Conditioning—The Best Teams are in the Best Shape! 2010 (Unrated)
Coach Alan Stein presents drills and exercises to improve your basketball team's agility and reaction time. 69m; DVD. **A:** Family. **P:** Education. **U:** Home, Institution. **Spo-Rec:** Basketball, Athletic Instruction/Coaching, Fitness/Exercise. **Acq:** Purchase. **Dist:** Championship Productions. $39.99.

Alan Stein: In-Season Training for Basketball Players 2007 (Unrated)
Coach Alan Stein presents exercises designed for basketball players to incorporate into their practices during the season. 72m; DVD. **A:** Family. **P:** Education. **U:** Home, Institution. **Spo-Rec:** Basketball, Fitness/Exercise. **Acq:** Purchase. **Dist:** Championship Productions. $39.99.

Alan Stein: Off-Season Training for Basketball 2006
Provides basketball players with conditioning, strength, and skill development techniques for the off-season by training expert Alan Stein. 75m; DVD. **A:** Sr. High-Adult. **P:** Instruction. **U:** Institution. **Spo-Rec:** Basketball. **Acq:** Purchase. **Dist:** Championship Productions. $39.95.

Alan Stein's Active Warm-Up and Core Training for Basketball Players 2008 (Unrated)
Coach Allan Stein demonstrates a warm-up and core training program developed for basketball players. 71m; DVD. **A:** Family. **P:** Education. **U:** Home, Institution. **Spo-Rec:** Basketball, Fitness/Exercise. **Acq:** Purchase. **Dist:** Championship Productions. $29.99.

Alan Stein's DeMatha Basketball: Agility & Conditioning 2011 (Unrated)
Coach Alan Stein presents drills for coaches of high school basketball whose teams need to increase their conditioning and reaction times. 63m; DVD. **A:** Family. **P:** Education. **U:** Home, Institution. **Spo-Rec:** Basketball, Athletic Instruction/Coaching. **Acq:** Purchase. **Dist:** Championship Productions. $39.99.

Alan Stein's DeMatha Basketball: Warm-Up & Flexibility 2011 (Unrated)
Coach Alan Stein demonstrates warm-up and flexibility exercises for high school basketball players needing to improve their range of motion. 67m; DVD. **A:** Family. **P:** Education. **U:** Home, Institution. **Spo-Rec:** Basketball, Athletic Instruction/Coaching. **Acq:** Purchase. **Dist:** Championship Productions. $39.99.

Alan Stein's Explosive Conditioning for Basketball Players 2006 (Unrated)
Coach Alan Stein presents a workout for basketball players designed to keep them in playing condition when they aren't in season. 30m; DVD. **A:** Family. **P:** Education. **U:** Home, Institution. **Spo-Rec:** Basketball, Fitness/Exercise. **Acq:** Purchase. **Dist:** Championship Productions. $29.99.

Alan Stein's Strength & Power Training for Basketball Players 2006 (Unrated)
Coach Alan Stein shares his workout program designed to increase a basketball team's players strength and physical fitness. 29m; DVD. **A:** Family. **P:** Education. **U:** Home, Institution. **Spo-Rec:** Basketball, Fitness/Exercise. **Acq:** Purchase. **Dist:** Championship Productions. $29.99.

Alan T.D. Wiggins & Band in Concert 1991
Filmed live at the Aaron Davis Hall in New York City. Songs include "Heaven," "Living for You," "I Shall Wear a Crown," and more. 60m; VHS. **A:** Jr. High-Adult. **P:** Entertainment. **U:** Home. **Mov-Ent:** Music Video, Religion. **Acq:** Purchase. **Dist:** Xenon Pictures; Music Video Distributors. $29.95.

Alan Watts Series 1971
Alan Watts shares his insights on life and living, gleaned from years of studying Eastern philosophies and religions. 30m; VHS, 3/4 U, Special order formats. **C:** Hosted by Alan Watts. **Pr:** Hartley Productions; Wishing Well. **A:** Jr. High-Adult. **P:** Education. **U:** Institution, CCTV, Home. **Gen-Edu:** Documentary Films, Buddhism, Yoga. **Acq:** Purchase. **Dist:** Hartley Film Foundation. $39.95.
Indiv. Titles: 1. The Art of Meditation 2. In the Flow Series 3. Zen Series 4. Clothing 5. Cosmic Drama 6. Death 7. Do You Smell? 8. Ego 9. God 10. Man in Nature 11. Meditation 12. The More It Changes 13. Nothingness 14. Time 15. Work as Play.

Alanis Morissette: Live at Montreux 2012 2013 (Unrated)
Live concert by Alanis Morissette recorded on her Guardian Angel Tour at Montreux. 98m; DVD, Blu-Ray. **A:** Primary-Adult. **P:** Entertainment. **U:** Home. **L:** English. **Mov-Ent:** Music--Performance, Music--Pop/Rock. **Acq:** Purchase. **Dist:** Eagle Rock Entertainment Inc. $19.98 14.98.

Alannah Myles 1990
The Canadian songstress performs her hit, "Black Velvet" plus "Lover of Mine," "Still Got This Thing" and "Love Is." 18m; VHS. **C:** Alannah Myles. **Pr:** Elektra Entertainment. **A:** Jr. High-Adult. **P:** Entertainment. **U:** Home. **Mov-Ent:** Music Video. **Acq:** Purchase. **Dist:** WarnerVision; Fast Forward; Music Video Distributors. $14.98.

Alarm 2008 (Unrated) — ★½
Irish psycho-thriller. Molly leaves Dublin a year after her father's death, the result of their being terrorized during a home invasion. She hopes for some peace and quiet in her country estate house but only experiences isolation. When her home is repeatedly broken into, Molly begins to have paranoid suspicions about everyone from her old friends to a new lover. 104m; DVD. **C:** Alan Howley; Tom Hickey; Ruth Bradley; Aidan Turner; Anita Reeves; Owen Roe; Directed by Gerard Stembridge; Written by Gerard Stembridge; Cinematography by Bruno de

Keyzer. **A:** Sr. High-Adult. **P:** Entertainment. **U:** Home. **Mov-Ent**: Mystery & Suspense. **Acq:** Purchase. **Dist:** MPI Media Group.

The Alarm: Blaze of Glory—Greatest Hits Live in Concert 1992
The last live concert of the Welsh rock group ended with singer Mike Peters announcing he was leaving the band. Featuring such favorites as "Sixty-Eight Guns," "Sold Me Down the River," and "Rescue Me." 70m; VHS. **A:** Sr. High-Adult. **P:** Entertainment. **U:** Home. **Mov-Ent:** Music Video, Music--Pop/Rock. **Acq:** Purchase. **Dist:** Anchor Bay Entertainment; Music Video Distributors. $14.98.

Alarm Clock 1982
The program shows some of the steps that took place in the evolution of telling time. It also illustrates problems that had to be overcome to perfect the device. Part of the "Inventive Child" series. 10m; VHS, 3/4 U. **Pr:** Film Polski. **A:** Primary-Jr. High. **P:** Education. **U:** Institution, SURA. **Chl-Juv**: Inventors & Inventions. **Acq:** Purchase, Rent/Lease, Trade-in. **Dist:** Encyclopedia Britannica.

Alarm: Spirit of '86 1986
A performance by the Welsh rock band at UCLA, featuring "Strength," "68 Guns," "Absolute Reality," "Spirit of '76," "Knocking on Heaven's Door," "Walk Forever By My Side" and seven more. 90m; VHS. **Pr:** Jay Boberg; Ian Wilson; International Record Syndicate Video Inc. **A:** Jr. High-Adult. **P:** Entertainment. **U:** Home. **Mov-Ent:** Music--Performance, Music--Pop/Rock. **Acq:** Purchase. **Dist:** Music Video Distributors. $19.95.

Alarm: Standards 198?
Early and recent material are combined in this video compilation. Song include "The Stand," "Where Were You Hiding When the Storm Broke," "Sold Me Down The River," "Love Don't Come Easy," "A New South Wales" and more. 60m; VHS. **A:** Jr. High-College. **P:** Entertainment. **U:** Home. **Mov-Ent:** Music Video. **Acq:** Purchase. **Dist:** Music Video Distributors. $19.98.

The Alarmist 1998 (Unrated) — ★★
Tommy Hudler (Arquette) is the eager beaver new employee at the L.A. home-security company owned by slick super-salesman Heinrich Grigoris (Tucci). But Tommy's soon shocked to learn that Heinrich makes certain clients continue to need his services by breaking into their homes. Tommy makes his first sale to fortysomething widow Gale (Capshaw), who enjoys seducing the boyish innocent, and the two embark on a torrid affair. Then Gale and her teenaged son are murdered after a home break-in and Tommy suspects Heinrich went a little too far. Arquette's amusingly geeky but Tucci steals the film as his sleazy boss. 93m; VHS, DVD. **C:** Stanley Tucci; David Arquette; Kate Capshaw; Ryan Reynolds; Mary McCormack; Tricia Vessey; Directed by Evan Dunsky; Written by Evan Dunsky; Cinematography by Alex Nepomniaschy; Music by Christophe Beck. **Pr:** Avalanche Releasing. **A:** Sr. High-Adult. **P:** Entertainment. **U:** Home. **Mov-Ent:** Comedy--Black. **Acq:** Purchase. **Dist:** Sony Pictures Home Entertainment Inc.

Alaska! 1967
The rugged people, treacherous trails, and giant glaciers of Alaska are the subject of this program. 52m; 3/4 U, Special order formats. **Pr:** National Geographic Society. **A:** Jr. High-Adult. **P:** Education. **U:** Institution, Home, SURA. **Gen-Edu:** U.S. States. **Acq:** Purchase, Trade-in, Duplication License. **Dist:** National Geographic Society.

Alaska 1988
Picturesque presentation of Alaska's past and present, using color footage and black and white still photography. Covers the state's industry, recreation, climate, geography, and history. 28m; VHS. **Pr:** Rainbow. **A:** Primary-Jr. High. **P:** Education. **U:** Institution. **Gen-Edu:** History--U.S., Arctic Regions, U.S. States. **Acq:** Purchase. **Dist:** Clear Vue Inc. $89.00.

Alaska 1989
The history of Alaska, from the time that the first Native Americans migrated there to the present day. 75m; VHS, 3/4 U. **Pr:** Alaska State Department of Education. **A:** Primary-Adult. **P:** Education. **U:** Institution, CCTV, CATV, BCTV. **Gen-Edu:** U.S. States, History--U.S. **Acq:** Purchase, Rent/Lease, Duplication License. **Dist:** Agency for Instructional Technology. $495.00.
Indiv. Titles: 1. The Mists of Time 2. Age of Discovery 3. Folly or Fortune 4. Mary Nell: Adventures of a Pioneer 5. The Silver Years.

Alaska 1996 (PG) — ★★½
Fourteen-year-old Vincent Barnes (Kartheiser) and his 12-year-old sister Jessie (Birch) try to rescue their bush pilot father Jake (Benedict) whose plane has crashed in the wilderness. They also rescue an orphaned polar bear cub from an evil poacher (Heston) that manages to help them out along the way. See this flick if only to enjoy the lush backdrop of Alaska and British Columbia and, of course, the absolutely adorable polar cub. Director Fraser C. Heston directs dad Charlton, appropriate payback for landing him the role as the infant Moses in "The Ten Commandments." 109m; VHS, DVD, CC. **C:** Thora Birch; Vincent Kartheiser; Dirk Benedict; Charlton Heston; Directed by Fraser Heston; Written by Andy Burg; Carol Fuchs; Cinematography by Tony Westman. **Pr:** Andy Burg; Carol Fuchs; Castle Rock Entertainment; Columbia Pictures. **A:** Family. **P:** Entertainment. **U:** Home. **Mov-Ent:** Action-Adventure, Family Viewing, Wilderness Areas. **Acq:** Purchase. **Dist:** Sony Pictures Home Entertainment Inc.

Alaska: An Hour Video Tour of the Inside Passage 1995
Features the Inside Passage of Southeast Alaska including Juneau and Glacier Bay, plus a variety of wildlife. 60m; VHS. **A:** Primary-Adult. **P:** Entertainment. **U:** Home. **Gen-Edu:** Wildlife, Arctic Regions, Travel. **Acq:** Purchase. **Dist:** Paragon Home Video. $19.95.

Alaska and Hawaii 1983
Involves a trip to the northernmost, westernmost, and southernmost points of the United States. Part of a 10 part series. 26m; VHS, 3/4 U. **A:** Primary-Jr. High. **P:** Education. **U:** Institution. **Gen-Edu:** Geography. **Acq:** Purchase. **Dist:** National Geographic Society. $79.00.

Alaska Centennial 1967
Presents the history of the development of Alaska, its statehood, and its role in assisting the U.S. in defense, resources, and manpower for peace. 29m; VHS, 3/4 U, Special order formats. **Pr:** Department of the Army. **A:** Sr. High-Adult. **P:** Education. **U:** Institution, CCTV, CATV, BCTV, Home. **Gen-Edu:** U.S. States. **Acq:** Purchase. **Dist:** National Audiovisual Center.

Alaska Classic Series 19??
Three-part series which showcases Alaska's natural wonders and history. Includes visits to wilderness areas and the natural habitats of some of Alaska's wildlife. 79m; VHS. **TV Std:** NTSC, PAL. **A:** Family. **P:** Education. **U:** Home. **Gen-Edu:** U.S. States, Wilderness Areas, Wildlife. **Acq:** Purchase. **Dist:** Alaska Video Postcards Inc. $9.95.
Indiv. Titles: 1. Glacier Bay National Park 2. Denali Wilderness 3. Voices from the Ice.

Alaska: Crude Awakening 1990
This special CBS "48 Hours" program takes a look at the Alaskan wildlife nearly destroyed by the 1989 Exxon Valdez oil spill in Prince William Sound. 47m; VHS. **Pr:** Films for the Humanities. **A:** Sr. High-Adult. **P:** Education. **U:** Institution. **Gen-Edu:** Documentary Films, Oil Industry, Ecology & Environment. **Acq:** Purchase. **Dist:** Films for the Humanities & Sciences. $179.00.

Alaska: Denali National Park 1993
Tour the majestic Denali wilderness along with the caribou, wolves, moose, and grizzly bears. See real life struggles of the inhabitants of this harsh land. 30m; VHS. **A:** Jr. High-Adult. **P:** Education. **U:** Home. **Gen-Edu:** Travel, National Parks & Reserves. **Acq:** Purchase. **Dist:** Finley Holiday Film Corp. $24.95.

The Alaska Earthquake, 1964 1990
A look at the devastation caused by the earthquake in 1964, including an explanation of the causes and the location of the principle fault zones. 20m; VHS. **Pr:** Crystal Productions. **A:** Jr. High-Sr. High. **P:** Education. **U:** Institution. **Hea-Sci:** Geology, Earthquakes, U.S. States. **Acq:** Purchase. **Dist:** Crystal Productions. $39.95.

The Alaska Experience 1991
This three cassette series explores the history, culture, wildlife and geography of Alaska with historic footage and colorful anecdotes. 180m; VHS. **Pr:** Fusion Video. **A:** Sr. High-Adult. **P:** Education. **U:** Home. **Gen-Edu:** Travel, Wildlife, History. **Acq:** Purchase. **Dist:** PBS Home Video; Fusion Video. $59.95.
Indiv. Titles: 1. Wild Alaska 2. Touring Alaska 3. Cruising Alaska's Inside Passage.

Alaska for Salmon and Halibut 19??
Gorgeous backdrop for snaring salmon and halibut as Dr. Jim Wright cruises North to Alaska to investigate the annual salmon run. Includes cooking section and bonus whale footage. ?m; VHS. **A:** Adult. **P:** Instruction. **U:** Home. **Spo-Rec:** Fishing. **Acq:** Purchase. **Dist:** Bennett Marine Video. $19.95.

Alaska Grizzlies 19??
Breathtaking adventure into the habitat of the grizzly bear of Alaska, illustrating how they survive and live their daily lives. Includes footage of cubs discovering their environment, a mother bear defending her cubs from attack, bears hunting and fishing for food, and a face-to-face encounter with an adult Kodiak brown bear. 60m; VHS. **TV Std:** NTSC, PAL. **A:** Family. **P:** Education. **U:** Home. **Gen-Edu:** Wilderness Areas, Wildlife. **Acq:** Purchase. **Dist:** Alaska Video Postcards Inc. $19.95.

The Alaska Highway 19??
Traces the construction and history of the Alcan with archival footage and photos as well as through a present trip along the highway, 50 years after its completion. 58m; VHS. **C:** Narrated by Hoyt Axton. **A:** Family. **P:** Entertainment. **U:** Home. **Gen-Edu:** U.S. States, Construction, Travel. **Acq:** Purchase. **Dist:** AnimEigo Inc. $29.95.

Alaska King Crab Cowboys 199?
Covers the hardships and rewards of one of the most dangerous occupations in the world—crab fishing. Climb aboard a fishing boat and witness the grueling work and harrowing conditions of the crab fisher; filmed entirely on location. 23m; VHS. **A:** Jr. High. **P:** Education. **U:** Home. **Gen-Edu:** Fishing, Documentary Films. **Acq:** Purchase. **Dist:** John Sabella & Associate. $19.95.

Alaska: Mystic Ice 1991
Travel program explores the largest, most remote state in the United States. The stunning natural beauty is supplemented by a dramatic musical score. Non-narrated. 40m; VHS. **C:** Directed by Gray Warriner. **A:** Adult. **P:** Entertainment. **U:** Home. **Gen-Edu:** Travel, U.S. States, Arctic Regions. **Acq:** Purchase. **Dist:** Camera One Productions. $30.00.

The Alaska Railroad 1980
The AuRoRa Streamliner is featured traveling amidst the natural beauty of Alaska. 90m; VHS. **Pr:** Pentrex Media Group L.L.C. **A:** Jr. High-Adult. **P:** Education. **U:** Home. **Gen-Edu:** Trains. **Acq:** Purchase. **Dist:** Pentrex Media Group L.L.C.; ESPN Inc. $59.95.

Alaska: Spirit of the Wild 1996
Narrated by Charlton Heston, this documentary explores the raw wilderness of Alaska from the Aurora Borealis to the power of a caribou stampede. 40m; DVD, Blu-Ray, CC. **A:** Family. **P:** Education. **U:** Home. **Gen-Edu:** U.S. States, Wilderness Areas, Animals. **Acq:** Purchase. **Dist:** Razor Digital.

Alaska: State of Extremes 1981
The history, natural beauty, and current social conditions of Alaska are explored. 16m; VHS, 3/4 U. **Pr:** Wolfgang Bayer. **A:** Jr. High-College. **P:** Education. **U:** Institution, SURA. **Gen-Edu:** U.S. States. **Acq:** Purchase. **Dist:** Phoenix Learning Group.

Alaska State Troopers: Season 1 2009
Follows the law enforcement agents who patrol the rugged terrain of Alaska through the wilderness and into remote villages. 5 episodes: "Ice Patrol," "Crime On the Kenai," "The Wild West," "Frontier Force," "Drug Bust." 225m; DVD. **A:** Jr. High-Adult. **P:** Entertainment. **U:** Home. **Gen-Edu:** Television Series, U.S. States. **Acq:** Purchase. **Dist:** National Geographic. $27.95.

Alaska State Troopers: Season 2 2010
Episodes offer a day-in-the-life look at the job as troopers response by land, sea, and air. 12 episodes, including "Spring Break Madness," "Manhunt," "Shots Fired," "Operation Moose Decoy," and "Anchorage Ubdercover." 585m; DVD. **A:** Jr. High-Adult. **P:** Entertainment. **U:** Home. **Gen-Edu:** Television Series, U.S. States. **Acq:** Purchase. **Dist:** National Geographic. $29.95.

Alaska State Troopers: Season 3 2011
Looks at more of what the approximately 400 troopers in Alaska deal with. 12 episdes, including "Beers & Bears," "Grizzly Showdown," "Spring Break Crazy," and "Cowboy Fugitive." 585m; DVD. **A:** Jr. High-Adult. **P:** Entertainment. **U:** Home. **Gen-Edu:** Television Series, U.S. States. **Acq:** Purchase. **Dist:** National Geographic. $29.95.

Alaska State Troopers: Season 4 2012
Crime investigations follow drug trafficking, accidents, natural disasters, and animal mayhem. 12 episodes, including "Alaska Chainsaw Massacre," "Grizzly-pendence Day," "Meth Dealer Manhunt," Total Inferno, and "Chopper Down." 585m; DVD. **A:** Jr. High-Adult. **P:** Entertainment. **U:** Home. **Gen-Edu:** Television Series, U.S. States. **Acq:** Purchase. **Dist:** National Geographic. $29.95.

Alaska: The 49th State—3rd Edition 1985
A visualization of the natural beauty of Alaska and development of its five geographic areas, showing the land, resources, the people, and their work. ?m; VHS, 3/4 U. **Pr:** Encyclopedia Britannica Educational Corporation. **A:** Family. **P:** Education. **U:** Institution, BCTV, SURA. **Gen-Edu:** U.S. States. **Acq:** Purchase, Rent/Lease, Trade-in. **Dist:** Encyclopedia Britannica. $89.00.

Alaska: The Last Frontier 1975
Travels throughout Alaska exploring the various aspects of the state, including its diverse culture, climate, and geography, as well as some of the top attractions. Includes visits to Ketchiken, Sitka, Juneau, Skagway, Valdez, Cordova, Anchorage, Fairbanks, Denali National Park, Glacier Bay, Prudhoe Bay, McNeil River, and Saint Michael. Also contains footage from a bush plane ride around Mt. McKinley, a sportfishing adventure, a dogsled race, and the famous Northern Lights. 75m; VHS. **TV Std:** NTSC, PAL. **A:** Family. **P:** Education. **U:** Home. **L:** English, Japanese. **Gen-Edu:** U.S. States, Travel, Wilderness Areas. **Acq:** Purchase. **Dist:** Alaska Video Postcards Inc. $29.95.

Alaska: The Story from the Top of the World 1983
This tape explores the history and beauty of the 49th State Alaska. 40m; VHS, 3/4 U. **Pr:** BBI Productions. **A:** Jr. High-Adult. **P:** Education. **U:** Institution, SURA. **Gen-Edu:** History--U.S. **Acq:** Purchase. **Dist:** Home Vision Cinema.

Alaska Wing Men: Season 1 & 2 2011
Looks at Alaska's bush pilots and the risks they face as they transpot supplies and rescue the lost and injured. 13 episodes, including "Explosive Cargo," "Ski Chopper Devils," "Grizzly 911," High Voltage Hazard," and "Man Down." 585m; DVD. **A:** Jr. High-Adult. **P:** Entertainment. **U:** Home. **Gen-Edu:** Aeronautics, Television Series, U.S. States. **Acq:** Purchase. **Dist:** National Geographic. $29.95.

Alaska Winter Wonder 19??
Outlines the many wonders available in Alaska during the winter season. Includes footage of the Northern Lights, Eskimos, the lifestyle along the Iditarod Trail from Anchorage to Nome, the gathering of the bald eagles in Haines, Anchorage's Fur Rendezvous festival, and skiing opportunities. 33m; VHS. **TV Std:** NTSC, PAL. **A:** Family. **P:** Entertainment. **U:** Home. **Gen-Edu:** U.S. States, Wildlife, Wilderness Areas. **Acq:** Purchase. **Dist:** Alaska Video Postcards Inc. $14.95.

The Alaskan Eskimo 1953
This award winning film looks at life in an Arctic eskimo village, including native customs and traditions. 47m; VHS, 3/4 U, EJ, Special order formats. **TV Std:** NTSC, PAL, SECAM. **A:** Primary-College. **P:** Education. **U:** Institution, CCTV, SURA. **Gen-Edu:** Native Americans. **Acq:** Purchase, Rent/Lease. **Dist:** Phoenix Learning Group. $250.00.

Alaskan Heritage 1967
This tape describes Alaska's history and development, focusing on the important role of the U.S. armed forces in Alaska and shows Alaska's present day status and strategic importance as she celebrates her centennial. 20m/B/W; VHS, 3/4 U, Special order formats. **Pr:** Department of Defense. **A:** Sr. High-Adult. **P:** Education. **U:** Institution, CCTV, CATV, SURA. **Gen-Edu:** U.S. States. **Acq:** Purchase. **Dist:** National Audiovisual Center.

Alaskan Rainbow—The Fishing Adventure of a Lifetime! 19??
Ron Hayes hosts this visit to the Alaskan wilderness where he explores the world of fishing for the Alaskan Rainbow Salmon. Includes footage of the famous Rainbow Lodge and tips of wilderness fishing. 55m; VHS. **Pr:** Bennett Marine Video. **A:** Jr. High-Adult. **P:** Entertainment. **U:** Home. **Spo-Rec:** Fishing, Travel. **Acq:** Purchase. **Dist:** Bennett Marine Video. $29.95.

Alaska's Deadly Volcano 1994 (Unrated)
One hundred times more powerful than the eruption of Mount St. Helen's, the Alaskan volcano eruption of 1912 in the Katmai region created so much falling ash that it literally blacked out the sun for three days. In light of such devastation, it is almost unbelievable how the land has recovered and now sustains one of the world's largest brown bear populations, plentiful salmon runs, and a plant and grass environment that creates a stunning landscape. National Geographic shows how the ecology and environment in the region have renewed themselves so astoundingly in a relatively short time span. 50m; DVD. **A:** Family. **P:** Education. **U:** Institution, Home. **Mov-Ent:** Documentary Films, History--U.S., Animals. **Acq:** Purchase. **Dist:** National Geographic Society. $19.95.

Alaska's Denali Park 19??
Visits the Denali National Park located in Alaska, which includes Mt. McKinley. Contains footage of much of the wildlife found in this wilderness area, including Dall sheep, wolves, and bears. 55m; VHS. **TV Std:** NTSC, PAL. **A:** Family. **P:** Education. **U:** Home. **Gen-Edu:** U.S. States, Wildlife, Wilderness Areas. **Acq:** Purchase. **Dist:** Alaska Video Postcards Inc. $14.95.

Alaska's Gulf Coast 19??
Explores all the various tourist destinations and natural attractions located along Alaska's Gulf Coast in southcentral Alaska. Included are stops in Anchorage, Homer, Seaward, Kenai Fjords National Park, Katmai National Park, Prince Williams Sound, and Kodiak, as well as visits with brown bears, glacier watching, and fishing expeditions. 45m; VHS. **TV Std:** NTSC, PAL. **A:** Family. **P:** Entertainment. **U:** Home. **Gen-Edu:** U.S. States, Travel, Wildlife. **Acq:** Purchase. **Dist:** Alaska Video Postcards Inc. $19.95.

Alaska's Inside Passage 19??
Tours Alaska's Inside Passage, centering on the attractions, destinations, wildlife, and wilderness of the area. Includes stops in Glacier Bay National Park, Tracy Arm, Misty Fjords, Ketchikan, Sitka, Juneau, and Skagway. 40m; VHS. **TV Std:** NTSC, PAL. **A:** Family. **P:** Education. **U:** Home. **Gen-Edu:** U.S. States, Travel, Wilderness Areas. **Acq:** Purchase. **Dist:** Alaska Video Postcards Inc. $19.95.

Alaska's Kenai Peninsula 19??
Provides insight into the many recreational opportunities available in Alaska's Kenai Peninsula, one of the state's favorite recreation areas. Includes footage of fishing on the Kenai and Russian Rivers, kayaking in Kachemak Bay, Cook Inlet, Holgate Glacier located in the Kenai Fjords National Park, Hope, Homer, Seldovia, and Seward. 60m; VHS. **TV Std:** NTSC, PAL. **A:** Family. **P:** Entertainment. **U:** Home. **Gen-Edu:** U.S. States, Wildlife, Fishing. **Acq:** Purchase. **Dist:** Alaska Video Postcards Inc. $19.95.

Alaska's Last Oil 2008 (Unrated)
With the world's oil supplies steadily diminishing, the race is on to extract oil wherever it can be found. This increasingly includes the Arctic National Wildlife Refuge in Alaska, where oil companies are pressuring the U.S. government to be allowed to extract the oil found there. Also included is a review of the history of oil and how it was first created millions of years ago. 52m; DVD. **A:** Family. **P:** Education. **U:** Institution, Home. **Mov-Ent:** Documentary Films, Animals, Arctic Regions. **Acq:** Purchase. **Dist:** National Geographic Society. $19.95.

Alaska's Portage Glacier 19??
Visits Alaska's Portage Glacier with footage from both a tourboat and a helicopter. Special attention is given to the falling ice and the many aquamarine icebergs surrounding the glacier. Also furnishes informatiopn on the history and geology of this glacial region. 37m; VHS. **TV Std:** NTSC, PAL. **A:** Family. **P:** Education. **U:** Home. **Gen-Edu:** U.S. States, Wilderness Areas, Travel. **Acq:** Purchase. **Dist:** Alaska Video Postcards Inc. $14.95.

Alaska's Rain Forest: The Tongass 1993
Surveys the plant, animal, and human life that coexist in the Tongass National Forest in southeast Alaska, the largest rain forest located in a temperate climate anywhere in the world. 26m; VHS, 3/4 U. **Pr:** Capital Community Broadcasting. **A:** Jr. High-Adult. **P:** Education. **U:** Institution. **Gen-Edu:** Arctic Regions, Ecology & Environment, Forests & Trees. **Acq:** Purchase, Rent/Lease. **Dist:** New Dimension Media. $270.00.

Alaska's Whales and Wildlife 1990
Visual journey through spectacular Alaskan wilderness, guided by naturalists. Includes views of natural wonders and wildlife, such as black and brown bears, bald eagles, and humpback whales. 46m; VHS. **A:** Sr. High-Adult. **P:** Education. **U:** Institution, Home. **Gen-Edu:** Documentary Films, Ecology & Environment, Wildlife. **Acq:** Purchase, Rent/Lease. **Dist:** The Video Project. $59.95.

Alaska's Wildlife 19??
Experience an Alaskan wildlife safari and track brown bears, caribou, Dall sheep, bull moose, puffins, walrusses, bald eagles, and more. 30m; VHS. **A:** Family. **P:** Entertainment. **U:** Home. **Gen-Edu:** Wilderness Areas, Animals, U.S. States. **Acq:** Purchase. **Dist:** AnimEigo Inc. $14.95.

Alateen Tells It Like It Is 19??
Young people talk about growing up with an alcoholic in the home and how the Alateen program helped them. 16m; VHS. **A:** Jr. High-Sr. High. **P:** Education. **U:** Institution. **Hea-Sci:** Alcoholism. **Acq:** Purchase. **Dist:** Hazelden Publishing. $39.95.

Albanian Journey: End of an Era 1991
Looks at the history of the country of Albania, from its communistic beginning in 1944 to the country's first multi-party elections in 1991. Utilizes archival footage and interviews with Albanian citizens. 60m; VHS. **C:** Directed by Paul Jay. **A:** Sr. High-Adult. **P:** Education. **U:** Institution. **Gen-Edu:** Documentary Films. **Acq:** Purchase, Rent/Lease. **Dist:** The Cinema Guild. $350.00.

The Albatross 19??
Dr. Harvey I. Fischer of the University of Southern Illinois, an authority on the Laysan albatross, presents a detailed study of the life cycle of this unusual species of birds. 38m; 3/4 U, Special order formats. **Pr:** University of Southern Illinois. **A:** Jr. High-College. **P:** Education. **U:** Institution, CCTV, CATV, BCTV. **Hea-Sci:** Birds. **Acq:** Purchase, Rent/Lease. **Dist:** Education Development Center.

Albatross 2011 (Unrated) — ★½
Cliff House is a family-run hotel on England's south coast that is also the title of the one successful novel by owner Jonathan Fischer (Koch). His frustrated wife Joa (Ormond) isn't happy with the disruptive influence of new teenage maid Emelia (Findlay), who has writing aspirations and is supposedly being mentored by Jonathan, or her friendship with their serious daughter Beth (Jones). Nor should she be, since Emelia is doing more than sharpening her literary skills with Jonathan. 90m; DVD. **C:** Jessica Brown-Findlay; Sebastian Koch; Julia Ormond; Felicity Jones; Harry Treadway; Thomas Brodie-Sangster; Directed by Niall MacCormick; Written by Tamzin Rafn; Cinematography by Jan Jonaeus; Music by Jack C. Arnold. **A:** Sr. High-Adult. **P:** Entertainment. **U:** Home. **L:** English. **Mov-Ent:** Hotels & Hotel Staff Training, Marriage, Great Britain. **Acq:** Purchase. **Dist:** IFC Films.

Albert Camus 19??
Offers an examination of the works of the Algerian-born author. 21m; VHS. **A:** Jr. High-Adult. **P:** Education. **U:** Institution. **Gen-Edu:** Biography, Literature, Documentary Films. **Acq:** Purchase. **Dist:** Thomas S. Klise Co. $58.00.

Albert Einstein: How I See the World 19??
Provides in-depth look at the life and work of Albert Einstein. 60m; VHS. **A:** Jr. High-Adult. **P:** Education. **U:** Institution. **Hea-Sci:** Science, Biography. **Acq:** Purchase. **Dist:** Educational Video Network. $49.95.

Albert Einstein: The Education of a Genius 198?
A profile of the genius of physics, as told mostly in his own words. 44m; VHS, 3/4 U. **Pr:** Harold Mantell. **A:** College-Adult. **P:** Education. **U:** Institution, SURA. **Gen-Edu:** Scientists. **Acq:** Purchase, Rent/Lease. **Dist:** Films for the Humanities & Sciences.

Albert Ellis: A Demonstration with a Family 1989
This session, using the Rational-Emotive approach, chiefly focuses on parental conflict with some interaction problems involving the children. 45m; VHS, 3/4 U. **Pr:** Institute for Rational Living. **A:** Adult. **P:** Education. **U:** Institution, CCTV, Home, SURA. **Hea-Sci:** Psychology, Family. **Acq:** Purchase. **Dist:** Albert Ellis Institute. $65.00.

Albert Ellis: A Demonstration with a Woman Fearful of Expressing Emotion 1970
Dr. Ellis helps a woman who wants to modify her behavior, by uncovering her illogical belief system. 30m; VHS, 3/4 U, Special order formats. **Pr:** Educational Films. **A:** College-Adult. **P:** Professional. **U:** Institution, SURA. **Hea-Sci:** Psychology, Psychiatry. **Acq:** Purchase. **Dist:** Psychological & Educational Films.

Albert Ellis: A Demonstration with a Woman with Sexual and Weight Problems 1989
A session that has Ellis dealing with a woman with weight and sexual problems, followed by the woman's comments on the session. 60m; VHS, 3/4 U. **Pr:** Institute for Rational Living. **A:** Sr. High-Adult. **P:** Education. **U:** Institution, CCTV, Home, SURA. **Hea-Sci:** Psychology, Eating Disorders, Sex & Sexuality. **Acq:** Purchase. **Dist:** Albert Ellis Institute. $65.00.

Albert Ellis: A Demonstration with a Young Divorced Woman 1970
Ellis counsels a 29-year-old woman recovering from a traumatic divorce. The techniques of Rational Emotive Therapy are discussed. 30m; VHS, 3/4 U, Special order formats. **Pr:** Educational Films. **A:** College-Adult. **P:** Professional. **U:** Institution, SURA. **Hea-Sci:** Psychology, Psychiatry. **Acq:** Purchase. **Dist:** Psychological & Educational Films.

Albert Ellis: A Demonstration with a Young Woman with Problem of Loneliness 1989
A discussion with a young divorced mother which shows her how to deal with her fear of dependency, and through the use of rational emotive imagery, shows her how to get from intellectual to emotional insight. 45m; VHS, 3/4 U. **Pr:** Institute for Rational Living. **A:** Adult. **P:** Education. **U:** Institution, CCTV, Home, SURA. **Hea-Sci:** Psychology. **Acq:** Purchase. **Dist:** Albert Ellis Institute. $65.00.

Albert Ellis: A Demonstration with a Young Woman with Sexual and Overweight Problems 1978
This Rational-Emotive session shows a non-orgasmic client how she tends to block her sexuality by negatively talking to herself instead of focusing on sex enjoyment. 60m; 3/4 U, EJ, Special order formats. **Pr:** Institute for Rational Living. **A:** Adult. **P:** Education. **U:** Institution, CCTV, Home, SURA. **Hea-Sci:** Psychology, Sex & Sexuality. **Acq:** Purchase. **Dist:** Albert Ellis Institute.

Albert Ellis: A Demonstration with an Elementary School-Age Child 1970
A demonstration of Ellis'controversial Rational Emotive Therapy (RET) with a nine-year-old boy. Ellis comments afterwards on the session. 30m; VHS, 3/4 U, Special order formats. **Pr:** Educational Films. **A:** College-Adult. **P:** Professional. **U:** Institution, SURA. **Hea-Sci:** Psychology. **Acq:** Purchase. **Dist:** Psychological & Educational Films.

Albert Ellis: Interview with a Man Anxious About Love Problems 1989
A man comes to Dr. Ellis to discuss his problems with his lover. Then they talk about how they feel about each other. 45m; VHS, 3/4 U. **Pr:** Institute for Rational Living. **A:** Sr. High-Adult. **P:** Education. **U:** Institution, CCTV, Home, SURA. **Hea-Sci:** Psychology. **Acq:** Purchase. **Dist:** Albert Ellis Institute. $65.00.

Albert Ellis: Rational Emotive Psychotherapy 1970
Dr. Albert Ellis gives a thorough explanation of Rational Emotive Therapy, which is based on the idea that people continue to endure pain and unhappiness in their lives because of a self-defeating belief system, rather than specific activating events. 30m; VHS, 3/4 U, Special order formats. **Pr:** Educational Films. **A:** College-Adult. **P:** Professional. **U:** Institution, SURA. **Hea-Sci:** Psychology, Psychiatry. **Acq:** Purchase. **Dist:** Psychological & Educational Films.

Albert Ellis: Rational Emotive Psychotherapy Applied to Groups 1970
The reknowned doctor guides us through the RET approach, and its uses in a group setting. 30m; VHS, 3/4 U, Special order formats. **Pr:** Educational Films. **A:** College-Adult. **P:** Professional. **U:** Institution, SURA. **Hea-Sci:** Psychology, Psychiatry. **Acq:** Purchase. **Dist:** Psychological & Educational Films.

Albert Ellis: RET Group Therapy Demonstration 1989
Dr. Albert Ellis conducts a group therapy session, during the course of which he applies a wide variety of rational-emotive techniques, including rational-emotive imagery. 60m; VHS, 3/4 U. **Pr:** Institute for Rational Living. **A:** Adult. **P:** Education. **U:** Institution, CCTV, Home, SURA. **Hea-Sci:** Psychology. **Acq:** Purchase. **Dist:** Albert Ellis Institute. $65.00.

Albert Fish 2007
Docudrama chronicles the life of the Depression-era New York City serial killer and cannibal who preyed on children. 86m; DVD. **A:** Sr. High-Adult. **P:** Entertainment. **U:** Home. **Gen-Edu:** Documentary Films. **Acq:** Purchase. **Dist:** Facets Multimedia Inc.

Albert Herring—Glyndebourne 1995
Contains Benjamin Britten's comic opera about life in an English market town at the turn of the century. Features John Graham-Hall in the leading role and music by the London Philharmonic Orchestra as conducted by Bernard Haitink. 170m; VHS. **A:** Family. **P:** Entertainment. **U:** Home. **Fin-Art:** Opera, Performing Arts, Music--Performance. **Acq:** Purchase. **Dist:** Kultur International Films Ltd., Inc. $14.95.

Albert Lee: Advanced Country Guitar 19??
Lee performs and discusses "Travis picking," chord voicings, scalar ideas, lines based off chord shapes, and more. 80m; VHS. **A:** Jr. High-Adult. **P:** Entertainment. **U:** Home. **How-Ins:** How-To, Music--Instruction. **Acq:** Purchase. **Dist:** Music Video Distributors. $49.95.

Albert Lee: Country Guitar Instruction 1990
Learn how to pick the country chords in this guitar lesson. 40m; VHS. **A:** Jr. High-Adult. **P:** Instruction. **U:** Home. **How-Ins:** Music--Instruction. **Acq:** Purchase. **Dist:** Music Video Distributors. $44.95.

Albert Lewin 1966
Profiles the producer/writer/director who worked during Hollywood's Golden Era. Includes excerpts from his work including "Portrait of Dorian Gray" and "Pandora and the Flying Dutchman." 28m/B/W; VHS, 3/4 U. **A:** Sr. High-Adult. **P:** Education. **U:** Home. **Gen-Edu:** Filmmaking. **Acq:** Purchase. **Dist:** Camera Three Productions, Inc.

Albert Nobbs 2011 (R) — ★★½
A passion project by Close results in one of the best film performances of her career as a 19th-century Irish woman who has to disguise herself as the title character to work as a hotel butler. When she meets a man (McTeer) who turns out to also be a woman in disguise, Albert is thrown out of her routine by the concept that she could have more happiness than her predictable life has provided, maybe even love with a co-worker (Wasikowska). Close and McTeer are subtle and often spectacular but the overall piece is relatively slight. 113m; DVD, Blu-Ray. **C:** Glenn Close; Mia Wasikowska; Aaron Taylor-Johnson; Janet McTeer; Pauline Collins; Brenda Fricker; Jonathan Rhys Meyers; Brendan Gleeson; Mark Williams; Bronagh Gallagher; Directed by Rodrigo Garcia; Written by Glenn Close; John Banville; Gabriella Prekop; Cinematography by Michael McDonough. **Pr:** Glenn Close; Bonnie Curtis; Julie Lynn; Alan Moloney; Glenn Close; Mockingbird Pictures; Parallel Films; Roadside Attractions. **A:** Sr. High-Adult. **P:** Entertainment. **U:** Home. **L:** English. **Mov-Ent:** Hotels & Hotel Staff Training. **Acq:** Purchase. **Dist:** Lionsgate.

Albert Schweitzer: Called to Africa 2006
Biography of Dr. Albert Schweitzer, the Nobel Peace Prize-winning humanitarian who built a hospital in Gabon, West Africa, and offered needed medical services in Africa. Takes the

perspective of his wife, Helene, a nurse who was left in Europe with their daughter as Schweitzer focused on his work in Africa. 52m; DVD. **A:** Jr. High-Adult. **P:** Entertainment. **U:** Home. **Mov-Ent:** Biography: Science & Medical, Documentary Films, Africa. **Acq:** Purchase. **Dist:** First Run Features. $24.95.

Albert Szent-Gyorgyi: A Special Gift 1985
Examines the life and work of Albert Szent-Gyorgyi, winner of the Nobel Prize in Medicine in 1937, and one of the world's leading physiological and cancer researchers. 30m; VHS, 3/4 U. **TV Std:** NTSC, PAL, SECAM. **Pr:** Joel Sucher. **A:** Sr. High-Adult. **P:** Education. **U:** Institution, SURA. **Gen-Edu:** Cancer, Biography. **Acq:** Purchase, Rent/Lease. **Dist:** The Cinema Guild.

Alberta Bound 19??
A family moves from a Prince Edward Island fishing village to Edmonton, Alberta. Family discusses why they left and the adjustments they had to make. 29m; VHS. **Pr:** National Film Board of Canada. **A:** Sr. High-Adult. **P:** Education. **U:** Institution. **Gen-Edu:** Immigration, Canada. **Acq:** Purchase. **Dist:** Access The Education Station. $49.00.

Alberta Elementary Physical Education 19??
Eight programs providing an insight into the seven dimensions of physical education and how they should be balanced for an effective program. Run times vary. Manual available separately. ?m; VHS. **A:** College-Adult. **P:** Teacher Education. **U:** Institution. **Gen-Edu:** Education, Fitness/Exercise. **Acq:** Purchase. **Dist:** Access The Education Station. $29.00.
Indiv. Titles: 1. Introduction 2. Fitness 3. Games 4. Gymnastics 5. Dance 6. Outdoor Pursuits 7. Aquatics 8. Track and Field.

Alberta Hunter 1978
Hunter performs "One Hundred Years From Today," "Get Yourself a Working Man," "The Best Things in Life are Free," and others. 29m; VHS, 3/4 U. **A:** Jr. High-Adult. **P:** Entertainment. **U:** Home. **Mov-Ent:** Music--Performance. **Acq:** Purchase. **Dist:** Camera Three Productions, Inc.

Alberta Hunter: My Castle's Rockin' 1988
Portrays the life of Hunter, a blues singer and songwriter in the 1920s and '30s, who later lapsed into obscurity. She left show business to become a nurse but made her triumphant comeback at age 82. Features many of her hit songs, including "The Love I Have for You," "Handy Man," "Downhearted Blues," and "Darktown Strutters Ball." 60m; VHS, DVD. **C:** Narrated by Billy Taylor; Directed by Stuart Goldman. **A:** Jr. High-Adult. **P:** Entertainment. **U:** Home. **Gen-Edu:** Biography, Black Culture. **Acq:** Purchase. **Dist:** V.I.E.W. Inc./Arkadia Entertainment Corp.; Facets Multimedia Inc. $19.98.

Alberto Express 1992 (Unrated) — ★★½
Black comedy explores the debts children owe their parents—literally. Alberto's family has a peculiar tradition. It seems that now he's married and about to become a father, he's expected to pay back every cent spent on his own upbringing. Cash poor (and panicky) Alberto hops a train from Paris to Rome and frantically tries to raise the necessary cash by preying, in a series of increasingly bizarre ways, on his fellow passengers before he faces his father once again. In French and Italian with English subtitles. 90m; VHS. **C:** Sergio Castellitto; Nino Manfredi; Marie Trintignant; Jeanne Moreau; Michel Aumont; Dominique Pinon; Marco Messeri; Eugenia Marruzzo; Directed by Arthur Joffe; Written by Arthur Joffe. **Pr:** Maurice Bernart; MK2. **A:** College-Adult. **P:** Entertainment. **U:** Home. **L:** French, Italian, English. **Mov-Ent:** Comedy--Black, Trains. **Acq:** Purchase. **Dist:** Wellspring Media. $89.95.

Alberto Moravia 1976
A profile/interview with Moravia about his writing, his social concerns, views on fascism and Italy, accompanied by dramatic readings from his novels. 55m; VHS. **C:** Alberto Moravia; Bernardo Bertolucci. **A:** Sr. High-Adult. **P:** Education. **U:** Home. **Gen-Edu:** Literature--Modern, Interviews. **Acq:** Purchase. **Dist:** Facets Multimedia Inc.

Albert's Last Stand 1980
In the third episode of "The Backstreet Six," the gang convinces Luke, who sees mysteries everywhere, that Albert is being held prisoner and must be rescued. 26m; VHS, 3/4 U. **Pr:** Les Productions Prisma. **A:** Primary-Jr. High. **P:** Entertainment. **U:** Institution, SURA. **Chl-Juv.** **Acq:** Purchase. **Dist:** Phoenix Learning Group.

Albert's Memorial 2009 (Unrated) — ★★½
In London, aged Harry and Frank agree to honor their dying friend Albert's last wish to be buried on the German hill where they fought together during WWII. The duo (and Albert's dead body) set off in Harry's cab but get lost in France and then rely on German hitchhiker Vicki to help them. She also uncovers a 55-year-old secret (revealed in flashbacks) that still haunts the men. 68m; DVD. **C:** David Jason; David Warner; Judith Hoersch; Michael Jayston; Nick Bennett; Scott Harrison; Adam Flynn; Directed by David Richards; Written by Thomas Ellice; Cinematography by Tony Coldwell; Music by Hal Lindes. **A:** Sr. High-Adult. **P:** Entertainment. **U:** Home. **Mov-Ent:** TV Movies, Aging, France. **Acq:** Purchase. **Dist:** BFS Video.

Albino 1976 (R) — **Bomb!**
Albino chief leads African terrorists to murder white settlers, one of whom is an ex-policeman's fiancee. So the ex-cop pursues the bad guys, who are fairly easy to identify (just look for the big group hanging with the albino). Danning, Lee, and Howard only briefly show faces and collect checks. 85m; VHS. **TV Std:** NTSC, PAL. **C:** Christopher Lee; Trevor Howard; Sybil Danning; Horst Frank; James Faulkner; Directed by Jurgen Goslar. **Pr:** Jurgen Goslar; Jurgen Goslar. **A:** Adult. **P:** Entertainment. **U:** Home. **Mov-Ent:** Africa. **Acq:** Purchase. **Dist:** No Longer Available.

Albino Alligator 1996 (R) — ★★
Three small-time crooks bungle a robbery and inadvertently run down a federal officer in Academy Award-winning actor Spacey's directorial debut. The trio, consisting of leader Dova (Dillon), brains Milo (Sinise) and brawn Law (Fichtner) hole up in a seedy bar and grab the occupants as hostages. The police soon surround the dive, and the crooks begin arguing among themselves and with brash barmaid Janet (Dunaway) about their chances and means for escape. All, however, is not as it seems. The claustrophobic setting seems more suitable for the stage than the screen, and the plot twists don't bend very far from predictable. Screenwriter Forte is the son of '60s teen idol Fabian. 94m; VHS, DVD, Blu-Ray, CC. **C:** Matt Dillon; Gary Sinise; Faye Dunaway; William Fichtner; Joe Mantegna; Viggo Mortensen; John Spencer; Skeet Ulrich; M. Emmet Walsh; Directed by Kevin Spacey; Written by Christian Forte; Cinematography by Mark Plummer; Music by Michael Brook. **Pr:** Brad Krevoy; Brad Jenkel; Motion Picture Corporation of America; Miramax Film Corp. **A:** Sr. High-Adult. **P:** Entertainment. **U:** Home. **Mov-Ent:** Crime Drama. **Acq:** Purchase. **Dist:** Buena Vista Home Entertainment.

Albino Farm 2009 (R) — ★½
College kids travel to the Ozarks to research an urban legend and run afoul of inbred mutant rednecks. 90m; DVD. **C:** Chris Jericho; Richard Christy; Duane Whitaker; Sunkrish Bala; Nick Richey; Kevin Blair Spirtas; Tammin Sursok; Directed by Joe Sanderson; Written by Joe Sanderson; Sean McEwen; Cinematography by Rene Jung; Music by Scott Rockenfield. **A:** Sr. High-Adult. **P:** Entertainment. **U:** Home. **L:** English, Spanish. **Mov-Ent.** **Acq:** Purchase. **Dist:** MTI Home Video. $24.95.

The Albula Swiss Mountain Railroad 1991
A one-of-a-kind ride from Thusis to St. Moritz, rising 410 meters in only 12.5km. This technically demanding track is laid out with five ingenious hairpin turns. 50m; VHS. **A:** Jr. High-Adult. **P:** Education. **U:** Home. **Gen-Edu:** Documentary Films, Trains, Travel. **Acq:** Purchase. **Dist:** Pentrex Media Group L.L.C. $39.95.

The ALCAN Highway—Adventure Road to Alaska 19??
Traces the history and path of the ALCAN highway, which runs from Canada into Alaska. Also features footage of the actual highway construction, the highway itself, residents along the highway, wildlife along the highway, and the Kluane National Park. 60m; VHS. **A:** Family. **P:** Education. **U:** Home. **Gen-Edu:** Travel, Wildlife, Canada. **Acq:** Purchase. **Dist:** Trailwood Films. $24.95.

Alcatraz 1977
A documentary outlining the history, security, and denizens of the notorious prison. 54m; VHS, 3/4 U. **TV Std:** NTSC, PAL. **C:** Narrated by William Conrad; Directed by Paul Krasny. **Pr:** Tom Thayer. **A:** Jr. High-Adult. **P:** Education. **U:** Home. **Gen-Edu:** Documentary Films. **Acq:** Purchase. **Dist:** MPI Media Group. $29.95.

Alcatraz: Metallic Live '84 in Japan 1984
This Japanese import has the legendary Yngwie Malmsteen leading such songs as "Too Young to Die, Too Drunk to Live," "Something Else" and many more. ?m; VHS. **A:** Jr. High-College. **P:** Entertainment. **U:** Home. **Mov-Ent:** Music Video. **Acq:** Purchase. **Dist:** Music Video Distributors. $129.95.

Alcatraz: Power Live 19??
Yngwie Malmsteen leads a string of 16 headbanging classics in this Japanese live import. ?m; VHS. **A:** Jr. High-College. **P:** Entertainment. **U:** Home. **Mov-Ent:** Music Video, Music--Performance. **Acq:** Purchase. **Dist:** Music Video Distributors. $119.95.

The Alchemist 1981 (R) — **Bomb!**
See humans transformed into murderous zombies! A bewitched man seeks revenge upon the evil magician who placed a curse on him, causing him to live like an animal. Painfully routine, with a few chills along the way. Amonte is an alias for Charles Band. Filmed in 1981 and released four years later. 86m; VHS, DVD. **C:** Robert Ginty; Lucinda Dooling; John Sanderford; Viola Kate Stimpson; Bob Glaudini; Directed by Charles Band; Written by Alan J. Adler; Music by Richard Band. **A:** Sr. High-Adult. **P:** Entertainment. **U:** Home. **Mov-Ent:** Magic, Death. **Acq:** Purchase. **Dist:** Synergy Entertainment, Inc. $79.98.

The Alchemist Sea 1975
For nearly 200 million years the Earth's surface has broken up into massive plates that shift and move. Examines how plate motion is relatd to ore deposits on the sea floor. 10m; VHS, 3/4 U. **A:** College-Adult. **P:** Education. **U:** Institution, SURA. **Hea-Sci:** Oceanography. **Acq:** Purchase. **Dist:** Capital Communications.

The Alchemists 1999 (PG-13) — ★½
The world's leading pharmaceutical company is covering up the fact that their fertility drug has some serious side effects. Employees Show and Gemmell try to expose the corporate conspiracy. Based on the novel by Peter James. 150m; VHS, DVD. **C:** Grant Show; Ruth Gemmell; Edward Hardwicke; Directed by Peter Smith; Cinematography by Peter Middleton; Music by Rick Wentworth. **A:** Jr. High-Adult. **P:** Entertainment. **U:** Home. **Mov-Ent:** Science Fiction, Conspiracies or Conspiracy Theories. **Acq:** Purchase. **Dist:** Bedford Entertainment Inc.

Alchemy 2005 (PG-13) — ★★½
Slight romantic comedy that gets a little extra oomph from its appealing leads. Professor Mal Downey (Cavanaugh) uses his new computer software to woo struggling actress Samantha Rose (Chalke) based on the responses the program generates. 85m; DVD. **C:** Sarah Chalke; Nadia Dajani; Illeana Douglas; Celeste Holm; Tom Cavanaugh; James Barbour; Anna Belknap; Erik Palladino; Directed by Evan Oppenheimer; Written by Evan Oppenheimer; Cinematography by Luke Geissbuhler; Music by Peter Lurye. **A:** Jr. High-Adult. **P:** Entertainment. **U:** Home. **Mov-Ent:** Computers, Comedy--Romantic. **Acq:** Purchase. **Dist:** Monarch Home Video.

ALCO Shortlines in the Northeast 2007
Footage from 2005-6 captures locomotives on thirteen passenger and freight lines throughout New York, Pennsylvania, and Ohio, including the New York & Lake Erie, the Buffalo Southern, the Tioga Central, the Western New York & Pennsylvania, the Ontario Midland, and the Delaware & Ulster. 95m; DVD. **A:** Family. **P:** Education. **U:** Home. **L:** English. **Gen-Edu:** Trains, U.S. States. **Acq:** Purchase. **Dist:** Plet's Express; The Civil War Standard. $34.95.

Alcohol 1993
Explains the effects of alcohol on the central nervous system and other body systems. 30m; VHS. **A:** Adult. **P:** Education. **U:** Institution. **Gen-Edu:** Health Education. **Acq:** Purchase. **Dist:** RMI Media. $99.00.

Alcohol: A New Focus 1973
A new look at important facts and attitudes about this abused drug, designed to make young people think twice before drinking. 17m; VHS, 3/4 U. **C:** Narrated by James Brolin. **Pr:** American Educational Films. **A:** Jr. High-Sr. High. **P:** Education. **U:** Institution, SURA. **Hea-Sci:** Alcoholism. **Acq:** Purchase. **Dist:** Capital Communications.

Alcohol and Attitudes: Where Do You Stand? 1993
Eight scenarios depict common adolescent involvement with alcohol, challenging students to consider the risks and consequences of alcohol use and change their destructive attitudes. Includes teacher's guide. 28m; VHS. **A:** Jr. High-Sr. High. **P:** Education. **U:** Institution. **Gen-Edu:** Alcoholic Beverages, Adolescence. **Acq:** Purchase. **Dist:** Sunburst Digital Inc. $189.00.

Alcohol and Drug Abuse 1988
The physical and emotional problems of people with an addiction, as well as the effectiveness of treatment programs, are the main topics of this video. 30m; VHS. **Pr:** Cambridge Career Productions. **A:** Jr. High-Adult. **P:** Education. **U:** Institution, Home. **Hea-Sci:** Drug Abuse, Alcoholism. **Acq:** Purchase. **Dist:** Cambridge Educational. $49.00.

Alcohol & Drug Testing Training/Awareness Program 19??
Helps a company organize, set up, and manage a company program which complies with DOT's new requirements for 60 minutes of training on alcohol misuse and 60 minutes of training on drug use. Covers such topics as the general requirements, drug and alcohol testing, and awareness. Comes with facilitator's guide, participant's handbooks, training log, DOT breath alcohol testing forms, and much more. 25m; VHS. **A:** Adult. **P:** Vocational. **U:** Institution. **Bus-Ind:** Job Training, Management, Drug Abuse. **Acq:** Purchase. **Dist:** J.J. Keller and Associates Inc. $189.00.

Alcohol and Drugs in the Workplace 1995
Features a variety of options available to handle substance abuse in the workplace. 12m; VHS. **A:** Adult. **P:** Professional. **U:** Institution. **Bus-Ind:** Job Training, Management, Alcoholism. **Acq:** Purchase, Rent/Lease. **Dist:** National Safety Council, California Chapter, Film Library. $195.00.

Alcohol and Human Physiology 1984
A detailed look at the effects excessive alcohol abuse has on the human body. 27m; VHS, 3/4 U. **Pr:** National Safety Council. **A:** College-Adult. **P:** Education. **U:** Institution. **Hea-Sci:** Alcoholism. **Acq:** Rent/Lease. **Dist:** National Safety Council, California Chapter, Film Library.

Alcohol and Pregnancy: Fetal Alcohol Syndrome and Fetal Alcohol Effects 1994
Discusses the dangers of alcohol use during pregnancy. Emphasizes the fetus' vulnerability and the struggles of FAS/FAE children, their families and caregivers. 20m; VHS. **A:** Adult. **P:** Education. **U:** Institution. **Hea-Sci:** Alcoholic Beverages, Pregnancy. **Acq:** Purchase. **Dist:** Milner-Fenwick, Inc.

Alcohol and Pregnancy: The Effects of Alcohol on the Unborn Fetus 1987
Effects and prevention of fetal alcohol syndrome are explained by a pediatrician. 28m; VHS. **A:** Adult. **P:** Education. **U:** Institution. **Hea-Sci:** Health Education, Alcoholic Beverages, Pregnancy. **Acq:** Purchase. **Dist:** Media Center/Munroe-Meyer Institute for Genetics and Rehabilitation. $75.00.

Alcohol and Red Flares 1971
A young man finds out about the dangers of driving under the influence after he's arrested and thrown into the drunk tank. 20m; VHS, 3/4 U. **Pr:** National Safety Council. **A:** College-Adult. **P:** Education. **U:** Institution. **Hea-Sci:** Alcoholism. **Acq:** Rent/Lease. **Dist:** National Safety Council, California Chapter, Film Library.

Alcohol and the Commercial Driver 19??
Graphically examines the affect alcohol has on a driver's abilities. 13m; VHS. **A:** Adult. **P:** Education. **U:** Institution. **Gen-Edu:** Driver Education, Safety Education, Alcoholism. **Acq:** Purchase, Rent/Lease. **Dist:** AMS Distributors, Inc.

Alcohol and You 1969
This documented treatment of drinking explores the social pressures and the drinking habits that can lead an individual into becoming an alcoholic. 28m; VHS, 3/4 U. **Pr:** Max Miller Productions. **A:** Jr. High-Sr. High. **P:** Education. **U:** Institution, SURA. **Hea-Sci:** Alcoholism. **Acq:** Purchase. **Dist:** Phoenix Learning Group.

Alcohol and Your Body: Assessing the Damage 1997
Reveals the latest information on the ways drinking alcohol can damage bodily systems and cause disease. Warns young women on the dangers of mixing alcohol and pregnancy. Includes Teacher's Resource Book. 30m; VHS. **A:** Jr. High-Sr. High. **P:** Education. **U:** Institution. **Hea-Sci:** Alcoholic Beverages, Alcoholism, Health Education. **Acq:** Purchase. **Dist:** HRM Video. $189.00.

Alcohol: Brain Under the Influence 1998
Uses live demonstrations, reenactments and 3-D computer animation to explain why drinking alcohol is pleasurable, how field sobriety tests work and why driving skills become impaired. Features two-time Indy 500 champ Arie Luyendyk. ?m; VHS. **A:** Sr. High-Adult. **P:** Education. **U:** Home. **Gen-Edu:** Documentary Films, Alcoholic Beverages. **Acq:** Purchase. **Dist:** Tapeworm Video Distributors Inc. $29.95.

Alcohol: Crisis for the Unborn 1980
Dealing with Fetal Alcohol Syndrome, shows the potentially tragic outcome of drinking alcohol during pregnancy. 8m; 3/4 U. **Pr:** March of Dimes. **A:** Sr. High-Adult. **P:** Education. **U:** Institution, CCTV, CATV. **Hea-Sci:** Pregnancy. **Acq:** Free Loan. **Dist:** March of Dimes.

Alcohol, Drugs & Senior: Tarnished Dreams 1987
A look for the layman at the hazards implicit in drug and alcohol abuse by senior citizens. 23m; VHS, 3/4 U, Special order formats. **Pr:** Telford-Clark Productions. **A:** Adult. **P:** Education. **U:** Institution. **Hea-Sci:** Drug Abuse, Aging. **Acq:** Purchase, Rent/Lease. **Dist:** Terra Nova Films. $295.00.

Alcohol: Facts, Myths and Decisions 1992
Depicts a typical scenario involving a partying teen who pressures his classmates to drink alcohol. A host teen speaks to the camera after each scene to instruct the viewer on the proper behavior. Comes with catalog kit and teacher's guide. 20m; VHS. **A:** Jr. High-Sr. High. **P:** Education. **U:** Institution. **Gen-Edu:** Alcoholism, Adolescence. **Acq:** Purchase. **Dist:** Sunburst Digital Inc. $149.00.

The Alcohol Film for "Kids" 1988
Viewed through the eyes of a preteen, the effects that alcohol has on the body are displayed. 18m; VHS, 3/4 U. **Pr:** Lucerne Films. **A:** Primary-Jr. High. **P:** Education. **U:** Institution, SURA. **Hea-Sci:** Alcoholism, Health Education, Adolescence. **Acq:** Purchase. **Dist:** Lucerne Media. $165.00.

Alcohol: It's Serious Business 19??
Outlines the effects of underage drinking, both physical and emotional. Explores alternatives to dealing with stress besides alcohol. Provides exercises that help deal with peer pressure and discusses self-help organizations. Includes teacher's guide, interactive masters, and reproducible masters. ?m; VHS. **A:** Primary-Jr. High. **P:** Education. **U:** Institution. **Hea-Sci:** Health Education, Alcoholism. **Acq:** Purchase, Duplication License. **Dist:** Educational Activities Inc. $79.00.

Alcohol: Legal Drug 1994
In-depth look at alcohol, its history, uses, science and effects. 28m; VHS, CC. **A:** Jr. High-Adult. **P:** Education. **U:** Institution. **Gen-Edu:** Alcoholism. **Acq:** Purchase. **Dist:** National Geographic Society. $110.

Alcohol, Pills and Recovery 1977
This program introduces Dick and Jane, an average American couple, raised in the age of anxiety and living in the age of sedativism-combining booze and pills. 27m; 3/4 U. **Pr:** FMS Productions. **A:** Sr. High-Adult. **P:** Education. **U:** Institution, SURA. **Hea-Sci:** Drug Abuse. **Acq:** Purchase. **Dist:** FMS Productions, Inc.

Alcohol: Pink Elephant 1976
A cartoon program in which a pink elephant meets a drunk and convinces him that he has an alcohol problem. 15m; VHS, 3/4 U. **Pr:** Encyclopedia Britannica Educational Corporation. **A:** Jr. High-Sr. High. **P:** Education. **U:** Institution, SURA. **Hea-Sci:** Alcoholism. **Acq:** Purchase, Rent/Lease, Trade-in. **Dist:** Encyclopedia Britannica.

Alcohol Plus Auto Equals Arraignment 1975
Examines the motivation of three drivers who were arrested for driving while intoxicated. 13m; VHS, 3/4 U. **Pr:** National Safety Council. **A:** College-Adult. **P:** Education. **U:** Institution. **Hea-Sci:** Alcoholism. **Acq:** Rent/Lease. **Dist:** National Safety Council, California Chapter, Film Library.

The Alcohol Problem 1973
Society's most popular drug is examined in several ways-the social aspect of drinking, the history of alcohol usage, the psychological effects, and physical dependency. 18m; VHS, 3/4 U. **Pr:** Encyclopedia Britannica Educational Corporation. **A:** Jr. High-Adult. **P:** Education. **U:** Institution, SURA. **Hea-Sci:** Alcoholism. **Acq:** Purchase, Rent/Lease, Trade-in. **Dist:** Encyclopedia Britannica.

Alcohol: The Accepted Drug 199?
Tackles alcohol use and abuse, outlining its effects, how to say no, and where to find help. 10m; VHS. **A:** Jr. High. **P:** Education. **U:** Institution. **Gen-Edu:** Alcoholic Beverages, Alcoholism. **Dist:** Marshmedia. $59.95.

Alcohol: The First Decision 1972
Young people are confronted with invitations to drink at every turn. This film suggest to students that they must make their own decision about drinking. 9m; VHS, 3/4 U. **Pr:** Don Dickerson. **A:** Jr. High-Sr. High. **P:** Education. **U:** Institution, SURA. **Hea-Sci:** Alcoholism. **Acq:** Purchase. **Dist:** Phoenix Learning Group.

Alcohol: The Social Drug, Personal Problem 1984
This program looks at the psychological and physiological effects of alcohol use and abuse. 39m; VHS, 3/4 U. **Pr:** Guidance Associates. **A:** Jr. High-Adult. **P:** Education. **U:** Institution, SURA. **Hea-Sci:** Alcoholism. **Acq:** Purchase. **Dist:** Center for Humanities, Inc./Guidance Associates.

Alcohol: What About It? ????
Discusses the effects of alcohol use and abuse, assertiveness skills, ways to deal with stress, conflict, or negative feelings, and the importance of supportive personal relationships. 16m; VHS; Closed Captioned. **A:** Primary. **P:** Education. **U:** Institution. **Chl-Juv:** Alcoholic Beverages, Health Education. **Acq:** Purchase. **Dist:** Marshmedia. $69.95.

Alcohol Withdrawal 1971
A demonstration of a patient with prominent neuromuscular excitability secondary to alcohol withdrawal. 9m; VHS, 3/4 U, Special order formats. **Pr:** Ohio State University Health Sciences AV Center. **A:** College-Adult. **P:** Professional. **U:** Institution, SURA. **Hea-Sci:** Neurology, Alcoholism. **Acq:** Purchase, Rent/Lease. **Dist:** Ohio State University.

Alcohol Withdrawal 1982
This program describes treatment of acute alcoholism and its withdrawal symptoms. 21m; VHS, 3/4 U. **Pr:** Emory University. **A:** College-Adult. **P:** Professional. **U:** Institution, CCTV, Home, SURA. **Hea-Sci:** Alcoholism. **Acq:** Purchase, Rent/Lease, Subscription. **Dist:** Emory Medical Television Network.

Alcohol Withdrawal Syndrome 1985
A series of three 20 minute videos that can be used by detox and other rehabilitation centers. 60m; VHS, 3/4 U. **Pr:** Alcoholism and Drug Addiction Research. **A:** Adult. **P:** Professional. **U:** Institution, CCTV. **Hea-Sci:** Alcoholism. **Acq:** Purchase. **Dist:** Centre for Addiction and Mental Health. $250.00.

The Alcoholic: A Woman's Perspective 1981
The challanges and rewards of women who try to kick their drinking habits. 27m; VHS, 3/4 U. **Pr:** University of California at Los Angeles. **A:** Sr. High-Adult. **P:** Education. **U:** Institution. **Hea-Sci:** Women, Alcoholism. **Acq:** Purchase. **Dist:** University of California at Los Angeles Neuropsychiatric Institute. $250.00.

The Alcoholic Within Us 1973
With the use of symbolic figures, this film portrays how the mind gives in to emotions and how the emotions can lead one to alcohol. Written and narrated by a young alcoholic. 25m; VHS, 3/4 U. **Pr:** Noel Nosseck. **A:** College-Adult. **P:** Education. **U:** Institution, Home, SURA. **Hea-Sci:** Alcoholism. **Acq:** Purchase, Rent/Lease. **Dist:** Pyramid Media.

Alcoholism 1982
The problem of alcoholism is looked at from a religious viewpoint in these three programs, each available separately. 30m; VHS, 3/4 U. **A:** Adult. **P:** Religious. **U:** Institution, SURA. **Hea-Sci:** Alcoholism. **Acq:** Purchase. **Dist:** St. Anthony Messenger Press.
Indiv. Titles: 1. The Alcoholic Marriage 2. Female Alcoholism 3. Alcoholism in the Professions.

Alcoholism and Addiction Series 1985
Three programs examine various aspects of alcohol and chemical addiction among health professionals. Features interviews with such individuals, their colleagues, and families. Also provides intervention guidelines. 23m; VHS, 3/4 U. **TV Std:** NTSC, PAL, SECAM. **Pr:** HSC. **A:** College-Adult. **P:** Education. **U:** Institution, CCTV, SURA. **Hea-Sci:** Documentary Films, Alcoholism, Drug Abuse. **Acq:** Purchase, Rent/Lease, Subscription. **Dist:** Emory Medical Television Network.
Indiv. Titles: 1. Alcoholism: A Treatable Disease 2. It Could Never Happen to Me 3. Intervention: Rescue from Destruction.

Alcoholism and Chemical Dependency in Women 19??
Offers information on the prevalence of drug and alcohol dependency in our society, including the effects of society on the female addict, the different effects of chemical dependency on men and women, fetal alcohol syndrome, and the overall growth of addiction in society. Also discusses educational programs and support systems that can help prevent chemical dependency and its related problems in women. Includes study guide. 28m; VHS. **A:** College-Adult. **P:** Education. **U:** Institution. **Hea-Sci:** Nursing, Drug Abuse, Alcoholism. **Acq:** Purchase, Rent/Lease. **Dist:** AJN Video Library/Lippincott Williams & Wilkins. $285.00.

Alcoholism and the Family 1977
This program points out the effects of alcoholism on the family before and after sobriety. 42m; 3/4 U. **C:** Fr. Joseph Martin. **Pr:** FMS Productions. **A:** Sr. High-Adult. **P:** Education. **U:** Institution, SURA. **Hea-Sci:** Alcoholism. **Acq:** Purchase. **Dist:** FMS Productions, Inc.

Alcoholism and the Physician 19??
An information-packed video, this piece shows physicians how to diagnose alcohol abuse in their patients. It outlines the physicians' responsibilities at each stage of alcohol rehabilitation, and is an accredited video program for medical professionals. 80m; VHS. **A:** Adult. **P:** Education. **U:** Institution. **L:** English. **Hea-Sci:** Psychology. **Acq:** Purchase. **Dist:** Hazelden Publishing. $225.

Alcoholism: I Was Going to School Drunk 198?
A study of teenage alcoholism emphasizing the double standard society has about drinking. Often, mostly through mass media, the pleasurable aspects of alcohol are stressed, but according to doctors and experts in the field, alcohol's physical and emotional effects can be dangerous. 26m; 3/4 U, Special order formats. **Pr:** Hobel Leiterman Productions. **A:** College-Adult. **P:** Education. **U:** Institution. **Gen-Edu:** Alcoholism. **Acq:** Purchase. **Dist:** The Cinema Guild.

Alcoholism in Industry 1977
This program was designed to help the professional appeal to the employer's emotional, financial, and humanistic character with regard to alcoholism. 16m; 3/4 U. **C:** Fr. Joseph Martin. **Pr:** FMS Productions. **A:** Adult. **P:** Professional. **U:** Institution, SURA. **Bus-Ind:** Alcoholism. **Acq:** Purchase. **Dist:** FMS Productions, Inc.

Alcoholism in Industry: How to Handle the Problem Drinker 1974
How to take advantage of the best motivational tool known to date-the desire of the alcoholic employee to hold down his job. Provides supervisors with the key needed to prevent the problem drinker interfering with on-the-job effectiveness. 30m; VHS, 3/4 U. **Pr:** Bureau of Business Practice. **A:** College-Adult. **P:** Professional. **U:** Institution, CCTV. **Bus-Ind:** Employee Counseling, Alcoholism, Management. **Acq:** Purchase, Rent/Lease. **Dist:** Aspen Publishers, Inc. $495.00.

Alcoholism in the Workplace 1995
Explains warning signs of alcoholism, recognizing symptoms, long-term effects of alcohol, and how to help the alcoholic. 10m; VHS. **A:** Adult. **P:** Professional. **U:** Institution. **L:** Spanish. **Bus-Ind:** Job Training, Management, Alcoholism. **Acq:** Purchase. **Dist:** National Safety Council, California Chapter, Film Library. $195.00.

Alcoholism: Life Under the Influence 1984
This program looks at the nation's largest and least admitted disease, alcoholism. 57m; VHS, 3/4 U, Special order formats. **Pr:** WGBH Boston. **A:** Sr. High-Adult. **P:** Education. **U:** Institution, SURA. **Hea-Sci:** Alcoholism. **Acq:** Purchase, Rent/Lease. **Dist:** Time-Life Video and Television.

Alcoholism: The Drink that Destroys Series 1990
A series about the horrors of alcoholism and its impact on families and society in general. The series emphasizes treatment and recovery. 72m; VHS, 3/4 U. **Pr:** Altschul Group. **A:** Jr. High-Adult. **P:** Education. **U:** Institution, SURA. **Hea-Sci:** Alcoholism, Health Education, Adolescence. **Acq:** Purchase, Rent/Lease. **Dist:** United Learning Inc. $1325.00.
Indiv. Titles: 1. Alcoholism and Teenagers 2. Conquering the Bottle 3. Impact on the Family 4. Surviving Sobriety 5. The Truth About Alcoholism.

Alcoholism: The Hidden Epidemic 1988
A group of experts discuss the physical, emotional, and social problems caused by excessive drinking. 60m; VHS. **Pr:** Cambridge Career Productions. **A:** Jr. High-Adult. **P:** Education. **U:** Institution, Home. **Hea-Sci:** Alcoholism. **Acq:** Purchase. **Dist:** Cambridge Educational. $39.95.

Alcoholism's Children: ACoAs in Priesthood and Religious Life 19??
Clinical psychologist Brother Sean Sammon, provides a thorough look at the difficulties AcoAs face and what they must do to recover. Includes discussions on alcoholism, intervention, and recovery. 120m; VHS. **A:** Jr. High-Adult. **P:** Religious. **U:** Institution, Home. **Gen-Edu:** Religion, Alcoholism, Self-Help. **Acq:** Purchase. **Dist:** Alba House Media Center. $34.95.
Indiv. Titles: 1. Disease of Alcoholism 2. Rules and Roles in Alcoholic Families 3. Details of Roles in Alcoholic Families, Intervention 4. Recovery.

Alcos, Iron Ore and More! 19??
Pays tribute to the Alco and Baldwin diesels that served on the railways of Michigan's Upper Peninsula as Jim Boyd, Editor of Railfan & Railroad Magazine films along the Lake Superior and Ishpeming, Escanaba & Lake Superior, and the Green Bay & Western. 60m; DVD. **A:** Family. **P:** Education. **U:** Home. **L:** English. **Gen-Edu:** Trains, U.S. States. **Acq:** Purchase. **Dist:** Mark 1 Video; The Civil War Standard. $29.95.

Alden for Pittsburgh 1982
This program documents the consecration of The Rt. Rev. Alden M. Hathaway as Bishop of Pittsburgh. 60m; VHS, 3/4 U. **Pr:** WPXI Pittsburgh. **A:** Family. **P:** Religious. **U:** Institution, CCTV, CATV, BCTV, Home. **Gen-Edu:** Religion. **Acq:** Purchase, Rent/Lease. **Dist:** Alliance for Christian Media.

Aldo Ciccolini In Concert 1992
Contains a rare taped concert performance of pianist Aldo Ciccolini as he performs selections by Chopin and Mozart. 89m; VHS. **A:** Jr. High-Adult. **P:** Entertainment. **U:** Home. **Fin-Art:** Performing Arts, Music--Performance, Music--Classical. **Acq:** Purchase. **Dist:** Kultur International Films Ltd., Inc. $14.95.

Aldous Huxley: The Gravity of Light 1996
Hockenhull uses archival footage, animation, and visual effects to explore the social prophecies and cultural criticisms of the writer/thinker. 70m; VHS. **C:** Directed by Oliver Hockenhull. **A:** Sr. High-Adult. **P:** Entertainment. **U:** Home. **Gen-Edu:** Biography. **Acq:** Purchase. **Dist:** Water Bearer Films Inc.

Aldrich Ames: Traitor Within 1998 (PG) — ★★1/2
Hutton stars as Aldrich Ames, a longtime, second-rate CIA employee with an expensive Colombian-born second wife, Rosario (Pena), and a lot of debts. So Ames turns weasel and begins to sell secrets to the Russians in the mid-'80s, which resulted in the deaths of at least 10 agents. Plowright is the CIA analyst in charge of plugging the leak. Both Ames' were arrested and sent to prison in 1994; Rosario was released in 1999 and returned to Bogota. 97m; VHS. **C:** Timothy Hutton; Joan Plowright; Elizabeth Pena; Eugene Lipinski; C. David Johnson; Directed by John MacKenzie; Written by Michael Burton; Cinematography by Walter McGill. **Pr:** Showtime Net-

works. **A:** Jr. High-Adult. **P:** Entertainment. **U:** Home. **Mov-Ent:** Intelligence Service. **Acq:** Purchase. **Dist:** Paramount Pictures Corp.

Alec McCowen in St. Mark's Gospel 1990
Presents a recording of Alec McCowen's solo performance of St. Mark's Gospel. 105m; VHS. **A:** Adult. **P:** Education. **U:** Institution. **Fin-Art:** Theater. **Acq:** Purchase. **Dist:** Insight Media. $139.00.

Alefbet Parade Video 1993
Language arts lesson in the sounds and names of the Hebrew alphabet according to the Sefardic pronunciation. Children learn 31 common words. 30m; VHS. **A:** Primary. **P:** Education. **U:** Institution. **Gen-Edu:** Language Arts. **Acq:** Purchase. **Dist:** Ktav Publishing House Inc. $24.95.

Alejandra Guzman: La Diva del Rock 19??
Guzman performs eight songs including "Estoy Tiener" and "Provocacion." ?m; VHS. **A:** Jr. High-Adult. **P:** Entertainment. **U:** Home. **Mov-Ent:** Music Video. **Acq:** Purchase. **Dist:** Music Video Distributors. $14.95.

Alejandra Guzman: Lo Mejor de Alejandra Guzman 19??
Top Mexican performer Guzman sings "La Playa," "Luz de Luna," "Buena Onda," and "Reina de Corazones." 60m; VHS. **A:** Jr. High-Adult. **P:** Entertainment. **U:** Home. **Mov-Ent:** Music Video, Music--Performance. **Acq:** Purchase. **Dist:** Music Video Distributors. $24.95.

Alejandro Obregon Paints a Fresco 1965
The Colombian painter demonstrates fresco techniques. 21m; VHS, 3/4 U. **Pr:** Museum of Modern Art of Latin America. **A:** Jr. High-Adult. **P:** Education. **U:** Institution, SURA. **Fin-Art:** Art & Artists, Painting. **Acq:** Purchase. **Dist:** Art Museum of The Americas.

Alejo Carpentier: El Derecho De Aslilo 198? — ★
The almost humorous story of an escapee who hides from officials in the residence of a moronic ambassador and his beautiful wife. 60m; VHS. **A:** Jr. High-Adult. **P:** Education. **U:** Institution, SURA. **L:** Spanish. **Mov-Ent. Acq:** Purchase. **Dist:** Films for the Humanities & Sciences.

Aleksandr's Price 2013 (Unrated) — ★½
Illegal Russian emigre Aleksandr doesn't know where to turn after his mother's death so he gets work dancing in gay clubs for the money and the feeling of being desired. Soon, he's working asa prostitute and becoming increasingly troubled as his desperate search for love turns into just another sexual encounter. Low-budget indie wth a familar story. 110m; DVD. **C:** Pau Maso; Josh Berresford; Directed by Pau Maso; Written by Pau Maso; Cinematography by David Damen; Music by Dave Klotz. **A:** Adult. **P:** Entertainment. **U:** Home. **L:** English. **Mov-Ent:** Homosexuality, Prostitution. **Acq:** Purchase. **Dist:** Breaking Glass Pictures.

Aletheia 19??
Looks at how the concept of beauty has been conveyed in the Western culture and the fascination of cosmetic surgery among Asian women. Contains graphic footage. 16m; VHS, 3/4 U, Special order formats. **P:** Education. **U:** Institution. **Gen-Edu:** Asia, Sociology, Health Education. **Acq:** Purchase, Rent/Lease. **Dist:** Third World Newsreel. $180.00.

Alex 1992 (Unrated) — ★★½
Inspirational story about 15-year-old New Zealand swimmer Alex Archer (Jackson), who is working towards a spot at the 1960 Rome Olympics. But her goal is threatened by an accident and a new rival and Alex struggles to overcome her obstacles with the help of her boyfriend Andy (Picker). Based on the novel by Tessa Duder. 92m; VHS. **C:** Lauren Jackson; Chris Haywood; Josh Picker; Catherine Godbold; Elizabeth Hawthorne; Directed by Megan Simpson. **A:** Jr. High-Adult. **P:** Entertainment. **U:** Home. **Mov-Ent:** Adolescence, Swimming, Sports--Olympic. **Acq:** Purchase. **Dist:** MGM Studios Inc.

Alex & Emma 2003 (PG-13) — ★½
The original unwieldy title was "Loosely Based on a True Love Story" because it's loosely based on writer Fyodor Dostoyevsky's story "The Gambler," which was based on a true incident in his life. Or at least that's what the original hype for the movie maintained. Writer Alex (Wilson) has big gambling debts so he takes an advance from his publisher (Reiner) in exchange for churning out a book in 30 days. He hires stenographer Emma (Hudson) to take dictation of his very bad novel, which is set in 1924 and comes to life as Alex spins a story that Emma heartily criticizes. Lame romantic comedy wastes its leads, who have been much more charming in other films (and who have no chemistry together). Lovely blond Hudson is forced into a drab brunette persona that's as unappealing as her wardrobe. 96m; VHS, DVD. **C:** Luke Wilson; Kate Hudson; Sophie Marceau; David Paymer; Francois Giroday; Rob Reiner; Cloris Leachman; Rip Taylor; Directed by Rob Reiner; Written by Jeremy Leven; Cinematography by Gavin Finney; Music by Marc Shaiman. **Pr:** Alan Greisman; Todd Black; Elie Samaha; Jeremy Leven; Rob Reiner; Jeremy Leven; Franchise Pictures; Escape Artists; Warner Bros. **A:** Jr. High-Adult. **P:** Entertainment. **U:** Home. **Mov-Ent:** Comedy--Romantic, Gambling. **Acq:** Purchase. **Dist:** Warner Home Video, Inc.

Alex and Leo 2010 (Unrated) — ★½
Low-budget gay German rom com. Leo finally admits to his longtime girlfriend that he's gay and then immediately begins pursuing Alex, whom he meets in a Berlin bar. Alex has just found out that his boyfriend has not only been cheating but videotaping his sexual encounters so Alex isn't too interested in getting immediately involved with another guy. German with subtitles. 96m; DVD. **C:** Marcel Schlutt; Andre Schneider; Sascia Haj; Udo Lutz; Barbara Kowa; Beate Kurecki; Hans Hendrick Trost; Directed by Ives-Yuri Garate; Written by Andre Schneider; Cinematography by Matthias Stockloew; Music by Leonard Lasry. **A:** College-Adult. **P:** Entertainment. **U:** Home. **L:** German. **Mov-Ent:** Comedy--Romantic. **Acq:** Purchase. **Dist:** Breaking Glass Pictures.

Alex Cross 2012 (PG-13) — **Bomb!**
A future MST3K entry from reel one, Perry's attempt to step into the shoes of the character made popular by Morgan Freeman in the first two films adapted from James Patterson's novels is laughable. The half-asleep Perry plays Cross as he tries to track down a maniacal assassin played with bug-eyed intensity by Fox in what is easily one of the most ridiculous performances of the young decade. At least Fox seems to be concerned with keeping the action moving, which is more than can be said for everyone else involved, especially the lackluster direction by Cohen. 101m; DVD, Blu-Ray; Closed Captioned. **C:** Tyler Perry; Matthew Fox; Edward Burns; Rachel Nichols; Jean Reno; Cicely Tyson; Carmen Ejogo; Directed by Rob Cohen; Written by Kerry Williamson; Marc Moss; Cinematography by Ricardo Della Rosa; Music by John Debney. **Pr:** Bill Block; Paul Hanson; James Patterson; Summit Entertainment; Emmett/Furla Films. **A:** Jr. High-Adult. **P:** Entertainment. **U:** Home. **L:** English. **Mov-Ent:** Crime Drama. **Acq:** Purchase. **Dist:** Summit Entertainment.

Alex Grey & the Chapel of Sacred Mirrors: Cosm the Movie 2006 (Unrated)
Painter, sculptor and author Alex Grey gives a guided tour of the artworks of the Chapel of Sacred Mirrors gallery in New York. 80m; DVD. **A:** Sr. High-Adult. **P:** Education. **U:** Home. **Gen-Edu:** Documentary Films, Art & Artists. **Acq:** Purchase. **Dist:** Docurama. $26.95.

Alex Haley 1992
The author reminisces about his life while newsreel footage captures the changing status of blacks over the years. 50m; VHS. **Pr:** RTSI-Swiss Television. **A:** Sr. High-Adult. **P:** Education. **U:** Institution. **Gen-Edu:** Biography, Black Culture. **Acq:** Purchase. **Dist:** California Newsreel; Films for the Humanities & Sciences. $49.00.

Alex Haley: The Search for Roots 197?
Haley discusses his background, his own life, and his journey to Africa. 18m; VHS, 3/4 U. **C:** Alex Haley. **Pr:** Tony Brown; Black Journal. **A:** College. **P:** Education. **U:** Institution, SURA. **Gen-Edu:** Genealogy. **Acq:** Purchase, Rent/Lease. **Dist:** Films for the Humanities & Sciences.

Alex in Love 2004
Alex is a 13-year old boy living near the futile Persian border and dealing with his lustful feelings for a visiting relative from Poland. In Hebrew with English subtitles. 88m; DVD. **A:** Adult. **P:** Entertainment. **U:** Home. **L:** Hebrew. **Mov-Ent:** Middle East. **Acq:** Purchase. **Dist:** SISU Home Entertainment, Inc. $29.95.

Alex in Wonderland 1970 (R) — ★★½
A semi-autobiographical and satirical look at Hollywood from the standpoint of a young director who's trying to follow up his recent hit (in real life, "Bob & Carol & Ted & Alice") with a picture of some integrity that will keep the mass audience away. The confused plot provides obvious parallels to Fellini (who appears in a cameo) and some sharp, often bitter insights into the Hollywood of the early '60s. Strong performances by Sutherland and Burstyn compensate somewhat for the patience-trying self-indulgent arty whining of the script. 109m; VHS, DVD. **C:** Donald Sutherland; Ellen Burstyn; Paul Mazursky; Cameo(s) Jeanne Moreau; Federico Fellini; Directed by Paul Mazursky; Written by Larry Tucker; Paul Mazursky. **Pr:** MGM. **A:** College-Adult. **P:** Entertainment. **U:** Home. **Mov-Ent:** Satire & Parody, Biography: Show Business. **Acq:** Purchase. **Dist:** WarnerArchive.com; Facets Multimedia Inc. $19.98.

Alex Katz Painting 1979
Katz's paintings are featured along with the story of his creation of the Time Square billboards. 22m; VHS, 3/4 U, Special order formats. **C:** Directed by Randy Burckhardt. **Pr:** Randy Burckhardt. **A:** Jr. High-Adult. **P:** Education. **U:** Institution, Home. **Fin-Art:** Documentary Films, Art & Artists, Painting. **Acq:** Purchase, Rent/Lease. **Dist:** Museum of Modern Art.

Alex Kovalev: My Training Methods 2008 (Unrated)
Professional hockey player Alex Kovalev and personal trainer Tommy Sheehan combine both on-ice and off-ice exercises in a total fitness and strength program designed to benefit hockey players and other athletes. 180m; DVD. **A:** Jr. High-Adult. **P:** Instruction. **U:** Home. **Hea-Sci:** Fitness/Exercise, Hockey. **Dist:** Lions Gate Entertainment Inc. $15.98.

Alex Mack: In the Nick of Time 199?
Episodes from the Nickelodeon series find Alex, an average 13 year-old with a slight problem—she's electric and can turn herself into water. ?m; VHS. **A:** Family. **P:** Entertainment. **U:** Home. **Chl-Juv:** Children, Family Viewing, Family. **Acq:** Purchase. **Dist:** Viacom International Inc.

Alex Rider: Operation Stormbreaker 2006 (PG) — ★★
Horowitz adapted the story from the first book in his own young adult series about 14-year-old Alex Rider (newcomer Pettyfer), who's basically a junior James Bond. Alex is orphaned and living with his spy uncle Ian (McGregor), who's quickly killed off, thus leaving Alex himself to be recruited by MI-6 boss Blunt (Nighy). Good thing the teen's already had all that special ops training. The villain is the ever-creepy Rourke, here playing some evil tycoon with a grudge, and Silverstone is Alex's helpful housekeeper, Jack. There's gadgets and action galore for the undemanding youngster while the adults can stick with Ian Fleming. 93m; DVD. **C:** Ewan McGregor; Mickey Rourke; Bill Nighy; Sophie Okonedo; Alex Pettyfer; Alicia Silverstone; Missi Pyle; Sarah Bolger; Damian Lewis; Andy Serkis; Robbie Coltrane; Stephe Fry; Directed by Geoffrey Sax; Written by Anthony Horowitz; Cinematography by Chris Seager; Music by Alan Parker. **Pr:** Marc Samuelson; Peter Samuelson; Steve Christian; Andreas Grosch; Rising Star; Medienfonds 4. **A:** Jr. High-Adult. **P:** Entertainment. **U:** Home. **L:** English. **Mov-Ent:** Adoption, Adolescence. **Acq:** Purchase. **Dist:** Weinstein Company L.L.C.

Alex Stein's DeMatha Basketball: Strength & Power 2011 (Unrated)
Coach Alan Stein presents exercises and drills for basketball players to increase ankle and core strength. 113m; DVD. **A:** Family. **P:** Education. **U:** Home, Institution. **Spo-Rec:** Basketball, Athletic Instruction/Coaching. **Acq:** Purchase. **Dist:** Championship Productions. $39.99.

Alexander 2004 (R) — ★★
Looooong and somewhat farcical bio of Macedonian conqueror Alexander the Great. In Stone's depiction, Alexander (Farrell) is the pawn in a marital war between his swaggering, drunken father Philip (Kilmer) and his snake-worshipping mother Olympias (a sultry Jolie), who implies that her boy is really the progeny of the god Zeus. Tutored by Aristotle (Plummer), Alexander believes it's his destiny to subjugate as much of the known world as is possible. Lots of big battles ensue as Alexander forcibly unites the squabbling Greek city-states before challenging the might of the Persian empire. He does take some time out to marry hot-blooded Eastern princess, Roxanne (Dawson), while the ruler's relationship with constant companion Hephaistion (Leto) is reduced to meaningful glances. Farrell cannot overcome the fact that he isn't forceful enough to portray an epic figure. 175m; VHS, DVD, Blu-Ray. **C:** Colin Farrell; Angelina Jolie; Val Kilmer; Christopher Plummer; Jared Leto; Rosario Dawson; Anthony Hopkins; Brian Blessed; Jonathan Rhys Meyers; Tim Pigott-Smith; Gary Stretch; John Kavanagh; Ian Beattie; Feodor Atkine; Connor Paolo; Nick Dunning; Marie Meyer; Elliot Cowan; Joseph Morgan; Denis Conway; Neil Jackson; Rory McCann; Raz Degan; Annelise Hesme; Directed by Oliver Stone; Written by Oliver Stone; Laeta Kalogridis; Christopher Kyle; Cinematography by Rodrigo Prieto; Music by Vangelis. **Pr:** Jon Kilik; Iain Smith; Thomas Schuhly; Moritz Borman; Warner Bros. **A:** Sr. High-Adult. **P:** Entertainment. **U:** Home. **Mov-Ent:** Drama, Biography: Military, War--General. **Acq:** Purchase. **Dist:** Warner Home Video, Inc.

Alexander and the Car with a Missing Headlight 1967
An animated film about Alexander's adventures with his little old car, a ferocious dog, a woodpecker, a baby elephant, and an African princess. Available in Swedish. 13m; VHS, 3/4 U. **Pr:** Peter Fleischmann. **A:** Primary. **P:** Entertainment. **U:** Institution, SURA. **L:** English, Swedish. **Chl-Juv. Acq:** Purchase. **Dist:** Weston Woods Studios.

Alexander and the Terrible, Horrible, No Good, Very Bad Day 1989
Judith Viorst's book about a kid who has everything go wrong one day, is brought to life. 30m; VHS. **A:** Primary. **P:** Entertainment. **U:** Home. **Chl-Juv:** Animation & Cartoons, Children, Literature--Children. **Acq:** Purchase. **Dist:** Golden Book Video. $9.95.

Alexander Calder ????
Retrospective of Calder's 16,000 captivating works ranging in size from a matchbox to monuments over seven stories high. 60m; VHS. **A:** Sr. High-Adult. **P:** Education. **U:** Home, Institution. **Gen-Edu:** Art & Artists. **Acq:** Purchase. **Dist:** Crystal Productions. $19.98.

Alexander Calder 1998
A biographical exploration of the life and work of twentieth-century artist Alexander Calder, who devised the mobile as an art form. 57m; DVD. **A:** Sr. High-Adult. **P:** Entertainment. **U:** Home. **Mov-Ent:** Biography: Artists, Documentary Films. **Acq:** Purchase. **Dist:** First Run Features. $24.95.

Alexander Calder: Calder's Universe ????
Features exhibits of Calder's rotating spheres, spinning mobiles, animated wire sculpture, and more. 30m; VHS. **A:** Sr. High-Adult. **P:** Education. **U:** Home, Institution. **Gen-Edu:** Art & Artists. **Acq:** Purchase. **Dist:** Crystal Productions. $19.95.

Alexander Hamilton 1987
From his boyhood through his work with the Washington administration to his death by duel with Aaron Burr, this important American political figure is chronicled. 18m; VHS, 3/4 U. **A:** Primary-Sr. High. **P:** Education. **U:** Institution, SURA. **Gen-Edu:** Biography, History--U.S. **Acq:** Purchase, Trade-in. **Dist:** Encyclopedia Britannica. $240.00.

Alexander Nevsky 19??
The Sydney Orchestra plays the great film score, as well as Tchaikovsky's First Symphony and Beethoven's Third. 134m; VHS. **C:** Conducted by Jose Serebrier. **A:** Adult. **P:** Entertainment. **U:** Home. **Fin-Art:** Music--Classical. **Acq:** Purchase. **Dist:** Music Video Distributors. $29.95.

Alexander Nevsky 1938 — ★★★½
A story of the invasion of Russia in 1241 by the Teutonic Knights of Germany and the defense of the region by good old Prince Nevsky. Eisenstein's first completed project in nearly ten years, it was widely regarded as an artistic disappointment upon release and as pro-war propaganda for the looming conflict with the Nazis. Fabulous Prokofiev score illuminates the classic battle scenes, which used thousands of Russian army regulars. Russian with subtitles. 110m/B/W; VHS, DVD. **TV Std:** NTSC, PAL. **C:** Nikolai Cherkassov; Nikolai P. Okhlopkov; Andrei Abrikosov; Alexandra Danilova; Dmitri Orlov; Vera Ivasheva; Sergei Blinnikov; Lev Fenin; Vladimir Yershov; Nikolai Arsky;

Naum Rogozhin; Varvara O. Massalitinova; Vasili Novikov; Ivan Lagutin; Directed by Sergei Eisenstein; Written by Sergei Eisenstein; Pyotr Pavlenko; Cinematography by Eduard Tisse; Music by Sergei Prokofiev. **A:** Sr. High-Adult. **P:** Entertainment. **U:** Home. **L:** Russian. **Mov-Ent**: Action-Adventure, War--General, Classic Films. **Acq:** Purchase. **Dist:** Image Entertainment Inc.; BMG Entertainment; White Star.

Alexander O'Neal: Live in London 1991
Filmed at Wembley Arena in London during his annual sold out shows, the musician plays "Alex 9000," "Fake," "Criticize," "Time is Running Out," and five more. 60m; VHS. **A:** Jr. High-Adult. **P:** Entertainment. **U:** Home. **Mov-Ent**: Music--Performance. **Acq:** Purchase. **Dist:** Music Video Distributors; Sony Music Entertainment Inc. $19.98.

Alexander Solzhenitsyn: One Word of Truth 1976
Based on the Nobel Prize Acceptance speech the Soviet government refused to let him give, the film is Alexander Solzhenitsyn's personal denouncement of totalitarism and faith in justice: "One word of truth outweighs the whole world." 29m; VHS, 3/4 U. **C:** Narrated by Tom Courtenay. **A:** Sr. High-Adult. **P:** Education. **U:** Institution, SURA. **Gen-Edu**: Literature. **Acq:** Purchase. **Dist:** Films for the Humanities & Sciences.

Alexander Technique: First Lesson 2000
Actor William Hurt and certified Alexander Technique teacher Jane Kominsky teach the posture exercises discovered by F.M. Alexander to beginners. 75m; VHS, DVD. **A:** Sr. High-Adult. **P:** Instruction. **U:** Home. **Hea-Sci**: Yoga. **Acq:** Purchase. **Dist:** Wellspring Media. $24.98.

Alexander Technique: Solutions for Back Pain 2000
Certified Alexander Technique teacher Deborah Caplan posture techniques to help alleviate and prevent back pain. 75m; VHS, DVD. **A:** Sr. High-Adult. **P:** Instruction. **U:** Home. **Hea-Sci**: Yoga. **Acq:** Purchase. **Dist:** Wellspring Media. $24.98.

Alexander the Great 1955 — ★★½
A lavish epic about the legendary Greek conqueror of the fourth century B.C., which provides Burton a rare chance at an adventure role. Here we find Alexander is the product of a dysfunctional royal family who hopes to create an idealized world modeled after Greek culture to make up for the love he lacks from daddy. This he does by conquering everything before dying at the age of 33. The great cast helps to overcome the sluggish pacing of the spectacle, while numerous battle scenes featuring loads of spears and arrows are staged effectively. 135m; VHS, DVD, Wide. **C:** Richard Burton; Fredric March; Claire Bloom; Harry Andrews; Peter Cushing; Danielle Darrieux; Helmut Dantine; Directed by Robert Rossen; Cinematography by Robert Krasker. **Pr:** Rossen Films; United Artists. **A:** Jr. High-Adult. **P:** Entertainment. **U:** Home. **Mov-Ent**: Drama, Biography: Military, War--General. **Acq:** Purchase. **Dist:** MGM Home Entertainment; Facets Multimedia Inc. $19.98.

Alexander the Great 1982
Offers instruction on specific aspects of true and mythological saints and legends. 30m; VHS. **A:** Adult. **P:** Education. **U:** Institution. **Gen-Edu**: History. **Acq:** Purchase. **Dist:** RMI Media. $69.95.

Alexander the Great: Conquerors ????
Reenactments, location footage, and historical artwork follow the rise of a young general on a quest for world domination. 26m; VHS; Closed Captioned. **A:** Jr. High-Sr. High. **P:** Education. **U:** Institution. **Gen-Edu**: History--Ancient, Biography. **Acq:** Purchase. **Dist:** Zenger Media. $39.95.

Alexander the Last 2009 (Unrated) — ★½
Brief mumblecore drama from Swanberg with a lot of improvised dialogue by the actors that may be more realistic but isn't very interesting. Married actress Alex is rehearsing a very-Off Broadway play with costar Jamie in which the director needs them to simulate a sex scene and make it seem hot. With her husband out of town, Alex starts getting increasingly uncomfortable about her attraction to the other man. 72m; DVD. **C:** Jess Weixler; Barlow Jacobs; Justin M. Rice; Jane Adams; Josh Hamilton; Amy Seimetz; Jo Schornikow; Directed by Joe Swanberg; Written by Joe Swanberg; Cinematography by Joe Swanberg; Music by Justin M. Rice; Jo Schornikow. **A:** Sr. High-Adult. **P:** Entertainment. **U:** Home. **Mov-Ent. Acq:** Purchase. **Dist:** MPI Media Group.

Alexander: The Other Side of Dawn 1977 — ★★
Tired sequel to the television movie "Dawn: Portrait of a Teenage Runaway." A young man turns to prostitution to support himself on the street of Los Angeles. 100m; VHS, DVD. **C:** Leigh McCloskey; Eve Plumb; Earl Holliman; Juliet Mills; Jean Hagen; Lonny (Lonnie) Chapman; Directed by John Erman. **Pr:** Douglas Cramer Productions. **A:** Jr. High-Adult. **P:** Entertainment. **U:** Home. **Mov-Ent**: TV Movies, Prostitution. **Acq:** Purchase. **Dist:** East West.

Alexander von Humboldt: Venezuela, 1799 1976
From the "Ten Who Dared" series, recalls the explorations of the "Father of Geography" who came to observe the forces of nature and their effect on plant and animal life in uncharted zones. 49m; VHS, 3/4 U, Special order formats. **C:** Narrated by Anthony Quinn. **Pr:** British Broadcasting Corporation; Time-Life Multimedia. **A:** Jr. High-Sr. High. **P:** Education. **U:** Institution, SURA. **Gen-Edu**: Explorers. **Acq:** Purchase, Rent/Lease. **Dist:** Time-Life Video and Television.

Alexander's Ragtime Band 1938 — ★★★
Energetic musical that spans 1915 to 1938 and has Power and Ameche battling for Faye's affections. Power is a society nabob who takes up ragtime. He puts together a band, naming the group after a piece of music (hence the title), and finds a singer (Faye). Ameche is a struggling composer who brings a Broadway producer to listen to their performance. Faye gets an offer to star in a show and becomes an overnight success. Over the years the trio win and lose success, marry and divorce, and finally end up happy. Corny but charming. 105m/B/W; VHS, DVD. **C:** Tyrone Power; Alice Faye; Don Ameche; Ethel Merman; Jack Haley; Jean Hersholt; Helen Westley; John Carradine; Paul Hurst; Joe King; Ruth Terry; Directed by Henry King; Written by Kathryn Scola; Lamar Trotti; Music by Irving Berlin. **Pr:** Darryl F. Zanuck; 20th Century-Fox. **A:** Jr. High-Adult. **P:** Entertainment. **U:** Home. **Mov-Ent**: Musical, Romance, Theater. **Awds:** Oscars '38: Score. **Acq:** Purchase. **Dist:** Fox Home Entertainment. $19.98.
Songs: Alexander's Ragtime Band; All Alone; Blue Skies; Easter Parade; Everybody's Doin' It; Everybody Step; For Your Country and My Country; Heat Wave; I Can Always Find a Little Sunshine at the YMCA; Marie; My Walking Stick; Now It Can Be Told; Oh, How I Hate to Get Up In the Morning; Pack Up Your Sins and Go to the Devil; A Pretty Girl Is Like a Melody; Ragtime Violin; Remember; Say It With Music; That International Rag; This Is the Life; We're On Our Way to France; What'll I Do?; When the Midnight Choo-Choo Leaves for Alabam'.

Alexandria Again and Forever 1990 (Unrated) — ★★
Yehia (Chahine) remembers his win as best director at the Berlin Film Festival a decade before for his political film "Alexandria...Why?" and thinks about that film's leading man with whom he fell in love. But when he meets and falls for Nadia, Yehia decides he will launch her career as the star of his new film. The final part of Chahine's Alexandria trilogy, following "Alexandria...Why?" and "An Egyptian Story." Arabic with subtitles. 105m; VHS, DVD, Wide. **C:** Youssef Chahine; Zaki Abdel Wahab; Menha Batraoui; Teheya Cariocca; Amr Abdel Guelil; Yousra; Directed by Youssef Chahine; Written by Youssef Chahine; Cinematography by Ingy Assolh; Music by Mohammed Nouh. **A:** College-Adult. **P:** Entertainment. **U:** Home. **L:** Arabic. **Mov-Ent**: Documentary Films, Filmmaking. **Acq:** Purchase. **Dist:** Wellspring Media.

The Alexandria Trilogy 19??
Three films of love, politics and cinema from Egyptian filmmaker Youssef Chahine. DVD features include Interactive Menus, Scene Access, Filmographies and Awards and Weblinks. ?m; VHS, DVD. **A:** Adult. **P:** Entertainment. **U:** Home. **Mov-Ent**: Drama, Romance. **Acq:** Purchase. **Dist:** Arab Film Distribution. $49.99.
Indiv. Titles: 1. Alexandria Why 2. An Egyptian Story 3. Alexandria Again and Forever.

Alexandria. . . Why? 1978 (Unrated) — ★★
Schoolboy (director Chahine uses his adolescent recollections) tries to ignore the war in Alexandria in 1942 by escaping into the movies and his dreams of becoming a star. He also witnesses two love affairs—one between a Muslim man and a Jewish woman and the second betweeen an Arab nationalist and an English soldier. Part 1 of Chahine's Alexandria trilogy, followed by "An Egyptian Story" and "Alexandria Again and Forever." Arabic with subtitles. 133m; VHS, DVD, Wide. **C:** Gerry Sundquist; Naglaa Fathi; Farid Shawqi; Mohsen Mohiedine; Directed by Youssef Chahine; Written by Youssef Chahine; Cinematography by Mohsen Nasr; Music by Foad El Zaheri. **A:** College-Adult. **P:** Entertainment. **U:** Home. **L:** Arabic. **Mov-Ent**: World War Two. **Acq:** Purchase. **Dist:** Wellspring Media.

Alexi Lalas: Teaches Soccer's Instep Drive 1997
Professional soccer player Alexi Lalas teaches children the instep drive. Also contains music written and performed by Lalas. ?m; VHS. **A:** Family. **P:** Instruction. **U:** Home. **Spo-Rec**: Sports--General, Soccer. **Acq:** Purchase. **Dist:** Tapeworm Video Distributors Inc. $16.95.

Alexia 2002 (Unrated)
Experimental video exploring word blindness, a condition that afflicts people who have suffered a stroke causing them to lose visual recognition of individual letters but perceive the whole word or vice versa. 10m; DVD. **A:** Adult. **P:** Education. **U:** Institution. **Gen-Edu**: Stroke, Blindness. **Acq:** Purchase. **Dist:** Third World Newsreel. $175.

Alexis Sklarevski: Slap Bass Program 198?
Choking, damping, percussive right-hand tapping, funk patterns, machine gun triplets and more are covered in this video. Highly recommended by Guitar Player and Guitar World magazines. 83m; VHS. **A:** Sr. High-Adult. **P:** Instruction. **U:** Home. **How-Ins**: Music--Instruction. **Acq:** Purchase. **Dist:** Music Video Distributors. $49.95.

Alf Landon at 90 1978
Provides an interview with Alfred M. Landon, former Bull Moose Progressive, former governor of Kansas, and Republican candidate for president in 1936. He retains political interest, runs his radio stations and oil business, and rides his horse every morning. 30m; 3/4 U, EJ. **Pr:** NETCHE. **A:** College-Adult. **P:** Education. **U:** Institution, CCTV, BCTV, SURA. **Gen-Edu**: Politics & Government. **Acq:** Purchase, Rent/Lease, Subscription. **Dist:** NETCHE.

ALF: Project ALF 2005 (Unrated)
Follow-up to the 1986-1990 NBC television comedy about ALF (short for "alien life form")?a brown furry extraterrestrial from the planet Melmac whose real name is Gordon Shumway—after he leaves the Tanner family to return to his home planet only to held hostage by the Alien Task Force with Colonel Milfoil (Sheen) who's bent on getting rid of him while two doctors (O'Leary and Daggett) try to get him out of the mess. 91m; DVD. **C:** Martin Sheen; Jensen (Jennifer) Daggett; William O'Leary; Benji Gregory. **A:** Family. **P:** Entertainment. **U:** Home. **Mov-Ent**: Television Series, Family, Science Fiction. **Acq:** Purchase. **Dist:** Music Video Distributors. $14.98.

ALF: Season 1 2004 (Unrated)
Features the debut season of the 1986-1990 NBC television comedy about ALF (short for "alien life form")?a brown furry extraterrestrial from the planet Melmac whose real name is Gordon Shumway—and his life with the Tanner family who keeps his identity under wraps after he crash-lands on their garage. Includes: ALF tries his hand at telephone cosmetic sales, dad Willie (Wright) gets angry at ALF at a family camping outing, a blow to the head makes ALF think he's actually an insurance salesman, and ALF must take over the wheel for an airplane pilot who becomes ill. 26 episodes. 616m; DVD. **C:** Max Wright; Ann Schedeen; Andrea Elson; Benji Gregory; Paul Fusco. **A:** Family. **P:** Entertainment. **U:** Home. **Mov-Ent**: Television Series, Family, Science Fiction. **Acq:** Purchase. **Dist:** Lions Gate Entertainment Inc. $39.98.

ALF: Season 2 2005
Four-disc set of the sitcom starring a furry alien stranded on earth. DVD. **A:** Family. **P:** Entertainment. **U:** Home. **Mov-Ent**: Television. **Acq:** Purchase. **Dist:** Lions Gate Home Entertainment; CinemaNow Inc. $39.98.

ALF: Season 3 2006 (Unrated)
Features the third season of the 1986-1990 NBC television comedy about ALF (short for "alien life form")?a brown furry extraterrestrial from the planet Melmac whose real name is Gordon Shumway—and his life with the Tanner family who keeps his identity under wraps after he crash-lands on their garage. Includes: a two-parter of ALF hosting "The Tonight Show" with sidekick Ed McMahon, a magic trick goes awry when ALF makes Brian (Gregory) disappear, and ALF thinks their neighbor is actually Elvis. 26 episodes. 600m; DVD. **C:** Max Wright; Ann Schedeen; Andrea Elson; Benji Gregory; Paul Fusco. **A:** Family. **P:** Entertainment. **U:** Home. **Mov-Ent**: Television Series, Family, Science Fiction. **Acq:** Purchase. **Dist:** Lions Gate Entertainment Inc. $39.98.

ALF: Season 4 2006 (Unrated)
Features the fourth season of the 1986-1990 NBC television comedy about ALF (short for "alien life form")?a brown furry extraterrestrial from the planet Melmac whose real name is Gordon Shumway—and his life with the Tanner family who keeps his identity under wraps after he crash-lands on their garage. Includes: the Tanners scramble to recover pictures taken of ALF, Willie (Wright) is visited by his brother irking ALF who has to hide, and ALF leaves Earth and the Tanners only to be caught by the Alien Task Force. 22 episodes. 500m; DVD. **C:** Max Wright; Ann Schedeen; Andrea Elson; Benji Gregory; Paul Fusco. **A:** Family. **P:** Entertainment. **U:** Home. **Mov-Ent**: Television Series, Family, Science Fiction. **Acq:** Purchase. **Dist:** Lions Gate Entertainment Inc. $39.98.

ALF Tales: ALF and the Beanstalk and Other Classic Fairy Tales 2006 (Unrated)
Includes episodes from the animated 1987-1990 television series with AL (short for "alien life form"), a brown furry extraterrestrial from the planet Melmac whose real name is Gordon Shumway—as he tells classic children's stories such as "Robin Hood," "Sleeping Beauty," and "Jack and the Beanstalk." 7 episodes. 163m; DVD. **C:** Paul Fusco; Peggy Mahon; Paulina Gillis; Thick Wilson. **A:** Family. **P:** Entertainment. **U:** Home. **Mov-Ent**: Television Series, Science Fiction, Animation & Cartoons. **Acq:** Purchase. **Dist:** Lions Gate Entertainment Inc. $14.98.

ALF: The ALF Files 2002 (Unrated)
Features various episodes from the 1986-1990 NBC television comedy about ALF (short for "alien life form")?a brown furry extraterrestrial from the planet Melmac whose real name is Gordon Shumway—and his life with the Tanner family who keeps his identity under wraps after he crash-lands on their garage. Includes: ALF gets amnesia and thinks he's an insurance salesman, ALF is mistaken for a toy and given away while the Tanners are on a Christmas holiday at a cabin, and ALF joins Ed McMahon on "The Tonight Show." 3 episodes. 144m; DVD. **C:** Max Wright; Ann Schedeen; Andrea Elson; Benji Gregory; Paul Fusco. **A:** Family. **P:** Entertainment. **U:** Home. **Mov-Ent**: Television Series, Family, Science Fiction. **Acq:** Purchase. **Dist:** Lions Gate Entertainment Inc. $19.98.

ALF: The Animated Series - 20,000 Years in Driving School 2006 (Unrated)
Contains episodes from the animated 1987-1990 NBC television series on ALF (short for "alien life form"), a brown furry extraterrestrial from the planet Melmac whose real name is Gordon Shumway—and his life on his home planet prior to crash-landing on Earth. Includes "Phantom Pilot," "Hair Today, Bald Tomorrow," "Two for the Brig," "Gordon Ships Out," "Birdman of Melmac," "Pismo and the Orbit Gyro," "20,000 Years in Driving School," "Pride of the Shumways," and "Captain Bobaroo." 9 episodes. 198m; DVD. **C:** Paul Fusco; Thick Wilson; Peggy Mahon; Paulina Gillis. **A:** Family. **P:** Entertainment. **U:** Home. **Mov-Ent**: Television Series, Science Fiction, Animation & Cartoons. **Acq:** Purchase. **Dist:** Lions Gate Entertainment Inc. $9.98.

Alfie 1966 (PG) — ★★★
What's it all about, Alfie? Caine, in his first starring role, plays the British playboy out of control in mod London. Alfie is a despicable, unscrupulous and vile sort of guy who uses woman after woman to fulfill his basic needs and then casts them aside until...tragedy strikes. Though this box office hit was seen as a sophisticated take on current sexual mores upon release, it now seems a dated but engaging comedy, notable chiefly for its performances. From the play by Bill Naughton. The title song "Alfie," sung by Dionne Warwick, was a top ten hit. 114m; VHS, DVD, Wide. **C:** Michael Caine; Shelley Winters; Millicent Martin; Vivien Merchant; Julia Foster; Jane Asher; Shirley Anne Field; Eleanor Bron; Denholm Elliott; Alfie Bass; Graham Stark; Mur-

ray Melvin; Sydney Tafler; Directed by Lewis Gilbert; Written by Bill Naughton; Cinematography by Otto Heller; Music by Burt Bacharach; Sonny Rollins. **Pr:** Paramount Pictures. **A:** Jr. High-Adult. **P:** Entertainment. **U:** Home. **Mov-Ent:** Sex & Sexuality. **Awds:** Cannes '67: Grand Jury Prize; Golden Globes '67: Foreign Film; Natl. Bd. of Review '66: Support. Actress (Merchant); Natl. Soc. Film Critics '66: Actor (Caine). **Acq:** Purchase. **Dist:** Paramount Pictures Corp. $14.95.

Alfie 2004 (R) — ★★½
Law plays a kinder, gentler lothario in this contemporary update of the 1966 film (which helped make Michael Caine a star), although Alfie still engages in a somewhat self-conscious running commentary directed to the camera. The charming, handsome Alfie is now a limo driver in New York who indulges himself with as many beautiful birds as will put up with him. These include the lonely, married Dorie (Krakowski); single mom Julie (Tomei), who kicks him out after realizing Alfie is a horn-dog; sexy, self-destructive party girl Nikki (Miller); and foxy Lonette (Long), the ex-girlfriend of his best friend Marlon (Epps). But even Alfie must pay for his dalliances when he suffers a bout of impotence and then meets his sexual match in worldly mature beauty Liz (Sarandon). While Alfie remains a narcissist (though ever-so-appealing as played by Law) at least the women characters are no longer complaisant or compliant. 106m; VHS, DVD. **C:** Jude Law; Marisa Tomei; Omar Epps; Nia Long; Jane Krakowski; Sienna Miller; Susan Sarandon; Renee Taylor; Dick Latessa; Jefferson Mays; Gedde Watanabe; Directed by Charles Shyer; Written by Charles Shyer; Elaine Pope; Cinematography by Ashley Rowe; Music by Mick Jagger; David A. Stewart; John Powell. **Pr:** Charles Shyer; Charles Shyer; Elaine Pope; Paramount. **A:** Sr. High-Adult. **P:** Entertainment. **U:** Home. **Mov-Ent:** Comedy-Drama, Sex & Sexuality. **Awds:** Golden Globes '05: Song ("Old Habits Die Hard"). **Acq:** Purchase. **Dist:** Paramount Pictures Corp. $29.95.

Alfred G. Graebner Memorial High School Handbook of Rules and Regulations 1984
Also available in a 30 minute version, this film depicts a freshman girl's efforts to fit into high school life. 44m; VHS, 3/4 U. **Pr:** ABC Afterschool Special. **A:** Jr. High-Sr. High. **P:** Education. **U:** Institution. **Gen-Edu:** Adolescence. **Acq:** Purchase, Rent/Lease. **Dist:** Phoenix Learning Group.

Alfred Hitchcock 1972
Features the late great director discussing his life and work with television journalist Pia Lindstrom and film historian William Everson. Includes excerpts from many of his films and a montage of Hitchcock's cameo appearances in his own films. 58m; VHS, 3/4 U. **A:** Sr. High-Adult. **P:** Education. **U:** Home. **Gen-Edu:** Filmmaking, Film History. **Acq:** Purchase. **Dist:** Camera Three Productions, Inc.

Alfred Hitchcock Presents: Season Four 1958 (Unrated)
CBS 1955-60 mystery series. Includes such classics as "Poison" directed by Alfred Hitchcock, "Don't Interrupt" guest starring Cloris Leachman, "The Jokester" guest starring James Coburn, "Design for Loving" written by Ray Bradbury, "A Man with a Problem" guest starring Elizabeth Montgomery, "The Morning After" guest starring Fay Wray, "Out There - Darkness" directed by Paul Henreid, guest starring Bette Davis, "The Diamond Necklace" stars Claude Rains, "A Night with the Boys" directed by Norman Lloyd costarring Brian Keith, and "The Dusty Drawer" guest starring Dick York. 36 episodes. 930m; DVD. **C:** Alfred Hitchcock. **A:** Family. **P:** Entertainment. **U:** Home. **Mov-Ent:** Mystery & Suspense, Television Series. **Acq:** Purchase. **Dist:** Universal Studios Home Video. $39.99.

Alfred Hitchcock Presents: Season One 2005 (Unrated)
Offers the debut season of the 1955-1962 television series hosted by Alfred Hitchcock with short stories on a variety of topics, in particular horror, drama, suspense, and fantasy and highlighted by the host's commentary. Includes: during a woman's trip to Paris her mother disappears from their hotel room though no one else recalls her being there, a mobster has it out for a singer who murdered his brother, a death at vaudeville theater leaves a ventriloquist and his realistic puppet as a suspect, and a man takes a bet to stay overnight at a "haunted" manor. 39 episodes. 1003m; DVD. **C:** Alfred Hitchcock. **A:** Jr. High-Adult. **P:** Entertainment. **U:** Home. **Mov-Ent:** Television Series, Horror, Drama. **Acq:** Purchase. **Dist:** Universal Studios Home Video. $39.98.

Alfred Hitchcock Presents: Season Two 2006 (Unrated)
Offers the debut season of the 1955-1962 television series hosted by Alfred Hitchcock with short stories on a variety of topics, in particular horror, drama, suspense, and fantasy and highlighted by the host's commentary. Includes: a man wants to cash in on his rich aunt by pretending to be someone else and killing her, a mortgage banker isn't safe around two sisters who want to poison him, a son isn't too pleased when his widowed dad ties the knot, and a woman looks suspicious to her insurance company when she plans to remarry after her first two husbands died under questionable circumstances. 39 episodes. 1014m; DVD. **C:** Alfred Hitchcock. **A:** Jr. High-Adult. **P:** Entertainment. **U:** Home. **Mov-Ent:** Television Series, Horror, Drama. **Acq:** Purchase. **Dist:** Universal Studios Home Video. $39.98.

Alfred Hitchcock's Aventure Malgache 1944
Hitchcock worked with the Moliere Players on this propaganda piece about the French Resistance. He based this story on the experiences of the actor Clarousse. Working for the Resistance in occupied Madagascar, Clarousse is betrayed and sent to prison by the Vichy government. Rescued by the British he returns to resume his work. In French with English subtitles. 31m/B/W; VHS, DVD. **C:** Directed by Alfred Hitchcock; Cinematography by Gunther Krampf. **Pr:** British Ministry of Information. **A:** College-Adult. **P:** Entertainment. **U:** Home. **L:** French, English. **Mov-Ent:** World War Two, Propaganda. **Acq:** Purchase. **Dist:** Milestone Film & Video.

Alfred Hitchcock's Bon Voyage 1944
One of director Hitchcock's short propaganda pieces filmed as a tribute to the French Resistance. In London an RAF pilot is interrogated by the Free French about his escape from France. He was aided by a Polish agent who was actually working for the Gestapo to learn about the Resistance's movements. Flashbacks show the pilot's adventures from the spy's point-of-view. In French with English subtitles. 26m/B/W; VHS, DVD. **C:** John Blythe; Directed by Alfred Hitchcock; Written by J.O.C. Orton; Cinematography by Gunther Krampf. **Pr:** British Ministry of Information. **A:** College-Adult. **P:** Entertainment. **U:** Home. **L:** French, English. **Mov-Ent:** World War Two, Propaganda. **Acq:** Purchase. **Dist:** Milestone Film & Video. $39.95.

Alfred, Lord Tennyson: "The Charge of the Light Brigade": A Modern Reexamination 1993
Diverse views on Tennyson's famous poem. 25m; VHS. **A:** Sr. High. **P:** Education. **U:** Home. **Gen-Edu:** Education. **Acq:** Purchase. **Dist:** Films for the Humanities & Sciences. $149.00.

Alfred Stieglitz, Photographer 1982
Ansel Adams, Aaron Copeland, Isamu Noguichi and others narrate this tribute to Stieglitz, a pioneering photographer and a patron of the arts. 26m; 3/4 U, Special order formats. **C:** Directed by Paul Falkenberg; Hans Namuth. **Pr:** Paul Falkenberg; Hans Namuth. **A:** Sr. High-Adult. **P:** Education. **U:** Institution. **Gen-Edu:** Documentary Films, Photography. **Acq:** Purchase, Rent/Lease. **Dist:** Museum of Modern Art; Crystal Productions. $19.95.

Alfred Wallis: Artist and Mariner 1973
The primitive and passionate works of untrained painter Wallis are featured. 23m; 3/4 U, Special order formats. **C:** Directed by Christopher Mason. **Pr:** Arts Council of Great Britain. **A:** Sr. High-Adult. **P:** Education. **U:** Institution. **Fin-Art:** Documentary Films, Art & Artists, Painting. **Acq:** Purchase, Rent/Lease. **Dist:** Museum of Modern Art.

Alfredo, Alfredo 1972 (R) — ★★
Hoffman plays a mild-mannered bank clerk who regrets marrying a sexy woman. Lightweight domestic comedy. In Italian with English subtitles (Hoffman's voice was dubbed). 97m; VHS, DVD, CC. **C:** Dustin Hoffman; Stefania Sandrelli; Carla Gravina; Clara Colosimo; Daniela Patella; Dulio Del Prete; Directed by Pietro Germi; Written by Pietro Germi; Leonardo Benvenuti; Cinematography by Aiace Parolini; Music by Carlo Rustichelli. **A:** College-Adult. **P:** Entertainment. **U:** Home. **L:** Italian. **Mov-Ent:** Comedy--Romantic, Marriage. **Acq:** Purchase. **Dist:** Amazon.com Inc.; Paramount Pictures Corp.

Alfredo Kraus: Werther 1991
Alfredo Kraus returns to the site of his debut at the Teatro Sao Carlo in Lisbon and performs his favorite characterization, the title role of Jules Massenet's opera "Werther." 60m; VHS. **A:** Jr. High-Adult. **P:** Entertainment. **U:** Home. **Fin-Art:** Opera, Performing Arts, Music--Performance. **Acq:** Purchase. **Dist:** Kultur International Films Ltd., Inc. $24.95.

Alfred's Drum Method, Books 1 & 2 1990
Step-by-step instruction in percussion instruments, on two tapes. Tape one is an introduction to drums; tape two advances to a higher level and introduces accessory instruments. ?m; VHS. **Pr:** Alfred Publishing Company. **A:** Jr. High-Adult. **P:** Instruction. **U:** Institution, Home. **How-Ins:** How-To, Music--Instruction. **Acq:** Purchase. **Dist:** Alfred Music Publishing Company Inc. $39.95.

Algae 1988
A documentary about the five major groups of algae and their ecological and economic importance. 14m; VHS, 3/4 U. **Pr:** Indiana University Audio-Visual Center. **A:** Jr. High-Sr. High. **P:** Education. **U:** Institution, SURA. **Hea-Sci:** Biology, Plants. **Acq:** Purchase, Rent/Lease. **Dist:** Encyclopedia Britannica. $255.00.

Algebra 1 Series 1991
A six volume series teaching the ins and outs of basic through intermediate algebra, including graphing equations, quadratic equations, radicals, square roots, and more. Different length cassettes, depending on material covered. 395m; VHS. **A:** Jr. High-Adult. **P:** Instruction. **U:** Institution, Home. **How-Ins:** How-To, Mathematics. **Acq:** Purchase. **Dist:** Video Tutorial Service, Inc. $29.95.

Algebra: Elementary 1990
A four-tape instructional series which teaches you all the basics and some of the more advanced functions of algebra. 480m; VHS. **Pr:** VAI. **A:** Family. **P:** Education. **U:** Home. **Gen-Edu:** Education, Mathematics. **Acq:** Purchase. **Dist:** Video Aided Instruction Inc.; Moonbeam Publications Inc. $119.95.

Algebra: Intermediate 1991
A two-tape instructional series which teaches you some more advanced functions of algebra. 240m; VHS. **Pr:** VAI. **A:** Adult. **P:** Education. **U:** Home. **Gen-Edu:** Education. **Acq:** Purchase. **Dist:** Moonbeam Publications Inc.; Video Aided Instruction Inc. $59.95.

Algebraic Expressions 1993
Part of a series that offers instruction in algebra, covering expressions, exponents, real numbers, solving equations, polynomials, factoring, and graphing linear equations and inequalities. 45m; VHS. **A:** Jr. High-Sr. High. **P:** Education. **U:** Institution. **Gen-Edu:** Mathematics. **Acq:** Purchase. **Dist:** RMI Media. $50.00.

Algeria: Women at War 1992
Documents Algerian women and the role they played in their country's liberation struggle from the French 30 years ago. Examines their equally important place in today's politics and explores the balancing act between women's and national liberation struggles. 52m; VHS. **A:** College-Adult. **P:** Education. **U:** Institution. **Gen-Edu:** Women, Middle East, Violence. **Acq:** Purchase, Rent/Lease. **Dist:** Women Make Movies. $295.00.

Algiers 1938 (Unrated) — ★★★
Nearly a scene-for-scene Americanized remake of the 1937 French "Pepe Le Moko" about a beautiful rich girl (Lamarr) who meets and falls in love with a notorious thief (Boyer, then a leading sex symbol). Pursued by French police and hiding in the underworld-controlled Casbah, Boyer meets up with Lamarr in a tragically fated romance done in the best tradition of Hollywood. Boyer provides a measured performance as Le Moko, while Lamarr is appropriately sultry in her American film debut (which made her a star). Later remade as the semi-musical "Casbah." 96m/B/W; DVD, 3/4 U, Special order formats. **C:** Charles Boyer; Hedy Lamarr; Sigrid Gurie; Gene Lockhart; Joseph Calleia; Alan Hale; Directed by John Cromwell; Cinematography by James Wong Howe. **Pr:** Walter Wanger. **A:** Family. **P:** Entertainment. **U:** Home. **Mov-Ent:** Drama, Africa. **Acq:** Purchase. **Dist:** Synergy Entertainment, Inc.; Gotham Distributing Corp.; VCX Ltd. $9.95.

Ali 1998
Follows a young girl's battle with a rare form of cancer of the course of two years. 30m; VHS. **A:** Family. **P:** Education. **U:** Institution. **Hea-Sci:** Health Education, Patient Education, Cancer. **Acq:** Purchase. **Dist:** Aquarius Health Care Media. $150.00.

Ali 2001 (R) — ★★½
Mann, a notorious obsessive, couldn't have picked a more ambitious topic. The herculean task proves too much, yielding a film that lacks focus or insight into its subject. Ali is depicted during a contentious decade (1964-1974), in which he converted to Islam, befriended civil rights icons, refused the draft, was stripped of his title, married three times, and blurred lines between sport, ethics and society. Perhaps it's no coincidence that screenwriter Roth, who previously penned "Forrest Gump," was chosen to chronicle Ali amid such historic happenings. Mann's visual skills are apparent, and Smith gives an inspired performance in and out of the ring. Other noteworthies include Foxx as cornerman "Bundini" Brown, and Voight as verbose sportscaster Cosell. Despite the charisma of its subject (and its lead), film feels distant and subdued. Lands a few clean blows, but certainly not a knockout. 158m; VHS, DVD, Wide. **C:** Will Smith; Jamie Foxx; Jon Voight; Mario Van Peebles; Ron Silver; Jeffrey Wright; Mykelti Williamson; Jada Pinkett Smith; Michael Michele; Joe Morton; Paul Rodriguez; Nona Gaye; Bruce McGill; Barry (Shabaka) Henley; Giancarlo Esposito; Laurence Mason; LeVar Burton; Albert Hall; David Cubitt; Ted Levine; David Elliott; Michael Bentt; James N. Toney; Charles Shufford; Malick Bowens; Shari Watson; Victoria Dillard; Kim Robillard; Gailard Sartain; Rufus Dorsey; Robert Sale; Damien "Bolo" Wills; Michael Dorn; Directed by Michael Mann; Written by Michael Mann; Stephen J. Rivele; Christopher Wilkinson; Eric Roth; Cinematography by Emmanuel Lubezki; Music by Lisa Gerrard; Pieter Bourke. **Pr:** James Lassiter; Paul Ardaji; Jon Peters; A. Kitman Ho; Michael Mann; Michael Mann; Peters Entertainment; Forward Pass Productions; Overbrook Films; Columbia Pictures. **A:** Sr. High-Adult. **P:** Entertainment. **U:** Home. **Mov-Ent:** Boxing, Biography: Sports, Black Culture. **Acq:** Purchase. **Dist:** Sony Pictures Home Entertainment Inc.

Ali Baba 1954
Retells the classic story of Ali Baba who faces many dangers after stealing treasure from a magic cave. In French with English subtitles. 92m; VHS. **A:** Adult. **P:** Entertainment. **U:** Home. **L:** French. **Mov-Ent. Acq:** Purchase. **Dist:** Mercury International Productions Inc. $29.95.

Ali Baba and the Forty Thieves 1943 — ★★½
Ali Baba and his gang of thieves do battle against Hulagu Khan, leader of the Mongols, to save Baghdad and its citizens from ruin and death. 87m; VHS, DVD, CC. **C:** Jon Hall; Turhan Bey; Maria Montez; Andy Devine; Kurt Katch; Frank Puglia; Fortunio Bonanova; Moroni Olsen; Scotty Beckett; Directed by Arthur Lubin; Written by Edmund Hartmann; Cinematography by William Howard Greene. **A:** Jr. High-Adult. **P:** Entertainment. **U:** Home. **Mov-Ent:** Action-Adventure, Middle East. **Acq:** Purchase. **Dist:** Universal Studios Home Video; Facets Multimedia Inc. $14.98.

Ali Baba and the 40 Thieves 1954 — ★★★
French adaptation of the popular novel "A Thousand and One Nights." Servant boy Ali Baba discovers the magic cave holding the stolen treasure of Abdul and his 40 thieves. Shot on location in Morocco. Also available dubbed. 92m; VHS. **C:** Samia Gamal; Dieter Borsche; Henri Vilbert; Directed by Jacques Becker; Written by Jacques Becker. **A:** Sr. High-Adult. **P:** Entertainment. **U:** Home. **L:** French. **Mov-Ent:** Middle East. **Acq:** Purchase. **Dist:** Mercury International Productions Inc.; Facets Multimedia Inc. $59.95.

Ali Baba and the Forty Thieves 1991
The thieves of Ali-Baba are set loose in this animated classic based on Arabian folklore. 25m; VHS. **A:** Family. **P:** Entertainment. **U:** Home. **Chl-Juv:** Animation & Cartoons, Children. **Acq:** Purchase. **Dist:** Anchor Bay Entertainment. $14.95.

Ali Baba and the Pirates 1996
Animated children's show about the adventures of Ali Baba and his family. 80m; DVD. **A:** Family. **P:** Entertainment. **U:** Home,

Institution. **L**: English, Arabic, French. **Chl-Juv**: Children, Fantasy, Animation & Cartoons. **Acq**: Purchase, Rent/Lease. **Dist**: Arab Film Distribution. $19.99.

Ali Baba and the Seven Saracens 1964 (Unrated) — ★

The hero is either Sinbad or Ali Baba but it's never really clear (maybe it's the atrocious dubbing)?not that it matters anyway. The leaders of eight tribes must battle to the death until a winner is left to be the new ruler to the Golden Throne of the Majii. And whoever our hero is, he's a prime candidate. Dubbed. 92m; DVD. **C**: Gordon Mitchell; Bella Cortez; Bruno Piergentili; Carla Calo; Tony Di Mitri; Directed by Emmimo Salvi. **A**: Jr. High-Adult. **P**: Entertainment. **U**: Home. **Mov-Ent. Acq**: Purchase. **Dist**: Sinister Cinema.

Ali Baba's Revenge 1984

The efforts of Al Huck, his rodent side-kick, and a goofy genie combine to overthrow the tyrannical king of Alibaba. The Alibaban peasants (all cats) revolt behind Huck's leadership in response to unfair food and luxury taxes. 53m; VHS. **C**: Voice(s) by Jim Backus; Directed by H. Shidar. **Pr**: ATA Trading Corporation. **A**: Preschool-Jr. High. **P**: Entertainment. **U**: Home. **Chl-Juv**: Animation & Cartoons. **Acq**: Purchase. **Dist**: MPI Media Group.

Ali: Fear Eats the Soul 1974 (Unrated) — ★★★

A widow cleaning woman in her 60s has a love affair with a Moroccan man 30 years her junior. To no one's surprise, both encounter racism and moral hypocrisy in West Germany. Serious melodrama from Fassbinder, who wrote it and appears as the squirmy son-in-law. In German with English subtitles. 68m; VHS, DVD. **C**: Brigitte Mira; El Hedi Ben Salem; Irm Hermann; Directed by Rainer Werner Fassbinder; Written by Rainer Werner Fassbinder; Cinematography by Jurgen Jurges. **A**: Sr. High-Adult. **P**: Entertainment. **U**: Home. **L**: German, English. **Mov-Ent**: Drama, Germany. **Acq**: Purchase. **Dist**: New Yorker Video; Facets Multimedia Inc. $79.95.

Ali MacGraw's Yoga Mind & Body 1994

Low-impact, stress-reducing exercise regimen combining breathing exercises, stretches, and 13 Hatha-style yoga poses. 55m; VHS. **A**: Adult. **P**: Instruction. **U**: Home. **Hea-Sci**: Yoga, Fitness/Exercise. **Acq**: Purchase. **Dist**: Warner Home Video, Inc. $19.98.

Ali-Norton Trilogy: All Three Fights 1980

On March 31, 1973, these two legends first met. In 1976 they would fight their third and final battle. This is a chronicle of their unforgettable meetings. 74m; VHS. **Pr**: Top Rank Inc. **A**: Family. **P**: Entertainment. **U**: Home. **Spo-Rec**: Documentary Films, Boxing. **Acq**: Purchase. **Dist**: School-Tech Inc. $12.95.

Ali Rap 2006

A collection of Muhammad Ali's quips, quotes, and insults. Based on the book by George Lois. 44m; DVD. **A**: Jr. High-Adult. **P**: Entertainment. **U**: Home. **Gen-Edu**: Documentary Films. **Acq**: Purchase. **Dist**: Genius Entertainment.

Ali the Fighter 2005

In 1971 Muhammad Ali came to New York to face unbeaten Joe Frazier for the heavyweight title. Filmmaker William Greaves looks at the training, press conferences, and the controversial 15-round fight. 98m; DVD. **A**: Jr. High-Adult. **P**: Entertainment. **U**: Home. **Gen-Edu**: Documentary Films. **Acq**: Purchase. **Dist**: Anchor Bay Entertainment.

Ali Zaoua: Prince of the Streets 2000

Four young runaways on the streets of Casablanca rebel against the oppressive leader of their gang, running away a second time. With English subtitles. Available in 35mm for rent. 90m; VHS, DVD. **A**: Sr. High-Adult. **P**: Entertainment. **U**: Home, Institution. **L**: Arabic. **Mov-Ent**: Drama. **Acq**: Purchase, Rent/Lease. **Dist**: Arab Film Distribution. $14.99.

Alias 2005

Two girls witness the suicide of a young girl as she plunges to her death from a fourth floor window. They capture the event on video, which leads to a chain of events that will serious alter their lives. 98m; VHS, DVD. **A**: Adult. **P**: Entertainment. **U**: Home. **Mov-Ent**: Drama, Mystery & Suspense. **Acq**: Purchase. **Dist**: Vanguard International Cinema, Inc. $29.95.

Alias Betty 2001 (Unrated) — ★★

Writer Betty (Kiberlain) has recently returned to Paris after separating from her lover. She is uneasily waiting for the arrival of her mother Margot (Garcia), a disturbed woman who abused Betty as a child. Betty's own young son Joseph (Setbon) suddenly dies in an accidental fall and she suffers a breakdown. Jose (Chatrian) is the abused young son of single mother Carole (Seigner). When Margot notices Jose alone in the streets, she takes him back to Betty as a replacement child and Betty debates whether to go along or go to the cops. Based on the book "The Tree of Hands" by Ruth Rendell. French with subtitles. 101m; VHS, DVD. **C**: Sandrine Kiberlain; Nicole Garcia; Mathilde Seigner; Alexis Chatrian; Edouard Baer; Arthur Setbon; Luck Mervil; Stephane Freiss; Directed by Claude Miller; Written by Claude Miller; Cinematography by Christophe Pollock. **Pr**: Yves Marmion; Annie Miller; Go Films; Les Films de la Boissiere; Wellspring Media. **A**: College-Adult. **P**: Entertainment. **U**: Home. **L**: French. **Mov-Ent**: Child Abuse. **Acq**: Purchase. **Dist**: Wellspring Media.

Alias Billy the Kid 1946 (Unrated) — ★★

Western adventure with Carson posing as a famous outlaw to find out who's behind the scam involving the Denton City cattle trade. 54m/B/W; VHS, Streaming, CC. **C**: Sunset Carson; Peggy Stewart; Tom London; Roy Barcroft; Directed by Thomas Carr; Cinematography by Bud Thackery. **A**: Jr. High-Adult. **P**: Entertainment. **U**: Home. **Mov-Ent**: Western. **Acq**: Purchase. **Dist**: Lions Gate Entertainment Inc. $9.98.

Alias Jesse James 1959 (PG) — ★★

Insurance agent Milford Farnsworth (Hope) is an eastern tenderfoot who holds a policy on Jesse James (Corey). So he heads west to make certain the outlaw doesn't get killed. Only Jesse sets Milford up as himself, hoping to collect on his own policy. Fleming's the local beauty. A number of western stars have cameos, coming to Hope's rescue. 92m; VHS, DVD, CC. **C**: Bob Hope; Rhonda Fleming; Wendell Corey; Jim Davis; Gloria Talbott; Will Wright; Mary (Marsden) Young; Joseph (Joe) Vitale; Cameo(s) Hugh O'Brian; Ward Bond; James Arness; Roy Rogers; Fess Parker; Gail Davis; James Garner; Gene Autry; Jay Silverheels; Bing Crosby; Gary Cooper; Directed by Norman Z. McLeod; Written by William Bowers; D.D. Beauchamp; Cinematography by Lionel Lindon. **Pr**: Jack Hope; Hope Enterprises; United Artists. **A**: Jr. High-Adult. **P**: Entertainment. **U**: Home. **Mov-Ent**: Insurance. **Acq**: Purchase. **Dist**: MGM Home Entertainment.

Alias John Law 1935 — ★

The Good Guy fights for oil rights against the bad guys. Confused program western with an especially convoluted plot. 54m/B/W; VHS, DVD. **C**: Bob Steele; Directed by Robert North Bradbury. **A**: Family. **P**: Entertainment. **U**: Home. **Mov-Ent**: Western. **Acq**: Purchase. **Dist**: Movies Unlimited. $14.99.

Alias John Preston 1956 — ★½

Yet another one of those pseudo-psychological to sleep perchance to dream movies. Lee plays a man haunted by dreams in which he's a murderer, and soon starts to question whether his dreams might not imitate life. It's been done before, it's been done since, and it's been done better. 66m/B/W; VHS, DVD. **C**: Betta St. John; Alexander Knox; Christopher Lee; Sandra Dorne; Patrick Holt; Betty Ann Davies; John Longden; Bill Fraser; John Stuart; Directed by David MacDonald. **Pr**: Danzigers; British Lion. **A**: Jr. High-Adult. **P**: Entertainment. **U**: Home. **Mov-Ent**: Mystery & Suspense. **Acq**: Purchase. **Dist**: Sinister Cinema. $19.98.

Alias, La Gringa 1991 — ★★

Follows the adventures of La Gringa, a likeable criminal capable of escaping from any Peruvian jail. After being aided in his latest escape by a political prisoner, La Gringa decides to return in disguise to pay back the favor. But the prison is rocked by rioting and La Gringa finds himself in a situation out of his control. Spanish with subtitles. 100m; VHS. **C**: Orlando Sacha; German Gonzalez; Elsa Olivero; Juan Manuel Ochoa; Directed by Alberto Durant; Written by Alberto Durant; Cinematography by Mario Garcia Joya; Music by Pochi Marambio. **A**: College-Adult. **P**: Entertainment. **U**: Home. **L**: Spanish. **Mov-Ent. Acq**: Purchase. **Dist**: Facets Multimedia Inc. $59.95.

Alias Mary Smith 1932 (Unrated) — ★★

Drunken playboy (Darrow) saves a poor young woman (Mehaffey) from a purse-snatcher but their affair is troublesome since she's trying to declare a gangster is guilty of murder. Lots of laughs on a little budget. 61m/B/W; DVD. **C**: John Darrow; Blanche Mehaffey; Matthew Betz; Henry B. Walthall; Raymond Hatton; Jack Grey; Gwen Lee; Directed by E. Mason Hopper; Written by Edward T. Lowe; Cinematography by Jules Cronjager. **A**: Jr. High-Adult. **P**: Entertainment. **U**: Home. **Mov-Ent**: Crime Drama. **Acq**: Purchase. **Dist**: Sinister Cinema.

Alias Smith and Jones: Season One 2007 (Unrated)

Presents the debut season of the 1971-1973 television western series on two old West cousins, Hannibal Heyes (Duel) and Jed Kid Curry (Murphy)?now dubbed as Smith and Jones—who have forsaken their outlaw ways and are trying to earn amnesty from the governor though that doesn't matter to others who are hunting for them. Includes: Heyes and Curry get in the middle of a dispute for artwork and land, a no-good banker sets the pair up for his embezzling, and their good deed of returning lost gems goes sour when the owner finds out that the jewels are actually fake. 15 episodes. 783m; DVD. **C**: Peter Duel; Ben Murphy. **A**: Jr. High-Adult. **P**: Entertainment. **U**: Home. **Mov-Ent**: Television Series, Action-Adventure, Western. **Acq**: Purchase. **Dist**: Universal Studios Home Video. $39.98.

Alias Smith and Jones: Seasons Two & Three 1972 (Unrated)

ABC 1971-73 western comedy. Former Devil's Hole Gang leaders Kid Curry (Murphy) and Hannibal Heyes (Duel) settle in a small town and try to go straight after a lifetime of banditry. If they can keep their noses clean for a year the Governor may grant them a pardon but until then they are fair game for bounty hunters and lawmen. 35 episodes. 1765m; DVD. **C**: Ben Murphy; Pete Duel; Burl Ives; Walter Brennan; Roger Davis; Ralph Story. **A**: Jr. High-Adult. **P**: Entertainment. **U**: Home. **Mov-Ent**: Western, Drama, Television Series. **Acq**: Purchase. **Dist**: Timeless Media Group. $49.99.

Alias: The Complete Fifth Season 2006 (Unrated)

In the fifth and final season of the 2001-2006 ABC television action-drama with Sydney (Garner), who's now pregnant (as was Garner in real life) with boyfriend Michael Vaughn's (Vartan) baby though he has made a disturbing disclosure to her that has led to his apparent untimely demise leaving Sydney to search for answers. 17 episodes. 723m; DVD. **C**: Jennifer Garner; Victor Garber; Ron Rifkin; Kevin Weisman; Carl Lumbly; Michael Vartan. **A**: Jr. High-Adult. **P**: Entertainment. **U**: Home. **Mov-Ent**: Television Series, Drama, Action-Adventure. **Acq**: Purchase. **Dist**: Buena Vista Home Entertainment. $39.99.

Alias: The Complete First Season 2003

Features the 22-episode premiere season of the early 2000s TV suspense drama with Sydney Bristow (Jennifer Garner) as a young spy who discovers that the covert CIA division (SD-6) she believed she was working for is in fact a group trying to control the world. Sydney then becomes a double agent working for the real CIA to take down SD-6 along with handler Michael Vaughn (Michael Vartan) and estranged-father-double-agent Jack Bristow (Victor Garber). 999m; DVD. **C**: Jennifer Garner; Ron Rifkin; Michael Vartan; Victor Garber. **A**: Sr. High-Adult. **P**: Entertainment. **U**: Home. **Mov-Ent**: Television, Drama, Action-Adventure. **Acq**: Purchase. **Dist**: Buena Vista Home Entertainment. $69.99.

Alias: The Complete Fourth Season 2005

Features the 22-episode fourth season of the early 2000s TV suspense drama with Sydney Bristow (Jennifer Garner) as a young double agent who leaves the CIA to work for a covert secret operations group headed by now-good-guy Sloane (Ron Rifkin). Sydney must work with former handler Michael Vaughn (Michael Vartan) as he copes with the loss of his wife; meanwhile, she discovers that she has a half-sister whose father is Sloane. 931m; DVD. **C**: Jennifer Garner; Ron Rifkin; Michael Vartan; Victor Garber. **A**: Sr. High-Adult. **P**: Entertainment. **U**: Home. **Mov-Ent**: Television, Drama, Action-Adventure. **Acq**: Purchase. **Dist**: Buena Vista Home Entertainment. $59.99.

Alias: The Complete Second Season 2003

Features the 22-episode second season of the early 2000s TV suspense drama with Sydney Bristow (Jennifer Garner) as a young double agent working with the CIA and handler Michael Vaughn (Michael Vartan) along with estranged-father-double-agent Jack Bristow (Victor Garber) to take down the evil SD-6 group. Episodes include the introduction of Sydney's not-so-deceased mother, Irina Derevko (Lena Olin), an old agent of the KGB who shoots her daughter before deciding to join the CIA. 917m; DVD. **C**: Jennifer Garner; Ron Rifkin; Michael Vartan; Victor Garber; Lena Olin. **A**: Sr. High-Adult. **P**: Entertainment. **U**: Home. **Mov-Ent**: Television, Drama, Action-Adventure. **Acq**: Purchase. **Dist**: Buena Vista Home Entertainment. $69.99.

Alias: The Complete Third Season 2004

Features the 22-episode third season of the early 2000s TV suspense drama with Sydney Bristow (Jennifer Garner) as a young double agent working for the CIA against SD-6's boss Sloane (Rifkin). The season opens with Sydney in Hong Kong with no memory of the past two years of her life; since then, Sloane appears to now be a do-gooder while her romance with handler Michael Vaughn (Michael Vartan) is obviously over as he's happily married. Episodes revolve around her search for the Rambaldi device while coming to terms with the changes in her life. 968m; DVD. **C**: Jennifer Garner; Ron Rifkin; Michael Vartan; Victor Garber. **A**: Sr. High-Adult. **P**: Entertainment. **U**: Home. **Mov-Ent**: Television, Drama, Action-Adventure. **Acq**: Purchase. **Dist**: Buena Vista Home Entertainment. $69.99.

Alias the Doctor 1932 — ★½

Karl Brenner is the adopted son of Martha Brenner and both he and his drunken brother Stephan are studying medicine. He takes the blame for student Stephan's botched operation and goes to prison but Martha urges him to return to medicine upon his release. Since Stephan is dead, Karl passes himself off as his doctor brother and finds success in Vienna until his past is exposed. 69m/B/W; DVD. **C**: Richard Barthelmess; Norman Foster; Lucille LaVerne; Marian Marsh; Adrienne Dore; Oscar Apfel; John St. Polis; George Rosener; Claire Dodd; Directed by Michael Curtiz; Written by Houston Branch; Charles Kenyon; Cinematography by Barney McGill. **A**: Sr. High-Adult. **P**: Entertainment. **U**: Home. **Mov-Ent. Acq**: Purchase. **Dist**: WarnerArchive.com.

Alias Will James 1988

Documents the life of Will James, who went from cattle rustler to toast of Hollywood. 83m; VHS, 3/4 U. **Pr**: Eric Michel. **A**: Jr. High-Adult. **P**: Entertainment. **U**: Institution, SURA. **Gen-Edu**: Biography, Documentary Films. **Acq**: Purchase, Rent/Lease. **Dist**: National Film Board of Canada. $500.00.

Alias—The Bad Man 1931 — ★½

Maynard's help is sought to round up rustlers on his father's ranch. There he discovers his father has been murdered so Maynard goes undercover to infiltrate the outlaw gang. 64m/B/W; VHS. **C**: Ken Maynard; Virginia Brown Faire; Frank Mayo; Robert E. Homans; Irving Bacon; Lafe (Lafayette) McKee; Directed by Phil Rosen. **Pr**: Tiffany. **A**: Family. **P**: Entertainment. **U**: Home. **Mov-Ent**: Western. **Acq**: Purchase. **Dist**: Grapevine Video. $11.95.

Alibi 1929 — ★★

Low-budget crime drama from independent producer/director West. Gangster Chick Williams (Morris) reclaims his mob role after being released from prison. But when a cop is killed during a robbery, Williams is suspected of the crime and the detective squad will employ any method to bring him to justice. Noted for its experimental use of sound, its dazzling Art Deco sets, and its eccentric composition. 84m/B/W; VHS, DVD. **C**: Chester Morris; Mae Busch; Regis Toomey; Harry Stubbs; Directed by Roland West; Written by Roland West; C. Gardner Sullivan; Cinematography by Ray June; Music by Hugo Riesenfeld. **A**: Sr. High-Adult. **P**: Entertainment. **U**: Home. **Mov-Ent**: Crime Drama. **Acq**: Purchase. **Dist**: Kino on Video.

Alibi for Murder 1936 (Unrated) — ★½

Radio newsman Perry Travis (Gargan) turns amateur sleuth when his scientist interviewee is murdered and Travis becomes the prime suspect. 61m/B/W; DVD. **C**: William Gargan; Marguerite Churchill; Gene Morgan; John Gallaudet; Romaine Callender; Directed by David Ross Lederman; Written by Tom Van Dycke; Cinematography by George Meehan, Jr. **A**: Jr. High-Adult. **P**: Entertainment. **U**: Home. **Mov-Ent**: Mystery & Suspense. **Acq**: Purchase. **Dist**: Movies Unlimited.

Alibi Ike 1935 (Unrated) — ★★½

Baseball comedy about rookie Cubs pitcher Frank Farrell (rubbery-faced comedian Brown), who is known as "Alibi Ike" because he's always making excuses, driving his manager Cap (Frawley) and his teammates crazy. He can't even be straight with his gal, Dolly (de Havilland). Next, Frank gets into trouble with gamblers who want him to throw games but he comes through in the end. Adapted from a story by Ring Lardner. 73m/B/W; VHS, DVD. **C:** Joe E. Brown; Olivia de Havilland; William Frawley; Ruth Donnelly; Roscoe Karns; Joseph King; Paul Harvey; Selmer Jackson; Directed by Ray Enright; Written by William Wister Haines; Cinematography by Arthur L. Todd. **A:** Jr. High-Adult. **P:** Entertainment. **U:** Home. **Mov-Ent:** Baseball, Gambling, Sports--Fiction: Comedy. **Acq:** Purchase. **Dist:** WarnerArchive.com. $19.99.

Alice 1986 (Unrated) — ★★
A twist on the "Alice in Wonderland" tale. Alice witnesses an attempted murder, faints, and awakens in a weird, yet strangely familiar environment. Adapted from the stage production. 80m; VHS, DVD. **C:** Sophie Barjac; Susannah York; Jean-Pierre Cassel; Paul Nicholas; Directed by Jacek Bromski; Jerzy Gruza. **Pr:** Baudonin Mussche; Jerry Gruza. **A:** Jr. High-Adult. **P:** Entertainment. **U:** Home. **Mov-Ent:** Musical. **Acq:** Purchase. **Dist:** MGM Studios Inc. ; Warner Home Video, Inc. $59.95.

Alice 1988 (Unrated) — ★★★½
An acclaimed surreal version of Lewis Carroll's already surreal "Alice in Wonderland," with the emphasis on Carroll's obsessiveness. Utilizing animated puppets and a live actor for Alice, Czech director Svankmajer injects grotesque images and black comedy into Wonderland. Not for the kids. 84m; VHS, DVD, Blu-Ray. **C:** Kristina Kohoutova; Directed by Jan Svankmajer; Written by Jan Svankmajer; Cinematography by Svatopluk Maly. **Pr:** Jan Svankmajer. **A:** Sr. High-Adult. **P:** Entertainment. **U:** Institution, SURA, Home. **Mov-Ent:** Fantasy, Rabbits, Comedy--Black. **Acq:** Purchase. **Dist:** First Run/Icarus Films; Tapeworm Video Distributors Inc. $490.00.

Alice 1990 (PG-13) — ★★★
Farrow is "Alice," a woman plagued with doubts about her lifestyle, her religion, and her happiness. Her perfect children, husband, and apartment don't prevent her backaches, and she turns to an Oriental "herbalist" for aid. She finds his methods unusual and the results of the treatments surprising. Lightweight fairytale of Yuppiedom gone awry. Fine performances, but superficial and pointed story that may leave the viewer looking for more. (Perhaps that's Allen's point.) Farewell performance from charactor actor Luke, unbilled cameo from Judith Ivey, and first time out for Dylan O'Sullivan Farrow, adopted daughter of Allen and Farrow, as Kate. 106m; VHS, DVD, Wide, CC. **C:** Mia Farrow; William Hurt; Joe Mantegna; Keye Luke; Alec Baldwin; Cybill Shepherd; Blythe Danner; Gwen Verdon; Bernadette Peters; Judy Davis; Patrick O'Neal; Julie Kavner; Caroline Aaron; Holland Taylor; Robin Bartlett; David Spielberg; Bob Balaban; Dylan O'Sullivan Farrow; Elle Macpherson; Directed by Woody Allen; Written by Woody Allen; Cinematography by Carlo Di Palma. **Pr:** Robert Greenhut; Orion Pictures. **A:** Sr. High-Adult. **P:** Entertainment. **U:** Home. **Mov-Ent:** Drama, Family. **Awds:** Natl. Bd. of Review '90: Actress (Farrow). **Acq:** Purchase. **Dist:** MGM Studios Inc. ; Facets Multimedia Inc. $92.98.

The Alice 2004 (Unrated) — ★½
A disparate group of characters come from all corners of Australia to the outback town of Alice Springs in order to witness a total eclipse of the sun in hopes that it will changes their lives. Apparently intended as an Australian TV pilot although it never went any farther. 98m; DVD. **C:** Erik Thomson; Jessica Napier; Brett Stiller; Simon Burke; Caitlin McDougall; Luke Carroll; Kyas Sherriff; Directed by Kate Dennis; Written by Justin Mongo; Cinematography by Louis Irving. **A:** Jr. High-Adult. **P:** Entertainment. **U:** Home. **Mov-Ent:** Australia. **Acq:** Purchase. **Dist:** BFS Video.

Alice 2009 (Unrated) — ★★
Syfy pic derived from "Alice in Wonderland" goes psychedelic with uneven results. This time Alice (Scorsone) is not only an adult but a martial arts instructor who tumbles through a mirror with the help of a ring given to her by beau Jack (Winchester). Wonderland is under the totalitarian control of the Queen of Hearts (Bates) and Alice teams up with such rebels as the Hatter (Potts) and the White Knight (Frewer) to battle the regime, which tends to turn unwelcome guests into zombies. 180m; DVD. **C:** Caterina Scorsone; Kathy Bates; Philip Winchester; Andrew Lee Potts; Matt Frewer; Colm Meaney; Tim Curry; Allan Gray; Eugene Lipinski; Harry Dean Stanton; Directed by Nick Willing; Written by Nick Willing; Cinematography by Jon Joffin; Music by Ben Mink. **A:** Jr. High-Adult. **P:** Entertainment. **U:** Home. **Mov-Ent:** Science Fiction. **Acq:** Purchase. **Dist:** Lions Gate Entertainment Inc.

Alice Adams 1935 (Unrated) — ★★½
Based on the classic Booth Tarkington novel about a poor girl from a small Midwestern town who falls in love with a man from the upper level of society. She tries desperately to fit in and nearly alienates her family and friends. The sets may be dated, but the insight on human behavior is timeless. 99m/B/W; VHS, DVD. **C:** Katharine Hepburn; Fred MacMurray; Evelyn Venable; Fred Stone; Frank Albertson; Ann Shoemaker; Charley Grapewin; Grady Sutton; Hedda Hopper; Hattie McDaniel; Directed by George Stevens; Music by Max Steiner. **Pr:** Pandro S. Berman. **A:** Family. **P:** Entertainment. **U:** Home. **Mov-Ent:** Drama. **Acq:** Purchase. **Dist:** Critics' Choice Video & DVD; Turner Broadcasting System Inc. $14.98.

Alice Aycock 1983
Alice Aycock is interviewed about various facets of her sculpture within her sculpture "Celestial Amusement Park." 11m; VHS, 3/4 U. **Pr:** Department of Education. **A:** Jr. High-Adult. **P:** Education. **U:** Institution, Home. **Gen-Edu:** Sculpture, Women. **Acq:** Purchase, Rent/Lease. **Dist:** Museum of Modern Art. $275.00.

Alice Cooper: Brutally Live 2000 (Unrated)
Concert film of rocker Alice Cooper which emphasizes the theartricality of his live performances. 105m; DVD. **A:** Sr. High-Adult. **P:** Entertainment. **U:** Home. **Mov-Ent:** Music--Performance, Documentary Films, Music--Pop/Rock. **Acq:** Purchase. **Dist:** Eagle Rock Entertainment Inc. $9.99.

Alice Cooper: Super Duper Alice Cooper 2014 (Unrated)
Biographical documentary of Vincent Furnier and his musical alter ego Alice Cooper. 127m; DVD. **A:** Jr. High-Adult. **P:** Entertainment. **U:** Home. **Mov-Ent:** Biography: Music, Documentary Films, Music--Pop/Rock. **Acq:** Purchase. **Dist:** Eagle Rock Entertainment Inc. $14.98.

Alice Cooper: The Nightmare Returns 1986 (Unrated)
Taped at Detroit's Joe Louis Arena, Cooper performs his live Halloween-esque theatrics; songs included are: "School's Out," "Eighteen," "Be My Lover," "Welcome to My Nightmare," "No More Mr. Nice Guy," and more. 76m; VHS. **Pr:** MCA Entertainment. **A:** Jr. High. **P:** Entertainment. **U:** Home. **Mov-Ent:** Music--Performance. **Acq:** Purchase. **Dist:** Music Video Distributors. $19.95.

Alice Cooper: Trash These Videos 1990
Alice Cooper music videos, including "Poison," "House of Fire," and "Bed of Nails." 15m; VHS. **C:** Alice Cooper. **Pr:** CBS. **A:** Sr. High-Adult. **P:** Entertainment. **U:** Home. **Mov-Ent:** Music Video. **Acq:** Purchase. **Dist:** Music Video Distributors; Sony Music Entertainment Inc. $12.98.

Alice Cooper Trashes the World 1990
Glam horror king Alice Cooper performs some of his scariest songs including, "Trash," "Billion Dollar Babies," "I'm Eighteen," "House of Fire," "No More Mr. Nice Guy," "Welcome to My Nightmare," "Only Women Bleed," "Poison," "Muscle of Love," "Spark in the Dark," "Bed of Nails," "School's Out," "Under My Wheels," and seven more. 94m; VHS. **C:** Alice Cooper. **Pr:** CBS. **A:** Jr. High-Adult. **P:** Entertainment. **U:** Home. **Mov-Ent:** Music Video, Music--Performance, Music--Pop/Rock. **Acq:** Purchase. **Dist:** Music Video Distributors; Sony Music Entertainment Inc. $19.98.

Alice Cooper: Welcome to My Nightmare 1975 (Unrated)
The '70s glitter rock singer performs the hits that made him infamous, including: "Eighteen," "School's Out," and "Only Women Bleed." 84m; VHS, DVD. **C:** Alice Cooper. **Pr:** Tommy-J Productions. **A:** Jr. High-Adult. **P:** Entertainment. **U:** Home. **Mov-Ent:** Music--Performance. **Acq:** Purchase. **Dist:** Music Video Distributors; Rhino Entertainment Co. $19.95.

Alice Doesn't Live Here Anymore 1974 (PG) — ★★½
Scorsese marries road opera with pseudo-feminist semi-realistic melodrama and produces uneven but interesting results. When Alice's husband dies suddenly, leaving her with their 11-year-old son, she leaves for California, but finds herself stranded in Phoenix, down to her last few bucks. There she lands a job as a waitress in a diner where she meets kindly rancher Kristofferson. Notable for its female point of view, it was also the basis for the once-popular TV show "Alice." Burstyn and Ladd lend key performances, while Kristofferson is typically wooden. 105m; VHS, DVD, Wide. **C:** Ellen Burstyn; Kris Kristofferson; Diane Ladd; Jodie Foster; Harvey Keitel; Vic Tayback; Billy Green Bush; Laura Dern; Directed by Martin Scorsese; Written by Robert Getchell; Cinematography by Kent Wakeford; Music by Richard LaSalle. **Pr:** David Susskind; Audrey Maas. **A:** Jr. High-Adult. **P:** Entertainment. **U:** Home. **Mov-Ent:** Comedy-Drama, Romance, Women. **Awds:** Oscars '74: Actress (Burstyn); British Acad. '75: Actress (Burstyn), Film, Screenplay, Support. Actress (Ladd). **Acq:** Purchase. **Dist:** Warner Home Video, Inc.; Facets Multimedia Inc.; Baker and Taylor. $19.98.

Alice et Martin 1998 (R) — ★★½
Director Andre Techine examines the complexity of relationships through the lives of nervous violinist Alice (Binoche) and psychologically fragile model Martin (Loret). The story opens in Martin's childhood, when he is sent by his free-spirited mother to live with his cold and distant father Victor (Maguelon). Martin flees his father's house after an unrevealed trauma, showing up at the door of his half-brother Benjamin (Amalric), who is Alice's roommate. Despite initial reluctance from Alice, the pair become lovers. During a trip to Spain Alice tells Martin that she's pregnant, and he goes off the deep end, haunted by memories of his father and the fateful event that will continue to affect their lives. Slow-moving but beautifully filmed. 123m; VHS. **C:** Juliette Binoche; Alexis Loret; Carmen Maura; Pierre Maguelon; Mathieu Amalric; Directed by Andre Techine; Written by Andre Techine; Gilles Taurand; Olivier Assayas; Cinematography by Caroline Champetier; Music by Philippe Sarde. **Pr:** October Films. **A:** College-Adult. **P:** Entertainment. **U:** Home. **L:** French. **Mov-Ent:** Drama, France. **Acq:** Purchase.

Alice in Chains: Live Facelift 1991
Songs from the band include "Man in the Box," "Real Thing," "Sea of Sorrow," "Bleed in the Freak" and more. 45m; VHS. **Pr:** Sony Video. **A:** Sr. High-Adult. **P:** Entertainment. **U:** Home. **Mov-Ent:** Music--Performance, Music--Pop/Rock. **Acq:** Purchase. **Dist:** Sony Music Entertainment Inc. $17.99.

Alice in Effects Land 19??
A modern Alice explores the world of film special effects in this creative and highly recommended film. Features techniques such as front projection, rotoscoping and multilayer optical printing, miniatures and motion control, glass matting, and computerized streaking effects. 15m; VHS. **Pr:** Australian Film, Radio and Television School. **A:** College-Adult. **P:** Education. **U:** Home, Institution. **Gen-Edu:** Filmmaking. **Acq:** Purchase, Rent/Lease. **Dist:** TMW Media Group. $119.

Alice in the Cities 1974 — ★★★½
American and German culture are compared and contrasted in this early Wenders road work about a German journalist in the USA on assignment who suddenly finds himself custodian to a worldly nine-year-old girl abandoned by her mother. Together they return to Germany and search for the girl's grandmother. Along the way they learn about each other, with many distinctive and graceful Wenders moments. 110m/B/W; VHS. **C:** Ruediger Vogler; Yella Rottlaender; Elisabeth (Lisa) Kreuzer; Edda Kochl; Directed by Wim Wenders; Written by Wim Wenders. **Pr:** Wim Wenders; Wim Wenders. **A:** Sr. High-Adult. **P:** Entertainment. **U:** Home. **L:** English, German. **Mov-Ent:** Germany, Parenting, Journalism. **Acq:** Purchase. **Dist:** Facets Multimedia Inc.; German Language Video Center; Tapeworm Video Distributors Inc. $29.95.

Alice in Wonderland 198?
Alice meets the Cheshire Cat, March Hare, Queen of Hearts, and other fabulous characters after falling down the rabbit hole in this animated version of the Lewis Carroll classic. 30m; VHS. **Pr:** R&G Comm. **A:** Family. **P:** Entertainment. **U:** Home. **Chl-Juv:** Animation & Cartoons, Fairy Tales. **Acq:** Purchase. **Dist:** Anchor Bay Entertainment. $6.95.

Alice in Wonderland 1933 (Unrated) — ★★½
Early black-and-white version of Lewis Carroll's classic with what was an all-star cast at the time. It's somewhat pressed for time as it includes both of Carroll's works, and is presented as more of a series of episodes then a standard plot. 77m/B/W; DVD, Streaming. **C:** Richard Arlen; Gary Cooper; Cary Grant; Charlotte Henry; Directed by Norman Z. McLeod; Written by Joseph L. Mankiewicz; William Cameron Menzies; Cinematography by Bert Glennon; Henry Sharp; Music by Dimitri Tomkin. **A:** Family. **P:** Entertainment. **U:** Home. **L:** English, French, Spanish. **Mov-Ent. Acq:** Purchase, Rent/Lease. **Dist:** Universal Studios Home Video. $14.98 9.99.

Alice in Wonderland 1950 (Unrated) — ★★½
Another version of the Lewis Carroll classic which combines the usage of Lou Bunin's puppets and live action to tell the story. Released independently to cash in on the success of the Disney version. Takes a more adult approach to the story and is worth viewing on its own merits. 83m; VHS, DVD, Blu-Ray. **C:** Carol Marsh; Stephen Murray; Pamela Brown; Felix Aylmer; Ernest Milton; Directed by Dallas Bower. **Pr:** Leo Hurwitz; Souvaine Selective Pictures. **A:** Family. **P:** Entertainment. **U:** Home. **Mov-Ent:** Animation & Cartoons, Puppets, Fairy Tales. **Acq:** Purchase. **Dist:** Walt Disney Studios Home Entertainment. $24.95.

Alice in Wonderland 1951 (G) — ★★★
Classic Disney dream version of Lewis Carroll's famous children's story about a girl who falls down a rabbit hole into a magical world populated by strange creatures. Beautifully animated with some startling images, but served with a strange dispassion warmed by a fine batch of songs. Wynn's Mad Hatter and Holloway's Cheshire Cat are among the treats in store. 75m; VHS, DVD, CC. **C:** Voice(s) by Kathryn Beaumont; Ed Wynn; Sterling Holloway; Jerry Colonna; Directed by Hamilton Luske; Wilfred Jackson; Clyde Geronimi. **Pr:** Walt Disney Studios. **A:** Family. **P:** Entertainment. **U:** Home. **L:** English, French. **Mov-Ent:** Animation & Cartoons, Children, Classic Films. **Acq:** Purchase. **Dist:** Walt Disney Studios Home Entertainment; Facets Multimedia Inc.; Knowledge Unlimited, Inc. $24.99.
Songs: Alice in Wonderland; I'm Late; A Very Merry Un-Birthday.

Alice in Wonderland 1966 — ★★★
Minimalist re-telling of the classic story set in old mansions with the main characters in Victorian period costumes. The BBC decided for a darker more surrealistic tone for the film as opposed to what had been done before. 72m/B/W; DVD. **C:** Anne-Marie Mallik; Michael Redgrave; Peter Cook; Michael Gough; Peter Sellers; Directed by Jonathan Miller; Written by Jonathan Miller; Cinematography by Dick Bush; Music by Ravi Shankar. **A:** Jr. High-Adult. **P:** Entertainment. **U:** Home. **L:** English. **Mov-Ent. Acq:** Purchase. **Dist:** BBC Worldwide Publishing Ltd. $14.98.

Alice in Wonderland 1985 — ★★½
All-star updated adaptation of the Lewis Carroll classic. This time instead of Alice falling down a rabbit hole she falls through her television set. But her adventures still include the White Rabbit, Mad Hatter, March Hare, Cheshire Cat, and the King and Queen of Hearts. Followed by "Alice Through the Looking Glass." 90m; VHS, DVD. **C:** Natalie Gregory; Anthony Newley; Ringo Starr; Telly Savalas; Robert Morley; Sammy Davis, Jr.; Steve Allen; Steve Lawrence; Eydie Gorme; Red Buttons; Ann Jillian; Scott Baio; Sid Caesar; Ernest Borgnine; Beau Bridges; Lloyd Bridges; Tom McLoughlin; Harvey Korman; Patrick Duffy; Donald O'Connor; Arte Johnson; Carol Channing; Sherman Hemsley; Roddy McDowall; Donna Mills; Imogene Coca; Karl Malden; Noriyuki "Pat" Morita; Sally Struthers; Martha Raye; Merv Griffin; Jack Warden; Louis Nye; Shelley Winters; John Stamos; Jonathan Winters; George Savalas; Directed by Harry Harris; Written by Paul Zindel; Cinematography by Fred W. Koenekamp; Music by Morton Stevens. **Pr:** Irwin Allen. **A:** Family. **P:** Entertainment. **U:** Home. **Mov-Ent:** Fantasy, Children, Pets. **Acq:** Purchase. **Dist:** Facets Multimedia Inc. $19.98.

Alice in Wonderland 1999 — ★★½
Visually elaborate but somewhat tedious version of the popular Lewis Carroll tale filled with scenery chewing by the real actors and the welcome presence of animatronic wonders from the Jim

Henson Creature Shop. This time Alice is the poised Majorino, who seems more annoyed by the denizens of Wonderland than amazed at her adventures. 129m; VHS, DVD, CC. **C:** Tina Majorino; Martin Short; Miranda Richardson; Whoopi Goldberg; Ben Kingsley; Gene Wilder; Christopher Lloyd; Pete Postlethwaite; Peter Ustinov; George Wendt; Robbie Coltrane; Directed by Nick Willing; Written by Peter Barnes; Cinematography by Giles Nuttgens; Music by Richard Hartley. **Pr:** Dyson Lovell; Robert Halmi, Sr.; Hallmark Entertainment; National Broadcasting Company. **A:** Family. **P:** Entertainment. **U:** Home. **Mov-Ent:** Rabbits, Fantasy, Pets. **Acq:** Purchase. **Dist:** Alpha Video; Movies Unlimited.

Alice in Wonderland 2010 (PG) — ★★½
Burton's visually stunning flick combines Lewis Carroll's novels of Wonderland with his poem "The Jabberwocky" to tell the tale of an older Alice (Wasikowska). Now 19 years old and resisting an arranged marriage to an upper-class twit, Alice flees her engagement party and once again falls down the rabbit hole. She's reunited with her old friends the Mad Hatter (Depp) and the White Queen (Hathaway), as well as her old enemy the Red Queen (Bonham-Carter). The climactic battle scene seems forced and cribbed from other recent fantasy epics, but the characters retain their demented quirkiness. The movie was not actually shot in 3-D, which makes its release in this format (with sub-par results) seem curiouser and curiouser. 108m; Blu-Ray, Wide, CC. **C:** Mia Wasikowska; Johnny Depp; Anne Hathaway; Helena Bonham Carter; Crispin Glover; Michael Sheen; Alan Rickman; Christopher Lee; Stephen Fry; Matt Lucas; Marton Csokas; Lindsay Duncan; Directed by Tim Burton; Written by Linda Woolverton; Cinematography by Dariusz Wolski; Music by Danny Elfman. **Pr:** Tim Burton; Richard D. Zanuck; Joe Roth; Jennifer Todd; Suzanne Todd; Tim Burton; Roth Films; Zanuck Company; Walt Disney Pictures. **A:** Primary-Adult. **P:** Entertainment. **U:** Home. **L:** English. **Mov-Ent:** Fantasy. **Awds:** Oscars '10: Art Dir./Set Dec., Costume Des.; British Acad. '10: Costume Des., Makeup. **Acq:** Purchase. **Dist:** Alpha Video; Buena Vista Home Entertainment; Movies Unlimited.

Alice in Wonderland: A Dance Fantasy 1993
Highly stylized dance version of the Lewis Carroll classic as interpreted by the Prague Chamber Ballet, with music composed by Viktor Kalabis and performed by the Czech Philharmonic. Performance includes dance, music, art, mime, theatre, and acrobatics. 30m; VHS. **A:** Family. **P:** Entertainment. **U:** Home. **Fin-Art:** Dance--Ballet. **Acq:** Purchase. **Dist:** V.I.E.W. Inc./Arkadia Entertainment Corp.; Facets Multimedia Inc. $19.98.

Alice Neel 1978
Chronicles Alice Neel's career, a profound portrait painter of the modern era, her early marriage to a Cuban painter, through the Depression, her work with the WPA, and life in Spanish Harlem. 19m; VHS. **A:** College-Adult. **P:** Education. **U:** Institution. **Gen-Edu:** Women, Art & Artists. **Acq:** Purchase, Rent/Lease. **Dist:** Women Make Movies. $195.00.

Alice Neel: Collector of Souls 1978
The artist is seen with a work in progress, along with scenes from a reception at New York's Graham Gallery, where some of her subjects are seen with their portraits. 30m; 3/4 U, Special order formats. **C:** Directed by Nancy Baer. **Pr:** Nancy Baer. **A:** Sr. High-Adult. **P:** Education. **U:** Institution, Home. **Fin-Art:** Documentary Films, Art & Artists, Painting. **Acq:** Purchase, Rent/Lease. **Dist:** Museum of Modern Art.

Alice of Wonderland in Paris 1965
Alice takes a trip to Paris in this animated fantasy. ?m; VHS. **C:** Voice(s) by Carl Reiner. **A:** Preschool-Primary. **P:** Entertainment. **U:** Home. **Chl-Juv:** Animation & Cartoons, Fantasy. **Acq:** Purchase. **Dist:** Sinister Cinema. $16.95.

Alice Sweet Alice 1976 (R) — ★½
Mediocre, gory who-killed-her, best remembered as the debut of Shields (in a small role). 112m; VHS, DVD. **C:** Linda Miller; Paula Sheppard; Mildred Clinton; Niles McMaster; Jane Lowry; Rudolph Willrich; Brooke Shields; Alphonso de Noble; Gary Allen; Tom Signorelli; Lillian Roth; Directed by Alfred Sole; Written by Alfred Sole; Rosemary Ritvo; Cinematography by John Friberg; Chuck Hall; Music by Stephen Lawrence. **Pr:** Allied Artists International. **A:** Sr. High-Adult. **P:** Entertainment. **U:** Home. **Mov-Ent:** Horror, Religion. **Acq:** Purchase. **Dist:** Anchor Bay Entertainment; Baker and Taylor.

Alice: Television Favorites 2006 (Unrated)
Features episodes from the 1976-1985 television comedy show centered around Alice (Lavin), a recent widow who takes her 12-year-old son across the country to resume her singing career dreams. She gets stuck in Arizona though and working at Mel's Diner with acerbic owner Mel (Tayback) and fellow waitresses Flo (Holliday)?a sassy redhead whose favorite saying was "Mel, kiss my grits!"?and the ditzy Vera (Howland). Includes: "Alice Gets a Pass" (1976), "The Odd Couple" (1977), "Close Encounters of the Worst Kind" (1978), "Block Those Kicks" (1978), "Cabin Fever" (1979), and "Flo's Farewell" (1980). Drawn from the 1975 Martin Scorsese film "Alice Doesn't Live Here Anymore." 6 episodes. 151m; DVD. **C:** Linda Lavin; Vic Tayback; Polly Holliday; Beth Howland. **A:** Family. **P:** Entertainment. **U:** Home. **Mov-Ent:** Television Series. **Acq:** Purchase. **Dist:** Warner Home Video, Inc. $9.98.

Alice Through the Looking Glass 1966 (Unrated) — ★★½
Based on Lewis Carroll's classic adventure. Follows the further adventures of young Alice. After a chess piece comes to life, it convinces Alice that excitement and adventure lie through the looking glass. 72m; VHS, DVD. **C:** Judi Rolin; Ricardo Montalban; Nanette Fabray; Robert Coote; Agnes Moorehead; Jack Palance; Jimmy Durante; Tom Smothers; Roy Castle; Richard Denning; Directed by Alan Handley. **Pr:** Bob Wynn; Alan Handley; National Broadcasting Company. **A:** Family. **P:** Entertainment. **U:** Home. **Mov-Ent:** Fantasy, Chess. **Acq:** Purchase. **Dist:** Infinity Entertainment Group. $14.98.

Alice Through the Looking Glass 1985
In this continuation of "Alice in Wonderland" Alice is stuck in the bizarre world on the reverse side of the mirror. She must stay away from the fearsome Jabberwocky if she wants to return home, and runs into a number of eccentric figures, including Tiger Lily, a mock turtle, Humpty Dumpty, and Tweedledum and Tweedledee. 90m; VHS. **C:** Ringo Starr; Sally Struthers; Jack Warden; Jonathan Winters; Steve Lawrence; Karl Malden; Beau Bridges; Lloyd Bridges; Written by Paul Zindel. **A:** Family. **P:** Entertainment. **U:** Home. **Chl-Juv:** Fantasy, Children. **Acq:** Purchase. **Dist:** Facets Multimedia Inc. $19.98.

Alice to Nowhere 1986 — ★★
Concerns a running argument in the Outback over a fortune in gems unknowingly carried by a young woman. Based on a novel by Evan Green. 210m; VHS. **C:** Rosie Jones; Steve Jacobs; John Waters; Ruth Cracknell; Directed by John Power. **Pr:** Crawford Productions. **A:** Jr. High-Adult. **P:** Entertainment. **U:** Home. **Mov-Ent:** TV Movies. **Acq:** Purchase. **Dist:** Paramount Pictures Corp. $59.95.

Alice Upside Down 2007 (Unrated) — ★★½
Preteen Alice McKinley (Stoner) and her older brother Lester (Grabeel) struggle when their widowed dad Ben (Perry) decides to make a fresh start in St. Louis. Alice has a tough time adjusting to her new school and gets into trouble with her stern homeroom teacher Mrs. Plotkin (Marshall). But Alice learns two important lessons as adolescence hits: don't be judgmental and don't jump to conclusions. Adapted from Phyllis Reynolds Naylor's "Alice" novels. 90m; DVD. **C:** Alyson Stoner; Luke Perry; Lucas Grabeel; Penny Marshall; Ann Dowd; Dylan McLaughlin; Parker McKenna Posey; Directed by Stanley Tung; Written by Stanley Tung; Meghan Heritage; Cinematography by Mark Mervis. **A:** Family. **P:** Entertainment. **U:** Home. **Mov-Ent:** Adolescence. **Acq:** Purchase. **Dist:** Anchor Bay Entertainment.

Alice Walker: Possessing the Secret of Joy ????
Interview with the womanist writer discussing her novel "Possessing the Secret of Joy." Includes archival footage, dramatized scenes from the book, and additional interviews with Gloria Steinem and others, relating Ms. Walker's work to issues of womanhood worldwide. 53m; VHS. **A:** Sr. High-Adult. **P:** Education. **U:** Institution. **Gen-Edu:** Black Culture, Women, Literature--American. **Acq:** Purchase, Rent/Lease. **Dist:** Films for the Humanities & Sciences. $149.00.

Alice's Adventures in Wonderland 1972
Musical adaptation of Lewis Carroll's timeless fantasy of a young girl who meets new friends when she falls into a rabbit hole. 96m; VHS. **C:** Fiona Fullerton; Michael Crawford; Ralph Richardson; Flora Robson; Peter Sellers; Robert Helpmann; Dudley Moore; Michael Jayston; Spike Milligan; Michael Hordern; Directed by William Sterling; Written by William Sterling; Cinematography by Geoffrey Unsworth; Music by John Barry. **Pr:** American National Enterprises. **A:** Family. **P:** Entertainment. **U:** Home. **Chl-Juv:** Children, Fantasy, Fairy Tales. **Acq:** Purchase. **Dist:** Mill Creek Entertainment L.L.C.

Alice's Adventures in Wonderland 1981
An animated version of Lewis Carroll's classic story. 22m; VHS, 3/4 U. **Pr:** Greatest Tales, Inc. **A:** Primary. **P:** Education. **U:** Institution, SURA. **Chl-Juv:** Literature. **Acq:** Purchase. **Dist:** Phoenix Learning Group.

Alice's Restaurant 1969 (PG) — ★★½
Based on the popular and funny 20-minute Arlo Guthrie song "Alice's Restaurant Massacre" about a Flower Child during the Last Big War who gets hassled for littering, man. Step back in time and study the issues of the hippie era, including avoiding the draft, dropping out of college, and dealing with the local pigs. Sort of a modern movie in the cinematic ambling genre, in that nothing really happens. 111m; VHS, DVD, Wide. **C:** Arlo Guthrie; James Broderick; Pat Quinn; Geoff Outlaw; Pete Seeger; Lee Hays; Michael McClanathan; Tina Chen; Kathleen Dabney; William Obanhein; Graham Jarvis; M. Emmet Walsh; Directed by Arthur Penn; Written by Arthur Penn; Venabel Herndon; Cinematography by Michael Nebbia; Music by Arlo Guthrie; Garry Sherman. **Pr:** United Artists. **A:** Sr. High-Adult. **P:** Entertainment. **U:** Home. **Mov-Ent:** Comedy-Drama. **Acq:** Purchase. **Dist:** Music Video Distributors; MGM Home Entertainment. $19.95.

Alice's World 1975
Portrays the life and career of Alice Awten, who produced thousands of photographs depicting life at the turn of the century. 26m; VHS, 3/4 U. **C:** Narrated by Helen Hayes. **Pr:** WNET New York. **A:** Sr. High-Adult. **P:** Education. **U:** Institution, CCTV, Home. **Fin-Art:** Photography. **Acq:** Purchase, Rent/Lease. **Dist:** WNET/Thirteen Non-Broadcast.

Alicia Alonso: Alicia 1976
A profile of the life and work of ballerina Alicia Alonso, with excerpts from "Giselle," "Carmen," "Grand Pas de Quatre" and "Swan Lake." 70m; VHS. **A:** Jr. High-Adult. **P:** Entertainment. **U:** Home. **Fin-Art:** Dance, Biography. **Acq:** Purchase. **Dist:** Stagestep; Music Video Distributors; Corinth Films Inc. $49.95.

Alien 1979 (R) — ★★★½
Terse direction, stunning sets and special effects, and a well-seasoned cast save this from being another "Slimy monster from Outerspace" story. Instead it's a grisly rollercoaster of suspense and fear (and a huge boxoffice hit). Intergalactic freighter's crew is invaded by an unstoppable carnivorous alien intent on picking off the crew one by one. While the cast mostly bitches and banters while awaiting the horror of their imminent departure, Weaver is exceptional as Ripley, a self-reliant survivor who goes toe to toe with the Big Ugly. Futuristic, in the belly of the beast visual design creates a vivid sense of claustrophobic doom enhanced further by the ominous score. Oscar-winning special effects include the classic baby alien busting out of the crew guy's chest routine, a rib-splitting ten on the gore meter. Successfully followed by "Aliens" and "Alien 3." 116m; VHS, DVD, Blu-Ray. **C:** Tom Skerritt; Sigourney Weaver; Veronica Cartwright; Yaphet Kotto; Harry Dean Stanton; Ian Holm; John Hurt; Bolaji Badejo; Voice(s) by Helen Horton; Directed by Ridley Scott; Written by Dan O'Bannon; Cinematography by Derek Vanlint; Music by Jerry Goldsmith. **Pr:** 20th Century-Fox. **A:** Sr. High-Adult. **P:** Entertainment. **U:** Home. **Mov-Ent:** Science Fiction, Space Exploration, Pets. **Awds:** Oscars '79: Visual FX; Natl. Film Reg. '02. **Acq:** Purchase. **Dist:** Movies Unlimited; Alpha Video; Fox Home Entertainment. $19.98.

Alien 3 1992 (R) — ★★
Picks up where "Aliens" left off as Ripley crash lands on Fiorina 161, a planet that serves as a penal colony for 25 celibate but horny men who smell bad. Ripley is forced to shave her head because of the planet's lice problem, and she sets out to survive on the cold, unfriendly planet until a rescue ship can come for her. Fending off sexual advances from the men, Ripley soon discovers she wasn't the only survivor of the crash—the alien survived too and has somehow implanted her with an alien of her own. Dark and disturbing, filled with religious allegories, and a universe removed from the two earlier Aliens. Intended as the final installment of the series. 135m; VHS, DVD, Blu-Ray, Wide, CC. **C:** Sigourney Weaver; Charles S. Dutton; Charles Dance; Paul McGann; Brian Glover; Ralph Brown; Danny (Daniel) Webb; Christopher John Fields; Holt McCallany; Lance Henriksen; Directed by David Fincher; Cinematography by Alex Thomson; Music by Elliot Goldenthal. **A:** Sr. High-Adult. **P:** Entertainment. **U:** Home. **Mov-Ent:** Science Fiction, Pregnancy, Suicide. **Acq:** Purchase. **Dist:** Fox Home Entertainment.

The Alien Agenda: Endangered Species 1997 — ★½
Tabloid TV reporter Megan Cross has a too-close encounter with extraterrestrials that frightens her enough to have her join a secret organization that keeps tabs on alien activity. Along with mercenary Cope Ransom and operative Fritz, Megan is sent to infiltrate the mutant wasteland that used to be Florida and see what the aliens are plotting. 102m; VHS. **C:** Debbie Rochon; Joel D. Wynkoop; Joe Zaso; Candice Meade; Directed by Kevin J. Lindenmuth; Ron Ford; Gabriel Campisi; Tim Ritter; Written by Kevin J. Lindenmuth; Ron Ford; Gabriel Campisi; Tim Ritter. **A:** Sr. High-Adult. **P:** Entertainment. **U:** Home. **Mov-Ent.** **Acq:** Purchase. **Dist:** Brimstone Media Productions.

The Alien Agenda: Out of the Darkness 1996 — **Bomb!**
Cheesy sci-fi with a narrator who ruminates about mysterious aliens who enjoy tormenting humans and can travel through time (and send humans back and forth). You won't care. 80m; VHS. **C:** Sasha Graham; Michael (Mick) McCleery; Scooter McCrae; T.J. Miller; Marcus Zanders; Directed by Michael (Mick) McCleery; Kevin J. Lindenmuth; Written by Michael (Mick) McCleery; Kevin J. Lindenmuth. **A:** Jr. High-Adult. **P:** Entertainment. **U:** Home. **Mov-Ent:** Science Fiction. **Acq:** Purchase. **Dist:** Tapeworm Video Distributors Inc.; Brimstone Media Productions. $29.95.

The Alien Agenda: Under the Skin 1997 — ★½
Scientist Alfred Malone is kidnapped by the mystery guys in black and taken to their hideaway in Puerto Rico, where vicious aliens roam around outside just looking for a tasty earthling snack. Then there's Victor who's a smalltime hood who's not only got the cops after him but the new head of Chicago's crime syndicate, who's not exactly what he seems. 75m; VHS. **C:** Nick Kostopoulos; Arthur Lundquist; Leslie Body; Steven Jon White; Conrad Brooks; Directed by Kevin J. Lindenmuth; Mike Legge; Written by Kevin J. Lindenmuth; Mike Legge. **A:** Sr. High-Adult. **P:** Entertainment. **U:** Home. **Mov-Ent:** Science. **Acq:** Purchase. **Dist:** Brimstone Media Productions.

Alien Agent 2007 (R) — ★½
Agent Rykker (Dacascos) is sent to stop a renegade military unit that is building a portal between its dying homeworld and Earth. Seem Saylon (Zane), Isis (Cooke), and their band have decided they will exterminate the humans and move in. Good fights (director Johnson got his start as a stunt coordinator) but not much true sci-fi despite the plot. 95m; DVD. **C:** Mark Dacascos; Billy Zane; Kim Coates; Amelia Cooke; Emma Lahana; Directed by Jesse Johnson; Written by Vlady Pildysh; Cinematography by C. Kim Miles; Music by Michael Richard Plowman. **A:** Sr. High-Adult. **P:** Entertainment. **U:** Home. **Mov-Ent:** Science Fiction. **Acq:** Purchase. **Dist:** Allumination Filmworks.

Alien Apocalypse 2005 (Unrated) — ★
A group of astronauts return to Earth after 40 years in suspended animation to discover that humanity is enslaved by giant termite aliens. Unsurprisingly, despite being outnumbered, outgunned, and just out everything'd, they lead a slave revolt to free humanity. 88m; DVD. **C:** Bruce Campbell; Renee O'Connor; Remington Franklin; Michael Cory Davis; Peter Jason; Directed by Josh Becker; Written by Josh Becker; Joseph LoDuca; Cinematography by David Worth. **A:** Sr. High-Adult. **P:** Entertainment. **U:** Home. **L:** English. **Mov-Ent.** **Acq:** Purchase. **Dist:** Anchor Bay Entertainment Inc. $9.98.

Alien Autopsy: Fact or Fiction? 1995
Film supposedly showing footage of an autopsy performed by the government on an alien being discovered after an unexplained crash in Roswell, New Mexico. 70m; VHS. **C:** Hosted by Jonathan Frakes. **A:** Jr. High-Adult. **P:** Entertainment. **U:** Home.

Gen-Edu: Science. **Acq:** Purchase. **Dist:** Lions Gate Home Entertainment; CinemaNow Inc. $19.95.

Alien Avengers 1996 (R) — ★★½
Naive, poor Joseph Collins (Brown) inherits a rundown rooming-house and before he knows it, he has his first tenants—Charlie (Wendt), Rhonda (Reed), and their teenaged daughter Daphne (Sakelaris). What Joseph doesn't know is the friendly trio are aliens (on vacation), who are fond of killing lowlifes and bringing home human parts for snacks. Goofy and gory cable movie. 120m; VHS, DVD. **C:** George Wendt; Shanna Reed; Christopher Brown; Anastasia Sakelaris; Directed by Lev L. Spiro; Written by Michael James McDonald; Cinematography by Christopher Baffa; Music by Tyler Bates. **Pr:** Michael Amato; Roger Corman; Concorde Pictures; Showtime. **A:** Sr. High-Adult. **P:** Entertainment. **U:** Home. **Mov-Ent**: TV Movies, Violence. **Acq:** Purchase. **Dist:** Movies Unlimited.

Alien Cargo 1999 (PG) — ★
The crew of a Mars transport ship has just awakened from eight months in hypersleep to discover something they're off-course and in big trouble. Standard issue plot makes for boring entertainment. 89m; VHS, CC. **C:** Jason London; Missy (Melissa) Crider; Simon Westaway; Elizabeth (Liz) Alexander; Directed by Mark Haber. **A:** Jr. High-Adult. **P:** Entertainment. **U:** Home. **Mov-Ent**: Space Exploration. **Acq:** Purchase. **Dist:** Paramount Pictures Corp.

Alien Chaser 1996 (R) — ★★
Alien android Zagarino, who crashed in the African desert 5000 years ago, returns to life thanks to the unwitting aid of archeologists Jensen and MacDonald. They literally hold the key to stopping his destruction of mankind. 95m; VHS, DVD. **C:** Frank Zagarino; Todd Jensen; Jennifer MacDonald; Brian O'Shaughnessy; Directed by Mark Roper; Written by B.J. Nelson; Cinematography by Rod Stewart; Music by Robert O. Ragland. **Pr:** Danny Lerner; Avi Lerner; Trevor Short; Dan Dimbort; Nu Image Films. **A:** Sr. High-Adult. **P:** Entertainment. **U:** Home. **Mov-Ent**: Science Fiction. **Acq:** Purchase. **Dist:** Image Entertainment Inc.

Alien Contamination 1981 (R) — **Bomb!**
Tale of two astronauts who return to Earth from an expedition on Mars carrying some deadly bacterial eggs. Controlled by a Martian intent on conquering the world, the eggs squirt a gloppy juice that makes people explode on contact (a special effect). A cheap and sloppy attempt to cash in on the success of "Alien." Dubbed. 90m; VHS, DVD. **C:** Ian McCulloch; Louise Monroe; Martin Mase; Siegfried Rauch; Lisa Hahn; Louise Marleau; Directed by Luigi Cozzi; Written by Luigi Cozzi. **Pr:** Independent. **A:** Sr. High-Adult. **P:** Entertainment. **U:** Home. **Mov-Ent**: Science Fiction. **Acq:** Purchase. **Dist:** Movies Unlimited. $22.49.

Alien Dead 1979 (R) — ★
The teenage victims of a bizarre meteor crash reincarnate as flesh-eating ghouls anxious for a new supply of human food in this extremely low-budget sleep inducer. 75m; VHS, DVD. **C:** Buster Crabbe; Linda Lewis; Ray Roberts; Mike Bonavia; Dennis Underwood; Directed by Fred Olen Ray; Written by Fred Olen Ray; Martin Allen Nicholas; Cinematography by Fred Olen Ray. **Pr:** Cannon Films. **A:** Sr. High-Adult. **P:** Entertainment. **U:** Home. **Mov-Ent**: Horror. **Acq:** Purchase. **Dist:** Unknown Distributor.

Alien Deep With Bob Ballard 2012 (PG)
Dr. Robert Ballard, the famed international explorer who found the Titanic's final resting place, takes viewers on an amazing journey thousands of feet below the ocean's surface to reveal sea life and geographic elements that have never been seen before. Among the areas he explores are lava vents on the ocean floor where red-hot magma still pours out of the earth to build amazing rock formations and create an unexpectedly warm environment where any number of bizarre sea creatures live. 240m; DVD, Blu-Ray. **A:** Family. **P:** Education, Entertainment. **U:** Home, Institution. **Mov-Ent**: Documentary Films, Oceanography, Science. **Acq:** Purchase. **Dist:** $32.95 44.95.

The Alien Factor 1978 (PG) — ★½
Another low-budget crazed critter from outerspace dispatch, this one featuring multiple aliens, one of whom is good, who have the misfortune of crash landing near Baltimore. The grotesque extraterrestrials jolt a small town out of its sleepy state by wreaking havoc (except for the good one, of course). Decent special effects. 82m; VHS, DVD. **C:** Don Leifert; Tom Griffith; Mary Mertens; Richard Dyszel; Richard Geiwitz; Eleanor Herman; Anne Frith; Christopher Gummer; George Stover; John Walker; Donald M. Dohler; Directed by Donald M. Dohler; Written by Donald M. Dohler; Music by Ken Walker. **Pr:** Cinemagic. **A:** Jr. High-Adult. **P:** Entertainment. **U:** Home. **Mov-Ent**: Science Fiction. **Acq:** Purchase. **Dist:** Movies Unlimited. $59.99.

Alien Factor 2: The Alien Rampage 2001 (Unrated) — ★½
An alien traps a town inside a force field and runs about shooting the inhabitants at will. 75m; DVD. **C:** Patrick Bussink; Jonas Grey; Steven King; Bill Ulrich; George Stover; Joe Ripple; Richard Ruxton; Donna Sherman; Jaime Kulman; LauraLee O'Shell; Anne Frith; Directed by Don Dohler; Written by Don Dohler. **A:** Sr. High-Adult. **P:** Entertainment. **U:** Home. **L:** English. **Mov-Ent**. **Acq:** Purchase. **Dist:** Image Entertainment Inc. $9.98.

Alien 51 2004 (R) — ★
A monster escapes from Area 51 and is adopted by a traveling freak show. 90m; DVD. **C:** Layton Matthews; Heidi Fleiss; Mia Riverton; Directed by Brennon Jones; Paul Wynne; Written by Brennon Jones; Cinematography by Roderick E. Stevens; Music by Collin Simon. **A:** Sr. High-Adult. **P:** Entertainment. **U:** Home. **L:** English. **Mov-Ent**. **Acq:** Purchase. **Dist:** York Pictures Inc. $12.95.

Alien Fireballs 2010 (Unrated)
In this documentary, National Geographic examines one of the largest meteorite falls in recent history. More cameras, radar, and listening equipment documented the event than any that had come before it, leading scientists to hope they would learn new information about our universe. Also documents the coverage of a meteorite from Mars, which contained key information about the beginning of our solar system. 50m; DVD. **A:** Family. **P:** Education, Entertainment. **U:** Home, Institution.: Documentary Films, Astronomy, Nature. **Acq:** Purchase. **Dist:** $19.95.

Alien from L.A. 1987 (PG) — **Bomb!**
Awesomely inept comedy about a California girl who unwittingly stumbles onto the famed continent of Atlantis and can't find a yogurt stand. Weakly plotted and acted and filmed. Like, really. 88m; VHS, DVD. **C:** Kathy Ireland; Thom Mathews; Don Michael Paul; Linda Kerridge; William R. Moses; Richard Haines; Janie du Plessis; Russel Savadier; Simon Poland; Locher de Kock; Deep Roy; Directed by Albert Pyun; Written by Albert Pyun; Debra Ricci; Regina Davis; Cinematography by Tom Fraser; Music by James Saad. **Pr:** Cannon Films. **A:** Jr. High-Adult. **P:** Entertainment. **U:** Home. **Mov-Ent**: Action-Adventure, Fantasy, Science Fiction. **Acq:** Purchase. **Dist:** Movies Unlimited. $13.49.

Alien Fury: Countdown to Invasion 2000 (PG-13) — ★
Bill Templer (Midkiff) is upset when budget cuts threaten to close his government defense office, which sends probes into space looking for aliens. So he fakes some satellite photos of an alien armada poised to attack Earth from the dark side of the moon. Only, ha ha, the threat turns out to be real. This movie is so lame, you'll hope the aliens do attack and wipe these fools out. 88m; VHS. **C:** Dale Midkiff; Stephen Tobolowsky; Dondre T. Whitfield; Joanie Laurer; Grace Phillips; Scott Lowell; Paul Schulze; Troy Evans; Directed by Rob Hedden; Written by Rob Hedden; Cinematography by John Newby; Music by John Beal; Dennis McCarthy. **A:** Jr. High-Adult. **P:** Entertainment. **U:** Home. **Mov-Ent**: The Moon. **Acq:** Purchase. **Dist:** Parenting Pictures.

Alien Hunter 2003 (R) — ★½
Cobbled together compilation of a dozen sci fi movies. A cryptozoologist is called to the Antarctic to translate messages from an alien artifact in a plot that in no way owes a massive homage to "The Thing." Okay, actually it owes it in every way. 92m; DVD, Streaming. **C:** James Spader; Janine Eser; John Lynch; Nikolai Biney; Leslie Stefanson; Directed by Ron Krauss; Written by Boaz Davidson; J.S. Cardone; Cinematography by Darko Suvac; Music by Tim Jones. **A:** Sr. High-Adult. **P:** Entertainment. **U:** Home. **L:** English, French. **Mov-Ent**. **Acq:** Purchase, Rent/Lease. **Dist:** Sony Pictures Home Entertainment Inc. $9.99 9.99.

Alien Intruder 1993 (R) — ★★
What happens when an evil demon appears before the soldiers of the future in the guise of a beautiful woman? Futuristic trash B-movie emerges from the depths. 90m; VHS, DVD, On Demand, CC. **C:** Billy Dee Williams; Tracy Scoggins; Maxwell Caulfield; Directed by Ricardo Jacques Gale. **A:** Sr. High-Adult. **P:** Entertainment. **U:** Home. **L:** English, Spanish. **Mov-Ent**: Science Fiction. **Acq:** Purchase. **Dist:** Amazon.com Inc. $89.95.

Alien Invasion Arizona 2007 (R) — ★
A group of death row inmates manage an escape from their prison bus, only to end up in a deserted town. Deserted, that is, except for the military covering up their experiments with alien life forms. A bad idea since they get freaked out and eat whatever's in reach. 87m; DVD. **C:** Dan Southworth; Avery Clyde; Sam McConkey; James Luca McBride; Larry Jones; Directed by Dustin Rikert; Written by Dustin Rikert; Soon Hee Newbold; Cinematography by Brian Lataille; Music by Carl Rydlund. **A:** Sr. High-Adult. **P:** Entertainment. **U:** Home. **L:** English, Spanish. **Mov-Ent**. **Acq:** Purchase. **Dist:** Lions Gate Entertainment Inc. $14.98.

Alien Lockdown 2004 (R) — ★
Special Forces are required to infiltrate a genetics lab when it's super soldier experiment gets loose and goes on a killing spree. 92m; DVD, Streaming. **C:** James Marshall; John Savage; Martin Kove; Michelle Goh; Directed by Tim Cox; Written by Kenneth M. Badish; Boaz Davidson; Ross Helford; T. M. Van Ostrand; Cinematography by John S. Bartley; Music by John Dickson. **A:** Sr. High-Adult. **P:** Entertainment. **U:** Home. **L:** English. **Mov-Ent**. **Acq:** Purchase, Rent/Lease. **Dist:** First Look Studios Inc. $9.98 4.99.

Alien Massacre 1967 (Unrated) — **Bomb!**
One of the worst films of all time—five short horror stories about zombies and vampires. Goes by many names—stinks in all of them. 90m; VHS, DVD. **C:** Lon Chaney, Jr.; John Carradine; Rochelle Hudson; Roger Gentry; Mitch Evans; Joey Benson; Vic McGee; Directed by David L. Hewitt; Written by Gary Heacock; David Prentiss; Cinematography by Austin McKinney. **Pr:** Dorad Corporation; Borealis Productions. **A:** Jr. High-Adult. **P:** Entertainment. **U:** Home. **Mov-Ent**. **Acq:** Purchase. **Dist:** $19.95.

Alien Nation 1988 (R) — ★★½
A few hundred thousand alien workers land accidentally on Earth and slowly become part of its society, although widely discriminated against. One of the "newcomers" teams with a surly and bigoted human cop to solve a racially motivated murder. An inconsistent and occasionally transparent script looks at race conflicts and includes some humorous parallels with contemporary American life. Basis for the TV series. Producer Hurd was also the force behind "The Terminator" and "Aliens." 89m; VHS, DVD, Wide, CC. **C:** James Caan; Mandy Patinkin; Terence Stamp; Kevyn Major Howard; Peter Jason; Jeff Kober; Leslie Bevis; Directed by Graham Baker; Written by Rockne S. O'Bannon; Cinematography by Adam Greenberg; Music by Curt Sobel. **Pr:** Gale Anne Hurd; 20th Century-Fox. **A:** Sr. High-Adult. **P:** Entertainment. **U:** Home. **Mov-Ent**: Science Fiction, Drug Abuse. **Acq:** Purchase. **Dist:** Alpha Video; Movies Unlimited; Fox Home Entertainment. $19.98.

Alien Nation: Body and Soul 1995 — ★★½
The second TV movie sequel to the series finds detectives Francisco (Pierpoint) and Sykes (Graham) on a murder investigation that leads to a Newcomer scientist whose secret research deals with interspecies breeding. Meanwhile, Sykes' romance with Cathy (Treas) is heating up and he's becoming painfully aware of the sexual differences between humans and Newcomers. 87m; VHS, DVD. **C:** Gary (Rand) Graham; Eric Pierpoint; Terri Treas; Michelle Scarabelli; Sean Six; Lauren Woodland; Kristin Davis; Tiny Ron; Directed by Kenneth Johnson; Cinematography by Shelly Johnson; Music by David Kurtz. **Pr:** Paul Kurta; Kenneth Johnson; Kenneth Johnson; National Studios, Inc. **A:** Jr. High-Adult. **P:** Entertainment. **U:** Home. **Mov-Ent**: Science Fiction, TV Movies, Sex & Sexuality. **Acq:** Purchase. **Dist:** Fox Home Entertainment.

Alien Nation: Dark Horizon 1994 (PG) — ★★½
The alien Newcomers have successfully adapted to life on Earth but face continuing dangers when a human-supremacy group develops a virus to wipe them out and an alien infiltrator is plotting to return them to slavery on Tencton. Naturally, it's up to detectives Sykes and Francisco to save the day. Based on the TV series. Part of the 'Alien Nation: Ultimate Movie Collection'. 90m; VHS, DVD, CC. **C:** Gary (Rand) Graham; Eric Pierpoint; Scott Patterson; Terri Treas; Michelle Scarabelli; Lee Bryant; Sean Six; Lauren Woodland; Ron Fassler; Jeff Marcus; Directed by Kenneth Johnson; Written by Diane Frolov; Andrew Schneider; Music by David Kurtz. **Pr:** Kenneth Johnson; Kenneth Johnson; Diane Frolov; Andrew Schneider. **A:** Jr. High-Adult. **P:** Entertainment. **U:** Home. **Mov-Ent**: Science Fiction, TV Movies, Prejudice. **Acq:** Purchase. **Dist:** Amazon.com Inc.; Fox Home Entertainment.

Alien Nation: Millennium 1996 — ★★½
In this third TV sequel Matt (Graham) and George's (Pierpoint) latest police investigation hits very close to the Francisco home. Rebellious teenager Buck (Six) gets involved with a suspicious cult, lead by Newcomer Jennifer (Keane), that offers spiritual enlightenment at a very heavy price. 120m; VHS, DVD. **C:** Eric Pierpoint; Gary (Rand) Graham; Sean Six; Kerrie Keane; Michelle Scarabelli; Terri Treas; Lauren Woodland; Jeff Marcus; Jenny Gago; David Faustino; Directed by Kenneth Johnson; Written by Kenneth Johnson; Cinematography by Shelly Johnson; Music by David Kurtz. **Pr:** Kenneth Johnson; Paul Kurta; Kenneth Johnson; National Studios, Inc. **A:** Jr. High-Adult. **P:** Entertainment. **U:** Home. **Mov-Ent**: Science Fiction, TV Movies, Family. **Acq:** Purchase. **Dist:** Fox Home Entertainment.

Alien Nation: The Complete Series 2006 (Unrated)
Features all episodes of the science fiction television series spun off of the 1988 movie of the same name. LAPD detective Matthew Sikes (Graham) is teamed with George Francisco (Pierpoint) who is part of a group of bright and powerful alien slaves—Tenctonese, or "Newcomers"?that crashed their spaceship into the Mojave Desert and are now trying to live among the humans though as a minority. Meanwhile, the slave owners, or "Overseers," search to reclaim and enslave them. 22 episodes. 989m; DVD. **C:** Gary (Rand) Graham; Eric Pierpoint; Michelle Scarabelli. **A:** Jr. High-Adult. **P:** Entertainment. **U:** Home. **Mov-Ent**: Television Series, Science Fiction, Action-Adventure. **Acq:** Purchase. **Dist:** Fox Home Entertainment. $49.98.

Alien Nation: The Enemy Within 1996 — ★★½
George (Pierpont) must deal with his own bigotry when he and Matt (Graham) investigate the death of an Eenos Newcomer. The underground-dwelling Eenos are shunned as an ignorant and savage subclass by other Newcomers but the detectives gradually discover some sinister goings-on involving a fierce Eenos/Newcomer mutant. Meanwhile, George's wife Susan (Scarabelli) is feeling neglected and Cathy (Treas) and Matt find living together causes a strain on their relationship. The fourth TV movie from the series. 120m; VHS, DVD. **C:** Eric Pierpoint; Gary (Rand) Graham; Michelle Scarabelli; Terri Treas; Sean Six; Lauren Woodland; Joe Lando; Kerrie Keane; Tiny Ron; Ron Fassler; Directed by Kenneth Johnson. **Pr:** Kenneth Johnson; Kenneth Johnson. **A:** Jr. High-Adult. **P:** Entertainment. **U:** Home. **Mov-Ent**: Science Fiction, TV Movies, Family. **Acq:** Purchase. **Dist:** Fox Home Entertainment.

Alien Outlaw 1985 (Unrated) — ★
Disappointing hybrid of sci fi and westerns that's not the corny entertainment it should be given the plot. Sharpshooter Jesse Jamison (Anderson) has fallen on hard times when a trio of aliens lands their spaceship in a remote desert area with the intention of hunting and killing humans. And co-star Lash LaRue doesn't even have his bullwhip! 90m; DVD. **C:** Kari Anderson; Lash LaRue; Sunset Carson; Directed by Phil Smoot; Written by Phil Smoot; Cinematography by Paul Hughen; Music by Marcus Kearns. **A:** Jr. High-Adult. **P:** Entertainment. **U:** Home. **Mov-Ent**. **Acq:** Purchase. **Dist:** VCI Entertainment.

Alien Predators 1980 (R) — **Bomb!**
Three friends encounter a malevolent alien in this dull reworking of the plot of "The Andromeda Strain" with laughable special effects tossed in for those outwitted by the script. 92m; VHS. **C:**

Dennis Christopher; Martin Hewitt; Lynn-Holly Johnson; Luis Prendes; Directed by Deran Sarafian. **A:** College-Adult. **P:** Entertainment. **U:** Home. **Mov-Ent**: Science Fiction. **Acq:** Purchase. **Dist:** Anchor Bay Entertainment. $79.95.

Alien Prey 1978 (R) — ★½
Two lesbians are making love when they are unexpectedly devoured by a hungry and indiscreet alien. No safe sex there. Graphic sex, violence, and cannibalism abound. Interesting twist to the old eat 'em and leave 'em genre. 85m; VHS, DVD. **C:** Barry Stokes; Sally Faulkner; Glory Annen; Sandy Chinney; Directed by Norman J. Warren; Written by Max Cuff; Cinematography by Derek V. Browne; Music by Ivor Slaney. **Pr:** American International Pictures. **A:** College-Adult. **P:** Entertainment. **U:** Home. **Mov-Ent**: Horror, Great Britain. **Acq:** Purchase. **Dist:** Amazon.com Inc.

Alien Private Eye 1987 (Unrated) — ★★
An extraterrestrial detective searches Los Angeles for a missing magic disk while investigating an intergalactic crime ring. 90m; VHS. **C:** Nikki Fastinetti; Directed by Nik Rubenfeld. **Pr:** Rae Don. **A:** College-Adult. **P:** Entertainment. **U:** Home. **Mov-Ent**: Science Fiction. **Acq:** Purchase. **Dist:** Amazon.com Inc.

Alien Raiders 2008 (R) — ★★
A family-owned supermarket in a small Arizona town is getting ready to close when it is taken over by armed men. They aren't robbers but scientists who have tracked an alien infestation to that store. Now the scientists have to discover who among the employees and customers were infected. Fast-paced and reasonably clever with a few twists. 85m; DVD. **C:** Matthew St. Patrick; Rockmond Dunbar; Jeff(rey) Licon; Bonita Friedericy; Carlos Bernard; Courtney Ford; Derek Basco; Bryan Krasner; Directed by Ben Rock; Written by David Simkins; Julia Fair; Cinematography by Walt Lloyd; Music by Kays Alatrakchi. **A:** Sr. High-Adult. **P:** Entertainment. **U:** Home. **Mov-Ent**: Science. **Acq:** Purchase. **Dist:** Warner Home Video, Inc.

Alien: Resurrection 1997 (R) — ★★★
Despite her fiery end in the last film, Ripley is brought back, through cloning, by a team of scientist anxious to get their hands on the alien embryo that invaded her. A more buffed and equally strange Ripley (Weaver) results as some of her DNA gets mixed with her alien friend. Injecting new life into the franchise, director Jeunet creates a freaky and macabre journey as the aliens get loose on board the mysterious space craft Auriga and create messy havoc for new alien appetizers including Call (Ryder), who has a personal agenda of her own with Ripley. Ryder may be somewhat out of place, but the humor and energy from the supporting cast, along with the film's dank look raises this one from the bowels of formulaic action/horror. Includes some decent scares with a tense underwater sequence. 108m; VHS, DVD, Blu-Ray, Wide, CC. **C:** Sigourney Weaver; Winona Ryder; Ron Perlman; Dominique Pinon; Michael Wincott; Kim Flowers; Leland Orser; Brad Dourif; Dan Hedaya; J.E. Freeman; Raymond Cruz; Directed by Jean-Pierre Jeunet; Written by Joss Whedon; Cinematography by Darius Khondji; Music by John (Gianni) Frizzell. **Pr:** David Giler; Walter Hill; Gordon Carroll; Bill Badalato; Brandywine; 20th Century-Fox. **A:** Jr. High-Adult. **P:** Entertainment. **U:** Home. **Mov-Ent**: Science Fiction, Basketball, Handicapped. **Acq:** Purchase. **Dist:** Fox Home Entertainment.

Alien Rights 19??
Serena Chen and Donald Yee discuss the rights of aliens and the problems immigrants face; instructs on how to file the alien registration form. 30m/B/W; EJ. **Pr:** KTVU Oakland. **A:** Adult. **P:** Education. **U:** Institution, CCTV. **Gen-Edu**: Immigration. **Acq:** Loan. **Dist:** Chinese for Affirmative Action.

Alien Seed 1989 (Unrated) — ★
Aliens kidnap a woman and impregnate her. Estrada is the government scientist hot on her trail. (How far could a woman carrying alien offspring wander?) 88m; VHS, DVD. **C:** Erik Estrada; Heidi Paine; Steven Blade; Directed by Bob James. **A:** Adult. **P:** Entertainment. **U:** Home. **Mov-Ent**: Horror. **Acq:** Purchase. **Dist:** Movies Unlimited. $12.74.

Alien Sex Fiend: A Purple Glistener 19??
Horror rock includes songs "Ignore the Machine," "R.I.P." and more. ?m; VHS. **A:** Jr. High-College. **P:** Entertainment. **U:** Home. **Mov-Ent**: Music Video. **Acq:** Purchase. **Dist:** Music Video Distributors. $29.95.

Alien Sex Fiend: Edit 19??
The British band featured in clips "Wild Women," "Get Into It," "Manic Depression" and plenty more. ?m; VHS. **A:** Jr. High-College. **P:** Entertainment. **U:** Home. **Mov-Ent**: Music Video. **Acq:** Purchase. **Dist:** Music Video Distributors. $29.95.

Alien Sex Fiend: Overdose 19??
British import includes "April Showers," "I Walk the Line," "R.I.P.," "I Wish I Woz a Dog" and more. 40m; VHS. **A:** Jr. High-College. **P:** Entertainment. **U:** Home. **Mov-Ent**: Music Video. **Acq:** Purchase. **Dist:** Music Video Distributors. $29.95.

Alien Siege 2005 (R) — ★½
Aliens descend upon Earth seeking human blood, which is the only cure for a virus killing their race. They destroy some cities to show they mean business. Since they need 8 million bodies, a lottery system is devised and the unlucky get to become alien vaccine. Scientist Steven Chase (Johnson) decides no fair when his only child, Heather (Ross), is chosen. Naturally, there's a resistance group that feels earthlings should be fighting the alien fiends and Steve joins. A Sci-Fi Channel original. 90m; DVD. **C:** Brad Johnson; Carl Weathers; Nathan Anderson; Erin Ross; Lilas Lane; Directed by Robert Stadd; Written by Robert Stadd; Cinematography by Lorenzo Senatore; Music by Matthias Weber; Chris Walden. **A:** Sr. High-Adult. **P:** Entertainment. **U:** Home. **Mov-Ent**. **Acq:** Purchase. **Dist:** Image Entertainment Inc.

Alien Space Avenger 1991 (Unrated) — ★½
A spaceship piloted by four alien convicts crash lands in New York City. Stalked by an intergalatic bounty hunter whose job is to kill them, the aliens attack and hide inside human bodies to avoid discovery. It's a race against time as the preservation of the human race depends on the avenger's ability to seek and destroy the alien invaders. Bland ripoff of "Aliens" is reminiscent of old-time "B" sci-fi flicks , with more gore and violence. Shot with the old 3-strip Technicolor method. 88m; VHS. **C:** Robert Prichard; Mike McClerie; Charity Staley; Gina Mastrogiacomo; Kick Fairbanks Fogg; Angela Nicholas; Marty Roberts; James Gillis; Directed by Richard W. Haines; Written by Richard W. Haines; Linwood Sawyer; Music by Richard Fiocca. **A:** Sr. High-Adult. **P:** Entertainment. **U:** Home. **Mov-Ent**: Science Fiction. **Acq:** Purchase. **Dist:** Unknown Distributor.

Alien Terminator 1995 (R) — ★
Scientists experimenting with DNA find themselves creating an organism capable of instant regeneration that also likes to nosh on living flesh. To make matters worse, the scientists are trapped in their lab complex, which happens to be located five miles below Los Alamos. 95m; VHS, DVD. **C:** Maria Ford; Kevin Alber; Rodger Halston; Cassandra Leigh; Emile Levisetti; Directed by Dave Payne. **A:** Sr. High-Adult. **P:** Entertainment. **U:** Home. **Mov-Ent**: Science Fiction. **Acq:** Purchase. **Dist:** New Horizons Picture Corp.

Alien 3000 2004 (R) — **Bomb!**
This woofer is dull as well as stupid. A commando unit is sent into the forest to search for an invisible alien creature that is supposed to be guarding an unknown treasure in a cave no one can find. Ummm, maybe that's because it's really hard to tell what's going on and not worth the effort anyway. 81m; DVD. **C:** Lorenzo Lamas; Priscilla Barnes; Corbin Timbrook; Scott Schwartz; Directed by Jeff Leroy; Written by Garrett Clancy; Cinematography by Rachel Wyn Dunn; Music by Collin Simon. **A:** Sr. High-Adult. **P:** Entertainment. **U:** Home. **Mov-Ent**: Forests & Trees. **Acq:** Purchase. **Dist:** Lions Gate Entertainment Inc.

Alien Trespass 2009 (PG) — ★★½
In 1957, a spaceship crash-lands in the Mohave desert, witnessed only by a waitress and an astronomer. The occupants are a vicious omnivorous alien, Ghota, and its captor, Urp. In order to save mankind, Urp (McCormack) must take over the astronomer's body and capture the beast, with the waitress's help. Earnest tribute to 1950s drive-in movie monster flicks. 90m; Blu-Ray, On Demand, Wide. **C:** Eric McCormack; Robert Patrick; Dan Lauria; Jenni Baird; Jody Thompson; Aaron Brooks; Sarah Smyth; Andrew Dunbar; Directed by R.W. Goodwin; Written by Steve(n) Fisher; Cinematography by David Moxness; Music by Louis Febre. **A:** Primary-Adult. **P:** Entertainment. **U:** Home. **L:** English. **Mov-Ent**: Satire & Parody. **Acq:** Purchase. **Dist:** Image Entertainment Inc.; Amazon.com Inc.; Movies Unlimited.

Alien 2 on Earth 1980 (Unrated) — **Bomb!**
In this obscure, cheap Italian sci fi rip-off, telepathic speleologist Thelma Joyce discovers a space capsule that crashed to Earth has littered the coast with rocks that are actually alien life forms. After taking time out to go bowling (!), Thelma and her team get trapped in an underground cavern teaming with these alien/rock forms, which like to burrow inside humans. 84m; DVD. **C:** Belinda Mayne; Michele (Michael) Soavi; Judy Perrin; Roberto Barrese; Benedetta Fantoli; Directed by Ciro Ippolito; Written by Ciro Ippolito; Cinematography by Silvio Fraschetti; Music by Guido de Angelis; Maurizio de Angelis. **A:** Sr. High-Adult. **P:** Entertainment. **U:** Home. **Mov-Ent**: Bowling. **Acq:** Purchase. **Dist:** Midnight Legacy.

Alien Uprising 2012 (R) — **Bomb!**
Slow-moving, low-budget Brit sci fi. Friends have a drunken night out and wake the next day to discover the city has no power and no communications. Yes, aliens have invaded. They decide to find recluse survivalist George to help them out. Van Damme apparently took this small role because daughter Bianca Bree is one of the leads. Nice daddy gesture but it didn't help--the pic is still dumb and dreadful. 101m; DVD. **C:** Sean Brosnan; Bianca Bree; Jazz Lintott; Simon Phillips; Maya Grant; Jean-Claude Van Damme; Sean Pertwee; Directed by Dominic Burns; Written by Dominic Burns; Cinematography by Luke Bryant; Music by Si Begg. **A:** Sr. High-Adult. **P:** Entertainment. **U:** Home. **L:** English. **Mov-Ent**: Science Fiction. **Acq:** Purchase. **Dist:** Phase 4/kaBOOM Entertainment.

Alien vs. Predator 2004 (PG-13) — ★
How to classify "AvP?" Is it an "Alien" or "Predator" movie? It doesn't really matter since it's the worst offering that either franchise has produced to date. Predictable, effects-laden prequel to the four-part "Alien" saga and a sequel to the two "Predator" films has a bunch of humans finding an arctic training base for adolescent Predators that uses Aliens as their prey. Of course, the silly humans get caught between them and bad things happen. Monster fest fails to enhance either franchise. 110m; VHS, DVD, Blu-Ray, UMD. **C:** Sanaa Lathan; Raoul Bova; Lance Henriksen; Ewen Bremner; Colin Salmon; Tommy Flanagan; Joseph Rye; Agathe de la Boulaye; Carsten Norgaard; Sam Troughton; Ian Whyte; Directed by Paul W.S. Anderson; Written by Paul W.S. Anderson; Dan O'Bannon; Cinematography by David C(lark) Johnson; Music by Harald Kloser. **Pr:** John Davis; Gordon Carroll; David Giler; Walter Hill; Brandywine; Davis Entertainment Company; 20th Century-Fox. **A:** Jr. High-Adult. **P:** Entertainment. **U:** Home. **Mov-Ent**: Science Fiction, Science, Arctic Regions. **Acq:** Purchase. **Dist:** Fox Home Entertainment.

Alien Visitor 1995 (PG-13) — ★★
Beautiful alien woman lands on Earth in the Australian outback where she meets a guy and is disappointed in her destination since Earth is considered so backwards. But he manages to show her some things that make Earth life worth living. 92m; VHS, DVD, Wide, CC. **C:** Syd Brisbane; Alethea McGrath; Chloe Ferguson; Phoebe Ferguson; Ulli Birve; Directed by Rolf de Heer; Written by Rolf de Heer; Cinematography by Tony Clark; Music by Graham Tardif. **A:** Jr. High-Adult. **P:** Entertainment. **U:** Home. **Mov-Ent**: Australia, Romance. **Acq:** Purchase. **Dist:** Buena Vista Home Entertainment.

Alien Warrior 1985 (R) — **Bomb!**
An extraterrestrial fights a street pimp to save a crime-ridden Earth neighborhood. Low-brain rip-off of Superman. 92m; VHS. **C:** Brett (Baxter) Clark; Pamela Saunders; Directed by Ed(ward) Hunt. **Pr:** Shapiro Ent. **A:** Sr. High. **P:** Entertainment. **U:** Home. **Mov-Ent**: Science Fiction, Prostitution. **Acq:** Purchase. **Dist:** Lions Gate Television Corp. $79.98.

Alienator 1989 (R) — ★
In the improbable future, an unstoppable android killer is sent after an intergalactic villain. An intentional "Terminator" rip-off. 93m; VHS, DVD. **C:** Jan-Michael Vincent; John Phillip Law; Ross Hagen; Dyana Ortelli; Dawn Wildsmith; P.J. Soles; Teagan Clive; Robert Clarke; Leo Gordon; Robert Quarry; Fox Harris; Hoke Howell; Jay Richardson; Directed by Fred Olen Ray. **Pr:** Majestic; Amazing Movies. **A:** College-Adult. **P:** Entertainment. **U:** Home. **Mov-Ent**: Science Fiction. **Acq:** Purchase. **Dist:** Unknown Distributor.

Aliens 1986 (R) — ★★★½
The bitch is back, some 50 years later. Popular sequel to "Alien" amounts to non-stop, ravaging combat in space. Contact with a colony on another planet has mysteriously stopped. Fresh from deep space sleep, Ripley and a slew of pulsar-equipped Marines return to confront the mother alien at her nest, which is also inhabited by a whole bunch of the nasty critters spewing for a fight. Something's gotta give, and the Oscar-winning special effects are especially inventive (and messy) in the alien demise department. Dimension (acting biz talk) is given to our hero Ripley, as she discovers maternal instincts lurking within her space suit while looking after a young girl, the lone survivor of the colony. Tension-filled gore blaster. Followed by "Aliens 3." 138m; VHS, DVD, Blu-Ray, Wide, CC. **C:** Sigourney Weaver; Michael Biehn; Lance Henriksen; Bill Paxton; Paul Reiser; Carrie Henn; Jenette Goldstein; William Hope; Al Matthews; Mark Rolston; Ricco Ross; Colette Hiller; Directed by James Cameron; Written by James Cameron; Walter Hill; Cinematography by Adrian Biddle; Music by James Horner. **Pr:** Gale Anne Hurd; 20th Century-Fox. **A:** Sr. High-Adult. **P:** Entertainment. **U:** Home. **Mov-Ent**: Science Fiction, Parenting, Adoption. **Awds:** Oscars '86: Sound FX Editing, Visual FX. **Acq:** Purchase. **Dist:** Movies Unlimited; Alpha Video; Fox Home Entertainment. $19.98.

Aliens and Archetypes 1989
Terrence McKenna, leading authority on alternative realities, offers his theory on the existence of UFOs and the like, re: they stem from psychic projections from our own minds. Their function is to offset the imbalance of the rationalist thought in contemporary culture. 30m; VHS. **Pr:** Thinking Allowed Productions. **A:** Sr. High-Adult. **P:** Education. **U:** Home. **Gen-Edu**: Psychology. **Acq:** Purchase. **Dist:** Thinking Allowed Productions. $29.95.

Aliens Are Coming 1980 — ★½
A spaceship crash lands on Earth, and its devious denizens begin invading human bodies. TV movie that's a dull echo of "Invasion of the Body Snatchers." 100m; VHS. **C:** Tom Mason; Melinda Fee; Max Gail; Eric Braeden; Matthew Laborteaux; Directed by Harvey Hart; Music by William Goldstein. **Pr:** Quinn Martin Productions. **A:** Jr. High-Adult. **P:** Entertainment. **U:** Home. **Mov-Ent**: Science Fiction, TV Movies. **Acq:** Purchase. **Dist:** $9.95.

Aliens, Dragons, Monsters & Me: The Fantasy Film World of Ray Harryhausen 1992
A look at the career of special effects whiz Ray Harryhausen. Harryhausen discusses his career and techniques, including his work on such films as "King Kong," "Clash of the Titans," "7th Voyage of Sinbad," and others. Includes film footage. 48m; VHS. **A:** Family. **P:** Entertainment. **U:** Home. **Gen-Edu**: Documentary Films. **Acq:** Purchase. **Dist:** Fusion Video. $19.95.

Aliens from Inner Space 1984
This episode from "The Living Planet" examines the form, movement and communication of the cuttlefish, squid and octopus. 25m; VHS, 3/4 U. **C:** Narrated by David Attenborough. **Pr:** British Broadcasting Corporation. **A:** Jr. High-Adult. **P:** Education. **U:** Institution, SURA. **Hea-Sci**: Animals. **Acq:** Purchase, Rent/Lease. **Dist:** Home Vision Cinema.

Aliens from Inner Space/The Fastest Claw in the West 1990
"Aliens from Inner Space" dives into the amazing world of cuttlefish, squid, and octopi, to see how they communicate. "The Fastest Claw in the West" takes a look at shrimp with attack and defense systems that have been studied by the Pentagon. Both episodes on one cassette. 48m; VHS. **Pr:** British Broadcasting Corporation. **A:** Jr. High-Adult. **P:** Education. **U:** Home. **Gen-Edu**: Documentary Films, Oceanography. **Acq:** Purchase. **Dist:** Home Vision Cinema. $24.95.

Aliens from Spaceship Earth 1977 — ★½
Are strange, celestial forces invading our universe? If they are, is man prepared to defend his planet against threatening aliens of unknown strength? Lame docudrama featuring the Hurdy Gurdy man himself, Donovan. 107m; VHS, DVD. **C:** Donovan; Lynda Day George; Directed by Don Como. **Pr:** International TF

Productions. **A:** Jr. High-Adult. **P:** Entertainment. **U:** Home. **Mov-Ent:** Science Fiction. **Acq:** Purchase. **Dist:** UFO Central.

Aliens in the Attic 2009 (PG) — ★½
Youngsters will probably be at least mildly entertained by this live-action/(mediocre) CGI concoction. The extended Pearson family is staying at their vacation home in Michigan although the teens are less than thrilled about being there. Then brainiac Tom (Jenkins) discovers four pint-sized aliens have taken over the attic. The nasty aliens have a device (resembling a videogame joystick) that can control the minds and actions of the adults so it's up to the kids to improvise and save the planet. Silly and generally harmless, although Roberts as a martial arts-kicking granny is somewhat unnerving. 86m; Blu-Ray, Wide. **C:** Carter Jenkins; Ashley Tisdale; Austin Butler; Ashley Boettcher; Doris Roberts; Robert Hoffman, III; Kevin Nealon; Andy Richter; Tim Meadows; Henri Young; Regan Young; Malese Jow; Maggie VandenBerghe; Megan Parker; Voice(s) by Thomas Haden Church; Josh Peck; Ashley Peldon; Kari Wahlgren; J.K. Simmons; Directed by John Schultz; Written by Mark Burton; Adam F. Goldberg; Cinematography by Don Burgess; Music by John Debney. **Pr:** Barry Josephson; Regency Enterprises; Josephson Entertainment; 20th Century-Fox. **A:** Family. **P:** Entertainment. **U:** Home. **L:** English. **Mov-Ent. Acq:** Purchase. **Dist:** Fox Home Entertainment; Movies Unlimited; Alpha Video.

Aliens of the Sea 1999
Documentary featuring ocean reefs around Australia. 50m; VHS. **A:** Family. **P:** Education. **U:** Home. **Hea-Sci:** Documentary Films, Oceanography, Wildlife. **Acq:** Purchase. **Dist:** Instructional Video. $24.99.

Aliens vs. Predator: Requiem 2007 (R) — ★½
In this sequel to the 2004 flick, the extraterrestrial beasties are cool and the humans are interchangeable incubators and fodder. A mutant alien-predator crash-lands near a small Colorado town and begins using convenient humans for procreation vessels and a super-Predator shows up to dispatch the new critters. The locals are collateral damage. Everything moves along at a snappy pace and there's some action pieces that are watchable, which means if you're a fan you probably won't be disappointed. 86m; Blu-Ray, Wide. **C:** Reiko Aylesworth; Johnny Lewis; Ariel Gade; Steven Pasquale; Sam Trammell; Robert Joy; John Ortiz; Directed by Colin Strause; Greg Strause; Written by Shane Salerno; Cinematography by Daniel Pearl; Music by Brian Tyler. **Pr:** John Davis; David Giler; Walter Hill; Brandywine; Dune Entertainment; 20th Century-Fox. **A:** Sr. High-Adult. **P:** Entertainment. **U:** Home. **L:** English. **Mov-Ent:** Science Fiction. **Acq:** Purchase. **Dist:** Fox Home Entertainment; Movies Unlimited; Alpha Video.

Aligned and Well—Biomechanics for Bad Backs 2009 (Unrated)
Biomechanics expert Katy Bowman demonstrates a combination of lifestyle changes and exercises designed to help people with back problems. 40m; DVD, Streaming. **A:** Jr. High-Adult. **P:** Entertainment. **U:** Home. **Hea-Sci:** Health Education, Fitness/Exercise. **Acq:** Purchase, Rent/Lease. **Dist:** Janson Media. $14.95.

Aligned and Well—Biomechanics for Strong Bones 2009 (Unrated)
Katy Bowman continues her series on using biomechanics exercises to promote health and reduce bodily problems due to lifestyles; this volume deals with strengthening bones in key load-bearing areas. 40m; DVD, Streaming. **A:** Jr. High-Adult. **P:** Entertainment. **U:** Home. **Hea-Sci:** Health Education, Fitness/Exercise. **Acq:** Purchase, Rent/Lease. **Dist:** Janson Media. $14.95.

Aligned and Well—Easy Rx...ercise for Diabetics 2009 (Unrated)
Workout program by Katy Bowman designed for diabetics to increase blood flow and health in their lower body. 40m; DVD, Streaming. **A:** Jr. High-Adult. **P:** Entertainment. **U:** Home. **Hea-Sci:** Health Education, Diabetes, Fitness/Exercise. **Acq:** Purchase, Rent/Lease. **Dist:** Janson Media. $14.95.

Aligned and Well—Fix Your Feet 2009 (Unrated)
Katy Bowman designs a workout for people with foot problems such as fallen arches, fasciitis, and others. 40m; DVD, Streaming. **A:** Jr. High-Adult. **P:** Entertainment. **U:** Home. **Hea-Sci:** Health Education, Fitness/Exercise. **Acq:** Purchase, Rent/Lease. **Dist:** Janson Media. $14.95.

Aligned and Well—From the Shoulders Up 2009 (Unrated)
Katy Bowman introduced head and neck exercises for people with problems gained from sitting long hours at the computer. 40m; DVD, Streaming. **A:** Jr. High-Adult. **P:** Entertainment. **U:** Home. **Hea-Sci:** Health Education, Fitness/Exercise. **Acq:** Purchase, Rent/Lease. **Dist:** Janson Media. $14.95.

Aligned and Well—Get Your Balance Back 2009 (Unrated)
Katy Bowman uses biomechanics to design a workout to increase your balance. 40m; DVD. **A:** Jr. High-Adult. **P:** Entertainment. **U:** Home. **Hea-Sci:** Health Education, Fitness/Exercise. **Acq:** Purchase. **Dist:** Janson Media. $14.95.

Aligned and Well—Knees and Hips 2009 (Unrated)
Katy Bowman presents exercises for strengthening the knees and hips for runners or people with hip disorders. 40m; DVD, Streaming. **A:** Jr. High-Adult. **P:** Entertainment. **U:** Home. **Hea-Sci:** Health Education, Fitness/Exercise. **Acq:** Purchase, Rent/Lease. **Dist:** Janson Media. $14.95.

Aligned and Well—My Hands Hurt: From Elbows to Fingers 2009 (Unrated)
Video on exercises and lifestyle changes for people who have hand and arm issues due to occupational hazards such as long hours spent typing. 40m; DVD, Streaming. **A:** Jr. High-Adult. **P:** Entertainment. **U:** Home. **Hea-Sci:** Health Education, Fitness/Exercise. **Acq:** Purchase, Rent/Lease. **Dist:** Janson Media. $14.95.

Aligned and Well—Smart Digestion 2009 (Unrated)
Katy Bowman discusses lifestyle changes and presents some exercises for people with acid reflux and similar digestive disorders. 40m; DVD, Streaming. **A:** Jr. High-Adult. **P:** Entertainment. **U:** Home. **Hea-Sci:** Health Education, Fitness/Exercise. **Acq:** Purchase, Rent/Lease. **Dist:** Janson Media. $14.95.

Aligned and Well—When You Can't Breathe 2009 (Unrated)
Katy Bowman discusses the mechanics of breathing and how to properly synch it with exercise. 40m; DVD, Streaming. **A:** Jr. High-Adult. **P:** Entertainment. **U:** Home. **Hea-Sci:** Health Education, Fitness/Exercise. **Acq:** Purchase, Rent/Lease. **Dist:** Janson Media. $14.95.

Aligned and Well—When You Hurt All Over 2009 (Unrated)
Katy Bowman discusses stretching exercises for improving blood flow among patients who are in pain but need to exercise. 40m; DVD, Streaming. **A:** Jr. High-Adult. **P:** Entertainment. **U:** Home. **Hea-Sci:** Health Education, Fitness/Exercise. **Acq:** Purchase, Rent/Lease. **Dist:** Janson Media. $14.95.

Aligned and Well—When Your Doctor Prescribes Exercise 2009 (Unrated)
Katy Bowman crafts a workout for those who have been prescribed exercise by their doctor but can't do high intensity workouts or have physical problems. 40m; DVD, Streaming. **A:** Jr. High-Adult. **P:** Education. **U:** Home. **Hea-Sci:** Health Education, Fitness/Exercise. **Acq:** Purchase, Rent/Lease. **Dist:** Janson Media. $14.95.

Aligned and Well?"Below the Belt" for Men 2009 (Unrated)
Biomechanics expert Katy Bowman takes a look at pelvic ailments in men—and lifestyle changes and exercises that can be made to correct them. 40m; DVD, Streaming. **A:** Jr. High-Adult. **P:** Education. **U:** Home. **Hea-Sci:** Health Education, Fitness/Exercise. **Acq:** Purchase, Rent/Lease. **Dist:** Janson Media. $14.95.

Aligned and Well?"Down There" for Women 2009 (Unrated)
A companion video for Katy Bowman's video for pelvic problems for men but designed for women. 40m; DVD, Streaming. **A:** Jr. High-Adult. **P:** Education. **U:** Home. **Hea-Sci:** Health Education, Fitness/Exercise. **Acq:** Purchase, Rent/Lease. **Dist:** Janson Media. $14.95.

Alignment Adjustment Locations Chrysler K-Car 1987
Offers instruction on specific aspects of automotive maintenance and repair. 4m; VHS. **A:** Adult. **P:** Instruction. **U:** Institution. **How-Ins:** Automobiles. **Acq:** Purchase. **Dist:** RMI Media. $45.00.

Alignment Adjustment Locations Ford Products 1987
Offers instruction on specific aspects of automotive maintenance and repair. 6m; VHS. **A:** Adult. **P:** Instruction. **U:** Institution. **How-Ins:** Automobiles. **Acq:** Purchase. **Dist:** RMI Media. $51.00.

Alignment Adjustment Locations Ford Products With Strut Rod 1987
Offers instruction on specific aspects of automotive maintenance and repair. 4m; VHS. **A:** Adult. **P:** Instruction. **U:** Institution. **How-Ins:** Automobiles. **Acq:** Purchase. **Dist:** RMI Media. $47.00.

Alignment Adjustment Locations General Motors 1987
Offers instruction on specific aspects of automotive maintenance and repair. 6m; VHS. **A:** Adult. **P:** Instruction. **U:** Institution. **How-Ins:** Automobiles. **Acq:** Purchase. **Dist:** RMI Media. $51.00.

Alimony Madness 1933 — ★½
Architect John Thurman is desperate to divorce his greedy wife Eloise, so he agrees to her excessive alimony demands. When the depression causes his business to collapse, he gets into legal trouble for non-payment. His frantic second wife Joan finally confronts Eloise--and winds up on trial for her murder. 66m/B/W; DVD. **C:** Helen Chandler; Leon Ames; Charlotte Merriam; Edward Earle; Directed by B. Reeves Eason; Written by John Thomas "Jack" Neville; Cinematography by Ernest Miller. **A:** Adult. **P:** Entertainment. **U:** Home. **L:** English. **Mov-Ent:** Divorce, Law. **Acq:** Purchase. **Dist:** Alpha Video.

Alison's Birthday 1979 (Unrated) — ★★
A teenage girl learns that some of her family and friends are Satan worshipers at a terrifying birthday party. Meanwhile, the ghost of her dad hovers about, asking for more lines. 99m; VHS. **C:** Joanne Samuel; Lou Brown; Bunny Brooke; Directed by Ian Coughlan. **Pr:** David Hannay. **A:** Sr. High-Adult. **P:** Entertainment. **U:** Home. **Mov-Ent:** Horror. **Acq:** Purchase. **Dist:** Unknown Distributor.

Alive 1993 (R) — ★★½
Recounts the true-life survival story of a group of Uruguayan rugby players in 1972. After their plane crashes in the remote,

snowy Andes (in a spectacular sequence) they're forced to turn to cannibalism during a 10-week struggle to stay alive. Marshall doesn't focus on the gruesome idea, choosing instead to focus on all aspects of their desperate quest for survival. The special effects are stunning, but other parts of the film are never fully realized, including the final scene. Based on the nonfiction book by Piers Paul Read. 127m; VHS, DVD, Wide, CC. **C:** Ethan Hawke; Vincent Spano; Josh Hamilton; Bruce Ramsay; John Haymes Newton; David Kriegel; Kevin Breznahan; Sam Behrens; Illeana Douglas; Jack Noseworthy; Christian Meoli; Jake Carpenter; Narrated by John Malkovich; Directed by Frank Marshall; Written by John Patrick Shanley; Cinematography by Peter James; Music by James Newton Howard. **Pr:** Buena Vista. **A:** Sr. High-Adult. **P:** Entertainment. **U:** Home. **Mov-Ent:** Action-Adventure. **Acq:** Purchase. **Dist:** Buena Vista Home Entertainment. $19.99.

Alive 2002 (Unrated) — ★½
Tenshu Yashiro (Sakaki) has been sent to the chair for murdering the gang who raped and killed his girlfriend. Surviving his initial shock in the electric chair, he is given the choice of being jolted again or sharing a cell with another inmate who has also survived the chair. He'll be given anything he wants (within reason), as long as he stays in the cell. At first this doesn't seem like too bad a deal until he learns his cellmate is a violent serial rapist. 119m; DVD. **C:** Shun Sugata; Hideo Sakaki; Erika Oda; Ryo; Koyuki; Directed by Ryuhei Kitamura; Written by Ryuhei Kitamura; Yudai Yamaguchi; Isao Kiriyama; Daisuke Yano; Cinematography by Takumi Furuya; Music by Nobuhiko Morino. **A:** Sr. High-Adult. **P:** Entertainment. **U:** Home. **L:** English, Japanese. **Mov-Ent:** Science Fiction. **Acq:** Purchase. **Dist:** Media Blasters Inc. $29.95.

Alive Again 1986
Attitudes and stereotypes about alcoholics are discussed. 15m; VHS. **Pr:** New Dimension Films. **A:** Sr. High-Adult. **P:** Education. **U:** Institution. **Hea-Sci:** Alcoholism. **Acq:** Purchase, Rent/Lease. **Dist:** New Dimension Media. $295.00.

Alive and Kicking 1996 (R) — ★★½
Tonio (Flemyng) is a handsome, vain ballet dancer with AIDS, who hides his emotions beneath a witty facade and his work. At a club he meets the older, equally driven Jack (Sher), an AIDS counselor, who pursues him. Though they become lovers, Tonio's obsession with his latest (and last) dance role causes a rift between them. Subplot between Tonio and lesbian dancer Millie (Parish) is self-conscious and Tonio's theatrics can become annoying but both Flemyng and Sher do their best in somewhat one-note roles. 100m; VHS, DVD. **C:** Jason Flemyng; Anthony Sher; Dorothy Tutin; Anthony (Corlan) Higgins; Diane Parish; Bill Nighy; Directed by Nancy Meckler; Written by Martin Sherman; Cinematography by Chris Seager; Music by Peter Salem. **Pr:** Martin Pope; Channel Four Film; First Look Pictures. **A:** Sr. High-Adult. **P:** Entertainment. **U:** Home. **Mov-Ent:** Drama, AIDS, Dance--Ballet. **Acq:** Purchase. **Dist:** Movies Unlimited.

Alive and Well: A Guide to Sustainable Soil Management 19??
Visits five different farming operations where sustainable soil management practices have been successfully implemented. Contains interviews with the farmers and demonstrations of their methods, including soil aeration, minimum disturbance after aeration, composting, soil amendments, cover cropping, biological diversity, and economic strategies. 35m; VHS. **A:** Adult. **P:** Vocational. **U:** Institution, SURA. **Bus-Ind:** Agriculture. **Acq:** Purchase. **Dist:** San Luis Video Publishing. $79.00.

Alive Day Memories: Home from Iraq 2007
Looks at the physical and emotional toll of the war in Iraq on wounded veterans as they remember the day they escaped death and their feelings on their future. 66m; DVD. **A:** Sr. High-Adult. **P:** Education. **U:** Home. **Gen-Edu:** Armed Forces--U.S., Documentary Films. **Acq:** Purchase. **Dist:** Home Box Office Inc. $19.98.

Alive in the Nuclear Age 19??
Twelve-part series featuring short programs about nuclear issues and the arms race. Includes contributions from Gwynne Dyer and David Suzuki. Hosted by young peace activists Desiree McGraw and Maxime Faille who are both rather well-known for their travels throughout Canada holding discussions with high school students on various issues associated with the use of nuclear power and weapons. 172m; VHS. **Pr:** National Film Board of Canada. **A:** Jr. High-Sr. High. **P:** Education. **U:** Institution. **Gen-Edu:** Canada, Nuclear Energy, Nuclear Warfare. **Acq:** Purchase. **Dist:** Xenon Pictures Inc. ; Lucerne Media.
Indiv. Titles: 1. What Canadian Youth are Saying 2. What Soviet Youth are Saying 3. The Road to Total War 4. The First Atomic Bombs 5. No More Hiroshima 6. Canada's Nuclear Technology 7. Push Button Weapons 8. How Nuclear War Might Start 9. The End of War: Nuclear Winter 10. The International Peace Movement 11. Guns or Shoes 12. Bombs Away.

Alive or Dead 2008 (R) — ★
After wrecking her car in a sordid and unique manner, a woman comes across the bloody aftermath of a crime scene on a deserted bus before being kidnapped by a mutant freak. 83m; DVD, Streaming. **C:** Ann Henson; Angelica May; Directed by Stephen Goetsch; Written by Stephen Goetsch; Cinematography by Stephen Goetsch; Music by William Anderson. **A:** Sr. High-Adult. **P:** Entertainment. **U:** Home. **L:** English. **Mov-Ent. Acq:** Purchase, Rent/Lease. **Dist:** Lions Gate Entertainment Inc. $14.98 9.99.

Alive: 20 Years Later 1993
With the release of the big-screen fictional version comes this follow-up documentary with the survivors of the 1972 mountain

plane crash telling their own story. 51m; VHS, CC. **C:** Narrated by Martin Sheen; Directed by Jill Fullerton-Smith. **Pr:** Frank Marshall; Robert Watts; Bruce Cohen; Jill Fullerton-Smith. **A:** Jr. High-Adult. **P:** Entertainment. **U:** Home. **Mov-Ent:** Documentary Films. **Acq:** Purchase. **Dist:** Buena Vista Home Entertainment. $39.95.

Alive with Yoga 19??
Teaches the 6000-year-old art of yoga; increasing flexibility, stamina and longevity. Instructor Lilias guides both the beginning and intermediate students. 60m; VHS. **A:** Jr. High-Adult. **P:** Instruction. **U:** Home. **Hea-Sci:** Yoga, Fitness/Exercise. **Acq:** Purchase. **Dist:** Hartley Film Foundation. $39.95.

All Aboard: A Collection of Music Videos for Children 1991
A set of programs designed to get children involved in building friendships, self-confidence, and safety awareness, all while promoting physical fitness. 30m; VHS. **C:** Directed by Lauritz Kjerulff. **Pr:** CRM Productions. **A:** Preschool-Primary. **P:** Education. **U:** Institution, Home. **Hea-Sci:** Music Video, Children, Safety Education. **Acq:** Purchase. **Dist:** Learning Station. $14.95.

All Aboard America ???? (Unrated)
Children's animated/musical program that follows a giant bald eagle named Rudy across the United States visiting some of the nation's most historic landmarks; includes anthems such as "Grand Old Flag," "Yankee Doodle Dandy," "I've Been Working on the Railroad," and "Home on the Range." ??m; DVD. **A:** Family. **P:** Education. **U:** Institution, Home. **Mov-Ent:** Children, Children's Shows, Animation & Cartoons. **Acq:** Purchase. **Dist:** Bridgestone Multimedia Group Inc. $11.96.

All Aboard: Volume 1 1997
Episodes 1 and 2 of the PBS series All Aboard takes you on a trip to the Colorado Railroad Museum, three Colorado narrow gauge tourist railroads, and then for a ride on Amtrak's California Zephyr on its route from Chicago to Oakland. 56m; DVD. **A:** College-Adult. **P:** Education. **U:** Home. **Gen-Edu:** Trains. **Acq:** Purchase. **Dist:** The Civil War Standard. $19.95.

All Aboard: Volume 2 1997
Episodes 3 and 4 of the PBS series All Aboard brings you to the Florida East Coast Railway to rail yards and repair shops, and highlights elements unique to North American railroading, like Canada's Godrich Exeter short line and steam excursion trains. 56m; DVD. **A:** College-Adult. **P:** Education. **U:** Home. **Gen-Edu:** Trains. **Acq:** Purchase. **Dist:** The Civil War Standard. $19.95.

All Aboard: Volume 3 1997
Episodes 5 and 6 of the PBS series All Aboard shows the railroad history of Atlanta, the railroad capitol of the South; also looks at privately owned passenger cars. 56m; DVD. **A:** College-Adult. **P:** Education. **U:** Home. **Gen-Edu:** Trains. **Acq:** Purchase. **Dist:** The Civil War Standard. $19.95.

All Aboard: Volume 4 1997
Episodes 7 and 8 of the PBS series All Aboard shows the final days of the Denver & Rio Grande Western's narrow gauge operations between Alamosa and Chama, and 1950s footage of steam power locomotives. 56m; DVD. **A:** College-Adult. **P:** Education. **U:** Home. **Gen-Edu:** Trains. **Acq:** Purchase. **Dist:** The Civil War Standard. $19.95.

All Aboard: Volume 5 1997
Episodes 9 and 10 of the PBS series All Aboard features a look at Norfolk Southern's Georgia Division and the 1960s rail activity in Detroit. 56m; DVD. **A:** College-Adult. **P:** Education. **U:** Home. **Gen-Edu:** Trains. **Acq:** Purchase. **Dist:** The Civil War Standard. $19.95.

All Aboard: Volume 6 1997
Episodes 11 and 12 of the PBS series All Aboard features rail activity in Chicago in the 1980s, including commuter trains; then looks at the Detroit, Toledo & Ironton Railroad from 1963 to the 1980s. 56m; DVD. **A:** College-Adult. **P:** Education. **U:** Home. **Gen-Edu:** Trains. **Acq:** Purchase. **Dist:** The Civil War Standard. $19.95.

All Aboard: Volume 7 1997
Episodes 13 and 14 of the PBS series All Aboard shows the Union Pacific Railroad's Wyoming coal trains and western mountain region operations, followed by rail in the 1960s in St. Louis. 56m; DVD. **A:** College-Adult. **P:** Education. **U:** Home. **Gen-Edu:** Trains. **Acq:** Purchase. **Dist:** The Civil War Standard. $19.95.

All Aboard: Volume 8 1997
Episodes 15 and 16 of the PBS series All Aboard takes a ride on Amtrak's Empire Builder, featuring scenic views and interviews with crew, then features Canada's steam locomotives of the 1950s. 56m; DVD. **A:** College-Adult. **P:** Education. **U:** Home. **Gen-Edu:** Trains. **Acq:** Purchase. **Dist:** The Civil War Standard. $19.95.

All Aboard: Volume 9 1997
Episodes 17 and 18 of the PBS series All Aboard features the Pennsylvania Railroad from 1952 to 1969, and rail activity in Pittsburgh in the 1980s. 56m; DVD. **A:** College-Adult. **P:** Education. **U:** Home. **Gen-Edu:** Trains. **Acq:** Purchase. **Dist:** The Civil War Standard. $19.95.

All Aboard: Volume 10 1997
Episodes 19 and 20 of the PBS series All Aboard features a 1965 Rocky Mountain Railroad Club narrow gauge passenger train, and the Illinois Central Railroad in the 1950s through 1970s. 56m; DVD. **A:** College-Adult. **P:** Education. **U:** Home. **Gen-Edu:** Trains. **Acq:** Purchase. **Dist:** The Civil War Standard. $19.95.

All Aboard: Volume 11 1997
Episodes 21 and 22 of the PBS series All Aboard shows the link between railroads and NASA space programs, and the history of the East Broad Top Railroad. 56m; DVD. **A:** College-Adult. **P:** Education. **U:** Home. **Gen-Edu:** Trains. **Acq:** Purchase. **Dist:** The Civil War Standard. $19.95.

All Aboard: Volume 12 1997
Episodes 23 and 24 of the PBS series All Aboard shows Norfolk Southern's steam locomotive restoration efforts, and Santa Fe rail travel from the 1950s through the 1980s. 56m; DVD. **A:** College-Adult. **P:** Education. **U:** Home. **Gen-Edu:** Trains. **Acq:** Purchase. **Dist:** The Civil War Standard. $19.95.

All Aboard: Volume 13 1997
Episodes 25 and 26 of the PBS series All Aboard features the Chicago, Rock Island & Pacific Railway in Chicago from the 1950s through the 1970s, then visit revitalized narrow gauge steamers. 56m; DVD. **A:** College-Adult. **P:** Education. **U:** Home. **Gen-Edu:** Trains. **Acq:** Purchase. **Dist:** The Civil War Standard. $19.95.

All About a Hole in the World 1990
Richard Rhodes, Pulitzer-Prize winning author, relates his abused childhood in his latest work, "Hole in the World." 29m; VHS. **A:** Sr. High-Adult. **P:** Education. **U:** Institution. **Gen-Edu:** Biography, Child Abuse. **Acq:** Purchase. **Dist:** University of Washington Educational Media Collection. $15.00.

All About Ah Long 1989 (Unrated) — ★★
The saga of an ex-gang member, following his imprisonment, divorce, and final reunion with his son and true love. In Cantonese with English subtitles. 99m; VHS, DVD. **C:** Sylvia Chang; Chow Yun-Fat; To Kai-Fung; Directed by To Kai-Fung; Written by Cheng Chung Tai. **A:** Sr. High-Adult. **P:** Entertainment. **U:** Home. **L:** Chinese. **Mov-Ent:** Family, Marriage. **Acq:** Purchase. **Dist:** Facets Multimedia Inc. $39.95.

All About Anger 1993
Presents children in situations where they must grapple with angry feelings, and includes questions to stimulate discussion and problem-solving skills. 16m; VHS. **A:** Primary. **P:** Education. **U:** Institution. **Chl-Juv:** Education, Children. **Acq:** Purchase. **Dist:** Sunburst Digital Inc. $89.00.

All About Attention Deficit Disorder, Part 1: Symptoms, Development, Prognosis and Causes 1990
The symptoms, development, prognosis and causes of the common child behavioral disorder known as ADD are examined. 108m; VHS. **A:** Family. **P:** Education. **U:** Home. **Hea-Sci:** Children, Diagnosis, Psychology. **Acq:** Purchase. **Dist:** Parent Magic, Inc. $29.95.

All About Attention Deficit Disorder, Part 2: Diagnosis and Treatment 1990
The diagnosis and treatment of the common child behavioral disorder known as ADD are examined. 85m; VHS. **A:** Family. **P:** Entertainment. **U:** Home. **Hea-Sci:** Children, Psychology, Medical Education. **Acq:** Purchase. **Dist:** Parent Magic, Inc. $29.95.

All About Babies: A Guide to the First Two Years of Life 1986
A comprehensive guide to parenting and caregiving infants. 45m; VHS. **Pr:** Deborah Koons. **A:** Adult. **P:** Education. **U:** Institution, Home. **Hea-Sci:** Infants. **Acq:** Purchase, Rent/Lease. **Dist:** Clear Vue Inc.

All About Bears 1989
The characteristics and habits of bears in their natural habitat are shown. 12m; VHS, 3/4 U. **Pr:** Dennis Sawyer. **A:** Family. **P:** Education. **U:** Institution, SURA. **Gen-Edu:** Animals. **Acq:** Purchase, Rent/Lease. **Dist:** National Film Board of Canada.

All About Clauses 19??
Explains independent clauses, subordinate clauses, noun clauses, adjective clauses, adverb clauses, and how clauses work in a sentence. 20m; VHS. **A:** Primary. **P:** Education. **U:** Institution. **Gen-Edu:** Language Arts. **Acq:** Purchase. **Dist:** Thomas S. Klise Co. $58.00.

All about Darfur 2005
Documentary on Sudan from the perspective of people living there. 82m; VHS, DVD. **A:** Sr. High-Adult. **P:** Education. **U:** Home, Institution. **L:** Arabic. **Gen-Edu:** Documentary Films, Africa. **Acq:** Purchase. **Dist:** California Newsreel. $49.95.

All About Dinosaurs 1990
Children in grade school can learn all about the prehistoric creatures that fascinate them so. ?m; VHS. **Pr:** United Learning Inc. **A:** Primary. **P:** Education. **U:** Institution, CCTV, CATV, Home, SURA. **Gen-Edu:** Documentary Films, Dinosaurs. **Acq:** Purchase, Duplication. **Dist:** United Learning Inc. $150.00.
Indiv. Titles: 1. Dinosaurs: What Were They? 2. How Dinosaurs Lived 3. Digging Up Bones 4. What Happened to Dinosaurs.

All About Elections: A Two-Part Set 19??
Explores the importance of voting, how candidates are selected, and how elections are carried out. 28m; VHS. **A:** Primary-Sr. High. **P:** Education. **U:** Institution. **Gen-Edu:** Law, Politics & Government. **Acq:** Purchase. **Dist:** Thomas S. Klise Co. $98.00.

All About Eve 1950 (Unrated) — ★★★★
One of the wittiest (and most cynical) flicks of all time follows aspiring young actress Eve Harrington (Baxter) as she ingratiates herself with a prominent group of theatre people so she can become a Broadway star without the usual years of work. The not-so-innocent babe becomes secretary to aging star Margo Channing (Davis) and ruthlessly uses everyone in her climb to the top, much to Davis' initial disbelief and eventual displeasure. Satirical, darkly funny view of the theatre world features exceptional work by Davis, Sanders, and Ritter. Based on "The Wisdom of Eve" by Mary Orr. Later staged as the musical "Applause." 138m/B/W; VHS, DVD. **C:** Bette Davis; Anne Baxter; George Sanders; Celeste Holm; Gary Merrill; Thelma Ritter; Marilyn Monroe; Hugh Marlowe; Gregory Ratoff; Eddie Fisher; Directed by Joseph L. Mankiewicz; Written by Joseph L. Mankiewicz; Cinematography by Milton Krasner; Music by Alfred Newman. **Pr:** 20th Century-Fox. **A:** Family. **P:** Entertainment. **U:** Home. **Mov-Ent:** Classic Films. **Awds:** Oscars '50: Costume Des. (B&W), Director (Mankiewicz), Film, Screenplay, Sound, Support. Actor (Sanders); AFI '98: Top 100; British Acad. '50: Film; Cannes '51: Actress (Davis), Grand Jury Prize; Directors Guild '50: Director (Mankiewicz); Golden Globes '51: Screenplay; Natl. Film Reg. '90; N.Y. Film Critics '50: Actress (Davis), Director (Mankiewicz), Film. **Acq:** Purchase. **Dist:** Baker and Taylor; Home Vision Cinema. $19.98.

All About Fire 1976
Fred Calvert (who created segments for "Sesame Street" and "Electric Circus") uses colorful animation and a friendly but somewhat cynical cat to bring home a message on fire prevention. 10m; VHS. **Pr:** Farmhouse Films. **A:** Primary-Jr. High. **P:** Education. **U:** Institution, Home, SURA. **L:** Dutch, French, Spanish. **Gen-Edu:** Safety Education, Fires. **Acq:** Purchase, Rent/Lease. **Dist:** Pyramid Media. $195.00.

All About Kids' Safety 19??
Three cartoons teach children about bike, fire, and pedestrian rules of safety. 40m; VHS. **A:** Family. **P:** Instruction. **U:** Home. **Gen-Edu:** Safety Education, Children. **Acq:** Purchase. **Dist:** Facets Multimedia Inc. $19.95.

All About Lily Chou-Chou 2001 (Unrated) — ★★★
Yuichi's (Hayato Ichihara) mother has remarried, and he doesn't exactly like it. At school he is bullied horrifically, and he has to resort to crime to pay off the demands of his assailants, one of whom pimps out the other school boys to older men. His only respite is the website he runs about his favorite singer Lily Chou-Chou. Pic boasts some of the most beautiful cinematography to come out of Japan, but its subject matter is brutal and unforgiving, and the nonlinear story will cause some confusion. 146m; DVD. **C:** Hayato Ichihara; Yu Aoi; Shugo Oshinari; Ayumi Ito; Takao Osawa; Miwako Ichikawa; Izumi Inamori; Kazusa Matsuda; Ryo Katsuji; Directed by Shunji Iwai; Written by Shunji Iwai; Cinematography by Noboru Shinoda; Music by Takeshi Kobayashi. **A:** Sr. High-Adult. **P:** Entertainment. **U:** Home. **L:** English, Japanese. **Mov-Ent:** Rape, Suicide, Adolescence. **Acq:** Purchase. **Dist:** Image Entertainment Inc. $29.95.

All About Motions ????
A visual encyclopedia of most of the motions in Robert's Rules of Order. 140m; VHS. **A:** Adult. **P:** Education. **U:** Institution. **Gen-Edu:** Business, How-To. **Acq:** Purchase. **Dist:** Robert McConnell Productions. $114.50.

All About Music 1977
An introduction to the origin and basic elements of music, this animated film follows a caveman through his discovery of the principles of rhythm, melody, and harmony. 10m; VHS, 3/4 U, Special order formats. **Pr:** Farmhouse Films. **A:** Preschool-Primary. **P:** Education. **U:** Institution, Home, SURA. **L:** Swedish. **Chl-Juv. Acq:** Purchase, Rent/Lease. **Dist:** Pyramid Media. $195.00.

All About My Mother 1999 (R) — ★★★
Manuela (Roth) is a single mom, emotionally dependent on her 17-year-old son, Esteban (Azorin). After seeing him killed in a car accident, the grief-stricken mom seeks to find Esteban's father—now a transvestite named Lola (Canto)?and meets an old friend, tranvestite prostitute Agrado (San Juan), who offers comfort. Adding to the female roundelay are Huma Rojo (Paredes), Esteban's favorite actress, and Sister Rosa (Cruz), a pregnant nun who runs a shelter. As Manuela encounters each of them, they help give her a renewed sense of hope and the strength to carry on. Spanish with subtitles. 102m; VHS, DVD, Wide, CC. **C:** Cecilia (Celia) Roth; Penelope Cruz; Marisa Paredes; Eloy Azorin; Toni Canto; Antonia San Juan; Candela Pena; Directed by Pedro Almodovar; Written by Pedro Almodovar; Cinematography by Affonso Beato; Music by Alberto Iglesias. **Pr:** Sony Pictures Classics. **A:** College-Adult. **P:** Entertainment. **U:** Home. **L:** Spanish. **Mov-Ent:** Melodrama, Death, Pregnancy. **Awds:** Oscars '99: Foreign Film; British Acad. '99: Director (Almodovar), Foreign Film; Cannes '99: Director (Almodovar); Cesar '00: Foreign Film; Golden Globes '00: Foreign Film; L.A. Film Critics '99: Foreign Film; N.Y. Film Critics '99: Foreign Film; Broadcast Film Critics '99: Foreign Film. **Acq:** Purchase. **Dist:** Sony Pictures Home Entertainment Inc.

All About Myself 1984
This video helps children talk about their feelings. 30m; VHS. **Pr:** HAL. **A:** Family. **P:** Education. **U:** Home. **Gen-Edu:** Children, Communication. **Acq:** Purchase. **Dist:** Karol Media. $7.00.

All About Pedestrian Safety 1982
An animated story that instructs children on the rules of safe walking. 10m; VHS, 3/4 U. **A:** Primary-Jr. High. **P:** Education. **U:** Institution, Home, SURA. **Chl-Juv:** Safety Education. **Acq:** Purchase, Rent/Lease, Duplication License. **Dist:** Pyramid Media. $195.00.

All About Rocks and Minerals 1992
This well-made video defines minerals as a naturally formed inorganic crystal, and rocks as mixtures of two or more minerals. Also proposes the idea that rocks and minerals are an ever-lessening natural resource which need to be conserved and recycled. Includes teacher's guide and blackline mas-

ters. 17m; VHS. **A:** Primary-Jr. High. **P:** Education. **U:** Institution. **Chl-Juv:** Science. **Acq:** Purchase. **Dist:** United Learning Inc. $89.00.

All About Santa Claus 2007
Holiday tale for children. Also includes "Magic Gift of the Snowman." ?m; DVD. **A:** Preschool-Primary. **P:** Entertainment. **U:** Home. **Chl-Juv:** Animation & Cartoons, Children. **Acq:** Purchase. **Dist:** Acorn Media Group Inc. $9.98.

All About Seeds 1993
Part of the 14-part First Time Science Series that uses animation to illustrate how plants, vegetables, and trees start out as seeds, placing emphasis on the actual growing cycle of each. 9m; VHS. **Pr:** Film Ideas, Inc. **A:** Preschool-Primary. **P:** Education. **U:** Institution. **Chl-Juv:** Science. **Acq:** Purchase. **Dist:** Film Ideas, Inc. $37.50.

All About Steve 2009 (PG-13) — ★
Mary Magdalene Horowitz is a boring, clingy, delusional, cruciverbalist (crossword-puzzle designer) who after one blind date with cable news cameraman Steve (Cooper) misinterprets an innocent comment that leads her to relentlessly follow him across the country, egged on by a self-serving reporter, Hartman Hughes (Church). Amid the trek she befriends a variety of socially inept characters like herself that bring nothing but more uncomfortable irritation. Feature debut from director Traill falls seriously short of anything remotely funny, even with his notable cast, while writer Barker vies for the "most annoying character ever created" award. Even Bullock's charm and Cooper's hunky-ness can't spare this from being, in a five-letter word-- "awful." 98m; Blu-Ray, On Demand, Wide. **C:** Sandra Bullock; Bradley Cooper; Thomas Haden Church; Ken Jeong; DJ Qualls; Katy Mixon; Directed by Phil Traill; Written by Kim Barker; Cinematography by Tim Suhrstedt; Music by Christophe Beck. **Pr:** Sandra Bullock; Mary McLaglen; Sandra Bullock; Fortis Films; Fox 2000 Pictures; Radar Pictures; 20th Century-Fox. **A:** Jr. High-Adult. **P:** Entertainment. **U:** Home. **L:** English. **Mov-Ent:** Comedy--Romantic. **Awds:** Golden Raspberries '09: Worst Actress (Bullock). **Acq:** Purchase. **Dist:** Fox Home Entertainment; Amazon.com Inc.; Movies Unlimited.

All About the Benjamins 2002 (R) — ★★
Cube and Epps re-team (2000's "Next Friday") as bounty hunter Bucum (Ice Cube) and two-bit con Reggie (Epps) who meet mobsters and mayhem in Miami in this hip-hop buddy flick. Bucum, who dreams of opening his own private-eye agency, is sent to track down Reggie, who seeks a lost lottery tickets which gets the mismatched duo mixed up in a diamond heist. As usual, Cube, straight man to Epps's clown, have the usual chemistry and deliver some amusing moments in this light caper comedy, but the director's penchant for gory violence interrupts the otherwise slapstick mood. The two leads would shine if not for being stuck in this nod to "Miami Vice" and Elmore Leonard without the character development and plot. Cube co-wrote with Levy. 98m; VHS, DVD. **C:** Ice Cube; Mike Epps; Tommy Flanagan; Eva Mendes; Carmen Chaplin; Roger Guenveur Smith; Anthony Michael Hall; Valarie Rae Miller; Bow Wow; Directed by Kevin Bray; Written by Ice Cube; Ronald Lang; Cinematography by Glen MacPherson; Music by John Murphy. **Pr:** Ice Cube; Matt Alvarez; Cube Vision; New Line Cinema. **A:** Sr. High-Adult. **P:** Entertainment. **U:** Home. **Mov-Ent:** Black Culture. **Acq:** Purchase. **Dist:** New Line Home Video.

All About Welfare 1972
Examination of merits and weaknesses of public welfare and ways in which needs of people who genuinely require assistance may be met. 29m; VHS, 3/4 U. **C:** Margaret Mead. **Pr:** WITF Hershey. **A:** College-Adult. **P:** Education. **U:** Institution, CCTV, CATV. **Gen-Edu:** Poverty. **Acq:** Purchase, Rent/Lease, Off-Air Record. **Dist:** PBS Home Video.
Indiv. Titles: 1. All American Poverty Show 2. Lingering Depression 3. Save the Children 4. What is Work? 5. Occupant U.S.A. 6. Superfluous Citizen.

All About You 2001 (PG) — ★1/2
Tired tale takes Nicole from lost love Robbie in L.A. to blossoming romance with Brian in San Fran. Naturally the new guy is the old guy's alienated brother. 100m; VHS, DVD. **C:** Terron Brooks; Debbie Allen; LisaRaye; Renee Goldsberry; Lou Myers; Vanessa Bell Calloway; Bobby Hosea; Chris Spencer; Tico Wells; Adam Lazarre-White; Emily Liu; Directed by Christine Swanson; Written by Christine Swanson; Cinematography by Wolf Baschung; David Scardina; Music by John Bickerton. **A:** Primary-Adult. **P:** Entertainment. **U:** Home. **Mov-Ent:** Black Culture, Drama. **Acq:** Purchase. **Dist:** Ventura Distribution Inc. $14.99.

All Access Agility and Conditioning Workout for Lacrosse 2012 (Unrated)
Coach Lesley Moser and the Stanford women's lacrosse team participate in a conditioning workout. 46m; DVD. **A:** Family. **P:** Education. **U:** Home, Institution. **Spo-Rec:** Lacrosse, Fitness/Exercise. **Acq:** Purchase. **Dist:** Championship Productions. $39.99.

All Access Arizona Basketball Practice with Sean Miller 2011 (Unrated)
Basketball coach Sean Miller lets cameras record his practice sessions and warm-up drills, with a slight emphasis on using the transition offense. 327m; DVD. **A:** Family. **P:** Education. **U:** Home, Institution. **Spo-Rec:** Basketball, Athletic Instruction/Coaching. **Acq:** Purchase. **Dist:** Championship Productions. $119.99.

All Access Baseball Practice with Ed Servais 2012 (Unrated)
Coach Ed Servais discusses his philosophy for running a baseball practice during two of his live practice sessions. 280m;

DVD. **A:** Family. **P:** Education. **U:** Home. **L:** English. **Spo-Rec:** Athletic Instruction/Coaching, Baseball, How-To. **Acq:** Purchase. **Dist:** Championship Productions. $119.99.

All Access Baseball Practice with Nathan Blackwood 2010 (Unrated)
Coach Nathan Blackwood presents two full practice sessions of the Lubbock Christian University's baseball team. 132m; DVD. **A:** Family. **P:** Education. **U:** Home, Institution. **Spo-Rec:** Baseball, Athletic Instruction/Coaching. **Acq:** Purchase. **Dist:** Championship Productions. $49.99.

All Access Basketball Practice with Andy Toole 2012
Coach Andy Toole invites All Access to film three days of practices by Robert Morris University's basketball team. 407m; DVD. **A:** Jr. High-Adult. **P:** Education. **U:** Home, Institution. **L:** English. **Gen-Edu:** Athletic Instruction/Coaching, Basketball, Education. **Acq:** Purchase. **Dist:** Championship Productions. $149.99.

All Access Basketball Practice with Bob Hurley 2013 (Unrated)
All Access Cameras follow Coach Bob Hurley through three of his basketball team's practice sessions. 251m; DVD. **A:** Family. **P:** Education. **U:** Home. **L:** English. **Spo-Rec:** Athletic Instruction/Coaching, Basketball. **Acq:** Purchase. **Dist:** Championship Productions. $119.99.

All Access Basketball Practice with Ed Madec 2013
All Access cameras follow Coach Ed Madec as he puts the Fresno City College basketball team through several training sessions. DVD. **A:** Jr. High-Adult. **P:** Education. **U:** Home, Institution. **L:** English. **Gen-Edu:** Athletic Instruction/Coaching, Basketball, Education. **Acq:** Purchase. **Dist:** Championship Productions. $149.99.

All Access Basketball Practice with Geno Auriemma 2012
All Access cameras follow the University of Connecticut's women's basketball head coach, Geno Auriemma, through his basketball team's practice sessions. 679m; DVD. **A:** Jr. High-Adult. **P:** Education. **U:** Home, Institution. **L:** English. **Gen-Edu:** Athletic Instruction/Coaching, Basketball, Education. **Acq:** Purchase. **Dist:** Championship Productions. $149.99.

All Access Basketball Practice with Keno Davis 2012
Central Michigan Head Coach Keno Davis lets All Access cameras follow him through three practice sessions as he teaches his basketball team his fast-break philosophy. 260m; DVD. **A:** Jr. High-Adult. **P:** Education. **U:** Home, Institution. **L:** English. **Gen-Edu:** Athletic Instruction/Coaching, Basketball, Education. **Acq:** Purchase. **Dist:** Championship Productions. $119.99.

All Access Basketball Practice with Larry Brown 2013
SMU head basketball coach Larry Brown lets cameras follow him through a few of his basketball team's practice sessions. DVD. **A:** Jr. High-Adult. **P:** Education. **U:** Home, Institution. **L:** English. **Gen-Edu:** Athletic Instruction/Coaching, Basketball, Education. **Acq:** Purchase. **Dist:** Championship Productions. $149.99.

All Access Basketball Practice with Seth Greenberg 2011 (Unrated)
Virginia Tech Head Coach Seth Greenberg shows the drills he uses for building fundamental skills among his basketball players, as well as the motion and transition offenses. 619m; DVD. **A:** Family. **P:** Education. **U:** Home, Institution. **Spo-Rec:** Basketball, Athletic Instruction/Coaching. **Acq:** Purchase. **Dist:** Championship Productions. $119.99.

All Access Basketball Practice with Steve Alford 2011 (Unrated)
University of New Mexico's Basketball Coach Steve Alford lets cameras follow him through his team's warm-up drills as well as their offense/defense training. 397m; DVD. **A:** Family. **P:** Education. **U:** Home, Institution. **Spo-Rec:** Basketball, Athletic Instruction/Coaching. **Acq:** Purchase. **Dist:** Championship Productions. $119.99.

All Access Basketball Practice with Tubby Smith 2013 (Unrated)
All Access cameras follow Coach Tubby Smith and the Texas Tech basketball team as they go through two mid-season practices. 462m; DVD. **A:** Family. **P:** Education. **U:** Home. **L:** English. **Spo-Rec:** Athletic Instruction/Coaching, Basketball. **Acq:** Purchase. **Dist:** Championship Productions. $119.99.

All Access Baylor Basketball Practice 2013 (Unrated)
Cameras follow 3 days of practice sessions by Coach Scott Drew and the Baylor basketball team. 233m; DVD. **A:** Family. **P:** Education. **U:** Home. **L:** English. **Spo-Rec:** Athletic Instruction/Coaching, Basketball. **Acq:** Purchase. **Dist:** Championship Productions. $119.99.

All Access Baylor Practice with Steve Smith 2013 (Unrated)
Coach Steve Smith allows cameras to film five live practice sessions of the Baylor University baseball team. 527m; DVD. **A:** Family. **P:** Education. **U:** Home. **L:** English. **Spo-Rec:** Athletic Instruction/Coaching, Baseball, How-To. **Acq:** Purchase. **Dist:** Championship Productions. $119.99.

All Access Blair Academy Wrestling Practice with Jeff Buxton 2011 (Unrated)
Coach Jeff Buxton has cameras follow him for five in-season practices of the Blair Academy wrestling team. 408m; DVD. **A:** Family. **P:** Education. **U:** Home, Institution. **Spo-Rec:** Athletic Instruction/Coaching. **Acq:** Purchase. **Dist:** Championship Productions. $119.99.

All Access Boston College Basketball Practice with Steve Donahue 2011 (Unrated)
Coach Steve Donahue covers the man-to-man offensive and defensive systems at his basketball team's practice sessions. 316m; DVD. **A:** Family. **P:** Education. **U:** Home, Institution. **Spo-Rec:** Basketball, Athletic Instruction/Coaching. **Acq:** Purchase. **Dist:** Championship Productions. $119.99.

All Access Brandon High School Wrestling Practice with Russ Cozart 2012 (Unrated)
Coach Russ Cozart allows cameras to film his wrestling team during a four-day practice week. DVD. **A:** Family. **P:** Education. **U:** Home. **L:** English. **Spo-Rec:** Athletic Instruction/Coaching, Sports--General, How-To. **Acq:** Purchase. **Dist:** Championship Productions. $119.99.

All Access Butterfly with Matt Kredich featuring Christine Magnuson 2010 (Unrated)
Coach Matt Kredich and Olympian silver medalist Christine Magnusson present drills and techniques for swimmers wishing to improve their butterfly stroke. 190m; DVD. **A:** Family. **P:** Education. **U:** Home, Institution. **Spo-Rec:** Swimming, Athletic Instruction/Coaching. **Acq:** Purchase. **Dist:** Championship Productions. $79.99.

All Access BYU Basketball Practice with Dave Rose 2012
Brigham Young University Head Coach Dave Rose demonstrates transition drills and other exercises during his basketball team's training sessions. 275m; DVD. **A:** Jr. High-Adult. **P:** Education. **U:** Home, Institution. **L:** English. **Gen-Edu:** Athletic Instruction/Coaching, Basketball, Education. **Acq:** Purchase. **Dist:** Championship Productions. $119.99.

All Access College Wartburg College Wrestling Practice with Jim Miller 2012 (Unrated)
Coach Jim Miller allows cameras to follow him through the Wartburg College Wrestling teams practice sessions and discusses wrestling techniques and training. 179m; Streaming. **A:** Family. **P:** Education. **U:** Home, Institution. **Spo-Rec:** Athletic Instruction/Coaching. **Acq:** Purchase. **Dist:** Championship Productions. $99.99.

All Access Cornell Hockey Practice with Mike Schafer 2012 (Unrated)
Coach Mike Schafer gets followed by cameras for three live practice sessions of the Cornell University hockey team. 336m; DVD. **A:** Family. **P:** Education. **U:** Home. **L:** English. **Spo-Rec:** Athletic Instruction/Coaching, Hockey, How-To. **Acq:** Purchase. **Dist:** Championship Productions. $119.99.

All Access Cornell Wrestling Practice with Rob Koll 2010 (Unrated)
Coach Rob Koll presents three practices from the Cornell Wrestling team's 2010 season. 250m; DVD. **A:** Family. **P:** Education. **U:** Home, Institution. **Spo-Rec:** Athletic Instruction/Coaching. **Acq:** Purchase. **Dist:** Championship Productions. $99.99.

All Access Creighton Basketball Practice 2013 (Unrated)
Coach Greg McDermott and his team are taped live during four of their basketball practice sessions. 336m; DVD. **A:** Family. **P:** Education. **U:** Home. **L:** English. **Spo-Rec:** Athletic Instruction/Coaching, Basketball. **Acq:** Purchase. **Dist:** Championship Productions. $119.99.

All Access DeMatha Catholic High School Basketball Practice 2011 (Unrated)
Coaches Mike Jones and Alan Stein provide the exercise routines and development drills they use to get their basketball teams in shape for the season. 334m; DVD. **A:** Family. **P:** Education. **U:** Home, Institution. **Spo-Rec:** Basketball, Athletic Instruction/Coaching. **Acq:** Purchase. **Dist:** Championship Productions. $119.99.

All Access Denver Hockey Practice 2012 (Unrated)
Coach George Gwozdecky teaches small ice games, defensive zone coverage, and other concepts during three practice sessions. DVD. **A:** Family. **P:** Education. **U:** Home. **L:** English. **Spo-Rec:** Athletic Instruction/Coaching, Hockey, How-To. **Acq:** Purchase. **Dist:** Championship Productions. $99.99.

All Access Duke Basketball Practice 2010-2011 Season 2011 (Unrated)
Coach Mike Krzyzewski let the All Access Cameras follow Duke University's basketball team through some early practice sessions of the season. 419m; DVD. **A:** Family. **P:** Education. **U:** Home, Institution. **Spo-Rec:** Basketball, Athletic Instruction/Coaching. **Acq:** Purchase. **Dist:** Championship Productions. $119.99.

All Access Duke Basketball Practice: National Championship Season 2009-2010 2010 (Unrated)
Coach Mike Krzyzewski allows cameras to follow him for three full practice sessions of his basketball team as well as several clinics. ??m; DVD. **A:** Family. **P:** Education. **U:** Home, Institution. **Spo-Rec:** Basketball, Athletic Instruction/Coaching. **Acq:** Purchase. **Dist:** Championship Productions. $149.99.

All Access Duke Basketball Practice with Mike Krzyzewski 2009 (Unrated)
Taped presentation of Mike Kyrzyzewski leading the Duke University basketball team through two full practice sessions and several clinic sessions. 438m; DVD. **A:** Family. **P:** Education. **U:** Home, Institution. **Spo-Rec:** Basketball, Athletic Instruction/Coaching. **Acq:** Purchase. **Dist:** Championship Productions. $119.99.

All Access Duke Field Hockey Practice with Beth Bozman 2010 (Unrated)
Duke University Head Coach Beth Bozman lets cameras tape her field hockey team as they work their way through the first three practices of the season. 139m; DVD. **A:** Family. **P:** Education. **U:** Home, Institution. **Spo-Rec:** Hockey, Athletic Instruction/Coaching. **Acq:** Purchase. **Dist:** Championship Productions. $79.99.

All Access Duke Lacrosse, Volume 1: One-on One and Team Drills 2010 (Unrated)
Coach John Danowski lets cameras record the first four practices of his team's 2009-10 season. 390m; DVD. **A:** Family. **P:** Education. **U:** Home, Institution. **Spo-Rec:** Lacrosse, Athletic Instruction/Coaching. **Acq:** Purchase. **Dist:** Championship Productions. $119.99.

All Access Duke Lacrosse, Volume 2: Individual Skills and Full Field Drills 2010 (Unrated)
In this companion volume, Coach Danowski lectures on the principles being taught in the first volume while showing how the practices themselves are put together. 312m; DVD. **A:** Family. **P:** Education. **U:** Home, Institution. **Spo-Rec:** Lacrosse, Athletic Instruction/Coaching. **Acq:** Purchase. **Dist:** Championship Productions. $119.99.

All Access Florida Basketball Practice with Billy Donovan 2012
University of Florida Head Coach Billy Donovan has cameras follow him through three of his basketball team's practice sessions. DVD. **A:** Jr. High-Adult. **P:** Education. **U:** Home, Institution. **L:** English. **Spo-Rec:** Athletic Instruction/Coaching, Basketball, How-To. **Acq:** Purchase. **Dist:** Championship Productions. $149.99.

All Access Florida Soccer Practice 2014 (Unrated)
All Access Cameras follow Coach Becky Burleigh and the University of Florida through four of their soccer training sessions. 291m; DVD. **A:** Family. **P:** Education. **U:** Home. **L:** English. **Spo-Rec:** Athletic Instruction/Coaching, Soccer. **Acq:** Purchase. **Dist:** Championship Productions. $119.99.

All Access Florida Softball Practice with Tim Walton 2012 (Unrated)
All Access cameras follow Coach Tim Walton through three days of practice sessions by the University of Florida softball team. 678m; DVD. **A:** Family. **P:** Education. **U:** Home. **L:** English. **Spo-Rec:** Athletic Instruction/Coaching, Softball, How-To. **Acq:** Purchase. **Dist:** Championship Productions. $119.99.

All Access Florida Volleyball Practice with Mary Wise 2012 (Unrated)
Coach Mary Wise and the University of Florida volleyball team are filmed during three days of live practice sessions. 263m; DVD. **A:** Family. **P:** Education. **U:** Home. **L:** English. **Spo-Rec:** Athletic Instruction/Coaching, Volleyball, How-To. **Acq:** Purchase. **Dist:** Championship Productions. $119.99.

All Access Football Practice with J.T. Curtis 2011 (Unrated)
High school coach J. T. Curtis lets cameras follow him through seven practices and several staff meetings of his football team. 794m; DVD. **A:** Family. **P:** Education. **U:** Home, Institution. **Spo-Rec:** Football, Athletic Instruction/Coaching. **Acq:** Purchase. **Dist:** Championship Productions. $199.99.

All Access George Mason Basketball Practice with Jim Larranaga 2010 (Unrated)
385m; DVD. **A:** Family. **P:** Education. **U:** Home, Institution. **Spo-Rec:** Basketball, Athletic Instruction/Coaching. **Acq:** Purchase. **Dist:** Championship Productions. $119.99.

All Access Gold Medal Wrestling Camp with Ken Chertow 2012 (Unrated)
Coach Ken Chertow allows cameras to follow his winter break training camp for several days of practices. 203m; DVD. **A:** Family. **P:** Education. **U:** Home. **L:** English. **Spo-Rec:** Athletic Instruction/Coaching, Sports--General, How-To. **Acq:** Purchase. **Dist:** Championship Productions. $99.99.

All Access High School Baseball Practice with Mike Woods 2012 (Unrated)
Coach Mike Woods prepares his baseball team for their upcoming season while the cameras roll. 250m; DVD. **A:** Family. **P:** Education. **U:** Home. **L:** English. **Spo-Rec:** Athletic Instruction/Coaching, Baseball, How-To. **Acq:** Purchase. **Dist:** Championship Productions. $99.99.

All Access High School Hockey Practice 2013 (Unrated)
Coach Kenneth Pauly and the Benilde-St. Margaret's High school hockey team are taped during their practice sessions. 263m; DVD. **A:** Family. **P:** Education. **U:** Home. **L:** English. **Spo-Rec:** Athletic Instruction/Coaching, Hockey. **Acq:** Purchase. **Dist:** Championship Productions. $263.

All Access Hockey Practice with Tim Coghlin 2013 (Unrated)
Coach Tim Coghlin lets All Access cameras follow his hockey team through the beginning of the season as well as practice routines. 229m; DVD. **A:** Family. **P:** Education. **U:** Home. **L:** English. **Spo-Rec:** Athletic Instruction/Coaching, Hockey. **Acq:** Purchase. **Dist:** Championship Productions. $79.99.

All Access Houston Softball Practice with Kyla Holas 2012 (Unrated)
Coach Kyla Holas allows cameras to film three days of the University of Houston softball team's practices. 402m; DVD. **A:** Family. **P:** Education. **U:** Home. **L:** English. **Spo-Rec:** Athletic Instruction/Coaching, Softball, How-To. **Acq:** Purchase. **Dist:** Championship Productions. $119.99.

All Access Huntington Prep High School Basketball Practice 2013 (Unrated)
Cameras follow Coach Rob Halford through three of his basketball practice sessions: one for skill development, one for strength and conditioning, and the last for defensive drills. 137m; DVD. **A:** Family. **P:** Education. **U:** Home. **L:** English. **Spo-Rec:** Athletic Instruction/Coaching, Basketball. **Acq:** Purchase. **Dist:** Championship Productions. $39.99.

All-Access Illinois Basketball Practice with Bruce Weber 2010 (Unrated)
Cameras follow Basketball Coach Bruce Weber as he takes his team through several practice sessions, including their game day set-up. 398m; DVD. **A:** Family. **P:** Education. **U:** Home, Institution. **Spo-Rec:** Basketball, Athletic Instruction/Coaching. **Acq:** Purchase. **Dist:** Championship Productions. $119.99.

All Access Indoor Baseball Practice with Dr. Dirk Baker 2013 (Unrated)
Dr. Dirk Baker has cameras record three days of the Worcester State University baseball team's practice sessions. 245m; DVD. **A:** Family. **P:** Education. **U:** Home. **L:** English. **Spo-Rec:** Athletic Instruction/Coaching, Baseball, How-To. **Acq:** Purchase. **Dist:** Championship Productions. $119.99.

All Access Indoor Softball Practice 2009 (Unrated)
Coach George Wares allows cameras to accompany him on an indoor practice session held for his softball team. ??m; DVD. **A:** Family. **P:** Education. **U:** Home, Institution. **Spo-Rec:** Softball, Athletic Instruction/Coaching. **Acq:** Purchase. **Dist:** Championship Productions. $79.99.

All Access Indoor Softball Practice with John Tschida 2012 (Unrated)
Coach John Tschida brings the All Access cameras along for three practice sessions by the University of St. Thomas softball team. 314m; DVD. **A:** Family. **P:** Education. **U:** Home. **L:** English. **Spo-Rec:** Athletic Instruction/Coaching, Softball, How-To. **Acq:** Purchase. **Dist:** Championship Productions. $119.99.

All Access Kansas Basketball Practice with Bill Self 2010 (Unrated)
Coach Bill Self allows cameras to record the first four full practice sessions of the 2009-2010 season of the University of Kansas basketball program. 424m; DVD. **A:** Family. **P:** Education. **U:** Home, Institution. **Spo-Rec:** Basketball, Athletic Instruction/Coaching. **Acq:** Purchase. **Dist:** Championship Productions. $119.99.

All Access Kansas State Basketball Practice with Frank Martin 2011 (Unrated)
Coach Frank Martin discusses the motion offense and man-to-man defense while running his basketball team through their practice sessions. 486m; DVD. **A:** Family. **P:** Education. **U:** Home, Institution. **Spo-Rec:** Basketball, Athletic Instruction/Coaching. **Acq:** Purchase. **Dist:** Championship Productions. $119.99.

All Access Kentucky Basketball Practice 2010-2011 Season 2011 (Unrated)
Basketball coach John Calipari lets cameras follow him through several team practices as they study transition, man-to-man defense, and the dribble drive motion offense. 248m; DVD. **A:** Family. **P:** Education. **U:** Home, Institution. **Spo-Rec:** Basketball, Athletic Instruction/Coaching. **Acq:** Purchase. **Dist:** Championship Productions. $119.99.

All Access Kentucky Basketball Practice with John Calipari 2010 (Unrated)
Coach John Calipari is followed by the All Access cameras during the first several practice sessions of his University of Kentucky basketball team's season. ??m; DVD. **A:** Family. **P:** Education. **U:** Home, Institution. **Spo-Rec:** Basketball, Athletic Instruction/Coaching. **Acq:** Purchase. **Dist:** Championship Productions. $119.99.

All Access Lacrosse Practice with Bill Tierney 2011 (Unrated)
Lacrosse coach Bill Tierney allows cameras to follow his team through three days worth of practice sessions. 346m; DVD. **A:** Family. **P:** Education. **U:** Home, Institution. **Spo-Rec:** Lacrosse, Athletic Instruction/Coaching. **Acq:** Purchase. **Dist:** Championship Productions. $119.99.

All-Access Lacrosse Practice with Cindy Timchal 2009 (Unrated)
Coach Cindy Timchal narrates this overview of two of her lacrosse teams' practice sessions, including footage of an entire game. 232m; DVD. **A:** Family. **P:** Education. **U:** Home, Institution. **Spo-Rec:** Lacrosse, Athletic Instruction/Coaching. **Acq:** Purchase. **Dist:** Championship Productions. $79.99.

All Access Lacrosse Practice with Mike Pressler 2010 (Unrated)
Bryant University head coach Mike Pressler lets cameras follow his team through three of their 2010 practice sessions. 315m; DVD. **A:** Family. **P:** Education. **U:** Home, Institution. **Spo-Rec:** Lacrosse, Athletic Instruction/Coaching. **Acq:** Purchase. **Dist:** Championship Productions. $119.99.

All Access Lacrosse Practice with Rick Sowell 2011 (Unrated)
Coach Rick Sowell lets the All Access cameras follow him for three practice sessions of the Stony Brook University lacrosse team. 354m; DVD. **A:** Family. **P:** Education. **U:** Home, Institution. **Spo-Rec:** Lacrosse, Athletic Instruction/Coaching. **Acq:** Purchase. **Dist:** Championship Productions. $119.99.

All Access Louisville Baseball Practice 2014 (Unrated)
Coach Dan McDonnell lets cameras follow his college baseball team as they move through their practice sessions. 97m; DVD. **A:** Family. **P:** Education. **U:** Home. **L:** English. **Spo-Rec:** Athletic Instruction/Coaching, Baseball. **Acq:** Purchase. **Dist:** Championship Productions. $79.99.

All Access Louisville Women's Basketball Practice with Jeff Walz 2010 (Unrated)
Coach Jeff Walz lets cameras follow him and his team for the first four practices of their college basketball 2010 season. 380m; DVD. **A:** Family. **P:** Education. **U:** Home, Institution. **Spo-Rec:** Basketball, Athletic Instruction/Coaching. **Acq:** Purchase. **Dist:** Championship Productions. $119.99.

All Access Martensdale: St. Mary's Baseball Practice with Justin Dehmer 2012 (Unrated)
Coach Justin Dehmer allows a three-day look into his baseball program at Martensdale-St. Mary's. 423m; DVD. **A:** Family. **P:** Education. **U:** Home. **L:** English. **Spo-Rec:** Athletic Instruction/Coaching, Baseball, How-To. **Acq:** Purchase. **Dist:** Championship Productions. $119.99.

All Access Maryland Field Hockey Practice with Missy Meharg 2010 (Unrated)
Cameras follow Missy Meharg and her team through three practices and various exercise sessions and team meetings along with a full hockey game. 373m; DVD. **A:** Family. **P:** Education. **U:** Home, Institution. **Spo-Rec:** Hockey, Athletic Instruction/Coaching. **Acq:** Purchase. **Dist:** Championship Productions. $79.99.

All-Access Maryland Women's Basketball Practice with Brenda Frese 2010 (Unrated)
Cameras follow Coach Brenda Frese as she puts her basketball team through their strength and conditioning training, preseason practice sessions, and a lecture on what it means to be a leader. 597m; DVD. **A:** Family. **P:** Education. **U:** Home, Institution. **Spo-Rec:** Basketball, Athletic Instruction/Coaching. **Acq:** Purchase. **Dist:** Championship Productions. $119.99.

All-Access Men's Basketball Practice with Bruce Pearl 2010 (Unrated)
Cameras show off Basketball Coach Bruce Pearl's practice sessions, along with game-day footage that shows the results of the drills and concepts he teaches his team. ??m; DVD. **A:** Family. **P:** Education. **U:** Home, Institution. **Spo-Rec:** Basketball, Athletic Instruction/Coaching. **Acq:** Purchase. **Dist:** Championship Productions. $119.99.

All Access Miami of Ohio Hockey Practice with Enrico Blasi 2011 (Unrated)
Coach Enrico Blasi allows cameras to follow the Miami of Ohio hockey team for three of their practice sessions. 150m; DVD. **A:** Family. **P:** Education. **U:** Home, Institution. **Spo-Rec:** Hockey, Athletic Instruction/Coaching. **Acq:** Purchase. **Dist:** Championship Productions. $79.99.

All Access Miami of Ohio Hockey Practice with Enrico Blasie 2011 (Unrated)
Coach Enrico Blasi allows cameras to follow his hockey team through three practices, a film scouting session, and a game film breakdown session. 150m; DVD. **A:** Family. **P:** Education. **U:** Home, Institution. **Spo-Rec:** Hockey, Athletic Instruction/Coaching. **Acq:** Purchase. **Dist:** Championship Productions. $79.99.

All Access Michigan State Basketball Practice with Tom Izzo 2010 (Unrated)
Coach Tom Izzo lets cameras follow three practice sessions of the Michigan State basketball team during their 2010-11 season. 440m; DVD. **A:** Family. **P:** Education. **U:** Home, Institution. **Spo-Rec:** Basketball, Athletic Instruction/Coaching. **Acq:** Purchase. **Dist:** Championship Productions. $119.99.

All Access Mississippi State Baseball Practice with John Cohen 2011 (Unrated)
Mississippi State Head Baseball Coach John Cohen presents the drills he uses in baseball practice sessions while he and his staff explain why each one is necessary. 179m; DVD. **A:** Family. **P:** Education. **U:** Home, Institution. **Spo-Rec:** Baseball, Athletic Instruction/Coaching. **Acq:** Purchase. **Dist:** Championship Productions. $79.99.

All Access NC State Basketball Practice with Mark Gottfried 2012
Coach Mark Gottfried lets cameras follow him through two of the Wolfpack's practice sessions. 197m; DVD. **A:** Jr. High-Adult. **P:** Education. **U:** Home, Institution. **L:** English. **Gen-Edu:** Athletic Instruction/Coaching, Basketball, Education. **Acq:** Purchase. **Dist:** Championship Productions. $99.99.

All Access Nebraska Volleyball Practice with John Cook 2012 (Unrated)
Coach John Cook allows cameras to follow his college's volleyball team through five of their recent practices. 631m; DVD. **A:** Family. **P:** Education. **U:** Home, Institution. **Spo-Rec:** Volleyball, Athletic Instruction/Coaching. **Acq:** Purchase. **Dist:** Championship Productions. $119.99.

All Access North Carolina Basketball Practice with Roy Williams 2013 (Unrated)
Cameras follow Coach Roy WIliams and the University of North Carolina basketball team through three practice sessions. 380m; DVD. **A:** Family. **P:** Education. **U:** Home. **L:** English. **Spo-Rec:** Athletic Instruction/Coaching, Basketball. **Acq:** Purchase. **Dist:** Championship Productions. $119.99.

All Access North Carolina Softball Practice with Donna Papa 2011 (Unrated)
Coach Donna Papa allows cameras to film two of her softball practices during the 2010 season. 176m; DVD. **A:** Family. **P:** Education. **U:** Home, Institution. **Spo-Rec:** Softball, Athletic Instruction/Coaching. **Acq:** Purchase. **Dist:** Championship Productions. $119.99.

All Access Northwestern Lacrosse Practice with Kelly Amonte Hiller 2012 (Unrated)
Coach Kelly Amonte Hiller has cameras film three of her lacrosse team's practice sessions. 229m; DVD. **A:** Family. **P:** Education. **U:** Home. **L:** English. **Spo-Rec:** Athletic Instruction/Coaching, Lacrosse, How-To. **Acq:** Purchase. **Dist:** Championship Productions. $119.99.

All Access Notre Dame Practice with Mike Brey 2012 (Unrated)
Basketball coach Mike Brey demonstrates drills and his offensive and defensive philosophies in this three-DVD set. 323m; DVD. **A:** Family. **P:** Education. **U:** Home, Institution. **Spo-Rec:** Basketball, Athletic Instruction/Coaching. **Acq:** Purchase. **Dist:** Championship Productions. $119.99.

All Access Oklahoma Men's Basketball Practice with Jeff Capel 2011 (Unrated)
Coach Jeff Capel demonstrates his basketball team's offensive and defensive systems at three of their 2011 season practices. 358m; DVD. **A:** Family. **P:** Education. **U:** Home, Institution. **Spo-Rec:** Basketball, Athletic Instruction/Coaching. **Acq:** Purchase. **Dist:** Championship Productions. $119.99.

All Access Oklahoma State Basketball Practice with Travis Ford 2013 (Unrated)
Travis Ford lets All Access cameras follow him and the Oklahoma State University basketball team through their practices. 388m; DVD. **A:** Family. **P:** Education. **U:** Home. **L:** English. **Spo-Rec:** Athletic Instruction/Coaching, Basketball. **Acq:** Purchase. **Dist:** Championship Productions. $119.99.

All Access Oklahoma State Cross Country Practice 2012 (Unrated)
Coach Dave Smith discusses his training program for cross country runners while allowing cameras along for four workout sessions. 115m; DVD. **A:** Family. **P:** Education. **U:** Home. **L:** English. **Spo-Rec:** Athletic Instruction/Coaching, Sports--Track & Field, How-To. **Acq:** Purchase. **Dist:** Championship Productions. $49.99.

All Access Oklahoma State Softball Practice 2012 (Unrated)
Coach Rich Wieligman presents two days of practice sessions of the Oklahoma State University's softball team. 236m; DVD. **A:** Family. **P:** Education. **U:** Home, Institution. **Spo-Rec:** Softball, Athletic Instruction/Coaching. **Acq:** Purchase. **Dist:** Championship Productions. $119.99.

All Access Oklahoma State Wrestling Practice with John Smith 2012 (Unrated)
Cameras follow Coach John Smith and his wrestling team for the first three practices of their 2011-12 season. 223m; DVD. **A:** Family. **P:** Education. **U:** Home. **L:** English. **Spo-Rec:** Athletic Instruction/Coaching, Sports--General, How-To. **Acq:** Purchase. **Dist:** Championship Productions. $119.99.

All Access Practice with Bobby Clark 2009 (Unrated)
University of Notre Dame Head Coach Bobby Clark allows cameras to follow and record two of their soccer practice sessions. 178m; DVD. **A:** Family. **P:** Education. **U:** Home, Institution. **Spo-Rec:** Soccer, Athletic Instruction/Coaching. **Acq:** Purchase. **Dist:** Championship Productions. $39.99.

All Access Practice with Ed Servais 2012 (Unrated)
Coach Ed Servais lets cameras follow the Creighton University baseball team through individual and group practices as well as their weight training program. 280m; DVD. **A:** Family. **P:** Education. **U:** Home, Institution. **Spo-Rec:** Baseball, Athletic Instruction/Coaching. **Acq:** Purchase. **Dist:** Championship Productions. $119.99.

All Access Practice With Pat Summit 2010 (Unrated)
Coach Pat Summit allows cameras to record the Lady Vols Basketball team in their initial practice sessions for the 2009-2010 season. 155m; DVD. **A:** Family. **P:** Education. **U:** Home, Institution. **Spo-Rec:** Basketball, Athletic Instruction/Coaching. **Acq:** Purchase. **Dist:** Championship Productions. $119.99.

All Access RPI Hockey Practice with Seth Appert 2012 (Unrated)
All Access cameras follow Coach Seth Appert through four days of practice sessions with the Rensselaer Polytechnic Institute hockey team. 450m; DVD. **A:** Family. **P:** Education. **U:** Home. **L:** English. **Spo-Rec:** Athletic Instruction/Coaching, Hockey, How-To. **Acq:** Purchase. **Dist:** Championship Productions. $119.99.

All Access: Running an Efficient Softball Practice 2013 (Unrated)
Coach Francis Troyan allows cameras to follow him through five Lehigh University softball practices. 95m; DVD. **A:** Family. **P:** Education. **U:** Home. **L:** English. **Spo-Rec:** Athletic Instruction/Coaching, Softball, How-To. **Acq:** Purchase. **Dist:** Championship Productions. $39.99.

All Access Rutgers Basketball Practice with Mike Rice 2012
Cameras follow Coach Mike Rice through several of his basketball teams practice sessions as he presents his offensive philosophy. 441m; DVD. **A:** Jr. High-Adult. **P:** Education. **U:** Home, Institution. **L:** English. **Gen-Edu:** Athletic Instruction/Coaching, Basketball, Education. **Acq:** Purchase. **Dist:** Championship Productions. $149.99.

All Access Single Coach Track & Field Practice 2013 (Unrated)
Coach Bob Sanger walks cameras through two practice sessions: one early in the season, and one just before a meet. 141m; DVD. **A:** Family. **P:** Education. **U:** Home. **L:** English. **Spo-Rec:** Athletic Instruction/Coaching, Sports--Track & Field, How-To. **Acq:** Purchase. **Dist:** Championship Productions. $39.99.

All Access Skill Development & Conditioning Drills with Billy Donovan 2011 (Unrated)
University of Florida head basketball coach Billy Donovan lets cameras follow him through three separate practice sessions—each one focusing on a different part of the game. 253m; DVD. **A:** Family. **P:** Education. **U:** Home, Institution. **Spo-Rec:** Basketball, Athletic Instruction/Coaching. **Acq:** Purchase. **Dist:** Championship Productions. $119.99.

All Access Soccer Practice with Bobby Clark 2009 (Unrated)
Notre Dame Coach Bobby Clark walks a camera crew through two of his team's soccer practices. 178m; DVD. **A:** Family. **P:** Education. **U:** Home, Institution. **Spo-Rec:** Soccer, Athletic Instruction/Coaching. **Acq:** Purchase. **Dist:** Championship Productions. $49.99.

All Access Stanford Lacrosse Practice with Amy Bokker 2012 (Unrated)
Coach Amy Bokker lets All Access cameras follow her and her lacrosse team for three days of practice sessions. 284m; DVD. **A:** Family. **P:** Education. **U:** Home. **L:** English. **Spo-Rec:** Athletic Instruction/Coaching, Lacrosse, How-To. **Acq:** Purchase. **Dist:** Championship Productions. $119.99.

All Access Stanford Women's Basketball Practice with Tara VanDerveer 2011 (Unrated)
Coach Tara VanDerveer lets cameras follow the Stanford University women's basketball team as they prepare for their 2010-2011 season. 607m; DVD. **A:** Family. **P:** Education. **U:** Home, Institution. **Spo-Rec:** Basketball, Athletic Instruction/Coaching. **Acq:** Purchase. **Dist:** Championship Productions. $119.99.

All Access Stanford Women's Volleyball Practice with John Dunning 2011 (Unrated)
All Access cameras follow Coach John Dunning for three days as he puts the Stanford Women's Volleyball team through their practice sessions. 308m; DVD. **A:** Family. **P:** Education. **U:** Home, Institution. **Spo-Rec:** Volleyball, Athletic Instruction/Coaching. **Acq:** Purchase. **Dist:** Championship Productions. $119.99.

All Access Swimming Practice with Sam Freas 2012 (Unrated)
Coach Sam Freas invites All Access cameras to follow him through several training sessions with his swim team. 342m; DVD. **A:** Family. **P:** Education. **U:** Home. **L:** English. **Spo-Rec:** Athletic Instruction/Coaching, Swimming, How-To. **Acq:** Purchase. **Dist:** Championship Productions. $99.99.

All Access Syracuse Lacrosse Practice with John Desko 2012 (Unrated)
Coach John Desko lets cameras film four days of his team's practice sessions. 529m; DVD. **A:** Family. **P:** Education. **U:** Home. **L:** English. **Gen-Edu:** Athletic Instruction/Coaching, Lacrosse, How-To. **Acq:** Purchase. **Dist:** Championship Productions. $119.99.

All Access TCU Baseball Practice with James Schlossnagle 2012 (Unrated)
Coach James Schlossnagle runs the Texas Christian University baseball team through three practice sessions. 324m; DVD. **A:** Family. **P:** Education. **U:** Home. **L:** English. **Spo-Rec:** Athletic Instruction/Coaching, Baseball, How-To. **Acq:** Purchase. **Dist:** Championship Productions. $119.99.

All Access UCLA Softball Practice with Kelly Inouye-Perez 2011 (Unrated)
UCLA Coaches Lisa Fernandez and Kelly Inouye-Perez walk the camera team through one of their team's 2011 practice sessions. 194m; DVD. **A:** Family. **P:** Education. **U:** Home, Institution. **Spo-Rec:** Softball, Athletic Instruction/Coaching. **Acq:** Purchase. **Dist:** Championship Productions. $119.99.

All Access UCLA Volleyball Practice with Al Scates 2012 (Unrated)
Coach Al Scates starts off three days of practice sessions with volleyball blocking drills, along with the introduction of a new drill to his team. 518m; DVD. **A:** Family. **P:** Education. **U:** Home. **L:** English. **Spo-Rec:** Athletic Instruction/Coaching, Volleyball, How-To. **Acq:** Purchase. **Dist:** Championship Productions. $119.99.

All Access University of Missouri Basketball Practice 2013 (Unrated)
Coach Frank Haith allows the All Access cameras to follow him and the University of Missouri basketball team through three of their early season practices. 427m; DVD. **A:** Family. **P:** Education. **U:** Home. **L:** English. **Spo-Rec:** Athletic Instruction/Coaching, Basketball. **Acq:** Purchase. **Dist:** Championship Productions. $119.99.

All Access USA Basketball Practice 2011 (Unrated)
Coaches Don Showalter and Mike Jones, along with St. Louis Basketball Club President Rich Gray, have cameras follow them as they whittle the USA Developmental National Team from 27 members to 12 through drills and practice sessions. 858m; DVD. **A:** Family. **P:** Education. **U:** Home, Institution. **Spo-Rec:** Basketball, Athletic Instruction/Coaching. **Acq:** Purchase. **Dist:** Championship Productions. $39.99.

All Access USC Tennis Practice with Peter Smith 2011 (Unrated)
Coach Peter Smith has cameras follow him as he takes his tennis players through their paces. 261m; DVD. **A:** Family. **P:** Education. **U:** Home, Institution. **Spo-Rec:** Tennis, Athletic Instruction/Coaching. **Acq:** Purchase. **Dist:** Championship Productions. $79.99.

All Access USC Volleyball Practice with Mick Haley 2012 (Unrated)
Coach Mick Haley demonsrates various drills during several days of practice sessions. 805m; DVD. **A:** Family. **P:** Education. **U:** Home. **L:** English. **Spo-Rec:** Athletic Instruction/Coaching, Volleyball, How-To. **Acq:** Purchase. **Dist:** Championship Productions. $119.99.

All Access USC Water Polo Practice 2012 (Unrated)
USC water polo Head Coach Jovan Vavic lets cameras film him and his team through over ten hours of drills and practice sessions. 622m; DVD. **A:** Family. **P:** Education. **U:** Home, Institution. **L:** English. **Spo-Rec:** Sports--Water, Athletic Instruction/Coaching. **Acq:** Purchase. **Dist:** Championship Productions. $119.99.

All Access UT-Arlington Basketball Practice 2013 (Unrated)
Coach Scott Cross allows All Access cameras to follow the University of Texas-Arlington basketball team as they go through their practices. 387m; DVD. **A:** Family. **P:** Education. **U:** Home. **L:** English. **Spo-Rec:** Athletic Instruction/Coaching, Basketball. **Acq:** Purchase. **Dist:** Championship Productions. $119.99.

All Access UTEP Basketball Practice with Tim Floyd 2013 (Unrated)
Coach Tim Floyd allows All Access cameras to follow him and his basketball team through three of their practice sessions. 476m; DVD. **A:** Family. **P:** Education. **U:** Home. **L:** English. **Spo-Rec:** Athletic Instruction/Coaching, Basketball. **Acq:** Purchase. **Dist:** Championship Productions. $119.99.

All Access Virginia Lacrosse Practice with Dom Starsia 2010 (Unrated)
Coach Al Dom Starsia allows the All Access cameras to film three of his lacrosse teams' practices along with him providing perspective on what he believes makes a successful coach. 261m; DVD. **A:** Family. **P:** Education. **U:** Home, Institution. **Spo-Rec:** Lacrosse, Athletic Instruction/Coaching. **Acq:** Purchase. **Dist:** Championship Productions. $119.99.

All Access Virginia Soccer Practice with Greg Gelnovatch 2010 (Unrated)
University of Virginia Coach Greg Gelnovatch lets cameras follow him for his team's training and drills while discussing his philosophy on coaching soccer. 143m; DVD. **A:** Family. **P:** Education. **U:** Home, Institution. **Spo-Rec:** Soccer, Athletic Instruction/Coaching. **Acq:** Purchase. **Dist:** Championship Productions. $39.99.

All Access Virginia Soccer Practice with Greg Gelnovatch 2010 (Unrated)
Coach Greg Gelnovatch allows the All Access cameras to follow him and film his soccer team during their practice sessions. 143m; DVD. **A:** Family. **P:** Education. **U:** Home, Institution. **Spo-Rec:** Soccer, Athletic Instruction/Coaching. **Acq:** Purchase. **Dist:** Championship Productions. $39.99.

All Access Virginia Tennis: First Match of the Season 2012 (Unrated)
Tennis coach Brian Boland allows cameras to follow his college team's first match of the season as well as their pre-match warm-up while he discusses his early season training strategy. 43m; DVD. **A:** Family. **P:** Education. **U:** Home. **L:** English. **Spo-Rec:** Athletic Instruction/Coaching, Tennis, How-To. **Acq:** Purchase. **Dist:** Championship Productions. $29.99.

All Access Volleyball Practice with Kevin Hambly 2013 (Unrated)
Coach Kevin Hambly and the University of Illinois volleyball team perform in a preseason practice session. 549m; DVD. **A:** Adult. **P:** Education. **U:** Home. **L:** English. **Spo-Rec:** Athletic Instruction/Coaching, Volleyball, How-To. **Acq:** Purchase. **Dist:** Championship Productions. $119.99.

All Access Volleyball Practice with Russ Rose 2011 (Unrated)
Coach Russ Rose has cameras follow him for three days of the Penn State Volleyball team's practice sessions. 498m; DVD. **A:** Family. **P:** Education. **U:** Home, Institution. **Spo-Rec:** Volleyball, Athletic Instruction/Coaching. **Acq:** Purchase. **Dist:** Championship Productions. $119.99.

All Access Wartburg College Wrestling Practice with Jim Miller 2012 (Unrated)
Coach Jim Miller shows the warm-up exercises and training drills he teaches the Wartburg College wrestling team. 179m; DVD. **A:** Family. **P:** Education. **U:** Home. **L:** English. **Spo-Rec:**

Athletic Instruction/Coaching, Sports--General, How-To. **Acq:** Purchase. **Dist:** Championship Productions. $119.99.

All Access West Virginia Basketball Practice with Bob Huggins 2011 (Unrated)
Cameras follow Coach Bob Huggins as he conducts his first three practices of the 2011 college basketball season. 352m; DVD. **A:** Family. **P:** Education. **U:** Home, Institution. **Spo-Rec:** Basketball, Athletic Instruction/Coaching. **Acq:** Purchase. **Dist:** Championship Productions. $119.99.

All Access Williams College Basketball Practice with Mike Maker 2012 (Unrated)
Basketball coach Mike Maker lets cameras follow him through several live sessions as he teaches his version of the Princeton Offense to the Williams College team. 286m; DVD. **A:** Family. **P:** Education. **U:** Home, Institution. **Spo-Rec:** Basketball, Athletic Instruction/Coaching. **Acq:** Purchase. **Dist:** Championship Productions. $119.99.

All Access Wisconsin Hockey Practice 2013 (Unrated)
Coach Mike Eaves allows the All Access cameras to follow him and the Wisconsin Badgers hockey team through their practice sessions. 281m; DVD. **A:** Family. **P:** Education. **U:** Home. **L:** English. **Spo-Rec:** Athletic Instruction/Coaching, Hockey. **Acq:** Purchase. **Dist:** Championship Productions. $119.99.

All Access Women's Basketball Practice with Sherri Coale 2011 (Unrated)
Cameras follow Coach Sherri Coale as she goes through a pre-practice session with her basketball team discussing what they need to improve before moving on to the actual drills and practice sessions; also contains the 2010 Oklahoma Coaches Clinic. ??m; DVD. **A:** Family. **P:** Education. **U:** Home, Institution. **Spo-Rec:** Basketball, Athletic Instruction/Coaching. **Acq:** Purchase. **Dist:** Championship Productions. $119.99.

All Access Xavier Basketball Practice with Chris Mack 2011 (Unrated)
Xavier University's basketball head coach Chris Mack and the Musketeers are followed for their practice sessions of the 2009-10 season. 462m; DVD. **A:** Family. **P:** Education. **U:** Home, Institution. **Spo-Rec:** Basketball, Athletic Instruction/Coaching. **Acq:** Purchase. **Dist:** Championship Productions. $119.99.

All, All and All 1976
A program that explores self-identity through the combined efforts of poetry and film leaving the viewer with a serene feeling of being one with the universe. 6m; VHS, 3/4 U. **C:** Narrated by Claudine Longet. **Pr:** Marv Albert. **A:** Family. **P:** Education. **U:** Institution, SURA. **Gen-Edu.** **Acq:** Purchase. **Dist:** Phoenix Learning Group.

All American Baseball Series 19??
13-tape series features renown coaches sharing their drills and techniques. 1130m; VHS. **A:** Adult. **P:** Instruction. **U:** Institution. **How-Ins:** Baseball, Sports--General, How-To. **Acq:** Purchase. **Dist:** Championship Productions. $379.95.
Indiv. Titles: 1. Pitching Drills for Total Body Control 2. The "Power" Curve Ball 3. Preseason Pitching Program and Drills 4. Fielding for Pitchers 5. Maximizing the Fastball 6. Baserunning Strategies and Drills 7. Power Hitting Drills 8. Bunting Drills & Techniques 9. Contact Hitting & Plate Coverage 10. Double Play Tactics & Drills 11. Outfield Drills 12. Individual Drills 13. Catching Drills & Mechanics.

The All-American Boy 1973 (Unrated) — ★
Voight plays one of the most unpleasant characters seen on screen in this sports drama that was shot in 1969. Manipulative, self-centered, petulant amateur boxer Vic Bealer has dreams of going to the Olympics but he doesn't have the talent or the heart. Instead he's just a user, especially with the women in his life. 118m; DVD. **C:** Jon Voight; Anne Archer; Carol Androsky; Gene Borkan; Jeanne Cooper; Rosalind Cash; Ron Burns; Directed by Charles Eastman; Written by Charles Eastman; Cinematography by Philip H. Lathrop. **A:** Sr. High-Adult. **P:** Entertainment. **U:** Home. **Mov-Ent:** Boxing, Pregnancy, Sports--Fiction: Drama. **Acq:** Purchase. **Dist:** WarnerArchive.com.

All-American Crashes 1990
See the most gut-wrenching racing crashes in history. 60m; VHS. **A:** Jr. High-Adult. **P:** Entertainment. **U:** Home. **Spo-Rec:** Sports--General, Automobiles--Racing. **Acq:** Purchase. **Dist:** ESPN Inc.; Powersports - Powerdocs. $39.95.

All-American Girl: The Complete Series 2006 (Unrated)
Taken from her own life experiences, comedienne Margaret Cho stars as Margaret Kim as the Americanized San Franciscan must deal with her traditional Korean family in this television sitcom that ran from 1994-1995. Includes: her mother doesn't like her boyfriend Kyle so Margaret decides to move in with him, Margaret's mother fills in at the cosmetics counter with her, and she gets cold feet when a nude sculpture of her is displayed to her family. Several celebrities made guest appearances such as Oprah Winfrey and Quentin Tarantino. 19 episodes. 450m; DVD. **C:** Margaret Cho; Amy Hill; Jodi Long; Clyde Kusatsu; J.B. Quon. **A:** Jr. High-Adult. **P:** Entertainment. **U:** Home. **Mov-Ent:** Television Series, Family, Drama. **Acq:** Purchase. **Dist:** Shout! Factory. $39.95.

All American Girls: Cheerleading & Dance 19??
Learn cheerleading and dance from the All American Girls. ?m; VHS. **A:** Jr. High-Adult. **P:** Instruction. **U:** Home. **Hea-Sci:** Fitness/Exercise. **Acq:** Purchase. **Dist:** Inspired Corp. $14.98.

All American Girls: Dance Funk Workout 19??
Enjoy a funky workout with the All American Girls. ?m; VHS. **A:** Jr. High-Adult. **P:** Instruction. **U:** Home. **Hea-Sci:** Fitness/Exercise. **Acq:** Purchase. **Dist:** Inspired Corp. $14.98.

All American High 1987
A foreign exchange student from Finland experiences his senior year of high school in middle-class suburban America. 60m; VHS, 3/4 U. **Pr:** Keva Rosenfeld. **A:** Jr. High-Adult. **P:** Education. **U:** Institution, SURA. **Gen-Edu:** Adolescence. **Acq:** Purchase, Rent/Lease. **Dist:** Direct Cinema Ltd.

All-American Murder 1991 (R) — ★★
A rebellious young man is enrolled in a typical, all-American college for one last shot at mainstream life. Things start out okay, as he meets an attractive young coed. Hours later, he finds himself accused of her grisly murder. The youth is then given 24 hours to prove his innocence by a canny homicide detective. Average performances highlight this film, which isn't able to rise above the mediocre. 94m; VHS, DVD, CC. **C:** Christopher Walken; Charlie Schlatter; Josie Bissett; Joanna Cassidy; Richard Kind; Woody Watson; J.C. Quinn; Amy Davis; Directed by Anson Williams; Written by Barry Sandler. **Pr:** Greenwich Films; Prism Entertainment. **A:** Sr. High-Adult. **P:** Entertainment. **U:** Home. **Mov-Ent:** Mystery & Suspense. **Acq:** Purchase. **Dist:** Unknown Distributor.

All Around Us: Radiation 1983
Explains he nature of radiation and discusses questions and concerns concerning it use. 28m; VHS, SVS, 3/4 U. **Pr:** United Kingdom Atomic Energy Authority. **A:** Sr. High-Adult. **P:** Education. **U:** Institution. **Hea-Sci:** Nuclear Energy. **Acq:** Purchase. **Dist:** Encyclopedia Britannica. $59.00.

All Ashore 1953 (Unrated) — ★1/2
Generally mediocre Columbia Pictures musical comedy about three sailors on shore leave. They head to Catalina Island for some girl chasing fun but Rooney's gullible sailor is constantly being taken advantage of by his two supposed pals (Haynes, McDonald) and that's not a lot of laughs. 80m; DVD. **C:** Mickey Rooney; Dick Haymes; Ray McDonald; Barbara Bates; Jody Lawrance; Peggy Ryan; Directed by Richard Quine; Written by Richard Quine; Blake Edwards; Cinematography by Charles Lawton, Jr. **A:** Jr. High-Adult. **P:** Entertainment. **U:** Home. **L:** English. **Mov-Ent:** Musical, Armed Forces--U.S. **Acq:** Purchase. **Dist:** Sony Pictures Home Entertainment Inc.

All But Forgotten: Holman Francis Day, Filmmaker 1977
A look at the career of filmmaker and author Day, whose work includes "My Lady of the Pines" with Mary Astor. 30m; VHS. **A:** Jr. High-Adult. **P:** Education. **U:** Institution, Home. **Gen-Edu:** Filmmaking, Biography. **Acq:** Purchase. **Dist:** Northeast Historic Film. $24.95.

All Change: The Management of Change 1988
An explanation of why change is not always bad in the business world. Part One examines the pitfalls of staying with the status quo. Part Two shows how to implement change effectively. 27m; VHS, 8 mm, 3/4 U, Special order formats. **C:** John Cleese; Geoffrey Palmer; Simon Cadell; Directed by Robert Knights. **Pr:** Video Arts. **A:** College-Adult. **P:** Education. **U:** Institution, SURA. **Bus-Ind:** Business, Management, Office Practice. **Acq:** Purchase, Rent/Lease. **Dist:** Video Arts, Inc. $790.00.
Indiv. Titles: 1. Change for the Better 2. The Shape of Things to Come.

All Creatures Great and Small 1974 (Unrated) — ★★★
Taken from James Herriot's bestselling novels, this is a delightful, quiet drama of a veterinarian's apprentice in rural England. Fine performance by Hopkins. Followed by "All Things Bright and Beautiful" and a popular British TV series. 92m; VHS, DVD, CC. **C:** Simon Ward; Anthony Hopkins; Lisa Harrow; Brian Stirner; Freddie Jones; T.P. McKenna; Directed by Claude Whatham; Written by Hugh Whitemore; Cinematography by Peter Suschitzky; Music by Wilfred Josephs. **Pr:** EMI Media. **A:** Jr. High-Adult. **P:** Entertainment. **U:** Home. **Mov-Ent:** Animals. **Acq:** Purchase. **Dist:** Reader's Digest Home Video; Home Vision Cinema; Video Collectibles. $29.97.

All Creatures Great and Small: Series 1 2002 (Unrated)
Presents episodes from the first season of the 1978-1980 run of the drama-comedy television series based on books by James Herriot (Timothy), a 1940s veterinarian in a village in Yorkshire, England, working with Siegfried Farnon (Hardy). Includes: James' introduction to the interesting and eclectic townspeople, his troubles taking care of a pig, and his new relationship with Helen Alderson (Drinkwater), who had been seeing another man. 13 episodes. 646m; DVD. **C:** Christopher Timothy; Robert Hardy; Peter Davison; Carol Drinkwater. **A:** Family. **P:** Entertainment. **U:** Home. **Mov-Ent:** Television Series, Nature, Drama. **Acq:** Purchase. **Dist:** Warner Home Video, Inc. $79.98.

All Creatures Great and Small: Series 2 2002 (Unrated)
Presents episodes from the second season of the 1978-1980 run of the drama-comedy television series based on books by James Herriot (Timothy), a 1940s veterinarian in a village in Yorkshire, England, working with Siegfried Farnon (Hardy). Includes: the locals become less wary of James as the new vet in town, James finds strength with his now-wife Helen (Drinkwater), and Christmas Day is a busy one at the clinic. 14 episodes. 700m; DVD. **C:** Christopher Timothy; Robert Hardy; Peter Davison; Carol Drinkwater. **A:** Family. **P:** Entertainment. **U:** Home. **Mov-Ent:** Television Series, Nature, Drama. **Acq:** Purchase. **Dist:** Warner Home Video, Inc. $79.98.

All Creatures Great and Small: Series 3 2003 (Unrated)
Presents episodes from the third season of the 1978-1980 run of the drama-comedy television series based on books by James Herriot (Timothy), a 1940s veterinarian in a village in Yorkshire, England, working with Siegfried Farnon (Hardy). Includes: James and Helen (Drinkwater) attempt to rescue a cow from being killed, the couple struggles financially to celebrate their wedding anniversary after a goat munches on the contents of their checkbook, and James and Siegfried abandon the practice to join the Royal Air Force during WWII (at which point there is an eight-year break). 14 episodes. 722m; DVD. **C:** Christopher Timothy; Robert Hardy; Peter Davison; Carol Drinkwater. **A:** Family. **P:** Entertainment. **U:** Home. **Mov-Ent:** Television Series, Nature, Drama. **Acq:** Purchase. **Dist:** Warner Home Video, Inc. $79.98.

All Creatures Great and Small: Series 4 2004 (Unrated)
Presents episodes from the 1988-1990 second run of the drama-comedy television series based on books by James Herriot (Timothy), a 1940s veterinarian in a village in Yorkshire, England, working with Siegfried Farnon (Hardy). Includes: James and Siegfried return from their time in the Royal Air Force serving in WWI and their workload is heavier than ever while another, more prosperous, animal hospital tries to lure James to their practice. Lynda Bellingham replaced Carol Drinkwater and John McGlynn is added to the cast as Calum Buchanan, a new assistant to James. 10 episodes. 546m; DVD. **C:** Christopher Timothy; Robert Hardy; Peter Davison; John McGlynn; Linda Bellingham. **A:** Family. **P:** Entertainment. **U:** Home. **Mov-Ent:** Television Series, Nature, Drama. **Acq:** Purchase. **Dist:** Warner Home Video, Inc. $79.98.

All Creatures Great and Small: Series 5 2005 (Unrated)
Presents episodes from the 1988-1990 second run of the drama-comedy television series based on books by James Herriot (Timothy), a 1940s-50s veterinarian in a village in Yorkshire, England, working with Siegfried Farnon (Hardy). Includes: James makes housecalls on skis during a blizzard, he gets invited as the guest of honor to a wealthy woman's Pekinese's birthday party, and the Herriots struggle as Helen (Bellingham) endures through a severe back injury. 12 episodes. 449m; DVD. **C:** Christopher Timothy; Robert Hardy; Peter Davison; Linda Bellingham; John McGlynn. **A:** Family. **P:** Entertainment. **U:** Home. **Mov-Ent:** Television Series, Nature, Drama. **Acq:** Purchase. **Dist:** Warner Home Video, Inc. $79.98.

All Creatures Great and Small: Series 6 2006 (Unrated)
Presents episodes from the 1988-1990 second run of the drama-comedy television series based on books by James Herriot (Timothy), a 1940s-50s veterinarian in a village in Yorkshire, England, working with Siegfried Farnon (Hardy). Includes: James and Siegfried try to convince the townspeople of the benefits of a more modern scientific approach to treating animals. 12 episodes. 600m; DVD. **C:** Christopher Timothy; Robert Hardy; Peter Davison; Linda Bellingham; John McGlynn. **A:** Family. **P:** Entertainment. **U:** Home. **Mov-Ent:** Television Series, Nature, Drama. **Acq:** Purchase. **Dist:** Warner Home Video, Inc. $79.98.

All Creatures Great and Small: The Complete Collection 2007
Based on James Herriot's best-selling books about a country veterinarian in Yorkshire Dales town of Darrowby from the 1930's through World War II. 324m; DVD. **C:** Christopher Timothy; Robert Hardy; Peter Davison; Linda Bellingham. **A:** Family. **P:** Entertainment. **U:** Home. **Mov-Ent:** Drama, Animals, History. **Acq:** Purchase. **Dist:** BBC Worldwide Publishing Ltd.

All Creatures Great and Small: Two Post War Specials 2003 (Unrated)
Features special episodes (1983 and 1985) that appeared after the first run ended (in 1980) of the drama-comedy television series based on books by James Herriot (Timothy), a 1940s veterinarian in a village in Yorkshire, England, working with Siegfried Farnon (Hardy). Includes: (1983 special) James returns from his wartime service six years later and has trouble adjusting to civilian life and (1985 special) James struggles to balance outdated medical procedures versus more modern medicine. 2 episodes. 179m; DVD. **C:** Christopher Timothy; Robert Hardy; Peter Davison; Carol Drinkwater. **A:** Family. **P:** Entertainment. **U:** Home. **Mov-Ent:** Television Series, Nature, Drama. **Acq:** Purchase. **Dist:** Warner Home Video, Inc. $24.98.

All Day Long 1987
Documentary segments explore daycare from the perspectives of professionals, daycare workers, parents, and children. 41m; VHS, 3/4 U. **Pr:** RMI Media Productions. **A:** Adult. **P:** Education. **U:** Institution. **Gen-Edu:** Children, Child Care. **Acq:** Purchase. **Dist:** RMI Media.

All Dogs Christmas Carol 1998 (G)
Holiday grumbling turns to holiday merriment with a little help from some canine Santas. 73m; VHS, DVD, CC. **C:** Voice(s) by Steven Weber; Dom DeLuise; Sheena Easton; Ernest Borgnine; Charles Nelson Reilly; Bebe Neuwirth; Directed by Paul Sabella; Written by Jymn Magon; Music by Mark Watters; Lorraine Feather. **A:** Family. **P:** Entertainment. **U:** Home. **Chl-Juv:** Animation & Cartoons, Christmas, Pets. **Acq:** Purchase. **Dist:** MGM Home Entertainment.

All Dogs Go to Heaven 1989 (G) — ★★
Somewhat heavy-handed animated musical (Reynolds sings) about a gangster dog who is killed by his partner in business. On the way to Heaven, he discovers how to get back to Earth to seek his revenge. When he returns to Earth, he is taken in by a

little girl and learns about something he missed in life the first time around: Love. Expertly animated, but the plot may not keep the grown-ups engrossed, and the kids may notice its lack of charm. 85m; VHS, DVD, Blu-Ray, 8 mm, CC. **C:** Voice(s) by Burt Reynolds; Judith Barsi; Dom DeLuise; Vic Tayback; Charles Nelson Reilly; Melba Moore; Candy Devine; Loni Anderson; Directed by Don Bluth; Written by Don Bluth; David N. Weiss; Music by Ralph Burns. **Pr:** MGM Home Entertainment; United Artists. **A:** Family. **P:** Entertainment. **U:** Home. **Mov-Ent:** Animation & Cartoons, Children, Pets. **Acq:** Purchase. **Dist:** MGM Home Entertainment; Reader's Digest Home Video. $14.95.

All Dogs Go to Heaven 2 1995 (G) — ★★½
Animated musical finds lovable scamp Charlie (Sheen) the dog discovering that the afterlife is not all it's cracked up to be and pining for dysfunction aplenty back on earth. He gets his chance when Gabriel's Horn is stolen and Charlie is assigned to retrieve it. Charlie teams up again with old buddy Itchy (Deluise) as the two come down from Dog Heaven to stop the villainous Carface (Borgnine) and demonic cat Red (Hearn). Along the way, Charlie falls in love with sexy Irish Setter Sasha (Easton), and finds a chance for redemption by helping a little boy in trouble. Animation not outstanding, but should keep the attention of small children. 82m; VHS, DVD, Blu-Ray, CC. **C:** Voice(s) by Charlie Sheen; Sheena Easton; Ernest Borgnine; Dom DeLuise; George Hearn; Bebe Neuwirth; Hamilton Camp; Wallace Shawn; Bobby DiCicco; Adam Wylie; Directed by Paul Sabella; Larry Leker; Written by Arne Olsen; Kelly Ward; Mark Young; Music by Mark Watters; Barry Mann; Cynthia Weil. **Pr:** Kelly Ward; Kelly Ward; Mark Young; Paul Sabella; Jonathan Dern; Metro-Goldwyn-Mayer Pictures; MGM Home Entertainment. **A:** Family. **P:** Entertainment. **U:** Home. **Mov-Ent:** Animation & Cartoons, Animals, Pets. **Acq:** Purchase. **Dist:** MGM Home Entertainment.

All Dogs Go to Heaven: The Series - Dogs Undercover 2006 (Unrated)
Offers the animated adventures of canine pals Charlie (Weber) and Itchy (DeLuise) from the 1996-1999 television series—drawn from the 1989 movie—as they perform missions given by canine angel leader, Annabelle (Neuwirth). Includes: "The Magical Misery Tour," "La Doggie Vita," "Fearless Fido," and "The Big Fetch." 4 episodes. 88m; DVD. **C:** Steven Weber; Dom DeLuise; Sheena Easton; Ernest Borgnine; Bebe Neuwirth. **A:** Primary. **P:** Entertainment. **U:** Home. **Chl-Juv:** Television Series, Animation & Cartoons, Children's Shows. **Acq:** Purchase. **Dist:** MGM Home Entertainment. $9.95.

All Dogs Go to Heaven: The Series - Friends to the Rescue 2006 (Unrated)
Offers the animated adventures of canine pals Charlie (Weber) and Itchy (DeLuise) from the 1996-1999 television series—drawn from the 1989 movie—as they perform missions given by canine angel leader, Annabelle (Neuwirth). Includes: "Field Trip," "Cyrano de Barkinac," "Mutts Ado About Nothing," and "Heaven Inning Stretch." 4 episodes. 88m; DVD. **C:** Steven Weber; Dom DeLuise; Sheena Easton; Ernest Borgnine; Bebe Neuwirth. **A:** Primary. **P:** Entertainment. **U:** Home. **Chl-Juv:** Television Series, Animation & Cartoons, Children's Shows. **Acq:** Purchase. **Dist:** MGM Home Entertainment. $9.95.

All Fall Down 1962 (Unrated) — ★★½
A young man (de Wilde) idolizes his callous older brother (Beatty) until a tragedy forces him to grow up. Saint plays the older woman taken in by the brothers' family, who is seduced and abandoned. When she finds herself pregnant and alone, she commits suicide causing the younger brother, who loved her from afar, to vow to kill his older sibling. A well-acted melodrama. Also available colorized. 111m/B/W; VHS, DVD. **C:** Eva Marie Saint; Brandon de Wilde; Warren Beatty; Karl Malden; Angela Lansbury; Constance Ford; Barbara Baxley; Directed by John Frankenheimer; Written by William Inge; Cinematography by Lionel Lindon; Music by Alex North. **A:** College-Adult. **P:** Entertainment. **U:** Home. **Mov-Ent:** Melodrama. **Acq:** Purchase. **Dist:** MGM Home Entertainment. $19.98.

All Fired Up 1995
Presents a humorous adaptation discussing the serious problem of fire safety. 15m; VHS. **A:** Adult. **P:** Professional. **U:** Institution. **Bus-Ind:** Safety Education, Management, Occupational Training. **Acq:** Purchase, Rent/Lease. **Dist:** National Safety Council, California Chapter, Film Library. $195.00.

All Fit 1988
Slim Goodbody explains all sorts of things that can help people be healthier in this 15-tape series. A teacher's guide is included. Tapes can be purchased individually or as a set. 15m; VHS, 3/4 U. **C:** Hosted by Slim Goodbody. **Pr:** Slim Goodbody Corporation. **A:** Family. **P:** Education. **U:** Institution, CCTV, CATV, BCTV. **Chl-Juv:** Fitness/Exercise, Health Education, Nutrition. **Acq:** Purchase, Rent/Lease, Duplication License. **Dist:** Agency for Instructional Technology. $39.00.
Indiv. Titles: 1. Fitness 2. Body Design 3. Training Principles 4. Warm-Up & Cool-Down 5. Flexibility 6. Strength & Endurance 7. Cardiorespiratory Fitness 8. Body Composition 9. Balance 10. Posture 11. Coordination & Agility 12. Speed & Power 13. Stress & Relaxation 14. Lifetime Fitness 15. All Fit Workout.

All God's Children 1980 — ★★½
Drama about the controversial forced busing issue and two families who must face it. Top-notch cast is occasionally mislead by meandering script attempting to stay true to a sensitive issue. 100m; VHS. **C:** Richard Widmark; Ned Beatty; Ossie Davis; Ruby Dee; Mariclare Costello; George Spell; Trish Van Devere; Ken Swofford; Directed by Jerry Thorpe; Music by Billy Goldenberg. **A:** Adult. **P:** Entertainment. **U:** Home. **Mov-Ent:** TV Movies, Education. **Acq:** Purchase. **Dist:** No Longer Available.

All Good Things 2010 (R) — ★★½
Fictional account of the true crime story involving Robert A. Durst and the (unsolved) disappearance of his wife Kathie in 1982. David Marks (Gosling) doesn't want to follow his wealthy father Sanford (Langella) into the family's New York real estate business. He tries rebelling, including through his marriage to Katie (Dunst), but finally succumbs to parental pressure. As David gets increasingly angry, his marriage falls apart. Then Katie goes missing. Dunst is appealing but Gosling is stuck playing a repellent cipher. 101m; DVD. **C:** Ryan Gosling; Kirsten Dunst; Frank Langella; Lily Rabe; Kristen Wiig; Diane Venora; Philip Baker Hall; Michael Esper; Nick Offerman; John Cullum; Directed by Andrew Jarecki; Written by Marcus Hinchey; Marc Smerling; Cinematography by Michael Seresin; Music by Rob Simonsen. **Pr:** Bruno Papandrea; Michael London; Andrew Jarecki; Marc Smerling; Groundswell Productions; Hit the Ground Running Films; Magnolia Pictures. **A:** Sr. High-Adult. **P:** Entertainment. **U:** Home. **L:** English. **Mov-Ent:** Real Estate, Mystery & Suspense. **Acq:** Purchase. **Dist:** Magnolia Home Entertainment.

All Grown Up! Dude, Where's My Horse? 2005 (Unrated)
The "Rugrats" gang is now approaching their teenage years with all the usual complications and crises in this animated Nick Jr. series that began in 2003. Includes "Dude, Where's My Horse?," "Blind Man's Buff," and "Yu-Gotta-Go". 3 episodes. 92m; DVD. **C:** Voice(s) by Elizabeth Daily; Tara Strong; Nancy Cartwright; Dionne Quan; Cheryl Chase; Cree Summer; Jack Riley; Melanie Chartoff; Michael Bell; Kath Soucie; Joe Alaskey. **A:** Family. **P:** Entertainment. **U:** Home. **Chl-Juv:** Television Series, Family, Animation & Cartoons. **Acq:** Purchase. **Dist:** Paramount Pictures Corp. $9.99.

All Grown Up! Growing Up Changes Everything 2003 (Unrated)
The "Rugrats" gang is now approaching their teenage years with all the usual complications and crises in this animated Nick Jr. series that began in 2003. Includes "Susie Sings the Blues" and "Coup Deville" along with two "Rugrats" shows ("All Growed Up" and "My Fair Babies"). 4 episodes. 101m; DVD. **C:** Voice(s) by Elizabeth Daily; Tara Strong; Nancy Cartwright; Dionne Quan; Cheryl Chase; Cree Summer; Jack Riley; Melanie Chartoff; Michael Bell; Kath Soucie; Joe Alaskey. **A:** Family. **P:** Entertainment. **U:** Home. **Chl-Juv:** Television Series, Family, Animation & Cartoons. **Acq:** Purchase. **Dist:** Paramount Pictures Corp. $19.99.

All Grown Up! Interview with a Campfire 2005 (Unrated)
The "Rugrats" gang is now approaching their teenage years with all the usual complications and crises in this animated Nick Jr. series that began in 2003. Includes "Interview with a Campfire," "River Rats," and "Bad Aptitude." 3 episodes. 91m; DVD. **C:** Voice(s) by Elizabeth Daily; Tara Strong; Nancy Cartwright; Dionne Quan; Cheryl Chase; Cree Summer; Jack Riley; Melanie Chartoff; Michael Bell; Kath Soucie; Joe Alaskey. **A:** Family. **P:** Entertainment. **U:** Home. **Chl-Juv:** Television Series, Family, Animation & Cartoons. **Acq:** Purchase. **Dist:** Paramount Pictures Corp. $16.99.

All Grown Up! O' Brother 2004 (Unrated)
The "Rugrats" gang is now approaching their teenage years with all the usual complications and crises in this animated Nick Jr. series that began in 2003. Includes "Brother Can You Spare the Time?," "Tommy Foolery," "The Old and the Restless," and "Bad Kimi." 4 episodes. 95m; DVD. **C:** Voice(s) by Elizabeth Daily; Tara Strong; Nancy Cartwright; Dionne Quan; Mark Crowdy; Cree Summer; Jack Riley; Melanie Chartoff; Michael Bell; Kath Soucie; Joe Alaskey. **A:** Family. **P:** Entertainment. **U:** Home. **Chl-Juv:** Television Series, Family, Animation & Cartoons. **Acq:** Purchase. **Dist:** Paramount Pictures Corp. $16.99.

All Grown Up! R.V. Having Fun Yet? 2005 (Unrated)
The "Rugrats" gang is now approaching their teenage years with all the usual complications and crises in this animated Nick Jr. series that began in 2003. Includes "R.V. Having Fun Yet?," "The Science Pair," and "It's Karma, Dude." 3 episodes. 93m; DVD. **C:** Voice(s) by Elizabeth Daily; Tara Strong; Nancy Cartwright; Dionne Quan; Cheryl Chase; Cree Summer; Jack Riley; Melanie Chartoff; Michael Bell; Kath Soucie; Joe Alaskey. **A:** Family. **P:** Entertainment. **U:** Home. **Mov-Ent:** Television Series, Family, Animation & Cartoons. **Acq:** Purchase. **Dist:** Paramount Pictures Corp. $16.99.

All Grown Up...And Loving It! 2005
The Rugrats are all grown up. When Cupid strikes, Chuckie, Tommy, Dil and the rest of the gang discover that love can be confusing for kids and grownups alike. Part of Nickelodeon's "All Grown Up" television series. 91m; VHS, DVD. **A:** Primary-Family. **P:** Entertainment. **U:** Home. **Chl-Juv:** Animation & Cartoons. **Acq:** Purchase. **Dist:** Paramount Pictures Corp. $19.99.

All Hands on Deck 1961 — ★½
Silly Naval comedy has young Lt. Victor Donald (Boone) assigned to keep crazy sailor Shrieking Eagle Garfield (Hackett)--and his pet turkey--out of trouble. Meanwhile, reporter Sally Hobson (Eden) wants a story, sneaks aboard, and falls for the crooning officer. 98m; DVD. **C:** Pat Boone; Buddy Hackett; Dennis O'Keefe; Warren Berlinger; Gale Gordon; Directed by Norman Taurog; Written by Jay Sommers; Cinematography by Barbara Eden; Leo Tover; Music by Cyril Mockridge. **A:** Jr. High-Adult. **P:** Entertainment. **U:** Home. **L:** English. **Mov-Ent:** Armed Forces--U.S., Birds. **Acq:** Purchase. **Dist:** Fox Home Entertainment.

All Hat 2007 (R) — ★★½
And no particular brains or heart. Hot-head Ray Doakes (Kirby) just got out of prison. He returns to his Ontario hometown to find that lowdown land developer Sonny Stanton (Jenkins), who helped put Ray away, is still up to no good. When an expensive thoroughbred from Stanton's racing stables goes missing, the scumball uses it as an excuse to squeeze the local farmers into selling their property for his golf resort. Only Ray comes up with a plan to stop him. 91m; DVD. **C:** Rachael Leigh Cook; Luke Kirby; Noam Jenkins; Keith Carradine; Ernie Hudson; David Alpay; Graham Greene; Gary Farmer; Lisa Ray; Stephen McHattie; Michelle Nolden; Directed by Leonard Farlinger; Written by Brad Smith; Cinematography by Paul Sarossy; Music by Bill Frisell. **A:** Sr. High-Adult. **P:** Entertainment. **U:** Home. **Mov-Ent:** Canada, Horses. **Acq:** Purchase. **Dist:** Movies Unlimited; Alpha Video.

All Hell Broke Loose 2009 (PG-13) — ★½
Worth a bone just to see Carradine in a western. Ian McHenry was a sharpshooter during the Civil War and becomes a hired gun after the fighting ends. Only he eventually decides to redeem himself by hunting the outlaws he once rode with. 90m; DVD. **C:** David Carradine; Jim Hilton; Jerry Chesser; Alex Daniel; Michael Hilton; Scotty Sparks; Directed by Christopher Forbes; Written by Jim Hilton; Christopher Forbes; Cinematography by Christopher Forbes; Music by Christopher Forbes. **A:** Jr. High-Adult. **P:** Entertainment. **U:** Home. **Mov-Ent:** Western. **Acq:** Purchase. **Dist:** North American Motion Pictures, LLC.

All I Desire 1953 (Unrated) — ★★★½
Estranged wife and mother (Stanwyck) returns to her hometown after fleeing years ago to pursue a stage career. She desires a new beginning with her family, but finds things have changed in her absence. The story examines the will of a strong woman and small town values. Director Sirk disagreed with the happy ending demanded by producers, but the drama is still noteworthy. 80m/B/W; VHS, DVD, CC. **C:** Barbara Stanwyck; Richard Carlson; Lyle Bettger; Maureen O'Sullivan; Directed by Douglas Sirk; Written by James Gunn; Robert Blees; Carl Guthrie; Gina Kaus; Music by Joseph Gershenson. **Pr:** Ross Hunter; Universal Pictures. **A:** Family. **P:** Entertainment. **U:** Home. **Mov-Ent.** **Acq:** Purchase. **Dist:** Universal Studios Home Video. $14.98.

All I See 199?
A young boy and a painter strike up a friendship in this story by Cynthia Rylant. An iconographic presentation of illustrations by Peter Catalanotto. 8m; VHS. **A:** Primary-Jr. High. **P:** Entertainment. **U:** Institution. **Chl-Juv:** Children. **Acq:** Purchase. **Dist:** Facets Multimedia Inc. $33.00.

All I Wanna Do 1998 (PG-13) — ★★½
The students of an exclusive, and financially troubled, East Coast girls' school, circa 1963, are vigorously opposed to the merger of their school with a boys' academy. So they decide to stage a protest strike. Rather typical coming of age tale with a notable cast of up-and-comers. Film was briefly released in 1998 at 110 minutes under the title "Strike" and then re-edited and re-released under its current title in 2000. 94m; VHS, DVD, Wide. **C:** Kirsten Dunst; Gaby Hoffman; Heather Matarazzo; Rachael Leigh Cook; Monica Keena; Merritt Wever; Lynn Redgrave; Vincent Kartheiser; Tom Guiry; Matthew Lawrence; Robert Bockstael; Directed by Sarah Kernochan; Written by Sarah Kernochan; Cinematography by Anthony C. "Tony" Jannelli; Music by Graeme Revell. **Pr:** Ira Deutchman; Peter Newman; Robert Lantos; Andras Hamori; Nora Ephron; Redeemable Features; Alliance Communications Corporation; Miramax Film Corp. **A:** Jr. High-Adult. **P:** Entertainment. **U:** Home. **Mov-Ent:** Education. **Acq:** Purchase. **Dist:** Buena Vista Home Entertainment.

All I Want 2002 (R) — ★★
Jones Dillon (Wood) is a 17-year-old wide-eyed Kansas university freshman who soon decides that dorm life is not for him. So he moves into the boarding house of Ma Mabley (Harry) and is soon pining after a couple of his neighbors--sweet would-be actress Lisa (Moore) and experienced photographer Jane (Potente). Coming of ager hasn't anything new to say but the three leads do well with their limited material. 96m; VHS, DVD, CC. **C:** Elijah Wood; Franka Potente; Mandy Moore; Deborah Harry; Aaron Pearl; Elizabeth Perkins; Directed by Jeffrey Porter; Written by Charles Kephart; Cinematography by Blake T. Evans; Music by Andrew Gross. **A:** Sr. High-Adult. **P:** Entertainment. **U:** Home. **Mov-Ent:** Romance. **Acq:** Purchase. **Dist:** Sony Pictures Home Entertainment Inc.

All I Want for Christmas 1991 (G) — ★★
Low-budget, sappy holiday tale of a young girl (Birch) who wants to reunite her divorced parents. Determined to fulfill her Christmas wish, Hallie seeks out the Santa Claus at Macy's department store to tell him the one thing she truly wants for Christmas. Birch is charming as are Bacall as her grandmother and Nielsen as Santa but the story is too squishy and bland to be believable. 92m; VHS, DVD. **C:** Thora Birch; Leslie Nielsen; Lauren Bacall; Jamey Sheridan; Harley Jane Kozak; Ethan (Randall) Embry; Kevin Nealon; Andrea Martin; Directed by Ron Lieberman; Written by Richard Kramer; Thom Eberhardt; Neal Israel; Gail Parent; Cinematography by Robbie Greenberg; Music by Bruce Broughton. **A:** Family. **P:** Entertainment. **U:** Home. **Mov-Ent:** Comedy-Drama, Family, Christmas. **Acq:** Purchase. **Dist:** Paramount Pictures Corp. $19.95.

All I Want for Christmas 2007 (Unrated) — ★★½
Wanting to help out his overworked, widowed mom Sarah (O'Grady), young Jesse (Pinchak) enters a national contest sponsored by a toy company with an essay about wanting a new husband to take care of his mom. When Jesse wins, it thrusts them into a national spotlight and Sarah just may wind up with the wrong guy. A Hallmark Channel original. 89m; DVD. **C:** Gail O'Grady; Robert Mailhouse; Greg Germann; Amanda

Foreman; Jimmy Pinchak; Bess Meyer; Robert Pine; Directed by Harvey Frost; Written by Marc Rey; Cinematography by Dane Peterson; Music by Stephen Graziano. **A:** Family. **P:** Entertainment. **U:** Home. **Mov-Ent:** Christmas. **Acq:** Purchase. **Dist:** Genius.com Incorporated.

All In 2006 (R) — ★
Alice "Ace" Anderson (Swain) has been raised by her poker-playing father (Madsen) in the world of backstreet gambling. With mounting debts from med school, Ace decides to recruit some fellow students to take on the best players and win at the World Series of Poker. Lame effort with some confusing and unnecessary subplots. ?m; DVD. **C:** Dominique Swain; Michael Madsen; James Russo; Louis Gossett, Jr.; Kristen Miller; Colleen Porch; Scott Whyte; Michelle Lombardo; Chris Backus; Johann Urb; Hayley DuMond; Directed by Nick Vallelonga; Written by Loren Comitor; Cinematography by Jeff Baustert; Music by Harry Manfredini. **A:** Sr. High-Adult. **P:** Entertainment. **U:** Home. **Mov-Ent:** Gambling. **Acq:** Purchase. **Dist:** Bedford Entertainment Inc.

All in a Night's Work 1961 — ★★½
The founder of a one-man publishing empire is found dead with a smile on his face. His nephew inherits the business and finds himself caught in a series of big and small business misunderstandings. He's also falling in love with the woman he suspects was responsible for his uncle's grin. Nicely paced sex and business comedy with warm performances. 94m; DVD. **C:** Dean Martin; Shirley MacLaine; Cliff Robertson; Charlie Ruggles; Directed by Joseph Anthony; Written by Sidney Sheldon; Cinematography by Joseph LaShelle; Music by Andre Previn. **Pr:** Paramount Pictures; Hal Wallis Productions. **A:** Family. **P:** Entertainment. **U:** Home. **L:** English, Spanish. **Mov-Ent:** Comedy--Screwball. **Acq:** Purchase. **Dist:** WarnerArchive.com. $19.95.

All In: Building a Great Football Program 2013 (Unrated)
Coach Jeffrey Steinberg discusses building a successful football program. 61m; DVD. **A:** Family. **P:** Education. **U:** Home. **L:** English. **Spo-Rec:** Athletic Instruction/Coaching, Volleyball, How-To. **Acq:** Purchase. **Dist:** Championship Productions. $39.99.

All-in-One Complete Player Workout 2014 (Unrated)
Basketball coach Lyndsey Fennelly presents a series of workout drills that can be done individually, in teams, or in groups. 57m; DVD. **A:** Family. **P:** Education. **U:** Home. **L:** English. **Spo-Rec:** Athletic Instruction/Coaching, Basketball. **Acq:** Purchase. **Dist:** Championship Productions. $39.99.

All in the Family 3-Pack 1998
Three volume set, with each tape featuring three episodes of the classic television program "All in the Family." Titles include: "In the Family Way," "Archie Meets Meathead" and "Sammy Takes Bunker Hill." 75m; VHS. **A:** Jr. High-Adult. **P:** Entertainment. **U:** Home. **Mov-Ent.** **Acq:** Purchase. **Dist:** Sony Pictures Home Entertainment Inc. $29.85.

All in the Family 20th Anniversary Special 1991
A hilarious, loving tribute to one of the most important, groundbreaking television programs of all time. In addition to scenes from the show's most memorable moments, the original cast members offer their views on the characters they portrayed. Also, an assortment of viewers give their opinions on the show's effect on the general public. Originally aired on CBS February 16, 1991. 74m; VHS, CC. **C:** Carroll O'Connor; Jean Stapleton; Rob Reiner; Sally Struthers; Hosted by Norman Lear; Directed by David S. Jackson; Written by David S. Jackson. **Pr:** Norman Lear; Norman Lear; Act III Productions; Columbia Pictures Television. **A:** Jr. High-Adult. **P:** Entertainment. **U:** Home. **Mov-Ent:** TV Movies, Family, Prejudice. **Acq:** Purchase. **Dist:** Sony Pictures Home Entertainment Inc.; Fusion Video. $14.95.

All in the Family: Fan Favorites 1971 (Unrated)
CBS 1971-79 family sitcom. Working-class family man Archie Bunker has a bigoted and conservative view on the world and isn't afraid to share it. Includes "The Blockbuster," "The Insurance is Canceled," "Christmas Day at the Bunkers," "The Man in the Street," "Cousin Maude's Visit," "Edith's Problem," "The Elevator Story," and "Archie and the FBI." 192m; DVD. **C:** Carroll O'Connor; Jean Stapleton; Rob Reiner; Sally Struthers. **A:** Family. **P:** Entertainment. **U:** Home. **Mov-Ent:** Family, Television Series. **Acq:** Purchase. **Dist:** Sony Pictures Home Entertainment Inc. $14.99.

All in the Family: In the Family Way 1998
Part of the "TV Screen Gems" line, this video contains three episodes of the classic television comedy "All in the Family." Episodes include: "Gloria's Pregnancy," "The First and Last Supper" and "The Bunkers and the Swingers." 75m; VHS. **A:** Jr. High-Adult. **P:** Entertainment. **U:** Home. **Mov-Ent.** **Acq:** Purchase. **Dist:** Sony Pictures Home Entertainment Inc. $9.95.

All in the Family: The Complete Fifth Season 2006 (Unrated)
Features the fifth season of the 1971-1979 family television sitcom with grumpy, strong-willed, and politically-incorrect patriarch Archie (O'Connor), his loyal, good-natured, yet somewhat flighty wife Edith (Stapleton), their feminist daughter Gloria (Struthers), and her socially and politically conscious husband Michael (Reiner)?or, as Archie dubs him, Meathead. Includes: the Bunkers struggle when Archie's union is on strike in a four-part arc, Lionel stays with the Bunkers when his father, George Jefferson, goes on a rant when Lionel wants to marry a bi-racial girl who has a white father, and in a three-parter Archie winds up missing which stresses the family and makes Edith doubt his fidelity. 24 episodes. 620m; DVD. **C:** Carroll O'Connor; Jean Stapleton; Rob Reiner; Sally Struthers. **A:** Family. **P:** Entertainment. **U:** Home. **Mov-Ent:** Television Series, Family. **Acq:** Purchase. **Dist:** Sony Pictures Home Entertainment Inc. $29.95.

All in the Family: The Complete First Season 1971
This groundbreaking comedy follows the Bunker family as they navigate topics such as politics, sex, and race. Archie Bunker makes no excuses for his bigoted opinions. His wife Edith is sweet and unintelligent. Their daughter Gloria and son-in-law Michael are liberal-minded activists. In "Meet the Bunkers", Archie and Edith celebrate their wedding anniversary, Mike and Archie write opposing letters to President Nixon in "Writing the President," Archie suffers whiplash in "Oh, My Aching Back," Archie donates blood in "Archie Gives Blood," and in "Judging Books By Covers," Mike and Gloria defend their gay friend. 13 episodes. 338m; DVD. **C:** Rob Reiner. **A:** Family. **P:** Entertainment. **U:** Home. **Mov-Ent:** Television Series. **Acq:** Purchase. **Dist:** Sony Electronics Inc. $39.95.

All in the Family: The Complete Fourth Season 2005
Includes the fourth season of the classic 1970s television comedy known for addressing social issues of the day with cranky, socially intolerant Archie Bunker (O'Connor) and his naive-yet-warm-hearted wife Edith (Stapleton), along with daughter Gloria (Struthers) and her liberal husband Mike (Reiner); Archie is rankled when a Mexican family moves in the area, Gloria discovers she has breast cancer, and the Bunkers rekindle their romance as they celebrate their 25th anniversary. 608m; DVD. **A:** Family. **P:** Entertainment. **U:** Home. **Mov-Ent:** Television, Family. **Acq:** Purchase. **Dist:** Sony Pictures Home Entertainment Inc. $29.95.

All in the Family: The Complete Second Season 2003 (Unrated)
Features the second season of the 1971-1979 family television sitcom with grumpy, strong-willed, and politically-incorrect patriarch Archie (O'Connor), his loyal, good-natured, yet somewhat flighty wife Edith (Stapleton), their feminist daughter Gloria (Struthers), and her socially and politically conscious husband Michael (Reiner)?or, as Archie dubs him, Meathead. Includes: Gloria sets Archie off by wanting to pose nude and for a Hungarian artist no less, the family recalls Archie's reaction to first meeting Mike on the couple's first anniversary, Edith coaxes Archie into talking to Mike about his temporary impotency, and Archie takes an extra job driving a taxi and winds up with Sammy Davis Jr. as a passenger which triggers his inner bigot. 24 episodes. 528m; DVD. **C:** Carroll O'Connor; Jean Stapleton; Rob Reiner; Sally Struthers. **A:** Family. **P:** Entertainment. **U:** Home. **Mov-Ent:** Television Series, Family. **Acq:** Purchase. **Dist:** Sony Pictures Home Entertainment Inc. $29.95.

All in the Family: The Complete Sixth Season 2007 (Unrated)
Features the sixth season of the 1971-1979 family television sitcom with grumpy, strong-willed, and politically-incorrect patriarch Archie (O'Connor), his loyal, good-natured, yet somewhat flighty wife Edith (Stapleton), their feminist daughter Gloria (Struthers), and her socially and politically conscious husband Michael (Reiner)?or, as Archie dubs him, Meathead. Includes: on the day that Gloria and Mike prepare to leave the Bunker house for their own home Gloria finds out she's pregnant and Mike isn't overjoyed at the news, Edith's volunteerism makes Archie feel lonely and he demands she quit though she refuses, and while Gloria is having her baby her parents create a scene at the hospital. 24 episodes. 612m; DVD. **C:** Carroll O'Connor; Jean Stapleton; Rob Reiner; Sally Struthers. **A:** Family. **P:** Entertainment. **U:** Home. **Mov-Ent:** Television Series, Family. **Acq:** Purchase. **Dist:** Sony Pictures Home Entertainment Inc. $29.95.

All in the Family: The Complete Third Season 2004 (Unrated)
Features the third season of the 1971-1979 family television sitcom with grumpy, strong-willed, and politically-incorrect patriarch Archie (O'Connor), his loyal, good-natured, yet somewhat flighty wife Edith (Stapleton), their feminist daughter Gloria (Struthers), and her socially and politically conscious husband Michael (Reiner)?or, as Archie dubs him, Meathead. Includes: Archie and Mike argue about gun control, Archie's racism is in full swing when his niece has a thing for their black neighbors' son Lionel, Archie orders a new TV using insurance money from Edith's missing jewelry only to have the insurance adjuster pop by the house, and Archie is surprised to find out a hospital roommate he's been talking to is black. 24 episodes. 610m; DVD. **C:** Carroll O'Connor; Jean Stapleton; Rob Reiner; Sally Struthers. **A:** Family. **P:** Entertainment. **U:** Home. **Mov-Ent:** Television Series, Family. **Acq:** Purchase. **Dist:** Sony Pictures Home Entertainment Inc. $29.95.

All in the Genes 19??
Documentary of genetic science in medicine and its effect on humankind. Presents genetics breakthroughs, such as cloning, the benefits, and the dangers that some scientists and people feel may be forthcoming. 52m; VHS. **A:** Adult. **P:** Education. **U:** Home. **Gen-Edu:** Documentary Films, Genetics, Science. **Acq:** Purchase, Rent/Lease. **Dist:** Filmakers Library Inc. $350.

All in the Morning Early: A Scottish Folktale 1969
In this traditional Scottish accumulative counting rhyme, Sandy sets forth on an errand "all in the morning early" and meets many amiable companions along the way. Adapted from Sorche Nic Leodhas's book. 11m; VHS, 3/4 U. **Pr:** Stephen Bosustow. **A:** Primary. **P:** Education. **U:** Institution, SURA. **Chl-Juv:** Folklore & Legends, Scotland. **Acq:** Purchase. **Dist:** Phoenix Learning Group.

All in the Same Boat 19??
In this long range cruising videotape, a couple build their own ocean cruiser and takes their children on a trip around the world. 49m; VHS. **A:** Adult. **P:** Entertainment. **U:** Home. **Spo-Rec:** Boating. **Acq:** Purchase. **Dist:** Bennett Marine Video. $29.95.

All Is But a Beginning 1972
This two-lesson sequence represents an autobiography in conversation with Dr. John G. Neihardt, poet Laureate of the State of Nebraska; author of "Black Elk Speaks,"" The Death of Crazy Horse," and others. In two untitled programs. 30m; 3/4 U, EJ. **Pr:** NETCHE. **A:** College-Adult. **P:** Education. **U:** Institution, CCTV, BCTV, SURA. **Gen-Edu:** Literature--English. **Acq:** Purchase, Rent/Lease, Subscription. **Dist:** NETCHE.

All is Lost 2013 (PG-13) — ★★★
Devastating in its brutal lack of Hollywoodization, writer/director Chandor's drama captures what it must really be like to be trapped alone with a seemingly inevitable death coming soon. A nameless man (played perfectly by Redford) is forced to deal with water, sun, and sharks when his boat is struck by a drifting cargo container in a sailing trip far from shore. With only about 45 seconds of dialogue, Chandor and Redford have crafted a film that desperately displays a portrait of human struggle against its most notable enemy, Mother Nature. Redford proves he still has the acting chops in a performance that feels completely real. 106m; DVD, Blu-Ray. **C:** Robert Redford; Directed by J.C. Chandor; Written by J.C. Chandor; Cinematography by Frank DeMarco; Peter Zuccarini; Music by Alex Ebert. **Pr:** Neal Dodson; Anna Gerb; Justin Nappi; Teddy Schwarzman; Lions Gate Entertainment Inc; Black Bear. **A:** Sr. High-Adult. **P:** Entertainment. **U:** Home. **L:** English. **Mov-Ent:** Boating, Men. **Awds:** Golden Globes '14: Orig. Score. **Acq:** Purchase. **Dist:** Lions Gate Home Entertainment.

All is Well on the Border Front 1997
Explores issues of representation within the occupied zone of South Lebanon through staged interviews with Lebanese prisoners. Subtitled in English. 43m; VHS. **A:** Adult. **P:** Education. **U:** Institution, BCTV. **L:** Arabic. **Gen-Edu:** Documentary Films, Middle East. **Acq:** Purchase, Rent/Lease. **Dist:** Arab Film Distribution. $150.00.

All Men Are Brothers 1975 (Unrated) — ★★
Based on the book of the same name, and a sequel to 'The Water Margin'. The 108 rebels from the original film are pardoned by the Emperor, and asked by him to find a way for his armies to enter a fortress that has been commandeered by a rebel army. 102m; DVD, Blu-Ray. **C:** David Chiang; Lung Ti; Betty Chung; Kuan Tai Chen; Directed by Cheh Chang; Ma Wu; Written by Cheh Chang; Kuang Ni; Guanzhong Luo; Cinematography by Han Le Kuang; Music by Yung-Yu Chen. **A:** Sr. High-Adult. **P:** Entertainment. **U:** Home. **Mov-Ent:** Martial Arts. **Acq:** Purchase. **Dist:** Well Go USA, Inc. $14.98.

All Mine to Give 1956 — ★★½
Sad saga of a Scottish family of eight who braved frontier hardships, epidemics, and death in the Wisconsin wilderness more than a century ago. Midway through, mom and dad die, leaving the oldest child struggling to keep the family together. A strange, though often effective, combination of pioneer adventures and tearjerking moments that avoids becoming hopelessly soapy due to fine performances. Unless you're pretty weathered, you'll need some hankies. Based on the reminiscences of Dale and Katherine Eunson as detailed in a "Cosmopolitan" magazine article. 102m; VHS, DVD. **C:** Glynis Johns; Cameron Mitchell; Rex Thompson; Patty McCormack; Ernest Truex; Hope Emerson; Alan Hale, Jr.; Royal Dano; Reta Shaw; Rita Johnson; Ellen Corby; Jon(athan) Provost; Directed by Allen Reisner; Music by Max Steiner. **Pr:** RKO. **A:** Family. **P:** Entertainment. **U:** Home. **Mov-Ent:** Melodrama, Homeless, Wilderness Areas. **Acq:** Purchase. **Dist:** Turner Broadcasting System Inc.

All My Friends: Celebrating the Songs & Voice of Gregg Allman 2014 (Unrated)
Various musical performers pay tribute to well-known rock artist Gregg Allman. 161m; DVD, Blu-Ray. **A:** Jr. High-Adult. **P:** Entertainment. **U:** Home. **L:** English. **Gen-Edu:** Music--Performance, Music--Pop/Rock. **Acq:** Purchase. **Dist:** Rounder Records Corp. $24.98 19.98.

All My Good Countrymen 1968 — ★★½
A lyrical, funny film about the eccentric denizens of a small Moravian village soon after the socialization of Czechoslovakia in 1948. Completed during the Soviet invasion of 1968 and immediately banned. In Czech with English subtitles. 115m; VHS, DVD. **C:** Vladimir Mensik; Radoslav Brozobohaty; Pavel Pavlovsky; Directed by Vojtech Jasny. **Pr:** Vojtech Jasny; Vojtech Jasny. **A:** Jr. High-Adult. **P:** Entertainment. **U:** Home. **L:** Czech. **Mov-Ent:** Comedy-Drama. **Awds:** Cannes '69: Director (Jasny). **Acq:** Purchase. **Dist:** Facets Multimedia Inc. $59.95.

All My Loved Ones 2000 (Unrated) — ★★
Moving fictionalized account by director Minac of his mother's recollections of being one of nearly 700 Czech Jewish children saved in the Kindertransport trains. Briton Nicholas Winton (Graves) is on holiday in Prague in 1938; recognizing the worsening situation for the Jews in Czechoslovakia, he discovers that both Sweden and Britain are willing to take in child refugees if he can transport them out of the country. One of these potential transportees is 10-year-old David (Holicek), a member of a weathy family who fail to recognize the seriousness of their situation. Czech with subtitles. 91m; VHS, DVD. **C:** Rupert Graves; Libuse Safrankova; Josef Abrham; Jiri Bartoska; Brano Holicek; Jiri Menzel; Directed by Matej Minac; Written by Jiri Hubac; Cinematography by Dodo Simoncic;

Music by Janusz Stoklosa. **A:** College-Adult. **P:** Entertainment. **U:** Home. **L:** Czech. **Mov-Ent**: Judaism. **Acq:** Purchase. **Dist:** Wellspring Media.

All My Sons 1948 (Unrated) — ★★★
Joe Keller (Robinson) is a small-town manufacturer enjoying the profits he made from his WWII contracts. But his family is pulled apart by guilt and shame when son Chris (Lancaster) discovers his father sold defective parts to the military that resulted in loss of life and then covered up the crime. Excellent performances; adapted from the play by Arthur Miller. Remade in 1986 with James Whitmore and Aidan Quinn. 94m/B/W; VHS. **C:** Edward G. Robinson; Burt Lancaster; Mady Christians; Louisa Horton; Howard Duff; Frank Conroy; Arlene Francis; Harry (Henry) Morgan; Directed by Irving Reis; Written by Chester Erskine; Cinematography by Russell Metty; Music by Randall Keith Horton. **Pr:** Chester Erskine; Chester Erskine; Universal International. **A:** Jr. High-Adult. **P:** Entertainment. **U:** Home. **Mov-Ent**: Suicide. **Acq:** Purchase.

All My Sons 1986 — ★★★
A wealthy family is distraught when their eldest son is listed as missing-in-action during WWII. They must cope with guilt, as well as grief, because the father's business reaped profits from the war. Adapted from the acclaimed Arthur Miller play. 122m; VHS. **C:** James Whitmore; Aidan Quinn; Joan Allen; Michael Learned; Directed by John Power. **Pr:** Brandman Productions. **A:** Jr. High-Adult. **P:** Entertainment. **U:** Home. **Mov-Ent**: TV Movies. **Acq:** Purchase. **Dist:** $39.95.

All New Adventures of Laurel and Hardy: For Love or Mummy 1998 (PG) — ★★½
Stan Laurel (Pinchot) and Oliver Hardy (Sartain) are the equally bumbling nephews of the original comedic duo. The would-be movers are hired to transport an Egyptian mummy to an American museum, where archeologist Leslie (Danford) is the unwitting object of an ancient curse that fortells her marrying the reanimated corpse. 84m; VHS, DVD. **C:** Bronson Pinchot; Gailard Sartain; F. Murray Abraham; Susan Danford; Directed by John R. Cherry, III; Larry Harmon. **A:** Family. **P:** Entertainment. **U:** Home. **Mov-Ent**: Comedy--Slapstick. **Acq:** Purchase. **Dist:** Monarch Home Video.

All-New Fly Casting Techniques 1989
A new approach to fly casting is explained by world-class fly fisherman, Lefty Kreh. 36m; VHS. **Pr:** Outdoor Safari International. **A:** Jr. High-Adult. **P:** Instruction. **U:** Home. **Spo-Rec**: Fishing. **Acq:** Purchase. **Dist:** Bennett Marine Video. $39.95.

The All New Not-So-Great Moments in Sports 1988
Another compilation of nonsensical blunders in various professional sports arenas. 56m; VHS. **Pr:** HBO. **A:** Family. **P:** Entertainment. **U:** Home. **Spo-Rec**: Sports--General, Outtakes & Bloopers. **Acq:** Purchase. **Dist:** Reader's Digest Home Video. $14.98.

The All-New Super Friends Hour: Season 1, Volume 1 1977
The SuperFriends are joined by Wonder Twins Zan and Jayna from the planet Exxor. Professor Fearo takes revenge on the Academy of Science for expelling him in "Will the World Collide?" Professor Comstock needs a "Time Rescue" when his time machine takes him 2000 years in the future to a desert planet of slaves. Floridians are being turned into green leafy vegetable beings in "Day of the Plant Creatures" after a meteor lands in an Everglades swamp. 7 episodes. 352m; DVD. **C:** Voice(s) by Kathy Garver; Norman Alden; Olan Soule; Jack Angel; Michael Bell. **A:** Family. **P:** Entertainment. **U:** Home. **Chl-Juv**: Animation & Cartoons, Action-Adventure. **Acq:** Purchase. **Dist:** Warner Home Video, Inc.

The All-New Super Friends Hour: Volume Two 2005 (Unrated)
From the DC Comics series "Justice League of America" are superheroes Superman, Batman & Robin, Aquaman, and Wonder Woman, among others, who battle against the Legion of Doom. 16 episodes. 365m; DVD. **C:** Voice(s) by Norman Alden; Jack Angel; Michael Bell; Kathy Garver; William Woodson; Danny Dark; Shannon Farnon; Casey Kasem; Buster Jones; Olan Soule; Michael Rye; Liberty Williams. **A:** Family. **P:** Entertainment. **U:** Home. **Mov-Ent**: Television Series, Animation & Cartoons, Action-Adventure. **Acq:** Purchase. **Dist:** Warner Home Video, Inc. $26.99.

The All New Trollies Musical Adventure 1993
When the Trouble Trollies plot sadness and misery for the fun-loving Trollie friends, R.T., Cherry, Olaf, and the others protect their forest. Filled with the delightful songs children love to sing. ?m; VHS. **A:** Primary. **P:** Entertainment. **U:** Home. **Chl-Juv**: Animation & Cartoons, Music--Children. **Acq:** Purchase. **Dist:** Inspired Corp. $12.98.

All Night 1918 (Unrated) — ★★
A rare comedy starring newcomer Valentino. Struggling William and Maude Harcourt invite young friends Richard and Elizabeth to a dinner party, with the Harcourts pretending to be servants since their own hired help have walked out. But the joke is on them when millionaire Bradford suddenly decides to take the Harcourts up on a previous invitation. So they have Richard and Elizabeth host instead and Bradford is so charmed by the faux-Harcourts that it causes more trouble, including a quite suggestive bedroom scene. 57m/B/W; Silent; DVD. **C:** Rudolph Valentino; Carmel Myers; Charles Dorian; Mary Warren; William J. Dyer; Wadsworth Harris; Directed by Paul Powell; Written by Edgar Franklin; Fred Myton. **A:** Sr. High-Adult. **P:** Entertainment. **U:** Home. **Mov-Ent**: Silent Films. **Acq:** Purchase. **Dist:** Movies Unlimited.

All Night Long 1962 (Unrated) — ★★
Brit jazz version of Shakespeare's "Othello." Black pianist/band leader Aurelius Rex (Harris) is married to white, now-retired singer Delia (Stevens). They are celebrating their anniversary in a London club where ambitious drummer Johnny (McGoohan) is determined to cause trouble. If he can break them up and get Delia back singing, he can secure a contract for his own group and so the lies begin. 91m/B/W; DVD. **C:** Patrick McGoohan; Paul Harris; Marti Stevens; Keith Michell; Richard Attenborough; Betsy Blair; Bernard Braden; Directed by Basil Dearden; Written by Paul Jarrico; Nel King; Cinematography by Edward (Ted) Scaife; Music by Philip Green. **A:** Sr. High-Adult. **P:** Entertainment. **U:** Home. **Mov-Ent**: Nightclubs, Music--Jazz. **Acq:** Purchase. **Dist:** Criterion Collection Inc.

All Night Long 1981 (R) — ★★★
Offbeat middle-age crisis comedy about a burned-out and recently demoted drugstore executive in L.A. who leaves his wife, takes up with his fourth cousin by marriage, and begins a humorous rebellion, becoming an extremely freelance inventor while joining the drifters, weirdos and thieves of the night. An obscure, sometimes uneven little gem with Hackman in top form and an appealing supporting performance by Streisand. Highlighted by delightful malapropisms and sataric inversion of the usual cliches. 100m; VHS, DVD. **C:** Gene Hackman; Barbra Streisand; Diane Ladd; Dennis Quaid; Kevin Dobson; William Daniels; Directed by Jean-Claude Tramont; Written by W.D. Richter; Music by Ira Newborn. **Pr:** Mark Huffam. **A:** Sr. High-Adult. **P:** Entertainment. **U:** Home. **Mov-Ent**: Comedy--Romantic. **Acq:** Purchase. **Dist:** Movies Unlimited; Universal Studios Home Video. $14.95.

All Night Long/Smile Please 1924
Two classic comedies by the most overlooked of the great silent clowns, both produced by slapstick progenitor Mack Sennett. 66m/B/W; Silent; VHS. **C:** Harry Langdon; Natalie Kingston; Jack Cooper; Alberta Vaughn. **Pr:** Mack Sennett. **A:** Family. **P:** Entertainment. **U:** Home. **Mov-Ent**: Comedy--Slapstick, Silent Films. **Acq:** Purchase. **Dist:** Image Entertainment Inc. $24.95.

All Nothing: Tout Rien 19??
Purports that man's urge to dominate nature has led to destroying it. 10m; VHS. **A:** Sr. High-Adult. **P:** Education. **U:** Home. **Gen-Edu**. **Acq:** Purchase. **Dist:** Direct Cinema Ltd. $24.95.

All of Me 1984 (PG) — ★★½
A wealthy woman (Tomlin) dies and her guru accidentally transfers her soul to the right side of her lawyer's body, a modern version of existential hell. Lawyer Martin indulges in some funny slapstick as he discovers that his late client is waging an internal war for control of his body. Flat and cliched at times, but redeemed by the inspired clowning of Martin and witty Martin/Tomlin repartee. Based on the novel "Me Too" by Ed Davis. 93m; VHS, DVD. **C:** Steve Martin; Lily Tomlin; Victoria Tennant; Madolyn Smith; Richard Libertini; Dana Elcar; Selma Diamond; Jason Bernard; Eric Christmas; Peggy (Margaret) Feury; Directed by Carl Reiner; Written by Phil Alden Robinson; Cinematography by Richard H. Kline; Music by Patrick Williams. **Pr:** Mark Huffam. **A:** Jr. High-Adult. **P:** Entertainment. **U:** Home. **Mov-Ent**: Comedy--Slapstick, Death. **Awds:** N.Y. Film Critics '84: Actor (Martin); Natl. Soc. Film Critics '84: Actor (Martin). **Acq:** Purchase. **Dist:** Facets Multimedia Inc. $19.98.

All of Our Lives 1984
A celebration of elderly women who have achieved much despite their situation, banding together to fight for senior citizen's rights. 29m; VHS, 3/4 U. **Pr:** Laura Sky; NFBC. **A:** Sr. High-Adult. **P:** Education. **U:** Institution. **Gen-Edu**: Women, Aging. **Acq:** Purchase, Rent/Lease. **Dist:** National Safety Council, California Chapter, Film Library; Filmakers Library Inc.

All of Us 2003
Examines efforts being made to keep the disabled involved and participating in their communities. Explores the benefits of group homes as an alternative to traditional institutions for the disabled. 28m; VHS. **A:** Adult. **P:** Vocational. **U:** Institution. **Hea-Sci**: Handicapped, Medical Care, Occupational Training. **Acq:** Purchase. **Dist:** Aquarius Health Care Media. $125.00.

All of Us and AIDS 1988
Nine teenagers made this video which contains information about how NOT to get AIDS and discussions about sexual decisions, conflicting attitudes and personal fears. A challenging, assertive AIDS education program. 30m; VHS, 3/4 U. **Pr:** Peer Education Health Resources. **A:** Jr. High-Adult. **P:** Education. **U:** Institution, SURA. **Gen-Edu**: AIDS, Adolescence. **Acq:** Purchase. **Dist:** New Day Films Library.

All of Us: Talking Together 1999
Presents a sex education course geared for developmentally disabled youth. Covers reproductive anatomy, pregnancy, contraception, disease prevention, the difference between love and friendship, and public/private behavior. Available in Spanish version. 24m; VHS. **A:** Jr. High-Sr. High. **P:** Education. **U:** Institution. **Hea-Sci**: Learning Disabilities, Sex & Sexuality, Health Education. **Acq:** Purchase. **Dist:** Aquarius Health Care Media. $195.00.

All or Nothing 2002 (R) — ★★
A depressing tale about depressed and desperate people set in a grotty housing project in South London. Hangdog minicab driver Phil (Spall) can't even earn a decent wage to support his family, cashier common-law wife Penny (Manville), and their layabout son Rory (Corden) and misfit daughter Rachel (Garland). Their neighbors aren't any better off—stuck with abusive boyfriends, unplanned pregnancy, alcoholism, and the general dreariness of their daily lives. Leigh is known for his slice-of-life dramas but this just stays one-dimensional. 128m; VHS, DVD. **C:** Timothy Spall; Lesley Manville; Alison Garland; James Corden; Paul Jesson; Ruth Sheen; Marion Bailey; Sally Hawkins; Ben Crompton; Helen Coker; Daniel Mays; Directed by Mike Leigh; Written by Mike Leigh; Cinematography by Dick Pope; Music by Andrew Dickson. **Pr:** Simon Channing-Williams; Alain Sarde; Thin Man; United Artists. **A:** College-Adult. **P:** Entertainment. **U:** Home. **Mov-Ent**: Poverty. **Acq:** Purchase. **Dist:** MGM Home Entertainment.

All or Nothing at All 1993 (Unrated) — ★★
Leo Hopkins (Laurie) is a charming con man with a successful career and a wife and kids. He's also a gambling addict who can't help living life on the edge, until he finds himself about to fall off. 150m; DVD. **C:** Hugh Laurie; Bob Monkhouse; Pippa Guard; Caroline Quentin; Jessica Turner; Steve Steen; Phyllida Law; Directed by Andrew Grieve; Written by Guy Andrews. **A:** Sr. High-Adult. **P:** Entertainment. **U:** Home. **Mov-Ent**: Gambling. **Acq:** Purchase. **Dist:** Video Collectibles.

All Orientals Look the Same 1986
This tape confronts the prejudices and inconsistencies of the title phrase through the use of experimental images of Asians. 2m; VHS, 3/4 U. **Pr:** Valerie Soe. **A:** Jr. High-Adult. **P:** Education. **U:** Institution, SURA. **Gen-Edu**: Asia. **Acq:** Rent/Lease. **Dist:** Video Out Distribution; Women Make Movies.

All Our Children 1991
Bill Moyers takes a look at the state of education in the US, where up to 800,000 students leave school early or lack the skills needed to compete. 90m; VHS, CC, 3/4 U. **C:** Hosted by Bill Moyers. **Pr:** Public Affairs Television. **A:** College-Adult. **P:** Education. **U:** Institution, CCTV, CATV, SURA. **Gen-Edu**: Documentary Films, Education, Children. **Acq:** Purchase, Rent/Lease, Duplication License, Off-Air Record. **Dist:** PBS Home Video. $39.95.

. . .All Our Lives 1986
A personal history of the Spanish Civil War as remembered by several women who actively participated in the revolution. English subtitles. 54m; VHS, 3/4 U. **TV Std:** NTSC, PAL, SECAM. **Pr:** Lisa Berger. **A:** Jr. High-Adult. **P:** Education. **U:** Institution, SURA. **L:** English, Spanish. **Gen-Edu**: Spain, Women. **Acq:** Purchase, Rent/Lease. **Dist:** The Cinema Guild.

All Our Sons: Fallen Heroes of 9/11 2003 (Unrated)
Profiles twelve African American firefighters who were victims in the World Trade Center attacks September 11, 2001. 28m; DVD. **A:** Adult. **P:** Education. **U:** Institution. **Gen-Edu**: U.S. States, World Affairs. **Acq:** Purchase. **Dist:** Third World Newsreel. $59.95.

All Out 1975
A Christian video that probes the psychodynamics of selling one's soul. Theme: dehumanizing effects of greed. 27m; VHS, 3/4 U, Special order formats. **C:** Bob Hastings; Nan Martin. **Pr:** Paulist Productions. **A:** Sr. High-Adult. **P:** Religious. **U:** Institution, CCTV, SURA. **Gen-Edu**: Religion. **Acq:** Purchase, Rent/Lease. **Dist:** Paulist Productions.

All Over Me 1996 (R) — ★★★
Teen angst/coming of age set in New York's Hell's Kitchen. Ungainly wanna-be guitarist, 15-year-old Claudia-AKA-Claude (Folland), is best friends with flirty blonde Ellen (Subkoff). But their relationship changes when Ellen begins dating the macho older Mark (Hauser) and is soon into sex and drugs, while Claude's sexual quandries lead her to a lesbian bar and an interest in singer Lucy (Hailey). Good performances but a moody and somewhat awkward first feature from Sichel, whose sister wrote the screenplay. 90m; VHS, DVD. **C:** Alison Folland; Tara Subkoff; Cole Hauser; Wilson Cruz; Leisha Hailey; Pat Briggs; Ann Dowd; Directed by Alex Sichel; Written by Sylvia Sichel; Cinematography by Joe DeSalvo; Music by Miki Navazio. **Pr:** Dolly Hall; Andreas Buhler; Stephen X. Graham; Nina M. Benton; Medusa Pictures; Fine Line Features. **A:** Sr. High-Adult. **P:** Entertainment. **U:** Home. **Mov-Ent**: Adolescence. **Acq:** Purchase. **Dist:** New Line Home Video.

All Over the Guy 2001 (R) — ★★½
Writer/director Roos served as executive producer on this film, which re-unites some of the personnel from his hit "The Opposite of Sex." Unfortunately, the quality of that film isn't reproduced here. Eli (writer Bucatinsky adapted from his play) and Tom (Ruccolo) are two gay men who are set up on a blind date by Brett (Goldberg) and Jackie (Alexander). They don't really get along, but they find themselves very attracted to one another. The film then explores the ups and downs of their courtship, as each tries to deal with the baggage from the past which keeps them from succeeding in the present. The problem is it's incredibly unoriginal. There doesn't seem to be any real chemistry between the couple, so whether or not they stay together may become a moot point to some viewers. Some of the performances are good (Goldberg has some good lines), but Ruccolo looks very uncomfortable at times. 95m; VHS, DVD, Wide. **C:** Dan Bucatinsky; Richard Ruccolo; Adam Goldberg; Sasha Alexander; Doris Roberts; Andrea Martin; Tony Abatemarco; Joanna Kerns; Nicolas Surovy; Christina Ricci; Lisa Kudrow; Directed by Julie Davis; Written by Dan Bucatinsky; Cinematography by Goran Paviceric; Music by Peter Stuart; Andrew Williams. **Pr:** Lions Gate Films. **A:** Sr. High-Adult. **P:** Entertainment. **U:** Home. **Mov-Ent**: Comedy--Romantic. **Acq:** Purchase. **Dist:** Movies Unlimited; Alpha Video. $24.99.

All Over Town 1937 — ★★½
Two vaudevillians with a trained seal find themselves involved in a murder when they are kidnapped by a gang of thugs. A lesser Olsen and Johnson comedy with scattered funny moments. 52m/B/W; VHS, DVD. **C:** Ole Olsen; Chic Johnson; Mary Howard; Franklin Pangborn; James Finlayson; Directed by James W. Horne; Written by Jack Townley; Jerome Chodorov. **Pr:** Republic Pictures. **A:** Family. **P:** Entertainment.

U: Home. **Mov-Ent:** Comedy--Slapstick. **Acq:** Purchase. **Dist:** Movies Unlimited; Alpha Video. $19.95.

All Passion Spent 1986 (Unrated) — ★★½
BBC TV production based on Vita Sackville-West's 1931 novel. After the death of her politically prominent husband, 85-year-old Lady Slane no longer wishes to be part of London society. Ignoring her children's expectations, she moves to a cottage in the country and intends to do as she pleases and keep company with only those people she likes (which doesn't include most of her family). 158m; DVD. **C:** Wendy Hiller; Harry Andrews; Maurice Denham; Jane Snowden; Eileen Way; David Waller; Directed by Martyn Friend; Written by Peter Buckman; Cinematography by Trevor Wimlett; Music by Nigel Hess. **A:** Adult. **P:** Entertainment. **U:** Home. **L:** English. **Mov-Ent:** Aging, Family. **Acq:** Purchase. **Dist:** Acorn Media Group Inc.

All Power to the People! 199?
Documentary featuring the establishment of the 1960s civil rights movement. Includes activism by The Black Panther Party, Martin Luther King, Malcolm X, Fred Hamptom, and others. 115m; VHS. **A:** Adult. **P:** Education. **U:** Home. **Gen-Edu:** Documentary Films, Black Culture, Civil Rights. **Acq:** Purchase, Rent/Lease. **Dist:** Filmakers Library Inc. $350.

All Pro 1981
A new motivational film with conversations with five top all pros. They discuss their careers and the traits that make a top professional. 29m; VHS, 3/4 U. **Pr:** Cally Curtis. **A:** Adult. **P:** Instruction. **U:** Institution, SURA. **Bus-Ind:** Sales Training. **Acq:** Purchase, Rent/Lease. **Dist:** Aspen Publishers, Inc.

All-Pro Punting Techniques 1992
Ray Pelfrey and Steve Hoffman propel you to kicking excellence by teaching you the techniques and fundamentals of this gridiron art. Learn the proper stance and alignment, as well as kicking strategies to put your opponent at a great disadvantage. 90m; VHS. **A:** Jr. High-Sr. High. **P:** Instruction. **U:** Institution, Home. **Spo-Rec:** Football. **Acq:** Purchase. **Dist:** Cambridge Educational. $69.50.

All Quiet on the Western Front 1930 — ★★★★
Extraordinary and realistic anti-war epic based on the novel by Erich Maria Remarque. Seven patriotic German youths go together from school to the battlefields of WWI. They experience the horrors of war first-hand, stuck in the trenches and facing gradual extermination. Centers on experiences of one of the young men, Paul Baumer, who changes from enthusiastic war endorser to battle-weary veteran in an emotionally exact performance by Ayres. Boasts a gigantic budget (for the time) of $1.25 million, and features more than 2000 extras swarming about battlefields set up on ranchland in California. Relentless anti-war message is emotionally draining and startling with both graphic shots and haunting visual poetry. Extremely controversial in the U.S. and Germany upon release, the original version was 140 minutes long (some versions are available with restored footage) and featured ZaSu Pitts as Ayres mother (later reshot with Mercer replacing her). Remarque, who had fought and been wounded on the Western Front, was eventually forced to leave Germany for the U.S. due to the film's ongoing controversy. 103m/B/W; VHS, DVD, Blu-Ray. **TV Std:** NTSC, PAL. **C:** Lew Ayres; Louis Wolheim; John Wray; Slim Summerville; Russell Gleason; Raymond Griffith; Ben Alexander; Beryl Mercer; Arnold Lucy; William "Billy" Bakewell; Scott Kolk; Owen Davis, Jr.; Walter Rodgers; Richard Alexander; Harold Goodwin; G. Pat Collins; Edmund Breese; Directed by Lewis Milestone; Written by Maxwell Anderson; George Abbott; Del Andrews; Cinematography by Arthur Edeson; Karl Freund; Music by David Broekman. **Pr:** Carl Laemmle; Mark Huffam. **A:** Family. **P:** Entertainment. **U:** Home. **Mov-Ent:** World War One, Classic Films. **Awds:** Oscars '30: Director (Milestone), Film; AFI '98: Top 100; Natl. Film Reg. '90. **Acq:** Purchase. **Dist:** Facets Multimedia Inc.; German Language Video Center; Baker and Taylor. $19.98.

All Quiet on the Western Front 1979 — ★★½
A big-budget TV remake of the 1930 masterpiece starring John Boy. Sensitive German youth Thomas plunges excitedly into WWI and discovers its terror and degradation. Nowhere near the original's quality. 150m; VHS, DVD. **C:** Richard Thomas; Ernest Borgnine; Donald Pleasence; Patricia Neal; Directed by Delbert Mann; Written by Paul Monash; Cinematography by John Coquillon; Music by Allyn Ferguson. **Pr:** Norman Rosemont Productions; Marble Arch Productions; Universal Pictures. **A:** Jr. High-Adult. **P:** Entertainment. **U:** Home. **Mov-Ent:** World War One, TV Movies. **Acq:** Purchase. **Dist:** Lions Gate Television Corp.; Facets Multimedia Inc.

All Roads Lead Home 2008 (PG) — ★★½
Twelve-year-old Belle (Cardone) begins acting out after her mother's death in a car accident. She thinks her father Cody (London), who must euthanize unwanted pets as part of his animal control job, is in some way responsible. Cody decides to send Belle to her maternal grandfather Hock's (Coyote) farm but Hock is having trouble dealing with his own grief and it has turned him indifferent to the plight of the animals on the property. Of course as Belle helps care for the various critters, she and her family begin to reach out to one another. Boyle's last film role. 112m; DVD. **C:** Vivien Cardone; Peter Coyote; Jason London; Evan Dexter Parke; Peter Boyle; Patton Oswalt; Vanessa Branch; Shannon Knopke; Directed by Dennis Fallon; Written by Douglas Delaney; Cinematography by Fred Paddock; Music by Korey Ireland. **A:** Family. **P:** Entertainment. **U:** Home. **Mov-Ent:** Agriculture, Animals. **Acq:** Purchase. **Dist:** Anchor Bay Entertainment.

All Saint's Day 1998 (Unrated) — ★★
Tired of his going-nowhere life, Marco (Blatt) recruits four of his screw-up friends to help him rob the Brooklyn fish market where he works. Of course, since they're all losers this doesn't work out as planned. 82m; VHS, DVD. **C:** Mickey Blatt; Thomas J. La Sorsa; James Patrick McArdle; Mark Love; Christopher Lynn; Anthony Mangano; Ray Garvey; Howard Simon; Directed by Thomas J. La Sorsa; Written by Thomas J. La Sorsa; Christopher Lynn; Cinematography by Daniel Marracino. **A:** Sr. High-Adult. **P:** Entertainment. **U:** Home. **Mov-Ent.** **Acq:** Purchase. **Dist:** Wellspring Media.

All Screwed Up 1974 — ★★★
A group of young immigrants come to Milan and try to adjust to city life; they soon find that everything is in its place, but nothing is in order. Wertmuller in a lighter vein than usual. Part of 'Kino Classics Lina Wertmuller' collection. 104m; VHS, DVD, Blu-Ray. **C:** Luigi Diberti; Lina Polito; Directed by Lina Wertmuller; Written by Lina Wertmuller. **Pr:** New Line Cinema. **A:** College-Adult. **P:** Entertainment. **U:** Home. **Mov-Ent:** Comedy-Drama, Italy, Film--Avant-Garde. **Acq:** Purchase. **Dist:** Kino International Corporation.

All Singing, All Dancing 19??
A collection of classic song and dance scenes. 60m; VHS. **C:** Fred Astaire; Jane Powell; Cab Calloway; Cary Grant; Alexis Smith; Ann Sheridan. **A:** Family. **P:** Entertainment. **U:** Home, Institution. **Mov-Ent:** Dance, Singing. **Acq:** Purchase. **Dist:** Video Resources.

All Souls Day 2005 (Unrated) — ★½
Vargas Diaz's 1892 brutal rampage in a small Mexican town on the symbolic "Day of the Dead" causes his murderous soul to haunt the locals for years, leading them to perform certain acts to keep the zombies at bay. First up to be terrorized is a 1950's family with a sick boy and a hot teenaged girl who takes the standard "something-bad-is-about-to-happen" steamy bath. Then, in the present, Joss (Wester) and Alicia (Ramirez) seem doomed when they unknowingly interrupt the long-standing rite and must flee the same creepy hotel. Sci-Fi Channel original should have let the walking dead lie. 90m; DVD. **C:** Travis Wester; Nichole Hiltz; Laz Alonso; Laura Elena Harring; Marisa Ramirez; David Keith; Jeffrey Combs; Ellie Cornell; Julia Vera; Daniel Burgio; Mircea Monroe; Danny Trejo; Noah Luke; Directed by Jeremy Kasten; Written by Mark Altman; Cinematography by Christopher Duddy; Music by Joseph Gutowski. **A:** Sr. High-Adult. **P:** Entertainment. **U:** Home. **Mov-Ent:** Horror, Mexico. **Acq:** Purchase. **Dist:** Anchor Bay Entertainment. $14.99.

All-Star Batting Tips 1975
Tony Kubek moderates an All-Star panel as they discuss their philosophies on hitting and teach the six essential steps necessary to become a better hitter. 28m; VHS. **Pr:** Major League Baseball Productions. **A:** Primary-Sr. High. **P:** Instruction. **U:** Institution, Home, SURA. **Spo-Rec:** Baseball. **Acq:** Purchase. **Dist:** Major League Baseball Productions, On Moratorium. $39.95.

All-Star Cartoon Parade 19??
A collection of popular vintage cartoons, starring such favorites as Little Lulu, Casper the Friendly Ghost, Betty Boop and Raggedy Ann and Andy. 54m; VHS. **Pr:** Famous Studios. **A:** Family. **P:** Entertainment. **U:** Home. **Mov-Ent:** Animation & Cartoons. **Acq:** Purchase. **Dist:** Lions Gate Entertainment Inc. $29.98.

All-Star Catching and Base Stealing Tips 1975
The fine points of catching and the art of stealing bases are the featured topics on this program. Game-action footage of today's stars is presented in an easy-to-understand manner. 28m; VHS. **Pr:** Major League Baseball Productions. **A:** Primary-Sr. High. **P:** Instruction. **U:** Institution, Home, SURA. **Spo-Rec:** Baseball. **Acq:** Purchase. **Dist:** Major League Baseball Productions, On Moratorium.

All-Star Country Music Fair 1982 (Unrated)
From the 1982 Nashville Fan Fair comes live performances from Charley Pride, Sylvia, Razzy Bailey and Earl Thomas Conley. 83m; VHS. **A:** Family. **P:** Entertainment. **U:** Home. **Mov-Ent:** Music--Performance, Music--Country/Western. **Acq:** Purchase. **Dist:** BMG Entertainment; Music Video Distributors. $14.95.

All-Star Game, 1967 1967
Tony Perez' 15th inning home run off Catfish Hunter gives the National League a 2-1 victory in the longest All-Star game ever played. Young Mets' pitcher Tom Seaver gets credit for the victory. 30m; VHS. **Pr:** Winik Films. **A:** Family. **P:** Entertainment. **U:** Institution, Home, SURA. **Spo-Rec:** Baseball. **Acq:** Purchase. **Dist:** Major League Baseball Productions, On Moratorium.

All-Star Game, 1970: What Makes an All-Star 1970
The National League wins its eighth straight midsummer classic, 5-4, in 12 innings. Pete Rose barrels into American League catcher Ray Fosse at home plate to score the winning run on Jim Hickman's single. 30m; VHS. **Pr:** W and W Productions. **A:** Family. **P:** Entertainment. **U:** Institution, Home, SURA. **Spo-Rec:** Baseball. **Acq:** Purchase. **Dist:** Major League Baseball Productions, On Moratorium.

All-Star Game, 1971: Home Run Heroes 1971
Some or the great home run sluggers of the past are paid tribute, including Babe Ruth, Hank Greenberg, Mel Ott, and Mickey Mantle. The game itself produces six home runs, one of them a mammoth blast by Oakland's Reggie Jackson, and the American League goes on to a 6-4 victory. 26m; VHS. **Pr:** W and W Productions. **A:** Family. **P:** Entertainment. **U:** Institution, Home, SURA. **Spo-Rec:** Baseball. **Acq:** Purchase. **Dist:** Major League Baseball Productions, On Moratorium.

All-Star Game, 1972: Years of Tradition, Night of Pride 1972
Highlights from the first All-Star Game in 1933 to the present ones are shown prior to the National League's 10-inning, 4-3 victory at Atlanta Stadium. Hank Aaron thrills the home-team crowd with a dramatic home run. 26m; VHS. **Pr:** W and W Productions. **A:** Family. **P:** Entertainment. **U:** Institution, Home, SURA. **Spo-Rec:** Baseball. **Acq:** Purchase. **Dist:** Major League Baseball Productions, On Moratorium.

All-Star Game, 1973: A New Generation of Stars 1973
The great Willie Mays plays in his last All-Star Game, while the up-and-coming stars such as Bobby Bonds and Johnny Bench lead the National League to victory. 26m; VHS. **Pr:** W and W Productions. **A:** Family. **P:** Entertainment. **U:** Institution, Home, SURA. **Spo-Rec:** Baseball. **Acq:** Purchase. **Dist:** Major League Baseball Productions, On Moratorium.

All-Star Game, 1974: Mid-Summer Magic 1974
Write-in candidate Steve Garvey leads the National League to its third straight victory at Pittsburgh's Three Rivers Stadium. A sequence of ironic dream game performances by All-Stars throughout the years is included. 26m; VHS. **Pr:** W and W Productions. **A:** Family. **P:** Entertainment. **U:** Institution, Home, SURA. **Spo-Rec:** Baseball. **Acq:** Purchase. **Dist:** Major League Baseball Productions, On Moratorium.

All-Star Game, 1975: All-Star Fever 1975
National League home runs by Steve Garvey and Jimmy Wynn give them an early lead. Carl Yastrzemski's homer ties the game for the American leaguers. The Nationals score three times in the ninth inning with Bill Madlock's single the key hit in a 6-3 victory at County Stadium in Milwaukee. 28m; VHS. **Pr:** Major League Baseball Productions. **A:** Family. **P:** Entertainment. **U:** Institution, Home, SURA. **Spo-Rec:** Baseball. **Acq:** Purchase. **Dist:** Major League Baseball Productions, On Moratorium.

All-Star Game, 1976: Champions of Pride 1976
The National League celebrates its 100th anniversary with another victory over the American League. Unusual viewpoints are featured, including Randy Jones' sinkerball, the many motions of Luis Tiant, the aggressive play of Pete Rose and Mickey Rivers, and the zany antics of Tigers' pitcher, "The Bird," Mark Fidrych. 28m; VHS. **Pr:** Major League Baseball Productions. **A:** Family. **P:** Entertainment. **U:** Institution, Home, SURA. **Spo-Rec:** Baseball. **Acq:** Purchase. **Dist:** Major League Baseball Productions, On Moratorium.

All-Star Game, 1977: Man Behind the Mask 1977
Highlights the game and the individual stars of the National League's 7-5 victory over the American League, while featuring the work of home plate umpire Bill Kunkel, from his pre-game preparation to the final out. 29m; VHS. **Pr:** Major League Baseball Productions. **A:** Family. **P:** Entertainment. **U:** Institution, Home, SURA. **Spo-Rec:** Baseball. **Acq:** Purchase. **Dist:** Major League Baseball Productions, On Moratorium.

All-Star Game, 1978: What Makes an All-Star 1978
Los Angeles Dodger first baseman Steve Garvey collects two hits, two RBI's, and the game's MVP award as the National League defeats the American League 7-3 in San Diego. "Mr. Cub," Ernie Banks, comments from the stands along with the youngsters who won the "Pitch, Hit, and Run" competition. 26m; VHS. **Pr:** Major League Baseball Productions. **A:** Family. **P:** Entertainment. **U:** Institution, Home, SURA. **Spo-Rec:** Baseball. **Acq:** Purchase. **Dist:** Major League Baseball Productions, On Moratorium.

All-Star Game, 1979: Inches and Jinxes 1979
The National League is victorious again. A 7-6 win in Seattle's Kingdome is highlighted by Lee Mazzili's home run and Dave Parker's throw to home plate to nail Brian Downing, a potentially important run for the American League. Ron Guidry walks Mazzili to force in the winning run. 30m; VHS. **Pr:** Major League Baseball Productions. **A:** Family. **P:** Entertainment. **U:** Institution, Home, SURA. **Spo-Rec:** Baseball. **Acq:** Purchase. **Dist:** Major League Baseball Productions, On Moratorium.

All-Star Game, 1980: Heroes to Remember 1980
Cubs' relief pitcher Bruce Sutter wins the game's MVP award, as he nails down yet another victory for the National League in the Midsummer's Classic. 30m; VHS. **Pr:** Major League Baseball Productions. **A:** Family. **P:** Entertainment. **U:** Institution, Home, SURA. **Spo-Rec:** Baseball. **Acq:** Purchase. **Dist:** Major League Baseball Productions, On Moratorium.

All-Star Game, 1981 1981
In the first baseball game played since the great strike, Gary Carter of the Expos captures the MVP award by crashing two home runs in leading the National League to still another victory over the American League, at Cleveland's Municipal Stadium. 30m; VHS. **Pr:** Major League Baseball Productions. **A:** Family. **P:** Entertainment. **U:** Institution, Home, SURA. **Spo-Rec:** Baseball. **Acq:** Purchase. **Dist:** Major League Baseball Productions, On Moratorium.

All-Star Game, 1982 1982
The National League wins again. Cincinnati Reds' shortstop Dave Concepcion homers and is named MVP of this All-Star Game at Montreal. Montreal's own Steve Rogers is the winning pitcher, and Boston's Dennis Eckersley takes the 4-1 loss for manager Billy Martin's American League squad. Detroit catcher Lance Parrish stars in defeat, throwing out three NL runners attempting to steal bases. 30m; VHS. **Pr:** Major League Baseball Productions. **A:** Family. **P:** Entertainment. **U:** Institution, Home, SURA. **Spo-Rec:** Baseball. **Acq:** Purchase. **Dist:** Major League Baseball Productions, On Moratorium.

All-Star Game, 1983: Golden Memories 1983
The American League wins the All-Star Game for the first time in 12 years by a score of 13 to 3. Fred Lynn hits the first grand slam home run in the 50-year history of the game. 25m; VHS. **Pr:** Major League Baseball Productions. **A:** Family. **P:** Entertainment. **U:** Institution, Home, SURA. **Spo-Rec**: Baseball. **Acq:** Purchase. **Dist:** Major League Baseball Productions, On Moratorium.

All-Star Game, 1984: Something Special 1984
Highlights from the 1984 mid-summer classic, where the National League triumphed over the American League once again. 25m; VHS. **Pr:** Major League Baseball Productions. **A:** Family. **P:** Entertainment. **U:** Institution, Home, SURA. **Spo-Rec**: Baseball. **Acq:** Purchase. **Dist:** Major League Baseball Productions, On Moratorium.

The All-Star Game: From Ruth to Mays 1933-1956 1956
Restored from the original 16mm films. Includes highlights from almost every All-Star Game, from the first at Comiskey Park in 1933 to the 1956 game at Washington's Griffith Stadium. 40m; VHS. **A:** Family. **P:** Entertainment. **U:** Home. **Spo-Rec**: Baseball. **Acq:** Purchase. **Dist:** Baseball Direct. $29.95.

All-Star Gospel Session 1987
A soul-moving session with some of the biggest names in gospel. Featuring Paul Simon, Andrae Crouch, the Edwin Hawkins Singers, the Mighty Clouds of Joy, Jennifer Holliday, the Oak Ridge Boys, Luther Vandross, and many more. Songs include "Amazing Grace," "Can't Nobody Do Me Like Jesus," "His Eye Is On the Sparrow," "I Would Crawl All the Way (to the River)," "Slip Slidin' Away," "Oh Happy Day," "Change Is Gonna Come," "Right Now," "Still Waters Run Deep/Bridge Over Troubled Water," "Steal Away to Jesus," "I Made a Step," and "Gone at Last." 60m; VHS. **C:** Music by Paul Simon; Andrae Crouch. **Pr:** HBO. **A:** Family. **P:** Entertainment. **U:** Home. **Mov-Ent**: Music--Performance, Singing, Black Culture. **Acq:** Purchase. **Dist:** Music Video Distributors; WarnerVision; Facets Multimedia Inc. $19.95.

All Star Guitar Night 199?
Nashville's Caffe Milano concert featuring Muriel Anderson, Peppino D'Agostino, Alex de Grassi, Ed Gerhard, Tommy Jones, Laurence Juber, Phil Keaggy, Gayla Drake Paul, Preston Reed, Martin Taylor, and The Richard Smith Trio. 60m; VHS. **A:** Sr. High-Adult. **P:** Entertainment. **U:** Home. **Fin-Art**: Music--Performance, Music--Country/Western. **Acq:** Purchase. **Dist:** Hal Leonard Corp. $24.95.

The All-Star Jazz Show 1976
Television special broadcast featuring Count Basie, Lionel Hampton, Dizzy Gillespie, Herbie Hancock, Max Roach, Stan Getz, and Gerry Mulligan. 47m; VHS. **A:** Sr. High-Adult. **P:** Entertainment. **U:** Home. **Gen-Edu**: TV Movies, Music--Jazz. **Acq:** Rent/Lease. **Dist:** The Cinema Guild. $295.00.

All Star Piano Extravaganza: The Verbier Festival 2004
In celebration of Switzerland's Verbier Festival's tenth year, renown pianists from around the world gathered to play classical favorites by Mozart, Wagner, Rimsky-Korsakov, Smetana, Sousa, and Gottschalk, with four to 16 hands on one to eight pianos. Another festival highlight is Bach's "Concerto in A Minor" for four pianos performed by the Verbier Birthday Festival Orchestra. 100m; DVD. **A:** Adult. **P:** Entertainment. **U:** Home, Institution. **Fin-Art**: Music--Performance, Music--Classical. **Acq:** Purchase. **Dist:** WGBH/Boston. $19.95.

All-Star Pitching Tips 1975
The basics of pitching are explained by host and Hall of Famer Whitey Ford, along with helpful hints from many major league pitching stars. 28m; VHS. **Pr:** Major League Baseball Productions. **A:** Primary-Sr. High. **P:** Instruction. **U:** Institution, Home, SURA. **Spo-Rec**: Baseball. **Acq:** Purchase. **Dist:** Major League Baseball Productions, On Moratorium.

The All-Star Reggae Session 1988
Star-studded live performance of reggae music recorded at Fort Charles in Jamaica. Features Jimmy Cliff, The Neville Brothers, Ziggy Marley and the Melody Makers, Toots Hibbert, Chrissie Hynde, Grace Jones, The I-Threes, Carlos Santana, Sly & Robbie and Bunny Wailer, Coati Mundi, Tyrone Downie, Stephen "Cat" Coore, the 809 Band, Solomonic All Stars, and Dallol & Oneness. Songs: "Buffalo Soldier," "Rise and Shine," "Roots, Radics, Rockers, and Reggae," "Conscious Party," "Waiting In Vain," "Steppin' Razor," "Country Roads," "5446 Was My Number," "My Jamaican Guy," "My Blood in South Africa," "Hanging Fire," "Love Me, Love Me," and "The Harder They Come." 60m; VHS. **Pr:** HBO. **A:** Family. **P:** Entertainment. **U:** Home. **Mov-Ent**: Music--Performance. **Acq:** Purchase. **Dist:** Music Video Distributors; Image Entertainment Inc.; Fast Forward. $19.95.

All-Star Swing Festival 1972
Doc Severinsen hosts this once-in-a-lifetime teaming of jazz greats, taped at Lincoln Center's Philharmonic Hall. A highlight of the concert was the reunion of the original Benny Goodman Quartet: Benny, Lionel Hampton, Teddy Wilson, and Gene Krupa. 52m; VHS. **Pr:** Lincoln Center. **A:** Family. **P:** Entertainment. **U:** Home. **Mov-Ent**: Music--Performance, Music--Jazz. **Acq:** Purchase. **Dist:** Music Video Distributors. $29.95.

All-Star Tripleheader ????
Features highlights from All-Star Games in 1948, 1952, and 1955. 35m; VHS. **A:** Adult. **P:** Entertainment. **U:** Home. **Spo-Rec**: Baseball, Sports--General. **Acq:** Purchase. **Dist:** Baseball Direct. $29.95.

All Strings Attached 1987
John Abercrombie, Larry Carlton, John Scofield, Tal Farrow and Larry Coryell play great jazz music together. 59m; VHS. **A:** College-Adult. **P:** Entertainment. **U:** Home. **Mov-Ent**: Music--Performance, Music--Jazz. **Acq:** Purchase. **Dist:** Music Video Distributors. $19.95.

All Summer in a Day 1982
Ray Bradbury's famous story tells about a group of children living on Venus where it rains nearly all the time. One day, the children are told that the sun will appear for a few minutes. 25m; VHS, 3/4 U. **Pr:** Learning Corporation of America. **A:** Jr. High-Sr. High. **P:** Education. **U:** Institution, SURA. **Gen-Edu**: Literature. **Acq:** Purchase, Rent/Lease. **Dist:** Phoenix Learning Group.

All Superheroes Must Die 2011 (Unrated) — ★
Four superheroes are abducted by a man who steals their powers and makes them take part in horrific challenges to save a whole town of people he's kidnapped. 78m; DVD, Blu-Ray. **C:** Jason Trost; Lucas Till; James Remar; Sophie Merkley; Lee Valmassy; Directed by Jason Trost; Written by Jason Trost; Cinematography by Amanda Treyz; Music by George Holdcroft. **A:** Sr. High-Adult. **P:** Entertainment. **U:** Home. **L:** English. **Mov-Ent. Acq:** Purchase. **Dist:** Image Entertainment Inc. $29.97 27.97.

All Systems Go 199?
Teaches children some of the major systems within their bodies, and how they work. 13m; VHS. **A:** Primary. **P:** Education. **U:** Institution. **Chl-Juv**: Health Education, Biology. **Acq:** Purchase. **Dist:** The Video Project. $295.00.

All Systems Go: Motivating for Excellence 1993
Presents the Four Seasons Hotel as an example of how highly motivated employees have made a positive impact in their organization. 30m; VHS. **A:** Adult. **P:** Professional. **U:** Institution. **Bus-Ind**: Business, Management. **Acq:** Purchase. **Dist:** RMI Media. $99.00.

All That Bach ????
Performance of works by J.S. Bach featuring Keith Jarrett, The Canadian Brass, Maureen Forrester, and Christopher Hogwood. ?m; VHS. **A:** Adult. **P:** Entertainment. **U:** Home. **Fin-Art**: Music--Classical, Music--Performance. **Acq:** Purchase. **Dist:** Video Artists International. $29.95.

All That Heaven Allows 1955 (Unrated) — ★★★
Attractive, wealthy middleaged widow Cary Scott (Wyman) falls for her 15-years-younger gardener, Ron Kirby (Hudson), and becomes the target of small-minded gossips and her disapproving family. Ron's no gigolo or fortune-hunter but societal pressure still gets to Cary and she breaks things off. But loneliness makes her realize what she's missing and she decides to make things up with Ron and forget her critics. Hopeful Sirk romance that still takes some jabs at conformity. 89m/B/W; VHS, DVD, Blu-Ray, Wide. **C:** Jane Wyman; Rock Hudson; Conrad Nagel; Agnes Moorehead; Virginia Grey; Gloria Talbott; William Reynolds; Directed by Douglas Sirk; Written by Peggy Fenwick; Cinematography by Russell Metty; Music by Frank Skinner; Joseph Gershenson. **Pr:** Ross Hunter; Universal Studios. **A:** Sr. High-Adult. **P:** Entertainment. **U:** Home. **Mov-Ent**: Drama. **Awds:** Natl. Film Reg. '95. **Acq:** Purchase. **Dist:** Criterion Collection Inc.

All That I Marry 1978
An examination of the attitudes that women in American culture have toward their past, present, and future marriages. 24m; 3/4 U. **Pr:** Carol Coren. **A:** Adult. **P:** Education. **U:** Institution, SURA. **Gen-Edu**: Marriage, Women. **Acq:** Purchase, Rent/Lease. **Dist:** Temple University Dept. of Film and Media Arts.

All That Jazz 1979 (R) — ★★★1/2
Fosse's autobiographical portrait with Scheider fully occupying his best role as the obsessed, pill-popping, chain-smoking choreographer/director dancing simultaneously with love and death. But even while dying, he creates some great dancing. Vivid and imaginative with exact editing, and an eerie footnote to Fosse's similar death almost ten years later. Egocentric and self-indulgent for sure, but that's entertainment. 120m; VHS, DVD, Wide, CC. **C:** Roy Scheider; Jessica Lange; Ann Reinking; Leland Palmer; Cliff Gorman; Ben Vereen; Erzebet Foldi; John Lithgow; Max Wright; Deborah Geffner; Michael (Lawrence) Tolan; Keith Gordon; David Margulies; Nicole Fosse; Anthony Holland; Directed by Bob Fosse; Written by Bob Fosse; Robert Alan Aurthur; Cinematography by Giuseppe Rotunno; Music by Ralph Burns. **A:** Sr. High-Adult. **P:** Entertainment. **U:** Home. **Mov-Ent**: Musical, Dance, Biography: Show Business. **Awds:** Oscars '79: Art Dir./Set Dec., Costume Des., Film Editing, Orig. Song Score and/or Adapt.; Cannes '80: Film; Natl. Film Reg. '01. **Acq:** Purchase. **Dist:** Facets Multimedia Inc., On Moratorium. $19.98.
Songs: On Broadway; Everything Old is New Again; After You've Gone; There'll Be Some Changes Made; Some of These Days; Bye Bye Love.

All the Best 1988
Great football action through the years is compiled on this tape. 60m; VHS. **Pr:** NFL Films. **A:** Family. **P:** Entertainment. **U:** Institution, Home. **Spo-Rec**: Football. **Acq:** Purchase. **Dist:** NFL Films Video. $29.95.

All the Best: Steve Allen 1986
From Steve Allen's hit TV show, "The Steve Allen Show." Some of the funniest bits ever seen on TV, with wacky and unpredictable Steve Allen hosting it all. Not to be missed. 48m/B/W; VHS. **C:** Steve Allen; Jerry Lewis; Johnny Carson; Don Knotts; Jonathan Winters; Zsa Zsa Gabor; Sammy Davis, Jr; Tom Poston; Charlton Heston. **A:** Jr. High-Adult. **P:** Entertainment. **U:** Home. **Mov-Ent**: Television Series. **Acq:** Purchase. **Dist:** Image Entertainment Inc.

All the Boys Love Mandy Lane 2006 (R) — ★1/2
Throwback indie slasher flick shelved for seven years until the studios dusted it off for reasons unknown, and unimportant. Titular character Mandy Lane (Heard) walks in slow motion through her Texas high school hallways, oozing untouchable sexuality and mystery. During a weekend blowout at a remote cattle ranch, her dimwitted classmates are picked off one-by-one as she's left to take the killer on alone. A juicy twist ending can't undo its otherwise formulaic blah. Nothing worth the seven-year wait. 90m; DVD, Blu-Ray. **C:** Amber Heard; Anson Mount; Aaron Himelstein; Luke Grimes; Whitney Able; Melissa Price; Edwin Hodge; Michael Welch; Directed by Jonathan Levine; Written by Jacob Forman; Cinematography by Darren Genet; Music by Mark Schulz. **Pr:** Radius-TWC. **A:** Sr. High-Adult. **P:** Entertainment. **U:** Home. **L:** English. **Mov-Ent**: Adolescence, Horror. **Acq:** Purchase. **Dist:** Anchor Bay Entertainment Inc.

All the Brothers Were Valiant 1953 — ★★1/2
Brothers Taylor and Granger are New England whaling captains but Granger decides to treasure hunt instead. He finds a priceless cache of black pearls on an island but angers the locals who regard the gems as sacred. When Taylor rescues him, Granger promptly turns his brother's crew into mutineers in order to return to the island and retrieve his prize. Lots of brawling and there's an incidental love story with Blyth desired by both men (she's married Taylor and just happens to be aboard). Last role for Stone. Based on the novel by Ben Ames Williams. 101m; VHS, DVD. **C:** Robert Taylor; Stewart Granger; Ann Blyth; Betta St. John; Keenan Wynn; James Whitmore; Kurt Kasznar; Lewis Stone; Robert Burton; Peter Whitney; John Lupton; Billie Dove; Directed by Richard Thorpe; Written by Harry Brown; Cinematography by George J. Folsey; Music by Miklos Rozsa. **Pr:** Pandro S. Berman; MGM. **A:** Jr. High-Adult. **P:** Entertainment. **U:** Home. **Mov-Ent**: Boating. **Acq:** Purchase. **Dist:** WarnerArchive.com. $19.98.

All the Colors of the Dark 1972 (R) — ★★
Re-imagining of "Rosemary's Baby" in which a Satanic cult attempts to seduce a hysterical woman so they can claim her inheritance. 88m; DVD. **C:** George Hilton; Ivan Rassimov; Julian Ugarte; George Rigaud; Edwige Fenech; Nieves Navarro; Marina Malfatti; Directed by Sergio Martino; Written by Ernesto Gastaldi; Santiago Moncada; Sauro Scavolini, Bruno Nicolai; Cinematography by Giancarlo Ferrando; Miguel Fernandez Mila. **A:** Sr. High-Adult. **P:** Entertainment. **U:** Home. **L:** English. **Mov-Ent. Acq:** Purchase. **Dist:** Media Blasters Inc. $29.90.

All the Fine Young Men 1984
This documentary recreates the two most dramatic WWII air battles that took place in Germany: The October, 1943 attack on the Schweinfurt ball bearing plant and the March 1944 Berlin air raid. 52m; VHS, 3/4 U. **Pr:** National Broadcasting Company. **A:** Sr. High-Adult. **P:** Entertainment. **U:** Institution, SURA. **Gen-Edu**: World War Two. **Acq:** Purchase, Rent/Lease. **Dist:** Home Vision Cinema.

All the Good Ones Are Married 2007 (Unrated) — ★1/2
Alex (Hannah) is going through an amicable divorce from Ben (McGowan) until his mistress (Douglas) shows up at her door. Having been dumped herself, she thinks the two women scorned should team up, but Alex is naturally wary. Lifetime drama. 89m; DVD. **C:** Daryl Hannah; Deborah Odell; Matthew Knight; Nick Baillie; James McGowan; Joanna Douglas; Matthew Broderick; Brittany Snow; Maura Tierney; Peter Facinelli; Directed by Terry Ingram; Cinematography by Marcus Elliott. **A:** Jr. High-Adult. **P:** Entertainment. **U:** Home. **Mov-Ent**: Divorce. **Acq:** Purchase. **Dist:** Lions Gate Entertainment Inc.

All the Kids Do It 1989
This film dramatizes the dangers of drinking and driving from a teenage point of view. 30m; VHS, 3/4 U. **C:** Scott Baio; Directed by Henry Winkler. **Pr:** Henry Winkler; Henry Winkler. **A:** Primary-Jr. High. **P:** Education. **U:** Institution, Home, SURA. **Gen-Edu**: Alcoholism, Adolescence. **Acq:** Purchase. **Dist:** Pyramid Media. $395.00.

All the Kind Strangers 1974 (Unrated) — ★★
Traveling photographer Keach picks up a young hitchhiker and takes him to the boy's home. He discovers six other children there who want him as a father, his alternative being death. He and "Mother" Eggar plot their escape from the dangerous orphans. Thriller short on suspense. 72m; VHS, DVD, CC. **C:** Stacy Keach; Robby Benson; John Savage; Samantha Eggar; Directed by Burt Kennedy. **Pr:** Cinemation Industries. **A:** Jr. High-Adult. **P:** Entertainment. **U:** Home. **Mov-Ent**: Mystery & Suspense, Children, TV Movies. **Acq:** Purchase. **Dist:** Movies Unlimited. $59.98.

All the King's Horses 1983
This tape is designed to give an accurate understanding of the needs of the disabled. 54m; VHS, 3/4 U. **Pr:** WMAQ Chicago. **A:** Jr. High-Adult. **P:** Special Education. **U:** Institution, SURA. **Hea-Sci**: Handicapped. **Acq:** Purchase. **Dist:** Home Vision Cinema.

All the King's Horses 1986 (Unrated)
The tensions faced by the modern family are explored when a young couple's own self-interest comes between themselves and their children. 80m; VHS. **C:** Directed by Frank Tuttle. **Pr:** Heartland Productions. **A:** Family. **P:** Religious. **U:** Home. **Mov-Ent**: Religion, Family. **Acq:** Purchase. **Dist:** Russ Doughten Films Inc. $69.95.

All the King's Men 1949 (Unrated) — ★★★★
Grim and graphic classic set in the Depression follows the rise of a Louisiana farm-boy from angry and honest political hopeful to powerful but corrupt governor. Loosely based on the life (and

death) of Huey Long and told by a newsman who's followed his career (Ireland). Willy Stark (Crawford, in his break-through role) is the politician who, while appearing to improve the state, rules dictatorially, betraying friends and constituents and proving once again that power corrupts. In her first major role, McCambridge delivers a powerful performance as the cunning political aide. Potent morality play based on the Robert Penn Warren book. 109m/B/W; VHS, DVD, Blu-Ray. **C:** Broderick Crawford; Mercedes McCambridge; John Ireland; Joanne Dru; John Derek; Anne Seymour; Shepperd Strudwick; Directed by Robert Rossen; Written by Robert Rossen; Cinematography by Burnett Guffey; Music by Louis Gruenberg. **Pr:** Robert Rossen; Robert Rossen. **A:** Family. **P:** Entertainment. **U:** Home. **Mov-Ent:** Classic Films, Ethics & Morals. **Awds:** Oscars '49: Actor (Crawford), Film, Support. Actress (McCambridge); Golden Globes '50: Actor--Drama (Crawford), Director (Rossen), Film--Drama, Support. Actress (McCambridge); Natl. Film Reg. '01; N.Y. Film Critics '49: Actor (Crawford), Film. **Acq:** Purchase. **Dist:** Sony Pictures Home Entertainment Inc.; Baker and Taylor. $19.95.

All the King's Men 1999 — ★★½
In 1915, Frank Beck (Jason), the manager of the royal estate of Sandringham, trains a company of servants to be volunteer soldiers. Unfortunately, the raw recruits are posted to the disaster of Gallipoli and a battle against the Turks. The true fate of the company was unknown for many years and their disappearance became the stuff of myth (recent discoveries proved much grimmer) but the storyline is muddled and it's not easy to distinguish one youthful character from another (although the veterans do a notable job). Based on the novel by Nigel McCrery. 110m; VHS, DVD, CC. **C:** David Jason; Maggie Smith; Stuart Bunce; William Ash; James Murray; Sonya Walger; Eamon Boland; David Troughton; Emma Cunniffe; Adam Kotz; Patrick Malahide; Ed Waters; Tom Burke; Ben Crompton; Jo Stone-Fewings; James Hillier; Ian McDiarmid; Phyllis Logan; Directed by Julian Jarrold; Written by Alma Cullen; Cinematography by David Odd; Music by Adrian Johnston. **A:** Sr. High-Adult. **P:** Entertainment. **U:** Home. **Mov-Ent:** World War One, Middle East. **Acq:** Purchase. **Dist:** WGBH/Boston.

All the King's Men 2006 (PG-13) — ★½
Based on Robert Penn Warren's 1946 novel, this bungled remake of the 1949 film focuses on the rise and fall of a Huey P. Long-like politician, with Penn all bug-eyed sputterings as southern demagogue Willie Stark. Besides the out-of-place Penn, there's a bunch of miscast Brits, including narrator Law as boozy journalist Jack Burden, Winslet as Stark's unrequited love Anne, and Hopkins as a judge that Willie wants dirt on. Louisiana native Clarkson and former child actor Haley are about the only two actors who probably won't make you squirm. 128m; DVD, Blu-Ray. **C:** Sean Penn; Jude Law; Kate Winslet; James Gandolfini; Mark Ruffalo; Patricia Clarkson; Kathy Baker; Jackie Earle Haley; Anthony Hopkins; Kevin Dunn; Frederic Forrest; Talia Balsam; Glenn Morshower; Directed by Steven Zaillian; Written by Steven Zaillian; Cinematography by Pawel Edelman; Music by James Horner. **Pr:** Mike Medavoy; Ken Lemberger; Arnold W. Messer; Steven Zaillian; Steven Zaillian; Rising Star; Relativity Media; Phoenix Pictures; Columbia Pictures; Sony Pictures Home Entertainment Inc. **A:** Jr. High-Adult. **P:** Entertainment. **U:** Home. **L:** English. **Mov-Ent:** Politics & Government, Political Campaigns. **Acq:** Purchase. **Dist:** Sony Pictures Home Entertainment Inc.

All the Light in the Sky 2013 (Unrated) — ★★★
Ultra-low-budget filmmaker Swanberg includes even less dramatic thrust than normal in this practically short film about aging actress Marie (Adams, a character-driven performer doing very personal work here) who spends a few days with her visiting niece Faye (Takal) in her apartment. They don't do much. The movie doesn't say much. And yet Swanberg and his cast develop a nice, gentle charm with their dialogue, particularly in scenes that suggest the woman realizes she's entering the twilight period of her life. It's a small film that's slow but immensely likable. 79m; DVD. **C:** Jane Adams; Sophia Takal; Kent Osborne; Larry Fessenden; Directed by Joe Swanberg; Written by Jane Adams; Joe Swanberg; Cinematography by Joe Swanberg; Music by Orange Mighty Trio. **Pr:** Adam Donaghey; Joe Swanberg; Factory 25. **A:** Sr. High-Adult. **P:** Entertainment. **U:** Home. **L:** English. **Mov-Ent:** Drama, Family, Aging. **Acq:** Purchase.

All the Little Animals 1998 (R) — ★★½
Twenty-four-year old Bobby (Bale) is brain damaged from a childhood accident. After his mother's death, he's left in the less-than-tender care of his malevolent stepfather, De Winter (Benzali), who's only interested in Bobby's inheritance. So Bobby runs away and is taken in by hermit, Mr. Summers (Hurt), who is devoted to burying the remains of animals killed in road accidents. But Bobby's idyll cannot last when his stepfather finds him—and Mr. Summers is also not quite what he seems. Based on the novel by Walker Hamilton. 104m; VHS, DVD, CC. **C:** John Hurt; Christian Bale; Daniel Benzali; James Faulkner; Amy Robbins; Directed by Jeremy Thomas; Written by Eski Thomas; Cinematography by Mike Molloy; Music by Richard Hartley. **Pr:** Chris Auty; Jeremy Thomas; J & M Entertainment; BBC Films; Recorded Pictures Company; Lions Gate Films. **A:** Sr. High-Adult. **P:** Entertainment. **U:** Home. **Mov-Ent:** Mental Retardation. **Acq:** Purchase. **Dist:** Movies Unlimited; Alpha Video.

All the Lovin' Kinfolk 1970 (R) — ★
Two recent Hillbilly High graduates decide to take on the big city, but find themselves in dire situations. For those with time to kill. 80m; VHS. **C:** Mady Maguire; Jay Scott; Anne Ryan; John Denis; Donna Young; Marland Proctor; Uschi Digart; Directed by John Hayes; Written by John Hayes. **A:** College-Adult. **P:** Entertainment. **U:** Home. **Mov-Ent:** Action-Adventure. **Acq:** Purchase. **Dist:** Movies Unlimited.

. . .All the Marbles 1981 (R) — ★★
A manager of two beautiful lady wrestlers has dreams of going to the top. Aldrich's last film, and an atypical one, with awkward pacing and a thin veil of sex exploitation. Falk provides needed grace and humor as the seedy manager, with Young contributing his usual competent bit as a hustling promoter dabbling in criminal activity. One of the few tag-team women wrestling pictures, it builds to a rousing finale match in the "Rocky" tradition, although the shift in tone and mounting cliches effectively body slam the intent. 113m; VHS, DVD. **C:** Peter Falk; Burt Young; Richard Jaeckel; Vicki Frederick; Claudette Nevins; Lenny Montana; Directed by Robert Aldrich; Cinematography by Joseph Biroc. **Pr:** MGM. **A:** Jr. High-Adult. **P:** Entertainment. **U:** Home. **Mov-Ent.** **Acq:** Rent/Lease. **Dist:** WarnerArchive.com, On Moratorium.

All the Nights to Come 19??
The poet Yehuda Amichai decries war and affirms life amid scenes from Jewish history. 15m; VHS, 3/4 U, Special order formats. **TV Std:** NTSC, PAL, SECAM. **Pr:** Alden Films. **A:** Jr. High-Adult. **P:** Education. **U:** Institution, Home, SURA. **Gen-Edu:** Judaism, Israel, History. **Acq:** Purchase, Rent/Lease. **Dist:** Alden Films.

All the President's Men 1976 (PG) — ★★★½
True story of the Watergate break-in that led to the political scandal of the decade, based on the best-selling book by Washington Post reporters Bob Woodward and Carl Bernstein. Intriguing, terse thriller is a nail-biter even though the ending is no secret. Expertly paced by Pakula with standout performances by Hoffman and Redford as the reporters who slowly uncover and connect the seemingly isolated facts that ultimately lead to criminal indictments of the Nixon Administration. Deep Throat Holbrook and Robards as executive editor Ben Bradlee lend authenticity to the endeavor, a realistic portrayal of the stop and go of journalistic investigations. 135m; VHS, DVD, Blu-Ray, Wide. **C:** Robert Redford; Dustin Hoffman; Jason Robards, Jr.; Martin Balsam; Jane Alexander; Hal Holbrook; F. Murray Abraham; Stephen Collins; Lindsay Crouse; Meredith Baxter; Ned Beatty; Penny Fuller; Dominic Chianese; David Arkin; Polly Holliday; James Karen; Directed by Alan J. Pakula; Written by William Goldman; Cinematography by Gordon Willis; Music by David Shire. **A:** Jr. High-Adult. **P:** Entertainment. **U:** Home. **Mov-Ent:** Journalism, Presidency, Conspiracies or Conspiracy Theories. **Awds:** Oscars '76: Adapt. Screenplay, Art Dir./Set Dec., Sound, Support. Actor (Robards); Natl. Bd. of Review '76: Director (Pakula), Support. Actor (Robards); Natl. Film Reg. '10; N.Y. Film Critics '76: Director (Pakula), Film, Support. Actor (Robards); Natl. Soc. Film Critics '76: Film, Support. Actor (Robards); Writers Guild '76: Adapt. Screenplay. **Acq:** Purchase. **Dist:** Warner Home Video, Inc.; Baker and Taylor. $19.98.

All the Pretty Horses 2000 (PG-13) — ★★
John Grady Cole (Damon) is a dispossessed Texas cowboy in the late 1940s who, along with his buddy Lacey Rawlins (Thomas) and teen misfit Blevins (Black), crosses the border for, he hopes, a better life in Mexico. What he finds is an ill-fated romance with the beautiful daughter (Cruz) of a possessive rancher (Blades). It's pretty, all right. But thanks to Thornton's uneven pacing and inability to settle on a visual style, the story, and splendor, of the book is lost somewhere along the way. Of the young (and also pretty) cast, Damon and especially Black fare the best. Based on the first book of Cormac McCarthy's Border Trilogy. 117m; VHS, DVD, Wide, CC. **C:** Matt Damon; Penelope Cruz; Ruben Blades; Lucas Black; Henry Thomas; Robert Patrick; Julio Oscar Mechoso; Miriam Colon; Bruce Dern; Sam Shepard; Directed by Billy Bob Thornton; Written by Ted Tally; Cinematography by Barry Markowitz; Music by Marty Stuart. **Pr:** Miramax Film Corp; Columbia Pictures; Miramax; Sony Pictures Home Entertainment Inc. **A:** Sr. High-Adult. **P:** Entertainment. **U:** Home. **Mov-Ent:** Western, Mexico, Horses. **Awds:** Natl. Bd. of Review '00: Screenplay. **Acq:** Purchase. **Dist:** Sony Pictures Home Entertainment Inc.

All the Queen's Men 2002 (Unrated) — ★★
After his mission to steal a German Enigma encoding machine is torpedoed by an arrogant British officer, American OSS agent O'Rourke (LeBlanc) is assigned to multinational commando team to try again. Only this time they'll be infiltrating a Nazi factory—as female workers. Cross-dressing comic Izzard, as team member Tony, is invaluable here, as he's the only one who looks comfortable in a dress or supplies any comic flair. Jumbled plot and bumbled comedic opportunities combine to thwart a good premise and excellent cast. 99m; VHS, DVD. **C:** Matt LeBlanc; Eddie Izzard; James Cosmo; Udo Kier; Edward Fox; Nicolette Krebitz; David Birkin; Oliver Korittke; Karl Markovics; Directed by Stefan Ruzowitzky; Written by David Schneider; Cinematography by Wedigo von Schultzendorff; Music by Joern-ewe Fahrenkrog-Petersen. **A:** Sr. High-Adult. **P:** Entertainment. **U:** Home. **Mov-Ent:** Germany, World War Two. **Acq:** Purchase. **Dist:** Strand Releasing.

All the Real Girls 2003 (R) — ★★★½
Sophomore effort of writer-director Green is a sincere and poignant look at youthful love. Paul (Schneider), a twentysomething Romeo who's broken more than a few hearts in town, finds the real thing in Noel (played wonderfully by Deschanel), the 18-year-old sister of his best friend, fresh out of boarding school. Fully captures the real and often awkward moments of young love and the pain and confusion that can come with it. Schneider also helped conceive and write the story. 108m; VHS, DVD, CC. **C:** Paul Schneider; Zooey Deschanel; Patricia Clarkson; Maurice Compte; Benjamin Mouton; Shea Whigham; Danny McBride; Directed by David Gordon Green; Written by Paul Schneider; David Gordon Green; Cinematography by Tim Orr; Music by David Wingo; Michael Linnen. **Pr:** Jean Doumanian; Lisa Muskat; Sony Pictures Classics. **A:** Sr. High-Adult. **P:** Entertainment. **U:** Home. **Mov-Ent:** Drama, Adolescence. **Acq:** Purchase. **Dist:** Sony Pictures Home Entertainment Inc.

All the Right Moves 1983 (R) — ★★½
Cruise is the high school football hero hoping for a scholarship so he can vacate pronto the dying Pennsylvania mill town where he grew up. At least he thinks that's what he wants to do. Further mixing up his own mixed feelings are his pushy, ambitious coach (Nelson, doing what he does best), his understanding dad (Cioffi) and supportive girlfriend (Thompson, in a notable early role). Strong performances push the relatively cliched melodrama into field goal range. Cinematographer Chapman's directorial debut. 90m; VHS, DVD, Wide, CC. **C:** Tom Cruise; Lea Thompson; Craig T. Nelson; Christopher Penn; Charles Cioffi; Paul Carafotes; Dick Miller; Directed by Michael Chapman; Written by Michael Kane; Cinematography by Jan De Bont; Music by David (Richard) Campbell. **Pr:** 20th Century-Fox. **A:** Sr. High-Adult. **P:** Entertainment. **U:** Home. **Mov-Ent:** Football, Sports--Fiction: Drama. **Acq:** Purchase. **Dist:** Fox Home Entertainment. $14.98.

All the Right Moves: Techniques for Transferring Patients 1996
Discusses the proper techniques and competencies required to transfer patients. 25m; VHS. **A:** Adult. **P:** Education. **U:** Institution. **Hea-Sci:** Nursing, Health Education. **Acq:** Purchase, Rent/Lease. **Dist:** AJN Video Library/Lippincott Williams & Wilkins. $295.00.

All The Right Moves: To Beat and Get Past Your Opponent ????
Features a variety of soccer techniques by Roby Stahl with footage of international players. 35m; VHS, DVD. **A:** Jr. High-Adult. **P:** Instruction. **U:** Home. **Spo-Rec:** Soccer. **Acq:** Purchase. **Dist:** Soccer Learning Systems. $24.95.

All the Right Skills—Soccer Skills to Make it Happen 2010 (Unrated)
Introduction to the eight basic skills needed by soccer players and how to develop them in both experienced and newer players. 45m; DVD. **A:** Family. **P:** Education. **U:** Home, Institution. **Spo-Rec:** Soccer, Athletic Instruction/Coaching. **Acq:** Purchase. **Dist:** Championship Productions. $24.99.

All the Rivers Run 1984 — ★★½
First made-for-cable miniseries. A young Australian girl spends her inheritance on a river boat and becomes the first female river captain in Australian history. Directed by George Miller of "Man from Snowy River" fame. 400m; VHS. **C:** Sigrid Thornton; John Waters; Diane Craig; Charles "Bud" Tingwell; Gus Mercurio; Directed by George Miller; Pino Amenta; Cinematography by David Connell. **Pr:** HBO Films. **A:** Sr. High-Adult. **P:** Entertainment. **U:** Home. **Mov-Ent:** Action-Adventure, TV Movies. **Acq:** Purchase. **Dist:** $79.95.

All the Unsung Heroes: The Story of the Vietnam Veterans Memorial 1990
Video tour of Washington's most visited monument. Includes an interview with the designer, a discussion of the monument's symbolism and scenes from its construction, mixed together with combat footage. 30m; VHS. **A:** Jr. High-Adult. **P:** Education. **U:** Institution. **Gen-Edu:** Vietnam War, Sculpture, Art & Artists. **Acq:** Purchase. **Dist:** Cambridge Educational. $24.95.

All the Vermeers in New York 1991 (Unrated) — ★★★½
A stressed-out Wall Street broker flees to the soothing recesses of the Metropolitan Museum's Vermeer Room. There he meets a beautiful, manipulative French actress dreaming of success in Manhattan. Amidst the opulent art world of New York, the two pursue their relationship to an ultimately tragic end. Jost offers an inside look at the collision of commerce and art and the corrupt underside of New York in this elegant contemporary film. 87m; VHS, DVD, Wide. **C:** Emmanuelle Chaulet; Stephen Lack; Grace Phillips; Katherine Bean; Laurel Lee Kiefer; Gracie Mansion; Gordon Joseph Weiss; Roger Ruffin; Directed by Jon Jost; Written by Jon Jost. **Pr:** Henry S. Rosenthal. **A:** College-Adult. **P:** Entertainment. **U:** Home. **Mov-Ent:** Drama, Art & Artists, Finance. **Acq:** Purchase. **Dist:** $24.98.

All the Way, Boys 1973 (PG) — ★½
Two inept adventurers crash-land a plane in the Andes in the hope of discovering slapstick, but find none. "Trinity" cast up to no good. 105m; VHS, DVD, Streaming. **C:** Terence Hill; Bud Spencer; Cyril Cusack; Michel Antoine; Directed by Giuseppe Colizzi. **Pr:** Joseph E. Levine; Italo Zingarelli. **A:** Sr. High-Adult. **P:** Entertainment. **U:** Home. **Mov-Ent:** Action-Adventure. **Acq:** Purchase. **Dist:** Unknown Distributor.

All the Way Up There 1980
A 24-year-old cerebral palsy victim realizes his dream of climbing a mountain, aided by one of the world's best mountaineers. The two men inspire each other in striving to reach a common goal. 27m; VHS, 3/4 U. **Pr:** Encyclopedia Britannica Educational Corporation. **A:** Jr. High-Adult. **P:** Education. **U:** Institution, SURA. **Gen-Edu:** Handicapped. **Acq:** Purchase, Rent/Lease, Trade-in. **Dist:** Encyclopedia Britannica.

All the Wonderful Things That Fly 1974
Demonstrates the many different special types of aircraft that have been developed. 14m; VHS, 3/4 U. **Pr:** Flight Plan I, Inc. **A:** Primary. **P:** Education. **U:** Institution, SURA. **Chl-Juv:** Aeronautics. **Acq:** Purchase, Rent/Lease, Trade-in. **Dist:** Encyclopedia Britannica.

All the World's a Stage 1975
A view of the Juilliard School of Drama's role in developing talents and turning out "thinking" actors. 20m; VHS, 3/4 U. **Pr:** Carlton Moss. **A:** Sr. High-Adult. **P:** Education. **U:** Institution, Home, SURA. **Fin-Art:** Theater. **Acq:** Purchase, Rent/Lease. **Dist:** Pyramid Media.

All the Wrong Clues for the Solution 1981 (Unrated) — ★
Another parody of American films from Hong Kong. This time Hong Kong is set to resemble Prohibition-era Chicago, complete with a gangster named Ah Capone. In Cantonese with English subtitles. ?m; VHS. **C:** Carl Mak; Directed by Tsui Hark. **A:** Sr. High-Adult. **P:** Entertainment. **U:** Home. **L:** English, Chinese. **Mov-Ent:** Satire & Parody. **Acq:** Purchase. **Dist:** Facets Multimedia Inc. $49.95.

All the Wrong Moves 1986
A video which explains how to handle sexual harassment in the workplace. Workshop materials are available. 23m; VHS, 3/4 U, Special order formats. **Pr:** Dartnell. **A:** College-Adult. **P:** Instruction. **U:** Institution, Home. **How-Ins:** How-To, Business, Management. **Acq:** Purchase, Rent/Lease. **Dist:** Excellence in Training Corp. $495.00.

All the Wrong Places 2000 (Unrated) — ★1/2
Twenty-somethings Marisa (Hillis) and Paul (Klavens), the children of successful parents, are struggling to find their own identities and careers. Marisa is trying to make it as a filmmaker, while spending much of her time on her therapist's couch, while Paul is working on his first novel. They've got a lot in common but most of it is little above slacker whining. 95m; DVD. **C:** Ali Hillis; Alyce LaTourelle; Brian Patrick Sullivan; Jeremy Klavens; Judy Del Guidice; Directed by Martin Edwards; Written by Martin Edwards; Cinematography by Bing Rao; Music by Jody Elff. **A:** Sr. High-Adult. **P:** Entertainment. **U:** Home. **Mov-Ent:** Comedy--Romantic, Filmmaking. **Acq:** Purchase. **Dist:** Vanguard International Cinema, Inc.

All the Years 1989
Based on a short story by Morley Callaghan, this film tells the story of the relationship between a son and his mother. 24m; VHS, 3/4 U. **A:** Jr. High-Adult. **P:** Education. **U:** Institution, SURA. **Gen-Edu:** Parenting, Family. **Acq:** Purchase, Rent/Lease. **Dist:** National Film Board of Canada.

All the Young Men 1960 (Unrated) — ★★★
Fairly powerful men-uniting-in-battle story with an interesting cast, highlighted by Poitier in an early role. A tiny marine squadron overrun by the Chinese in the Korean War attempts to resist the numerous attackers. In their spare time, the men confront racial prejudice when a black man (guess who) takes command. 86m/B/W; VHS. **C:** Alan Ladd; Sidney Poitier; James Darren; Glenn Corbett; Mort Sahl; Ana St. Clair; Paul (E.) Richards; Richard (Dick) Davalos; Lee Kinsolving; Joseph (Joe) Gallison; Paul Baxley; Charles Quinlivan; Directed by Hall Bartlett; Written by Hall Bartlett; Cinematography by Daniel F. Fapp; Music by George Duning. **Pr:** Hall Bartlett; Hall Bartlett; Columbia Pictures. **A:** Jr. High-Adult. **P:** Entertainment. **U:** Home. **Mov-Ent:** Korean War. **Acq:** Purchase. **Dist:** Sony Pictures Home Entertainment Inc. $14.99.

All Things Connected: Native Americans and the Environment 1994
Examines 19th century Native American life in relatively unexploited lands. The guide "This Land is Sacred" is available at additional cost. 15m; VHS. **A:** Jr. High-College. **P:** Education. **U:** Institution, Home. **Gen-Edu:** Native Americans. **Acq:** Purchase. **Dist:** Environmental Media. $19.95.

All Things Considered: Ancel Nunn 1979
A look at the Texas artist Ancel Nunn, with emphasis on his philosophy, technique, inspiration, and the effect Texas has had on his attitudes and approach to painting. 26m; VHS, 3/4 U. **Pr:** Institute of Texan Cultures. **A:** Sr. High-Adult. **P:** Education. **U:** Institution, CCTV. **Fin-Art:** Art & Artists. **Acq:** Purchase. **Dist:** University of Texas Institute of Texan Cultures.

All Things Fair 1995 — ★★1/2
Coming of age story set in neutral Sweden in 1943. Fifteen-year-old Stig (Widerberg, the director's son) has just arrived in Malmo to begin classes at his all-male school—a situation filled with sexual curiosity and repression. Stig is attracted to his beautiful teacher Viola (Lagercrantz), whose marriage to alcoholic traveling salesman Frank (von Bromssen) is less than ideal, and the duo begin an affair. Frank not only seems not to care but befriends his wife's youthful lover, although the situation is ripe for tragedy. Excellent performances, sensual air, though somewhat lacking in logical narrative. Swedish with subtitles. 128m; VHS, DVD. **C:** Johan Widerberg; Marika Lagercrantz; Tomas von Bromssen; Bjorn Kjellman; Charles A. Palmer; Directed by Bo Widerberg; Written by Bo Widerberg; Cinematography by Morten Bruus. **Pr:** Per Holst. **A:** College-Adult. **P:** Entertainment. **U:** Home. **L:** Swedish. **Mov-Ent:** Marriage, Adolescence, Education. **Acq:** Purchase. **Dist:** Home Vision Cinema.

All Things to All Men 2013 (Unrated) — ★★
Brit crime drama with an ordinary story and a good cast. In London, crooked cop Parker, his partner Sands, and rookie detective Dixon nab a drug dealer who turns out to be the son of crime boss Joseph Corso. So they leverage the son's arrest to have Corso set up safecracker/jewel thief Riley, who's about to pull another job. Of course nothing goes according to plan, but that's because the plan isn't so clear. 84m; DVD. **C:** Rufus Sewell; Toby Stephens; Gabriel Byrne; Terence Maynard; Leo Gregory; Julian Sands; Directed by George Isaac; Written by George Isaac; Cinematography by Howard Atherton; Music by Thomas Wanker. **A:** Sr. High-Adult. **P:** Entertainment. **U:** Home. **L:** English. **Mov-Ent:** Crime Drama. **Acq:** Purchase. **Dist:** Screen Media Ventures, LLC.

All This and Heaven Too 1940 — ★★★
When a governess arrives at a Parisian aristocrat's home in the 1840s, she causes jealous tension between the husband and his wife. The wife is soon found murdered. Based on Rachel Field's best-seller. 141m/B/W; VHS, DVD. **C:** Charles Boyer; Bette Davis; Barbara O'Neil; Virginia Weidler; Jeffrey Lynn; Helen Westley; Henry Daniell; Harry Davenport; June Lockhart; Montagu Love; Anne Howard; Directed by Anatole Litvak; Music by Max Steiner. **Pr:** Warner Bros. **A:** Jr. High-Adult. **P:** Entertainment. **U:** Home. **Mov-Ent:** Drama, Classic Films, Marriage. **Acq:** Purchase. **Dist:** Warner Home Video, Inc. $19.95.

All This and Tex Avery, Too! 1992 (Unrated)
Fourteen cartoons from the great Tex Avery are featured here, including "What Price Freedom," "Doggone Tired," "Wags to Riches," "The Screwy Truant," "King-Size Canary," "House of Tomorrow," and eight others. 120m. **C:** Directed by Tex Avery. **Pr:** Warner Bros. **A:** Primary-Jr. High. **P:** Entertainment. **U:** Home. **Mov-Ent:** Animation & Cartoons. **Acq:** Purchase. **Dist:** MGM Home Entertainment. $34.98.

All Through the Night 1942 (Unrated) — ★★★
A very funny spy spoof as well as a thrilling crime story with Bogart playing a gambler who takes on a Nazi spy ring. Features memorable double-talk and a great auction scene that inspired the one with Cary Grant in "North by Northwest." Suspense builds throughout the film as Lorre appears in a sinister role as Pepi and Veidt gives a fine performance as the spymaster. 107m/B/W; VHS, DVD, CC. **C:** Humphrey Bogart; Conrad Veidt; Karen Verne; Jane Darwell; Frank McHugh; Peter Lorre; Judith Anderson; William Demarest; Jackie Gleason; Phil Silvers; Barton MacLane; Martin Kosleck; Wallace Ford; Directed by Vincent Sherman; Cinematography by Sidney Hickox; Music by Adolph Deutsch. **Pr:** Hal B. Wallis. **A:** Sr. High-Adult. **P:** Entertainment. **U:** Home. **Mov-Ent:** Satire & Parody. **Acq:** Purchase. **Dist:** MGM Home Entertainment. $19.98.

All Tied Up 1992 (R) — ★★1/2
Ladies man Brian (Galligan) thinks he's found true love with Linda (Hatcher) but that doesn't mean he's stopped seeing other women. And when Linda finds out, she breaks it off. So Brian goes over to her house to work things out and gets tied up—literally—by Linda and her girlfriends. Talk about teaching a guy a lesson. 90m; VHS, DVD. **C:** Zach Galligan; Teri Hatcher; Tracy Griffith; Lara Harris; Directed by John Mark Robinson; Written by Robert Madero; I. Markie Lane; Music by Bernardo Bonezzi. **Pr:** Isabel Mula; Irongate Entertainment Group. **A:** Sr. High-Adult. **P:** Entertainment. **U:** Home. **Mov-Ent:** Comedy--Romantic. **Acq:** Purchase. **Dist:** Sony Pictures Home Entertainment Inc. $89.95.

All-Time A's 1994
Profiles some of the most memorable players and teams in Oakland A's team history, from the early 1970s dynasty of Reggie Jackson, Sal Bando, Rollie Fingers, Catfish Hunter, and Vida Blue to the late 1980s powerhouse incarnation with Jose Canseco, Mark McGwire, Dennis Eckersley, and Dave Stewart. 45m; VHS. **A:** Family. **P:** Entertainment. **U:** Home. **Spo-Rec:** Sports--General, Baseball. **Acq:** Purchase. **Dist:** Major League Baseball Productions. $19.95.

The All-Time Greatest Animal Foul-Ups 19??
Animals steal the show in a compilation of television outtakes. 30m; VHS. **A:** Family. **P:** Entertainment. **U:** Home. **Mov-Ent:** Outtakes & Bloopers, Animals. **Acq:** Purchase. **Dist:** Rhino Entertainment Co.

The All-Time Greatest Kids Foul-Ups 19??
Bloopers by kids in a collection of various programs. 30m; VHS. **A:** Family. **P:** Entertainment. **U:** Home. **Mov-Ent:** Outtakes & Bloopers, Children. **Acq:** Purchase. **Dist:** Rhino Entertainment Co.

The All-Time Greatest TV Foul-Ups 19??
Television's funniest blunders. 30m; VHS. **A:** Family. **P:** Entertainment. **U:** Home. **Mov-Ent:** Outtakes & Bloopers, Television. **Acq:** Purchase. **Dist:** Rhino Entertainment Co.

All Together Now 1973
Pauline Lee of the Social Security Office talks about the problems faced by Chinese immigrants in this program. Kathy Fong talks of her involvement with her organization, Chinese for Affirmative Action. Also includes a musical number, "Horse with No Name" performed by Asian Wood. 30m/B/W; EJ. **Pr:** KPIX San Francisco. **A:** Adult. **P:** Education. **U:** Institution, CCTV. **Gen-Edu:** Minorities. **Acq:** Loan. **Dist:** Chinese for Affirmative Action.

All Together Now—Asian Americans on the Political Scene 19??
In this program, four local Bay Area Asian American politicians speak on the political process. Represented are Floyd Mori, Gordon Lau, John Chin, and Kiyoshi Matso. 17m; 3/4 U. **Pr:** KPIX Oakland. **A:** Adult. **P:** Education. **U:** Institution, CCTV. **Gen-Edu:** Minorities. **Acq:** Loan. **Dist:** Chinese for Affirmative Action.

All Under Heaven 1996
Involves life in a north China village from the human perspective of the people who live, work, worship, build families and die there. 58m; VHS. **A:** Jr. High-Adult. **P:** Education. **U:** Home, Institution. **Gen-Edu:** China, Sociology. **Acq:** Purchase, Rent/Lease. **Dist:** New Day Films Library. $250.00.

All Washed Up 1995
Features safety showers and eyewashes in a humorous manner. 12m; VHS. **A:** Adult. **P:** Professional. **U:** Institution. **Bus-Ind:** Job Training, Safety Education, Management. **Acq:** Purchase, Rent/Lease. **Dist:** National Safety Council, California Chapter, Film Library. $195.00.

All Water Has A Perfect Memory 2001
Filmmaker Natalia Almada, her North American mother, Mexican father and brother share personal recollections of the drowning accident in Mexico that killed her then two-year old sister. Subtitled. 19m; VHS. **A:** Adult. **P:** Education. **U:** Institution. **Gen-Edu:** Death, Family. **Acq:** Purchase, Rent/Lease. **Dist:** Women Make Movies. $250.00.

All Women Have Periods 1979
Designed to help the mentally retarded girl and her family prepare for menstruation. It is written to fit the comprehension level of a retarded girl. 11m; CC, 3/4 U, Special order formats. **Pr:** Life Crisis Services; Norman Film Productions. **A:** Jr. High-Adult. **P:** Education. **U:** Institution, Home, SURA. **Hea-Sci:** Gynecology. **Acq:** Purchase, Rent/Lease, Trade-in, Duplication License. **Dist:** United Learning Inc.

All Year Round Series 1988
An introduction for primary school students to a wide variety of scientific observations on plant and animal life, designed to increase their curiosity and understanding of the processes necessary to life. 15m; VHS, 3/4 U, Special order formats. **Pr:** Altschul Group. **A:** Primary. **P:** Education. **U:** Institution, SURA. **Chl-Juv:** Education, Science. **Acq:** Purchase, Rent/Lease. **Dist:** New Dimension Media. $225.00.
Indiv. Titles: 1. Families 2. Harvesting 3. Breathing 4. Feeding 5. Resting 6. Cold Days 7. Keeping Clean 8. Keeping Healthy 9. Growing 10. Homes 11. Playing with Air 12. Beginning Again 13. Moving.

All You Have to Do Is Ask 1993
Geri Jewell, a disabled actress and consultant, talks about successful interaction with disabled people, and helps one come to grips fear and misconceptions about disabled people. Focuses on hearing, vision, and speech impairment, and the use of a wheelchair. Includes leader's guide. 16m; VHS, CC. **A:** Adult. **P:** Professional. **U:** Institution. **Bus-Ind:** Handicapped, Business, Employee Counseling. **Acq:** Purchase, Rent/Lease. **Dist:** American Media, Inc. $550.00.

All You Need Is Cash 1978 (Unrated) — ★★★
"The Rutles" star in this parody of The Beatles' legend, from the early days of the "Pre-Fab Four" in Liverpool to their worldwide success. A marvelous pseudo-documentary, originally shown on NBC-TV and with various SNL alumni, which captures the development of the Beatles and '60s rock with devastating effect. Served as the inspiration for "This Is Spinal Tap." 70m; VHS, DVD, Blu-Ray. **C:** Eric Idle; Neil Innes; Ricky Fataar; Dan Aykroyd; Gilda Radner; John Belushi; George Harrison; Paul Simon; Mick Jagger; John Halsey; Michael Palin; Bianca Jagger; Bill Murray; Gwen Taylor; Ron Wood; Jeannette Charles; Al Franken; Lorne Michaels; Tom Davis; Directed by Eric Idle; Gary Weis; Written by Eric Idle; Cinematography by Gary Weis; Music by Neil Innes. **Pr:** Lorne Michaels; Lorne Michaels. **A:** Family. **P:** Entertainment. **U:** Home. **Mov-Ent:** Satire & Parody, TV Movies. **Acq:** Purchase. **Dist:** Music Video Distributors; Music for Little People. $14.95.

All You Need Is Love: The Story of Popular Music 19??
Director Tony Palmer tells the story behind different popular music genres, including jazz, folk, blues, country, and rock. Includes performances and interviews. 17 episodes. 840m; DVD. **A:** Sr. High-Adult. **P:** Entertainment. **U:** Home. **Music:** Interviews, Music. **Acq:** Purchase. **Dist:** Acorn Media Group Inc. $99.95.

All You Need to Know About Cigars! 19??
Covers the history of cigars, the cigar lifestyle, and advice for both novices and connoisseurs. 60m; VHS. **A:** Adult. **P:** Instruction. **U:** Home. **How-Ins:** Smoking. **Acq:** Purchase. **Dist:** Tapeworm Video Distributors Inc. $19.95.

Allah Tantou 1991
Using home movies, newsreels, dramatizations, a prison journal, and a forced confession, director Achkar traces the life and imprisonment of his father, Marof Achkar, and the corruption of the Toure regime ruling over Africa's Guinea. Not unlike Guinea itself, Marof Achkar was a confident and charismatic leader stripped of his identity, position, and family for the sake of European colonization. In French with English subtitles. 62m; VHS, 3/4 U. **C:** Directed by David Achkar. **Pr:** David Achkar. **A:** College-Adult. **P:** Education. **U:** Institution. **L:** French, English. **Gen-Edu:** Documentary Films, Africa, Human Rights. **Acq:** Purchase, Rent/Lease. **Dist:** California Newsreel. $195.00.

Allan Hoffenblum's Seminar: The 5 Factors Essential for a Winning Campaign 1994
Three-tape set, filmed before a live audience, offers practical advice on how to determine the potential of a campaign and outlines Hoffenblum's strategies for success, including fund raising, volunteers, and how to deal with the media. Campaign manual available separately. 120m; VHS. **A:** Adult. **P:** Instruction. **U:** Institution. **Gen-Edu:** Politics & Government, How-To. **Acq:** Purchase. **Dist:** Allan Hoffenblum & Associates. $89.95.

Allan Quartermain and the Temple of Skulls 2008 (R) — ★1/2
Passably enjoyable adventure (filmed in South Africa) is a retelling of H. Rider Haggard's "King Solomon Mines." Desperately in need of money, washed-up adventurer Allan Quartermain (Michael) is trying to sell his half of a treasure map to baddie Hartford (Adamson). Along comes Lady Anna (Stone) and her silly brother Sir Henry (Bonjour) with the other half of the map and the trio reluctantly agree to team up, which doesn't make Hartford too happy. 90m; DVD. **C:** Sean Cameron

Michael; Chris(topher) Adamson; Natalie Stone; Daniel Boujour; Wittly Jourdan; Nick Everhart; Directed by Mark Atkins; Written by David Michael Latt; Cinematography by Mark Atkins; Music by Kays Al-Atrakchi. **A:** Sr. High-Adult. **P:** Entertainment. **U:** Home. **Mov-Ent**: Africa. **Acq:** Purchase. **Dist:** The Asylum.

Allan Quatermain and the Lost City of Gold 1986 (PG) — ★½
While trying to find his brother, Quatermain discovers a lost African civilization, in this weak adaptation of an H. Rider Haggard adventure. An ostensible sequel to the equally shallow "King Solomon's Mines." 100m; VHS, DVD, CC. **C:** Richard Chamberlain; Sharon Stone; James Earl Jones; Directed by Gary Nelson; Written by Gene Quintano; Lee Reynolds; Cinematography by Frederick Elmes. **Pr:** Cannon Films. **A:** Jr. High-Adult. **P:** Entertainment. **U:** Home. **Mov-Ent**: Action-Adventure, Africa. **Acq:** Purchase. **Dist:** Anchor Bay Entertainment. $9.99.

Allan Ruppersberg: The Secret Life and Death 1991
Ruppersberg conducts a tour of his own exhibition at the Museum of Contemporary Art in L.A. 29m; VHS. **A:** Sr. High-Adult. **P:** Education. **U:** Home. **Fin-Art**: Documentary Films, Art & Artists. **Acq:** Purchase. **Dist:** Facets Multimedia Inc. $39.95.

Allan Stein: Pre-Season Strength & Conditioning—The Foundation of a Championship Team 2010 (Unrated)
Coach Alan Stein demonstrates drills to develop speed, reaction time, and physical and mental agility for basketball teams. 74m; DVD. **A:** Family. **P:** Education. **U:** Home. **Spo-Rec**: Basketball, Athletic Instruction/Coaching, Fitness/Exercise. **Acq:** Purchase. **Dist:** Championship Productions. $39.99.

Alle Jahre Wieder: 1983 1983
Singers, groups, and choirs present a program of Christmas music from Ramsau, Nuernberg, Koenigsee, Dinkelsbuehl and other picturesque locales. In German only. 60m; VHS. **TV Std:** NTSC, PAL. **C:** Heino; Lolita; Franzl Lang. **A:** Family. **P:** Entertainment. **U:** Home. **L:** German. **Mov-Ent**: Christmas, Singing, Germany. **Acq:** Purchase, Rent/Lease. **Dist:** German Language Video Center. $39.95.

Al'leessi....an African Actress 2004 (Unrated)
Chronicles the cinematic career of Zalika Souley, Africa's first professional female actress who was legendary for her bad girl roles in African films. Souley who now lives with her four children in a small apartment in Naimey with no electricity or water speaks candidly about the way audiences confused her with the characters she portrayed and as she gained celebrity abroad she was chastised in her own country. 69m; DVD. **A:** Adult. **P:** Education. **U:** Institution. **L:** French. **Gen-Edu**: Africa, Film History, Women. **Acq:** Purchase. **Dist:** Women Make Movies. $295.00.

Alleged 2010 (Unrated) — ★½
Simplistic drama with an emphasis on the movie's religious intentions. In 1925, ambitious Dayton, Tennessee newspaper reporter Charles Anderson becomes part of the media circus surrounding the so-called Scopes 'Monkey' Trial. Cynical columnist H.L. Mencken becomes Charles' mentor, much to the dismay of his fiance and fellow reporter Rose, who feels Charles isn't thinking for himself. 91m; DVD. **C:** Nathan West; Colm Meaney; Ashley Johnson; Fred Dalton Thompson; Brian Dennehy; Jamie Kolacki; Directed by Tom Hines; Written by Brian Godawa; Cinematography by John Samaras; Music by John R. Graham. **A:** Jr. High-Adult. **P:** Entertainment. **U:** Home. **Mov-Ent**: Journalism, Law. **Acq:** Purchase. **Dist:** Image Entertainment Inc.

Allegheny Rail, Volume II: The Western Maryland 19??
Classic train footage. Western Maryland 2-10-0 Decapods, 4-6-6-4 Challengers, 4-8-4 Potomacs and first generation diesels journey the Connellsville mainline and the Elkins subdivision through the Salisbury Viaduct, Big Savage Tunnel, and the arduous Black Fork grade. 52m; DVD. **A:** Family. **P:** Education. **U:** Home. **L:** English. **Gen-Edu**: Trains, U.S. States. **Acq:** Purchase. **Dist:** The Civil War Standard; WB Video Productions. $39.95.

Allegheny Rails: The Western Maryland ????
Watch diesels power their way through rugged terrain across Western Maryland. 52m; VHS, DVD. **A:** College-Adult. **P:** Education. **U:** Home. **Gen-Edu**: Trains. **Acq:** Purchase. **Dist:** The Civil War Standard. $39.95.

Allegheny Rails, Volume 1: The Baltimore & Ohio 19??
Steam leviathans from Baltimore & Ohio such as the "Big Six" 2-10-2, EM1 Class 2-8-8-4, and Q1BA Class 2-8-2 ride the Pittsburgh Division, over the Sand Patch grade, and through the Cumberland Division. 55m; DVD. **A:** Family. **P:** Education. **U:** Home. **L:** English. **Gen-Edu**: Trains, U.S. States. **Acq:** Purchase. **Dist:** WB Video Productions; The Civil War Standard. $39.95.

Allegheny Uprising 1939 (Unrated) — ★★½
Set in 1759, the story of a frontiersman who clashes with a British military commander in order to stop the sale of firearms to Indians. The stars of "Stagecoach" are back on board in this lesser effort. Also available colorized. 81m/B/W; VHS, DVD, CC. **C:** John Wayne; Claire Trevor; George Sanders; Brian Donlevy; Chill Wills; Moroni Olsen; Directed by William A. Seiter. **Pr:** RKO. **A:** Family. **P:** Entertainment. **U:** Home. **Mov-Ent**: Western. **Acq:** Purchase. **Dist:** Turner Broadcasting System Inc. $14.98.

Allegiance 2012 (R) — ★½
One-dimensional drama set over a single day in 2004. White National Guard Lt. Danny Sefton (Gabel) gets homefront duty while his unit is being deployed to Iraq, thanks to his politican dad's intervention. Feeling guilty, he tries to help black medic Chris Reyes (Bow Wow), who can't get a transfer even though his young son is dying. 91m; DVD, Blu-Ray. **C:** Seth Gabel; Bow Wow; Aidan Quinn; Pablo Schreiber; Malik Yoba; Directed by Michael Connors; Written by Michael Connors; Cinematography by Daniel Vecchione. **A:** Sr. High-Adult. **P:** Entertainment. **U:** Home. **L:** English. **Mov-Ent**: Armed Forces--U.S. **Acq:** Purchase. **Dist:** ARC Entertainment, LLC.

Allegra's Christmas 1997
Christmas stories featuring characters from the Nickelodeon animated series. 26m; VHS. **A:** Primary. **P:** Entertainment. **U:** Home. **Chl-Juv**: Animation & Cartoons, Christmas. **Acq:** Purchase. **Dist:** Paramount Pictures Corp. $12.95.

Allegra's Window: Sing Along with Allegra and Lindi 1998
Contains seven sing-along songs from the Nickelodeon children's show. 28m; VHS. **A:** Preschool-Primary. **P:** Entertainment. **U:** Home. **Chl-Juv**: Music--Children. **Acq:** Purchase. **Dist:** Paramount Pictures Corp. $9.95.

Allegro 2005 (Unrated) — ★½
Emotionally frigid pianist Zetterstrom (Thomson) is unable to tell his girlfriend Andrea (Christensen) that he loves her, which causes some bizarre time rupture. He loses his memories, which are sealed-off in a special section of Copenhagen called the Zone. When Zetterstrom returns to Copenhagen after ten years, he's instructed to go to Zone and see if he can recapture his past. Since the romantic leads have zero chemistry, this doesn't seem too important but the visual effects are kinda cool. Danish with subtitles. 88m; DVD. **C:** Ulrich Thomsen; Henning Moritzen; Helena Christensen; Svetoslav Korolev; Directed by Christoffer Boe; Written by Christoffer Boe; Mikawel Wulff; Cinematography by Manuel Alberto Claro; Music by Thomas Knak. **A:** College-Adult. **P:** Entertainment. **U:** Home. **L:** Danish. **Mov-Ent**: Science Fiction. **Acq:** Purchase. **Dist:** Entertainment One US LP.

Allegro Non Troppo 1976 (PG) — ★★★
An energetic and bold collection of animated skits set to classical music in this Italian version of Disney's "Fantasia." Watch for the evolution of life set to Ravel's Bolero, or better yet, watch the whole darn movie. Features Nichetti (often referred to as the Italian Woody Allen, particularly by people in Italy) in the non-animated segments, who went on to write, direct, and star (he may have sold concessions in the lobby as well) in "The Icicle Thief." 75m; VHS, DVD. **C:** Maurizio Nichetti; Nestor Garay; Maria Giovannini; Directed by Bruno Bozzetto; Written by Maurizio Nichetti; Bruno Bozzetto; Guido Manuli; Cinematography by Mario Masini. **Pr:** Specialty. **A:** Family. **P:** Entertainment. **U:** Home. **Mov-Ent**: Animation & Cartoons. **Acq:** Purchase. **Dist:** BMG Entertainment; Image Entertainment Inc.; Baker and Taylor. $29.95.

The Alleluia Kid 1977
Black all-American quarterback on the way to a brilliant career is ashamed of his humble origins and religious upbringing. Rides high until illness shatters his life. Theme: the fullness of life only comes by passing through death. 25m; VHS, 3/4 U, Special order formats. **C:** Philip Michael Thomas; Helen Martin. **Pr:** Paulist Productions. **A:** Sr. High-Adult. **P:** Religious. **U:** Institution, CCTV, SURA. **Gen-Edu**: Death. **Acq:** Purchase, Rent/Lease. **Dist:** Paulist Productions.

Allen & Rossi Comedy Special 1994
Classic comedy routines performed by the duo of Marty Allen and Steve Rossi. 40m; VHS. **A:** Adult. **P:** Entertainment. **U:** Home. **Mov-Ent**: Comedy--Performance. **Acq:** Purchase. **Dist:** White Star. $19.95.

Allen Ginsberg 19??
Part of the Moveable Feast: Profiles of Contemporary American Authors Series. Allen Ginsberg discusses his past, the "Beat Generation" and other writers, including Jack Kerouac, William Burroughs, and William Carlos Williams. 30m; VHS. **Pr:** Atlas Video. **A:** Family. **P:** Education. **U:** Institution. **Gen-Edu**: Biography, Literature, Language Arts. **Acq:** Purchase. **Dist:** Instructional Video. $19.95.

The Allen Smart Scope Explained 1987
The Allen Smart Scope, which tests automotive systems, is demonstrated. 15m; VHS. **Pr:** Bergwall Productions. **A:** Sr. High-Adult. **P:** Instruction. **U:** Institution. **How-Ins**: Automobiles, Education. **Acq:** Purchase. **Dist:** Bergwall Productions, Inc. $119.00.
Indiv. Titles: 1. Basic Parts 2. Testing and Maintenance.

Allen Toussaint: Melody 19??
Composer Allen Toussaint demonstrates musical contour and explains how repetition, variation, and contrast are used in creating melodies. Provides in-class activities to help students learn about musical creativity. Includes teacher's guide. 30m; VHS, CC. **A:** Primary. **P:** Education. **U:** Institution. **Chl-Juv**: Performing Arts, Education. **Acq:** Purchase. **Dist:** GPN Educational Media. $23.95.

Allen's Strange and Lonely World: The Story of an Autistic Child 1979
This program focuses on Allen, a six and a half-year-old autistic child who attends a special school where training is based on behavior modification plus parental involvement in the training procedure. 29m; VHS, 3/4 U. **Pr:** Health Communications Network. **A:** College-Adult. **P:** Education. **U:** Institution, SURA. **Hea-Sci**: Handicapped. **Acq:** Purchase, Rent/Lease, Subscription.

Allergic Aspergillosis: Growing Recognition of a Problem 1986
An analysis for doctors of the entitled lung-degenerative condition. 53m; VHS, 3/4 U. **A:** Adult. **P:** Professional. **U:** Institution, CCTV, Home, SURA. **Hea-Sci**: Respiratory System. **Acq:** Purchase, Rent/Lease, Subscription. **Dist:** Emory Medical Television Network.

Allergy 1975
The numerous substances most commonly causing allergies and hay fever are explored, as well as the problems of asthma and the ways of living with these ailments. 10m; VHS, 3/4 U. **Pr:** Professional Research. **A:** Adult. **P:** Education. **U:** Institution, CCTV, SURA. **Hea-Sci**: Allergy. **Acq:** Purchase, Rent/Lease. **Dist:** Discovery Education. $99.00.

Allergy and Immunotherapy 1989
Viewers are taught about the range in the seriousness of allergies, from annoying to life-threatening. 26m; VHS, 3/4 U. **Pr:** Films for the Humanities. **A:** Jr. High-Adult. **P:** Education. **U:** Institution, SURA. **Hea-Sci**: Allergy. **Acq:** Purchase, Rent/Lease. **Dist:** Films for the Humanities & Sciences. $149.00.

Allergy Immunotherapy: Principles, Practice, and Prospects for the Future 1983
This program explains that allergy immunotherapy is effective for some types of allergic rhinitis and anaphylaxis. 58m; VHS, 3/4 U. **Pr:** Emory University. **A:** College-Adult. **P:** Professional. **U:** Institution, CCTV, Home, SURA. **Hea-Sci**: Allergy, Immunology. **Acq:** Purchase, Rent/Lease, Subscription. **Dist:** Emory Medical Television Network.

Alles umsonst 1983 (Unrated)
After 30 years of a less-than-perfect marriage, baker Schmidt finds joy only in the companionship of his assistant. When his shrewish wife is found dead, he becomes the prime suspect. An episode of the "Tatort" series. In German only. 90m; VHS. **TV Std:** NTSC, PAL. **Pr:** German Language Video Center. **A:** Jr. High-Adult. **P:** Entertainment. **U:** Home. **L:** German. **Mov-Ent**: Mystery & Suspense, TV Movies. **Acq:** Purchase, Rent/Lease. **Dist:** German Language Video Center. $33.95.

Alleviating Stress Associated with Nursing Home Admission 19??
Examines the anxiety and stress patients and their families face when admission into a nursing home is necessary. Three residents discuss their fears and anxieties prior to being admitted into the nursing home and how they have adjusted their lives. Emphasis is placed on how staff can ease the transition. 20m; VHS. **Pr:** John Hopkins. **A:** Adult. **P:** Education. **U:** Institution. **Hea-Sci**: Aging, Medical Care, Patient Care. **Acq:** Purchase, Rent/Lease. **Dist:** University of Maryland. $300.00.

Alley Cat 1984 (R) — ★
Woman uses martial arts to fight back against a street gang that attacked her. 82m; VHS, DVD. **C:** Karin Mani; Robert Torti; Brit Helfer; Michael Wayne; Jon Greene; Directed by Edward Victor. **Pr:** Film Ventures International. **A:** Adult. **P:** Entertainment. **U:** Home. **Mov-Ent**: Martial Arts. **Acq:** Purchase. **Dist:** Lions Gate Television Corp. $69.98.

The Alley Cats 1965 — ★★
Leslie, a part of Berlin's swinging '60s set, is being ignored by fiance Logan in favor of his affair with her friend Agnes. So Leslie decides to retaliate by having an affair with a painter, Christian, but since Leslie just can't stand to be alone, when Christian is called away on business, she succumbs to the charms of socialite Irena. 83m/B/W; VHS, DVD. **C:** Anna Arthur; Sabrina Koch; Karin (Karen) Field; Chaz Hickman; Harold Baerow; Uta Levka; Directed by Radley Metzger; Written by Radley Metzger. **Pr:** Radley H. Metzger. **A:** College-Adult. **P:** Entertainment. **U:** Home. **Mov-Ent**: Sex & Sexuality. **Acq:** Purchase. **Dist:** First Run Features.

Alley Cats Strike 2000 (Unrated) — ★★½
Four teen misfits have an interest in bowling that makes them outcasts among their hipper classmates. But then their skills could win them a major trophy and school glory. 88m; VHS, CC. **C:** Robert Ri'chard; Kyle Schmid; Kaley Cuoco; Mimi Paley; Daphne Maxwell; Directed by Rod Daniel. **A:** Family. **P:** Entertainment. **U:** Home. **Mov-Ent**: Education, Bowling. **Acq:** Purchase. **Dist:** Buena Vista Home Entertainment.

Alley of Alley 1984
A visual tour of some of the poorer but colorful urban dwellings of Japan. 15m; VHS, 3/4 U. **Pr:** Akira Matsumoto. **A:** Jr. High-Adult. **P:** Education. **U:** Institution, SURA. **Gen-Edu**: Japan. **Acq:** Purchase, Rent/Lease. **Dist:** Video Out Distribution.

Allie & Me 1997 — ★★
Gullible beautician Allie (Baron) wants to make some changes in her life but doesn't quite expect what happens when she teams up with wronged wife Michelle (Benson). They decide to take out their frustrations by committing a burglary but find the Beverly Hills abode occupied by stud Rodney (Wilder), whom they take as a hostage, and then Allie decides to fall in love with him. Lots of recognizable faces but the comedy doesn't quite come together. 86m; VHS, DVD. **C:** Joanne Baron; Lyndie Benson; James Wilder; Steven Prince; Ed Lauter; Lainie Kazan; Dyan Cannon; Harry Hamlin; Julianne Phillips; Directed by Michael Rymer; Written by Michael Rymer; Cinematography by Rex Nicholson. **A:** Sr. High-Adult. **P:** Entertainment. **U:** Home. **Mov-Ent**. **Acq:** Purchase. **Dist:** Vanguard International Cinema, Inc.

Allies at War 2002
An historical documentary between three would-be World War II allies: American President Franklin Delano Roosevelt, British Prime Minister Winston Churchill, and French general and statesman Charles de Gaulle, whom the other two men came to

distrust. 125m; DVD. **A:** Adult. **P:** Entertainment. **U:** Home. **Gen-Edu:** Documentary Films, Biography: Politics, World War Two. **Acq:** Purchase. **Dist:** MPI Media Group. $24.98.

Alligator 1980 (R) — ★★★
Dumped down a toilet 12 long years ago, lonely alligator Ramon resides in the city sewers, quietly eating and sleeping. In addition to feasting on the occasional stray human, Ramon devours the animal remains of a chemical plant's experiment involving growth hormones and eventually begins to swell at an enormous rate. Nothing seems to satisfy Ramon's ever-widening appetite: not all the people or all the buildings in the whole town, but he keeps trying, much to the regret of the guilt-ridden cop and lovely scientist who get to know each other while trying to nab the gator. Mediocre special effects are only a distraction in this witty eco-monster take. 94m; VHS, DVD. **C:** Robert Forster; Robin Riker; Jack Carter; Henry Silva; Dean Jagger; Michael V. Gazzo; Perry Lang; Bart Braverman; Angel Tompkins; Sue Lyon; Sydney Lassick; James Ingersoll; John Lisbon Wood; Robert Doyle; Patti Jerome; Directed by Lewis Teague; Written by John Sayles; Frank Ray Perilli; Cinematography by Joseph Mangine; Music by Craig Hundley. **Pr:** Group I. **A:** Jr. High-Adult. **P:** Entertainment. **U:** Home. **Mov-Ent:** Horror. **Acq:** Purchase. **Dist:** Lions Gate Television Corp. $14.98.

Alligator 2: The Mutation 1990 (PG-13) — ★★
Not a sequel to 1980's surprisingly good "Alligator," but a bland rehash with a decent cast. Once again a toxic alligator grows to enormous size and menaces a community. A Donald-Trump-like villain and pro wrestlers (!) bring this up to date, but it's all on the level of a TV disaster movie; even the PG-13 rating is a bit too harsh. 92m; VHS. **C:** Steve Railsback; Dee Wallace; Joseph Bologna; Woody Brown; Bill Daily; Brock Peters; Richard Lynch; Holly Gagnier; Directed by Jon Hess; Written by Curt Allen; Cinematography by Joseph Mangine. **Pr:** New Line Cinema. **A:** Sr. High-Adult. **P:** Entertainment. **U:** Home. **Mov-Ent:** Horror. **Acq:** Purchase. **Dist:** Sony Pictures Home Entertainment Inc.; New Line Home Video. $19.98.

Alligator Alley 1972 (Unrated) — ★
When two young divers witness a major drug deal, they become entangled in a web of danger they never expected. 92m; VHS, DVD. **C:** Steve Alaimo; John Davis Chandler; Willie Pastrano; Jeremy Slate; Cece Stone; Directed by William Grefe. **A:** Adult. **P:** Entertainment. **U:** Home. **Mov-Ent:** Action-Adventure. **Acq:** Purchase. **Dist:** Unknown Distributor.

Alligator Aquaculture 19??
Looks at the world of alligator farming. Discusses such topics as alligator biology, habitat, behavior, facility requirements, egg incubation, feeding, harvesting, and marketing. 18m; VHS. **A:** Jr. High-Adult. **P:** Education. **U:** Institution. **Bus-Ind:** Agriculture, Business, Animals. **Acq:** Purchase. **Dist:** CEV Multimedia. $69.95.

Alligator Eyes 1990 (R) — ★★½
Stranger wearing trouble like a cheap perfume enters the midst of a vacationing trio of New Yorkers. Their vulnerabilities are exposed by a young hitchhiker sporting a slinky polka dot ensemble and way cool sunglasses who insinuates herself into their vacation plans (not to mention their private lives), before the three realize she's blind and full of manipulative and vindictive tricks, thanks to the usual brutal childhood. Psycho-sexo-logical thriller has some fine performances and a promising beginning, before fizzling into celluloid cotton candy. 101m; VHS, DVD. **C:** Annabelle Larsen; Roger Kabler; Mary McLain; Allen McCullough; John MacKay; Directed by John Feldman; Written by John Feldman; Music by Sheila Silver. **Pr:** John Feldman; John Feldman; Castle Hill Productions. **A:** College-Adult. **P:** Entertainment. **U:** Home. **Mov-Ent:** Mystery & Suspense, Mystery & Suspense, Blindness. **Acq:** Purchase. **Dist:** Unknown Distributor.

An Alligator Named Daisy 1955 (Unrated) — ★★½
And what a troublesome reptile she turns out to be! Peter (Sinden) is set to marry wealthy Vanessa (Dors) when he suddenly acquires a baby alligator from another ferry boat passenger. He tries to dispose of Daisy in various ways but she's like a boomerang and keeps returning, as does zoo worker Moira (Carson) who urges Peter just to keep Daisy. But Vanessa gives him an ultimatum. 85m; DVD. **C:** Donald Sinden; Diana Dors; Jeannie Carson; James Robertson Justice; Roland Culver; Avice Landone; Margaret Rutherford; Stanley Holloway; Directed by J. Lee Thompson; Written by Jack Davies; Cinematography by Reg Wyer; Music by Stanley Black. **A:** Jr. High-Adult. **P:** Entertainment. **U:** Home. **Mov-Ent:** Comedy--Romantic, Zoos. **Acq:** Purchase. **Dist:** VCI Entertainment.

Alligators 1996
Examines the lives of alligators as they battle for territory and mates, hatch their young, swim under water, walk and even run on land, and rule the Everglades. Hosted by nature expert Rich Kern. 30m; VHS. **A:** Family. **P:** Education. **U:** Home. **Gen-Edu:** Animals. **Acq:** Purchase. **Dist:** Ivy Classics Video; Education 2000, Inc. $29.95.

Alligators All Around 1978
An animated family of alligators clowns its way through the alphabet. 2m; VHS, 3/4 U. **Pr:** Sheldon Riss. **A:** Preschool. **P:** Entertainment. **U:** Institution, SURA. **Chl-Juv:** Language Arts. **Acq:** Purchase. **Dist:** Weston Woods Studios.

The Allman Brothers Band: Brothers of the Road 1985
A performance concert by the legendary band, featuring "Pony Boy," "Jessica," "Ramblin' Man," "Whippin Post," "Crazy Love," "One Way Out" and many more. 113m; VHS, DVD. **Pr:** RCA Video Productions. **A:** Family. **P:** Entertainment. **U:** Home. **Mov-Ent:** Music--Performance, Music--Pop/Rock. **Acq:** Purchase. **Dist:** Music Video Distributors; Sony Pictures Home Entertainment Inc. $14.95.

The Allnighter 1987 (PG-13) — ★
A college coed searches through the hypersexed beach-party milieu of her senior year for Mr. Right. Bangle Hoffs is directed by her mom, to no avail. 95m; VHS, DVD. **C:** Susanna Hoffs; John Terlesky; Joan Cusack; Michael Ontkean; Directed by Tamar Simon Hoffs; Written by Tamar Simon Hoffs; Cinematography by Joseph D. Urbanczyk; Music by Charles Bernstein. **Pr:** Nancy Israel; Tamar Simon Hoffs; Tamar Simon Hoffs. **A:** Jr. High-Adult. **P:** Entertainment. **U:** Home. **Mov-Ent:** Comedy--Romantic, Sex & Sexuality, Prostitution. **Acq:** Purchase. **Dist:** Movies Unlimited; Universal Studios Home Video. $79.95.

Allo 'Allo: Complete Series 9 1990 (Unrated)
British television sitcom series from 1982-1992. Rene lures the Germans into a windmill marked for target practice in "Gone with the Windmill," escapes Communist capture in "A Tour de France," and turns himself in faking amnesia in "Dead Man Marching." Gruber, von Klinkerhoffen, and the Colonel go to Berlin to assassinate Hitler in "A Fishy Sendoff," and more trouble comes at the Fishmongers Parade in "Tarts and Flickers." A painting hidden at the end of the war is now worth millions but how will the shares be divided in "A Wrinkle in Time." 7 episodes. 180m; DVD. **A:** Sr. High-Adult. **P:** Entertainment. **U:** Home. **Mov-Ent:** Drama, World War Two, Television Series. **Acq:** Purchase. **Dist:** BBC Worldwide Publishing Ltd.

'Allo 'Allo! Complete Series Five 2006 (Unrated)
Presents the fifth season of the 1982-1992 British comedy series about Rene (Kaye), a cafe owner in France during World War II, who has trouble being faithful to wife Edith (Silvera) as he deals with Nazis who are searching for a priceless painting that is hidden in a sausage, two British airmen who won't leave, and the fact that he was shot and seemingly killed. Includes: Rene continues to help the French Resistance by trying to get his hands on the German's invasion plans while still having trouble fending off his lady pursuers. 26 episodes. ?m; DVD. **C:** Gordon Kaye; Carmen Silvera; Vicki Michelle; Richard Marner; Kim Hartman; Guy Siner; Kirsten Cooke. **A:** Sr. High-Adult. **P:** Entertainment. **U:** Home. **Mov-Ent:** Television Series, War--General, France. **Acq:** Purchase. **Dist:** Warner Home Video, Inc. $69.92.

'Allo 'Allo! Complete Series Four 2006 (Unrated)
Presents the fourth season of the 1982-1992 British comedy series about Rene (Kaye), a cafe owner in France during World War II, who has trouble being faithful to wife Edith (Silvera) as he deals with Nazis who are searching for a priceless painting that is hidden in a sausage, two British airmen who won't leave, and the fact that he was shot and seemingly killed. Includes: Rene is trapped in a POW camp and plots to escape, Rene and Edit must fill a waitress position when one winds up missing, and more mayhem occurs with a mix-up involving painting-filled sausages. 6 episodes. ?m; DVD. **C:** Gordon Kaye; Carmen Silvera; Vicki Michelle; Richard Marner; Kim Hartman; Guy Siner; Kirsten Cooke. **A:** Sr. High-Adult. **P:** Entertainment. **U:** Home. **Mov-Ent:** Television Series, War--General, France. **Acq:** Purchase. **Dist:** Warner Home Video, Inc. $24.98.

'Allo 'Allo! Complete Series Six 2007 (Unrated)
Presents the sixth season of the 1982-1992 British comedy series about Rene (Kaye), a cafe owner in France during World War II, who has trouble being faithful to wife Edith (Silvera) as he deals with Nazis who are searching for a priceless painting that is hidden in a sausage, two British airmen who won't leave, and the fact that he was shot and seemingly killed. Includes: Rene must rescue the British airmen after they are caught by the Germans and he tries to deal the priceless painting. 8 episodes. ?m; DVD. **C:** Gordon Kaye; Carmen Silvera; Vicki Michelle; Richard Marner; Kim Hartman; Guy Siner; Kirsten Cooke. **A:** Sr. High-Adult. **P:** Entertainment. **U:** Home. **Mov-Ent:** Television Series, War--General, France. **Acq:** Purchase. **Dist:** Warner Home Video, Inc. $34.98.

Allo! Allo! Complete Series Three 2005
World War II sitcom. DVD. **A:** Adult. **P:** Entertainment. **U:** Home. **Mov-Ent:** Television. **Acq:** Purchase. **Dist:** Warner Home Video, Inc. $34.98.

'Allo 'Allo! Complete Series Two 2005 (Unrated)
Presents the second season of the 1982-1992 British comedy series about Rene (Kaye), a cafe owner in France during World War II, who has trouble being faithful to wife Edith (Silvera) as he deals with Nazis who are searching for a priceless painting that is hidden in a sausage, two British airmen who won't leave, and the fact that he was shot and seemingly killed. Includes: Edith goes wild with her inheritance as Rene's sole beneficiary, posing as Rene's twin he must decide whether to win Edith back or move on with one of the waitresses, and Rene must help blow up a train supposedly carrying the art-filled sausage to Hitler. 7 episodes. 230m; DVD. **C:** Vicki Michelle; Richard Marner; Guy Siner; Gordon Kaye; Carmen Silvera; Kim Hartman; Kirsten Cooke. **A:** Sr. High-Adult. **P:** Entertainment. **U:** Home. **Mov-Ent:** Television Series, War--General, France. **Acq:** Purchase. **Dist:** Warner Home Video, Inc. $34.98.

'Allo 'Allo: Series I 1982
Britcom set in occupied France features Rene, a small cafe proprietor who works to deceive German Army members that frequent his bar. 2400m; DVD, CC. **A:** Adult. **P:** Entertainment. **U:** Home. **Mov-Ent:** Television. **Acq:** Purchase. **Dist:** Warner Home Video, Inc. $34.98.

Allonsanfan 1973 — ★★★½
Early Taviani, in which a disillusioned Jacobin aristocrat in 1816, after Napoleon has fallen, struggles with his revolutionary ideals and his accustomed lifestyle. Exciting score. In Italian with English subtitles. 115m; VHS. **C:** Marcello Mastroianni; Laura Betti; Renato de Carmine; Lea Massari; Mimsy Farmer; Claudio Cassinelli; Bruno Cirino; Michael Berger; Directed by Paolo Taviani; Vittorio Taviani; Written by Paolo Taviani; Vittorio Taviani; Cinematography by Giuseppe Ruzzolini; Music by Ennio Morricone. **Pr:** Italtoons Corporation; Wonder Movies. **A:** Jr. High-Adult. **P:** Entertainment. **U:** Home. **L:** Italian. **Mov-Ent.** **Acq:** Purchase. **Dist:** Facets Multimedia Inc.; Water Bearer Films Inc. $29.95.

Allosaurus: A Walking With Dinosaurs Special 2001 (Unrated)
Reconstructs the world of an Allosaurus dinosaur—dubbed "Big Al"?in this television special using digital technology and animatronics from television specials to detail the 15 years of its life. 1 episode. 60m; DVD. **C:** Narrated by Kenneth Branagh; Avery Brooks; Andre Dussollier. **A:** Family. **P:** Entertainment. **U:** Home. **Mov-Ent:** Television Series, Dinosaurs, Documentary Films. **Acq:** Purchase. **Dist:** Warner Home Video, Inc. $14.98.

Allosaurus: A Walking with Dinosaurs Special 2005
Scientists piece together the story of the Jurassic age dinosaur from a nearly-complete skeleton discovered in Wyoming. Computer graphics and animatronics recreated its life. ?m; DVD. **A:** Jr. High-Adult. **P:** Entertainment. **U:** Home. **Gen-Edu:** Documentary Films. **Acq:** Purchase. **Dist:** Warner Home Video, Inc.

All's Fair 1989 (Unrated) — ★
Silly and predictable comedy about executives who take on their spouses at weekend war games. An unfortunate waste of a good cast. 89m; VHS, CC. **C:** George Segal; Sally Kellerman; Robert Carradine; Jennifer Edwards; Jane Kaczmarek; John Kapelos; Lou Ferrigno; Directed by Rocky Lane; Cinematography by Peter Lyons Collister. **A:** Adult. **P:** Entertainment. **U:** Home. **Mov-Ent:** Comedy--Romantic. **Acq:** Purchase. **Dist:** No Longer Available.

All's Fair in Love and War 1997
Classic crime drama about the clash of two underworld mob families. 117m; VHS. **A:** Adult. **P:** Entertainment. **U:** Home. **Mov-Ent.** **Acq:** Purchase. **Dist:** Tapeworm Video Distributors Inc. $89.95.

All's Faire in Love 2009 (Unrated) — ★½
Wannabe actress Kate (Ricci) takes a summer job at a Renaissance Faire where college quarterback Will (Benjamin) has been assigned to work by his irate professor as a punishment for blowing off class. There's a social hierarchy, headed by a Queen (Ann-Margret) who instills competition among her somewhat crazy subjects even as Kate and Will find romance. 108m; DVD, Blu-Ray. **C:** Christina Ricci; Owen Benjamin; Ann-Margret; Cedric the Entertainer; Matthew Lillard; Bill Engvall; Directed by Scott Marshall; Written by Scott Marshall; Cinematography by Mark Irwin; Music by Jeff Cardoni; Julian Jackson. **A:** Jr. High-Adult. **P:** Entertainment. **U:** Home. **Mov-Ent:** Comedy--Romantic. **Acq:** Purchase. **Dist:** Hannover House.

All's Well That Ends Well 1981
Clever characters and delightful scenes highlight this comedy in which Shakespeare uses one of his favorite devices-trickery. The new wife of a young count resorts to chicanery to win her husband's respect. Part of the "Shakespeare Plays" series. 141m; VHS. **C:** Ian Charleson; Angela Down; Celia Johnson; Peter Jeffrey; Donald Sinden; Rosemary Leach; Pippa Guard; Michael Hordern. **Pr:** Cedric Messina; Dr. Jonathan Miller; British Broadcasting Corporation. **A:** Sr. High-Adult. **P:** Entertainment. **U:** Institution. **Fin-Art:** TV Movies. **Acq:** Purchase. **Dist:** Ambrose Video Publishing, Inc. $249.95.

Ally McBeal: Ally on Sex and the Single Life 2000 (Unrated)
Presents various episodes from the 1997-2002 offbeat comedy-drama-romance television series about the life of lawyer Ally McBeal (Flockhart) as she tries to get over her feelings for her old boyfriend Billy (Bellows) who's now married and a colleague. Includes: "Pilot," "The Attitude," "Cro-Magnon," "Silver Bells," "Theme of Life," and "The Playing Field." 6 episodes. 264m; DVD. **C:** Calista Flockhart; Peter MacNichol; Greg Germann; Jane Krakowski; Gil Bellows; Lisa Nicole Carson. **A:** Sr. High-Adult. **P:** Entertainment. **U:** Home. **Mov-Ent:** Television Series, Drama, Law. **Acq:** Purchase. **Dist:** Fox Home Entertainment. $39.98.

Ally McBeal: The Complete Fifth Season 2001 (Unrated)
Fox Television 1997-2002 legal dramedy. In the first episode, "Friends and Lovers", Cage misunderstands Ally and thinks she loves him. The governor offers Ling a position as a judge in "Judge Ling," John confesses his feelings for Ally and she tells him they will only be platonic in "Neutral Corners." Ally and Glenn alternately flirt with each other and avoid each other during the episode "Fear of Flirting," and Ling continues to have a gift of the dramatic by adding an orchestra to her courtroom in "I Want Love." 22 episodes. DVD. **A:** Jr. High-Adult. **P:** Entertainment. **U:** Home. **Acq:** Purchase. **Dist:** Sony Pictures Home Entertainment Inc. $39.98.

Ally McBeal: The Complete First Season 1997 (Unrated)
Fox Television 1997-2002 legal dramedy. Ally is a talented lawyer who got into the profession for all the wrong reasons, a man, who dumped her before they matriculated law school. She now works for the Boston firm Cage & Fish along with the former love and his current wife, which makes for many awkward moments and fantasies. Ally represents a Jewish woman seeking spiritual release from her comatose husband in "The Attitude," defends a repeat offending prostitute who turns out to be a transgender man in "Boy to the World," and

co-councils a case with Billy involving an aging artist battling heirs over the control of his estate in "Once in a Lifetime." 23 episodes. 969m; DVD. **C:** Calista Flockhart; Greg Germann; Jane Krakowski; Peter MacNichol. **A:** Jr. High-Adult. **P:** Entertainment. **U:** Home. **Mov-Ent:** Television Series, Law, Comedy-Drama. **Acq:** Purchase. **Dist:** Fox Home Entertainment. $39.99.

Ally McBeal: The Complete Fourth Season 2000 (Unrated)
Fox Television 1997-2002 legal dramedy. In "Sex, Lies, and Second Thoughts," Brian asks Ally to move in with him and she is unsure. "Girls' Night Out" has Ally scheduling a night out at a club, and "Two's A Crowd" shows Ally juggling two different men who are related. Ally makes fun of an old college friend and is then sued for defamation in "Without a Net," and she is nervous about kissing Larry for the first time in "The Last Virgin". 23 episodes. 964m; DVD. **A:** Jr. High-Adult. **P:** Entertainment. **U:** Home. **Mov-Ent:** Television Series. **Acq:** Purchase. **Dist:** Sony Pictures Home Entertainment Inc. $39.98.

Ally McBeal: The Complete Second Season 2010 (Unrated)
Fox Television 1997-2002 legal dramedy. In "The Real World," Ally and John defend a woman who had an affair with a minor, Georgia and John defend a restaurant that served horse meat in "They Eat Horses, Don't They?," a priest seeks the firm's legal counsel in "Fool's Night Out," feminist issues are front and center in "It's My Party," and a love triangle develops in the office between George, Ally, and Elaine in "The Story of Love." 23 episodes. 1080m; DVD. **A:** Jr. High-Adult. **P:** Entertainment. **U:** Home. **Mov-Ent:** Television Series. **Acq:** Purchase. **Dist:** $39.98.

Ally McBeal: The Complete Series 1997 (Unrated)
Fox Television 1997-2002 legal dramedy. Ally McBeal had loved Billy Thomas since they were children and eventually followed him to law school. When he decided to pursue a career apart from her Ally tried desperately to overcome her disappointment and broken heart. Now employed as an associate at Boston's Cage & Fish firm she's achieved much success in the courtroom but not so much in love, to make matters worse Billy has now come to work at her firm with his new wife in tow. 112 episodes. Soundtrack CD. 1271m; DVD. **C:** Calista Flockhart; Greg Germann; Jane Krakowski; Peter MacNichol. **A:** Sr. High-Adult. **P:** Entertainment. **U:** Home. **Mov-Ent:** Television Series, Law, Comedy-Drama. **Acq:** Purchase. **Dist:** Fox Home Entertainment. $199.99.

Ally McBeal: The Complete Third Season 1999 (Unrated)
Fox Television 1997-2002 legal dramedy. Ally sleeps with a man at a car wash in "Car Wash," Ally and Ling kiss but realize they miss male genitalia in "Buried Pleasures," in "Seeing Green," Ally falls in love with her fantasy Al Green, "Heat Wave" shows Ally being sued because of the ramifications of her tryst in the car wash, and "Troubled Water" shows the gang's antics on the day before Thanksgiving. 21 episodes. 945m; DVD. **A:** Adult. **P:** Entertainment. **U:** Home. **Mov-Ent:** Television Series. **Acq:** Purchase. **Dist:** Fox Home Entertainment. $39.98.

Almanac of Fall 1985 — ★★
Set in a claustrophobic apartment, where the occupants reveal all their deepest hostilities, fears, and obsessions. In Hungarian with English subtitles. 119m; VHS, DVD. **C:** Hedi Temessy; Erika Bodnar; Miklos B. Szekely; Pal Hetenyi; Janos Derzsi; Directed by Bela Tarr; Written by Bela Tarr. **A:** Sr. High-Adult. **P:** Entertainment. **U:** Home. **L:** Hungarian. **Mov-Ent:** Mystery & Suspense. **Acq:** Purchase. **Dist:** Facets Multimedia Inc. $59.95.

Almighty: Soul Destruction Live 19??
Almighty performs 16 songs live from London's Town & Country club. Titles include "Destroyed," "Love Religion," and "Crucify." 65m; VHS. **A:** Jr. High-Adult. **P:** Entertainment. **U:** Home. **Mov-Ent:** Music--Pop/Rock, Music--Performance. **Acq:** Purchase. **Dist:** Music Video Distributors. $64.95.

Almighty Thor 2011 (Unrated) — **Bomb!**
Almighty mess. The Asylum's boring rip-off of "Thor" debuted on the Syfy Channel. Evil Loki wants the Hammer of Invincibility so he can destroy Earth. Odin refuses, so Loki destroys Asgard and then heads to Earth anyway (specifically L.A.). A constantly whining Thor gets some extra training to battle his brother from Valkyrie Jarnsaxa, who eventually just gives the big lug an Uzi to cap anyone who gets in his way. 90m; DVD, Blu-Ray. **C:** Richard Grieco; Patricia Velasquez; Kevin Nash; Cody Deal; Jess Allen; Directed by Christopher Ray; Written by Erik Estenberg; Cinematography by Alexander Yellen; Music by Chris Ridenhour. **A:** Jr. High-Adult. **P:** Entertainment. **U:** Home. **Mov-Ent:** Fantasy, Folklore & Legends. **Acq:** Purchase. **Dist:** The Asylum.

Almonds & Raisins: A History of the Yiddish Cinema 1983
The phenomenon of Yiddish cinema is remembered by the actors, directors and producers who made it happen. Excerpts from the great filmworks of Maurice Schwartz, Molly Picon, Moishe Oysher and others provide a glimpse of this lost era. 90m/B/W; VHS. **C:** Narrated by Orson Welles; Directed by Russ Karel. **Pr:** Ergo Media. **A:** Family. **P:** Entertainment. **U:** Home. **Gen-Edu:** Documentary Films, Judaism, Film History. **Acq:** Purchase. **Dist:** Ergo Media Inc.; Tapeworm Video Distributors Inc. $79.95.

Almos' a Man 1978
Richard Wright's story of a black teenage farm worker in the late 1930s who must endure the pains of growing up. From the "American Short Story" series. 51m; VHS. **C:** LeVar Burton; Madge Sinclair; Robert DoQui. **Pr:** Learning in Focus, Inc. **A:** Sr. High-College. **P:** Entertainment. **U:** Home. **Mov-Ent:** Family Viewing, Literature--American, Black Culture. **Acq:** Purchase. **Dist:** Karol Media; Monterey Home Video; Facets Multimedia Inc. $24.95.

. . .Almost 1990 (PG) — ★★
Arquette plays a curiously giddy bookworm with a vivid imagination. When her husband disappears on their anniversary, the man of her dreams shows up to sweep her off her feet. Is he real or is he simply another daydream? Almost a good time. 87m; VHS, DVD. **C:** Rosanna Arquette; Bruce Spence; Directed by Michael Pattinson. **A:** Jr. High-Adult. **P:** Entertainment. **U:** Home. **Mov-Ent:** Comedy--Romantic, Fantasy, Romance. **Acq:** Purchase. **Dist:** Movies Unlimited. $49.99.

Almost an Angel 1990 (PG) — ★½
Another in a recent spate of angels and ghosts assigned back to earth by the head office. A life-long criminal (Hogan) commits a heroic act and finds himself a probationary angel returned to earth to gain permanent angel status. He befriends a wheelchair-bound man, falls in love with the guy's sister, and helps her out at a center for potential juvenile delinquents. Melodramatic and hokey in places, relying too much on Hogan's crocodilian charisma. 98m; VHS, DVD, CC. **C:** Paul Hogan; Linda Kozlowski; Elias Koteas; Doreen Lang; Charlton Heston; David Alan Grier; Larry Miller; Douglas Seale; Parley Baer; Hank Worden; Directed by John Cornell; Written by Paul Hogan; Cinematography by Russell Boyd; Music by Maurice Jarre. **Pr:** Paramount Pictures. **A:** Jr. High-Adult. **P:** Entertainment. **U:** Home. **Mov-Ent:** Comedy--Romantic. **Acq:** Purchase. **Dist:** Paramount Pictures Corp.

Almost Angels 1962 (Unrated) — ★★
Two boys romp in Austria as members of the Vienna Boys Choir. Lesser sentimental Disney effort that stars the actual members of the Choir; not much of a draw for today's Nintendo-jaded young viewers. 85m; VHS, DVD. **C:** Vincent Winter; Peter Weck; Hans Holt; Directed by Steve Previn. **Pr:** Walt Disney Studios. **A:** Family. **P:** Entertainment. **U:** Home. **Mov-Ent:** Musical, Children. **Acq:** Purchase. **Dist:** Walt Disney Studios Home Entertainment. $69.95.

Almost Blue 1993 (R) — ★½
A gigantic, slow-moving, movie cliche. Madsen is a sulky, hard-living sax player going off the deep end because of his wife's death. Walden is the good woman who comes along to save him from himself. Tenor saxman Ernie Watts doubles for Madsen. Do yourself a favor—skip the movie and listen to some good jazz instead. 98m; VHS, Streaming. **C:** Michael Madsen; Lynette Walden; Garrett Morris; Gale Mayron; Yaphet Kotto; Directed by Keoni Waxman. **A:** Sr. High-Adult. **P:** Entertainment. **U:** Home. **Mov-Ent:** Drama, Music--Jazz. **Acq:** Purchase. **Dist:** Lions Gate Television Corp. $89.98.

Almost Dead 1994 (Unrated) — ★★½
Psychiatrist Katherine Roshak's (Doherty) mother committed suicide four years ago and suddenly her corpse is appearing to Katherine. When she visits Mom's grave, Katherine finds an empty coffin. So she teams up with a skeptical cop (Mandylor) to figure out what's going on. Lots of loose ends. Based on the novel "Resurrection" by William Valtos. 92m; VHS, Streaming. **C:** Shannen Doherty; Costas Mandylor; William R. Moses; Directed by Ruben Preuss; Written by Miguel Tejada-Flores; Cinematography by Zoran Hochstatter. **A:** Sr. High-Adult. **P:** Entertainment. **U:** Home. **Mov-Ent:** Mystery & Suspense, Psychiatry. **Acq:** Purchase. **Dist:** Amazon.com Inc.; Monarch Home Video. $89.95.

Almost Famous 2000 (R) — ★★★
Fifteen-year-old budding rock critic William Miller's (Fugit) dream comes true after he bluffs his way into a Rolling Stone writing assignment covering a rising '70s rock band on tour. This ode to the music and youth culture of that decade may lack grit, but its sympathetic treatment of young Miller's coming-of-age amid groupies, drugs, rock and roll, and a worried, undupable mother (McDormand) achieves director Crowe's ends. The film's adoration of the music's energy and emotion appear to be the headliner here, but it never outperforms its devotion to character and relationship. Delicate performances by first-timer Fugit, and by Hudson as the more-than-a-groupie groupie, plus a memorable portrayal of the wise and slightly surly critic Lester Bangs by Hoffman. Based on Crowe's own experiences. 202m; VHS, DVD, Blu-Ray, Wide. **C:** Patrick Fugit; Philip Seymour Hoffman; Frances McDormand; Jason Lee; Billy Crudup; Kate Hudson; John Fedevich; Mark Kozelek; Fairuza Balk; Bijou Phillips; Anna Paquin; Noah Taylor; Jimmy Fallon; Zooey Deschanel; Liz Stauber; Eion Bailey; Mark Pellington; Terry Chen; Peter Frampton; Zack (Zach) Ward; Cameo(s) Jann Wenner; Directed by Cameron Crowe; Written by Cameron Crowe; Cinematography by John Toll; Music by Nancy Wilson. **A:** Sr. High-Adult. **P:** Entertainment. **U:** Home. **Mov-Ent:** Comedy--Romantic, Music--Pop/Rock. **Awds:** Oscars '00: Orig. Screenplay; Golden Globes '01: Film--Mus./Comedy, Support. Actress (Hudson); L.A. Film Critics '00: Support. Actress (McDormand); Broadcast Film Critics '00: Orig. Screenplay, Support. Actress (McDormand). **Acq:** Purchase. **Dist:** DreamWorks Home Entertainment.

Almost Heaven 2006 (Unrated) — ★★
Alcoholic Canadian director Mark Brady (Logue) is hired for a low-rated fishing program in Scotland that's hosted by his bitter ex-wife Taya (Collins). The village is filled with the usual quirky characters and Mark finds romance with independent fishing guide Nicki (Mitchell) but is she enough to help keep him sober? 102m; DVD. **C:** Donal Logue; Tom Conti; Kirsty Mitchell; Joely Collins; Erin Karpluk; Directed by Shel Piercy; Written by Shel Piercy; Richard Beattie; Cinematography by Oliver Cheesman; Music by Richard G. Mitchell. **A:** Sr. High-Adult. **P:** Entertainment. **U:** Home. **Mov-Ent:** Alcoholism, Scotland, Fishing. **Acq:** Purchase. **Dist:** Entertainment One US LP.

Almost Heroes 1997 (PG-13) — ★½
Farley's last screen appearance teams him with Perry as explorers Edwards and Hunt, who are racing Lewis and Clark to the Pacific Ocean in 1804. Edwards (Perry) is a glory-seeking fop who's totally out of his league, Hunt (Farley) is a slovenly, clumsy tracker with a soft spot for toilet (or would that be outhouse?) humor. Along with a team of misfits and losers, the duo wreaks havok on the American frontier. Perry and Farley show some flashes of comic chemistry, but their left to fend for themselves by a script that's lost in the wilderness, sadly relying too much on Farley's patented self-destructive schtick. 87m; VHS, DVD. **C:** Chris Farley; Matthew Perry; Eugene Levy; Bokeem Woodbine; Lisa Barbuscia; Kevin Dunn; Hamilton Camp; Lewis Arquette; Voice(s) by Harry Shearer; Directed by Christopher Guest; Written by Tom Wolfe; Mark Nutter; Boyd Hale; Cinematography by Adam Kimmel; Kenneth Macmillan; Music by C.J. Vanston. **Pr:** Denise Di Novi; Warner Bros. **A:** Jr. High-Adult. **P:** Entertainment. **U:** Home. **Mov-Ent:** Wilderness Areas, Explorers, Bears. **Acq:** Purchase. **Dist:** Warner Home Video, Inc.

Almost Human 1979 (R) — **Bomb!**
An Italian Mafia gorefest about a second-class don who kidnaps a businessman's daughter, and then has trouble trying to collect a ransom. For aficionados of Italian Mafia gorefests only (check your weapons at the door). 90m; VHS, DVD. **C:** Henry Silva; Tomas Milian; Laura Belli; Directed by Umberto Lenzi; Music by Ennio Morricone. **Pr:** Taurus Partners. **A:** Sr. High-Adult. **P:** Entertainment. **U:** Home. **Mov-Ent. Acq:** Purchase. **Dist:** Unknown Distributor.

Almost Like You and Me 19??
Documentary that highlights the life of Mary Taubier and how she overcame her severe behavior disorders to become a productive member of society. Also outlines the life of Jane Salzano, an elementary school teacher whose son has autism, and how she discovered a new, humane way to help autistic people. 27m; VHS. **A:** College-Adult. **P:** Education. **U:** Institution. **Gen-Edu:** Documentary Films, Psychology, Learning Disabilities. **Acq:** Purchase, Rent/Lease. **Dist:** CC-M Inc. $60.00.

Almost Partners 1987
Grandpa's ashes are in trouble. His urn and remains have been stolen. Fortunately, his teenage granddaughter and a detective are on the case. From the PBS "Wonderworks" series. 58m; VHS, DVD, CC. **C:** Paul Sorvino; Royana Black; Mary Wickes; Directed by Alan Kingsberg. **Pr:** PBS. **A:** Family. **P:** Entertainment. **U:** Home. **Mov-Ent:** Mystery & Suspense, Family Viewing, TV Movies. **Acq:** Purchase. **Dist:** Timeless Media Group; Facets Multimedia Inc. $29.95.

Almost Peaceful 2002 (Unrated) — ★★★
In 1946, a Jewish tailor is restarting his business and attempting to regain a life of normalcy. Deville quietly follows the Jewish employees—some who have survived the camps, some who have escaped the horrors but have fought their own war—as they stitch, sew, and try to restore themselves. Intertwined stories flow marvelously, providing poignant observation of the Holocaust aftermath. 90m; DVD. **C:** Simon Abkarian; Zabou Breitman; Denis Podalydes; Vincent Elbaz; Lubna Azabal; Stanislas Merhar; Clotilde Courau; Julie Gaynet; Malik Zidi; Directed by Michel DeVille; Cinematography by Andre Diot. **A:** Sr. High-Adult. **P:** Entertainment. **U:** Home. **L:** French. **Mov-Ent:** Drama, Holocaust, Judaism. **Acq:** Purchase. **Dist:** Movies Unlimited. $24.29.

Almost Perfect 2011 (Unrated) — ★★
Vanessa is a 34-year-old New Yorker who heads the philanthropic foundation at her family's company. She has no life of her own because she caters to everyone else's whims until she runs into old friend Dwayne, who admits he's always had a crush on her. Just as the romantic sparks are igniting, Vanessa's self-absorbed family comes to her with various crises and she has to decide whether to focus or their lives or her own. 106m; DVD. **C:** Kelly Hu; Ivan Shaw; Christina Chang; Edson Chen; Tina Chen; Roger Rees; Directed by Bertha Bay-Sa Pan; Written by Bertha Bay-Sa Pan; Cinematography by Sam Chase; Music by Jeff Martin. **A:** Sr. High-Adult. **P:** Entertainment. **U:** Home. **L:** English. **Mov-Ent:** Comedy-Drama, Family, Romance. **Acq:** Purchase. **Dist:** Virgil Films & Entertainment.

An Almost Perfect Affair 1979 (PG) — ★★
Taxing romantic comedy about an ambitious independent American filmmaker who, after finishing a movie about an executed murderer, travels to the Cannes festival and proceeds to fall in love or lust with the wife of an Italian producer. Numerous inside jokes and capable performances nearly overcome script lethargy. 92m; VHS, DVD. **C:** Keith Carradine; Monica Vitti; Raf Vallone; Christian de Sica; Dick Anthony Williams; Directed by Michael Ritchie; Written by Walter Bernstein; Music by Georges Delerue. **Pr:** Terry Carr; Paramount Pictures. **A:** Sr. High-Adult. **P:** Entertainment. **U:** Home. **Mov-Ent:** Comedy-Drama, Romance, Filmmaking. **Acq:** Purchase. **Dist:** Paramount Pictures Corp. $59.95.

Almost Pregnant 1991 (R) — ★★½
Linda Anderson (Roberts) desperately wants a baby, but her husband, Charlie (Conaway) is unable to get her pregnant. Dead set against artificial insemination, Linda decides to take a lover. Charlie doesn't want to lose her, so he goes along with her idea. Linda falls in love with the new guy; discovers he's had a vasectomy and takes yet another lover while continuing to see the other two guys. Hilarious complications abound in her outrageous quest for a baby. An unrated version containing explicit scenes is also available. 90m; VHS, CC. **C:** Tanya

Roberts; Jeff Conaway; Joan Severance; Dom DeLuise; Directed by Michael DeLuise; Written by Fred Stroppel. **Pr:** Ray Haboush. **A:** College-Adult. **P:** Entertainment. **U:** Home. **Mov-Ent**: Comedy--Romantic, Pregnancy, Sex & Sexuality. **Acq:** Purchase. **Dist:** Sony Pictures Home Entertainment Inc. $19.95.

Almost Royal Family 1984
All kinds of problems arise when a family inherits an island on the St. Lawrence River embargoed by the United States and Canada. 52m; VHS. **C:** Sarah Jessica Parker; John Femia; Garrett M. Brown; Frederick Koehler; Directed by Claude Kerven. **Pr:** Scholastic Productions, Inc. **A:** Family. **P:** Entertainment. **U:** Home. **Mov-Ent**. **Acq:** Purchase. **Dist:** Warner Home Video, Inc. $39.95.

Almost Strangers 2001 (Unrated) — ★★★
Compelling thriller about family ties. Ernest Symon (Howell) arranges a complicated three-day family reunion at a London hotel, which is reluctantly attended by black sheep Raymond (Gambon) and his curious son Daniel (Macfadyen). Both see family photos of events neither of them can remember and then Daniel meets his up-to-no-good cousins Rebecca (Skinner) and Charles (Stephens). Are those family skeletons we hear rattling? 237m; DVD. **C:** Michael Gambon; Matthew MacFadyen; Claire Skinner; Toby Stephens; Lindsay Duncan; Peter Howell; Anton Lesser; Directed by Stephen Poliakoff; Written by Stephen Poliakoff; Cinematography by Cinders Forshaw; Music by Adrian Johnston. **A:** Jr. High-Adult. **P:** Entertainment. **U:** Home. **Mov-Ent**: Hotels & Hotel Staff Training. **Acq:** Purchase. **Dist:** Alpha Video; Hallmark Hall of Fame.

Almost You 1985 (R) — ★★
Normal marital conflicts and uncertainties grow exponentially when a wealthy New York City 30-something couple hires a lovely young nurse to help care for the wife after a car accident. An unsentimental marital comedy with a good cast that still misses. 91m; VHS, DVD, CC. **C:** Brooke Adams; Griffin Dunne; Karen Young; Marty Watt; Christine Estabrook; Josh Mostel; Laura Dean; Dana Delany; Miguel Pinero; Joe Silver; Suzzy Roche; Spalding Gray; Directed by Adam Brooks; Music by Jonathan Elias. **Pr:** 20th Century-Fox. **A:** Sr. High-Adult. **P:** Entertainment. **U:** Home. **Mov-Ent**: Comedy--Romantic, Marriage. **Acq:** Purchase. **Dist:** $79.98.

Aloha, Bobby and Rose 1974 (PG) — ★★½
A mechanic and his girlfriend in L.A. become accidentally involved in an attempted robbery and murder and go on the run for Mexico, of course. Semi-satisfying drama in the surf, with fine location photography. 90m; VHS, DVD. **C:** Paul LeMat; Dianne Hull; Robert Carradine; Tim McIntire; Noble Willingham; Leigh French; Directed by Floyd Mutrux; Written by Floyd Mutrux; Cinematography by William A. Fraker. **A:** Sr. High-Adult. **P:** Entertainment. **U:** Home. **Mov-Ent**: Action-Adventure. **Acq:** Purchase. **Dist:** Movies Unlimited. $21.24.

Aloha Hawaii 1988
The beautiful Hawaiian islands are displayed in this video travel guide. 30m; VHS. **Pr:** Visual Horizons. **A:** Jr. High-Adult. **P:** Education. **U:** Institution, Home. **Gen-Edu**: Travel, U.S. States. **Acq:** Purchase. **Dist:** Visual Horizons. $39.95.

Aloha Summer 1988 (PG) — ★★
Six surfing teenagers of various ethnic backgrounds learn of love and life in 1959 Hawaii while riding the big wave of impending adulthood, with a splash of Kung Fu thrown in for good measure. Sensitive and bland. 97m; VHS. **C:** Chris Makepeace; Lorie Griffin; Don Michael Paul; Sho Kosugi; Yuji Okumoto; Tia Carrere; Directed by Tommy Lee Wallace; Written by Bob Benedetto. **Pr:** Spectrafilm. **A:** Jr. High-Adult. **P:** Entertainment. **U:** Home. **Mov-Ent**: Comedy-Drama, Romance, Martial Arts. **Acq:** Purchase. **Dist:** Warner Home Video, Inc.; MGM Studios Inc. $19.98.

Alone 1982
This experimental video portrays what it is like to be ultimately alone. 3m; VHS, 3/4 U. **Pr:** Julie Harrison. **A:** College-Adult. **P:** Education. **U:** Institution. **Fin-Art**: Video. **Acq:** Rent/Lease. **Dist:** Video Out Distribution.

Alone 2002 (R) — ★½
A murder investigation crosses paths with a psychiatric patient who is obsessed with a local woman. 110m; DVD. **C:** John Shrapnel; Miriam Margolyes; Laurel Holloman; Isabel Brook; Caroline Carver; Claire Goose; Susan Vidler; Claudia Harrison; Directed by Phil Claydon; Written by Edgar Allan Poe; Paul Hart-Wilden; Cinematography by Peter Thornton; Music by Jonathan Rudd; Phil Claydon; Jim Betteridge. **A:** Sr. High-Adult. **P:** Entertainment. **U:** Home. **L:** English, Spanish. **Mov-Ent**. **Acq:** Purchase. **Dist:** MTI Home Video. $9.98.

Alone Against Rome 1962 — ★½
A muscle-bound warrior takes on the forces of Rome to avenge himself against a scornful woman. 100m/B/W; VHS. **C:** Lang Jeffries; Rossana Podesta; Phillippe LeRoy; Directed by Herbert Wise. **Pr:** Medallion Pictures. **A:** Jr. High-Adult. **P:** Entertainment. **U:** Home. **Mov-Ent**: Fantasy, War--General, Drama. **Acq:** Purchase. **Dist:** Sinister Cinema. $16.95.

Alone in Tehran 1999
Portrays the challenges a young aspiring actress living alone faces in Iranian society. In Farsi, subtitled in English. 25m; VHS. **A:** Adult. **P:** Education. **U:** Institution, BCTV. **Gen-Edu**: Women, Middle East. **Acq:** Purchase, Rent/Lease. **Dist:** Arab Film Distribution. $150.00.

Alone in the Dark 1982 (R) — ★★
Slash and dash horror attempt featuring four escaped patients from a mental hospital who decide that they must kill their doctor because they don't like him. Conveniently, a city-wide blackout provides the opportunity, as the good doctor defends home and family against the aging stars intent on chewing up as much scenery as possible. 92m; VHS, DVD. **C:** Jack Palance; Donald Pleasence; Martin Landau; Dwight Schultz; Directed by Jack Sholder; Written by Jack Sholder. **Pr:** Robert Shaye; New Line Cinema. **A:** College-Adult. **P:** Entertainment. **U:** Home. **Mov-Ent**: Horror. **Acq:** Purchase. **Dist:** New Line Home Video; Sony Pictures Home Entertainment Inc. $19.95.

Alone in the Dark 2005 (R) — **Bomb!**
If there's any justice, Tim Burton's grandson will one day film a lovingly campy biopic about director Uwe Boll. Heir apparent to Ed Wood, Boll follows up 2003's "House of the Dead" with yet another incoherent video game adaptation. Paranormal detective Edward Carnby (Slater) represses memories of an orphanage trauma as he travels the globe collecting mystical chotchkies and fighting poorly-lit bad guys. When his fellow orphans start disappearing, Carnby and his scientist girlfriend (Reid) team up to battle bargain-basement CGI terror dogs. The monsters are somehow tied to an extinct Indian tribe, but you'll be too busy groaning at Reid's phonetically sounded-out science talk or the ridiculously inane opening crawl to care. 96m; DVD. **C:** Christian Slater; Tara Reid; Stephen Dorff; Matthew (Matt) Walker; Will Sanderson; Darren Shahlavi; Karin Konoval; Ed Anders; Frank C. Turner; Mark Acheson; Craig Bruhnanski; Kwesi Ameyaw; Catherine Lough Haggquist; Directed by Uwe Boll; Written by Elan Mastai; Michael Roesch; Peter Scheerer; Cinematography by Mathias Neumann; Music by Bernd Wendlandt. **Pr:** Shawn Williamson; Boll KG Prods; Lions Gate Films. **A:** Sr. High-Adult. **P:** Entertainment. **U:** Home. **L:** English. **Mov-Ent**: Horror, Adoption, Occult Sciences. **Acq:** Purchase. **Dist:** CinemaNow Inc. $27.98.

Alone in the Dark 2 2008 (PG-13) — **Bomb!**
Private eye Edward Carnby (Yune) gets caught in a feud between a group of witch hunters and witch Elizabeth Dexter (Lange) over a stolen (and cursed) dagger. Lead character Carnby has the same name as the character in the videogame (and the 2005 movie) but that's all and the plot actually makes little to no sense whatsoever. Infamously bad director Uwe Boll only produced this time around but it didn't seem to make any difference. 90m; DVD. **C:** Rick Yune; Allison Lange; Rachel Specter; Bill Moseley; Ralph (Ralf) Moeller; Michael Pare; Jason Connery; P.J. Soles; Danny Trejo; Lance Henriksen; Natassia Malthe; Zack (Zach) Ward; Directed by Michael Roesch; Peter Scheerer; Written by Michael Roesch; Peter Scheerer; Cinematography by Zoran Popovic; Music by Jessica de Rooij. **A:** Jr. High-Adult. **P:** Entertainment. **U:** Home. **Mov-Ent**. **Acq:** Purchase. **Dist:** Vivendi Visual Entertainment.

Alone in the Dark: Living with Choices—Drinking and Driving 1994
Features the story of Tasha, a teenage girl who gets drunk one night after sneaking out of the house and attempts to drive home before her parents discover she is missing. With the help of a mysterious "Assistant Controller" in a "Control Room," she is shown the consequences of what she has chosen to do. Comes with teacher's guide and blackline masters. 27m; VHS. **C:** Christopher Stone; Dee Wallace. **A:** Primary-Adult. **P:** Education. **U:** Institution. **Gen-Edu**: Adolescence, Family, Alcoholism. **Acq:** Purchase. **Dist:** United Learning Inc. $99.00.

Alone in the Neon Jungle 1987 (Unrated) — ★★
A glamorous big-city police captain is assigned to clean up the most corrupt precinct in town. Pleshette is untypically cast but still manages to make her role believable in a serviceable TV cop drama with more dialogue than action. 90m; VHS, DVD. **C:** Suzanne Pleshette; Danny Aiello; Georg Stanford Brown; Frank Converse; Joe Morton; Directed by Georg Stanford Brown. **Pr:** Brademan-Self Productions. **A:** Sr. High-Adult. **P:** Entertainment. **U:** Home. **Mov-Ent**: TV Movies. **Acq:** Purchase. **Dist:** New Line Home Video. $14.98.

Alone in the T-Shirt Zone 1986 (Unrated) — ★
A maniacal T-shirt designer lands in a mental institution. 81m; VHS. **C:** Michael Barrack; Taylor Gilbert; Bill Barron; Directed by Mikel B. Anderson; Written by Mikel B. Anderson. **Pr:** New World Pictures. **A:** College-Adult. **P:** Entertainment. **U:** Home. **L:** Spanish. **Mov-Ent**: Comedy--Black. **Acq:** Purchase. **Dist:** Unknown Distributor.

Alone in the Woods 1995 (PG) — ★★
Ten-year-old Justin mistakenly gets into the wrong van while on his way to his family's annual mountain vacation. Turns out the duo in the van are would-be kidnappers after Chelsea Stuart, the daughter of a toy magnate and now Justin must escape and rescue Chelsea. 81m; VHS, DVD. **C:** Brady Bluhm; Chick Vennera; Matthias Hues; Laraine Newman; Daniel McVicar; Krystee Clark; Directed by John Putch; Written by J. Riley Lagesen; Cinematography by Frank Johnson; Music by David Lawrence. **Pr:** Concorde Pictures. **A:** Jr. High-Adult. **P:** Entertainment. **U:** Home. **Mov-Ent**. **Acq:** Purchase. **Dist:** New Horizons Picture Corp.

Alone Together 1984
The innovative singles programs that three San Francisco churches run are examined. 26m; VHS, 3/4 U. **Pr:** Herbert Danska. **A:** Sr. High-Adult. **P:** Education. **U:** Institution. **Gen-Edu**: Human Relations. **Acq:** Purchase. **Dist:** Filmakers Library Inc.

Alone Together: Young Adults & HIV 19??
Contains interviews of young people (straight, gay, men, women, and minorities) who have been infected by the HIV virus in their teen years. They provide insight on their condition, their feelings, and how they became infected. 18m; VHS. **A:** Jr. High-College. **P:** Education. **U:** Institution, Home. **Hea-Sci**: Health Education, AIDS, Adolescence. **Acq:** Purchase, Rent/Lease. **Dist:** Fanlight Productions. $195.00.

Alone with a Stranger 1999 (R) — ★★
Long lost Evil Twin (Moses) learns that he has a rich brother. Evil Twin and girlfriend (Peeples) plan to kidnap Good Twin, sell his company, and scoot with the loot. But what about Good Twin's wife (Niven) and family? 90m; DVD. **C:** William R. Moses; Barbara Niven; Priscilla Barnes; Nia Peeples; Mindy Cohn; Directed by Peter Paul Liapis; Written by Peter Paul Liapis; Richard Dana Smith; Cinematography by M. David Mullen; Music by Alan Howarth. **A:** Sr. High-Adult. **P:** Entertainment. **U:** Home. **Mov-Ent**. **Acq:** Purchase. **Dist:** New Horizons Picture Corp.

Alone With Her 2007 (Unrated) — ★½
Clumsy thriller with camera as voyeur. Doug (Hanks) is obsessed with Amy (Talancon) and sets up surveillance on her with hidden cameras after breaking into her apartment. He orchestrates nasty little surprises and then turns up as Amy's concerned friend but the tension never particularly increases, even when Doug goes to what should have been more creepy extremes. 78m; DVD. **C:** Ana Claudia Talancon; Colin Hanks; Jordana Spiro; Jonathan Trent; Directed by Eric Nicholas; Written by Eric Nicholas; Cinematography by Nathaniel Wilson; Music by David E. Russo. **Pr:** Tom Engelman; Bob Engelman; IFC First Take. **A:** Sr. High-Adult. **P:** Entertainment. **U:** Home. **L:** English. **Mov-Ent**: Mystery & Suspense. **Acq:** Purchase. **Dist:** IFC Films.

Alone Yet Not Alone 2013 (PG-13) — ★
Dreadful faith-based indie with historical inaccuracies and amateur ability in front of and behind the camera. In 1755 in the Ohio valley, frontier farms are under attack by hostile local tribes. During a raid, two sisters are taken but find comfort in their captivity through the titular hymn. After Barbara and her sister get separated, she decides to escape with other captives, but they must cross miles of wilderness to safety while being pursued. Based on the Tracey Leininger Craven "Alone Yet Not Alone: Their Faith Became Their Freedom." 103m; DVD. **C:** Kelly Greyson; Natalie Racoosin; Jenn Gotzon; Clay Walker; Ozzie Torres; Directed by Ray Bengston; George D. Escobar; Written by George D. Escobar; James Richards; Cinematography by James Suttles; Music by William Ross. **Pr:** James Richards; Bud Smith; Ken Wales; Enthuse Entertainment. **A:** Jr. High-Adult. **P:** Entertainment. **U:** Home. **L:** English. **Mov-Ent**: History--U.S., Religion, Family. **Acq:** Purchase.

Along Came a Spider 2001 (R) — ★★
Sequel to 1997's "Kiss the Girls" is actually a prequel storywise but Freeman does reprise his character of Detective Alex Cross. This time he must save a U.S. Senator's daughter who's been kidnapped by a serial killer. Freeman is easily the best thing in this convoluted, plot-deficient, murky mess. He makes every "yeah, right" moment (and there are many) palatable. Based on the novel by James Patterson. 103m; VHS, DVD, CC. **C:** Morgan Freeman; Monica Potter; Michael Wincott; Penelope Ann Miller; Michael Moriarty; Dylan Baker; Billy Burke; Jay O. Sanders; Kim Hawthorne; Mika Boorem; Anton Yelchin; Directed by Lee Tamahori; Written by Marc Moss; Cinematography by Matthew F. Leonetti; Music by Jerry Goldsmith. **Pr:** David Brown; Joe Wizan; Phase One; Revelations Entertainment; Paramount Pictures. **A:** Sr. High-Adult. **P:** Entertainment. **U:** Home. **Mov-Ent**: Federal Bureau of Investigation (FBI), Children, Secret Service. **Acq:** Purchase. **Dist:** Paramount Pictures Corp.

Along Came Jones 1945 (Unrated) — ★★★
Cowboy Cooper, who can't handle a gun and is saddled with grumpy sidekick Demarest, is the victim of mistaken identity as both the good guys and the bad guys pursue him thinking he is a vicious killer. Young is the woman who rides to his defense. Offbeat and charming western parody based on a novel by Alan le May. 93m/B/W; VHS, DVD. **C:** Gary Cooper; Loretta Young; Dan Duryea; William Demarest; Directed by Stuart Heisler; Written by Nunnally Johnson; Cinematography by Milton Krasner; Music by Arthur Lange. **Pr:** United Artists. **A:** Family. **P:** Entertainment. **U:** Home. **Mov-Ent**. **Acq:** Purchase. **Dist:** MGM Home Entertainment; Facets Multimedia Inc. $19.98.

Along Came Polly 2004 (PG-13) — ★★
There's something about Polly. Neurotic risk analyst (Stiller) meets wild child Polly (Aniston) and learns to let loose. Has the requisite number of sight gags involving bodily fluids and embarrassing situations (Stiller is a master at squeezing the humor out of both), but breaks no new ground and quickly become formulaic. Generic romantic comedy with a few laughs is otherwise forgettable. 91m; VHS, DVD. **C:** Ben Stiller; Jennifer Aniston; Philip Seymour Hoffman; Debra Messing; Alec Baldwin; Hank Azaria; Bryan Brown; Michele Lee; Jsu Garcia; Bob (Robert) Dishy; Missi Pyle; Judah Friedlander; Kym E. Whitley; Kevin Hart; Directed by John Hamburg; Written by John Hamburg; Cinematography by Seamus McGarvey; Music by Theodore Shapiro. **Pr:** Danny DeVito; Michael H. Shamberg; Stacey Sher; Jersey Films; Universal Pictures. **A:** Jr. High-Adult. **P:** Entertainment. **U:** Home. **Mov-Ent**: Comedy--Romantic, Insurance. **Acq:** Purchase. **Dist:** Movies Unlimited; Alpha Video.

Along for the Ride 2000 (R) — ★½
Seriously disturbed Lulu (Griffith) checks herself out of the mental hospital and informs old boyfriend Ben (Swayze) that when she was a teen, she gave birth to their son and put him up for adoption. Somehow she manages to persuade him on a cross-country journey to Wisconsin to meet the now-teenaged kid. Naturally, this idea doesn't sit that well with Ben's wife Claire (Miller) who decides to put a stop to the nonsense. Goopy sentiment. 99m; VHS, DVD. **C:** Melanie Griffith; Patrick Swayze; Penelope Ann Miller; Joseph Gordon-Levitt; Richard Schiff; Annie Corley; Lee Garlington; Michael J. Pollard; Steven Bauer; Directed by John Kaye; Written by John Kaye; Cinema-

tography by Dion Beebe; Music by Serge Colbert. **A:** Sr. High-Adult. **P:** Entertainment. **U:** Home. **Mov-Ent**. **Acq:** Purchase. **Dist:** Lions Gate Television Corp.

Along the Great Divide 1951 (Unrated) — ★★
A U.S. marshal and his deputy battle pursuing vigilantes and the untamed frontier to bring a falsely accused murderer to trial (and of course, find the real bad guy). Douglas' first western has the usual horse opera cliches supported by excellent cinematography. 88m/B/W; VHS, DVD. **C:** Kirk Douglas; John Agar; Walter Brennan; Virginia Mayo; Directed by Raoul Walsh. **A:** Family. **P:** Entertainment. **U:** Home. **Mov-Ent**: Western. **Acq:** Purchase. **Dist:** WarnerArchive.com; Time-Life Video and Television. $19.98.

Along the Hudson Division 1992
Chug north out of New York City to Albany on the Amtrak line. Encounter Harlem bustle, then watch the big Apple melt away into stately mansions and manicured lawns and finally, rolling farmland. 60m; VHS. **A:** Jr. High-Adult. **P:** Entertainment. **U:** Home. **Gen-Edu**: Trains. **Acq:** Purchase. **Dist:** Pentrex Media Group L.L.C. $39.95.

Along the Navaho Trail 1945 — ★★
A cattle syndicate is threatening the local ranchers and Roy, aided by a band of gypsies, helps thwart the bad guys. 66m/B/W; VHS, DVD. **C:** Roy Rogers; Dale Evans; George "Gabby" Hayes; Douglas Fowley; Directed by Frank McDonald; Written by Gerald Geraghty; Cinematography by William Bradford. **Pr:** Republic Pictures. **A:** Family. **P:** Entertainment. **U:** Home. **Mov-Ent**: Western. **Acq:** Purchase. **Dist:** Amazon.com Inc.; Movies Unlimited.

Along the Pocahontas District: Coal Trains & Time Freights 1996
Explores the historic Pocahontas District railroad located in the mountains of West Virginia. Emphasis is placed on the coal mining industry of the region and how it is affected by the railroad. 92m; VHS. **A:** Family. **P:** Education. **U:** Home. **Gen-Edu**: Trains, Miners & Mining. **Acq:** Purchase. **Dist:** Pentrex Media Group L.L.C. $29.95.

Along the Rio Grande 1941 (Unrated) — ★½
Ranch hands Jeff, Smokey, and Whopper's boss Pop Edwards is murdered and they are falsely accused of bank robbery and jailed. Rustler Doc Randall breaks one of his henchmen out of jail and they persuade him to let them join his gang with the intention of proving Randall's the real criminal. 65m/B/W; DVD. **C:** Tim Holt; Ray Whitley; Emmett Lynn; Robert (Fisk) Fiske; Betty Jane Rhodes; Carl Stockdale; Slim Whitaker; Monte Montague; Harry Humphrey; Hal Taliaferro; Ruth Clifford; Directed by Edward Killy; Written by Arthur V. Jones; Morton Grant; Cinematography by Frank Redman. **A:** Jr. High-Adult. **P:** Entertainment. **U:** Home. **Mov-Ent**: Western. **Acq:** Purchase. **Dist:** WarnerArchive.com.

Along the Silk Road 1993
Explores the East-West conduit and the exploits of Zhang Qian, Xuan Zang, and Marco Polo. 37m; VHS. **A:** Jr. High-Sr. High. **P:** Education. **U:** Institution. **Gen-Edu**: Japan, Explorers, History. **Acq:** Purchase. **Dist:** Zenger Media. $54.95.

Along the Sundown Trail 1942 — ★½
Standard western escapades as cowboy G-men round up the villains. 59m/B/W; VHS, DVD. **C:** William Boyd; Art Davis; Lee Powell; Julie Duncan; Kermit Maynard; Charles "Blackie" King; Directed by Sam Newfield. **Pr:** Producers Releasing Corporation. **A:** Family. **P:** Entertainment. **U:** Home. **Mov-Ent**: Western. **Acq:** Purchase. **Dist:** Alpha Video. $11.95.

Along with Ghosts 1969 (Unrated) — ★★
A young girl discovers proof of corruption in her town, and her grandfather is murdered because of it. She flees in search of her father. Because her grandfather was murdered on holy ground, the Yokai agree to protect her and take revenge on her behalf. This is the third film in the Yokai trilogy. The monsters are finally a little less cutesy looking for this sequel, which is fitting considering the mythological reputation of the Yokai. 90m; DVD. **C:** Kojiro Hongo; Bokuzen Hidari; Pepe Hozumi; Masami Burukido; Mutsuhiro; Yoshito Yamaji; Directed by Yoshiyuki Kuroda; Kimiyoshi Yasuda; Written by Tetsuro Yoshida; Cinematography by Hiroshi Imai; Music by Michiaki Watanabe. **A:** Primary-Adult. **P:** Entertainment. **U:** Home. **L:** English, Japanese. **Mov-Ent**: Horror, Puppets. **Acq:** Purchase. **Dist:** Movies Unlimited. $19.98.

Alouette 1989
This film contains single-frame animation of paper cut-outs. 3m; VHS, 3/4 U. **Pr:** Norman McLaren. **A:** Jr. High-Adult. **P:** Education. **U:** Institution, SURA. **Gen-Edu**: Filmmaking. **Acq:** Purchase, Rent/Lease. **Dist:** National Film Board of Canada.

Alpaca Breeders of Chimboya 1984
A portrait of a small community in the Peruvian Andes that depends on the exporting of alpaca fleece. 30m; 3/4 U. **Pr:** Kusi Films. **A:** Sr. High-Adult. **P:** Education. **U:** Institution, SURA. **Gen-Edu**: South America. **Acq:** Purchase. **Dist:** First Run/Icarus Films.

Alpha 1972
Algebraic equivalencies are presented in simple terms at high speed through the animated manipulation of formulas. 1m; VHS, 3/4 U. **Pr:** Charles Eames; Ray Eames. **A:** Jr. High-Sr. High. **P:** Instruction. **U:** Institution, Home, SURA. **Fin-Art**: Mathematics. **Acq:** Purchase, Rent/Lease, Duplication License. **Dist:** Pyramid Media.

Alpha and Omega 2010 (PG) — ★½
Unambitious but not unappealing 3D animated kiddie comedy finds disciplined Alpha wolf Kate and fun-loving Omega wolf Humphrey transported from their Canadian national park home to Idaho as part of a wolf-relocation project. They want to get home but it's a thousand mile journey of bears, a helpful golfing duck, squabbles, and predictable adventures. Little ones will be generally amused, though it's mostly forgettable. Grown-ups beware that some rather obvious sexual references might prompt questions. 88m; Blu-Ray, On Demand, Wide, CC. **C:** Voice(s) by Hayden Panettiere; Justin Long; Dennis Hopper; Danny Glover; Chris Carmack; Christina Ricci; Larry Miller; Eric Price; Vicki Lewis; Directed by Anthony Bell; Ben Gluck; Written by Chris Denk; Steve Moore; Music by Chris P. Bacon. **Pr:** Richard Rick; Ken Katsumoto; Steve Moore; Crest Animation; Lionsgate. **A:** Family. **P:** Entertainment. **U:** Home. **L:** English. **Mov-Ent**: Animation & Cartoons, Animals, Bears. **Acq:** Purchase. **Dist:** Lions Gate Entertainment Inc.; Amazon.com Inc.; Movies Unlimited.

Alpha Beta 1973 (Unrated) — ★★½
A stage production set to film studying the break-up of a marriage, where all the husband and wife have in common is the children. Finney and Roberts efficiently carry the load. 70m; VHS. **C:** Albert Finney; Rachel Roberts; Directed by Anthony Page. **Pr:** CINE III. **A:** Sr. High-Adult. **P:** Entertainment. **U:** Institution, Home. **Mov-Ent**: Parenting, Divorce. **Acq:** Purchase. **Dist:** No Longer Available.

Alpha Dog 2006 (R) — ★★
True crime saga resulting from sheer stupidity. Wannabe white gangsta drug dealer Johnny Truelove (Hirsch) feels dissed when customer Jake (Foster) refuses to pay his tab. So Johnny and his equally wasted posse take advantage of a run-in with Jake's naive 15-year-old half brother Zack (Yelchin) and decide to hold him as collateral. Cohort Frankie (a convincing Timberlake) becomes Zack's de-facto babysitter and introduces him to their indulgent SoCal life—that is until someone finally realizes that kidnapping is a serious crime. A "River's Edge" for 21st-century teens. 117m; DVD, Blu-Ray, HD-DVD. **C:** Emile Hirsch; Justin Timberlake; Ben Foster; Anton Yelchin; Shawn Hatosy; Bruce Willis; Sharon Stone; David Thornton; Fernando Vargas; Amanda Seyfried; Dominique Swain; Olivia Wilde; Lukas Haas; Vincent Kartheiser; Harry Dean Stanton; Alex Kingston; Heather Wahlquist; Directed by Nick Cassavetes; Written by Nick Cassavetes; Cinematography by Robert Fraisse; Music by Aaron Zigman. **Pr:** Sidney Kimmel; Chuck Pacheco; VIP Medianfonds 2; A-Mark Films; Universal Pictures. **A:** Sr. High-Adult. **P:** Entertainment. **U:** Home. **L:** English. **Mov-Ent**: Marijuana. **Acq:** Purchase. **Dist:** Movies Unlimited; Alpha Video; Universal Studios Home Video.

Alpha Fetoprotein Screening 1988
The uses and purposes of the alpha fetoprotein test on pregnant women are documented. 10m; VHS, 3/4 U. **Pr:** Milner-Fenwick. **A:** Jr. High-Adult. **P:** Education. **U:** Institution, CCTV. **Hea-Sci**: Pregnancy. **Acq:** Purchase. **Dist:** Milner-Fenwick, Inc. $200.00.

Alpha Helix Formation 19??
A polyglycine chain is shown folding into an alpha helix from the carboxylic and amino ends. The role of hydrogen bonding between CO and NH groups is stressed by showing a magnification of the alpha helices. 3m/B/W; 3/4 U, Special order formats. **Pr:** Joel de Rosnay. **A:** College-Adult. **P:** Education. **U:** Institution, CCTV, CATV, BCTV. **Hea-Sci**: Biology. **Acq:** Purchase, Rent/Lease. **Dist:** Education Development Center.

The Alpha Incident 1976 (PG) — ★½
Time-worn doomsday drama about an alien organism with the potential to destroy all living things. Government works hard to cover up. 86m; VHS, DVD. **C:** Ralph Meeker; Stafford Morgan; John Goff; Carol Irene Newell; John Alderman; Directed by Bill Rebane. **Pr:** Bill Rebane; Bill Rebane. **A:** Sr. High-Adult. **P:** Entertainment. **U:** Home. **Mov-Ent**: Science Fiction. **Acq:** Purchase. **Dist:** Amazon.com Inc. $9.95.

Alpha Male 2006 (Unrated) — ★★½
The time switch between the present and 10 years in the past can be confusing but this is an otherwise decent family drama. Wealthy Jim (Huston) has made a good life for wife Alice (Ehle) and their two children, despite his temper and domineering attitude. After Jim dies from cancer, officious son Jack (Wells) takes it badly when Alice decides to remarry, especially since widower Clive (Baladi) is his father's polar opposite. The situation comes to a boil when Alice throws Jack a lavish 21st birthday party. 100m; DVD. **C:** Danny Huston; Jennifer Ehle; Amelia Warner; Christopher Egan; Mark Wells; Patrick Baladi; Trudie Styler; Directed by Dan Wilde; Written by Dan Wilde; Cinematography by Shane Daly; Music by Stephen Warbeck. **A:** Sr. High-Adult. **P:** Entertainment. **U:** Home. **Mov-Ent**. **Acq:** Purchase. **Dist:** ThinkFilm Company Inc.

Alphabet 1970
In this educational short, each letter of the alphabet introduces itself by means of word associations and comical episodes. 6m/B/W; VHS, 3/4 U. **Pr:** Robert Verrall. **A:** Primary. **P:** Instruction. **U:** Institution, SURA. **Chl-Juv**: Language Arts. **Acq:** Purchase, Rent/Lease. **Dist:** National Film Board of Canada.

Alphabet & Numbers for ages 2.5-5 19??
Highly acclaimed program teaching children to draw and identify numbers. 30m; VHS. **A:** Preschool-Primary. **P:** Education. **U:** Institution, Home. **Chl-Juv**: Children, Singing. **Acq:** Purchase. **Dist:** Silver Mine Video Inc. $19.95.

Alphabet City 1984 (R) — ★★
A drug kingpin who runs New York's Lower East Side has decided to turn over a new leaf, but first he must survive his last night as a criminal while figuring out a way to pay off his large debts. Very stylish and moody, but light on content and plot. 85m; VHS, DVD. **C:** Vincent Spano; Michael Winslow; Kate Vernon; Jami Gertz; Zohra Lampert; Raymond Serra; Ken Marino; Daniel Jordano; Miguel Pinero; Directed by Amos Poe; Written by Amos Poe. **Pr:** Andrew Braunsberg; Atlantic Releasing. **A:** Sr. High-Adult. **P:** Entertainment. **U:** Home. **Mov-Ent**: Drugs. **Acq:** Purchase, Rent/Lease. **Dist:** Movies Unlimited; Alpha Video; MGM Home Entertainment. $79.98.

Alphabet Conspiracy 1959
From the Bell Telephone Science Hour, the story of human language is told in an "Alice and Wonderland" format. Combination live action and animation. 55m; VHS. **C:** Hans Conried; Directed by Isadore "Friz" Freleng. **A:** Family. **P:** Entertainment. **U:** Home. **Mov-Ent**: Television Series. **Acq:** Purchase. **Dist:** Moviecraft Home Video; Rhino Entertainment Co. $19.95.

The Alphabet Dragon 1979
A poor farmer releases an Alphabet Dragon from an evil spell. The farmer's reward is a wish for every letter of the alphabet. 16m; VHS, 3/4 U. **Pr:** David Christianson. **A:** Primary. **P:** Education. **U:** Institution, SURA. **Chl-Juv**: Language Arts. **Acq:** Purchase. **Dist:** Phoenix Learning Group.

The Alphabet in Art 1969
Lettering in combination with pictures is a strong force in communicating ideas. A contemporary designer selects letter forms to convey given moods. 13m; VHS, 3/4 U. **A:** Primary-Jr. High. **P:** Education. **U:** Institution, SURA. **Fin-Art**: Graphics. **Acq:** Purchase. **Dist:** Phoenix Learning Group.

The Alphabet Jungle Game 1998
Sesame Street characters Elmo, Zoe, and Telly explore the alphabet in this collection of segments from the popular children's show. 30m; VHS. **A:** Preschool-Primary. **P:** Entertainment. **U:** Home. **Chl-Juv**: Children. **Acq:** Purchase. **Dist:** SONY Wonder. $12.98.

The Alphabet Killer 2008 (R) — ★★
Loosely-based on the true story of a 1970s serial killer in Rochester, New York. Police detective Megan Paige (Dushku) becomes obsessed with a child killer case and has a breakdown after suffering hallucinations. Diagnosed as schizophrenic, Megan eventually returns to the force just as the killer, who chooses victims whose first and last names begin with the same letter, gets active again. Can she hold it together long enough to catch the killer this time? 100m; DVD, Blu-Ray. **C:** Eliza Dushku; Cary Elwes; Timothy Hutton; Tom Malloy; Michael Ironside; Martin Donovan; Melissa Leo; Bill Moseley; Carl Lumbly; Tom Noonan; Directed by Rob Schmidt; Written by Tom Malloy; Cinematography by Joe DeSalvo; Music by Eric Perlmutter. **A:** Sr. High-Adult. **P:** Entertainment. **U:** Home. **Mov-Ent**. **Acq:** Purchase. **Dist:** Anchor Bay Entertainment.

The Alphabet Murders 1965 (Unrated) — ★★
Picture this: Randall playing Agatha Christie's famous Belgian sleuth, Hercule Poirot, and Rutherford—in a cameo'as Miss Marple. As if that wouldn't be enough to make Dame Agatha roll over in her grave, there's plenty of cloying wisecracking and slapsticking throughout. An adaptation of "The ABC Murders" in which Poirot stalks a literate killer who snuffs out his victims in alphabetical order. Hardly a must-see, unless you're hellbent on viewing the entire Randall opus. 90m/B/W; VHS. **C:** Tony Randall; Anita Ekberg; Robert Morley; Maurice Denham; Guy Rolfe; Sheila Allen; Margaret Rutherford; Julian Glover; Directed by Frank Tashlin. **Pr:** MGM. **A:** Jr. High-Adult. **P:** Entertainment. **U:** Home. **Mov-Ent**: Satire & Parody, Mystery & Suspense. **Acq:** Purchase. **Dist:** MGM Home Entertainment; Facets Multimedia Inc. $19.98.

An Alphabet of Dinosaurs 1989
The eternal fascination of small children for dinosaurs is used by this video to teach those same tykes their alphabet through disnosaur-related topics. 13m; VHS, 8 mm, 3/4 U. **TV Std:** NTSC, PAL, SECAM. **Pr:** Christianson Productions; Coronet Films. **A:** Preschool. **P:** Education. **U:** Institution, CCTV, SURA. **Chl-Juv**: Language Arts. **Acq:** Purchase, Rent/Lease, Duplication License. **Dist:** Phoenix Learning Group. $79.00.

An Alphabet of Weather 1991
Gives youngsters a sprinkling of 26 weather terms complete with actual footage of the weather concepts. Includes teacher's guide. 13m; VHS, Special order formats. **A:** Primary. **P:** Education. **U:** Institution. **Chl-Juv**: Meteorology. **Acq:** Purchase, Rent/Lease. **Dist:** Phoenix Learning Group. $75.00.

Alphabet Soup: Learn the Letters 1992
Professor Wise Old Owl uses rhymes, music, and word pictures to teach young children the alphabet. Part of the "Look and Learn" series. 30m; VHS. **A:** Preschool. **P:** Education. **U:** Home. **Chl-Juv**: Animation & Cartoons, Education, Language Arts. **Acq:** Purchase. **Dist:** V.I.E.W. Inc./Arkadia Entertainment Corp. $14.98.

Alphabet, The Story of Writing 19??
Traces man's struggle for literacy from the beginning of civilization of Mesopotamia to the present day, and shows how writing became an art form. 25m; VHS. **A:** Sr. High. **P:** Education. **U:** Institution. **Gen-Edu**: Anthropology, Communication. **Acq:** Purchase. **Dist:** Filmakers Library Inc. $295.

The Alphabet Zoo 1989
This volume helps children learn the alphabet using familiar animals. Includes "Alphabet Zoo: Reading with You." 60m; VHS. **A:** Preschool. **P:** Education. **U:** Home. **Chl-Juv**: Children, Education. **Acq:** Purchase. **Dist:** School-Tech Inc. $17.95.

An Alphabetter Answer 1989
Features a fifth grade class that takes part in their school's drug-free program by putting together a play based on the alphabet. Dramatizes a child's viewpoint on alcoholic parents, truancy, smoking, single parent families, and delinquency. 31m; VHS, 3/4 U, Special order formats. **A:** Primary. **P:** Education. **U:** Institution. **Chl-Juv**: Health Education, Drug Abuse, Children. **Acq:** Purchase, Rent/Lease. **Dist:** Select Media, Inc. $39.95.

Alphas: Season One 2011
Syfy Channel 2011-2012 science fiction. "Pilot": Dr. Lee Rosen leads a group of humans with enhanced physical and mental abilities in solve baffling crimes. "Never Let Me Go": Dr. Rosen and the team investigate a series of sudden deaths at a Pennsylvania high school. "Original Sin ": The team don't know who to trust when Red Flag leader Stanton Parish escalates his war on the Department of Defense. 11 episodes. 497m; DVD. **C:** David Strathairn; John Pyper-Ferguson; Warren Christie; Malik Yoba; Laura Mennell. **A:** Jr. High-Adult. **P:** Entertainment. **U:** Home. **L:** English. **Mov-Ent**: Science Fiction, Television Series. **Acq:** Purchase. **Dist:** Universal Studios Home Video. $39.98.

Alphas: Season Two 2012
Syfy Channel 2011-2012 science fiction. "Wake Up Call": Discredited by the government after revealing the Alphas' existence, Dr. Rosen reassembles the team to rescue Rosen's estranged daughter Dani, who is supposedly carrying a message from Red Flag. "Falling": Kat goes undercover to investigate a street drug and Rosen thinks Dani's a mole for Parish and Red Flag. "God's Eye": Separated from the team, injured, and suffering from hallucinations, Dr. Rosen wants a final confrontation with Stanton Parish. 13 episodes. 562m; DVD. **C:** David Strathairn; John Pyper-Ferguson; Warren Christie; Laura Mennell; Summer Glau; Kathleen Munroe; Erin Way. **A:** Jr. High-Adult. **P:** Entertainment. **U:** Home. **L:** English. **Mov-Ent**: Science Fiction, Television Series. **Acq:** Purchase. **Dist:** Universal Studios Home Video. $44.98.

Alphaville 1965 — ★★★
Engaging and inimitable Godard attempt at science fiction mystery. P.I. Lemmy Caution searches for a scientist in a city (Paris as you've never seen it before) run by robots and overseen by a dictator. The futuristic techno-conformist society must be upended so that Caution may save the scientist as well as nonconformists everywhere. In French with subtitles. 100m/B/W; VHS, DVD. **C:** Eddie Constantine; Anna Karina; Akim Tamiroff; Howard Vernon; Laszlo Szabo; Michel Delahaye; Jean-Pierre Leaud; Directed by Jean-Luc Godard; Written by Jean-Luc Godard; Cinematography by Raoul Coutard; Music by Paul Misraki. **Pr:** Chaumiane; Filmstudio. **A:** Jr. High-Adult. **P:** Entertainment. **U:** Home. **Mov-Ent**: Science Fiction, Mystery & Suspense. **Awds:** Berlin Intl. Film Fest. '65: Golden Berlin Bear. **Acq:** Purchase. **Dist:** Home Vision Cinema; Sinister Cinema; Rex Miller Artisan Studio. $29.95.

Alpine Fire 1989 (R) — ★★½
Coming of age story about an adolescent girl and her deaf-mute brother living an isolated life in the Swiss Alps. When life on the mountain overwhelms them, they turn to each other for love. Sharply observed with a naturalistic style, elevating the proceedings above mere voyeurism. 119m; VHS. **C:** Thomas Knock; Johanna Lier; Dorothea Moritz; Rolf Illig; Directed by Fredi M. Murer. **A:** Sr. High-Adult. **P:** Entertainment. **U:** Home. **Mov-Ent**: Sex & Sexuality, Mountaineering. **Acq:** Purchase. **Dist:** Lions Gate Television Corp. $79.98.

Alpine Ski Schools Series 1983
This series combines instruction with the natural excitement of downhill skiing. 30m; VHS, 3/4 U. **Pr:** PBS Video. **A:** Family. **P:** Education. **U:** Institution, CCTV, CATV. **Spo-Rec**: Sports--Winter. **Acq:** Purchase, Rent/Lease, Off-Air Record. **Dist:** PBS Home Video.
Indiv. Titles: 1. The Mountain Awakens 2. Up and Down the Slopes 3. The Creative Christie 4. Dynamic Skiing 5. The Mountain is Yours.

Alpine Ski Technique 1981
All aspects of alpine skiing are discussed, from the use of the T-bar, to plowing, turning, and jumping. Filmed in the Rockies. 28m; 3/4 U. **Pr:** Douglas Sinclair Productions. **A:** Family. **P:** Instruction. **U:** Institution, SURA. **L:** English, French. **Spo-Rec**: Sports--Winter. **Acq:** Purchase, Rent/Lease. **Dist:** Kinetic Film Enterprises Ltd.

Alpine Skiing 1988
Everything from picking out the right equipment to the actual skiing itself is made simple. 76m; VHS, 3/4 U. **Pr:** Champions on Film. **A:** Primary-Adult. **P:** Instruction. **U:** Institution, CCTV, Home. **Spo-Rec**: Sports--Winter, Skiing. **Acq:** Purchase. **Dist:** School-Tech Inc. $29.95.

Already Dead 2007 (R) — ★½
Thomas Archer (Eldard) has a great job and a beautiful wife and son. Then the Archer home is robbed, his wife is brutalized, and his son is killed. The police can't find the criminals so Archer turns to a shadow group that promises to deliver those responsible and then give Archer the opportunity to deal with them as he sees fit. 93m; DVD. **C:** Ron Eldard; Til Schweiger; Christopher Plummer; Patrick Kilpatrick; Marisa Coughlan; Directed by Joe Otting; Written by Joe Chappelle; Cinematography by Eric Trageser; Music by Nathan Furst. **A:** Sr. High-Adult. **P:** Entertainment. **U:** Home. **Mov-Ent. Acq:** Purchase. **Dist:** Sony Pictures Home Entertainment Inc.

ALS and the Family 1986
The daughter of an amyotrophic lateral sclerosis patient describes her family's attitudes and reactions to this progressive disease. 55m; VHS, 3/4 U. **A:** Adult. **P:** Education. **U:** Institution. **Hea-Sci**: Diseases. **Acq:** Purchase, Rent/Lease. **Dist:** Boston University, GKM Instructional Resource Center. $100.00.

Alsino and the Condor 1982 (R) — ★★★
An acclaimed Nicaraguan drama about a young boy, caught in war-torn Nicaragua between the Somoza government and the Sandinista rebels, who dreams of flying above the human strife. In Spanish with English subtitles. 89m; VHS. **C:** Dean Stockwell; Alan Esquivel; Directed by Miguel Littin; Written by Miguel Littin. **Pr:** Almi Pictures. **A:** College-Adult. **P:** Entertainment. **U:** Home. **L:** Spanish. **Mov-Ent**: War--General. **Acq:** Purchase. **Dist:** Facets Multimedia Inc.; Tapeworm Video Distributors Inc. $29.95.

Altered 2006 (R) — ★★
Four men who were violated by aliens in the woods return 15 years later to get some revenge. 88m; DVD, Streaming. **C:** Adam Kaufman; Brad William Henke; Michael C. Williams; Paul McCarthy-Boyington; James Gammon; Catherine Mangan; Directed by Eduardo Sanchez; Written by Eduardo Sanchez; Jamie Nash; Cinematography by Steve Yedlin; Music by Tony Cora; Exiquio Talavera. **A:** Sr. High-Adult. **P:** Entertainment. **U:** Home. **L:** English, French, Spanish. **Mov-Ent. Acq:** Purchase, Rent/Lease. **Dist:** Universal Studios Home Video. $12.98 9.99.

Altered Environments: An Inquiry into the American Wildlands 1970
Raises questions about the values to be found in remaining wildlands and involves students in decisions about future use of our wild areas. 10m; VHS, 3/4 U. **Pr:** Bert Kempers. **A:** Jr. High-Sr. High. **P:** Education. **U:** Institution, SURA. **Gen-Edu**: Wilderness Areas. **Acq:** Purchase. **Dist:** Phoenix Learning Group.

Altered Environments: An Inquiry into the Growth of American Cities 1972
This show is designed to involve students in an analysis of the factors that must be considered in the design of cities. 10m; VHS, 3/4 U. **Pr:** Bert Kempers. **A:** Jr. High-Sr. High. **P:** Education. **U:** Institution, SURA. **Gen-Edu**: Cities & Towns. **Acq:** Purchase. **Dist:** Phoenix Learning Group.

Altered Landscapes 1989
Features the Environmental Biology Program at the Boyce Thompson Institute for Plant Research located at Cornell University. Covers scientific research involving air pollutants, acid rain and ozone. 18m; VHS. **A:** Sr. High-Adult. **P:** Education. **U:** Institution. **Hea-Sci**: Education, Ecology & Environment. **Acq:** Purchase, Rent/Lease. **Dist:** Cornell University. $50.00.

Altered States 1980 (R) — ★★★
Obsessed with the task of discovering the inner man, Hurt's ambitious researcher ignores his family while consuming hallucinogenic drugs and floating in an immersion tank. He gets too deep inside, slipping way back through the evolutionary order and becoming a menace in the process. Confusing script based upon Chayefsky's (alias Sidney Aaron) confusing novel is supported by great special effects and the usual self-indulgent and provocative Russell direction. Chayefsky eventually washed his hands of the project after artistic differences with the producers. Others who departed from the film include initial director William Penn and special effects genius John Dykstra (relieved ably by Bran Ferren). Hurt's a solemn hoot in his first starring role. 103m; VHS, DVD, Blu-Ray. **C:** William Hurt; Blair Brown; Bob Balaban; Charles Haid; Dori Brenner; Drew Barrymore; Miguel Godreau; Thaao Penghlis; Peter Brandon; Charles White Eagle; Meghan Jeffers; Jack Murdock; John Larroquette; Directed by Ken Russell; Written by Paddy Chayefsky; Sidney Aaron; Cinematography by Jordan Cronenweth; Music by John Corigliano. **A:** Adult. **P:** Entertainment. **U:** Home. **Mov-Ent**: Science Fiction, Drugs, Science. **Acq:** Purchase. **Dist:** Warner Home Video, Inc. $14.95.

Alternate Energy Sources: Geothermal, Wind and Water 1984
Witness some of the many ways to generate energy without pollutive consequences. 30m; VHS. **Pr:** Increase. **A:** Sr. High-Adult. **P:** Education. **U:** Home. **Gen-Edu**: Energy, Natural Resources. **Acq:** Purchase. **Dist:** Silver Mine Video Inc. $29.95.

Alternate Route 1997
Documentary following several youths who own their own businesses. 45m; DVD. **A:** Sr. High-Adult. **P:** Education. **U:** Institution. **Gen-Edu**: Documentary Films, Business. **Acq:** Purchase, Rent/Lease. **Dist:** The Cinema Guild. $165.00.

Alternate Work Sites: At Home, at Work 1988
This film features Control Data Corporation of Minneapolis and workers in an Alpine Swiss village showing how to create a work site. 30m; VHS, 3/4 U. **Pr:** National Educational Media Inc. **A:** College-Family. **P:** Professional. **U:** Institution, SURA. **Bus-Ind**: Business. **Acq:** Purchase, Rent/Lease, Trade-in. **Dist:** Encyclopedia Britannica. $395.00.

Alternating Current Fundamentals 1993
Tricky concepts of light, energy, and magnetism become clear with this illuminating set of five programs. ?m; VHS. **A:** Adult. **P:** Professional. **U:** Institution. **Bus-Ind**: Business, Electricity, Physics. **Acq:** Purchase. **Dist:** Bergwall Productions, Inc. $439.00.
Indiv. Titles: 1. Magnetism and Electromagnetism 2. Electrical Generators and Motors 3. Measuring AC 4. Capacitors, Inductors, and Transformers 5. Reactance and Electrical Power.

Alternative 1976 (Unrated) — ★★
A female magazine editor finds herself unmarried and quite pregnant. She is caught in a tug-of-war between the baby's father and her current lover. Dated liberated woman and career snoozer. 90m; VHS. **C:** Wendy Hughes; Peter Adams; Alwyn Kurts; Carla Hoogeveen; Tony Bonner; Directed by Paul Eddy; Written by Tony Morphett; Cinematography by Russell Boyd; Music by Bob Young. **Pr:** Grundy Organization. **A:** Sr. High-Adult. **P:** Entertainment. **U:** Home. **Mov-Ent**: Pregnancy. **Acq:** Purchase. **Dist:** No Longer Available.

Alternative Approaches to Algebra 1987
An educational music video for young people, instructing in arithmetic and algebraic math. 20m; VHS, 3/4 U. **C:** Hosted by Paul McGuire; Written by Paul McGuire. **Pr:** Multi-Media Mathematics. **A:** Primary-Sr. High. **P:** Education. **U:** Institution, CCTV, Home. **Gen-Edu**: Mathematics. **Acq:** Purchase. **Dist:** Multi-Media Mathematics. $30.00.
Indiv. Titles: 1. Source/Myth 2. Politics/Sex 3. Tragedy/Architecture 4. Science/Art 5. Ideas/War.

Alternative Billing Practices for Lawyers 1993
Offers alternative methods for client-billing which reduce client bills, but reward the lawyer. Includes study guide. 50m; VHS. **A:** Adult. **P:** Professional. **U:** Institution. **Bus-Ind**: Law. **Dist:** American Law Institute - Committee on Continuing Professional Education. $95.

Alternative Dispute Resolution Techniques: Incorporating ADR in Your Law Practice 1989
Practicing lawyers are offered techniques for Alternative Dispute Resolution. Discusses arbitration, mini-trials, summary jury trials, and more. Two-tape series complete with study materials. 210m; VHS. **A:** Adult. **P:** Professional. **U:** Institution. **Bus-Ind**: Law, Supreme Court. **Dist:** American Law Institute - Committee on Continuing Professional Education. $150.

Alternative Energies 1993
Profiles different alternative energy sources including solar, wind, and geothermal resources. 20m; VHS. **Pr:** Film Ideas, Inc. **A:** Jr. High-Sr. High. **P:** Education. **U:** Institution. **Hea-Sci**: Science, Energy. **Acq:** Purchase. **Dist:** Film Ideas, Inc. $115.00.

Alternative Energy Sources 1984
All the different forms of power including geothermal, tidal, and wave energies are explained on this videocassette. 30m; VHS. **Pr:** Star Merchants. **A:** College-Adult. **P:** Education. **U:** Institution, Home. **Gen-Edu**: Energy. **Acq:** Purchase. **Dist:** Silver Mine Video Inc. $29.95.

Alternative Management Techniques for the Colorado Potato Beetle 1992
Demonstrates two non-chemical alternatives for managing the adult Colorado potato beetle: Trench Traps and Propane Flaming. Includes bulletins describing these techniques. 16m; VHS. **A:** Adult. **P:** Instruction. **U:** Institution. **Gen-Edu**: Agriculture, Insects. **Acq:** Purchase. **Dist:** Cornell University. $25.00.

Alternative Medicine 1997
Explores the various forms of alternative medicine that are being used in place of or in addition to traditional health care. 29m; VHS. **A:** Sr. High-Adult. **P:** Education. **U:** Institution. **Hea-Sci**: Health Education, Patient Education, Diseases. **Acq:** Purchase. **Dist:** Aquarius Health Care Media. $149.00.

Alternative to Formal Education 1990
This video examines the possibility of Catholic parents educating their children at home. 30m; VHS. **Pr:** KTF. **A:** Adult. **P:** Religious. **U:** Institution, Home. **Gen-Edu**: Education. **Acq:** Purchase. **Dist:** Keep the Faith Inc. $20.00.

Alternatives to Assembly Lines: Modern Times—Revisited 1988
In this program we visit assembly plants in Sweden and Italy to see how Volvo and Olivetti use self-pacing work teams, replacing the classic assembly line. 29m; VHS, 3/4 U. **Pr:** National Educational Media Inc. **A:** College-Family. **P:** Professional. **U:** Institution, SURA. **Bus-Ind**: Business, Industry & Industrialists. **Acq:** Purchase, Rent/Lease, Trade-in. **Dist:** Encyclopedia Britannica. $395.00.

Alternatives to Violence 199?
Students learn social skills to prevent violent situations. Includes a teacher's guide. ?m; VHS. **A:** Jr. High. **P:** Education. **U:** Institution. **Gen-Edu**: Violence, Sociology. **Acq:** Purchase. **Dist:** United Learning Inc. $245.00.

Alternatives to Violence: Conflict Resolution and Mediation 1994
Two-part presentation on alternative models for solving problems. Part one shares dramatized sequences demonstrating listening, oral expression, critical thinking, assertiveness, and teamwork skills. Part two explores youth-adult conflicts and encourages peer mediation programs. Complete with instructor's guide. 20m; VHS. **A:** Jr. High-Adult. **P:** Education. **U:** Institution. **Gen-Edu**: Communication, Violence. **Acq:** Purchase. **Dist:** United Learning Inc. $125.00.

The Alternator Explained 1981
On five tapes, automobile alternators are shown for what they are. 71m; VHS, 3/4 U. **Pr:** Bergwall Productions. **A:** Sr. High-Adult. **P:** Vocational. **U:** Institution. **Bus-Ind**: Automobiles. **Acq:** Purchase. **Dist:** Bergwall Productions, Inc.

Alternator Stator Testing 1988
Offers instruction on specific aspects of automotive maintenance and repair. 8m; VHS. **A:** Adult. **P:** Instruction. **U:** Institution. **How-Ins**: Automobiles. **Acq:** Purchase. **Dist:** RMI Media. $39.95.

Altitude 2010 (R) — ★★
Terror in the air. New pilot Sara persuades boyfriend Bruce and three friends that she can fly them to a concert. This is before the plane's instruments malfunction, they are forced into an uncontrolled climb, and they start seeing something horrible in the strange storm clouds that surround them. 90m; DVD. **C:** Jessica Lowndes; Landon Liboiron; Julianna Guill; Jake Weary; Ryan Donowho; Mike Dopud; Directed by Kaare Andrews; Written by Paul A. Birkett; Cinematography by Norm Li; Music by Jeff Tymoschuk. **A:** Sr. High-Adult. **P:** Entertainment. **U:** Home. **Mov-Ent**: Aeronautics, Horror. **Acq:** Purchase. **Dist:** Anchor Bay Entertainment.

The Altruists 19??
Looks at the lives and philosophies of four people who help others by giving of themselves. 28m; VHS. **A:** Family. **P:**

Entertainment. **U:** Home. **Gen-Edu:** Documentary Films. **Acq:** Purchase. **Dist:** Hartley Film Foundation. $29.95.

Alucard 2008 (Unrated) — ★
A modern day remake of "Dracula." 156m; DVD, Streaming. **C:** Jay Barber; Liam Smith; David Harscheid; Karthik Srinivasan; John VanPatten; Hal Handerson; John Johnson; Rebecca Taylor; Mariah Smith; Vicki Taylor; Directed by John Johnson; Written by Spenser Tomson; Cinematography by John Johnson; Sergio Lescari; Music by Lisa Hammer. **A:** Sr. High-Adult. **P:** Entertainment. **U:** Home. **L:** English. **Mov-Ent:** **Acq:** Purchase, Rent/Lease. **Dist:** Darkstone Entertainment. $14.98 9.99.

Alucarda 1977 (R) — ★★
A young girl is sent to a convent filled with vampires, bloody nuns, and the daughter of Satan. 74m; DVD. **C:** Claudio Brook; David Silva; Martin LaSalle; Tina Romero; Susana Kamini; Lili Garza; Tina French; Birgitta Segerskog; Adriana Roel; Directed by Juan Lopez Moctezuma; Written by Juan Lopez Moctezuma; Alexis T. Arroyo; Tita Arroyo; Yolanda Lopez Moctezuma; Cinematography by Xavier Cruz; Music by Anthony Guefen. **A:** Sr. High-Adult. **P:** Entertainment. **U:** Home. **L:** English, Spanish. **Mov-Ent:** **Acq:** Purchase. **Dist:** Mondo Macabro. $24.95.

Alva Boyz: Backyard Annihilation 1989
The Alva Skate Team, plus rad pool skating, plus hardcore skate tunes equals one hot video! 40m; VHS. **C:** Tony Alva; Bill Danforth. **Pr:** NSI. **A:** Jr. High-Adult. **P:** Entertainment. **U:** Home. **Spo-Rec:** Sports--General. **Acq:** Purchase. **Dist:** NSI Sound & Video Inc. $29.95.

Alvarez Kelly 1966 — ★★½
Offbeat western with Holden as the Mexican-Irish Kelly who has just sold a herd of cattle to the North during the Civil War. Confederate officer Widmark kidnaps Holden in an effort to have the cattle redirected to the South. Aided by the traditional women in the midst of men intent on double-crossing each other, a fierce hatred develops between the two, erupting into violence. Sleepy performance by Holden is countered by an intensive Widmark. Based on a true Civil War incident, the script occasionally wanders far afield with the cattle, who cleverly heighten the excitement by stampeding. 109m; VHS, DVD, Wide. **C:** William Holden; Richard Widmark; Janice Rule; Patrick O'Neal; Harry Carey, Jr.; Victoria Shaw; Roger C. Carmel; Indus Arthur; Directed by Edward Dmytryk; Written by Elliott Arnold; Franklin Coen; Cinematography by Joe MacDonald; Music by Johnny Green. **Pr:** Sol C. Siegel. **A:** Family. **P:** Entertainment. **U:** Home. **Mov-Ent:** Western, Civil War. **Acq:** Purchase. **Dist:** Sony Pictures Home Entertainment Inc. $14.95.

Alveolar and Mixed CO2 Tensions 1970
A demonstration and discussion of endtidal and mixed venous CO_2 tension in the dynamic situation, utilizing the pneumotachograph and an infrared CO_2 analyzer. 21m; VHS, 3/4 U, Special order formats. **Pr:** Ohio State University Health Sciences AV Center. **A:** College-Adult. **P:** Professional. **U:** Institution, SURA. **Hea-Sci:** Anatomy & Physiology. **Acq:** Purchase, Rent/Lease. **Dist:** Ohio State University.

Alvin Ailey: Ailey Dances 1987
Four different performances of the Ailey troupe are shown. Taped in New York City, 1982. Includes "Night Creatures," "Revelations," "The Lark Ascending," and "Cry." 85m; VHS. **Pr:** Princeton/Dance Horizons. **A:** Family. **P:** Entertainment. **U:** Institution, Home. **Fin-Art:** Dance--Ballet, Dance--Performance, Performing Arts. **Acq:** Purchase. **Dist:** Music Video Distributors; Princeton Book Company Publishers; Kultur International Films Ltd., Inc. $39.95.

Alvin Ailey American Dance Theater: Beyond the Steps 2007 (Unrated)
Documentary presenting a backstage view of the Alvin Ailey American Dance Theater and its performers. 86m; DVD. **A:** Sr. High-Adult. **P:** Education. **U:** Home. **Gen-Edu:** Documentary Films, Dance. **Acq:** Purchase. **Dist:** Docurama. $26.95.

Alvin Ailey: Memories and Visions 1974
An introduction to the artistry of the Alvin Ailey City Center Dance Theater. Features selections from the major works of choreographer Ailey, performed to music which ranges from modern blues to classical to traditional spirituals. 54m; VHS, 3/4 U. **Pr:** WNET New York. **A:** Jr. High-Adult. **P:** Entertainment. **U:** Institution, SURA. **Fin-Art:** Dance. **Acq:** Purchase. **Dist:** Phoenix Learning Group. $39.95.

Alvin and the Chipmunks 2007 (PG) — ★★½
Alvin, Simon, and Theodore (now digitally rendered) bring their chipmunk schtick into the twenty-first century, and mostly pull it off. Dave Seville (Lee) finds the trio in a muffin basket, quickly discovering their ability not only to speak, but to sing. Soon enough, a hustling promoter (Cross) takes their act on the road, where, sadly, the chipmunks fall victim to burn-out and must lip-sync the rest of their shows. (It ain't the '50s.) Lots of fun for nostalgic baby-boomers and kiddies alike; featuring techno and hip-hop remixes of the Chipmunks' classics. 92m; Blu-Ray, On Demand, Wide. **C:** Jason Lee; David Cross; Cameron Richardson; Jane Lynch; Voice(s) by Justin Long; Matthew Gray Gubler; Jesse McCartney; Directed by Tim Hill; Written by Jon Vitti; Will McRobb; Chris Viscardi; Cinematography by Peter Lyons Collister; Music by Christopher Lennertz. **Pr:** Janice Karman; Ross Bagdasarian, Jr.; Bagdasarian Productions; Regency Enterprises; Fox 2000 Pictures; 20th Century-Fox. **A:** Family. **P:** Entertainment. **U:** Home. **L:** English. **Mov-Ent:** Christmas, Music--Pop/Rock. **Acq:** Purchase. **Dist:** Fox Home Entertainment; Amazon.com Inc.; Movies Unlimited.

Alvin & the Chipmunks: A Chipmunk Christmas 1981
The classic Chipmunk Christmas tale has Alvin giving away his beloved harmonica to a little boy. Unfortunately, Dave has booked the trio for a Christmas concert at Carnegie Hall and expects Alvin to perform a harmonica solo. The Chipmunks perform "Christmas Don't Be Late" and more traditional Christmas carols. 25m; VHS, CC. **Pr:** Bagdasarian Productions. **A:** Family. **P:** Entertainment. **U:** Home. **Chl-Juv:** Animation & Cartoons, Christmas. **Acq:** Purchase. **Dist:** Buena Vista Home Entertainment. $12.99.

Alvin & the Chipmunks: A Christmas Celebration 1995
Alvin, Simon, and Theodore have invited the Seville clan to a family reunion so they can watch the boys perform at a community play. But when things go wrong, the trio try to figure out a way to get out of the show without disappointing the family. 25m; VHS. **A:** Family. **P:** Entertainment. **U:** Home. **Chl-Juv:** Animation & Cartoons. **Acq:** Purchase. **Dist:** Buena Vista Home Entertainment. $12.99.

Alvin & the Chipmunks: Alvin's Christmas Carol 19??
Dicken's "A Christmas Carol" is given the Chipmunk spin when Alvin is a Scroogelike little chipmunk visited by three ghosts. It's up to ghostly visitors Dave, Simon, and Theodore to teach Alvin the true spirit of the holiday. 30m; VHS. **Pr:** Bagdasarian Productions. **A:** Family. **P:** Entertainment. **U:** Home. **Chl-Juv:** Animation & Cartoons, Christmas. **Acq:** Purchase. **Dist:** Buena Vista Home Entertainment. $12.99.

Alvin and the Chipmunks: Alvin's Thanksgiving Celebration 1983 (Unrated)
Children's animated television series. Alvin, Simon, and Theodore celebrate Turkey Day, deal with Dave's marriage, care for a kitten, overview famous times in American History and get parts in a play on this comical collection. 88m; DVD. **A:** Primary. **P:** Entertainment. **U:** Home. **Chl-Juv:** Animation & Cartoons. **Acq:** Purchase. **Dist:** Paramount Pictures Corp.

Alvin & the Chipmunks: Back to Alvin's Future 199?
Eccentric Professor Clyde Crashcup takes the Chipmunks back in time to 1957 to try and persuade the Alvin of the Past not to give up his musical career. Because if he does the present-day Alvin and the Chipmunks won't exist! 25m; VHS, CC. **Pr:** Bagdasarian Productions. **A:** Family. **P:** Entertainment. **U:** Home. **Chl-Juv:** Animation & Cartoons. **Acq:** Purchase. **Dist:** Buena Vista Home Entertainment. $12.99.

Alvin & the Chipmunks: Batmunk 199?
The Chipmunks spoof of "Batman" features Simon as Batmunk, the Caped Crimefighter, and Alvin as the villianous Jokester, whose criminal cohorts have been stealing all the toys in the city. But Batmunk will teach these baddies a lesson! 25m; VHS, CC. **Pr:** Bagdasarian Productions. **A:** Family. **P:** Entertainment. **U:** Home. **Chl-Juv:** Animation & Cartoons. **Acq:** Purchase. **Dist:** Buena Vista Home Entertainment. $12.99.

Alvin and the Chipmunks: Chipwrecked 2011 (G) — ★½
This third Chipmunks adventure is more of the silly same and modestly acceptable kiddy fare. The Chipmunks and Chipettes plus human minder Dave and nemesis Ian are onboard a cruise ship until they become 'chipwrecked' on an island thanks to Alvin's misbehavior. It's not as deserted as they thought since they find long-stranded treasure hunter Zoe (who's gone a little crazy). They practice some survival skills and then a volcano starts rumbling. 87m; DVD, Blu-Ray. **C:** Jason Lee; Alyssa Milano; David Cross; Andy Buckley; Voice(s) by Justin Long; Matthew Gray Gubler; Jesse McCartney; Amy Poehler; Anna Faris; Christina Applegate; Directed by Mike Mitchell; Written by Jonathan Aibel; Glenn Berger; Cinematography by Thomas Ackerman. **Pr:** Janice Karman; Ross Bagdasarian, Jr.; Regency Enterprises; Fox 2000 Pictures; 20th Century-Fox. **A:** Family. **P:** Entertainment. **U:** Home. **L:** English. **Mov-Ent:** Action-Adventure, Volcanos. **Acq:** Purchase. **Dist:** Fox Home Entertainment.

Alvin and the Chipmunks: Christmas with the Chipmunks 1992 (Unrated)
Four digitally restored Christmas cartoons featuring Alvin and the Chipmunks, including: A Chipmunk Christmas, It's a Wonderful Life, Dave, Alvin's Christmas Carol, and A Chipmunk Celebration. 88m; DVD. **A:** Family. **P:** Entertainment. **U:** Home. **L:** English. **Mov-Ent:** Animation & Cartoons, Music--Pop/Rock. **Acq:** Purchase. **Dist:** Bagdasarian Productions. $14.99.

Alvin & the Chipmunks: Dayton Jones and the Pearl of Wisdom 1990 (Unrated)
The chipmunks spoof Indiana Jones with Alvin as Daytona Jones and Simon as Seri-Toga, Batman with Simon as Brice Wayne/Batmunk, Theodore as Happy the Butler, and Alvin-The Jokester, and Robocop with Alvin playing Officer Mallone, Brittany as Violet, and Simon as Dr. Simonize. 3 episodes. 66m; DVD. **A:** Primary. **P:** Entertainment. **U:** Home. **Chl-Juv:** Animation & Cartoons, Action-Adventure. **Acq:** Purchase. **Dist:** Paramount Pictures Corp.

Alvin & the Chipmunks: Funny, We Shrunk the Adults 199?
Alvin and his friends make a giant mess with their indoor musical skateboarding rally—not to mention they've managed to shrink Dave and Mrs. Miller to miniscule size thanks to Simon's shrinking machine! 25m; VHS, CC. **Pr:** Bagdasarian Productions. **A:** Family. **P:** Entertainment. **U:** Home. **Chl-Juv:** Animation & Cartoons. **Acq:** Purchase. **Dist:** Buena Vista Home Entertainment. $12.99.

Alvin & the Chipmunks Go to the Movies: Star Wreck 1990 (Unrated)
Three episodes from the 8th and final season of the animated series that ran from 1982-1990 and spoofed a box-office hit in each episode. "Star Wreck" features Alvin as Captain Dirk commander of the S.S. Boobyprize, "Chip Tracy" is a mystery of kidnapped girlfriend Bess played by Jeanette, and in "Elementary My Dear Simon" Alvin and Simon play Holmes and Watson trying to find a museum thief. 66m; DVD. **C:** Voice(s) by Ross Bagdasarian; Janice Karman. **A:** Preschool-Primary. **P:** Entertainment. **U:** Home. **Chl-Juv:** Animation & Cartoons, Children's Shows. **Acq:** Purchase. **Dist:** Paramount Pictures Corp. $16.99.

Alvin & the Chipmunks: Hair-Raising Chipmunk Tales 1993
A trio of tales from the three troublemakers. "Babysitter Fright Night" has Dave away overnight so he hires a gruesome governess to look after Alvin, Simon, and Theodore. A full moon is causing Theodore to behave even stranger than usual in "Theodore's Life As Dog." "Unfair Science" has the three competing in a science fair but Alvin can't seem to find a project to enter. 35m; VHS. **Pr:** Bagdasarian Productions. **A:** Family. **P:** Entertainment. **U:** Home. **Chl-Juv:** Animation & Cartoons. **Acq:** Purchase. **Dist:** Buena Vista Home Entertainment. $12.99.

Alvin & the Chipmunks: It's a Wonderful Life, Dave 19??
The Chipmunks homage to the classic Christmas movie "It's a Wonderful Life" has Dave wishing he'd never been born after a string of back luck leaves him blue. It's up to Alvin, Simon, and Theodore to show Dave just how important he really is. 30m; VHS. **Pr:** Bagdasarian Productions. **A:** Family. **P:** Entertainment. **U:** Home. **Chl-Juv:** Animation & Cartoons, Christmas. **Acq:** Purchase. **Dist:** Buena Vista Home Entertainment. $12.99.

Alvin & the Chipmunks: I've Been Working on the Railroad 1994
Sing-a-long with the chipmunk trio to 10 favorite children's songs. 30m; VHS, CC. **A:** Preschool-Primary. **P:** Entertainment. **U:** Home. **Chl-Juv:** Animation & Cartoons, Music--Children. **Acq:** Purchase. **Dist:** Buena Vista Home Entertainment. $15.99.
Songs: Down in the Valley; Whistle While You Work; Home on the Range; The Band Played On; I Wish I Had a Horse; On Top of Old Smokey; Row, Row, Row Your Boat; Swing Low, Sweet Chariot; Working on the Railroad; Sing a Goofy Song.

Alvin & the Chipmunks: Kong 199?
Alvin plays a Broadway producer looking for his next hot hit. Kiki, a helpful jungle guide, introduces Alvin to the giant gorilla Kong and Alvin makes the ape the toast of Broadway. But Kiki and Kong learn friendship is more important than fame when Kong can't handle all his newfound acclaim. 25m; VHS, CC. **Pr:** Bagdasarian Productions. **A:** Family. **P:** Entertainment. **U:** Home. **Chl-Juv:** Animation & Cartoons. **Acq:** Purchase. **Dist:** Buena Vista Home Entertainment. $12.99.

Alvin & the Chipmunks: Love Potion #9 1993
Features Alvin, Simon, and Theodore and their Valentine's Day antics. 30m; VHS. **A:** Preschool-Primary. **P:** Entertainment. **U:** Home. **Chl-Juv:** Animation & Cartoons. **Acq:** Purchase. **Dist:** Buena Vista Home Entertainment. $12.99.

Alvin & the Chipmunks Meet Frankenstein 1998 (G)
Alvin and his brothers are performing in a movie studio theme park but become distracted by all the park's attractions, including Frankenstein's Castle, where it seems the doctor and his monster are really alive. 78m; DVD, CC. **A:** Family. **P:** Entertainment. **U:** Home. **Chl-Juv:** Animation & Cartoons. **Acq:** Purchase. **Dist:** Universal Studios Home Video.

Alvin & the Chipmunks Meet the Wolfman 2000
Children's animated Halloween adventure featuring chipmunks Alvin, Simon, and Theodore as they meet the notorious Wolfman. 78m; DVD. **A:** Family. **P:** Entertainment. **U:** Home. **Chl-Juv:** Animation & Cartoons, Halloween. **Acq:** Purchase. **Dist:** Universal Studios Home Video. $14.98.

Alvin & the Chipmunks: Nightmare on Seville Street 1993
Three spooky tales to make you jump from Alvin, Simon, and Theodore. "Nightmare on Seville Street" is what the boys have when they watch a hideous horror movie right before bedtime. "Psychic Alvin" has everyone thinking he sees and knows all. The boys learn "No Chipmunk is an Island" when they each want their own room. 35m; VHS. **Pr:** Bagdasarian Productions. **A:** Family. **P:** Entertainment. **U:** Home. **Chl-Juv:** Animation & Cartoons. **Acq:** Purchase. **Dist:** Buena Vista Home Entertainment. $12.99.

Alvin & the Chipmunks: Robomunk 19??
Alvin and the Chipmunks offer up their rendition of Robocop with Alvin starring in the lead role of Robomunk. 25m; VHS. **Pr:** Buena Vista. **A:** Family. **P:** Entertainment. **U:** Home. **Chl-Juv:** Animation & Cartoons, Comedy--Screwball. **Acq:** Purchase. **Dist:** Buena Vista Home Entertainment. $12.99.

Alvin & the Chipmunks: Rockin' with the Chipmunks 199?
Alvin, Simon, and Theodore sing the songs of such rock legends as Little Richard, Elvis Presley, Elton John, The Beatles, The Beach Boys, and The Rolling Stones. Alvin also dances with Michael Jackson to "Beat It." 25m; VHS, CC. **Pr:** Bagdasarian Productions. **A:** Family. **P:** Entertainment. **U:** Home. **Chl-Juv:** Animation & Cartoons. **Acq:** Purchase. **Dist:** Buena Vista Home Entertainment. $12.99.

Alvin & the Chipmunks: School's Out for Summer 1994
Two animated Alvin stories and a Chipmunks musical version of "School's Out for Summer." In "Alvin's Summer Job," he's working at the zoo and in "The Thinking Cap Trap," the boys try to win big on a TV game show. A companion audiocassette offers nine more Chipmunk tunes. 30m; VHS, CC. **A:** Preschool-Primary. **P:** Entertainment. **U:** Home. **Chl-Juv:** Animation & Cartoons. **Acq:** Purchase. **Dist:** Buena Vista Home Entertainment. $15.99.

Alvin & the Chipmunks: Sing-Alongs 1993
Favorite songs done in the fun-filled chipmunk style, including "Ragtime Cowboy Joe," "Witch Doctor," "Git Along Little Doggies," "Where Oh Where Has My Little Dog Gone," and others. 30m; VHS, CC. **Pr:** Bagdasarian Productions. **A:** Preschool-Primary. **P:** Entertainment. **U:** Home. **Chl-Juv:** Animation & Cartoons, Music--Children. **Acq:** Purchase. **Dist:** Buena Vista Home Entertainment. $12.99.

Alvin & the Chipmunks: The Alvinnn! Edition 2007 (Unrated)
Children's animated television series. Collection of Alvin's mischievous adventures from Hawaii to army boot camp, on the ski slopes and more. 14 episodes. 165m; DVD. **A:** Primary. **P:** Entertainment. **U:** Home. **Chl-Juv:** Animation & Cartoons. **Acq:** Purchase. **Dist:** Paramount Pictures Corp.

Alvin & the Chipmunks: The Chipettes 1983 (Unrated)
The chipmunk trio meet their female matches as high-spirited diva Brittany keeps Alvin in line, Jeanette gets cozy with fellow brainiac Simon, and the athletic Eleanor sets her sights on Theodore. 66m; DVD. **A:** Preschool-Primary. **P:** Entertainment. **U:** Home. **Chl-Juv:** Animation & Cartoons. **Acq:** Purchase. **Dist:** Paramount Pictures Corp. $16.99.

Alvin and the Chipmunks: The Complete Holiday Gift Set 1994 (Unrated)
Children's animated television series. Includes "Alvin's Thanksgiving Celebration," "Trick or Treason," and "A Chipmunk Christmas." 221m; DVD. **A:** Primary. **P:** Entertainment. **U:** Home. **Chl-Juv:** Animation & Cartoons. **Acq:** Purchase. **Dist:** Paramount Pictures Corp.

Alvin and the Chipmunks: The Easter Chipmunk 1995 (Unrated)
Alvin thinks his grandfather was the inspiration for the Easter Bunny and sets out to prove it in court in "The Easter Chipmunk." The Chipmunks and Chipettes become part of a Snow White production in "Snow Wrong," Alvin coaches a "Special Kind of Champion," Simon creates a hat that will give others around him higher intelligence in "Thinking Cap Trap," and Alvin thinks he'll make a mint when a classmate claims to have connections with a lucky leprechaun in "Luck O' the Chipmunks." 5 episodes. 66m; DVD. **A:** Preschool-Primary. **P:** Entertainment. **U:** Home. **Chl-Juv:** Animation & Cartoons, Children's Shows. **Acq:** Purchase. **Dist:** Paramount Pictures Corp. $16.99.

Alvin and the Chipmunks: The Squeakuel 2009 (PG) — ★½
The unruly rodent trio of Alvin, Simon, and Theodore are back! This time around, Dave Seville (Lee) is laid up in a French hospital (thanks to Alvin) and the boys are inevitably left in the care of Dave's lazy video-game playing cousin Toby (Levi). Former promoter Ian (Cross) is angry that the Chipmunks aren't his to manage anymore but soon comes across the female Chipettes—Eleanor, Jeanette, and Brittany—who he pits against the boys. Mayhem ensues with plenty of pop music mixes to entertain the kiddies though its weak and predictable plot makes it a far squeak from the original. 88m; Blu-Ray, Wide. **C:** Jason Lee; Zachary Levi; David Cross; Bridgit Mendler; Wendie Malick; Voice(s) by Justin Long; Matthew Gray Gubler; Jesse McCartney; Anna Faris; Christina Applegate; Amy Poehler; Directed by Betty Thomas; Written by Jonathan Aibel; Glenn Berger; Ross Bagdasarian; Jon Vitti; Cinematography by Anthony B. Richmond; Music by David Newman. **Pr:** Ross Bagdasarian, Jr.; Janice Karman; Bagdasarian Productions; Fox 2000 Pictures; Regency Enterprises; 20th Century-Fox. **A:** Family. **P:** Entertainment. **U:** Home. **L:** English. **Mov-Ent:** Musical. **Acq:** Purchase. **Dist:** Fox Home Entertainment; Movies Unlimited.

Alvin & the Chipmunks: Trick or Treason 1996
Alvin and his brothers Simon and Theodore learn that friendship is more important than popularity as Alvin tries to enter the Monster Club. Includes the Chipmunks' rendition of the hit song, "Monster Mash." 25m; VHS. **Pr:** Buena Vista. **A:** Family. **P:** Entertainment. **U:** Home. **Chl-Juv:** Animation & Cartoons, Holidays. **Acq:** Purchase. **Dist:** Buena Vista Home Entertainment. $12.99.

Alvin Purple 1973 (R) — ★½
Pedestrian comedy about a Mr. Purple, an ordinary Aussie who sells waterbeds and is for some reason constantly being pursued by throngs of sexually insatiable women. Fortunately, he too enjoys sex, even though complications abound. Sexual situations, double entendres, and a script that aims for cleverness (but rarely attains it) somehow made the lust romp a hit in its native Australia, while worldwide it helped establish a market for Down Under cinema. Shot in Melbourne, and followed by "Alvin Rides Again." 97m; VHS. **C:** Graeme Blundell; George Whaley; Ellie MacLure; Penne Hackforth-Jones; Directed by Tim Burstall; Written by Alan Finney; Alan Hopgood; Tim Burstall. **Pr:** Hexagon Productions. **A:** Sr. High-Adult. **P:** Entertainment. **U:** Home. **Mov-Ent:** Comedy--Slapstick, Sex & Sexuality, Australia. **Acq:** Purchase. **Dist:** No Longer Available.

Alvin Rides Again 1974 (Unrated) — ★★
The sexually insatiable Alvin Purple is asked to impersonate an American gangster who was accidentally killed. Another Aussie sex farce from the original writers, who conspire to create a decent sequel to "Alvin Purple," with much of the same cast and crew. 89m; VHS. **C:** Graeme Blundell; Alan Finney; Briony Behets; Frank Thring, Jr.; Jeff Ashby; Chantal Contouri; Directed by David Bilcock; Robin Copping; Written by Alan Finney; Tim Burstall; Alan Hopgood; Cinematography by Robin Copping. **Pr:** Hexagon Productions. **A:** Sr. High-Adult. **P:** Entertainment. **U:** Home. **Mov-Ent:** Comedy--Slapstick, Sex & Sexuality. **Acq:** Purchase. **Dist:** Unknown Distributor.

The Alvin Show: The Very First Alvin Show 1961 (Unrated)
CBS 1961-62 original animated series. Energetic rodents Alvin, Theodore, and Simon put their manager-father Dave Seville through the best of times and the worst of times. Includes "Rockin Through the Decades" and "A Chipmunks Reunion" as extras. 74m; DVD. **C:** Voice(s) by Ross Bagdasarian; Shepard Menken; June Foray. **A:** Preschool-Primary. **P:** Entertainment. **U:** Home. **Chl-Juv:** Animation & Cartoons, Children's Shows. **Acq:** Purchase. **Dist:** Paramount Pictures Corp. $16.99.

Always 1985 (R) — ★★★
Jaglom fictionally documents his own divorce and reconciliation with Patrice Townsend: set in the director's home and starring his friends and family, the film provides comic insight into the dynamics of married/about-to-be-married/and used-to-be-married relationships. Set at a Fourth of July barbecue, this bittersweet romantic comedy is a veritable feast for Jaglom fans, but not everyone will find the director's free-form narrative to their taste. 105m; VHS, DVD, CC. **C:** Henry Jaglom; Patrice Townsend; Bob Rafelson; Melissa Leo; Andre Gregory; Michael Emil; Joanna Frank; Alan Rachins; Jonathan Kaufer; Directed by Henry Jaglom; Written by Henry Jaglom; Cinematography by Hanania Baer. **Pr:** Samuel Goldwyn Company. **A:** Sr. High-Adult. **P:** Entertainment. **U:** Home. **Mov-Ent:** Comedy-Drama, Marriage. **Acq:** Purchase. **Dist:** Lions Gate Television Corp. $79.98.

Always 1989 (PG) — ★★½
A hotshot pilot (Dreyfuss) meets a fiery end and finds that his spirit is destined to become a guardian angel to the greenhorn fire-fighting flyboy (Johnson) who steals his girl's heart. Warm remake of "A Guy Named Joe," one of Spielberg's favorite movies. Sparks between Dreyfuss and Hunter eventually ignite, but Goodman delivers the most heat. Hepburn makes an appearance as the angel who guides Dreyfuss. An old-fashioned tree-burner romance that includes actual footage of the 1988 Yellowstone fire. 123m; VHS, DVD, Wide, CC. **C:** Holly Hunter; Richard Dreyfuss; John Goodman; Audrey Hepburn; Brad Johnson; Marg Helgenberger; Keith David; Roberts Blossom; Dale Dye; Directed by Steven Spielberg; Written by Jerry Belson; Cinematography by Mikael Salomon; Music by John Williams. **Pr:** Mark Huffam; United Artists; Amblin Entertainment. **A:** Jr. High-Adult. **P:** Entertainment. **U:** Home. **Mov-Ent:** Drama, Aeronautics, Fires. **Acq:** Purchase. **Dist:** Facets Multimedia Inc. $19.95.

Always a Bridesmaid 2000
At the outset, we are lead to believe that filmmaker Nina Davenport has made a film about the pressures that women face concerning marriage, but from there, she places the emphasis solely on herself and her relationship with boyfriend Nick. While she does fit into the demographic which the film purports to study, Davenport's story is quite boring and difficult to watch. She interviews family members and ex-boyfriends, all of who look directly into the camera and list off her faults—all of which make Davenport sound like a very troubled person. A documentary on society's views of unmarried women would be very interesting, but this doesn't fit that bill. 98m; DVD. **C:** Directed by Nina Davenport; Written by Nina Davenport; Cinematography by Nina Davenport. **A:** Sr. High-Adult. **P:** Entertainment. **U:** Home. **Mov-Ent:** Documentary Films, Women, Marriage. **Acq:** Purchase. **Dist:** New Video Group. $24.95.

Always Afternoon 1987
World War I madness strikes Australia as Australians of German descent and German immigrants are sent to internment camps. However, a young violinist still manages to fall in love with a local girl. 210m; VHS. **C:** Lisa Harrow; Jochen Horst; Tushka Bergen; Directed by David Stevens. **A:** Jr. High-Adult. **P:** Entertainment. **U:** Home. **Mov-Ent:** Australia, World War One, Drama. **Acq:** Purchase. **Dist:** BFS Video.

Always for Pleasure 1978
An insider's look at Mardi Gras and the myriad musical traditions the annual celebration supports in New Orleans. 58m; VHS, 3/4 U. **A:** Family. **P:** Education. **U:** Institution, Home. **Gen-Edu:** Documentary Films, Parades & Festivals, Black Culture. **Acq:** Purchase. **Dist:** Flower Films; Music Video Distributors; Baker and Taylor. $49.95.

Always Goodbye 1938 (Unrated) — ★★
Typical '30s melodrama. Unmarried tough cookie Margot Weston (Stanwyck) gives up her baby for adoption to Phil Marshall (Hunter) and his wife. After becoming a successful businesswoman, Margot accidentally meets her son and learns his mother has died and his dad is getting remarried. Margot pushes her way into their lives, doesn't like Phil's fiance (Bari), and aims to break them up. 75m/B/W; DVD. **C:** Barbara Stanwyck; Ian Hunter; Lynn Bari; Herbert Marshall; Cesar Romero; Binnie Barnes; Directed by Sidney Lanfield; Written by Kathryn Scola; Cinematography by Robert Planck; Music by Cyril Mockridge. **A:** Adult. **P:** Entertainment. **U:** Home. **L:** English. **Mov-Ent:** Adoption, Family. **Acq:** Purchase. **Dist:** Twentieth Century Fox Film Corp.

Always Outnumbered Always Outgunned 1998 (R) — ★★★
Character study follows ex-con Socrates Fortlow (Fishburne in a dynamic performance). A convicted murderer, he's now trying to lead a non-violent life on the violent streets of L.A.'s Watts, maintain his dignity, and find a job. But none of this is easy. Adapted from the book by Mosley, who wrote the teleplay. 110m; VHS, DVD, CC. **C:** Laurence Fishburne; Bill Cobbs; Natalie Cole; Daniel Williams; Laurie Metcalf; Bill Nunn; Cicely Tyson; Isaiah Washington, IV; Directed by Michael Apted; Written by Walter Mosley; Cinematography by John Bailey; Music by Michael Franti. **Pr:** Laurence Fishburne; Walter Mosley; Laurence Fishburne; Walter Mosley; HBO; Palomar Pictures International. **A:** Sr. High-Adult. **P:** Entertainment. **U:** Home. **Mov-Ent:** TV Movies, Black Culture, Poverty. **Acq:** Purchase. **Dist:** Movies Unlimited; Alpha Video.

Always Ready: The United States Coast Guard Story 1990
The history of the Coast Guard is documented here, from its fouding in 1789 to end smuggling and collect tarriffs to the present day position as a valuable force of the U.S. Navy. 45m; VHS. **Pr:** MPI Media Group. **A:** Sr. High-Adult. **P:** Entertainment. **U:** Home. **Gen-Edu:** Documentary Films, Armed Forces--U.S. **Acq:** Purchase. **Dist:** MPI Media Group; Fusion Video. $29.95.

Always Roses 1991
A Latino city-boy is sent to Arizona to stay with his grandparents while his parents sort out their marital problems. During his stay, Mike is introduced to his Mexican heritage and forms everlasting bonds with his family. 29m; VHS. **A:** Primary. **P:** Education. **U:** Institution. **Gen-Edu:** Mexico, Adolescence, Family. **Acq:** Purchase, Rent/Lease. **Dist:** Direct Cinema Ltd. $195.00.

Always Wear the Right Stuff! 1994
Demonstrates to pesticide users how they can reduce the risk of pesticide problems and contamination by wearing certain protective clothing, and equipment. 26m; VHS. **A:** Adult. **P:** Instruction. **U:** Institution. **Gen-Edu:** Poisons, Clothing & Dress. **Acq:** Purchase. **Dist:** Cornell University. $24.95.

Always Will 2006 (PG) — ★★½
High-school senior Will discovers his elementary school's time capsule and it allows him to revisit his past and change decisions he now regrets. But his changes impact his present in unexpected ways and Will wonders if selfishness is the true problem and if he needs to accept his past and move on. 95m; DVD. **C:** Andrew Baglini; John Schmidt; Mark Schroeder; Noelle Meixell; Bart Mallard; Jody Seymour; Directed by Michael Sammaciccia; Written by Michael Sammaciccia; Cinematography by Michael Sammaciccia; Music by Michael Aharon. **A:** Family. **P:** Entertainment. **U:** Home. **Mov-Ent:** Adolescence. **Acq:** Purchase. **Dist:** Bedford Entertainment Inc.

Alyssa Milano: Look in My Heart 1989
The television actress takes her stab at the music world in this three clip compilation. 24m; VHS. **C:** Alyssa Milano. **A:** Jr. High-Sr. High. **P:** Entertainment. **U:** Home. **Mov-Ent:** Music Video. **Acq:** Purchase. **Dist:** Music Video Distributors. $49.95.

Alyssa Milano's Teen Steam 1988
A dance workout tape for teenagers, featuring rhythmic exercises set to top hits. 60m; VHS. **Pr:** J2 Communications. **A:** Jr. High-Sr. High. **P:** Instruction. **U:** Home. **Hea-Sci:** Fitness/Exercise. **Acq:** Purchase. **Dist:** j2 Global.

The Alzheimer Care Kit ????
Presentation for professionals and family caregivers explains ways to minimize stress and implement positive care procedures for handling those with dementia. 89m; VHS. **A:** Adult. **P:** Vocational. **U:** Institution. **Hea-Sci:** Mental Health, Occupational Training, Medical Education. **Acq:** Purchase. **Dist:** University of Maryland. $400.00.
Indiv. Titles: 1. Signs and Symptoms of Alzheimer Disease 2. Alzheimer Disease: Responsive Care Plans 3. Alzheimer Disease: Minimizing Care Problems.

Alzheimer's: A Personal Story 1992
Dramatically conveys the progression of the disease on three individuals and the impact it has on their families. 29m; VHS. **A:** College-Adult. **P:** Education. **U:** Institution. **Hea-Sci:** Diseases, Health Education, Nursing. **Acq:** Purchase, Rent/Lease. **Dist:** Terra Nova Films. $145.00.

Alzheimer's: A True Story 1999
A true look at the demise due to Alzheimer's through documentation of Malcolm Pointon's (husband, father, Cambridge Professor and gifted pianist) descent into dementia. He was diagnosed at the age of 51 and his wife stood by him "in sickness and in health." Note: Objectionable content. 75m; VHS. **A:** Adult. **P:** Professional. **U:** Institution. **Hea-Sci:** Aging, Diseases, Health Education. **Acq:** Purchase. **Dist:** Aquarius Health Care Media. $179.00.

Alzheimer's Disease 1988
The history of this disease is summarized. 10m; VHS, 3/4 U. **Pr:** Ohio State University Health Sciences AV Center. **A:** College-Adult. **P:** Professional. **U:** Institution, CCTV. **Hea-Sci:** Neurology, Aging, Diseases. **Acq:** Purchase, Rent/Lease. **Dist:** Discovery Education. $295.00.

Alzheimer's Disease 1988
Alzheimer's patients are seen, so nurses can get an idea of what they have to deal with. 28m; VHS, 3/4 U. **Pr:** Hospital Satellite Network. **A:** Adult. **P:** Professional. **U:** Institution, CCTV, SURA. **Hea-Sci:** Nursing, Diseases, Aging. **Acq:** Purchase, Rent/Lease. **Dist:** AJN Video Library/Lippincott Williams & Wilkins. $275.00.
Indiv. Titles: 1. Coping with Confusion 2. Discharge Planning.

Alzheimer's Disease 1997
Discusses the symptoms and difficulties of the patient afflicted with Alzheimer's Disease and their families. 28m; VHS. **A:** Sr. High-Adult. **P:** Education. **U:** Institution. **Hea-Sci**: Health Education, Aging, Mental Health. **Acq:** Purchase. **Dist:** Aquarius Health Care Media. $149.00.

Alzheimer's Disease: A Daughter's Perspective 1986
A daughter relates her family's realization that their father had the disease and would need support and custodial care. 45m; VHS, 3/4 U. **A:** Adult. **P:** Education. **U:** Institution. **Hea-Sci**: Diseases. **Acq:** Purchase, Rent/Lease. **Dist:** Boston University, GKM Instructional Resource Center. $100.00.

Alzheimer's Disease: A Family Perspective 1984
Family members of patients with Alzheimer's Disease share experiences, frustrations and optimism. 30m; VHS, 3/4 U. **Pr:** Good Samaritan Hospital. **A:** Family. **P:** Education. **U:** Institution, CCTV, Home. **Hea-Sci**: Diseases. **Acq:** Purchase, Rent/Lease. **Dist:** Good Samaritan Hospital & Medical Center.

Alzheimer's Disease: A Son's Perspective 1986
This interview reveals how the son comes to accept his father's condition and the responsibility for his future care. 40m; VHS, 3/4 U. **A:** Adult. **P:** Education. **U:** Institution. **Hea-Sci**: Diseases. **Acq:** Purchase, Rent/Lease. **Dist:** Boston University, GKM Instructional Resource Center. $100.00.

Alzheimer's Disease Series 1988
This series discusses the horrendous problems faced by victims of Alzheimer's Disease and their families in obtaining proper care and treatment. The availability of resources to help victims is examined as well. 11m; VHS, 3/4 U. **Pr:** Altschul Group. **A:** Jr. High-Adult. **P:** Education. **U:** Institution, SURA. **Hea-Sci**: Health Education, Nursing, Diseases. **Acq:** Purchase, Rent/Lease. **Dist:** Discovery Education. $295.00.
Indiv. Titles: 1. Advocacy & Support Groups 2. Alternative Care 3. Home Care & Problem Solving 4. An Introduction for Caregivers.

Alzheimer's Disease: The Long Nightmare 1989
The emotional and financial problems that people caring for Alzheimer's victims suffer are highlighted. 19m; VHS, 3/4 U. **Pr:** Films for the Humanities. **A:** Jr. High-Adult. **P:** Education. **U:** Institution, SURA. **Hea-Sci**: Aging, Neurology, Diseases. **Acq:** Purchase, Rent/Lease. **Dist:** Films for the Humanities & Sciences. $149.00.

Alzheimer's Disease: You Are Not Alone 1985
What type of help is available for Alzheimer's Disease victims and their families? Gives case examples of patients who were just diagnosed to those who are in later stages of the disease. 28m; VHS. **Pr:** Elias S. Cohen; Anne Stanaway. **A:** Sr. High-Adult. **P:** Education. **U:** Home, Institution. **Hea-Sci**: Patient Education, Aging, Diseases. **Acq:** Purchase. **Dist:** WITF-TV.

Alzheimer's 101: The Basics for Caregiving 1992
Nursing students will benefit from this in-depth outline to the basics of caregiving for the Alzheimer's patient. Eighteen segments centered around six topics deal with issues from personal care to caregiver stress. Includes two workbooks, trainer's manual, and a learner's guide. 85m; VHS. **Pr:** South Carolina ETV Commission; Independent. **A:** College-Adult. **P:** Education. **U:** Institution. **Hea-Sci**: Diseases, Nursing, Health Education. **Acq:** Purchase, Rent/Lease. **Dist:** Terra Nova Films. $295.00.

The Alzheimer's Project 2009
Provides an in-depth look at scientific advances being made in research and medical understanding of the progressive brain disorder. 298m; DVD. **A:** Adult. **P:** Education. **U:** Home. **Hea-Sci**: Alzheimer's/Dementia, Documentary Films. **Acq:** Purchase. **Dist:** Home Box Office Inc. $19.98.

An Alzheimer's Story 1985
This powerful program, filmed over the course of two years, follows the decline of Anna Jasper from Alzheimer's disease, and the reaction of her husband and daughter. 28m; VHS, 3/4 U. **Pr:** Kenneth Paul Rosenburg; Ruth Neuwald. **A:** Jr. High-Adult. **P:** Education. **U:** Institution, Home, SURA. **Gen-Edu**: Aging, Family. **Acq:** Purchase, Rent/Lease, Duplication. **Dist:** Filmakers Library Inc.

Alzheimer's: The Myths and the Facts 1985
Burton Reifler, associate professor of psychiatry and behavioral sciences at the University of Washington, discusses the long- and short-term effects of Alzheimer's disease. 29m; VHS. **A:** Sr. High-Adult. **P:** Education. **U:** Institution. **Hea-Sci**: Health Education, Diseases. **Acq:** Purchase. **Dist:** University of Washington Educational Media Collection. $15.00.

Am Brunnen vor dem Tore 1952 (Unrated)
The young owner of a Gasthaus falls in love with an English ex-pilot. Filmed in Dinkelsbuehl. In German only. 88m; VHS. **TV Std:** NTSC, PAL. **C:** Sonja Ziemann; Willy Fritsch; Paul Klinger. **A:** Family. **P:** Entertainment. **U:** Home. **L:** German. **Mov-Ent**: Drama. **Acq:** Purchase, Rent/Lease. **Dist:** German Language Video Center. $49.95.

Am I Happy? 1979
This is a collection of video shorts expressing the opinions of video artist Shawn Preus. 31m; VHS, 3/4 U. **Pr:** Shawn Preus; Open Space. **A:** College-Adult. **P:** Entertainment. **U:** Institution. **Fin-Art**: Video. **Acq:** Rent/Lease. **Dist:** Video Out Distribution.

Am I Normal? 1979
Focusing on three fictional characters, this program presents the facts about male sexual development, while raising important questions about masculinity, identity and peer pressure. 24m; VHS, Special order formats. **Pr:** Copperfield Films. **A:** Jr. High-Sr. High. **P:** Education. **U:** Home. **Hea-Sci**: Adolescence, Sex & Sexuality. **Acq:** Purchase, Rent/Lease. **Dist:** EcuFilm; MGM Home Entertainment; New Day Films Library. $39.95.

Am I Wife, Mother. . .Or Me? 1975
A deeply discerning look at modern marriage emerges in the story of Karen-a woman determined to establish her own identity. Edited from "I Love You...Goodbye." 31m; VHS, 3/4 U. **C:** Hope Lange; Earl Holliman. **Pr:** Learning Corporation of America; Tomorrow Entertainment Inc. **A:** Adult. **P:** Entertainment. **U:** Institution, SURA. **Gen-Edu**: Women. **Acq:** Purchase, Rent/Lease. **Dist:** Phoenix Learning Group.

Am I Worthwhile? Identity and Self-Image 1974
This program stresses the importance of a positive self-image in developing a healthy personality, and examines literature which concerns itself with independence, self-esteem, and inner feelings. 29m; VHS, 3/4 U. **Pr:** Center for Humanities. **A:** Jr. High-Adult. **P:** Education. **U:** Institution, SURA. **Gen-Edu**: Human Relations, Personality. **Acq:** Purchase. **Dist:** Center for Humanities, Inc./Guidance Associates.

A.M. Klein: The Poet as Landscape 1979
A portrait of Anglo-Jewish writer Klein, with a description of the social forces that moved him to the creation of his poetry. 58m; VHS, 3/4 U. **Pr:** David Kaufman. **A:** Sr. High-Adult. **P:** Education. **U:** Institution, SURA. **Gen-Edu**: Documentary Films, Literature. **Acq:** Purchase. **Dist:** Ergo Media Inc. $39.95.

AM Radio Was His Only Friend 1977
This experimental video features video artist Rodney Werden talking over a macro close-up of two people making love. 17m; VHS, 3/4 U. **Pr:** Rodney Werden. **A:** College-Adult. **P:** Education. **U:** Institution. **Fin-Art**: Video. **Acq:** Rent/Lease. **Dist:** Video Out Distribution.

AMA Healthy Heart Series 1994
Four-tape series covering cardiovascular topics. Each program includes booklet. 15m; VHS, CC. **A:** Adult. **P:** Education. **U:** Institution. **Hea-Sci**: Heart, Patient Education, Medical Care. **Acq:** Purchase. **Dist:** Milner-Fenwick, Inc.
Indiv. Titles: 1. Guide to Your Healthy Heart 2. Guide to Controlling Your Cholesterol 3. Guide to High Blood Pressure Control 4. Guide to Stop Smoking.

The AMA Home Video Guide to Controlling Your Cholesterol 1996
Answers questions and covers topics related to cholesterol and how to control it through diets that don't have to be bland and boring. 33m; VHS. **A:** Adult. **P:** Education. **U:** Home. **Gen-Edu**: Health Education, Heart. **Acq:** Purchase. **Dist:** Milner-Fenwick, Inc. $19.98.

Amadeus 1984 (PG) — ★★★½
Entertaining adaptation by Shaffer of his play about the intense rivalry between 18th century composers Antonio Salieri and Wolfgang Amadeus Mozart. Abraham's Salieri is a man who desires greatness but is tortured by envy and sorrow. His worst attacks of angst occur when he comes into contact with Hulce's Mozart, an immature, boorish genius who, despite his gifts, remains unaffected and delighted by the beauty he creates while irking the hell out of everyone around him. Terrific period piece filmed on location in Prague; excellent musical score, beautiful sets, nifty billowy costumes, and realistic American accents for the 18th century Europeans. 158m; VHS, DVD, Blu-Ray. **C:** F. Murray Abraham; Tom Hulce; Elizabeth Berridge; Simon Callow; Roy Dotrice; Christine Ebersole; Jeffrey Jones; Kenny Baker; Cynthia Nixon; Vincent Schiavelli; Directed by Milos Forman; Written by Peter Shaffer; Cinematography by Miroslav Ondricek; Music by John Strauss. **Pr:** Saul Zaentz; Orion Pictures. **A:** Jr. High-Adult. **P:** Entertainment. **U:** Home. **Mov-Ent**: Drama, Biography: Music. **Awds:** Oscars '84: Actor (Abraham), Adapt. Screenplay, Art Dir./Set Dec., Costume Des., Director (Forman), Film, Makeup, Sound; AFI '98: Top 100; Cesar '85: Foreign Film; Directors Guild '84: Director (Forman); Golden Globes '85: Actor--Drama (Abraham), Director (Forman), Film--Drama, Screenplay; L.A. Film Critics '84: Director (Forman), Film, Screenplay. **Acq:** Purchase. **Dist:** Baker and Taylor; Home Vision Cinema; Facets Multimedia Inc. $14.98.
Songs: Concert No. 27 for Pianoforte and Orchestra in B Flat Major; Ave Verum Corpus; A Quintet For Strings in E Flat; A Concerto for Clarinet and Orchestra in A Major; Number 39 in E Flat Major; Number 40 in G Minor; Number 41 in C Major.

Amahl and the Night Visitors 1978
A performance of Gian Carlo Menotti's popular holiday opera, written expressly for TV in 1951, featuring the Philharmonic Orchestra and conductor Jesus Lopez-Cobos. 120m; VHS. **C:** Teresa Stratas; Giorgio Tozzi; Willard White; Robert Sapolsky. **Pr:** Arvin Brown; Giancarlo Menotti; National Broadcasting Company. **A:** Jr. High-Adult. **P:** Entertainment. **U:** Home. **Fin-Art**: Opera, Christmas, Religion. **Acq:** Purchase. **Dist:** Home Vision Cinema; Music Video Distributors; Karol Media. $19.95.

Amanda and the Alien 1995 (R) — ★½
Dumb saga finds flaky Californian Amanda (Eggert) taking care of a sex-starved, shape-changing extraterrestrial (Meneses) while a couple of feds hunt him down. Based on a story by Robert Silverberg. 94m; VHS, CC. **C:** Alex Meneses; Nicole Eggert; Michael Dorn; Stacy Keach; Michael C. Bendetti; Richard Speight, Jr.; David Millbern; Directed by Jon Kroll; Written by Jon Kroll. **Pr:** Showtime. **A:** Sr. High-Adult. **P:** Entertainment. **U:** Home. **Mov-Ent**: TV Movies. **Acq:** Purchase. **Dist:** Lions Gate Entertainment Inc.

Amanda Knox: Murder on Trail in Italy 2011 (Unrated) — ★
Lifetime usually does a better job with its true crime efforts, but this one is apparently pasted together from tabloid headlines. In 2007, Seattle exchange student Amanda Knox is accused by Italian authorities of murdering her British roommate Meredith Kercher, aided by her boyfriend and another male friend. The evidence is likely tainted and Prosecutor Mignini has been accused of misconduct but the trial goes on anyway. 92m; DVD. **C:** Hayden Panettiere; Marcia Gay Harden; Vincent Riotta; Paolo Romio; Djirbi Kebe; Amanda Fernando Stevens; Clive Walton; Directed by Robert Dornhelm; Written by Wendy Battles; Music by Zack Ryan. **A:** Sr. High-Adult. **P:** Entertainment. **U:** Home. **Mov-Ent**: TV Movies, Italy, Law. **Acq:** Purchase. **Dist:** A&E Television Networks L.L.C.

The Amanda Show: Volume 1 - Amanda, Please! 2004 (Unrated)
Features episodes from the 1999-2002 Nick Jr. sketch comedy show starring teenager Amanda Byne including Judge Trudy goes on a reality show (episode 214), customers beware when the Klutzes operate a restaurant (episode 217), Amanda struggles to find someone with enough brawn to open a bag of chips (episode 222), and the garage guy is bummed out about bug bites (episode 226). 4 episodes. 88m; DVD. **C:** Amanda Bynes; Drake Bell; Josh Peck; Nancy Sullivan. **A:** Primary-Jr. High. **P:** Entertainment. **U:** Home. **Chl-Juv**: Television Series, Children's Shows, Family. **Acq:** Purchase. **Dist:** Paramount Pictures Corp. $16.99.

The Amanda Show: Volume 2 - The Girls' Room 2004 (Unrated)
Features episodes from the 1999-2002 Nick Jr. sketch comedy show starring teenager Amanda Byne including "the girls' room" hosts a competition (episode 216), Amanda takes to the street with microphone in hand (episode 219), a wacky cereal parody (episode 224), and Judge Trudy and the Dancing Lobsters head to school (episode 228). 4 episodes. 88m; DVD. **C:** Amanda Bynes; Drake Bell; Josh Peck; Nancy Sullivan. **A:** Primary-Jr. High. **P:** Entertainment. **U:** Home. **Chl-Juv**: Television Series, Children's Shows, Family. **Acq:** Purchase. **Dist:** Paramount Pictures Corp. $16.99.

Amanita 1974
A journey through the magnificent world of mushrooms with the use of ultra close-up photography and electronic music. 9m; 3/4 U. **Pr:** Vic Atkinson. **A:** Family. **P:** Entertainment. **U:** Institution, SURA. **Fin-Art**: Fantasy. **Acq:** Purchase, Rent/Lease. **Dist:** Pyramid Media.

Amantes Salvajes 2005 (Unrated) — ★
Softcore porn attempting to be a murder mystery. 82m; DVD. **C:** Todd White; Belinds Gavin; Tamara Landry; kerry windsor; Directed by Dante Giove; Written by David Ciesielsky; Cinematography by Chuck d'Ayala; Music by Jay Harris. **A:** Sr. High-Adult. **P:** Entertainment. **U:** Home. **L:** English. **Mov-Ent.** **Acq:** Purchase. **Dist:** Navarre Corp. $9.98.

Amarcord 1974 (R) — ★★★½
Semi-autobiograpical Fellini fantasy which takes place in the village of Rimini, his birthplace. Focusing on the young Zanin's impressions of his town's colorful slices of life, Fellini takes aim at fascism, family life, and religion in 1930s Italy. Visually ripe, delivering a generous, occasionally uneven mix of satire, burlesque, drama, and tragicomedic lyricism. Considered by people in the know as one of Fellini's best films and the topic of meaningful discussions among art film students everywhere. 124m; VHS, DVD. **C:** Magali Noel; Bruno Zanin; Pupella Maggio; Armando Brancia; Directed by Federico Fellini; Written by Federico Fellini; Tonino Guerra; Cinematography by Giuseppe Rotunno; Music by Nino Rota. **Pr:** Franco Cristaldi. **A:** College-Adult. **P:** Entertainment. **U:** Home. **L:** Italian. **Mov-Ent**: Comedy-Drama, Italy, Biography. **Awds:** Oscars '74: Foreign Film; N.Y. Film Critics '74: Director (Fellini), Film. **Acq:** Purchase. **Dist:** Home Vision Cinema. $39.95.

Amarilly of Clothesline Alley 1918 (Unrated) — ★★½
Amarilly (Pickford) gets a job as a New York dance hall cigarette girl and is around to help wealthy slumming playboy Gordon Phillips (Kerry) after he gets into a fight. Phillips becomes convinced he loves Amarilly, despite her social inferiority, but Amarilly comes to realize she should stick with those that know her best, including neighborhood beau, Terry (Scott). 77m/B/W; Silent; VHS, DVD. **C:** Mary Pickford; William Scott; Norman Kerry; Ida Waterman; Kate Price; Margaret Landis; Directed by Marshall Neilan; Written by Frances Marion; Cinematography by Walter Stradling. **A:** Jr. High-Adult. **P:** Entertainment. **U:** Home. **Mov-Ent**: Silent Films, Comedy--Romantic. **Acq:** Purchase. **Dist:** Milestone Film & Video.

Amass Composite 1976
A ballerina dances against the background of the Quebec skyline in this experimental video. 20m/B/W; VHS, 3/4 U. **Pr:** Paul Wong; Valerie Hammer. **A:** College-Adult. **P:** Entertainment. **U:** Institution. **Fin-Art**: Video, Dance. **Acq:** Rent/Lease. **Dist:** Video Out Distribution.

Amate: The Great Fig Tree 1986
A documentary profiling the Central American fig tree and its cohabitating wildlife. 30m; VHS, 3/4 U. **Pr:** Benchmark Films. **A:** Family. **P:** Education. **U:** Institution, CCTV. **Gen-Edu**: Forests & Trees, Wildlife. **Acq:** Purchase, Rent/Lease. **Dist:** Benchmark Media.

The Amateur 1982 (R) — ★½
Computer technologist for the CIA dives into a plot of international intrigue behind the Iron Curtain when he investigates the death of his girlfriend, murdered by terrorists. Confused and ultimately disappointing spy drama cursed with a wooden script written by Littell, based on his novel. 112m; VHS, DVD. **C:** John Savage; Christopher Plummer; Marthe Keller; Arthur Hill; Ed Lauter; Directed by Charles Jarrott; Written by Robert Littell. **Pr:** 20th Century-Fox. **A:** Sr. High-Adult. **P:** Entertainment. **U:**

Home. **Mov-Ent**: Mystery & Suspense, Intelligence Service, Terrorism. **Acq:** Purchase. **Dist:** Anchor Bay Entertainment. $59.98.

Amateur 1994 (R) — ★★★
Former nun Huppert, trying to make a living writing pornography, hooks up with an amnesiac (Donovan) who turns out to have a criminal past and a porno actress wife (Lowensohn) who wants him dead. Blackmail plot has oddball characters racing through dark and evocative settings while unfolding a tale loaded with offbeat oppositions and an irresistibly bizarre romantic triangle. Lively and playful without becoming pretentious, Hartley's self-described "action thriller... with one flat tire" evokes his typical deadpan subtle style. 105m; VHS, DVD, CC. **C:** Isabelle Huppert; Martin Donovan; Elina Lowensohn; Damian Young; Chuck Montgomery; David Simonds; Pamela Stewart; Terry Alexander; Directed by Hal Hartley; Written by Hal Hartley; Cinematography by Michael Spiller; Music by Hal Hartley; Jeff Taylor. **Pr:** Hal Hartley; Ted Hope; Hal Hartley; Lindsay Law; Jerome Brownstein; Scott Meek; Yves Marmion; UGC; Zenith Productions; True Fiction Pictures; Sony Pictures Classics. **A:** College-Adult. **P:** Entertainment. **U:** Home. **Mov-Ent**: Pornography. **Acq:** Purchase. **Dist:** Sony Pictures Home Entertainment Inc.

Amateur Crook 1937 (Unrated) — ★½
Mining engineer Jerry Cummings uses a diamond as collateral with loan sharks Crone and Jaffin. When his daughter Betsey realizes they—ve stolen the gem and are off to Mexico, she poses as a crook to steal it back only to be first hindered—and then helped—by confused artist Jimmy Baxter. 62m/B/W; DVD. **C:** Bruce Bennett; Joan Barclay; Monte Blue; Jack Mulhall; Vivien Oakland; Jimmy Aubrey; Forrest Taylor; Fuzzy Knight; Directed by Sam Katzman; Written by Basil Dickey; Cinematography by William (Bill) Hyer. **A:** Sr. High-Adult. **P:** Entertainment. **U:** Home. **Mov-Ent**: Crime Drama. **Acq:** Purchase. **Dist:** Sinister Cinema.

The Amateur Naturalist 1989
Naturalist Charles Durrell and zoologist Lee Durrell demonstrate how to observe, record, interpret and help conserve the features of each habitat. 24m; VHS, 3/4 U. **Pr:** Landmark Films, Inc. **A:** Jr. High-Adult. **P:** Education. **U:** Institution, SURA. **Hea-Sci**: Ecology & Environment, Wilderness Areas, Wildlife. **Acq:** Purchase, Rent/Lease. **Dist:** Landmark Media. $250.00. **Indiv. Titles:** 1. Creatures of the Sun 2. Living on the Edge 3. Wetland Wilderness 4. A Monarchy of Trees 5. Between Ice and Fire 6. Feast of Grass 7. Guardian of the Meadows 8. Upstream, Downstream 9. The Cost of High Living 10. Tapestry of the Tropics.

Amateur Night 1985 (Unrated) — ★
Sloppy musical comedy about the backstage bickering occuring during the amateur night at a famous nightclub. 91m; VHS. **C:** Geoffrey Deuel; Dennis Cole; Allen Kirk; Directed by Eddie Beverly, Jr.; Written by Tom Dempsey. **Pr:** Snowbird Productions. **A:** Jr. High-Adult. **P:** Entertainment. **U:** Home. **Mov-Ent**: Musical, Nightclubs. **Acq:** Purchase. **Dist:** Lions Gate Television Corp. $69.98.

Amatzia: The Bar Kochba Caves 1990
Fascinating look at the Bar Kochba caves, from which the Jews of ancient Israel launched an attack against Rome in 132 C.E. The Kochba Caves are the only caves which have been completely excavated to date, and feature an olive press room, a ritual bath (mikvah), a huge water cistern and more. 12m; VHS. **A:** Sr. High-Adult. **P:** Education. **U:** Home. **Gen-Edu**: Documentary Films, Archaeology, Israel. **Acq:** Purchase. **Dist:** Ergo Media Inc. $29.95.

Amaurosis 2002 (Unrated)
Documents the life of Nguyen Duc Dat, a blind, American Asian, impoverished orphan, guitarist from Little Saigon, California. 28m; DVD. **A:** Adult. **P:** Education. **U:** Institution. **Gen-Edu**: Documentary Films, Identity. **Acq:** Purchase. **Dist:** Third World Newsreel. $175.

An Amazin' Era: New York Mets 1986
The story of the 1986 World Series as won by the New York Mets, plus highlights from the team's first 25 years. 71m; VHS. **Pr:** Major League Baseball Productions. **A:** Family. **P:** Entertainment. **U:** Home. **Spo-Rec**: Baseball. **Acq:** Purchase. **Dist:** Major League Baseball Productions. $19.95.

Amazing Advantages for Kids 1995
Instructs proper manners for children to use in everyday situations. Offers examples on how they should behave in different social situations that will improve the childs' confidence. ?m; VHS. **A:** Family. **P:** Education. **U:** Institution, Home. **Gen-Edu**: Children, Family, Parenting. **Acq:** Purchase. **Dist:** Cambridge Educational. $54.95.

Amazing Adventure 1937 — ★★
A millionaire wins a bet when he rises from a chauffeur's position to the executive board room without using his wealth. Though not particularly amazing, lightweight English comedy has Grant working hard to charm over and above the demands of the dated formula, a performance he undertook during a vacation from Hollywood. Adapted from a novel by E. Phillips Oppenheim. 63m; VHS, DVD. **C:** Cary Grant; Mary Brian; Henry Kendall; Leon M. Lion; Ralph Richardson; Directed by Alfred Zeisler. **A:** Family. **P:** Entertainment. **U:** Home. **Mov-Ent**: Comedy--Screwball. **Acq:** Purchase. **Dist:** Movies Unlimited; Alpha Video. $19.95.

Amazing Alaska Animals 1997
Features Monty the Moose and his sidekick Captain Patrick Puffin on an Arctic tundra adventure. 40m; VHS. **A:** Primary. **P:** Education. **U:** Home. **Chl-Juv**: Arctic Regions, Animals. **Acq:** Purchase. **Dist:** 411 Video Information. $19.95.

The Amazing Apes 1977
This feature reveals never-before-known facts about these fascinating primates through absorbing highlights such as monkey worship, life-style of snow monkeys in Japan, and studies of gorillas and chimps in the wild. 93m; VHS. **Pr:** Bill Burrud Productions. **A:** Family. **P:** Entertainment. **U:** Home. **Gen-Edu**: Documentary Films, Animals. **Acq:** Purchase. **Dist:** Walt Disney Studios Home Entertainment. $19.95.

Amazing Ball Choreography 2003
A fast-paced cardio workout led by Patrick Goudeau includes a variety of exercises (some with core toning benefits) using a stability ball. Fun and easy to follow. 42m; DVD. **A:** Adult. **P:** Instruction. **U:** Home. **Hea-Sci**: Fitness/Exercise. **Acq:** Purchase. **Dist:** Collage Video Specialties, Inc.

Amazing Ball Choreography II 2004
Fun cardio workout using a stability ball with more intensity than the first volume. Many moves have toning benefits as well. Led by Patrick Goudeau. 53m; DVD. **A:** Adult. **P:** Instruction. **U:** Home. **Hea-Sci**: Fitness/Exercise. **Acq:** Purchase. **Dist:** Collage Video Specialties, Inc.

Amazing Birds of America 1999
Features over 150 different species of North American birds with bird expert Steve Maslowski. Includes woodpeckers, pheasants, swallows, meadowlarks and others. 60m; VHS. **A:** Family. **P:** Education. **U:** Home. **Gen-Edu**: Birds, Wildlife, Nature. **Acq:** Purchase. **Dist:** Instructional Video. $19.95.

Amazing Bone and Other Stories 1988
Four animated stories narrated by John Lithgow. Included are "The Amazing Bone," "John Brown, Rose and the Midnight Cat," "A Picture for Harold's Room," and "The Trip." Recommended for children ages 3-10. 32m; VHS. **C:** Narrated by John Lithgow. **Pr:** CC Studios. **A:** Preschool-Primary. **P:** Entertainment. **U:** Home. **Chl-Juv**: Children, Animation & Cartoons, Storytelling. **Acq:** Purchase. **Dist:** Facets Multimedia Inc.; Baker and Taylor; Weston Woods Studios. $14.95.

The Amazing Book ???? (Unrated)
Children's animated religious program that introduces the Bible and its teachings using characters such as Doc Dickory, Dewey Decimole, Rikki, and Revver; first part of the "Amazing Bible Series." ??m; DVD. **A:** Family. **P:** Education. **U:** Institution, Home. **Mov-Ent**: Religion, Children, Children's Shows. **Acq:** Purchase. **Dist:** Bridgestone Multimedia Group Inc. $6.36.

The Amazing Captain Nemo 1978 (Unrated) — ★½
Captain Nemo (Ferrer) is awakened after a 100-year cryogenic freeze with the help of scientist Waldo Cunningham (Meredith) after Navy divers discover the Nautilus and take it to DC. Since Waldo is nuts, he decides to use Nemo and the Nautilus, threatening to destroy the capitol unless he gets a billion in gold. Originally broadcast as a three-part TV pilot from producer Irwin Allen and then re-cut for an international film release. 98m; DVD. **C:** Jose Ferrer; Burgess Meredith; Mel Ferrer; Burr DeBenning; Horst Buchholz; Tom Hallick; Lynda Day George; Directed by Alex March; Written by Robert Bloch; Robert C. Dennis; Norman Katkov; Cinematography by Lamar Boren; Music by Richard LaSalle. **A:** Family. **P:** Entertainment. **U:** Home. **Mov-Ent**: Science, Science Fiction. **Acq:** Purchase. **Dist:** WarnerArchive.com.

The Amazing Chan and the Chan Clan: The Complete Series 1972
Hanna-Barbera Studios animated series shown on CBS. Chinese-American detective Charlie Chan and his kids travel the world solving mysteries. 16 episodes. 344m; DVD. **A:** Family. **P:** Entertainment. **U:** Home. **L:** English. **Chl-Juv**: Animation & Cartoons, Television Series. **Acq:** Purchase. **Dist:** WarnerArchive.com. $35.99.

The Amazing Children ???? (Unrated)
Children's animated religious program that introduces the Bible and its teachings using characters such as Doc Dickory, Dewey Decimole, Rikki, and Revver; second part of the "Amazing Bible Series." 26m; DVD. **A:** Family. **P:** Education. **U:** Institution, Home. **Mov-Ent**: Religion, Children, Children's Shows. **Acq:** Purchase. **Dist:** Bridgestone Multimedia Group Inc. $6.36.

The Amazing Colossal Man 1957 (Unrated) — ★★
A standard '50s sci-fi film about atomic radiation. Colonel Manning is exposed to massive doses of plutonium when an experiment backfires (literally). The former good-guy grows to 70 feet and starts taking out his anger on a helpless Las Vegas. Can anything stop his murderous rampages? Followed by "War of the Colossal Beast." 79m/B/W; VHS. **C:** Glenn Langan; Cathy Downs; William (Bill) Hudson; James Seay; Russ Bender; Lyn Osborn; Frank Jenks; Hank Patterson; Directed by Bert I. Gordon; Written by Bert I. Gordon; Mark Hanna; Cinematography by Joseph Biroc; Music by Albert Glasser. **Pr:** Bert I. Gordon; Bert I. Gordon; American International Pictures. **A:** Family. **P:** Entertainment. **U:** Home. **Mov-Ent**: Science Fiction. **Acq:** Purchase. **Dist:** Sony Pictures Home Entertainment Inc.; Fusion Video. $9.95.

The Amazing Cosmic Awareness of Duffy Moon 197?
Story of the class shrimp who overcomes the teasing of others with imagination and ingenuity. 32m; VHS, 3/4 U, Special order formats. **Pr:** Daniel Wilson Productions. **A:** Primary-Sr. High. **P:** Entertainment. **U:** Institution, SURA. **Chl-Juv**. **Acq:** Purchase, Rent/Lease. **Dist:** Time-Life Video and Television.

The Amazing Dobermans 1976 (G) — ★★
Family-oriented pooch performance piece featuring Astaire in one of his lesser roles. Ex-con man Astaire and his five trained Dobermans assist an undercover agent in foiling a small-time criminal's gambling and extortion racket. The last in a series that includes "The Daring Dobermans" and "The Doberman Gang." 96m; VHS. **C:** Fred Astaire; Barbara Eden; James Franciscus; Jack Carter; Billy Barty; Parley Baer; Directed by Byron Ross Chudnow; Music by Alan Silvestri. **Pr:** Golden Films. **A:** Family. **P:** Entertainment. **U:** Institution, Home. **Mov-Ent**: Action-Adventure, Pets, Family Viewing. **Acq:** Purchase. **Dist:** Amazon.com Inc. $9.95.

Amazing Dr. Clitterhouse 1938 — ★★★
Satirical gangster saga has criminologist Dr. Clitterhouse (Robinson) so fascinated by crime that he commits a few jewel robberies just to test out that bad guy rush. He contacts a fence, luscious Jo Keller (Trevor), who gets Clitterhouse an in with gangster Rocks Valentine (Bogart). Clitterhouse sucessfully masterminds some heists for Valentine—who becomes jealous of Clitterhouse's brain power and things just get more wacky from there (including a farcical trial). This is definitely Robinson's show. 87m/B/W; VHS, DVD. **C:** Edward G. Robinson; Claire Trevor; Humphrey Bogart; Gale Page; Donald Crisp; Maxie "Slapsie" Rosenbloom; Thurston Hall; Allen Jenkins; John Litel; Henry O'Neill; Ward Bond; Curt Bois; Directed by Anatole Litvak; Written by John Huston; John Wexley; Cinematography by Gaetano Antonio "Tony" Gaudio; Music by Max Steiner. **Pr:** Anatole Litvak; Robert Lord; Anatole Litvak; Warner Bros. **A:** Jr. High-Adult. **P:** Entertainment. **U:** Home. **Mov-Ent**: Satire & Parody. **Acq:** Purchase. **Dist:** Warner Home Video, Inc.

The Amazing Feats of Young Hercules 1997
A teenaged Hercules is banished from Mt. Oylmpus to Earth by dad Zeus for abusing his powers and must face four deadly challenges to prove himself worthy to return home. This animated adventure will provide kids with lots of action and some good lessons about loyalty and friendship. 60m; DVD. **A:** Family. **P:** Entertainment. **U:** Home. **Chl-Juv**: Animation & Cartoons. **Acq:** Purchase. **Dist:** Allumination Filmworks.

Amazing Grace 19??
Portrays the story of Amazing Grace, a little girl who wants to be Peter Pan. Spotlights on women who have gone past stereotyping to pursue their dreams. Narrated by Tyne Daly. Hosted by LeVar Burton. Features Whoopi Goldberg as she shares her story of success. Includes teacher's guide. 30m; VHS, CC. **C:** Narrated by Tyne Daly; Hosted by LeVar Burton. **A:** Jr. High. **P:** Education. **U:** Institution. **Chl-Juv**: Literature--Children, Women, Education. **Acq:** Purchase. **Dist:** GPN Educational Media. $39.95.

Amazing Grace 1974 (Unrated) — ★★
Some righteous mothers led by Moms Mabley go up against corrupt city politics in this extremely dated comedy that was cast with a sense of the absurd. 99m; VHS, DVD, Wide, CC. **C:** Moms (Jackie) Mabley; Slappy (Melvin) White; Moses Gunn; Rosalind Cash; Dolph Sweet; Butterfly McQueen; Stepin Fetchit; Directed by Stan Lathan; Written by Matt Robinson; Cinematography by Edward R. Brown; Sol Negrin. **Pr:** Platinum Pictures. **A:** Adult. **P:** Entertainment. **U:** Home. **Mov-Ent**: Parenting. **Acq:** Purchase. **Dist:** MGM Home Entertainment.

Amazing Grace 1979
Filmed in the Sequoia National Park in California, this program gives an enchanting look at the giant Sequoia in all seasons. 10m; VHS, 3/4 U, Special order formats. **Pr:** National Park Service. **A:** Primary-Adult. **P:** Entertainment. **U:** Institution, SURA. **Spo-Rec**: National Parks & Reserves. **Acq:** Purchase. **Dist:** National Audiovisual Center.

Amazing Grace 1992 — ★★
Eighteen-year-old Jonathan leaves home to share his friend Mickey's apartment. He meets Thomas, who has just returned to Israel after years in New York, and they begin a tentative relationship. But Thomas is hiding the fact that he may be HIV-positive and tries to keep a distance from the eager Jonathan. Hebrew with subtitles. 95m; VHS. **C:** Rivka Michaely; Sharon Alexander; Gal Hoyberger; Hina Rozovska; Directed by Amos Guttman. **A:** College-Adult. **P:** Entertainment. **U:** Home. **L:** Hebrew. **Mov-Ent**: AIDS, Israel. **Acq:** Purchase.

Amazing Grace 1994
Adaptation of Mary Hoffman's Amazing Grace featuring narrator Alfre Woodard. 10m; VHS. **A:** Primary. **P:** Education. **U:** Institution. **Chl-Juv**. **Acq:** Purchase. **Dist:** Weston Woods Studios. $90.00.

Amazing Grace 2006 (PG) — ★★★
Sincere and forceful bio of evangelical Christian William Wilberforce (Gruffudd), a member of the House of Commons, who spent his years in the British Parliament introducing antislavery legislation. Tells the crusader's story with flashbacks, introducing both foes and friends, including former slave trader John Newton (Finney), who wrote the title hymn (rousingly sung by Gruffudd), as part of his atonement. Senegalese singer N'Dour makes his film debut as freed slave and author Oloudah Equiano. 111m; DVD. **C:** Ioan Gruffudd; Romola Garai; Albert Finney; Michael Gambon; Rufus Sewell; Ciaran Hinds; Toby Jones; Nicholas Farrell; Sylvestria Le Touzel; Stephan Campbell Moore; Benedict Cumberbatch; Youssou N'Dour; Directed by Michael Apted; Written by Steven Knight; Cinematography by Remi Adefarasin; Music by David Arnold. **Pr:** Edward B. Pressman; Terrence Malick; David Hunt; Michelle Murdocca; Roadside Attractions; Bristol Bay Prods; Samuel Goldwyn Films. **A:** Jr. High-Adult. **P:** Entertainment. **U:** Home. **L:** English. **Mov-Ent**: Drama, Biography: Politics, Blindness. **Acq:** Purchase. **Dist:** Fox Home Entertainment.

Amazing Grace & Chuck 1987 (PG) — ★★
Perhaps the only anti-war/sports fantasy ever made. After a visit to a Minuteman missile site in Montana, 12-year-old Little Leaguer Chuck learns of the dangers of nuclear arms. He begins a protest by refusing to play until the nations come to a

peace agreement. In a sudden surge of social conscience, athletes worldwide put down their equipment and join in droves, starting with pro-basketball star Amazing Grace Smith (Denver Nugget English). Capra-like fantasy has good intentions but ultimately lacks two key elements: coherency and plausibility. 115m; VHS, DVD, CC. **C:** Jamie Lee Curtis; Gregory Peck; William L. Petersen; Joshua Zuehlke; Alex English; Directed by Mike Newell; Cinematography by Robert Elswit; Music by Elmer Bernstein. **Pr:** Tri-Star Pictures. **A:** Family. **P:** Entertainment. **U:** Home. **Mov-Ent:** Nuclear Warfare, Baseball, Youth Sports. **Acq:** Purchase. **Dist:** Sony Pictures Home Entertainment Inc.; Alpha Video. $19.99.

Amazing Grace with Bill Moyers 1990
Bill Moyers hosts a study of the most popular hymn in the English language, written by an 18th-century ship captain. Performers such as Judy Collins, Johnny Cash, Jessye Norman, and Marion Williams tell how the song has effected their lives. Includes performances by Jean Ritchie and the Boys Choir of Harlem and readings by Jeremy Irons. 87m; VHS, CC. **C:** Hosted by Bill Moyers. **Pr:** PBS Video. **A:** Family. **P:** Entertainment. **U:** Institution, CCTV, Home, SURA. **Gen-Edu:** Religion, Music--Performance, Black Culture. **Acq:** Purchase, Duplication License, Off-Air Record. **Dist:** PBS Home Video; Karol Media; Signals Video. $19.95.

Amazing Grains ????
Tours the world of grains: rice, wheat, corn, buckwheat, kasha, and quinoa. Discusses their importance in the food pyramid. 20m; VHS. **A:** Adult. **P:** Professional. **U:** Institution, CCTV. **Hea-Sci:** Nutrition, Fitness/Exercise. **Acq:** Purchase. **Dist:** The Learning Seed. $89.00.

The Amazing Howard Hughes 1977 — ★★½
Reveals the full story of the legendary millionaire's life and career, from daring test pilot to inventor to Hollywood film producer to isolated wealthy paranoiac with a germ phobia. Lingers on the rich guy with big problems theme. Big-budget TV drama with a nice performance by Jones. 119m; VHS, DVD. **C:** Tommy Lee Jones; Ed Flanders; James Hampton; Tovah Feldshuh; Lee Purcell; Directed by William A. Graham. **Pr:** Roger Gimbel Productions; EMI Media. **A:** Sr. High-Adult. **P:** Entertainment. **U:** Home. **Mov-Ent:** Biography: Show Business, TV Movies. **Acq:** Purchase. **Dist:** Facets Multimedia Inc. $19.95.

Amazing Insect Warriors 1998
Explains how warrior insects use camouflage and chemicals to find a mate, food, and protection. 23m; VHS; Closed Captioned. **A:** Primary. **P:** Education. **U:** Home, Institution. **Chl-Juv:** Insects, Biology, Science. **Acq:** Purchase. **Dist:** Library Video Inc. $12.95.

Amazing Mallika 19??
Part of a curriculum plan designed to teach elementary students the importance of coping with anger through the story of Mallika the tiger of India. Includes storybook and teaching guide. 15m; VHS. **A:** Primary. **P:** Education. **U:** Institution. **Chl-Juv:** Ethics & Morals, Education. **Acq:** Purchase. **Dist:** Marshmedia. $79.95.

Amazing Masters of the Martial Arts 1985
Learn the secrets of martial arts masters Sonny Chiba, Bruce Lei, and Carter Wong. 60m; VHS. **C:** Hosted by Ken Howard; Directed by Domonic Paris. **Pr:** Paris Productions. **A:** Jr. High-Adult. **P:** Entertainment. **U:** Home. **Spo-Rec:** Martial Arts. **Acq:** Purchase. **Dist:** Lions Gate Television Corp. $59.98.

The Amazing Miracles ???? (Unrated)
Children's animated religious program that introduces the Bible and its teachings using characters such as Doc Dickory, Dewey Decimole, Rikki, Revver, and Giant Cat; third part of the "Amazing Bible Series." ??m; DVD. **A:** Family. **P:** Education. **U:** Institution, Home. **Mov-Ent:** Religion, Children, Children's Shows. **Acq:** Purchase. **Dist:** Bridgestone Multimedia Group Inc. $6.36.

The Amazing Mrs. Holiday 1943 (Unrated) — ★★½
Pleasant Durbin outing finds the star playing the daughter of missionaries working in China. Ruth accompanies a group of Chinese orphans aboard a ship bound for San Francisco, aided by steward Timothy (Fitzgerald). She wants the children to stay together, so Timothy passes Ruth off as the wife of a shipping magnate, who's been lost at sea. Ruth admits her deception to the man's grandson Tom (O'Brien) and convinces him that it's okay that she and the children stay in the family mansion. 98m/B/W; VHS, CC. **C:** Deanna Durbin; Edmond O'Brien; Barry Fitzgerald; Arthur Treacher; Harry Davenport; Grant Mitchell; Frieda Inescort; Elisabeth Risdon; Directed by Bruce Manning; Written by Frank Ryan; John Jacoby; Cinematography by Elwood "Woody" Bredell; Music by Frank Skinner; Hans J. Salter. **Pr:** Universal Pictures. **A:** Jr. High-Adult. **P:** Entertainment. **U:** Home. **Mov-Ent:** Comedy-Drama, Adoption. **Acq:** Purchase.

The Amazing Mr. Bean: Series I, II, III 1998
British actor and comedian Rowan Atkinson brings portrays his character Mr. Bean in a series of slapstick comedy episodes. Five hours and fifty four minutes on six videocassettes. 59m; VHS; Closed Captioned. **A:** Jr. High-Adult. **P:** Entertainment. **U:** Home. **Mov-Ent:** Comedy--Slapstick. **Acq:** Purchase. **Dist:** PBS Home Video. $99.95.

The Amazing Mr. Bean: Series IV 1998
Rowan Atkinson reprises his Mr. Bean character in two new videos, "Unseen Bean" and "The Best Bits of Mr. Bean," a compilation of his funniest skits. Two hours on two videocassettes. 60m; VHS; Closed Captioned. **A:** Jr. High-Adult. **P:** Entertainment. **U:** Home. **Mov-Ent:** Comedy--Slapstick. **Acq:** Purchase. **Dist:** PBS Home Video. $39.95.

Amazing Mr. Blunden 1972 (G) — ★★½
Solid kidvid about two youngsters aided by a ghost who travel back in time to save the lives of two murdered children. Adapted by Jeffries from Antonia Barber's novel, "The Ghosts." 100m; VHS, DVD. **C:** Laurence Naismith; Lynne Frederick; Garry Miller; Marc Granger; Rosalyn London; Diana Dors; Directed by Lionel Jeffries; Music by Elmer Bernstein. **Pr:** Media. **A:** Family. **P:** Entertainment. **U:** Home. **Mov-Ent:** Fantasy, Mystery & Suspense, Great Britain. **Acq:** Purchase. **Dist:** Unknown Distributor.

The Amazing Mr. X 1948 (Unrated) — ★★½
When a woman's husband dies, she tries to contact him via a spiritualist. Things are not as they seem however, and the medium may just be part of an intricate scheme to defraud the woman. 79m/B/W; VHS, DVD. **C:** Turhan Bey; Lynn Bari; Cathy O'Donnell; Richard Carlson; Donald Curtis; Virginia Gregg; Directed by Bernard Vorhaus; Written by Ian McLellan Hunter; Muriel Roy Boulton; Cinematography by John Alton. **Pr:** Eagle Lion. **A:** Jr. High-Adult. **P:** Entertainment. **U:** Home. **Mov-Ent:** Mystery & Suspense, Occult Sciences. **Acq:** Purchase. **Dist:** Sinister Cinema; Rex Miller Artisan Studio. $19.95.

The Amazing Newborn 1975
Presents three normal infants from one to seven days of age who are shown reacting to visual, tactile, and auditory stimuli. Helps parents recognize not only when their child is alert, but also its individuality. 25m; VHS, 3/4 U. **Pr:** Case Western Reserve University. **A:** Adult. **P:** Education. **U:** Institution. **Hea-Sci:** Infants. **Acq:** Purchase, Rent/Lease. **Dist:** Polymorph Films, Inc.

The Amazing Normal Story 1998
Documentary of childhood sexual abuse and the filmmaker, Flavyn Feller, who became sexually involved with a much older man at the age of 12. Includes her childhood diaries and interviews with family and friends. 57m; VHS. **A:** Adult. **P:** Education. **U:** Home. **Gen-Edu:** Documentary Films, Children, Sexual Abuse. **Acq:** Purchase, Rent/Lease. **Dist:** Filmakers Library Inc. $295.

Amazing North America 1994
Spin, National Geographic's animated globe, takes a coast-to-coast cruise through North America. He seeks out the multitude of wildlife that life in this great region as he explores from the tundras of the north to the swamps of the south. 52m; VHS, CC. **Pr:** National Geographic Society. **A:** Family. **P:** Education. **U:** Institution, Home. **Gen-Edu:** Documentary Films, Wildlife, Wilderness Areas. **Acq:** Purchase. **Dist:** Sony Pictures Home Entertainment Inc. $14.95.

Amazing Ocean 3D 2013 (Unrated)
Universal Studios' 3D film about coral reef life. 50m; DVD, Blu-Ray, Streaming. **A:** Family. **P:** Entertainment. **U:** Home. **L:** English, Arabic, Chinese, Czech, Danish, French, German, Greek, Hungarian, Italian, Japanese, Korean, Norwegian, Polish, Portuguese, Russian, Spanish, Swedish. **Gen-Edu:** Documentary Films, Nature. **Acq:** Purchase, Rent/Lease. **Dist:** Universal Studios Home Video. $29.98 29.98 11.99.

The Amazing Panda Adventure 1995 (PG) — ★★½
Ryan (Slater) is off to China during his spring break to visit dad Michael (Lang), who's working on a project to rescue the dwindling panda population. But there's poacher trouble and Ryan and young translator Ling (Ding) decide to rescue the preserve's panda cub, which has been animal-napped (where's Ace Ventura when you need him). Family fare, with a mixture of totally adorable real and animatronic pandas; filmed in the Sichuan province of China, home to the Wolong Nature Reserve which is famous for its successful breeding of the endangered giant pandas. Slater, in his first starring role, is the younger brother of Christian. 84m; DVD, CC. **C:** Ryan Slater; Stephen Lang; Yi Ding; Wang Fei; Directed by Christopher Cain; Written by Laurice Elehwany; Jeff Rothberg; Cinematography by Jack N. Green; Music by William Ross. **Pr:** Gary Foster; Gabriella Martinelli; Lee Rich; Beijing Film Studio; Warner Bros. **A:** Family. **P:** Entertainment. **U:** Home. **Mov-Ent:** Action-Adventure, China, Animals. **Acq:** Purchase. **Dist:** Warner Home Video, Inc. $19.98.

Amazing Planet: Explosive Earth 1996 (Unrated)
Captain Rip Rayon and his fellow explorers investigate all manner of naturally explosive situations on Earth, including volcanoes, geysers, tsunamis, earthquakes and more. 52m; VHS, DVD. **A:** Family. **P:** Entertainment. **U:** Institution, Home. **Mov-Ent:** Documentary Films, Volcanos, National Parks & Reserves. **Acq:** Purchase. **Dist:** National Geographic Society. $19.95.

The Amazing Race: The First Season 2005 (Unrated)
Offers the debut season of the television reality-game show hosted by Phil Keoghan that followed 11 teams of 22 contestants as they travel worldwide in search of clues that will lead them to the eventual finish line with a $1 million prize. Some destinations included Thailand, China, Italy, Alaska, and Zambia with competitors such as two circus clowns, a gay married couple, a father and son, a separated couple, and best friends. 13 episodes. 769m; DVD. **C:** Hosted by Phil Keoghan. **A:** Jr. High-Adult. **P:** Entertainment. **U:** Home. **Mov-Ent:** Television Series, Action-Adventure, Game Show. **Acq:** Purchase. **Dist:** Paramount Pictures Corp. $39.98.

The Amazing Race: The Seventh Season 2005 (Unrated)
Offers the seventh season of the television reality-game show hosted by Phil Keoghan that followed 11 teams of 22 contestants as they travel worldwide in search of clues that will lead them to the eventual finish line with a $1 million prize. Some destinations included Long Beach, California, Buenos Aires,

South Africa, and London with competitors such as Rob and Amber of "Survivor" fame, an older married couple, a mother and son, and brothers. 12 episodes. 650m; DVD. **C:** Hosted by Phil Keoghan. **A:** Jr. High-Adult. **P:** Entertainment. **U:** Home. **Mov-Ent:** Television Series, Action-Adventure, Game Show. **Acq:** Purchase. **Dist:** Paramount Pictures Corp. $39.98.

Amazing Special Effects You Can Do with Your Camcorder 1990
Special effects expert Harry Joyner shows how to make impressive effects for the home camcorder. 60m; VHS. **Pr:** Multi-Video. **A:** Jr. High-Adult. **P:** Instruction. **U:** Home. **How-Ins:** How-To, Video. **Acq:** Purchase. **Dist:** Multi-Video, Inc. $29.95.

The Amazing Spider-Man 1977 (Unrated) — ★★
The Marvel Comics superhero's unique powers are put to the test when he comes to the rescue of the government by preventing an evil scientist from blackmailing the government for big bucks. The wall-walking web-slinger has his origins probed (a grad student bit by a radioactive spider develops super-human powers) in his live-action debut, which led to a short-lived TV series. 94m; VHS, CC. **C:** Nicholas Hammond; David White; Lisa Eilbacher; Michael Pataki; Directed by E.W. Swackhamer. **Pr:** Edward S. Montagne. **A:** Family. **P:** Entertainment. **U:** Home. **Mov-Ent:** Fantasy, TV Movies. **Acq:** Purchase. **Dist:** Image Entertainment Inc. $24.98.

The Amazing Spider-Man 2012 (PG-13) — ★★★
The Marvel Comics franchise gets a fine (if a little long) 3D film reboot as awkward science nerd Peter Parker (Garfield) goes back to his high school outcast teen years, his crush on Gwen Stacy (Stone), and his family issues. Peter gets bitten by a spider at genetics research company Oscorp--where his dad's ex-partner, Dr. Curt Connors (Ifans) works. (Connors has a second identity as the villainous Lizard.) Spidey is perceived as a weirdo vigilante by Gwen's police captain dad (Leary). There's the usual big action sequences, including a rescue, and battling the destructive baddie. The end-credits give a peek at the inevitable sequel's villain. 136m; DVD, Blu-Ray. **C:** Andrew Garfield; Rhys Ifans; Emma Stone; Martin Sheen; Sally Field; Denis Leary; Irrfan Khan; Chris Zylka; Campbell Scott; Embeth Davidtz; Directed by Marc Webb; Written by James Vanderbilt; Alvin Sargent; Steve Kloves; Cinematography by John Schwartzman; Music by James Horner. **Pr:** Laura Ziskin; Avi Arad; Matthew Tolmach; Marvel Studios; Columbia Pictures; Sony Pictures Home Entertainment Inc. **A:** Jr. High-Adult. **P:** Entertainment. **U:** Home. **L:** English. **Mov-Ent:** Acq: Purchase. **Dist:** Sony Pictures Home Entertainment Inc.

The Amazing Spider-Man 2 2014 (PG-13) — ★★
Peter Parker/Spider-man (Garfield) is back along with his girlfriend Gwen Stacy (Stone) and troubled friend Harry Osborn (DeHaan). Beleaguered Max Dillon (Foxx) suffers an accident at work that has electrifying consequences as he takes on his own alter ego, Electro. Besides this new threat, Spidey has to confront even more enemies--The Green Goblin, Rhino, and his own emotional drama. Some of the rapport between Garfield and Stone works (and Field steals the movie as Aunt May) but it's mostly too cluttered down with subplots and villains that it can't take flight. 142m; DVD, Blu-Ray. **C:** Andrew Garfield; Emma Stone; Jamie Foxx; Dane DeHaan; Paul Giamatti; Colm Feore; Sally Field; Felicity Jones; Directed by Marc Webb; Written by Alex Kurtzman; Roberto Orci; Jeff Pinkner; Cinematography by Dan(iel) Mindel; Music by Hans Zimmer. **Pr:** Avi Arad; Matthew Tolmach; Columbia Pictures Industries Inc; Marvel Entertainment L.L.C. **A:** Jr. High-Adult. **P:** Entertainment. **U:** Home. **L:** English. **Mov-Ent:** Action-Adventure. **Acq:** Purchase.

Amazing Sports Bloopers 1988
Sports bloopers so hilarious you may throw away all your other sports bloopers videos. 45m; VHS. **C:** Hosted by Roy Firestone. **Pr:** Sports Illustrated. **A:** Family. **P:** Instruction. **U:** Home. **Spo-Rec:** Sports--General, Outtakes & Bloopers. **Acq:** Purchase. **Dist:** ESPN Inc. $9.95.

Amazing Stories 1985 (Unrated)
From the Steven Spielberg produced TV series. "The Mission" sees a WWII turret gunner trapped in an unusual predicament. In "The Wedding Ring," a man gives his wife a strange ring and bizarre situations ensue. 70m; VHS. **C:** Kevin Costner; Casey Siemaszko; Kiefer Sutherland; Danny DeVito; Rhea Perlman; Directed by Danny DeVito; Steven Spielberg. **Pr:** Steven Spielberg; Steven Spielberg; Amblin Entertainment; Universal City Studios. **A:** Jr. High-Adult. **P:** Entertainment. **U:** Home. **Mov-Ent:** Science Fiction, Fantasy, Serials. **Acq:** Purchase. **Dist:** Movies Unlimited; Facets Multimedia Inc. $19.98.

Amazing Stories, Book 3 1993 (Unrated)
Three stories from the short-lived series produced by Steven Spielberg. In "Life on Death Row," Patrick Swayze is a criminal who acquires a great new power. Gregory Hines is "The Amazing Falsworth," a nightclub psychic who uncovers a mass murderer by accident. Then an army outcast, played by Charlie Sheen, performs a miracle to save his fellow soldiers from certain death in "No Day at the Beach." 73m; VHS. **C:** Patrick Swayze; James Callahan; Gregory Hines; Richard Masur; Charlie Sheen; Ralph Seymour; Philip McKeon; Steven Gethers; Tom (Thomas E.) Hodges; Directed by Mick Garris; Peter Hyams; Leslie Linka Glatter. **Pr:** Steven Spielberg; Amblin Entertainment. **A:** Jr. High-Adult. **P:** Entertainment. **U:** Home. **Mov-Ent:** Science Fiction, Serials, TV Movies. **Acq:** Purchase. **Dist:** Universal Studios Home Video. $19.98.

Amazing Stories, Book 4 1985 (Unrated)
Three fantastic tales from the Speilberg-produced TV show. "Mirror, Mirror" (1985; directed by Martin Scorsese) finds a director of horror films tormented by the very monsters he created. "Blue Man Down" (1986; directed by Paul Michael

Glaser) tells of a cop who is helped by a mysterious young woman after his partner is shot dead. In "Mr. Magic" (1985; directed by Donald Petrie), an aging magician has his powers revitalized thanks to a strange deck of cards. 71m; VHS, CC. **C:** Sam Waterston; Helen Shaver; Dick Cavett; Max Gail; Kate McNeil; Chris Nash; Sid Caesar; Leo Rossi; Directed by Martin Scorsese; Paul Michael Glaser; Donald Petrie. **Pr:** Steven Spielberg; Amblin Entertainment; Universal City Studios. **A:** Family. **P:** Entertainment. **U:** Home. **Mov-Ent:** Fantasy, TV Movies, Serials. **Acq:** Purchase. **Dist:** Universal Music and Video Distribution. $19.95.

Amazing Stories, Book 5 1985 (Unrated)
More Spielberg-produced tales from the TV series. "The Pumpkin Competition" is a comedy about a parsimonious widow who enters a pumpkin growing contest. A young girl vanishes for two decades in "Without Diana," and a gang of space travellers collide head on with a trio of high school students working on a science project in "Fine Tuning." 73m; VHS. **C:** June Lockhart; Polly Holliday; J.A. Preston; Billy Green Bush; Dianne Hull; Gennie James; Matthew Laborteaux; Gary Riley; Jimmy Gatherum; Milton Berle; Directed by Norman Reynolds; Leslie Linka Glatter; Bob Balaban. **Pr:** Steven Spielberg; Amblin Entertainment. **A:** Family. **P:** Entertainment. **U:** Home. **Mov-Ent:** Fantasy, Science Fiction, TV Movies. **Acq:** Purchase. **Dist:** Universal Studios Home Video. $19.98.

Amazing Stories: The Complete First Season 1985
Created and produced by Steven Spielberg, the 24 episodes of this anthology cover horror, sci-fi, and fantasy. Guest stars include Kevin Costner, Sid Caesar, John Lithgow, Tim Robbins, Milton Berle, and many more. Directors include Spielberg, Martin Scorsese, Clint Eastwood, Paul Bartel, and Joe Dante. 683m; DVD. **A:** Jr. High-Adult. **P:** Entertainment. **U:** Home. **Mov-Ent:** Television Series. **Acq:** Purchase. **Dist:** Universal Studios Home Video.

Amazing Surf Stories 198?
Six surfing stories that try to capture surfing and surfers from every angle. 85m; VHS. **A:** Jr. High-Adult. **P:** Entertainment. **U:** Home. **Spo-Rec.** **Acq:** Purchase. **Dist:** ESPN Inc. $39.95.

Amazing Things, Vol. 1 1985
Shows how everyday household items can become amusing toys for your children. Hosted by Dr. Misterio. 60m; VHS. **Pr:** Maljack Productions Inc. **A:** Family. **P:** Entertainment. **U:** Home. **Chl-Juv:** Animation & Cartoons. **Acq:** Purchase. **Dist:** MPI Media Group.

Amazing Things, Vol. 2 1985
Dr. Misterio shows your children how to make incredible toys out of common household objects. 60m; VHS. **Pr:** MPI Media Group. **A:** Family. **P:** Entertainment. **U:** Home. **Chl-Juv:** Family Viewing, Crafts, Inventors & Inventions. **Acq:** Purchase. **Dist:** MPI Media Group. $19.95.

The Amazing Transparent Man 1960 — **Bomb!**
A mad scientist makes a crook invisible in order to steal the radioactive materials he needs. The crook decides to rob banks instead. Shot at the Texas State Fair for that elusive futuristic look. For Ulmer fans only. 58m/B/W; VHS, DVD, Blu-Ray, Wide. **C:** Douglas Kennedy; Marguerite Chapman; James J. Griffith; Ivan Triesault; Boyd 'Red' Morgan; Carmel Daniel; Jonathan Ledford; Norman Smith; Patrick Cranshaw; Kevin Kelly; Directed by Edgar G. Ulmer; Written by Jack Lewis; Cinematography by Meredith Nicholson; Music by Darrell Calker. **Pr:** American International Pictures. **A:** Adult. **P:** Entertainment. **U:** Home. **Mov-Ent.** **Acq:** Purchase. **Dist:** Sinister Cinema. $16.95.

The Amazing Transplant 1970 (Unrated) — **Bomb!**
A sleaze-bag psycho has a "love enhancing" transplant, much to the pleasure of his sexual partners. Much to their and our dismay, however, he then kills them and bores us. 90m; VHS, DVD. **C:** Juan Fernandez; Linda Southern; Larry Hunter; Kim Pope; Directed by Doris Wishman; Written by Doris Wishman; Cinematography by C. Davis Smith. **A:** Adult. **P:** Entertainment. **U:** Home. **Mov-Ent:** Horror, Sex & Sexuality. **Acq:** Purchase. **Dist:** Tapeworm Video Distributors Inc. $24.95.

Amazing Underground Secrets 2012
Three episodes from Reader's Digest cover natural and manmade wonders, including cave painitngs, underground rivers, hiding places for treasure from the Saxons to the Nazis, and various tunnels, including one constructed beneath the Swiss Alps. 180m; DVD. **A:** Family. **P:** Entertainment. **U:** Home. **Gen-Edu:** Construction, Nature. **Acq:** Purchase. **Dist:** Acorn Media Group Inc.; Questar Inc. $29.99.

The Amazing Voyages of Nikki Piper: An Alligator Tale 1998
Combines live-action and puppets to present an engaging tale of alligators for children. Includes an activity guide. 32m; VHS. **A:** Preschool-Primary. **P:** Entertainment. **U:** Home. **Chl-Juv:** Children, Animals. **Acq:** Purchase. **Dist:** Tapeworm Video Distributors Inc. $14.95.

Amazing Wheat 2001
Presents a history of wheat, how it is grown, harvested, milled, and manufactured. Also explains the many unique wheat food products made around the world. For use with grades 3 to 5. 16m; VHS. **A:** Primary. **P:** Education. **U:** Institution. **Gen-Edu:** Agriculture, Food Industry, Gardening. **Acq:** Purchase. **Dist:** University of Idaho. $25.00.

The Amazing World Below 1988
All of the underground life of Blanchard Springs Caverns, Arkansas is featured, with some additional animated sequences of cavern formation. 20m; VHS. **A:** Family. **P:** Education. **U:** Institution, Home. **Gen-Edu:** Documentary Films, Geology. **Acq:** Purchase. **Dist:** Karol Media. $24.95.

Amazon 1968
A look at the size and the course of the mighty Amazon River. 52m; 3/4 U, Special order formats. **Pr:** National Geographic Society. **A:** Primary-Jr. High. **P:** Education. **U:** Institution, Home, SURA. **Gen-Edu:** Ecology & Environment. **Acq:** Purchase, Trade-in, Duplication License. **Dist:** National Geographic Society.

Amazon 1983
Documentary study of Australia's wildlife resources. 59m; VHS. **A:** Primary-Adult. **P:** Education. **U:** Institution. **Gen-Edu:** Documentary Films, Animals, Australia. **Acq:** Purchase. **Dist:** National Geographic Society. $50.

Amazon 1990 (R) — ★★
An adventure movie filmed in the Brazilian rainforest with an environmental message. A businessman being chased by the police in the Amazon jungle is rescued by a bush pilot who dreams of mining the Amazon's riches. A Brazilian woman enters the picture and persuades the businessman to help save the rainforest. Portions of the proceeds from the sale of this film go to the Rainforest Action Network. 88m; VHS, CC. **C:** Kari Vaananen; Robert Davi; Rae Dawn Chong; Directed by Mika Kaurismaki. **Pr:** Pentti Kouri Productions; Villealfa Filmproductions. **A:** Sr. High-Adult. **P:** Entertainment. **U:** Home. **Mov-Ent:** Action-Adventure, South America, Ecology & Environment. **Acq:** Purchase. **Dist:** Lions Gate Television Corp. $89.98.

The Amazon: A Vanishing Rainforest 1988
The destruction of the Amazon tropical rainforest is documented. Examines clear cutting of the forest to raise beef cattle, the planned construction of a hydroelectric dam, and the effects these and other man-made developments is having on the whole eco-system. 29m; VHS, 3/4 U. **TV Std:** NTSC, PAL, SECAM. **Pr:** Bradford Brooks. **A:** Jr. High-Adult. **P:** Education. **U:** Institution, SURA. **Gen-Edu:** Ecology & Environment, Forests & Trees, South America. **Acq:** Purchase, Rent/Lease, Duplication. **Dist:** The Cinema Guild.

Amazon Diary 19??
A young Amazonian boy discovers the threat facing his rain forest home. 16m; VHS. **A:** Primary. **P:** Education. **U:** Home. **Chl-Juv:** Forests & Trees, Ecology & Environment. **Acq:** Purchase. **Dist:** Direct Cinema Ltd. $24.95.

Amazon Dreams 1990
A tour of the Amazon rain forest, accompanied by New Age music. 30m; VHS. **Pr:** MNTEX Ent. **A:** Family. **P:** Entertainment. **U:** Home. **Mov-Ent:** Music Video, Forests & Trees, South America. **Acq:** Purchase. **Dist:** Karol Media; MNTEX Entertainment, Inc. $14.95.

Amazon Jail 1985 (Unrated) — ★
Scantily clad women go over the wall and promptly get caught by devil worshiping men in the jungle. They should have known better. Redeemed only by lingerie selection. 94m; VHS, DVD. **C:** Elisabeth Hartmann; Mauricio Do Valle; Sondra Graffi; Directed by Oswald De Oliveira. **A:** Adult. **P:** Entertainment. **U:** Home. **Mov-Ent.** **Acq:** Purchase. **Dist:** Movies Unlimited. $18.99.

Amazon Journal 1995
Provides a perspective on the explosive changes of this era starting with the assassination of Chico Mendes in 1988 and ending with a return trip to Yanomani Territory in 1995. 58m; VHS. **A:** College-Adult. **P:** Education. **U:** Institution. **Gen-Edu:** Politics & Government, Documentary Films, Violence. **Acq:** Purchase, Rent/Lease. **Dist:** Filmakers Library Inc. $395.00.

Amazon: Land of the Flooded Forest 199?
American scientist Michael Goulding shares his discoveries in this investigation of underwater ecosystems. 60m; VHS. **A:** Jr. High-Adult. **P:** Education. **U:** Institution. **Gen-Edu:** Ecology & Environment, Africa, Biology. **Acq:** Purchase. **Dist:** Sony Pictures Home Entertainment Inc. $19.98.

The Amazon: People and Resources of Northern Brazil 1968
Typical family scenes illustrate the ways people gain a living from the river and the jungle. 17m; VHS, 3/4 U. **Pr:** Encyclopedia Britannica Educational Corporation. **A:** Primary-Sr. High. **P:** Education. **U:** Institution, SURA. **L:** English, Spanish. **Gen-Edu:** Ecology & Environment. **Acq:** Purchase, Rent/Lease, Trade-in. **Dist:** Encyclopedia Britannica.

Amazon Rain Forest, Vol. 1 19??
Two volume set which offers a portrait of the Amazon rain forest, its rivers, wildlife and flora. 40m; VHS. **A:** Jr. High-Adult. **P:** Education. **U:** Institution. **Gen-Edu:** Forests & Trees, Africa. **Acq:** Purchase. **Dist:** Ark Media Group Ltd.

Amazon Sisters 1992
Focuses on the work of women inhabitants of Amazonia to save their environment and rebuild regions of the rainforest suffering from inappropriate development. Subtitled. 60m; VHS. **A:** Adult. **P:** Education. **U:** Institution, BCTV. **Gen-Edu:** Women, Ecology & Environment. **Acq:** Purchase, Rent/Lease. **Dist:** Women Make Movies. $275.00.

Amazon Warrior 1997 — ★★
Tara is a mercenary in a future world ruled by violence. The last survivor of her Amazon tribe, she sells her fighting skills to the highest bidder while searching for the leader of the rebel Marauder army, which massacred her people. Tara's well-equipped when that final showdown comes. 85m; VHS. **C:** J.J. Rodgers; Christine Lydon; Jimmy Jerman; Al Spencer; Raymond Storti; Directed by Dennis Devine; Written by Steve Jarvis; Music by David De Palo. **A:** Sr. High-Adult. **P:** Entertainment. **U:** Home. **Mov-Ent.** **Acq:** Purchase. **Dist:** Unknown Productions Inc.

Amazon Women on the Moon 1987 (R) — ★★
A plotless, irreverent media spoof, depicting the programming of a slipshod TV station as it crams weird commercials and shorts around a comical '50s science fiction film. Inconsistent, occasionally funny anthology hangs together very loosely. Produced by Landis, with the usual amount of in-joke cameos and allusions to his other works of art. 85m; VHS, DVD. **C:** Rosanna Arquette; Steve Guttenberg; Steve Allen; B.B. King; Michelle Pfeiffer; Arsenio Hall; Andrew Silverstein; Howard Hesseman; Lou Jacobi; Carrie Fisher; Griffin Dunne; Sybil Danning; Henny Youngman; Monique Gabrielle; Paul Bartel; Kelly Preston; Ralph Bellamy; Russ Meyer; Steve Forrest; Joey Travolta; Ed Begley, Jr.; Forrest J Ackerman; Archie Hahn; Phil Hartman; Peter Horton; Charlie Callas; T.K. Carter; Dick Miller; Roxie Roker; Directed by John Landis; Joe Dante; Carl Gottlieb; Robert Weiss; Peter Horton; Written by Michael Barrie; Jim Mulholland; Cinematography by Daniel Pearl; Music by Ira Newborn. **Pr:** Westward Productions. **A:** Sr. High-Adult. **P:** Entertainment. **U:** Home. **Mov-Ent:** Satire & Parody. **Acq:** Purchase. **Dist:** Movies Unlimited; Alpha Video. $14.98.

Amazonia 2001
An artful portrayal of the battle over breast cancer. Narrative about fighting the disease is complemented with images of Amazon warrior women and body geography. 8m; VHS. **A:** Adult. **P:** Education. **U:** Institution. **Gen-Edu:** Cancer, Women. **Acq:** Purchase, Rent/Lease. **Dist:** Women Make Movies. $195.00.

Amazonia: A Celebration of Life 1992
Profiles Amazonia. In equal size to the U.S. and harboring the mightiest river system in the world, Amazonia inhabitants equal more than one million species, including ocelot, tapir, scarlet macaw, and much more. Discusses the impact of deforestation. 23m; VHS. **A:** Primary-Sr. High. **P:** Education. **U:** Institution. **Gen-Edu:** Geography, Documentary Films, South America. **Acq:** Purchase. **Dist:** Landmark Media. $195.00.

Amazonia: The Road to the End of the Forest 19??
Provides a comprehensive survey of the global catastrophe escalating in the Amazon basin, focusing upon the burning of the tropical rainforest, which contributes to the greenhouse effect. 48m; VHS. **A:** Sr. High. **P:** Education. **U:** Institution. **Gen-Edu:** Natural Resources, South America, Ecology & Environment. **Acq:** Purchase. **Dist:** Filmakers Library Inc. $495.

Amazonia: The Road to the End of the Forest 1990
Overviews the current problems in the Amazon basin surrounding a failed massive resettlement program. 94m; VHS. **A:** Sr. High-Adult. **P:** Education. **U:** Institution. **Gen-Edu:** South America, Forests & Trees, Ecology & Environment. **Acq:** Purchase. **Dist:** University of Washington Educational Media Collection. $32.00.

Amazonia: Voices From the Rainforest 1991
Documents the lifestyles of the native people of the Amazon, how they depend on its resources, and their struggle for survival. 70m; VHS. **A:** Sr. High-Adult. **P:** Education. **U:** Institution, Home. **Gen-Edu:** Documentary Films, Natural Resources, South America. **Acq:** Purchase, Rent/Lease. **Dist:** The Video Project. $95.00.

The Amazons 1984 — ★½
Goofy drama about a beautiful doctor who discovers an underground organization of Amazon-descended women bent on taking over the world or at least making life hard for men while investigating a Congressman's mysterious death. 100m; VHS. **C:** Tamara Dobson; Jack Scalia; Stella Stevens; Madeleine Stowe; Jennifer Warren; Directed by Paul Michael Glaser; Music by Basil Poledouris. **Pr:** ABC Circle Films. **A:** Jr. High-Adult. **P:** Entertainment. **U:** Home. **Mov-Ent:** Action-Adventure, TV Movies. **Acq:** Purchase. **Dist:** No Longer Available.

Amazons 1986 (R) — ★
Tall, strong women who occasionally wander around nude search for a magical talisman that will overthrow an evil magician. 76m; VHS, DVD. **C:** Mindi Miller; Penelope Reed; Joseph Whipp; Willie Nelson; Danitza Kingsley; Directed by Alex Sessa. **Pr:** New Horizons Pictures. **A:** Sr. High. **P:** Entertainment. **U:** Home. **Mov-Ent:** Fantasy. **Acq:** Purchase. **Dist:** MGM Home Entertainment. $79.95.

Amazons and Gladiators 2001 (R) — ★★
The title just says it all, doesn't it? Beautiful slave girl joins up with an Amazon queen and her band of warriors to fight an evil Roman governor. 89m; VHS, DVD, Wide. **C:** Jennifer Rubin; Patrick Bergin; Nichole Hiltz; Wendi Winburn; Melanie Gutteridge; Richard Norton; Directed by Zachary Weintraub; Written by Zachary Weintraub; Cinematography by Thomas Hencz; Music by Timothy S. (Tim) Jones. **A:** Sr. High-Adult. **P:** Entertainment. **U:** Home. **Mov-Ent.** **Acq:** Purchase. **Dist:** Movies Unlimited; Alpha Video.

The Ambassador 1984 (Unrated) — ★★½
An American ambassador (Mitchum) is sent to the Middle East to try to solve the area's deep political problems. He quickly becomes the target of terrorist attacks, and is blamed for the nation's unrest. To make matters worse, his wife is having an affair with a PLO leader. The President ignores him, forcing the ambassador to fend for himself. Talk about your bad days. Hudson's last feature. Based on Elmore Leonard's "52 Pickup," and remade a year later under its own title. 97m; VHS, DVD. **C:** Robert Mitchum; Ellen Burstyn; Rock Hudson; Fabio Testi; Donald Pleasence; Directed by J. Lee Thompson. **Pr:** Cannon Productions. **A:** Sr. High-Adult. **P:** Entertainment. **U:** Home. **Mov-Ent:** Mystery & Suspense, Middle East. **Acq:** Purchase. **Dist:** MGM Home Entertainment. $79.95.

The Ambassador 2005 (Unrated)
Offers the complete 1998-1999 British television political drama series on the life of Harriet Smith (Collins), who takes on the daunting task of becoming Britain's newest ambassador to Ireland and must confront a variety of issues including corruption, criminal activities, and scandals along with handling personal family dilemmas. Includes: the Ambassador places the safety of an abusive Saudi diplomat's wife over a potential windfall aircraft contract for her country, on the brink of civil war she requests assistance from MI6 agent John Stone (Lawson), and she falls in love but he gets kidnapped. 12 episodes. 300m; DVD. **C:** Pauline Collins; Denis Lawson. **A:** Sr. High-Adult. **P:** Entertainment. **U:** Home. **Mov-Ent**: Television Series, Drama, Politics & Government. **Acq:** Purchase. **Dist:** BFS Video. $49.98.

Ambassador Bill 1931 — ★★
An Oklahoma rancher is appointed ambassador to a country in revolt. Rogers, of course, saves the day with his rustic witticisms. Based on the story "Ambassador from the United States" by Vincent Sheean. 68m/B/W; VHS, DVD. **C:** Will Rogers; Marguerite Churchill; Greta Nissen; Ray Milland; Tad Alexander; Gustav von Seyffertitz; Directed by Sam Taylor. **Pr:** 20th Century-Fox. **A:** Family. **P:** Entertainment. **U:** Home. **Mov-Ent**: Comedy--Screwball, International Relations. **Acq:** Purchase. **Dist:** Fox Home Entertainment. $19.98.

Ambassador: Inside the Embassy 2002 (Unrated)
In most countries around the world, there is one small patch of land that is actually American soil, as the U.S. has established diplomatic embassies almost everywhere. This National Geographic documentary offers a behind-the-scenes look at how the embassies work and what the daily lives of diplomats are like. In addition, the film examines how the role of diplomat has changed since the terrorist attacks on the United States on September 11, 2011. 60m; DVD. **A:** Family. **P:** Education, Entertainment. **U:** Home, Institution. **Mov-Ent**: Documentary Films, International Relations, Intelligence Service. **Acq:** Purchase. **Dist:** $24.95.

The Ambassador's Boots 1985
In this chapter of the "Partners in Crime" made-for-television series, the Beresfords aid the American Ambassador to England in answering some curious queries regarding the handling of his luggage. 60m; VHS. **C:** James Warwick; Francesca Annis; Directed by Peter Duffell; Written by Agatha Christie. **A:** Family. **P:** Entertainment. **U:** Home. **Mov-Ent**: Mystery & Suspense, Television. **Acq:** Purchase. **Dist:** Tapeworm Video Distributors Inc. $14.95.

The Ambassador's Daughter 1956 — ★★
The Parisian adventures of an American ambassador's daughter De Havilland and soldier Forsythe, who, unaware of her position, falls in love with her. Faltering comedy is supported by an expert cast (although nearly 40, De Havilland is charming as the young woman) with especially good performances from Menjou and Loy. 102m; VHS, DVD. **C:** Olivia de Havilland; John Forsythe; Myrna Loy; Adolphe Menjou; Edward Arnold; Francis Lederer; Tommy Noonan; Minor Watson; Directed by Norman Krasna; Written by Norman Krasna. **Pr:** MGM Home Entertainment. **A:** Adult. **P:** Entertainment. **U:** Home. **Mov-Ent**: Comedy--Romantic, France. **Acq:** Purchase. **Dist:** Education 2000, Inc.

Amber Waves 1982 (Unrated) — ★★½
Credible drama about a generation-gap conflict between a Midwestern farmer (Weaver) and an irresponsible male model (Russell) who has coasted through life on con and charm. 98m; VHS. **C:** Dennis Weaver; Kurt Russell; Rossie (Ross) Harris; Mare Winningham; Wilford Brimley; Directed by Joseph Sargent. **A:** Preschool. **P:** Entertainment. **U:** Institution, SURA. **Mov-Ent**: TV Movies. **Acq:** Purchase, Rent/Lease. **Dist:** Time-Life Video and Television.

Amberjack: The Backbreaker 19??
Learn to locate, lure, and land this ruthless gamefish that deserves its reputation as one of the toughest challlenges for the saltwater sportfisher. 40m; VHS. **A:** Adult. **P:** Instruction. **U:** Home. **Spo-Rec**: Fishing. **Acq:** Purchase. **Dist:** Bennett Marine Video. $29.95.

Ambition 1991 (R) — ★½
Scriptwriter/star Phillips gets a bone for chutzpah by taking an unsavory lead role; his character torments a paroled psycho so that the killer will kill again and inspire a true-crime bestseller. The plot looks good on paper, but onscreen it's padded and unconvincing. 99m; VHS, CC. **C:** Lou Diamond Phillips; Clancy Brown; Cecilia Peck; Richard Bradford; Willard Pugh; Grace Zabriskie; Katherine Armstrong; John David (J.D.) Cullum; Haing S. Ngor; Directed by Scott Goldstein; Written by Lou Diamond Phillips; Music by Leonard Rosenman. **Pr:** Gwen Field; Richard E. Johnson; Spirit Productions; Diamond Unicorn Productions. **A:** College-Adult. **P:** Entertainment. **U:** Home. **Mov-Ent**: Mystery & Suspense. **Acq:** Purchase. **Dist:** Anchor Bay Entertainment. $92.98.

Amblyopia 19??
Part of the three-part Pediatric Ophthalmology Series on childhood eye problems. Uses clear graphics to discuss amblyopia, or lazy eye, usually caused by strabismus, muscle imbalance, corneal scarring, or cataracts. Also offers various methods of treatment, including patching, medication, and eye glasses. 7m; VHS. **A:** College-Adult. **P:** Education. **U:** Institution. **Hea-Sci**: Medical Education, Pediatrics, Eye. **Acq:** Purchase, Rent/Lease. **Dist:** AJN Video Library/Lippincott Williams & Wilkins. $100.00.

Amblyopia 1983
The causes, diagnostic procedures, and courses of treatment for amblyopia are outlined in this program. 15m; VHS, 3/4 U. **Pr:** Milner-Fenwick. **A:** College-Adult. **P:** Education. **U:** Institution, CCTV. **L:** English, Spanish. **Hea-Sci**: Eye. **Acq:** Purchase. **Dist:** Milner-Fenwick, Inc.

Ambrose Bierce's The Man and the Snake and the Return 1996
Features a film adaptation of classic literature. 65m; VHS. **A:** Family. **P:** Entertainment. **U:** Home. **Mov-Ent**: Literature. **Acq:** Purchase. **Dist:** Monterey Home Video. $24.95.

Ambulance 196?
A non-dialogue drama about the Holocaust, in which innocent school children are carted to the gas chambers by way of an ambulance, usually seen as a symbol of goodness. 10m/B/W; VHS. **Pr:** Alden Films. **A:** Primary-Jr. High. **P:** Education. **U:** Institution. **Chl-Juv**: World War Two, Children. **Acq:** Purchase, Rent/Lease. **Dist:** Alden Films.

The Ambulance 1990 (R) — ★★½
A New York cartoonist witnesses a mysterious ambulance at work and decides to investigate. His probings uncover a plot to sell the bodies of dying diabetics. A surprisingly good no-money feature from low-budget king Cohen. Includes an appearance by Marvel Comics' Stan Lee as himself. 95m; VHS, DVD, CC. **C:** Eric Roberts; James Earl Jones; Megan Gallagher; Richard Bright; Janine Turner; Eric Braeden; Red Buttons; Laurene Landon; Jill Gatsby; Nick (Nicholas) Chinlund; James Dixon; Stan Lee; Directed by Larry Cohen; Written by Larry Cohen; Cinematography by Jacques Haitkin; Music by Jay Chattaway. **Pr:** Robert Katz. **A:** Sr. High-Adult. **P:** Entertainment. **U:** Home. **Mov-Ent**: Horror, Anatomy & Physiology. **Acq:** Purchase. **Dist:** Epic Records; MGM Home Entertainment. $19.95.

Ambulation with Assistance 19??
Part of the Restorative Care Series. Demonstrates various techniques for ambulation of patients. Stresses the importance of positioning and safety. 27m; VHS. **A:** Adult. **P:** Education. **U:** Institution. **Hea-Sci**: Aging, Medical Care, Patient Care. **Acq:** Purchase, Rent/Lease. **Dist:** University of Maryland. $200.00.

Ambush 1950 (Unrated) — ★★
Director Sam Wood's last film is a tough, lean western. Civilian scout Ward Kinsman is asked by Major Breverty to find Mary Carlyle, who was taken in an Apache raid. Ward refuses until Mary's beautiful sister Ann pleads and then insists on coming along. Ward learns where Mary is being held and reports her whereabouts to Capt. Lorrison who prepares to attack. First he and Ward have to settle their jealousy issues since both have fallen for Ann. 89m/B/W; DVD. **C:** Robert Taylor; Arlene Dahl; John Hodiak; Leon Ames; Charles Stevens; Don Taylor; Jean Hagen; Bruce Cowling; Chief Thundercloud; John McIntire; Marta Mitrovich; Directed by Sam Wood; Written by Marguerite Roberts; Cinematography by Harold Lipstein; Music by Rudolph Kopp. **A:** Sr. High-Adult. **P:** Entertainment. **U:** Home. **Mov-Ent**: Native Americans. **Acq:** Purchase. **Dist:** WarnerArchive.com.

Ambush 1999 (Unrated) — ★★★
Young lieutenant Eero is serving in the Finnish Army in 1941 pursuing Russian troops along the border. During his mission, Eero is able to briefly spend some time with his lovely fiancee Irina but must soon leave to go on a recon. He receives word that Irina has been killed by Russian soldiers and seeks revenge on any Russians he finds—turning from innocent soldier to dehumanized killer. Co-writer Tuuri adapted from his novel. Finnish with subtitles. 117m; VHS, DVD, Wide. **C:** Peter Franzen; Irina Bjorklund; Kari Vaananen; Kari Heiskanen; Taisto Reimalvoto; Directed by Olli Saarela; Written by Olli Saarela; Antti Tuuri; Cinematography by Kjell Lagerros; Music by Tuomas Kantelinen. **A:** College-Adult. **P:** Entertainment. **U:** Home. **L:** Finnish. **Mov-Ent**: World War Two, Scandinavia. **Acq:** Purchase. **Dist:** Vanguard International Cinema, Inc.

Ambush at Masai Mara 1982
This program looks at the characteristics of the African lion during the annual wildebeest migration. 25m; VHS, 3/4 U. **Pr:** British Broadcasting Corporation. **A:** Jr. High-Adult. **P:** Education. **U:** Institution, SURA. **Hea-Sci**: Wildlife. **Acq:** Purchase. **Dist:** Home Vision Cinema.

Ambush at Tomahawk Gap 1953 (Unrated) — ★★
Three released prisoners go in search of hidden loot and tempers rise when the goods don't turn up. Then the Apaches show up. 73m; DVD. **C:** John Hodiak; John Derek; David Brian; Maria Elena Marques; Ray Teal; Directed by Fred F. Sears. **Pr:** Columbia Pictures. **A:** Jr. High-Adult. **P:** Entertainment. **U:** Home. **Mov-Ent**: Western. **Acq:** Purchase. **Dist:** Alpha Video.

The Ambush Murders 1982 — ★★½
True story of a stalwart white attorney defending a black activist accused of killing two cops. Not the compelling TV drama it could be, but still enjoyable. From Ben Bradlee Jr.'s novel. 100m; VHS, Streaming. **C:** James Brolin; Dorian Harewood; Alfre Woodard; Louis Giambalvo; John McLiam; Teddy Wilson; Antonio Fargas; Amy Madigan; Directed by Steven Hilliard Stern. **Pr:** Charles Fries Productions. **A:** Jr. High-Adult. **P:** Entertainment. **U:** Home. **Mov-Ent**: TV Movies. **Acq:** Purchase. **Dist:** Lions Gate Television Corp. $49.95.

Ambush Trail 1946 — ★★
Stranger-in-town Steele metes out justice to help local ranchers while sidekick Saylor leaves 'em laughing. 60m/B/W; VHS, DVD. **C:** Bob Steele; Syd Saylor; I. Stanford Jolley; Lorraine Miller; Charles "Blackie" King; Kermit Maynard; Directed by Harry Fraser. **Pr:** Producers Releasing Corporation. **A:** Jr. High-Adult. **P:** Entertainment. **U:** Home. **Mov-Ent**: Western. **Acq:** Purchase. **Dist:** Alpha Video. $19.95.

Ambush Valley 1936
Cattleman kill a homesteader and his mother vows to avenge her son's death. 58m/B/W; VHS. **C:** Bob Custer; Victoria Vinton; Eddie (Edward) Phillips; Wally Wales; Directed by Franklin Shamray. **A:** Family. **P:** Entertainment. **U:** Home. **Mov-Ent**: Western. **Acq:** Purchase. **Dist:** Grapevine Video. $11.95.

amBushed 19??
Depicts a brutal act by police against a young teeange boy as a mother and child look on and illustrates the problems associated with inner city life for black youths today. 12m/B/W; VHS, 3/4 U, Special order formats. **A:** College-Adult. **P:** Education. **U:** Institution. **Gen-Edu**: Violence, Black Culture. **Acq:** Purchase, Rent/Lease. **Dist:** Third World Newsreel. $125.00.

Ambushed 2013 (R) — ★½
A couple of low-level L.A. coke dealers get in big trouble with their mobster boss and their antics bring in the DEA, including an undercover agent, as well as a crooked LAPD officer. The big action names (Lundgren, Jones, Couture) actually have supporting roles and leads Capaldi and Bonjour aren't nearly as interesting amidst the clichés. 96m; DVD, Blu-Ray. **C:** Gianni Capaldi; Daniel Bonjour; Dolph Lundgren; Vinnie Jones; Randy Couture; Carly Pope; Cinthya Carmona; Directed by Giorgio Serafini; Written by Augustin; Cinematography by Marco Cappetta. **A:** Sr. High-Adult. **P:** Entertainment. **U:** Home. **L:** English. **Mov-Ent**: Crime Drama, Drug Enforcement Agency (DEA), Drug Trafficking/Dealing. **Acq:** Purchase. **Dist:** Anchor Bay Entertainment Inc.

The Ambushers 1967 — **Bomb!**
Martin's third Matt Helm farce finds him handling a puzzling case involving the first United States spacecraft. When the craft is hijacked with Rule on board, it's Matt to the rescue, regaining control before unfriendly forces can take it back to Earth. Tired formula seems to have worn Martin out while the remainder of the cast goes to camp. Followed by "The Wrecking Crew." 102m; VHS, DVD. **C:** Dean Martin; Janice Rule; James Gregory; Albert Salmi; Senta Berger; Kurt Kasznar; Beverly Adams; Directed by Henry Levin; Written by Herbert Baker; Cinematography by Burnett Guffey; Edward Colman; Music by Hugo Montenegro. **Pr:** Irving Allen. **A:** Jr. High-Adult. **P:** Entertainment. **U:** Home. **Mov-Ent**: Action-Adventure. **Acq:** Purchase. **Dist:** Sony Pictures Home Entertainment Inc. $14.95.

Amelia 2009 (PG) — ★★½
Good-looking, if old-fashioned, biography of famed celebrity aviatrix Amelia Earhart based on Susan Butler's "East to the Dawn" and Elgin Long's "Amelia Earhart: The Mystery Solved." Director Nair highlights the wonder (and danger) of flying in the 1920s and 30s through Swank's sparkling lead performance and how the adventuresome Amelia dealt with worldwide fame as well as her unconventional marriage to New York publisher George Putnam (Gere). 111m; DVD, Blu-Ray, On Demand. **C:** Hilary Swank; Richard Gere; Ewan McGregor; Christopher Eccleston; Mia Wasikowska; Directed by Mira Nair; Written by Ronald Bass; Anna Hamilton Phelan; Cinematography by Stuart Dryburgh; Music by Gabriel Yared. **Pr:** Ted Waitt; Lydia Dean Pilcher; Kevin Hyman; AE Electra Productions; Avalon Pictures; Fox Searchlight. **A:** Jr. High-Adult. **P:** Entertainment. **U:** Home. **L:** English. **Mov-Ent**: Biography, Aeronautics, Marriage. **Acq:** Purchase. **Dist:** Fox Home Entertainment; Amazon.com Inc.; Movies Unlimited.

Amelia Earhart 1994
Kathy Bates narrates documentary on the great aviator, focusing on her career rather than her mysterious death. 60m; VHS. **A:** Sr. High-Adult. **P:** Education. **U:** Institution. **Gen-Edu**: Aeronautics. **Acq:** Purchase. **Dist:** PBS Home Video. $69.95.

Amelia Earhart: The Final Flight 1994 — ★★½
Investigates the mysterious disappearance of pioneering aviatrix Amelia Earhart's 1937 flight to become the first pilot to circumnavigate the globe. Earhart (Keaton) and her navigator Fred Noonan (Hauer) disappeared over the Pacific Ocean and their fate has never been determined. Dern plays Earhart's husband, publisher George B. Putnam, who served as Amelia's manager and publicist. Based on the biography by Doris L. Rich. 95m; DVD. **C:** Diane Keaton; Rutger Hauer; Bruce Dern; Paul Guilfoyle; Denis Arndt; David Carpenter; Diana Bellamy; Directed by Yves Simoneau; Written by Anna Sandor; Cinematography by Lauro Escorel; Music by George S. Clinton. **Pr:** Turner Network Television. **A:** Jr. High-Adult. **P:** Entertainment. **U:** Home. **Mov-Ent**: TV Movies, Aeronautics, Women. **Acq:** Purchase. **Dist:** WarnerArchive.com.

Amelia Fry on Oral History 1979
Amelia Fry, veteran participant in the University of California at Berkeley Oral History Project, discusses the problems and prospects of the flourishing field of oral history. 30m; 3/4 U. **C:** Hosted by Dr. Helen Hawkins. **Pr:** Dr. Helen Hawkins; KPBS Humanities Office. **A:** Sr. High-Adult. **P:** Education. **U:** Institution, CCTV. **Gen-Edu**: History--U.S. **Acq:** Purchase. **Dist:** KPBS-TV.

Amelie 2001 (R) — ★★★½
Paris waitress Amelie (Tautou) has led a solitary, but not wholly unpleasant, existence. When she finds a box of childhood treasures behind a wall in her apartment, she sets out to return them to their original owner. Accomplishing this, she begins to secretly intervene in the lives of neighbors and coworkers, helping some find romance, others retribution for past wrongs. When her "missions" bring her into contact with a quirky local (Kassovitz), she begins a roundabout courtship involving a treasure hunt instead of approaching him directly. Director Jeunet leaves intact his stunning, and very stylized visual talents, but marshals them in service of a fresh, lighthearted comedy, in contrast to his previous, downcast work. Tautout has no problem carrying the movie and has the look of a budding major star. 120m; VHS, DVD, Blu-Ray. **C:** Audrey Tautou; Mathieu Kassovitz; Rufus; Yolande Moreau; Dominique Pinon; Maurice Benichou; Artus de Penguern; Urbain Cancellier; Isabelle Nanty; Claire Maurier; Claude Perron; Clothilde Mollet;

Serge Merlin; Jamel Debbouze; Flora Guiet; Narrated by Andre Dussollier; Directed by Jean-Pierre Jeunet; Written by Jean-Pierre Jeunet; Guillaume Laurant; Cinematography by Bruno Delbonnel; Music by Yann Tiersen. **Pr:** Claudie Ossard; France 3 Cinema; MMC Independent; Victoires Productions; Tapioca Films; Miramax Film Corp. **A:** Sr. High-Adult. **P:** Entertainment. **U:** Home. **L:** French. **Mov-Ent**: Romance, Photography, Philanthropy. **Awds:** British Acad. '01: Orig. Screenplay; Cesar '01: Art Dir./Set Dec., Director (Jeunet), Film, Score; Broadcast Film Critics '01: Foreign Film. **Acq:** Purchase. **Dist:** Buena Vista Home Entertainment.

Amen 2002 (R) — ★★★
Costa-Gavras dramatizes a Holocaust story with a somewhat heavy hand. SS. Lt. Kurt Gerstein (Tukur) is a chemist who uses prussic acid Zyklon B for fumigating camp barracks. Sent to a Polish concentration camp, he witnesses the deaths of Jewish prisoners by the gas. Appalled, Gerstein rishes reprisals by informing various church leaders, although no one is willing to speak out until he reaches the young Italian priest, Father Riccardo Fontana (Kassovitz), who has family ties to Pope Pius XII (Iures). As head of the the Hygiene Institute, the SS expects Gerstein to continue to eliminate vermin of all kinds while Father Fontana heads to the Vatican in the hopes of getting the Pope to expose the genocide. An adaptation of Rolf Hochhuth's 1963 play, "The Deputy." 130m; DVD, Blu-Ray. **C:** Ulrich Tukur; Mathieu Kassovitz; Marcel Iures; Ulrich Muhe; Michel Duchaussoy; Ion Caramitru; Directed by Constantin Costa-Gavras; Written by Constantin Costa-Gavras; Jean-Claude Grumberg; Cinematography by Patrick Blossier; Music by Armand Amar. **Pr:** Claude Berri; Renn Productions; TF-1 Films; KC Medien; Canal Plus; Kino International Corporation. **A:** College-Adult. **P:** Entertainment. **U:** Home. **Mov-Ent**: Holocaust. **Acq:** Purchase. **Dist:** Kino on Video.

Amenaza Nuclear 19?? (Unrated) — ★
A Mexican farce about two idiots who try to stop mysterious Chinamen from stealing nuclear arms. 106m; VHS. **C:** Emeterio Y. Felipes; Lydia Zamora; Ki Jeong Lee. **A:** Jr. High-Adult. **P:** Entertainment. **U:** Home. **L:** Spanish. **Mov-Ent**: Action-Adventure. **Acq:** Purchase. **Dist:** Spanishmultimedia. $59.95.

The Amendments to the Constitution 1998
Seven-part program provides a detailed analysis of each Amendment using live action, historical artwork, archival footage, and expert commentary. 47m; VHS. **A:** Jr. High-Sr. High. **P:** Education. **U:** Institution. **Gen-Edu**: Politics & Government, U.S. States. **Acq:** Purchase. **Dist:** Zenger Media. $250.00.
Indiv. Titles: 1. Amendment 1 2. Amendment 2 3. Amendment 3 4. Amendment 4 5. Amendment 5-8 6. Amendment 9 7. Amendment 10.

America 1924 — ★★½
Young patriot Nathan Holden (Hamilton) is torn between his political beliefs and his love for the daughter of a Virignia Tory (Dempster). Meanwhile, evil redcoat Captain Butler (Barrymore) and his band of murderous Mohawks ruthlessly attack the colonists. 141m/B/W; Silent; VHS, DVD. **C:** Neil Hamilton; Carol Dempster; Lionel Barrymore; Erville Alderson; Charles Bennett; Arthur Donaldson; Charles Emmet Mack; Frank McGlynn; Henry O'Neill; Ed Roseman; Harry Semels; Louis Wolheim; Hugh Baird; Lee Beggs; Downing Clarke; Sydney Deane; Arthur Dewey; Michael Donavan; Paul Doucet; John Dunton; Riley Hatch; Emil Hoch; Edwin Holland; W.W. Jones; William S. Rising; Frank Walsh; Directed by D.W. Griffith; Written by Robert W. Chambers; Cinematography by Marcel Le Picard; Hendrik Sartov; Billy (G.W.) Bitzer. **A:** College-Adult. **P:** Entertainment. **U:** Home. **Mov-Ent**: Action-Adventure, Romance, Revolutionary War. **Acq:** Purchase. **Dist:** Kino on Video.

America 1969 (Unrated)
Interviews with Vietnam vets, teenagers, and African American militants provides new insight to the anti-war movement as the Vietnam War escalated. 30m/B/W; VHS, DVD. **A:** Adult. **P:** Education. **U:** Institution. **Gen-Edu**: Vietnam War, History. **Acq:** Purchase. **Dist:** Third World Newsreel. $175.

America 1973
Cooke digs up America's roots, finding reason and order in the tangled trails of our past. 52m; VHS, 3/4 U, Special order formats. **C:** Narrated by Alistair Cooke. **Pr:** British Broadcasting Corporation; Time-Life Films. **A:** Sr. High-College. **P:** Education. **U:** Institution, Home, SURA. **Gen-Edu**: History--U.S. **Acq:** Purchase, Rent/Lease. **Dist:** Time-Life Video and Television.
Indiv. Titles: 1. The New-Found Land 2. Home From Home 3. Making A Revolution 4. Inventing A Nation 5. Gone West 6. A Firebell in the Night 7. Domesticating a Wilderness 8. Money on the Land 9. The Huddled Masses 10. The Promise Fulfilled and the Promise Broken 11. The Arsenal 12. The First Impact 13. The More Abundant Life.

America 1986 (R) — ★½
New York cable station receives worldwide fame when their signal bounces off of the moon. Uninspired piece of fluff from otherwise talented director Downey. 83m; VHS. **C:** Zack Norman; Tammy Grimes; Michael J. Pollard; Monroe Arnold; Richard Belzer; Liz Torres; Howard Thomashefsky; Laura Ashton; Robert Downey, Jr.; Directed by Robert Downey. **A:** Adult. **P:** Entertainment. **U:** Home. **Mov-Ent**: Comedy--Screwball, Mass Media. **Acq:** Purchase. **Dist:** No Longer Available.

America 2009 (Unrated) — ★★½
Outstanding performance by newcomer Philip Johnson in the title role highlights this message movie that's based on the novel by E.R. Frank. Therapist Dr. Marie Brennan (O'Donnell) tries to help sullen 17-year-old America (Johnson), who's caught up in the overburdened foster care system. Flashbacks detail some of the abuse he's suffered while in the present America struggles to adjust to a group home. 90m; DVD. **C:** Rosie O'Donnell; Phil Johnson; Raquel Castro; Timothy Edward Rhoze; Jade Yorker; Ruby Dee; Directed by Yves Simoneau; Written by Joyce Eliason; Cinematography by John Aronson; Music by Normand Corbeil. **A:** Jr. High-Adult. **P:** Entertainment. **U:** Home. **Mov-Ent**: Adolescence, Child Abuse, Psychiatry. **Acq:** Purchase. **Dist:** Sony Pictures Home Entertainment Inc.

America: A Tribute to Heroes 2001 (Unrated)
Presents a rock and pop music telethon by a variety of actors and musicians held ten days after the September 11, 2001, terrorist attacks with the proceeds for victims. Included performances by Bruce Springsteen, Neil Young, Tom Petty, Stevie Wonder, Faith Hill, Billy Joel, Paul Simon, Willie Nelson, and the Dixie Chicks. 1 episode. 120m; DVD. **A:** Family. **P:** Entertainment. **U:** Home. **Mov-Ent**: Television Series, Music--Performance. **Acq:** Purchase. **Dist:** Genius.com Incorporated. $19.97.

America After Vietnam 1979
The veteran broadcast journalist examines the continuing impact of the crisis in Vietnam on American society. Political, economic, cultural, and personal changes resulting from Vietnam are explored. 29m; VHS, 3/4 U. **C:** Hosted by Daniel Schorr. **Pr:** KTCA St. Paul/Minneapolis. **A:** College-Adult. **P:** Education. **U:** Institution, CCTV, CATV. **Gen-Edu**: Vietnam War. **Acq:** Purchase, Rent/Lease, Off-Air Record. **Dist:** PBS Home Video.
Indiv. Titles: 1. America and Its Political Institutions 2. America's Face to the World 3. American Talks to Herself 4. America's Disrupted Lives.

America America 1963 (Unrated) — ★★½
Over-long and slow-moving, but very personal, immigrant drama that Kazan adapted from his own book and based on his uncle's life. In 1896, young Stavros is sent by his family from Anatolia, Turkey--where the Greeks are an oppressed minority--to Constantinople. After various tribulations, Stavros decides to realize his own dream and emigrate to America but his idealism soon gives way to a frequently harsh reality. 177m/B/W; DVD. **C:** Stathis Giallelis; Harry Davis; Elena Karam; Frank Wolff; Estelle Hemsley; Lou Antonio; John Marley; Directed by Elia Kazan; Written by Elia Kazan; Cinematography by Haskell Wexler; Music by Manos Hadjidakis. **A:** Jr. High-Adult. **P:** Entertainment. **U:** Home. **Mov-Ent**: Immigration. **Awds:** Oscars '63: Art Dir./Set Dec., B&W. **Acq:** Purchase. **Dist:** Fox Home Entertainment.

America and Its Political Institutions 1979
A discussion of the political changes resulting from United States involvement in the Vietnam War. 29m; VHS, 3/4 U. **Pr:** KTCA St. Paul/Minneapolis. **A:** Jr. High-Adult. **P:** Education. **U:** Institution, CCTV, CATV. **Gen-Edu**: Politics & Government, Vietnam War, Comedy--Black. **Acq:** Purchase, Rent/Lease, Off-Air Record. **Dist:** PBS Home Video.

America and Lewis Hine 1984
The life and work of social photographer Lewis Hines (1874-1940), who pioneered this new medium in the United States, is documented in this absorbing video. His photographs captured the human side of the industrial revolution and featured the recently arrived immigrants who worked in the country's factories, mills, mines, and sweatshops. 56m; VHS, 3/4 U. **TV Std:** NTSC, PAL, SECAM. **C:** Narrated by Jason Robards, Jr; Maureen Stapleton. **Pr:** Nina Rosenblum. **A:** Jr. High-Adult. **P:** Education. **U:** Institution, SURA. **Fin-Art**: History--U.S., Photography. **Acq:** Purchase, Rent/Lease. **Dist:** The Cinema Guild; New Video Group.

America and the Holocaust: Deceit and Indifference 1994
Uses archival photos, documents, and interviews to look at anti-Semitism in America from the turn of the century to the tragedy in the 1940s when the U.S. government delayed action, suppressed information, and blocked large-scale efforts to rescue Jews from Hitler. 90m; VHS. **C:** Narrated by Hal Linden. **A:** Sr. High-Adult. **P:** Education. **U:** Home. **Gen-Edu**: Documentary Films, Holocaust, History--U.S. **Acq:** Purchase. **Dist:** Shanachie Entertainment. $19.95.

America at the Movies 1976 — ★★½
Scenes from more than 80 of the finest American motion pictures fly by in an effort to tell the story of the cinema and provide a portrait of America as it has been seen on screen for half a century. Clips from "The Birth of a Nation," "Citizen Kane," "Dr. Strangelove," "East of Eden," "The French Connection," and "From Here to Eternity" are among the many included. Some black-and-white scenes; produced by the American Film Institute. 116m; VHS. **C:** John Wayne; Orson Welles; Peter Sellers; James Dean; Gene Hackman; Burt Lancaster; Julie Harris; Deborah Kerr; Al Pacino; Robert De Niro; Narrated by Charlton Heston; Music by Nelson Riddle. **Pr:** George Stevens; American Film Institute. **A:** Family. **P:** Entertainment. **U:** Home. **Mov-Ent**: Film History. **Acq:** Purchase. **Dist:** Sony Pictures Home Entertainment Inc.; Image Entertainment Inc. $59.95.

America at War: 1941-1945 1983
This program highlights all the events of World War Two from Pearl Harbor to V-J Day. 16m/B/W; VHS, 3/4 U. **Pr:** WGBH Boston. **A:** Jr. High-Adult. **P:** Education. **U:** Institution, SURA. **Gen-Edu**: World War Two, History--U.S. **Acq:** Purchase, Rent/Lease. **Dist:** Hearst Entertainment/King Features.

America at War: The Home Front ????
Examines the major war movement in America during the 1940s and 1950s using wartime newsreels, propaganda documentaries, movies, music and humor. 300m; VHS. **A:** Adult. **P:** Education. **U:** Home. **Gen-Edu**: War--General, U.S. States, History--U.S. **Acq:** Purchase. **Dist:** Janson Media. $39.95.
Indiv. Titles: 1. While the Storm Clouds Gather 2. Praise the Lord and Pass the Ammunition 3. Sacrifice and Shortages 4. A String of Pearls 5. On the Shady Side of the Street 6. Right in der Fuehrer's Face 7. Thanks for the Memories 8. Accentuating the Positive 9. Mood Indigo: Blacks and Whites 10. It's Been A Long, Long Time.

America at War: The Revolutionary and Civil Wars 1988
The main events of these two wars are recounted in this tape. 40m; VHS, 3/4 U. **Pr:** SVE. **A:** Jr. High-Adult. **P:** Education. **U:** Institution, CCTV, Home. **Gen-Edu**: Revolutionary War, Civil War, History--U.S. **Acq:** Purchase, Duplication. **Dist:** Clear Vue Inc. $99.00.

America at War: World Wars I and II 1988
This is a video overview of America's involvement in the two major wars of the 20th century. 40m; VHS, 3/4 U. **Pr:** SVE. **A:** Jr. High-Adult. **P:** Education. **U:** Institution, CCTV, Home. **Gen-Edu**: World War One, World War Two, History--U.S. **Acq:** Purchase, Duplication. **Dist:** Clear Vue Inc. $99.00.

America Becoming 1991
A look at the history of the Immigration and Nationality Act from 1965 to the present, focusing on the lives of ordinary people—both newcomers and long-time residents. 90m; VHS, CC, 3/4 U. **A:** Jr. High-Adult. **P:** Education. **U:** Institution, CCTV, CATV. **Gen-Edu**: History--U.S., Immigration, Sociology. **Acq:** Purchase, Duplication License, Off-Air Record. **Dist:** PBS Home Video. $79.95.

America Before Columbus 2009 (Unrated)
A journey into American history that seeks to disprove the current notion of Columbus discovering a mostly uninhabited, undeveloped country. 90m; DVD. **A:** Family. **P:** Education. **U:** Institution, Home. **Gen-Edu**: Documentary Films, History--U.S. **Acq:** Purchase. **Dist:** National Geographic Society. $24.95.

America Betrayed 2008
This exposé shows the depth of corruption, misappropriation, and waste among federal government agencies, such as the Army Corps of Engineers, which has negatively impacted the infrastructure of the United States. 94m; DVD. **A:** Sr. High-Adult. **P:** Entertainment. **U:** Home. **Mov-Ent**: Politics & Government, Documentary Films. **Acq:** Purchase. **Dist:** First Run Features. $24.95.

America Between the Great Wars 1978
Covers celebrations and tragedies from the Roaring '20s. Includes the Century of Progress Exposition in Chicago, the Prohibition era, the Hindenburg disaster, and the off-screen activities of Charlie Chaplin. 60m/B/W; VHS. **Pr:** Blackhawk Films. **A:** Family. **P:** Entertainment. **U:** Home. **Gen-Edu**: Documentary Films, History--U.S. **Acq:** Purchase. **Dist:** Critics' Choice Video & DVD. $29.98.

America by Air 19??
Three-volume set offers aerial footage of America's natural beauty. 145m; VHS. **A:** Jr. High-Adult. **P:** Education. **U:** Institution. **Gen-Edu**: U.S. States. **Acq:** Purchase. **Dist:** Ark Media Group Ltd.

America by Air: Treasures of the West 1989
A grand aerial tour of the Western U.S. Included are views of Alaskan volcanoes, the Pacific Northwest coastline, deserts of the Great Basin, canyons of Arizona and Utah, farmlands of Washington, Idaho and Oregon, the San Andreas fault zone, ancient Indian sites in Utah, Colorado, New Mexico and Arizona and the Sierra Nevada range. 47m; VHS. **C:** Directed by Douglas Kahan; Music by Grant Reeves. **A:** Sr. High-Adult. **P:** Entertainment. **U:** Home. **Gen-Edu**: Documentary Films, Aeronautics, Wilderness Areas. **Acq:** Purchase. **Dist:** Music Video Distributors. $29.95.

America by Design 1987
Examines the architectural history of the U.S. 60m; VHS, 3/4 U. **C:** Hosted by Spiro Kostof. **Pr:** Werner Schumann; PBS. **A:** College-Adult. **P:** Education. **U:** Institution, CCTV, Home, SURA. **Gen-Edu**: Architecture, History--U.S., Technology. **Acq:** Purchase, Rent/Lease, Duplication, Off-Air Record. **Dist:** PBS Home Video. $59.95.
Indiv. Titles: 1. The House 2. Public Places and Monuments 3. The Shape of the Land 4. The Street 5. The Workplace.

America: Discovery to Revolution: Puritans-The English Frontier ????
Discusses the Lost Colony, Jamestown, the relations between colonists and Native Americans, and the arrivals of other groups such as Quakers and Jews. 25m; VHS. **A:** Sr. High. **P:** Education. **U:** Institution. **Gen-Edu**: History--U.S., Explorers. **Acq:** Purchase. **Dist:** Zenger Media. $99.95.

America: Discovery to Revolution: The American Revolution ????
Discusses the Stamp Act of 1765 and examines the conflicts at Lexington and Concord from soldiers fighting on both sides, and civilians involved in the fighting. 25m; VHS. **A:** Sr. High. **P:** Education. **U:** Institution. **Gen-Edu**: War--General, History--U.S. **Acq:** Purchase. **Dist:** Zenger Media. $99.95.

America: Discovery to Revolution: The Dutch Frontier ????
Discusses explorations of Henry Hudson, founder of New Netherland, contributions of Stuyvesant and Minuet, and the takeover of the Dutch colony in 1664 by England. 25m; VHS. **A:** Sr. High. **P:** Education. **U:** Institution. **Gen-Edu**: Explorers, History. **Acq:** Purchase. **Dist:** Zenger Media. $99.95.

America: Discovery to Revolution: The French Frontier ????
Examines the exploits of LaSalle and other claimants, colonial rivalry, and how Napoleon altered the course of North American settlement. 25m; VHS. **A:** Sr. High. **P:** Education. **U:** Institution. **Gen-Edu:** France, Explorers, History. **Acq:** Purchase. **Dist:** Zenger Media. $99.95.

America: Discovery to Revolution: The Pilgrim Frontier ????
Discusses the pilgrim voyage from England, stories of William Bradford and William Brewster, relations between settlers and Natives and more. 25m; VHS. **A:** Sr. High. **P:** Education. **U:** Institution. **Gen-Edu:** Explorers, History. **Acq:** Purchase. **Dist:** Zenger Media. $99.95.

America: Discovery to Revolution: The Spanish Frontier ????
Explores the religious and political competition during Spain's quest for glory and examines achievements of Columbus, Cabeza de Vaca, Hernando de Soto, Coronado, Ponce de Leon, and others. 25m; VHS. **A:** Sr. High. **P:** Education. **U:** Institution. **Gen-Edu:** Spain, Explorers, History. **Acq:** Purchase. **Dist:** Zenger Media. $99.95.

America Fights Back 1989
Features quality control expert Dr. W. Edward Deming as he explains philosophies that helped an industry regain a competitive edge in the international marketplace. 60m; VHS. **A:** Adult. **P:** Professional. **U:** Institution. **Bus-Ind:** Business, Management. **Acq:** Purchase. **Dist:** RMI Media. $99.95.

America First 1970 (Unrated) — ★½
A group of seven travelers try to build an "Eden" with the inhabitants of an Appalachian hollow. 90m; VHS. **C:** Michael Kennedy; Walter Keller; Pat Estrin; Lois McGuire; Directed by Joseph L. Anderson. **Pr:** Optos Ltd. **A:** Adult. **P:** Entertainment. **U:** CATV, Home. **Mov-Ent. Acq:** Purchase, Rent/Lease. **Dist:** No Longer Available.

America: Freedom to Fascism 2006
Producer Aaron Russo sets out to learn which law requires American citizens to pay income tax, from the creation of the Federal Reserve in 1913 to the present day. 105m; DVD. **A:** Sr. High-Adult. **P:** Entertainment. **U:** Home. **Gen-Edu:** Documentary Films. **Acq:** Purchase. **Dist:** Cinema Libre Studio.

America Goes to War: The Home Front—WWII 1989
This series examines the shifts in American society and culture brought on by its entry into WWII. Each tape consists of two half-hour programs. 30m; VHS, 3/4 U. **C:** Narrated by Eric Sevareid. **A:** Jr. High-Adult. **P:** Education. **U:** Institution, CCTV, CATV. **Gen-Edu:** World War Two, History--U.S. **Acq:** Purchase, Duplication License, Off-Air Record. **Dist:** PBS Home Video. $59.95.
Indiv. Titles: 1. While the Storm Clouds Gather/Praise the Lord and Pass the Ammunition 2. Sacrifice & Shortages/A String of Pearls 3. On the Shady Side of the Street/Right in Der Fuehrer's Face 4. Thanks for the Memories/Accentuating the Positive 5. Mood Indigo/It's Been a Long, Long Time.

America Goes to War: World War II ????
Six-volume set examines the effects WWII had on the continental U.S. Includes a bonus program, The Story of GI Joe. 300m; VHS. **A:** Jr. High-Sr. High. **P:** Education. **U:** Institution. **Gen-Edu:** History--U.S., World War Two. **Acq:** Purchase. **Dist:** Zenger Media. $39.95.

America Held Hostage: The Iran Crisis 1990
Examine the days when Iran was overtaken by radicals and exposed hostages to brutal scenes of barbarism on camera. 60m; VHS. **Pr:** Fusion Video. **A:** Sr. High-Adult. **P:** Education. **U:** Home. **Gen-Edu:** Documentary Films, Middle East. **Acq:** Purchase. **Dist:** Fusion Video. $29.98.

America: Home from Home 1973
Documents the regional and cultural differences of Colonial America people, merchants, social dissenters, Quakers, Puritans, and the landed gentry of the South. Written and narrated by Alistair Cooke who worked in America as a foreign correspondent for three decades researching the country's history. 52m; VHS. **A:** Sr. High. **P:** Education. **U:** Institution. **Gen-Edu:** History--U.S., History. **Acq:** Purchase. **Dist:** Zenger Media. $99.95.

America: Hooked on Drugs 1986
Ted Koppel hosts this look at the destructive power of mind-altering chemicals. 20m; VHS, 8 mm, 3/4 U. **TV Std:** NTSC, PAL, SECAM. **Pr:** ABC Nightline. **A:** Sr. High-Adult. **P:** Education. **U:** Institution, CCTV, SURA. **Gen-Edu:** Drug Abuse. **Acq:** Purchase, Rent/Lease, Duplication License. **Dist:** Phoenix Learning Group. $400.00.

America Hurts: The Drug Epidemic 1987
Even though widespread drug abuse is best described as an endemic condition, rather than an epidemic, this film uses the more shocking word in its quest for a new Prohibition. 34m; VHS, 8 mm, 3/4 U. **TV Std:** NTSC, PAL, SECAM. **Pr:** Dystar Television. **A:** Jr. High-Adult. **P:** Education. **U:** Institution, CCTV, SURA. **Gen-Edu:** Drug Abuse. **Acq:** Purchase, Rent/Lease, Duplication License. **Dist:** Phoenix Learning Group. $595.00.

America, I Love You! 1987
Using the familiar man/woman in the street interview, this film examines the lives and feelings of American Jews. 30m/B/W; VHS. **Pr:** Alden Films. **A:** Family. **P:** Education. **U:** Institution, Home. **Gen-Edu:** Judaism, History. **Acq:** Purchase, Rent/Lease. **Dist:** Alden Films.

America in Black & White 1990
Three videocasssettes featuring work by director Scott Jacobs. "Pug 'n Pols" includes short films about a boxer, and election night and election day in Chicago. "The Las Vegas Tapes" is a four day and night sojourn into the lives of underground inhabitants of Las Vegas. "The Real Realness of the Higher Highness" celebrates the Bio-Centennial Unity Fair in Golden Gate Park. Tapes are also available individually for $19.95. 89m/B/W; VHS. **C:** Directed by Scott Jacobs. **A:** College-Adult. **P:** Education. **U:** Home. **Gen-Edu:** Film--Avant-Garde. **Acq:** Purchase. **Dist:** Facets Multimedia Inc. $39.95.

America in Black and White: The Secret Game 1997
Ted Koppel interviews players from two basketball teams, one all black from North Carolina College for Negros and one all white from Duke University who participated in an illegal game in 1944 that held serious consequence according to the Jim Crow laws of that time. 21m; VHS; Closed Captioned. **A:** Jr. High-Sr. High. **P:** Education. **U:** Institution. **Gen-Edu:** Basketball, Black Culture, History--U.S. **Acq:** Purchase. **Dist:** Zenger Media. $79.95.

America in 1968: Government and Politics 1979
Political upheaval and disorientation are historically presented in this program from the "Years of Change" series. Issues discussed include Vietnam, civil rights, crime, protest, and dissent, all of which were indicative of a nation politically divided. 23m; VHS, 3/4 U. **Pr:** BFA Educational Media. **A:** Jr. High-Adult. **P:** Education. **U:** Institution, SURA. **Gen-Edu:** History--U.S. **Acq:** Purchase. **Dist:** Phoenix Learning Group.

America in 1968: People and Culture 1979
Cultural and social outcries of alienation, racism, and poverty thrust our nation into a review of its values and priorities. The first successful heart transplant became a medical victory. Part of the "Years of Change" series. 20m; VHS, 3/4 U. **Pr:** BFA Educational Media. **A:** Jr. High-Adult. **P:** Education. **U:** Institution, SURA. **Gen-Edu:** History--U.S. **Acq:** Purchase. **Dist:** Phoenix Learning Group.

America in 1968: World Affairs 1979
The unresolved questions of United States foreign affairs and policy stemming from 1968 are presented and analyzed in this program from the "Years of Change" series. 20m; VHS, 3/4 U. **Pr:** BFA Educational Media. **A:** Jr. High-Adult. **P:** Education. **U:** Institution, SURA. **Gen-Edu:** History--U.S., International Relations. **Acq:** Purchase. **Dist:** Phoenix Learning Group.

America in Portrait 1990
From the "Heritage Collection" comes an anthology of poetry and verse dramatically read by some of the great actors of recent years. Selections include authors such as: Robert Frost, Oliver Wendell Holmes, Edgar Allen Poe, Carl Sandburg, Edgar Lee Masters, and Geoffrey Chaucer. 45m; VHS. **C:** James Whitmore; Henry Fonda; William Shatner. **Pr:** Monterey Home Video. **A:** Family. **P:** Entertainment. **U:** Home. **Mov-Ent:** Performing Arts, Literature. **Acq:** Purchase. **Dist:** Karol Media; Monterey Home Video. $24.95.

America in Search of Itself 1982
This tape explores the social and political reasons why Ronald Reagan won the presidency. 43m; VHS, 3/4 U. **Pr:** National Broadcasting Company. **A:** Sr. High-Adult. **P:** Education. **U:** Institution, SURA. **Gen-Edu:** Politics & Government, Presidency. **Acq:** Purchase. **Dist:** Home Vision Cinema.

America in Space 1989
A history of the American space program from its inauspicious beginnings to the era of the space shuttle. 30m; VHS. **Pr:** Simitar. **A:** Family. **P:** Entertainment. **U:** Home. **Gen-Edu:** Space Exploration, History--U.S. **Acq:** Purchase. **Dist:** Karol Media. $9.95.

America in Space: The First 25 Years 1984
A comprehensive NASA documentary about the first 25 years of space travel. 50m; VHS. **Pr:** National Aeronautics and Space Administration. **A:** Family. **P:** Education. **U:** Home. **Gen-Edu:** Documentary Films, Space Exploration, History--U.S. **Acq:** Purchase. **Dist:** Finley Holiday Film Corp. $24.95.

America in the '40s--A Sentimental Journey 1998
Nostalgic look at the decade of the '40s, including powerful wartime footage, home movies and original stories interspersed with music made famous during that time. Available with softcover book for an additional price. 60m; VHS; Closed Captioned. **A:** Family. **P:** Education. **U:** Home. **Gen-Edu:** History, History--U.S., World War Two. **Acq:** Purchase. **Dist:** PBS Home Video. $49.98.

America in the Age of AIDS 1988
A sensitive look at how Americans are coping with this deadly disease. 60m; VHS, 3/4 U. **Pr:** KCTS-TV. **A:** Jr. High-Adult. **P:** Education. **U:** Institution, CCTV, CATV, BCTV. **Hea-Sci:** AIDS. **Acq:** Purchase. **Dist:** GPN Educational Media. $44.95.

America in the 21st Century 1990
A symposium on the future of America, focusing on business, education, the family, economics, and immigration. 30m; VHS, 3/4 U. **C:** Hosted by Hodding Carter. **Pr:** Robert Gardner. **A:** Jr. High-Adult. **P:** Education. **U:** Institution, CCTV, CATV. **Gen-Edu:** Public Affairs, Politics & Government, Sociology. **Acq:** Purchase, Duplication License, Off-Air Record. **Dist:** PBS Home Video. $49.95.

America in Transition 1983
This series examines the changing social, financial and urban conditions of five American cities. 20m; VHS, 3/4 U. **Pr:** British Broadcasting Corporation. **A:** Sr. High-Adult. **P:** Education. **U:** Institution, SURA. **Gen-Edu:** Cities & Towns. **Acq:** Purchase, Rent/Lease. **Dist:** Home Vision Cinema.

Indiv. Titles: 1. Great Lakes City: Cleveland, Ohio 2. Sunbeltcity: Phoenix, Arizona 3. Farming Country: LaFayette County, Missouri 4. Energy Boom: Evanston, Wyoming 5. Deep South Town: Greenville, Mississippi.

America Is #1: Thanks to Our Veterans 1984
This video documents the 1983 Veterans' Day ceremony at the Arlington National Cemetary. 10m; VHS, 3/4 U. **Pr:** USVA. **A:** Family. **P:** Entertainment. **U:** Institution, SURA. **Gen-Edu:** U.S. States. **Acq:** Purchase. **Dist:** National Audiovisual Center. $80.00.

America Lost and Found 1980
Compilation of rare footage conveying the psychological impact of the Great Depression of the 1930s. 59m/B/W; VHS, 3/4 U, Special order formats. **C:** Narrated by Pat Hingle. **Pr:** Tom Johnson; Lance Bird. **A:** Jr. High-Adult. **P:** Education. **U:** Institution, Home, SURA. **Gen-Edu:** History--U.S. **Acq:** Purchase, Rent/Lease. **Dist:** Direct Cinema Ltd.

America Lost and Found: The Depression Decade ????
Discusses the political and social history of the 1930s and analyzes the psychological impact of the Great Depression. 58m/B/W; VHS. **A:** Jr. High-Sr. High. **P:** Education. **U:** Institution. **Gen-Edu:** History--U.S., Politics & Government. **Acq:** Purchase. **Dist:** Zenger Media. $95.00.

America, Love It or Leave It 1990
Twenty years after, a look back at those who left the United States for Canada rather than be drafted to fight in Vietnam. 60m; VHS, 3/4 U. **Pr:** Canadian Broadcasting Corp. **A:** Jr. High-Adult. **P:** Education. **U:** Institution, CCTV, CATV. **Gen-Edu:** Documentary Films, History--U.S., Vietnam War. **Acq:** Purchase, Duplication License, Off-Air Record. **Dist:** PBS Home Video. $59.95.

America on the Road 1982
Bill Moyers shows how the auto became not only a means of transportation, but a new vision of ourselves. 58m; VHS, 3/4 U. **Pr:** The Corporation for Entertainment and Learning. **A:** Jr. High-Sr. High. **P:** Education. **U:** Institution, CCTV, CATV. **Gen-Edu:** History--U.S., Automobiles. **Acq:** Purchase, Rent/Lease, Off-Air Record. **Dist:** PBS Home Video.

America on the Rocks 1973
This program focuses on the dimensions of the alcoholism problem in the U.S. today. 29m; VHS, 3/4 U, Special order formats. **C:** Narrated by Robert Mitchum. **Pr:** National Institute on Alcohol Abuse. **A:** Family. **P:** Education. **U:** Institution, SURA. **Hea-Sci:** Alcoholism. **Acq:** Purchase. **Dist:** National Audiovisual Center.

America Past 1987
Different people from America's past are documented. 15m; VHS, 3/4 U. **C:** Narrated by Jim Fleet. **Pr:** KRMA-TV. **A:** Primary-Adult. **P:** Education. **U:** Institution, CCTV, CATV, BCTV. **Gen-Edu:** History--U.S. **Acq:** Purchase, Rent/Lease, Duplication License. **Dist:** Agency for Instructional Technology. $125.00.
Indiv. Titles: 1. New Spain 2. New France 3. Southern Colonies 4. New England Colonies 5. Canals & Steamboats 6. Roads & Railroads 7. The Artist's View 8. The Writer's View 9. The Abolitionists 10. The Role of Women 11. Utopias 12. Religion 13. Social Life 14. Moving West 15. The Industrial North 16. The Antebellum South.

America Screams 1987
A dazzling, nail-biting look at the history of the American rollercoaster featuring the country's scariest rides! 30m; VHS. **C:** Hosted by Vincent Price. **A:** Adult. **P:** Entertainment. **U:** Home. **Spo-Rec:** Documentary Films, Fairs & Expositions. **Acq:** Purchase. **Dist:** Rhino Entertainment Co. $14.95.

America Since World War II 1990
The United States is examined in the years following the second World War, including the nuclear age, Vietnam, technology and societal norms. ?m; VHS. **Pr:** United Learning Inc. **A:** Jr. High-Sr. High. **P:** Education. **U:** Institution, CCTV, CATV, Home, SURA. **Gen-Edu:** Documentary Films, History--U.S., World War Two. **Acq:** Purchase, Duplication. **Dist:** United Learning Inc. $250.00.
Indiv. Titles: 1. The Superpowers Emerge 2. Tension in the Nuclear Age 3. The War in Vietnam 4. Continued Involvement in Global Affairs 5. New Deal to New Federalism 6. A Society in Upheaval 7. Technology: On the Threshold of the Future 8. Economic Ups and Downs.

America Staying Alive 1985
A dissertation on the modern breakthroughs in disease care and prevention. In two parts: cancer and heart disease. 18m; VHS, 3/4 U. **C:** Tony Randall. **Pr:** Professional Research. **A:** Sr. High-Adult. **P:** Education. **U:** Institution, CCTV. **Hea-Sci:** Patient Care, Diseases. **Acq:** Purchase, Rent/Lease. **Dist:** Discovery Education.
Indiv. Titles: 1. Winning the Battle Against Cancer 2. Winning the Battle Against Heart Disease.

America Talks to Itself 1979
A discussion of the way the Vietnam War was reported by the news media, in the history books and in fiction. 29m; VHS, 3/4 U. **Pr:** KTCA St. Paul/Minneapolis. **A:** Jr. High-Adult. **P:** Education. **U:** Institution, CCTV, CATV. **Gen-Edu:** Vietnam War, Mass Media. **Acq:** Purchase, Rent/Lease, Off-Air Record. **Dist:** PBS Home Video.

America the Beautiful: The National Forests of Utah 1994
Seven of the state's most popular National Forests provide the beautiful setting for this visual exploration, accompanied by the musical of Rachmaninov, Gounod, Adam, and others. 30m;

VHS. **A:** Family. **P:** Entertainment. **U:** Home. **Mov-Ent:** Music--Classical, National Parks & Reserves, U.S. States. **Acq:** Purchase. **Dist:** V.I.E.W. Inc./Arkadia Entertainment Corp. $19.98.

America the Beautiful: The Natural Splendors of Florida 1994
A celebration of Florida's diversity of landscape and wildlife. Covers the flora, birds, and underwater life from the Everglades to the Keys. 35m; VHS. **A:** Family. **P:** Entertainment. **U:** Home, SURA. **Gen-Edu:** Travel, U.S. States. **Acq:** Purchase. **Dist:** V.I.E.W. Inc./Arkadia Entertainment Corp. $14.98.

America the Bountiful 1992
Six-part historical documentary on American agriculture. Historical re-enactments are interspersed throughout. Teaching Guide included. Also available individually. 22m; VHS, CC. **C:** Narrated by Ed Begley, Jr. **A:** Jr. High-Adult. **P:** Education. **U:** Institution, Home, SURA. **Gen-Edu:** Documentary Films, History--U.S., Agriculture. **Acq:** Purchase. **Dist:** CEV Multimedia. $375.00.
Indiv. Titles: 1. Horn of Plenty 2. Land 3. Swords and Plowshares 4. Torchlight 5. The Ever-Normal Granary 6. Whereby We Thrive.

America/The Fall of Babylon 1924 — ★★★
A double feature containing abridged versions; in "America," a Boston patriot and the daughter of an aristocratic Virginia Tory fall in love during the Revolutionary War; "The Fall of Babylon" is one of the stories in D.W. Griffith's "Intolerance." Silent. 56m/B/W; Silent; VHS. **C:** Neil Hamilton; Lionel Barrymore; Constance Talmadge; Elmer Clifton; Alfred Paget. **Pr:** D.W. Griffith. **A:** Family. **P:** Entertainment. **U:** Home. **Mov-Ent:** Silent Films, Revolutionary War. **Acq:** Purchase. **Dist:** $29.98.

America the Homeless 1991
Three-part series offers insight on the homeless dilemma in America today. Interviews with congressmen, church officials, and the homeless themselves shed light on difficult questions and provide hopeful suggestions for the future. 28m; VHS, Special order formats. **A:** Jr. High-Adult. **P:** Education. **U:** Institution. **Gen-Edu:** Homeless, Sociology. **Acq:** Rent/Lease. **Dist:** EcuFilm.
Indiv. Titles: 1. The New Faces of Homelessness 2. Caregivers...Who and Where? 3. Will the Sun Come Out Tommorrow?.

America the Living Dream: The History of Our Nation 2000
Six-volume set provides an overview of American history from the country's beginnings to the present day. Uses photos, historical artwork, film and video footage to illustrate the narrative. Each episode is available separately. 288m; VHS. **A:** Jr. High-Sr. High. **P:** Education. **U:** Home, Institution. **Gen-Edu:** History--U.S. **Acq:** Purchase. **Dist:** Social Studies School Service; Zenger Media. $159.95.
Indiv. Titles: 1. America's Beginnings 2. The Revolution in America 3. Growth of a Nation 4. The Civil War & the Move West 5. WWI, Prohibition, Roaring Twenties, Great Depression, WWII, Cold War 6. Space Race, Vietnam, Watergate, 21st Century.

America, The Way We Were: The Home Front, 1940-1945 1989
A three-part look at America during WWII, featuring numerous cameos of important political figures as well as celebrity entertainers. 180m; VHS. **Pr:** PBS. **A:** Primary-Adult. **P:** Education. **U:** Home. **Gen-Edu:** Documentary Films, History--U.S., World War Two. **Acq:** Purchase. **Dist:** PBS Home Video. $59.95.

America 3000 1986 (PG-13) — ★
Hundreds of years in the holocaust-torn future, men rebel against a brutal, overpowering race of women, with predictable results. 94m; VHS. **C:** Chuck Wagner; Laurene Landon; Directed by David Engelbach. **Pr:** Cannon Films. **A:** Jr. High-Adult. **P:** Entertainment. **U:** Home. **Mov-Ent:** Fantasy, Satire & Parody. **Acq:** Purchase. **Dist:** MGM Home Entertainment. $79.95.

America Tropical 1971
The story of a controversial mural painted by Mexican artist David Alfaro Siquieros on an Los Angeles building. 30m; VHS, DVD. **A:** Sr. High-Adult. **P:** Education. **U:** Home, Institution. **Gen-Edu:** Documentary Films, Art & Artists. **Acq:** Purchase, Rent/Lease. **Dist:** The Cinema Guild. $99.95.

America Undercover: CatHouse 2005 (Unrated)
Takes a peek inside the inner workings of the Bunny Ranch, a legal brothel, in an HBO television special in 2002 with hidden cameras that catch the dealings of both the working girls and their customers. 1 episode. 60m; DVD. **A:** Sr. High-Adult. **P:** Entertainment. **U:** Home. **Mov-Ent:** Television Series, Documentary Films, Drama. **Acq:** Purchase. **Dist:** Warner Home Video, Inc. $19.97.

America Undercover: The Autopsy Files 2005 (Unrated)
Features the reality-based HBO television series hosted by forensic pathologist Dr. Michael Baden including "Confessions of a Medical Examiner" (1994) and "Voices from the Dead" (1995). 2 episodes. 120m; DVD. **C:** Hosted by Michael Baden. **A:** Sr. High-Adult. **P:** Entertainment. **U:** Home. **Mov-Ent:** Television Series, Documentary Films, Science. **Acq:** Purchase. **Dist:** Warner Home Video, Inc. $19.97.

America, Where Are Your Heroes? 19??
Past New Mexico FFA Prepared and Extemporaneous Public Speaking Contest winner Ernest Cummings talks about what it takes to be a hero and how to set examples for others. 12m; VHS. **A:** Sr. High-Adult. **P:** Education. **U:** Institution. **Gen-Edu:** Speech. **Acq:** Purchase. **Dist:** CEV Multimedia. $19.95.

America Works 1984
A series of programs depicting the American workforce, and its attitude toward jobs and the economy as a whole. 30m; VHS, 3/4 U, EJ, Q. **Pr:** AFL-CIO. **A:** Sr. High-Adult. **P:** Education. **U:** Institution, SURA. **Gen-Edu:** Labor & Unions. **Acq:** Duplication, Free Duplication.
Indiv. Titles: 1. Plant Closings 2. Services to the Unemployed 3. Pay Equity for Women 4. Voter Registration 5. Toxics in the Workplace 6. Job Restraining 7. Senior Citizens' Health Care 8. Industrial Policy 9. Gas Decontrol 10. The New Hungry 11. Health Cost Containment 12. Financing Education.

America Works . . . America Sings 1990
American folk classics are performed in their respective historic and geographic contexts. Includes a lyric booklet. 20m; VHS, 3/4 U, EJ, Special order formats. **TV Std:** NTSC, PAL, SECAM. **A:** Primary-Sr. High. **P:** Education. **U:** Institution, CCTV, SURA. **Gen-Edu:** Geography, History. **Acq:** Purchase, Rent/Lease. **Dist:** Phoenix Learning Group. $250.00.

America Works When America Works 1980
As industrial change accelerates in the 1980s, can the American manpower system keep pace? When companies are forced out of the economy, unemployed workers whose skills are no longer valued are left behind, putting a strain on the American economy and the workers themselves. 78m; VHS, 3/4 U. **Pr:** Ray Lockhart. **A:** Sr. High-Adult. **P:** Education. **U:** Institution, SURA. **Gen-Edu:** Economics. **Acq:** Purchase. **Dist:** Home Vision Cinema.

America—A Look Back: End of the Trail 19??
Walter Brennan narrates the tragic fall of the American Indian. 60m; VHS. **A:** Sr. High-Adult. **P:** Entertainment. **U:** Institution. **Gen-Edu:** History--U.S. **Acq:** Purchase. **Dist:** Ambrose Video Publishing, Inc. $99.95.

America—A Look Back: Journals of Lewis and Clark 19??
The story of explorers Lewis and Clark's 18-month journey to find a western route to the Pacific ocean. 60m; VHS. **A:** Sr. High-Adult. **P:** Entertainment. **U:** Institution. **Gen-Edu:** History--U.S. **Acq:** Purchase. **Dist:** Ambrose Video Publishing, Inc. $99.95.

America—A Look Back: Life in the Thirties 19??
Examines the decade of the Great Depression. 60m; VHS. **A:** Sr. High-Adult. **P:** Entertainment. **U:** Institution. **Gen-Edu:** History--U.S. **Acq:** Purchase. **Dist:** Ambrose Video Publishing, Inc. $99.95.

America—A Look Back: Mark Twain's America 19??
Profiles the life and times of Mark Twain. 60m; VHS. **A:** Sr. High-Adult. **P:** Entertainment. **U:** Institution. **Gen-Edu:** History--U.S. **Acq:** Purchase. **Dist:** Ambrose Video Publishing, Inc. $99.95.

America—A Look Back: Meet George Washington 19??
Profiles the life of George Washington. 60m; VHS. **A:** Sr. High-Adult. **P:** Entertainment. **U:** Institution. **Gen-Edu:** History--U.S. **Acq:** Purchase. **Dist:** Ambrose Video Publishing, Inc. $99.95.

America—A Look Back: Not So Long Ago 19??
Looks at the Atomic Age, 1945 to 1950, when GIs returned home, employment increased, and there was a renewed sense of pride in America. 60m; VHS. **A:** Sr. High-Adult. **P:** Entertainment. **U:** Institution. **Gen-Edu:** History--U.S. **Acq:** Purchase. **Dist:** Ambrose Video Publishing, Inc. $99.95.

America—A Look Back: That War Korea 19??
Explores the Korean War, McCarthyism, and the red scare that shaped the future of America as a superpower. 60m; VHS. **A:** Sr. High-Adult. **P:** Entertainment. **U:** Institution. **Gen-Edu:** History--U.S. **Acq:** Purchase. **Dist:** Ambrose Video Publishing, Inc. $99.95.

America—A Look Back: The Civil War 19??
Offers tribute to Abraham Lincoln, Ulysses S. Grant, and Robert E. Lee. 60m; VHS. **A:** Sr. High-Adult. **P:** Entertainment. **U:** Institution. **Gen-Edu:** History--U.S. **Acq:** Purchase. **Dist:** Ambrose Video Publishing, Inc. $99.95.

America—A Look Back: The Great War 19??
A portrait of World War I (1914-18). 60m; VHS. **A:** Sr. High-Adult. **P:** Entertainment. **U:** Institution. **Gen-Edu:** History--U.S. **Acq:** Purchase. **Dist:** Ambrose Video Publishing, Inc. $99.95.

America—A Look Back: The Innocent Years 19??
Looks at the age of the first automobiles, motion pictures, robber barons and suffragettes. 60m; VHS. **A:** Sr. High-Adult. **P:** Entertainment. **U:** Institution. **Gen-Edu:** History--U.S. **Acq:** Purchase. **Dist:** Ambrose Video Publishing, Inc. $99.95.

America—A Look Back: The Jazz Age 19??
A look at 1920s America and the birth of jazz. 60m; VHS. **A:** Sr. High-Adult. **P:** Entertainment. **U:** Institution. **Gen-Edu:** History--U.S. **Acq:** Purchase. **Dist:** Ambrose Video Publishing, Inc. $99.95.

America—A Look Back: The Real West 19??
The story of the real pioneers, miners, gamblers, and gunslingers as narrated by Gary Cooper. 60m; VHS. **A:** Sr. High-Adult. **P:** Entertainment. **U:** Institution. **Gen-Edu:** Computers. **Acq:** Purchase. **Dist:** Ambrose Video Publishing, Inc. $99.95.

America—A Look Back: The West of Charles Russell 19??
Charles Marion Russell, cowboy and artist, captures mid-1800s frontier life in his art. 60m; VHS. **A:** Sr. High-Adult. **P:** Entertainment. **U:** Institution. **Gen-Edu:** History--U.S., Art & Artists. **Acq:** Purchase. **Dist:** Ambrose Video Publishing, Inc. $99.95.

America—A Look Back: Victory at Sea 19??
A look at World War II naval battles. 60m; VHS. **A:** Sr. High-Adult. **P:** Entertainment. **U:** Institution. **Gen-Edu:** History--U.S. **Acq:** Purchase. **Dist:** Ambrose Video Publishing, Inc. $99.95.

America—A Look Back: Will Rogers 19??
Bob Hope narrates the story of Will Rogers. 60m; VHS. **A:** Sr. High-Adult. **P:** Entertainment. **U:** Institution. **Gen-Edu:** History--U.S. **Acq:** Purchase. **Dist:** Ambrose Video Publishing, Inc. $99.95.

America—Catch the Spirit! 1986
This is a tourist program designed to lure foreign nationals into taking their vacations in America. 30m; VHS, 3/4 U. **Pr:** USDCP. **A:** Adult. **P:** Education. **U:** Institution, SURA. **Gen-Edu:** U.S. States, Travel. **Acq:** Purchase. **Dist:** National Audiovisual Center. $110.00.

America3 "Cubed": The Power to Create 19??
Relates tale of how the U.S. team won the America's Cup yacht race. Yacht owner Bill Koch explains that the victory was a result of teamwork rather than superlative skill. Intended to be a motivational lesson to workers. Contains exciting footage of the race. 28m; VHS. **A:** College-Adult. **P:** Professional. **U:** Institution. **Bus-Ind:** Business, Management, Boating. **Acq:** Purchase. **Dist:** Enterprise Media. $795.00.

The American 2001 — ★★
Heavy-handed adaptation of Henry James's 1877 novel. Christopher Newman (Modine) makes a fortune in California and heads to Paris in the 1870s where he hopes to acquire both culture and a wife. He meets mysterious widow Claire de Cintre (Sullivan) but his proposal is rejected by her snobby aristocratic family, which is headed by Claire's imperious mother, Madame de Bellegarde (Rigg). Then Newman learns a family secret that could win him Claire's hand. 90m; VHS, DVD, CC. **C:** Matthew Modine; Aisling O'Sullivan; Diana Rigg; Brenda Fricker; Andrew Scott; Eva Birthistle; Directed by Paul Unwin; Written by Michael Hastings. **A:** Sr. High-Adult. **P:** Entertainment. **U:** Home. **Mov-Ent:** Drama. **Acq:** Purchase. **Dist:** PBS Home Video.

The American 2010 (R) — ★★
A cold-blooded weapons-making assassin goes soft in this adaptation of the Martin Booth novel "A Very Private Gentleman." Knowing he's being hunted, Jack (Clooney) hides out in the Italian countryside. His lone wolf instincts are changed when he indulges the interest of Father Benedetto (Bonacelli) and moves from a client relationship with hooker Clara (Placido) to something more emotional. Neither situation is very believable but Clooney can certainly sell the cool. 105m; Blu-Ray, Wide. **C:** George Clooney; Paolo Bonacelli; Bruce Altman; Violante Placido; Thekla Reuten; Johan Leysen; Directed by Anton Corbijn; Written by Rowan Joffe; Cinematography by Martin Ruhe; Music by Herbert Gronemeyer. **Pr:** Ann Wingate; Grant Heslov; George Clooney; Anne Carey; Jill Green; George Clooney; A This Is That; Greenlit; Smokehouse; Twins Financing; Focus Features L.L.C. **A:** Sr. High-Adult. **P:** Entertainment. **U:** Home. **L:** English. **Mov-Ent:** Italy. **Acq:** Purchase. **Dist:** Movies Unlimited; Universal Studios Home Video.

American Adobo 2002 (R) — ★★½
An adobo is the Philippines' national dish, a savory concoction that must marinate to bring its flavors together. As it does five Filipino-American long-time friends around a dinner table in Queens. They are all doing well professionally but their personal lives could definitely use work. 99m; VHS, DVD. **C:** Dina Bonnevie; Randy Becker; Cherry Pie Picache; Sol Ocoa; Christopher De Leon; Susan Valdez-LeGoff; Ricky Davao; Wayne Maugans; Paolo Montalban; Gloria Romero; Directed by Laurice Guillen; Written by Vincent R. Nebrida; Cinematography by Lee Meily. **A:** Sr. High-Adult. **P:** Entertainment. **U:** Home. **Mov-Ent:** Food Industry. **Acq:** Purchase.

An American Adventure: The Rocket Pilot 1981
This tape looks at three rocket test pilots who were involved in the experimental X-15 rocket aircraft program during the space race. 77m; VHS, 3/4 U. **Pr:** National Broadcasting Company. **A:** Sr. High-Adult. **P:** Education. **U:** Institution, SURA. **Gen-Edu:** Space Exploration. **Acq:** Purchase. **Dist:** Home Vision Cinema.

American Adventures U.S.A.: A Fun-Filled Journey Across the United States 1996
Provides a fun filled journey across the United States visiting National Parks and exploring outdoor adventure sports for the entire family. Includes visits to coastal areas, Yellowstone Park, the Everglades, the Blue Ridge Mountains, Lake Powell, Niagara Falls, Yosemite, and Washington D.C. Covers such outdoor activities as mountain biking, river rafting, skiiing, snowboarding, windsurfing, surfing, rock climbing, sand buggies, dirtbikes, and hot air ballooning. 50m; VHS. **A:** Family. **P:** Entertainment. **U:** Home. **Gen-Edu:** Travel, National Parks & Reserves, Sports--General. **Acq:** Purchase. **Dist:** Tapeworm Video Distributors Inc. $19.95.

An American Affair 1999 (Unrated) — ★½
Washington, D.C., District Attorney Sam Brady (Bernsen) marries Genevieve (D'Abo) even though he's having an affair with her best friend, Barbara (Heitmeyer). But after Genevieve is murdered, her ghost begins to haunt him. And to make things more complicated, a senator seems to have it in for Sam. The two plotlines take too long to intersect, so the story never makes much sense. 90m; VHS, DVD. **C:** Corbin Bernsen; Maryam D'Abo; Jayne Heitmeyer; Robert Vaughn; Directed by Sebastian Shah. **A:** Sr. High-Adult. **P:** Entertainment. **U:** Home. **Mov-Ent.** **Acq:** Purchase. **Dist:** York Entertainment.

An American Affair 2009 (R) — ★½
In 1963, 13-year-old Adam (Bright), suffering from raging teen hormones, takes to peeping on his beautiful new Washington, DC neighbor Catherine (Mol), even working odd jobs in order to be near her. She's got lots of problems, including over-indulging in drugs and alcohol. Catherine, a divorced socialite artist, is also having an affair with the President and is a pawn for the CIA. Mol gives off that Marilyn Monroe vibe but the story is probably drawn from a tryst JFK had with a Washington socialite who was later murdered. 93m; DVD. **C:** Gretchen Mol; Cameron Bright; Perrey Reeves; Noah Wyle; James Rebhorn; Mark Pellegrino; Kris Arnold; Directed by William Sten Olsson; Written by Alex Metcalf; Cinematography by David Insley; Music by Dustin O'Halloran. **A:** Sr. High-Adult. **P:** Entertainment. **U:** Home. **Mov-Ent:** Alcoholism, Adolescence, Presidency. **Acq:** Purchase. **Dist:** Universal Studios Home Video.

American Agriculture 1987
Covers the changing patterns of crop production and livestock across the Nation as well as other aspects of America's production agriculture. 11m; VHS. **A:** Sr. High-Adult. **P:** Education. **U:** Institution. **Gen-Edu:** Agriculture. **Acq:** Rent/Lease. **Dist:** Cornell University. $16.00.

The American Alligator 1987
Presents a portrait of the American alligator and its place in Florida's history and ecology. ?m; VHS. **A:** Jr. High-College. **P:** Education. **U:** Institution. **Gen-Edu:** Animals, Wildlife, Ecology & Environment. **Acq:** Purchase. **Dist:** Educational Images Ltd. $49.50.

The American Angels: Baptism of Blood 1989 (R) — ★
Three beautiful young women, each with a personal dream, strive to make it in the world of professional wrestling. Hackneyed plot devices, but those simply watching for the wrestling scenes won't be disappointed. 99m; VHS, CC. **C:** Jan MacKenzie; Tray Loren; Mimi Lesseos; Trudy Adams; Patricia Cavoti; Susan Sexton; Jean Kirkland; Jeff Lundy; Lee Marshall; Directed by Beverly Sebastian; Ferd Sebastian. **Pr:** Sebastian International Pictures. **A:** Sr. High-Adult. **P:** Entertainment. **U:** Home. **Mov-Ent. Acq:** Purchase. **Dist:** Paramount Pictures Corp. $79.95.

American Anthem 1986 (PG-13) — ★
A young gymnast must choose between family responsibilities or the parallel bars. Olympic gymnast Gaylord makes his movie debut but doesn't get the gold. Good fare for young tumblers, but that's about it. Followed by two of the films' music videos and tape-ads featuring Max Headroom. 100m; VHS, DVD, CC. **C:** Mitch Gaylord; Janet Jones; Michelle Phillips; Michael Pataki; Directed by Albert Magnoli; Written by Evan P. Archerd; Jeff Benjamin; Music by Alan Silvestri. **Pr:** Lorimar Productions. **A:** Jr. High-Adult. **P:** Entertainment. **U:** Home. **Mov-Ent:** Gymnastics, Sports--Fiction: Drama, Sports--Olympic. **Acq:** Purchase. **Dist:** WarnerArchive.com; Warner Home Video, Inc. $19.98.

American Apartheid ????
Discusses issues of African-American equality in today's society, such as continuing segregation of American communities, violence in black communities, and substandard minority housing. 35m; VHS. **A:** Sr. High-Adult. **P:** Education. **U:** Institution. **Gen-Edu:** Civil Rights, Black Culture, History--U.S. **Acq:** Purchase. **Dist:** Films for the Humanities & Sciences. $99.00.

American Aristocracy 1917 — ★★½
A silent comic romp in which Fairbanks, an old moneyed dandy, wreaks havoc on an island resort whose clientele is composed of the nouveau well-to-do. 52m/B/W; Silent; VHS, DVD. **C:** Douglas Fairbanks, Sr.; Jewel Carmen; Albert Parker; Directed by Lloyd Ingraham. **Pr:** Triangle Film Corporation. **A:** Jr. High-Adult. **P:** Entertainment. **U:** Home. **Mov-Ent:** Comedy--Slapstick, Silent Films. **Acq:** Purchase. **Dist:** Grapevine Video. $16.95.

American Art '85 1985
A document of the special 1985 art exhibit at the Whitney Museum, including work and commentary by Dara Birnbaum, Robert Breer, Eric Fisch, Donald Judd, Susan Rothenberg and others. 28m; VHS, 3/4 U, Special order formats. **Pr:** Whitney Museum. **A:** Family. **P:** Entertainment. **U:** Home. **Fin-Art:** Art & Artists, Museums. **Acq:** Purchase. **Dist:** Home Vision Cinema. $29.95.

American Art and Architecture 19??
Explains how American art and architecture helps to reflect the history of the country. Includes footage of paintings, sculptures, folk art, and photography. Also available in a version for middle school students ($139.00). ?m; VHS. **A:** Sr. High. **P:** Education. **U:** Institution. **Fin-Art:** History--U.S., Art & Artists, Architecture. **Acq:** Purchase. **Dist:** Crystal Productions. $219.00.

American Art from the National Gallery of Art 1993
A still-frame archive of over 2,600 works by American artists including Gilbert Stuart, Winslow Homer, and Jackson Pollock. Features several details of each work. Also contains motion photography of selected works. Comes with index. ?m. **A:** Sr. High-Adult. **P:** Education. **U:** SURA. **Gen-Edu:** Art & Artists. **Acq:** Free Loan. **Dist:** National Gallery of Art; Crystal Productions. $99.95.

American Art in the Sixties 1973
Andy Warhol, George Segal, Roy Lichtenstein, John Cage, Claes Oldenberg, and Leo Castelli are just some of the people who offer their works and their views on American art in the '60s. 57m; VHS, 3/4 U. **C:** Narrated by Barbara Rose. **Pr:** Michael Blackwood Productions. **A:** Sr. High-Adult. **P:** Education. **U:** Institution. **Fin-Art:** Art & Artists. **Acq:** Purchase, Rent/Lease. **Dist:** Michael Blackwood Productions.

American Art Since 1945 1984
A series examing the rise and variations of modern American art. 58m; VHS, 3/4 U. **Pr:** Michael Blackwood Productions. **A:** Sr. High-Adult. **P:** Education. **U:** Institution, SURA. **Fin-Art:** Art & Artists. **Acq:** Purchase, Rent/Lease. **Dist:** Michael Blackwood Productions.
Indiv. Titles: 1. The New York School 2. Masters of Modern Sculpture 3. The 1960's 4. The 1970's 5. A New Spirit in Painting: Six Painters of the 1980's.

American Art Today: Whitney Biennial Exhibitions 1987
A survey of the Whitney Museum's biennial exhibitions of new American art, with work and talk by Nam June Paik, Tzhar Patkin, Ross Bleckner, Judy Pfaff, and others. 28m; VHS. **Pr:** Whitney Museum. **A:** Jr. High-Adult. **P:** Entertainment. **U:** Home. **Fin-Art:** Documentary Films, Art & Artists, Museums. **Acq:** Purchase. **Dist:** Home Vision Cinema; Crystal Productions. $29.95.
Indiv. Titles: 1. Whitney 1985 Biennial Exhibition 2. Whitney 1987 Biennial Exhibition 3. Whitney 1989 Biennial Exhibition.

The American as Artist: A Portrait of Bob Penn 1976
An essay on American Indian artist Penn and his experimental work, examining both the art and his position as a Native American artist. 29m; VHS, 1C, 3/4 U, Q. **Pr:** South Dakota ETV; Midwestern Educational Television. **A:** Jr. High-Adult. **P:** Education. **U:** Institution, BCTV, SURA. **Fin-Art:** Art & Artists, Native Americans. **Acq:** Purchase, Rent/Lease. **Dist:** Vision Maker Media.

American Autobahn 1984 (Unrated) — ★½
A low-budget independent actioner about a journalist who discovers an underworld weapons ring that hits the highway in pursuit of him. 90m; VHS. **C:** Jan Jalenak; Michael von der Goltz; Jim Jarmusch; Directed by Andre Degas. **Pr:** Ping Bismark; Michael von der Goltz. **A:** Preschool. **P:** Entertainment. **U:** Home. **Mov-Ent:** Journalism. **Acq:** Purchase. **Dist:** Amazon.com Inc.

American Avant Garde Films 1989
A collection of controversial and influential films including Fall of the House of Usher (1928), Lot in Sodom (1933), and Life and Death of a Hollywood Extra (1928). ?m; VHS. **A:** Sr. High-Adult. **P:** Entertainment. **U:** Home. **Mov-Ent:** Film--Avant-Garde. **Acq:** Purchase. **Dist:** Festival Films. $49.95.

American Baby: A Journey Through the First Year of Life 1994
Educational psychologist Dr. Burton L. White and "American Baby" editor Judith Nolte offer information and advice on caring for your baby during the first year of life. 45m; VHS. **A:** Adult. **P:** Education. **U:** Home, Institution. **Hea-Sci:** Parenting, Infants, Child Care. **Acq:** Purchase. **Dist:** Baker and Taylor. $14.95.

American Baby: Journey Through First Year 1990
The experts at "American Baby" magazine offer insights into the first year of a baby's growth and development. 60m; VHS. **Pr:** American Baby Magazine. **A:** Family. **P:** Education. **U:** Home. **Gen-Edu:** Infants, Child Care, Parenting. **Acq:** Purchase. **Dist:** Karol Media. $19.95.

American Ballet Theatre: A Close-Up in Time ????
A compilation of six major dance pieces performed by the American Ballet Theatre with choreographer interviews. Selections include "Les Sylphides," "Rodeo," "Pillar of Fire," "Swan Lake," "The River," and "Etudes." 90m; VHS. **A:** Adult. **P:** Entertainment. **U:** Institution, Home. **Fin-Art:** Dance--Ballet, Dance--Performance. **Acq:** Purchase. **Dist:** Stagestep. $39.95.

American Ballet Theatre at the Met 1985
Four ballets by the famed dance company: "Les Sylphides," "Paquita," "Sylvia" and "Triad," with choreography by Balanchine, Fokine and Makarova. In hi-fi Stereo. 100m; VHS. **C:** Mikhail Baryshnikov; Cynthia Gregory; Cynthia Harvey. **Pr:** NVC Arts International. **A:** Family. **P:** Entertainment. **U:** Home. **Fin-Art:** Dance. **Acq:** Purchase. **Dist:** Music Video Distributors; Home Vision Cinema; Stagestep. $39.95.

American Ballet Theatre in San Francisco 1987
Scenes from "Swan Lake," "Romeo and Juliet," and "Jardin aux Lilas" highlight this tape. 105m; VHS. **C:** Natalia Makarova; Fernando Bujones; Cynthia Gregory. **Pr:** Princeton/Dance Horizons. **A:** Jr. High-Adult. **P:** Entertainment. **U:** Institution, Home. **Fin-Art:** Dance--Ballet, Dance--Performance, Dance. **Acq:** Purchase. **Dist:** Music Video Distributors; Home Vision Cinema. $39.95.

American Ballet Theatre Now ????
Principal dancers perform romantic, classical and contemporary excerpts from major ballets including "Sleeping Beauty," "Swan Lake," and "Romeo and Juliet." 83m; VHS. **A:** Adult. **P:** Entertainment. **U:** Institution, Home. **Fin-Art:** Dance--Ballet, Dance--Performance. **Acq:** Purchase. **Dist:** Stagestep. $29.95.

American Bandits: Frank and Jesse James 2010 (PG) — ★½
Falls into the category of poorly acted, unexciting westerns. After Jesse (Stults) is shot, brother Frank (Abell) splits up the gang, planning to meet up again in four days. However, U.S. Marshal Kane (Fonda) is in pursuit and someone in the gang isn't loyal so a showdown is looming. 86m; DVD. **C:** George Stults; Tim Abell; Peter Fonda; Jeffrey Combs; Anthony Tyler Quinn; Michael Gaglio; Directed by Fred Olen Ray; Written by Fred Olen Ray; Cinematography by Theo Angell; Music by Jason Solowsky. **A:** Jr. High-Adult. **P:** Entertainment. **U:** Home. **Mov-Ent:** Western. **Acq:** Purchase. **Dist:** Entertainment One US LP.

American Barbecue and Grilling 1986
Rich Davis explains the difference between grilling and barbecuing, and how to do each of them properly. 30m; VHS. **Pr:** Cambridge Career Productions. **A:** Sr. High-Adult. **P:** Instruction. **U:** Institution, Home. **How-Ins:** Cooking. **Acq:** Purchase. **Dist:** ESPN Inc.; Cambridge Educational. $19.95.

American Beauty 1999 (R) — ★★★½
Lester Burnham (Spacey) is dead. This isn't any shock—Lester tells you this himself in his opening narration. It's the time leading up to his death Lester wants to remember. Lester is a middle-aged drone with a brittle, status-conscious wife, Carolyn (Bening), and a sullen teenaged daughter, Jane (Birch). Lester's world is rocked when he meets Jane's Lolita-like friend, Angela (Suvari), and his fantasies find him quitting his job, pumping iron, and smoking dope with Ricky (Bentley), the voyeuristic kid next door who has a thing for videotaping Jane. It's a suburban nightmare writ large with an excellent cast and some unexpected twists. 118m; VHS, DVD, Blu-Ray, Wide, CC. **C:** Kevin Spacey; Annette Bening; Mena Suvari; Thora Birch; Wes Bentley; Peter Gallagher; Chris Cooper; Allison Janney; Scott Bakula; Sam Robards; Directed by Sam Mendes; Written by Alan Ball; Cinematography by Conrad L. Hall; Music by Thomas Newman. **Pr:** Bruce Cohen; DreamWorks SKG. **A:** Sr. High-Adult. **P:** Entertainment. **U:** Home. **Mov-Ent:** Marriage, Sex & Sexuality, Adolescence. **Awds:** Oscars '99: Actor (Spacey), Cinematog., Director (Mendes), Film, Orig. Screenplay; British Acad. '99: Actor (Spacey), Actress (Bening), Cinematog., Film, Film Editing, Score; Directors Guild '99: Director (Mendes); Golden Globes '00: Director (Mendes), Film--Drama, Screenplay; L.A. Film Critics '99: Director (Mendes); Natl. Bd. of Review '99: Film; Screen Actors Guild '99: Actor (Spacey), Actress (Bening), Cast; Writers Guild '99: Orig. Screenplay; Broadcast Film Critics '99: Director (Mendes), Film, Orig. Screenplay. **Acq:** Purchase. **Dist:** DreamWorks Home Entertainment.

American Beer 2005
Four buddies road trip to California but their car breaks down in the Dakota badlands, when they split up to search for help each has a dangerous, hilarious and bizarre episode with the dimwitted locals. 89m; VHS, DVD. **A:** Adult. **P:** Entertainment. **U:** Home. **Mov-Ent:** Drama. **Acq:** Purchase. **Dist:** Vanguard International Cinema, Inc. $19.95.

American Bike Grand Prix 1988 1988
Fast action at the racetrack with this tape of second series of races in California. ?m; VHS. **A:** Adult. **P:** Entertainment. **U:** Home. **Spo-Rec:** Sports--General, Motorcycles. **Acq:** Purchase. **Dist:** Powersports - Powerdocs.

The American Bill of Rights 19??
The Bill of Rights is analyzed. 16m; VHS. **A:** Primary-Sr. High. **P:** Education. **U:** Institution. **Gen-Edu:** History--U.S., History, Politics & Government. **Acq:** Purchase. **Dist:** Thomas S. Klise Co. $58.00.

American Blackout 2006 (Unrated)
Documentary following congress woman Cynthia McKinney, and voting irregularities in recent elections that appear to be intended to disenfranchise black voters. 92m; DVD. **A:** Sr. High-Adult. **P:** Education. **U:** Home. **Gen-Edu:** Documentary Films, Politics & Government. **Acq:** Purchase. **Dist:** Disinformation. $14.95.

American Blue Note 1989 (PG-13) — ★★
Loosely plotted, bittersweet account of a struggling jazz quartet in the early 1960s, as its leader (MacNicol) must decide if their fruitless tours of sleazy bars and weddings are still worth it. The debut of director Toporoff. 96m; VHS. **C:** Peter MacNichol; Carl Capotorto; Tim Guinee; Bill Christopher-Myers; Jonathan Walker; Charlotte d'Amboise; Louis Guss; Zohra Lampert; Trini Alvarado; Sam Behrens; Directed by Ralph Toporoff; Written by Gilbert Girion; Larry Schanker. **Pr:** Panorama Entertainment. **A:** Sr. High-Adult. **P:** Entertainment. **U:** Home. **Mov-Ent:** Music--Jazz. **Acq:** Purchase. **Dist:** Sony Pictures Home Entertainment Inc.; Baker and Taylor. $89.95.

American Born 1989 (Unrated) — ★½
Murder Inc. returns to the dismay of one idealist who embarks on a battle he doesn't intend to lose. The mob had better look out. 90m; VHS, DVD, Streaming. **C:** Joey Travolta; Andrew Zeller; Directed by Raymond Martino; Written by Raymond Martino. **Pr:** PM Films. **A:** College-Adult. **P:** Entertainment. **U:** Home. **Mov-Ent. Acq:** Purchase. **Dist:** Madacy Entertainment; Echo Bridge Home Entertainment.

American Boyfriends 1989 (PG-13) — ★★
An ostensible sequel to "My American Cousin," in which two Canadian girls go to California and discover innocent romance and friendship. 90m; VHS; Open Captioned. **C:** Margaret Langrick; John Wildman; Jason Blicker; Lisa Repo Martell; Directed by Sandy Wilson; Written by Sandy Wilson; Cinematography by Brenton Spencer. **Pr:** Telefilm Canada; National Film Board of Canada. **A:** Jr. High-Adult. **P:** Entertainment. **U:** Home. **Mov-Ent:** Comedy-Drama, Romance, Canada. **Acq:** Purchase. **Dist:** Lions Gate Television Corp. $79.95.

American Buffalo 1995 (R) — ★★½
Somewhat lackluster but decent screen adaptation of a classic American drama. Franz's junk shop owner Donny plans to steal back a rare Buffalo-head nickel that he feels he was swindled out of, with the help of his protege Bobby (Nelson). Hoffman's ferret-like Teach, one of Donny's card-playing buddies and an arrogant opportunist, tries to weasel in on the plan that never comes to fruition. Set in Corrente's hometown of Pawtucket, the

director's reverence for the material is obvious and he plays it too safe. Top-notch performances raise the level. Mamet adapts his play for the screen. 88m; VHS, DVD, Wide, CC. **C:** Dustin Hoffman; Dennis Franz; Sean Nelson; Directed by Michael Corrente; Written by David Mamet; Cinematography by Richard Crudo; Music by Thomas Newman. **Pr:** Gregory Mosher; John Sloss; Capitol Films; Punch Productions; Samuel Goldwyn Company. **A:** Sr. High-Adult. **P:** Entertainment. **U:** Home. **Mov-Ent:** Poverty. **Acq:** Purchase. **Dist:** MGM Home Entertainment.

American Bullfighter I: The Bullfighting Clowns 1998
Takes a look at the world of rodeo clowns from their roles as rodeo cowboy protectors to their crowd pleasing antics. Also shows bullfighting athletes as they compete for the title of "World Champion Bullfighter." 60m; DVD. **A:** Family. **P:** Entertainment. **U:** Home. **Spo-Rec:** Rodeos. **Acq:** Purchase. **Dist:** Allumination Filmworks. $19.95.

American Bullfighter II: Dances With Bulls 1998
Features highlights from five years of National Finals Bullfighting action. Also contains a segment where cowboy Rex Dunn exhibits his Bullfighting School for the cameras. 60m; DVD. **A:** Family. **P:** Entertainment. **U:** Home. **Spo-Rec:** Rodeos. **Acq:** Purchase. **Dist:** Allumination Filmworks. $19.95.

American Business English/ESL: The Fundamentals 1998
Two volume interactive course was designed for native speakers of other languages who want to learn American Business English correctly. 113m; VHS. **A:** Sr. High-Adult. **P:** Education. **U:** Home. **Gen-Edu:** Education, Language Arts, Study Skills. **Acq:** Purchase. **Dist:** Video Aided Instruction Inc. $79.95.

American Business History 1981
A ten-program course in American business history spanning colonial times to the present day. Study guide and book of readings are available. 30m; VHS, 3/4 U, Special order formats. **A:** College-Adult. **P:** Education. **U:** Institution, CCTV, CATV, BCTV, SURA. **Bus-Ind:** Business, History--U.S. **Acq:** Rent/Lease, Duplication License. **Dist:** GPN Educational Media. $300.00.
Indiv. Titles: 1. The Browns of Providence and Merchant Capitalism 2. Samuel Slater and the Industrial Revolution 3. James J. Hill and the Transportation Revolution 4. Andrew Carnegie and Business Ideology 5. John D. Rockefeller and the Rise of Oligopoly 6. J. P. Morgan and Finance Capitalism 7. Herbert Hoover and Political Capitalism 8. Henry Ford and Mass Consumption Society 9. Alfred Sloan and Corporate Bureaucracy 10. IBM and the Communications Revolution.

American Business Management Series 19??
Management training series offers instruction on many of today's business and management issues. ?m; VHS. **A:** College-Adult. **P:** Professional. **U:** Home. **Bus-Ind:** Business, Management, Job Training. **Acq:** Purchase. **Dist:** Instructional Video.
Indiv. Titles: 1. Building a Successful Business Plan 2. Finding New Customers for Your Business 3. How to Start & Operate Your Own Business 4. Dealing with Sexual Harassment in the Work Place 5. Hiring & Firing - Things You Need to Know.

American Business Sales Series 19??
Business education series aimed at improving phone-selling skills. ?m; VHS. **A:** College-Adult. **P:** Professional. **U:** Home. **Bus-Ind:** Sales Training. **Acq:** Purchase. **Dist:** Instructional Video.
Indiv. Titles: 1. Asking for the Order and Closing the Sale 2. Making Cold Calls Easy & Profitable 3. Fundamentals of Effective Selling 4. Advanced Selling - Consultative Sales Techniques/Behavioral Styles 5. Making Unhappy Customers Love You 6. Effective Telephone Selling.

An American Carol 2008 (PG-13) — Bomb!
An anti-American filmmaker named Michael Malone (Farley)--a shameless parody of real-life documentarian Michael Moore, down to the ubiquitous baseball cap—is out to abolish the 4th of July holiday when he is visited by three ghostly historic figures who try to get him to appreciate his country ala "A Christmas Carol." An overtly biased skewering of supposedly "liberal" politics and ideologies is ultimately a smear campaign masquerading as entertainment—and it's not even funny. Kevin Farley is the brother of the late Chris Farley. 84m; Blu-Ray, On Demand, Wide. **C:** Kevin Farley; Kelsey Grammer; Jon Voight; Robert Davi; Chriss Anglin; Leslie Nielsen; Gail O'Grady; Trace Adkins; Directed by David Zucker; Written by David Zucker; Lewis Freidman; Myrna Sokoloff; Cinematography by Brian Baugh; Music by James L. Venable. **Pr:** David Zucker; John Shepherd; Stephen McEveety; David Zucker; Mpower Pictures; Vivendi Visual Entertainment. **A:** Jr. High-Adult. **P:** Entertainment. **U:** Home. **L:** English. **Mov-Ent:** Satire & Parody, Holidays, History--U.S. **Acq:** Purchase. **Dist:** Alpha Video; Vivendi Visual Entertainment; Amazon.com Inc.

American Chai 2001 (R) — ★★
Indian-American college student Sureel is caught between pleasing his traditional parents, who think he's studying pre-med, and his own desires to be a professional musician. He meets another first generation student, the beautiful Maya, who's equally determined to pursue her career as a dancer. Now Sureel has to find the correct fusion in his personal life that he strives for in his music--a harmonious blending of East and West. 92m; DVD. **C:** Aalok Mehta; Paresh Rawal; Sheetal Sheth; Josh Ackerman; Ajay Naidu; Aasif Mandvi; Bharati Desai; Jamie Hurley; Anand Chulani; Reena Shah; Directed by Anurag Mehta; Written by Anurag Mehta; Cinematography by John Matkowsky; Music by Aalok Mehta; Jack Bowden Faulkner. **Pr:** Taylor MacCrae; Dream Merchants Pictures;

Fusion Films. **A:** Sr. High-Adult. **P:** Entertainment. **U:** Home. **L:** English. **Mov-Ent:** Family, India. **Acq:** Purchase. **Dist:** Amazon.com Inc.

American Chain Gang 1999
Follows guards and prisoners who, 30 years after its abolishment, are part of the chain gang, which has been reinstated into the modern-day prison system. 56m; DVD. **A:** Sr. High-Adult. **P:** Entertainment. **U:** Home. **Gen-Edu:** Documentary Films. **Acq:** Purchase. **Dist:** Cinema Libre Studio.

American Chainsaw 2012
Chainsaw sculptor Jesse Green and his crew carve 'eco art' in his New England-based studio. 8 epsides, including "Salem Witch Project," "Bat Man," Getting Squirrelly," and "Clown Town." 175m; DVD. **A:** Jr. High-Adult. **P:** Entertainment. **U:** Home. **Gen-Edu:** Art & Artists, Television Series. **Acq:** Purchase. **Dist:** National Geographic. $19.95.

American Challenge: Alone Against the Atlantic 1982
The intimate on-board story of seven solo sailors facing the ultimate challenge of the Observer Singlehanded TransAtlantic Race, filmed during the actual event. 57m; VHS. **Pr:** Chris Knight; New Film Company. **A:** Family. **P:** Entertainment. **U:** Institution, Home. **Spo-Rec:** Documentary Films, Boating. **Acq:** Purchase, Rent/Lease. **Dist:** The New Film Co., Inc.

The American Character Toy Company 1959
Late '60s and early '70s commercials and sales films for American Character Toy Company products. ?m; VHS. **A:** Family. **P:** Entertainment. **U:** Home. **Mov-Ent:** Television Series, Commercials. **Acq:** Purchase. **Dist:** Video Resources.

American Cheerleading Federation: Advanced Stunts Volume 7 2003 (Unrated)
The American Cheerleading Federation demonstrates 14 new stunts for cheerleaders at the advanced level. 30m; VHS. **A:** Family. **P:** Education. **U:** Home, Institution. **Spo-Rec:** Cheerleaders, Athletic Instruction/Coaching. **Acq:** Purchase. **Dist:** Championship Productions. $39.99.

American Cheerleading Federation: Advanced Stunts Volume 8 2004 (Unrated)
The American Cheerleading Foundation demonstrates 10 new stunts for cheerleaders to use after they have mastered more basic stunts. 20m; VHS, DVD. **A:** Family. **P:** Education. **U:** Home, Institution. **Spo-Rec:** Cheerleaders, Athletic Instruction/Coaching. **Acq:** Purchase. **Dist:** Championship Productions. $29.99.

American Cheerleading Federation: Advanced Stunts Volume 9 2005 (Unrated)
The American Cheerleading Foundation demonstrates 12 new stunts for cheerleaders at the advanced level. ??m; DVD. **A:** Family. **P:** Education. **U:** Home, Institution. **Spo-Rec:** Cheerleaders, Athletic Instruction/Coaching. **Acq:** Purchase. **Dist:** Championship Productions. $29.99.

American Cheerleading Federation: Beginning Stunts Volume 8 2009 (Unrated)
The American Cheerleading Foundation demonstrates 11 new stunts for beginning cheerleaders. 71m; DVD. **A:** Family. **P:** Education. **U:** Home, Institution. **Spo-Rec:** Cheerleaders, Athletic Instruction/Coaching. **Acq:** Purchase. **Dist:** Championship Productions. $39.99.

American Cheerleading Federation: Beginning Stunts Volume 9 2005 (Unrated)
The American Cheerleading Foundation demonstrates 10 new stunts for cheerleaders at the beginning level. ??m; DVD. **A:** Family. **P:** Education. **U:** Home, Institution. **Spo-Rec:** Cheerleaders, Athletic Instruction/Coaching. **Acq:** Purchase. **Dist:** Championship Productions. $29.99.

American Cheerleading Federation: Cheers & Chants Volume 8 2004 (Unrated)
The American Cheerleading Foundation demonstrates six cheers and twelve chants for cheerleaders to use. 18m; DVD. **A:** Family. **P:** Education. **U:** Home, Institution. **Spo-Rec:** Cheerleaders, Athletic Instruction/Coaching. **Acq:** Purchase. **Dist:** Championship Productions. $29.99.

American Cheerleading Federation: Cheers & Chants Volume 9 2005 (Unrated)
The American Cheerleading Foundation demonstrates twelve chants and six cheers, as well as discussing the best drills for sharp motions in cheerleading routines. ??m; DVD. **A:** Family. **P:** Education. **U:** Home, Institution. **Spo-Rec:** Cheerleaders, Athletic Instruction/Coaching. **Acq:** Purchase. **Dist:** Championship Productions. $29.99.

American Cheerleading Federation: Dances & Quick Dances Volume 8 2004 (Unrated)
The American Cheerleading Foundation demonstrates three 8-8 count dances and four 4-8 count dances for cheerleaders to use. 51m; DVD. **A:** Family. **P:** Education. **U:** Home, Institution. **Spo-Rec:** Cheerleaders, Athletic Instruction/Coaching. **Acq:** Purchase. **Dist:** Championship Productions. $29.99.

American Cheerleading Federation: Dances & Quick Dances Volume 9 2005 (Unrated)
The American Cheerleading Foundation demonstrates more sets of three 8-8 count dances and four 4-8 count dances. 47m; DVD. **A:** Family. **P:** Education. **U:** Home, Institution. **Spo-Rec:** Cheerleaders, Athletic Instruction/Coaching. **Acq:** Purchase. **Dist:** Championship Productions. $29.99.

American Chinatown 1996 (Unrated) — ★½
Orphaned tough guy is taken in by a powerful Chinatown mob family but gets into trouble when he falls for the head man's

sister. He has a chance to redeem himself when he learns about a plot to overthrow the triad clan but will he take it? 90m; VHS, DVD. **C:** Henry Lee; Robert Z'Dar; Liat Goodson; Directed by Richard W. Park. **A:** Sr. High-Adult. **P:** Entertainment. **U:** Home. **Mov-Ent:** Martial Arts. **Acq:** Purchase.

American Chopper: The Series - Black Widow 2003 (Unrated)
From the Discovery Channel's reality show that began in 2003 as the wild Teutel gang battles tight deadlines to build custom motorcycles and choppers in their New York workshop. Includes the construction of the Black Widow Bike. 2 episodes. 592m; DVD. **C:** Paul Teutul, Sr; Paul Teutul, Jr; Michael Teutul; Vince DeMartino; Cody Conelly; Rick Petko. **A:** Jr. High-Adult. **P:** Entertainment. **U:** Home. **Mov-Ent:** Television Series, Motorcycles. **Acq:** Purchase. **Dist:** Sony Pictures Home Entertainment Inc. $14.98.

American Chopper: The Series - Complete 1st Season 2005 (Unrated)
From the debut season of the Discovery Channel's reality show that began in 2003 as the wild Teutel gang battles tight deadlines to build custom motorcycles and choppers in their New York workshop. Includes: a chopper for a NASCAR event, the Firebike for firefighters affected by 9/11, and a vacation in Daytona, Florida. 13 episodes. 583m; DVD. **C:** Paul Teutul, Sr; Paul Teutul, Jr; Michael Teutul; Vince DeMartino; Cody Conelly; Rick Petko. **A:** Jr. High-Adult. **P:** Entertainment. **U:** Home. **Mov-Ent:** Television Series, Motorcycles. **Acq:** Purchase. **Dist:** Sony Pictures Home Entertainment Inc. $29.96.

American Chopper: The Series - Complete 2nd Season 2005 (Unrated)
From the second season of the Discovery Channel's reality show that began in 2003 as the wild Teutel gang battles tight deadlines to build custom motorcycles and choppers in their New York workshop. Includes: Tool Bike, a bike for enthusiastic TV host Jay Leno, and patriotic Liberty Bike. 13 episodes. 582m; DVD. **C:** Paul Teutul, Sr; Paul Teutul, Jr; Michael Teutul; Vince DeMartino; Cody Conelly; Rick Petko. **A:** Jr. High-Adult. **P:** Entertainment. **U:** Home. **Mov-Ent:** Television Series, Motorcycles. **Acq:** Purchase. **Dist:** Sony Pictures Home Entertainment Inc. $29.96.

American Chopper: The Series - Complete 3rd Season 2005 (Unrated)
From the third season of the Discovery Channel's reality show that began in 2003 as the wild Teutel gang battles tight deadlines to build custom motorcycles and choppers in their New York workshop. Includes: Caterpillar Bike, Gillette Bike, Yankees Bike, and Space Shuttle Bike. 13 episodes. 575m; DVD. **C:** Paul Teutul, Sr; Paul Teutul, Jr; Michael Teutul; Vince DeMartino; Cody Conelly; Rick Petko. **A:** Jr. High-Adult. **P:** Entertainment. **U:** Home. **Mov-Ent:** Television Series, Motorcycles. **Acq:** Purchase. **Dist:** Sony Pictures Home Entertainment Inc. $29.96.

American Chopper: The Series - Fire Bike 2003 (Unrated)
From the Discovery Channel's reality show that began in 2003 as the wild Teutel gang battles tight deadlines to build custom motorcycles and choppers in their New York workshop. Includes the construction of the Fire Bike. 2 episodes. 92m; DVD. **C:** Paul Teutul, Sr; Paul Teutul, Jr; Michael Teutul; Vince DeMartino; Cody Conelly; Rick Petko. **A:** Jr. High-Adult. **P:** Entertainment. **U:** Home. **Mov-Ent:** Television Series, Motorcycles. **Acq:** Purchase. **Dist:** Sony Pictures Home Entertainment Inc. $14.98.

American Chopper: The Series—Honoring the Uniform 2002 (Unrated)
Family Home Entertainment (FHE) 2002-? sport family reality show. In the three-part "POW/MIA" Paul Sr. works on a chopper to honor fallen American military heroes, while in "Jr/Sr Military Tribute Bikes 1 & 2" father and son each build a bike to be auctioned off to benefit wounded and fallen troops. 5 episodes. 222m; DVD. **C:** Paul Teutul, Sr; Paul Teutul, Jr; Michael Teutul. **A:** Family. **P:** Entertainment. **U:** Home. **Mov-Ent:** Motorcycles, Television Series. **Acq:** Purchase. **Dist:** Image Entertainment Inc. $14.99.

An American Christmas Carol 1979 (Unrated) — ★★
Charles Dickens' classic story is retold with limited charm in a TV effort. This time a greedy American financier (Winkler) learns about the true meaning of Christmas. 98m; VHS, DVD, Blu-Ray. **C:** Henry Winkler; David Wayne; Dorian Harewood; Directed by Eric Till; Music by Hagood Hardy. **Pr:** Smith-Hemion Productions. **A:** Family. **P:** Entertainment. **U:** Home. **Mov-Ent:** Christmas, Family, TV Movies. **Acq:** Purchase. **Dist:** Lions Gate Television Corp. $12.98.

American Cinema: 100 Years of Filmmaking 1994
Ten-part series covering the roughly 100 years of cinema history through a look at the Hollywood film. Lots of clips and interviews with each part providing an overview of a particular feature of the movie industry from stars to studios to independent filmmakers. Available as a five-tape boxed set or individually. 500m; VHS, DVD. **C:** Narrated by Robert Altman; Clint Eastwood; Harrison Ford; Spike Lee; John Lithgow; George Lucas; Sidney Lumet; Julia Roberts; Martin Scorsese; Steven Spielberg; Oliver Stone; Quentin Tarantino. **Pr:** Lawrence Pitkethly; New York Center for Visual History. **A:** Jr. High-Adult. **P:** Entertainment. **U:** Home. **Gen-Edu:** Film History, Documentary Films. **Acq:** Purchase. **Dist:** Image Entertainment Inc.; Zenger Media. $124.98.
Indiv. Titles: 1. The Hollywood Style 2. The Star 3. Romantic Comedy 4. The Studio System 5. The Western 6. The Combat Film 7. Film in the Television Age 8. Film Noir 9. The Film School Generation 10. The Edge of Hollywood.

The American City Series 1982
Former New York City Mayor John Lindsay examines major issues of U.S. urban history by contrasting and comparing an important episode from New York City's history to that of another city. 30m; VHS, 3/4 U. **Pr:** WNET; New York. **A:** Sr. High-Adult. **P:** Education. **U:** Institution, SURA. **Gen-Edu:** History--U.S., Cities & Towns. **Acq:** Purchase, Rent/Lease. **Dist:** Home Vision Cinema.
Indiv. Titles: 1. The City Aflame 2. Women in the City 3. City Within a City.

The American Colonies 1996
Examines the beginnings of the colonies, key people, places and reasons the Pilgrims, Puritans, and Quakers came to the New World. 27m; VHS. **A:** Primary-Sr. High. **P:** Education. **U:** Institution. **Gen-Edu:** History--U.S. **Acq:** Purchase. **Dist:** Knowledge Unlimited, Inc. $98.00.

The American Colonies: A Two-Part Set 19??
Highlights the beginning of the original 13 colonies to the settling of Savannah, Georgia in 1733. 27m; VHS. **A:** Primary-Sr. High. **P:** Education. **U:** Institution. **Gen-Edu:** History, Documentary Films. **Acq:** Purchase. **Dist:** Thomas S. Klise Co. $98.00.

American Colony: Meet the Hutterites 2012 (Unrated)
A series that documents the lives of the Hutterites, a religious colony of 59 people who live in rural Montana. All 59 members of the King Colony are related, and all worship and live together every day of the year, a closeness that often leads to conflicts as the small group tries to merge their traditional way of life with the modern world. 450m; DVD. **A:** Family. **P:** Education. **U:** Home, Institution. **L:** English. **Mov-Ent:** Documentary Films, Ethics & Morals, Family. **Acq:** Purchase. **Dist:** $19.95.

American Commandos 1984 (R) — ★
An ex-Green Beret slaughters the junkies who killed his son and raped his wife, and then joins his old buddies for a secret, Rambo-esque mission in Vietnam providing a tired rehash of Vietnam movie cliches. 96m; VHS, DVD. **C:** Chris Mitchum; John Phillip Law; Franco Guerrero; Directed by Bobby Suarez. **Pr:** Panorama Entertainment. **A:** Sr. High-Adult. **P:** Entertainment. **U:** Home. **Mov-Ent:** Rape, Vietnam War. **Acq:** Purchase. **Dist:** Lions Gate Television Corp. $79.98.

American Cop 1994 (PG-13) — ★½
Elmo LaGrange is an ordinary cop taking a vacation, when his layover in the Moscow airport becomes a lesson in mistaken identities. He teams up with the pre-requisite beautiful woman to outwit and outrun the Russian mafia. 91m; VHS. **C:** Wayne Crawford; Ashley Laurence; Daniel Quinn; William Katt; Olga Vodin; Vladimir Shpoudeiko; Nickolai Nedovodin; Directed by Wayne Crawford; Written by Carlos Brooks; Cinematography by Nicholas Josef von Sternberg. **Pr:** Gregory Small; Joel Levine; Infinite Productions; Heatherwood Film Productions. **A:** Jr. High-Adult. **P:** Entertainment. **U:** Home. **Mov-Ent:** USSR. **Acq:** Purchase. **Dist:** $92.95.

American Cousins 2002 (Unrated) — ★★½
New Jersey gangsters Gino and Settimo Bazaglia get into trouble with the Ukrainian mob while in Europe and are instructed to lay low in Glasgow with their distant cousin Roberto. Roberto is a mild-mannered, stamp-collecting fish & chips shop proprietor, who is clueless about his American cousins' true business. But they decide to repay his hospitality by helping Roberto out with some local thugs who are trying to muscle in on his business. Light-hearted culture clash comedy. 89m; DVD. **C:** Danny Nucci; Dan Hedaya; Shirley Henderson; Vincent Pastore; Gerald Lepkowski; Russell Hunter; Stevan Rimkus; Directed by Donald Coutts; Written by Sergio Casci; Cinematography by Jerry Kelly; Music by Don Shaw. **A:** Sr. High-Adult. **P:** Entertainment. **U:** Home. **Mov-Ent. Acq:** Purchase. **Dist:** BFS Video.

The American Cowboy 1979
After the Civil War, cowboys became key figures in exploration and settlement of the west. 17m; VHS, 3/4 U. **Pr:** Capricorn Film Productions. **A:** Jr. High-Sr. High. **P:** Education. **U:** Institution, SURA. **Gen-Edu:** History--U.S. **Acq:** Purchase. **Dist:** Phoenix Learning Group.

American Cowslip 2009 (R) — ★½
Overly quirky indie. Agoraphobic heroin addict Ethan lives in a remote California desert town. He's obsessed with his garden and is determined to win first prize in a gardening contest by growing a rare American cowslip. 107m; DVD. **C:** Diane Ladd; Cloris Leachman; Lin Shaye; Rip Torn; Hanna Hall; Bruce Dern; Val Kilmer; Peter Falk; Priscilla Barnes; Ronnie Gene Blevins; Directed by Mark David; Written by Mark David; Ronnie Gene Blevins; Cinematography by Mark David; Music by Joseph Blaustein. **A:** Sr. High-Adult. **P:** Entertainment. **U:** Home. **Mov-Ent:** Gardening, Drug Abuse. **Acq:** Purchase. **Dist:** Entertainment One US LP.

American Crime 2004 (R) — ★½
A reporter disappears while researching a serial killer who films his victims, and her colleagues waste no time running to her aid in the tradition of amateur would-be cops everywhere. 92m; DVD. **C:** Cary Elwes; Kip Pardue; Annabella Sciorra; Rachael Leigh Cook; Directed by Dan Mintz; Written by Jeff Ritchie; Cinematography by Dan Mintz; Music by Kurt Oldman. **A:** Sr. High-Adult. **P:** Entertainment. **U:** Home. **L:** English. **Mov-Ent. Acq:** Purchase. **Dist:** Lions Gate Entertainment Inc. $14.98.

An American Crime 2007 (R) — ★★
A cringing, sordid true crime story set in 1965 in Indianapolis. Sylvia (Page) and her younger sister Jennie (McFarland) are left by their carny parents in the paid care of single mother Gertrude (Keener), who already has seven kids. Gert needs the money but she's soon over the edge (although booze and drugs help). Soon, the crazy sadist accuses Sylvia of all sorts of crimes and locks her in the basement. Then the real abuse starts until things end tragically with a trial. 92m; DVD, Wide. **C:** Catherine Keener; Ellen Page; James Franco; Bradley Whitford; Ari Gaynor; Nick Searcy; Michael O'Keefe; Romy Rosemont; Hayley McFarland; Directed by Tommy O'Haver; Written by Tommy O'Haver; Irene Turner; Cinematography by Byron Shah; Music by Alan Ari Lazar. **A:** Sr. High-Adult. **P:** Entertainment. **U:** Home. **Mov-Ent:** Child Abuse, Poverty. **Acq:** Purchase. **Dist:** Movies Unlimited; Alpha Video.

American Crude 2007 (R) — ★
That would be crude as in unfunny sex comedy and not as in oil production. Johnny (Livingston) is married to Jane (Watros) and they are both throwing separate engagement parties for their friends Bill (Schneider) and Olivia (Detmer) on the same night. There's also a bunch of other characters, including an amateur porn maker, a ho, and a runaway teen, and of course their stories will converge but you won't care in the slightest. 98m; DVD. **C:** Ron Livingston; Cynthia Watros; Rob Schneider; Amanda Detmer; Jennifer Esposito; Michael Clarke Duncan; Missi Pyle; Raymond J. Barry; Sarah Foret; Nancy Marlow; Directed by Craig Sheffer; Written by Craig Sheffer; Cinematography by James Mathers; Music by Dennis Hamlin. **A:** Sr. High-Adult. **P:** Entertainment. **U:** Home. **Mov-Ent. Acq:** Purchase. **Dist:** Sony Pictures Home Entertainment Inc.

American Cultures for Children: African-American Heritage 1997
Examines the diverse cultures, history, and geography of west Africa. 25m; VHS; Closed Captioned. **A:** Primary. **P:** Education. **U:** Home, Institution. **Chl-Juv:** Ethnicity, Africa. **Acq:** Purchase. **Dist:** Library Video Inc. $29.95.

American Cultures for Children: Arab-American Heritage 1997
Examines the diverse cultures, history, and geography of Arab countries and the cultural influences Arab people have brought to the United States. 25m; VHS; Closed Captioned. **A:** Primary. **P:** Education. **U:** Home, Institution. **Chl-Juv:** Ethnicity, India. **Acq:** Purchase. **Dist:** Library Video Inc. $29.95.

American Cultures for Children: Central American Heritage 1997
Examines the diverse cultures, history, and geography of the seven Central American countries and the cultural influences their people have brought to the United States. 25m; VHS; Closed Captioned. **A:** Primary. **P:** Education. **U:** Home, Institution. **Chl-Juv:** Ethnicity, Central America. **Acq:** Purchase. **Dist:** Library Video Inc. $29.95.

American Cultures for Children: Chinese-American Heritage 1997
Examines the diverse cultures, history, and geography of China and the cultural influences Chinese people have brought to the United States. 25m; VHS; Closed Captioned. **A:** Primary. **P:** Education. **U:** Home, Institution. **Chl-Juv:** Ethnicity, China. **Acq:** Purchase. **Dist:** Library Video Inc. $29.95.

American Cultures for Children: Irish-American Heritage 1997
Examines the customs, history, and geography of Ireland and the cultural influences its people's immigration brought to the United States. 25m; VHS; Closed Captioned. **A:** Primary. **P:** Education. **U:** Home, Institution. **Chl-Juv:** Ethnicity, Ireland. **Acq:** Purchase. **Dist:** Library Video Inc. $29.95.

American Cultures for Children: Japanese-American Heritage 1997
Examines the diverse cultures, history, and geography of Japan and the cultural influences Japanese people have brought to the United States. 25m; VHS; Closed Captioned. **A:** Primary. **P:** Education. **U:** Home, Institution. **Chl-Juv:** Ethnicity, Japan. **Acq:** Purchase. **Dist:** Library Video Inc. $29.95.

American Cultures for Children: Jewish-American Heritage 1997
Examines the history of Jewish Americans, their traditions, and journey to the United States. 25m; VHS; Closed Captioned. **A:** Primary. **P:** Education. **U:** Home, Institution. **Chl-Juv:** Ethnicity, Judaism. **Acq:** Purchase. **Dist:** Library Video Inc. $29.95.

American Cultures for Children: Korean-American Heritage 1997
Examines the traditions, history, and geography of Korea and the cultural influences Korean people have brought to the United States. 25m; VHS; Closed Captioned. **A:** Primary. **P:** Education. **U:** Home, Institution. **Chl-Juv:** Ethnicity, Geography. **Acq:** Purchase. **Dist:** Library Video Inc. $29.95.

American Cultures for Children: Mexican-American Heritage 1997
Examines the diverse cultures, history, and geography of Mexico and the cultural influences Mexican people have brought to the United States. 25m; VHS; Closed Captioned. **A:** Primary. **P:** Education. **U:** Home, Institution. **Chl-Juv:** Ethnicity, Mexico, Hispanic Culture. **Acq:** Purchase. **Dist:** Library Video Inc. $29.95.

American Cultures for Children: Native American Heritage 1997
Examines the cultures, history, and diverse groups of the first inhabitants in North America. 25m; VHS; Closed Captioned. **A:** Primary. **P:** Education. **U:** Home, Institution. **Chl-Juv:** Ethnicity, Native Americans. **Acq:** Purchase. **Dist:** Library Video Inc. $29.95.

American Cultures for Children: Puerto Rican Heritage 1997
Examines the unique cultures, history, and geography of the United States Commonwealth of Puerto Rico. 25m; VHS; Closed Captioned. **A:** Primary. **P:** Education. **U:** Home, Institution. **Chl-Juv:** Ethnicity, Geography, Hispanic Culture. **Acq:** Purchase. **Dist:** Library Video Inc. $29.95.

American Cultures for Children: Vietnamese-American Heritage 1997
Examines the diverse cultures, history, and geography of Vietnam and how the people there live, work, and play. 25m; VHS; Closed Captioned. **A:** Primary. **P:** Education. **U:** Home, Institution. **Chl-Juv:** Ethnicity, Geography. **Acq:** Purchase. **Dist:** Library Video Inc. $29.95.

American Cyborg: Steel Warrior 1994 (R) — ★★½
Basic evil-machine-bent-on-mankind's-destruction movie—with a hero bent on rescuing the world. 95m; VHS, Streaming. **C:** Joe Lara; John P. Ryan; Directed by Boaz Davidson; Written by Bill Crounse. **A:** Sr. High-Adult. **P:** Entertainment. **U:** Home. **Mov-Ent:** Science Fiction. **Acq:** Purchase. **Dist:** Unknown Distributor.

American Dad! Volume Eight 2011 (Unrated)
Presents the animated television series that began in 2005 with CIA agent Stan Smith (Seth MacFarlane) who gets overly sensitive when it comes to possible terrorist threats—even if it's only his toast popping up. Stan tries to protect his loving wife Francine (Schaal) and teenage kids Hayley (Rachael MacFarlane) and Steve (Grimes) along with an alien and a German-speaking goldfish. In "Hot Water," Stan buys a hot tub to alleviate his stress but it starts murdering his friends and family; "Hurricane!" has Stan's efforts to protect his family from a hurricane causing them more harm than good; Roger becomes Steve's guardian in "A Ward Show"; Stan is worried he will never be a best man and therefore convinces Principal Lewis to get married in "The Worst Stan". "Virtual In-Stanity" Stan creates an alternate avatar with whom Steve plans to have sex. 18 episodes. 394m; DVD. **A:** Adult. **P:** Entertainment. **U:** Home. **Mov-Ent:** Television Series. **Acq:** Purchase. **Dist:** 20th Century Fox Animation. $39.98.

American Dad! Volume Five 2009 (Unrated)
Fox Television animated comedy. Seth Green puts a move on Steve's plus-size girlfriend in "Bar Mitzvah Hustle," Stan announces he's chosen a backup wife in the case of Francine's demise in "Wife Insurance," "Daddy Queerest" has Stan posing as gay, and Extraterrestrial Roger finds out he was not sent to decide whether Earth is to be destroyed or not in "The Wiener of Our Discontent," and sabotages the CIA telethon for the tortured program in "Phantom of the Telethon." 14 episodes. 280m; DVD. **C:** Rachael MacFarlane; Voice(s) by Seth MacFarlane; Scott Grimes; Wendy Schaal. **A:** Sr. High-Adult. **P:** Entertainment. **U:** Home. **Mov-Ent:** Animation & Cartoons, Television Series. **Acq:** Purchase. **Dist:** Fox Home Entertainment. $39.99.

American Dad: Volume Four 2005 (Unrated)
Fox television's 2005-? animated family parody. Random collection of shows from various seasons starting the spoof "Tearjerker" which has Stan Smith and others taking on Bondian personas to take down an arch villain/failed actor with a diabolical scheme to create a movie so sad people will cry themselves to death. In "Pulling Double Booty" Stan's daughter gets hot and heavy with his CIA body double much to wife Francine's projectile disgust. "Oedipal Panties" takes a moment to celebrate the series' 1,000th vagina joke and "1600 Candles" is Roger's 1,600th birthday. 14 episodes. 411m; DVD. **C:** Voice(s) by Seth MacFarlane; Wendy Schaal; Dee Bradley Baker; Scott Grimes; Rachael MacFarlane; Mike Barker. **A:** Sr. High-Adult. **P:** Entertainment. **U:** Home. **Mov-Ent:** Animation & Cartoons, Television Series. **Acq:** Purchase. **Dist:** Fox Home Entertainment. $39.99.

American Dad! Volume One 2006 (Unrated)
Presents the animated television series that began in 2005 with CIA agent Stan Smith (Seth MacFarlane), who gets overly sensitive when it comes to possible terrorist threats—even if it's only his toast popping up. Stan tries to protect his loving wife Francine (Schaal) and teenage kids Hayley (Rachael MacFarlane) and Steve (Grimes) along with an alien and a German-speaking goldfish. Includes: Stan aides Steve in becoming class president while the Hayley calls on the alien to do her schoolwork, Stan gets bent out of shape when Francine's real estate job nets her a higher income than him, things go awry for Stan at the company picnic, and when Francine won't throw Stan's boss a dinner party he takes on the task with disastrous results. 13 episodes. 292m; DVD. **C:** Wendy Schaal; Dee Bradley Baker; Scott Grimes; Seth MacFarlane; Rachael MacFarlane. **A:** Jr. High-Adult. **P:** Entertainment. **U:** Home. **Mov-Ent:** Television Series, Animation & Cartoons, Family. **Acq:** Purchase. **Dist:** Fox Home Entertainment. $39.98.

American Dad! Volume Seven 2011 (Unrated)
Presents the animated television series that began in 2005 with CIA agent Stan Smith (Seth MacFarlane) who gets overly sensitive when it comes to possible terrorist threats—even if it's only his toast popping up. In "100 A.D.," Jeff and Hayley run away and get married, much to Stan and Francine's displeasure; "Son of Stan" shows Stan and Francine revisiting their parenting style and having a BMX race to determine how to raise Steve. "Best Little Horror House in Langley Falls" finds Stan upset because Buckle's haunted house is scarier than his. "Stan's Fast Food Restaurant" has Roger and Stan facing off against each other in the restaurant business, and "White Rice" focuses on Stan and Francine trying to solve their marriage problems by seeing a hypnotist. 19 episodes. 418m; DVD. **A:**

Adult. **P:** Entertainment. **U:** Home. **Mov-Ent:** Television Series. **Acq:** Purchase. **Dist:** 20th Century Fox Animation. $39.98.

American Dad! Volume Six 2010 (Unrated)
Presents the animated television series that began in 2005 with CIA agent Stan Smith (Seth MacFarlane) who gets overly sensitive when it comes to possible terrorist threats—even if it's only his toast popping up. Stan tries to protect his loving wife Francine (Schaal) and teenage kids Hayley (Rachael MacFarlane) and Steve (Grimes) along with an alien and a German-speaking goldfish. Includes: "In Country...Club" where Steve participates in a war re-enactment; "Moon Over Isla Island," an episode focused on how often Stan takes advantage of Roger; "Home Adrone" features the mishaps of Steve when he is left home alone; "Brains, Brains and Automobiles" has Stan worried about Francine leaving him; and "Man in the Moonbounce" features Stan having an emotional breakdown in an inflatable bouncehouse. 18 episodes. 396m; DVD. **A:** Adult. **P:** Entertainment. **U:** Home. **Acq:** Purchase. **Dist:** $39.98.

American Dad! Volume Three 2007 (Unrated)
Presents the animated television series that began in 2005 with CIA agent Stan Smith (Seth MacFarlane) who gets overly sensitive when it comes to possible terrorist threats—even if it's only his toast popping up. Stan tries to protect his loving wife Francine (Schaal) and teenage kids Hayley (Rachael MacFarlane) and Steve (Grimes) along with an alien and a German-speaking goldfish. Includes the remaining ten episodes from Season 3 and 8 episodes from Season 4. "The Most Adequate Christmas Ever" is not included on this DVD. "Bush Comes to Dinner" shows President Bush smoothing things over between liberal-minded Hayley and her Republican father. In "The Vacation Goo," Francine insists on taking a real vacation after realizing all of her vacation memories were manufactured. "Haylias" reveals that Hayley is brainwashed and "The 42-Year-Old Virgin" reveals that Stan has never actually killed anyone. 18 episodes. 418m; DVD. **A:** Adult. **P:** Entertainment. **U:** Home. **Acq:** Purchase. **Dist:** 20th Century Fox Animation. $39.98.

American Dad! Volume Two 2007 (Unrated)
Presents the animated television series that began in 2005 with CIA agent Stan Smith (Seth MacFarlane) who gets overly sensitive when it comes to possible terrorist threats—even if it's only his toast popping up. Stan tries to protect his loving wife Francine (Schaal) and teenage kids Hayley (Rachael MacFarlane) and Steve (Grimes) along with an alien and a German-speaking goldfish. Includes: the kids get on Francine's nerves with their gun control debate, Francine befriends the neighborhood wives by lying to fit in, and Stan tries to help Steve from being the high school dweeb. 19 episodes. 418m; DVD. **C:** Seth MacFarlane; Wendy Schaal; Dee Bradley Baker; Scott Grimes; Rachael MacFarlane. **A:** Jr. High-Adult. **P:** Entertainment. **U:** Home. **Mov-Ent:** Television Series, Animation & Cartoons, Family. **Acq:** Purchase. **Dist:** Fox Home Entertainment. $39.98.

American Dance Theater 1974
The American Dance Theater performs a dance choreographed to the music of Duke Ellington and excerpts from Lawrence Ferlinghetti's poem "Autobiography." 30m/B/W; VHS, 3/4 U, EJ, Q. **Pr:** WCBS New York; Camera Three Productions. **A:** Sr. High-Adult. **P:** Entertainment. **U:** Institution, SURA. **Fin-Art:** Dance. **Acq:** Duplication, Free Duplication. **Dist:** Camera Three Productions, Inc.

American Dances! 1897-1948: A Collector's Edition of Social Dance in Film 2003
A collection of 60 historical dance film clips overviews the changing traditions in dance through the early part of the century. 75m; VHS. **A:** Adult. **P:** Education. **U:** Home. **Gen-Edu:** Dance, History. **Acq:** Purchase, Rent/Lease. **Dist:** Dancetime Publications. $49.95.

American Documents 1989
A series of American history programs for people who want to review or learn it for the first time. 75m; VHS, 3/4 U. **Pr:** Learning Corporation of America. **A:** Jr. High-Adult. **P:** Education. **U:** Institution, SURA. **Gen-Edu:** History--U.S. **Acq:** Purchase, Rent/Lease. **Dist:** Phoenix Learning Group. $570.00.
Indiv. Titles: 1. Martin Luther King, Jr.: Letter from Birmingham Jail 2. Roosevelt: The Fireside Chats and the New Deal 3. Roosevelt: The Making of a Super Power.

American Documents Series 1976
This patriotic series documents America's history through rare newsreels, archive photographs and excerpts from Hollywood films. Each program is available individually. 55m; VHS. **C:** Narrated by Lowell Thomas; Theodore Bikel; Gloria Swanson; Ossie Davis; Jean Stapleton; William Shatner. **Pr:** Post Newsweek Stations. **A:** Jr. High-Adult. **P:** Education. **U:** Home. **Gen-Edu:** Documentary Films, History--U.S. **Acq:** Purchase. **Dist:** Lions Gate Entertainment Inc. $19.98.
Indiv. Titles: 1. The Age of Ballyhoo 2. Black Shadows on a Silver Screen 3. The Building of the Capitol 4. The Empty Frame 5. How We Got the Vote 6. Inaugural Souvenir 7. Just Around the Corner 8. We All Came to America 9. A Moment in Time 10. Patent Pending 11. The Legendary West 12. Working for the Lord 13. America's Romance with Space.

American Doomsday 2011 (PG)
At the height of the Cold War between the United States and the Soviet Union in the 1960s, the U.S. government developed what was known as its "Doomsday plan," a guide to what each branch of the government would do if the worst happened and the Soviets—or some other nation--attacked. The plan included a command, control, and communications airplane that would serve as Air Force One during the early stages of a crisis, as well as the creation of well-stocked bunkers that would house government officials. Although tensions were high in the 1960s, no parts of the plan were ever implemented until the terrorist attacks on September 11, 2011. 45m; DVD. **A:** Family. **P:** Education, Entertainment. **U:** Home, Institution. **Mov-Ent:** Documentary Films, Terrorism, Politics & Government. **Acq:** Purchase. **Dist:** $19.95.

An American Dream 1966 (Unrated) — ★½
Stephen Rojack (Whitman) says his wife Deborah (Parker) committed suicide but the cops think it's murder and he's the prime suspect. Because the ruthless TV talk show host has been targeting police corruption, they may be prejudiced so Stephen turns to ex-flame Cherry (Leigh) for help. But you know what they say about a woman scorned. Adapted from the Norman Mailer bestseller. 103m; DVD. **C:** Stuart Whitman; Janet Leigh; Eleanor Parker; Barry Sullivan; Lloyd Nolan; Murray Hamilton; J.D. Cannon; George Takei; Directed by Robert Gist; Written by Mann Rubin; Cinematography by Sam Leavitt; Music by Johnny Mandel. **A:** Jr. High-Adult. **P:** Entertainment. **U:** Home. **Mov-Ent:** Crime Drama, Mass Media. **Acq:** Purchase. **Dist:** WarnerArchive.com.

American Dream 1981 (Unrated) — ★★★
A midwestern family leaves the suburbs and moves into a Chicago inner-city neighborhood. Good TV-movie pilot for the short-lived series that was Emmy nominated for direction and writing. 90m; VHS. **C:** Stephen Macht; Karen Carlson; John Karlen; Andrea Smith; John Malkovich; John McIntire; Directed by Mel Damski; Music by Artie Butler. **Pr:** Mace Neufeld. **A:** Family. **P:** Entertainment. **U:** Home. **Mov-Ent:** Family. **Acq:** Purchase. **Dist:** $29.95.

American Dream 1990 — ★★★
Kopple's account of the Hormel labor strike, which devastated the small company town of Austin, Minnesota in the 1980s, makes a compelling documentary of big business versus worker demands. A mixture of interviews with major participants and location footage of the strikers and their families focuses also on the dispute between the local meatpackers and their parent union's lack of support and on the ultimately futile efforts of the union organizers. 100m; VHS, DVD, CC. **C:** Directed by Barbara Kopple; Cinematography by Phil Parmet. **Pr:** Prestige Pictures Releasing Corporation. **A:** Sr. High-Adult. **P:** Education. **U:** Home. **Gen-Edu:** Documentary Films, Sociology, Labor & Unions. **Awds:** Oscars '90: Feature Doc.; Natl. Soc. Film Critics '92: Feature Doc.; Sundance '91: Aud. Award, Grand Jury Prize. **Acq:** Purchase. **Dist:** Baker and Taylor; Miramax Film Corp.; Warner Home Video, Inc. $19.98.

American Dream Contest 1990
The results of a contest among 9- to 17-year-olds to produce a short feature about what's worthwhile in America. 47m; VHS. **C:** Hosted by Michael Landon. **A:** Jr. High-Adult. **P:** Education. **U:** Institution, Home. **Gen-Edu:** Documentary Films. **Acq:** Purchase. **Dist:** Pyramid Media. $95.00.

The American Dream Deferred 1991
Discusses the reactions of African Americans to their denied equality. 30m; VHS. **A:** Adult. **P:** Education. **U:** Institution. **Gen-Edu:** History--U.S. **Acq:** Purchase. **Dist:** RMI Media. $99.00.

The American Dream: Puerto Ricans and Mexicans in New York City 2003
Documentary exploring the differences in the experiences of Latin immigrants from Latin America and the Caribbean. 30m; VHS, DVD. **A:** Sr. High-Adult. **P:** Education. **U:** Home, Institution. **Gen-Edu:** Documentary Films, Immigration. **Acq:** Purchase, Rent/Lease. **Dist:** The Cinema Guild. $195.00.

American Dreamer 1984 (PG) — ★★
A housewife wins a trip to Paris as a prize from a mystery writing contest. Silly from a blow on the head, she begins living the fictional life of her favorite literary adventure. Sporadic comedy with a good cast wandering about courtesy of a clumsy screenplay. 105m; VHS, DVD, CC. **C:** JoBeth Williams; Tom Conti; Giancarlo Giannini; Coral Browne; James Staley; Directed by Rick Rosenthal; Music by Lewis Furey. **Pr:** CBS Films; Warner Bros. **A:** Sr. High-Adult. **P:** Entertainment. **U:** Home. **Mov-Ent:** Comedy--Romantic. **Acq:** Purchase. **Dist:** Movies Unlimited; Alpha Video; Paramount Pictures Corp. $19.98.

American Dreaming: Atlantic City's Casino Gamble 1991
Examines the issues associated with casino gambling and its proposal to cure current urban problems. Winner of the CINE Golden Eagle, 1991; Bronze Apple, National Educational Film & Video Festival, 1991. 57m; VHS. **A:** College-Adult. **P:** Education. **U:** Institution. **Gen-Edu:** Documentary Films, Sociology, Gambling. **Acq:** Purchase, Rent/Lease. **Dist:** Filmakers Library Inc. $295.00.

American Dreams 1983
Features an appreciation for baseball. 56m; VHS, Special order formats. **A:** Family. **P:** Entertainment. **U:** Institution. **Spo-Rec:** Sports--General, Baseball. **Acq:** Purchase, Rent/Lease. **Dist:** First Run/Icarus Films. $390.00.

American Dreams: Season One 2004 (Unrated)
Features the first season of the 2002-2005 television drama about Pryor family as they experience all of the social changes of the 1960s era as the teenaged Meg (Snow) aspires to become an "American Bandstand" dancer to ditch her clean-cut image, mother Helen (O'Grady) returns to school, dad Jack (Verica) grapples with running for city council, JJ's (Estes) football success is tempered by his romantic woes. The two younger siblings also have their struggles as Patty (Ramos) excels in school but has trouble socially while Will (Dampf) has polio surgery. Includes much music of the time performed by modern singers in various roles such as Usher, Ashanti, and Vanessa Carlton. 25 episodes. 1094m; DVD. **C:** Gail O'Grady; Tom Verica; Brittany Snow; Will Estes; Ethan Dampf; Sarah Ramos. **A:** Jr. High-Adult. **P:** Entertainment. **U:** Home. **Mov-Ent:** Television Series, Drama, Music. **Acq:** Purchase. **Dist:** Universal Studios Home Video. $89.98.

American Dreamz 2006 (PG-13) — ★★
Weitz's obvious satire has self-loathing, smarmy Brit Martin Tweed (Grant) hosting the universally popular reality show of the title. This latest version will be highlighted by the appearance of dim-witted, affable American President Staton (Quaid) as a guest judge. He has the time because the country is actually being run by his power-hungry chief of staff (Dafoe). Vying for celebrity status are small-town blonde Sally Kendoo (Moore), who hides her unholy ambitions behind a girl-next-door smile, and Omer (Golzari), a showtune-loving Iraqi who has been chosen as a suicide bomber. Grant and Moore fare best as conniving players who recognize and respect the dark streak in each other. 107m; DVD, Wide. **C:** Hugh Grant; Dennis Quaid; Mandy Moore; Willem Dafoe; Chris Klein; Jennifer Coolidge; Marcia Gay Harden; John Cho; Sam Golzari; Seth Meyers; Judy Greer; Shohreh Aghdashloo; Bernie (Bernard) White; Tony Yalda; Marley Shelton; Lawrence Pressman; Noureen DeWulf; Directed by Paul Weitz; Written by Paul Weitz; Cinematography by Robert Elswit; Music by Stephen Trask. **Pr:** Paul Weitz; Rodney Liber; Andrew Miano; Depth of Field; Universal. **A:** Jr. High-Adult. **P:** Entertainment. **U:** Home. **L:** English. **Mov-Ent:** Presidency, Satire & Parody, Terrorism. **Acq:** Purchase. **Dist:** Movies Unlimited; Alpha Video.

American Drive-In 1988 (Unrated) — ★
A guffaw-laden teenage comedy about a suburban drive-in theatre. The movie being shown at the theater looks suspiciously like the director's previous film, "Hard Rock Zombies." Never released theatrically, for good reason. 92m. **C:** Emily Longstreth; Joel Bennett; Giancarlo Giannini; Pat Kirton; Rhonda Snow; Directed by Krishna Shah. **Pr:** Patel/Shah Film Company. **A:** Sr. High-Adult. **P:** Entertainment. **U:** Home. **Mov-Ent:** Satire & Parody, Sex & Sexuality, Adolescence. **Acq:** Purchase. **Dist:** Lions Gate Television Corp. $79.98.

American Eagle 1990 (R) — ★½
A veteran goes crazy and seeks sadistic, bloody revenge on his war buddies. Now his war buddies are the only ones who can stop him. 92m; VHS, DVD. **C:** Asher Brauner; Robert F. Lyons; Vernon Wells; Kai Baker; Directed by Robert J. Smawley. **Pr:** Vidmark Entertainment. **A:** College-Adult. **P:** Entertainment. **U:** Home. **Mov-Ent:** Veterans. **Acq:** Purchase. **Dist:** CinemaNow Inc. $89.95.

American East 2007 (R) — ★★
Arab-American Moustafa is having a very bad day. He has problems with his children and sister and the customers at his rundown L.A. diner insist on arguing about politics. Then when he goes to pick up his cousin at the airport, Moustafa is detained and questioned by an FBI agent. His one dream is to open a classy Middle Eastern restaurant with his Jewish pal Sam (Shalhoub), but no one believes he can do that either. 110m; DVD. **C:** Sayed Badreya; Tony Shalhoub; Anthony Azizi; Kais Nashef; Amanda Detmer; Erik Avari; Ray Wise; Tay Blessey; Sarah Shahi; Directed by Hesham Issawi; Written by Sayed Badreya; Hesham Issawi; Cinematography by Michael G. Wojciechowski; Music by Tony Humecke. **A:** Sr. High-Adult. **P:** Entertainment. **U:** Home. **Mov-Ent:** Federal Bureau of Investigation (FBI), Arab-America. **Acq:** Purchase. **Dist:** Fox Home Entertainment.

American Empire 1942 (Unrated) — ★★½
Two Civil War heroes struggle to build a cattle empire in Texas and are hampered by rustlers, one of whom was their partner. A fine, veteran cast and a tight script keep things moving, including the cattle. 82m/B/W; VHS, DVD, 3/4 U, Special order formats. **C:** Preston Foster; Richard Dix; Frances Gifford; Leo Carrillo; Directed by William McGann. **Pr:** Harry R. Sherman; United Artists. **A:** Family. **P:** Entertainment. **U:** Home. **Mov-Ent:** Western, Action-Adventure. **Acq:** Purchase. **Dist:** Grapevine Video; Gotham Distributing Corp. $16.95.

The American English in Modern Situations Series 1978
This series for English as a second language students has international and American students portraying common social situations. Programs available individually. 11m; VHS, 3/4 U, Special order formats. **Pr:** Paul S. Karr Productions. **A:** Sr. High-College. **P:** Education. **U:** Institution, CCTV, Home, SURA. **Gen-Edu:** Language Arts. **Acq:** Purchase, Rent/Lease. **Dist:** Alpine Film & Video Exchange.
Indiv. Titles: 1. Meeting New People 2. Eating in New Places 3. Classroom Conduct and Culture 4. Business Beginnings: Buying and Selling 5. Conversation Skills in American Culture 6. Misunderstandings and Apologies 7. Adjusting to a New Community 8. More Understanding, Please 9. Legal & Medical Emergencies 10. Effective Study Skills for ESL Writers 11. More Efficient Reading for ESL Readers 12. American Patterns of Writing for ESL Writers.

The American Entrepreneur Today 1991
A 14-part course focuses on the creativity and dedication needed to making a good idea work. Six successful entrepreneurs offer insight into their business success. Course text is "New Venture Creation: Entrepreneurship in the 1990s" by Jeffry A. Timmons. 30m; VHS. **A:** College-Adult. **P:** Education. **U:** Institution. **Bus-Ind:** Business. **Acq:** Purchase. **Dist:** GPN Educational Media. $785.00.

The American Experience 1990
A wide-ranging anthology on the American scene, focusing on government, the economy, and the ups and downs in the lives of ordinary citizens. 60m; VHS, CC, 3/4 U. **Pr:** PBS Video. **A:** Family. **P:** Education. **U:** Institution, CCTV, CATV, Home. **Gen-**

Edu: Documentary Films, Sociology, Politics & Government. **Acq:** Purchase. **Dist:** PBS Home Video. $59.95.
Indiv. Titles: 1. The 54th Colored Infantry 2. Ballad of a Mountain Man 3. Coney Island 4. The Crash of 1929 5. Demon Rum 6. Do You Mean There Are Still Real Cowboys? 7. Eric Sevareid's "Not So Wild a Dream" 8. A Family Gathering 9. Forever Baseball 10. Geronimo and the Apache Resistance 11. God Bless America and Poland, Too 12. The Great Air Race of 1924 13. The Great San Francisco Earthquake 14. The Great War - 1918 15. Ida B. Wells - A Passion for Justice 16. Indians, Outlaws and Angie Debo 17. Insanity on Trial 18. The Iron Road 19. Journey to America 20. Lindbergh 21. Los Mineros 22. Mr. Sears' Catalogue 23. Nixon 24. Radio Bikini 25. The Radio Priest 26. Roots of Resistance - A Story of the Underground Railroad 27. The Satellite Sky 28. The Sins of Our Mothers 29. That Rhythm, Those Blues 30. The World That Moses Built.

American Experience: 1964 2014 (Unrated)
While the entire 1960s were a tumultuous time in America, perhaps no year was wilder than 1964. In the wake of President John F. Kennedy's assassination in November 1963, the country was thrust into a period of immense social changes. New president Lyndon B. Johnson presided over the rise of the civil rights movement in Harlem and in the South, as three civil rights workers were murdered in Mississippi. This documentary also covers the rise of Barry Goldwater's conservative views, the enormous growth of the youth counterculture on campuses across the country, the birth of the Beatles, and much more. Includes a timeline, photo gallery, further reading list, and more. 120m; DVD. **A:** Family. **P:** Entertainment. **U:** Home. **Mov-Ent**: Documentary Films, Civil Rights, Presidency. **Acq:** Purchase. **Dist:** WGBH/Boston. $24.99.

The American Experience: A Brilliant Madness 2002
Biography of John Nash, a mathematical genius whose proof written at age 20 became the foundation for modern economic theory. His triumph was overshadowed by a descent into paranoid schizophrenia, as he claimed to be a special messenger for aliens that were communicating though him. Includes interviews with Nash himself, his wife Alicia, friends, colleagues and experts in game theory and mental illness. ?m; DVD. **A:** Sr. High-Adult. **P:** Education. **U:** Home. **Gen-Edu**: Biography, Mathematics. **Acq:** Purchase. **Dist:** WGBH/Boston. $19.95.

American Experience: A Class Apart 2009 (PG)
In 1954, Hispanic attorneys Gus Garcia and Carlos Cardena argued before the U.S. Supreme Court and forever changed the lives of Mexican-Americans. In the landmark case Hernandez v. Texas, the pair argued that Mexican-Americans lived as "a class apart" in the United States and that, as a result, Pedro Hernandez, the defendant in a murder trial in Texas, could not receive a fair trial if he was tried by an all Anglo jury instead of a true jury of his peers. When the Supreme Court ruled that Hernandez must receive a new trial, it helped put an end to the Jim Crow-style laws facing Hispanics in America. Includes a photo gallery, further reading list, bonus video footage, teacher's resources, and more. 60m; DVD. **A:** Family. **P:** Education, Entertainment. **U:** Home, Institution. **Mov-Ent**: Documentary Films, Law, History--U.S. **Acq:** Purchase. **Dist:** WGBH/Boston. $19.99.

American Experience: Abraham and Mary Lincoln: A House Divided 2001
Examines the family life of President Lincoln, who experienced both the fracturing of the union as well as division in his own home when his aristocratic Southern-born wife remained loyal to her slave owner father, as did her two brothers who fought for the Confederates. 360m; DVD. **A:** Adult. **P:** Education. **U:** Home. **Gen-Edu**: Biography, Presidency, History--U.S. **Acq:** Purchase. **Dist:** WGBH/Boston. $59.95.

American Experience: Alexander Hamilton 2007
Examines the life of Alexander Hamilton, who served as secretary of the treasury during the nation's expansion and helped turn the country into an industrial powerhouse. Unfortunately, his stubbornness, overzealous candor, and arrogance were the keys to eventual scandal and political demise. 120m; DVD; Closed Captioned. **A:** Adult. **P:** Education. **U:** Home. **Gen-Edu**: Biography, Politics & Government, History--U.S. **Acq:** Purchase. **Dist:** WGBH/Boston. $24.95.

The American Experience: Amelia Earhart: The Price of Courage 199?
Portrait of the first female aviator to cross the continent and the Atlantic solo nonstop, and the first to earn the Distinguished Flying Cross. Details Earhart's life from her first flight to her mysterious disappearance somewhere over the Pacific. 60m; VHS, CC. **C:** Narrated by Kathy Bates. **A:** Sr. High-Adult. **P:** Entertainment. **U:** Home. **Gen-Edu**: Aeronautics, Women. **Acq:** Purchase. **Dist:** Signals Video. $19.95.

American Experience: America and the Holocaust 1995
Examines the anti-Semitism experienced in the U.S. as the government suppressed information about the horrors of Kristallnacht in 1938 and struggled with political, economic, and social problems of the Depression. 85m; VHS, DVD; Closed Captioned. **A:** Sr. High-Adult. **P:** Education. **U:** Home. **Gen-Edu**: Documentary Films, History--U.S., Holocaust. **Acq:** Purchase. **Dist:** WGBH/Boston. $19.95.

The American Experience: America and the Holocaust: Deceit and Indifference 1994
Depicts the U.S.'s slow response to the victimization of Jews in Nazi Europe through the story of a Jewish boy whose efforts to bring his family to America at the start of World War II are stalled by red tape and anti-Semitism. Includes commentary by government officials and historians, texts of letters and State Department documents, and footage from newsreels and archival films. 90m; VHS, CC. **C:** Narrated by Hal Linden; Directed by Marty Ostrow. **Pr:** Jean-Jacques Annaud. **A:** Sr. High-Adult. **P:** Education. **U:** Institution, Home. **Gen-Edu**: Holocaust, World War Two, History--U.S. **Acq:** Purchase. **Dist:** PBS Home Video. $69.95.

American Experience: Annie Oakley 2006
Examines the legend and contradictions of the sharpshooter, who was the star attraction of Buffalo Bill's Wild West Show. 60m; DVD. **A:** Jr. High-Adult. **P:** Entertainment. **U:** Home. **Gen-Edu**: Documentary Films, Biography: Show Business. **Acq:** Purchase. **Dist:** Paramount Pictures Corp.

American Experience: Ansel Adams: A Documentary Film 2002
Archival footage, photos, dramatic readings of Ansel's own writings, plus interviews with photographers, historians, curators, naturalists, and Adams's family, friends, and colleagues provide an intimate and intellectual portrait of this visionary pioneer and ardent environmentalist. 90m; DVD. **A:** Adult. **P:** Education. **U:** Home. **Gen-Edu**: Biography, Photography. **Acq:** Purchase. **Dist:** WGBH/Boston. $24.95.

American Experience: Around the World in 72 Days 1997
Biographer and historian interviews plus turn-of-the-century photographs and engravings examine the life and career of Nellie Bly, including her journey around the world in 72 days to beat Jules Verne's fictional escapade, her 10 days "undercover" in an insane asylum doing research for an expose, and her clever job-hunting ruse. 56m; VHS, DVD; Closed Captioned. **A:** Jr. High-Adult. **P:** Education. **U:** Home. **Gen-Edu**: Documentary Films, Women. **Acq:** Purchase. **Dist:** WGBH/Boston. $24.95.

American Experience: Bataan Rescue 2003
Recounts the daring rescue mission by an elite force of Army Rangers during WWII to rescue more than 500 American prisoners of war who had been held in brutal captivity in a Japanese prison camp in the Philippines. 60m; VHS. **A:** Sr. High-Adult. **P:** Education. **U:** Home. **Gen-Edu**: Military History, World War Two. **Acq:** Purchase. **Dist:** WGBH/Boston. $24.95.

The American Experience: Becoming an American 1975
This show presents the experiences of three American families to illustrate the process of change and assimilation which all immigrants face. 23m; VHS, 3/4 U. **Pr:** Forum. **A:** Jr. High-Sr. High. **P:** Education. **U:** Institution, SURA. **Gen-Edu**: Immigration. **Acq:** Purchase. **Dist:** Phoenix Learning Group.

American Experience: Billy the Kid 2012 (PG)
Although he was only 21-years-old when he died, the young gunslinger known as Billy the Kid was already one of the most famous—and hunted—outlaws in the American Southwest. Born Henry McCarty in New York City, he moved west with his mother and was orphaned when she died in New Mexico in 1874. Quickly falling in with a gang of gamblers, McCarty changed his name to William H. Bonney—also known as Billy the Kid—after he killed a man in a bar fight. He formed a group known as "The Regulators," who helped defend the land owned by rancher John Tunstall during the famous Lincoln County War of the late 1870s. Revered by the local Hispanic community for his Robin Hood-like ways, Billy was gunned down and killed by sheriff Pat Garrett on July 14, 1881. Includes a timeline, photo gallery, teacher's resources, and more. 60m; DVD. **A:** Family. **P:** Education, Entertainment. **U:** Home, Institution. **Mov-Ent**: Documentary Films, History--U.S., Gambling. **Acq:** Purchase. **Dist:** WGBH/Boston. $19.99.

American Experience: Buffalo Bill's Wild West 2008
Documents the career of master showman William Cody, who brought the Wild West to life in 1883 with his "Buffalo Bill's Wild West" show, which toured for three decades and performed for enthusiastic crowds throughout the U.S. and Europe. 60m; DVD; Closed Captioned. **A:** Adult. **P:** Education. **U:** Home. **Gen-Edu**: Biography, Western, History--U.S. **Acq:** Purchase. **Dist:** WGBH/Boston. $24.95.

American Experience: Building the Alaska Highway 2005
Documents the American soldiers who battled mud, muskeg, mosquitoes, ice, snow, and bitter cold in 1942 to forge through primeval forest and build a 1,520-mile road across one of the harshest landscapes in the world. 60m; DVD. **A:** Jr. High-Adult. **P:** Education. **U:** Home. **Gen-Edu**: Documentary Films, History--U.S. **Acq:** Purchase. **Dist:** WGBH/Boston. $29.95.

American Experience: Chicago: City of the Century 2003
History of Chicago's development from swampy fur-trading frontier town to mass metropolis of innovation and ingenuity with all its hardships, architectural achievements, political corruption, and labor upheavals. 3-disc set. 270m; VHS, DVD; Closed Captioned. **A:** Jr. High-Adult. **P:** Education. **U:** Home. **Gen-Edu**: Documentary Films, Cities & Towns, History--U.S. **Acq:** Purchase. **Dist:** WGBH/Boston. $79.95.

American Experience: Citizen King 2004
Friends, movement associates, journalists, policemen, and historians reflect on the last five years of Martin Luther King's life as he ignored political cautions and moved beyond the civil rights movement in an attempt to "transform and re-structure the whole of American society." 120m; DVD. **A:** Jr. High-Adult. **P:** Education. **U:** Home. **Gen-Edu**: Biography, Civil Rights, Black Culture. **Acq:** Purchase. **Dist:** WGBH/Boston. $24.95.

American Experience: Clinton 2012 (Unrated)
A look back at the life and presidency of William Jefferson Clinton, elected president in 1992 and reelected in 1996. After enduring a difficult childhood that saw his parents divorce, Clinton worked his way up through local and state politics in Arkansas before winning the Democratic presidential nomination in 1992. As president, Clinton alternated between remarkable achievements, such as balancing the federal budget, and major scandals, including his sordid affair with White House intern Monica Lewinsky, all while dealing with harsh partisan politics and the increasing threat terrorism posed to the United States. Includes bonus video footage and an interview with Clinton. 240m; DVD. **A:** Family. **P:** Education, Entertainment. **U:** Home, Institution. **Mov-Ent**: Documentary Films, Presidency, Politics & Government. **Acq:** Purchase. **Dist:** WGBH/Boston. $19.99.

American Experience: Custer's Last Stand 2012 (Unrated)
This documentary explores the infamous events that unfolded in the Montana Territory on June 25-26, 1876, that became known as "Custer's Last Stand." Over the course of those two days, Civil War hero General George Armstrong Custer led the Seventh Cavalry Regiment into battle against a group of Cheyenne, Lakota, and Arapaho warriors. Badly outgunned, the group of warriors managed to trap Custer and his men along the Little Bighorn River and preceded to kill 268 of the 700 U.S. soldiers, including Custer. It was easily the worst defeat suffered by American forces during the Great Sioux War of 1876, and the circumstances surrounding the massacre captured the attention of an engrossed American public and became a larger-than-life myth that remains one of the iconic events from America's westward expansion. Includes a timeline, further reading list, photo gallery, teacher's resources, and a map. 120m; DVD. **A:** Family. **P:** Education, Entertainment. **U:** Home, Institution. **Mov-Ent**: Documentary Films, History--U.S., Native Americans. **Acq:** Purchase. **Dist:** WGBH/Boston. $19.99.

American Experience: D-Day 1994
Chronicles the historic D-Day landings in Normandy, utilizing archival footage, interviews, and narrative history. 60m; VHS. **A:** Adult. **P:** Education. **U:** Home. **Gen-Edu**: France, World War Two. **Acq:** Purchase. **Dist:** PBS Home Video. $69.95.

American Experience: Daughter from Danang 2003
As part of an evacuation program known as "Operation Babylift," Mai Thi Kim sent her 7-year old daughter (whose father was an American naval officer) over to the United States in 1975 to be adopted by a woman in Tennessee and raised as American. Program documents the tense mother and daughter reunion twenty-two years later in Danang. 90m; DVD. **A:** Sr. High-Adult. **P:** Education. **U:** Home. **Gen-Edu**: Biography, Adoption, Vietnam War. **Acq:** Purchase. **Dist:** WGBH/Boston. $24.95.

The American Experience: Demon Rum ????
Analyzes motivating factors behind the 18th Amendment and its repeal. Discusses temperance, police raids, whiskey runs, Mafia involvement, and more. 57m; VHS; Closed Captioned. **A:** Sr. High. **P:** Education. **U:** Institution. **Gen-Edu**: History--U.S., U.S. States. **Acq:** Purchase. **Dist:** Zenger Media. $49.00.

American Experience: Dinosaur Wars 2011 (Unrated)
In post-Civil War America, the American West was home to perhaps one of the largest collections of dinosaur fossils in the world. As scientists explored the West, two American paleontologists—Othniel Charles Marsh and Edward Drinker Cope—rose to the forefront and uncovered hundreds of bones and fossils as they put American science on the map. Unfortunately, the two men were incredibly competitive, and their battle to be the leading American scientists of that era left them alone and almost penniless. This documentary tells the story of the personal battle between the two men, and also how their work provided important evidence to back up Charles Darwin's famous "On the Origin of Species." Includes a timeline, primary resource materials, a photo gallery, map, and more. 60m; DVD. **A:** Family. **P:** Education, Entertainment. **U:** Home, Institution. **Mov-Ent**: Documentary Films, Dinosaurs, Science. **Acq:** Purchase. **Dist:** WGBH/Boston. $19.99.

American Experience: Dolley Madison 2010 (Unrated)
This biography of Dolley Madison, the wife of the fourth U.S. president James Madison, is widely recognized as the initial "First Lady" of American politics, as her leadership and political skills helped solidify Washington's role as the American capitol and also defined how the wives of future presidents would act while their spouses were in office. As First Lady, Madison opened up the President's House to the public while also holding weekly socials intended solely for Washington's elite so that they would have somewhere to meet and discuss important issues of the day in a bipartisan setting. When she passed away in 1849, Madison was honored by the largest state funeral ever held for a woman. Includes bonus video, a further reading list, teacher's resources, and more. 90m; DVD. **A:** Family. **P:** Education, Entertainment. **U:** Home, Institution. **Mov-Ent**: Documentary Films, Presidency, History--U.S. **Acq:** Purchase. **Dist:** WGBH/Boston. $19.99.

American Experience: Earth Days 2010 (Unrated)
In the United States, Earth Day and other environmental events are now widely celebrated, but that was not always the case. It was not until the early 1950s and 1960s that pioneers such as politician Stewart Udall, Whole Earth Catalog founder Stewart Brand, author Rachel Carson, and others helped spread the idea to the general public that man had a drastic impact on the

environment and that guidelines needed to be put in place to protect it. The result of that early movement was a three-year period from 1972 to 1974 that saw the passage of the Clean Water Act, Endangered Species Act, and several other important pieces of environmental legislation. Includes a timeline, further resources, a photo gallery, a further reading list, and more. 120m; DVD. **A:** Family. **P:** Education, Entertainment. **U:** Home, Institution. **Mov-Ent:** Documentary Films, Ecology & Environment, History--U.S. **Acq:** Purchase. **Dist:** WGBH/Boston. $19.99.

The American Experience: Edison's Miracle of Light ????
Examines the competition between Edison' General Electric Company and current distribution systems from George Westinghouse and Nikola Tesla. 60m; VHS; Closed Captioned. **A:** Jr. High-Sr. High. **P:** Education. **U:** Institution, Home. **Gen-Edu:** Inventors & Inventions, Industry & Industrialists, History--U.S. **Acq:** Purchase. **Dist:** Zenger Media. $19.95.

The American Experience: Eisenhower 19??
Two-part documentary on America's WWII soldier/leader and cold war President. Based on declassified Eisenhower records and featuring extensive archival footage, excerpts from Ike's letters and diaries, and interviews with historians, friends, and family. 150m; VHS. **A:** Sr. High-Adult. **P:** Education. **U:** Home. **Gen-Edu:** Biography, Presidency, Armed Forces--U.S. **Acq:** Purchase. **Dist:** Signals Video. $39.95.

American Experience: Eleanor Roosevelt 200?
Explores the private life of the former First Lady who worked as an advocate for the disadvantaged, influenced social policies, and fought for the first human rights international charter. 150m; DVD; Closed Captioned. **A:** Adult. **P:** Education. **U:** Home. **Gen-Edu:** Biography, Presidency, Women. **Acq:** Purchase. **Dist:** WGBH/Boston. $24.95.

American Experience: Emma Goldman 2004
Examines the life of Emma Goldman, a Russian immigrant and expatriate who was noted to be the sponsor of anarchy and revolution, and deemed "the most dangerous woman in America." 90m; DVD; Closed Captioned. **A:** Jr. High-Adult. **P:** Education. **U:** Home. **Gen-Edu:** Biography, Women. **Acq:** Purchase. **Dist:** WGBH/Boston. $29.95.

American Experience: Eugene O'Neill 2006
Director Ric Burns profiles the American playwright's life and award-winning career, from his troubled childhood until his death at age 65. ?m; DVD. **A:** Sr. High-Adult. **P:** Entertainment. **U:** Home. **Fin-Art:** Documentary Films. **Acq:** Purchase. **Dist:** Paramount Pictures Corp.

American Experience: Eyes on the Prize: America's Civil Rights Years 1954-1965 2009 (Unrated)
This award-winning documentary covers the grassroots civil rights movement in the 1950s and 1960s that transformed the United States. Divided into six episodes, the series covers the very beginnings of the movement, including Rosa Parks historic refusal to give up her bus seat to a white passenger in Montgomery, Alabama, and chronicles every major event, culminating in the passage of the Voting Rights Act and more. The shows strive to tell the story from the perspective of the men and women who lived through the harrowing struggle and features interviews with those who took part in key parts of the movement, as well as readings of important source materials. Episodes include: "Awakenings (1954-1956)," "Fighting Back (1957-1962)," "Ain't Scared of Your Jails (1960-1961)," "No Easy Walk (1961-1963)," "Mississippi: Is This America? (1962-1964)," and "Bridge to Freedom (1965)." Narrated by Julian Bond. 360m; DVD. **A:** Family. **P:** Education, Entertainment. **U:** Home, Institution. **Mov-Ent:** Documentary Films, Civil Rights, History--U.S. **Acq:** Purchase. **Dist:** WGBH/Boston. $29.99.

The American Experience: FDR 1994
A warts and all portrayal of the 32nd U.S. President Franklin Delano Roosevelt, from his leadership during the Depression through WWII, discusses his political career as well as his polio and his marital infidelity. Includes archival film footage, home movies, and audio clips. On four cassettes. 270m; VHS. **A:** Jr. High-Adult. **P:** Education. **U:** Home, Institution. **Gen-Edu:** Documentary Films, Presidency. **Acq:** Purchase. **Dist:** Shanachie Entertainment; Zenger Media.

American Experience: Fidel Castro 2005
Relatives, childhood friends, rebel leaders, Bay of Pigs veterans, human rights activists, and journalists discuss the Cuban leader, who remained resilient despite CIA assassination attempts, ongoing U.S. hostility, an economic embargo, and an invasion. 120m; DVD. **A:** Adult. **P:** Education. **U:** Home. **Gen-Edu:** Biography, Military History. **Acq:** Purchase. **Dist:** WGBH/Boston. $24.95.

American Experience: Fly Girls 2006
Profiles women who took the opportunity to become the first female military pilots to fly for the United States during World War II. 56m; DVD. **A:** Jr. High-Adult. **P:** Entertainment. **U:** Home. **Gen-Edu:** Documentary Films. **Acq:** Purchase. **Dist:** WGBH/Boston.

American Experience: Freedom Riders 2011 (Unrated)
Based in part on Raymond Arsenault's book "Freedom Riders: 1961 and the Struggle for Racial Justice," this documentary tells the story of the brave college students willing to buy bus tickets to the Deep South to help African Americans fight for the civil rights they deserved. Known as Freedom Riders, the young men and women who made the trip south helped show the American public just how horrible segregation was and thus helped bring about a change in the way many people viewed

the struggle for equality. 120m; DVD. **A:** Family. **P:** Education, Entertainment. **U:** Home, Institution. **Mov-Ent:** Documentary Films, Civil Rights, History--U.S. **Acq:** Purchase. **Dist:** WGBH/Boston. $19.99.

The American Experience: George Washington: The Man Who Wouldn't Be King 1992
PBS presentation that uses battle reenactments, interviews, and visits to historical sites to disspell myths about George Washington, General and U.S. President. Offering information that points out his flaws and great strengths, this documentary paints a very human portrait of an important historical figure. 60m; VHS. **A:** Jr. High-Sr. High. **P:** Education. **U:** Institution. **Gen-Edu:** Biography, Presidency, History--U.S. **Acq:** Purchase. **Dist:** PBS Home Video. $59.95.

The American Experience: Geronimo and the Apache Resistance 199?
Chronicles the Apache resistance led by Geronimo in 1886 to preserve their ancestral land. Part of the PBS American Indian series. 60m; VHS. **A:** Family. **P:** Education. **U:** Institution. **Gen-Edu:** Native Americans, History--U.S. **Acq:** Purchase. **Dist:** PBS Home Video.

American Experience: God in America 2010 (Unrated)
The producers of American Experience and Frontline combine to provide a look back at 400 years of the religious experience in the United States, covering the arrival of the Pilgrims and other European settlers up to the 2008 Presidential election. Over the course of six hours, the series explains how the religious dissidents who helped found this country ensured that the ideas of liberty and individualism existed together with strong religious faith, and that religious freedom would always be part of the American experience. Also covered is the importance of religion in social reform and in the political arena. Episodes include: "A New Adam," "A New Eden," "A Nation Reborn," "A New Light," "Soul of a Nation," "Of God and Caesar." Narrated by Campbell Scott. 360m; DVD. **A:** Family. **P:** Education, Entertainment. **U:** Home, Institution. **Mov-Ent:** Documentary Films, History--U.S., Religion. **Acq:** Purchase. **Dist:** WGBH/Boston. $24.99.

American Experience: Golden Gate Bridge 2004
Overviews the design, political finagling and environmental challenges of constructing one of the longest suspension bridges in the world, completed in 1937. 60m; VHS, DVD; Closed Captioned. **A:** Jr. High-Adult. **P:** Education. **U:** Home. **Gen-Edu:** Documentary Films, Architecture, History--U.S. **Acq:** Purchase. **Dist:** WGBH/Boston. $29.95.

American Experience: Grand Central 2008
Explains how a tragedy on January 8, 1902, when two commuter trains crashed in a NYC tunnel, birthed Grand Central Terminal, which by 1947 had over 65 million people travel through it. 60m; DVD; Closed Captioned. **A:** Adult. **P:** Education. **U:** Home. **Gen-Edu:** Documentary Films, Trains. **Acq:** Purchase. **Dist:** WGBH/Boston. $24.95.

The American Experience: Hawaii's Last Queen 1998
Depicts the life of Lili'uokalani, the charismatic leader of the Hawaiian people who was forced to surrender her kingdom at gunpoint in 1893. Also describes the epidemics and alcoholism that nearly destroyed the Hawaiian islanders, and the missionary fervor that nearly destroyed their culture. 60m; VHS; Closed Captioned. **A:** Family. **P:** Education. **U:** Home. **Gen-Edu:** History, History--U.S., U.S. States. **Acq:** Purchase. **Dist:** PBS Home Video. $19.98.

American Experience: Henry Ford 2013 (Unrated)
A biography of the man who did more to change the industrial landscape in the United States than any other man by creating the assembly line and, with it, the modern American auto. Born on a farm, Henry Ford went on to create the first industrial assembly line for use in producing the company's iconic Model T automobile. In doing so, he had a huge influence in how life was lived in America, affecting everything from labor relations to how people worked and traveled. Includes a timeline, further reading list, photo gallery, and more. 120m; DVD. **A:** Family. **P:** Education, Entertainment. **U:** Home, Institution. **Mov-Ent:** Documentary Films, Biography: Politics, Presidency. **Acq:** Purchase. **Dist:** WGBH/Boston. $19.99.

American Experience: Hijacked 2006
Producer Ilan Ziv interviews Popular Front for the Liberation of Palestine (P.F.L.P.) militant leaders that carried out the hijacking of four commercial airplanes in September 1970, attempting to bring attention to the Palestinian cause and secure release of their comrades. Crew members and passengers also relay their experiences. Though none of the 600 hostages was killed, all four planes were blown up and a door was opened for militant groups to use civilians as pawns in their terrorist endeavors. 60m; DVD; Closed Captioned. **A:** Adult. **P:** Education. **U:** Home. **Gen-Edu:** Documentary Films, Terrorism, History. **Acq:** Purchase. **Dist:** WGBH/Boston. $19.95.

American Experience: Hoover Dam 1999
Presents the dramatic endeavor of an ambitious engineer who took an army of unemployed workers and molded them into a creative force that constructed a dam rising 700 feet above the Colorado River. 56m; DVD; Closed Captioned. **A:** Jr. High-Adult. **P:** Education. **U:** Home. **Gen-Edu:** Agriculture, History--U.S. **Acq:** Purchase. **Dist:** WGBH/Boston. $19.95.

The American Experience: In the White Man's Image 1991
Explores the cultural genocide that occured in the Carlisle School for Indian Students which impacted on generations of Native Americans. At the school, students were taught to read

and write English, and were placed in uniforms and drilled like soldiers in order to "civilize" them. Includes interviews with former students. 51m; VHS, 1C, 3/4 U. **Pr:** Native American Public Broadcasting Consortium; Nebraska Educational Television Network. **A:** Sr. High-Adult. **P:** Education. **U:** Institution, SURA. **Gen-Edu:** Documentary Films, Native Americans, Education. **Acq:** Purchase, Rent/Lease. **Dist:** Vision Maker Media. $59.95.

American Experience: Influenza 1918: The Worst Epidemic in American History 1999
Examines the epidemic that raged as the nation mobilized for war, killing 675,000 people of all ages during 1918 then leaving as suddenly as it came. 60m; VHS, DVD; Closed Captioned. **A:** Sr. High-Adult. **P:** Education. **U:** Home. **Gen-Edu:** Documentary Films, Diseases, History--U.S. **Acq:** Purchase. **Dist:** WGBH/Boston. $24.95.

American Experience: Into the Deep--America, Whaling, & the World 2010
Historical documentary on the lives of American whalers, and on the whaling industry's role in the country. 120m; DVD. **A:** Family. **P:** Education. **U:** Home. **L:** English. **Gen-Edu:** Documentary Films, Whales, Television. **Acq:** Purchase. **Dist:** $29.99 24.99.

American Experience: Jesse James 2005 (Unrated)
Jesse James is a true American paradox. Viewed by many as an American version of Robin Hood, a poor Civil War veteran who struggled to survive by robbing from the rich and sharing his "profits" with other poor people. In reality, however, he was little more than a brutal outlaw who used violence whenever it suited him and who was an equal opportunity robber of both the rich and poor; no matter who he robbed, he always made sure he got to keep the lion's share of the profits instead of sharing it with others. This documentary attempts to dispel the popular myths and paint a portrait of the real Jesse James. Includes a further reading list, primary resource materials, and more. 60m; DVD. **A:** Family. **P:** Education, Entertainment. **U:** Home, Institution. **Mov-Ent:** Documentary Films, Civil War, History--U.S. **Acq:** Purchase. **Dist:** WGBH/Boston. $17.99.

American Experience: Jesse Owens 2012 (Unrated)
With the entire world watching, Jesse Owens became perhaps the most famous athlete in the world when he almost single-handedly made a mockery of Adolf Hitler's ideas regarding racial superiority while competing at the 1936 Olympics in Berlin. At the young age of 22, the son of a poor sharecropper became a worldwide hero when he claimed four gold medals in track and field events, all while enduring racial slurs from the largely German audience. Unfortunately, Owens learned that the U.S. also still had plenty of work to do when it came to race relations, as he quickly discovered that even four gold medals didn't earn him a seat at the front of a bus or at a white's only lunch counter. Includes a further reading list, teacher's resources, bonus video footage, and more. 60m; DVD. **A:** Family. **P:** Education, Entertainment. **U:** Home, Institution. **Mov-Ent:** Documentary Films, Sports Documentary, Civil Rights. **Acq:** Purchase. **Dist:** WGBH/Boston. $9.99.

American Experience: JFK 2013 (Unrated)
With his presidency and his life cut tragically short by an assassin's bullet, President John F. Kennedy is revered as one of the most beloved—albeit controversial—political figures of the 20th century. That reverence has led some political scientists to wonder if the memory of the charismatic leader matches his actual accomplishments, or if the way he was killed has led to the memory of what he accomplished failing to match what he really did while in office. As this documentary shows, there is no doubt that he did lead the nation through the Cuban missile crisis and that he was preparing landmark legislation regarding civil rights and a sweeping tax cut when Lee Harvey Oswald ended his life in Dallas, TX, in November 1963. Includes a timeline, teacher's resources, a further reading list, and more. 240m; DVD. **A:** Family. **P:** Education, Entertainment. **U:** Home, Institution. **Mov-Ent:** Documentary Films, Presidency, Politics & Government. **Acq:** Purchase. **Dist:** WGBH/Boston. $29.99.

American Experience: Jimmy Carter 2002 (PG)
In 1976, Jimmy Carter was elected President of the United States, serving just one term before being soundly defeated by Ronald Reagan in 1980. Instead of letting that defeat define him, Carter became one of the most respected international statesmen in the world, leading humanitarian projects and consistently working to resolve international conflicts wherever they arose. In 2002, he was rewarded for his efforts when he was named the winner of the Nobel Prize for Peace. The video includes interviews with members of his political team and those who have worked with him in the years following his presidency. Includes bonus video footage and several essays about Carter. 180m; DVD. **A:** Family. **P:** Education, Entertainment. **U:** Home, Institution. **Mov-Ent:** Documentary Films, Presidency, History--U.S. **Acq:** Purchase. **Dist:** WGBH/Boston. $17.99.

American Experience: John and Abigail 2006
Reviews letters exchanged by the second president and his wife, portraying a glimpse into the tumultuous revolutionary era and a marriage of true companions. 120m; VHS, DVD; Closed Captioned. **A:** Adult. **P:** Education. **U:** Home. **Gen-Edu:** Biography, Presidency. **Acq:** Purchase. **Dist:** WGBH/Boston. $24.95.

American Experience: Jonestown 2007
Investigates the story behind the headlines of the People's Temple, its leader Jim Jones, and the mass murder-suicide of 900 Jonestown settlers in November 1978. 90m; DVD; Closed

Captioned. **A:** Adult. **P:** Education. **U:** Home. **Gen-Edu:** Documentary Films, Cults, History. **Acq:** Purchase. **Dist:** WGBH/Boston. $24.95.

American Experience: Kinsey 2005
A collection of interviews with professional and personal relations examines the achievements of biologist Alfred Kinsey, whose breakthrough report on the sexual practices of men and women caused a stir in the 1940s. 90m; VHS, DVD. **A:** Adult. **P:** Education. **U:** Home. **Gen-Edu:** Biography, Biology, Sex & Sexuality. **Acq:** Purchase. **Dist:** WGBH/Boston. $19.95.

American Experience: Kit Carson 199?
Examines the life of Kit Carson, master of America's western frontier who was inspiration for dozens of dime store novels and an unwitting agent in the migration that transformed and ultimately destroyed the West he knew and loved. 90m; DVD. **A:** Adult. **P:** Education. **U:** Home. **Gen-Edu:** Biography, History--U.S. **Acq:** Purchase. **Dist:** WGBH/Boston. $24.95.

The American Experience: Knute Rockne and His Fighting Irish 1993
Profiles the charismatic football coach (University of Notre Dame, 1914-31) who is credited for heavily influencing how football was played. 52m; VHS. **Pr:** Florentine Films. **A:** Sr. High-Adult. **P:** Education. **U:** Institution. **Spo-Rec:** Football, Biography. **Acq:** Purchase. **Dist:** Direct Cinema Ltd. $95.00.

American Experience: Las Vegas: An Unconventional History 2005
Documents the history of America's playground, a city of excess and reckless abandon, as it celebrates its 100th anniversary. 180m; DVD; Closed Captioned. **A:** Adult. **P:** Education. **U:** Home. **Gen-Edu:** Cities & Towns, History--U.S. **Acq:** Purchase. **Dist:** WGBH/Boston. $24.95.

The American Experience: Last Stand at Little Big Horn 1992
Take a look at the historical battle of June 25, 1876: Little Big Horn. While Custer had designed the battle against the Cheyenne and Lakota Indians to make himself a hero, his scouts warned him everyone would be killed. Ties in themes of manifest destiny and the white/Natvie American relationship during the Westward expansion, when Native Americans were seen simply as obstacles to progress. 60m; VHS, CC. **A:** Jr. High-College. **P:** Education. **U:** Institution. **Gen-Edu:** Native Americans, History--U.S., War--General. **Acq:** Purchase. **Dist:** PBS Home Video; Baker and Taylor. $59.95.

American Experience: Lost in the Grand Canyon 199?
Tells the story of John Wesley Powell's 99 day expedition down the Colorado River into uncharted territory in the spring of 1869, an experience that would transform how America viewed the West. President Theodore Roosevelt visited in 1902 and declared the Grand Canyon to be "a natural wonder unparalleled in the world." 53m; DVD; Closed Captioned. **A:** Jr. High-Adult. **P:** Education. **U:** Home. **Gen-Edu:** Documentary Films, National Parks & Reserves, History--U.S. **Acq:** Purchase. **Dist:** WGBH/Boston. $19.95.

The American Experience: MacArthur 1999
Follows MacArthur's military career from World War I to his retirement after receiving orders to return home from the Far East. Two-volume set. 240m/B/W; VHS; Closed Captioned. **A:** Jr. High-Sr. High. **P:** Education. **U:** Institution. **Gen-Edu:** Biography, Military History. **Acq:** Purchase. **Dist:** Zenger Media. $29.98.

American Experience: Mary Pickford 2005
Archive footage, stills, original audio interviews with Pickford, and movie clips present the career and achievements of the respected actress, creative producer, and shrewd businesswoman. 90m; VHS, DVD. **A:** Jr. High-Adult. **P:** Education. **U:** Home. **Gen-Edu:** Biography, Film History, Biography: Show Business. **Acq:** Purchase. **Dist:** WGBH/Boston. $24.95.

American Experience: Minik, the Lost Eskimo 200?
Examines the events that unfolded when Robert Peary brought five Eskimos from the Arctic back to New York with him in 1897 to study them at the American Museum of Natural History. Within several months four of them died, leaving a young boy, Minik, to adjust to his new surroundings alone, as race, culture, and fledgling science collided at the turn of the 20th century. 60m; DVD. **A:** Adult. **P:** Education. **U:** Home. **Gen-Edu:** Biography, Eskimos. **Acq:** Purchase. **Dist:** WGBH/Boston. $24.95.

American Experience: Mount Rushmore 200?
Story of Mount Rushmore's divergent Danish American creator, Gutzon Borglum, who many considered insane, and his relentless pursuits despite economic depression to complete his monstrous masterpiece. 60m; DVD. **A:** Adult. **P:** Education. **U:** Home. **Gen-Edu:** Documentary Films, Art & Artists, History--U.S. **Acq:** Purchase. **Dist:** WGBH/Boston. $19.95.

American Experience: My Lai 2010 (Unrated)
On March 16, 1968, the men of Charlie Company entered the small village of My Lai in central Vietnam. Exhausted and mentally strung out after suffering waves of horrific casualties, the U.S. soldiers were told that My Lai would contain only enemy combatants and that they should go in shooting. Unfortunately, that intelligence was outdated, and what followed was a horrific massacre of anywhere from 300 to 500 Vietnamese civilians, mostly women, children, and the elderly. When reporter Seymour Hersh finally broke the story about the "My Lai Massacre" 16 months later, the way most Americans viewed the conflict in Vietnam was changed forever. Includes a further reading list, timeline, photo gallery, and more. 90m; DVD. **A:** Family. **P:** Education, Entertainment. **U:** Home, Institution. **Mov-Ent:** Documentary Films, Vietnam War, Intelligence Service. **Acq:** Purchase. **Dist:** WGBH/Boston. $19.99.

American Experience: New Orleans 2006
Historical portrait of New Orleans focuses on Reconstruction to the desegregation of schools in the 1960s and explores the distinct culture that resides at the mouth of the mighty Mississippi. 120m; DVD; Closed Captioned. **A:** Adult. **P:** Education. **U:** Home. **Gen-Edu:** Documentary Films, Cities & Towns, History--U.S. **Acq:** Purchase. **Dist:** WGBH/Boston. $24.95.

American Experience: New York 1999
Chronicles the history of New York from is Dutch trading post founding in 1624 to the leading city of culture and economy in the world. Eight discs. 1050m; VHS, DVD; Closed Captioned. **A:** Jr. High-Adult. **P:** Education. **U:** Home. **Gen-Edu:** Documentary Films, Cities & Towns, History--U.S. **Acq:** Purchase. **Dist:** WGBH/Boston. $139.95.

The American Experience: New York Underground 1998
Documentary examines the construction of the New York subway system, which was considered the new century's most amazing engineering achievement at the time, and the events that led to it. 60m; VHS; Closed Captioned. **A:** Family. **P:** Education. **U:** Home. **Gen-Edu:** Documentary Films, History. **Acq:** Purchase. **Dist:** PBS Home Video. $19.98.

American Experience: Nixon 1990 (Unrated)
When Richard Nixon resigned as U.S. president on August 8, 1974, he brought to a close one of the most famous—and notorious—political careers in U.S. history. Covering his early run for Senate in California and culminating with his resignation, this documentary covers all of the highs and lows of Nixon's career, including his troubled record in Vietnam, his improvement of U.S. and Soviet relations, and the role he played in opening up relations with Communist China for the first time. Despite his foreign policy successes, the quagmire that was Vietnam, along with Nixon's thirst for power and paranoia, combined to bring an end to his presidency following the infamous Watergate break-in and ensuing scandal. Includes teacher's resources, primary resource materials, and more. 170m; DVD. **A:** Family. **P:** Education, Entertainment. **U:** Home, Institution. **Mov-Ent:** Documentary Films, History--U.S., Presidency. **Acq:** Purchase. **Dist:** WGBH/Boston. $19.99.

The American Experience: One Woman, One Vote 1995
A history of women's suffrage from Seneca Falls in 1848 to the installation of the 19th Amendment in 1920. 106m; VHS; Closed Captioned. **A:** Jr. High-Sr. High. **P:** Education. **U:** Institution. **Gen-Edu:** Women, History--U.S., Civil Rights. **Acq:** Purchase. **Dist:** Zenger Media. $94.95.

American Experience: Oswald's Ghost 200?
Rare archival footage and interviews investigates Kennedy's assassination, the public's reaction, and the loss of trust in the government that ensued. 90m; DVD; Closed Captioned. **A:** Adult. **P:** Education. **U:** Home. **Gen-Edu:** Documentary Films, Presidency, History--U.S. **Acq:** Purchase. **Dist:** WGBH/Boston. $24.95.

The American Experience: Our Living Traditions 1975
Young Americans are rediscovering their roots and revitalizing their ethnic heritage. 19m; VHS, 3/4 U. **Pr:** Hanna Roman Productions. **A:** Jr. High-Sr. High. **P:** Education. **U:** Institution, SURA. **Gen-Edu:** Genealogy. **Acq:** Purchase. **Dist:** Phoenix Learning Group.

American Experience: Panama Canal 2011 (Unrated)
With the completion of the Panama Canal on August 15, 1914, the United States took a giant leap forward as an international superpower, both militarily and economically. The canal, which connects the Atlantic and Pacific Oceans, took more than a decade to build and came at an incredibly high price: $375 million and more than 5,000 workers killed during construction, which is in addition to the estimated 20,000 who died when the French originally attempted to build the canal in the 1880s. In the end, the 48-mile canal was the most expensive project ever undertaken at that time, it was actually completed for $23 million less than originally budgeted. While the project was overseen by three American presidents, it is Theodore Roosevelt who is given the most credit for ensuring the Panama Canal would be completed. Includes teacher's resources, primary resource materials, bonus video footage, photo gallery, and more. 90m; DVD. **A:** Family. **P:** Education, Entertainment. **U:** Home, Institution. **Mov-Ent:** Documentary Films, History--U.S., Military History. **Acq:** Purchase. **Dist:** WGBH/Boston. $19.99.

American Experience: Partners of the Heart 2003
Recounts the partnership of Vivien Thomas, a gifted black doctor, and Alfred Blalock, a white surgeon, during the height of segregation in the United States. Together they pioneered a procedure that cured the heart defect causing "blue baby syndrome." 60m; VHS; Closed Captioned. **A:** Jr. High-Adult. **P:** Education. **U:** Home. **Gen-Edu:** Biography, Medical Education, History--U.S. **Acq:** Purchase. **Dist:** WGBH/Boston. $24.95.

American Experience: Race for the Superbomb 1999 (Unrated)
In August 1945, the United States changed the face of warfare when it detonated two atomic bombs in Japan. Far more powerful than any weapon previously used during wartime, the bombs wiped out the cities of Nagasaki and Hiroshima and did exactly what they were intended to do—forced Japan to surrender, thus ending the war sooner than expected and with far fewer Allied casualties. On the negative side, the bombs touched off an arms race with the Soviet Union that lasted the duration of the Cold War that lead to the creation of the hydrogen fusion bomb, a nuclear weapon that was a thousand times more powerful than the bomb dropped on Hiroshima. In 1952, the United States conducted the first test of a live H-bomb, with the Soviets following suit in 1955, thus setting in motion the nuclear arms race. Includes a timeline, teacher's resources, and more. 60m; VHS, DVD. **A:** Family. **P:** Education, Entertainment. **U:** Home, Institution. **Mov-Ent:** Documentary Films, World War Two, Japan. **Acq:** Purchase. **Dist:** WGBH/Boston.

American Experience: Race to the Moon 2005
Documents the entrance of Apollo 8 into lunar orbit on December 25, 1968, the first manned moon mission. 60m; DVD; Closed Captioned. **A:** Adult. **P:** Education. **U:** Home. **Gen-Edu:** Documentary Films, Space Exploration, History. **Acq:** Purchase. **Dist:** WGBH/Boston. $29.95.

The American Experience: Rachel Carson's Silent Spring 1993
Profiles environmental activist Rachel Carson and her book that helped propel the environmental movement, "Silent Spring." Documentary uses interviews, television footage, old photos, and excerpts from Carson's writings and letters. 60m; VHS. **A:** Jr. High-College. **P:** Education. **U:** Institution. **Gen-Edu:** Documentary Films, Ecology & Environment, Women. **Acq:** Purchase. **Dist:** PBS Home Video. $59.95.

American Experience: Reagan 2004
Biography of Ronald Wilson Reagan, an actor, ideologue, and eventual president of the United States whose charisma and charm served well his values of optimism, lower taxes, less government, and anti-communism. 270m; VHS, DVD; Closed Captioned. **A:** Jr. High-Adult. **P:** Education. **U:** Home. **Gen-Edu:** Biography, Presidency. **Acq:** Purchase. **Dist:** WGBH/Boston. $19.95.

American Experience: Reconstruction: The Second Civil War 2004
Narrates the stories of white and black Americans of southern and northern descent that stood out in the struggle to reshape the nation from 1863 to 1877: Tunis Campbell, a former minister who claimed Georgia's Sea Islands as a black colony off-limits to whites; Frances Butler, who negotiated labor contracts with her family's former slaves to keep their Georgia rice plantation operating; John Roy Lynch, a former Mississippi slave elected to Congress; plus presidents Andrew Johnson and Ulysses S. Grant along with General William Tecumseh Sherman. 180m; VHS, DVD. **A:** Jr. High-Adult. **P:** Education. **U:** Home. **Gen-Edu:** Documentary Films, Slavery, History--U.S. **Acq:** Purchase. **Dist:** WGBH/Boston. $19.95.

The American Experience: Religious Diversity 1976
Meet young Americans involved in seven of America's major religious groups. 19m; VHS, 3/4 U. **Pr:** Moctesuma Esparza Productions. **A:** Jr. High-Sr. High. **P:** Education. **U:** Institution, SURA. **Gen-Edu:** Religion. **Acq:** Purchase. **Dist:** Phoenix Learning Group.

American Experience: Remember the Alamo 2004
Explores the efforts made by Tejano leader Jose Antonio Navarro and his followers to protect the sovereignty of his Texas homeland. ?m; VHS, DVD. **A:** Jr. High-Adult. **P:** Education. **U:** Home. **Gen-Edu:** Biography, Documentary Films, History--U.S. **Acq:** Purchase. **Dist:** WGBH/Boston. $24.95.

American Experience: Rescue at Sea 199?
Recounts the tragedy of January 23, 1909, when a ship carrying Italian immigrants to New York and an American tourist ship heading to Europe collided in a dense fog off the Nantucket coast. 60m; VHS. **A:** Adult. **P:** Education. **U:** Home. **Gen-Edu:** Documentary Films, History, Emergencies. **Acq:** Purchase. **Dist:** WGBH/Boston. $19.95.

American Experience: Return with Honor 2001
First-person accounts describe the transformation of 461 American airmen to war prisoners in North Vietnam until the signing of the Paris Peace Accords in 1973; covers their shoot downs, solitary confinement, and excruciating tortures and touches on the home front and the women left behind, unsure if they were widows or wives. ?m; VHS, DVD; Closed Captioned. **A:** Sr. High-Adult. **P:** Education. **U:** Home. **Gen-Edu:** Documentary Films, Vietnam War, History. **Acq:** Purchase. **Dist:** WGBH/Boston. $19.95.

American Experience: RFK 2004
Examines the tragic yet remarkable life of Robert F. Kennedy and the essential role he played in the Cuban Missile Crisis, the civil right movement, and the war in Vietnam. 120m; DVD; Closed Captioned. **A:** Jr. High-Adult. **P:** Education. **U:** Home. **Gen-Edu:** Biography, Politics & Government, History--U.S. **Acq:** Purchase. **Dist:** WGBH/Boston. $24.95.

The American Experience: Riding the Rails 1997
Footage, letters, folk songs, and interviews recount the lives of some 25,000 Depression-era teenagers who hopped aboard freight trains in search of a better life. 72m; VHS, DVD. **C:** Directed by Michael Uys; Lexy Lovell. **A:** Sr. High-Adult. **P:** Entertainment. **U:** Home. **Gen-Edu:** Documentary Films, Trains, Poverty. **Awds:** L.A. Film Critics '97: Feature Doc. **Acq:** Purchase. **Dist:** WGBH/Boston; The Civil War Standard. $19.95.

American Experience: Roads to Memphis 2010 (Unrated)
This documentary tells the stories of both civil rights icon Martin Luther King Jr. and James Earl Ray, the lifelong criminal who became infamous when he shot and killed Dr. King on April 4, 1968, in Memphis, Tennessee. Mixed in with interviews of those

closest to King about what happened that fateful day is the story of the two-month international manhunt that ultimately led to Ray's arrest in the country of Rhodesia. Includes a further reading list, bonus video footage, a photo gallery, a timeline, and more. 90m; DVD. **A:** Family. **P:** Education, Entertainment. **U:** Home, Institution. **Mov-Ent:** Documentary Films, Civil Rights, History--U.S. **Acq:** Purchase. **Dist:** WGBH/Boston. $19.99.

American Experience: Robert E. Lee 2011 (Unrated)
This documentary is a profile of Robert E. Lee, the leader of the Confederate Army during the American Civil War. As a young man, Lee was the head of his family's household after his father ran off to the West Indies to escape his heavy debt. Disgraced by his father's actions, Lee set out to lead an exemplary life. He attended West Point, finishing second in his class, and fought with great distinction in the Mexican-American War in the 1840s. When the Civil War first broke out, President Abraham Lincoln recruited Lee to take over as leader of the Union Army; Lee declined, not wanting to attack the South, and instead was named commander of Virginia's army and, ultimately, head of all Confederate forces. Lee fought with distinction in the Civil War but was done in by superior Union resources and manpower. After the war, he took over as president of Washington University until dying of a massive stroke in 1870. Includes a timeline, teacher's resources, a further reading list, and more. 90m; DVD. **A:** Family. **P:** Education, Entertainment. **U:** Home, Institution. **Mov-Ent:** Documentary Films, Biography: Military, Military History. **Acq:** Purchase. **Dist:** WGBH/Boston. $9.99.

American Experience: Roberto Clemente 2008 (PG)
A profile of the first, and still one of the greatest, Latin American baseball players of all-time, Roberto Clemente was a superstar from Puerto Rico whose career was tragically cut short at age 38 when he was killed in a plane crash while helping earthquake victims in Nicaragua on December 31, 1972. A member of the Pittsburgh Pirates from 1955 until his death, he was an all-star 12 times, won four batting titles, two World Series, and one Most Valuable Player award. In the final at bat of his career, he collected his 3,000th hit, still one of only 28 players to achieve that feat. A great humanitarian, Clemente also fought racism in the United States and worked passionately in support of human rights around the world, especially in Latin American countries. Includes primary resource materials, teacher's resources, and more. 60m; DVD. **A:** Family. **P:** Education, Entertainment. **U:** Home, Institution. **Mov-Ent:** Documentary Films, Hispanic Culture, Sports Documentary. **Acq:** Purchase. **Dist:** WGBH/Boston. $19.99.

American Experience: Roots of Resistance 1990
Documents the risks taken by black and white men and women to develop a network of escape routes for slaves which became known as the Underground Railroad. 56m; DVD; Closed Captioned. **A:** Jr. High-Adult. **P:** Education. **U:** Home. **Gen-Edu:** Documentary Films, Slavery, History--U.S. **Acq:** Purchase. **Dist:** WGBH/Boston. $19.95.

American Experience: Scottsboro--An American Tragedy 2001 (Unrated)
In March 1931, nine African American teenagers riding a freight train as hoboes got into a fight with a group of white hoboes who were also aboard the train. When the train is stopped by an angry mob in Paint Rock, Alabama, the fight is all but forgotten when two women—one black and one white—come forward and say they were raped by the nine African Americans. When the teens deny raping anyone, the case touches off the biggest racial divide in the United States since the Civil War. Originally convicted and sentenced to death, the nine boys would be at the center of legal maneuverings and cases over the next decade that resulted in two landmark U.S. Supreme Court cases and touch off the beginnings of the modern civil rights movement. Includes a further reading list, primary resource materials, and more. 90m; DVD. **A:** Family. **P:** Education, Entertainment. **U:** Home, Institution. **Mov-Ent:** Documentary Films, Minorities, History--U.S. **Acq:** Purchase. **Dist:** WGBH/Boston. $17.99.

American Experience: Seabiscuit 2003
Examines the world of thoroughbred racing through the experience of Seabiscuit, one of the most remarkable racehorses in history, as well as his owner Charles Howard, trainer Tom Smith, and the two jockeys that rode him to glory in Depression-era America. 60m; VHS, DVD. **A:** Jr. High-Adult. **P:** Education. **U:** Home. **Gen-Edu:** Biography, Horses--Racing, Horses. **Acq:** Purchase. **Dist:** WGBH/Boston. $19.95.

American Experience: Silicon Valley 2013 (Unrated)
While many people think that modern computer companies such as Apple and Intuit are responsible for founding the area in northern California known as Silicon Valley, it actually became known as the home of cutting edge technology in America in 1957. At that time, 29-year-old Robert Noyce and seven other men defected from the Shockley Semiconductor Company and formed a competitor known as Fairchild Semiconductor. By developing state of the art (and never before seen) products for both the space industry and the new personal computer industry, Fairchild grew rapidly and was the first of many technology companies to open in what became known as Silicon Valley. Includes a timeline, bonus video footage, and more. 90m; DVD. **A:** Family. **P:** Education, Entertainment. **U:** Home, Institution. **Mov-Ent:** Documentary Films, Space Exploration, Technology. **Acq:** Purchase. **Dist:** WGBH/Boston. $19.99.

The American Experience: Simple Justice 1993
Describes events which led up to the outlawing of segregated education in the U.S. Focusses on Thurgood Marshall and the U.S. Supreme Court's landmark decision in Brown v. Board of Education in 1954. Comes with guide. 140m; VHS, CC. **Pr:**

Avon Kirkland. **A:** Sr. High-Adult. **P:** Education. **U:** Institution. **Gen-Edu:** Politics & Government, Law, History--U.S. **Acq:** Purchase. **Dist:** PBS Home Video. $89.95.

American Experience: Sister Aimee 2007
Presents an illuminating portrait of controversial evangelist Aimee McPherson through interviews with historians and scholars. 60m; DVD; Closed Captioned. **A:** Adult. **P:** Education. **U:** Home. **Gen-Edu:** Biography, Women. **Acq:** Purchase. **Dist:** WGBH/Boston. $24.95.

American Experience: Soundtrack for a Revolution 2010 (Unrated)
During the civil rights movement of the 1960s, music played an important role in the difficult struggle for equality. During the freedom rides and at every rally and march, protesters sang the "freedom songs" that provided hope to all those fighting for equality and justice. In this documentary, interviews with civil rights leaders—including Harry Belafonte and Julian Bond--and protestors from the front lines across the American South talk about the role music played in the protests, about how former slave chants evolved into songs that gave protestors the courage to stand up in the fight against racism. Mixed in with the interviews are musical performances by contemporary stars such as John Legend, the Roots, and Wyclef Jean, who sing some of the most popular songs of that era. Includes a timeline, further reading list, and more. 82m; DVD. **A:** Family. **P:** Education, Entertainment. **U:** Home, Institution. **Mov-Ent:** Documentary Films, Civil Rights, Music. **Acq:** Purchase. **Dist:** WGBH/Boston. $19.99.

American Experience: Spy in the Sky 1996
Explains and further investigates one of the greatest spy stories of all time, the development and use of the U-2 that flew its first mission in 1956 and revealed Russia's bluff of bomb development. 60m; VHS, DVD; Closed Captioned. **A:** Jr. High-Adult. **P:** Education. **U:** Home. **Gen-Edu:** Documentary Films, Military History. **Acq:** Purchase. **Dist:** WGBH/Boston. $19.95.

American Experience: Stephen Foster 200?
Narrates the tale of America's first great songwriter, Stephen Foster, responsible for "Camptown Races," "Beautiful Dreamer," and "Oh! Susanna" among others, set to a score of lively 19th century music. 60m; VHS. **A:** Adult. **P:** Education. **U:** Home. **Gen-Edu:** Biography, Music, History--U.S. **Acq:** Purchase. **Dist:** WGBH/Boston. $19.95.

American Experience: Stonewall Uprising 2011 (Unrated)
In the 1960s, lesbian, gay, bisexual, and transgendered (LGBT) Americans lived their lives mostly in the shadows, as they were largely forced to keep their sexuality to themselves or else face discrimination in every aspect of their lives, even violence. That began to change on June 28, 1969, when police raided the Stonewall Inn in New York's Greenwich Village, a self-proclaimed dive bar where LGBT patrons felt safe socializing and dancing. Raids at the Stonewall happened regularly, but on that June night, patrons of the bar and residents of the surrounding neighborhood fought back against the police, touching off six nights of riots and protests. In the years that followed, the Stonewall Uprising became known as the turning point. Based in part on the book "Stonewall: The Riots that Sparked the Gay Revolution, Stonewall Uprising" by David Carter. Includes primary resource materials, a timeline, photo gallery, and more. 90m; DVD. **A:** Family. **P:** Education, Entertainment. **U:** Home, Institution. **Mov-Ent:** Documentary Films, Civil Rights, History--U.S. **Acq:** Purchase. **Dist:** WGBH/Boston. $19.99.

American Experience: Summer of Love 2007
Examines the counter-culture movement following the drug abuse, disillusionment, and violence that grew in San Francisco's Haight-Ashbury district after the 1967 hippie boon. 60m; DVD; Closed Captioned. **A:** Adult. **P:** Education. **U:** Home. **Gen-Edu:** Documentary Films, History--U.S., Drug Abuse. **Acq:** Purchase. **Dist:** WGBH/Boston. $24.95.

American Experience: Surviving the Dust Bowl 199?
Presents the stories of those determined to hold onto their homes and way of life during the 1930s in the "Dust Bowl," enduring drought, dust, disease, and death for close to a decade as the rains stopped and the "black blizzards" blazed. 56m; DVD; Closed Captioned. **A:** Jr. High-Adult. **P:** Education. **U:** Home. **Gen-Edu:** Documentary Films, History--U.S., U.S. States. **Acq:** Purchase. **Dist:** WGBH/Boston. $19.95.

American Experience: Test Tube Babies 2006
Chronicles the experiences of doctors, researchers, and hopeful couples in 1978 who took science beyond its limits and revolutionized the process of human reproduction with repercussions still under debate. 60m; DVD. **A:** Adult. **P:** Education. **U:** Home. **Gen-Edu:** Documentary Films, Medical Education, History. **Acq:** Purchase. **Dist:** WGBH/Boston. $24.95.

American Experience: The Abolitionists 2013 (Unrated)
Leading up to the U.S. Civil War, abolitionists fought to abolish all slavery in the United States, an idea that was unpopular with a large segment of the nation and led to the leaders of the abolitionist movement being labeled as radicals, troublemakers, agitators, and much worse. This documentary shows how men and women such as Frederick Douglass, William Lloyd Garrison, Angelina Grimké, Harriet Beecher Stowe and John Brown fought the nation's first civil rights battle, leading a crusade that was powered by both religious fervor and a desire to question the very meaning of the U.S. Constitution. Includes teacher's resources, bonus video footage, and more. 180m; DVD. **A:** Family. **P:** Education, Entertainment. **U:** Home, Institution. **Mov-Ent:** Documentary Films, Civil War, Slavery. **Acq:** Purchase. **Dist:** WGBH/Boston. $2013.

American Experience: The Amish 2012 (PG)
This documentary takes an unprecedented, in-depth look at the Amish community in America, which has existed since the first Amish settled in Pennsylvania in the 1730s. Given full access to an Amish community for more than a year, producer Mark Samels examines the group's history in America and attempts to explain how the Amish have maintained their core values through both the Industrial Revolution and the more recent Information Age. Includes a timeline, primary resources material, and more. 120m; DVD. **A:** Family. **P:** Education, Entertainment. **U:** Home, Institution. **Mov-Ent:** Documentary Films, Religion, Amish. **Acq:** Purchase. **Dist:** WGBH/Boston. $19.99.

American Experience: The Assassination of Abraham Lincoln 2009 (PG)
On April 9, 1865, just five days after the end of the Civil War, President Abraham Lincoln was shot and killed by assassin John Wilkes Booth while watching a play at Washington's Ford Theatre. This documentary chronicles how Booth's obsession with Lincoln took such a tragic turn and how, in death, Lincoln became a universally beloved leader and a true American hero. Also covered is the remarkable 1700-mile journey Lincoln's casket took by train from Washington to his home of Springfield, Illinois, which was viewed by more than seven million people, as well as the 12-day manhunt that led to Booth's eventual capture and death in Virginia. Includes a timeline, further reading list, and more. Narrated by Chris Cooper. 82m; DVD. **A:** Family. **P:** Education, Entertainment. **U:** Home, Institution. **Mov-Ent:** Documentary Films, Civil War, Presidency. **Acq:** Purchase. **Dist:** WGBH/Boston. $19.99.

American Experience: The Battle of the Bulge: The Deadliest Battle of World War II 2004
In December 1944, Hitler's forces counterattacked the allies in the biggest battle U.S. forces were to experience. Includes archival and army footage and eyewitness accounts. 90m; DVD. **A:** Sr. High-Adult. **P:** Entertainment. **U:** Home. **Gen-Edu:** Documentary Films, World War Two. **Acq:** Purchase. **Dist:** WGBH/Boston.

The American Experience: The Battle Over Citizen Kane 2000
120m; VHS. **A:** Jr. High-Adult. **P:** Education. **U:** Home. **Gen-Edu:** Film History. **Acq:** Purchase. **Dist:** WGBH/Boston. $19.95.

American Experience: The Berlin Airlift 2006
First-hand accounts explain the detriment of the 1948 Soviet Union blockade of West Berlin's supply access and commerce as Allied forces kept civilians and soldiers alive by air-dropping supplies for nearly a year, refusing to allow the city to be lost during this early cold war conflict. 90m; DVD; Closed Captioned. **A:** Adult. **P:** Education. **U:** Home. **Gen-Edu:** Germany, History. **Acq:** Purchase. **Dist:** WGBH/Boston. $24.95.

American Experience: The Bombing of Germany 2010 (Unrated)
When it first entered World War II in late 1941, the U.S. military had a policy that no civilian targets would be attacked during bombing raids, only military targets. However, when the German military stepped up its air raids on British cities and killed tens of thousands of civilians, things changed. In retaliation and in an attempt to break the Germans' will to fight, the United States and its allies began nighttime raids that included civilian targets. Devastating attacks against Dresden, Berlin, and other cities paved the way for more large-scale bombing raids in Japan, including the dropping of the two atomic bombs in 1945. Includes a timeline, further reading list, teacher's resources, and more. 60m; DVD. **A:** Family. **P:** Education, Entertainment. **U:** Home, Institution. **Mov-Ent:** Documentary Films, World War Two, Germany. **Acq:** Purchase. **Dist:** WGBH/Boston. $19.99.

American Experience: The Boy in the Bubble 2006
Questions the intent of doctors who treated David Vetter, who died at the age of 12 after living his life sequestered in a plastic bubble. 60m; DVD. **A:** Adult. **P:** Education. **U:** Home. **Gen-Edu:** Biography, Documentary Films, Medical Care. **Acq:** Purchase. **Dist:** WGBH/Boston. $29.95.

American Experience: The Carter Family: Let the Circle Be Unbroken 2005
Rare family photographs, memorabilia, and archival footage chronicle the life and music career of A.P., Sara, and Maybelle Carter, whose songs and performances lifted the nation's spirits during the darkest days of the Depression. 60m; DVD. **A:** Adult. **P:** Education. **U:** Home. **Gen-Edu:** Biography, Music--Country/ Western, History--U.S. **Acq:** Purchase. **Dist:** WGBH/Boston. $19.95.

American Experience: The Civilian Conservation Corps 2009 (Unrated)
With America trapped in the throes of the Great Depression, President Franklin Roosevelt did everything in his power to put Americans back to work, including creating the Civilian Conservation Corps (CCC). Designed to create jobs in all natural resource conservation fields, the program employed more than three million Americans. Among their jobs were planting more than three billion trees, building flood barriers and fire breaks, maintaining roads, working in national parks, and more. Designed for men 18 to 25, the CCC jobs paid $30 per month--$25 of which each man had to send to his family. In addition, classes were offered that were intended to teach men job skills and trades to which they otherwise might not have had access. Includes teacher's resources, a photo gallery, an interactive map, bonus video, and more. 60m; DVD. **A:** Family. **P:** Education, Entertainment. **U:** Home, Institution. **Mov-Ent:** Documentary Films, History--U.S., Presidency. **Acq:** Purchase. **Dist:** WGBH/Boston. $19.99.

American Experience: The Crash of 1929 1991
The contrast between the Roaring '20s and the Great Depression is presented here through a combination of narrative, historical footage, and expert commentary. 59m; VHS. **A:** Sr. High. **P:** Education. **U:** Institution. **Chl-Juv:** History--Modern. **Acq:** Purchase. **Dist:** PBS Home Video. $59.95.

The American Experience: The Donner Party 1992
A group of 87 settlers, heading for California in 1846, make the disastrous mistake of taking a shortcut through the Sierra Nevada mountains. Trapped by snow for five months in what is now known as Donner Pass, some of the group resort to cannabalism in order to survive. Burns (brother of "The Civil War" Ken Burns) uses readings from journals, archival photos, and photography of the sites to show the heartbreak and self-sacrifice of this ill-fated expedition. 86m; VHS. **C:** Directed by Ric Burns. **A:** Family. **P:** Education. **U:** Home. **Gen-Edu:** Documentary Films, History--U.S. **Acq:** Purchase. **Dist:** Direct Cinema Ltd. $39.95.

The American Experience: The Fall of Saigon 1983
Commemoration of the 20th aniversary offers a vivid account of the last three days (April 27th to April 30, 1975) before the surrender of South Vietnam to the North Vietnamese. Includes newsreel clips and first-person accounts (both American and Vietnamese). 120m; VHS. **C:** Narrated by Garrick Utley; Directed by Michael Dutfield. **Pr:** Discovery Channel. **A:** Jr. High-Adult. **P:** Education. **U:** Home. **Gen-Edu:** History--U.S., Vietnam War. **Acq:** Purchase. **Dist:** Discovery Home Entertainment. $19.95.

American Experience: The Fight 2004
Considers the political and social significance across the globe surrounding the rematch between African American heavyweight Joe Louis and German Nazi Party challenger Max Schmeling on June 22, 1938. 90m; VHS, DVD; Closed Captioned. **A:** Jr. High-Adult. **P:** Education. **U:** Home. **Gen-Edu:** Documentary Films, Boxing, History. **Acq:** Purchase. **Dist:** WGBH/Boston. $24.95.

American Experience: The Gold Rush 2006
Overviews the seminal event in America's history that sent a once-sleepy village of 800 people on track to become the fast-moving city of San Francisco in 1853. 120m; DVD; Closed Captioned. **A:** Adult. **P:** Education. **U:** Home. **Gen-Edu:** Documentary Films, History--U.S., Cities & Towns. **Acq:** Purchase. **Dist:** WGBH/Boston. $24.95.

American Experience: The Great Famine 2011 (Unrated)
In 1921, just as the Soviet Union was taking form in the wake of the Bolshevik Revolution of 1917, a terrible famine swept across the enormous nation that ultimately killed more than five million people. As horrible as the famine was—cannibalism was widespread at one point—many more deaths would have occurred if not for the efforts of American politician (and future president) Herbert Hoover. As leader of the American Relief Administration (ARA), Hoover convinced American leaders to provide food to the Soviets in hopes of enhancing their view of Americans while, more importantly, saving millions of lives. Vladimir Lenin and the Communists initially viewed Hoover's actions with great suspicion, they ultimately helped him distribute food and aid, thus achieving the ARA's goal to save millions of people. In fact, Hoover is credited with saving more people than any other person in history. Includes a photo gallery, timeline, primary resource materials, and more. 60m; DVD. **A:** Family. **P:** Education, Entertainment. **U:** Home, Institution. **Mov-Ent:** Documentary Films, USSR, Death. **Acq:** Purchase. **Dist:** WGBH/Boston. $19.99.

American Experience: The Great San Francisco Earthquake 1987
Rare, newly restored movie footage and personal eyewitness accounts retell the tale of San Francisco's disastrous April 18, 1906, earthquake, the firestorms that raged for days following, and the determination of the people to rebuild their city and their livelihoods. 56m; DVD; Closed Captioned. **A:** Jr. High-Adult. **P:** Education. **U:** Home. **Gen-Edu:** History--U.S., Cities & Towns, Earthquakes. **Acq:** Purchase. **Dist:** WGBH/Boston. $19.95.

American Experience: The Great Transatlantic Cable 2005
Documents the endeavor of New York paper merchant Cyrus Field in the 1850s to carry out the laying of a 2,000-mile long transatlantic cable three miles beneath the Atlantic to connect the U.S. and Europe, a 13-year endeavor that cost him almost everything. 60m; DVD; Closed Captioned. **A:** Adult. **P:** Education. **U:** Home. **Gen-Edu:** Documentary Films, Inventors & Inventions, History--U.S. **Acq:** Purchase. **Dist:** WGBH/Boston. $29.95.

American Experience: The Great War—1918 2006
Offers recollections of the experiences of American doughboys and others fighting in France in World War I. 56m; DVD. **A:** Jr. High-Adult. **P:** Entertainment. **U:** Home. **Gen-Edu:** Documentary Films. **Acq:** Purchase. **Dist:** WGBH/Boston.

American Experience: The Greely Expedition 2011 (PG)
In the summer of 1881, First Lieutenant Adolphus Greely led a team of 24 additional men on an journey to the Arctic called the Lady Franklin Bay Expedition. The trip was intended to gather significant scientific data over the next two years, as well as beat the long-standing British record for having a team go the "Farthest North." As it turned out, Greeley's team achieved both goals, but in doing so, all but Greely and five of his men were killed when no rescue boats showed up as planned to extract the expedition. In an attempt to stay alive until rescuers did arrive, Greeley and his men sailed south to Cape Sabine, all the while enduring madness, death, and even cannibalism. Includes a timeline, interactive map, teacher's resources, bonus video footage, and more. 60m; DVD. **A:** Family. **P:** Education, Entertainment. **U:** Home, Institution. **Mov-Ent:** Documentary Films, Arctic Regions, Explorers. **Acq:** Purchase. **Dist:** WGBH/Boston. $19.99.

American Experience: The Hurricane of '38 1993
Chronicles the experience of fishermen, residents, and vacationers caught in one of the greatest natural disasters to hit the eastern seaboard, claiming 700 lives, property damages near $300 million, 8,000 homes destroyed, and 6,000 boats ruined. 53m; DVD; Closed Captioned. **A:** Jr. High-Adult. **P:** Education. **U:** Home. **Gen-Edu:** Documentary Films, Nature, History--U.S. **Acq:** Purchase. **Dist:** WGBH/Boston. $19.95.

The American Experience: The Iron Road 1992
Chronicles the building of the Trans-Continental Railroad after the Civil War, a six year, 1800 mile endeavor linking California to the rest of the United States. Period photographs are combined with live re-enactments. 58m; VHS. **A:** Family. **P:** Entertainment. **U:** Home. **Gen-Edu:** Documentary Films, Trains. **Acq:** Purchase. **Dist:** Acorn Media Group Inc.; PBS Home Video. $19.95.

American Experience: The Kennedys 2003
Family members, friends, and first-hand witnesses document the legacy of America's own royal family from Joseph Kennedy's rise on Wall Street to his sons? political trials and triumphs. ?m; DVD. **A:** Jr. High-Adult. **P:** Education. **U:** Home. **Gen-Edu:** Biography, History--U.S., Presidency. **Acq:** Purchase. **Dist:** WGBH/Boston. $24.95.

The American Experience: The Kennedys, 1900-1980 1992
A two-part look at the triumphs and tragedies of the Kennedy family, from patriarch Joseph to Teddy at Chappaquidick. Shown on the PBS series "The American Experience." On two cassettes. 240m; VHS, CC. **A:** Sr. High-Adult. **P:** Entertainment. **U:** Home. **Gen-Edu:** Documentary Films, Politics & Government, Family. **Acq:** Purchase. **Dist:** Signals Video; Shanachie Entertainment; PBS Home Video. $39.95.
Indiv. Titles: 1. The Early Years 2. The Later Years.

American Experience: The Living Weapon 2007
Examines the challenges and moral dilemmas surrounding the development of biological weapons during World War II. 60m; DVD; Closed Captioned. **A:** Adult. **P:** Education. **U:** Home. **Gen-Edu:** Documentary Films, Military History, World War Two. **Acq:** Purchase. **Dist:** WGBH/Boston. $24.95.

American Experience: The Lobotomist 199?
Tells the story of neurologist Walter J. Freeman's medical intervention, which came to be considered a barbaric mistake in the treatment of mental illness. 60m; DVD; Closed Captioned. **A:** Adult. **P:** Education. **U:** Home. **Gen-Edu:** Documentary Films, Medical Education, Mental Health. **Acq:** Purchase. **Dist:** WGBH/Boston. $24.95.

American Experience: The Man Behind Hitler: The Goebbels Experiment 2004
Joseph Goebbels (1897-1945) was the propaganda genius behind the workings of the Third Reich. This documentary uses his own extensive diaries, written from 1924 to 1945, to reveal a psychological portrait of a manic-depressive man who eventually took his own life along with those of his wife and children. 107m; DVD; Closed Captioned. **A:** Adult. **P:** Education. **U:** Home. **Gen-Edu:** Biography, Politics & Government, Germany. **Acq:** Purchase. **Dist:** WGBH/Boston. $29.95.

American Experience: The Massachusetts 54th Colored Infantry 1991
Retells the adventures of the brave shopkeepers, farmers, musicians, blacksmiths, doctors, and lawyers from Massachusetts and neighboring states that banded together as the first northern black regiment to join the battle against slavery and returned to Boston victorious in the fall of 1865. 56m; DVD; Closed Captioned. **A:** Jr. High-Adult. **P:** Education. **U:** Home. **Gen-Edu:** Documentary Films, Civil War, History--U.S. **Acq:** Purchase. **Dist:** WGBH/Boston. $19.95.

American Experience: The Mormons 2006 (PG)
Founded in 1830 by Joseph Smith, the Church of Jesus Christ of Latter-day Saints, better known as the Mormons, has been one of the most controversial. Persecuted mercilessly in its early years (founder Smith was killed by anti-Mormon protestors in 1844 in Nauvoo, Illinois, after which Brigham Young led believers to Utah, still the church's base today), the Mormons survived the early bloodshed and eventually began to thrive. While still controversial today for their opposition to anything seen as "anti-family," including equal rights for women and homosexuality, the Mormons are one of the fastest growing religions in the world. Includes a timeline, teacher's resources, and more. 240m; DVD. **A:** Family. **P:** Education, Entertainment. **U:** Home, Institution. **Mov-Ent:** Documentary Films, History--U.S., Religion. **Acq:** Purchase. **Dist:** WGBH/Boston. $19.99.

American Experience: The Murder of Emmett Till 2005
Examines the murder of Emmett Till, a teen from Chicago who was beaten and shot by two white men days after whistling at a white woman in a Mississippi grocery store in 1955. The killers were acquitted by an all-white, all-male jury and unabashedly shared the details of the event with a journalist. Till's death helped spark the civil rights movement. 60m; VHS, DVD; Closed Captioned. **A:** Sr. High-Adult. **P:** Education. **U:** Home. **Gen-Edu:** Documentary Films, History--U.S., Civil Rights. **Acq:** Purchase. **Dist:** WGBH/Boston. $29.95.

American Experience: The Nuremberg Trials 2006
Recreates the military tribunal of November 20, 1945, at the Palace of Justice in Nuremberg, Germany wherein surviving representatives of the Nazi elite were charged with the murders of millions of people. 60m; VHS, DVD; Closed Captioned. **A:** Adult. **P:** Education. **U:** Home. **Gen-Edu:** History, Germany, Law. **Acq:** Purchase. **Dist:** WGBH/Boston. $29.95.

American Experience: The Orphan Trains 199?
Living "Orphan Train" riders share their memories of going from begging on the streets of New York to traveling across the country in trains between 1854 and 1929 to live with foster families in the Midwest. 60m; DVD; Closed Captioned. **A:** Jr. High-Adult. **P:** Education. **U:** Home. **Gen-Edu:** Documentary Films, History--U.S. **Acq:** Purchase. **Dist:** WGBH/Boston. $19.95.

American Experience: The Pill 2003 (Unrated)
Until the 1950s, American women feared that becoming sexually active would lead to multiple pregnancies. All that changed in May 1960 when, thanks to the efforts of activists Margaret Sanger and Katherine McCormick and scientist Gregory Pincus, the U.S. Food and Drug Administration approved the sale of the first contraceptive pill. While the Catholic Church strongly opposed the new drug, it was widely accepted by American women, and, in fact, touched off a social revolution. Interviews with some of the first women to take "the Pill" show how the drug gave them a sexual freedom they had never before experienced and also made it easier for them to have a career, since they would no longer need to worry about unexpected pregnancies. Includes teacher's resources, primary source material, and more. 60m; VHS, DVD. **A:** Family. **P:** Education, Entertainment. **U:** Home, Institution. **Mov-Ent:** Documentary Films, History--U.S., Pregnancy. **Acq:** Purchase. **Dist:** WGBH/Boston.

American Experience: The Poisoner's Handbook 2014 (Unrated)
In the earliest years of the 20th century, the surest way a person could get away with murder was to poison his or her victim. This was true largely due to one simple reason—police investigative techniques had not kept pace with the rapid changes in society brought about by the Industrial Revolution, meaning almost everyone had easy access to previously unknown deadly chemicals such as radioactive radium, thallium, and morphine, just to name a few. In 1918 that started to change, as New York City hired Charles Norris, its first medical examiner to have received scientific training, and Alexander Gettler, who worked as Norris's chief toxicologist. Together, the two men made forensic chemistry an important tool for every police department to rely on. Includes a timeline, photo gallery, further reading list, teacher's resources, and more. 60m; DVD. **A:** Family. **P:** Education, Entertainment. **U:** Home, Institution. **Mov-Ent:** Documentary Films, Poisons, Death. **Acq:** Purchase. **Dist:** WGBH/Boston. $24.99.

American Experience: The Polio Crusade 2009 (PG)
By 1950, a full-scale polio epidemic devastated tens of thousands of Americans, many under the age of 10. This documentary includes interviews with historians, doctors, polio patients, parents, and more to show how terrifying the disease became and how urgent was the search for a cure. President Franklin Roosevelt, himself a polio survivor, had his law partner, Basil O'Connor lead the fight to find a cure, a fight that led to the founding of the March of Dimes organization. With O'Connor's backing, Dr. Jonas Salk used a killed virus approach to develop what turned out to be the vaccine for polio. Field tested in 1954 and approved for use in 1955, the vaccine reduced the number of polio cases in the United States to mere thousands by the mid-1960s. Includes a further reading list, teacher's resources, and more. 60m; DVD. **A:** Family. **P:** Education, Entertainment. **U:** Home, Institution. **Mov-Ent:** Documentary Films, History--U.S., Diseases. **Acq:** Purchase. **Dist:** WGBH/Boston. $19.99.

American Experience: The Richest Man in the World: Andrew Carnegie 1997 (Unrated)
Born in Scotland in 1835, Andrew Carnegie emigrated with his family to the United States in 1848 when steam-powered looms cost his father Will his job. Carnegie proved a hard worker who quickly rose through the ranks of industry. Using money earned from successful investments in railroads and oil, Carnegie became one of the leading businessmen in the United States and one of the richest and most powerful men in the world. In 1900, he held the title of "the richest man in the world" when he sold his Carnegie Steel company to financier J. P. Morgan for $480 million. Before his death in 1919, Carnegie gave away most of his vast fortune through one philanthropic endeavor after another. Includes a timeline, teacher's resources, and more. Narrated by David Ogden Stiers. 60m; VHS, DVD. **A:** Family. **P:** Education, Entertainment. **U:** Home, Institution. **Mov-Ent:** Documentary Films, Biography, History--U.S. **Acq:** Purchase. **Dist:** WGBH/Boston.

American Experience: The Rockefellers 2007 (Unrated)
The closest thing America has ever had to a royal family, the Rockefellers are one of the wealthiest and most influential families to ever live in the United States. After ruthless oil baron John D. Rockefeller built one of the largest private fortunes ever starting in the late 1800s--the family changed the way America did business by at one point owning 90 percent of the world's oil refineries and 90 percent of the marketing of oil—it was left to John's son John Jr. to salvage the family's reputation by donating much of the family fortune to charity. Since those early years, the large family has remained a fixture on the world business scene and in American politics. Includes a timeline, bonus video footage, and more. 210m; VHS, DVD. **A:** Family. **P:**

Education, Entertainment. **U:** Home, Institution. **Mov-Ent:** Documentary Films, Politics & Government, Oil Industry. **Acq:** Purchase. **Dist:** WGBH/Boston.

The American Experience: The Scandalous Mayor 1991
Profiles James Michael Curley, four-term Boston mayor between the world wars. Regarded as a scoundrel by some, and a hero by others, this program combines interviews, footages, newspaper clips and more to create an in-depth portrait of Curley. 60m; VHS, CC. **Pr:** WNET. **A:** Jr. High-Adult. **P:** Education. **U:** Institution. **Gen-Edu:** History--U.S., Biography, Politics & Government. **Acq:** Purchase. **Dist:** PBS Home Video. $59.95.

American Experience: The Telephone 1997 (Unrated)
When he debuted the first telephone on March 10, 1876, at the American Centennial Exposition in Philadephia, Alexander Graham Bell thought there would be little—or no—interest. In fact, both scientists and the general public were fascinated by the device; President Rutherford B. Hayes even said its debut was "one of the greatest events since creation." By 1900, more than 2 million were in operation in the United States, forever changing the way business was done and the speed and accuracy of interpersonal communications. Includes a timeline, teacher's resources, and more. 60m; VHS, DVD. **A:** Family. **P:** Education, Entertainment. **U:** Home, Institution. **Mov-Ent:** Documentary Films, Inventors & Inventions, History. **Acq:** Purchase. **Dist:** WGBH/Boston.

American Experience: The Trials of J. Robert Oppenheimer 2009 (Unrated)
As the end of World War II drew near, a group of scientists working in secret at Los Alamos, New Mexico, desperately tried to become the first to utilize nuclear energy and create the world's most powerful bomb. Thanks to the work of the brilliant, yet troubled, scientist J. Robert Oppenheimer, that group succeeded, leading to the bombings of Hiroshima and Nagasaki, Japan, which forced Japan to surrender to the United States, ending the war. Initially hailed as an American hero, Oppenheimer endured a fall from grace in which his fellow scientists and Americans in general turned on him and humiliated him. This documentary features interviews with former colleagues and uses reenactments of key moments from Oppenheimer's life to try to determine why he was so successful and yet was ultimately thrown aside by the scientific community. Produced by David Grubin, extras include a further reading list, teacher's resources, primary resource materials, and more. 120m; DVD. **A:** Family. **P:** Education, Entertainment. **U:** Home, Institution. **Mov-Ent:** Documentary Films, World War Two, Nuclear Energy. **Acq:** Purchase. **Dist:** WGBH/Boston. $19.99.

The American Experience: The Wright Stuff—The Wright Brothers and the Invention of the Airplane ????
Examines the lives of Orville and Wilbur Wright from their childhood to their celebrity following Kitty Hawk using archival film and photos, interviews with historians, relative remembrances, letter readings, and reenactments. 60m; VHS. **A:** Jr. High-Sr. High. **P:** Education. **U:** Institution, Home. **Gen-Edu:** Biography, Aeronautics, Inventors & Inventions. **Acq:** Purchase. **Dist:** Zenger Media. $19.95.

American Experience: TR, The Story of Theodore Roosevelt 1996 (Unrated)
This documentary covers the life of Theodore Roosevelt, primarily his two terms as President of the United States from 1901 to 1909. A war hero best known for leading the famous 1898 charge up San Juan Hill in Cuba during the Spanish-American War, Roosevelt was President William McKinley's Vice President for the election of 1900. When McKinley was assassinated in September 2001, Roosevelt, at age 42, became the youngest president ever. During his eight years in office (he was reelected in 1904), Roosevelt was known as a strong, progressive leader on domestic issues and one of the strongest presidents ever when it came to foreign policy. Known for the famous slogan "walk softly and carry a big stick," Roosevelt sought peaceful solutions to conflicts, becoming the first president to win the Nobel Peace Prize in 1906. Includes a further reading list, primary resource materials, and more. Narrated by Jason Robards. 225m; DVD. **A:** Family. **P:** Education, Entertainment. **U:** Home, Institution. **Mov-Ent:** Documentary Films, Presidency, Politics & Government. **Acq:** Purchase. **Dist:** WGBH/Boston. $19.99.

American Experience: Transcontinental Railroad 2006 (Unrated)
The building of the first transcontinental railroad in America featured both positive and negative aspects that were unlike those seen on any other large-scale project undertaken in the United States. On May 10, 1869, the ceremonial Golden Spike was driven to signal the railroad's completion in Promontory Summit, Utah. The engineering technique of working from both east and west to meet up was a striking positive. In contrast stood two major negatives: first, the displacement of tens of thousands of Native Americans who stood in the railroad's path; and second, the unbridled greed displayed by almost every company working on the railroad, as crews of Chinese laborers and other immigrants were paid near-slave wages to work in often harsh conditions they were pushed to the breaking point. Includes a timeline, bonus articles, and more. 120m; DVD. **A:** Family. **P:** Education, Entertainment. **U:** Home, Institution. **Mov-Ent:** Documentary Films, Industry & Industrialists, History--U.S. **Acq:** Purchase. **Dist:** WGBH/Boston.

American Experience: Triangle Fire 2011 (Unrated)
On March 25, 1911, a tragic fire at the Triangle Shirtwaist Factory in New York City killed 146 people, most of them women and roughly half of them just teenagers. Just one year earlier, workers at the Triangle Factory and almost every other company in the city's garment district had fought for shorter work hours, higher wages, union representation, and other improvements. While they did not allow a union, Triangle owners Max Blanck and Isaac Harris did cut hours and raise their workers' pay. Despite those concessions, conditions were still deplorable at the time of the fire. In the blaze's aftermath, 36 new laws were passed in New York State governing workplace conditions in general and fire safety specifically. Those laws would serve as a template for new laws passed around the United States. Includes a timeline, an interactive map, primary resource materials, and more. 60m; DVD. **A:** Family. **P:** Education, Entertainment. **U:** Home, Institution. **Music:** Documentary Films, Minorities, History--U.S. **Acq:** Purchase. **Dist:** WGBH/Boston. $19.99.

American Experience: Tupperware! 2004 (Unrated)
This documentary tells the unlikely story of the small company started by Earl Silas Tupper that was turned into a business phenomenon by marketing wizard Brownie Wise. Tupper invented the plastic bowls that bore his name—Tupperware. After a slow start, things began to change rapidly when Wise met Tupper and convinced him that U.S. women were looking for a way to stay in the workforce and make money after their experiences as working women during World War II. Together, the two men created a business empire that allowed women to sell products from the comfort of their own homes, and almost overnight, the "Tupperware party" became an American institution. The documentary includes home videos of actual Tupperware parties, a look at the annual Tupperware Jubilee, and interviews with the Tupperware executives who oversaw the company's meteoric rise. Includes primary resource materials and more. 60m; DVD. **A:** Family. **P:** Education, Entertainment. **U:** Home, Institution. **Mov-Ent:** Documentary Films, Business, Marketing. **Acq:** Purchase. **Dist:** WGBH/Boston.

American Experience: Two Days in October 200?
Recounts two days in October 1967 when a U.S. battalion in Vietnam marched into a trap that killed 61 of them, and a world away a University of Wisconsin protest went tragically out of control. Based on the Pulitzer Prize winning book "They Marched into Sunlight" and told almost exclusively by individuals involved in both events. 90m; DVD; Closed Captioned. **A:** Adult. **P:** Education. **U:** Home. **Gen-Edu:** Documentary Films, Vietnam War. **Acq:** Purchase. **Dist:** WGBH/Boston. $29.95.

American Experience: U.S. Grant--Warrior President 2002 (Unrated)
Leading the Union to its victory over the Confederacy in the Civil War, General Ulysses S. Grant also served as President of the United States and was one of the greatest American leaders of the 19th century. After taking Robert E. Lee's surrender at Appamatox, Grant served two terms as President during one of the most important periods in U.S. history. Not only did he help define how the United States handled fundamental issues regarding the end of slavery and the role of freed African Americans, he also helped guide the country out of a severe economic depression, and, perhaps most importantly, healed the national psyche from the horrible wounds inflicted by the bloody Civil War. Includes a biography, teacher's resources, and more. 240m; DVD. **A:** Family. **P:** Education, Entertainment. **U:** Home, Institution. **Mov-Ent:** Documentary Films, Presidency, History--U.S. **Acq:** Purchase. **Dist:** WGBH/Boston. $17.99.

American Experience: Victory in the Pacific 2005
Looks at the final months of World War II in the Pacific as bloodletting from both the Americans and Japanese escalated and leaders made the ultimate decisions that brought the war to an end. 120m; VHS, DVD. **A:** Adult. **P:** Education. **U:** Home. **Gen-Edu:** Documentary Films, World War Two. **Acq:** Purchase. **Dist:** WGBH/Boston. $24.95.

The American Experience: Vietnam: A Television History 1983
Analyzes the causes, costs, and consequences of the Vietnam conflict from the 1945 revolution against the French to the U.S. evacuation of Saigon in 1975. On seven cassettes. 120m; VHS, CC, 3/4 U. **Pr:** WGBH Boston. **A:** Sr. High-Adult. **P:** Education. **U:** Institution, SURA, Home. **Gen-Edu:** Documentary Films, Vietnam War, Military History. **Acq:** Purchase. **Dist:** Signals Video; Home Vision Cinema; Time-Life Video and Television. $99.95.

Indiv. Titles: 1. Roots of War/The First Vietnam, 1946-1954 2. America's Mandarin, 1954-1963/LBJ Goes to War, 1964-1965 3. America Takes Charge, 1965-1967/With America's Enemy, 1954-1967 4. TET, 1968/Vietnamizing the War, 1969-1973 5. No Neutral Ground: Cambodia and Laos/Peace is at Hand 6. Homefront, U.S.A./The End of the Tunnel, 1973-1975 7. Legacies (60 min.).

American Experience: Vietnam: The Fall of Saigon 2006
Offers footage and eyewitness accounts of Saigon's 1975 collapse into North Vietnamese hands. 60m; DVD. **A:** Jr. High-Adult. **P:** Entertainment. **U:** Home. **Gen-Edu:** Documentary Films. **Acq:** Purchase. **Dist:** WGBH/Boston.

American Experience: Walt Whitman 2007
Overviews the life of Walt Whitman, including his Long Island childhood, his work as a Brooklyn newspaper reporter, his poetry, and his death in 1892 at the age of 69. ?m; DVD. **A:** Adult. **P:** Education. **U:** Home. **Gen-Edu:** Biography, Literature--American. **Acq:** Purchase. **Dist:** WGBH/Boston. $24.95.

American Experience: War Letters 2002 (Unrated)
From the American Revolution all the way to the current incursions in Afghanistan and elsewhere in the Middle East, American servicemen and women have written letters to their loved ones at home trying to describe the day-to-day realities of war and military experience as they see it. This documentary features some of the best, real-life letters received from the different wars in which Americans have served. Special features include a photo gallery, primary resources, a timeline, and general articles related to wartime correspondence. 60m; DVD. **A:** Family. **P:** Education, Entertainment. **U:** Home, Institution. **Mov-Ent:** Documentary Films, War--General, Military History. **Acq:** Purchase. **Dist:** WGBH/Boston.

American Experience: War of the Worlds 2013 (Unrated)
This documentary examines the events that unfurled across the nation on the night before Halloween in 1938 when a radio program performed by Orson Welles was mistaken for news reports describing a real alien invasion. Intended to be nothing more than a Halloween-themed radio performance of author H. G. Wells' "War of the Worlds," the show instead triggered isolated instances of panicked reactions as some people thought the fake news broadcasts that made up the show were real and that the earth was being invaded by creatures from Mars. Includes a timeline, photo gallery, further reading list, and more. 60m; DVD. **A:** Family. **P:** Education, Entertainment. **U:** Home, Institution. **Mov-Ent:** Documentary Films, Halloween, Space Exploration. **Acq:** Purchase. **Dist:** WGBH/Boston. $24.99.

American Experience: We Shall Remain 2009 (Unrated)
A five-part series that examines the history of Native Americans in the United States, dating from the Wampanoag tribe in the 1600s to the new generation of leaders who emerged in the 1970s to guide Native Americans into the future. The main focus of the series is how all Native American people were eventually forced off their ancestral land, which in turn led to severe damage to, and in some cases, the destruction of, their entire culture and way of life. The five episodes include: "After the Mayflower," "Tecumseh's Vision," "Trail of Tears," "Geronimo," and "Wounded Knee." 450m; DVD. **A:** Family. **P:** Education, Entertainment. **U:** Home, Institution. **Mov-Ent:** Documentary Films, History--U.S., Native Americans. **Acq:** Purchase. **Dist:** WGBH/Boston. $44.99.

American Experience: Woodrow Wilson 2001
Explores the transformation of Woodrow Wilson from a history professor to one of America's most respected presidents. 285m; DVD; Closed Captioned. **A:** Jr. High-Adult. **P:** Education. **U:** Home. **Gen-Edu:** Biography, Presidency. **Acq:** Purchase. **Dist:** WGBH/Boston. $34.95.

American Experience: Wyatt Earp 2010 (Unrated)
This documentary examines the complicated life of famed Western hero, Wyatt Earp, most famous for his role in the legendary "Shootout at the OK Corral" in Tombstone, Arizona, on October 26, 1881. Most modern accounts of Earp's life focus on his successes as a lawman, painting him as a folk hero for his willingness to wear the sheriff's badge in any number of Western towns that were largely lawless before his arrival. In reality, Earp worked any number of jobs as he traveled across the West and often found himself flirting with the wrong side of the law, as he definitely enjoyed gambling and visiting brothels. That said, police work was definitely Earp's specialty, and he cemented his legacy as one of the West's "good guys" when he and his brothers (and good friend Doc Holiday) finished off their feud with the notorious Cowboys gang with the bloody OK Corral shootout. Includes a timeline, further reading list, photo gallery, teacher's resources, and more. 60m; DVD. **A:** Family. **P:** Education, Entertainment. **U:** Home, Institution. **Mov-Ent:** Documentary Films, History--U.S., Gambling. **Acq:** Purchase. **Dist:** WGBH/Boston. $19.99.

American Fabulous 1992 (Unrated) — ★★½
The posthumously released autobiography of an eccentric homosexual who lived life in the fast lane. Jeffrey Strouth performs his monologue from the back seat of a 1957 Cadillac, where the images of small-town America are seen to contrast sharply with his flamboyant style. His grotesque and candid recollections include his alcoholic Elvis-impersonator father, a stint as a teenage prostitute, drag queen friends, and drug addiction in New York. Strouth puts a comic twist on even the most brutal of his memories. He died of AIDS at the age of 33 in 1992. 105m; VHS. **C:** Jeffrey Strouth; Directed by Reno Dakota; Written by Jeffrey Strouth. **A:** College-Adult. **P:** Entertainment. **U:** Home. **Mov-Ent:** Documentary Films, Drug Abuse. **Acq:** Purchase. **Dist:** First Run Features. $59.95.

The American Family: An Endangered Species Series 1979
"The American Family" series focuses on a variety of family units through a series of intimate film essays. Covers a wide social, economic, racial, and geographic range. All are available individually. Running times vary. 9m; VHS, 3/4 U. **Pr:** Marion Lear Swaybill. **A:** Sr. High-Adult. **P:** Education. **U:** Institution, SURA. **Gen-Edu:** Family. **Acq:** Purchase. **Dist:** Home Vision Cinema.

Indiv. Titles: 1. The Merinos 2. The Edholms 3. Sean's Story 4. The Gleghorns 5. The Hartmans 6. Peggy Collins 7. The Kreimeik and Bosworth Families 8. The Sorianos 9. The Schuster/Isaacson Family 10. Share-A-Home.

An American Family: Anniversary Edition 2011 (Unrated)
A retrospective on the groundbreaking reality series "An American Family," featuring best moments from the series. 120m;

DVD, Streaming. **A:** Jr. High-Adult. **P:** Entertainment. **U:** Home. **L:** English.: Documentary Films, Television, Drama. **Acq:** Purchase, Rent/Lease. **Dist:** Acorn Media Group Inc. $24.99 11.99.

American Family Revisited 1983
Updated portrait of the William Loud family of Santa Barbara, the subjects of the PBS 12-hour series "An American Family." 60m; VHS. **A:** Sr. High-Adult. **P:** Education. **U:** Institution, Home. **Gen-Edu:** Family. **Acq:** Purchase, Rent/Lease. **Dist:** DeepFocus Productions Film Library.

American Family: The Complete First Season 2003 (Unrated)
Presents the debut season of the 2002-2004 PBS television drama series on the American-Latino Gonzalez family as father Jess (Olmos) and his grown children endure the loss of wife and mother, Berta (Braga). Includes: daughter Nina (Marie) moves back in to her parents' home following Berta's death to help out though this doesn't please everyone, a family reunion provides an opportunity for Jess to share stories of his grandmother who served as a soldier during the Mexican Revolution, and the tragedy of the September 11, 2001, terrorist attacks causes emotional flashbacks for Jess of his time in the Korean War. 22 episodes. 1001m; DVD. **C:** Edward James Olmos; Constance Marie; Sonia Braga; Kurt Cacares; Austin Marques; A.J. Lamas. **A:** Jr. High-Adult. **P:** Entertainment. **U:** Home. **Mov-Ent:** Television Series, Family, Drama. **Acq:** Purchase. **Dist:** Fox Home Entertainment. $69.98.

An American Farmer 1983
This program profiles a midwestern farmer, his life and his work. 14m; VHS, 3/4 U. **Pr:** WGBH Boston. **A:** Jr. High-Adult. **P:** Education. **U:** Institution, SURA. **Gen-Edu:** Agriculture, Interviews. **Acq:** Purchase, Rent/Lease. **Dist:** Hearst Entertainment/King Features.

American Fashion. . .Rags and Riches 1981
An inside look at how new fashions are dreamed up by famous designers and skillfully promoted to influence American consumers. Designers Halston, Bill Blass and Calvin Klein are interviewed. 52m; VHS, 3/4 U. **Pr:** National Broadcasting Company. **A:** Jr. High-Adult. **P:** Education. **U:** Institution, SURA. **Gen-Edu:** Clothing & Dress. **Acq:** Purchase, Rent/Lease. **Dist:** Home Vision Cinema.

American Fever 1994
A 19th century Norwegian woman prepares to immigrate to America. 15m; VHS. **A:** Jr. High. **P:** Education. **U:** Institution. **Gen-Edu:** Immigration. **Acq:** Purchase. **Dist:** Her Own Words Productions. $95.00.

The American Field Trip—the Career 1994
Four-part vocational guidance series that uses on-site footage and interviews with different employees to look at career opportunities in communications, journalism, marine biology, and space technology. Emphasis is placed on job qualifications, proper study habits, and getting the job. 112m; VHS. **A:** Sr. High-Adult. **P:** Education. **U:** Institution. **Gen-Edu:** Occupations, Job Training, Journalism. **Acq:** Purchase. **Dist:** HRM Video. $490.00.

American Film Institute's Life Achievement Awards: Alfred Hitchcock 1979
The American Film Institute honors Hitchcock's varied filmmaking career. Includes excerpts from "The 39 Steps," "Vertigo," and "Psycho." 72m; VHS. **Pr:** Worldvision Enterprises. **A:** Family. **P:** Entertainment. **U:** Home. **Mov-Ent:** Documentary Films, Filmmaking. **Acq:** Purchase. **Dist:** Movies Unlimited. $19.95.

American Film Institute's Life Achievement Awards: Bette Davis 1977
The American Film Institute honors Davis' long and colorful film career. Excerpts include "Now Voyager," "Dark Victory," "Forever Amber," and others. 68m; VHS. **Pr:** Worldvision Enterprises. **A:** Family. **P:** Entertainment. **U:** Home. **Mov-Ent:** Documentary Films, Biography: Show Business. **Acq:** Purchase. **Dist:** Movies Unlimited. $19.95.

American Film Institute's Life Achievement Awards: Billy Wilder 1986
Writer, director, and cynic, Wilder's film career includes "The Apartment," "Some Like it Hot," and "Sunset Boulevard." Wilder is saluted by Jack Lemmon, Audrey Hepburn, Fred MacMurray, Walter Matthau, and Tony Curtis. 72m; VHS. **Pr:** Worldvision Enterprises. **A:** Family. **P:** Entertainment. **U:** Home. **Mov-Ent:** Documentary Films, Filmmaking. **Acq:** Purchase. **Dist:** Movies Unlimited. $19.99.

American Film Institute's Life Achievement Awards: Frank Capra 1982
The populist director of films for the common man is honored by Bette Davis, Claudette Colbert, Jimmy Stewart, Donna Reed, and other stars, as are his films, including "It's a Wonderful Life," "Lost Horizon," "You Can't Take It with You," and "It Happened One Night." 71m; VHS. **Pr:** Worldvision Enterprises. **A:** Family. **P:** Entertainment. **U:** Home. **Mov-Ent:** Documentary Films, Filmmaking. **Acq:** Purchase. **Dist:** Movies Unlimited. $19.99.

American Film Institute's Life Achievement Awards: Fred Astaire 1981
The master innovator of the song-and-dance film is saluted with footage from "Roberta," "Top Hat," "Funny Face," and other movies. 93m; VHS. **Pr:** Worldvision Enterprises. **A:** Family. **P:** Entertainment. **U:** Home. **Mov-Ent:** Documentary Films, Biography: Show Business. **Acq:** Purchase. **Dist:** Movies Unlimited. $19.99.

American Film Institute's Life Achievement Awards: Gene Kelly 1985
Dancer, actor, director, and screen legend, Kelly is honored by Fred Astaire, Shirley MacLaine, Leslie Caron, and others. Films clips include "An American in Paris," "The Pirate," and "Singin' in the Rain." 71m; VHS. **Pr:** Worldvision Enterprises. **A:** Family. **P:** Entertainment. **U:** Home. **Mov-Ent:** Documentary Films, Biography: Show Business. **Acq:** Purchase. **Dist:** Movies Unlimited. $19.99.

American Film Institute's Life Achievement Awards: Henry Fonda 1978
The American Film Institute honors Henry Fonda for his exceptional film career, including such films as "The Grapes of Wrath," "Jezebel," "Young Mr. Lincoln," and "Mr. Roberts." Presenters include Jane and Peter Fonda, Jack Lemmon, and Lucille Ball. 97m; VHS. **Pr:** Worldvision Enterprises. **A:** Family. **P:** Entertainment. **U:** Home. **Mov-Ent:** Documentary Films, Biography: Show Business. **Acq:** Purchase. **Dist:** Movies Unlimited. $19.95.

American Film Institute's Life Achievement Awards: Jack Lemmon 1988
Anecdotes from Julie Andrews, Walter Matthau, Neil Simon, and Janet Leigh and highlights from "The Odd Couple," "The Fortune Cookie," and "The Apartment" are included in this salute. 70m; VHS. **Pr:** Worldvision Enterprises. **A:** Family. **P:** Entertainment. **U:** Home. **Mov-Ent:** Documentary Films, Biography: Show Business. **Acq:** Purchase. **Dist:** Movies Unlimited. $19.99.

American Film Institute's Life Achievement Awards: James Cagney 1974
The American Film Institute honors James Cagney for his wide and exceptional film career. Includes excerpts from "Yankee Doodle Dandy," "The Seven Little Foys," and "Love Me or Leave Me." 74m; VHS. **Pr:** Worldvision Enterprises. **A:** Family. **P:** Entertainment. **U:** Home. **Mov-Ent:** Documentary Films, Biography: Show Business. **Acq:** Purchase. **Dist:** Movies Unlimited. $19.95.

American Film Institute's Life Achievement Awards: Jimmy Stewart 1980
A tribute to one of America's best loved actors, featuring film clips and interviews with many of Hollywood's biggest names. Includes excerpts from "It's a Wonderful Life," "Harvey," "Vertigo," and others. 71m; VHS. **C:** Hosted by Henry Fonda. **Pr:** Worldvision Enterprises. **A:** Family. **P:** Entertainment. **U:** Home. **Mov-Ent:** Documentary Films, Biography: Show Business. **Acq:** Purchase. **Dist:** Movies Unlimited. $19.95.

American Film Institute's Life Achievement Awards: John Ford 1973
The recipient of the very first Life Achievement Award, director Ford is honored by John Wayne, Maureen O'Hara, Charlton Heston, and others. Films clips include "Stagecoach," "Fort Apache," and "The Grapes of Wrath." 75m; VHS. **C:** Hosted by Danny Kaye. **Pr:** Worldvision Enterprises. **A:** Family. **P:** Entertainment. **U:** Home. **Mov-Ent:** Documentary Films, Filmmaking. **Acq:** Purchase. **Dist:** Movies Unlimited. $19.99.

American Film Institute's Life Achievement Awards: John Huston 1983
Writer, director, actor, and adventurer Huston is feted by fans Lauren Bacall, Orson Welles, Jack Nicholson, and Robert Mitchum. Film clips include "Key Largo," "The Maltese Falcon," and "The Treasure of Sierra Madre." 96m; VHS. **Pr:** Worldvision Enterprises. **A:** Family. **P:** Entertainment. **U:** Home. **Mov-Ent:** Documentary Films, Filmmaking. **Acq:** Purchase. **Dist:** Movies Unlimited. $19.99.

American Film Institute's Life Achievement Awards: Lillian Gish 1984
The silent screen legend is honored with clips from "The Birth of a Nation," "Duel in the Sun," "The Scarlet Letter," and other films, as well as with testimonials by Douglas Fairbanks Jr., Mary Martin, Sally Fields, and Jennifer Jones. 73m; VHS. **Pr:** Worldvision Enterprises. **A:** Family. **P:** Entertainment. **U:** Home. **Mov-Ent:** Documentary Films, Biography: Show Business. **Acq:** Purchase. **Dist:** Movies Unlimited. $19.99.

American Film Institute's Life Achievement Awards: Orson Welles 1975
Auteur Welles is saluted by Frank Sinatra, Ingrid Bergman, Charlton Heston, and Joseph Cotten. Film clips include "Citizen Kane," "Touch of Evil," and "The Magnificent Ambersons," as well as Welles as actor in "The Third Man" and other films. 75m; VHS. **Pr:** Worldvision Enterprises. **A:** Family. **P:** Entertainment. **U:** Home. **Mov-Ent:** Documentary Films, Biography: Show Business, Filmmaking. **Acq:** Purchase. **Dist:** Movies Unlimited. $19.99.

The American Film Theatre: Series 1 1973
Five "plays-on-film" including 'The Iceman Cometh' and 'The Maids.' Stars Gene Wilder, Alan Bates, Glenda Jackson, Dame Judi Dench and many others. 677m; VHS, DVD. **A:** Adult. **P:** Entertainment. **U:** Home. **Mov-Ent:** Theater, Performing Arts. **Acq:** Purchase. **Dist:** Kino on Video. $119.95.

The American Film Theatre: Series 2 1973
Five "plays-on-film" including 'A Delicate Balance' and 'Three Sisters.' Stars Katherine Hepburn, Laurence Olivier, Joan Plowright and many others. 655m; VHS, DVD. **A:** Adult. **P:** Entertainment. **U:** Home. **Mov-Ent:** Theater, Performing Arts. **Acq:** Purchase. **Dist:** Kino on Video. $119.95.

The American Film Theatre: Series 3 1973
Four "plays-on-film" including 'Galileo' and 'Jacques Brel Is Alive and Well and Living in Paris.' Stars Topol and Sir John Gielgud, Jacques Brel and many others. 427m; VHS, DVD. **A:** Adult. **P:** Entertainment. **U:** Home. **Mov-Ent:** Theater, Performing Arts. **Acq:** Purchase. **Dist:** Kino on Video. $89.95.
Indiv. Titles: 1. Philadelphia Here I Come! 2. Jacques Brel Is Alive and Well and Living in Paris 3. Lost in the Stars 4. Galileo.

American Film Theatre Set I 1973
Collection of "plays-on-film" featuring top stars from stage and screen. Five works including The Iceman Cometh, The Maids, and Rhinoceros. 677m; VHS, DVD. **A:** Adult. **P:** Entertainment. **U:** Home. **Mov-Ent:** Classic Films, Drama. **Acq:** Purchase. **Dist:** Kino on Video. $119.95.

American Film Theatre Set II 1973
Collection of "plays-on-film" featuring top stars from stage and screen. 655m; VHS, DVD. **A:** Adult. **P:** Entertainment. **U:** Home. **Mov-Ent:** Classic Films, Drama. **Acq:** Purchase. **Dist:** Kino on Video. $119.95.
Indiv. Titles: 1. The Homecoming 2. Three Sisters 3. In Celebration 4. The Man in the Glass Booth 5. A Delicate Balance.

American 1st and 9th Armies: Aachen to the Ruhr River 1945
Uncensored combat footage of Americans fighting the Nazis in 1944 in Klenheim, Stolberg, Mausbach and the Hurtigen Forest comprise this tape. 58m/B/W; VHS, 3/4 U. **TV Std:** NTSC, PAL. **Pr:** U.S. War Department. **A:** Sr. High-Adult. **P:** Education. **U:** Institution, Home. **Gen-Edu:** Documentary Films, War--General, Military History. **Acq:** Purchase. **Dist:** International Historic Films Inc.; German Language Video Center. $29.95.

The American Flag: Story of Old Glory—Revised 2nd Edition 1970
A visual study of the country's flag, reviewing changes in its appearance through the years. 14m; VHS, 3/4 U. **Pr:** Encyclopedia Britannica Educational Corporation. **A:** Primary-Jr. High. **P:** Education. **U:** Institution, SURA. **Gen-Edu:** Philosophy & Ideology. **Acq:** Purchase, Rent/Lease, Trade-in. **Dist:** Encyclopedia Britannica.

American Flyers 1985 (PG-13) — ★★½
Two competitive brothers train for a grueling three-day bicycle race in Colorado while tangling with personal drama, including the spectre that one of them may have inherited dad's tendency for cerebral aneurisms and is sure to drop dead during a bike race soon. Written by bike movie specialist Tesich ("Breaking Away") with a lot of the usual cliches (the last bike ride, battling bros, eventual understanding), which are gracefully overridden by fine bike-racing photography. Interesting performances, especially Chong as a patient girlfriend and Amos as the trainer. 113m; VHS, DVD, Wide, CC. **C:** Kevin Costner; David Marshall Grant; Rae Dawn Chong; Alexandra Paul; John Amos; Janice Rule; Robert Townsend; Jennifer Grey; Luca Bercovici; Directed by John Badham; Written by Steve Tesich; Music by Lee Ritenour; Greg Mathieson. **Pr:** Gareth Wigan; Paula Weinstein; Warner Bros. **A:** Jr. High-Adult. **P:** Entertainment. **U:** Home. **Mov-Ent:** Bicycling, Sports--Fiction: Drama. **Acq:** Purchase. **Dist:** Warner Home Video, Inc. $19.98.

American Folk Music 19??
Outlines the history of American folk music, discussing how the ballads of Britain and Ireland, brought over by immigrants, have influenced their heritage. 21m; VHS. **A:** Family. **P:** Education. **U:** Institution. **Gen-Edu:** History--U.S., Folklore & Legends. **Acq:** Purchase. **Dist:** Educational Video Network. $39.95.

American Folklife Company 1971
The American Folklife Company is a group of folk artists who represent the diversity of American cultural life. The program begins with a slave story and progresses to a conclusion with traditional blues songs. 30m; EJ. **Pr:** NETCHE. **A:** College-Adult. **P:** Education. **U:** Institution, CCTV, BCTV, SURA. **Fin-Art:** Folklore & Legends. **Acq:** Purchase, Rent/Lease, Subscription. **Dist:** NETCHE.

American Folklore Series 197?
This ten-part series is a lesson in American folklore, a product of our people and national history. Tales of heroes are creatively told relating to regions and occupations. Programs are available individually. 11m; VHS, 3/4 U. **Pr:** BFA Educational Media. **A:** Primary. **P:** Education. **U:** Institution, SURA. **Chl-Juv:** Folklore & Legends. **Acq:** Purchase. **Dist:** Phoenix Learning Group.
Indiv. Titles: 1. Captain Stormalong 2. Casey Jones 3. Glooskap 4. Joe Margarac 5. Tepozton 6. John Henry 7. Johnny Appleseed 8. Paul Bunyan 9. Pecos Bill 10. Steamboat Bill.

American Foreign Policy Series 1981
Using Movietone newsreel footage with added narration, this series of four programs documents historical events and decisions that determined America's foreign policy from 1940 to 1963. Programs are available individually. 16m/B/W; VHS, 3/4 U. **Pr:** Encyclopedia Britannica Educational Corporation. **A:** Sr. High-Adult. **P:** Education. **U:** Institution, SURA. **Gen-Edu:** History--U.S., International Relations. **Acq:** Purchase, Rent/Lease, Trade-in. **Dist:** Encyclopedia Britannica.
Indiv. Titles: 1. FDR and World War II 2. Truman and Containment 3. Eisenhower and the Cold War 4. Kennedy and Confrontation.

American Foundations 1980
This film traces the development of American life and values, from the nation's discovery and exploration through the stresses and tensions of the 20th century. 25m; VHS, 3/4 U. **Pr:** Video Knowledge, Inc. **A:** Sr. High-Adult. **P:** Education. **U:** Institution, SURA. **Gen-Edu:** History--U.S. **Acq:** Purchase. **Dist:** Cambridge Educational; Video Knowledge, Inc.; Knowledge Unlimited, Inc. $49.95.
Indiv. Titles: 1. Birth of the Nation — The Thirteen Colonies 2. Colonists Become Citizens — The Evolution of Freedom 3. Technology and Environment — The Economic Development of

America 4. American Ideals in the 20th Century 5. Crossroads of the Cold War 6. The New Immigrant 7. Women and the American Family.

The American Friend 1977 — ★★★½
Tribute to the American gangster film helped introduce Wenders to American moviegoers. Young Hamburg picture framer thinks he has a terminal disease and is set up by American expatriate Hopper to become a hired assassin in West Germany. The lure is a promise of quick money that the supposedly dying man can then leave his wife and child. After the first assasination, the two bond. Hopper is the typical Wenders protagonist, a strange man in a strange land looking for a connection. Great, creepy thriller adapted from Patricia Highsmith's novel "Ripley's Game." Fuller and Ray (better known as directors) appear briefly as gangsters. 127m; VHS, DVD. **C:** Bruno Ganz; Dennis Hopper; Elisabeth (Lisa) Kreuzer; Gerard Blain; Jean Eustache; Samuel Fuller; Nicholas Ray; Daniel Schmid; Lou Castel; Rudolf Schuendler; Sandy Whitelaw; Cameo(s) Wim Wenders; Directed by Wim Wenders; Written by Wim Wenders; Cinematography by Robby Muller; Music by Jurgen Knieper. **Pr:** Wim Wenders; Wim Wenders. **A:** Sr. High-Adult. **P:** Entertainment. **U:** Home. **L:** German, English. **Mov-Ent**: Mystery & Suspense, Cult Films. **Acq:** Purchase. **Dist:** Anchor Bay Entertainment; Facets Multimedia Inc.; German Language Video Center.

American Friends 1991 (PG) — ★★
Genteel story masquerades as high comedy. Palin is a fussy middle-aged Oxford classics tutor. On a holiday he meets American Hartley (Booth) and her adopted daughter, Elinor (Alvarado). Both women are immensely attracted to the don (for reasons that are unclear) and follow him back to Oxford, where he's engaged in a battle of succession with his rival Molina. Dismal screenplay lacks logic and urgency, making it difficult to care about the story or the characters. Script is said to have been inspired by an incident in the life of Palin's great-grandfather. If this sounds like your cup of tea, save your time and watch a Merchant Ivory film instead. 95m; VHS, Streaming. **C:** Michael Palin; Connie Booth; Trini Alvarado; Alfred Molina; Directed by Tristam Powell; Written by Michael Palin; Tristam Powell; Music by Georges Delerue. **Pr:** Castle Hill Productions. **A:** Sr. High-Adult. **P:** Entertainment. **U:** Home. **Mov-Ent**: Comedy Romantic, Great Britain, Education. **Acq:** Purchase. **Dist:** CinemaNow Inc.; Facets Multimedia Inc. $92.95.

The American Frontier: Jamestown 1996
Looks at the voyage to Jamestown and the trials and hardships of the first settlers. 27m; VHS. **A:** Primary-Adult. **P:** Education. **U:** Institution. **Gen-Edu**: History, History--U.S. **Acq:** Purchase. **Dist:** Knowledge Unlimited, Inc. $75.00.

American Fusion 2005 (PG-13) — ★★½
Charming romance in a culture clash comedy. Middle-aged, divorced Yvonne (Chang) is the frustrated daughter in a crazy Chinese-American family. She falls in love with Hispanic dentist Jose (Morales) but her family disapproves and his family isn't too happy with the cultural diversity either. 107m; DVD. **C:** Sylvia Chang; Esai Morales; Collin Chou; James Hong; Lan Yeung; Noriyuki "Pat" Morita; Randall Park; Directed by Frank Lin; Written by Randall Park; Frank Lin; Cinematography by Jason Inouye; Music by Dave Iwataki. **A:** Jr. High-Adult. **P:** Entertainment. **U:** Home. **Mov-Ent**: Hispanic Culture, Comedy--Romantic. **Acq:** Purchase. **Dist:** Image Entertainment Inc.

The American Gangster 1992
Documentary look at the beginnings of organized crime and the rise of the gangster in American society. Includes vintage film and photographs. Profiles include Bugsy Siegel, Al Capone, John Dillinger, Pretty Boy Floyd, and Lucky Luciano. 45m; VHS. **A:** Sr. High-Adult. **P:** Entertainment. **U:** Home. **Gen-Edu**: Documentary Films. **Acq:** Purchase. **Dist:** Sony Pictures Home Entertainment Inc. $14.95.

American Gangster 2007 (R) — ★★★
Director Ridley Scott's shot at the gangster genre hits the mark, transcending the tough-guy norm in its purposeful juxtaposition of the two main characters: Frank Lucas (Washington), the near-perfect, respectable, yet cold-blooded criminal genius who is pursued by the unkempt, womanizing, but razor-straight cop, Ritchie Roberts (Crowe). Washington and Crowe are mesmerizing in this powerful story of the brutality and excess of the '70s era Harlem drug trade that would be over-the-top if it weren't true, and that revolutionized both the drug trade and the law enforcement of the period. 157m; DVD, Blu-Ray. **C:** John Ortiz; Denzel Washington; Russell Crowe; Chiwetel Ejiofor; Cuba Gooding, Jr.; Josh Brolin; Ted Levine; Armand Assante; Clarence Williams, III; Lymari Nadal; RZA; Ruby Dee; Idris Elba; Carla Gugino; Common; Joe Morton; Jon Polito; Kevin Corrigan; Ruben Santiago-Hudson; Roger Bart; KaDee Strickland; Directed by Ridley Scott; Written by Steven Zaillian; Cinematography by Harris Savides; Music by Marc Streitenfeld. **Pr:** Brian Grazer; Ridley Scott; Ridley Scott; Scott Free; Imagine Films; Universal. **A:** Sr. High-Adult. **P:** Entertainment. **U:** Home. **L:** English. **Mov-Ent**: Black Culture, Crime Drama, Drug Trafficking/Dealing. **Awds:** Screen Actors Guild '07: Support. Actress (Dee). **Acq:** Purchase. **Dist:** Movies Unlimited; Alpha Video; Universal Studios Home Video.

American Gangster: The Complete 1st Season 2006
Documentary series explores the lives of nine African American criminals, including Stanley "Tookie" Williams, co-founder of the Crips gang, who was nominated for a Nobel Peace Prize for trying to end gang warfare and was ultimately executed for multiple murders; Ricky "Freeway" Ross, a would-be pro tennis player who built a successful cocaine empire with Iran-Contra connections; Lorenzo "Fat Cat" Nichols, who modeled his crime organization after the General Motors management structure; and Dino and Troy Smith, who studied gemology to blend in with elite jewelers and high end collectors. 180m; DVD. **C:** Narrated by Ving Rhames. **A:** Adult. **P:** Entertainment. **U:** Home. **Mov-Ent**: Documentary Films. **Acq:** Purchase. **Dist:** Paramount Pictures Corp.

American Gigolo 1979 (R) — ★★
A Los Angeles loner who sexually services the rich women of Beverly Hills becomes involved with the wife of a California state senator and is then framed for a murder he did not commit. A highly stylized but empty view of seamy low lives marred by a contrived plot, with decent romp in the hay readiness displayed by Gere. 117m; VHS, DVD, Wide. **C:** Richard Gere; Lauren Hutton; Hector Elizondo; Nina Van Pallandt; Bill Duke; K. Callan; Cameo(s) Paul Schrader; Directed by Paul Schrader; Written by Paul Schrader; Cinematography by John Bailey; Music by Giorgio Moroder. **Pr:** Jerry Bruckheimer. **A:** Sr. High-Adult. **P:** Entertainment. **U:** Home. **Mov-Ent**: Mystery & Suspense, Sex & Sexuality, Prostitution. **Acq:** Purchase. **Dist:** Paramount Pictures Corp. $59.95.

American Girl: Chrissa Stands Strong 2009 (Unrated) — ★★½
When fourth-grader Chrissa's family moves in to help out her recently-widowed grandma, she's most afraid that she won't make friends at her new school. Chrissa's fears seem well-founded when Tara, queen of the mean girl clique, starts tormenting Chrissa and turns out to be her main rival on the swim team. Chrissa must figure out the best way to stand up to Tara's bullying. 90m; DVD. **C:** Michael Learned; Annabeth Gish; Timothy Bottoms; Jennifer Tilly; Don Franklin; Sammi Hanratty; Adair Tishler; Austin Thomas; Directed by Martha Coolidge; Written by Christine Coyle Johnson; Julie Prendiville Roux; Cinematography by Johnny E. Jensen; Music by Jennie Muskett. **A:** Family. **P:** Entertainment. **U:** Home. **Mov-Ent. Acq:** Purchase. **Dist:** Warner Home Video, Inc.

An American Girls Author Series 1991
Series of interviews with some of the most popular names in childrens' literature. Especially intended for girls, each program comes with 35 copies of an author's biography. Also available separately. 18m; VHS. **A:** Primary. **P:** Education. **U:** Institution. **Chl-Juv**: Interviews, Literature--Children. **Acq:** Purchase. **Dist:** Pleasant Co. Publications. $24.00.
Indiv. Titles: 1. Meet Valerie Tripp 2. Meet Janet Shaw.

American Gladiators Ultimate Workout 2008 (Unrated)
Television's American Gladiators provide an extreme physical fitness workout, designed to help lose weight and build muscles. 89m; DVD. **A:** Jr. High-Adult. **P:** Instruction. **U:** Home. **Hea-Sci**: Fitness/Exercise. **Dist:** Lions Gate Entertainment Inc. $12.98.

American Gothic 1988 (R) — **Bomb!**
Three couples headed for a vacation are instead stranded on an island and captured by a demented family headed by Steiger and De Carlo, a scary enough proposition in itself. Even worse, Ma and Pa have three middle-aged moronic offspring who still dress as children and are intent on killing the thwarted vacationers (who are none too bright themselves) one by bloody one. A stultifying career low for all involved. 89m; VHS, DVD. **C:** Rod Steiger; Yvonne De Carlo; Michael J. Pollard; Sarah Torgov; Fiona Hutchinson; William Hootkins; Terry Kelly; Mark Ericksen; Caroline Barclay; Mark Lindsay Chapman; Directed by John Hough; Written by Michael Vines; Bert Wetanson; Cinematography by Harvey Harrison; Music by Alan Parker. **Pr:** Independent. **A:** Adult. **P:** Entertainment. **U:** Home. **Mov-Ent**: Horror, Family. **Acq:** Purchase. **Dist:** CinemaNow Inc. $89.95.

American Gothic: The Complete Series 1995
Contains 22 episodes starring Gary Cole, Jake Weber and Paige Turco. Includes over 45 minutes of deleted scenes. 1002m; DVD. **A:** Adult. **P:** Entertainment. **U:** Home. **Mov-Ent**: Television, Drama. **Acq:** Purchase. **Dist:** Universal Studios Home Video. $49.98.

American Government: Standard Deviants 1999
Overviews the origins and characteristics of U.S. government, the writing of the Constitution and Bill of Rights, the three branches of government, how a bill becomes a law, the electoral college and the Pendleton Act. Two-video set, appropriate for Grades 7-12. 225m; VHS. **A:** Jr. High-Sr. High. **P:** Education. **U:** Institution. **Gen-Edu**: Politics & Government. **Acq:** Purchase. **Dist:** Zenger Media; Social Studies School Service. $33.99.

American Government Super Pack 2001
The Standard Deviants group uses humor and historical film to explain parts and function of American government. Ten-volume series. ?m; VHS. **A:** Jr. High-Sr. High. **P:** Education. **U:** Institution. **Gen-Edu**: Politics & Government, U.S. States. **Acq:** Purchase. **Dist:** Zenger Media. $449.99.
Indiv. Titles: 1. Introduction to Government 2. The U.S. Constitution 3. Federalism 4. Civil Rights 5. Civil Liberties 6. The Three Branches of Government 7. The Congress 8. The Executive Branch 9. The Bureaucracy 10. The Judicial System.

American Graffiti 1973 (PG) — ★★★½
Atmospheric, episodic look at growing up in the innocence of America before the Kennedy assassination and the Vietnam War. It all takes place on one hectic but typical night in the life of a group of recent California high school grads unsure of what the next big step in life is. So they spend their time cruising, listening to Wolfman Jack, and meeting at the drive-in. Slice of '60s life boasts a prudent script, great set design, authentic soundtrack, and consistently fine performances by the young cast. Catapulted Dreyfuss, Ford, and Somers to stardom, branded Lucas a hot directorial commodity with enough leverage to launch "Star Wars," and steered Howard and Williams towards continued age-of-innocence nirvana on "Happy Days." 112m; VHS, DVD, Blu-Ray. **C:** Richard Dreyfuss; Ron Howard; Cindy Williams; MacKenzie Phillips; Paul LeMat; Charles Martin Smith; Suzanne Somers; Candy Clark; Harrison Ford; Bo Hopkins; Joe Spano; Kathleen Quinlan; Wolfman Jack; Directed by George Lucas; Written by George Lucas; Gloria Katz; Willard Huyck; Cinematography by Jan D'Alquen; Ron Everslage. **Pr:** Mark Huffam; Francis Ford Coppola. **A:** Family. **P:** Entertainment. **U:** Home. **Mov-Ent**: Comedy-Drama, Automobiles--Racing, Adolescence. **Awds:** AFI '98: Top 100; Golden Globes '74: Film--Mus./Comedy; Natl. Film Reg. '95; N.Y. Film Critics '73: Screenplay; Natl. Soc. Film Critics '73: Screenplay. **Acq:** Purchase. **Dist:** Facets Multimedia Inc. $14.95.

American Guerrilla in the Philippines 1950 — ★½
Listless war drama whose title says it all. After his boat is sunk, Ensign Chuck Palmer (Power) is among those stranded in the Philippines after the islands surrender to the Japanese invasion in 1942. Plamer joins the guerilla movement as they wait for Gen. Douglas MacArthur's promised return. 105m; DVD. **C:** Tyrone Power; Micheline Presle; Tom Ewell; Tommy Cook; Juan Torena; Robert Barrat; Directed by Fritz Lang; Written by Lamar Trotti; Cinematography by Harry Jackson; Music by Cyril Mockridge. **A:** Adult. **P:** Entertainment. **U:** Home. **L:** English. **Mov-Ent**: World War Two. **Acq:** Purchase. **Dist:** Fox Home Entertainment.

American Gun 2002 (R) — ★★★
Coburn, in his last performance, is Martin Tillman, an anguished father whose daughter has recently been killed during a violent crime. He decides to trace the history of the gun that was used, and along the way deals with an incident from his service in the Korean War that still haunts him. Coburn's performance is magnificent, even if the material itself is a little uneven. 89m; VHS, DVD. **C:** James Coburn; Barbara Bain; Virginia Madsen; Alexandra Holden; Directed by Alan Jacobs; Written by Alan Jacobs; Cinematography by Phil Parmet; Music by Anthony Marinelli. **A:** Sr. High-Adult. **P:** Entertainment. **U:** Home. **Mov-Ent**: Christmas, Korean War, Runaways. **Acq:** Purchase. **Dist:** Buena Vista Home Entertainment. $29.99.

American Gun 2005 (R) — ★½
Three generally uninvolving stories about guns from debuting director Avelino. In Oregon, Janet (Harden) and her teen son David (Marquete) are guilt-wracked community outcasts three years after her older son participated in a high school shooting rampage. At a gang-ridden Chicago school, Principal Carter (Whitaker) expels student Jay (Escarpeta) for having a handgun, and the pic follows the teen to his convenience store job where he tries to use the (fake) weapon as intimidation against would-be thieves. In Virginia, co-ed Mary Ann (Cardellini) sets aside her dislike of firearms and learns to shoot after a friend is date-raped. 94m; DVD. **C:** Donald Sutherland; Forest Whitaker; Marcia Gay Harden; Linda Cardellini; Tony Goldwyn; Christopher Marquette; Nikki Reed; Garcelle Beauvais; Amanda Seyfried; Melissa Leo; Arlen Escarpeta; Directed by Aric Avelino; Written by Aric Avelino; Steven Bagatourian; Cinematography by Nancy Schreiber; Music by Peter Golub. **Pr:** Ted Kroeber; IFC Films; Participant Films. **A:** Sr. High-Adult. **P:** Entertainment. **U:** Home. **L:** English. **Mov-Ent**: Rape. **Acq:** Purchase. **Dist:** Genius Entertainment.

An American Haunting 2005 (PG-13) — ★½
Fictionalized account of Tennessee's "Bell Witch," adapted from Brent Monahan's novel. In 1818, a neighbor curses the prosperous Bell family for their greed and soon they are haunted by a poltergeist that eventually takes possession of pretty teen daughter Betsy (Hurd-Ward). Parents John (Sutherland) and Lucy (Spacek) try to fight the evil spirit. Lots of hokum, not many frights. 82m; DVD. **C:** Donald Sutherland; Sissy Spacek; Rachel Hurd-Wood; James D'Arcy; Matthew Marsh; Thom Fell; Gaye Brown; Directed by Courtney Solomon; Written by Courtney Solomon; Cinematography by Adrian Biddle; Music by Caine Davidson. **Pr:** Andre Rouleau; Courtney Solomon; Christopher Milburn; Courtney Solomon; Remstar; Midsummer Films; SC MediaPro Pictures; After Dark Films. **A:** Jr. High-Adult. **P:** Entertainment. **U:** Home. **L:** English. **Mov-Ent**: Horror, Horror, Interviews. **Acq:** Purchase. **Dist:** Lions Gate Entertainment Inc.

American Haute: Skiing the High-Country Huts 1984
Skiing cross-country through the Aspen-to-Vail trail. 15m; VHS. **Pr:** Video Travel, Inc. **A:** Jr. High-Adult. **P:** Entertainment. **U:** Home. **Spo-Rec**: Sports--Winter. **Acq:** Purchase. **Dist:** Vivid Publisher.

American Health 1986
An expanding series of programs, based on the popular magazine, dealing with subjects such as stress, fitness and nutrition. 60m; VHS, CC. **Pr:** American Health. **A:** Family. **P:** Education. **U:** Home. **Hea-Sci**: Health Education. **Acq:** Purchase. **Dist:** MGM Studios Inc.

American Health: Relaxed Body 198?
Learn how to relax tight muscles to prevent injuries caused by a fast-paced life. This video features an anti-tension workout. 60m; VHS, CC. **Pr:** Karl/Lorimar. **A:** Sr. High-Adult. **P:** Instruction. **U:** Home. **Hea-Sci**: Sports--General, Fitness/Exercise. **Acq:** Purchase. **Dist:** MGM Studios Inc. $19.95.

American Heart 1992 (R) — ★★★½
Jack (Bridges) is a suspicious ex-con, newly released from prison, with few prospects and little hope. He also has a teenage son, Nick (Furlong), he barely remembers but who desperately wants to have his father back in his life. Jack is reluctantly persuaded to let Nick stay with him in his cheap hotel where Nick befriends fellow resident, Molly (Kaprisky), a teenage hooker, and other castoff street kids. Superb performances by both male leads—Furlong, both yearning and frustrated as

he pursues his dream of having a family, and Bridges as the tough parolee, unwilling to open his heart. Hardboiled, poignant, and powerful. 114m; VHS, DVD. **C:** Jeff Bridges; Edward Furlong; Lucinda Jenney; Tracey Kapisky; Don Harvey; Margaret Welsh; Directed by Martin Bell; Written by Peter Silverman; Cinematography by James R. Bagdonas; Music by James Newton Howard. **Pr:** Rosilyn Heller; Jeff Bridges; Jeff Bridges; Triton Pictures. **A:** Sr. High-Adult. **P:** Entertainment. **U:** Home. **Mov-Ent:** Parenting, Prostitution. **Awds:** Ind. Spirit '94: Actor (Bridges). **Acq:** Purchase. **Dist:** Baker and Taylor; Lions Gate Television Corp. $19.98.

The American Hero Show 1981
This is a high-spirited film that tells the story of the founding of Chicago. 30m; VHS, 3/4 U. **Pr:** KCET Los Angeles. **A:** Primary-Adult. **P:** Education. **U:** Institution, CCTV, CATV, BCTV. **Gen-Edu:** History--U.S., Cities & Towns. **Acq:** Purchase, Rent/Lease, Off-Air Record. **Dist:** GPN Educational Media. $65.00.

American Heroes: 18th Century, The Age of Revolution 1980
This program includes a look at George Washington, Benjamin Franklin, Patrick Henry, and Thomas Jefferson. 25m; VHS, 3/4 U. **Pr:** Video Knowledge, Inc. **A:** Primary-Adult. **P:** Education. **U:** Institution, Home. **Gen-Edu:** History--U.S. **Acq:** Purchase. **Dist:** Video Knowledge, Inc.

American Heroes: 19th Century, The Growth of America 1980
This video includes a look at Lewis & Clark, Daniel Boone, Andrew Jackson, and Abraham Lincoln. 25m; VHS, 3/4 U. **Pr:** Video Knowledge, Inc. **A:** Primary-Adult. **P:** Education. **U:** Institution, Home. **Gen-Edu:** History--U.S. **Acq:** Purchase. **Dist:** Video Knowledge, Inc.

American Heroes: 20th Century, Recent Times 1980
This video features a look at Woodrow Wilson, Franklin D. Roosevelt, John F. Kennedy and Dr. Martin Luther King. 25m; VHS, 3/4 U. **Pr:** Video Knowledge, Inc. **A:** Jr. High-Adult. **P:** Education. **U:** Institution, Home. **Gen-Edu:** History--U.S. **Acq:** Purchase. **Dist:** Video Knowledge, Inc.

American Heroes & Legends: John Henry 1992
Investigates the legend of John Henry, a man who could drive steel faster than a steam drill. 30m; VHS. **C:** Narrated by Denzel Washington; Music by B.B. King. **A:** Jr. High-Adult. **P:** Education. **U:** Institution, Home. **Gen-Edu:** Storytelling. **Acq:** Purchase. **Dist:** Baker and Taylor. $9.98.

American Heroes & Legends: Mose the Fireman 199?
Keaton shares the turn of the century legend of New York fireman Mose. ?m; VHS. **C:** Narrated by Michael Keaton. **A:** Preschool-Primary. **P:** Entertainment. **U:** Home. **Gen-Edu:** Storytelling. **Acq:** Purchase. **Dist:** BMG Entertainment. $9.98.

American Heroes & Legends Series 1996
Enlightens children with an animated, look at classic children's literature and ethnic folktales. 200m; VHS. **A:** Primary. **P:** Entertainment. **U:** Institution, Home. **Chl-Juv:** Animation & Cartoons, Folklore & Legends. **Acq:** Purchase. **Dist:** Knowledge Unlimited, Inc. $99.50.
Indiv. Titles: 1. Annie Oakley 2. Brer Rabbit and Boss Lion 3. Davy Crockett 4. Follow the Drinking Gourd: The Story of the Underground Railroad 5. Johnny Appleseed 6. Princess Scargo and the Birthday Pumpkin 7. Rip Vn Winkle 8. The Song of Sacajawea 9. Squanto and the First Thanksgiving 10. Stormalong.

American Heroes: Christopher Columbus 1992
Brief overview of the life and voyages of explorer Christopher Columbus, touching on his interest in sailing, his father's disapproval, discussions with mapmakers, fundraising, the first voyage, the loss of the Santa Maria, and the Indian discovery. 30m; VHS. **Pr:** AVCEL. **A:** Primary-Jr. High. **P:** Education. **U:** Institution. **Gen-Edu:** History, Explorers, Holidays. **Acq:** Purchase. **Dist:** Clear Vue Inc. $79.00.

American Heroes: The Future Belongs to the Educated 1993
Spotlights winners of the National Educator's Awards from urban, suburban, and rural schools. They talk about teacher/student interactions, teaching styles, and sensitivity to cultural diversity. 57m; VHS. **A:** Adult. **P:** Education. **U:** Institution. **Gen-Edu:** Education. **Acq:** Purchase. **Dist:** PBS Home Video. $59.95.

American History: A Bilingual Study 1981
The history of the U.S., from the explorers and the Revolution to the World Wars, is chronicled in this series. All programs available individually. Available in English, Spanish, or bilingual. 60m; VHS, 3/4 U. **Pr:** Video Knowledge, Inc. **A:** Primary. **P:** Education. **U:** Institution, Home. **L:** English, Spanish. **Gen-Edu:** History--U.S. **Acq:** Purchase. **Dist:** Video Knowledge, Inc.
Indiv. Titles: 1. Expansion and Growth-Nineteenth Century America 2. The Divided House-The Second American Revolution 3. Industrial America-The Third American Revolution 4. Becoming a Modern Nation 5. The Transformation of American Society 6. Twentieth Century America 7. Discovery and Exploration 8. The First American Revolution: 1750-1789.

American History: A Visual Perspective 1980
In this series, the major events in American history are presented from a historical perspective, allowing the viewer to understand those events, and to see their relationship to the growth of the United States from the earliest days to the present. 25m; VHS, 3/4 U. **Pr:** Video Knowledge, Inc. **A:** Sr. High-Adult. **P:** Education. **U:** Institution, Home. **Gen-Edu:** History--U.S. **Acq:** Purchase. **Dist:** Video Knowledge, Inc.

American History: Birth of a Nation Series 1967
History and meaning of American heritage. Programs available individually, or combined on four laserdiscs. 17m; VHS, 3/4 U. **Pr:** AIMS. **A:** Primary-Jr. High. **P:** Education. **U:** Institution, SURA. **Gen-Edu:** History--U.S. **Acq:** Purchase, Duplication License. **Dist:** Knowledge Unlimited, Inc.; Clear Vue Inc.
Indiv. Titles: 1. Colonial America in the 1760's 2. Taxation Without Representation 3. Prelude to Revolution 4. Lexington, Concord, and Independence 5. Fighting for Freedom 6. A Nation in Crisis 7. The Living Constitution.

American History for Children: African American Life 1995
Familiarizes youngsters with African life in America, including indentured servitude and slavery, resistance, abolition, the Emancipation Proclamation, segregation, and the civil rights movement with, Martin Luther King Jr. 25m; VHS. **A:** Preschool-Primary. **P:** Education. **U:** Institution. **Gen-Edu:** History. **Acq:** Purchase. **Dist:** Library Video Inc. $29.95.

American History for Children: American Independence 1995
Explores the Declaration of Independence, Thomas Jefferson, Liberty Bell, Independence Hall, and much more. 25m; VHS. **A:** Preschool-Primary. **P:** Education. **U:** Institution. **Gen-Edu:** History. **Acq:** Purchase. **Dist:** Library Video Inc. $29.95.

American History for Children: Early Settlers 1995
Documents the history of the Mayflower, Pilgrims, Plymouth Rock, Squanto, Thanksgiving, The Mayflower Compact, and the life of colonial children. 25m; VHS. **A:** Preschool-Primary. **P:** Education. **U:** Institution. **Gen-Edu:** History, History--U.S. **Acq:** Purchase. **Dist:** Library Video Inc. $29.95.

American History for Children: Equal Rights for All 1995
Illustrates the history of the Bill of Rights, abolitionists, Abraham Lincoln, Emancipation Proclamation, Susan B. Anthony, and women's suffrage. 25m; VHS. **A:** Preschool-Primary. **P:** Education. **U:** Institution. **Gen-Edu:** History. **Acq:** Purchase. **Dist:** Library Video Inc. $29.95.

American History for Children: National Observances 1995
Familiarizes children with the reasons why American celebrate Veterans Day, Memorial Day, Labor Day, Election Day, and the history of voting. 25m; VHS. **A:** Preschool-Primary. **P:** Education. **U:** Institution. **Gen-Edu:** History. **Acq:** Purchase. **Dist:** Library Video Inc. $29.95.

American History for Children: Native American Life 1995
Covers Native American historical figures such as Pocahontas, Tecumseh, The Trail of Tears, and Mother Earth/Father Sky. 25m; VHS. **A:** Preschool-Primary. **P:** Education. **U:** Institution. **Gen-Edu:** History, Native Americans. **Acq:** Purchase. **Dist:** Library Video Inc. $29.95.

American History for Children: United States Expansion 1995
Spotlights the travels of Lewis and Clark and Sacajawea, forced relocation of Native Americans, and life for children in pioneer days. 25m; VHS. **A:** Preschool-Primary. **P:** Education. **U:** Institution. **Gen-Edu:** History. **Acq:** Purchase. **Dist:** Library Video Inc. $29.95.

American History for Children: United States Flag 1995
Chronicles the history of the U.S. flag, Betsy Ross, "The Star Spangled Banner," "The Pledge of Allegiance," and other flag issues. 25m; VHS. **A:** Preschool-Primary. **P:** Education. **U:** Institution. **Gen-Edu:** History. **Acq:** Purchase. **Dist:** Library Video Inc. $29.95.

American History for Children: United States Independence 1995
Introduces youngsters to the Constitution, George Washington, Benjamin Franklin, the Great Seal of the U.S., and the bald eagle. 25m; VHS. **A:** Preschool-Primary. **P:** Education. **U:** Institution. **Gen-Edu:** History. **Acq:** Purchase. **Dist:** Library Video Inc. $29.95.

American History for Children: U.S. Songs and Poems 1995
Covers the meaning of such songs as "The Star-Spangled Banner," "American the Beautiful," "My Country 'Tis of Thee," "Pledge of Allegiance," " Yankee Doodle," "John Henry," " Hiawatha," "Dreams," and "This Land is Your Land." 25m; VHS. **A:** Preschool-Primary. **P:** Education. **U:** Institution. **Gen-Edu:** History. **Acq:** Purchase. **Dist:** Library Video Inc. $29.95.

American History for Children: Washington D.C. 1995
Investigates important structures and institutions of historic Washington D.C., including the White House, the Capitol, Lincoln Memorial, Jefferson Memorial, Vietnam Memorial, and the Supreme Court Building. 25m; VHS. **A:** Preschool-Primary. **P:** Education. **U:** Institution. **Gen-Edu:** History. **Acq:** Purchase. **Dist:** Library Video Inc. $29.95.

American History of the Children: Immigration to the U.S. 1995
Explores the reasons why people migrate to the U.S., from different countries and cultural diversity today. Also looks at the life of an immigrant child in a new country. 25m; VHS. **A:** Preschool-Primary. **P:** Education. **U:** Institution. **Gen-Edu:** History. **Acq:** Purchase. **Dist:** Library Video Inc. $29.95.

The American History Series 197?
In this series political cartoons, billboards, old prints, and early film footage re-create history. All programs are available individually. 25m; VHS, 3/4 U. **A:** Jr. High-Sr. High. **P:** Education. **U:** Institution, CCTV, SURA. **Gen-Edu:** History--U.S. **Acq:** Purchase. **Dist:** Knowledge Unlimited, Inc. $64.95.
Indiv. Titles: 1. Colonial America: The Beginnings 2. Colonial Economy 3. Negro Slavery 4. The Civil War: A House Divided 5. The Years of Reconstruction: 1865-1877 6. Westward Expansion 7. The United States Becomes a World Power 8. America Becomes an Industrial Nation 9. The Rise of the Industrial Giants 10. Trusts and Trust Busters 11. Immigration 12. The Progressives 13. World War I 14. The Twenties 15. The New Deal 16. The American People in World War II.

American History Series 1982
An overview of American history on tapes, this series examines the evolution of the United States from Colonial America in the 1500s through WWII. 60m; VHS. **A:** Jr. High-Adult. **P:** Education. **U:** Institution. **Gen-Edu:** History--U.S. **Acq:** Purchase. **Dist:** Knowledge Unlimited, Inc.
Indiv. Titles: 1. 1500-1600: Colonial America 2. 1700: The Roots of Democracy 3. 1840-1914: Gathering Strength 4. 1850-1900: America Grows Up 5. 1860-1900: Opening the West 6. 1860: The War Between the States 7. 1870-1914: The Game of Monopoly 8. 1914-1929: Warring and Roaring 9. 1935-1945: Two Great Crusades.

American History: The Civil War 1983
The descendants of Northern and Southern forces that fought in the Civil War discuss the historical factors that led up to the war. 25m; VHS. **Pr:** Star Merchants. **A:** Jr. High-Adult. **P:** Education. **U:** Institution, Home. **Gen-Edu:** Civil War, History--U.S. **Acq:** Purchase. **Dist:** Silver Mine Video Inc. $29.95.

American History: The Navy—War of 1812 1989
The historic water battles and memorable quotes of the War of 1812 are recalled. 30m; VHS. **Pr:** Increase. **A:** Jr. High-Adult. **P:** Education. **U:** Institution, Home. **Gen-Edu:** History--U.S. **Acq:** Purchase. **Dist:** Silver Mine Video Inc. $29.95.

American History X 1998 (R) — ★★½
Former skinhead Derek (Norton) is released from prison after a three-year stint for killing two black teens. He returns home having renounced his neo-Nazi ideology and lifestyle, only to find his younger brother Danny (Furlong) involved in a skinhead gang. Controversial not only due to its touchy subject matter and startling violence, but also because director Kaye waged a public war with New Line to remove his name from the film, believing his vision had been compromised by the studio. Ultimately, the fuss is much ado about not much, as the film falls short of expectations. The story is predictable and rather simplistic, the script uneven and sometimes preachy, and most of the characters are wafer-thin. Only Norton's mesmerizing, forceful performance and a commendable job by Furlong as the impressionable younger brother lend credibility. 118m; VHS, DVD, Blu-Ray, CC. **C:** Edward Norton; Edward Furlong; Fairuza Balk; Beverly D'Angelo; Avery Brooks; Stacy Keach; Jennifer Lien; Elliott Gould; William Russ; Joe Cortese; Ethan Suplee; Guy Torry; Giuseppe Andrews; Jordan Marder; Anne Lambton; Paul LeMat; Directed by Tony Kaye; Written by David McKenna; Cinematography by Tony Kaye; Music by Anne Dudley. **Pr:** John Morrissey; Lawrence Turman; Steve Tisch; William C. Carraro; New Line Cinema. **A:** Sr. High-Adult. **P:** Entertainment. **U:** Home. **Mov-Ent. Acq:** Purchase. **Dist:** New Line Home Video.

American Horror Story: Asylum 2012 (Unrated)
FX series. American Horror Story: Asylum is the second season of the American Horror Story series, with all new characters and a new location. "Welcome to Briarcliff" features a reporter trying to expose the Briarcliff asylum. "Tricks and Treats" has an exorcism as well as three patients' attempted escape from the asylum. "Nor'easter" has an extremely violent storm hitting the asylum, causing some patients to consider another escape attempt during this distraction. "I Am Anne Frank" is a two-part episode revealing the identity of Bloody Face. A 911 phone call directs the authorities to the evil doings within the asylum, in "The Origins of Monstrosity". 13 episodes., FX television series. The second season of The American Horror Story series takes place in a different location from the first season, with all new characters. American Horror Story: Asylum takes place in 1964 mental institution, focusing on the patients, nuns, and doctors. The stories are interspersed with tales from the past and present. Episodes include: "Welcome to Briarcliff" where a reporter tries to expose the horrible goings-on in the Briarcliff mental institution; "Tricks and Treats" has an exorcism, as well as attempted escapes by several inmates. "Nor'easter" features a violent storm allowing a possible distraction for another escape attempt. "I Am Anne Frank" is a two-part episode revealing the identity of Bloody Face. In "The Origins of Monstrosity", a 911 call leads the authorities to the asylum. 13 episodes. 572m; DVD, Blu-Ray. **A:** College-Adult. **P:** Entertainment. **U:** Home. **Acq:** Purchase. **Dist:** 20th Century Fox Home Entertainment. $49.98.

American Horror Story: The Complete First Season 2012 (Unrated)
FX psychosexual horror/drama series. Follows the Harmon family (Ben, Vivien and daughter Violet) as they settle in to their gorgeous restored Los Angeles mansion after a move from Boston. Their own demons follow them, but they've got new ones to contend with as the house and its cast of characters come alive. Ben's Boston fling calls to tell him she's pregnant in "Home Invasion." Violet learns the truth about Tate and Vivien grows fearful about her pregnancy in "Piggy Piggy." In "Birth," the former inhabitants, now ghosts, assist Vivien in childbirth. 12 episodes. 534m; DVD, Blu-Ray. **C:** Dylan McDermott; Connie Britton; Jessica Lange; Taissa Farmiga; Denis O'Hare. **A:** College-Adult. **P:** Entertainment. **U:** Home. **Mov-Ent:** Horror, Television Series. **Acq:** Purchase. **Dist:** 20th Century Fox Home Entertainment. $19.99.

The American Horse and Horseman TV Series 1980
A selection of episodes from the popular TV series involving the nation's most exciting races, trainers and riders, celebrity owners and horsemanship history. 60m; VHS. **Pr:** Mercedes Maharis Productions. **A:** Sr. High-Adult. **P:** Education. **U:** Home. **Spo-Rec:** Horses. **Acq:** Purchase. **Dist:** , On Moratorium.

American Hostage 2011 (Unrated)
Twenty years ago, American Terry Anderson lived through the nightmare of being kidnapped by a terrorist group of radical Muslims, who held him hostage and tortured him for almost seven years. On the 20th anniversary of Anderson's release, National Geographic interviews Anderson as well as those who were held hostage with him, his family, and the one man who put his own freedom at risk to help free him to fully understand Anderson's experiences. 45m; DVD. **A:** Family. **P:** Education, Entertainment. **U:** Home, Institution. **Mov-Ent:** Documentary Films, Terrorism, Religion. **Acq:** Purchase. **Dist:** $19.95.

The American House: A Guide to Architectural Styles 1992
Guide to architectural styles features homes in the neoclassical, Queen Anne, bungalow, simple ranch, prairie, colonial revival, and contemporary styles. Despite a corny first-person approach ("I am the Queen Anne style"), this is a comprehensive overview for students and home buyers. 23m; VHS. **A:** Sr. High-Adult. **P:** Education. **U:** Home, Institution. **Gen-Edu:** Architecture. **Acq:** Purchase. **Dist:** The Learning Seed. $89.00.

American Hustle 2013 (R) — ★★★½
Director Russell brilliantly turns the '70s Abscam scandal into a story about the American ability to lie to survive. Irving Rosenfeld (Bale) and his lover Sydney Prosser (Adams) run cons in the art world when FBI agent Richie DiMaso (Cooper) catches them, making them employees of the federal government in his narcissistic quest to "get a big fish." The trio sets their sights on entrapping Atlantic City Mayor Carmine Polito (Renner) in a bribery scam that involves the mob as well as Irving's emotionally turbulent wife Rosalyn (a feisty Lawrence). And we get to see this truly dazzling ensemble don gaudy clothes of the era, and the boys' stunningly bad 'dos. 138m; DVD, Blu-Ray. **C:** Christian Bale; Bradley Cooper; Amy Adams; Jennifer Lawrence; Jeremy Renner, Louis CK; Jack Huston; Michael Pena; Shea Wigham; Alessandro Nivola; Elisabeth Rohm; Directed by David O. Russell; Written by David O. Russell; Eric Singer; Cinematography by Linus Sandgren; Music by Danny Elfman. **Pr:** Megan Ellison; Jonathan Gordon; Charles Roven; Richard Suckle; Annapurna Pictures; Columbia Pictures Industries Inc. **A:** Sr. High-Adult. **P:** Entertainment. **U:** Home. **Mov-Ent:** Politics & Government, Drama, Crime Drama. **Awds:** British Acad. '13: Actress--Supporting (Lawrence), Makeup, Orig. Screenplay; Golden Globes '14: Actress--Mus./Comedy (Adams), Actress--Supporting (Lawrence), Film--Mus./Comedy; Screen Actors Guild '13: Cast. **Acq:** Purchase. **Dist:** Sony Pictures Home Entertainment Inc.

American Ideals in the Twentieth Century 1980
This tape reviews the major historical developments of the 20th century as they affected our policies and our changing philosophy regarding our government and our role in the world as a nation. 25m; VHS, 3/4 U. **Pr:** Video Knowledge, Inc. **A:** Sr. High-Adult. **P:** Education. **U:** Institution, SURA. **Gen-Edu:** History--U.S., International Relations, Politics & Government. **Acq:** Purchase. **Dist:** Video Knowledge, Inc.

American Idol: The Search for a Superstar 2002 (Unrated)
Provides excerpts of the popular Fox television game show from 2002 hosted by Ryan Seacrest as contestants sing songs of their choice and are first judged by Simon Cowell, Paula Abdul, and Randy Jackson prior to receiving votes from the general public to determine the winner—who receives a recording contract—over the course of the season's run. Includes winner Kelly Clarkson and runner-up Justin Guarini. 1 episode. 90m; DVD. **C:** Paula Abdul; Simon Cowell; Randy Jackson; Hosted by Ryan Seacrest. **A:** Family. **P:** Entertainment. **U:** Home. **Mov-Ent:** Television Series, Game Show, Music--Performance. **Acq:** Purchase. **Dist:** Ventura Distribution Inc. $19.99.

The American Image 1967
A tour of the Whitney Museum, and through a history of American art. 60m; VHS, 3/4 U. **C:** Hosted by E.G. Marshall. **Pr:** National Broadcasting Company. **A:** Family. **P:** Education. **U:** Institution. **Gen-Edu:** Art & Artists, Museums. **Acq:** Purchase. **Dist:** Social Studies School Service.

An American Image: 150 Years of Photography 1990
A chronicle of American history as seen through the eyes of her most prominent photographers. Includes the works of Ansel Adams, Jacob Riis, Steiglitz and others. 60m; VHS. **Pr:** Wood Knapp Video. **A:** Family. **P:** Entertainment. **U:** Home. **Gen-Edu:** Photography, History--U.S. **Acq:** Purchase. **Dist:** Karol Media; Crystal Productions. $24.95.

The American Imagination: The Lives and Works of Twelve Great American Writers 19??
Examines the lives and works of 12 of the most influential American writers in history. Includes Edgar Allan Poe, Henry David Thoreau, Walt Whitman, Mark Twain, Emily Dickinson, Willa Cather, Robert Frost, F. Scott Fitzgerald, Ernest Hemingway, John Steinbeck, Richard Wright, and J.D. Salinger. 243m; VHS. **A:** Jr. High-Adult. **P:** Education. **U:** Institution, CCTV, SURA. **Gen-Edu:** Literature--American. **Acq:** Purchase. **Dist:** Thomas S. Klise Co.
Indiv. Titles: 1. Creating the American Dream 2. Innovation and Imagination.

American Impressionist: Richard Earl Thompson 1992
Landscapist Richard Earl Thompson's work, often compared to Monet, is displayed. 30m; VHS. **A:** Jr. High-Adult. **P:** Entertainment. **U:** Home, Institution. **Fin-Art:** Art & Artists. **Acq:** Purchase. **Dist:** Crystal Productions; Cambridge Educational. $29.95.

An American in Paris 1951 (Unrated) — ★★★★
Lavish, imaginative musical features a sweeping score, and knockout choreography by Kelly. Ex-G.I. Kelly stays on in Paris after the war to study painting, supported in his efforts by rich American Foch, who hopes to acquire a little extra attention. But Kelly loves the lovely Caron, unfortunately engaged to an older gent. Highlight is an astonishing 17-minute ballet which holds the record for longest movie dance number—and one of the most expensive, pegged at over half a million for a month of filming. For his efforts, the dance king won a special Oscar citation. While it sure looks like Paris, most of it was filmed in MGM studios. 113m; VHS, DVD, 8 mm. **C:** Gene Kelly; Leslie Caron; Oscar Levant; Nina Foch; Georges Guetary; Directed by Vincente Minnelli; Written by Alan Jay Lerner; Cinematography by John Alton; Lyrics by Ira Gershwin. **Pr:** MGM. **A:** Family. **P:** Entertainment. **U:** Home. **Mov-Ent:** Musical, Romance, Classic Films. **Awds:** Oscars '51: Art Dir./Set Dec., Color, Color Cinematog., Costume Des. (C), Film, Scoring/Musical, Story & Screenplay; AFI '98: Top 100; Golden Globes '52: Film--Mus./Comedy; Natl. Film Reg. '93. **Acq:** Purchase. **Dist:** MGM Home Entertainment; Time-Life Video and Television; Baker and Taylor. $14.95.
Songs: S'Wonderful; I Got Rhythm; Embraceable You; Love Is Here To Stay; Tra-La-La; I'll Build a Stairway to Paradise; Nice Work If You Can Get It; By Strauss; Concerto in F (3rd Movement); An American in Paris; Piano Concerto in F.

American Independence 1776 1989
Describes the events that led to the secession of the colonies from British rule and discusses the social complexity of that era. 28m; VHS, SVS, 3/4 U. **A:** Jr. High-Adult. **P:** Education. **U:** Institution. **Gen-Edu:** History--U.S., Revolutionary War. **Acq:** Purchase, Rent/Lease. **Dist:** Encyclopedia Britannica. $99.00.

The American Indian 19??
Outlines the history of the American Indian, considered by most to be the first and original American settler. Contains photographs and footage of Indian cave dwellings, archaeological digs, tools and artifacts. 12m; VHS. **A:** Jr. High-Adult. **P:** Education. **U:** Institution, CCTV, SURA. **Gen-Edu:** History--U.S., Native Americans, Archaeology. **Acq:** Purchase. **Dist:** Thomas S. Klise Co. $58.00.

American Indian: A Brief History 1985
Offers a history of Native American life from the time American settlers landed on the continent from Asia. 22m; VHS. **A:** Primary. **P:** Education. **U:** Institution. **Gen-Edu:** Native Americans. **Acq:** Purchase. **Dist:** National Geographic Society. $80.

American Indian Artists, Part 1 1976
A series looking at the work and lifestyle of six American Indian artists. Tapes are sold as a series or individually. 29m; VHS, 1C, 3/4 U, Q. **C:** Narrated by Rod McKuen. **Pr:** KAET-Phoenix. **A:** Jr. High-Adult. **P:** Education. **U:** Institution, BCTV, SURA. **Fin-Art:** Art & Artists, Native Americans. **Acq:** Purchase, Rent/Lease. **Dist:** Vision Maker Media; PBS Home Video. $69.95.
Indiv. Titles: 1. Allan Houser/Fritz Scholder 2. Charles Loloma/Helen Hardin 3. Medicine Flower & Lonewolf/R. C. Gorman.

American Indian Artists, Part 2 1982
Three more American Indian artists display and discuss their work. Tapes are available individually or as a series for $104.95. 29m; VHS, 1C, 3/4 U, Q. **Pr:** Native American Public Broadcasting Consortium; South Dakota ETV. **A:** Jr. High-Adult. **P:** Education. **U:** Institution, BCTV, SURA. **Fin-Art:** Art & Artists, Native Americans. **Acq:** Purchase, Rent/Lease. **Dist:** Vision Maker Media. $49.95.
Indiv. Titles: 1. Larry Golsh 2. Juane Quick-to-See Smith 3. Dan Namingha.

American Indian Collection: Geronimo and the Apache Resistance 1991
Chronicles the years of unfair treatment handed out to the Apache tribe and the efforts of American soldiers to apprehend Geronimo and his warriors after their revolt against this tyranny. 60m; VHS. **Pr:** PBS Video. **A:** Family. **P:** Education. **U:** Home. **Gen-Edu:** Documentary Films, War--General, Native Americans. **Acq:** Purchase. **Dist:** PBS Home Video; Signals Video; Cambridge Educational. $19.95.

American Indian Collection: Myths and Moundbuilders 1991
Recently, archeologists discovered that huge earthen mounds scattered throughout the central U.S. were built by Indians. Part of the "Odyssey" series. 60m; VHS. **Pr:** Public Broadcasting Associates. **A:** Sr. High-College. **P:** Education. **U:** Institution, Home. **Gen-Edu:** Documentary Films, Native Americans, Archaeology. **Acq:** Purchase, Rent/Lease, Off-Air Record. **Dist:** PBS Home Video; Signals Video; Cambridge Educational. $19.95.

American Indian Collection: Seasons of the Navajo 1991
An extended Navajo family deals with modern life through tribal communion in this documentary. 60m; VHS. **Pr:** Peace River Films; KAET-Phoenix. **A:** Jr. High-Adult. **P:** Education. **U:** Institution, Home. **Gen-Edu:** Documentary Films, Native Americans. **Acq:** Purchase, Rent/Lease. **Dist:** Vision Maker Media; PBS Home Video; Signals Video. $19.95.

American Indian Collection: Spirit of Crazy Horse 1991
This documentary explores the culture, customs, and legacy of the great Sioux tribe and their efforts to retain their traditions and honor in a modern world. 54m; VHS. **Pr:** PBS Video. **A:** Family. **P:** Education. **U:** Home. **Gen-Edu:** Documentary Films, Native Americans. **Acq:** Purchase. **Dist:** PBS Home Video; Signals Video; Cambridge Educational. $19.95.

American Indian Collection: Winds of Change—A Matter of Promises 1991
This documentary examines the problems facing Native Americans as they try to hold onto ancient customs and values in a modern society. The ways of the Navajo nation in Arizona and New Mexico, the Lummi tribe in Washington State, and the Onondaga in New York are detailed. 60m; VHS. **C:** Hosted by N. Scott Momaday. **Pr:** PBS Video. **A:** Family. **P:** Education. **U:** Home. **Gen-Edu:** Documentary Films, Native Americans. **Acq:** Purchase. **Dist:** PBS Home Video; Signals Video; Cambridge Educational. $19.95.

American Indian Dance Theatre: Dances for the New Generations 19??
Follows the American Indian Dance Theatre as they travel across the country to learn many of the traditional Native American dances, including some of those from the Makah, Kwakiuti, Penobscot, and Iroquis Indian tribes. Filmed at ceremonials in Alert Bay, British Columbia, a pow wow in New Town, and at a live performance in Boston. Nominated for an Emmy with its "Great Performances" airing. 60m; VHS. **A:** Jr. High-Adult. **P:** Education. **U:** Home. **Gen-Edu:** Performing Arts, Native Americans, Dance. **Acq:** Purchase. **Dist:** Stagestep. $29.95.

American Indian Dance Theatre "Finding A Circle" ????
Performances of Native dances on stage and reservation, including the Eagle Dance, the Hoop Dance, Fancy Dance, Women's Fancy Shawl Dance and the Apache Crown Dance. 60m; VHS. **A:** Adult. **P:** Education. **U:** Institution. **Fin-Art:** Dance, Dance--Performance, Native Americans. **Acq:** Purchase. **Dist:** Stagestep. $30.00.

American Indian Influence on the United States 1972
A look at how life in the U.S has been influenced by the Indian-economically, sociologically, philosophically, and culturally. 20m; VHS, 3/4 U, EJ, Special order formats. **C:** Narrated by Barry Sullivan. **Pr:** Alan Saparoff. **A:** Primary-Jr. High. **P:** Education. **U:** Institution, SURA. **Gen-Edu:** Native Americans. **Acq:** Purchase. **Dist:** Dana Productions.

American Indian Sacred Sweat Lodge 1989
Explores the sacred native American ceremonies. 87m; VHS. **A:** Adult. **P:** Education. **U:** Home. **Gen-Edu:** Native Americans. **Acq:** Purchase. **Dist:** Artistic Video. $39.95.

The American Indian Speaks 1973
This powerful documentary lets the Indian speak about his people and heritage, about the white man and the future. 23m; VHS, 3/4 U. **Pr:** Encyclopedia Britannica Educational Corporation. **A:** Jr. High-College. **P:** Education. **U:** Institution, SURA. **Gen-Edu:** Native Americans. **Acq:** Purchase, Rent/Lease, Trade-in. **Dist:** Encyclopedia Britannica.

American Indian Sweat Lodge Ceremony 1987
The entire ceremony, which is one of North America's oldest, is shown. 90m; VHS. **Pr:** Bob Klein. **A:** Family. **P:** Education. **U:** Institution, Home. **Gen-Edu:** Native Americans. **Acq:** Purchase. **Dist:** Artistic Video. $39.95.

American Indians: A Brief History 1985
Centers on the first Americans who came from Asia and settled throughout the New World. Details that when white settlers arrived and forced the Indians onto reservations, the Indians' spirit remained strong and proud. 22m; VHS, 3/4 U. **A:** Primary-Sr. High. **P:** Education. **U:** Institution. **Gen-Edu:** Native Americans, History--U.S. **Acq:** Purchase. **Dist:** National Geographic Society. $79.00.

American Indians: Sacred Ground 19??
Visits ancestral Indian lands from New York to Oregon, explaining why they are considered sacred to the Native Americans and the history behind them. Includes teacher's manual. 49m; VHS. **A:** Family. **P:** Education. **U:** Institution. **Gen-Edu:** History--U.S., Native Americans. **Acq:** Purchase. **Dist:** Educational Video Network. $49.95.

The American Industrial Revolution 1997
Documents development in the United States from 1865 to 1900: railroads, steel, oil industry, agriculture, mining, cattlemen, urbanization. Recommended for Grades 7-12. 27m; VHS. **A:** Jr. High-Sr. High. **P:** Education. **U:** Institution. **Gen-Edu:** History--U.S., U.S. States, Industry & Industrialists. **Acq:** Purchase. **Dist:** Zenger Media; Social Studies School Service. $95.00.

American Institute of Small Business: Advertising and Sales Promotion 199?
Magazine, newspaper, radio, television, direct mail, trade shows, and all other media advertising is covered, along with selecting the right media, choosing an ad theme, and budgeting. ?m; VHS. **A:** Adult. **P:** Professional. **U:** Institution. **Bus-Ind:** Business, Advertising. **Acq:** Purchase. **Dist:** American Institute of Small Business. $69.95.

American Institute of Small Business: Marketing 199?
Know who your customers are and how to generate new business. ?m; VHS. **A:** Adult. **P:** Professional. **U:** Institution.

Bus-Ind: Marketing, Business. **Acq**: Purchase. **Dist**: American Institute of Small Business. $69.95.

American Institute of Small Business: Setting Up a Home-Based Business 199?
Step-by-step guide to operating a business out of your home. ?m; VHS. **A**: Adult. **P**: Professional. **U**: Institution. **Bus-Ind**: Business. **Acq**: Purchase. **Dist**: American Institute of Small Business. $69.95.

American Institute of Small Business: Starting a Business—Advice from Experts 199?
Business commentators from Money, Fortune, and Newsweek magazines give tips on taxes, obtaining financing, and other issues. ?m; VHS. **A**: Adult. **P**: Education. **U**: Home. **Bus-Ind**: Business, Finance. **Acq**: Purchase. **Dist**: American Institute of Small Business. $69.95.

American Institute of Small Business: The Business Plan 199?
The key elements of a business plan are discussed. Includes a study guide. ?m; VHS. **A**: Adult. **P**: Professional. **U**: Institution. **Bus-Ind**: Business. **Acq**: Purchase. **Dist**: American Institute of Small Business. $69.95.

American Institute of Small Business: The Internet 199?
The Internet, electronic mail, world wide web, and Newsgroups are explained. Includes computer diskettes for PCs and Macs, as well as a study guide. ?m; VHS. **A**: Adult. **P**: Professional. **U**: Home. **Bus-Ind**: Computers. **Acq**: Purchase. **Dist**: American Institute of Small Business. $69.95.

American Institute of Small Business: Women in Business 199?
Female small business owners discuss success, overcoming stereotypes, obtaining financing, and other issues. ?m; VHS. **A**: Adult. **P**: Professional. **U**: Home. **Bus-Ind**: Business, Women. **Acq**: Purchase. **Dist**: American Institute of Small Business. $69.95.

American Institute of Small Business: Your Own Business Getting Started 199?
Covers financial sources, writing your own business plan, knowing your market and competition, and other issues. 45m; VHS. **A**: Adult. **P**: Professional. **U**: Home. **Bus-Ind**: Business, Finance. **Acq**: Purchase. **Dist**: American Institute of Small Business. $69.95.

American Institute of Small Business: Your Personal Financial Guide to Success, Power & Security 199?
Covers money management, financial planning, budgeting, record keeping, and spending and savings plans. ?m; VHS. **A**: Adult. **P**: Education. **U**: Home. **Bus-Ind**: Finance, Management. **Acq**: Purchase. **Dist**: American Institute of Small Business. $69.95.

The American Island 1970
A discussion of one of America's last unspoiled resources; her islands. Shows how intelligent planning for use provides a variety of recreational activities and protects the environment for future generations. 29m; VHS, 3/4 U, Special order formats. **Pr**: Department of Transportation. **A**: Sr. High-Adult. **P**: Education. **U**: Institution, SURA. **Spo-Rec**: Wilderness Areas. **Acq**: Purchase. **Dist**: National Audiovisual Center.

An American Ism: Joe McCarthy 1979
A portrait of the former U.S. Senator, who exploited America's irrational fear of communists during the post-war era. McCarthy's unlikely rise to power is told in this film by friends, victims and politicians. 84m; 3/4 U. **Pr**: Glenn Silber. **A**: Jr. High-Adult. **P**: Education. **U**: Institution, SURA. **Gen-Edu**: Documentary Films, Biography, History--Modern. **Acq**: Purchase. **Dist**: First Run/Icarus Films.

American Jobs 2005 (Unrated)
A documentary exploring the impact low-wage earning foreign workers have on American communities and workplaces. 62m; DVD. **A**: Sr. High-Adult. **P**: Education. **U**: Home. **Gen-Edu**: Documentary Films, Economics. **Acq**: Purchase. **Dist**: Disinformation. $14.95.

American Journey 1986
The experiences of 16 Americans who returned home to an indifferent, sometimes hostile community, after fighting in Nicaragua are shared with the viewer. 60m; 3/4 U. **Pr**: Lisa Maya Knauer. **A**: Jr. High-Adult. **P**: Education. **U**: SURA. **Gen-Edu**: Documentary Films. **Acq**: Purchase. **Dist**: First Run/Icarus Films.

American Justice 199?
Collection includes the most significant crimes of the 20th century from the Boston Strangler to Son of Sam. Reveals the criminal, his motives, and the methods used to solve each case. On four cassettes. 420m; VHS. **A**: Sr. High-Adult. **P**: Education. **U**: Home. **Gen-Edu**: U.S. States, Law. **Acq**: Purchase. **Dist**: A&E Television Networks L.L.C.; New Video Group. $99.95.

American Justice 1986 (R) — ★★
Two cops, one of whom looks suspiciously like a Simon of "Simon and Simon," fight political corruption and white slavery near the Mexican border. The chief white slaver bears a full resemblance to the other Simon. Sufficient action but less than original. 96m; VHS, DVD. **C**: Jameson Parker; Gerald McRaney; Wilford Brimley; Jack Lucarelli; Directed by Gary Grillo. **Pr**: Moviestore Entertainment. **A**: Jr. High-Adult. **P**: Entertainment. **U**: Home. **Mov-Ent**: Prostitution. **Acq**: Purchase. **Dist**: Lions Gate Television Corp. $79.98.

American Justice: Hunting Bambi: The Laurie Bembenek Story ????
Presents the A&E cable channel special on Lawrencia "Bambi" Bembenek, who was convicted of murdering her husband's ex-wife in 1981, though many questioned the validity of the verdict due to possible police corruption; Bembenek fled jail after nine years though was captured three months later. Includes interviews with Bembenek, the victim's boyfriend, the police detective in charge, and a reporter with the "Chicago Tribune." 50m; DVD. **A**: Jr. High-Adult. **P**: Entertainment. **U**: Home, CATV. **Mov-Ent**: Television Series, Documentary Films, Biography. **Acq**: Purchase. **Dist**: A&E Television Networks L.L.C. $24.95.

American Justice: Matthew Shepard: Death in the High Desert ????
Presents the A&E cable channel special on the 1998 beating death of 21-year-old University of Wyoming student Matthew Shepard by Aaron McKinney and Russell Henderson, who killed him because of his homosexuality; includes interviews with Shepard's mother, Judy Shepard, the trial attorneys, and Senator Michael Massie and discusses hate-crime legislation introduced as a result. 50m; DVD. **A**: Sr. High-Adult. **P**: Entertainment. **U**: Home, CATV. **Mov-Ent**: Television Series, Documentary Films, Biography. **Acq**: Purchase. **Dist**: A&E Television Networks L.L.C. $24.95.

American Justice: Mob Hitmen 2006
An expose of the mob wars in Philadelphia, including interviews with police, prosecutors, and mob triggermen. 50m; DVD. **A**: Jr. High-Adult. **P**: Entertainment. **U**: Home. **Gen-Edu**: Documentary Films. **Acq**: Purchase. **Dist**: A&E Television Networks L.L.C.

American Justice: The Doctor's Wife 2004
Presents the A&E cable channel special on the investigation into the death of Dr. David Stephens as suspicion moves to Stephens' wife, Stephanie, who is revealed to have a classic home-wrecker profile. Bill Curtis hosts this detailed investigation, which features interviews with police investigators and attorneys involved in the case. 50m; DVD. **A**: Jr. High-Adult. **P**: Entertainment. **U**: Home, Institution. **Mov-Ent**: Television Series, Documentary Films, Biography. **Acq**: Purchase. **Dist**: A&E Television Networks L.L.C. $24.95.

American Justice: The Donnie Brasco Story 2006
FBI special agent Joseph Pistone went undercover in 1976 to investigate the Bonnano crime family using the alias of thief Donnie Brasco. Interviews trace the five-year investigation and how Pistone's story became a best-selling book and movie. 50m; DVD. **A**: Jr. High-Adult. **P**: Entertainment. **U**: Home. **Gen-Edu**: Documentary Films. **Acq**: Purchase. **Dist**: A&E Television Networks L.L.C.

American Justice: The John Lennon Assassination 2006
Profiles Mark David Chapman and his fascination with Lennon, which lead to murder and incarceration. 50m; DVD. **A**: Jr. High-Adult. **P**: Entertainment. **U**: Home. **Gen-Edu**: Documentary Films. **Acq**: Purchase. **Dist**: A&E Television Networks L.L.C.

American Justice: The Quiz Show Scandal and Other Frauds 2006
Examines some of the most recent hoaxes, why they were perpetrated, and how they were uncovered, from the 1950s game show scandals to Clifford Irving's fake biography of Howard Hughes and beyond. 50m; DVD. **A**: Jr. High-Adult. **P**: Entertainment. **U**: Home. **Gen-Edu**: Documentary Films. **Acq**: Purchase. **Dist**: A&E Television Networks L.L.C.

American Justice: The Sting ????
Presents the A&E cable channel special on various well-known sting operations, including former Washington D.C. mayor Marion Barry and his 1990 arrest for cocaine possession; the entrapment defense used by wealthy automaker John DeLorean after cocaine trafficking charges were brought in 1982; and the Abscam front in the late 1970s involving the bribery of public officials by an "Arab Sheik." 50m; DVD. **A**: Sr. High-Adult. **P**: Entertainment. **U**: Home, CATV. **Mov-Ent**: Television Series, Documentary Films, Drug Trafficking/Dealing. **Acq**: Purchase. **Dist**: A&E Television Networks L.L.C. $24.95.

American Justice: The Witness and the Hitman 2002
Presents the A&E cable channel special on the life of Bob Lowe, a witness to a mob murder, whose life was destroyed by his testimony against the killer. Lowe entered the Witness Protection Program but the killer, Harry Aleman, was acquitted by a corrupt judge, bringing Lowe into a spiral of drugs and alcohol which ended with him going to jail for larceny. Finally, 25 years later, Lowe's testimony put Aleman in prison for life. 50m; DVD. **A**: Jr. High-Adult. **P**: Entertainment. **U**: Home, Institution. **Mov-Ent**: Television Series, Documentary Films. **Acq**: Purchase. **Dist**: A&E Television Networks L.L.C. $24.95.

American Kickboxer 1 1991 (R) — ★½
Barrett stars as B.J. Quinn, a down on his luck kickboxing champion who spends much of his time onscreen aimlessly wandering (apparently searching for the meaning of his life). Lackluster script and performances will make this one trying—even for kickboxing fans. Barrett is Chuck Norris' former workout partner, but there isn't enough action often enough for him to show off his formidable skills. 93m; VHS, DVD. **C**: John Barrett; Keith Vitali; Brad Morris; Terry Norton; Ted Leplat; Directed by Frans Nel; Written by Emil Kolbe; Music by Frank Becker. **Pr**: Anant Singh; Distant Horizon. **A**: College-Adult. **P**: Entertainment. **U**: Home. **L**: English, Spanish. **Mov-Ent**: Martial Arts, Sports--Fiction: Drama. **Acq**: Purchase. **Dist**: Warner Home Video, Inc. $13.49.

American Kickboxer 2: To the Death 1993 (R) — ★½
Lillian must find a way to get her cop ex-husband and her kickboxer ex-lover to work together to save her kidnapped daughter's life. 91m; VHS, DVD, CC. **C**: Dale "Apollo" Cook; Evan Lurie; Kathy Shower; Ted Markland; Directed by Jeno Hodi. **A**: Sr. High-Adult. **P**: Entertainment. **U**: Home. **L**: English. **Mov-Ent**: Martial Arts. **Acq**: Purchase. **Dist**: CinemaNow Inc. $92.95.

American Legacy 1983
This series emphasizes the concept of interdependence as it examines the development of the U.S., region by region. 15m; VHS, 3/4 U, Q. **C**: Hosted by John Rugg. **Pr**: KRMA Denver; Agency for Instructional Television. **A**: Primary. **P**: Education. **U**: Institution, CCTV, CATV, BCTV. **Gen-Edu**: History--U.S. **Acq**: Purchase, Rent/Lease, Duplication License. **Dist**: Agency for Instructional Technology.
Indiv. Titles: 1. Our Federal District 2. Seaports and Ships 3. Megalopolis 4. Tidewater to Piedmont 5. The Tennessee Valley 6. Our Bread Basket 7. We Make Anything 8. By Ship, Train, or Plane 9. A Great River 10. Cattle Country 11. Storehouse of Minerals 12. National Parks 13. The Problem of Water 14. The Northwest 15. Our 49th State 16. The Islands.

American Light: The Luminist Movement, 1850-1875 1989
A look at the landscape paintings of American artists during the second half of the 19th century. These paintings, which are particularly notable for their poetic and dramatic light, are interspersed with photographs of the same landscapes and commentary. 32m; VHS, 3/4 U, Special order formats. **Pr**: National Gallery of Art. **A**: Family. **P**: Entertainment. **U**: Institution, SURA. **Fin-Art**: Documentary Films, Art & Artists, Museums. **Acq**: Free Loan. **Dist**: National Gallery of Art.

American Loser 2007 (R) — ★★
Adapted from comic Jeff Nichols' memoir "The Little Yellow Bus." New Yorker Jeff (Scott) is dyslexic, suffers from attention-deficit disorder and a mild case of Tourette's, and is a recovering alcoholic. He has little idea what a normal life is but Jeff likes to talk, so he attends multiple 12-step programs for a chance to share (truthfully or not). He meets down-on-her luck Lynn (Mol) at one meeting and she actually befriends him and tries to cope with his foibles while helping Jeff manage his life. 94m; DVD. **C**: Seann William Scott; Gretchen Mol; Jeff Garlin; Deirdre O'Connell; Denis O'Hare; Kevin Conway; Ian Buchanan; Directed by Tod Harrison Williams; Written by Tod Harrison Williams; Cinematography by Michael Simmonds; Music by Marcelo Zarvos. **A**: Sr. High-Adult. **P**: Entertainment. **U**: Home. **Mov-Ent**: Handicapped. **Acq**: Purchase. **Dist**: Lions Gate Entertainment Inc.

An American Love Story 1999
Presents the story of a 30-year love affair between a black man and a white woman, as well as the stories of their families and children. Ten hours on five videocassettes. Comes with a Teacher's Guide and closed-circuit and public performance rights. 120m; VHS. **A**: Sr. High-Adult. **P**: Education. **U**: Home, Institution. **Gen-Edu**: Documentary Films, Sociology, Interviews. **Acq**: Purchase, Rent/Lease. **Dist**: First Run/Icarus Films. $349.00.

American Made: Marysville and the Honda Plant 1984
This program examines why Honda chose the town of Marysville, Ohio as its first site for an assembly plant in America and the effect it had on the town. 30m; 3/4 U. **Pr**: Ohio University Telecommunications Center. **A**: Sr. High-College. **P**: Education. **U**: Institution, CCTV, SURA. **Gen-Edu**: Automobiles, Business. **Acq**: Purchase, Rent/Lease. **Dist**: WOUB Public Media.

American Madness 1932 — ★★½
Benevolent banker Dickson (Huston) has been making loans without sufficient collateral. The bank's board of directors give him a warning and then a robbery causes a run on the bank. The directors are ready to oust Dickson when the small businessmen he's helped rally to his defense. Tedious romantic subplot has Dickson's unhappy wife (Johnson) accusing him of neglect and dallying with unscrupulous bank clerk Cluett (Gordon). 75m/B/W; VHS, DVD. **C**: Walter Huston; Pat O'Brien; Kay Johnson; Gavin Gordon; Constance Cummings; Robert Ellis; Walter Walker; Arthur Hoyt; Directed by Frank Capra; Written by Robert Riskin; Cinematography by Joseph Walker. **Pr**: Columbia Pictures. **A**: Sr. High-Adult. **P**: Entertainment. **U**: Home. **Mov-Ent**: Finance. **Acq**: Purchase. **Dist**: Sony Pictures Home Entertainment Inc.

The American Mall 2008 (Unrated) — ★★½
An MTV-produced teen musical that finds songwriter Ally (Dobrev) working at her mother's failing mall music store. She falls for janitor/musician Joey (Mayes) and they would make beautiful music together if not for rich witch Madison (Reeser), whose daddy owns the property. A would-be fashion designer, Madison wants Joey to be her model and she wants to kick out Ally's mom so she can have the space to expand her own store. Satisfyingly chipper—if predictable—with cute leads and bright songs. 100m; DVD. **C**: Nina Dobrev; Autumn Reeser; Al Sapienza; Rob Mayes; Yassmin Alers; Wade Allain-Marcus; Neil Haskell; Brooke Lyons; Directed by Shawn Ku; Written by Margaret Grieco Oberman; Cinematography by Matthew Williams. **A**: Jr. High-Adult. **P**: Entertainment. **U**: Home. **Mov-Ent**. **Acq**: Purchase. **Dist**: Paramount Pictures Corp.

American Masters: Alfred Steiglitz: The Eloquent Eye 2001
Documents the creative genius of the man who came to be known as "the father of modern photography," propelling the craft to be recognized as an art form. 60m; DVD. **A:** Adult. **P:** Education. **U:** Home, Institution. **Gen-Edu:** Biography, Photography, Art & Artists. **Acq:** Purchase. **Dist:** WGBH/Boston. $24.95.

American Masters: Alice Waters and Her Delicious Revolution 2003
Biography of Alice Waters, world-famous chef and owner of Chez Panisse restaurant. 60m; VHS. **A:** Adult. **P:** Education. **U:** Home, Institution. **Gen-Edu:** Biography, Cooking. **Acq:** Purchase. **Dist:** WGBH/Boston. $19.95.

American Masters: Andy Warhol: A Documentary Film 2006
Confidants from art dealers to fellow artists reveal the insecurities behind the man who was focused on achieving fame while he redefined our views of art and culture. The spectrum of Warhol's development is explored, from his humble upbringing in Pittsburgh to his apprenticeship in New York on through his Factory days and untimely death in 1987. 240m; DVD. **A:** Adult. **P:** Education. **U:** Home, Institution. **Gen-Edu:** Biography, Art & Artists. **Acq:** Purchase. **Dist:** WGBH/Boston. $24.95.

American Masters: Atlantic Records: The House That Ahmet Built 2007
Follows the career of record mogul Ahmet Ertegun from the start of his label in 1947. Features rare and classic clips, including performances and studio sessions of Atlantic artists. 120m; DVD. **A:** Adult. **P:** Education. **U:** Home. **Gen-Edu:** Documentary Films, Music. **Acq:** Purchase. **Dist:** WGBH/Boston. $19.95.

American Masters: Balanchine 2004
Documents the career of the "father of the American ballet" and celebrates his ballet themes, beginning at the Maryinsky Theater in Russia and proceeding to his work in Hollywood and on Broadway, concluding with the formation of the New York City Ballet. 156m; DVD. **A:** Adult. **P:** Education. **U:** Home, Institution. **Gen-Edu:** Documentary Films, Biography, Dance--Ballet. **Acq:** Purchase. **Dist:** WGBH/Boston. $29.95.

American Masters: Charlotte Church: Enchantment from Cardiff, Wales 2002
Hometown performance recorded at St. David's Hall on September 19, 2001. Accompanied by the National Orchestra of Wales, Church performs songs from Broadway musicals, arias, Gaelic airs, pop music, and her own "Enchantment"album. 116m; DVD. **A:** Adult. **P:** Entertainment. **U:** Home. **Fin-Art:** Opera, Music--Performance. **Acq:** Purchase. **Dist:** WGBH/Boston. $14.95.

American Masters: Ella Fitzgerald: Something to Live For 1999
Exclusive interviews and newly discovered performance footage capture the Grammy Award-winning performer from her life in Depression-era New York and her discovery at the Apollo Theater to her reign as the top jazz vocal stylist of all time. 86m; DVD. **A:** Jr. High-Adult. **P:** Education. **U:** Home, Institution. **Gen-Edu:** Biography, Documentary Films, Music--Jazz. **Acq:** Purchase. **Dist:** WGBH/Boston. $24.95.

American Masters: Ernest Hemingway: Rivers to the Sea 2005
Explores Hemingway's work and storytelling style, with perspective from his close friend A.E. Hotchner, daughter-in-law Valerie Hemingway, son Peter, and Peter Viertel. 90m; DVD. **A:** Adult. **P:** Education. **U:** Home. **Gen-Edu:** Biography, Literature--American. **Acq:** Purchase. **Dist:** WGBH/Boston. $24.95.

American Masters: F. Scott Fitzgerald: Winter Dreams 2002
Provides an in-depth look at the literary icon's life and work, from his poor upbringing in a well-to-do neighborhood, his obsession with class and money, his marriage to a mentally disturbed socialite, and his own notorious partying and abuse of alcohol. 90m; DVD. **A:** Adult. **P:** Education. **U:** Home, Institution. **Gen-Edu:** Biography, Documentary Films, Literature--American. **Acq:** Purchase. **Dist:** WGBH/Boston. $24.95.

American Masters: Gene Kelly: Anatomy of a Dancer 2002
Betsy Blair (Gene's first wife), Debbie Reynolds, Andre Previn, and other family members and Hollywood colleagues reflect on Kelly's talents and shortcomings. Includes rare footage of Kelly's breakthrough Broadway role as Pal Joey, his solo in "Summer Stock," his double-exposure "Alter Ego" number from "Cover Girl," and the unsurpassable "Singin' in the Rain." 85m; DVD. **A:** Family. **P:** Education. **U:** Home, Institution. **Gen-Edu:** Biography, Dance. **Acq:** Purchase. **Dist:** WGBH/Boston. $24.95.

American Masters: Good Rockin' Tonight: The Legacy of Sun Records 2002
Explores the roots of American pop culture through the endeavors of music entrepreneur Sam Phillips, who started Sun Records in Memphis, Tennessee, and is responsible for the discovery of such seminal artists as Elvis Presley, Carl Perkins, Johnny Cash, and Jerry Lee Lewis. Includes live reprisals performed by current artists, many accompanied by Elvis' original band mates, Scotty Moore and D.J. Fontana. 112m; DVD. **A:** Adult. **P:** Education. **U:** Home, Institution. **Gen-Edu:** Documentary Films, Music--Pop/Rock, History. **Acq:** Purchase. **Dist:** WGBH/Boston. $24.95.

American Masters: Hank Williams: Honky Tonk Blues 2004
Profiles the personal and professional life of country music's first superstar with a first-ever on-camera interview with Williams? widow and exclusives with son Hank Williams Jr. and grandson Hank Williams III. Author Rick Bragg also provides his research findings about the legend's life, accompanied by rare audio and film clips of early performances. 60m; DVD. **A:** Adult. **P:** Education. **U:** Home, Institution. **Gen-Edu:** Biography, Music--Country/Western. **Acq:** Purchase. **Dist:** WGBH/Boston. $19.95.

American Masters: Inventing David Geffen 2012 (Unrated)
Biographical documentary on record producer David Geffen, focusing more on his pre-success life than the controversy which would accompany him later. DVD, Blu-Ray. **A:** Jr. High-Adult. **P:** Entertainment. **U:** Home. **L:** English. **Mov-Ent:** Biography: Music, Documentary Films. **Acq:** Purchase. **Dist:** PBS Home Video. $29.99 24.99.

American Masters: Isaac Stern: Life's Virtuoso 2000
Archival footage, home movies, and interviews with friends and colleagues present a distinguished portrait of the renowned violinist, teacher, emissary, and humanitarian. During his 60-year career, Stern toured for the U.S.O. in WWII, provided music for Hollywood films, shared the stage with Jack Benny, performed in the Soviet Union and communist China, and orchestrated a fundraiser that saved Carnegie Hall from the wrecker's ball. 60m; DVD. **A:** Adult. **P:** Education. **U:** Home, Institution. **Gen-Edu:** Biography, Music--Classical. **Acq:** Purchase. **Dist:** WGBH/Boston. $24.95.

American Masters: John James Audubon: Drawn from Nature 2007
Documents the self-taught artistry and self-made endeavors of America's best know naturalist. 60m; DVD; Closed Captioned. **A:** Adult. **P:** Education. **U:** Home. **Gen-Edu:** Documentary Films, Art & Artists, Birds. **Acq:** Purchase. **Dist:** WGBH/Boston. $24.95.

American Masters: Julia Child: America's Favorite Cook 2004
Interview with Ms. Child in her fabled kitchen intermixed with family photos provides tribute to an American icon and her two great loves, her husband Paul and cooking. 60m; VHS, DVD. **A:** Jr. High-Adult. **P:** Education. **U:** Home. **Gen-Edu:** Biography, Cooking. **Acq:** Purchase. **Dist:** WGBH/Boston. $19.95.

American Masters: Merce Cunningham: A Lifetime of Dance 2001
Retrospective of modern dance pioneer Merce Cunnigham is a masterful mix of performances pieces, interviews both past and present, troupe members? memories of long-time musical collaborator John Cage, and clips of company rehearsals. 90m; DVD. **A:** Adult. **P:** Education. **U:** Home, Institution. **Gen-Edu:** Documentary Films, Dance--History, Dance. **Acq:** Purchase. **Dist:** WGBH/Boston. $24.95.

American Masters: Muddy Waters: Can't Be Satisfied 2003
Fieldhand, bootlegger, and part-time musician McKinley Morganfield rose from his rural roots in Mississippi to become the undisputed King of the Blues of the Chicago club circuit and eventually the globe with such songs as "Hoochie Coochie Man," "I Just Want to Make Love to You," "Still a Fool," and "Rolling Stone." 60m; DVD. **A:** Jr. High-Adult. **P:** Education. **U:** Home, Institution. **Gen-Edu:** Biography, Music, History. **Acq:** Purchase. **Dist:** WGBH/Boston. $24.95.

American Masters: Pete Seeger: The Power of Song 2007
Joan Baez, Arlo Guthrie, Natalie Maines, Tom Paxton, Bonnie Raitt, Toshi Seeger, Tommy Smothers, Bruce Springsteen, Marty Travers, and Peter Yarrow perform songs by and with the legendary artist and political activist. Includes rarely-seen clips and off-stage footage of a 1960s Around-the-World-Tour. ?m; DVD. **A:** Adult. **P:** Education. **U:** Home. **Mov-Ent:** Music--Performance, Music, History--U.S. **Acq:** Purchase. **Dist:** WGBH/Boston. $24.95.

American Masters: Quincy Jones: In the Pocket 2002
Interviews, photos, and film clips document the 50-year career of composer, record/TV/film producer, arranger, instrumentalist, magazine founder, and multi-media entrepreneur Quincy Jones, from his days playing trumpet with Lionel Hampton, to producing music for Michael Jackson, Ray Charles, and Frank Sinatra. Covers his experiences with two failed marriages, an aneurysm and nervous breakdown, arranging and producing "We Are the World," as well as composing for a multitude of movies and TV shows. 90m; DVD. **A:** Adult. **P:** Education. **U:** Home, Institution. **Gen-Edu:** Biography, Music, Art & Artists. **Acq:** Purchase. **Dist:** WGBH/Boston. $24.95.

American Masters: Respect Yourself: The Stax Records Story 2007
Documents the rise and fall of Memphis-based Stax Records, founded in 1957 as Satellite Records and renamed in 1961, to sign and produce some of the most popular soul/R&B artists of the time. But detrimental contract negotiations with Atlantic Records and personal disasters brought dark days to the label. 113m; DVD. **A:** Adult. **P:** Education. **U:** Home, Institution. **Gen-Edu:** Documentary Films, Music, History--U.S. **Acq:** Purchase. **Dist:** WGBH/Boston. $19.95.

American Masters: Sidney Poitier: One Bright Light 2000
Poitier discusses his upbringing in the Caribbean, obstacles of racism, living in poverty in America, and his incessant desire to succeed as an actor. Includes film clips from all phases of his career. Quincy Jones, James Earl Jones, Denzel Washington, and director Stanley Kramer provide their own insights of the actor and the man that pioneered the way for black actors. 60m; DVD. **A:** Adult. **P:** Education. **U:** Home, Institution. **Gen-Edu:** Biography, Art & Artists, Biography: Show Business. **Acq:** Purchase. **Dist:** WGBH/Boston. $24.95.

American Masters: Sweet Honey in the Rock: Raise Your Voice 2005
Background information and performance clips of the African-American female a capella sextet that uses their voices to raise awareness about those suffering from abuse, civil inequities, or economically challenged situations. 90m; DVD. **A:** Adult. **P:** Education. **U:** Home, Institution. **Gen-Edu:** Music--Performance, Music. **Acq:** Purchase. **Dist:** WGBH/Boston. $26.95.

American Masters: The Artists 2004
Six profiles of influential artists: Richard Avedon, Alexander Calder, Robert Rauschenberg, Man Ray, Norman Rockwell, and Alfred Stieglitz. 440m; DVD. **A:** Sr. High-Adult. **P:** Entertainment. **U:** Home. **Gen-Edu:** Documentary Films. **Acq:** Purchase. **Dist:** Genius Entertainment.

American Masters: Willa Cather: The Road Is All 2005
Pays homage to the great American writer, whose novels "O Pioneer," "My Antonia," "Death Comes for the Archbishop," and "One of Ours" exquisitely render life on the Nebraskan prairies. 90m; DVD; Closed Captioned. **A:** Adult. **P:** Education. **U:** Home. **Gen-Edu:** Biography, Literature--American. **Acq:** Purchase. **Dist:** WGBH/Boston. $24.95.

American Masters: Woody Guthrie 2007
Biography of Guthrie and his leftist patriotic music rooted in the Dust Bowl of Depression-era America. 90m; DVD. **A:** Adult. **P:** Education. **U:** Home. **Gen-Edu:** Documentary Films, Music. **Acq:** Purchase. **Dist:** WGBH/Boston. $24.95.

American Matchmaker 1940 (Unrated) — ★★½
Nat Silver decides to go into the matchmaking business, after his own marriages fail miserably, hoping to experience happiness vicariously. However, he soon begins to realize that one of his clients is a better match for him than the man he chose for her. In Yiddish with English subtitles. 87m/B/W; VHS, DVD. **C:** Leo Fuchs; Judith Abarbanel; Rosetta Bialis; Yudel Dubinsky; Abe Lax; Directed by Edgar G. Ulmer; Written by S. (Shirley Ulmer) Castle; Cinematography by Edgar G. Ulmer. **A:** Jr. High-Adult. **P:** Entertainment. **U:** Home. **L:** Yiddish. **Mov-Ent:** Comedy--Romantic, Judaism, Marriage. **Acq:** Purchase. **Dist:** Ergo Media Inc. $69.95.

American Me 1992 (R) — ★★★
Violent and brutal depiction of more than 30 years of gang wars and drugs in East Los Angeles. Santana founded a street gang as a teenager, but has spent the last 18 years in prison, where he's the boss of the so-called Mexican Mafia, which oversees the drugs, scams, murders, and violence that are an everyday fact of prison life. Released from Folsom, Santana goes back to his old neighborhood and attempts to distance himself from his old life but finds his gang ties are stronger than any other alliance. Unsparing and desolate directorial debut from Olmos. 119m; VHS, DVD, HD-DVD, CC. **C:** Edward James Olmos; William Forsythe; Pepe Serna; Danny De La Paz; Evelina Fernandez; Daniel Villarreal; Cary-Hiroyuki Tagawa; Sal Lopez; Tony Giorgio; Directed by Edward James Olmos; Written by Floyd Mutrux; Desmond Nakano; Cinematography by Reynaldo Villalobos; Music by Dennis Lambert. **Pr:** Universal Pictures. **A:** Sr. High-Adult. **P:** Entertainment. **U:** Home. **Mov-Ent:** Crime Drama, Violence. **Acq:** Purchase. **Dist:** Movies Unlimited; Alpha Video. $19.98.

American Meltdown 2004 (Unrated) — ★★
In this tense thriller six terrorists take over the San Juan nuclear power plant and the government tries to figure out how to respond to the threat without it leading to a meltdown. However, the terrorists aren't exactly who they seem. 90m; DVD. **C:** Bruce Greenwood; Leslie Hope; Arnold Vosloo; James Remar; Susan Merson; Will Lyman; Directed by Jeremiah S. Chechik; Written by Larry Barber; Paul Barber; Cinematography by Douglas Koch; Music by tomandandy. **A:** Jr. High-Adult. **P:** Entertainment. **U:** Home. **Mov-Ent:** Federal Bureau of Investigation (FBI), Terrorism, Nuclear Warfare. **Acq:** Purchase. **Dist:** Morningstar Entertainment.

American Movie 1999 (R) — ★★★½
Would-be filmmaker Mark Borchardt's American Dream is to make his own independent film in his home of Menomonee Falls, Wisconsin. He doesn't have the money (or a particularly workable idea) but he does have lots of self-confidence and enthusiasm, as well as his mom, his 82-year-old Uncle Bill, and a cast of eccentrics. Smith's unlimited access shows Borchardt's almost limitless failures and obstacles, making the whole affair seem like a "Spinal Tap"-esque spoof, even though the people are sometimes painfully, sometimes hilariously real. 104m; VHS, DVD, CC. **C:** Mike Schank; Mark Borchardt; Directed by Chris Smith; Cinematography by Chris Smith; Music by Mike Schank. **Pr:** Sony Pictures Classics. **A:** College-Adult. **P:** Entertainment. **U:** Home. **Mov-Ent:** Documentary Films, Filmmaking. **Acq:** Purchase. **Dist:** Sony Pictures Home Entertainment Inc.

American Muscle Car: '53-'62 Chevrolet Corvette Chevrolet Camaro SS 396 2005
Traces the development of the original 1953 roadster and concept vehicles plus the introduction of the 1967-'69 Chevrolet Camaro SS 396. 60m; DVD. **A:** Jr. High-Adult. **P:** Entertainment. **U:** Home. **Gen-Edu:** Documentary Films, Automobiles. **Acq:** Purchase. **Dist:** MPI Media Group. $9.98.

American Muscle Car: '63-'67 Corvette Sting Ray, Camaro Z28 2006
Explores the development of the Camaro Z28 for the SCCA Trans Am road race plus the introduction of the 1963 redesigned Sting Ray Chevrolet Corvette. 50m; DVD. **A:** Jr. High-Adult. **P:** Entertainment. **U:** Home. **Gen-Edu:** Documentary Films, Automobiles. **Acq:** Purchase. **Dist:** MPI Media Group. $9.98.

American Muscle Car: '64 Ford Fairlane Thunderbolt & The Shelby Mustangs 2006
Looks at the '64 Ford Fairlane Thunderbolt and its 427 engine as well as Carroll Shelby's tenure with the Ford Motor Company and the introduction of the GT-350 and GT-500KR. 50m; DVD. **A:** Jr. High-Adult. **P:** Entertainment. **U:** Home. **Gen-Edu:** Documentary Films, Automobiles. **Acq:** Purchase. **Dist:** MPI Media Group. $9.98.

American Muscle Car: '64 Pontiac GTO & Pontiac GTO Judge 2006
Introduction of the 1964 Gran Turismo Omologato with its 389 engine plus the 1969 GTO Judge and its Ram Air IV engine. 50m; DVD. **A:** Jr. High-Adult. **P:** Entertainment. **U:** Home. **Gen-Edu:** Documentary Films, Automobiles. **Acq:** Purchase. **Dist:** MPI Media Group. $9.98.

American Muscle Car: American Motors AMX, AAR, 'Cuda, Challenger TA 2006
Looks at the two manufacturing years of the two-seater AMX sports car plus Chrysler's road racers. 50m; DVD. **A:** Jr. High-Adult. **P:** Entertainment. **U:** Home. **Gen-Edu:** Documentary Films, Automobiles. **Acq:** Purchase. **Dist:** MPI Media Group. $9.98.

American Muscle Car: Boss 302 & 429 Mustang: The Saleen Mustangs 2006
Examines the 1980s road racing Saleen Mustangs, popular with endurance racing competitions and Trans Am racing. 50m; DVD. **A:** Jr. High-Adult. **P:** Entertainment. **U:** Home. **Gen-Edu:** Documentary Films, Automobiles. **Acq:** Purchase. **Dist:** MPI Media Group. $9.98.

American Muscle Car: Buick Gran Sport and Oldsmobile 442 2006
A look at the Buick Gran Sport, made in Flint, Michigan, and the 1969-'71 Hurst Oldsmobile 442. 50m; DVD. **A:** Jr. High-Adult. **P:** Entertainment. **U:** Home. **Gen-Edu:** Documentary Films, Automobiles. **Acq:** Purchase. **Dist:** MPI Media Group. $9.98.

American Muscle Car: Buick Regal GNX, '55-'57 Chevrolet Bel Air 2006
Check out the late 1980s introduction of the Buick Regal with its turbocharged V-6 engine as well as Chevrolet's introduction of the V-8 Bel Air model. 50m; DVD. **A:** Jr. High-Adult. **P:** Entertainment. **U:** Home. **Gen-Edu:** Documentary Films, Automobiles. **Acq:** Purchase. **Dist:** MPI Media Group. $9.98.

American Muscle Car: Chevrolet Chevelle SS & Chevrolet Impala 409 2006
Looks at Chevrolet's Chevelle Super Sport 396 and 454 models and the '61-'64 Chevrolet Impala 409. 50m; DVD. **A:** Jr. High-Adult. **P:** Entertainment. **U:** Home. **Gen-Edu:** Documentary Films, Automobiles. **Acq:** Purchase. **Dist:** MPI Media Group. $9.98.

American Muscle Car: Chrysler 300, The Ramchargers 2006
Looks at the introduction of the Hemi engine with the Chrysler 300 in the 1950s and Chrysler's advanced engineering department's development of the Ramchargers for drag racing. 50m; DVD. **A:** Jr. High-Adult. **P:** Entertainment. **U:** Home. **Gen-Edu:** Documentary Films, Automobiles. **Acq:** Purchase. **Dist:** MPI Media Group. $9.98.

American Muscle Car: Dart GTS, Plymouth Roadrunner 2006
Looks at the Dodge Dart GTS 426 Hemi and Chrysler's Plymouth Roadrunner. 50m; DVD. **A:** Jr. High-Adult. **P:** Entertainment. **U:** Home. **Gen-Edu:** Documentary Films, Automobiles. **Acq:** Purchase. **Dist:** MPI Media Group. $9.98.

American Muscle Car: Dodge Charger, Dodge Viper 2006
Looks at the 1966-1970 models of the Dodge Charger and the sports racing car, the Dodge Viper. 50m; DVD. **A:** Jr. High-Adult. **P:** Entertainment. **U:** Home. **Gen-Edu:** Documentary Films, Automobiles. **Acq:** Purchase. **Dist:** MPI Media Group. $9.98.

American Muscle Car: Dodge Daytona & Plymouth Superbird: The Mopar Super Stockers 2006
Examines the 1969 and '70 Dodge Daytona and the 1970 Plymouth Superbird with its 440 Magnum or 425 Hemi engine plus the 1963-1966 Mopar Super Stockers: Plymouth Belvedere and Dodge Coronet. 50m; DVD. **A:** Jr. High-Adult. **P:** Entertainment. **U:** Home. **Gen-Edu:** Documentary Films, Automobiles. **Acq:** Purchase. **Dist:** MPI Media Group. $9.98.

American Muscle Car: Ford Fairlane GT, Ford Talladega, 427 Cobra 2006
Looks at Ford's 427 Fairlane and Torino Talladega models plus Carroll Shelby's LeMans 427 Cobras. 50m; DVD. **A:** Jr. High-Adult. **P:** Entertainment. **U:** Home. **Gen-Edu:** Documentary Films, Automobiles. **Acq:** Purchase. **Dist:** MPI Media Group. $9.98.

American Muscle Car: Ford Thunderbird, Chevrolet El Camino, Ford Ranchero 2006
An introduction to the 1955 Ford Thunderbird plus a look at the half-pickup/half-car El Camino and Ranchero models. 50m; DVD. **A:** Jr. High-Adult. **P:** Entertainment. **U:** Home. **Gen-Edu:** Documentary Films, Automobiles. **Acq:** Purchase. **Dist:** MPI Media Group. $9.98.

American Muscle Car: Plymouth Hemi 'Cuda, Dodge Hemi Challenger, Chevrolet Nova SS 2006
Looks at the introduction of the Plymouth Hemi Barracuda and the Dodge Challenger plus the 1968 Chevrolet Nova SS 396. 50m; DVD. **A:** Jr. High-Adult. **P:** Entertainment. **U:** Home. **Gen-Edu:** Documentary Films, Automobiles. **Acq:** Purchase. **Dist:** MPI Media Group. $9.98.

American Muscle Car: Season 1 2006 (Unrated)
Presents the 1998-2001 television series that profiles a variety of vintage muscle cars such as the 1964 Pontiac GTO, 1953-62 Chevrolet Corvette, and 1968 Chevrolet Nova SS 396. 12 episodes. 300m; DVD. **A:** Family. **P:** Entertainment. **U:** Home. **Mov-Ent:** Television Series, Documentary Films, Automobiles. **Acq:** Purchase. **Dist:** MPI Media Group. $29.98.

American Muscle Car: Season 2 2006 (Unrated)
Presents the 1998-2001 television series that profiles a variety of vintage muscle cars such as the 1959-63 Pontiac Firebird Trans Am, Ford Fairlane GT, and Camaro Z28. 12 episodes. 300m; DVD. **A:** Family. **P:** Entertainment. **U:** Home. **Mov-Ent:** Television Series, Documentary Films, Automobiles. **Acq:** Purchase. **Dist:** MPI Media Group. $29.98.

American Muscle Car: Season 3 2006 (Unrated)
Presents the 1998-2001 television series that profiles a variety of vintage muscle cars such as the 1986-2001 Chevrolet Corvette, the Saleen Mustangs, and Plymouth Roadrunner. 12 episodes. 300m; DVD. **A:** Family. **P:** Entertainment. **U:** Home. **Mov-Ent:** Television Series, Documentary Films, Automobiles. **Acq:** Purchase. **Dist:** MPI Media Group. $29.98.

American Museum of Natural History 1987
A look at the exhibits of the largest natural history museum in the world, complete with a peek at behind-the-scenes work. A teaching guide is included. 30m; VHS. **Pr:** Video Tours. **A:** Family. **P:** Entertainment. **U:** Institution, CCTV, Home. **Gen-Edu:** Documentary Films, Museums. **Acq:** Purchase. **Dist:** VT Entertainment. $24.95.

The American Musical Theater 1986
Provides history, commentary, and excerpts from classical musicals. 94m; VHS. **A:** Adult. **P:** Education. **U:** Institution. **Fin-Art:** Theater, Musical. **Acq:** Purchase. **Dist:** Insight Media. $350.00.
Indiv. Titles: 1. Part 1: 1800s to 1960s 2. Part 2: 1970s.

The American Navy in Vietnam 1967
A documentary film emphasizing aircraft carrier operations, bombing strikes, and naval bombardments. 29m; VHS. **TV Std:** NTSC, PAL. **C:** Narrated by Chet Huntley. **A:** Jr. High-Adult. **P:** Education. **U:** Institution, Home. **Gen-Edu:** Documentary Films, Vietnam War, Armed Forces--U.S. **Acq:** Purchase. **Dist:** International Historic Films Inc. $24.95.

American Needlework Collection 1987
Describes various needlework techniques, including cross stitching, custom framing, and crocheting. 60m; VHS, 3/4 U. **Pr:** RMI Media Productions. **A:** Jr. High-Adult. **P:** Instruction. **U:** Institution. **How-Ins:** Crafts, Sewing. **Acq:** Purchase. **Dist:** RMI Media. $29.95.
Indiv. Titles: 1. Learn to Cross Stitch 2. Basic Cross Stitching Design 3. Basic Cross Stitch on Linen 4. Finishing Your Cross Stitch Project 5. Basic Custom Framing for Needlework 6. Learn to Crochet.

American Nightmare 1981 (Unrated) — ★1/2
Young man searches for his missing sister against a background of pornography, drug peddling, and prostitution in the slums of a city. The usual titillating squalid urban drama. 85m; VHS. **C:** Lawrence S. Day; Lora Staley; Lenore Zann; Michael Ironside; Alexandra Paul; Directed by Don McBrearty. **Pr:** Ray Sager. **A:** Adult. **P:** Entertainment. **U:** Home. **Mov-Ent:** Prostitution, Exploitation. **Acq:** Purchase. **Dist:** No Longer Available.

American Nightmare 2000 (R) — ★1/2
To commemorate the killings of four college students on Halloween the year before, pirate radio show "American Nightmare" is broadcasting all night. The program's host, Caligari (Ryan), has listeners calling in with their worst fears and seven friends take turns calling. Too bad, the killer is also listening and decides to make their nightmares come true. 91m; VHS, DVD. **C:** Debbie Rochon; Brandy Little; Johnny Sneed; Christopher Ryan; Brinke Stevens; Directed by Jon Keeyes; Written by Jon Keeyes; Cinematography by Brad Walker; Music by Peter Gannan; David Rosenblad. **A:** Sr. High-Adult. **P:** Entertainment. **U:** Home. **Mov-Ent:** Halloween. **Acq:** Purchase. **Dist:** Monarch Home Video.

The American Nightmare 2004 (Unrated)
Documentary covering the rise and rebirth of American horror films since the 1960s, with interviews of John Carpenter, Wes Craven, David Cronenberg, and Tobe Hooper. 73m; DVD. **A:** Sr. High-Adult. **P:** Entertainment. **U:** Home. **Gen-Edu:** Documentary Films, Horror. **Acq:** Purchase. **Dist:** Docurama. $24.95.

An American Nile 1997
Examines the history of the Colorado River from its "wild" days to its use as a controlled resource. 55m; VHS; Closed Captioned. **A:** Jr. High-Sr. High. **P:** Education. **U:** Institution. **Gen-Edu:** Ecology & Environment, Geography, U.S. States. **Acq:** Purchase. **Dist:** Zenger Media. $29.95.

American Ninja 1985 (R) — ★★
American Dudikoff is G.I. Joe, a martial-arts expert stationed in the Philippines who alienates most everyone around him (he's a rebel). Deadly black-belt war begins with Joe confronting the army which is selling stolen weapons to the South American black market. Aided by one faithful pal, Joe uses his head-kicking martial arts skills to stop hundreds of ninja combatants working for the corrupt arms dealer. In his spare time he romances the base chief's daughter. Efficient rib-crunching chop-socky action wrapped in no-brainer plot and performed by nonactors. Cannon epic mercilessly followed by at least three sequels. 96m; VHS, DVD, Wide, CC. **C:** Michael Dudikoff; Guich Koock; Judie Aronson; Steve James; Directed by Sam Firstenberg; Written by Gideon Amir; Cinematography by Hanania Baer; Music by Michael Linn. **Pr:** Cannon Productions. **A:** Sr. High-Adult. **P:** Entertainment. **U:** Home. **Mov-Ent:** Martial Arts. **Acq:** Purchase. **Dist:** MGM Home Entertainment. $14.95.

American Ninja 2: The Confrontation 1987 (R) — ★★
Soldiers Dudikoff and James are back again using their martial arts skills (in lieu of any acting) to take on a Caribbean drug-lord. Apparently he has been kidnapping Marines and taking them to his island, where he genetically alters them to become fanatical ninja assassins eager to do his dirty work. The script hardly gets in the way of the rib-crunching action, but is an improvement upon Ninja Number One. 90m; VHS, DVD, CC. **C:** Michael Dudikoff; Steve James; Larry Poindexter; Gary Conway; Directed by Sam Firstenberg; Written by Gary Conway; James Booth. **Pr:** Cannon Films. **A:** Jr. High. **P:** Entertainment. **U:** Home. **Mov-Ent:** Martial Arts. **Acq:** Purchase. **Dist:** MGM Home Entertainment. $19.95.

American Ninja 3: Blood Hunt 1989 (R) — **Bomb!**
Second sequel in the American Ninja series. Bradley replaces Dudikoff as the martial arts good guy fighting the martial arts bad guys on a Caribbean island. He's pursued by ex-evangelist Marjoe, who wants to inject him with a nasty virus before unloading the germs to bad buys worldwide. Less ninjitsu; more uninspired martial arts. 90m; VHS, DVD. **C:** David Bradley; Steve James; Marjoe Gortner; Michele Chan; Calvin Jung; Directed by Cedric Sundstrom; Written by Paul DeMielche; Gary Conway; Music by George S. Clinton. **Pr:** Cannon Films. **A:** Sr. High-Adult. **P:** Entertainment. **U:** Home. **Mov-Ent:** Martial Arts. **Acq:** Purchase. **Dist:** MGM Home Entertainment. $14.95.

American Ninja 4: The Annihilation 1991 (R) — **Bomb!**
Dudikoff returns after noticeable absence in last sequel. He should have stayed away from #4—it's a rehash of tired ideas that never gets off the ground. Forget this and see "American Ninja 2: The Confrontation," the best of this series. 99m; VHS, DVD, CC. **C:** Michael Dudikoff; David Bradley; James Booth; Dwayne Alexandre; Robin Stille; Ken Gampu; Directed by Cedric Sundstrom; Written by David Geeves; Music by Nicolas Tenbroek. **Pr:** Cannon Productions. **A:** Sr. High-Adult. **P:** Entertainment. **U:** Home. **L:** English, Spanish. **Mov-Ent:** Martial Arts. **Acq:** Purchase. **Dist:** Movies Unlimited. $7.50.

An American Nurse at War ????
Overviews events during WWI through photographs and letters to home from American Red Cross nurse Marion McCune Rice. 36m/B/W; VHS. **A:** Jr. High-Adult. **P:** Education. **U:** Institution. **Gen-Edu:** History--Modern, World War One. **Acq:** Purchase. **Dist:** Zenger Media. $29.95.

American Oompah 1983
A documentary about the rigors a high school marching band must go through to participate in a national pageant. 30m; VHS, 3/4 U. **Pr:** New Jersey Network. **A:** Sr. High-Adult. **P:** Education. **U:** Institution. **Gen-Edu:** Documentary Films. **Acq:** Purchase, Rent/Lease. **Dist:** New Jersey Network.

American Outlaws 2001 (PG-13) — ★
Look kids, it's N'Sync as the James Gang! Remember "Young Guns" (1988)? By the end of this, you'll be begging for Emilio Estevez's constant mugging and Kiefer Sutherland's ridiculous brooding. Jesse (Farrell) and Frank James (Macht), along with cousins Cole (Caan), Bob (McCormack) and Jim Younger (Smith) return from the Civil War to find Ma (Bates) and the family farm threatened by the railroad. So they commence to robbin' banks to help out the poor folk who been done wrong. Along the way Jesse courts purty young filly Zee (Larter). People have been writing the obituary of the Western for a few years now, but "Outlaws" may be the bullet in the genre's back. 95m; VHS, DVD, Wide. **C:** Colin Farrell; Gabriel Macht; Scott Caan; Gregory Edward Smith; Will McCormack; Timothy Dalton; Kathy Bates; Nathaniel Arcand; Ali Larter; Ronny Cox; Harris Yulin; Terry O'Quinn; Ty O'Neal; Joe Stevens; Directed by Les Mayfield; Written by John Rogers; Roderick Taylor; Cinematography by Russell Boyd; Music by Trevor Rabin. **Pr:** James G. Robinson; Morgan Creek Productions; Warner Bros. **A:** Jr. High-Adult. **P:** Entertainment. **U:** Home. **Mov-Ent:** Western. **Acq:** Purchase. **Dist:** Warner Home Video, Inc.

American Outrage 2008
Issues of land rights and Native American rights are considered by looking at the federal persecution of Carrie and Mary Dunn in this documentary. The Western Shoshone sisters faced legal action and the loss of their horses and cattle for grazing them on nearby open range claimed by their tribe. 56m; DVD. **A:** Sr.

High-Adult. **P:** Entertainment. **U:** Home. **Mov-Ent**: Law, Family, Documentary Films. **Acq:** Purchase. **Dist:** First Run Features. $24.95.

The American Parade: F.D.R.?Man Who Changed America 1976
The program shows the charismatic leadership of F.D.R. even when America was going through its worst economic crisis. 30m/B/W; VHS, 3/4 U. **C:** Narrated by Henry Fonda. **Pr:** CBS News. **A:** Jr. High-Sr. High. **P:** Education. **U:** Institution, SURA. **Gen-Edu**: Presidency. **Acq:** Purchase. **Dist:** Phoenix Learning Group.

The American Parade: Power and the Presidency 1974
The nation's history has been profoundly affected by strong men who used their power to shape the character of the office. 28m; VHS, 3/4 U. **C:** Narrated by George C. Scott. **Pr:** CBS News. **A:** Sr. High-College. **P:** Education. **U:** Institution, SURA. **Gen-Edu**: Presidency. **Acq:** Purchase. **Dist:** Phoenix Learning Group.

The American Parade: Second Revolution 1977
Tony Randall explores this often overlooked aspect of our history: the industrial revolution. Both live action and animation. 28m; VHS, 3/4 U. **C:** Tony Randall. **Pr:** CBS News. **A:** Jr. High-Sr. High. **P:** Education. **U:** Institution, SURA. **Gen-Edu**: History--U.S. **Acq:** Purchase. **Dist:** Phoenix Learning Group.

The American Parade: Song of Myself 1976
Walt Whitman (played by Rip Torn) reminisces about his life, from the time he started writing "Leaves of Grass" until he had to return to his family again after a paralytic stroke. 31m; VHS, 3/4 U. **C:** Rip Torn. **Pr:** CBS News. **A:** Sr. High-College. **P:** Education. **U:** Institution, SURA. **Gen-Edu**: Literature--American. **Acq:** Purchase. **Dist:** Phoenix Learning Group.

The American Parade: Stop Thief 1976
"Stop Thief" is a colorful, sometimes comic dramatization of one of America's outstanding scoundrels-Boss Tweed. Howard de Silva creates the character of Tweed. 32m; VHS, 3/4 U. **C:** Howard da Silva. **Pr:** CBS News. **A:** Jr. High-Sr. High. **P:** Education. **U:** Institution, SURA. **Gen-Edu**: Politics & Government. **Acq:** Purchase. **Dist:** Phoenix Learning Group.

The American Parade: 34th Star 1975
The show portrays the Simpson family, who represent an American generation that settled Kansas Territory; we see the life-styles and social, political, and economic aspects of an era. 34m; VHS, 3/4 U. **Pr:** CBS News. **A:** Jr. High-Sr. High. **P:** Education. **U:** Institution, SURA. **Gen-Edu**: History--U.S. **Acq:** Purchase. **Dist:** Phoenix Learning Group.

The American Parade: We the Women 1974
Narrated by Mary Tyler Moore, the program traces the history of the women's movement. 30m; VHS, 3/4 U. **C:** Narrated by Mary Tyler Moore. **Pr:** CBS News. **A:** Sr. High-College. **P:** Education. **U:** Institution, SURA. **Gen-Edu**: Women. **Acq:** Purchase. **Dist:** Phoenix Learning Group.

The American Parade: With All Deliberate Speed 1976
This show dramatizes the courage and suffering of two individuals who stood for what they believed was right. 32m; VHS, 3/4 U. **Pr:** CBS News. **A:** Jr. High-Sr. High. **P:** Education. **U:** Institution, SURA. **Gen-Edu**: Psychology. **Acq:** Purchase. **Dist:** Phoenix Learning Group.

American Patchwork: Appalachian Journey 1990
Documentary which traces the roots of country music from mountain to mouthblow to bluegrass. Some of the creators of country music are interviewed. 60m; VHS. **A:** Family. **P:** Entertainment. **U:** Home. **Gen-Edu**: Music--Country/Western, History. **Acq:** Purchase. **Dist:** PBS Home Video. $14.95.

American Patchwork: Cajun Country 1990
The rich history of the Cajun peoples of Louisiana. Their music, song, dance, story-telling, food and folk beliefs are examined in this colorful documentary. 58m; VHS. **A:** Family. **P:** Entertainment. **U:** Home. **Gen-Edu**: Documentary Films, History--U.S., U.S. States. **Acq:** Purchase. **Dist:** PBS Home Video; Facets Multimedia Inc.; Music Video Distributors. $14.95.

American Patchwork: Dreams and Songs of the Noble Old 1991
Explore the musical and cultural contributions of older Americans. Includes interviews with Janie Hunter, an 80-year-old woman, who leads her church in early American spirituals. 60m; VHS. **Pr:** PBS. **A:** Family. **P:** Entertainment. **U:** Home. **Gen-Edu**: Documentary Films. **Acq:** Purchase. **Dist:** PBS Home Video. $14.95.

American Patchwork: Jazz Parades 1990
A history and exhibition of America's jazz musicians. 60m; VHS. **Pr:** PBS Video. **A:** Jr. High-Adult. **P:** Entertainment. **U:** Home. **Gen-Edu**: Documentary Films, Music--Jazz, History--U.S. **Acq:** Purchase. **Dist:** PBS Home Video. $14.95.

American Patchwork: Land Where Blues Began 1990
An historical evaluation of the development of blues music. 60m; VHS. **Pr:** PBS Video. **A:** Jr. High-Adult. **P:** Entertainment. **U:** Home. **Gen-Edu**: Documentary Films, Music--Performance. **Acq:** Purchase. **Dist:** PBS Home Video. $14.98.

American Photography: A Century of Images ????
Looks at how photography has affected American history from the early 20th century to the present. 90m; VHS. **A:** Adult. **P:** Instruction. **U:** Home, Institution. **How-Ins**: Photography, Art & Artists. **Acq:** Purchase. **Dist:** Crystal Productions. $49.98.

American Pickers: Civil War Pickings 2011 (Unrated)
History Channel Reality Series featuring antique collectors Mike Wolfe and Frank Fritz. This special edition shows Mike and Frank on special assignment from the Gettysburg Museum, looking for Civil War relics. Along the way, the duo participate in a Civil War reenactment. 47m; DVD. **A:** Family. **P:** Entertainment. **U:** Home. **Acq:** Purchase. **Dist:** A&E Television Networks L.L.C. $14.99.

American Pickers: Picks From the Back of the Van 2011 (Unrated)
History Channel Reality Series featuring antique collectors Mike Wolfe and Frank Fritz. This "best of" collection features eight fan favorites from the first season of American Pickers, including "Big Bear", "Super Scooter", "White Castle on the Farm", "Invisible Pump", "Back Breaker", "Mole Man", "Frank's Gamble", and "5 Acres of Junk". 8 episodes. 360m; DVD. **A:** Family. **P:** Entertainment. **U:** Home. **Acq:** Purchase. **Dist:** A&E Television Networks L.L.C. $19.98.

American Pickers: The Complete Season 1 2009 (Unrated)
History Channel 2010-? reality documentary. Mike Wolfe, owner of Antique Archaeology in Iowa, and his business partner Frank Fritz track down historical and collectible objects that have been long forgotten by their owners such as a rare Vespa Ape "Super Scooter." In "Invisible Pump" the guys discover a circa 1920s 'visible' gas pump and visit an 1879 opera house now a home for vintage movie posters. 12 episodes. 453m; DVD. **C:** Mike Wolfe; Frank Fritz. **A:** Family. **P:** Entertainment. **U:** Home. **Mov-Ent**: Documentary Films, Antiques, Television Series. **Acq:** Purchase. **Dist:** A&E Television Networks L.L.C. $29.99.

American Pickers: Volume Three 2010 (Unrated)
History Channel Reality Series. In "Hobo Jack", Mike and Frank find numerous treasures in a retired chimney sweep's collection. "Laurel and Hardy" has the duo visiting a couple living in a geodesic dome with lots of valuables including large Laurel and Hardy masks. Frank and Mike visit a Wisconsin farm inhabited by a man called Hippie Tom in "Frank Flips". The van shows signs of engine trouble which Mike ignores in "Mike's Breakdown", and in "Pint-Sized Picker" they explore an opera singer's homestead. 8 episodes. 336m; DVD. **A:** Family. **P:** Entertainment. **U:** Home. **Acq:** Purchase. **Dist:** A&E Television Networks L.L.C. $19.98.

American Pie 1999 (R) — ★★★
And you thought you loved dessert! Four high school seniors led by pastry molesting Jim (Biggs) vow to lose their virginity before the Prom. Unfortunately for them, the girls that they're chasing aren't your usual teenage sex comedy tarts. These smart little cookies make sure that the boys' quest is chock full of humiliation. The sensitivity to the female point-of-view is balanced by a heapin' helpin' of crude and disgusting humor for the guys. An absolute must-see for baked goods and the men who love them. 95m; VHS, DVD, Blu-Ray, UMD, Wide, CC. **C:** Jason Biggs; Thomas Ian Nicholas; Chris Owen; Chris Klein; Natasha Lyonne; Tara Reid; Mena Suvari; Alyson Hannigan; Shannon Elizabeth; Eugene Levy; Seann William Scott; Jennifer Coolidge; Eddie Kaye Thomas; Lawrence Pressman; Eric Lively; Molly Cheek; Clyde Kusatsu; John Cho; Eli Marienthal; Casey Affleck; Tara Subkoff; Christina Milian; Directed by Chris Weitz; Paul Weitz; Written by Adam Herz; Cinematography by Richard Crudo; Music by David Lawrence. **Pr:** Warren Zide; Chris Moore; Universal Studios. **A:** Sr. High-Adult. **P:** Entertainment. **U:** Home. **Mov-Ent**: Sex & Sexuality. **Acq:** Purchase. **Dist:** Universal Studios Home Video.

American Pie 2 2001 (R) — ★★½
No pie is abused in this movie, although everyone (including exec producers Chris and Paul Weitz) is back for a second helping. The story picks up a year later while everyone is on summer vacation from college and sharing a beach house. Jim (Biggs) is nervously anticipating a visit from Nadia, while getting sex tips from band camp geek Michelle (Hannigan). Entertaining sequel shares the original's appealing and effective combination of gross-out situations and sweet silliness, and while it's not quite as good, it doesn't miss by much. 105m; VHS, DVD, UMD, Wide. **C:** Jason Biggs; Shannon Elizabeth; Alyson Hannigan; Chris Klein; Natasha Lyonne; Thomas Ian Nicholas; Tara Reid; Chris Owen; Seann William Scott; Mena Suvari; Eddie Kaye Thomas; Eugene Levy; Jennifer Coolidge; Christopher Penn; Eli Marienthal; Casey Affleck; Denise Faye; Molly Cheek; Directed by James B. Rogers; Written by Adam Herz; Cinematography by Mark Irwin; Music by David Lawrence. **Pr:** Warren Zide; Chris Moore; Craig Perry; Universal Pictures. **A:** Sr. High-Adult. **P:** Entertainment. **U:** Home. **Mov-Ent**: Adolescence, Sex & Sexuality. **Acq:** Purchase. **Dist:** Alpha Video; Movies Unlimited.

American Pie Presents Band Camp 2005 (Unrated) — ★
Stiffler's equally obnoxious and horny younger brother Matt (Hilgenbrink) is sent to summer band camp as punishment for a prank gone wrong. He decides to liven up his stay by shooting "girls gone wild"-type videos of the band chicks, only to have a change of heart when he hooks up with old friend Elyse (Kebbel). Levy's the only original cast member to sheepishly show up in this drivel. 94m; DVD, Wide. **C:** Tad Hilgenbrink; Arielle Kebbel; Crystle Lightning; Eugene Levy; Jason Earles; Directed by Steve Rash; Written by Brad Riddell; Cinematography by Victor Kemper; Music by Robert Folk. **A:** Sr. High-Adult. **P:** Entertainment. **U:** Home. **Mov-Ent**: Camps & Camping. **Acq:** Purchase. **Dist:** Movies Unlimited; Alpha Video.

American Pie Presents: Beta House 2007 (R) — ★
And the franchise just gets lamer and grosser. Dwight Stifler is the head of the infamous Beta frat, just pledged by his cousin Erik and his buds. But their house superiority is challenged by newcomer Geek House and power-hungry nerd Edgar. 89m; DVD. **C:** Jake Siegel; John White; Steven Talley; Meghan Heffern; Nic Nac; Tyrone Savage; Sarah Power; Eugene Levy; Christopher McDonald; Directed by Andrew Waller; Written by Erik Lindsay; Music by Jeff Cardoni. **A:** Sr. High-Adult. **P:** Entertainment. **U:** Home. **Mov-Ent**. **Acq:** Purchase. **Dist:** Movies Unlimited; Alpha Video.

American Pie Presents: Book of Love 2009 (R) — ★
The seventh entry in the impossibly lame series finds high-school virgins Rob, Nathan, and Lube discovering the legendary love manual hidden in the school's library. So they vow to test its wisdom on various babes. None of the characters are appealing and this is merely a crude wannabe comedy. 94m; DVD. **C:** Bug Hall; Brandon Hardesty; Kevin M. Horton; John Patrick Jordan; Eugene Levy; Cindy Busby; Jennifer Holland; Beth Behrs; Rosanna Arquette; Directed by John Putch; Written by David H. Steinberg; Cinematography by Ross Berryman. **A:** Sr. High-Adult. **P:** Entertainment. **U:** Home. **Mov-Ent**. **Acq:** Purchase. **Dist:** Universal Studios Home Video.

American Pie Presents: The Naked Mile 2006 (R) — ★★
Raunchy and surprisingly funny sex comedy. Erik Stifler (White) is a high school virgin since sweet girlfriend Tracy (Schram) won't put out. Erik and his buddies are visiting his cousin Dwight (Talley) at college for the weekend in order to run in the annual naked mile. Feeling guilty, Tracy gives him a free pass to do whatever he wants—and then worries that what Erik wants is sex with some other girl. Humiliation and a wide variety of bodily fluids follow. Also available unrated. 97m; DVD, Wide. **C:** John White; Steven Talley; Ross Thomas; Christopher McDonald; Jessy Schram; Jake Siegel; Eugene Levy; Candace Kroslak; Directed by Joe Nussbaum; Written by Erik Lindsay; Cinematography by Eric Haase; Music by Jeff Cardoni. **A:** Sr. High-Adult. **P:** Entertainment. **U:** Home. **Mov-Ent**. **Acq:** Purchase. **Dist:** Movies Unlimited; Alpha Video.

American Pimp 1999 (R)
The Hughes brothers take a break from conventional features ("Menace 2 Society," "From Hell") to spin out a modest documentary about pimps. They combine interview footage with film clips to let the likes of Rosebudd, C-Note, and Gorgeous Dre tell their own stories. Those already interested in the subject may find it fascinating. Others will see it as all flash and no style. 87m; DVD, Wide. **C:** Directed by Albert Hughes; Written by Allen Hughes; Cinematography by Albert Hughes. **A:** College-Adult. **P:** Entertainment. **U:** Home. **Mov-Ent**: Documentary Films, Prostitution. **Acq:** Purchase. **Dist:** MGM Home Entertainment.

The American Pioneering Experience ????
Series of five videos charts the pioneer movements across the Appalachians, the Sante Fe and Oregon trails through a series of reenactments, historic artwork, and quotes from historic source materials. 130m; VHS; Closed Captioned. **A:** Jr. High. **P:** Education. **U:** Institution. **Gen-Edu**: History--U.S., U.S. States. **Acq:** Purchase. **Dist:** Zenger Media. $450.00.

Indiv. Titles: 1. Daniel Boone & the First American Pioneers 2. Ohio Boatman & the Pioneering Farmers 3. Mountain Men & Gold Seekers 4. Old Texas & the Trail Drivers 5. Covered Wagon & Westward Expansion.

American Pioneers 1989
This tape describes the independent of American poetry British styles with examinations of Edgar Allan Poe's poetry as musical art, Walt Whitman's bravado, E.A Robinson's modernism, and Emily Dickinson. 28m; VHS, 3/4 U. **Pr:** Films for the Humanities and Sciences. **A:** College. **P:** Education. **U:** Institution, CCTV, CATV, BCTV. **Fin-Art**: Literature--American. **Acq:** Purchase, Rent/Lease, Duplication License. **Dist:** Films for the Humanities & Sciences.

American Pluck 1925 (Unrated) — ★★
Before he can inherit anything, a playboy millionaire's son must go out into the world and prove he can make his own way. He meets a beautiful princess, who is pursued by a villainous count. Walsh, as the dashing hero, was the younger brother of director Raoul. Silent with original organ music. 91m/B/W; Silent; VHS, DVD. **C:** George Walsh; Wanda (Petit) Hawley; Frank Leigh; Sidney De Grey; Directed by Richard Stanton. **Pr:** Video Yesteryear. **A:** Family. **P:** Entertainment. **U:** Home. **Mov-Ent**: Comedy--Slapstick, Silent Films. **Acq:** Purchase. **Dist:** Televista. $24.95.

American Pop 1981 (R) — ★★
Animated story of four generations of men told in music. Immigrant Zalmie starts off in vaudeville and winds up involved in the mob, his pianist son Benny gets killed in WWII, Benny's son Tony winds up in the early psychedelic rock scene in Haight-Asbury, and Tony's son Little Pete becomes a rock idol. 95m; VHS, DVD, CC. **C:** Voice(s) by Ron Thompson; Marya Small; Lisa Jane Persky; Roz Kelly; Richard Singer; Jeffrey Lippa; Directed by Ralph Bakshi; Written by Ronni Kern; Music by Lee Holdridge. **A:** Sr. High-Adult. **P:** Entertainment. **U:** Home. **Mov-Ent**: Animation & Cartoons, Music--Pop/Rock, Family. **Acq:** Purchase. **Dist:** Sony Pictures Home Entertainment Inc.

Songs: A Hard Rain's A-Gonna Fall; Don't Think Twice It's All Right; People Are Strange; Purple Haze; Hell is for Children; Free Bird; I'm Waiting for the Man; Night Moves; You Send Me; This Train; California Dreamin'; Cantelope Island; I Got Rhythm; Somebody Loves Me; Summertime; Our Love is Here to Stay; Anything Goes.

The American Presidency 1989
The powers, importance, and the relationship between the Congress and the President are explained. 30m; VHS, 3/4 U. **Pr:** SVE. **A:** Jr. High. **P:** Education. **U:** Institution, CCTV, Home. **Gen-Edu:** Presidency, Politics & Government. **Acq:** Purchase, Duplication. **Dist:** Clear Vue Inc. $79.00.

The American President 1995 (PG-13) — ★★★
Widower president Andrew Shepherd (Douglas) decides it's time to get back into the dating game. But just what woman wants to find her romance in the public eye? Well, it turns out to be feisty environmental lobbyist Sydney Wade (the ever-charming Bening). But the Prez also has to put up with nasty opponent Bob Rumson (Dreyfuss), who's using their courtship as political fodder, approval ratings, and a nosy press. Glossy fairytale material expertly handled by both cast and director. 114m; VHS, DVD, Blu-Ray, Wide, CC. **C:** Michael Douglas; Annette Bening; Martin Sheen; Michael J. Fox; David Paymer; Samantha Mathis; John Mahoney; Anna Deavere Smith; Nina Siemaszko; Wendie Malick; Shawna Waldron; Richard Dreyfuss; Gabe Jarret; Anne Haney; Gail Strickland; Joshua Malina; Ron Canada; Jennifer Crystal Foley; Taylor Nichols; Directed by Rob Reiner; Written by Aaron Sorkin; Cinematography by John Seale; Music by Marc Shaiman. **Pr:** Jeffrey Stott; Charles Newirth; Rob Reiner; Castle Rock Entertainment; Universal Pictures. **A:** Sr. High-Adult. **P:** Entertainment. **U:** Home. **Mov-Ent:** Comedy--Romantic, Politics & Government, Presidency. **Acq:** Purchase. **Dist:** Sony Pictures Home Entertainment Inc.

The American President 2000
Five-volume collection provides brief profiles on 41 of America's presidents. Appropriate for Grades 7-12. 600m; VHS, DVD; Closed Captioned. **A:** Jr. High-Sr. High. **P:** Education. **U:** Institution. **Gen-Edu:** Politics & Government, Presidency. **Acq:** Purchase. **Dist:** Social Studies School Service; Zenger Media. $99.98.

The American Professionals Series 1984
In this series of 21 half hour programs, various occupations are examined in depth, including a day in the life of each worker. 30m; VHS, 3/4 U. **Pr:** WTBS Atlanta. **A:** Sr. High-Adult. **P:** Education. **U:** Institution, CCTV, Home. **Gen-Edu:** Business, Occupations. **Acq:** Purchase. **Dist:** RMI Media; Cambridge Educational.
Indiv. Titles: 1. Nurse 2. Fireman 3. Stuntman 4. Mother 5. Coal Miner 6. Parole Agent 7. Jockey 8. Photojournalist 9. Farmer 10. Referee 11. Oil Driller 12. Hockey Coach 13. Pilot 14. Fisherman 15. Chips 16. Veterinarian 17. Doctor 18. Coast Guard Pilot 19. Horse Trainer 20. Paramedic 21. Auto Assembly Line General Repairman.

An American Prophet: The Lowdermilk Story 1988
A celebration of the accomplishments of the man who is responsible for Israeli agriculture. 46m; VHS. **Pr:** Alden Films. **A:** Primary-Adult. **P:** Education. **U:** Institution, Home. **Gen-Edu:** Agriculture, Middle East. **Acq:** Purchase, Rent/Lease. **Dist:** Alden Films. $59.95.

American Psycho 1999 (R) — ★★
Trimmed-down and (slightly) cleaned-up version of Bret Easton Ellis's widely hated 1991 novel has Bale as '80s hotshot Wall Street exec and apparent serial-killer Patrick Bateman. Bateman is the poster child for Reagan-era excess and preference for style over substance, a theme with which the film, while shooting for satire, beats you over the head. Like the decade it portrays, "Psycho" is far from subtle, and the characters barely register as two-dimensional, let alone three. They got the look right, but then, that's the point, isn't it? The production drew protests in Toronto, where some scenes were shot, and Leo DiCaprio was rumored to be in line to play the lead for a time. 103m; VHS, DVD, Blu-Ray, UMD, Wide, CC. **C:** Christian Bale; Willem Dafoe; Jared Leto; Reese Witherspoon; Samantha Mathis; Chloe Sevigny; Justin Theroux; Josh(ua) Lucas; Guinevere Turner; Matt Ross; William Sage; Cara Seymour; Directed by Mary Harron; Written by Guinevere Turner; Mary Harron; Cinematography by Andrzej Sekula; Music by John Cale. **A:** Sr. High-Adult. **P:** Entertainment. **U:** Home. **Mov-Ent:** Satire & Parody, Prostitution. **Acq:** Purchase. **Dist:** Movies Unlimited; Alpha Video; Lions Gate Entertainment Inc.

American Psycho 2: All American Girl 2002 (R) — ★★
Rachelle Newman (Kunis) is the only victim who managed to escape from serial killer Patrick Bateman. But her ordeal left her obsessed with such killers and when she learns that college prof Robert Strickland (Shatner) was an FBI profiler specializing in the subject, Rachelle is determined to become his teaching assistant. Even if it means killing the competition. 88m; VHS, DVD, CC. **C:** Mila Kunis; William Shatner; Geraint Wyn Davies; Lindy Booth; Robin Dunne; Directed by Morgan J. Freeman; Written by Karen Craig; Alex Sanger; Cinematography by Vanja Cernjul; Music by Norman Orenstein. **A:** Sr. High-Adult. **P:** Entertainment. **U:** Home. **Mov-Ent. Acq:** Purchase. **Dist:** CinemaNow Inc.

American Queen: St. Louis to St. Paul on the Upper Mississippi River ????
Provides a ride aboard the American Queen, the world's largest steam riverboat, for its 685-mile trip northward on the Mississippi River from St. Louis to St. Paul, Minnesota as it passes through locks and dams and visits several river towns. 104m; VHS, DVD. **A:** College-Adult. **P:** Education. **U:** Home. **Gen-Edu:** Trains, Boating. **Acq:** Purchase. **Dist:** The Civil War Standard; Herron Rail Video. $29.95.

American Radical: The Trials of Norman Finkelstein 2009 (Unrated)
Documentary on controversial author Norman Finklestein. DVD. **A:** Jr. High-Adult. **P:** Education. **U:** Home, Institution. **L:** Arabic, English. **Gen-Edu:** Documentary Films, Biography, Literature. **Acq:** Purchase. **Dist:** Arab Film Distribution. $19.99 300.00.

American Railroad Collection Vol. 1 2002
A collection of promotional, safety, and training films including "Portrait of a Railroad" (1973), "Switches-Hand Brakes and YOU" (1974), "Mo-Pac Delivers" (1975), and "TLC (Tender Loving Care)" (1967). 76m; VHS, DVD. **A:** Family. **P:** Entertainment. **U:** Home. **Gen-Edu:** Trains. **Acq:** Purchase. **Dist:** Pentrex Media Group L.L.C. $19.95.

American Railroad Collection Vol. 2 2002
A collection of promotional, safety, and training films including "The Freight Goes Through" (1952), "The Right to Compete" (1956), "New Direction in Modern Railroading" (1966), and "The Right Track" (1967). 95m; VHS, DVD. **A:** Family. **P:** Entertainment. **U:** Home. **Gen-Edu:** Trains. **Acq:** Purchase. **Dist:** Pentrex Media Group L.L.C. $19.95.

American Railroad Memories 1955
Short train films are featured on this video, including "Big Trains Rolling (1952)," "Mainline USA (1955)" and "The Passenger Train (1955)" 55m; VHS. **Pr:** Moviecraft Entertainment. **A:** Sr. High-Adult. **P:** Entertainment. **U:** Home. **Gen-Edu:** Trains. **Acq:** Purchase. **Dist:** Moviecraft Home Video. $24.95.

American Railroads in the 20th Century 2003
Archival footage and narration present a comprehensive history of railroad trains and systems. 52m; VHS. **A:** Family. **P:** Entertainment. **U:** Home. **Gen-Edu:** Trains. **Acq:** Purchase. **Dist:** Pentrex Media Group L.L.C. $29.95.

American Red Cross Emergency Test 1990
Presents 20 questions to viewers about the proper way for non-professionals to handle life-threatening medical emergencies. Then takes viewers through procedures recommended by the Red Cross. Comes with test score card. 50m; VHS. **A:** Sr. High-Adult. **P:** Instruction. **U:** Institution, Home. **Hea-Sci:** Health Education. **Acq:** Purchase. **Dist:** Cambridge Educational. $39.95.

An American Retrospective Through Animation 1948
Classic cartoons made between 1948 and 1954 tell the story of business in America by following "King Joe," the American worker. He learns how an idea can lead to a product, how higher wages for him can actually cost him money, how he can lose freedoms to big government, and more. 60m; VHS. **A:** Family. **P:** Entertainment. **U:** Home. **Mov-Ent:** Animation & Cartoons, Business. **Acq:** Purchase. **Dist:** Moviecraft Home Video. $19.95.

American Reunion 2012 (R) — ★★
The fourth film to feature the characters from 1999's "American Pie" also features the stalest comedy in the franchise. Jim (Biggs), Oz (Klein), Kevin (Nicholas), Finch (Thomas), and Stifler (Scott) are all back for some raunchy action (and are ably assisted by many of the supporting characters like Levy and Coolidge) but they forgot to write an interesting story for them. In typical fashion, the quintet of guys show up for their reunion in Michigan and sexually-charged hijinks ensue. Except for the occasional jolt of comic energy from Scott or Levy, the entire affair is like an actual reunion with people you never wanted to see again. 113m; DVD, Blu-Ray, Streaming. **C:** Jason Biggs; Alyson Hannigan; Chris Klein; Thomas Ian Nicholas; Tara Reid; Seann William Scott; Mena Suvari; Eddie Kaye Thomas; Jennifer Coolidge; Eugene Levy; Natasha Lyonne; Shannon Elizabeth; Chris Owen; Directed by Jon Hurwitz; Hayden Schlossberg; Written by Jon Hurwitz; Hayden Schlossberg; Cinematography by Daryn Okada; Music by Lyle Workman; JoJo Villanueva. **Pr:** Adam Herz; Chris Moore; Craig Perry; Warren Zide; Universal Pictures; Practical Pictures; Relativity Media. **A:** Sr. High-Adult. **P:** Entertainment. **U:** Home. **L:** English. **Mov-Ent:** Comedy--Screwball. **Acq:** Purchase, Rent/Lease. **Dist:** Universal Studios Home Video. $29.98 22.98 9.99.

The American Revolution 1953
Explains the strategy, struggle, movement for forces, important military engagements, and the meaning of the war for independence. 16m; VHS, 3/4 U. **Pr:** Encyclopedia Britannica Educational Corporation. **A:** Jr. High-Sr. High. **P:** Education. **U:** Institution, SURA. **L:** English, Spanish. **Gen-Edu:** History--U.S. **Acq:** Purchase, Rent/Lease, Trade-in. **Dist:** Encyclopedia Britannica.

The American Revolution 1994
Comprehensive account of the War of Independence, with the words and deeds of George Washington, Thomas Jefferson, Benjamin Franklin, John Adams, Aaron Burr, and others. Includes battle recreations filmed at actual on-site locations. On six cassettes. 300m; VHS. **A:** Jr. High-Adult. **P:** Entertainment. **U:** Home. **Gen-Edu:** History--U.S., Revolutionary War. **Acq:** Purchase. **Dist:** A&E Television Networks L.L.C.

The American Revolution 1995
Features battle reenactments, archival photos, and rare documents to trace the story of the American Revolution. Includes teacher's guide. 30m; VHS. **A:** Jr. High-Adult. **P:** Education. **U:** Institution. **Gen-Edu:** Revolutionary War, Politics & Government. **Acq:** Purchase. **Dist:** Knowledge Unlimited, Inc. $99.95.

The American Revolution: Cause of Liberty 1972
A real-life drama of the Revolutionary era, based on actual correspondence between John Laurens and his father, Henry, who was president of the First Continental Congress. 24m; VHS, 3/4 U. **C:** Michael Douglas. **Pr:** Robert Saudek; Learning Corporation of America. **A:** Jr. High-Adult. **P:** Education. **U:** Institution, SURA. **L:** English, Spanish. **Gen-Edu:** History--U.S. **Acq:** Purchase, Rent/Lease. **Dist:** Phoenix Learning Group.

The American Revolution: Impossible War 1972
A sequel to "The Cause of Liberty," with John Laurens' experiences in the American Revolution. 25m; VHS, 3/4 U. **C:** Michael Douglas; Keene Curtis. **Pr:** Robert Saudek; Learning Corporation of America. **A:** Jr. High-Adult. **P:** Education. **U:** Institution, SURA. **L:** English, Spanish. **Gen-Edu:** History--U.S. **Acq:** Purchase, Rent/Lease. **Dist:** Phoenix Learning Group.

An American Rhapsody 2001 (PG-13) — ★★★
A mother/daughter conflict steeped in history and based on the experiences of writer/director Gardos. Margit (Kinski) and her family flee Hungary during the communist takeover of the 1950s but she is forced to leave her infant daughter behind. While the family settles in L.A., Suzanne is being raised in the country by adoptive parents and knows nothing of her origins. She gets a rude awakening at the age of 6 when her grandmother Helen (Banfalvy) makes arrangements to reunite Suzy with her unknown "real" family. The child grows into a sullen teenager (Johansson) who longs to return to Budapest. Her father finally agrees to a solo trip and Suzanne learns just what her family suffered and where she truly belongs. 106m; VHS, DVD, Wide, CC. **C:** Nastassja Kinski; Scarlett Johansson; Tony Goldwyn; Kelly Endresz-Banlaki; Agnes Banfalvy; Zsuzsi Czinkoczi; Balazs Galko; Zoltan Seress; Mae Whitman; Lisa Jane Persky; Emmy Rossum; Directed by Eva Gardos; Written by Eva Gardos; Cinematography by Elemer Ragalyi; Music by Cliff Eidelman. **Pr:** Bonnie Timmerman; Colleen Camp; Fireworks Pictures; Seven Arts Pictures; Paramount Classics. **A:** Jr. High-Adult. **P:** Entertainment. **U:** Home. **Mov-Ent:** Family, Adolescence, Immigration. **Acq:** Purchase. **Dist:** Paramount Pictures Corp.

American Rider 1990
The lure of motorcycles and the type of people who ride them are examined. Documentary focuses on the Black Hills Motor Classic in Sturgis, S.D., where bikers congregate from all over the nation. Also available in an adult version. 60m; VHS. **C:** Gary Busey; Hosted by Joe Estevez. **Pr:** Monterey Home Video. **A:** Jr. High-Adult. **P:** Entertainment. **U:** Home. **Spo-Rec:** Documentary Films, Motorcycles. **Acq:** Purchase. **Dist:** Monterey Home Video. $29.95.

An American Romance 1944 (Unrated) — ★★
That would be a romance with the country and not your typical love match. Czech immigrant Steve Dangos (Donlevy) believes in the American Dream and strives to better himself. He eventually starts his own auto manufacturing company in Chicago, marries Ann (Richards), and raises a family. But the industrialist has a problem when his workers want to unionize and Steve's son Teddy (McNally) takes their side. Vidor's expensive propaganda piece was cut by the studio by some 30 minutes and Vidor himself eventually dismissed the movie. 121m; DVD. **C:** Brian Donlevy; Ann Richards; Stephen McNally; John Qualen; Walter Abel; Mary McLeod; Bob Lowell; Directed by King Vidor; Written by Herbert Dalmas; William Ludwig; Cinematography by Harold Rosson; Music by Louis Gruenberg. **A:** Sr. High-Adult. **P:** Entertainment. **U:** Home. **Mov-Ent:** Labor & Unions, Family. **Acq:** Purchase. **Dist:** WarnerArchive.com.

American Roulette 1988 (R) — ★
Garcia is the exiled president of a Latin American country living in London in this thin political thriller. A plot riddled with weaknesses and poor direction make this potentially interesting film dull and lifeless. 102m; VHS. **C:** Andy Garcia; Kitty Aldridge; Robert Stephens; Al Matthews; Susannah York; Directed by Maurice Hatton; Music by Michael Gibbs. **A:** Adult. **P:** Entertainment. **U:** Home. **Mov-Ent:** Action-Adventure, International Relations. **Acq:** Purchase. **Dist:** Movies Unlimited. $12.99.

American Samurai 1992 (R) — ★½
Drew is the adopted son of a Japanese samurai, who gives him the family's sacred sword. This gesture angers his stepbrother who gets involved with Japanese gangsters and illegal live-blade fighting, and who also vows revenge on this American upstart. Lots of sword play to go with the chop-socky action. 89m; VHS, DVD, CC. **C:** David Bradley; Mark Dacascos; John Fujioka; Valarie Trapp; Directed by Sam Firstenberg; Written by John Corcoran. **Pr:** Allan Greenblatt; Cannon Films. **A:** Sr. High-Adult. **P:** Entertainment. **U:** Home. **Mov-Ent:** Martial Arts. **Acq:** Purchase. **Dist:** Warner Home Video, Inc. $89.99.

American Scenes 1985
This series is designed to aid students in improving comprehension and in mastering the structures and functions of colloquial English. Each program contains skits that show scenes of American life, providing a context for the highlighted text. Created for the intermediate student in English as a Second or Foreign Language courses. 55m; VHS, 3/4 U. **Pr:** Elliot Glass; Paul Arcario. **A:** Jr. High-Adult. **P:** Education. **U:** Institution, Home. **Gen-Edu:** Language Arts. **Acq:** Purchase. **Dist:** Crossroads Video.
Indiv. Titles: 1. Getting Around 2. Home Sweet Home 3. Eat to Your Heart's Content 4. Hitting the Books 5. An Ounce of Prevention 6. Getting Along 7. Out on the Town.

American Scrapbook 1977
This lesson takes students to monuments in history-places and moments. They can gain a new insight into the importance of some of the nation's memorable events through a visit to locales as varied as the events of the past. For grades 4-6. Programs are available individually. 15m; VHS, 3/4 U, Special order formats. **Pr:** WVIZ Cleveland. **A:** Primary. **P:** Education. **U:** Institution, CCTV, CATV, BCTV. **Gen-Edu:** History--U.S. **Acq:** Purchase, Rent/Lease, Duplication License, Off-Air Record. **Dist:** GPN Educational Media. $433.10.
Indiv. Titles: 1. The First Americans 2. James Forte at Jamestown 3. The Acadians 4. The World Turned Upside Down 5. 5. A Man to Ride the River With 6. 6. An American Village,

1840 7. 7. Mountain Men 8. 8. Fort Laramie 9. 9. Pioneers of the Southwest 10. 10. Louisiana Plantation 11. 11. North to Freedom 12. 12. Appomattox Courthouse: August 1865 13. 13. A Great Public Park 14. 14. Rodeo 1 5. The Steam Engine Comes to the Farm 1 6. The Circus Is Coming.

The American Scream 1988 (Unrated) — ★½
An innocent family vacationing in the mountains stumbles on to a satanic cult. And that can really ruin a vacation. 85m; VHS. **C:** Jennifer Darling; Pons Marr; Blackie Dammott; Kimberly Kramer; Jean Sapienza; Kevin Kaye; Matt Borlenghi; James Cooper; Directed by Mitchell Linden. **A:** Jr. High-Adult. **P:** Entertainment. **U:** Home. **Mov-Ent:** Action-Adventure, Occult Sciences. **Acq:** Purchase. **Dist:** Amazon.com Inc. $59.95.

American Serengeti 2010 (Unrated)
The American Great Plains once teemed with herds of bison and other animals that thrived in the sweeping grasslands, and now scientists and others are working hard to create a three-million acre wildlife preserve that would preserve and restore the area known as —America's Serengeti.? Narrated by Tom Selleck. 50m; DVD, Blu-Ray. **A:** Family. **P:** Education. **U:** Institution, Home. **Mov-Ent:** Documentary Films, Ecology & Environment, Explorers. **Acq:** Purchase. **Dist:** National Geographic Society. $32.95.

American Shaolin: King of the Kickboxers 2 1992 (PG-13) — ★½
When Drew gets his butt kicked in a karate tournament he decides to head to China and learn some fight-winning moves from a group of warrior monks. 103m; VHS, CC. **C:** Reese Madigan; Trent Bushy; Daniel Dae Kim; Billy Chang; Cliff Lenderman; Zhang Shi Yen; Kim Chan; Alice Zhang Hung; Directed by Lucas Lowe. **Pr:** Ng See Yuen; Seasonal Film Productions. **A:** Jr. High-Adult. **P:** Entertainment. **U:** Home. **Mov-Ent:** Martial Arts. **Acq:** Purchase. **Dist:** Movies Unlimited. $39.99.

The American Short Story Series, Part 1 1978
Nine short stories, each depicting a particular time in American culture. 45m; VHS, 3/4 U. **Pr:** Learning in Focus, Inc. **A:** Sr. High-College. **P:** Education. **U:** Institution, CCTV, SURA. **Gen-Edu:** Literature--American. **Acq:** Purchase. **Dist:** Moonbeam Publications Inc.

Indiv. Titles: 1. Parker Adderson, Philosopher 2. The Jolly Corner 3. The Blue Hotel 4. I'm a Fool 5. Soldier's Home 6. Bernice Bobs Her Hair 7. Almos' a Man 8. The Displaced Person 9. The Music School.

The American Short Story Series, Part 2 1980
The second season of film adaptations of great short stories by American authors, that appeared on PBS. The authors include Hawthorne, Faulkner, Twain, Cather, Lardner, Thurber, Porter, and Gaines. 50m; VHS, 3/4 U. **C:** James Whitmore; Eric Roberts; Brad Davis; Kathleen Beller; Geraldine Fitzgerald; Tommy Lee Jones. **Pr:** Learning in Focus, Inc. **A:** Sr. High-Adult. **P:** Education. **U:** Institution, CCTV, SURA. **Gen-Edu:** Literature--American. **Acq:** Purchase. **Dist:** Moonbeam Publications Inc.

Indiv. Titles: 1. The Golden Honeymoon 2. Paul's Case 3. The Greatest Man in the World 4. Rappaccini's Daughter 5. Jilting of Granny Weatherall 6. The Sky Is Grey 7. The Man That Corrupted Hadleyburg 8. Born Burning.

American Society for Testing Materials 1991
A five-tape program showing the specifics of materials testing. 8m; VHS, 3/4 U. **TV Std:** NTSC, PAL, SECAM. **Pr:** Gulf Publishing Co. **A:** Adult. **P:** Vocational. **U:** Institution, SURA. **Bus-Ind:** How-To, Industrial Arts, Engineering. **Acq:** Purchase. **Dist:** Gulf Publishing Co. $295.00.

Indiv. Titles: 1. D524-Carbon Residue 2. D96-The Determination of Sediment and Water 3. D93-The Determination of Flash Point 4. Aniline 5. Sulfur.

The American Soldier 1970 (Unrated) — ★★½
Fassbinder's homage to the American gangster film tells the story of Ricky, a charismatic hit man. Ricky always wears a gun in a shoulder holster, sports a fedora and a white double-breasted suit, and drinks Scotch straight from the bottle. He also carries out his assigned murders with complete efficiency and no emotion. In German with English subtitles. 80m; VHS, DVD. **C:** Rainer Werner Fassbinder; Karl Scheydt; Elga Sorbas; Jan George; Ingrid Caven; Ulli Lommel; Kurt Raab; Directed by Rainer Werner Fassbinder; Written by Rainer Werner Fassbinder; Cinematography by Dietrich Lohmann; Music by Peer Raben. **A:** College-Adult. **P:** Entertainment. **U:** Home. **Mov-Ent.** **Acq:** Purchase. **Dist:** New Yorker Video. $79.95.

The American Soldier in Combat 1988
From the Revolution to the Korean War, the efforts and sacrifices of our soldiers are looked at. 29m/B/W; VHS. **Pr:** Fireworks Pictures. **A:** Jr. High-Adult. **P:** Education. **U:** Institution, Home. **Gen-Edu:** Armed Forces--U.S., History--U.S. **Acq:** Purchase. **Dist:** Silver Mine Video Inc.; OnDeck Home Entertainment. $14.95.

American Soldiers 2005 (R) — **Bomb!**
Incompetent mess mangles a serious subject and is only worth a groan for its ineptitude. In April 2004, an army platoon is ambushed by insurgents in Iraq and the surviving soldiers must make their way back to base through enemy territory. Filmed in Hamilton, Ontario, which cannot in any way pass for Iraq. 103m; DVD. **C:** Curtis Morgan; Zan Calabretta; Jordan Brown; Eddie Della Siepe; Directed by Sidney J. Furie; Written by Greg Mellott. **A:** Sr. High-Adult. **P:** Entertainment. **U:** Home. **Mov-Ent:** Persian Gulf War. **Acq:** Purchase. **Dist:** Velocity Home Entertainment.

American Son 2008 (R) — ★★½
Well-done drama focuses on the personal rather than the military aspects of the Iraq War. Marine Pvt. Mike Holland (Cannon) gets a four-day Thanksgiving leave before shipping out to Iraq. While taking the bus from Camp Pendleton to Bakersfield, Mike is instantly smitten by fellow passenger Cristina (Diaz), a Mexican-American college student. Mike keeps postponing the moment he has to tell his troubled family he's leaving while dealing with his volatile friend, drug dealer Jake (O'Leary), who's upset that Mike has changed. Meanwhile, Mike tries to persuade Cristina to be his girlfriend despite his upcoming departure. 86m; DVD. **C:** Nick Cannon; Melonie Diaz; Matt O'Leary; Jay Hernandez; Chi McBride; Tom Sizemore; April Grace; Directed by Neil Abramson; Written by Eric Schmid; Cinematography by Kris Kachikis; Music by Tim Bolland; Sam Retzer. **A:** Sr. High-Adult. **P:** Entertainment. **U:** Home. **Mov-Ent:** Persian Gulf War. **Acq:** Purchase. **Dist:** Buena Vista Home Entertainment.

American Songfest 1976
Hosted by Robert McCloskey, presents interviews with professional Illustrators and Excerpts from four children's films based on folk music. 42m; VHS, 3/4 U. **C:** Hosted by Robert McCloskey. **Pr:** Morton Schindel; C.B. Wismar. **A:** Adult. **P:** Education. **U:** Institution, SURA. **Gen-Edu:** Folklore & Legends. **Acq:** Purchase. **Dist:** Weston Woods Studios.

An American Songster: John Jackson 1989
A musical portrait of the singer/guitarist/banjo player from Virginia, filmed over a seven year span at Jackson's home and at concerts. 30m; VHS. **C:** Directed by Renato Tonelli. **A:** Jr. High-Adult. **P:** Entertainment. **U:** Home. **Mov-Ent:** Documentary Films. **Acq:** Purchase. **Dist:** Rhapsody Films, Inc. $14.95.

The American Space Shuttle from Landing to Launch 1991
An inside look at how the space shuttle's boosters, external fuel tank, and orbiter work together for launch at the Kennedy Space Center. 30m; VHS, CC. **A:** Family. **P:** Education. **U:** Home. **Gen-Edu:** Space Exploration. **Acq:** Purchase. **Dist:** Baker and Taylor. $19.95.

American Splendor 2003 (R) — ★★★½
Giamatti is brilliant as Harvey Pekar, a life-long file clerk in Cleveland who authored the R. Crumb-illustrated autobiographical graphic novels of the film's title. The unlikely courtship of misfits Pekar and his third wife Joyce Brabner (Davis) is comically portrayed as the two kindred souls mysteriously come together. Their unlikely romance mirrors the unlikelihood that a comic filled with the pessimism, cynicism, and wry comic observations of Pekar's admitted hum-drum life would somehow translate just as well onto the big screen. But it does. Documentarian directors Berman and Pulcini weave fiction with fact as the real Pekar narrates and cameos. They also make use of illustrated comic segments and footage from Pekar's frequent appearances on David Letterman's show. 101m; VHS, DVD. **C:** Paul Giamatti; Hope Davis; Harvey Pekar; Joyce Brabner; Earl Billings; James Urbaniak; Judah Friedlander; Donal Logue; Molly Shannon; James McCaffrey; Shari Springer Berman; Robert Pulcini; Directed by Shari Springer Berman; Robert Pulcini; Written by Shari Springer Berman; Robert Pulcini; Cinematography by Terry Stacey; Music by Mark Suozzo. **Pr:** Ted Hope; HBO Films; Good Machine; Fine Line Features. **A:** Sr. High-Adult. **P:** Entertainment. **U:** Home. **Mov-Ent:** Biography. **Awds:** L.A. Film Critics '03: Film, Screenplay; N.Y. Film Critics '03: Actress (Davis); Natl. Soc. Film Critics '03: Film, Screenplay; Writers Guild '03: Adapt. Screenplay. **Acq:** Purchase. **Dist:** Movies Unlimited; Alpha Video.

The American Story 1985
A series of 15 programs relating the story of our country from its beginnings through the Centennial celebration of the United States in 1876 told against the backdrop of nationally significant sites. Teacher's guide available. Programs available individually. 30m; VHS. **Pr:** Dallas County Community College. **A:** Sr. High-College. **P:** Education. **U:** Institution. **Gen-Edu:** History--U.S. **Acq:** Purchase. **Dist:** GPN Educational Media. $394.70.

Indiv. Titles: 1. Road to Revolution 2. Declaring Independence 3. Creating a Republic 4. Experiment in Government 5. The Federalist Era 6. Nationalism 7. The Emerging Nation 8. Expansion and Removal 9. Social Reform 10. Manifest Destiny 11. Eve of Conflict 12. The Blue and the Gray 13. Road to Appomattox 14. Reconstruction 15. Rebuilding the Union.

An American Story 1992 (PG) — ★★½
Earnest but predictable story based on an actual incident. Six WWII vets return to their small Texas town as heroes. But when they find a corrupt mayor and a brutal sheriff running things they decide to campaign to unseat the local politicos, in spite of some dire warnings. Meade (Johnson), their commanding officer in Europe, is the designated leader in the plan but his ambitious wife and father-in-law want him to align himself with the status quo instead. Hallmark Hall of Fame production is enjoyable and better than most made for TV movies, but fails to reach the heights of many other HHF offerings. 97m; VHS, CC. **C:** Brad Johnson; Kathleen Quinlan; Tom Sizemore; Josef Sommer; Patricia Clarkson; Lisa Blount; G.W. Bailey; John M. Jackson; Directed by John Gray; Written by John Gray; Cinematography by Johnny E. Jensen. **Pr:** Alan Jacobs; Robert Halmi, Jr.; Hallmark Hall of Fame; RHI Entertainment Inc; Signboard Hill Productions, Inc. **A:** Jr. High-Adult. **P:** Entertainment. **U:** Home. **Mov-Ent:** Politics & Government. **Acq:** Purchase. **Dist:** Lions Gate Entertainment Inc. $89.98.

American Strays 1996 (R) — ★½
Episodic black comedy about various oddballs (most of them violent) who cross paths (usually in Kane's roadside diner) in an isolated desert town. There's a masochist who wants help committing suicide, an unemployed family man on the verge of a breakdown, a serial killer, and more—mostly strange. 97m; VHS, DVD. **C:** Carol Kane; Jennifer Tilly; Eric Roberts; John Savage; Luke Perry; Joe (Johnny) Viterelli; James Russo; Vonte Sweet; Sam Jones; Brion James; Toni Kalem; Melora Walters; Jack Kehler; Directed by Michael Covert; Written by Michael Covert; Cinematography by Sead Muhtarevic; Music by John Graham. **Pr:** Rod Dean; Kirk Hassig; Douglas Textor; Frank Agrama; Canned Pictures. **A:** Sr. High-Adult. **P:** Entertainment. **U:** Home. **Mov-Ent:** Comedy--Black, Suicide. **Acq:** Purchase. **Dist:** Movies Unlimited; Alpha Video.

American Streetfighter 1996 — ★★
Martial arts expert Jake Tanner gets involved with an illegal streetfighting ring to rescue his brother, Randy, who's the target of a drug courier. But what happens when his next opponent is his sibling? 80m; VHS, DVD. **C:** Gary Daniels; Ian Jacklin; Tracy Dali; Directed by Steven Austin. **A:** Sr. High-Adult. **P:** Entertainment. **U:** Home. **Mov-Ent:** Martial Arts. **Acq:** Purchase. **Dist:** Trinity Films.

American Streetfighter 2: The Full Impact 1997 (Unrated) — ★½
Ex-cop becomes a bounty hunter tracking a serial killer who likes to kill his victims with his bare hands. 90m; VHS, DVD. **C:** Gary Daniels; Graciela Casillas; Directed by Marc Messenger. **A:** Sr. High-Adult. **P:** Entertainment. **U:** Home. **Mov-Ent.** **Acq:** Purchase.

American Success Stories: Franklin Chang-Diaz 1989
Profiles Franklin Chang-Diaz, a half-Chinese, half-Hispanic, scientist-astronaut. Discusses his successful completion of his Ph.D. and how he overcame the language barrier to gain a college scholarship. Part of the American Success Stories Series. 14m; VHS, SVS, 3/4 U. **A:** Jr. High-Sr. High. **P:** Education. **U:** Institution. **Gen-Edu:** Science, Space Exploration. **Acq:** Purchase. **Dist:** Encyclopedia Britannica. $59.00.

American Success Stories: Jewel Lafontant 1989
Details the success story of Jewel Lafontant, a Chicago attorney and the first Black and first woman Deputy Solicitor General of the U.S. Part of the American Success Stories Series. 14m; VHS, SVS, 3/4 U. **A:** Jr. High-Sr. High. **P:** Education. **U:** Institution. **Gen-Edu:** Law. **Acq:** Purchase. **Dist:** Encyclopedia Britannica. $59.00.

American Success Stories: Mrs. Fields 1989
Outlines the story of Debbie Fields and how she became successful in the cookie business. Part of the American Success Stories Series. 15m; VHS, SVS, 3/4 U. **A:** Jr. High-Sr. High. **P:** Education. **U:** Institution. **Gen-Edu:** Business. **Acq:** Purchase. **Dist:** Encyclopedia Britannica. $59.00.

American Success Stories: Yue-Sai Kan 1989
Summarizes the success story of China-born Yue-Sai Kan, well-known New York television producer and personality. Part of the American Success Stories Series. 18m; VHS, SVS, 3/4 U. **A:** Jr. High-Sr. High. **P:** Education. **U:** Institution. **Gen-Edu:** Television. **Acq:** Purchase. **Dist:** Encyclopedia Britannica. $59.00.

American Suite 1990
Country music by Roy Clark, Merle Haggard, and others accompanies video footage of a professional rodeo in Cheyenne, Wyoming. 45m; VHS. **C:** Music by Merle Haggard; Roy Clark; Tex Ritter. **Pr:** Sony Pictures Home Entertainment Inc. **A:** Family. **P:** Entertainment. **U:** Home. **Mov-Ent:** Music Video, Rodeos, Music--Country/Western. **Acq:** Purchase. **Dist:** Karol Media. $19.95.

An American Summer 1990 — ★★
A Chicago kid spends a summer with his aunt in beach-rich Los Angeles in this coming-of-age tale filled with '90s teen idols. 100m; VHS, DVD, CC. **C:** Brian Austin Green; Joanna Kerns; Michael Landes; Tony Crane; Brian Krause; Wayne Pere; Amber Susa; Directed by James Slocum; Written by James Slocum; Cinematography by Bruce Dorfman; Music by Roger Neill. **Pr:** Jane Hamsher. **A:** Family. **P:** Entertainment. **U:** Home. **Mov-Ent:** Adolescence. **Acq:** Purchase. **Dist:** Unknown Distributor.

An American Tail 1986 (G) — ★★½
While emigrating to New York in the 1880s, a young Russian mouse (Fievel) is separated from his family. He matures as he learns to live on the Big Apple's dirty boulevards. The bad guys are of course cats. Excellent animation and a high-minded (though sentimental and stereotypical) plot keep it interesting for adults. Produced by Spielberg and the first big hit for the Bluth factory, a collection of expatriate Disney artists. Knowing better than to let a money-making mouse tale languish, Bluth followed with "An American Tale: Fievel Goes West." 81m; VHS, DVD, Blu-Ray, CC. **C:** Voice(s) by Dom DeLuise; Madeline Kahn; Phillip Glasser; Christopher Plummer; Nehemiah Persoff; Will Ryan; John Finnegan; Cathianne Blore; Directed by Don Bluth; Music by James Horner. **Pr:** Steven Spielberg; Kathleen Kennedy; Frank Marshall. **A:** Family. **P:** Entertainment. **U:** Home. **L:** English, Spanish. **Mov-Ent:** Animation & Cartoons, Family Viewing, Immigration. **Acq:** Purchase. **Dist:** Alpha Video; Movies Unlimited. $24.98.

Indiv. Titles: 1. Somewhere Out There 2. There Are No Cats in America 3. Never Say Never 4. A Duo.

An American Tail: Fievel Goes West 1991 (G) — ★★
Fievel and the Mousekewitz family continue their pursuit of the American dream by heading West, where the intrepid mouse seeks to become a famous lawman while his sister looks to make it big as a dance hall singer. The score is performed by the London Symphony Orchestra. Unfortunately released at the same time as "Beauty and the Beast," "Fievel Goes West"

suffers from comparison. Worthwhile viewing for the whole family, but it won't ever reach the heights of "B&B." The laser edition is letterboxed and features chapter stops. 75m; VHS, DVD, Wide, CC. **C:** Voice(s) by John Cleese; Dom DeLuise; Phillip Glasser; Amy Irving; Jon Lovitz; Catherine Cavadini; Nehemiah Persoff; Erica Yohn; James Stewart; Directed by Phil Nibbelink; Simon Wells; Written by Flint Dille; Music by James Horner. **Pr:** Steven Spielberg; Mark Huffam. **A:** Family. **P:** Entertainment. **U:** Home. **Mov-Ent:** Animation & Cartoons, Family Viewing. **Acq:** Purchase. **Dist:** Movies Unlimited; Alpha Video. $24.98.

Indiv. Titles: 1. Somewhere Out There 2. Way Out West 3. Rawhide 4. Dreams to Dream 5. The Girl I Left Behind.

An American Tail: The Mystery of the Night Monster 2000
Follows the animated adventures of Fievel Mousekewitz and his pals Tiger and Tony as they try to solve the mystery of a night "monster" terrorizing their neighborhood. 76m; VHS. **A:** Family. **P:** Entertainment. **U:** Home. **Chl-Juv:** Fiction--Children, Animation & Cartoons. **Acq:** Purchase. **Dist:** Sony Pictures Home Entertainment Inc. $14.98.

An American Tail: The Treasure of Manhattan Island 1998 (G)
Fieval and his family are visiting New York when Fieval and his friends discover an underground civilization of Native American mice who hve built a series of tunnels beneath Manhattan. Fieval has a map thinking it will lead to buried treasure, instead it leads the little mouse to the beautiful princess Cholena. 78m; DVD, CC. **A:** Family. **P:** Entertainment. **U:** Home. **Chl-Juv:** Animation & Cartoons. **Acq:** Purchase. **Dist:** Universal Studios Home Video.

American Tall Tales and Legends: Annie Oakley 1998
Jamie Lee Curtis and Brian Dennehy star in this adaptation of the classic story. 52m; VHS. **A:** Family. **P:** Entertainment. **U:** Home. **Chl-Juv:** Children. **Acq:** Purchase. **Dist:** HIT Entertainment Ltd. $9.99.

American Tall Tales and Legends: Casey at the Bat 1998
Elliot Gould stars as Casey Frank in this adaptation of the classic story. 52m; VHS. **A:** Family. **P:** Entertainment. **U:** Home. **Chl-Juv:** Children. **Acq:** Purchase. **Dist:** HIT Entertainment Ltd. $9.99.

American Tall Tales and Legends: Davy Crockett 1998
Mac Davis stars as Davy Crockett in this adaptation of the classic story. 49m; VHS. **A:** Family. **P:** Entertainment. **U:** Home. **Chl-Juv:** Children. **Acq:** Purchase. **Dist:** HIT Entertainment Ltd. $9.99.

American Tall Tales and Legends: Johnny Appleseed 1998
Martin Short and Molly Ringwald star in this adaptation of the classic story. 52m; VHS. **A:** Family. **P:** Entertainment. **U:** Home. **Chl-Juv:** Children. **Acq:** Purchase. **Dist:** HIT Entertainment Ltd. $9.99.

American Tapestry Today: An Exhibition 1990
A delightful exhibition of American tapestry from all over the country in Palo Alto, California—and you're invited! 25m; VHS. **A:** Family. **P:** Entertainment. **U:** Home. **Gen-Edu:** Crafts. **Acq:** Purchase. **Dist:** Victorian Video/Yarn Barn of Kansas, Inc. $25.00.

American Teacher 2011 (Unrated)
To explore the state of the public school system in the United States, the documentary follows five teachers working in various parts of the country. 81m; DVD. **A:** Jr. High-Adult. **P:** Entertainment. **U:** Home. **Mov-Ent:** Education, Documentary Films. **Acq:** Purchase. **Dist:** First Run Features; Eagle Rock Entertainment Inc. $24.95.

American Teen 2008 (PG-13) — ★★1/2
Slick documentary following four teens through their senior year of high school in Warsaw, Indiana. Director Burstein shot 1000 hours of footage over 10 months, piecing together her version of "The Breakfast Club" for MTV. The popular girl, the basketball star, the band geek, and the art chick all suspiciously play exactly to stereotype, making it seem more like reality TV than a documentary. Nothing too thought provoking or unusual (zits, prom jitters, the big game, Internet drama) but it still touches a nerve and may bring back a few memories, good or bad. 95m; On Demand. **C:** Directed by Nanette Burstein; Cinematography by Laela Kilbourn; Wolfgang Held; Robert Hanna; Music by Michael Penn. **Pr:** Jordan Roberts; Eli Gonda; Chris Huddleston; Nanette Burstein; Firehouse Films; Quasiworld Entertainment; 57th and Irving. **A:** Jr. High-Adult. **P:** Entertainment. **U:** Home. **L:** English. **Mov-Ent:** Documentary Films, Adolescence. **Acq:** Purchase. **Dist:** Amazon.com Inc.; Movies Unlimited; Alpha Video.

American Theater Conversations: The Actors' Studio 1963
Documents discussions with Paul Newman, Geraldine Page, Frank Corsaro, Michael Wager, Rip Torn, and Fred Stewart about their training and the goals of the Actor's Studio. 30m; VHS. **A:** Adult. **P:** Education. **U:** Institution. **Fin-Art:** Theater. **Acq:** Purchase. **Dist:** Insight Media. $129.00.

American Tickler 1976 (R) — ★1/2
A thigh-slappin' (or is it head-whacking?) series of satirical pastiches in the grand style of "Kentucky Fried Movie," only more sophomoric. A tasteless collection of yearning to be funny sketches about American institutions. 77m; VHS. **C:** W.P. Dremak; Joan Sumner; Marlow Ferguson; Jeff Allin; Joe Piscopo; Directed by Chuck Vincent. **Pr:** Chuck Vincent; Chuck Vincent. **A:** Sr. High-Adult. **P:** Entertainment. **U:** Home. **Mov-Ent:** Satire & Parody. **Acq:** Purchase. **Dist:** Unknown Distributor.

American Tiger 1989 (R) — ★★
The collegiate hero of "American Tiger" is, like so many college students, framed for murder, and he applies himself to clearing his sullied name. Somewhere during this process, he finds himself in the middle of a battle between good and evil on a football field. About what you'd expect from a supernatural kung-fu teen-action drama. 93m; VHS. **C:** Mitch Gaylord; Donald Pleasence; Daniel Greene; Victoria Prouty; Directed by Sergio Martino. **Pr:** Academy Entertainment. **A:** College-Adult. **P:** Entertainment. **U:** Home. **L:** Spanish. **Mov-Ent:** Action-Adventure. **Acq:** Purchase. **Dist:** Unknown Distributor.

An American Time Capsule 1968
With the use of the "quick cutting" technique, this film takes you on a high-speed trip through the history of the United States. 4m; VHS, 3/4 U. **Pr:** Charles Braverman. **A:** Family. **P:** Education. **U:** Institution, Home, SURA. **Gen-Edu:** Documentary Films, History--U.S. **Acq:** Purchase, Rent/Lease. **Dist:** Pyramid Media. $125.00.

American Tongues 1987
Americans voice their opinions on their own and others' accents and dialects. Speakers from all parts of the country are profiled and the development of regional and social accents is charted. 56m; VHS, 3/4 U. **C:** Narrated by Polly Holliday. **A:** College-Adult. **P:** Education. **U:** Institution, Home. **Gen-Edu:** Speech, Language Arts. **Acq:** Purchase, Rent/Lease. **Dist:** Center for New American Media.

American Tradition Series: Milestones in America's Past 19??
Six-part series which explores different aspects of American history. 360m; VHS. **A:** Jr. High-Adult. **P:** Education. **U:** Home. **Gen-Edu:** History--U.S. **Acq:** Purchase. **Dist:** Cole Media Group.

Indiv. Titles: 1. Vol. 1: Great Steamboat Race 2. Vol. 2: Golden Spike 3. Vol. 3: Mississippi River Roads 4. Vol. 4: Oregon Trail 5. Vol. 5: Route 66 6. Vol. 6: Pony Express.

An American Tragedy 1931 (Unrated) — ★★
Straightforward retelling of the Theodore Dreiser novel (although Dreiser sued Paramount because he didn't approve of the script). Ambitious factory boss Clyde Griffiths (Holmes) takes advantage of his distant connection to some wealthy relatives to hang around the fringes of high society. He romances moneyed beauty Sondra (Dee) but his plans are thrown into disarray when working-class Roberta (Sidney) tells Clyde she's pregnant. After a boating trip, Clyde becomes a criminal suspect leading to a long trial sequence. Remade as 1951's "A Place in the Sun." 96m/B/W; DVD. **C:** Phillips Holmes; Sylvia Sidney; Frances Dee; Irving Pichel; Lucille LaVerne; Frederick Burton; Charles Middleton; Emmett Corrigan; Directed by Irving Pichel; Josef von Sternberg; Written by Samuel Hoffenstein; Cinematography by Lee Garmes. **A:** Sr. High-Adult. **P:** Entertainment. **U:** Home. **Mov-Ent**. **Acq:** Purchase. **Dist:** Movies Unlimited.

American Tragedy 2000 (PG-13) — ★★1/2
Remember the O.J. Simpson trial? Well, if you don't, this cable drama is here to remind you as it explores the egos and infighting of Simpson's four defense lawyers: Johnny Cochran (Rhames), Bob Shapiro (Silver), F. Lee Bailey (Plummer), and Barry Scheck (Kirby). Based on the book by Schiller, who also directed. 170m; VHS, DVD, Wide. **C:** Ving Rhames; Ron Silver; Christopher Plummer; Bruno Kirby; Nicholas Pryor; Robert LuPone; Ruben Santiago-Hudson; Richard Cox; Clyde Kusatsu; Jeff Kober; Directed by Lawrence Schiller; Written by Norman Mailer; Cinematography by Bruce Surtees; Music by Bill Conti. **A:** Jr. High-Adult. **P:** Entertainment. **U:** Home. **Mov-Ent:** Law, Mass Media. **Acq:** Purchase. **Dist:** CinemaNow Inc.

American Vampire 1997 (R) — ★★1/2
Teenager Frankie (Lussauer) has been left alone while his parents are on vacation. One night on the beach, he and his friend Bogie (Hitt) meet Moondoggie (Venokur), who promises to help them party the summer away. He soon reappears with two babes (Electra and Xavier) who appear to be undead. Frankie must turn to The Big Kahuna (West) to stop the vampires. Yes, the plot strictly follows the formula, but the effects are not bad for a low-budget production; the photography is better than it needs to be; and the humor is intentional. 99m; VHS, DVD. **C:** Trevor Lissauer; Danny Hitt; Johnny Venokur; Carmen Electra; Debora Xavier; Adam West; Sydney Lassick; Directed by Luis Esteban; Written by Rollin Jarrett; Cinematography by Jurgen Baum; Goran Paviceric. **A:** Sr. High-Adult. **P:** Entertainment. **U:** Home. **Mov-Ent**. **Acq:** Purchase. **Dist:** York Entertainment.

American Venus 2007 (Unrated) — ★1/2
Celia Lane (De Mornay) is the ultimate in crazy, controlling mothers. When her ice skating daughter Jenna (McGregor) chokes during a national-level competition, Jenna decides she's had enough and quits for good—much to coach/mom Celia's fury. So Jenna sneaks out of Spokane to live the college life in Vancouver, British Columbia—until Celia tracks her down. Celia's also the ultimate in ugly Americans in a foreign country and the viewer is never quite sure if Sweeney is aiming for satire or not. 80m; DVD. **C:** Rebecca De Mornay; Jane McGregor; Matt Craven; Nicholas Lea; Agam Darshi; Anna Amoroso; Directed by Bruce Sweeney; Written by Bruce Sweeney; Cinematography by David Pelletier; Music by James Jandrisch. **A:** Jr. High-Adult. **P:** Entertainment. **U:** Home. **Mov-Ent:** Skating. **Acq:** Purchase. **Dist:** IFC Films.

American Violet 2009 (PG-13) — ★★1/2
Docudrama of Dee Roberts (Beharie), a 24 year-old African-American single mother of four young girls living in a small Texas town barely able to make ends meet. While police drag Dee from work in handcuffs on trumped-up charges, dumping her in the women's county prison, the powerful local district attorney (O'Keefe) leads an extensive drug bust, sweeping her housing project and ultimately charging Dee as a drug dealer. With few choices, Dee and her ACLU attorney decide to sue the DA for unjust practices. Predictable outcome but does well in its portrayal of the plight of poor minorities caught up, legitimately or not, in a racially tainted justice system. Newcomer Beharie shines alongside veterans Woodard, Dutton, and Blake Nelson. Based on a true story that's set during the 2000 presidential campaign. 103m; Blu-Ray, On Demand, Wide. **C:** Michael O'Keefe; Tim Blake Nelson; Will Patton; Alfre Woodard; Nicole Beharie; Xzibit; Scott A. Martin; Directed by Tim Disney; Written by Bill Haney; Cinematography by Steve Yedlin. **Pr:** Samuel Goldwyn Films. **A:** Jr. High-Adult. **P:** Entertainment. **U:** Home. **L:** English. **Mov-Ent:** Black Culture, Law. **Acq:** Purchase. **Dist:** Movies Unlimited; Alpha Video; Image Entertainment Inc.

American Virgin 1998 (R) — ★
Ronny Bartoloti (Loggia) is a successful Hollywood adult film director who has upset his virginal 18-year-old daughter, Katrina (Suvari), with his double-standard attitudes. So she decides to get even by sharing her first sexual experience with millions—by going live on camera on closed-circuit—with the help of Ronny's rival Joey Quinn (Hoskins). But can daddy get his determined little darling to change her mind? Exploitative would-be satire falls flat. 87m; VHS, DVD, On Demand. **C:** Mena Suvari; Robert Loggia; Bob Hoskins; Gabriel Mann; Sally Kellerman; Bobbie Phillips; Lamont Johnson; Rick Peters; O-lan Jones; Alexandra Wentworth; Directed by Jean Pierre Marois; Written by Jean Pierre Marois; Ira Israel; Cinematography by Eagle Egilsson. **A:** Sr. High-Adult. **P:** Entertainment. **U:** Home. **Mov-Ent:** Sex & Sexuality, Adolescence. **Acq:** Purchase. **Dist:** Amazon.com Inc.; Echo Bridge Home Entertainment.

American Virgin 2009 (R) — ★
Yeah, it's a stupid, low-budget, direct-to-DVD college sex comedy (and the female leads keep their clothes on) but said female leads try hard and even Schneider isn't completely offensive. Chaste college freshman Priscilla (Dewan) is horrified that her roommate Natalie (Davis) is the biggest slut on campus. Then Priscilla gets drunk (thanks to Natalie) at a frat party and displays her ta-tas for a "Girls Gone Crazy" video. Humiliated, she scrambles to get the footage back from sleazy producer Ed (Schneider), who's now down in New Orleans filming more unseemly behavior at Mardi Gras. 88m; DVD. **C:** Jenna Dewan; Brianne Davis; Rob Schneider; Ebon Moss-Bachrach; Chase Ryan Jeffery; Ben Marten; Ashley Schneider; Bo Burnham; Directed by Clare Kilner; Written by Lucas Jarach; Jason Price; Jeff Seeman; Cinematography by Oliver Curtis; Music by John Hunter. **A:** Sr. High-Adult. **P:** Entertainment. **U:** Home. **Mov-Ent**. **Acq:** Purchase. **Dist:** Echo Bridge Home Entertainment.

The American Vision 1981
Pictures from the National Gallery of Art give a broad view of American painting from pre-revolutionary days to the beginning of the 20th century. 35m; VHS, 3/4 U, Special order formats. **C:** Narrated by Burgess Meredith. **Pr:** National Gallery of Art. **A:** Jr. High-Adult. **P:** Education. **U:** Institution, Home, SURA. **Fin-Art:** Documentary Films, Painting, Museums. **Acq:** Free Loan. **Dist:** National Gallery of Art.

American Visions: The History of American Art and Architecture 1997
Hosted by art critic and author Robert Hughes, this eight-tape series provides a view of American history as reflected by its arts and artists, in every medium and genre, from the Colonial era to the present day. 480m; VHS, CC. **A:** Sr. High-Adult. **P:** Education. **U:** Home. **Fin-Art:** Art & Artists, History--U.S., Architecture. **Acq:** Purchase. **Dist:** PBS Home Video; Crystal Productions.

American Voices: 200 Years of Speaking Out 1989
Dramatizes concerns of Americans based on letters to the government from a National Archives exhibit. 29m; VHS. **A:** Adult. **P:** Education. **U:** Institution. **Gen-Edu:** Politics & Government, U.S. States. **Acq:** Purchase. **Dist:** Zenger Media. $49.95.

American Warship 2012 (Unrated) — ★1/2
The Asylum changed the title from American Battleship when it ran into some legal trouble but this low-budget copycat military adventure is surprisingly watchable. The USS Iowa, a WWII-era destroyer, is on its final voyage when Capt. Winston (Van Peebles) and his crew run into trouble. Naval vessels have been disappearing in the South Pacific and the enemy turn out to be aliens. 90m; DVD, Blu-Ray. **C:** Mario Van Peebles; Carl Weathers; Brandon Clark; Johanna Watts; Nikki McCauley; Elijah Chester; Directed by Thunder Levin; Written by Thunder Levin; Cinematography by Stuart Brereton; Music by Chris Ridenhour. **A:** Jr. High-Adult. **P:** Entertainment. **U:** Home. **L:** English. **Mov-Ent:** Science Fiction. **Acq:** Purchase. **Dist:** The Asylum.

American Warships 2001 (Unrated) — ★
The U.S. Navy takes on aliens in the Asylum's mockbuster salute to "Battleship." 90m; DVD, Blu-Ray. **C:** Mario Van Peebles; Carl Weathers; Johanna Watts; Nikki McCauley; Elijah Chester; Directed by Thunder Levin; Written by Thunder Levin; Cinematography by Stuart Brereton; Music by Chris Ridenhour. **A:** Sr. High-Adult. **P:** Entertainment. **U:** Home. **L:** English. **Mov-Ent**. **Acq:** Purchase. **Dist:** The Asylum. $24.95 14.95.

American Wedding 2003 (R) — ★★½
In the finale of the epic trilogy Annakin and Amidala, no, wait. Frodo and Gollum...no, Neo and Trinity...that's not it either. Jim and Michelle are getting married, with the dubious help of most of the gang. Kevin and Finch are still around, but it's Stifler who has the biggest impact, throwing the bachelor party, battling Finch for the affections of Michelle's sister Cadence (Jones), and almost putting the kibosh on the whole wedding. Like the other two, it's pretty gross in parts, uproarious in others, but still has its sweet, charming moments. Levy and Willard make the most of their scenes as the father of the groom and bride, respectively. 96m; VHS, DVD, UMD, Wide. **C:** Jason Biggs; Alyson Hannigan; Seann William Scott; Eddie Kaye Thomas; January Jones; Eugene Levy; Thomas Ian Nicholas; Fred Willard; Molly Cheek; Eric Allen Kramer; Deborah Rush; Jennifer Coolidge; Angela Paton; Lawrence Pressman; Amanda Swisten; Nikki Schieler Ziering; Directed by Jesse Dylan; Written by Adam Herz; Cinematography by Lloyd Ahern, II; Music by Christophe Beck. **Pr:** Adam Herz; Warren Zide; Craig Perry; Chris Moore; Adam Herz; Chris Bonder; Universal Pictures. **A:** Sr. High-Adult. **P:** Entertainment. **U:** Home. **Mov-Ent**: Family. **Acq:** Purchase. **Dist:** Movies Unlimited; Alpha Video.

American Weed 2012 (Unrated)
The medical marijuana industry is thriving in Colorado and its life-changing effects are examined in these 10 episodes. From growers, to patients, to law enforcement, explore the many issues presented by a newly legalized culture. Episodes include Marijuana Dream, Weed-Jacked! , War Over Weed, Buds on the Ballot, Pot or Not? Marijuana Under Fire, Green Rush, Rocky Mountain Medicine, 4/20 or Bust, and Banned and Busted. 180m; DVD. **A:** Family. **P:** Entertainment. **U:** Home. **L:** English. **Mov-Ent**: Diseases, Documentary Films, Drug Enforcement Agency (DEA). **Acq:** Purchase. **Dist:** $19.95.

An American Werewolf in London 1981 (R) — ★★★
Strange, darkly humorous version of the classic man-into-wolf horror tale became a cult hit, but never clicked with most American critics. Two American college students, David (Naughton) and Jack (Dunne), are backpacking through England when thy're viciously attacked by a werewolf one foggy night. Jack is killed, but keeps appearing (in progressively decomposed form) before the seriously wounded David, warning him of impending werewolfdom when the moon is full, Jack advises suicide. Seat-jumping horror and gore, highlighted by intensive metamorphosis sequences orchestrated by Rick Baker, are offset by wry humor, though the shifts in tone don't always work. Great moon songs permeate the soundtrack, including CCR's "Bad Moon Rising" and Van Morrison's "Moondance." Followed by "An American Werewolf in Paris" (1997). 97m; VHS, DVD, Blu-Ray, HD-DVD. **C:** David Naughton; Griffin Dunne; Jenny Agutter; Frank Oz; Brian Glover; Lila Kaye; David Schofield; John Woodvine; Don McKillop; Paul Kember; Colin Fernandes; Rik Mayall; Paddy Ryan; Directed by John Landis; Written by John Landis; Cinematography by Robert Paynter; Music by Elmer Bernstein. **Pr:** Mark Huffam. **A:** Sr. High-Adult. **P:** Entertainment. **U:** Home. **Mov-Ent**: Horror, Cult Films. **Awds:** Oscars '81: Makeup. **Acq:** Purchase. **Dist:** Lions Gate Television Corp.

An American Werewolf in Paris 1997 (R) — ★★
More of a remake than a sequel, horror-comedy fails to live up to the wit and quirkiness of the original. Andy (Scott) is on a daredevil tour of Europe along with buddies Brad (Vieluf) and Chris (Buckman). As he attempts to bungee jump off of the Eiffel Tower, he spots a French femme attempting to plungee jump nearby. He saves her and immediately falls in love with her. The girl, Serafine (Delpy) warns him to stay away, but he keeps sniffing around. They tail her to a creepy house she shares with a guy named Claude (Cosso), where Andy secures a date and his friends are invited to a dinner party. Claude, however, is top dog in a pack of racist werewolves, and Andy's pals end up as the main course. Bitten himself, Andy learns that he's now a werewolf. Brad and the other victims pop up now and again to remind Andy that they're doomed to walk the earth until the werewolves that killed them are destroyed. Special effects have advanced a long way since the original and it shows, although the computer generated wolves are difficult to tell apart. 100m; VHS, DVD, CC. **C:** Julie Delpy; Tom Everett Scott; Julie Bowen; Anthony Waller; Pierre Cosso; Thierry Lhermitte; Vince Vieluf; Phil Buckman; Tom Novembre; Isabelle Constantini; Directed by Anthony Waller; Written by Anthony Waller; Tim Burns; Tom Stern; Cinematography by Egon Werdin; Music by Wilbert Hirsch. **Pr:** Richard Claus; Miramax Film Corp. **A:** Sr. High-Adult. **P:** Entertainment. **U:** Home. **Mov-Ent**: France. **Acq:** Purchase. **Dist:** Buena Vista Home Entertainment.

American Women 2000 (PG-13) — ★★
Poor schlub County Donegal lads, weary of their lack of female companionship, send an ad to the Miami Herald, looking for young, nubile American women to come over and "see what happens." Hoping to see the American lasses in time for the social event of the season, the St. Martha's Day dance, they're disappointed when the day arrives but the girls don't. To make matters worse, the local ladies have brought in some Spanish fishermen to play music at the dance. Old fashioned ethnic comedy tries to cash in on the successes of "The Full Monty" and "Waking Ned Devine," but contains a wee bit too many Irish cliches, and the charm is squeezed out by the patronizing view of what is supposed to be modern-day Ireland. 90m; VHS, DVD, CC. **C:** Ian Hart; Sean McGinley; Niamh Cusack; Ruth McCabe; Ewan Stewart; Maureen O'Brien; Pat Laffan; Britta Smith; Pat Shortt; Cathleen Bradley; Sean McDonagh; Risteard Cooper; Directed by Aileen Ritchie; Written by William Ivory; Cinematography by Robert Alazraki; Music by Rachel Portman. **Pr:** Fox Searchlight. **A:** Jr. High-Adult. **P:** Entertainment. **U:** Home. **Mov-Ent**: Comedy--Romantic, Ireland. **Acq:** Purchase. **Dist:** Fox Home Entertainment.

American Women of Achievement 1995
Set of ten videos highlights the lives and contributions of notable women. 300m; VHS. **A:** Jr. High-Sr. High. **P:** Education. **U:** Institution. **Gen-Edu**: Women, History--U.S. **Acq:** Purchase. **Dist:** Zenger Media. $399.50.

Indiv. Titles: 1. Abigail Adams 2. Jane Addams 3. Marian Anderson 4. Susan B. Anthony 5. Clara Barton 6. Emily Dickinson 7. Amelia Earhart 8. Helen Keller 9. Sandra Day O'Connor 10. Wilma Rudolph.

The American Women of Achievement Video Collection 1995
Ten-part series, based on Chelsea House books, that profiles notable women of America's past. Includes interviews from academics, historians, and family members. 300m; VHS, CC. **Pr:** Schlessinger Video Productions. **A:** Jr. High-Sr. High. **P:** Education. **U:** Institution, SURA. **Gen-Edu**: History--U.S., Women, Biography. **Acq:** Purchase. **Dist:** Library Video Inc. $399.50.

American Wonders 19??
Features the beauty of Yellowstone, Grand Canyon, Big Sur, Glacier, Yosemite, Bryce, Zion and Alaskan National Parks. 40m; VHS. **A:** Jr. High-Adult. **P:** Education. **U:** Institution. **Gen-Edu**: National Parks & Reserves, Music Video. **Acq:** Purchase. **Dist:** Ark Media Group Ltd.

American Yakuza 1994 (R) — ★★
FBI agent Nick Davis (Mortensen) is sent to L.A. to infiltrate the American arm of the Yakuza, Japan's dangerous criminal underworld. He rises through the ranks and is adopted into the powerful Tendo family. Now Davis finds himself caught between the FBI, the Yakuza, and the vengeful American mafia. 95m; VHS, DVD, CC. **C:** Viggo Mortensen; Michael Nouri; Ryo Ishibashi; Franklin Ajaye; Directed by Frank Cappello; Written by Max Strom; John Allen Nelson; Cinematography by Richard Clabaugh; Music by David Williams. **Pr:** Michael Leahy; Aki Komine; Joel Soisson; Taka Ichise; W.K. Border; First Look Pictures; Neo Motion Pictures; Ozla Pictures. **A:** Sr. High-Adult. **P:** Entertainment. **U:** Home. **Mov-Ent**: Federal Bureau of Investigation (FBI). **Acq:** Purchase. **Dist:** Sony Pictures Home Entertainment Inc.

American Zombie 2007 (Unrated) — ★★
Mockumentary covering a small community of the living dead in Los Angeles and their attempts to fit in despite obvious discrimination, shortly before the usual social uprising. 91m; DVD, Streaming. **C:** Austin Basis; Al Vicente; John Solomon; Andrew Amondson; Kevin Michael Walsh; Paul Eiding; Jose Solomon; Philip Newby; Grace Lee; Jane Edith Wilson; Suzy Nakamura; Amy Higgins; Directed by Grace Lee; Written by Grace Lee; Rebecca Sonnenshine; Cinematography by Matthias Grunsky; Music by Woody Pak. **A:** Sr. High-Adult. **P:** Entertainment. **U:** Home. **L:** English. **Mov-Ent**. **Acq:** Purchase, Rent/Lease. **Dist:** Cinema Libre Studio. $24.95 9.99.

Americana 1981 (PG) — ★★½
A troubled Vietnam vet tries to restore himself by rebuilding a merry-go-round in a small midwestern town, while dealing with opposition from the local residents. Offbeat, often effective post-Nam editorial that was produced and directed in 1973 by Carradine and then shelved. Hershey and Carradine were a couple back then. 90m; VHS, DVD. **C:** David Carradine; Barbara Hershey; Michael Greene; John Drew (Blythe) Barrymore, Jr.; Directed by David Carradine; Written by Richard Carr. **Pr:** David Carradine; David Carradine. **A:** Sr. High-Adult. **P:** Entertainment. **U:** Home. **Mov-Ent**: Vietnam War, Veterans. **Acq:** Purchase. **Dist:** Lions Gate Television Corp. $69.98.

Americana Trail 1981
This program looks at the fascinating history of the northeastern portion of the United States. 23m; VHS, 3/4 U. **Pr:** AB/Energy Productions. **A:** Sr. High-Adult. **P:** Education. **U:** Institution, SURA. **Gen-Edu**: History--U.S., Travel. **Acq:** Purchase. **Dist:** Home Vision Cinema.

Americaner Schadchen 1940
Restored Yiddish feature film combines Hollywood comedy with the Yiddish theatre experience. Yiddish with English subtitles. 87m/B/W; VHS. **A:** Sr. High-Adult. **P:** Entertainment. **U:** Home. **Mov-Ent**: Comedy--Romantic. **Acq:** Purchase. **Dist:** National Center for Jewish Film.

The Americanization of Emily 1964 — ★★★
A happy-go-lucky American naval officer (Garner) with no appetite for war discovers to his horror that he may be slated to become the first casualty of the Normandy invasion as part of a military PR effort in this black comedy-romance. Meanwhile, he spreads the charisma in an effort to woo and uplift Emily (Andrews), a depressed English woman who has suffered the loss of her husband, father, and brother during the war. A cynical, often funny look at military maneuvers and cultural drift that was adapted by Paddy Chayefsky from William Bradford Huie's novel. Also available colorized. 117m/B/W; VHS, DVD, Blu-Ray, Wide. **C:** James Garner; Julie Andrews; Melvyn Douglas; James Coburn; Joyce Grenfell; Keenan Wynn; Edward Binns; Liz Fraser; William Windom; Directed by Arthur Hiller; Written by Paddy Chayefsky. **Pr:** MGM. **A:** Jr. High-Adult. **P:** Entertainment. **U:** Home. **Mov-Ent**: Comedy--Black, World War Two. **Acq:** Purchase. **Dist:** MGM Home Entertainment. $19.95.

The Americano 1917 — ★★½
Ever-suave Fairbanks frees a South American politician locked in a dungeon, returns him to political success, and captures the heart of his beautiful daughter. Based on Eugene P. Lyle Jr.'s "Blaze Derringer." 58m/B/W; Silent; VHS, DVD. **C:** Douglas Fairbanks, Sr.; Alma Rubens; Spottiswoode Aitken; Lillian Langdon; Carl Stockdale; Tom Wilson; Directed by John Emerson. **Pr:** Triangle Film Corporation. **A:** Jr. High-Adult. **P:** Entertainment. **U:** Home. **Mov-Ent**: Action-Adventure, Romance, South America. **Acq:** Purchase. **Dist:** Alpha Video. $16.95.

Americano 1955 — ★★
A cowboy travelling to Brazil with a shipment of Brahma bulls discovers the rancher he's delivering them to has been murdered. An odd amalgam of western cliches and a South American setting. 85m; DVD, Blu-Ray. **C:** Glenn Ford; Frank Lovejoy; Abbe Lane; Cesar Romero; Directed by William Castle. **Pr:** RKO; Robert Stillman Productions. **A:** Family. **P:** Entertainment. **U:** Home. **Mov-Ent**: Western, South America. **Acq:** Purchase. **Dist:** Olive Films. $19.98.

Americano 2005 (R) — ★★
Recent college grad Chris (Jackson) and his friends Ryan (Sharp) and Michelle (Ruthanna Hopper) have been backpacking through Europe and wind up at the end of their trip in Pamplona, Spain, for the annual running of the bulls. Chris meets beautiful Adela (Varela), who takes pity on him and lets Chris stay at her house after his backpack is stolen. His feelings quickly turn romantic. Dennis Hopper plays an ex-pat bar owner proffering advice when Chris wonders if he's really ready to return home. 95m; DVD. **C:** Joshua Jackson; Leonor Varela; Dennis Hopper; Timm Sharp; Ruthanna Hopper; Directed by Kevin Noland; Written by Kevin Noland; Cinematography by Robert Christopher Webb; Music by Peter Golub. **A:** Sr. High-Adult. **P:** Entertainment. **U:** Home. **Mov-Ent**: Spain. **Acq:** Purchase. **Dist:** Bedford Entertainment Inc.

Americano 2011 (Unrated) — ★★
Demy makes his feature directorial debut and also stars in this melancholy drama that features clips from his mother Agnes Varda's 1981 film "Documenteur" that show him as a child and are used as flashbacks. Martin, who has lived in France for years, returns to Los Angeles to sort out his estranged mom's estate. He knows little of her life but a letter and a photo has Martin searching in Tijuana for Lola (Hayek), who's working in a strip club called the Americano. English, French, and Spanish with subtitles. 106m; DVD, Blu-Ray. **C:** Mathieu Demy; Salma Hayek; Geraldine Chaplin; Chiara Mastroianni; Carlos Bardem; Directed by Mathieu Demy; Written by Mathieu Demy; Cinematography by Georges Lechaptois; Music by Gregoire Hetzel. **A:** Sr. High-Adult. **P:** Entertainment. **U:** Home. **L:** English, French, Spanish. **Mov-Ent**: Drama, Mexico. **Acq:** Purchase. **Dist:** MPI Media Group.

The Americano/Variety 1925
The two silent classics in abridged form: "The Americano," (1917) about a soldier-of-fortune who aids a revolt-ridden Caribbean country, and "Variety," (1925) a classic German masterpiece about the career of a trapeze artist . 54m/B/W; Silent; VHS. **C:** Douglas Fairbanks, Sr.; Emil Jannings; Directed by John Emerson; E.A. Dupont. **Pr:** Fine Arts Triangle. **A:** Family. **P:** Entertainment. **U:** Home. **Mov-Ent**: Silent Films. **Acq:** Purchase. **Dist:** $39.95.

American's Greatest Monuments: Washington D.C. 2007 (Unrated)
Tours the nation's capitol from the war memorials to monuments honoring our founding fathers, providing information that clarifies many a myth and mystery. 530m; DVD. **A:** Family. **P:** Entertainment. **U:** Home. **Mov-Ent**: U.S. States, Cities & Towns, History--U.S. **Acq:** Purchase. **Dist:** Infinity Entertainment Group.

Americans on Everest 1967
Norman Dyhrenfurth films his expedition to the top of Mt. Everest over the dangerous and previously untried west ridge. 50m; VHS, 3/4 U. **C:** Narrated by Orson Welles. **Pr:** Norman Dyhrenfurth. **A:** Family. **P:** Entertainment. **U:** Institution, Home, SURA. **Gen-Edu**: Mountaineering. **Acq:** Purchase, Rent/Lease. **Dist:** Pyramid Media.

The Americans: 1776 1975
A view of everyday life during the time of the American Revolution. The crafts, lifestyles, and different opinions and attitudes of Colonists are portrayed. 28m; VHS, 3/4 U, Special order formats. **Pr:** National Park Service. **A:** Family. **P:** Education. **U:** Institution, SURA. **Gen-Edu**: History--U.S. **Acq:** Purchase. **Dist:** National Audiovisual Center; Harpers Ferry Historical Association. $24.99.

The Americans with Disabilities Act: Commonsense Compliance 19??
Explains ways to meet the standards set by the Americans with Disabilities Act. 24m; VHS. **A:** Sr. High-Adult. **P:** Professional. **U:** Institution. **Bus-Ind**: Business, Law, Handicapped. **Acq:** Purchase. **Dist:** National Safety Council, California Chapter, Film Library. $225.00.

The Americans with Disabilities Act: New Access to the Workplace 19??
Covers a broad scope of information through interviews with government officials. Intended mainly for employers. 40m; VHS. **A:** Sr. High-Adult. **P:** Professional. **U:** Institution. **Bus-Ind**: Business, Law, Handicapped. **Acq:** Purchase. **Dist:** Phoenix Learning Group. $495.00.

The Americans With Disabilities Act of 1990: What Employers Need to Know about Provisions Affecting the Workplace 1991
Examines the effects of the 1990 Americans with Disabilities Act on employers and employees alike. Complete with study guide. 50m; VHS. **A:** Adult. **P:** Professional. **U:** Institution. **Bus-Ind**: Law, Handicapped. **Dist:** American Law Institute - Committee on Continuing Professional Education. $95.

Americas 1992
Series of 10 programs first broadcast on PBS are arranged topically and feature various facets of life in Latin America, including contemporary history, politics, culture, religion, ethnic identity and the evolving role of women, among others. Includes text, anthology, study guide, and faculty guide. Can be purchased as a set or separately. 60m; VHS, CC. **Pr:** WGBH Boston. **A:** Sr. High-Adult. **P:** Education. **U:** Institution. **Gen-Edu:** South America, Sociology, Women. **Acq:** Purchase. **Dist:** Annenberg Media. $275.00.
Indiv. Titles: 1. The Garden of Forking Paths: Dilemmas of National Development 2. Continent on the Move: Migration and Urbanization 3. Mirrors of the Heart: Race and Identity 4. In Women's Hands: The Changing Role of Women 5. Miracles Are Not Enough: Continuity and Change in Religion 6. Builders of Images: Latin American Cultural Identity 7. Get Up, Stand Up: Problems of Sovereignty 8. Fire in the Mind: Revolutions and Revolutionaries 9. The Americas: The Latin American and Caribbean Presence in the United States 10. Capital Sins: Authoritarianism and Democratization.

America's Ancient Forests 1990
Environmentalists and loggers debate the future of the U.S. National Forest. 11m; VHS, 3/4 U. **Pr:** Capital Cities/ABC Video Productions. **A:** Jr. High-Adult. **P:** Education. **U:** Institution. **Gen-Edu:** Documentary Films, Forests & Trees, Ecology & Environment. **Acq:** Rent/Lease. **Dist:** New Dimension Media. $25.00.

America's Atomic Bomb Tests 1998
This compilation of formerly top secret government footage chronicles the atomic detonation experiments that went on for nearly 50 years, spanning the full story of atomic testing. Five hours and 30 minutes on five videocassettes. 66m; DVD. **A:** Family. **P:** Education. **U:** Home. **Gen-Edu:** Nuclear Warfare, Military History. **Acq:** Purchase. **Dist:** Image Entertainment Inc. $49.98.

America's Best: Gymnastics Championships 1992
Some of the biggest names in the sport compete for the title of national champion. These athletes have trained for their entire lives to succeed at this moment. Viewers are treated to an awesome display of talent. 50m; VHS. **Pr:** National Broadcasting Company; Lynch Entertainment; Laurel Canyon Productions. **A:** Family. **P:** Entertainment. **U:** Home. **Spo-Rec:** Gymnastics. **Acq:** Purchase. **Dist:** Fast Forward. $14.95.

America's Best Kept Secret 198?
This documentary discusses the reasons, preventions and cures for devil worship in America. This tape is designed as a teaching resource. 60m; VHS. **A:** Sr. High-Adult. **P:** Education. **U:** Home. **Gen-Edu:** Documentary Films, Religion. **Acq:** Purchase. **Dist:** Blockbuster L.L.C. $49.95.

America's Castles 1994
Showcases the fabulous homes and estates built by America's industrial magnates during the Gilded Age of the late 19th century. Includes the various Vanderbilt homes—The Breakers, Marble House, and Biltmore—as well as William Randolph Hearst's San Simeon, John Ringling's Ca d'Zan, Jay Gould's Lyndhurst, and more. 100m; VHS. **Pr:** A&E (Arts & Entertainment) Network. **A:** Family. **P:** Entertainment. **U:** Home. **Gen-Edu:** Architecture, U.S. States. **Acq:** Purchase. **Dist:** A&E Television Networks L.L.C.; New Video Group. $29.95.

America's Castles 2 1995
A further look at America's grandest mansions, built between 1913 and 1929 by some of the country's best-known millionaires. Included are Kykuit, the Rockefeller country estate; Henry Ford's Fair Lane; the Edsel & Eleanor Ford house; Meadow Brook Hall, built for Alice Dodge; Marjorie Merriweather Post's Hillwood; Stan Hywet Hall, the mansion of tire baron Frank Seiberling; and more. 100m; VHS. **A:** Family. **P:** Entertainment. **U:** Home. **Gen-Edu:** Architecture, U.S. States. **Acq:** Purchase. **Dist:** A&E Television Networks L.L.C.; PBS Home Video. $29.95.

America's Castles: California Dreamers: The Winchester Mystery House and Scotty's Castle 2006
Profiles two of California's strangest homes. The 160-room, never-finished, Winchester mansion was built by Sara Pardee Winchester for the spirits of those killed by the famed weapon. Walter Scott built a 20-room Spanish style castle in the middle of Death Valley. 50m; DVD. **A:** Jr. High-Adult. **P:** Entertainment. **U:** Home. **Gen-Edu:** Documentary Films. **Acq:** Purchase. **Dist:** A&E Television Networks L.L.C.

America's Castles: Grand Plantations 2006
A tour of the American South along the Mississippi and the region's mansions that sugar, cotton, and cane built. 50m; DVD. **A:** Jr. High-Adult. **P:** Entertainment. **U:** Home. **Gen-Edu:** Documentary Films. **Acq:** Purchase. **Dist:** A&E Television Networks L.L.C.

America's Castles: Hearst Castle at San Simeon 2006
A look at the 165-room mansion built, starting in 1918, by newspaper mogul William Randolph Hearst. 50m; DVD. **A:** Jr. High-Adult. **P:** Entertainment. **U:** Home. **Gen-Edu:** Documentary Films. **Acq:** Purchase. **Dist:** A&E Television Networks L.L.C.

America's Children: Poorest in a Land of Plenty 1989
Still photos and videotakes document the neglect of America's most valuable resource: her children. Solutions to this dilemma are sought through church and community organizations who are working together to give children a better future. 52m; VHS. **A:** Sr. High-Adult. **P:** Religious. **U:** Institution. **Gen-Edu:** Children, Child Abuse, Poverty. **Acq:** Rent/Lease. **Dist:** EcuFilm.

America's Crown Jewels: Grand Canyon, Yosemite, Yellowstone National Parks 19??
Presents the stories of America's three great natural wonders. 48m; DVD, Blu-Ray. **A:** Sr. High. **P:** Education. **U:** Home. **L:** English. **Gen-Edu:** Wilderness Areas. **Acq:** Purchase. **Dist:** Questar Inc. $24.98.

America's Cultural Kaleidoscope 19??
Through visuals and folk songs the viewer sees why people from different countries came to America, learn about some of the problems they face in adjusting to their new land, and discover the contributions they've made to American culture. 15m; VHS, Q, Special order formats. **Pr:** Western Instructional Television. **A:** Jr. High. **P:** Education. **U:** Institution, CCTV, CATV, BCTV, SURA. **Gen-Edu:** History--U.S. **Acq:** Purchase, Rent/Lease. **Dist:** Western Instructional Television.
Indiv. Titles: 1. The Irish: Why They Came 2. The Irish American 3. Latin America Emerges 4. The Mexican-American 5. From Africa to the New World 6. The Black American 7. Religion in Colonial America 8. The Protestant in America 9. The Jews in America 10. The Mormon in America 11. The Catholic in America 12. From Eastern Europe and the Mediterranean 13. From Northern Europe 14. The American Indian 15. From The Orient.

America's Cup '88: The Official Video 1988
Using footage taken from ESPN's coverage of the contest, highlights of the American catamaran's destruction of the New Zealander's monster boat is shown. Also included is behind the scenes action of the boats' construction and the legal maneuvering on both sides. 60m; VHS. **C:** Hosted by Gary Jobson. **Pr:** ESPN. **A:** Family. **P:** Entertainment. **U:** Home. **Spo-Rec:** Sports--Water, Boating. **Acq:** Purchase. **Dist:** Bennett Marine Video. $24.95.

America's Cup: The Walter Cronkite Report 1987
Chronicles the 1987 America's Cup and Dennis Conner's challenge of recapturing the cup from Australia. 109m; VHS. **C:** Narrated by Walter Cronkite. **A:** Jr. High-Adult. **P:** Entertainment. **U:** Home. **Spo-Rec:** Documentary Films, Boating, Sports--Water. **Acq:** Purchase. **Dist:** Anchor Bay Entertainment; Bennett Marine Video. $19.98.

America's Cup, Vol. 1 1962
A film record of the 1958 and 1962 America's Cup races. 76m; VHS. **Pr:** Thomas J. Lipton Inc. **A:** Family. **P:** Entertainment. **U:** Institution, Home. **Spo-Rec:** Boating. **Acq:** Purchase. **Dist:** Mystic Seaport.

America's Cup, Vol. 2 1967
A record of the 1964 and 1967 America's Cup race. 80m; VHS. **Pr:** Thomas J. Lipton Inc. **A:** Family. **P:** Entertainment. **U:** Institution, Home. **Spo-Rec:** Boating. **Acq:** Purchase. **Dist:** Mystic Seaport.

America's Cup, Vol. 3 1984
This tape offers the official filmed record of the 1970 race, as well as a behind-the-scenes view. 120m; VHS. **Pr:** Thomas J. Lipton Inc; Time-Life Films. **A:** Family. **P:** Entertainment. **U:** Institution, Home. **Spo-Rec:** Boating. **Acq:** Purchase. **Dist:** Mystic Seaport.

America's Cup, Vol. 4 1974
A film record of the suspenseful 1974 race. 85m; VHS. **Pr:** James C. Lipscomb; Time-Life Films. **A:** Family. **P:** Entertainment. **U:** Institution, Home. **Spo-Rec:** Boating. **Acq:** Purchase. **Dist:** Mystic Seaport.

America's Cup, Vol. 5 1980
A film record of the provocative 1977 & 1980 races. 109m; VHS. **Pr:** Thomas J. Lipton Inc; Offshore. **A:** Family. **P:** Entertainment. **U:** Institution, Home. **Spo-Rec:** Boating. **Acq:** Purchase. **Dist:** Mystic Seaport.

America's Cup, Vol. 6: The 25th Defense, End of an Era 1984
A film record of the 1983 America's Cup race, featuring footage taken from the Goodyear blimp. 57m; VHS. **Pr:** Thomas J. Lipton Inc. **A:** Family. **P:** Entertainment. **U:** Institution, Home. **Spo-Rec:** Boating. **Acq:** Purchase. **Dist:** Mystic Seaport.

America's Deadliest Home Video 1991 (Unrated) — ★★
Camp spoof about America's obsession with videotaping everything in sight. Video enthusiast Doug is taken hostage by the Clint Dryer gang who want him to tape their crime spree. Every aspect is only seen through the lens of the video camera. 90m; VHS. **C:** Danny Bonaduce; Mick Wynhoff; Mollena Williams; Melora Walters; Directed by Jack Perez; Written by Jack Perez. **Pr:** Michael L. Wynhoff; Randum Film Group; Video Vigilantes. **A:** Sr. High-Adult. **P:** Entertainment. **U:** Home. **Mov-Ent:** Comedy--Black, Satire & Parody, Video. **Acq:** Purchase. **Dist:** Facets Multimedia Inc. $39.95.

America's Defense Monitor 1990
Series of videos which impartially examine different aspects of military policy. Produced by the U.S. Armed Services, this presentation supports defense, but opposes waste, mismanagement, and policies that increase chances of war. Complete with teacher's guide. 30m; VHS. **A:** Sr. High-College. **P:** Education. **U:** Institution. **Gen-Edu:** Armed Forces--U.S., Politics & Government. **Acq:** Purchase. **Dist:** Cambridge Educational. $29.95.
Indiv. Titles: 1. Changing Times in Charlottesville 2. Retooling the Arms Industry 3. The Great Arms Debate 4. Scrambling for Dollars 5. The Politics of Military Spending 6. The Aftermath of War with Iraq 7. Military Spending After War with Iraq 8. Treating the Casualties of War with Iraq 9. Sandstorm in the Gulf: Digging Out 10. Alternatives to War in the Middle East 11. Oil, Arms & the Gulf.

America's Defense Monitor: War with Iraq 19??
Six-part series which explains, in easily understood terminology, the military affairs associated with the Gulf War with Iraq and explains how they affected our lives. Covers such topics as the aftermath, military spending, casualties, alternatives, and the causes. Features interviews with top experts and governmental officials. Comes with teacher's guides. 180m; VHS. **A:** Jr. High-Adult. **P:** Education. **U:** Institution. **Gen-Edu:** War--General, History--U.S., Politics & Government. **Acq:** Purchase. **Dist:** Cambridge Educational. $169.95.
Indiv. Titles: 1. The Aftermath of War with Iraq 2. Military Spending After War with Iraq 3. Treating the Casualties of War with Iraq 4. Sandstorm in the Gulf: Digging Out 5. Alternatives to War in the Middle East 6. Oil, Arms, & the GUlf.

America's Disrupted Lives 1979
An examination of those people most directly affected by the Vietnam War veterans, refugees and antiwar dissenters—focusing on how America is dealing with these "living victims." 29m; VHS, 3/4 U. **Pr:** KTCA St. Paul/Minneapolis. **A:** Jr. High-Adult. **P:** Education. **U:** Institution, CCTV, CATV. **Gen-Edu:** Vietnam War. **Acq:** Purchase, Rent/Lease, Off-Air Record. **Dist:** PBS Home Video.

America's Dream 1995 (PG-13) — ★★★
Trilogy of short stories covering black life from 1938 to 1958. In "Long Black Song," based on a short story by Richard Wright, Alabama farmer Silas (Glover) lives with lonely wife Sarah (Lifford), who succumbs to the charms of white travelling salesman, David (Donovan). "The Boy Who Painted Christ Black" is young Aaron (Golden), who gives the drawing to his teacher, Miss Williams (Calloway). But the portrait causes a great deal of controversy in Aaron's 1948 Georgia school, especially for ambitious principal George Du Vaul (Snipes). Based on a story by John Henrich Clarke. The last story is Maya Angelou's "The Reunion," about Chicago jazz pianist Philomena (Toussaint), who encounters her childhood nemesis, Beth Ann (Thompson), the daughter of the white family who employed her parents as servants. 87m; VHS, DVD. **C:** Danny Glover; Tina Lifford; Tate Donovan; Dan Kamin; Wesley Snipes; Jasmine Guy; Vanessa Bell Calloway; Norman D. Golden, II; Timothy Carhart; Yolanda King; Rae'ven (Alyia Larrymore) Kelly; Lorraine Toussaint; Susanna Thompson; Carl Lumbly; Phyllis Cicero; Directed by Bill Duke; Kevin Rodney Sullivan; Paris Barclay; Written by Ron Stacker Thompson; Ashley Tyler; Cinematography by Karl Herrmann; Music by Patrice Rushen. **Pr:** David Knoller; Danny Glover; Carolyn McDonald; Danny Glover; Carrie Productions. **A:** Jr. High-Adult. **P:** Entertainment. **U:** Home. **Mov-Ent:** Black Culture, TV Movies. **Acq:** Purchase. **Dist:** Home Box Office Inc.

America's Endangered Species: Don't Say Goodbye 1998 (Unrated)
Photographers Susan Middleton and David Liittschwager travel across the United States capturing on film some of the country's most endangered species. A black-footed ferret, red wolves, and a baby bald eagle are just a few of the creatures photographed in an effort to bring more attention to the plight of America's threatened creatures. 56m; VHS, DVD. **A:** Family. **P:** Education. **U:** Institution, Home. **Mov-Ent:** Documentary Films, Animals, Birds. **Acq:** Purchase. **Dist:** National Geographic Society. $19.95.

America's Fabulous Black Marlin Fishing 19??
Find out exactly where to go in the U.S. for what many consider to be the world's finest sportfish. Includes footage of the backbreaking work involved in reeling in a world champion specimen. 40m; VHS. **A:** Adult. **P:** Instruction. **U:** Home. **Spo-Rec:** Fishing. **Acq:** Purchase. **Dist:** Bennett Marine Video. $29.95.

America's Face to the World 1979
A look at the effects American participation in the Vietnam War has had on our national psyche. 29m; VHS, 3/4 U. **Pr:** KTCA St. Paul/Minneapolis. **A:** Jr. High-Adult. **P:** Education. **U:** Institution, CCTV, CATV. **Gen-Edu:** Vietnam War. **Acq:** Purchase, Rent/Lease, Off-Air Record. **Dist:** PBS Home Video.

America's Family Doctor: C. Everett Koop 1991
Former Surgeon General C. Everett Koop discusses his lifelong work in his book, "Koop: The Memoirs of America's Family Doctor," and how he wishes to be remembered. 28m; VHS. **A:** Sr. High-Adult. **P:** Education. **U:** Institution. **Gen-Edu:** Biography. **Acq:** Purchase. **Dist:** University of Washington Educational Media Collection. $17.00.

America's Favorite Jokes 1987
A series of on-the-street interviews with a cross-section of the American public, all telling their favorite jokes. 30m. **Pr:** Rick Traum; Tony Nassour. **A:** Jr. High-Adult. **P:** Entertainment. **U:** Home. **Mov-Ent:** Comedy--Performance. **Acq:** Purchase. **Dist:** Rhino Entertainment Co. $16.95.

America's Favorite Sportfish with Uncle Homer 19??
Uncle Homer, the angling editor of "Sports Afield" magazine, teaches you all the details to hook the top six freshwater game fish. 38m; VHS. **A:** Sr. High-Adult. **P:** Instruction. **U:** Home. **Spo-Rec:** Sports--Water. **Acq:** Purchase. **Dist:** Bennett Marine Video. $19.95.

America's Favorite Sports Cars 1991
Legendary sportscars of the world are collected in this video, including Corvettes, Mustangs, T-Birds and more. Also included is a history of the design process and the test drive of the 1963 Corvette Sting Ray. 60m; VHS. **Pr:** Sony Pictures Home

Entertainment Inc. **A:** Sr. High-Adult. **P:** Entertainment. **U:** Home. **Spo-Rec:** Documentary Films, Automobiles, Hobbies. **Acq:** Purchase. **Dist:** Sony Music Entertainment Inc.; Sony Pictures Home Entertainment Inc. $19.98.

America's 58 National Parks 2012
Reveals the beauty of each of the 58 national parks in the U.S., including Yellowstone, Yosemite, Denali, Grand Teton, Biscayne, and Dry Tortugas. 395m; DVD. **A:** Family. **P:** Entertainment. **U:** Home. **Gen-Edu:** National Parks & Reserves. **Acq:** Purchase. **Dist:** Acorn Media Group Inc.; Questar Inc. $39.99.

America's First City: Teotihuacan 1976
The city of Teotihuacan is revered by Mexicans as an example of the skills and artistry of their forefathers. Although the city was abandoned in 800 AD, its lavish archeology remains. Spanish version also available. 17m; VHS, 3/4 U. **Pr:** Joe Kelley Film Productions. **A:** Primary-Jr. High. **P:** Education. **U:** Institution, SURA. **L:** English, Spanish. **Gen-Edu:** Archaeology, Mexico. **Acq:** Purchase. **Dist:** Home Vision Cinema.

America's Funniest Animal Foul-Ups 1991
What will those crazy animals do next? Watch some of the most hilarious antics pulled off by our friends in the animal kingdom. Fun for the whole family! 30m; VHS. **C:** Hosted by Kelly Monteith. **A:** Family. **P:** Entertainment. **U:** Home. **Mov-Ent:** Animals, Outtakes & Bloopers. **Acq:** Purchase. **Dist:** Universal Music and Video Distribution; Rhino Entertainment Co. $9.95.

America's Funniest Families 1992
The funniest skits covering family life are featured in this collection of comedy direct from the TV show "America's Funniest Home Videos." ?m; VHS, CC. **C:** Hosted by Bob Saget. **Pr:** ABC Video Enterprises, Inc; CBS/Fox. **A:** Family. **P:** Entertainment. **U:** Home. **Mov-Ent:** Family, Television. **Acq:** Purchase. **Dist:** Fox Home Entertainment. $14.98.

America's Funniest Home Videos: Animal Antics 1999 (Unrated)
Compiles various clips from the long-running comedy television program (1990-) that shows home viewer videos of animal tricks and bloopers that are set to dialogue from host Bob Saget. 1 episode. 51m; DVD. **C:** Hosted by Bob Saget. **A:** Family. **P:** Entertainment. **U:** Home. **Mov-Ent:** Television Series, Outtakes & Bloopers. **Acq:** Purchase. **Dist:** Shout! Factory. $19.99.

America's Funniest Home Videos: Athletic Supporters 2006 (Unrated)
Compiles various clips from the long-running comedy television program (1990-) that shows home viewer videos of sports-related tricks and bloopers that are set to dialogue. 1 episode. 120m; DVD. **A:** Family. **P:** Entertainment. **U:** Home. **Mov-Ent:** Television Series, Outtakes & Bloopers. **Acq:** Purchase. **Dist:** Shout! Factory. $9.98.

America's Funniest Home Videos: Best of Kids and Animals 2005 (Unrated)
Compiles various clips from the long-running comedy television program (1990-) that shows home viewer videos of animal and kid tricks and bloopers that are set to dialogue from hosts Bob Saget and Tom Bergeron. 5 episodes. ?m; DVD. **C:** Hosted by Bob Saget; Tom Bergeron. **A:** Family. **P:** Entertainment. **U:** Home. **Mov-Ent:** Television Series, Outtakes & Bloopers. **Acq:** Purchase. **Dist:** Shout! Factory. $29.98.

America's Funniest Home Videos: Deluxe Uncensored 1999 (Unrated)
Compiles various clips that could not be aired on the long-running comedy television program (1990-) due to mature content that shows home viewer videos of tricks and bloopers that are set to dialogue. 1 episode. 61m; DVD. **A:** Sr. High-Adult. **P:** Entertainment. **U:** Home. **Mov-Ent:** Television Series, Outtakes & Bloopers. **Acq:** Purchase. **Dist:** Shout! Factory. $17.99.

America's Funniest Home Videos: Guide to Parenting 199? (Unrated)
Amateur home video clips capture kiddie gaffes and funny moments. 80m; DVD. **C:** Hosted by Bob Saget. **A:** Family. **P:** Entertainment. **U:** Home. **Mov-Ent:** Family. **Acq:** Purchase. **Dist:** Shout! Factory.

America's Funniest Home Videos: Home for the Holidays 2005 (Unrated)
Compiles various clips from the long-running comedy television program (1990-) that shows home viewer videos of holiday-time tricks and bloopers that are set to dialogue from hosts Bob Saget and Tom Bergeron. 1 episode. 80m; DVD. **C:** Hosted by Bob Saget; Tom Bergeron. **A:** Family. **P:** Entertainment. **U:** Home. **Mov-Ent:** Television Series, Outtakes & Bloopers. **Acq:** Purchase. **Dist:** Shout! Factory. $9.98.

America's Funniest Home Videos: Motherhood Madness 199? (Unrated)
Collection of amateur-filmed antics of children falling, bumping into things, acting outrageous, and generally finding ways to annoy and humor their mothers. 80m; DVD. **C:** Hosted by Bob Saget. **A:** Family. **P:** Entertainment. **U:** Home. **Mov-Ent:** Family. **Acq:** Purchase. **Dist:** Shout! Factory.

America's Funniest Home Videos: Nincompoops & Boneheads 2006 (Unrated)
Compiles various clips from the long-running comedy television program (1990-) that shows home viewer videos of individuals' tricks and bloopers that are set to dialogue from hosts Bob Saget and Tom Bergeron. 1 episode. 80m; DVD. **C:** Hosted by Bob Saget; Tom Bergeron. **A:** Family. **P:** Entertainment. **U:** Home. **Mov-Ent:** Television Series, Outtakes & Bloopers. **Acq:** Purchase. **Dist:** Shout! Factory. $9.98.

America's Funniest Home Videos: Salute to Romance 2007 (Unrated)
Compiles various clips from the long-running comedy television program (1990-) that shows home viewer videos of romantic bloopers including weddings that are set to dialogue from host D.L. Hughley. 1 episode. 85m; DVD. **C:** Hosted by D.L. Hughley. **A:** Family. **P:** Entertainment. **U:** Home. **Mov-Ent:** Television Series, Outtakes & Bloopers. **Acq:** Purchase. **Dist:** Shout! Factory. $9.98.

America's Funniest Home Videos: Vol. 1 2005
Twelve one-hour episodes from the 2002 season, featuring host Tom Bergeron. Includes the "300th Episode Celebration," which aired in two parts. DVD. **A:** Family. **P:** Entertainment. **U:** Home. **Gen-Edu. Acq:** Purchase. **Dist:** Shout! Factory. $39.98.

America's Funniest Kid Foul-Ups 1991
See some of the most hilarious gags and bloopers featuring children. 30m; VHS. **Pr:** Rhino Video. **A:** Family. **P:** Entertainment. **U:** Home. **Mov-Ent:** Children, Outtakes & Bloopers. **Acq:** Purchase. **Dist:** Rhino Entertainment Co. $9.95.

America's Funniest Pets 1992
Join host Saget in this collection of hilarious pet scenes from the hit TV show "America's Funniest Home Videos." ?m; VHS, CC. **C:** Hosted by Bob Saget. **Pr:** ABC Video Enterprises, Inc; CBS/Fox. **A:** Family. **P:** Entertainment. **U:** Home. **Mov-Ent:** Pets, Television. **Acq:** Purchase. **Dist:** Fox Home Entertainment. $14.98.

America's Great Indian Leaders 1994
Assesses four Indian leaders who fought to preserve their land and culture in the American West in the late nineteenth century. 65m; VHS. **A:** Sr. High-Adult. **P:** Education. **U:** Institution. **Gen-Edu:** Native Americans. **Acq:** Purchase. **Dist:** Questar Inc. $29.99.

America's Great National Parks 1991
Close up look at our National Treasures including Yosemite, Yellowstone, the Grand Canyon and smaller parks. Beautiful photography of the diverse landscape, flora and fauna. A donation to America's National Parks is made with each purchase. Titles available individually for $29.95. 270m; VHS. **Pr:** Questar Inc. **A:** Family. **P:** Entertainment. **U:** Home, SURA. **Gen-Edu:** National Parks & Reserves, Wilderness Areas. **Acq:** Purchase. **Dist:** Questar Inc.; Facets Multimedia Inc.; Home Vision Cinema. $89.95.
Indiv. Titles: 1. Yellowstone National Park 2. Yosemite National Park 3. Grand Canyon National Park 4. Hidden Treasures of America's National Parks.

America's Great Volcanoes 19??
Provides information on the formation of some of America's great volcanoes and how they affect the environment around them. Comes with teacher's manual. 60m; VHS. **A:** Jr. High-Adult. **P:** Education. **U:** Institution. **Gen-Edu:** Geography, Volcanos. **Acq:** Purchase. **Dist:** Educational Video Network. $59.95.

America's Great Volcanoes 1992
Discusses some of the best known volcanoes in North America, including Mt. St. Helens, Mt. Rainier, Crater Lake, Katmai, and Kilauea. Contains footage of these volcanoes as well as historical data. 60m; VHS. **A:** Jr. High-Adult. **P:** Education. **U:** Institution. **Hea-Sci:** Volcanos, Geology. **Acq:** Purchase. **Dist:** Cambridge Educational. $29.95.

America's Greatest Battles 2005
Provides an overview of U.S. military conflicts from the Civil War to the Iraqi invasion with battles such as the Civil War's Battle of Perryville and World War II's Battle of Normandy. 180m; DVD. **A:** Sr. High-Adult. **P:** Entertainment. **U:** Home. **Gen-Edu:** Documentary Films, War--General, Terrorism. **Acq:** Purchase. **Dist:** Ventura Distribution Inc. $24.99.

America's Greatest Roller Coaster Thrills—In 3-D! 1995
Features front car rides on 14 of the most exciting roller coasters in the nation. Includes 3-D glasses for depth perception. 60m; VHS, DVD. **A:** Family. **P:** Entertainment. **U:** Home. **Gen-Edu. Acq:** Purchase. **Dist:** Paragon Home Video. $19.95.

America's Greatest Victories 2002
Chronicles America's most significant military battles through rare archival footage and interviews with historians and strategists. 150m; VHS. **A:** Adult. **P:** Education. **U:** Home. **Gen-Edu:** Documentary Films, History--U.S., War--General. **Acq:** Purchase. **Dist:** A&E Television Networks L.L.C. $29.95.

America's Gymnastic Stars 1998
Two-video set that features highlights in the American gymnastics program. "Gymnastics Golden Moments" shows highlights from the careers of Cathy Rigby, Kurt Thomas, Bart Conner, Julianne McNamara, Peter Vidmar, among others. "Atlanta's Magnificent Seven" features the U.S.A. Women's Gymnastic Team as they won their very first Olympic gold medal. One hour and 30 minutes on two videos. 45m; VHS. **A:** Family. **P:** Entertainment. **U:** Home. **Spo-Rec:** Gymnastics, Sports--Olympic. **Acq:** Purchase. **Dist:** PBS Home Video. $39.95.

America's Hardest Bounty Hunters: Bail Jumpers Beware 2006 (Unrated)
Profiles the lives of several bounty hunters who track down fugitives and bail-jumpers using unique and highly aggressive techniques. 5 episodes. 125m; DVD. **C:** Fred Slack; Robert Slack; Ben Hoppes; Rob Webb. **A:** Sr. High-Adult. **P:** Entertainment. **U:** Home. **Mov-Ent:** Television Series, Action-Adventure, Documentary Films. **Acq:** Purchase. **Dist:** Direct Source Special Products, Inc.

America's Hardest Bounty Hunters: Criminals Meet Your Maker! 2006 (Unrated)
Profiles the lives of several bounty hunters who track down fugitives and bail-jumpers using unique and highly aggressive techniques. 5 episodes. 125m; DVD. **C:** Fred Slack; Robert Slack; Ben Hoppes; Rob Webb. **A:** Sr. High-Adult. **P:** Entertainment. **U:** Home. **Mov-Ent:** Television Series, Action-Adventure, Documentary Films. **Acq:** Purchase. **Dist:** Direct Source Special Products, Inc. $5.98.

America's Heart and Soul 2004 (PG) — ★★
Series of vignettes seeks to capture the diversity and indomitable spirit of America, as a saccharine and ineffective answer to "Fahrenheit 9/11." Viewers literally fly over the U.S. and swoop down to meet a cowboy in Colorado, a rug weaver in Appalachia, a dairy farmer in Vermont, a trombone prodigy in Louisiana, a Methodist pastor in San Francisco, an Olympic boxer in Chicago and so on. Although the scenery is gorgeous and the people compelling, you're never with them for very long or reach any sort of depth. 84m; DVD. **C:** Directed by Louis Schwartzberg; Cinematography by Louis Schwartzberg; Music by Joel McNeely. **A:** Primary-Adult. **P:** Entertainment. **U:** Home. **Mov-Ent:** Documentary Films, Interviews, Music--Gospel. **Acq:** Purchase. **Dist:** Buena Vista Home Entertainment. $19.99.

America's Historic Trails ????
Six volume set follows the footsteps and wagon ruts of the frontiering pioneers as they explored, settled and worked the land. 360m; VHS; Closed Captioned. **A:** Jr. High-Adult. **P:** Education. **U:** Institution. **Gen-Edu:** History--U.S., Explorers. **Acq:** Purchase. **Dist:** Zenger Media. $39.95.
Indiv. Titles: 1. The Old Post Road 2. The Great Wagon Road & the Wilderness Trail 3. The River Road & the Natchez Trace 4. The California Trail & El Camino Real 5. The Mormon Trail & California's Mission Trail 6. Seattle & the Gold Rush Trail.

Americas in Transition 1982
This program provides an introduction to U.S. relations with Latin America, and the underlying causes of unrest there. 29m; 3/4 U. **Pr:** Obie Benz. **A:** Sr. High-Adult. **P:** Education. **U:** Institution, SURA. **Gen-Edu:** International Relations. **Acq:** Purchase. **Dist:** First Run/Icarus Films.

America's Jews 19??
Explores American Jewish life, examining such movies as "Hester Street," "The Way We Were," and "The Frisco Kid." Complete with guide. 60m; VHS. **A:** Primary-Adult. **P:** Religious. **U:** Institution. **Gen-Edu:** Judaism. **Acq:** Purchase. **Dist:** Ergo Media Inc. $39.95.

America's Library 1980
The Library of Congress contains some 76 million items. It serves scholars, other libraries, and copyright applicants along with its primary role as a research and reference arm of Congress. 18m; VHS, 3/4 U. **Pr:** Library of Congress; The Roberts Fund. **A:** Jr. High-Adult. **P:** Education. **U:** Institution, SURA. **Gen-Edu:** Information Science. **Acq:** Purchase, Rent/Lease. **Dist:** Home Vision Cinema.

America's Lost Mustangs 2001 (Unrated)
Narrated by actor William Shatner this film focuses on the efforts of "horse whisperer" Pat Parelli and scientists as they work with wranglers to round up and breed back from extinction the last descendants of America's first mustangs. 56m; VHS, DVD. **A:** Family. **P:** Education. **U:** Institution, Home. **Mov-Ent:** Documentary Films, History--U.S., Animals. **Acq:** Purchase. **Dist:** National Geographic Society. $19.95.

America's Lost Valley: Craters of the Moon 1989
Explores the Moon National Monument in Pocatello, Idaho, which is made up of an unusual assortment of mini-volcanoes and expansive lava flows. The impact of high volcanic activity offers unique geology and plant life, as well as the lore of the surrounding area. 25m; VHS. **A:** Jr. High-Adult. **P:** Education. **U:** Institution, Home. **Gen-Edu:** National Parks & Reserves, Geology, Volcanos. **Acq:** Purchase. **Dist:** GPN Educational Media. $29.95.

America's Money Vault 2012 (PG)
Host Jake Ward takes viewers behind the scenes at some of the biggest—and most secretive—financial institutions in the United States. Among the places Ward visits are the Federal Reserve Bank's Manhattan branch, where more than 25 percent of all the gold in the world is stored on a daily basis; New York City's Diamond District, where $24 billion changes hands every year; and the Bureau of Engraving and Printing, which mints and prints new American currency and monitors the flow of new bills into the economy. 45m; DVD. **A:** Family. **P:** Education, Entertainment. **U:** Home, Institution. **Mov-Ent:** Documentary Films, Finance, Business. **Acq:** Purchase. **Dist:** $19.95.

America's Monumental Story 1990
The story of how America was decorated with granite and stone, with particular emphasis placed on Mount Vernon, the Washington Monument, the Jefferson Memorial, the Lincoln Memorial and other sites of historical significance. 30m; VHS. **Pr:** Video Vacation. **A:** Sr. High-Adult. **P:** Education. **U:** Home. **Gen-Edu:** Travel, History--U.S. **Acq:** Purchase. **Dist:** Cole Media Group. $24.95.

America's Most Scenic Drives 2002
Spectacular drives from Maine's rocky coastline to Key Largo, Florida, Iowa's Bridges of Madison County and the Arizona Grand Canyon. 210m; VHS, DVD. **A:** Adult. **P:** Entertainment. **U:** Home. **Gen-Edu:** U.S. States, Travel. **Acq:** Purchase. **Dist:** Questar Inc. $29.99.

America's Multicultural Heroes 1993
Series of four videos focusing on major figures in American history. Explores their generation, the adversity they faced, and

their contributions to society. Includes teacher information and skill sheets. 15m; VHS. **A:** Primary-Jr. High. **P:** Education. **U:** Institution. **Gen-Edu:** Black Culture, History--U.S., Women. **Acq:** Purchase. **Dist:** Clear Vue Inc. $89.00.

Indiv. Titles: 1. Susan B. Anthony Tells Her Own Story 2. Harriet Tubman Tells Her Own Story 3. Chief Seattle Tells His Own Story 4. Frederick Douglass Tells His Own Story.

America's Music: Chicago and All That Jazz 1987
The history of jazz in Chicago, with exemplary playing from Chicago's greatest. 60m; VHS. **A:** Jr. High-Adult. **P:** Entertainment. **U:** Home. **Mov-Ent:** Music--Performance. **Acq:** Purchase. **Dist:** Music Video Distributors. $19.98.

America's Music, Vol. 1: Country & Western 1 1987
A series of programs featuring vintage musical appearances by veterans of basically American styles of music-gospel, jazz, country, folk, blues and rock. 60m. **Pr:** Sandra Turbow; Herb Silvers. **A:** Preschool. **P:** Entertainment. **U:** Home. **Mov-Ent:** Music--Country/Western. **Acq:** Purchase. **Dist:** Music Video Distributors. $19.98.

America's Music, Vol. 2: Country & Western 2 1981
The series continues with performances from Moe Bandy, Jerry Lee Lewis, Terry Gregory and Ricky Skaggs. 59m; VHS. **Pr:** Sandra Turbow; Herb Silvers. **A:** Family. **P:** Entertainment. **U:** Home. **Mov-Ent:** Music--Performance, Music--Country/Western. **Acq:** Purchase. **Dist:** Music Video Distributors. $19.95.

America's Music, Vol. 3: Blues 1 1987
Featured in this blues retrospective are B.B. King performing, "Payin' the Cost to the Boss," Eddie "Cleanhead" Vinson performing, "Cleanhead Blues," plus Linda Hopkins, Vi Redd, Bessie Smith and more. 60m; VHS. **A:** Jr. High-Adult. **P:** Entertainment. **U:** Home. **Mov-Ent:** Music--Performance. **Acq:** Purchase. **Dist:** Music Video Distributors. $19.95.

America's Music, Vol. 4: Blues 2 1987
Videos of blues great Mamie Smith, Count Basie, Big Joe Turner, Joe Williams, Bobby McGee, Buddy Guy, Junior Wells and more. 60m; VHS. **A:** Sr. High-Adult. **P:** Entertainment. **U:** Home. **Mov-Ent:** Music Video, Black Culture. **Acq:** Purchase. **Dist:** Music Video Distributors; Facets Multimedia Inc. $19.95.

America's Music, Vol. 5: Rhythm and Blues 1 1987
Footage of R&B greats includes Ruth Brown, Billy Preston, Gloria Lynne, Sheer Delight, Billy Eckstine and more. 60m; VHS. **C:** Hosted by Billy Eckstine. **A:** Jr. High-Adult. **P:** Entertainment. **U:** Home. **Mov-Ent:** Music--Performance, Black Culture. **Acq:** Purchase. **Dist:** Music Video Distributors; Facets Multimedia Inc. $19.95.

America's Music, Vol. 6: Rhythm and Blues 2 1987
The R&B greats featured here include, Brook Benton, Mary Wells, O.C. Smith and Scatman Crothers. 60m; VHS. **C:** Hosted by Billy Eckstine. **A:** Jr. High-Adult. **P:** Entertainment. **U:** Home. **Mov-Ent:** Music--Performance, Black Culture. **Acq:** Purchase. **Dist:** Music Video Distributors; Facets Multimedia Inc. $19.95.

America's Music, Vol. 7: Folk 1 1987
The folk performers highlighted here include, Leadbelly and the Limeliters, Hoyt Axton, Glenn Yarbrough and the New Christy Minstrels. 60m; VHS. **A:** Jr. High-Adult. **P:** Entertainment. **U:** Home. **Mov-Ent:** Music--Performance. **Acq:** Purchase. **Dist:** Music Video Distributors. $19.95.

America's Music, Vol. 8: Folk 2 1987
Featured folk performers include the Limeliters, Josh White Jr., Doc Watson, and Jean Richie. 60m; VHS. **A:** Jr. High-Adult. **P:** Entertainment. **U:** Home. **Mov-Ent:** Music--Performance. **Acq:** Purchase. **Dist:** Music Video Distributors. $19.95.

America's Music, Vol. 9: Jazz Then Dixieland 1 1987
The masters of jazz include, Louis Armstrong, Al Hirt, Woody Herman and Della Reese. 60m; VHS. **A:** Jr. High-Adult. **P:** Entertainment. **U:** Home. **Mov-Ent:** Music--Performance, Music--Jazz. **Acq:** Purchase. **Dist:** Music Video Distributors. $19.95.

America's Music, Vol. 10: Dixieland 2 1987
Musical greats include Scatman Crothers, Bob Crosby, Fats Waller, Teddy Buckner and more. 60m; VHS. **A:** Family. **P:** Entertainment. **U:** Home. **Mov-Ent:** Music Video. **Acq:** Purchase. **Dist:** Music Video Distributors. $19.95.

America's Music, Vol. 11: Soul 1 1987
Featured artists in this retrospective are, James Brown, Ben E. King, Tyrone Davis and Maxine Nightingale. 60m; VHS. **Pr:** Video Associates. **A:** Jr. High-Adult. **P:** Entertainment. **U:** Home. **Mov-Ent:** Music--Performance, Documentary Films, Black Culture. **Acq:** Purchase. **Dist:** Music Video Distributors; Facets Multimedia Inc. $19.95.

America's Music, Vol. 12: Soul 2 1987
This volume contains clips of soul greats Gladys Knight, Rufus Thomas, Jerry Butler, Carla Thomas, Freda Payne, Percy Sledge and more. 60m; VHS. **A:** Sr. High-Adult. **P:** Entertainment. **U:** Home. **Mov-Ent:** Music Video, Black Culture. **Acq:** Purchase. **Dist:** Music Video Distributors; Facets Multimedia Inc. $19.95.

America's Music, Vol. 13: Gospel 1 1987
Featured artists in this retrospective are, Andre Crouch, The Winans, Marion Williams and Mahalia Jackson. 60m; VHS. **C:** Hosted by LeVar Burton. **A:** Jr. High-Adult. **P:** Entertainment. **U:** Home. **Mov-Ent:** Music--Performance, Religion, Black Culture. **Acq:** Purchase. **Dist:** Music Video Distributors; Facets Multimedia Inc. $19.95.

America's Music, Vol. 14: Gospel 2 1987
The artists profiled in this edition include Linda Hopkins, Wentley Phipps and Sandra Crouch and Friends. 60m; VHS. **A:** Jr. High-Adult. **P:** Entertainment. **U:** Home. **Mov-Ent:** Music--Performance, Religion, Black Culture. **Acq:** Purchase. **Dist:** Music Video Distributors; Facets Multimedia Inc. $19.95.

America's Music, Vol. 15: Rock 'n' Roll 1 19??
Features material from some of the greatest rock stars of the '50s and '60s, including the Coasters, Chubby Checker, Fabian, Lou Christie, and Leslie Gore. 57m; VHS. **C:** Hosted by Fabian. **A:** Jr. High-Adult. **P:** Entertainment. **U:** Home. **Mov-Ent:** Music Video, Music--Pop/Rock. **Acq:** Purchase. **Dist:** Music Video Distributors. $14.95.

America's Music, Vol. 16: Rock 'n' Roll 2 19??
Includes material from Bo Diddley, the Diamonds, Fabian, the Crystals, and Little Anthony. 60m; VHS. **C:** Hosted by Fabian. **A:** Jr. High-Adult. **P:** Entertainment. **U:** Home. **Mov-Ent:** Music Video, Music--Pop/Rock. **Acq:** Purchase. **Dist:** Music Video Distributors. $14.95.

America's Mysterious Places 19??
A documentary investigation into America's unexplained civilizations and most mysterious ancient sites. 60m; VHS. **A:** Sr. High-Adult. **P:** Entertainment. **U:** Home. **Mov-Ent:** Native Americans, History--U.S., History--Ancient. **Acq:** Purchase. **Dist:** Hartley Film Foundation. $19.95.

Indiv. Titles: 1. Mysteries of America's Historic Sites 2. Mysteries of Ancient America.

America's National Monuments: The Geologic West 2009
A guide to 11 National Monuments of the Pacific Northwest, including mountain ranges, fossil beds, and plant and animal diversity. 150m; DVD, CC. **A:** Jr. High-Adult. **P:** Education. **U:** Institution. **Gen-Edu:** Documentary Films, U.S. States, Ecology & Environment. **Acq:** Purchase. **Dist:** Ambrose Video Publishing, Inc. $129.99.

America's National Parks 1988
See Mount Rushmore, the redwood forests and many more of the nation's wildlife reserves. 30m; VHS. **Pr:** Visual Horizons. **A:** Jr. High-Adult. **P:** Education. **U:** Institution, Home. **Gen-Edu:** Travel, National Parks & Reserves, Wilderness Areas. **Acq:** Purchase. **Dist:** Visual Horizons. $39.95.

America's National Parks: An Eagle's View 2013 (G)
Documentary presenting an aerial view of several of America's national parks. Blu-Ray. **A:** Family. **P:** Entertainment. **U:** Home. **L:** English. **Gen-Edu:** Documentary Films, Nature, U.S. States. **Acq:** Purchase. **Dist:** Mill Creek Entertainment L.L.C. $9.98.

America's Next Top Model: Cycle One 2004
Features the first season of the reality show hosted by supermodel Tyra Banks with 20 young female contestants as they vie for the top prize of a modeling contract, "Marie Claire Magazine" spread, and a Revlon cosmetics contract; the winner is decided by a panel of judges based on a variety of different photo shoots. ?m; DVD. **A:** Sr. High-Adult. **P:** Entertainment. **U:** Home. **Mov-Ent:** Television, Documentary Films. **Acq:** Purchase. **Dist:** Paramount Pictures Corp. $38.99.

America's Next Top Model: Cycle One 2005 (Unrated)
Features the television game show with host supermodel Tyra Banks who prepares 10 young women for competitive photo shoots as they vie for the prize of a modeling contract and to be signed by a top agency and are graded and "eliminated" by celebrity judges. 9 episodes. 380m; DVD. **C:** Kimora Lee Simmons; Janet Dickenson; Beau Quillan; Hosted by Tyra Banks. **A:** Sr. High-Adult. **P:** Entertainment. **U:** Home. **Mov-Ent:** Television Series, Game Show, Documentary Films. **Acq:** Purchase. **Dist:** Paramount Pictures Corp. $49.99.

America's Out Islands: The Florida Keys 19??
Ace boating destination for vacationers looking for something close to the U.S. mainland. Different perspectives from sea level and from above add something extra to this guide. 60m; VHS. **A:** College-Adult. **P:** Entertainment. **U:** Home. **Spo-Rec:** Boating, Travel. **Acq:** Purchase. **Dist:** Bennett Marine Video. $39.95.

America's Past: Early American History 1992
Two programs cover crucial periods in American history: the Revolutionary War and the Civil War. Available on one tape or separately. 15m; VHS. **A:** Primary-Jr. High. **P:** Education. **U:** Institution. **Chl-Juv:** History--U.S., Civil War, Revolutionary War. **Acq:** Purchase. **Dist:** January Productions. $34.95.

America's People: Our Ethnic Heritage 1977
A look at how our country has been built by people who have come from all over the world searching for freedom and rights. 11m; VHS, 3/4 U, EJ, Special order formats. **Pr:** Albert Saparoff. **A:** Primary-Jr. High. **P:** Education. **U:** Institution, SURA. **Gen-Edu:** History--U.S. **Acq:** Purchase. **Dist:** Dana Productions.

America's Polka King: Frankie Yankovic "One More Time" 1993
Best Selling Polka Recording Artist, Polka Hall of Famer, and Polka Grammy Award Winner Frank Yankovic celebrates his retirement. Three-volume set. ?m; VHS. **A:** Adult. **P:** Entertainment. **U:** Home. **Mov-Ent.** **Acq:** Purchase. **Dist:** Universal Productions International/Gaming Tapes, Inc. $19.95.

America's Presidents 1983
This program presents the history of the Presidency from George Washington to Jimmy Carter with many rare stills and films incorporated in the program. 15m; VHS, 3/4 U. **Pr:** WGBH Boston. **A:** Jr. High-Adult. **P:** Education. **U:** Institution, SURA. **Gen-Edu:** Presidency. **Acq:** Purchase, Rent/Lease. **Dist:** Hearst Entertainment/King Features.

America's Public Enemies/Dealers in Death 1986
Using authentic footage, this is a look at the careers of John Dillinger, Bonnie & Clyde, Al Capone, and other notorious crooks. 60m/B/W; VHS, 3/4 U. **TV Std:** NTSC, PAL. **C:** Narrated by Broderick Crawford. **Pr:** MPI Media Group. **A:** Jr. High-Adult. **P:** Education. **U:** Home. **Gen-Edu:** Documentary Films. **Acq:** Purchase. **Dist:** MPI Media Group. $19.95.

America's Railroads: How the Iron Horse Shaped Our Nation 1986
For students, a historical survey of the role railroads have played in American history, from their inception to the present day. 22m; VHS, 3/4 U. **Pr:** Cypress Films Productions. **A:** Primary-Jr. High. **P:** Education. **U:** Institution, Home, SURA. **Gen-Edu:** History--U.S., Trains. **Acq:** Purchase. **Dist:** Clear Vue Inc.

America's Railroads: The Steam Train Legacy 1998
This comprehensive series records the golden age of steam trains in America, with segments which relive journeying aboard old-time passenger cars and operations of actual rail lines. Seven hours on seven videocassettes. 60m; VHS, DVD. **A:** Family. **P:** Education. **U:** Home. **Gen-Edu:** Trains, History--U.S. **Acq:** Purchase. **Dist:** PBS Home Video. $69.95.

America's Railroads: The Steam Train Legacy, Volume 2 19??
Collection of promotional films used by various railroads along with historical information about railroading service. Footage features steam engines on the Delaware & Hudson, World War II troop trains, the California Zephyr and more. 420m; DVD. **A:** Family. **P:** Education. **U:** Home. **L:** English. **Gen-Edu:** Trains, U.S. States. **Acq:** Purchase. **Dist:** Timeless Media Group; The Civil War Standard. $29.95.

America's Railroads: The Steam Train Legacy Volume II ????
More than seven hours of footage of America's railroads and steam trains, with both documentary footage and promotional films shot by the railroad companies. 420m; VHS, DVD. **A:** College-Adult. **P:** Education. **U:** Home. **Gen-Edu:** Trains. **Acq:** Purchase. **Dist:** The Civil War Standard. $29.95.

America's Rainforest 1992
Interviews and narrated scenes illustrate the threat facing the only temperate rainforest in the U.S., located in Washington's Olympia Peninsula. Informative presentation explores a variety of aspects, including deforestation, differences found in various rainforests, their precious natural resources, how their disappearance is affecting the world, and more. 20m; VHS. **A:** Jr. High-Sr. High. **P:** Education. **U:** Institution. **Hea-Sci:** Ecology & Environment, Forests & Trees, Natural Resources. **Acq:** Purchase. **Dist:** Cambridge Educational. $49.95.

America's Romance with Space 1990
The American Space Program is chronicled with former astronaut William Anders and the widow of one of the founders of the project, Dr. Robert H. Goddard. 60m/B/W; VHS. **Pr:** Republic Pictures. **A:** Sr. High-Adult. **P:** Education. **U:** Home. **Gen-Edu:** Documentary Films, Space Exploration, History--U.S. **Acq:** Purchase. **Dist:** Lions Gate Entertainment Inc.

America's Scenic Rail Journeys 2005
A documentary looking at America as the filmmakers travel from one coast to the other by railroad. 324m; DVD. **A:** Jr. High-Adult. **P:** Entertainment. **U:** Home. **Gen-Edu:** Documentary Films, Education. **Acq:** Purchase. **Dist:** Acorn Media Group Inc. $39.99.

America's Schools: Who Gives a Damn? 1991
Two programs feature a distinguished panel answering questions posed by Harvard law professors on the state of public education. Explores the tough issues of peer intervention programs, equalizing funds for substandard schools, dropout prevention, and more. 60m; VHS. **A:** Adult. **P:** Education. **U:** Institution. **Gen-Edu:** Education. **Acq:** Purchase. **Dist:** PBS Home Video. $120.00.

America's Special Days 199?
Ten-part series for children which teaches the traditions and history of certain holidays. Viewers are taken to different parts of the country throughout different times in history so that they may see the celebrations associated with the holidays. 150m; VHS. **A:** Primary. **P:** Education. **U:** Institution, BCTV, CATV, CCTV. **Chl-Juv:** History, Holidays, Travel. **Acq:** Purchase. **Dist:** GPN Educational Media. $199.50.

Indiv. Titles: 1. New Year's Day 2. Martin Luther King, Jr./Black History Month 3. President's Day 4. Women's History Month 5. Arbor Day/Earth Day 6. Memorial Day/Veterans' Day 7. Flag Day/Citizenship Day 8. Independence Day(s) 9. Native American Day 10. Thanksgiving Day.

America's Sweethearts 2001 (PG-13) — ★★
This just in: Hollywood is shallow and fake, Julia Roberts is pretty, and entertainment reporters are freeloading numbskulls. These are the themes covered in this disappointing romantic comedy in which America's favorite on- and off-screen couple Eddie (Cusack) and Gwen (Zeta-Jones) pretend to reconcile during a disaster-filled press junket cooked up by desparate publicist Lee (Crystal). Complicating matters are the developing relationship between Gwen's sister and assistant Kiki (Roberts)

and Eddie. Roth hasn't directed a film in over 10 years, and it shows here. But beneath the rust, there are some funny moments, mostly including Walken as the crazy director who has taken his own film hostage. 103m; VHS, DVD, Wide, CC. **C:** Julia Roberts; Catherine Zeta-Jones; John Cusack; Billy Crystal; Hank Azaria; Christopher Walken; Seth Green; Stanley Tucci; Cameo(s) Larry King; Directed by Joe Roth; Written by Billy Crystal; Peter Tolan; Cinematography by Phedon Papamichael; Music by James Newton Howard. **Pr:** Billy Crystal; Susan Arnold; Donna Roth; Billy Crystal; Revolution Studios; Face; Columbia Pictures. **A:** Jr. High-Adult. **P:** Entertainment. **U:** Home. **Mov-Ent:** Comedy--Romantic, Marriage, Hotels & Hotel Staff Training. **Acq:** Purchase. **Dist:** Sony Pictures Home Entertainment Inc.

America's Team: Being a U.S. Air Force Thunderbird 2008 (Unrated)
A behind-the-scenes documentary following the U.S. Air Force Thunderbirds as they get ready for a show. 81m; DVD. **A:** Jr. High-Adult. **P:** Entertainment. **U:** Home. **Gen-Edu:** Documentary Films. **Acq:** Purchase. **Dist:** Janson Media. $24.95.

America's Toughest Sheriff 2006
Follows the controversial career of Joe Arpaio, the Sheriff of Maricopa County in Arizona, and his views on incarceration, including female chain gangs and inmate tent cities. His unorthodox methods have been questioned by civil rights groups, including Amnesty International. 50m; DVD. **A:** Sr. High-Adult. **P:** Entertainment. **U:** Home. **Gen-Edu:** Documentary Films, U.S. States, Biography: Law Enforcement. **Acq:** Purchase. **Dist:** MPI Media Group. $14.98.

America's Unsung Heroes of WWII 2001
Four volumes of untold true stories of WWII: Charles Bowers, the greatest submariner ever; civilian correspondents joining assault forces on D-Day; daring wartime escapes of Colonel Merritt, and much more. ?m; VHS. **A:** Adult. **P:** Education. **U:** Home. **Gen-Edu:** World War Two, History, Documentary Films. **Acq:** Purchase. **Dist:** A&E Television Networks L.L.C. $39.95.

America's Victoria: The Victoria Woodhull Story 1995
Chronicles the life of Victoria Woodhull, who became the first women to campaign for U.S. president. Profiles the radical suffragist who refused to restrict her presidential campaign to the issue of women's suffrage. 52m; VHS. **A:** College-Adult. **P:** Education. **U:** Institution. **Gen-Edu:** Women, History--U.S. **Acq:** Purchase, Rent/Lease. **Dist:** Women Make Movies. $250.00.

America's Weirdest Homes 1999
Four-tape series features unusual homes in the U.S. Includes houses decorated with bottles, button, and beer cans; a junk castle; an underground grotto; and more. 240m; VHS. **A:** Family. **P:** Entertainment. **U:** Home. **Gen-Edu:** Architecture, Art & Artists. **Acq:** Purchase. **Dist:** Instructional Video. $99.95.

America's Western National Parks 1992
Views of national parks including the Sierra Nevada of California, the Badlands of South Dakota, the Grand Canyon, and the Olympic Mountains. Panoramic overviews and intimate details of wildlife. 60m; VHS. **A:** Family. **P:** Entertainment. **U:** Home. **Gen-Edu:** Travel, National Parks & Reserves. **Acq:** Purchase. **Dist:** Finley Holiday Film Corp. $24.95.

America's Westward Expansion 1996
Explores the key events that spurred America's westward expansion in 1805. 20m; VHS. **A:** Primary-Sr. High. **P:** Education. **U:** Institution. **Gen-Edu:** History--U.S., Native Americans, Wilderness Areas. **Acq:** Purchase. **Dist:** Knowledge Unlimited, Inc. $55.00.

America's Wings 1978
A historical overview of the ideas that made manned flight possible, from Kitty Hawk to the present. Contains information on some of the great inventors of this century, including Igor Skorsky, who developed the helicopter; Adolph Busemann, who developed the swept-wing aircraft; and Richard Whitcomb, who invented the modern shape of commercial jet aircraft. 30m; 1C, 3/4 U, Q. **Pr:** National Aeronautics and Space Administration. **A:** Primary-Adult. **P:** Education. **U:** BCTV, SURA. **Hea-Sci:** Aeronautics. **Acq:** Free Loan. **Dist:** NASA Lyndon B. Johnson Space Center. $24.99.

America's Wonderlands: The National Parks 1968
A visit to America's national parks reveals nature at its most beautiful. 52m; 3/4 U, Special order formats. **Pr:** National Geographic Society. **A:** Primary. **P:** Education. **U:** Institution, Home, SURA. **Chl-Juv:** National Parks & Reserves. **Acq:** Purchase, Trade-in, Duplication License. **Dist:** National Geographic Society.

Americathon 1979 (PG) — **Bomb!**
It is the year 1998 and the United States is almost bankrupt, so President Chet Roosevelt decides to stage a telethon to keep the country from going broke. Interesting satiric premise with a diverse cast, but a poor script and slack pacing spoil all the fun. The soundtrack features music by The Beach Boys and Elvis Costello while the narration is by George Carlin. 85m; VHS, DVD. **C:** Peter Riegert; John Ritter; Nancy Morgan; Harvey Korman; Fred Willard; Meat Loaf Aday; Elvis Costello; Chief Dan George; Howard Hesseman; Jay Leno; Terence McGovern; Allan Arbus; David Opatoshu; John Lone; Cybill Shepherd; Dorothy Stratten; Cameo(s) Tommy Lasorda; Peter Marshall; Narrated by George Carlin; Directed by Neal Israel; Written by Monica Johnson; Neal Israel; Music by Earl Brown, Jr. **Pr:** Lorimar Productions. **A:** Sr. High-Adult. **P:** Entertainment. **U:** Home. **Mov-Ent:** Satire & Parody, Politics & Government. **Acq:** Purchase. **Dist:** WarnerArchive.com; Warner Home Video, Inc. $59.95.

Amerikanauk: The Basques of the American West 1990
Examines the migration patterns, history, and culture of the Basques. Shows how the Basques have contributed to our diverse ethnic heritage. 28m; VHS, 3/4 U. **A:** Jr. High-Adult. **P:** Education. **U:** Institution. **Gen-Edu:** Ethnicity. **Acq:** Rent/Lease. **Dist:** New Dimension Media. $40.00.

Ameslan: ASL 1988
A sign language course with Ella Lentz and Frieda Norman including practice sentences, dialogues, poems, songs and stories. Includes a textbook by Lou Fant. 60m; VHS, 3/4 U. **Pr:** Joyce Media. **A:** Jr. High-Adult. **P:** Education. **U:** Institution, Home. **Gen-Edu:** Deafness, Communication, Education. **Acq:** Purchase. **Dist:** Joyce Media Inc. $69.00.

Amici Dance 1987
A group of mentally handicapped people perform a dance. 29m; VHS, 3/4 U. **Pr:** CTVC. **A:** Jr. High-Adult. **P:** Religious. **U:** Institution, SURA. **Gen-Edu:** Mental Retardation, Dance. **Acq:** Purchase, Rent/Lease. **Dist:** St. Anthony Messenger Press. $29.95.

Amie 1987
A journalist gets involved with helping the poor. 17m; VHS, 3/4 U. **Pr:** Franciscan Communications. **A:** Jr. High-Adult. **P:** Religious. **U:** Institution, SURA. **L:** Spanish. **Gen-Edu. Acq:** Purchase, Rent/Lease. **Dist:** St. Anthony Messenger Press. $160.00.

Amigos 1990
Number of programs to boost Spanish as a second language proficiency and familiarize students with Hispanic culture and geography. Uses the FLEX (Foreign Language Experience) approach to learning. Programs may be purchased individually or as series. Teacher's guide available at additional cost. 15m; VHS, CC. **Pr:** Center for Telecommunications and Video. **A:** Preschool-Primary. **P:** Education. **U:** Institution. **L:** Spanish. **Gen-Edu:** Language Arts, Hispanic Culture, Communication. **Acq:** Purchase, Rent/Lease. **Dist:** Agency for Instructional Technology. $125.00.

Indiv. Titles: 1. Perro Pepe encuentra su casa (Perro Pepe Finds a Home) 2. Perro Pepe tiene seis anos (Perro Pepe is 6 Years Old) 3. Perro Pepe es un perro (Perro Pepe is a Dog) 4. Fernandez's Funky Fonda: la gran inauguracion (Fernandez's Funky Fonda: The Grand Opening) 5. El gran secreto de Perro Pepe (Perro Pepe's Big Secret) 6. El cumpleanos de Perro Pepe (Perro Pepe's Birthday) 7. La caperucita roja (Little Red Riding Hood) 8. El sueno de Perro Pepe (Perro Pepe's Dream) 9. El regalo de Lu (Lu's Gift) 10. La escuela de Perro Pepe (Perro Pepe's School) 11. Mark va a la escuela? (Is Mark Going to School?) 12. La senorita y su perro (The Lady & Her Dog) 13. Vamos al cine (Let's Go to the Movies) 14. Las flores (The Flowers) 15. Lunes de tormenta (Stormy Monday) 16. Los colores de Miriam (Miriam's Colors) 17. Ir o no ir (To Go or Not to Go) 18. Buen viaje, Senorita Fernandez (Good Trip, Senorita Fernandez) 19. En cual direccion doblar? (Which Way to Turn?) 20. Es magia (It's Magic) 21. El problema de Miriam (Miriam's Problem) 22. Ir de compras (Going Shopping) 23. Mi casa es su casa (My House is Your House) 24. Donde esta el perro? (Where Is the Dog?) 25. El cocinero (The Chef) 26. Perro Pepe en la television (Perro Pepe on Television) 27. A Perro Pepe le duele un diente (Perro Pepe Has a Toothache) 28. Las formas (The Shapes) 29. La reunion (The Reunion) 30. Mi hogar, dulce hogar (Home Sweet Home).

Amin: The Rise and Fall 1982 — **Bomb!**
Excessively violent and ultimately pointless dramatization of Idi Amin's eight-year reign of terror in Uganda, which resulted in the deaths of a half million people and the near ruin of a nation. 101m; VHS. **C:** Joseph Olita; Geoffrey Keen; Directed by Sharad Patel. **Pr:** Sharad Patel. **A:** Sr. High-Adult. **P:** Entertainment. **U:** Home. **Mov-Ent:** Biography: Politics, Africa. **Acq:** Purchase. **Dist:** No Longer Available.

Amino Acids and Proteins 19??
The creation of a protein is followed from the formation of the peptide bonds through the folding of the polypeptide. The details of the step-by-step formations of a dipeptide, (glycylglycine) are shown. The difference between random coils of polypeptide chains and helices is illustrated. The enormous amount of possible configurations of polypeptide chains in proteins is emphasized by showing dihedral angle rotation. Finally the three-dimensional structure of two proteins shows the location of active sides, alpha helical sections, and pleated sheets. 6m/B/W; 3/4 U, Special order formats. **Pr:** Joel de Rosnay. **A:** College-Adult. **P:** Education. **U:** Institution, CCTV, CATV, BCTV. **Hea-Sci:** Biology. **Acq:** Purchase, Rent/Lease. **Dist:** Education Development Center.

Amiotte 1976
A film outlining the career and life of Native American artist Arthur Amiotte. 29m; VHS, 1C, 3/4 U, Q. **Pr:** South Dakota ETV. **A:** Jr. High-Adult. **P:** Education. **U:** Institution, BCTV, SURA. **Fin-Art:** Native Americans, Art & Artists. **Acq:** Purchase, Rent/Lease. **Dist:** Vision Maker Media.

Amir: An Afghan Refugee Musician's Life in Peshawar, Pakistan 1986
Westerner John Baily explores the urban music of Afghanistan as practiced by Amir, a refugee who is a professional musician. Includes his performance of a song of protest. Study guide included. 52m; VHS. **TV Std:** NTSC, PAL. **Pr:** John Baily. **A:** Sr. High-Adult. **P:** Education. **U:** Institution. **Gen-Edu:** Asia. **Acq:** Purchase, Rent/Lease. **Dist:** Documentary Educational Resources. $245.00.

The Amish: A People of Preservation 1992
This tape examines the history of the Amish people, their beliefs, the attitudes of the younger members, and their relationship to the neighboring community. Also available in a 28-minute edited version. 53m; VHS, 3/4 U. **Pr:** John A. Hostetler; Encyclopedia Britannica Educational Corporation. **A:** Jr. High-Adult. **P:** Education. **U:** Institution, SURA. **Gen-Edu:** Religion. **Acq:** Purchase, Rent/Lease, Trade-in. **Dist:** Encyclopedia Britannica; Cambridge Educational. $29.95.

The Amish and Us 1998
Takes an offbeat look at the growing commerce between the traditional Amish community of Lancaster, Pennsylvania and the millions of tourists who come to gawk at them and buy their wares. 57m; VHS. **A:** Jr. High-Adult. **P:** Education. **U:** Home. **Gen-Edu:** Documentary Films, Amish, Business. **Acq:** Purchase. **Dist:** Direct Cinema Ltd. $24.95.

Amish Grace 2010 (Unrated) — ★★½
Fact-based Lifetime movie taken from a book on the 2006 shootings of Amish schoolgirls in Pennsylvania. Ida Graber (Paisley-Williams), whose daughter was killed, grapples with the demands of her Old Order Amish faith that she forgive the sinner. Amy Roberts (Blanchard), a mother herself, must deal with the inexplicable and horrible aftermath that her husband was the killer. 90m; DVD. **C:** Kimberly Williams; Tammy Blanchard; Matt Letscher; Fay Masterson; John Churchill; Madison Mason; Gary (Rand) Graham; Directed by Gregg Champion; Written by Sylvie White; Teena Booth; Cinematography by Ross Berryman; Music by Joseph Conlan. **A:** Jr. High-Adult. **P:** Entertainment. **U:** Home. **Mov-Ent:** TV Movies, Amish. **Acq:** Purchase. **Dist:** Fox Home Entertainment.

The Amish: Not to Be Modern 1985
Provides a rare portrait of the Amish and the simple agrarian lifestyle they have maintained for almost 300 years. 57m; VHS, 3/4 U. **Pr:** MPI Media Group. **A:** Primary-Adult. **P:** Education. **U:** Institution, Home, SURA. **Gen-Edu:** Sociology, Religion. **Acq:** Purchase, Rent/Lease, Duplication. **Dist:** Filmakers Library Inc.; Cambridge Educational. $29.98.

Amish Riddle 19??
Shows a dynamic people, who, contrary to popular belief, are not relics frozen in time. The audience meets an Amish family and learns how they conduct their daily lives. 50m; VHS. **A:** Sr. High. **P:** Education. **U:** Institution. **Gen-Edu:** Human Relations. **Acq:** Purchase. **Dist:** Filmakers Library Inc. $395.

Amistad 1997 (R) — ★★★
Spielberg again creates an epic from another historic example of man's inhumanity, although not quite as effectively this time around. In 1839, African captives aboard the slaveship Amistad, led by a Mende tribesman named Cinque (Hounsou), free themselves and take over the ship in a bloody mutiny. Property attorney Robert Baldwin (McConaughey) must prove in lengthy court battles that the Africans were rightfully freed individuals in the eyes of the law. John Quincy Adams (Hopkins) presents the Africans' defense to the Supreme Court. Sequences depicting the horrors of slavery are bogged down with heavy handed musical orchestrations that elicit emotion, but at the price of storytelling. McConaughey seems a bit too Californian to be colonial and Morgan Freeman is reduced to periodic cameos as an abolitionist. Fortunately, thanks to an eye for rich detail and superb acting by dynamic newcomer Hounsou, the film nearly escapes the clutches of melodrama to emerge educational and moving. Film's release was marred by a French author accusing Spielberg and his Dreamworks studio of plagiarism. 152m; VHS, DVD, Blu-Ray. **C:** Djimon Hounsou; Anthony Hopkins; Matthew McConaughey; Morgan Freeman; Nigel Hawthorne; David Paymer; Pete Postlethwaite; Stellan Skarsgard; Anna Paquin; Austin Pendleton; Tomas Milian; Paul Guilfoyle; Directed by Steven Spielberg; Written by David Franzoni; Cinematography by Janusz Kaminski; Music by John Williams. **Pr:** Colin Wilson; Debbie Allen; Steven Spielberg; Steven Spielberg; HBO; DreamWorks SKG. **A:** Jr. High-Adult. **P:** Entertainment. **U:** Home. **Mov-Ent:** Slavery, History--U.S., Law. **Awds:** Broadcast Film Critics '97: Support. Actor (Hopkins). **Acq:** Purchase. **Dist:** DreamWorks Home Entertainment.

The Amistad Revolt: "All We Want Is Make Us Free" 1995
Overviews the kidnapping of 53 Mende men, women, and children, their revolt, foiled escape, victory in Supreme Court, and return voyage to Africa. 33m; VHS. **A:** Jr. High-Sr. High. **P:** Education. **U:** Institution. **Gen-Edu:** History--U.S., Slavery. **Acq:** Purchase. **Dist:** Zenger Media. $39.95.

The Amityville Horror 1979 (R) — ★★
Sometimes a house is not a home. Ineffective chiller that became a boxoffice biggie, based on a supposedly real-life occurrence in Amityville, Long Island. The Lutz family moves into the house of their dreams only to find it full of nightmares. Once the scene of a grisly mass murder, the house takes on a devilish attitude, plunging the family into supernatural terror. Pipes and walls ooze icky stuff, flies manifest in the strangest places, and doors mysteriously slam while exorcist Steiger staggers from room to room in scene-chewing prayer. Based on the Jay Anson book and followed by a number of sequels. 117m; VHS, DVD, Blu-Ray, Wide. **C:** James Brolin; Margot Kidder; Rod Steiger; Don Stroud; Murray Hamilton; Helen Shaver; Amy Wright; Val Avery; Natasha Ryan; John Larch; K.C. Martel; Meeno Peluce; Directed by Stuart Rosenberg; Written by Sandor Stern; Cinematography by Fred W. Koenekamp; Music by Lalo Schifrin. **Pr:** American International Pictures. **A:** Adult. **P:** Entertainment. **U:** Home. **Mov-Ent:** Horror, Death. **Acq:** Purchase. **Dist:** Warner Home Video, Inc., On Moratorium.

Amityville 2: The Possession 1982 (R) — **Bomb!**
More of a prequel than a sequel to "The Amityville Horror" (1979). Relates the story of the house's early years as a haven for demonic forces intent on driving a father to beat the kids, a mother to prayer, and a brother to lust after his sister (before he murders them all). Young etc. portray an obnoxious family that you're actually glad to see wasted by the possessed son. A stupid, clumsy attempt to cash in on the success of the first film, which was also stupid and clumsy but could at least claim novelty in the bad housing development genre. Followed by "Amityville 3: The Demon" in 1983. 110m; VHS, DVD, Blu-Ray. **C:** James Olson; Burt Young; Andrew Prine; Moses Gunn; Rutanya Alda; Jack Magner; Diane Franklin; Directed by Damiano Damiani; Written by Tommy Lee Wallace; Cinematography by Franco Di Giacomo; Music by Howard Blake; Lalo Schifrin. **Pr:** Dino De Laurentiis. **A:** Sr. High-Adult. **P:** Entertainment. **U:** Home. **Mov-Ent:** Horror, Death. **Acq:** Purchase. **Dist:** MGM Home Entertainment. $14.24.

Amityville 3: The Demon 1983 (R) — ★1/2
America's worst real-estate value dupes another funky buyer. The infamous Amityville house is once again restless with terror and gore, though supported with even less plot than the usual smidgin. Cynical reporter Roberts moves in while trying to get to the bottom of the story by way of the basement. Courtesy of 3-D technology, monsters sprang at theatre patrons but the video version is strictly two-dimensional, forcing the viewer to press his or her face directly onto the TV screen in order to derive similar effect. 98m; VHS, DVD, Blu-Ray. **C:** Tony Roberts; Tess Harper; Robert Joy; Candy Clark; John Beal; Leora Dana; John Harkins; Lori Loughlin; Meg Ryan; Rikke Borge; Jack Cardiff; Directed by Richard Fleischer; Written by William Wales; David Ambrose; Cinematography by Fred Schuler; Music by Howard Blake. **Pr:** Stephen F. Kesten. **A:** Sr. High-Adult. **P:** Entertainment. **U:** Home. **Mov-Ent:** Horror, Death. **Acq:** Purchase. **Dist:** Lions Gate Television Corp. $79.98.

Amityville 4: The Evil Escapes 1989 (R) — ★1/2
It's an unusual case of house-to-house transference as the horror from Amityville continues, now lodged in a Californian residence. The usual good-house-gone-bad story has the place creating a lot of unusual creaks and rattles before deciding to use its inherited powers to attack and possess a little girl. Special effects from Richard Stutsman ("The Lost Boys" and "Jaws"). 95m; VHS, DVD. **C:** Patty Duke; Jane Wyatt; Norman Lloyd; Frederic Lehne; Brandy Gold; Directed by Sandor Stern; Written by Sandor Stern; Music by Rick Conrad. **A:** Adult. **P:** Entertainment. **U:** Home. **Mov-Ent:** Horror, TV Movies, Death. **Acq:** Purchase. **Dist:** CinemaNow Inc. $89.95.

Amityville: A New Generation 1993 (R) — ★1/2
And the bad sequels just go on and on and on. Terry is a young photographer who's given an old mirror by a crazy homeless man (tell me why he took it). He shares a loft with three friends and all begin experiencing vivid and terrifying dreams of murder. Seems the mirror is tied to Amityville and its evil legacy and Terry is the designated inheritor. 92m; VHS, DVD, CC. **C:** Ross Partridge; Julia Nickson-Soul; David Naughton; Richard Roundtree; Terry O'Quinn; Directed by John Murlowski; Written by Christopher DeFaria; Antonio Toro. **Pr:** Christopher DeFaria; Steve White; Barry Bernardi; Christopher DeFaria. **A:** Sr. High-Adult. **P:** Entertainment. **U:** Home. **Mov-Ent:** Horror. **Acq:** Purchase. **Dist:** Lions Gate Entertainment Inc. $14.98.

The Amityville Curse 1990 (R) — **Bomb!**
The possessed house is yet again purchased by a pathetically uninformed family. The usual ghostly shenanigans occur with low-budget regularity in this fifth film in the series. Never released theatrically, for good reason. 91m; VHS. **C:** Kim Coates; Dawna Wightman; Helen Hughes; David Stein; Cassandra Gava; Jan Rubes; Directed by Tom Berry; Written by Michael Krueger; Norvell Rose. **A:** Sr. High-Adult. **P:** Entertainment. **U:** Home. **Mov-Ent:** Canada, Death. **Acq:** Purchase. **Dist:** Lions Gate Home Entertainment; Anchor Bay Entertainment. $9.99.

Amityville Dollhouse 1996 (R) — ★1/2
Family moves into their Victorian dream home in Amityville, which comes complete with a replica dollhouse that charms the daughter. But the Amityville curse inhabits the plaything and soon the poltergeists make their nasty appearance. 97m; VHS, DVD, CC. **C:** Robin Thomas; Starr Andreeff; Allen (Culter) Cutler; Rachel Duncan; Jarrett Lennon; Clayton Murray; Frank Ross; Lenora Kasdorf; Lisa Robin Kelly; Directed by Steve White; Written by Joshua Michael Stern; Cinematography by Thomas Callaway. **Pr:** Republic Entertainment Inc. **A:** Sr. High-Adult. **P:** Entertainment. **U:** Home. **Mov-Ent:** Horror, Occult Sciences, Family. **Acq:** Purchase. **Dist:** Lions Gate Entertainment Inc.

The Amityville Horror 2005 (R) — ★★1/2
Revamp of the Amityville tale swaps the understated chills of the original 1979 film with faster editing, more gore, and lots of goth imagery. George and Kathy Lutz (Reynolds and George) learn the meaning of "buyer beware" when they move their family into a lakeside colonial home, a real bargain thanks to the house's history of bone-chilling mass murders. After a series of strange incidents and ghostly visitations, Kathy begins catching on, just in time to watch her husband start channeling Jack Nicholson in "The Shining." The scares are familiar, but Douglas does an admirable job of creating a pervasively creepy, claustrophobic atmosphere throughout. 89m; DVD, Blu-Ray, UMD. **C:** Ryan Reynolds; Melissa George; Jesse James; Jimmy Bennett; Rachel Nichols; Philip Baker Hall; Rich Komenich; Scott Kosar; Brendan Donaldson; Annabel Armour; Chloe Grace Moretz; Isabel Conner; Jose Taitano; David Gee; Danny McCarthy; Nancy Lollar; Directed by Andrew Douglas; Cinematography by Peter Lyons Collister; Music by Steve Jablonsky. **Pr:** Michael Bay; Andrew Form; Brad Fuller; Platinum Dunes; MGM. **A:** Sr. High-Adult. **P:** Entertainment. **U:** Home. **L:** English. **Mov-Ent:** Horror, Exorcism & Exorcists. **Acq:** Purchase. **Dist:** MGM Home Entertainment.

Amityville 1992: It's About Time 1992 (R) — ★★
Time is of the essence in the sixth installment of the Amityville flicks. A vintage clock (from Amityville, of course), causes creepy goings-on in a family's house. Actually a halfway decent horror film with high-grade special effects, and much, much better than previous Amityville sequels, which isn't saying much. 95m; VHS, DVD, CC. **C:** Stephen Macht; Shawn Weatherly; Megan Ward; Damon Martin; Nita Talbot; Dick Miller; Directed by Tony Randel; Written by Christopher DeFaria; Antonio Toro. **Pr:** Republic Pictures. **A:** Sr. High-Adult. **P:** Entertainment. **U:** Home. **Mov-Ent:** Horror, Death. **Acq:** Purchase. **Dist:** Lions Gate Entertainment Inc. $14.98.

The Ammeter and Its Use 1976
Introduces correct methods for using DC ammeter in a typical series DC circuit. 13m; VHS. **A:** Adult. **P:** Education. **U:** Institution. **Gen-Edu:** Electricity. **Acq:** Purchase. **Dist:** RMI Media. $89.95.

Amnesia 1996 (R) — ★★
Minister Paul Keller (Walker) is having an affair with his son's teacher, Veronica Dow (Tomanovich). Paul decides to fake his death, leaving wife Martha (Sheedy) with the insurance money, and allowing him to start a new life with Veronica. Only he has an accident that causes amnesia and runs into more trouble than he can imagine. Has more humor than you might imagine, thanks to its wacky characters, but as usual Kirkland is way over the top as a love-starved motel owner. 92m; VHS, DVD. **C:** Nicholas Walker; Ally Sheedy; Sally Kirkland; John Savage; Dara Tomanovich; Vincent Berry; Directed by Kurt Voss. **A:** Sr. High-Adult. **P:** Entertainment. **U:** Home. **Mov-Ent:** Mystery & Suspense, Marriage, Insurance. **Acq:** Purchase.

Amnestic Syndrome 1972
The history of encephalitis is presented. 16m; VHS, 3/4 U, Special order formats. **Pr:** Ohio State University Health Sciences AV Center. **A:** College-Adult. **P:** Professional. **U:** Institution, SURA. **Hea-Sci:** Neurology. **Acq:** Purchase, Rent/Lease. **Dist:** Ohio State University.

Amniocentesis 1993
The amniocentesis procedure is explained, showing samples of amniotic fluid and stressing that the birth of children with defects can be avoided by early detection. 15m; VHS, 3/4 U. **Pr:** Milner-Fenwick. **A:** Adult. **P:** Education. **U:** Institution, CCTV. **L:** English, French, Spanish. **Hea-Sci:** Pregnancy. **Acq:** Purchase. **Dist:** Milner-Fenwick, Inc.

Amniocentesis and Chorionic Villus Sampling 1992
Thoroughly covers two prenatal tests for detecting chromosonal abnormalities. Presents solid reasons for pursuing prenatal testing and expounds on causes of birth defects, amniocentesis, CVS, risks involved, discomfort, and much more. 16m; VHS. **A:** Adult. **P:** Education. **U:** Institution. **Hea-Sci:** Pregnancy, Medical Education, Medical Care. **Acq:** Purchase. **Dist:** Milner-Fenwick, Inc. $250.00.

The Amoeba 1981
An in-depth look at the amoeba. Live sequences with high-magnification photography show ameboid motion, encirclement and ingestion of food, elimination of wastes, reproduction and responses to stimuli. 30m; VHS, 3/4 U. **Pr:** Educational Materials and Equipment. **A:** Jr. High-Adult. **P:** Education. **U:** Institution, Home, SURA. **Hea-Sci:** Science, Microbiology. **Acq:** Purchase. **Dist:** EME Corp.

Among Brothers 2005 (Unrated) — ★★
A "what if" based on a true crime from 1994. South Carolina frat boy Ethan doesn't take it well when co-ed Jennifer just wants to be friends, and she winds up dead in her apartment. Ethan whines to frat brothers Miles and Billy that it was an accident, so they torch the place to cover things up. Only the cops figure out Jennifer was murdered, so the boys try to shift the blame elsewhere. The real crime remains unsolved. 85m; DVD. **C:** Matt Mercer; Lauren Schneider; Corey Cicci; Daniel J. Watts; Directed by John Schwert; Written by John Schwert; Cinematography by Brad Hoover. **A:** Sr. High-Adult. **P:** Entertainment. **U:** Home. **Mov-Ent. Acq:** Purchase. **Dist:** Vanguard International Cinema, Inc.

Among Brothers: Politics in New Orleans 1987
Examines the new urban politics where blacks often run for elected office against other blacks. The tape also examines new coalition building. 60m; VHS, 3/4 U. **Pr:** Center for New American Media; Deep South Productions; PBS. **A:** Sr. High-Adult. **P:** Education. **U:** Institution, CCTV, Home, SURA. **Gen-Edu:** Black Culture, Politics & Government. **Acq:** Purchase, Rent/Lease, Duplication, Off-Air Record. **Dist:** PBS Home Video.

Among Equals 1991
Part six in the "Childhood" series examines the role of peer relationships in a child's development. 57m; VHS. **A:** Sr. High-Adult. **P:** Education. **U:** Institution. **Gen-Edu:** Parenting, Children. **Acq:** Purchase. **Dist:** University of Washington Educational Media Collection. $17.00.

Among Fish 1989
The daily life of a fish is revealed in this film, geared towards junior science classes. 11m; VHS, 3/4 U. **Pr:** Rene Johnson. **A:** Jr. High-Sr. High. **P:** Education. **U:** Institution, SURA. **Gen-Edu:** Fish. **Acq:** Purchase, Rent/Lease. **Dist:** National Film Board of Canada.

Among Giants 1998 (R) — ★★
Postlethwaite is Ray, the foreman of a crew of painters assigned to slap a new coat on the electrical towers that line the Yorkshire countryside. When a female Australian rock climber (Griffiths) wanders into town, joins the crew, and starts sleeping with Ray, she causes static between him and his best friend (Thornton). Understated to the point of being comatose, nothing much happens with the romance or the dangerous occupation angle. Postlethwaite does a fine job as the unlikely romantic lead, though. 93m; VHS, Streaming. **C:** Pete Postlethwaite; Rachel Griffiths; James Thornton; Lennie James; Andy Serkis; Rob Jarvis; Directed by Sam Miller; Written by Simon Beaufoy; Cinematography by Witold Stok; Music by Tim Atack. **Pr:** 20th Century-Fox. **A:** Sr. High-Adult. **P:** Entertainment. **U:** Home. **Mov-Ent:** Great Britain. **Acq:** Purchase. **Dist:** Amazon.com Inc.; Fox Home Entertainment.

Among Good Christian People 1991
Co-director Woodson documents her story as a Black lesbian raised as a Jehovah Witness as she comes to terms with her sexuality, lifestyle, and spiritual yearnings. 30m; VHS, 3/4 U. **C:** Directed by Catherine Saalfield; Jacqueline Woodson. **A:** College-Adult. **P:** Education. **U:** Institution. **Gen-Edu:** Documentary Films, Black Culture, Homosexuality. **Acq:** Purchase, Rent/Lease. **Dist:** Third World Newsreel; Frameline.

Among the Cinders 1983 — ★★
Sometimes interesting coming of age drama about a 16-year-old New Zealand boy who runs away to his grandfather's farm to forget about his friend's accidental death. At the farm, he meets an older woman and compromises his virtue. 103m; VHS. **C:** Paul O'Shea; Derek Hardwick; Rebecca Gibney; Yvonne Lawley; Amanda Jones; Directed by Rolf Haedrich. **Pr:** New World Pictures. **A:** Sr. High-Adult. **P:** Entertainment. **U:** Home. **Mov-Ent. Acq:** Purchase. **Dist:** Anchor Bay Entertainment. $9.95.

Among the First to Die 2005
Stark memorial to a 28-year-old Guatemalan man who joined the Marines and quickly lost his life, only then receiving his citizenship from President Bush. 10m; VHS. **A:** Jr. High-Adult. **P:** Education. **U:** Institution, Home. **Gen-Edu:** Ethnicity. **Acq:** Purchase. **Dist:** Third World Newsreel. $25.00.

Among the Wild Chimpanzees 19??
Looks at the habitat and lifestyle of the wild chimpanzee. 59m; VHS, 3/4 U. **A:** Primary-Adult. **P:** Education. **U:** Institution. **Gen-Edu:** Animals. **Acq:** Purchase. **Dist:** National Geographic Society. $24.20.

Among Women 1996
Using interviews and experimental techniques, explores the social and medical perceptions of pregnancy and midwifery as a healthy political choice for care and delivery. 32m; VHS. **A:** Adult. **P:** Education. **U:** Home. **Gen-Edu:** Documentary Films, Pregnancy. **Acq:** Purchase, Rent/Lease. **Dist:** Third World Newsreel. $175.00.

Amongst Friends 1993 (R) — ★★
Three boyhood buddies, Trevor (McGaw), Billy (Lindsey), and Andy (Parlavecchio), from a nice Long Island neighborhood turn to crime out of boredom. Trevor gets busted and goes to prison for two years. Upon getting out, he finds his old cronies still share the taste for crime and general aimlessness but also still want that one big score. Trevor finally agrees to join Andy and Billy in a drug deal but the jealous Billy, who wants Trevor's old girlfriend Laura (Sorvino), plans a double-cross that will affect them all. Filled with cutting attacks on the society that spawns aimless youth. Debut of then 26-year-old writer/director Weiss. 88m; VHS, DVD, CC. **C:** Patrick McGaw; Steve Parlavecchio; Joseph Lindsey; Mira Sorvino; David Stepkin; Michael Artura; Louis Lombardi; Directed by Rob Weiss; Written by Rob Weiss; Cinematography by Michael Bonvillain; Music by Mick Jones. **Pr:** Matt Blumberg; Robert K. Weiss; Last Outlaw Films; Fine Line Features. **A:** Sr. High-Adult. **P:** Entertainment. **U:** Home. **Mov-Ent:** Drugs. **Acq:** Purchase. **Dist:** Sony Pictures Home Entertainment Inc.

Amongst Women 1998 (Unrated) — ★★
Embittered ex-IRA soldier Michael Moran (Doyle) is desperate to keep his family together, but the widower's brutality only succeeds in driving his children to strong measures to make their own lives. Set in 1950s rural Ireland; based on the novel by John McGahern. 219m; DVD. **C:** Tony Doyle; Susan Lynch; Ger Ryan; Geraldine O'Rawe; Anne-Marie Duff; Brian F. O'Byrne; Directed by Tom Cairns; Written by Adrian Hodges; Cinematography by Sue Gibson; Music by Niall Byrne. **A:** Jr. High-Adult. **P:** Entertainment. **U:** Home. **Mov-Ent:** Ireland. **Acq:** Purchase. **Dist:** BFS Video.

Amor Bandido 1979 (Unrated) — ★★1/2
When cab drivers in Rio are turning up dead, a young prostitute is torn between her detective father and her prime suspect boyfriend. Drama based on a true story. In Portuguese with English subtitles. 95m; VHS. **C:** Paulo Gracindo; Cristina Ache; Paulo Guarniero; Directed by Bruno Barreto. **A:** College-Adult. **P:** Entertainment. **U:** Home. **L:** Portuguese. **Mov-Ent:** Prostitution, Adolescence. **Acq:** Purchase. **Dist:** Wellspring Media; Image Entertainment Inc.; Facets Multimedia Inc. $19.98.

Amor de Hombre 1997 — ★★
Ramon is a gay man with a lot of bedroom action. His best friend is Esperanza, who goes home alone since she always falls for gay guys. Trouble starts when Ramon meets Esperanza's fellow teacher Roberto and their relationship turns into more than a one-night stand. Suddenly, Esperanza is really the odd woman out. Spanish with subtitles. 88m; VHS, DVD. **C:** Andrea Occhipinti; Pedro Mari Sanchez; Armando Del Rio; Directed by Juan Luis Iborra; Yolanda Garcia Serrano; Written by Juan Luis Iborra; Yolanda Garcia Serrano; Cinematography

by Paco Femenia. **A:** College-Adult. **P:** Entertainment. **U:** Home. **L:** Spanish. **Mov-Ent:** Comedy--Romantic. **Acq:** Purchase. **Dist:** TLA Releasing.

Amor, Dolor y Vica Versa 2008 (Unrated) — ★★
Desperate to find the lover she dreams of nightly, a woman concocts a rape story to get the police to find him. He turns out to be having nightmares about being killed by a woman who looks a lot like his accuser. 85m; DVD, Streaming. **C:** Leonardo Sbaraglia; Joaquin Cosio; Barbara Mori; Marina de Tavira; Irene Azuela; Directed by Alfonso Pineda Ulloa; Written by Alex Marino; Blas Valdez; Cinematography by Damian Garcia; Music by Roque Banos. **A:** Sr. High-Adult. **P:** Entertainment. **U:** Home. **L:** English, Spanish. **Mov-Ent. Acq:** Purchase, Rent/Lease. **Dist:** Lions Gate Entertainment Inc. $14.98 9.99.

Amore 1948 (Unrated) — ★★★
Rossellini's tribute to actress Magnani consists of the short films "The Human Voice" and "The Miracle." In "The Human Voice," Magnani is shown alone, speaking to her lover on the telephone. Based on Jean Cocteau's one-act drama. In "The Miracle," she is a simple peasant girl who believes her illegitimate child is acutally the new Messiah. In Italian with English subtitles. 78m/B/W; VHS. **C:** Anna Magnani; Directed by Roberto Rossellini. **A:** College-Adult. **P:** Entertainment. **U:** Home. **L:** Italian. **Mov-Ent. Acq:** Purchase. **Dist:** Facets Multimedia Inc. $59.95.

Amore! 1993 (PG-13) — ★★½
Wealthy investment banker Saul Schwartz (Scalia) hates his job, his wife, and his life. The only way he loses himself is by watching movies starring Italian matinee idol Rudolfo Carbonera (Hamilton). So Saul gets divorced and decides to change his life—by going to Hollywood and becoming an actor like his debonair idol. With the help of some newfound friends he transforms himself into suave leading man material (under the name of Salvatore Guiliano III) but promptly winds up falling for a writer (Ireland), who couldn't care less. 93m; VHS, CC. **C:** Jack Scalia; Kathy Ireland; Elliott Gould; George Hamilton; Brenda Epperson; James Doohan; Katherine Helmond; Betsy Russell; Norm Crosby; Frank Gorshin; Directed by Lorenzo Doumani; Written by Lorenzo Doumani. **A:** Jr. High-Adult. **P:** Entertainment. **U:** Home. **Mov-Ent:** Comedy--Romantic. **Acq:** Purchase. **Dist:** $89.95.

Amores Perros 2000 (R) — ★★★
A Mexico City car accident and the fortunes of a dog bring together three stories of love, loss, and redemption in director/producer Gonzalez Inarritu's impressive feature debut. Octavio's love for his brother's wife leads him to enter his dog, Cofi, in a dogfight for elopement money. When Cofi is wounded, it leads to a car chase, and the central accident. A woman, Valeria, is injured and permanently scarred in the accident. This affects her beau, who has just left his family to be with her. A homeless man, a former revolutionary turned hitman, witnesses the crash and rescues the dog, who becomes a part of his search for his estranged daughter. The plot structure invites comparisons to Tarantino, but these characters inhabit a more consequences-and-morality-oriented world than Q's characters ever did. Film came under fire from animal rights activists for the dogfight scenes, although it was made clear from the start that no animals were actually harmed. 153m; VHS, DVD, Wide. **C:** Vanessa Bauche; Emilio Echeverria; Gael Garcia Bernal; Goya Toledo; Alvaro Guerrero; Jorge Salinas; Marco Perez; Rodrigo Murray; Humberto Busto; Gerardo Campbell; Rosa Maria Bianchi; Dunia Saldivar; Adriana Barraza; Directed by Alejandro Gonzalez Inarritu; Written by Guillermo Arriaga; Cinematography by Rodrigo Prieto; Music by Gustavo Santaolalla. **Pr:** Alejandro Gonzalez Inarritu; Altavista; Zeta Films; Lions Gate Films. **A:** Sr. High-Adult. **P:** Entertainment. **U:** Home. **L:** Spanish. **Mov-Ent:** Mexico, Homeless, Pets. **Awds:** British Acad. '01: Foreign Film; Natl. Bd. of Review '01: Foreign Film. **Acq:** Purchase. **Dist:** Lions Gate Home Entertainment; CinemaNow Inc.

The Amorous Adventures of Moll Flanders 1965 (Unrated) — ★★
An amusing romp set in 18th century England focusing on a poor orphan girl who seeks wealth. Moll plots to get ahead through an advantageous series of romances and marriages. Her plan is ruined when she falls in love and he turns out to be a wanted highwayman, landing her in prison. Not surprisingly, love (and money) conquers all. Based on the novel by Daniel Defoe. Novak tries in this female derivative of "Tom Jones," but this period piece isn't her style. 126m; VHS, Streaming. **C:** Kim Novak; Richard Johnson; Angela Lansbury; Vittorio De Sica; Leo McKern; George Sanders; Lilli Palmer; Directed by Terence Young; Cinematography by Ted Moore; Music by John Addison. **A:** Jr. High-Adult. **P:** Entertainment. **U:** Home. **Mov-Ent:** Comedy--Romantic, Sex & Sexuality. **Acq:** Purchase. **Dist:** Paramount Pictures Corp. $19.95.

Amos 1985 — ★★½
Douglas is Amos, an aging baseball coach confined most reluctantly to a nursing home. He's disturbed by recent suspicious events there, his concern causing him to take on Montgomery, the staunch head nurse. Well-acted drama produced by Douglas's son Peter, offering an echo of "One Flew Over the Cuckoo's Nest," which Dad starred in on Broadway and son Michael helped produced as a movie classic. 100m; VHS. **C:** Kirk Douglas; Elizabeth Montgomery; Dorothy McGuire; Noriyuki "Pat" Morita; James Sloyan; Ray Walston; Directed by Michael Tuchner; Music by Georges Delerue. **A:** Jr. High-Adult. **P:** Entertainment. **U:** Home. **Mov-Ent:** TV Movies, Aging. **Acq:** Purchase. **Dist:** No Longer Available.

Amos and Andrew 1993 (PG-13) — ★½
Embarrassing attempt at comedy stops short of endorsing the stereotypes it tries to parody. Prizewinning African-American author Andrew Sterling (Jackson) is seen moving into a house on an island previously reserved for the uptight white, and the neighbors call the cops, assuming he's a thief. Chief of police (Coleman) eagerly gets into the act, then exploits drifter Amos (Cage) in a cover-up attempt when he realizes his mistake. Talented cast can't overcome lame jokes and transparent plot that serves as an opportunity to bring black and white together for a "see how much we have in common" bonding session. 96m; VHS, DVD, CC. **C:** Nicolas Cage; Samuel L. Jackson; Michael Lerner; Margaret Colin; Giancarlo Esposito; Dabney Coleman; Bob Balaban; Aimee Graham; Brad Dourif; Chelcie Ross; Jodi Long; Directed by E. Max Frye; Written by E. Max Frye; Music by Richard Gibbs. **Pr:** Gary Goetzman; Castle Rock Entertainment. **A:** Jr. High-Adult. **P:** Entertainment. **U:** Home. **Mov-Ent:** Comedy--Slapstick, Prejudice. **Acq:** Purchase. **Dist:** Sony Pictures Home Entertainment Inc.; Image Entertainment Inc.; New Line Home Video. $14.95.

Amos Fortune, Free Man 1986
A prince who was sold into slavery finally regains his freedom. From a story by Elizabeth Yates. 46m; VHS. **Pr:** Random House Inc. **A:** Primary-Jr. High. **P:** Entertainment. **U:** Institution. **Chl-Juv:** Literature. **Acq:** Purchase, Subscription. **Dist:** Facets Multimedia Inc.; Zenger Media. $69.95.

Amos 'n' Andy: Anatomy of a Controversy 1983
A documentary examining both sides of the racial argument surrounding the old sitcom, including interviews with Jesse Jackson and Redd Foxx. A complete episode of the show is included. 60m; VHS. **C:** Narrated by George Kirby. **Pr:** CBS. **A:** Family. **P:** Entertainment. **U:** Home. **Mov-Ent:** Documentary Films, Interviews, Television Series. **Acq:** Purchase. **Dist:** Facets Multimedia Inc. $19.95.

Amos 'n' Andy Comedy Classics 195?
Three complete and uncut episodes from the popular TV series of the early 1950s are featured on this tape, with original commercials included. 70m/B/W; VHS. **C:** Alvin Childress; Tim Moore; Spencer Williams, Jr; Ernestine Wade; Amanda Randolph. **Pr:** CBS. **A:** Family. **P:** Entertainment. **U:** Home. **Mov-Ent:** Television Series. **Acq:** Purchase. **Dist:** Lions Gate Entertainment Inc. $28.00.

Amos 'n' Andy: The Boarder/Insurance Policy 195?
Two half-hour episodes of this vintage television show are featured. Good print quality. 54m/B/W; VHS. **C:** Alvin Childress; Spencer Williams, Jr.; Tim Moore; Ernestine Wade; Directed by Charles T. Barton. **A:** Family. **P:** Entertainment. **U:** Home. **Mov-Ent:** Television Series, Black Culture. **Acq:** Purchase. **Dist:** Grapevine Video. $9.95.

Amour 2012 (PG-13) — ★★★
Writer/director Haneke's clinical approach to filmmaking takes on his most emotional subject matter in this tale of the inevitable common bond of life--the cruelty of death. Georges (Trintignant) and Anne (Riva) are a happy couple in their 80s until Anne has a stroke and goes unresponsive for long periods of time. The film merely chronicles, often like a fly on the wall, the final days of a decades-old relationship. Riva and Trintignant are stunningly real, adding to the feeling that this is so truthful, so private, and so emotionally raw that we shouldn't even be watching. 125m; DVD, Blu-Ray. **C:** Jean-Louis Trintignant; Emmanuelle Riva; Isabelle Huppert; Alexandre Tharaud; William Shimell; Directed by Michael Haneke; Written by Michael Haneke; Cinematography by Darius Khondji; Music by Cecile Lenoir. **Pr:** Margaret Menegoz; Michael Katz; Veit Heiduschka; Stefan Arndt; Sony Pictures Classics. **A:** Jr. High-Adult. **P:** Entertainment. **U:** Home. **L:** French. **Mov-Ent:** Aging, Death, Marriage. **Awds:** Oscars '12: Foreign Film; British Acad. '12: Actress (Riva), Foreign Film; Golden Globes '13: Foreign Film; Ind. Spirit '13: Foreign Film. **Acq:** Purchase. **Dist:** Sony Pictures Home Entertainment Inc.

Amphibian Embryo: Frog, Toad, and Salamander 1963
Illustrates the developmental process by which a single-celled amphibian egg is transformed into a multicellular adult organism. 16m; VHS, 3/4 U. **Pr:** K.T. Rogers; Encyclopedia Britannica Educational Corporation. **A:** Sr. High. **P:** Education. **U:** Institution, SURA. **L:** English, Spanish. **Hea-Sci:** Embryology. **Acq:** Purchase, Rent/Lease, Trade-in. **Dist:** Encyclopedia Britannica.

The Amphibian Man 1961 (Unrated) — ★★
What does a scientist do once he's created a young man with gills? Plunge him in the real world of aqua pura to experience life and love, albeit underwater. Trouble is, the protagonist, who's come to be known as the Sea Devil, takes a dive for a young pretty he's snatched from the jaws of death. A '60s Soviet sci-fi romance originally seen on American TV. 93m; VHS, DVD. **C:** K. Korieniev; M. Virzinskaya; Mikhail Kozakov; Vladlen Davydov; Directed by Y. Kasancki; Written by Aleksei Kapler. **Pr:** Sovexportfilm USSR; Lenfilm. **A:** Primary-Adult. **P:** Entertainment. **U:** Home. **Mov-Ent:** Fantasy, Romance. **Acq:** Purchase. **Dist:** Sinister Cinema; Image Entertainment Inc. $19.98.

Amphibians: Frogs, Toads, and Salamanders—Revised 1980
The program explores through a microscope the frog's development, and serves to introduce the differences between kinds of amphibians. 11m; VHS, 3/4 U. **A:** Primary-Sr. High. **P:** Education. **U:** Institution, SURA. **Hea-Sci:** Animals. **Acq:** Purchase. **Dist:** Phoenix Learning Group.

Amplitude Modulation 1981
Basic AM theory is explained to electronics students or anyone needing a better understanding of the subject. Single and double sideband, suppressed carrie, and vestigial sideband are discussed. 16m; VHS, 3/4 U. **Pr:** Hewlett Packard. **A:** College-Adult. **P:** Education. **U:** Institution, CCTV, Home. **Bus-Ind:** Electronics. **Acq:** Purchase. **Dist:** Hewlett-Packard Media Solutions.

Amputee Gait Activities 1974
A brief explanation and demonstration of the mauch S-N-S hydraulic knee unit for an above knee amputee. 22m; VHS, 3/4 U, Special order formats. **Pr:** Ohio State University Health Sciences AV Center. **A:** College-Adult. **P:** Professional. **U:** Institution, SURA. **Hea-Sci:** Amputation. **Acq:** Purchase, Rent/Lease. **Dist:** Ohio State University.

Amputee with an Axe 1973 (R) — ★½
A young boy murders his father with a tractor for no apparent reason, and amputates his own arm in the process. After a long stay in the wacky bin, he relapses upon being released. Upon finding out his mother has remarried, he decides to replace her with a succession easily kidnapped women. 90m; DVD, Streaming. **C:** Fred Holbert; Robert Knox; Angus Scrimm; Leigh Mitchell; Suzette Hamilton; Directed by Marc B. Ray; Written by Marc B. Ray; Larry Alexander; Cinematography by Stephen Burum. **A:** Sr. High-Adult. **P:** Entertainment. **U:** Home. **L:** English. **Mov-Ent. Acq:** Purchase, Rent/Lease. **Dist:** Apprehensive Films. $12.95 9.99.

Amreeka 2009 (PG-13) — ★★★
Palestinian divorced mom Muna (Faour), who lives on the West Bank, decides she and her 16-year-old son Fadi (Muallem) will have a better life joining her married sister Raghda (Abbass) in suburban Chicago. However, the U.S. has just invaded Iraq so all Arabs are under suspicion and Muna and her family face a number of indignities. Despite her professional background, the only job Muna can find is working at White Castle (a fact she keeps from her family) while Fadi tries to make his way through the hazards of high school. The cast is excellent with Faour expressing a particularly warm, bright, and strong presence. English and Arabic with subtitles. 96m; DVD, Wide. **C:** Nisreen Faour; Melkar Muallem; Hiam Abbass; Yussef Abu-Warda; Alia Shawkat; Joseph Ziegler; Directed by Cherien Dabis; Written by Cherien Dabis; Cinematography by Tobias Datum; Music by Kareem Roustom. **Pr:** Christina Piovesan; Paul Barkin; Alcina Pictures; Buffalo Gals Pictures; Eagle Vision Media Group; First Generation Films; National Geographic Cinema Ventures. **A:** Sr. High-Adult. **P:** Entertainment. **U:** Home. **L:** English, Arabic. **Mov-Ent:** Arab-America. **Acq:** Purchase. **Dist:** Virgil Films & Entertainment; Movies Unlimited. $9.99.

The Amsterdam Connection 1978 (Unrated) — ★
Film company acts as a cover for prostitution and drug smuggling, with the girls acting as international couriers. 90m; VHS, DVD. **C:** Chen Shing; Kid Sherrif; Yeung Sze; Jason Pai Piu; Fang Mui San; Directed by Fang Mui San; Lo Ke. **Pr:** K.K. Wong. **A:** Sr. High-Adult. **P:** Entertainment. **U:** Home. **Mov-Ent:** Martial Arts, Drugs, Prostitution. **Acq:** Purchase. **Dist:** Movies Unlimited. $17.99.

The Amsterdam Kill 1978 (R) — ★★
A washed-up ex-agent of the U.S. Drug Enforcement Agency is hired by a desperate U.S. Drug Enforcement Agency to hunt down the kingpin of a narcotics syndicate in Hong Kong. Tedious pace with occasional spells of violence fails to awaken somnambulent Mitchum. Shot on location in Hong Kong. 93m; VHS. **C:** Robert Mitchum; Richard Egan; Keye Luke; Leslie Nielsen; Bradford Dillman; Directed by Robert Clouse; Written by Robert Clouse. **Pr:** Columbia Pictures. **A:** Sr. High-Adult. **P:** Entertainment. **U:** Home. **Mov-Ent:** Drugs. **Acq:** Purchase. **Dist:** $9.95.

Amsterdamned 1988 (R) — ★★
A crime thriller taking place on the canals of Amsterdam featuring a serial skindiver killer who surfaces periodically to slash and splash. A steely detective fishes for clues. Dubbed. 114m; VHS, Wide. **C:** Monique Van De Ven; Huub Stapel; Hidde Maas; Serge-Henri Valcke; Wim Zomer; Tatum Dagelet; Directed by Dick Maas; Written by Dick Maas; Cinematography by Marc Felperlaan. **A:** Sr. High-Adult. **P:** Entertainment. **U:** Home. **L:** English, Spanish. **Mov-Ent:** Mystery & Suspense. **Acq:** Purchase. **Dist:** Lions Gate Television Corp. $89.98.

Amtrack: Trackside ????
Footage of more than 200 Amtrak trains filmed from 1979 through the mid-1990s. No narration or music so rail fans can hear the engines and whistles. 80m; VHS. **A:** College-Adult. **P:** Education. **U:** Home. **Gen-Edu:** Trains. **Acq:** Purchase. **Dist:** The Civil War Standard. $21.95.

Amtrak Across America: 25th Anniversary 1996
Explores the 25-year history of the passenger train service provided by Amtrak. Travels through many of the companies passenger lines while exploring the many changes the company has undertaken through its history. 30m; VHS. **A:** Jr. High-Adult. **P:** Education. **U:** Home. **Gen-Edu:** Travel, Trains, History. **Acq:** Purchase. **Dist:** Pentrex Media Group L.L.C. $19.95.

Amtrak 30: 1991-2001 ????
Watch Amtrak change from its first decades and learn about how the company is positioning itself for the future. Features footage of modern and new high-speed trains. 90m; VHS, DVD. **A:** College-Adult. **P:** Education. **U:** Home. **Gen-Edu:** Trains. **Acq:** Purchase. **Dist:** The Civil War Standard. $24.95.

Amtrak 20: 1971-1991 ????
Covers Amtrak's creation and first 20 years, including the maiden voyage from Chicago's Union Station. 95m; VHS, DVD. **A:** College-Adult. **P:** Education. **U:** Home. **Gen-Edu:** Trains. **Acq:** Purchase. **Dist:** The Civil War Standard. $24.95.

Amtrak's Auto Train 1994
Join passengers from Virginia, travelling to Florida, who not only travel with their luggage but their cars as well. Ride with the crew and get a look at not only the special carriers but other train cars. 75m; VHS. **A:** Family. **P:** Entertainment. **U:** Home. **Gen-Edu:** Trains. **Acq:** Purchase. **Dist:** Pentrex Media Group L.L.C. $39.95.

Amtrak's California Zephyr ????
Ride from Chicago to the West Coast in the cab of a California Zephyr, meeting train crew and viewing famous landmarks along the way. 48m; VHS, DVD. **A:** College-Adult. **P:** Education. **U:** Home. **Gen-Edu:** Trains. **Acq:** Purchase. **Dist:** The Civil War Standard. $24.95.

Amtrak's Northeast Corridor: Cab Ride—Washington D.C. to Philadelphia 1992
Ride along in the cab of an Amtrak train at speeds of up to 125 mph from Washington, D.C. to Philadelphia. 85m; VHS. **A:** Jr. High-Adult. **P:** Entertainment. **U:** Home. **Gen-Edu:** Trains, Travel. **Acq:** Purchase. **Dist:** Pentrex Media Group L.L.C. $29.95.

Amtrak's Northeast Corridor: New York City to Philadelphia 1992
Glide along the southern section of this Amtrak track that mixes modern technology with turn-of-the-century equipment. Also visit towers in New York and Philadelphia that will soon be replaced. 80m; VHS. **A:** Jr. High-Adult. **P:** Entertainment. **U:** Home. **Gen-Edu:** Trains, Travel. **Acq:** Purchase. **Dist:** Pentrex Media Group L.L.C. $39.95.

Amtrak's Northeast Corridor: Philadelphia to Washington, D.C. 1992
Explore this section of one of Amtrak's most traveled lines. Includes a tour of a state-of-the-art computer dispatching center, a ride in the cab of an AEM7 locomotive, and visits to a variety of stops along the way, including Wilmington, Delaware, Eddystone, Pennsylvania, and Baltimore, Maryland. 80m; VHS. **A:** Jr. High-Adult. **P:** Entertainment. **U:** Home. **Gen-Edu:** Trains, Travel. **Acq:** Purchase. **Dist:** Pentrex Media Group L.L.C. $39.95.

Amtrak's Turbo Trains—Cab Ride 1992
All aboard for a scenic trip in the countryside of New York State. On this journey, you'll speed through a tunnel carved out of the hillside, and behold glorious bridges spanning one of this country's most praised rivers, the Hudson. 30m; VHS. **A:** Jr. High-Adult. **P:** Entertainment. **U:** Home. **Gen-Edu:** Trains. **Acq:** Purchase. **Dist:** Pentrex Media Group L.L.C. $19.95.

Amuck! 1971 (Unrated) — ★★½
Vintage early '70s Euro-sleaze makes a belated debut on home video. Greta (Bouchet) is hired to be a secretary to world-famous author Richard Stuart (Granger). But Stuart's wife Eleanora (Neri) has designs on the young woman, and Greta has secrets of her own. Nostalgic treat for fans of the era. 98m; DVD. **C:** Farley Granger; Barbara Bouchet; Rosalba Neri; Umberto Raho; Patrizia Viotti; Dino Mele; Petar Martinovic; Nino Segurini; Directed by Silvio Amandio; Written by Silvio Amandio; Cinematography by Aldo Giordani; Music by Teo Usuelli. **A:** College-Adult. **P:** Entertainment. **U:** Home. **Mov-Ent.** **Acq:** Purchase. **Dist:** Luminous Film & Video Wurks.

Amusement 2008 (R) — ★
There's nothing amusing about it. Longtime friends Tabitha, Shelby, and Lisa are held hostage in a maze of cells and traps as someone wants revenge for a long-past incident from their school days. 85m; DVD, Blu-Ray. **C:** Katheryn Winnick; Laura Breckenridge; Jessica Lucas; Tad Hilgenbrink; Reid Scott; Directed by John Simpson; Written by Jake Wade Hall; Cinematography by Mark Garret; Music by Marco Beltrami. **A:** Sr. High-Adult. **P:** Entertainment. **U:** Home. **Mov-Ent:** Horror. **Acq:** Purchase. **Dist:** Warner Home Video, Inc.

Amusement Parks: The Pursuit of Fun ????
History and tours of amusement parks throughout the United States. 54m; VHS. **A:** Family. **P:** Entertainment. **U:** Home. **Gen-Edu:** Circuses. **Acq:** Purchase. **Dist:** Janson Media. $19.95.

Amy 198?
This film teaches young people how to become safety conscious baby sitters through demonstrations on fire safety, injury prevention and first aid. 17m; VHS, 3/4 U. **Pr:** National Safety Council. **A:** College-Adult. **P:** Education. **U:** Institution. **Gen-Edu:** Safety Education. **Acq:** Rent/Lease. **Dist:** National Safety Council, California Chapter, Film Library.

Amy 1981 (G) — ★★½
Set in the early 1900s, the story follows the experiences of a woman after she leaves her well-to-do husband to teach at a school for the deaf and blind. Eventually she organizes a football game between the handicapped kids and the other children in the neighborhood. Good Disney family fare. 100m; VHS, DVD, Streaming. **C:** Jenny Agutter; Barry Newman; Kathleen Nolan; Margaret O'Brien; Nanette Fabray; Chris Robinson; Louis Fant; Directed by Vincent McEveety; Music by Robert F. Brunner. **Pr:** Walt Disney Studios. **A:** Family. **P:** Entertainment. **U:** Home. **Mov-Ent:** Blindness, Deafness, Education. **Acq:** Purchase. **Dist:** Walt Disney Studios Home Entertainment. $69.95.

Amy 1998 — ★★½
Quirky to say the least. Nine-year-old Amy (De Roma) has been an elective deaf-mute since witnessing the death of her rock star father Will (Barker), who was electrocuted during a concert. The only way Amy does communiate is through music—something discovered by luckless musician Robert (Mendelsohn). Meanwhile, Amy's bitter mom Tanya (Griffiths) is trying to avoid the welfare authorities who want to take charge of Amy's schooling and treatment. Uneasy mix of genres but the performance by child actress De Roma is remarkable. 103m; VHS. **C:** Rachel Griffiths; Alana De Roma; Ben Mendelsohn; Nick Barker; Kerry Armstrong; Directed by Nadia Tass; Written by David Parker; Cinematography by David Parker; Music by Phil Judd. **Pr:** Nadia Tass; David Parker; Nadia Tass; David Parker; Cascade Films; Village Roadshow Pictures. **A:** Sr. High-Adult. **P:** Entertainment. **U:** Home. **Mov-Ent:** Comedy-Drama, Handicapped. **Acq:** Purchase. **Dist:** Not Yet Released.

Amy! and Frida Kahlo and Tina Modotti 1980 (Unrated)
"Amy!" is a documentary on Amy Johnson, the first woman to fly solo from Great Britain to Australia, and features newsreel footage of her arrival, dramatic recreations of pivotal events in her life, and contemporary feminist discussions. "Frida Kahlo and Tina Modotti" is a short film examining the painter's and photographer's themes and styles as they worked during the aftermath of the Mexican Revolution. 59m; DVD. **A:** Adult. **P:** Education. **U:** Institution. **Gen-Edu:** Women, Art & Artists, Aeronautics. **Acq:** Purchase. **Dist:** Women Make Movies. $295.00.

Amy and the Angel 1982
Depressed about her parents' divorce and her own lack of a social life, Amy contemplates suicide. Her guardian angel then appears and shows her what things would have been like if she had never been born. 46m; VHS, CC. **C:** Helen Slater; James Earl Jones; Hermione Gingold; Matthew Modine. **Pr:** Learning Corporation of America. **A:** Jr. High-Sr. High. **P:** Education. **U:** Home. **Gen-Edu:** Adolescence, Literature, Suicide. **Acq:** Purchase. **Dist:** Phoenix Learning Group.

Amy Bento's "A Team" Boot Camp 2006
Bento leads a series of six challenging cardio/toning intervals for advanced exercisers. Uses a variety of equipment, including a step, dumbbells, barbell, stability ball, and X-ertube. 64m; DVD. **A:** Adult. **P:** Instruction. **U:** Home. **Hea-Sci:** Fitness/Exercise. **Acq:** Purchase. **Dist:** Collage Video Specialties, Inc.

Amy Bento's Advanced Step Challenge 2006
Intense, high-energy workout, with Bento leading advanced exercisers through challenging step sequences, ending with seven minutes of plyometric drills. 55m; DVD. **A:** Adult. **P:** Instruction. **U:** Home. **Hea-Sci:** Fitness/Exercise. **Acq:** Purchase. **Dist:** Collage Video Specialties, Inc.

Amy Bento's Cardio Pump Hi/Lo 2006
Bento combines an intense, compact cardio segment with a toning segment that uses a variety of equipment, including dumbbells, X-ertube, stability ball, and step. 49m; DVD. **A:** Adult. **P:** Instruction. **U:** Home. **Hea-Sci:** Fitness/Exercise. **Acq:** Purchase. **Dist:** Collage Video Specialties, Inc.

The Amy Fisher Story 1993 (Unrated) — ★★
Amy Fisher wishes she looked this good. Perhaps if she did, she could be acting in TV movies like Barrymore instead of providing fodder for them. The ABC account draws from a variety of sources to dramatize the relationship between Amy and her married, ahem, friend, and Amy's subsequent attack on his wife. Although it tries not to take sides, it does include some pretty hot sex scenes which could be why this docudrama garnered the highest ratings of the three network productions released on TV. See also: "Casualties of Love: The 'Long Island Lolita' Story" and "Lethal Lolita—Amy Fisher: My Story." 93m; VHS, DVD. **C:** Drew Barrymore; Anthony John (Tony) Denison; Harley Jane Kozak; Tom Mason; Laurie Paton; Ken Pogue; Linda Darlow; Garry Davey; Dwight McFee; Gabe Khouth; Philip Granger; Stephen Cooper; Directed by Andy Tennant; Written by Janet Brownell; Cinematography by Glen MacPherson; Music by Michael Hoenig. **Pr:** George Perkins; Andrew Adelson; Andrew Adelson Company; ABC Productions. **A:** Sr. High-Adult. **P:** Entertainment. **U:** Home. **Mov-Ent:** Documentary Films, TV Movies, Sex & Sexuality. **Acq:** Purchase. **Dist:** Anchor Bay Entertainment.

Amy Grant: Age to Age 1985 (Unrated)
Amy Grant performs such contemporary gospel favorites as "El Shadai" and "Sing Your Praise to the Lord" in this concert, which is available in VHS Dolby hi-fi Stereo and Beta hi-fi Stereo. 90m; VHS. **C:** Amy Grant. **Pr:** A&M Video. **A:** Jr. High-Adult. **P:** Entertainment. **U:** Home. **Mov-Ent:** Music--Performance, Religion, Music Video. **Acq:** Purchase. **Dist:** Music Video Distributors; Sony Pictures Home Entertainment Inc. $19.95.

Amy Grant: Find a Way 1985
Amy Grant delivers her own brand of gospel rock in this collection of three music videos from her "Unguarded" album. In VHS Dolby Hi-Fi Stereo and Beta Hi-Fi Stereo. 30m; VHS. **Pr:** A&M Video. **A:** Jr. High-Adult. **P:** Religious. **U:** Home. **Mov-Ent:** Music Video, Religion. **Acq:** Purchase. **Dist:** Sony Pictures Home Entertainment Inc.; Music Video Distributors. $14.98.

Amy Grant: Heart in Motion 1991
Amy Grant videos, including her most recent, "That's What Love is For." Interview footage and three more videos, including her big commercial hit "Next Time I Fall in Love," the duet with Peter Cetera. 30m; VHS. **C:** Amy Grant. **Pr:** A&M Video. **A:** Jr. High-Adult. **P:** Entertainment. **U:** Home. **Mov-Ent:** Music Video. **Acq:** Purchase. **Dist:** Music Video Distributors. $14.95.

Amy-on-the-Lips 1987
This tape focuses on society's changing attitudes and the issues surrounding education for the handicapped. 32m; VHS, 3/4 U, EJ, Special order formats. **TV Std:** NTSC, PAL, SECAM. **A:** Primary-Adult. **P:** Education. **U:** Institution, CCTV, SURA. **Hea-Sci:** Handicapped. **Acq:** Purchase, Rent/Lease. **Dist:** Phoenix Learning Group. $495.00.

Amyotrophic Lateral Sclerosis 1971
A demonstration of atrophy of the arms and hands, fasciculations of the tongue, biceps and hand. (Also known as Lou Gehrig's Disease.) 23m; VHS, 3/4 U, Special order formats. **Pr:** Ohio State University Health Sciences AV Center. **A:** College-Adult. **P:** Professional. **U:** Institution, SURA. **Hea-Sci:** Neurology, Diseases. **Acq:** Purchase, Rent/Lease. **Dist:** Ohio State University.

Amy's O 2002 (Unrated) — ★★
Amy (Davis) is a twentysomething L.A. single who has penned a self-help book about why women don't need men to feel complete. She's successful but doesn't believe her own work and is lonely and looking. She meets radio shock jock Matthew Starr (Chinlund), who turns out to be a pretty decent guy, although he's got some personal quirks Amy comes to resent. And Matthew finds some things about Amy he could live without. Of course, they're meant to be together if they could just get past their own egos. 87m; VHS, DVD. **C:** Julie Davis; Nick (Nicholas) Chinlund; Caroline Aaron; Mitchell Whitfield; Mary Ellen Trainor; Charles Cioffi; Tina Lifford; Jennifer Bransford; Directed by Julie Davis; Written by Julie Davis; Cinematography by Mark Mervis; Goran Paviceric. **A:** Sr. High-Adult. **P:** Entertainment. **U:** Home. **Mov-Ent:** Comedy--Romantic. **Acq:** Purchase. **Dist:** Showtime Networks Inc.

An I for An I 1987
Lawrence Andrews' work confronts racist culture and its effects on the mind and the body as it pleads for an alternative to violence. 18m; VHS, 3/4 U. **A:** College-Adult. **P:** Entertainment. **U:** Institution. **Fin-Art:** Video. **Acq:** Purchase, Rent/Lease. **Dist:** Video Data Bank.

Ana Gabriel: Altos de Chavon-Los Dos Conciertos 2013 (Unrated)
Live concert performance by Ana Gabriel divided between traditional Mariachi music and her more standard pop offerings. 175m; DVD, Blu-Ray. **A:** Primary-Adult. **P:** Entertainment. **U:** Home. **L:** English. **Mov-Ent:** Music--Performance, Music--Pop/Rock. **Acq:** Purchase. **Dist:** Sony Pictures Home Entertainment Inc. $24.98 18.98.

Ana In the Rainforest 1992
Features Ana's dream, which takes her to a rainforest where she learns its inhabitants, beauty, and life cycle. Reveals the danger our rainforests are in. Received recognition from: N. American Association for Environmental Education Film Festival; KidFilm/USA Film Festival. 11m; VHS, Special order formats. **A:** Primary. **P:** Education. **U:** Institution. **Chl-Juv:** Forests & Trees, Animals. **Acq:** Purchase, Rent/Lease. **Dist:** Bullfrog Films, Inc. $195.00.

Ana Mendieta: Fuego de Tierre 1987
Life and work of Cuban-born American artist Ana Mendieta. Interview footage and the artist's own filmed records of her earthworks and performances reveal her feminist political consciousness and poetic vision. 52m; VHS. **A:** Adult. **P:** Education. **U:** Institution, BCTV. **Gen-Edu:** Women, Art & Artists. **Acq:** Purchase, Rent/Lease. **Dist:** Women Make Movies. $225.00.

Anabolic Steroids 1992
Demonstrates that teens can attain their personal goals without resorting to drug use. 21m; VHS. **A:** Jr. High-Sr. High. **P:** Education. **U:** Institution, Home. **Gen-Edu:** Education, Drugs. **Acq:** Purchase. **Dist:** Cambridge Educational. $99.95.

Anabolic Steroids: Bound to Lose 1989
Teens share their experiences with steroids, emphasizing adverse side effects and encouraging alternative routes to better athletic performance and body image. Includes discussion guide. 21m; VHS. **A:** Jr. High-Sr. High. **P:** Education. **U:** Institution. **Hea-Sci:** Health Education, Drug Abuse. **Acq:** Purchase. **Dist:** United Learning Inc. $95.00.

Anabolic Steroids: The Quest for Superman 1992
The dangers of steroid use are highlighted in this revealing program. Features interviews with professionals and scientists. Granted an award at the American Film & Video Festival, the International Non-Broadcast Media Competition, and a CINDY award. 30m; VHS. **A:** Jr. High-Sr. High. **P:** Instruction. **U:** Institution, Home. **Spo-Rec:** Weight Lifting. **Acq:** Purchase. **Dist:** Cambridge Educational; Human Relations Media. $149.95.

Anaconda 1996 (PG-13) — ★★½
Snakes—lots and lots of snakes. Teeny baby snakes, little snakes, medium-sized snakes, large snakes, and one gigantic 40-foot long snake that likes to swallow people and then vomit them up again (the better to have room to swallow somebody else). Oh yeah, the minimal plot concerns a documentary film crew traveling the Amazon River looking for a legendary Indian tribe. They not only have to contend with the snakes but with crazy, snake-obsessed guide Paul Sarone (Voight). The actors react appropriately to becoming snake food. 90m; VHS, DVD, Blu-Ray, CC. **C:** Jon Voight; Jennifer Lopez; Ice Cube; Eric Stoltz; Owen Wilson; Kari Wuhrer; Jonathan Hyde; Vincent Castellanos; Danny Trejo; Directed by Luis Llosa; Written by Jim Cash; Jack Epps, Jr.; Hans Bauer; Cinematography by Bill Butler; Music by Randy Edelman. **Pr:** Verna Harrah; Leonard Rabinowitz; Carole Little; Susan Ruskin; CL Cinema Line Films Corp; Columbia Pictures. **A:** Jr. High-Adult. **P:** Entertainment. **U:** Home. **Mov-Ent.** **Acq:** Purchase. **Dist:** Sony Pictures Home Entertainment Inc.

Anaconda 3: The Offspring 2008 (R) — ★
It was filmed in Romania, has bad CGI, and a nonsensical plot—yep, it's another Sci-Fi Channel treasure. Scientist Amanda (Allen) has been working with Murdoch (Rhys-Davies), who has done some genetic tinkering that resulted in a mutated 60-foot long anaconda with a machete growing out of its tail

(good for the gore factor but really silly looking). Of course the beastie gets loose and must be eradicated, which is where Hammett (Hasselhoff) and his mercenaries come in. 91m; DVD. **C:** John Rhys-Davies; David Hasselhoff; Anthony Green; Crystal Allen; Patrick Regis; Directed by Don E. Fauntleroy; Written by Nicholas Davidoff; David C. Olson; Cinematography by Don E. Fauntleroy; Music by Peter Meisner. **A:** Sr. High-Adult. **P:** Entertainment. **U:** Home. **Mov-Ent.** **Acq:** Purchase. **Dist:** Sony Pictures Home Entertainment Inc.

Anacondas: The Hunt for the Blood Orchid 2004 (PG-13) — ★★
An enjoyably trashy quasi-sequel to the 1997 flick finds even more (and bigger) snakes to swallow the generally no-name cast. A pharmaceutical company sponsors a scientific expedition along a Borneo river to hunt for the rare title flower, which may extend life and youth. There's the usual mix of characters: fearless riverboat captain (Messner), arrogant scientist (Marsden), computer geek (Bryd), babe (Strickland), etc., and the standard situations: ramshackle boat, dense jungle, hungry snakes, and a really clever monkey for a little variety. The director and cast handle their parts efficiently and they know enough not to take it too seriously. Neither should you. 93m; VHS, DVD, UMD. **C:** Johnny Messner; KaDee Strickland; Matthew Marsden; Eugene Byrd; Denis Arndt; Morris Chestnut; Salli Richardson-Whitfield; Nicholas Gonzalez; Directed by Dwight Little; Written by Michael Miner; John Claflin; Daniel Zelman; Edward Neumeier; Cinematography by Stephen Windon; Music by Nerida Tyson-Chew. **Pr:** Verna Harrah; Middle Fork; Screen Gems; Sony Pictures Entertainment. **A:** Jr. High-Adult. **P:** Entertainment. **U:** Home. **Mov-Ent:** South America, Rivers & Streams. **Acq:** Purchase. **Dist:** Sony Pictures Home Entertainment Inc. $26.96.

Anacondas: Trail of Blood 2009 (R) — ★
Yep, SciFi Channel does it again with cheap CGI that can't even get the snakes right (there's a couple of decent deaths which is why this isn't a woofer). In this fourth entry, scientist Amanda (Allen) has turned into a good girl and is trying to foil a corporate plot to get the super-snake's priceless venom. 88m; DVD. **C:** John Rhys-Davies; Linden Ashby; Crystal Allen; Calin Stanciu; Danny Midwinter; Ana Ularu; Directed by Don E. Fauntleroy; Written by David C. Olson; Cinematography by Don E. Fauntleroy; Music by Peter Meisner. **A:** Sr. High-Adult. **P:** Entertainment. **U:** Home. **Mov-Ent:** Science. **Acq:** Purchase. **Dist:** Sony Pictures Home Entertainment Inc.

Anaerobic Digestion: Is It Right for Your Farm? 1990
Covers anaerobic digestion and six major issues one should consider in utilizing this technology. Also contains both positive and negative views on operation of a digestive system. 22m; VHS. **A:** Sr. High-Adult. **P:** Education. **U:** Institution. **Hea-Sci:** Digestive System, Agriculture. **Acq:** Purchase, Rent/Lease. **Dist:** Cornell University. $18.00.

Anaheim Angels: Vintage World Series Films 20??
Presents the A&E cable channel special on the Major League Baseball Anaheim Angels and their 2002 victory over the San Francisco Giants, which marked the first occurrence of two wild card teams facing off in the World Series. 93m; DVD. **A:** Family. **P:** Entertainment. **U:** Home, CATV. **Spo-Rec:** Television Series, Documentary Films, Biography: Sports. **Acq:** Purchase. **Dist:** A&E Television Networks L.L.C. $19.95.

Anais Nin: Her Diary 197?
Erotic writer Anais Nin recreates her impressions of Europe in the 1930s as she reads passages from her diary. 30m/B/W; VHS, 3/4 U, EJ, Q. **Pr:** WCBS New York; Camera Three Productions. **A:** Sr. High-Adult. **P:** Education. **U:** Institution, SURA. **Gen-Edu:** Literature--Modern. **Acq:** Duplication, Free Duplication. **Dist:** Camera Three Productions, Inc.; Creative Arts Television Archive.

Anais Nin Observed 19??
Series of interviews, completed in 1973, where diarist and erotica writer Nin discusses her life and philosophy as well as her friendships with Henry Miller, D.H. Lawrence, Martha Graham, Frank Lloyd Wright, and others. 60m; VHS. **A:** Adult. **P:** Education. **U:** Home. **Gen-Edu:** Documentary Films, Biography, Literature--Modern. **Acq:** Purchase. **Dist:** Mystic Fire Video; Direct Cinema Ltd. $29.95.

Analgesic Therapy for Problem Patients 1973
The comparative pharmacology of aspirin and acetominophen is presented in this program. 30m; VHS, 3/4 U, Special order formats. **Pr:** Ohio State University Health Sciences AV Center. **A:** College-Adult. **P:** Professional. **U:** Institution, SURA. **Hea-Sci:** Drugs. **Acq:** Purchase, Rent/Lease. **Dist:** Ohio State University.

Analog IC Layout Design Considerations 1982
These lectures consider most aspects of analog IC layout design. 75m/B/W; VHS, 3/4 U, EJ. **Pr:** University of Arizona. **A:** College. **P:** Vocational. **U:** Institution, CCTV, Home. **Gen-Edu:** Electronics. **Acq:** Purchase, Rent/Lease. **Dist:** University of Arizona.
Indiv. Titles: 1. An Introduction, High Current Metal Considerations and Dedicated Crossunders 2. Dedicated Crossunders, Pinched Resistors and Popular Merged Devices with a Parasitic Latch 3. Merged Latches and the Substrate Injection of Electrons 4. Substrate Injection of Electrons, Miscellaneous Topics and Matching 5. Matching 6. MOSFETS, OSFETS and High Power Layout.

Analysis of Behavior 1993
Part 10 of the 11-part Biology, Brain, and Behavior Series. Provides exercises in the observation and interpretation of animal behavior with an emphasis on behavior patterns that may not be immediately detectable. Uses a group of gulls for the exercises. 40m; VHS, SVS, 3/4 U. **A:** College-Adult. **P:** Education. **U:** Institution. **Hea-Sci:** Biology, Birds, Animals. **Acq:** Purchase. **Dist:** Encyclopedia Britannica. $149.00.

Analysis of Dental Malpractice—Current Medical and Legal Perspectives 19??
Describes the legal responsibility of the dentist and dental treatments. Covers surgical complications, dental implants, root canals, crown and bridge procedures, myofascial pain, lack of informed consent, brain injuries, death, failure to advise, and patient care. Includes program syllabus. 120m; VHS. **A:** College-Adult. **P:** Education. **U:** Institution. **Hea-Sci:** Dentistry, Law--Medical. **Acq:** Purchase. **Dist:** MediLegal Institute. $295.00.

Analyze That 2002 (R) — ★½
Woefully inferior sequel finds shrink Dr. Sobel (Crystal, becoming more irritating with every film), who's trying to deal with his father's death, also helping out mobster Vitti (De Niro), whose life is being threatened by mob factions with boundary issues. After Vitti fakes a breakdown to escape jailhouse hitmen, Sobel is forced by the FBI to house and rehabilitate him, incurring the wrath of his loving but running-out-of patience wife Laura (the sadly underused Kudrow). There are a few laughs to be had, mostly compliments of De Niro, but not enough to keep the inevitable "Analyze the Other Thing" off the Least Wanted list. 95m; VHS, DVD. **C:** Billy Crystal; Robert De Niro; Lisa Kudrow; Joe (Johnny) Viterelli; Reg Rogers; Cathy Moriarty; John Finn; Kyle Sabihy; Callie (Calliope) Thorne; Pat Cooper; Frank Gio; Donnamarie Recco; Directed by Harold Ramis; Written by Harold Ramis; Peter Steinfeld; Peter Tolan; Cinematography by Ellen Kuras; Music by David Holmes. **Pr:** Paula Weinstein; Jane Rosenthal; Village Roadshow Pictures; NPV Entertainment; Tribeca Productions; Face; Baltimore Spring Creek Pictures; Warner Bros. **A:** Sr. High-Adult. **P:** Entertainment. **U:** Home. **Mov-Ent:** Psychiatry, Federal Bureau of Investigation (FBI). **Acq:** Purchase. **Dist:** Warner Home Video, Inc.

Analyze This 1998 (R) — ★★★
Robert De Niro stars as anxiety-stricken mob boss Paul Vitti. He begins to see suburban shrink Ben (Crystal), and is so pleased with the results that he strong-arms the doc into seeing him whenever he wants. Unfortunately for Ben and fiance Laura (Kudrow), that usually happens to be when they're trying to get married. Palminteri is a rival gangster with whom Vitti "seeks closure." De Niro expertly winks at the mob genre (which he helped create) without losing the air of menace that surrounds the good fella character. His performance carries the movie despite the somewhat hokey ending. It's De Niro's underworld, Billy's just living in it. 110m; VHS, DVD, CC. **C:** Robert De Niro; Billy Crystal; Lisa Kudrow; Chazz Palminteri; Joe (Johnny) Viterelli; Bill Macy; Leo Rossi; Rebecca Schull; Molly Shannon; Max Casella; Pat Cooper; Richard C. Castellano; Jimmie Ray Weeks; Elizabeth Bracco; Tony Darrow; Kyle Sabihy; Donnamarie Recco; Directed by Harold Ramis; Written by Harold Ramis; Peter Tolan; Kenneth Lonergan; Cinematography by Stuart Dryburgh; Music by Howard Shore. **Pr:** Paula Weinstein; Jane Rosenthal; Baltimore Pictures; Spring Creek Productions; Tribeca Productions; Warner Bros. **A:** Sr. High-Adult. **P:** Entertainment. **U:** Home. **Mov-Ent:** Psychiatry, Federal Bureau of Investigation (FBI). **Acq:** Purchase. **Dist:** Warner Home Video, Inc.

Analyzing for Training 1981
Supervisors are shown how to establish performance standards for jobs and how to do a simple task analysis. From the "Supervisor and OJT" series. 12m; VHS, 3/4 U. **Pr:** Resources for Education and Management. **A:** Adult. **P:** Professional. **U:** Institution, CCTV. **Bus-Ind:** Personnel Management. **Acq:** Purchase. **Dist:** Resources for Education & Management, Inc.

Analyzing Our Time Usage 1972
Two methods for managing time-breaking down the types of work we do and setting priorities-are discussed. 11m; VHS, 3/4 U. **Pr:** Resources for Education and Management. **A:** Adult. **P:** Professional. **U:** Institution, CCTV. **Bus-Ind:** Management. **Acq:** Purchase. **Dist:** Resources for Education & Management, Inc.

Analyzing the Communication Environment ACE: An Inventory of Ways to Encourage Communication in Functional Activities 199?
By evaluating and adjusting the classroom environment using the ACE method, students from pre-school age through adolescence are motivated to communicate and participate in activities within a safe and familiar atmosphere. 90m; VHS. **A:** Adult. **P:** Education. **U:** Institution. **Gen-Edu:** Deafness, Speech, Communication. **Acq:** Purchase. **Dist:** Communication Therapy Skill Builders. $99.00.

Anamorph 2007 (R) — ★½
Psycho-thriller gets too arty for its own good. Stan Aubray (Dafoe) is an OCD NYC police detective assigned to the case of a serial killer who arranges his victims using an artistic technique called anamorphosis (manipulating perspective). The killings may be related to a closed case where Aubray killed the prime suspect. Are the new murders being done by a copycat or did Aubray kill the wrong person? 107m; DVD. **C:** Willem Dafoe; Scott Speedman; Clea DuVall; James Rebhorn; Peter Stormare; Amy Carlson; Directed by H.S. Miller; Written by H.S. Miller; Tom Phelan; Cinematography by Fred Murphy; Music by Reinhold Heil; Johnny Klimek. **A:** Sr. High-Adult. **P:** Entertainment. **U:** Home. **Mov-Ent:** Mystery & Suspense, Art & Artists. **Acq:** Purchase. **Dist:** Genius.com Incorporated.

Ananse's Farm 1989
A folktale from Ghana about a spider with good intentions, who uses the wrong means to try to achieve the desired result. 8m; VHS, 3/4 U. **Pr:** Rene Jodoin. **A:** Jr. High-Adult. **P:** Education. **U:** Institution, SURA. **Gen-Edu:** Folklore & Legends. **Acq:** Purchase, Rent/Lease. **Dist:** National Film Board of Canada.

Anansi 1991
Anansi is a spider who manages to outwit a prideful snake but then gets caught up in his own lies. Adaptation of a Jamaican folktale which features the reggae music of UB40. 30m; VHS. **C:** Narrated by Denzel Washington. **Pr:** Rabbit Ears Productions. **A:** Family. **P:** Entertainment. **U:** Home. **Chl-Juv:** Animation & Cartoons, Folklore & Legends, Family Viewing. **Acq:** Purchase. **Dist:** Facets Multimedia Inc.; Music for Little People. $9.95.

Anansi and the Moss-Covered Rock 1990
Anansi, a trickster, uses a magical rock to fool his neighbors and steal their food. Then Little Bush Deer arrives and tricks the trickster. Shot directly from the book by Eric A. Kimmel. 11m; VHS. **Pr:** Live Oak Media. **A:** Preschool-Primary. **P:** Entertainment. **U:** Institution, Home. **Chl-Juv:** Storytelling. **Acq:** Purchase. **Dist:** Live Oak Media. $36.95.

Anansi Goes Fishing 1992
Anansi's plans to let Turtle do all the work while fishing are challenged when Turtle teaches the spider how to fish and make nets. Shot directly from the book by Eric A. Kimmel. 11m; VHS. **Pr:** Live Oak Media. **A:** Preschool-Primary. **P:** Entertainment. **U:** Home, Institution. **Chl-Juv:** Storytelling. **Acq:** Purchase. **Dist:** Live Oak Media. $36.95.

Anansi the Spider 1969
Anansi, a folk hero of Ghana's Ashanti people, falls into a river and is swallowed by a fish. His six sons attempt to save him. 10m; VHS, 3/4 U, Special order formats. **Pr:** Gerald McDermott. **A:** Primary-Jr. High. **P:** Entertainment. **U:** Institution. **Chl-Juv:** Folklore & Legends. **Acq:** Purchase. **Dist:** Home Vision Cinema.

Anarchism in America 1982
The influence of the anarchist philosophy on recent American political struggles. The film shows how the movement began in the United States, fusing with 19th century traditions of individualism and affecting modern conflicts such as the anti-Vietnam and nuclear movements. 75m; 3/4 U, Special order formats. **Pr:** Pacific Street Films. **A:** Sr. High-Adult. **P:** Education. **U:** Institution. **Gen-Edu:** Philosophy & Ideology, History--U.S. **Acq:** Purchase. **Dist:** The Cinema Guild.

Anasazi: The Ancient Ones 19??
Provides insight into the heritage and history of the Anasazi tribe, showing how their traditions are still alive in the Hopi and Pueblo Indians of the American Southwest. 24m; VHS. **A:** Jr. High-Adult. **P:** Education. **U:** Institution. **Gen-Edu:** History--U.S., Native Americans. **Acq:** Purchase. **Dist:** Educational Video Network. $39.95.

Anastasia 1956 — ★★★½
Bergman won her second Oscar, and deservedly so, for her classic portrayal of the amnesia victim chosen by Russian expatriate Brynner to impersonate Anastasia, the last surviving member of the Romanoff dynasty. As such, she becomes part of a scam to collect millions of rubles deposited in a foreign bank by her supposed father, the now-dead Czar. But is she just impersonating the princess? Brynner as the scheming White General and Hayes as the Grand Duchess who needs to be convinced turn in fine performances as well. Based on Marcelle Maurette's play. 105m; VHS, DVD, Wide. **C:** Ingrid Bergman; Yul Brynner; Helen Hayes; Akim Tamiroff; Martita Hunt; Felix Aylmer; Ivan Desny; Sacha (Sascha) Pitoeff; Directed by Anatole Litvak; Written by Arthur Laurents; Cinematography by Jack Hildyard. **Pr:** Fox. **A:** Sr. High-Adult. **P:** Entertainment. **U:** Home. **Mov-Ent:** Drama, Classic Films, USSR. **Awds:** Oscars '56: Actress (Bergman); Golden Globes '57: Actress--Drama (Bergman); N.Y. Film Critics '56: Actress (Bergman). **Acq:** Purchase. **Dist:** Wellspring Media.

Anastasia 1996
Tells the story of Anastasia, the young princess who must regain her identity when Rasputin betrays her royal family during the Russian Revolution. 48m; VHS. **A:** Preschool. **P:** Entertainment. **U:** Home. **Gen-Edu:** Fiction--Children. **Acq:** Purchase. **Dist:** Random House of Canada Ltd. $9.98.

Anastasia 1997 (G) — ★★½
Let's face it, this is a pretty weird story to turn into a cartoon fairy tale. Fox's first entry into the Disney-dominated full-length animated musical fray is the story of Princess Anastasia and the fall of the Romanov empire. She has been missing ever since the evil Rasputin put a curse on the Romanov family and started the Russian Revolution (Lenin must have flunked the screen test. Not "toon" enough). Ten years later, con artist Dimitri and ex-aristocrat Vladimir try to convince orphaned 18-year-old Anya that she's the ex-royal so they can claim a reward from the princess' grandmother. Little do they know that she actually is the lost princess, but they must battle Rasputin and his albino bat henchman to put things right. Among the big names lending their voices are Meg Ryan, John Cusack (Cossack?), and Christopher Lloyd. Now let me tell you how the Katzenjammer Kids started WWII. . . 90m; VHS, DVD. **C:** Voice(s) by Meg Ryan; John Cusack; Kelsey Grammer; Angela Lansbury; Christopher Lloyd; Hank Azaria; Bernadette Peters; Kirsten Dunst; Directed by Don Bluth; Gary Goldman; Written by Bruce Graham; Susan Gauthier; Bob Tzudiker; Noni White; Music by David Newman. **Pr:** 20th Century-Fox. **A:** Family. **P:** Entertainment. **U:** Home. **Mov-Ent:** Animation & Cartoons, Family Viewing, USSR. **Acq:** Purchase. **Dist:** Fox Home Entertainment.

Anastasia: The Mystery of Anna 1986 (Unrated) — ★★½
Irving stars as Anna Anderson, a woman who claimed to be the Grand Duchess Anastasia, the sole surviving daughter of

Russian Czar Nicholas II. A powerful epic reliving her experience of royalty, flight from execution, and struggle to retain her heritage. The story of Anastasia remains as one of the greatest dramatic mysteries of the 20th century. Adapted from the book "Anastasia: The Riddle of Anna Anderson" by Peter Kurth. 190m; VHS, DVD. **C:** Amy Irving; Olivia de Havilland; Jan Niklas; Nicolas Surovy; Susan Lucci; Elke Sommer; Edward Fox; Claire Bloom; Omar Sharif; Rex Harrison; Directed by Marvin J. Chomsky; Written by James Goldman. **Pr:** Telecom Entertainment. **A:** Sr. High-Adult. **P:** Entertainment. **U:** Home. **Mov-Ent:** Drama, USSR, TV Movies. **Acq:** Purchase, Rent/Lease. **Dist:** PBS Home Video; Fusion Video. $79.95.

Anatomical Transurethral Resection of the Prostate 1975
The program gives maximum unobstructed viewing of this procedure as well as its anatomical considerations. 22m; 3/4 U. **Pr:** New Jersey Medical School. **A:** College-Adult. **P:** Education. **U:** Institution, CCTV. **Hea-Sci:** Urology. **Acq:** Purchase. **Dist:** New Jersey Medical School.

Anatomy 2000 (R) — ★★★
Medical student Paula Henning (Potente) is accepted into a prestigious Heidelberg anatomy class. She's carrying on the family tradition of her grandfather, who's dying in the hospital he built, and her father, with whom she disagrees on almost everything. But when she gets to the new university, she finds that very creepy stuff is going on. Medical horror/thriller is right up there with "Coma." It's inventive, grotesque, and the special effects work very well. Franka Potente shows that the impression she made in "Run, Lola, Run" was no fluke. 100m; VHS, DVD, Blu-Ray, Wide. **C:** Franka Potente; Benno Furmann; Anna Loos; Holger Spechhahn; Sebastian Blomberg; Directed by Stefan Ruzowitzky; Written by Stefan Ruzowitzky; Cinematography by Peter von Haller; Music by Marius Ruhland. **A:** Sr. High-Adult. **P:** Entertainment. **U:** Home. **Mov-Ent:** Conspiracies or Conspiracy Theories. **Acq:** Purchase. **Dist:** Sony Pictures Home Entertainment Inc.

Anatomy 2 2003 (R) — ★1/2
A cabal of mad scientists are implanting synthetic muscles into willing interns, only to learn the drugs needed to prevent their bodies from rejecting the foreign tissues drive them to insanity and murder. 101m; DVD, Blu-Ray. **C:** Ariane Schnug; August Diehl; Herbert Knaup; Birgit von Ronn; Barnaby Metschurat; Directed by Stefan Ruzowitsky; Written by Stefan Ruzowitsky; Cinematography by Andreas Berger; Music by Marius Ruhland. **A:** Sr. High-Adult. **P:** Entertainment. **U:** Home. **L:** English, French, German. **Mov-Ent. Acq:** Purchase. **Dist:** Sony Pictures Home Entertainment Inc. $9.98 24.98.

Anatomy and Injuries of the Knee 1985
Anatomical and clinical view of knee injuries and various treatments are presented. 60m; VHS, 3/4 U. **Pr:** Medi-Legal Institute. **A:** Adult. **P:** Professional. **U:** Institution, SURA. **Hea-Sci:** Anatomy & Physiology. **Acq:** Purchase. **Dist:** MediLegal Institute.

Anatomy and Injuries of the Low Back 1983
This program presents frequently seen injuries to the lower back. A descriptive anatomical overview is also provided. 120m; VHS, 3/4 U. **Pr:** Medi-Legal Institute. **A:** Sr. High-Adult. **P:** Education. **U:** Institution, SURA. **Hea-Sci:** Anatomy & Physiology, Back Disorders. **Acq:** Purchase. **Dist:** MediLegal Institute.

Anatomy and Injuries of the Lower Limbs 19??
Discusses the anatomy of the hip, knee, and pelvic regions. Covers fractures, dislocations, treatments, history and physcial examination of the knee joint, diagnostic and treatment techniques, arthrogram, conventional x-rays, MRI, arthroscopy, and foot and ankle anatomy. Includes program syllabus. 120m; VHS. **A:** College-Adult. **P:** Education. **U:** Institution. **Hea-Sci:** Law--Medical, Medical Care, Anatomy & Physiology. **Acq:** Purchase. **Dist:** MediLegal Institute. $295.00.

Anatomy and Injuries of the Neck 1985
Anatomical and clinical views of neck injuries and treatment are presented. 60m; VHS, 3/4 U. **Pr:** Medi-Legal Institute. **A:** Adult. **P:** Professional. **U:** Institution, SURA. **Hea-Sci:** Anatomy & Physiology. **Acq:** Purchase. **Dist:** MediLegal Institute.

Anatomy and Injuries of the Upper Limbs 19??
Illustrates the anatomy of the shoulder, elbow, wrist, and hand. Covers orthopedic history, physical examination techniques, dislocations, separations, rotator cuff injuries, thoracic outlet syndrome, carpal tunnel syndrome, wrist fractures, tendon and nerve injuries, and diagnosis and treatment. Includes program syllabus. 120m; VHS. **A:** College-Adult. **P:** Education. **U:** Institution. **Hea-Sci:** Law--Medical, Medical Care, Anatomy & Physiology. **Acq:** Purchase. **Dist:** MediLegal Institute. $295.00.

Anatomy and Physiology of Hearing 1985
A taped lecture about the auditory canal and outer and inner ears. 12m; VHS, 3/4 U. **Pr:** House Ear Institute. **A:** Adult. **P:** Professional. **U:** Institution, CCTV. **Hea-Sci:** Ear. **Acq:** Purchase. **Dist:** House Research Institute. $30.00.

Anatomy and Physiology of Pregnancy 1984
This revised program examine the functions of reproductive organs and outlines fertilization, sex determination, embryo development, fetus growth and physiologic development. 6m; VHS, 3/4 U, CV. **Pr:** Professional Research. **A:** College-Adult. **P:** Education. **U:** Institution, CCTV, SURA. **L:** English, Spanish. **Hea-Sci:** Pregnancy. **Acq:** Purchase, Rent/Lease. **Dist:** Discovery Education. $199.00.

Anatomy and Physiology of the Larynx 1974
The basic anatomy of the larynx is reviewed. 27m; VHS, 3/4 U, Special order formats. **Pr:** Ohio State University Health Sciences AV Center. **A:** College-Adult. **P:** Professional. **U:** Institution, SURA. **Hea-Sci:** Anatomy & Physiology. **Acq:** Purchase, Rent/Lease. **Dist:** Ohio State University.

Anatomy As a Master Image in Training Dancers 1988
Includes fundmental movement principles that complement any dance style or technique. Each exercise is broken down into components, then put together and brought up to tempo, with an explanatory narrative and musical accompaniment. 59m; VHS. **A:** Adult. **P:** Instruction. **U:** Institution. **How-Ins:** Dance--Instruction. **Acq:** Purchase. **Dist:** Princeton Book Company Publishers. $275.00.

Anatomy Examination 1971
A self evaluation including histology, cell biology, and musculoskeletal system. 30m; VHS, 3/4 U, Special order formats. **Pr:** Ohio State University Health Sciences AV Center. **A:** College-Adult. **P:** Professional. **U:** Institution, SURA. **Hea-Sci:** Anatomy & Physiology. **Acq:** Purchase, Rent/Lease. **Dist:** Ohio State University.

Anatomy of a Crisis 1983
This video documents a large-scale hazardous chemicals spill from the point of view of the authorities and agencies who dealt with the situation and cleaned it up. 23m; VHS, 3/4 U. **Pr:** USEPAP. **A:** Adult. **P:** Instruction. **U:** Institution, SURA. **Gen-Edu:** Action-Adventure. **Acq:** Purchase. **Dist:** National Audiovisual Center. $110.00.

Anatomy of a Fall 198?
The most common excuses for slips and falls in industry and hospitals are examined. 15m; VHS, 3/4 U, Special order formats. **Pr:** Altschul Group. **A:** College-Adult. **P:** Education. **U:** Institution, SURA. **Bus-Ind:** Safety Education. **Acq:** Purchase, Rent/Lease. **Dist:** National Safety Council, California Chapter, Film Library. $430.00.

Anatomy of a Filmmaker 19??
Examines the life and career of controversial director Otto Preminger. Includes film clips and interviews with Frank Sinatra, James Stewart, Michael Caine, Deborah Kerr, and others. 119m; VHS. **C:** Hosted by Burgess Meredith. **A:** College-Adult. **P:** Entertainment. **U:** Home. **Mov-Ent:** Documentary Films, Film History, Filmmaking. **Acq:** Purchase. **Dist:** Warner Home Video, Inc. $19.98.

Anatomy of a Leveraged Buyout 1989
Now everyone can pull off a leveraged buyout, because Terry Greve, a man who has been involved with eight of them, tells his secrets in this video. 60m; VHS, 3/4 U. **Pr:** Chesney Communications. **A:** Adult. **P:** Education. **U:** Institution, Home. **Bus-Ind:** Finance. **Acq:** Purchase. **Dist:** Chesney Communications. $49.95.

Anatomy of a Libel Case: Business vs. the Media 19??
Features a panel of journalists, major corporation heads, and members of the legal profession as they discuss the law and the libel suit process. Emphasis is placed on head-to-head confrontations between business and the media. 120m; VHS, 3/4 U. **A:** College-Adult. **P:** Education. **U:** Institution. **Gen-Edu:** Law, Business, Journalism. **Acq:** Purchase. **Dist:** PBS Home Video.

Anatomy of a Libel Trial: Carol Burnett vs. National Enquirer 1983
This program examines and analyzes the elements of a public figure libel trial, the 1981 Carol Burnett vs. National Enquirer, which was videotaped as an experiment by the California court system. 240m; VHS, 3/4 U. **Pr:** Practicing Law Institute. **A:** Sr. High-Adult. **P:** Education. **U:** Institution, Home. **Bus-Ind:** Law. **Acq:** Purchase, Rent/Lease. **Dist:** Practising Law Institute. $65.00.

Anatomy of a Murder 1959 — ★★★★
Considered by many to be the best courtroom drama ever made. Small-town lawyer in northern Michigan faces an explosive case as he defends an army officer who has killed a man he suspects was his philandering wife's rapist. Realistic, cynical portrayal of the court system isn't especially concerned with guilt or innocence, focusing instead on the interplay between the various courtroom characters. Classic performance by Stewart as the down home but brilliant defense lawyer who matches wits with Scott, the sophisticated prosecutor; terse and clever direction by Preminger. Though tame by today's standards, the language used in the courtroom was controversial. Filmed in upper Michigan; based on the bestseller by judge Robert Traver. 161m/B/W; VHS, DVD, Blu-Ray. **C:** James Stewart; George C. Scott; Arthur O'Connell; Ben Gazzara; Lee Remick; Orson Bean; Eve Arden; Duke Ellington; Kathryn Grant; Murray Hamilton; Joseph Welch; Directed by Otto Preminger; Written by Wendell Mayes; Cinematography by Sam Leavitt; Music by Duke Ellington. **Pr:** Otto Preminger; Otto Preminger. **A:** Jr. High-Adult. **P:** Entertainment. **U:** Home. **Mov-Ent:** Classic Films, Law. **Awds:** Natl. Film Reg. '12; N.Y. Film Critics '59: Actor (Stewart), Screenplay. **Acq:** Purchase. **Dist:** Sony Pictures Home Entertainment Inc.; Criterion Collection Inc.

The Anatomy of a Piano: How Your Grand Piano Works 1992
Familiarizes the viewer with basic information about the workings of a grand piano. Identifies its parts, their working motion, care and maintenance. Also explores common problems, their causes, and remedies. 75m; VHS. **Pr:** JMC Productions. **A:** Jr. High-Adult. **P:** Education. **U:** Institution, Home. **Gen-Edu. Acq:** Purchase. **Dist:** Instructional Video. $39.95.

Anatomy of a Psycho 1961 (Unrated) — ★
A man plans to avenge his gas chambered brother by committing mass murder. Very cheaply and poorly produced. 75m/B/W; VHS, DVD. **C:** Ronnie Burns; Pamela Lincoln; Darrell Howe; Russ Bender; Directed by Boris L. Petroff. **A:** Jr. High-Adult. **P:** Entertainment. **U:** Home. **Mov-Ent:** Mystery & Suspense. **Acq:** Purchase. **Dist:** Sinister Cinema. $16.95.

Anatomy of a Seduction 1979 — ★★
TV formula melodrama of a middle-aged divorcee's affair with her son's best friend. Age knows no boundaries when it comes to television lust. 100m; VHS, Streaming. **C:** Susan Flannery; Jameson Parker; Rita Moreno; Ed Nelson; Michael LeClair; Directed by Steven Hilliard Stern; Music by Hagood Hardy. **A:** Adult. **P:** Entertainment. **U:** Home. **Mov-Ent:** Drama, TV Movies. **Acq:** Purchase. **Dist:** $79.99.

Anatomy of a Song 1978
The cast members of "Pacific Overtures" along with composer Stephen Sondheim discuss how one song became written into the show. 30m; VHS, 3/4 U, EJ, Q. **Pr:** WCBS New York; Camera Three Productions. **A:** Sr. High-Adult. **P:** Education. **U:** Institution, SURA. **Fin-Art:** Theater. **Acq:** Duplication, Free Duplication. **Dist:** Camera Three Productions, Inc.; Creative Arts Television Archive.

Anatomy of a Springroll 1993
Paul Kwan remembers life in Saigon when he smells his mother's cooking at their new home in California. To pay his respects to his recently deceased father, he returns to his homeland to perform the rituals in the temple, visit his childhood home, and reflect on his gratitude to his parents. 56m; VHS. **A:** Sr. High-Adult. **P:** Entertainment. **U:** Institution. **Mov-Ent:** Asia, Immigration, Family. **Acq:** Purchase, Rent/Lease. **Dist:** Filmakers Library Inc. $395.00.

Anatomy of a Strike 1983
An illustration of the stages of a strike. 82m; VHS, 3/4 U. **Pr:** University of Toronto. **A:** Sr. High-Adult. **P:** Education. **U:** Institution, CCTV. **Gen-Edu:** Business, Labor & Unions. **Acq:** Purchase, Rent/Lease. **Dist:** University of Toronto.

Anatomy of a Volcano 1981
The events leading up to the eruption of Mt. St. Helens are analyzed. This production shows how scientists' instruments gave them a better understanding of how to prevent a natural wonder from inflicting catastrophic damage. 57m; VHS, 3/4 U. **Pr:** WGBH Boston. **A:** Jr. High-College. **P:** Education. **U:** Institution, SURA. **Gen-Edu:** Volcanos. **Acq:** Purchase, Rent/Lease. **Dist:** Time-Life Video and Television.

The Anatomy of an Accident 1977
This program from Allied Chemical examines the fact that most accidents are caused by several factors and, usually, several people. 15m; VHS, 3/4 U. **Pr:** Allied Chemical Corporation. **A:** College-Adult. **P:** Professional. **U:** Institution, SURA. **Bus-Ind:** Safety Education. **Acq:** Purchase, Rent/Lease. **Dist:** Learning Communications L.L.C.

Anatomy of an Embargo 1986
A look at the good and bad results that economic sanctions have had over the years. 30m; VHS, 3/4 U. **Pr:** Learning Corporation of America. **A:** Sr. High-Adult. **P:** Education. **U:** Institution, SURA. **Gen-Edu:** Economics, History--U.S. **Acq:** Purchase, Rent/Lease. **Dist:** Phoenix Learning Group. $310.00.

Anatomy of Desire 1995
Documentary examines the debate surrounding the origins of sexual orientation. 48m; VHS. **A:** College. **P:** Education. **U:** Institution. **Hea-Sci:** Documentary Films, Sex & Sexuality. **Acq:** Purchase, Rent/Lease. **Dist:** The Cinema Guild. $295.

The Anatomy of Eloquence: Making the Sounds of Speech 19??
Offers an examination of the physiology of speech and looks at human's vocal tracts, and explains our ability to understand speech. 31m; VHS. **A:** Sr. High. **P:** Education. **U:** Institution. **Gen-Edu:** Speech. **Acq:** Purchase. **Dist:** Filmakers Library Inc. $295.

Anatomy of Hell 2004 (Unrated) — **Bomb!**
French pretentiousness at its most full-blown. An unnamed straight woman (Casar)?bored, stupid, mentally unbalanced or all three—slits her wrists in a gay disco and is attended to by a nameless gay man (Italian porn stud Siffredi) whom she then propositions. She'll pay him to accompany her to her creepy isolated house and look at her naked. This will help her confront her problems with intimacy or sexuality or something. Unless you're as masochistic as the characters, you won't care. Oh, and Casar has a body double for the more, ummm, close-up views but that's all Siffredi all the time. Adapted from Breillat's novel "Pornocratie"; French with subtitles. 87m; DVD. **C:** Amira Casar; Rocco Siffredi; Catherine Breillat; Directed by Catherine Breillat; Written by Catherine Breillat; Cinematography by Yorgos Arvanitis; Guillaume Schiffman; Miguel Malherios; Pedro da Santos; Music by D'juiz. **A:** College-Adult. **P:** Entertainment. **U:** Home. **L:** French. **Mov-Ent:** Sex & Sexuality, Women, France. **Acq:** Purchase. **Dist:** TLA Releasing. $24.99.

Anatomy of Japan 1988
A vivid presentation of Japan's current economy, industry and relations with the world. 60m; VHS, 3/4 U. **Pr:** Landmark Films, Inc. **A:** Jr. High-Adult. **P:** Education. **U:** Institution, SURA. **Gen-Edu:** Japan. **Acq:** Purchase, Rent/Lease. **Dist:** Landmark Media. $350.00.
Indiv. Titles: 1. Postwar Japan: 40 Years of Economic Recovery 2. An Economy in Transition: Japanese Business Goes Abroad 3. The Shacho: A Japanese President and His Company 4. The Company Man: Myths and Realities of Lifetime Employment 5. MiTI: Guiding Hand of the Japanese Economic Miracle 6. Small Companies: True Heroes of Japanese Industry 7. Quality Control: An American Idea Takes Root in Japan 8. A

Test of Japanese Management: Japanese Cars Made in the U.S.A. 9. Breaking Barriers: Foreign Companies That Succeed in Japan 10. Japan and the Future: A Time for Choice.

Anatomy of Love 1994
Follows the trials and tribulations of real people and the subject of love from courtship to marriage to adultery to breaking up and staying together. Couples are from North America, Japan, and Africa. Based on the book by Helen Fisher. 190m; VHS. **C:** Directed by Katherine Gilday; Written by Katherine Gilday; Rachel Low. **Pr:** W. Patterson Ferns; Rachel Low; TBS; Primedia Productions. **A:** College-Adult. **P:** Education. **U:** Home. **Hea-Sci:** Marriage, Sex & Sexuality. **Acq:** Purchase. **Dist:** Turner Broadcasting System Inc.

Anatomy of Muscles and Related Muscle Tissues 19??
Furnishes close-up footage of the muscles of a pig carcass being dissected from the skeleton to illustrate the location, relative size, shape, and function of each. Also identifies and discusses the location and functions of other tissues, such as major blood vessels, nerves, fat deposits, and bones. 32m; VHS. **A:** Sr. High-Adult. **P:** Education. **U:** Institution. **Hea-Sci:** Agriculture, Animals, Science. **Acq:** Purchase. **Dist:** CEV Multimedia. $49.95.

Anatomy of Shoulder Arthroscopy Cadaver Demonstration 1983
An orthopedic surgeon dissects a cadaver to show the surface and deep anatomy of the shoulder. 29m; VHS, 3/4 U. **Pr:** Emory University. **A:** College-Adult. **P:** Education. **U:** Institution, CCTV, Home, SURA. **Hea-Sci:** Joints, Anatomy & Physiology. **Acq:** Purchase, Rent/Lease, Subscription. **Dist:** Emory Medical Television Network.

Anatomy of Terror 1974 (Unrated) — ★
Drama about an army vet going bonkers (what? really?) and revealing espionage secrets in his home life. 73m; VHS. **C:** Paul Burke; Polly Bergen; Dinsdale Landen; Basil Henson; Roger Hume; William Job; Directed by Brian Clemens; Peter Jefferies; Music by Laurie Johnson. **Pr:** John Sichel; Cecil Clarke. **A:** Jr. High-Adult. **P:** Entertainment. **U:** Home. **Mov-Ent:** TV Movies, Veterans. **Acq:** Purchase. **Dist:** Lions Gate Television Corp. $29.95.

Anatomy of the Adult Tooth 1978
A review of the basic structures which compose the adult tooth, to better prepare the student for the study of odontogenesis. 10m; VHS, 3/4 U, EJ, Q, Special order formats. **Pr:** University of Oklahoma. **A:** College. **P:** Professional. **U:** Institution, CCTV. **Hea-Sci:** Tooth & Mouth. **Acq:** Purchase. **Dist:** University of Oklahoma.

Anatomy of the Alimentary Canal and Organs 19??
Concentrates on the anatomy associated with the alimentary canals of meat animals. Includes dissection footage of different animals and shows the major cavities, organs, glands, muscles, and reproductive tracts of these animals. 41m; VHS. **A:** Sr. High-Adult. **P:** Education. **U:** Institution. **Hea-Sci:** Agriculture, Animals, Science. **Acq:** Purchase. **Dist:** CEV Multimedia. $49.95.

Anatomy of the Chest and Abdomen 19??
Outlines the anatomy of the thoracic cavity. Covers areas of the mediastinum subject to blunt trauma, lung and respiratory tract injuries and anatomy, the concept of pneumothorax, and the anatomy and physiology of the gastrointestinal tract, liver, and gall bladder. Includes program syllabus. 120m; VHS. **A:** College-Adult. **P:** Education. **U:** Institution. **Hea-Sci:** Law--Medical, Medical Care, Anatomy & Physiology. **Acq:** Purchase. **Dist:** MediLegal Institute. $295.00.

Anatomy of the Face and Skin 19??
Outlines the anatomy of the facial areas and the skin. Covers pain reception and how it relates to soft tissue injuries. Examines inflammation and wound healing principles, the structural makeup of the face, skull, and eye, and types of facial injuries. Includes program syllabus. 120m; VHS. **A:** College-Adult. **P:** Education. **U:** Institution. **Hea-Sci:** Law--Medical, Medical Care, Anatomy & Physiology. **Acq:** Purchase. **Dist:** MediLegal Institute. $295.00.

Anatomy of the Forearm and Hand 1985
A training film depicting a dissection of a fresh cadaver's hand and forearm for anatomical purposes. 60m; VHS, 3/4 U. **Pr:** American Society for Surgery of the Hand. **A:** Adult. **P:** Professional. **U:** Institution, CCTV, SURA. **Hea-Sci:** Anatomy & Physiology. **Acq:** Purchase. **Dist:** American Society for Surgery of the Hand.

Anatomy of the Head and Vertebral Column 19??
Outlines the anatomy of the scalp and skull. Discusses blowout fractures of the eye, TMJ injuries and their anatomical basis, cervical and lumbar spine analysis, radiological diagnosis, radiculopathy, compression fractures, disc degeneration, cervical lordosis, and cauda equina syndrome. Includes program syllabus. 120m; VHS. **A:** College-Adult. **P:** Education. **U:** Institution. **Hea-Sci:** Law--Medical, Medical Care, Anatomy & Physiology. **Acq:** Purchase. **Dist:** MediLegal Institute. $295.00.

Anatomy of the Heart and Cardiovascular System 19??
Furnishes information on the major components of the heart and cardiovascular system. Covers the principles of coronary circulation and cardiac conduction, blood vessels and their purposes, heart enlargement, and emergency procedures. Includes program syllabus. 120m; VHS. **A:** College-Adult. **P:**

Education. **U:** Institution. **Hea-Sci:** Medical Care, Anatomy & Physiology, Heart. **Acq:** Purchase. **Dist:** MediLegal Institute. $295.00.

Anatomy of the Orbit and Related Structures 1979
This tape looks at the structures of the orbit, the eyelids and lacrimal apparatus. 62m; VHS, 3/4 U. **TV Std:** NTSC, PAL, SECAM. **Pr:** McGill University. **A:** Adult. **P:** Professional. **U:** Institution, CCTV. **Hea-Sci:** Eye. **Acq:** Purchase, Rent/Lease. **Dist:** McGill University.

Anatomy of the Skull with Clinical Correlations 1973
The anatomy of the skull from the standpoint of the otolaryngologist. 23m; VHS, 3/4 U, Special order formats. **Pr:** Ohio State University Health Sciences AV Center. **A:** College-Adult. **P:** Professional. **U:** Institution, SURA. **Hea-Sci:** Anatomy & Physiology. **Acq:** Purchase, Rent/Lease. **Dist:** Ohio State University.

Anatomy of the Whiplash Injury 19??
Uses footage to demonstrate how non-bony tissues are involved in cervical sprain (whiplash) injuries. Covers the fasciae, joint capsules, ligaments, tendons, skeletal muscles, nerves, and vessels in the neck region. Includes cadaver demonstration to explain the vertebral disc segments and soft tissue structures of the cervical spine. 30m; VHS. **A:** College-Adult. **P:** Education. **U:** Institution. **Hea-Sci:** Back Disorders, Medical Care, Anatomy & Physiology. **Acq:** Purchase. **Dist:** MediLegal Institute. $165.00.

Anchor of the Soul 1994
Illustrates the struggles and triumphs of an African American community in Portland, Maine. 60m; VHS. **A:** Jr. High. **P:** Education. **U:** Home. **Gen-Edu:** Minorities. **Acq:** Purchase. **Dist:** Northeast Historic Film. $24.95.

Anchorage! Alaska 19??
Showcases the sights and sounds of Alaska's largest city, Anchorage. Combines historical photographs with modern footage to detail the history of the growth of the city. Includes coverage of the many events which take place in the city, such as the Fur Rendezvous festival and the World Champion Sled Dog Races. 40m; VHS. **TV Std:** NTSC, PAL. **A:** Family. **P:** Entertainment. **U:** Home. **Gen-Edu:** U.S. States, Travel, Cities & Towns. **Acq:** Purchase. **Dist:** Alaska Video Postcards Inc. $19.95.

Anchorages 199?
Covers general rules for identifying anchorage points and guidelines for safe hookup. 17m; VHS. **A:** Adult. **P:** Vocational. **U:** Institution. **L:** English, Spanish. **Bus-Ind:** Safety Education. **Acq:** Purchase, Rent/Lease. **Dist:** Audio Graphics Training Systems. $450.00.

Anchorages: Make the Connection 1955
Demonstrates that proper anchoring is necessary to make personal fall protection devices effective. Also covers safety rules. 17m; VHS. **A:** Adult. **P:** Professional. **U:** Institution. **Bus-Ind:** Job Training, Safety Education. **Acq:** Rent/Lease. **Dist:** National Safety Council, California Chapter, Film Library.

Anchoress 1993 (Unrated) — ★★
Young Christine (Morse) is a 14th-century woman who decides to devote her life to the Virgin Mary after seeing visions. The local priest (Eccleston) encourages the girl to become an anchoress—a walled-in recluse—whose blessings are asked for by pilgrims. The priest treats Christine as a religious trophy, conveying power on himself, while she slowly realizes she's escaped the outside world only to trade one sort of bondage for another. Based on the true story of the Anchoress of Shere. Stylized images heighten the sense of otherworldliness. 108m/ B/W; VHS, DVD. **C:** Natalie Morse; Christopher Eccleston; Gene Bervoets; Toyah Willcox; Pete Postlethwaite; Directed by Chris Newby; Written by Judith Stanley-Smith; Christine Watkins; Cinematography by Michel Baudour. **Pr:** Ben Gibson; Paul Breuls. **A:** College-Adult. **P:** Entertainment. **U:** Institution. **Mov-Ent:** Religion. **Acq:** Purchase. **Dist:** International Film Circuit, Inc. $195.00.

Anchorman 2: The Legend Continues 2013 (PG-13) — ★★½
Less inspired than the original, McKay's follow-up to his cult hit still connects with the funny bone. Ron Burgundy (Ferrell) is back, pushed out of the New York news scene just as a company is about to create 24-hour news like CNN in the early '80s. Burgundy is called back in, reuniting with partners Brian (Rudd), Champ (Koechner), and Brick (Carell) in an effort to rise to the top of his form again. Not every joke works but they come fast enough that the laughs outnumber the duds. 119m; DVD, Blu-Ray. **C:** Will Ferrell; Steve Carell; Paul Rudd; David Koechner; Christina Applegate; Meagan Good; Directed by Adam McKay; Written by Will Ferrell; Adam McKay; Cinematography by Oliver Wood; Music by Andrew Feltenstein; John Nau. **Pr:** Adam McKay; Judd Apatow; Apatow Productions; Paramount Pictures Corp. **A:** Jr. High-Adult. **P:** Entertainment. **U:** Home. **Mov-Ent:** Comedy--Screwball, Television, Black Culture. **Acq:** Purchase. **Dist:** Paramount Pictures Corp.

Anchorman: The Legend of Ron Burgundy 2004 (PG-13) — ★★½
Back in the '80s, Chevy Chase specialized in clueless all-American goofs who thought they were smarter than they were. The crown has now been passed to Ferrell. Here, he plays Ron Burgundy, the top-rated anchorman in '70s-era San Diego. Ron is the booze swilling, cigarette smoking, female ogling, narcissistic leader of an all-male news team whose world is rocked by the arrival of a new female reporter—beautiful, talented, and ambitious Veronica Corningstone (Applegate). Ron falls for the babe even as he tries to retain his chauvinistic place at the top

of the news chain. It's amusing shtick and a fair send-up of a time when men were pigs and women decided to bring home the bacon themselves. Besides Applegate, Ferrell is well supported by Koechner, Carell, and Rudd as his equally macho-wannabe news boys. 91m; DVD, Blu-Ray, HD-DVD, Wide. **C:** Will Ferrell; Christina Applegate; David Koechner; Steve Carell; Paul Rudd; Fred Willard; Vince Vaughn; Chad Everett; Tara Subkoff; Stephen (Steve) Root; Danny Trejo; Jack Black; Ben Stiller; Missi Pyle; Chris Parnell; Tim Robbins; Luke Wilson; Laura Kightlinger; Kevin Corrigan; Fred Armisen; Directed by Adam McKay; Written by Will Ferrell; Adam McKay; Cinematography by Thomas Ackerman; Music by Alex Wurman. **Pr:** Judd Apatow; DreamWorks SKG. **A:** Jr. High-Adult. **P:** Entertainment. **U:** Home. **Mov-Ent:** Comedy--Romantic. **Acq:** Purchase. **Dist:** Movies Unlimited; Alpha Video; DreamWorks Home Entertainment. $29.99.

Anchors Aweigh 1945 — ★★★
Snappy big-budget (for then) musical about two horny sailors, one a girl-happy dancer and the other a shy singer. While on leave in Hollywood they return a lost urchin to his sister. The four of them try to infiltrate a movie studio to win an audition for the girl from maestro Iturbi. Kelly's famous dance with Jerry the cartoon Mouse (of "Tom and Jerry" fame) is the second instance of combining live action and animation. The young and handsome Sinatra's easy crooning and Grayson's near operatic soprano are blessed with music and lyrics by Styne and Cahn. Lots of fun, with conductor-pianist Iturbi contributing and Hollywood-style Little Mexico also in the brew. 139m; VHS, DVD, CC. **C:** Frank Sinatra; Gene Kelly; Kathryn Grayson; Jose Iturbi; Dean Stockwell; Carlos Ramirez; Pamela Britton; Sharon McManus; Leon Ames; Directed by George Sidney; Music by Jule Styne; Lyrics by Sammy Cahn. **Pr:** MGM. **A:** Family. **P:** Entertainment. **U:** Home. **Mov-Ent:** Musical, Classic Films, Dance. **Awds:** Oscars '45: Scoring/Musical. **Acq:** Purchase. **Dist:** MGM Home Entertainment. $19.98.

Songs: We Hate to Leave; I Fall in Love Too Easily; The Charm of You; The Worry Song; Jalousie; All of a Sudden My Heart Sings; I Begged Her; What Makes the Sun Set?; Waltz Serenade.

Anchors Aweigh: The United States Navy Story 1990
The two century history of the U.S. Navy is explored through historic footage. 45m; VHS. **Pr:** MPI Media Group. **A:** Sr. High-Adult. **P:** Entertainment. **U:** Home. **Gen-Edu:** Documentary Films, Armed Forces--U.S., Military History. **Acq:** Purchase. **Dist:** MPI Media Group; Fusion Video. $29.98.

Ancient Africans 1970
Traces the roots of African history from Stone Age ruins to the fabled Kingdoms of Kush and Zimbabwe in the east and Ghana, Mali, and Songhai in the west. 27m; 3/4 U, Special order formats. **Pr:** International Film Foundation. **A:** Primary-Adult. **P:** Education. **U:** Institution, SURA. **L:** English, French, Spanish. **Gen-Edu:** History--Ancient, Africa. **Acq:** Purchase, Rent/Lease. **Dist:** International Film Foundation.

Ancient America: Indians of the Eastern Woodlands 19??
Wes Studi narrates this look at the Eastern Woodland Indian. Investigates Effigy Mounds, road systems of the Ohio Valley, Monks Mound and Woodhenge. 60m; VHS. **A:** Jr. High-Adult. **P:** Education. **U:** Institution. **Gen-Edu:** Archaeology, History--Ancient. **Acq:** Purchase. **Dist:** Ark Media Group Ltd.

Ancient America: Indians of the Northwest 19??
Investigates the life, culture and customs of the Northwest Indian. Introduces totem pole origin, legends, Ming Dynasty and more. 60m; VHS. **A:** Jr. High-Adult. **P:** Education. **U:** Institution. **Gen-Edu:** China. **Acq:** Purchase. **Dist:** Ark Media Group Ltd.

Ancient America: Indians of the Southwest 19??
Explores southwest Native American culture. Introduces Chimney Rocks, Mesa Verde, and more. Studies teh Anasazi, Mimbres, and Salado. 60m; VHS. **A:** Jr. High-Adult. **P:** Education. **U:** Institution. **Gen-Edu:** Native Americans. **Acq:** Purchase. **Dist:** Ark Media Group Ltd.

Ancient America: More Than Bows and Arrows 19??
Doctor N. Scott Momaday narrates this look at Native American traditions of the Anasazi and Iriqouis tribes. Introduces the Iriqouis League of Nations, the first democracy, ceremonial mounds and more. 60m; VHS. **A:** Jr. High-Adult. **P:** Education. **U:** Institution. **Gen-Edu:** Native Americans. **Acq:** Purchase. **Dist:** Ark Media Group Ltd.

Ancient America: Nomadic Indians of the West 19??
Explores the life and customs of the Plains Indians. Introduces the Medicine Wheel, smoke signals, sign language, and much more. 60m; VHS. **A:** Jr. High-Adult. **P:** Education. **U:** Institution. **Gen-Edu:** Native Americans. **Acq:** Purchase. **Dist:** Ark Media Group Ltd.

Ancient American Indian Civilizations 1972
A series that examines the religious, political, and economic life of three ancient Indian civilizations, and compares their artistic and technological achievements. 8m; VHS, 3/4 U. **Pr:** Encyclopedia Britannica Educational Corporation. **A:** Primary-Jr. High. **P:** Education. **U:** Institution, SURA. **Gen-Edu:** History--Ancient. **Acq:** Purchase, Rent/Lease, Trade-in. **Dist:** Encyclopedia Britannica.

Indiv. Titles: 1. Ancient Aztec Indians of North America 2. Ancient Maya Indians of Central America 3. Ancient Inca Indians of South America.

Ancient Americans-The Mayas and Aztecs 1998
Overviews Mayan life, their buildings, and intricate calendar. Examines the Aztec empire from its forebearers to its collapse once in contact with the Spanish. 32m; VHS; Closed Captioned. **A:** Jr. High. **P:** Education. **U:** Institution. **Gen-Edu:** History--Ancient, Native Americans. **Acq:** Purchase. **Dist:** Zenger Media. $135.00.

Ancient and Modern: The Fall and Rise of the Middle East 1984
Examines the geography, natural resources, religion, politics and economy of the Middle East in a historical perspective from the Golden Age of Islam to the 20th century. 25m; VHS. **A:** Jr. High-Sr. High. **P:** Education. **U:** Institution. **Gen-Edu:** Middle East, Geography. **Acq:** Purchase. **Dist:** Zenger Media. $59.00.

The Ancient Art of Belly Dancing 1977
The program features an historical account of belly dancing, given in both still and moving images. Modern history follows belly dancing to the Islamic nations, Europe, and the Chicago World's Fair. 30m; VHS, 3/4 U. **Pr:** Stewart Lippe. **A:** College-Adult. **P:** Education. **U:** Institution, SURA. **Fin-Art:** Dance. **Acq:** Purchase. **Dist:** Phoenix Learning Group.

The Ancient Art of Pottery: Daughters of the Anasazi 19??
Provides detailed examination of ancient Native American pottery techniques still used today by Acoma potter Lucy Lewis and her daughters. 28m; VHS. **A:** Jr. High-Adult. **P:** Education. **U:** Institution, Home. **Gen-Edu:** Art & Artists, How-To, Crafts. **Acq:** Purchase. **Dist:** Crystal Productions. $24.95.

Ancient Aztec Indians of North America 1972
Describes the Aztec invasion of Mexico and the subsequent rise of their civilization. From the "Ancient American Indian Civilizations" series. 8m; VHS, 3/4 U. **Pr:** Encyclopedia Britannica Educational Corporation. **A:** Primary-Jr. High. **P:** Education. **U:** Institution, SURA. **Gen-Edu:** Anthropology. **Acq:** Purchase, Rent/Lease, Trade-in. **Dist:** Encyclopedia Britannica.

Ancient Chinese 1974
Presents the history of China's great dynasties from the earliest days to Sun Yat-Sen. 24m; 3/4 U, Special order formats. **Pr:** International Film Foundation. **A:** Primary-Adult. **P:** Education. **U:** Institution, SURA. **L:** English, French. **Gen-Edu:** China, History--Ancient. **Acq:** Purchase, Rent/Lease. **Dist:** International Film Foundation.

Ancient Civilizations ????
Six-video set on architecture and events involving Athens, Rome, Pompeii, Cleopatra's Egypt, the pyramids, the Aztecs, the Maya, and the Seven Wonders of the World. Contains nudity in classical art, recommended for Grades 7-12. 420m; VHS. **A:** Jr. High-Sr. High. **P:** Education. **U:** Institution. **Gen-Edu:** History--Ancient, Archaeology. **Acq:** Purchase. **Dist:** Zenger Media; Social Studies School Service. $39.95.

Ancient Civilizations 1978
Reveals the history, monuments, and everyday life of ancient civilizations such as: Africa Mesopotamia and Egypt, Greece, Rome, and China. ?m; VHS. **A:** Primary-Sr. High. **P:** Education. **U:** Institution. **Gen-Edu:** History--Ancient, Sociology, Asia. **Acq:** Purchase. **Dist:** National Geographic Society. $120.00.

Ancient Civilizations 2002
Three-dimensional animation recreates daily life of ancient Greece, Aztec culture, Cleopatra's kingdom and more. 403m; VHS, DVD. **A:** Adult. **P:** Education. **U:** Home. **Gen-Edu:** History, Documentary Films. **Acq:** Purchase. **Dist:** Questar Inc. $24.98.

Ancient Civilizations for Children: Ancient Aegean 1998
Provides a history of the Minoan and Mycenaean civilizations that lived on the islands and mainland of what is now Greece. 23m; VHS; Closed Captioned. **A:** Primary-Jr. High. **P:** Education. **U:** Home, Institution. **Chl-Juv:** History--Ancient. **Acq:** Purchase. **Dist:** Library Video Inc. $29.95.

Ancient Civilizations for Children: Ancient Africa 1998
Discusses two ancient African civilizations, the Great Zimbabwe from the south and the Swahili from the eastern coast. 23m; VHS; Closed Captioned. **A:** Primary-Jr. High. **P:** Education. **U:** Home, Institution. **Chl-Juv:** History--Ancient, Africa. **Acq:** Purchase. **Dist:** Library Video Inc. $29.95.

Ancient Civilizations for Children: Ancient China 1998
Discusses the history behind the building of the Great Wall, the "Silk Road" trade route, Chinese inventions, and Emperor Qin's tomb of clay soldiers. 23m; VHS; Closed Captioned. **A:** Primary-Jr. High. **P:** Education. **U:** Home, Institution. **Chl-Juv:** History--Ancient, China. **Acq:** Purchase. **Dist:** Library Video Inc. $29.95.

Ancient Civilizations for Children: Ancient Egypt 1998
Discusses the mysteries of the pyramids and pharaohs, hieroglyphics, daily life in the Nile, Egyptian art and architecture. 23m; VHS; Closed Captioned. **A:** Primary-Jr. High. **P:** Education. **U:** Home, Institution. **Chl-Juv:** History--Ancient, Africa. **Acq:** Purchase. **Dist:** Library Video Inc. $29.95.

Ancient Civilizations for Children: Ancient Greece 1998
Discusses the culture, democracy, theatre, Olympic Games philosophy, the Parthenon, and other aspects of life in ancient Greece. 23m; VHS; Closed Captioned. **A:** Primary-Jr. High. **P:** Education. **U:** Home, Institution. **Chl-Juv:** History--Ancient. **Acq:** Purchase. **Dist:** Library Video Inc. $29.95.

Ancient Civilizations for Children: Ancient Inca 1998
Discusses the daily life, religion, farming and food of the Inca through visits to ruins of the lost city of Machu Picchu and other remains. 23m; VHS; Closed Captioned. **A:** Primary-Jr. High. **P:** Education. **U:** Home, Institution. **Chl-Juv:** History--Ancient, South America. **Acq:** Purchase. **Dist:** Library Video Inc. $29.95.

Ancient Civilizations for Children: Ancient Maya 1998
Discusses the culture, food, religious beliefs, inventions, and hieroglyphics of the ancient Mayans. 23m; VHS; Closed Captioned. **A:** Primary-Jr. High. **P:** Education. **U:** Home, Institution. **Chl-Juv:** History--Ancient, South America. **Acq:** Purchase. **Dist:** Library Video Inc. $29.95.

Ancient Civilizations for Children: Ancient Mesopotamia 1998
Discusses the culture, customs and history of the Sumerians, Babylonians and Assyrians. 23m; VHS; Closed Captioned. **A:** Primary-Jr. High. **P:** Education. **U:** Home, Institution. **Chl-Juv:** History--Ancient, Religion. **Acq:** Purchase. **Dist:** Library Video Inc. $29.95.

Ancient Civilizations for Children: Ancient Rome 1998
Discusses the architecture, trade system, art, and governing body of the Roman Empire. 23m; VHS; Closed Captioned. **A:** Primary-Jr. High. **P:** Education. **U:** Home, Institution. **Chl-Juv:** History--Ancient. **Acq:** Purchase. **Dist:** Library Video Inc. $29.95.

Ancient Egypt ????
Reenactments and footage of artifacts and archaeological sites present a history of the Nile, the pyramids of Giza, and the origins of hieroglyphics. Recommended for use with grades 3 to 8. 23m; VHS. **A:** Primary-Jr. High. **P:** Education. **U:** Institution. **Gen-Edu:** History--Ancient, Africa. **Acq:** Purchase. **Dist:** Zenger Media. $49.95.

Ancient Egypt 1971
Takes us back through history to the most picturesque and exciting of all early civilizations. We learn of the people who created these monuments, about their zest for living, their love of sports, their religion. 51m; VHS, 3/4 U, Special order formats. **C:** Narrated by Ken Clark. **Pr:** Brian Brake; Time-Life Films. **A:** Sr. High-College. **P:** Education. **U:** Institution, SURA. **L:** English, Spanish. **Gen-Edu:** History--Ancient. **Acq:** Purchase, Rent/Lease. **Dist:** Time-Life Video and Television.

Ancient Egypt: The Gift of the Nile ????
Discusses the culture and agricultural development of ancient Egypt. Recommended for Grades 4-8. 28m; VHS; Closed Captioned. **A:** Primary-Jr. High. **P:** Education. **U:** Institution. **Gen-Edu:** History--Ancient, Africa. **Acq:** Purchase. **Dist:** Zenger Media. $135.00.

Ancient Egypt—Alarion 19??
Explores the art and architecture of ancient Egypt. Includes footage of paintings and sculptures of kings, queens, noble persons, temples, tombs, pyramids, and Tutankhamun's tomb. Also available in versions for elementary students ($89.00) and middle school students ($119.00). ?m; VHS. **A:** Sr. High. **P:** Education. **U:** Institution. **Fin-Art:** History--Ancient, Art & Artists, Architecture. **Acq:** Purchase. **Dist:** Crystal Productions. $199.00.

The Ancient Egyptian 1963
This film brings the ancient Egyptian alive through his own art and through Philip Stapp's inspired animation. 27m; 3/4 U, Special order formats. **Pr:** International Film Foundation. **A:** Primary-College. **P:** Education. **U:** Institution, SURA. **Gen-Edu:** History--Ancient, Middle East. **Acq:** Purchase, Rent/Lease. **Dist:** International Film Foundation.

Ancient Empire 1987
The lifestyles and customs of the Roman Empire are the subject of this tape. 25m; VHS, 3/4 U. **Pr:** SVE. **A:** Jr. High. **P:** Education. **U:** Institution, CCTV, Home. **Gen-Edu:** History--Ancient. **Acq:** Purchase, Duplication. **Dist:** Clear Vue Inc. $99.00.

Ancient Evil: Scream of the Mummy 2000 (R) — ★½
Six archeology students discover accidentally revive an Aztec mummy and unleash a deadly curse that could destroy mankind. 86m; VHS, DVD. **C:** Ariauna Albright; Jeff Peterson; Russell Richardson; Christopher Cullen; Directed by David DeCoteau. **A:** Sr. High-Adult. **P:** Entertainment. **U:** Home. **Mov-Ent:** Archaeology. **Acq:** Purchase. **Dist:** Bedford Entertainment Inc.

Ancient Forests 1992
National Geographic visits the Pacific Northwest to examine the ecosystem of the forests and the impact of the logging industry on them. 25m; VHS. **A:** Jr. High-Adult. **P:** Education. **U:** Institution. **Gen-Edu:** Forests & Trees, Ecology & Environment. **Acq:** Purchase. **Dist:** National Geographic Society. $110.00.

Ancient Graves: Voices of the Dead 1998
Scientific look at ancient grave exploration. 60m; VHS. **A:** Jr. High-Adult. **P:** Education. **U:** Home. **Hea-Sci:** History, Science. **Acq:** Purchase. **Dist:** Instructional Video. $19.95.

Ancient Greece ????
Explores the roots of Western Man through architecture, temples, and sculpture of the Golden Age. 49m; VHS. **A:** Sr. High-Adult. **P:** Education. **U:** Home, Institution. **Gen-Edu:** Art & Artists, History--Ancient. **Acq:** Purchase. **Dist:** Crystal Productions. $127.50.

Ancient Greece 19??
Two-part series, filmed on location in Greece, which examines the religion, architecture, art, and customs of Greek culture over the past 4,000 years. 120m; VHS. **A:** Jr. High-Adult. **P:** Education. **U:** Home, Institution. **Gen-Edu:** Art & Artists, Architecture, Religion. **Acq:** Purchase. **Dist:** Kultur International Films Ltd., Inc. $29.95.
Indiv. Titles: 1. Vol. 1: Art in Ancient Greece/Mining in Ancient Greece 2. Vol. 2: Bacchus, The God of Wine/Fire Walking in Greece.

Ancient Greece—Alarion 19??
Looks at the basic concepts of Greek architecture and illustrates how they relate to Stonehenge, Crete, and Archaic Greek temples. Includes footage of the temples on the Acropolis and Greek sculptures. Also available in versions for elementary students ($89.00) and middle school students ($109.00). ?m; VHS. **A:** Sr. High. **P:** Education. **U:** Institution. **Fin-Art:** History--Ancient, Art & Artists, Architecture. **Acq:** Purchase. **Dist:** Crystal Productions. $189.00.

Ancient Greek Art and Architecture 19??
Examines the development of classical Greek art and the orders of Greek temples. 22m; VHS. **A:** Adult. **P:** Education. **U:** Institution. **Fin-Art:** Art & Artists, History--Ancient, Architecture. **Acq:** Purchase. **Dist:** Educational Video Network. $49.95.

Ancient Healing 2000
Investigates how Chinese medicine is used for treatment of chronic sciatica and how native healers in Guatemala use drums, music, and deep reverence of nature to heal people and the earth. 27m; VHS, DVD. **A:** Adult. **P:** Professional. **U:** Institution. **Hea-Sci:** Health Education, Medical Education. **Acq:** Purchase. **Dist:** Aquarius Health Care Media. $99.00.

Ancient History: America's Prehistoric Civilizations: The Mound Builders 2007
Looks at the mound building cultures of the eastern United States, including their development, achievements, and decline. 30m; DVD, CC. **A:** Jr. High-Adult. **P:** Education. **U:** Institution. **Gen-Edu:** Documentary Films, History--Ancient, History--U.S. **Acq:** Purchase. **Dist:** Ambrose Video Publishing, Inc. $49.99.

Ancient History: Ancient Britain: Stonehenge to Celtic Iron Age Forts 2007
Looks at the 7,000 year evolution of Great Britain's people from Stone Age clans and Bronze and Iron Age tribes to modern, castle-building kings and queens. 30m; DVD, CC. **A:** Jr. High-Adult. **P:** Education. **U:** Institution. **Gen-Edu:** Documentary Films, Great Britain, History. **Acq:** Purchase. **Dist:** Ambrose Video Publishing, Inc. $49.99.

Ancient History: Ancient Pueblo People: The Anasazi 2007
The history of the Pueblo people from the four corners region of the western United States, including their structures, rock art, and pottery. 30m; DVD, CC. **A:** Jr. High-Adult. **P:** Education. **U:** Institution. **Gen-Edu:** Documentary Films, History--U.S., Native Americans. **Acq:** Purchase. **Dist:** Ambrose Video Publishing, Inc. $49.99.

Ancient History: Greek Accomplishments 2007
A history of Greek thinkers from Homer in 700 BC to Ptolemy in 150 AD. 30m; DVD, CC. **A:** Jr. High-Adult. **P:** Education. **U:** Institution. **Gen-Edu:** Documentary Films, History--Ancient, Philosophy & Ideology. **Acq:** Purchase. **Dist:** Ambrose Video Publishing, Inc. $49.99.

Ancient History: Rome Reexamined 2008
Four-part series on the growth and development of ancient Rome, including the rise and decline of the Roman Republic. 120m; DVD, CC. **A:** Jr. High-Adult. **P:** Education. **U:** Institution. **Gen-Edu:** Documentary Films, History--Ancient. **Acq:** Purchase. **Dist:** Ambrose Video Publishing, Inc. $99.99.

Ancient History: The Greek City-State and Democracy 2007
Looks at the golden age of the Greek city-state and its ideas of democracy, liberty, and freedom. 30m; DVD, CC. **A:** Jr. High-Adult. **P:** Education. **U:** Institution. **Gen-Edu:** Documentary Films, History--Ancient. **Acq:** Purchase. **Dist:** Ambrose Video Publishing, Inc. $49.99.

Ancient History: The Incas 2007
Examines the empire of the Inca people, located in present-day Peru, and its architectural wonders. 30m; DVD, CC. **A:** Jr. High-Adult. **P:** Education. **U:** Institution. **Gen-Edu:** Documentary Films, Architecture, History--Ancient. **Acq:** Purchase. **Dist:** Ambrose Video Publishing, Inc. $49.99.

Ancient History: The Maya 2008
Refutes the misconceptions of this ancient civilization as a bloodthirsty warrior society by looking at their thriving agricultural culture. 30m; DVD, CC. **A:** Jr. High-Adult. **P:** Education. **U:** Institution. **Gen-Edu:** Documentary Films, History--Ancient, Agriculture. **Acq:** Purchase. **Dist:** Ambrose Video Publishing, Inc. $49.99.

Ancient Inca Indians of South America 1972
Describes the largest ancient empire and most advanced civilization in the Western Hemisphere. From the "Ancient American Indian Civilizations" series. 8m; VHS, 3/4 U. **Pr:** Encyclopedia Britannica Educational Corporation. **A:** Primary-Jr. High. **P:** Education. **U:** Institution, SURA. **Gen-Edu:** Anthropology. **Acq:** Purchase, Rent/Lease, Trade-in. **Dist:** Encyclopedia Britannica.

Ancient India ????
Examines religious tensions between Hinduism, Buddhism, and Islam and discusses historical events that shaped the great

civilizations of India. 48m; VHS. **A:** Sr. High-Adult. **P:** Education. **U:** Institution. **Gen-Edu:** India, History. **Acq:** Purchase, Rent/Lease. **Dist:** Films for the Humanities & Sciences. $129.00.

Ancient Indian Cultures of Northern Arizona 1985
Concentrates on the Sinagua and Anasazi people and how they survived under harsh conditions. Also looks at five national monuments: Montezuma Castle, Wupatki, Tuzigoot, Walnut Canyon and Sunset Crater. 30m; VHS. **Pr:** Finley-Holiday Film Corporation. **A:** Family. **P:** Education. **U:** Home. **Gen-Edu:** Documentary Films, History--U.S., Native Americans. **Acq:** Purchase. **Dist:** Finley Holiday Film Corp.; Karol Media; Cambridge Educational. $29.95.

Ancient Lives 1984 (Unrated)
Historical documentary miniseries aired on public television 1984. Examines the mysteries of daily life in ancient Egypt: the pharaohs, their scribes, tomb building, high priests who presided over the city, their meals, love lives, fights, and dreams. 205m; DVD. **C:** John Romer. **A:** Family. **P:** Entertainment. **U:** Home. **Mov-Ent:** History--Ancient, Documentary Films. **Acq:** Purchase. **Dist:** Acorn Media Group Inc. $49.99.

Ancient Lives 1985
A survey of ancient civilizations and their cultures. Available separately as well as a package. 27m; VHS, 3/4 U. **Pr:** Films for the Humanities. **A:** Jr. High-Adult. **P:** Education. **U:** Institution, SURA. **Gen-Edu:** History. **Acq:** Purchase, Rent/Lease. **Dist:** Films for the Humanities & Sciences.
Indiv. Titles: 1. The Village of the Craftsmen 2. The Valley of the Kings 3. An Artist's Life 4. Temple Priests & Civil Servants 5. Woman's Place 6. Dreams & Rituals 7. The Year of the Hyena 8. The Deserted Village.

The Ancient Mariners 1981
Ancient shipbuilding and the development of nautical archaeology are examined by two master craftsmen who lived and worked 23 centuries apart. Part of the "Odyssey" series. 60m; VHS, 3/4 U. **Pr:** Public Broadcasting Associates. **A:** College-Adult. **P:** Education. **U:** Institution, CCTV, CATV. **Gen-Edu:** Boating. **Acq:** Purchase, Rent/Lease, Off-Air Record. **Dist:** PBS Home Video.

Ancient Maya Indians of Central America 1972
This tape shows how the Mayan civilization, mainly agrarian, reached its peak of power during periods of peaceful expansion. From the "Ancient American Indian Civilizations" series. 9m; VHS, 3/4 U. **Pr:** Encyclopedia Britannica Educational Corporation. **A:** Primary-Jr. High. **P:** Education. **U:** Institution, SURA. **Gen-Edu:** Anthropology. **Acq:** Purchase, Rent/Lease, Trade-in. **Dist:** Encyclopedia Britannica.

Ancient Moderns: Greek Island Art and Culture 2000-3000 B.C. 1979
Shot on location on the Cycladic Islands, this program examines the sculpture, pottery, tools, and jewelry of this mysterious civilization which some consider to be the birthplace of ancient Greek art. 19m; VHS, 3/4 U, Special order formats. **C:** Narrated by Rex Harrison. **Pr:** Encyclopedia Britannica Educational Corporation. **A:** Sr. High-Adult. **P:** Education. **U:** Institution, SURA. **Gen-Edu:** Documentary Films, History--Ancient. **Acq:** Purchase, Rent/Lease, Trade-in. **Dist:** Encyclopedia Britannica. $335.00.

Ancient Mysteries: Ancient Prophecy 2006
Prophecy has been used to divine the future since ancient times and in cultures throughout the world. This program examines prophecy from the Greeks to Nostrodamus and Native America. 50m; DVD. **A:** Jr. High-Adult. **P:** Entertainment. **U:** Home. **Gen-Edu:** Documentary Films. **Acq:** Purchase. **Dist:** A&E Television Networks L.L.C.

Ancient Mysteries: Ancient Rome and Its Mysterious Cities 2006
Wherever the Romans conquered, they built a city to solidify their power and influence. Explore why so many of these ancient cities flourished and how the Romans kept control. 50m; DVD. **A:** Jr. High-Adult. **P:** Entertainment. **U:** Home. **Gen-Edu:** Documentary Films. **Acq:** Purchase. **Dist:** A&E Television Networks L.L.C.

Ancient Mysteries: Ark of the Covenant 2005
This sacred symbol is said to contain the tablets of the Ten Commandments and to possess incredible power. Follow the clues from biblical texts to the present day to decide if the Ark ever existed and what became of it. 50m; DVD. **A:** Jr. High-Adult. **P:** Entertainment. **U:** Home. **Gen-Edu:** Documentary Films. **Acq:** Purchase. **Dist:** A&E Television Networks L.L.C.

Ancient Mysteries: Astrology: Secrets in the Stars 2005
Do the movements of the stars and planets determine one's character and predict their destiny? Experts explore the 4,000-year-old origins of astrology as it was developed by the Babylonians and what influence it has on cultures worldwide. 50m; DVD. **A:** Jr. High-Adult. **P:** Entertainment. **U:** Home. **Gen-Edu:** Documentary Films. **Acq:** Purchase. **Dist:** A&E Television Networks L.L.C.

Ancient Mysteries: Atlantis—The Lost Civilization 2006
Examines the myths surrounding the underwater city, including historical stories and current speculation. 50m; DVD. **A:** Jr. High-Adult. **P:** Entertainment. **U:** Home. **Gen-Edu:** Documentary Films. **Acq:** Purchase. **Dist:** A&E Television Networks L.L.C.

Ancient Mysteries: Bigfoot 2005 (Unrated)
Presents the 1994 A&E television program hosted by Leonard Nimoy that explores the Pacific Northwest attempting to locate proof of the mythical Bigfoot, also known as Sasquatch. 1 episode. 50m; DVD. **C:** Hosted by Leonard Nimoy. **A:** Family. **P:** Entertainment. **U:** Home. **Gen-Edu:** Television Series, Documentary Films, Education. **Acq:** Purchase. **Dist:** A&E Television Networks L.L.C. $24.95.

Ancient Mysteries: Camelot 2005 (Unrated)
Presents the 1995 A&E television program hosted by actress Kathleen Turner that explores the legend of King Arthur as historians and archeologists attempt to find proof of his existence in England and Wales. 1 episode. 50m; DVD. **C:** Hosted by Kathleen Turner. **A:** Family. **P:** Entertainment. **U:** Home. **Gen-Edu:** Television Series, Documentary Films, Education. **Acq:** Purchase. **Dist:** A&E Television Networks L.L.C. $24.95.

Ancient Mysteries: Curse of the Hope Diamond 2005
At 45.5 carats, it is the largest blue diamond in the world, said to stolen from the eye of a Hindu god. It's alleged curse has followed anyone in possession of the gemstone, including the ill-fated Hope family. Has the curse ended now that the stone resides at the Smithsonian? 50m; DVD. **A:** Jr. High-Adult. **P:** Entertainment. **U:** Home. **Gen-Edu:** Documentary Films. **Acq:** Purchase. **Dist:** A&E Television Networks L.L.C.

Ancient Mysteries: Dragons: Myths and Legends 2006
Interviews and art explore the legendary creature that is featured in stories from around the world. 50m; DVD. **A:** Jr. High-Adult. **P:** Entertainment. **U:** Home. **Gen-Edu:** Documentary Films. **Acq:** Purchase. **Dist:** A&E Television Networks L.L.C.

Ancient Mysteries: Guardian of the Ages: The Great Sphinx 2006
Examines the famous desert ruin through expert opinion, computer graphics, and the latest scientific discoveries, including which pharaoh is supposed to be the model for the sphinx's head. 50m; DVD. **A:** Jr. High-Adult. **P:** Entertainment. **U:** Home. **Gen-Edu:** Documentary Films. **Acq:** Purchase. **Dist:** A&E Television Networks L.L.C.

Ancient Mysteries: Human Sacrifice 2006
The ancients believed that human blood was the ultimate gift to the gods. Explore cultures that practiced human sacrifice, including the Aztecs and followers of the Indian goddess Kali. 50m; DVD. **A:** Jr. High-Adult. **P:** Entertainment. **U:** Home. **Gen-Edu:** Documentary Films. **Acq:** Purchase. **Dist:** A&E Television Networks L.L.C.

Ancient Mysteries: Legends of the Arabian Nights 2006
Explores the origins and impact of the 1001 tales and such characters as Sinbad, Ali Baba, and Aladdin from myths to movies. 50m; DVD. **A:** Jr. High-Adult. **P:** Entertainment. **U:** Home. **Gen-Edu:** Documentary Films. **Acq:** Purchase. **Dist:** A&E Television Networks L.L.C.

Ancient Mysteries: Lost Castles of England 2006
Scholars explore the locations of the vanished timber castles that once provided protection and what life was like within their walls. 50m; DVD. **A:** Jr. High-Adult. **P:** Entertainment. **U:** Home. **Gen-Edu:** Documentary Films. **Acq:** Purchase. **Dist:** A&E Television Networks L.L.C.

Ancient Mysteries: Magic of Alchemy 1997
Presents the A&E cable channel special on the shadowy group known as alchemists from 2,000 years ago who worked in primitive laboratories pursuing the magical ability to make gold, seek divine wisdom, and to unlock the secrets of immortality. Sir Isaac Newton's possible involvement is explored. 50m; DVD. **A:** Jr. High-Adult. **P:** Entertainment. **U:** Home, Institution. **Mov-Ent:** Television Series, Documentary Films, Biography. **Acq:** Purchase. **Dist:** A&E Television Networks L.L.C. $24.95.

Ancient Mysteries: Miraculous Canals of Venice 2006
The first inhabitants were escaping the barbarian hordes of Attila the Hun. But how did people build a city in a lagoon and how has Venice survived continuous flooding? 50m; DVD. **A:** Jr. High-Adult. **P:** Entertainment. **U:** Home. **Gen-Edu:** Documentary Films. **Acq:** Purchase. **Dist:** A&E Television Networks L.L.C.

Ancient Mysteries: Mystical Monuments of Ancient Greece 2006
What was the purpose of the ancient Greek temples built on Athens' Acropolis? This program explores whether they were built as symbols of democracy or as a cult tribute to Athena, the goddess of wisdom and war. 50m; DVD. **A:** Jr. High-Adult. **P:** Entertainment. **U:** Home. **Gen-Edu:** Documentary Films. **Acq:** Purchase. **Dist:** A&E Television Networks L.L.C.

Ancient Mysteries: Pompeii: Buried Alive 2005
Mount Vesuvius erupted on August 24, 79 AD, and covered the cities of Pompeii and Herculaneum, thus preserving a look into daily life during the Roman Empire. Learn about ongoing excavations and the latest discoveries. 50m; DVD. **A:** Jr. High-Adult. **P:** Entertainment. **U:** Home. **Gen-Edu:** Documentary Films. **Acq:** Purchase. **Dist:** A&E Television Networks L.L.C.

Ancient Mysteries: Sacred Places 2006
Explores the world's most sacred and mysterious sites, including Easter Island, Stonehenge, and Machu Picchu. 50m; DVD. **A:** Jr. High-Adult. **P:** Entertainment. **U:** Home. **Gen-Edu:** Documentary Films. **Acq:** Purchase. **Dist:** A&E Television Networks L.L.C.

Ancient Mysteries: Secrets of the Aztec Empire 2006
Scholars and archeologists examine the achievements and mysteries of the Aztec civilization, which flourished between the 14th and 16th centuries. 50m; DVD. **A:** Jr. High-Adult. **P:** Entertainment. **U:** Home. **Gen-Edu:** Documentary Films. **Acq:** Purchase. **Dist:** A&E Television Networks L.L.C.

Ancient Mysteries: Seven Wonders of the Ancient World 2005
What are the stories behind such ancient accomplishments as the Hanging Gardens of Babylon, the Colossus of Rhodes, and the pyramids? Period art, fragmentary remains, and modern reconstructions bring them to life again. 100m; DVD. **A:** Jr. High-Adult. **P:** Entertainment. **U:** Home. **Gen-Edu:** Documentary Films. **Acq:** Purchase. **Dist:** A&E Television Networks L.L.C.

Ancient Mysteries: Tattooing 2005
For thousands of years, people have decorated their bodies. Examines the origins of the practice and its continuing popularity. 50m; DVD. **A:** Jr. High-Adult. **P:** Entertainment. **U:** Home. **Gen-Edu:** Documentary Films. **Acq:** Purchase. **Dist:** A&E Television Networks L.L.C.

Ancient Mysteries: The Black Death 2005
Scientist explore the origins of the 52-year plague, which began in 542 AD and claimed 100 million lives. How was a cure discovered and are the remnants of the disease with us today? 50m; DVD. **A:** Jr. High-Adult. **P:** Entertainment. **U:** Home. **Gen-Edu:** Documentary Films. **Acq:** Purchase. **Dist:** A&E Television Networks L.L.C.

Ancient Mysteries: The Fate of the Neandertals 2006
Interviews with paleontologists and other experts offer facts and theories into the Neandertal race. 50m; DVD. **A:** Jr. High-Adult. **P:** Entertainment. **U:** Home. **Gen-Edu:** Documentary Films. **Acq:** Purchase. **Dist:** A&E Television Networks L.L.C.

Ancient Mysteries: The Forbidden City: Dynasty & Destiny 2005
The Ming Emperor began construction in 1403 and it took more than 14 years to complete a royal city spread over 250 acres in what is now Beijing. Explore the history of this hidden world, which 24 emperors ruled until 1924. 50m; DVD. **A:** Jr. High-Adult. **P:** Entertainment. **U:** Home. **Gen-Edu:** Documentary Films. **Acq:** Purchase. **Dist:** A&E Television Networks L.L.C.

Ancient Mysteries: The Great Pyramid 1995
Studies the mystery of the Great Pyramid of Egypt, looking for insight to its secrets. 100m; VHS. **A:** Jr. High-Adult. **P:** Education. **U:** Institution. **Gen-Edu:** History--Ancient. **Acq:** Purchase. **Dist:** A&E Television Networks L.L.C. $19.95.

Ancient Mysteries: The Hidden City of Petra 2005
This ancient city was literally carved into the mountains in Jordan. But what desert people accomplished this feat and what happened to them? Archeologists lead an exploration along some 35 miles of streets and buildings in Petra. 50m; DVD. **A:** Jr. High-Adult. **P:** Entertainment. **U:** Home. **Gen-Edu:** Documentary Films. **Acq:** Purchase. **Dist:** A&E Television Networks L.L.C.

Ancient Mysteries: The Incredible Monuments of Rome 2006
Explores the imperial monuments of Rome, including arenas, palaces, and places of worship. 50m; DVD. **A:** Jr. High-Adult. **P:** Entertainment. **U:** Home. **Gen-Edu:** Documentary Films. **Acq:** Purchase. **Dist:** A&E Television Networks L.L.C.

Ancient Mysteries: The Odyssey of Troy 1995
Examination of the legends and fables of the Fall of Troy. 50m; VHS. **A:** Sr. High-Adult. **P:** Education. **U:** Institution. **Gen-Edu:** History--Ancient. **Acq:** Purchase. **Dist:** A&E Television Networks L.L.C. $19.95.

Ancient Mysteries: The Quest for the Fountain of Youth 2006
Explores the origins of water mythology and immortality, including 16th century Spanish explorer Ponce de Leon's ill-fated journey to Florida. 50m; DVD. **A:** Jr. High-Adult. **P:** Entertainment. **U:** Home. **Gen-Edu:** Documentary Films. **Acq:** Purchase. **Dist:** A&E Television Networks L.L.C.

Ancient Mysteries: The Sacred Waters of Lourdes 2006
A peasant girl claimed to have seen a vision of the Virgin Mary and ever since, the waters in the mountain village of Lourdes are thought by pilgrims to have healing properties. Scholars, doctors, and theologians explore both the sacred and secular evidence. 50m; DVD. **A:** Jr. High-Adult. **P:** Entertainment. **U:** Home. **Gen-Edu:** Documentary Films. **Acq:** Purchase. **Dist:** A&E Television Networks L.L.C.

Ancient Mysteries: The Vikings in North America 2006
Investigates the claim that the Vikings landed in North America some 1,000 years ago, following Eric the Red and Leif Ericsson across the North Atlantic to a settlement in Vinland. 50m; DVD. **A:** Jr. High-Adult. **P:** Entertainment. **U:** Home. **Gen-Edu:** Documentary Films. **Acq:** Purchase. **Dist:** A&E Television Networks L.L.C.

Ancient Mysteries: Tombs of the Gods: The Great Pyramids of Giza 2006
Egyptologists tell of the pharaohs, engineers, and architects who built the Great Pyramids of Giza, Hatshepsut's Temple in Thebes, and the Temple of Amun at Karnak. 50m; DVD. **A:** Jr.

High-Adult. **P:** Entertainment. **U:** Home. **Gen-Edu:** Documentary Films. **Acq:** Purchase. **Dist:** A&E Television Networks L.L.C.

Ancient Mysteries: UFOs: The First Encounters 2005
Looks at the monuments and texts that reference the stars, flying objects, and strange civilizations. 50m; DVD. **A:** Jr. High-Adult. **P:** Entertainment. **U:** Home. **Gen-Edu:** Documentary Films. **Acq:** Purchase. **Dist:** A&E Television Networks L.L.C.

Ancient Mysteries: Vampires 1994
Presents the A&E cable channel special on the history of vampires. From Bram Stoker's penning of "Dracula" to the real history of the horrible Transylvanian ruler, Vlad the Impaler, vampires have fascinated throughout history. Visit vampire lore in Transylvania, Greece, China, and the United States to see if the stories are really only dark tales. 50m; DVD. **A:** Jr. High-Adult. **P:** Entertainment. **U:** Home, Institution. **Mov-Ent:** Television Series, Documentary Films, Death. **Acq:** Purchase. **Dist:** A&E Television Networks L.L.C. $24.95.

Ancient Mysteries: Witchcraft in America 1993
Presents the A&E cable channel special on witchcraft, following its origins in America with the Salem witch trials 300 years ago in Massachusetts, to a voodoo queen's rituals in 19th century New Orleans and a witch doctor in 1928 Pennsylvania, to a modern day Wiccan ceremony. Includes interviews with descendents of the Salem witches. 50m; DVD. **A:** Jr. High-Adult. **P:** Entertainment. **U:** Home, Institution. **Mov-Ent:** Television Series. **Acq:** Purchase. **Dist:** A&E Television Networks L.L.C. $24.95.

Ancient Mysteries: Witches 2006
Looks at the history of the witch from healer to caster of magic spells, including the Inquisition of the Middle Ages and the Salem, Massachusetts witch trials conducted by the Puritans. 50m; DVD. **A:** Jr. High-Adult. **P:** Entertainment. **U:** Home. **Gen-Edu:** Documentary Films. **Acq:** Purchase. **Dist:** A&E Television Networks L.L.C.

The Ancient New World 1986
An animated film visualizing early civilization in Central America, leading up to the Mayan and Aztec cultures. For kids. 16m; VHS, 3/4 U. **Pr:** Churchill Films. **A:** Primary-Jr. High. **P:** Education. **U:** Institution, Home, SURA. **Chl-Juv:** History--Ancient, Central America. **Acq:** Purchase. **Dist:** Clear Vue Inc.

The Ancient Ones 1984
Presents a history of the Anasazi Indians, Native Americans who lived 800 years ago and built stone cities in the Southwest, as revealed by archaeological finds. 24m; VHS. **A:** Family. **P:** Education. **U:** Institution. **Gen-Edu:** Native Americans, History--U.S. **Acq:** Purchase. **Dist:** Knowledge Unlimited, Inc. $19.95.

The Ancient Peruvian 1968
Provides a study of the civilization of pre-Columbian America. 29m; 3/4 U, Special order formats. **Pr:** International Film Foundation. **A:** Primary-Adult. **P:** Education. **U:** Institution, SURA. **Gen-Edu:** History--Ancient, South America. **Acq:** Purchase, Rent/Lease. **Dist:** International Film Foundation.

Ancient Relic 2002 (R) — ★½
Confusing German miniseries focuses on a startling archeological discovery. Steffen Vogt is helping out at a dig site in Israel when he finds a 2,000-year-old skeleton holding instructions for a video camera. He leaps to the conclusion that the skeleton belongs to a time traveler who got actual footage of Jesus. His crackpot idea is given credence by expert Kaun, who's convinced the camera is hidden somewhere in Jerusalem's Wailing Wall. Then Steffen is abducted by your basic secret Vatican society who doesn't want the status quo upset. German with subtitles. 182m; DVD. **C:** Naike Rivelli; Hans Diehl; Matthias Koeberlin; Heinrich Giskes; Directed by Sebastian Niemann; Written by Martin Ritzenhoff; Cinematography by Gerhard Schirlo; Music by Egon Riedel. **A:** Sr. High-Adult. **P:** Entertainment. **U:** Home. **L:** German. **Mov-Ent:** Archaeology, Israel, Religion. **Acq:** Purchase. **Dist:** Genius Entertainment.

Ancient Rome ????
Explores the development of architecture and sculpture in Ancient Rome. Also examines the Age of Augustus, Age of Trajan, and the time of Hadrian. 40m; VHS. **A:** Sr. High-Adult. **P:** Education. **U:** Home, Institution. **Gen-Edu:** Art & Artists, History--Ancient. **Acq:** Purchase. **Dist:** Crystal Productions. $127.50.

Ancient Rome 1993
Re-creates daily life in Rome circa A.D. 300, offering comparisons with modern urban life. 15m; VHS. **A:** Jr. High-Sr. High. **P:** Education. **U:** Institution. **Gen-Edu:** History--Ancient, Cities & Towns, Italy. **Acq:** Purchase. **Dist:** Encyclopedia Britannica. $99.00.

Ancient Rome: The Rise and Fall of Rome 1991
Traces the history of the center of ancient civilization—Rome. Looks at the development of the Roman Republic, tours ancient ruins, and discusses ancient Roman lifestyles and customs, focusing on the inevitable destruction of the city. Five program series. 15m; VHS. **A:** Sr. High-College. **P:** Education. **U:** Institution. **Gen-Edu:** History--Ancient, Cities & Towns. **Acq:** Purchase. **Dist:** Cambridge Educational. $59.95.
Indiv. Titles: 1. The Rise of Rome: 750 B.C.-300 B.C. 2. The Roman Empire: 300 B.C.-200 A.D. 3. Fall of the Roman Empire: 200-400 A.D. 4. Ancient Rome: Lifestyles and Customs 5. The Roman Renaissance.

Ancient Rome: The Story of an Empire that Ruled the World 2000
Four volume set examines the lives and legends of Nero, Ceasar, and Ptolemy; Romulus and Remus and the rise of Christianity; and reveals treasures and secret sites throughout Europe and the Near East, foremost Pompeii. ?m; VHS. **A:** Adult. **P:** Education. **U:** Home. **Gen-Edu:** History--Ancient. **Acq:** Purchase. **Dist:** A&E Television Networks L.L.C. $39.95.

Ancient Rome—Alarion 19??
Explores the art and architecture of ancient Rome. Explains how the arch, vault, and dome relate to the aqueduct. Includes footage of the Coliseum, Baths, Pantheon, sculptures, and mosaics. Also available in versions for elementary students ($89.00) and middle school students ($109.00). ?m; VHS. **A:** Sr. High. **P:** Education. **U:** Institution. **Fin-Art:** History--Ancient, Art & Artists, Architecture. **Acq:** Purchase. **Dist:** Crystal Productions. $189.00.

Ancient Roots 1987
See a boat that Jesus might have used, what might actually be Christ's tomb, caves where Jews hid from the Romans, and other ancient religious sites. 28m; VHS. **Pr:** Alden Films. **A:** Jr. High-Adult. **P:** Education. **U:** Institution, Home, SURA. **Gen-Edu:** Religion, History--Ancient. **Acq:** Purchase, Rent/Lease. **Dist:** Alden Films. $50.00.

Ancient Sea Monsters 2010 (Unrated)
Deep in Nevada's Augusta Mountains, scientists recently discovered the fossilized remains of a 35-foot long ichthyosaur that is acknowledged to be the largest sea reptile known to exist during the time of the dinosaurs 240-million years ago. 45m; DVD. **A:** Family. **P:** Education. **U:** Institution, Home. **Mov-Ent:** Documentary Films, History--Ancient, Dinosaurs. **Acq:** Purchase. **Dist:** National Geographic Society. $19.95.

The Ancient Sea Turtles: Last Voyage? 1991
A look at the history of sea turtles, plus an examination of the threats to their habitat posed by modern society. 25m; VHS, 3/4 U, Special order formats. **A:** Jr. High-Adult. **P:** Education. **U:** Institution, CCTV, CATV, BCTV, Home, SURA. **Gen-Edu:** Ecology & Environment, Wildlife. **Acq:** Purchase, Rent/Lease. **Dist:** The Video Project. $59.95.

The Ancient Spirit, Living Word: Oral Tradition 1983
An exploration of the Native American oral story-telling tradition. 58m; VHS, 1C, 3/4 U, Q. **Pr:** Daniel Salazar; KBDI Broomfield. **A:** Jr. High-Adult. **P:** Education. **U:** Institution, BCTV, SURA. **Gen-Edu:** Native Americans, Folklore & Legends. **Acq:** Purchase, Rent/Lease. **Dist:** Vision Maker Media.

Ancient Tales from a Promised Land 1993
Fourteen classic Old Testament stories are narrated from locations in the Holy Land. On seven cassettes, available separately or as a set. 30m; VHS. **C:** Narrated by Tony Robinson. **A:** Family. **P:** Entertainment. **U:** Home. **Mov-Ent:** Bible, Storytelling. **Acq:** Purchase. **Dist:** Acorn Media Group Inc.; Baker and Taylor. $19.95.
Indiv. Titles: 1. Joshua Smashes Jericho/Joshua in Trouble Valley 2. Deborah and the Headbanger/Gideon Gets His Woolly Wet 3. Gideon's Exploding Pickle Pots/Samson Gets Knotted 4. Samson Gets a Haircut/Samuel and the Spooky Godbox 5. Saul Rips Up His Camel/David Gets a Good Gig 6. David and the Hairy Man Mountain/Saul Goes Bonkers 7. Saul Bumps into a Witch/David Gets to Number One.

Ancient Traditions in Modern Society 1989
Gaer Luce offers suggestions for reverting back to the ways of ancient cultures, honoring their respect for nature and the harmony with the body and soul. 30m; VHS. **Pr:** Thinking Allowed Productions. **A:** Sr. High-Adult. **P:** Education. **U:** Home. **Gen-Edu:** Documentary Films, History--Ancient, History--Modern. **Acq:** Purchase. **Dist:** Thinking Allowed Productions. $29.95.

Ancient Treasures From the Deep 19??
Underwater archaeologists discover and retrieve ivory, amber, copper, myrrh, and frankincense from a merchant ship that sank in the eastern Mediterranean around 1300 B.C. The findings have helped scientists better understand the advancements of the Bronze Age. A Nova presentation. 57m. **Pr:** Nova Productions. **A:** Primary-Adult. **P:** Education. **U:** Home, Institution. **Gen-Edu:** History--Ancient, Boating, Science. **Acq:** Purchase. **Dist:** Clear Vue Inc. $30.00.

Ancient Voices, Modern World: Colombia & Amazon 2009 (Unrated)
Anthropologist Wade Davis is tour guide for two trips that explore ancient tribes of South America. In the "Colombia" episode, he meets with the Elder Brothers, a group that claims to be the last members of the Tairona, a civilization dating back to at least the first century A.D. "Amazon" focuses on the Barasana, a group thought to be descended from the "lost" Amazonian tribe and explores their ancestors and rituals. 90m; DVD. **A:** Family. **P:** Education. **U:** Institution, Home. **Mov-Ent:** Documentary Films, South America, Anthropology. **Acq:** Purchase. **Dist:** National Geographic Society. $19.95.

Ancient Voices, Modern World: Mongolia & Australia 2008 (Unrated)
Noted anthropologist Wade Davis again leads expeditions to study the descendants of the world's oldest civilizations. In the "Mongolia" episode, Davis visits Central Asia to examine the lives of present-day relatives of Genghis Khan, the founder of the Mongol Empire. In the next episode, "Australia," Davis travels to the far-reaches of the outback to study the Aborigines, the reasons for their dwindling numbers, and the difficulties they face trying to maintain their traditions for future generations. 90m; DVD. **A:** Family. **P:** Education. **U:** Institution, Home. **Mov-Ent:** Documentary Films, Australia, Asia. **Acq:** Purchase. **Dist:** National Geographic Society. $19.95.

Ancient Voices of Children 1976
Images of life and death and the relationship between a mother and her child are contrasted in seven poems by Federico Garcia Lorca. Set to music by George Crumb, sung in Spanish. 27m; 3/4 U. **Pr:** Allen Miller. **A:** Family. **P:** Entertainment. **U:** Institution, SURA. **Fin-Art:** Performing Arts. **Acq:** Purchase, Rent/Lease. **Dist:** Pyramid Media; Creative Arts Television Archive.

Ancient Warriors 1994
Three-volume series covers the history of such militaristic societies as the Spartans, Janissaries, and Shaolin Monks, and how they lived, trained, and fought. Tapes available as a boxed set or individually. ?m; VHS. **A:** Jr. High-Adult. **P:** Education. **U:** Home. **Gen-Edu:** History--Ancient. **Acq:** Purchase. **Dist:** Discovery Home Entertainment. $49.95.
Indiv. Titles: 1. Barbarian Forces 2. Soldiers of the East 3. Classical Warriors.

And a Nightingale Sang 1991 (Unrated) — ★★½
WWII England is the scene of this sweet romance, a sad and humorous tale of a woman who gives everything for the war effort. Stunning recreation of the final days of the Blitzkreig. Originally produced for Masterpiece Theatre. 90m; VHS, CC. **C:** Joan Plowright; Tom Watt; Phyllis Logan; John Woodvine; Pippa Hinchley; Stephen Tompkinson; Directed by Robert Knights. **Pr:** Public Broadcasting Service. **A:** Sr. High-Adult. **P:** Entertainment. **U:** Home. **Mov-Ent:** Drama, World War Two, Great Britain. **Acq:** Purchase. **Dist:** PBS Home Video; Fusion Video; Wellspring Media. $19.95.

And Access for All: ADA and Your Library 1993
Visits libraries in compliance with the Americans with Disabilities Act, and includes interviews with librarians who discuss how to meet the needs of their disabled patrons. Guide included. 47m; VHS, CC. **A:** Adult. **P:** Education. **U:** Institution. **Gen-Edu:** Information Science, Handicapped, Law. **Acq:** Purchase. **Dist:** Library Video Network. $130.00.

And Another Honky Tonk Girl Says She Will 1990
A Tennessee farm girl's dreams are destroyed when she moves to Nashville to become a big star. 30m; VHS. **C:** Directed by Michelle Paymar. **A:** Jr. High-Adult. **P:** Entertainment. **U:** Home. **Mov-Ent. Acq:** Purchase. **Dist:** The Cinema Guild. $59.95.

And Baby Makes Six 1979 — ★★½
An unexpected pregnancy creates new challenges for a couple with grown children. Dewhurst is excellent as usual. Followed by "Baby Comes Home." 100m; VHS, DVD. **C:** Colleen Dewhurst; Warren Oates; Maggie Cooper; Mildred Dunnock; Timothy Hutton; Allyn Ann McLerie; Directed by Waris Hussein; Written by Shelley List. **A:** College-Adult. **P:** Entertainment. **U:** Home. **Mov-Ent:** Comedy--Screwball, Comedy-Drama, TV Movies. **Acq:** Purchase. **Dist:** Direct Source Special Products, Inc.

And Baby Makes Three: Balancing Everyone's Needs 1985
Describes how two couples face common problems in adjusting to parenthood. Also shows how parents' personalities can affect how they raise their children. 27m; VHS. **A:** Sr. High-Adult. **P:** Education. **U:** Institution. **Gen-Edu:** Documentary Films, Parenting, Children. **Acq:** Purchase, Rent/Lease. **Dist:** Filmakers Library Inc. $295.00.

And Baby Makes Two 1978
The problems of teenage pregnancy are discussed openly by girls in a school for pregnant teens. No answers or morals are stated but both boys and girls express their feelings about this individual and societal burden. 27m; VHS, 3/4 U. **C:** Hosted by Valerie Bertinelli. **Pr:** KNBC Los Angeles. **A:** Jr. High-Sr. High. **P:** Education. **U:** Institution, SURA. **Chl-Juv:** Pregnancy. **Acq:** Purchase. **Dist:** Home Vision Cinema.

And Baby Makes Two 1982
Follows the lives of five single women who are raising their children alone. 30m; VHS, 3/4 U. **Pr:** Maryland Public Television; PBS. **A:** Sr. High-Adult. **P:** Education. **U:** Institution, CCTV, Home, SURA. **Gen-Edu:** Children, Parenting, Women. **Acq:** Purchase, Rent/Lease, Duplication, Off-Air Record. **Dist:** PBS Home Video.

And Baby Makes Two 2007 (Unrated)
Follows eight single women in New York City as they pursue dreams of motherhood. 60m; DVD. **A:** Sr. High-Adult. **P:** Entertainment. **U:** Home. **Mov-Ent:** Pregnancy, Documentary Films, Family. **Acq:** Purchase. **Dist:** First Run Features; Eagle Rock Entertainment Inc. $24.95.

And Baby Makes Two: A Look at Teenage Single Parenting 1987
This video covers a teen father's responsibilities, sex education, peer pressure and an array of programs designed to give the teen mother ways of becoming a successful and productive adult. 25m; VHS, 3/4 U. **Pr:** Centre Productions, Inc. **A:** Sr. High-Adult. **P:** Education. **U:** Institution, SURA. **Gen-Edu:** Parenting, Pregnancy, Adolescence. **Acq:** Purchase. **Dist:** Clear Vue Inc.

. . .And Everything Nice 1974
The program shows the process of consciousness-raising (CR) during which women develop new expectations. In an actual CR group, Gloria Steinem and Shirley Chisholm provide insights. 20m; VHS, 3/4 U. **C:** Gloria Steinem; Shirley Chisholm. **Pr:** Norma Adams. **A:** Sr. High-College. **P:** Education. **U:** Institution, SURA. **Gen-Edu:** Women. **Acq:** Purchase. **Dist:** Phoenix Learning Group.

And God Created Whales 1979
This program provides detailed information on the habits of the killer whale. 28m; VHS, 3/4 U. **Pr:** Canadian Broadcasting Corp. **A:** Family. **P:** Education. **U:** Institution. **Gen-Edu:** Animals. **Acq:** Purchase. **Dist:** Filmakers Library Inc.

And God Created Woman 1957 (PG) — ★★½
Launching pad for Bardot's career as a sex siren, as she flits across the screen in a succession of scanty outfits and hangs out at the St. Tropez beach in what is euphemistically known as a swimsuit while turning up the heat for the males always in attendance. The plot concerns an 18-year-old nymphomaniac who is given a home by a local family with three handsome young sons. A cutting-edge sex film in its time that was boffo at the boxoffice. In French with English subtitles. 93m; VHS, DVD, Wide. **C:** Brigitte Bardot; Curt Jurgens; Jean-Louis Trintignant; Christian Marquand; Directed by Roger Vadim; Written by Roger Vadim; Raoul Levy; Cinematography by Armand Thirard; Music by Paul Misraki. **Pr:** Raoul J. Levy. **A:** Adult. **P:** Entertainment. **U:** Home. **Mov-Ent:** Sex & Sexuality. **Acq:** Purchase. **Dist:** Movies Unlimited. $25.49.

And God Created Woman 1988 (R) — ★½
Loose, dull remake by Vadim of his own 1957 softcore favorite about a free-spirited woman dodging men and the law while yearning for rock and roll stardom. DeMornay is a prisoner who hopes to marry one of the local hunks (Spano) so she can be paroled. They marry, she strips, he frets, while political hopeful Langella smacks his lips in anticipation. Available in an unrated 100-minute version. 98m; VHS, DVD. **C:** Rebecca De Mornay; Vincent Spano; Frank Langella; Donovan Leitch; Judith Chapman; Thelma Houston; Directed by Roger Vadim; Music by Tom Chase; Steve Rucker. **Pr:** Braunstein and Hamady; Crow Productions. **A:** Sr. High-Adult. **P:** Entertainment. **U:** Home. **L:** English, Spanish. **Mov-Ent:** Sex & Sexuality. **Acq:** Purchase. **Dist:** Lions Gate Television Corp. $89.98.

And God Said to Cain 1969 (Unrated) — ★
Another Biblically titled western from the prolific Kinski, about a put-upon gunman who must fight for his life. 95m; VHS, DVD. **C:** Klaus Kinski; Antonio Cantafora; Peter Carsten; Marcella Michelangeli; Alan Collins; Giuliano Raffaelli; Directed by Anthony M. Dawson; Written by Anthony M. Dawson; Giovanni Addessi; Cinematography by Riccardo (Pallton) Pallottini; Luciano Trasatti; Music by Carlo Savina. **A:** Jr. High-Adult. **P:** Entertainment. **U:** Home. **Mov-Ent. Acq:** Purchase. **Dist:** Mill Creek Entertainment L.L.C. $29.95.

. . .And God Spoke 1994 (R) — ★★
Low budget spoof takes on both religion and moviemaking with two schlockmeisters filming a biblical epic. Since the duo have no budget and are basic hacks with pretensions, they have to settle...so Sales plays Moses, "The Incredible Hulk" Ferrigno gets cast as Cain, while Plumb ("Jan" on "The Brady Bunch") does Mrs. Noah. Has some lulls but also covers very recognizable territory. Directorial debut of Borman. 82m; VHS, DVD. **C:** Michael Riley; Stephen Rappaport; Soupy Sales; Lou Ferrigno; Eve Plumb; Andy Dick; R(ichard) C(arlos) Bates; Fred Kaz; Daniel Tisman; Directed by Arthur Borman; Written by Gregory S. Malins; Michael Curtis; Cinematography by Lee Daniel. **Pr:** Mark Borman; Richard Raddon; LIVE Entertainment. **A:** Sr. High-Adult. **P:** Entertainment. **U:** Home. **Mov-Ent:** Satire & Parody, Filmmaking. **Acq:** Purchase. **Dist:** Lions Gate Entertainment Inc.

And Hope to Die 1972 (Unrated) — ★★½
Moody, muddled crime drama with a good cast about a fleeing Frenchman who joins a gang of hardened criminals in Canada. They go ahead with their plans to kidnap a retarded girl even though she is already dead. Standard caper film is enhanced by arty camera work and some unusual directorial touches. 95m; VHS. **C:** Robert Ryan; Jean-Louis Trintignant; Aldo Ray; Tisa Farrow; Lea Massari; Directed by Rene Clement. **Pr:** 20th Century-Fox. **A:** Sr. High-Adult. **P:** Entertainment. **U:** Home. **Mov-Ent. Acq:** Purchase. **Dist:** No Longer Available.

And I Alone Survived 1978 (Unrated) — ★★
True story of a woman who survives a leisure-plane crash in the Sierra Nevadas and her struggle to get to the village below. Brown does her best to elevate the proceedings above the usual I-hope-I-don't-die cliches. 90m; VHS. **C:** Blair Brown; David Ackroyd; Vera Miles; G.D. Spradlin; Directed by William A. Graham; Cinematography by Jordan Cronenweth. **A:** Jr. High-Adult. **P:** Entertainment. **U:** Home. **Mov-Ent:** Action-Adventure, Aeronautics, TV Movies. **Acq:** Purchase. **Dist:** No Longer Available.

And I'm a Rapist: A Story About Rage 1991
Based on convicted rapists' testimonies, this dramatization is a composite portrait of a rapist, Anthony, who calmly explains the way he selects, tracks, and rapes his victims. Flashbacks tell the story of one of his victims, Christina, including her work with a rape counselor. 24m; VHS. **A:** Sr. High-Adult. **P:** Education. **U:** Institution. **Gen-Edu:** Rape. **Acq:** Purchase, Rent/Lease. **Dist:** Pyramid Media. $295.00.

And Justice for All 19??
Documentary that highlights the problems of providing legal help to the needy of Baltimore. Provides information on Baltimore's legal system including the public defender's office and legal clinics. Features interviews with members of the Homeless Persons Representation Project, Baltimore Legal Aid Bureau, and Maryland Legal Services Corporation. 60m; VHS, 3/4 U. **A:** Sr. High-Adult. **P:** Education. **U:** Institution, BCTV, CATV, CCTV. **Gen-Edu:** Documentary Films, Law, Poverty. **Acq:** Purchase, Rent/Lease. **Dist:** Maryland Public Television. $19.95.

And Justice for All 1979 (R) — ★★½
Earnest attorney Pacino questions the law and battles for justice in and out of the courtroom. He's hired to defend a detested judge from a rape charge, while dealing with a lost-soul caseload of eccentric and tragedy-prone clients. Overly melodramatic, an odd mix of satire, cynicism, and seemingly sincere drama that hits with a club when a stick will do. Jewison aims for black surrealism, permitting both Pacino and Warden (as a judge losing his sanity) to veer into histrionics, to the detriment of what is essentially a gripping behind-the-scenes story. Excellent cast creates sparks, including Lahti in her film debut. And Baltimore never looked lovelier. 120m; VHS, DVD, Wide. **C:** Al Pacino; Jack Warden; Christine Lahti; Thomas G. Waites; Craig T. Nelson; John Forsythe; Lee Strasberg; Jeffrey Tambor; Dominic Chianese; Directed by Norman Jewison; Written by Barry Levinson; Valerie Curtin; Cinematography by Victor Kemper; Music by Dave Grusin. **Pr:** Norman Jewison; Norman Jewison; Patrick Palmer. **A:** College-Adult. **P:** Entertainment. **U:** Home. **Mov-Ent:** Rape, Law, Ethics & Morals. **Acq:** Purchase. **Dist:** Sony Pictures Home Entertainment Inc. $14.95.

. . .and Justice for Whom? 2001 (Unrated)
Examines how legislation geared towards domestic security will affect communities throughout the United States and the globe post 9/11. 11m; VHS, DVD. **A:** Adult. **P:** Education. **U:** Institution. **Gen-Edu:** U.S. States, World Affairs. **Acq:** Purchase. **Dist:** Third World Newsreel. $30.

And Life Goes On: Severe Seizures of Early Childhood 1991
Three families explain how they have adjusted to the needs of an epileptic family member. Discusses feelings, life changes and helpful resources. 16m; VHS. **A:** Adult. **P:** Education. **U:** Institution. **Hea-Sci:** Epilepsy, Family. **Acq:** Purchase. **Dist:** Epilepsy Foundation of America. $14.95.

And Man Created Dog 2010 (Unrated)
The first dogs evolved from wolves more than 100,000 years ago and soon formed a special bond with humans, who found the animals to be excellent companions, workers, and hunters. Over time, man used selective breeding to create dogs that best suit their various needs, a process that also gave dogs a unique ability to communicate with humans. 90m; DVD. **A:** Family. **P:** Education. **U:** Institution, Home. **Mov-Ent:** Documentary Films, Pets, History. **Acq:** Purchase. **Dist:** National Geographic Society. $19.95.

And Never Let Her Go 2001 (Unrated) — ★★½
CBS true crime miniseries based on the book by Ann Rule. Powerful Delaware lawyer Thomas Capano (Harmon) has an affair with vulnerable secretary Anne Marie Fahey (Morris) as well as keeping his longtime mistress, Christine (Ward). She breaks things off, but the obsessed, manipulative Capano won't let her go. Then Anne Marie disappears. The investigation is hindered because there's no body and by the sensational release of her diaries, but the detectives refuse to give up. 170m; DVD. **C:** Mark Harmon; Kathryn Morris; Rachel Ward; Steven Eckholdt; Paul Michael Glaser; Rick Roberts; Olympia Dukakis; Directed by Peter Levin; Written by Adam Greenman; Cinematography by Bruce Surtees; Music by Harald Kloser. **A:** Sr. High-Adult. **P:** Entertainment. **U:** Home. **L:** English. **Mov-Ent:** Crime Drama, TV Movies. **Acq:** Purchase. **Dist:** Genius Entertainment; Movies Unlimited.

And Nothing But the Truth 1982 (Unrated) — ★★½
A multinational corporation is out to ruin the investigative TV report team trying to do a story on the company. 90m; VHS. **C:** Glenda Jackson; Jon Finch; Kenneth Colley; James Donnelly; Directed by Karl Francis. **Pr:** Castle Hill Productions. **A:** Sr. High-Adult. **P:** Entertainment. **U:** Home. **Mov-Ent:** Mass Media. **Acq:** Purchase. **Dist:** Unknown Distributor.

And Now a Word From Our Sponsor 2013 (Unrated) — ★½
Satire on the ad world is badly in need of new ideas. Chicago exec Adan Kundle (Greenwood) has a breakdown, lands in the hospital, and responds only by spouting commercial slogans. Widowed hospital volunteer Karen (Posey), who once attended a Kundle seminar, believes he's misunderstood and decides to take him in thus upsetting her teen daughter Meghan (MacDonald) and ruthless agency prez Lucas Foster (Blue) who wants Kundle declared incompetent. Debut director Bernbam doesn't seem to know how to make the cliches fresh. 87m; DVD, Streaming. **C:** Bruce Greenwood; Parker Posey; Callum Blue; Allie MacDonald; Directed by Zack Bernbaum; Written by Michael Hamilton-Wright; Cinematography by Stephen Whitehead; Music by Erica Procunier. **Pr:** Michael Hamilton-Wright. **A:** Adult. **P:** Entertainment. **U:** Home. **L:** English. **Mov-Ent:** Mental Health, Advertising, Satire & Parody. **Acq:** Purchase, Rent/Lease. **Dist:** Amazon.com Inc.; Virgil Films & Entertainment.

And Now for Something Completely Different 1972 (PG) — ★★★
A compilation of skits from BBC-TV's "Monty Python's Flying Circus" featuring Monty Python's own weird, hilarious brand of humor. Sketches include "The Upper Class Twit of the Year Race," "Hell's Grannies," and "The Townswomen's Guild Reconstruction of Pearl Harbour." A great intro to Python for the uninitiated, or a chance for the converted to see their favorite sketches again. 89m; VHS, DVD. **C:** John Cleese; Michael Palin; Eric Idle; Graham Chapman; Terry Gilliam; Terry Jones; Carol Cleveland; Connie Booth; Directed by Terry Gilliam; Ian McNaughton; Written by John Cleese; Michael Palin; Eric Idle; Graham Chapman; Terry Gilliam; Terry Jones; Cinematography by David Muir; Music by Douglas Gamley. **Pr:** Patricia Casey. **A:** Sr. High-Adult. **P:** Entertainment. **U:** Home. **Mov-Ent:** Television Series. **Acq:** Purchase. **Dist:** Sony Pictures Home Entertainment Inc. $19.95.

And Now Ladies and Gentlemen 2002 (PG-13) — ★★
Englishman Valentin (Irons) is a jewel thief who likes disguises and is suffering from mysterious blackouts. In Paris, jazz singer Jane Lester (Kaas) is also suffering from blackouts. They both wind up in Morocco, staying at the same hotel and seeing the same doctor (both turn out to have brain tumors). They flirt, there's a robbery at the hotel, a cop investigates...and the film continues to meander on and on. It all looks lovely but doesn't amount to much. English and French with subtitles. 126m; VHS, DVD. **C:** Jeremy Irons; Patricia Kaas; Alessandra Martines; Thierry Lhermitte; Ticky Holgado; Yvan Attal; Claudia Cardinale; Amidou; Jean-Marie Bigard; Directed by Claude Lelouch; Written by Claude Lelouch; Pierre Uytterhoeven; Pierre Leroux; Cinematography by Pierre William Glenn; Music by Michel Legrand. **Pr:** Claude Lelouch; Claude Lelouch; Les Films 13; France 2 Cinema; Gemka; L&G Productions Ltd; Paramount Classics. **A:** College-Adult. **P:** Entertainment. **U:** Home. **L:** French, English. **Mov-Ent:** Africa, Hotels & Hotel Staff Training, Singing. **Acq:** Purchase. **Dist:** Paramount Pictures Corp.

And Now Miguel 1966 (Unrated) — ★★
Plodding tale of a young boy who wants to take over as head shepherd of his family's flock. Filmed in New Mexico, but the over-long outdoor shots make it drag a bit in spite of Cardi's competent performance. 95m; VHS. **C:** Pat Cardi; Michael Ansara; Guy Stockwell; Clu Gulager; Joe De Santis; Pilar Del Rey; Buck Taylor; Directed by James B. Clark. **Pr:** Mark Huffam. **A:** Family. **P:** Entertainment. **U:** Home. **Mov-Ent. Acq:** Purchase. **Dist:** No Longer Available.

And Now My Love 1974 (PG) — ★★½
A French couple endeavor to maintain their romance despite interfering socio-economic factors—she's a millionaire and he's an ex-con filmmaker. Keller plays three roles spanning three generations, as Lelouch invests autobiographical details to invent a highly stylized, openly sentimental view of French folks in love with love. Along the way he comments on social mores and changing attitudes through the years. Dubbed in English. 121m; VHS, DVD. **C:** Marthe Keller; Andre Dussollier; Carla Gravina; Directed by Claude Lelouch; Written by Claude Lelouch. **Pr:** Joseph E. Levine. **A:** Sr. High-Adult. **P:** Entertainment. **U:** Home. **Mov-Ent:** Drama. **Awds:** L.A. Film Critics '75: Foreign Film. **Acq:** Purchase. **Dist:** Sony Pictures Home Entertainment Inc. $19.95.

And Now the Screaming Starts 1973 (R) — ★★½
The young bride-to-be of the lord of a British manor house is greeted by bloody faces at the window, a severed hand, and five corpses. Then Cushing shows up to investigate. Good-looking, sleek production with genuine chills. 91m; VHS, DVD, Wide. **C:** Peter Cushing; Herbert Lom; Patrick Magee; Ian Ogilvy; Stephanie Beacham; Rosalie Crutchley; Guy Rolfe; Janet Key; Gillian Lind; Directed by Roy Ward Baker; Written by Roger Marshall; Cinematography by Denys Coop; Music by Douglas Gamley. **Pr:** Cinerama Releasing. **A:** Sr. High-Adult. **P:** Entertainment. **U:** Institution, Home. **Mov-Ent:** Horror. **Acq:** Purchase. **Dist:** Movies Unlimited. $79.95.

And Now the Truth 1980
In this experimental program video artist Vera Frankel reveals her true feelings about life and art. 30m; VHS, 3/4 U. **Pr:** Vera Frankel. **A:** College-Adult. **P:** Education. **U:** Institution. **Fin-Art:** Video. **Acq:** Rent/Lease. **Dist:** Video Out Distribution.

And on the Seventh Day 1967
Three Israelis visit Jerusalem the day after the Six Day War and give their impressions and thoughts. 27m; VHS, 3/4 U, Special order formats. **TV Std:** NTSC, PAL, SECAM. **Pr:** Alden Films. **A:** Adult. **P:** Education. **U:** Institution, Home, SURA. **Gen-Edu:** Israel, War--General. **Acq:** Purchase, Rent/Lease. **Dist:** Alden Films.

And Sew On 1986
A home economics series consisting of 15 programs which offers demonstrated techniques to a variety of sewing projects. A study guide includes objectives, program summaries, suggested activities and patterns or instructions for some projects. 15m; VHS. **A:** Jr. High-Sr. High. **P:** Instruction. **U:** Institution. **Gen-Edu:** Sewing, Clothing & Dress. **Acq:** Purchase. **Dist:** GPN Educational Media. $365.40.
Indiv. Titles: 1. What'll I Wear? 2. Now You See It...Now You Don't 3. Getting It Together 4. Sewing Room Surgery 5. Matching Magic 6. Whoops! 7. The Inside Story 8. Facings, Bindings, Bands 9. Com-Pleat Confidence 10. Setting in Sleeves 11. Zippety Can Do 12. Waistbands and Casings 13. Hems 14. Play It Again, Sam! 15. STRETCH It Out.

And So It Goes 2014
Self-centered real estate agent Oren (Douglas) is shocked when his estranged son dumps his previously unknown granddaughter Sarah (Jerins) on his doorstep. He turns to his determined neighbor Leah (Keaton) for help. DVD. **C:** Michael Douglas; Diane Keaton; Sterling Jerins; Directed by Rob Reiner; Written by Mark Andrus; Cinematography by Reed Morano. **Pr:** Castle Rock Entertainment Inc. **P:** Entertainment. **U:** Home. **L:** English. **Mov-Ent:** Children, Family. **Acq:** Purchase. **Dist:** Not Yet Released.

And So They Were Married 1936 — ★★½
Amusing rom com with winning performances by the leads. Widower Stephen Blake (Douglas) and divorcee Edith Farnham (Astor) are temporarily stuck at a winter resort lodge at Christmas because of the weather. They begin an unexpected romance but their respective children have taken an instant dislike to each other and are determined to break them up. After succeeding, the kids have a change of heart and then scheme to get the adults back together. 74m/B/W; DVD. **C:** Melvyn Douglas; Mary Astor; Edith Fellows; Jackie Moran; Donald

Meek; Directed by Elliott Nugent; Written by Doris Anderson; Joseph Anthony; Cinematography by Henry Freulich; Music by Howard Jackson. **A:** Adult. **P:** Entertainment. **U:** Home. **L:** English. **Mov-Ent:** Children, Christmas, Comedy--Romantic. **Acq:** Purchase. **Dist:** Sony Pictures Home Entertainment Inc.

And Soon the Darkness 1970 (PG) — ★★
One of two vacationing young nurses disappears in France where a teenager was once murdered and the search is on. Predictable, ineffective suspenser. 94m; VHS, DVD, Wide. **C:** Pamela Franklin; Michele Dotrice; Sandor Eles; John Nettleton; Claire Kelly; Hanna-Marie Pravda; Directed by Robert Fuest; Written by Brian Clemens; Terry Nation; Cinematography by Ian Wilson; Music by Laurie Johnson. **Pr:** Albert Fennell; EMI Media. **A:** Jr. High-Adult. **P:** Entertainment. **U:** Home. **Mov-Ent:** Mystery & Suspense, France, Bicycling. **Acq:** Purchase. **Dist:** Anchor Bay Entertainment. $59.99.

And Soon the Darkness 2010 (R) — ★
Too many horror cliches make for boring viewing in this remake of the 1970 British film. Stephanie and Ellie go to rural Argentina on vacation but Ellie goes missing and the police seem to be indifferent. Stephanie turns to ex-pat American Michael, who's staying at the same hotel, but he may not be so trustworthy. 91m; DVD, Blu-Ray. **C:** Amber Heard; Odette Annable; Karl Urban; Ceasar Vianco; Directed by Marcos Efron; Written by Marcos Efron; Jennifer Derwingson; Cinematography by Gabriel Beristain; Music by tomandandy. **A:** Sr. High-Adult. **P:** Entertainment. **U:** Home. **Mov-Ent:** South America. **Acq:** Purchase. **Dist:** Anchor Bay Entertainment.

And Spare the Child 1982
From toddler to adolescence, this film examines the process of instilling values in children. 11m; VHS, 3/4 U. **Pr:** Professional Research. **A:** Adult. **P:** Education. **U:** Institution, CCTV, SURA. **Hea-Sci:** Parenting, Children. **Acq:** Purchase, Rent/Lease. **Dist:** Discovery Education. $199.00.

And Starring Pancho Villa as Himself 2003 (Unrated) — ★★★
It's 1914, and Mexican revolutionary Pancho Villa finds himself in dire need of funding for his campaign against the military-run government. He strikes a deal with American filmmakers D.W. Griffith (Feore) and Harry Aiken (Broadbent) that provides them with full access to his war. Based upon actual events, their efforts resulted in the first feature length film. Splendid portrayal by the charismatic and superbly-cast Banderas in the title role of the complex and compelling Villa. 115m; VHS, DVD, Wide. **C:** Antonio Banderas; Eion Bailey; Alan Arkin; Jim Broadbent; Matt(hew) Day; Colm Feore; Michael McKean; Alexa Davalos; Anthony Head; Kyle Chandler; Saul Rubinek; Damian Alcazar; Pedro Armendariz, Jr.; Directed by Bruce Beresford; Written by Larry Gelbart; Cinematography by Andre Fleuren; Peter James; Music by Joseph Vitarelli. **A:** College-Adult. **P:** Entertainment. **U:** Home. **Mov-Ent:** War--General, Mexico, Documentary Films. **Acq:** Purchase. **Dist:** Movies Unlimited; Alpha Video. $19.99.

And Still I Rise 1993
Compilation of film clips, interviews, and performances exploring and exposing stereotypes against African-American women. 30m; VHS. **A:** Adult. **P:** Education. **U:** Institution. **Gen-Edu:** Documentary Films, Women, Black Culture. **Acq:** Rent/Lease. **Dist:** Women Make Movies.

And Still the Turtle Watches 19??
Native American story that points out our responsibility to nature and the environment. Hosted by LeVar Burton who discusses various things being done to preserve our environment. Includes teacher's guide. 30m; VHS, CC. **A:** Jr. High. **P:** Education. **U:** Institution. **Chl-Juv:** Literature--Children, Ecology & Environment, Education. **Acq:** Purchase. **Dist:** GPN Educational Media. $39.95.

And the Band Played On 1993 (PG-13) — ★★★
Randy Shilts's monumental, and controversial, 1987 book on the AIDS epidemic comes to TV in an equally controversial cable movie. Details the intricate medical research undertaken by doctors in France and the U.S. who fought to isolate and identify the mystery virus despite governmental neglect, red tape, clashing egos, and lack of funding. Various aspects of gay life are shown objectively, without sensationalizing. Celebrity cameos are somewhat distracting though most acquit themselves well. The script went through numerous rewrites; director Spottiswoode reportedly objected to HBO interference at the editing stage. 140m; VHS, DVD, Wide, CC. **C:** Matthew Modine; Alan Alda; Ian McKellen; Lily Tomlin; Glenne Headly; Richard Masur; Saul Rubinek; Charles Martin Smith; Patrick Bauchau; Nathalie Baye; Christian Clemenson; Cameo(s) Richard Gere; David Clennon; Phil Collins; Alex Courtney; David Dukes; David Marshall Grant; Ronald Guttman; Anjelica Huston; Ken Jenkins; Richard Jenkins; Tcheky Karyo; Swoosie Kurtz; Jack Laufer; Steve Martin; Dakin Matthews; Peter McRobbie; Lawrence Monoson; B.D. Wong; Donal Logue; Jeffrey Nordling; Stephen Spinella; Directed by Roger Spottiswoode; Written by Arnold Schulman; Cinematography by Paul Elliott; Music by Carter Burwell. **Pr:** Midge Sanford; Sarah Pillsbury; Aaron Spelling; E. Duke Vincent; HBO. **A:** Sr. High-Adult. **P:** Entertainment. **U:** Home. **Mov-Ent:** AIDS, Documentary Films, TV Movies. **Acq:** Purchase. **Dist:** Home Box Office Inc. $49.99.

And the Children Shall Lead 1985
A young black girl is moved by the coming of the civil rights movement to her small Mississippi town. Part of the "Wonderworks" series. 60m; VHS. **C:** Danny Glover; LeVar Burton; Pam Potillo; Denise Nicholas; Andrew Prine; Directed by Michael Pressman. **Pr:** Topper Carew; Rainbow Television Works. **A:** Family. **P:** Entertainment. **U:** Home. **Chl-Juv:** Family Viewing,

Children, Civil Rights. **Acq:** Purchase. **Dist:** Home Vision Cinema; Facets Multimedia Inc. $29.95.

And the Children Shall Lead: Wonderworks ????
A friendship between a white sheriff and a black carpenter is tested during the civil rights movement in Mississippi, 1964. 58m; VHS. **A:** Jr. High. **P:** Education. **U:** Institution. **Gen-Edu:** Drama, Civil Rights. **Acq:** Purchase. **Dist:** Zenger Media. $14.95.

And the Dish Ran Away with the Spoon 1994
Shows how Caribbean inhabitants receive a distorted view of the world that alienates them from their cultural heritage by primarily U.S. television programs that they receive. Reveals how Cuba tackled the problem and the U.S. response in the form of Radio Marti. 49m; VHS, Special order formats. **A:** Sr. High-Adult. **P:** Education. **U:** Institution. **Gen-Edu:** Communication, Television, Caribbean. **Acq:** Purchase, Rent/Lease. **Dist:** Bullfrog Films, Inc. $150.00.

. . .And the Door Was Opened 1988
Four alcoholics share the experiences they have had, both about drinking and getting help. 40m; VHS, 3/4 U. **Pr:** Alcoholism and Drug Addiction Research. **A:** Sr. High-Adult. **P:** Education. **U:** Institution, CCTV. **Hea-Sci:** Alcoholism. **Acq:** Purchase. **Dist:** Centre for Addiction and Mental Health. $275.00.

. . .And the Earth Did Not Swallow Him 1994 (Unrated) — ★★½
Family trials of migrant farm workers from the perspective of 12-year-old Marcos, who travels with his parents on their annual (it's 1952) move from Texas throughout the midwest during harvest season. Balances their struggles with the strong family bonds that allow them to endure. Based on the semi-autobiographical novel by Tomas Rivera. 99m; VHS, DVD. **C:** Jose Alcala; Rose Portillo; Marco Rodriguez; Directed by Severo Perez; Written by Severo Perez; Cinematography by Virgil Harper; Music by Marcos Loya. **Pr:** Kino International Corporation. **A:** Sr. High-Adult. **P:** Entertainment. **U:** Home. **Mov-Ent:** Agriculture. **Acq:** Purchase. **Dist:** Kino on Video; Facets Multimedia Inc.

And the Ship Sails On 1983 (PG) — ★★★
On the eve of WWI, a group of devoted opera lovers take a luxury cruise to pay their respects to a recently deceased opera diva. Also on board is a group of fleeing Serbo-Croation freedom fighters. A charming and absurd autumnal homage-to-life by Fellini shot entirely in the studio. 130m; VHS, DVD. **C:** Freddie Jones; Barbara Jefford; Janet Suzman; Peter Cellier; Philip Locke; Victor Poletti; Norma West; Directed by Federico Fellini; Written by Federico Fellini; Tonino Guerra; Cinematography by Giuseppe Rotunno; Music by Gianfranco Plenizio. **Pr:** Triumph Films. **A:** College-Adult. **P:** Entertainment. **U:** Home. **L:** Italian. **Mov-Ent:** Boating. **Acq:** Purchase. **Dist:** Home Vision Cinema.

. . .and the Spirit of God Dances 1990
A vignette recognizing the power of God, followed by a report on the 1990 Student Congress on Global Issues and a reading from Colossians 4 by Isaac Canales, pastor of Mission Ebenezer Baptist Church in California. Presented at the InterVarsity 16th Triennial Student Mission Convention. 80m; VHS. **Pr:** TwentyOneHundred Productions. **A:** Sr. High-College. **P:** Religious. **U:** Institution. **Gen-Edu:** Acq: Purchase. **Dist:** InterVarsity Video. $14.95.

And the Walls Came Tumblin' Down 1977
Retired tailor gives up on life and awaits death. One day a young man representing God appears to the old man and gives him a reason to live. Theme: experiencing God makes us alive, hope-filled and loving. 27m; VHS, 3/4 U, Special order formats. **C:** Jack Albertson; Martin Sheen. **Pr:** Paulist Productions. **A:** Jr. High-Adult. **P:** Religious. **U:** Institution, CCTV, SURA. **Gen-Edu:** Death. **Acq:** Purchase, Rent/Lease. **Dist:** Paulist Productions.

And the Wild, Wild Women 1959 (Unrated) — ★★
Italian women-behind-bars potboiler. Young Lina (Masina) is falsely convicted of robbery and sent to the slammer in Rome, where seasoned cellmate Egle (Magnani) decides to look after her. Lina is finally exonerated but, to Egle's regret, that doesn't mean Lina's life gets any better. Dubbed. 85m/B/W; DVD. **C:** Anna Magnani; Giulietta Masina; Renato Salvatori; Alberto Sordi; Myriam Bru; Cristina Gaioni; Directed by Renato Castellani; Written by Renato Castellani; Cinematography by Leonida Barboni; Music by Roman Vlad. **A:** Sr. High-Adult. **P:** Entertainment. **U:** Home. **Mov-Ent:** Acq: Purchase. **Dist:** Sinister Cinema.

. . .And The Word Was God 1987
A poetic narrative video focusing on the Cree-speaking natives of northern Saskatchewan. 28m; VHS, 3/4 U. **Pr:** Ruby Truly. **A:** Jr. High-Adult. **P:** Education. **U:** Institution, SURA. **Gen-Edu:** Native Americans, Religion. **Acq:** Rent/Lease. **Dist:** Video Out Distribution.

And Then 1978
A young married filmmaking couple has their feature film script accepted by a big Hollywood producer, who wants them to rewrite it his way. 21m; VHS, 3/4 U. **Pr:** Caroline Mouris; Frank Mouris. **A:** Sr. High-Adult. **P:** Education. **U:** Institution, SURA. **Gen-Edu:** Filmmaking. **Acq:** Purchase. **Dist:** Phoenix Learning Group.

And Then Came John 1987
An inspiring film about overcoming life's obstacles. John McGough, born with Down's syndrome, has grown up to be a well-regarded artist, musician, and beloved member of his community. 36m; VHS, 3/4 U. **Pr:** Scott Andrews; Telesis Productions. **A:** Jr. High-Adult. **P:** Education. **U:** Institution,

Home, SURA. **Gen-Edu:** Handicapped, Birth Defects. **Acq:** Purchase, Rent/Lease, Duplication. **Dist:** Filmakers Library Inc.

And Then Came Lola 2009 (Unrated) — ★★
Lesbian rom com inspired by the 1998 German film "Run, Lola, Run." This Lola is a talented but unreliable San Francisco photographer who is asked by her girlfriend to deliver some important photos to a meeting. Lola has three chances but gets waylaid by a no-nonsense meter maid, crazy dog owners, and beautiful babes, which could ruin both her personal and professional lives if she screws up. 70m; DVD. **C:** Ashleigh Sumner; Jill Bennett; Cathy DeBuono; Jessica Graham; Candy Tolentino; Linda Ignazi; Angelyna Martinez; Jenoa Harlow; Directed by Ellen Seidler; Megan Siler; Written by Ellen Seidler; Megan Siler; Cinematography by Jennifer Derbin. **A:** College-Adult. **P:** Entertainment. **U:** Home. **Mov-Ent:** Photography, Comedy--Romantic. **Acq:** Purchase. **Dist:** Wolfe Video.

And Then Came Love 2007 (Unrated) — ★★
When Julie (Williams) decides to search for the anonymous sperm donor father of her six-year old son, her idyllic world is suddenly turned upside-down. This color-blind romantic comedy provides unadulterated insight into complex relationships without being overly sappy or contrary. 98m; DVD, CC. **C:** Vanessa L(ynne) Williams; Kevin Daniels; Ben Vereen; Michael Boatman; Eartha Kitt; Tommy Nelson; Stephen Spinella; Directed by Richard Schenkman; Written by Caytha Jentis; Cinematography by Timothy Naylor; Music by Rebecca Lloyd. **P:** Entertainment. **U:** Home. **Mov-Ent:** Black Culture, Comedy--Romantic. **Acq:** Purchase. **Dist:** Warner Home Video, Inc.

And Then I'll Stop: Does Any of This Sound Familiar? 1989
Six different people with chemical dependancy problems narrate their individual stories of recovery. 20m; VHS, 3/4 U. **A:** Jr. High-Adult. **P:** Education. **U:** Institution, Home, SURA. **Hea-Sci:** Alcoholism, Drug Abuse. **Acq:** Purchase, Rent/Lease. **Dist:** Pyramid Media. $325.00.

And Then There Was One 1991
A look at the effect of accidents on the families of workers, using four case studies. The importance of safety awareness, protective equipment and understanding potential hazards are all emphasized. ?m; VHS, 3/4 U. **Pr:** Mobil Oil Productions. **A:** College-Adult. **P:** Vocational. **U:** Institution. **Bus-Ind:** Safety Education, Job Training, Personnel Management. **Acq:** Rent/Lease. **Dist:** Learning Communications L.L.C. $175.00.

And Then There Was Voyager: Jupiter, Uranus, Saturn & Neptune 19??
Spotlights solar system discoveries made by the Voyagers 1 and 2, including swirling atmospheres, rings of ice and rock, and more. Explains scientific theories behind these discoveries via computer generated graphics. 30m; VHS. **A:** Sr. High-College. **P:** Education. **U:** Institution. **Hea-Sci:** Astronomy. **Acq:** Purchase. **Dist:** Cambridge Educational. $34.95.

And Then There Were None 1945 (Unrated) — ★★★½
An all-star cast makes up the ten colorful guests invited to a secluded estate in England by a mysterious host. What the invitations do not say, however, is the reason they have been specifically chosen to visit—to be murdered, one by one. Cat and mouse classic based on Agatha Christie's book with an entertaining mix of suspense and black comedy. Remade in 1966 and again in 1975 as "Ten Little Indians," but lacking the force and gloss of the original. 97m/B/W; VHS, DVD, Blu-Ray. **C:** Louis Hayward; Barry Fitzgerald; Walter Huston; Roland Young; Sir C. Aubrey Smith; Judith Anderson; Mischa Auer; June Duprez; Directed by Rene Clair; Written by Rene Clair; Dudley Nichols; Cinematography by Lucien N. Andriot; Music by Mario Castelnuovo-Tedesco. **Pr:** 20th Century-Fox. **A:** Family. **P:** Entertainment. **U:** Home. **Mov-Ent:** Mystery & Suspense. **Acq:** Purchase. **Dist:** Image Entertainment Inc.; VCI Entertainment; Tapeworm Video Distributors Inc.

. . .And Then There Were Two 198?
The correct work procedures and safety rules for erecting scaffolds and platforms are explained. 22m; VHS, 3/4 U. **A:** College-Adult. **P:** Education. **U:** Institution. **Bus-Ind:** Safety Education. **Acq:** Rent/Lease. **Dist:** National Safety Council, California Chapter, Film Library.

And Then What Happened, Paul Revere? ????
A video portrayal of Jean Fritz's American history biography. Recommended for use with grades 3 to 6. 24m; VHS. **A:** Primary. **P:** Education. **U:** Institution. **Gen-Edu:** History--U.S., Biography. **Acq:** Purchase. **Dist:** Zenger Media. $39.95.

And Then You Die 1988 (R) — ★★★
An intense crime drama about a Canadian drug lord who amasses a fortune from the cocaine and marijuana trade. His empire is threatened as the Mafia, Hell's Angels, and the police try to bring him down. 115m; VHS. **C:** Kenneth Welsh; R.H. Thomson; Wayne Robson; Tom Harvey; George Bloomfield; Graeme Campbell; Directed by Francis Mankiewicz. **Pr:** Brian McKenna. **A:** Sr. High-Adult. **P:** Entertainment. **U:** Home. **Mov-Ent:** Drugs, Canada. **Acq:** Purchase. **Dist:** CinemaNow Inc. $79.95.

And There Was Light 1987
The story of the Bible—how it was formed, its various translators, and other key points in its history. 60m; VHS. **Pr:** Clifton Bible Classics. **A:** Family. **P:** Education. **U:** Institution, Home. **Gen-Edu:** History--Ancient, Bible. **Acq:** Purchase. **Dist:** Alden Films. $79.95.

And They All Fall Down 1975
A young hobbyist creates amazingly elaborate designs with dominoes. 6m/B/W; 3/4 U. **Pr:** Bonnie Cutler; Sheri Herman. **A:**

Family. **P:** Education. **U:** Institution, SURA. **Spo-Rec:** Games. **Acq:** Purchase, Rent/Lease. **Dist:** Temple University Dept. of Film and Media Arts.

And They Lived Happily Ever After? 1981
A look at teenage marriages—why they fail and what is special about the ones that succeed. 46m; VHS, 3/4 U. **Pr:** Guidance Associates. **A:** Jr. High-Adult. **P:** Education. **U:** Institution, SURA. **Gen-Edu:** Marriage, Adolescence. **Acq:** Purchase. **Dist:** Center for Humanities, Inc./Guidance Associates.

And They're Off 2011 (PG-13) — ★½
What's really off here is the so-called comedy. Dusty Sanders (Astin) is a losing horse trainer with no horses, a volatile jockey girlfriend (Oteri), and a documentary crew following him around. A meeting with his former English teacher and her husband may change his luck because they're about to buy a horse and give Dusty the opportunity to train it. 90m; DVD. **C:** Sean Astin; Cheri Oteri; Mark Moses; Gigi Rice; Martin Mull; Peter Jacobson; Mo Collins; Kevin Nealon; Directed by Rob Schiller; Written by Alan Grossbard; Cinematography by Ulf Soderqvist; Music by Lawrence Brown. **A:** Jr. High-Adult. **P:** Entertainment. **U:** Home. **L:** English. **Mov-Ent:** Horses, Horses--Racing. **Acq:** Purchase. **Dist:** Screen Media Ventures, LLC.

And This Is Free 1995
Cult classic of award winning photographer Mike Shea which provides a personal vision of life around Chicago's Maxwell Street open air market in 1964. Captures the flavor and texture of the urban landscape which was known as the home of Chicago Blues. This was the last year of life for this historical section of Chicago as shortly following this filming the section was razed and replaced by a parking lot. 50m/B/W; VHS. **A:** Jr. High-Adult. **P:** Entertainment. **U:** Home. **Mov-Ent:** Documentary Films, History--U.S., Cities & Towns. **Acq:** Purchase. **Dist:** Shanachie Entertainment. $19.95.

And Thou Shalt Honor 2002
Resource covering all issues concerning caregiving. 116m; VHS, DVD. **A:** Adult. **P:** Vocational. **U:** Institution. **Hea-Sci:** Health Education, Medical Care, Occupational Training. **Acq:** Purchase. **Dist:** Aquarius Health Care Media. $285.00.

And Time Passes 1984
A look at the lives of four elderly people who refuse to retire. 55m; VHS, 3/4 U. **Pr:** Pasia Schonberg. **A:** Sr. High-Adult. **P:** Education. **U:** Institution. **Gen-Edu:** Aging. **Acq:** Purchase. **Dist:** Filmakers Library Inc.

And We Knew How to Dance: Women in World War I 19??
Contains the stories of 12 different women as they recall their entry into the world of traditional men's jobs in this celebration of Canada's "other veterans." 56m; VHS. **Pr:** National Film Board of Canada. **A:** Family. **P:** Education. **U:** Home. **Gen-Edu:** Documentary Films, Canada, Women. **Acq:** Purchase. **Dist:** Direct Cinema Ltd. $34.95.

And What of the Future? 1981
A prediction for the future-what will the effects of microelectronics be on jobs and the way people will live in the next few decades? 40m; VHS, 3/4 U. **Pr:** BBC Horizon. **A:** Jr. High-Adult. **P:** Education. **U:** Institution, SURA. **Hea-Sci:** Technology, Electronics. **Acq:** Purchase, Rent/Lease. **Dist:** Home Vision Cinema.

And While We Were Here 2013 (R) — ★★
Young American writer Jane (Bosworth) and her violinist husband Leonard (Goldberg) travel to the island of Ischia, off the Amalfi Coast, as he prepares for a concert. Reading her grandmother's memoir about her WWII experiences (narrated by Bloom), Jane questions the mundane nature of her marriage contrasted against the passion in what she reads and what she feels far away from home. A romantic affair with younger man Caleb (Blackley) seems inevitable. Too slight and forgettable but the location-shooting captures the ability of beautiful places to crack people out of their well-worn patterns. 83m; DVD, Blu-Ray. **C:** Kate (Catherine) Bosworth; Iddo Goldberg; Jamie Blackley; Voice(s) by Claire Bloom; Directed by Kat Coiro; Written by Kat Coiro; Cinematography by Doug Chamberlain; Music by Mateo (Matt) Messina. **Pr:** Well Go USA, Inc. **A:** Sr. High-Adult. **P:** Entertainment. **U:** Home. **L:** English. **Mov-Ent:** Italy, Marriage, Romance. **Acq:** Purchase. **Dist:** Well Go USA, Inc.

...And Woman Wove It in a Basket... 1989
Explores Klickitat river culture by portraying basketweaver Nettie Jackson Kuneki and her family. 70m; VHS. **A:** College-Adult. **P:** Education. **U:** Institution. **Gen-Edu:** Women, Native Americans, Ethnicity. **Acq:** Purchase, Rent/Lease. **Dist:** Women Make Movies. $350.00.

And Yet It Moves 1981
This fascinating look at the artistry of animation demonstrates the tools and techniques used by the animator. 8m; VHS, 3/4 U. **Pr:** Romania Films. **A:** Sr. High-Adult. **P:** Education. **U:** Institution, SURA. **Fin-Art:** Art & Artists. **Acq:** Purchase. **Dist:** Phoenix Learning Group.

And You Thought Your Parents Were Weird! 1991 (PG) — ★★½
A pair of introverted, whiz kid brothers invent a lovable robot to provide fatherly guidance as well as companionship for their widowed mother. Surprisingly charming, sentimental film is only slightly hampered by low-budget special effects. 92m; VHS, Streaming, CC. **C:** Marcia Strassman; Joshua John Miller; Edan Gross; John Quade; Sam Behrens; Susan Gibney; Gustav Vintas; Eric Walker; Voice(s) by Alan Thicke; Richard Libertini; Directed by Tony Cookson; Written by Tony Cookson; Cinematography by Paul Elliott; Music by Randy Miller. **Pr:** Just Betzer; Panorama Entertainment. **A:** Jr. High-Adult. **P:** Entertainment. **U:** Home. **Mov-Ent:** Comedy--Romantic, Gifted Children, Family Viewing. **Acq:** Purchase. **Dist:** Lions Gate Home Entertainment; CinemaNow Inc. $92.95.

Anderson, Bruford, Wakeman and Howe: In the Big Dream 1990
Former members of "Yes" perform their original music, including "Brother of Mine," "Starship Trooper," "Order of the Universe" plus rare behind the scenes. 30m; VHS. **Pr:** RCA. **A:** Jr. High-Adult. **P:** Entertainment. **U:** Home. **Mov-Ent:** Music Video. **Acq:** Purchase. **Dist:** Music Video Distributors. $14.98.

The Anderson Platoon 1967
A French documentary following the activities of an integrated platoon in Vietnam. 62m/B/W; VHS, 3/4 U. **TV Std:** NTSC, PAL. **C:** Directed by Pierre Schoendoerffer. **Pr:** Pierre Schoendoerffer; Pierre Schoendoerffer. **A:** Sr. High-Adult. **P:** Education. **U:** Institution, SURA. **Gen-Edu:** Documentary Films, War--General, Vietnam War. **Awds:** Oscars '67: Feature Doc. **Acq:** Purchase. **Dist:** Home Vision Cinema; International Historic Films Inc.; Facets Multimedia Inc. $19.95.

The Anderson Tapes 1971 (PG) — ★★★
Newly released from prison, an ex-con assembles his professional pals and plans the million-dollar robbery of an entire luxury apartment house on NYC's upper east side. Of course, he's unaware that a hoard of law men from federal, state, and local agencies are recording their activities for a wide variety of reasons, though none of the surveillance is coordinated and it has nothing to do with the planned robbery. Based on the novel by Lawrence Sanders, the intricate caper is effectively shaped by Lumet, who skillfully integrates broad satire with suspense. Shot on location in New York City. Walken is The Kid, his first major role. 100m; VHS, DVD, Blu-Ray. **C:** Sean Connery; Dyan Cannon; Martin Balsam; Christopher Walken; Alan King; Ralph Meeker; Garrett Morris; Margaret Hamilton; Val Avery; Dick Anthony Williams; Richard B. Shull; Conrad Bain; Paul Benjamin; Directed by Sidney Lumet; Written by Frank Pierson; Music by Quincy Jones. **Pr:** Columbia Pictures. **A:** Family. **P:** Entertainment. **U:** Home. **Mov-Ent:** Mystery & Suspense. **Acq:** Purchase. **Dist:** Sony Pictures Home Entertainment Inc. $9.95.

Andersonville 1995 (Unrated) — ★★★
Andersonville was an infamous Confederate prison camp in Georgia that by August, 1864 contained more than 32,000 Union POWs—and was planned to hold 8,000 men. One in four soldiers died in the camp. The story is told through the eyes of Massachusetts Corporal Josiah Day (Emick), who is captured in 1864 and struggles to survive the hellish conditions. The commander of the Andersonville was a deranged German-Swiss captain named Wirz (Triska)?who became the only Civil War soldier to be hanged for war crimes (depicted in "The Andersonville Trial"). The TV miniseries was filmed some 150 miles from the original site. 168m; VHS, DVD. **C:** Jarrod Emick; Frederic Forrest; Ted Marcoux; Jan Triska; Cliff DeYoung; Tom Aldredge; Frederick Coffin; Justin Henry; Kris Kamm; William H. Macy; Gabriel Olds; William Sanderson; Bud Davis; Carmen Argenziano; Peter Murnik; Thomas F. Wilson; Directed by John Frankenheimer; Written by David W. Rintels; Cinematography by Ric Waite; Music by Gary Chang. **Pr:** David W. Rintels; John Frankenheimer; David W. Rintels; John Frankenheimer; Ethel Winant; Turner Network Television. **A:** Jr. High-Adult. **P:** Entertainment. **U:** Home. **Mov-Ent:** Civil War, TV Movies. **Acq:** Purchase. **Dist:** Facets Multimedia Inc.; Warner Home Video, Inc.; Turner Broadcasting System Inc.

The Andersonville Trial 1970 — ★★★½
Details the atrocities experienced by captured Union soldiers who were held in the Confederacy's notorious Andersonville prison during the American Civil War. Provides an interesting account of the war-crimes trial of the Georgia camp's officials, under whom more than 14,000 prisoners died. Moving, remarkable TV drama based on the book by Pulitzer prize-winner MacKinlay Kantor. 150m; VHS, DVD. **C:** Martin Sheen; William Shatner; Buddy Ebsen; Jack Cassidy; Richard Basehart; Cameron Mitchell; Directed by George C. Scott. **A:** Sr. High-Adult. **P:** Entertainment. **U:** Home. **Mov-Ent:** Civil War, TV Movies. **Acq:** Purchase. **Dist:** Lions Gate Television Corp. $59.95.

Andragogy 1972
Andragogy means the art and science of helping adults learn; it implied a redefinition of the teacher's role. The instructor becomes a facilitator and resource person and the learning process become one of inquiry instead of simple absorption and regurgitation. 30m; EJ. **Pr:** NETCHE. **A:** College-Adult. **P:** Teacher Education. **U:** Institution, CCTV, BCTV, SURA. **Gen-Edu:** Education. **Acq:** Purchase, Rent/Lease, Subscription. **Dist:** NETCHE.

Andre 1994 (PG) — ★★½
More human-animal interaction from the director of "The Man from Snowy River," telling the true story of an orphaned seal that was adopted by the local Maine harbormaster (Carradine) and his family. As they raise their houseguest, the question arises whether Andre should be returned to the wild. It'll remind you of "Free Willy" with an appealing smaller sea mammal and the equally appealing Majorino, as the youngster who befriends Andre. For those who are sticklers for accuracy, Andre is actually portrayed by a sea lion and not a seal. 94m; VHS, DVD, Wide, CC. **C:** Keith Carradine; Tina Majorino; Chelsea Field; Keith Szarabajka; Shane Meier; Joshua Jackson; Directed by George Miller; Written by Dana Baratta; Cinematography by Thomas Burstyn; Music by Bruce Rowland. **Pr:** Annette Handley; Adam Shapiro; Andre Productions; Paramount Pictures. **A:** Family. **P:** Entertainment. **U:** Home. **Mov-Ent:** Animals, Family Viewing, Adoption. **Acq:** Purchase. **Dist:** Paramount Pictures Corp. $14.95.

Andre Agassi and Nick Bollettieri: Attack 1992
1992 Wimbledon Champ Agassi and professional tennis coach Bollettieri team up for an instructional video program offering techniques, strategies, and inspiration to the tennis enthusiast. 45m; VHS. **A:** Jr. High-Adult. **P:** Instruction. **U:** Home. **Spo-Rec:** Tennis, Sports--General. **Acq:** Purchase. **Dist:** Fast Forward; Sony Pictures Home Entertainment Inc. $19.95.

Andre Malraux 1989
A portrait of French novelist, Andre Malraux who boasted of fictional exploits while keeping secret his truly heroic deeds. 26m; VHS, 3/4 U. **Pr:** Films for the Humanities and Sciences. **A:** College. **P:** Education. **U:** Institution, CCTV, CATV, BCTV. **L:** French. **Fin-Art:** Literature. **Acq:** Purchase, Rent/Lease, Duplication License. **Dist:** Films for the Humanities & Sciences. $275.00.

Andre und Ursula 19?? (Unrated)
Set during WWII, this is the story of two lovers reunited by a diary found on a dying soldier. In German only. 82m/B/W; VHS. **TV Std:** NTSC, PAL. **C:** Ivan Desny; Elisabeth Mueller; Walter Clemens; Ina Peters; Maria V. Tasnady; Denise Command; Ulrich Bettac. **Pr:** German Language Video Center. **A:** Sr. High-Adult. **P:** Entertainment. **U:** Home. **L:** German. **Mov-Ent:** Drama, World War Two. **Acq:** Purchase, Rent/Lease. **Dist:** German Language Video Center. $33.95.

Andre Walton: Arise Skates 1990
Get ready for the most stunning skateboarding you've ever seen. Set to rap, thrash and metal music. 60m; VHS. **A:** Adult-Family. **P:** Entertainment. **U:** Home. **Mov-Ent:** Music Video, Music--Rap. **Acq:** Purchase. **Dist:** Chordant Distribution Group. $19.95.

Andre Watts in Concert 1985
The noted pianist performs pieces by Beethoven, Lizst, Scarlatti and Gershwin, taped live at Lincoln Center in 1985. 90m; VHS. **Pr:** Paramount Pictures. **A:** Family. **P:** Entertainment. **U:** Home. **Fin-Art:** Music--Classical. **Acq:** Purchase. **Dist:** Music Video Distributors; Paramount Pictures Corp.; Home Vision Cinema. $29.95.

Andrea: A Friend in Need 1987
This documentary focuses on the problem of teenage suicide in America. 40m; VHS, 3/4 U. **Pr:** Centre Productions, Inc. **A:** Jr. High-Adult. **P:** Education. **U:** Institution, SURA. **Gen-Edu:** Suicide, Adolescence. **Acq:** Purchase. **Dist:** Clear Vue Inc.

Andrea Chenier 1978
A performance by La Scala of the Umberto Giordano opera. In Italian with subtitles. 128m; VHS. **C:** Jose Carreras; Eva Marton. **A:** Family. **P:** Entertainment. **U:** Home. **L:** Italian. **Fin-Art:** Opera. **Acq:** Purchase. **Dist:** Home Vision Cinema; Facets Multimedia Inc. $39.95.

Andrea Chenier 1987
A performance of the Giordano opera taped at the Royal Opera House, Covent Garden. English subtitles. 118m; VHS. **C:** Placido Domingo; Anna Tomowa-Sintow; Giorgio Zancanaro. **Pr:** National Video Corporation Ltd. **A:** Family. **P:** Entertainment. **U:** Home. **L:** Italian. **Fin-Art:** Opera. **Acq:** Purchase. **Dist:** Home Vision Cinema; Music Video Distributors. $39.95.

Andrea's Story: A Hitchhiking Tragedy 1990
Andrea hitches a ride home and becomes the victim of a rapist on a deserted road. Sensitively adapted from the novel by Gloria D. Miklowitz, it deals with anger, loneliness, and confusion from a student's perspective. Winner of five Emmy awards and a special Jury Award in the San Francisco Film Festival. Based on the novel "Did You Hear What Happened to Andrea?" by Gloria Miklowitz. 30m; VHS, 3/4 U, EJ, Special order formats. **TV Std:** NTSC, PAL, SECAM. **Pr:** Martin Tahse; Disney Educational Productions. **A:** Primary-College. **P:** Education. **U:** Institution, CCTV, SURA. **Mov-Ent:** Rape, Adolescence. **Acq:** Purchase, Rent/Lease. **Dist:** Phoenix Learning Group; New Kid Home Video. $39.95.

Andrei Rublev 1966 — ★★★★
A 15th-century Russian icon painter must decide whether to record history or participate in it as Tartar invaders make life miserable. During the black and white portion, he becomes involved in a peasant uprising, killing a man in the process. After a bout of pessimism and a vow of silence, he goes forth to create artistic beauty as the screen correspondingly blazes with color. A brilliant historical drama censored by Soviet authorities until 1971. In Russian with English subtitles. 185m; VHS, DVD. **C:** Anatoli (Otto) Solonitzin; Ivan Lapikov; Nikolai Grinko; Nikolai Sergeyev; Directed by Andrei Tarkovsky; Written by Andrei Tarkovsky; Andrei Konchalovsky; Cinematography by Vadim Yusov; Music by Vyacheslav Ovchinnikov. **Pr:** Mosfilm. **A:** College-Adult. **P:** Entertainment. **U:** Home. **L:** Russian. **Mov-Ent:** Drama, Art & Artists. **Acq:** Purchase. **Dist:** Wellspring Media; Facets Multimedia Inc. $19.98.

Andre's Lives 1998
Explores the life of Andre Steiner, an architect who saved over seven thousand Slovak Jews from being deported to Auschwitz during World War II. 62m; VHS. **A:** Sr. High-Adult. **P:** Education. **U:** Home, Institution. **Gen-Edu:** Documentary Films, World War Two, Judaism. **Acq:** Purchase, Rent/Lease. **Dist:** First Run/Icarus Films. $275.00.

Andres Lopez: Me Pido La Ventana 2007 (Unrated)
Live performance by comedian Andres Lopez, considered the pioneer of stand-up comedy in Colombia. 160m; DVD. **A:** Sr. High-Adult. **P:** Entertainment. **U:** Home. **Mov-Ent:** Comedy--Performance, Television. **Acq:** Purchase. **Dist:** Comedy Central. $14.98.

Andres Orozco of Mexico 1994
Shows how young Andres Orozco of San Luis Potosi, Mexico, lives his life in a day to day scenario. 12m; VHS. **A:** Primary. **P:** Education. **U:** Institution. **Chl-Juv:** Children, Mexico, Sociology. **Acq:** Purchase. **Dist:** United Learning Inc. $79.95.

Andres Segovia: The Song of the Guitar 1976
Classsical guitarist Andres Segovia performs music by Albenz, Granados, Scarlatti, Rameau, Sar, Ponce, Aguado, Bach, Chopin, and Torroba. Filmed in Granada at the Palaces of Alhambra. 52m; VHS. **A:** Family. **P:** Entertainment. **U:** Home. **Mov-Ent:** Music--Classical. **Acq:** Purchase. **Dist:** Music Video Distributors. $29.95.

Andrew Carnegie and the Age of Steel: Empires of American Industry 1997
Presents a history of the iron and steel industry in America from the colonial era to modern times with emphasis on the contributions and technologies instituted by Andrew Carnegie. 50m; VHS. **A:** Sr. High-Adult. **P:** Education. **U:** Institution. **Gen-Edu:** Inventors & Inventions, Industry & Industrialists, History--U.S. **Acq:** Purchase. **Dist:** Zenger Media. $19.95.

Andrew Carnegie: The Gospel of Wealth 1974
Fascinating portrait of the legendary tycoon and a remarkable insight into the power games of big business. 267m; VHS, 3/4 U. **C:** Bramwell Fletcher. **Pr:** Robert Saudek; Learning Corporation of America. **A:** Jr. High-Adult. **P:** Entertainment. **U:** Institution, SURA. **Gen-Edu:** Documentary Films, Biography. **Acq:** Purchase, Rent/Lease. **Dist:** Phoenix Learning Group.

Andrew Dice Clay & His Gang in the Valentine's Day Massacre 1995
Andrew Dice Clay's stand-up shows which features traditional "Diceman" comedy. Includes comedy performances from two other comedians, John Mulrooney and Paul Mooney. Contains graphic language. 105m; VHS. **C:** Andrew Silverstein. **A:** College-Adult. **P:** Entertainment. **U:** Home. **Mov-Ent:** Comedy--Performance. **Acq:** Purchase. **Dist:** MPI Media Group. $19.98.

Andrew Dice Clay: Dice Rules 1991
Foul-mouthed, alleged comedian Clay in his Madison Square Garden performances. 87m; VHS. **C:** Andrew Silverstein; Maria Parkinson; "Noodles" Levenstein; Directed by Jay Dubin. **Pr:** Seven Arts Pictures. **A:** Adult. **P:** Entertainment. **U:** Home. **Mov-Ent:** Comedy--Performance. **Acq:** Purchase. **Dist:** Lions Gate Television Corp. $89.98.

Andrew Dice Clay: No Apologies 1993
The Dice-Man returneth with his usual controversial humor. Filmed live at Long Island's Westbury Music Fair. 65m; VHS, DVD. **A:** Adult. **P:** Entertainment. **U:** Home. **Mov-Ent:** Comedy--Performance. **Acq:** Purchase. **Dist:** BMG Entertainment; Music Video Distributors. $29.98.

Andrew Dice Clay: One Night With Dice 1991
The Diceman returneth with more of his patented raunchy humor. "Guaranteed to offend." 60m; VHS. **C:** Andrew Silverstein. **Pr:** Vestron Video. **A:** Adult. **P:** Entertainment. **U:** Home. **Mov-Ent:** Comedy--Performance. **Acq:** Purchase. **Dist:** Lions Gate Television Corp. $39.98.

Andrew Dice Clay: The Diceman Cometh 1989
It's no wonder women refused to appear with Clay on "Saturday Night Live." See what all the uproar is about. 60m; VHS. **C:** Andrew Silverstein. **A:** Adult. **P:** Entertainment. **U:** Home. **Mov-Ent:** Comedy--Performance. **Acq:** Purchase. **Dist:** Lions Gate Television Corp. $19.98.

Andrew J. Russell: A Visual Historian 1983
Documentary that focuses on the life and works of photography Andrew J. Russell, one of the most prominent photographers of 19th century American history. 29m; VHS, SVS, 3/4 U. **Pr:** Brigham Young University. **A:** Jr. High-Adult. **P:** Education. **U:** Institution. **Gen-Edu:** Documentary Films, History--U.S., Photography. **Acq:** Purchase, Rent/Lease. **Dist:** Encyclopedia Britannica. $59.00.

Andrew Lloyd Webber: Requiem 1985
Webber's masterpiece is performed beautifully. The work is assisted by his friends Placido Domingo, Sarah Brightman, the Choirs of St. Thomas' Church and Winchester Cathedral and the Orchestra of St. Luke conducted by Lorin Maazel. 60m; VHS. **C:** Placido Domingo; Sarah Brightman; Conducted by Lorin Maazel. **Pr:** Really Useful Company, Ltd. **A:** Jr. High-Family. **P:** Entertainment. **U:** Home. **Fin-Art:** Music--Classical, Music--Performance. **Acq:** Purchase. **Dist:** Home Vision Cinema; Kultur International Films Ltd., Inc.; Music Video Distributors. $19.95.

Andrew Wyeth: The Helga Pictures 1987
A close examination of the 44 most important Helga pictures, placing them in perspective with Wyeth's career, his artistic development, and art history as a whole. The laserdisc edition features still shots of all 237 of the Helga paintings. Filmed in Chadds Ford on the Kuerner farm and also at Wyeth's home. 36m; VHS. **C:** Narrated by Charlton Heston. **Pr:** Videodisc Publishing Inc. **A:** Family. **P:** Education. **U:** Institution, Home. **Fin-Art:** Documentary Films, Art & Artists, Painting. **Acq:** Purchase. **Dist:** Crystal Productions. $29.95.

Androcles and the Lion 1952 — ★★½
Stage-bound Hollywood version of the George Bernard Shaw story about a tailor in Imperial Rome who saves Christians from a hungry lion he had previously befriended. Sharp dialogue and a plot that's relatively (within the bounds of Hollywood) faithful help a great play become a semi-satisfying cinematic morsel. Harpo Marx was originally cast as Androcles, but was fired by producer Howard Hughes five weeks into the shooting. 105m/B/W; VHS, DVD. **C:** Jean Simmons; Alan Young; Victor Mature; Robert Newton; Maurice Evans; Elsa Lanchester; Directed by Chester Erskine; Cinematography by Harry Stradling, Sr. **Pr:** Gabriel Pascal. **A:** Jr. High-Adult. **P:** Entertainment. **U:** Home. **Mov-Ent:** Comedy-Drama, Religion, History--Ancient. **Acq:** Purchase. **Dist:** Criterion Collection Inc. $19.95.

Android 1982 (PG) — ★★½
When an android who has been assisting a quirky scientist in space learns that he is about to be permanently retired, he starts to take matters into his own synthetic hands. Combines science fiction, suspense and cloned romance. A must for Kinski fans. 80m; VHS, DVD. **C:** Klaus Kinski; Don Opper; Brie Howard; Norbert Weisser; Crofton Hardester; Kendra Kirchner; Directed by Aaron Lipstadt; Written by Don Opper; James Reigle; Cinematography by Tim Suhrstedt; Music by Don Preston. **Pr:** Mary Ann Fisher. **A:** Sr. High-Adult. **P:** Entertainment. **U:** Home. **Mov-Ent:** Science Fiction, Mystery & Suspense, Cult Films. **Acq:** Purchase. **Dist:** Movies Unlimited. $19.99.

The Android Affair 1995 (PG-13) — ★★½
Karen Garrett (Kozak) is studying at the Institute for Surgical Research where doctors practice experimental techniques on lifelike androids. Her next patient is William (Dunne), a handsome and charming android with a heart defect, who doesn't want to "die" during Karen's risky surgical procedure. What's worse is Karen finds this 'droid all too humanly appealing and decides to help him escape the Institute. From a story by Isaac Asimov and screenwriter Kletter. 90m; VHS, DVD, CC. **C:** Harley Jane Kozak; Griffin Dunne; Ossie Davis; Saul Rubinek; Peter Outerbridge; Natalie Radford; Directed by Richard Kletter; Written by Richard Kletter; Cinematography by Berhard Salzmann; Music by Simon Boswell. **Pr:** Joan Carson; Thom Colwell; Jana Sue Memel; Chanticleer Films; MTE, Inc. **A:** Jr. High-Adult. **P:** Entertainment. **U:** Home. **Mov-Ent:** Science Fiction, Technology, Romance. **Acq:** Purchase. **Dist:** Universal Studios Home Video.

Android Cop 2014 (Unrated) — ★½
90m; DVD, Blu-Ray. **C:** Michael Jai White; Randy Wayne; Kadeem Hardison; Larissa Vereza; Charles S. Dutton; Directed by Mark Atkins; Written by Mark Atkins; Cinematography by Mark Atkins; Music by Chris(topher) Cano. **A:** Jr. High-Adult. **P:** Entertainment. **U:** Home. **L:** English. **Mov-Ent:** Science Fiction. **Acq:** Purchase. **Dist:** The Asylum.

Android Kikaider: The Animation - Volume 1: Lonely Soul 2000 (Unrated)
Features the animated science fiction television series on Kikaider, a humanoid robot, designed by Dr. Komyoji to ensure the safety of his children, Mitsuko and Masaru, against the evil forces of DARK—a group that is led by Professor Gill with menacing robots and monsters who use extreme violence to dominate Japan. 4 episodes. 100m; DVD. **C:** Voice(s) by Michael Gregory; Christopher Carroll; Lia Sargent; Dave Wittenberg. **A:** Jr. High-Adult. **P:** Entertainment. **U:** Home. **Mov-Ent:** Television Series, Animation & Cartoons, Science Fiction. **Acq:** Purchase. **Dist:** Bandai Entertainment Inc. $29.98.

Android Kikaider: The Animation - Volume 2: Conflicting Hearts 2000 (Unrated)
Features the animated science fiction television series on Kikaider, a humanoid robot, designed by Dr. Komyoji to ensure the safety of his children, Mitsuko and Masaru, against the evil forces of DARK—a group that is led by Professor Gill with menacing robots and monsters who use extreme violence to dominate Japan. 4 episodes. 100m; DVD. **C:** Voice(s) by Christopher Carroll; Michael Gregory; Lia Sargent; Dave Wittenberg. **A:** Jr. High-Adult. **P:** Entertainment. **U:** Home. **Mov-Ent:** Television Series, Animation & Cartoons, Science Fiction. **Acq:** Purchase. **Dist:** Bandai Entertainment Inc. $29.98.

Android Kikaider: The Animation - Volume 3: Unveiled Past 2000 (Unrated)
Features the animated science fiction television series on Kikaider, a humanoid robot, designed by Dr. Komyoji to ensure the safety of his children, Mitsuko and Masaru, against the evil forces of DARK—a group that is led by Professor Gill with menacing robots and monsters who use extreme violence to dominate Japan. 3 episodes. 75m; DVD. **C:** Voice(s) by Christopher Carroll; Michael Gregory; Lia Sargent; Dave Wittenberg. **A:** Jr. High-Adult. **P:** Entertainment. **U:** Home. **Mov-Ent:** Television Series, Animation & Cartoons, Science Fiction. **Acq:** Purchase. **Dist:** Bandai Entertainment Inc. $29.98.

Android Kikaider: The Animation - Volume 4: Silent Journey 2000 (Unrated)
Features the animated science fiction television series on Kikaider, a humanoid robot, designed by Dr. Komyoji to ensure the safety of his children, Mitsuko and Masaru, against the evil forces of DARK—a group that is led by Professor Gill with menacing robots and monsters who use extreme violence to dominate Japan. 3 episodes. 75m; DVD. **C:** Voice(s) by Christopher Carroll; Michael Gregory; Lia Sargent; Dave Wittenberg. **A:** Jr. High-Adult. **P:** Entertainment. **U:** Home. **Mov-Ent:** Television Series, Animation & Cartoons, Science Fiction. **Acq:** Purchase. **Dist:** Bandai Entertainment Inc. $24.98.

Andromeda: Season 1 2003 (Unrated)
Features the 2000-2005 futuristic science fiction television series about the crew of the Andromeda Ascendant that awoke from a 300-year slumber to witness the collapse of their perfect government—the Systems Commonwealth—and the subsequent mayhem that has erupted throughout the universe causing Captain Dylan Hunt (Sorbo) to rally them to overcome the militant Nietzscheans. Includes: the crew goes back in time 300 years just prior to the Nietzscheans overthrow of the Commonwealth and Dylan receives a life sentence on Azaria and Harper (Woolvett) mistakenly replaces Andromeda's with an older version causing it to revert to a previous mission which killed the former crew members. 22 episodes. 1100m; DVD. **C:** Kevin Sorbo; Lisa Ryder; Lexa Doig; Gordon Michael Woolvett; Laura Bertram; Keith Hamilton Cobb; Brent Stait. **A:** Jr. High-Adult. **P:** Entertainment. **U:** Home. **Mov-Ent:** Television Series, Science Fiction, Fantasy. **Acq:** Purchase. **Dist:** Amazon.com Inc. $69.98.

Andromeda: Season 1 Volume 1 2002 (Unrated)
Features the 2000-2005 futuristic science fiction television series about the crew of the Andromeda Ascendant that awoke from a 300-year slumber to witness the collapse of their perfect government—the Systems Commonwealth—and the subsequent mayhem that has erupted throughout the universe causing Captain Dylan Hunt (Sorbo) to rally them to overcome the militant Nietzscheans. 5 episodes. 260m; DVD. **C:** Kevin Sorbo; Lisa Ryder; Lexa Doig; Gordon Michael Woolvett; Brent Stait; Laura Bertram; Keith Hamilton Cobb. **A:** Jr. High-Adult. **P:** Entertainment. **U:** Home. **Mov-Ent:** Television Series, Science Fiction, Fantasy. **Acq:** Purchase. **Dist:** Amazon.com Inc. $39.98.

Andromeda: Season 1 Volume 2 2002 (Unrated)
Features the 2000-2005 futuristic science fiction television series about the crew of the Andromeda Ascendant that awoke from a 300-year slumber to witness the collapse of their perfect government—the Systems Commonwealth—and the subsequent mayhem that has erupted throughout the universe causing Captain Dylan Hunt (Sorbo) to rally them to overcome the militant Nietzscheans. Includes: the crew goes back in time 300 years just prior to the Nietzscheans overthrow of the Commonwealth and Dylan receives a life sentence on Azaria. 5 episodes. 265m; DVD. **C:** Kevin Sorbo; Lisa Ryder; Lexa Doig; Gordon Michael Woolvett; Laura Bertram; Keith Hamilton Cobb; Brent Stait. **A:** Jr. High-Adult. **P:** Entertainment. **U:** Home. **Mov-Ent:** Television Series, Science Fiction, Fantasy. **Acq:** Purchase. **Dist:** Amazon.com Inc. $39.98.

Andromeda: Season 1 Volume 3 2002 (Unrated)
Features the 2000-2005 futuristic science fiction television series about the crew of the Andromeda Ascendant that awoke from a 300-year slumber to witness the collapse of their perfect government—the Systems Commonwealth—and the subsequent mayhem that has erupted throughout the universe causing Captain Dylan Hunt (Sorbo) to rally them to overcome the militant Nietzscheans. Includes: the Andromeda shipmates come across a similar ship—the Pax Magellanic. 4 episodes. 200m; DVD. **C:** Kevin Sorbo; Lisa Ryder; Lexa Doig; Gordon Michael Woolvett; Laura Bertram; Keith Hamilton Cobb; Brent Stait. **A:** Jr. High-Adult. **P:** Entertainment. **U:** Home. **Mov-Ent:** Television Series, Science Fiction, Fantasy. **Acq:** Purchase. **Dist:** Amazon.com Inc. $39.98.

Andromeda: Season 1 Volume 4 2003 (Unrated)
Features the 2000-2005 futuristic science fiction television series about the crew of the Andromeda Ascendant that awoke from a 300-year slumber to witness the collapse of their perfect government—the Systems Commonwealth—and the subsequent mayhem that has erupted throughout the universe causing Captain Dylan Hunt (Sorbo) to rally them to overcome the militant Nietzscheans. Includes: a humanoid robot tries to force them to meet its leader. 4 episodes. 200m; DVD. **C:** Kevin Sorbo; Lisa Ryder; Lexa Doig; Gordon Michael Woolvett; Laura Bertram; Keith Hamilton Cobb; Brent Stait. **A:** Jr. High-Adult. **P:** Entertainment. **U:** Home. **Mov-Ent:** Television Series, Science Fiction, Fantasy. **Acq:** Purchase. **Dist:** Amazon.com Inc. $39.98.

Andromeda: Season 1 Volume 5 2003 (Unrated)
Features the 2000-2005 futuristic science fiction television series about the crew of the Andromeda Ascendant that awoke from a 300-year slumber to witness the collapse of their perfect government—the Systems Commonwealth—and the subsequent mayhem that has erupted throughout the universe causing Captain Dylan Hunt (Sorbo) to rally them to overcome the militant Nietzscheans. Includes: Harper (Woolvett) mistakenly replaces Andromeda's with an older version causing it to revert to a previous mission which killed the former crew members. 4 episodes. 200m; DVD. **C:** Kevin Sorbo; Lisa Ryder; Lexa Doig; Gordon Michael Woolvett; Laura Bertram; Keith Hamilton Cobb; Brent Stait. **A:** Jr. High-Adult. **P:** Entertainment. **U:** Home. **Mov-Ent:** Television Series, Science Fiction, Fantasy. **Acq:** Purchase. **Dist:** Amazon.com Inc. $39.98.

Andromeda: Season 2 2004 (Unrated)
Features the 2000-2005 science fiction television series about the crew of the Andromeda Ascendant that awoke from a 300-year slumber to witness the collapse of their perfect government—the Systems Commonwealth—and the subsequent mayhem that has erupted throughout the universe causing Captain Dylan Hunt (Sorbo) to rally them to overcome the militant Nietzscheans. Includes: the Andromeda is damaged, the Eureka Maru goes out to get parts to repair the Andromeda but smashes into a frozen planet, Dylan receives a note from his deceased fiance which send him out on a personal journey, Harper (Woolvett) and the crew take their first trip back to Earth to rescue it from Nietzschean. 22 episodes. 1100m; DVD. **C:** Kevin Sorbo; Lisa Ryder; Lexa Doig; Gordon Michael Woolvett; Laura Bertram; Keith Hamilton Cobb; Brent Stait. **A:** Jr. High-Adult. **P:** Entertainment. **U:** Home. **Mov-Ent:** Television Series, Science Fiction, Fantasy. **Acq:** Purchase. **Dist:** Amazon.com Inc. $69.98.

Andromeda: Season 2 Volume 1 2002 (Unrated)
Features the 2000-2005 futuristic science fiction television series about the crew of the Andromeda Ascendant that awoke from a 300-year slumber to witness the collapse of their perfect government—the Systems Commonwealth—and the subsequent mayhem that has erupted throughout the universe causing Captain Dylan Hunt (Sorbo) to rally them to overcome the

militant Nietzscheans. Includes: the Andromeda is damaged, the Eureka Maru goes out to get parts to repair the Andromeda but smashes into a frozen planet, and Trance (Bertram) is taken prisoner on Inaris under suspicion of starting a civil war there years before. 5 episodes. 260m; DVD. **C:** Kevin Sorbo; Lisa Ryder; Lexa Doig; Gordon Michael Woolvett; Laura Bertram; Keith Hamilton Cobb; Brent Stait. **A:** Jr. High-Adult. **P:** Entertainment. **U:** Home. **Mov-Ent:** Television Series, Science Fiction. Fantasy. **Acq:** Purchase. **Dist:** Amazon.com Inc. $39.98.

Andromeda: Season 2 Volume 2 2003 (Unrated)
Features the 2000-2005 futuristic science fiction television series about the crew of the Andromeda Ascendant that awoke from a 300-year slumber to witness the collapse of their perfect government—the Systems Commonwealth—and the subsequent mayhem that has erupted throughout the universe causing Captain Dylan Hunt (Sorbo) to rally them to overcome the militant Nietzscheans. Includes: Tyr's (Cobb) questioned by Dylan after the remnants of the Drago Musevini are uncovered and Dylan receives a note from his deceased fiancee which send him out on a personal journey. 4 episodes. 200m; DVD. **C:** Kevin Sorbo; Lisa Ryder; Lexa Doig; Gordon Michael Woolvett; Laura Bertram; Keith Hamilton Cobb; Brent Stait. **A:** Jr. High-Adult. **P:** Entertainment. **U:** Home. **Mov-Ent:** Television Series, Science Fiction, Fantasy. **Acq:** Purchase. **Dist:** Amazon.com Inc. $39.98.

Andromeda: Season 2 Volume 3 2003 (Unrated)
Features the 2000-2005 futuristic science fiction television series about the crew of the Andromeda Ascendant that awoke from a 300-year slumber to witness the collapse of their perfect government—the Systems Commonwealth—and the subsequent mayhem that has erupted throughout the universe causing Captain Dylan Hunt (Sorbo) to rally them to overcome the militant Nietzscheans. Includes: Harper (Woolvett) and the crew take their first trip back to Earth to rescue it from Nietzschean forces and to avoid an ambush Dylan comes aboard another ship—with a rookie female captain who intrigues Dylan. 5 episodes. 260m; DVD. **C:** Kevin Sorbo; Lisa Ryder; Lexa Doig; Gordon Michael Woolvett; Laura Bertram; Keith Hamilton Cobb; Brent Stait. **A:** Jr. High-Adult. **P:** Entertainment. **U:** Home. **Mov-Ent:** Television Series, Science Fiction, Fantasy. **Acq:** Purchase. **Dist:** Amazon.com Inc. $39.98.

Andromeda: Season 2 Volume 4 2003 (Unrated)
Features the 2000-2005 futuristic science fiction television series about the crew of the Andromeda Ascendant that awoke from a 300-year slumber to witness the collapse of their perfect government—the Systems Commonwealth—and the subsequent mayhem that has erupted throughout the universe causing Captain Dylan Hunt (Sorbo) to rally them to overcome the militant Nietzscheans. Includes: the crew is threatened by a biological infection by sick citizens of a drifter colony and Dylan is knocked out only to awaken to a wife and child but he doesn't know whether its reality or not. 4 episodes. 200m; DVD. **C:** Kevin Sorbo; Lisa Ryder; Lexa Doig; Gordon Michael Woolvett; Laura Bertram; Keith Hamilton Cobb; Brent Stait. **A:** Jr. High-Adult. **P:** Entertainment. **U:** Home. **Mov-Ent:** Television Series, Science Fiction, Fantasy. **Acq:** Purchase. **Dist:** Amazon.com Inc. $39.98.

Andromeda: Season 2 Volume 5 2003 (Unrated)
Features the 2000-2005 futuristic science fiction television series about the crew of the Andromeda Ascendant that awoke from a 300-year slumber to witness the collapse of their perfect government—the Systems Commonwealth—and the subsequent mayhem that has erupted throughout the universe causing Captain Dylan Hunt (Sorbo) to rally them to overcome the militant Nietzscheans. Includes: a giant space monster terrifies the people of Savion causing Dylan and Trance (Bertram) to go protect them but that leaves the Andromeda at risk and the Commonwealth's delegates attempt to sign a charter is hampered by a strange and deadly force. 4 episodes. 200m; DVD. **C:** Kevin Sorbo; Lisa Ryder; Lexa Doig; Gordon Michael Woolvett; Laura Bertram; Keith Hamilton Cobb; Brent Stait. **A:** Jr. High-Adult. **P:** Entertainment. **U:** Home. **Mov-Ent:** Television Series, Science Fiction, Fantasy. **Acq:** Purchase. **Dist:** Amazon.com Inc. $39.98.

Andromeda: Season 3 2005 (Unrated)
Features the 2000-2005 futuristic science fiction television series about the crew of the Andromeda Ascendant that awoke from a 300-year slumber to witness the collapse of their perfect government—the Systems Commonwealth—and the subsequent mayhem that has erupted throughout the universe causing Captain Dylan Hunt (Sorbo) to rally them to overcome the militant Nietzscheans. Includes: Dylan faces a difficult decision when the crew comes across a unique spaceship sent from Earth over 3,000 years ago, a good friend of Dylan is in jeopardy from a killer named "The Leper," the crew is prompted into action when bizarre attacks happen on nearby planets and an historic Commonwealth ship—the first in more than 300 years—is suspiciously destroyed before it can take its maiden voyage, and Tyr (Cobb) is confronted with either aiding the Andromeda or a group of Nietzscheans that he's pulled together under his son. 22 episodes. 1100m; DVD. **C:** Kevin Sorbo; Lisa Ryder; Lexa Doig; Gordon Michael Woolvett; Laura Bertram; Keith Hamilton Cobb. **A:** Jr. High-Adult. **P:** Entertainment. **U:** Home. **Mov-Ent:** Television Series, Science Fiction, Fantasy. **Acq:** Purchase. **Dist:** Amazon.com Inc. $69.98.

Andromeda: Season 3 Volume 1 2003 (Unrated)
Features the 2000-2005 futuristic science fiction television series about the crew of the Andromeda Ascendant that awoke from a 300-year slumber to witness the collapse of their perfect government—the Systems Commonwealth—and the subsequent mayhem that has erupted throughout the universe causing Captain Dylan Hunt (Sorbo) to rally them to overcome the

militant Nietzscheans. Includes: during his run for Commonwealth leader Beka's (Ryder) uncle Sid becomes an assassination target and Dylan faces a difficult decision when the crew comes across a unique spaceship sent from Earth over 3,000 years ago. 5 episodes. 250m; DVD. **C:** Kevin Sorbo; Lisa Ryder; Lexa Doig; Gordon Michael Woolvett; Laura Bertram; Keith Hamilton Cobb. **A:** Jr. High-Adult. **P:** Entertainment. **U:** Home. **Mov-Ent:** Television Series, Science Fiction, Fantasy. **Acq:** Purchase. **Dist:** Amazon.com Inc. $39.98.

Andromeda: Season 3 Volume 2 2003 (Unrated)
Features the 2000-2005 futuristic science fiction television series about the crew of the Andromeda Ascendant that awoke from a 300-year slumber to witness the collapse of their perfect government—the Systems Commonwealth—and the subsequent mayhem that has erupted throughout the universe causing Captain Dylan Hunt (Sorbo) to rally them to overcome the militant Nietzscheans. Includes: the Andromeda crew must disarm a planet's nova bombs and a good friend of Dylan is in jeopardy from a killer named "The Leper." 4 episodes. 200m; DVD. **C:** Kevin Sorbo; Lisa Ryder; Lexa Doig; Gordon Michael Woolvett; Laura Bertram; Keith Hamilton Cobb. **A:** Jr. High-Adult. **P:** Entertainment. **U:** Home. **Mov-Ent:** Television Series, Science Fiction, Fantasy. **Acq:** Purchase. **Dist:** Amazon.com Inc. $39.98.

Andromeda: Season 3 Volume 3 2004 (Unrated)
Features the 2000-2005 futuristic science fiction television series about the crew of the Andromeda Ascendant that awoke from a 300-year slumber to witness the collapse of their perfect government—the Systems Commonwealth—and the subsequent mayhem that has erupted throughout the universe causing Captain Dylan Hunt (Sorbo) to rally them to overcome the militant Nietzscheans. Includes: the crew is prompted into action when bizarre attacks happen on nearby planets and an historic Commonwealth ship—the first in more than 300 years—is suspiciously destroyed before it can take its maiden voyage. 4 episodes. 200m; DVD. **C:** Kevin Sorbo; Lisa Ryder; Lexa Doig; Gordon Michael Woolvett; Laura Bertram; Keith Hamilton Cobb. **A:** Jr. High-Adult. **P:** Entertainment. **U:** Home. **Mov-Ent:** Television Series, Science Fiction, Fantasy. **Acq:** Purchase. **Dist:** Amazon.com Inc. $39.98.

Andromeda: Season 3 Volume 4 2004 (Unrated)
Features the 2000-2005 futuristic science fiction television series about the crew of the Andromeda Ascendant that awoke from a 300-year slumber to witness the collapse of their perfect government—the Systems Commonwealth—and the subsequent mayhem that has erupted throughout the universe causing Captain Dylan Hunt (Sorbo) to rally them to overcome the militant Nietzscheans. Includes: Beka's (Ryder) old love interest is in peril but the truth behind his story becomes murky and only Dylan hears a woman's plea for help from an unknown planet. 5 episodes. 250m; DVD. **C:** Kevin Sorbo; Lisa Ryder; Lexa Doig; Gordon Michael Woolvett; Laura Bertram; Keith Hamilton Cobb. **A:** Jr. High-Adult. **P:** Entertainment. **U:** Home. **Mov-Ent:** Television Series, Science Fiction, Fantasy. **Acq:** Purchase. **Dist:** Amazon.com Inc. $39.98.

Andromeda: Season 3 Volume 5 2004 (Unrated)
Features the 2000-2005 futuristic science fiction television series about the crew of the Andromeda Ascendant that awoke from a 300-year slumber to witness the collapse of their perfect government—the Systems Commonwealth—and the subsequent mayhem that has erupted throughout the universe causing Captain Dylan Hunt (Sorbo) to rally them to overcome the militant Nietzscheans. Includes: the crew stumbles upon a woman in a hibernation capsule with the illusion that she's a princess and Tyr (Cobb) is confronted with either aiding the Andromeda or a group of Nietzscheans that he's pulled together under his son. 4 episodes. 200m; DVD. **C:** Kevin Sorbo; Lisa Ryder; Lexa Doig; Gordon Michael Woolvett; Laura Bertram; Keith Hamilton Cobb. **A:** Jr. High-Adult. **P:** Entertainment. **U:** Home. **Mov-Ent:** Television Series, Science Fiction, Fantasy. **Acq:** Purchase. **Dist:** Amazon.com Inc. $39.98.

Andromeda: Season 4 2005 (Unrated)
Features the 2000-2005 futuristic science fiction television series about the crew of the Andromeda Ascendant that awoke from a 300-year slumber to witness the collapse of their perfect government—the Systems Commonwealth—and the subsequent mayhem that has erupted throughout the universe causing Captain Dylan Hunt (Sorbo) to rally them to overcome the militant Nietzscheans. Includes: Dylan leads the crew on a rescue mission for an abducted Commonwealth Triumvirate member, Trance (Bertram) comes forward with her true identity in order to safeguard the Andromeda, Dylan receives an ultimatum or else risk civil war and he is stuck in an alternate reality due a failed experiment by Harper (Woolvett), the words of a dying man connected to Beka (Ryder) cause the crew to search for answers, and the season-ending two-parter where conflict divides the crew—possibly permanently. 22 episodes. 1100m; DVD. **C:** Kevin Sorbo; Lisa Ryder; Lexa Doig; Gordon Michael Woolvett; Laura Bertram; Steve Bacic. **A:** Jr. High-Adult. **P:** Entertainment. **U:** Home. **Mov-Ent:** Television Series, Science Fiction, Fantasy. **Acq:** Purchase. **Dist:** Amazon.com Inc. $69.98.

Andromeda: Season 4 Volume 1 2004 (Unrated)
Features the 2000-2005 futuristic science fiction television series about the crew of the Andromeda Ascendant that awoke from a 300-year slumber to witness the collapse of their perfect government—the Systems Commonwealth—and the subsequent mayhem that has erupted throughout the universe causing Captain Dylan Hunt (Sorbo) to rally them to overcome the militant Nietzscheans. Includes: Dylan leads the crew on a rescue mission for an abducted Commonwealth Triumvirate member and Harper (Woolvett) struggles to decommission a

potent mind-erasing device and keeping it out of enemy hands. 5 episodes. 250m; DVD. **C:** Kevin Sorbo; Lisa Ryder; Lexa Doig; Gordon Michael Woolvett; Laura Bertram; Steve Bacic. **A:** Jr. High-Adult. **P:** Entertainment. **U:** Home. **Mov-Ent:** Television Series, Science Fiction, Fantasy. **Acq:** Purchase. **Dist:** Amazon.com Inc. $39.98.

Andromeda: Season 4 Volume 2 2004 (Unrated)
Features the 2000-2005 futuristic science fiction television series about the crew of the Andromeda Ascendant that awoke from a 300-year slumber to witness the collapse of their perfect government—the Systems Commonwealth—and the subsequent mayhem that has erupted throughout the universe causing Captain Dylan Hunt (Sorbo) to rally them to overcome the militant Nietzscheans. Includes: Trance (Bertram) comes forward with her true identity in order to safeguard the Andromeda and an assembled group of the universe's greatest minds meets without realizing the danger they're in—including Harper (Woolvett). 4 episodes. 200m; DVD. **C:** Kevin Sorbo; Lisa Ryder; Lexa Doig; Gordon Michael Woolvett; Laura Bertram; Steve Bacic. **A:** Jr. High-Adult. **P:** Entertainment. **U:** Home. **Mov-Ent:** Television Series, Science Fiction, Fantasy. **Acq:** Purchase. **Dist:** Amazon.com Inc. $39.98.

Andromeda: Season 4 Volume 3 2004 (Unrated)
Features the 2000-2005 futuristic science fiction television series about the crew of the Andromeda Ascendant that awoke from a 300-year slumber to witness the collapse of their perfect government—the Systems Commonwealth—and the subsequent mayhem that has erupted throughout the universe causing Captain Dylan Hunt (Sorbo) to rally them to overcome the militant Nietzscheans. Includes: Dylan receives an ultimatum or else risk civil war and he is stuck in an alternate reality due a failed experiment by Harper (Woolvett). 4 episodes. 200m; DVD. **C:** Kevin Sorbo; Lisa Ryder; Lexa Doig; Gordon Michael Woolvett; Laura Bertram; Steve Bacic. **A:** Jr. High-Adult. **P:** Entertainment. **U:** Home. **Mov-Ent:** Television Series, Science Fiction, Fantasy. **Acq:** Purchase. **Dist:** Amazon.com Inc. $39.98.

Andromeda: Season 4 Volume 4 2005 (Unrated)
Features the 2000-2005 futuristic science fiction television series about the crew of the Andromeda Ascendant that awoke from a 300-year slumber to witness the collapse of their perfect government—the Systems Commonwealth—and the subsequent mayhem that has erupted throughout the universe causing Captain Dylan Hunt (Sorbo) to rally them to overcome the militant Nietzscheans. Includes: Dylan becomes ill with a plague when leaders of a civil war come aboard and the capture of Dylan, Rhade, and Harper leads to Harper being forced to create a time machine. 4 episodes. 200m; DVD. **C:** Kevin Sorbo; Lisa Ryder; Lexa Doig; Gordon Michael Woolvett; Laura Bertram; Steve Bacic. **A:** Jr. High-Adult. **P:** Entertainment. **U:** Home. **Mov-Ent:** Television Series, Science Fiction, Fantasy. **Acq:** Purchase. **Dist:** Amazon.com Inc. $39.98.

Andromeda: Season 4 Volume 5 2005 (Unrated)
Features the 2000-2005 futuristic science fiction television series about the crew of the Andromeda Ascendant that awoke from a 300-year slumber to witness the collapse of their perfect government—the Systems Commonwealth—and the subsequent mayhem that has erupted throughout the universe causing Captain Dylan Hunt (Sorbo) to rally them to overcome the militant Nietzscheans. Includes: the words of a dying man connected to Beka (Ryder) cause the crew to search for answers and the season-ending two-parter where conflict divides the crew—possibly permanently. 5 episodes. 250m; DVD. **C:** Kevin Sorbo; Lisa Ryder; Lexa Doig; Gordon Michael Woolvett; Laura Bertram; Steve Bacic. **A:** Jr. High-Adult. **P:** Entertainment. **U:** Home. **Mov-Ent:** Television Series, Science Fiction, Fantasy. **Acq:** Purchase. **Dist:** Amazon.com Inc. $39.98.

Andromeda: Season 5 2006 (Unrated)
Features the finale of the 2000-2005 futuristic science fiction television series about the crew of the Andromeda Ascendant that awoke from a 300-year slumber to witness the collapse of their perfect government—the Systems Commonwealth—and the subsequent mayhem that has erupted throughout the universe causing Captain Dylan Hunt (Sorbo) to rally them to overcome the militant Nietzscheans. Includes: the crew is separated and Dylan's life is in the balance meanwhile an old message from Beka (Ryder) leads him to an inactive Andromeda, Dylan experiences a trip through time that answers many questions, Trance (Bertram) slips away when she realizes the crew hold her accountable for their present condition, and the final battle between the Andromeda and the Nietzscheans. 22 episodes. 1100m; DVD. **C:** Kevin Sorbo; Lisa Ryder; Lexa Doig; Gordon Michael Woolvett; Laura Bertram; Steve Bacic. **A:** Jr. High-Adult. **P:** Entertainment. **U:** Home. **Mov-Ent:** Television Series, Science Fiction, Fantasy. **Acq:** Purchase. **Dist:** Amazon.com Inc. $69.98.

Andromeda: Season 5 Volume 1 2005 (Unrated)
Features the 2000-2005 futuristic science fiction television series about the crew of the Andromeda Ascendant that awoke from a 300-year slumber to witness the collapse of their perfect government—the Systems Commonwealth—and the subsequent mayhem that has erupted throughout the universe causing Captain Dylan Hunt (Sorbo) to rally them to overcome the militant Nietzscheans. Includes: the crew is separated and Dylan's life is in the balance meanwhile an old message from Beka (Ryder) leads him to an inactive Andromeda. 5 episodes. 250m; DVD. **C:** Kevin Sorbo; Lisa Ryder; Lexa Doig; Gordon Michael Woolvett; Laura Bertram; Steve Bacic. **A:** Jr. High-Adult. **P:** Entertainment. **U:** Home. **Mov-Ent:** Television Series, Science Fiction, Fantasy. **Acq:** Purchase. **Dist:** Amazon.com Inc. $39.98.

Andromeda: Season 5 Volume 2 2005 (Unrated)
Features the 2000-2005 futuristic science fiction television series about the crew of the Andromeda Ascendant that awoke from a 300-year slumber to witness the collapse of their perfect government—the Systems Commonwealth—and the subsequent mayhem that has erupted throughout the universe causing Captain Dylan Hunt (Sorbo) to rally them to overcome the militant Nietzscheans. Includes: Dylan experiences a trip through time that answers many questions and Trance (Bertram) slips away when she realizes the crew hold her accountable for their present condition. 5 episodes. 250m; DVD. **C:** Kevin Sorbo; Lisa Ryder; Lexa Doig; Gordon Michael Woolvett; Laura Bertram; Steve Bacic. **A:** Jr. High-Adult. **P:** Entertainment. **U:** Home. **Mov-Ent:** Television Series, Science Fiction, Fantasy. **Acq:** Purchase. **Dist:** Amazon.com Inc. $39.98.

Andromeda: Season 5 Volume 3 2006 (Unrated)
Features the 2000-2005 futuristic science fiction television series about the crew of the Andromeda Ascendant that awoke from a 300-year slumber to witness the collapse of their perfect government—the Systems Commonwealth—and the subsequent mayhem that has erupted throughout the universe causing Captain Dylan Hunt (Sorbo) to rally them to overcome the militant Nietzscheans. Includes: Beka's (Ryder) has a new boyfriend with an evil past and Trance (Bertram) is taken with Ione, the Sun God. 4 episodes. 200m; DVD. **C:** Kevin Sorbo; Lisa Ryder; Lexa Doig; Gordon Michael Woolvett; Laura Bertram; Steve Bacic. **A:** Jr. High-Adult. **P:** Entertainment. **U:** Home. **Mov-Ent:** Television Series, Science Fiction, Fantasy. **Acq:** Purchase. **Dist:** Amazon.com Inc. $39.98.

Andromeda: Season 5 Volume 4 2006 (Unrated)
Features the 2000-2005 futuristic science fiction television series about the crew of the Andromeda Ascendant that awoke from a 300-year slumber to witness the collapse of their perfect government—the Systems Commonwealth—and the subsequent mayhem that has erupted throughout the universe causing Captain Dylan Hunt (Sorbo) to rally them to overcome the militant Nietzscheans. Includes: Dylan is in danger again from the avatar of the black hole that had held him hostage. 4 episodes. 200m; DVD. **C:** Kevin Sorbo; Lisa Ryder; Lexa Doig; Gordon Michael Woolvett; Laura Bertram; Steve Bacic. **A:** Jr. High-Adult. **P:** Entertainment. **U:** Home. **Mov-Ent:** Television Series, Science Fiction, Fantasy. **Acq:** Purchase. **Dist:** Amazon.com Inc. $39.98.

Andromeda: Season 5 Volume 5 2006 (Unrated)
Features the finale of 2000-2005 futuristic science fiction television series about the crew of the Andromeda Ascendant that awoke from a 300-year slumber to witness the collapse of their perfect government—the Systems Commonwealth—and the subsequent mayhem that has erupted throughout the universe causing Captain Dylan Hunt (Sorbo) to rally them to overcome the militant Nietzscheans. Includes: the final battle between the Andromeda and the Nietzscheans. 4 episodes. 200m; DVD. **C:** Kevin Sorbo; Lisa Ryder; Gordon Michael Woolvett; Lexa Doig; Laura Bertram; Steve Bacic. **A:** Jr. High-Adult. **P:** Entertainment. **U:** Home. **Mov-Ent:** Television Series, Science Fiction, Fantasy. **Acq:** Purchase. **Dist:** Amazon.com Inc. $39.98.

The Andromeda Strain 1971 (G) — ★★½
A satellite falls back to earth carrying a deadly bacteria that must be identified in time to save the population from extermination. The tension inherent in the bestselling Michael Crichton novel is talked down by a boring cast. Also available in letterbox format. 131m; VHS, DVD, Wide. **C:** Arthur Hill; David Wayne; James Olson; Kate Reid; Paula Kelly; Ramon Bieri; George Mitchell; Directed by Robert Wise; Written by Nelson Gidding; Cinematography by Richard H. Kline; Music by Gil Melle. **Pr:** Mark Huffam; Robert Wise; Robert Wise. **A:** Family. **P:** Entertainment. **U:** Home. **Mov-Ent:** Mystery & Suspense, Science. **Acq:** Purchase. **Dist:** Movies Unlimited; Alpha Video; Universal Studios Home Video. $59.95.

The Andromeda Strain 2008 (Unrated) — ★★
Creepy, updated, but over-extended adaptation of Michael Crichton's 1969 novel that was previously filmed for the big screen in 1971. An alien pathogen—code-named Andromeda—hitches a ride aboard a satellite that crashes near a small desert town in Utah. It either quickly kills the inhabitants or turns them into homicidal zombies. Dr. Jeremy Stone (Bratt) and his team are responsible for finding a cure but their efforts are hindered by government conspiracies as well as environmental activism and potential bioterrorism. Then a military snafu leads to an outbreak within the scientists' underground lab. 177m; DVD. **C:** Benjamin Bratt; Christa Miller; Rick Schroder; Andre Braugher; Eric McCormack; Viola Davis; Justin Louis; Daniel Dae Kim; Directed by Mikael Salomon; Written by Robert Schenkkan; Cinematography by Jim Joffin; Music by Joel J. Richard. **A:** Jr. High-Adult. **P:** Entertainment. **U:** Home. **Mov-Ent:** Science, Action-Adventure, Conspiracies or Conspiracy Theories. **Acq:** Purchase. **Dist:** Movies Unlimited; Alpha Video.

Andromedia 2000 (Unrated) — ★½
Horribly sappy teen romance drama from director Takashi Miike featuring two Japanese pop bands as actors. A father resurrects his dead teen daughter as a computer program only to be murdered by a mega-corporation hell-bent on world domination. How they intend to achieve said domination with the archived memories of a dead teenager is anyone's guess. 109m; DVD. **C:** Hiroko Shimabukoro; Eriko Imai; Takako Uehara; Hitoe Arakaki; Kenji Harada; Ryo Karato; Christopher Doyle; Tomorowo Taguchi; Issa Hentona; Shinobu Miyara; Yukinari Tamaki; Ken Okumoto; Directed by Takashi Miike; Written by Itaru Era; Masa Nakamura; Kozy Watanabe; Cinematography by Christopher Doyle; Hideo Yamamoto. **A:** Sr. High-Adult. **P:** Entertainment. **U:** Home. **L:** English, Japanese. **Mov-Ent:** Science Fiction. **Acq:** Purchase. **Dist:** Pathfinder Pictures. $14.98.

Andros Bahamas 19??
Relatively inaccessible due to the small number of dive resorts, the waters at Andros are teeming with exotic marine life. It is said that the Whale Sharks nip at the divers' heels. 30m; VHS. **A:** Sr. High-Adult. **P:** Entertainment. **U:** Home. **Spo-Rec:** Scuba, Travel. **Acq:** Purchase. **Dist:** Bennett Marine Video. $19.95.

Andy and the Airwave Rangers 1989 (Unrated) — ★★
Andy is whisked into the TV!! He finds adventure and excitement—car chases, intergalactic battles, and cartoons. 75m; VHS, DVD. **C:** Dianne Kay; Vince Edwards; Bo Svenson; Richard Thomas; Erik Estrada; Randy Josselyn; Jessica Puscas; Chuck Kovacic; Directed by Deborah Brock. **Pr:** RCA. **A:** Family. **P:** Entertainment. **U:** Home. **Mov-Ent:** Action-Adventure, Children, Television. **Acq:** Purchase. **Dist:** Sony Pictures Home Entertainment Inc. $79.95.

Andy and the Lion 1955
An iconographic film about the friendship between a lion and a boy and the favors they exchange. Available in several languages. 10m; VHS, 3/4 U. **Pr:** Morton Schindel. **A:** Preschool-Primary. **P:** Entertainment. **U:** Institution, SURA. **L:** English, Italian, Spanish. **Chl-Juv:** Human Relations. **Acq:** Purchase. **Dist:** Weston Woods Studios.

Andy Andrews: The Seven Decisions 2005
PBS special by the novelist and speaker Andy Andrews. ??m; DVD. **A:** Adult. **P:** Instruction. **U:** Home. **Gen-Edu:** Self-Help, Documentary Films. **Acq:** Purchase. **Dist:** Acorn Media Group Inc. $19.99.

Andy Barker P.I.: The Complete Series 2007 (Unrated)
NBC 2007 detective comedy. Critically-acclaimed but short-lived comedy about a CPA who's new office used to be one of a private detective. When a beautiful woman shows up dropping cash on his desk and demanding he find her husband, Andy Barker suddenly finds himself in a whole new career. 6 episodes. 100m; DVD. **C:** Andy Richter; Clea Lewis; Tony Hale; Marshall Manesh. **A:** Jr. High-Adult. **P:** Entertainment. **U:** Home. **Mov-Ent:** Television Series. **Acq:** Purchase. **Dist:** Shout! Factory. $24.99.

Andy Enfield: Up-Tempo Transition Game 2013 (Unrated)
Coach Andy Enfield demonstrates the particular offensive philosophy he teaches his basketball teams. 74m; DVD. **A:** Family. **P:** Education. **U:** Home. **L:** English. **Spo-Rec:** Athletic Instruction/Coaching, Basketball. **Acq:** Purchase. **Dist:** Championship Productions. $39.99.

Andy Griffith Show 1960
Life in Mayberry with smalltown sheriff Andy (Griffith), inept deputy Barney Fife (Knotts), Andy's son Opie (Howard), Aunt Bee (Bavier) and all the other townsfolk in the first of the rural comedy series. Two episodes: "Barney's Sidecar" and "The Darlings Are Coming." Additional episodes are available. 52m/B/W; VHS, DVD. **C:** Andy Griffith; Don Knotts; Ron Howard; Jim Nabors; Frances Bavier; George Lindsey; Howard McNear; Hal Smith; Howard Morris. **A:** Family. **P:** Entertainment. **U:** Home. **Mov-Ent:** Television Series. **Acq:** Purchase. **Dist:** Movies Unlimited.

Andy Griffith Show: Barney the Love God 196?
Three episodes highlighting Barney's misadventures with love. 90m/B/W; DVD. **C:** Andy Griffith; Don Knotts; Ron Howard; Jim Nabors; Frances Bavier; George Lindsey; Howard McNear; Hal Smith; Howard Morris. **A:** Family. **P:** Entertainment. **U:** Home. **Mov-Ent:** Television Series. **Acq:** Purchase. **Dist:** Paramount Pictures Corp.

Andy Griffith Show: Best of Barney, Vol. 1 196?
The second-in-command at the Mayberry Sheriff's Department takes center stage in four episodes from the popular comedy series. The installments are entitled "Barney's First Car," "Up in Barney's Room," "Barney's Sidecar," and "Lucky Letter." 104m/B/W; VHS. **C:** Andy Griffith; Don Knotts; Ron Howard; Frances Bavier; George Lindsey; Jim Nabors; Howard McNear; Hal Smith; Howard Morris. **A:** Family. **P:** Entertainment. **U:** Home. **Mov-Ent:** Television, Television Series. **Acq:** Purchase. **Dist:** Fusion Video.

Andy Griffith Show: Best of Barney, Vol. 2 196?
Four more installments of the beloved comedy series which spotlight the shenanigans of the second fiddle of the Mayberry Sheriff's Department. The episodes are "Return of Barney Fife," "Legend of Barney Fife," "Visit to Barney Fife," and "Barney Hosts a Summit Meeting." 104m/B/W; VHS. **C:** Andy Griffith; Don Knotts; Ron Howard; Frances Bavier; George Lindsey; Jim Nabors; Howard McNear; Hal Smith; Howard Morris. **A:** Family. **P:** Entertainment. **U:** Home. **Mov-Ent:** Television Series, Television. **Acq:** Purchase. **Dist:** Fusion Video.

Andy Griffith Show: Floyd's Hair-Raising Adventures 196?
Three television episodes starring Mayberry's favorite barber. 90m/B/W; DVD. **C:** Andy Griffith; Don Knotts; Ron Howard; Jim Nabors; Frances Bavier; George Lindsey; Howard McNear; Hal Smith; Howard Morris. **A:** Family. **P:** Entertainment. **U:** Home. **Mov-Ent:** Television Series. **Acq:** Purchase. **Dist:** Paramount Pictures Corp.

Andy Griffith Show: Misadventures of Opie 196?
Opie learns that mistakes are a part of growing up. Three television episodes. 90m/B/W; DVD. **C:** Andy Griffith; Don Knotts; Ron Howard; Jim Nabors; Charlie Daniels; George Lindsey; Howard McNear; Hal Smith; Howard Morris. **A:** Family. **P:** Entertainment. **U:** Home. **Mov-Ent:** Television Series. **Acq:** Purchase. **Dist:** Paramount Pictures Corp.

The Andy Griffith Show: The Complete Fifth Season 2006
Presents the 32-episode fifth season of the 1960s family classic TV show. Includes episodes "Goodbye, Sheriff Taylor" (Don Knotts left the show after this season), "TV or Not TV," and "Banjo Playing Deputy." 814m/B/W; DVD. **C:** Andy Griffith; Ron Howard; Don Knotts; Frances Bavier; Howard McNear. **A:** Family. **P:** Entertainment. **U:** Home. **Mov-Ent:** Television, Family. **Acq:** Purchase. **Dist:** Paramount Pictures Corp. $38.99.

The Andy Griffith Show: The Complete Final Season 2006 (Unrated)
Presents the final season of the 1960s family classic TV show with Andy Griffith as big-hearted, down-to-Earth town sheriff who's left to care for son Opie (Ron Howard) after his wife dies along with spinster Aunt Bee (Frances Bavier). Set in (made-up) small-town Mayberry, North Carolina. Episodes include Opie falls in love, his grades slide in school once he becomes part of a rock band, and Andy helps Opie get a job at the drugstore along with special guest appearances Don Knotts, Teri Garr, and Howard Hesseman. 30 episodes. 733m/B/W; DVD. **C:** Andy Griffith; Ron Howard; Frances Bavier; Jack Dodson. **A:** Family. **P:** Entertainment. **U:** Home. **Mov-Ent:** Television Series, Family. **Acq:** Purchase. **Dist:** Paramount Pictures Corp. $49.99.

The Andy Griffith Show: The Complete First Season 2004
Presents the 32-episode first season of the 1960s family classic TV show with Andy Griffith as big-hearted, down-to-Earth town sheriff Andy Taylor, who's left to care (along with spinster Aunt Bee, played by Frances Bavier) for son Opie (Ron Howard) after his wife dies. Set in (made-up) small-town Mayberry, North Carolina. Don Knotts also stars as Andy's cousin and quirky deputy sheriff Barney Fife. ?m/B/W; DVD, Blu-Ray. **C:** Andy Griffith; Ron Howard; Don Knotts; Frances Bavier; Howard McNear. **A:** Family. **P:** Entertainment. **U:** Home. **Mov-Ent:** Television, Family. **Acq:** Purchase. **Dist:** Paramount Pictures Corp. $38.99.

The Andy Griffith Show: The Complete Fourth Season 2005
Presents the 32-episode fourth season of the 1960s family classic TV show. Includes episodes "Opie the Birdman," "Citizen's Arrest," and "The Haunted House." 801m/B/W; DVD. **C:** Andy Griffith; Ron Howard; Don Knotts; Frances Bavier; Howard McNear. **A:** Family. **P:** Entertainment. **U:** Home. **Mov-Ent:** Television, Family. **Acq:** Purchase. **Dist:** Paramount Pictures Corp. $38.99.

The Andy Griffith Show: The Complete Second Season 2005
Presents the 31-episode second season of the 1960s family classic TV show with Andy Griffith as sheriff of Mayberry, North Carolina. Includes episodes such as "The Pickle Story," "Barney and the Choir," and "Andy on Trail." 782m/B/W; DVD. **C:** Andy Griffith; Ron Howard; Don Knotts; Frances Bavier; Howard McNear. **A:** Family. **P:** Entertainment. **U:** Home. **Mov-Ent:** Television, Family. **Acq:** Purchase. **Dist:** Paramount Pictures Corp. $38.99.

The Andy Griffith Show: The Complete Series 1960
Includes all 249 episodes on 40 discs of the down-home comedy that ran for eight seasons with widower Andy Taylor raising his young son, Opie and upholding his duties as sheriff and justice of the peace in Mayberry, North Carolina, with the help of Aunt Bee and his deputy sheriff, Barney Fife. 6395m; DVD. **C:** Andy Griffith; Ron Howard; Frances Bavier; Don Knotts. **A:** Family. **P:** Entertainment. **U:** Home. **Mov-Ent:** Television Series, Family. **Acq:** Purchase. **Dist:** Paramount Pictures Corp.

The Andy Griffith Show: The Complete Seventh Season 2006
Presents the 30-episode seventh season of the 1960s family classic TV show. Set in (made-up) small-town Mayberry, North Carolina. Episodes include "The Darling Fortune," "A Visit to Barney Fife," and "Barney Comes to Mayberry" and feature special guest appearances by Jack Nicholson and Rob Reiner. 780m; DVD. **C:** Andy Griffith; Ron Howard; Frances Bavier; Howard McNear. **A:** Family. **P:** Entertainment. **U:** Home. **Mov-Ent:** Television, Family. **Acq:** Purchase. **Dist:** Paramount Pictures Corp. $38.99.

The Andy Griffith Show: The Complete Sixth Season 2006
Presents the 30-episode sixth season of the 1960s family classic TV show. Episodes include "Malcolm at the Crossroads," "The Taylors in Hollywood," and "Otis the Artist." Warren Ferguson was cast to replace Don Knotts character but only appeared in a third of the season's episodes. 767m; DVD. **C:** Andy Griffith; Ron Howard; Frances Bavier; Howard McNear; Jack Burns. **A:** Family. **P:** Entertainment. **U:** Home. **Mov-Ent:** Television, Family. **Acq:** Purchase. **Dist:** Paramount Pictures Corp. $38.99.

The Andy Griffith Show: The Complete Third Season 2005
Presents the 32-episode third season of the 1960s family classic TV show with Andy Griffith as the sheriff of Mayberry, North Carolina. Includes episodes "Barney's First Car," "Mountain Wedding," and "The Darlings Are Coming." 808m/B/W; DVD. **C:** Andy Griffith; Ron Howard; Don Knotts; Frances

Bavier. **A:** Family. **P:** Entertainment. **U:** Home. **Mov-Ent:** Television, Family. **Acq:** Purchase. **Dist:** Paramount Pictures Corp. $38.99.

Andy Hardy Comes Home 1958 — ★½
After a 12-year hiatus, Rooney and MGM tried to restart the Andy Hardy franchise to no effect. Andy's now married to bland Jane, has two trouble-prone young sons, and is a lawyer for an aviation factory in California. He and his family come back to Carvel to explore building a new plant. There's a crooked businessman who causes trouble but, since Judge Hardy has died, Andy must now make the moral choices. 80m/B/W; DVD. **C:** Mickey Rooney; Patricia Breslin; Fay Holden; Cecilia Parker; Sara Haden; Frank Ferguson; Vaughn Taylor; Directed by Howard W. Koch; Written by Edward Everett Hutshing; Robert Morris Donley; Cinematography by William W. Spencer; Music by Van Alexander. **A:** Family. **P:** Entertainment. **U:** Home. **L:** English. **Mov-Ent:** Business, Family. **Acq:** Purchase. **Dist:** WarnerArchive.com.

Andy Hardy Gets Spring Fever 1939 — ★★
Andy falls for a beautiful acting teacher, and then goes into a funk when he finds she's engaged. Judge Hardy and the gang help heal the big wound in his heart. A lesser entry (and the seventh) from the popular series. 88m/B/W; DVD, Streaming. **C:** Mickey Rooney; Lewis Stone; Ann Rutherford; Fay Holden; Cecilia Parker; Sara Haden; Helen Gilbert; Directed by W.S. Van Dyke; Written by Kay Van Riper; Cinematography by Lester White; Music by David Snell; Edward Ward. **Pr:** MGM. **A:** Family. **P:** Entertainment. **U:** Home. **Mov-Ent:** Comedy-Drama, Family, Adolescence. **Acq:** Purchase. **Dist:** WarnerArchive.com. $19.95.

Andy Hardy Meets Debutante 1940 (Unrated) — ★★½
Seems like there should be an article in that title. Garland's second entry in series, wherein Andy meets and falls foolishly for glamorous debutante Lewis with Betsy's help while family is on visit to New York. Judy/Betsy sings "I'm Nobody's Baby" and "Singing in Rain." 86m/B/W; DVD, Streaming. **C:** Mickey Rooney; Judy Garland; Lewis Stone; Ann Rutherford; Fay Holden; Sara Haden; Cecilia Parker; Diana Lewis; Tom Neal; Directed by George B. Seitz; Written by Tom Seller; Annalee Whitmore; Cinematography by Charles Lawton, Jr.; Sidney Wagner; Music by David Snell. **Pr:** MGM. **A:** Family. **P:** Entertainment. **U:** Home. **Mov-Ent:** Musical, Adolescence, Family. **Acq:** Purchase. **Dist:** WarnerArchive.com. $19.95.

Andy Hardy's Blonde Trouble 1944 — ★★
Andy's antics are sillier than usual in this 15th entry in the series as he deals with being a freshman at Wainwright College, his dad's alma mater that's just gone co-ed. Andy befriends Kay, who's more interested in faculty advisor, Mr. Standish, and is bewildered by a pert blonde who flirts with him one minute and ignores him the next. Andy's slow to discover these are the trouble-making Walker twins who cause hm to believe he should give up and go home until Judge Hardy comes to visit. 107m/B/W; DVD. **C:** Mickey Rooney; Bonita Granville; Lee Wilde; Lyn Wilde; Herbert Marshall; Lewis Stone; Directed by George B. Seitz; Written by Agnes Christine Johnston; William Ludwig; Harry Ruskin; Cinematography by Lester White; Music by David Snell. **A:** Family. **P:** Entertainment. **U:** Home. **L:** English. **Mov-Ent:** Education, Family. **Acq:** Purchase. **Dist:** WarnerArchive.com.

Andy Hardy's Double Life 1942 — ★★½
In this entertaining installment from the Andy Hardy series, Andy proposes marriage to two girls at the same time and gets in quite a pickle when they both accept. Williams makes an early screen splash. 91m/B/W; DVD, Streaming. **C:** Mickey Rooney; Lewis Stone; Ann Rutherford; Fay Holden; Sara Haden; Cecilia Parker; Esther Williams; William Lundigan; Susan Peters; Robert (Bobby) Blake; Directed by George B. Seitz; Written by Agnes Christine Johnston; Cinematography by John Mescall; George J. Folsey; Music by Daniele Amfitheatrof. **Pr:** MGM. **A:** Family. **P:** Entertainment. **U:** Home. **Mov-Ent:** Comedy-Drama, Adolescence, Family. **Acq:** Purchase. **Dist:** WarnerArchive.com. $19.95.

Andy Hardy's Private Secretary 1941 — ★★
After Andy fails his high school finals he gets help from a sympathetic faculty member. As the secretary, Grayson makes a good first impression in one of her early screen appearances. The Hardy series was often used as a training ground for new MGM talent. 101m/B/W; DVD, Streaming. **C:** Mickey Rooney; Kathryn Grayson; Lewis Stone; Fay Holden; Ian Hunter; Gene Reynolds; Ann Rutherford; Directed by George B. Seitz; Written by Jane Murfin; Harry Ruskin; Cinematography by Lester White. **Pr:** MGM. **A:** Family. **P:** Entertainment. **U:** Home. **Mov-Ent:** Comedy-Drama, Adolescence, Family. **Acq:** Purchase. **Dist:** WarnerArchive.com. $19.95.

Andy Kaufman: I'm from Hollywood 19??
A look at the bizarre comedic career of Kaufman, from his days on "Taxi" to his career as the "Inter-Gender Wrestling Champion of the World." Includes performances footage and interviews with his costars. 60m; VHS, DVD. **A:** Sr. High-Adult. **P:** Entertainment. **U:** Home. **Mov-Ent:** Comedy--Performance. **Acq:** Purchase. **Dist:** Shanachie Entertainment.

Andy Kaufman Plays Carnegie Hall 2000
Filmed at the pinnacle of comedian Andy Kaufman's career, this performance also features interviews with influential figures in his life, and a bizarre turn where he takes the entire audience out for milk and cookies. 78m; VHS. **A:** Jr. High-Adult. **P:** Entertainment. **U:** Home. **Mov-Ent:** Comedy--Performance, Interviews. **Acq:** Purchase. **Dist:** Paramount Pictures Corp. $12.95.

Andy Kennedy: Communication and Conditioning Drills 2009 (Unrated)
Coach Andy Kennedy demonstrates drills for basketball players to use to increase their skills at ball handling, rebounding, ball screens, fast breaks, closeouts, and helping the defense. 66m; DVD. **A:** Family. **P:** Education. **U:** Home, Institution. **Spo-Rec:** Basketball, Athletic Instruction/Coaching. **Acq:** Purchase. **Dist:** Championship Productions. $39.99.

Andy Landers: Freeze & 4-Out Zone Offense 2007
Coach Andy Landers demonstrates two variations on the Zone Offense used by his basketball team. 70m; DVD. **A:** Family. **P:** Education. **U:** Home, Institution. **Spo-Rec:** Basketball, Athletic Instruction/Coaching. **Acq:** Purchase. **Dist:** Championship Productions. $39.99.

Andy Laverne and John Abercrombie In Concert 1996
Presents a superb set of live jazz, as they explore and expand the inspiring duo format. Includes backstage interviews and conversation. 70m; VHS. **A:** Family. **P:** Entertainment. **U:** Home. **Fin-Art:** Music--Jazz. **Acq:** Purchase. **Dist:** Homespun Tapes Ltd. $24.95.

Andy Laverne's Guide to Modern Jazz Piano, Vol. 1 1990
The jazz pianist demonstrates techniques designed to enhance any player's style, including improvisation, chord voicing, rhythm and other techniques in solo and band formats. 90m; VHS. **Pr:** Homespun Video. **A:** Sr. High-Adult. **P:** Instruction. **U:** Home. **How-Ins:** How-To, Music--Instruction. **Acq:** Purchase. **Dist:** Homespun Tapes Ltd. $49.95.

Andy Laverne's Guide to Modern Jazz Piano, Vol. 2 1994
Laverne analyzes various aspects of his compositions and illustrates them in performances. 90m; VHS. **A:** Jr. High-Adult. **P:** Instruction. **U:** Home. **How-Ins:** How-To, Music--Instruction. **Acq:** Purchase. **Dist:** Homespun Tapes Ltd. $49.95.

Andy Milonakis Show: The Complete First Season 2005 (Unrated)
Features the debut season of the MTV television comedy series featuring energetic stand-up comedian Andy Milonakis as he performs skits and does man on-the-street interviews with guest stars such as Snoop Dogg and the Black Eyed Peas. 8 episodes. 160m; DVD. **C:** Andy Milonakis. **A:** Jr. High-Adult. **P:** Entertainment. **U:** Home. **Mov-Ent:** Television Series. **Acq:** Purchase. **Dist:** Paramount Pictures Corp. $26.99.

Andy Milonakis Show: The Complete Second Season 2006 (Unrated)
Features the second season of the MTV television comedy series featuring energetic stand-up comedian Andy Milonakis as he performs skits and does man-on-the-street interviews with guest stars. 8 episodes. 163m; DVD. **C:** Andy Milonakis. **A:** Jr. High-Adult. **P:** Entertainment. **U:** Home. **Mov-Ent:** Television Series. **Acq:** Purchase. **Dist:** Paramount Pictures Corp. $26.99.

Andy Richter Controls the Universe: The Complete Series 2002 (Unrated)
Fox television's 2002-03 workplace comedy. Andy (Richter) is a tech manual writer for a Chicago conglomerate and is prone to fantasies, daydreams, and flashbacks such as turning a boring office meeting into a Broadway musical. Jessica (Brewster) is Andy's high-strung, career-obsessed boss, Byron (Slavin), his socially awkward illustrator officemate, and receptionist Wendy (Molloy) is the one he adores from afar. Andy is required to take sensitivity training in "We're All the Same, Only Different." Conan O'Brien makes a guest appearance in "Crazy in Rio" as an off-kilter executive. 19 episodes. 417m; DVD. **C:** Andy Richter; Paget Brewster; Irene Molloy; Jonathan Slavin. **A:** Jr. High-Adult. **P:** Entertainment. **U:** Home. **Mov-Ent:** Television Series. **Acq:** Purchase. **Dist:** Paramount Pictures Corp. $39.99.

The Andy Rooney Television Collection 1993
Three-volume set captures Rooney's unique perspective on the little things in life in clips from the award-winning news series, "60 Minutes." Each tape available separately. 180m; VHS. **A:** Jr. High-Adult. **P:** Entertainment. **U:** Institution, Home. **Gen-Edu:** Journalism, Television, Satire & Parody. **Acq:** Purchase. **Dist:** Facets Multimedia Inc. $39.98.
Indiv. Titles: 1. His Best Minutes, Vol. 1 2. His Best Minutes, Vol. 2 3. A Bird's Eye View of America.

Andy Toole: Individual and Team Shooting Drills 2014 (Unrated)
Coach Andy Toole presents various competitive shooting drills for basketball. 71m; DVD. **A:** Family. **P:** Education. **U:** Home. **L:** English. **Spo-Rec:** Athletic Instruction/Coaching, Basketball. **Acq:** Purchase. **Dist:** Championship Productions. $39.99.

Andy Warhol 1973
A portrait of the best-known of the pop artists, with excerpts from some of his own movies. 53m; VHS, 3/4 U. **C:** Narrated by Andy Warhol; Emile DeAntonio; Henry Geldzahler; Clement Greenberg; Paul Morrissey; Bridgit Polk; Viva. **Pr:** Michael Blackwood Productions. **A:** Jr. High-Adult. **P:** Education. **U:** Institution. **Fin-Art:** Documentary Films, Biography, Art & Artists. **Acq:** Purchase, Rent/Lease. **Dist:** Michael Blackwood Productions. $290.00.

Andy Warhol 1988
This comprehensive profile of Warhol includes interviews, film clips, and art from his entire career. 78m; VHS, DVD. **C:** Andy Warhol; Directed by Kim Evans. **A:** Sr. High-Adult. **P:** Entertainment. **U:** Institution, Home. **Fin-Art:** Biography, Film--Avant-Garde, Art & Artists. **Acq:** Purchase. **Dist:** Home Vision Cinema; Educational Video Network. $39.95.

Andy Warhol 2006
Director Ric Burns offers a look at Warhol's artistic output from the late 1940s to his death in 1987, and from his Pittsburgh childhood to Warhol's work as a commercial artist and his celebrity status. 180m; DVD. **A:** Jr. High-Adult. **P:** Entertainment. **U:** Home. **Fin-Art:** Documentary Films, Art & Artists. **Acq:** Purchase. **Dist:** Paramount Pictures Corp.; PBS Home Video.

Andy Warhol: Life and Death 2007
Interviews with Warhol, his brother, and others about his life and work. 81m; DVD. **A:** Jr. High-Adult. **P:** Entertainment. **U:** Home. **Fin-Art:** Documentary Films, Art & Artists. **Acq:** Purchase. **Dist:** Entertainment One US LP.

Andy Warhol's Bad 1977 (R) — ★★★
In the John Waters' school of "crime is beauty," a Queens housewife struggles to make appointments for both her home electrolysis clinic and her all-female murder-for-hire operation, which specializes in children and pets (who are thrown out of windows and knived, respectively). Her life is further complicated by a boarder (King) who's awaiting the go-ahead for his own assignment, an autistic child unwanted by his mother. One of Warhol's more professional-appearing films, and very funny if your tastes run to the tasteless. 100m; VHS, DVD. **C:** Perry King; Carroll Baker; Susan Tyrrell; Stefania Casini; Cyrinda Foxe; Lawrence Tierney; Tito Goya; Directed by Jed Johnson; Cinematography by Alan Metzger; Music by Michael Bloomfield. **Pr:** Andy Warhol. **A:** Sr. High-Adult. **P:** Entertainment. **U:** Home. **Mov-Ent:** Cult Films. **Acq:** Purchase. **Dist:** Cheezy Flicks Entertainment, Inc. $59.95.

Andy Warhol's Dracula 1974 (R) — ★★★
Sex and camp humor, as well as a large dose of blood, highlight Warhol's treatment of the tale. As Dracula can only subsist on the blood of pure, untouched maidens ("were-gins"), gardener Dallesandro rises to the occasion in order to make as many women as he can ineligible for Drac's purposes. Very reminiscent of Warhol's "Frankenstein," but with a bit more spoofery. Look for Roman Polanski in a cameo peek as a pub patron. Available in R and unrated versions. 106m; VHS, DVD. **C:** Udo Kier; Maxine McKendry; Joe Dallesandro; Vittorio De Sica; Milena Vukotic; Dominique Darel; Stefania Casini; Silvia Dionisio; Cameo(s) Roman Polanski; Directed by Paul Morrissey; Anthony M. Dawson; Written by Paul Morrissey; Cinematography by Luigi Kuveiller; Music by Claudio Gizzi. **Pr:** Bryanston Pictures. **A:** Adult. **P:** Entertainment. **U:** Home. **Mov-Ent:** Satire & Parody, Cult Films. **Acq:** Purchase. **Dist:** Movies Unlimited. $18.99.

Andy Warhol's Factory People 2009 (Unrated)
Documentary on the life and career of artist Andy Warhol, focusing on his time in the Silver Factory in New York with interviews of his acquaintances, and rare personal photos and footage. 156m; DVD. **A:** Sr. High-Adult. **P:** Entertainment. **U:** Home. **Gen-Edu:** Documentary Films, Biography: Artists. **Acq:** Purchase. **Dist:** Docurama. $26.95.

Andy Warhol's Frankenstein 1974 (X) — ★★½
A most outrageous parody of Frankenstein, featuring plenty of gore, sex, and bad taste in general. Baron von Frankenstein (Kier) derives sexual satisfaction from his corpses (he delivers a particularly thought-provoking philosphy on life as he lustfully fondles a gall bladder); his wife seeks her pleasure from the monster himself (Dallesandro). Originally made in 3-D, this is one of Warhol's campiest outings. Also available on video in an R-rated version. 95m; VHS, DVD. **C:** Udo Kier; Monique Van Vooren; Joe Dallesandro; Dalia di Lazzaro; Srdjan Zelenovic; Nicoletta Elmi; Marco Liofredi; Cristina Gajoni; Carla Mancini; Liu Bozizio; Directed by Paul Morrissey; Written by Paul Morrissey; Cinematography by Luigi Kuveiller; Music by Claudio Gizzi. **Pr:** Bryanston Pictures. **A:** Adult. **P:** Entertainment. **U:** Home. **Mov-Ent:** Cult Films, Satire & Parody. **Acq:** Purchase. **Dist:** Movies Unlimited; Alpha Video. $79.95.

Andy Warhol's Last Love 1978-82 19??
A video work by Bruce Kurtz. 30m/B/W; EJ. **Pr:** Bruce Kurtz. **A:** Adult. **P:** Entertainment. **U:** Institution, Home. **Fin-Art:** Video. **Acq:** Rent/Lease. **Dist:** Kitchen Center for Video, Music & Dance.

Andy West: Creative Musical Approaches for 6-String Bass 1990
Bass guitar improvisational techniques for solo or band play. ?m; VHS. **A:** Jr. High-Adult. **P:** Instruction. **U:** Home. **How-Ins:** Music--Instruction. **Acq:** Purchase. **Dist:** Music Video Distributors. $49.95.

The Andy Williams Christmas Show: Live from the Moon River Theatre 2001 (Unrated)
Brings the live 1993 performance of classic Christmastime music by the legendary Andy Williams at his theater in Branson, Missouri, with guests Lorrie Morgan and the Osmond Brothers. 1 episodes. 80m; DVD. **C:** Andy Williams; Lorrie Morgan. **A:** Family. **P:** Entertainment. **U:** Home. **Mov-Ent:** Television Series, Christmas, Music Video. **Acq:** Purchase. **Dist:** Kultur International Films Ltd., Inc. $19.95.

Andy's Gang with Andy Devine, Vol. 2 1956
Two episodes of the vintage television show. 60m/B/W; VHS. **C:** Andy Devine. **A:** Family. **P:** Entertainment. **U:** Home. **Mov-Ent:** Television Series. **Acq:** Purchase. **Dist:** Video Resources.

Andy's Gang with Andy Devine, Vol. 3 1956
Two episodes from the '50s television show. 60m/B/W; VHS. **C:** Andy Devine. **A:** Family. **P:** Entertainment. **U:** Home. **Mov-Ent:** Television Series. **Acq:** Purchase. **Dist:** Video Resources.

Andy's Gang with Milton Berle 1955
Features musical and comedy segments with Midnight the Cat, Squeaky the Mouse, and Froggie the Gremlim. 60m/B/W; VHS.

C: Hosted by Andy Devine. **A:** Family. **P:** Entertainment. **U:** Home. **Mov-Ent:** Television Series. **Acq:** Purchase. **Dist:** Video Resources.

Anecdotes About Fidel 2010 (Unrated)
Documentary interviewing various politicians, stars, writers, and other famous people about their experiences meeting Fidel Castro. 47m; DVD. **A:** Jr. High-Adult. **P:** Entertainment. **U:** Home, Institution. **Gen-Edu:** Documentary Films, Biography: Politics. **Acq:** Purchase, Rent/Lease. **Dist:** The Cinema Guild. $195.

Anemia of Chronic Disease 1971
A look at a patient whose history is that of chronic anemia which varies in severity with the state of her rheumatoid arthritis. 10m; VHS, 3/4 U, Special order formats. **Pr:** Ohio State University Health Sciences AV Center. **A:** College-Adult. **P:** Professional. **U:** Institution, SURA. **Hea-Sci:** Blood. **Acq:** Purchase, Rent/Lease. **Dist:** Ohio State University.

Anemia of Chronic Disease: A Disorder or an Adjustment? 1982
This program explains the mechanisms behind the anemia that is often seen in patients with chronic disease. 40m; VHS, 3/4 U. **Pr:** Emory University. **A:** College-Adult. **P:** Professional. **U:** Institution, CCTV, Home, SURA. **Hea-Sci:** Blood, Diseases. **Acq:** Purchase, Rent/Lease, Subscription. **Dist:** Emory Medical Television Network.

Anesthesia and You 1980
An introduction for the patient to events before and after surgery. 17m; VHS, 3/4 U, Special order formats. **Pr:** Ohio State University Health Sciences AV Center. **A:** College-Adult. **P:** Education. **U:** Institution, SURA. **Hea-Sci:** Anesthesia, Patient Education. **Acq:** Purchase, Rent/Lease. **Dist:** Ohio State University.

Anesthesiology 1972
Designed for physicians and medical institutions for continuing professional education. Each program features a professor of medicine. Programs available individually. 40m; VHS, 3/4 U, CV, Special order formats. **Pr:** Professional Research. **A:** Adult. **P:** Professional. **U:** Institution, CCTV. **Hea-Sci:** Anesthesia. **Acq:** Purchase, Rent/Lease. **Dist:** Discovery Education.
Indiv. Titles: 1. Neuromuscular Blocking Agents 2. Use of Large Doses of Morphine in Anesthetic Practice 3. Central Venous Pressure Monitoring Techniques 4. Common Problems in Obstetric Anesthesia 5. Recent Advances in Pediatric Anesthesia 6. Current Status of Neuroleptanalgesia 7. The Hazards of Nitrous Oxide 8. Resuscitation Practices-Pitfalls, Problems and the Law.

Angano. . .Angano. . .Tales from Madagascar 1989
Myths and oral traditions are highlighted with these tales of rural life which explain the creation of man and woman, the origin of rice cultivation, and the reason for animal sacrifice. In Malagasy and French with English subtitles. 64m; VHS. **C:** Directed by Cesar Paes. **A:** College-Adult. **P:** Entertainment. **U:** Institution. **Mov-Ent:** Folklore & Legends, Africa, Black Culture. **Acq:** Purchase, Rent/Lease. **Dist:** California Newsreel. $195.00.

Angel 1937 — ★★½
Melodrama finds Maria Barker (Dietrich) the bored wife of British diplomat Sir Frederick (Marshall). So she heads off to Paris to visit a friend and meets the dashing Anthony Halton (Douglas), with whom she has a fling. Too bad Halton's next stop is jolly old England where he runs into an old military chum (Sir Fred, of course). High gloss but no heart. 91m/B/W; VHS. **C:** Marlene Dietrich; Herbert Marshall; Melvyn Douglas; Edward Everett Horton; Laura Hope Crews; Directed by Ernst Lubitsch; Written by Guy Bolton; Samson Raphaelson; Russell Medcraft; Cinematography by Charles B(ryant) Lang, Jr.; Music by Frederick "Friedrich" Hollander. **Pr:** Ernst Lubitsch; Ernst Lubitsch; Paramount Pictures. **A:** Sr. High-Adult. **P:** Entertainment. **U:** Home. **Mov-Ent:** Drama, Marriage. **Acq:** Purchase. **Dist:** Universal Music and Video Distribution. $14.98.

Angel 1982 — ★★
Angel (Maniatis) falls for a sailor (Xanthos) who promises a better life away from his abusive father and the poverty that surrounds him. Instead, Angel winds up on the Athens' streets as a transvestite prostitute, a situation that eventually lead the distraught young man to a shocking act of violence. Explicit but not prurient and based on a true story. Greek with subtitles. 126m; VHS, DVD. **C:** Michael Maniatis; Dionyssis Xanthos; Maria Alkeou; Katerina Helmy; Directed by George Katakouzinos; Written by George Katakouzinos; Cinematography by Tassos Alexakis; Music by Stamatis Spanoudakis. **A:** College-Adult. **P:** Entertainment. **U:** Home. **L:** Greek. **Mov-Ent:** Prostitution, Poverty. **Acq:** Purchase. **Dist:** Water Bearer Films Inc.

Angel 1984 (R) — ★½
Low-budget leerer about a 15-year-old honor student who attends an expensive Los Angeles private school during the day and by night becomes Angel, a streetwise prostitute making a living amid the slime and sleaze of Hollywood Boulevard. But wait, all is not perfect. A psycho is following her, looking for an opportunity. 94m; VHS, DVD. **C:** Donna Wilkes; Cliff Gorman; Susan Tyrrell; Dick Shawn; Rory Calhoun; Elaine Giftos; Ross Hagen; Directed by Robert Vincent O'Neil; Written by Joseph M. Cala. **Pr:** Roy Watts; Donald P. Borchers. **A:** Sr. High-Adult. **P:** Entertainment. **U:** Home. **L:** Spanish. **Mov-Ent:** Adolescence, Prostitution. **Acq:** Purchase. **Dist:** Anchor Bay Entertainment. $19.95.

Angel 2007 (Unrated) — ★½
Over-ripe costumed melodrama set in Edwardian Britain and based on the 1957 novel by Elizabeth Taylor. Angel, the daughter of a provincial grocer, wants more from life and, through her writing of purple prose bestselling novels, she becomes wealthy. After buying a country mansion and hiring adoring secretary Lucy, Angel marries Lucy's brother Esme (a tortured artist, naturally) but World War I intrudes. Angel is remarkably unlikeable and almost every other character (with the exception of those of Neill and Rampling) is a cliché. 134m; DVD. **C:** Romola Garai; Sam Neill; Michael Fassbender; Lucy Russell; Charlotte Rampling; Jacqueline Tong; Janine Duvitsky; Christopher Benjamin; Tom Georgeson; Directed by Francois Ozon; Written by Francois Ozon; Martin Crimp; Cinematography by Denis Lenoir; Music by Philippe Rombi. **A:** Sr. High-Adult. **P:** Entertainment. **U:** Home. **Mov-Ent:** Drama, Art & Artists, Great Britain. **Acq:** Purchase. **Dist:** IFC Films.

Angel 3: The Final Chapter 1988 (R) — **Bomb!**
Former hooker Angel hits the streets to save her newly discovered sister from a life of prostitution. Trashy sequel with a better cast to tepid "Avenging Angel," which was the inept 1985 follow-up to 1984's tasteless "Angel." 100m; VHS, DVD. **C:** Maud Adams; Mitzi Kapture; Richard Roundtree; Mark Blankfield; Kin Shriner; Tawny (Ellis) Fere; Toni Basil; Directed by Tom De Simone; Music by Eric Allaman. **Pr:** Donald P. Borchers; Roy Watts. **A:** College-Adult. **P:** Entertainment. **U:** Home. **Mov-Ent:** Prostitution. **Acq:** Purchase. **Dist:** Anchor Bay Entertainment; Image Entertainment Inc. $19.95.

Angel-A 2005 (R) — ★★
Andre (Debbouze), a small-time crook, owes thugs all over Paris and he's at the end of the line. Contemplating a leap from a bridge to end his woes, a gorgeous blonde in a miniskirt beats him to it and leaps first. Of course he saves her. Of course she's his angel (a la "It's a Wonderful Life") and it's really her mission to save him. The spectacular Angela (Rasmussen) and Andre then traipse around town fixing Andre's mistakes, as well as Andre himself. Shot in black and white, with stunning images of Paris; the film's plot and actors, alas, do not fare as well. 91m/B/W; DVD. **C:** Jamel Debbouze; Rie Rasmussen; Gilbert Melki; Serge Riaboukine; Directed by Luc Besson; Written by Luc Besson; Cinematography by Thierry Arbogast. **Pr:** Luc Besson; Luc Besson; Europacorp; TF-1 Films; Apipoulai Productions; Sony Pictures Classics. **A:** College-Adult. **P:** Entertainment. **U:** Home. **L:** French. **Mov-Ent:** Fantasy, Crime Drama. **Acq:** Purchase. **Dist:** Sony Pictures Home Entertainment Inc.

Angel and Big Joe 1975
Story of the deep friendship that develops between Angel, a young Hispanic migrant worker, and Big Joe, a telephone lineman. 27m; VHS, 3/4 U; Open Captioned. **C:** Paul Sorvino; Dadi Pinero; Directed by Bert Salzman. **Pr:** Learning Corporation of America. **A:** Family. **P:** Entertainment. **U:** Institution, SURA. **L:** English, Spanish. **Gen-Edu.** **Acq:** Purchase, Rent/Lease. **Dist:** Phoenix Learning Group.

Angel and the Badman 1947 — ★★★
When notorious gunslinger Wayne is wounded during a shoot-out, a pacifist family takes him in and nurses him back to health. While he's recuperating, the daughter in the family (Russell) falls for him. She begs him not to return to his previous life. But Wayne, though smitten, thinks that a Duke's gotta do what a Duke's gotta do. And that means finding the dirty outlaw (Cabot) who killed his pa. Predictable but nicely done, with a good cast and script. Wayne provides one of his better performances (and also produced). 100m/B/W; VHS, DVD, Blu-Ray. **C:** John Wayne; Gail Russell; Irene Rich; Harry Carey, Sr.; Bruce Cabot; Directed by James Edward Grant; Written by James Edward Grant; Cinematography by Archie Stout; Music by Richard Hageman. **Pr:** Republic. **A:** Family. **P:** Entertainment. **U:** Home. **Mov-Ent:** Western, Romance. **Acq:** Purchase. **Dist:** Lions Gate Entertainment Inc.; Anchor Bay Entertainment; Karol Media. $19.98.

Angel and the Badman 2009 (PG-13) — ★½
Wounded gunslinger Quirt Evans (Phillips) takes refuge with a family of Quakers and immediately starts romancing eldest daughter Temperance (Unger). But if he really expects to win her heart, he has to lay down his gun and not take revenge against bad guy Loredo (Perry). Dull remake of the 1947 western, which starred John Wayne, features Wayne's grandson Brendan in a small role. 92m; DVD. **C:** Lou Diamond Phillips; Deborah Kara Unger; Luke Perry; Brendan Wayne; Directed by Terry Ingram; Written by Jack Nasser; Cinematography by Anthony C. Metchie; Music by Stu Goldberg. **A:** Jr. High-Adult. **P:** Entertainment. **U:** Home. **Mov-Ent:** Western. **Acq:** Purchase. **Dist:** Lions Gate Entertainment Inc.

The Angel and the Soldier Boy 1990
A wonderful Christmas story for the whole family, featuring the animation of Alison De Vere and based on Peter Collington's book about a little girl, pirates, a soldier, and an angel. Soundtrack performed by Clannad. 25m; VHS. **Pr:** VPI. **A:** Family. **P:** Entertainment. **U:** Home. **Chl-Juv:** Animation & Cartoons, Children, Family Viewing. **Acq:** Purchase. **Dist:** BMG Entertainment; Ignatius Press. $7.98.

An Angel at My Table 1989 (R) — ★★★★
New Zealand TV miniseries chronicling the life of Janet Frame, New Zealand's premiere writer/poet. At once whimsical and tragic, the film tells of how a mischievious, free-spirited young girl was wrongly placed in a mental institution for eight years, yet was ultimately able to cultivate her incredible storytelling gifts, achieving success, fame and happiness. Adapted from three of Frame's novels: "To the Is-land," "An Angel at My Table," and "The Envoy From Mirror City." Highly acclaimed the world over, winner of over 20 major international awards. 157m; VHS, DVD. **C:** Kerry Fox; Alexia Keogh; Karen Fergusson; Iris Churn; K.J. Wilson; Martyn Sanderson; Directed by Jane Campion; Written by Laura Jones; Cinematography by Stuart Dryburgh. **Pr:** Hibiscus Films; New Zealand Film Commission. **A:** Sr. High-Adult. **P:** Entertainment. **U:** Home. **Mov-Ent:** TV Movies. **Awds:** Ind. Spirit '92: Foreign Film. **Acq:** Purchase. **Dist:** Sony Pictures Home Entertainment Inc.; New Line Home Video. $19.95.

Angel Baby 1961 (Unrated) — ★★½
A mute girl struggles to re-define her faith when she is cured by preacher, but then sees him fail with others. Fine performances all around, notably Reynolds in his screen debut. Adapted from "Jenny Angel" by Elsie Oaks Barber. 97m/B/W; VHS, DVD. **C:** George Hamilton; Salome Jens; Mercedes McCambridge; Joan Blondell; Henry Jones; Burt Reynolds; Directed by Paul Wendkos; Hubert Cornfield; Cinematography by Haskell Wexler. **Pr:** Allied Artists International. **A:** Adult. **P:** Entertainment. **U:** Home. **Mov-Ent:** Religion. **Acq:** Purchase. **Dist:** WarnerArchive.com.

Angel Baby 1995 (R) — ★★★
Psychiatric out patients Kate (McKenzie) and Harry (Lynch) fall in love and move in together despite some misgivings from family and the medical bureaucracy. When Kate becomes pregnant, they decide to stop taking their medication so the baby has a better chance of being born healthy. Kate's doctors believe she's not capable of dealing with a child, although she is equally determined to have her baby, while Harry struggles to make a life for all of them. Strong performances and an assured debut by writer/director Rymer. Film won all seven of the Australian Film Institute Awards for which it was nominated. 101m; VHS, CC. **C:** John Lynch; Jacqueline McKenzie; Colin Friels; Deborra-Lee Furness; Robyn Nevin; Directed by Michael Rymer; Written by Michael Rymer; Cinematography by Ellery Ryan; Music by John Clifford Ryan. **Pr:** Timothy White; Australian Film Finance Corp. **A:** College-Adult. **P:** Entertainment. **U:** Home. **Mov-Ent:** Drama, Pregnancy, Mental Health. **Awds:** Australian Film Inst. '95: Actor (Lynch), Actress (McKenzie), Cinematog., Director (Rymer), Film, Film Editing, Orig. Screenplay. **Acq:** Purchase. **Dist:** Lions Gate Entertainment Inc.

Angel Blue 1997 (Unrated) — ★½
All-around married nice guy Dennis Cromwell (Bottoms) lives with his wife, Jill (Eichhorn) and newborn child in his California hometown. He befriends newcomer Enrique (Rodriguez) and soon Enrique's daughter Angela (Behrens) is babysitting for the infant Cornwell. David should really know better when his friendship with the teen turns sexual and their secret gets out. 91m; VHS, DVD. **C:** Sam Bottoms; Yeniffer Behrens; Lisa Eichhorn; Marco Rodriguez; Karen Black; Sandor Tecsy; Directed by Steven Kovacs; Written by Steven Kovacs; Cinematography by Mickey Freeman; Music by Joel Lindheimer. **A:** Sr. High-Adult. **P:** Entertainment. **U:** Home. **Mov-Ent:** Sex & Sexuality. **Acq:** Purchase. **Dist:** Vanguard International Cinema, Inc.

Angel City 1980 (Unrated) — ★★½
A Florida labor camp is the setting for this made-for-TV drama. A family of rural West Virginia migrant workers find themselves trapped inside the camp and exploited by the boss-man. Adapted from Patricia Smith's book. 90m; VHS. **C:** Ralph Waite; Paul Winfield; Jennifer Warren; Jennifer Jason Leigh; Mitchell Ryan; Directed by Philip Leacock; Written by James Lee Barrett. **Pr:** Factor-Newland Productions. **A:** Jr. High-Adult. **P:** Entertainment. **U:** Home. **Mov-Ent:** Slavery, TV Movies. **Acq:** Purchase. **Dist:** Xenon Pictures Inc. $59.95.

Angel City 1984 (Unrated)
An experimental parody of film mysteries where a detective investigates the nature of visual truth in and about Hollywood. 75m; VHS. **C:** Bob Glaudini; Directed by Jon Jost. **Pr:** Jon Jost; Jon Jost. **A:** Sr. High-Adult. **P:** Entertainment. **U:** Home. **Fin-Art:** Satire & Parody, Film--Avant-Garde. **Acq:** Purchase. **Dist:** Facets Multimedia Inc.

Angel Crafts Video Vol. 1 1996
Kathy Peterson provides instruction for creating six heirloom angels. 60m; VHS. **A:** Adult. **P:** Instruction. **U:** Home. **How-Ins:** Crafts. **Acq:** Purchase. **Dist:** Tapeworm Video Distributors Inc. $19.95.

Angel Death 1979
The more serious consequences of "angel dust" (PCP) are shown in this sobering documentary. This program is ideal for law enforcement agencies, social services, and schools. 33m; VHS, 3/4 U. **C:** Narrated by Paul Newman; Joanne Woodward. **Pr:** Dave Bell Productions. **A:** Adult. **P:** Education. **U:** Institution, CCTV, SURA. **Gen-Edu:** Drug Abuse. **Acq:** Purchase, Rent/Lease. **Dist:** Home Vision Cinema.

Angel Dust 1996 (Unrated) — ★★
Nightmare noir about a serial killer who haunts Tokyo's subways. Setsuko (Minami) is a criminal psychologist investigating the murders of several young women, all committed during rush hour at various commuter stops. Each victim has been killed with a poisonous injection. Setsuko learns the first victim was psychologically deprogrammed after leaving a religious cult and contacts her ex-lover, Rei (Wakamatsu), who runs a clinic specializing in such deprogramming. But Rei also becomes the chief suspect when he begins to play sadistic mind games with Setsuko. Is she paranoid or truly in danger? Japanese with subtitles. 116m; VHS. **C:** Kaho Minami; Takeshi Wakamatsu; Directed by Sogo Ishii; Written by Sogo Ishii; Yorozu Ikuta; Cinematography by Norimichi Kasamatsu; Music by Hiroyuki Nagashima. **A:** College-Adult. **P:** Entertainment. **U:** Home. **L:** Japanese. **Mov-Ent:** Mystery & Suspense, Psychiatry. **Acq:** Purchase. **Dist:** New Yorker Video.

Angel Dusted 1981 (Unrated) — ★½
This made-for-TV flick about the dangers of drug use looks sorta hysterical and dated but check out the performances by Stapleton and real-life son Putch as unsuspecting housewife/mom Betty Eaton and college boy Owen who winds up in

restraints after smoking some PCP-laced reefer. He's had a major violent freakout and is committed to a psych hospital but his complete recovery is uncertain. Based on the book by Ursula Etons. 97m; DVD. **C:** John Putch; Maureen Stapleton; Arthur Hill; Percy Rodriguez; Darlene Craviotto; Patrick Cassidy; Helen Hunt; Directed by Dick Lowry; Written by Darlene Craviotto; Music by James Horner. **A:** Jr. High-Adult. **P:** Entertainment. **U:** Home. **Mov-Ent:** Drug Abuse, Marijuana, Psychiatry. **Acq:** Purchase. **Dist:** WarnerArchive.com.

The Angel Effect 2011 (PG)
At times of great peril when they are near certain death, many people seem to share a very similar experience in which a mysterious "stranger" or presence calms them and guides them to safety. Depending on one's personal beliefs, these incidents have been ascribed to angels, phantoms, or nothing more than the brain reacting in a positive manner during a stressful, threatening situation. With so many such incidents reported through the centuries, today's scientists are studying the phenomenon dubbed the "Third Man Factor" to try to determine what could make the human brain flip the so-called "angel switch" to summon help at a time when death appears inevitable. 45m; DVD. **A:** Family. **P:** Education, Entertainment. **U:** Home, Institution. **Mov-Ent:** Documentary Films, Death, Folklore & Legends. **Acq:** Purchase. **Dist:** $19.95.

Angel Eyes 2001 (R) — ★★½
Although the film's marketing campaign implied some supernatural elements, there's nothing unworldly about this romantic drama. And despite some capable performances by the leads, the film is utterly predictable as well. Tough Chicago police officer Sharon Pogue (Lopez) is still dealing with the effects of an abusive childhood when she meets another lost soul, Catch (Caviezel), who's grappling with the death of his wife and child. He saves her life, they fall for each other, but things are hardly that simple. They both have emotional issues and a past connection that's all too easy to determine. 104m; DVD, Wide. **C:** Jennifer Lopez; James (Jim) Caviezel; Sonia Braga; Terrence Howard; Jeremy Sisto; Monet Mazur; Victor Argo; Shirley Knight; Jeremy Ratchford; Peter MacNeill; Stephen Kay; Directed by Luis Mandoki; Written by Gerald Di Pego; Cinematography by Piotr Sobocinski; Music by Marco Beltrami. **Pr:** Elie Samaha; Mark Canton; Warner Bros; Morgan Creek Productions; Franchise Pictures. **A:** Sr. High-Adult. **P:** Entertainment. **U:** Home. **Mov-Ent:** Drama, Domestic Abuse, Death. **Acq:** Purchase. **Dist:** Warner Home Video, Inc.

Angel Face 1952 (Unrated) — ★★★
An angel's face with a devil's heart is psycho rich girl Diane (Simmons), who wants to get rid of her hated stepmommy (O'Neil) so she can have daddy (Marshall) all to herself. Diane is infatuated with new chauffeur Frank (Mitchum) and he becomes an unwitting accomplice in her deadly scheme. Both are brought up on murder charges but Frank doesn't realize how far this crazy chick will go to keep what—and who'she wants. Wild noir melodrama from Preminger that gave good girl Simmons a chance to unleash her inner bad femme. Mitchum is his usual cool self. 92m/B/W; DVD, CC. **C:** Jean Simmons; Robert Mitchum; Herbert Marshall; Mona Freeman; Leon Ames; Barbara O'Neil; Kenneth Tobey; Directed by Otto Preminger; Written by Frank Nugent; Oscar Millard; Cinematography by Harry Stradling, Sr.; Music by Dimitri Tiomkin. **A:** Jr. High-Adult. **P:** Entertainment. **U:** Home. **Mov-Ent**. **Acq:** Purchase. **Dist:** Warner Home Video, Inc.

An Angel for Satan 1966 — ★½
Steele plays a dual role in her last major, Italian horror film. She gives a strong performance as a woman possessed by the spirit of a statue. In Italian with no subtitles. 90m/B/W; VHS, DVD. **C:** Barbara Steele; Anthony Steffen; Aldo Berti; Mario Brega; Ursula Davis; Claudio Gora; Directed by Camillo Mastrocinque; Written by Camillo Mastrocinque; Music by Francesco De Masi. **A:** Sr. High-Adult. **P:** Entertainment. **U:** Home. **L:** Italian. **Mov-Ent:** Horror. **Acq:** Purchase. **Dist:** Sinister Cinema. $16.95.

Angel Force 1994 (Unrated) — ★
A rescue team named Angel Force is given orders to save an agent from ruthless drug traffickers in Bangkok. The team, led by a female agent, carries out their orders through the jungles of Thailand with the bad guys hot on their trail. The final confrontation is a fierce, cartridge-spewing, bullet-ripping battle between the drug traffickers and the Angel Force team. ?m; VHS. **C:** Si-Fong Lee; Gewen-Shen Lin. **Pr:** Youngtze Film & Video. **A:** Adult. **P:** Entertainment. **U:** Home. **Mov-Ent:** Martial Arts. **Acq:** Purchase. **Dist:** Tapeworm Video Distributors Inc. $44.95.

Angel Heart 1987 (R) — ★★½
Exotic, controversial look at murder, voodoo cults, and sex in 1955 New Orleans. Bonet defiantly sheds her image as a young innocent (no more Cosby Show for you, young lady). Rourke is slimy as marginal NYC private eye Angel, hired by the devilish De Niro to track a missing big band singer who violated a "contract." His investigation leads him to the bizarre world of the occult in New Orleans, where the blood drips to a different beat. Visually stimulating, with a provocative sex scene between Bonet and Rourke, captured in both R-rated and unrated versions. Adapted by Parker from "Falling Angel" by William Hjortsberg. 112m; VHS, DVD, Blu-Ray. **C:** Mickey Rourke; Robert De Niro; Lisa Bonet; Charlotte Rampling; Michael Higgins; Charles Gordone; Kathleen Wilhoite; Stocker Fountelieu; Brownie McGhee; Elizabeth Whitcraft; Eliott Keener; Dann Florek; Directed by Alan Parker; Written by Alan Parker; Cinematography by Michael Seresin; Music by Trevor Jones. **Pr:** Tri-Star Pictures. **A:** Sr. High-Adult. **P:** Entertainment. **U:** Home. **Mov-Ent:** Mystery & Suspense, Death. **Acq:** Purchase. **Dist:** Facets Multimedia Inc.; Lions Gate Television Corp. $19.95.

Angel in a Taxi 1959 (Unrated) — ★★
A six-year-old boy in an orphanage decides to choose his own mother, a beautiful ballerina he sees in a magazine, when an ugly couple try to adopt him. Italian film dubbed in English. 89m/B/W; VHS, 8 mm. **C:** Wera Cecova; Ettore Manni; Vittorio De Sica; Marietto; Gabriele Ferzetti; Directed by Antonio Leonviola. **Pr:** Video Yesteryear. **A:** Family. **P:** Entertainment. **U:** Home. **Mov-Ent:** Comedy-Drama, Adoption, Dance--Ballet. **Acq:** Purchase. **Dist:** Facets Multimedia Inc. $24.95.

Angel in the House 2011 (PG) — ★★½
The Morrison's marriage is rocky after the death of their child and their problems conceiving another. They decide to become foster parents instead and seven-year-old Eli suddenly appears on their doorstep, saying the agency sent him. Eli seems wise beyond his years and is not only a good listener but offers sound advice to put the Morrson's marriage back together. It's reliably charming and suitable for family viewing. 90m; DVD. **C:** Toni Collette; Ioan Gruffudd; Maurice Cole; Hayley Mills; Richard E. Grant; Anne Reid; Directed by Jonathan Newman; Written by Jonathan Newman; Cinematography by Dirk Nel; Music by Mark Thomas. **A:** Family. **P:** Entertainment. **U:** Home. **L:** English. **Mov-Ent:** Children, Comedy-Drama, Family. **Acq:** Purchase. **Dist:** Screen Media Ventures, LLC.

Angel Island 1980
A look at the San Francisco area island where many Chinese immigrants were treated harshly. 30m; EJ. **Pr:** Chinese for Affirmative Action. **A:** Jr. High-Adult. **P:** Education. **U:** Institution, CCTV. **Gen-Edu:** Ethnicity, Immigration. **Acq:** Rent/Lease. **Dist:** Chinese for Affirmative Action. $25.00.

The Angel Levine 1970 (PG) — ★★½
Morris (Mostel) is an old Jewish man who has lost his faith in God after a series of personal and professional losses. Alexander Levine (Belafonte) is a black angel who can earn his wings if he can convince Morris that his life does have meaning. As sentimental as it sounds but the leads are pros. Based on a story by Bernard Malamud. 104m; VHS, DVD. **C:** Zero Mostel; Harry Belafonte; Ida Kaminska; Milo O'Shea; Gloria Foster; Eli Wallach; Anne Jackson; Directed by Jan Kadar; Written by Bill Gunn; Ronald Ribman; Cinematography by Richard Kratina; Music by William Eaton. **A:** Jr. High-Adult. **P:** Entertainment. **U:** Home. **Mov-Ent:** Black Culture, Judaism, Aging. **Acq:** Purchase. **Dist:** Critics' Choice Video & DVD.

Angel Links: Avenging Angel—Vol. 1 2001 (Unrated)
Features the animated science fiction television series about Meifon Li, a saucy 16-year-old girl of extraordinary talents including running a company along with the Angel Links, a group that fends off the evils of the galaxy, such as pirates, as a free service. Includes: "Guardian Angel," "A Wasted Fairy Tale," "The Proud Dragon," and "Lief-Living Ether Flier." A spin-off of "Outlaw Star." 4 episodes. 100m; DVD. **C:** Voice(s) by Ryoka Yuzuki; Elizabeth Stepkowski; Tommy Campbell. **A:** Sr. High-Adult. **P:** Entertainment. **U:** Home. **Mov-Ent:** Television Series, Animation & Cartoons, Action-Adventure. **Acq:** Purchase. **Dist:** Bandai Entertainment Inc. $29.98.

Angel Links: Broken Angel—Vol. 3 2001 (Unrated)
Features the animated science fiction television series about Meifon Li, a saucy 16-year-old girl of extraordinary talents including running a company along with the Angel Links, a group that fends off the evils of the galaxy, such as pirates, as a free service. Includes: "My Ship," "A Pheasant Chooses Its Tree," and "The Ones Who Were Left." A spin-off of "Outlaw Star." 3 episodes. 75m; DVD. **C:** Voice(s) by Ryoka Yuzuki; Elizabeth Stepkowski; Tommy Campbell. **A:** Sr. High-Adult. **P:** Entertainment. **U:** Home. **Mov-Ent:** Television Series, Animation & Cartoons, Action-Adventure. **Acq:** Purchase. **Dist:** Bandai Entertainment Inc. $29.98.

Angel Links: Eternal Angel—Vol. 4 2001 (Unrated)
Features the animated science fiction television series about Meifon Li, a 16-year-old girl of extraordinary talents including running a company along with the Angel Links, a group that fends off the evils of the galaxy, such as pirates, as a free service. Includes: "At the Binary Interval," "All My Soul," and "Fragment of an Angel." A spin-off of "Outlaw Star." 4 episodes. 75m; DVD. **C:** Voice(s) by Ryoka Yuzuki; Elizabeth Stepkowski; Tommy Campbell. **A:** Sr. High-Adult. **P:** Entertainment. **U:** Home. **Mov-Ent:** Television Series, Animation & Cartoons, Action-Adventure. **Acq:** Purchase. **Dist:** Bandai Entertainment Inc. $29.98.

Angel Links: Fallen Angel—Vol. 2 2001 (Unrated)
Features the animated science fiction television series about Meifon Li, a saucy 16-year-old girl of extraordinary talents including running a company along with the Angel Links, a group that fends off the evils of the galaxy, such as pirates, as a free service. Includes: "The Rain Upon the Stars," "Crossroads," and "The Angel and The Fallen Angel." A spin-off of "Outlaw Star." 3 episodes. 75m; DVD. **C:** Voice(s) by Ryoka Yuzuki; Elizabeth Stepkowski; Tommy Campbell. **A:** Sr. High-Adult. **P:** Entertainment. **U:** Home. **Mov-Ent:** Television Series, Animation & Cartoons, Action-Adventure. **Acq:** Purchase. **Dist:** Bandai Entertainment Inc. $29.98.

Angel Negro 2000 (Unrated) — ★★
Hyped as Chile's first horror film, it starts with the usual group of high school students celebrating in a manner that ends in one's inevitable death. Just as inevitably the survivors start getting murdered one by one years later by someone they assume is the dead girl. 85m; DVD. **C:** Alvaro Morales; Andrea Freund; Blanca Lewin; Directed by Jorge Olguin; Written by Jorge Olguin; Cinematography by Arnaldo Rodriquez; Music by Juan Francisco Cueto. **A:** Sr. High-Adult. **P:** Entertainment. **U:** Home. **L:** English. **Mov-Ent**. **Acq:** Purchase. **Dist:** Troma Entertainment. $19.98.

Angel of Death 1986 (R) — **Bomb!**
A small mercenary band of Nazi hunters attempt to track down Josef Mengele in South America. Stupid entry in the minor "let's find the darn Nazi before he really causes trouble" genre. Director Franco is also known as A. Frank Drew White. 92m; VHS, DVD. **C:** Chris Mitchum; Fernando Rey; Susan Andrews; Directed by Jess (Jesus) Franco. **Pr:** New World Pictures. **A:** Sr. High-Adult. **P:** Entertainment. **U:** Home. **L:** Spanish. **Mov-Ent**. **Acq:** Purchase. **Dist:** Televista. $19.95.

Angel of Death 2002 (Unrated) — ★
Detective Maria Delgado (Sorvino) comes to Seville during Holly Week to investigate a series of ritual killings. With cops Quemada (Martinez) and Torillo (Atkine) assisting, Maria discovers a mysterious religious order, The Brotherhood of Christ, and an old woman (Valli) keeping a secret since the Spanish Civil War. Lackluster, miscast thriller adapted from the novel by David Hewson. 94m; DVD. **C:** Mira Sorvino; Olivier Martinez; Feodor Atkine; Alida Valli; Luis Tosar; Directed by Pepe Danquart; Written by Roy Mitchell; Cinematography by Ciro Cappellari; Music by Andrea Guerra. **A:** Sr. High-Adult. **P:** Entertainment. **U:** Home. **Mov-Ent:** Religion, Spain. **Acq:** Purchase. **Dist:** MGM Home Entertainment.

Angel of Death 2009 (R) — ★½
Originally a 10-episode web series starring Bell as remorseless assassin Eve. After suffering severe head trauma, the hitwoman begins to hallucinate and is haunted by her victims. So Eve decides to seek revenge on her mob employers, who ordered the hits. 90m; DVD. **C:** Zoe Bell; Lucy Lawless; Doug Jones; Vail Bloom; Theodore (Ted) Raimi; Brian Poth; Justin Huen; Jake Abel; Directed by Paul Etheredge-Ouzts; Written by Ed Brubaker; Cinematography by Carl Herse. **A:** Sr. High-Adult. **P:** Entertainment. **U:** Home. **Mov-Ent**. **Acq:** Purchase. **Dist:** Sony Pictures Home Entertainment Inc.

Angel of Destruction 1994 (R) — ★½
Undercover cop is assigned to protect controversial rock star from psycho fan. Cop gets killed and cop's sister decides to go after the killer. 80m; VHS, DVD. **C:** Maria Ford; Charlie Spradling; Directed by Charles Philip Moore. **A:** College-Adult. **P:** Entertainment. **U:** Home. **Mov-Ent**. **Acq:** Purchase. **Dist:** New Horizons Picture Corp.

Angel of Fury 1993 (R) — ★★½
Rothrock plays the head of security of a computer corporation who must battle terrorists after the company's top-secret computer. And there's no one she can trust. Lots of martial arts action with the competent Rothrock. 91m; VHS, CC. **C:** Cynthia Rothrock; Christopher Barnes; Peter O'Brien; Directed by Ackyl Anwary. **A:** Sr. High-Adult. **P:** Entertainment. **U:** Home. **Mov-Ent:** Martial Arts, Terrorism. **Acq:** Purchase. **Dist:** Imperial Entertainment Corp. $92.95.

Angel of H.E.A.T. 1982 (R) — **Bomb!**
Porn-star Chambers is Angel, a female super-agent on a mission to save the world from total destruction. Sex and spies abound with trashy nonchalance. 90m; VHS, DVD. **C:** Marilyn Chambers; Mary Woronov; Steve Johnson; Directed by Helen Sanford; Myrl A. Schreibman. **Pr:** Myrl A. Schreibman; Hal Kant; Myrl A. Schreibman. **A:** College-Adult. **P:** Entertainment. **U:** Home. **Mov-Ent:** Action-Adventure, Sex & Sexuality, Exploitation. **Acq:** Purchase. **Dist:** $69.95.

Angel of the Night 1998 (R) — ★★
Rebecca inherits her grandmother's creepy mansion and invites her best friend and her boyfriend for a visit. While exploring, Rebecca discovers that great-grandpa Rico was a vampire and she inadvertently releases him from his tomb. Dubbed from Danish. 98m; VHS, DVD, Wide. **C:** Ulrich Thomsen; Maria Karlsen; Erik Holmey; Directed by Shakey Gonzaless; Written by Shakey Gonzaless; Cinematography by Jacob Kusk; Music by Soren Hyldgaard. **A:** Sr. High-Adult. **P:** Entertainment. **U:** Home. **Mov-Ent**. **Acq:** Purchase. **Dist:** Bedford Entertainment Inc.

Angel on My Shoulder 1946 — ★★★
A murdered convict makes a deal with the Devil (Rains) and returns to earth for revenge as a respected judge who's been thinning Hell's waiting list. Occupying the good judge, the murderous Muni has significant problems adjusting. Amusing fantasy with Muni in a rare and successful comic role. Co-written by Segall, who scripted "Here Comes Mr. Jordan," in which Rains played an angel. Remade in 1980. 101m/B/W; VHS, DVD, 3/4 U, Special order formats. **C:** Paul Muni; Claude Rains; Anne Baxter; Onslow Stevens; Directed by Archie Mayo; Written by Harry Segall; Cinematography by James Van Trees; Music by Dimitri Tiomkin. **Pr:** United Artists. **A:** Family. **P:** Entertainment. **U:** Institution, Home. **Mov-Ent:** Fantasy, Death. **Acq:** Purchase. **Dist:** Gotham Distributing Corp.; VCI Entertainment; VCX Ltd. $9.95.

Angel on My Shoulder 1980 (Unrated) — ★★
A small-time hood wrongfully executed for murder comes back as district attorney. He owes the devil, but he's finding it tough to be evil enough to repay his debt. O.K. TV remake of the better 1946 film starring Paul Muni. 96m; VHS. **C:** Peter Strauss; Richard Kiley; Barbara Hershey; Janis Paige; Directed by John Berry; Music by Artie Butler. **Pr:** Mace Neufeld. **A:** Jr. High-Adult. **P:** Entertainment. **U:** Home. **Mov-Ent:** Law, Death, TV Movies. **Acq:** Purchase. **Dist:** No Longer Available.

Angel Rodriguez 2005 (Unrated) — ★★½
Unsentimental story about the problems facing the trouble-prone title character. Angel (Everett) is a smart Brooklyn high schooler whose temper often gets the best of him. After getting into a fight with his dad's girlfriend, he's thrown out of the house and taken in for the night by his pregnant guidance counselor Nicole (Griffiths). But good intentions have a way of going wrong. 87m; DVD, Wide. **C:** Rachel Griffiths; Denis O'Hare;

David Zayas; Jonan Everett; Wallace Little; Jon Norman Schneider; Denise Burse; Directed by Jim McKay; Written by Jim McKay; Hannah Weyer; Cinematography by Chad Davidson. **A:** Jr. High-Adult. **P:** Entertainment. **U:** Home. **Mov-Ent**: Adolescence, Adolescence, Pregnancy. **Acq:** Purchase. **Dist:** Movies Unlimited; Alpha Video.

Angel: Season Five 2005 (Unrated)
Spin-off television series (1999-2004) of the popular "Buffy the Vampire Slayer" as Angel (Boreanaz) relocates to Los Angeles and renews his vow to right the wrongs of his past by protecting the innocent. Includes: Cordelia (Carpenter) can't believe that Angel is in control of Wolfram & Hart once she awakens from a coma and Angel and the gang face their biggest battle ever in the series finale. 22 episodes. 990m; DVD. **C:** David Boreanaz; Alexis Denisof; J. August Richards; Charisma Carpenter; Andy Hallett; Amy Acker; James Marsters. **A:** Sr. High-Adult. **P:** Entertainment. **U:** Home. **Mov-Ent**: Television Series, Horror, Drama. **Acq:** Purchase. **Dist:** Fox Home Entertainment. $59.98.

Angel: Season Four 2004 (Unrated)
Spin-off television series (1999-2004) of the popular "Buffy the Vampire Slayer" as Angel (Boreanaz) relocates to Los Angeles and renews his vow to right the wrongs of his past by protecting the innocent. Includes: Angel's search for Cordelia (Carpenter) takes him to Las Vegas but when she is found she's lost all memory though once pieces of her past slowly return to her she has a horrific insight that the end of the world is quickly approaching; meanwhile, Cordelia has another child that ends up being an alluring grown woman. 22 episodes. 990m; DVD. **C:** David Boreanaz; Alexis Denisof; J. August Richards; Charisma Carpenter; Amy Acker; Andy Hallett; James Marsters. **A:** Sr. High-Adult. **P:** Entertainment. **U:** Home. **Mov-Ent**: Television Series, Horror, Drama. **Acq:** Purchase. **Dist:** Fox Home Entertainment. $59.98.

Angel: Season One 2003 (Unrated)
Spin-off television series (1999-2004) of the popular "Buffy the Vampire Slayer" as Angel (Boreanaz) relocates to Los Angeles and renews his vow to right the wrongs of his past by protecting the innocent. Includes: Angel receives his first mission to save a young girl as seen in Doyle's vision, a woman's neurosurgeon appears to be stalking her, and Buffy (Sarah Michelle Gellar) finds Angel and the two fend off a demon but not before its blood gets on Angel and he becomes fully human. 22 episodes. 1080m; DVD. **C:** David Boreanaz; Alexis Denisof; Charisma Carpenter; Glenn Quinn; J. August Richards. **A:** Sr. High-Adult. **P:** Entertainment. **U:** Home. **Mov-Ent**: Television Series, Horror, Drama. **Acq:** Purchase. **Dist:** Fox Home Entertainment. $59.98.

Angel: Season Three 2004 (Unrated)
Spin-off television series (1999-2004) of the popular "Buffy the Vampire Slayer" as Angel (Boreanaz) relocates to Los Angeles and renews his vow to right the wrongs of his past by protecting the innocent. Includes: Angel stakes a female vampire from his soulless past—200 years ago'leading her lover to avenge her death and Angel's old betrayal and Angel finds out that Darla (Benz) is having his child but the infant boy is in danger from many demons who are out to possess him though, later, the boy ages to a teenager in another dimension who becomes hostile toward Angel for his violent past. 22 episodes. 990m; DVD. **C:** David Boreanaz; Alexis Denisof; J. August Richards; Charisma Carpenter; Julie Benz; Amy Acker. **A:** Sr. High-Adult. **P:** Entertainment. **U:** Home. **Mov-Ent**: Television Series, Horror, Drama. **Acq:** Purchase. **Dist:** Fox Home Entertainment. $59.98.

Angel: Season Two 2003 (Unrated)
Spin-off television series (1999-2004) of the popular "Buffy the Vampire Slayer" as Angel (Boreanaz) relocates to Los Angeles and renews his vow to right the wrongs of his past by protecting the innocent. Includes: Angel helps a woman reign in her telekinetic powers, his insomnia leads to painful memories in his dreams that cause concern that he'll return to his old evil vampire ways, and Angel must deal with an old flame who was returned into a vampire state. 22 episodes. 1080m; DVD. **C:** David Boreanaz; Alexis Denisof; J. August Richards; Charisma Carpenter. **A:** Sr. High-Adult. **P:** Entertainment. **U:** Home. **Mov-Ent**: Television Series, Horror, Drama. **Acq:** Purchase. **Dist:** Fox Home Entertainment. $59.98.

Angel Square 1992 — ★★
A Canadian production from the director of the acclaimed "Bye Bye Blues." When the father of a neighborhood boy is brutally attacked, the community bands together to search for the culprit. 106m; VHS. **C:** Ned Beatty; Directed by Anne Wheeler; Written by James DeFelice. **A:** Jr. High-Adult. **P:** Entertainment. **U:** Home. **Mov-Ent**: Drama, Canada. **Acq:** Purchase. **Dist:** No Longer Available.

Angel Stories 1 & 2 19??
Presents encounters with angels experienced by ordinary people through the use of special effects and re-creations. 47m; VHS. **A:** Jr. High-Adult. **P:** Entertainment. **U:** Home. **Gen-Edu**: Religion. **Acq:** Purchase. **Dist:** Hartley Film Foundation. $39.95.

Angel: The Collector's Set 1999
Springing from the character's popularity on the show "Buffy the Vampire Slayer," 240-year-old vampire-with-a-conscience Angel now carries his own show wherein he resides in Los Angeles and starts his own Angel Investigations to "help the helpless" along with Cordelia and Doyle. Many of the battles involve the supernatural law firm Wolfram and Hart and over the course of the series former Buffy regulars join the cast, including Watcher Wesley, demon street fighter Gunn, physicist Fred, and soulful vampire Spike. Angel's old flame Darla also returns and their son Connor surges a revenge driven quest against his father. Includes all 110 episodes on 30 discs. 5130m; DVD. **C:** David Boreanaz; Charisma Carpenter; Glenn Quinn. **A:** Sr. High-Adult. **P:** Entertainment. **U:** Home. **Mov-Ent**: Drama, Fantasy. **Acq:** Purchase. **Dist:** Fox Home Entertainment.

Angel Town 1989 (R) — ★
A foreign exchange student, who happens to be a champion kick-boxer, is forced into combat with LA street gangs. 90m; VHS, DVD. **C:** Olivier Gruner; Theresa Saldana; Frank Aragon; Tony Valentino; Peter Kwong; Mike Moroff; Directed by Eric Karson. **Pr:** Imperial Entertainment. **A:** Sr. High-Adult. **P:** Entertainment. **U:** Home. **Mov-Ent**: Martial Arts. **Acq:** Purchase. **Dist:** Imperial Entertainment Corp. $89.95.

Angel Unchained 1970 — ★1/2
Typical biker exploitation flick has bikers and hippies joining together to fend off small-town redneck hostility. 92m; VHS, DVD. **C:** Don Stroud; Tyne Daly; Luke Askew; Larry Bishop; Aldo Ray; Bill McKinney; Directed by Lee Madden; Written by Jeffrey Alladin Fiskin. **Pr:** Hal Klein; American International Pictures. **A:** Sr. High-Adult. **P:** Entertainment. **U:** Home. **Mov-Ent**: Motorcycles. **Acq:** Purchase. **Dist:** MGM Studios Inc. $14.98.

Angel with the Trumpet 1950 (Unrated) — ★★
Depressing character study of a woman who marries to please her family, rather than herself. When the Gestapo finds out about her Jewish ancestry, she must make the most important decision of her life. Currently only available as part of a collection 'The Nifty Fifties'. 98m/B/W; VHS, DVD. **C:** Eileen Herlie; Basil Sydney; Norman Wooland; Maria Schell; Olga Edwards; Oskar Werner; Anthony Bushell; Wilfrid Hyde-White; Directed by Anthony Bushell. **Pr:** London Films Productions; British Lion. **A:** Sr. High-Adult. **P:** Entertainment. **U:** Home. **Mov-Ent. Acq:** Purchase. **Dist:** Mill Creek Entertainment L.L.C.; Movies Unlimited. $29.98.

Angela 1977 (Unrated) — ★
Twisted love story about a young man (Railsback) who jumps the bones of an older woman, unaware that she is the mother he's been separated from for 23 long years. Seems that way back when, the boy was kidnapped by crime boss Huston from mom Loren, an ex-prostitute, who then turned in the boy's dad, who was something of a criminal. Mom thought son was dead, dad vowed revenge from prison, and son went about his unwitting business. It all comes together insipidly, at the expense of the cast and viewer. 91m; VHS. **C:** Sophia Loren; Steve Railsback; John Huston; John Vernon; Directed by Boris Sagal; Music by Henry Mancini. **Pr:** 20th Century-Fox. **A:** Sr. High-Adult. **P:** Entertainment. **U:** Home. **Mov-Ent**: Canada. **Acq:** Purchase. **Dist:** No Longer Available.

Angela 1994 — ★★
Exceedingly mystical film focuses on religiously obsessed 10-year-old Angela (Rhyne), who tells her six-year-old sister Ellie (Blythe) that unless they are very good the Devil will come to take them away. Meanwhile, she tries to cope with volatile family relationships, including their unstable mother. Good performances in a sometimes sluggish and abstract drama. 105m; VHS, DVD. **C:** Miranda Stuart Rhyne; Charlotte Blythe; Anna Thomson; John Ventimiglia; Vincent Gallo; Directed by Rebecca Miller; Written by Rebecca Miller; Cinematography by Ellen Kuras; Music by Michael Rohatyn. **Pr:** Ron Kastner; Tree Farm Pictures. **A:** College-Adult. **P:** Entertainment. **U:** Home. **Mov-Ent**: Religion. **Awds:** Sundance '95: Cinematog., Filmmakers Trophy. **Acq:** Purchase. **Dist:** New Video Group.

Angela 2002 (R) — ★★
Angela (Finochiarro) is married to the older Saro (Pupella), who runs the mob in Palermo. Angela helps out by using her shoe store as a front for his drug deals, but she's frustrated by being shut out of all the business decisions. Then hunky hood Masino (di Stefano) is hired and the two are soon hitting the sheets. A bad idea, not only because of what Saro will do but because it gives the cops, who have the mobsters under surveillance, the leverage they need to take Saro down. Italian with subtitles. 100m; DVD. **C:** Andrea Di Stefano; Donatella Finochiarro; Mario Pupella; Toni Gambino; Directed by Roberta Torre; Written by Roberta Torre; Massimo D'Anolfi; Cinematography by Daniele Cipri; Music by Andrea Guerra. **A:** College-Adult. **P:** Entertainment. **U:** Home. **L:** Italian. **Mov-Ent**: Italy. **Acq:** Purchase. **Dist:** Movies Unlimited.

Angela Lansbury: Two Tape Collector's Set 19??
Two classic television performances from the 1950s, "The Indiscreet Mrs. Jarvis" and "A String of Pearls." 25m; VHS. **A:** Family. **P:** Entertainment. **U:** Home. **Mov-Ent**: Television, Television Series. **Acq:** Purchase. **Dist:** Rhino Entertainment Co.

Angela Lansbury's Positive Moves 1988
The actress demonstrates fitness techniques and explains her outlook for a healthy lifestyle. 50m; VHS, CC. **C:** Angela Lansbury. **Pr:** Wood Knapp Video. **A:** Family. **P:** Instruction. **U:** Home. **Hea-Sci**: Fitness/Exercise. **Acq:** Purchase. **Dist:** Karol Media; Reader's Digest Home Video.

Angela's Airplane 1993
Two five year-old girls find themselves in the middle of exciting adventures. Angela sneaks into a plane and flies it with the help of Ralph, her stuffed rabbit co-pilot, and in "The Fire Station" Sheila talks Michael into hiding in a fire engine that gets sent out to a fire. 25m; VHS. **A:** Preschool-Primary. **P:** Entertainment. **U:** Home. **Chl-Juv**: Animation & Cartoons, Children, Aeronautics. **Acq:** Purchase. **Dist:** Golden Book Video. $12.95.

Angela's Ashes 1999 (R) — ★★1/2
Frank McCourt's devastating memoir covers growing up poverty-stricken in Limerick during the 1930s, with an alcoholic father (Carlyle) and a mother (Watson) struggling to hold the family together while dealing with her own deep depression. The book had the saving graces of lyricism and wit. Unfortunately, the film misses all that and is merely bleak despite the talented cast (including the three actors who play Frank through the years). 145m; DVD, CC. **C:** Emily Watson; Robert Carlyle; Joe Breen; Ciaran Owens; Michael Legge; Ronnie Masterson; Pauline McLynn; Narrated by Andrew Bennett; Directed by Alan Parker; Written by Robert Carlyle; Laura Jones; Cinematography by Michael Seresin; Music by John Williams. **Pr:** Scott Rudin; David Brown; Alan Parker; Adam Schroeder; Alan Parker; Paramount Pictures. **A:** Sr. High-Adult. **P:** Entertainment. **U:** Home. **Mov-Ent**: Ireland, Poverty, Alcoholism. **Acq:** Purchase. **Dist:** WarnerArchive.com.

Angele 1934 — ★★★
A lovely, naive country girl is lured to the city by a cunning pimp who knows that she wants to escape her oppressive father. With her illegitimate baby, she's discovered in a whorehouse and taken in disgrace back home to dad, who promptly locks her in the barn. One special guy, however, appreciates her purity and plots to rescue her. What he lacks in material resources he makes up for in character. An overlong but moving story of lost innocence and intolerence. In French with English subtitles. Based on the novel "Un de Baumugnes" by Jean Giono. 130m/B/W; VHS. **C:** Orane Demazis; Fernandel; Henri Poupon; Edouard Delmont; Directed by Marcel Pagnol. **A:** Sr. High-Adult. **P:** Entertainment. **U:** Home. **L:** French, English. **Mov-Ent. Acq:** Purchase. **Dist:** Interama, Inc. $59.95.

Angelic Conversation 1985 (Unrated)
Fourteen of William Shakespeare's versifications on love are combined with industrial music and delicate visuals to create an ode to homosexuality. 78m; VHS. **C:** Paul Reynolds; Philip Williamson; Voice(s) by Judi Dench; Directed by Derek Jarman. **Pr:** Derek Jarman; Derek Jarman. **A:** Adult. **P:** Entertainment. **U:** Home. **Mov-Ent**: Homosexuality, Literature--English. **Acq:** Purchase. **Dist:** Mystic Fire Video. $29.95.

Angelic Gospel Singers: Gospel in Motion 198? (Unrated)
The singers perform ten gospel greats. ?m; VHS. **A:** Family. **P:** Entertainment. **U:** Home. **Mov-Ent**: Music--Performance. **Acq:** Purchase. **Dist:** Music Video Distributors. $29.95.

Angelica Knows Best 1998
Angelica and the rest of the Rugrats gang entertain children in five cartoons: "Psycho Angelica," "Angelica Nose Best," "Angelica's Last Stand," "Ransom of Cynthia," and "Word of the Day." 57m; VHS. **A:** Preschool-Primary. **P:** Entertainment. **U:** Home. **Chl-Juv**: Children, Animation & Cartoons. **Acq:** Purchase. **Dist:** Paramount Pictures Corp. $12.95.

Angelina Ballerina: Angelina in the Wings 2002
Features four 11-minute episodes about the adventures and mishaps of a young mouse-girl who dreams of stardom in the ballet. Includes "The Cheese Ball Cup," "Two Mice in a Boat," "Treasure Tandems," and the title episode. 44m; VHS, DVD. **A:** Primary. **P:** Entertainment. **U:** Home. **Chl-Juv**: Television, Animation & Cartoons. **Acq:** Purchase. **Dist:** HIT Entertainment Ltd. $14.95.

Angelina Ballerina: Friends Forever 2002
Presents four 11-minute stories about friendship and features two live-actions segments with young dancers from the Royal Academy of Dance in London. 48m; VHS, DVD. **A:** Preschool. **P:** Entertainment. **U:** Home. **Chl-Juv**: Animation & Cartoons, Television. **Acq:** Purchase. **Dist:** HIT Entertainment Ltd. $14.99.

Angelina Ballerina: Lights, Camera, Action! 2004
Four animated stories starring Angelina teach children lessons about friendship, forgiveness, teamwork and honesty. DVD includes many extras including live-action segments with students from the Royal Academy of Dance in London plus a Matching and Dress-Up game. 52m; VHS, DVD. **A:** Primary. **P:** Entertainment. **U:** Home. **Chl-Juv**: Animation & Cartoons, Children. **Acq:** Purchase. **Dist:** HIT Entertainment Ltd. $16.99.

Angelina Ballerina: Rose Fairy Princess 2002
Features four 11-minute episodes about the adventures and mishaps of a young mouse-girl who dreams of stardom in the ballet. Includes "Angelina at the Fair," "The Ballet Tickets," and "Midnight Muddle" as well as the title episode. 44m; VHS, DVD. **A:** Primary. **P:** Entertainment. **U:** Home. **Chl-Juv**: Television, Animation & Cartoons. **Acq:** Purchase. **Dist:** HIT Entertainment Ltd. $14.95.

Angelina Ballerina: The Lucky Penny 2002
In four animated stories Angelina learns about the value of practicing, tolerance and kindness for others, helps a friend overcome a fear, and searches for her Grandfather's lost war medal. 53m; VHS, DVD. **A:** Preschool. **P:** Entertainment. **U:** Home. **Chl-Juv**: Animation & Cartoons, Television. **Acq:** Purchase. **Dist:** HIT Entertainment Ltd. $14.99.

Angelique 1964 (Unrated) — ★★1/2
The first of a five-picture series of mildly racy, bodice-ripping costumed pulp. Beautiful Angelique (Mercier) is forced to leave her lover Nicolas (Gemma) to marry wealthy (but disfigured) Count Joffrey de Peyrac (Hossein). A marriage of convenience turns into true love but Joffrey has powerful enemies, including a jealous Louis XIV (Toja), who accuses Joffrey of sorcery. Loosely based on the novels by Anne and Serge Colon; French with subtitles. 117m; DVD. **C:** Michele Mercier; Robert Hossein; Jean Rochefort; Claude Giraud; Giuliano Gemma; Charles Regnier; Jacques Toja; Directed by Bernard Borderie; Written by Claude Brule; Francis Cosne; Cinematography by Henri Persin; Music by Michel Magne. **A:** Sr. High-Adult. **P:** Entertainment. **U:** Home. **L:** French. **Mov-Ent**: France. **Acq:** Purchase. **Dist:** Lions Gate Entertainment Inc.

Angelique and the King 1966 (Unrated) — ★★½
The third in the series following "Angelique: The Road to Versailles." The Persian ambassador (Frey) falls in love with Angelique and holds her captive, hoping that she'll return his affections. When she finally returns to the court of King Louis (Toja) it's to rumors that she's his new mistress. Followed by "Untamable Angelique." French with subtitles. 104m; DVD. **C:** Michele Mercier; Robert Hossein; Sami Frey; Jean Rochefort; Estella Blain; Jacques Toja; Directed by Bernard Borderie; Written by Bernard Borderie; Francis Cosne; Alain Decaux; Cinematography by Henri Persin; Music by Michel Magne. **A:** Sr. High-Adult. **P:** Entertainment. **U:** Home. **L:** French. **Mov-Ent:** France. **Acq:** Purchase. **Dist:** Lions Gate Entertainment Inc.

Angelique and the Sultan 1968 (Unrated) — ★★½
The fifth and last in the series, following "Untamable Angelique." Angelique continues to be threatened by d'Escrainville, who holds her aboard his ship. A battle ensues between the kidnapper and Joffrey but Angelique has already been sold to the Sultan of Morocco, so Joffrey must go rescue his wife. French with subtitles. 97m; DVD. **C:** Michele Mercier; Robert Hossein; Roger Pigaut; Ettore Manni; Helmuth Schneider; Jean-Claude Pascal; Jacques Santi; Aly Ben-Ayed; Directed by Bernard Borderie; Written by Bernard Borderie; Francis Cosne; Cinematography by Henri Persin; Music by Michel Magne. **A:** Sr. High-Adult. **P:** Entertainment. **U:** Home. **L:** French. **Mov-Ent:** France. **Acq:** Purchase. **Dist:** Lions Gate Entertainment Inc.

Angelique: The Road to Versailles 1965 (Unrated) — ★★½
The second in the series, following "Angelique." Believing her husband Joffrey is dead, Angelique hides out in Paris with her old love Nicolas but discovers he's changed from a sweet youth to a ruthless criminal. Still, Nicolas offers her protection and when Angelique is reunited with her children, she decides to try respectability by becoming a shop owner under an assumed name. Followed by "Angelique and the King." French with subtitles. 105m; DVD. **C:** Michele Mercier; Robert Hossein; Giuliano Gemma; Claude Giraud; Jean Rochefort; Charles Regnier; Claire Maurier; Jacques Toja; Jean-Louis Trintignant; Directed by Bernard Borderie; Written by Claude Brule; Francis Cosne; Cinematography by Henri Persin; Music by Michael Magne. **A:** Sr. High-Adult. **P:** Entertainment. **U:** Home. **L:** French. **Mov-Ent:** France. **Acq:** Purchase. **Dist:** Lions Gate Entertainment Inc.

The Angelmakers 2005
Documentary on a small village in Hungary in which over 140 men were poisoned by their wives after returning home from WWI. 34m; VHS, DVD. **A:** Sr. High-Adult. **P:** Education. **U:** Home, Institution. **Gen-Edu:** Documentary Films. **Acq:** Purchase, Rent/Lease. **Dist:** The Cinema Guild. $195.00.

Angelo My Love 1983 (R) — ★★★
Compassionate docudrama about New York's modern gypsy community. Follows the adventures of 12-year-old Angelo Evans, the streetwise son of a fortune teller, who, with a fresh view, explores the ups and downs of his family's life. Duvall financed the effort and cast non-professional actors in this charming tale of reality and fairy-tale. 91m; VHS. **C:** Angelo Evans; Michael Evans; Steve "Patalay" Tsiginoff; Cathy Kitchen; Millie Tsiginoff; Directed by Robert Duvall; Music by Michael Kamen. **Pr:** Cinecom Pictures. **A:** Sr. High-Adult. **P:** Entertainment. **U:** Home. **Mov-Ent. Acq:** Purchase. **Dist:** Sony Pictures Home Entertainment Inc. $59.95.

Angel's Advent Lesson 19??
Teaches children the true meaning of Advent and Christmas. Emphasis is placed on knowing how to prepare for the coming of Jesus. Comes with Teacher's Guide. 12m; VHS. **A:** Primary. **P:** Religious. **U:** Institution. **Chl-Juv:** Christmas, Children. **Acq:** Purchase. **Dist:** Twenty-Third Publications. $29.95.

Angels & Demons 2009 (PG-13) — ★★
Sequel/prequel to Dan Brown's "The Da Vinci Code," is just as ridiculously plotted as the original, but is thankfully faster-paced and less exposition-intensive. Harvard symbologist Robert Langdon (Hanks) is in Rome trying to prevent the secret society, the Illuminati, from destroying the Vatican. It all adds up to a semi-entertaining mess that can be enjoyed if you don't think about it too much. 138m; DVD, Blu-Ray. **C:** Tom Hanks; Ayelet Zurer; Ewan McGregor; Stellan Skarsgard; Armin Mueller-Stahl; Directed by Ron Howard; Written by Akiva Goldsman; David Koepp; Cinematography by Salvatore Totino; Music by Hans Zimmer. **Pr:** Columbia Pictures. **P:** Entertainment. **U:** Home. **L:** English. **Mov-Ent:** Mystery & Suspense, Religion. **Acq:** Purchase. **Dist:** Sony Pictures Home Entertainment Inc.

Angels and Insects 1995 (R) — ★★★
Very strange Victorian-era romantic drama is definitely an acquired taste. The mysteries of nature are nothing compared to the mysteries of human life as naturalist William Adamson (Rylance) comes to discover when he takes up a position at the home of amateur insect collector, Sir Harald Alabaster (Kemp). He falls in love and quickly marries blondly beautiful Eugenia (Kensit), whose outward propriety hides a sensual nature and some decadent family secrets. Based on A.S. Byatt's novella "Morpho Eugenia." Take particular note of the costumes by Paul Brown, which mimic the exoticness of insects. 116m; VHS, DVD, Wide, CC. **C:** Mark Rylance; Patsy Kensit; Kristin Scott Thomas; Jeremy Kemp; Douglas Henshall; Chris Larkin; Annette Badland; Anna Massey; Saskia Wickham; Directed by Philip Haas; Written by Belinda Haas; Philip Haas; Cinematography by Bernard Zitzermann; Music by Alexander Balanescu. **Pr:** Joyce Herlihy; Lindsay Law; Belinda Haas; Playhouse International Pictures; Samuel Goldwyn Company. **A:** College-Adult. **P:** Entertainment. **U:** Home. **Mov-Ent:** Drama, Family, Insects. **Acq:** Purchase. **Dist:** MGM Home Entertainment.

Angels & Miracles 19??
In this interview, author Joan Wester Anderson relates stories about angels and miracles, as well as instructing the viewer on the keys to opening up the miraculous in their lives. 58m; VHS. **A:** Jr. High-Adult. **P:** Entertainment. **U:** Home. **Gen-Edu:** Interviews, Religion. **Acq:** Purchase. **Dist:** Hartley Film Foundation. $29.95.

Angel's Brigade 1979 (PG) — ★★
Seven models get together to stop a big drug operation. Drive-in vigilante movie fare fit for a rainy night. 97m; VHS. **C:** Jack Palance; Peter Lawford; Jim Backus; Arthur Godfrey; Directed by Greydon Clark; Written by Greydon Clark; Cinematography by Dean Cundey. **Pr:** Arista Films. **A:** Jr. High. **P:** Entertainment. **U:** Home. **Mov-Ent:** Drugs. **Acq:** Purchase. **Dist:** Lions Gate Television Corp. $19.98.

Angels Crest 2011 (R) — ★½
Based on Leslie Schwartz's novel, this drama centers on the loss of a child, often a foundation for manipulative histrionics. Set in the titular Rocky Mountain town, Dellal's film is another tale of working class, already-troubled people dealing with intense, unimaginable tragedy. Young father Ethan (Dekker) is trying to take care of his son instead of the boy's alcoholic mother (Collins) but this snow-covered film quickly turns to melodrama. The cast seems up for the soap operatic challenge but the piece never develops the realism for the grave subject matter to have any weight. 92m; DVD, Blu-Ray. **C:** Tom Decker; Jeremy Piven; Lynn Collins; Mira Sorvino; Elizabeth McGovern; Joseph Morgan; Kate Walsh; Barbara Williams; Julian Domingues; Ameko Eks Mass Carroll; Directed by Gaby Dellal; Written by Catherine Triescmann; Cinematography by David Johnson; Music by Stephen Warbeck. **Pr:** Leslie Cowan; Shirleysse Vercruysse; Harrow Films; Magnolia Pictures. **A:** Sr. High-Adult. **P:** Entertainment. **U:** Home. **L:** English. **Mov-Ent:** Death. **Acq:** Purchase. **Dist:** Magnolia Home Entertainment.

Angel's Dance 1999 (R) — ★★½
Tony (Chandler) works for mobster Uncle Vinnie (Polito) and wants to be a hit man. So, Vinnie sends him to L.A. for training with Stevie Rossellini (Belushi) who, despite appearances, is an expert. Part of Tony's education is to choose and kill a victim at random and he selects Angel (Lee). This is Tony's big mistake, since this Angel is turns out to be the avenging kind. Gets a little too goofy but does provide some action. 102m; VHS, DVD. **C:** James Belushi; Sheryl Lee; Kyle Chandler; Jon Polito; Ned Bellamy; Mac Davis; Frank John Hughes; Mark Carlton; Directed by David Corley; Written by David Corley; Cinematography by Michael G. Wojciechowski; Music by Tim Truman. **A:** Sr. High-Adult. **P:** Entertainment. **U:** Home. **Mov-Ent. Acq:** Purchase. **Dist:** York Entertainment.

Angels Die Hard 1970 (R) — ★★
Novel biker story with the cyclists as the good guys intent on helping a town during a mining disaster. Grizzly Adams makes an early film appearance. 86m; VHS, DVD. **C:** Tom Baker; R.G. Armstrong; Dan Haggerty; William (Bill) Smith; Directed by Richard Compton; Written by Richard Compton; Music by Bill Cone. **Pr:** New World Pictures. **A:** Adult. **P:** Entertainment. **U:** Home. **Mov-Ent:** Motorcycles, Miners & Mining. **Acq:** Purchase. **Dist:** Unknown Distributor.

Angels Don't Have Headlights: Children's Reaction to Death in the Family 1992
Shows how the child's conception of death and the child's grieving process differ from those of an adult and in fact, vary considerably with each developmental stage. 25m; VHS. **A:** Adult. **P:** Education. **U:** Institution. **Gen-Edu:** Death, Children. **Acq:** Purchase. **Dist:** Filmakers Library Inc.

Angels Don't Sleep Here 2000 (Unrated) — ★★
Forensic pathologist Michael Daniels returns to his hometown when his twin brother disappears. He gets involved with district attorney Kate, who was his brother's childhood girlfriend, and whose father is the town's mayor. Michael thinks his brother is stalking him and when the mayor is killed, he believes his brother is the culprit. But local detective Russell Stark thinks Michael is the real criminal. 97m; VHS, DVD, CC. **C:** Dana Ashbrook; Robert Patrick; Roy Scheider; Susan Allison; Gary Farmer; Kelly Rutherford; Christina Pickles; Directed by Paul Cade. **A:** Sr. High-Adult. **P:** Entertainment. **U:** Home. **Mov-Ent. Acq:** Purchase. **Dist:** Movies Unlimited; Alpha Video.

Angels Fall 2007 (Unrated) — ★★½
Reece Gilmore (Locklear) was the sole survivor of a mass killing at the Boston restaurant where she worked. Desperate for a fresh start, Reece hits the road until her car breaks down in a Wyoming town and she takes a diner job to get some cash. Settling in, Reece becomes interested in writer Brody (Schaech), who is the only one to help her when Reece claims she witnessed a murder, although the cops don't find any evidence of a crime. A Lifetime original movie based on the novel by Nora Roberts. 95m; DVD, CC. **C:** Heather Locklear; Johnathon Schaech; Gary Hudson; Derek Hamilton; Linda Darlow; Directed by Ralph Hamecker; Written by Janet Brownell; Cinematography by Joel Ransom; Music by Chris P. Bacon; Stuart M. Thomas. **A:** Jr. High-Adult. **P:** Entertainment. **U:** Home. **Mov-Ent. Acq:** Purchase. **Dist:** Sony Pictures Home Entertainment Inc.

Angels from Hell 1968 (Unrated) — ★
Early application in the nutso 'Nam returnee genre. Disillusioned Vietnam veteran forms a massive biker gang for the sole purpose of wreaking havoc upon the Man, the Establishment and anyone else responsible for sending him off to war. The big gang invades a town, with predictably bloody results. Sort of a follow-up to "Hell's Angels on Wheels." 86m; VHS, Streaming. **C:** Tom Stern; Arlene Martel; Ted Markland; Stephen Oliver; Paul Bertoya; James Murphy; Jack Starrett; Pepper Martin; Luana Talltree; Directed by Bruce Kessler. **Pr:** American International Pictures. **A:** Adult. **P:** Entertainment. **U:** Home. **Mov-Ent:** Motorcycles, Veterans. **Acq:** Purchase. **Dist:** No Longer Available.

Angels: Good or Evil 2005
From such winged messengers as Hermes and Mercury to biblical archangels Gabriel and Michael, angels and demons have been immortalized in religion and art. Explore the phenomena and hear testimony from those who claim to have had firsthand encounters. 100m; DVD. **A:** Jr. High-Adult. **P:** Entertainment. **U:** Home. **Gen-Edu:** Documentary Films. **Acq:** Purchase. **Dist:** A&E Television Networks L.L.C.

Angels Hard As They Come 1971 (R) — ★★
Opposing Hell's Angels leaders clash in a hippie-populated ghost town. A semi-satiric spoof of the biker genre's cliches features an early Glenn appearance and Busey's film debut. 86m; VHS, DVD. **C:** Gary Busey; Scott Glenn; James Iglehart; Gary Littlejohn; Charles Dierkop; Larry Tucker; Gilda Texter; Janet Wood; Brendan Kelly; Directed by Joe Viola; Written by Jonathan Demme; Joe Viola; Music by Richard Hieronymous. **Pr:** Jonathan Demme; Jonathan Demme. **A:** Sr. High-Adult. **P:** Entertainment. **U:** Home. **Mov-Ent:** Action-Adventure, Motorcycles. **Acq:** Purchase. **Dist:** Movies Unlimited. $29.99.

Angels in America 2003 (Unrated) — ★★★
Kushner exquisitely adapts his two-part award-winning play into this six-part miniseries that vividly intertwines the lives and sufferings of several New Yorkers as they grapple with such issues as AIDS, drug addiction, homosexuality, and abandonment during the mid-80s. Masterfully directed by Nichols, it presents a spiritual perspective featuring Thompson as an angel of mercy to a man dying of AIDS while Streep appears as an apparition to another. 360m; DVD. **C:** Meryl Streep; Emma Thompson; Justin Kirk; Ben Shenkman; Mary-Louise Parker; Jeffrey Wright; Patrick Wilson; James Cromwell; Michael Gambon; Simon Callow; Brian Markinson; Directed by Mike Nichols; Written by Al Pacino; Tony Kushner; Cinematography by Stephen Goldblatt; Music by Thomas Newman. **A:** College-Adult. **P:** Entertainment. **U:** Home. **Mov-Ent:** AIDS, Marriage, Divorce. **Acq:** Purchase. **Dist:** Warner Home Video, Inc. $39.98.

Angels in the Endzone 1998 (Unrated) — ★★½
TV follow-up to Disney's 1994 "Angels in the Outfield" finds the heavenly troops trying to aid a failing high school football squad, especially the leading players (Gallagher and Lawrence) who are also trying to also handle the death of their father. 85m; VHS, DVD, CC. **C:** Matthew Lawrence; David Gallagher; Paul Dooley; Christopher Lloyd; Directed by Gary Nadeau. **A:** Family. **P:** Entertainment. **U:** Home. **Mov-Ent:** TV Movies, Football, Education. **Acq:** Purchase. **Dist:** Buena Vista Home Entertainment.

Angels in the Infield 2000 (Unrated) — ★★½
Third in the Disney series finds former baseball player Bob "The Bungler" Bugler (Grier) trying to earn his Guardian Angels wings by looking out for pitcher Eddie Everett (Warburton) who's lost his self-confidence. But with daughter Laurel (Irvin) praying for some heavenly intervention, things are certainly looking up. 93m; VHS, DVD, CC. **C:** David Alan Grier; Patrick Warburton; Kurt Fuller; Rebecca Jenkins; Colin Fox; Peter Keleghan; Duane Davis; Brittney Irvin; Directed by Robert King. **A:** Family. **P:** Entertainment. **U:** Home. **Mov-Ent:** Baseball, Sports--Fiction: Comedy. **Acq:** Purchase. **Dist:** Buena Vista Home Entertainment.

Angels in the Outfield 1951 (Unrated) — ★★★
Enjoyable comedy fantasy about the lowly Pittsburgh Pirates who get a little celestial help in their race for the pennant. Naturally, it takes the prayers of young Bridget (Corcoran) to get the angel Gabriel to assist. Oh yeah, only the kid can actually see the angels (no special effects in this movie). Great performances all around, especially Douglas as gruff losing manager Guffy McGovern, with Janet Leigh as the reporter he makes a play for. Based on a story by Richard Conlin. 102m/B/W; DVD. **C:** Paul Douglas; Janet Leigh; Keenan Wynn; Donna Corcoran; Lewis Stone; Spring Byington; Bruce Bennett; Marvin Kaplan; Ellen Corby; Jeff Richards; Directed by Clarence Brown; Written by Dorothy Kingsley; George Wells; Cinematography by Paul Vogel. **Pr:** MGM. **A:** Jr. High-Adult. **P:** Entertainment. **U:** Home. **Mov-Ent:** Baseball. **Acq:** Purchase. **Dist:** WarnerArchive.com. $14.95.

Angels in the Outfield 1994 (PG) — ★★½
Remake of the 1951 fantasy about a lowly baseball team who, along with some heavenly animated help find themselves on a winning streak. The new lineup includes Glover as manager of the hapless California Angels, Danza as a washed-up pitcher, and Lloyd as captain of the celestial spirits. Gordon-Levitt plays the foster child who believes he'll get his family back together if the Angels win the pennant. Familar ground still yields good, heartfelt family fare. Oakland A's third baseman Carney Lansford served as technical advisor, molding actors into fair semblance of baseball team. 105m; DVD, Wide, CC. **C:** Danny Glover; Tony Danza; Christopher Lloyd; Brenda Fricker; Ben Johnson; Joseph Gordon-Levitt; Jay O. Sanders; Dermot Mulroney; Directed by William Dear; Written by Holly Goldberg Sloan; Cinematography by Matthew F. Leonetti; Music by Randy Edelman. **Pr:** Roger Birnbaum; Irby Smith; Joe Roth; Walt Disney Pictures; Buena Vista. **A:** Family. **P:** Entertainment. **U:** Home. **Mov-Ent:** Baseball, Sports--Fiction: Comedy, Family Viewing. **Acq:** Purchase. **Dist:** Walt Disney Studios Home Entertainment. $19.99.

Angels Memories: The Greatest Moments in Angels Baseball History 2011 (Unrated)
Video containing highlights from the history of the Los Angeles Angels baseball team. 84m; DVD. **A:** Family. **P:** Entertainment. **U:** Home. **Spo-Rec**: Baseball, Sports--General. **Acq:** Purchase. **Dist:** A&E Television Networks L.L.C. $19.95.

Angels of the City 1989 (Unrated) — ★★
What's a girl got to do to join a sorority? A house prank turns vicious when two coeds take a walk on the wild side and accidentally observe a murder, making them the next targets. Credible exploitation effort, if that's not an oxymoron. 90m; VHS, DVD. **C:** Lawrence-Hilton Jacobs; Cynthia Cheston; Kelly Galindo; Sandy Gershman; Directed by Lawrence-Hilton Jacobs; Written by Lawrence-Hilton Jacobs; Raymond Martino; Joseph Merhi. **A:** Adult. **P:** Entertainment. **U:** Home. **Mov-Ent**: Action-Adventure, Exploitation. **Acq:** Purchase. **Dist:** Echo Bridge Home Entertainment. $29.95.

Angels of War 1982
This tape studies the role the natives of Papua, New Guinea played in the fighting of WWII. 54m; VHS, 3/4 U. **Pr:** Andrew Pike; Hank Nelson; Gavan Daws. **A:** Jr. High-Adult. **P:** Education. **U:** Institution. **Gen-Edu**: World War Two. **Acq:** Purchase. **Dist:** Filmakers Library Inc.

Angels on High 19??
Instructs how to create full-size window patterns, cut glass, work with copper foil, solder and frame in zinc came. 30m; VHS. **A:** Adult. **P:** Instruction. **U:** Home. **How-Ins**: Crafts, Hobbies, How-To. **Acq:** Purchase. **Dist:** Cutters Productions. $19.95.

Angels One Five 1954 (Unrated) — ★★
A worm's-eye view of British air power in WWII. What little "excitement" there is, is generated by flashing lights, plotting maps, and status boards. Hawkins and Denison are the only bright spots. 97m/B/W; VHS, DVD. **C:** Jack Hawkins; Michael Denison; Dulcie Gray; John Gregson; Cyril Raymond; Veronica Hurst; Geoffrey Keen; Vida Hope; Andrew Osborn; Directed by George More O'Ferrall; Written by Derek Twist; Cinematography by Christopher Challis; Stanley Grant; Music by John Wooldridge. **Pr:** John Gossage; Derek N. Twist; Pathe. **A:** Jr. High-Adult. **P:** Entertainment. **U:** Home. **Mov-Ent**: World War Two, Great Britain, Aeronautics. **Acq:** Purchase. **Dist:** Lions Gate Entertainment Inc. $18.99.

Angels Over Broadway 1940 (Unrated) — ★★★
Slick, fast-paced black comedy about con man Fairbanks, who plans to hustle suicidal thief Qualen during a poker game, but has a change of heart. With the help of call-girl Hayworth and drunken playwright Mitchell, he helps Qualen turn his life around. Ahead of its time with an offbeat morality, but a delight in the '90s. 80m/B/W; VHS, DVD. **C:** Douglas Fairbanks, Jr.; Rita Hayworth; Thomas Mitchell; John Qualen; George Watts; Directed by Ben Hecht; Lee Garmes; Written by Ben Hecht; Cinematography by Lee Garmes. **Pr:** Ben Hecht; Ben Hecht; Columbia Pictures. **A:** Family. **P:** Entertainment. **U:** Home. **Mov-Ent**: Comedy--Black, Philanthropy, Suicide. **Acq:** Purchase. **Dist:** Facets Multimedia Inc.; Sony Pictures Home Entertainment Inc. $19.95.

Angels Sing 2013 (PG) — ★★½
Austin, Texas set Christmas tale. Because of a holiday tragedy in his childhood, Michael Walker (Connick, Jr.) is a decidedly bah-humbug guy. The struggling family gets a great deal on a house from an elderly man named Nick (Nelson) but the catch is it's located in a neighborhood known for its elaborate Christmas displays. The neighbors besiege the Walkers to participate, meaning Michael finally has to make peace with his past. Cheerfully sentimental without the sappiness. 86m; DVD, Blu-Ray. **C:** Harry Connick, Jr.; Connie Britton; Chandler Canterbury; Lyle Lovett; Fionnula Flanagan; Kris Kristofferson; Willie Nelson; Dana Wheeler-Nicholson; Directed by Tim McCanlies; Written by Lou Berney; Cinematography by Kamal Derkaoui; Music by Carl Thiel; Scott Warren. **A:** Family. **P:** Entertainment. **U:** Home. **L:** English. **Mov-Ent**: Christmas, Family. **Acq:** Purchase. **Dist:** Lions Gate Home Entertainment.

Angels Wash Their Faces 1939 (Unrated) — ★½
Warner Bros. tried to cash in on the 1938 James Cagney classic "Angels With Dirty Faces," which also featured the Dead End Kids, to little success. Newcomer Gabe (Thomas) is framed for arson by some local mobsters and the gang plan to clear his name with the help of Assistant District Attorney Patrick Remson (Reagan) who happens to love Gabe's sister Joy (Sheridan). 86m/B/W; DVD. **C:** Billy Halop; Leo Gorcey; Bobby Jordan; Huntz Hall; Gabriel Dell; Bonita Granville; Frankie Thomas, Jr.; Ann Sheridan; Ronald Reagan; Bernard Punsley; Eduardo Ciannelli; Bernard Nedell; Margaret Hamilton; Marjorie Main; Directed by Ray Enright; Written by Michael Fessier; Robert Buckner; Niven Busch; Cinematography by Arthur L. Todd; Music by Adolph Deutsch. **A:** Jr. High-Adult. **P:** Entertainment. **U:** Home. **Mov-Ent**: Crime Drama. **Acq:** Purchase. **Dist:** WarnerArchive.com.

Angels Watch Over Me: Jim, Gerri and Jason's Story 1996
Witnesses the struggles and pain involved as infant son and father die of AIDS. 58m; VHS. **A:** Adult. **P:** Education. **U:** Institution, Home. **Gen-Edu**: AIDS, Death. **Acq:** Purchase. **Dist:** Aquarius Health Care Media. $175.00.

Angels' Wild Women 1972 (Unrated) — **Bomb!**
From the man who brought you "Dracula vs. Frankenstein" comes an amalgamation of hippies, motorcycle dudes, evil desert gurus and precious little plot. 85m; VHS, DVD. **C:** Kent Taylor; Regina Carrol; Ross Hagen; Maggie Bemby; Vicki Volante; Directed by Al Adamson. **Pr:** VidAmerica, Inc. **A:** Adult. **P:** Entertainment. **U:** Home. **Mov-Ent**: Motorcycles. **Acq:** Purchase. **Dist:** Movies Unlimited. $15.99.

Angels with Dirty Faces 1938 (Unrated) — ★★★★
Rousing classic with memorable Cagney twitches and the famous long walk from the cell to the chair. Two young hoods grow up on NYC's lower East Side with diverse results—one enters the priesthood and the other opts for crime and prison. Upon release from the pen, famed gangster Cagney sets up shop in the old neighborhood, where Father O'Brien tries to keep a group of young toughs (the Dead End Kids) from following in his footsteps. Bogart's his unscrupulous lawyer and Bancroft a crime boss intent on double-crossing Cagney. Reportedly they were blasting real bullets during the big shootout, no doubt helping Cagney's intensity. Adapted from a story by Rowland Brown. 97m/B/W; VHS, DVD. **C:** James Cagney; Pat O'Brien; Humphrey Bogart; Ann Sheridan; George Bancroft; Billy Halop; Leo Gorcey; Huntz Hall; Bobby Jordan; Bernard Punsley; Gabriel Dell; Adrian Morris; Directed by Michael Curtiz; Written by John Wexley; Warren Duff; Rowland Brown; Cinematography by Sol Polito; Music by Max Steiner. **A:** Family. **P:** Entertainment. **U:** Home. **Mov-Ent**: Crime Drama, Adolescence, Classic Films. **Awds:** N.Y. Film Critics '38: Actor (Cagney). **Acq:** Purchase. **Dist:** MGM Home Entertainment. $19.98.

Anger 1979
This program looks at parents' reactions to their children's expressions of anger and frustration and discusses how children can find an acceptable outlet for their anger. 29m; VHS, 3/4 U. **Pr:** South Carolina ETV Commission. **A:** Adult. **P:** Education. **U:** Institution, CCTV, CATV. **Hea-Sci**: Psychology. **Acq:** Purchase, Rent/Lease, Off-Air Record. **Dist:** PBS Home Video.

Anger 1984
An examination of anger and, when involving parents, how it affects the children. An ABC 20/20 report. 15m; VHS, 3/4 U. **Pr:** ABC 20/20. **A:** Jr. High-Sr. High. **P:** Education. **U:** Institution. **Gen-Edu**: Family. **Acq:** Purchase, Rent/Lease. **Dist:** Phoenix Learning Group. $160.00.

Anger 1989
Features interviews with different "angry" people, including a four time murderer who has never been caught, a woman who has been raped and stabbed, a hermaphrodite who feels she betrayed herself by becoming a woman, a Wall Street sadist, a New York City detective who was framed by police, skinheads who are junkies, and others. Segment of the feature film "Seven Women-Seven Sins." Winner of Best Short Film at the Montreal Festival of New Cinema, the Award of Special Distinction at the Tokyo Video Festival, and the Special Jury Award at the San Francisco Film and Video Festival. 20m; VHS, 3/4 U. **Pr:** Maxi Cohen. **A:** Adult. **P:** Entertainment. **U:** Institution, SURA. **Gen-Edu**: Documentary Films, Violence, Drug Abuse. **Acq:** Purchase, Rent/Lease. **Dist:** Maxi Cohen Film & Video Productions.

Anger Management 2003 (PG-13) — ★★
Disappointing comedy has mild-mannered, confrontation-averse Dave (Sandler) forced to attend anger management therapy after a misunderstanding on an airplane. Crazed anger therapist Dr. Buddy Rydell (Nicholson) is of the opinion that Dave isn't angry enough on the outside, so he proceeds, in increasingly ridiculous ways, to make him...angry, disrupting Dave's life and his relationship with girlfriend Linda (Tomei). While attempting to play off the two leads' screen and public personas, it succeds only rarely, due mainly to a weak script that takes the easy way out whenever it's offered, and by-the-numbers direction. Nicholson's obvious glee at not having to be restrained makes some scenes work on a pure comic level, while Sandler seems right at home, back in his element, after the smart comedy of "Punch-Drunk Love." 101m; VHS, DVD, Blu-Ray, UMD. **C:** Adam Sandler; Jack Nicholson; Marisa Tomei; Luis Guzman; Allen Covert; Lynne Thigpen; Kurt Fuller; Jonathan Loughran; Krista Allen; January Jones; Woody Harrelson; John Turturro; Heather Graham; John C. Reilly; Kevin Nealon; Harry Dean Stanton; Cameo(s) Bobby Knight; John McEnroe; Directed by Peter Segal; Written by David Dorfman; Cinematography by Donald McAlpine; Music by Teddy Castellucci. **Pr:** Jack Giarraputo; Barry Bernardi; Revolution Studios; Happy Madison Productions; Sony Pictures Classics. **A:** Jr. High-Adult. **P:** Entertainment. **U:** Home. **Mov-Ent**: Psychiatry. **Acq:** Purchase. **Dist:** Sony Pictures Home Entertainment Inc.

Anger Management for Parents: The RETHINK Method 199?
Parent training program introduces the seven-step RETHINK Method for managing anger. Also includes interviews with parents who share their own experiences. 25m; VHS. **A:** Adult. **P:** Education. **U:** Institution. **Gen-Edu**: Parenting, Self-Help. **Acq:** Purchase. **Dist:** Research Press. $200.00.

Anger, Rage and You 1996
Provides techniques for dealing with anger and to differentiate between angry feelings and behavior and shows how to regain control. Includes teacher's guide. 23m; VHS. **A:** Primary-Jr. High. **P:** Education. **U:** Institution. **Gen-Edu**: Adolescence, Self-Help. **Acq:** Purchase. **Dist:** Sunburst Digital Inc. $189.00.

Anger: The Turbulent Emotion 1983
Examines anger and issues surrounding it, such as what causes it, whether it's better to vent or stuff it in, and more. Granted an award by the Learning/Curriculum Product Review. ?m; VHS, Special order formats. **A:** Sr. High. **P:** Education. **U:** Institution. **Hea-Sci**: Mental Health. **Acq:** Purchase. **Dist:** HRM Video. $145.00.

Anger: You Can Handle It 1995
Explains that anger is a human emotion and teaches students how to gain control and deal with anger in safe, constructive ways. Teacher's guide included. 24m; VHS. **A:** Jr. High-Sr. High. **P:** Education. **U:** Institution. **Chl-Juv**: Children, Education, Human Relations. **Acq:** Purchase. **Dist:** Sunburst Digital Inc. $169.00.

Angi Vera 1978 — ★★★★
Naive 18-year-old Angi (Papp) is living in 1948 Hungary during the early days of socialism. Sent to a re-education school, she falls in love with her married Party leader but gradually loses her personal integrity to a corrupt system. Hungarian with subtitles. 96m; VHS. **C:** Veronika Papp; Erszi Pasztor; Eva Szabo; Tamas Dunai; Laszlo Horvath; Directed by Pal Gabor; Written by Pal Gabor; Cinematography by Lajos Koltai; Music by Gyorgy Selmeczi. **A:** College-Adult. **P:** Entertainment. **U:** Home. **L:** Hungarian. **Mov-Ent**: Politics & Government. **Acq:** Purchase. **Dist:** No Longer Available.

Angie 1994 (R) — ★★
Brassy Angie finds herself pregnant and unmarried. Tired of the advice and criticism she receives from her close knit neighborhood she strikes out of Brooklyn to find a new life for herself. Average "woman's movie" wrought with messages of pregnancy, childbirth, friendship, love, and family has far too much going on and relies too heavily on formula soap. Davis, in what could have been a juicy (read "Oscar") role is strong, but her performance is drowned by all the melodrama. Madonna was originally cast as Angie, but was bounced when the filming of "Snake Eyes" conflicted. Adapted from the book "Angie, I Says" by Avra Wing. 108m; VHS, DVD, Blu-Ray, Wide, CC. **C:** Geena Davis; Aida Turturro; Stephen Rea; Philip Bosco; James Gandolfini; Jenny O'Hara; Directed by Martha Coolidge; Written by Todd Graff. **Pr:** Larry Brezner; Patrick McCormick; Buena Vista. **A:** Sr. High-Adult. **P:** Entertainment. **U:** Home. **Mov-Ent**: Comedy-Drama, Pregnancy, Family. **Acq:** Purchase. **Dist:** Disney Educational Productions.

Angina 1988
This tape covers the types, pathophysiology, evaluation, risk factors, and diagnostic modalities used in angina. 10m; VHS, 3/4 U. **Pr:** Marshfield Regional Video Network. **A:** College-Adult. **P:** Professional. **U:** Institution, CCTV. **Hea-Sci**: Diseases, Heart. **Acq:** Purchase, Rent/Lease. **Dist:** Discovery Education. $295.00.

Angina Coma, Drop Attacks 1971
An interview and brief examination of a patient with angina, basilar artery ischemic attacks, and exercise pain in legs due to radiculopathy. 18m; VHS, 3/4 U, Special order formats. **Pr:** Ohio State University Health Sciences AV Center. **A:** College-Adult. **P:** Professional. **U:** Institution, SURA. **Hea-Sci**: Neurology, Heart. **Acq:** Purchase, Rent/Lease. **Dist:** Ohio State University.

The Angina Patient: Maintaining Optimal Function 1976
Beta-adrenergic blocking therapy is described, and its proper use under various circumstances is explained. 30m; 3/4 U. **Pr:** Ayerst Laboratories. **A:** College-Adult. **P:** Professional. **U:** Institution, CCTV. **Hea-Sci**: Heart. **Acq:** Purchase, Free Loan. **Dist:** Pfizer Inc.

Angina Pectoris 1990
Animation is used to demonstrate the blood supply and demand problems of the heart due to arteriosclerosis and to explain how to check the progress of the underlying disease and treat the angina symptoms. 15m; VHS, 3/4 U. **Pr:** Milner-Fenwick. **A:** Adult. **P:** Education. **U:** Institution, CCTV. **L:** English, French, Spanish. **Hea-Sci**: Heart. **Acq:** Purchase. **Dist:** Milner-Fenwick, Inc.

Angina Update: Diagnosis and Management 1981
Five distinguished cardiologists discuss and demonstrate the latest technologic aids for diagnosing and evaluating angina. 30m; 3/4 U. **Pr:** Ayerst Laboratories. **A:** Adult. **P:** Professional. **U:** Institution, CCTV. **Hea-Sci**: Heart. **Acq:** Purchase, Free Loan. **Dist:** Pfizer Inc.

Angiography: A Gentle Look 19??
Patient education video that covers the angiography procedure, including information on the insertion of the catheter, the different dyes used, the different instruments used and their sounds and movements, and what the patient should feel during each step of the procedure. 7m; VHS. **A:** College-Adult. **P:** Education. **U:** Institution. **Hea-Sci**: Medical Education, Patient Education, Surgery. **Acq:** Purchase, Rent/Lease. **Dist:** AJN Video Library/Lippincott Williams & Wilkins. $200.00.

Angioimmunoblastic Lymphadenopathy with Dysprotinemia: What Was It and Where Did It Go? 1987
A look at the uncommon immunologic disease AILD, its history and etiologic factors. 47m; VHS, 3/4 U. **C:** Samuel R. Newcom. **Pr:** Emory University. **A:** Adult. **P:** Professional. **U:** Institution, CCTV, Home, SURA. **Hea-Sci**: Immunology, Diseases, AIDS. **Acq:** Purchase, Rent/Lease, Subscription. **Dist:** Emory Medical Television Network.

Angioplasty: An Available Alternative 19??
Patient education video that walks the viewer, step-by-step, through the diagnostic and treatment stages of angioplasty. Describes the benefits of the procedure. Also provides information on patient-doctor interaction, cardiac catheterization, patient preparation, equipment, and diagnostic results. 10m; VHS. **A:** College-Adult. **P:** Education. **U:** Institution. **Hea-Sci**: Nursing, Medical Education, Patient Education. **Acq:** Purchase, Rent/Lease. **Dist:** AJN Video Library/Lippincott Williams & Wilkins. $200.00.

Angiosperms 19??
Explains the different biological theories associated with angiosperms. 12m; VHS. **A:** Jr. High-Adult. **P:** Education. **U:**

Institution. **Hea-Sci**: Biology, Science, Plants. **Acq:** Purchase. **Dist:** Educational Video Network. $49.95.

Angiosperms: The Flowering Plants 1962
Details the characteristic, differences between angiosperms and other plants. Spotlights the angiosperms processes of pollination, seed and fruit formation, seed dispersal, and growth. 21m; VHS, SVS, 3/4 U. **A:** Sr. High. **P:** Education. **U:** Institution. **L:** English, Spanish, Arabic. **Hea-Sci**: Plants, Biology. **Acq:** Purchase. **Dist:** Encyclopedia Britannica. $79.00.

AngKor: Cambodia Express 1981 (Unrated) — ★
An American journalist travels back to Vietnam to search for his long lost love. 96m; VHS, DVD. **C:** Robert Walker, Jr.; Christopher George; Directed by Lek Kitiparaporn. **Pr:** Monarex Hollywood Corporation. **A:** Sr. High-Adult. **P:** Entertainment. **U:** Home. **Mov-Ent**: Journalism, Romance. **Acq:** Purchase. **Dist:** Lions Gate Television Corp. $69.98.

Angle-Closure Glaucoma 1989
Angle-closure glaucoma is hard to diagnose and can destroy the patient's vision if not corrected in time. 30m; VHS, 3/4 U. **Pr:** American Academy of Ophthalmology. **A:** Adult. **P:** Professional. **U:** Institution, Home, SURA. **Hea-Sci**: Eye. **Acq:** Purchase, Rent/Lease. **Dist:** American Academy of Ophthalmology. $85.00.

Angle Defense 1978
The coach whose University of Michigan school has captured eight Big Ten titles in 11 years describes the philosophy and techniques of his rugged defensive unit, with execution demonstrated and reinforced with game examples. 15m; VHS, 3/4 U. **C:** Bo Schembechler. **Pr:** Champions on Film. **A:** Sr. High-Adult. **P:** Instruction. **U:** Institution, CCTV, Home. **Spo-Rec**: Football. **Acq:** Purchase, Rent/Lease. **Dist:** School-Tech Inc. $19.95.

Angler's Autumn 1977
A lyrical, non-narrated portrait of the intricate balance of nature present in a northwestern river and the respect fishermen have for it. 11m; VHS, 3/4 U. **Pr:** Terr Aqua Productions. **A:** Sr. High-Adult. **P:** Education. **U:** Institution, Home, SURA. **Gen-Edu**: Ecology & Environment. **Acq:** Purchase, Rent/Lease, Duplication License. **Dist:** Pyramid Media.

Anglo-Saxon Attitudes 1992 (Unrated) — ★½
Dreary TV adaptation of the 1956 Angus Wilson novel. At age 60, retired historian Gerald Middleton is estranged from his family and looks back over the mess he's made of his life. In 1912, Gerald is one of a group excavating a bishop's grave that also contains a pagan fertility idol, a find that is kept secret. The young Gerald also has an affair with Dollie, his friend Gilbert's fiance, and she will continue to be his mistress for years though he marries another woman. Everyone is miserable and not very interesting to watch. 229m; DVD. **C:** Richard Johnson; Dorothy Tutin; Elizabeth Spriggs; Douglas Hodge; Tara Fitzgerald; Briony Glassco; Daniel Craig; Directed by Diarmuid Lawrence; Written by Andrew Davies; Cinematography by Clive Tickner; Music by Colin Towns. **A:** Adult. **P:** Entertainment. **U:** Home. **L:** English. **Mov-Ent**: Aging, Marriage. **Acq:** Purchase. **Dist:** Acorn Media Group Inc.

Angola 1988
A vivid portrait of daily life during the civil war in Angola. 30m; VHS, 3/4 U. **Pr:** DCTV. **A:** Jr. High-Adult. **P:** Education. **U:** Institution, SURA. **Gen-Edu**: Documentary Films, War--General, Africa. **Acq:** Purchase, Rent/Lease. **Dist:** Downtown Community TV Center. $200.00.

Angola 1991
Provides an overview of Angolan society and culture, including a brief history of the war for independence from Portugal, a look at rural and urban life, and the economy. Angolans offer their perspective and opinions on civil war and apartheid in South Africa. 55m; VHS, 3/4 U. **A:** Jr. High-Adult. **P:** Education. **U:** Institution. **Gen-Edu**: Africa. **Acq:** Purchase, Rent/Lease. **Dist:** Third World Newsreel. $225.00.

Angola Is Our Country 1988
Documentary highlighting the contribution women make to the reconstruction of a country where war has consumed more than half the national budget, and produced at least a million internal refugees. 45m; VHS. **A:** College-Adult. **P:** Education. **U:** Institution. **Gen-Edu**: Women, War--General. **Acq:** Purchase, Rent/Lease. **Dist:** Women Make Movies. $275.00.

Angola: Saudades from the One Who Loves You 2006
A documentary on Angola, a former Portuguese colony in Africa trying to recover after nearly three decades of civil war. 60m; VHS, DVD. **A:** Sr. High-Adult. **P:** Education. **U:** Home, Institution. **L:** English, Polish. **Gen-Edu**: Africa, Documentary Films. **Acq:** Purchase, Rent/Lease. **Dist:** The Cinema Guild. $295.00.

Angola: Victory of Hope 1976
The history of Angola from colonization by Portugal to the Declaration of Independence in 1976. Subtitled and narrated in English. 72m; VHS, 3/4 U. **TV Std:** NTSC, PAL, SECAM. **Pr:** Jose Massip. **A:** Sr. High-Adult. **P:** Education. **U:** Institution, SURA. **L:** English, Portuguese. **Gen-Edu**: Africa, Black Culture. **Acq:** Purchase, Rent/Lease, Duplication. **Dist:** The Cinema Guild.

Angoon One Hundred Years Later 1982
A commemoration of the destruction of the Tlingit Indian village of Angoon, Alaska in 1882 by the U.S. Naval Force. 30m; VHS, 1C, 3/4 U, Q. **Pr:** KTOO Juneau. **A:** Jr. High-Adult. **P:** Education. **U:** Institution, BCTV, SURA. **Gen-Edu**: Native Americans, History--U.S. **Acq:** Purchase, Rent/Lease. **Dist:** Vision Maker Media.

The Angry Beavers: The Best of Season 1 1997 (Unrated)
Nickelodeon 1997-2001 animated comedy. Norbert and Dagget Beaver strike out on their own after their parents have yet another litter. Their new lakeside home in the middle of a forest becomes disturbed on a daily basis by crazy government scientists, 100-foot walking splinters, a fish big enough to eat a Swede, mind-controlling pond scum, Mexican wrestlers, a fat hairy naked Canadian and so much more. 20 episodes. 253m; DVD. **C:** Charlie Brissette; Voice(s) by Richard Steven Horovitz; Nick Bakay. **A:** Primary-Jr. High. **P:** Entertainment. **U:** Home. **Chl-Juv**: Animation & Cartoons, Television Series. **Acq:** Purchase. **Dist:** Viacom International Inc. $35.99.

The Angry Eye 2001
Documentary revisiting the famous 1968 Brown Eyes/Blue Eyes Exercise by Jane Elliot. 35m; VHS, DVD. **A:** Sr. High-Adult. **P:** Education. **U:** Institution. **Gen-Edu**: Prejudice, Documentary Films. **Acq:** Purchase. **Dist:** California Newsreel. $295.00.

Angry Harvest 1985 — ★★★
During the WWII German occupation of Poland, a gentile farmer shelters a young Jewish woman on the run, and a serious, ultimately interdependent relationship forms. Acclaimed; Holland's first film since her native Poland's martial law imposition made her an exile to Sweden. In German with English subtitles. Contains nudity and violence. 102m; VHS, DVD. **C:** Armin Mueller-Stahl; Elisabeth Trissenaar; Wojciech Pszoniak; Margit Carstensen; Kurt Raab; Kathe Jaenicke; Hans Beerhenke; Isa Haller; Directed by Agnieszka Holland; Written by Agnieszka Holland. **Pr:** CCC-Filmkunst; Admiral. **A:** Sr. High-Adult. **P:** Entertainment. **U:** Home. **L:** German. **Mov-Ent**: World War Two, Judaism. **Awds:** Montreal World Film Fest. '85: Actor (Mueller-Stahl). **Acq:** Purchase. **Dist:** Facets Multimedia Inc.; Tapeworm Video Distributors Inc.; German Language Video Center. $69.95.

Angry Joe Bass 1976 (Unrated) — ★
Contemporary Native American Joe Bass faces government officials who continually usurp his fishing rights. Something like "Billy Jack" without the intelligence. 82m; VHS, DVD. **C:** Henry Bal; Molly Mershon; Directed by Thomas G. Reeves. **Pr:** Thomas G. Reeves. **A:** Jr. High-Adult. **P:** Entertainment. **U:** Home. **Mov-Ent**: Native Americans. **Acq:** Purchase. **Dist:** Unknown Distributor.

Angry John 1994
Children learn how to deal with their anger. 23m; VHS. **A:** Primary. **P:** Education. **U:** Institution. **Chl-Juv**: Children. **Acq:** Purchase. **Dist:** Pyramid Media. $295.00.

Angry Monk 2005
A biography of Gendun Choephel, a Tibetan Buddhist monk who left his monastery in 1934 and traveled extensively in Tibet and India. Focusing on intellectual and artistic pursuits, Choepel became an outspoken critic of Tibet and its government. 97m; DVD. **A:** Jr. High-Adult. **P:** Entertainment. **U:** Home. **Mov-Ent**: Religion, Buddhism, India. **Acq:** Purchase. **Dist:** First Run Features. $24.95.

The Angry Red Planet 1959 (Unrated) — ★★
An unintentionally amusing sci-fi adventure about astronauts on Mars fighting off aliens and giant, ship-swallowing amoebas. Filmed using bizarre "Cinemagic" process, which turns almost everything pink. Wild effects have earned the film cult status. 83m; VHS, DVD. **C:** Gerald Mohr; Les Tremayne; Jack Kruschen; Nora Hayden; Paul Hahn; J. Edward McKinley; Tom Daly; Don Lamond; Directed by Ib Melchior; Written by Ib Melchior; Sidney W. Pink; Cinematography by Stanley Cortez; Music by Paul Dunlap. **Pr:** Sid Pink; Norman Maurer. **A:** Family. **P:** Entertainment. **U:** Home. **Mov-Ent**: Science Fiction, Cult Films, Hypnosis & Hypnotists. **Acq:** Purchase. **Dist:** Movies Unlimited. $12.74.

The Angry Skies 2004
Documentary following human rights activist Blake Kerr as he explores the rise of the Khmer Rouge, and its enduing legacy. 60m; VHS, DVD. **A:** Sr. High-Adult. **P:** Education. **U:** Institution. **Gen-Edu**: Documentary Films, Asia. **Acq:** Purchase, Rent/Lease. **Dist:** The Cinema Guild. $295.00.

Anguilla 19??
Five shipwrecks off the coast of this British colony lure divers and salvagers. 30m; VHS. **A:** Sr. High-Adult. **P:** Entertainment. **U:** Home. **Spo-Rec**: Scuba, Travel. **Acq:** Purchase. **Dist:** Bennett Marine Video. $19.95.

Anguish 1988 (R) — ★★½
Well-done horror thriller about a lunatic who, inspired to duplicate the actions of an eyeball-obsessed killer in a popular film, murders a movie audience as they watch the movie. Violence and gore abound. 89m; VHS, DVD, Wide, CC. **C:** Zelda Rubinstein; Michael Lerner; Talia Paul; Clara Pastor; Directed by Bigas Luna; Written by Bigas Luna; Cinematography by Josep Civit; Music by J(ose) M(anuel) Pagan. **Pr:** Spectra Film. **A:** Sr. High-Adult. **P:** Entertainment. **U:** Home. **Mov-Ent**: Horror. **Acq:** Purchase. **Dist:** Anchor Bay Entertainment.

Angular Modulation 1981
A comprehensive overview of frequency and phase modulation is presented. Spectrum width and power distribution in angular modulated signals are covered. 18m; VHS, 3/4 U. **Pr:** Hewlett Packard. **A:** College-Adult. **P:** Professional. **U:** Institution, CCTV, Home. **Bus-Ind**: Electronics. **Acq:** Purchase. **Dist:** Hewlett-Packard Media Solutions.

Angus 1995 (PG-13) — ★★
Dull teen comedy about self-esteem revolves around the overweight Angus (Talbert), a friendly kid tormented by the usual school bullies. His best bud is twerp Troy (Owen), who tries to help Angus out with his crush on cute blonde Melissa (Ariana). There's even a schmaltzy prom scene. The profanity, though mild, and the boys sexual interests make this questionable for the pre-teen audience that could actually enjoy it. 87m; VHS, DVD. **C:** Charlie Talbert; Kathy Bates; George C. Scott; Chris Owen; Ariana Richards; Lawrence Pressman; Rita Moreno; James Van Der Beek; Anna Thomson; Directed by Patrick Read Johnson; Written by Jill Gordon; Cinematography by Alexander Grusynski; Music by David E. Russo. **Pr:** Dawn Steel; Charles Miller; New Line Cinema. **A:** Jr. High-Adult. **P:** Entertainment. **U:** Home. **Mov-Ent**: Family, Adolescence. **Acq:** Purchase. **Dist:** WarnerArchive.com.

Angus Lost 1982
Angus is a very curious, very clever Scottish terrier, whose curiosity gets him into a number of close scrapes in this tale. 11m; VHS, 3/4 U. **A:** Preschool-Primary. **P:** Entertainment. **U:** Institution, SURA. **Chl-Juv**: Action-Adventure, Pets. **Acq:** Purchase. **Dist:** Phoenix Learning Group.

Angus, Thongs and Perfect Snogging 2008 (PG-13) — ★★½
Angus is a feral cat and 'snogging' is kissing in Brit-speak in this cheerful adaptation of the first two books in Louise Rennison's teen girl series. Plain 14-year-old Georgia (Groome) is obsessed with both her looks and inexperience with boys, which she writes about in her diary. Things look up in the boy department when two handsome brothers move into the neighborhood and she and Robbie (Johnson) bond over their fondness for cats. Too bad that he's already been claimed by her school rival Lindsay (Nixon). 100m; DVD. **C:** Aaron Taylor-Johnson; Kimberly Nixon; Eleanor Tomlinson; Sean Bourke; Liam Hess; Alan J. Dachman; Karen Taylor; Manjeevan Grewal; Georgia Henshaw; Eva Drew; Directed by Gurinder Chadha; Written by Gurinder Chadha; Paul Mayeda Berges; Will McRobb; Chris Viscardi; Cinematography by Richard Pope; Music by Joby Talbot. **A:** Jr. High-Adult. **P:** Entertainment. **U:** Home. **Mov-Ent**: Pets. **Acq:** Purchase. **Dist:** Paramount Pictures Corp.

Anhydrous Ammonia 1988
An anhydrous ammonia accident could happen anytime or anywhere, so you had better be prepared to deal with it. 27m; VHS, 3/4 U. **Pr:** Emergency Film. **A:** Adult. **P:** Instruction. **U:** Institution. **Bus-Ind**: Emergencies. **Acq:** Purchase, Rent/Lease. **Dist:** Emergency Film Group. $375.00.

Anima 1998 (Unrated) — ★★
Sam and Iris have long left their pasts in Nazi Germany behind them for a secluded life in a New England farmhouse. At least until young journalist Bill discovers them while researching an article on taxidermy and mummification and sees their bizarre private world. 88m; VHS, DVD. **C:** Bray Poor; George Bartenieff; Jacqueline Bertrand; Directed by Craig Richardson; Written by Craig Richardson; Cinematography by Randy Drummond; Music by Joel Diamond; Adam Hurst. **A:** College-Adult. **P:** Entertainment. **U:** Home. **Mov-Ent**: Aging, Journalism. **Acq:** Purchase. **Dist:** Vanguard International Cinema, Inc.

The Animal 2001 (PG-13) — ★★½
Meek clerk Schneider is injured in a serious car accident and is rescued by a mad scientist who surgically replaces his damaged organs with animal parts. These animalistic traits tend to surface at the worst possible time for Schneider, just as he's realizing his dream of becoming a supercop. Haskell (from TV's first "Survivor") is pleasant in her big screen debut as the animal-rights advocate girlfriend, but Schneider is the one who makes this surprisingly enjoyable comedy work with his affable loser persona and willingness to go with the joke. 83m; VHS, DVD, Wide, CC. **C:** Rob Schneider; Guy Torry; John C. McGinley; Colleen Haskell; Michael Caton; Louis Lombardi; Ed Asner; Michael (Mike) Papajohn; Directed by Luke Greenfield; Written by Rob Schneider; Tom Brady; Cinematography by Peter Lyons Collister; Music by Teddy Castellucci. **Pr:** Barry Bernardi; Carr D'Angelo; Todd Garner; Revolution Studios; Columbia Pictures. **A:** Jr. High-Adult. **P:** Entertainment. **U:** Home. **Mov-Ent**: Animals. **Acq:** Purchase. **Dist:** Sony Pictures Home Entertainment Inc.

Animal 2005 (R) — ★★½
James "Animal" Allen is a violent gangsta sent to prison, leaving behind young son Darius (Howard), who grows up following in pop's footsteps. When Animal emerges from prison reformed, he attempts to get Darius out of the life. Thoughtful and intelligent, with excellent performances by leads Howard and Rhames. 93m; DVD. **C:** Ving Rhames; Terrence Howard; Jim Brown; Chazz Palminteri; Paula Jai Parker; Faizon Love; Wes Studi; Beverly Todd; Directed by David J. Burke; Written by David C(lark) Johnson. **A:** Sr. High-Adult. **P:** Entertainment. **U:** Home. **Mov-Ent**. **Acq:** Purchase. **Dist:** Movies Unlimited. $26.98.

Animal 2 2007 (Unrated) — ★★
Lifer James "Animal" Allen's (Rhames) prison transfer finds him doing time with younger son James Jr. (Collins), who was framed for murder by Animal's old foe Kasada (Dunn), who wants Animal to get back into the prison fight game. On the outside, elder son Darius (Shannon) is trying to find the evidence to clear his bro. 93m; DVD. **C:** Ving Rhames; Vicellous Shannon; Conrad Dunn; K.C. Collins; Directed by Ryan Combs; Written by Jacob L. Adams; Music by Craig McConnell. **A:** Sr. High-Adult. **P:** Entertainment. **U:** Home. **Mov-Ent**: Boxing, Family. **Acq:** Purchase. **Dist:** Phase 4/kaBOOM Entertainment.

Animal ABCs 1989
This video teaches small children about animals through the use of the alphabet. 30m; VHS. **Pr:** Creative Video Concepts.

A: Preschool-Primary. P: Education. U: Institution. Chl-Juv: Animals. Acq: Purchase. Dist: Rainbow Educational Media, Inc.

Animal Adaptations in a Northern Environment 1970
Animals that live in the Arctic must be able to live in summer temperatures of 90 degrees Fahrenheit, as well as in the extreme cold of long winters. 12m; VHS, 3/4 U. **Pr:** S and I Films. **A:** Jr. High-Sr. High. **P:** Education. **U:** Institution, SURA. **Hea-Sci:** Arctic Regions. **Acq:** Purchase. **Dist:** Phoenix Learning Group.

Animal Adaption 19??
Learning program for young students looks at how animals have survived by adapting to their environments, using a variety of animals as examples. Part of the "Biology Studies" series. 25m; VHS. **A:** Jr. High-Adult. **P:** Education. **U:** Home, Institution. **Chl-Juv:** Science, Animals, Evolution. **Acq:** Purchase. **Dist:** Educational Activities Inc. $89.00.

Animal Alphabet 1985
The cassettes in this series feature live action and animated sequences designed to help youngsters learn the alphabet. Broadway composer Elizabeth Swados wrote a special song for each letter; animal footage adds a mnemonic device. 30m; VHS. **A:** Preschool. **P:** Education. **U:** Home. **Chl-Juv:** Language Arts, Children. **Acq:** Purchase. **Dist:** MGM Studios Inc. ; Warner Home Video, Inc. $14.95.

Animal Antics 199?
Professor Iris is on safari looking for elephants. Puppetry. 40m; VHS. **A:** Preschool. **P:** Education. **U:** Home. **Chl-Juv:** Animals, Children, Puppets. **Acq:** Purchase. **Dist:** Discovery Home Entertainment. $12.95.

Animal Appetites 19??
Satire focusing on two Cambodian immigrants who were put on trial in California for slaughtering their pet dog for food. Depicts a hypocrisy among the American culture that is associated with such issues as race relations and animal rights. 18m; VHS, 3/4 U, Special order formats. **A:** College-Adult. **P:** Education. **U:** Institution. **Gen-Edu:** Documentary Films, Animals, Law. **Acq:** Purchase, Rent/Lease. **Dist:** Third World Newsreel. $175.00.

Animal Architecture 1977
Many animals build structures for shelter and food gathering. This show features the structures that animals build from the simple to the complex. 9m; VHS, 3/4 U. **Pr:** Allied Artists International. **A:** Jr. High-Sr. High. **P:** Education. **U:** Institution, SURA. **Gen-Edu:** Animals. **Acq:** Purchase. **Dist:** Phoenix Learning Group.

Animal Babies 1981
Investigates animal offspring, comparing size, number of babies born, habitat and parental care. 15m; VHS. **A:** Primary. **P:** Education. **U:** Institution. **Gen-Edu:** Animals. **Acq:** Purchase. **Dist:** National Geographic Society. $70.

Animal Babies 1987
A variety of familiar and exotic animals and their offspring are compared for size, habitat, and parental care. 10m; VHS, 3/4 U. **Pr:** National Geographic Society. **A:** Primary. **P:** Education. **U:** Institution, SURA. **Hea-Sci:** Animals. **Acq:** Purchase, Trade-in, Duplication License. **Dist:** Encyclopedia Britannica. $190.00.

Animal Babies in the Wild 1987
National Geographic footage of baby animals in their natural habitats as songs, stories, and dialogue familiarize children with less often seen wildlife. 30m; VHS. **A:** Preschool-Primary. **P:** Education. **U:** Home. **Chl-Juv:** Animals. **Acq:** Purchase. **Dist:** Music for Little People. $15.98.

Animal Behavior 1989 (PG) — ★
An animal researcher and a music professor fall in love on a college campus. Bowen's (she actually released it under the alias Riley H. Anne) comedy was filmed in 1985 and edited/shelved for over four years, with good reason. 79m; VHS; Open Captioned. **C:** Karen Allen; Armand Assante; Holly Hunter; Josh Mostel; Richard Libertini; Directed by Jenny (H. Anne Riley) Bowen; Written by Susan Rice; Cinematography by Richard Bowen; Music by Cliff Eidelman. **Pr:** Millimeter Films. **A:** Jr. High-Adult. **P:** Entertainment. **U:** Home. **Mov-Ent:** Comedy--Romantic. **Acq:** Purchase. **Dist:** $89.99.

Animal Behavior: A First Film 1973
The animal behavior is triggered by some initial action. The program points out how we can learn to be better observers of animal behavior by describing exactly what we see them do. 11m; VHS, 3/4 U. **Pr:** Norman Bean. **A:** Primary. **P:** Education. **U:** Institution, SURA. **Hea-Sci:** Animals. **Acq:** Purchase. **Dist:** Phoenix Learning Group.

Animal Behavior: Babies and their Parents 1991
Observe various creatures of the the animal kingdom nurture their young. Comes with teacher's guide. 12m; VHS. **Pr:** Coronet Films. **A:** Primary. **P:** Education. **U:** Institution. **Chl-Juv:** Animals. **Acq:** Purchase, Rent/Lease. **Dist:** Phoenix Learning Group. $75.00.

Animal Behavior: Finding and Building Homes 1991
Watch nature's engineers build, find or borrow homes for themselves and their families. Animals featured include bats, hermit crabs, ant lions, spiders, prairie dogs, and others. 12m; VHS. **A:** Primary. **P:** Education. **U:** Institution. **Chl-Juv:** Animals, Wildlife. **Acq:** Purchase, Rent/Lease. **Dist:** Phoenix Learning Group. $250.00.

Animal Behavior: Partnerships, 2nd ed. 1991
Features an explanation of commensalism, mutualism, and parasitism, and provides examples in nature of all three. 15m; VHS. **A:** Primary-Jr. High. **P:** Education. **U:** Institution. **Hea-Sci:** Animals, Science. **Acq:** Purchase, Rent/Lease. **Dist:** Phoenix Learning Group. $250.00.

Animal Behavior Series 1981
This series explores various aspects of animal behavior and learning. All programs are available individually. 15m; 3/4 U, Special order formats. **Pr:** National Geographic Society. **A:** Jr. High-Adult. **P:** Education. **U:** Institution, Home, SURA. **Hea-Sci:** Animals. **Acq:** Purchase, Trade-in, Duplication License. **Dist:** National Geographic Society.
Indiv. Titles: 1. Invertebrates: Conditioning or Learning? 2. Do Animals Reason? 3. The Function of Beauty in Nature 4. Konrad Lorenz: Science of Animal Behavior 5. The Tool Users.

Animal Called Man 1972 (Unrated) — ★
Two crooked buddies join a big western gang in pillaging a small town and get in too deep. 83m; VHS. **C:** Vassilli Karis; Craig Hill; Gillian Bray; Directed by Robert (Roberto) Mauri; Written by Robert (Roberto) Mauri; Cinematography by Luis Ciccarese; Music by Carlo Savina. **A:** Jr. High-Adult. **P:** Entertainment. **U:** Home. **Mov-Ent:** Western. **Acq:** Purchase. **Dist:** No Longer Available.

Animal Camouflage 1977
For many animals, the interaction with their environment has resulted in colors and patterns that allow them protection and disguise from their prey. 9m; VHS, 3/4 U. **Pr:** Allied Artists International. **A:** Jr. High-Sr. High. **P:** Education. **U:** Institution, SURA. **Hea-Sci:** Animals. **Acq:** Purchase. **Dist:** Phoenix Learning Group.

Animal Communication 1971
Looks at the variety of communication signals used by a dozen species of animals from insects to primates. From "Life Around Us." 30m; VHS, 3/4 U, Special order formats. **Pr:** Time-Life Films. **A:** Jr. High-Sr. High. **P:** Education. **U:** Institution, SURA. **L:** English, Spanish. **Hea-Sci:** Communication. **Acq:** Purchase, Rent/Lease. **Dist:** Time-Life Video and Television.

The Animal Contract 1991
A look at the changing relationship between man and animals. 60m; VHS, 3/4 U. **A:** Jr. High-Adult. **P:** Education. **U:** Institution, CCTV, CATV, BCTV, SURA. **Gen-Edu:** Wildlife, Animals. **Acq:** Purchase, Duplication. **Dist:** Ambrose Video Publishing, Inc. $275.00.

Animal Crackers 1930 (G) — ★★★½
The second and possibly the funniest of the 13 Marx Brothers films, "Animal Crackers" is a screen classic. Groucho is a guest at the house of wealthy matron Margaret Dumont and he, along with Zeppo, Chico, and Harpo, destroy the tranquility of the estate. Complete with the Harry Ruby music score—including Groucho's "Hooray for Captain Spaulding" with more quotable lines than any other Marx Brothers film: "One morning I shot an elephant in my pajamas. How he got into my pajamas, I'll never know." Based on a play by George S. Kaufman. 98m/B/W; VHS, DVD. **C:** Groucho Marx; Chico Marx; Harpo Marx; Zeppo Marx; Lillian Roth; Margaret Dumont; Louis Sorin; Hal Thompson; Robert Greig; Margaret Irving; Edward Metcalf; Kathryn Reece; Directed by Victor Heerman; Written by Morrie Ryskind; Cinematography by George J. Folsey; Music by Bert Kalmar; Harry Ruby. **Pr:** Paramount Pictures. **A:** Family. **P:** Entertainment. **U:** Home. **Mov-Ent:** Comedy--Slapstick, Classic Films. **Acq:** Purchase. **Dist:** Facets Multimedia Inc. $14.98.

Animal Crackers 1989
This film helps managers remember basic management fundamentals when they're on the firing line and haven't time to review their seminar notes or management books. 15m; VHS, 3/4 U. **Pr:** Cally Curtis Company. **A:** Family. **P:** Education. **U:** Institution, SURA. **Bus-Ind:** Management. **Acq:** Purchase, Rent/Lease. **Dist:** Aspen Publishers, Inc.

Animal Faces, Animal Places 1991
Rhyming format helps to teach children about animals and their habitats. Includes information the beluga whales and the Arctic Ocean, rhinos and the plains of Africa, and marmosets and the Amazon rainforests. 20m; VHS. **A:** Primary. **P:** Education. **U:** Institution. **Chl-Juv:** Science, Geography, Animals. **Acq:** Purchase. **Dist:** Rainbow Educational Media, Inc. $85.00.

Animal Factory 2000 (R) — ★★½
When first-time felon Ron Decker (Furlong) is sentenced to two years in a decaying prison, he is introduced to a world where violence is a way of life. After witnessing a riot, Ron is taken under the wing of Earl Copen (Dafoe), the main-man on the cellblock, but the younger man soon discovers that life in prison is not about rehabilitation, it's about survival. Bunker wrote the screenplay based on his novel of the same name. 94m; VHS, DVD, Wide, CC. **C:** Willem Dafoe; Edward Furlong; Danny Trejo; John Heard; Mickey Rourke; Tom Arnold; Mark Boone, Jr.; Steve Buscemi; Edward (Eddie) Bunker; Seymour Cassel; Directed by Steve Buscemi; Written by Edward (Eddie) Bunker; John Steppling; Cinematography by Phil Parmet; Music by John Lurie. **A:** Sr. High-Adult. **P:** Entertainment. **U:** Home. **Mov-Ent.** **Acq:** Purchase. **Dist:** Sony Pictures Home Entertainment Inc.

Animal Farm 1955 (Unrated) — ★★★
An animated version of George Orwell's classic political satire about a barnyard full of animals who parallel the growth of totalitarian dictatorships. Not entirely successful, but probably best translation of Orwell to film. 73m; VHS, DVD, 8 mm, 3/4 U, Special order formats. **TV Std:** NTSC, PAL. **C:** Voice(s) by Maurice Denham; Gordon Heath; Directed by John Halas; Joy Batchelor. **Pr:** Louis de Rochemont; Halas and Batchelor Studios. **A:** Family. **P:** Entertainment. **U:** Home. **Mov-Ent:** Animation & Cartoons, Satire & Parody, Animals. **Acq:** Purchase. **Dist:** Amazon.com Inc.; Knowledge Unlimited, Inc.; Anchor Bay Entertainment. $24.95.

Animal Farm 1999 — ★½
Orwell's political satire is given the "Babe" treatment in this live-action version. Drunken farmer Mr. Jones (Postlethwaite) has his power overthrown by his barnyard animals, who in turn are ruled by the farm's pig population. Only porker Napoleon (Stewart) turns out to be as big a tyrant as his human counterpart. Far beyond the scope of children, this retelling is clunky and its propaganda value has certainly come and gone. (Orwell was originally satirizing Stalinist Russia.) 91m; DVD. **C:** Pete Postlethwaite; Voice(s) by Patrick Stewart; Kelsey Grammer; Ian Holm; Julia Ormond; Julia Louis-Dreyfus; Paul Scofield; Peter Ustinov; Directed by John Stephenson; Written by Martyn Burke; Alan Janes; Cinematography by Mike Brewster; Music by Richard Harvey. **A:** Jr. High-Adult. **P:** Entertainment. **U:** Home. **Mov-Ent:** Agriculture, Satire & Parody. **Acq:** Purchase. **Dist:** Movies Unlimited; Alpha Video.

Animal Follies 1984
Famous characters, such as Ruff 'n Ready, Snagglepuss, Touche Turtle, Augie Doggie, and Yippee, Yappee and Yahooey, are featured in several episodes of their own shows. 90m; VHS. **C:** Voice(s) by Daws Butler. **Pr:** Hanna-Barbera Productions. **A:** Family. **P:** Entertainment. **U:** Home. **Mov-Ent:** Animation & Cartoons, Television Series, Family Viewing. **Acq:** Purchase. **Dist:** Image Entertainment Inc.; Turner Broadcasting System Inc. $29.95.

Animal Friends 1956
Tells of the friendship between a kitten and a big white dog. They play and even eat together. 10m; VHS, 3/4 U. **Pr:** BFA Educational Media. **A:** Primary. **P:** Entertainment. **U:** Institution, SURA. **Chl-Juv:** Animals. **Acq:** Purchase. **Dist:** Phoenix Learning Group.

Animal Guessing Games 1988
Introduces students to a number of animals and their features. 15m; VHS. **A:** Preschool-Primary. **P:** Education. **U:** Institution. **Gen-Edu:** Animals. **Acq:** Purchase. **Dist:** National Geographic Society. $80.

Animal Habitats 1956
By illustrating the specific adaptations of animals to the varying conditions, this show serves as a simple introduction to the principles of ecology. 11m; VHS, 3/4 U; Open Captioned. **Pr:** BFA Educational Media. **A:** Jr. High-Sr. High. **P:** Education. **U:** Institution, SURA. **L:** English, French. **Hea-Sci:** Ecology & Environment. **Acq:** Purchase. **Dist:** Phoenix Learning Group.

Animal Homes 1955
Shows where various animals live-above the ground, in the ground, and in the water-and explains why animals build their homes where they do. 11m/B/W; VHS, 3/4 U. **Pr:** Encyclopedia Britannica Educational Corporation. **A:** Primary. **P:** Education. **U:** Institution, SURA. **Hea-Sci:** Animals. **Acq:** Purchase, Rent/Lease, Trade-in. **Dist:** Encyclopedia Britannica.

Animal Homes 1988
This new program illustrates the many ways in which animals provide shelter for themselves. 12m; VHS, 3/4 U. **Pr:** Morse-Allen, Inc. **A:** Jr. High-Adult. **P:** Education. **U:** Institution, CCTV, SURA. **Gen-Edu:** Animals, Wildlife. **Acq:** Purchase, Rent/Lease. **Dist:** Phoenix Learning Group.

Animal Homes 2 1979
This program looks at a variety of animals and the shelters they call home. 11m; VHS, 3/4 U, Special order formats. **Pr:** Ken Nelson. **A:** Primary. **P:** Education. **U:** Institution, Home, SURA. **Gen-Edu:** Animals. **Acq:** Purchase, Duplication License. **Dist:** Clear Vue Inc.

Animal Hormones 1 and 2 1987
Examines the function and regulation of hormone systems. 60m; VHS. **Pr:** University of California, Davis. **A:** Jr. High-College. **P:** Education. **U:** Institution. **Hea-Sci:** Biology. **Acq:** Purchase. **Dist:** Educational Images Ltd.

Animal Instincts 1992 (R) — ★★
A woman takes a prescription drug that makes her a nymphomaniac, and her police officer husband discovers that he's turned on by videotaping her in bed with other men and women. One of the many in her constant stream of lovers is a politician whose campaign is based on shutting down all the town's sex clubs. Another in the string of sexual thrillers riding on the coattails of "Basic Instinct." 94m; VHS, DVD, CC. **C:** Maxwell Caulfield; Jan-Michael Vincent; Mitch Gaylord; Shannon Whirry; Delia Sheppard; John Saxon; David Carradine; Directed by Alexander Gregory (Gregory Dark) Hippolyte; Written by Jon Robert Samsel; Georges des Esseintes; Cinematography by Paul Desatoff; Music by Joseph Smith. **Pr:** Andrew Garroni; Axis Films International. **A:** Sr. High-Adult. **P:** Entertainment. **U:** Home. **Mov-Ent:** Mystery & Suspense, Sex & Sexuality, Nightclubs. **Acq:** Purchase. **Dist:** Unknown Distributor.

Animal Instincts 2 1994 (R) — ★★
Joanna leaves her overbearing husband and moves into a supposedly quiet community. Neighbor Steve is a security expert—and a voyeur. He's hidden a camera in Joanna's bedroom but she knows he's watching. 92m; VHS, DVD, CC. **C:** Shannon Whirry; Woody Brown; Elizabeth Sandifer; Al Sapienza; Directed by Alexander Gregory (Gregory Dark) Hippolyte. **Pr:** Magnum. **A:** College-Adult. **P:** Entertainment. **U:** Home. **Mov-Ent:** Mystery & Suspense, Sex & Sexuality. **Acq:** Purchase. **Dist:** No Longer Available.

Animal Instincts 3: The Seductress 1995 (R) — ★
Joanna (Schumacher) finds a new kind of sexual excitement when she gets involved with rock music promoter Alex (Mathew), whose kicks include feining blindness. The unrated version contains 12 more minutes of footage. 96m; VHS, DVD. **C:** Wendy Schumacher; James Matthew; Marcus Graham;

John Bates; Anthony Lesa; Directed by Alexander Gregory (Gregory Dark) Hippolyte; Written by Selwyn Harris; Cinematography by Ernest Paul Roebuck. **Pr:** Andrew Garroni; Walter Gernert; Axis Films International. **A:** Sr. High-Adult. **P:** Entertainment. **U:** Home. **Mov-Ent:** Sex & Sexuality. **Acq:** Purchase. **Dist:** Image Entertainment Inc. $92.95.

Animal Intelligence 1994
Explores many issues associated with animal intelligence and answers such questions as: Can animals actually think?; Are they problem solvers?; and Can they be taught?. Includes footage of different animals at Busch Gardens in Tampa Bay and Sea World in Orlando, both located in Florida. Comes with teacher's guide and blackline masters. 15m; VHS. **A:** Primary-Jr. High. **P:** Education. **U:** Institution. **Hea-Sci:** Science, Animals, Biology. **Acq:** Purchase. **Dist:** United Learning Inc. $89.95.

The Animal Kingdom 1932 (Unrated) — ★★★
A romantic triangle develops when Howard, married to Loy, has an affair with Harding. The problem is Harding acts more like a wife and Loy a mistress. Intelligently written and directed, with a marvelous performance from veteran character actor Gargan. 95m/B/W; VHS, DVD. **C:** Ann Harding; Leslie Howard; Myrna Loy; Neil Hamilton; William Gargan; Henry Stephenson; Ilka Chase; Directed by Edward H. Griffith; Written by Horace Jackson; Cinematography by George J. Folsey. **Pr:** David O. Selznick; RKO. **A:** Sr. High-Adult. **P:** Entertainment. **U:** Home. **Mov-Ent:** Drama. **Acq:** Purchase. **Dist:** Facets Multimedia Inc. $29.95.

Animal Kingdom 2009 (R) — ★★★
Feature debut from writer/director Michod is a contemporary noir following the disintegration of the Codys, a Melbourne family of criminals, ruled by monstrous mom Smurf whose specialty is the armed robberies she plans with her three psycho sons. When his mother ODs, teenaged grandson Joshua is brought into the fold but his allegiance might not lay where everyone thinks it should. Increasing violence and some cops getting killed brings too much scrutiny and trouble increases amidst the brutality and tension that Michod and his cast play with assurance. 112m; Blu-Ray, On Demand, Wide, CC. **C:** Jacki Weaver; Guy Pearce; Ben Mendelsohn; Joel Edgerton; James Frecheville; Luke Ford; Sullivan Stapleton; Daniel Wyllie; Anthony Hayes; Justin Rosniak; Susan Prior; Anne Lise Phillips; Laura Wheelwright; Mirrah Foulkes; Clayton Jacobson; Directed by David Michod; Written by David Michod; Cinematography by Adam Arkapaw; Music by Antony Partos. **Pr:** Liz Watts; Porchlight Films Prod; Screen Australia; Sony Pictures Classics; Paladin. **A:** Sr. High-Adult. **P:** Entertainment. **U:** Home. **L:** English. **Mov-Ent:** Crime Drama, Australia, Family. **Acq:** Purchase. **Dist:** Movies Unlimited; Alpha Video; Amazon.com Inc.

Animal Life Spans 1992
Investigates life spans in animals and describes how scientists determine the ages of wild animals and their life expectancy. 15m; VHS. **A:** Preschool-Primary. **P:** Education. **U:** Institution. **Gen-Edu:** Animals. **Acq:** Purchase. **Dist:** National Geographic Society. $80.

Animal Magic with Fran ????
Shows how to make cartoon figures using basic shapes and letters. 30m; VHS. **A:** Primary. **P:** Instruction. **U:** Home, Institution. **How-Ins:** Art & Artists, How-To. **Acq:** Purchase. **Dist:** Crystal Productions. $19.95.

Animal Migration 1977
One of the most spectacular and mysterious animal behaviors-migration-is explored. 12m; VHS, 3/4 U. **Pr:** Allied Artists International. **A:** Jr. High-Sr. High. **P:** Education. **U:** Institution, SURA. **Hea-Sci:** Animals. **Acq:** Purchase. **Dist:** Phoenix Learning Group.

Animal Migration 1992
Explores spectacular and mysterious animal migration behaviors. 22m; VHS, 3/4 U; Closed Captioned. **A:** Primary. **P:** Education. **U:** Institution. **Chl-Juv:** Science, Animals. **Acq:** Purchase. **Dist:** National Geographic Society. $99.00.

The Animal Movie 1970 — ★★★
A boy sees that animals move differently than he does, and, unlike man, are limited in the ways they can accomplish tasks. This cartoon explores the differences. 10m; VHS, 3/4 U. **Pr:** Sidney Goldsmith. **A:** Primary. **P:** Education. **U:** Institution, SURA. **Chl-Juv:** Animals. **Acq:** Purchase, Rent/Lease. **Dist:** National Film Board of Canada.

Animal Navigation 1970
A series of experiments suggest that all migrating animals orientate themselves by means of the sun. 14m; VHS, 3/4 U. **Pr:** Celebrity Concert Corporation Film. **A:** Jr. High-Sr. High. **P:** Education. **U:** Institution, SURA. **Hea-Sci:** Animals. **Acq:** Purchase. **Dist:** Phoenix Learning Group.

Animal Nutrition 1978
Discusses lipids, carbohydrates and proteins. 29m; VHS. **A:** Adult. **P:** Education. **U:** Institution. **Hea-Sci:** Biology. **Acq:** Purchase. **Dist:** RMI Media. $75.00.

Animal Populations: Nature's Checks and Balances 1987
Climate, food supply, and predators play a key factor in limiting the number of a group of animals in a certain area. 22m; VHS, 3/4 U. **A:** Jr. High-Sr. High. **P:** Education. **U:** Institution, SURA. **Hea-Sci:** Animals. **Acq:** Purchase, Trade-in. **Dist:** Encyclopedia Britannica. $300.00.

Animal Profiles 19??
Zookeepers at the Washington Park Zoo and Oregon Wildlife Safari talk about the habits and lifestyles of particular animals. Volume one, Animal Profiles: Primates, contains four cassettes; volume two, Animal Profiles: Endangered Species, contains five. Teacher's guide included. 13m; VHS. **Pr:** Rainbow. **A:** Primary. **P:** Education. **U:** Institution. **Gen-Edu:** Animals, Zoos. **Acq:** Purchase. **Dist:** Clear Vue Inc. $229.00.
Indiv. Titles: 1. Gorillas 2. Golden Monkeys 3. Chimpanzees 4. Mandrills 5. Ring-Tailed Lemurs 6. Orangutans 7. Rhinoceroses 8. Red Pandas 9. Snow Leopards.

Animal Quiz 1 1984
This series is an invitation to children and their parents to test their animal expertise. This volume features "Looney Gooney," a look at the comical aerodynamics of the Gooney bird of Midway Island; the dragon-like lizards of Indonesia in "Komodo Dragons"; and the San Diego Zoo's collection of animal infants in "Zoo Babies." 60m; VHS. **Pr:** Walt Disney. **A:** Family. **P:** Entertainment. **U:** Home. **Chl-Juv:** Animals. **Acq:** Purchase. **Dist:** Walt Disney Studios Home Entertainment. $39.95.

Animal Quiz 2 1984
This volume takes viewers to the arid state of Chihuahua, Mexico, for a glimpse of the "Mexican Grizzly," an oasis-like watering hole in Africa for "Kenya's Spring of Life"; and the frigid, desolate realm of the Emperor penguin in "Adventure Antarctica." 60m; VHS. **Pr:** Walt Disney. **A:** Family. **P:** Entertainment. **U:** Home. **Chl-Juv:** Animals. **Acq:** Purchase. **Dist:** Walt Disney Studios Home Entertainment. $39.95.

Animal Quiz 3 1984
The third volume provides insights to "The Strange Creatures of the Galapagos," and traces the training and breeding of racehorses in "Thoroughbred" and the monkeyshines performed by "The Apes of Gibraltar." 60m; VHS. **Pr:** Walt Disney. **A:** Family. **P:** Entertainment. **U:** Home. **Chl-Juv:** Documentary Films, Animals, Pacific Islands. **Acq:** Purchase. **Dist:** Walt Disney Studios Home Entertainment. $39.95.

Animal Quiz 4 1984
Viewers are shown the creatures of the Sonoran desert, visit the famed Masai warriors of Africa and participate in a Pacific shark watch. 84m; VHS. **Pr:** Walt Disney Productions. **A:** Preschool-Adult. **P:** Education. **U:** Home. **Chl-Juv:** Animals. **Acq:** Purchase. **Dist:** Walt Disney Studios Home Entertainment. $39.95.

Animal Quiz 5 1984
Viewers witness unique structures built by animals, visit the Mexican desert where jaguars roam and observe the crocodile population of the Nile. 84m; VHS. **Pr:** Walt Disney Productions. **A:** Primary-Adult. **P:** Education. **U:** Home. **Chl-Juv:** Animals. **Acq:** Purchase. **Dist:** Walt Disney Studios Home Entertainment. $39.95.

Animal Quiz 6 1984
The big cats of South Africa are filmed in their habitat, as are Japan's snow monkeys. 84m; VHS. **Pr:** Walt Disney Productions. **A:** Primary-Adult. **P:** Education. **U:** Home. **Chl-Juv:** Animals. **Acq:** Purchase. **Dist:** Walt Disney Studios Home Entertainment. $39.95.

Animal Quiz 7 1985
Here's a chance to test your knowledge about the jungle jaguar, the brown bears of Alaska, and New Zealand sheep dogs. 83m; VHS. **Pr:** Walt Disney Productions. **A:** Primary-Adult. **P:** Entertainment. **U:** Home. **Chl-Juv:** Animals. **Acq:** Purchase. **Dist:** Walt Disney Studios Home Entertainment. $39.95.

Animal Quiz 8 1985
This volume visits the Yagua Indian tribe and looks at the various animals who inhabit a Kenyan game reserve. 83m; VHS. **Pr:** Walt Disney Productions. **A:** Primary-Adult. **P:** Entertainment. **U:** Home. **Chl-Juv:** Animals. **Acq:** Purchase. **Dist:** Walt Disney Studios Home Entertainment. $39.95.

Animal Quiz 9 1985
In this volume, find out about the elephants of Thailand, Kenya's pink flamingos, and a colony of fur seals on the Pribilof Islands. 83m; VHS. **Pr:** Walt Disney Productions. **A:** Primary-Adult. **P:** Entertainment. **U:** Home. **Chl-Juv:** Animals. **Acq:** Purchase. **Dist:** Walt Disney Studios Home Entertainment. $39.95.

Animal Room 1995 (Unrated) — ★★
When high school student Arnold Mosk (Harris) is caught using drugs, he's place in the school's controversial isolation program that's nicknamed "The Animal Room." There are no rules and Arnold's life is threatened by delinquent thug, Doug (Lillard). But if Arnold expects to survive, he's going to have to learn how to fight. 98m; VHS, DVD. **C:** Neil Patrick Harris; Matthew Lillard; Gabriel Olds; Catherine Hicks; Brian Vincent; Directed by Craig Singer. **A:** Sr. High-Adult. **P:** Entertainment. **U:** Home. **Mov-Ent. Acq:** Purchase. **Dist:** Vanguard International Cinema, Inc.

Animal Safari: A Learning Journey-Vol. 3: Born in a Barnyard 1999
Discusses the characteristics and behaviors of farm animals. Shows children holding and observing bunnies, chicks, and ducklings. 31m; VHS. **A:** Primary. **P:** Education. **U:** Home, Institution. **Chl-Juv:** Animals, Biology, Science. **Acq:** Purchase. **Dist:** Coyote Creek Productions. $19.95.

Animal Safari: A Learning Journey-Vol. 3: Creepy Critters 1999
Discusses the characteristics and behaviors of bugs, spiders and other small creatures. Shows children holding and observing a spider and a scorpion. 32m; VHS. **A:** Primary. **P:** Education. **U:** Home, Institution. **Chl-Juv:** Insects, Biology, Science. **Acq:** Purchase. **Dist:** Coyote Creek Productions. $19.95.

Animal Safari: A Learning Journey-Vol. 5: Tongues, Tails, and Scales 2000
Discusses the characteristics and behaviors of several reptiles including turtles, a bearded dragon lizard and an alligator. Shows children holding and observing an albino Burmese python. 51m; VHS. **A:** Primary. **P:** Education. **U:** Home, Institution. **Chl-Juv:** Animals, Biology, Science. **Acq:** Purchase. **Dist:** Coyote Creek Productions. $19.95.

Animal Safari: A Learning Journey-Vol. 6: Animals and Man 2000
Discusses how the relationship between man and animals has changed over time. Animals shown include a chinchilla, llamas, a capuchin monkey, and a North American opossum. 33m; VHS. **A:** Primary. **P:** Education. **U:** Home, Institution. **Chl-Juv:** Animals, Biology, Science. **Acq:** Purchase. **Dist:** Coyote Creek Productions. $19.95.

Animal Safari: A Learning Journey-Vol. 7: Wild Wetlands 2000
Discusses how animals such as tarantulas, tree frogs, caiman turtles, hermit crabs, and snakes help maintain the balance in wetland ecosystems. 33m; VHS. **A:** Primary. **P:** Education. **U:** Home, Institution. **Chl-Juv:** Animals, Biology, Science. **Acq:** Purchase. **Dist:** Coyote Creek Productions. $19.95.

Animal Safari: A Learning Journey-Vol. 8: Exploration Dinosaur 2000
Discusses connections between modern day creatures and dinosaurs. Animals shown include an emu, a macaw and a tegu. 26m; VHS. **A:** Primary. **P:** Education. **U:** Home, Institution. **Chl-Juv:** Dinosaurs, Animals, Science. **Acq:** Purchase. **Dist:** Coyote Creek Productions. $19.95.

Animal Safari, Vol. 1: Wild World Habitats 1999
Features wildlife education for children. Includes exotic animals from around the world. 38m; VHS. **A:** Primary. **P:** Education. **U:** Home. **Chl-Juv:** Children, Education, Wildlife. **Acq:** Purchase. **Dist:** Instructional Video. $19.95.

Animal Safari, Vol. 2: Animals of the Amazon 1999
Features wildlife education for children. Features creatures from the Amazon, including a boa constrictor, a tarantula, and a scarlet macaw. 40m; VHS. **A:** Primary. **P:** Education. **U:** Home. **Chl-Juv:** Children, Education, Animals. **Acq:** Purchase. **Dist:** Instructional Video; Coyote Creek Productions. $19.95.

Animal Safety Is Fun! 1992
Veterinarian Michael Cornwall shares safety tips for children and adults when dealing with dogs. Suggestions include avoiding stray dogs and standing still if approached by a dog, plus more. 15m; VHS. **A:** Family. **P:** Education. **U:** Home, Institution. **Hea-Sci:** Safety Education, Pets. **Acq:** Purchase. **Dist:** Glencoe Animal Hospital. $49.95.

Animal Sculptures 1987
A talk by John Bedford on how he creates sculptures, his own creative process and the messages he hopes his sculpture will convey. 8m; VHS, 3/4 U. **C:** John Bedford. **Pr:** Paulle Clarke. **A:** Family. **P:** Education. **U:** Institution, Home, SURA. **Gen-Edu:** Sculpture. **Acq:** Purchase, Duplication License. **Dist:** Bullfrog Films, Inc.

Animal Sounds: Concert at the Pond 1992
Enjoy the simple beauty of a pond at sunrise, and view the daily cycle of plants and wildlife. 14m; VHS. **A:** Primary. **P:** Education. **U:** Institution. **Chl-Juv:** Wildlife, Children. **Acq:** Purchase. **Dist:** Encyclopedia Britannica. $250.00.

Animal Stories 1984
An animated collection of animal stories for the young: "Andy and the Lion," "Why Mosquitos Buzz in People's Ears" and "Petunia." 30m; VHS. **Pr:** CC Studios. **A:** Preschool. **P:** Entertainment. **U:** Home. **Chl-Juv:** Animation & Cartoons, Children, Animals. **Acq:** Purchase. **Dist:** Facets Multimedia Inc.

Animal Stories: The Complete 52 Episode Series 1998 (Unrated)
Independent Television (ITV) 1998-? animated tales. Collection of modern-day Aesop Fables written in humorous rhyming couplets explain why penguins can't fly, what life is like for a pig who thinks he's too fat, and what to do if you're a dog with bad breath. 52 episodes. 261m; DVD. **C:** Voice(s) by Nigel Hawthorne; Alan Marriott. **A:** Preschool-Primary. **P:** Entertainment. **U:** Home. **Chl-Juv:** Animation & Cartoons, Children's Shows, Television Series. **Acq:** Purchase. **Dist:** Mill Creek Entertainment L.L.C. $14.99.

Animal Studies Series 1987
A charming cameo of wildlife for classrooms and public library programs. 60m; VHS, 3/4 U. **Pr:** Paulle Clarke. **A:** Family. **P:** Education. **U:** Institution, Home, SURA. **Gen-Edu:** Animals. **Acq:** Purchase, Duplication License. **Dist:** Bullfrog Films, Inc.

Animal Town of the Prairie: Prairie Dogs and Their Neighbors 1960
This tape shows how the prarie dog modifies his environment to suit his needs by digging a network of underground tunnels which provide shelter, protection, and a place to rest. 11m; VHS, 3/4 U. **Pr:** Charles C. Carpenter; Encyclopedia Britannica Educational Corporation. **A:** Primary-Sr. High. **P:** Education. **U:** Institution, SURA. **Hea-Sci:** Wildlife. **Acq:** Purchase, Rent/Lease, Trade-in. **Dist:** Encyclopedia Britannica.

Animal Tracks and Signs 1987
Points out how animals can be identified by the tracks they leave. 60m; VHS, 3/4 U. **Pr:** James R. Wailes; Encyclopedia Britannica Educational Corporation. **A:** Primary. **P:** Education. **U:** Institution. **Hea-Sci:** Animals. **Acq:** Purchase, Rent/Lease, Trade-in. **Dist:** Educational Images Ltd. $59.95.

Animal, Vegetable, Mineral 1976
Modern man is constantly finding new uses for the Over 2500 minerals found in the earth's crust and seas, without which human life would have remained primitive, at best. 29m; VHS, 3/4 U. **Pr:** Ontario Education Communication Authority. **A:** Sr. High-College. **P:** Education. **U:** Institution, SURA. **Gen-Edu:** Natural Resources. **Acq:** Purchase. **Dist:** Home Vision Cinema.

Animal Vision: Eyes of the Beholder 19??
Illustrates sight patterns of different animals emphasizing that animals' eyes vary depending on their environment and that their eyes vary from species to species. Provides activities that allow students to try out various ways of seeing. Includes teacher's guide. ?m; VHS. **Pr:** Children's Television Workshop. **A:** Primary-Jr. High. **P:** Education. **U:** Institution. **Chl-Juv:** Science, Animals, Eye. **Acq:** Purchase. **Dist:** GPN Educational Media. $15.00.

Animal Wonder Down Under Series 1986
A series of programs exploring the wildlife of Australia. 50m; VHS, 3/4 U. **Pr:** Centre Productions, Inc. **A:** Primary-Adult. **P:** Education. **U:** Institution, SURA. **Gen-Edu:** Australia, Wildlife. **Acq:** Purchase. **Dist:** Clear Vue Inc. $24.95.
Indiv. Titles: 1. Bandicoots 2. World of Koala 3. Crocodiles 4. Reptiles 5. Fauna of Australia 6. Platypus 7. The Islands 8. Silver Gulls 9. Mallee Fowl 10. Little Marsupials 11. Kangaroos 12. Tiny Carnivores 13. Wombats.

The Animal World 1990
Animal biology and survial are examined, and Darwin's theory of "Natural Selection" is discussed. ?m; VHS. **Pr:** United Learning Inc. **A:** Primary-Jr. High. **P:** Education. **U:** Institution, CCTV, CATV, Home, SURA. **Gen-Edu:** Documentary Films, Animals, Biology. **Acq:** Purchase, Duplication. **Dist:** United Learning Inc. $180.00.
Indiv. Titles: 1. Invertebrates (Part 1) 2. Invertebrates (Part 2): The Arthropods 3. The First Vertebrates 4. Conquering the Land 5. Animal Adaptation.

Animaland 1948
Features four film shorts by Disney animator David Hand, known for the classics "Snow White" and "Bambi." 69m; VHS, DVD. **C:** Directed by David Hand. **A:** Family. **P:** Entertainment. **U:** Home. **Mov-Ent:** Animation & Cartoons, Animals, Family Viewing. **Acq:** Purchase. **Dist:** Tapeworm Video Distributors Inc. $14.95.
Indiv. Titles: 1. Ginger Nutt's Forest Dragon 2. Ginger Nutt's Bee Bother 3. Fantasy on London 4. It's a Lovely Day.

Animalia Volume One: Welcome to the Kingdom 2007 (Unrated)
Zoe and Alex travel from their library into a magical world of talking animals that need their help to solve mysteries and bring peace back to the kingdom. 4 episodes. 96m; DVD. **A:** Primary. **P:** Entertainment. **U:** Home. **Chl-Juv:** Animation & Cartoons, Children's Shows. **Acq:** Purchase. **Dist:** Porchlight Home Entertainment.

Animals 1987
A child and his father visit an inner-city neighborhood zoo. 4m; VHS, SVS, 1C, 3/4 U. **Pr:** Julius Kohanyi. **A:** Primary-Sr. High. **P:** Education. **U:** Institution, CATV, BCTV, Home, SURA. **Chl-Juv:** Zoos. **Acq:** Purchase, Duplication License. **Dist:** Green Acre Video. $19.95.

Animals 1988
These non-narrated programs show the lives of five different animals. 12m; VHS, 3/4 U. **Pr:** Dimension Films. **A:** Primary-Sr. High. **P:** Education. **U:** Institution, Home, SURA. **Hea-Sci:** Animals. **Acq:** Purchase, Rent/Lease, Duplication License. **Dist:** Clear Vue Inc. $500.00.
Indiv. Titles: 1. Chick, Chick, Chick 2. The Cow 3. Dogs 4. Pigs! 5. Sheep Sheep Sheep.

Animals 2008 (Unrated) — ★
Lots of gratuitous nudity and sex scenes to make up for the stupid plot and lack of actual acting skills. Syd (Blucas) gets picked up by Nora (Aycox) in a small town Nevada bar. After a night of rough sex he wakes up infected by lycanthropy (that Nora was a biter). They keep hooking up but Nora's jealous and vicious lycan sire Vic (Andrews) wants her back. 93m; DVD. **C:** Marc Blucas; Nicki Aycox; Naveen Andrews; Eva Amurri; Andy Comeau; Bart Johnson; Ron Rogge; Directed by Douglas Aarniokoski; Written by Craig Spector; Cinematography by Matthew Williams; Music by Alan Brewer. **A:** Sr. High-Adult. **P:** Entertainment. **U:** Home. **Mov-Ent. Acq:** Purchase. **Dist:** Maverick Entertainment.

Animals A to Z 1988
Introduces familiar and not-so-familiar animals that begin with letters from th e alphabet starting with letters from A to Z. 15m; VHS. **A:** Preschool-Primary. **P:** Education. **U:** Institution. **Gen-Edu:** Animals. **Acq:** Purchase. **Dist:** National Geographic Society. $80.

Animals and Angels: Spirituality in Recovery 19??
Dr. Abraham Twerski defines the foundations of spirituality and tools to pursue recovery from drug addiction. 30m; VHS. **A:** Adult. **P:** Education. **U:** Institution. **Hea-Sci:** Alcoholism, Drug Abuse. **Acq:** Purchase. **Dist:** Hazelden Publishing. $69.95.

Animals and How They Grow 1993
Shows how young animals grow and change. Involves mammals, fish, birds, amphibians and reptiles, and insects ?m; VHS. **A:** Preschool-Primary. **P:** Education. **U:** Institution. **Chl-Juv:** Animals, Biology, Science. **Acq:** Purchase. **Dist:** National Geographic Society. $75.00.

Animals and Plants of North America 1981
This series promotes an understanding of plants and animals as individual entities, as population, as parts of communities, and the relationships of living things to their environment. Programs are available individually. 15m; VHS, 3/4 U. **Pr:** Karvonen Films Ltd. **A:** Primary-Adult. **P:** Education. **U:** Institution, SURA. **Hea-Sci:** Ecology & Environment. **Acq:** Purchase, Rent/Lease. **Dist:** Phoenix Learning Group.
Indiv. Titles: 1. Lakeside Habitat 2. Osprey's Domain 3. Boreal Forest (Fall and Winter) 4. Boreal Forest (Spring and Summer) 5. Below the Ramparts 6. Loons of Amisk.

Animals Are Beautiful People 1984
A profile of the animal communities in the African wilderness. From the director of "The Gods Must Be Crazy." 92m; VHS. **C:** Narrated by Paddy O'Byrne; Directed by Jamie Uys. **Pr:** Mimosa Films. **A:** Family. **P:** Entertainment. **U:** Home. **Gen-Edu:** Documentary Films, Animals, Africa. **Acq:** Purchase. **Dist:** Warner Home Video, Inc. $14.95.

The Animals Are Crying 1973
Focuses on the overpopulations of dogs and cats. Sixteen-minute version also available. 28m; VHS, 3/4 U. **C:** Directed by Peter A. Beltz. **Pr:** Learning Corporation of America. **A:** Jr. High-Adult. **P:** Education. **U:** Institution, SURA. **Gen-Edu:** Animals. **Acq:** Purchase, Rent/Lease. **Dist:** Phoenix Learning Group.

Animals Around You Series 1992
Series of three videos discusses a variety of concepts related to animals. "Animal Life Spans" explains factors involved with life span, and birth and mortality rates. "Sizing Up Animals" compares and contrasts animals of differents sizes, from plankton to blue whales, from ants to dinosaurs, and uses a six-year-old girl as a point of reference. "Animals on the Farm" visits different farms and emphasizes the connection between farm products and what is available in the grocery store. All the videos contain much more interesting and well-presented information, and have a variety of applications. 45m; VHS. **A:** Primary. **P:** Education. **U:** Institution. **Chl-Juv:** Animals, Science. **Acq:** Purchase. **Dist:** National Geographic Society. $245.00.
Indiv. Titles: 1. Animals on the Farm 2. Sizing Up Animals 3. Animal Life Spans.

Animals at Night 1963
Tells the story of nocturnal animals-how they differ in their physical characteristics and behavior from animals that are active during the day. 11m; VHS, 3/4 U. **Pr:** Margaret McKibben Lawler; Encyclopedia Britannica Educational Corporation. **A:** Primary. **P:** Education. **U:** Institution, SURA. **Hea-Sci:** Animals. **Acq:** Purchase, Rent/Lease, Trade-in. **Dist:** Encyclopedia Britannica.

Animals at Work in Nature 1956
Shows that animals have special body parts which enable them to perform specialized functions: building their homes, raising young, and finding and storing food. 11m; VHS, 3/4 U. **Pr:** Encyclopedia Britannica Educational Corporation. **A:** Primary. **P:** Education. **U:** Institution, SURA. **Hea-Sci:** Animals. **Acq:** Purchase, Rent/Lease, Trade-in. **Dist:** Encyclopedia Britannica.

Animals Breathe in Many Ways 1964
Animals from insects to whales breathe air to sustain life. This program demonstrates the diverse methods animals utilize to breathe. 11m; VHS, 3/4 U. **Pr:** Norman Bean. **A:** Primary-Jr. High. **P:** Education. **U:** Institution, SURA. **Hea-Sci:** Animals. **Acq:** Purchase. **Dist:** Phoenix Learning Group.

Animals Can Bite 1976
Caution rather than fear is used in this film to teach youngsters how to avoid being bitten by dogs or scratched by cats, and what to do if injury does occur. 13m; VHS, 3/4 U. **Pr:** John Hart. **A:** Preschool-Primary. **P:** Education. **U:** Institution, Home, SURA. **Chl-Juv:** Safety Education. **Acq:** Purchase, Rent/Lease. **Dist:** Pyramid Media. $195.00.

Animals Eat in Many Ways 1971
Every animal has feeding habits and physical features that enable it to eat particular kinds of foods. 10m; VHS, 3/4 U. **Pr:** Amitai. **A:** Primary-Jr. High. **P:** Education. **U:** Institution, SURA. **Hea-Sci:** Animals. **Acq:** Purchase. **Dist:** Phoenix Learning Group.

Animals Film 1981
A gruesome, unflinching document of the cruelties man inflicts on animals in the name of commerce and science. Banned from television. 120m; VHS. **C:** Narrated by Julie Christie; Directed by Victor Schonfeld. **Pr:** Slick Pix. **A:** Sr. High-Adult. **P:** Education. **U:** Home. **Gen-Edu:** Documentary Films, Animals, Science. **Acq:** Purchase. **Dist:** MPI Media Group. $60.00.

Animals Growing Up 1949
Shows growth and development of puppies, a calf, and chicks during the first few weeks of life and shows how mother animals care for their young. 11m/B/W; VHS, 3/4 U. **Pr:** Encyclopedia Britannica Educational Corporation. **A:** Primary. **P:** Education. **U:** Institution, SURA. **Hea-Sci:** Animals. **Acq:** Purchase, Rent/Lease, Trade-in. **Dist:** Encyclopedia Britannica.

Animals Hear in Many Ways 1968
Hearing is an important sense and animals hear in many ways. 12m; VHS, 3/4 U. **Pr:** Norman Bean. **A:** Primary-Jr. High. **P:** Education. **U:** Institution, SURA. **L:** English, Spanish. **Hea-Sci:** Animals. **Acq:** Purchase. **Dist:** Phoenix Learning Group.

Animals in Action, Vol. 1: How Animals Move 1986
The wonderfully photographed series for children aged 4-12 continues with the world of animal movement, how creatures learn to creep, crawl, climb, burrow and more. 30m; VHS. **Pr:** Eastman Kodak Company. **A:** Preschool-Primary. **P:** Education. **U:** Home. **Chl-Juv:** Children, Education, Wildlife. **Acq:** Purchase. **Dist:** Facets Multimedia Inc. $14.95.

Animals in Action, Vol. 2: Mountain Animals 1986
This episode in the splendidly photographed series from Eastman Kodak explores the world of mountainous animals, and what it takes for them to survive in their airy terrain. 30m; VHS. **Pr:** Eastman Kodak Company. **A:** Preschool-Primary. **P:** Education. **U:** Home. **Chl-Juv:** Children, Education, Wildlife. **Acq:** Purchase. **Dist:** Facets Multimedia Inc. $14.95.

Animals in Action, Vol. 3: Tree Living Animals 1986
Animals, who for one reason or another, seek food, shelter, and sometimes safety in the friendly branches of trees, are examined in this segment from the series. 30m; VHS. **Pr:** Eastman Kodak Company. **A:** Preschool-Primary. **P:** Education. **U:** Home. **Chl-Juv:** Children, Education, Wildlife. **Acq:** Purchase. **Dist:** Facets Multimedia Inc. $14.95.

Animals in Action, Vol. 4: Turtle Family 1986
In this segment from the series created for children aged 4 to 12, kids can learn the differences among turtles, tortoises and terrapins. 30m; VHS. **Pr:** Eastman Kodak Company. **A:** Preschool-Primary. **P:** Education. **U:** Home. **Chl-Juv:** Children, Education, Wildlife. **Acq:** Purchase. **Dist:** Facets Multimedia Inc. $14.95.

Animals in Action, Vol. 5: Fresh Water Animals 1986
The series for children aged 4-12 continues with an episode dealing with the lives of beavers, otters and racoons. Again, excellent photography is a hallmark. 30m; VHS. **Pr:** Eastman Kodak Company. **A:** Preschool-Primary. **P:** Education. **U:** Home. **Chl-Juv:** Children, Animals, Education. **Acq:** Purchase. **Dist:** Facets Multimedia Inc. $14.95.

Animals in Action, Vol. 6: Spiders 1986
The world of the spider is explored in this segment of the series created for 4- to 12-year-olds. Meet some of the more than 30,000 species of web-spinners, and learn how they spin traps as strong as steel in the insect world. 30m; VHS. **Pr:** Eastman Kodak Company. **A:** Preschool-Primary. **P:** Education. **U:** Home. **Chl-Juv:** Children, Education, Wildlife. **Acq:** Purchase. **Dist:** Facets Multimedia Inc. $14.95.

Animals in Action, Vol. 7: How Animals "Talk" 1986
A fascinating look at various methods of animal communication. Another superbly photographed segment from the series produced by Eastman Kodak. 30m; VHS. **Pr:** Eastman Kodak Company. **A:** Preschool-Primary. **P:** Education. **U:** Home. **Chl-Juv:** Children, Animals, Education. **Acq:** Purchase. **Dist:** Facets Multimedia Inc. $14.95.

Animals in Action, Vol. 8: Record-Breaking Animals 1986
This entry in the series for children aged 4-12 might be titled the "Animal Olympics." Record-breakers in air, on land, and in water are profiled with superb photography and excellent narration. 30m; VHS. **Pr:** Eastman Kodak Company. **A:** Preschool-Primary. **P:** Education. **U:** Home. **Chl-Juv:** Children, Wildlife, Animals. **Acq:** Purchase. **Dist:** Facets Multimedia Inc. $14.95.

Animals in Action, Vol. 9: Frogs and Toads 1986
The exciting world of amphibious frogs and toads, and their journeys from water to land, is examined in this segment from the series produced by Kodak. Geared to children ages 4 to 12. 30m; VHS. **Pr:** Eastman Kodak Company. **A:** Preschool-Primary. **P:** Education. **U:** Home. **Chl-Juv:** Children, Wildlife, Animals. **Acq:** Purchase. **Dist:** Facets Multimedia Inc. $14.95.

Animals in Action, Vol. 10: Desert Animals and Plants 19??
Another in the series about nature and animals created for children aged 4 to 12. The desert, its animals and plants, are the focus in this segment. 30m; VHS. **Pr:** Eastman Kodak Company. **A:** Preschool-Primary. **P:** Education. **U:** Home. **Chl-Juv:** Children, Education, Wildlife. **Acq:** Purchase. **Dist:** Facets Multimedia Inc. $14.95.

Animals in Action, Vol. 11: Animals of the Night 19??
A series created for the 4-12 year-old set, which explores and teaches children about feeding habits, survival techniques, and the everyday life of animals in the wild. This volume focuses on animals of the nocturnal world. 30m; VHS. **Pr:** Eastman Kodak Company. **A:** Family. **P:** Education. **U:** Home. **Chl-Juv:** Children, Wildlife, Education. **Acq:** Purchase. **Dist:** Facets Multimedia Inc. $14.95.

Animals in Action, Vol. 12: Baby Birds 19??
Another volume in the series created for children aged 4-12, which explores the animal world. The world of baby birds, and why they stay in the nest, or eventually leave, is explored. 30m; VHS. **Pr:** Eastman Kodak Company. **A:** Preschool-Primary. **P:** Entertainment. **U:** Home. **Chl-Juv:** Children, Wildlife, Education. **Acq:** Purchase. **Dist:** Facets Multimedia Inc. $14.95.

Animals in All Kinds of Weather 1989
Travels from the Arctic to Africa to investigate how animals survive and adapt to weather patterns across the globe. 15m; VHS. **A:** Preschool-Primary. **P:** Education. **U:** Institution. **Gen-Edu:** Animals. **Acq:** Purchase. **Dist:** National Geographic Society. $80.

Animals in Autumn and Winter 1982
The program demonstrates how animals and insects prepare for the winter. Also shown are the changes insects undergo during the fall life cycles. 11m; VHS, 3/4 U. **Pr:** Wolfgang Bayer Productions. **A:** Primary-Jr. High. **P:** Education. **U:** Institution, SURA. **Hea-Sci:** Animals, Seasons. **Acq:** Purchase, Rent/Lease, Trade-in. **Dist:** Encyclopedia Britannica.

Animals in Spring and Summer 1983
Depicts the hatching of eggs, the emergence of a moth from its cocoon, and animals feeding and protecting their young. 13m; VHS, 3/4 U. **Pr:** Encyclopedia Britannica Educational Corporation. **A:** Primary. **P:** Education. **U:** Institution, SURA. **Hea-Sci:** Animals, Seasons. **Acq:** Purchase, Rent/Lease, Trade-in. **Dist:** Encyclopedia Britannica.

Animals in the City 1978
Studies animals that are constantly searching for suitable homesites and sources of food in the city: birds, dogs, cats, insects, and rodents. 10m; VHS, 3/4 U. **Pr:** Encyclopedia Britannica Educational Corporation. **A:** Primary. **P:** Education. **U:** Institution, SURA. **Chl-Juv:** Animals. **Acq:** Purchase, Rent/ Lease, Trade-in. **Dist:** Encyclopedia Britannica.

Animals Move in Many Ways 1958
Utilizing the dramatic skills of photography this program illustrates the movement of diverse animals and insects. 11m; VHS, 3/4 U. **Pr:** BFA Educational Media. **A:** Primary. **P:** Education. **U:** Institution, SURA. **Hea-Sci:** Animals. **Acq:** Purchase. **Dist:** Phoenix Learning Group.

The Animals Nobody Loved 1975
Coyotes, rattlesnakes, and mustangs-students learn both sides of the controversy surrounding each of these animals. 52m; 3/4 U, Special order formats. **Pr:** National Geographic Society. **A:** Primary-Adult. **P:** Education. **U:** Institution, Home, SURA. **Hea-Sci:** Animals. **Acq:** Purchase, Trade-in, Duplication License. **Dist:** National Geographic Society.

Animals of Africa: Africa in Flight 1988
At an African waterhole shared by prey and predator, host Joan Embery shows how the animals interact. Also, see how the hornbill lives among elephants, and visit a rare pink pelican on the island of Madagascar. 70m; VHS. **C:** Hosted by Joan Embery. **Pr:** Harmony Gold Productions. **A:** Family. **P:** Education. **U:** Home. **Chl-Juv:** Documentary Films, Africa, Wildlife. **Acq:** Purchase. **Dist:** Facets Multimedia Inc. $14.99.

Animals of Africa: Big Cats of the Kalahari 1988
Joan Embery hosts as this edition of the wildlife series spends a day with lions and cheetahs. 70m; VHS. **C:** Hosted by Joan Embery. **Pr:** Harmony Gold Productions. **A:** Family. **P:** Education. **U:** Home. **Chl-Juv:** Documentary Films, Wildlife, Africa. **Acq:** Purchase. **Dist:** Facets Multimedia Inc. $14.99.

Animals of the Bible 1995
Introduces 18 animals which appear in the Old and New Testaments of the Bible. Offers Biblical stories which help to answer the question "Where did I come from?" 33m; VHS. **A:** Preschool. **P:** Education. **U:** Home. **Chl-Juv:** Bible, Animals. **Acq:** Purchase. **Dist:** Acorn Media Group Inc. $14.95.

Animals of the Desert 1964
The wild life of the desert is depicted, which emphasizes the need for adaptation to living with very little water and a great deal of warmth. 12m; VHS, 3/4 U; Open Captioned. **Pr:** Justin Byers; Geraldine Byers. **A:** Primary. **P:** Education. **U:** Institution, SURA. **Hea-Sci:** Ecology & Environment. **Acq:** Purchase. **Dist:** Phoenix Learning Group.

Animals on the Farm 1992
Visits the farms to learn about livestock, their special characteristics and care. 15m; VHS. **A:** Preschool-Primary. **P:** Education. **U:** Institution. **Gen-Edu:** Animals. **Acq:** Purchase. **Dist:** National Geographic Society. $80.

Animals See in Many Ways—Revised 1980
Eye structure and position are significantly demonstrated as viewers witness the visual scope of a snail, fly, squirrel, snake, and chamelon. 13m; VHS, 3/4 U. **Pr:** Norman Bean. **A:** Primary-Sr. High. **P:** Education. **U:** Institution, SURA. **Hea-Sci:** Animals. **Acq:** Purchase. **Dist:** Phoenix Learning Group.

The Animal's Story 1990
This controversial program shows the darker side of animal experimentation. Not for the squeamish. 120m; VHS. **Pr:** MPI Media Group. **A:** Sr. High-Adult. **P:** Education. **U:** Home. **Gen-Edu:** Documentary Films, Animals, Scientists. **Acq:** Purchase. **Dist:** MPI Media Group. $79.95.

Animals That Build 1983
This program introduces young viewers to animals that build their homes, including beavers, birds, wasps, sticklebacks and African termites. 15m; 3/4 U, Special order formats. **Pr:** National Geographic Society. **A:** Primary. **P:** Education. **U:** Institution, Home, SURA. **Hea-Sci:** Animals. **Acq:** Purchase, Trade-in, Duplication License. **Dist:** National Geographic Society.

Animals That Fly 1961
The wings and motion of insects, birds, and bats are studied in flight. 11m; VHS, 3/4 U. **Pr:** BFA Educational Media. **A:** Primary-Sr. High. **P:** Education. **U:** Institution, SURA. **Gen-Edu:** Animals. **Acq:** Purchase. **Dist:** Phoenix Learning Group.

Animals That Live in Groups 1989
Focuses on animals who travel in packs and their banding ways of survival. 15m; VHS. **A:** Preschool-Primary. **P:** Education. **U:** Institution. **Gen-Edu:** Animals. **Acq:** Purchase. **Dist:** National Geographic Society. $80.

Animals That Live in the City 1988
Travels the city in search of wild animals and finds raccoons, pigeons, ducks, squirrels and more. 15m; VHS. **A:** Preschool-Primary. **P:** Education. **U:** Institution. **Gen-Edu:** Animals. **Acq:** Purchase. **Dist:** National Geographic Society. $80.

Animals Useful to Man 1960
Shows how animals have played an important role as a source of food, clothing, and work power in the history of civilization. 11m; VHS, 3/4 U. **Pr:** Encyclopedia Britannica Educational

Corporation. **A:** Primary. **P:** Education. **U:** Institution, SURA. **Gen-Edu:** Animals. **Acq:** Purchase, Rent/Lease, Trade-in. **Dist:** Encyclopedia Britannica.

Animals: Ways They Eat 1956
Illustrates the use of specially adapted body parts which enable various animals to catch and eat food. 11m; VHS, 3/4 U. **Pr:** Encyclopedia Britannica Educational Corporation. **A:** Primary. **P:** Education. **U:** Institution, SURA. **Hea-Sci:** Animals. **Acq:** Purchase, Rent/Lease, Trade-in. **Dist:** Encyclopedia Britannica.

Animals: Ways They Move 1956
Pictures the different means of movement by animals: running, hopping, crawling, climbing, swimming, gliding, and flying. 11m; VHS, 3/4 U. **Pr:** Encyclopedia Britannica Educational Corporation. **A:** Primary. **P:** Education. **U:** Institution, SURA. **Hea-Sci:** Animals. **Acq:** Purchase, Rent/Lease, Trade-in. **Dist:** Encyclopedia Britannica.

Animalympics 1979
Children from ages 5 to 12 will enjoy seeing animals compete in traditional Olympic events. 30m; VHS. **C:** Voice(s) by Gilda Radner; Billy Crystal; Harry Shearer; Michael Fremer; Directed by Steven Lisberger. **Pr:** Family Home Entertainment. **A:** Primary-Jr. High. **P:** Entertainment. **U:** Home. **Chl-Juv:** Animation & Cartoons, Sports--General, Animals. **Acq:** Purchase. **Dist:** Lions Gate Television Corp. $14.95.

Animaniacs: Volume 1 2006 (Unrated)
Presents the 1993-1998 animated television children's series about a wide-ranging cast of kooky characters—too kooky for TV—including the "original" Warner brothers, Yakko and Wakko, and their sister Dot. 25 episodes. 550m; DVD. **C:** Voice(s) by Tress MacNeille; Rob Paulsen; Jess Harnell. **A:** Primary. **P:** Entertainment. **U:** Home. **Chl-Juv:** Television Series, Animation & Cartoons, Children's Shows. **Acq:** Purchase. **Dist:** Warner Home Video, Inc. $44.98.

Animaniacs: Volume 2 2006 (Unrated)
Presents the 1993-1998 animated television children's series about a wide-ranging cast of kooky characters—too kooky for TV—including the "original" Warner brothers, Yakko and Wakko, and their sister Dot. 25 episodes. 531m; DVD. **C:** Voice(s) by Tress MacNeille; Rob Paulsen; Jess Harnell. **A:** Primary. **P:** Entertainment. **U:** Home. **Chl-Juv:** Television Series, Animation & Cartoons, Children's Shows. **Acq:** Purchase. **Dist:** Warner Home Video, Inc. $44.98.

Animaniacs: Volume 3 2006 (Unrated)
Presents the 1993-1998 animated television children's series about a wide-ranging cast of kooky characters—too kooky for TV—including the "original" Warner brothers, Yakko and Wakko, and their sister Dot. 25 episodes. 750m; DVD. **C:** Tress MacNeille; Rob Paulsen; Jess Harnell. **A:** Primary. **P:** Entertainment. **U:** Home. **Chl-Juv:** Television Series, Animation & Cartoons, Children's Shows. **Acq:** Purchase. **Dist:** Warner Home Video, Inc. $44.98.

The Animated Almanac 19??
Brief overview of general almanacs and how to use them, including indices, read and use tables, headings, and captions. Also introduces how almanacs are created. Includes teacher's guide and skill sheets. 18m; VHS. **A:** Primary. **P:** Education. **U:** Institution. **Gen-Edu:** Education. **Acq:** Purchase. **Dist:** Clear Vue Inc. $79.00.

The Animated Atlas 19??
Animated tool to help youngsters understand the contents of an atlas and how to use it, including locating and decoding information, identifying and reading maps, and use indices and coordinates. Includes teacher's guide and skill sheets. 18m; VHS. **A:** Primary. **P:** Education. **U:** Institution. **Gen-Edu:** Animation & Cartoons, Education. **Acq:** Purchase. **Dist:** Clear Vue Inc. $79.00.

Animated Atlas: Expansion West and the Mexican War 2000
Explains the fight between the United States and Mexico over Texas using animated maps and period artwork. Briefly discusses history of Latin American and the Texas Revolution. Appropriate for Grades 5-12. 30m; VHS. **A:** Primary-Sr. High. **P:** Education. **U:** Institution. **Gen-Edu:** History--U.S., Mexico. **Acq:** Purchase. **Dist:** Social Studies School Service; Zenger Media. $69.95.

An Animated Atlas of the World 197?
"Rocky"-like strongman Atlas takes us on a worldwide trip to explore many different geographies and weather patterns. 8m; VHS, 3/4 U, EJ, Special order formats. **TV Std:** NTSC, PAL, SECAM. **Pr:** Disney Educational Productions. **A:** Primary-Jr. High. **P:** Education. **U:** Institution, CCTV, SURA. **Chl-Juv:** Geography, Animation & Cartoons. **Acq:** Purchase, Rent/ Lease. **Dist:** Phoenix Learning Group; Disney Educational Productions. $165.00.

Animated Atlas: The Revolutionary War 1999
Video world map shows the movements and battlefields of armies and fleets during the conflict between France and England. Physical relief map of North America shows the war's campaigns for its territories. For Grades 5-12. 20m; VHS. **A:** Primary-Sr. High. **P:** Education. **U:** Institution. **Gen-Edu:** Revolutionary War, History. **Acq:** Purchase. **Dist:** Social Studies School Service; Zenger Media. $69.95.

The Animated Dictionary 1992
Four claymation dictionaries (a general dictionary, an unabridged dicitonary, a thesaurus, and a biographicl dictionary) teach a boy the fundamentals of using their helpful resources. Although the presentation does explain basics of dictionary usage, the claymations' pontification detracts from its primary focus. Includes teacher's guide and skill sheets. 21m; VHS. **A:**

Primary. **P:** Education. **U:** Institution. **Gen-Edu:** Education. **Acq:** Purchase. **Dist:** Clear Vue Inc. $79.00.

The Animated Encyclopedia 19??
Overview of how to use the encyclopedia, including guide words, indices, pictures, maps, graphs, charts, headings and subheadings, cross-referencing, and study aids. Comes with skill sheets and guide. 18m; VHS. **A:** Primary. **P:** Education. **U:** Institution. **Gen-Edu:** Animation & Cartoons, Education. **Acq:** Purchase. **Dist:** Clear Vue Inc. $79.00.

Animated Hero Classics: Alexander Graham Bell 1995
Presents an animated portrait of the life and accomplishments of Alexander Graham Bell. 30m; VHS; Closed Captioned. **A:** Primary-Jr. High. **P:** Education. **U:** Home, Institution. **L:** Spanish. **Chl-Juv:** Biography, History--U.S., Inventors & Inventions. **Acq:** Purchase. **Dist:** Library Video Inc. $29.95.

Animated Hero Classics: Benjamin Franklin: Scientist & Inventor 1993
Presents an animated portrait of the life and accomplishments of Ben Franklin including his work with electricity and his involvement in publishing. 30m; VHS; Closed Captioned. **A:** Primary-Jr. High. **P:** Education. **U:** Home, Institution. **L:** Spanish. **Chl-Juv:** Biography, History--U.S., Inventors & Inventions. **Acq:** Purchase. **Dist:** Library Video Inc. $29.95.

Animated Hero Classics: Christopher Columbus 1991
Chronicles how Columbus persuaded Queen Isabella of Spain to support his quest of the new world. 30m; VHS; Closed Captioned. **A:** Primary-Jr. High. **P:** Education. **U:** Home, Institution. **L:** Spanish. **Chl-Juv:** Biography, History--U.S., Explorers. **Acq:** Purchase. **Dist:** Library Video Inc. $29.95.

Animated Hero Classics: Florence Nightingale 1993
Presents an animated portrait of the life and accomplishments of Florence Nightingale who helped injured soldiers during the Crimean War and made a profound effect on the science and practice of nursing. 30m; VHS; Closed Captioned. **A:** Primary-Jr. High. **P:** Education. **U:** Home, Institution. **L:** Spanish. **Chl-Juv:** Biography, History, Nursing. **Acq:** Purchase. **Dist:** Library Video Inc. $29.95.

Animated Hero Classics: Galileo 1997
Presents an animated portrait of the life and accomplishments of 16th century Italian astronomer Galileo. 30m; VHS; Closed Captioned. **A:** Primary-Jr. High. **P:** Education. **U:** Home, Institution. **L:** Spanish. **Chl-Juv:** Biography, Astronomy, Scientists. **Acq:** Purchase. **Dist:** Library Video Inc. $29.95.

Animated Hero Classics: General George Washington 1992
Presents an animated portrait of the life and military accomplishments of General George Washington. 30m; VHS; Closed Captioned. **A:** Primary-Jr. High. **P:** Education. **U:** Home, Institution. **L:** Spanish. **Chl-Juv:** Biography, History--U.S., Military History. **Acq:** Purchase. **Dist:** Library Video Inc. $29.95.

Animated Hero Classics: Harriet Tubman 1996
Presents an animated portrait of the life and accomplishments of Harriet Tubman, known for helping over 300 slaves escape to the North from 1849 to 1860 using the Underground Railroad. 30m; VHS; Closed Captioned. **A:** Primary-Jr. High. **P:** Education. **U:** Home, Institution. **L:** Spanish. **Chl-Juv:** Biography, History--U.S., Slavery. **Acq:** Purchase. **Dist:** Library Video Inc. $29.95.

Animated Hero Classics: Helen Keller 1996
Chronicles the communication challenges Helen Keller faced due to her being rendered deaf and blind by a childhood illness. 30m; VHS; Closed Captioned. **A:** Primary-Jr. High. **P:** Education. **U:** Home, Institution. **L:** Spanish. **Chl-Juv:** Biography, History--U.S. **Acq:** Purchase. **Dist:** Library Video Inc. $29.95.

Animated Hero Classics: Joan of Arc 1996
Presents an animated portrait of the life and accomplishments of Joan of Arc who rose from anonymity to guide her French countrymen to victory over the English in 1429. 30m; VHS; Closed Captioned. **A:** Primary-Jr. High. **P:** Education. **U:** Home, Institution. **L:** Spanish. **Chl-Juv:** Biography, History, Military History. **Acq:** Purchase. **Dist:** Library Video Inc. $29.95.

Animated Hero Classics: Leonardo da Vinci 1996
Presents an animated portrait of the life and accomplishments of Leonardo da Vinci a master painter and scientist. 30m; VHS; Closed Captioned. **A:** Primary-Jr. High. **P:** Education. **U:** Home, Institution. **L:** Spanish. **Chl-Juv:** Biography, Art & Artists, History. **Acq:** Purchase. **Dist:** Library Video Inc. $29.95.

Animated Hero Classics: Louis Pasteur 1995
Presents an animated portrait of the life and accomplishments of Louis Pasteur known for solving some of the greatest medical mysteries of all time. 30m; VHS; Closed Captioned. **A:** Primary-Jr. High. **P:** Education. **U:** Home, Institution. **L:** Spanish. **Chl-Juv:** Biography, Scientists, History. **Acq:** Purchase. **Dist:** Library Video Inc. $29.95.

Animated Hero Classics: Maccabees: The Story of Hanukkah 1995
Chronicles the origins of the celebration of Hanukkah in second century B.C. Palestine. 30m; VHS; Closed Captioned. **A:** Primary-Jr. High. **P:** Education. **U:** Home, Institution. **L:** Spanish. **Chl-Juv:** Judaism, Religion. **Acq:** Purchase. **Dist:** Library Video Inc. $29.95.

Animated Hero Classics: Marco Polo 1997
Presents an animated portrait of the life and accomplishments of Marco Polo who traveled throughout Asia and helped open

new worlds for contemporaries in Europe. 30m; VHS; Closed Captioned. **A:** Primary-Jr. High. **P:** Education. **U:** Home, Institution. **L:** Spanish. **Chl-Juv:** Biography, History. **Acq:** Purchase. **Dist:** Library Video Inc. $29.95.

Animated Hero Classics: Marie Curie 1997
Presents an animated portrait of the life and accomplishments of Marie Curie, known for her work with radium and plutonium. 30m; VHS; Closed Captioned. **A:** Primary-Jr. High. **P:** Education. **U:** Home, Institution. **L:** Spanish. **Chl-Juv:** Biography, Scientists, History. **Acq:** Purchase. **Dist:** Library Video Inc. $29.95.

Animated Hero Classics: Pocahontas 1995
Presents an animated portrait of the life and accomplishments of Pocahontas who helped the English settlers at Jamestown and promoted a peaceful interchange between two very different cultures in early America. 30m; VHS; Closed Captioned. **A:** Primary-Jr. High. **P:** Education. **U:** Home, Institution. **L:** Spanish. **Chl-Juv:** Biography, History--U.S. **Acq:** Purchase. **Dist:** Library Video Inc. $29.95.

Animated Hero Classics: President Abraham Lincoln 1993
Presents an animated portrait of the life and accomplishments of Abraham Lincoln from Civil War days to his assassination by John Wilkes Booth. 30m; VHS; Closed Captioned. **A:** Primary-Jr. High. **P:** Education. **U:** Home, Institution. **L:** Spanish. **Chl-Juv:** Biography, History--U.S., Presidency. **Acq:** Purchase. **Dist:** Library Video Inc. $29.95.

Animated Hero Classics: The Wright Brothers 1996
Presents an animated portrait of the life and accomplishments of Orville and Wilbur Wright who followed their dream of making powered flight possible. 30m; VHS; Closed Captioned. **A:** Primary-Jr. High. **P:** Education. **U:** Home, Institution. **L:** Spanish. **Chl-Juv:** Biography, History--U.S., Inventors & Inventions. **Acq:** Purchase. **Dist:** Library Video Inc. $29.95.

Animated Hero Classics: Thomas Edison and the Electric Light 1993
Presents an animated portrait of the life and accomplishments of Thomas Edison best known for inventing the electric lightbulb. 30m; VHS; Closed Captioned. **A:** Primary-Jr. High. **P:** Education. **U:** Home, Institution. **L:** Spanish. **Chl-Juv:** Biography, Inventors & Inventions, History--U.S. **Acq:** Purchase. **Dist:** Library Video Inc. $29.95.

Animated Hero Classics: William Bradford: The First Thanksgiving 1992
Chronicles the Mayflower crossing and the friendship William Bradford and the Pilgrims made with the Native Americans. 30m; VHS; Closed Captioned. **A:** Primary-Jr. High. **P:** Education. **U:** Home, Institution. **L:** Spanish. **Chl-Juv:** History--U.S., Holidays. **Acq:** Purchase. **Dist:** Library Video Inc. $29.95.

Animated Motion: Part 1 19??
First of the five-part series which deals with various aspects of animated motion by showing a disc travelling in one move from A to B, and then progressively moving at slower tempos. 9m; VHS. **Pr:** National Film Board of Canada. **A:** Jr. High-Adult. **P:** Education. **U:** Institution. **Gen-Edu:** Animation & Cartoons, How-To. **Acq:** Purchase. **Dist:** National Film Board of Canada.

Animated Motion: Part 2 19??
Second part of the five-part series which teaches different aspects associated with animated motion. This section discusses three of the five categories of motion: constant, accelerated, and decelerated. Provides examples of acceleration and deceleration and explains how these types of motions may be applied in regard to gesture, gravity, and perspective. 8m; VHS. **Pr:** National Film Board of Canada. **A:** Jr. High-Adult. **P:** Education. **U:** Institution. **Gen-Edu:** Animation & Cartoons, How-To. **Acq:** Purchase. **Dist:** National Film Board of Canada.

Animated Motion: Part 3 19??
Third part of the five-part series which covers various aspects of motion and how it can be used in animation. Covers zero motion and irregular motion and demonstrates how both these types of motions can be applied in the creation of animation. 10m; VHS. **Pr:** National Film Board of Canada. **A:** Jr. High-Adult. **P:** Education. **U:** Institution. **Gen-Edu:** Animation & Cartoons, How-To. **Acq:** Purchase. **Dist:** Xenon Pictures Inc.

Animated Motion: Part 4 19??
Fourth part of the five-part series which teaches the use of motion in animation. Explains composite motion, where two or more different types of motion are occurring at the same time. Includes information on human gesturing in animation and also the action of animation known as strobing. 7m; VHS. **Pr:** National Film Board of Canada. **A:** Jr. High-Adult. **P:** Education. **U:** Institution. **Gen-Edu:** Animation & Cartoons, How-To. **Acq:** Purchase. **Dist:** National Film Board of Canada.

Animated Motion: Part 5 19??
Final part of the five-part series which deals with the use of different types of motion in animation. Deals with the use of change, paying special attention to the amount and color of light used in an otherwise static screen. 7m; VHS. **Pr:** National Film Board of Canada. **A:** Jr. High-Adult. **P:** Education. **U:** Institution. **Gen-Edu:** Animation & Cartoons, How-To. **Acq:** Purchase. **Dist:** National Film Board of Canada.

Animated Musical Stories & Songs 4 Kids in 3 Dimensions 1993
Computer animated rhymes and stories set to original music. 31m; VHS. **A:** Primary. **P:** Entertainment. **U:** Home. **Chl-Juv:** Animation & Cartoons, Music--Children. **Acq:** Purchase. **Dist:** M3D Studios, Inc. $14.95.

Animated Science Collection ????
Educational Collection concentrates on environmental themes such as evolving earth, weather, life cycle in plants, and recycling. 40m; VHS; Closed Captioned. **A:** Primary. **P:** Education. **U:** Institution. **Chl-Juv:** Science, Education. **Acq:** Purchase. **Dist:** Disney Educational Productions. $299.00.
Indiv. Titles: 1. Harold and His Amazing Green Plants 2. Winnie the Pooh Discovers the Seasons 3. Recycle Rex 4. Animated Earth: Forces That Shape Our Planet.

Animation: Basic Camera Techniques 19??
Teaching aid for art education introduces and demonstrates the basic principles of animation and discusses career opportunities in animation. 20m; VHS. **A:** Jr. High-College. **P:** Education. **U:** Institution. **Gen-Edu:** Art & Artists, Animation & Cartoons. **Acq:** Purchase. **Dist:** Crystal Productions. $24.95.

Animation Celebration, Vol. 1 1991
Twenty-three animated titles from many of today's up-and-coming artists. Features the Academy Award-nominee "Second Class Mail," Osamu Tequka's "Broken Down Film," Paul Vester's "Sunbeam," Sally Cruikshank's "Quasi's Cabaret Trailer," George Griffin's "It's an OK Life," Jane Aaron's "Traveling Light," Brett Koth's "Happy Hour," Stephen Weston's "Wreck of the Julie Plante," and more. 90m; VHS. **Pr:** Expanded Entertainment. **A:** Family. **P:** Entertainment. **U:** Home. **Mov-Ent:** Animation & Cartoons. **Acq:** Purchase. **Dist:** Tapeworm Video Distributors Inc. $39.95.

Animation Celebration, Vol. 2 1992
A collection of 18 videos from animators worldwide, including Bulgaria, Hungary, Cuba, Italy, and the U.S. ?m; VHS. **A:** College-Adult. **P:** Entertainment. **U:** Home. **Mov-Ent:** Animation & Cartoons. **Acq:** Purchase. **Dist:** Tapeworm Video Distributors Inc. $39.95.
Indiv. Titles: 1. ASIFA Children's Film 2. Beat Dedication 3. A Crushed World 4. Eternity 5. Finger Wave 6. Goodnight Norma...Goodnight Milton 7. Lady and the Lamp 8. Lazar 9. Paradisia 10. Pencil Dance 11. Propagandance 12. Quinoscopio #2 13. Salome 14. Sature to Olive Jar 15. Scaredy Cat 16. Suspicious Circumstances 17. Quit Smoking 18. Umbabararuma.

Animation Celebration, Vol. 3 1992
Twenty videos from animators worldwide, including Jan Svankmajer, Bruno Bozzetto, and Bill Plympton. ?m; VHS. **A:** College-Adult. **P:** Entertainment. **U:** Home. **Mov-Ent:** Animation & Cartoons. **Acq:** Purchase. **Dist:** Tapeworm Video Distributors Inc. $39.95.
Indiv. Titles: 1. The Animated Star-Spangled Banner 2. Bonehead 3. Darkness, Light, Darkness 4. Fumo 5. Lava, Jr. 6. Mr. Tao 7. New Fangled 8. Nice Day in the Country 9. Personality Software 10. Plymptoons 11. Poumse 12. Prehistoric Beast 13. The Reading Room 14. Snowie and The Seven Dorps 15. Still Life 16. This is Not Frank's Planet 17. War Story 18. Welcome 19. The Wiseman 20. Zeno Reads a Newspaper.

Animation Celebration, Vol. 4 1992
Nineteen animated shorts from Armenia, Bulgaria, the United Kingdom, Italy, Cuba, Holland, the U.S., and other countries. ?m; VHS. **A:** College-Adult. **P:** Entertainment. **U:** Home. **Mov-Ent:** Animation & Cartoons. **Acq:** Purchase. **Dist:** Tapeworm Video Distributors Inc. $39.95.
Indiv. Titles: 1. The Boss 2. The Button 3. Canfilm 4. Dancing 5. Fantastic Person 6. Green Beret 7. The Hunter 8. Madcap 9. Office Space 10. Okay Tex 11. Pre-Hysterical Daze 12. Quinoscopio 13. RRRINGG! 14. A Smaller World "Big Baby" 15. The Song of Wolfgang the Intrepid 16. The Tale of Nippoless Nippleby 17. Tarzan 18. Unsavory Avery 19. Weeds.

Animation for Fallen Catholics 1992
Animation and live action combine in ten short films in this irreverent look at Catholicism. Includes a nun on wheels, whirling Virgins, a priest in purgatory, and more. 60m; VHS. **A:** Sr. High-Adult. **P:** Entertainment. **U:** Home. **Mov-Ent:** Animation & Cartoons, Religion. **Acq:** Purchase. **Dist:** Next Gen Video. $24.95.
Indiv. Titles: 1. Opening Dance 2. Divine Miracle 3. Regina Coeli 4. Heavenly Taste 5. Landscape with Fallen Icarus 6. Intermission Song 7. Alterations 8. Simply Divine 9. Divine Departure 10. Finale Dance.

Animation from Cape Dorset 1989
A collection of short animated sequences designed to introduce northern people to a new and novel form of creative expression. 19m; VHS, 3/4 U. **Pr:** Joanasie Salamonie. **A:** Jr. High-Adult. **P:** Education. **U:** Institution, SURA. **Gen-Edu:** Animation & Cartoons. **Acq:** Purchase, Rent/Lease. **Dist:** National Film Board of Canada.

Animation Games 19??
Presents an overview of animation techniques and ideas, including puppet animation, cutout animation, and pixilation. 51m; VHS. **Pr:** Australian Film, Radio and Television School. **A:** College-Adult. **P:** Education. **U:** Home, Institution. **Gen-Edu:** Animation & Cartoons. **Acq:** Purchase, Rent/Lease. **Dist:** TMW Media Group. $149.

Animation in the Classroom 1997
Teaches students to make objects grow or shrink, vanish or appear, speed up or slow down, and the difference between limited and full animation. 20m; VHS. **A:** Primary-Sr. High. **P:** Education. **U:** Institution. **Fin-Art:** Art & Artists. **Acq:** Purchase. **Dist:** Crystal Productions. $29.95.

Animation in the Netherlands 1990
Take your visual capabilities to the limit as you relax to the incredible animation found in the Netherlands. 30m; VHS. **Pr:** Expanded Entertainment. **A:** Family. **P:** Entertainment. **U:** Home. **Mov-Ent:** Animation & Cartoons. **Acq:** Purchase. **Dist:** Tapeworm Video Distributors Inc. $39.95.

Animation Legend: Winsor McCay 1993
All the surviving films of pioneer turn-of-the-century cartoonist and animator McCay, the creator of Little Nemo and Gertie the Dinosaur. 100m; VHS, DVD. **A:** Sr. High-Adult. **P:** Entertainment. **U:** Home. **Mov-Ent:** Animation & Cartoons. **Acq:** Purchase. **Dist:** Milestone Film & Video; Baker and Taylor. $39.95.
Indiv. Titles: 1. Little Nemo (1911) 2. A Mosquito Operates (1912) 3. Gertie the Dinosaur (1914) 4. The Sinking of the Lusitania (1918) 5. Bug Vaudeville (1921) 6. The Pet (1921) 7. The Flying House (1921) 8. Gertie On Tour 9. The Centaurs 10. Flip's Circus.

Animation of the Apocalypse 1991
A compilation of animated features dealing with death and destruction. Features "Loop of Doom," where toy soldiers are exposed to the horrors of the Vietnam war. 60m; VHS. **A:** College-Adult. **P:** Entertainment. **U:** Home. **Mov-Ent:** Animation & Cartoons, Death, Filmmaking. **Acq:** Purchase. **Dist:** Next Gen Video; Facets Multimedia Inc.; Tapeworm Video Distributors Inc. $29.95.

Animation—Animation 1987
Three animated shorts have been compiled on this tape: "The Unicycle Race," "Ink, Paint, Scratch" and "Kick Me." 30m; VHS, 3/4 U. **A:** Primary-Jr. High. **P:** Entertainment. **U:** Institution, SURA. **Gen-Edu:** Animation & Cartoons. **Acq:** Purchase, Trade-in. **Dist:** Encyclopedia Britannica. $300.00.

Animaux du Monde 19??
Aimed at helping the beginning French student improve their vocabulary with the use of the animals of the world. 18m; VHS. **A:** Adult. **P:** Instruction. **U:** Institution. **L:** French. **How-Ins:** Language Arts, France. **Acq:** Purchase. **Dist:** Educational Video Network. $49.95.

Animorphs Part 3: The Enemy Among Us 1999
Follows the animated adventures of Jake, Rachel, Marco, Cassie and Tobias, teens with the ability to morph into any animal they touch, as they battle the evil Yeerk's plans to take over the world. This volume contains the episodes "The Stranger," "The Leader Part 1," and "The Leader Part 2." 74m; VHS. **A:** Family. **P:** Entertainment. **U:** Home. **Chl-Juv:** Animation & Cartoons. **Acq:** Purchase. **Dist:** Sony Pictures Home Entertainment Inc. $12.95.

Animorphs Part 4: The Legacy Survives 1999
Follows the animated adventures of Jake, Rachel, Marco, Cassie and Tobias, teens with the ability to morph into any animal they touch, as they battle the evil Yeerk's plans to take over the world. This volume contains the episodes "Not My Problem," "The Capture: Part 1," and "The Capture: Part 2." 74m; VHS. **A:** Family. **P:** Entertainment. **U:** Home. **Chl-Juv:** Animation & Cartoons. **Acq:** Purchase. **Dist:** Sony Pictures Home Entertainment Inc. $12.95.

Animorphs—Part 1: The Invasion Begins 1998
Relates the adventures of five teenagers on a mission to save the world from an alien invasion. Empowered with the ability to transform themselves into any animal they touch, these five young heroes must use their brains and newly acquired abilities to outsmart the evil aliens known as Yeerks. Contains three uncut episodes: "My Name Is Jake: Part 1," "My Name Is Jake: Part 2" and "The Underground." 79m; VHS. **A:** Family. **P:** Entertainment. **U:** Home. **Chl-Juv:** Animals, Animation & Cartoons. **Acq:** Purchase. **Dist:** Sony Pictures Home Entertainment Inc. $14.95.

Animotion: Video EP 1986
This energetic video features songs from their debut and follow-up albums such as "I Engineer," "I Want You" and "Obsession." 24m; VHS. **Pr:** Sony Video. **A:** Sr. High-Adult. **P:** Entertainment. **U:** Home. **Mov-Ent:** Music Video. **Acq:** Purchase. **Dist:** Music Video Distributors.

Anita 2014 (Unrated) — ★★
Director Mock's documentary is a riveting reminder of the story that shook the world over 20 years ago when Anita Hill accused Supreme Court nominee Clarence Thomas of sexual harassment. In detailed testimony not really publicly available in the early '90s, she speaks openly in front of a Senate committee about horrendous behavior in a sexist environment. While Hill disappeared from the public spotlight after the testimony, painted by too many as a liar, her case had an amazing impact on workplace restrictions. She returns for the first time in 22 years to discuss what happened then and how she dealt with the fallout. 91m; DVD. **C:** Anita Hill; Directed by Frieda Lee Mock; Written by Frieda Lee Mock; Cinematography by Bestor Cram; Don Lenzer; Music by Lili Haydn. **Pr:** Frieda Lee Mock; Samuel Goldwyn Films. **A:** Adult. **P:** Entertainment. **U:** Home. **L:** English. **Mov-Ent:** Documentary Films, Politics & Government, Supreme Court. **Acq:** Purchase.

Anita Baker: One Night of Rapture 1987
The Grammy-winning singer performs "Mystery," "You've Changed," "Sweet Love," "Caught Up in the Rapture," "Been So Long," "No One in the World," "Watch Your Step," "You Bring Me Joy," and "Same Ole Love." 46m; VHS. **Pr:** Warner Reprise Video. **A:** Jr. High-Adult. **P:** Entertainment. **U:** Home. **Mov-Ent:** Music Video. **Acq:** Purchase. **Dist:** Music Video Distributors. $19.98.

Anita, Dances of Vice 1987 (Unrated) — ★★
German avant-garde film celebrates Anita Berber, the "most scandalous woman in 1920s Berlin." Berber was openly bisexual, used drugs, and danced nude in public. In von Praunheim's film, she rises from the dead and creates yet more scandal. 85m; VHS, 3/4 U. **C:** Lotti Huber; Ina Blum; Mikhael Honesseau; Directed by Rosa von Praunheim. **Pr:** Rosa von

Praunheim. **A:** Sr. High-Adult. **P:** Entertainment. **U:** Institution, SURA. **Mov-Ent:** Film--Avant-Garde, Biography. **Acq:** Purchase. **Dist:** First Run Features; German Language Video Center; Tapeworm Video Distributors Inc. $49.95.

Anita O'Day: Live at Ronnie Scotts 1987
The jazz great plays her best live in the small venue. 56m; VHS. **A:** College-Adult. **P:** Entertainment. **U:** Home. **Mov-Ent:** Music--Performance, Music--Jazz. **Acq:** Purchase. **Dist:** Music Video Distributors. $19.95.

Anja Schreiner's Lower Body Workout 1991
The fitness expert demonstrates her personal routine, using both circuit-training and free weights to tone the lower body. 30m; VHS. **Pr:** ESPN. **A:** Sr. High-Adult. **P:** Instruction. **U:** Home. **Hea-Sci:** Fitness/Exercise, Weight Lifting. **Acq:** Purchase. **Dist:** ESPN Inc.; Fast Forward. $9.95.

Anja Schreiner's Upper Body Workout 1991
The fitness expert demonstrates her personal method to tone the chest, shoulders and arms through a system of circuit training and free weights. 30m; VHS. **Pr:** ESPN. **A:** Sr. High-Adult. **P:** Instruction. **U:** Home. **Hea-Sci:** Fitness/Exercise. **Acq:** Purchase. **Dist:** ESPN Inc.; Fast Forward. $9.95.

The Ann Jillian Story 1988 (Unrated) — ★1/2
Jillian stars as herself in this melodrama recounting her battle with breast cancer. Several musical numbers are included. 96m; VHS, Streaming. **C:** Ann Jillian; Tony LoBianco; Viveca Lindfors; Leighton Bewley; Directed by Corey Allen. **Pr:** 9J Inc; ITC Entertainment Group. **A:** Family. **P:** Entertainment. **U:** Home. **Mov-Ent:** Biography: Show Business, Autobiography, Diseases. **Acq:** Purchase. **Dist:** Lions Gate Entertainment Inc.

Ann Marie Series 1980
Ann Marie, a popular ventriloquist, and her dummy Jackie illustrate how each person can use his God-given talents to do what God wants him to do, in these four programs, each available individually. 12m; VHS, 3/4 U. **C:** Ann Marie. **Pr:** Broadman. **A:** Family. **P:** Religious. **U:** Institution, CCTV. **Gen-Edu:** Religion, Self-Help. **Acq:** Purchase. **Dist:** Broadman & Holman Publishers.
Indiv. Titles: 1. God Can Use Me 2. God Has a Plan 3. In Tune with God 4. Who Is Pulling Your Strings.

Ann Rule Presents: The Stranger Beside Me 2003 (Unrated) — ★★
Crime writer Ann Rule (Hershey) is working at a Seattle crisis center in 1971 alongside charming volunteer Ted Bundy (Campbell). When Bundy comes under suspicion as a serial killer, Rule has trouble believing the accusations—until the truth comes out. Based on Rule's 1983 nonfiction bestseller about Bundy. 88m; DVD. **C:** Barbara Hershey; Billy Campbell; Kevin Dunn; Jay Brazeau; Benjamin Ratner; Matthew Bennett; Suki Kaiser; Directed by Paul Shapiro; Written by Matthew McDuffie; Matthew Tabak; Cinematography by Ronald Orieux; Music by Joseph Conlan. **A:** Jr. High-Adult. **P:** Entertainment. **U:** Home. **Mov-Ent:** TV Movies. **Acq:** Purchase. **Dist:** Echo Bridge Home Entertainment.

Ann Vickers 1933 (Unrated) — ★★1/2
A dashing young army captain wins over the heart of a dedicated social worker. Okay adaptation of a Sinclair Lewis novel, with Dunne suffering more than usual. 76m/B/W; VHS. **C:** Irene Dunne; Walter Huston; Bruce Cabot; Conrad Nagel; Edna May Oliver; Directed by John Cromwell; Music by Max Steiner. **Pr:** RKO. **A:** Family. **P:** Entertainment. **U:** Home. **Mov-Ent:** Drama. **Acq:** Purchase. **Dist:** Turner Broadcasting System Inc. $19.98.

Anna 1951 — ★★
Novitiate nun Anna (Mangano) is forced to confront her sordid past (as a nightclub entertainer), and her love for two very different men, when her seriously injured former fiancee is brought to the hospital where she is a nurse. Anna must finally deal with her feelings and decide which path her life will take. Dubbed in English. 111m/B/W; VHS. **C:** Silvana Mangano; Raf Vallone; Vittorio Gassman; Directed by Alberto Lattuada; Cinematography by Otello Martelli; Music by Nino Rota. **A:** College-Adult. **P:** Entertainment. **U:** Home. **Mov-Ent:** Drama, Religion. **Acq:** Purchase. **Dist:** Facets Multimedia Inc. $29.95.

Anna 1987 (PG-13) — ★★★
Age, envy, and the theatrical world receive their due in an uneven but engrossing drama about aging Czech film star Anna, making a sad living in New York doing commercials and trying for off-Broadway roles. She takes in Krystyna, a young Czech peasant girl who eventually rockets to model stardom. Modern, strongly acted "All About Eve" with a story partially based on a real Polish actress. Kirkland drew quite a bit of flak for shamelessly self-promoting for the Oscar. She still lost. 101m; VHS, DVD, CC. **C:** Sally Kirkland; Paulina Porizkova; Robert Fields; Stefan Schnabel; Larry Pine; Ruth Maleczech; Directed by Yurek Bogayevicz; Written by Yurek Bogayevicz; Agnieszka Holland; Cinematography by Bobby Bukowski; Music by Greg Hawkes. **Pr:** Vestron Pictures; Magnus Films. **A:** Jr. High-Adult. **P:** Entertainment. **U:** Home. **Mov-Ent:** Women, Aging. **Awds:** Golden Globes '88: Actress--Drama (Kirkland); Ind. Spirit '88: Actress (Kirkland); L.A. Film Critics '87: Actress (Kirkland). **Acq:** Purchase. **Dist:** Lions Gate Television Corp. $79.98.

Anna 1993 (Unrated) — ★★★1/2
Director Nikhalkov follows Russian history from the early 1980s through the early 1990s by following the development of his daughter during these years. He does this by annually asking her a series of questions about her views, likes, loves, hates, and outlook. Effectively paints a portrait of a country and a person experiencing life and the accompanying growing pains and triumphs. 99m; VHS. **C:** Nikita Mikhalkov; Nadia Mikhalkov; Anna Mikhalkov; Directed by Nikita Mikhalkov; Written by Nikita Mikhalkov; Cinematography by Pavel Lebeshev; Vadim Yusov; Music by Eduard Artemyev. **A:** Jr. High-Adult. **P:** Entertainment. **U:** Home. **L:** Russian. **Mov-Ent:** Documentary Films, USSR. **Acq:** Purchase. **Dist:** New Yorker Video.

The Anna Akhmatova File 1989
Documentary of Soviet poet Akhmatova, whose work, though banned for 17 years, became an underground rallying point for Russians victimized by Stalin. Film utilizes her diaries as a script. In Russian with English subtitles. 65m; VHS. **C:** Directed by Simeon Aranovitch. **A:** Family. **P:** Education. **U:** Home. **L:** Russian, English. **Gen-Edu:** USSR, Documentary Films. **Acq:** Purchase. **Dist:** Facets Multimedia Inc.; The Video Project. $39.95.

Anna and Bella 1986 (Unrated)
Two elderly sisters spend an afternoon pouring over the family photo album. 8m; VHS, 3/4 U. **Pr:** Ring Borge. **A:** Primary-Adult. **P:** Entertainment. **U:** Institution, SURA. **Mov-Ent:** Animation & Cartoons. **Acq:** Purchase, Rent/Lease. **Dist:** Direct Cinema Ltd. $150.00.

Anna and Poppy 1976
Sensitive treatment of a young girl's first experience with death. Theme: a life shared in love gives meaning and hope to death. 13m; VHS, 3/4 U, Special order formats. **Pr:** Paulist Productions. **A:** Primary. **P:** Religious. **U:** Institution, CCTV, SURA. **Chl-Juv:** Death. **Acq:** Purchase, Rent/Lease. **Dist:** Paulist Productions.

Anna and the King 1999 (PG-13) — ★★1/2
Based on the story of English widow and schoolteacher Anna Leonowens (Foster) who, in 1862, is hired by the King Mongkut of Siam (Yun-Fat) to introduce his 58 children to the ideas of the West. The film looks stunning (it was filmed in Malaysia) and Yun-Fat is regal and charismatic but Foster is too stiff upper-lipped and remote and there's respect rather than any hint of romance. Previously filmed as 1946's "Anna and the King of Siam" and the 1956 musical "The King and I." 147m; VHS, DVD, Wide, CC. **C:** Jodie Foster; Chow Yun-Fat; Bai Ling; Tom Felton; Syed Alwi; Directed by Andy Tennant; Written by Steve Meerson; Peter Krikes; Cinematography by Caleb Deschanel; Music by George Fenton. **Pr:** Lawrence Bender; Fox 2000 Pictures; 20th Century-Fox. **A:** Jr. High-Adult. **P:** Entertainment. **U:** Home. **Mov-Ent:** Asia. **Acq:** Purchase. **Dist:** Fox Home Entertainment.

Anna and the King of Siam 1946 — ★★★1/2
Splendid adaptation, from the book by Margaret Landon, about the true life adventures of 33-year-old English widow Anna Leonowens. In 1862 Anna and her son travelled to the exotic kingdom of Siam to educate the harem and children of the king. Dunne is splendid as the strong-willed governess as is Harrison (in his first American film) as the authoritarian eastern ruler. Remade as the musical "The King and I." 128m/B/W; VHS, DVD. **C:** Irene Dunne; Rex Harrison; Linda Darnell; Lee J. Cobb; Gale Sondergaard; Mikhail Rasumny; Dennis Hoey; Richard Lyon; John Abbott; Directed by John Cromwell; Written by Sally Benson; Talbot Jennings; Cinematography by Arthur C. Miller; Music by Bernard Herrmann. **Pr:** Louis D. Lighton; 20th Century-Fox. **A:** Jr. High-Adult. **P:** Entertainment. **U:** Home. **Mov-Ent:** Education. **Awds:** Oscars '46: Art Dir./Set Dec., B&W, B&W Cinematog. **Acq:** Purchase. **Dist:** Fox Home Entertainment. $19.98.

Anna Bolena: Donizetti 1969
Features Joan Sutherland singing the role of Anna Bolena in a 1984 production by the Canadian Opera Company. Sung in Italian with English subtitles. 157m; VHS. **A:** Adult. **P:** Entertainment. **U:** Home. **L:** Italian. **Fin-Art:** Music--Classical, Music--Performance. **Acq:** Purchase. **Dist:** Video Artists International. $39.95.

Anna Christie 1923 (Unrated) — ★★★1/2
Silent production of Eugene O'Neill's play that even he liked. A young girl is sent away by her father, a seaman, and finds her way to Chicago, where she becomes a prostitute. Later she visits her father's barge and falls for a sailor. She shares her past life story, hoping they will understand. This film was acclaimed when it was released, and still remains a touching work of art. Remade in 1930. 75m/B/W; Silent; VHS, DVD. **C:** Blanche Sweet; George F. Marion, Sr.; William Russell; Eugenie Besserer; Chester Conklin; George Siegmann; Victor Potel; Fred Kohler, Sr.; Directed by John Griffith Wray. **Pr:** Thomas H. Ince. **A:** Sr. High-Adult. **P:** Entertainment. **U:** Home. **Mov-Ent:** Drama, Prostitution, Silent Films. **Acq:** Purchase. **Dist:** Warner Home Video, Inc.; Grapevine Video; Facets Multimedia Inc. $34.95.

Anna Christie 1930 (Unrated) — ★★1/2
Garbo is the ex-prostitute who finds love with sailor Bickford. Bickford is unaware of his lover's tarnished past and she does her best to keep it that way. Garbo's first sound effort was advertised with the slogan "Garbo Talks." Adapted from the classic Eugene O'Neill play, the film is a slow but rewarding romantic drama. 90m/B/W; VHS, DVD. **C:** Greta Garbo; Marie Dressler; Charles Bickford; George F. Marion, Sr.; Directed by Clarence Brown; Cinematography by William H. Daniels. **Pr:** MGM. **A:** Sr. High-Adult. **P:** Entertainment. **U:** Home. **Mov-Ent:** Comedy--Romantic, Prostitution, Classic Films. **Acq:** Purchase. **Dist:** MGM Home Entertainment. $19.98.

Anna from Benin 2000
17-year-old Anna receives a scholarship to study music in France, a rare opportunity for a girl in Central Africa. Documents her struggles being an independent teenager with a domineering father in Africa and living without the protection of her 30 siblings and 5 mothers in France. Subtitled. 45m; VHS. **A:** Adult. **P:** Education. **U:** Institution, BCTV. **L:** German. **Gen-Edu:** Africa, Adolescence, Family. **Acq:** Purchase, Rent/Lease. **Dist:** Women Make Movies. $195.00.

Anna Karenina 1935 (Unrated) — ★★★1/2
Cinematic Tolstoy with Garbo as sad, moody, married Anna willing to give up everything to be near Vronsky (March), the cavalry officer she's obsessed with. And since it's Russian, expect tragedy. A classic Garbo vehicle with March and Rathbone (as the cuckhold husband) providing excellent support. Interestingly, a remake of the Garbo and John Gilbert silent, "Love." 85m/B/W; VHS, DVD. **C:** Greta Garbo; Fredric March; Freddie Bartholomew; Maureen O'Sullivan; May Robson; Basil Rathbone; Reginald Owen; Reginald Denny; Directed by Clarence Brown; Written by S.N. Behrman; Clemence Dane; Salka Viertel; Cinematography by William H. Daniels; Music by Herbert Stothart. **Pr:** MGM. **A:** Jr. High-Adult. **P:** Entertainment. **U:** Home. **Mov-Ent:** Comedy--Romantic. **Awds:** N.Y. Film Critics '35: Actress (Garbo). **Acq:** Purchase. **Dist:** MGM Home Entertainment. $19.98.

Anna Karenina 1948 — ★★1/2
Stiff version of Tolstoy's passionate story of illicit love between a married woman and a military officer. In spite of exquisite costumes, and Leigh and Richardson as leads, still tedious. 123m; VHS, DVD. **C:** Vivien Leigh; Ralph Richardson; Kieron Moore; Sally Ann Howes; Niall MacGinnis; Martita Hunt; Michael Gough; Directed by Julien Duvivier; Written by Julien Duvivier; Cinematography by Henri Alekan; Music by Constant Lambert. **Pr:** Korda. **A:** Jr. High-Adult. **P:** Entertainment. **U:** Home. **Mov-Ent:** Drama, War--General. **Acq:** Purchase. **Dist:** Facets Multimedia Inc.; Monterey Home Video. $39.95.

Anna Karenina 1985 (PG) — ★★1/2
TV version of Tolstoy's novel of betrayal, intrigue, and forbidden love. Anna, defying all social practices of the time, falls into the arms of a dashing count. Features an excellent performance from Paul "A Man for All Seasons" Scofield. 96m; VHS. **C:** Jacqueline Bisset; Christopher Reeve; Paul Scofield; Ian Ogilvy; Anna Massey; Judi Bowker; Directed by Simon Langton. **A:** Jr. High-Adult. **P:** Entertainment. **U:** Home. **Mov-Ent:** Drama, TV Movies. **Acq:** Purchase. **Dist:** $89.95.

Anna Karenina 1996 (PG-13) — ★★1/2
The third film version of Tolstoy's tempestuous, tragic romance certainly looks good, even if the performances don't engender the passion the story demands. Beautiful Anna (Marceau) leaves stuffy husband Karenin (Fox) to travel to 1880 Moscow and mend the marriage of her philandering brother Stiva (Huston). She meets dashing soldier, Count Alexei Vronsky (Bean), who pursues the beauty, and the two begin an all-encompassing affair, leading to tragedy. This version also includes the secondary, contrasting romance between young Kitty (Kirshner) and Tolstoy's alter ego, aristo Levin (Molina). Filmed on location in St. Petersburg, Russia. 120m; VHS, DVD. **C:** Sophie Marceau; Sean Bean; Alfred Molina; Mia Kirshner; James Fox; Danny Huston; Fiona Shaw; Phyllida Law; David Schofield; Saskia Wickham; Directed by Bernard Rose; Written by Bernard Rose; Cinematography by Daryn Okada. **Pr:** Bruce Davey; Icon Productions; Warner Bros. **A:** Sr. High-Adult. **P:** Entertainment. **U:** Home. **Mov-Ent:** Drama, Marriage. **Acq:** Purchase. **Dist:** Warner Home Video, Inc.

Anna Karenina 2000 — ★★1/2
Well-done British adaptation of the familiar Tolstoy drama although, frankly, Anna (McCrory) is a pill. Less tragic than headstrong, this willful Russian beauty runs from her passionless marriage to Karenin (Dillane) straight into the arms of dashing seducer Vronsky (McKidd). Of course, once they turn each other's lives to misery, what else is left but a tragic end. This version also includes the secondary love affair of Kitty (Baeza) and Levin (Henshall). 240m; VHS, DVD. **C:** Helen McCrory; Kevin McKidd; Stephen (Dillon) Dillane; Douglas Henshall; Paloma Baeza; Amanda Root; Mark Strong; Directed by David Blair; Written by Allan Cubitt; Cinematography by Ryszard Lenczewski; Music by John Keane. **A:** Sr. High-Adult. **P:** Entertainment. **U:** Home. **Mov-Ent:** Drama. **Acq:** Purchase. **Dist:** PBS Home Video.

Anna Karenina 2012 (R) — ★1/2
Director Wright found such creative success with his costume-heavy literary adaptations of "Pride & Prejudice" and "Atonement" that it makes sense that he would try to go for three hits with leading lady Knightley. Sadly, the umpteenth version of Tolstoy's 1877 drama is easily his worst film as his decision to present the entire piece as an elaborate stage play (complete with sets that fly in and visible light rigs) makes an already-cold story even more frigid. Knightley makes it out unscathed but Wright can't save a lot of the supporting cast, including a remarkably bad performance from Taylor-Johnson as Anna's paramour Vronsky. 130m; DVD, Blu-Ray. **C:** Keira Knightley; Jude Law; Aaron Taylor-Johnson; Kelly Macdonald; Matthew MacFadyen; Emily Watson; Olivia Williams; Domhnall Gleeson; Alicia Vikander; Directed by Joe Wright; Written by Tom Stoppard; Cinematography by Seamus McGarvey; Music by Dario Marianelli. **Pr:** Tim Bevan; Paul Webster; Focus Features L.L.C; Universal Pictures; Working Title. **A:** Sr. High-Adult. **P:** Entertainment. **U:** Home. **L:** English. **Mov-Ent:** Marriage, Romance. **Awds:** Oscars '12: Costume Des.; British Acad. '12: Costume Des. **Acq:** Purchase. **Dist:** Universal Studios Home Video.

Anna Karenina: Bolshoi Ballet 1974
The Bolshoi Ballet performs their version of the Tolstoy novel. 81m; VHS. **Pr:** Princeton/Dance Horizons. **A:** Family. **P:** Entertainment. **U:** Institution, Home. **Fin-Art:** Dance--Ballet, Dance--Performance, Dance. **Acq:** Purchase. **Dist:** Kultur International Films Ltd., Inc.; Music Video Distributors; Princeton Book Company Publishers. $29.95.

Anna Kournikova Fitness 2004 (Unrated)
Professional tennis player and model Anna Kournikova demonstrates her all-ages workout designed to help tennis players increase stamina and improve their game. Nonplayers can also benefit from the fitness regime. ??m; DVD. **A:** Jr. High-Adult. **P:** Instruction. **U:** Home. **Hea-Sci:** Fitness/Exercise. **Dist:** Lions Gate Entertainment Inc. $7.98.

Anna Livia: Dublin, a City of Splendor 19??
Outlines the history of Dublin, Ireland. Covers everything from Medieval times up to the modern city of today. Includes rare footage of the city from the 1916-21 period. Hosted by Late, Late Show host Gay Byrne. 73m; VHS. **A:** Family. **P:** Education. **U:** Home. **Gen-Edu:** Documentary Films, Ireland, History. **Acq:** Purchase. **Dist:** Rego Irish Records. $29.95.

Anna Moffo in Opera and Song 1990
Anna Moffo sings arias from "Faust," "Madame Butterfly," "I Pagliacci," "La Boheme" as well as songs by Rodgers & Hammerstein and others. 30m; VHS. **C:** Music by Richard Rodgers; Oscar Hammerstein. **Pr:** Video Artists International. **A:** Family. **P:** Entertainment. **U:** Home. **Fin-Art:** Opera. **Acq:** Purchase. **Dist:** Video Artists International; Facets Multimedia Inc. $19.95.

Anna Moffo in Verdi's La Traviata 1991
Giuseppi Patane conducts the Rome Opera Orchestra and Chorus in this production of Verdi's classic. Anna Moffo and Franco Bonisolli star. 113m; VHS. **C:** Anna Moffo; Franco Bonisolli. **Pr:** VAI. **A:** Jr. High-Adult. **P:** Entertainment. **U:** Home. **Fin-Art:** Opera. **Acq:** Purchase. **Dist:** Video Artists International; Facets Multimedia Inc. $39.95.

Anna Moffo'Bell Telephone Hour Telecasts, 1962-1967 ????
Excerpts from operas performed by soprano Anna Moffo with the Bell Telephone Orchestra and Chorus directed by Donald Voorhees. Includes selections from "La Traviata," "La Boheme," and "Romeo and Juliet." 42m; VHS. **A:** Adult. **P:** Entertainment. **U:** Home. **Fin-Art:** Music--Classical, Music--Performance. **Acq:** Purchase. **Dist:** Video Artists International. $24.95.

Anna Nicole 2013 (Unrated) — ★½
The rags-to-riches tragedy of Anna Nicole Smith (Bruckner) gets a tacky biopic treatment from Lifetime. The small town Texas single mom becomes a buxom blonde with Marilyn Monroe as her idol and dreams of fame that lead to modeling, men, and a prescription drug habit. While working at a strip club, Anna Nicole meets elderly oil tycoon J. Howard Marshall (Landau), who's some 60 years her senior, but a willing sugar daddy to the young woman, whom he marries. His death leads to an ugly court battle with Marshall's family over his money and Anna Nicole's continuing decline. 89m; DVD. **C:** Agnes Bruckner; Martin Landau; Cary Elwes; Adam Goldberg; Virginia Madsen; Directed by Mary Harron; Written by Joe Batteer; John Rice; Cinematography by Michael Simmonds; Music by Zack Ryan. **A:** Sr. High-Adult. **P:** Entertainment. **U:** Home. **L:** English. **Mov-Ent:** TV Movies, Biography: Show Business, Drug Abuse. **Acq:** Purchase. **Dist:** Sony Pictures Home Entertainment Inc.

The Anna Nicole Show: The First Season 2003 (Unrated)
Offers the reality television show from the E! cable network with former model and tabloid sensation Anna Nicole Smith that follows the often comedic ongoings in her life at the time. 13 episodes. 336m; DVD. **C:** Anna Nicole Smith; Daniel E. Smith; Howard Stern; Kim Walther. **A:** Sr. High-Adult. **P:** Entertainment. **U:** Home. **Mov-Ent:** Television Series, Documentary Films. **Acq:** Purchase. **Dist:** Lions Gate Entertainment Inc. $19.98.

Anna Pavlova: A Woman for All Time ????
Full-length feature film captures the life story of world renown ballerina Anna Pavlova, from her training with the Imperial Ballet School to performances with dance legends Diaghilev and Fokine, and a world tour with her own ballet troupe. 135m; VHS. **A:** Adult. **P:** Education. **U:** Institution, Home. **Fin-Art:** Dance, Dance--History. **Acq:** Purchase. **Dist:** Stagestep. $19.95.

Anna Russell: The Clown Princess of Comedy ????
Interviews and performance footage of the failed diva dubbed "the world's funniest woman" by the London Times. ?m; VHS. **A:** Adult. **P:** Entertainment. **U:** Home. **Fin-Art:** Music--Classical, Music--Performance. **Acq:** Purchase. **Dist:** Video Artists International. $29.95.

Anna Russell: The First Farewell Concert 1984
Anna Russell performs her unique version of Wagners "Ring Cycle" and "Wind Instruments I Have Known" in this concert recorded at Baltimore's Museum of Art. 85m; VHS. **Pr:** Philip Byrd; Maryland Public Television. **A:** Family. **P:** Entertainment. **U:** Home. **Fin-Art:** Music--Performance, Satire & Parody. **Acq:** Purchase. **Dist:** Video Collectibles; Music Video Distributors; Home Vision Cinema. $49.95.

Anna Russell's Farewell Special 1988 (Unrated)
Russell parodies Wagnerian operas and Gilbert and Sullivan tunes. Songs include "Wind Instruments I Have Known," "How to Become a Singer," and "Three Parody Fold Tunes." 90m; VHS, 3/4 U. **Pr:** Maryland Center for Public Broadcasting. **A:** Jr. High-Adult. **P:** Entertainment. **U:** Institution, CCTV, CATV, BCTV. **Mov-Ent:** Music--Performance, Satire & Parody. **Acq:** Purchase. **Dist:** Maryland Public Television. $39.95.

Anna Sokolow: Choreographer 1991
The famous modern dance choreographer is profiled in this career retrospective, featuring interviews, photos and clips of her work. 20m; VHS. **Pr:** Princeton Visual Communications. **A:** Sr. High-Adult. **P:** Education. **U:** Home. **Gen-Edu:** Documentary Films, Dance, Biography. **Acq:** Purchase. **Dist:** Princeton Book Company Publishers. $39.95.

Anna to the Infinite Power 1984 — ★★½
Sci fi based on the book of the same name follows a young girl with telepathic powers. When the girl discovers that she has sisters as the result of a strange scientific experiment, she sets out to find them, drawing on her own inner strength. 101m; VHS, DVD. **C:** Dina Merrill; Martha Byrne; Mark Patton; Directed by Robert Wiemer. **Pr:** Bruce Graham; Blue Marble Company Films. **A:** Sr. High-Adult. **P:** Entertainment. **U:** Home. **Mov-Ent:** Science Fiction. **Acq:** Purchase. **Dist:** Amazon.com Inc.; Sony Pictures Home Entertainment Inc. $59.95.

Annabel Takes a Tour/Maid's Night Out 1938
A delightful comedy double feature. In "Annabel Takes a Tour," a fading movie star falls in love with a writer while on a tour to boost her career, and in "Maids Night Out," an heiress and a millionaire fall in love. 131m/B/W; VHS. **C:** Lucille Ball; Jack Oakie; Ruth Donnelly; Joan Fontaine; Allan "Rocky" Lane; Hedda Hopper; Alice White; Directed by Lew Landers. **Pr:** RKO. **A:** Family. **P:** Entertainment. **U:** Home. **Mov-Ent:** Comedy--Romantic. **Acq:** Purchase. **Dist:** Turner Broadcasting System Inc. $34.95.

Annabelle's Wish 1997
Based on a legend that Santa Claus gives voices to animals at Christmas. In this animated story, young calf Annabelle dreams of being one of Santa's reindeer; her unselfish wish brings joy to the little boy she loves instead. 54m; DVD. **C:** Voice(s) by Randy Travis; Cloris Leachman; Jerry Van Dyke; Jim Varney; Rue McClanahan. **A:** Family. **P:** Entertainment. **U:** Home. **Chl-Juv:** Animation & Cartoons, Christmas. **Acq:** Purchase. **Dist:** SONY Wonder.

Annapolis 1928 — ★
Life's in the pink for two guys at the U.S. naval academy until jealousy rears its loathsome head when they fall for the same gal. Just when it's beginning to look like love and honor is an either-or proposition, the lovelorn rivals find that although love transcends all, a guy's gotta do what a guy's gotta do, even if it means sticking up for his romantic nemesis. Lots of sub-par male bonding. 63m/B/W; Silent; VHS. **C:** Johnny Mack Brown; Hugh Allan; Hobart Bosworth; William "Billy" Bakewell; Charlotte Walker; Jeanette Loff; Directed by Christy Cabanne. **Pr:** Pathe. **A:** Sr. High-Adult. **P:** Entertainment. **U:** Home. **Mov-Ent:** Drama, Silent Films, Boating. **Acq:** Purchase. **Dist:** Grapevine Video; Facets Multimedia Inc. $19.95.

Annapolis 2006 (PG-13) — ★½
Predictable military/boxing flick finds hot-headed, working-class Jake Huard (Franco) set on entering the U.S. Naval Academy at Annapolis. He's finally accepted and finds himself subjected to the berating of disciplinarian Lt. Cole (Gibson), who is certain Jake doesn't have what it takes. However, Jake is a really good boxer and starts training for the Academy's Brigades competition, hoping for a shot at the reigning champ—Cole. The fetching Brewster serves as Jake's superior officer, questionable trainer, and romantic object. 108m; DVD, Blu-Ray. **C:** James Franco; Tyrese Gibson; Jordana Brewster; Donnie Wahlberg; Vicellous Shannon; Roger Fan; Chi McBride; Brian Goodman; Charles Napier; Zachery Ty Bryan; Directed by Justin Lin; Written by Dave Collard; Cinematography by Phil Abraham; Music by Brian Tyler. **Pr:** Damien Saccani; Mark Vahradian; Touchstone Pictures; Buena Vista. **A:** Jr. High-Adult. **P:** Entertainment. **U:** Home. **L:** English. **Mov-Ent:** Boxing, Sports--Fiction: Drama. **Acq:** Purchase. **Dist:** Walt Disney Studios Home Entertainment.

The Annapolis Book of Seamanship: Powerboat Navigation 1988
Every aspect of powerboat navigating is covered. 75m; VHS. **Pr:** U.S. Coast Guard. **A:** Jr. High-Adult. **P:** Instruction. **U:** Home. **How-Ins:** Boating. **Acq:** Purchase. **Dist:** Bennett Marine Video. $49.95.

Annapolis Book of Seamanship, Vol. 1: Cruising Under Sail 1989
Demonstration and instruction for open water sailings. Includes information about sailing techniques, as well as lessons in crew management and navigation. 72m; VHS. **Pr:** Creative Programming, Inc. **A:** Sr. High-Adult. **P:** Instruction. **U:** Home. **How-Ins:** How-To, Boating. **Acq:** Purchase. **Dist:** Bennett Marine Video. $49.95.

Annapolis Book of Seamanship, Vol. 2: Heavy Weather Sailing 1989
This volume highlights the approaches to the mastery of sailing during inclimate weather. Narrator John Rousmaniere discloses tips on everything from preparedness to steering through a storm. 55m; VHS. **Pr:** Bennett Marine Video. **A:** Sr. High-Adult. **P:** Instruction. **U:** Home. **Spo-Rec:** Boating. **Acq:** Purchase. **Dist:** Bennett Marine Video. $49.95.

Annapolis Book of Seamanship, Vol. 3: Safety at Sea 1989
What to do in a marine emergency? Panic no more. This impressive installation in the "Book of Seamanship" series has come to the rescue. Detailed enactments of possible accidents include the appropriate measures to handle them. Included are liferaft operation, rescue, help signals, injuries, and much more. 94m; VHS. **Pr:** Bennett Marine Video. **A:** Sr. High-Adult. **P:** Instruction. **U:** Home. **Spo-Rec:** Boating. **Acq:** Purchase. **Dist:** Bennett Marine Video. $49.95.

Annapolis Book of Seamanship, Vol. 4: Sailboat Navigation 1989
The Coast Guard coordinated the episode of this helpful series. Navigation is explored in a wide range of possible contexts. From electronics to conventional to foul weather navigation is detailed in a comprehensive and concise way. 70m; VHS. **Pr:** Bennett Marine Video. **A:** Sr. High-Adult. **P:** Entertainment. **U:** Home. **Spo-Rec:** Boating. **Acq:** Purchase. **Dist:** Bennett Marine Video. $49.95.

Annapolis Book of Seamanship, Vol. 5: Daysailers Sailing and Racing 1989
A comprehensive video packed full of information for the beginning boater. This video covers safety, navigation, racing tips, and mechanics of a boat. 75m; VHS. **Pr:** Bennett Marine Video. **A:** Sr. High-Adult. **P:** Instruction. **U:** Home. **Spo-Rec:** Boating. **Acq:** Purchase. **Dist:** Bennett Marine Video. $49.95.

An Annapolis Story 1955 (Unrated) — ★½
Cliche-ridden WWII drama about two naval cadets romancing the same lucky girl. Low-rent time for director Siegel which wastes a decent cast. 81m; VHS. **C:** John Derek; Kevin McCarthy; Diana Lynn; Pat Conway; L.Q. Jones; Alvy Moore; Betty Lou Gerson; Robert Osterloh; George Eldredge; Dabbs Greer; Sam Peckinpah; William Schallert; Directed by Donald Siegel; Written by Daniel Mainwaring; Daniel Ullman; Cinematography by Sam Leavitt; Music by Marlin Skiles. **Pr:** Allied Artists International. **A:** Adult. **P:** Entertainment. **U:** Home. **Mov-Ent:** Drama, World War Two. **Acq:** Purchase. **Dist:** $19.98.

Annapurna: A Woman's Place 1979
An all-woman crew of filmmakers followed ten female athletes up Annapurna, one of the world's tallest and most dangerous peaks. 45m; VHS, 3/4 U. **Pr:** Dyanna Taylor; Marie Ashton. **A:** Jr. High-Adult. **P:** Education. **U:** Institution, SURA. **Gen-Edu:** Women, Mountaineering. **Acq:** Purchase, Rent/Lease. **Dist:** Women Make Movies. $275.00.

Anna's Storm 2007 (Unrated) — ★
Silly disaster flick finds Mayor Anna's (Wilson) small town being hit by meteor storms (with low-budget CGI) that are destroying everything in sight. This doesn't stop her from fretting more over her bothersome marriage. 90m; DVD. **C:** Sheree J. Wilson; Peter Lacroix; Scott Hylands; Aaron Pearl; Desiree Loewen; Graham Wardle; Sarah Jane Redmond; Directed by Kristoffer Tabori; Written by Steven B. Frank; Julie Ferber Frank; Music by Michael Neilsen. **A:** Jr. High-Adult. **P:** Entertainment. **U:** Home. **Mov-Ent:** Action-Adventure. **Acq:** Purchase. **Dist:** A&E Television Networks L.L.C.

Anne Braden: Southern Patriot 2012 (Unrated)
Biographical documentary of organizer and journalist Anne Braden who became famous during her participation in the Civil Rights movement. 77m; DVD, Streaming. **A:** Jr. High-Adult. **P:** Entertainment. **U:** Home, Institution. **L:** English, Spanish. **Mov-Ent:** Biography: Politics, Documentary Films, Civil Rights. **Acq:** Purchase, Rent/Lease. **Dist:** California Newsreel. $24.95 49.95 195.00 195.00.

Anne Frank: A Legacy for Our Time 1988
Anne Frank's story is used to make students question their own feelings about prejudice. 39m; VHS, 3/4 U. **Pr:** SVE. **A:** Jr. High. **P:** Education. **U:** Institution, CCTV, Home. **Gen-Edu:** Dance, Judaism, Prejudice. **Acq:** Purchase, Duplication. **Dist:** Clear Vue Inc. $99.00.

The Anne Frank Ballet 1989
The famous diary of Anne Frank, the young girl who hid from the Nazis with her family in Holland during WWII, is translated into dance in this video. In HiFi Dolby sound. 30m; VHS. **Pr:** Kultur. **A:** Primary-Adult. **P:** Entertainment. **U:** Home. **Fin-Art:** Dance--Ballet, Performing Arts, Judaism. **Acq:** Purchase. **Dist:** Music Video Distributors. $19.95.

Anne Frank in Maine 1983
This tape looks at a group of youngsters who spend a year studying the Holocaust. 28m; VHS, 3/4 U. **Pr:** Anti-Defamation League of B'nai B'rith. **A:** Primary-Adult. **P:** Education. **U:** Institution, CCTV, CATV, BCTV, Home. **Gen-Edu:** World War Two, Judaism. **Acq:** Purchase. **Dist:** Anti-Defamation League of B'nai B'rith.

Anne Frank Remembered 1995 (PG)
Eyewitness chronicle of the life and legacy of the 15-year-old Jewish girl who symbolized the children exterminated in the Holocaust through the publication of her diary in 1947. Includes archival footage, photos, family letters, and personal testimony. 117m; VHS, CC. **C:** Narrated by Kenneth Branagh; Directed by Jon Blair; Written by Jon Blair; Cinematography by Barry Ackroyd; Music by Carl Davis. **Pr:** British Broadcasting Corporation. **A:** Jr. High-Adult. **P:** Education. **U:** Home, Institution. **Gen-Edu:** Documentary Films, Biography, Holocaust. **Awds:** Oscars '95: Feature Doc. **Acq:** Purchase. **Dist:** Sony Pictures Home Entertainment Inc.

Anne Frank: The Whole Story 2001 (Unrated) — ★★★
Solid made-for-TV entry into the pantheon of Anne Frank pathos, legend, or tragedy—take your pick. Romanian-born director Robert Dornhelm does his best work to date by taking a more intimate look at the day-to-day life of the young Anne Frank (played with great precision by Hannah Taylor-Gordon) during the years she and her family spent in hiding from the German invaders. Anne, as a human being, is fleshed out and painted with more detail than in other bio-pics covering the same ground (story is based on Melissa Muller's biography, and not on the famous diary). This has the effect of making her ultimate fate at Auschwitz all the more painful. 189m; DVD. **C:** Ben Kingsley; Brenda Blethyn; Hannah Taylor Gordon; Joachim Krol; Lili Taylor; Tatjana Blacher; Directed by Richard Dornhelm; Written by Kirk Ellis; Cinematography by Elemer Ragalyi; Music by Graeme Revell. **Pr:** David Kappes; Touchstone Television. **A:** Jr. High-Adult. **P:** Entertainment. **U:** Home, Institution. **Mov-**

Ent: Holocaust, Biography, World War Two. **Acq:** Purchase. **Dist:** Walt Disney Studios Home Entertainment.

Anne Frank—The Life of a Young Girl: Biography 1998
Readings from Anne's diary plus comments from young friends and her father provide a unique historical perspective of the Holocaust. 44m; VHS. **A:** Jr. High-Sr. High. **P:** Education. **U:** Institution. **Gen-Edu:** Biography, World War Two, Holocaust. **Acq:** Purchase. **Dist:** Zenger Media. $14.95.

Anne Murray 1990
The Canadian country singer is featured in clips "Who's Leaving Who," "If Ever I Fall in Love Again (duo with Kenny Roger)," "Flying on Your Own," "Now and Forever" and more. 30m; VHS, DVD. **A:** Sr. High-Adult. **P:** Entertainment. **U:** Home. **Mov-Ent:** Music--Country/Western. **Acq:** Purchase. **Dist:** Music Video Distributors. $15.98.

Anne Murray's Classic Christmas 2000
Songstress Anne Murray and special guests perform at The Old Mill in Toronto. 48m; VHS, DVD. **A:** Adult. **P:** Entertainment. **U:** Home. **Mov-Ent:** Music--Performance, Holidays. **Acq:** Purchase. **Dist:** Wellspring Media. $14.95.

Anne of Avonlea 1987 (Unrated) — ★★★½
Equally excellent miniseries sequel to "Anne of Green Gables" in which the romantic heroine grows up and discovers romance. The same cast returns and Sullivan continues his tradition of lavish filming on Prince Edward Island and beautiful costumes. Based on the characters from L.M. Montgomery's classic novels "Anne of Avonlea," "Anne of the Island," and "Anne of Windy Poplars." CBC, PBS, and Disney worked together on this WonderWorks production. 224m; VHS, DVD, CC. **C:** Megan Follows; Colleen Dewhurst; Wendy Hiller; Frank Converse; Patricia Hamilton; Schuyler Grant; Jonathan Crombie; Rosemary Dunsmore; Directed by Kevin Sullivan; Written by Kevin Sullivan; Music by Hagood Hardy. **Pr:** Kevin Sullivan; Trudy Grant; Kevin Sullivan; Walt Disney Co; Canadian Broadcasting Corp; PBS; Sullivan Entertainment. **A:** Family. **P:** Entertainment. **U:** Home. **Mov-Ent:** Drama, Canada, TV Movies. **Acq:** Purchase. **Dist:** Ignatius Press; Signals Video; Knowledge Unlimited, Inc. $29.95.

Anne of Green Gables 1934 (Unrated) — ★★★
A lonely Canadian couple adopts an orphan who keeps them on their toes with her animated imagination, and wins a permanent place in their hearts. Warm (but loose) adaptation of Lucy Maud Montgomery's popular novel is entertaining although 1985 remake is far superior. Followed by "Anne of Windy Poplars." 79m/B/W; VHS, DVD. **C:** Anne Shirley; Tom Brown; O.P. Heggie; Helen Westley; Sara Haden; Charley Grapewin; Directed by George Nicholls, Jr.; Music by Max Steiner. **Pr:** Kenneth McGowan; RKO. **A:** Family. **P:** Entertainment. **U:** Home. **Mov-Ent:** Adoption, Family, Canada. **Acq:** Purchase. **Dist:** Allied Artists International. $19.98.

Anne of Green Gables 1985 (Unrated) — ★★★½
Splendid production of the famous Lucy Maud Montgomery classic about a young orphan girl growing to young adulthood with the help of a crusty brother and sister duo. The characters come to life under Sullivan's direction, and the movie is enhanced by the beautiful Prince Edward Island scenery and wonderful costumes. One of the few instances where an adaptation lives up to (if not exceeds) the quality of the original novel. A WonderWorks presentation that was made with the cooperation of the Disney channel, CBC, and PBS. Followed by "Anne of Avonlea." On two tapes. 197m; VHS, DVD, CC. **C:** Megan Follows; Colleen Dewhurst; Richard Farnsworth; Patricia Hamilton; Schuyler Grant; Jonathan Crombie; Marilyn Lightstone; Charmion King; Rosemary Radcliffe; Jackie Burroughs; Robert E. Collins; Joachim Hansen; Cedric Smith; Paul Bown; Miranda de Pencier; Jennifer Inch; Wendy Lyon; Christiane Kruger; Trish Nettleton; Morgan Chapman; Directed by Kevin Sullivan; Written by Kevin Sullivan; Joe Wiesenfeld; Cinematography by Rene Ohashi; Music by Hagood Hardy. **Pr:** Kevin Sullivan; Ian McDougall; Walt Disney; Kevin Sullivan; Canadian Broadcasting Corp; PBS; Sullivan Entertainment. **A:** Family. **P:** Entertainment. **U:** Home. **Mov-Ent:** Family Viewing, Adoption, TV Movies. **Acq:** Purchase. **Dist:** Knowledge Unlimited, Inc.; Buena Vista Home Entertainment; Ignatius Press. $29.95.

Anne of Green Gables: The Continuing Story 1999 — ★★½
Anne (Follows) learns that fiance Gilbert (Blythe) has accepted a job in a New York hospital. She takes a job in a publishing house where she meets fast-living journalist Jack Garrison (Daddo). Gilbert and Anne return to Avonlea to marry just before WWI and Gilbert joins the army as a doctor and is sent to France. When he's declared MIA, Anne heads overseas with the Red Cross to search for him and runs into Jack again, who leads Anne into numerous intrigues. This far-fetched story is not based on one of Lucy Maud Montgomery's books but Anne at least retains her spunkiness and determination. 185m; VHS, DVD, CC. **C:** Megan Follows; Jonathan Crombie; Cameron Daddo; Schuyler Grant; Patricia Hamilton; Rosemary Radcliffe; Miranda de Pencier; Barry Morse; Martha Henry; Janet-Laine Green; Nigel Bennett; Shannon Lawson; Directed by Stefan Scaini; Written by Kevin Sullivan; Laurie Pearson; Cinematography by Robert Saad; Music by Peter Breiner. **Pr:** Kevin Sullivan; Kevin Sullivan; Trudy Grant; Sullivan Entertainment; Canadian Broadcasting Corp. **A:** Jr. High-Adult. **P:** Entertainment. **U:** Home. **Mov-Ent:** World War One, International Relations. **Acq:** Purchase. **Dist:** PBS Home Video.

Anne of the Thousand Days 1969 (PG) — ★★★½
Lavish re-telling of the life and loves of Henry the VIII. In 1526, Henry tosses aside his current wife for the young and devastat-ingly beautiful Anne Boleyn (Bujold). But after the birth of Princess Elizabeth, Henry tires of Anne and wishes to marry another. So he decides to rid himself of her presence—permanently. Burton's performance of the amoral king garnered him an Oscar nomination. Based on the 1948 play by Maxwell Anderson. Watch for Elizabeth Taylor as a masked courtesan at the costume ball. 145m; VHS, DVD. **C:** Richard Burton; Genevieve Bujold; Irene Papas; Anthony Quayle; John Colicos; Michael Hordern; Michael Johnson; Directed by Charles Jarrott; Written by Bridget Boland; John Hale; Music by Georges Delerue. **Pr:** Mark Huffam. **A:** Jr. High-Adult. **P:** Entertainment. **U:** Home. **Mov-Ent:** Drama, Great Britain. **Awds:** Oscars '69: Costume Des.; Directors Guild '70: Director (Jarrott); Golden Globes '70: Actress--Drama (Bujold), Director (Jarrott), Film--Drama, Screenplay. **Acq:** Purchase. **Dist:** Universal Studios Home Video. $19.98.

Anne Powell on Underwater Video 19??
A pioneer of underwater video offers expertise in a variety of formats first hand. 60m; VHS. **A:** College-Adult. **P:** Entertainment. **U:** Home. **Spo-Rec:** Scuba, Video. **Acq:** Purchase. **Dist:** Bennett Marine Video. $29.95.

Anne Rice: Birth of the Vampire 1994
Just in time for the big-screen release of Rice's novel "Interview with a Vampire," comes this BBC documentary on the best-selling author of "The Vampire Chronicles." Documents Rice's childhood in New Orleans and interviews with family, friends, and the author, along with short readings from her novels. 45m; VHS. **C:** Directed by Anand Tucker. **A:** Sr. High. **P:** Entertainment. **U:** Home. **Mov-Ent:** Biography, Women. **Acq:** Purchase. **Dist:** Fox Home Entertainment. $14.98.

Anne Rice's The Feast of All Saints 2001 — ★★½
It's not about vampires. Rice's novel is set in pre-Civil War New Orleans among free people of color. They enjoy certain privileges of middleclass society while still dealing with class, race, and sex. Cecil St. Marie (Rueben) is the mistress of white plantation owner Philippe Ferronnaire (Gallagher). He makes certain promises to his children by Cecil—Marcel (Ri'chard) and Marie (Lyn)?which he fails to keep, thus causing family dissension. As the children grow into adults they face romantic and societal dilemmas of their own. Excellent cast does well by the sometimes melodramatic story. Title refers to the day for remembering the dead. 212m; VHS, DVD, CC. **C:** Robert Ri'chard; Peter Gallagher; Gloria Reuben; Nicole Lyn; Jennifer Beals; Ossie Davis; Ruby Dee; Pam Grier; Jasmine Guy; Victoria Rowell; James Earl Jones; Eartha Kitt; Ben Vereen; Forest Whitaker; Bianca Lawson; Daniel Sunjata; Directed by Peter Medak; Written by John Wilder; Cinematography by Edward Pei; Music by Patrick Seymour. **A:** Sr. High-Adult. **P:** Entertainment. **U:** Home. **Mov-Ent:** Black Culture, Sex & Sexuality. **Acq:** Purchase. **Dist:** Showtime Networks Inc.

L'Annee Sainte 1976
A comedy about two gangsters that take on highjackers on an international flight to recover stolen money. In French with English subtitles. 90m; VHS. **A:** Adult. **P:** Entertainment. **U:** Home. **L:** French. **Mov-Ent:** Acq: Purchase. **Dist:** Mercury International Productions Inc. $29.95.

Annette: The 1957-1958 Limited Edition Collector's Edition 1957 (Unrated)
Documentary collection of 20 'Mickey Mouse Club' daily series shows featuring Annette Funicello as she moves to California to live with her aunt and uncle, do basic teenager stuff like hang out at the malt shop, go to a sock hop, and wrestle with pinning on a corsage. Film historian Leonard Maltin commentates noting that Annette was the only Mouseketeer hand-picked by Walt Disney himself and had a more "ethnic-look" than previous Mouseketeers on 1950s television. 240m; DVD. **C:** Annette Funicello; Steve Stevens. **A:** Family. **P:** Entertainment. **U:** Home. **Mov-Ent:** Children's Shows, Television Series. **Acq:** Purchase. **Dist:** Walt Disney Studios Home Entertainment. $32.99.

Annie 1982 (PG) — ★★
Stagy big-budget adaption of the Broadway musical, which was an adaptation of the comic strip. A major financial disaster upon release, still it's an entertaining enterprise curiously directed by Huston and engagingly acted by Finney and Quinn. 128m; VHS, DVD, Blu-Ray, 8 mm, Wide, CC. **C:** Aileen Quinn; Carol Burnett; Albert Finney; Bernadette Peters; Ann Reinking; Tim Curry; Directed by John Huston; Written by Thomas Meehan; Cinematography by Richard Moore; Music by Ralph Burns. **Pr:** Ray Stark; Columbia Pictures. **A:** Family. **P:** Entertainment. **U:** Home. **Mov-Ent:** Musical, Adoption. **Awds:** Golden Raspberries '82: Worst Support. Actress (Quinn). **Acq:** Purchase. **Dist:** Facets Multimedia Inc.; Music Video Distributors; Sony Pictures Home Entertainment Inc. $14.95.
Songs: Tomorrow; It's the Hard Knock Life; Maybe; I Think I'm Gonna Like It Here; Little Girls; We Got Annie; Let's Go to the Movies; You're Never Fully Dressed Without a Smile; Easy Street; I Don't Need Anything But You.

Annie 1999 — ★★★
Lively and amusing adaptation of the smash Broadway musical that will make you forget that dud 1982 movie version. Scrappy urchin Annie (newcomer Morton) is incarcerated in a Depression-era orphange run by despotic Miss Hannigan (Bates) when she's offered the chance to spend the holidays with chilly moneybags Oliver Warbucks (Garber). Naturally, Annie thaws his frosty demeanor. Able support is provided by Warbucks' faithful assistant Grace (McDonald) and Miss Hannigan's wastrel brother Rooster (Cumming) and his floozy Lily (Chenoweth). 120m; VHS, DVD. **C:** Alicia Morton; Victor Garber; Kathy Bates; Alan Cumming; Audra McDonald; Kristin Chenoweth; Cameo(s) Andrea McArdle; Directed by Rob Marshall; Written by Irene Mecchi; Cinematography by Ralf

Bode; Music by Charles Strouse; Lyrics by Martin Charnin. **A:** Family. **P:** Entertainment. **U:** Home. **Mov-Ent:** Musical, Adoption. **Acq:** Purchase. **Dist:** Buena Vista Home Entertainment.

Annie: A Royal Adventure 1995 (Unrated) — ★★½
TV sequel to "Annie" finds the red-haired heroine (Johnson) traveling to England with her Daddy Warbucks (Hearn), who's about to be knighted in London. But the evil Lady Edwina Hogbottom (played to a high-camp hilt by Collins) has a plan to blow up Buckingham Palace and take over as queen. Naturally, it's up to Annie to defeat her and have a happy ending. 92m; VHS, DVD. **C:** Ashley Johnson; George Hearn; Joan Collins; Emily Ann Lloyd; Camilla Belle; Ian McDiarmid; Directed by Ian Toynton; Written by Trish Soodik; Cinematography by Alan Hume; Music by David Michael Frank. **A:** Family. **P:** Entertainment. **U:** Home. **Mov-Ent:** TV Movies, Children. **Acq:** Purchase. **Dist:** Sony Pictures Home Entertainment Inc. $14.95.

Annie and the Old One 1976
The Old One is the beloved grandmother of a little Navajo girl named Annie. Annie questions the Old One about the cycle of life. Adapted from a book by Miska Miles. 24m; VHS, Special order formats. **Pr:** Greenhouse Films Productions. **A:** Family. **P:** Entertainment. **U:** Institution, SURA. **Chl-Juv:** Native Americans, Family. **Acq:** Purchase, Rent/Lease. **Dist:** Phoenix Learning Group; EcuFilm.

Annie Claus is Coming to Town 2011 (Unrated) — ★★½
In this Hallmark Channel holiday movie, Santa's (Jason) naive daughter Annie (Thayer) leaves the North Pole for the first time to experience the real world by heading to L.A. where she is befriended by single mom Lucy (Fox) and her daughter Mia (Kirby). Annie goes to work for struggling toy shop owner Ted (Page), who is not feeling the Christmas spirit, and she needs to bring it back. 87m; DVD. **C:** Maria Thayer; Sam Page; Vivica A. Fox; Nay Nay Kirby; Peter Jason; Vicki Lawrence; Directed by Kevin Connor; Written by Nina Weinman; Cinematography by Maximo Munzi; Music by Nathan Wang. **A:** Family. **P:** Entertainment. **U:** Home. **L:** English. **Mov-Ent:** Christmas, Family, Romance. **Acq:** Purchase. **Dist:** Gaiam Inc.

Annie Get Your Gun 1950 — ★★★
A lavish production of Irving Berlin's Broadway hit musical. Sharpshooting Annie Oakley (Hutton) is the queen of Buffalo Bill's Wild West show though her talents leave her loveless. Seems fellow marksman Frank Butler's (Keel) ego can't handle the fact that Annie keeps beating him. Lots of singing, with an enthusiastic lead performance by Hutton. 107m; VHS, DVD. **C:** Betty Hutton; Howard Keel; Keenan Wynn; Louis Calhern; J. Carrol Naish; Edward Arnold; Clinton Sundberg; Directed by George Sidney; Written by Sidney Sheldon; Cinematography by Charles Rosher; Music by Irving Berlin. **Pr:** MGM. **A:** Jr. High-Adult. **P:** Entertainment. **U:** Home. **Mov-Ent:** Musical. **Awds:** Oscars '50: Scoring/Musical. **Acq:** Purchase. **Dist:** Warner Home Video, Inc.
Songs: There's No Business Like Show Business; My Defenses Are Down; I'm an Indian Too; Doin' What Comes Natur'lly; Colonel Buffalo Bill; The Girl That I Marry; You Can't Get a Man with a Gun; They Say It's Wonderful; I Got the Sun in the Morning; Anything You Can Do.

Annie Hall 1977 (PG) — ★★★★
Acclaimed coming-of-cinematic-age film for Allen is based in part on his own life. His love affair with Hall/Keaton is chronicled as an episodic, wistful comedy commenting on family, love, loneliness, communicating, maturity, driving, city life, careers, and various other topics. Abounds with classic scenes, including future star Goldblum and his mantra at a cocktail party; Allen and the lobster pot; and Allen, Keaton, a bathroom, a tennis racket, and a spider. The film operates on many levels, as does Keaton's wardrobe, which started a major fashion trend. Don't blink or you'll miss several future stars in bit parts. Expertly shot by Gordon Willis. 94m; VHS, DVD, Wide. **C:** Woody Allen; Diane Keaton; Tony Roberts; Carol Kane; Paul Simon; Colleen Dewhurst; Janet Margolin; Shelley Duvall; Christopher Walken; Marshall McLuhan; Dick Cavett; John Glover; Jeff Goldblum; Beverly D'Angelo; Directed by Woody Allen; Written by Woody Allen; Marshall Brickman; Cinematography by Gordon Willis. **Pr:** Jack Rollins; Charles H. Joffe; United Artists. **A:** Sr. High-Adult. **P:** Entertainment. **U:** Home. **Mov-Ent:** Comedy--Romantic, Cult Films, Classic Films. **Awds:** Oscars '77: Actress (Keaton), Director (Allen), Film, Orig. Screenplay; AFI '98: Top 100; British Acad. '77: Actress (Keaton), Director (Allen), Film, Screenplay; Directors Guild '77: Director (Allen); Golden Globes '78: Actress--Mus./Comedy (Keaton); L.A. Film Critics '77: Screenplay; Natl. Bd. of Review '77: Support. Actress (Keaton); Natl. Film Reg. '92; N.Y. Film Critics '77: Actress (Keaton), Director (Allen), Film, Screenplay; Natl. Soc. Film Critics '77: Actress (Keaton), Film, Screenplay; Writers Guild '77: Orig. Screenplay. **Acq:** Purchase. **Dist:** Baker and Taylor; MGM Home Entertainment; Home Vision Cinema. $14.95.

Annie Leibovitz: Celebrity Photographer 1993
Looks at the career of Leibovitz, who started at "Rolling Stone" magazine in the '70s and who became "Vanity Fair's" first contributing photographer, with two nude covers of Demi Moore. Other celebrities include Yoko Ono and John Lennon, Whoppi Goldberg, and Clint Eastwood. 51m; VHS. **A:** Sr. High-Adult. **P:** Entertainment. **U:** Home. **Fin-Art:** Photography, Interviews, Biography. **Acq:** Purchase. **Dist:** Home Vision Cinema. $29.95.

Annie Lennox: Diva 1992
The former singer for "The Eurythmics" goes solo in this video featuring songs from her debut album. 35m; VHS. **A:** Jr. High-Adult. **P:** Entertainment. **U:** Home. **Mov-Ent:** Music Video, Music--Pop/Rock. **Acq:** Purchase. **Dist:** BMG Entertainment; Music Video Distributors. $14.98.

Annie O 1995 (PG) — ★★½
15-year-old Annie Rojas (Yares) runs into problems when she joins the boys' basketball team (since her school doesn't have a girls team). Her teammates are jealous and so are her brother and boyfriend. 93m; VHS, CC. **C:** Coco Yares; Chad Willet; Rob Stewart; Directed by Michael McClary. **A:** Primary-Adult. **P:** Entertainment. **U:** Home. **Mov-Ent**: Adolescence, Basketball, TV Movies. **Acq:** Purchase.

Annie Oakley 1935 (Unrated) — ★★★
Energetic biographical drama based on the life and legend of sharpshooter Annie Oakley and her on-off relationship with Wild Bill Hickok. Stanwyck makes a great Oakley. Later musicalized as "Annie Get Your Gun." 90m/B/W; VHS, DVD. **C:** Barbara Stanwyck; Preston Foster; Brad Johnson; Melvyn Douglas; Pert Kelton; Andy Clyde; Moroni Olsen; Chief Thundercloud; Directed by George Stevens. **Pr:** RKO. **A:** Family. **P:** Entertainment. **U:** Home. **Mov-Ent**: Biography. **Acq:** Purchase. **Dist:** Warner Home Video, Inc. $19.98.

Annie Oakley 1955
A package of episodes from the popular television Western series. Contains "Dutch Gunman," "Joker on Horseback," "Shadow at Sonoma," and "Annie and the Twisted Trails." 100m/B/W; VHS. **C:** Gail Davis; Billy Gray. **Pr:** ABC. **A:** Family. **P:** Entertainment. **U:** Home. **Mov-Ent**: Western, Television Series. **Acq:** Purchase. **Dist:** Shokus Video. $24.95.

Annie Oakley 1992
The adventures of real-life Western sharpshooter Annie Oakley are recounted. Features music by Los Lobos. 30m; VHS. **C:** Narrated by Keith Carradine. **A:** Preschool-Primary. **P:** Entertainment. **U:** Home. **Chl-Juv**: Folklore & Legends, Family Viewing. **Acq:** Purchase. **Dist:** Movies Unlimited. $9.95.

Annie Oakley, 2 195?
The first four episodes of the 1950s series are packaged together on this tape; includes "Bull's Eye," the original pilot for the series; "Annie Gets Her Man"; "Sharpshooting Annie"; and "Justice Guns." 100m/B/W; VHS. **C:** Gail Davis; Billy Gray; Clayton Moore. **Pr:** ABC. **A:** Primary-Adult. **P:** Entertainment. **U:** Home. **Mov-Ent. Acq:** Purchase. **Dist:** Shokus Video. $24.95.

Annie Oakley, 3 1956
The lovely Davis stars as the legendary distaff sharpshooter. Episodes from the series include "Annie and the Silver Ace," "Annie and the Chinese Puzzle," "Flint and Steel" and "Valley of the Shadows." 105m/B/W; VHS. **C:** Alan Hale, Jr; Keye Luke; Gail Davis. **Pr:** Shokus Video Productions. **A:** Family. **P:** Entertainment. **U:** Home. **Mov-Ent**: Western, Variety, Television Series. **Acq:** Purchase. **Dist:** Shokus Video. $24.95.

Annie Oakley, 4 1957
Contains episodes from the popular TV Western, including "Dead Man's Bluff," "The Tall Tale," "Annie and the First Phone," and "Annie Rings the Bell." 100m/B/W; VHS. **C:** Gail Davis. **A:** Family. **P:** Entertainment. **U:** Home. **Mov-Ent**: Television Series, Western. **Acq:** Purchase. **Dist:** Shokus Video. $24.95.

Annie Oakley/The Rebel 1957
Features an episode from each classic television show. 60m/B/W; VHS. **C:** Nick Adams; Gail Davis. **A:** Family. **P:** Entertainment. **U:** Home. **Mov-Ent**: Television Series. **Acq:** Purchase. **Dist:** Video Resources.

Annie's Point 2005 (G) — ★★½
Recent widow Annie intends to fulfill her husband's final request: to have his ashes scattered on a bluff in California they called Annie's Point. Resentful son Richard doesn't approve, so Annie takes off on a cross-country road trip from Chicago with Richard's free-spirited daughter Ella instead. A Hallmark Channel family drama. 87m; DVD. **C:** Betty White; Richard Thomas; Amy Davidson; Ellen A. Dow; Robert F. Lyons; John Dybdahl; James Keane; Rebecca Switzer; Directed by Michael Switzer; Written by Mike Leonardo; Cinematography by Amit Bhattacharya; Music by Steve Dorff. **A:** Family. **P:** Entertainment. **U:** Home. **Mov-Ent. Acq:** Purchase. **Dist:** RHI Entertainment.

The Annihilators 1985 (R) — **Bomb!**
A group of Vietnam vets band together in an extremely violent manner to protect their small town from a gang of thugs. 87m; VHS. **C:** Gerrit Graham; Lawrence-Hilton Jacobs; Paul Koslo; Christopher Stone; Andy Wood; Sid Conrad; Dennis Redfield; Directed by Charles E. Sellier. **Pr:** New World Pictures. **A:** Sr. High-Adult. **P:** Entertainment. **U:** Home. **L:** Spanish. **Mov-Ent**: Vietnam War, Veterans. **Acq:** Purchase. **Dist:** Anchor Bay Entertainment. $9.95.

The Anniversary 1968 (Unrated) — ★★
One-eyed monster mom Mrs. Taggart (Bette at her baddest) gives new meaning to the word "possessive." Thoroughly cowing her three grown sons, she manages to get them to come home each year on the wedding anniversary to the husband she despised. Only this time, the trio tell her they're going to live their own lives. Hah—not if mom has anything to do with it. Based on the play by Bill MacIlwraith. 93m; VHS, DVD. **C:** Bette Davis; Jack Hedley; James Cossins; Christian Roberts; Sheila Hancock; Elaine Taylor; Directed by Roy Ward Baker; Written by Jimmy Sangster; Cinematography by Henry Waxman; Music by Philip Martell. **Pr:** Jimmy Sangster; Jimmy Sangster; Hammer Films. **A:** Jr. High-Adult. **P:** Entertainment. **U:** Home. **Mov-Ent**: Comedy--Black. **Acq:** Purchase. **Dist:** Fox Home Entertainment. $19.98.

Anniversary Celebration of the German Railroad, Nurenberg 1985 1985
Over 250 railroad cars and engines of the Deutsche Bundesbahn parade past spectators in Nuernberg, where the world's first rail line opened in December 1835. Available in either German or English. 57m; VHS. **TV Std:** NTSC, PAL. **Pr:** German Language Video Center. **A:** Family. **P:** Entertainment. **U:** Home. **L:** English, German. **Gen-Edu**: Trains, History. **Acq:** Purchase, Rent/Lease. **Dist:** German Language Video Center; Pentrex Media Group L.L.C. $33.95.

The Anniversary Party 2001 (R) — ★★★
Leigh and Cumming co-write, co-direct, and star as the central couple in this impressive ensemble comedy-drama about a group of Hollywood friends celebrating said couple's sixth anniversary. Amid much career and personal angst, drug use, and sometimes nasty air-clearing, most of the characters are fleshed out nicely and the dialogue remains sharp throughout. The air is thick with genuine personal dread and interpersonal tension. Among the uniformly excellent performances, two especially stand out: Leigh as the aging actress on the cusp of career oblivion, and Cates as a former actress who's given up her career to focus on being a wife (to just-beyond-leading-man-status hubby Kline) and mother. Filmed in digital video in 19 days under the Dogme 95 guidelines. 117m; VHS, DVD, Wide. **C:** Jennifer Jason Leigh; Alan Cumming; Gwyneth Paltrow; Kevin Kline; Phoebe Cates; John C. Reilly; Jane Adams; John Benjamin Hickey; Parker Posey; Denis O'Hare; Jennifer Beals; Mina Badie; Michael Panes; Directed by Jennifer Jason Leigh; Alan Cumming; Written by Jennifer Jason Leigh; Alan Cumming; Cinematography by John Bailey; Music by Michael Penn. **Pr:** Jennifer Jason Leigh; Joanne Sellar; Alan Cumming; Jennifer Jason Leigh; Alan Cumming; Pas de Quoi; Fine Line Features. **A:** Sr. High-Adult. **P:** Entertainment. **U:** Home. **Mov-Ent**: Comedy-Drama, Drug Abuse, Marriage. **Acq:** Purchase. **Dist:** New Line Home Video.

Announcing...Carpal Tunnel Syndrome 19??
Centers on the importance of developing good work and health habits as a means to prevent carpal tunnel syndrome (CTS). Provides information on the causes and symptoms of CTS, work-related risk factors, the importance of proper posture and exercise, adjusting furniture and keyboards, modifying non-adjustable furniture, and the importance of early detection. Comes with instructional guide. 10m; VHS. **A:** College-Adult. **P:** Education. **U:** Institution. **Hea-Sci**: Medical Education, Office Practice, Safety Education. **Acq:** Purchase. **Dist:** Medfilms Inc. $230.00.

Ann's Kids in the Holy Land 1982
Ann Kiemel leads children through the settings of Old and New Testament events and reminds them of Bible stories. 30m; VHS. **Pr:** Gospel Films. **A:** Primary. **P:** Religious. **U:** Institution. **Gen-Edu**: Bible. **Acq:** Rent/Lease. **Dist:** Gospel Communications International.

Annual Fall Pension Law and Practice Update 1993
Series covering issues of interest to tax attorneys and other professions having to deal with pension plans and employee benefits. Covers IRA rollovers, the 1992 Revenue Reconciliation Act, and more. Includes study guide. 210m; VHS. **A:** Adult. **P:** Professional. **U:** Institution. **Bus-Ind**: Law, Finance. **Dist:** American Law Institute - Committee on Continuing Professional Education. $200.

Annual First Aid Review 1988
This is a first aid refresher, and includes an eight-step action plan for emergency situations. 18m; VHS, 8 mm, 3/4 U. **TV Std:** NTSC, PAL, SECAM. **Pr:** Mountain West. **A:** Adult. **P:** Education. **U:** Institution, CCTV, SURA. **Hea-Sci**: First Aid. **Acq:** Purchase, Rent/Lease, Duplication License. **Dist:** Phoenix Learning Group. $325.00.

Annual Spring Pension Law and Practice Update 1994
Two-tape series introducing lawyers to the IR determination letter program concerning pensions and employee benefits. Discusses VCR and CAP issues, Harris Bank v. John Hancock, and more. Includes study materials. 210m; VHS. **A:** Adult. **P:** Professional. **U:** Institution. **Bus-Ind**: Law. **Dist:** American Law Institute - Committee on Continuing Professional Education. $200.

Annual Spring Pension Law and Practice Update, Featuring the Latest Treaty and PBGC Regulations 1993
Series discussing pension employee benefit programs. Issues discussed include 401(a)(4) nondiscrimination regulation, IRS audit procedure, Unemployment Compensation Amendments of 1992, PBGC regulations, and more. Includes study guide. 210m; VHS. **A:** Adult. **P:** Professional. **U:** Institution. **Bus-Ind**: Law, Finance. **Dist:** American Law Institute - Committee on Continuing Professional Education. $200.

Annual Spring Pension Law and Practice Update—Highlights: Age-Based Profit Sharing Plans; New Proposed ERISA Section 404(c) Regs; and Timing 1991
Discusses ERISA Section 404(c), IRC Section 401(a)(4), SLOB, and Section 401(k). Two-tape series includes study materials. 210m; VHS. **A:** Adult. **P:** Professional. **U:** Institution. **Bus-Ind**: Law. **Dist:** American Law Institute - Committee on Continuing Professional Education. $200.

Annual Teleconference on Securities Regulation 1990
Recorded live, this video presents the ups and downs of current trends in the business and economic world. Also explores the many ways, both legal and illegal, in which attorneys aid the corporate cycle. Comes with course handbook. 210m; VHS. **Pr:** Practicing Law Institute. **A:** College-Adult. **P:** Professional. **U:** Institution, Home. **Bus-Ind**: Law, Business, Finance. **Acq:** Purchase. **Dist:** Practising Law Institute. $195.00.

Annuals/Hanging Baskets 1980
Syndicated columnist Ed Hume discusses the care of annuals and the preparation of hanging baskets. Part of the "Lawn and Garden" series. 60m; VHS, 3/4 U, Special order formats. **Pr:** Cinema Associates. **A:** Jr. High-Adult. **P:** Instruction. **U:** Institution, CCTV, CATV, BCTV, Home. **How-Ins**: Gardening. **Acq:** Purchase. **Dist:** RMI Media. $14.95.

Annunciation 1977
This is a dramatic symbiosis of dance and film which interweaves moments from a woman's life, traversing past, present and future, to create an archetypal experience of time and place. 16m; VHS, 3/4 U. **Pr:** Marcelo Epstein. **A:** Sr. High-Adult. **P:** Education. **U:** Institution, SURA. **Fin-Art**: Dance. **Acq:** Purchase. **Dist:** Phoenix Learning Group.

Ano Nuevo 1989
Documents the living and working conditions faced by illegal Mexican immigrants. 55m; VHS, 3/4 U. **TV Std:** NTSC, PAL, SECAM. **Pr:** Todd Darling. **A:** Jr. High-Adult. **P:** Education. **U:** Institution, SURA. **Gen-Edu**: Immigration, Sociology, Minorities. **Acq:** Purchase, Rent/Lease, Duplication. **Dist:** The Cinema Guild.

Anonymous 2011 (PG-13) — ★½
Weaves a political thriller around the conspiracy theory that William Shakespeare didn't write his own works. Rather it was actually Edward De Vere, Earl of Oxford (played exceptionally by Ifans), who was forced to keep his gift secret by a political structure that devalued art. Director Emmerich changes gears after his string of CGI-driven end-of-the-world blockbusters, though this melodramatic piece is just as absurd. A wasted effort for Redgrave as Queen Elizabeth I. 130m; DVD, Blu-Ray. **C:** Rhys Ifans; Vanessa Redgrave; Joely Richardson; David Thewlis; Jamie Campbell Bower; Rafe Spall; Xavier Samuel; Sebastian Armesto; Ed Hogg; Sam Reid; Directed by Roland Emmerich; Written by John Orloff; Cinematography by Anna Foerster; Music by Harald Kloser. **Pr:** Roland Emmerich; Larry J. Franco; Robert Leger; Roland Emmerich; Columbia Pictures; Centropolis Entertainment; Relativity Media; Sony Pictures Home Entertainment Inc. **A:** Jr. High-Adult. **P:** Entertainment. **U:** Home. **L:** English. **Mov-Ent**: Drama. **Acq:** Purchase. **Dist:** Sony Pictures Home Entertainment Inc.

Anonymous at Westbrook Hospital 197?
A doctor, hardened by his son's death, finds it hard to relate to his young patients until an orphan is admitted to the hospital with head injuries. 28m; VHS, 3/4 U. **A:** Jr. High-Adult. **P:** Religious. **U:** Institution, SURA. **Gen-Edu**: Ethics & Morals, Human Relations. **Acq:** Purchase, Rent/Lease. **Dist:** Faith for Today.

Anonymous Hero 1989
This program teaches emergency medical dispatchers about anxious callers, medical interrogation, and telephone treatment sequences for common emergencies. 33m; VHS, 3/4 U. **Pr:** Focal Point Productions. **A:** College-Adult. **P:** Professional. **U:** Institution, Home, SURA. **Hea-Sci**: Medical Care, Health Education, Emergencies. **Acq:** Purchase, Rent/Lease, Duplication License. **Dist:** Pyramid Media. $195.00.

Anonymous Rex 2004 (Unrated) — ★★
So dinosaurs didn't actually die off, they adapted and live side-by-side with humans. They wear holographic suits as disguises. Dino-detectives Vince Rubio and Ernie Watson are out to stop a mutant sect that wants to wipe out mankind. Based on the comic mysteries by Eric Garcia. 89m; DVD. **C:** Sam Trammell; Daniel Baldwin; Faye Dunaway; Isaac Hayes; Tamara Gorski; Stephanie Lemelin; Directed by Julian Jarrold; Written by Joe Menosky; Cinematography by Albert J. Dunk; Kit Whitmore; Music by David Bergeaud. **A:** Sr. High-Adult. **P:** Entertainment. **U:** Home. **Mov-Ent**: Dinosaurs. **Acq:** Purchase. **Dist:** Allumination Filmworks.

Anonymous Was a Woman 1977
Many great pieces of American folk art were made by women in their spare time who had no awareness of themselves as "artists." Part of the series, "The Originals." 30m; VHS, 3/4 U. **C:** Directed by Mirra Bank. **Pr:** Perry Miller Adato; WNET. **A:** College-Adult. **P:** Education. **U:** Institution, SURA. **Gen-Edu**: Documentary Films, Women, Art & Artists. **Acq:** Purchase. **Dist:** Home Vision Cinema. $198.00.

Anorexia and Bulimia 199?
Reviews self-starvation, discussing avoidance of eating disorders, medical care and psychological counseling. 10m; VHS. **A:** Primary. **P:** Education. **U:** Institution. **Gen-Edu**: Eating Disorders, Mental Health. **Dist:** Marshmedia. $59.95.

Anorexia Nervosa 1988
Different aspects of this particular eating disorder are examined. 10m; VHS, 3/4 U. **Pr:** Professional Research. **A:** Sr. High-Adult. **P:** Education. **U:** Institution, CCTV. **Hea-Sci**: Eating Disorders. **Acq:** Purchase, Rent/Lease. **Dist:** Discovery Education. $295.00.

Anorexia Nervosa 1992
Summarizes common causes of this eating disorder, such as low self-esteem, family problems, cultural factors, etc. A recovering anorexic shares her personal experiences. Encourages support groups. 11m; VHS. **A:** Jr. High-Adult. **P:** Education. **U:** Institution. **Hea-Sci**: Eating Disorders, Health Education. **Acq:** Purchase. **Dist:** Cambridge Educational. $59.95.

Anorexia: Thin Obsession 1990
The eating disorder anorexia is defined and described. Discusses symptoms, causes, and help available. ?m; VHS. **A:** Jr. High-Sr. High. **P:** Education. **U:** Institution. **Hea-Sci**: Eating Disorders. **Acq:** Purchase. **Dist:** Meridian Education Corp. $45.00.

Anosognosia 1972
A doctor describes the history of anosognosia. 16m; VHS, 3/4 U, Special order formats. **Pr:** Ohio State University Health Sciences AV Center. **A:** College-Adult. **P:** Professional. **U:** Institution, SURA. **Hea-Sci:** Neurology. **Acq:** Purchase, Rent/Lease. **Dist:** Ohio State University.

Another Africa: Wildlife and People in Conflict 1986
This production is highlighted by footage of African wildlife-elephants, giraffes, lions, hyenas, and more. Interviews with Masai and Kikuyu tribespeople, as well as English safari guides, dramatize the increasing conflict. 25m; VHS, 3/4 U. **Pr:** Centre Productions, Inc. **A:** Sr. High-Adult. **P:** Education. **U:** Institution, SURA. **Gen-Edu:** Africa, Anthropology, Wildlife. **Acq:** Purchase. **Dist:** Clear Vue Inc.

Another Brother 1998 (Unrated)
Photographs, audiotaped interviews, and archival footage portray the story of Vietnam veteran Clarence Fitch, an African American deeply entrenched and affected by racism, the Black civil rights movement, the Vietnam War and aftermath, the scourge of drugs, and AIDS crisis. 51m; VHS, DVD. **A:** Adult. **P:** Education. **U:** Institution. **Gen-Edu:** Vietnam War, Black Culture, History. **Acq:** Purchase. **Dist:** Third World Newsreel. $300.

Another Call from Home 1991
A training program that treats family matters as a business issue, showing how to help employees balance career and home life. Workshop materials are included. 28m; VHS, 3/4 U, Special order formats. **Pr:** Dartnell. **A:** College-Adult. **P:** Education. **U:** Institution. **Bus-Ind:** Employee Counseling, Business, Personnel Management. **Acq:** Purchase, Rent/Lease. **Dist:** Excellence in Training Corp. $635.00.

Another Chance 1988 (R) — ★★
Girl-crazy bachelor is returned from heaven for a second chance and has to choose between a "bad" girl and a "good" girl. What a choice! 99m; VHS. **C:** Bruce Greenwood; Frank Annese; Jeff East; Anne Ramsey; Barbara (Lee) Edwards; Directed by Jerry Vint. **Pr:** Republic. **A:** Adult. **P:** Entertainment. **U:** Home. **Mov-Ent:** Comedy--Romantic, Death. **Acq:** Purchase. **Dist:** Lions Gate Entertainment Inc. $9.98.

Another Cinderella Story 2008 (PG) — ★★½
Same basic plot as 2004's "A Cinderella Story" with different characters. Our Cinderella is Mary (Gomez), whose mean stepsisters are trying to stop her from putting on her dancing shoes and going to a costume ball. But Mary makes it and dances with Joey (Seeley), the most popular guy around, who recognizes that this is his dream girl even behind a mask. When Mary has to make a quick exit to meet her curfew, Joey's only clue is the phone she left behind. 90m; DVD, Blu-Ray. **C:** Jane Lynch; Katharine Isabelle; Emily Perkins; Marcus T. Paulk; Selena Gomez; Andrew Seeley; Jessica Parker Kennedy; Directed by Damon Santostefano; Written by Masahiro Asakawa; Jessica Scott; Cinematography by Jon Joffin; Music by John Paesano. **A:** Family. **P:** Entertainment. **U:** Home. **Mov-Ent. Acq:** Purchase. **Dist:** Warner Home Video, Inc.

Another Country 1984 (Unrated) — ★★½
Mitchell's adaptation of his play based on the life of Guy Burgess, who became a spy for the Soviet Union. Guy Bennett (Everett) is an English boarding school upperclassman whose affected mannerisms and barely disguised homosexuality cause dissension among his schoolmates, while his one friend, Tommy Judd (Firth), is a fervant Marxist. Rather fancifully depicted and loving recreation of 1930s English life. Although the film is inferior to the award-winning play, director Kanievska manages to transform a piece into a solid film, and Everett's performance as Bennett/Burgess is outstanding. 90m; VHS, DVD. **C:** Rupert Everett; Colin Firth; Michael Jenn; Robert Addie; Anna Massey; Betsy Brantley; Rupert Wainwright; Cary Elwes; Arthur Howard; Tristan Oliver; Frederick Alexander; Adrian Ross-Magenty; Geoffrey Bateman; Philip Dupuy; Jeffrey Wickham; Gideon Boulting; Ivor Howard; Charles Spencer; Directed by Marek Kanievska; Written by Julian Mitchell; Cinematography by Peter Biziou; Music by Michael Storey. **Pr:** Goldcrest Films. **A:** Sr. High-Adult. **P:** Entertainment. **U:** Home. **Mov-Ent. Acq:** Purchase. **Dist:** Unknown Distributor.

Another Day 1976
This program is a musical documentary with the artist as featured performer, combining documentary, musical, scripted, and improvised material. 14m/B/W; VHS, DVD, 3/4 U. **Pr:** Joel Gold. **A:** Sr. High-Adult. **P:** Entertainment. **U:** Institution, SURA. **Gen-Edu:** Video. **Acq:** Purchase, Rent/Lease. **Dist:** Maxi Cohen Film & Video Productions.

Another Day in Paradise 1998 (R) — ★★
Tulsa teen junkies Bobbie (Kartheiser) and Rosie (Wagner) team up with older junkie couple Mel (Woods) and Sidney (Griffith) and go from bad to worse. Mel's also a dealer and thief and is glad to add two would-be partners in crime to his and Sidney's traveling road to hell. Woods is all sly confidence while Griffith shows some seductive tough-chick grit and the younger twosome manage to hold their own nicely. Not a pic for the faint of heart or queasy of stomach. Based on the book by Eddie Little. 101m; VHS, DVD. **C:** James Woods; Melanie Griffith; Vincent Kartheiser; Natasha Gregson Wagner; Paul Hipp; Brent Briscoe; Lou Diamond Phillips; Directed by Larry Clark; Written by Christopher Landon; Stephen Chin; Cinematography by Eric Alan Edwards. **Pr:** Larry Clark; James Woods; James Woods; Larry Clark; Stephen Chin; Chinese Bookie Pictures; Trimark Pictures. **A:** Sr. High-Adult. **P:** Entertainment. **U:** Home. **Mov-Ent:** Crime Drama, Drug Abuse. **Acq:** Purchase. **Dist:** Lions Gate Home Entertainment; CinemaNow Inc.

Another Day of Cruising 1976
This program presents safety tips for recreational boating and discusses the essentials of basic boating courtesy and skill. 25m; VHS, 3/4 U, Special order formats. **Pr:** U.S. Coast Guard. **A:** Family. **P:** Education. **U:** Institution, SURA. **Spo-Rec:** Boating. **Acq:** Purchase. **Dist:** National Audiovisual Center.

Another Earth 2011 (PG-13) — ★★
Cahill's expressionistic low-budget flick is melodramatic and compelling at the same time. A 10th planet—a duplicate Earth—is discovered and young MIT student Rhoda (co-writer Marling) is so busy looking at Earth 2 that she plows her SUV into another car and kills all but one of the occupants. After serving a prison term, a penitent Rhoda tries making amends by secretly befriending the lone survivor, isolated and grief-stricken composer John (Mapother), while still being obsessed with the possibility of an alternate reality on the alternate planet. 92m; DVD, Blu-Ray, On Demand. **C:** Brit Marling; William Mapother; Jordan Baker; Flint Beverage; Kumar Pallana; Directed by Mike Cahill; Written by Brit Marling; Mike Cahill; Cinematography by Mike Cahill; Music by Fall on Your Sword. **Pr:** Nicholas Shumaker; Brit Marling; Mike Cahill; Hunter Gray; Artists Public Domain; Fox Searchlight. **A:** Sr. High-Adult. **P:** Entertainment. **U:** Home. **L:** English. **Mov-Ent:** Science. **Acq:** Purchase. **Dist:** Movies Unlimited; Fox Home Entertainment; Amazon.com Inc.

Another First Step—From Institution to Independence 1994
Tells the story of 26-year-old Michael Whalen after his grandfather asks him to assume responsibility for his 46-year-old disabled son. 51m; VHS. **A:** Adult. **P:** Education. **U:** Institution. **Gen-Edu:** Family, Handicapped. **Acq:** Purchase. **Dist:** Filmakers Library Inc. $295.00.

Another 48 Hrs. 1990 (R) — ★½
Continuing chemistry between Nolte and Murphy is one of the few worthwhile items in this stodgy rehash. Any innovation by Murphy seems lost, the story is redundant of any other cop thriller, and violence and car chases abound. Pointlessly energetic and occasionally fun for only the true devotee. 98m; VHS, DVD, 8 mm, CC. **C:** Eddie Murphy; Nick Nolte; Brion James; Kevin Tighe; Bernie Casey; David Anthony Marshall; Ed O'Ross; Tisha Campbell; Directed by Walter Hill; Written by Jeb Stuart; Cinematography by Matthew F. Leonetti; Music by James Horner. **Pr:** Paramount Pictures. **A:** College-Adult. **P:** Entertainment. **U:** Home. **Mov-Ent:** Action-Adventure. **Acq:** Purchase. **Dist:** Paramount Pictures Corp. $14.95.

Another Great Class 19??
Dance instructor David Howard and four dancers from the David Howard Center in New York City demonstrate a dance exercise which covers the entire barre and excerpts from all 13 combinations. 60m; VHS. **A:** Jr. High-Adult. **P:** Instruction. **U:** Home, Institution. **How-Ins:** Dance--Instruction. **Acq:** Purchase. **Dist:** Stagestep. $26.95.

Another Happy Day 2011 (R) — ★★
An angry dysfunctional family portrait that unfortunately mistakes drama for comedy. Neurotic mother Lynn (Barkin) hits the road with her two youngest sons to Annapolis for the marriage of her oldest son Dylan (Nardelli) to Heather (Coover). Inflated ego trips lead to the inevitable, and cliched, clash with the in-laws, setting the stage for excellent, if a bit over-the-top performances from a great cast. Moore is especially in overdrive as a goofy, sexed up second wife of Lynn's abusive ex-husband Paul (Church). A feast for the performers, but doesn't give the audience much to digest. 119m; DVD, Blu-Ray. **C:** Ellen Barkin; Kate (Catherine) Bosworth; Michael Nardelli; Daniel Yelsky; Ezra Miller; George Kennedy; Ellen Burstyn; Thomas Haden Church; Demi Moore; Laura Coover; Jeffrey DeMunn; Directed by Sam Levinson; Written by Sam Levinson; Cinematography by Ivan Strasburg; Music by Olafur Arnalds. **Pr:** Celine Rattray; Ellen Barkin; Johnny Lin; Salli Newman; Ellen Barkin; Michael Nardelli; Mandalay Vision; Cineric Inc; Filmula; Michigan Production Studios; Prop Blast Films; Phase 4. **A:** Sr. High-Adult. **P:** Entertainment. **U:** Home. **L:** English. **Mov-Ent:** Drug Abuse. **Acq:** Purchase. **Dist:** Phase 4.

Another Home for Mom 19??
Documentary follows a couple as they confront the decision of whether to place the husband's mother, who has Alzheimer's Disease, in a nursing home. 30m; VHS. **A:** College-Adult. **P:** Education. **U:** Institution. **Hea-Sci:** Documentary Films, Patient Care, Aging. **Acq:** Purchase, Rent/Lease. **Dist:** Fanlight Productions. $195.00.

Another Kind of Music 1978
Two young rock musicians and a catchy reggae sound track generate a symbol with which today's young people can easily identify. 24m; VHS, 3/4 U. **Pr:** Rebecca Yates. **A:** Jr. High-Sr. High. **P:** Education. **U:** Institution, SURA. **Fin-Art. Acq:** Purchase. **Dist:** Phoenix Learning Group.

Another Life 2001 (Unrated) — ★★½
Based on the 1920s Thompson-Bywaters criminal case. Fanciful Edith (Little) makes a grave mistake by marrying staid Percy Thompson (Moran), whom she soon feels is dull, resentful, and cold. When Edith re-connects with exciting family friend Frederick Bywaters (Gruffudd), she strays, eventually confessing to Freddy that she wishes Percy were dead. He soon is and the adulterers stand trial for his murder. 101m; DVD. **C:** Natasha Little; Nick Moran; Ioan Gruffudd; Imelda Staunton; Rachael Stirling; Tom Wilkinson; Liz McKechnie; Directed by Philip Goodhew; Written by Philip Goodhew; Cinematography by Simon Archer; Music by James McConnel. **A:** Jr. High-Adult. **P:** Entertainment. **U:** Home. **Mov-Ent. Acq:** Purchase. **Dist:** BFS Video.

Another Lonely Hitman 1995 (Unrated) — ★★
Character study rather than a typical gangster flick. Old-school yakuza and former junkie Tachibana (Ishibashi) finds his ways badly out-of-date after he's released from a 10-year prison stretch. He tries to do the right thing by helping young druggie/hooker Yuki (Sawada) clean up (and the withdrawal scenes aren't pretty) and teach the younger hoods some manners. Based on the book by Yamanouchi, who did the screenplay; Japanese with subtitles. 105m; DVD, Wide. **C:** Ryo Ishibashi; Asami Sawada; Kazuhiko Kanayama; Tatsuo Yamada; Directed by Rokuro Mochizuki; Written by Yukio Yamanouchi; Cinematography by Naoki Imaizumi; Music by Kazutoki Umezu. **A:** Sr. High-Adult. **P:** Entertainment. **U:** Home. **L:** Japanese. **Mov-Ent:** Aging, Drug Abuse, Prostitution. **Acq:** Purchase. **Dist:** Movies Unlimited; Alpha Video.

Another Man, Another Chance 1977 (PG) — ★★
Remake of Lelouch's "A Man and a Woman," set in the turn-of-the-century American West, pales by comparison to the original. Slow-moving tale casts widow Bujold and widower Caan as lovers. 132m; VHS, DVD. **C:** James Caan; Genevieve Bujold; Francis Huster; Jennifer Warren; Susan Tyrrell; Directed by Claude Lelouch; Written by Claude Lelouch. **Pr:** Wood Knapp Video. **A:** Jr. High-Adult. **P:** Entertainment. **U:** Home. **Mov-Ent:** Western, Romance. **Acq:** Purchase. **Dist:** MGM Home Entertainment.

Another Man's Poison 1952 (Unrated) — ★★½
Melodramatic crime drama with a showy, if stereotypical role, for Davis. She's mystery writer Janet Frobisher and lives on a secluded Yorkshire farm. Too bad her escaped con husband suddenly shows up (and gets killed by Janet). Her troubles aren't over. Hubby's partner, George Bates (Merrill), comes a-lookin' and agrees to dispose of the body if Janet will let him hide out. She tries to kill Bates as well but her scheming comes to an unexpected conclusion. Adapted from the play "Deadlock" by Leslie Sands. 90m/B/W; VHS, DVD. **C:** Bette Davis; Gary Merrill; Emlyn Williams; Anthony Steel; Barbara Murray; Reginald Beckwith; Edna Morris; Directed by Irving Rapper; Written by Val Guest; Cinematography by Robert Krasker; Music by Paul Sawtell. **A:** Sr. High-Adult. **P:** Entertainment. **U:** Home. **Mov-Ent:** Crime Drama. **Acq:** Purchase. **Dist:** Movies Unlimited.

Another Meeting 1978
Gives practical ideas on how to improve the results and time efficiency of meetings. A solid basis for analyzing the meeting process is explored. 60m; 3/4 U. **A:** College-Adult. **P:** Professional. **U:** Institution, CCTV. **Bus-Ind:** Management. **Acq:** Purchase. **Dist:** Exec-U-Service Associates.

Another 9 1/2 Weeks 1996 (R) — **Bomb!**
Uninteresting sequel finds suicidal John (Rourke) overwhelmed by his kinky memories of Elizabeth, so he flies to Paris determined to find her. Instead, he meets fashion designer Lea (Everhart), who claims to be Elizabeth's friend and who puts the sexual tease on the S/M devotee. Monotony sets in early and there's no real heat generated between the duo. 104m; VHS, DVD, CC. **C:** Mickey Rourke; Angie Everhart; Steven Berkoff; Agathe de la Fontaine; Dougray Scott; Directed by Anne Goursaud; Written by Mick Davis; Cinematography by Robert Alazraki; Music by Stephen Parsons; Francis Haines. **Pr:** Staffan Ahrenberg; Barry Barnholtz; Don Carmody; Trimark Pictures. **A:** Sr. High-Adult. **P:** Entertainment. **U:** Home. **Mov-Ent. Acq:** Purchase. **Dist:** Lions Gate Home Entertainment; CinemaNow Inc.

Another 101 Best Tries 19??
An entertaining look at rugby in Great Britain. 60m; VHS. **Pr:** British Broadcasting Corporation. **A:** Jr. High-Adult. **P:** Entertainment. **U:** Home. **Spo-Rec:** Sports--General. **Acq:** Purchase. **Dist:** Video Collectibles. $29.95.

Another Page 1984
This reading series is designed for adults whose performance on standardized tests falls within the range of fifth to eighth grade levels. Preceded by a 15-minute orientation. 30m; VHS, 3/4 U. **Pr:** Kentucky Educational Television. **A:** Adult. **P:** Education. **U:** Institution, CCTV, CATV. **Gen-Edu:** Language Arts. **Acq:** Purchase, Rent/Lease, Free Loan. **Dist:** KET, The Kentucky Network.

Indiv. Titles: 1. Practical Reading (6 tapes) 2. General Reading (4 tapes) 3. Prose Literature (4 tapes).

Another Page: General Reading 1981
This series helps adults whose performance on a standardized reading test falls within the range of fifth to eighth grade levels to understand materials of general adult interest as found in popular magazines and newspapers. 30m; VHS, 3/4 U. **Pr:** KET/Cambridge. **A:** Adult. **P:** Education. **U:** Institution, CCTV, CATV, BCTV. **Gen-Edu:** Language Arts. **Acq:** Purchase. **Dist:** Prentice Hall.

Indiv. Titles: 1. Reading for Literal Information; Finding the Main Idea 2. Using Context Clues 3. Making Inferences 4. Evaluating Reading Material.

Another Page: Practical Reading 1981
This series helps adults whose performance on a standardized reading test falls within the range of fifth to eight grade levels to understand utilitarian materials such as forms, leases, how-to articles, advertisements, recipes and reference books. 30m; VHS, 3/4 U. **Pr:** KET/Cambridge. **A:** Adult. **P:** Education. **U:** Institution, CCTV, CATV, BCTV. **Gen-Edu:** Language Arts. **Acq:** Purchase. **Dist:** Prentice Hall.

Indiv. Titles: 1. Finding Directly Stated Facts/Details 2. Finding the Main Idea 3. Finding the Main Idea; Putting Facts Together to Draw a Logical conclusion 4. Making Inferences 5. Practical Applications: Using Sources of Information 6. Practical Applications: Reading Forms.

Another Page: Prose Literature 1981
This series helps adults whose performance on a standardized reading test falls within the range of fifth to eighth grade levels to understand contemporary fiction, biography, and essays. 30m; VHS, 3/4 U. **Pr:** KET/Cambridge. **A:** Adult. **P:** Education. **U:** Institution, CCTV, CATV, BCTV. **Gen-Edu**: Language Arts. **Acq:** Purchase. **Dist:** Prentice Hall.
Indiv. Titles: 1. Finding Directly Stated Facts/Details 2. Literal versus Figurative Language 3. Finding the Main Idea 4. Making Inferences (About Character, Theme, Setting).

Another Pair of Aces: Three of a Kind 1991 (Unrated) — ★★★
Nelson and Kristofferson team up to clear the name of Torn, a Texas Ranger accused of murder. Video contains some scenes deemed too racy for TV. Sequel to "A Pair of Aces." 93m; VHS, DVD. **C:** Willie Nelson; Kris Kristofferson; Joan Severance; Rip Torn; Dan Kamin; Ken Farmer; Richard Jones; Directed by Bill Bixby. **Pr:** Vidmark Entertainment. **A:** College-Adult. **P:** Entertainment. **U:** Home. **Mov-Ent**: Western, TV Movies. **Acq:** Purchase. **Dist:** Lions Gate Home Entertainment. $89.95.

Another Public Enemy 2005 (R) — ★
Prosecutor Kang investigates corrupt businessman Han, who is laundering his ill-gotten real estate gains in the U.S. Only his superiors suspect Kang's motives since the two were bitter high school rivals. Really, really, really long, which dilutes any action and suspense. Korean with subtitles. 148m; DVD. **C:** Kyung-gu Sol; Jun-ho Jeong; Shin-il Kang; Directed by Woo-suk Kang; Written by Woo-suk Kang; Music by Jawe-kwon Han. **A:** Sr. High-Adult. **P:** Entertainment. **U:** Home. **L:** Korean. **Mov-Ent**. **Acq:** Purchase. **Dist:** Palisades Tartan Video.

Another Set of Eyes: Conferencing Skills 1988
School administrators learn how they can get their teachers to give a better lesson. 45m; VHS, 3/4 U, EJ. **Pr:** Association for Supervision and Curriculum. **A:** Adult. **P:** Teacher Education. **U:** Institution, SURA. **Bus-Ind**: Education. **Acq:** Purchase, Rent/Lease. **Dist:** Association for Supervision and Curriculum Development. $695.00.

Another Set of Eyes: Techniques for Classroom Observation 1987
School administrators are told how they can better evaluate teacher performances. 60m; VHS, 3/4 U, EJ. **Pr:** Association for Supervision and Curriculum. **A:** Adult. **P:** Teacher Education. **U:** Institution, SURA. **Gen-Edu**: Education. **Acq:** Purchase, Rent/Lease. **Dist:** Association for Supervision and Curriculum Development. $445.00.

Another Stakeout 1993 (PG-13) — ★★½
Sequel six years after the original finds Dreyfuss and Estevez partnered again for another stakeout, this time to keep an eye on Moriarty, a reluctant witness against the Mob. The two spying detectives find themselves in an upscale neighborhood where blending in is a hard thing to do. O'Donnell is a breath of fresh air as a wisecracking assistant district attorney. Stowe briefly reprises her role as Dreyfuss' girlfriend. Writer Kouf reportedly had difficulty penning the script, surprising since there isn't much new here. 109m; VHS, DVD, CC. **C:** Richard Dreyfuss; Emilio Estevez; Rosie O'Donnell; Cathy Moriarty; Madeleine Stowe; John Rubinstein; Marcia Strassman; Dennis Farina; Miguel Ferrer; Directed by John Badham; Written by Jim Kouf; Cinematography by Roy Wagner. **Pr:** Jim Kouf; Lynn Bigelow; Cathleen Summers; John Badham; Jim Kouf; John Badham; Buena Vista. **A:** Sr. High-Adult. **P:** Entertainment. **U:** Home. **Mov-Ent**: Action-Adventure. **Acq:** Purchase. **Dist:** Buena Vista Home Entertainment. $96.83.

Another Thin Man 1939 — ★★½
Powell and Loy team up for the third in the delightful "Thin Man" series. Slightly weaker series entry takes its time, but has both Powell and Loy providing stylish performances. Nick Jr. is also introduced as the newest member of the sleuthing team. Sequel to "After the Thin Man"; followed by "Shadow of the Thin Man." 105m/B/W; VHS, DVD, CC. **C:** William Powell; Myrna Loy; Virginia Grey; Otto Kruger; Sir C. Aubrey Smith; Ruth Hussey; Directed by W.S. Van Dyke. **Pr:** MGM. **A:** Jr. High-Adult. **P:** Entertainment. **U:** Home. **Mov-Ent**: Mystery & Suspense, Comedy--Romantic. **Acq:** Purchase. **Dist:** MGM Home Entertainment. $24.95.

Another Time, Another Place 1958 (Unrated) — ★★
Sappy melodrama about an American journalist who suffers an emotional meltdown when her married British lover is killed during WWII. So she heads for Cornwall to console the widow and family. 98m/B/W; VHS, DVD. **C:** Lana Turner; Barry Sullivan; Glynis Johns; Sean Connery; Terence Longdon; Directed by Lewis Allen; Cinematography by Jack Hildyard. **Pr:** Paramount Pictures. **A:** Family. **P:** Entertainment. **U:** Home. **Mov-Ent**: Melodrama, World War Two, Journalism. **Acq:** Purchase. **Dist:** Paramount Pictures Corp. $19.95.

Another Time, Another Place 1983 (R) — ★★★
Bored young Scottish housewife married to an older fella falls in love with an Italian prisoner-of-war who works on her farm during WWII. Occasionally quirky, always finely crafted view of wartime Britain and the little-known life of POWs in England. 101m; VHS, CC. **C:** Phyllis Logan; Giovanni Mauriello; Gian Luca Favilla; Paul Young; Tom Watson; Directed by Michael Radford; Written by Michael Radford; Cinematography by Roger Deakins. **Pr:** Samuel Goldwyn Company. **A:** Sr. High-Adult. **P:** Entertainment. **U:** Home. **Mov-Ent**: Drama, World War Two, Scotland. **Acq:** Purchase. **Dist:** No Longer Available.

Another Way 1982 — ★★★
The director of 1971's much-lauded "Love" sets this politically charged love story in Hungary in 1958. Opening with a view of a female corpse, the story flashes backward to look at the woman's journalistic career and her relationship with a women colleague. Candid love scenes between women in Hungary of 1958, considered a cinematic novelty in many places outside Hungary. In Hungarian with English subtitles. 100m; VHS, DVD. **C:** Jadwiga Jankowska Cieslak; Grazyna Szapolowska; Josef Kroner; Hernadi Judit; Andorai Peter; Directed by Karoly Makk. **A:** College-Adult. **P:** Entertainment. **U:** Home. **L:** Hungarian. **Mov-Ent**: Drama, Women. **Awds:** Cannes '82: Actress (Cieslak). **Acq:** Purchase. **Dist:** Facets Multimedia Inc.; New Yorker Video.

Another Way of Looking at the World 19??
Diane Circincione and Dr. Gerald Jampolsky teach you how to make important changes in your life by explaining four important concepts that have helped them turn their lives around. 62m; VHS. **A:** Sr. High-Adult. **P:** Education. **U:** Home. **Gen-Edu**: Self-Help, Philosophy & Ideology. **Acq:** Purchase. **Dist:** Hay House Inc. $19.98.

Another Way to Learn 1968
This program documents an early attempt to introduce the English "integrated day" approach in an American primary classroom in a first grade in Wellesley, Massachusetts. Children are shown going about their activities with great independence and responsibility, with guidance from a strong, unobtrusive teacher. 12m/B/W; 3/4 U, Special order formats. **Pr:** Education Development Center. **A:** College-Adult. **P:** Education. **U:** Institution, CCTV, CATV, BCTV. **Gen-Edu**: Education, Children. **Acq:** Purchase, Rent/Lease. **Dist:** Education Development Center.

Another Woman 1988 (PG) — ★★★
The study of an intellectual woman whose life is changed when she begins to eavesdrop. What she hears provokes her to examine every relationship in her life, finding things quite different than she had believed. Heavy going, with Rowlands effective as a woman coping with an entirely new vision of herself. Farrow plays the catalyst. Although Allen's comedies are more popular than his dramas, this one deserves a look. 81m; VHS, DVD, Wide, CC. **C:** Gena Rowlands; Gene Hackman; Mia Farrow; Ian Holm; Betty Buckley; Martha Plimpton; Blythe Danner; Harris Yulin; Sandy Dennis; David Ogden Stiers; John Houseman; Philip Bosco; Frances Conroy; Kenneth Welsh; Michael Kirby; Directed by Woody Allen; Written by Woody Allen; Cinematography by Sven Nykvist. **Pr:** Jack Rollins; Charles H. Joffe; Orion Pictures. **A:** Jr. High-Adult. **P:** Entertainment. **U:** Home. **Mov-Ent**: Women. **Acq:** Purchase. **Dist:** MGM Studios Inc. $14.98.

Another Woman 1994 (Unrated) — ★½
Lisa Temple (Bateman) was attacked and left for dead in an alley. She wakes up in the hospital with amnesia but her bitter husband Paul (Outerbridge) still wants a divorce. Lisa learns things about herself she doesn't like and vows to change but as her memories start to return she realizes just what put her in that alley in the first place. From the Harlequin Romance Series; adapted from the Margot Dalton novel. 91m; DVD. **C:** Justine Bateman; Peter Outerbridge; Amy Stewart; Kenneth Welsh; James Purcell; Jackie Richardson; Michael Copeman; Elizabeth Lennie; Directed by Alan Smythe; Written by Jim Henshaw; Lee Langley; Lyle Slack; Cinematography by Michael Storey; Music by David Blamires. **A:** Jr. High-Adult. **P:** Entertainment. **U:** Home. **Mov-Ent**. **Acq:** Purchase. **Dist:** Echo Bridge Home Entertainment.

Another Woman's Husband 2000 (Unrated) — ★★½
Traumatized as a child by the drowning death of her brother, Laurel (Rinna) finally decides to get over her fear of water by taking swimming lessons. Susan (O'Grady) is her swimming instructor and they become best friends. Until the women realize they also share the same man (Midkiff), who happens to be Susan's husband. Based on the novel "Swimming Lessons" by Anna Villegas and Lynne Hugo. 91m; VHS, DVD. **C:** Lisa Rinna; Gail O'Grady; Dale Midkiff; Sally Kirkland; Charlotte Rae; Directed by Noel Nosseck; Written by Susan Arnout Smith; Cinematography by Alan Caso; Music by Mark Snow. **A:** Sr. High-Adult. **P:** Entertainment. **U:** Home. **Mov-Ent**. **Acq:** Purchase. **Dist:** Movies Unlimited; Alpha Video.

Another Year 2010 (PG-13) — ★★★
Despite the PG13 rating, Leigh's film is all about adults—some who are and some who should be. This slice of life drama, set in North London, features a year (corresponding to the seasons) in an interconnected group of family and friends that longtime-marrieds Tom (Broadbent) and Gerri (Sheen) regularly see. Among them is increasingly desperate, self-pitying Mary (Manville, in a shockingly vulnerable performance) who drinks too much and embarrasses herself with inappropriate flirtations. 129m; Blu-Ray, On Demand. **C:** Jim Broadbent; Ruth Sheen; Lesley Manville; Oliver Maltman; Peter Wight; David Bradley; Martin Savage; Philip Davis; Imelda Staunton; Karina Fernandez; Michele Austin; Directed by Mike Leigh; Written by Mike Leigh; Cinematography by Dick Pope; Music by Gary Yershon. **Pr:** Georgina Lowe; Thin Man; Sony Pictures Classics. **A:** College-Adult. **P:** Entertainment. **U:** Home. **L:** English. **Mov-Ent**: Marriage. **Acq:** Purchase. **Dist:** Amazon.com Inc.; Movies Unlimited; Alpha Video.

Another You 1991 (R) — ★
Con man Wilder takes pathological liar Pryor under his care and decides to use his talents to his fullest advantage. Posing as successful businessmen, the duo initiate a scam so complicated that they may end up being double-crossed or worse yet, dead! Can the pair see their plan through without losing their lives? Sad to see how far these two gifted comedians have fallen. Their collaboration is tired and the movie generally dreadful. 98m; VHS, DVD, 8 mm, CC. **C:** Richard Pryor; Gene Wilder; Mercedes Ruehl; Vanessa L(ynne) Williams; Stephen Lang; Kevin Pollak; Directed by Maurice Phillips. **Pr:** Tri-Star Pictures. **A:** Sr. High-Adult. **P:** Entertainment. **U:** Home. **Mov-Ent**. **Acq:** Purchase. **Dist:** Sony Pictures Home Entertainment Inc. $19.95.

Ansel Adams: Photographer 1981
An appreciative retrospective interview with the premiere American landscape photographer. 60m; VHS. **A:** Jr. High-Adult. **P:** Education. **U:** Home. **Gen-Edu**: Documentary Films, Art & Artists, Photography. **Acq:** Purchase. **Dist:** Facets Multimedia Inc.; Crystal Productions; PBS Home Video.

Anson Dorrance: Guide to a Winning Culture 2014 (Unrated)
Coach Anson Dorrance discusses practice planning, motivating players, and what he believes it takes to make a championship soccer team. 91m; DVD. **A:** Family. **P:** Education. **U:** Home. **L:** English. **Spo-Rec**: Athletic Instruction/Coaching, Soccer. **Acq:** Purchase. **Dist:** Championship Productions. $39.99.

Anson Dorrance: Train Like a Champion 2014 (Unrated)
Coach Anson Dorrance demonstrates competitive drills and games for improving the performance of a soccer team. 79m; DVD. **A:** Family. **P:** Education. **U:** Home. **L:** English. **Spo-Rec**: Athletic Instruction/Coaching, Soccer. **Acq:** Purchase. **Dist:** Championship Productions. $39.99.

The Answer Is You 1980
The role of the March of Dimes volunteer is highlighted in this feature, which shows people donating their time and energy toward the March of Dimes' goal of crusading against birth defects. 4m; 3/4 U. **Pr:** March of Dimes. **A:** College-Adult. **P:** Education. **U:** Institution, CCTV, CATV. **Gen-Edu**: Voluntary Services. **Acq:** Free Loan. **Dist:** March of Dimes.

The Answer Man 2009 (R) — ★★
Arlen Faber (Daniels) has suffered for 20 years as the author of a spiritual self-help guide that became a mass-media sensation. Unable to handle the fame, Arlen is a misanthropic recluse with back trouble that drives him into the arms of single mom/chiropractor Elizabeth (Graham) who thinks maybe Arlen could also be the new dad figure in her young son's life. Also having father issues is bookstore owner Kris (Pucci), just out of alcohol rehab, who turns to the reluctant Arlen for guidance. Pic skates on the emotional surface of some big issues but does have some nice turns by the leads. 96m; Blu-Ray, On Demand, Wide, CC. **C:** Jeff Daniels; Lauren Graham; Lou Taylor Pucci; Olivia Thirlby; Kat Dennings; Nora Dunn; Tony Hale; Directed by John Hindman; Written by John Hindman; Cinematography by Oliver Bokelberg; Music by Teddy Castellucci. **Pr:** Kevin J. Messick; Jana Edelbaum; 120 db Films; iDeal Partners Film Fund; Magnolia Pictures. **A:** Sr. High-Adult. **P:** Entertainment. **U:** Home. **L:** English. **Mov-Ent**: Comedy--Romantic, Mass Media. **Acq:** Purchase. **Dist:** Magnolia Home Entertainment; Amazon.com Inc.; Movies Unlimited.

Answer This 2010 (PG-13) — ★½
Nerd comedy. Trivia whiz Paul Tarson (Gorham) doesn't know what he's going to do after grad school. He postpones his long-overdue dissertation yet again so he and some buddies can tackle the First Annual Ann Arbor Pub Trivia Tournament. 105m; DVD, CC. **C:** Christopher Gorham; Nelson Franklin; Evan Jones; Arielle Kebbel; Kip Pardue; Chris Parnell; Ralph Williams; Directed by Christopher Farah; Written by Christopher Farah; Cinematography by Christian Sprenger; Music by John Paesano. **A:** Jr. High-Adult. **P:** Entertainment. **U:** Home. **Mov-Ent**: Games. **Acq:** Purchase. **Dist:** Lions Gate Entertainment Inc.

Answers by Inspection 1 1980
A simplified expression for voltage gain is developed and demonstrations serve to illustrate the usefulness and effectiveness of this formula. Part of the "Practical Transistors" series. 43m; VHS, 3/4 U. **Pr:** Hewlett Packard. **A:** College-Adult. **P:** Professional. **U:** Institution, CCTV, Home. **Bus-Ind**: Electronics. **Acq:** Purchase. **Dist:** Hewlett-Packard Media Solutions.

Answers by Inspection 2 1980
Formulas for the calculation of voltage gain with feedback, input impedance, output impedance, and distortion in common emitter circuits. Part of the "Practical Transistors" series. 40m; VHS, 3/4 U. **C:** George Stanley, Jr. **Pr:** Hewlett Packard. **A:** College-Adult. **P:** Professional. **U:** Institution, CCTV, Home. **Bus-Ind**: Electronics. **Acq:** Purchase. **Dist:** Hewlett-Packard Media Solutions.

Answers by Inspection 3 1980
The program concentrates on the emitter follower circuit and develops expressions for its voltage gain, and input and output impedance. Part of the "Practical Transistors" series. 37m; VHS, 3/4 U. **C:** George Stanley, Jr. **Pr:** Hewlett Packard. **A:** College-Adult. **P:** Professional. **U:** Institution, CCTV, Home. **Bus-Ind**: Electronics. **Acq:** Purchase. **Dist:** Hewlett-Packard Media Solutions.

Answers to Nothing 2011 (R) — ★½
Competent but undistinguished drama. Stories about five days in the lives of some Los Angelenos suffering various crises converge around the highly publicized search for a kidnapped young girl, including the female detective assigned to the case and several suspects. There's a therapist with his family issues plus the problems of a couple of his patients and a recovering alcoholic who's the caregiver for her disabled brother. 124m; DVD. **C:** Dane Cook; Elizabeth Mitchell; Julie Benz; Barbara Hershey; Zach Gilford; Erik Palladino; Mark Kelly; Kali Hawk; Aja Volkman; Directed by Matthewer Leutwyler; Written by Matthewer Leutwyler; Gillian Vigman; Cinematography by David Robert Jones; Music by Craig Richey. **Pr:** Amanda Marshall; Sim Sara; Cold Iron Pictures; Ambush Entertainment;

Roadside Attractions. **A:** Sr. High-Adult. **P:** Entertainment. **U:** Home. **L:** English. **Mov-Ent:** Handicapped, Psychiatry. **Acq:** Purchase. **Dist:** Lions Gate Home Entertainment.

Ant--America's Ready 2006 (Unrated)
Live performance by standup comedian Ant. 60m; DVD. **A:** Sr. High-Adult. **P:** Entertainment. **U:** Home. **L:** English. **Mov-Ent:** Comedy--Performance, Television. **Acq:** Purchase. **Dist:** Comedy Central; Goldhill Home Media. $14.98.

The Ant and the Aardvark 1969
Five Ant & Aardvark cartoons from the Pink Panther canon, including "The Ant from Uncle," "Never Bug an Ant" and "Technology, Phooey." 32m; VHS. **Pr:** D.F; Mirisch Geoffrey Productions. **A:** Preschool-Jr. High. **P:** Entertainment. **U:** Home. **Chl-Juv:** Animation & Cartoons. **Acq:** Purchase. **Dist:** MGM Home Entertainment. $14.95.

The Ant and the Grasshopper 1980
This Aesop fable, part of the "Classic Tales Retold" series, depicts the lesson of the lack of foresight, as illustrated by the lazy grasshopper and the industrious ant. 11m; VHS, 3/4 U. **Pr:** BFA Educational Media. **A:** Primary. **P:** Entertainment. **U:** Institution, SURA. **Chl-Juv:** Fairy Tales. **Acq:** Purchase. **Dist:** Phoenix Learning Group.

The Ant Bully 2006 (PG) — ★★½
Warner Bros. entry in the CGI-created insect category comes eight years after Pixar and DreamWorks set the standard with "A Bug's Life" and "Antz," respectively, and delivers nothing new. New kid on the block and neighborhood punching-bag Lucas, vents his frustration by picking on something smaller than him—an ant colony in his yard—only to be magically shrunken and transported into the ant's world to face his victims. Predictable life lessons about acceptance and teamwork, along with uninspired voice work from the star-studded cast drag down this visually impressive but all too familiar story. Based on the book by John Nickle. 88m; DVD, Blu-Ray. **C:** Voice(s) by Zach Tyler; Jake T. Austin; Nicolas Cage; Bruce Campbell; Meryl Streep; Julia Roberts; Paul Giamatti; Myles Jeffrey; Regina King; Cheri Oteri; Lily Tomlin; Rob Paulsen; Allison Mack; Ricardo Montalban; Larry Miller; Austin Majors; Mark DeCarlo; Frank Welker; Nicole Sullivan; Vernee Watson-Johnson; Directed by John A. Davis; Written by John A. Davis; Music by John Debney. **Pr:** John A. Davis; Tom Hanks; Gary Goetzman; Playtone Picture; Warner Bros. **A:** Family. **P:** Entertainment. **U:** Home. **L:** English. **Mov-Ent:** Animation & Cartoons, Insects, Action-Adventure. **Acq:** Purchase. **Dist:** Warner Home Video, Inc.

Ant Farm Video 2004
Documentary including footage of performance artists Doug Michels and Chip Lord, who formed in 1968, such as "Media Burn" (1975) featuring Michels and Curtis Schreier in astronaut suits and plowing their Phantom Dream Car into a pyramid of televisions. 127m; DVD. **A:** Sr. High-Adult. **P:** Entertainment. **U:** Home. **Mov-Ent:** Documentary Films, Art & Artists. **Acq:** Purchase. **Dist:** Facets Multimedia Inc. $29.95.

Ant World 1972
Documents the life cycles of the common ant and their parallels to human patterns. Ants practice slavery, organize for war, grow plants, keep pets, and become hooked on their own kind of drug. 15m; VHS, 3/4 U. **Pr:** Robert Crandall. **A:** Family. **P:** Education. **U:** Institution, Home, SURA. **L:** English, French. **Gen-Edu:** Insects. **Acq:** Purchase, Rent/Lease. **Dist:** Pyramid Media.

Antaeus 1982
Borden Deal's story about a rural boy from Alabama who moves to New York City in 1940. Young T.J. convinces his new friends to plant a garden on the roof of their apartment house. From the "LCA Short Story Library." 20m; VHS, 3/4 U. **Pr:** Learning Corporation of America. **A:** Jr. High-Sr. High. **P:** Education. **U:** Institution, SURA. **Gen-Edu:** Literature. **Acq:** Purchase, Rent/Lease. **Dist:** Phoenix Learning Group.

Antarctic Animals: Living on the Edge 19??
Profiles the animals that have adapted to life in Antarctica, including penguins and seals. Provides activities to help students understand how animals adapted and survived in the Antarctic. Includes teacher's guide. ?m; VHS. **Pr:** Children's Television Workshop. **A:** Primary-Jr. High. **P:** Education. **U:** Institution. **Chl-Juv:** Animals, Antarctic Regions. **Acq:** Purchase. **Dist:** GPN Educational Media. $15.00.

Antarctic Odyssey 1991
Another from the "Mutual of Omaha's Spirit of Adventure" series, this time focusing on the barren continent Antarctica. 50m; VHS. **C:** Hosted by Sam Posey. **A:** Family. **P:** Education. **U:** Home. **Gen-Edu:** Documentary Films, Antarctic Regions. **Acq:** Purchase. **Dist:** MPI Media Group. $19.98.

Antarctic Wildlife Adventure ????
National Geographic documentary providing first hand accounts of geographic issues and exploration. 60m; VHS; Closed Captioned. **A:** Jr. High-Sr. High. **P:** Education. **U:** Institution. **Gen-Edu:** Geography, Arctic Regions, Animals. **Acq:** Purchase. **Dist:** Zenger Media. $19.98.

Antarctic Wildlife Adventure 1995
Joins a family of real-life explorers, on board the 50-foot schooner Damien II, as they travel through the Antarctic region in search of the wildlife. Includes footage of humpback whales, penguins, and young elephant seals. 60m; VHS, CC. **Pr:** National Geographic Society. **A:** Family. **P:** Education. **U:** Institution, Home. **Gen-Edu:** Documentary Films, Antarctic Regions, Wildlife. **Acq:** Purchase. **Dist:** Sony Pictures Home Entertainment Inc. $19.95.

Antarctica 1984 — ★★
Due to unfortunate circumstances, a group of scientists must leave their pack of huskies behind on a frozen glacier in the Antarctic. The film focuses on the dogs' subsequent struggle for survival. Dubbed. 112m; VHS, CC. **C:** Ken Takakura; Masako Natsume; Keiko Oginome; Directed by Koreyoshi Kurahara; Music by Vangelis. **Pr:** TLC Films. **A:** Family. **P:** Entertainment. **U:** Home. **Mov-Ent:** Arctic Regions, Pets. **Acq:** Purchase. **Dist:** $59.98.

Antarctica 1989
This tape explores Antarctica and the use of this continent as a garbage dump and details the geography of Antarctica and the discovery of the depletion of ozone layer in that region. 26m; VHS, 3/4 U. **Pr:** Films for the Humanities and Sciences. **A:** College. **P:** Education. **U:** Institution, CCTV, CATV, BCTV. **Hea-Sci:** Ecology & Environment. **Acq:** Purchase, Rent/Lease, Duplication License. **Dist:** Films for the Humanities & Sciences.

Antarctica 1991
Builds a case for prohibiting the exploitation of Antarctica through discussions of the effects of pollution, global warming, and the hole in the ozone layer. Also features footage of Greenpeace combating a Japanese whaling ship. 58m; VHS. **A:** Sr. High-Adult. **P:** Education. **U:** Institution. **Gen-Edu:** Ecology & Environment. **Acq:** Purchase. **Dist:** Landmark Media. $250.00.

Antarctica 2008 (R) — ★½
Various Tel Aviv residents look for love or merely a one-night stand in Hochner's interconnecting stories. Librarian Omer and dancer Danny are looking for commitment, journalist Ronen and choreographer Boaz prefer to play the field, and Shirley keeps trying to leave her girlfriend Michal. Hebrew with subtitles. 112m; DVD. **C:** Ofer Regirer; Guy Zoaretz; Tomer Ilan; Yiftach Mizrahi; Lucy Dubinchik; Liat Ekta; Directed by Yair Hochner; Written by Yair Hochner; Cinematography by Ziv Berkovich; Music by Eli Soorani. **A:** College-Adult. **P:** Entertainment. **U:** Home. **L:** Hebrew. **Mov-Ent:** Sex & Sexuality. **Acq:** Purchase. **Dist:** Liberty International Entertainment.

Antarctica: A Threatened Ecosystem 1992
Portrays Antarctica as an ecologically important but environmentally threatened region. 18m; VHS, SVS, 3/4 U. **A:** Jr. High-Sr. High. **P:** Education. **U:** Institution. **Gen-Edu:** Ecology & Environment, Geography, Antarctic Regions. **Acq:** Purchase, Rent/Lease. **Dist:** Encyclopedia Britannica. $89.00.

Antarctica: Exploring the Frozen Continent 1979
Provides a history of major expeditions to the remote, frozen polar world of Antarctica, where 12 nations have presently established research centers. 22m; VHS, 3/4 U. **Pr:** Alan P. Sloan; Avatar Learning. **A:** Primary-Sr. High. **P:** Education. **U:** Institution, SURA. **Gen-Edu:** Antarctic Regions. **Acq:** Purchase, Rent/Lease, Trade-in. **Dist:** Encyclopedia Britannica.

Antarctica: Frozen Ambitions 1990
A look at the last unclaimed territory in the world—the frozen continent of Antarctica. This program focuses on the contrast between scientific ideals and political reality as the Antarctic Treaty comes up for a review after 30 years. 60m; VHS, CC, 3/4 U. **Pr:** Channel 4. **A:** Jr. High-Adult. **P:** Education. **U:** Institution, CCTV, CATV, Home. **Gen-Edu:** Antarctic Regions, Science, Wilderness Areas. **Acq:** Purchase, Duplication License, Off-Air Record. **Dist:** PBS Home Video. $59.95.

Antarctica: Getting to the South Pole 19??
Profiles Antarctica giving a description of the area and following the routes taken by early explorers. Provides hands-on exercises to help students learn why polar regions are colder than places near the Equator. Includes teacher's guide. ?m; VHS. **Pr:** Children's Television Workshop. **A:** Primary-Jr. High. **P:** Education. **U:** Institution. **Chl-Juv:** Science, Antarctic Regions. **Acq:** Purchase. **Dist:** GPN Educational Media. $15.00.

Antarctica: The Last Frontier 19??
Examines the international tensions endangering a unique treaty, which has protected this continent from the effects of human interference. 46m; VHS. **A:** Sr. High. **P:** Education. **U:** Institution. **Gen-Edu:** Ecology & Environment, International Relations. **Acq:** Purchase. **Dist:** Filmakers Library Inc. $295.

Antarctica: The Last Great Wilderness 19??
IMAX presentation journeys exotic Antartica, probing into its ice peaks, caverns, and wildlife. 40m; VHS. **A:** Jr. High-Adult. **P:** Education. **U:** Institution. **Gen-Edu:** Antarctic Regions. **Acq:** Purchase. **Dist:** Ark Media Group Ltd.

Antelami, the Baptistery of Parma 1987
A look at the blend of architecture, painting, and sculpture, which came together in the 13th century baptistery of the Cathedral of Parma. 18m; VHS, 8 mm, Special order formats. **C:** Directed by Carlo L. Ragghianti. **A:** Sr. High-Adult. **P:** Education. **U:** Institution, Home. **Fin-Art:** Documentary Films, Architecture, Art & Artists. **Acq:** Purchase. **Dist:** The Roland Collection. $89.00.

Anthem 1991
Experimental music video on homoeroticism and the African-American male. 9m; VHS, Special order formats. **C:** Directed by Marlon Riggs. **A:** College-Adult. **P:** Entertainment. **U:** Institution. **Fin-Art:** Music Video, Black Culture. **Acq:** Purchase. **Dist:** Frameline. $150.00.

Anthony Adverse 1936 — ★★½
March is a young man in the 19th century who searches for manhood across America and Mexico. He grows slowly as he battles foes, struggles against adversity and returns home to find his lover in this romantic swashbuckler. A star-studded cast, lush costuming, and an energetic musical score. Highly acclaimed in its time, but now seems dated. Based on the novel by Hervey Allen. 141m/B/W; VHS. **C:** Fredric March; Olivia de Havilland; Anita Louise; Gale Sondergaard; Claude Rains; Edmund Gwenn; Louis Hayward; Anne Howard; Directed by Mervyn LeRoy; Cinematography by Gaetano Antonio "Tony" Gaudio; Music by Erich Wolfgang Korngold. **A:** Family. **P:** Entertainment. **U:** Home. **Mov-Ent:** Drama. **Awds:** Oscars '36: Cinematog., Film Editing, Score, Support. Actress (Sondergaard). **Acq:** Purchase. **Dist:** Baker and Taylor; MGM Home Entertainment. $19.98.

Anthony & Cleopatra 19??
Contains Shakespeare's story of two of history's most famous lovers and how they struggled for power against the rulers of the Roman world. 183m; VHS. **C:** Timothy Dalton; Lynn Redgrave; John Carradine; Anthony Geary. **A:** Jr. High-Adult. **P:** Entertainment. **U:** Home. **Mov-Ent:** Drama, Middle East, Africa. **Acq:** Purchase. **Dist:** Stagestep. $20.95.

Anthony Jeselnik: Caligula 2013 (Unrated)
Stand-up performance by comedian Anthony Jeselnik, including some of his material from Comedy Central roasts among the bonus features. 60m; DVD, Streaming. **A:** Sr. High-Adult. **P:** Entertainment. **U:** Home. **L:** English. **Mov-Ent:** Comedy--Performance, Television. **Acq:** Purchase, Rent/Lease. **Dist:** Comedy Central. $14.98 14.99.

Anthony Tudor 19??
Color and black & white film footage of Tudor classics "Pillar of Fire," "Dark Elegies," "Undertow," "Jardin aux Lilas," and "Romeo & Juliet." Also contains interviews with Tudor, Margaret Caraske, Agnes de Mille, Nora Kaye, and Martha Hill. 60m; VHS. **A:** College-Adult. **P:** Entertainment. **U:** Institution, Home. **Fin-Art:** Dance--Performance, Dance--Ballet. **Acq:** Purchase. **Dist:** Stagestep. $49.95.

Anthrax: Live Noize 1991
Contains live concert footage of Anthrax from their tour with Public Enemy. Songs include "Anti-Social," "I'm the Man," and "Parasite." 60m; VHS. **A:** Jr. High-Adult. **P:** Entertainment. **U:** Home. **Mov-Ent:** Music Video, Music--Pop/Rock. **Acq:** Purchase. **Dist:** Music Video Distributors. $19.95.

Anthrax: Through Time P.O.V. 1989
Perhaps the heaviest of all metal bands is here to destroy your conceptions about reality with songs "Metal Thrashing Mad," "Madhouse," "I'm the Man," "Anti-Social," "Who Cares Wins," "Got the Time" and "In My World." 60m; VHS. **Pr:** Island Visual Arts. **A:** Jr. High-Adult. **P:** Entertainment. **U:** Home. **Mov-Ent:** Music Video, Music--Pop/Rock. **Acq:** Purchase. **Dist:** Music Video Distributors. $19.95.

Anthropod Identification 19??
Identifies six classes and eight orders of anthropods, including ticks, mites, spiders, and scorpions. Centers on the physical characteristics of each, such as size, color, and unique features. Part of the "Entomology Series." 10m; VHS. **A:** Jr. High-Adult. **P:** Education. **U:** Institution. **Hea-Sci:** Insects, Science. **Acq:** Purchase. **Dist:** CEV Multimedia. $49.95.

Anthropology: A Study of People 1970
This show tells how anthropologists study groups of people and ancient cultures. 17m; VHS, 3/4 U. **Pr:** Wayne Mitchell. **A:** Jr. High-Sr. High. **P:** Education. **U:** Institution, SURA. **Gen-Edu:** Anthropology. **Acq:** Purchase. **Dist:** Phoenix Learning Group.

Anthropophagus: The Grim Reaper 1980 (Unrated) — ★★
Disturbing cult film about American tourists vacationing in Greece who stumble upon an island village that appears to be missing all its inhabitants. Infamously gory, and rarely available in its uncut form due to its graphic nature. 90m; DVD. **C:** George Eastman; Saverio Vallone; Mark Bodin; Bob Larson; Tisa Farrow; Serena Grandi; Margaret Mazzantini; Rubina Rey; Zora Kerova; Directed by Joe D'Amato; Written by George Eastman; Joe D'Amato; Cinematography by Enrico Biribicchi; Music by Marcello Giombini. **A:** Sr. High-Adult. **P:** Entertainment. **U:** Home. **L:** English. **Mov-Ent. Acq:** Purchase. **Dist:** Media Blasters Inc. $16.98.

Anti-Climax 1993
Safe sex presentation targeted at older male students. Rob and Kelly, both high on alcohol, consider having sex. Kelly questions Rob's sexual history, and after considering the one night stand, decides to pass. Humorous approach to a serious topic is successful. "Captain Condom" expounds important safe sex information. 20m; VHS. **Pr:** Benjamin/Steibal Productions. **A:** Sr. High-College. **P:** Education. **U:** Institution. **Hea-Sci:** Sex & Sexuality, AIDS, Birth Control. **Acq:** Purchase, Rent/Lease. **Dist:** Select Media, Inc. $189.00.

Anti-Friction Bearing Lubrication 1986
Part of a series offering instruction on installation and maintenance procedures for service life of common power transmission products. 21m; VHS. **A:** Adult. **P:** Vocational. **U:** Institution. **Gen-Edu:** Industrial Arts, Technology. **Acq:** Purchase. **Dist:** RMI Media. $132.50.

Anti-Friction Bearing Lubrication 1995
Covers the selection of proper lubricant for a given application, the amount necessary, the optimum frequency and problems with lubricant contamination. 21m; VHS. **A:** Adult. **P:** Professional. **U:** Institution. **Bus-Ind:** Job Training, Management, How-To. **Acq:** Rent/Lease. **Dist:** National Safety Council, California Chapter, Film Library.

Anti-Infective Medication Therapy-Nursing Implications 19??
Three video series is designed to provide the healthcare professional with the knowledge of the vital role of anti-infective agents in patient care and to illustrate the nurse's increased responsibilities when administering such drugs. Titles include:

"Assessment of an Infection," "Antibiotics" and "Antifungal, Antiviras, and Antitubercular Agents." ?m; VHS. **A:** College-Adult. **P:** Education. **U:** Institution. **Hea-Sci:** Nursing, Medical Education. **Acq:** Purchase. **Dist:** Concept Media.

Anti-Lock Brake Systems Explained 1989
The operation and repair of anti-lock brake systems are examined for the benefit of auto mechanics. This series is also available as a single tape for the same cost. ?m; VHS. **Pr:** Bergwall Productions. **A:** Sr. High-Adult. **P:** Instruction. **U:** Institution. **How-Ins:** Automobiles, Industrial Arts. **Acq:** Purchase. **Dist:** Bergwall Productions, Inc. $369.00.
Indiv. Titles: 1. How Automotive Brakes Work 2. Theory and Operation 3. Service and Troubleshooting 4. Diagnosis and Repair of Drum Brakes 5. Diagnosis and Repair of Disc Brakes.

Anti-Matter 1974
An examination of relativity, cloud chambers, atom smashers, and particle physics. 12m; VHS, 3/4 U. **Pr:** American Educational Films. **A:** College-Adult. **P:** Education. **U:** Institution, SURA. **Hea-Sci:** Physics. **Acq:** Purchase. **Dist:** Capital Communications. $49.99.

Anti-Microbial Resistance: Lessons from Clinical Epidemiology 1987
A look at a disease's ability to acquire resistance to an antibiotic, and what is being done to combat that problem. 53m; VHS, 3/4 U. **C:** John E. McGowan, Jr. **A:** Adult. **P:** Professional. **U:** Institution, CCTV, Home, SURA. **Hea-Sci:** Immunology, Diseases. **Acq:** Purchase, Rent/Lease, Subscription. **Dist:** Emory Medical Television Network.

Anti-Terrorism: Weapons and Tactics 1987
Peter Eliot, one of the world's top anti-terrorism weapons and tactics experts, gives the viewer an insight into the training of an anti-terrorist team. He demonstrates selected life-threatening scenarios, such as hostage releases, using live ammunition, plastic explosives and the most effective tactical handgun and positive-controlled room-entry techniques. Also includes essential anti-terrorist travel tips. 30m; VHS. **TV Std:** NTSC, PAL. **Pr:** Mark Schulze; New and Unique Videos. **A:** Adult. **P:** Instruction. **U:** Home. **Gen-Edu:** Documentary Films, Terrorism, Firearms. **Acq:** Purchase. **Dist:** New & Unique Videos; Gun Video. $39.95.

Anti-Terrorist Cell: Manhunt 2001 (Unrated) — ★
The ATC is an international covert organization that hunts terrorists who escape government, military, and police agencies although this case involves a group of greedy mercenaries. Made as a TV pilot for the European market, it failed to sell—probably because it's cheap and boring. 92m; DVD. **C:** Joe Penny; Michael Wincott; Arnold Vosloo; Michael Ironside; Ben Cross; Colin Salmon; Directed by Jerry Jameson; Written by Terry Thompson; Steven Whitney; Cinematography by Fernando Arguelles; Music by Martin Locker. **A:** Jr. High-Adult. **P:** Entertainment. **U:** Home. **Mov-Ent. Acq:** Purchase. **Dist:** Morningstar Entertainment.

Antibodies 2005 (Unrated) — ★★
Captured serial killer Gabriel Engel (Hennicke) admits to the murders of 13 boys and is suspected in the death of a young girl in a rural community. Naive local cop Michael Martens (Mohring) travels to the city to question the now wheelchair-bound Engel and close his case. But Engel tries to convince him that someone else killed the girl and Michael learns more about the killer and himself that he could have imagined. German with subtitles. 128m; DVD. **C:** Andre Hennicke; Wotan Wilke Mohring; Heinz Hoenig; Ulrike Krumbiegel; Jurgen Schornagel; Directed by Christian Alvart; Written by Christian Alvart; Cinematography by Hagen Bogdanski; Music by Michi Britsch. **A:** Sr. High-Adult. **P:** Entertainment. **U:** Home. **L:** German. **Mov-Ent. Acq:** Purchase. **Dist:** MPI Media Group.

Antibody 2002 (R) — ★★
Terrorist Moran (Vergov) has a nuclear bomb and the detonator chip is inside his body. He's shot and if he dies, the chip will go off. So it's up to security expert Richard Gaynes (Henriksen) and a team of scientists to send an experimental tracking craft inside Moran's bloodstream to find and extract the chip in time. 90m; VHS, DVD. **C:** Lance Henriksen; Robin Givens; William Zabka; Julian Vergov; Directed by Christian McIntire; Written by Micheal Baldwin; Cinematography by Adolfo Bartoli; Music by Scott Clausen. **A:** Sr. High-Adult. **P:** Entertainment. **U:** Home. **Mov-Ent:** Terrorism. **Acq:** Purchase. **Dist:** Movies Unlimited; Alpha Video.

Antichrist 2009 (Unrated) — ★
Challenging in all the wrong ways, Von Tier's self-conscious, symbolic, misogynistic, psychosexual arthouse horror is divided into four chapters and begins with the accidental death of a toddler. The nameless traumatized mother (Gainsbourg) and her domineering husband (Dafoe), a professional therapist, go to their isolated home in the country in an effort to deal with their grief. Soon, her sanity is in question and Von Tier eventually tips over the edge in a graphically-depicted mutilation scene. In black and white and color. 105m; Blu-Ray, On Demand, Wide. **C:** Charlotte Gainsbourg; Willem Dafoe; Directed by Lars von Trier; Written by Lars von Trier; Cinematography by Anthony Dod Mantle. **Pr:** Meta Louise Foldanger; Zentropa Entertainment; Memfis Film Intl; Lucky Red; Zentropa Intl. Kohn; Slot Machine; IFC Films. **A:** Adult. **P:** Entertainment. **U:** Home. **L:** English. **Mov-Ent:** Forests & Trees. **Acq:** Purchase. **Dist:** Criterion Collection Inc.; Amazon.com Inc.; Movies Unlimited.

The Antichrist Revisited and Updated 19??
Father Vincent P. Miceli offers his insights on the great apostasy. ?m; VHS. **A:** Jr. High-Adult. **P:** Religious. **U:** Institution. **Gen-Edu:** Religion. **Acq:** Purchase. **Dist:** Keep the Faith Inc. $20.00.

The Antichrist/The Plight of Papist Catholics 1990
Two programs: one about the Antichrist and the other about public support of the Pope. 30m; VHS. **Pr:** Keep the Faith, Inc. **A:** Family. **P:** Religious. **U:** Institution, Home. **Gen-Edu:** Religion. **Acq:** Purchase. **Dist:** Keep the Faith Inc. $20.00.

Anticipation: Rx for Crisis Management 1991
A guide for supervisors on analyzing daily work situations in order to avoid trouble before it happens. 20m; VHS, 3/4 U. **Pr:** Bureau of Business Practice. **A:** Adult. **P:** Professional. **U:** Institution. **Bus-Ind:** How-To, Management. **Acq:** Purchase, Rent/Lease. **Dist:** Aspen Publishers, Inc. $495.00.

Antietam 1990
This re-enactment of the bloodiest day in the history of the Civil War tells the story of the first invasion of the North by Robert E. Lee. Also available as part of a set entitled "Mr. Lincoln's Army." 52m; VHS. **C:** Directed by Jack Foley. **Pr:** Classic Images Productions. **A:** Jr. High-Adult. **P:** Education. **U:** Institution, Home. **Gen-Edu:** War--General, History--U.S., Civil War. **Acq:** Purchase. **Dist:** Fusion Video. $39.95.

Antietam: The Bloodiest Day in American History 1987
Join the soldiers of the Civil War in this re-enactment of a well known battle. Graphic maps and a historical narration help to embellish this video. Narrated by Dr. Jay Luvass. 60m; VHS. **C:** Directed by Mike Wicklein. **Pr:** Parade. **A:** Jr. High-Adult. **P:** Education. **U:** Home. **Gen-Edu:** Civil War, History--U.S. **Acq:** Purchase. **Dist:** Inspired Corp.; Cambridge Educational. $14.95.

Antietam Visit 1979
A look at the Battle of Antietam and its historical impact. This program reenacts Abraham Lincoln's actual visit to Antietam two weeks after the battle. Through the President's "eyes" the viewer learns of the bloodiest single day in the Civil War—its strategy, its aftermath and its consequences. 30m; VHS. **Pr:** National Park Service. **A:** Jr. High-Adult. **P:** Education. **U:** Institution, SURA. **Gen-Edu:** History--U.S., Civil War. **Acq:** Purchase. **Dist:** Harpers Ferry Historical Association.

Antietam Visit 1982
This is a dramatic re-enactment of the encounter that stopped General Robert E. Lee's movement towards the North. 27m; VHS, 3/4 U. **Pr:** U.S. Government. **A:** Sr. High-Adult. **P:** Education. **U:** Institution, Home. **Gen-Edu:** History--U.S., Civil War. **Acq:** Purchase. **Dist:** National Audiovisual Center. $19.95.

Antigone 19??
Provides an analysis of Sophocles' "Antigone," considered by many to be his most popular work. Also introduces the form and ethical nature of Greek tragedy and delves into the techniques used in Greek theatre while exploring Greek theatre's dual role as religious ritual and theatre. 21m; VHS. **A:** Jr. High-Adult. **P:** Education. **U:** Institution, CCTV, SURA. **Gen-Edu:** Literature, Theater, Language Arts. **Acq:** Purchase. **Dist:** Thomas S. Klise Co. $58.00.

Antigone 1962 (Unrated)
Greek production of the Sophocles tragedy. Papas plays Oedipus' daughter who achieves greatness by defying the king. In Greek with English subtitles. 86m/B/W; VHS. **C:** Irene Papas; Manos Katrakis; Directed by Dinos Katsourides. **A:** Sr. High-Adult. **P:** Entertainment. **U:** Home. **L:** Greek. **Mov-Ent:** Folklore & Legends, Literature. **Acq:** Purchase. **Dist:** Hen's Tooth Video; Ivy Classics Video; Tapeworm Video Distributors Inc. $59.95.

Antigone 1987
A staged version of one of the most accessible of all the great classical tragedies with its clear and up-to-date theme of the conflict between moral and political law. 120m; VHS, 3/4 U. **Pr:** Films for the Humanities and Sciences. **A:** College-Adult. **P:** Entertainment. **U:** Institution, SURA. **Fin-Art:** Theater. **Acq:** Purchase. **Dist:** Films for the Humanities & Sciences.

Antigone: Lesson 6 1994
Discusses whether a citizen's first duty is to the law of the state or law of religion. 58m; VHS. **A:** Adult. **P:** Education. **U:** Institution. **Gen-Edu:** Literature. **Acq:** Purchase. **Dist:** RMI Media. $89.95.

Antigone: Rites for the Dead 1991
Sophocles' classic tragedy interpreted through dance and modern music. 85m; VHS, DVD. **C:** Bertram Ross; Janet Eilber; Amy Greenfield; Directed by Amy Greenfield; Music by Glenn Branca; Paul Lemos; Elliot Sharp; Diamanda Galas; David Van Tiegham. **Pr:** Mystic Fire Video. **A:** Jr. High-Adult. **P:** Entertainment. **U:** Home. **Fin-Art:** Musical, Dance, Literature--Modern. **Acq:** Purchase. **Dist:** Mystic Fire Video. $29.95.

Antigua Guatemala: American Monument 1978
A documentary program on one of the oldest cities in the Americas. 23m; VHS, 3/4 U. **Pr:** Museum of Modern Art of Latin America. **A:** Jr. High-Adult. **P:** Education. **U:** Institution, SURA. **Fin-Art:** Central America, Art & Artists. **Acq:** Purchase. **Dist:** Art Museum of The Americas.

Antimatter 19??
Uses animation to help explain theories associated with antimatter. 14m; VHS. **A:** Jr. High-Adult. **P:** Education. **U:** Institution. **Hea-Sci:** Science, Chemistry. **Acq:** Purchase. **Dist:** Educational Video Network. $39.95.

Antiobiotic Selection 1987
A tape which presents a doctor's opinion of the major factors that people should consider when deciding which antibiotic to use. 50m; VHS, 3/4 U. **A:** Adult. **P:** Education. **U:** Institution, CCTV, Home, SURA. **Hea-Sci:** Infection, Patient Education, Drugs. **Acq:** Purchase, Rent/Lease, Subscription. **Dist:** Emory Medical Television Network.

Antipasto: A Sampling of Italy 1988
This tape brings you the sights and sounds of Italy. 30m; VHS. **Pr:** Around the World in Sight & Sound. **A:** Jr. High-Adult. **P:** Education. **U:** Institution, Home. **Gen-Edu:** Travel, Italy. **Acq:** Purchase, Rent/Lease. **Dist:** Visual Horizons. $39.95.

Antique Shopping in Britain 199?
Tour some of the most famous shops and markets of Britain and learn how to train your eye to spot that perfect bargain and protect yourself from fakes. 90m; VHS. **A:** Adult. **P:** Entertainment. **U:** Home. **Gen-Edu:** Antiques, Great Britain. **Acq:** Purchase. **Dist:** Fusion Video. $19.98.

Antisocial Behavior 2007 (Unrated) — ★
A man known for his mental instability because he committed murder as a young boy is tomented by a gang of teens. The cops prove worthless to help him, and he falls back on old habits. 90m; DVD. **C:** Simon Brewer; Aidan Cross; Okezie Morro; David Watkins; Posey Brewer; Directed by Vinson Pike; Written by Vinson Pike; Kevin Ault; Cinematography by John Wilson; Music by Steven Wilson. **A:** Sr. High-Adult. **P:** Entertainment. **U:** Home. **L:** English. **Mov-Ent. Acq:** Purchase. **Dist:** Image Entertainment Inc. $24.98.

Antitrust 2000 (PG-13) — ★½
Supernerd code writer Milo (Phillippe) leaves the garage for a Pacific Northwest software giant only to discover the company's mega-monied leader, Winston (Robbins), may not be on the up and up—in fact, the things he's doing to maintain industry supremacy could be downright evil. Robbins's bespectacled techie villain is spot-on Bill Gates, but the film borrows heavily from its paranoid predecessors and offers little of its own to the field. A mediocre thriller among other mediocre thrillers. 120m; VHS, DVD, Wide. **C:** Ryan Phillippe; Tim Robbins; Rachael Leigh Cook; Claire Forlani; Douglas McFerran; Richard Roundtree; Yee Jee Tso; Tygh Runyan; Directed by Peter Howitt; Written by Howard Franklin; Cinematography by John Bailey; Music by Don Davis. **Pr:** Keith Addis; David Nicksay; Nick Wechsler; Hyde Park Entertainment; Industry Entertainment; Metro-Goldwyn-Mayer Pictures. **A:** Sr. High-Adult. **P:** Entertainment. **U:** Home. **Mov-Ent:** Computers. **Acq:** Purchase. **Dist:** MGM Home Entertainment.

Antiviral 2012 (Unrated) — ★★
Brandon Cronenberg (son of director David) debuts with some creepy ick of his own. In a star-obsessed, slightly near-future culture, the latest craze has Syd and the employees at Lucas Clinic injecting rabid fans with non-contagious viruses bought from the famous. Syd also runs a black-market sideline in live viruses, which backfires when he injects himself with some exotica taken from starlet Hannah. He quickly realizes something's gone wrong after Hannah dies and Syd himself becomes terminal. Not for those with weak stomachs as needles and bodily fluids are rampant. 109m; DVD, Blu-Ray. **C:** Caleb Landry Jones; Sarah Gadon; Malcolm McDowell; Nicholas (Nick) Campbell; Sheila McCarthy; Joe Pingue; Wendy Crewson; Directed by Brandon Cronenberg; Written by Brandon Cronenberg; Cinematography by Karim Hussain; Music by E.C. Woodley. **A:** Sr. High-Adult. **P:** Entertainment. **U:** Home. **L:** English. **Mov-Ent. Acq:** Purchase. **Dist:** MPI Media Group.

Antlers Big and Small 19??
Treks the wilderness of North America for an intimate portrait of the deer family, including moose to caribou. ?m; VHS. **A:** Jr. High-Adult. **P:** Education. **U:** Institution, Home. **Gen-Edu:** Animals, Wildlife. **Acq:** Purchase. **Dist:** Baker and Taylor. $14.95.

Antoine et Antoinette 1947 — ★★½
Antoine (Pigaut) is a shop foreman and his wife, Antoinette (Maffei), a clerk, who lead a somewhat tempestuous life in Paris. Then the situation worsens when Antoine loses the couple's winning lottery ticket. The first of Becker's romantic trilogy, followed by "Rendez-vous de Juillet" and "Edward and Caroline." French with subtitles; originally released at 95 minutes. 78m/B/W; VHS. **C:** Roger Pigaut; Claire Maffei; Noel Roquevert; Directed by Jacques Becker; Written by Jacques Becker; Maurice Griffe; Francoise Giroud; Cinematography by Pierre Montazel; Music by Jean Jacques Grunenwald. **A:** College-Adult. **P:** Entertainment. **U:** Home. **L:** French. **Mov-Ent:** Comedy--Romantic, Marriage. **Acq:** Purchase. **Dist:** Water Bearer Films Inc.

Anton Chekhov: A Writer's Life 1974
A portrait of the Russian writer whose genius for the short story was surpassed only by his plays, such as "The Cherry Orchard," "Uncle Vanya," and "The Seagull." 37m/B/W; VHS, 3/4 U. **Pr:** Mosfilm. **A:** College-Adult. **P:** Education. **U:** Institution, SURA. **Gen-Edu:** Literature. **Acq:** Purchase, Rent/Lease. **Dist:** Films for the Humanities & Sciences.

Anton Chekhov's The Duel 2009 (Unrated) — ★½
Adaptation of Chekov's 1891 novella. Self-absorbed aristocrat Laevsky has come to a seaside town with his married mistress Nadya. But now that they are together all the time, Laevsky grows bored and the flirtatious Nadya looks for other romantic prospects. Another visitor, zoologist Van Koren, becomes increasingly enraged by Laevsky's neurotic behavior and maneuvers him into a duel in a seeming reaction to the notion of survival of the fittest. 95m; DVD. **C:** Andrew Scott; Tobias Menzies; Niall Buggy; Fiona Glascott; Michelle Fairley; Nicholas (Nick) Rowe; Jeremy Swift; Directed by Dover Kosashvili; Written by Mary Bing; Cinematography by Paul Sarossy; Music by Angelo Milli. **A:** Sr. High-Adult. **P:** Entertainment. **U:** Home. **Mov-Ent:** Drama, USSR. **Acq:** Purchase. **Dist:** Music Box Films.

Anton, the Magician 1978 — ★★
Anton likes to live by his wits. A car mechanic, he marries the boss' daughter, Liesel, and uses his skills to make a pile of illegal dough that he hides at the home of the widowed Sabine,

with whom he's also involved. When Anton's schemes catch up with him, he ends up in prison, and Sabine takes off to Switzerland with the cash. But this isn't the end of their story. German with subtitles. 101m; VHS. **C:** Ulrich Thein; Barbara Dittus; Anna Dymna; Erwin Geschonneck; Erik S. Klein; Directed by Guenther Reisch; Written by Guenther Reisch; Karl-Georg Egel; Cinematography by Gunter Haubold; Music by Wolfram Heicking. **Pr:** Deutsche Film-Aktiengesellschaft. **A:** College-Adult. **P:** Entertainment. **U:** Home. **L:** German. **Mov-Ent. Acq:** Purchase.

Antonia: A Portrait of a Woman 1974
A portrait of Antonia Brico, who in the 1930s, established an international reputation as an accomplished orchestra conductor. Explores her life and work. 58m; VHS, 3/4 U. **C:** Antonia Brico; Directed by Judy Collins; Jill Godmilow. **Pr:** Rocky Mountain Productions Inc. **A:** Jr. High-Adult. **P:** Education. **U:** Institution, SURA. **Fin-Art. Awds:** Natl. Film Reg. '03. **Acq:** Purchase. **Dist:** Phoenix Learning Group.

Antonia and Jane 1991 (R) — ★★★
Enjoyable film tells the story of a longstanding, heavily tested friendship between two women. From the very beginning, they are a study in contrasts—Jane as rather plain, frumpy, and insecure; Antonia as glamorous, elegant, and successful. Both believe that each other's lives are more interesting and exciting than their own. Kidron, who directed this smart witty comedy for British TV, offers an honest look into the often complex world of adult friendships. 75m; VHS, CC. **C:** Imelda Staunton; Saskia Reeves; Patricia Leventon; Alfred Hoffman; Maria Charles; John Bennett; Richard Hope; Alfred Marks; Lila Kaye; Bill Nighy; Brenda Bruce; Directed by Beeban Kidron; Written by Marcy Kahan; Cinematography by Rex Maidment; Music by Rachel Portman. **Pr:** Miramax; British Broadcasting Corporation. **A:** Sr. High-Adult. **P:** Entertainment. **U:** Home. **Mov-Ent:** Women, TV Movies. **Acq:** Purchase. **Dist:** Paramount Pictures Corp.

Antonia's Line 1995 (R) — ★★½
90-year-old Antonia (Van Ammelrooy) has decided that she is going to die today and so begins a 50-year-long flashback of her nonconformist life in a Dutch village. Her lesbian daughter Danielle (Dottermans) wants a child without bothering about a husband and Antonia obliging arranges a brief interlude that produces child prodigy Therese (Van Overloop), who eventually has her own daughter, Sarah (Ravesteijn). Lots of female bonding (the male characters are mostly on the periphery of the action) and a certain magic realism abound. Dutch with subtitles. 102m; VHS, DVD. **C:** Willeke Van Ammelrooy; Els Dottermans; Veerle Van Overloop; Thyrza Ravesteijn; Jan Decleir; Mil Seghers; Jan Steen; Marina De Graaf; Directed by Marleen Gorris; Written by Marleen Gorris; Cinematography by Willy Stassen; Music by Ilona Sekacz. **Pr:** Hans De Weers; First Look Pictures. **A:** College-Adult. **P:** Entertainment. **U:** Home. **L:** Dutch. **Mov-Ent:** Comedy-Drama. **Awds:** Oscars '95: Foreign Film. **Acq:** Purchase. **Dist:** BMG Entertainment.

Antonio 1973 (Unrated) — ★★
A Texas millionaire on the run from his wife and her divorce lawyer alights in a small Chilean village and turns it upside down. 89m; VHS, DVD. **C:** Larry Hagman; Trini Lopez; Noemi Guerrero; Pedro Becker; Directed by Claudio Guzman. **Pr:** Profilms; Platinum Pictures. **A:** Family. **P:** Entertainment. **U:** Home. **Mov-Ent:** Comedy--Screwball. **Acq:** Purchase. **Dist:** Movies Unlimited.

Antonio Carlos Jobim: An All-Star Tribute 1994
Last recorded concert appearance of the Brazilian bossa nova master who died in December, 1994. Features Herbie Hancock, Shirley Horn, Gal Costa, Jon Hendricks, and others. 60m; VHS, DVD. **A:** Adult. **P:** Entertainment. **U:** Home. **Mov-Ent:** Music--Jazz, Music--Performance. **Acq:** Purchase. **Dist:** V.I.E.W. Inc./Arkadia Entertainment Corp. $19.98.
Songs: Girl from Ipanema; No More Blues; Once I Loved; A Felicidade; Se Todos Fossem; Chega de Saudad; Wave; Luiza.

Antonio Das Mortes 1968 — ★★½
Antonio is a savage mercenary hired to kill rebels against the Brazilian government. Belatedly he realizes he sympathizes with the targets and turns his guns the other way for an incredible shootout finale. A visually lavish poltical polemic, espousing revolutionary guerrilla action within the format of a South American western. In Portuguese with English subtitles. 100m; VHS. **C:** Mauricio Do Valle; Odete Lara; Jofre Soares; Othon Bastos; Directed by Glauce Rocha; Written by Glauce Rocha; Cinematography by Affonso Beato. **A:** Jr. High-Adult. **P:** Entertainment. **U:** Home. **L:** English, Portuguese. **Mov-Ent:** Folklore & Legends, Politics & Government. **Acq:** Purchase. **Dist:** Facets Multimedia Inc. $79.95.

Antony and Cleopatra 1973 (PG) — ★★
Heston wrote, directed, and starred in this long, dry adaptation of the Shakespeare play that centers on the torrid romance between Mark Antony and Cleopatra. 150m; VHS, DVD. **C:** Charlton Heston; Hildegard(e) Neil; Fernando Rey; Eric Porter; John Castle; Freddie Jones; Warren Clarke; Julian Glover; Directed by Charlton Heston. **Pr:** Peter Snell. **A:** Sr. High-Adult. **P:** Entertainment. **U:** Home. **Mov-Ent:** Drama, Biography, Romance. **Acq:** Purchase. **Dist:** Unknown Distributor.

Antony and Cleopatra 1981
A sequel to Shakespeare's great tragedy, Julius Caesar, this play is known for its memorable poetry, intricate planning, and remarkable characterizations. Part of the "Shakespeare Plays" series. 171m; VHS. **C:** Colin Blakely; Jane Lapotaire; Ian Charleson; Esmond Knight; Donald (Don) Sumpter; George Innes; Lynn Farleigh; Emrys James; Jonathan Adams; Geoffrey Collins; Janet Key; Cassie McFarlane; Anthony Pedley. **Pr:** Dr. Jonathan Miller; Cedric Messina; British Broadcasting Corporation. **A:** Sr. High-Adult. **P:** Entertainment. **U:** Institution. **Fin-Art:** History--Ancient, TV Movies. **Acq:** Purchase. **Dist:** Ambrose Video Publishing, Inc. $249.95.

Antony Tudor 1985
A 1983 tribute to this insightful, spiritual dancer/choreographer. Interviews and dance footage from some of his works, including "Dark Elegies," "Leaves are Fading," and "Pillar of Fire." 60m; VHS. **Pr:** Swedish TV. **A:** Sr. High-Adult. **P:** Education. **U:** Institution, Home. **Gen-Edu:** Dance--Performance, Biography. **Acq:** Purchase. **Dist:** Princeton Book Company Publishers. $49.95.

Antonyms, Synonyms, and Homonyms 19??
Examples of antonyms, synonyms, and homonyms are provided. 13m; VHS. **A:** Primary. **P:** Education. **U:** Institution. **Gen-Edu:** Language Arts. **Acq:** Purchase. **Dist:** Thomas S. Klise Co. $58.00.

Ants 1977 — ★½
A mad bug parable for our planet-obsessed society. Insecticide-infected ants turn militant and check into a local hotel to vent their chemically induced foul mood on the unsuspecting clientele. The guest register includes a gaggle of celebrities who probably wish they'd signed on the Love Boat instead. Made for TV (an ant farm would probably be just too horrible on the big screen). 100m; VHS, DVD. **C:** Suzanne Somers; Robert Foxworth; Myrna Loy; Lynda Day George; Gerald Gordon; Bernie Casey; Barry Van Dyke; Karen Lamm; Anita Gillette; Moosie Drier; Steve Franken; Brian Dennehy; Bruce French; Stacy Keach, Sr.; Rene Enriquez; James Storm; Directed by Robert Scheerer; Written by Guerdon (Gordon) Trueblood; Cinematography by Bernie Abramson; Music by Ken Richmond. **Pr:** Alan Landsburg Productions. **A:** Jr. High-Adult. **P:** Entertainment. **U:** Home. **Mov-Ent:** Horror, TV Movies, Hotels & Hotel Staff Training. **Acq:** Purchase. **Dist:** Lions Gate Television Corp.

Ants: Backyard Science—Revised 1978
In this show, we see in detail what an ant's body is like and how this structure aids the ant in obtaining food and carrying on daily activities. 13m; VHS, 3/4 U. **Pr:** Norman Bean; Marjorie Bean. **A:** Primary-Jr. High. **P:** Education. **U:** Institution, SURA. **Hea-Sci:** Insects. **Acq:** Purchase. **Dist:** Phoenix Learning Group.

Ants: Hunters and Gardeners 1977
A close-up look at ant behavior. 11m; 3/4 U, Special order formats. **Pr:** National Geographic Society. **A:** Primary. **P:** Education. **U:** Institution, Home, SURA. **Hea-Sci:** Insects. **Acq:** Purchase, Trade-in, Duplication License. **Dist:** National Geographic Society.

Antwone Fisher 2002 (PG-13) — ★★★
Washington's directorial debut is a drama based on the true story of Antwone Fisher, who also wrote the screenplay. Washington also stars as Jerome Davenport, the naval psychiatrist who helps the angry young Fisher (Luke) get past the demons of his foster childhood. The two knock heads and are both forced to change their own ideas, slowly coming to understand and trust one another. Davenport learns that Fisher was born in prison, his father murdered and his mother a convict. Davenport urges Fisher to confront his past, and some of the best scenes are with Fisher's aunt (Johnson), uncle (Billings) and mother (Davis), which resonate. Subplot with Davenport and wife Berta (Richardson) shows they have their own issues to work out, as well. A tearjerker in the best sense, the simply told tale is a triumph for Luke, who is impressive in his debut role. 113m; VHS, DVD, Blu-Ray. **C:** Derek Luke; Denzel Washington; Joy Bryant; Salli Richardson-Whitfield; Earl Billings; Kevin Connolly; Viola Davis; Rainoldo Gooding; Novella Nelson; Vernee Watson-Johnson; Kente Scott; Yolonda Ross; Stephen Snedden; Malcolm David Kelly; Directed by Denzel Washington; Written by Antwone Fisher; Cinematography by Philippe Rousselot; Music by Mychael Danna. **Pr:** Todd Black; Randa Haines; Denzel Washington; Denzel Washington; Mundy Lane Entertainment; Fox Searchlight. **A:** Jr. High-Adult. **P:** Entertainment. **U:** Home. **Mov-Ent:** Biography: Military, Psychiatry, Black Culture. **Awds:** Ind. Spirit '03: Actor (Luke). **Acq:** Purchase. **Dist:** Fox Home Entertainment.

Antz 1998 (PG) — ★★★
Malcontent worker ant, Z (Allen), moans to his therapist about his insignificance and the depressing anonymity of "being born in the middle of five million." But after meeting the colony's princess, Bala (Stone), who is facing her own bleak future thanks to an arranged marriage with the colony's power-hungry General Mandible (Hackman), Z and Princess Bala embark on a dangerous mission to the surface in search of the mythical "Insectopia." Only the second film ever created entirely through computer animation ("Toy Story" being the first), pic is visually amazing. The fact that the ant characters do not resemble their performers' appearances makes the relationship between Z and the princess plausible, and actually adds depth to the characters' personalities. An interesting, rather elaborate storyline, along with excellent voice performances (even Stallone!) make this one fun for all ages. 83m; VHS, DVD. **C:** Voice(s) by Woody Allen; Sharon Stone; Sylvester Stallone; Anne Bancroft; Danny Glover; Christopher Walken; Jane Curtin; Jennifer Lopez; John Mahoney; Dan Aykroyd; Paul Mazursky; Gene Hackman; Directed by Eric Darnell; Tim Johnson; Written by Chris Weitz; Paul Weitz; Todd Alcott; Music by Harry Gregson-Williams; John Powell. **Pr:** Aron Warner; Patty Wooton; Brad Lewis; Penney Finkelman Cox; Sandra Rabins; Carl Rosendahl; DreamWorks SKG. **A:** Family. **P:** Entertainment. **U:** Home. **Mov-Ent:** Animation & Cartoons, Insects. **Acq:** Purchase. **Dist:** Movies Unlimited; Alpha Video.

Anuncios Comerciales 19??
Contains Spanish-language commericals for both the American and Mexican television markets that help provide language practice while showing the different cultures involved. Comes with teacher's manual. 45m; VHS. **A:** Jr. High-Adult. **P:** Education. **U:** Institution. **L:** Spanish. **Gen-Edu:** Hispanic Culture, Language Arts, Advertising. **Acq:** Purchase. **Dist:** Educational Video Network. $49.95.

Anvil! The Story of Anvil 2009 (Unrated) — ★★
Rockumentary about the aging, working-class Canadian metal band that seemed on the brink of stardom in the mid-1980s and instead faded into obscurity. Lead vocalist Steve 'Lips' Kudlow and drummer Robb Reiner have been playing together since the age of 14 and their early LPs influenced more successful speed-metal bands. But with only modest hits and a mismanaged European tour, they were dropped by their label. Still playing clubs (with two additional rotating members), they have day jobs to support their families while working on a comeback album. You have to admire their persistence and optimism if nothing else. 90m; DVD. **C:** Steve "Lips" Kudlow; Robb Reiner; Directed by Sacha Gervasi; Cinematography by Christopher Soos. **Pr:** Rebecca Yeldham; A Little Dean and Ahimsa Films; Abramorama Films. **A:** Sr. High-Adult. **P:** Entertainment. **U:** Home. **L:** English. **Mov-Ent:** Documentary Films, Interviews, Music--Pop/Rock. **Awds:** Ind. Spirit '10: Feature Doc. **Acq:** Purchase. **Dist:** Paramount Pictures Corp.

Anxiety 1984
The causes and manifestations of anxiety and the roots of anxiety found in childhood are explored. 25m; VHS, 3/4 U. **Pr:** Trainex. **A:** College-Adult. **P:** Education. **U:** Institution. **Hea-Sci:** Psychology. **Acq:** Purchase, Rent/Lease. **Dist:** Medcom Inc.

Anxiety and Stress 1990
Discusses stress and anxiety, and their effects on a person's psychological and physical well-being. Also includes role-playing coping strategies. ?m; VHS. **A:** Jr. High-Sr. High. **P:** Education. **U:** Institution. **Hea-Sci:** Stress, Health Education. **Acq:** Purchase. **Dist:** Meridian Education Corp. $45.00.

Anxiety: Panic Disorder 1988
A layman's look at this form of psychological depression. 10m; VHS, 3/4 U. **Pr:** Professional Research. **A:** Sr. High-Adult. **P:** Education. **U:** Institution, CCTV. **Hea-Sci:** Psychology. **Acq:** Purchase, Rent/Lease. **Dist:** Discovery Education.

Anxiety/Panic Disorders: Use and Side Effects of Medication 1988
The different medications used to treat anxiety are looked at. 10m; VHS, 3/4 U. **Pr:** Professional Research. **A:** Sr. High-Adult. **P:** Education. **U:** Institution, CCTV. **Hea-Sci:** Medical Care, Psychology. **Acq:** Purchase, Rent/Lease. **Dist:** Discovery Education. $295.00.

Any Child Is My Child 1989
The oppression of children by the apartheid regime in South Africa is the focus of this film. 54m; VHS, 3/4 U. **Pr:** International Defense and Aid Fund. **A:** Family. **P:** Education. **U:** Institution. **Gen-Edu:** Apartheid, Children, Music--Performance. **Acq:** Purchase. **Dist:** The Cinema Guild. $350.00.

Any Day Now 2012 (R) — ★★★
Rudy (Cumming) and Paul (Dillahunt) are a loving gay couple who take in teenager Marco (Leyva) with Down syndrome and give him the acceptance and family that he's never found. When authorities try to take Marco away from them, a court battle ensues. Dillahunt and Cumming are two great actors who are allowed a timely showcase in this true story of gay parenthood in the '70s, and how the issues then remain ones today. 97m; DVD, Blu-Ray. **C:** Alan Cumming; Garret Dillahunt; Isaac Leyva; Frances Fisher; Gregg Henry; Jamie Anne Allman; Kelli Williams; Chris Mulkey; Alan Rachins; Directed by Travis Fine; Written by Travis Fine; George Arthur Bloom; Cinematography by Rachel Morrison; Music by Joey Newman. **Pr:** Travis Fine; Kristine Fine; Music Box Films; PFM Pictures. **A:** Sr. High-Adult. **P:** Entertainment. **U:** Home. **L:** English. **Mov-Ent:** Homosexuality, Parenting, Family. **Acq:** Purchase. **Dist:** Not Yet Released.

Any Family 19??
A northern California family of third generation gypsies raises every type of horse and tours the country with a mini big top circus and Royal Horse Fair. 18m; VHS. **Pr:** Jay Miracle. **A:** Family. **P:** Entertainment. **U:** Home. **Gen-Edu:** Family, Animals. **Acq:** Purchase. **Dist:** , On Moratorium.

Any Friend of Nicholas Nickelby Is a Friend of Mine 1985
Based on the Ray Bradbury story, a made-for-television film about a small-town family taking in a stranger who claims to be Charles Dickens. 54m; VHS. **C:** Fred Gwynne; Ralph Rosenblum. **A:** Family. **P:** Entertainment. **U:** Home. **Mov-Ent:** TV Movies. **Acq:** Purchase. **Dist:** Film Ideas, Inc.; Monterey Home Video. $59.95.

Any Given Sunday 1999 (R) — ★★★
Stone sets aside his conspiracy theories on war and politics and effectively shines a spotlight on a different kind of battlefield to come up with the most commerical and entertaining film of his career. Pacino heads an all-star cast as the battered, yet wise and resilient coach of a struggling Miami football team who locks horns with not only young quarterback Foxx, but ruthless, ballbuster team owner Diaz. Epic-like runtime (which sprints along thanks to Stone's potent mix of raw camera work and hip-hop soundtrack) allows much of the cast plenty of room, with comedian Foxx holding his own with the big boys in a star-making performance as the hotdog player with a bad case of ego. With an intelligent script and a perfect cast, Stone creates the most realistic look at pro football since 1979's "North Dallas Forty." 170m/B/W; VHS, DVD, Blu-Ray, Wide. **C:** Al Pacino; Dennis Quaid; Cameron Diaz; Jamie Foxx; Charlton Heston; James Woods; Matthew Modine; Ann-Margret; Lauren Holly; Lela Rochon; LL Cool J; Aaron Eckhart; Jim Brown; Bill

Bellamy; Elizabeth Berkley; John C. McGinley; Directed by Oliver Stone; Written by Oliver Stone; John Logan; Cinematography by Salvatore Totino; Music by Robbie Robertson. **A:** Adult. **P:** Entertainment. **U:** Home. **Mov-Ent**: Football, Sports--Fiction: Drama. **Acq:** Purchase. **Dist:** Warner Home Video, Inc.

Any Gun Can Play 1967 — ★
Typical spaghetti western. Three men (banker, thief, and bounty hunter) compete for a treasure of gold while wandering about the Spanish countryside. 103m; VHS, DVD. **C:** Edd Byrnes; Gilbert Roland; George Hilton; Kareen O'Hara; Pedro Sanchez; Gerard Herter; Directed by Enzo G. Castellari. **Pr:** RAF. **A:** Jr. High-Adult. **P:** Entertainment. **U:** Home. **Mov-Ent. Acq:** Purchase. **Dist:** Movies Unlimited. $8.99.

Any Human Heart 2011 (Unrated) — ★★
Boyd adapts his own novel, which follows three stages (and three actors) in the life of minor British writer Logan Mountstuart from his 1920s youth (Claflin) through WWII (Macfadyen) and his old age (Broadbent) in the 1970s. Various historical personages flit through (Hemingway, Ian Fleming, the Duke and Duchess of Windsor) while Logan endures a series of romantic encounters that are recounted through his journals. Melancholy and too long, though not as dismal as may be imagined. 240m; DVD. **C:** Sam Claflin; Matthew MacFadyen; Jim Broadbent; James Musgrave; Ed Stoppard; Freddie Fox; Samuel West; Hayley Atwell; Holliday Grainger; Kim Cattrall; Charity Wakefield; Emerald Fennell; Tom Hollander; Gillian Anderson; Tobias Menzies; Julian Ovenden; Directed by Michael Samuels; Written by William Boyd; Cinematography by Wojciech Szepel; Music by Dan (Daniel) Jones. **A:** Sr. High-Adult. **P:** Entertainment. **U:** Home. **Mov-Ent**: Marriage, France, Aging. **Acq:** Purchase. **Dist:** PBS Home Video.

Any Man's Death 1990 (R) — ★★
Savage is a globe-trotting reporter on the trail of a worldwide conspiracy who accidentally uncovers a Nazi war criminal in Africa. Well-meaning but confused tale. 105m; VHS, DVD. **C:** John Savage; William Hickey; Mia Sara; Ernest Borgnine; Michael Lerner; Directed by Tom Clegg. **Pr:** Paramount Pictures. **A:** Sr. High-Adult. **P:** Entertainment. **U:** Home. **Mov-Ent**: Mystery & Suspense, Ethics & Morals. **Acq:** Purchase. **Dist:** Movies Unlimited.

Any Number Can Play 1949 — ★★½
Fast-moving drama about an ailing gambler who faces a series of crises. Gable gives a commanding performance as the noble dice-roller. Based on the novel by Edward Harris Heath. 102m/B/W; VHS, DVD. **C:** Clark Gable; Alexis Smith; Wendell Corey; Audrey Totter; Frank Morgan; Mary Astor; Lewis Stone; Barry Sullivan; Directed by Mervyn LeRoy; Written by Richard Brooks. **Pr:** Arthur Freed; MGM; MGM/UA Entertainment Company. **A:** Sr. High-Adult. **P:** Entertainment. **U:** Home. **Mov-Ent**: Gambling. **Acq:** Purchase. **Dist:** WarnerArchive.com; MGM Home Entertainment. $19.98.

Any Number Can Win 1963 — ★★
Two ex-convicts, aging Charles (Gabin) and his former cellmate Francis (Delon), risk their lives and freedom for one last major heist: a gambling casino on the French Riviera. French with English subtitles. 118m/B/W; VHS, DVD. **C:** Jean Gabin; Alain Delon; Viviane Romance; Maurice Biraud; Carla Marlier; Jose-Luis De Villalonga; Jean Carmet; Claude Cerval; Directed by Henri Verneuil; Written by Henri Verneuil; Michel Audiard; Albert Simonin; Cinematography by Louis Page; Music by Michel Magne. **A:** College-Adult. **P:** Entertainment. **U:** Home. **L:** French. **Mov-Ent**: Mystery & Suspense, Gambling, Aging. **Acq:** Purchase. **Dist:** Vanguard International Cinema, Inc.; Facets Multimedia Inc.

Any Place But Home 1997 (PG-13) — ★★½
Roberta (Keller) and Lucas (Lando) Dempsey find themselves in big trouble when Roberta's sister Carrie Miller (Conway) and her low-life hubby Carl (Midkiff) try to involve them in a plan to kidnap 12-year-old John Danforth (Norris), figuring John's rich dad August (Thicke) will be happy to pay the ransom. Roberta manages to get the kid and the money away from the Millers but she and Lucas discover John is an abused child and terrified of his father. The threesome go on the run with the Millers, August's hired help, and the FBI on their trail. 90m; VHS. **C:** Joe Lando; Mary Page Keller; Alan Thicke; Dale Midkiff; Cristie Conway; Richard Roundtree; Directed by Rob Hedden; Written by Bart Baker. **Pr:** Bart Baker; John L. Roman; Kevin Kelly Brown; USA Network. **A:** Jr. High-Adult. **P:** Entertainment. **U:** Home. **Mov-Ent**: TV Movies, Child Abuse. **Acq:** Purchase. **Dist:** Universal Music and Video Distribution.

Any Questions?: The Universal Precautions Explained 19??
A presentation for hospital workers on the latest CDC guidelines governing protection from HIV infection. 15m; VHS, 3/4 U. **A:** College-Adult. **P:** Education. **U:** Institution. **Hea-Sci**: AIDS, Hospitals, Job Training. **Acq:** Purchase, Rent/Lease. **Dist:** Leo Media, Inc. $295.00.

Any Wednesday 1966 — ★★½
Okay sex farce about powerful industrialist Robards' use of his mistress's apartment as a tax write-off. When a young company executive learns of the "company" apartment, he meets Robards' nonchalant wife for a tryst of their own. Based on Muriel Resnik's Broadway play; similar to the 1960 "The Apartment." 110m; VHS, DVD. **C:** Jane Fonda; Jason Robards, Jr.; Dean Jones; Rosemary Murphy; Directed by Robert Ellis Miller; Written by Julius J. Epstein; Music by George Duning. **A:** Sr. High-Adult. **P:** Entertainment. **U:** Home. **Mov-Ent**: Satire & Parody, Marriage, Sex & Sexuality. **Acq:** Purchase. **Dist:** WarnerArchive.com. $19.98.

Any Which Way You Can 1980 (PG) — ★★
Bad brawler Philo Beddoe and his buddy Clyde, the orangutan, are back again in the sequel to "Every Which Way But Loose." This time Philo is tempted to take part in a big bout for a large cash prize. Clyde steals scenes, brightening up the no-brainer story. 116m; VHS, DVD, Wide. **C:** Clint Eastwood; Sondra Locke; Ruth Gordon; Harry Guardino; William (Bill) Smith; Geoffrey Lewis; Barry Corbin; Directed by Buddy Van Horn; Written by Stanford Sherman; Cinematography by David Worth. **A:** Jr. High-Adult. **P:** Entertainment. **U:** Home. **Mov-Ent**: Comedy--Slapstick, Boxing. **Acq:** Purchase. **Dist:** Warner Home Video, Inc. $19.98.

Anybody's Bike Video: Bike Repair 1990
Learn how to repair common bike problems (flat tires, wheel alignments, etc.) and how to keep up regular maintenance. 76m; VHS. **Pr:** Do It Yourself Inc. **A:** Jr. High-Adult. **P:** Instruction. **U:** Home. **How-Ins**: How-To, Bicycling. **Acq:** Purchase. **Dist:** Do It Yourself, Inc./D.I.Y. Video Corp.; Cambridge Educational. $39.95.

Anyone Around My Base Is It 1987
Examines the modern relevance of religion. 28m/B/W; VHS. **Pr:** Alden Films. **A:** Family. **P:** Religious. **U:** Institution, Home. **Gen-Edu**: Religion, Judaism. **Acq:** Purchase, Rent/Lease. **Dist:** Alden Films.

Anyone Can Be a Genius 1985
The title comes from a catchphrase used by Dr. Luis Alberto Machado, Minister of State for the Development of Human Intelligence in Venezuela. Machado has engineered a revolution in education through various creative techniques, which have raised the level of intelligence throughout Venezuela. His goal is to accomplish this throughout the world. 46m; 3/4 U. **Pr:** Julian Russell. **A:** Jr. High-Adult. **P:** Education. **U:** Institution, SURA. **Gen-Edu**: Documentary Films, South America, Education. **Acq:** Purchase. **Dist:** First Run/Icarus Films.

Anyone Can Dance: Freestyle 199?
Provides instruction on how to dance freestyle; geared toward the beginning dancer. ?m; VHS. **A:** Adult. **P:** Instruction. **U:** Home. **How-Ins**: Dance--Instruction. **Acq:** Purchase. **Dist:** Dance Vision. $19.95.

Anyone Can Dance: Slow Dancing 199?
Provides instruction on how to slow dance; geared toward the beginning dancer. ?m; VHS. **A:** Adult. **P:** Instruction. **U:** Home. **How-Ins**: Dance--Instruction. **Acq:** Purchase. **Dist:** Dance Vision. $19.95.

Anyone Can Earn Big Money in T.V. Commercials 1991
Practical advice for those looking to work in the TV commercial industry from Bob Collier, veteran announcer and commercial actor. 90m; VHS. **Pr:** Bob Collier. **A:** Sr. High-Adult. **P:** Instruction. **U:** Home. **How-Ins**: How-To, Television, Advertising. **Acq:** Purchase. **Dist:** Video Learning Library L.L.C. $39.95.

Anything But Love 2002 (PG-13) — ★★½
Predictable Hollywood love story. Writer/actor Isabel Rose plays Billie Golden, a not-so-young wanna-be torch singer wrestling with the choice of whether to marry her old high school crush (Bancroft) for security, or stay with her anguished true love (McCarthy), who better understands her. Meager budget is best spent on the elaborate dream sequences. Eartha Kitt appears as herself, providing crucial advice and a shining example of a true star. 99m; VHS, DVD. **C:** Isabel Rose; Andrew McCarthy; Cameron Bancroft; Alix Korey; Victor Argo; Ilana Levine; Sean Arbuckle; Eartha Kitt; Directed by Robert Cary; Written by Isabel Rose; Robert Cary; Cinematography by Horacio Marquinez; Music by Andrew Hollander; Steven Lutvak. **Pr:** Aimee Schoof; Isen Robbins; Samuel Goldwyn Films. **A:** Jr. High-Adult. **P:** Entertainment. **U:** Home. **Mov-Ent**: Comedy--Romantic, Singing, Nightclubs. **Acq:** Purchase. **Dist:** Wellspring Media.

Anything But Love: Volume One 2007 (Unrated)
Features the first season of the 1989-1992 television comedy series about a writer named Marty (Lewis) who helps out Hannah (Curtis) by getting her a job at his magazine publisher's office and it's not long before the pair can't seem to resist one another. Includes: Hannah's first assignment is in jeopardy due to PC problems and they go on a "not date" night for Hannah's birthday after Marty breaks up with his girlfriend. 28 episodes. 732m; DVD. **C:** Jamie Lee Curtis; Richard Lewis; Richard Frank; Sandy Faison. **A:** Jr. High-Adult. **P:** Entertainment. **U:** Home. **Mov-Ent**: Television Series, Comedy--Romantic. **Acq:** Purchase. **Dist:** Fox Home Entertainment. $39.98.

Anything Else 2003 (R) — ★½
With his last few outings, Allen has shown that he's a shadow of his former creative self, so he's logically picked Biggs to play a shadow of his former self. Biggs doesn't seem comfortable in his role as a neurotic psychoanalyst-dependent joke-writer trying to break up with the quirky, torturing girlfriend (Ricci) he's smitten with. The Woodman shows up as his alter-ego's paranoid, mean-spirited mentor and confidant. Flick is so short on new ideas that the young couple can only agree on their love of Bogie and old jazz records. Ricci spends most of the film walking around her apartment in her underwear, which isn't bad if you can keep the image of Allen leering just off-camera out of your head. If you insist on a Woody Allen movie, make it almost anything else but this mess. 108m; VHS, DVD. **C:** Jason Biggs; Christina Ricci; Woody Allen; Stockard Channing; Danny DeVito; Jimmy Fallon; Erica Leerhsen; David Conrad; KaDee Strickland; Adrian Grenier; Directed by Woody Allen; Written by Woody Allen; Cinematography by Darius Khondji. **Pr:** Letty Aronson; Gravier Productions; Perdido; DreamWorks SKG. **A:** Sr. High-Adult. **P:** Entertainment. **U:** Home. **Mov-Ent**: Comedy--Romantic. **Acq:** Purchase. **Dist:** DreamWorks Home Entertainment.

Anything for a Thrill 1937 — ★
Two kids save a cameraman's career, make friends with a millionairess, and foil some crooks. 59m/B/W; VHS, DVD. **C:** Frankie Darro; Kane Richmond; Directed by Leslie Goodwins. **Pr:** Maurice Conn. **A:** Family. **P:** Entertainment. **U:** Home. **Mov-Ent. Acq:** Purchase. **Dist:** Alpha Video. $24.95.

Anything for Love 1993 (Unrated) — ★½
Teen musician is the object of a school bully's rage so he decides to dress up as a girl to escape the guy's fists. 90m; VHS, DVD. **C:** Corey Haim; Nicole Eggert; Cameron Bancroft; Kevin McNulty; Wendy Van Riesen; Lochlyn Munro; Rachel Hayward; Molly Parker; Directed by Michael Keusch; Music by Amin Bhatia. **A:** Jr. High-Adult. **P:** Entertainment. **U:** Home. **Mov-Ent**: Adolescence. **Acq:** Purchase. **Dist:** CinemaNow Inc. $92.95.

Anything Goes 1956 — ★★
Listless Paramount musically occasionally highlighted by the Cole Porter songs. Veteran Broadway star Bill Benson (Crosby) teams up with TV entertainer Ted Adams (O'Connor) for a new musical but they need a leading lady. Thanks to plot contrivances, each separately finds the perfect dame in Europe and the quartet meet up on the ocean liner heading home. However, their show is only designed for one female star. 106m; DVD. **C:** Bing Crosby; Donald O'Connor; Mitzi Gaynor; Zizi Jeanmaire; Phil Harris; Kurt Kasznar; Directed by Robert Lewis; Written by Sidney Sheldon; Cinematography by John F. Warren. **A:** Sr. High-Adult. **P:** Entertainment. **U:** Home. **L:** English. **Mov-Ent**: Musical, Romance. **Acq:** Purchase. **Dist:** WarnerArchive.com.

Anything You Want To Be 1996
Features a humorous vignette with sex-role stereotypes as told by a teenage girl. 8m; VHS. **A:** Jr. High. **P:** Entertainment. **U:** Home, Institution. **Gen-Edu**: Adolescence. **Acq:** Purchase, Rent/Lease. **Dist:** New Day Films Library. $99.00.

Anyuta: Bolshoi Ballet 1982
This memorable ballet production is replete with grace and wit. The best of the best ballet companies join forces here to perform an unprecedented interpretation of the lovable Anyuta and her apathetic nuptials. 68m; VHS. **C:** Ekaterina Maximova; Vladimir Vasiliev. **A:** Family. **P:** Entertainment. **U:** Home. **Fin-Art**: Dance. **Acq:** Purchase. **Dist:** Corinth Films Inc.; Kultur International Films Ltd., Inc.; Music Video Distributors. $39.95.

Anywhere But Here 1999 (PG-13) — ★★½
Just who's the Mom here? It certainly doesn't seem to be flaky Adele (Sarandon), who suddenly uproots teen daughter Ann (Portman) from provincial Wisconsin to relocate in sunny L.A., where Adele wants Ann to become an actress. Ann's definitely the practical one of the duo and she tries to rein in Adele's loopier flights of fantasy. Of course, Ann does have some plans (and dreams) of her own. The leads are both pros and there are enough tear-jerking moments to satisfy in this somewhat stereotypical drama. Based on the 1986 novel by Mona Simpson. 114m; VHS, DVD. **C:** Susan Sarandon; Natalie Portman; Shawn Hatosy; Hart Bochner; Bonnie Bedelia; Eileen Ryan; Ray Baker; Caroline Aaron; Paul Guilfoyle; Mary Ellen Trainor; Ashley Johnson; Directed by Wayne Wang; Written by Alvin Sargent; Cinematography by Roger Deakins; Music by Danny Elfman. **Pr:** Laurence Mark; Fox 2000 Pictures; 20th Century-Fox. **A:** Jr. High-Adult. **P:** Entertainment. **U:** Home. **Mov-Ent**: Adolescence. **Acq:** Purchase. **Dist:** Fox Home Entertainment.

Anzacs: The War Down Under 1985 — ★★★
Well-made Australian TV miniseries about the Australian and New Zealand Army Corps during WWI. Follows the men from the time they enlist to the campaigns in Gallipoli and France. 165m; VHS. **C:** Paul Hogan; Andrew Clarke; Jon Blake; Megan Williams; Directed by George Miller. **Pr:** Geoff Burrows. **A:** Jr. High-Adult. **P:** Entertainment. **U:** Home. **Mov-Ent**: Action-Adventure, World War One, Australia. **Acq:** Purchase. **Dist:** $19.95.

Anzio 1968 — ★★
The historic Allied invasion of Italy during WWII as seen through the eyes of American war correspondent Mitchum. Fine cast waits endlessly to leave the beach, though big battle scenes are effectively rendered. Based on the book by Wynford Vaughan Thomas. 117m; VHS, DVD, Wide. **C:** Robert Mitchum; Peter Falk; Arthur Kennedy; Robert Ryan; Earl Holliman; Mark Damon; Reni Santoni; Patrick Magee; Giancarlo Giannini; Directed by Edward Dmytryk; Written by H.A.L. Craig; Frank De Felitta; Cinematography by Giuseppe Rotunno; Music by Riz Ortolani. **Pr:** Columbia Pictures. **A:** Jr. High-Adult. **P:** Entertainment. **U:** Home. **Mov-Ent**: World War Two, Journalism. **Acq:** Purchase. **Dist:** Movies Unlimited. $11.99.

Ao Dai 1991
Considers the resurgence of the Ao Dai, the traditional Vietnamese tunic dress, in relation to the growing prosperity of the country. 13m; VHS. **C:** Directed by Le Trac. **A:** Sr. High-Adult. **P:** Education. **U:** Institution. **Gen-Edu**: Asia, Documentary Films, Clothing & Dress. **Acq:** Purchase, Rent/Lease, Duplication. **Dist:** First Run/Icarus Films. $160.00.

Aortic and Mitral Stenosis 1982
This program discusses many ramifications of stenotic valves. 51m; VHS, 3/4 U. **Pr:** Emory University. **A:** College-Adult. **P:** Professional. **U:** Institution, CCTV, Home, SURA. **Hea-Sci**: Heart. **Acq:** Purchase, Rent/Lease, Subscription. **Dist:** Emory Medical Television Network.

AOTA: The Professional Edge 1992
The benefits of joining the American Occupational Therapy Association are listed. 11m; VHS, 3/4 U. **Pr:** American Occupational Therapy Association. **A:** Adult. **P:** Education. **U:** Institution, CCTV. **Bus-Ind:** Labor & Unions. **Acq:** Free Loan. **Dist:** American Occupational Therapy Association.

The APA Rehearses 197?
This program goes behind the scenes of the APA Repertory Company's production of Ibsen's "The Wild Duck." 30m/B/W, VHS, 3/4 U, EJ, Q. **Pr:** WCBS New York; Camera Three Productions. **A:** Sr. High-Adult. **P:** Education. **U:** Institution, SURA. **Fin-Art:** Theater. **Acq:** Free Duplication, Duplication License. **Dist:** Camera Three Productions, Inc.; Creative Arts Television Archive.

Apache 1954 (Unrated) — ★★½
Lancaster is the only Indian in Geronimo's outfit who refuses to surrender in this chronicle of a bitter battle between the Indians and the U.S. cavalry in the struggle for the West. First western for Aldrich is a thoughtful piece for its time that had the original tragic ending reshot (against Aldrich's wishes) to make it more happy. Adapted from "Bronco Apache" by Paul I. Wellman. 91m; VHS, DVD. **C:** Burt Lancaster; John McIntire; Jean Peters; Charles Bronson; John Dehner; Paul Guilfoyle; Directed by Robert Aldrich; Cinematography by Ernest Laszlo. **Pr:** United Artists. **A:** Jr. High-Adult. **P:** Entertainment. **U:** Home. **Mov-Ent:** Western. **Acq:** Purchase. **Dist:** MGM Home Entertainment; Facets Multimedia Inc. $19.98.

Apache: Attack Helicopter 1990
The incredible destructive potential of the Apache attack helicopter, that was so instrumental to the Gulf War effort, is revealed. 30m; VHS. **A:** Jr. High-Family. **P:** Entertainment. **U:** Home. **Gen-Edu:** Documentary Films, Armed Forces--U.S., Aeronautics. **Acq:** Purchase. **Dist:** MNTEX Entertainment, Inc.

Apache Blood 1975 (R) — ★½
An Indian Brave, the lone survivor of an Indian massacre by the U.S. Army, squares off with a cavalry scout in the forbidding desert. 92m; VHS, DVD. **C:** Ray Danton; DeWitt Lee; Troy Neighbors; Diane Taylor; Eva Kovacs; Jason Clark; Directed by Thomas Quillen. **Pr:** Key International; Platinum Pictures. **A:** College-Adult. **P:** Entertainment. **U:** Home. **Mov-Ent:** Western, Native Americans. **Acq:** Purchase. **Dist:** Mill Creek Entertainment L.L.C. $19.99.

Apache Chief 1950 — ★
Two Apache tribe leaders, one good, the other evil clash. Ultimately, and perhaps predictably, they face each other in hand-to-hand combat and peace prevails. 60m/B/W; VHS. **C:** Alan Curtis; Tom Neal; Russell Hayden; Carol Thurston; Fuzzy Knight; Directed by Frank McDonald. **Pr:** Lippert Productions. **A:** Family. **P:** Entertainment. **U:** Home. **Mov-Ent:** Western, Native Americans. **Acq:** Purchase. **Dist:** Movies Unlimited. $14.99.

Apache Kid's Escape 1930 — ★
The Apache Kid leads the cavalry on a wild chase across the plains in this saga of the old west. 60m/B/W; VHS, DVD. **C:** Jack Perrin; Fred Church; Josephine Hill; Virginia Ashcroft; Bud Osborne; Henry Roquemore; Buzz Barton; Directed by Robert J. Horner. **Pr:** Republic Pictures. **A:** Family. **P:** Entertainment. **U:** Home. **Mov-Ent:** Western. **Acq:** Purchase, Rent/Lease. **Dist:** Alpha Video; Mill Creek Entertainment L.L.C. $19.95.

Apache Mountain Spirit 1985
When Robert takes up with a bad crowd, the Gaan, Apache Mountain spirits, touch and test him. He allows the spirits to direct his life and use his powers within for good purposes. 59m; VHS, 1C, 3/4 U. **Pr:** Silvercloud Video Productions. **A:** Jr. High-Adult. **P:** Entertainment. **U:** Institution, BCTV, SURA. **Gen-Edu:** Native Americans, Folklore & Legends. **Acq:** Purchase, Rent/Lease. **Dist:** Vision Maker Media. $59.95.

Apache Rifles 1964 (Unrated) — ★★
Army Captain Jeff Stanton delivers a message to renegade Apache chief Victorio that if his tribe go back to the reservation, miners won't be allowed on their land. When gold is discovered, the miners break the treaty. Jeff has fallen in love with half-white, half-Comanche missionary Dawn and wants to restore the peace to prove himself to her. 92m; DVD. **C:** Audie Murphy; Linda Lawson; Michael Dante; L.Q. Jones; Joseph (Joe) Vitale; Directed by William Witney; Written by Charles B. Smith; Cinematography by Arch R. Dalzell; Music by Richard LaSalle. **A:** Jr. High-Adult. **P:** Entertainment. **U:** Home. **Mov-Ent:** Western, Native Americans, Miners & Mining. **Acq:** Purchase. **Dist:** VCI Entertainment.

Apache Rose 1947 (Unrated) — ★★
Gambling boat owner plots to gain control of oil found on Vegas Ranch. Roy and Dale oppose the idea. First of the series in color; the original, unedited version of the film. 75m/B/W; VHS, DVD. **C:** Roy Rogers; Dale Evans; Olin Howlin; George Meeker; Directed by William Witney. **Pr:** Republic. **A:** Family. **P:** Entertainment. **U:** Home. **Mov-Ent:** Western. **Acq:** Purchase. **Dist:** Movies Unlimited; Alpha Video. $9.99.

Apache Territory 1958 (Unrated) — ★½
Drifter Logan Cates (Calhoun) takes refuge with a group of settlers at Papago Wells who are fending off an Apache attack. But as the food and water run out, the settlers turn on each other while Cates decides to use the cover of a dust storm to strike back. Based on the Louis L'Amour novel "Last Stand at Papago Wells." 71m; DVD. **C:** Rory Calhoun; Barbara Bates; John Dehner; Carolyn Craig; Tom Pitman; Leo Gordon; Myron Healey; Directed by Ray Nazarro; Written by George W. George; Charles Marion; Cinematography by Irving Lippman. **A:** Sr. High-Adult. **P:** Entertainment. **U:** Home. **Mov-Ent:** Western. **Acq:** Purchase. **Dist:** Sony Pictures Home Entertainment Inc.

Apache Uprising 1966 (Unrated) — ★½
A standard western with Calhoun as the lawman up against gunfighters and stagecoach robbers as well as the usual Indians. 90m; VHS, Streaming, CC. **C:** Rory Calhoun; Corinne Calvet; DeForest Kelley; John Russell; Lon Chaney, Jr.; Gene Evans; Richard Arlen; Robert H. Harris; Arthur Hunnicutt; Jean Parker; Johnny Mack Brown; Directed by R.G. Springsteen. **Pr:** Paramount Pictures. **A:** Family. **P:** Entertainment. **U:** Home. **Mov-Ent:** Western. **Acq:** Purchase. **Dist:** Paramount Pictures Corp.

Apache Woman 1955 (Unrated) — ★½
Bridges stars as a government agent sent to investigate some crimes committed by a group of Apache Indians. As he tries to calm the townspeople, Bridges discovers that the group is made up of white people led by an educated half-breed. He instigates the help of the half-breed's sister (and also Bridges' love interest) to stop the gang. Some good action, but lots of dull spots. 82m; VHS. **C:** Lloyd Bridges; Joan Taylor; Lance Fuller; Morgan Jones; Paul Birch; Jonathan Haze; Paul Dubov; Lou Place; Directed by Roger Corman. **Pr:** Roger Corman; Roger Corman. **A:** Jr. High-Adult. **P:** Entertainment. **U:** Home. **Mov-Ent:** Western, Native Americans. **Acq:** Purchase. **Dist:** Facets Multimedia Inc.; Sony Pictures Home Entertainment Inc. $19.95.

Apache's Last Battle 1964 — ★★
A boundary scout discovers the ward of an Apache chief has been framed for murder by a cavalry officer who wants to start an Indian war in this exciting Euro western. 122m; VHS, DVD. **C:** Lex Barker; Pierre Brice; Daliah Lavi; Guy Madison; Ralf Wolter; Gustavo Rojo; Rick (Rik) Battaglia; Bill Ramsey; Directed by Hugo Fregonese; Written by Ladislas Fodor; Robert A. Stemmle; Cinematography by Siegfried Hold; Music by Riz Ortolani. **A:** Jr. High-Adult. **P:** Entertainment. **U:** Home. **Mov-Ent. Acq:** Purchase. **Dist:** Amazon.com Inc.; Sinister Cinema. $16.95.

Aparajito 1958 — ★★★½
The second of the Apu trilogy, about a boy growing up in India, after "Pather Panchali," and before "The World of Apu." Apu is brought to Benares and his education seriously begins. The work of a master; in Bengali with English subtitles. 108m/B/W; VHS, DVD. **C:** Pinaki Sen Gupta; Karuna Bannerjee; Kanu Bannerjee; Ramani Sen Gupta; Directed by Satyajit Ray; Written by Satyajit Ray; Cinematography by Subrata Mitra; Music by Ravi Shankar. **Pr:** Epic Films Private. **A:** Family. **P:** Entertainment. **U:** Home. **L:** Bengali. **Mov-Ent:** India. **Awds:** Venice Film Fest. '57: Film. **Acq:** Purchase. **Dist:** Facets Multimedia Inc.; Tapeworm Video Distributors Inc. $29.95.

Apart from Hugh 1994 (Unrated) — ★★
Collin and Hugh have been living together for a year and to celebrate the occasion, Hugh decides to plan an anniversary party. Unfortunately, Collin hasn't told Hugh he's having second thoughts about their relationship. Directorial debut of FitzGerald. 87m/B/W; VHS, DVD. **C:** Steve Arnold; David Merwin; Jennifer Reed; Directed by Jon FitzGerald; Written by Jon FitzGerald; Cinematography by Randy Allred; Music by James Clarke. **Pr:** Jon FitzGerald. **A:** College-Adult. **P:** Entertainment. **U:** Home. **Mov-Ent:** Drama. **Acq:** Purchase. **Dist:** Water Bearer Films Inc. $39.95.

Apart from the Crowd 1983
A documentary about people who have left their line of work to make a living from personal hobbies. 30m; VHS, 3/4 U. **Pr:** New Jersey Network. **A:** Sr. High-Adult. **P:** Education. **U:** Institution. **Gen-Edu:** Occupations. **Acq:** Purchase, Rent/Lease. **Dist:** New Jersey Network.

Apartheid 1990
Apartheid as seen through the eyes of a young South African. 10m; VHS. **A:** Sr. High-Adult. **P:** Education. **U:** Home. **Gen-Edu:** Documentary Films, Africa, Apartheid. **Acq:** Rent/Lease. **Dist:** The Cinema Guild. $150.00.

Apartheid, Part 5 1987
A documentary with rare footage of the 1987 confrontations between dissident white Africaners and black leaders from the outlawed African National Congress (ANC) in racially torn South Africa. 60m; VHS, 3/4 U. **Pr:** PBS. **A:** Jr. High-Adult. **P:** Education. **U:** Institution, SURA. **Gen-Edu:** Apartheid, Documentary Films, Africa. **Acq:** Purchase, Rent/Lease. **Dist:** PBS Home Video. $300.00.

Apartheid Revisited: Confronting History ????
Follows a group of students on a field trip across South Africa. Visits include key landmarks, veterans of the anti-apartheid movement, a Zulu village, museums, and meetings with student leaders of today for an exchange of ideas and experiences. 38m; VHS. **A:** Sr. High-Adult. **P:** Education. **U:** Institution. **Gen-Edu:** Africa, Apartheid. **Acq:** Purchase. **Dist:** Films for the Humanities & Sciences. $79.00.

The Apartment 1960 — ★★★½
Lowly insurance clerk C.C. Baxter (Lemmon) tries to climb the corporate ladder by "loaning" his apartment out to executives having affairs. Problems arise, however, when he unwittingly falls for sweet elevator operator Fran Kubelik (MacLaine), the most recent girlfriend of his unfeeling boss J.D. Sheldrake (MacMurray). Highly acclaimed social satire. 125m/B/W; VHS, DVD, Wide. **C:** Jack Lemmon; Shirley MacLaine; Fred MacMurray; Ray Walston; Jack Kruschen; Joan Shawlee; Edie Adams; Hope Holiday; David Lewis; Directed by Billy Wilder; Written by I.A.L. Diamond; Billy Wilder; Cinematography by Joseph LaShelle; Music by Adolph Deutsch. **Pr:** United Artists. **A:** Sr. High-Adult. **P:** Entertainment. **U:** Home. **Mov-Ent:** Comedy--Romantic, Classic Films, Sex & Sexuality. **Awds:** Oscars '60: Art Dir./Set Dec., B&W, Director (Wilder), Film, Film Editing, Story & Screenplay; AFI '98: Top 100; British Acad. '60: Actor (Lemmon), Actress (MacLaine), Film; Directors Guild '60: Director (Wilder); Golden Globes '61: Actor--Mus./Comedy (Lemmon), Actress--Mus./Comedy (MacLaine), Film--Mus./Comedy; Natl. Film Reg. '94; N.Y. Film Critics '60: Director (Wilder), Film, Screenplay. **Acq:** Purchase. **Dist:** Baker and Taylor; MGM Home Entertainment. $19.98.

Apartment Complex 1998 (R) — ★★½
An assortment of Hollywood weirdos occupy Dr. Caligari's Wonder View Apartments where psych grad student Stan Warden (Lowe) has just taken a job as the building manager. There's a hot-to-trot psychic, a paranoid ex-government agent, and a recluse, among others and then Stan discovers the body of the previous super. Strange things begin happening (including the appearance of a giant snake), even as hapless Stan becomes the prime suspect and potential victim. Creepy and comic. 99m; VHS, CC. **C:** Chad Lowe; Fay Masterson; Obba Babatunde; Patrick Warburton; Ron Canada; Amanda Plummer; Miguel (Michael) Sandoval; Jon Polito; R. Lee Ermey; Charles Martin Smith; Directed by Tobe Hooper; Written by Karl Schaefer; Cinematography by Jacques Haitkin; Music by Mark Adler. **A:** Sr. High-Adult. **P:** Entertainment. **U:** Home. **Mov-Ent:** Mystery & Suspense. **Acq:** Purchase. **Dist:** Paramount Pictures Corp.

Apartment for Peggy 1948 (Unrated) — ★★½
Touching postwar drama. WWII vet Jason Taylor (Holden) is going to college on the GI Bill while he and his pregnant wife Peggy (Crain) struggle to find affordable housing in the postwar boom. Peggy charms elderly, depressed Henry Barnes (Gwenn) and he allows them to renovate his attic into an apartment. Their optimism about the future also gives the old man a new lease on life. 96m; DVD. **C:** Jeanne Crain; William Holden; Edmund Gwenn; Gene Lockhart; Directed by George Seaton; Written by George Seaton; Cinematography by Harry Jackson; Music by David Raskin. **A:** Sr. High-Adult. **P:** Entertainment. **U:** Home. **L:** English. **Mov-Ent:** Drama, Aging, Marriage. **Acq:** Purchase. **Dist:** Fox Home Entertainment.

Apartment For Rent 1991
Follows three individuals on their quests for apartments. Introduces terms and questions that should be asked before signing a lease. Outlines basic considerations to be explored by the individual, including size needs, cost effectiveness, etc. 15m; VHS. **A:** Sr. High-College. **P:** Education. **U:** Institution. **Gen-Edu:** Housing, Consumer Education. **Acq:** Purchase. **Dist:** Cambridge Educational. $89.00.

Apartment Renting 101: What Happened to My Security Deposit? 1998
Dramatized vignettes explain the do's and don'ts for first time renters such as budgeting, understanding leases, insuring possessions, and other needs and wants that should be assessed. 30m; VHS. **A:** Sr. High. **P:** Education. **U:** Institution. **Gen-Edu:** Real Estate, Consumer Education, Economics. **Acq:** Purchase. **Dist:** Zenger Media. $79.95.

Apartment 1303 2007 (Unrated) — ★★
Sayaka throws an apartment-warming party, during which she freaks out and throws herself from the balcony after sucking down some dog food for no apparent reason, leaving her friends to wonder what the heck they just witnessed as the little kid from the hall says, "There goes another one". Sayaka's curious sister learns suicides happen pretty regularly among the tenants in that building, and of course there are ghosts involved. 94m; DVD. **C:** Eriko Hatsune; Yuka Itaya; Naoko Otani; Directed by Byeong-ki Ahn; Written by Byeong-ki Ahn; Brian O'Hara; Cinematography by Seok-hyeon Lee; Music by Tae-beon Lee. **A:** Sr. High-Adult. **P:** Entertainment. **U:** Home. **L:** English, Japanese, Spanish. **Mov-Ent:** Horror, Suicide. **Acq:** Purchase. **Dist:** Palisades Tartan Video. $19.95.

Apt. 3 1977
Two brothers search for the origin of the wistful harmonica music they hear and discover beauty in this iconographic film. 8m; VHS, 3/4 U. **Pr:** Alexander Cochran. **A:** Primary. **P:** Entertainment. **U:** Institution, SURA. **L:** English, Spanish. **Chl-Juv:** Language Arts. **Acq:** Purchase. **Dist:** Weston Woods Studios.

Apartment 12 2006 (R) — ★★½
Artisan Alex (Ruffalo) is stunned when a gallery curator trashes his work and pulls his show, causing his shallow bombshell of a girlfriend to lose interest. Dejected and homeless, he takes a pizza shop job and moves into more affordable digs where he meets several interesting characters, including goofy and loveable Lori (Ulrich). They start dating but Alex's cold feet mess things up, though the neighbors can't avoid one another. Solid work by leads Ruffalo and Ulrich keep this average romantic tale from getting evicted. 90m; DVD. **C:** Mark Ruffalo; Alan Gelfant; Manuel Cabral; Beth Ulrich; Mary Coleston; Directed by Dan Bootzin; Written by Dan Bootzin; Elizabeth Rivera Bootzin. **A:** Sr. High-Adult. **P:** Entertainment. **U:** Home. **Mov-Ent:** Comedy--Romantic. **Acq:** Purchase. **Dist:** Bedford Entertainment Inc. $24.95.

Apartment Zero 1988 (R) — ★★★½
A decidedly weird, deranged psychological drama about the parasite/host-type relationship between two roommates in downtown Buenos Aires: one, an obsessive British movie nut, the other, a sexually mesmerizing stud who turns out to be a cold-blooded psycho. 124m; VHS, DVD. **C:** Hart Bochner; Colin Firth; Fabrizio Bentivoglio; Liz Smith; Dora Bryan; James Telfer; Mirella D'Angelo; Juan Vitale; Francesca D'Aloja; Miguel Ligero; Elvia Andreoli; Marikeva Monti; Directed by Martin

Donovan; Written by Martin Donovan; David Koepp; Cinematography by Miguel Rodriguez; Music by Elia Cmiral. **Pr:** Skouras Pictures; Summit Company Ltd. **A:** College-Adult. **P:** Entertainment. **U:** Home. **Mov-Ent:** Mystery & Suspense, Cult Films, South America. **Acq:** Purchase. **Dist:** Wellspring Media; Image Entertainment Inc.; Facets Multimedia Inc. $14.95.

The Ape 1940 — ★★
When his daughter dies of a crippling disease, Karloff becomes fixated with the mission to cure paralysis. Obviously distraught, he begins donning the hide of an escaped circus ape whose spinal fluid is the key to the serum. Hide-bedecked, he slays unknowing townspeople to tap them of their spinal fluid and cure his latest patient. 62m/B/W; VHS, DVD. **C:** Boris Karloff; Maris Wrixon; Henry Hall; Gertrude Hoffman; Directed by William Nigh. **Pr:** Monogram. **A:** Family. **P:** Entertainment. **U:** Home. **Mov-Ent:** Horror. **Acq:** Purchase. **Dist:** Sinister Cinema; Facets Multimedia Inc.; Rex Miller Artisan Studio. $19.95.

A*P*E* 1976 (PG) — **Bomb!**
A*P*E* is 36 feet tall and ten tons of animal fury who destroys anything that comes between him and the actress he loves. Cheap rip-off of Kong. 87m; VHS, DVD, Wide. **C:** Rod Arrants; Joanna Kerns; Alex Nicol; Francis Lee; Directed by Paul Leder; Written by Paul Leder; Reuben Leder. **Pr:** Worldwide Entertainment; Korean. **A:** Sr. High-Adult. **P:** Entertainment. **U:** Home. **Mov-Ent:** Horror. **Acq:** Purchase. **Dist:** Unknown Distributor.

The Ape 2005 (Unrated) — ★
In search of solitude as he struggles to write his first great novel, Harry (Franco, also debuting as writer and director) leaves his wife and child for a studio apartment in NYC, where he is shocked to find that an ape already lives there—one that talks and wears a gaudy Hawaiian t-shirt. He somehow serves as Harry's inspiration despite stooping to lowbrow jokes and gags such as throwing poop. 93m; DVD. **C:** James Franco; Brian Lally; Allison Bibicoff; Stacey Miller; Vince Jolivette; Directed by James Franco; Written by James Franco; Merriwether Williams. **A:** Jr. High-Adult. **P:** Entertainment. **U:** Home. **Mov-Ent:** Comedy--Black. **Acq:** Purchase. **Dist:** TLA Releasing. $19.99.

The Ape Man 1943 — ★★
With the aid of a secret potion, a scientist turns himself into a murderous ape. The only way to regain his human side is to ingest human spinal fluid. Undoubtedly inspired by Boris Karloff's 1940 film, "The Ape." 64m/B/W; VHS, DVD, 3/4 U, Special order formats. **C:** Wallace Ford; Bela Lugosi; Louise Currie; Henry Hall; Minerva Urecal; Wheeler Oakman; J. Farrell MacDonald; Directed by William Beaudine; Written by Barney A. Sarecky; Cinematography by Mack Stengler. **Pr:** Prime Television. **A:** Family. **P:** Entertainment. **U:** Home. **Mov-Ent:** Horror. **Acq:** Purchase. **Dist:** Gotham Distributing Corp.; Sinister Cinema; Rex Miller Artisan Studio. $19.95.

Ape Man: The Story of Human Evolution 1994
A four-video set assessing man's origins from the first appearance of the Neanderthals to an anthropological view of mankind's past, present, and future. 200m; VHS. **C:** Hosted by Walter Cronkite. **A:** Jr. High-Adult. **P:** Education. **U:** Home. **Gen-Edu:** Documentary Films, Anthropology, Evolution. **Acq:** Purchase. **Dist:** A&E Television Networks L.L.C.; New Video Group. $79.95.
Indiv. Titles: 1. The Human Puzzle 2. Giant Strides 3. All in the Mind 4. Science and Fiction.

A.P.E. Surfshop Accounting Videos 1992
Four tapes use a real life illustration to introduce and explain the Attache 4 Integrated Accounting Software. 105m; VHS. **A:** Adult. **P:** Education. **U:** Institution. **Bus-Ind:** Business, Computers, Finance. **Acq:** Purchase. **Dist:** Cambridge Educational. $199.00.

Ape to Man 2005
Examines the search for the origins of humanity, from the first discovery of bones from Neanderthal man in 1856 to the present. 100m; DVD. **A:** Jr. High-Adult. **P:** Entertainment. **U:** Home. **Gen-Edu:** Documentary Films, Archaeology. **Acq:** Purchase. **Dist:** A&E Television Networks L.L.C.

APELCO 460/560 Fishfinder 19??
Illustrates the steps to follow when properly using the APELCO 460/560 Fishfinder. ?m; VHS. **Pr:** Bennett Marine Video. **A:** Adult. **P:** Instruction. **U:** Home. **Spo-Rec:** Boating, How-To, Electronics. **Acq:** Purchase. **Dist:** Bennett Marine Video. $29.95.

APELCO GPS 15 19??
Demonstrates how to properly use the APELCO GPS 15 navigational unit. ?m; VHS. **Pr:** Bennett Marine Video. **A:** Adult. **P:** Instruction. **U:** Home. **Spo-Rec:** Boating, How-To, Electronics. **Acq:** Purchase. **Dist:** Bennett Marine Video. $29.95.

Apelco'Marine Electronics 1992
Instruction in marine electronics for this company's models. Each model has its own program. ?m; VHS, Special order formats. **A:** Adult. **P:** Instruction. **U:** Home. **How-Ins:** Boating. **Acq:** Purchase. **Dist:** Bennett Marine Video. $29.95.
Indiv. Titles: 1. Apelco 6100/6600 2. Apelco DXL 6000 3. Apelco DXL 6300 4. Apelco DXL 6500 5. Apelco DXL 6510 6. Apelco 6800 7. Apelco DXL 6350 Loran C 8. Apelco LFC-6550 Loran/FF/Plot 9. Apelco GXL-1100 Compact GPS.

A.P.E.X. 1994 (R) — ★★
Nicholas Sinclair (Keats), a researcher from 2073, time travels back to 1973 to retrieve a faulty robot probe called A.P.E.X. (Advanced Prototype Extermination Unit). Unwittingly he has been infected with a mysterious virus and when he returns it's to a version of his own time where humans are dying from the virus and robots are sent to eradicate the few survivors. It also seems Sinclair is now a guerilla in an anti-robot army. Yes, it

sounds like "The Terminator" but the action moves and though the budget is limited the special effects are still impressive. 103m; VHS, CC. **C:** Richard Keats; Mitchell Cox; Lisa Ann Russell; Marcus Aurelius; Adam Lawson; Directed by Phillip J. Roth; Written by Phillip J. Roth; Ronald Schmidt; Music by Jim Goodwin. **Pr:** Gary Jude Barkart; Talaat Captan; Green Communications, Inc; Republic Pictures. **A:** Sr. High-Adult. **P:** Entertainment. **U:** Home. **Mov-Ent:** Science Fiction. **Acq:** Purchase. **Dist:** Lions Gate Entertainment Inc. $9.98.

Aphakic Spectacles in Perspective 1980
This program reviews the optics of aphakic correction and aspheric correction, and describes lens prescription and patient management techniques. 50m; VHS, 3/4 U. **Pr:** American Academy of Ophthalmology. **A:** College-Adult. **P:** Professional. **U:** Institution, Home, SURA. **Hea-Sci:** Eye. **Acq:** Purchase, Rent/Lease. **Dist:** American Academy of Ophthalmology.

Apheresis 1981
This program explains the procedure of apheresis and its importance in blood component therapy. 28m; VHS, 3/4 U. **Pr:** Health Communications Network. **A:** College-Adult. **P:** Professional. **U:** Institution, SURA. **Hea-Sci:** Blood. **Acq:** Purchase, Rent/Lease, Subscription.

The Aphid Eaters: Eve's Research Project 1976
A young girl follows the development of ladybird beetles from the egg stage through the larva stage while recording her observations and researching the insects. 15m; VHS, 3/4 U. **Pr:** Amitai. **A:** Primary-Jr. High. **P:** Education. **U:** Institution, SURA. **Hea-Sci:** Insects. **Acq:** Purchase, Rent/Lease. **Dist:** Clear Vue Inc.

APHIS-First Line of Defense 1983
Aimed at airline catering employees, this video explains the role of the Animal and Plant Health Inspection Service of the U.S. Department of Agriculture in quarantine and inspection proceedings. 12m; VHS, 3/4 U. **Pr:** USDA. **A:** Adult. **P:** Instruction. **U:** Institution, Home. **Gen-Edu:** Agriculture, Politics & Government. **Acq:** Purchase. **Dist:** National Audiovisual Center. $95.00.

Aphrodite 1983 (Unrated) — ★
Steamy drama based on Pierre Louy's masterpiece of erotic literature. 89m; VHS. **C:** Valerie Kaprisky; Directed by Robert Fuest. **Pr:** Adolphe Viezzi. **A:** Sr. High-Adult. **P:** Entertainment. **U:** Home. **Mov-Ent:** Sex & Sexuality. **Acq:** Purchase. **Dist:** Lions Gate Television Corp. $69.98.

Apocalipsis Joe 1965 (Unrated) — ★★¹/₂
A lonely gunfighter looks to kick an evil criminal out of a small town. 90m; VHS. **C:** Eduardo Fajardo; Mary Paz Pondal; Fernando Ceruli; Fernando Bilbao. **Pr:** Madera. **A:** Preschool. **P:** Entertainment. **U:** Home. **L:** Spanish. **Mov-Ent:** Western. **Acq:** Purchase. **Dist:** Spanishmultimedia. $34.90.

Apocalypse 1988
This program features an intimate interview with German physicist/ philosopher Carl-Fredrich von Weizsacker. 29m; VHS, DVD, 3/4 U. **Pr:** Centre Productions, Inc. **A:** Sr. High-Adult. **P:** Education. **U:** Institution, SURA. **Gen-Edu:** International Relations. **Acq:** Purchase. **Dist:** Clear Vue Inc.

The Apocalypse 1996 (R) — ★★
Space pilot J.T. Wayne (Bernhard) teams up with salvage operator Suarez (McCoy) and his crew to retrieve a cargo ship lost in space for 25 years. But crewman Vendler (Zagarino) hijacks the cargo for himself, with only Wayne and Lennon (Dye) as survivors. But it turn's out the ship is one big booby-trap rigged to crash into earth. Now Wayne and Lennon must not only save themselves but the planet as well. Low-budget, with a confusing plot. 96m; VHS, DVD. **C:** Sandra Bernhard; Laura San Giacomo; Cameron Dye; Frank Zagarino; Matt McCoy; Directed by Hubert de la Bouillerie; Cinematography by Greg Gardiner. **A:** Sr. High-Adult. **P:** Entertainment. **U:** Home. **Mov-Ent:** Science Fiction, Space Exploration. **Acq:** Purchase. **Dist:** Movies Unlimited.

The Apocalypse 2007 (Unrated) — **Bomb!**
There's some kind of end of days nonsense attached to this dreck but not even anyone interested in apocalyptic prophecies will be able to watch. Multiple asteroids trigger a series of disasters so Ashley and Jason decide they must travel to L.A. to spend their last four days with daughter Lindsey before an even bigger asteroid wipes out the planet. 90m; DVD. **C:** Rhett Giles; Jill Stapley; Kristen Quintrall; Tom Nagel; Kim Little; Sarah Lieving; Shaley Scott; Amol Shah; Erica Roby; Michael Tower; Directed by Justin Jones; Written by David Michael Latt; Cinematography by Adam Silver. **A:** Sr. High-Adult. **P:** Entertainment. **U:** Home. **Mov-Ent:** Action-Adventure. **Acq:** Purchase. **Dist:** The Asylum.

Apocalypse Now 1979 (R) — ★★★★
Coppola's $40 million epic vision of the Vietnam War was inspired by Joseph Conrad's novella "Heart of Darkness," and continues to be the subject of debate. Disillusioned Army captain Sheen travels upriver into Cambodia to assassinate overweight renegade colonel Brando. His trip is punctuated by surrealistic battles and a terrifying descent into a land where human rationality seems to have slipped away. Considered by some to be the definitive picture of war in its overall depiction of chaos and primal bloodletting; by others, over-wrought and unrealistic. May not translate as well to the small screen, yet worth seeing if for nothing more than Duvall's ten minutes of scenery chewing as a battle-obsessed major ("I love the smell of napalm in the morning!"), a study in manic machismo. Stunning photography by Vittorio Storaro, awe-inspiring battle scenes, and effective soundtrack montage. Both Sheen and Coppola suffered emotional breakdowns during the prolonged filming, and that's a very young Fishburne in his major film

debut. Available in a remastered version in letterbox on VHS with a remixed soundtrack that features Dolby Surround stereo. In 1991 a documentary detailing the making of the film, "Hearts of Darkness: A Filmmaker's Apocalypse," was released. 153m; VHS, DVD, Blu-Ray, CD-I, Wide. **C:** Marlon Brando; Martin Sheen; Robert Duvall; Frederic Forrest; Sam Bottoms; Scott Glenn; Albert Hall; Laurence Fishburne; Harrison Ford; G.D. Spradlin; Dennis Hopper; Cynthia Wood; Colleen Camp; Francis Ford Coppola; Linda Carpenter; Tom Mason; James Keane; Damien Leake; Jack Thibeau; R. Lee Ermey; Vittorio Storaro; Directed by Francis Ford Coppola; Written by Francis Ford Coppola; John Milius; Michael Herr; Cinematography by Vittorio Storaro; Music by Carmine Coppola. **Pr:** Francis Ford Coppola; Francis Ford Coppola; United Artists. **A:** College-Adult. **P:** Entertainment. **U:** Home. **Mov-Ent:** Action-Adventure, Vietnam War, Cult Films. **Awds:** Oscars '79: Cinematog., Sound; AFI '98: Top 100; British Acad. '79: Director (Coppola), Support. Actor (Duvall); Cannes '79: Film; Golden Globes '80: Director (Coppola), Score, Support. Actor (Duvall); Natl. Film Reg. '00; Natl. Soc. Film Critics '79: Support. Actor (Forrest). **Acq:** Purchase. **Dist:** Paramount Pictures Corp. $29.95.

Apocalypse Planet Earth 1991
Events preceding the dramatic Apocalypse as prophesied in the Bible are compared to recent occurrences in today's world. 45m; VHS. **C:** Hosted by Hal Lindsey. **Pr:** Jeremiah Films. **A:** Family. **P:** Religious. **U:** Home. **Gen-Edu:** Speculation, Religion, World Affairs. **Acq:** Purchase. **Dist:** Jeremiah Films. $39.95.

Apocalypse Pompeii 2014 (Unrated) — ★¹/₂
Mt. Vesuvius blows its top again just when the wife and daughter of a Special Ops commando are playing tourist. So Jeff calls his former teammates to rescue his trapped family. Cheese all the way but consistent for a release from The Asylum. 87m; DVD, Blu-Ray. **C:** Adrian Paul; Georgina Beedle; John Rhys-Davies; Jhey Castles; Dylan Vox; Directed by Ben Demaree; Written by Jacob Cooney; Bill Hanstock; Cinematography by Ben Demaree; Music by Joseph Metcalfe. **A:** Jr. High-Adult. **P:** Entertainment. **U:** Home. **L:** English. **Mov-Ent:** Action-Adventure, Italy, Volcanos. **Acq:** Purchase. **Dist:** The Asylum.

The Apocalypse Watch 1997 (Unrated) — ★★
CIA analyst Drew (Bergin) takes over his field agent brother's assignment when the latter is killed. Drew hooks up with his bro's girlfriend/partner (Madsen) and their spying leads to a neo-Nazi organization. Based on the novel by Ludlum. 176m; VHS, DVD, CC. **C:** Patrick Bergin; Virginia Madsen; John Shea; Benedick Blythe; Christopher Neame; Malcolm Tierney; Directed by Kevin Connor; Written by John Goldsmith; Christopher Canaan; Cinematography by Dennis C. Lewiston; Music by Ken Thorne. **A:** Jr. High-Adult. **P:** Entertainment. **U:** Home. **Mov-Ent:** **Acq:** Purchase. **Dist:** Lions Gate Television Corp.

Apocalypto 2006 (R) — ★★★
Set during ancient times against a lavish, peaceful backdrop in the Yucatan Peninsula. Producer/director/co-writer Gibson unleashes a savage nightmare that somehow surpasses the bloodbaths of his other works, "Passion of the Christ" and "Braveheart." Jaguar Paw (Youngblood, part of the all-native cast) and his forest tribe are viciously rounded up by Mayan attackers as their rulers desperately attempt to save their decaying civilization by sacrificing Paw's people to the gods. As the graphic slaughter begins, Paw slips away and triggers an intense 45-minute jungle chase as he tries to outrun his captors and return to his pregnant wife and young son who he'd hidden in a village well. Gibson's talent at creating no-holds-barred action is on full display. In the Mayan language of the Yucatec, with English subtitles. 137m; DVD, Blu-Ray. **C:** Rudy Youngblood; Dalia Hernandez; Jonathan Brewer; Morris Birdyellowhead; Carlos Emilio Baez; Raoul Trujillo; Rodolfo Palacios; Directed by Mel Gibson; Written by Mel Gibson; Farhad Safinia; Cinematography by Dean Semler; Music by James Horner. **Pr:** Mel Gibson; Bruce Davey; Mel Gibson; Icon Productions; Touchstone Pictures; Buena Vista. **A:** Sr. High-Adult. **P:** Entertainment. **U:** Home. **L:** English. **Mov-Ent:** Action-Adventure, Drama, Central America. **Acq:** Purchase. **Dist:** Buena Vista Home Entertainment.

Apogee: Life in Motion 1994
Time-lapse photography provides images from China, Japan, Singapore, India, East Africa, Canada, and the U.S., accompanied by original music. 45m; VHS. **A:** Adult. **P:** Entertainment. **U:** Home. **Mov-Ent:** Travel. **Acq:** Purchase. **Dist:** V.I.E.W. Inc./Arkadia Entertainment Corp. $19.98.

Apollo 8: Leaving the Cradle 2002
Contains hours of exclusive footage from NASA archives filmed during groundbreaking space programs during the 1950s and 60s. 240m; DVD. **A:** Adult. **P:** Education. **U:** Home. **Gen-Edu:** Space Exploration, Science. **Acq:** Purchase. **Dist:** Fox Home Entertainment. $49.98.

Apollo 9: Space Duet of Spider and Gumdrop 1969
Set to music, presents a remarkable look at Apollo 9's launch, the docking of the command module (Gumdrop) with the lunar module (Spider), and the return and recovery of the astronauts. 28m; 3/4 U, Q. **Pr:** National Aeronautics and Space Administration. **A:** Primary-Adult. **P:** Education. **U:** BCTV, SURA. **Hea-Sci:** Space Exploration. **Acq:** Free Loan. **Dist:** NASA Lyndon B. Johnson Space Center; JEF Films, Inc. $29.95.

Apollo 10: Green Light for a Lunar Landing 1969
This documentary provides highlights of the Apollo 10 flight, including the lunar module's close encounter with the surface of the Moon. 28m; 3/4 U. **Pr:** National Aeronautics and Space

Administration. **A:** Primary-Adult. **P:** Education. **U:** BCTV, SURA. **Hea-Sci:** Space Exploration. **Acq:** Free Loan. **Dist:** NASA Lyndon B. Johnson Space Center; JEF Films, Inc. $39.95.

Apollo 11: A Night to Remember 2009 (Unrated)
Documentary following the Apollo 11 mission from the British perspective. Includes some archival footage and demonstrations of space technology. 118m; DVD. **A:** Sr. High-Adult. **P:** Entertainment. **U:** Home. **Gen-Edu:** Documentary Films. **Acq:** Purchase. **Dist:** Acorn Media Group Inc. $24.99.

Apollo 11: Man's 1st Moon Landing 1973
An indepth look at the first lunar landing. 28m; 3/4 U. **Pr:** National Aeronautics and Space Administration. **A:** Family. **P:** Education. **U:** Institution, Home. **Gen-Edu:** Space Exploration. **Acq:** Free Loan. **Dist:** NASA Lyndon B. Johnson Space Center; JEF Films, Inc. $39.95.

Apollo 12: Pinpoint for Science 1969
Highlights the scientific achievements of the Apollo 12 mission to the Moon, including the inspection of the unmanned spacecraft Surveyor. 28m; 3/4 U, Q. **Pr:** National Aeronautics and Space Administration. **A:** Primary-Adult. **P:** Education. **U:** BCTV, SURA. **Hea-Sci:** Space Exploration. **Acq:** Free Loan. **Dist:** NASA Lyndon B. Johnson Space Center; JEF Films, Inc. $39.95.

Apollo 13 1995 (PG) — ★★★½
Realistic big-budget reenactment of the 1970 Apollo lunar mission that ran into a "problem" 205,000 miles from home reunites Hanks and Sinese from "F. Gump" and Howard and Hanks from "Splash." And an enjoyable reunion it is. Explosion in one of two oxygen tanks helping power the spacecraft leaves the three astronauts (led by Hanks) tumbling through space. With the electrical system kaput and oxygen running low, the men seek refuge in the Lunar Excursion Module. Since it's based on the real event and the outcome is known, director Howard concentrates on the personalities and the details of the seven-day adventure at Mission Control and in space, in the process delivering the dramatic payload. Weightless shots are the real deal as crew filmed for ten days and made 600 parabolic loops in a KC-135 jet, NASA's "Vomit Comet," the long plunge creating 25 seconds of weightlessness. Special effects (by James Cameron's Digital Domain) and set design do the rest; no NASA footage is used, though original TV footage is used to dramatic effect. Script, with an uncredited rewrite by John Sayles, is based on the 1994 book, "Lost Moon," written by 13's Jim Lovell (who has a cameo as the Navy captain welcoming the astronauts aboard the recovery ship), while Apollo 15 commander David Scott served as a consultant. 140m; VHS, DVD, Blu-Ray, HD-DVD, CC. **C:** Tom Hanks; Kevin Bacon; Bill Paxton; Gary Sinise; Ed Harris; Kathleen Quinlan; Brett Cullen; Emily Ann Lloyd; Miko Hughes; Max Elliott Slade; Jean Speegle Howard; Tracy Reiner; Michelle Little; David Andrews; Mary Kate Schellhardt; Gabe Jarret; Chris Ellis; Joe Spano; Xander Berkeley; Marc McClure; Clint Howard; Loren Dean; Todd Louiso; Directed by Ron Howard; Written by William Broyles, Jr.; Al Reinert; Cinematography by Dean Cundey; Music by James Horner. **Pr:** Brian Grazer; Todd Hallowell; Mark Huffam; Imagine Entertainment. **A:** Jr. High-Adult. **P:** Entertainment. **U:** Home. **Mov-Ent:** Action-Adventure, Space Exploration, Explorers. **Awds:** Oscars '95: Film Editing, Sound; Directors Guild '95: Director (Howard); Screen Actors Guild '95: Cast, Support. Actor (Harris); Blockbuster '96: Drama Actor, T. (Hanks). **Acq:** Purchase. **Dist:** Universal Music and Video Distribution. $22.98.

Apollo 13: "Houston, We've Got a Problem" 1970
Half way to the Moon, Apollo 13 was rocked by an explosion in the service module. Documents the crew's and Mission Control's reaction to the accident as well as the life-saving measures that were taken. Also includes the worldwide reaction to the near tragedy. 28m; 3/4 U. **Pr:** National Aeronautics and Space Administration. **A:** Primary-Adult. **P:** Education. **U:** BCTV, SURA. **Hea-Sci:** Space Exploration. **Acq:** Free Loan. **Dist:** NASA Lyndon B. Johnson Space Center.

Apollo 14: Mission to Fra Mauro 1971
A documentary on Apollo 12's mission to the moon. Includes scenes of the geological surveys and experiments made by the astronauts. 28m; 3/4 U. **Pr:** National Aeronautics and Space Administration. **A:** Primary-Adult. **P:** Education. **U:** BCTV, SURA. **Hea-Sci:** Space Exploration. **Acq:** Free Loan. **Dist:** NASA Lyndon B. Johnson Space Center.

Apollo 15: In Mountains of the Moon 1971
This program details the successful landing of the fourth lunar mission, including information of the lunar and orbital experiments carried out by the astronauts. 28m; 3/4 U. **Pr:** National Aeronautics and Space Administration. **A:** Primary-Adult. **P:** Education. **U:** BCTV, SURA. **Hea-Sci:** Space Exploration. **Acq:** Free Loan. **Dist:** NASA Lyndon B. Johnson Space Center. $24.99.

Apollo 16: Nothing So Hidden 1972
A visual documentation of Apollo 16's mission to the moon. Highlights include the exploration of the lunar surface near the Descartes crater It also captures the anxieties and joy experienced by members of Mission Control and the Science Support Room. 28m; 3/4 U, Q. **Pr:** National Aeronautics and Space Administration. **A:** Primary-Adult. **P:** Education. **U:** BCTV, SURA. **Hea-Sci:** Space Exploration. **Acq:** Free Loan. **Dist:** NASA Lyndon B. Johnson Space Center. $24.99.

Apollo 17: On the Shoulders of Giants 1973
A documentary on Apollo 17, America's last manned mission to the Moon. Contains highlights of the journey, the Apollo/Soyuz mission, and the Shuttle program. 23m; 3/4 U, Q. **Pr:** National Aeronautics and Space Administration. **A:** Primary-Adult. **P:**

Education. **U:** BCTV, SURA. **Hea-Sci:** Aeronautics, Space Exploration. **Acq:** Free Loan. **Dist:** ESPN Inc.; NASA Lyndon B. Johnson Space Center. $19.95.

Apollo and Dionysus: Two Fundamental Human Alternatives 198?
Two documentaries make up this program which is part of the "Art of Being Human" series. "The Sunlit Chariot" is a venture into exploring Apollo as a symbol of order. "Dionysus: Ecstasy and Renewal" is a look at a time of reaction against all traditions and a celebration of life. Both documentaries feature sequences to dramatize their objects. 60m; VHS, 3/4 U. **Pr:** Miami Dade Community College. **A:** Sr. High-Adult. **P:** Education. **U:** Institution, SURA. **Gen-Edu:** Philosophy & Ideology. **Acq:** Purchase. **Dist:** Home Vision Cinema.

Apollo 18 2011 (PG-13) — ★
Shot in quasi-documentary style, this gimmicky, tedious sci fi wannabe thriller shows found classified film of a secret moon mission in 1974 that NASA later denied. American astronauts (two on the ground and one piloting the space module) find disturbing evidence of very unfriendly alien life forms on the dark side of the moon along with a Soviet spacecraft and a dead cosmonaut. Much of the plot isn't coherent and we're not just talking about the grainy footage beamed back to Earth. 90m; DVD, Blu-Ray. **C:** Warren Christie; Ryan Robbins; Directed by Lloyd Owen; Gonzalo Lopez-Gallego; Written by Brian Miller; Cinematography by Jose David Montero. **Pr:** Timur Bekamambetov; Michele Wolkoff; Dimension Films; Weinstein Co; Bekmambetov Projects. **A:** Sr. High-Adult. **P:** Entertainment. **U:** Home. **L:** English. **Mov-Ent:** Science Fiction, The Moon, Conspiracies or Conspiracy Theories. **Acq:** Purchase. **Dist:** Weinstein Company L.L.C.; Anchor Bay Entertainment Inc.

Apollo Kids 2000 (Unrated)
Gio misses the number 6 train in Spanish Harlem and subsequently endures humiliation by his teacher, suspension from school, and harassment by law enforcement, all due to forces beyond his control. 5m; DVD. **A:** Adult. **P:** Education. **U:** Institution. **Gen-Edu:** Documentary Films. **Acq:** Purchase. **Dist:** Third World Newsreel. $79.95.

Apology 1986 (Unrated) — ★★
A psychotic killer stalks Warren, an experimental artist, In Manhattan while a detective stalks the killer. Written by Medoff, author of "Children of a Lesser God." 98m; VHS. **C:** Lesley Ann Warren; Peter Weller; John Glover; George Loros; Jimmie Ray Weeks; Chris Noth; Harvey Fierstein; Directed by Robert Bierman; Written by Mark Medoff; Music by Maurice Jarre. **A:** College-Adult. **P:** Entertainment. **U:** Home. **Mov-Ent:** Mystery & Suspense, TV Movies, Mystery & Suspense. **Acq:** Purchase. **Dist:** Movies Unlimited. $14.99.

An Apology to Elephants 2013
A look at how elephants live in the wild and the problems caused by humans, including habitat destruction, poaching, and captivity in zoos and circuses. 40m; DVD. **C:** Narrated by Lily Tomlin. **A:** Jr. High-Adult. **P:** Education. **U:** Home. **Gen-Edu:** Animals, Documentary Films. **Acq:** Purchase. **Dist:** Home Box Office Inc. $19.98.

The Apostate 1998 (R) — ★★
A young Jesuit priest, whose gay prostitute brother has been murdered by a serial killer, heads home to Puerto Rico and offers his assistance to his police inspector uncle in catching the killer, who seems driven by religious torment. But the priest himself is torn by spiritual doubts about his calling and is plunged into a world of temptation and vengeance. 94m; VHS, DVD, CC. **C:** Richard Grieco; Dennis Hopper; Kristin Minter; Frank Medrano; Michael Cole; Efrain Figueroa; Bridget Ann White; Directed by Bill Gove; Written by Bill Gove; Cinematography by Reinhart Pesche; Music by Thomas Morse. **A:** Sr. High-Adult. **P:** Entertainment. **U:** Home. **Mov-Ent. Acq:** Purchase. **Dist:** Alpha Video.

The Apostle 1997 (PG-13) — ★★★
No-holds-barred look at one man's search for religious redemption. Eulis Dewey (Duvall) is a devout, middle-aged, Pentecostal preacher in Texas, with a true gift for inspiring his congregation. Unfortunately, he's not so inspiring to his wife Jessie (Fawcett), who's cheating on him with younger minister, Horace (Allen). When Eulis discovers the infidelity, he strikes Horace with a bat, sending the man into a coma. Eulis escapes and winds up in the predominantly black town of Bayou Boutte, Louisiana, having shed his old identity for that of E.F., "The Apostle" of God. He zealously starts up a new church, seeking salvation, but his past comes back to haunt him. 134m; VHS, DVD, CC. **C:** Robert Duvall; Miranda Richardson; Farrah Fawcett; John Beasley; Todd Allen; June Carter Cash; Billy Bob Thornton; Rick Dial; Walton Goggins; Billy Joe Shaver; Directed by Robert Duvall; Written by Robert Duvall; Cinematography by Barry Markowitz; Music by David Mansfield. **Pr:** Rob Carliner; Robert Duvall; Robert Duvall; Butchers Run Films; October Films. **A:** Sr. High-Adult. **P:** Entertainment. **U:** Home. **Mov-Ent:** Religion. **Awds:** Ind. Spirit '98: Actor (Duvall), Director (Duvall), Film; L.A. Film Critics '97: Actor (Duvall), Natl. Soc. Film Critics '97: Actor (Duvall). **Acq:** Purchase. **Dist:** Movies Unlimited; Alpha Video.

Apostle of Divine Mercy: Sister Faustina 19??
The biography of Helen Kowolska of Poland, who later became the Apostle of Divine Mercy as Sister Faustina, after receiving the revelations of mercy from Christ. 60m; VHS. **A:** Jr. High-Adult. **P:** Religious. **U:** Home. **Gen-Edu:** Religion, Biography. **Acq:** Purchase. **Dist:** Ignatius Press. $39.95.

Appalachia: No Man's Land 1988
The lives of people affected by the mining lay-offs in Kentucky and West Virginia are studied in this tape. 28m; VHS. **Pr:**

Maryknoll World Productions. **A:** Jr. High-Adult. **P:** Education. **U:** Institution. **Gen-Edu:** Poverty, Labor & Unions. **Acq:** Purchase. **Dist:** Maryknoll Sisters. $19.95.

Appalachian Genesis 1971
The issues facing young Appalachians, such as coal mining, the educational system, job opportunities, and health facilities, are discussed. 29m; VHS, 3/4 U. **Pr:** Appalshop Films. **A:** College-Adult. **P:** Education. **U:** Institution, Home. **Gen-Edu:** Sociology. **Acq:** Purchase. **Dist:** Appalshop Films & Video.

Appalachian Journey 19??
Documents the birth and growth of southern, country music. 60m; VHS. **C:** Hosted by Alan Lomax. **A:** Jr. High-Adult. **P:** Entertainment. **U:** Home. **Gen-Edu:** Music--Country/Western. **Acq:** Purchase. **Dist:** Music Video Distributors. $19.95.

Appalachian Spring 1944
A performance of Martha Graham's interpretation in dance of Aaron Copland's music. 31m/B/W; VHS, 3/4 U. **C:** Martha Graham. **A:** Jr. High-Adult. **P:** Entertainment. **U:** Institution, SURA. **Fin-Art:** Dance, Dance--Performance. **Acq:** Purchase. **Dist:** Phoenix Learning Group.

Appalachian Spring: Copeland 1993
Ballet performance illustrating an early 19th century newlywed couple setting up a Pennsylvania home. Complete with teacher's guide. 23m; VHS. **A:** Primary-Jr. High. **P:** Education. **U:** Institution. **Fin-Art:** Dance--Performance, History--U.S. **Acq:** Purchase. **Dist:** Clear Vue Inc. $45.00.

The Appalachian Story 1988
Explains how mountains are created and demonstrates how geologists can solve the giant jigsaw puzzle of the earth's history from the slender evidence found in rocks. 52m; VHS. **A:** Family. **P:** Education. **U:** Home, Institution. **Gen-Edu:** Geology, Science. **Acq:** Purchase. **Dist:** Moving Images Distribution.

Appalachian Trail 2009 (Unrated)
Join National Geographic and explore the outer reaches of the Appalachian Trail. 50m; DVD. **A:** Family. **P:** Education. **U:** Institution, Home. **Gen-Edu:** Documentary Films, National Parks & Reserves. **Acq:** Purchase. **Dist:** National Geographic Society. $19.95.

The Appalachians 2005
PBS documentary recalling the history of the Appalachian mountain region and its role in the development of the country; includes interviews with everyday citizens and scholars along with, among others, legendary country musicians Loretta Lynn and Johnny Cash. 180m; VHS, DVD. **A:** Sr. High-Adult. **P:** Entertainment. **U:** Home. **Gen-Edu:** Documentary Films, History--U.S., Music--Country/Western. **Acq:** Purchase. **Dist:** PBS Home Video. $44.95.

The Appaloosa 1966 (Unrated) — ★★½
A lamenting loner who decides to begin anew by breeding Appaloosas is ripped off by a desperate woman who steals his horse in order to get away from her abusive amour. Brando falls in love with the girl and the two amazingly survive a wealth of obstacles in their battle against Mexican bandits. 99m; VHS, DVD. **C:** Marlon Brando; Anjanette Comer; John Saxon; Directed by Sidney J. Furie; Written by James Bridges; Cinematography by Russell Metty. **Pr:** Mark Huffam. **A:** Jr. High-Adult. **P:** Entertainment. **U:** Home. **Mov-Ent:** Western, Romance, Horses. **Acq:** Purchase. **Dist:** Movies Unlimited; Alpha Video. $14.95.

Appaloosa 2008 (R) — ★★★
Director, co-writer, co-producer, and star Harris brings the 2005 Robert B. Parker novel to the big screen with grit and grandeur. In 1880s New Mexico, two friends, Virgil Cole (Harris) and Everett Hitch (Mortensen), are hired to uphold the law in a small town overtaken by a tyrannical rancher (Irons). Their duty, as well as their friendship, is put to the test as a fetching young widow (Zellweger) strolls into town, stirring the hearts of both men. Beautifully shot and perfectly acted, with a smart and funny screenplay that keeps it above the genre cliches. 114m; Blu-Ray, Wide. **C:** Ed Harris; Viggo Mortensen; Renee Zellweger; Jeremy Irons; Rex Linn; Tom Bower; Timothy Spall; James Gammon; Lance Henriksen; Ariadna Gil; Directed by Ed Harris; Written by Ed Harris; Robert Knott; Cinematography by Dean Semler; Music by Jeff Beal. **Pr:** Robert Knott; Ed Harris; Ginger Sledge; Ed Harris; Groundswell Productions; Axon Films; New Line Cinema. **A:** Sr. High-Adult. **P:** Entertainment. **U:** Home. **L:** English. **Mov-Ent:** Western. **Acq:** Purchase. **Dist:** New Line Home Video; Movies Unlimited; Alpha Video.

Apparel and Textile Careers 19??
Outlines the various career opportunities available in the apparel and textile industries. Breaks down into four separate categories: clothing services; clothing production and management; textile and clothing design; and merchandising and retailing. Provides information on the market, the industry, and the requirements. 41m; VHS. **A:** Jr. High-Adult. **P:** Education. **U:** Institution. **Bus-Ind:** Textile Industry, Occupations. **Acq:** Purchase. **Dist:** CEV Multimedia. $89.95.

Apparition 1982 (Unrated)
Wryly explores the issues of faith and ignorance. With color sequences. 8m/B/W; VHS. **C:** Directed by Pascal Aubier. **Pr:** Flower Films. **A:** Sr. High-Adult. **P:** Entertainment. **U:** Institution, Home. **Mov-Ent:** Film--Avant-Garde. **Acq:** Purchase. **Dist:** Flower Films.

The Apparition 2012 (PG-13) — Bomb!
The scariest thing about this turgid mess is the thought of having to sit through it again. The creators of this absolute disaster did the bare minimum of work to produce an Asian horror rip-off years after most people thought that trend had mercifully ended. A boring couple is haunted by a boring ghost

in a boring retread of better movies. Without a single memorable line of dialogue, scary moment, or actual twist, it's almost a non-horror movie, only terrifying when one considers that any effort was put into making it. 82m; DVD, Blu-Ray. **C:** Ashley Greene; Sebastian Stan; Tom Felton; Julianna Guill; Luke Pasqualino; Rick Gomez; Directed by Todd Lincoln; Written by Todd Lincoln; Cinematography by Daniel Pearl; Music by tomandandy. **Pr:** Joel Silver; Andrew Rona; Alex Heineman; Todd Lincoln; Warner Bros; Dark Castle Entertainment. **A:** Jr. High-Adult. **P:** Entertainment. **U:** Home. **L:** English. **Mov-Ent:** Horror. **Acq:** Purchase. **Dist:** Warner Home Video, Inc.

An Appeal to the Jews of the World 1941
Exemplifies the brief uniting of Jews and non-Jews in the Soviet Union during Stalin's reign. Explores the signed appeal of Jewish writers and artists asking the Soviet people to unite against Fascism. Yiddish with English subtitles. 6m/B/W; VHS. **A:** Jr. High-Adult. **P:** Education. **U:** Institution. **Gen-Edu:** Holocaust, USSR. **Acq:** Purchase. **Dist:** National Center for Jewish Film.

The Appeared 2007 (Unrated) — ★★
Siblings Malena and Pablo are in a Buenos Aires hospital to deal with their comatose father. Pablo suddenly decides he wants to visit their rural childhood home and then finds a journal in their father's car detailing 20-year-old murders. Everywhere the siblings travel, they are haunted by the ghosts of the victims and then stalked by a killer who doesn't want any secrets revealed. Spanish with subtitles. 120m; DVD. **C:** Ruth Diaz; Javier Pereira; Pablo Cedron; Leonara Balearce; Directed by Paco Cabezas; Written by Paco Cabezas; Cinematography by Andreu Rebes; Music by Oscar Araujo. **A:** College-Adult. **P:** Entertainment. **U:** Home. **L:** Spanish. **Mov-Ent:** South America, Horror. **Acq:** Purchase. **Dist:** MPI Media Group.

Appellate Advocacy 1987
A series for law students in the techniques of appellate court trials. 40m; VHS, 3/4 U. **Pr:** National Institute for Trial Advocacy. **A:** Adult. **P:** Professional. **U:** Institution. **Gen-Edu:** Law. **Acq:** Purchase, Rent/Lease. **Dist:** National Institute for Trial Advocacy.
Indiv. Titles: 1. Appellate Argument: Purposes, Preparation & Introduction 2. Appellate Argument: Argument 3. Appellate Argument: Rebuttal, Problems, Court Conference.

Appetite 1998 (R) — ★★
Try to stick with this slow-moving suspenser because it's got a wicked ending. A group of strangers, staying at the same hotel, play a game of cards where the loser must sleep in the reputedly haunted Room 207. 99m; VHS, DVD. **C:** Ute Lemper; Trevor Eve; Christien Anholt; Edward Hardwicke; Directed by George Milton; Written by Dominik Scherrer; Cinematography by Peter Thwaites. **A:** Sr. High-Adult. **P:** Entertainment. **U:** Home. **Mov-Ent:** Horror, Hotels & Hotel Staff Training. **Acq:** Purchase. **Dist:** Movies Unlimited.

Appetizers, Soups, and Salads 199?
Covers the techniques of preparing table-side appetizers, soups and salads for food service employees and wait staff. Part of the Table-Side Service Series. 29m; VHS. **A:** Sr. High-Adult. **P:** Instruction. **U:** Home. **How-Ins:** Cooking, Food Industry, How-To. **Acq:** Purchase. **Dist:** Culinary Institute of America. $75.00.

Applause! 197?
Noted speech consultant Dr. Georgette McGregor teaches seven steps for achieving effective speech. 26m; VHS, 3/4 U. **Pr:** Cally Curtis. **A:** Adult. **P:** Education. **U:** Institution, SURA. **Gen-Edu:** Language Arts. **Acq:** Purchase, Rent/Lease. **Dist:** Aspen Publishers, Inc.

Applause 1929 (Unrated) — ★★★
Morgan plays a down-and-out burlesque star trying to protect her fresh from the convent daughter. Definitely dated, but a marvelous performance by Morgan. Film buffs will appreciate this early talkie. 78m/B/W; VHS, DVD. **C:** Helen Morgan; Joan Peers; Fuller Mellish, Jr.; Henry Wadsworth; Dorothy (Dorothy G. Cummings) Cumming; Directed by Rouben Mamoulian; Cinematography by George J. Folsey. **Pr:** Paramount Pictures. **A:** Jr. High-Adult. **P:** Entertainment. **U:** Home. **Mov-Ent. Awds:** Natl. Film Reg. '06. **Acq:** Purchase. **Dist:** Paramount Pictures Corp.

The Apple 1964 (Unrated)
An animated parable about a man's desire to capture an evasive apple takes an ironic turn. 8m; VHS. **Pr:** Janus Films. **A:** Sr. High-Adult. **P:** Entertainment. **U:** Institution. **Mov-Ent:** Animation & Cartoons, Ethics & Morals. **Acq:** Purchase. **Dist:** Pyramid Media.

The Apple 1980 (PG) — ★1/2
Futuristic musical filmed in Berlin that features a young, innocent, folk-singing couple who nearly become victims of the evil, glitzy record producer who tries to recruit the couple into a life of sex and drugs. 90m; VHS, DVD. **C:** Catherine Mary Stewart; Alan Love; Joss Ackland; Directed by Menahem Golan; Written by Menahem Golan. **Pr:** Independent. **A:** Jr. High-Adult. **P:** Entertainment. **U:** Home. **Mov-Ent:** Musical. **Acq:** Purchase. **Dist:** Movies Unlimited.

An Apple, An Orange 1988
Two immigrant women find it difficult to live together. 90m; VHS, 3/4 U. **Pr:** Maryland Center for Public Broadcasting. **A:** Jr. High-Adult. **P:** Education. **U:** Institution, CCTV, CATV, BCTV. **Gen-Edu:** Women, Immigration. **Acq:** Purchase. **Dist:** Maryland Public Television. $29.95.

Apple Dolls 1988
Urve Buffey demonstrates the art of apple-doll making, a pleasurable and creative hobby for the pioneers of North America. 18m; VHS, 3/4 U. **Pr:** Labyrinth. **A:** Jr. High-Adult. **P:**

Education. **U:** Institution, SURA. **How-Ins:** Crafts. **Acq:** Purchase. **Dist:** Lucerne Media. $205.00.

The Apple Dumpling Gang 1975 (G) — ★★
Three frisky kids strike it rich and trigger the wildest bank robbery in the gold-mad West. Unmistakably Disney, a familial subplot and a wacky duo are provided. Mediocre yet superior to its sequel, "The Apple Dumpling Gang Rides Again." 100m; VHS, DVD, CC. **C:** Bill Bixby; Susan Clark; Don Knotts; Tim Conway; David Wayne; Slim Pickens; Harry (Henry) Morgan; Directed by Norman Tokar; Music by Buddy (Norman Dale) Baker. **Pr:** Walt Disney Studios. **A:** Family. **P:** Entertainment. **U:** Home. **Mov-Ent:** Family Viewing. **Acq:** Purchase. **Dist:** Walt Disney Studios Home Entertainment. $19.99.

The Apple Dumpling Gang Rides Again 1979 (G) — ★★
Two lovable hombres terrorize the West in their bungling attempt to go straight. Fans of Conway or Knotts may appreciate this sequel to Disney's "The Apple Dumpling Gang." 88m; VHS, DVD. **C:** Tim Conway; Don Knotts; Tim Matheson; Kenneth Mars; Harry (Henry) Morgan; Jack Elam; Directed by Vincent McEveety; Music by Buddy (Norman Dale) Baker. **Pr:** Walt Disney Studios. **A:** Family. **P:** Entertainment. **U:** Home. **Mov-Ent:** Family Viewing. **Acq:** Purchase. **Dist:** Walt Disney Studios Home Entertainment. $69.95.

Apple II Repair, Maintenance and Expansion 1987
Many different repair techniques and applications for the Apple II are explored. 13m; VHS. **Pr:** Bergwall Productions. **A:** Sr. High-Adult. **P:** Instruction. **U:** Institution. **How-Ins:** Computers, How-To. **Acq:** Purchase. **Dist:** Bergwall Productions, Inc. $249.00.
Indiv. Titles: 1. Introduction to Computer Repair 2. Troubleshooting Disk Drives 3. Motherboard and Main Computer Testing 4. Peripheral Diagnosis and Expansion.

Apple Packing House Operations ????
Explains handling and sorting techniques, equipment operation, packing line maintenance, employee supervision and more. 15m; VHS. **A:** Adult. **P:** Education. **U:** Home. **Gen-Edu:** Agriculture, Food Industry. **Acq:** Purchase. **Dist:** Michigan State University. $15.00.

Apple Tree of Paradise 1985
In this sequel to "The Girls of Nowopilki," the young heroines attempt to sort out their lives in post-war Warsaw. In Polish only, no English subtitles. 112m; VHS. **C:** Directed by Barbara Sass. **Pr:** Polish. **A:** Adult. **P:** Entertainment. **U:** Home. **L:** Polish. **Mov-Ent. Acq:** Purchase. **Dist:** Facets Multimedia Inc. $49.95.

The Applegates 1989 (R) — ★★1/2
Ecologically correct Amazonian beetles are more than a little miffed about the slash-and-burn tactics in their home and decide to establish a kinder, gentler habitat. Bug Begley and his brood transform themselves into average Americans, but then don't want to leave their decadent life: even insects aren't immune to the lure of sex, drugs, and cable shopping networks. Imaginative, often quite funny one-joke flick should've been shorter. Fits quite well as a double feature with Lehmann's earlier "Heathers." 90m; VHS, CC. **C:** Ed Begley, Jr.; Stockard Channing; Dabney Coleman; Camille (Cami) Cooper; Bobby Jacoby; Glenn Shadix; Susan Barnes; Adam Biesk; Savannah Smith Boucher; Directed by Michael Lehmann; Written by Michael Lehmann; Redbeard Simmons; Cinematography by Mitchell Dubin; Music by David Newman. **Pr:** Denise Di Novi. **A:** College-Adult. **P:** Entertainment. **U:** Home. **Mov-Ent:** Comedy--Black, Ecology & Environment, Terrorism. **Acq:** Purchase. **Dist:** Anchor Bay Entertainment. $89.98.

Apples 1997
Teaches about this favorite fruit through the stories of Johnny Appleseed, orchard tours, demonstrations of how to make apple crafts, and food products. 30m; VHS; Closed Captioned. **A:** Preschool-Primary. **P:** Education. **U:** Institution. **Gen-Edu:** Children, Nutrition. **Acq:** Purchase. **Dist:** DeBeck Educational Video. $35.00.

Apples of Gold 1980
The history and struggles of the Jewish people from the early Zionist movement to the present state of Israel is documented. 80m; VHS. **Pr:** Crossroads Christian Communications. **A:** College-Adult. **P:** Education. **U:** Institution, Home. **Gen-Edu:** Judaism, Middle East. **Acq:** Purchase, Rent/Lease. **Dist:** Alden Films. $50.00.

Appleseed 1988
Humans and bioroids live peacefully together in the futuristic city of Olympus. However, when a terrorist group invades, the harmony is shattered. In Japanese with English subtitles. 70m; VHS, UMD. **A:** Sr. High-Adult. **P:** Entertainment. **U:** Home. **L:** Japanese. **Mov-Ent:** Animation & Cartoons, Terrorism. **Acq:** Purchase. **Dist:** Tapeworm Video Distributors Inc. $34.95.

The Application of Good Design 19??
Outlines techniques in creating graphic designs that sell. Provides demonstrations by professional designers working on rough layouts, comprehensives, and dummies. Also discusses computer aids. 45m; VHS. **A:** Jr. High-Adult. **P:** Instruction. **U:** Institution. **How-Ins:** Graphics, Education, How-To. **Acq:** Purchase. **Dist:** Instructional Video. $39.95.

Application of Pre-Woven Cane 1992
Step-by-step look at one of the easier methods of chair weaving for both the groove and the frame type chair, including not only clear instructions but the proper tools necessary for each step. 42m; VHS. **A:** Jr. High-Adult. **P:** Instruction. **U:** Home. **How-Ins:** How-To. **Acq:** Purchase. **Dist:** Interlace Productions. $27.95.

Application of the Mental Status Exam 1982
This program discusses the procedures for a nurse making a mental status assessment. 12m; 3/4 U. **Pr:** Margaret L. Larson. **A:** Adult. **P:** Professional. **U:** Institution. **Hea-Sci:** Nursing. **Acq:** Purchase, Rent/Lease. **Dist:** University of Washington Educational Media Collection.

Applications of Conic Sections: The Eccentric Professor 1994
Provides introduction to the mathematical processes associated with conic sections. Uses tongue-in-cheek approach as an aging professor teaches students who are either distracted or asleep. Covers such topics as circles, ellipses, hyperbolas, and parabolas. Comes with teacher's guide. 23m; VHS. **A:** Sr. High. **P:** Education. **U:** Institution. **Gen-Edu:** Mathematics, Education. **Acq:** Purchase. **Dist:** HRM Video. $189.00.

Applications of Distillation Control 199?
An instrument technology training program on the applications of distillation control. Includes a manual. 30m; VHS. **A:** Adult. **P:** Instruction. **U:** Institution. **Bus-Ind:** Technology, Job Training. **Acq:** Purchase. **Dist:** ISA -The International Society of Automation. $95.00.

Applications of Heat Exchanger Control 199?
An instrument technology training program on the applications of heat exchanger control. Includes a manual. 30m; VHS. **A:** Adult. **P:** Instruction. **U:** Institution. **Bus-Ind:** Technology, Job Training. **Acq:** Purchase. **Dist:** ISA -The International Society of Automation. $95.00.

Applications of Logarithms 19??
Provides comprehensive information on the mathematical functions associated with algebra and logarithms. Uses examples of carbon dating of dinosaur fossils, nuclear decay, population models, interest and amortization, seismology, and learning curves. 25m; VHS. **Pr:** HRM. **A:** Sr. High. **P:** Education. **U:** Institution. **Gen-Edu:** Mathematics. **Acq:** Purchase. **Dist:** HRM Video. $175.00.

Applications of pH Control 199?
An instrument technology training program on the applications of pH control. Includes a manual. 30m; VHS. **A:** Adult. **P:** Instruction. **U:** Institution. **Bus-Ind:** Technology, Job Training. **Acq:** Purchase. **Dist:** ISA -The International Society of Automation. $95.00.

Applications of Trigonometry 19??
Combines student-friendly language, footage, and graphics to explain the properties of various trigonometric functions and how they apply in everyday life. Includes examples of their uses in surveying, navigation, astronomy, amusement park design, and oceanography. Comes with worksheets and transparencies. 25m; VHS. **Pr:** HRM. **A:** Sr. High. **P:** Education. **U:** Institution. **Gen-Edu:** Mathematics. **Acq:** Purchase. **Dist:** HRM Video. $175.00.

Applied Communication 1988
A tape of drills that students can use to practice their communication skills. 100m; VHS, CC, 3/4 U. **Pr:** Agency for Instructional Television. **A:** Jr. High-Adult. **P:** Education. **U:** Institution, CCTV, CATV, BCTV. **Gen-Edu:** Communication, Education, Language Arts. **Acq:** Purchase, Rent/Lease, Duplication License. **Dist:** Agency for Instructional Technology.

Applied Communication Skills 1986
For beginning and advanced students, examines the theory and application of communication skills. 28m; VHS. **Pr:** WMVS Milwaukee. **A:** Sr. High-Adult. **P:** Education. **U:** Institution, CCTV, BCTV, SURA. **Gen-Edu:** Communication. **Acq:** Purchase, Rent/Lease, Loan. **Dist:** Wisconsin Technical College System Foundation.
Indiv. Titles: 1. What It's All About 2. It's Up to You 3. Discussion for Democracy 4. Forms of Discussion 5. Discussing the Problem 6. Solving the Problem 7. The Discussion Leader 8. The Discussion Group 9. Putting It All Together 10. Endless Discussion 11. Persuasion Appeals 12. Persuasion Gone Awry 13. Speaking Persuasively 14. Basic Writing Skills 15. Writing It Right 16. The Research Paper 17. Using the Library 18. The Business Leader 19. The Job Application 20. The Many Modes of Media 21. The 23-Inch World 22. Viewing the News 23. The Film 24. The Novel 25. Poets and Poetry 26. What It Was About.

Applied Genetics 19??
Discusses ways that genetics can be applied in everyday life, including cloning, karyo-typing, genetic counseling, and the use of genetic profiles by law enforcement. Comes with activity masters and teacher's guide. 30m; VHS. **A:** Jr. High-Sr. High. **P:** Education. **U:** Institution. **Hea-Sci:** Genetics, Education. **Acq:** Purchase. **Dist:** Educational Activities Inc. $79.00.

Applied Leadership 1982
This program discusses good leadership behavior patterns and reveals six fundamental leadership activities that can help a person become a leader. 18m; VHS, 3/4 U. **Pr:** Resources for Education and Management. **A:** Adult. **P:** Professional. **U:** Institution, CCTV. **Bus-Ind:** Management. **Acq:** Purchase. **Dist:** Resources for Education & Management, Inc.

The Applied Management Series 1984
This series of four six hour programs will train people in current effective management techniques. 360m; 3/4 U. **Pr:** Organizational Dynamics Inc. **A:** College-Adult. **P:** Education. **U:** Institution. **Bus-Ind:** Management, Business. **Acq:** Purchase, Rent/Lease. **Dist:** SkillSoft.
Indiv. Titles: 1. Managing Conflict 2. Problem Solving and Decision Making 3. Performance Review 4. Managing Time.

Applied Physics for Nurses 197?
This series creates an awareness and stimulates thinking of physical principles as part of routine nursing procedures. 15m;

VHS, 3/4 U. **Pr:** Trainex. **A:** College-Adult. **P:** Professional. **U:** Institution. **Hea-Sci:** Nursing, Physics. **Acq:** Purchase. **Dist:** Medcom Inc.

Indiv. Titles: 1. Liquids 2. Gases 3. Force and Motion 4. Heat 5. Electricity.

Applique and Mola Design 1982
Designing and applying appliques are demonstrated in this tape from the "Crafts and Decorating" series. 60m; VHS, 3/4 U, Special order formats. **C:** Lee Mahor. **Pr:** Cinema Associates. **A:** Jr. High-Adult. **P:** Instruction. **U:** Institution, CCTV, CATV, BCTV, Home. **How-Ins:** Crafts. **Acq:** Purchase, Rent/Lease. **Dist:** RMI Media; Morris Video. $39.95.

Applique: Traditional, Stained Glass and Shadow 1988
Three different projects are used to teach you this fun and delicate craft. 57m; VHS. **A:** Jr. High-Adult. **P:** Instruction. **U:** Home. **How-Ins:** How-To, Crafts, Sewing. **Acq:** Purchase. **Dist:** Victorian Video/Yarn Barn of Kansas, Inc. $39.95.

Applique—5 Techniques 1989
Applying fabric to fabric is the center of attention here. 60m; VHS. **C:** Theta Happ. **Pr:** Nancy's Notions Ltd. **A:** Jr. High-Adult. **P:** Instruction. **U:** Institution, Home. **How-Ins:** Sewing. **Acq:** Rent/Lease. **Dist:** Nancy's Notions Ltd.

Apply Methods of Evaluating Learner Part Two 1994
Part of a series offering instruction on training the nursing assistant trainer. 25m; VHS. **A:** Adult. **P:** Professional. **U:** Institution. **Hea-Sci:** Nursing. **Acq:** Purchase. **Dist:** RMI Media. $89.95.

Applying a Tourniquet 1983
This video graphically depicts the proper use and placement of a tourniquet, and gives precautions for its use. From the EMT video: group two series. 5m; VHS, 3/4 U. **Pr:** USAAHS. **A:** Adult. **P:** Instruction. **U:** Institution, SURA. **Hea-Sci:** Emergencies, First Aid. **Acq:** Purchase. **Dist:** National Audiovisual Center. $80.00.

Applying Communication Theory to Work with Patients 1979
Major theories of communication are presented by Dr. Scheflen. Communication as a mutually influencing and regulating process is focused upon. 50m; VHS, 3/4 U, EJ. **Pr:** Dr. Milton M. Berger. **A:** College-Adult. **P:** Professional. **U:** Institution, CCTV, SURA. **Hea-Sci:** Psychiatry, Communication. **Acq:** Purchase, Rent/Lease. **Dist:** Health & Education Multimedia, Inc.

Applying for a Job 1971
Demonstrates how proper attention to dress and manner can affect the outcome of a job interview. From the "Careers in the Office" series. 13m; VHS, 3/4 U. **Pr:** Encyclopedia Britannica Educational Corporation. **A:** Jr. High-Sr. High. **P:** Education. **U:** Institution, SURA. **L:** English, Spanish. **Gen-Edu:** Occupations. **Acq:** Purchase, Rent/Lease, Trade-in. **Dist:** Encyclopedia Britannica.

Applying Modifiers for Geometric Dimensioning and Tolerancing 1990
Explains modifiers used in geometric tolerancing including material condition, least material condition, and regardless-of-feature size. 30m; VHS. **A:** Adult. **P:** Education. **U:** Institution. **Gen-Edu:** Engineering. **Acq:** Purchase. **Dist:** RMI Media. $79.95.

Applying Pressure with 3-Deep Zone Blitzes 2008 (Unrated)
Coach/Defensive Coordinator Dave Doeren demonstrates drills for improving a football team's defensive abilities as well as help with using blitzes to pressure the opposing team. 48m; DVD. **A:** Sr. High-Adult. **P:** Education. **U:** Home. **Spo-Rec:** Football, Athletic Instruction/Coaching. **Acq:** Purchase. **Dist:** Championship Productions. $39.99.

Applying Splints to the Leg 1983
This video demonstrates how to use all of the major types of splints, as well as how to make a splint out of at-hand materials. From the EMT video: group two series. 30m; VHS, 3/4 U. **Pr:** USAAHS. **A:** Adult. **P:** Instruction. **U:** Institution, SURA. **How-Ins:** Emergencies. **Acq:** Purchase. **Dist:** National Audiovisual Center. $110.00.

Applying the Model Rules of Professional Conduct 1984
A panel of lawyers applies the new American Bar Association's Model Rules of Professional Conduct to 12 hypothetical problems that lawyers face. 120m; VHS, 3/4 U. **Pr:** Practicing Law Institute. **A:** Sr. High-Adult. **P:** Education. **U:** Institution, Home. **Gen-Edu:** Law. **Acq:** Purchase, Rent/Lease. **Dist:** Practising Law Institute.

The Appointment 197?
Portrays what it's like to go alone to a business appointment. You're not really alone if you've used all the resources and support your company makes available to you. 3m; VHS, 3/4 U. **Pr:** Cally Curtis. **A:** Adult. **P:** Professional. **U:** Institution, SURA. **Bus-Ind:** Management. **Acq:** Purchase, Rent/Lease. **Dist:** Aspen Publishers, Inc.

The Appointment 1982 (Unrated) — **Bomb!**
A supernatural force enters the bodies and minds of people and suddenly everyone goes crazy. 90m; VHS, 8 mm. **C:** Edward Woodward; Jane Merrow; Directed by Lindsey C. Vickers; Cinematography by Carlo Di Palma. **A:** Jr. High-Adult. **P:** Entertainment. **U:** Home. **Mov-Ent:** Horror, Horror. **Acq:** Purchase. **Dist:** No Longer Available.

Appointment in Honduras 1953 (Unrated) — ★★
An adventurer goes on a dangerous trek through the Central American jungles to deliver funds to the Honduran President. 79m; VHS, DVD. **C:** Glenn Ford; Ann Sheridan; Zachary Scott; Directed by Jacques Tourneur. **Pr:** RKO. **A:** Family. **P:** Entertainment. **U:** Home. **Mov-Ent:** Central America. **Acq:** Purchase. **Dist:** Unknown Distributor.

Appointment in London 1953 (Unrated) — ★★½
In 1943, Wing Commander Tim Mason is trying to complete 90 German bombing missions before being consigned to desk duty. Under increasing strain, his superior officers ground him after his 89th mission but when another bomber pilot is injured, Mason defies orders and takes his place. 96m; DVD. **C:** Dirk Bogarde; Ian Hunter; Bill Kerr; Bryan Forbes; William Sylvester; Dinah Sheridan; Walter Fitzgerald; Directed by Philip Leacock; Written by Robert Westerby; John Wooldridge; Cinematography by Stephen Dade; Music by John Wooldridge. **A:** Jr. High-Adult. **P:** Entertainment. **U:** Home. **Mov-Ent:** Aeronautics, World War Two. **Acq:** Purchase. **Dist:** Movies Unlimited.

Appointment with Crime 1945 (Unrated) — ★★½
After serving a prison sentence, an ex-con sets out to avenge himself against the colleagues who double crossed him. Well done, highlighted by superior characterizations. Based on the story by Michael Leighton. 91m/B/W; VHS, Streaming. **C:** William Hartnell; Raymond Lovell; Robert Beatty; Herbert Lom; Joyce Howard; Alan Wheatley; Cyril Smith; Directed by John Harlow; Written by John Harlow. **Pr:** British National. **A:** Sr. High-Adult. **P:** Entertainment. **U:** Home. **Mov-Ent:** Action-Adventure. **Acq:** Purchase. **Dist:** Sinister Cinema. $16.95.

Appointment With Danger 1951 — ★★
Postal Inspection Service detective Al Goddard (Ladd) goes undercover to get the gang who murdered his partner after persuading the only witness, Sister Augustine (Calvert), to identity the killer. But psychotic gang member Joe (Webb) decides to take care of any loose ends that will prevent them from going after a million dollar mail heist. 89m/B/W; DVD, Blu-Ray. **C:** Alan Ladd; Phyllis Calvert; Jack Webb; Harry (Henry) Morgan; Paul Stewart; Jan Sterling; Directed by Lewis Allen; Written by Richard L. Breen; Warren Duff; Cinematography by John Seitz; Music by Victor Young. **A:** Sr. High-Adult. **P:** Entertainment. **U:** Home. **Mov-Ent:** Mailmen. **Acq:** Purchase. **Dist:** Olive Films.

Appointment with Death 1988 (PG) — ★½
Disappointing Agatha Christie mystery with Hercule Poirot solving the murder of a shrewish widow in 1937 Palestine. 103m; VHS, CC. **C:** Peter Ustinov; Lauren Bacall; Carrie Fisher; John Gielgud; Piper Laurie; Hayley Mills; Jenny Seagrove; David Soul; Directed by Michael Winner; Written by Anthony Shaffer; Peter Buckman; Michael Winner; Music by Pino Donaggio. **Pr:** Cannon Films. **A:** Jr. High-Adult. **P:** Entertainment. **U:** Home. **Mov-Ent:** Mystery & Suspense. **Acq:** Purchase. **Dist:** Warner Home Video, Inc.; Facets Multimedia Inc. $19.98.

Appointment With Death 2010 (Unrated) — ★★½
Vacationing in Syria, Hercule Poirot (Suchet) joins in visiting the archeological expedition of Lord Greville Boynton (Curry), which is financed by his loathed second wife, domineering, wealthy American Lady Boynton (Campbell). It's no wonder she becomes a murder victim and the Belgian detective has numerous suspects, but his final act denouncement by gathering them all together proves somewhat long and tedious. Based on the Agatha Christie mystery. 90m; DVD. **C:** David Suchet; Tim Curry; Cheryl Campbell; Tom Riley; Zoe Boyle; Emma Cunniffe; John Hannah; Elizabeth McGovern; Angela Pleasence; Paul Freeman; Beth Goddard; Mark Gatiss; Christian McKay; Christina Cole; Directed by Ashley Pearce; Written by Guy Andrews; Cinematography by Peter Greenhalgh; Music by Stephen McKeon. **A:** Jr. High-Adult. **P:** Entertainment. **U:** Home. **Mov-Ent:** Archaeology, Child Abuse, Middle East. **Acq:** Purchase. **Dist:** PBS Home Video.

Appointment with Fear 1985 (R) — ★
A tough detective investigates a murder and all of the clues lead him mysteriously to a comatose asylum inmate. 95m; VHS. **C:** Michael Wyle; Michelle Little; Kerry Remsen; Douglas Rowe; Garrick Dowhen; Deborah Voorhees; Directed by Alan Smithee; Razmi Thomas; Written by Gideon Davis; Bruce Meade. **Pr:** Tom Boutross. **A:** Sr. High-Adult. **P:** Entertainment. **U:** Home. **Mov-Ent:** Mystery & Suspense. **Acq:** Purchase. **Dist:** Lions Gate Television Corp. $14.95.

Appointment With Murder 1948 (Unrated) — ★½
In this low-budget mystery, private detective Michael Watling (Calvert) is hired by an insurance firm to locate two stolen paintings. The trail leads first to Italy and back to L.A. 65m/B/W; DVD. **C:** John Calvert; Catherine Craig; Jack Reitzen; Lyle Talbot; Robert Conte; Directed by Jack Bernhard; Written by Don Martin; Cinematography by Walter Strenge; Music by Karl Hajos. **A:** Sr. High-Adult. **P:** Entertainment. **U:** Home. **L:** English. **Mov-Ent:** Mystery & Suspense. **Acq:** Purchase. **Dist:** Movies Unlimited.

Appointment With Venus 1951 (Unrated) — ★★
In this silly WWII comedy, the Germans occupy the Channel Island of Armorel. The British Ministry of Agriculture and the War Office plan an operation to smuggle out a valuable, pedigreed Gurnsey milk cow named Venus via the Royal Navy. German commander Weiss wants Venus shipped to the Fatherland. 89m/B/W; DVD. **C:** David Niven; Glynis Johns; George Coulouris; Kenneth More; Noel Purcell; Bernard Lee; Directed by Ralph Thomas; Written by Nicholas Phipps; Cinematography by Ernest Steward; Music by Benjamin Frankel. **A:** Jr. High-Adult. **P:** Entertainment. **U:** Home. **Mov-Ent:** World War Two, Animals. **Acq:** Purchase. **Dist:** WarnerArchive.com.

Appomattox 1990
Another re-enactment of a famous battle of the Civil War. Also available as a part of a set entitled "Embattled Nation." 30m; VHS. **C:** Directed by Jack Foley. **Pr:** Classic Images Productions. **A:** Jr. High-Adult. **P:** Education. **U:** Institution, Home. **Gen-Edu:** War--General, History--U.S., Civil War. **Acq:** Purchase. **Dist:** Fusion Video. $29.95.

The Appraisal Interview 1979
A film outlining steps to be taken in an appraisal interview, and offers some practical means for increasing its effectiveness. 9m; VHS, 3/4 U. **Pr:** Resources for Education and Management. **A:** Adult. **P:** Professional. **U:** Institution, CCTV. **Bus-Ind:** Personnel Management. **Acq:** Purchase. **Dist:** Resources for Education & Management, Inc.

Appraisals in Action: 7PD-D99 1979
Part of an integrated course for supervisors and managers who are concerned about the "why" and "how" of a good performance appraisal and developmental planning system. 30m; 3/4 U. **Pr:** Professional Development. **A:** College-Adult. **P:** Professional. **U:** Institution. **Bus-Ind:** Management. **Acq:** Purchase, Rent/Lease. **Dist:** SkillSoft.

Indiv. Titles: 1. What's in It for You? (7PD-D01) 2. Preparing for the Review (7PD-D02) 3. Conducting the Review (7PD-D03) 4. Developmental Planning (7PD-D04).

Appreciating Yourself 1992
Features Tuggy, a character that learns that being himself is better than pretending to be something that he isn't. 28m; VHS. **A:** Primary. **P:** Education. **U:** Institution. **Chl-Juv:** Children, Psychology. **Acq:** Purchase. **Dist:** Rainbow Educational Media, Inc. $59.95.

The Apprentice 1971 (Unrated) — ★½
A directionless young French-Canadian man, growing up in Montreal, is involved with both his fanatical French separatist girlfriend and a free-spirited English-Canadian model. It's a love triangle that doesn't end well. An early role for Sarandon and a time capsule of the '70s separatist movement in Quebec. English and French with subtitles. 81m; DVD. **C:** Susan Sarandon; Carole Laure; Gerard Parkes; Steve Fiset; Celine Bernier; Jean-Pierre Cartier; Directed by Larry Kent; Written by Edward Steward; Cinematography by Jean-Claude Labrecque. **A:** Sr. High-Adult. **P:** Entertainment. **U:** Home. **L:** French, English. **Mov-Ent:** Drama. **Acq:** Purchase. **Dist:** Entertainment One US LP.

The Apprentice 1991
Animated story set in medieval times about two fools who seek different paths to get to their castle. The story is a metaphor for the different processes that different people bring to a challenge. Notable for its amusing content. 9m; VHS, Special order formats. **A:** Sr. High. **P:** Education. **U:** Institution. **Chl-Juv:** Animation & Cartoons, Ethics & Morals. **Acq:** Purchase, Rent/Lease. **Dist:** National Film Board of Canada. $40.00.

The Apprentice: The Complete First Season 2004 (Unrated)
Presents the debut season of the NBC television reality series-game show as 16 contestants compete for an executive position at one of host-businessman Donald Trump's companies. Split into teams, various business-related tasks must be performed with the results judged by Trump and one player exiting every week with his trademark "you're fired!"; Bill Rancic prevailed as the first winner. 15 episodes. 718m; DVD. **C:** Donald Trump; Carolyn Kepcher; George Ross. **A:** Jr. High-Adult. **P:** Entertainment. **U:** Home. **Mov-Ent:** Television Series, Documentary Films, Business. **Acq:** Purchase. **Dist:** Amazon.com Inc. $59.98.

Apprentice to Murder 1988 (PG-13) — ★★
A small Pennsylvania Dutch town is shaken by a series of murders, thought to be associated with a bizarre local mystic and healer. Based on a true story, sort of. 97m; VHS, CC. **C:** Donald Sutherland; Mia Sara; Chad Lowe; Eddie Jones; Directed by Ralph L. (R.L.) Thomas; Written by Allan Scott; Wesley Moore. **Pr:** New World Pictures. **A:** Jr. High-Adult. **P:** Entertainment. **U:** Home. **L:** Spanish. **Mov-Ent:** Mystery & Suspense, Occult Sciences. **Acq:** Purchase. **Dist:** Anchor Bay Entertainment. $19.95.

The Apprenticeship of Duddy Kravitz 1974 (PG) — ★★★½
Young Jewish man in Montreal circa 1948 is driven by an insatiable need to be the "somebody" everyone has always told him he will be. A series of get-rich-quick schemes backfire in different ways, and he becomes most successful at driving people away. Young Dreyfuss is at his best. Made in Canada with thoughtful detail, and great cameo performances. Script by Richler, from his novel. 121m; VHS, DVD. **C:** Richard Dreyfuss; Randy Quaid; Denholm Elliott; Jack Warden; Micheline Lanctot; Joe Silver; Directed by Ted Kotcheff; Written by Mordecai Richler; Lionel Chetwynd. **Pr:** Paramount Pictures. **A:** Jr. High-Adult. **P:** Entertainment. **U:** Home. **Mov-Ent:** Comedy-Drama, Family, Judaism. **Awds:** Berlin Intl. Film Fest. '74: Golden Berlin Bear; Writers Guild '74: Adapt. Screenplay. **Acq:** Purchase. **Dist:** Paramount Pictures Corp. $14.95.

Approach to Growth: East and West 1989
Gestsalt theory, Sufism and Buddhism are examined to point out their parallels. Claudio Naranjo also describes his experiences with a Chilean Sufi teacher. 30m; VHS. **Pr:** Thinking Allowed Productions. **A:** College-Adult. **P:** Instruction. **U:** Home. **Gen-Edu:** Psychology, Philosophy & Ideology. **Acq:** Purchase. **Dist:** Thinking Allowed Productions. $29.95.

Approach to the Burn Patient 1977
The stabilization and management of the burn patient in the first few hours following burn injury is covered. A clinical example of

a severely burned patient in the Emergency Department and Burn Center is included. 5m; VHS, 3/4 U, Special order formats. **Pr:** Health Sciences Learning Resources. **A:** College-Adult. **P:** Professional. **U:** Institution, CCTV. **Hea-Sci:** Burns, Patient Care. **Acq:** Purchase. **Dist:** Health Sciences Center for Educational Resources.

Approach to the Critically Injured Patient 1977
An introductory program which emphasizes initial resuscitation of a trauma victim and subsequent diagnostic and therapeutic procedures. 10m; VHS, 3/4 U, Special order formats. **Pr:** Health Sciences Learning Resources. **A:** College-Adult. **P:** Professional. **U:** Institution, CCTV. **Hea-Sci:** Emergencies, Patient Care. **Acq:** Purchase. **Dist:** Health Sciences Center for Educational Resources.

An Approach to the Prediction of Earthquakes 1971
A look at a small Japanese village whose daily earthquakes have attracted scientists from around the world. 27m; VHS, 3/4 U. **Pr:** American Educational Films. **A:** College-Adult. **P:** Education. **U:** Institution, SURA. **Hea-Sci:** Earthquakes. **Acq:** Purchase. **Dist:** Capital Communications.

Approach to Urinary Incontinence in the Elderly 19??
Outlines bladder mechanics and functional status in the assessment and treatment of urinary incontinence in elderly patients. Also covers treatment plans, determining mental status, the Folstein Mine-Mental State procedure, the Katz ADL State procedure, exercise, drug therapy, and surgery. Includes study guide. Approved for CE credit. 28m; VHS. **A:** College-Adult. **P:** Education. **U:** Institution. **Hea-Sci:** Nursing, Medical Education, Aging. **Acq:** Purchase, Rent/Lease. **Dist:** AJN Video Library/ Lippincott Williams & Wilkins. $285.00.

Approach to Ventricular Tachycardia 1986
A primer for doctors in diagnosing tachycardia. 57m; VHS, 3/4 U. **A:** Adult. **P:** Professional. **U:** Institution, CCTV, Home, SURA. **Hea-Sci:** Heart. **Acq:** Purchase, Rent/Lease, Subscription. **Dist:** Emory Medical Television Network.

Approaches and Actions to get the Responses You want 19??
By viewing this videotape, teachers will learn and understand the four primary causes of misbehavior. They will also see a variety of techniques used in actual classroom situations and how these techniques will affect student behavior. 50m; VHS. **A:** Adult. **P:** Teacher Education. **U:** Institution. **L:** English. **Gen-Edu:** Education. **Acq:** Purchase. **Dist:** Master Teacher Inc. $129.95.

Approaches in Psychosocial Rehabilitation 1984
A tape aimed at helping community agencies to develop comprehensive rehabilitation programs for the mentally and emotionally handicapped. 60m; VHS, 3/4 U; Signed. **TV Std:** NTSC, PAL. **Pr:** Fellowship Foundation. **A:** Adult. **P:** Professional. **U:** Institution. **L:** English, Spanish. **Gen-Edu:** Psychology. **Acq:** Purchase, Rent/Lease. **Dist:** Fellowship House.
Indiv. Titles: 1. Introduction to Psychosocial Programs 2. Staff Rule: The Generalist Model 3. Social Rehabilitation Program 4. Pre-Vocational Rehabilitation Programs 5. Transitional Employment 6. Residential Continuum in the Community 7. Parents and Concerned Friends Organizations 8. Involvement of Community Groups 9. Choices for People.

Approaches to Acting 1975
Lee Strasberg and Andre Gregory discuss how to train actors in this series of two untitled programs. 30m; VHS, 3/4 U, EJ, Q. **Pr:** WCBS New York; Camera Three Productions. **A:** Sr. High-Adult. **P:** Education. **U:** Institution, SURA. **Fin-Art:** Theater. **Acq:** Duplication, Free Duplication.

Approaches to Consciousness 19??
Four program study of the mind conducted by medical professionals. ?m; VHS. **A:** College-Adult. **P:** Education. **U:** Institution. **Gen-Edu:** Psychology. **Acq:** Purchase. **Dist:** Thinking Allowed Productions. $69.95.
Indiv. Titles: 1. The Evolution of Consciousness 2. The Nervous System and the Soul 3. Working With Comas 4. When Nietzsche Wept.

Approaches to Growth: East and West 199?
Psychiatrist Claudio Naranjo, M.D., shares his experiences training under the Arica systems with Chilean Sufi teacher Dr. Oscar Ichazo and compares it with western psychotherapy methods. 30m; DVD. **A:** Adult. **P:** Education. **U:** Home, Institution. **Gen-Edu:** Psychology, Psychiatry. **Acq:** Purchase. **Dist:** Thinking Allowed Productions. $29.95.

Approaches to Hamlet 1984
A young actor's attempts to master the role of Hamlet are intercut with footage of the four greatest Hamlets of this century: John Barrymore, Laurence Oliver, John Gielgud, and Nicol Williamson. Narrated by Gielgud. 45m; VHS, 3/4 U. **C:** Narrated by John Gielgud. **Pr:** Granada International Productions Ltd. **A:** Jr. High-Adult. **P:** Education. **U:** Institution, SURA. **Fin-Art:** Theater. **Acq:** Purchase, Rent/Lease. **Dist:** Films for the Humanities & Sciences.

Approaches to Organization Development 1973
This program illustrates the approaches that have been implemented in the past, and some of their basic shortcomings. 18m; VHS, 3/4 U. **Pr:** Resources for Education and Management. **A:** Adult. **P:** Professional. **U:** Institution, CCTV. **Bus-Ind:** Management. **Acq:** Purchase. **Dist:** Resources for Education & Management, Inc.

Approaches to Organizational Behavior Modification 1978
Using actual training sessions of OBM as case studies, serves as a guide to increasing efficiency in any company. The viewer learns how to use proven techniques to identify, analyze, and change problem behavior patterns. 26m; 3/4 U, Special order formats. **Pr:** Hobel Leiterman Productions. **A:** College-Adult. **P:** Professional. **U:** Institution. **Bus-Ind:** Personnel Management. **Acq:** Purchase. **Dist:** The Cinema Guild.

Approaches to Therapy 1990
Part of a series offering instruction on the study of human behavior. 30m; VHS. **A:** Adult. **P:** Education. **U:** Institution. **Gen-Edu:** Psychology. **Acq:** Purchase. **Dist:** RMI Media. $89.95.

Approaching Corporations for Donations 1989
A selected panel discusses how non-profit organizations can entice corporations into donating. 30m; VHS. **A:** Adult. **P:** Professional. **U:** Institution. **Bus-Ind:** Business, Management. **Acq:** Purchase. **Dist:** RMI Media. $89.95.

Appropriate Adult 2011 (Unrated) — ★★
Chilling Brit true crime story finds unassuming social worker Janet Leach (West) brought in to monitor the police interrogations of serial killer Fred West (West) in 1994. Pleased to be so needed, Janet is out of her depth with the manipulative sociopath, caught between his evasions and the frustrations of the police in the highly publicized case. 135m; DVD. **C:** Emily Watson; Dominic West; Robert Glenister; Sylvestria Le Touzel; Monica Dolan; Directed by Julian Jarrold; Written by Neil McKay; Cinematography by Tony Slater-Ling; Music by Dan Jones, PhD. **A:** Sr. High-Adult. **P:** Entertainment. **U:** Home. **L:** English. **Mov-Ent:** Crime Drama, TV Movies, Great Britain. **Acq:** Purchase. **Dist:** Inception Media Group.

Appropriate Behavior 2014 (Unrated) — ★★½
Writer/director/star Akhavan makes a confident debut with this story of a bisexual Persian dealing with life half-in and half-out of the closet in New York City. Shirin's (Akhavan) old-fashioned, Iranian parents would never accept their daughter's sexuality were she to come out to them, but the act of hiding herself has created a lack of self-confidence, which pushes her into an unhealthy relationship with lesbian Maxine. The film takes place on the day of their break-up, flashing back to the highlights of it and then pushing forward to her getting past it. Solid, if not a little too familiar. 82m; DVD. **C:** Desiree Akhavan; Rebecca Henderson; Halley Feiffer; Scott Adsit; Directed by Desiree Akhavan; Written by Desiree Akhavan; Cinematography by Chris Teague; Music by Josephine Wiggs. **A:** Sr. High-Adult. **P:** Entertainment. **U:** Home. **L:** English. **Mov-Ent:** Family, Romance, Immigration. **Acq:** Purchase.

Appropriate Technologists 1979
Appropriate technology is a new attitude toward technology in our time. Its purpose is to serve people in a meaningful way that is understandable, ecological, and participatory. Citizen groups band together in this effort. Part of the "Are You Listening" series. 28m; 3/4 U, Q. **Pr:** Martha Stuart Communications. **A:** Sr. High-Adult. **P:** Education. **U:** Institution, CCTV, CATV, BCTV, Home. **Gen-Edu:** Technology, Public Affairs. **Acq:** Purchase, Rent/Lease. **Dist:** Communication for Change, Inc.

Apres Lui 2007 (Unrated) — ★★
Divorcee Camille (Deneuve) is devastated when her 20-year-old son Mathieu (Jolivet) is killed in a car accident. She turns to her son's grief-stricken best friend Franck (Dumerchez), who was the driver of the car, and starts helping the less-privileged young man out with college, also giving him a job in her bookstore. Franck's bewildered by her concern, which becomes obsessive, especially when Camille follows him on vacation. French with subtitles. 89m; DVD. **C:** Catherine Deneuve; Guy Marchand; Elodie Bouchez; Adrien Jolivet; Thomas Dumerchez; Directed by Gael Morel; Written by Gael Morel; Christophe Honore; Cinematography by Jean-Max Bernard; Music by Louis Sclavis. **A:** College-Adult. **P:** Entertainment. **U:** Home. **L:** French. **Mov-Ent. Acq:** Purchase. **Dist:** MPI Media Group.

Apres-Vous 2003 (R) — ★★
Sometimes you should just mind your own business. Parisian maitre d' Antoine (Auteuil) saves depressive loser Louis (Garcia) from hanging himself in a park and then feels responsible for making the man happy. He gets Louis a wine steward job, though he has no abilities whatsoever, and seeks to reconcile the sad sack with ex-lover Blanche (Kiberlain), except that Antoine falls for her himself. Auteuil is so good he can make any character believable (even this overzealous nice guy), but this familiar farce doesn't do much to stretch his talents. French with subtitles. 110m; DVD. **C:** Daniel Auteuil; Jose Garcia; Sandrine Kiberlain; Marilyne Canto; Michele Moretti; Garance Clavel; Fabio Zenoni; Ange Ruze; Directed by Pierre Salvadori; Written by Pierre Salvadori; Benoit Graffin; David Colombo Leotard; Cinematography by Gilles Henry; Music by Camille Bazbaz. **Pr:** Philippe Martin; Omri Maron; Tovo Films. **A:** Sr. High-Adult. **P:** Entertainment. **U:** Home. **L:** French. **Mov-Ent:** Comedy--Romantic, France, Suicide. **Dist:** Paramount Pictures Corp. $29.99.

April Fool 1926 — ★★½
A man makes a fortune in the umbrella business and then discovers his daughter has fallen in love with the son of a nouveaux riche neighbor, resulting in all sorts of complications. 63m/B/W; Silent; VHS, DVD. **C:** Alexander Carr; Mary Alden; Raymond Keane; Snitz Edwards; Directed by Nat Ross; Written by Zion Myers. **A:** Sr. High-Adult. **P:** Entertainment. **U:** Home. **Mov-Ent:** Comedy--Romantic, Silent Films. **Acq:** Purchase. **Dist:** Grapevine Video; Facets Multimedia Inc. $14.95.

April Fools 1969 (PG) — ★★
A bored stockbroker falls in love with a beautiful woman who turns out to be married to his boss. 95m; DVD. **C:** Jack Lemmon; Catherine Deneuve; Sally Kellerman; Peter Lawford; Harvey Korman; Melinda Dillon; Kenneth Mars; Directed by Stuart Rosenberg; Music by Marvin Hamlisch. **Pr:** National General Pictures; Cinema Center. **A:** Sr. High-Adult. **P:** Entertainment. **U:** Home. **Mov-Ent:** Comedy--Romantic. **Acq:** Purchase. **Dist:** Paramount Pictures Corp. $19.98.

April Fools 2007 (Unrated) — ★
A teen is killed by a prank gone wrong, causing yet another killing spree to occur later when the group responsible begin to wonder who saw what they did. 72m; DVD. **C:** Darrin Dewitt Henson; Aaliyah Franks; Dava Vaidya; Directed by Nancy Norman; Written by Nancy Norman; Cinematography by Jeff Brown; Music by Donald Hayes; Kenneth Hampton. **A:** Sr. High-Adult. **P:** Entertainment. **U:** Home. **L:** English. **Mov-Ent. Acq:** Purchase. **Dist:** Toucan Cove. $6.95.

April Fool's Day 1986 (R) — ★½
Rich girl Muffy (Foreman) invites eight college friends to spend the April Fool's weekend with her at her family's isolated island mansion. Everyone is subjected to an endless series of practical jokes when things apparently turn deadly and several of the kids begin disappearing. Twist ending. Lame spoof of "Friday the 13th" and other teenagers-in-peril slasher films. 90m; VHS, DVD, CC. **C:** Deborah Foreman; Jay Baker; Pat Barlow; Lloyd Berry; Deborah Goodrich; Ken Olandt; Griffin O'Neal; Tom Heaton; Mike Nomad; Leah K. Pinsent; Clayton Rohner; Amy Steel; Thomas F. Wilson; Directed by Fred Walton; Written by Danilo Bach; Cinematography by Charles Minsky; Music by Charles Bernstein. **Pr:** Frank Mancuso, Jr.; Paramount Pictures. **A:** Sr. High-Adult. **P:** Entertainment. **U:** Home. **Mov-Ent. Acq:** Purchase. **Dist:** Paramount Pictures Corp. $19.95.

April Fool's Day 2008 (R) — **Bomb!**
You'll be the fool if you're conned into watching this dreck done by the duo appropriately calling themselves the Butcher Brothers. Rich bitch Desiree (Cole) plays a prank on rival Milan (Aldridge) at a party, only things go way too far and Milan dies. A year later, the partygoers receive invitations to Milan's gravesite and are then warned that they too will die unless someone accepts responsibility for Milan's death. Shares nothing but the title with the 1986 slasher flick. 91m; DVD. **C:** Sabrina Aldridge; Josh Henderson; Scout Taylor-Compton; Joe Egender; Samuel Child; Jennifer Siebel (Newsom); Joseph McKelheer; Directed by Phil Flores; Mitchell Altieri; Written by Phil Flores; Mitchell Altieri; Cinematography by Michael Maley; Music by James Stemple. **A:** Sr. High-Adult. **P:** Entertainment. **U:** Home. **Mov-Ent. Acq:** Purchase. **Dist:** Sony Pictures Home Entertainment Inc.

April in Paris 1952 — ★★
Dynamite Jackson (Day), a chorus girl accidentally sent by the State Department to perform in Paris, meets S. Winthrop Putnam (Bolger), a timid fellow trapped in an unpleasant marriage. They eventually sing and dance their way to warm feelings as they begin a lifelong romance and live happily ever after. 100m; VHS, DVD. **C:** Doris Day; Ray Bolger; Claude Dauphin; Eve Miller; George Givot; Paul Harvey; Directed by David Butler; Written by Jack Rose; Melville Shavelson. **Pr:** Warner Home Video, Inc. **A:** Family. **P:** Entertainment. **U:** Home. **Mov-Ent:** Musical, Romance, Dance. **Acq:** Purchase. **Dist:** Warner Home Video, Inc.; Music Video Distributors. $19.98.

April Love 1957 (Unrated) — ★★½
Simple, pleasant romance/musical with Boone as the nicest juvenile delinquent you'll ever meet. After he's placed on probation for car theft in Chicago, Nick (Boone) is sent to stay at his Aunt Henrietta's (Nolan) and Uncle Jed's (O'Connell) Kentucky horse farm. The city boy is out of his element as he prefers horsepower to horses but he learns to train a horse and drive a racing sulky as well as romance pretty neighbor Liz (Jones)?once he gets over his crush on her sister Fran (Michaels). Filmed on location in Lexington, Kentucky. 97m; DVD. **C:** Pat Boone; Shirley Jones; Jeannette Nolan; Arthur O'Connell; Dolores Michaels; Matt Crowley; Brandon T. Jackson; Directed by Henry Levin; Written by Winston Miller; Cinematography by Wilfred M. Cline; Music by Sammy Fain; Alfred Newman. **A:** Jr. High-Adult. **P:** Entertainment. **U:** Home. **Mov-Ent:** Horses. **Acq:** Purchase. **Dist:** Fox Home Entertainment; Screen Archives Entertainment.

April Morning 1988 (Unrated) — ★★½
A Hallmark Hall of Fame presentation based on the Howard Fast novel. April 19, 1775 marked the beginning of the American Revolution as British troops clashed with American militia. Moses Cooper (Jones) and his teenage son Adam (Lowe) are part of the Lexington Minutemen who oppose Major John Pitcairn (Colvey) and his redcoats in this well-done family/ historical drama. 99m; DVD. **C:** Tommy Lee Jones; Chad Lowe; Robert Urich; Peter Colvey; Rip Torn; Susan Blakely; Meredith Salenger; Vlasta Vrana; Directed by Delbert Mann; Written by James Lee Barrett; Cinematography by Frank Tidy; Music by Allyn Ferguson. **A:** Family. **P:** Entertainment. **U:** Home. **Mov-Ent:** Drama, History--U.S., Revolutionary War. **Acq:** Purchase. **Dist:** MGM Home Entertainment.

April's Shower 2003 (R) — ★½
April's about to get married, but what few know is that April's been a lesbian most of her life. Her ex-lover, and now bridesmaid, has even kept it a secret. Up until now. A slew of one-dimensional stereotypes parade across the screen, almost like they're at a John Waters audition, to ruin the emotional core. Tries too hard to be comedic and outrageous and oh, so culturally hip, assuming it can elude criticism by playing the indie card. Nope. Even the gay and lesbian crowds will find little

amusement. 98m; DVD. **C:** Maria Cina; Zack (Zach) Ward; Lara Harris; Molly Cheek; Trish Doolan; Frank Grillo; Randall Batinkoff; Arly Jover; Directed by Trish Doolan; Written by Trish Doolan; Cinematography by Kristian Bernier; Rory King; Music by Jeff Cardoni. **Pr:** Honey Labrador; William Shaffer; Christopher Racster; Trish Doolan; Silver Leaf Prods; ConQuest Entertainment. **P:** Entertainment. **U:** Home. **L:** English. **Mov-Ent:** Comedy--Romantic, Marriage. **Acq:** Purchase. **Dist:** Genius Entertainment.

Apt Pupil 1997 (R) — ★★
In 1984, high school senior Todd Bowden (Renfro) becomes fascinated by the Holocaust during a school project and is able to discern from an old photo that neighbor Kurt Dussander (McKellen) was a Nazi concentration camp commander and is a war criminal. Todd agrees to keep quiet if the old man will tell exactly what he did during the war. But Dussander hasn't stayed quiet all these years to have his secrets revealed by a nosy teen, so Todd gets an up close and personal lesson about the nature of evil. Very creepy adaptation of the Stephen King novella with a standout performance by McKellen. 111m; VHS, DVD, CC. **C:** Ian McKellen; Brad Renfro; Jan Triska; Bruce Davison; Joe Morton; Elias Koteas; David Schwimmer; Michael Byrne; Heather McComb; Ann Dowd; Joshua Jackson; Michael Artura; Directed by Bryan Singer; Written by Brandon Boyce; Cinematography by Newton Thomas (Tom) Sigel; Music by John Ottman. **Pr:** Jane Hamsher; Bryan Singer; Don Murphy; Tim Harbert; Bryan Singer; TriStar Pictures; Phoenix Films; Sony Pictures Home Entertainment Inc. **A:** Sr. High-Adult. **P:** Entertainment. **U:** Home. **Mov-Ent:** Adolescence. **Acq:** Purchase. **Dist:** Sony Pictures Home Entertainment Inc.

Apu Condor: The Condor God 1992
Provides the first western look at the sacred Peruvian "Yawar Fiesta of the Apu Condor," the Fiesta of Blood of the Condor God. Stresses the themes of social stratification, ritual reversal, and political relationships. The Fiesta is filmed in Cotabambas, a tiny village located in the Peruvian Andes. Winner of multiple awards. 28m; VHS. **A:** Adult. **P:** Education. **U:** Institution, Home. **Gen-Edu:** Documentary Films, Hispanic Culture, South America. **Acq:** Purchase, Rent/Lease. **Dist:** Documentary Educational Resources. $195.00.

Aqabat Jaber: Passing Through 1988
Aqabat Jaber is a Palestinian relocation camp that was "temporarily" constructed by the United Nations in the 1950s. This video offers the perspective of its inhabitants, which include several generations, who have been for decades mired in political limbo. Arabic dialouge is subtitled in English. 52m; VHS. **Pr:** The Cinema Guild. **A:** Jr. High-Adult. **P:** Education. **U:** Institution, Home. **L:** Arabic. **Gen-Edu:** Documentary Films, Middle East, United Nations. **Acq:** Purchase. **Dist:** The Cinema Guild. $350.00.

Aqabat Jaber: Peace with No Return? 1995
Examines the situation of 3,000 inhabitants at Aqabat Jaber, a 50-year-old Palestinian refugee camp just outside of Jericho, addressing the possibility of peace while there are so many victims of political or ethnic conflicts. 60m; VHS. **A:** Adult. **P:** Education. **U:** BCTV, Institution. **Gen-Edu:** Middle East, Documentary Films. **Acq:** Purchase, Rent/Lease. **Dist:** First Run/Icarus Films. $390.00.

AQP: Computer Aided Relationship Strategies 1990
Larry C. Bobbert lectures on the computer program he created which shows individuals how to sell their ideas and products by analyzing society's behavior. 36m; VHS. **A:** Adult. **P:** Education. **U:** Institution. **Bus-Ind:** Computers, Business. **Acq:** Purchase. **Dist:** Geographical Studies and Research Center, Department of Geography and Planning.

Aqua Aerobics for Shallow and Deep Pools 19??
Offers aqua aerobics exercises that help the individual prevent injuries, shin splints, and other discomforts associated with jogging or walking. Also contains exercises that help increase strength and endurance. 30m; VHS. **P:** Instruction. **U:** Institution, Home. **Hea-Sci:** Fitness/Exercise, Sports Medicine. **Acq:** Purchase. **Dist:** Distinctive Home Video Productions. $29.99.

Aqua Exercise for Multiple Sclerosis 19??
Demonstrates aquatic exercises aimed at individuals suffering from multiple sclerosis. 15m; VHS. **P:** Instruction. **U:** Institution, Home. **Hea-Sci:** Fitness/Exercise, Handicapped. **Acq:** Purchase. **Dist:** Distinctive Home Video Productions. $19.99.

Aqua Teen Hunger Force Colon Movie Film for Theaters 2007 (R) — ★½
As intentionally nonsensical as its title. This component of the Cartoon Network's "Adult Swim" feature has New Jersey roomies (and fast-food items) Frylock, Master Shake, and Meatwad going full-length and big screen, battling the Insane-O-Flex home exercise machine that's actually an alien (the outer space kind). Familiar characters like Carl, Dr. Weird, Err, and others make their appearances. Only for those who already know "Aqua Teen" or just can't stand to be out of the pop culture loop. 86m; DVD. **C:** Voice(s) by Bruce Campbell; Matt Maiellaro; Dave Willis; Dana Snyder; Carey Means; Mike Schatz; Andy Merrill; C. Martin Croker; Directed by Matt Maiellaro; Dave Willis; Written by Matt Maiellaro; Dave Willis. **Pr:** Jay Wade Edwards; David Willis; Ned Hastings; Matt Maiellaro; Williams Street; Adult Swim; First Look Pictures. **A:** Sr. High-Adult. **P:** Entertainment. **U:** Home. **L:** English. **Mov-Ent:** Animation & Cartoons, Food Industry. **Acq:** Purchase. **Dist:** Warner Home Video, Inc.

Aqua Teen Hunger Force: Volume 5 2004
Master Shake moves in with a legendary New Jersey monster in "Dirtfoot" and Carl fears he's losing his manhood in "Dickesode," while Frylock, Meatwad, and Carl find other troubles in "Moonajuana," "Hand Banana," and more installments of Adult Swim's original show. 180m; DVD. **C:** Voice(s) by Dave Willis; Carey Means; Dana Snyder. **A:** Adult. **P:** Entertainment. **U:** Home. **Mov-Ent:** Animation & Cartoons. **Acq:** Purchase. **Dist:** Warner Home Video, Inc.

Aqua Teen Hunger Force: Volume Four 2005 (Unrated)
Offers the Cartoon Network's animated comedy television series with fast-food menu items—Master Shake, Meatwad, and Frylock—who join together to solve mysteries that typically deal with Dr. Evil while confronting the usual adolescence dramas. 13 episodes. 150m; DVD. **C:** Voice(s) by Carey Means; C. Martin Croker; Dana Snyder; Dave Willis. **A:** Sr. High-Adult. **P:** Entertainment. **U:** Home. **Mov-Ent:** Television Series, Animation & Cartoons, Action-Adventure. **Acq:** Purchase. **Dist:** Warner Home Video, Inc. $29.98.

Aqua Teen Hunger Force: Volume One 2003 (Unrated)
Offers the Cartoon Network's animated comedy television series with fast-food menu items—Master Shake, Meatwad, and Frylock—who join together to solve mysteries that typically deal with Dr. Evil while confronting the usual adolescence dramas. 16 episodes. 187m; DVD. **C:** Voice(s) by Carey Means; C. Martin Croker; Dana Snyder; Dave Willis. **A:** Sr. High-Adult. **P:** Entertainment. **U:** Home. **Mov-Ent:** Television Series, Animation & Cartoons, Action-Adventure. **Acq:** Purchase. **Dist:** Warner Home Video, Inc. $29.98.

Aqua Teen Hunger Force: Volume Seven 2007 (Unrated)
Cartoon Network and Adult Swim 2000-? adult animated comedy. More surreal adventures down by the Jersey Shore as Frylock creates a monster duck in "Rubberman," Master Shake accidentally forms a legion of Meatwads in "Multiple Meats," and Adolf Hitler gets reincarnated as a balloon in "Der Inflatable Fuhrer" with Bill Hader guest voicing. 20 episodes. 143m; DVD. **C:** Voice(s) by Dave Willis; Dana Snyder; Carey Means; Martin Croker. **A:** Sr. High-Adult. **P:** Entertainment. **U:** Home. **Mov-Ent:** Animation & Cartoons, Television Series. **Acq:** Purchase. **Dist:** Warner Home Video, Inc. $29.99.

Aqua Teen Hunger Force: Volume Three 2004 (Unrated)
Offers the Cartoon Network's animated comedy television series with fast-food menu items—Master Shake, Meatwad, and Frylock—who join together to solve mysteries that typically deal with Dr. Evil while confronting the usual adolescence dramas. 13 episodes. 150m; DVD. **C:** Voice(s) by Carey Means; C. Martin Croker; Dana Snyder; Dave Willis. **A:** Sr. High-Adult. **P:** Entertainment. **U:** Home. **Mov-Ent:** Television Series, Animation & Cartoons, Action-Adventure. **Acq:** Purchase. **Dist:** Warner Home Video, Inc. $29.98.

Aqua Teen Hunger Force: Volume Two 2004 (Unrated)
Offers the Cartoon Network's animated comedy television series with fast-food menu items—Master Shake, Meatwad, and Frylock—who join together to solve mysteries that typically deal with Dr. Evil while confronting the usual adolescence dramas. 13 episodes. 156m; DVD. **C:** Voice(s) by Carey Means; C. Martin Croker; Dana Snyder; Dave Willis. **A:** Sr. High-Adult. **P:** Entertainment. **U:** Home. **Mov-Ent:** Television Series, Animation & Cartoons, Action-Adventure. **Acq:** Purchase. **Dist:** Warner Home Video, Inc. $29.98.

Aquaculture and Follow-Up Discussion 1979
The program "Aquaculture: Farming Under Water" is presented, followed by a panel discussion wherein experts tell what they consider to be the future of this new agricultural science. 60m; 3/4 U. **Pr:** Washington Sea Grant Program. **A:** College-Adult. **P:** Education. **U:** Institution. **Hea-Sci:** Agriculture. **Acq:** Rent/Lease. **Dist:** University of Washington Educational Media Collection.

Aquaculture: Farming the Waters 19??
Outlines the history of aquaculture by discussing cultural practices, nutritional requirements, and species selection. Also talks about the financial and environmental considerations associated with aquaculture. 30m; VHS. **A:** Sr. High-Adult. **P:** Education. **U:** Institution, SURA. **Gen-Edu:** Agriculture, Food Industry, Ecology & Environment. **Acq:** Purchase. **Dist:** San Luis Video Publishing. $90.00.

Aquaculture: Farming Under Water 1979
This program focuses on developments in the Pacific in research being done in aquaculture, the problems encountered, and the prospects for the future. 60m; 3/4 U. **Pr:** Washington Sea Grant Program. **A:** College-Adult. **P:** Education. **U:** Institution. **Hea-Sci:** Agriculture. **Acq:** Rent/Lease. **Dist:** University of Washington Educational Media Collection.

Aquaculture Processing Safety and Quality 19??
Oultines measures which can help preserve the safety and provide good quality production in the aquaculture processing industry. 20m; VHS. **A:** Jr. High-Adult. **P:** Education. **U:** Institution. **Bus-Ind:** Agriculture, Safety Education, Quality Control. **Acq:** Purchase. **Dist:** CEV Multimedia. $69.95.

Aquae Sulis: The City of Bath 19??
Tour this ancient town, founded by the Romans, and its famous hot springs, as well as exploring Bath Abbey and visiting the Bath International Festival. 29m; VHS. **A:** Sr. High-Adult. **P:** Entertainment. **U:** Home. **Gen-Edu:** Travel, Great Britain. **Acq:** Purchase. **Dist:** Fusion Video. $19.98.

Aquaman 1967
A collection of eight animated adventures featuring that mighty superhero, Aquaman. 60m; VHS. **Pr:** Filmation Associates. **A:** Family. **P:** Entertainment. **U:** Home. **Mov-Ent:** Animation & Cartoons. **Acq:** Purchase. **Dist:** Warner Home Video, Inc. $12.95.

Aquaman: The Adventures of: The Complete Collection 1968
Aquaman, King of the Seven Seas combats villainous foes that threaten the peace of the undersea world in the city of Atlantis. Aquadlad and Mera have good intentions to assist with the safeguarding but more times than not become a hindrance. Black Manta, Mer Queen Vassa, the Fisherman, and the Brain keep the Sea King busy in this set with a throng of vile sea monsters, space aliens, and an unknown race set on shrinking ocean life forms for collection. Contains 36 seven-minute shorts. 264m; DVD. **C:** Voice(s) by Bud Collyer; Tommy Cook; Marvin Miller; Jerry Dexter. **A:** Primary-Jr. High. **P:** Entertainment. **U:** Home. **Chl-Juv:** Animation & Cartoons, Television Series. **Acq:** Purchase. **Dist:** Warner Home Video, Inc.

Aquamarine 2006 (PG) — ★★½
Sweet tweener flick about best friends and a girl with a tail. Mermaid Aquamarine (Paxton) washes into a Florida beach club pool after a storm. She's discovered by 13-year-olds Claire (Roberts) and Hailey (Levesque) and the trio make a pact: Aqua needs to prove to her stern father that true love exists within three days or she will be forced to marry, and the girls want her to grant their wish to stop Hailey from moving away. Fortunately, Aqua is a blonde babe (her tail can conveniently vanish during daylight) who falls for cute lifeguard, Raymond (McDorman)?a romance the younger girls eagerly encourage. Generally comic calamities ensue. Based on the book by Alice Hoffman. 109m; DVD. **C:** Sara Paxton; Emma Roberts; Arielle Kebbel; Claudia Karvan; Joanna "JoJo" Levesque; Jake McDorman; Bruce Spence; Roy Billing; Tammin Sursok; Julia Blake; Shaun Micallef; Directed by Elizabeth Allen; Written by Jessica Bendinger; John Quaintance; Cinematography by Brian J. Breheny; Music by David Hirschfelder. **Pr:** Susan Carsonis; Fox 2000 Pictures; Storefront Pictures; 20th Century-Fox. **A:** Primary-Adult. **P:** Entertainment. **U:** Home. **L:** English. **Mov-Ent:** Fantasy. **Acq:** Purchase. **Dist:** Fox Home Entertainment.

The Aquarium: Classroom Science 1967
Shows that not only fish, but insects, salamanders, and a variety of other interesting living things can be raised in an aquarium. 12m; VHS, 3/4 U. **Pr:** Norman Bean. **A:** Primary. **P:** Education. **U:** Institution, SURA. **Hea-Sci:** Biology. **Acq:** Purchase. **Dist:** Phoenix Learning Group.

An Aquarium in Action 1972
A look at how the different fish in an aquarium each play a vital role in the balance of nature. 11m; VHS, 3/4 U. **Pr:** Bobwin Associates. **A:** Primary. **P:** Education. **U:** Institution, SURA. **Hea-Sci:** Fish. **Acq:** Purchase. **Dist:** Center for Humanities, Inc./Guidance Associates.

Aquarium Relaxation Video 19??
Features the relaxing music of Harold Blanchard, world renowned composer and musician, set to the sights of a colorful tropical aquarium. 20m; VHS. **A:** Adult. **P:** Entertainment. **U:** Home. **Gen-Edu:** Stress. **Acq:** Purchase, Duplication License. **Dist:** Crawford Productions, Inc. $24.95.

Aquasize I 1992
When you combine aerobics and water, you protect your body from muscle strain without sacrificing a vigorous workout. Watch the program on land, then try the exercises out on the water. Includes instructional guide for easy reference. 40m; VHS. **A:** Sr. High-Adult. **P:** Instruction. **U:** Institution, Home. **Hea-Sci:** Swimming, Fitness/Exercise. **Acq:** Purchase. **Dist:** Cambridge Educational. $19.95.

Aquatic Cross Training 19??
Offers aquatic training techniques aimed at keeping the individual healthy, injury free, and motivated while emphasizing the need to overcome training blues and overuse injuries. 18m; VHS. **P:** Instruction. **U:** Institution, Home. **Spo-Rec:** Sports Medicine, Fitness/Exercise. **Acq:** Purchase. **Dist:** Distinctive Home Video Productions. $29.99.

Aquatic Ecosystems Series 1993
Series of programs overviewing the planet's natural water systems. Focusing on aquatic ecosystem life cycles, each program takes a glimpse at mysterious plants and animals, the food chain, human effects on the environment, land form change, tidal activity, and more. Teacher's guide included. 12m; VHS. **Pr:** Coronet Films. **A:** Jr. High-College. **P:** Education. **U:** Institution. **Hea-Sci:** Ecology & Environment, Science. **Acq:** Purchase, Rent/Lease. **Dist:** Phoenix Learning Group. $250.00.
Indiv. Titles: 1. Freshwater 2. Marine 3. Estuaries 4. Freshwater Wetlands.

Aquatic Exercise for Back Pain 19??
Offers aquatic workout exercises for individuals who are suffering from chronic back pain. Emphasis is placed on traction, stretching, flexibility, ease of movement, and strengthening of the back. 15m; VHS. **P:** Instruction. **U:** Institution, Home. **Hea-Sci:** Fitness/Exercise, Back Disorders. **Acq:** Purchase. **Dist:** Distinctive Home Video Productions. $19.99.

Aquatic Games for Children 2002 (Unrated)
Elementary school PE teacher shares swimming pool games and activities designed to teach swimming and manipulative skills. 38m; VHS. **A:** Family. **P:** Education. **U:** Home, Institution. **Gen-Edu:** Physical Education, Swimming. **Acq:** Purchase. **Dist:** Championship Productions. $34.99.

Aquatic Pest Control: Applicator Training 1993
Teaches the basic knowledge necessary to be certified as a restricted use pesticide applicator in aquatic pest control. 58m;

VHS. **A:** Adult. **P:** Instruction. **U:** Institution. **Gen-Edu:** Poisons, Plants, Biology. **Acq:** Rent/Lease. **Dist:** Cornell University. $36.00.

Aquatic Therapy for the Athletes Lower Body 19??
Describes aquatic therapy techniques aimed at the lower body that will help to maintain the current fitness level and increase lower body strength. 18m; VHS. **P:** Instruction. **U:** Home, Institution. **Spo-Rec:** Sports Medicine, Fitness/Exercise. **Acq:** Purchase. **Dist:** Distinctive Home Video Productions. $29.99.

Aquatic Therapy for the Athletes Upper Body 19??
Offers techniques that help the individual rehabilitate an upper body injury with the use of aquatic therapy. Emphasis is placed on the use of buoyancy to help maintain or improve range of motion and strength following an injury. 18m; VHS. **P:** Instruction. **U:** Institution, Home. **Spo-Rec:** Sports Medicine, How-To. **Acq:** Purchase. **Dist:** Distinctive Home Video Productions. $29.99.

Aqueduct 1982
The program demonstrates the need for plumbing and sewage disposal in the home. Visualized in a humorous way are the related technological and ecological problems. Part of the "Inventive Child" Series. 11m; VHS, 3/4 U. **Pr:** Film Polski. **A:** Primary-Jr. High. **P:** Education. **U:** Institution, SURA. **Chl-Juv:** Technology. **Acq:** Purchase, Rent/Lease, Trade-in. **Dist:** Encyclopedia Britannica.

Aqui Se Habla Espanol 1983
The social and language problems of the Hispanic New Jersey resident are examined in this documentary. 60m; VHS, 3/4 U. **Pr:** New Jersey Network. **A:** Sr. High-Adult. **P:** Education. **U:** Institution. **Gen-Edu:** Minorities. **Acq:** Purchase, Rent/Lease. **Dist:** New Jersey Network.

A.R. Mitchell's West 1990
The last days of the Old West are captured in the art of Arthur Roy Mitchell. 28m; VHS, 3/4 U. **Pr:** Centre Productions, Inc. **A:** Sr. High-Adult. **P:** Education. **U:** Institution, SURA. **Fin-Art:** Documentary Films, History--U.S. **Acq:** Purchase, Rent/Lease. **Dist:** Clear Vue Inc. $295.00.

The Arab-American Comedy Tour 2006
Documentary following three popular Arab-American comedians. 95m; DVD. **A:** Adult. **P:** Entertainment. **U:** Home, Institution. **Gen-Edu:** Documentary Films, Comedy--Performance, Prejudice. **Acq:** Purchase, Rent/Lease. **Dist:** Arab Film Distribution. $19.99.

Arab and Jew: Wounded Spirits in a Promised Land 1989
The ongoing battle between the Arabs and the Jews is explored in this program, based on Shipier's Pulitzer Prize-winning book. 120m; VHS, CC, 3/4 U. **C:** David K. Shipier. **Pr:** Robert Gardner. **A:** Jr. High-Adult. **P:** Education. **U:** Institution, CCTV, Home, SURA. **Gen-Edu:** History, Middle East, Islam. **Acq:** Purchase, Rent/Lease, Duplication. **Dist:** PBS Home Video. $59.95.

The Arab Conspiracy 1976 (R) — ★★
Sharpe plays a hit-woman conspiring with assassins from all over the world to kill Arab leaders. One problem—she falls in love with Saudi Arabian ambassador Connery as he tries to gain peace with Palestine. 108m; VHS, DVD. **C:** Sean Connery; Cornelia Sharpe; Albert Paulsen; Adolfo Celi; Charles Cioffi; Directed by Richard Sarafian; Written by Alan R. Trustman; Cinematography by Michael Chapman; Music by Michael Kamen. **A:** Sr. High-Adult. **P:** Entertainment. **U:** Home. **Mov-Ent:** Action-Adventure, Middle East. **Acq:** Purchase. **Dist:** Movies Unlimited; Alpha Video. $9.95.

The Arab Experience Series 1976
Arab culture, customs, and architecture, which are widely unknown to westerners, are presented in this series. Programs are available individually. 27m; VHS, 3/4 U. **Pr:** Antony Thomas. **A:** Sr. High-Adult. **P:** Education. **U:** Institution, SURA. **Gen-Edu:** Middle East. **Acq:** Purchase, Rent/Lease. **Dist:** Phoenix Learning Group.
Indiv. Titles: 1. The Arab Identity: Who Are the Arabs 2. Egypt: The Struggle for Stability 3. Saudi Arabia: The Oil Revolution.

The Arab Identity: Who Are the Arabs? 1976
Illustrates the fascinating diversity of 125 million Arabs and the unifying power of their centuries-old heritage. 26m; VHS, 3/4 U. **Pr:** EL, SP Learning Corporation of America; Yorkshire Television. **A:** Sr. High-College. **P:** Education. **U:** Institution, SURA. **Gen-Edu:** Middle East. **Acq:** Purchase, Rent/Lease. **Dist:** Phoenix Learning Group.

Arab-Israeli Struggle for Peace 1993 (Unrated)
Documentary on conflict in the Middle East beginning with the founding of Israel in 1948. 55m; VHS, DVD. **A:** Jr. High-Adult. **P:** Education. **U:** Institution. **L:** English. **Gen-Edu:** Documentary Films, Middle East. **Acq:** Purchase. **Dist:** Arab Film Distribution. $250.00.

The Arab Jews 1976
The program shows how the Arab Jews have been absorbed into their new homelands and how Jewish refugees from Moslem Arab countries make up a majority of the population of the State of Israel. 28m; VHS, 3/4 U. **Pr:** Verite Film Productions. **A:** Jr. High-Adult. **P:** Education. **U:** Institution, SURA. **Gen-Edu:** Middle East. **Acq:** Purchase. **Dist:** Phoenix Learning Group.

Arab Stereotypes 19??
Four-part series gives examples of common stereotypes of Arabs in western media and entertainment during the early part of the century. 200m; VHS. **A:** Adult. **P:** Education. **U:** Institution, BCTV. **Gen-Edu:** Documentary Films, Middle East, Identity. **Acq:** Purchase, Rent/Lease. **Dist:** Arab Film Distribution. $450.00.
Indiv. Titles: 1. Tom & Jerry: Gypped in Egypt 2. Hal Roach: Grief in Baghdad 3. George Melies: Palace of the Arabian Nights 4. Outposts of the Foreign Legion.

The Arab World 1988
A complete discussion of current politics in the Middle East. 20m; VHS. **A:** Jr. High-Adult. **P:** Education. **U:** Institution. **Gen-Edu:** Middle East, Islam, Politics & Government. **Acq:** Purchase. **Dist:** Knowledge Unlimited, Inc. $55.00.

The Arab World 1991
Thorough investigation of the Arab world discusses the role of religion, artistic achievements, and the historical forces that shaped it, from the medieval Crusades to Operation Desert Storm. Five-part series. 30m; VHS. **C:** Hosted by Bill Moyers. **A:** Sr. High-College. **P:** Education. **U:** Institution. **Gen-Edu:** Middle East, History. **Acq:** Purchase. **Dist:** Cambridge Educational. $50.00.
Indiv. Titles: 1. Who They Are 2. The Historic Memory 3. The Image of God 4. The Bonds of Pride 5. Arabs and the West.

Arabella 1984
A recording of Richard Strauss' opera at the Glyndebourne Festival Opera, conducted by Bernard Haitink. 154m; VHS. **C:** Ashley Putnam; Gianna Rolandi; Regina Sarfaty; Directed by John Cox. **Pr:** Glyndebourne Productions Ltd. **A:** Family. **P:** Entertainment. **U:** Home. **Fin-Art:** Opera. **Acq:** Purchase. **Dist:** Music Video Distributors; Home Vision Cinema. $39.95.

Arabella 1992
Sir Georg Solti conducts the Vienna Philharmonic Orchestra. Featured singers are Gundula Janowitz, Bernd Weikel, Rene Kollo, and Sona Ghazarian. 149m; VHS. **A:** Jr. High-Adult. **P:** Entertainment. **U:** Home. **Mov-Ent:** Music Video, Music--Performance. **Acq:** Purchase. **Dist:** Music Video Distributors. $34.95.

Arabesque 1966 — ★★½
A college professor is drawn into international espionage by a beautiful woman and a plot to assassinate an Arab prince. Stylish and fast moving. From the novel "The Cipher" by Gordon Cotler. 105m; VHS, DVD. **C:** Gregory Peck; Sophia Loren; George Coulouris; Alan Badel; Kieron Moore; Directed by Stanley Donen; Music by Henry Mancini. **Pr:** Stanley Donen; Mark Huffam; Stanley Donen. **A:** Jr. High-Adult. **P:** Entertainment. **U:** Home. **Mov-Ent:** Romance, Mystery & Suspense. **Acq:** Purchase. **Dist:** Facets Multimedia Inc.; Universal Studios Home Video. $14.95.

Arabesque 1976
Playing musical notes into a computer produces wave combinations that visually compose this film set to contemporary Eastern music. One will enjoy bright colors and constantly changing patterns. 7m; VHS. **Pr:** John Witney. **A:** Family. **P:** Entertainment. **U:** Institution, Home, SURA. **Fin-Art:** Film--Avant-Garde. **Acq:** Purchase, Rent/Lease, Duplication License. **Dist:** Pyramid Media.

Arabia: Sand, Sea & Sky 19??
Explores the beauty of Arabia's land and coast. 80m; VHS, 3/4 U; Closed Captioned. **A:** Primary-Adult. **P:** Education. **U:** Institution. **Gen-Edu.** **Acq:** Purchase. **Dist:** National Geographic Society. $24.20.

Arabian Adventure 1979 (G) — ★★
Pleasant enough fantasy adventure for the family. A prince enlists the aid of a peasant in order to prevent an evil wizard from obtaining a magical rose and taking over the kingdom. 98m; DVD. **C:** Christopher Frank Carandini Lee; Milo O'Shea; Oliver Tobias; Emma Samms; Peter Cushing; Directed by Kevin Connor; Written by Brian Hayles; Cinematography by Alan Hume; Music by Ken Thorne. **A:** Family. **P:** Entertainment. **U:** Home. **L:** English. **Mov-Ent.** **Acq:** Purchase. **Dist:** Televista. $24.95.

The Arabian Horse: A Gift from the Desert 2012 (Unrated)
A documentary on the history and development of the Arabian horse breed. 60m; DVD. **A:** Family. **P:** Education, Entertainment. **U:** Home, Institution. **L:** English. **Gen-Edu:** Documentary Films, Horses, Television. **Acq:** Purchase. **Dist:** Janson Media. $24.95.

Arabian Nights 198?
A tale based on the stories by Scheherazade with Genies, flying carpets, exotic lands, and the Thief of Bagdad. 30m; VHS. **Pr:** R&G Comm. **A:** Family. **P:** Entertainment. **U:** Home. **Chl-Juv:** Animation & Cartoons. **Acq:** Purchase. **Dist:** Anchor Bay Entertainment. $6.95.

Arabian Nights 1942 — ★★
Two brothers fight for the throne of Turkey and the affection of the sultry dancing girl Scheherazade. Enchanting costumes and lavish sets augment the fantasy atmosphere. 87m; VHS, DVD, CC. **C:** Jon Hall; Maria Montez; Sabu; Leif Erickson; Edgar Barrier; Richard Lane; Turhan Bey; Directed by John Rawlins; Written by Michael Hogan; Cinematography by Milton Krasner. **A:** Jr. High-Adult. **P:** Entertainment. **U:** Home. **Mov-Ent:** Middle East. **Acq:** Purchase. **Dist:** Facets Multimedia Inc. $14.98.

Arabian Nights 1974 — ★★★
The third of Pasolini's epic, explicit adaptations of classic portmanteau, featuring ten of the old Scheherazade favorites adorned by beautiful photography, explicit sex scenes and homoeroticism. In Italian with English subtitles; available dubbed. 130m; VHS, DVD, Blu-Ray, Wide. **C:** Ninetto Davoli; Franco Merli; Ines Pellegrini; Luigina Rocchi; Franco Citti; Directed by Pier Paolo Pasolini; Written by Pier Paolo Pasolini; Cinematography by Giuseppe Ruzzolini; Music by Ennio Morricone. **Pr:** Alberto Grimaldi. **A:** College-Adult. **P:** Entertainment. **U:** Home. **L:** English, Italian. **Mov-Ent:** Comedy-Drama. **Acq:** Purchase. **Dist:** Water Bearer Films Inc.

Arabian Nights 2000 — ★★½
Lavish spectacle and good casting overcomes the somewhat sluggish storytelling that combines a number of familiar tales. Sultan Schahriar's (Scott) grip on reality is slim ever since his greedy brother (Frain) and his first (and now late) wife plotted to assassinate him. Although he agrees to marry lovely Scheherezade (Avital), he also plans to kill her the morning after. But the lady is bright and desperate, she sooths her savage sultan with a number of stories involving genies, flying carpets, 40 thieves, and magic in order to stay alive until his sanity returns. Filmed on location in Turkey and Morocco. 175m; VHS, DVD, CC. **C:** Mili Avital; Dougray Scott; James Frain; John Leguizamo; Rufus Sewell; Jason Scott Lee; Alan Bates; Tcheky Karyo; Directed by Steven Barron; Written by Peter Barnes; Cinematography by Remi Adefarasin; Music by Richard Harvey. **Pr:** Robert Halmi, Sr.; Robert Halmi, Jr.; Hallmark Entertainment. **A:** Jr. High-Adult. **P:** Entertainment. **U:** Home. **Mov-Ent:** Middle East, Magic, Marriage. **Acq:** Purchase. **Dist:** Lions Gate Television Corp.

Arabian, Palomino and Saddlebred 19??
Four separate programs about different breeds of horses comprise this tape. "The Proud Breed" is about Arabians; "The Color of Gold" covers Palomino history; and "Showtime for Saddlebreds" and "A Horse of History" look at Saddlebreds. 77m; VHS. **Pr:** International Arabian Horse Association; Palomino Horse Breeders of America; American Saddlebred Horse Association. **A:** Jr. High-Adult. **P:** Education. **U:** Home. **Gen-Edu:** Documentary Films, Horses. **Acq:** Purchase. **Dist:** , On Moratorium. $69.95.

Arabian Sands 1997
Documentary based on the memoirs of its subject, Wilfred Thesiger, a British explorer who crossed the Arabian desert and discovered unknown tribes in previously uncharted territory (now Oman). Now retired in Kenya, Thesiger recalls his days of living with the Bedouin. 52m; VHS. **A:** Adult. **P:** Education. **U:** Home. **Gen-Edu:** Documentary Films, Middle East, Explorers. **Acq:** Purchase, Rent/Lease. **Dist:** Filmakers Library Inc. $295.

The Arabs: A Living History 1988
The rich variety of life, opinion and history in the Arab land is explored. 50m; VHS, DVD, 3/4 U. **Pr:** Landmark Films, Inc. **A:** Jr. High-Adult. **P:** Education. **U:** Institution, SURA. **Gen-Edu:** Middle East. **Acq:** Purchase, Rent/Lease. **Dist:** Landmark Media. $395.00.
Indiv. Titles: 1. The Making of the Arabs 2. Between Two Worlds 3. The City Victorious? 4. The Power of the World 5. New Knowledge For Old 6. Ways of Faith 7. The Shadow of the West 8. Building a Nation 9. Family Ties 10. The Arabs Now.

Arabs and Israelis 1974
This joint Israeli-Arab-produced series focuses on both sides of the political and emotional questions surrounding the Mideast conflict. 30m; VHS, 3/4 U. **Pr:** WGBH Boston. **A:** Jr. High-Adult. **P:** Education. **U:** Institution, CCTV, CATV. **Gen-Edu:** Middle East, International Relations. **Acq:** Purchase, Rent/Lease, Off-Air Record. **Dist:** PBS Home Video.
Indiv. Titles: 1. Ali Darwish and Hanna Meron 2. Golan 3. Jerusalem 4. The Palestinian Question, Part I 5. The Palestinian Question, Part II 6. Sinai 7. Two Families.

Arabs and Terrorism 2006
Multi-part documentary on terrorism filmed in 11 countries. 135m; DVD. **A:** Adult. **P:** Education. **U:** Home, Institution. **L:** English, Arabic, French, Hebrew, Spanish. **Gen-Edu:** Documentary Films, Middle East, Terrorism. **Acq:** Purchase, Rent/Lease. **Dist:** Arab Film Distribution. $24.99.

Arachnia 2003 (R) — ★½
Giant stop motion spider puppets invade a farm as all that stands between them and the rest of Arizona are a paleontologist and his bumbling assistants. 82m; DVD. **C:** David Bunce; Directed by Brett Piper; Written by Brett Piper; Music by David Giancola; Cheryl Friberg; Chuck Harding. **A:** Sr. High-Adult. **P:** Entertainment. **U:** Home. **L:** English. **Mov-Ent.** **Acq:** Purchase. **Dist:** Bedford Entertainment Inc. $9.98.

Arachnid 2001 (R) — ★½
Plane carrying a rescue crew on a mission to find a downed pilot crashes on a tropical island that contains a gigantic, carnivorous alien spider. Nothing that hasn't been seen before. 95m; VHS, DVD, Wide. **C:** Chris Potter; Neus Asensi; Jose Sancho; Alex Reid; Directed by Jack Sholder; Written by Mark Sevi; Cinematography by Carlos Gonzalez; Music by Francesc Gener. **A:** Sr. High-Adult. **P:** Entertainment. **U:** Home. **Mov-Ent.** **Acq:** Purchase. **Dist:** CinemaNow Inc.

Arachnoiditis 1971
An interview and examination of an interesting patient with a localized spinal cord disorder secondary to arachnoiditis of unknown etiology. 23m; VHS, 3/4 U, Special order formats. **Pr:** Ohio State University Health Sciences AV Center. **A:** College-Adult. **P:** Professional. **U:** Institution, SURA. **Hea-Sci:** Neurology. **Acq:** Purchase, Rent/Lease. **Dist:** Ohio State University.

Arachnophobia 1990 (PG-13) — ★★½
Big-budget big-bug horror story has a few funny moments as lots and lots of spiders wreak havoc in a white picket fence community somewhere off the beaten track. Lethal South American spider makes a trek to sunny California, meets up with local spiders, and rapidly multiplies. Utterly arachnophobic (read: totally scared of spiders) town doctor Daniels pairs with gung-ho exterminator Goodman to try and track down the

culprits. The script's a bit yawn-inspiring but the cast and effects will keep you from dozing off. Directorial debut for Marshall, a longtime friend and producer for Spielberg. 109m; VHS, DVD, Blu-Ray, Wide, CC. **C:** Jeff Daniels; John Goodman; Harley Jane Kozak; Julian Sands; Roy Brocksmith; Stuart Pankin; Brian McNamara; Mark L. Taylor; Henry Jones; Peter Jason; James Handy; Directed by Frank Marshall; Written by Wesley Strick; Don Jakoby; Cinematography by Mikael Salomon; Music by Trevor Jones. **Pr:** Amblin Entertainment. **A:** Adult. **P:** Entertainment. **U:** Home. **Mov-Ent**. **Acq:** Purchase. **Dist:** Walt Disney Studios Home Entertainment.

The Aral Sea: Environment Under Siege 1993
Outlines the ecological damage in the Aral Sea. 16m; VHS, SVS, 3/4 U. **A:** Jr. High-Sr. High. **P:** Education. **U:** Institution. **Hea-Sci**: Science, Ecology & Environment. **Acq:** Purchase. **Dist:** Encyclopedia Britannica. $99.00.

Ararat 2002 (R) — ★★★
The slaughter of more than one million Armenians by the Turks in 1915 is the difficult subject matter of Canadian/Armenian director Egoyan's historically-themed drama. Excellent ensemble cast portrays characters in modern-day Toronto who deal with pasts that have been affected by the event in different ways. A director (Aznavour) revisits his roots by making a movie about the Armenian genocide. An expert (Egoyan's wife Khanjian) on Armenian painter Gorky deals with her son (Alpay), whose father was killed after attempting to assassinate a Turkish diplomat, and stepdaughter (Croze), who's father committed suicide. Frequent Egoyan collaborator Greenwood turns up as an actor portraying a real-life U.S. doctor in Turkey during that era who published a book about the events. Stylistically intricate, which may leave some confused, but the heartfelt message is not lost in the crowd. 116m; VHS, DVD. **C:** Charles Aznavour; Eric Bogosian; Brent Carver; David Alpay; Marie Josee Croze; Arsinee Khanjian; Bruce Greenwood; Elias Koteas; Christopher Plummer; Simon Abkarian; Directed by Atom Egoyan; Written by Atom Egoyan; Cinematography by Paul Sarossy; Music by Mychael Danna. **Pr:** Robert Lantos; Atom Egoyan; Alliance Atlantis Communications; Serendipity Point Films; Miramax Film Corp. **A:** Sr. High-Adult. **P:** Entertainment. **U:** Home. **Mov-Ent**: Filmmaking, History, Canada. **Awds:** Genie '02: Actress (Khanjian), Costume Des., Film, Score, Support. Actor (Koteas). **Acq:** Purchase. **Dist:** Buena Vista Home Entertainment.

Ararat Beckons 1991
The first expedition led by Armenians to Mt. Ararat in Turkey. Photographs which make up the film had to be smuggled out of the country. 49m; VHS. **C:** Narrated by Mike Connors. **Pr:** J. Michael Hagopian; Atlantis Productions. **A:** Sr. High-Adult. **P:** Entertainment. **U:** Home, Institution. **Gen-Edu**: Travel, Mountaineering, Asia. **Acq:** Purchase. **Dist:** Armenian Film Foundation. $39.00.

Arata Isozaki 1985
A film which tells the story of the influential Japanese architect. 58m; VHS, 3/4 U. **Pr:** Michael Blackwood Productions. **A:** Jr. High-Adult. **P:** Education. **U:** Institution. **Gen-Edu**: Architecture. **Acq:** Purchase, Rent/Lease. **Dist:** Michael Blackwood Productions. $290.00.

Arata Isozaki 2 1992
Presents Isozaki's new work including The Museum of Contemporary Art in Los Angeles, Disney Headquarters Building in Orlando, the Mito Cultural Complex near Tokyo, the Palladium discotheque in New York, and many other projects. 58m; VHS, 3/4 U. **Pr:** Michael Blackwood Productions. **A:** Sr. High-Adult. **P:** Education. **U:** Home, Institution. **Gen-Edu**: Architecture, Animals. **Acq:** Purchase, Rent/Lease. **Dist:** Michael Blackwood Productions. $290.

Araucanians of Ruca Choroy 1974
Explores the present day life of the Araucanian Indians of the Ruca Choroy valley, a life of poverty, shepherding, baking, sowing, dancing, and exquisite weaving. 50m; VHS, 3/4 U. **Pr:** Jorge Preloran. **A:** Sr. High-Adult. **P:** Education. **U:** Institution, SURA. **Gen-Edu**: Anthropology. **Acq:** Purchase. **Dist:** Phoenix Learning Group.

Araya 1959 (Unrated) — ★★
Ethnographic documentary with separate narrations done in Spanish and French with subtitles. In 1957, writer/director Margo Benacerraf discovers the Araya peninsula, an isolated region in Northern Venezuela. The entire community is based on salt mining from the marshes next to the ocean and the exporting of the product. Trucks bring in the only fresh water and the inhabitants either fish or work in the communal salt production. Even as Benacerraf was making her only film, mechanization was being introduced, which would change a centuries-old way of life. 82m/B/W; DVD. **C:** Narrated by Laurent Terzieff; Jose Ignacio Cabrujas; Directed by Margot Benacerraf; Written by Margot Benacerraf; Pierre Seghers; Cinematography by Giuseppe Nisoli; Music by Guy Bernard. **A:** College-Adult. **P:** Entertainment. **U:** Home. **L:** Spanish, French. **Mov-Ent**: Documentary Films, Miners & Mining, South America. **Acq:** Purchase. **Dist:** Milestone Film & Video.

Arbitrage 2012 (R) — ★★★
Investment guru Robert Miller (Gere) comes off as an untouchable tycoon, with a beautiful wife (Sarandon), amped to sell his trading empire for a fortune. However, he's secretly millions in debt, trying to hush his spitfire mistress (Casta), and elude a detective (Roth) breathing down his neck. Soon enough, his world begins to collapse, leaving him running on empty. First-time feature director Jarecki pulls off a modern-day Hitchcockian miracle, making financial struggles chilling and exciting in this dense thriller. Leading the top-notch cast is Gere, whose portrayal of a desperate man is powerful. 107m; DVD, Blu-Ray. **C:** Richard Gere; Susan Sarandon; Tim Roth; Brit Marling; Laetitia Casta; Nate Parker; Directed by Nicholas Jarecki; Written by Nicholas Jarecki; Cinematography by Yorick Le Saux; Music by Cliff Martinez. **Pr:** Laura Bickford; Robert Salerno; Kevin Turen; Justin Nappi; Alvernia Studios; Parlay Films; Lionsgate; Roadside Attractions. **A:** Sr. High-Adult. **P:** Entertainment. **U:** Home. **L:** English. **Mov-Ent**: Business. **Acq:** Purchase. **Dist:** Lionsgate.

Arbitration: Seven Tests of Just Cause 1991
An in-depth presentation on how to determine whether or not an employee is being discharged or disciplined for just cause. 50m; VHS, 3/4 U. **Pr:** BNA Communications. **A:** College-Adult. **P:** Vocational. **U:** Institution. **Bus-Ind**: How-To, Personnel Management, Law. **Acq:** Rent/Lease. **Dist:** Learning Communications L.L.C. $175.00.

Arbitration III: The Proof of the Matter 199?
When labor and management are in conflict, cool heads must prevail. Dramatizes an intense situation involving substance abuse on the job by an aircraft mechanic and a near-disaster involving aircraft passengers. 75m; VHS. **A:** Adult. **P:** Professional. **U:** Institution. **Bus-Ind**: Labor & Unions, Management. **Acq:** Purchase. **Dist:** Learning Communications L.L.C. $875.00.

Arbitration: Truth of the Matter 1978
This program discusses topics relating to supervision, discipline, union-management relations, preparation for hearings on grievances and arbitration and development and enforcement of company policies. 50m; VHS, 3/4 U. **A:** College-Adult. **P:** Professional. **U:** Institution, SURA. **Bus-Ind**: How-To, Personnel Management, Law. **Acq:** Purchase, Rent/Lease. **Dist:** Learning Communications L.L.C.

Arbuckle & Keaton, Vol. 1: 1917-19 2000
These two discs present some of his best films, two reel comedies that feature a young Buster Keaton as his co-star. Their physical humor contains beautifully timed gags and some of their slapstick is superb. The overt racism of "Out West" is offputting, but it's not unknown in films of that time. 125m/B/W; DVD. **C:** Fatty Arbuckle; Buster Keaton; Directed by Fatty Arbuckle. **A:** Family. **P:** Entertainment. **U:** Home. **Mov-Ent**: Comedy--Slapstick. **Acq:** Purchase. **Dist:** Kino on Video.

Arbuckle & Keaton, Vol. 2: 1918-1920 2000
Contents: "Back Stage," "Good Night Nurse!," "Coney Island," "The Rough House," "The Garage." 121m/B/W; DVD. **C:** Fatty Arbuckle; Buster Keaton; Directed by Fatty Arbuckle. **A:** Family. **P:** Entertainment. **U:** Home. **Mov-Ent**: Comedy--Slapstick. **Acq:** Purchase. **Dist:** Kino on Video.

Arc 2006 (Unrated) — ★
Former L.A. cop Paris Pritchert (Facinelli) is now a junkie and drug dealer. In a last ditch effort at redemption, he tries to find a missing child, which leads to deceit, betrayal, and his own past. First-time director Gunnerson drags out the story and gets overly self-important for what should be a tight crime drama. 113m; DVD. **C:** Peter Facinelli; Jonah Blechman; Ann Cusack; Logan Grove; Mel Harris; Ken Howard; Simone Moore; Directed by Robert Ethan Gunnerson; Written by Robert Ethan Gunnerson; Cinematography by David J. Frederick; Music by Monte Montgomery. **A:** Sr. High-Adult. **P:** Entertainment. **U:** Home. **Mov-Ent**: Crime Drama, Drug Abuse, Drug Trafficking/Dealing. **Acq:** Purchase. **Dist:** Well Go USA, Inc.

ARC: Across the Atlantic 1988
Scenes from an event which featured sailors who decided to race across the Atlantic Ocean in small sailboats. 52m; VHS. **Pr:** Bennett Marine Video. **A:** Family. **P:** Entertainment. **U:** Home. **Spo-Rec**: Boating, Sports--Water. **Acq:** Purchase. **Dist:** Bennett Marine Video. $29.95.

ARC Across the Atlantic/Transatlantic Rally 1987
"ARC Across the Atlantic" covers the 1986 and '87 races, focusing on the people involved in sailing. "Transatlantic Rally" looks at the 1986 race, which ran from Las Palmas, Gran Canaria, and ended in Bridgetown, Barbados. 102m; VHS, 8 mm. **A:** Jr. High-Adult. **P:** Entertainment. **U:** Home, Institution. **Spo-Rec**: Boating. **Acq:** Purchase. **Dist:** Mystic Seaport. $34.95.

Arc Cutting 1995
Features safety rules and various techniques of arc cutting and gouging. 13m; VHS. **A:** Adult. **P:** Professional. **U:** Institution. **Bus-Ind**: Job Training, Safety Education, How-To. **Acq:** Purchase, Rent/Lease. **Dist:** National Safety Council, California Chapter, Film Library. $195.00.

Arc Welding 1995
Features seven key issues involving arc welding: the workshop; personal safety; equipment safety; striking the arc; welding faults; gives examples of types of welds. 23m; VHS. **A:** Adult. **P:** Professional. **U:** Institution. **Bus-Ind**: Job Training, Safety Education, How-To. **Acq:** Purchase, Rent/Lease. **Dist:** National Safety Council, California Chapter, Film Library. $195.00.

Arc Welding Electrode Identification 1978
Offers instruction on specific aspects of arc and MIG welding. 10m; VHS. **A:** Adult. **P:** Vocational. **U:** Institution. **Bus-Ind**: Welding. **Acq:** Purchase. **Dist:** RMI Media. $62.00.

Arc Welding Lab Orientation 1978
Offers instruction on specific aspects of arc and MIG welding. 19m; VHS. **A:** Adult. **P:** Vocational. **U:** Institution. **Bus-Ind**: Welding. **Acq:** Purchase. **Dist:** RMI Media. $84.00.

Arc Welding: Safety and Operation 198?
The basic fundamentals and safety precautions of arc welding are demonstrated. 14m; VHS, 3/4 U. **A:** College-Adult. **P:** Education. **U:** Institution. **L:** English, Spanish. **Bus-Ind**: Welding, Safety Education. **Acq:** Rent/Lease. **Dist:** National Safety Council, California Chapter, Film Library; CEV Multimedia. $49.95.

Arc Welding Series 1980
Close-up photography is used to demonstrate the techniques of each type of welding including the exact procedures necessary to produce the perfect weld. Programs are available individually. 10m; VHS, 3/4 U, EJ, Q. **Pr:** Cornell University. **A:** Sr. High-Adult. **P:** Instruction. **U:** Institution, CCTV, CATV, BCTV, Home. **How-Ins**: Welding. **Acq:** Purchase, Rent/Lease. **Dist:** Cornell University.
Indiv. Titles: 1. Running a Stringer Bead in Flat Position/Running Weave Beads in Flat Position/Padding 2. Cutting, Piercing Holes, Chamfering and Gouging 3. Making a Horizontal Tee Weld 4. Making a Flat Position Open Butt Weld/Making a Flat Position Closed Butt Weld/Butt Welding Steel Rods End to End 5. Braze Welding Galvanized Iron Sheet Metal.

Arcade 1993 (R) — ★½
All the kids in town are desperate to play the new virtual reality game Arcade, only the game is just a little too real. Seems it can transport you into another world with its stunning graphics and sound effects but you really put your life on the line. Only Alex (Ward) worries when kids start to disappear and she decides to battle the game for their lives. 85m; VHS, DVD, CC. **C:** Megan Ward; Peter Billingsley; John de Lancie; Sharon Farrell; Seth Green; Humberto Ortiz; Jonathan Fuller; Norbert Weisser; Directed by Albert Pyun; Written by David S. Goyer; Music by Alan Howarth. **Pr:** Cathy Gesualdo; Charles Band; Full Moon Entertainment. **A:** Sr. High-Adult. **P:** Entertainment. **U:** Home. **Mov-Ent**: Science Fiction, Games, Children. **Acq:** Purchase. **Dist:** Full Moon Pictures.

Arcadia 1990
Ex-Duran Duran members perform their hits in this Japanese import. 60m; VHS. **A:** Jr. High-College. **P:** Entertainment. **U:** Home. **Mov-Ent**: Music Video, Music--Pop/Rock. **Acq:** Purchase. **Dist:** Music Video Distributors. $99.95.

Arcadia of My Youth 1982
In the 30th century the evil Illumidus Empire has conquered Earth and only the heroic Captain Harlock and his friends can battle their tyranny. Based on Matsumoto Leiji's comic book series. Draws parallels to the post-WWII occupation of Japan. Animated; in Japanese with English subtitles. 130m; VHS. **C:** Directed by Anthony M. Dawson. **A:** Sr. High-Adult. **P:** Entertainment. **U:** Home. **L:** Japanese, English. **Mov-Ent**: Animation & Cartoons. **Acq:** Purchase. **Dist:** AnimEigo Inc. $39.95.

Arch Books on Video 1984
These are Bible stories on video for the religious instruction of children. 15m; VHS, 3/4 U. **Pr:** CPH. **A:** Family. **P:** Religious. **U:** Institution, Home. **Chl-Juv**: Bible. **Acq:** Purchase. **Dist:** Concordia Publishing House. $74.00.
Indiv. Titles: 1. The World God Made/The Story of Noah's Ark 2. Daniel in the Lion's Den/Samson's Secret 3. The Princess and the Baby (Moses)/The Great Escape (Exodus) 4. The Little Sleeping Beauty (Jairus' Daughter)/Boy Who Gave His Lunch Away (Feeding of 5000) 5. Mary's Story/Clem the Clumsy Camel (Christmas) 6. The Little Boat That Almost Sank/The Man Who Couldn't Wait.

Arch of Triumph 1948 — ★★★
In Paris, an Austrian refugee doctor falls in love just before the Nazis enter the city. Big-budget boxoffice loser featuring fine cast but sluggish pace. Based on the Erich Maria Remarque novel. 120m/B/W; VHS, DVD. **C:** Ingrid Bergman; Charles Boyer; Charles Laughton; Louis Calhern; Ruth Warrick; Directed by Lewis Milestone; Written by Lewis Milestone; Harry Brown; Cinematography by Russell Metty. **Pr:** United Artists; Enterprise. **A:** Jr. High-Adult. **P:** Entertainment. **U:** Home. **Mov-Ent**: Drama, World War Two, France. **Acq:** Purchase. **Dist:** Paramount Pictures Corp. $129.98.

Arch of Triumph 1985 (Unrated) — ★★½
A refugee doctor falls in love with a mystery woman as the Nazis enter Paris. TV remake of the 1948 film. 95m; VHS, DVD. **C:** Anthony Hopkins; Lesley-Anne Down; Donald Pleasence; Frank Finlay; Directed by Waris Hussein; Written by Charles Israel; Music by Georges Delerue. **A:** Jr. High-Adult. **P:** Entertainment. **U:** Home. **Mov-Ent**: Drama, World War Two, TV Movies. **Acq:** Purchase. **Dist:** Facets Multimedia Inc. $19.95.

Archaeological Dating: Retracing Time 1976
Explores relative and absolute dating techniques archeologists use to date their finds. 18m; VHS, 3/4 U. **Pr:** Encyclopedia Britannica Educational Corporation. **A:** Sr. High. **P:** Education. **U:** Institution, SURA. **Hea-Sci**: Archaeology. **Acq:** Purchase, Rent/Lease, Trade-in. **Dist:** Encyclopedia Britannica.

Archaeologists at Work 19??
In this show two archaeologists excavate a site in the Southwest. 13m; VHS, 3/4 U. **Pr:** Wayne Mitchell. **A:** Jr. High-Sr. High. **P:** Education. **U:** Institution, SURA. **Gen-Edu**: Archaeology. **Acq:** Purchase. **Dist:** Phoenix Learning Group.

Archaeology: Evidence of the Past 1994
Documents a Mesa Verde archaeology study to explain Carbon 14 dating, stratigraphy, dendrochronology, ground probes, and more. Complete with study guide. 20m; VHS. **A:** Jr. High-College. **P:** Education. **U:** Institution. **Gen-Edu**: Archaeology. **Acq:** Purchase. **Dist:** Lucerne Media. $195.

Archaeology in Mesopotamia 19??
Dr. Robert Adams discusses the findings of ancient mounds in Mesopotamia and explains how they were formed, how archaeologists dug them up, and the problems these scientists encountered in their digging. 16m; 3/4 U, Special order formats. **Pr:** Education Development Center. **A:** Jr. High-College. **P:**

Education. **U:** Institution, CCTV, CATV, BCTV. **Gen-Edu:** Archaeology. **Acq:** Purchase, Rent/Lease. **Dist:** Education Development Center.

Archangel 2005 (R) — ★★½
Based on the novel by Robert Harris, this thriller follows British historian Kelso (Craig), an expert on the Stalin-era USSR, to a Moscow conference. He's approached by an elderly man (Chernvak) claiming to know the whereabouts of Stalin's lost diary and he's plausible enough to have Kelso haring off to the port city of Archangel, accompanied by the man's daughter Zinaida (Rednikova) and reporter O'Brian (Macht). Only their search leads them to a dangerous underground movement to restore Stalinism to modern Russia. Originally broadcast as a BBC miniseries. 120m; DVD. **C:** Daniel Craig; Yekaterina Rednikova; Gabriel Macht; Valery Chernvak; Directed by Jon Jones; Written by Dick Clement; Ian La Frenais; Cinematography by Chris Seager; Music by Robert (Rob) Lane. **A:** Sr. High-Adult. **P:** Entertainment. **U:** Home. **Mov-Ent:** USSR, Politics & Government. **Acq:** Purchase. **Dist:** Bedford Entertainment Inc.

Archbishop Desmond Tutu and the Rainbow Nation ????
A day in the life of Archbishop Desmond Tutu as he begins a tour through his Cape Town diocese and ends with a trip to Johannesburg to greet his mentor, Trevor Huddleston. 54m; VHS. **A:** Sr. High-Adult. **P:** Education. **U:** Institution. **Gen-Edu:** Africa, Apartheid. **Acq:** Purchase, Rent/Lease. **Dist:** Films for the Humanities & Sciences. $149.00.

Archbishop Desmond Tutu with Bill Moyers ????
Candid discussion of Tutu's life, work, and thoughts on justice, truth, and forgiveness. 57m; VHS. **A:** Sr. High-Adult. **P:** Education. **U:** Institution. **Gen-Edu:** Africa, Apartheid. **Acq:** Purchase. **Dist:** Films for the Humanities & Sciences. $89.95.

Archbishop Fulton Sheen 19??
Archbishop Sheen delivers his message of inspiration, centering on Christ and his mission. 60m; VHS. **Pr:** Ignatius Press. **A:** Jr. High-Adult. **P:** Religious. **U:** Institution, Home. **Gen-Edu:** Religion, Ethics & Morals. **Acq:** Purchase. **Dist:** Ignatius Press. $34.95.

Archbishop O'Connor Scores Pornography as Major Threat to Family Life/Father Ritter Fights "Teen Sex Industry" in New York City 1987
These two programs outline major problems facing family life today. 60m; VHS. **Pr:** Keep the Faith, Inc. **A:** Family. **P:** Religious. **U:** Institution, Home. **Gen-Edu:** Prostitution, Pornography, Religion. **Acq:** Purchase. **Dist:** Keep the Faith Inc. $20.00.

Archer: The Fugitive from the Empire 1981 (Unrated) — ★
A young warrior battles the forces of evil. Lots of strange names to learn even if you already know who's going to win the final battle. 97m; VHS. **C:** Lane Caudell; Belinda Bauer; George Kennedy; Victor Campos; Kabir Bedi; George Innes; Marc Alaimo; Allan Rich; John Hancock; Priscilla Pointer; Sharon Barr; Directed by Nicholas J. Corea. **Pr:** Universal Television. **A:** Primary-Jr. High. **P:** Entertainment. **U:** Home. **Mov-Ent:** TV Movies. **Acq:** Purchase. **Dist:** $39.95.

Archer's Adventure 1985 — ★½
An Australian family film based on a true story. A horsetrainer's young apprentice delivers a prize racehorse to Melbourne, through 600 miles of tough frontier, devious bush rangers, and disaster. 120m; VHS, DVD. **C:** Brett Climo; Nicole Kidman; Directed by Denny Lawrence. **A:** Jr. High-Adult. **P:** Entertainment. **U:** Home. **L:** Spanish. **Mov-Ent:** Action-Adventure, Horses--Racing. **Acq:** Purchase. **Dist:** Anchor Bay Entertainment. $14.95.

Archery 1978
Progressive techniques in archery are demonstrated including nock, anchor, release, and pre-gap and sight methods of aiming. Presented in two parts. 10m; VHS, 3/4 U. **C:** Directed by Fred Shuette. **Pr:** Champions on Film. **A:** Sr. High-Adult. **P:** Instruction. **U:** Institution, CCTV, Home. **Spo-Rec:** Sports--General. **Acq:** Purchase, Rent/Lease. **Dist:** School-Tech Inc.

Archery Elk: The Dream Hunt 19??
Features bow hunting for bull elk in New Mexico, Colorado, and Montana with Mike Lapinski and Paul Brunner. 84m; VHS. **A:** Adult. **P:** Entertainment. **U:** Home. **Spo-Rec:** Hunting. **Acq:** Purchase. **Dist:** Stoney-Wolf Productions, Inc. $49.95.

Archery Fundamentals 1961
Designed to give beginning archers basic knowledge about shooting equipment and proper methods of choosing and using it, by showing step-by-step procedures. 11m; VHS, 3/4 U. **Pr:** D.L. Richardson. **A:** Jr. High-Sr. High. **P:** Instruction. **U:** Institution, SURA. **Spo-Rec:** Sports--General. **Acq:** Purchase. **Dist:** Phoenix Learning Group.

Archery Gobblers 19??
Professional bowhunters Mike McClendon and John Whelan demonstrate their master bowhunting techniques as they hunt turkey. 68m; VHS. **A:** Adult. **P:** Instruction. **U:** Home. **Spo-Rec:** Hunting. **Acq:** Purchase. **Dist:** Stoney-Wolf Productions, Inc. $49.95.

Archery Techniques 1971
Mrs. Wells examines the equipment and basic techniques of the ancient sport of archery. 30m; EJ. **Pr:** NETCHE. **A:** College-Adult. **P:** Education. **U:** Institution, CCTV, BCTV, SURA. **Spo-Rec:** Sports--General. **Acq:** Purchase, Rent/Lease, Subscription. **Dist:** NETCHE.

Arches National Park 1991
This well-filmed travel video displays the beauty of the natural arches found in this federal preserve, and explains the erosive forces that created this landscape. 30m; VHS. **Pr:** Finley-Holiday Film Corporation. **A:** Jr. High-Adult. **P:** Education. **U:** Home. **Gen-Edu:** Travel, National Parks & Reserves, U.S. States. **Acq:** Purchase. **Dist:** Finley Holiday Film Corp. $14.95.

Archetypal Forms and Forces 199?
Cross-cultural anthropologist Angeles Arrien, Ph.D., presents ways to activate one's archetypal energies as healers, warriors, visionaries, and teachers, through song, dance, storytelling, and meditation. 90m; DVD. **A:** Adult. **P:** Education. **U:** Home, Institution. **Gen-Edu:** Anthropology, Psychology. **Acq:** Purchase. **Dist:** Thinking Allowed Productions. $49.95.

Archetypal Psychology 1989
Jungian analyst and author of "The Tao of Psychology" and "Goddesses in Every Woman, Gods in Every Man," Jean Shinoda Bolen, M.D., explains the synchronicity of the ego and an archetypal self much like the ancient Chinese Tao, and deities imprint powerful projections on the psyche. With knowledge of myths of the gods we can learn more about ourselves. 90m; DVD. **A:** Adult. **P:** Education. **U:** Home, Institution. **Gen-Edu:** Psychology, Psychiatry. **Acq:** Purchase. **Dist:** Thinking Allowed Productions. $49.95.

Archie & Friends: Archie's TV Funnies 2004 (Unrated)
Presents the animated 1960s-1970s television cartoon with high-schooler Archie and the gang including Jughead, Reggie, Betty, Veronica, and Sabrina. Includes: "Riverdale Grand Auto Race," "The Riverdale Air Circus," "The Ghost of Swedlow Swamp," and "U.S. of Archie." 4 episodes. 90m; DVD. **C:** Voice(s) by Dallas McKennon; Howard Morris; Jane Webb; John Erwin. **A:** Family. **P:** Entertainment. **U:** Home. **Mov-Ent:** Television Series, Animation & Cartoons. **Acq:** Purchase. **Dist:** Radio Archives. $12.98.

Archie Bunker's Place: The Complete First Season 2006 (Unrated)
Presents the debut season of the 1979-1983 spin-off comedy television series with Archie (O'Connor) from "All in the Family" as he now operates a restaurant bar along with business partner Murray Klein (Balsam) and cook Veronica (Meara) with occasional appearances by wife Edith (Stapleton) and niece Stephanie (Brisebois). Includes: Archie can't handle when Harry (Wingreen) wants to sell his stake in the bar to Jewish liberal Murray, a robber has struck in their neighborhood which worries Archie and Murray, and Sammy Davis Jr. stops by per Archie's invitation. 24 episodes. 590m; DVD. **C:** Carroll O'Connor; Jason Wingreen; Anne Meara; Martin Balsam; Danielle Brisebois; Bill Quinn; Jean Stapleton; Allan Melvin. **A:** Family. **P:** Entertainment. **U:** Home. **Mov-Ent:** Television Series. **Acq:** Purchase. **Dist:** Sony Pictures Home Entertainment Inc. $29.95.

Archie Carr: In Praise of Wild Florida 1993
Authors Peter Matthiessen and Russell Hoban summarize the work of award-winning conservationist philosopher Dr. Archie Carr. They take a look at his views of Florida as a pristine wilderness that should be cherished and enjoyed. Includes study guide. 29m; VHS. **Pr:** Ironwood Productions. **A:** Jr. High-Adult. **P:** Education. **U:** Home, Institution. **Gen-Edu:** Ecology & Environment, Literature. **Acq:** Purchase. **Dist:** Ivy Classics Video. $195.00.

Archie Miller: Off-Season Skill Development 2013 (Unrated)
Coach Archie Miller discusses developing a basketball team's abilities during the off season. 64m; DVD. **A:** Family. **P:** Education. **U:** Home. **L:** English. **Spo-Rec:** Athletic Instruction/Coaching, Basketball. **Acq:** Purchase. **Dist:** Championship Productions. $39.99.

Archie: Return to Riverdale 1990 (PG) — ★★½
Archie, Reggie, Betty, Veronica, and Jughead return to Riverdale for their 15-year class reunion. Made for TV; based on the comic book. 85m; VHS. **C:** Christopher Rich; Lauren Holly; Karen Kopins; Sam Whipple; Gary Kroeger; Matt McCoy; David Doyle; Fran Ryan; Directed by Dick Lowry; Cinematography by Frank Byers; Music by Mark Snow. **Pr:** Concorde Pictures. **A:** Jr. High-Adult. **P:** Entertainment. **U:** Home. **Mov-Ent:** TV Movies. **Acq:** Purchase. **Dist:** New Horizons Picture Corp.

Archie Shepp: "I Am Jazz. . .It's My Life" 1984
Jazz musician Archie Shepp has been playing music since the 1950s and throughout the years has developed political and social theories related to jazz music as a movement. In addition to performing in this film, he speaks on the African origins of jazz, and on what he perceives as the revolutionary purpose of jazz. He also talks about the invisibility and isolation of black people in society. 52m; VHS. **C:** Directed by Frank Cassenti; Music by Archie Shepp. **Pr:** Hubert Niogret. **A:** Family. **P:** Entertainment. **U:** Home. **Mov-Ent:** Music--Jazz, Biography, Black Culture. **Acq:** Purchase. **Dist:** Music Video Distributors; Rhapsody Films, Inc. $29.95.

The Archie Show: The Complete Series 1968
Vintage animated series produced by Lou Scheimer captures Archie, Veronica, Betty, Reggie, Jughead, and Hot Dog as they live, love, and flub their way through high school. "The Added Distraction," "Beauty Is Only Fur Deep," "Hot Rod Drag," "Groovy Ghosts," and "Hard Day's Knight" are among the collection's 32 episodes. 363m; DVD. **C:** Voice(s) by Dallas McKennon; Howard Morris; Jane Webb; John Erwin. **A:** Jr. High-Sr. High. **P:** Entertainment. **U:** Home. **Chl-Juv:** Animation & Cartoons, Television Series. **Acq:** Purchase. **Dist:** Classic Media.

Archie's Fun House: The Complete Series 1970
Archie, Betty, Veronica, and Jughead sing catchy ditties like "Lucky Me," "Love Vibrations," "Candy Kisses," and the anti-pollution "Mr. Factory" while enjoying fun in the sun and high school. Reggie demonstrates his inept abilities at magic, bronco-busting, rope twirling, and surfing. "Mr. Weatherbee's Camping Corner" has the principal teaching the kids how to build a tree house and Big Ethel goes over the top to catch Jughead. 16 episodes. 336m; DVD. **C:** Voice(s) by Howard Morris; John Erwin; Jane Webb; Dal McKennon; Ron Dante. **A:** Primary-Jr. High. **P:** Entertainment. **U:** Home. **Chl-Juv:** Animation & Cartoons. **Acq:** Purchase. **Dist:** Classic Media.

Archimedes Principle 1979
An historical dramatization of how Archimedes developed and demonstrated his principle of physics. 7m; VHS, 3/4 U, Special order formats. **Pr:** Paul S. Karr Productions. **A:** Primary-Jr. High. **P:** Education. **U:** Institution, CCTV, Home, SURA. **Hea-Sci:** Physics. **Acq:** Purchase, Rent/Lease. **Dist:** Alpine Film & Video Exchange.

The Architect 2006 (R) — ★★
Rickety construction undermines the cast. Affluent white architect Leo Waters (LaPaglia) lives with his dysfunctional family on Chicago's North Shore. Black activist Tonya Neely (Davis) is an occupant of a South Side housing tower that Leo designed, which in now gang-controlled and falling apart. Tonya, who has her own family issues, wants the towers torn down for new housing and thinks Leo's signature on her petition will help her efforts, but he's reluctant to participate. Based on a play by David Grieg. 82m; DVD. **C:** Anthony LaPaglia; Viola Davis; Isabella Rossellini; Hayden Panettiere; Sebastian Stan; Paul James; Serena Reeder; Walton Goggins; Directed by Matt Tauber; Written by Matt Tauber; Cinematography by John Bailey; Music by Marcelo Zarvos. **A:** Sr. High-Adult. **P:** Entertainment. **U:** Home. **Mov-Ent:** Architecture. **Acq:** Purchase. **Dist:** Magnolia Home Entertainment.

Architects/Architecture 1977
A discussion of American architectural design, and the problems and opportunities that face students and architects. 36m; VHS, Special order formats. **Pr:** International Masonry Institute. **A:** College-Adult. **P:** Education. **U:** Institution, Home. **Gen-Edu:** Documentary Films, Architecture. **Acq:** Rent/Lease. **Dist:** American Institute of Architects. $20.00.

Architects' Compensation: Challenge for the Profession—Grassroots '85 Conference 1985
Features the panel discussion, held at the end of the Grassroots 1985 Conference, on the issues associated with the compensation of architects. 90m; VHS. **A:** Adult. **P:** Professional. **U:** Institution, Home. **Bus-Ind:** Architecture, Education. **Acq:** Purchase, Rent/Lease. **Dist:** American Institute of Architects. $75.00.

The Architects: DEFA Collection 1990
When East Berlin-based architect Daniel Brenner is chosen to create a design for a new small city, his vexations with Communist rule in East Germany are somewhat eased, though he continues to struggle in his personal and professional life. 97m; DVD. **A:** Sr. High-Adult. **P:** Entertainment. **U:** Home. **Mov-Ent:** Architecture, Germany, Politics & Government. **Acq:** Purchase. **Dist:** First Run Features. $24.95.

Architects in Industry: Career Alternatives 1986
Explores the field of architecture and looks at the benefits, possibilities, and qualifications. 20m; VHS. **A:** College-Adult. **P:** Professional. **U:** Institution, Home. **Bus-Ind:** Architecture, Education, Occupations. **Acq:** Rent/Lease. **Dist:** American Institute of Architects.

The Architect's Office of the Future 1981
Illustrates some of the more pronounced changes taking place in the architect's office. 20m; VHS, 3/4 U. **A:** Adult. **P:** Professional. **U:** Institution, Home. **Bus-Ind:** Architecture, Education. **Acq:** Rent/Lease. **Dist:** American Institute of Architects.

Architectural Drafting 2 1986
Advanced drafting techniques and applications are examined. 10m; VHS. **Pr:** Bergwall Productions. **A:** College-Adult. **P:** Instruction. **U:** Institution. **How-Ins:** Architecture, Education. **Acq:** Purchase. **Dist:** Bergwall Productions, Inc. $269.00.
Indiv. Titles: 1. Blueprints and Exterior Walls 2. Interior Partitions and Doors 3. Blocking in the Windows 4. Broadening the Object Lines.

Architectural Drawing 1986
The basics of drafting are demonstrated. 10m; VHS. **Pr:** Bergwall Productions. **A:** Sr. High-Adult. **P:** Instruction. **U:** Institution. **How-Ins:** Architecture, Education. **Acq:** Purchase. **Dist:** Bergwall Productions, Inc. $269.00.
Indiv. Titles: 1. Blueprints and How They Are Used 2. Setting up the Drafting Table 3. Equipment and Determining Sheet Size 4. How to Lay Out Border Lines and Title Box.

Architecture 1984
The various aspects of this complex career are explored, including the different levels of education available. 15m; VHS. **Pr:** Morris Video. **A:** Sr. High-Adult. **P:** Instruction. **U:** Home. **How-Ins:** How-To, Occupations, Architecture. **Acq:** Purchase. **Dist:** Morris Video. $24.95.

Architecture: Career Profile 1988
Outlines the various activities of an architect and emphasizes the scope and complexity of the profession. Based on the Canadian architectural system, it contains examples of architectural design work. 10m; VHS. **A:** College. **P:** Professional. **U:** Institution, Home. **Bus-Ind:** Architecture, Education, Occupations. **Acq:** Rent/Lease. **Dist:** American Institute of Architects.

Architecture: Choosing a Future 1988
Profiles women in the architecture profession by illustrating how they represent a diversity of roles. Also discusses the skills needed by an architect. 13m; VHS. **A:** Sr. High-Adult. **P:** Professional. **U:** Institution, Home. **Bus-Ind**: Architecture, Education, Women. **Acq:** Purchase, Rent/Lease. **Dist:** American Institute of Architects. $75.00.

Architecture in America: The Work of a Younger Generation 1993
Features the work of a younger generation dealing with a more realistic, less universal theory of modernism. These architects all hold the belief that less is more meaningful to late 20th century America. 58m; VHS. **Pr:** Michael Blackwood Productions. **A:** College-Adult. **P:** Education. **U:** Home, Institution. **Gen-Edu**: Architecture. **Acq:** Purchase, Rent/Lease. **Dist:** Michael Blackwood Productions.

The Architecture of Cells: Special Structure, Special Function 1983
By examining a variety of cells from different organisms, students learn how different cell structures contribute to different cell functions. ?m; VHS, Special order formats. **A:** Jr. High-College. **P:** Education. **U:** Institution. **Hea-Sci**: Science, Biology. **Acq:** Purchase. **Dist:** HRM Video. $175.00.

The Architecture of Doom 1991
Examines the Third Reich from the view of the Nazi cult of the beautiful and Hitler's eccentric cultural ambitions and obsessions to "beautify" the world. 119m/B/W; VHS, DVD. **C:** Directed by Peter Cohen. **A:** College-Adult. **P:** Education. **U:** Institution, Home. **Gen-Edu**: World War Two, Holocaust. **Acq:** Purchase. **Dist:** First Run Features. $59.95.

The Architecture of Frank Lloyd Wright 1984
Biographic portrait of Frank Lloyd Wright, showing his architectural works and explaining his concepts of form and function. 90m; VHS. **A:** Sr. High-Adult. **P:** Professional. **U:** Institution, Home. **Fin-Art**: Architecture, History, Biography. **Acq:** Purchase, Rent/Lease. **Dist:** American Institute of Architects.

The Architecture of Frank Lloyd Wright 1988
One of America's greatest architects is profiled in this documentary. Through visuals of Wright's creations, recordings of Wright himself and narration by his granddaughter, we are shown how a young man from Wisconsin helped define modern architecture. 75m; VHS. **C:** Narrated by Anne Baxter; Directed by Murray Grigor. **Pr:** NVC Arts International. **A:** Jr. High-Adult. **P:** Education. **U:** Home. **Fin-Art**: Documentary Films, Biography, Architecture. **Acq:** Purchase. **Dist:** Home Vision Cinema; Direct Cinema Ltd. $39.95.

Architectures IV 2005
Looks at the historical and social functions of the Royal Saltworks of Arc and Senans; Bilboa's Guggenheim Museum; Jean Pouve's House; the St. Foy Abbey; and the Sendai Mediatheque. English, French, and German with subtitles. 160m; DVD. **A:** Sr. High-Adult. **P:** Entertainment. **U:** Home. **L:** French, German. **Fin-Art**: Documentary Films, Architecture. **Acq:** Purchase. **Dist:** Facets Multimedia Inc.

Archives of the Mossad: Josef Mengele—The Final Account 1998
Looks back at the crimes and life of the SS doctor who sent over 400,000 people to the gas chambers in the horrifying pursuit of racial purification. 60m; VHS. **A:** Sr. High-Adult. **P:** Education. **U:** Home. **Gen-Edu**: Documentary Films, Judaism, Intelligence Service. **Acq:** Purchase. **Dist:** Direct Cinema Ltd. $24.95.

Archives of the Mossad: Mikdad—Into the Mind of a Terrorist 1998
Tells the story of Hussein Mikdad, a terrorist sent to bestow mass destruction on Israel who ends up the only victim of his own bomb. Also reveals a web of terrorism that stretches from the Middle East to Europe to America. 52m; VHS. **A:** Sr. High-Adult. **P:** Education. **U:** Home. **Gen-Edu**: Documentary Films, Judaism, Intelligence Service. **Acq:** Purchase. **Dist:** Direct Cinema Ltd. $24.95.

Archives of the Mossad: Shaheed—The Making of a Suicide Bomber 1998
Probes the minds of suicide bombers and examines the reasons why the young men sacrifice their lives to become "shaheed" or holy martyrs. 52m; VHS. **A:** Sr. High-Adult. **P:** Education. **U:** Home. **Gen-Edu**: Documentary Films, Judaism, Intelligence Service. **Acq:** Purchase. **Dist:** Direct Cinema Ltd. $24.95.

Archives of the Mossad: The Disappearance of Martin Bormann 1998
Examines the rumors and theories concerning the fate of Martin Bormann, Hitler's right hand man, following his disappearance after World War II. 52m; VHS. **A:** Sr. High-Adult. **P:** Education. **U:** Home. **Gen-Edu**: Documentary Films, Judaism, Intelligence Service. **Acq:** Purchase. **Dist:** Direct Cinema Ltd. $24.95.

Archives of the Mossad: The Hunt for Adolf Eichmann 1998
Presents a firsthand account by the Mossad agents who planned and implemented the covert operation to capture Nazi war criminal Adolf Eichmann. 90m; VHS. **A:** Sr. High-Adult. **P:** Education. **U:** Home. **Gen-Edu**: Documentary Films, Judaism, Intelligence Service. **Acq:** Purchase. **Dist:** Direct Cinema Ltd. $29.95.

Archives of War: 3-Volume Box Set 1999
Volume 1: "World War I and the Interwar Years" covers the three WWI battles fought outside Ypres, Belgium; the Spanish Civil War; the Sino-Japanese War; and the rise of the Nazi party. "World War II - The Leaders": Includes Hitler, Mussolini, Hirohito, Roosevelt, Churchill, and Stalin. Volume 2: "The Battles": from the 1939 outbreak of war in Europe to the dropping of the atomic bomb in Japan in 1945. "The Cold War": the rise of atomic weapons and the increased postwar tensions between the U.S. and U.S.S.R. Volume 3: "Korea": covers the invasion of South Korea, the Inchon landing, the resignation of General Douglas MacArthur, and POW exchanges. "Vietnam": includes several phases of the conflict from the French struggle with the communist Viet Minh through the beginning of the 1968 Paris peace negotiations. 1720m; DVD. **A:** Sr. High-Adult. **P:** Entertainment. **U:** Home. **Gen-Edu**: Documentary Films, Vietnam War, Korean War. **Acq:** Purchase. **Dist:** MPI Media Group. $69.98.

Archology: City in the Image of Man 198?
Architect William Kirsch and design consultant Christopher Alexander offer alternative building designs to those of metropolitan modern cities because it is believed high buildings make one feel isolated from society and emotionally detached. 19m; 3/4 U, Special order formats. **Pr:** Hobel Leiterman Productions. **A:** College-Adult. **P:** Education. **U:** Institution. **Gen-Edu**: Architecture, Cities & Towns. **Acq:** Purchase. **Dist:** The Cinema Guild.

The Arctic Adventure 1980
A documentary look at "the Polar Goddess," "mistress" to the famous explorers who have crossed the borders of her icy domain. 120m; 3/4 U. **Pr:** Lyle Bebensee. **A:** Primary-Adult. **P:** Education. **U:** Institution, SURA. **Gen-Edu**: Documentary Films, Arctic Regions, Explorers. **Acq:** Purchase, Rent/Lease. **Dist:** Kinetic Film Enterprises Ltd.

Arctic Blue 1993 (R) — ★½
Alaskan biologist Walsh gets stuck being the local lawman when he's the only one willing to escort Hauer, a homicidal trapper, to a Fairbanks jail. But nothing's that easy—their plane crashes atop a glacier and the duo must battle each other and the elements to survive, while Hauer's brutal partners hunt Walsh. 95m; VHS, DVD, CC. **C:** Dylan Walsh; Rutger Hauer; Richard Bradford; Directed by Peter Masterson; Written by Ross LaManna; Cinematography by Thomas Burstyn; Music by Peter Melnick. **Pr:** Rick Stevenson; John Flock; Paul L. Newman; New City Releasing. **A:** Sr. High-Adult. **P:** Entertainment. **U:** Home. **Mov-Ent**: Action-Adventure, Arctic Regions, Wilderness Areas. **Acq:** Purchase. **Dist:** Sony Pictures Home Entertainment Inc.

Arctic Engineering 1981
A course in 35 hours on advanced particulars involving engineering in the polar areas. 60m; VHS, 3/4 U. **Pr:** Univ of Alaska. **A:** Adult. **P:** Special Education. **U:** Institution, Home, SURA. **Gen-Edu**: Engineering. **Acq:** Purchase, Rent/Lease. **Dist:** University of Alaska Fairbanks.

Arctic Heat and Mass Transfer ME-685 1983
A course in 42 one-hour tapes of advanced training in Arctically mass transfer and engineering. 60m; VHS, 3/4 U. **Pr:** Univ of Alaska. **A:** Adult. **P:** Special Education. **U:** Institution, Home, SURA. **Hea-Sci**: Engineering, Arctic Regions. **Acq:** Purchase, Rent/Lease. **Dist:** University of Alaska Fairbanks.

Arctic Kingdom ????
National Geographic documentary providing first hand accounts of geographic issues and exploration. 60m; VHS; Closed Captioned. **A:** Jr. High-Sr. High. **P:** Education. **U:** Institution. **Gen-Edu**: Geography, Arctic Regions. **Acq:** Purchase. **Dist:** Zenger Media. $19.98.

Arctic Kingdom: Life at the Edge 1996 (Unrated)
While the frozen Arctic land is among the most forbidding in the world, there is actually a vast array of wildlife that survives there. Watch as animals as diverse as the ferocious 1700-pound polar bear and the stealthy arctic fox hunt their prey while also avoiding animals that are tracking them. 84m; DVD. **A:** Family. **P:** Education. **U:** Institution, Home. **Mov-Ent**: Documentary Films, Arctic Regions, Bears. **Acq:** Purchase. **Dist:** National Geographic Society. $19.95.

Arctic Mirror 1979
This is a chronicle of the six-month, 600-mile trek of two young filmmakers into the arctic area of Alaska. 19m; VHS, 3/4 U. **Pr:** Jay Coggeshall. **A:** Sr. High-Adult. **P:** Education. **U:** Institution, SURA. **Gen-Edu**: Arctic Regions. **Acq:** Purchase. **Dist:** Phoenix Learning Group.

Arctic Mission: The Great Adventure 2011 (Unrated)
Documentary following scientists on a five-month trek through Canada as they study global warming. 681m; DVD, Blu-Ray. **A:** Jr. High-Adult. **P:** Entertainment. **U:** Home. **L:** English. **Mov-Ent**: Documentary Films, Ecology & Environment, Meteorology. **Acq:** Purchase. **Dist:** Madacy Entertainment L.P.; Acorn Media Group Inc. $17.97 14.98.

Arctic Oil Spills 1977
Explores research currently being conducted by Canada on the properties of oil under Arctic conditions. Part of the Discovery Series. 7m; VHS. **A:** Adult. **P:** Education. **U:** Institution, Home. **Gen-Edu**: Canada, Science, Oil Industry. **Acq:** Purchase. **Dist:** University of Toronto. $9.00.

Arctic Refuge: A Vanishing Wilderness 1990
The coastal plain of the Arctic National Wildlife Refuge is a 100-mile stretch of wilderness which provides a springtime gathering site for a number of animals. The area is threatened by the oil and gas industries which want to begin drilling on the same site. 60m; VHS. **C:** Narrated by Meryl Streep. **A:** Family. **P:** Education. **U:** Home. **Gen-Edu**: Documentary Films, Ecology & Environment, Wilderness Areas. **Acq:** Purchase. **Dist:** Baker and Taylor. $14.98.

Arctic River: The Mackenzie 1988
A look at Canada's Mackenzie River which is home to a great variety of wildlife and plants. All of this is threatened by increasing exploitation of the Arctic for its oil and minerals. 22m; VHS, 3/4 U. **Pr:** National Film Board of Canada. **A:** Family. **P:** Education. **U:** Institution, Home, SURA. **Gen-Edu**: Geography, Ecology & Environment. **Acq:** Purchase, Duplication License. **Dist:** Bullfrog Films, Inc.

Arctic Son 2008 (Unrated)
Documentary following Stanley Njootli Jr. as he travels to the Arctic Circle to meet the father he hasn't seen in nearly 25 years. 75m; DVD. **A:** Sr. High-Adult. **P:** Education. **U:** Home. **Mov-Ent**: Documentary Films, Family. **Acq:** Purchase. **Dist:** Docurama. $26.95.

Arctic Tale 2007 (G) — ★★½
We love pretending animals are just like us, don't we? Just add some disco music ("We Are Family") and a narrator (Queen Latifah) we all recognize and watch those wacky things animals do in the wild (like fart). Flick follows a polar bear and a walrus over six years, starting with their birth. The message is clear beyond our compulsion to humanize them, however; climate change, possibly caused by us, is dramatically affecting their habitat. Lush (if not chilly) backdrops and the directors' passion make this a fine family film. 96m; DVD, Blu-Ray, HD-DVD. **C:** Narrated by Queen Latifah; Directed by Adam Ravetch; Sarah Robertson; Written by Linda Woverton; Moses Richards; Kristin Gore; Cinematography by Adam Ravetch; Music by Joby Talbot. **Pr:** Adam Leipzip; Keenan Smart; National Geographic Society; Visionbox Pictures; Paramont Vantage. **A:** Family. **P:** Entertainment. **U:** Home. **L:** English. **Mov-Ent**: Documentary Films, Ecology & Environment, Antarctic Regions. **Acq:** Purchase. **Dist:** Paramount Pictures Corp.

Arctic to Amazonia ?
Native people from North and South America talk about the impact of industrial development upon their land and cultures. Special pricing available to high schools, libraries and community organizations. 21m; VHS. **A:** Family. **P:** Education. **U:** Institution. **Gen-Edu**: Native Americans, Documentary Films. **Acq:** Purchase, Rent/Lease. **Dist:** Turning Tide Productions. $189.00.

Arde Amor 2000 (Unrated) — ★½
Two lovers commit suicide and as their respective old flames pick through their belongings they decide to begin a romance with each other. 90m; DVD, Streaming. **C:** Serge Lopez; Chete Lera; Miguel Pernas; Rosana Pastor; Maria Bouzas; Directed by Raul Veiga; Written by Raul Veiga; Cinematography by Juan Carlos Gomez; Music by Carles Cases. **A:** Sr. High-Adult. **P:** Entertainment. **U:** Home. **L:** English, Spanish. **Mov-Ent. Acq:** Purchase, Rent/Lease. **Dist:** Venevision International. $14.98 9.99.

ARDS: Adult Respiratory Distress Syndrome 1988
The many factors which cause this malady are accompanied by an explanation of why it's important that it be detected early. 28m; VHS, 3/4 U. **Pr:** Hospital Satellite Network. **A:** Adult. **P:** Professional. **U:** Institution, CCTV, SURA. **Hea-Sci**: Nursing, Diseases. **Acq:** Purchase, Rent/Lease. **Dist:** $275.00.

Are Current Reforms Going to Improve American Education? 19??
Discusses the current educational system and whether or not current reforms are going to make changes to this system. Discussion guide included. 60m; VHS. **A:** Adult. **P:** Education. **U:** Institution. **Gen-Edu**: Education. **Acq:** Purchase. **Dist:** Instructivision Inc. $44.95.

Are Parents People? 1925 — ★★
Lighthearted silent comedy about a young girl's successful attempts to reunite her feuding parents. It all begins as she runs away and spends the night in the office of a doctor she has grown to like. After a frantic night of searching, her parents are reunited through their love for her. 60m/B/W; Silent; VHS, DVD. **C:** Betty Bronson; Adolphe Menjou; Florence Vidor; Andre Beranger; Lawrence Gray; Mary Beth Milford; Emily Fitzroy; William Courtwright; Directed by Malcolm St. Clair; Written by Frances Agnew; Alice Duer Miller; Cinematography by Bert Glennon. **Pr:** Famous Players Company. **A:** Family. **P:** Entertainment. **U:** Home. **Mov-Ent**: Comedy--Romantic, Silent Films. **Acq:** Purchase. **Dist:** Grapevine Video; Paramount Pictures Corp. $16.95.

Are People All the Same? 1977
This part of the "Who We Are" series features live action and animation showing children the meaning of race and the uniqueness of each and every person. 9m; VHS, 3/4 U. **Pr:** John Korty. **A:** Primary-Jr. High. **P:** Education. **U:** Institution, Home, SURA. **Gen-Edu**: Minorities. **Acq:** Purchase, Rent/Lease, Duplication License. **Dist:** Pyramid Media.

Are the United States Courts Handcuffing the Press? 1980
This program in the "Issues in World Communications 1980" discusses the relationship between the courts and the press. 30m; VHS, 3/4 U. **C:** H. L. Stevensen; Murray Baron; James C. Goodall; Dale Spencer. **Pr:** Ohio University Telecommunications Center. **A:** College-Adult. **P:** Education. **U:** Institution, CCTV, SURA. **Gen-Edu**: Mass Media, Law. **Acq:** Purchase, Rent/Lease. **Dist:** WOUB Public Media.

Are Vows Made to Be Broken? 1990
Dr. Marra explores the Catholic conception of the nature of vows, particularly those of marriage and religion. 30m; VHS. **Pr:** KTF. **A:** Adult. **P:** Religious. **U:** Institution, Home. **Gen-Edu**. **Acq:** Purchase. **Dist:** Keep the Faith Inc. $20.00.

Are We Alone? 197?
Authors Will Ley and Walter Sullivan discuss the possibilities of life on other planets such as the Moon and Mars in this program. 30m/B/W; VHS, 3/4 U, EJ, Q. **Pr:** WCBS New York; Camera Three Productions. **A:** Family. **P:** Education. **U:** Institution, SURA. **Hea-Sci:** Science. **Acq:** Duplication, Free Duplication. **Dist:** Camera Three Productions, Inc.; Creative Arts Television Archive.

Are We Different? 19??
Interviews black teens about their racial experiences and other cultural issues. 27m; VHS. **A:** Jr. High-Adult. **P:** Education. **U:** Institution. **Gen-Edu:** Black Culture, Interviews. **Acq:** Purchase, Rent/Lease. **Dist:** Filmakers Library Inc. $295.00.

Are We Done Yet? 2007 (PG) — ★½
Apparently this sequel to "Are We There Yet?" is based on the 1948 Cary Grant comedy "Mr. Blandings Builds His Dream House" but don't count on it. Nick's (Ice Cube) married to divorcee-with-kids Suzanne (Long) and she announces she's preggers. Nick decides the family needs larger digs and leaves city life for a deceptively beautiful country house sold to them by slick/crazy contractor/building inspector/real estate salesman Chuck (scene-stealer McGinley). Of course their new abode is actually a homeowner's worst nightmare. If you liked the first Ice Cube family flick, this is more of the same. 92m; DVD, Blu-Ray. **C:** Ice Cube; Nia Long; John C. McGinley; Aleisha Allen; Philip Daniel Bolden; Directed by Steve Carr; Written by Hank Nelken; Cinematography by Jack N. Green; Music by Teddy Castellucci. **Pr:** Ted Hartley; Ice Cube; Matt Alvarez; Todd Garner; Revolution Studios; RKO Pictures; Cube Vision; Sony Pictures Home Entertainment Inc. **A:** Family. **P:** Entertainment. **U:** Home. **L:** English. **Mov-Ent:** Pregnancy, Real Estate. **Acq:** Purchase. **Dist:** Sony Pictures Home Entertainment Inc.

Are We Scaring Ourselves to Death? 1994
ABC News' John Stossel examines fears, including crime, toxic waste, cancer, and food, to see how likely they are to cause general harm and whether the press is exacerbating matters. 50m; VHS. **Pr:** ABC News. **A:** College-Adult. **P:** Education. **U:** Home, Institution. **Gen-Edu:** Journalism, Consumer Education. **Acq:** Purchase. **Dist:** MPI Media Group. $19.98.

Are We There Yet? 2005 (PG) — ★
Ice Cube is Nick Persons, an easygoing, charming ladies' man with a self-professed hatred of kids, when in walks his dream woman in the form of Suzanne (Long), an event planner. Suzanne, unfortunately for Nick, is a divorcee with two children, 11-year-old Lindsey (Allen) and 8-year-old Kevin (Bolden). Nick reconsiders his anti-kid rule, and decides to court Suzanne anyway. However, the two kids, who stubbornly believe that their parents will get back together, have decided to thwart any of their mother's would-be boyfriends. As luck would have it, their mother is needed in Vancouver to plan a New Year's Eve party and needs Nick to bring the kids to her. While Ice Cube is certainly enjoyable to watch, the kids are so obnoxious that the obvious question is, "is this movie done yet?" 91m; DVD, UMD. **C:** Ice Cube; Nia Long; Jay Mohr; M.C. Gainey; Aleisha Allen; Philip Daniel Bolden; Tracy Morgan; Nichelle Nichols; Directed by Brian Levant; Written by Steven Banks; Claudio Grazioso; J. David Stem; David N. Weiss; Cinematography by Thomas Ackerman; Music by David Newman. **Pr:** Dan Kolsrud; Ice Cube; Matt Alvarez; Cube Vision; Sony Pictures Entertainment. **A:** Primary-Adult. **P:** Entertainment. **U:** Home. **L:** English. **Mov-Ent. Acq:** Purchase. **Dist:** Sony Pictures Home Entertainment Inc. $28.95.

Are You Addicted? 1992
Two medical experts discuss symptoms, addictions, and the road back, and talk with three young people currently in recovery: a 24-year-old gambling addict, a 16-year-old girl with an eating disorder, and an 18-year-old drug and alcohol addict. 29m; VHS. **A:** Jr. High-Adult. **P:** Education. **U:** Institution. **Gen-Edu:** Health Education, Drugs, Alcoholism. **Acq:** Purchase. **Dist:** HRM Video; Human Relations Media. $189.00.

Are You Afraid of the Dark? The Complete 1st Season 1992
Features the Nickelodeon 1992-1996 television program about kids in the Midnight Society who gather in the woods to share scary stories. A strange man in the woods forces two lost brothers to solve riddles before letting them go, a girl's cousin makes her sleep over by herself in a haunted house or else she won't hang out with her, and two kids try to heal the aching heart of the ghost of a girl killed by a hit-and-run driver as she waited for her prom date. 13 episodes. 325m; DVD. **C:** Daniel Desanto; Joanna Garcia; Rose Hull; Jodie Resther; Raine Pare-Coull; Jason Alisharan. **A:** Family. **P:** Entertainment. **U:** Home. **Mov-Ent:** Television Series, Family, Children's Shows. **Acq:** Purchase. **Dist:** Direct Source Special Products, Inc. $29.99.

Are You Afraid of the Dark? The Complete 2nd Season 1993
Features the Nickelodeon 1992-1996 television program about kids in the Midnight Society who gather in the woods to share scary stories. A teenaged girl who wants to live in a fairy tale land finds it's not all that it appears, the ghost of a girl killed in a school chemistry-room accident lurks about her old locker, and after a boy's friend drowns he is haunted by his ghost. 13 episodes. 375m; DVD. **C:** Rose Hull; Jodie Resther; Jason Alisharan; Daniel Desanto; Raine Pare-Coull; Joanna Garcia. **A:** Family. **P:** Entertainment. **U:** Home. **Mov-Ent:** Television Series, Family, Children's Shows. **Acq:** Purchase. **Dist:** Direct Source Special Products, Inc. $29.99.

Are You Afraid of the Dark? The Complete 3rd Season 1994
Features the Nickelodeon 1992-1996 television program about kids in The Midnight Society who gather in the woods to share scary stories. Two lost campers stumble upon a wicked force in Watcher's Woods, a babysitter makes reading fun as she's able to bring books to life, and a house's ghost takes a girl and threatens two brothers who move in. 13 episodes. 325m; DVD. **C:** Rose Hull; Jodie Resther; Raine Pare-Coull; Jason Alisharan; Daniel Desanto; Joanna Garcia. **A:** Family. **P:** Entertainment. **U:** Home. **Mov-Ent:** Television Series, Family, Children's Shows. **Acq:** Purchase. **Dist:** Direct Source Special Products, Inc. $29.99.

Are You Being Served? 1991
The long-running British comedy series about the hapless denizens of Grace Brothers Department Store. Six episodes on two cassettes. 177m; VHS, DVD. **A:** Family. **P:** Entertainment. **U:** Home. **Mov-Ent:** Television Series. **Acq:** Purchase. **Dist:** Signals Video; Video Collectibles. $39.95.
Indiv. Titles: 1. Dear Sexy Knickers 2. Our Figures are Slipping 3. Camping In 4. Big Brother 5. His and Hers 6. Cold Comfort.

Are You Being Served? Christmas Special 1997
Four episodes starring the nutty employees of the Grace Brothers Department Store getting into serious high-jinks not only with each other, but with the frenzied Christmas shoppers. 120m; DVD, CC. **A:** Adult. **P:** Entertainment. **U:** Home. **Mov-Ent:** Comedy--Screwball, Christmas. **Acq:** Purchase. **Dist:** Warner Home Video, Inc. $14.98.

Are You Being Served? Volume 1 1972
Presents episodes from the 1972-1985 British television satire with the wacky goings-on of the Grace Brothers Department Store. The store decides to merge men's and women's clothing led by Mr. Grainger (Brough) and Mrs. Slocombe (Sugden) (the pilot); a drop in sales leads to an all-night-yet-unproductive meeting ("Our Figures Are Slipping"); and a new fragrance display causes problems ("His and Hers"), as well as "Dear Sexy Knickers," "Camping In," and "Diamonds Are a Man's Best Friend." 6 episodes. 180m; DVD. **C:** John Inman; Frank Thornton; Nicholas C. Smith; Mollie Sugden; Wendy Richard; Arthur Brough. **A:** Jr. High-Adult. **P:** Entertainment. **U:** Home. **Mov-Ent:** Television Series, Great Britain, Satire & Parody. **Acq:** Purchase. **Dist:** Warner Home Video, Inc. $19.98.

Are You Being Served? Volume 2 1974
Presents episodes from the 1972-1985 British television satire with the wacky goings-on of the Grace Brothers Department Store. Mr. Grainger (Brough) is worried that an anniversary dinner might really mean an early retirement ("The Clock"); things get cold at the store during a widespread fuel shortage ("Cold Comfort"); and Mr. Grainger and Mrs. Slocombe (Sugden) discover shoplifting is afoot which leads to the installation of intrusive security cameras ("Big Brother"), as well as "Think Tank," "Hoorah for Holidays," and "The Hand of Fate." 6 episodes. 180m; DVD. **C:** John Inman; Mollie Sugden; Frank Thornton; Wendy Richard; Nicholas C. Smith; Arthur Brough. **A:** Jr. High-Adult. **P:** Entertainment. **U:** Home. **Mov-Ent:** Television Series, Great Britain, Satire & Parody. **Acq:** Purchase. **Dist:** Warner Home Video, Inc. $19.98.

Are You Being Served? Volume 3 1975
Presents episodes from the 1972-1985 British television satire with the wacky goings-on of the Grace Brothers Department Store. Chaos ensues when Mr. Grainger's (Brough) slightly late lunch causes management to crack down on everyone's breaks ("Coffee Morning"); the ladies' department is remodeling and the men aren't so thrilled about making space for them ("Shoulder to Shoulder"); and the store has a sale on German goods but the Germans aren't pleased ("German Week") as well as "Up Captain Peacock," "Cold Store," and "Wedding Bells." 6 episodes. 180m; DVD. **C:** John Inman; Mollie Sugden; Frank Thornton; Wendy Richard; Nicholas C. Smith; Arthur Brough. **A:** Jr. High-Adult. **P:** Entertainment. **U:** Home. **Mov-Ent:** Television Series, Great Britain, Satire & Parody. **Acq:** Purchase. **Dist:** Warner Home Video, Inc. $19.98.

Are You Being Served? Volume 4 1975
Presents episodes from the 1972-1985 British television satire with the wacky goings-on of the Grace Brothers Department Store. Includes: the staff begrudgingly dons holiday attire ("Christmas Crackers"); early store hours prompt a revolt ("No Sale"); and Mr. Grainger (Brough) lets his temporary time as store manager get to his head ("Forward Mr. Grainger"), as well as "New Look," "Top Hat and Tails," and "Fire Practice." 6 episodes. 180m; DVD. **C:** John Inman; Mollie Sugden; Frank Thornton; Wendy Richard; Nicholas C. Smith; Arthur Brough. **A:** Jr. High-Adult. **P:** Entertainment. **U:** Home. **Mov-Ent:** Television Series, Great Britain, Satire & Parody. **Acq:** Purchase. **Dist:** Warner Home Video, Inc. $19.98.

Are You Being Served? Volume 5 197?
Presents episodes from the 1972-1985 British television satire with the wacky goings-on of the Grace Brothers Department Store. The staff wants to surprise Mrs. Solcombe (Sugden) with a 50th birthday party ("Fifty Years On"); Mrs. Solcombe's coworkers are shocked when they believe that she's pregnant when in fact it's her cat ("Mrs. Solcombe Expects"); and jobs get switched around at the store with some happy results ("A Change Is as Good as a Rest"), as well as "Oh What a Tangled Web" and "The Father Christmas Affair." 5 episodes. 150m; DVD. **C:** John Inman; Mollie Sugden; Frank Thornton; Wendy Richard; Nicholas C. Smith. **A:** Jr. High-Adult. **P:** Entertainment. **U:** Home. **Mov-Ent:** Television Series, Great Britain, Satire & Parody. **Acq:** Purchase. **Dist:** Warner Home Video, Inc. $19.98.

Are You Being Served? Volume 6 197?
Presents episodes from the 1972-1985 British television satire with the wacky goings-on of the Grace Brothers Department Store. Another company tries to acquire the store ("Takeover"); the staff can't take a grumpy Mr. Grainger (Brough) and decide to send him packing ("Goodbye, Mr. Grainger"), as well as "Founder's Day," "The Old Order Changes," and "It Pays to Advertise." 5 episodes. 150m; DVD. **C:** John Inman; Mollie Sugden; Frank Thornton; Wendy Richard; Nicholas C. Smith; Arthur Brough. **A:** Jr. High-Adult. **P:** Entertainment. **U:** Home. **Mov-Ent:** Television Series, Great Britain, Satire & Parody. **Acq:** Purchase. **Dist:** Warner Home Video, Inc. $19.98.

Are You Being Served? Volume 8 1981
Presents episodes from the 1972-1985 British television satire with the wacky goings-on of the Grace Brothers Department Store. A royal visit comes to a quick end ("By Appointment") and to save money someone must lose their job ("Shedding the Load"), as well as "The Club," "Do You Take This Man," "A Bliss Girl," and "Happy Returns." 6 episodes. 180m; DVD. **C:** John Inman; Mollie Sugden; Frank Thornton; Wendy Richard; Nicholas C. Smith. **A:** Jr. High-Adult. **P:** Entertainment. **U:** Home. **Mov-Ent:** Television Series, Great Britain, Satire & Parody. **Acq:** Purchase. **Dist:** Warner Home Video, Inc. $19.98.

Are You Being Served? Volume 9 1983
Presents episodes from the 1972-1985 British television satire with the wacky goings-on of the Grace Brothers Department Store. The staff panics about their insurance physicals while eavesdropping ("Strong Stuff This Insurance") and they must take on food detail after complaining to the caterers ("Anything You Can Do"), as well as "The Junior," "The Apartment," "Mrs. Solcombe, Senior Person," and "The Hero." 6 episodes. 180m; DVD. **C:** John Inman; Mollie Sugden; Frank Thornton; Wendy Richard; Nicholas C. Smith. **A:** Jr. High-Adult. **P:** Entertainment. **U:** Home. **Mov-Ent:** Television Series, Great Britain, Satire & Parody. **Acq:** Purchase. **Dist:** Warner Home Video, Inc. $19.98.

Are You Being Served? Volume 10 1985
Presents episodes from the 1972-1985 British television satire with the wacky goings-on of the Grace Brothers Department Store. Some staff are tempted to leave the store for another opportunity ("The Agent") and they might be sent down to the bargain basement, which sparks a rooftop rally ("Sit Out"), as well as "The Punch and Judy Affair," "Is It Catching?," "A Personal Problem," and "Front Page Story." 6 episodes. 180m; DVD. **C:** John Inman; Mollie Sugden; Frank Thornton; Wendy Richard; Nicholas C. Smith. **A:** Jr. High-Adult. **P:** Entertainment. **U:** Home. **Mov-Ent:** Television Series, Great Britain, Satire & Parody. **Acq:** Purchase. **Dist:** Warner Home Video, Inc. $19.98.

Are You Being Served? Volume 11 1981
Presents episodes from the 1972-1985 British television satire with the wacky goings-on of the Grace Brothers Department Store. Mrs. Solcombe (Sugden) has fantasies about Mr. Humphries (Inman) and then makes a move on him ("The Erotic Dreams of Mrs. Solcombe") and Mr. Humphries is accused of stealing from the store ("Conduct Unbecoming"), as well as "Heir Apparent," "Closed Circuit," "Roots?," and "The Sweet Smell of Success." 6 episodes. 180m; DVD. **C:** John Inman; Mollie Sugden; Frank Thornton; Wendy Richard; Nicholas C. Smith. **A:** Jr. High-Adult. **P:** Entertainment. **U:** Home. **Mov-Ent:** Television Series, Great Britain, Satire & Parody. **Acq:** Purchase. **Dist:** Warner Home Video, Inc. $19.98.

Are You Being Served? Volume 12 1983
Presents episodes from the 1972-1985 British television satire with the wacky goings-on of the Grace Brothers Department Store. Mrs. Solcombe (Sugeden) gets knocked for a loop ("Memories Are Made of This") and she switches her affections from her cat after it goes missing to Mr. Humphries (Inman) ("Lost and Found"), as well as "Calling All Customers," "Monkey Business," "Goodbye, Mrs. Slocombe," and "Grounds for Divorce." 6 episodes. 180m; DVD. **C:** John Inman; Mollie Sugden; Frank Thornton; Wendy Richard; Nicholas C. Smith. **A:** Jr. High-Adult. **P:** Entertainment. **U:** Home. **Mov-Ent:** Television Series, Great Britain, Satire & Parody. **Acq:** Purchase. **Dist:** Warner Home Video, Inc. $19.98.

Are You Being Served? Volume 13 1985
Presents episodes from the 1972-1985 British television satire with the wacky goings-on of the Grace Brothers Department Store. Includes: the staff tries to track down a thief ("The Hold Up") and the store becomes a nightclub though things don't proceed quite as planned ("The Night Club"), as well as "Gambling Fever," "Friends and Neighbors," and "The Pop Star." 5 episodes. 150m; DVD. **C:** John Inman; Mollie Sugden; Frank Thornton; Wendy Richard; Nicholas C. Smith. **A:** Jr. High-Adult. **P:** Entertainment. **U:** Home. **Mov-Ent:** Television Series, Great Britain, Satire & Parody. **Acq:** Purchase. **Dist:** Warner Home Video, Inc. $19.98.

Are You in the House Alone? 1978 — ★★
Adaptation of Richard Peck's award-winning novel. Story of a high school coed who becomes the target of a terror campaign. 100m; VHS. **C:** Blythe Danner; Kathleen Beller; Tony Bill; Scott Colomby; Directed by Walter Grauman; Music by Charles Bernstein. **Pr:** Charles Fries Productions. **A:** Jr. High-Adult. **P:** Entertainment. **U:** Home. **Mov-Ent:** Mystery & Suspense, TV Movies. **Acq:** Purchase. **Dist:** $49.95.

Are You Listening? 1932 (Unrated) — ★½
Haines' last film on his MGM contract turns out to be a more somber affair as wise-cracking radio writer Bill is tricked into confessing to the accidental death of his greedy wife Alice (Morley) on a phone-in program. 73m/B/W; DVD. **C:** William Haines; Karen Morley; Madge Evans; Anita Page; John Miljan; Neil Hamilton; Joan Marsh; Wallace Ford; Jean Hersholt; Directed by Harry Beaumont; Written by Dwight Taylor; Cinematography by Harold Rosson. **A:** Sr. High-Adult. **P:** Entertainment. **U:** Home. **Mov-Ent. Acq:** Purchase. **Dist:** WarnerArchive.com.

Are You Listening? 1979
Part of an integrated course designed to stimulate talking and thinking about human concerns within the organizational set-

ting. The ability to listen is emphasized throughout. 30m; 3/4 U. **Pr:** Martha Stuart Communications. **A:** College-Adult. **P:** Professional. **U:** Institution. **Bus-Ind:** Communication. **Acq:** Purchase, Rent/Lease. **Dist:** SkillSoft.
Indiv. Titles: 1. Women in Management (7MS-A01) 2. Women in Middle Management (7MS-A02) 3. Men Who Work with Women in Management (7MS-A03) 4. Shop Stewards (7MS-A04) 5. Older People (7MS-A05).

Are You Lonesome Tonight 1992 (PG-13) — ★★½
Suspense thriller casts Seymour as a wealthy socialite who discovers her husband is having an affair with a phone-sex girl. His sudden and mysterious disappearance forces her to hire a private detective (Stevenson) to track him down, with only the taped conversations as clues. Average cable TV fare. 91m; VHS, CC. **C:** Jane Seymour; Parker Stevenson; Beth Broderick; Joel Brooks; Robert Pine; Directed by E.W. Swackhamer; Written by Wesley Moore. **Pr:** Gordon Wolf; Wilshire Court Productions; OTML Productions Inc; The Mahoney Company. **A:** Sr. High-Adult. **P:** Entertainment. **U:** Home. **Mov-Ent:** Mystery & Suspense, Romance. **Acq:** Purchase, Rent/Lease. **Dist:** Paramount Pictures Corp. $19.95.

Are You My Mother?/Go, Dog, Go!/The Best Nest 1991
Three unrelated popular stories by P.D. Eastman are put to animation and narrated by various voices. 25m; VHS. **A:** Preschool. **P:** Entertainment. **U:** Home. **Chl-Juv:** Animation & Cartoons. **Acq:** Purchase. **Dist:** Random House of Canada Ltd. $9.95.

Are You Ready for Parenthood? 19??
Having a child and becoming a parent is one of the most important decisions a person can make. Issues surrounding the decision to become a parent are the focus of this video, which includes valid and invalid reasons for becoming a parent and the associated responsibilities. 12m; VHS. **A:** Sr. High. **P:** Education. **U:** Institution. **L:** English. **Gen-Edu:** Child Care. **Acq:** Purchase. **Dist:** Meridian Education Corp. $49.

Are You Ready for Sex? 1978
Depicts high school students discussing and dramatizing questions concerning teenage sexuality. 24m; 3/4 U, Special order formats. **Pr:** Mayor and Espar. **A:** Sr. High. **P:** Education. **U:** Institution, Home, SURA. **Hea-Sci:** Sex & Sexuality. **Acq:** Purchase, Rent/Lease, Trade-in, Duplication License. **Dist:** United Learning Inc.

Are You Ready for the Postpartum Experience? 1975
This is a parent education program that depicts the first weeks at home with a new baby. Designed for high school, adult, and professional use. 17m; VHS, 3/4 U, Special order formats. **Pr:** Courter Films. **A:** Sr. High-Adult. **P:** Education. **U:** Institution, CCTV, Home. **Gen-Edu:** Women, Parenting. **Acq:** Purchase. **Dist:** Parenting Pictures.

Are You Really Listening? 1991
A program designed to help managers and employers learn to listen actively—hearing not only words, but feelings and attitudes as well. 15m; VHS, 3/4 U, Special order formats. **Pr:** Britannica Films. **A:** College-Adult. **P:** Vocational. **U:** Institution. **Bus-Ind:** How-To, Business, Management. **Acq:** Purchase, Rent/Lease. **Dist:** Excellence in Training Corp. $495.00.

Are You Really There? 19??
Features a video for the song "Are You Really There?" written by George Blackburn during World War II, a love song that captures the feelings of a serviceman longing for home. 5m; VHS. **A:** Jr. High-Adult. **P:** Education. **U:** Home. **Gen-Edu:** War--General, Music Video. **Acq:** Purchase. **Dist:** The War Amps. $10.00.

Are You Satisfied? 1989
Ditka, football coach and master motivator, demonstrates the powers of motivation as a means of attaining all of your goals. Includes one discussion guide and one set of Blackline Masters. 35m; VHS, 3/4 U. **C:** Hosted by Mike Ditka. **A:** Sr. High-Adult. **P:** Education. **U:** Institution, CCTV, CATV, Home, SURA. **Gen-Edu:** Adolescence, Self-Help, Family. **Acq:** Purchase, Rent/Lease. **Dist:** United Learning Inc. $125.00.

Are You Scared 2 2009 (R) — ★
A group of young people competing in an online reality show involving treasure hunting are pursued by psychopaths sent by someone wishing to take advantage of their fame by murdering them all. 93m; DVD, Streaming. **C:** Adam Busch; Tony Todd; Andrea Monier; Kathy Gardiner; Directed by John Lands; Russell Appling; Written by John Lands; Russell Appling; Cinematography by John Lands; Music by Kevin Gradnigo. **A:** Sr. High-Adult. **P:** Entertainment. **U:** Home. **L:** English, Spanish. **Mov-Ent. Acq:** Purchase, Rent/Lease. **Dist:** Image Entertainment Inc. $14.98 9.93.

Are You Scared? 2006 (Unrated) — **Bomb!**
Scared only by this movie—a dire rip-off/combination of "Saw" and TV's "Fear Factor." Six young people wake up in an abandoned factory and learn they are contestants on the reality TV show of the title. They all have to face their worst fear—or die trying. 79m; DVD. **C:** Aletha Kutscher; Erin Consolvi; Carlee Avers; Soren Bowie; Kariem Marbury; Brad Ashten; Caia Coley; Brent Fidler; Directed by Andy Hurst; Written by Andy Hurst; Cinematography by Jeffrey Smith. **A:** Sr. High-Adult. **P:** Entertainment. **U:** Home. **Mov-Ent. Acq:** Purchase. **Dist:** Lions Gate Entertainment Inc.

Are You Talking to Me? 1990
Features more than 300 students from some 50 high schools performing in 60 real-life scenes portraying different levels of drug and alcohol involvement, focusing on awareness, confrontation, and self-help. 26m; VHS. **A:** Jr. High-Sr. High. **P:** Education. **U:** Institution. **Gen-Edu:** Education, Alcoholic Beverages, Drugs. **Acq:** Purchase. **Dist:** GPN Educational Media; Baker and Taylor. $195.00.

Are You with Me? 1989
Part of the AIDSFILMS Series. An urban teenager, whose friend dies of AIDS, and her mother discuss ways of becoming more assertive about safe sex, including asking their partners about past sexual experiences and the use of condoms. Includes guidebook. 17m; VHS, 3/4 U, Special order formats. **A:** Sr. High-Adult. **P:** Education. **U:** Institution. **Hea-Sci:** Health Education, AIDS, Sex & Sexuality. **Acq:** Purchase, Rent/Lease. **Dist:** Select Media, Inc. $65.00.

Area 51: America's Most Secret Base 1997
Investigates the mystery base in the Nevada desert that has attracted interested people worldwide and features never-before-seen footage of flying objects. 60m; VHS. **A:** Adult. **P:** Education. **U:** Home. **Gen-Edu:** Military History, Documentary Films. **Acq:** Purchase. **Dist:** Vanguard International Cinema, Inc. $24.98.

Area 88, Act I: The Blue Skies of Betrayal 1985 — ★★★½
Shin Kazuma is the best pilot in a mercenary air force fighting a war he doesn't care about in a middle eastern country he barely knew existed until he found himself legally bound to it. He must stay for two years... unless he can earn enough money to buy out his contract. With thrilling aerial combat scenes and contrasting portraits of Shin as a civilian and as a mercenary, this is a great beginning to a memorable three-part series. What makes the series unforgettable is the careful depiction of the physical, mental and emotional price Shin pays as he becomes an ace in his desperation to go home. If the character designs are slightly dated, the story is not and it remains among the best anime has to offer. Based on the comic book series by Kaoru Shintani. 50m; DVD. **A:** Sr. High-Adult. **P:** Entertainment. **U:** Home. **L:** Japanese, English. **Mov-Ent:** Anime, Animation & Cartoons. **Acq:** Purchase. **Dist:** Amazon.com Inc. $34.95.

Area 51 2011 (R) — ★½
Syfy Channel feature that keeps all its sci-fi cliches briskly moving along. Public and political pressure finally forces the Air Force to allow selected journalists limited access to their Area 51 base. Of course, this proves to be a disaster when one alien captive uses the visit to free itself and some other aliens and they go on a killing spree. 90m; DVD. **C:** Bruce Boxleitner; John Shea; Vanessa Branch; Lena Clark; Rachel Miner; Jason London; Damon Lipari; Billy Slaughter; Directed by Jason Connery; Written by Lucy Mukerjee; Cinematography by Yaron Levy; Music by Ian Honeyman. **A:** Sr. High-Adult. **P:** Entertainment. **U:** Home. **Mov-Ent:** TV Movies, Journalism, Science Fiction. **Acq:** Purchase. **Dist:** Lions Gate Entertainment Inc.

Area 51 Declassified 2011 (Unrated)
Some Americans think the infamous Area 51 is a figment of the collective imagination of alien conspiracy crackpots, and in a way, they're right—the famous military base does not officially exist. That said, the very real, but secret base was home to important, covert operations during the Cold War between the United States and Soviet Union, among other things. In this documentary, people with direct knowledge of Area 51 go on record and reveal, for the first time, what they know about all secret activities at the base, including those involving supposed extraterrestrials. 45m; DVD. **A:** Family. **P:** Education, Entertainment. **U:** Home, Institution. **Mov-Ent:** Documentary Films, Conspiracies or Conspiracy Theories, Military History. **Acq:** Purchase. **Dist:** $19.95.

The Arena 1973 (R) — ★★
Ancient Romans capture beautiful women from around the world and force them to compete in gladiatorial games. New World exploitation gem featuring mostly Italian cast, including Bay, who starred in the previous year's "Lady Frankenstein." 75m; VHS, DVD. **C:** Margaret Markov; Pam Grier; Lucretia Love; Paul Muller; Daniel Vargas; Marie Louise; Mary Count; Rosalba Neri; Vic Karis; Sid Lawrence; Peter Cester; Anna Melita; Directed by Steve Carver; Written by John W. Corrington; Joyce H. Corrington; Cinematography by Joe D'Amato; Music by Francesco De Masi. **Pr:** New World Pictures. **A:** Sr. High-Adult. **P:** Entertainment. **U:** Home. **Mov-Ent:** Slavery. **Acq:** Purchase. **Dist:** MGM Home Entertainment. $79.95.

Arena 1989 (PG-13) — ★★
Remember old boxing melodramas about good-natured palookas, slimy opponents, gangsters and dames? This puts those cliches in a garish sci-fi setting, with handsome Steve Armstrong battling ETs and the astro-mob to be the first human pugilistic champ in decades. A really cute idea (from the screenwriters of "The Rocketeer"), but it conks out at the halfway point. Worth a look for buffs. 97m; VHS, CC. **C:** Paul Satterfield; Claudia Christian; Hamilton Camp; Marc Alaimo; Armin Shimerman; Shari Shattuck; Jack Carter; Directed by Peter Manoogian; Written by Danny Bilson; Paul DeMeo; Music by Richard Band. **Pr:** Empire Pictures. **A:** Sr. High-Adult. **P:** Entertainment. **U:** Home. **Mov-Ent:** Science Fiction, Boxing. **Acq:** Purchase. **Dist:** Sony Pictures Home Entertainment Inc. $14.95.

The Arena 2001 (R) — ★★★
Recently, Roger Corman has been re-making the exploitation pictures he produced in the 1960s and '70s. The results have generally lacked the freshness and verve of the originals. This one is an exception. The Russian production is stylishly filmed and inventively edited. It looks like it cost much more than the Pam Grier version, though the story is just as silly. (Playboy Playmates are cast in the leads.) 92m; DVD. **C:** Lisa Dergan; Karen McDougal; Jennifer Murphy; Georgina Stoll; Solanie Keenan; Viktor Verzhbitsky; Anatoly Mambetrov; Directed by Timur Bekmambetov; Written by John W. Corrington; Cinematography by Olugbeck Khamraev; Music by Pavel Karmanov. **A:** College-Adult. **P:** Entertainment. **U:** Home. **Mov-Ent. Acq:** Purchase. **Dist:** New Horizons Picture Corp.

Arena 2011 (R) — ★½
What is Jackson doing in this violent, uninspired foolishness? A sadistic businessman (Jackson) runs an underground gladiatorial arena that kidnaps would-be fighters and forces them into death matches for online bettors. David's (Lutz) the latest combatant but winning becomes more than just a matter of survival for him. 94m; DVD. **C:** Kellan Lutz; Samuel L. Jackson; Nina Dobrev; Daniel Dae Kim; Johnny Messner; James Remar; Directed by Jonah Loop; Written by Robert Martinez; Martin Hultqvist; Cinematography by Nelson Cragg; Music by Jeff Danna. **A:** Sr. High-Adult. **P:** Entertainment. **U:** Home. **Mov-Ent. Acq:** Purchase. **Dist:** Sony Pictures Home Entertainment Inc.

Aretha Franklin: Greatest Hits 1980-1994 1994
Pop songstress' tunes include "Freeway of Love," "Who's Zoomin' Who," and more. 60m; VHS. **A:** Jr. High-Adult. **P:** Entertainment. **U:** Home. **Mov-Ent:** Music--Pop/Rock, Music--Performance. **Acq:** Purchase. **Dist:** Arista Records. $19.98.

Aretha Franklin: Ridin' on the Freeway 1987
A collection of Franklin's recent videos, including "I Know You Were Waiting (For Me)," "Freeway of Love," and "Jumpin' Jack Flash." In HiFi Stereo. 25m; VHS. **Pr:** Music Vision. **A:** Family. **P:** Entertainment. **U:** Home. **Mov-Ent:** Music Video. **Acq:** Purchase. **Dist:** Music Video Distributors; Sony Pictures Home Entertainment Inc. $14.95.

Aretha Franklin: The Queen of Soul 1989
Aretha's musical career is traced, beginning with her days as a Detroit gospel singer to clips of the performances which earned her her nickname "the Queen of Soul." Includes interviews with Aretha, as well as her family, friends and colleagues. 60m; VHS. **C:** Aretha Franklin; Rev. Cecil Franklin; Rev. James Cleveland; Clive Davis; Keith Richards; Ray Charles; Dionne Warwick; George Michael; Whitney Houston; Eric Clapton. **Pr:** Pacific Arts. **A:** Family. **P:** Entertainment. **U:** Home. **Mov-Ent:** Music--Performance, Biography. **Acq:** Purchase. **Dist:** WarnerVision; Music Video Distributors; Image Entertainment Inc. $19.95.

Argentina 1981
This experimental video examines the relationship between two producers and a third person of indeterminate sexuality. 7m; VHS, 3/4 U. **Pr:** Daniel Dion; Philippe Poloni. **A:** College-Adult. **P:** Education. **U:** Institution. **Fin-Art:** Video. **Acq:** Rent/Lease. **Dist:** Video Out Distribution.

Argentina 1991
A look at Argentina's geography and population. 40m; VHS. **A:** Primary-Sr. High. **P:** Education. **U:** Institution. **Gen-Edu:** South America, Geography, Population. **Acq:** Purchase. **Dist:** QUSA. $49.95.

Argentina: Recuerdos del Noroeste 19??
Bilingual program that outlines the influence of the gauchos in the land of the Pampas. Comes with teacher's manual. 34m; VHS. **A:** Jr. High-Adult. **P:** Education. **U:** Institution. **L:** English, Spanish. **Gen-Edu:** Hispanic Culture, South America, History. **Acq:** Purchase. **Dist:** Educational Video Network. $39.95.

Argentina's Jews: Days of Awe 1990
A depiction of Argentine Jewry, including attempts to cope with anti-Semitism and loss of identity. 55m; VHS. **Pr:** Ergo Media. **A:** Sr. High-Adult. **P:** Education. **U:** Home. **Gen-Edu:** Judaism, South America. **Acq:** Purchase. **Dist:** Ergo Media Inc. $34.95.

Argentine Nights 1940 (Unrated) — ★½
The Ritz Brothers arrive broke in Argentina with their all-girl band and try to save a local hotel from a con man. Debut of The Andrews Sisters. 75m/B/W; VHS. **C:** Al Ritz; Andrews Sisters; George Reeves; Peggy Moran; Anne Nagel; Constance Moore; Harry Ritz; Jimmy Ritz; Directed by Albert Rogell; Written by Ray Golden; Arthur T. Horman; Sid Kuller; Cinematography by Elwood "Woody" Bredell. **A:** Jr. High-Adult. **P:** Entertainment. **U:** Home. **Mov-Ent:** Hotels & Hotel Staff Training, Comedy--Screwball, South America. **Acq:** Purchase. **Dist:** Nostalgia Family Video/Hollywood's Attic. $19.99.

Argentine Tango Instructional Video I 1992
Two dancers discuss and demonstrate the steps of the Argentine Tango, stressing improvisation when dancing salon-style. 43m; VHS. **A:** College-Adult. **P:** Instruction. **U:** Home. **How-Ins:** How-To, Dance--Instruction. **Acq:** Purchase. **Dist:** Tanguero Productions. $29.95.

Argentinian Grotesque Theatre 1983
Argentinian actor Osvaldo Terranova performs three short dramatic pieces. 30m; VHS, 3/4 U. **Pr:** New Jersey Network. **A:** Sr. High-Adult. **P:** Entertainment. **U:** Institution. **L:** Spanish. **Fin-Art:** Theater. **Acq:** Purchase, Rent/Lease. **Dist:** New Jersey Network.

Argento Soma - Volume 1: Another Reality 2000
Presents episodes from the anime series set in the year 2058 after ornery aliens have inhabited the Earth; during a scientific experiment based on the aliens a tragic accident occurs that leaves Takuto disfigured and his girlfriend dead, causing him to reinvent himself as Lt. Ryu Soma and plotting revenge. Includes: "Rebirth and Death," "Death and the Maiden," "The Maiden and the Meeting," "The Meeting and the Hatred," and "Hatred and War." 5 episodes. 125m; DVD. **A:** Jr. High-Adult. **P:** Entertainment. **U:** Home. **Mov-Ent:** Television Series, Anime, Action-Adventure. **Acq:** Purchase. **Dist:** Bandai Entertainment Inc. $29.98.

Argento Soma - Volume 2: Getting Even 2000
Presents episodes from the anime series set in the year 2058 after ornery aliens have inhabited the Earth; during a scientific experiment based on the aliens a tragic accident occurs that leaves Takuto disfigured and his girlfriend dead, causing him to reinvent himself as Lt. Ryu Soma and plotting revenge. Includes: "War and Escape," "Escape and Memory," "Memory and Loneliness," "Loneliness and Sorrow," and "Sorrow and Malice." 5 episodes. 125m; DVD. **A:** Jr. High-Adult. **P:** Entertainment. **U:** Home. **Mov-Ent**: Television Series, Anime, Action-Adventure. **Acq**: Purchase. **Dist**: Bandai Entertainment Inc. $29.98.

Argento Soma - Volume 3: No Tears 2000
Presents episodes from the anime series set in the year 2058 after aliens have inhabited the Earth; during a scientific experiment based on the aliens a tragic accident occurs that leaves Takuto disfigured and his girlfriend dead, causing him to reinvent himself as Lt. Ryu Soma and plotting revenge. Includes: "Malice and Betrayal," "Betrayal and Despair," "Despair and Hope," and "Hope and Chaos."4 episodes. 100m; DVD. **A:** Jr. High-Adult. **P:** Entertainment. **U:** Home. **Mov-Ent**: Television Series, Anime, Action-Adventure. **Acq**: Purchase. **Dist**: Bandai Entertainment Inc. $29.98.

Argento Soma - Volume 4: Outside Sanity 2000
Presents episodes from the anime series set in the year 2058 after ornery aliens have inhabited the Earth; during a scientific experiment based on the aliens a tragic accident occurs that leaves Takuto disfigured and his girlfriend dead, causing him to reinvent himself as Lt. Ryu Soma and plotting revenge. Includes: "Chaos and Confusion," "Confusion and Answers," "Answers and the Past," and "The Past and Crimes." 4 episodes. 100m; DVD. **A:** Jr. High-Adult. **P:** Entertainment. **U:** Home. **Mov-Ent**: Television Series, Anime, Action-Adventure. **Acq**: Purchase. **Dist**: Bandai Entertainment Inc. $29.98.

Argento Soma - Volume 5: Our Memories 2000
Presents episodes from the anime series set in the year 2058 after ornery aliens have inhabited the Earth; during a scientific experiment based on the aliens a tragic accident occurs that leaves Takuto disfigured and his girlfriend dead causing him to reinvent himself as Lt. Ryu Soma and plotting revenge. Includes: "Crimes and Punishment," and "Punishment and Awakening," "Awakening and Truth," and "Truth and Destruction." 5 episodes. 100m; DVD. **A:** Jr. High-Adult. **P:** Entertainment. **U:** Home. **Mov-Ent**: Television Series, Anime, Action-Adventure. **Acq**: Purchase. **Dist**: Bandai Entertainment Inc. $29.98.

Argento Soma - Volume 6: Annihilation 2000
Presents episodes from the anime series set in the year 2058 after ornery aliens have inhabited the Earth; during a scientific experiment based on the aliens a tragic accident occurs that leaves Takuto disfigured and his girlfriend dead causing, him to reinvent himself as Lt. Ryu Soma and plotting revenge. Includes: "Destruction and Courage," "Courage and Love," and "Love and Rebirth." 3 episodes. 100m; DVD. **A:** Jr. High-Adult. **P:** Entertainment. **U:** Home. **Mov-Ent**: Television Series, Anime, Action-Adventure. **Acq**: Purchase. **Dist**: Bandai Entertainment Inc. $29.98.

Argento's Dracula 3D 2013 (Unrated) — ★
Schlocky kitsch horror filled with sex, gore, and cheap effects (just wait until Dracula turns into a giant praying mantis). Argento sticks to the basics of the Bram Stoker novel with Jonathan Harker coming to work for the bloodsucker who soon has designs on Harker's sweet wife, Mina. Meanwhile, Mina's sexy friend, Lucy, becomes a victim and Dracula is hunted by vampire slayer Van Helsing. 106m; Blu-Ray, On Demand. **C:** Thomas Kretschmann; Marta Gastini; Asia Argento; Unax Ugalde; Rutger Hauer; Miriam Giovanelli; Giovanni Franzoni; Directed by Dario Argento; Written by Dario Argento; Enrique Cerezo; Cinematography by Luciano Tovoli; Music by Claudio Simonetti. **Pr:** IFC Midnight. **A:** Sr. High-Adult. **P:** Entertainment. **U:** Home. **L:** English. **Mov-Ent**: Horror. **Acq**: Rent/Lease. **Dist**: Amazon.com Inc.

Argo 2012 (R) — ★★★★
Affleck's skillful retelling of a recently declassified aspect of the Iranian hostage crisis offers impressive attention to detail, but never loses sight of the emotional journey of the characters involved. The film details the invention of a faux Hollywood production in order to "exfiltrate" six Americans from Iran during the crisis. Affleck stars as the man with the daring plan, giving a remarkably strong if reserved performance that allows supporting players like Cranston, Arkin, and Goodman to shine. Producing tension in a story for which most viewers know the ending, Affleck proves his first two directorial efforts to be no mere flukes. 120m; DVD, Blu-Ray. **C:** Ben Affleck; Alan Arkin; Bryan Cranston; John Goodman; Kyle Chandler; Rory Cochrane; Tate Donovan; Titus Welliver; Richard Kind; Victor Garber; Clea DuVall; Taylor Schilling; Directed by Ben Affleck; Written by Chris Terrio; Cinematography by Rodrigo Prieto; Music by Alexandre Desplat. **Pr:** George Clooney; Grant Heslov; Ben Affleck; GK Films; Smokehouse Pictures; Warner Bros. **A:** Sr. High-Adult. **P:** Entertainment. **U:** Home. **L:** English. **Mov-Ent**: Iran, Intelligence Service. **Awds**: Oscars '12: Adapt. Screenplay, Film, Film Editing; British Acad. '12: Director (Affleck), Film, Film Editing; Directors Guild '12: Director, Director (Affleck); Golden Globes '13: Director (Affleck), Film--Drama; Screen Actors Guild '12: Cast; Writers Guild '12: Adapt. Screenplay. **Acq**: Purchase. **Dist**: Warner Home Video, Inc.

The Argon Laser in Otology 1981
Basic laser science, laser biologic effects on tissue, instrumentation, and current clinical applications in stapedectomy for otosclerosis, myringotomy, myringoplasty, and other reconstructive surgery uses for the new argon microsurgical laser are presented in this program. 59m; VHS, 3/4 U. **Pr:** House Ear Institute. **A:** College-Adult. **P:** Professional. **U:** Institution, CCTV. **Hea-Sci**: Ear. **Acq**: Purchase. **Dist**: House Research Institute.

Arguing the World 1998
Irving Howe, Daniel Bell, Nathan Glazer, and Irving Kristol were young radicals at New York's City College in the 1930s. They've spent the next 40 years arguing ideas and politics—from Marxism to McCarthyism to the New Left. 109m; VHS, DVD. **C:** Directed by Joseph Dorman; Written by Joseph Dorman. **A:** College-Adult. **P:** Education. **U:** Home, Institution. **Gen-Edu**: Interviews, Philosophy & Ideology. **Acq**: Purchase. **Dist**: First Run Features.

An Argument About a Marriage 1969
The complexities of marriage rules and bride-service in a kinship system are presented. 18m; 3/4 U. **Pr:** Laurence Marshall; John Marshall. **A:** Sr. High-Adult. **P:** Education. **U:** Institution, SURA. **Gen-Edu**: Africa, Anthropology. **Acq**: Purchase. **Dist**: Documentary Educational Resources.

Aria 1988 (R) — ★★
Ten directors were given carte blanche to interpret ten arias from well-known operas. Henry and D'Angelo star in Julian Temple's rendition of Verdi's "Rigoletto." In Fonda's film debut, she and her lover travel to Las Vegas and eventually kill themselves in the bathtub, just like "Romeo & Juliet." Jarman's piece (a highlight) shows an aged operatic star at her last performance remembering an early love affair. "I Pagliacci" is the one aria in which the director took his interpretation in a straightforward manner. 90m; VHS, DVD. **C:** Theresa Russell; Anita Morris; Bridget Fonda; Beverly D'Angelo; Buck Henry; John Hurt; Directed by Ken Russell; Charles Sturridge; Robert Altman; Bill Bryden; Jean-Luc Godard; Bruce Beresford; Nicolas Roeg; Franc Roddam; Derek Jarman; Julien Temple; Written by Ken Russell; Charles Sturridge; Robert Altman; Bill Bryden; Jean-Luc Godard; Bruce Beresford; Nicolas Roeg; Franc Roddam; Derek Jarman; Julien Temple; Cinematography by Caroline Champetier; Oliver Stapleton; Gale Tattersall. **Pr:** Don Boyd; Miramax. **A:** College-Adult. **P:** Entertainment. **U:** Home. **Mov-Ent**: Film--Avant-Garde. **Acq**: Purchase. **Dist**: Facets Multimedia Inc.; Lightyear Entertainment. $29.95.

Ariel 1989 (Unrated) — ★★★
Refreshing, offbeat Finnish comedy by highly praised newcomer Kaurismaki. Hoping to find work in Southern Finland, an out-of-work miner from Northern Finland (Pajala) jets off in his white Cadillac convertible given to him in a cafe by a friend, who promptly shoots himself. There's no linear progression toward a happy ending, although antiheroic subject does find employment and romances a meter maid. Mostly, though, he's one of those it's hell being me guys who wouldn't have any luck if it weren't for bad luck. Strange slice-of-life sporting film noir tendencies, although essentially anti-stylistic. 74m; VHS, DVD. **C:** Susanna Haavisto; Turo Pajala; Matti Pellonpaa; Directed by Aki Kaurismaki; Written by Aki Kaurismaki; Cinematography by Timo Salminen. **A:** Jr. High-Adult. **P:** Entertainment. **U:** Home. **Mov-Ent**: Comedy--Black. **Awds**: Natl. Soc. Film Critics '90: Foreign Film. **Acq**: Purchase. **Dist**: Criterion Collection Inc.; Facets Multimedia Inc. $79.95.

Ariel's Undersea Adventure, Vol. 1: Whale of a Tale 1992
Join Ariel and her friends in two exciting undersea adventures. In "A Whale of a Tale," Ariel adopts a lost baby whale, and with the help of Sebastian and Flounder, tries to hide him from her father until the whale's family can find him. In "Urchin," Ariel makes friends with a mer-boy who has been swimming with gangsters and their friendship is put to the test. 44m; VHS. **Pr:** Disney. **A:** Family. **P:** Entertainment. **U:** Home. **Chl-Juv**: Animation & Cartoons, Family Viewing. **Acq**: Purchase. **Dist**: Walt Disney Studios Home Entertainment. $12.99.

Ariel's Undersea Adventure, Vol. 2: Stormy the Wild Seahorse 1993
Join Ariel in two exciting undersea adventures! In "Stormy the Wild Seahorse," Ariel tries to tame a wild seahorse against her father's and Sebastian's words to the wise. "The Great Sebastian" follows Sebastian as he travels through shark-infested waters with Ariel and Flounder in tow. 44m; VHS. **Pr:** Walt Disney Productions. **A:** Preschool-Primary. **P:** Entertainment. **U:** Home. **Chl-Juv**: Animation & Cartoons, Family Viewing. **Acq**: Purchase. **Dist**: Buena Vista Home Entertainment. $12.99.

Ariel's Undersea Adventure, Vol. 3: Double Bubble 1993
Join Ariel and friends in two exciting undersea adventures! "Double Bubble" finds Ariel with her hands full babysitting mer-twins, while at the same time trying to foil the kidnapping schemes of Lobster Mobster and Da Shrimp. In "Message in a Bottle," Ariel meets Simon the Sea Monster. He's so boisterous that everyone is afraid of him, that is until he saves the day by protecting the castle from sea-enemies. 44m; VHS. **A:** Preschool-Primary. **P:** Entertainment. **U:** Home. **Chl-Juv**: Animation & Cartoons, Family Viewing. **Acq**: Purchase. **Dist**: Buena Vista Home Entertainment. $12.99.

Ariel's Undersea Adventure, Vol. 4: In Harmony 1993
Two more adventures from the popular series. "In Harmony" finds Ariel mistakenly freeing the Evil Manta from a dormant undersea volcano and the creature tries to destoy Atlantica. Fortunately, Ariel and Flounder's friendship saves the day. Ariel is warned by her father Triton never to play with things from the human world in "Charmed." But when she finds a beautiful charm bracelet she can't resist putting it on and it leads her into all sorts of trouble. 44m; VHS, CC. **A:** Preschool-Primary. **P:** Entertainment. **U:** Home. **Chl-Juv**: Animation & Cartoons. **Acq**: Purchase. **Dist**: Walt Disney Studios Home Entertainment. $12.99.

Ariel's Undersea Adventure, Vol. 5: Ariel's Gift 1993
A magic youth stone turns King Triton into a young boy who calls himself "Red" and Ariel tries to keep him out of mischief until she can find a way to remove the magic spell. In "Trident True" Ariel wants to give Triton a special gift for Father's Day but she winds up in trouble as usual. 44m; VHS, CC. **A:** Preschool-Primary. **P:** Entertainment. **U:** Home. **Chl-Juv**: Animation & Cartoons. **Acq**: Purchase. **Dist**: Walt Disney Studios Home Entertainment. $12.99.

Aries Spears: Hollywood, Look I'm Smiling 2011 (Unrated)
Taped performance of former Mad TV star Aries Spears as he riffs on controversial topics. 90m; DVD. **A:** Sr. High-Adult. **P:** Entertainment. **U:** Home, Institution. **Gen-Edu**: Comedy--Performance, Performing Arts. **Acq**: Purchase. **Dist**: Comedy Central; Vivendi Visual Entertainment. $19.97.

Arise from Darkness 19??
Fr. Benedict Groeschel presents this inspirational program that examines the religious factors that have helped people overcome handicaps in order to lead good lives. 180m; VHS. **A:** Family. **P:** Religious. **U:** Home. **Gen-Edu**: Religion, Handicapped. **Acq**: Purchase. **Dist**: Ignatius Press. $19.95.

Aristide and the Endless Revolution 2006
Explores the life of popular Haitian president Jean-Bertrand Aristide, focusing on the later years of his presidency before going into exile in 2004. 82m; DVD. **A:** Sr. High-Adult. **P:** Entertainment. **U:** Home. **Mov-Ent**: Biography: Politics, Documentary Films, Caribbean. **Acq**: Purchase. **Dist**: First Run Features. $24.95.

The Aristocats 1970 — ★★★
Typically entertaining Disney animated story about pampered pussy Duchess (Gabor) and her three kittens, who are left a fortune in their mistress' will. The fortune goes to the butler if the cats don't survive, so he dumps them in the country hoping they won't find their way home. The cats are aided by tough alley denizen O'Malley (Harris)?it's kind of the feline version of "Lady and the Tramp." Maurice Chevalier sings the title tune. 78m; VHS, DVD, Blu-Ray. **C:** Voice(s) by Eva Gabor; Phil Harris; Sterling Holloway; Roddy Maude-Roxby; Bill Thompson; Hermione Baddeley; Carol(e) Shelley; Pat Buttram; Nancy Kulp; Paul Winchell; Directed by Wolfgang Reitherman; Music by George Bruns. **Pr:** Wolfgang Reitherman; Wolfgang Reitherman; Buena Vista. **A:** Family. **P:** Entertainment. **U:** Home. **Mov-Ent**: Animation & Cartoons, Pets, Family Viewing. **Acq**: Purchase. **Dist**: Walt Disney Studios Home Entertainment. $26.99.

Aristocrats 1999 (Unrated) — ★★½
Lavish BBC historical drama based on Stella Tillyard's biography about aristocratic life in 18th-century Britain and Ireland as seen through the eyes of the Lennox sisters. Daughters of the Duke of Richmond and great-granddaughters of Charles II (via an illegitimate son), the sisters find marriage, politics, and family ties intertwining. 293m; DVD. **C:** Serena Gordon; Geraldine Somerville; Anne-Marie Duff; Jodhi May; Alun Armstrong; Ben Daniels; Julian Fellowes; Toby Jones; Narrated by Sian Phillips; Directed by David Caffrey; Written by Harriet O'Carroll; Cinematography by James Welland; Music by Mark Thomas. **A:** Sr. High-Adult. **P:** Entertainment. **U:** Home. **L:** English. **Mov-Ent**: Family, Marriage, TV Movies. **Acq**: Purchase. **Dist**: Acorn Media Group Inc.

The Aristocrats 1999 — ★★½
True story of the scandalous 18th-century aristocratic Lennox family, including the four beautiful sisters whose elopements, liaisons, and intrigues provided ample English gossip. Based on the novel by Stella Tillyard. Three cassettes. 255m; VHS, DVD, CC. **C:** Jodhi May; Geraldine Somerville; Serena Gordon; Anne-Marie Duff; Alun Armstrong; Julian Fellowes; Ben Daniels; Diane Fletcher; Clive Swift; Sian Phillips; Richard Dempsey; Directed by David Caffrey; Written by Harriet O'Carroll. **A:** Sr. High-Adult. **P:** Entertainment. **U:** Home. **Mov-Ent**: Marriage. **Acq**: Purchase. **Dist**: Movies Unlimited; Alpha Video.

The Aristocrats 2005 (Unrated) — ★★★
"A family walks into a talent agency..." and so begins the raunchiest joke in cinematic history. It might seem odd to dedicate an entire documentary to one joke, but co-directors Provenza and Jillette excel at demonstrating how different comedians bring their own unique interpretations to the same material. The all-star interviewees (George Carlin, Chris Rock, and Robin Williams, among many others) speak elegantly about the joys of working "blue," although the true tour-de-force performances come from Bob Saget, Gilbert Gottfried, and Sarah Silverman, who all give blisteringly filthy renditions of the titular joke that you'll be talking about for weeks to come. 87m; DVD. **C:** Directed by Paul Provenza; Music by Gary Stockdale. **Pr:** Peter Adam Golden; Mighty Cheese. **A:** College-Adult. **P:** Entertainment. **U:** Home. **L:** English. **Mov-Ent**: Documentary Films, Comedy--Performance. **Acq**: Purchase. **Dist**: Velocity Home Entertainment.

Aristotle's Ethics: Theory of Happiness 1963
A discussion of the philosophical problems of what makes a human life good. 36m; VHS, 3/4 U. **Pr:** Encyclopedia Britannica Educational Corporation. **A:** Sr. High-College. **P:** Education. **U:** Institution, SURA. **Gen-Edu**: Philosophy & Ideology. **Acq**: Purchase, Rent/Lease, Trade-in. **Dist**: Encyclopedia Britannica.

Arithmetic Disabilities 1976
The relationship of arithmetic disorders to memory, perception, reading comprehension, and written language disorders is demonstrated by children experiencing these problems. 30m; VHS, 3/4 U. **Pr:** Learning Disabilities Council. **A:** College-Adult. **P:** Education. **U:** Institution, SURA. **Gen-Edu:** Mathematics, Learning Disabilities. **Acq:** Purchase. **Dist:** Home Vision Cinema.

Arithmetic Review 1987
This film is a 2-hour review of arithmetic, including whole numbers, fractions, decimals, ratios, and percents. 120m; VHS. **Pr:** VAI. **A:** Sr. High-Adult. **P:** Education. **U:** Home. **Gen-Edu:** Education, Mathematics. **Acq:** Purchase. **Dist:** Moonbeam Publications Inc.; Video Aided Instruction Inc. $29.95.

Arizona 1931 (Unrated) — ★★
Wayne's inexperience shows in this romantic drama. West Point cadet Bob Gunton (Wayne) refuses to commit to girlfriend Evelyn (La Plante) and she marries his mentor Frank Bonham (Stanley). The Bonhams move to an Arizona Army post where Bob is also posted. Instead of being upset, Bob starts wooing Evelyn's younger sister Bonnie (Clyde), which definitely angers Evelyn. 70m/B/W; DVD. **C:** Laura La Plante; John Wayne; Forrest Stanley; June Clyde; Directed by George B. Seitz; Written by Robert Riskin; Cinematography by Ted Tetzlaff. **A:** Adult. **P:** Entertainment. **U:** Home. **L:** English. **Mov-Ent:** Armed Forces--U.S., Marriage, Romance. **Acq:** Purchase. **Dist:** Warner Home Video, Inc.

Arizona 1940 — ★★½
Arthur is a hellion in wild 1860 Tucson who falls for the wandering Holden. He's headed for California and she can't keep him in town so Arthur throws herself into business by establishing a freight line. Only warring Apaches try to burn her out and Holden rides in to save the day (with the cavalry and a stampeding cattle herd). Holden's first western is lively but long. 121m/B/W; VHS, DVD. **C:** Jean Arthur; William Holden; Warren William; Porter Hall; Paul Harvey; George Chandler; Regis Toomey; Edgar Buchanan; Directed by Wesley Ruggles; Written by Claude Binyon; Music by Victor Young. **Pr:** Wesley Ruggles; Wesley Ruggles; Columbia Pictures. **A:** Jr. High-Adult. **P:** Entertainment. **U:** Home. **Mov-Ent:** Western, Women, Romance. **Acq:** Purchase. **Dist:** Sony Pictures Home Entertainment Inc. $14.95.

Arizona 1986 (Unrated) — ★½
A group of illegal aliens struggle for survival after they cross the border into the harsh desert. 94m; VHS. **C:** Roberto "Flaco" Guzman; Juan Valentin; Anna De Sade; Gilberto Trujillo; Directed by Fernando Duran Rojas; Written by Hector Kiev; Cinematography by Manuel Tejada; Music by Gustavo Cesar Carrion. **A:** College-Adult. **P:** Entertainment. **U:** Home. **Mov-Ent:** Immigration. **Acq:** Purchase. **Dist:** Amazon.com Inc.

Arizona Bad Man 1935 (Unrated) — ★½
Cattleman's Association detective Steve Donovan is sent after cattle rustler Bart Dunston and his henchman Pedro who are working with outlaw Sonny Karns. Bart is also evil enough to mistreat his two stepchildren, whom Steve tries to help. Steve gets into trouble but help comes from some unexpected sources. 58m/B/W; DVD. **C:** Reb Russell; Lois January; Slim Whitaker; Dick Botiller; Edmund Cobb; Tommy Bupp; Directed by S. Roy Luby; Written by Oliver Drake; Cinematography by James S. Brown, Jr. **A:** Jr. High-Adult. **P:** Entertainment. **U:** Home. **Mov-Ent:** Western. **Acq:** Purchase. **Dist:** Sinister Cinema.

Arizona Badman 1935 — ★½
There is a bad man in Arizona, and he must be gotten rid of. 60m/B/W; VHS. **C:** Reb Russell; Directed by S. Roy Luby. **A:** Family. **P:** Entertainment. **U:** Home. **Mov-Ent:** Western. **Acq:** Purchase, Rent/Lease. **Dist:** Sinister Cinema. $19.95.

Arizona Bound 1941 — ★
Mesa City is infested with a villain and our "Rough Rider" trio must rid the town of him. 57m/B/W; VHS, DVD. **C:** Buck Jones; Tim McCoy; Raymond Hatton; Dennis Moore; Luana Walters; Directed by Spencer Gordon Bennet. **Pr:** Monogram. **A:** Family. **P:** Entertainment. **U:** Home. **Mov-Ent:** Western. **Acq:** Purchase. **Dist:** Movies Unlimited; Alpha Video. $19.95.

Arizona Bushwackers 1967 — ★½
Routine western that has Confederate spy Keel taking job as sheriff in small Arizona town. Once there, he has to straighten out a few bad guys who have been selling weapons to the Apaches. Notable for presence of old western-movie veterans Ireland, Donlevy, Brady, and MacLane. Based on a story by Steve Fisher. 87m; VHS, Streaming. **C:** Howard Keel; Yvonne De Carlo; John Ireland; Marilyn Maxwell; Scott Brady; Brian Donlevy; Barton MacLane; Directed by Lesley Selander. **Pr:** Paramount Pictures. **A:** Jr. High-Adult. **P:** Entertainment. **U:** Home. **Mov-Ent:** Western. **Acq:** Purchase. **Dist:** Paramount Pictures Corp. $14.95.

Arizona Cyclone 1941 (Unrated) — ★½
Tom Baxter runs the freight lines for George Randolph and his daughter Claire against competitor Quirt Crenshaw. Town banker Adam Draper, in cahoots with Crenshaw, wants to discredit the Randolphs because he knows a lucrative hauling contract is about to be awarded. So he hires a gang of outlaws to steal a gold shipment and Baxter must save the day. 59m/B/W; DVD. **C:** Johnny Mack Brown; Fuzzy Knight; Nell O'Day; Herbert Rawlinson; Dick Curtis; Robert Strange; Glenn Strange; Kathryn Adams; Directed by Joseph H. Lewis; Written by Sherman Lowe; Cinematography by Charles Van Enger. **A:** Family. **P:** Entertainment. **U:** Home. **Mov-Ent:** Western. **Acq:** Purchase. **Dist:** Movies Unlimited.

Arizona Days 1937 — ★½
Cowboys join a minstrel group and rescue the show when a group of toughs try to break it up. 56m/B/W; VHS, DVD. **C:** Tex Ritter; Eleanor Stewart; Syd Saylor; Snub Pollard; Directed by John English. **Pr:** Grand National Productions. **A:** Family. **P:** Entertainment. **U:** Home. **Mov-Ent:** Western. **Acq:** Purchase. **Dist:** VCI Entertainment. $19.95.

The Arizona Diamondbacks 2001 World Series: Collector's Edition 20??
Presents the A&E cable channel special on the stunning seven-game victory by the 2001 Arizona Diamondbacks over the New York Yankees in the World Series, which had been delayed to late October after the September 11 terrorist attacks. 1129m; DVD. **A:** Family. **P:** Entertainment. **U:** Home, CATV. **Spo-Rec:** Television Series, Documentary Films, Biography: Sports. **Acq:** Purchase. **Dist:** A&E Television Networks L.L.C. $19.95.

Arizona Dream 1994 (R) — ★★
Alex (Depp) is a New York drifter who gets stuck working for his uncle's (Lewis) car dealership in a small Arizona town. He meets an eccentric older woman (Dunaway) with a homemade plane and some dreams of her own. Tends toward the surreal and confusing. 119m; VHS, DVD, CC. **C:** Johnny Depp; Faye Dunaway; Jerry Lewis; Lili Taylor; Paulina Porizkova; Tricia Leigh Fisher; Vincent Gallo; Directed by Emir Kusturica; Written by Emir Kusturica; David Atkins; Cinematography by Vilko Filac. **Pr:** Claudie Ossard. **A:** Sr. High-Adult. **P:** Entertainment. **U:** Home. **Mov-Ent:** Comedy-Drama. **Acq:** Purchase. **Dist:** WarnerArchive.com.

Arizona Gunfighter 1937 — ★
A young cowhand seeks revenge against the man who murdered his father in this western. 60m/B/W; VHS, DVD. **C:** Bob Steele; Ted Adams; Ernie Adams; Directed by Sam Newfield. **Pr:** Republic Pictures. **A:** Family. **P:** Entertainment. **U:** Home. **Mov-Ent:** Western. **Acq:** Purchase, Rent/Lease. **Dist:** Movies Unlimited; Alpha Video. $19.95.

Arizona Heat 1987 (R) — ★★
A violent cop is teamed up with a tough, but tender female cop in this all-too-familiar tale of two cops chasing a cop killer. 91m; VHS. **C:** Michael Parks; Denise Crosby; Hugh Farrington; Directed by John G. Thomas. **Pr:** Independent. **A:** College-Adult. **P:** Entertainment. **U:** Home. **Mov-Ent:** Action-Adventure. **Acq:** Purchase. **Dist:** Lions Gate Entertainment Inc. $79.98.

Arizona Kid 1939 — ★
Another sagebrush saga featuring Roy in singin' and fightin' action. 54m/B/W; VHS, DVD. **C:** Roy Rogers; George "Gabby" Hayes; Directed by Joseph Kane. **Pr:** Republic. **A:** Family. **P:** Entertainment. **U:** Home. **Mov-Ent:** Western. **Acq:** Purchase. **Dist:** Movies Unlimited; Alpha Video. $9.99.

Arizona Mahoney 1936 — ★
Weird mixture of circus adventure and serious western doesn't work too well. Confused film with farfetched reasons for having the paths of circus performers and cowboys cross. Based on a Zane Grey novel. 58m/B/W; VHS, DVD. **C:** Joe Cook; Robert Cummings; June Martel; Marjorie Gateson; John Miljan; Directed by James Hogan; Written by Robert Yost; Stuart Anthony. **Pr:** Paramount Pictures. **A:** Jr. High-Adult. **P:** Entertainment. **U:** Home. **Mov-Ent:** Western, Circuses. **Acq:** Purchase. **Dist:** Movies Unlimited. $19.99.

Arizona Raiders 1965 (Unrated) — ★★
Arizona rangers hunt down killers who have been terrorizing the territory. 88m; VHS, DVD, Streaming. **C:** Audie Murphy; Buster Crabbe; Gloria Talbott; Directed by William Witney. **Pr:** Grant Whytock; Columbia Pictures. **A:** Family. **P:** Entertainment. **U:** Home. **Mov-Ent:** Western. **Acq:** Purchase. **Dist:** Sony Pictures Home Entertainment Inc. $19.95.

Arizona Roundup 1942 — ★½
Good vs. bad amid tumbleweed, bleached-white chaps, bloodless shoot-outs and happy endings. 54m/B/W; VHS, DVD. **C:** Tom Keene; Sugar Dawn; Jack Ingram; Directed by Robert Emmett Tansey. **Pr:** Monogram. **A:** Family. **P:** Entertainment. **U:** Home. **Mov-Ent:** Western. **Acq:** Purchase. **Dist:** Alpha Video; Mill Creek Entertainment L.L.C. $19.95.

Arizona Sky 2008 (Unrated) — ★★
Kyle and Jake were teenaged best friends who could never follow through with their feelings for each other because of hometown prejudice. A stressed-out Jake returns to their desert community after 20 years and discovers Kyle hasn't been happy with his choices either. So the men decide to see if those old emotions are worth pursuing. 91m; DVD. **C:** Patricia Place; Eric Dean; Jayme McCabe; Bernadette Murray; Directed by Jeff London; Written by Jeff London; Cinematography by Matthew Skala. **A:** Sr. High-Adult. **P:** Entertainment. **U:** Home. **Mov-Ent:** Drama. **Acq:** Purchase. **Dist:** Wolfe Video.

Arizona Stagecoach 1942 — ★
The Range Busters set out to bust a notorious, guiltless, devil-may-care outlaw gang. 58m/B/W; VHS, DVD. **C:** Ray Corrigan; Max Terhune; Kermit Maynard; Charles "Blackie" King; John "Dusty" King; Directed by S. Roy Luby. **Pr:** Monogram. **A:** Family. **P:** Entertainment. **U:** Home. **Mov-Ent:** Western, Mystery & Suspense. **Acq:** Purchase. **Dist:** Movies Unlimited. $14.99.

Arizona Strip 1972
The old days of the American West are seen in horse-driven round-ups, chuck wagons, and branding. Working cowboys express their views about the life of cattlemen. 29m; VHS, 3/4 U, Special order formats. **Pr:** National Park Service. **A:** Family. **P:** Education. **U:** Institution, SURA. **Gen-Edu:** History--U.S. **Acq:** Purchase. **Dist:** National Audiovisual Center.

Arizona Summer 2003 (PG) — ★★½
Brent (Barnett) makes friends and gets some life lessons at a summer camp run by Travers (Majors). Simple family entertainment. 90m; DVD. **C:** Lee Majors; Greg Evigan; Morgan Fairchild; Bug Hall; Gemini Barnett; David Henrie; Lorenzo Henrie; Scott Clifton; Directed by Joey Travolta; Written by Bill Blair. **A:** Family. **P:** Entertainment. **U:** Home. **Mov-Ent:** Camps & Camping, Family Viewing. **Acq:** Purchase. **Dist:** Bedford Entertainment Inc.

Arizona Terror 1931 — ★½
Our hero is on a quest for vengeance, seeking the posse that killed his partner. 64m/B/W; VHS, DVD, Streaming. **C:** Ken Maynard; Lena Basquette; Hooper Atchley; Michael Visaroff; Tom London; Jack Natteford; Directed by Phil Rosen; Written by Jack Natteford; Cinematography by Arthur Reed. **Pr:** Tiffany. **A:** Family. **P:** Entertainment. **U:** Home. **Mov-Ent:** Western. **Acq:** Purchase. **Dist:** Sinister Cinema.

Arizona's Shortline Railroads 1992
Big trains crossing vast western desert landscapes. Could anything be more serene? Complete with all those sounds associated with old-fashioned diesel locomotives-the rhythmic beat of the engine churning, the clackety-clack of the wheels along the tracks, the low-pitched whine of the locomotive's horn. Great for train fans young and old. 100m; VHS. **A:** Jr. High-Adult. **P:** Entertainment. **U:** Home. **Gen-Edu:** Trains. **Acq:** Purchase. **Dist:** Pentrex Media Group L.L.C. $39.95.

The Ark 1991
Features a management team moving in and slashing expenditures, including 90 people and 40% of the zoo's stock, after the "ark in the park" was told it must pay its own way. 240m; VHS. **A:** Jr. High-Adult. **P:** Education. **U:** Institution. **Gen-Edu:** Zoos, Animals, Economics. **Acq:** Purchase, Rent/Lease. **Dist:** First Run/Icarus Films. $590.00.
Indiv. Titles: 1. Survival of the Fittest 2. Natural Selection 3. The Political Animal 4. Tooth & Claw.

Ark of the Covenant 1995
Reveals new possibilities of the whereabouts of the lost ark. 50m; VHS. **Pr:** A&E (Arts & Entertainment) Network. **A:** Family. **P:** Entertainment. **U:** Home. **Gen-Edu:** Archaeology, Religion. **Acq:** Purchase. **Dist:** New Video Group. $19.95.

Ark of the Sun God 1982 (Unrated) — ★
Another adventurer battles the Nazis and nutsies for a 2000-year-old ark buried in the Sahara. 95m; VHS, DVD. **C:** David Warbeck; John Steiner; Susie Sudlow; Alan Collins; Riccardo Palacio; Directed by Anthony M. Dawson. **Pr:** Flora Film; UFM Studio. **A:** Jr. High-Adult. **P:** Entertainment. **U:** Home. **Mov-Ent. Acq:** Purchase. **Dist:** Unknown Distributor.

Arkansas, Tennessee, and South Carolina 19??
A great tour of the Blue Ridge Mountains, Appalachias and other lush areas to be found in these three states. 53m; VHS. **A:** Family. **P:** Education. **U:** Home. **Gen-Edu:** Travel. **Acq:** Purchase. **Dist:** Christy's Editorial Film and Video Supply. $29.95.

Arkansas Track & Field Common Errors & Corrections Discus 2013 (Unrated)
Coach Travis Geopfert demonstrates drills for maximizing distance on the discus throw. 55m; DVD. **A:** Family. **P:** Education. **U:** Home. **L:** English. **Spo-Rec:** Athletic Instruction/Coaching, Sports--Track & Field, How-To. **Acq:** Purchase. **Dist:** Championship Productions. $39.99.

Arkansas Track & Field Common Errors & Corrections High Jump 2013 (Unrated)
Coach Travis Geopfert discusses how to fix common errors that cost high jumpers height. 29m; DVD. **A:** Family. **P:** Education. **U:** Home. **L:** English. **Spo-Rec:** Athletic Instruction/Coaching, Sports--Track & Field, How-To. **Acq:** Purchase. **Dist:** Championship Productions. $39.99.

Arkansas Track & Field Common Errors & Corrections Javelin 2013 (Unrated)
Coach Travis Geopfert discusses the mechanics of javelin throwing and how to correct common problems. 39m; DVD. **A:** Family. **P:** Education. **U:** Home. **L:** English. **Spo-Rec:** Athletic Instruction/Coaching, Sports--Track & Field, How-To. **Acq:** Purchase. **Dist:** Championship Productions. $39.99.

Arkansas Track & Field Common Errors & Corrections Long Jump 2013 (Unrated)
Coach Travis Geopfert discuses correcting problems in athletes performing the long jump and demonstrates training drills. 41m; DVD. **A:** Family. **P:** Education. **U:** Home. **L:** English. **Spo-Rec:** Athletic Instruction/Coaching, Sports--Track & Field, How-To. **Acq:** Purchase. **Dist:** Championship Productions. $39.99.

Arkansas Track & Field Common Errors & Corrections Shot Put 2013 (Unrated)
Coach Travis Geopfert discusses drills and techniques for shot putters wishing to extend their throwing distance. 65m; DVD. **A:** Family. **P:** Education. **U:** Home. **L:** English. **Spo-Rec:** Athletic Instruction/Coaching, Sports--Track & Field, How-To. **Acq:** Purchase. **Dist:** Championship Productions. $39.99.

Arkansas Track & Field Presents Common Errors & Corrections Men's Hurdles 2013 (Unrated)
Coach Doug Case addresses common errors male hurdlers make before introducing drills to correct them. 43m; DVD. **A:** Family. **P:** Education. **U:** Home. **L:** English. **Spo-Rec:** Athletic Instruction/Coaching, Sports--Track & Field, How-To. **Acq:** Purchase. **Dist:** Championship Productions. $43.

Arkansas Track & Field Presents Common Errors and Corrections Sprints 2013 (Unrated)
Coach Doug Case highlights common errors made by sprinters and gives suggestions for how they can be fixed. 39m; DVD. **A:**

Family. **P:** Education. **U:** Home. **L:** English. **Spo-Rec:** Athletic Instruction/Coaching, Sports--Track & Field, How-To. **Acq:** Purchase. **Dist:** Championship Productions. $39.99.

Arkansas Track & Field Presents Common Errors & Corrections Triple Jump 2013 (Unrated)
Coach Travis Geopfert presents more than 10 drills to help athletes performing in the triple jump. 34m; DVD. **A:** Family. **P:** Education. **U:** Home. **L:** English. **Spo-Rec:** Athletic Instruction/Coaching, Sports--Track & Field, How-To. **Acq:** Purchase. **Dist:** Championship Productions. $39.99.

Arkansas Track & Field Presents Common Errors & Corrections Women's Hurdles 2013 (Unrated)
Coach Rolando Greene presents a companion piece to Arkansas' DVD for fixing mistakes hurdlers make, this time with an emphasis on women. 49m; DVD. **A:** Family. **P:** Education. **U:** Home. **L:** English. **Spo-Rec:** Athletic Instruction/Coaching, Sports--Track & Field, How-To. **Acq:** Purchase. **Dist:** Championship Productions. $39.99.

Arkelope 19??
Parody of nature documentaries which traces the fictional history of the arkelope, an imaginary endangered species used to illustrate the mechanisms of species extinction and the struggle for survival. 5m; VHS. **A:** Jr. High-Adult. **P:** Education. **U:** Institution. **Gen-Edu:** Animation & Cartoons, Wildlife, Ecology & Environment. **Acq:** Purchase. **Dist:** Bullfrog Films, Inc.; National Film Board of Canada.

Arlen Roth Band: Live in England 198? (Unrated)
Roth plays live in England with Kjell Benner, Joe Dalton, and Michael Braun. 90m; VHS. **A:** Jr. High-College. **P:** Entertainment. **U:** Home. **Mov-Ent:** Music--Performance. **Acq:** Purchase. **Dist:** Music Video Distributors. $29.95.

Arlen Roth Guitar Instruction Series 1990
The guitarist demonstrates and teaches his world-famous technique in this seven-video collection. 60m; VHS. **A:** Jr. High-Adult. **P:** Instruction. **U:** Home. **How-Ins:** Music--Instruction. **Acq:** Purchase. **Dist:** Music Video Distributors. $44.95.
Indiv. Titles: 1. Advanced Rock Guitar 2. Beginning Electric Guitar 3. Chicago Blues Guitar 4. Hot Country Lead Guitar 5. Rhythm Guitar and R & B Styles 6. Rock/Metal Guitar 7. Slide Guitar.

Arlene Siegel's Sculpture Classroom 19??
Demonstrates the basics of sculpture using a young boy's head as an example. Identifies needed tools. 53m; VHS. **A:** Jr. High-Adult. **P:** Instruction. **U:** Institution. **How-Ins:** How-To, Sculpture, Art & Artists. **Acq:** Purchase. **Dist:** Cambridge Educational. $59.95.

Arli$$: The Best of Arli$$ Volume 1 2003
Highlights episodes from the 1996-2002 television comedy-drama series about sports agent Arliss (Wuhl) as he works with athletes in this high-stakes, high-octane, and sometimes morally-questionable field. Includes appearances by Dave Winfield, Ernie Banks, Tommy Lasorda, and attorney Bob Shapiro. 13 episodes. 390m; DVD. **C:** Robert Wuhl; Sandra Oh; Jim Turner; Michael Boatman. **A:** Sr. High-Adult. **P:** Entertainment. **U:** Home. **Mov-Ent:** Television Series, Comedy-Drama, Sports--General. **Acq:** Purchase. **Dist:** Warner Home Video, Inc. $39.98.

Arlington Cemetery: Field of Honor 2004 (Unrated)
Once nothing more than a potter's field, Arlington National Cemetery is now one of the most revered locations in America. Located near Washington, DC, in Arlington, Virginia, the cemetery is home to the famous, including U.S. presidents and the tombs of the Unknown Soldiers, and average, working-class soldiers from across the country. Includes first-hand accounts from the employees who keep the facility in pristine condition and stirring accounts of the heroic actions taken by some of the soldiers who are now interred there. 60m; DVD. **A:** Family. **P:** Education, Entertainment. **U:** Home, Institution. **Mov-Ent:** Documentary Films, Death, U.S. States. **Acq:** Purchase. **Dist:** $24.95.

Arlington National Cemetery 1992
Visits and tours Arlington National Cemetery, looking at such things as the Changing of the Guard Ceremony at the Tomb of the Unknowns and the stories behind the many men and women buried in this national monument. 30m; VHS. **A:** Jr. High-Adult. **P:** Education. **U:** Institution. **Gen-Edu:** History--U.S., Travel. **Acq:** Purchase. **Dist:** Cambridge Educational. $24.95.

Arlington Road 1999 (R) — ★★½
The tranquility of surburban life is shattered for college professor Faraday (Bridges) when he suspects the picket fence and overly friendliness of new neighbor Lang (Robbins) is a cover for his right-wing terrorism. As Faraday slowly uncovers Lang's true identity, it becomes harder for him to convince friends to believe the conspiracy. Impressive nail-biter with an interesting twist has a solid performance from Bridges as the paranoid professor, and an eerie one from the otherwise affable Robbins. Director Pellington, with the aide of Badalamenti's haunting score maintains the film's objective of showing how evil can come from the most unlikely place. 119m; VHS, DVD, Blu-Ray, CC. **C:** Jeff Bridges; Tim Robbins; Joan Cusack; Hope Davis; Mason Gamble; Stanley Anderson; Robert Gossett; Spencer Treat Clark; Directed by Mark Pellington; Written by Ehren Kruger; Cinematography by Bobby Bukowski; Music by Angelo Badalamenti; tomandandy. **Pr:** Peter Samuelson; Marc Samuelson; Tom Gorai; Polygram Filmed Entertainment. **A:** Adult. **P:** Entertainment. **U:** Home. **Mov-Ent:** Terrorism. **Acq:** Purchase. **Dist:** Sony Pictures Home Entertainment Inc.

Arlit: Deuxieme Paris 2004
Documentary on environmental destruction and racism set in the uranium mining town of Arlit. In French, Bariba, Hausa, and Tamashek with English subtitles. 75m; VHS, DVD. **A:** Sr. High-Adult. **P:** Education. **U:** Institution. **L:** French. **Gen-Edu:** Africa, Documentary Films. **Acq:** Purchase. **Dist:** California Newsreel. $49.95.

The Arm and Elbow Joint 1984
The humerous and muscles of the human arm are medically discussed. 15m; 3/4 U. **Pr:** McMaster University. **A:** Adult. **P:** Professional. **U:** Institution, SURA. **Hea-Sci:** Joints. **Acq:** Purchase, Rent/Lease. **Dist:** McMaster University.

Arm Spins & Shoulder Throws 2010 (Unrated)
Coach Rob Koll discusses two different takedown techniques in wrestling and how to enter them from various positions. 39m; DVD. **A:** Family. **P:** Education. **U:** Home, Institution. **Spo-Rec:** Athletic Instruction/Coaching. **Acq:** Purchase. **Dist:** Championship Productions. $39.99.

Arm Swing Progressions for High Power Attacking 2011 (Unrated)
Coach Kevin Hambly discusses the body mechanics of volleyball with drills designed to make teams better at offense. 40m; Streaming. **A:** Family. **P:** Education. **U:** Home, Institution. **Spo-Rec:** Volleyball, Athletic Instruction/Coaching. **Acq:** Purchase. **Dist:** Championship Productions. $39.99.

Armageddon 1998 (PG-13) — ★★½
A Texas-sized asteroid is hurtling towards earth, NASA gets nervous, and it's up to oil driller Harry Stamper (Willis) and his misfit crew to turn astronaut, blast off into space, land on that rock, and blow the sucker to kingdom come. Ya get a little romance as hotshot A.J. Frost (Affleck) smooches with babe Grace (Tyler), who's Harry's nubile daughter. Lots of action (naturally), some humor, and some sappy, heart-tugging moments for perfect put-your-brain-on-hold entertainment. The second "space rock hits earth" movie, following the somber "Deep Impact." 150m; VHS, DVD, Blu-Ray, Wide, CC. **C:** Bruce Willis; Ben Affleck; Billy Bob Thornton; Steve Buscemi; Liv Tyler; Will Patton; Peter Stormare; Keith David; Owen Wilson; William Fichtner; Jessica Steen; Grayson McCouch; Jason Isaacs; Michael Clarke Duncan; Erik Per Sullivan; Directed by Michael Bay; Written by Jonathan Hensleigh; J.J. (Jeffrey) Abrams; Cinematography by John Schwartzman; Music by Trevor Rabin. **Pr:** Jerry Bruckheimer; Gale Anne Hurd; Michael Bay; Jim Van Wyck; Chad Oman; Michael Bay; Jonathan Hensleigh; Valhalla Motion Pictures; Touchstone Pictures. **A:** Jr. High-Adult. **P:** Entertainment. **U:** Home. **Mov-Ent:** Action-Adventure. **Awds:** MTV Movie Awards '99: Action Seq., Song ("I Don't Want to Miss a Thing"); Golden Raspberries '98: Worst Actor (Willis). **Acq:** Purchase. **Dist:** Criterion Collection Inc.; Buena Vista Home Entertainment.

Armageddon Express 198?
Contains two films on peace protests. "The Healing of Brian Wilson" is a tribute to the protester who had both his legs cut off by a train carrying munitions. "The Arms Race Within" uses the music of Bob Dylan to tell the story of a group of activists who plan to protest nuclear weaponry. 90m; VHS. **C:** Kris Kristofferson; Joan Baez; Music by Jackson Browne; Bob Dylan. **A:** Sr. High-Adult. **P:** Education. **U:** Home. **Gen-Edu:** Documentary Films. **Acq:** Purchase. **Dist:** MPI Media Group. $19.98.

Armageddon: The Final Challenge 1994 — ★½
After a nuclear holocaust, evil forces rule the Earth in the guise of "The Future Bank." They send out Fear-Permutator Clones to keep order and kill undesirables but naturally there's a rebel ready to do battle. 85m; VHS. **C:** Todd Jensen; Graham Clarke; Tony Caprari; Joanna Rowlands; Directed by Michael Garcia; Written by George Garcia; Michael Garcia; Music by Johan Lass. **A:** Sr. High-Adult. **P:** Entertainment. **U:** Home. **Mov-Ent:** Science Fiction, Technology. **Acq:** Purchase. **Dist:** York Entertainment.

The Armaments: War Game 198?
Nuclear proliferation and the United States' plan to turn the responsibility of launching a retaliation over to computers are examined. 18m; 3/4 U, Special order formats. **Pr:** Hobel Leiterman Productions. **A:** College-Adult. **P:** Education. **U:** Institution. **Gen-Edu:** Nuclear Warfare. **Acq:** Purchase. **Dist:** The Cinema Guild.

Armauer Hansen: Discoverer of the Leprosy Bacillus 1976
Armauer Hansen, a young surgeon during the height of the leprosy epidemic in Norway, set out to discover the cause of the disease. 11m; VHS, 3/4 U; Open Captioned. **Pr:** Svekon Film Productions. **A:** Jr. High-Sr. High. **P:** Education. **U:** Institution, SURA. **Hea-Sci:** Scientists. **Acq:** Purchase. **Dist:** Phoenix Learning Group.

Armchair Fitness 1984
Exercise expert Betty Switkes leads her group through an aerobic work especially designed for senior citizens. 60m; VHS. **Pr:** CCM Productions. **A:** Adult. **P:** Instruction. **U:** Home. **Hea-Sci:** Fitness/Exercise, Aging. **Acq:** Purchase. **Dist:** CC-M Inc. $39.95.

Armchair Thriller—Set 1 1984 (Unrated)
PBS Mystery! 1984 series. A man's attempts to save his life may cost his sanity in "Dying Day." A wife disappears with no trace in "The Limbo Connection." A girl searching for her father is captured by a terrorist in "Rachel in Danger," and an industrialist uses all his resources to find his kidnapped daughter in "The Victim." 4 episodes. 487m; DVD. **C:** Ian McKellen; John Shrapnel; James Bolam. **A:** Jr. High-Adult. **P:** Entertainment. **U:** Home. **Mov-Ent:** Mystery & Suspense, Drama, Television Series. **Acq:** Purchase. **Dist:** Acorn Media Group Inc. $49.99.

Armed and Dangerous 1986 (PG-13) — ★★
Candy and Levy are incompetent security guards assigned to a do-nothing job. Things get spiced up when a mobster tries to run a crime ring under their nose. Candy catches on and winds up in a full-fledged chase. Not as funny as it sounds, though occasionally has moments of genuine comedy. 88m; VHS, DVD, CC. **C:** John Candy; Eugene Levy; Kenneth McMillan; Brion James; Robert Loggia; Meg Ryan; Don Stroud; Jonathan Banks; Steve Railsback; Bruce Kirby; Tony Burton; Larry Hankin; Judy Landers; David Wohl; Directed by Mark L. Lester; Written by Harold Ramis; Peter Torokvei; James Keach; Brian Grazer. **Pr:** Frostbacks. **A:** Jr. High-Adult. **P:** Entertainment. **U:** Home. **Mov-Ent:** Comedy--Slapstick, Security Officer Training. **Acq:** Purchase. **Dist:** Sony Pictures Home Entertainment Inc. $14.95.

Armed and Dangerous with Andre Houle: Shape, Define, Strengthen ????
A beginner to advanced workout designed to develop lean arms, shoulders, and back. 30m; VHS. **A:** Adult. **P:** Instruction. **U:** Home. **Hea-Sci:** Fitness/Exercise, How-To. **Acq:** Purchase. **Dist:** Body Bar Systems. $14.95.

Armed for Action 1992 — ★★
Routine action thriller casts Estevez as Sgt. Phil Towers who gets more than he bargained for when his prisoner, Mafia hitman David Montel, escapes while en route from New York to Los Angeles. When he finally catches up with them, Towers leads a small army of locals on a brutal assault. 88m; VHS, CC. **C:** Joe Estevez; Rocky Patterson; Barri Murphy; David Harrod; J. Scott Guy; Directed by Shane Spaulding. **A:** Sr. High-Adult. **P:** Entertainment. **U:** Home. **Mov-Ent. Acq:** Purchase. **Dist:** Unknown Distributor.

Armed Forces Workout 1984
A U.S. Marine Corps drill instructor instructs a program of daily exercises designed to strengthen one's body and attitude toward working-out. 54m; VHS. **Pr:** K Tel International Inc. **A:** College-Adult. **P:** Instruction. **U:** Home. **Hea-Sci:** Fitness/Exercise. **Acq:** Purchase. **Dist:** ESPN Inc.; Lions Gate Television Corp.; Cambridge Educational. $19.98.

Armed Response 1986 (R) — ★★
Carradine leads a group of mercenaries in a battle against Chinatown mobsters. They race to locate a priceless jade statue before it can fall into the wrong hands. 86m; VHS, DVD. **C:** David Carradine; Lee Van Cleef; Mako; Lois Hamilton; Ross Hagen; Brent Huff; Directed by Fred Olen Ray; Cinematography by Paul Elliott. **Pr:** Cinetel Films. **A:** Sr. High-Adult. **P:** Entertainment. **U:** Home. **Mov-Ent:** Exploitation. **Acq:** Purchase. **Dist:** Unknown Distributor.

Armenia: Bittersweet Freedom 1993
Details Armenia's struggle for survival since its independence from the former Soviet Union. Outlines the many events which have affected the country including blockades, earthquakes, armed conflict with Azerbaijan and chronicles the relief efforts being conducted by Armenian-American groups. Winner of many awards including CINE Golden Eagle and Silver Plaque at the International Communication Film and Video Festival. 47m; VHS. **C:** Narrated by Mike Connors. **A:** Jr. High-Adult. **P:** Education. **U:** Institution. **Gen-Edu:** Documentary Films, Sociology, USSR. **Acq:** Purchase, Rent/Lease. **Dist:** The Cinema Guild. $295.00.

The Armenian Case 1989
An edited version of "The Forgotton Genocide" and "Supplement to The Forgotton Genocide." 45m; VHS. **C:** Narrated by Mike Connors. **Pr:** Armenian Film Foundation. **A:** Jr. High-Adult. **P:** Education. **U:** Institution, Home. **Gen-Edu:** History--Modern, Asia. **Acq:** Purchase. **Dist:** Armenian Film Foundation. $55.00.

The Armenian Genocide 1991
Tells the story of the slaughter of the Armenian people of the Ottoman Empire from 1915-23. Draws comparisons between this episode and modern human rights violations. Comes with teacher's guide. 24m; VHS. **Pr:** Atlantis Productions. **A:** Sr. High. **P:** Education. **U:** Home, Institution. **Gen-Edu:** History--Modern, War--General, Human Rights. **Acq:** Purchase. **Dist:** Armenian Film Foundation. $39.00.

Arming Dictators 1992
Examines the government policy of arming dictators friendly to the U.S. in the 1980s, pro and con. 28m; VHS. **A:** Sr. High-Adult. **P:** Education. **U:** Institution, Home. **Gen-Edu:** Documentary Films, Military History, War--General. **Acq:** Purchase. **Dist:** The Video Project. $25.00.

The Arming of the Earth 1982
Bill Moyers traces the evolution of three significant weapons: the machine gun, the submarine and the bomber plane. 58m; VHS, 3/4 U. **Pr:** The Corporation for Entertainment and Learning. **A:** Jr. High-Sr. High. **P:** Education. **U:** Institution, CCTV, CATV. **Gen-Edu:** Technology. **Acq:** Purchase, Rent/Lease, Off-Air Record. **Dist:** PBS Home Video.

Armistead Maupin's More Tales of the City 1997 — ★★½
More risque and odd adventures for the inhabitants of Barbary Lane. Sequel picks up some six weeks after the first adventures. In 1977 San Francisco, Mary Ann (Linney) and Mouse (Hopkins) hunt for romance on a Mexican cruise. Mary Ann falls for handsome amnesiac Burke (Ferguson) and tries to help him regain his memory, while Mouse reunites with ex-lover, Dr. Jon (Campbell). Meanwhile, Mona (Siemszko) searches for her roots, which leads to revelations from Mrs. Madrigal (Dukakis). Brian (Hubley) becomes a voyeur and DeDe (Garrick) awaits the birth of twins—whose father is not her supercilious husband Beauchamp (Gibson). 330m; VHS, DVD. **C:** Laura Linney; Olympia Dukakis; Colin Ferguson; Billy Campbell; Paul

Hopkins; Whip Hubley; Thomas Gibson; Barbara Garrick; Nina Siemaszko; Jackie Burroughs; Swoosie Kurtz; Francoise Robertson; Dan E. Butler; Cameo(s) Parker Posey; Ed Asner; Paul Bartel; Brian Bedford; Sheila McCarthy; Scott Thompson; Directed by Pierre Gang; Written by Nicholas Wright; Cinematography by Serge Ladouceur; Music by Richard Gregoire. **Pr:** Alan Poul; Suzanne Girard; Tim Bevan; Showtime Networks; Propaganda Films. **A:** Sr. High-Adult. **P:** Entertainment. **U:** Home. **Mov-Ent:** Comedy-Drama, Sex & Sexuality, Pregnancy. **Acq:** Purchase. **Dist:** Movies Unlimited; Alpha Video.

Armistead Maupin's Tales of the City 1993 — ★★½
Carefree '70s San Francisco is the setting for the interconnected stories of the inhabitants of 28 Barbary Lane. There's mysterious landlady Mrs. Madrigal (Dukakis); free-spirit Mona Ramsey (Webb); her gay roomie, Michael "Mouse" Tolliver (D'Amico); hetero lawyer-turned-waiter Brian (Gross); nerdy, secretive Norman (DeSantis); and the naively sweet Mary Ann Singleton (Linney). Definite time-warp factor in this pre-AIDS depiction of sex and drugs, but also the timeless search for love and happiness. Maupin first wrote the stories as an ongoing serial for the "San Francisco Chronicle" and they were later turned into six novels. Made for British TV. 360m; VHS, DVD. **C:** Olympia Dukakis; Donald Moffat; Chloe Webb; Laura Linney; Marcus D'Amico; Billy Campbell; Thomas Gibson; Paul Gross; Barbara Garrick; Nina Foch; Edie Adams; Meagen Fay; Lou Liberatore; Country Joe McDonald; Mary Kay Place; Parker Posey; Kevin Sessums; McLean Stevenson; Stanley DeSantis; Cynda Williams; Karen Black; Michael Jeter; Paul Bartel; Lance Loud; Ian McKellen; Bob Mackie; Marissa Ribisi; Mother Love; Don Novello; Rod Steiger; Janeane Garofalo; Armistead Maupin; Directed by Alastair Reid; Written by Richard Kramer; Music by John Keane. **Pr:** Alan Poul; Antony Root; Working Title Productions; Channel 4; Propaganda Films. **A:** Sr. High-Adult. **P:** Entertainment. **U:** Home. **Mov-Ent:** Comedy-Drama, Sex & Sexuality, Drug Abuse. **Acq:** Purchase. **Dist:** Acorn Media Group Inc. $59.95.

Armored 2009 (PG-13) — ★★½
Unpretentious but generic heist movie. A six-man crew at an L.A. armored transport security firm are in on a robbery against their company with a $42 million dollar payoff. If only planner Coohrane (Dillon) can persuade Iraqi war vet Hackett (Short) to go along by reassuring him that nobody will get hurt. Of course, that turns out to be wrong and a conflicted Hackett then tries to do the right thing. 88m; Blu-Ray, On Demand, Wide. **C:** Columbus Short; Jean Reno; Laurence Fishburne; Skeet Ulrich; Amaury Nolasco; Fred Ward; Matt Dillon; Milo Ventimiglia; Andre Jamal Kinney; Directed by Nimrod Antal; Written by James V. Simpson; Cinematography by Andrzej Sekula; Music by John Murphy. **Pr:** Josh Donen; Dan Farah; Stars Road Entertainment; Screen Gems. **A:** Jr. High-Adult. **P:** Entertainment. **U:** Home. **L:** English. **Mov-Ent:** Crime Drama, Veterans. **Acq:** Purchase. **Dist:** Amazon.com Inc.; Movies Unlimited; Sony Pictures Home Entertainment Inc.

Armored Car Robbery 1950 — ★★
Talman and his buddies plot to rob an armored car but are foiled by McGraw and his crimefighters. Surprisingly good B-crime drama. 68m/B/W; VHS, DVD. **C:** Charles McGraw; Adele Jergens; William Talman; Steve Brodie; Douglas Fowley; Don McGuire; James Flavin; Gene Evans; Directed by Richard Fleischer; Written by Gerald Drayson Adams; Earl Felton; Cinematography by Guy Roe; Music by Paul Sawtell. **Pr:** RKO. **A:** Jr. High-Adult. **P:** Entertainment. **U:** Home. **Mov-Ent. Acq:** Purchase. **Dist:** Warner Home Video, Inc.

Armored Command 1961 — ★½
A beautiful German spy infiltrates an American outpost during the Battle of the Bulge. Tepid WWII fare made too long after the fact. 105m/B/W; VHS. **C:** Burt Reynolds; Tina Louise; Howard Keel; Earl Holliman; Warner Anderson; Carleton Young; Directed by Byron Haskin. **Pr:** Allied Artists International. **A:** Sr. High-Adult. **P:** Entertainment. **U:** Home. **Mov-Ent. Acq:** Purchase. **Dist:** Facets Multimedia Inc. $19.98.

Armored Saint: A Trip Thru Red Times 1991
Metal band, Armored Saint, rips through some of its best tunes: "Chemical Euphoria," "Lesson Well Learned," "Long Before I Die," "Human Vulture," "Book of Blood," "Nervous Fear," "Can U Deliver," "Raising Fear," "Aftermath," "Striken By Fate," and "March of the Saint." Also includes interviews. Rock on, Metal heads! 60m; VHS. **Pr:** Warner Reprise Video. **A:** Jr. High-Adult. **P:** Entertainment. **U:** Home. **Mov-Ent:** Music Video, Music--Performance, Interviews. **Acq:** Purchase. **Dist:** Music Video Distributors. $19.98.

Armory Show 1963
This program recreates the first art show in America, the Armory Show of 1913 and the influence the show has had on modern art is discussed. 59m/B/W; VHS, 3/4 U, EJ, Q. **Pr:** Educational Broadcasting Corporation. **A:** College-Adult. **P:** Education. **U:** Institution, SURA. **Fin-Art:** Art & Artists. **Acq:** Duplication, Free Duplication.

A.R.M.S. Concert: Complete 1991
Both volumes of the concert to benefit Multiple Sclerosis, performed at London's Royal Albert Hall in 1983. 118m; VHS. **Pr:** Glyn Johns. **A:** Jr. High-Adult. **P:** Entertainment. **U:** Home. **Mov-Ent:** Music--Performance. **Acq:** Purchase. **Dist:** Music Video Distributors. $24.95.

A.R.M.S. Concert: Part 1 1983
An ensemble of rock-n-roll stars, from Eric Clapton to Bill Wyman, perform in this live benefit concert. 59m; VHS. **Pr:** Glyn Johns. **A:** Family. **P:** Entertainment. **U:** Home. **Mov-Ent:** Music--Performance, Music--Pop/Rock. **Acq:** Purchase. **Dist:** Music Video Distributors. $14.95.

A.R.M.S. Concert: Part 2 1984
Further compilation of British rock from these four consecutive benefit concerts includes staples like "Stairway to Heaven," "Layla," and "Who's to Blame." 59m; VHS. **Pr:** Glyn Johns. **A:** Jr. High-Adult. **P:** Entertainment. **U:** Home. **Mov-Ent:** Music--Performance, Music--Pop/Rock. **Acq:** Purchase. **Dist:** Music Video Distributors. $14.95.

The Armstrong Lie 2013 (R) — ★★★
Expert documentarian Gibney just happened to be shooting a documentary on the life of infamous cyclist Lance Armstrong when his life and public persona collapsed, thereby changing the focus of the film that would be released. As Armstrong continuously tried to defend the now-revealed fact that he used performance enhancing drugs to become an international champion, Gibney holds him over the flame via interview segments, ultimately painting a portrait of a deeply troubled man who not only cheated but tried to ruin the lives of those who knew about it. It's too long for its own good but fascinating at times. 124m; DVD, Blu-Ray. **C:** Lance Armstrong; Narrated by Alex Gibney; Directed by Alex Gibney; Written by Alex Gibney; Cinematography by Maryse Alberti; Music by David Kahne. **Pr:** Alex Gibney; Frank Marshall; Matthew Tolmach; Sony Pictures Classics. **A:** Sr. High-Adult. **P:** Entertainment. **U:** Home. **L:** English. **Mov-Ent:** Sports Documentary, Bicycling, Biography: Sports. **Acq:** Purchase. **Dist:** Sony Pictures Home Entertainment Inc.

Armswing Progressions 2004 (Unrated)
Coach Chris Lamb presents armswing progressions for improving volleyball technique. 37m; DVD. **A:** Family. **P:** Education. **U:** Home, Institution. **Spo-Rec:** Volleyball, Athletic Instruction/Coaching. **Acq:** Purchase. **Dist:** Championship Productions. $39.99.

Army Ants: A Study in Social Behavior 1966
Presents the basic structure of an ant colony, shows the behavior of ants, and presents evidence of stimuli which influence their behavior. 19m; VHS, 3/4 U. **Pr:** Encyclopedia Britannica Educational Corporation. **A:** Sr. High-College. **P:** Education. **U:** Institution, SURA. **Hea-Sci:** Insects. **Acq:** Purchase, Rent/Lease, Trade-in. **Dist:** Encyclopedia Britannica.

Army Brats 1984 — ★½
In this Dutch film a military family goes bloodily and comically to war with itself. Even in a welfare state, parents can't control their wee ones. 105m; VHS. **C:** Akkemay; Frank Schaafsma; Peter Faber; Directed by Ruud Van Hemert. **Pr:** Chris Brouwer; Haig Balian. **A:** Sr. High-Adult. **P:** Entertainment. **U:** Home. **Mov-Ent:** Comedy--Black, Family. **Acq:** Purchase. **Dist:** Warner Home Video, Inc. $59.95.

The Army Forced Them to be Violent 2002
Provides eyewitness footage of the violent clashes between the Indonesia student movement and the military/police during their fight for reform. 43m; VHS. **A:** Adult. **P:** Education. **U:** Institution. **Gen-Edu:** Documentary Films, Asia, History. **Acq:** Purchase, Rent/Lease. **Dist:** Third World Newsreel. $225.00.

Army-Navy Screen Magazine 199?
Compilation of the biweekly news and information shows that were shown to U.S. troops during World War II. 58m; VHS. **A:** Jr. High-Adult. **P:** Education. **U:** Home. **Gen-Edu:** World War Two, Armed Forces--U.S., Cult Films. **Acq:** Purchase. **Dist:** OnDeck Home Entertainment. $19.95.

The Army of Crime 2010 (Unrated) — ★★
Semi-fictional historical drama about French communists, the Resistance movement, and the Nazis. Armenian-born poet and militant Communist Missak Manouchian becomes the leader of a group of anti-fascist partisans. The Nazis begin a crackdown and Manouchian's group is eventually rounded up to be executed. French and German with subtitles. 139m; DVD. **C:** Simon Abkarian; Virginie Ledoyen; Robinson Stevenin; Gregoire Leprince-Ringuet; Lola Naymark; Yann Tregouet; Ariane Ascaride; Jean-Pierre Darroussin; Directed by Robert Guediguian; Written by Robert Guediguian; Serge Le Peron; Gilles Taurand; Cinematography by Pierre Milon; Music by Alexandre Desplat. **A:** College-Adult. **P:** Entertainment. **U:** Home. **L:** French, German. **Mov-Ent:** World War Two. **Acq:** Purchase. **Dist:** Kino on Video.

Army of Darkness 1992 (R) — ★★★
Campbell returns for a third "Evil Dead" round as the square-jawed, none too bright hero, Ash in this comic book extravaganza. He finds himself hurled back to the 14th-century through the powers of an evil book. There he romances a babe, fights an army of skeletons, and generally causes all those Dark Age knights a lot of grief, as he tries to get back to his own time. Raimi's technical exuberance is apparent and, as usual, the horror is graphic but still tongue-in-cheek. 77m; VHS, DVD, Blu-Ray, HD-DVD, Wide, CC. **C:** Bruce Campbell; Embeth Davidtz; Marcus Gilbert; Ian Abercrombie; Richard Grove; Michael Earl Reid; Tim Quill; Bridget Fonda; Patricia Tallman; Theodore (Ted) Raimi; Ivan Raimi; Donald Campbell; William Lustig; Josh Becker; Directed by Sam Raimi; Written by Sam Raimi; Ivan Raimi; Cinematography by Bill Pope; Music by Joseph LoDuca; Danny Elfman. **Pr:** Mark Huffam; Robert Tapert; Bruce Campbell; Bruce Campbell. **A:** Sr. High-Adult. **P:** Entertainment. **U:** Home. **Mov-Ent:** Occult Sciences. **Acq:** Purchase. **Dist:** Anchor Bay Entertainment.

Army of One 1994 (R) — ★½
Santee (Lundgren) and his pal are hauling stolen cars across the desert when a cop pulls them over. Soon there's two dead bodies and Santee's in big trouble. An unrated version is also available. 102m; VHS, DVD. **C:** Dolph Lundgren; George Segal; Kristian Alfonso; Geoffrey Lewis; Michelle Phillips; Directed by Vic Armstrong; Written by Steven Pressfield; Joel Goldsmith. **Pr:** Illana Diamant; Andy Armstrong; Vision International. **A:** Sr. High-Adult. **P:** Entertainment. **U:** Home. **Mov-Ent. Acq:** Purchase. **Dist:** Lions Gate Television Corp. $92.98.

Army of Shadows 1969 (Unrated) — ★★★½
Melville's stunning adaptation of the 1943 Joseph Kessel novel focuses on members of the French Resistance in 1942. They lead shadow lives under false identities, struggling to survive while living in fear of betrayal. The head of this cell is Luc Jardie (Meurisse) but the most necessary of its members is field commander Philippe Gerbier (Ventura,) who metes out punishment for such betrayals. It's grim and dangerous and morally ambivalent and no one has time to be heroic (though they are) because there's too much at stake. You can't look away even if you want to. Melville himself was a member of the Resistance. French with subtitles. 140m; DVD, Blu-Ray. **C:** Lino Ventura; Simone Signoret; Paul Meurisse; Jean-Pierre Cassel; Claude Mann; Paul Crauchet; Christian Barbier; Alain Libolt; Jean-Marie Robain; Directed by Jean-Pierre Melville; Written by Jean-Pierre Melville; Cinematography by Pierre Lhomme; Music by Eric Demarsen. **Pr:** Jacques Dorfmann; Rialto Pictures. **A:** Sr. High-Adult. **P:** Entertainment. **U:** Home. **L:** French. **Mov-Ent:** Drama, World War Two, France. **Acq:** Purchase. **Dist:** Lions Gate Home Entertainment; Alpha Video; Movies Unlimited.

Army of the Dead 2008 (R) — ★
Some college students awaken a small army of dead spanish guys who are guarding a buried treasure. 89m; DVD. **C:** Mike Hatfield; Malcolm Madera; Ross Kelly; Miguel Martinez; Audrey Anderson; Stefani Marchesi; Directed by Joseph Conti; Written by Tom Woosley; Michael Ciccolini; Cinematography by John Grace; Music by William T. Stromberg. **A:** Sr. High-Adult. **P:** Entertainment. **U:** Home. **L:** English, Spanish. **Mov-Ent. Acq:** Purchase. **Dist:** Maverick Entertainment. $24.98.

Army on Wheels 1938
The various military uses of trucks during peacetime activities at American military bases are shown in this period documentary. 27m/B/W; VHS. **TV Std:** NTSC, PAL. **Pr:** U.S. War Department; Dodge Motor Company. **A:** Jr. High-Adult. **P:** Education. **U:** Institution, Home. **Gen-Edu:** Documentary Films, Armed Forces--U.S. **Acq:** Purchase. **Dist:** International Historic Films Inc. $19.95.

Army Wives: Season Six, Part One 2012
Lifetime 2007-? drama. "Winds of War": The wives are preparing to leave Fort Marshall until a hurricane devastates the community. "True Colors": Fort Marshall may be combined with another base and Claudia Joy has problems with the arrival of General Clarke. "Blood Relative": Denise offers a kidney to an ill Claudia Joy but Frank has misgivings and Joan and Roland are warned about legal issues after meeting their son's biological father. Episodes 1-13. 551m; DVD. **C:** Catherine Bell; Kim Delaney; Brigid Brannagh; Wendy Davis; Sally Pressman; Brian McNamara; Sterling K. Brown; Drew Fuller; Terry Serpico; Jeremy Davidson. **A:** Sr. High-Adult. **P:** Entertainment. **U:** Home. **Mov-Ent:** Armed Forces--U.S., Marriage, Television Series. **Acq:** Purchase. **Dist:** Buena Vista Home Entertainment. $39.99.

Army Wives: Season Six, Part Two 2012
Lifetime 2007-? drama. "Battle Scars": Claudia Joy decides to use her legal practice to help vets and Roxy worries about Trevor's injured buddy, Cory. "Centennial": Everyone prepares for Fort Marshall's 100th birthday as the base welcomes dignitaries to the celebration. "Onward": Fort Marshall is combining with an Air Force base and the troops must deploy earlier than expected. Episodes 14-23. 426m; DVD. **C:** Catherine Bell; Kim Delaney; Brigid Brannagh; Wendy Davis; Sally Pressman; Brian McNamara; Sterling K. Brown; Drew Fuller; Terry Serpico; Jeremy Davidson. **A:** Sr. High-Adult. **P:** Entertainment. **U:** Home. **Mov-Ent:** Armed Forces--U.S., Marriage, Television Series. **Acq:** Purchase. **Dist:** Buena Vista Home Entertainment. $29.99.

Army Wives: The Complete Fifth Season 2011
Lifetime 2007-? drama. "Command Presence": Claudia Joy graduates fromm law school as Pamela decides whether to stay or leave for a job in Atlanta. "Solider On": Denise has trouble coping after Jeremy's death and Roxy makes a decision about keeping the bar. "Counter Measures": The 23rd airborne troops come home but Roxy is afraid to tell Trevor about her truck stop business and Joan and Roland decide to adopt. 13 episodes. 551m; DVD. **C:** Catherine Bell; Kim Delaney; Brigid Brannagh; Wendy Davis; Sally Pressman; Brian McNamara; Sterling K. Brown; Drew Fuller; Terry Serpico; Jeremy Davidson. **A:** Sr. High-Adult. **P:** Entertainment. **U:** Home. **Mov-Ent. Acq:** Purchase. **Dist:** Buena Vista Home Entertainment. $39.99.

Army Wives: The Complete First Season 2007
Lifetime 2007-? drama. "A Tribe Is Born": Single mom Roxy impulsively marries Pvt. Trevor LeBlanc and moves to his Army post at Fort Marshall where she meets other Army wives, including Claudia Joy Holden, Denise Sherwood, and pregnant Pamela Moran. "One of Our Own": Denise's husband Frank is MIA in Iraq as she must also deal with her son Jeremy's abusive behavior. "Rules of Engagement": Colonel Holden gets a promotion, Roland knows jis marriage to Joan is in trrouble, and Trevor wants Roxy to quit her job at the Hump Bar after a brawl. 13 episodes. 552m; DVD. **C:** Catherine Bell; Kim Delaney; Brigid Brannagh; Wendy Davis; Sally Pressman; Brian McNamara; Drew Fuller; Terry Serpico; Jeremy Davidson; Sterling K. Brown. **A:** Sr. High-Adult. **P:** Entertainment. **U:** Home. **Mov-Ent:** Television Series, Armed Forces--U.S., Marriage. **Acq:** Purchase. **Dist:** Buena Vista Home Entertainment. $23.99.

Army Wives: The Complete Fourth Season 2010
Lifetime 2007-? drama. "Collateral Damage": Jeremy gets psychiatric care after a gun incident, Pamela takes the kids and leaves Chase, and Roland learns the extent of Joan's injuries. "Guns and Roses": Claudia Joy prepares for the annual Mother's Day brunch but other celebrations don't go as planned. "Army Strong": Nearly everyone in the 23rd airborne division will be deployed to Afghanistan but Joan is suffering from a traumatic brain injury. 18 epsiodes. 765m; DVD. **C:** Catherine Bell; Kim Delaney; Brigid Brannagh; Wendy Davis; Sally Pressman; Brian McNamara; Sterling K. Brown; Drew Fuller; Terry Serpico; Jeremy Davidson. **A:** Sr. High-Adult. **P:** Entertainment. **U:** Home. **Mov-Ent:** Armed Forces--U.S., Marriage, Television Series. **Acq:** Purchase. **Dist:** Buena Vista Home Entertainment. $23.99.

Army Wives: The Complete Second Season 2008
Lifetime 2007-? drama. "Would You Know My Name": The bombing at the Hump Bar throws a number of lives into turmoil. "Thicker Than Water": Trevor is uncomfortable being declared a hero, Denise's behavior causes gossip, and Pamela reacts when she's censored by the Army brass on her radio program. "Departures, Arrivals": Since Denise and Frank have separated, she openly dates Mac whle the Holdens have to decide about moving to Belgium for a new posting. 18 episodes. 811m; DVD. **C:** Catherine Bell; Kim Delaney; Brigid Brannagh; Wendy Davis; Sally Pressman; Brian McNamara; Sterling K. Brown; Drew Fuller; Terry Serpico; Jeremy Davidson. **A:** Sr. High-Adult. **P:** Entertainment. **U:** Home. **Mov-Ent:** Armed Forces--U.S., Television Series, Marriage. **Acq:** Purchase. **Dist:** Buena Vista Home Entertainment. $23.99.

Army Wives: The Complete Third Season 2009
Lifetime 2007-? drama. "Disengagement": Roxy has problems at the Hump Bar's reopening, Frank and Denise go to a mediator, and Joan spends time with her baby daughter before her deployment to Iraq. "Operation: Tango": Trevor is promoted to sergeant and Roxy needs to make a good impression on the principal of the private school she hopes her gifted son Finn will attend. "Fields of Fire": Another brawl at the bar makes it off-limits to the troops, putting Roxy anf Trevor in financial straits. Pamela thinks her marriage to Chase is over and Michael worries about the base closing. 18 episodes. 759m; DVD. **C:** Catherine Bell; Kim Delaney; Brigid Brannagh; Wendy Davis; Sally Pressman; Brian McNamara; Sterling K. Brown; Drew Fuller; Terry Serpico; Jeremy Davidson. **A:** Sr. High-Adult. **P:** Entertainment. **U:** Home. **Mov-Ent:** Armed Forces--U.S., Marriage, Television Series. **Acq:** Purchase. **Dist:** Buena Vista Home Entertainment. $23.99.

Arn: The Knight Templar 2007 (R) — ★★
Historical epic that doesn't have as much action as the plot implies. In the 12th century, young Swedish nobleman Arn is being trained as a warrior when he impregnates love Cecilia. As penance for this scandal, Arn is sent to Jerusalem to join the Crusades, where his fighting ability will eventually be used to unify rival clans back home. 139m; DVD. **C:** Joakim Natterqvist; Sofia Helin; Stellan Skarsgard; Michael Nyqvist; Bibi Andersson; Simon Callow; Vincent Perez; Sven-Bertil Taube; Milind Soman; Lina Englund; Directed by Peter Flinth; Written by Hans Gunnarsson; Cinematography by Eric Kress; Music by Tuomas Kantelinen. **A:** Sr. High-Adult. **P:** Entertainment. **U:** Home. **Mov-Ent:** Drama, Pregnancy, Scandinavia. **Acq:** Purchase. **Dist:** Entertainment One US LP.

Arnold 1973 (PG) — ★★½
Outrageous black comedy involving a woman who marries a cadaver to gain his large inheritance. Lots of bizarre and creative deaths in this horror spoof. Unusual wedding scene is a must-see. 96m; VHS. **C:** Stella Stevens; Roddy McDowall; Elsa Lanchester; Victor Buono; Bernard Fox; Farley Granger; Shani Wallis; Jamie Farr; Patric Knowles; John McGiver; Norman Stuart; Directed by Georg Fenady; Written by Jameson Brewer; John Fenton Murray; Cinematography by William B. Jurgensen; Music by George Duning. **Pr:** Bing Crosby Productions. **A:** Family. **P:** Entertainment. **U:** Home. **Mov-Ent:** Comedy--Black, Marriage. **Acq:** Purchase. **Dist:** No Longer Available.

Arnold of the Ducks 1985
Charming animation adventure of a lost boy rescued by ducks and raised as one of their own. 25m; VHS. **C:** Hosted by Bob Keeshan. **A:** Family. **P:** Entertainment. **U:** Home. **Chl-Juv:** Children, Animation & Cartoons. **Acq:** Purchase. **Dist:** Knowledge Unlimited, Inc. $14.98.

Arnold Palmer, Vol. 1: Mastering the Fundamentals 1983
Arnie lends all his knowledgable tips in an attempt to improve your game. 53m; VHS. **C:** Arnold Palmer. **Pr:** Champions on Film. **A:** Family. **P:** Entertainment. **U:** Home. **Spo-Rec:** Sports--General, Golf. **Acq:** Purchase. **Dist:** School-Tech Inc.; Lions Gate Television Corp. $19.98.

Arnold Palmer, Vol. 2: Course Strategy 1983
Arnie takes it to the green to see if you can apply your knowledge in the field of battle. 55m; VHS. **C:** Arnold Palmer. **Pr:** Champions on Film. **A:** Family. **P:** Instruction. **U:** Home. **How-Ins:** How-To, Sports--General, Golf. **Acq:** Purchase. **Dist:** Lions Gate Television Corp.; School-Tech Inc. $19.98.

Arnold Palmer, Vol. 3: The Scoring Zone 1989
Arnie helps you put the finishing touches on your game, allowing you to crush all who would oppose you. 53m; VHS. **C:** Hosted by Arnold Palmer. **A:** Adult. **P:** Entertainment. **U:** Home. **Spo-Rec:** Golf. **Acq:** Purchase. **Dist:** Lions Gate Television Corp. $19.98.

Arnold Palmer, Vol. 4: Practice Like a Pro 1989
The Master himself helps you improve your game and shares a little laughter along the way. 52m; VHS. **C:** Hosted by Arnold Palmer. **A:** Adult. **P:** Entertainment. **U:** Home. **Spo-Rec:** Golf. **Acq:** Purchase. **Dist:** Lions Gate Television Corp. $39.98.

Arnstein's Miracle 1977
Aging violinist is totally consumed with his own importance and refuses to play a charity concert. Chance meeting with an old man shatters his egomania. Theme: we must share the gifts God has given us in thanks to Him. 25m; VHS, 3/4 U, Special order formats. **C:** Howard da Silva. **Pr:** Paulist Productions. **A:** Sr. High-Adult. **P:** Religious. **U:** Institution, CCTV, SURA. **Gen-Edu:** Psychology, Religion. **Acq:** Purchase, Rent/Lease. **Dist:** Paulist Productions.

Aromatherapy Journeys 1998
Two tape set features the history and healing aspects of flowers from aromatherapist Kendra Grace. Includes jasmine, bitter orange blossom, lavender and others. 80m; VHS. **A:** Adult. **P:** Instruction. **U:** Home. **Hea-Sci:** Health Education, Flowers. **Acq:** Purchase. **Dist:** Instructional Video. $24.95.

Aromatic and Flavoring Combinations 199?
Teaches food industry and kitchen workers the fundamentals of prepping mirepoix, matignon, chili powder, marinades and more. Part of the Kitchen Preparation Series. 18m; VHS. **A:** Sr. High-Adult. **P:** Instruction. **U:** Home. **How-Ins:** Cooking, Food Industry, How-To. **Acq:** Purchase. **Dist:** Culinary Institute of America. $75.00.

Aroostook County, 1920s 19??
Maine's northernmost county, Aroostook, is known for agriculture, outdoor recreation, and congenial towns. This video is a record of life in and around the town of Presque Isle in the 1920s. The music of the film is from the period, and compiled by silent film accompanist Danny Patt. 20m; VHS. **A:** Family. **P:** Education. **U:** Institution. **L:** English. **Gen-Edu:** History. **Acq:** Purchase. **Dist:** Northeast Historic Film. $14.95.

Around a Small Mountain 2009 (Unrated) — ★★
Melancholy, talky Rivette pic follows Kate as she returns to her late father's small traveling circus after a 15-year absence. When Vittorio helps her with her stalled car, Kate invites him to a village performance and he ingratiates himself with the troupe. His (non-romantic) interest in Kate makes Vittorio want to learn about the trouble that made her leave her family and life behind and why she came back. French with subtitles. 85m; DVD. **C:** Jane Birkin; Sergio Castellitto; Andre Marcon; Jacques Bonnaffe; Julie-Marie Parmentier; Helene De Vallombreuse; Valintino Orsini; Vimala Pons; Directed by Jacques Rivette; Written by Sergio Castellitto; Jacques Rivette; Cinematography by Irina Lubtchansky; Music by Pierre Allio. **A:** College-Adult. **P:** Entertainment. **U:** Home. **L:** French. **Mov-Ent:** France, Circuses. **Acq:** Purchase. **Dist:** The Cinema Guild.

Around Alone 19??
Explains the story of how businessman Dodge Morgan fulfilled his dream and sailed nonstop around the world alone. Places one in the position of the sailor's companion as he confronts his fears and copes with loneliness, gear failures, fierce storms, and rough seas. 58m; VHS. **Pr:** Bennett Marine Video. **A:** Jr. High-Adult. **P:** Entertainment. **U:** Home. **Spo-Rec:** Boating, Travel. **Acq:** Purchase. **Dist:** Bennett Marine Video; The New Film Co., Inc. $39.95.

Around Cape Horn 1992
A 1929 film shot by Irving Johnson on board a tall ship. Longest surviving footage from on board a sailing vessel known to exist. 37m; VHS. **A:** Family. **P:** Education. **U:** Home. **Gen-Edu:** Boating. **Acq:** Purchase. **Dist:** Bennett Marine Video. $29.95.

Around Every Corner 1982
The causes of accidents in the workplace are thoroughly uncovered. 16m; VHS, 3/4 U. **Pr:** Educational Resources Foundation. **A:** Adult. **P:** Vocational. **U:** Institution, SURA. **Bus-Ind:** Safety Education. **Acq:** Purchase, Rent/Lease. **Dist:** ERI Safety Videos.

Around Friends: An Alcohol Decisions Program 19??
Addresses the problems of peer pressure teens face regarding drug and alcohol use. 13m; VHS. **A:** Jr. High-Sr. High. **P:** Education. **U:** Institution. **Hea-Sci:** Alcoholism, Drug Abuse, Adolescence. **Acq:** Purchase. **Dist:** Hazelden Publishing. $225.00.

Around June 2008 (Unrated) — ★★
Ever since June's (Armstrong) mother died when she was a girl, her grief-stricken father Murry (Gries) has dominated her life. But things change when June meets illegal immigrant Juan (Guerrero), who offers her a chance at happiness. 93m; DVD. **C:** Samaire Armstrong; Oscar H. Guerrero; Jon(athan) Gries; Brad William Henke; Michael Goorjian; Directed by James Savoca; Written by James Savoca; Cinematography by Peter Hawkins; Music by Didier Rachou. **A:** Sr. High-Adult. **P:** Entertainment. **U:** Home. **L:** English. **Mov-Ent:** Family, Romance. **Acq:** Purchase. **Dist:** Indican Pictures.

Around South America 1992
Video tour of South America presents some of the country's historical, geographical, and cultural background. Visits include the Galapagos Islands, Machu Picchu, Buenos Aires, Devil's Island, and Curacao. 57m; VHS. **A:** Jr. High-Sr. High. **P:** Education. **U:** Institution. **Gen-Edu:** South America, Geography. **Acq:** Purchase. **Dist:** Zenger Media. $50.00.

Around the Bend 2004 (R) — ★★
Dying patriarch Henry Lair (Caine) is being cared for by his grandson Jason (Lucas), who is also looking after his own young son, Zach (Bobo). Jason's black sheep father, Turner (Walken), abandoned him to Henry's care when he was a child. But Turner suddenly shows up, just in time to fulfill Henry's last request—he wants to be buried in a bizarre ritual that will mean a generational road trip from L.A. to Albuquerque. So does some male bonding occur? Boy, howdy, you betcha, but with Walken around the trip is never completely mundane. Feature debut of director/writer Roberts. 83m; DVD. **C:** Christopher Walken; Josh(ua) Lucas; Michael Caine; Glenne Headly; Jonah Bobo; Directed by Jordan Roberts; Written by Jordan Roberts; Cinematography by Michael Grady; Music by David Baerwald. **Pr:** Elliott Lewitt; Julie Kirkham; Kirkham-Lewitt; Warner Independent Pictures. **A:** Sr. High-Adult. **P:** Entertainment. **U:** Home. **Mov-Ent:** Aging, Archaeology. **Dist:** Warner Home Video, Inc. $27.95.

Around the Clock: Parenting the Delayed ADHD Child 1994
Insightful portrayal of the problems and frustrations two families contend with when they are raising children who suffer from ADHD. Provides parents and professionals with a helpful look at how to deal with the many problems that may arise in such an environment. 45m; VHS. **Pr:** Guilford Publication, Inc. **A:** Adult. **P:** Special Education. **U:** Home, Institution. **How-Ins:** Child Care, Mental Health, Mental Retardation. **Acq:** Purchase. **Dist:** Guilford Publications, Inc. $150.00.

Around the Fire 1998 (R) — ★★
At boarding school, Simon (Sawa) tries to escape his emotional troubles by getting in with the school druggies, including Andrew (Mabius). He also begins a foray into the neo-hippie world of the Grateful Dead, where he falls for the free-spirited Jennifer (Reid). Simon does wind up in rehab, looking back on his life. 107m; VHS, DVD, Wide. **C:** Devon Sawa; Eric Mabius; Bill Smitrovich; Tara Reid; Charlaine Woodard; Michael McKeever; Directed by John Jacobsen; Written by John Comerford; Tommy Rosen; Music by B.C. Smith. **A:** Sr. High-Adult. **P:** Entertainment. **U:** Home. **Mov-Ent:** Adolescence, Education, Drug Abuse. **Acq:** Purchase. **Dist:** Alpha Video; Movies Unlimited.

Around the Narrow Gauge Circle 19?? (Unrated)
Renowned rail cinematographer Otto Perry captures narrow gauge equipment and operations in the Colorado Rocky Mountains including the Denver & Rio Grande Western, the Rio Grande Southern, and Colorado Southern. 55m; DVD. **A:** Family. **P:** Education. **U:** Home. **Gen-Edu:** Trains, U.S. States. **Acq:** Purchase. **Dist:** The Civil War Standard. $24.95.

Around the World 1943 — ★½
Kyser leads a USO-like tour to entertain troops. Interesting only in a historical sense. 80m/B/W; VHS. **C:** Kay Kyser; Ish Kabibble; Mischa Auer; Joan Davis; Marcy McGuire; Directed by Allan Dwan. **Pr:** Allan Dwan; Allan Dwan; RKO. **A:** Family. **P:** Entertainment. **U:** Home. **Mov-Ent:** Musical, World War Two. **Acq:** Purchase. **Dist:** Turner Broadcasting System Inc. $19.98. **Songs:** Doodle-Ee-Doo; He's Got a Secret Weapon; Candlelight and Wine; Great News in the Making; They Chopped Down the Old Apple Tree; A Moke from Shamokin.

Around the World in 80 Days 1956 (G) — ★★★
Niven is the unflappable Victorian Englishman who wagers that he can circumnavigate the earth in four-score days. With his faithful manservant Cantinflas they set off on a spectacular journey. A perpetual favorite providing ample entertainment. Star-gazers will particularly enjoy the more than 40 cameo appearances by many of Hollywood's biggest names. Adapted from the novel by Jules Verne. 178m; VHS, DVD, CC. **C:** David Niven; Shirley MacLaine; Cantinflas; Robert Newton; Charles Boyer; Joe E. Brown; Martine Carol; John Carradine; Charles Coburn; Ronald Colman; Cameo(s) Melville Cooper; Noel Coward; Andy Devine; Reginald Denny; Fernandel; Marlene Dietrich; Hermione Gingold; Cedric Hardwicke; Trevor Howard; Glynis Johns; Buster Keaton; Evelyn Keyes; Peter Lorre; John Gielgud; Victor McLaglen; John Mills; Robert Morley; Jack Oakie; George Raft; Cesar Romero; Gilbert Roland; Red Skelton; Frank Sinatra; Beatrice Lillie; Ava Gardner; Directed by Michael Anderson, Sr.; Written by James Poe; John Farrow; S.J. Perelman; Cinematography by Lionel Lindon; Music by Victor Young. **Pr:** Michael Todd. **A:** Family. **P:** Entertainment. **U:** Home. **Mov-Ent:** Action-Adventure. **Awds:** Oscars '56: Adapt. Screenplay, Color Cinematog., Film, Film Editing, Orig. Dramatic Score; Golden Globes '57: Actor--Mus./Comedy (Cantinflas), Film--Drama; N.Y. Film Critics '56: Film, Screenplay. **Acq:** Purchase. **Dist:** Warner Home Video, Inc.; Baker and Taylor; Home Vision Cinema. $29.98.

Around the World in 80 Days 1984
Phineas Fogg and Passepartout set out to travel around the world in a balloon within 80 days. 80m; VHS. **C:** Directed by Stephen MacLean. **Pr:** API. **A:** Family. **P:** Entertainment. **U:** Home. **L:** English, Spanish. **Mov-Ent:** Animation & Cartoons, Children. **Acq:** Purchase. **Dist:** New Line Home Video. $19.95.

Around the World in 80 Days 1989 — ★★½
TV adaptation of the Jules Verne adventure novel that finds Victorian gentleman Phineas Fogg (Brosnan) wagering that he can circle the globe in 80 days. He's pursued by private detective Fix (Ustinov), who suspects him of a daring bank robbery, and faces many trials and much excitement along the way. On two cassettes. 270m; VHS, DVD. **C:** Pierce Brosnan; Peter Ustinov; Eric Idle; Arielle Dombasle; Henry Gibson; John Hillerman; Jack Klugman; Christopher Lee; Patrick Macnee; Roddy McDowall; Darren McGavin; John Mills; Robert Morley; Lee Remick; Pernell Roberts; James B. Sikking; Jill St. John; Robert Wagner; Julia Nickson-Soul; Directed by Buzz Kulik. **Pr:** Renne Valente. **A:** Family. **P:** Entertainment. **U:** Home. **Mov-Ent:** Action-Adventure, TV Movies. **Acq:** Purchase. **Dist:** Trinity Films.

Around the World in 80 Days 1990
Monty Python alumnus Palin recreates the globe-trotting journey of Jules Verne's character Phineas Fogg, using the same route and modes of travel from the 1872 novel and accompa-

nied by a four-member film crew. An visual feast for armchair travelers and accidental tourists, laced with Palin's wit. The set of four cassettes runs nearly six hours, but never becomes boring. 330m; VHS. **C:** Hosted by Michael Palin; Written by Michael Palin. **Pr:** British Broadcasting Corporation. **A:** Family. **P:** Entertainment. **U:** Home. **Gen-Edu:** Travel. **Acq:** Purchase. **Dist:** Video Collectibles; Home Vision Cinema; Fusion Video. $49.95.

Around the World in 80 Days 1991
The Jules Verne classic is brought to life via animation. 47m; VHS. **A:** Family. **P:** Entertainment. **U:** Home. **Chl-Juv:** Animation & Cartoons. **Acq:** Purchase. **Dist:** Anchor Bay Entertainment. $9.99.

Around the World in 80 Days 2004 (PG) — ★★
Phileas Fogg (Coogan) bets the London science community that he can circumnavigate the earth in 80 days, aided by assistant Passpartout (Chan). Surprising no one, a few people don't want him to make it. This time around Passpartout steals the show as a martial arts expert trying to return a stolen sacred heirloom to his village in China. In fact, Fogg's unworldly inventor seems at times like the sidekick. While departing wildly from the source material, it's lightweight fun better suited to the lowered expectations of a rental. As in the previous version, entertaining cameos add to the humor. Schwarzenegger is especially silly as an over-the-top lusty Turkish prince. 125m; DVD. **C:** Steve Coogan; Jackie Chan; Cecile de France; Jim Broadbent; Kathy Bates; Arnold Schwarzenegger; John Cleese; Ian McNeice; Luke Wilson; Owen Wilson; Ewen Bremner; Rob Schneider; Mark Addy; Sammo Hung; Roger Hammond; David Ryall; Macy Gray; Daniel Wu; Will Forte; Robert Fyfe; Karen Joy Morris; Richard Branson; Directed by Frank Coraci; Written by David Benullo; David Titcher; David Goldstein; Cinematography by Phil Meheux; Music by Trevor Jones. **Pr:** Hal Lieberman; Bill Badalato; Revere Pictures; Spanknyce; Walden Media; Walt Disney Pictures; Buena Vista. **A:** Primary-Adult. **P:** Entertainment. **U:** Home. **Mov-Ent:** Action-Comedy, Trains. **Acq:** Purchase. **Dist:** Buena Vista Home Entertainment.

Around the World in 80 Waves 1990
Awesome surf action set to the music of Agent Orange, Drivin' N' Cryin', Tony Creed, the Hoodoo Guru's and more. 85m; VHS. **Pr:** NSI. **A:** Jr. High-Adult. **P:** Entertainment. **U:** Home. **Spo-Rec:** Sports--General. **Acq:** Purchase. **Dist:** NSI Sound & Video Inc. $59.95.

Around the World in 80 Ways 1986 (R) — ★★½
Sometimes clever, sometimes crude Australian comedy about an aging man rescued from a nursing home and taken on a phony trip around the world by his sons. Odd, but genuinely funny at times. 90m; VHS. **C:** Philip Quast; Alan Penney; Diana Davidson; Kelly Dingwall; Gosia Dobrowolska; Directed by Stephen MacLean; Written by Stephen MacLean; Paul Leadon; Music by Chris Neal. **A:** College-Adult. **P:** Entertainment. **U:** Home. **Mov-Ent:** Comedy--Slapstick, Travel, Australia. **Acq:** Purchase. **Dist:** New Line Home Video. $19.98.

Around the World in a Daze 1963 (Unrated) — ★★½
The Stooges are servants for Phileas Fogg's great-grandson, who has decided to repeat his ancestor's famous feat. Mayhem ensues when the three help out in their usual efficient, competent way. 93m/B/W; VHS, DVD. **C:** Moe Howard; Larry Fine; Joe DeRita; Jay Sheffield; Directed by Norman Maurer. **A:** Jr. High-Adult. **P:** Entertainment. **U:** Home. **Mov-Ent:** Comedy--Slapstick, Travel. **Acq:** Purchase. **Dist:** Sony Pictures Home Entertainment Inc. $14.95.

Around the World Under the Sea 1965 — ★★
Bunch of men and one woman scientist plunge under the ocean in an experiment to predict earthquakes. They plant earthquake detectors along the ocean floor and discover the causes of tidal waves. They have men-women battles. They see big sea critters. 111m; VHS, DVD, Streaming. **C:** David McCallum; Shirley Eaton; Gary Merrill; Keenan Wynn; Brian Kelly; Lloyd Bridges; Directed by Andrew Marton. **Pr:** Ivan Tors Productions. **A:** Family. **P:** Entertainment. **U:** Home. **Mov-Ent:** Science Fiction, Fishing, Science. **Acq:** Purchase. **Dist:** WarnerArchive.com; MGM Home Entertainment. $59.95.

Around the World with Orson Welles 1955
Five episodes of a 1950s documentary series that Welles made for the BBC. Though far from his finest work, Welles's screen presence alone gives a lot of oomph to the rather average presentations. 134m; DVD. **C:** Hosted by Orson Welles; Directed by Orson Welles. **A:** Jr. High-Adult. **P:** Entertainment. **U:** Home. **Mov-Ent:** Documentary Films, Travel. **Acq:** Purchase. **Dist:** Image Entertainment Inc. $29.99.

Aroused 1966 (Unrated) — ★
Hollister is an apparently dedicated policeman who commits a number of blunders in the pursuit of a serial killer, including leaving his wife with the sociopath while he cavorts with the prostitute assigned to his protection. Director Holden's psychothriller was gorily ahead of its time. Includes heart-stopping castration sequence. 78m/B/W; VHS, DVD. **C:** Janine Lenon; Steve Hollister; Fleurette Carter; Joanna Mills; Tony Palladino; Ted Gelanza; Directed by Anton Holden. **A:** College-Adult. **P:** Entertainment. **U:** Home. **Mov-Ent:** Prostitution. **Acq:** Purchase. **Dist:** Something Weird Video; Tapeworm Video Distributors Inc. $23.00.

The Arousers 1970 — **Bomb!**
Hunk Hunter stars as a handsome, repressed California psycho in this cult item. Eddie travels the coast searching for a woman he is able to make love to; those who fail to arouse him come to tragic, climactic ends. Dreary, cheap exploitation with Roger Corman as executive producer for New World Pictures. 85m; DVD. **C:** Tab Hunter; Cherie Latimer; Nadyne Turney; Isabel Jewell; Directed by Curtis Hanson; Written by Curtis Hanson; Cinematography by Daniel Lacambre; Music by Charles Bernstein. **Pr:** New World Pictures. **A:** College-Adult. **P:** Entertainment. **U:** Home. **Mov-Ent:** Mystery & Suspense, Cult Films, Sex & Sexuality. **Acq:** Purchase. **Dist:** Shout! Factory. $24.98.

Arpeggios for the Lead Guitarist 199?
Paul Hanson presents a step-by-step demonstration of a variety of arpeggios, sweep picking, triads, 7th chords, and more. 30m; VHS. **A:** Sr. High-Adult. **P:** Instruction. **U:** Home. **How-Ins:** Music--Instruction. **Acq:** Purchase. **Dist:** Hal Leonard Corp. $9.95.

The Arrangement 1969 (R) — ★½
Veteran advertising executive Douglas attempts suicide and then sets out to search for the meaning of life. Along the way he attempts to patch up his "arrangements" with his wife, his mistress and his father. Forced, slow, and self-conscious, though well acted. Adapted by Kazan from the director's own novel. 126m; VHS, DVD. **C:** Kirk Douglas; Faye Dunaway; Deborah Kerr; Richard Boone; Hume Cronyn; Directed by Elia Kazan; Written by Elia Kazan; Cinematography by Robert L. Surtees; Music by David Amram. **Pr:** Elia Kazan; Elia Kazan; Warner Bros. **A:** Sr. High-Adult. **P:** Entertainment. **U:** Home. **Mov-Ent:** Suicide, Family. **Acq:** Purchase. **Dist:** Warner Home Video, Inc. $59.95.

The Arrangement 1999 (R) — ★★★
Jake (Keskhemnu) lives in Los Angeles. Luhann (James) is in New York. They're engaged until he admits to a one-night stand and invites her to experiment herself before the wedding. When she accepts, he is not pleased. Low-budget independent production is a bit obvious and slow moving in some respects, much more sophisticated in others. The details of everyday life are well observed and ring true. Editing is zippy and the characters are treated seriously. 90m; DVD, Wide. **C:** Billie James; Keskhemnu; Directed by H.H. Cooper; Written by H.H. Cooper; Cinematography by Douglas W. Shannon; Music by Michael Bearden. **A:** Sr. High-Adult. **P:** Entertainment. **U:** Home. **Mov-Ent:** Comedy--Romantic. **Acq:** Purchase. **Dist:** Bedford Entertainment Inc.

Arrangements Made Easy 1995
Instructs how to make a wreath, swag or flower arrangements look professional. 150m; VHS. **A:** Family. **P:** Instruction. **U:** Home. **Gen-Edu:** How-To, Hobbies. **Acq:** Purchase. **Dist:** Paragon Home Video. $59.95.

Arrest and Trial: Best of 1963
Precursor to today's popular crime and courtroom series features LAPD detective Sgt. Nick Anderson gathering evidence and tracking and arresting a suspect during the first half of the show, while defense attorney John Egan fights to exonerate the accused during the second half. 9 episodes. 675m; DVD. **C:** Chuck Connors; Ben Gazzara; John Larch. **A:** Adult. **P:** Entertainment. **U:** Home. **Mov-Ent:** Drama. **Acq:** Purchase. **Dist:** Timeless Media Group.

Arrest Bulldog Drummond 1938 — ★★
Captain Drummond is accused of killing the inventor of a futuristic detonator machine and must track down the real killers. Part of the "Bulldog Drummond" series. 57m/B/W; VHS, DVD. **C:** John Howard; Heather Angel; George Zucco; H.B. Warner; E.E. Clive; Reginald Denny; John Sutton; Directed by James Hogan. **Pr:** Paramount Pictures. **A:** Adult. **P:** Entertainment. **U:** Home. **Mov-Ent. Acq:** Purchase. **Dist:** Paramount Pictures Corp.; Rex Miller Artisan Studio; Sinister Cinema. $16.95.

Arrest Control Techniques 19??
A demonstration of how to control a prisoner physically and psychologically without risk to others. 15m; VHS. **A:** College-Adult. **P:** Instruction. **U:** Institution, Home. **How-Ins:** How-To, Police Training. **Acq:** Purchase. **Dist:** Gun Video. $99.95.

Arrested Development: Home Video 1992
Three songs, "Tennessee," "People Everyday," and "Mr. Wendal," plus live performance footage and a profile of the band are included in this video. 90m; VHS. **A:** Jr. High-Adult. **P:** Entertainment. **U:** Home. **Mov-Ent:** Music--Pop/Rock, Music Video. **Acq:** Purchase. **Dist:** Music Video Distributors. $14.98.

Arrested Development: The Complete First Season 2003
Patriarch George Bluth Sr. (Tambor) made a fortune in tract housing and his crazy family is used to spending lavishly, except for responsible Michael (Bateman). He's the son who's forced to look after everyone when dad is accused of tax fraud and their assets are frozen. 491m; DVD. **C:** Jason Bateman; Jeffrey Tambor; Jessica Walter; Portia de Rossi; David Cross; Will Arnett. **A:** Jr. High-Adult. **P:** Entertainment. **U:** Home. **Mov-Ent:** Television Series, Comedy--Black. **Acq:** Purchase. **Dist:** Fox Home Entertainment.

Arrested Development: The Complete Second Season 2005
Presents the entire second season of the quirky television comedy following the down-and-out Bluth family as son Michael tries to keep the dysfunctional family financially and emotionally afloat; often-drunk matriarch Lucille searches for fugitive hubby George Sr. while her kids coordinate efforts to get her into rehab. 396m; DVD. **A:** Sr. High-Adult. **P:** Entertainment. **U:** Home. **Mov-Ent:** Television, Comedy--Black, Family. **Acq:** Purchase. **Dist:** Fox Home Entertainment. $39.98.

Arrested Development: The Complete Third Season 2005
Uncle Oscar is actually the one doing time while George Sr. is on the lam but when Michael tracks him down, George blames their troubles on the Iraqis. Michael and Buster go to Iraq to save Gob and Michael learns who's been manipulating the situation all along. 286m; DVD. **C:** Jason Bateman; Jeffrey Tambor; Jessica Walter; Portia de Rossi; David Cross; Will Arnett. **A:** Jr. High-Adult. **P:** Entertainment. **U:** Home. **Mov-Ent:** Television Series, Comedy--Black. **Acq:** Purchase. **Dist:** Fox Home Entertainment.

The Arrival 1990 (R) — ★
An never-seen alien parasite turns an old man into a vampiric young stud after female blood. Plot and characterizations never do arrive. Horror director Stuart Gordon cameos as a hairy biker. 107m; VHS. **C:** John Saxon; Joseph Culp; Robert Sampson; Michael J. Pollard; Cameo(s) David Schmoeller; Directed by David Schmoeller; Written by David Schmoeller; Music by Richard Band. **Pr:** Ron Matonak. **A:** College-Adult. **P:** Entertainment. **U:** Home. **Mov-Ent:** Science Fiction. **Acq:** Purchase. **Dist:** Movies Unlimited. $19.99.

The Arrival 1996 (PG-13) — ★★½
Radio astronomer Zane (Sheen) picks up a message from deep space and discovers a planned alien invasion. When he brings evidence of such to his boss Gordian (Silver) he finds himself on the run from both government operatives and morphing aliens. Starts off slow, but an intelligent script and premise makes this a grade above cheesy. The aliens, with their kooky flaps of skin and back bending knees, are fun to watch. Directorial debut for Twohy. 109m; VHS, DVD, CC. **C:** Charlie Sheen; Ron Silver; Lindsay Crouse; Teri Polo; Directed by David N. Twohy; Written by David N. Twohy; Cinematography by Hiro Narita; Music by Arthur Kempel. **Pr:** Thomas G. Smith; Jim Steele; LIVE Entertainment; Orion Pictures. **A:** Jr. High-Adult. **P:** Entertainment. **U:** Home. **Mov-Ent:** Science Fiction, Astronomy, Conspiracies or Conspiracy Theories. **Acq:** Purchase. **Dist:** Lions Gate Television Corp.

The Arrival 2 1998 (R) — ★★
Computer programmer Muldoon receives information describing an extraterrestrial conspiracy against earth. Dull story, dull cast. 101m; VHS, DVD, CC. **C:** Patrick Muldoon; Michael Sarrazin; Jane Sibbett; Directed by Kevin S. Tenney; Written by Mark David Perry; Cinematography by Bruno Philip; Music by Ned Bouhalassa. **A:** Sr. High-Adult. **P:** Entertainment. **U:** Home. **Mov-Ent:** Science Fiction, Conspiracies or Conspiracy Theories. **Acq:** Purchase. **Dist:** Lions Gate Television Corp.

Arrivederci, Baby! 1966 (Unrated) — ★
An unfunny sex comedy with Curtis as a modern Bluebeard who weds rich women and kills them for their money. His last mate plans to turn the tables and kill him first. 100m; VHS, CC. **C:** Tony Curtis; Rosanna Schiaffino; Lionel Jeffries; Zsa Zsa Gabor; Nancy Kwan; Fenella Fielding; Anna Quayle; Warren Mitchell; Mischa Auer; Directed by Ken Hughes; Written by Ken Hughes. **Pr:** Paramount Pictures. **A:** Jr. High-Adult. **P:** Entertainment. **U:** Home. **Mov-Ent:** Comedy--Black, Marriage, Sex & Sexuality. **Acq:** Purchase. **Dist:** Paramount Pictures Corp.

Arriving 1991
Part one in the "Trials of Life" series, this program discusses the struggles of birth and surviving in the animal kingdom. 49m; VHS. **A:** Sr. High-Adult. **P:** Education. **U:** Institution. **Gen-Edu:** Animals, Wildlife. **Acq:** Purchase. **Dist:** University of Washington Educational Media Collection. $17.00.

The Arrogant 1991 (R) — **Bomb!**
A man on the run meets his only hope while travelling through the desert. Originally shown on the Playboy Channel. 86m; VHS. **C:** Sylvia Kristel; Gary (Rand) Graham; Directed by Philippe Blot; Written by Philippe Blot. **Pr:** Warner. **A:** Sr. High-Adult. **P:** Entertainment. **U:** Home. **Mov-Ent:** Romance, TV Movies. **Acq:** Purchase. **Dist:** Warner Home Video, Inc. $89.98.

Arrow 1974
A group of boys engage in an arrow fight to practice their aim and to learn how to dodge other arrows. 10m; 3/4 U. **Pr:** Timothy Asch; Napoleon Chagnon. **A:** Jr. High-College. **P:** Education. **U:** Institution, SURA. **Gen-Edu:** South America, Anthropology. **Acq:** Purchase. **Dist:** Documentary Educational Resources.

Arrow: The Complete First Season 2012
The CW 2012-? action-sci fi based on the DC Comics superhero Green Arrow. "Pilot" Oliver Queen returns home after five years of being marooned on an island. But the former playboy's purpose now is to clean-up Starling City as a hooded vigilante with deadly skills. "Vendetta": Oliver attempts to train Helena (Jessica De Gouw), hoping she will join him but she has her own ideas about justice and becomes the lethal Huntress. "Sacrifice": Malcolm Merlyn (John Barrowman) accelerates his plan to destroy the Glades with a man-made earthquake and Oliver isn't able to stop him. 23 episodes. 1020m; DVD, Blu-Ray. **C:** Stephen Amell; Katie Cassidy; David Ramsey; Paul Blackthorne; Willa Holland; Susanna Thompson; Emily Bett Rickards. **A:** Jr. High-Adult. **P:** Entertainment. **U:** Home. **Mov-Ent:** Action-Adventure, Science Fiction, Television Series. **Acq:** Purchase. **Dist:** Warner Home Video, Inc. $59.98.

Arrow to the Sun 1973
A tale from the Acoma Pueblo Indians: A boy's search for his father leads him to take a voyage upon an arrow to the sun. 12m; VHS, 3/4 U, Special order formats. **Pr:** Gerald McDermott. **A:** Primary-Jr. High. **P:** Entertainment. **U:** Institution. **Chl-Juv:** Folklore & Legends. **Acq:** Purchase. **Dist:** Home Vision Cinema.

Arrowhead 1953 — ★★½
A long-running argument between a tough Cavalry scout and an Apache chief pits the cowboys against the Indians in this western fantasy. The personal battles that become all-out wars turn back to fist-fights before the matter is finally settled. 105m; VHS, DVD, CC. **C:** Charlton Heston; Jack Palance; Katy

Jurado; Brian Keith; Milburn Stone; Directed by Charles Marquis Warren; Cinematography by Ray Rennahan. **Pr:** Paramount Pictures. **A:** Family. **P:** Entertainment. **U:** Home. **Mov-Ent**: Western. **Acq**: Purchase. **Dist:** Paramount Pictures Corp. $14.95.

Arrows Against the Wind 1993
Tells the story of two tribes, the Dani and Asmat, of West Papua, and how they and other tribes lived in spiritual harmony with the land. Reveals the story of their social, political and environmental upheaval. Received the following awards: Silver Apple, NEFVF; Finalist, Birmingham International Education Film Festival; Vermont Int'l. Film Festival; Dreamspeakers Festival. 52m; VHS, Special order formats. **A:** Sr. High-Adult. **P:** Education. **U:** Institution. **Gen-Edu**: Anthropology, Ecology & Environment, Sociology. **Acq**: Purchase, Rent/Lease. **Dist:** Bullfrog Films, Inc. $250.00.

Arrowsmith 1932 (Unrated) — ★★½
A small-town medical researcher battles his conscience as he juggles his selfish and unselfish motivations for the work he does. He travels to the West Indies to confront the issues of his life and come to terms with himself once and for all. A talented cast takes their time. Based on the classic Sinclair Lewis novel. Two edited versions available (99 and 89 minutes), both of which delete much of Loy. 95m/B/W; VHS, DVD. **C:** Ronald Colman; Helen Hayes; Myrna Loy; Directed by John Ford. **Pr:** Samuel Goldwyn. **A:** Family. **P:** Entertainment. **U:** Home. **Mov-Ent**: Caribbean, Science. **Acq**: Purchase. **Dist:** Movies Unlimited. $14.99.

Arsenal 1929 (Unrated) — ★★★
Classic Russian propagandist drama about strikes affecting the Russian home front during WWI, marking Dovzhenko's first great achievement in the realm of Eisenstein and Pudovkin. Silent. 75m/B/W; Silent; VHS, DVD. **C:** Semyon Svashenko; Luciano Albertini; Directed by Alexander Dovzhenko; Written by Alexander Dovzhenko; Cinematography by Daniil Demutsky. **Pr:** VUFKU. **A:** College-Adult. **P:** Entertainment. **U:** Home. **Mov-Ent**: Silent Films, World War One, Propaganda. **Acq**: Purchase. **Dist:** Kino on Video; International Historic Films Inc.; Glenn Video Vistas Ltd.

The Arsenal 1973
This episode of the "America" series traces the American way of war from Colonial times to the modern armed forces. 52m; VHS, 3/4 U, Special order formats. **C:** Narrated by Alistair Cooke. **Pr:** British Broadcasting Corporation; Time-Life Films. **A:** Sr. High-College. **P:** Education. **U:** Institution, SURA. **L:** English, Spanish. **Gen-Edu**: History--U.S. **Acq**: Purchase, Rent/Lease. **Dist:** Time-Life Video and Television.

Arsenal 1886-1986 1990
A look at the wonderful history of the Arsenal F.C. 91m; VHS. **A:** Family. **P:** Entertainment. **U:** Home. **Gen-Edu**: Sports--General, Soccer. **Acq**: Purchase. **Dist:** Video Collectibles. $29.95.

Arsenal Centurions DVD: 100 Goals Each From Dennis Bergkamp and Thierry Henry ????
On two DVDs, chronicles the careers of soccer greats Dutchman Dennis Bergkamp and Frenchman Thierry Henry, including each player's milestone 100th goal for London's Arsenal Football Club. 115m; DVD. **A:** Sr. High-Adult. **P:** Entertainment. **U:** Home. **Spo-Rec**: Soccer, Great Britain. **Acq**: Purchase. **Dist:** Soccer Learning Systems. $29.95.

Arsenal 501 Goals ????
Covers four decades and 501 soccer goals by England's Arsenal Football Club featuring goals by legends such as Thierry Henry, Frank Stapleton, and Dennis Bergkamp. 173m; DVD. **A:** Sr. High-Adult. **P:** Entertainment. **U:** Home. **Spo-Rec**: Soccer, Great Britain. **Acq**: Purchase. **Dist:** Soccer Learning Systems. $24.95.

The Arsenal Stadium Mystery 1939 (Unrated) — ★★½
Inspector Banks of Scotland Yard tracks down the killer of a football star in this clever but unassuming murder mystery. 85m/B/W; DVD. **C:** Leslie Banks; Greta Gynt; Ian MacLean; Liane Linden; Anthony Bushell; Esmond Knight; Directed by Thorold Dickinson. **A:** Adult. **P:** Entertainment. **U:** Home. **L:** English. **Mov-Ent**: Mystery & Suspense. **Acq**: Purchase. **Dist:** VCI Entertainment; Sinister Cinema. $16.95.

Arsenal 02/03 Review 200?
Provides highlights from the English soccer team Arsenal's 200-2003 season including career 100th goals by Dennis Bergkamp and Thierry Henry. 115m; VHS. **A:** Sr. High-Adult. **P:** Entertainment. **U:** Home. **Spo-Rec**: Soccer, Great Britain. **Acq**: Purchase. **Dist:** Soccer Learning Systems. $9.95.

Arsene Lupin 1932 — ★★★
The scene-stealing Barrymore brothers team up for this early talkie about a suave international jewel thief (John) and the police detective (Lionel) who relentlessly pursues him. This time Guerchard hears rumors that Lupin is going to try and steal the Mona Lisa from the Louvre. Followed by 1938's "Arsene Luoin Returns" with a different cast and played with more comedy. 64m/B/W; DVD. **C:** John Barrymore; Lionel Barrymore; Karen Morley; John Miljan; Directed by Jack Conway; Written by Lenore Coffee; Bayard Veiller; Cinematography by Oliver T. Marsh. **A:** Adult. **P:** Entertainment. **U:** Home. **L:** English. **Mov-Ent**: Crime Drama. **Acq**: Purchase. **Dist:** WarnerArchive.com.

Arsene Lupin Returns 1938 — ★★½
Having faked his death, the former jewel thief is living the life of a gentleman farmer. Despite his protests that he's retired, insurance detective Steve Emerson (William) is certain Lupin (Douglas) is behind the theft of a necklace owned by beautiful Lorraine De Grissac (Bruce). Played with more comic/mystery elements than 1932's "Arsene Lupin," which starred the Barrymore brothers. 81m/B/W; DVD. **C:** Melvyn Douglas; Warren William; Virginia Bruce; John Halliday; Monty Woolley; Nat Pendleton; Directed by George Fitzmaurice; Written by James Kevin McGuinness; George Harmon Coxe; Howard Emmett Rogers; Cinematography by George J. Folsey; Music by Franz Waxman. **A:** Adult. **P:** Entertainment. **U:** Home. **L:** English. **Mov-Ent**: Mystery & Suspense. **Acq**: Purchase. **Dist:** WarnerArchive.com.

Arsenic and Old Lace 1944 — ★★★½
Set-bound but energetic adaptation of the classic Joseph Kesselring play. Easy-going drama critic Mortimer Brewster (Grant) is caught in a sticky situation when he learns of his aunts' favorite pastime. Apparently the kind, sweet, lonely spinsters lure gentlemen to the house and serve them elderberry wine with a touch of arsenic, then they bury the bodies in the cellar—a cellar which also serves as the Panama Canal for Mortimer's cousin (who thinks he's Theodore Roosevelt). Massey, as Brewster cousin Jonathan, and Lorre, as his plastic surgeon, excel in their sinister roles. One of the best madcap comedies of all time—a must-see. Shot in 1941 and released a wee bit later. 118m/B/W; VHS, DVD, CC. **C:** Cary Grant; Josephine Hull; Jean Adair; Raymond Massey; Jack Carson; Priscilla Lane; John Alexander; Edward Everett Horton; Peter Lorre; James Gleason; John Ridgely; Directed by Frank Capra; Written by Julius J. Epstein; Philip G. Epstein; Cinematography by Sol Polito; Music by Max Steiner. **Pr:** Warner Bros. **A:** Family. **P:** Entertainment. **U:** Home. **Mov-Ent**: Comedy--Black, Classic Films, Poisons. **Acq**: Purchase. **Dist:** MGM Home Entertainment; Home Vision Cinema. $19.95.

Arsenic Polyneuropathy 1970
A brief interview and pertinent examination. 9m; VHS, 3/4 U, Special order formats. **Pr:** Ohio State University Health Sciences AV Center. **A:** College-Adult. **P:** Professional. **U:** Institution, SURA. **Hea-Sci**: Neurology. **Acq**: Purchase, Rent/Lease. **Dist:** Ohio State University.

Arshile Gorky 19??
Combines extensive interviews with family and friends with footage of Gorky at work in his studio to explore the tragic life of the Armenian-born artist. 29m; VHS. **A:** Sr. High-Adult. **P:** Education. **U:** Home. **Gen-Edu**: Documentary Films, Biography, Art & Artists. **Acq**: Purchase. **Dist:** Direct Cinema Ltd. $29.95.

Arson: Communities Fight Back 1980
Arson is a problem in many communities. This program examines the attempts in cites to combat this crisis. Community groups and legislative bodies should be aware of how to deal with this situation. Topics discussed are conviction of arsonists, identifying arsonists, creating public awareness, and cooperation with police, fire insurance, and media institutions. 25m; VHS, 3/4 U. **Pr:** National Fire Protection Association. **A:** College-Adult. **P:** Education. **U:** Institution, CCTV, Home. **Gen-Edu**: Fires. **Acq**: Purchase. **Dist:** National Fire Protection Association.

Arson Investigation 1980
Robert Carter, chief fire and arson investigation specialist, demonstrates (in a simulated arson-related fire) the procedure and investigative techniques used in dealing with arson cases. 22m; VHS, 3/4 U. **Pr:** National Fire Protection Association. **A:** Sr. High-Adult. **P:** Education. **U:** Institution, CCTV, Home. **Gen-Edu**: Fires. **Acq**: Purchase. **Dist:** National Fire Protection Association.

Arson Investigation 1984
This program describes techniques for deciding whether or not a fire was set intentionally. 38m; VHS, 3/4 U. **TV Std**: NTSC, PAL, SECAM. **Pr:** Gulf Publishing Co. **A:** Sr. High-Adult. **P:** Education. **U:** Institution, SURA. **Gen-Edu**: Fires. **Acq**: Purchase. **Dist:** Gulf Publishing Co.

Art a la Carte - Delivering Images of Hope 19??
Health professions film from the University of Calgary Learning Commons. ?m; VHS. **A:** Adult. **P:** Education. **U:** Institution. **Hea-Sci**: Health Education, Medical Education. **Acq**: Purchase. **Dist:** University of Calgary Library, Visual Resources Centre.

Art Ache 1990
A three-volume series exploring the world of art through the perspective of the marketplace, including museums, galleries, dealers, investors, and the media. Tapes available individually. 45m; VHS. **A:** College-Adult. **P:** Education. **U:** Home, Institution. **Fin-Art**: Art & Artists. **Acq**: Purchase. **Dist:** Baker and Taylor; Home Vision Cinema. $39.95.
Indiv. Titles: 1. Art is Long—Life is Short? 2. The Game of Art and How to Play it 3. The Image of an Artist.

Art Adventure Series 1979
A series designed to introduce young children to the world of art and handicraft. 11m; VHS. **Pr:** Coronet Films. **A:** Sr. High-Adult. **P:** Education. **U:** Institution, Home. **Fin-Art**: Art & Artists, Education. **Acq**: Purchase, Rent/Lease. **Dist:** Phoenix Learning Group. $185.00.
Indiv. Titles: 1. Block Printing 2. Fabric Dyeing 3. Making Baskets 4. Sand Casting.

Art Advocacy Something Special 199?
Develops awareness of the arts for an overall education by showing children in visual arts, music, dance, and theatre classes. 28m; VHS. **A:** Primary-College. **P:** Teacher Education. **U:** Institution, Home. **Gen-Edu**: Art & Artists, Theater, Dance. **Acq**: Purchase. **Dist:** Crystal Productions. $39.95.

Art America 1976
This series traces the achievements of Americans in the visual arts from colonial times to the present focusing on painting and sculpture with supplemental information on architecture and photography. In 20 untitled programs. 30m; 3/4 U, Q. **Pr:** Children's Television International. **A:** Sr. High-Adult. **P:** Education. **U:** Institution, CCTV, CATV, BCTV, Home. **Fin-Art**: Art & Artists. **Acq**: Purchase, Rent/Lease. **Dist:** Children's Television International.

Art and Anatomy 1989
Discusses terminology and orientation, skeletal structure, joints, muscles and tendons in an attempt toward accurate renditions. 40m; VHS. **A:** Adult. **P:** Education. **U:** Institution. **Fin-Art**: Art & Artists. **Acq**: Purchase. **Dist:** RMI Media. $69.95.

Art and Dance 1993
Three teen artists discuss the importance of art in their lives as a form of self-expression and as a career opportunity. Serves to emphasize the importance of the arts in education. Part of the Arts and You(th) Series. 15m; VHS. **A:** Jr. High-Adult. **P:** Education. **U:** Institution. **Gen-Edu**: Art & Artists, Education. **Acq**: Purchase. **Dist:** Films for the Humanities & Sciences. $89.95.

Art and Jazz in Animation 1985
Four programs exploring the animated works of John and Faith Hubley. Covers "The Hole" and "Tender Game" from the 60s, "Voyage to Next" and "Dig" of the 70s, and "The Cosmic Eye" of the 80s. Features the music of Dizzy Gillespie and Quincy Jones. 245m; VHS, DVD. **C:** Narrated by Maureen Stapleton; Dudley Moore. **A:** Jr. High-Adult. **P:** Education. **U:** Institution. **Gen-Edu**: Animation & Cartoons. **Acq**: Purchase. **Dist:** Lightyear Entertainment. $59.95.

Art and Motion 1952
Explains motion as an integral element of the visual arts. 17m; VHS, 3/4 U. **Pr:** Virginia Purcell; Encyclopedia Britannica Educational Corporation. **A:** Sr. High-College. **P:** Education. **U:** Institution, SURA. **Fin-Art**: Art & Artists. **Acq**: Purchase, Rent/Lease, Trade-in. **Dist:** Encyclopedia Britannica. $140.00.

Art and Music in America 1990
A two-part program designed to teach art and music appreciation to school children by critiquing pieces by Cole and MacDowell. ?m; VHS. **Pr:** Crystal Productions. **A:** Primary-Jr. High. **P:** Education. **U:** Institution. **Gen-Edu**: Education, Art & Artists. **Acq**: Purchase. **Dist:** Crystal Productions. $99.00.
Indiv. Titles: 1. Looking at Art 2. Listening to Music.

Art and Perception: Learning to See 1970
The viewer is encouraged to look for the visual elements of art such as color, line, light qualities, texture, and form with the eye of an artist. 17m; VHS, 3/4 U. **Pr:** A. Paul Burnford. **A:** Sr. High-College. **P:** Instruction. **U:** Institution, SURA. **How-Ins**: Art & Artists. **Acq**: Purchase. **Dist:** Phoenix Learning Group.

Art and Recreation in Latin America 1980
This video presents the games people play and the art and architecture they enjoy are presented. The focus is on the Spanish and Indian influences to be found today. 25m; VHS, 3/4 U. **Pr:** Video Knowledge, Inc. **A:** Jr. High-Adult. **P:** Education. **U:** Institution, Home. **Gen-Edu**: South America, Architecture, Art & Artists. **Acq**: Purchase. **Dist:** Video Knowledge, Inc.

Art and Remembrance: The Legacy of Felix Nussbaum 1993
Examines the art of Felix Nussbaum, a German-Jewish artist who spent most of the Holocaust in hiding, creating paintings. Nussbaum was turned into the Gestapo right before the end of the war and died at Auschwitz. Students in Berlin face the Holocaust and their feelings about this period of history through Nussbaum's art. 30m; VHS. **C:** Directed by Barbara Pfeffer. **A:** Sr. High-Adult. **P:** Education. **U:** Institution. **Gen-Edu**: Holocaust, Documentary Films, War--General. **Acq**: Purchase. **Dist:** First Run/Icarus Films. $280.00.

Art and Revolution in Mexico 198?
A study of the painters whose work was a result and a cause of the 1910 Mexican revolution. 60m; VHS, 3/4 U. **C:** Octavio Paz. **A:** Sr. High-Adult. **P:** Education. **U:** Institution, SURA. **Fin-Art**: Art & Artists, Mexico. **Acq**: Purchase. **Dist:** Films for the Humanities & Sciences.

Art & Science of Punkin' Chunkin' 1998
Documents Delaware's annual post-Halloween pumpkin propelling competition. Teaches scientific, physical principles in a fun manner. 18m; VHS. **A:** Primary. **P:** Education. **U:** Home. **Chl-Juv**: Children, Education, Science. **Acq**: Purchase. **Dist:** Instructional Video. $19.95.

The Art and Science of Translation 197?
The roles that translators play in the worlds of culture, business and politics is explained in this program. 30m/B/W; VHS, 3/4 U, EJ, Q. **Pr:** WCBS New York; Camera Three Productions. **A:** Sr. High-Adult. **P:** Education. **U:** Institution, SURA. **Gen-Edu**: Language Arts. **Acq**: Duplication, Free Duplication. **Dist:** Camera Three Productions, Inc.

Art and Society: The Revolt of William Morris 1974
An account of Morris' life based on his writings, presenting his political and artistic philosophies. From the "Victorians" series. 30m; VHS, 3/4 U. **Pr:** University of Toronto. **A:** Sr. High-Adult. **P:** Education. **U:** Institution, CCTV. **Gen-Edu**: Great Britain. **Acq**: Purchase, Rent/Lease. **Dist:** University of Toronto.

Art and Technique of the Ballet 1967
Explains the visual meaning of ballet. 11m/B/W; VHS, 3/4 U. **TV Std**: NTSC, PAL, SECAM. **Pr:** Lehrfilm-Institut. **A:** Jr. High-Adult. **P:** Education. **U:** Institution, SURA. **Fin-Art**: Dance--Ballet. **Acq**: Purchase, Rent/Lease, Duplication. **Dist:** The Cinema Guild.

Art and the Artist Series 1969
Leon Moburg, a ceramic artist, explains and demonstrates various techniques and styles utilized in making ceramic vessels. Programs in this series are available individually. 14m; VHS, 3/4 U. **C:** Leon Moburg. **Pr:** Cinecrafters. **A:** Jr. High-Adult. **P:** Education. **U:** Institution, SURA. **Fin-Art:** Crafts. **Acq:** Purchase. **Dist:** Phoenix Learning Group.
Indiv. Titles: 1. Art of Ceramic Decorating 2. Art of Ceramic Firing 3. Art of Ceramic Glazing 4. Art of the Potter 5. Art of Thrown Sculpture 6. Covered Jars 7. Pitchers, Spouts, and Handles.

Art and the Exceptional Student 1979
From the "Stretch" series developed by educators to facilitate mainstreaming. Introduces art as an important motivational force for students since it focuses on their strengths and nurtures their creative spirit. 30m; VHS, 3/4 U, EJ. **Pr:** Metropolitan Cooperative Educationa. **A:** College-Adult. **P:** Teacher Education. **U:** Institution, CCTV. **Gen-Edu:** Handicapped. **Acq:** Purchase. **Dist:** American Educational Products LLC.

Art and Therapy 198?
This use of art therapy in helping the mentally ill is explored. Filmed at the South Bronx Community Mental Health Center. 22m; VHS, 3/4 U. **Pr:** Hughes Lavergne. **A:** Jr. High-Adult. **P:** Education. **U:** Institution, Home, SURA. **Gen-Edu:** Psychology. **Acq:** Purchase, Rent/Lease, Duplication. **Dist:** Filmakers Library Inc.

Art and Worship 1987
An exploration of how a place of worship can have a positive effect on people. 28m; VHS, 3/4 U. **Pr:** Real to Reel Productions. **A:** Jr. High-Adult. **P:** Religious. **U:** Institution, SURA. **Gen-Edu:** Art & Artists. **Acq:** Purchase, Rent/Lease. **Dist:** St. Anthony Messenger Press. $19.95.

Art Appreciation 1991
Four programs designed to teach an appreciation of various styles of art of the 20th century. Topics covered are Fauvism, Expressionism, Cubism & Nonobjective Art, and Surrealism. Works of Matisse, Kokoschka, Kandinsky, Dali, and Picasso are featured. ?m; VHS. **Pr:** Crystal Productions. **A:** Jr. High-Adult. **P:** Education. **U:** Institution, Home. **Fin-Art:** Art & Artists, Painting, Education. **Acq:** Purchase. **Dist:** Crystal Productions. $59.95.
Indiv. Titles: 1. Fauvism & Expressionism 2. Cubism & Nonobjective Art and Surrealism.

The Art Awareness Collection 197?
Documents the lives, styles, and works of eight artists from different countries and different eras. Programs available individually. 7m; VHS, 3/4 U. **Pr:** National Gallery of Art; WETA Washington. **A:** Jr. High-College. **P:** Education. **U:** Institution, SURA. **Fin-Art:** Art & Artists. **Acq:** Purchase, Rent/Lease, Trade-in. **Dist:** Encyclopedia Britannica.
Indiv. Titles: 1. Rembrandt 2. Fragonard 3. Goya 4. John Singleton Copley 5. Joseph Mallord William Turner, R.A. 6. A Nation of Painters 7. Degas 8. Renoir.

Art Blakey & the Jazz Messengers: Japan 1961 19??
Blakey & The Jazz Messengers perform in a 1961 TV appearance. Includes the hits "The Summit," "A Night in Tunisia," "Yama," and "Blues March." 48m; VHS. **A:** Jr. High-Adult. **P:** Entertainment. **U:** Home. **Mov-Ent:** Music Video, Music--Performance, Music--Jazz. **Acq:** Purchase. **Dist:** Music Video Distributors. $59.95.

Art Blakey: Live at Ronnie Scotts 19??
The jazz legend plays live at the well-known small club in this British import. 60m; VHS. **A:** College-Adult. **P:** Entertainment. **U:** Home. **Mov-Ent:** Music--Jazz. **Acq:** Purchase. **Dist:** Music Video Distributors. $19.95.

Art Blakey: The Jazz Life 1982
The jazz great performs music with Wynton Marsalis and other greats. 55m; VHS. **A:** College-Adult. **P:** Entertainment. **U:** Home. **Mov-Ent:** Music--Performance, Music--Jazz. **Acq:** Purchase. **Dist:** Music Video Distributors.

Art Blakey: The Jazz Messenger 1989
A look at Blakey's past contributions to jazz and his commitment to the future of the music. 78m; VHS. **C:** Directed by Dick Fontaine; Pat Hartley. **Pr:** Kino International Corporation. **A:** Sr. High-Adult. **P:** Entertainment. **U:** Home. **Mov-Ent:** Music--Jazz, Black Culture. **Acq:** Purchase. **Dist:** Music Video Distributors; Facets Multimedia Inc.; Rhapsody Films, Inc. $29.95.

Art Briles: Shield Punt & Offensive Schemes 2013 (Unrated)
Coach Art Briles discusses his football coaching philosophy on both offense and special teams play. 56m; DVD. **A:** Family. **P:** Education. **U:** Home. **L:** English. **Spo-Rec:** Athletic Instruction/Coaching, Football. **Acq:** Purchase. **Dist:** Championship Productions. $29.99.

Art Careers 1991
A look at career possibilities in both fine arts and commercial art. Topics covered include painting, pottery, sculpture, cartooning, and photography. Tapes can be purchased individually or as a set. 30m; VHS. **Pr:** Crystal Productions. **A:** Jr. High-College. **P:** Education. **U:** Institution. **Gen-Edu:** Job Hunting, Occupations, Art & Artists. **Acq:** Purchase. **Dist:** Crystal Productions. $39.95.
Indiv. Titles: 1. Fine Art: General, Vol. 1 2. Fine Art: Production, Vol. 2 3. Fine Art: Education, Vol. 3 4. Commercial Art: General, Vol. 1 5. Commercial Art: Media, Vol. 2 6. Commercial Art: Design, Vol. 3.

Art: Ceramic Techniques 1992
Provides art teachers with skills and techniques needed to help students translate creative ideas into actual projects using the medium of ceramics. Emphasizes understanding the work of past and contemporary ceramicists through appreciation, designing, hand-building, decoration, and wheel techniques. Series of ten programs with teacher's guide. 30m; VHS. **A:** Adult. **P:** Teacher Education. **U:** Institution. **Gen-Edu:** Art & Artists, How-To. **Acq:** Purchase. **Dist:** GPN Educational Media. $275.00.
Indiv. Titles: 1. Introduction to Ceramic Techniques 2. Pinch Construction 3. Coil Construction 4. Slab Construction 5. Slab Structure 6. Fantasy Sculpture 7. Wheel Techniques: Centering/Cylinder/Bowl 8. Wheel Techniques: Trimming Foot/Spout/Handles 9. Tiles and Murals 10. Decorating, Glazing and Firing.

The Art Chest 19??
Emphasizes creative expression while building the child's confidence and enjoyment in simple art projects. Provides easy-to-follow techniques in drawing, painting, paper folding, paper cutting, sculpturing, and introduces new art projects. 15m; VHS, Q, Special order formats. **Pr:** Western Instructional Television. **A:** Primary. **P:** Instruction. **U:** Institution, CCTV, CATV, BCTV, SURA. **How-Ins:** Art & Artists. **Acq:** Purchase, Rent/Lease. **Dist:** Western Instructional Television.
Indiv. Titles: 1. Beginning Free Brush 2. Drawing Without Lines 3. Beginning Designs 4. Drawing Animals 5. Colored Chalk 6. Sponge Painting 7. Face Decorations 8. Paper Tearing 9. Like Van Gogh 10. Stylized People 11. Making It With Paper Strips 12. Clay Bowls 13. Making Your Own Wrapping Paper 14. Santa Claus Christmas Tree 15. What's Going On At Your House? 16. Scrap Printing 17. Fold Painting 18. Blow Painting 19. String Painting 20. Finger Paint Designs 21. Your Very Own Mail Box 22. Wet Chalk 23. Free Drawing 24. Free Painting 25. Pipe Cleaner People 26. Paper Bag Puppets 27. Our Bunny Friends 28. Corsage for Mom 29. Egg Decorations 30. Paper Sculptured Birds 31. T-Shirt Designs 32. Summer Craft Ideas.

Art City: A Ruling Passion 2006
Focuses on artists who use their art to explore emotional issues, including Louise Bourgeois, Richard Burton, David Deutsch, Elizabeth Peyton, and others. 58m; DVD. **A:** Sr. High-Adult. **P:** Entertainment. **U:** Home. **Fin-Art:** Documentary Films, Art & Artists. **Acq:** Purchase. **Dist:** Microcinema International.

Art City: Simplicity 2006
A look at the lives and studios of such artists as Richard Tuttle, Agnes Martin, Robert Williams, Amy Adler, and others. 59m; DVD. **A:** Sr. High-Adult. **P:** Entertainment. **U:** Home. **Fin-Art:** Documentary Films, Art & Artists. **Acq:** Purchase. **Dist:** Microcinema International.

Art Com Video 1: Scandinavia 1992 (Unrated)
Diverse collection of videos from Scandanavia. Includes "Char, en Oversattning," "Cricket," "Elastic Party," "The Hu, man Race," "Johnny-A Modern Interpretation of Slavology," "Menschen," "R.E.M.," and others. 92m; VHS. **A:** Jr. High-Adult. **P:** Entertainment. **U:** Home. **Mov-Ent:** Art & Artists, Video, Scandinavia. **Acq:** Purchase. **Dist:** Facets Multimedia Inc. $54.95.

Art Com Video 2: Video Japan 1992
A collection of videos from artists in Japan, representing nature, culture traditions, and the romance of new technology. Includes "Mt. Fuji," "Flow (3) Part 2," "Koto Buki," "Listen the Body," "My Gaijin Tengoky," and "Alley o Alley." 57m; VHS. **A:** Jr. High-Adult. **P:** Entertainment. **U:** Home. **Mov-Ent:** Art & Artists, Video, Japan. **Acq:** Purchase. **Dist:** Facets Multimedia Inc. $49.95.

Art Com Video 3: Max Almy 1989
A collection of videos by Almy which probe unseen and unexpected sides of contemporary American life. Includes "Modern Times," "Deadline," "Leaving the 20th Century," "Perfect Leader," "Drake's Equation," and "Lost in the Pictures." 52m; VHS. **A:** Jr. High-Adult. **P:** Entertainment. **U:** Home. **Mov-Ent:** Art & Artists, Video. **Acq:** Purchase. **Dist:** Facets Multimedia Inc. $49.95.

Art Commission Hearings 1 1973
Part I of the "Art Commission Hearings" explains how the Kearny Street Workshop and the Bay Area Arts Club serve their communities in California. 30m/B/W; EJ. **A:** Adult. **P:** Education. **U:** Institution, CCTV. **Gen-Edu:** Cities & Towns. **Acq:** Loan. **Dist:** Chinese for Affirmative Action.

The Art Critic 1995
The role of the art critic is explored. 29m; VHS. **P:** Professional. **U:** Home. **Bus-Ind:** Art & Artists, Occupations. **Acq:** Purchase. **Dist:** Crystal Productions. $29.95.

Art Education in Action, Vol. 1: Aesthetics 19??
Part of a five-volume teaching aid for art education that observes teachers and students of art in diverse communities. Each tape includes a teaching guide and student activities. 40m; VHS. **A:** Jr. High-College. **P:** Education. **U:** Institution. **Gen-Edu:** Art & Artists, Education. **Acq:** Purchase. **Dist:** Crystal Productions. $15.00.

Art Education in Action, Vol. 2: Integrating the Art Disciplines 19??
Part of a five-volume teaching aid for art education that observes teachers and students of art in diverse communities. Each tape includes a teaching guide and student activities. 40m; VHS. **A:** Jr. High-College. **P:** Education. **U:** Institution. **Gen-Edu:** Art & Artists, Education. **Acq:** Purchase. **Dist:** Crystal Productions. $15.00.

Art Education in Action, Vol. 3: Making Art 19??
Part of a five-volume teaching aid for art education that observes teachers and students of art in diverse communities. Each tape includes a teaching guide and student activities. 40m; VHS. **A:** Jr. High-College. **P:** Education. **U:** Institution. **Gen-Edu:** Art & Artists, Education. **Acq:** Purchase. **Dist:** Crystal Productions. $15.00.

Art Education in Action, Vol. 4: Art History and Art Criticism 19??
Part of a five-volume teaching aid for art education that observes teachers and students of art in diverse communities. Each tape includes a teaching guide and student activities. 40m; VHS. **A:** Jr. High-College. **P:** Education. **U:** Institution. **Gen-Edu:** Art & Artists, Education. **Acq:** Purchase. **Dist:** Crystal Productions. $15.00.

Art Education in Action, Vol. 5: School-Museum Collaboration 19??
Part of a five-volume teaching aid for art education that observes teachers and students of art in diverse communities. Each tape includes a teaching guide and student activities. 40m; VHS. **A:** Jr. High-College. **P:** Education. **U:** Institution. **Gen-Edu:** Art & Artists, Education. **Acq:** Purchase. **Dist:** Crystal Productions. $15.00.

Art Elements: An Introduction 1981
An introduction and review of the basic elements of two-dimensional art. 18m; VHS, 3/4 U. **Pr:** Sal Bruno. **A:** Jr. High-Sr. High. **P:** Education. **U:** Institution, SURA. **Fin-Art:** Art & Artists. **Acq:** Purchase. **Dist:** Phoenix Learning Group.

Art Ensemble of Chicago: Live from the Jazz Showcase 1981
Listen to jazz of all types. From New Orleans jazz to ballads, from be-bop to funk, enjoy one of the greatest jazz groups of our time perform these memorable hits. 50m; VHS. **A:** Sr. High-Adult. **P:** Entertainment. **U:** Home. **Fin-Art:** Performing Arts, Music--Jazz, Music--Performance. **Acq:** Purchase. **Dist:** Music Video Distributors; Rhapsody Films, Inc. $29.95.

Art Explorations: Mexican Folk Art 1992
Presents a variety of Mexican art forms, influenced by pre-Columbian designs and Spanish colonial and mestizo motifs. Examines the historical overview as well as ceremonial and utilitarian purposes. 22m; VHS. **A:** Jr. High-Sr. High. **P:** Education. **U:** Home. **Gen-Edu:** Art & Artists, Mexico. **Acq:** Purchase. **Dist:** SRA/McGraw-Hill. $83.

Art Farmer 1982
Trumpet player Art Farmer, with Fred Hersch on piano, Dennis Irwin on bass, and Billy Hart on drums, performs classic jazz tunes. 60m; VHS. **A:** Family. **P:** Entertainment. **U:** Home. **Fin-Art:** Music--Performance, Music--Jazz. **Acq:** Purchase. **Dist:** Kultur International Films Ltd., Inc. $29.95.

Art for Teachers of Children 1995 (Unrated) — ★★
Autobiographical account of 14-year-old Jennifer (McDonnell) who becomes a model for married photographer John (Hannah), who's also her boarding school dorm advisor. He's well-known for his nude portraits of young women as well as his affairs with his models and Jennifer's both confused and excited by her emerging sexuality as she and John become lovers. Remarkably detached considering the provocative subject matter. 82m/B/W; VHS. **C:** Caitlin Grace McDonnell; Duncan Hannah; Coles Burroughs; Bryan Keane; Directed by Jennifer Montgomery; Written by Jennifer Montgomery; Cinematography by Jennifer Montgomery. **Pr:** Zeitgeist Films Ltd. **A:** College-Adult. **P:** Entertainment. **U:** Home. **Mov-Ent:** Sex & Sexuality, Adolescence, Photography. **Acq:** Purchase. **Dist:** Zeitgeist Films Ltd.; Water Bearer Films Inc.

Art for Whose Sake? 1987
A discussion of whether art exists for the sake of the artist or the viewer. 14m; VHS, 8 mm, Special order formats. **C:** Directed by Sam Napier-Bell. **A:** Jr. High-Adult. **P:** Education. **U:** Institution, Home. **Fin-Art:** Art & Artists, Philosophy & Ideology. **Acq:** Purchase. **Dist:** The Roland Collection. $79.00.

Art from Found Materials 1971
Many artists use "found materials" with imagination. They use such natural materials as seeds and shells as well as scrap materials. Both the collage and assemblage are illustrated. 12m; VHS, 3/4 U. **A:** Jr. High-Sr. High. **P:** Education. **U:** Institution, SURA. **Fin-Art:** Crafts. **Acq:** Purchase. **Dist:** Phoenix Learning Group.

Art Galleries 1995
Ways artists can get their work into a gallery and related concerns. 31m; VHS. **A:** Adult. **P:** Professional. **U:** Home. **Bus-Ind:** Art & Artists. **Acq:** Purchase. **Dist:** Crystal Productions. $29.95.

Art Heist 2005 (R) — ★★½
The theft of a precious painting from a Barcelona art gallery causes art expert Sandra (Pompeo) to leave New York to work with Daniel (Folk), an old love interest, to investigate the crime. This doesn't sit well with her tough-guy ex-husband Bruce (Baldwin), an NYPD cop, who tracks Sandra down, only to find her in over her head with the menacing Russian mafia. 98m; VHS, DVD, Wide. **C:** Ellen Pompeo; William Baldwin; Abel Folk; Simon Andreu; Ed Lauter; Written by Diane Fine; Evan Spiliotopolos; Cinematography by Jacques Haitkin. **A:** Sr. High-Adult. **P:** Entertainment. **U:** Home. **Mov-Ent:** Acq: Purchase. **Dist:** Movies Unlimited; Alpha Video. $14.94.

Art History 1: A Century of Modern Art 1989
The story of the last one hundred years of art is told. 15m; VHS, 3/4 U. **Pr:** WDCN-TV. **A:** Primary-Adult. **P:** Education. **U:** Institution, CCTV, CATV, BCTV. **Fin-Art:** Art & Artists, Painting.

Acq: Purchase, Rent/Lease, Duplication License. **Dist:** Agency for Instructional Technology. $995.00.
Indiv. Titles: 1. Impressionism 2. The Fauves 3. Expressionism 4. Cubism 5. Surrealism 6. Modern Mavericks 7. American Landscapes 8. Realism 9. Abstract Expressionism 10. Pop.

Art History 2: A Survey of the Western World 1989
Series of 12 programs studying the art of the western world. Titles may be purchased individually or as a series. Teacher's guide available at additional cost. 15m; VHS. **Pr:** WDCN Nashville. **A:** Jr. High-Sr. High. **P:** Education. **U:** Institution. **Fin-Art:** Art & Artists, History, Italy. **Acq:** Purchase, Rent/Lease. **Dist:** Agency for Instructional Technology. $125.00.
Indiv. Titles: 1. Ash Can Plus 2. Cosmopolitan: Looking Toward Europe 3. Colonials: Realistic and Romantic 4. English Painting 5. Spain 6. German Painting 7. Seventeenth Century Dutch Masters 8. Flemish Painting 9. Italian Renaissance Painting 10. Mannerism: Italy 11. Italian Architecture 12. Chateaux of the Loire.

Art House 1998 (R) — ★½
Ray (O'Donahue) and his irritating pal Weston (irritating Hardwick) aspire to be filmmakers, but the road to success is blocked by rocky relationships, money problems, and lack of talent. The comic elements are fitfully funny but the image is so rough that only the most dedicated fans of low-budget ($200,000 according to the director) independent productions will be willing to stick with it. Those hoping to see a lot of Internet babe Weber will be disappointed. 89m; DVD. **C:** Dan O'Donahue; Chris Hardwick; Luigi Amodeo; Rebecca McFarland; Adam Carolla; Cheryl Pollak; Amy Weber; Directed by Leigh Slawner; Written by Dan O'Donahue; Leigh Slawner; Cinematography by Billy Beaird; Music by Christopher Lennertz. **A:** Sr. High-Adult. **P:** Entertainment. **U:** Home. **Mov-Ent:** Filmmaking. **Acq:** Purchase. **Dist:** York Entertainment.

Art in an Age of Mass Culture 1992
Prepared as a response to the much discussed exhibition "High & Low: High Art and Popular Culture," which opened at the Museum of Modern Art in New York in 1990. Includes interviews with many of the artists featured in the exhibition. 30m; VHS, 3/4 U. **Pr:** Michael Blackwood Productions. **A:** College-Adult. **P:** Education. **U:** Home, Institution. **Gen-Edu:** Art & Artists. **Acq:** Purchase, Rent/Lease. **Dist:** Michael Blackwood Productions. $250.

Art in Architecture 1989
Contains on-site commentary and design evaluation of five Denver-area buildings. Includes comments by design professionals. 30m; VHS. **Pr:** University of Colorado. **A:** College-Adult. **P:** Professional. **U:** Institution, Home. **Fin-Art:** Architecture, Education. **Acq:** Rent/Lease. **Dist:** American Institute of Architects.

Art in Motion Volume 1: Warm Up/ Progressions ????
Joe Istre's complete jazz course with warm-up, center exercises, turn combination, floor routines, and a complete lyrical piece, with in-depth analysis and demonstration. 72m; VHS. **A:** Adult. **P:** Teacher Education. **U:** Institution. **How-Ins:** Dance, Dance--Instruction. **Acq:** Purchase. **Dist:** Stagestep. $59.95.

Art in Motion Volume 2: Intermediate Progressions ????
Joe Istre's complete jazz course using all traveling combinations, starting with a simple level and increasing in difficulty. Designed to help younger dancers improve their flexibility, speed and coordination. Concludes with analysis and demonstration of a complete jazz number. 60m; VHS. **A:** Adult. **P:** Teacher Education. **U:** Institution. **How-Ins:** Dance, Dance--Instruction. **Acq:** Purchase. **Dist:** Stagestep. $59.95.

Art in Motion Volume 3: Advanced Progressions ????
Joe Istre's complete jazz course for the advanced dancer includes four battement combinations; multiple head, shoulder, rib, and hip isolations; turn combinations; five floor routines and two long jump passes. 68m; VHS. **A:** Adult. **P:** Teacher Education. **U:** Institution. **How-Ins:** Dance, Dance--Instruction. **Acq:** Purchase. **Dist:** Stagestep. $59.95.

Art in Stations: Detroit People Mover 1989
Illustrates the 15 commissioned works of art located in the 13 transit stations of the Detroit People Mover system in downtown Detroit. 30m; VHS. **P:** Education. **U:** Institution, Home. **Fin-Art:** Art & Artists. **Acq:** Purchase. **Dist:** Museum of Arts and Design. $29.95.

Art in the Cultural Revolution 1997
Documentary examines the effect of the art policies enforced during China's Cultural Revolution. 33m; VHS. **A:** College. **P:** Education. **U:** Institution. **Fin-Art:** Documentary Films, Art & Artists, China. **Acq:** Purchase, Rent/Lease. **Dist:** The Cinema Guild. $250.

Art in the Public Eye: The Making of Dark Star Park 1988
A documentary on the construction of Dark Star Park, a functional public sculpture outside Washington, D.C., including interviews with the artist and footage of the sculpture being constructed. 33m; VHS, 3/4 U. **Pr:** Nancy Holt. **A:** Jr. High-Adult. **P:** Education. **U:** Institution, Home. **Gen-Edu:** Sculpture, Women. **Acq:** Purchase, Rent/Lease. **Dist:** Museum of Modern Art.

Art in the Stations 1989
Promotes public art as artists discuss the planning, execution, and installation of 15 major works of art in downtown Detroit's people mover stations. Narrated by Sam Sachs, director of the Detroit Institute of Arts. Includes more than two years of footage

artist's studios, workplaces, and installation sites. 29m; VHS, 3/4 U, Special order formats. **P:** Education. **U:** Institution, SURA. **Fin-Art:** Art & Artists. **Acq:** Purchase, Rent/Lease. **Dist:** Sue Marx Films, Inc.

Art in the 20th Century Series 1990
Four-part art education series that focuses on the four post-war art trends: constructivism, dadaism, new objectivity, and surrealism. Emphasizes how the gruesome reality of modern war shaped the thinking and work of a new generation of artists. 118m; VHS, SVS, 3/4 U. **A:** Sr. High-Adult. **P:** Education. **U:** Institution. **Gen-Edu:** Art & Artists. **Acq:** Purchase, Rent/Lease. **Dist:** Encyclopedia Britannica. $285.00.
Indiv. Titles: 1. Constructivism 2. Dadaism 3. New Objectivity 4. Surrealism.

Art in the Western World 1958
Surveys Western painting from the 13th through the early 20th century, providing a comprehensive view of the many periods and styles of art. From the National Gallery of Art in Washington, D. C. 30m; VHS, 3/4 U. **Pr:** Encyclopedia Britannica Educational Corporation; National Gallery of Art. **A:** Sr. High-College. **P:** Education. **U:** Institution, SURA. **Fin-Art:** Painting. **Acq:** Purchase, Rent/Lease, Trade-in. **Dist:** Encyclopedia Britannica. $16.50.

Art Is ... The Permanent Revolution 2012
Ideas of social protest and revolution have been depicted by graphic artists and printmakers for centuries. These art forms are explored with the contemporary assistance and perspective of three artists and a master printer. 82m; DVD. **A:** Sr. High-Adult. **P:** Entertainment. **U:** Home. **Mov-Ent:** Art & Artists, Sociology, Documentary Films. **Acq:** Purchase. **Dist:** First Run Features. $27.95.

Art Journaling with Marianne Hieb, RSM 19??
Marianne Hieb lectures on art-journaling as a modality for prayer and dialogue with the Holy and the self. 30m; VHS. **A:** Jr. High-Adult. **P:** Religious. **U:** Institution, Home. **Gen-Edu:** Religion, Self-Help. **Acq:** Purchase. **Dist:** Alba House Media Center. $19.95.

Art Lessons for Children, Vol. 1: Easy Watercolor Techniques in 4 Lessons 1991
Presents easy instructions on how to create beautiful watercolors using simple and inexpensive materials. 50m; VHS. **A:** Primary. **P:** Instruction. **U:** Home, Institution. **How-Ins:** How-To, Art & Artists. **Acq:** Purchase. **Dist:** Crystal Productions; Coyote Creek Productions. $29.95.

Art Lessons for Children, Vol. 2: Easy Art Projects in 3 Lessons 1991
Demonstrates simple techniques for children to use in creating oil pastel paintings, foil bas relief hangings, and watercolor prints. 50m; VHS. **A:** Primary. **P:** Instruction. **U:** Home, Institution. **How-Ins:** How-To, Art & Artists. **Acq:** Purchase. **Dist:** Crystal Productions; Coyote Creek Productions. $29.95.

Art Lessons for Children, Vol. 4: Felt Pen Fun in 4 Lessons 1992
Donna Hugh demonstrates how to draw colorful pictures with felt tip pens using various techniques and suggestions. 58m; VHS. **A:** Primary. **P:** Instruction. **U:** Home, Institution. **How-Ins:** Drawing, Children, Art & Artists. **Acq:** Purchase. **Dist:** Coyote Creek Productions; Crystal Productions. $29.95.

Art Lessons for Children, Vol. 5: Animals of the Rain Forest 199?
By seeing live animals from the rain forest, children learn to produce art. 58m; VHS. **A:** Primary. **P:** Instruction. **U:** Home, Institution. **How-Ins:** How-To, Art & Artists. **Acq:** Purchase. **Dist:** Crystal Productions; Coyote Creek Productions. $29.95.

Art Lessons for Children, Vol. 6: Plants of the Rain Forest 199?
Donna Hugh shows, through living plants, how to create artwork. 48m; VHS. **A:** Primary. **P:** Instruction. **U:** Home, Institution. **How-Ins:** How-To, Art & Artists. **Acq:** Purchase. **Dist:** Coyote Creek Productions; Crystal Productions. $29.95.

Art Lessons for Children with Donna Hugh, Vol. 5: Animals of the Rain Forest 1994
Donna Hugh demonstrates step-by-step procedures for children on how to paint different types of animals. Contains three lessons: (1) The Toucan; (2) The Iguana; and (3) The Tamandua. 58m; VHS. **A:** Primary. **P:** Instruction. **U:** Institution, Home. **How-Ins:** How-To, Art & Artists, Animals. **Acq:** Purchase. **Dist:** Coyote Creek Productions.

Art Lessons for Children with Donna Hugh, Vol. 6: Plants of the Rain Forest 1994
Art teacher Donna Hugh provides examples of live rain forest plants and then demonstrates step-by-step procedures, aimed at children, on how to paint these plants. Contains three lessons: (1) Tillandsias; (2) Bromeliads; and (3) Orchids. 48m; VHS. **A:** Primary. **P:** Instruction. **U:** Home, Institution. **How-Ins:** How-To, Art & Artists, Plants. **Acq:** Purchase. **Dist:** Coyote Creek Productions.

Art Linkletter on Positive Aging 1994
Eighty-one-year-old Art Linkletter shares research and interviews on aging. Two-tape program discusses fractured families, and the importance of grandparents. Also features gerontologist, physician/nutritionist, psychotherapist and others who speak on the physical and emotional well-being of the elderly. 45m; VHS. **A:** Adult. **P:** Education. **U:** Institution. **Hea-Sci:** Aging. **Acq:** Purchase. **Dist:** PBS Home Video. $125.

Art Machine 2012 (Unrated) — ★
Declan has had great success as a teenaged art prodigy but now he's old news. He's struggling to find something new to

present, but seems stuck until he meets up with an art collective that includes Cassandra. Declan's inspired but the same can't be said for the movie, which is an uneasy satire that feels unfinished. 89m; DVD. **C:** Joseph Cross; Jessica Szohr; Joey Lauren Adams; Damian Young; Directed by Doug Karr; Written by Doug Karr; Nuno Viera Faustino; Cinematography by Adriana Correia; Music by Mark Stephan Kondracki. **A:** Sr. High-Adult. **P:** Entertainment. **U:** Home. **L:** English. **Mov-Ent:** Art & Artists. **Acq:** Purchase. **Dist:** Virgil Films & Entertainment.

Art Maker 1982
This series develops skills in free brush, crayon drawing, the use of chalk and charcoal, paper cutting and folding, and more. 15m; VHS, Q, Special order formats. **C:** Hosted by Dan Mihuta. **Pr:** Western Instructional Television. **A:** Primary. **P:** Instruction. **U:** Institution, CCTV, CATV, BCTV, SURA. **Gen-Edu:** Art & Artists. **Acq:** Purchase, Rent/Lease. **Dist:** Western Instructional Television.
Indiv. Titles: 1. Free Brush Strokes 2. Flat Crayon Drawing 3. Mandala Designs 4. Drawing People 5. Chalk Stencils 6. Dry Brush 7. Mask Making 8. Paper Weaving 9. Sponge Paint Turkeys 10. Paper Sculpture Animals 11. Clay Plaques 12. Christmas Crafts 13. Spray Painting 14. Beginning Charcoal 15. Value Painting 16. Paint Over Crayon 17. Crayon Etching 18. Old Fashioned Valentine 19. Transparent Water Color 20. Finger Painting 21. Mono Printing 22. Cardboard Printing 23. Clay Animals 24. Using Texture 25. Crayon Mosaics 26. Easter Lilies 27. Twirlers 28. Mixed Media 29. Cartooning 30. Paper Plate Art 31. Stuffed Paper Animals 32. Beginning Sculpture.

Art Makes the Difference 1991
Features Jeff Daniels, Phil Benton, Mitch Albom, Mort Crim, and others as they try to raise the consciousness about the importance of art in our lives. 10m; VHS, 3/4 U, Special order formats. **P:** Education. **U:** Institution, SURA. **Fin-Art:** Art & Artists. **Acq:** Purchase, Rent/Lease. **Dist:** Sue Marx Films, Inc.

Art Meets Science & Spirituality in a Changing Economy, Vol. 1: From Fragmentation to Wholeness 1993
The Dalai Lama, quantum physicist David Bohm, and artist Robert Rauschenberg gather to discuss creativity, wholeness, coherence, and the theory of "the implicate order." 52m; VHS. **A:** Sr. High-College. **P:** Education. **U:** Institution. **Gen-Edu:** Philosophy & Ideology, Art & Artists, Science. **Acq:** Purchase. **Dist:** Baker and Taylor; Mystic Fire Video. $95.00.

Art Meets Science & Spirituality in a Changing Economy, Vol. 2: The Chaotic Universe 1993
Thermodynamic physicist Ilya Prigogine, composer John Cage, and philosopher Huston Smith discuss the nature and organization of all living systems at an Amsterdam conference. 52m; VHS. **A:** Sr. High-College. **P:** Education. **U:** Institution. **Gen-Edu:** Philosophy & Ideology, Art & Artists, Science. **Acq:** Purchase. **Dist:** Baker and Taylor; Mystic Fire Video. $95.00.

Art Meets Science & Spirituality in a Changing Economy, Vol. 3: Crisis of Perception 1993
Group discussion focusing on reality and non-reality features Carmelite nun Mother Tesa Bielecki, artist Jacques van der Heyden, and cognitive scientist Francisco Verela. 52m; VHS. **A:** Sr. High-College. **P:** Education. **U:** Institution. **Gen-Edu:** Art & Artists, Science, Religion. **Acq:** Purchase. **Dist:** Baker and Taylor; Mystic Fire Video. $95.00.

Art Meets Science & Spirituality in a Changing Economy, Vol. 4: The Transforming World 1993
Biologist Ruper Sheldrake, Director of Credit Lyonnais J.M. Leveque, and artist lawrence Weiner discuss reincarnation, art and entropy, the Third World, and more. 52m; VHS. **A:** Sr. High-College. **P:** Education. **U:** Institution. **Gen-Edu:** Philosophy & Ideology, Art & Artists, Science. **Acq:** Purchase. **Dist:** Baker and Taylor; Mystic Fire Video. $95.00.

Art Meets Science & Spirituality in a Changing Economy, Vol. 5: The Shifting Paradigm 1993
Discusses ecology, existentialism, and reality in an everchanging world. 52m; VHS. **A:** Sr. High-College. **P:** Education. **U:** Institution. **Gen-Edu:** Philosophy & Ideology, Art & Artists, Economics. **Acq:** Purchase. **Dist:** Baker and Taylor; Mystic Fire Video. $95.00.

ART/New York, Vol. 1 1980
An ongoing video magazine, this edition features Andy Warhol's Portraits of the '70s at the Whitney Museum; Ned Smyth's Thomas Lanaghan Schmidt at the Holly Solomon Gallery; Mel Bochner at Sonnabend Gallery; and Joseph Beuys at the Ronald Feldman Gallery. Included is an interview with Joseph Beuys. 30m; VHS, 3/4 U. **C:** Tom Wolfe. **Pr:** Paul Tschinkel. **A:** Jr. High-Adult. **P:** Education. **U:** Institution, Home, SURA. **Fin-Art:** Art & Artists. **Acq:** Purchase, Subscription. **Dist:** ART/new york.

ART/New York, Vol. 2 1980
An ongoing video magazine, this edition features a group show at the Leo Castelli Gallery, including Robert Rauschenberg, Robert Morris, Frank Stella, Donald Judd, Richard Serra, Bruce Nauman, and Roy Lichtenstein; Vito Acconci, Robert Morris, and Dennis Oppenheim at the Sonnabend Gallery; Vito Acconi at The Kitchen; and Jenny Snider at Artist's Space. Included is an interview with Vito Acconi and a film by Jenny Snider. 30m; VHS, 3/4 U. **C:** Tom Wolfe. **Pr:** Paul Tschinkel. **A:** Jr. High-Adult. **P:** Education. **U:** Institution, Home, SURA. **Fin-Art:** Art & Artists. **Acq:** Purchase, Subscription. **Dist:** ART/new york.

ART/New York, Vol. 3 1980
An ongoing video magazine, this edition features a group show, "Illustration and Allegory," at the Brooke Alexander Gallery including Richard Bosman, Ken Goodman, Thomas Lawson, Robert Longo, Philip Smith, and Michael Zwack; Jim Sullivan at

the Nancy Hoffman Gallery; Claes Oldenburg at the Whitney Museum and Leo Castelli Gallery; and Lynda Benglis at the Paula Cooper Gallery. Included is an interview with Lynda Benglis. 30m; VHS, 3/4 U. **C:** Tom Wolfe. **Pr:** Paul Tschinkel. **A:** Jr. High-Adult. **P:** Education. **U:** Institution, Home, SURA. **Fin-Art:** Art & Artists. **Acq:** Purchase, Subscription. **Dist:** ART/new york.

ART/New York, Vol. 4 1980
An ongoing video magazine, this edition features Duane Hanson at the OK Harris Gallery; Anthony Caro at Acquavella Gallery; Allain Kirili at Sonnabend Gallery; and Jonathan Borofsky at the Paula Cooper Gallery. Included is an interview with Borofsky. 30m; VHS, 3/4 U. **C:** Tom Wolfe. **Pr:** Paul Tschinkel. **A:** Jr. High-Adult. **P:** Education. **U:** Institution, Home, SURA. **Fin-Art:** Art & Artists. **Acq:** Purchase, Subscription. **Dist:** ART/new york.

ART/New York, Vol. 5 1980
An ongoing video magazine, this edition features "New York New Wave at P.S.1," an exhibition organized by Diego Cortez. Guest commentator for this tape is Marc Miller. An interview with Curt Hoppi and Diego Cortez is included. 30m; VHS, 3/4 U. **C:** Hosted by Tom Wolfe. **Pr:** Paul Tschinkel. **A:** Jr. High-Adult. **P:** Education. **U:** Institution, Home, SURA. **Fin-Art:** Art & Artists. **Acq:** Purchase, Subscription. **Dist:** ART/new york.

ART/New York, Vol. 6 1980
An ongoing video magazine, this edition covers the Whitney Biennial-the survey of current American painting and sculpture. Included is an interview with Patterson Sims, curator. 30m; VHS, 3/4 U. **C:** Tom Wolfe. **Pr:** Paul Tschinkel. **A:** Jr. High-Adult. **P:** Education. **U:** Institution, Home, SURA. **Fin-Art:** Art & Artists, Museums. **Acq:** Purchase, Subscription. **Dist:** ART/new york.

ART/New York, Vol. 7 1980
An ongoing video magazine, this edition covers a selection of photographs in the Whitney Biennial and also looks at the Whitney's Video and Film installations. An interview with John Hanhardt, Film and Video Curator, is included. 30m; VHS, 3/4 U. **C:** Tom Wolfe. **Pr:** Paul Tschinkel. **A:** Jr. High-Adult. **P:** Education. **U:** Institution, Home, SURA. **Fin-Art:** Art & Artists, Museums. **Acq:** Purchase, Subscription. **Dist:** ART/new york.

ART/New York, Vol. 8 1980
An ongoing video magazine, this edition is a survey of the multiplicity of trends in contemporary painting. 30m; VHS, 3/4 U. **C:** Tom Wolfe. **Pr:** Paul Tschinkel. **A:** Jr. High-Adult. **P:** Education. **U:** Institution, Home, SURA. **Fin-Art:** Painting, Art & Artists. **Acq:** Purchase, Subscription. **Dist:** ART/new york.

ART/New York, Vol. 9 1982
Covers pop and neo-pop exhibits: "Roy Lichtenstein 1970-1980" at the Whitney; "Myths by Andy Warhol" at the Ron Feldman Gallery; and "Paintings by Jack Goldstein" at Metro Pictures. Also includes interviews with Lichtenstein and Goldstein. Foreign language versions can be arranged. 30m; VHS, 3/4 U. **C:** Hosted by Tom Wolfe. **Pr:** Paul Tschinkel. **A:** Sr. High-Adult. **P:** Entertainment. **U:** Institution, Home, SURA. **Fin-Art:** Art & Artists. **Acq:** Purchase, Subscription. **Dist:** ART/new york.

ART/New York, Vol. 10 1982
This tape covers exhibits concerned with aspects of pattern and decoration: "Homework" at the Henry Street Settlement; "Useable Art" at the Queens Museum; and a visit to the Holly Solomon Gallery. Also includes interviews with Miriam Schapiro, art critic John Perrault and art dealer Holly Solomon. Foreign languages available. 30m; VHS, 3/4 U. **C:** Hosted by Tom Wolfe. **Pr:** Paul Tschinkel. **A:** Sr. High-Adult. **P:** Entertainment. **U:** Institution, Home, SURA. **Fin-Art:** Art & Artists. **Acq:** Purchase, Subscription. **Dist:** ART/new york.

ART/New York, Vol. 11 1982
This tape covers photography exhibitions, including exhibits and interviews with Hans Namuth, Cindy Sherman, Robert Rauschenberg. Foreign language versions can be made available. 30m; VHS, 3/4 U. **C:** Hosted by Tom Wolfe. **Pr:** Paul Tschinkel. **A:** Sr. High-Adult. **P:** Entertainment. **U:** Institution, Home, SURA. **Fin-Art:** Photography, Art & Artists. **Acq:** Purchase, Subscription. **Dist:** ART/new york.

ART/New York, Vol. 12 1982
This tape covers directions in painting, including exhibits by Frank Stella and exhibits and interviews by David Salle and Leon Galub. Foreign language versions can be arranged. 30m; VHS, 3/4 U. **C:** Hosted by Tom Wolfe. **Pr:** Paul Tschinkel. **A:** Sr. High-Adult. **P:** Entertainment. **U:** Institution, Home, SURA. **Fin-Art:** Painting, Art & Artists. **Acq:** Purchase, Subscription. **Dist:** ART/new york.

ART/New York, Vol. 13 1982
This tape covers performance art with Sam Hsieh, Robert Longo, and Colette. Foreign language versions can be made available. 30m; VHS, 3/4 U. **C:** Hosted by Tom Wolfe. **Pr:** Paul Tschinkel. **A:** Sr. High-Adult. **P:** Entertainment. **U:** Institution, Home, SURA. **Fin-Art:** Art & Artists. **Acq:** Purchase, Subscription. **Dist:** ART/new york.

ART/New York, Vol. 14 1983
This program examines the art of public sculpture and including the McGraw-Hill building, Citicorp Center, Maiden Lane Plaza and Federal Plaza. Interviews with Louise Nevelson and Richard Serra are included. 28m; VHS, 3/4 U. **C:** Hosted by Tom Wolfe. **Pr:** Paul Tschinkel. **A:** College-Adult. **P:** Education. **U:** Institution, Home, SURA. **Fin-Art:** Art & Artists. **Acq:** Purchase. **Dist:** ART/new york.

ART/New York, Vol. 15 1983
This program explores New York public art from the city streets to the subways. Interviews with Joyce Kozloff, Keith Haring, and

Henry Geldzahler are featured. 28m; VHS, 3/4 U. **C:** Hosted by Tom Wolfe. **Pr:** Paul Tschinkel. **A:** College-Adult. **P:** Education. **U:** Institution, Home, SURA. **Fin-Art:** Art & Artists. **Acq:** Purchase. **Dist:** ART/new york.

ART/New York, Vol. 16 1980
This program discusses video as art, through interviews with Nam June Paik, Ernest Gusella and M.O.M.A. curator Barbara London. These programs can be made in French, German and Japanese. 30m; VHS, 3/4 U. **C:** Tom Wolfe. **Pr:** Paul Tschinkel. **A:** College-Adult. **P:** Education. **U:** Institution, Home, SURA. **Fin-Art:** Art & Artists. **Acq:** Purchase, Subscription. **Dist:** ART/new york.

ART/New York, Vol. 17 1980
This program looks at geometric abstraction. Interviews with Al Held and Brice Marden. 30m; VHS, 3/4 U. **C:** Tom Wolfe. **Pr:** Paul Tschinkel. **A:** College-Adult. **P:** Education. **U:** Institution, Home, SURA. **Fin-Art:** Art & Artists. **Acq:** Purchase, Subscription. **Dist:** ART/new york.

Art/New York, Vol. 18 1982
The art of expressionist painters Lee Krasner and Malcolm Morley are examined in this program. 30m; VHS, 3/4 U. **C:** Hosted by Tom Wolfe. **Pr:** Paul Tschinkel. **A:** College-Adult. **P:** Education. **U:** Institution, Home, SURA. **Fin-Art:** Art & Artists. **Acq:** Purchase, Subscription. **Dist:** ART/new york.

Art/New York, Vol. 19 1982
The art of expressionist painters Jean-Michel Basquait, Franceso Clemente, and Julian Schnabel are examined in this program. 30m; VHS, 3/4 U. **C:** Hosted by Tom Wolfe. **Pr:** Paul Tschinkel. **A:** College-Adult. **P:** Education. **U:** Institution, Home, SURA. **Fin-Art:** Art & Artists. **Acq:** Purchase, Subscription. **Dist:** ART/new york.

Art/New York, Vol. 20 1982
The pop art works of James Rosenquist, Robert Rauschenberg, and Tom Wesselmann are examined in this program. 30m; VHS, 3/4 U. **C:** Hosted by Tom Wolfe. **Pr:** Paul Tschinkel. **A:** College-Adult. **P:** Education. **U:** Institution, Home, SURA. **Fin-Art:** Art & Artists. **Acq:** Purchase, Subscription. **Dist:** ART/new york.

ART/New York, Vol. 21 1985
The role of graffiti art in culture with Lady Pink, Crash and Kieth Haring. 30m; VHS, 3/4 U. **C:** Hosted by Tom Wolfe. **Pr:** Paul Tschinkel. **A:** College-Adult. **P:** Entertainment. **U:** Institution, Home, SURA. **Fin-Art:** Painting, Art & Artists. **Acq:** Purchase, Subscription. **Dist:** ART/new york.

ART/New York, Vol. 22 1985
A view of the New Narrative art, with paintings and interviews by Jennifer Bartleh, Jonathon Borofsky and Robert Longo. 30m; VHS, 3/4 U. **C:** Hosted by Tom Wolfe. **Pr:** Paul Tschinkel. **A:** College-Adult. **P:** Entertainment. **U:** Institution, Home, SURA. **Fin-Art:** Painting, Art & Artists. **Acq:** Purchase, Subscription. **Dist:** ART/new york.

ART/New York, Vol. 23 1985
A look at women's art with Nancy Graves, Judy Rifka, Marisol and Patsey Norvell. 30m; VHS, 3/4 U. **C:** Hosted by Tom Wolfe. **Pr:** Paul Tschinkel. **A:** College-Adult. **P:** Entertainment. **U:** Institution, Home, SURA. **Fin-Art:** Painting, Art & Artists. **Acq:** Purchase, Subscription. **Dist:** ART/new york.

ART/New York, Vol. 24 1985
Recent paintings at the Phyllis Kind Gallery, the Mary Boone Gallery and the O.K. Harris Galleryare shown, accompanied by interviews with Ed Paschke, Eric Fischl and art dealer Ivan Karp. 28m; VHS, 3/4 U. **C:** Hosted by Tom Wolfe. **Pr:** Paul Tschinkel. **A:** College-Adult. **P:** Education. **U:** Institution, Home, SURA. **Fin-Art:** Art & Artists. **Acq:** Purchase. **Dist:** ART/new york.

ART/New York, Vol. 25 1985
This program focuses on new young painters Bobby G. at the Semaphore East/Soho Galleries and interviews with Mark Kostabi and Kenny Scharf. 28m; VHS, 3/4 U. **Pr:** Paul Tschinkel. **A:** College-Adult. **P:** Education. **U:** Institution, Home, SURA. **Fin-Art:** Art & Artists. **Acq:** Purchase. **Dist:** ART/new york.

ART/New York, Vol. 26 1988
This program explores optical realism in the art of features Alex Katz at the Whitney Museum of American Art and the Robert Miller Gallery, and Janet Fish at the Robert Miller Gallery. 28m; VHS, 3/4 U. **Pr:** Paul Tschinkel. **A:** College-Adult. **P:** Education. **U:** Institution, Home, SURA. **Fin-Art:** Art & Artists. **Acq:** Purchase. **Dist:** ART/new york.

ART/New York, Vol. 27 1988
This program focuses on Louise Bourgeois and features two of her most recent sculpture shows at the Robert Miller Gallery. Also included is an interview in which Bourgeois talks about her work. 28m; VHS, 3/4 U. **Pr:** Paul Tschinkel. **A:** College-Adult. **P:** Education. **U:** Institution, Home, SURA. **Fin-Art:** Art & Artists. **Acq:** Purchase. **Dist:** ART/new york.

ART/New York, Vol. 29 1988
This program features the most recent works of Elizabeth Murray, as well as an interview with the artist in which she explains how she creates her uniquely shaped canvases. 28m; VHS, 3/4 U. **Pr:** Paul Tschinkel. **A:** College-Adult. **P:** Education. **U:** Institution, Home, SURA. **Fin-Art:** Art & Artists. **Acq:** Purchase. **Dist:** ART/new york.

ART/New York, Vol. 30 1988
Covers the brief but dazzling career of Jean-Michel Basquiat (1960-88), featuring the only existing video interview with the late French artist. 28m; VHS, 3/4 U. **Pr:** Paul Tschinkel. **A:**

College-Adult. **P:** Education. **U:** Institution, Home, SURA. **Fin-Art:** Art & Artists. **Acq:** Purchase. **Dist:** ART/new york.

ART/New York, Vol. 31 1988
Covers recent shows by Larry Rivers and Tom Wesselmann, whose style evolved from the Abstract Expressionist movement of the 1950s. Interviews with the artists and Queens Museum curator Marc Miller are featured. 28m; VHS, 3/4 U. **Pr:** Paul Tschinkel. **A:** College-Adult. **P:** Education. **U:** Institution, Home, SURA. **Fin-Art:** Art & Artists. **Acq:** Purchase. **Dist:** ART/new york.

Art Nouveau 1987
A look at the impact of the Art Nouveau movement on art, architecture and design. 14m; VHS, 8 mm. **C:** Directed by Maurice Rheims; Monique Lepeuve. **A:** Sr. High-Adult. **P:** Education. **U:** Institution, Home. **Fin-Art:** Documentary Films, Art & Artists, Architecture. **Acq:** Purchase, Rent/Lease. **Dist:** The Roland Collection. $79.00.

The Art of Action: Martian Arts in the Movies 2005
Host Samuel L. Jackson looks at more than 100 movies depicting martial arts, from vintage releases to modern-day pictures by Ang Lee, John Woo, and others. 96m; DVD. **A:** Jr. High-Adult. **P:** Entertainment. **U:** Home. **Fin-Art:** Documentary Films, Filmmaking, Martial Arts. **Acq:** Purchase. **Dist:** Sony Pictures Home Entertainment Inc.

The Art of Acupressure & Massage 19??
This two-part workshop teaches the basic techniques of Japanese massage & acupressure. Part One illustrates the meridians and acupressure points and how and where to apply pressure. Part Two is a nonstop sequence for developing pacing, timing and style. 120m; VHS. **A:** Sr. High-Adult. **P:** Instruction. **U:** Home. **Hea-Sci:** Massage. **Acq:** Purchase. **Dist:** Hartley Film Foundation. $29.95.

The Art of Advocacy: Expert Witnesses 1988
Intended to train the attorney in the art of examining expert witnesses. Provides information on the selection, preparation, and examination of the witness as well as case demonstrations of the techniques described within the program. 60m; VHS, 3/4 U. **Pr:** National Institute for Trial Advocacy. **A:** Adult. **P:** Professional. **U:** Institution. **Gen-Edu:** Law. **Acq:** Purchase, Rent/Lease. **Dist:** National Institute for Trial Advocacy. $1795.00.
Indiv. Titles: 1. Expert Witnesses: An Overview 2. Introducing Experts in Opening Statements 3. Qualifying the Expert 4. Examining the Medical Doctor 5. Examining the Materials Engineer 6. Examining the Hospital Administrator 7. Examining the Economist 8. Effective Use of Expert Testimony in Closing Argument 9. Discovery of Expert Witnesses Under the Federal Rules of Civil Procedure 10. Testimony of Expert Witnesses Under the Federal Rules of Evidence.

The Art of Advocacy: Opening Statements and Closing Arguments 1987
An extended series which instructs law students and lawyers in opening and closing statements. 60m; VHS, 3/4 U. **Pr:** National Institute for Trial Advocacy. **A:** Adult. **P:** Professional. **U:** Institution. **Gen-Edu:** Law. **Acq:** Purchase, Rent/Lease. **Dist:** National Institute for Trial Advocacy.

The Art of Advocacy: Selecting and Persuading the Jury 1989
Lawyers are shown how to get a jury that will be most favorable to their side of the case. 55m; VHS, 3/4 U. **Pr:** ABA. **A:** Adult. **P:** Professional. **U:** Institution, CCTV, Home, SURA. **Bus-Ind:** Law. **Acq:** Purchase, Rent/Lease. **Dist:** American Bar Association. $895.00.
Indiv. Titles: 1. An Overview 2. Selecting the Jury in a Civil Case 3. Persuading the Jury in a Civil Case: Opening Statements for the Plaintiff 4. Persuading the Jury in a Civil Case: Opening Statements for the Defense 5. Selecting the Jury in a Criminal Case 6. Persuading the Jury in a Criminal Case: Opening Statements for the Prosecution 7. Persuading the Jury in a Criminal Case: Opening Statements for the Defendant 8. Using Focus Groups to Identify Attitudes Towards a Case 9. The Contribution of the Social Sciences.

The Art of Africa 19??
Part of a multicultural art series that explores five major cultural areas of the world. Includes art reproduction prints and a teacher's guide. ?m; VHS. **A:** Jr. High-College. **P:** Education. **U:** Institution. **Gen-Edu:** Art & Artists, Africa. **Acq:** Purchase. **Dist:** Crystal Productions. $74.95.

The Art of Asia: India, Southeast Asia, China, Korea, and Japan 19??
Part of a multicultural art series that explores five major cultural areas of the world. Includes art reproduction prints and a teacher's guide. ?m; VHS. **A:** Jr. High-College. **P:** Education. **U:** Institution. **Gen-Edu:** Art & Artists, Asia. **Acq:** Purchase. **Dist:** Crystal Productions. $74.95.

The Art of Ballet 2010
Includes four ballet-related documentaries, "Ballerina," "The Dancer," "Etoiles: Dancers of the Paris Opera Ballet," and "Prima Ballerina." Each highlights the hard work and training required to achieve dance greatness. 325m; DVD. **A:** Jr. High-Adult. **P:** Entertainment. **U:** Home. **Mov-Ent:** Dance-Ballet, Documentary Films. **Acq:** Purchase. **Dist:** First Run Features. $59.95.

The Art of Baserunning: Strategy and Technique 2008 (Unrated)
Coach Loren Hibbs discusses baserunning, and presents techniques fro improving ones skill and performance. 61m; DVD. **A:** Family. **P:** Education. **U:** Home, Institution. **How-Ins:** Baseball, Athletic Instruction/Coaching. **Acq:** Purchase. **Dist:** Championship Productions. $34.99.

Art of Batting 1989
Improve your offensive skills in cricket by following two masters. 62m; VHS. **C:** Sunil Gavaskar; Garfield Sobers. **Pr:** Trace Video. **A:** Jr. High-Adult. **P:** Instruction. **U:** Institution, Home, SURA. **Spo-Rec:** Sports--General. **Acq:** Purchase, Rent/Lease, Subscription. **Dist:** Reedswain Inc.

The Art of Being Human 1978
This interdisciplinary series is based on the premise that knowledge and understanding of the humanities are key factors in leading a more fulfilled and enriched existence in a technological age. Each module contains two 30-minute documentaries using varying formats. The series is nonchronological; programs are available individually. 60m; VHS, 3/4 U. **Pr:** Miami Dade Community College. **A:** Sr. High-College. **P:** Education. **U:** Institution, SURA. **Gen-Edu:** Philosophy & Ideology. **Acq:** Purchase. **Dist:** Home Vision Cinema.
Indiv. Titles: 1. The Essence of Being Human 2. Man, the Esthetic Being 3. The Way of the Artist 4. The Way of Music 5. Myths and Identity 6. Apollo and Dionysus 7. Philosophy and Moral Values 8. Philosophy and Faith 9. Philosophy-Eastern/Western Consciousness 10. Two Masks-One Face 11. Media and Message 12. The Art of Living-What Is Love? 13. The Art of Living-What Is Happiness? 14. The Art of Living-Coping with Death 15. Contemporary Views of Human Nature.

The Art of Being Indian: Filmed Aspects of the Culture of the Sioux 1976
The refined art of being truly Sioux is thoroughly surveyed, past, present and future. Features art by Bob Penn, Seth Eastman, Stanley Morrow and George Catlin. 29m; VHS, 1C, 3/4 U, Q. **Pr:** South Dakota ETV. **A:** Jr. High-Adult. **P:** Education. **U:** Institution, BCTV, SURA. **Gen-Edu:** Native Americans. **Acq:** Purchase, Rent/Lease. **Dist:** Vision Maker Media.

The Art of Buster Keaton 1995
Features the best of Buster Keaton, including "The General," "Steamboat Bill Jr.," and "College," as well as seven shorts in a three-tape series. ?m; VHS. **A:** Adult. **U:** Home. **Gen-Edu:** Comedy--Slapstick. **Acq:** Purchase. **Dist:** Kino on Video. $29.95.

The Art of Central America and Panama 196?
Central American artists are shown with their paintings in their native environment. 29m; VHS, 3/4 U. **Pr:** Museum of Modern Art of Latin America. **A:** Jr. High-Adult. **P:** Education. **U:** Institution, SURA. **Fin-Art:** Art & Artists, Painting. **Acq:** Purchase. **Dist:** Art Museum of The Americas.

The Art of Ceramic Decorating 1968
Ceramic artist Leon Moburg shows two students his approach to various techniques and styles of decorating ceramic greenware. 16m; VHS, 3/4 U. **Pr:** Cinecrafters. **A:** Sr. High-College. **P:** Instruction. **U:** Institution, SURA. **How-Ins:** Crafts. **Acq:** Purchase. **Dist:** Phoenix Learning Group.

The Art of Ceramic Firing 1968
Ceramic artist Leon Moburg shows in detail the steps-and pitfalls-in successful firing of greenware and glazed bisqueware. Demonstrates proper methods of firing pots. 15m; VHS, 3/4 U. **Pr:** Cinecrafters. **A:** Jr. High-Sr. High. **P:** Instruction. **U:** Institution, SURA. **How-Ins:** Crafts. **Acq:** Purchase. **Dist:** Phoenix Learning Group.

The Art of Ceramic Glazing 1968
Ceramic artist Leon Moburg discusses and demonstrates design techniques for glazing; feataures live dialogue in preference to conventional narration. 16m; VHS, 3/4 U. **Pr:** Cinecrafters. **A:** Jr. High-Sr. High. **P:** Instruction. **U:** Institution, SURA. **How-Ins:** Crafts. **Acq:** Purchase. **Dist:** Phoenix Learning Group.

The Art of Chinese Cooking 1989
Sylvia Shulman and Madame Wong teach chinese cuisine preparation step-by-step. 30m; VHS. **Pr:** Gary Youngman. **A:** Jr. High-Adult. **P:** Education. **U:** Home. **How-Ins:** Cooking, China, How-To. **Acq:** Purchase, Rent/Lease. **Dist:** Silver Mine Video Inc. $29.95.

The Art of Claude Lorrain 1970
Discusses Lorrain's landscapes and the Classicist and pre-Impressionist styles used in them. 25m; 3/4 U, Special order formats. **Pr:** Balfour Films. **A:** Sr. High-Adult. **P:** Education. **U:** Institution. **Fin-Art:** Art & Artists. **Acq:** Purchase, Rent/Lease. **Dist:** Museum of Modern Art.

The Art of Clinical Instruction 1988
Academicians are taught how to better communicate their message and therefore be a better teacher. 14m; VHS, 3/4 U. **Pr:** University of Minnesota. **A:** Adult. **P:** Instruction. **U:** Institution. **How-Ins:** Communication, Education. **Acq:** Purchase, Rent/Lease. **Dist:** University of Minnesota. $195.00.

The Art of Communicating 1989
Noted philospher Jacob Needleman explains how to communicate more openly with others by exploring the depths within oneself. 30m; VHS. **Pr:** Thinking Allowed Productions. **A:** Sr. High-Adult. **P:** Instruction. **U:** Home. **How-Ins:** How-To, Communication. **Acq:** Purchase. **Dist:** Thinking Allowed Productions. $29.95.

The Art of Communication 19??
Discusses effective communication techniques between parents and children of different ages. Also illustrates the effects of verbal abuse on children. A pretest and activities list accompany the program. 30m; VHS. **A:** Adult. **P:** Education. **U:** Home, Institution. **Gen-Edu:** Communication, Parenting, Children. **Acq:** Purchase. **Dist:** Alliance for Children and Families. $95.00.

The Art of Communication Series 1979
The subtleties of good communication are explored in this series. 14m; VHS, 3/4 U. **Pr:** Coronet Films. **A:** Sr. High-Adult. **P:** Education. **U:** Institution, SURA. **Gen-Edu:** Communication, Meeting Openers. **Acq:** Purchase, Rent/Lease. **Dist:** Phoenix Learning Group. $250.00.
Indiv. Titles: 1. Communication by Voice and Action 2. Many Hear, Some Listen 3. Aids to Speaking 4. Stage Fright 5. Planning Your Speech 6. How to Conduct a Meeting 7. Reporting and Briefing.

The Art of Compassion 1995
Presents the stories of two men who have transformed painful experiences into sources of creative inspiration. Their stories resonate with themes of healing, appreciation for nature and spiritual growth. 52m; VHS. **A:** Family. **P:** Entertainment. **U:** Home, Institution. **Gen-Edu:** Art & Artists. **Acq:** Purchase. **Dist:** Moving Images Distribution.

Art of Computer Animation 19??
Spotlights the work of 30 computer animation artists. 70m; VHS. **A:** Jr. High-Adult. **P:** Education. **U:** Institution. **Gen-Edu:** Art & Artists, Computers. **Acq:** Purchase. **Dist:** Ark Media Group Ltd.

The Art of Conducting: Great Conductors of the Past 1994
Rare footage of 16 legendary conductors in rehearsal and performance, including Arturo Toscanini, Leonard Bernstein, Leopold Stokowski, Herbert Von Karajan, George Szell, Bruno Walter, Otto Klemperer, Sir Thomas Beecham, Arthur Nikisch, Richard Strauss, Felix Weingartner, Fritz Busch, Wilhelm Furtwangler, Serge Koussevitzky, and Fritz Reiner. 117m; VHS. **A:** Adult. **P:** Entertainment. **U:** Home. **Fin-Art:** Music--Classical. **Acq:** Purchase. **Dist:** Music Video Distributors. $29.98.

Art of Creating Crafts 1989
Things that can be given as gifts or kept around the home are made. 49m; VHS. **C:** Hosted by Lee Hanson. **Pr:** Increase. **A:** Family. **P:** Instruction. **U:** Institution, Home. **How-Ins:** Crafts, Art & Artists, How-To. **Acq:** Purchase. **Dist:** Silver Mine Video Inc. $29.95.

The Art of Creating Monotypes 199?
Four artists demonstrate a variety of methods for making a monotype. Includes hardcover textbook. 120m; VHS. **A:** Primary-College. **P:** Instruction. **U:** Institution, Home. **How-Ins:** Art & Artists. **Acq:** Purchase. **Dist:** Crystal Productions. $99.00.

The Art of Crime 1975 (Unrated) — ★★½
A gypsy/detective is drawn into a homicide case when one of his fellow antique dealers is charged with murder. Maintains an atmospheric edge over others of the crime art genre. A pilot for a prospective TV series based on the novel "Gypsy in Amber." 72m; VHS. **C:** Ron Leibman; Jose Ferrer; David Hedison; Jill Clayburgh; Directed by Richard Irving; Written by Bill Davidson; Martin Smith. **Pr:** Mark Huffam. **A:** Jr. High-Adult. **P:** Entertainment. **U:** Home. **Mov-Ent:** Mystery & Suspense. **Acq:** Purchase. **Dist:** Movies Unlimited.

The Art of Crosspicking 199?
Steve Kaufman teaches arrangements of seven songs that use the classic bluegrass flatpicking style. 60m; VHS. **A:** Sr. High-Adult. **P:** Education. **U:** Home. **How-Ins:** Music--Instruction. **Acq:** Purchase. **Dist:** Hal Leonard Corp. $39.95.

The Art of Dancing: An Introduction to Baroque Dance 1979
Produced with authentic 18th-century costumes, this program presents the minuet as a dancing lesson, based on Kellom Tomlinson's 1720 dance manual, "The Art of Dancing." Selection include the Ballroom Minuet and the Minuet d'Omphalle. 21m/B/W; VHS, 3/4 U, EJ. **Pr:** New York Baroque Dance Company; ARC Videodance. **A:** College-Adult. **P:** Education. **U:** Institution, CCTV, Home, SURA. **Fin-Art:** Dance, Video. **Acq:** Purchase. **Dist:** Eye on the Arts.

Art of Darkness 19??
Shows such landmark institutions as the National Gallery, the Tate Gallery, and the British Museum, and how they were all funded by money made from the slave trade. Documented through letters, paintings, and poetry, the 18th century is shown to be a period of high culture and an age of cruelty. 52m; VHS. **A:** Sr. High. **P:** Education. **U:** Institution. **Gen-Edu:** Slavery. **Acq:** Purchase. **Dist:** Filmakers Library Inc. $295.

The Art of Decorating Cakes 1984
This series of 26 half hour programs goes in depth to explain various aspects of cake decorating. 30m; VHS, 3/4 U. **Pr:** RMI Media Productions. **A:** Sr. High-Adult. **P:** Instruction. **U:** Institution, CCTV, Home. **How-Ins:** Cooking. **Acq:** Purchase. **Dist:** RMI Media.
Indiv. Titles: 1. Introduction 2. Border and Stems 3. Rose and Daisy 4. Carnation 5. Parrot 6. Chrysanthemum 7. Rose Gumpaste 8. Writing and Stems 9. Sugar Molding 10. Sea Scapes 11. Sea Lion Figure Piping 12. Scene Building 13. Bear 14. Spatula, Palette Knife Painting 15. Daisy, Daffodil, Mushroom, Thistle 16. Basketweave and Tea Pitcher 17. Geometric Top Border Designs 18. Foliage 19. Wedding Cake Construction 20. Wedding Cake Designs 21. Wedding Cake Borders 22. Wedding Cake Assembly 23. Presidential and State Designs 24. Orchids 25. Pentunia 26. Daisy.

The Art of Decoying Whitetail 19??
Demonstrates techniques for hunting whitetail deer using decoys. Features hunting footage, including an actual decoy attack. 70m; VHS. **A:** Adult. **P:** Instruction. **U:** Home. **Spo-Rec:** Hunting. **Acq:** Purchase. **Dist:** Stoney-Wolf Productions, Inc. $49.95.

The Art of Dining 1990
Consists of two programs about important dining situations. The viewer will learn the proper etiquette in both business lunches and social occasions and avoid potentially embarassing situations. 30m; VHS. **C:** Hosted by Marjabelle Young Stewart. **Pr:** Home Vision. **A:** Jr. High-Adult. **P:** Education. **U:** Home. **Gen-Edu:** Etiquette. **Acq:** Purchase. **Dist:** MPI Media Group. $14.95.
Indiv. Titles: 1. The Formal Dinner 2. The Business Lunch.

The Art of Diplomacy, Part 1 1983
In this program, the beginnings of American diplomacy from the Declaration of Independence to the Monroe Doctrine are highlighted. 12m; VHS, 3/4 U. **Pr:** WGBH Boston. **A:** Jr. High-Adult. **P:** Education. **U:** Institution, SURA. **Gen-Edu:** Politics & Government. **Acq:** Purchase, Rent/Lease. **Dist:** Hearst Entertainment/King Features.

The Art of Diplomacy, Part 2 1983
This program traces the development of American diplomacy from 1830 to 1905. 12m; VHS, 3/4 U. **Pr:** WGBH Boston. **A:** Jr. High-Adult. **P:** Education. **U:** Institution, SURA. **Gen-Edu:** Politics & Government. **Acq:** Purchase, Rent/Lease. **Dist:** Hearst Entertainment/King Features.

The Art of Diplomacy, Part 3 1983
This program examines American diplomacy from World War One to World War Two and the period in between. 14m/B/W; VHS, 3/4 U. **Pr:** WGBH Boston. **A:** Jr. High-Adult. **P:** Education. **U:** Institution, SURA. **Gen-Edu:** Politics & Government. **Acq:** Purchase, Rent/Lease. **Dist:** Hearst Entertainment/King Features.

The Art of Doll Repair and Restoration 1: Bisque and Parian Doll Heads 1991
Marty Westfall's best-seller comes to video as she demonstrates how to assess damage and make repairs to bisque, parian, and porcelain doll heads. 94m; VHS. **A:** Sr. High-Adult. **P:** Instruction. **U:** Home. **How-Ins:** How-To, Hobbies, Puppets. **Acq:** Purchase. **Dist:** Concept Videos. $49.95.

The Art of Dying 1990 (Unrated) — ★★★
A loony videophile decides to start staging productions of his all-time favorite scenes. Trouble is, his idea of a fabulous film moment calls for lots of blood and bile as he lures teenage runaways to his casting couch. Director Hauser stars as the cop who's none too impressed with the cinematic remakes, while cult favorite Pollard is his partner. If you like a little atmosphere and psychological depth in your slashers, you'll find this to be the stuff that populates film noir nightmares. 90m; VHS, DVD. **C:** Wings Hauser; Michael J. Pollard; Sarah Douglas; Kathleen Kinmont; Sydney Lassick; Mitch Hara; Gary Werntz; Directed by Wings Hauser. **A:** Adult. **P:** Entertainment. **U:** Home. **Mov-Ent:** Mystery & Suspense. **Acq:** Purchase. **Dist:** Echo Bridge Home Entertainment. $19.95.

The Art of Eating 1976
A visit to le Club Prosper Montagne, one of the oldest gastronomic societies in North America. A shorter version of "La Gastronomie." 11m; VHS, 3/4 U. **Pr:** National Film Board of Canada. **A:** Jr. High-Adult. **P:** Education. **U:** Institution, SURA. **Gen-Edu:** Cooking. **Acq:** Purchase, Rent/Lease. **Dist:** National Film Board of Canada.

The Art of Ecstasy 199?
Founder and director of the Skydancing Institute, Margo Anand, explains Western traditions that divide carnal and spiritual knowledge, breaking down our natural conscious abilities to create a blissful state; she then describes techniques couples can use to open new dimensions of their sexuality. 60m; DVD. **A:** Adult. **P:** Education. **U:** Home, Institution. **Gen-Edu:** Sex & Sexuality, New Age. **Acq:** Purchase. **Dist:** Thinking Allowed Productions. $34.95.

The Art of Entertaining 1989
Methods of Christian hospitality are demonstrated. 56m; VHS. **Pr:** Bob Jones University. **A:** Family. **P:** Religious. **U:** Institution, SURA. **Gen-Edu. Acq:** Purchase. **Dist:** Bob Jones University. $24.95.

Art of Fiber Dyeing 19??
Features Sandy Sitzman as she discusses techniques in fiber dyeing. She covers three different dye procedures: (1) union dyes; (2) uses acid dyes to create a rainbow dye bath; (3) uses acid dyes to demonstrate injection dyeing. Focuses on unspun fiber dyeing. Includes written outline and source list. 53m; VHS. **Pr:** Victorian Video Productions. **A:** Jr. High-Adult. **P:** Instruction. **U:** Home, Institution. **How-Ins:** Crafts, How-To. **Acq:** Purchase. **Dist:** Victorian Video/Yarn Barn of Kansas, Inc. $29.50.

The Art of Flatpick Guitar 1989
Russ Barenberg teaches guitar playing techniques including keeping solid time, composing solos, improvising, and achieving better control, good tone, and stronger technique. Provides exercises and original instrumentals. Includes tab. 90m; VHS. **A:** Jr. High-Adult. **P:** Instruction. **U:** Home, Institution. **How-Ins:** Music--Instruction. **Acq:** Purchase. **Dist:** Homespun Tapes Ltd. $49.95.

The Art of Folding Table Napkins 199?
Teaches food service employees and wait staff how to transform ordinary table napkins into artistic decorations suitable for any dining setting. 33m; VHS. **A:** Sr. High-Adult. **P:** Instruction. **U:** Home. **How-Ins:** Customer Service, Food Industry, How-To. **Acq:** Purchase. **Dist:** Culinary Institute of America. $75.00.

The Art of Getting By 2011 (PG-13) — ★½
Upper Manhattan prep school senior George (Highmore) is another rebel without a cause: privileged on paper, lonely in life. His life changes forever when he becomes friends with the

like-minded Sally (Roberts), a beautiful yet troubled popular girl. This indie, coming of age story reads more as a self-important drama without any real, original substance. Inconsistent and shallow writing aside, Highmore and Roberts just don't have the magnetic presences that are vital to sell this. Teen angst flicks are a dime a dozen, and this one doesn't stand out. Debut of writer/director Wisesen. 84m; Blu-Ray, Wide. **C:** Freddie Highmore; Emma Roberts; Michael Angarano; Elizabeth Reaser; Blair Underwood; Alicia Silverstone; Sam Robards; Rita Wilson; Directed by Gavin Wiesen; Written by Gavin Wiesen; Cinematography by Ben Kutchins; Music by Alec Puro. **Pr:** Jennifer Dana; Kara Baker; Gia Welsh; Darren Goldberg; Gigi Films; Goldcrest Pictures; Fox Searchlight. **A:** Jr. High-Adult. **P:** Entertainment. **U:** Home. **L:** English. **Mov-Ent**: Adolescence. **Acq:** Purchase. **Dist:** Fox Home Entertainment; Movies Unlimited.

Art of Glass Engraving 1999
Features the art of glass engraving with glass artists Wayland H. Cato, III. Five-tape series includes instruction for using glass engraving tools for artistic or business endeavors. 150m; VHS. **A:** Adult. **P:** Instruction. **U:** Home. **How-Ins:** Crafts, How-To, Art & Artists. **Acq:** Purchase. **Dist:** Instructional Video. $105.

The Art of Guitar Crosspicking 1996
Describes step-by-step, the flatpicking movements that define this distinctive way of playing. Provides exercises, speed drills, slowed-down and up-to-speed examples, invaluable advice and breathtaking arrangements. Includes music and tab. 60m; VHS. **A:** Adult. **P:** Instruction. **U:** Home. **How-Ins**: How-To, Music--Instruction. **Acq:** Purchase. **Dist:** Homespun Tapes Ltd. $39.95.

The Art of Haiti 1982
A look at the internationally influential painters of Haiti. The film traces the roots of the Haitian art movement showing the painters, their work, and how history and environment influenced them. 26m; VHS, Special order formats. **Pr:** Mark Mamalakis. **A:** Family. **P:** Education. **U:** Institution, Home. **Fin-Art**: Documentary Films, Drawing, Art & Artists. **Acq:** Purchase, Rent/Lease. **Dist:** Museum of Modern Art; Facets Multimedia Inc. $39.95.

The Art of Hawaiian Slack Key Guitar 1996
Introduces tunings and sounds of traditional Hawaiian guitar. Teaches seven instrumentals involved with the special tunings used in slack key playing. 80m; VHS. **A:** Adult. **P:** Instruction. **U:** Home. **How-Ins**: How-To, Music--Instruction. **Acq:** Purchase. **Dist:** Homespun Tapes Ltd. $39.95.

The Art of High-Impact Kicking 1982
Master Hwang Jang Lee demonstrates fundamental techniques using the feet as weaponry. 69m; VHS. **Pr:** Ng See Yuen; Roy Horan. **A:** Sr. High-Adult. **P:** Instruction. **U:** Home. **Spo-Rec**: Martial Arts. **Acq:** Purchase. **Dist:** World Video & Supply, Inc.

The Art of Hitting 1980
Ex-Cincinnati Reds batting star Vada Pinson offers tips on improving your hitting. 60m; VHS, 3/4 U, Special order formats. **C:** Vada Pinson. **Pr:** Cinema Associates. **A:** Primary-Adult. **P:** Instruction. **U:** Institution, CCTV, CATV, BCTV, Home. **Spo-Rec**: Baseball. **Acq:** Purchase. **Dist:** RMI Media; School-Tech Inc.

The Art of Hitting Slow-Pitch Softball 1991
Bob "Mr. Softball" Campbell is joined by baseballer Mike Marshall in demonstrating methods for improving softball hitting. 55m; VHS. **A:** Jr. High-Adult. **P:** Instruction. **U:** Home. **Spo-Rec**: Baseball. **Acq:** Purchase. **Dist:** Navarre Corp. $14.99.

The Art of Hitting .300 1989
Don Drysdale joins self-proclaimed "supercoach" Charley Lau to explain the "Ten Absolutes of Hitting" and take a look at the best hitters of all time. 50m; VHS. **Pr:** BFV. **A:** Family. **P:** Instruction. **U:** Home. **Spo-Rec**: Baseball. **Acq:** Purchase. **Dist:** Karol Media. $29.95.

The Art of Huckleberry Finn 1965
Discusses point of view, theme, and major symbols in Mark Twain's novel "Huckleberry Finn." 25m; VHS, 3/4 U. **Pr:** Encyclopedia Britannica Educational Corporation. **A:** Sr. High-College. **P:** Education. **U:** Institution, SURA. **Gen-Edu**: Literature--American. **Acq:** Purchase, Rent/Lease, Trade-in. **Dist:** Encyclopedia Britannica.

The Art of Huckleberry Finn, II 1965
Clifton Fadiman identifies three unifying sections in the Huckleberry Finn novel: the central point of view, the theme, and the development of two major symbols (the river and the shore). 25m; VHS, SVS, 3/4 U. **A:** Sr. High-College. **P:** Education. **U:** Institution. **Gen-Edu**: Literature--American. **Acq:** Purchase, Rent/Lease. **Dist:** Encyclopedia Britannica. $89.00.

Art of Indonesia: Tales from the Shadow World 1991
Documentary explores the ancient treasures of the 13,000 islands of Indonesia, and the rituals and myths which continue in importance today. 28m; VHS. **Pr:** National Gallery of Art; Metropolitan Museum of Art. **A:** Jr. High-Adult. **P:** Education. **U:** Home. **Fin-Art**: Documentary Films, Art & Artists, Pacific Islands. **Acq:** Purchase. **Dist:** Facets Multimedia Inc.; Crystal Productions. $29.95.

The Art of Influencing People Positively 1993
Dr. Tony Alessandra explains behavioral styles and how to deal with any type of person. 30m; VHS. **A:** Adult. **P:** Professional. **U:** Institution. **Bus-Ind**: Business, Management. **Acq:** Purchase. **Dist:** RMI Media. $95.00.

The Art of Interior Decorating 1988
Learn professional techniques for decorating a room or a whole house. Discusses colors, style, furniture, and accessories. A workbook is included. 90m; VHS. **A:** Adult. **P:** Instruction. **U:** Home. **How-Ins**: Interior Decoration, How-To. **Acq:** Purchase. **Dist:** Cambridge Educational. $49.95.

The Art of Jean-Pierre Rampal, Vol 1 ????
CBC, Montreal archival footage from 1956-1961 featuring performances of flutist Jean-Pierre Rampal with various orchestras. 69m/B/W; VHS. **A:** Adult. **P:** Entertainment. **U:** Home. **Fin-Art**: Music--Classical, Music--Performance. **Acq:** Purchase. **Dist:** Video Artists International. $24.95.

The Art of Jean-Pierre Rampal, Vol 2 ????
CBC, Montreal archival footage from 1966 featuring performances of flutist Jean-Pierre Rampal with various orchestras. 52m/B/W; VHS. **A:** Adult. **P:** Entertainment. **U:** Home. **Fin-Art**: Music--Classical, Music--Performance. **Acq:** Purchase. **Dist:** Video Artists International. $24.95.

Art of Job Negotiation 1987
Interview skills that will help people land a better job are covered. 16m; VHS, 3/4 U. **Pr:** Brigham Young University. **A:** College-Adult. **P:** Education. **U:** Institution, SURA. **Bus-Ind**: Interviews. **Acq:** Purchase, Trade-in. **Dist:** Encyclopedia Britannica. $300.00.

The Art of Landscaping 19??
Two-part series that provides advice from Howard Garrett on professional landscape design, covering such topics as predesign, conceptual design, design development, budgeting, site analysis, layout, irrigation, buying, and planting. 112m; VHS. **A:** Sr. High-Adult. **P:** Education. **U:** Institution. **Gen-Edu**: Landscaping, Occupational Training. **Acq:** Purchase. **Dist:** CEV Multimedia. $160.00.
Indiv. Titles: 1. Design 2. Shopping & Planting.

The Art of Landscaping 1988
Two program series overviews various topics of landscape architecture, including budgeting, layout, site analysis, irrigation, lighting, grading, plant selection, and planting procedures. 52m; VHS. **A:** Adult. **P:** Education. **U:** Institution. **Gen-Edu**: Landscaping. **Acq:** Purchase. **Dist:** American Nurseryman Publishing Co. $94.99.
Indiv. Titles: 1. Design 2. Shopping and Planting.

The Art of Leadership 1995
Centers on how leadership is a skill that can be developed. Also presents managers with strategies to develop and improve their leadership skills. 30m; VHS. **A:** Adult. **P:** Professional. **U:** Institution. **Bus-Ind**: Management, Occupational Training. **Acq:** Purchase, Rent/Lease. **Dist:** National Safety Council, California Chapter, Film Library. $250.00.

The Art of Learning 1984
This series is designed to inform prospective students about the study skills needed to sucessfully complete a college education. 20m; VHS, 3/4 U, Special order formats. **Pr:** WCVE Richmond. **A:** Sr. High-Adult. **P:** Education. **U:** Institution. **Gen-Edu**: Education. **Acq:** Rent/Lease, Duplication License. **Dist:** GPN Educational Media. $199.50.
Indiv. Titles: 1. The Efficient Learner 2. Getting the Message 3. The College Classroom 4. Using the Library 5. The Written Word 6. Test Taking.

The Art of Listening 1992
Constructively outlines seven "laws" of listening (spend more time listening, less time talking; find something interesting in the speaker; don't interrupt; listen to what a person means, not what they say; take notes; assume proper posture; be aware of your filters, i.e. women value communication for its own sake, men see it as information) via a simulated video production. Complete with teacher's guide. 28m; VHS. **A:** Jr. High-Sr. High. **P:** Education. **U:** Institution. **Gen-Edu**: Communication. **Acq:** Purchase. **Dist:** The Learning Seed. $89.00.

The Art of Living: Coping with Death 1978
Two half-hour documentaries, "For Everything a Season" and "Phoenix and Finnegan" are combined on this tape. Both explore ideas of death and immortality in Western society. 60m; VHS, 3/4 U. **Pr:** Miami Dade Community College. **A:** College. **P:** Education. **U:** Institution, SURA. **Gen-Edu**: Death. **Acq:** Purchase. **Dist:** Home Vision Cinema.

The Art of Living: What Is Happiness? 1978
Two half-hour documentaries, "In Search of Happiness" and "The Pursuit of the Ideal," are combined on this tape. Both programs examine man's dreams of creating an earthly paradise. 60m; VHS, 3/4 U. **Pr:** Miami Dade Community College. **A:** College. **P:** Education. **U:** Institution, SURA. **Gen-Edu**: Philosophy & Ideology. **Acq:** Purchase. **Dist:** Home Vision Cinema.

The Art of Living: What Is Love? 1978
Two half-hour documentaries, "Love: Myth and Mystery" and "Roles We Play," are included in this tape. Both shows focus on aspects of love and sexual role-playing. 60m; VHS, 3/4 U. **Pr:** Miami Dade Community College. **A:** College. **P:** Education. **U:** Institution, SURA. **Gen-Edu**: Human Relations. **Acq:** Purchase. **Dist:** Home Vision Cinema.

The Art of Living With Change 19??
Earnie Larsen uses situational role playing to talk about changing behaviors and supporting those changes. 45m; VHS. **A:** Adult. **P:** Education. **U:** Institution. **Hea-Sci**: Self-Help. **Acq:** Purchase. **Dist:** Hazelden Publishing. $29.95.

The Art of Love and Struggle 2006 (Unrated)
Twelve female artists, singers, emcees, activists, poets, and writers share the greatest challenges they've faced in terms of poverty, politics, personal sacrifice, love, identity, and culture, all of which helped shape their artistic and personal endeavors. 78m; DVD. **A:** Adult. **P:** Education. **U:** Institution. **Gen-Edu**: Women, Art & Artists. **Acq:** Purchase. **Dist:** Third World Newsreel. $275.

The Art of Making Pictures 1985
Artist Lee Hanson demonstrates how to create pictures using various art media such as watercolor, pen and pencil and collage. 51m; VHS. **Pr:** Western Video. **A:** Family. **P:** Instruction. **U:** Institution, Home. **How-Ins**: How-To, Art & Artists. **Acq:** Purchase. **Dist:** Silver Mine Video Inc. $29.95.

The Art of Meditation 1972
An easy and direct step-by-step demonstration of meditative posture, breathing control, and concentration. 28m; VHS. **A:** Adult. **P:** Instruction. **U:** Home. **Gen-Edu**: New Age. **Acq:** Purchase. **Dist:** Hartley Film Foundation. $39.95.

The Art of Memory 197?
An experimental video piece by Vasulka about the memory of war, juxtaposing images from various wars against images of American desert. 30m; VHS. **C:** Directed by Woody Vasulka. **Pr:** Woody Vasulka. **A:** Sr. High-Adult. **P:** Entertainment. **U:** Home. **Fin-Art**: Film--Avant-Garde, War--General. **Acq:** Purchase. **Dist:** Facets Multimedia Inc. $59.95.

The Art of Mexico, Central America, and South America 19??
Part of a multicultural art series that explores five major cultural areas of the world. Includes art reproduction prints and a teacher's guide. ?m; VHS. **A:** Jr. High-College. **P:** Education. **U:** Institution. **Gen-Edu**: Art & Artists, Central America, Mexico. **Acq:** Purchase. **Dist:** Crystal Productions. $74.95.

The Art of Mixing 199?
David Gibson shows viewers the techniques of sound mixing for music recording, along with other production and engineering techniques. Two video set. ?m; VHS. **A:** Family. **P:** Instruction. **U:** Home. **How-Ins**: Music--Instruction, Occupational Training. **Acq:** Purchase. **Dist:** Hal Leonard Corp. $89.95.

The Art of Murder 1999 (R) — ★★
Married Elizabeth (Pacula) has a wealthy hubby (Moriarty) and a younger lover (Kesnter) to keep her motor running. But then sleazy Willie (Onorati) threatens to show her husband dirty pictures of the affair and blackmail is just the beginning. 97m; VHS, DVD. **C:** Joanna Pacula; Michael Moriarty; Boyd Kestner; Peter Onorati; Directed by Ruben Preuss; Written by Anthony Stark; Cinematography by John Tarver. **A:** Sr. High-Adult. **P:** Entertainment. **U:** Home. **Mov-Ent**. **Acq:** Purchase. **Dist:** Movies Unlimited; Lions Gate Entertainment Inc.

The Art of Navajo Weaving 1988
Watch as skilled veterans perform the art of Navajo weaving. Also shows the Durango Collection, the world's largest private collection of Navajo weaving. 56m; VHS. **A:** Family. **P:** Education. **U:** Institution, Home. **Gen-Edu**: Documentary Films, Native Americans, Crafts. **Acq:** Purchase. **Dist:** Victorian Video/ Yarn Barn of Kansas, Inc.; Finley Holiday Film Corp.; Karol Media. $29.95.

The Art of Negotiating 1991
Supervisors and managers will learn how to get what they want with seven basic strategies in the fine art of negotiation. Hosted by master negotiator and world renowned counselor Gerard Nierenberg. 20m; VHS, 3/4 U. **Pr:** Bureau of Business Practice. **A:** Adult. **P:** Professional. **U:** Institution. **Bus-Ind**: How-To, Management, Communication. **Acq:** Purchase, Rent/Lease. **Dist:** Aspen Publishers, Inc. $495.00.

The Art of Noise: In Visible Silence 198?
Live from the Hammersmith Odeon, the group performs "Close to the Edit," "Paranoia," "Legs," "Moments in Love," "Beat Box," "Instruments of Darkness," "Back Beat" and more. 60m; VHS. **A:** Jr. High-College. **P:** Entertainment. **U:** Home. **Mov-Ent**: Music--Performance. **Acq:** Purchase. **Dist:** Music Video Distributors. $29.95.

The Art of Parenting Video Series 19??
Three-part series that outlines practical parenting tips and solutions to today's parental problems. Covers areas such as bedtime, whining children, TV viewing, sibling rivalry, potty training, and hyperactivity for infants through five years old; homework, friends, self-esteem, divorce, latch key kids, sex, discipline, and attention deficit disorder for school-age children; and curfews, step families, jobs, parental stress, conflict, driving, and love for teenagers. Includes comprehensive leader's guide with discussion questions, recommended reading, program texts, and developmental information. 156m; VHS, 3/4 U. **A:** Adult. **P:** Education. **U:** Home, Institution, CCTV, SURA. **Gen-Edu**: Parenting, Child Care. **Acq:** Purchase, Rent/Lease. **Dist:** Program Source. $209.85.
Indiv. Titles: 1. Volume 1: The Young Child 2. Volume 2: School Age Children 3. Volume 3: Teenagers.

The Art of Photo 197?
This program tells how a photographer and a writer went around the United States researching for a book on poor people. 30m; VHS, 3/4 U, EJ, Q. **Pr:** WCBS New York; Camera Three Productions. **A:** Sr. High-Adult. **P:** Education. **U:** Institution, SURA. **Gen-Edu**: Photography. **Acq:** Duplication, Free Duplication. **Dist:** Camera Three Productions, Inc.

The Art of Political Cartooning 197?
Political cartoonists David Levine and Draper Hill discuss graphic illustration and cartooning in this program. 30m/B/W; VHS, 3/4 U, EJ, Q. **Pr:** WCBS New York; Camera Three Productions. **A:** Family. **P:** Education. **U:** Institution, SURA. **Gen-Edu**: Animation & Cartoons, Politics & Government. **Acq:** Duplication, Free Duplication. **Dist:** Camera Three Productions, Inc.; Creative Arts Television Archive.

The Art of Psychotherapy/When Nietzsche Wept 199?
Stanford University psychiatry professor Irvin Yalom, M.D., discloses how initial symptoms mask deeper fears when patients first begin therapy and further explains "talking cure" origins as presented in his fictional work 'When Nietzsche Wept.' 60m; DVD. **A:** Adult. **P:** Education. **U:** Home, Institution. **Gen-Edu:** Psychology, Psychiatry. **Acq:** Purchase. **Dist:** Thinking Allowed Productions. $34.95.

The Art of Radio Advertising 19??
Successful radio commercial producers Bert Berdis and Alan Bartzman discuss their approach to concept development, copywriting, and directing for radio ads. 20m; VHS. **Pr:** Australian Film, Radio and Television School. **A:** Sr. High-Adult. **P:** Education. **U:** Home, Institution. **Gen-Edu:** Advertising, Commercials. **Acq:** Purchase, Rent/Lease. **Dist:** TMW Media Group. $119.

The Art of Reading/Speed Learning 1984
In this 30-hour series of nine programs, advanced reading, thinking and learning skills are developed for those who must read on the job. 120m; 3/4 U. **Pr:** Learn Inc. **A:** College-Adult. **P:** Education. **U:** Institution. **How-Ins:** Education, Business. **Acq:** Purchase, Rent/Lease. **Dist:** SkillSoft.
Indiv. Titles: 1. The Art of Reading 2. Getting It All Together 3. It's All Right to Be Wrong 4. Four on the Floor 5. A Competition with Yourself 6. An Active Mind 7. Surveying for Hidden Treasure 8. Rapid Reading 9. The Payoff.

The Art of Resistance 1994
Combines archival footage with interviews of Chicano artists to trace the development of contemporary Chicano art during the height of political activism in the late '60s and '70s. Includes information on the Chicano Moratorium, the United Farm Workers struggle, political prisoners' defense campaigns, and the fight for civil rights and ethnic identity. 26m; VHS. **A:** Jr. High-Adult. **P:** Education. **U:** Institution. **Gen-Edu:** Documentary Films, Art & Artists, Hispanic Culture. **Acq:** Purchase, Rent/Lease. **Dist:** The Cinema Guild. $250.00.

The Art of Resolving Conflicts in the Workplace 2000
Presents strategies for dealing with contention and conflict in the workplace brought about by growth and change, including segments on building cooperation, handling non-performing coworkers and resolving conflicting job assignments. Includes study guide. 37m; VHS. **A:** Sr. High-Adult. **P:** Education. **U:** Home. **Bus-Ind:** Business, Employee Counseling. **Acq:** Purchase. **Dist:** Advantage Media. $89.95.

The Art of Ribbon Craft 1988
Covers all possible ground in the craft, from tools and materials, to silk roses and embroidery. 68m; VHS. **C:** Susan Sirkis. **A:** Jr. High-Adult. **P:** Instruction. **U:** Home. **How-Ins:** How-To, Crafts, Sewing. **Acq:** Purchase. **Dist:** Victorian Video/Yarn Barn of Kansas, Inc.; Concept Videos; Cambridge Educational. $29.95.

The Art of Sabicas 197?
Flamenco guitarist Sabicas accompanies the Alba Spanish Dance Company in a performance of flamenco dancing. 30m/B/W; VHS, 3/4 U, EJ, Q. **Pr:** WCBS New York; Camera Three Productions. **A:** Sr. High-Adult. **P:** Education. **U:** Institution, SURA. **Fin-Art:** Dance. **Acq:** Duplication, Free Duplication. **Dist:** Camera Three Productions, Inc.

The Art of Satisfying Customers 19??
Addresses proper care of the customer and building repeat business. 15m; VHS. **A:** Adult. **P:** Professional. **U:** Institution. **Bus-Ind:** Customer Service. **Acq:** Purchase. **Dist:** Service Quality Institute. $149.95.

The Art of Seeing 19??
Presentation promoting the awareness of details, patterns, and shadows in art. Two programs each complete with teacher's guide. 36m; VHS. **A:** Jr. High-Sr. High. **P:** Education. **U:** Institution. **Gen-Edu:** Art & Artists. **Acq:** Purchase. **Dist:** Cambridge Educational. $130.00.

The Art of Seeing 1971
The program serves as an introduction to "The Art of Seeing" series and focuses on using the eyes for artistic perception of color, shape, pattern, and texture. 10m; VHS, 3/4 U. **Pr:** American Federation of Arts. **A:** Primary-Jr. High. **P:** Education. **U:** Institution, SURA. **Gen-Edu:** Art & Artists. **Acq:** Rent/Lease. **Dist:** Home Vision Cinema.

The Art of Sensual Massage 1986
A step-by-step instruction program about massage, how to do it, and how it can liven up a relationship. 37m; VHS, CC. **Pr:** Robert Bahr; Playboy Enterprises. **A:** Family. **P:** Entertainment. **U:** Home. **How-Ins:** Massage. **Acq:** Purchase. **Dist:** MGM Studios Inc. ; Warner Home Video, Inc. $29.95.

The Art of Sewage Treatment 1977
Designed for students with no background in the field, this program examines some of the physical, biological, and chemical processes which take place in a water purification sewage treatment plant. 20m; VHS, 3/4 U. **Pr:** University of Toronto. **A:** Jr. High-College. **P:** Education. **U:** Institution, CCTV. **Gen-Edu:** Public Health. **Acq:** Purchase, Rent/Lease. **Dist:** University of Toronto.

The Art of Silence 197?
Kenneth and Suzanne Martin perform pantomime in this program. 30m/B/W; VHS, 3/4 U, EJ, Q. **Pr:** WCBS New York; Camera Three Productions. **A:** Family. **P:** Entertainment. **U:** Institution, SURA. **Gen-Edu:** Mime. **Acq:** Duplication, Free Duplication. **Dist:** Camera Three Productions, Inc.

The Art of Silence: Pantomimes with Marcel Marceau 1975
A series of 13 shows in which Marcel Marceau introduces and then performs a pantomime. Programs available individually. 10m; VHS, 3/4 U. **C:** Marcel Marceau. **Pr:** Encyclopedia Britannica Educational Corporation. **A:** Jr. High-College. **P:** Education. **U:** Institution, SURA. **Fin-Art:** Mime. **Acq:** Purchase, Rent/Lease, Trade-in. **Dist:** Encyclopedia Britannica.
Indiv. Titles: 1. Pantomime: The Language of the Heart 2. Bip Hunts Butterflies 3. The Sideshow 4. Bip at a Society Party 5. The Painter 6. Bip as a Skater 7. The Cage 8. The Hands 9. The Dream 10. Bip as a Soldier 11. The Maskmaker 12. Youth, Maturity, Old Age, Death 13. The Creation of the World.

The Art of Slap Hitting 2006 (Unrated)
Coach Steve Miner discusses slap-hitting, and presents training drills for softball coaches wishing to train their batters in the technique. 36m; DVD. **A:** Family. **P:** Education. **U:** Home, Institution. **Spo-Rec:** Softball, Athletic Instruction/Coaching. **Acq:** Purchase. **Dist:** Championship Productions. $39.99.

The Art of Stone Carving 1989
Scupltor Luis Montoya offers a how-to on stone sculpting: how to pick a stone, how to make and use templates, safety equipment, hand and power tools, stone finishing, adhesives, and scuplture mounting. 85m; VHS. **A:** College-Adult. **P:** Instruction. **U:** Institution. **How-Ins:** Art & Artists, How-To. **Acq:** Purchase. **Dist:** GPN Educational Media. $79.95.

The Art of Storytelling: Tall Tales 1988
Students are introduced to the art of telling good tall tales. Pecos Bill and Annie Christmas are used as classic examples. 21m; VHS, 3/4 U. **Pr:** SVE. **A:** Primary-Jr. High. **P:** Education. **U:** Institution, CCTV, Home. **Gen-Edu:** Storytelling. **Acq:** Purchase, Duplication. **Dist:** Clear Vue Inc. $49.00.

The Art of Table Napkin Folding 19??
Step-by-step demonstration of 23 napkin folding styles. Covers the Fan, Angelfish, Lily, Fleur-de-lis, Orchid, Waterfall, Straight Pocket, Diagonal Pocket, French Fold, Wings, Candle I and II, Bird of Paradise, Rabbit, Graduation Cap, Frog, Bishop's Hat, Cinderella's Slipper, Artichoke, Lazy Butler, Large Poinsettia, Small Poinsettia, and Rose. 35m; VHS. **A:** Jr. High-Adult. **P:** Instruction. **U:** Institution. **How-Ins:** How-To, Home Economics. **Acq:** Purchase. **Dist:** Cambridge Educational. $29.95.

Art of the American West Series 19??
Three-part series which presents the story of the American West through art. Contains footage of many of the works reflecting this historical period. 60m; VHS. **A:** Primary-College. **P:** Education. **U:** Institution. **Fin-Art:** Art & Artists, History--U.S., Western. **Acq:** Purchase. **Dist:** Crystal Productions. $79.95.
Indiv. Titles: 1. Before the White Man 2. Westward Expansion 3. The Old West is Dead.

Art of the American West, Vol. 1: Before the White Man 19??
Reflects on the romantic and realistic styles from romantic paintings associated with the American West. Includes paintings from Bierstadt, Russell, Moran, Wimar, Farney, Hill, Whittredge, and Remington. 20m; VHS. **A:** Primary-College. **P:** Education. **U:** Institution. **Fin-Art:** Art & Artists, History--U.S., Western. **Acq:** Purchase. **Dist:** Crystal Productions. $29.95.

Art of the American West, Vol. II: Westward Expansion 19??
Includes paintings and sculpture that depicts the exploration of the American west. Contains works by Bingham, Johnson, Nahl, Dunton, Borein, Schreyvogel, Farny, Schoonover, and others. 20m; VHS. **A:** Primary-College. **P:** Education. **U:** Institution. **Fin-Art:** Art & Artists, History--U.S., Western. **Acq:** Purchase. **Dist:** Crystal Productions. $29.95.

Art of the American West, Vol. III: The Old West Is Dead 19??
Contains works by such notable artists as Blumenschein, Higgins, Wood, Benton, Scholder, and O'Keeffe, while trying to explain how these artists interpreted the "death" of the Old West. 20m; VHS. **A:** Primary-College. **P:** Education. **U:** Institution. **Fin-Art:** Art & Artists, History--U.S., Western. **Acq:** Purchase. **Dist:** Crystal Productions. $29.95.

The Art of the Animator, Part 1 19??
Offers a behind-the-scenes glimpse at the work of three animators, including Ishu Patel, Caroline Leaf and John Weldon. 24m; VHS. **A:** Jr. High-Adult. **P:** Education. **U:** Institution. **Gen-Edu:** Animation & Cartoons. **Acq:** Purchase, Rent/Lease. **Dist:** National Film Board of Canada. $195.

The Art of the Animator, Part 2 19??
Introduces animation techniques employed by three animators, inclding 3-dimensional sets, scratchboarding, and more. 24m; VHS. **A:** Jr. High-Adult. **P:** Education. **U:** Institution. **Gen-Edu:** Animation & Cartoons. **Acq:** Purchase, Rent/Lease. **Dist:** National Film Board of Canada. $195.

The Art of the Baltic States 1975
A collection of folk art, music, theatre, and dances of Estonia, Latvia, and Lithuania. English subtitles. 30m; VHS. **A:** Sr. High-Adult. **P:** Education. **U:** Institution, Home. **Fin-Art:** Art & Artists. **Acq:** Purchase. **Dist:** International Historic Films Inc.

The Art of the Book: Persian Miniatures from the Shahnameh 198?
The Iranian epic, Shahnameh, has been interpreted by three centuries of painters using a miniature style. The film offers a comparison to other kinds of art popular at the time the miniatures were done, and examines the culture that influenced them. 30m; VHS, 3/4 U. **Pr:** Fogg Art Museum. **A:** Sr. High-Adult. **P:** Education. **U:** Institution, SURA. **Fin-Art:** Art & Artists. **Acq:** Purchase. **Dist:** Films for the Humanities & Sciences.

The Art of the Bullwhip 1991
The history and techniques of the bullwhip, featuring tricks, interviews and exhibitions by the best. 60m; VHS. **A:** Sr. High-Adult. **P:** Instruction. **U:** Home. **Spo-Rec:** Documentary Films. **Acq:** Purchase. **Dist:** Gun Video. $49.95.

Art of the Cocktail, Part 1 19??
Offers instruction on cocktail mixing and preparation. ?m; VHS. **A:** Adult. **P:** Instruction. **U:** Home. **How-Ins:** Alcoholic Beverages, How-To. **Acq:** Purchase. **Dist:** Tapeworm Video Distributors Inc. $29.95.

Art of the Cocktail, Part 2 19??
Offers instruction on cocktail mixing and preparation. ?m; VHS. **A:** Adult. **P:** Instruction. **U:** Home. **How-Ins:** Alcoholic Beverages, How-To. **Acq:** Purchase. **Dist:** Tapeworm Video Distributors Inc. $29.95.

Art of the Devil 2004 (Unrated) — ★½
A pregnant woman is not surprised when her lover refuses to leave his family for her, and hires a witch doctor to get revenge via black magic. 95m; DVD. **C:** Tin Settachoke; Isara Ochakul; Nirut Sutchart; Somchai Satuthum; Krongthong Rachatawan; Arisa Wills; Supakson Chaimongkol; Krittayod Thimnate; Directed by Tanit Jitnukul; Written by Ghost Gypsy; Cinematography by Tanai Nimchareonpong; Thaya Nimchareonpong. **A:** Sr. High-Adult. **P:** Entertainment. **U:** Home. **L:** English, Thai. **Mov-Ent. Acq:** Purchase. **Dist:** Media Blasters Inc. $16.98.

The Art of the Dogon 1988
Footage from the Lester Wunderman collection at the Metropolitan Museum of Art presents the art and ritual of the Dogon people in Mali, West Africa. 24m; VHS. **Pr:** Metropolitan Museum of Art. **A:** Sr. High-Adult. **P:** Education. **U:** Home. **Fin-Art:** Documentary Films, Africa, Sculpture. **Acq:** Purchase. **Dist:** Home Vision Cinema; Facets Multimedia Inc.; Crystal Productions. $29.95.

Art of the Doll Maker 1999
Features a look at doll collecting. Includes interviews with doll artists at their studios and over 160 dolls are shown. 80m; VHS. **A:** Family. **P:** Education. **U:** Home. **Gen-Edu:** Crafts, Hobbies. **Acq:** Purchase. **Dist:** Instructional Video. $29.95.

The Art of the Middle Ages 1963
A discussion of the art of the Middle Ages—art that projects mysticism, the medieval approach to life and death. 30m; VHS, 3/4 U. **Pr:** Encyclopedia Britannica Educational Corporation. **A:** Sr. High-College. **P:** Education. **U:** Institution, SURA. **Fin-Art:** Documentary Films, History--Medieval, Art & Artists. **Acq:** Purchase, Rent/Lease, Trade-in. **Dist:** Encyclopedia Britannica. $410.00.

The Art of the Motion Picture 1970
Defines and gives examples of the five basic elements in filmmaking that lend themselves to artistic control by the filmmaker and to critical analysis by the viewer. 20m; VHS, 3/4 U. **A:** Jr. High-Sr. High. **P:** Education. **U:** Institution, SURA. **Fin-Art:** Filmmaking. **Acq:** Purchase. **Dist:** Phoenix Learning Group.

The Art of the Near East and Ancient Egypt 19??
Part of a multicultural art series that explores five major cultural areas of the world. Includes art reproduction prints and a teacher's guide. ?m; VHS. **A:** Jr. High-College. **P:** Education. **U:** Institution. **Gen-Edu:** Art & Artists. **Acq:** Purchase. **Dist:** Crystal Productions. $74.95.

The Art of the Potter 1967
Throwing a pot is the terminology used to cover the work of the potter from the time he begins work until he finishes. This film illustrates the proper techniques. 15m; VHS, 3/4 U. **Pr:** Cinecrafters. **A:** Jr. High-Sr. High. **P:** Instruction. **U:** Institution, SURA. **Fin-Art:** Crafts. **Acq:** Purchase. **Dist:** Phoenix Learning Group.

The Art of the Potter 1977
Traces the entire process of pottery-making while presenting the works of two of the most repected potters ever, Bernard Leach and the late Shoji Hamada. 50m; VHS, 3/4 U. **Pr:** Sidney Reichman. **A:** Sr. High-Adult. **P:** Education. **U:** Institution, SURA. **Fin-Art:** Crafts. **Acq:** Purchase. **Dist:** Phoenix Learning Group.

The Art of the Sixties 1968
Art in the first years of the 1960s graduated from the two-dimensional picture frame concept to sculpture merged in color, represented by the work of Segal and Oldenburg. 30m; VHS, 3/4 U. **C:** Narrated by Barnett Newmann. **Pr:** WCBS New York. **A:** Sr. High-College. **P:** Education. **U:** Institution, SURA. **Fin-Art:** Sculpture. **Acq:** Purchase. **Dist:** Phoenix Learning Group.

The Art of the Steal 2010
Chronicles the troubles of the Barnes Foundation, founded in 1922 in Lower Merion, Pennsylvania to house the private art collection of Albert C. Barnes. Barnes' will stipulated that the collection could not be sold, loaned, or moved after his 1951 death but politicians and philanthropists would like to see the works moved to Philadelphia and installed as a public museum. 101m; DVD. **A:** Adult. **P:** Entertainment. **U:** Home. **Gen-Edu:** Documentary Films, Art & Artists, Museums. **Acq:** Purchase. **Dist:** MPI Media Group. $24.98.

The Art of the Steal 2013 (R) — ★★
A fitfully amusing, overly complicated crime comedy held together by Russell's enjoyable performance as semi-reformed art thief Crunch Calhoun. The ex-con is working as a low-rent motorcycle daredevil when he reluctantly agrees to a heist with his untrustworthy brother, Nicky (Dillon). The plan is to steal a

rare book from a Niagara Falls border customs station but eager Interpol agent Bick's (Jones) out to stop them with Stamp delightfully disdainful as the thief coerced into helping him. 90m; DVD, Blu-Ray. **C:** Kurt Russell; Matt Dillon; Jay Baruchel; Kenneth Welsh; Terence Stamp; Jason Jones; Katheryn Winnick; Chris Diamantopoulos; Directed by Jonathan Sobol; Written by Jonathan Sobol; Cinematography by Adam Swica; Music by Grayson Matthews. **Pr:** Nicholas D. Tabarrok; Radius-TWC. **A:** Sr. High-Adult. **P:** Entertainment. **U:** Home. **L:** English. **Mov-Ent:** Family. **Acq:** Purchase. **Dist:** Radius-TWC.

Art of the Western World, Vol. 1: Greece & Rome 1989

Part one of the 10-part PBS art history series. Focuses on Greek and Roman art, covering Greek sculpture and architecture, including the Parthenon, and Roman art and architecture, including the Acropolis, the Colosseum, and the Pantheon. 55m; VHS. **Pr:** Educational Broadcasting Corporation; PBS. **A:** College-Adult. **P:** Education. **U:** Home, Institution. **Fin-Art:** Art & Artists, Architecture, History--Ancient. **Acq:** Purchase. **Dist:** Crystal Productions. $100.00.

Art of the Western World, Vol. 2: Romanesque & Gothic 1989

Part two of the 10-part PBS art history series. Outlines the art of the Middle Ages, including Gothic cathedrals and Romanesque churches. Includes footage of Chartres, Notre Dame, and St. Denis cathedrals. 55m; VHS. **Pr:** Educational Broadcasting Corporation; PBS. **A:** College-Adult. **P:** Education. **U:** Home, Institution. **Fin-Art:** Art & Artists, Architecture, History--Medieval. **Acq:** Purchase. **Dist:** Crystal Productions. $100.00.

Art of the Western World, Vol. 3: The Early Renaissance 1989

Part 3 of the ten-part PBS art history series. Profiles the histroy of art during the early Renaissance period, covering Italian, Flemish, and German artists including Giotto, Masaccio, Donatello, Botticello, Bellini, van Eyck and Durer. 55m; VHS. **Pr:** Educational Broadcasting Corporation; PBS. **A:** College-Adult. **P:** Education. **U:** Home, Institution. **Fin-Art:** Art & Artists, Italy, Germany. **Acq:** Purchase. **Dist:** Crystal Productions. $100.00.

Art of the Western World, Vol. 4: The High Renaissance 1989

Part 4 of the ten-part PBS art history series. Centers on the art and artists of the Renaissance, including Leonardo da Vinci, Michelangelo, Raphael, and Palladio. Contains footage of da Vinci's "The Last Supper," Michelangelo's "David," Sistine Chapel, and St. Peter's, and Raphael's "School of Athens," located in the Vatican Library. 55m; VHS. **Pr:** Educational Broadcasting Corporation; PBS. **A:** College-Adult. **P:** Education. **U:** Home, Institution. **Fin-Art:** Art & Artists, History--Renaissance. **Acq:** Purchase. **Dist:** Crystal Productions. $100.00.

Art of the Western World, Vol. 5: The Baroque 1989

Part 5 of the 10-part PBS art history series. Focuses on art from the Baroque period featuring the fountains of Rome, Madrid's Prado Museum, and Rubens' baronial museum in Flanders. Includes insight from leading art historians on the importance and context of the art of this time. 55m; VHS. **Pr:** Educational Broadcasting Corporation; PBS. **A:** College-Adult. **P:** Education. **U:** Home, Institution. **Fin-Art:** Art & Artists, History. **Acq:** Purchase. **Dist:** Crystal Productions. $100.00.

Art of the Western World, Vol. 6: An Age of Passion 1989

Part 6 of the 10-part PBS art history series. Features art from one of the most turbulent and revolutionary periods in history, including the works of Rococo, Fragonard, Delacroix, Ingres, Goya, Constable, and Turner. 55m; VHS. **Pr:** Educational Broadcasting Corporation; PBS. **A:** College-Adult. **P:** Education. **U:** Home, Institution. **Fin-Art:** Art & Artists, History. **Acq:** Purchase. **Dist:** Crystal Productions. $100.00.

Art of the Western World, Vol. 7: Realism and Impressionism 1989

Part 7 of the ten-part PBS art history series. Focuses on the great artists during the realism and impressionism era, including Monet, Degas, Manet, van Gogh, Cezanne, Seurat, Gauguin, England's Millais and Rosetti, and Americans Homer, Eakins, and Whistler. 55m; VHS. **Pr:** Educational Broadcasting Corporation; PBS. **A:** College-Adult. **P:** Education. **U:** Home, Institution. **Fin-Art:** Art & Artists, History. **Acq:** Purchase. **Dist:** Crystal Productions. $100.00.

Art of the Western World, Vol. 8: Into the Twentieth Century 1989

Part 8 of the 10-part PBS art history series. Picks up the history of art at the beginning of the 20th century, including the Cubism of Picasso and Braque, Vienna's avant-garde styles of Klimpt, Schiele, and Kokoshka, and the Modernism styles of Matisse, Leger, Miro, Calder, Mondrian, and Frank Lloyd Wright. 55m; VHS. **Pr:** Educational Broadcasting Corporation; PBS. **A:** College-Adult. **P:** Education. **U:** Home, Institution. **Fin-Art:** Art & Artists, History--Modern. **Acq:** Purchase. **Dist:** Crystal Productions. $100.00.

Art of the Western World, Vol. 9: World War II and Beyond 1989

Part 9 of the 10-part PBS art history series. Outlines art from after World War II, including minimalism, pop art, abstract, expressionism, and other modern artistic styles. Also covers Jackson Pollock's Action Painting, analyzes the satyrical pop works of Andy Warhol and Claes Oldenburg, and looks at the exciting international art world of the 1970s and 1980s. 55m; VHS. **Pr:** Educational Broadcasting Corporation; PBS. **A:** College-Adult. **P:** Education. **U:** Home, Institution. **Fin-Art:** Art & Artists, History--Modern. **Acq:** Purchase. **Dist:** Crystal Productions. $100.00.

Art of the Western World, Vol. 10: The Picture Gallery 1989

Final part of the 10-part PBS art history series. Combines all the still pictures of the first nine volumes into one huge "Picture Gallery" of over 5,500 pictures of some of western art's most important and greatest creations in painting, sculpture, and architecture. 55m; VHS. **Pr:** Educational Broadcasting Corporation; PBS. **A:** College-Adult. **P:** Education. **U:** Home, Institution. **Fin-Art:** Art & Artists, History. **Acq:** Purchase. **Dist:** Crystal Productions. $175.00.

Art of the Wild 1999

Features interviews with 14 writers who express their philosophy, backgrounds, and deep devotion to the land and all its inhabitants. 57m; VHS. **A:** Jr. High-Adult. **P:** Entertainment. **U:** Home. **Gen-Edu:** Ecology & Environment, Art & Artists. **Acq:** Purchase. **Dist:** Global Mindshift. $20.00.

The Art of Thrown Sculpture 1968

The film directs itself toward the freely expressive side of ceramic production. 12m; VHS, 3/4 U. **Pr:** Cinecrafters. **A:** Jr. High-Sr. High. **P:** Education. **U:** Institution, SURA. **Gen-Edu:** Crafts. **Acq:** Purchase. **Dist:** Phoenix Learning Group.

The Art of Tom & Jerry 1940

Enjoy the adventures of the cat and mouse adversaries with this five-disc set containing every Tom & Jerry cartoon from 1940 through 1953. 540m. **Pr:** MGM. **A:** Family. **P:** Entertainment. **U:** Home. **Mov-Ent:** Animation & Cartoons. **Acq:** Purchase. **Dist:** MGM Home Entertainment. $89.95.

The Art of Tom & Jerry, Vol. 3: The Chuck Jones Years 19??

Three-disc boxed set features all 35 Tom & Jerry shorts made during the Jones era. 300m. **A:** Family. **P:** Entertainment. **U:** Home. **Mov-Ent:** Animation & Cartoons, Pets, Family Viewing. **Acq:** Purchase. **Dist:** MGM Home Entertainment. $69.98.

The Art of Traditional Armenian Cooking 1989

Become an expert on Armenian cooking. This tape comes with or without a cookbook. 60m; VHS. **Pr:** Armenian Film Foundation. **A:** Jr. High-Adult. **P:** Instruction. **U:** Institution, Home. **How-Ins:** Cooking. **Acq:** Purchase. **Dist:** Armenian Film Foundation. $35.00.

The Art of Travel 2008 (R) — ★★

When Conner Layne (Masterson) finds his fiancee cheating, he dumps her at the altar and takes off for a solo Central American honeymoon. First he gets robbed, but then he's befriended by adventure junkies Darlene (Burns) and Christopher (Messner), who are planning to cross Darien Gap, 100 miles of roadless jungle separating Panama and Columbia. They invite Conner along and he's soon hooked on the travel and decides not to stop. 101m; DVD, On Demand. **C:** Christopher K. Masterson; Brooke Burns; Johnny Messner; James Duval; Angelika Baran; Jake Muxworthy; Maria Conchita Alonso; Shalim Ortiz; Directed by Thomas Whelan; Written by Thomas Whelan; Brian LaBelle; Cinematography by Lawson Deming; Music by Steve Bartek. **A:** Sr. High-Adult. **P:** Entertainment. **U:** Home. **Mov-Ent:** Central America. **Acq:** Purchase. **Dist:** Amazon.com Inc.

Art of Trolling for Salmon 1991

Learn how to rig bait fish plugs, troll lures, locate salmon, use downriggers and select gear with Gary Cooper. 60m; VHS. **Pr:** Bennett Marine Video. **A:** Sr. High-Adult. **P:** Instruction. **U:** Home. **How-Ins:** Sports--General, Fishing, How-To. **Acq:** Purchase. **Dist:** Bennett Marine Video. $29.95.

The Art of Turkey Calling 1986

National Turkey Calling Champion Leroy Braungardt shares his secrets for success. 42m; VHS. **Pr:** BFV. **A:** Adult. **P:** Instruction. **U:** Home. **Spo-Rec:** Hunting, Birds. **Acq:** Purchase. **Dist:** Best Video. $49.95.

The Art of War 2000 (R) — ★1/2

Disappointingly formulaic thriller has Snipes starring as top-secret U.N. operative Neil Shaw, who is framed for the assassination of a Chinese ambassador (Hong). Also involved is his boss, Eleanor Hooks (Archer), Chinese power broker David Chan (Tagawa), and interpreter Julia (Matiko), whom Shaw kidnaps to help him prove his innocence. Plot is both convoluted and obvious (you can pretty much guess what's coming) and you learn so little about the players that you won't be very interested in what happens to them. 117m; VHS, DVD, Wide. **C:** Wesley Snipes; Marie Matiko; Cary-Hiroyuki Tagawa; Anne Archer; Maury Chaykin; Michael Biehn; Donald Sutherland; Liliana Komorowska; James Hong; Directed by Christian Duguay; Written by Wayne Beach; Simon Davis Barry; Cinematography by Pierre Gill; Music by Normand Corbeil. **Pr:** Wesley Snipes; Elie Samaha; Dan Halstead; Wesley Snipes; Nicholas Clermont; Morgan Creek Productions; Amen Ra; Filmline International; Warner Bros. **A:** Sr. High-Adult. **P:** Entertainment. **U:** Home. **Mov-Ent:** Politics & Government, Federal Bureau of Investigation (FBI). **Acq:** Purchase. **Dist:** Warner Home Video, Inc.

Art of War 2: The Betrayal 2008 (R) — ★

Dull plot isn't even redeemed by any good action and everyone looks bored. Neil Shaw (Snipes) is called out of retirement by his friend Garret (Munro), a senatorial candidate. Seems senators with oversight on defense spending are either being blackmailed or killed and Garret doesn't want to wind up a statistic. 103m; DVD. **C:** Wesley Snipes; Lochlyn Munro; Athena Karkanis; Winston Rekert; Clifford W. Stewart; Ryan McDonald; Directed by Josef Rusnak; Written by Jason Bourque; Keith Shaw; Cinematography by Neil Cerrin; Music by Peter Allen. **A:** Sr. High-Adult. **P:** Entertainment. **U:** Home. **Mov-Ent:** Politics & Government. **Acq:** Purchase. **Dist:** Sony Pictures Home Entertainment Inc.

The Art of War 3: Retribution 2008 (R) — ★1/2

Agent Shaw is on a mission to prevent North Korean terrorists from obtaining a nuclear bomb. Framed for murder and hunted on the streets, Shaw has to stop the terrorists before they can detonate the bomb at a U.N. peace conference. 88m; DVD. **C:** Treach; Sung Hi Lee; Warren DeRosa; Directed by Gerry Lively; Written by Joe Halpin; Cinematography by Suki Medencevic; Music by James Bairian; Louis Castle. **A:** Sr. High-Adult. **P:** Entertainment. **U:** Home. **Mov-Ent:** Terrorism. **Acq:** Purchase. **Dist:** Sony Pictures Home Entertainment Inc.

Art Party 199?

Professor Iris creates a masterpiece. Puppetry. 40m; VHS. **A:** Preschool. **P:** Education. **U:** Home. **Chl-Juv:** Children, Puppets, Art & Artists. **Acq:** Purchase. **Dist:** Discovery Home Entertainment. $12.95.

Art, People, Feelings 1971

Using historical and contemporary art works including film, billboards, posters, and television, this show illustrates the communication of feeling through visual arts. 15m; VHS, 3/4 U. **Pr:** Michael Lyon. **A:** Sr. High-Adult. **P:** Entertainment. **U:** Institution, Home, SURA. **Fin-Art:** Film--Avant-Garde. **Acq:** Purchase, Rent/Lease, Duplication License. **Dist:** Pyramid Media.

Art Reveals Culture 1992

A five-part series examing the history and diversity of worldwide art in its cultural context. Teacher's guide available. 15m; VHS. **A:** Jr. High-Sr. High. **P:** Education. **U:** Institution. **Gen-Edu:** Art & Artists. **Acq:** Purchase. **Dist:** GPN Educational Media. $99.95.

Art School Confidential 2006 (R) — ★★

Underdeveloped and frequently flat satire about the art world. Idealistic Jerome (Minghella) wants to be the next Picasso when he enters art school. He soon learns it's not about art, it's about hype and commerce. Generic character types include pretentious professor Sandiford (Malkovich), no-talent filmmaker Vince (Suplee), shallow-but-beautiful artists' model Audrey (Myles), drunken failed artist Jimmy (Broadbent), and Jerome's own cynical guide Bardo (Moore). Jerome becomes disillusioned and desperate, and not just because a serial killer is working the neighborhood. Clowes adapted from his comic strip. Buscemi is uncredited as trendy restaurant owner Broadway Bob. 102m; DVD. **C:** Max Minghella; Sophia Myles; John Malkovich; Jim Broadbent; Matt Keeslar; Ethan Suplee; Anjelica Huston; Joel David Moore; Nick Swardson; Steve Buscemi; Directed by Terry Zwigoff; Written by Daniel Clowes; Cinematography by Jamie Anderson; Music by David Kitay. **Pr:** Lianne Halfon; John Malkovich; Russell Smith; John Malkovich; United Artists; Mr. Mudd; Sony Pictures Classics. **A:** Sr. High-Adult. **P:** Entertainment. **U:** Home. **L:** English. **Mov-Ent:** Art & Artists, Education, Comedy--Black. **Acq:** Purchase. **Dist:** Sony Pictures Home Entertainment Inc.

Art: Seeing and Creating 1991

Offers art instruction tips to K through 12 teachers. Covers ideas such as paper sculpture, puppet making, mounting artwork and creating imaginative bulletin boards. Comes in a series of 10 30-minute tapes, or each tape can be purchased individually. Includes a detailed course guide. 30m; VHS. **Pr:** Florida Instructional Television Center. **A:** Adult. **P:** Teacher Education. **U:** Institution. **Gen-Edu:** How-To, Art & Artists, Children. **Acq:** Purchase. **Dist:** GPN Educational Media. $275.00.

Art Series 1986

Three programs with Harold Riley, demonstrating artistic techniques. 30m; VHS. **Pr:** Morris Video. **A:** Jr. High-Adult. **P:** Instruction. **U:** Home. **How-Ins:** Art & Artists. **Acq:** Purchase. **Dist:** Morris Video.

Indiv. Titles: 1. Landscape Painting 2. Portrait Painting 3. Drawing.

Art Since Pop 19??

Two-part art appreciation program explores a number of debatable questions, such as What is art and who is qualified to say? Profiles the works of such popular artists as Warhol, Rothko, Olitski, and others. Discusses hard-edge painting, image reduction, video art, Superrealism, earth works, kinetic art, holograms, and much more. 29m; VHS. **A:** Primary-College. **P:** Education. **U:** Institution. **Fin-Art:** Art & Artists. **Acq:** Purchase. **Dist:** Cambridge Educational. $110.00.

Art Smart 1989

An arts and crafts series aimed at adults. 30m; VHS, 3/4 U. **Pr:** Great Plains National. **A:** Jr. High-Adult. **P:** Education. **U:** Institution. **Gen-Edu:** Art & Artists. **Acq:** Rent/Lease, Duplication License. **Dist:** Cambridge Educational. $49.95.

Indiv. Titles: 1. Wheel Thrown Pottery 2. Handbuilt Clay Sculpture 3. Handbuilt Pottery 4. Glazing and Firing.

Art Smart Drawing: Figure Drawing 1991

Illustrates figure study drawing techniques, including gesture poses, positive/negative space, rendering, proportion, and mood. 28m; VHS. **A:** Primary-Adult. **P:** Instruction. **U:** Institution. **How-Ins:** How-To, Drawing, Art & Artists. **Acq:** Purchase. **Dist:** Cambridge Educational. $49.95.

Art Smart Drawing: Fundamentals of Drawing 1990

Artist Carroll Erlandson demonstrates still-life drawing with charcoal. 26m; VHS. **A:** Jr. High-Adult. **P:** Instruction. **U:** Home. **How-Ins:** How-To, Drawing, Art & Artists. **Acq:** Purchase. **Dist:** Cambridge Educational. $49.95.

Art Smart Drawing: Portrait Drawing 1991
Introduces three basic portrait drawings: frontal, profile, and 3/4 view. Also provides historical information on protrait drawing. 26m; VHS. **A:** Primary-Adult. **P:** Instruction. **U:** Institution, Home. **How-Ins:** How-To, Art & Artists, Drawing. **Acq:** Purchase. **Dist:** Cambridge Educational. $49.95.

Art Surprises 1998
Donna Erickson presents creative projects for children of all ages, including Fish Prints and Potato Jewelry. 36m; VHS. **A:** Family. **P:** Instruction. **U:** Home. **Chl-Juv:** Art & Artists, Children. **Acq:** Purchase. **Dist:** Tapeworm Video Distributors Inc. $29.95.

The Art Teacher Series: Drawing Made Easy 19??
Part of the art education series featuring Dan Mihuta. Encourages beginning artists to use everyday articles to help them learn to draw. 55m; VHS. **A:** Family. **P:** Instruction. **U:** Institution, Home. **How-Ins:** Art & Artists, How-To, Drawing. **Acq:** Purchase. **Dist:** Crystal Productions. $24.95.

The Art Teacher Series: Painting Made Easy 19??
Part of Dan Mihuta's art education series. Covers instruction on basic techniques in painting. Includes demonstrations of brush techniques. 55m; VHS. **A:** Family. **P:** Instruction. **U:** Institution, Home. **How-Ins:** Art & Artists, How-To. **Acq:** Purchase. **Dist:** Crystal Productions. $24.95.

The Art Teacher Series: Paper Sculpture Projects 19??
Part of the art education series by Dan Mihuta. Provides step-by-step instruction on paper sculpturing techniques, covering folding, tearing, punching, curling, slotting, and scoring. Includes projects that can duplicated by the viewer. 55m; VHS. **A:** Family. **P:** Instruction. **U:** Institution, Home. **How-Ins:** Art & Artists, How-To. **Acq:** Purchase. **Dist:** Crystal Productions. $24.95.

The Art Teacher Series with Dan Mihuta 19??
Three-part series, featuring Dan Mihuta, that encourages the beginning artist to create through drawing, painting, and paper art projects. 165m; VHS. **A:** Family. **P:** Instruction. **U:** Institution, Home. **How-Ins:** Art & Artists, How-To. **Acq:** Purchase. **Dist:** Crystal Productions. $69.95.
Indiv. Titles: 1. Drawing Made Easy 2. Painting Made Easy 3. Paper Sculpture Projects.

Art: The Creative Young Child 1991
Emphasizes teaching art to very young children. Drawing, fingerpainting, painting with a brush, tearing and cutting, printmaking, constructing puppets, tips for displaying art and teaching art appreciation are covered. Comes in a series of 10 30-minute tapes, or each tape can be purchased individually. Includes a detailed course guide. 30m; VHS. **Pr:** Florida Instructional Television Center. **A:** Adult. **P:** Teacher Education. **U:** Institution. **Gen-Edu:** Art & Artists, How-To, Children. **Acq:** Purchase. **Dist:** GPN Educational Media. $275.00.

Art vs. Art 1983
The title refers to artist A. Hummer's run in Toronto's mayoral race in 1983, where she came in second to incumbent Art Eggleton. 60m; VHS, 3/4 U. **Pr:** Video Out. **A:** Jr. High-Adult. **P:** Education. **U:** Institution, SURA. **Gen-Edu:** Politics & Government, Art & Artists. **Acq:** Rent/Lease. **Dist:** Video Out Distribution.

Art: What Is It? Why Is It? 1963
An analysis of art that does much to unravel the mystery surrounding man's urge to paint, carve, and build. 30m; VHS, 3/4 U. **Pr:** Encyclopedia Britannica Educational Corporation. **A:** Sr. High-College. **P:** Education. **U:** Institution, SURA. **L:** English, Spanish, Arabic. **Gen-Edu:** Documentary Films, Art & Artists. **Acq:** Purchase, Rent/Lease, Trade-in. **Dist:** Encyclopedia Britannica. $410.00.

Art with the Elders in Long-Term Care 1985
Filmed at Hillhaven Convalescent Hospital, this film describes the art program developed for people over 80 years old. 10m; VHS, 3/4 U. **Pr:** Mary Ann Merker-Benton. **A:** Jr. High-Adult. **P:** Professional. **U:** Institution, Home, SURA. **Gen-Edu:** Aging, Art & Artists. **Acq:** Purchase, Rent/Lease, Duplication. **Dist:** Filmakers Library Inc.

Art—Who Needs It? 19??
Two-part program encourages viewers to reconstruct their ideas about art by debating tough questions such as "What is good and bad art?" Also examines the role of artists in society. Complete with teacher's guide. 36m; VHS. **A:** Jr. High-College. **P:** Education. **U:** Institution. **Fin-Art:** Art & Artists. **Acq:** Purchase. **Dist:** Cambridge Educational. $119.00.

Artemisia 1997 (R) — ★★
Artemisia (Cervi) is the teenaged daughter of well-known artist Orazio Gentileschi (Serrault), who encourages her artistic pursuits. He bullies the local art academy to admit Artemisia, a no-no in 17th-century Rome, and she even tries the forbidden territory of the male nude. Soon her artistic passion is matched by a sexual passion for fellow artist Agostino Tassi (Manojlovic), but this time her father isn't so understanding and Artemisia becomes the center of a rape trial. The real Artemisia is considered to be the first known female artist. French with subtitles. 95m; VHS, DVD, CC. **C:** Valentina Cervi; Michel Serrault; Miki (Predrag) Manojlovic; Luca Zingaretti; Brigitte Catillon; Frederic Pierrot; Maurice Garrel; Yann Tregouet; Jacques Nolot; Directed by Agnes Merlet; Written by Agnes Merlet; Cinematography by Benoit Delhomme; Music by Krishna Levy. **Pr:** Patrice Haddad; Premiere Heure; Miramax. **A:** College-Adult. **P:** Entertainment. **U:** Home. **L:** French. **Mov-Ent:** Drama, Art & Artists, Romance. **Acq:** Purchase. **Dist:** Buena Vista Home Entertainment.

Arterial Puncture 1977
This program discusses the anatomy of three sites for arterial puncture; the radial, brachial, and femoral arteries. A clinicl example of radial artery puncture is shown. 11m; VHS, 3/4 U, Special order formats. **Pr:** Health Sciences Learning Resources. **A:** College-Adult. **P:** Professional. **U:** Institution, CCTV. **Hea-Sci:** Circulatory System. **Acq:** Purchase. **Dist:** Health Sciences Center for Educational Resources.

Artful History: A Restoration Comedy 1988
Examines the business of art restoration: how paintings can suffer more harm from restorers than if left alone and how profit can determine the work. 28m; VHS. **C:** Directed by Jason Simon; Mark Dion. **A:** College-Adult. **P:** Education. **U:** Institution. **Fin-Art:** Art & Artists. **Acq:** Purchase, Rent/Lease. **Dist:** First Run/Icarus Films. $280.00.

Arthritic Joints 1979
A discussion on replacement of joints damaged by arthritis and the physical therapy needed to use the new joints. 30m; VHS, 3/4 U. **Pr:** WNET New York. **A:** Sr. High-Adult. **P:** Education. **U:** Institution, CCTV, Home. **Hea-Sci:** Arthritis. **Acq:** Purchase, Rent/Lease. **Dist:** WNET/Thirteen Non-Broadcast.

Arthritis: A Dialogue with Pain 1982
A look at arthritis its victims, the different forms of treatment available and personal formulas for coping with pain. 56m; VHS, 3/4 U. **Pr:** National Film Board of Canada. **A:** Sr. High-Adult. **P:** Education. **U:** Institution, SURA. **Hea-Sci:** Arthritis. **Acq:** Purchase, Rent/Lease. **Dist:** National Film Board of Canada. $24.99.

Arthritis: Best Use of the Hands 1988
Produced by medical professionals, these tapes enlighten arthritis sufferers on hand anatomy, principles of joint protection, ways to reduce stress on the joints of the hand, and general methods of dealing with arthritis. 40m; VHS. **Pr:** Video Education Specialists. **A:** College-Adult. **P:** Education. **U:** Institution. **Hea-Sci:** How-To, Arthritis, Patient Education. **Acq:** Purchase. **Dist:** Silver Mine Video Inc. $70.00.
Indiv. Titles: 1. Osteoarthritis 2. Rheumatoid Arthritis.

The Arthritis Foundation's Pool Exercise Program—P.E.P. 1992
The Arthritis Foundation's aquatic exercise program aimed at the individual suffering from arthritis. Emphasis is placed on increasing and maintaining joint flexibility, muscle strength, and endurance. 35m; VHS. **P:** Instruction. **U:** Institution, Home. **Hea-Sci:** Fitness/Exercise, Arthritis. **Acq:** Purchase. **Dist:** Distinctive Home Video Productions.

Arthrocentesis of the Knee 1978
The anatomy and pathophysiology of the swollen knee are presented in a step-by-step analysis. 6m; VHS, 3/4 U, Special order formats. **Pr:** Health Sciences Learning Resources. **A:** College-Adult. **P:** Professional. **U:** Institution, CCTV. **Hea-Sci:** Joints. **Acq:** Purchase. **Dist:** Health Sciences Center for Educational Resources.

Arthroplasty of the Shoulder: Cadaver Demonstration 1 1983
An orthopedic surgeon dissects a cadaver to demonstrate how to insert various devices into the shoulder joint. 38m; VHS, 3/4 U. **Pr:** Emory University. **A:** College-Adult. **P:** Education. **U:** Institution, CCTV, Home, SURA. **Hea-Sci:** Anatomy & Physiology, Joints, Health Education. **Acq:** Purchase, Rent/Lease, Subscription. **Dist:** Emory Medical Television Network.

Arthroplasty of the Shoulder: Cadaver Demonstration 2 1983
An orthopedic surgeon continues his exploration of the shoulder joint to insert prosthetic devices. 45m; VHS, 3/4 U. **Pr:** Emory University. **A:** College-Adult. **P:** Education. **U:** Institution, CCTV, Home, SURA. **Hea-Sci:** Anatomy & Physiology, Joints, Health Education. **Acq:** Purchase, Rent/Lease, Subscription. **Dist:** Emory Medical Television Network.

Arthroplasty of the Shoulder: Unipolar and Total 1983
An orthopedic surgeon discusses the various arthroplasty procedures. 56m; VHS, 3/4 U. **Pr:** Emory University. **A:** College-Adult. **P:** Education. **U:** Institution, CCTV, Home, SURA. **Hea-Sci:** Joints. **Acq:** Purchase, Rent/Lease, Subscription. **Dist:** Emory Medical Television Network.

Arthroscopy and Arthroscopic Surgery 1980
This program is a primer in the use of the arthroscope in diagnosis and surgical treatment. 53m; VHS, 3/4 U. **Pr:** Emory University. **A:** College-Adult. **P:** Professional. **U:** Institution, CCTV, Home, SURA. **Hea-Sci:** Surgery. **Acq:** Purchase, Rent/Lease, Subscription. **Dist:** Emory Medical Television Network.

Arthroscopy of the Knee 1982
This program covers knee anatomy and the effects of injury and disease; it also outlines a typical diagnostic work-up and shows how arthroscopy can be used for diagnosis and treatment. 15m; VHS, 3/4 U, CV. **Pr:** Professional Research. **A:** Adult. **P:** Education. **U:** Institution, CCTV, SURA. **Hea-Sci:** Joints. **Acq:** Purchase, Rent/Lease. **Dist:** Discovery Education. $295.00.

Arthroscopy of the Shoulder 1983
A discussion of the techniques used to perform shoulder arthroscopy. 20m; VHS, 3/4 U. **Pr:** Emory University. **A:** College-Adult. **P:** Education. **U:** Institution, CCTV, Home, SURA. **Hea-Sci:** Joints. **Acq:** Purchase, Rent/Lease, Subscription. **Dist:** Emory Medical Television Network.

Arthur 1981 (PG) — ★★★
Spoiled, alcoholic billionaire Moore stands to lose everything he owns when he falls in love with a waitress. He must choose between wealth and a planned marriage, or poverty and love. Surprisingly funny, with an Oscar for Gielgud as Moore's valet, and great performance from Minnelli. Arguably the best role Moore's ever had, and he makes the most of it, taking the one-joke premise to a Oscar nomination. 97m; VHS, DVD, 8 mm, CC. **C:** Dudley Moore; Liza Minnelli; John Gielgud; Geraldine Fitzgerald; Stephen Elliott; Jill Eikenberry; Lou Jacobi; Ted Ross; Barney Martin; Directed by Steve Gordon; Written by Steve Gordon; Cinematography by Fred Schuler; Music by Burt Bacharach; Peter Allen; Lyrics by Peter Allen. **Pr:** Orion Pictures. **A:** Jr. High-Adult. **P:** Entertainment. **U:** Home. **L:** English, Spanish. **Mov-Ent:** Comedy--Romantic, Alcoholism. **Awds:** Oscars '81: Song ("Arthur's Theme"), Support. Actor (Gielgud); Golden Globes '82: Actor--Mus./Comedy (Moore), Film--Mus./Comedy, Song ("Arthur's Theme"), Support. Actor (Gielgud); L.A. Film Critics '81: Support. Actor (Gielgud); N.Y. Film Critics '81: Support. Actor (Gielgud); Writers Guild '81: Orig. Screenplay. **Acq:** Purchase. **Dist:** Facets Multimedia Inc.; Baker and Taylor; Warner Home Video, Inc. $19.98.
Songs: Arthur's Theme; Blue Moon; If You Knew Susie; Santa Claus Is Coming to Town.

Arthur 2011 (PG-13) — ★★
Controversial funnyman Brand takes over the title role that Dudley Moore made famous in 1981. Arthur Bach is the punch-drunk zillionaire content with partying and always picking up the check. However, his controlling mother informs him that he'll be marrying rich young woman Susan (Garner) and finding a job to maintain the inheritance. All this just as he meets working girl Naomi (Gerwig), a woman with soul. Mirren puts more muscle into the part of the playboy's caretaker, previously filled by Arthur's aloof brother. A fairly faithful adaptation, with Brand never going over-the-top or doing a Moore impression. 110m; Blu-Ray, On Demand, Wide. **C:** Russell Brand; Greta Gerwig; Jennifer Garner; Helen Mirren; Nick Nolte; Geraldine James; Leslie Hendrix; Luis Guzman; Directed by Jason Winer; Written by Peter Baynham; Cinematography by Uta Briesewitz; Music by Theodore Shapiro. **Pr:** Chris Bender; JC Spink; Russell Brand; Larry Brezner; Kevin McCormick; Michael Tadross; Russell Brand; Benderspink; Morra, Brezner, Steinberg & Tenenbaum Entertainment, Inc; Langley Park Productions; Warner Bros. **A:** Jr. High-Adult. **P:** Entertainment. **U:** Home. **L:** English. **Mov-Ent:** Comedy--Romantic, Alcoholism. **Acq:** Purchase. **Dist:** Amazon.com Inc.; Movies Unlimited; Alpha Video.

Arthur 2: On the Rocks 1988 (PG) — ★½
When Arthur finally marries his sweetheart, it may not be "happily ever after" because the father of the girl he didn't marry is out for revenge. When Arthur discovers that he is suddenly penniless, a bit of laughter is the cure for the blues and also serves well when the liquor runs out. A disappointing sequel with few laughs. 113m; VHS, DVD, 8 mm, CC. **C:** Dudley Moore; Liza Minnelli; John Gielgud; Geraldine Fitzgerald; Stephen Elliott; Ted Ross; Barney Martin; Jack Gilford; Directed by Bud Yorkin; Written by Andy Breckman; Cinematography by Stephen Burum; Music by Burt Bacharach. **A:** Adult. **P:** Entertainment. **U:** Home. **Mov-Ent:** Comedy--Romantic, Romance, Alcoholism. **Awds:** Golden Raspberries '87: Worst Actress (Minnelli). **Acq:** Purchase. **Dist:** Warner Home Video, Inc.; Facets Multimedia Inc. $14.95.

Arthur and Lillie 1976
A film about Arthur and Lillie Mayer, their memories of the early Hollywood industry and their own lives, which have remained open throughout their life. 30m; VHS. **Pr:** Jon Else; Kristine Samuelson; Steven Kouvacs. **A:** College-Adult. **P:** Entertainment. **U:** Institution, Home, SURA. **Mov-Ent:** Documentary Films, Film History. **Acq:** Purchase, Rent/Lease, Duplication License. **Dist:** Pyramid Media.

Arthur and the Invisibles 2006 (PG) — ★
Maybe it makes sense to the French. Besson tackles kiddie fantasy in this mishmash combo of CGI and live-action. Arthur (Highmore) lives with his grandma (Farrow), who is about to lose their debt-ridden home. Arthur needs to follow clues left by grandpa to some rubies hidden in the land of the Minimoys, who look like fairies and happen to live in the backyard. A little hocus-pocus, and Arthur becomes mini, gets some help from the inhabitants, and goes after the gems, which are held by evil Maltazard (Bowie). Film's voices are frequently out of sync (it was dubbed from French) and since it's remarkably talky, this is a notable distraction (at least to adult eyes). 102m; DVD. **C:** Freddie Highmore; Mia Farrow; Adam LeFevre; Douglas Rand; Penny Balfour; Voice(s) by David Bowie; Madonna; Jimmy Fallon; Robert De Niro; Anthony Anderson; Chazz Palminteri; Snoop Dogg; Jason Bateman; Harvey Keitel; Emilio Estevez; Directed by Luc Besson; Written by Luc Besson; Celine Garcia; Cinematography by Thierry Arbogast; Music by Eric Serra. **Pr:** Luc Besson; Luc Besson; Emmanuel Prevost; Apipoulai Productions; IFC Films; Europacorp; Avalanche Productions. **A:** Family. **P:** Entertainment. **U:** Home. **L:** English. **Mov-Ent:** Fantasy, Miniaturization. **Acq:** Purchase. **Dist:** Genius Entertainment; Weinstein Company L.L.C.

Arthur: Arthur Cracks the Case 2003
Children's animated PBS television series taken from Marc Brown's books about the life and learnings of young aardvark Arthur, his family, and friends; includes: "D.W.'s Snow Mystery," "Arthur's Mystery Envelope," and "Finder's Key-pers." 3 episodes. 40m; DVD. **A:** Family. **P:** Entertainment. **U:** Home. **Chl-Juv:** Television Series, Animation & Cartoons, Children's Shows. **Acq:** Purchase. **Dist:** SONY Wonder. $5.98.

Arthur: Arthur Gets Spooked 2003
Children's animated PBS television series taken from Marc Brown's books about the life and learnings of young aardvark Arthur, his family, and friends; includes: "The Scare Your Pants Off Club," "Friday the 13th," and "The Boy Who Cried Comet." 3

episodes. 40m; DVD. **A:** Family. **P:** Entertainment. **U:** Home. **Chl-Juv:** Television Series, Animation & Cartoons, Children's Shows. **Acq:** Purchase. **Dist:** SONY Wonder. $12.98.

Arthur: Arthur Goes to Hollywood 2003
Children's animated PBS television series taken from Marc Brown's books about the life and learnings of young aardvark Arthur, his family, and friends; includes: "And Now Let's Talk to Some Kids," "The Contest," and "That's a Baby Show!" 3 episodes. 40m; DVD. **A:** Family. **P:** Entertainment. **U:** Home. **Chl-Juv:** Television Series, Animation & Cartoons, Children's Shows. **Acq:** Purchase. **Dist:** SONY Wonder. $12.98.

Arthur: Arthur Goes to the Doctor 2002
Children's animated PBS television series taken from Marc Brown's books about the life and learnings of young aardvark Arthur, his family, and friends; includes: "Arthur's Knee," "Buster's Breathless," and "The Lousy Week." 3 episodes. 40m; DVD. **A:** Family. **P:** Entertainment. **U:** Home. **Chl-Juv:** Television Series, Animation & Cartoons, Children's Shows. **Acq:** Purchase. **Dist:** SONY Wonder. $12.98.

Arthur: Arthur Makes the Team 2004
Children's animated PBS television series taken from Marc Brown's books about the life and learnings of young aardvark Arthur, his family, and friends; includes: "Arthur Makes the Team," "Meek for a Week," and "Arthur the Loser." 3 episodes. 40m; DVD. **A:** Family. **P:** Entertainment. **U:** Home. **Chl-Juv:** Television Series, Animation & Cartoons, Children's Shows. **Acq:** Purchase. **Dist:** SONY Wonder. $12.98.

Arthur: Arthur Saves the Day 2004
Children's animated PBS television series taken from Marc Brown's books about the life and learnings of young aardvark Arthur, his family, and friends; includes: "Buster Baxter, Cat Saver," "D.W. All Wet," and "The Big Blow-Up." 3 episodes. 40m; DVD. **A:** Family. **P:** Entertainment. **U:** Home. **Chl-Juv:** Television Series, Animation & Cartoons, Children's Shows. **Acq:** Purchase. **Dist:** SONY Wonder. $12.98.

Arthur: Arthur the Good Sport 2002
Children's animated PBS television series taken from Marc Brown's books about the life and learnings of young aardvark Arthur, his family, and friends; includes: "The Good Sport," "Muffy's Soccer Shocker," and "Francine Frensky, Olympic Rider." 3 episodes. 40m; DVD. **A:** Family. **P:** Entertainment. **U:** Home. **Chl-Juv:** Television Series, Animation & Cartoons, Children's Shows. **Acq:** Purchase. **Dist:** SONY Wonder. $12.98.

Arthur: Arthur Writes a Story 2003
Children's animated PBS television series taken from Marc Brown's books about the life and learnings of young aardvark Arthur, his family, and friends; includes: "Arthur Writes a Story," "Locked in the Library," and "I'd Rather Read It Myself." 3 episodes. 40m; DVD. **A:** Family. **P:** Entertainment. **U:** Home. **Chl-Juv:** Television Series, Animation & Cartoons, Children's Shows. **Acq:** Purchase. **Dist:** SONY Wonder. $12.98.

Arthur: Arthur's Baby 2003
Children's animated PBS television series taken from Marc Brown's books about the life and learnings of young aardvark Arthur, his family, and friends; includes: "Arthur's Baby," "D.W.'s Baby," and "Arthur Babysits." 3 episodes. 40m; DVD. **A:** Family. **P:** Entertainment. **U:** Home. **Chl-Juv:** Television Series, Animation & Cartoons, Children's Shows. **Acq:** Purchase. **Dist:** SONY Wonder. $12.98.

Arthur: Arthur's Best Friends 2003
Children's animated PBS television series taken from Marc Brown's books about the life and learnings of young aardvark Arthur, his family, and friends; includes: "D.W.'s Deer Friend," "Arthur's Faraway Friend," and "Buster's Back." 3 episodes. 40m; DVD. **A:** Family. **P:** Entertainment. **U:** Home. **Chl-Juv:** Television Series, Animation & Cartoons, Children's Shows. **Acq:** Purchase. **Dist:** SONY Wonder. $12.98.

Arthur: Arthur's Best School Days 2002
Children's animated PBS television series taken from Marc Brown's books about the life and learnings of young aardvark Arthur, his family, and friends; includes: "Arthur and the Square Dance," "Team Trouble," and "Buster Hits the Books." 3 episodes. 40m; DVD. **A:** Family. **P:** Entertainment. **U:** Home. **Chl-Juv:** Television Series, Animation & Cartoons, Children's Shows. **Acq:** Purchase. **Dist:** SONY Wonder. $12.98.

Arthur: Arthur's Celebration 2002
Children's animated PBS television series taken from Marc Brown's books about the life and learnings of young aardvark Arthur, his family, and friends; includes: "Arthur's Birthday," "Arthur's New Year's Eve," "Grandma Thora Appreciation Day," and "D.W.'s Perfect Wish." 4 episodes. 50m; DVD. **A:** Family. **P:** Entertainment. **U:** Home. **Chl-Juv:** Television Series, Animation & Cartoons, Children's Shows. **Acq:** Purchase. **Dist:** SONY Wonder. $12.98.

Arthur: Arthur's Chicken Pox 2004
Children's animated PBS television series taken from Marc Brown's books about the life and learnings of young aardvark Arthur, his family, and friends; includes: "Arthur's Chicken Pox," "Arthur and the True Francine," and "Double Tibble Trouble." 3 episodes. 40m; DVD. **A:** Family. **P:** Entertainment. **U:** Home. **Chl-Juv:** Television Series, Animation & Cartoons, Children's Shows. **Acq:** Purchase. **Dist:** SONY Wonder. $12.98.

Arthur: Arthur's Computer Adventure 1999
Children's animated PBS television series taken from Marc Brown's books about the life and learnings of young aardvark Arthur, his family, and friends; includes: "Arthur's Computer Adventure," "Arthur vs. the Piano," and "Arthur's Lucky Pencil." 3 episodes. 46m; DVD. **A:** Family. **P:** Entertainment. **U:** Home.

Chl-Juv: Television Series, Animation & Cartoons, Children's Shows. **Acq:** Purchase. **Dist:** SONY Wonder. $12.95.

Arthur: Arthur's Eyes 2004
Children's animated PBS television series taken from Marc Brown's books about the life and learnings of young aardvark Arthur, his family, and friends; includes: "Arthur's Eyes," "Francine's Bad Hair Day," and "Draw!" 3 episodes. 40m; DVD. **A:** Family. **P:** Entertainment. **U:** Home. **Chl-Juv:** Television Series, Animation & Cartoons, Children's Shows. **Acq:** Purchase. **Dist:** SONY Wonder. $12.98.

Arthur: Arthur's Family Fun 2003
Children's animated PBS television series taken from Marc Brown's books about the life and learnings of young aardvark Arthur, his family, and friends; includes: "Arthur and Los Vecinos (the Neighbors)," "Sue Ellen's Little Sister," and "Arthur's Family Feud." 3 episodes. 40m; DVD. **A:** Family. **P:** Entertainment. **U:** Home. **Chl-Juv:** Television Series, Animation & Cartoons, Children's Shows. **Acq:** Purchase. **Dist:** SONY Wonder. $12.98.

Arthur: Arthur's Family Ties 2005
Children's animated PBS television series taken from Marc Brown's books about the life and learnings of young aardvark Arthur, his family, and friends; includes: "Cast Away," "Bitzi's Break-Up," and "Francine's Split Decision." 3 episodes. 45m; DVD. **A:** Family. **P:** Entertainment. **U:** Home. **Chl-Juv:** Television Series, Animation & Cartoons, Children's Shows. **Acq:** Purchase. **Dist:** SONY Wonder. $14.98.

Arthur: Arthur's Family Vacation 2004
Children's animated PBS television series taken from Marc Brown's books about the life and learnings of young aardvark Arthur, his family, and friends; includes: "Arthur's Family Vacation," "Grandpa Dave's Old Country Farm," and "Arthur's Almost Boring Day." 3 episodes. 40m; DVD. **A:** Family. **P:** Entertainment. **U:** Home. **Chl-Juv:** Television Series, Animation & Cartoons, Children's Shows. **Acq:** Purchase. **Dist:** SONY Wonder. $12.98.

Arthur: Arthur's Famous Friends 2003
Children's animated PBS television series taken from Marc Brown's books about the life and learnings of young aardvark Arthur, his family, and friends; includes: "Arthur Meets Mister Rogers," "I'm a Poet," and "My Music Rules." 3 episodes. 40m; DVD. **A:** Family. **P:** Entertainment. **U:** Home. **Chl-Juv:** Television Series, Animation & Cartoons, Children's Shows. **Acq:** Purchase. **Dist:** SONY Wonder. $12.98.

Arthur: Arthur's First Crush 2005
Children's animated PBS television series taken from Marc Brown's books about the life and learnings of young aardvark Arthur, his family, and friends; includes: "Arthur's First Crush," "What Is That Thing?," and "1001 Dads." 3 episodes. 45m; DVD. **A:** Family. **P:** Entertainment. **U:** Home. **Chl-Juv:** Television Series, Animation & Cartoons, Children's Shows. **Acq:** Purchase. **Dist:** SONY Wonder. $12.95.

Arthur: Arthur's Great Summer 2002
Children's animated PBS television series taken from Marc Brown's books about the life and learnings of young aardvark Arthur, his family, and friends; includes: "Arthur Goes to Camp," "The Shore Thing," and "The Short Quick Summer." 3 episodes. 40m; DVD. **A:** Family. **P:** Entertainment. **U:** Home. **Chl-Juv:** Television Series, Animation & Cartoons, Children's Shows. **Acq:** Purchase. **Dist:** SONY Wonder. $12.98.

Arthur: Arthur's Lost Library Book 2003
Children's animated PBS television series taken from Marc Brown's books about the life and learnings of young aardvark Arthur, his family, and friends; includes: "Arthur's Lost Library Book," "D.W.'s Imaginary Friend," and "D.W.'s Library Card." 3 episodes. 40m; DVD. **A:** Family. **P:** Entertainment. **U:** Home. **Chl-Juv:** Television Series, Animation & Cartoons, Children's Shows. **Acq:** Purchase. **Dist:** SONY Wonder. $12.95.

Arthur: Arthur's Music Medley 2004
Children's animated PBS television series taken from Marc Brown's books about the life and learnings of young aardvark Arthur, his family, and friends; includes: "Arthur Plays the Blues," "Brother, Can You Spare a Clarinet?," and "To Beat or Not to Beat." 3 episodes. 40m; DVD. **A:** Family. **P:** Entertainment. **U:** Home. **Chl-Juv:** Television Series, Animation & Cartoons, Children's Shows. **Acq:** Purchase. **Dist:** SONY Wonder. $12.98.

Arthur: Arthur's New Puppy 2003
Children's animated PBS television series taken from Marc Brown's books about the life and learnings of young aardvark Arthur, his family, and friends; includes: "Arthur's New Puppy," "Buster's Dino Dilemma," and "Binky Barnes, Wingman." 3 episodes. 40m; DVD. **A:** Family. **P:** Entertainment. **U:** Home. **Chl-Juv:** Television Series, Animation & Cartoons, Children's Shows. **Acq:** Purchase. **Dist:** SONY Wonder. $12.98.

Arthur: Arthur's Perfect Christmas 2002
Children's animated PBS television series taken from Marc Brown's books about the life and learnings of young aardvark Arthur, his family, and friends; includes a holiday-themed episode where Arthur discovers the real meaning of the season. 1 episode. 60m; DVD. **A:** Family. **P:** Entertainment. **U:** Home. **Chl-Juv:** Television Series, Animation & Cartoons, Children's Shows. **Acq:** Purchase. **Dist:** SONY Wonder. $12.98.

Arthur: Arthur's Pet Business 2003
Children's animated PBS television series taken from Marc Brown's books about the life and learnings of young aardvark Arthur, his family, and friends; includes: "Arthur's Pet Business," "D.W. the Copycat," and "Pet Peeved." 3 episodes. 40m; DVD. **A:** Family. **P:** Entertainment. **U:** Home. **Chl-Juv:** Television

Series, Animation & Cartoons, Children's Shows. **Acq:** Purchase. **Dist:** SONY Wonder. $12.98.

Arthur: Arthur's Pet Follies 2004
Children's animated PBS television series taken from Marc Brown's books about the life and learnings of young aardvark Arthur, his family, and friends; includes: "Francine and the Feline," "Hide and Snake," and "So Long, Spanky." 3 episodes. 40m; DVD. **A:** Family. **P:** Entertainment. **U:** Home. **Chl-Juv:** Television Series, Animation & Cartoons, Children's Shows. **Acq:** Purchase. **Dist:** SONY Wonder. $12.98.

Arthur: Arthur's Scary Stories 2002
Children's animated PBS television series taken from Marc Brown's books about the life and learnings of young aardvark Arthur, his family, and friends; includes: "Night Fright," "What Scared Sue Ellen," and "The Fright Stuff." 3 episodes. 40m; DVD. **A:** Family. **P:** Entertainment. **U:** Home. **Chl-Juv:** Television Series, Animation & Cartoons, Children's Shows. **Acq:** Purchase. **Dist:** SONY Wonder. $12.98.

Arthur: Arthur's School of Hard Knocks 2004
Children's animated PBS television series taken from Marc Brown's books about the life and learnings of young aardvark Arthur, his family, and friends; includes: "Arthur Vs. The Very Mean Crossing Guard," "Buster Makes the Grade," and "D.W. All Fired Up." 3 episodes. 40m; DVD. **A:** Family. **P:** Entertainment. **U:** Home. **Chl-Juv:** Television Series, Animation & Cartoons, Children's Shows. **Acq:** Purchase. **Dist:** SONY Wonder. $12.98.

Arthur: Arthur's Snow Day 2003
Children's animated PBS television series taken from Marc Brown's books about the life and learnings of young aardvark Arthur, his family, and friends; includes: "The Rat Who Came to Dinner," "The Long, Dull Winter," and "The Blizzard." 3 episodes. 40m; DVD. **A:** Family. **P:** Entertainment. **U:** Home. **Chl-Juv:** Television Series, Animation & Cartoons, Children's Shows. **Acq:** Purchase. **Dist:** SONY Wonder. $12.98.

Arthur: Arthur's Tasty Treats 2003
Children's animated PBS television series taken from Marc Brown's books about the life and learnings of young aardvark Arthur, his family, and friends; includes: "Buster's Sweet Success," "Dad's Dessert Dilemma," and "How the Cookie Crumbles." 3 episodes. 40m; DVD. **A:** Family. **P:** Entertainment. **U:** Home. **Chl-Juv:** Television Series, Animation & Cartoons, Children's Shows. **Acq:** Purchase. **Dist:** SONY Wonder. $12.98.

Arthur Ashe: Citizen of the World 1994
Ashe tribute includes friends and admirers sharing their insights into his life and career. 59m; DVD. **C:** Narrated by Ossie Davis. **A:** Jr. High-Adult. **P:** Entertainment. **U:** Home. **Spo-Rec:** Biography, Tennis, Black Culture. **Acq:** Purchase. **Dist:** Home Box Office Inc. $19.98.

Arthur C. Clarke 1989
Biography of science fiction writer Arthur C. Clarke. The author is interviewed in Sri Lanka and discusses the influences on his life, the work of H.G. Wells and Jules Verne, and the relationship between science and spirituality. 53m; VHS, 3/4 U. **Pr:** Films for the Humanities and Sciences. **A:** College. **P:** Education. **U:** Institution, CCTV, CATV, BCTV. **Gen-Edu:** Biography. **Acq:** Purchase, Rent/Lease, Duplication License. **Dist:** Films for the Humanities & Sciences. $14.95.

Arthur C. Clarke's Mysterious Universe 1995
Author Arthur Clarke and a team of scientific experts travel the world exploring the truths behind mythical creatures, ancient legends and bizarre rituals. 150m; VHS, DVD. **A:** Adult. **P:** Entertainment. **U:** Home. **Mov-Ent:** Science Fiction, Science. **Acq:** Purchase. **Dist:** BFS Video. $19.98.

Arthur C. Clarke's Mysterious World 1989 (Unrated)
The author of "2001" and inventor of the communications satellite explores some of the great mysteries of the universe. 80m; VHS. **Pr:** Pacific Arts. **A:** Primary-Adult. **P:** Education. **U:** Home. **Mov-Ent:** Documentary Films, Science, Speculation. **Acq:** Purchase. **Dist:** Image Entertainment Inc. $9.95.

Arthur Christmas 2011 (PG) — ★★½
Charming 3D animated Christmas fare from Aardman studios. Santa's youngest son, klutzy and kind Arthur, just loves the holiday and is in charge of the Letters to Santa department. However, Santa is now a figurehead as his impatient elder son Steve has turned the North Pole into a high-tech operation and is dismissive when one present gets left behind. Arthur is horrified and decides to personally deliver Gwen's bicycle (she wrote a letter, after all) aboard their old-fashioned wooden sleigh, accompanied by his opinionated Grandsanta and elf Bronwyn. 97m; DVD, Blu-Ray. **C:** Voice(s) by James McAvoy; Hugh Laurie; Jim Broadbent; Bill Nighy; Imelda Staunton; Ashley Jensen; Directed by Sarah Smith; Written by Sarah Smith; Peter Baynham. **Pr:** Peter Lord; David Sproxton; Carla Shelley; Steve Pegram; Aardman Features; Sony Pictures Home Entertainment Inc. **A:** Family. **P:** Entertainment. **U:** Home. **L:** English. **Mov-Ent:** Animation & Cartoons, Christmas. **Acq:** Purchase. **Dist:** Sony Pictures Home Entertainment Inc.

The Arthur Dong Collection: Stories from the War on Homosexuality 2008 (Unrated)
A collection of three documentaries on the gay rights struggle in America: "Coming Out Under Fire" is about the persecution of gays by the military in WWII; "Family Fundamentals" examines fundamentalist religious families who oppose gay rights despite having children who are gay; "Licensed to Kill" is about seven men whose hatred of gays led them to commit murder. 132m; DVD. **A:** Sr. High-Adult. **P:** Education. **U:** Home. **Gen-Edu:** Documentary Films, World War Two, Homosexuality. **Acq:** Purchase. **Dist:** Docurama. $69.95.

Arthur: Double Dare 2004
Children's animated PBS television series taken from Marc Brown's books about the life and learnings of young aardvark Arthur, his family, and friends; includes: "Double Dare," "Arthur's Dummy Disaster," and "The Cave." 3 episodes. 40m; DVD. **A:** Family. **P:** Entertainment. **U:** Home. **Chl-Juv:** Television Series, Animation & Cartoons, Children's Shows. **Acq:** Purchase. **Dist:** SONY Wonder. $12.98.

Arthur: D.W. Thinks Big 2004
Children's animated PBS television series taken from Marc Brown's books about the life and learnings of young aardvark Arthur, his family, and friends; includes: "D.W. Thinks Big," "Arthur and D.W. Clean Up," and "For Whom the Bell Tolls." 3 episodes. 40m; DVD. **A:** Family. **P:** Entertainment. **U:** Home. **Chl-Juv:** Television Series, Animation & Cartoons, Children's Shows. **Acq:** Purchase. **Dist:** SONY Wonder. $12.98.

Arthur: D.W.'s Blankie 2004
Children's animated PBS television series taken from Marc Brown's books about the life and learnings of young aardvark Arthur, his family, and friends; includes: "D.W.'s Blankie," "The Perfect Brother," and "Go to Your Room, D.W." 3 episodes. 40m; DVD. **A:** Family. **P:** Entertainment. **U:** Home. **Chl-Juv:** Television Series, Animation & Cartoons, Children's Shows. **Acq:** Purchase. **Dist:** SONY Wonder. $12.98.

Arthur Frommer's Best Places to Retire
Contains ratings of favorite retirement areas for climate, housing, recreation, cost of living, and security. Includes information on Costa Rica, Mexico, Arizona, Florida, and the Carolinas. 60m; VHS. **A:** Adult. **P:** Education. **U:** Home. **Gen-Edu:** Travel, Aging, Self-Help. **Acq:** Purchase. **Dist:** Cole Media Group.

The Arthur Godfrey Show/Amos 'n' Andy 1951
Includes one episode from each of the popular '50s programs. 55m/B/W; VHS. **C:** Arthur Godfrey. **Pr:** CBS. **A:** Family. **P:** Entertainment. **U:** Home. **Mov-Ent:** Television Series. **Acq:** Purchase. **Dist:** Video Resources.

Arthur Godfrey's Talent Scouts 1954
One episode from the classic television show, with original commercials. 30m/B/W; VHS. **A:** Family. **P:** Entertainment. **U:** Home. **Mov-Ent:** Television Series. **Acq:** Purchase. **Dist:** Video Resources.

Arthur: It's Only Rock and Roll Starring the Backstreet Boys 2002
Children's animated PBS television series taken from Marc Brown's books about the life and learnings of young aardvark Arthur, his family, and friends; includes: pop boy band the Backstreet Boys visits the gang and Francine decides to rebel and starts her own band. 1 episode. 60m; DVD. **A:** Family. **P:** Entertainment. **U:** Home. **Chl-Juv:** Television Series, Animation & Cartoons, Children's Shows. **Acq:** Purchase. **Dist:** SONY Wonder. $14.98.

Arthur Makes the Team 1998
Features Arthur and the gang getting ready for baseball season. 30m; DVD, CC. **A:** Primary. **P:** Entertainment. **U:** Home. **Chl-Juv:** Animation & Cartoons, Children. **Acq:** Purchase. **Dist:** SONY Wonder. $12.95.

Arthur Miller 1982
This program explores the works of Arthur Miller with emphasis on his concern for freedom. 25m; VHS, 3/4 U. **Pr:** British Broadcasting Corporation. **A:** Sr. High-Adult. **P:** Education. **U:** Institution, SURA. **Fin-Art:** Literature--American. **Acq:** Purchase. **Dist:** Home Vision Cinema.

Arthur Miller's Salesman 1999
Examines the literary contributions of playwright Arthur Miller, including "Death of a Salesman," "All My Sons" and "After the Fall." 17m; VHS. **A:** Sr. High-Adult. **P:** Education. **U:** Home, Institution. **Gen-Edu:** Education, Art & Artists, Fiction. **Acq:** Purchase. **Dist:** Thomas S. Klise Co. $64.00.

Arthur Murray Dance Lessons 1990
A 12-volume series teaching the basic steps of various dance styles. Tapes are available individually. 30m; VHS, CC. **A:** Jr. High-Adult. **P:** Instruction. **U:** Home. **How-Ins:** Dance--Instruction. **Acq:** Purchase. **Dist:** Baker and Taylor. $9.95.

Indiv. Titles: 1. Cha Cha 2. Dancin' Dirty 3. Foxtrot 4. Mambo 5. Merengue 6. Nightclub Disco 7. Rumba 8. Salsa 9. Samba 10. Swing 11. Tango 12. Waltz.

Arthur Murray: Swing 1991
Learn how to dance the Swing, one of America's most popular dances. Can be used in the ballroom, nightclub or disco. 30m; VHS. **C:** Hosted by Terry Leone; Directed by Del Jack. **Pr:** Pathe. **A:** Sr. High-Adult. **P:** Instruction. **U:** Home. **How-Ins:** Dance--Instruction. **Acq:** Purchase. **Dist:** Reader's Digest Home Video.

Arthur Murray's Dance Magic Series 1990
Twelve instructional tape series which carries the viewer into the magical world of ballroom dancing. 30m; VHS. **A:** Family. **P:** Instruction. **U:** Institution. **How-Ins:** Dance--Instruction. **Acq:** Purchase. **Dist:** Princeton Book Company Publishers. $19.95.

Arthur: Nerves of Steel 2005
Children's animated PBS television series taken from Marc Brown's books about the life and learnings of young aardvark Arthur, his family, and friends; includes: "Nerves of Steel," "Prunella's Prediction," and "Sue Ellen and the Brainasaurus." 3 episodes. 45m; DVD. **A:** Family. **P:** Entertainment. **U:** Home. **Chl-Juv:** Television Series, Animation & Cartoons, Children's Shows. **Acq:** Purchase. **Dist:** SONY Wonder. $12.95.

Arthur: Parents Are from Pluto 2004
Children's animated PBS television series taken from Marc Brown's books about the life and learnings of young aardvark Arthur, his family, and friends; includes: "Kids Are from Earth, Parents Are from Pluto," "My Dad, the Garbage Man," and "Mom and Dad Have a Great Big Fight." 3 episodes. 40m; DVD. **A:** Family. **P:** Entertainment. **U:** Home. **Chl-Juv:** Television Series, Animation & Cartoons, Children's Shows. **Acq:** Purchase. **Dist:** SONY Wonder. $12.98.

Arthur Rubinstein—Tribute to Chopin 1950
Great pianist performs Chopin: Scherzo in C-sharp Minor, Nocturne in F-sharp, Grand Polonaise in A-flat, and Mazurka in C-sharp Minor. ?m; VHS. **A:** Adult. **P:** Entertainment. **U:** Home. **Fin-Art:** Music--Classical, Music--Performance. **Acq:** Purchase. **Dist:** Video Artists International. $19.95.

Arthur: Season 11 2006 (Unrated)
Arthur and his pals learn valuable lessons and have loads of fun in "Mind Your Manners," "Germophobia," "Baby Kate and the Imaginary Myster," "The Making of Arthur" featuring Matt Damon along with bonus downloadable materials. 11 episodes. 260m; DVD. **C:** Voice(s) by Cameron Ansell; Daniel Brochu; Jodie Resther; Arthur Holden. **A:** Primary. **P:** Entertainment. **U:** Home. **Chl-Juv:** Animation & Cartoons, Children's Shows, Television Series. **Acq:** Purchase. **Dist:** WGBH/Boston.

Arthur: The Music Video 1999
Music and education, featuring the children's character Arthur. 40m; VHS. **A:** Primary. **P:** Education. **U:** Home. **Chl-Juv:** Children, Education, Music--Children. **Acq:** Purchase. **Dist:** Instructional Video. $9.98.

Arthur Writes a Story 1997
Arthur the aardvark wants to write the best story in class and gets an idea when his dog has puppies but he also lets his imagination run away with him. In the second story, "Locked in the Library!," Arthur and Francine are working together on a project at the library and forget about the time, so the library closes and they're stuck inside. 29m; DVD. **A:** Preschool-Primary. **P:** Entertainment. **U:** Home. **Chl-Juv:** Animation & Cartoons. **Acq:** Purchase. **Dist:** SONY Wonder.

Arthur's First Sleepover 1998
D.W. has some alien fun during Arthur's sleepover with his friends. 30m; DVD, CC. **A:** Primary. **P:** Entertainment. **U:** Home. **Chl-Juv:** Animation & Cartoons, Children. **Acq:** Purchase. **Dist:** SONY Wonder. $12.95.

Arthur's Hallowed Ground 1984 (Unrated) — ★
A cricket field caretaker battles the board of directors over the fate of his favorite plot of sod. 75m; VHS. **C:** Jimmy Jewel; Jean Boht; Michael Elphick; Directed by Frederick A. (Freddie) Young. **Pr:** David Puttnam; Techno Sunley Leisure Ltd. **A:** Jr. High-Adult. **P:** Entertainment. **U:** Home. **Mov-Ent:** Sports--General. **Acq:** Purchase. **Dist:** MGM Home Entertainment. $59.95.

Arthur's Quest 1999 (PG) — ★★½
In this switcheroo on Mark Twain's "A Connecticut Yankee in King Arthur's Court" a five-year-old Arthur is transported by Merlin from his medieval home to the modern age because the wizard fears for the boy's safety. Merlin doesn't reappear for 10 years, so Arthur has become a typical American teen. Now, how do you convince a 15-year-old that he's really a medieval monarch who must return to save Camelot? 91m; VHS, DVD, On Demand. **C:** Kevin Elston; Zach Galligan; Arye Gross; Clint Howard; Brion James; Katie Johnston; Neil Mandt; Directed by Neil Mandt. **A:** Family. **P:** Entertainment. **U:** Home. **Mov-Ent:** Adolescence. **Acq:** Purchase. **Dist:** Amazon.com Inc.; Screen Media Ventures, LLC.

Article 99 1992 (R) — ★★
Doctors in a Kansas City Veteran's Administration hospital try to heal patients while putting up with bureaucratic red tape and a stingy administrator. When rogue physician Sturgess (Liotta) is dismissed, the patients hold a siege. Sort of son of "M.A.S.H." (Big Daddy Sutherland did Hawkeye) that gets its title from a fictional rule that says veterans can be treated only for conditions related to military service. Erstwhile cast labors to combine comedic and dramatic intentions of script. 100m; VHS, DVD, CC. **C:** Ray Liotta; Kiefer Sutherland; Forest Whitaker; Lea Thompson; John C. McGinley; John Mahoney; Keith David; Kathy Baker; Eli Wallach; Noble Willingham; Julie Bovasso; Troy Evans; Lynne Thigpen; Jeffrey Tambor; Rutanya Alda; Directed by Howard Deutch; Written by Ron Cutler; Cinematography by Rick Bota; Music by Danny Elfman. **A:** Sr. High-Adult. **P:** Entertainment. **U:** Home. **Mov-Ent:** Comedy-Drama, Hospitals, Veterans. **Acq:** Purchase. **Dist:** MGM Studios Inc. $14.98.

Articulateds 19??
Footage of Union Pacific's 4-6-6-4 Challenger 3985 and Norfolk & Western's 2-6-6-4 Class A 1218, two of the largest steam locomotives in operation presently plus information about their restoration, performance, and technical differences. 60m; DVD. **A:** Family. **P:** Education. **U:** Home. **L:** English. **Gen-Edu:** Trains, U.S. States. **Acq:** Purchase. **Dist:** The Civil War Standard.

Artifacts 2008 (R) — ★★
A young blonde has just broken up with her boyfriend to devote herself to her work. Then all her friends get murdered by their own look-alikes, and the boyfriend suddenly doesn't look so bad. Oh, and they both have the same weird chest implant that all their dead friends have. Is it the aliens? Is it the government? Will the boyfriend get wise and ditch her when he realizes he's being used as a meat shield? 75m; DVD. **C:** Mary Stockley; Cecile Boland; Max Digby; Jason Morell; Felix Scott; Martin Swabey; Veronique Van de Ven; Directed by Giles Daoust; Emmanuel Jespers; Written by Giles Daoust; Emmanuel Jespers; Cinematography by Bernard Vervoort; Music by Ernst Meinrath. **A:** Sr. High-Adult. **P:** Entertainment. **U:** Home. **L:** English, Spanish. **Mov-Ent:** Science Fiction, Horror. **Acq:** Purchase. **Dist:** Lions Gate Entertainment Inc. $26.98.

Artificial Body Parts 1989
The mixture of biology and technology, resulting in artificial body parts, is spotlighted. 28m; VHS, 3/4 U. **Pr:** Films for the Humanities. **A:** Jr. High-Adult. **P:** Education. **U:** Institution, SURA. **Hea-Sci:** Biology, Technology. **Acq:** Purchase, Rent/Lease. **Dist:** Films for the Humanities & Sciences. $149.00.

Artificial Intelligence 199?
John McCarthy, Ph.D., inventor of the AI language LSP, overviews the history of artificial intelligence and its future. 30m; DVD. **A:** Adult. **P:** Education. **U:** Home, Institution. **Gen-Edu:** Technology. **Acq:** Purchase. **Dist:** Thinking Allowed Productions. $29.95.

Artimus and Old Laces 1975
The distributive principle (long multiplication) is illustrated in this fanciful tale about the multiplication problems of tax collector Cyrus Sneeze. Part of "Math That Counts" series. 13m; VHS, 3/4 U. **Pr:** Davidson Films. **A:** Primary. **P:** Education. **U:** Institution, SURA. **Chl-Juv:** Mathematics. **Acq:** Purchase, Rent/Lease, Trade-in. **Dist:** Encyclopedia Britannica.

Artist 1999
Examines how mainstream media perceives the creative process and the creators themselves. 10m; VHS. **A:** Adult. **P:** Education. **U:** Institution, BCTV. **Gen-Edu:** Art & Artists. **Acq:** Purchase, Rent/Lease. **Dist:** Women Make Movies. $250.00.

The Artist 2011 (PG-13) — ★★★★
A brilliant hybrid of homage to the golden age of Hollywood while also being a film that could, with only few alterations, have been released in the silent film era as well. George Valentin (Dujardin) refuses to give in to the next wave of cinema as talkies threaten to make the silent film star irrelevant. As his star falls, that of the stunning newcomer (Bejo) he discovered rises. The risky artistic decision to make a '20s silent film in 2011 pays off for director Hazanavicius, as the result is a delightful, alluring comedy that works on multiple levels. 100m/B/W; Silent; DVD, Blu-Ray. **C:** Jean Dujardin; Berenice Bejo; John Goodman; James Cromwell; Penelope Ann Miller; Missi Pyle; Malcolm McDowell; Beth Grant; Ed Lauter; Ken Davitian; Directed by Michel Hazanavicius; Written by Michel Hazanavicius; Cinematography by Guillaume Schiffman; Music by Ludovic Bource. **Pr:** Thomas Langmann; La Petite Reine; Studio 37; Weinstein Co. **A:** Jr. High-Adult. **P:** Entertainment. **U:** Home. **L:** English. **Mov-Ent:** Comedy--Romantic, Silent Films. **Awds:** Oscars '11: Actor (Dujardin), Costume Des., Director (Hazanavicius), Film, Orig. Score; British Acad. '11: Actor (Dujardin), Cinematog., Costume Des., Director (Hazanavicius), Film, Orig. Score, Orig. Screenplay, Sound; Directors Guild '11: Director (Hazanavicius); Golden Globes '12: Actor--Mus./Comedy (Dujardin), Film--Mus./Comedy, Orig. Score; Ind. Spirit '12: Actor (Dujardin), Cinematog., Director (Hazanavicius), Film; Screen Actors Guild '11: Actor (Dujardin). **Acq:** Purchase. **Dist:** Weinstein Company L.L.C.

The Artist and His Environment 1991
A series of six short films focusing on a single theme or story and representing artists from different centuries and schools of art. Covers artists Brueghel and Arent Arentsz, 17th century Flemish and Dutch masters, the theme of youth through paintings by Van Dyck and Langetti, the portrayal of women in the 19th century, and an 18th century look at romantic landscape in England. 30m; VHS, SVS, 1C, 3/4 U. **Pr:** Julius Kohanyi. **A:** Jr. High-Sr. High. **P:** Education. **U:** Institution, CATV, BCTV, Home, SURA. **Fin-Art:** Art & Artists. **Acq:** Purchase, Duplication License. **Dist:** Green Acre Video. $69.95.

Indiv. Titles: 1. The Peasant's Wedding 2. Skaters on the Amstel 3. The Lowlands 4. Youth 5. Women of the 19th Century 6. Romantic Landscape in England.

Artist as a Reporter: Franklin McMahon 1978
Artist-reporter Franklin McMahon discusses his work and the inspirations and interests which lead him to cover particular people and events. 29m; VHS, 3/4 U. **Pr:** Bill Hare. **A:** Jr. High-Adult. **P:** Education. **U:** Institution, SURA. **Fin-Art:** Art & Artists. **Acq:** Purchase. **Dist:** Phoenix Learning Group.

The Artist as Witness 1987
Artists talk about the important role religion plays in their lives. 29m; VHS, 3/4 U. **Pr:** Real to Reel Productions. **A:** Jr. High-Adult. **P:** Religious. **U:** Institution, SURA. **Gen-Edu:** Art & Artists. **Acq:** Purchase, Rent/Lease. **Dist:** St. Anthony Messenger Press. $19.95.

Artist in the Tetons 19??
Outlines the different ways that artists choose scenes and angles for photography or painting. Features footage of paintings and original lithographs by Quinten Gregory. 30m; VHS. **A:** Family. **P:** Instruction. **U:** Institution. **How-Ins:** Art & Artists, Education, How-To. **Acq:** Purchase. **Dist:** Instructional Video. $19.95.

Artist on Fire: Joyce Wieland 1987
Joyce Weiland, pioneer of feminist avant-garde cinema, discusses how she explored the crux of nationalism, feminine sexuality, and ecology for more than 30 years in her films. 54m; VHS. **A:** College-Adult. **P:** Education. **U:** Institution. **Gen-Edu:** Women, Filmmaking. **Acq:** Purchase, Rent/Lease. **Dist:** Women Make Movies. $250.00.

Artist Unknown: The Search for African History ????
A young British man of African decent uncovers a tale of early African civilization and attempts to reconcile the wrongs he

discovers. 50m; VHS. **A:** Sr. High-Adult. **P:** Education. **U:** Institution. **Gen-Edu**: Documentary Films, Africa, History. **Acq:** Purchase, Rent/Lease. **Dist:** Films for the Humanities & Sciences. $129.00.

The Artist Was a Woman: Women Painters, 1550-1950 1988
A documentary about both renowned and lesser-known women artists from the Renaissance to 1950. Includes quotes from the letters and diaries of the artists as well as comments from their contemporary critics and admirers. 58m; VHS, 3/4 U, Special order formats. **C:** Narrated by Jane Alexander. **Pr:** Suzanne Bauman; Mary Bell. **A:** Jr. High-Adult. **P:** Education. **U:** Institution, Home. **Fin-Art**: Documentary Films, Painting, Women. **Acq:** Purchase. **Dist:** Filmakers Library Inc. $49.95.

Artists and Models 1937 (Unrated) — ★★
Mac Brewster's (Benny) struggling advertising agency lands a big ad campaign for Townsend Silver, and Mac promises his client that their spokesmodel will be queen of the Artists and Models Ball. But Alan Townsend (Arlen) rejects Mac's model girlfriend Paula (Lupino) because he wants someone from the social register. An angry Paula pretends to be a debutante while numerous variety acts perform at the event. Followed by "Artists and Models Abroad." 97m/B/W; DVD. **C:** Jack Benny; Ida Lupino; Richard Arlen; Gail Patrick; Ben Blue; Directed by Raoul Walsh; Written by Francis Martin; Walter DeLeon; Cinematography by Victor Milner; Music by Victor Young. **A:** Adult. **P:** Entertainment. **U:** Home. **L:** English. **Mov-Ent**: Musical, Advertising. **Acq:** Purchase. **Dist:** Turner Broadcasting System Inc.

Artists and Models 1955 — ★★½
Martin is a struggling comic book artist and Lewis his idiot roommate. The pair become mixed up in both romance and intrigue when Lewis begins talking in his sleep about spys and such. One of the duo's more pleasant cinematic outings. 109m; VHS, CC. **C:** Dean Martin; Jerry Lewis; Shirley MacLaine; Dorothy Malone; Eddie Mayehoff; Eva Gabor; Anita Ekberg; George Winslow; Jack Elam; Herbert Rudley; Nick Castle; Directed by Frank Tashlin; Written by Frank Tashlin; Hal Kanter; Herbert Baker; Cinematography by Daniel F. Fapp. **Pr:** Hal B. Wallis; Paramount Pictures. **A:** Family. **P:** Entertainment. **U:** Home. **Mov-Ent**: Musical, Romance, Art & Artists. **Acq:** Purchase. **Dist:** Paramount Pictures Corp. $14.95.
Songs: Inamorata; Lucky Song; You Look So Familiar; Why You Pretend.

Artists and Models Abroad 1938 (Unrated) — ★½
Tedious in-name-only sequel to 1937's "Artists and Models." Buck Boswell (Benny) and his all-girl troupe of entertainers are stranded in Paris. Buck gets them jobs as fashion models, including newcomer Patricia Harper (Bennett), who's just pretending to be penniless as is her wealthy father James (Grapewin). The truth comes out when Buck's financial problems multiply. May be of some interest for the fashions on display from then-current French designers. 90m/B/W; DVD. **C:** Jack Benny; Joan Bennett; Charley Grapewin; Mary Boland; Joyce Compton; Fritz Feld; Monty Woolley; Directed by Mitchell Leisen; Written by Ken Englund; Howard Lindsay; Cinematography by Ted Tetzlaff. **A:** Sr. High-Adult. **P:** Entertainment. **U:** Home. **Mov-Ent**: Clothing & Dress, Musical. **Acq:** Purchase. **Dist:** Nostalgia Family Video/Hollywood's Attic.

Artists at Work: The New Deal Art Projects 1985
Several artists, including Lee Krasner, James Brooks, and Jacob Lawrence, recount their experiences working with the WPA during the '30s, along with a look at some of the art of the era. 35m; VHS, 3/4 U, Special order formats. **C:** Directed by Mary Lance. **Pr:** Mary Lance. **A:** Sr. High-Adult. **P:** Education. **U:** Institution, Home. **Fin-Art**: Documentary Films, Art & Artists. **Acq:** Purchase, Rent/Lease. **Dist:** New Day Films Library; Direct Cinema Ltd.; Crystal Productions. $275.00.

Artists in Exile 1994
Four-part series which profiles the life and work of four of Cuba's most accomplished artists in exile. Contains both oral and visual history of their life and work and explains their involvement in politics. 120m; VHS. **A:** Jr. High-Adult. **P:** Education. **U:** Institution. **Gen-Edu**: Documentary Films, Art & Artists, Biography. **Acq:** Purchase, Rent/Lease. **Dist:** The Cinema Guild. $495.00.
Indiv. Titles: 1. Carmen Herrera 2. Roberto Estopinan 3. Agustin Fernandez 4. Daniel Serra-Badue.

Artists in the Lab 1982
A study of high tech art forms, including the ways in which computers and lasers are being used to produce a unique artistic expression. 57m; VHS, 3/4 U. **Pr:** WGBH Boston. **A:** College-Adult. **P:** Education. **U:** Institution, SURA. **Hea-Sci**: Technology, Art & Artists. **Acq:** Purchase, Rent/Lease. **Dist:** Time-Life Video and Television.

Artists of America Series: Michael Earney 1994
The artist discusses his work. 30m; VHS. **A:** Jr. High. **P:** Education. **U:** Home. **Gen-Edu**: Art & Artists. **Acq:** Purchase. **Dist:** Chip Taylor Communications. $140.00.

Artists of America's Southwest: Robert Rivera 1993
Features artist Robert Rivera decorating gourds in the style of the Anasazi and Hohokam Indians. 15m; VHS. **A:** Jr. High-Adult. **P:** Education. **U:** Institution. **Gen-Edu**: Art & Artists, Native Americans, Painting. **Acq:** Purchase. **Dist:** Chip Taylor Communications. $145.00.

The Artist's Revolution: 10 Days in Prague 1995
Documentary chronicles the ten days during November 1989, when dissident artists and students successfully overthrew the Czechoslovakian Communist regime. Narrated by Rod Steiger. 30m; VHS. **A:** College. **P:** Education. **U:** Institution. **Gen-Edu**: Documentary Films, Revolutionary War. **Acq:** Purchase, Rent/Lease. **Dist:** The Cinema Guild. $250.

The Artist's Studio 1973
A series examining the careers of various modern artists. 35m; VHS, 3/4 U. **Pr:** Michael Blackwood Productions. **A:** Sr. High-Adult. **P:** Education. **U:** Institution, SURA. **Fin-Art**: Art & Artists. **Acq:** Purchase, Rent/Lease. **Dist:** Michael Blackwood Productions.
Indiv. Titles: 1. Christo: Ten Works in Progress 2. Jim Dine, London 3. Sam Francis 4. Philip Guston 5. Motherwell/Aberti: A La Pintura 6. George Segal.

Artist's Studio Secrets 1964 (Unrated) — ★
An artist from Greenwich Village only gets aroused by clothed models, so his wife jealously arranges for him to only work with nude women. 78m/B/W; VHS. **A:** Adult. **P:** Entertainment. **U:** Home. **Mov-Ent**: Exploitation, Painting. **Acq:** Purchase. **Dist:** Tapeworm Video Distributors Inc. $19.95.

Artists Workshop 1966
A visual arts center where ordinary people are taught various medium, including life drawing, dance, puppetry, and clay sculpture. 26m/B/W; VHS, SVS, 1C, 3/4 U. **Pr:** Julius Kohanyi. **A:** Jr. High-Sr. High. **P:** Education. **U:** Institution, CATV, BCTV, Home, SURA. **Fin-Art**: Art & Artists. **Acq:** Purchase, Duplication License. **Dist:** Green Acre Video. $49.95.

Artpark People 1977
Mary Miss, Lynda Benglis, James Surls, and others are featured working in a park and mingling with the people. 53m; VHS, 3/4 U. **C:** Narrated by Brian O'Doherty. **Pr:** Michael Blackwood Productions. **A:** Sr. High-Adult. **P:** Education. **U:** Institution. **Fin-Art**: Art & Artists. **Acq:** Purchase, Rent/Lease. **Dist:** Michael Blackwood Productions.

The Arts 1970
A documentary on modern art. 18m; VHS, 3/4 U. **TV Std:** NTSC, PAL, SECAM. **Pr:** Document Associates Productions. **A:** Jr. High-Adult. **P:** Education. **U:** Institution, SURA. **Fin-Art**: Art & Artists. **Acq:** Purchase, Rent/Lease, Duplication. **Dist:** The Cinema Guild.

Arts-A-Bound! 1985
A series for students depicting real artists in the process of creating. 15m, VHS, 3/4 U. **Pr:** WVIZ Cleveland. **A:** Primary-Jr. High. **P:** Education. **U:** Institution, CCTV, CATV, BCTV. **Fin-Art**: Art & Artists. **Acq:** Purchase, Rent/Lease, Off-Air Record. **Dist:** GPN Educational Media. $319.20.

Arts Alive 1984
This series is designed to help students to participate in the arts and teach them where the arts are regarded in their society. Programs in this series are also available individually. 15m; VHS, 3/4 U, Q. **Pr:** Agency for Instructional Television. **A:** Jr. High. **P:** Education. **U:** Institution, CCTV, CATV, BCTV. **Fin-Art**: Education, Art & Artists. **Acq:** Purchase, Rent/Lease, Duplication License. **Dist:** Agency for Instructional Technology. $125.00.
Indiv. Titles: 1. Alive with the Arts 2. Elements of Visual Arts 3. Creating Visual Arts 4. Elements of Dance 5. Creating Dance 6. Elements of Music 7. Creating Music 8. Elements of Drama 9. Creating Theatre 10. Arts and Social Messages 12.Arts and Technology 13.Arts and Work.

Arts and Crafts in West Africa 1969
The arts and crafts of West Africa have an ancient heritage. Like those of most societies, they have developed in response to the need for domestic utensils, tools, and clothing, as well as religion. 11m; VHS, 3/4 U. **Pr:** Wayne Mitchell. **A:** Jr. High-Sr. High. **P:** Education. **U:** Institution, SURA. **Fin-Art**: Crafts. **Acq:** Purchase. **Dist:** Phoenix Learning Group.

Arts and Crafts Lantern: Using a Glass Saw 19??
Details how to use a glass saw, create your designs, work with copper foil, solder, etc. Teaches how to replace your outdoor lights with stained glass panels. 30m; VHS. **A:** Adult. **P:** Instruction. **U:** Home. **How-Ins**: Crafts, Hobbies, How-To. **Acq:** Purchase. **Dist:** Cutters Productions. $12.95.

Arts and Crafts of Mexico 1961
A series on the handicrafts of Mexican pottery, weaving, basketry, stone, wood onyx carving, guitar making, silverwork, and other crafts. 13m; VHS, 3/4 U, Special order formats. **C:** Directed by Daniel F. Rubin. **Pr:** Museo Nacional de Artes e Industrio. **A:** Jr. High-Adult. **P:** Education. **U:** Institution, Home. **Fin-Art**: Crafts, Mexico. **Acq:** Purchase, Rent/Lease. **Dist:** Encyclopedia Britannica; Educational Video Network. $195.00.
Indiv. Titles: 1. Pottery and Weaving 2. Basketry, Stone, Wood, and Metals.

Arts and Youth 1993
Three five-minute profiles feature Canadian students candidly explaining how education helped them realize their artistic interests. Supports arts in the schools and explores occupational choices. 15m; VHS. **Pr:** TV Ontario. **A:** Jr. High-Adult. **P:** Education. **U:** Institution. **Gen-Edu**: Art & Artists, Education, Occupations. **Acq:** Purchase. **Dist:** Films for the Humanities & Sciences. $89.95.

Arts Express 1983
This series introduces children to visual arts, music and dance. 15m; VHS, 3/4 U. **Pr:** Kentucky Educational Television. **A:** Preschool-Primary. **P:** Education. **U:** Institution, CCTV, CATV. **Chl-Juv**: Art & Artists. **Acq:** Purchase, Rent/Lease, Free Loan. **Dist:** KET, The Kentucky Network.
Indiv. Titles: 1. What Is Communication? 2. Living Creatures 3. The World We Live In 4. Arts Look at the World 5. Appearances, Portraits, and Lifestyles 6. Cultures and Customs 7. The Past 8. Fantasies, Dreams, and Wishes 9. Feelings 10. Line 11. Shape and Form 12. Space 13. Texture 14. Light 15. Visual Arts 16. Rhythm 17. Melody and Timbre 18. Music 19. Dance 20. Animation.

The Arts of Afghanistan 195?
A discussion with Faiz Khairzade about Afghan art in the 20th century. 30m/B/W; VHS, 3/4 U, EJ, Q. **Pr:** WCBS New York; Camera Three Productions. **A:** Sr. High-Adult. **P:** Education. **U:** Institution, SURA. **Fin-Art**: Asia, Art & Artists. **Acq:** Duplication, Free Duplication. **Dist:** Camera Three Productions, Inc.

The Arts of Criticism 2000
Teaches business professionals how to give criticism professionally and how to take criticism constructively. Includes study guide. 22m; VHS. **A:** Sr. High-Adult. **P:** Education. **U:** Home. **Bus-Ind**: Business, Employee Counseling. **Acq:** Purchase. **Dist:** Advantage Media. $89.95.

Arts on the Line 1988
An imaginative documentary about Massachusetts's project of creating and displaying public art in the subways. 28m; VHS, 3/4 U. **Pr:** Northern Light Productions. **A:** Jr. High-Adult. **P:** Education. **U:** Institution. **Gen-Edu**: Art & Artists. **Acq:** Purchase, Rent/Lease. **Dist:** Northern Lights Productions. $125.00.

ArtSmart 1989
Various arts and crafts, such as pottery and jewelry making, are taught. 30m; VHS, 3/4 U. **Pr:** IBEX. **A:** Jr. High-Adult. **P:** Instruction. **U:** Institution, CCTV, CATV, BCTV. **How-Ins**: Crafts. **Acq:** Purchase. **Dist:** GPN Educational Media. $300.00.

ARTSPECTRUM 1987
An overview of 65 films from The Roland Collection on Film Art that are available for sale or rental by the general public. 120m; VHS, 8 mm. **A:** Sr. High-Adult. **P:** Education. **U:** Home. **Fin-Art**: Art & Artists, Video. **Acq:** Purchase, Rent/Lease. **Dist:** The Roland Collection. $29.00.

Artur Rubinstein 1981
Rare footage never before seen showcases this great pianist in his home and in the recording studio. Rubinstein is featured in two solo spots and in a trio with cellist Gregor Piatigorsky and violinist Jascha Heifetz. 74m/B/W; VHS. **C:** Artur Rubinstein; Gregor Piatigorsky; Jascha Heifetz. **Pr:** Kultur. **A:** Family. **P:** Entertainment. **U:** Home. **Fin-Art**: Music--Performance. **Acq:** Purchase. **Dist:** Kultur International Films Ltd., Inc.; Music Video Distributors. $19.95.

Artur Rubinstein: In Concert 1975
The master performer plays the Chopin 2nd Piano Concerto, Grieg's Piano Concerto and Saint-Saens 2nd Concerto live from London. 93m; VHS. **A:** Adult. **P:** Entertainment. **U:** Home. **Fin-Art**: Music--Classical. **Acq:** Purchase. **Dist:** Music Video Distributors. $24.95.

Artus Moser of Buckeye Cove 1985
A portrait of the established folklorist, storyteller, performer, gardener, naturalist et al., based in North Carolina. 28m; VHS, 3/4 U. **Pr:** Headwaters Television. **A:** Jr. High-Adult. **P:** Education. **U:** Institution, Home. **Gen-Edu**: Biography. **Acq:** Purchase. **Dist:** Appalshop Films & Video.

ARTV 1989
This is an art history series aimed at seventh to ninth graders. 30m; VHS, 3/4 U. **Pr:** Brad Powell. **A:** Jr. High-Sr. High. **P:** Education. **U:** Institution, CCTV, CATV, BCTV. **Gen-Edu**: Art & Artists, History. **Acq:** Purchase. **Dist:** GPN Educational Media; Crystal Productions. $290.40.
Indiv. Titles: 1. Late Gothic to Early Renaissance 2. High Renaissance 3. 17th Century 4. Neo-Classicism and Romanticism 5. Realism 6. Impressionism 7. Post-Impressionism 8. Post-Impressionism to Cubism 9. Fantastic Art, Dada, Pop Art 10. Abstract Expressionism.

ARUSI Persian Wedding 2008 (Unrated)
Alex, an Iranian-American man, travels to Iran with his betrothed to have a traditional Persian wedding, with his filmmaker sister Marjan Tehrani capturing it all. Their Iranian father and American mother held their wedding in Iran during a time when the United States were close allies but as a tense dinner party reveals, relations between the countries has altered immensely over 50 years. Historical footage, intelligence documents, and photos provide a history of Iran far beyond politics. 63m; DVD. **A:** Adult. **P:** Education. **U:** Institution. **Gen-Edu**: Middle East, Marriage. **Acq:** Purchase. **Dist:** Women Make Movies. $295.

Arvis Strickling Jones: From the Inside Out 1992
Jones performs his gospel hits live from the First Union Baptist Church in San Francisco. 60m; VHS. **A:** Family. **P:** Entertainment. **U:** Home. **Mov-Ent**: Music Video, Religion. **Acq:** Purchase. **Dist:** Xenon Pictures; Music Video Distributors. $29.95.

As a Blind Person 1985
A documentary about a blind high school principal and how he handles his handicap on the job. 29m; VHS, 3/4 U. **Pr:** BFA Educational Media. **A:** Jr. High-Adult. **P:** Education. **U:** Institution, SURA. **Gen-Edu**: Blindness. **Acq:** Purchase. **Dist:** Phoenix Learning Group.

As a Wife Has a Cow 1985
This video breaks the traditional stereotypes of Westerns through its imagery of the "Marlboro Woman." 45m; VHS, 3/4 U. **Pr:** Cornelia Wyngaarden. **A:** Jr. High-Adult. **P:** Education. **U:** Institution, SURA. **Gen-Edu**: Western, Women. **Acq:** Rent/Lease. **Dist:** Video Out Distribution.

A's All-Star Almanac 1986
A visual survey of the Major League team's star players through the years. 30m; VHS. **Pr:** Major League Baseball Productions.

A: Family. P: Entertainment. U: Home. Spo-Rec: Sports--General, Baseball. Acq: Purchase. Dist: Major League Baseball Productions. $19.95.

As Children Saw It 1967
A fascinating look at the Six Day War, as depicted by the drawings of young children who were there. 15m; VHS, 3/4 U, Special order formats. **TV Std:** NTSC, PAL, SECAM. **Pr:** Alden Films. **A:** Family. **P:** Education. **U:** Institution, Home, SURA. **Gen-Edu:** Israel, War--General, Children. **Acq:** Purchase, Rent/Lease. **Dist:** Alden Films. $50.00.

As Cool As I Am 2013 (R) — ★
Clunky, melodramatic coming-of-age drama. Teen Lucy (Bolger) is realizing her parents, who had her when they were teenagers, have yet to become grown-ups. Lainee (Danes) suffers the effects of a long-distance marriage to lumberjack husband Chuck (Marsden) and the tension is affecting Lucy, who starts acting out. She and best friend Kenny (Mann) start experimenting sexually, which shocks their parents and causes more problems, especially for Lucy. 93m; DVD, Blu-Ray, Streaming. **C:** Sarah Bolger; Claire Danes; James Marsden; Thomas Mann; Jeremy Sisto; Jon Tenney; Peter Fonda; Anika Noni Rose; Directed by Max Mayer; Written by Virginia Korus Spragg; Cinematography by Tim Suhrstedt; Music by Christopher Lennertz. **Pr:** IFC Films. **A:** Sr. High-Adult. **P:** Entertainment. **U:** Home. **L:** English. **Mov-Ent:** Adolescence, Parenting, Sex & Sexuality. **Acq:** Purchase, Rent/Lease. **Dist:** Amazon.com Inc.; MPI Media Group.

As Far as I Can Go 1987
A look at the daily frustrations of Jack, Lorraine, and Michelle-three mildly retarded young adults. Discussion centers on their need for satisfying employment and for permanent relationships leading to marriage. 29m; VHS, 3/4 U. **Pr:** RMI Media Productions. **A:** Adult. **P:** Education. **U:** Institution. **Gen-Edu:** Mental Retardation. **Acq:** Purchase. **Dist:** RMI Media.

As Frozen Music 1980
A documentary featuring the renowned Sydney Opera House, with footage of its most popular stars in performance. 55m; VHS, 3/4 U. **C:** Luciano Pavarotti; Joan Sutherland; Janet Baker. **A:** Family. **P:** Entertainment. **U:** Institution, Home. **Gen-Edu:** Documentary Films, Opera, Architecture. **Acq:** Purchase. **Dist:** Facets Multimedia Inc. $49.95.

As Good as Dead 1995 (PG-13) — ★★½
A young woman allows her sick friend to assume her identity but when her friend is murdered, she realizes the killer was really after her. 88m; VHS, CC. **C:** Crystal Bernard; Traci Lords; Judge Reinhold; Directed by Larry Cohen; Written by Larry Cohen. **Pr:** Larry Cohen; Larry Cohen; Wilshire Court Productions. **A:** Jr. High-Adult. **P:** Entertainment. **U:** Home. **Mov-Ent:** Mystery & Suspense. **Acq:** Purchase. **Dist:** Paramount Pictures Corp.

As Good As Dead 2010 (R) — ★½
Grisly and confusing revenge thriller. New York journalist Ethan is held captive in his apartment and tortured by Southern Christian extremists who somehow believe he's responsible for the murder of their leader 10 years earlier. They try to force Ethan to confess but they may just have the wrong man. 92m; DVD, Wide. **C:** Cary Elwes; Andie MacDowell; Frank Whaley; Matt Dallas; Jess Weixler; Brian Cox; Nicole Ansari; Directed by Jonathan Mossek; Written by Eve Pomerance; Erez Mossek; Cinematography by Frank Barrera; Music by Greg Arnold. **A:** Sr. High-Adult. **P:** Entertainment. **U:** Home. **Mov-Ent:** Cults. **Acq:** Purchase. **Dist:** Movies Unlimited.

As Good As It Gets 1997 (PG-13) — ★★★
Entertaining and enjoyable outing from Brooks racked up an impressive list of Oscar noms (including Best Picture). Obsessive-compulsive romance novelist Melvin Udall (Nicholson) is also the meanest guy in New York, liked by nobody and hating all. The only exception is single-mother/waitress Carol (Hunt), who puts up with his annoying habits at the local restaurant where he dines. Forced to look after gay neighbor Kinnear's fussy-but-cute dog, Udall falls into an improbable quest for love, friendship, and a life as "normal as it gets" in this sort of extended-sitcom universe. Snappy dialogue by Brooks and co-writer Andrus, and an easy-going non-stereotypical performance by Kinnear are highlights, almost overshadowing both Hunt's Jodie Foster-like portrayal, and Nicholson's typical but delightful role (both of which won Oscars). 130m; VHS, DVD, Blu-Ray. **C:** Jack Nicholson; Helen Hunt; Greg Kinnear; Cuba Gooding, Jr.; Skeet Ulrich; Shirley Knight; Yeardley Smith; Lupe Ontiveros; Bibi Osterwald; Brian Doyle-Murray; Randall Batinkoff; Missi Pyle; Shane Black; Tara Subkoff; Danielle Brisebois; Harold Ramis; Jimmy Workman; Cameo(s) Lawrence Kasdan; Todd Solondz; Tom McGowan; Directed by James L. Brooks; Written by Mark Andrus; James L. Brooks; Cinematography by John Bailey; Music by Hans Zimmer. **Pr:** TriStar Pictures. **A:** Jr. High-Adult. **P:** Entertainment. **U:** Home. **Mov-Ent:** Comedy--Romantic, Pets, Art & Artists. **Awds:** Oscars '97: Actor (Nicholson), Actress (Hunt); Golden Globes '98: Actor--Mus./Comedy (Nicholson), Actress--Mus./Comedy (Hunt), Film--Mus./Comedy; Natl. Bd. of Review '97: Actor (Nicholson), Support. Actor (Kinnear); Screen Actors Guild '97: Actor (Nicholson), Actress (Hunt); Writers Guild '97: Orig. Screenplay; Broadcast Film Critics '97: Actor (Nicholson). **Acq:** Purchase. **Dist:** Sony Pictures Home Entertainment Inc.

As I Am 1989
TV star and Down's Syndrome victim David McFarlane hosts this look at the developmentally disabled and makes the point that they can often do more than people give them credit for, if only they are encouraged and allowed to try. 20m; VHS, 3/4 U. **Pr:** James Brodie. **A:** Jr. High-Adult. **P:** Education. **U:** Institution, SURA. **Gen-Edu:** Learning Disabilities, Documentary Films, Handicapped. **Acq:** Purchase, Rent/Lease. **Dist:** Fanlight Productions; National Film Board of Canada. $195.00.

As I Lay Dying 197?
William Faulkner's novel is adapted into a ballet-drama from which a short excerpt is performed in this program. 30m/B/W; VHS, 3/4 U, EJ, Q. **Pr:** WCBS New York; Camera Three Productions. **A:** Sr. High-Adult. **P:** Education. **U:** Institution, SURA. **Fin-Art:** Dance. **Acq:** Duplication, Free Duplication. **Dist:** Camera Three Productions, Inc.; Creative Arts Television Archive.

As I Remember It: A Portrait of Dorothy West 1991
A recollection of the life of African-American author Dorothy West who, although her father was born a slave, lived a middle class life in Boston during the early 1900s. The viewer learns not only about Ms. West but about other leaders of the Harlem Renaissance of the 1920s. 56m; VHS. **A:** Sr. High-Adult. **P:** Education. **U:** Institution. **Gen-Edu:** Documentary Films, Biography, Black Culture. **Acq:** Purchase. **Dist:** Women Make Movies. $325.00.

As If It Were Raining 1963 (Unrated) — ★★
Constantine gets involved in an embezzlement scheme in Spain in this espionage thriller. 85m; VHS. **C:** Eddie Constantine; Henri Cogan; Elisa Montes; Jose Nieto; Silvia Solar; Directed by Jose Monter. **A:** Jr. High-Adult. **P:** Entertainment. **U:** Home. **Mov-Ent. Acq:** Purchase. **Dist:** Sinister Cinema. $16.95.

As If It Were Yesterday 1980
Documents the efforts of the Belgian people to save 4,000 Jewish children during the Nazi occupation. Includes interviews with the adult survivors and the Belgians who hid them. In French and Flemish with English subtitles. 85m/B/W; VHS. **Pr:** Myriam Abromowicz; Esther Hoffenberg. **A:** Family. **P:** Education. **U:** Institution, Home, SURA. **Gen-Edu:** Documentary Films, Judaism, World War Two. **Acq:** Purchase. **Dist:** National Center for Jewish Film; Simon Wiesenthal Center. $90.00.

As Is 1985 (Unrated) — ★½
Two gay New Yorkers deal with a troubled romance and AIDS. Adapted from the William M. Hoffman play. 86m; VHS. **C:** Jonathan Hadary; Robert Carradine; Directed by Michael Lindsay-Hogg. **Pr:** Karl/Lorimar. **A:** Sr. High-Adult. **P:** Entertainment. **U:** Home. **Mov-Ent:** Drama, TV Movies, AIDS. **Acq:** Purchase. **Dist:** MGM Studios Inc. ; Warner Home Video, Inc. $19.98.

As It Is In Heaven 2004 (Unrated) — ★★
Well-known conductor Daniel Dareas returns to his northern Swedish village after a breakdown and is asked to give advice to the church choir. He's soon assuming the task of choirmaster and the group improves so much they are chosen for a prestigious competition. However, Daniel's role stirs up past jealousies and the problems of the isolated community as well as religious belief and romance. Swedish with subtitles. 132m; DVD. **C:** Michael Nyqvist; Frida Hallgren; Ingela Olsson; Niklas Falk; Lennart Jahkel; Helen Sjoholm; Directed by Kay Pollak; Written by Kay Pollak; Cinematography by Harald Gunnar Paalgard; Music by Stefan Nilsson. **A:** College-Adult. **P:** Entertainment. **U:** Home. **L:** Swedish. **Mov-Ent. Acq:** Purchase. **Dist:** Kino on Video.

As It Was in Colonial America 1990
Four part program exploring the simple life of colonial Americans. Visits Jamestown, Plymouth, Williamsburg, Van Cortlandt Manor, and Phillipsburg Manor to see how people worked, lived, and played. 60m; VHS. **Pr:** January Productions. **A:** Primary. **P:** Education. **U:** Institution. **Gen-Edu:** History--U.S. **Acq:** Purchase. **Dist:** Clear Vue Inc.; January Productions. $119.95.

As Long as He Can Count the Crows 1989
Ugey Dorji, from Bhutan, learns the lesson of success and failure. 29m; VHS. **A:** Primary. **P:** Education. **U:** Institution. **Chl-Juv:** Children, Education, Language Arts. **Acq:** Purchase, Rent/Lease. **Dist:** Phoenix Learning Group. $250.00.

As Long as the Rivers Flow 1991
Five programs about cultural genocide, or the replacement of Inuit and native American cultures by Europeans. Tribal members convey racist experiences through interviews which are interspersed with historians accounts of the gradual domination of their race and culture. Tapes are available separately. 59m; VHS. **Pr:** Tamarak Films. **A:** Jr. High-Sr. High. **P:** Education. **U:** Institution. **Gen-Edu:** Canada, Native Americans. **Acq:** Purchase, Rent/Lease. **Dist:** First Run/Icarus Films. $390.00.
Indiv. Titles: 1. The Learning Path 2. Time Immemorial 3. Flooding Job's Garden 4. Tikinqagan 5. Haudenosaunee: Way of the Longhouse.

As Seen By Both Sides: American and Vietnamese Artists Look at the War 1995
Explores the history and tour of an art exhibit which features the work of both American and Vietnamese veterans of the Indochina War. Combines archival footage, footage of the artwork, and interviews with the artists, historians, scholars, and veterans from both sides. Emphasis is placed on how the art has, and is changing the views of both sides involved in this war. 58m; VHS. **A:** Jr. High-Adult. **P:** Education. **U:** Institution. **Gen-Edu:** Documentary Films, Art & Artists, History. **Acq:** Purchase, Rent/Lease. **Dist:** The Cinema Guild. $350.00.

As Summers Die 1986 — ★★
Louisiana attorney Glenn fights in the late 1950s to protect the rights of a black family, against the wishes of a powerful local clan. Glenn finds support in surprising places, though. From Winston Groom's acclaimed novel. 100m; VHS. **C:** Scott Glenn; Jamie Lee Curtis; Penny Fuller; Bette Davis; John Randolph; Beah Richards; Ron O'Neal; John McIntire; Directed by Jean-Claude Tramont. **A:** Jr. High-Adult. **P:** Entertainment. **U:** Home. **Mov-Ent:** TV Movies, Civil Rights. **Acq:** Purchase. **Dist:** $14.95.

As Tears Go By 1988 (Unrated) — ★★★
A young gangster is visited by his pretty young cousin from the country because she needs medical treatment for her lung problems. He begins to fall for her but this is complicated by his unstable friend who has a habit of angering mob bosses. Soon he finds himself roped into a scheme to assassinate a witness before he can testify, in order to apologize for his friends' mistakes. 102m; DVD. **C:** Andy Lau; Maggie Cheung; Jacky Cheung; Directed by Kar-Wai Wong; Written by Kar-Wai Wong; Cinematography by Wai Keung (Andrew) Lau; Music by Teddy Robin Kwan; Ting Yat Chung. **A:** Sr. High-Adult. **P:** Entertainment. **U:** Home. **L:** English, Cantonese. **Mov-Ent. Acq:** Purchase. **Dist:** Kino on Video. $29.95.

As the Lab Turns: How Do You Use a Caliper? 1981
A demonstration of the two types of calipers, the micrometer and the vernier. 16m; VHS, 3/4 U. **Pr:** University of Toronto. **A:** Jr. High-College. **P:** Education. **U:** Institution, CCTV. **Hea-Sci:** Physics. **Acq:** Purchase, Rent/Lease. **Dist:** University of Toronto.

As the Lab Turns: How Do You Use an Oscilloscope? 1981
A demonstration of how an oscilloscope displays voltage and time axes. 16m; VHS, 3/4 U. **Pr:** University of Toronto. **A:** Jr. High-College. **P:** Education. **U:** Institution, CCTV. **Hea-Sci:** Physics. **Acq:** Purchase. **Dist:** University of Toronto.

As the Mirror Burns 1990
Examines Vietnamese women's role in the Vietnam War as part of the guerrilla forces, and not innocent bystanders. Shows how they were active participants in the struggle against foreign domination, and how the war still shapes their lives today. 58m; VHS. **A:** College-Adult. **P:** Education. **U:** Institution. **Gen-Edu:** Women, Vietnam War. **Acq:** Purchase, Rent/Lease. **Dist:** Women Make Movies. $275.00.

As the Mountains Round Jerusalem 19??
The spiritual and economic history of Jerusalem is reviewed, with a look at its multi-religious inhabitants and points of interest. 13m; VHS, 3/4 U, Special order formats. **TV Std:** NTSC, PAL, SECAM. **Pr:** Alden Films. **A:** Jr. High-Adult. **P:** Education. **U:** Institution, Home, SURA. **Gen-Edu:** Israel, Religion, History. **Acq:** Purchase, Rent/Lease. **Dist:** Alden Films. $50.00.

As the Petals Fall 1984
An amusing soap opera/psychodrama about high finance and family crises. 30m; VHS, 3/4 U. **Pr:** Video Out. **A:** Jr. High-Adult. **P:** Education. **U:** Institution, SURA. **Gen-Edu:** Satire & Parody. **Acq:** Rent/Lease. **Dist:** Video Out Distribution.

As the Twig Is Bent: How Our Children Learn 1972
The roles played by emotional security and environment in a child's learnign process are analyzed. Differences in learning between boys and girls, if any, are examined. 58m/B/W; VHS, 3/4 U. **C:** Dr. Jerome Kagan; B.F. Skinner. **Pr:** WNET New York. **A:** Sr. High-Adult. **P:** Education. **U:** Institution, CCTV, Home. **Gen-Edu:** Psychology. **Acq:** Purchase, Rent/Lease. **Dist:** WNET/Thirteen Non-Broadcast.

As the Wind Rocks the Wagon 1990
Recreates the experiences of families on the Oregon Trail between 1840 and 1870, based on eyewitness accounts taken from diaries, letters and memoirs written by pioneer women. Includes teacher's guide. 52m; VHS. **A:** Jr. High. **P:** Education. **U:** Institution. **Gen-Edu:** History--U.S., Women. **Acq:** Purchase. **Dist:** GPN Educational Media; Cambridge Educational. $149.00.

As Time Goes By: Complete Series 1 and 2 2002
Presents the first and second seasons of the 1992-2002 situation comedy about former nurse Jean Pargetter (Dench) and army officer Lionel Hardcastle (Palmer) who stumble upon one another 38 years after a brief affair ended when Lionel departed for the Korean War. Includes: Lionel and Jean meet after Lionel goes on a date with Jean's daughter Judith (Brooker); Lionel takes Jean on a tour of their old stomping grounds; and the two try to hide their past affair from Jean's late husband's sister. 13 episodes. 376m; DVD. **C:** Judi Dench; Geoffrey Palmer; Moira Booker; Philip Bretherton; Jenny Funnell. **A:** Jr. High-Adult. **P:** Entertainment. **U:** Home. **Mov-Ent:** Television Series, Comedy-Drama, Romance. **Acq:** Purchase. **Dist:** Warner Home Video, Inc. $39.98.

As Time Goes By: Complete Series 3 1994
Presents the third season of the 1992-2002 situation comedy about former nurse Jean Pargetter (Dench) and army officer Lionel Hardcastle (Palmer) who stumble upon one another 38 years after a brief affair ends when Lionel departed for the Korean War. Includes: they take a romantic journey to Paris only to be distracted by a lost young couple; a misunderstanding occurs when Jean and Lionel decide to move in together; and Lionel's book is adapted to a miniseries though the process gets off to a bumpy start. 10 episodes. 300m; DVD. **C:** Judi Dench; Geoffrey Palmer; Moira Booker; Philip Bretherton; Jenny Funnell. **A:** Jr. High-Adult. **P:** Entertainment. **U:** Home. **Mov-Ent:** Television Series, Comedy-Drama, Romance. **Acq:** Purchase. **Dist:** Warner Home Video, Inc. $39.98.

As Time Goes By: Complete Series 4 1995
Presents the fourth season of the 1992-2002 situation comedy about former nurse Jean Pargetter (Dench) and army officer Lionel Hardcastle (Palmer) who stumble upon one another 38

years after a brief affair ends when Lionel departed for the Korean War. Includes: Jean's sister-in-law moves in when she suspects her husband has been unfaithful; Lionel and Jean decide to get married; and filming begins for Lionel's miniseries. 10 episodes. 300m; DVD. **C:** Judi Dench; Geoffrey Palmer; Moira Booker; Philip Bretherton; Jenny Funnell. **A:** Jr. High-Adult. **P:** Entertainment. **U:** Home. **Mov-Ent:** Television Series, Comedy-Drama, Romance. **Acq:** Purchase. **Dist:** $39.98.

As Time Goes By: Complete Series 5 1996
Presents the fifth season of the 1992-2002 situation comedy about former nurse Jean Pargetter (Dench) and army officer Lionel Hardcastle (Palmer) who stumble upon one another 38 years after a brief affair ends when Lionel departed for the Korean War. Includes: Jean meets Lionel's ex-wife and Lionel doesn't want to preview his miniseries in the United States. 7 episodes. 210m; DVD. **C:** Judi Dench; Geoffrey Palmer; Moira Booker; Philip Bretherton; Jenny Funnell. **A:** Jr. High-Adult. **P:** Entertainment. **U:** Home. **Mov-Ent:** Television Series, Comedy-Drama, Romance. **Acq:** Purchase. **Dist:** Warner Home Video, Inc. $24.98.

As Time Goes By: Complete Series 6 1997
Presents the sixth season of the 1992-2002 situation comedy about former nurse Jean Pargetter (Dench) and army officer Lionel Hardcastle (Palmer) who stumble upon one another 38 years after a brief affair ends when Lionel departed for the Korean War. Includes: Jean can't seem to make the decision to retire from her business and Lionel has trouble surprising Jean with a trip. 7 episodes. 210m; DVD. **C:** Judi Dench; Geoffrey Palmer; Moira Booker; Philip Bretherton; Jenny Funnell. **A:** Jr. High-Adult. **P:** Entertainment. **U:** Home. **Mov-Ent:** Television Series, Comedy-Drama, Romance. **Acq:** Purchase. **Dist:** Warner Home Video, Inc. $24.98.

As Time Goes By: Complete Series 7 1998
Presents the seventh season of the 1992-2002 situation comedy about former nurse Jean Pargetter (Dench) and army officer Lionel Hardcastle (Palmer) who stumble upon one another 38 years after a brief affair ends when Lionel departed for the Korean War. Includes: while Jean thinks Lionel is having trouble hearing he thinks that she is having vision problems and Jean gathers everyone together to help out with the "old folks" party. 7 episodes. 210m; DVD. **C:** Judi Dench; Geoffrey Palmer; Moira Booker; Philip Bretherton; Jenny Funnell. **A:** Jr. High-Adult. **P:** Entertainment. **U:** Home. **Mov-Ent:** Television Series, Comedy-Drama, Romance. **Acq:** Purchase. **Dist:** Warner Home Video, Inc. $24.98.

As Time Goes By: Complete Series 8 and 9 2005
Presents the eighth and ninth seasons of the 1992-2002 situation comedy about former nurse Jean Pargetter (Dench) and army officer Lionel Hardcastle (Palmer) who stumble upon one another 38 years after a brief affair ends when Lionel departed for the Korean War. Includes: Lionel contemplates selling the country house to ensure their financial future and Jean's daughter Judith (Brooker) finally marries Lionel's publisher Alistair (Bretherton) despite all the odds. 10 episodes. 346m; DVD. **C:** Judi Dench; Geoffrey Palmer; Moira Booker; Philip Bretherton; Jenny Funnell. **A:** Jr. High-Adult. **P:** Entertainment. **U:** Home. **Mov-Ent:** Television Series, Comedy-Drama, Romance. **Acq:** Purchase. **Dist:** Warner Home Video, Inc. $34.98.

As Time Goes By: Reunion 2005
Presents a special 2005 episode of the 1992-2002 situation comedy about former nurse Jean Pargetter (Dench) and army officer Lionel Hardcastle (Palmer) who stumble upon one another 38 years after a brief affair ends when Lionel departed for the Korean War. Includes: Jean is eager for Judy (Booker) and Alistair (Bretherton) to produce some grandchildren though Alistair's possible medical condition might disappoint her. 120m; DVD. **C:** Judi Dench; Geoffrey Palmer; Moira Booker; Philip Bretherton; Jenny Funnell. **A:** Jr. High-Adult. **P:** Entertainment. **U:** Home. **Mov-Ent:** Television Series, Comedy-Drama, Romance. **Acq:** Purchase. **Dist:** Paramount Pictures Corp. $29.98.

As Time Goes By: Sets I-IV 1992
Judi Dench and Geoffrey Palmer star in this witty, romantic comedy series. Each set is also sold separately. 1920m; DVD, CC. **A:** Adult. **P:** Entertainment. **U:** Home. **Mov-Ent:** Comedy-Drama, Drama, Television. **Acq:** Purchase. **Dist:** Warner Home Video, Inc. $159.99.

As Time Goes By: You Must Remember This 2002
Presents a special episode after the end of the 1992-2002 situation comedy about former nurse Jean Pargetter (Dench) and army officer Lionel Hardcastle (Palmer) who stumble upon one another 38 years after a brief affair ends when Lionel departed for the Korean War. Includes: the couple—now married—reminisces about how they found one another again. 90m; DVD. **C:** Judi Dench; Geoffrey Palmer; Moira Booker; Philip Bretherton; Jenny Funnell. **A:** Jr. High-Adult. **P:** Entertainment. **U:** Home. **Mov-Ent:** Television Series, Comedy-Drama, Romance. **Acq:** Purchase. **Dist:** Warner Home Video, Inc. $14.98.

As Told By Ginger: Far from Home 2005
Features the 2000-2006 animated Nicktoon television series about Ginger, an awkward girl who goes through the ups and downs of being a teenager along with her friends Dodie, Macie, and Darren as well as her "new" friend, the popular Courtney, and Courtney's best pal Miranda, who resents the time Courtney is spending with Ginger. Includes: Ginger is headed out of town for a semester on a fellowship which makes her friends sad—but not Miranda—along with "The Party" (pilot) and "Ginger the Juvey." 3 episodes. 104m; DVD. **A:** Family. **P:** Entertainment. **U:** Home. **Chl-Juv:** Television Series, Animation & Cartoons, Children's Shows. **Acq:** Purchase. **Dist:** Paramount Pictures Corp. $16.99.

As Told by Ginger: The Wedding Frame 2004
Features the 2000-2006 animated Nicktoon television series about Ginger, an awkward girl who goes through the ups and downs of being a teenager along with her friends Dodie, Macie, and Darren as well as her "new" friend, the popular Courtney, and Courtney's best pal Miranda, who resents the time Courtney is spending with Ginger. Includes: the three-part series finale as Dr. Dave and Lois are married but someone is plotting against them; also "Stealing First" and "Dare I, Darren?" 5 episodes. 115m; DVD. **A:** Family. **P:** Entertainment. **U:** Home. **Chl-Juv:** Television Series, Animation & Cartoons, Children's Shows. **Acq:** Purchase. **Dist:** Paramount Pictures Corp. $16.99.

As We Are 1973
Documents an art program being conducted for retarded children, during which the children encounter a wide range of creative experiences to which they respond with a new awareness. 29m; VHS, 3/4 U. **Pr:** Marty Gross. **A:** Sr. High-Adult. **P:** Education. **U:** Institution, SURA. **Gen-Edu:** Handicapped. **Acq:** Purchase. **Dist:** Phoenix Learning Group.

As We Learn to Fall 1988
This program portrays a young girl's struggle to learn about and accept the death of a young friend. 30m; VHS, 3/4 U. **Pr:** Centre Productions, Inc. **A:** Jr. High-Sr. High. **P:** Education. **U:** Institution, SURA. **Gen-Edu:** Death, Adolescence. **Acq:** Purchase. **Dist:** Clear Vue Inc.

As Women See It 1983
Five-part series examines women in Third World countries, including India, Senegal, Nicaragua, Peru, and Egypt. Explores environmental issues, political struggles, and community problems. 150m; VHS. **A:** College-Adult. **P:** Education. **U:** Institution. **Gen-Edu:** Women, Human Rights, Ethnicity. **Acq:** Purchase, Rent/Lease. **Dist:** Women Make Movies. $495.00.
Indiv. Titles: 1. Sudesha 2. Selbe 3. Bread and Dignity 4. Women of El Planeta 5. Permissible Dreams.

As You Desire Me 1932 (Unrated) — ★★★
Garbo plays an amnesia victim who returns to a husband she doesn't even remember after an abusive relationship with a novelist. An interesting, if not down-right bizarre movie, due to the pairing of the great Garbo and the intriguing von Stroheim. An adaption of Luigi Pirandello's play. 71m/B/W; VHS. **C:** Greta Garbo; Melvyn Douglas; Erich von Stroheim; Owen Moore; Hedda Hopper; Directed by George Fitzmaurice. **Pr:** MGM. **A:** Jr. High-Adult. **P:** Entertainment. **U:** Home. **Mov-Ent:** Marriage. **Acq:** Purchase. **Dist:** MGM Home Entertainment; Facets Multimedia Inc. $19.98.

As You Like It 1936 (Unrated) — ★★½
A Duke's banished daughter poses as a man to win the attentions of one of her father's attendants in this highly stylized Shakespearean comedy adapted by J.M. Barrie and Robert Cullen. Early Shakespearean Olivier. 96m/B/W; VHS, DVD, 3/4 U, Special order formats. **TV Std:** NTSC, PAL. **C:** Elisabeth Bergner; Laurence Olivier; Henry Ainley; Felix Aylmer; Directed by Paul Czinner; Written by J.M. Barrie; Robert Cullen; Cinematography by Jack Cardiff; Harold Rosson; Music by William Walton. **Pr:** Inter Allied. **A:** Family. **P:** Entertainment. **U:** Home. **Mov-Ent:** Comedy--Screwball. **Acq:** Purchase. **Dist:** Synergy Enterprises Inc.; Gotham Distributing Corp.; Critics' Choice Video & DVD. $19.95.

As You Like It 1979
Shakespeare's lighthearted comedy about all kinds of love—physical and intellectual, sentimental and cynical, enduring love between friends, and romantic love at first sight. Play features the "Seven Ages of Man" speech. Part of the "Shakespeare Plays" series. 150m; VHS. **C:** Helen Mirren; Brian Stirner; Richard Pasco; Angharad Rees; James Bolam; Clive Francis; Richard Easton; David Prowse; John Quentin; Marilyn LeConte; Maynard Williams; Victoria Plucknett; Tony Church; Directed by Basil Coleman. **Pr:** Cedric Messina; Dr. Jonathan Miller; British Broadcasting Corporation. **A:** Sr. High-Adult. **P:** Entertainment. **U:** Institution. **Fin-Art:** Comedy-Drama, Romance, TV Movies. **Acq:** Purchase. **Dist:** Ambrose Video Publishing, Inc. $249.95.

As You Like It 1984
Presents Laurence Olivier's screen production of the famous play. 183m; VHS. **A:** Adult. **P:** Education. **U:** Institution. **Fin-Art:** Theater. **Acq:** Purchase. **Dist:** Insight Media. $69.00.

As You Like It 2006 (PG) — ★★½
Branagh sets this version of Shakespeare's romantic fantasy in 18th-century Japan with a group of Europeans who live in a trade colony. Because of a family conflict, Rosalind (Howard) and her entourage are forced to flee into the enchanted forest of Arden. Disguising herself (fetchingly unconvincingly) as a boy, Rosalind then proceeds to confuse the heck out of would-be love interest Orlando (Oyelowo). Kline is along as the melancholy Jacques with the "all the world's a stage" speech. 135m; DVD, Wide. **C:** Bryce Dallas Howard; David Oyelowo; Kevin Kline; Alfred Molina; Adrian Lester; Brian Blessed; Janet McTeer; Romola Garia; Jade Jefferies; Directed by Kenneth Branagh; Written by Kenneth Branagh; Cinematography by Roger Lanser; Music by Patrick Doyle. **A:** Jr. High-Adult. **P:** Entertainment. **U:** Home. **Mov-Ent:** Japan, Forests & Trees. **Acq:** Purchase. **Dist:** Movies Unlimited; Alpha Video.

As You Like It: An Introduction 1969
Brief narrative bridges connect the performances of key scenes, forming a compact and dramatic introduction to "As You Like It." 24m; VHS, 3/4 U. **Pr:** BHE Education Ltd; Seabourne Enterprises Ltd. **A:** Sr. High-College. **P:** Education. **U:** Institution, SURA. **Gen-Edu:** Literature--English. **Acq:** Purchase. **Dist:** Phoenix Learning Group.

As You Were 1951 — ★
A girl with a photographic memory enlists in the Army, becoming both a nuisance and comedic victim to her sergeant. 57m/B/W; VHS. **C:** Joseph (Joe) Sawyer; William Tracy; Sondra Rogers; Joan Vohs; Russell Hicks; John Ridgely; Directed by Bernard Girard; Written by Edward E. Seabrook. **Pr:** Lippert Productions. **A:** Family. **P:** Entertainment. **U:** Home. **Mov-Ent:** Comedy--Screwball. **Acq:** Purchase. **Dist:** No Longer Available.

As Young As You Feel 1951 (Unrated) — ★★★
A 65-year-old man is forced to retire from his job. He poses as the head of the conglomerate and convinces them to repeal their retirement policy. He then gains national publicity when he makes a speech about the dignity of man. Watch for Monroe as the boss's secretary. Fine comic performances enhance the script; based on a story by Chayefsky. 77m; VHS, DVD. **C:** Monty Woolley; Thelma Ritter; David Wayne; Jean Peters; Constance Bennett; Marilyn Monroe; Allyn Joslyn; Albert Dekker; Clinton Sundberg; Minor Watson; Directed by Harmon Jones; Written by Paddy Chayefsky. **A:** Jr. High-Adult. **P:** Entertainment. **U:** Home. **Mov-Ent:** Satire & Parody, Aging, Industry & Industrialists. **Acq:** Purchase. **Dist:** Fox Home Entertainment. $14.98.

Asana: Sacred Dance of the Yogis 1998
Members of the Jivamukti Yoga Center explore the relationship of yoga and dance. 30m; VHS. **A:** Adult. **P:** Instruction. **U:** Home. **Hea-Sci:** Yoga, Fitness/Exercise, Dance. **Acq:** Purchase. **Dist:** Mystic Fire Video. $19.95.

Asante Market Women 1982
This program looks at the Asante tribe of Ghana, in which women are subordinate in all domestic matters except the market place, where the women have evolved their own power structure. 52m; VHS, 3/4 U. **A:** Sr. High-Adult. **P:** Education. **U:** Institution. **Gen-Edu:** Anthropology. **Acq:** Purchase. **Dist:** Filmakers Library Inc.

Asbestos: A Lethal Legacy 1984
This program examines the consequences of asbestos use and the controversy over who is responsible. 57m; VHS, 3/4 U, Special order formats. **Pr:** WGBH Boston Yorkshire Television. **A:** Sr. High-Adult. **P:** Education. **U:** Institution, SURA. **Gen-Edu:** Safety Education. **Acq:** Purchase, Rent/Lease. **Dist:** Time-Life Video and Television.

Asbestos and Pollution Exclusion 1989
Teaches techniques to architects which help them analyze, identify, and manage the risks associated with pollution and asbestos abatements. Part of the Professional Liability Loss Prevention series. 19m; VHS. **Pr:** Department of Energy. **A:** Adult. **P:** Professional. **U:** Institution, Home. **Bus-Ind:** Architecture, Education, Safety Education. **Acq:** Rent/Lease. **Dist:** American Institute of Architects.

Asbestos Building and Inspection 1995
Teaches basics on how to plan for an inspection and various techniques in asbestos inspections. 11m; VHS. **A:** Adult. **P:** Professional. **U:** Institution. **L:** Spanish. **Bus-Ind:** Management, Occupational Training. **Acq:** Purchase, Rent/Lease. **Dist:** National Safety Council, California Chapter, Film Library. $175.00.

Asbestos Safety 1995
Explains the hazards of working around asbestos, and the responsibilities to protect themselves. 20m; VHS. **A:** Adult. **P:** Professional. **U:** Institution. **Bus-Ind:** Safety Education, Occupational Training. **Acq:** Purchase, Rent/Lease. **Dist:** National Safety Council, California Chapter, Film Library.

The Asbestos Threat 1995
Features asbestos; what it is; where it's found; and what can be done to reduce exposure to this cancer-causing substance. 8m; VHS. **A:** Adult. **P:** Professional. **U:** Institution. **L:** Spanish. **Bus-Ind:** Safety Education, Occupational Training. **Acq:** Purchase, Rent/Lease. **Dist:** National Safety Council, California Chapter, Film Library. $175.00.

Asbestos Training for Operations and Maintenance Planning 1995
Designed to meet responsibilities of Operations and Maintenance Planning. 81m; VHS. **A:** Adult. **P:** Professional. **U:** Institution. **Bus-Ind:** Safety Education, Occupational Training. **Acq:** Purchase, Rent/Lease. **Dist:** National Safety Council, California Chapter, Film Library.
Indiv. Titles: 1. Introduction to Asbestos Operations and Maintenance Training 2. General Awareness Training 3. Asbestos Operations and Maintenance Training for Custodial and Maintenance Personnel 4. Asbestos Coordinator (Designated Person) Training.

The Ascent 1976 (Unrated) — ★★★
During WWII, two Soviet partisans leave their comrades in order to obtain supplies from a nearby farm. Only the Germans have gotten there first, forcing the Soviets deeper into occupied territory, which leads to their eventual capture and interrogation. Russian with subtitles. 105m/B/W; VHS, DVD. **C:** Boris Plotnikov; Vladimir Gostyukhin; Directed by Larisa Shepitko; Written by Larisa Shepitko; Yuri Klepikov; Cinematography by Pavel Lebeshev; Vladimir Chukhnov; Music by Alfred Schnittke. **A:** College-Adult. **P:** Entertainment. **U:** Home. **L:** Russian. **Mov-Ent:** World War Two, USSR. **Acq:** Purchase. **Dist:** Criterion Collection Inc.

The Ascent 1994 (PG) — ★★½
Based on the true story of Franco (Spano), a WWII Italian POW who's held in a camp in Africa. The prisoners enjoy making fun of the camp commander (Cross), who consistently fails at his

attempts to climb the 15,500 peak of Mt. Kenya. Meanwhile, Franco decides to escape and climb the mountain himself—with the commander right behind. Beware if you suffer from vertigo. 96m; VHS, CC. **C:** Vincent Spano; Ben Cross; Tony LoBianco; Rachel Ward; Directed by Donald Shebib; Cinematography by David Connell. **Pr:** RHI Entertainment Inc. **A:** Jr. High-Adult. **P:** Entertainment. **U:** Home. **Mov-Ent**: Action-Adventure, World War Two, Mountaineering. **Acq:** Purchase. **Dist:** Unknown Distributor.

The Ascent of Man 1976
In this series Dr. Jacob Bronowski traces man's progress from a scientific/philosophic point of view. The programs are available individually. 52m; VHS, 3/4 U, Special order formats. **Pr:** British Broadcasting Corporation; Time-Life Films. **A:** Sr. High-Adult. **P:** Education. **U:** Institution, SURA. **L:** English, Spanish. **Gen-Edu**: Philosophy & Ideology. **Acq:** Purchase, Rent/Lease. **Dist:** Time-Life Video and Television.
Indiv. Titles: 1. Lower than the Angels 2. The Harvest of the Seasons 3. The Grain in the Stone 4. The Hidden Structure 5. The Music of the Spheres 6. The Starry Messenger 7. The Majestic Clockwork 8. The Drive for Power 9. The Ladder of Creation 10. World within World 11. Knowledge or Certainty 12. Generation upon Generation 13. The Long Childhood.

The Ascent of Man: Parts 1-3 1987
This evocative video assaults and strips down the concepts of heroism and patriotism and explores the propaganda beneath them. 19m; VHS, 3/4 U. **Pr:** Jayce Salloum. **A:** Jr. High-Adult. **P:** Education. **U:** Institution, SURA. **Gen-Edu**: Philosophy & Ideology. **Acq:** Rent/Lease. **Dist:** Video Out Distribution.

Ascites, Pathogenesis, and Therapy 1983
A specialist in digestive diseases describes the pathophysiology of the interplay between kidney and liver resulting in ascites. 50m; VHS, 3/4 U. **Pr:** Emory University. **A:** College-Adult. **P:** Education. **U:** Institution, CCTV, Home, SURA. **Hea-Sci**: Digestive System, Anatomy & Physiology, Diseases. **Acq:** Purchase, Rent/Lease, Subscription. **Dist:** Emory Medical Television Network.

Asepsis/Protection: Using Correct Body Mechanics 1992
Demonstrates correct methods for standing, sitting, shifting weight, and moving objects. 17m; VHS. **A:** Adult. **P:** Professional. **U:** Institution. **Hea-Sci**: Nursing. **Acq:** Purchase. **Dist:** RMI Media. $175.00.

Asepsis/Protection: Using Protection Precautions 1992
Provides basic instruction on universal precautions. 29m; VHS. **A:** Adult. **P:** Professional. **U:** Institution. **Hea-Sci**: Nursing. **Acq:** Purchase. **Dist:** RMI Media. $175.00.

Asepsis/Protection: Washing Hands 1992
Discusses appropriate methods for washing, rinsing, and drying hands. 19m; VHS. **A:** Adult. **P:** Professional. **U:** Institution. **Hea-Sci**: Nursing. **Acq:** Purchase. **Dist:** RMI Media. $175.00.

Asepsis Series 1977
Covers the principles of aseptic practice which is designed for all members of the health care profession. Programs available individually. 15m; VHS, 3/4 U, CV, Special order formats. **Pr:** Professional Research. **A:** Adult. **P:** Professional. **U:** Institution, CCTV. **Hea-Sci**: Infection, Hygiene. **Acq:** Purchase, Rent/Lease. **Dist:** Discovery Education.
Indiv. Titles: 1. Principles of Microbiology: Bacteria, Part I 2. Principles of Microbiology: Bacteria, Part II 3. Principles of Microbiology: Viruses 4. Disinfection: Health Care Principles, Part I 5. Disinfection: Health Care Principles, Part II 6. Handwashing: The Keystone of Infection Control 7. Personal Appearance and Hygiene 8. Urinary Catheterization, Part I 9. Urinary Catheterization, Part II 10. Suctioning the Patient with a Tracheostomy 11. Essentials of Dressing Change 12. Essentials of Bedmaking.

Ash Wednesday 1973 (R) — ★
Taylor endures the pain of cosmetic surgery in an effort to rescue her floundering union with Fonda. Another undistinguished performance by Liz. Fonda is especially slimy as the philandering husband, but only appears in the latter stages of the film. 99m; VHS, DVD, Streaming, CC. **C:** Elizabeth Taylor; Henry Fonda; Helmut Berger; Keith Baxter; Margaret Blye; Maurice Teynac; Monique Van Vooren; Directed by Larry Peerce; Music by Maurice Jarre. **Pr:** Paramount Pictures. **A:** College-Adult. **P:** Entertainment. **U:** Home. **Mov-Ent**: Surgery--Plastic, Marriage. **Acq:** Purchase. **Dist:** Facets Multimedia Inc.; Lions Gate Entertainment Inc.; Paramount Pictures Corp. $14.95.

Ash Wednesday 2002 (R) — ★★
On Ash Wednesday, 1983, ex-Hell's Kitchen tough Francis Sullivan (Burns) is working in his bar when his younger brother Sean (Wood) suddenly turns up. Three years ago to the day, Sean killed some thugs after his bro and went into exile, allowing everyone to think he was dead, including his wife Grace (Dawson). In the intervening time, Grace and Francis have become more than just in-laws. Oh, and gangster Moran (Platt) still wants revenge on Sean for killing his goons. The penance references are all too obvious and Wood's an odd casting choice since he looks too young and innocent for his role. 98m; VHS, DVD, CC. **C:** Edward Burns; Elijah Wood; Rosario Dawson; Oliver Platt; Pat McNamara; James Handy; Michael Mulheren; Malachy McCourt; Directed by Edward Burns; Written by Edward Burns; Cinematography by Russell Fine; Music by David Shire. **A:** Sr. High-Adult. **P:** Entertainment. **U:** Home. **Mov-Ent. Acq:** Purchase. **Dist:** First Look Studios Inc.; CinemaNow Inc.

The Ashanti Kingdom: Ghana ????
Explains the beliefs of the Ashanti kingdom such as the strict hierarchical village organization, the importance of the characteristic kente garment, naming of children, religious beliefs, traditional values and festivals, and the protocol surrounding the paramount chief of the Ashanti. 14m; VHS. **A:** Sr. High-Adult. **P:** Education. **U:** Institution. **Gen-Edu**: Africa, Religion. **Acq:** Purchase. **Dist:** Films for the Humanities & Sciences. $89.95.

Ashanti, Land of No Mercy 1979 — ★★
Caine of the week movie with Michael portraying a doctor acting as a missionary in South Africa who finds himself alone in a battle to rescue his wife from a band of slave traders. The chase spans many Middle Eastern countries and begins to look bleak for our man. Talented cast and promising plot are undone by slow pace. Based on the novel "Ebano" by Alberto Vasquez-Figueroa. 117m; VHS, DVD, Blu-Ray. **C:** Michael Caine; Omar Sharif; Peter Ustinov; Rex Harrison; William Holden; Beverly Johnson; Directed by Richard Fleischer. **Pr:** Columbia Pictures. **A:** Jr. High-Adult. **P:** Entertainment. **U:** Home. **Mov-Ent. Acq:** Purchase. **Dist:** Unknown Distributor.

Ashes and Diamonds 1958 — ★★★½
In the closing days of WWII, young Polish resistance fighter Maciek (Cybulski) is sent to a small town to assassinate a Communist Party official. Waiting around in a hotel, Maciek romances the beautiful barmaid, Krystyna (Krzysewska), and questions the meaning of struggle. A seminal Eastern European masterpiece that defined a generation of pre-solidarity Poles. The last installment of the trilogy that includes "A Generation" and "Kanal" and based on a novel by Jerzy Andrzewski. Polish with subtitles. 105m/B/W; VHS, DVD. **C:** Zbigniew Cybulski; Eva Krzyzewska; Adam Pawlikowski; Bogumil Kobiela; Waclaw Zastrzezynski; Directed by Andrzej Wajda; Written by Andrzej Wajda; Jerzy Andrzejewski; Cinematography by Jerzy Wojcik; Music by Jan Krenz; Filip Nowak. **Pr:** Film Unit KADR. **A:** College-Adult. **P:** Entertainment. **U:** Home. **L:** Polish. **Mov-Ent**: World War Two. **Acq:** Purchase. **Dist:** Facets Multimedia Inc.; New Line Home Video; Home Vision Cinema.

Ashes and Embers 1982 — ★★
A black Vietnam vet in Los Angeles has trouble fitting into society, eventually running afoul of the police. Ethiopian-born director Gerima endows vital subject matter with a properly alienated mood. 120m; VHS, DVD. **C:** John Anderson; Evelyn Blackwell; Directed by Haile Gerima. **A:** Sr. High-Adult. **P:** Entertainment. **U:** Home. **Mov-Ent**: Vietnam War, Black Culture, Veterans. **Acq:** Purchase. **Dist:** Sankofa. $59.95.

Ashes in the River: Buddhism: The Great Wheel of Being ????
Explains the tenets and history of the belief system founded on the teachings of Buddha, and discusses the Four Noble Truths. 50m; VHS. **A:** Sr. High-Adult. **P:** Education. **U:** Institution. **Gen-Edu**: India, Buddhism, Religion. **Acq:** Purchase, Rent/Lease. **Dist:** Films for the Humanities & Sciences. $149.00.

Ashes in the River: Four Religions of India ????
Five-part series presents historical and cultural events of Jainism, Islam, Buddhism, and Hinduism, within the context of modern-day India. 250m; VHS. **A:** Sr. High-Adult. **P:** Education. **U:** Institution. **Gen-Edu**: India, Religion. **Acq:** Purchase, Rent/Lease. **Dist:** Films for the Humanities & Sciences. $649.00.
Indiv. Titles: 1. Spiritual India: A Guide to Jainism, Islam, Buddhism, and Hinduism 2. Jainism: Ascetics and Warriors 3. Islam: The Five Pillars of Faith 4. Buddhism: The Great Wheel of Being 5. Hinduism: Faith, Festivals, and Rituals.

Ashes in the River: Hinduism: Faith, Festivals, and Rituals ????
Shows devotional ceremonies and observances of Hinduism and sacred Hindu literature, and some of the religion's ornate temples. Also discusses the Hindu emphasis on right living, or dharma. 50m; VHS. **A:** Sr. High-Adult. **P:** Education. **U:** Institution. **Gen-Edu**: India, Hinduism, Religion. **Acq:** Purchase, Rent/Lease. **Dist:** Films for the Humanities & Sciences. $149.00.

Ashes in the River: Islam: The Five Pillars of Faith ????
Covers the Koran, the Pillars of Islam, the influence of Sharia, and traditional Muslim festivals and holy sites. 50m; VHS. **A:** Sr. High-Adult. **P:** Education. **U:** Institution. **Gen-Edu**: India, Islam, Religion. **Acq:** Purchase, Rent/Lease. **Dist:** Films for the Humanities & Sciences. $149.00.

Ashes in the River: Jainism: Ascetics and Warriors ????
Explores the concepts of Jainism such as espousing salvation by conquering material existence and ahimsa, the doctrine of non-injury to any living thing. 50m; VHS. **A:** Sr. High-Adult. **P:** Education. **U:** Institution. **Gen-Edu**: India, Religion. **Acq:** Purchase, Rent/Lease. **Dist:** Films for the Humanities & Sciences. $149.00.

Ashes in the River: Spiritual India: A Guide to Jainism, Islam, Buddhism, and Hinduism ????
Footage from around the subcontinent show monuments, shrines, temples, festivals and sacred rituals from four of India's prominent religions. 50m; VHS. **A:** Sr. High-Adult. **P:** Education. **U:** Institution. **Gen-Edu**: India, Religion. **Acq:** Purchase, Rent/Lease. **Dist:** Films for the Humanities & Sciences. $149.00.

Ashes of Doom 1982
An anti-smoking message that gives a twist to the Dracula story. 2m; VHS, 3/4 U. **Pr:** National Film Board of Canada. **A:** Jr. High-Adult. **P:** Education. **U:** Institution, SURA. **Hea-Sci**: Smoking. **Acq:** Purchase, Rent/Lease. **Dist:** National Film Board of Canada.

Ashes of the Cold War 1993
Examines the impact of downsizing the military to peacetime industry level on the manufacturers of defense equipment, and the economies of the states which draw revenue from that industry. 60m; VHS, CC. **A:** Adult. **P:** Education. **U:** Institution. **Gen-Edu**: Documentary Films, Military History, Economics. **Acq:** Purchase. **Dist:** PBS Home Video. $150.00.

Ashes of Time 1994 (Unrated) — ★★★
Mystical, brooding, and sumptiously lensed martial arts epic was filmed in mainland China, with respect paid to Sergio Leone. A swordsman, played by Tony Leung, is going blind and wants to see his wife one last time before the lights go out completely. Another, played by the other Tony Leung, possesses a magic wine that allows him to forget his haunted past. The two swordsmen are hired to kill and protect, respectively, the same person. The plot simmers and occasionally explodes into chaotic action peppered with sparkling geysers and such. 95m; DVD, Wide. **C:** Tony Leung Chiu-Wai; Tony Leung Ka-Fai; Brigitte Lin; Jacky Cheung; Leslie Cheung; Maggie Cheung; Carina Lau; Directed by Wong Kar-Wai; Written by Wong Kar-Wai; Cinematography by Christopher Doyle; Music by Frankie Chan. **A:** Sr. High-Adult. **P:** Entertainment. **U:** Home. **Mov-Ent**: Martial Arts, Blindness. **Acq:** Purchase. **Dist:** World Video & Supply, Inc. $29.95.

Ashes of Time Redux 2008 (R) — ★★
Hong Kong director Wong was never satisfied with his 1994 wuxia epic, feeling he didn't do his vision justice (though it originally took two years to film). Over the years the movie was subjected to various bootleg versions and the original negative was disintegrating, so Wong spent five years reassembling, restoring, color-correcting, and rescoring before releasing his updated cut. Not that the dense narrative is any easier to follow (though the subtitles are good). Set over five seasons, Ouyang (Cheung), disappointed that his true love married his brother, moves to the desert and becomes a middleman for those who want to hire a swordsman to settle a wrong. Chinese with subtitles. 93m; Blu-Ray, On Demand, Wide. **C:** Leslie Cheung; Maggie Cheung; Brigitte Lin; Carina Lau; Tony Leung Ka-Fai; Jacky Cheung; Tony Leung Chiu-Wai; Directed by Wong Kar-Wai; Written by Wong Kar-Wai; Cinematography by Christopher Doyle; Music by Wu Tong. **Pr:** Jeff Lau; Kar-Wai Wong; Block 2 Pictures Inc; Jet Tone Productions; Beijing Film Studio; Scholar Film Co; Sony Pictures Classics. **A:** Sr. High-Adult. **P:** Entertainment. **U:** Home. **L:** Chinese. **Mov-Ent**: China, Martial Arts. **Acq:** Purchase. **Dist:** Sony Pictures Home Entertainment Inc.; Amazon.com Inc.; Movies Unlimited.

Ashik Kerib 1988 — ★★★
Ashik Kerib is a wandering minstrel who is rejected by a rich merchant as his daughter's suitor. He then journeys for 1,000 days trying to earn enough money to marry his beloved. Along the way he's imprisoned by an evil sultan and rides a flying horse, among other adventures. Wonderful use of exotic makeup and costumes highlight this Arabian Nights tale. Adapted from a story by Mikhail Lermontov. Paradjanov's last film. In Russian with English subtitles. 75m; VHS, DVD. **C:** Yiur Mgoyan; Veronkia Metonidze; Levan Natroshvili; Sofiko Chiaureli; Directed by Dodo Abashidze; Sergei Paradjanov; Written by Giya Badridze; Music by Djavashir Kuliev. **Pr:** Georgia Film Studio. **A:** College-Adult. **P:** Entertainment. **U:** Home. **L:** Russian. **Mov-Ent**: Fantasy. **Acq:** Purchase. **Dist:** Kino on Video; Facets Multimedia Inc. $59.95.

The Ashkenaz: German Jewish Experience 1988
The entire history of the Jewish people in Germany is retold. 20m; VHS. **Pr:** Alden Films. **A:** Jr. High-Adult. **P:** Education. **U:** Institution, Home. **Gen-Edu**: Judaism, Germany, History. **Acq:** Purchase, Rent/Lease. **Dist:** Alden Films; Ergo Media Inc. $50.00.

Ashpet: An American Cinderella 1988
The popular folktale has been moved to the American South and set in the early 1940s. 45m; VHS, 3/4 U, Special order formats. **Pr:** Davenport Films. **A:** Primary-Jr. High. **P:** Entertainment. **U:** Institution, Home, SURA. **Chl-Juv**: Fairy Tales. **Acq:** Purchase, Rent/Lease. **Dist:** Facets Multimedia Inc.; Davenport Films. $35.00.

Ashtanga, NY 2004
Sri K. Pattabhi Jois gives his final North American workshop in New York City in September 2001. When the terrorist attacks took place during this event he used the Ashtanga practice to heal and fortify his followers. 60m; DVD. **A:** Adult. **P:** Education. **U:** Home. **Gen-Edu**: Yoga, Fitness/Exercise. **Acq:** Purchase. **Dist:** First Run/Icarus Films. $24.95.

Ashtanga Yoga "The Practice" with David Swenson 1996
Two-part series from expert David Swenson on the practices and techniques of Ashtanga Yoga. Includes instruction for both beginners and advanced yoga practitioners. 259m; VHS. **A:** Jr. High-Adult. **P:** Instruction. **U:** Home. **Hea-Sci**: Fitness/Exercise, Yoga, How-To. **Acq:** Purchase. **Dist:** Ashtanga Yoga Productions Headquarters. $45.95.

Ashura 2005 (Unrated) — ★★½
Set in what appears to be 19th century Japan, this Kabuki play turned film is centered on the life of Izumo (Somegoro Ichikawa), a Demon Slayer who has retired to become an actor after accidentally killing a child. A former comrade has gone over to the dark side in his absence however, and he has become the lover of a demon looking to resurrect her Queen Ashura who is now in human form. They believe an amnesiac thief that Izumo has fallen in love with may be the one they are looking for, and the inevitable sword battles ensue. 119m; DVD. **C:** Somegoro Ichikawa; Rie Miyazawa; Kanako Higuchi; Atsuro Watabe; Fumiyo Kohinata; Takashi Naito; Directed by Yojiro

Takita; Written by Sei Kawaguchi; Kazuki Nakashima; Masashi Todayama; Cinematography by Katsumi Yanagijima; Music by Yoko Kanno. **A:** Sr. High-Adult. **P:** Entertainment. **U:** Home. **L:** English, Japanese. **Mov-Ent:** Action-Adventure, Fantasy. **Acq:** Purchase. **Dist:** AnimEigo Inc. $14.98.

Asia 1991
Reveals Asia, the largest and most populated continent. Explores both remote places and teeming cities. Part of a six-part series. 25m; VHS, 3/4 U. **A:** Primary-Sr. High. **P:** Education. **U:** Institution. **Gen-Edu:** Geography, Asia. **Acq:** Purchase. **Dist:** National Geographic Society. $99.00.

Asia: An Introduction—Revised 1981
This show explores the unique characteristics of each major region in Asia. 21m; VHS, 3/4 U. **Pr:** Wayne Mitchell. **A:** Primary-Adult. **P:** Education. **U:** Institution, SURA. **Gen-Edu:** Asia. **Acq:** Purchase. **Dist:** Phoenix Learning Group.

Asia in Asia 1983
Fusion rock group Asia plays a concert at Budokan, Japan, including "Heat of the Moment," "Soul Survivor," "The Heat Goes On," "Eye to Eye," "Open Your Eyes" and more. 60m; VHS. **Pr:** Independent. **A:** Jr. High-Adult. **P:** Entertainment. **U:** Home. **Mov-Ent:** Music--Performance. **Acq:** Purchase. **Dist:** Music Video Distributors. $19.95.

Asia in Transition: Burma: In the Garden of the Crying Buddha ????
Gives insight to Burmese life, such as washing the sacred Buddha at the Maha Muni Pagoda, initiation of young Buddhist novices, and farming the floating gardens of Lake Inle. Also discusses Burma's 40-year civil war, roles of the railway and cinema, and problems with smuggling. 49m; VHS. **A:** Sr. High-Adult. **P:** Education. **U:** Institution. **Gen-Edu:** Asia, Anthropology. **Acq:** Purchase, Rent/Lease. **Dist:** Films for the Humanities & Sciences. $149.00.

Asia in Transition: China: The Dance Around the Golden Calf ????
Examines the effects of economic reform on Chinese society, from small villages to large cities, in terms of cultural values and traditional arts and sciences. 50m; VHS. **A:** Sr. High-Adult. **P:** Education. **U:** Institution. **Gen-Edu:** Asia, Anthropology. **Acq:** Purchase, Rent/Lease. **Dist:** Films for the Humanities & Sciences. $149.00.

Asia in Transition: Culture, Politics, and Economics ????
Seven-part series following the Transasian Highway through seven countries. Covers topics such as tensions between religious and other cultural traditions, political change, and dynamic developments effecting everyday life. 344m; VHS. **A:** Sr. High-Adult. **P:** Education. **U:** Institution. **Gen-Edu:** Asia, Anthropology. **Acq:** Purchase, Rent/Lease. **Dist:** Films for the Humanities & Sciences. $899.00.
Indiv. Titles: 1. Iran: Departure into the Unknown 2. Pakistan: Between the Chitralis and Pathans 3. India: The River of Life 4. Burma: In the Garden of the Crying Buddha 5. Thailand: King, Combat, and Ad Karaboa 6. Laos: In the Shadow of the Giants 7. China: The Dance Around the Golden Calf.

Asia in Transition: India: River of Life ????
Overviews the caste system as it exists in the holy Hindu town of Varanasi, arranged marriages, local trades in Agra, Sikhism in the city of Amritsar, the Indian/Pakistani tug-of-war for Kashmir, and the plight of small farmers being driven from their holdings by powerful landowners. 50m; VHS. **A:** Sr. High-Adult. **P:** Education. **U:** Institution. **Gen-Edu:** Asia, Anthropology. **Acq:** Purchase, Rent/Lease. **Dist:** Films for the Humanities & Sciences. $149.00.

Asia in Transition: Iran: Departure into the Unknown ????
Describes the effects of a modern fundamentalist society on Iran's diverse population of Muslims, Christians, and Jews. Also show the celebration of Sizdah Bedar, to welcome the spring. 49m; VHS. **A:** Sr. High-Adult. **P:** Education. **U:** Institution. **Gen-Edu:** Asia, Anthropology. **Acq:** Purchase, Rent/Lease. **Dist:** Films for the Humanities & Sciences. $149.00.

Asia in Transition: Laos: In the Shadow of the Giants ????
Examines the cultural and economic impact modern improvement to the country will have on Laotians and Hmong, such as the new highway being built by Swedish engineers. Also discusses foreign tourism, problems with antigovernment rebels, and the spiritual life in Laos. 47m; VHS. **A:** Sr. High-Adult. **P:** Education. **U:** Institution. **Gen-Edu:** Asia, Anthropology. **Acq:** Purchase, Rent/Lease. **Dist:** Films for the Humanities & Sciences. $149.00.

Asia in Transition: Pakistan: Between the Chitralis and Pathans ????
Examines Pakistan's relations with Iran, India, and the United States. Also explores the region's heritage as the seat of the Indus Valley civilization. 51m; VHS. **A:** Sr. High-Adult. **P:** Education. **U:** Institution. **Gen-Edu:** Asia, Anthropology. **Acq:** Purchase, Rent/Lease. **Dist:** Films for the Humanities & Sciences. $149.00.

Asia in Transition: Thailand: King, Combat, and Ad Karaboa ????
Examines Thailand's political independence, based on democracy and peaceful rule by a monarch that is supported culturally. Also addresses the influences of Thai boxing and Buddhism. 48m; VHS. **A:** Sr. High-Adult. **P:** Education. **U:** Institution. **Gen-Edu:** Asia, Anthropology. **Acq:** Purchase, Rent/Lease. **Dist:** Films for the Humanities & Sciences. $149.00.

Asia: Live in Moscow 1990
The 1990 concert of supergroup Asia includes such songs as "Kari-anne," "Days Like These," and "Heat of the Moment." 72m; VHS. **A:** Sr. High-Adult. **P:** Entertainment. **U:** Home. **Mov-Ent:** Music--Performance, Music--Pop/Rock. **Acq:** Purchase. **Dist:** Movies Unlimited; Rhino Entertainment Co.; Music Video Distributors. $14.99.

Asia: Live in the UK, 1990 1991
Live from Nottingham Palace in May, 1990, the group performs 13 of their songs. 62m; VHS. **A:** Jr. High-Adult. **P:** Entertainment. **U:** Home. **Mov-Ent:** Music Video, Music--Performance, Music--Pop/Rock. **Acq:** Purchase. **Dist:** Music Video Distributors. $69.95.

Asia Pacific 1998
Five-video set looks at five Asian economies by focusing on a single person or family to demonstrate how large economic trends affect ordinary people. Recommended for Grades 7-12. 20m; VHS. **A:** Jr. High-Sr. High. **P:** Education. **U:** Institution. **Gen-Edu:** Asia, Geography, Economics. **Acq:** Purchase. **Dist:** Zenger Media; Social Studies School Service. $129.95.
Indiv. Titles: 1. Korea 2. Philippines 3. Singapore 4. Thailand 5. Vietnam.

Asian American Cultures in the U.S.A. 1992
Classifies groups known as Asian Americans, and discusses their similarities and differences. 60m; VHS. **A:** Adult. **P:** Education. **U:** Institution. **Gen-Edu:** Prejudice. **Acq:** Purchase. **Dist:** RMI Media. $99.00.

Asian-American Stories Series 19??
Asian-American Robert Kikuchi-Yngojo uses comic body postures, rubber faces, hand gestures, and colorful costumes to bring to life many folktales, myths, legends, and music from throughout Asia. 90m; VHS. **A:** Preschool-Primary. **P:** Education. **U:** Home. **Chl-Juv:** Storytelling. **Acq:** Purchase. **Dist:** Curriculum Associates. $69.95.
Indiv. Titles: 1. Pre-K?-K 2. Primary 3. Intermediate.

Asian American Theater Workshop 1984
This program discusses the Asian American Theatre and the role of Asians in the theatre. 30m; 3/4 U, EJ. **Pr:** Chinese for Affirmative Action. **A:** Sr. High-Adult. **P:** Education. **U:** Institution, CCTV. **Gen-Edu:** Asia, Theater. **Acq:** Loan. **Dist:** Chinese for Affirmative Action.

Asian Boys 1994
Eleven different interviews with "Asian boys" are intercut with images of "fish out of water" in Chinatown and footage from the Miss Universe pageant in the Philippines. The interviewees respond to requests for childhood stories illustrating their emerging ideas. 19m; VHS. **A:** Sr. High-Adult. **P:** Entertainment. **U:** Home. **Gen-Edu:** Documentary Films. **Acq:** Purchase, Rent/Lease. **Dist:** Third World Newsreel. $175.00.

Asian Community Press Conference on the "Triad Report" 1974
"Triad: the Mafia of the East" is a booklet published by the Head of the State Department, Justice E. J. Younger. The report was said to depict all Chinese as smugglers or drug suppliers. This would then prejudice law enforcement officers against Chinese aliens. A lawsuit was filed to prohibit further publication of similar reports. 30m/B/W; EJ. **Pr:** GMC Productions. **A:** Adult. **P:** Education. **U:** Institution, CCTV. **Gen-Edu:** Immigration. **Acq:** Loan. **Dist:** Chinese for Affirmative Action.

Asian Concepts of Stage Discipline and Western Actor Training 1980
Explores aspects of Asian theatre and demonstrates the principles of T'ai Chi Ch'uan. 33m; VHS. **A:** Adult. **P:** Education. **U:** Institution. **Fin-Art:** Theater. **Acq:** Purchase. **Dist:** Insight Media. $179.00.

Asian Garden Strike 1972
In 1972 workers of the Asia Garden Restaurant went on strike. In this program the workers and employers discuss working conditions. 15m/B/W; EJ. **A:** Adult. **P:** Education. **U:** Institution, CCTV. **Gen-Edu:** Labor & Unions. **Acq:** Loan. **Dist:** Chinese for Affirmative Action.

Asian Health Secrets 1999
Letha Hadady provides health instruction and the power of herbs, foods, and other natural healing methods. Includes remedies for weight loss, arthritis, pain, high blood pressure, and other maladies. 50m; VHS. **A:** Adult. **P:** Instruction. **U:** Home. **Hea-Sci:** Health Education, Nutrition. **Acq:** Purchase. **Dist:** Instructional Video. $19.98.

Asian Heart 1987
Mail order brides from Asia are becoming an increasingly popular method of finding suitable mates for European men. This film examines a group of Danish men who have courted Philippine women exclusively by mail. While some marriages work, many of the women are often confused and alone, having little legal status in their new countries, and are unable to return to their old homes. 38m; VHS, 3/4 U. **Pr:** Kaerne Films. **A:** Sr. High-Adult. **P:** Education. **U:** Institution, Home, SURA. **Gen-Edu:** Marriage, Asia. **Acq:** Purchase, Rent/Lease, Duplication. **Dist:** Filmakers Library Inc.

Asian Power in the Richmond 1975
Will the Richmond District in San Francisco be a second Chinatown? Residents say it will not. This program explores this question and looks at the Richmond Asian Multi Service, Inc. (RAMS). 15m/B/W; EJ. **Pr:** KRON San Francisco. **A:** Adult. **P:** Education. **U:** Institution, CCTV. **Gen-Edu:** Minorities. **Acq:** Loan. **Dist:** Chinese for Affirmative Action.

Asian Stories 2006 (Unrated) — ★1/2
Not particularly interesting story about a man who thinks he wants to die. Chinese-American Jim (Lee) has been dumped by his fiancee two weeks before their Valentine's Day wedding. Depressed and in debt, Jim asks his hitman best friend Alex (Kishita) to kill him and they decide to head off to a mountain cabin for some quiet contemplation under the condition that the deed must be done before the dreaded lovers' holiday. Think Jim will change his mind? 98m; DVD. **C:** James Kyson Lee; Kirt Kishita; Kathy Uyen; Directed by Ron Oda; Kris Chin; Written by Ron Oda; Cinematography by Jonathan Hall; Music by Thomas' Apartment. **A:** Sr. High-Adult. **P:** Entertainment. **U:** Home. **Mov-Ent. Acq:** Purchase. **Dist:** Entertainment One US LP.

Asian Theatre Series: Acting Techniques of Kutiyattam, Sanskrit Theatre of India 1988
A brief introduction to the body postures and movements of this type of acting is presented. 55m; VHS, 3/4 U. **Pr:** Michigan State University. **A:** Sr. High-Adult. **P:** Education. **U:** Institution, CCTV. **Fin-Art:** Performing Arts, Theater. **Acq:** Purchase, Rent/Lease. **Dist:** Michigan State University.

Asian Theatre Series: Acting Techniques of the Noh Theatre of Japan 1988
Walking and turning movements, as well as hand gestures and symbolism are explained. 30m; VHS, 3/4 U. **Pr:** Michigan State University. **A:** Sr. High-Adult. **P:** Education. **U:** Institution, CCTV. **Fin-Art:** Performing Arts, Japan, Theater. **Acq:** Purchase, Rent/Lease. **Dist:** Michigan State University.

Asian Theatre Series: Acting Techniques of Topeng, Masked Theatre of Bali 1988
The masked theatre of this South Sea island is explained, with its characteristic style of movement. 39m; VHS, 3/4 U. **C:** John Emigh. **Pr:** Michigan State University. **A:** Sr. High-Adult. **P:** Education. **U:** Institution, CCTV. **Fin-Art:** Performing Arts. **Acq:** Purchase, Rent/Lease. **Dist:** Michigan State University.

Asian Theatre Series: Asian Concepts of Stage Discipline and Western Actor Training 1988
After spending years in the orient, A.C. Scott talks about the differences between American and Eastern actors. 33m; VHS, 3/4 U. **Pr:** Michigan State University. **A:** Sr. High-Adult. **P:** Education. **U:** Institution, CCTV. **Fin-Art:** Performing Arts. **Acq:** Purchase, Rent/Lease. **Dist:** Michigan State University.

Asian Theatre Series: Conversation with A.C. Scott 1988
Film clips in China and Japan of stage productions are combined with an i nterview in which Scott talks about those projects. 28m; VHS, 3/4 U. **Pr:** Michigan State University. **A:** Sr. High-Adult. **P:** Education. **U:** Institution, CCTV. **Fin-Art:** Performing Arts. **Acq:** Purchase, Rent/Lease. **Dist:** Michigan State University.

Asian Theatre Series: Kabuki Acting Techniques 1: The Body 1988
Male and female movement patterns are described as they apply to kabuki. 60m; VHS, 3/4 U. **Pr:** Michigan State University. **A:** Jr. High-Adult. **P:** Instruction. **U:** Institution, CCTV. **Fin-Art:** Performing Arts. **Acq:** Purchase, Rent/Lease. **Dist:** Michigan State University.

Asian Theatre Series: Kabuki Acting Techniques 2: The Voice 1988
The range of voices appropriate for portraying warriors, young children, elderly people and others is described. 29m; VHS, 3/4 U. **Pr:** Michigan State University. **A:** Sr. High-Adult. **P:** Instruction. **U:** Institution, CCTV. **Fin-Art:** Performing Arts. **Acq:** Purchase, Rent/Lease. **Dist:** Michigan State University.

Asian Theatre Series: Kalarippayatt, Martial Art of India 1988
The basic steps, kicks, and jumps of this unique type of martial art are demonstrated. 23m; VHS, 3/4 U. **Pr:** Michigan State University. **A:** Jr. High-Adult. **P:** Education. **U:** Institution, CCTV. **Gen-Edu:** Martial Arts. **Acq:** Purchase, Rent/Lease. **Dist:** Michigan State University.

Asian Theatre Series: Surpanakha, the Amorous Demoness 1980
A dramatization of incidents drawn from the "Ramayana," one of India's major epics. A love-sick demoness disguises herself as a beautiful woman and attempts to seduce her beloved, but when she fails she assumes her true form and tries to terrorize him into submission. 91m; VHS, 3/4 U. **Pr:** Michigan State University. **A:** College-Adult. **P:** Education. **U:** Institution, CCTV. **Fin-Art. Acq:** Purchase, Rent/Lease. **Dist:** Michigan State University.

Asian Theatre: Techniques and Application 1980
This series introduces information on Asian acting techniques. ?m; VHS, 3/4 U. **Pr:** Michigan State University. **A:** Sr. High-Adult. **P:** Education. **U:** Institution, CCTV. **Fin-Art:** Theater, Asia. **Acq:** Purchase, Rent/Lease. **Dist:** Michigan State University.
Indiv. Titles: 1. Kabuki: The Body 2. Kabuki: The Voice 3. Techniques of the NOH Theatre of Japan 4. Techniques of Toperg, Masked Theatre of Bali 5. Kalarippaya H, Martial Art of India 6. Techniques of Kutiyattam, Sanskirt Theatre of India 7. Asian Concepts of Stage Discipline and Western Actor Training 8. Conversation With A.C. Scott 9. Kabuki for Western Actors and Directors 10. Actor Training and Kalarippayatt, Martial Art of India 11. Adapting To Peng, the Masked Theatre of Bali 12. Seraikella Chhau, the Masked Dance of India 13. NOH the Classical Theatre of Japan 14. From India to East Lansing-Surpanakha-Producing a Sanskirt Drama 15. Surpanakha (The Amorous Demoness).

Asian Traditions 1999
Provides an overview of the cultures and people of India and the Himalayan countries. 35m; VHS. **A:** Jr. High-Adult. **P:** Education. **U:** Home, Institution. **Gen-Edu:** Education, Geography, Asia. **Acq:** Purchase. **Dist:** Thomas S. Klise Co. $64.00.

Asian Writers' Conference 1985
Highlights from the gathering of Asian writers are seen. 30m; EJ. **Pr:** Chinese for Affirmative Action. **A:** Jr. High-Adult. **P:** Education. **U:** Institution, CCTV. **Gen-Edu:** Literature, Asia. **Acq:** Rent/Lease. **Dist:** Chinese for Affirmative Action. $25.00.

The Asianization of America 1991
Takes a look at the role of Asians in American society and their successes in academic and business fields. 26m; VHS. **Pr:** Films for the Humanities. **A:** Sr. High-Adult. **P:** Education. **U:** Institution. **Gen-Edu:** Minorities, Business, Education. **Acq:** Purchase. **Dist:** Films for the Humanities & Sciences. $149.00.

Asians Now: International Women's Day 1975
"Asians Now-International Women's Day" discusses the significance of International Women's day for Chinese women. Two Asian women express the difficulties they encounter being a worker and a wife. 30m/B/W; EJ. **Pr:** KTVU Oakland. **A:** Adult. **P:** Education. **U:** Institution, CCTV. **Gen-Edu:** Minorities. **Acq:** Loan. **Dist:** Chinese for Affirmative Action.

Asiklar: Those Who Are in Love 1996
Documents the life of the Ashiks, Turkish minstrels in traditional Anatolian society. 37m; VHS. **A:** College. **P:** Education. **U:** Institution. **Gen-Edu:** Anthropology, Documentary Films. **Acq:** Purchase, Rent/Lease. **Dist:** Documentary Educational Resources. $195.

Ask a Policeman 1938 (Unrated) — ★1/2
The village of Turnbottom Round has been crime-free for so long that bumbling Sgt. Dudfoot (Hay) and his constables Brown (Moffatt) and Harbottle (Marriott) may soon be unemployed. The trio decides to stage some bogus crimes, only to uncover a real smuggling operation. 83m/B/W; DVD. **C:** Will Hay; Graham Moffatt; Moore Marriott; Glennis Lorimer; Peter Gawthorne; Charles Oliver; Directed by Marcel Varnel; Written by Val Guest; Marriott Edgar; Cinematography by Derick Williams. **A:** Jr. High-Adult. **P:** Entertainment. **U:** Home. **Mov-Ent:** Drug Trafficking/Dealing. **Acq:** Purchase. **Dist:** VCI Entertainment.

Ask a Simple Question 1988
All sorts of different problems that are common to teenagers are explored. 36m; VHS. **Pr:** Cambridge Career Productions. **A:** Jr. High-Adult. **P:** Education. **U:** Institution, Home. **Gen-Edu:** Adolescence. **Acq:** Purchase. **Dist:** Cambridge Educational. $149.00.

Ask Any Girl 1959 (Unrated) — ★★1/2
Lighthearted fluff about a small-town girl who moves to Manhattan. MacLaine plays the bright Meg who gets a job at an ad agency and decides to set her sights on marrying her boss (Young). She asks his older brother's (Niven) help in her quest and the inevitable happens. 101m; VHS. **C:** Shirley MacLaine; David Niven; Gig Young; Rod Taylor; Jim Backus; Claire Kelly; Elisabeth Fraser; Directed by Charles Walters. **Pr:** Joe Pasternak; Metro-Goldwyn-Mayer Pictures. **A:** Jr. High-Adult. **P:** Entertainment. **U:** Home. **Mov-Ent:** Comedy--Romantic, Marriage. **Awds:** British Acad. '59: Actress (MacLaine). **Acq:** Purchase. **Dist:** MGM Home Entertainment; Movies Unlimited. $19.98.

Ask Dr. Jim about Cats 1994
Veterinarian Jim Humphries discusses how to chose a cat, nutrition and obesity, vaccinations, behavior problems, human allergies, and more. 45m; VHS. **A:** Adult. **P:** Education. **U:** Home. **Gen-Edu:** Pets. **Acq:** Purchase. **Dist:** Tapeworm Video Distributors Inc. $19.95.

Ask Dr. Jim about Dogs 1994
Veterinarian Jim Humphries discusses crate training puppies and adult dogs, spay and neutering, lyme disease, pet health insurance, overweight pets, and more. 45m; VHS. **A:** Adult. **P:** Education. **U:** Home. **Gen-Edu:** Pets. **Acq:** Purchase. **Dist:** Tapeworm Video Distributors Inc. $19.95.

Ask for It 1986
Animal puppets help show children in grades K-2 how to make requests in an assertive, nonaggressive way. 20m; VHS. **A:** Primary. **P:** Education. **U:** Institution. **Gen-Edu:** Children, How-To, Communication. **Acq:** Purchase. **Dist:** United Learning Inc. $250.00.

Ask for the Order. . .and Get It! 1972
Hammers home a key principle of salesmanship—to get an order you must ask for it; from the "Tough-Minded Salesmanship" series. 30m; VHS, 3/4 U, Special order formats. **Pr:** Dartnell. **A:** Adult. **P:** Professional. **U:** Institution, CCTV. **Bus-Ind:** Sales Training. **Acq:** Purchase. **Dist:** Dartnell Corp.

Ask for the Order. . .and Get It!?Revised 1991
An updated look at the timeless issues of selling. 26m; VHS, 3/4 U, Special order formats. **Pr:** Dartnell. **A:** College-Adult. **P:** Instruction. **U:** Institution. **Bus-Ind:** How-To, Business, Sales Training. **Acq:** Purchase, Rent/Lease. **Dist:** Excellence in Training Corp. $469.00.

Ask the Dust 2006 (R) — ★★
Chasing an aspiring novelist's dream in 1930s Los Angeles, Arturo Bandini (Farrell)--the son of Italian immigrants but desperate to leave his heritage behind—collides into a turbulent love/hate affair with Camilla (Hayek), a Latina waitress with her own agenda to quickly ascend the social ladder. When Arturo comes into money to write his book, their relationship oddly cools off, while later he struggles with what success has cost him. Taken from John Fantes' 1939 novel of the same name and highlighted by brilliant desert scenery shot in South Africa. 117m; DVD. **C:** Colin Farrell; Salma Hayek; Donald Sutherland; Eileen Atkins; Idina Menzel; Justin Kirk; Jeremy Crutchley; Richard Schickel; Directed by Robert Towne; Written by Robert Towne; Cinematography by Caleb Deschanel; Music by Ramin Djawadi; Hector Pereira. **Pr:** Tom Cruise; Paula Wagner; Jonas McCord; Don Granger; Capitol Films; Cruise-Wagner Productions; VIP Medienfonds 3; Ascendant Production; Paramount Classics. **A:** Sr. High-Adult. **P:** Entertainment. **U:** Home. **L:** English. **Mov-Ent:** Drama, Immigration. **Acq:** Purchase. **Dist:** Paramount Pictures Corp.

Ask This Old House: The Complete First Season 2003
Contains the first season of the home improvement television series hosted by Kevin O'Connor with general contractor Tom Silva, plumbing and heating expert Richard Trethewey, and landscape contractor Roger Cook as they answer viewers' questions while providing some on-site assistance. Spin-off of Bob Vila's "This Old House." 26 episodes. 840m; DVD. **A:** Family. **P:** Entertainment. **U:** Home. **Gen-Edu:** Television Series, Home Improvement, Documentary Films. **Acq:** Purchase. **Dist:** Warner Home Video, Inc. $49.98.

Asking for Help 1992
Dramatization examines the problem of overcomeing pride and embarrassment to seek help with learning difficulties. 28m; VHS. **A:** Primary. **P:** Education. **U:** Institution. **Chl-Juv:** Children, Psychology. **Acq:** Purchase. **Dist:** Rainbow Educational Media, Inc. $59.95.

Asking Questions 19??
Shows students at a teacher training college in Tanzania working with materials and developing different kinds of questions to assist children in learning about science. 7m; 3/4 U, Special order formats. **Pr:** Education Development Center. **A:** Primary-Adult. **P:** Education. **U:** Institution, CCTV, CATV, BCTV. **Gen-Edu:** Education, Africa. **Acq:** Purchase, Rent/Lease. **Dist:** Education Development Center.

Asking the Right Questions 19??
Education film from the University of Calgary Learning Commons. ?m; VHS. **A:** Adult. **P:** Education. **U:** Institution. **Gen-Edu:** Education, Documentary Films. **Acq:** Purchase. **Dist:** University of Calgary Library, Visual Resources Centre.

ASL Literature: Collector's Edition 19??
Ben Bahan's Bird of a Different Feather and Sam Supalla's For a Decent Living told in American Sign Language. 60m; VHS. **A:** Family. **P:** Education. **U:** Home. **Gen-Edu:** Language Arts. **Acq:** Purchase. **Dist:** Dawn Sign Press. $19.95.

ASL Literature Series—Student Workbook & Videotext 199?
ASL literature, Birds of a Different Feather by Ben Bahan and For a Decent Living by Sam Supalla, for hearing-impaired students. 120m; VHS. **A:** Primary. **P:** Education. **U:** Home. **Gen-Edu:** Literature. **Acq:** Purchase. **Dist:** Dawn Sign Press. $29.95.

Aspara and All the Children of the World 19??
Takes a look at the world-wide fraternity represented by the Foster Parents Plan while following the struggles of eight-year-old Apsara Dital, a child living in a poor Nepalese community. 58m; VHS. **Pr:** National Film Board of Canada. **A:** Sr. High-Adult. **P:** Education. **U:** Institution. **Gen-Edu:** Parenting, Children, Documentary Films. **Acq:** Purchase. **Dist:** Indiana University; National Film Board of Canada.

Aspects of Central Place 1985
Using Cambridge, England as an example, this tape examines a small city's function as a center for a vast regional area. 20m; VHS, 3/4 U. **Pr:** Films for the Humanities. **A:** Jr. High-Adult. **P:** Education. **U:** Institution, SURA. **Gen-Edu:** Cities & Towns. **Acq:** Purchase, Rent/Lease. **Dist:** Films for the Humanities & Sciences.

Aspects of Ecology 19??
Five programs focusing on topics of major ecological importance, with basic concepts illustrated by showing scientists in action. Designed specifically for biology students. Teacher's guide available separately. 29m; VHS. **A:** Sr. High. **P:** Education. **U:** Institution. **Gen-Edu:** Ecology & Environment, Biology, Science. **Acq:** Purchase. **Dist:** Access The Education Station. $49.00.
Indiv. Titles: 1. Circles and Cycles 2. Ecosystems 3. Populations 4. Micro-organisms 5. Biomes.

Aspects of Neo-Classic Theater: Racine's "Phedre" 19??
Features actor/director Paul-Emile Deiber of the Comedie Francaise directing scenes from the French drama. 13m; VHS. **A:** Adult. **P:** Education. **U:** Institution. **Fin-Art:** Theater. **Acq:** Purchase. **Dist:** Insight Media. $129.00.

Aspects of Stravinsky 1989
Covers Stravinsky's work from the first piece he wrote which was the setting of the Lord's Prayer done in Latin to his last piece, which was the Lord's Prayer done in Russian. Also available in black and white. 166m; VHS. **Pr:** Kultur. **A:** Sr. High-Adult. **P:** Education. **U:** Home. **Fin-Art:** Documentary Films, Music--Classical. **Acq:** Purchase. **Dist:** Home Vision Cinema; Kultur International Films Ltd., Inc.; Music Video Distributors. $59.95.

Aspects of the Commedia Dell'Arte 19??
Focuses on the mask characters of commedia and demonstrates voice qualities and gestures of the characters Truffaldino and Pantalone. 14m; VHS. **A:** Adult. **P:** Education. **U:** Institution. **Fin-Art:** Theater. **Acq:** Purchase. **Dist:** Insight Media. $129.00.

Aspects of the Kabuki Theater of Japan 19??
Presents footage of actual performances and rehearsal as an introduction to aspects of traditional Japanese theatre. 12m; VHS. **A:** Adult. **P:** Education. **U:** Institution. **Fin-Art:** Theater. **Acq:** Purchase. **Dist:** Insight Media. $129.00.

Aspen 1974
The snowy town of Aspen, Colorado has become a haven and special retreat for musicians, dancers, artists, craftsmen, modern-day philosophers, and of course, skiers. 27m; VHS, 3/4 U, Special order formats. **Pr:** International Communication Agency. **A:** Jr. High-Adult. **P:** Education. **U:** Institution, SURA. **Gen-Edu:** Cities & Towns. **Acq:** Purchase. **Dist:** National Audiovisual Center.

Aspen 1991
Documentary takes a look at life in the Colorado town which was once famous for silver mining, but now makes its name as a playground for the rich and famous. 146m; VHS. **A:** Sr. High-Adult. **P:** Entertainment. **U:** Home, Institution. **Gen-Edu:** Documentary Films, Cities & Towns. **Acq:** Purchase, Rent/Lease. **Dist:** Zipporah Films. $350.00.

Aspen Camp School for the Deaf 1978
A documentary featuring a child with perfect hearing interacting and coexisting with deaf children, and his adjustment to such an environment. 14m; 3/4 U. **Pr:** Grass Roots. **A:** Sr. High-Adult. **P:** Education. **U:** Institution, CCTV. **Gen-Edu:** Deafness. **Acq:** Purchase, Rent/Lease. **Dist:** Grassroots Community Television.

Aspen Extreme 1993 (PG-13) — ★
Former Aspen ski instructor writes and directs a movie on (what else?) ski instructors in (where?) Aspen! Long on ski shots and short on plot, this movie never leaves the bunny hill. Two Detroiters leave Motown for Snowtown to pursue a life on the slopes. T.J (Gross) soon has his hands full with two beautiful women (Polo and Hughes) who encourage his dream of becoming a writer. His friend Dexter (Berg), however, acquires a few bad habits, and the whole movie just goes downhill from there. 128m; VHS, DVD, CC. **C:** Paul Gross; Peter Berg; Finola Hughes; Teri Polo; Martin Kemp; Nicolette Scorsese; William Russ; Will MacMillan; Directed by Patrick Hasburgh; Written by Patrick Hasburgh; Cinematography by Steven Fierberg; Music by Michael Convertino. **Pr:** Leonard Goldberg; Fred Gallo; Touchwood Pacific Partners I; Hollywood Pictures. **A:** Jr. High-Adult. **P:** Entertainment. **U:** Home. **Mov-Ent:** Drama, Skiing. **Acq:** Purchase. **Dist:** Buena Vista Home Entertainment. $94.95.

Aspen: Two Views 1977
Describes the town's struggle with land use issues in an attempt to preserve its extraordinary natural assets and unique quality of life. 55m; 3/4 U. **Pr:** Grass Roots. **A:** Sr. High-Adult. **P:** Education. **U:** Institution, CCTV. **Gen-Edu:** Cities & Towns. **Acq:** Purchase, Rent/Lease. **Dist:** Grassroots Community Television.

Asperger Syndrome: Living Outside the Bell Curve 2001
Dr. Iyama from the University of Wisconsin explains the causes of, symptoms and strategies for coping with Asperger Syndrome. 18m; VHS. **A:** Adult. **P:** Professional. **U:** Institution. **Hea-Sci:** Learning Disabilities, Mental Health, Medical Education. **Acq:** Purchase. **Dist:** Aquarius Health Care Media. $79.00.

The Asphalt Jungle 1950 (Unrated) — ★★★★
An aging criminal emerges from his forced retirement (prison) and assembles a gang for one final heist. Then things start to go awry. A very realistic story line and a superb cast make this one of the best crime films ever made. Highly acclaimed. 112m/B/W; VHS, DVD. **C:** Sterling Hayden; Louis Calhern; Jean Hagen; James Whitmore; Sam Jaffe; John McIntire; Marc Lawrence; Barry Kelley; Anthony Caruso; Teresa Celli; Marilyn Monroe; Brad Dexter; Strother Martin; Dorothy Tree; Directed by John Huston; Written by Ben Maddow; W.R. Burnett; Music by Miklos Rozsa. **Pr:** Loew's, Inc; MGM. **A:** Family. **P:** Entertainment. **U:** Home. **Mov-Ent:** Classic Films, Crime Drama. **Awds:** Natl. Bd. of Review '50: Director (Huston); Natl. Film Reg. '08; Venice Film Fest. '50: Actor (Hayden). **Acq:** Purchase. **Dist:** MGM Home Entertainment. $19.98.

The Asphyx 1972 (PG) — ★★★
Nineteenth century doctor Stephens is studying death when he discovers The Asphyx, an aura that surrounds a person just before they die. Stephens delves deeper into his research and finds the keys to immortality. However, his irresponsibility in unleashing the obscure supernatural power on the world brings a swarm of unforeseen and irreversible troubles. High-class sci fi. 98m; VHS, DVD, Blu-Ray, Wide. **C:** Robert Stephens; Robert Powell; Jane Lapotaire; Alex Scott; Ralph Arliss; Fiona Walker; John Lawrence; Paul Bacon; Terry Scully; Directed by Peter Newbrook; Written by Brian Comfort; Cinematography by Frederick A. (Freddie) Young; Music by Bill McGuffie. **Pr:** Paragon. **A:** Jr. High-Adult. **P:** Entertainment. **U:** Home. **Mov-Ent:** Science Fiction, Death. **Acq:** Purchase. **Dist:** Movies Unlimited. $19.99.

Aspic: Gellied Aspic Coating for Food Products 1986
Offers instruction on specific aspects of cooking and food preparation. 14m; VHS. **A:** Adult. **P:** Instruction. **U:** Institution. **Gen-Edu:** Cooking. **Acq:** Purchase. **Dist:** RMI Media. $89.95.

Aspire Higher: Sports Careers for Women 1992
Shows the options available in several career fields for sports-minded women and provides a dose of motivation along the

way. Looks at women athletes who have successfully made the transition out of sports and into a wide range of satisfying positions. 24m; VHS. **C:** Narrated by Debi Thomas. **A:** Sr. High-College. **P:** Instruction. **U:** Institution, Home. **Spo-Rec:** Sports--General. **Acq:** Purchase. **Dist:** Cambridge Educational. $29.95.

Ass Backwards 2013 (Unrated) — ★
An unfunny comedy about stupid people. Delusional Kate and Chloe are best friends who are about to be evicted from their New York apartment. Just then, they get an invitation to attend the 50th anniversary celebration of their hometown's children's beauty pageant where they were dual last-place finishers. The road trip consists of one calamity after another, before they arrive to get involved in even more ridiculousness. 86m; Streaming. **C:** June Diane Raphael; Casey Wilson; Jon Cryer; Vincent D'Onofrio; Brian Geraghty; Alicia Silverstone; Directed by Chris Nelson; Written by June Diane Raphael; Casey Wilson; Cinematography by Andre Lascaris; Music by Erica Weis. **Pr:** Gravitas Ventures L.L.C. **A:** Sr. High-Adult. **P:** Entertainment. **U:** Home. **L:** English. **Mov-Ent:** Women. **Acq:** Purchase, Rent/Lease. **Dist:** Amazon.com Inc.

Assassin 1986 (PG-13) — ★★
Made for TV drama about a mad scientist who creates a bionic killer for a bizarre plot to take over the world. He programs the cyborg to assassinate the President and other key people to help carry out his plan. A retired CIA operative emerges to stop the scientist by trying to destroy the robot. 94m; VHS, DVD. **C:** Robert Conrad; Karen Austin; Richard Young; Jonathan Banks; Robert Webber; Directed by Sandor Stern; Written by Sandor Stern; Cinematography by Chuck (Charles G.) Arnold; Music by Anthony Guefen. **Pr:** Sankan Productions. **A:** Jr. High-Adult. **P:** Entertainment. **U:** Home. **Mov-Ent:** Science Fiction, Mystery & Suspense, Technology. **Acq:** Purchase. **Dist:** Movies Unlimited. $13.49.

Assassin 1989 (R) — ★★
Fairly lame thriller about a CIA agent protecting a Senator who falls under suspicion when his charge is shot by an assassin. In investigating the killing the agent discovers the usual governmental conspiracy. 92m; VHS; Open Captioned. **C:** Steve Railsback; Nicholas Guest; Xander Berkeley; Elpidia Carrillo; Directed by Jon Hess. **Pr:** L.A. Film Group. **A:** Sr. High-Adult. **P:** Entertainment. **U:** Home. **Mov-Ent:** Mystery & Suspense, Intelligence Service. **Acq:** Purchase. **Dist:** Movies Unlimited. $71.99.

Assassin in Love 2007 (PG-13) — ★½
London hitman Milo decides he needs a career change after screwing up a job and making his boss angry. So he moves to a Welsh village and finds work as a baker. However, when the locals learn Milo's previous occupation they want him to settle their own petty problems. 86m; DVD. **C:** Damian Lewis; Kate Ashfield; Nikolaj Coster-Waldau; Dyfan Dwyfor; Michael Gambon; Anthony O'Donnell; Steve Speirs; Directed by Gareth Lewis; Written by Gareth Lewis; Cinematography by Sean Bobbitt; Music by Alex Wurman. **A:** Sr. High-Adult. **P:** Entertainment. **U:** Home. **Mov-Ent. Acq:** Purchase. **Dist:** Screen Media Ventures, LLC.

Assassin of Youth 1935 (Unrated) — ★½
Girl is introduced to marijuana and soon becomes involved in "the thrills of wild parties," and the horrors of the "killer weed." Camp diversion. 70m/B/W; VHS, DVD. **C:** Luana Walters; Arthur Gardner; Earl Dwire; Fern Emmett; Dorothy Short; Directed by Elmer Clifton. **A:** Family. **P:** Entertainment. **U:** Institution, Home. **Mov-Ent:** Exploitation, Drugs. **Acq:** Purchase. **Dist:** Gotham Distributing Corp.; Synergy Entertainment, Inc.; Something Weird Video. $16.95.

Assassination 1987 (R) — ★
A serious threat has been made to First Lady Ireland and no one is taking it lightly. Secret Service agent Bronson has been called as Ireland's personal bodyguard and suddenly they are both the target of terrorist attacks. Strangely though, the attacks seem to be directed from inside the White House. Bronson as you've seen him many times before. 93m; VHS, DVD, CC. **C:** Charles Bronson; Jill Ireland; Stephen Elliott; Michael Ansara; Directed by Peter Hunt; Written by Richard Sale; Cinematography by Hanania Baer. **Pr:** Cannon Films. **A:** Sr. High-Adult. **P:** Entertainment. **U:** Home. **Mov-Ent:** Action-Adventure, Secret Service, Presidency. **Acq:** Purchase. **Dist:** Anchor Bay Entertainment. $9.98.

The Assassination Bureau 1969 (Unrated) — ★★★
Set in Victorian-era London, this amusing farce concerns a society of international assassins led by the charming Reed. Rigg is an intrepid reporter who pays Reed to have his own organization try to kill him. Reed in turn will try to get them first. A cross-European chase ends in a battle aboard a Zeppelin. Tongue-in-cheek whimsey with a fine cast. Based on a short story by Jack London. 106m; DVD, CC. **C:** Oliver Reed; Diana Rigg; Telly Savalas; Curt Jurgens; Philippe Noiret; Warren Mitchell; Beryl Reid; Clive Revill; Kenneth Griffith; Vernon Dobtcheff; Annabella Incontrera; Directed by Basil Dearden; Cinematography by Geoffrey Unsworth. **Pr:** Michael Relph; Basil Dearden; Basil Dearden; Paramount Pictures. **A:** Jr. High-Adult. **P:** Entertainment. **U:** Home. **Mov-Ent:** Comedy--Black. **Acq:** Purchase. **Dist:** WarnerArchive.com.

The Assassination File 1996 (R) — ★★
FBI agent Lauren Jacobs (Fenn) quits the Bureau after the first African-American President (Winfield) is killed on her watch. But two years later, when she encounters former co-workers, there's talk of a conspiracy and things turn even more dangerous. 106m; VHS. **C:** Sherilyn Fenn; Dan E. Butler; Tom Verica; Victor Love; Kevin Corrigan; Paul Winfield; Diedrich Bader; Directed by John Harrison; Written by Bruce Miller; Cinematography by Rob Draper. **Pr:** Michael Joyce. **A:** Sr. High-Adult. **P:** Entertainment. **U:** Home. **Mov-Ent:** Mystery & Suspense, Federal Bureau of Investigation (FBI), Conspiracies or Conspiracy Theories. **Acq:** Purchase. **Dist:** Universal Music and Video Distribution.

The Assassination Game 1992 (R) — ★
Rookie CIA agent teams up with a veteran KGB agent to prevent the assassination of a world leader. 90m; VHS. **C:** Robert Rusler; Theodore Bikel; Doug Wert; Denise Bixler; Directed by Jonathan Winfrey. **A:** Sr. High-Adult. **P:** Entertainment. **U:** Home. **Mov-Ent:** Intelligence Service. **Acq:** Purchase. **Dist:** New Horizons Picture Corp. $89.98.

Assassination in Rome 1965 (Unrated) — ★★
American Shelley North (Charisse) and her husband are vacationing in Rome when he suddenly disappears. When she goes to the American embassy for help, Shelley is reunited with ex-lover, reporter Dick Sherman (O'Brian), who decides to help her out. A dead body in the Trevi fountain isn't the missing Mr. North but Dick thinks there's a connection and he and Shelley take their investigation to Venice. Available as a Drive-In Double Feature with "Espionage in Tangiers." 104m; DVD. **C:** Cyd Charisse; Hugh O'Brian; Mario Feliciani; Juliette Mayniel; Alberto Closas; Directed by Silvio Amadio; Written by Giovanni Simonelli; Silvio Amadio; Cinematography by Mario Pacheco; Music by Armando Trovajoli. **A:** Jr. High-Adult. **P:** Entertainment. **U:** Home. **Mov-Ent. Acq:** Purchase. **Dist:** MPI Media Group.

Assassination of a High School President 2008 (R) — ★★
Mainstream high school black comedy finds ambitious sophomore Bobby Funke (Thompson) assigned to write about seemingly perfect star jock and class president Paul Moore (Taylor). Bobby writes a school paper expose that puts Paul in a bad light and turns out to be riddled with errors. The wannabe journalist finally figures out that the high school's problems go far beyond what he first imagined. 99m; DVD. **C:** Reece Thompson; Mischa Barton; Bruce Willis; Patrick Taylor; Melonie Diaz; Luke Grimes; Josh Pais; Kathryn Morris; Michael Rapaport; Directed by Brett Simon; Written by Tim Calpin; Kevin Jakubowski; Cinematography by M. David Mullen. **A:** Sr. High-Adult. **P:** Entertainment. **U:** Home. **Mov-Ent:** Journalism. **Acq:** Purchase. **Dist:** Sony Pictures Home Entertainment Inc.

The Assassination of Jesse James by the Coward Robert Ford 2007 (R) — ★★★
Calling this film a western is like calling a transcontinental railroad journey a trip to the coast. Tightly wound epic, brooding and dark yet visually spectacular, unfolds at a deliberate pace as a case study of James (Pitt) and his clinging young sycophant admirer, Robert Ford (Affleck), who would become the man who finally takes James' life. Ford's hero worship turns into jealousy and then disdain in the shadow of James' tabloid celebrity. A true film lover's film, director Dominik brings a style and texture that transcends the genre. See it if you worship the craft or Pitt, or both. 152m; DVD. **C:** Brad Pitt; Casey Affleck; Sam Shepard; Mary-Louise Parker; Sam Rockwell; Paul Schneider; Jeremy Renner; Garret Dillahunt; Zooey Deschanel; Michael Parks; Ted Levine; Alison Elliott; James Carville; Tom Aldredge; Narrated by Hugh Ross; Directed by Andrew Dominik; Written by Andrew Dominik; Cinematography by Roger Deakins; Music by Nick Cave; Warren Ellis. **Pr:** Brad Pitt; Dede Gardner; Ridley Scott; David Valdes; Jules Daly; Brad Pitt; Scott Free; Plan B Entertainment; Virtual Studios; Warner Bros. **A:** Sr. High-Adult. **P:** Entertainment. **U:** Home. **L:** English. **Mov-Ent:** Western. **Acq:** Purchase. **Dist:** Warner Home Video, Inc.

The Assassination of JFK 1992
Chronicles the individuals and events surrounding the assassination of President John F. Kennedy. Includes conspiracy theories involving the FBI, CIA, organized crime, Cuba, the Vietnam war, the Warren Commission, and decisions made by the Kennedys themselves. 78m; VHS. **C:** Directed by Dennis Mueller. **A:** Sr. High-Adult. **P:** Entertainment. **U:** Home. **Gen-Edu:** Documentary Films, Presidency. **Acq:** Purchase. **Dist:** MPI Media Group. $79.98.

The Assassination of Martin Luther King, Jr. 1993
Alleges the F.B.I. played a role in the murder of the civil rights leader with the help of recently declassified supporting documents. Includes interviews with many intimates of Dr. King. 90m; VHS, DVD. **A:** Sr. High-Adult. **P:** Entertainment. **U:** Home. **Gen-Edu:** Documentary Films, Civil Rights. **Acq:** Purchase. **Dist:** MPI Media Group. $59.98.

The Assassination of President Kennedy 1980
A comprehensive examination of the actual events surrounding the assassination of John F. Kennedy through the reconstruction of this tragic and controversial historical moment. 80m; VHS, 3/4 U. **Pr:** Witness Productions; British Broadcasting Corporation. **A:** Jr. High-Adult. **P:** Education. **U:** Institution, SURA. **Gen-Edu:** Presidency. **Acq:** Purchase. **Dist:** Phoenix Learning Group.

The Assassination of Richard Nixon 2005 (R) — ★★½
Sam Bicke (Penn), a hopeless loser who shoots himself in the foot at every turn, ends up blaming Nixon for his downfall and decides to hijack a jet and fly it into the White House. Based on the true story of a failed plot, film focuses on showing Bicke's gradual but certain descent, played by Penn with gutwrenching nakedness. Incredibly dismal but revealing look at the making of a potential terrorist. 95m; DVD. **C:** Sean Penn; Don Cheadle; Naomi Watts; Jack Thompson; Michael Wincott; Mykelti Williamson; Nick Searcy; Brad William Henke; Lily Knight; Tracy Middendorf; April Grace; Eileen Ryan; Jared Dorrance; Directed by Niels Mueller; Written by Niels Mueller; Kevin Kennedy; Cinematography by Emmanuel Lubezki; Music by Steven Stern. **Pr:** Alfonso Cuaron; Jorge Vergara; Anhelo Producciones. **A:** Sr. High-Adult. **P:** Entertainment. **U:** Home. **L:** English. **Mov-Ent:** Politics & Government, Presidency, Divorce. **Acq:** Purchase. **Dist:** New Line Home Video. $27.95.

Assassination of Sarajevo 1967
The program focuses on the behind-the-scenes diplomatic intrigue in Vienna. Events move beyond the ability to control them and on June 28, 1914, Archduke Franz Ferdinand is assassinated. 16m/B/W; VHS, 3/4 U. **Pr:** CBS. **A:** Sr. High-College. **P:** Education. **U:** Institution, SURA. **Gen-Edu:** History--Modern. **Acq:** Purchase. **Dist:** Home Vision Cinema.

Assassination of Trotsky 1972 — ★★
Middling attempt to dramatize the last days of the Russian Revolutionary leader in Mexico before he's done in with an ice pick. 113m; VHS, DVD. **C:** Richard Burton; Alain Delon; Romy Schneider; Valentina Cortese; Jean Desailly; Directed by Joseph Losey; Cinematography by Pasqualino De Santis. **Pr:** Cinerama Releasing. **A:** Adult. **P:** Entertainment. **U:** Home. **Mov-Ent:** Drama, Documentary Films, USSR. **Acq:** Purchase. **Dist:** Lions Gate Entertainment Inc.; Facets Multimedia Inc. $19.98.

The Assassination Run 1984 — ★
A retired British spy is involved against his will in an intricate plot of terrorism, counter-terrorism and espionage. 111m; VHS. **C:** Malcolm Stoddard; Mary Tamm; Directed by Ken Hannam. **Pr:** Bob McIntosh; British Broadcasting Corporation. **A:** Jr. High-Adult. **P:** Entertainment. **U:** Home. **Mov-Ent:** Mystery & Suspense, Terrorism, TV Movies. **Acq:** Purchase. **Dist:** $19.98.

Assassination Tango 2003 (R) — ★★★
Aging Brooklyn hit man John J. (Duvall), who dotes on girlfriend Maggie (Baker), and her daughter Jenny (Miller), and likes to hang out at the local dance hall, is sent to Argentina to kill a general. When the hit is delayed, he meets and is enchanted by Tango instructor Manuela, as well as the dance she teaches to him. Deep character study, beautifully shown in Duvall's performance, redeems film's slow, at times maddening pace. Duvall's direction, while not perfect, makes the proceedings interesting to watch, but requires patience. 114m; VHS, DVD, CC. **C:** Robert Duvall; Ruben Blades; Kathy Baker; Luciana Pedraza; Julio Oscar Mechoso; James Keane; Frank Gio; Katherine Micheaux Miller; Directed by Robert Duvall; Written by Robert Duvall; Cinematography by Felix Monti; Music by Luis Bacalov. **Pr:** Robert Duvall; Rob Carliner; Robert Duvall; American Zoetrope; United Artists. **A:** Sr. High-Adult. **P:** Entertainment. **U:** Home. **Mov-Ent:** South America, Dance. **Acq:** Purchase. **Dist:** MGM Home Entertainment.

Assassinations That Changed the World ????
Two-volume set chronicles successful and unsuccessful assassinations throughout history, investigates reasons behind each attempt, analyzes the perpetrators, and considers repercussions. 200m; VHS. **A:** Sr. High. **P:** Education. **U:** Institution. **Gen-Edu:** History, Politics & Government. **Acq:** Purchase. **Dist:** Zenger Media. $39.95.

Assassins 1995 (R) — ★★½
Stallone gets to play elder statesman in the very deadly rivalry between two contract killers. Robert Rath (Stallone) is the man—number one with a bullet—whose reputation has caught up with him. Hot-headed Miguel Bain (the ever-smoldering Banderas) wants to off Rath and assume the position of top hitman. Caught in the middle of this macho posturing is surveillance expert—and potential murderee—Electra (Moore). It's Stallone to the rescue but his character pays more attention to Pearl, Electra's pampered Persian cat than to the lovely lady herself. But then romance isn't what this film is about—and director Donner does know his action. 132m; VHS, DVD, Blu-Ray. **C:** Sylvester Stallone; Antonio Banderas; Julianne Moore; Anatoly Davydov; Directed by Richard Donner; Written by Brian Helgeland; Andy Wachowski; Lana Wachowski; Cinematography by Vilmos Zsigmond; Music by Mark Mancina. **Pr:** Richard Donner; Joel Silver; Bruce A. Evans; Raynold Gideon; Lauren Shuler Donner; Dino De Laurentiis; Richard Donner; Silver Pictures; Donner/Shuler-Donner Productions; Warner Bros. **A:** Sr. High-Adult. **P:** Entertainment. **U:** Home. **Mov-Ent. Acq:** Purchase. **Dist:** Warner Home Video, Inc.

The Assassins 2012 (Unrated) — ★★
Set in China's Three Kingdoms Period, this follows the personal life of oft-used villain Cao Cao (Chow Yun-Fat) as opposed to the usual stories presenting him as a military tactician and villain. Cao Cao has grown in power so much that he dwarfs even the Emperor, and various factions are competing to see him dead. 103m; DVD, Blu-Ray, Streaming. **C:** Chow Yun-Fat; Yifei Liu; Hiroshi Tamaki; Alec Su; Directed by Linshan Zhao; Written by Bin Wang; Cinematography by Xiaoding Zhao; Music by Shigeru Umebayashi. **A:** Jr. High-Adult. **P:** Entertainment. **U:** Home. **L:** English, Chinese. **Mov-Ent. Acq:** Purchase, Rent/Lease. **Dist:** Well Go USA, Inc. $29.98 24.98 10.99.

The Assassin's Blade 2008 (Unrated) — ★½
A young woman disguises herself to enter an all male martial arts academy to learn the skills needed to defend her family. 102m; DVD, Blu-Ray. **C:** Charlene (Cheuk-Yin) Choi; Chun Wu; Ge Hu; Directed by Jingle Ma; Written by Jingle Ma; Po Chun Chan; Ka Keung Ng; Sin Ling Yeung; Cinematography by Jingle Ma; Chi Ying Chan; Music by Tsang-Hei Chiu. **A:** Jr. High-Adult. **P:** Entertainment. **U:** Home. **L:** English, Yue Chinese. **Mov-Ent. Acq:** Purchase. **Dist:** Well Go USA, Inc. $29.98 24.98.

Assassin's Bullet 2012 (R) — ★
Everyone tries hard not to look bored in this nondescript thriller. Former FBI agent Robert (Slater), retired after a personal

tragedy, is a cultural attache in Sofia, Bulgaria. American Ambassador Ashdown (Sutherland) gets Robert to go back to his former profession to find a woman (Portnoy) who's assassinating Muslim jihadists. 91m; DVD, Blu-Ray. **C:** Christian Slater; Elika Portnoy; Donald Sutherland; Timothy Spall; Directed by Isaac Florentine; Written by Hans Feuersinger; Cinematography by Ross Clarkson; Music by Simon Stevens. **A:** Sr. High-Adult. **P:** Entertainment. **U:** Home. **L:** English. **Mov-Ent:** Federal Bureau of Investigation (FBI), Psychiatry. **Acq:** Purchase. **Dist:** ARC Entertainment, LLC.

Assault 1970 (Unrated) — ★½
Violent sex murders in a girl's school have the police baffled. The school's pretty art teacher offers to act as bait in order to catch the murderer. 89m; VHS. **C:** Suzy Kendall; Frank Finlay; Freddie Jones; James Laurenson; Lesley-Anne Down; Tony Beckley; Directed by Sidney Hayers. **Pr:** Peter Rogers; Rank. **A:** Adult. **P:** Entertainment. **U:** Home. **Mov-Ent:** Mystery & Suspense, Sex & Sexuality. **Acq:** Purchase. **Dist:** Amazon.com Inc. $59.95.

The Assault 1986 (PG) — ★★★½
Powerful and disturbing drama about a Dutch boy who witnesses the arbitrary murder of his family by Nazis. The memory tortures him and leaves him empty as he matures. Years later he meets other victims and also the perpetrators of the incident, each of them changed forever by it. Thought-provoking consideration of WWII and the horrors of living in Nazi Germany from many points of view. Based on a novel by Harry Mulisch. Dutch language dubbed into English. 149m; VHS. **C:** Derek de Lint; Marc Van Uchelen; Monique Van De Ven; Directed by Fons Rademakers. **Pr:** Cannon Films. **A:** Jr. High-Adult. **P:** Entertainment. **U:** Home. **Mov-Ent:** World War Two, Ethics & Morals, Holocaust. **Awds:** Oscars '86: Foreign Film; Golden Globes '87: Foreign Film. **Acq:** Purchase. **Dist:** Simon Wiesenthal Center; MGM Home Entertainment. $19.98.

Assault and Matrimony 1987 — ★½
Real-life married people Tucker and Eikenberry play a married couple fighting tooth and nail. Lots of slapstick and general nonsense. Based on James Anderson's novel. 100m; VHS, CC. **C:** John Hillerman; Michelle Phillips; Joe Cortese; Michael Tucker; Jill Eikenberry; Directed by James Frawley; Cinematography by Dick Bush. **A:** Primary-Adult. **P:** Entertainment. **U:** Home. **Mov-Ent:** Comedy--Slapstick, Marriage, TV Movies. **Acq:** Purchase. **Dist:** CinemaNow Inc. $89.95.

Assault at West Point: The Court-Martial of Johnson Whittaker 1994 (PG-13) — ★★½
In 1880, Johnson C. Whittaker, a black West Point cadet, is found beaten, mutilated, and tied to his bed. Instead of seeking his attackers, the Academy sets up a court martial to expel Whittaker, claiming he faked his own attack. Clashes also ignite between Whittaker's defense counsel—white abolitionist lawyer Chamberlain, whose own racism is thinly disguised, and black lawyer Greener, who originally encouraged Whittaker to enroll at the Point. Interesting case but a shallow production. Based on a true story and adapted from the book by John Marszalek. 98m; VHS, CC. **C:** Seth Gilliam; Samuel L. Jackson; Sam Waterston; John Glover; Al Freeman, Jr.; Directed by Harry Moses; Written by Harry Moses; Music by Terence Blanchard. **Pr:** Bob Rubin; Bill Siegler; Harry Moses; Showtime. **A:** Jr. High-Adult. **P:** Entertainment. **U:** Home. **Mov-Ent:** Black Culture, TV Movies, Military History. **Acq:** Purchase. **Dist:** Lions Gate Entertainment Inc.

Assault of the Killer Bimbos 1988 (R) — ★½
A show girl gets framed for the murder of her boss and takes off for the border with a couple of girlfriends. On the way they get pursued by the expected dumb cops and meet up with horny, clean-cut hunks. In Mexico they encounter the villain and extract comic vengeance. Watchable mainly due to the likable female leads and pleasant, lightly camp execution, although it might prove too tame for most of its target audience. 85m; VHS, DVD. **C:** Patti Astor; Christina Whitaker; Elizabeth Kaitan; Griffin O'Neal; Nick Cassavetes; Clayton Landey; Eddie Deezen; Arell Blanton; David Marsh; Tammara Souza; Jamie Bozian; Mike Muscat; Jeffrey Orman; John Quern; Jay O. Sanders; Directed by Anita Rosenberg; Written by Ted Nicolaou; Cinematography by Thomas Callaway; Music by Fred Lapides; Marc Ellis. **Pr:** Patti Astor; David DeCoteau; John Schouweiler; Debra Dion; Titan Productions; Urban Classics. **A:** Sr. High-Adult. **P:** Entertainment. **U:** Home. **Mov-Ent:** Comedy--Black. **Acq:** Purchase. **Dist:** Full Moon Pictures. $14.99.

Assault of the Party Nerds 1989 (R) — ★
Nerds throw a wild party to try and attract new members to their fraternity, while a jock frat plots against them. Sound familiar? Little more than a ripoff of "Revenge of the Nerds" made especially for video. 82m; VHS, DVD. **C:** Linnea Quigley; Troy Donahue; Richard Gabai; C. Paul Demsey; Marc Silverberg; Robert Mann; Richard Rifkin; Deborah Roush; Michelle (McClellan) Bauer; Directed by Richard Gabai. **Pr:** Check Entertainment, Inc. **A:** Sr. High-Adult. **P:** Entertainment. **U:** Home. **Mov-Ent:** Comedy--Screwball. **Acq:** Purchase. **Dist:** Movies Unlimited. $16.99.

Assault of the Party Nerds 2: Heavy Petting Detective 1995 — ★
Detective tries to save a beauty from her scheming husband. 87m; VHS, DVD. **C:** Linnea Quigley; Richard Gabai; Michelle (McClellan) Bauer; Arte Johnson; Burt Ward; Directed by Richard Gabai; Written by Richard Gabai. **A:** College-Adult. **P:** Entertainment. **U:** Home. **Mov-Ent. Acq:** Purchase. **Dist:** VCI Entertainment. $49.95.

Assault of the Rebel Girls 1959 — ★½
A reporter gets involved with smuggling in Castro's Cuba. Flynn's last film, saving the worst for last. 66m/B/W; VHS, DVD. **C:** Errol Flynn; Beverly Aadland; John MacKay; Jackie Jackler; Marie Edmund; Directed by Barry Mahon; Written by Errol Flynn. **Pr:** Exploit Films; Barry Mahon Productions. **A:** Family. **P:** Entertainment. **U:** Home. **Mov-Ent. Acq:** Purchase. **Dist:** VCI Entertainment.

Assault of the Sasquatch 2009 (Unrated) — ★
Police arrest a bear poacher and impound his truck which contains an unconscious Sasquatch. Unfortunately they don't bother to notice Bigfoot, and when he wakes up with a hangover from being shot multiple times he attacks the city. Despite his ability to rip off people's arms and use uprooted street signs as weapons, the local cops shrug off calling for help because "we got this." 85m; DVD, Streaming. **C:** Kevin Shea; Greg Nutcher; Jason Criscoulo; Cristina Santiago; Andrea Saenz; Directed by Andrew Gernhard; Written by John Doolan; Cinematography by Colin Theys; Matthew Wauhkonen; Music by Shannon Gould; Matthew Llewellyn. **A:** Sr. High-Adult. **P:** Entertainment. **U:** Home. **L:** English. **Mov-Ent. Acq:** Purchase, Rent/Lease. **Dist:** Synthetic Cinema. $14.95 14.99.

Assault on a Queen 1966 (Unrated) — ★
Stupid Sinatra vehicle about a group of con men who plot together to rob the Queen Mary on one of her trips. Their attack vessel is a renovated WWII German U-boat. The producers tried to capitalize on the popularity of "Ocean's Eleven," but they didn't even come close. Based on a novel by Jack Finney. 106m; VHS, DVD, CC. **C:** Frank Sinatra; Virna Lisi; Anthony (Tony) Franciosa; Richard Conte; Reginald Denny; Directed by Jack Donohue; Written by Rod Serling; Cinematography by William H. Daniels. **Pr:** William Goetz. **A:** Sr. High-Adult. **P:** Entertainment. **U:** Home. **Mov-Ent:** Boating, Oceanography. **Acq:** Purchase. **Dist:** Olive Films; Paramount Pictures Corp. $14.95.

Assault on Affirmative Action 1986
The issue of reverse discrimination is explored in this video. 60m; VHS, 3/4 U. **Pr:** PBS. **A:** Jr. High-Adult. **P:** Education. **U:** Institution, SURA. **Gen-Edu. Acq:** Purchase, Rent/Lease. **Dist:** PBS Home Video. $300.00.

Assault on Agathon 1975 (PG) — ★★
Amid the scenic Greek isles, an "executed" WWII guerilla leader returns to lead a revolution, and bloodshed and bombings ensue. 95m; VHS. **C:** Nina Van Pallandt; Marianne Faithfull; John Woodvine; Nico Minardos; Directed by Laszlo Benedek. **Pr:** Heritage Enterprises Productions. **A:** Jr. High-Adult. **P:** Entertainment. **U:** Home. **Mov-Ent:** World War Two. **Acq:** Purchase. **Dist:** $59.95.

Assault on Big Brother: Regulating the Regulators 1984
This documentary examines the drive to change the rules that regulate automobile airbags and hazardous waste. 52m; VHS, 3/4 U. **Pr:** National Broadcasting Company. **A:** College-Adult. **P:** Education. **U:** Institution, SURA. **Gen-Edu:** Ecology & Environment, Politics & Government. **Acq:** Purchase, Rent/Lease. **Dist:** Home Vision Cinema.

Assault on Precinct 13 1976 (Unrated) — ★★★
Urban horror invades LA. Lt. Bishop (Stoker) is assigned to oversee the final shutdown of Precinct 13. Nearly abandoned, except for a couple of secretaries and a few officers, the phones and electricity have already been shut off. First problem: a busload of criminals and officers are forced to make a stop to look after a sick prisoner. Second problem: a father, who just witnessed his daughter's murder by a brutal street gang, stumbles in. Then said street gang surrounds the precinct to get the witness. Paranoia abounds as the police are attacked from all sides and can see no way out. Carpenter's musical score adds to the excitement of this low-budget police exploitation story. Semi-acclaimed cult feature and very gripping. 91m; VHS, DVD, Blu-Ray. **TV Std:** NTSC, PAL. **C:** Austin Stoker; Darwin Joston; Martin West; Tony Burton; Nancy Loomis; Kim Richards; Henry (Kleinbach) Brandon; Laurie Zimmer; Charles Cyphers; Peter Bruni; Directed by John Carpenter; Written by John Carpenter; Cinematography by Douglas Knapp; Music by John Carpenter. **Pr:** Irwin Yablans Company. **A:** Sr. High-Adult. **P:** Entertainment. **U:** Home. **L:** English, Spanish. **Mov-Ent:** Crime Drama. **Acq:** Purchase. **Dist:** Movies Unlimited. $15.99.

Assault on Precinct 13 2005 (R) — ★★½
Richet's remake of the Carpenter cult classic has the cons and cops, led by burned-out Sgt. Roenick (Hawke) and criminal kingpin Bishop (Fishburne) holed up in a soon-to-be-closed Precinct 13 on a snowy New Year's Eve against a squad of corrupt cops intent on eliminating Bishop, their not-quite-silent-enough partner. Generally solid, if standard, updating loses much credibility by plopping a forest in the middle of a heavily industrial part of Detroit, where this one is set. Hawke and Fishburne are appropriately conflicted and heroic as it's called for, but it's the supporting cast that gives this rendition its zest. Stick around for the helpful plot-summarizing rap song that plays over the closing credits. 109m; VHS, DVD, Blu-Ray, UMD, HD-DVD. **C:** Ethan Hawke; Laurence Fishburne; Brian Dennehy; Drea De Matteo; Maria Bello; Gabriel Byrne; Ja Rule; Matt Craven; John Leguizamo; Fulvio Cecere; Currie Graham; Dorian Harewood; Kim Coates; Hugh Dillon; Titus Welliver; Aisha Hinds; Directed by Jean-Francois Richet; Written by James DeMonaco; Cinematography by Robert Gantz; Music by Graeme Revell. **Pr:** Pascal Caucheteux; Jeffrey Silver; Stephane Sperry; Liaison Films; Biscayne Pictures; Rogue Pictures. **A:** Sr. High-Adult. **P:** Entertainment. **U:** Home. **L:** English. **Mov-Ent:** Crime Drama, Psychiatry. **Acq:** Purchase. **Dist:** Movies Unlimited; Alpha Video; Universal Studios Home Video. $29.98.

Assault on the Record—Powerboating 1992
Witness history in the making as Bud Davie and Gary Garbrecht blow the old outboard motor water speed record out of the water. 30m; VHS. **A:** Adult. **P:** Entertainment. **U:** Home. **Spo-Rec:** Boating, Sports--Water. **Acq:** Purchase. **Dist:** Bennett Marine Video. $24.95.

Assault on Time 19??
Exposes the damage done by looters and vandals to valuable archaeological sites in the United States. 28m; VHS. **A:** Sr. High-Adult. **P:** Education. **U:** Institution. **Gen-Edu:** Documentary Films, Archaeology. **Acq:** Purchase. **Dist:** University of Washington Educational Media Collection. $15.00.

Assault on Wall Street 2013 (R) — ★★
When level-headed New York security guard Jim (Purcell) hears that his wife, Rosie (Karpluk), is diagnosed with a rare disease requiring a $300-per-shot hormone treatment, he puts the tab on his credit card, assuming his investment with a broker will soon pay off. Sure enough, the firm tanks and Jim's money disappears. From here on out, Jim stops at nothing to exact revenge on the system he holds accountable. The title suggests a grindhouse-like political massacre, especially coming from normally-outlandish director Boll. Instead, this everyman vs. corporate greed thriller is disappointingly restrained and dull. ; DVD, Blu-Ray, CC. **C:** Dominic Purcell; Edward Furlong; John Heard; Keith David; Eric Roberts; Erin Karpluk; Michael Pare; Lochlyn Munro; Directed by Uwe Boll; Written by Uwe Boll; Cinematography by Mathias Neumann; Music by Jessica de Rooij. **A:** Sr. High-Adult. **P:** Entertainment. **U:** Home. **L:** English. **Mov-Ent:** Drama. **Acq:** Purchase. **Dist:** Phase 4/kaBOOM Entertainment.

Assault with a Deadly Weapon 1982 (Unrated) — ★
When the police budget is cutback, crime runs rampant in an unnamed American city. 86m; VHS. **C:** Sandra Foley; Richard Holliday; Lamont Jackson; Directed by Arthur Kennedy. **A:** Adult. **P:** Entertainment. **U:** Home. **Mov-Ent. Acq:** Purchase. **Dist:** Lions Gate Television Corp. $39.95.

Assemblage 19??
Artist Susan Pickering Rothamel explains the materials, methods, and framing techniques of assemblage in this teaching aid for art education. 40m; VHS. **A:** Jr. High-College. **P:** Education. **U:** Institution. **Gen-Edu:** Art & Artists. **Acq:** Purchase. **Dist:** Crystal Productions. $39.00.

Assembling Pre-Cut Lamp Kits 19??
Demonstrates how to assemble pre-cut lamp shade kits. 30m; VHS. **A:** Adult. **P:** Instruction. **U:** Home. **How-Ins:** Crafts, Hobbies, How-To. **Acq:** Purchase. **Dist:** Cutters Productions. $19.95.

Assembly Language with Z80 Programming 1984
On three tapes, the basics of Z80 computer language are deciphered. 45m; VHS, 3/4 U. **Pr:** Bergwall Productions. **A:** Sr. High-Adult. **P:** Vocational. **U:** Institution. **Bus-Ind:** Electronics. **Acq:** Purchase. **Dist:** Bergwall Productions, Inc.

Assembly of Plastic Parts: Mechanical Fasteners 1995
Avoid common pitfalls in designing with mechanical fasteners by examining techniques for insert assembly, design for assembly, and design for disassembly and recycling. 64m; VHS. **A:** Adult. **P:** Professional. **U:** Institution. **L:** English. **Bus-Ind:** Industry & Industrialists. **Acq:** Purchase. **Dist:** Society of Manufacturing Engineers. $495.

Assembly of Plastic Parts: Press Fits and Snap Fits 1995
This video teaches good press and snap fit designs, press fit concepts, setting correct press fit interfaces, and other topics related to the assembly of plastic parts. 54m; VHS. **A:** Adult. **P:** Professional. **U:** Institution. **L:** English. **Bus-Ind:** Industry & Industrialists. **Acq:** Purchase. **Dist:** Society of Manufacturing Engineers. $495.

Assembly of Plastic Parts: Welding and Adhesive Bonding 1995
Help improve part performance by choosing the best bonding methods and welding concepts, as well as learning the theory of adhesive bonding and solvent bonding. 86m; VHS. **A:** Adult. **P:** Professional. **U:** Institution. **L:** English. **Bus-Ind:** Industry & Industrialists. **Acq:** Purchase. **Dist:** Society of Manufacturing Engineers. $495.

Assertive Behavior in Nursing 1977
This series focuses on the need for assertiveness in the nursing profession. Programs are available individually. 28m; VHS, 3/4 U. **Pr:** Health Communications Network. **A:** College-Adult. **P:** Professional. **U:** Institution, SURA. **Hea-Sci:** Nursing. **Acq:** Purchase, Rent/Lease, Subscription.
Indiv. Titles: 1. Behavioral Components of Assertion 2. The Acquisition of Assertiveness 3. Applications of Assertiveness 4. Ethics and Responsibilities of Assertiveness.

Assertive Discipline in Action 1980
This program presents a step-by-step approach to "assertive disciplinary" action for teachers to use within the school environment. 25m; 3/4 U. **Pr:** Media Five. **A:** College-Adult. **P:** Teacher Education. **U:** Institution, CCTV, SURA. **Gen-Edu:** Education, Psychology. **Acq:** Purchase. **Dist:** Home Vision Cinema.

Assertive Discipline in the Classroom 1978
This "no nonsense" approach shows teachers how to gain self-confidence and master the specific competencies necessary to manage a classroom effectively. 29m; 3/4 U. **Pr:** Media Five. **A:** Adult. **P:** Teacher Education. **U:** Institution, CCTV, SURA. **Gen-Edu:** Education. **Acq:** Purchase. **Dist:** Home Vision Cinema.

Assessing ADHD in the Schools 1998
Depicts assessment as a collaborative problem-solving process that is linked to the planning of individualized interventions. Includes a 31-page manual. 35m; VHS. **A:** College-Adult. **P:** Teacher Education. **U:** Institution. **Gen-Edu:** Education, Learning Disabilities. **Acq:** Purchase. **Dist:** Guilford Publications, Inc. $95.00.

Assessing Breath Sounds 1989
Demonstrates techniques for assessing breath sounds. Reveals illustrations and computer graphics to help nurses understand the physiologic causes of the sounds. Includes a booklet. ?m; VHS. **A:** Adult. **P:** Education. **U:** Institution. **Hea-Sci:** Medical Care, Medical Education, Nursing. **Acq:** Purchase. **Dist:** Nursing Center. $36.95.

Assessing Chest Pain 1989
Reviews anatomy and physiology, critical assessment techniques, key assessment landmarks, and pain assessment. Looks at how to recognize the cardiac, respiratory, gastrointestinal, and musculoskeletal causes of chest pain. Includes a booklet. 30m; VHS. **A:** Adult. **P:** Education. **U:** Institution. **Hea-Sci:** Medical Care, Medical Education, Nursing. **Acq:** Purchase. **Dist:** Nursing Center. $36.95.

Assessing Childhood Trauma 19??
Jane Middleton-Moz, examines specific and cumulative traumas, including physical, sexual, or psychological, and offers guidelines to diagnose treatment. 60m; VHS. **A:** Adult. **P:** Education. **U:** Institution. **Hea-Sci:** Psychology, Psychiatry. **Acq:** Purchase. **Dist:** Hazelden Publishing. $295.00.

Assessing Employee Potential 1972
The problems of assessing and developing the potential of employees are considered; divided into five modules: General Problems in Assessing Employees; Matching People and Positions; Assessment Methods; On-the-Job Assessment; and The Assessment Center. 63m; VHS, 3/4 U. **Pr:** Resources for Education and Management. **A:** Adult. **P:** Professional. **U:** Institution, CCTV. **Bus-Ind:** Personnel Management. **Acq:** Purchase. **Dist:** Resources for Education & Management, Inc.

Assessing Fluids and Electrolytes 1989
Details all the major points of assessment of fluids and electrolytes. Includes a booklet. 30m; VHS. **A:** Adult. **P:** Education. **U:** Institution. **Hea-Sci:** Medical Care, Medical Education, Nursing. **Acq:** Purchase. **Dist:** Nursing Center. $36.95.

Assessing Heart Sounds 1989
Included are ways to determine critical descriptive factors used for documentation. Includes a booklet. 30m; VHS. **A:** Adult. **P:** Education. **U:** Institution. **Hea-Sci:** Medical Care, Medical Education, Nursing. **Acq:** Purchase. **Dist:** Nursing Center. $36.95.

Assessing Learning Difficulties in the Workplace 19??
Education film from the University of Calgary Learning Commons. ?m; VHS. **A:** Adult. **P:** Education. **U:** Institution. **Gen-Edu:** Education, Documentary Films. **Acq:** Purchase. **Dist:** University of Calgary Library, Visual Resources Centre.

Assessing the Adult Head to Toe 1995
Demonstrated head-to-toe assessments without wasting time or taxing patients. Includes practical advice that will help nurses fine-tune their assessment skills and correctly interpret normal findings. Includes a companion booklet. 60m; VHS. **A:** Adult. **P:** Education. **U:** Home. **Hea-Sci:** Medical Care, Medical Education, Nursing. **Acq:** Purchase. **Dist:** Nursing Center. $39.95.

Assessing the Mental Status of the Older Person 199?
Dr. Peter Rabins, Director of the Psychogeriatric Unit at the John Hopkins University School of Medicine, discusses the importance of correct diagnosis in the mental status of older people. Covers confusion, loss of memory, hallucinations, loss of cognitive skills, depression, and the use of the Mini Mental State Examinations. 34m; VHS. **A:** Adult. **P:** Education. **U:** Institution. **Hea-Sci:** Aging, Medical Care, Mental Health. **Acq:** Purchase, Rent/Lease. **Dist:** University of Maryland. $150.00.

Assessing the Unconscious Patient 1986
Nurses are instructed to be on the lookout for patients that either are already or might suddenly become unconscious. 20m; VHS, 3/4 U. **Pr:** Fairview Audio-Visuals. **A:** Adult. **P:** Professional. **U:** Institution, CCTV. **Hea-Sci:** Nursing. **Acq:** Purchase, Rent/Lease. **Dist:** Kinetic Film Enterprises Ltd.; Medcom Inc. $295.00.

Assessment 1979
From the "Stretch" series developed by educators to facilitate mainstreaming. Shows six ways to evaluate students objectively and gives other assessment procedures. 30m; VHS, 3/4 U, EJ. **Pr:** Metropolitan Cooperative Educationa. **A:** College-Adult. **P:** Teacher Education. **U:** Institution, CCTV. **Gen-Edu:** Handicapped. **Acq:** Purchase. **Dist:** American Educational Products LLC.

Assessment & Intervention: The Confused Elderly 1986
Two different ways of dealing with older people who have grown confused are suggested for health care pros. 25m; VHS, 3/4 U. **Pr:** Fairview Audio-Visuals. **A:** Sr. High-Adult. **P:** Professional. **U:** Institution, CCTV. **Hea-Sci:** Aging. **Acq:** Purchase. **Dist:** Kinetic Film Enterprises Ltd.; Medcom Inc. $295.00.

Assessment and Treatment Planning: An Adult Following Stroke 19??
Provides insight on assessing stroke patients. 49m; VHS. **A:** Adult. **P:** Education. **U:** Institution. **Hea-Sci:** Aging, Medical Care, Diagnosis. **Acq:** Purchase, Rent/Lease. **Dist:** University of Maryland. $200.00.

Assessment & Treatment Planning with Personality Disorders ????
Explains assessment and treatment planning for Axis II of DSM-IV. Taking a positive approach to complex problems is shown using the DCT model. 35m; VHS. **A:** Adult. **P:** Professional. **U:** Institution. **Hea-Sci:** Psychology, Mental Health. **Acq:** Purchase. **Dist:** Microtraining Associates, Inc. $129.00.

Assessment Center 1972
An exploration of the Assessment Center and how it surpasses other evaluation methods. Shows how an effective detailed program can be staged almost anywhere in any organization. 17m; VHS, 3/4 U. **Pr:** Resources for Education and Management. **A:** Adult. **P:** Professional. **U:** Institution, CCTV. **Bus-Ind:** Personnel Management. **Acq:** Purchase. **Dist:** Resources for Education & Management, Inc.

Assessment Centers: A Brief Orientation to the Process 1987
Assessment center participants involved in several exercises are observed by the viewers of the videotape. 33m; VHS, 3/4 U. **Pr:** Dennis A. Joiner. **A:** Adult. **P:** Professional. **U:** Institution, CCTV. **Bus-Ind:** Business, Management, Personnel Management. **Acq:** Purchase. **Dist:** Dennis A. Joiner & Associates.

Assessment Centers in the Fire Service 1984
This program was developed to fill the need for a brief, but informative introduction to the process as used in fire service promotional examinations. 36m; VHS, 3/4 U. **Pr:** Dennis A. Joiner. **A:** Adult. **P:** Education. **U:** Institution, CCTV. **Gen-Edu:** Fires. **Acq:** Purchase. **Dist:** Dennis A. Joiner & Associates.

Assessment Centers: What Are They? 1985
How and why assessment centers work for managerial hiring and promotion decisions is explained. 50m; VHS, 3/4 U. **Pr:** Dennis A. Joiner. **A:** Adult. **P:** Professional. **U:** Institution, CCTV. **Bus-Ind:** Management. **Acq:** Purchase. **Dist:** Dennis A. Joiner & Associates.

Assessment Methods 1972
Popular assessment techniques are shown. On-the-job assignments and various simulated situations are covered. 14m; VHS, 3/4 U. **Pr:** Resources for Education and Management. **A:** Adult. **P:** Professional. **U:** Institution, CCTV. **Bus-Ind:** Personnel Management. **Acq:** Purchase. **Dist:** Resources for Education & Management, Inc.

Assessment of Respiratory Distress in Infants and Children 19??
Nursing education video that provides information on how to perform a respiratory assessment of infants and children with mild, moderate, and severe distress. Covers respiratory distress and failure, the physical differences between pediatric and adult respiratory systems, and abnormal signs of distress (stridor, wheezing, grunting, and retractions). Divides the assessment into four parts: level of consciousness, respiratory rate, efforts and mechanics of respiration, and evaluation of skin and mucous membranes. 20m; VHS. **A:** College-Adult. **P:** Education. **U:** Institution. **Hea-Sci:** Nursing, Children, Respiratory System. **Acq:** Purchase, Rent/Lease. **Dist:** AJN Video Library/Lippincott Williams & Wilkins. $275.00.

Assessment of the Arthritic Elder 19??
Illustrates evaluation techniques for the functional level of activity in elderly arthritis patients. Covers examination of neck, back, low back, arms, wrists, fingers, hips, knees, ankles, and toes. 35m; VHS. **A:** Adult. **P:** Education. **U:** Institution. **Hea-Sci:** Aging, Medical Care, Diagnosis. **Acq:** Purchase, Rent/Lease. **Dist:** University of Maryland. $200.00.

Assessment of the Geriatric Patient with a Total Hip Replacement 19??
Provides information on assessing elderly hip replacement patients. 31m; VHS. **A:** Adult. **P:** Education. **U:** Institution. **Hea-Sci:** Aging, Medical Care, Diagnosis. **Acq:** Purchase, Rent/Lease. **Dist:** University of Maryland. $200.00.

Assessor Training: The Leaderless Group Discussion 1981
This tape assists assessor trainers in facilitating an understanding of how to best observe, record, classify and evaluate the types of behavior demonstrated by candidates. 33m; VHS, 3/4 U. **Pr:** Dennis A. Joiner. **A:** Adult. **P:** Professional. **U:** Institution, CCTV. **Bus-Ind:** Management. **Acq:** Purchase. **Dist:** Dennis A. Joiner & Associates.

Asset: A Social Skills Program for Adolescents 1981
This series is designed to teach social skills to adolescents who are uncommunicative, noncompliant, or aggressive. ?m; VHS, 3/4 U. **Pr:** Norman E. Baxley. **A:** Jr. High-Sr. High. **P:** Education. **U:** Institution. **Gen-Edu:** Adolescence, Psychology, Education. **Acq:** Purchase. **Dist:** Research Press. $1400.00.
Indiv. Titles: 1. Giving Positive Feedback 2. Giving Negative Feedback 3. Accepting Negative Feedback 4. Resisting Peer Pressure 5. Problem Solving 6. Negotiation 7. Following Instructions 8. Conversation.

The Assignment 1978 (Unrated) — ★★
The assassination of a high-ranking officer in an uneasy Latin American nation spurs violence and political instability. A Swedish diplomat is assigned the tremendous task of restoring peace and stability between the political factions. 92m; VHS. **C:** Christopher Plummer; Thomas Hellberg; Carolyn Seymour; Fernando Rey; Directed by Mats Arehn. **A:** Family. **P:** Entertainment. **U:** Home. **Mov-Ent. Acq:** Purchase. **Dist:** No Longer Available.

The Assignment 1997 (R) — ★★½
Workmanlike thriller is a case of deadly impersonation. Infamous terrorist Carlos the Jackal (Quinn) is shown plying his trade in Europe under the nose of CIA counterterrorism expert Jack Shaw (Sutherland). Later, in Israel, Mossad agent Amos (Kinglsey) captures a man whom he thinks is Carlos, only it's his double—U.S. Navy officer Annibal Ramirez (Quinn again). So Shaw and Amos decide to turn the seaman into the terrorist, in an elaborate plot to have Carlos' Russian handlers think the terrorist has betrayed them. There's a very long setup for a somewhat lame payoff. 115m; VHS, DVD, CC. **C:** Aidan Quinn; Donald Sutherland; Ben Kingsley; Liliana Komorowska; Claudia Ferri; Celine Bonnier; Vlasta Vrana; Von Flores; Al Waxman; Directed by Christian Duguay; Written by Don Gordon; Sabi H. Shabtai; Cinematography by David Franco; Music by Normand Corbeil. **Pr:** Tom Berry; Franco Battista; David Saunders; Allegro Films; Triumph Films. **A:** Sr. High-Adult. **P:** Entertainment. **U:** Home. **Mov-Ent:** Terrorism, Middle East, Violence. **Acq:** Purchase. **Dist:** Sony Pictures Home Entertainment Inc.

Assignment K 1968 (Unrated) — ★½
Uninspired spy thriller. While in Munich, British spy Philip Scott's (Boyd) cover as a toy manufacturer is blown and he's under surveillance by German intelligence. His girlfriend Toni (Sparv) is kidnapped to learn the names of his contacts. A lot of the so-called action takes place at a ski resort. 97m; DVD. **C:** Stephen Boyd; Camilla Sparv; Leo McKern; Michael Redgrave; Jeremy Kemp; Robert Hoffmann; Directed by Val Guest; Written by Val Guest; Maurice Foster; William Harold Strutton; Cinematography by Ken Hodges; Music by Basil Kirchin. **A:** Sr. High-Adult. **P:** Entertainment. **U:** Home. **L:** English. **Mov-Ent:** Skiing. **Acq:** Purchase. **Dist:** Sony Pictures Home Entertainment Inc.

Assignment Outer Space 1961 (Unrated) — ★
A giant spaceship with bytes for brains is on a collision course with Earth. A team of astronauts is sent to save the world from certain peril. Seems they take the task lightly, though, and their mission (and hence the plot) revolves more around saving sexy sultress Farinon from certain celibacy. If you're into stultifying Italian space operas with a gratuitous sex sub-plot then look up this assignment, but don't say we didn't warn you. Director Margheriti is also known as Anthony Dawson, not to be confused with the actor of the same name. 79m/B/W; VHS, DVD. **C:** Rik van Nutter; Gabriella Farinon; Archie Savage; Dave Montresor; Alan Dijon; Narrated by Jack Wallace; Directed by Anthony M. Dawson. **Pr:** Hugo Grimaldi; Ultra Films; Titanus; American International Pictures. **A:** Primary-Adult. **P:** Entertainment. **U:** Home. **Mov-Ent:** Science Fiction, Romance, Action-Adventure. **Acq:** Purchase. **Dist:** Sinister Cinema. $19.98.

Assignment: Paris 1952 (Unrated) — ★★½
Spy thriller finds reporter Jimmy Race (Andrews) sent from Paris to Budapest where his editor, Nick Strang (Sanders), assigns him to work with local Jeanne (Toren) on a potential political bombshell. Seems democratic elements within the Hungarian government are talking with Yugoslav president Tito about overthrowing the country's communist dictatorship. An incriminating photo is involved. 84m/B/W; DVD. **C:** Dana Andrews; Marta Toren; George Sanders; Audrey Totter; Herbert Berghof; Sandro Giglio; Donald Ranolph; Directed by Robert Parrish; Written by William Bowers; Cinematography by Burnett Guffey; Ray Cory; Music by George Duning. **A:** Sr. High-Adult. **P:** Entertainment. **U:** Home. **Mov-Ent:** Journalism. **Acq:** Purchase. **Dist:** Sony Pictures Home Entertainment Inc.

Assignment Smoking 1991
Part of the Time Challengers Series, featuring animated characters traveling through time to look at different issues facing society. Provides young viewer's with information on the short and long-term health risks associated with smoking. Emphasis is placed on the power of each individual to say "NO." 14m; VHS. **Pr:** LCA. **A:** Primary. **P:** Education. **U:** Institution, CCTV, SURA. **Chl-Juv:** Health Education, Smoking. **Acq:** Purchase, Rent/Lease, Duplication License. **Dist:** Phoenix Learning Group. $250.00.

Assignment to Kill 1969 (Unrated) — ★
Tedious thriller with only some pretty scenery (courtesy of Switzerland) to make it almost watchable. Insurance investigator Richard Cutting (O'Neal) is hired to find out why so many of shipping tycoon Curt Valayan's (Gielgud) vessels are sinking. It turns out to be sabotage. 98m; DVD. **C:** Patrick O'Neal; John Gielgud; Herbert Lom; Joan Hackett; Oscar Homolka; Peter Van Eyck; Kent Smith; Fifi d'Orsay; Eric Portman; Directed by Sheldon Reynolds; Written by Sheldon Reynolds; Cinematography by Enzo Barboni; Harold Lipstein; Music by William Lava. **A:** Sr. High-Adult. **P:** Entertainment. **U:** Home. **Mov-Ent:** Boating, Insurance. **Acq:** Purchase. **Dist:** WarnerArchive.com.

Assisi: Home of St. Francis 2004 (Unrated)
A tour of the town of Assisi, with an emphasis on sites important to the life of its most famous Saint. 50m; DVD. **A:** Jr. High-Adult. **P:** Entertainment. **U:** Home. **Gen-Edu:** Documentary Films, Travel, France. **Acq:** Purchase. **Dist:** Janson Media. $24.95.

The Assisi Underground 1984 — ★★
True but boringly told story of how the Catholic Church helped to save several hundred Italian Jews from being executed by the Nazis during the 1943 German occupation of Italy. Edited from 178 minutes, a good-will gesture from the producers. 115m; VHS, DVD. **C:** James Mason; Ben Cross; Maximilian Schell; Irene Papas; Angelo Infanti; Directed by Alexander Ramati; Music by Pino Donaggio. **Pr:** Cannon Productions. **A:** Sr. High-Adult. **P:** Entertainment. **U:** Home. **Mov-Ent:** Holocaust, Judaism, World War Two. **Acq:** Purchase. **Dist:** MGM Home Entertainment; Ignatius Press. $79.95.

The Assistant 1997 — ★★
The Jewish Bober family have escaped the anti-Semitism of their homeland and emigrated to the U.S. where they are struggling to run a small grocery store during the depression.

Drifter Frank (Bellows) hooks up with thief Ward (Woolvet) and they rob the store, with Ward attacking Morris Bober (Mueller-Stahl). A guilty Frank later returns and offers to help out. Morris doesn't know Frank was part of the robbery and agrees and Frank soons falls for the Bober's daughter, Helen (Greenhouse). Then Morris discovers the truth. Based on a novel by Bernard Malamud. 105m; VHS. **C:** Gil Bellows; Armin Mueller-Stahl; Joan Plowright; Kate Greenhouse; Jaimz Woolvett; Directed by Daniel Petrie; Written by Daniel Petrie; Cinematography by Philip Earnshaw. **A:** College-Adult. **P:** Entertainment. **U:** Home. **Mov-Ent:** Judaism, Romance, Poverty. **Acq:** Purchase. **Dist:** Facets Multimedia Inc.

The Assistant Professor: All About Angles 1992
Three lessons explain angles, demonstrate their uses, and show how they are formed. In addition, animated graphics show how to use the protractor and the compass. 18m; VHS. **Pr:** Allied Video Corporation. **A:** Primary-Jr. High. **P:** Education. **U:** Institution, BCTV, Home. **Gen-Edu:** Education, Mathematics. **Acq:** Purchase. **Dist:** Allied Video Corp. $29.95.

The Assistant Professor: Fractions and All Their Parts, Part 1 1992
Three mathematics lessons comprise the program. Using animated graphics, the concept of fractions is introduced by drawing on examples from everyday life. One of a three-part series. 23m; VHS. **Pr:** Allied Video Corporation. **A:** Primary. **P:** Education. **U:** Institution. **Gen-Edu:** Mathematics, Education. **Acq:** Purchase. **Dist:** Allied Video Corp. $29.95.

The Assistant Professor: How to Read Music 199?
Graphics and animation explicitly present the basics of reading and understanding music. 28m; VHS. **A:** Primary-Adult. **P:** Education. **U:** Institution, Home. **How-Ins:** Education, How-To. **Acq:** Purchase. **Dist:** Allied Video Corp. $29.95.

The Assistant Professor: Our Solar System—The Inner Planets/The Outer Planets 199?
Explore the solar system aboard a homemade spacecraft and learn of the planets' unique features. Fascinating photographs and animation. A two tape set. 28m; VHS. **A:** Preschool-Adult. **P:** Education. **U:** Institution. **Gen-Edu:** Astronomy, Education. **Acq:** Purchase. **Dist:** Allied Video Corp. $54.95.

The Assistant Professor: The Greenhouse Effect 1993
Paralells the Earth's atmosphere to a greenhouse and explains the affects of greenhouse gases on Earth life. 28m; VHS. **A:** Primary-Adult. **P:** Education. **U:** Home, Institution. **Gen-Edu:** Ecology & Environment. **Acq:** Purchase. **Dist:** Allied Video Corp. $29.95.

The Assistant Professor: The Pythagorean Theorem 1993
Animated two-lesson program depicts a cartoon Pythagoras presenting his famous theorem and solving sample problems. 16m; VHS. **A:** Jr. High-Sr. High. **P:** Education. **U:** Institution. **Gen-Edu:** Mathematics. **Acq:** Purchase. **Dist:** Allied Video Corp. $29.95.

The Assistant Professor: The World of Circles 1992
Three lessons teach youngsters all about circles using animated graphics. Prerequisites are basic math skills, including an understanding of decimals. 24m; VHS. **Pr:** Allied Video Corporation. **A:** Primary-Jr. High. **P:** Education. **U:** Institution, BCTV, Home. **Gen-Edu:** Education, Mathematics. **Acq:** Purchase. **Dist:** Allied Video Corp. $29.95.

The Assistant Professor: What Are Variables? 199?
Mathematics students are introduced to variables and transforming simple problems into mathematical sentences. 17m; VHS. **A:** Primary-Adult. **P:** Education. **U:** Home, Institution. **Gen-Edu:** Mathematics, Education. **Acq:** Purchase. **Dist:** Allied Video Corp. $29.95.

The Assistant Professor: What Is Area? 199?
For the mathematics student, this program demonstrates the development of formulas for measuring the area of a triangle, rectangle, and parallelogram with square units through the use of animated graphics. 17m; VHS. **A:** Primary-Adult. **P:** Education. **U:** Home, Institution. **How-Ins:** Mathematics, Education, How-To. **Acq:** Purchase. **Dist:** Allied Video Corp. $29.95.

The Assistant Professor: Which Way Is Minus? 1992
Provides answers for the math student to the questions "Why is a negative multiplied by a negative a positive?" and "How can you have something that is less than nothing?" 15m; VHS. **A:** Primary-Adult. **P:** Education. **U:** Home, Institution. **Gen-Edu:** Mathematics, Education. **Acq:** Purchase. **Dist:** Allied Video Corp. $29.95.

The Assistants 2009 (Unrated) — ★½
Jack and his film school grad friends find it difficult to get their big break as they work on the showbiz fringes. As a joke they fake a coverage report for a nonexistent script but Jack's producer boss Gary sees it and wants to buy the property. Now they have to make the fake real, which in Hollywood should be a breeze (with certain complications of course). 100m; DVD. **C:** Joe Mantegna; Stacy Keach; Aaron Himelstein; Chris Conner; Jane Seymour; Peter Douglas; Tate Hanyok; Kathleen Early; Jonathan Bennett; Reiko Aylesworth; Michael Grant Terry; Directed by Steve Morris; Written by Steve Morris; Cinematography by Aaron Torres; Music by Aaron R. Kaplan. **A:** Sr. High-Adult. **P:** Entertainment. **U:** Home. **Mov-Ent. Acq:** Purchase. **Dist:** Osiris Entertainment.

Assisting Families of Patients with Alzheimer's Disease 1991
A series of four videos that give information for social workers to assist families coping with Alzheimer's Disease. Gives information on emotional reactions and helping families find helpful resources. Tapes available individually or as a series. 15m; VHS, 3/4 U, Special order formats. **Pr:** Duke University Medical Center. **A:** Adult. **P:** Education. **U:** Institution. **Hea-Sci:** Social Service, Aging, Family. **Acq:** Purchase, Rent/Lease. **Dist:** Terra Nova Films. $69.95.

Assisting with a Physical Examination 1985
The nurse's role in a physical examination is reviewed, and emphasis is placed on preparation, positioning, and draping. 25m; VHS, 3/4 U. **Pr:** Trainex. **A:** College-Adult. **P:** Professional. **U:** Institution. **Hea-Sci:** Nursing. **Acq:** Purchase, Rent/Lease. **Dist:** Medcom Inc.

The Associate 1979 (R) — ★★
French farce about penniless financial consultant Julien Pardot (Serrault) who invents a fictitious partner, Mr. Davis, in order to get his business rolling. When his clients, his wife, and even his mistress are all more intrigued by the partner than Julien, he becomes so jealous he decides to "murder" his creation. Based on the novel "My Partner, Mr. Davis" by Jenaro Prieto. French with subtitles; remade in 1996 with Whoopi Goldberg. 93m; VHS, DVD. **C:** Michel Serrault; Claudine Auger; Catherine Alric; Matthieu Carriere; Directed by Rene Gainville; Written by Jean-Claude Carriere. **Pr:** Simone Allouche. **A:** Sr. High-Adult. **P:** Entertainment. **U:** Home. **L:** French. **Mov-Ent:** Satire & Parody. **Acq:** Purchase. **Dist:** Pathfinder Pictures.

The Associate 1996 (PG-13) — ★★
Whoopi drags a 20-minute premise over almost two hours when she invents an elderly, white, male business partner to give her fledgling financial consulting business some prestige. After having all her moneymaking ideas appropriated by male colleagues, Laurel Ayres (Goldberg) starts her own business, only to find that no one wants to hire her. She creates the genius and the money comes rolling in. Everyone clamors to meet the mystery man, so she goes undercover as the elusive Robert S. Cutty. The sight of Goldberg in old white guy garb and makeup is jarring, and the payoff doesn't merit the overlong build up. Based on the French film "L'Associate" and the Jenaro Prieto novel "El Socio." 113m; VHS, DVD. **C:** Whoopi Goldberg; Timothy Daly; Bebe Neuwirth; Dianne Wiest; Eli Wallach; Directed by Donald Petrie; Written by Nick Thiel; Cinematography by Alex Nepomniaschy; Music by Christopher Tyng. **Pr:** Frederic Golchan; Patrick Markey; Adam Leipzip; Interscope Comm; Polygram Filmed Entertainment; Buena Vista. **A:** Jr. High-Adult. **P:** Entertainment. **U:** Home. **Mov-Ent. Acq:** Purchase. **Dist:** Buena Vista Home Entertainment.

Association Fibers of the Cerebral Hemisphere 1978
The cerebral hemisphere is dissected to display the association fibers of the cerebral deep white matter. Structures related to the lateral ventricle are demonstrated. Part of the "Dissection of the Brain" series. 32m; VHS, 3/4 U, EJ, Q, Special order formats. **Pr:** University of Oklahoma. **A:** College. **P:** Professional. **U:** Institution, CCTV. **Hea-Sci:** Neurology. **Acq:** Purchase. **Dist:** University of Oklahoma.

Assorted Nazi Political Films: 1932-1943 1943
Three different speeches by Adolf Hitler at various times during the Nazi regime, plus one by Goebbels in 1943, are now available on one tape. In German with English subtitles. 31m/B/W; VHS, 3/4 U. **TV Std:** NTSC, PAL. **A:** Sr. High-Adult. **P:** Education. **U:** Institution, Home. **L:** German. **Gen-Edu:** Documentary Films, World War Two, Propaganda. **Acq:** Purchase. **Dist:** International Historic Films Inc.; German Language Video Center. $35.95.

Assorted U.S. Government War Films Program, Vol. 1 1943
Several newsreels are combined here to give a comprehensive look at WWII. Speeches by various political and military leaders are joined with actual combat fooage to present an overview of the war and its effects. 45m/B/W; VHS. **TV Std:** NTSC, PAL. **A:** Sr. High-Adult. **P:** Education. **U:** Institution, Home. **Gen-Edu:** War--General, World War Two, Propaganda. **Acq:** Purchase. **Dist:** International Historic Films Inc. $24.95.

Assorted U.S. Government War Films Program, Vol. 2 1944
Newsreel and combat footage are combined to display the efforts of Allied military units in defeating the enemy. Also included is the "Private Snafu" cartoon. 45m/B/W; VHS. **TV Std:** NTSC, PAL. **A:** Jr. High-Adult. **P:** Education. **U:** Institution, Home. **Gen-Edu:** Documentary Films, World War Two, Armed Forces--U.S. **Acq:** Purchase. **Dist:** International Historic Films Inc. $24.95.

Assunta Spina 1915 (Unrated) — ★★
A very early, very rare Italian epic about ancient Rome, the prototype for the Italian silent epics to come. 70m/B/W; Silent; VHS. **C:** Francesca Bertini; Directed by Francesca Bertini. **A:** Family. **P:** Entertainment. **U:** Home. **Mov-Ent:** Drama, Film History, Silent Films. **Acq:** Purchase. **Dist:** Facets Multimedia Inc. $39.98.

Assurances 1990
A successful young real estate entrepreneur, who wants to get married, thinks he's found the perfect woman but just what does she think? 28m; VHS. **C:** Directed by Jody Widelitz. **A:** Sr. High-Adult. **P:** Entertainment. **U:** Home, Institution. **Mov-Ent:** Comedy--Romantic, Marriage. **Acq:** Purchase. **Dist:** The Cinema Guild. $59.95.

Asterix: Asterix and Cleopatra 1968
The gallant warrior Asterix, and his friends, battle Queen Cleopatra in ancient Egypt. 72m; VHS. **Pr:** Productions Dargaud Films. **A:** Family. **P:** Entertainment. **U:** Home. **Chl-Juv:** Animation & Cartoons. **Acq:** Purchase. **Dist:** Walt Disney Studios Home Entertainment. $49.95.

Asterix: Asterix the Gaul 1967
Asterix the Gaul and his sidekick, Obelix, take on an inept legion of Roman warriors when they try to take over Asterix's Gallic territory. 67m; VHS. **Pr:** Productions Dargaud Films. **A:** Family. **P:** Entertainment. **U:** Home. **L:** English, French. **Chl-Juv:** Animation & Cartoons, Children. **Acq:** Purchase. **Dist:** Walt Disney Studios Home Entertainment. $49.95.

Asterix: The Twelve Tasks of Asterix 1976
The gallant warrior Asterix matches brains and brawn with Caesar and the entire Roman Empire. 81m; VHS. **Pr:** Productions Dargaud Films. **A:** Family. **P:** Entertainment. **U:** Home. **Chl-Juv:** Animation & Cartoons, War--General, Drama. **Acq:** Purchase. **Dist:** Walt Disney Studios Home Entertainment. $49.95.

Asteroid 1978
Dancer Steve Paxton and video artist Paul Wong collaborated on this experimental program that combines video and ballet. 19m; VHS, 3/4 U. **Pr:** Steve Paxton; Paul Wong. **A:** College-Adult. **P:** Entertainment. **U:** Institution. **Fin-Art:** Video, Dance. **Acq:** Rent/Lease. **Dist:** Video Out Distribution.

Asteroid 1997 — ★★
Re-edited version of the NBC TV miniseries emphasizes the special effects and action, which should help this routine disaster flick. Astronomer Lily McKee (Sciorra) discovers that several giant asteroids are on a collision course with Kansas City. She contacts FEMA and gets hotshot director Jack Wallach (Biehn) anxious to help out (and not just with the rock problem). Naturally, the citizens freak and one asteroid hits but there's an even bigger one on the way. 120m; VHS, DVD. **C:** Michael Biehn; Annabella Sciorra; Don Franklin; Anne-Marie Johnson; Anthony Zerbe; Carlos Gomez; Jensen (Jennifer) Daggett; Michael Weatherly; Frank McRae; Denis Arndt; Directed by Bradford May; Written by Robbyn Burger; Scott Sturgeon; Cinematography by David Hennings; Thomas Del Ruth; Music by Shirley Walker. **Pr:** Peter V. Ware; Davis Entertainment Company; National Broadcasting Company. **A:** Jr. High-Adult. **P:** Entertainment. **U:** Home. **Mov-Ent:** Action-Adventure, TV Movies. **Acq:** Purchase. **Dist:** Lions Gate Television Corp.

The Asteroid and the Dinosaur 1981
Scientists explain a theory that a giant asteroid collided with the earth millions of years ago, tossing a killing cloud of dust and debris into the atmosphere. 57m; VHS, 3/4 U, Special order formats. **Pr:** WGBH Boston. **A:** Jr. High-Sr. High. **P:** Education. **U:** Institution, SURA. **Hea-Sci:** Dinosaurs, Astronomy. **Acq:** Purchase, Rent/Lease. **Dist:** Time-Life Video and Television.

Asteroid vs. Earth 2014 (Unrated) — ★
Cheesy sci-fi disaster from The Asylum. An asteroid is on a collision course with Earth in this end of the world cheapie and the solution is to set off a series of nukes in the Pacific Ocean in the hope of wobbling the planet off its axis enough for the asteroid to pass harmlessly by. Yep, no consequences there. 91m; DVD, Blu-Ray. **C:** Jason Brooks; Tia Carrere; Robert Davi; Charles Byun; Tim Russ; Directed by Christopher Ray; Written by Adam Lipsius; Cinematography by Laura Beth Love; Music by Chris Ridenhour. **A:** Jr. High-Adult. **P:** Entertainment. **U:** Home. **L:** English. **Mov-Ent:** Science Fiction. **Acq:** Purchase. **Dist:** The Asylum.

Asteroids, Comets, and Meteorites 1960
The show illustrates the newest objects in the solar system: man-made or artificial satellites. 11m; VHS, 3/4 U. **Pr:** BFA Educational Media. **A:** Jr. High-Sr. High. **P:** Education. **U:** Institution, SURA. **L:** English, Spanish. **Hea-Sci:** Astronomy. **Acq:** Purchase. **Dist:** Phoenix Learning Group.

Asteroids: Deadly Impact 1997
Dr. Eugene Shoemaker explains the small but deadly space objects that have scarred planets throughout the solar system, and their past and future threats to the planet Earth. 60m; VHS; Closed Captioned. **A:** Jr. High-Adult-Sr. High. **P:** Education. **U:** Home, Institution. **Gen-Edu:** Science, Astronomy, Geography. **Acq:** Purchase. **Dist:** National Geographic; Zenger Media. $19.95 19.98.

Asthma 1980
A look at the causes of asthma including viral infections, pollution and stress. Also examined are the responsibilities incurred by the patient and family when using medication. 14m; VHS, 3/4 U. **Pr:** Altschul Group. **A:** Family. **P:** Education. **U:** Institution, SURA. **Hea-Sci:** Respiratory System, Health Education, Medical Care. **Acq:** Purchase, Rent/Lease. **Dist:** Discovery Education. $199.00.

Asthma 1989
An entertaining informative view of asthma and the problems it can trigger. 19m; VHS, 3/4 U. **Pr:** Professional Research. **A:** Adult. **P:** Education. **U:** Institution, SURA. **Hea-Sci:** Respiratory System, Diseases. **Acq:** Purchase, Rent/Lease. **Dist:** Films for the Humanities & Sciences. $149.00.

Asthma in Childhood 197?
This series covers the childhood disease and how to diagnose and treat it. Programs are available individually. 25m; VHS, 3/4 U. **Pr:** Trainex. **A:** College-Adult. **P:** Professional. **U:** Institution. **Hea-Sci:** Respiratory System. **Acq:** Purchase, Rent/Lease. **Dist:** Medcom Inc.

Indiv. Titles: 1. Etiology and Pathophysiology 2. Patient History and a Clinical View 3. Diagnosis Testing 4. Treatment, Blood Gases, Status Asthmaticus 5. Prevention and Hyposensitization.

Asthma Kids: A Parents' Video Support System 1992
Provides an explanation of chronic lung disease, including case histories, medication, and equipment. Offers support to caregivers of children with asthma and includes a presentation about helping children cope. 75m; VHS. **A:** Adult. **P:** Instruction. **U:** Institution, Home. **Hea-Sci:** Health Education, Children. **Acq:** Purchase. **Dist:** Cambridge Educational. $49.95.

Asthma Super Start 1996
Explains asthma for children and teens. Stresses the possibility of a complete and fulfilled life with asthma. 13m; VHS. **A:** Family. **P:** Education. **U:** Home, Institution. **Hea-Sci:** Health Education, Diseases, Patient Education. **Acq:** Purchase, Rent/Lease. **Dist:** AJN Video Library/Lippincott Williams & Wilkins. $200.00.

Asthma: What You Need to Know 1993
Ten million Americans struggle with asthma and more than a third of them are children. Sufferers learn to understand and manage the illness. 16m; VHS. **A:** Family. **P:** Education. **U:** Institution. **Hea-Sci:** Health Education. **Acq:** Purchase. **Dist:** Baker and Taylor. $59.95.

Astoria 2000 (R) — ★★
The Astoria section of Queens is heavily Greek-American with all its ethnic traditions. Alex (Stear) is 28 and wants to escape his stagnant life by joining an archeological expedition to find the lost tomb of Alexander the Great. His father Demo (Setrakian) expects Alex to help with the family business. Alex isn't happy until Greek art restorer Elena (Turco) pays a visit and suddenly things look a lot brighter. 103m; DVD. **C:** Rick Stear; Ed Setrakian; Paige Turco; Joseph (Joe) D'Onofrio; Directed by Nick Efteriades; Written by Nick Efteriades; Cinematography by Elia Lyssey; Music by Nikos Papazoglou. **A:** Sr. High-Adult. **P:** Entertainment. **U:** Home. **Mov-Ent. Acq:** Purchase.

The Astounding She-Monster 1958 — **Bomb!**
How can you not love a movie with a title like this? A bad script and snail-paced plot are a good start. A geologist wanting only to be left alone with his rocks survives a brush with the kidnappers of a wealthy heiress only to happen upon an alien spacecraft that's crashed nearby. At the helm is a very tall, high-heeled fem-alien in an obligatory skintight space outfit. Excellent, our rock jock thinks, but it seems she kills with the slightest touch. For connoisseurs of truly bad movies. 60m/B/W; VHS, DVD. **C:** Robert Clarke; Kenne Duncan; Marilyn Harvey; Jeanne Tatum; Shirley Kilpatrick; Ewing Miles Brown; Directed by Ronnie Ashcroft; Written by Frank Hall; Cinematography by William C. Thompson; Music by Guenther Kauer. **Pr:** American International Pictures. **A:** Jr. High-Adult. **P:** Entertainment. **U:** Home. **Mov-Ent:** Science Fiction, Women. **Acq:** Purchase. **Dist:** Image Entertainment Inc.; Sinister Cinema.

Astral Projection and Remote Viewing 1997
Video hypnosis to promote astral projection and clairvoyant perception. 90m; VHS. **A:** Adult. **P:** Instruction. **U:** Home. **Hea-Sci:** Self-Help. **Acq:** Purchase. **Dist:** Valley of the Sun Publishing. $29.95.

Astro Boy 2009 (PG) — ★★½
Energetic—if somewhat violent—adaptation of the Japanese manga books and the 1963 anime TV series. Set in Metro City, an orbiting world above a polluted Earth, robot Astro Boy (Highmore) is created by grieving scientist Dr. Tenma (Cage) as a replacement for his deceased son. When he can't fulfill his "father's" expectations, the rejected Astro Boy finds a home amidst Earth's scavengers but must return to Metro City when he learns everyone is in danger from polluting red energy (Astro Boy is powered by clean blue energy) and save the day. 94m; Blu-Ray, On Demand, Wide. **C:** Voice(s) by Freddie Highmore; Nicolas Cage; Donald Sutherland; Kristen Bell; Bill Nighy; Nathan Lane; Eugene Levy; Matt Lucas; Samuel L. Jackson; Narrated by Charlize Theron; Directed by David Bowers; Written by Timothy Harris; Cinematography by Pepe Valencia; Music by John Ottman. **Pr:** Maryann Garger; Imagi Animation Studios; Summit Entertainment. **A:** Family. **P:** Entertainment. **U:** Home. **L:** English. **Mov-Ent:** Animation & Cartoons, Science. **Acq:** Purchase. **Dist:** Summit Entertainment; Amazon.com Inc.; Movies Unlimited.

Astro Boy: The Lost Episode 1963 — ★★
In "The Beast From 20 Fathoms," a group of jewel thieves disappears near Lake Foggybottom. The lake is drained revealing a monster whose hypnotic venom allows it to make humans its slaves. Of course, Astro Boy, the boy robot, is immune and more than able to take on the monster. This is the episode that creator Osamu Tezuka threw in the trash, intending for it never to be seen. Also includes "The Snow Lion" which finds an unearthly snow shutting down all man-made sources of energy. Of course, it's really a clever alien invasion. Objectively, the second episode on the tape is better than the lost episode, but the lost episode is interesting. In the overall TV series, these episodes are numbers 34 and 52, respectively. 50m/B/W; VHS. **A:** College-Adult. **P:** Entertainment. **U:** Home. **Mov-Ent:** Animation & Cartoons, Animation & Cartoons, Television Series. **Acq:** Purchase. **Dist:** The Right Stuf Inc. $14.95.

Astro Boy, Vol. 1 1963 — ★★★
Grief-stricken after the loss of his son, a brilliant scientist creates a robot boy. For years things are wonderful, but then the scientist becomes distressed that his "son" can't grow like normal boys. He gives Astro Boy to a circus where a cruel ringmaster tries to force him to fight with other robots. "The Birth of Astro Boy," is a strangely troubled beginning for the sunny-natured robot seen later in the series. But this beginning lends a believability to Astro Boy's character and shows his first heroic impulses. Next in "The Monster Machine" a scientist gets plans for a strange device via a transmission from outer space. Astro Boy and his kindly guardian Dr. Elefun have misgivings, but no one will listen to them until the alien machine starts absorbing all the other machines. A good action-packed episode with lots of humor. The first volume of a 12-volume series. Some people will fondly remember this series from its run on North American TV during their youths. The animation is a little better than might be expected for TV fare from the 60s. 50m/B/W; VHS. **C:** Directed by Osamu Tezuka. **Pr:** Mushi Productions. **A:** College-Adult. **P:** Entertainment. **U:** Home. **Mov-Ent:** Animation & Cartoons, Animation & Cartoons, Television Series. **Acq:** Purchase. **Dist:** The Right Stuf Inc.; Tapeworm Video Distributors Inc. $19.95.

Astro Boy, Vol. 2 1963 — ★★
"The Terrible Time Gun" sends Dr. Elefun and his lab, plus Astro Boy back to the 12th century where Astro Boy faces some 21st century robots. Next, in "One Million Mammoth Snails," Astro Boy visits Professor Nuttyfruitcake who earns his name with a bunch of crazy experiments. The original episodes were dubbed for broadcast in the U.S. Some children might find the episodes rather dated, but the ones willing to give them a chance might be pleasantly surprised. 50m/B/W; VHS. **C:** Directed by Osamu Tezuka. **Pr:** Mushi Productions. **A:** College-Adult. **P:** Entertainment. **U:** Home. **Mov-Ent:** Animation & Cartoons, Animation & Cartoons, Television Series. **Acq:** Purchase. **Dist:** The Right Stuf Inc.; Tapeworm Video Distributors Inc. $19.95.

Astro Boy, Vol. 3 1963
Contains "Super Brain" and "Mystery of the Amless Dam," two vintage Japanese-animated films featuring super kid Astro Boy. 50m/B/W; VHS. **C:** Directed by Osamu Tezuka. **Pr:** Mushi Productions. **A:** Family. **P:** Entertainment. **U:** Home. **Mov-Ent:** Animation & Cartoons, Television Series, Science Fiction. **Acq:** Purchase. **Dist:** Tapeworm Video Distributors Inc. $19.95.

Astro Boy, Vol. 4 1963
Two more fly-boy adventures, "The Magic Punch Card" and "The Great Rocket Robbery." 50m/B/W; VHS. **C:** Directed by Osamu Tezuka. **Pr:** Mushi Productions. **A:** Family. **P:** Entertainment. **U:** Home. **Mov-Ent:** Animation & Cartoons, Science Fiction, Television Series. **Acq:** Purchase. **Dist:** Tapeworm Video Distributors Inc. $19.95.

Astro Boy, Vol. 5 1963
Includes "Shipwreck in Space" and "Gift of Zeo" from the vintage television series. 50m/B/W; VHS. **C:** Directed by Osamu Tezuka. **Pr:** Mushi Productions. **A:** Family. **P:** Entertainment. **U:** Home. **Mov-Ent:** Animation & Cartoons, Science Fiction, Television Series. **Acq:** Purchase. **Dist:** Tapeworm Video Distributors Inc. $19.95.

Astro Boy, Vol. 6 1963
Includes "Mystery of the Metal Men" and "Gangor, the Monster." 50m/B/W; VHS. **C:** Directed by Osamu Tezuka. **Pr:** Mushi Productions. **A:** Family. **P:** Entertainment. **U:** Home. **Mov-Ent:** Animation & Cartoons, Science Fiction, Television Series. **Acq:** Purchase. **Dist:** Tapeworm Video Distributors Inc. $19.95.

Astro Boy, Vol. 7 1963
Two more Japanese film features, "Brother Jetto" and "Dogma Palace." 50m/B/W; VHS. **C:** Directed by Osamu Tezuka. **Pr:** Mushi Productions. **A:** Family. **P:** Entertainment. **U:** Home. **Mov-Ent:** Animation & Cartoons, Science Fiction, Television Series. **Acq:** Purchase. **Dist:** Tapeworm Video Distributors Inc. $19.95.

Astro Boy, Vol. 8 1963
"The Mad Beltway" and "Mission to the Middle of the World" from the classic Japanese series. 50m/B/W; VHS. **C:** Directed by Osamu Tezuka. **Pr:** Mushi Productions. **A:** Family. **P:** Entertainment. **U:** Home. **Mov-Ent:** Animation & Cartoons, Science Fiction, Television Series. **Acq:** Purchase. **Dist:** Tapeworm Video Distributors Inc. $19.95.

Astro Boy, Vol. 9 1963
"The Hooligan Whodunit" and "Return of Cleopatra." 50m/B/W; VHS. **C:** Directed by Osamu Tezuka. **Pr:** Mushi Productions. **A:** Family. **P:** Entertainment. **U:** Home. **Mov-Ent:** Animation & Cartoons, Science Fiction, Television Series. **Acq:** Purchase. **Dist:** Tapeworm Video Distributors Inc. $19.95.

Astro Boy, Vol. 10 1963
Contains "Inca Gold Fever" and "Hullabaloo Land." 50m/B/W; VHS. **C:** Directed by Osamu Tezuka. **Pr:** Mushi Productions. **A:** Family. **P:** Entertainment. **U:** Home. **Mov-Ent:** Animation & Cartoons, Science Fiction, Television Series. **Acq:** Purchase. **Dist:** Tapeworm Video Distributors Inc. $19.95.

Astro Boy: Volume 1 200? (Unrated)
Japanese animated adventure series. During his grief Dr. Boynton creates a super-robot in the image of his deceased son. Astro Boy can swim oceans, leap mountains, and even fly but he still cannot replacement his real son so the doctor soon abandons his creation. Dr. Packadermus J. Elefun from the Institute of Science discovers and befriends Astro Boy and together they embark on many adventures as they crusade against evil forces in the world. 26 episodes. 550m; DVD. **A:** Primary-Jr. High. **P:** Entertainment. **U:** Home. **Chl-Juv:** Television Series, Animation & Cartoons, Action-Adventure. **Acq:** Purchase. **Dist:** The Right Stuf Inc. $49.99.

Astro Boy: Volume 1 2008 (Unrated)
Fox Television series with updated, latest technology animation based on the original 1963 series inspired by the comic created by the "father of anime," Osamu Tezuka. 10 episodes. 202m; DVD. **A:** Primary-Jr. High. **P:** Entertainment. **U:** Home. **Chl-Juv:** Anime. **Acq:** Purchase. **Dist:** Sony Pictures Home Entertainment Inc. $14.99.

Astro Boy: Volume 2 200? (Unrated)
Japanese animated adventure series. Astro Boy continues to use his strength, rocket-power, kindness, and courage as he battles aliens, rogue robots and evil geniuses for the sake of humankind's safety. 26 episodes. 594m; DVD. **A:** Primary-Jr. High. **P:** Entertainment. **U:** Home. **Chl-Juv:** Television Series, Animation & Cartoons, Action-Adventure. **Acq:** Purchase. **Dist:** The Right Stuf Inc. $59.99.

The Astro-Zombies 1967 (Unrated) — **Bomb!**
A contender as one of the worst movies of all time. Carradine plays a mad scientist creating zombies who eat people's guts. Cult favorite Satana stars. Co-written and co-produced by Rogers of "M*A*S*H" fame. 83m; VHS, DVD, Wide. **C:** Tura Satana; Wendell Corey; John Carradine; Tom Pace; Joan Patrick; Rafael Campos; William Bagdad; Joseph Hoover; Victor Izay; Vincent Barbi; Rod Wilmoth; Directed by Ted V. Mikels; Written by Ted V. Mikels; Wayne Rogers; Cinematography by Robert Maxwell; Music by Nico (Nicholas Carras) Karaski. **Pr:** T.V. Mikels Film Productions. **A:** College-Adult. **P:** Entertainment. **U:** Home. **Mov-Ent:** Science Fiction. **Acq:** Purchase. **Dist:** Movies Unlimited. $9.99.

Astro-Zombies M3: Cloned 2010 (Unrated) — ★
Eight years after the preceeding film, the government resurrects the Astro-Zombies to use in war not thinking that this is a B-movie and that bringing back monsters will bite them on the heinie. Had it not been shot on digital video cam it might have been much more fun. 104m; DVD. **C:** Fletcher Sharp; Sean Morelli; Francine York; Directed by Ted V. Mikels; Written by Ted V. Mikels; Cory Udler; Cinematography by Ted V. Mikels. **A:** Sr. High-Adult. **P:** Entertainment. **U:** Home. **L:** English. **Mov-Ent. Acq:** Purchase. **Dist:** Gotham Distributing Corp. $9.98.

Astro-Zombies M4: Invaders from Cyberspace 2012 (Unrated) — ★
The Astro-Zombies are pretty upset over the last film in the series. Armed with their own planet, some nifty UFOs, and the ability to kill people over the Internet, they invade once again. 120m; DVD. **C:** Sean Morelli; Jaime Preston Lynch; Ted V. Mikels; Directed by Ted V. Mikels; Written by Ted V. Mikels; Cory Udler; Cinematography by Ted V. Mikels. **A:** Sr. High-Adult. **P:** Entertainment. **U:** Home. **L:** English. **Mov-Ent. Acq:** Purchase. **Dist:** Gotham Distributing Corp. $9.98.

Astrodudes: Shooting for the Moon 19??
Five interracial pre-adolescents beam a news program on rocket science to planet Alpha Centaurus. Their show is a look at the history of space exploration, including information on U.S.-Russian experiments, clips of JFK, and Neil Armstrong's walk on the moon, and footage and data from NASA, mixed with some comedy and rap. 35m; VHS. **A:** Primary-Jr. High. **P:** Entertainment. **U:** Home. **Chl-Juv:** Space Exploration, Journalism, Education. **Acq:** Purchase. **Dist:** Golden Book Video. $9.95.

Astrology and Science 199?
Inventor and author Arthur M. Young explains the differences between the planets in astrological terms and discusses the measure formulea of physics as expressed in an isomorphic manner to the zodiac. Young used these angular relationships while developing the Bell Helicopter. 90m; DVD. **A:** Adult. **P:** Education. **U:** Home, Institution. **Gen-Edu:** Astrology, Science. **Acq:** Purchase. **Dist:** Thinking Allowed Productions. $49.95.

The Astronaut Farmer 2007 (PG) — ★★½
NASA engineer Charlie Farmer (Thornton) left the space program for his family's failing Texas ranch but never gave up his dream of being an astronaut. He's got his very own shiny silver space suit and is building an actual rocket in his barn. His family and friends see Charlie as a larger-than-life eccentric but when he tries to buy rocket fuel the feds think Charlie's some kind of homegrown terrorist. Film treats Charlie and his dreams matter-of-factly as does Thornton, with Madsen luminous as his devoted wife and Simmons blustering as his fed nemesis. 104m; DVD. **C:** Billy Bob Thornton; Virginia Madsen; Bruce Dern; J.K. Simmons; Tim Blake Nelson; Max Thieriot; Jon(athan) Gries; Mark Polish; Jasper Polish; Logan Polish; Cameo(s) Bruce Willis; Directed by Michael Polish; Written by Mark Polish; Michael Polish; Cinematography by M. David Mullen; Music by Stuart Matthewman. **Pr:** Paula Weinstein; Mark Polish; Michael Polish; Mark Polish; Michael Polish; Len Amato; Spring Creek Productions; Polish Brothers Construction; Warner Bros. **A:** Jr. High-Adult. **P:** Entertainment. **U:** Home. **L:** English. **Mov-Ent:** Federal Bureau of Investigation (FBI). **Acq:** Purchase. **Dist:** Warner Home Video, Inc.

Astronaut Training STS-1 Prime Crew 1981
A NASA news release on Space Shuttle astronaut training. Silent. 7m; 3/4 U. **Pr:** National Aeronautics and Space Administration. **A:** Jr. High-Adult. **P:** Education. **U:** BCTV, SURA. **Hea-Sci:** Space Exploration. **Acq:** Free Loan. **Dist:** NASA Lyndon B. Johnson Space Center.

Astronauts 1998
This up close and personal look at the crew of a NASA space shuttle follows the astronauts from the day they are selected to the completion of their mission. 90m; VHS; Closed Captioned. **A:** Jr. High-Adult. **P:** Education. **U:** Home. **Gen-Edu:** Documentary Films, Space Exploration. **Acq:** Purchase. **Dist:** PBS Home Video. $19.98.

Astronauts: United States Project Mercury 1980
Examines the selection, testing, and training of the Mercury Astronauts. 28m; 3/4 U. **Pr:** National Aeronautics and Space Administration. **A:** Primary-Adult. **P:** Education. **U:** BCTV,

SURA. **Hea-Sci**: Space Exploration. **Acq:** Free Loan. **Dist:** NASA Lyndon B. Johnson Space Center. $24.99.

An Astronaut's View of Earth 1992
Far out look at aerial photography, including footage taken by shuttle crew members. Stunning visual panoramas are a delight to behold. 60m; VHS. **C:** Narrated by William Shatner. **Pr:** Jean-Jacques Annaud. **A:** Jr. High-Adult. **P:** Entertainment. **U:** Home, Institution. **Gen-Edu**: Space Exploration, Photography. **Acq:** Purchase, Rent/Lease. **Dist:** Films for the Humanities & Sciences. $149.00.

The Astronaut's Wife 1999 (R) — ★½
Astronaut Spencer Armacost (Depp) just isn't the same guy after he returns from a nearly fatal space shuttle mission. He and his wife, Jillian (Theron), suddenly move to New York and she definitely notices some behavorial changes (he likes to listen to the test pattern on the TV screen). Oh, and then the little woman discovers she's pregnant and things get very "Rosemary's Baby." Theron's role is also very much like her beleagured wife in "The Devil's Advocate," since everyone seems to think Jillian's nuts. Disappointingly formulaic; Depp's more believable in quirky roles in quirky movies. 109m; VHS, DVD, Blu-Ray, Wide. **C:** Johnny Depp; Charlize Theron; Joe Morton; Tom Noonan; Blair Brown; Nick Cassavetes; Clea DuVall; Donna Murphy; Samantha Eggar; Directed by Rand Ravich; Written by Rand Ravich; Cinematography by Allen Daviau; Music by George S. Clinton. **Pr:** Andrew Lazar; Mark Johnson; New Line Cinema. **A:** Sr. High-Adult. **P:** Entertainment. **U:** Home. **Mov-Ent**: Mystery & Suspense, Marriage, Pregnancy. **Acq:** Purchase. **Dist:** New Line Home Video.

The Astronomers 1991
Richard Chamberlain narrates a 6-part look at the world of astronomy and the state of the technology being used to explore space. Tapes are available individually or as a boxed set. 60m; VHS, CC, 3/4 U. **C:** Narrated by Richard Chamberlain. **Pr:** PBS; KCET. **A:** Jr. High-Adult. **P:** Education. **U:** Institution, CCTV, CATV, Home. **Gen-Edu**: Documentary Films, Space Exploration, Science. **Acq:** Purchase. **Dist:** PBS Home Video; Facets Multimedia Inc.; University of Washington Educational Media Collection. $19.95.
Indiv. Titles: 1. Prospecting for Planets 2. Searching for Black Holes 3. Stardust 4. Waves of the Future 5. Where is the Rest of the Universe? 6. Window to Creation.

The Astronomers: Prospecting for Planets 1991
See how astronomers search for evidence of worlds beyond our own as well as a look at the accomplishments of the Voyager mission, including a fly-by of the planet Neptune. An episode from the PBS series. 60m; VHS, CC. **C:** Narrated by Richard Chamberlain. **Pr:** PBS. **A:** Jr. High-Adult. **P:** Education. **U:** Home. **Gen-Edu**: Documentary Films, Space Exploration, Astronomy. **Acq:** Purchase. **Dist:** PBS Home Video; Facets Multimedia Inc.; University of Washington Educational Media Collection. $19.95.

The Astronomers: Searching for Black Holes 1991
Search for black holes with world-renowned scientists in this beautifully produced episode from PBS' "Astronomers" series. 60m; VHS, CC. **C:** Narrated by Richard Chamberlain. **Pr:** PBS; KCET. **A:** Jr. High-Adult. **P:** Education. **U:** Home. **Gen-Edu**: Documentary Films, Space Exploration, Science. **Acq:** Purchase. **Dist:** PBS Home Video; Facets Multimedia Inc.; University of Washington Educational Media Collection. $19.95.

The Astronomers: Stardust 1991
Join scientist Leo Blitz as he and other scientists explore the lives and deaths of stars. Features the supernova of 1987. 60m; VHS, CC. **C:** Narrated by Richard Chamberlain. **Pr:** PBS; KCET. **A:** Jr. High-Adult. **P:** Education. **U:** Home. **Gen-Edu**: Documentary Films, Space Exploration, Astronomy. **Acq:** Purchase. **Dist:** PBS Home Video; Facets Multimedia Inc.; University of Washington Educational Media Collection. $19.95.

The Astronomers: Waves of the Future 1991
Soviet scientist Leonid Grishchuk and American scientist Kip Thorne explore the mystery of gravity waves. Gravity waves, a kind of bubble in space and time, could be the key to explaining supernovas and even the Big Bang. 60m; VHS, CC. **C:** Narrated by Richard Chamberlain. **Pr:** PBS; KCET. **A:** Jr. High-Adult. **P:** Education. **U:** Home. **Gen-Edu**: Documentary Films, Astronomy, Science. **Acq:** Purchase. **Dist:** PBS Home Video; Facets Multimedia Inc.; University of Washington Educational Media Collection. $19.95.

The Astronomers: Where Is the Rest of the Universe? 1991
Astronomers try to explain the other 90% of the universe or "Dark Matter" as those in the know call it in this installment of PBS' "Astronomers" series. 60m; VHS, CC. **C:** Narrated by Richard Chamberlain. **Pr:** PBS. **A:** Jr. High-Adult. **P:** Education. **U:** Home. **Gen-Edu**: Documentary Films, Space Exploration, Astronomy. **Acq:** Purchase. **Dist:** PBS Home Video; Facets Multimedia Inc.; University of Washington Educational Media Collection. $19.95.

The Astronomers: Window to Creation 1991
Berkeley professors explore the mysterious Big Bang in this episode of PBS' "Astronomers" series. 60m; VHS, CC. **C:** Narrated by Richard Chamberlain. **Pr:** PBS; KCET. **A:** Jr. High-Adult. **P:** Education. **U:** Home. **Gen-Edu**: Documentary Films, Astronomy, Science. **Acq:** Purchase. **Dist:** PBS Home Video; Facets Multimedia Inc.; University of Washington Educational Media Collection. $19.95.

Astronomy 1973
This two-part program takes the viewer through the universe to investigate the life cycles of stars and some of the newest techniques in astronomy. 30m; 3/4 U, EJ. **Pr:** NETCHE. **A:** College-Adult. **P:** Education. **U:** Institution, CCTV, BCTV, SURA. **Hea-Sci**: Astronomy. **Acq:** Purchase, Rent/Lease, Subscription. **Dist:** NETCHE.
Indiv. Titles: 1. Star Birth in Our Galaxy 2. Recent Results in X-Ray Astronomy.

Astronomy: A New View of the Universe 1989
This tape examines scientific knowledge of the solar system, through findings of American and Europena solar probes and details ancient and Renaissance discoveries in astronomy, progressively, powerful telescope, and journeys into space. 26m; VHS, 3/4 U. **Pr:** Films for the Humanities and Sciences. **A:** College. **P:** Education. **U:** Institution, CCTV, CATV, BCTV. **Hea-Sci**: Astronomy. **Acq:** Purchase, Rent/Lease, Duplication License. **Dist:** Films for the Humanities & Sciences.

Astronomy: Perspectives 1985
A broad view for laymen about astronomical influences on life on earth, and the new technology which enables us to learn more about it. 28m; VHS. **Pr:** New Dimension Films. **A:** Jr. High-Adult. **P:** Education. **U:** Institution. **Hea-Sci**: Astronomy. **Acq:** Purchase, Rent/Lease. **Dist:** New Dimension Media.

Asunder 1999 — ★★½
Slick thriller with a familiar storyline. Michael (Beach) and wife Lauren (Morgan) are at the fairground with best friends Chance (Underwood) and his pregnant wife Roberta (Hicks). Roberta is tragically killed in a fall while riding the Ferris wheel. Michael and Lauren invite Chance to stay with them and the viewer learns that Lauren and Chance once had an extramarital affair. Then Chance decides to wreck her marriage and get Lauren back. 102m; VHS, DVD. **C:** Blair Underwood; Debbi (Deborah) Morgan; Michael Beach; Marva Hicks; Directed by Tim Reid; Written by Eric Lee Bowers; Cinematography by Johnny (John W.) Simmons; Music by Lionel Cole. **A:** Sr. High-Adult. **P:** Entertainment. **U:** Home. **Mov-Ent**: Mystery & Suspense, Marriage. **Acq:** Purchase. **Dist:** Buena Vista Home Entertainment.

ASVAB Review 1986
Men and women who wish to join the armed forces must take the Armed Services Vocational Aptitude Battery. This video will sharpen the academic and technical skills of the viewer, and help him prepare for a career in the military. 120m; VHS. **Pr:** VAI. **A:** Adult. **P:** Education. **U:** Home. **Gen-Edu**: Education. **Acq:** Purchase. **Dist:** Moonbeam Publications Inc.; Video Aided Instruction Inc. $29.95.

Aswad: Always Wicked 1991
The British reggae band performs "Set Them Free," "Don't Turn Around" and more. 42m; VHS. **Pr:** Island Visual Arts. **A:** Jr. High-Adult. **P:** Entertainment. **U:** Home. **Mov-Ent**: Music Video, Music--Performance. **Acq:** Purchase. **Dist:** Music Video Distributors. $16.95.

Aswad & Pablo Moses: Reggae in the Hills 198? (Unrated)
The U.K.'s top reggae/rock band plays live with Pablo Moses. 90m; VHS. **A:** Jr. High-Adult. **P:** Entertainment. **U:** Home. **Mov-Ent**: Music--Performance. **Acq:** Purchase. **Dist:** Music Video Distributors. $39.95.

Aswad: Distant Thunder Live 1988
The British reggae band performs live at the Hammersmith Odeon, December 1988. Songs include the hits "Don't Turn Around" and "Give a Little Love." 70m; VHS. **Pr:** Island Visual Arts. **A:** Jr. High-Adult. **P:** Entertainment. **U:** Home. **Mov-Ent**: Music--Performance. **Acq:** Purchase. **Dist:** Music Video Distributors. $19.95.

Aswad: Live at Light House Studio 198?
The top reggae/rock band in Britain performs their best stuff live. 60m; VHS. **A:** Jr. High-Adult. **P:** Entertainment. **U:** Home. **Mov-Ent**: Music--Performance. **Acq:** Purchase. **Dist:** Music Video Distributors. $99.95.

Aswang 2003 (Unrated) — ★★
The Aswang are shapeshifting Filipino vampires with long tongues, who sit on the roofs of houses and drink blood from sleeping victims by inserting their tongues down the house into the sleeping occupants. Some are particularly fond of unborn children. Kat (Tina Ona Paukstelis) is unwed and pregnant, and would prefer to give her child up for adoption instead of having an abortion. A family of creepy rich eccentrics accepts her offer. You can pretty much see where this is going. 82m; DVD. **C:** Norman Moses; Tina Ona Paukstelis; John Kishline; Flora Coker; Mildred Nierras; Jamie Jacobs Anderson; Daniel Demarco; Rosalie Seifert; Directed by Wyre Martin; Barry Poltermann; Written by Wyre Martin; Barry Poltermann; Frank L. Anderson; Cinematography by Jim Zabilla; Music by Ken Brahmstedt. **A:** Sr. High-Adult. **P:** Entertainment. **U:** Home. **Mov-Ent**: Horror, Pregnancy. **Acq:** Purchase. **Dist:** Mondo Macabro, On Moratorium.

Asylum 19??
Profiles the patients and caretakers at an institution for the criminally insane. 60m; VHS. **A:** Sr. High-Adult. **P:** Entertainment. **U:** Institution. **Gen-Edu**: Psychology, Mental Health, Documentary Films. **Acq:** Purchase. **Dist:** Ambrose Video Publishing, Inc. $99.95.

Asylum 199?
Chronicles how patients try to deal with their illnesses at the Patten State Hospital for the criminally insane. 30m; VHS. **A:** Sr. High-Adult. **P:** Entertainment. **U:** Institution. **Gen-Edu**: Mental Health, Documentary Films. **Acq:** Purchase. **Dist:** Ambrose Video Publishing, Inc. $69.95.

Asylum 1972 (PG) — ★★½
Four strange and chilling stories weave together in this film. A murderer's victim seeks retribution. A tailor seems to be collecting his bills. A man who makes voodoo dolls...only to become one later on. A woman plagued by a double. A doctor visiting the asylum tells each tale. Horrifying and grotesque, not as humorless as American horror films. 100m; VHS, DVD. **C:** Peter Cushing; Herbert Lom; Britt Ekland; Barbara Parkins; Patrick Magee; Barry Morse; Robert Powell; Richard Todd; Charlotte Rampling; Ann(e) Firbank; Sylvia Syms; James Villiers; Geoffrey Bayldon; Megs Jenkins; Directed by Roy Ward Baker; Written by Robert Bloch; Cinematography by Denys Coop. **Pr:** Cinerama Releasing. **A:** Family. **P:** Entertainment. **U:** Home. **Mov-Ent**: Horror. **Acq:** Purchase. **Dist:** Movies Unlimited. $9.99.

Asylum 1988
The complex and controversial story of America's insane asylums is documented in this acclaimed, disturbing film. 57m; VHS, 3/4 U. **Pr:** Sarah Mondale. **A:** Jr. High-Adult. **P:** Education. **U:** Institution, SURA. **Gen-Edu**: Psychiatry, Public Affairs, Patient Care. **Acq:** Purchase, Rent/Lease. **Dist:** Direct Cinema Ltd. $350.00.

Asylum 1997 (R) — ★½
Unstable investigator Nick Tordone (Patrick) looks into his shrink's supposed suicide by become a patient at the doctor's mental hospital. By what he finds is serial killer Sullivan Rane (McDowell) and a doctor (Gibson) doing dangerous mind control experiments. Tension holds up well until the unfortunate finale. 92m; VHS. **C:** Robert Patrick; Malcolm McDowell; Henry Gibson; Sarah Douglas; Jason Schombing; Kevin Anthony Cole; Peter Brown; Directed by James Seale; Written by James Seale; Cinematography by David Rakoczy; Music by Alan Williams. **Pr:** Norstar Entertainment. **A:** College-Adult. **P:** Entertainment. **U:** Home. **Mov-Ent**: Mystery & Suspense, Suicide. **Acq:** Purchase. **Dist:** Monarch Home Video.

Asylum 2005 (R) — ★★
Sex in the loony bin. In 1959, frustrated Stella Raphael (Richardson) accompanies her hubby Max (Bonneville) to the titular Victorian heap where he is the new superintendent. Stella meets hottie patient Edgar (Csokas), who helps out around the grounds, and the two are soon helping themselves to each other. Despite the fact that Edgar's locked up because he beat his wife to death in a jealous rage. Add to the mix Edgar's manipulative doctor, Peter Cleave (McKellen), and you've got a melodrama at high boil, just waiting to bubble over. As over-the-top as it sounds; adapted from the novel by Patrick McGrath. 90m; DVD. **C:** Natasha Richardson; Ian McKellen; Marton Csokas; Hugh Bonneville; Judy Parfitt; Sean Harris; Gus Lewis; Wanda Ventham; Joss Ackland; Directed by David Mackenzie; Written by Patrick Marber; Chrys Balis; Cinematography by Giles Nuttgens; Music by Mark Mancina. **Pr:** Mace Neufeld; Laurence Borg; David E. Allen; Paramount Classics; Seven Arts Pictures. **A:** Sr. High-Adult. **P:** Entertainment. **U:** Home. **L:** English. **Mov-Ent**: Mystery & Suspense, Sex & Sexuality, Drama. **Dist:** Paramount Pictures Corp. $29.99.

Asylum of Satan 1972 (Unrated) — ★
A beautiful concert pianist is savagely tortured by a madman in the Asylum of Satan. Filmed on location in Louisville, Kentucky. 87m; VHS, DVD. **C:** Charles Kissinger; Carla Borelli; Nick Jolly; Sherry Steiner; Directed by William Girdler; Written by William Girdler. **Pr:** Majestic International Pictures. **A:** Sr. High-Adult. **P:** Entertainment. **U:** Home. **Mov-Ent**: Horror. **Acq:** Purchase. **Dist:** VCI Entertainment. $19.95.

Asylum of the Damned 2003 (R) — ★★
Naive psychologist believes he can tackle the worst offenders at the criminally insane asylum but isn't ready to deal with the hideous truth behind the high volume of vanishing inmates. 85m; VHS, DVD, Blu-Ray. **C:** Bruce Payne; Tracy Scoggins; Tommy (Tiny) Lister; Gregory Wagrowski; Bill McKinney; Randall England; Kyle T. Heffner; Michael Earl Reid; David Thomas; Matt Stasi; Julia Lee; Joe Sabatino; Deborah Flora; Stefan Marchand; Directed by Philip Jones; Written by Matthew McCombs; Cinematography by Mark Melville; Music by Valentine Leone; Steve Bauman. **A:** Sr. High-Adult. **P:** Entertainment. **U:** Home. **Mov-Ent**: Hospitals, Horror. **Acq:** Purchase. **Dist:** Sony Pictures Home Entertainment Inc. $24.99.

Asynchronous Transfer Mode (ATM) 199?
An overview of the standardized cell relay technique. 180m; VHS. **A:** Adult. **P:** Vocational. **U:** Institution. **Bus-Ind**: Technology. **Acq:** Purchase. **Dist:** Telcordia Technologies Inc. $695.00.

At Any Cost 2000 (R) — ★★½
Ah, the music business. Austin, Texas band Beyond Gravity has a shot at a major recording career in L.A. when they're signed by an indie label. Leader Lance (Mills) vows to wife/bandmember Chelsea (Flannigan) that they won't blow their big chance but problems arise quickly. Seems Lance's brother Mike (Franco) can't control his drug problem and ambitious pal Ben (Quinn) wants to strike out on his own when the band starts to go south. Typical price-of-fame cable drama. 92m; VHS, CC. **C:** Eddie Mills; James Franco; Glenn Quinn; Maureen Flannigan; Cyia Batten; Directed by Charles Winkler; Written by Bruce Taylor; Roderick Taylor; Cinematography by Robert Steadman. **A:** Sr. High-Adult. **P:** Entertainment. **U:** Home. **Mov-Ent**: Music--Pop/Rock, Drug Abuse. **Acq:** Purchase. **Dist:** Paramount Pictures Corp.

At Arm's Length 1996
Features the individual journey of aging and looks at the adjustments that society must make as generations of people live longer. 52m; VHS. **A:** Adult-Family. **P:** Education. **U:** Institution. **Gen-Edu**: Aging. **Acq:** Purchase. **Dist:** Aquarius Health Care Media. $195.00.

At Close Range 1986 (R) — ★★★
Based on the true story of Bruce Johnston Sr. and Jr. in Brandywine River Valley, Pennsylvania. Father, Walken, tempts his teenaged son, Penn, into pursuing criminal activities with

talk of excitement and high living. Penn soon learns that his father is extremely dangerous and a bit unstable, but he's still fascinated by his wealth and power. Sometimes overbearing and depressing, but good acting and fancy camera work. A young cast of stars includes Masterson as the girl Penn tries to impress. Features Madonna's "Live to Tell." 115m; VHS, DVD, Wide, CC. **C:** Sean Penn; Christopher Walken; Christopher Penn; Mary Stuart Masterson; Crispin Glover; Kiefer Sutherland; Candy Clark; Tracey Walter; Millie Perkins; Alan Autry; David Strathairn; Eileen Ryan; Directed by James Foley; Written by Nicholas Kazan; Cinematography by Juan Ruiz-Anchia; Music by Patrick Leonard. **Pr:** Orion Pictures. **A:** Sr. High-Adult. **P:** Entertainment. **U:** Home. **Mov-Ent:** Crime Drama. **Acq:** Purchase. **Dist:** Lions Gate Television Corp. $79.98.

At Dawn, Overcoming All Difficulties 198?
Vasco de Gama's trip around Africa's Cape of Good Hope to India is examined as the expedition leading to Portugal's dominance throughout the Indian Ocean while in South America the Spaniards conquer the Inca, Maya and Aztec empires, subduing the native population and plundering the continent's riches. 17m; 3/4 U, Special order formats. **Pr:** Hobel Leiterman Productions. **A:** Jr. High-Adult. **P:** Education. **U:** Institution. **Gen-Edu:** History--Medieval, Explorers. **Acq:** Purchase. **Dist:** The Cinema Guild.

At First Sight 1995 (R) — ★½
Yakky pedestrian comedy about schleppy Lenny (Silverman) and his best friend, macho Joey (Cortese), trying to help each other out with their romantic crises. Lenny meets cute when he picks up Rhonda (Smith) at the planetarium while Joey beds a string of girls, all of whom are named Cindy, in an effort to get over the first Cindy who broke his heart. It's been done before—and better. 90m; VHS. **C:** Jonathan Silverman; Dan Cortese; Allison Smith; Monte Markham; Kathleen Freeman; Directed by Steven Pearl; Written by Ken Copel; Cinematography by Glenn Kershaw; Music by Richard Gibbs. **Pr:** Craig Saavedra; Jonathan Baruch; Mark Amin; Richard Becker; Pro Filmworks; Trimark Pictures. **A:** Sr. High-Adult. **P:** Entertainment. **U:** Home. **Mov-Ent. Acq:** Purchase. **Dist:** CinemaNow Inc.

At First Sight 1998 (PG-13) — ★★½
Slow-paced romantic drama stars Kilmer as a blind masseuse who falls for high-strung architect Sorvino. She persuades him to have an operation that restores his sight, and he's forced to adapt to a world he has never seen. Excellent supporting performances by McGillis as Kilmer's sister and Lane as the doctor that eases his transition. Kilmer does an outstanding job in making his character neither pitiful nor over-sentimental, which is rare in movies that center on disabilities. Based loosely on a case study by Dr. Oliver Sacks, whose work was also the basis for "Awakenings." 128m; VHS, DVD. **C:** Val Kilmer; Mira Sorvino; Kelly McGillis; Steven Weber; Bruce Davison; Nathan Lane; Ken Howard; Directed by Irwin Winkler; Written by Steve Levitt; Cinematography by John Seale; Music by Mark Isham. **A:** Jr. High-Adult. **P:** Entertainment. **U:** Home. **Mov-Ent:** Blindness, Drama, Architecture. **Acq:** Purchase. **Dist:** MGM Home Entertainment.

At Gunpoint 1955 (Unrated) — ★★
A store owner becomes the town hero when, by accident, he shoots and kills a bank robber. 81m; VHS. **C:** Fred MacMurray; Dorothy Malone; John Qualen; Walter Brennan; Directed by Alfred Werker; Cinematography by Ellsworth Fredericks. **Pr:** Allied Artists International. **A:** Sr. High-Adult. **P:** Entertainment. **U:** Home. **Mov-Ent:** Western. **Acq:** Purchase. **Dist:** Lions Gate Entertainment Inc. $39.95.

At Gunpoint 1990 (Unrated) — ★½
A no-account bank robber spends his six year stint in the slammer plotting his revenge. Having gone thoroughly stircrazy, the vengeful criminal stalks the lawman who put him away, like so many vengeful criminals before him. Run of the mill addition to big list of bad-guy-hunting-for-revenge flicks. 90m; VHS. **C:** Frank Kanig; Tain Bodkin; Scott Claflin; Directed by Steven Harris; Written by Steven Harris. **Pr:** Commonwealth Films. **A:** Adult. **P:** Entertainment. **U:** Home. **Mov-Ent. Acq:** Purchase. **Dist:** No Longer Available.

At Home with Mother Earth: A Study of Earth Architecture 19??
Looks at the rich tradition of "earth architecture," explaining what it is and analyzing the prejudices which hinder its acceptance into the modern world. Chronicles the historic struggle of this field's pioneers as well as the innovative and ecologically sound methods of current earth builders. Also illustrates how this concept affects architects, builders, code officials, the construction industry, and inhabitants. 40m; VHS. **A:** Sr. High-Adult. **P:** Education. **U:** Institution, SURA. **Gen-Edu:** Agriculture, Construction, Housing. **Acq:** Purchase. **Dist:** San Luis Video Publishing. $99.95.

At Home with the Braithwaites: Complete First Series 2000
Features the 2000-2003 BBC television series about Allison (Redman), a British woman who wins the European lottery on her 40th birthday but tries to hide it from her untrustworthy husband David (Davison) and greedy children. Includes: Allison puts some of her winnings towards starting a charity; her daughters attempt to get money given to Allison by her mother; David's affair becomes public knowledge; and she finally finds it impossible to keep her good fortune a secret. 6 episodes. 292m; DVD. **C:** Peter Davison; Amanda Redman; Linda Bellingham; Sylvia Syms; Julie Graham; Kevin Doyle; Sarah Smart. **A:** Jr. High-Adult. **P:** Entertainment. **U:** Home. **Mov-Ent:** Television Series, Comedy-Drama, Family. **Acq:** Purchase. **Dist:** Acorn Media Group Inc. $39.99.

At Home with the Braithwaites: Complete Second Series 2001
Features the 2000-2003 BBC television series about Allison (Redman), a British woman who wins the European lottery on her 40th birthday but tries to hide it from her untrustworthy husband David (Davison) and greedy children. Includes: the family moves into a mansion though it doesn't mean happiness; Allison considers divorce and begins seeing David's brother Graham (Stevenson); and David and Graham's argument takes a tragic turn. 8 episodes. 384m; DVD. **C:** Peter Davison; Amanda Redman; Linda Bellingham; Sylvia Syms; Julie Graham; Kevin Doyle; Sarah Smart; Ray Stevenson. **A:** Jr. High-Adult. **P:** Entertainment. **U:** Home. **Mov-Ent:** Television Series, Comedy-Drama, Family. **Acq:** Purchase. **Dist:** Acorn Media Group Inc. $59.99.

At Home with the Range: Cake Baking & Decorating 1995
Cake baking and decoration instruction from caterer Sharon Solomon. Includes recipes and helpful hints. 120m; VHS. **A:** Adult. **P:** Instruction. **U:** Home. **How-Ins:** Cooking. **Acq:** Purchase. **Dist:** Instructional Video. $14.95.

At Home with the Range: Candy 1995
Candy making instruction, including toffee, peanut brittle, fudge, and caramel. 70m; VHS. **A:** Adult. **P:** Instruction. **U:** Home. **How-Ins:** Cooking. **Acq:** Purchase. **Dist:** Instructional Video. $14.95.

At Home with the Range: Yeast Rolls & Quicker Breads 1995
Cooking instruction featuring rolls and bread. 80m; VHS. **A:** Adult. **P:** Instruction. **U:** Home. **How-Ins:** Cooking. **Acq:** Purchase. **Dist:** Instructional Video. $14.95.

At Home with the Webbers 1994 (R) — ★★
Gerald, Emma, Johnny, and Miranda Webber win a contest to star in a cable TV series about their lives. What they don't expect is that the series will become a hit or that all the family idosyncrasies will be exaggerated by stardom (the manipulative TV producer doesn't help). Over-the-top comedy requires tolerance but does have some amusing performances. 109m; VHS, CC. **C:** Jeffrey Tambor; Rita Taggart; Jennifer Tilly; David Arquette; Robby Benson; Brian Bloom; Caroline Goodall; Directed by Brad (Sean) Marlowe; Written by Brad (Sean) Marlowe. **A:** Sr. High-Adult. **P:** Entertainment. **U:** Home. **Mov-Ent:** Comedy--Black, Mass Media. **Acq:** Purchase. **Dist:** Lions Gate Television Corp. $89.98.

At Home with Zoo Animals 1992
Describes how zoos strive to provide living conditions for animals that most closely match their natural habitats. Presents information on feeding and caretaking, as well as explaining the crucial roles zoos play in species preservation. 15m; VHS, Special order formats. **A:** Primary. **P:** Education. **U:** Institution. **Chl-Juv:** Animals, Zoos. **Acq:** Purchase. **Dist:** National Geographic Society. $245.00.

At Middleton 2013 (R) — ★★½
In this love story, uptight George (Garcia) and free-spirit Edith (Vera Farmiga) meet at the title college--as parents visiting with their teenage children. Once the mismatched pair gets separated from the campus tour, they must get over their differences and realize they might have more in common than they think. Meanwhile George's preppy son Conrad (Lofranco) and Edith's ambitious, perfectionist daughter Audrey (Farmiga's younger sister Taissa) explore their own struggles with leaving home and entering adulthood. Story is predictable and chock-full of cliches, but as George and Edith, Garcia and Farmiga put up strong, chemistry-filled performances. 100m; DVD, Blu-Ray. **C:** Andy Garcia; Vera Farmiga; Taissa Farmiga; Spencer Lofranco; Peter Riegert; Tom Skerritt; Directed by Adam Rodgers; Written by Adam Rodgers; Glenn German; Cinematography by Emmanuel (Manu) Kadosh; Music by Arturo Sandoval. **Pr:** Glenn German; Andy Garcia; Anchor Bay Entertainment Inc. **A:** Sr. High-Adult. **P:** Entertainment. **U:** Home. **L:** English. **Mov-Ent:** Comedy--Romantic, Adolescence, Education. **Acq:** Purchase. **Dist:** Anchor Bay Entertainment Inc.

At Midnight, I'll Take Your Soul 1963 — ★
Brazilian import about sadistic gravedigger Coffin Joe (alter ego of director Jose Mojica Marins), who wanders the streets of his hometown in order to meet a desirable woman. His mission is to sire a son to continue his legacy and wiggle his lips at screaming women. A study in psycho-sexual horror, this makes "Apocalypse Now" look like a beach party. Coffin Joe, or "Ze do Caixao," is a kind of South American Freddy or Jason; Mojica Marin's movies—which are graphically sadistic—were banned by the Brazilian government. In Portugese with English subtitles. Followed by "Tonight I'll Be Incarnated in Your Corpse." 92m/B/W; VHS, DVD. **C:** Jose Mojica Marins; Magda Mei; Nivaldo de Lima; Directed by Jose Mojica Marins; Written by Jose Mojica Marins; Cinematography by Giorgio Attili. **A:** College-Adult. **P:** Entertainment. **U:** Home. **L:** Spanish. **Mov-Ent:** Horror, Cult Films. **Acq:** Purchase. **Dist:** Something Weird Video; Facets Multimedia Inc.; Tapeworm Video Distributors Inc. $20.00.

At 99: A Portrait of Louise Tandy Murch 1974
A portrait of Louise Tandy Murch who, at 99 years of age, lives life to the fullest, practices yoga daily, volunteers for charity, and has a lively sense of humor. 24m; 3/4 U, Special order formats. **Pr:** Deepa Saltzman, Sunrise Films Ltd. **A:** Family. **P:** Education. **U:** Institution, Home, SURA. **Gen-Edu:** Aging. **Acq:** Purchase, Rent/Lease, Trade-in, Duplication License. **Dist:** United Learning Inc.

At One with the Wind 1990
This video by the Royal Yachting Association, covers the basics of sailing a small craft, progressing to more advanced skills. Both beginners and advanced sailors will enjoy this instructional video. 55m; VHS. **A:** Sr. High-Adult. **P:** Instruction. **U:** Home. **Spo-Rec:** Boating. **Acq:** Purchase. **Dist:** Video Collectibles. $29.95.

At Play in the Fields of the Lord 1991 (R) — ★★★
A thoughtful epic that never quite lives up to its own self-importance—or length. Two yankee missionary couples try to evangelize a fearsome tribe of Brazilian rain-forest dwellers. One of the Christian families suffers a crisis of faith that's well-acted but not as powerful as a co-plot regarding a modern American Indian (Berenger) who joins the jungle natives with calamitous results. Based on the novel by Peter Matthiessen. 186m; VHS, CC. **C:** Tom Berenger; Aidan Quinn; Kathy Bates; John Lithgow; Daryl Hannah; Tom Waits; Stenio Garcia; Nelson Xavier; Jose Dumont; Niilo Kivirinta; Directed by Hector Babenco; Written by Hector Babenco; Jean-Claude Carriere; Music by Zbigniew Preisner. **Pr:** Saul Zaentz Company. **A:** Jr. High-Adult. **P:** Entertainment. **U:** Home. **Mov-Ent:** Ecology & Environment, South America. **Acq:** Purchase. **Dist:** $19.98.

The At-Risk Students Video Series 1990
Students from the innovative "Tree of Learning" program discuss the tough issues facing teens in junior high and high school today, including teen sex, pregnancy, stress, low self-esteem, drugs, and more. 25m; VHS. **A:** Jr. High-Sr. High. **P:** Education. **U:** Institution. **Gen-Edu:** Adolescence, Stress, Drugs. **Acq:** Purchase. **Dist:** Cambridge Educational. $449.00. **Indiv. Titles:** 1. Staying in School: Going the Distance 2. Drug Abuse: Saying No! to Peer Pressure 3. Low Self-Esteem: Why Kids Hurt Themselves 4. Liking Yourself with No Strings Attached: Self-Esteem 5. Sex and Pregnancy: The Power of Choice and Consequences.

At-Risk Students: What Works? 1992
Demonstrates comprehensive, practical, and effective approaches to help teachers increase academic achievements of at risk students in grades 7-12 and to evaluate their own at risk programs. Includes a free instructor's guide. 210m; VHS. **A:** Adult. **P:** Teacher Education. **U:** Institution. **Gen-Edu. Acq:** Purchase. **Dist:** GPN Educational Media. $375.00.

At Risk Video Series: A Dropout's Life—Go Back for Your Future 19??
This series explains the consequences of "at-risk" behavior to young people in a frank and candid manner. In this volume, the future of a school dropout is covered. Comes with instructor's notes and activity worksheets. Complete series also available. ?m; VHS. **A:** Jr. High-Adult. **P:** Education. **U:** Home, Institution. **Gen-Edu:** Adolescence, Education. **Acq:** Purchase. **Dist:** Education Associates Inc. $99.00.

At Risk Video Series: Proms and Pacifiers—Teens As Parents 19??
This series explains the consequences of "at-risk" behavior to young people in a frank and candid manner. In this volume, the ramifications of teen pregnancy are examined. Comes with instructor's notes and activity worksheets. Complete series also available. ?m; VHS. **A:** Jr. High-Adult. **P:** Education. **U:** Home, Institution. **Gen-Edu:** Adolescence, Pregnancy. **Acq:** Purchase. **Dist:** Education Associates Inc. $99.00.

At Risk Video Series: Teen Decisions for a Lifetime 19??
This series explains the consequences of "at-risk" behavior to young people in a frank and candid manner. In this volume, responsible decisions about sexual activity is covered. Comes with instructor's notes, and activity worksheets. Complete series also available. ?m; VHS. **A:** Jr. High-Adult. **P:** Education. **U:** Home, Institution. **Gen-Edu:** Adolescence, Sex & Sexuality. **Acq:** Purchase. **Dist:** Education Associates Inc. $99.00.

At Risk Video Series: Teens, Temptations, Troubles 19??
This series explains the consequences of "at-risk" behavior to young people in a frank and candid manner. In this volume, the confusions that adolescents experience are examined. Comes with instructor's notes, and activity worksheets. Complete series also available. ?m; VHS. **A:** Jr. High-Adult. **P:** Education. **U:** Home, Institution. **Gen-Edu:** Adolescence. **Acq:** Purchase. **Dist:** Education Associates Inc. $99.00.

At Sword's Point 1951 (Unrated) — ★★
Adventure tale based on characters from Alexandre Dumas's "The Three Musketeers," although the story is original. The French Queen (Cooper) is disturbed by sinister Duke Lavalle (Douglas) who wishes to marry Princess Henriette (Gates) and gain power to the throne. But the children of the four original musketeers come to her rescue, including swordswoman Claire (O'Hara). 81m; VHS, DVD. **C:** Cornel Wilde; Maureen O'Hara; Robert Douglas; Dan O'Herlihy; Alan Hale, Jr.; Blanche Yurka; Gladys Cooper; June Clayworth; Nancy Gates; Directed by Lewis Allen; Written by Walter Ferris; Joseph Hoffman; Cinematography by Ray Rennahan; Music by Roy Webb. **Pr:** RKO. **A:** Family. **P:** Entertainment. **U:** Home. **Mov-Ent. Acq:** Purchase. **Dist:** WarnerArchive.com; Facets Multimedia Inc. $19.95.

At the Autumn River Camp, Parts 1 and 2 1967
The autumn existence of the Netsilik Eskimos is related in these programs. Hunting, fishing, sewing tent roofs, and igloo building are a few of the jobs that are handled by the natives. 30m; 3/4 U, Special order formats. **Pr:** National Film Board of Canada. **A:** Jr. High-College. **P:** Education. **U:** Institution, CCTV, CATV, BCTV. **Gen-Edu:** Eskimos. **Acq:** Purchase, Rent/Lease. **Dist:** Education Development Center.

"At the Beep" 1991
Instruction on the mental and physical aspects of firearms training from internationl champ J. Michael Plaxco. 150m; VHS.

A: College-Adult. P: Instruction. U: Home. How-Ins: How-To, Firearms. Acq: Purchase. Dist: Gun Video. $69.95.

At the Caribou Crossing Place, Parts 1 and 2 1967
A documentary of the day-to-day existence of a family of Netsilik Eskimos. 30m; 3/4 U, Special order formats. **Pr:** National Film Board of Canada. **A:** Jr. High-College. **P:** Education. **U:** Institution, CCTV, CATV, BCTV. **Gen-Edu:** Eskimos. **Acq:** Purchase, Rent/Lease. **Dist:** Education Development Center.

At the Circus 1939 (Unrated) — ★★½
Marx Brothers invade the circus to save it from bankruptcy and cause their usual comic insanity, though they've done it better before. Beginning of the end for the Marxes, a step down in quality from their classic work, though frequently darn funny. 87m/B/W; VHS, DVD. **C:** Groucho Marx; Chico Marx; Harpo Marx; Margaret Dumont; Kenny L. Baker; Florence Rice; Eve Arden; Nat Pendleton; Fritz Feld; James Burke; Barnett Parker; Directed by Edward Buzzell; Written by Irving Brecher; Cinematography by Leonard Smith; Music by Harold Arlen. **Pr:** MGM. **A:** Family. **P:** Entertainment. **U:** Home. **Mov-Ent:** Comedy--Slapstick, Circuses, Classic Films. **Acq:** Purchase. **Dist:** MGM Home Entertainment. $19.95.
Songs: Lydia the Tattooed Lady; Step Up and Take a Bow; Two Blind Loves; Blue Moon.

At the Crossroads: Abortion 19??
Offers a Christian perspective on abortion, emphasizing the responsibility of procreative creatures. Includes interviews. Complete with study guide. 25m; VHS. **A:** Jr. High-Sr. High. **P:** Religious. **U:** Institution. **Gen-Edu:** Abortion. **Acq:** Purchase. **Dist:** Harcourt Religion Publishers. $59.95.

At the Crossroads: Faith in Cuba 2000
Documentary featuring Cuba after the 1959 Revolution. Explores the religious and political atmosphere during the recent economic hardships. Features interviews with Cubans on these issues. 52m; VHS. **A:** Adult. **P:** Education. **U:** Home. **Gen-Edu:** Documentary Films, Politics & Government, War--General. **Acq:** Purchase, Rent/Lease. **Dist:** Filmakers Library Inc. $295.

At the Earth's Core 1976 (PG) — ★★
A Victorian scientist invents a giant burrowing machine, which he and his crew use to dig deeply into the Earth. To their surprise, they discover a lost world of subhuman creatures and prehistoric monsters. Based on Edgar Rice Burrough's novels. 90m; VHS, DVD, Wide. **C:** Doug McClure; Peter Cushing; Caroline Munro; Cy Grant; Godfrey James; Keith Barron; Directed by Kevin Connor; Written by Milton Subotsky; Cinematography by Alan Hume; Music by Michael Vickers. **Pr:** American International Pictures. **A:** Jr. High-Adult. **P:** Entertainment. **U:** Home. **Mov-Ent:** Science Fiction, Dinosaurs. **Acq:** Purchase. **Dist:** Warner Home Video, Inc., On Moratorium.

At the Edge of Conquest: The Journey of Chief Wai-Wai 1992
Focuses on Chief Wai-Wai of the Waiapi Indians, who tries to communicate with the bureaucratic and cultural Brazilian government, to defend his land. Winner of the Bronze Apple, National Educational Film & Video Festival, 1992; U.S. Environmental Film Festival, 1992; Chicago Latino Film Festival, 1992. 28m; VHS. **A:** Sr. High-Adult. **P:** Education. **U:** Institution. **Gen-Edu:** Documentary Films, Politics & Government, Sociology. **Acq:** Purchase, Rent/Lease. **Dist:** Filmakers Library Inc. $295.00.

At the Foot of the Tree: A Homage to Steinlen 1987
A look at the social commentary of Alexander Steinlen, as seen in his paintings and lithographs. 24m/B/W; VHS, 8 mm, Special order formats. **C:** Directed by Alan Saury. **A:** Sr. High-Adult. **P:** Education. **U:** Institution, Home. **Fin-Art:** Documentary Films, Art & Artists. **Acq:** Purchase, Rent/Lease. **Dist:** The Roland Collection. $89.00.

At the Green Line 2005
Documentary following the Courage to Refuse movement in Israel, which seeks to end compulsory military service. 53m; VHS, DVD. **A:** Sr. High-Adult. **P:** Education. **U:** Institution. **Gen-Edu:** Documentary Films, War--General, Israel. **Acq:** Purchase, Rent/Lease. **Dist:** The Cinema Guild. $295.00.

At the Haunted End of the Day. . . 1989
Work of art exploring the career of Sir William Walton, England's Court Composer for half a decade. This film is enlightening and compassionate. 100m; VHS. **Pr:** Kultur. **A:** Family. **P:** Entertainment. **U:** Home. **Gen-Edu:** Biography. **Acq:** Purchase. **Dist:** Kultur International Films Ltd., Inc.; Music Video Distributors. $59.95.

At the Helm: Styles of Leadership 1993
Presents leaders from the Ritz-Carlton Hotel Company, Harden Industries, and the Virgin Group of Companies to demonstrate different styles of leadership and their effectiveness. 30m; VHS. **A:** Adult. **P:** Professional. **U:** Institution. **Bus-Ind:** Business, Management. **Acq:** Purchase. **Dist:** RMI Media. $99.00.

At the Hotel 2006
Murder dramedy takes place at the Chateau Rousseau where chambermaid Jenny stumbles upon a murder scene at the hotel pool her first day on the job. The victim is closely tied to the drug-addicted owner and her ruthless brother Jacob, who is trying to convince his sister to sell the property for re-development, leaving an unknown assailant looking to silence Jenny. 270m; DVD. **C:** Diego Klatenhoff; Natalie Lisinska. **A:** Adult. **P:** Entertainment. **U:** Home. **Mov-Ent:** Drama, Musical--Drama. **Acq:** Purchase. **Dist:** Morningstar Entertainment.

At the Houston Women's Conference 1977
Participants active in women's issues discuss the media's impact on the women's movement. 29m; 3/4 U, Q. **Pr:** Martha Stuart Communications. **A:** College-Adult. **P:** Education. **U:** Institution, CCTV, CATV, BCTV, Home. **Gen-Edu:** Women. **Acq:** Purchase, Rent/Lease. **Dist:** Communication for Change, Inc.

At the Interview 1988
This program shows you how to prepare for three of the most common interview situations in the workplace: performance appraisals, team assignments, and discussions on improving performance. 20m; VHS, 3/4 U. **Pr:** Library Video Network. **A:** College-Adult. **P:** Education. **U:** Institution, CCTV, SURA. **Bus-Ind:** Interviews, Management, Information Science. **Acq:** Purchase, Subscription, Duplication. **Dist:** Library Video Network.

At the Jazz Band Ball 1994
Presents jazz and pop performers filmed between 1925 and 1933, including a brief solo from cornetist Bix Beiderbecke, as well as Duke Ellington and Louis Armstrong. 60m; VHS, DVD. **A:** Adult. **P:** Entertainment. **U:** Home. **Mov-Ent:** Music--Jazz. **Acq:** Purchase. **Dist:** Shanachie Entertainment. $19.95.

At the Louvre with the Masters 1993
Explores how the Louvre played an essential role in forming the styles of painters Courbet, Degas, and Cezanne through their notebooks, paintings, and studios. Also discusses Ingres, Delacroix, Zola, Durant, Matisse, Monet, Renoir, Manet, and Picasso. 60m; VHS. **A:** Sr. High-Adult. **P:** Entertainment. **U:** Home. **Fin-Art:** Art & Artists, Museums, France. **Acq:** Purchase. **Dist:** Home Vision Cinema. $29.95.

At the Met: Curator's Choice 198?
Six-part series of guided tours through the Metropolitan Museum of Art. Each tour features insights and interpretations that both connoisseurs and neophytes will appreciate. 25m; VHS. **Pr:** NVC Arts International. **A:** Jr. High-Adult. **P:** Education. **U:** Home. **Gen-Edu:** Art & Artists, Museums. **Acq:** Purchase. **Dist:** Home Vision Cinema; Crystal Productions. $29.95.
Indiv. Titles: 1. The Tournament 2. Metropolitan Cats 3. Olmsted and Central Park 4. Curator's Choice 5. Voyages: The Journey of the Magi 6. Flowers and Gardens.

At the Midnight Hour 1995 (Unrated) — ★½
Elizabeth Guinness (Kensit) is hired as the new nanny to care for the troubled young son of widowed scientist Richard Keaton (MacCorkindale). She finds herself falling in love but then uncovers a secret about the death of Keaton's wife. From the Harlequin Romance series; adapted from the novel by Alicia Scott. 95m; DVD. **C:** Patsy Kensit; Simon MacCorkindale; Keegan Macintosh; Lindsay Merrithew; Cynthia Dale; Kay Hawtrey; Directed by Charles Jarrott; Written by Joe Wiesenfeld; Cinematography by Robert Fresco; Music by Charles T. Cozens. **A:** Jr. High-Adult. **P:** Entertainment. **U:** Home. **Mov-Ent. Acq:** Purchase. **Dist:** Movies Unlimited; Alpha Video.

At the Moment of Death 2000
Those who are dying, bereaved family members and hospice workers present the idea of death as a "spiritual passage." 15m; VHS, DVD. **A:** Adult. **P:** Professional. **U:** Institution. **Hea-Sci:** Death, Patient Care. **Acq:** Purchase. **Dist:** Aquarius Health Care Media. $99.00.

At the River I Stand 1993
Details the strike of black garbage workers in Memphis, Tennessee, in the winter of 1968 that preceded the appearance of Martin Luther King Jr. in the spring. Strike was considered a benchmark for the shift in focus among protesters from fighting for civil rights to economic and political issues. Musical accompaniment by various artists. 58m; VHS. **A:** Jr. High-Adult. **P:** Education. **U:** Institution. **Gen-Edu:** Civil Rights, History--U.S. **Acq:** Purchase. **Dist:** California Newsreel.

At the Spring Sea Ice Camp, Parts 1-3 1967
A record of the everyday life of a family of Netsilik Eskimos, as they hunt seals through the sea-ice in the springtime. 27m; 3/4 U, Special order formats. **Pr:** National Film Board of Canada. **A:** Jr. High-College. **P:** Education. **U:** Institution, CCTV, CATV, BCTV. **Gen-Edu:** Eskimos. **Acq:** Purchase, Rent/Lease. **Dist:** Education Development Center.

At the Throttle Cab Ride Volume 1 2008 (Unrated)
A stack train heads eastbound with a camera secured to the front to capture the scenic landscapes of the BNSF San Bernardino Subdivision from an "at the throttle" view for 65 miles from Hobart Yard, LA to the city of San Bernardino. This is a heavily traveled line so you'll catch lots of Amtrak, Metrolink, and BNSF freight action along the way on this Spring 2008 ride. 177m; DVD. **A:** Family. **P:** Education. **U:** Home. **Gen-Edu:** Trains, U.S. States. **Acq:** Purchase. **Dist:** Pentrex Media Group L.L.C. $19.95.

At the Throttle Cab Ride Volume 2 2008 (Unrated)
Go through the Cajon Subdivision "at the throttle" for 70-miles from Devore to Barstow with a camera positioned on the front of a BNSF lead unit. This Z train has plenty of horsepower to handle the summit of Cajon Pass, the Upper and Lower Narrows, and make superb time through the desert. 110m; DVD. **A:** Family. **P:** Education. **U:** Home. **Gen-Edu:** Trains, U.S. States. **Acq:** Purchase. **Dist:** Pentrex Media Group L.L.C. $19.95.

At the Time of Whaling 1974
The art of whaling is presented in this very exciting program. 38m; 3/4 U. **Pr:** Leonard Kamerling. **A:** Jr. High-Sr. High. **P:** Education. **U:** Institution, SURA. **Gen-Edu:** U.S. States. **Acq:** Purchase. **Dist:** Documentary Educational Resources.

At the Turn of the Age: Hans Holbein 1987
Examining the changes brought on by the Renaissance, this video eventually leads to the stunning work of Hans Holbein, one of Henry VIII's greatest court painters. 13m; VHS, 8 mm, Special order formats. **Pr:** Applause Productions. **A:** Jr. High-Adult. **P:** Entertainment. **U:** Institution, Home. **Gen-Edu:** Documentary Films, History--Renaissance, Art & Artists. **Acq:** Purchase. **Dist:** The Roland Collection. $79.00.

At the Wheel 1989
This video series documents the consequences and after-effects of a serious automobile crash. 55m; VHS, 3/4 U. **A:** Sr. High-Adult. **P:** Education. **U:** Institution, SURA. **Gen-Edu:** Automobiles, Driver Education. **Acq:** Purchase, Rent/Lease. **Dist:** National Film Board of Canada. $400.00.
Indiv. Titles: 1. After the Crash 2. On the Road 3. Under the Influence 4. The Road Ahead.

At the Wheel: After the Crash 19??
First part of a four-part series which centers on different issues associated with driving. Details the effects serious injuries have had on the lives of five accident victims, their families, and their friends. 67m; VHS. **Pr:** National Film Board of Canada. **A:** Jr. High-Adult. **P:** Education. **U:** Institution. **Gen-Edu:** Driver Education. **Acq:** Purchase. **Dist:** National Film Board of Canada; Home Vision Cinema.

At the Wheel: On the Road 19??
Follows two highway patrolmen as they patrol the expressways surrounding metropolitan Montreal. They discuss the true dangers of highway traffic and illustrate how quickly a seemingly innocent mistake can result in a tragedy. Second part of a four-part series. 49m; VHS. **Pr:** National Film Board of Canada. **A:** Jr. High-Adult. **P:** Education. **U:** Institution. **Gen-Edu:** Driver Education. **Acq:** Purchase. **Dist:** National Film Board of Canada; Home Vision Cinema.

At the Wheel: The Road Ahead 19??
Explores many of the causes behind automobile accidents and offers advice on what can be done to prevent them. Includes material on poorly designed and constructed roads, unsafe cars, and careless drivers. Last part of a four-part series. 49m; VHS. **Pr:** National Film Board of Canada. **A:** Jr. High-Adult. **P:** Education. **U:** Institution. **Gen-Edu:** Driver Education. **Acq:** Purchase. **Dist:** National Film Board of Canada; Home Vision Cinema.

At the Wheel: Under the Influence 19??
Follows two people accused of murder as a result of drunk driving as they make their way through the legal system from the time of arrest to sentencing. Third part of four-part series. 69m; VHS. **Pr:** National Film Board of Canada. **A:** Jr. High-Adult. **P:** Education. **U:** Institution. **Gen-Edu:** Driver Education. **Acq:** Purchase. **Dist:** National Film Board of Canada; Home Vision Cinema.

At the Winter Sea Ice Camp, Parts 1-4 1967
A way of life that is no more is seen in the lifestyle of the Netsilik Eskimos. We see them at work during the frigid Canadian winter, when special care must be taken to survive. 35m; 3/4 U, Special order formats. **Pr:** National Film Board of Canada. **A:** Jr. High-College. **P:** Education. **U:** Institution, CCTV, CATV, BCTV. **Gen-Edu:** Eskimos. **Acq:** Purchase, Rent/Lease. **Dist:** Education Development Center.

At War with the Army 1950 (Unrated) — ★★
Serviceable comedy from Martin and Lewis in their first starring appearance, as the recruits get mixed up in all kinds of wild situations at their army base. Based on the play by James Allardice. 93m/B/W; VHS, DVD, 3/4 U, Special order formats. **C:** Dean Martin; Jerry Lewis; Polly Bergen; Mike Kellin; Directed by Hal Walker; Written by Fred Finklehoffe; Cinematography by Stuart Thompson; Music by Jerry Livingston. **Pr:** Paramount Pictures. **A:** Family. **P:** Entertainment. **U:** Home. **Mov-Ent:** Comedy--Slapstick. **Acq:** Purchase. **Dist:** Gotham Distributing Corp.; Rex Miller Artisan Studio. $24.95.

At Your Service 2000
Documentary featuring a look at the service industry in England, France, Canada and the U.S. Includes professional waitpersons in each country and the sociological factors involved. 52m; VHS. **A:** Adult. **P:** Education. **U:** Home. **Gen-Edu:** Documentary Films, Sociology, Food Industry. **Acq:** Purchase, Rent/Lease. **Dist:** Filmakers Library Inc. $350.

Atalia 1985 (Unrated) — ★★
Relates the love between Atalia, a war widow, and the younger man she loves. The problem stems from the fact that she lives in a Kibbutz, and the lifestyle contradicts sharply from that of her beliefs in love, forcing her to eventually make a momentous decision. 90m; VHS. **C:** Michal Bat-Adam; Yftach Katzur; Dan Toren; Directed by Akiva Tevet. **A:** Sr. High-Adult. **P:** Entertainment. **U:** Home. **Mov-Ent:** Drama, Judaism. **Acq:** Purchase. **Dist:** Ergo Media Inc. $79.95.

Ataturk, Founder of Modern Turkey 2001
Documentary profiling Ataturk, a Nobel Peace Prize nominee, who became the leader of Turkey after World War I, and then secularized Turkey by emancipating women, guaranteeing equal rights to minorities, and replacing the Arabic script with the Latin alphabet. 52m; VHS. **A:** Sr. High-Adult. **P:** Education. **U:** Institution. **Gen-Edu:** History--Modern. **Acq:** Purchase, Rent/Lease. **Dist:** Filmakers Library Inc. $350.00.

Athena 1954 — ★★½
Two sisters (Powell and Reynolds) from an eccentric, health-faddist family fall in love with their opposites. Purdom is the stuffy Boston lawyer who goes off with Powell and Reynolds entices a TV crooner (Damone). Routine romance with routine songs. Reeves, who would become a star as a movie muscleman, appears in a brief role. 96m; DVD. **C:** Jane Powell; Debbie Reynolds; Edmund Purdom; Vic Damone; Louis Calhern; Evelyn Varden; Linda Christian; Virginia Gibson; Nancy Kilgas; Dolores Starr; Jane Fischer; Cecile Rogers; Steve Reeves; Directed by Richard Thorpe; Written by William

Ludwig; Leonard Spigelgass; Music by Hugh Martin; Ralph Blane. **Pr:** Joe Pasternak; Metro-Goldwyn-Mayer Pictures. **A:** Jr. High-Adult. **P:** Entertainment. **U:** Home. **Mov-Ent:** Musical, Romance. **Acq:** Purchase. **Dist:** WarnerArchive.com. $19.98.

Songs: Love Can Change the Stars; The Girl Next Door; Imagine; Venezia; Chacun le Sait; I Never Felt Better; Vocalize.

Athenian Democracy 1993
Presents a brief portrait of historical Athens and its limited democracy. Includes a profile of Pericles, the author of much of Athenian democracy, and footage from archaeological digs. 15m; VHS. **A:** Jr. High-Sr. High. **P:** Education. **U:** Institution. **Gen-Edu:** Politics & Government, History--Ancient. **Acq:** Purchase. **Dist:** Encyclopedia Britannica. $99.00.

Athens, Georgia: Inside/Out 1987 (Unrated)
Documentary about the extraordinary number of successful musical groups that have come out of Athens, Georgia. Included are profiles of the B-52's and R.E.M. plus a look at the up-and-coming groups like Love Tractor, Flat Duo Jets, and Bar-B-Q Killers. 90m; VHS. **A:** Adult. **P:** Entertainment. **U:** Home. **Mov-Ent:** Documentary Films, Cities & Towns. **Acq:** Purchase. **Dist:** Music Video Distributors. $29.95.

Athens: The Golden Age 1963
A discussion of the recurring question: Why is 5th century Athens considered by many to have been the most civilized society that existed? 30m; VHS, 3/4 U. **Pr:** Encyclopedia Britannica Educational Corporation. **A:** Sr. High-College. **P:** Education. **U:** Institution, SURA. **Gen-Edu:** History--Ancient. **Acq:** Purchase, Rent/Lease, Trade-in. **Dist:** Encyclopedia Britannica.

Athletic Clinic: Foot Injuries 1984
NBA trainers offer advice on the best methods of preventing and treating foot injuries. 22m; VHS. **Pr:** NBA. **A:** Jr. High-Adult. **P:** Instruction. **U:** Home. **Spo-Rec:** Sports--General, Sports Medicine. **Acq:** Purchase. **Dist:** School-Tech Inc. $14.95.

Athletic Clinic: Knee Injuries 1984
NBA trainers review the best ways to prevent and if necessary, treat knee injuries. 22m; VHS. **Pr:** NBA. **A:** Jr. High-Adult. **P:** Instruction. **U:** Home. **Spo-Rec:** Sports--General, Sports Medicine. **Acq:** Purchase. **Dist:** School-Tech Inc. $14.95.

Athletic Clinic Series 1988
An in-depth look at the causes and treatments of sports injuries. 30m; VHS. **Pr:** Cambridge Career Productions. **A:** Jr. High-Adult. **P:** Education. **U:** Institution, Home. **Spo-Rec:** Sports Medicine, Sports--General. **Acq:** Purchase. **Dist:** Cambridge Educational. $29.95.

Indiv. Titles: 1. Ankle Injuries 2. Athletic Taping 3. Foot Injuries 4. Knee Injuries 5. Shoulder Injuries 6. Shoulder & Knee Injuries 7. Hand, Wrist & Elbow Injuries 8. Soft Tissue Injuries 9. Neck, Head & Facial Injuries.

Athletic Clinic: Shoulder Injuries 1984
A selection of NBA trainers offer advice on the prevention and treatment of shoulder injuries. 22m; VHS. **Pr:** NBA. **A:** Jr. High-Adult. **P:** Instruction. **U:** Home. **Spo-Rec:** Sports--General, Sports Medicine. **Acq:** Purchase. **Dist:** School-Tech Inc. $14.95.

Athletic Goalie Play 2006 (Unrated)
Coach Ray Finnegan discusses what he believes are the two cornerstones of any successful lacrosse goalie: athleticism and discipline. ??m; DVD. **A:** Family. **P:** Education. **U:** Home, Institution. **Spo-Rec:** Lacrosse, Athletic Instruction/Coaching. **Acq:** Purchase. **Dist:** Championship Productions. $39.99.

Athletic Interval Training Program 1992
Aerobic conditioning combined with rope jumping will help develop flexibility and coordination. ?m; VHS. **A:** Jr. High-Sr. High. **P:** Instruction. **U:** Institution, Home. **Hea-Sci:** Fitness/Exercise. **Acq:** Purchase. **Dist:** Cambridge Educational. $49.95.

Athletic Taping 1984
This program presents some of the techniques used by professional trainers for taping up some of the best athletes in the world. 40m; VHS, 3/4 U. **Pr:** Champions on Film. **A:** Family. **P:** Education. **U:** Institution, CCTV, Home. **Hea-Sci:** Sports--General, Fitness/Exercise. **Acq:** Purchase, Rent/Lease. **Dist:** School-Tech Inc.

Athletic Trainer 1972
To the trainer, an athlete is a group of pressure sensitive joints, each of which is liable to injury. Some of these joints and the ways of protecting and rehabilitating them are examined. 30m; 3/4 U, EJ. **Pr:** NETCHE. **A:** Adult. **P:** Education. **U:** Institution, CCTV, BCTV, SURA. **Spo-Rec:** Sports Medicine. **Acq:** Purchase, Rent/Lease, Subscription. **Dist:** NETCHE.

Indiv. Titles: 1. The Ankle 2. The Knee 3. Miscellaneous Taping.

Athleticism in Dance 1984
These selections from "Eye on Dance" concern modern dance's relation to sports. 120m; VHS, 3/4 U, EJ. **Pr:** ARC Videodance. **A:** Sr. High-Adult. **P:** Entertainment. **U:** Institution, CCTV, Home, SURA. **Fin-Art:** Dance. **Acq:** Purchase. **Dist:** Eye on the Arts.

Indiv. Titles: 1. Arnie Zane & Elisa Monte 2. Catherine Turocy 3. Nancy Stark-Smith & Christopher Gillis 4. Robin Cousins & Toby Towson.

Athletics and Academics: An Uneasy Alliance 1988
Panel discussion profiles big-money college sports and the effect they have on academics and standards. Panelists include Joe Paterno, head football coach at Penn State University, James Brown, CBS Sports, Congressman Tom McMillan, Steve Robinson from Sports Illustrated, and Eamon Kelly, President of Tulane University. 90m; VHS, 3/4 U. **A:** College-Adult. **P:** Education. **U:** Institution. **Spo-Rec:** Sports--General, Education. **Acq:** Purchase. **Dist:** PBS Home Video.

Ati Athian 1986
Portrays an impromptu celebration of the Marcos regime, captured in cinema verite style. 8m; VHS, 3/4 U. **Pr:** Video Out. **A:** Jr. High-Adult. **P:** Education. **U:** Institution, SURA. **Gen-Edu:** Documentary Films, Politics & Government. **Acq:** Rent/Lease. **Dist:** Video Out Distribution.

ATL 2006 (PG-13) — ★★
A pack of roller-skating Atlanta outsiders battle the streets and get their groove on to a bumpin' soundtrack (certain to be the perfect corporate tie-in). High-octane dazzle should satisfy most looking for a safe urban-teen flick not loaded with the normally obligatory f-bomb. But the poor-boy-meets-rich-girl romance is too fluffy, and an evil drug-dealer conflict still doesn't add the bite it needs. Music-video director Chris Robinson makes his wildly disobedient big-screen debut with bling and hoopla, but a lack of grit and coherence is all too apparent. 105m; DVD, Blu-Ray, UMD, HD-DVD. **C:** Lonette McKee; Mykelti Williamson; Keith David; Jason Weaver; Tip "T.I." Harris; Lauren London; Evan Ross; Antwan Andre Patton; Jackie Long; Albert Daniels; Malika Khadijah; Tyree Simmons; Directed by Chris Robinson; Written by Tina Gordon Chism; Antwone Fisher; Music by Aaron Zigman. **Pr:** James Lassiter; Will Smith; Overbrook Entertainment; Warner Bros. **A:** Sr. High-Adult. **P:** Entertainment. **U:** Home. **L:** English. **Mov-Ent:** Adolescence, Skating. **Acq:** Purchase. **Dist:** Warner Home Video, Inc.

Atlanta 1990
This re-enactment captures your attention with the invasion of Atlanta by General Sherman. Animated maps add to this retelling of the Civil War. Also available as part of a set entitled "Field of Honor." 60m; VHS. **C:** Directed by Jack Foley. **Pr:** Classic Images Productions. **A:** Jr. High-Adult. **P:** Education. **U:** Institution, Home. **Gen-Edu:** War--General, History--U.S., Civil War. **Acq:** Purchase. **Dist:** Fusion Video. $39.95.

Atlanta Braves: Team Highlights 1984
This series highlights the many shining moments from the Atlanta Braves' past seasons. 30m; VHS. **Pr:** Major League Baseball Productions. **A:** Family. **P:** Entertainment. **U:** Institution, Home, SURA. **Spo-Rec:** Baseball. **Acq:** Purchase. **Dist:** Major League Baseball Productions, On Moratorium.

Indiv. Titles: 1. 1966: Here Come The Braves 2. 1982: Coming To America 3. 1983: The A Team 4. 1984: Ready To Rebound.

Atlanta Cyclorama: Battle of Atlanta 1991
This presentation takes viewers on a tour of the Cyclorama in Atlanta and recounts the bloody Battle of Atlanta, which was of major importance to the Civil War. The documentary also discusses efforts to renovate the Cyclorama. 30m; VHS. **Pr:** Finley-Holiday Film Corporation. **A:** Jr. High-Adult. **P:** Education. **U:** Institution, Home. **Gen-Edu:** Documentary Films, Civil War, History--U.S. **Acq:** Purchase. **Dist:** Finley Holiday Film Corp. $24.95.

Atlanta Falcons 1986: Falcon Fever 1987
Highlights of the Falcs' '86 season which saw marked improvement from previous years. 23m; VHS. **Pr:** NFL Films. **A:** Family. **P:** Entertainment. **U:** Home. **Spo-Rec:** Football. **Acq:** Purchase. **Dist:** NFL Films Video. $14.98.

Atlanta Falcons 1987: Preview of the '88 Falcons 1988
The Atlanta Falcons are one team that demands to be taken seriously after a mass overhaul on both offence and defence. 22m; VHS. **Pr:** NFL Films. **A:** Family. **P:** Entertainment. **U:** Home. **Spo-Rec:** Football. **Acq:** Purchase. **Dist:** NFL Films Video. $14.98.

Atlanta Falcons 1988: Fighting Falcons 1989
Highlights of the 1988 season. Led by quarterback Chris Miller and Pro Bowl running back John Settle, the Falcons finished with a 5-11 mark. 22m; VHS. **Pr:** NFL Films. **A:** Family. **P:** Entertainment. **U:** Home. **Spo-Rec:** Football. **Acq:** Purchase. **Dist:** NFL Films Video. $14.95.

Atlanta Falcons 1989: Special Moments: 25 Years of Falcon Football 1990
"Special Moments: 25 Years of Falcon Football" provides an overview of the franchise since its inception in 1966, plus highlights of the '89 season. 22m; VHS. **Pr:** NFL Films. **A:** Family. **P:** Entertainment. **U:** Home. **Spo-Rec:** Football. **Acq:** Purchase. **Dist:** NFL Films Video. $14.98.

The Atlanta Railroads: Their History and Their Story 19?? (Unrated)
Documents the railroading history of Atlanta from the state-owned Western & Atlantic days to the development of Louisville & Nashville, Southern Railway, Central of Georgia, and the Atlantic Coast Line plus investigates the city's modern day operations. 60m; DVD. **A:** Family. **P:** Education. **U:** Home. **Gen-Edu:** Trains, U.S. States, History. **Acq:** Purchase. **Dist:** The Civil War Standard. $24.95.

Atlanta Steam Celebration 1994
Covers the events and festivities of the National Railway Historical Society's 1994 convention in Atlanta, Georgia. Highlights include the Frisco 1522 and N&K 611 engine excursions. The Norfolk Southern's McDonough training center tour includes a look at locomotive simulators, signalmen training, welding centers, repair areas, a ride on a training track. 90m; VHS. **A:** Family. **P:** Entertainment. **U:** Home. **Gen-Edu:** Trains. **Acq:** Purchase. **Dist:** Pentrex Media Group L.L.C.

Atlanta's Olympic Glory 1998
This documentary by Bud Greenspan chronicles the drama and performances by athletes in the 1996 Atlanta Summer Olympics. Featured are Carl Lewis, Michael Johnson, Jackie Joyner-Kersee, Naim Suleymanoglu, Michelle Smith among many others. Three hours and 30 minutes on two videocassettes. 70m; VHS. **A:** Family. **P:** Entertainment. **U:** Home. **Spo-Rec:** Sports--Olympic. **Acq:** Purchase. **Dist:** PBS Home Video. $39.98.

Atlanta's Railroads ????
Historical background of Atlanta's railroad system—the largest in the southern United States—from the early days of Western & Atlantic to current-day operations. 60m; VHS, DVD. **A:** College-Adult. **P:** Education. **U:** Home. **Gen-Edu:** Trains. **Acq:** Purchase. **Dist:** The Civil War Standard. $24.95.

The Atlantic Circle: A One-Year Cruise Around the Pond 1989
Follows author Jimmy Cornell on a year-long circular tour of the North Atlantic about his 40-foot sloop. Gives tips on the best routes and landfalls, and the points of seamanship that make a cruise like this safe and practical. 52m; VHS, 8 mm. **A:** Jr. High-Adult. **P:** Entertainment. **U:** Home, Institution. **Spo-Rec:** Boating, Travel. **Acq:** Purchase. **Dist:** Mystic Seaport. $24.95.

Atlantic City 1944 (Unrated) — ★★
Bradford Taylor (Brown) learns a hard lesson in humility when he decides to build a boardwalk amusement pier in 1915's Atlantic City and transform the sleepy town into a vacation destination. While his ventures are successful, he alienates himself from his family and friends. Probably more interesting for the popular featured performers, including Louis Armstrong, Paul Whiteman, Dorothy Dandridge, Buck and Bubbles, and Gallagher and Sheen among others. 86m/B/W; DVD. **C:** Stanley Brown; Constance Moore; Charley Grapewin; Jerry Colonna; Robert Castaine; Directed by Ray McCarey; Written by Gilbert Doris; Frank Gill, Jr.; George Carleton Brown; Cinematography by John Alton. **A:** Sr. High-Adult. **P:** Entertainment. **U:** Home. **Mov-Ent.** **Acq:** Purchase. **Dist:** Movies Unlimited.

Atlantic City 1981 (R) — ★★★½
A small-time, aging Mafia hood falls in love with a young clam bar waitress, and they share the spoils of a big score against the backdrop of Atlantic City. Wonderful character study that becomes something more, a piercing declaration about a city's transformation and the effect on the people who live there. Lancaster, in a sterling performance, personifies the city, both of them fading with time. 104m; VHS, DVD, Wide. **C:** Burt Lancaster; Susan Sarandon; Kate Reid; Michel Piccoli; Hollis McLaren; Robert Joy; Al Waxman; Directed by Louis Malle; Written by John Guare; Cinematography by Richard Ciupka; Music by Michel Legrand. **Pr:** Dennis Heroux; Cine Neighbor; Selta Films. **A:** Adult. **P:** Entertainment. **U:** Home. **Mov-Ent:** Aging, Gambling, Canada. **Awds:** British Acad. '81: Actor (Lancaster), Director (Malle); Genie '81: Support. Actress (Reid); L.A. Film Critics '81: Actor (Lancaster), Film, Screenplay; Natl. Film Reg. '03; N.Y. Film Critics '81: Actor (Lancaster), Screenplay; Natl. Soc. Film Critics '81: Actor (Lancaster), Director (Malle), Film, Screenplay. **Acq:** Purchase. **Dist:** Paramount Pictures Corp. $14.95.

Atlantic City: Roulette of Power 1983
How casino gambling in Atlantic City has affected the Hispanic community in terms of jobs and housing is explored. 30m; VHS, 3/4 U. **Pr:** New Jersey Network. **A:** Sr. High-Adult. **P:** Education. **U:** Institution. **Gen-Edu:** Cities & Towns, Minorities. **Acq:** Purchase, Rent/Lease. **Dist:** New Jersey Network.

Atlantic City: The Queen Takes a Chance 1981
How Atlantic City saved itself from extinction through urban renewal is the subject of this documentary. 60m; VHS, 3/4 U. **Pr:** New Jersey Network. **A:** Sr. High-Adult. **P:** Education. **U:** Institution. **Gen-Edu:** Cities & Towns. **Acq:** Purchase, Rent/Lease. **Dist:** New Jersey Network.

Atlantic City Trolley Days ????
Provides a historic overview of Atlantic City's trolley system with a look at the whole route and cabs used. 42m; VHS. **A:** College-Adult. **P:** Education. **U:** Home. **Gen-Edu:** Trains. **Acq:** Purchase. **Dist:** The Civil War Standard. $29.95.

Atlantic Flight 1937 (Unrated) — ★★★
In 1937 Monogram pictures had just reformed after a troubled merger with Republic, and needed to make some quick money. Dick Merrill had just done the first two commercial transatlantic flights, and was one of the most famous men of his day. So the idea was made to make a film starring him and his co pilot Jack Lambie. Not surprisingly they're secondary characters, and the focus is on a romantic triangle (one of the members of which sabotages his plane). 58m/B/W; DVD. **C:** Dick Merrill; Jack Lambie; Paula Stone; Weldon Heyburn; Milburn Stone; Ivan Lebedeff; Lyle Moraine; Directed by William Nigh; Written by Scott Darling; Erna Lazarus; Cinematography by Paul Ivano. **A:** Sr. High-Adult. **P:** Entertainment. **U:** Home. **Mov-Ent:** Drama, Musical--Drama. **Acq:** Purchase. **Dist:** Alpha Video. $7.98.

Atlantic Records: The House That Ahmet Built 2007 (Unrated)
Follows the career of record mogul Ahmet Ertegun from the start of his label in 1947 featuring rare, private and classic clips, performances and studio sessions of Atlantic artists including Solomon Burke, Ray Charles, Eric Clapton, Phil Collins, Aretha Franklin, Mick Jagger, Kid Rock, Ben E. King, and Led Zeppelin. 120m; DVD. **A:** Adult. **P:** Education. **U:** Home. **Gen-Edu:** Documentary Films, Music. **Acq:** Purchase. **Dist:** Rhino Entertainment Co. $19.99.

The Atlantic Salmon 1978
This tape looks at the life cycle of the Atlantic salmon and the measures taken to protect this necessary resource. 28m; VHS, 3/4 U. **Pr:** National Film Board of Canada. **A:** Jr. High-Adult. **P:** Education. **U:** Institution, SURA. **Hea-Sci:** Fish, Ecology & Environment. **Acq:** Purchase, Rent/Lease. **Dist:** National Film Board of Canada.

Atlantic Speedsters: Bonito and False Albacore 1989
Come along with sportsman Pete Barrett as he tackles these popular game fish. 60m; VHS. **C:** Hosted by Pete Barrett. **Pr:** Salt Water Sportsman. **A:** Jr. High-Adult. **P:** Instruction. **U:** Home. **Spo-Rec:** Fishing. **Acq:** Purchase. **Dist:** Bennett Marine Video. $39.95.

Atlantis 1977
New archaeological discoveries in the southern Aegean Sea suggest the existence of the lost city of Atlantis. 41m; 3/4 U. **Pr:** Orpheus Films. **A:** Jr. High-Adult. **P:** Education. **U:** Institution, SURA. **Gen-Edu:** Speculation. **Acq:** Purchase, Rent/Lease. **Dist:** Kinetic Film Enterprises Ltd.

Atlantis 2010 (Unrated)
Plato described the city of Atlantis as a naval power from approximately 9600 B.C. and said that it disappeared into the ocean in a single day. National Geographic investigates whether or not this advanced society really existed as well as the legends that attribute its destruction to the corruption and immoral behavior of its inhabitants. 52m; DVD. **A:** Family. **P:** Education. **U:** Institution, Home. **Mov-Ent:** Documentary Films, Folklore & Legends, History--Ancient. **Acq:** Purchase. **Dist:** National Geographic Society. $19.95.

Atlantis: Season One 2013
BBC 2013--? adventure fantasy. Jason washes up on the shores of Atlantis while searching for his missing father. He's helped by new friends Pythagoras and a drunken Hercules as well as Medusa as they battle such mythological foes as the Minotaur and Circe and her sirens. 13 episodes. 585m; DVD, Blu-Ray. **C:** Jack Donnelly; Robert Emms; Mark Addy; Jemima Rooper. **A:** Jr. High-Adult. **P:** Entertainment. **U:** Home. **L:** English. **Mov-Ent:** Action-Adventure, Fantasy, Folklore & Legends. **Acq:** Purchase. **Dist:** BBC Worldwide Ltd. $29.98.

Atlantis, the Lost Continent 1961 — ★
If anything could sink the fabled lost continent of Atlantis it's this cheap fantasy flick. A greek sailor saves a princess and takes her back to her Atlantis home where he's promptly enslaved by the island's evil ruler. But this hero won't put up with any nonsense so he leads his fellow slaves in a revolt and gains his freedom before sinking both evil ruler and island (using atomic power no less!). 90m; VHS, DVD. **C:** Anthony Hall; Joyce Taylor; John Dall; William (Bill) Smith; Edward Platt; Frank De Kova; Narrated by Paul Frees; Directed by George Pal; Written by Daniel Mainwaring; Cinematography by Harold E. Wellman; Music by Russell Garcia. **Pr:** George Pal; George Pal; MGM. **A:** Family. **P:** Entertainment. **U:** Home. **Mov-Ent:** Fantasy. **Acq:** Purchase. **Dist:** WarnerArchive.com; Facets Multimedia Inc. $14.98.

Atlantis: The Lost Empire 2001 (PG) — ★★½
Fast-paced and action-packed animated Disney adventure about inexperienced explorer Milo Thatch (Fox) who uses his grandfather's secret journals to discover the whereabouts of the submerged city of Atlantis. Submarine Captain Rourke (Garner) leads the expedition, but the eccentric and multi-ethnic crew are not entirely who or what they seem to be. Once found, the city holds a love interest (Summer) for Milo, and treasures to tempt the less benevolent members of the crew. The animation is old-fashioned and the plotting is reminiscent of adventure movies such as "Raiders of the Lost Ark" and "20,000 Leagues Under the Sea," but these should be considered merits instead of liabilities, especially if you're under 13 years old. 95m; VHS, DVD, Blu-Ray, Wide. **C:** Voice(s) by Michael J. Fox; James Garner; Claudia Christian; Cree Summer; John Mahoney; Leonard Nimoy; David Ogden Stiers; Jim Varney; Phil Morris; Don Novello; Corey Burton; Jacqueline Obradors; Directed by Gary Trousdale; Kirk Wise; Written by Tab Murphy; Music by James Newton Howard. **Pr:** Don Hahn; Walt Disney Pictures; Buena Vista. **A:** Family. **P:** Entertainment. **U:** Home. **Mov-Ent:** Animation & Cartoons, Explorers, Fantasy. **Acq:** Purchase. **Dist:** Buena Vista Home Entertainment.

Atlas 197?
A quasi-animated map of the ancient Roman empire shifts and alters in accordance with world history as summarized by a narrator. 6m; VHS, 3/4 U. **Pr:** Charles Eames; Ray Eames. **A:** Jr. High-Adult. **P:** Education. **U:** Institution, Home, SURA. **Gen-Edu:** Geography. **Acq:** Purchase, Rent/Lease. **Dist:** Pyramid Media. $145.00.

Atlas 1960 (Unrated) — ★
The mighty Atlas takes on massive armies, one of which includes director Corman, in a bid to win the hand of a princess. About as cheap as they come, although it is one of the few Sword & Sandal epics that isn't dubbed. 84m; VHS, DVD. **C:** Michael Forest; Frank Wolff; Barboura Morris; Walter Maslow; Christos Exarchos; Miranda Kounelaki; Theodore Dimitriou; Charles B. Griffith; Roger Corman; Dick Miller; Directed by Roger Corman; Written by Charles B. Griffith; Cinematography by Basil Maros; Music by Ronald Stein. **Pr:** Roger Corman; Roger Corman; Filmgroup. **A:** Primary-Adult. **P:** Entertainment. **U:** Home. **Mov-Ent:** Fantasy, War--General, History--Ancient. **Acq:** Purchase. **Dist:** Sinister Cinema. $19.95.

Atlas in the Land of the Cyclops 1961 — **Bomb!**
Atlas takes on a hideous one-eyed monster to save a baby from an evil queen. Not a divorce custody drama. 100m; VHS, DVD. **C:** Mitchell Gordon; Chelo Alonso; Vira (Vera) Silenti; Directed by Antonio Leonviola. **Pr:** Medallion Pictures. **A:** Primary-Adult. **P:** Entertainment. **U:** Home. **Mov-Ent:** Fantasy, Folklore & Legends. **Acq:** Purchase. **Dist:** Alpha Video; Mill Creek Entertainment L.L.C.; Image Entertainment Inc. $19.98.

Atlas Shrugged II: The Strike 2012 (PG-13) — **Bomb!**
The second part of the Ayn Rand novel is a cinematic nightmare with a different cast and director. Business moguls Dagny Taggart (Mathis) and Henry Rearden (Beghe) fiercely object to the government takeover of their industries just because the world's economy has gone to hell. Sadly, the movie that is clearly designed to invoke conversation about modern politics and ideals is just so deadly dull that it's more likely to start conversation about the failure of its creators. A bizarre piece of work that even its director can't seem to keep track of the storyline. 111m; DVD, Blu-Ray. **C:** Samantha Mathis; Jason Beghe; Esai Morales; Patrick Fabian; Kim Rhodes; Diedrich Bader; Richard T. Jones; D.B. Sweeney; John Rubinstein; Robert Picardo; Directed by John Putch; Written by Brian Patrick O'Toole; Duke Sandefur; Duncan Scott; Cinematography by Ross Berryman; Music by Chris Bacon. **Pr:** Jeff Freilich; Harmon Kaslow; John Aglialoro; Atlas Distribution Co. **A:** Sr. High-Adult. **P:** Entertainment. **U:** Home. **L:** English. **Mov-Ent:** Drama, Politics & Government, Business. **Acq:** Purchase. **Dist:** Fox Home Entertainment.

Atlas Shrugged: Part 1 2011 (PG-13) — ★
Low-budget, simplistic, and rushed adaptation of the 1957 Ayn Rand novel, the first in a supposed trilogy of films, tackles only the first third of the book and sets it in 2016. Tough railroad heiress Dagny (Schilling) is merely a pretty-but-bland blonde businesswoman who gets involved with visionary manufacturer Hank Reardon (Bowler), whose formula for a new steel is expected to transform the nation's current economic crisis through free enterprise and rebuilding big business. 97m; Blu-Ray, Wide. **C:** Taylor Schilling; Grant Bowler; Matthew Marsden; Edi Gathegi; Graham Beckel; Jsu Garcia; Jon Polito; Michael Lerner; Neill Barry; Rebecca Wisocky; Paul Johansson; Directed by Paul Johansson; Written by Brian Patrick O'Toole; John Aglialoro; Cinematography by Ross Berryman; Music by Elia Cmiral. **Pr:** John Aglialoro; Harmon Koslow; Rocky Mountain Pictures. **A:** Jr. High-Adult. **P:** Entertainment. **U:** Home. **L:** English. **Mov-Ent:** Inventors & Inventions, Trains, Romance. **Acq:** Purchase. **Dist:** Fox Home Entertainment; Movies Unlimited.

ATM 2012 (R) — ★½
In the tradition of thrillers such as "Speed" and "Phone Booth," director Brooks takes one common location and attempts to turn it into a nail-biting nightmare. This time it's a late-night ATM in a deserted parking lot. Three young urban professionals (Geraghty, Eve, Peck) enter the barely lit chamber after parking ridiculously far away only to turn around and see a hulking shadow in a parka. What does he want? And did he really just kill that guy who was walking his dog? As a series of unbelievable events pile up, the gimmick is out of order. 90m; DVD, Blu-Ray. **C:** Brian Geraghty; Alice Eve; Josh Peck; Mike O'Brian; Directed by David Brooks; Written by Chris Sparling; Cinematography by Bengt Jonsson; Music by David Buckley. **Pr:** Paul Brooks; Peter Safran; IFC Films; Gold Circle Films; Buffalo Gals Pictures. **A:** Sr. High-Adult. **P:** Entertainment. **U:** Home. **L:** English. **Mov-Ent:** Horror, Christmas. **Acq:** Purchase. **Dist:** MPI Media Group.

ATME-I 1982 1982
A survey of the technical progress exhibited at the American Textile Machinery Exhibition-International in Greenville, South Carolina. 23m; VHS, 3/4 U. **Pr:** North Carolina State University. **A:** Adult. **P:** Education. **U:** Institution, CCTV, Home. **Bus-Ind:** Textile Industry. **Acq:** Purchase, Rent/Lease. **Dist:** No Longer Available.

The Atmosphere in Motion 1973
Explains convection cells, the Coriolis Effect, and the composition and structure of the atmosphere. 20m; VHS, 3/4 U. **Pr:** Encyclopedia Britannica Educational Corporation; American Geological Institute. **A:** Jr. High. **P:** Education. **U:** Institution, SURA. **Hea-Sci:** Meteorology. **Acq:** Purchase, Rent/Lease, Trade-in. **Dist:** Encyclopedia Britannica.

Atmosphere: On the Air 1993
Offers an animated tour of the atmosphere to learn about its layers and their functions, wind, clouds, and precipitation. Radio science show format features scientist responses. 20m; VHS. **A:** Jr. High-Adult. **P:** Education. **U:** Institution. **Gen-Edu:** Science. **Acq:** Purchase. **Dist:** National Geographic Society. $80.

Atmospheric Science Series 1985
This series outlines atmospheric phenomena for the layman. 14m; VHS, 3/4 U, Special order formats. **Pr:** Bill Walker Productions. **A:** Jr. High-Adult. **P:** Education. **U:** Institution, CCTV, SURA. **Hea-Sci:** Meteorology. **Acq:** Purchase, Rent/Lease, Duplication License. **Dist:** Phoenix Learning Group.
Indiv. Titles: 1. The Earth's Atmosphere 2. Winds & Air Currents 3. Global Winds 4. Clouds and Precipitation 5. Weather Systems in Motion 6. Violent Storms 7. Global Forecasting 8. The Energy Balance.

Atmospheric Testing 199?
Covers atmospheric hazards, procedures for proper pre-testing, and how to respond when air is unsafe. 17m; VHS. **A:** Adult. **P:** Vocational. **U:** Institution. **Bus-Ind:** Documentary Films, How-To. **Acq:** Purchase, Rent/Lease. **Dist:** Audio Graphics Training Systems. $495.00.

Atmospheric Testing for Enclosed Spaces 19??
Discusses atmospheric testing equipment and testing procedures, the importance of planning a job, proper ventilation, and on-going testing. Includes Leader's Guide and 25 Program Guides. 12m; VHS, 3/4 U. **A:** Adult. **P:** Education. **U:** Institution. **Bus-Ind:** Safety Education. **Acq:** Purchase. **Dist:** Williams Learning Network.

Atocha: Quest for Treasure 2000 (Unrated)
For more than 300 years, the shipwreck of the Spanish galleon Nuestra Senora de Atocha was the most sought-after wreck in the salvage community thanks to its cargo of gold, silver, and emeralds. In this documentary, National Geographic follows famous shipwreck hunter Mel Fisher as his 16-year search for the Atocha comes to a successful conclusion when he locates the ship and its more than 40 tons of gold. 58m; DVD. **A:** Family. **P:** Education, Entertainment. **U:** Home, Institution. **Mov-Ent:** Documentary Films, Hunting, History. **Acq:** Purchase. **Dist:** $19.95.

Atom 2010
In this three-part BBC series, scientists completely re-examine their idea of how the universe was created with the discovery of the atom and such concepts as quarks and anti-matter. 180m; DVD, CC. **A:** Jr. High-Adult. **P:** Education. **U:** Institution. **Gen-Edu:** Documentary Films, Science, Scientists. **Acq:** Purchase. **Dist:** Ambrose Video Publishing, Inc. $99.99.

The Atom: A Closer Look 1990
Nuclear energy and how we use it in the future, in relation to the atom, is explored. 30m; VHS, 3/4 U, EJ, Special order formats. **TV Std:** NTSC, PAL, SECAM. **Pr:** Disney Educational Productions. **A:** Primary-Sr. High. **P:** Education. **U:** Institution, CCTV, SURA. **Hea-Sci:** Nuclear Energy. **Acq:** Purchase, Rent/Lease. **Dist:** Phoenix Learning Group. $250.00.

Atom Age Vampire 1961 (Unrated) — **Bomb!**
Mad scientist doing research on Japanese nuclear bomb victims falls in love with a woman disfigured in an auto crash. To remove her scars, he treats her with a formula derived from the glands of freshly killed women. English dubbed. Not among the best of its kind (a low-rent district if ever there was one), but entertaining in a mischievous, boy-is-this-a-stupid-film sort of way. 71m/B/W; VHS, DVD. **C:** Alberto Lupo; Susanne Loret; Sergio Fantoni; Franca Parisi Strahl; Ivo Garrani; Andrea Scotti; Rina Franchetti; Directed by Anton Giulio Majano; Written by Anton Giulio Majano; Alberto Bevilacqua; Gino De Santis; Cinematography by Aldo Giordani. **Pr:** Mario Bava; Topaz Film Corporation. **A:** Sr. High-Adult. **P:** Entertainment. **U:** Home. **Mov-Ent:** Horror. **Acq:** Purchase. **Dist:** Rhino Entertainment Co. $16.95.

The Atom and Eve 1984
A short anti-nuclear-war film. 15m; VHS, Special order formats. **Pr:** Green Mountain Post Films. **A:** Jr. High-Adult. **P:** Education. **U:** Institution, CATV, BCTV, SURA. **Gen-Edu:** Nuclear Warfare. **Acq:** Purchase, Rent/Lease. **Dist:** Green Mountain Post Films.

Atom Ant 196?
Eight episodes in which the ant with atomic strength battles Ferocious Flea and Karate Ant. 53m; VHS. **Pr:** Hanna-Barbera Productions. **A:** Family. **P:** Entertainment. **U:** Home. **Chl-Juv:** Animation & Cartoons. **Acq:** Purchase. **Dist:** Turner Broadcasting System Inc. $19.95.

Atom Ant, Vol. 2 1965
The mightiest little hero in the universe, Atom Ant, is back to fight crime in this collection of six episodes from the series. 40m; VHS. **Pr:** Hanna-Barbera Productions. **A:** Family. **P:** Entertainment. **U:** Home. **Chl-Juv:** Animation & Cartoons. **Acq:** Purchase. **Dist:** Turner Broadcasting System Inc. $19.95.

The Atom Bomb 1987
The development of nuclear science leading to the atom bomb, and the political conditions surrounding that event are the focus of this video, which features historic pictures of the first atomic explosion, Roosevelt, Einstein, and more. ?m; VHS. **A:** Jr. High-College. **P:** Education. **U:** Institution. **Gen-Edu:** Nuclear Warfare, World War Two. **Acq:** Purchase. **Dist:** Educational Images Ltd. $42.95.

Atom Man vs. Superman 1950 — ★★
Superman saves Metropolis from the machinations of his deadly foe, Atom Man, in this long-unseen second theatrical serial. Contains all 15 episodes on two tapes. 251m/B/W; VHS, DVD. **C:** Kirk Alyn; Lyle Talbot; Noel Neill; Tommy "Butch" Bond; Pierre Watkin; Directed by Spencer Gordon Bennet. **Pr:** Sam Katzman; Columbia Pictures. **A:** Family. **P:** Entertainment. **U:** Home. **Mov-Ent:** Science Fiction, Serials. **Acq:** Purchase. **Dist:** Warner Home Video, Inc. $29.98.

Atom Nine Adventures 2007 (Unrated) — ★½
An astrophysicist and his homemade robot are pestered by terrorists after finding a meteorite with an alien organism in it. Fairly average sci fi thriller. 78m; DVD. **C:** Christopher Farley; Paul Meade; Jennifer Ferguson; Colin Armstrong; Directed by Christopher Farley; Written by Christopher Farley; Cinematography by Dave Arnold; Laura Beth Love; Music by Robert Gulya. **A:** Jr. High-Adult. **P:** Entertainment. **U:** Home. **L:** English. **Mov-Ent. Acq:** Purchase. **Dist:** Seminal Films. $19.95.

Atomic Artist 1983
A portrait of Tony Price, a painter and sculptor from New York who has lived and worked near the Los Alamos National Laboratory in New Mexico for almost 20 years. 29m; VHS, 3/4 U, Special order formats. **Pr:** Glenn Silber; Claudia Vianello. **A:** Sr. High-Adult. **P:** Education. **U:** Institution, SURA. **Gen-Edu:** Documentary Films, Art & Artists, Painting. **Acq:** Purchase, Rent/Lease. **Dist:** First Run/Icarus Films. $290.00.

Atomic Attack 1950
Nuclear bomb is dropped on New York City and a family living 50 miles away must escape. Gentlemen, start your engines. 50m/B/W; VHS. **TV Std:** NTSC, PAL. **C:** Walter Matthau.

A: Sr. High-Adult. **P:** Education. **U:** Institution, Home. **Mov-Ent:** Nuclear Warfare, Family. **Acq:** Purchase. **Dist:** International Historic Films Inc. $29.95.

Atomic Betty: Volume 1—Betty, Set, Go! 2005
Features the children's animated television cartoon about Betty, a seemingly ordinary schoolgirl who takes on galactic evil-doers such as Supreme Overlord Maximus I.Q. as her alter-ego Atomic Betty along with her pals Sparky and robot X-5. Episodes include: "Toxic Talent," "Spindly Tam Kanushu," "Atomic Roger," "Furball for the Sneeze," "Really Big Game," "But the Cat Came Back," "The Doppelganger," and "The Incredible Shrinking Betty." 8 episodes. 88m; DVD. **C:** Kristina Nicoll; Adrian Truss; Voice(s) by Robin Duke; Laura Elliott; Colin Fox; Bruce Hunter; Peter Oldring; William Shatner; Tajja Isen; Len Carlson. **A:** Family. **P:** Entertainment. **U:** Home. **Chl-Juv:** Television Series, Animation & Cartoons, Children's Shows. **Acq:** Purchase. **Dist:** Warner Home Video, Inc. $14.97.

Atomic Betty: Volume 2—Betty to the Rescue! 2005
Features the children's animated television cartoon about Betty, a seemingly ordinary schoolgirl who takes on galactic evil-doers such as Supreme Overlord Maximus I.Q. as her alter-ego Atomic Betty along with her pals Sparky and robot X-5. Episodes include: "Maximus Displeasure," "Cosmic Cake," "Attack of the Evil Baby," "Crass Menagerie," "The Trouble With Triplets," "The Substitute," "Infantor Rules," and "Best (Mis)Laid Plans." 8 episodes. 88m; DVD. **C:** Voice(s) by Tajja Isen; Len Carlson; Robin Duke; Laura Elliott; Colin Fox; Bruce Hunter; Kristina Nicoll; Lindsay Younce; Adrian Truss; William Shatner. **A:** Family. **P:** Entertainment. **U:** Home. **Chl-Juv:** Television Series, Animation & Cartoons, Children's Shows. **Acq:** Purchase. **Dist:** $19.97.

The Atomic Bomb: Truman's Decision 19??
Highlights the discovery and controversy over the atomic bomb and President Harry Truman's famous August 6, 1945 speech regarding his decision to use the bomb. 16m; VHS. **A:** Jr. High-Sr. High. **P:** Education. **U:** Institution. **Gen-Edu:** History--U.S. **Acq:** Purchase. **Dist:** Thomas S. Klise Co. $58.00.

The Atomic Brain 1964 (Unrated) — **Bomb!**
An old woman hires a doctor to transplant her brain into the body of a beautiful young girl. Of the three girls who are abducted, two become homicidal zombies and the third starts to act catty when she is given a feline brain. A must-see for bad-brain movie fans. 72m/B/W; VHS, DVD. **C:** Frank Gerstle; Erika Peters; Judy Bamber; Marjorie Eaton; Frank Fowler; Margie Fisco; Directed by Joseph Mascelli; Written by Jack Pollexfen; Vivian Russell; Dean Dillman, Jr; Sue Bradford. **Pr:** Emerson Film Enterprises. **A:** Primary-Adult. **P:** Entertainment. **U:** Home. **Mov-Ent:** Science Fiction, Scientists. **Acq:** Purchase. **Dist:** Sinister Cinema. $19.98.

The Atomic Cafe 1982 (Unrated) — ★★★
A chillingly humorous compilation of newsreels and government films of the 1940s and '50s that show America's preoccupation with the A-Bomb. Some sequences are in black and white. Includes the infamous training film "Duck and Cover," which tells us what to do in the event of an actual bombing. 92m; VHS, DVD. **C:** Directed by Kevin Rafferty; Jayne Loader; Pierce Rafferty; Music by Miklos Rozsa. **Pr:** Archives Project Inc. **A:** Jr. High-Adult. **P:** Entertainment. **U:** Home. **Mov-Ent:** Documentary Films, Propaganda, Nuclear Warfare. **Acq:** Purchase. **Dist:** First Run Features.

The Atomic City 1952 (Unrated) — ★★½
Barry plays a nuclear physicist at Los Alamos whose son is kidnapped by terrorists who want his bomb-making formulas. The bad guys hide out in the nearby mountains which at least makes for some pleasant scenery in this average thriller. 84m/B/W; VHS, DVD, Blu-Ray. **C:** Gene Barry; Lee Aaker; Michael D. Moore; Lydia Clarke; Nancy Gates; Milburn Stone; Directed by Jerry Hopper. **Pr:** Joseph Sistrom; Paramount Pictures. **A:** Jr. High-Adult. **P:** Entertainment. **U:** Home. **Mov-Ent:** Mystery & Suspense, Science. **Acq:** Purchase. **Dist:** Paramount Pictures Corp.

Atomic Dog 1998 (PG-13) — ★½
The Yates family (Hugh-Kelly and Pickett) move to a new town near a nuclear power plant. Soon, the family dog is having puppies—only the sire turns out to be a radioactive hound who wants his offspring and he's a very determined doggie indeed. 86m; VHS, CC. **C:** Daniel Hugh-Kelly; Isabella Hofmann; Cindy Pickett; Katie Stuart; Micah Gardener; Directed by Brian Trenchard-Smith; Written by Miguel Tejada-Flores; Cinematography by David Lewis; Music by Peter Bernstein. **A:** Jr. High-Adult. **P:** Entertainment. **U:** Home. **Mov-Ent:** Pets, TV Movies. **Acq:** Purchase. **Dist:** Paramount Pictures Corp.

Atomic Energy: Inside the Atom—2nd Edition 1982
Presents evidence that there is energy inside the atom, and shows ways in which radioactive substances can be used. 14m; VHS, 3/4 U. **Pr:** Albert V. Baez; Encyclopedia Britannica Educational Corporation. **A:** Jr. High. **P:** Education. **U:** Institution, SURA. **Hea-Sci:** Chemistry. **Acq:** Purchase, Rent/Lease, Trade-in. **Dist:** Encyclopedia Britannica.

The Atomic Kid 1954 — ★½
A man survives an atomic blast because of a peanut butter sandwich he was eating. As a result, he himself becomes radioactive and discovers that he has acquired some strange new powers which get him into what pass for hilarious predicaments. 86m/B/W; DVD, Blu-Ray. **C:** Mickey Rooney; Robert Strauss; Elaine Davis; Bill Goodwin; Whit Bissell; Directed by Leslie Martinson; Written by Blake Edwards; Cinematography by John L. "Jack" Russell; Music by Van Alexander. **Pr:** Republic. **A:** Jr. High-Adult. **P:** Entertainment. **U:** Home. **Mov-Ent:** Comedy--Black, Nuclear Warfare. **Acq:** Purchase. **Dist:** Olive Films. $19.98.

The Atomic Man 1956 (Unrated) — ★½
Owing to radioactive experimentation, a scientist exists for a short time in the future. Once there, both good and evil forces want to use him for their own purposes. 78m/B/W; VHS, DVD. **C:** Gene Nelson; Faith Domergue; Joseph Tomelty; Peter Arne; Directed by Ken Hughes. **A:** Primary-Adult. **P:** Entertainment. **U:** Home. **Mov-Ent:** Science Fiction, Science. **Acq:** Purchase. **Dist:** Sinister Cinema. $16.95.

Atomic Memories 1950
A nostalgic look at the sincere efforts of the U.S. Government to inform its citizens of safety procedures during the Atomic Era. Includes "Duck and Cover," "The Effects of Atomic Bomb Explosions," and "Survival under Atomic Attack." 60m/B/W; VHS. **Pr:** U.S. Government. **A:** Jr. High-Adult. **P:** Education. **U:** Home. **Gen-Edu:** Nuclear Warfare, Safety Education. **Acq:** Purchase. **Dist:** Facets Multimedia Inc.; Moviecraft Home Video. $19.95.

Atomic Rulers of the World 1965 (Unrated) — ★½
An alien council of robots concerned that possible nuclear war on Earth will contaminate the universe sends one of their own to oversee the planet in the form of superhero Starman. In this particular installment he fights criminals from a foreign land who intend to use A-bombs to rule the world. Campy sci fi fun. 83m/B/W; DVD. **C:** Ken Utsui; Directed by Koreyoshi Akasaka; Teruo Ishii; Akira Mitsuwa; Written by Ichiro Miyagawa; Cinematography by Takashi Watanabe; Music by Michiaki Watanabe. **A:** Family. **P:** Entertainment. **U:** Home. **L:** English. **Mov-Ent. Acq:** Purchase. **Dist:** Gotham Distributing Corp. $7.98.

Atomic Submarine 1959 (Unrated) — ★★
Futuristic sci fi plots government agents against alien invaders. The battle, however, takes place in the ocean beneath the Arctic and is headed by an atomic-powered submarine clashing with a special alien underwater saucer. We all live on the atomic submarine: fun for devotees. 80m; VHS, DVD. **C:** Arthur Franz; Dick Foran; Bob Steele; Brett Halsey; Joi Lansing; Tom Conway; Paul Dubov; Directed by Spencer Gordon Bennet; Written by Orville H. Hampton; Cinematography by Gilbert Warrenton; Music by Alexander Laszlo. **Pr:** Alex Gordon. **A:** Jr. High-Adult. **P:** Entertainment. **U:** Home. **Mov-Ent:** Science Fiction, Arctic Regions. **Acq:** Purchase. **Dist:** Sinister Cinema. $39.95.

Atomic Theory and Chemistry 1987
This tape shows how atoms and molecules behave, and how this knowledge can be used. 19m; VHS, 3/4 U. **A:** Sr. High-College. **P:** Education. **U:** Institution, SURA. **Hea-Sci:** Chemistry. **Acq:** Purchase, Trade-in. **Dist:** Encyclopedia Britannica. $300.00.

Atomic Train 1999 (PG-13) — ★½
Silly two-part TV mini about a runaway train that's packed with toxic waste and a nuclear bomb, which is headed straight for Denver. Lowe (who makes a surprisingly good action hero) is National Transportation Safety Board investigator John Seger, who must derail the disaster. Meanwhile, the relentless media coverage has brought on widespread panic (those fiends!). 168m; VHS, DVD. **C:** Rob Lowe; Kristin Davis; Esai Morales; John Finn; Mena Suvari; Sean Smith; Edward Herrmann; Erik King; Blu Mankuma; Directed by Dick Lowry; David S. Jackson; Cinematography by Steven Fierberg; Music by Lee Holdridge. **Pr:** Trimark Pictures. **A:** Jr. High-Adult. **P:** Entertainment. **U:** Home. **Mov-Ent:** TV Movies, Trains, Action-Adventure. **Acq:** Purchase. **Dist:** CinemaNow Inc.

Atomic TV, Vol. 1 19??
Inventions, issues, and discoveries of the '50s and '60s are discussed. 60m; VHS. **C:** Narrated by Edward R. Murrow. **A:** Family. **P:** Entertainment. **U:** Home. **Gen-Edu:** Documentary Films. **Acq:** Purchase. **Dist:** Video Resources.
Indiv. Titles: 1. Duck and Cover: Survival Under Nuclear Attack 2. A Is For Atom.

Atoms 19??
Explains theories associated with atoms such as the release and control of atomic energy, radioactivity, and the nature of alpha, beta, and gamma rays. 60m; VHS. **A:** Jr. High-Sr. High. **P:** Education. **U:** Institution. **Hea-Sci:** Education, Science, Nuclear Energy. **Acq:** Purchase. **Dist:** Educational Activities Inc. $79.00.

Atoms and Starlight 1994
Explains how the study of light evolved, how transitions of electrons between energy levels produce photons of different wavelengths, and the Doppler effect. 30m; VHS. **A:** Adult. **P:** Education. **U:** Institution. **Hea-Sci:** Astronomy. **Acq:** Purchase. **Dist:** RMI Media. $89.95.

Atonement 2007 (R) — ★★★
In 1935 England, 13-year-old Briony (Ronan) sees her sister Cecilia (Knightley) and their cook's son Robbie (McAvoy) together (literally) and, out of jealousy, accuses Robbie of a crime he didn't commit. The once beloved Robbie is sent to jail and the family, who had been paying for him to attend college, rejects him. Only Cecilia believes he is innocent, and cannot forgive her sister. Five years later, the now grown Briony (Garai) and Cecilia are nurses in London and Robbie has been released from prison to fight in the war. Desperate for forgiveness for ruining Robbie's life, Briony tries to find a way to fix her mistake, but it may be too late. Knightley and McAvoy shine as the long-lost lovers, and Ronan's Briony is stellar. Beautifully shot period film is faithful to McEwan's novel, and to the tone and style of 1930s and '40s-era melodramas. 122m; Blu-Ray, On Demand, Wide. **C:** James McAvoy; Keira Knightley; Saoirse Ronan; Romola Garai; Vanessa Redgrave; Brenda Blethyn; Juno Temple; Patrick Kennedy; Benedict Cumberbatch; Harriet Walter; Gina McKee; Directed by Joe Wright; Written by Christopher Hampton; Cinematography by Seamus McGarvey; Music by Dario Marianelli. **Pr:** Tim Bevan; Eric Fellner; Paul Webster; Universal Pictures; StudioCanal; Working Title Productions; Relativity Media; Focus Features L.L.C. **A:** Sr. High-Adult. **P:** Entertainment. **U:** Home. **L:** English. **Mov-Ent:** Drama, World War Two. **Awds:** Oscars '07: Orig. Score; British Acad. '07: Film; Golden Globes '08: Film--Drama, Orig. Score. **Acq:** Purchase. **Dist:** Amazon.com Inc.; Movies Unlimited; Alpha Video.

The Atonement of Gosta Berling 1924 (Unrated) — ★★★
A priest, forced to leave the priesthood because of his drinking, falls in love with a young married woman. Garbo shines in the first role which brought her critical acclaim; Hanson's performance also makes this a memorable drama. Adapted from the novel by Selma Lagerlof. 91m/B/W; Silent; VHS, DVD. **C:** Lars Hanson; Greta Garbo; Ellen Cederstrom; Mona Martenson; Jenny Hasselqvist; Gerda Lundequist; Directed by Mauritz Stiller. **A:** Sr. High-Adult. **P:** Entertainment. **U:** Home. **L:** Swedish. **Mov-Ent:** Drama, Silent Films. **Acq:** Purchase. **Dist:** Movies Unlimited; Alpha Video.

Ator the Fighting Eagle 1983 (PG) — **Bomb!**
Styled after "Conan The Barbarian" this mythical action fantasy stars O'Keeffe as Ator, son of Thorn. Ator must put an end to the tragic Dynasty of the Spiders, thereby fulfilling the legend of his family at the expense of the viewer. Goofy low-budget sword and sandal stuff. D'Amato used the pseudonym David Hills. Followed by "The Blade Master." 98m; VHS, DVD. **C:** Miles O'Keeffe; Sabrina Siani; Ritza Brown; Edmund Purdom; Laura Gemser; Directed by Joe D'Amato. **Pr:** Comworld. **A:** Primary-Adult. **P:** Entertainment. **U:** Home. **Mov-Ent:** Fantasy. **Acq:** Purchase. **Dist:** Unknown Distributor.

Atragon 1963 (Unrated) — ★★½
The lost continent of Mu invades the surface world in order to reclaim its colonies. An embittered WWII veteran is asked to return to service in Japan's navy to construct the super-weapon intended to reverse Japan's fortunes before they surrendered to the Allies. 96m; DVD. **C:** Tadao Takashima; Yoko Fujiyama; Yu Fujiki; Ken Uehara; Jun Tazaki; Directed by Ishiro Honda; Written by Shinichi Sekizawa; Cinematography by Hajime Koizumi; Music by Akira Ifukube. **A:** Jr. High-Adult. **P:** Entertainment. **U:** Home. **L:** English, Japanese. **Mov-Ent. Acq:** Purchase. **Dist:** Media Blasters Inc. $19.97.

The Attached Solar Greenhouse 1982
The film explains the basic principles of solar greenhouse design, shows one being built and deals with costs. 28m; VHS, 3/4 U. **Pr:** Rodale Press; Bullfrog Films. **A:** Jr. High-Adult. **P:** Education. **U:** Institution, SURA. **Hea-Sci:** Solar Energy. **Acq:** Purchase, Duplication License. **Dist:** Bullfrog Films, Inc.

An Attachment 19??
Presents a real-life episode of genteel romance in the life of a Victorian cleric, the Rev. Francis Kilvert. Contracts extracts from the Reverend's diary and period photographs to help illustrate what romance was like in Victorian times. 29m/B/W; VHS. **A:** Sr. High-Adult. **P:** Education. **U:** Institution. **Gen-Edu:** Sociology, History, Literature. **Acq:** Purchase. **Dist:** University of Toronto.

Attachments for Hobart: Mixer/Food Chopper 1986
Offers instruction on specific aspects of cooking and food preparation. 11m; VHS. **A:** Adult. **P:** Instruction. **U:** Institution. **Gen-Edu:** Cooking. **Acq:** Purchase. **Dist:** RMI Media. $49.95.

Attack! 1956 — ★★★
Cowardly Captain Cooney (Albert) is order to move one of his platoons into a forward position in 1944 Belgium. They are slowly surrounded by the enemy as platoon leader, Lt. Costa (Palance), calls headquarters for reinforcements. But Cooney won't commit his reserves even as the platoon is decimated. Expert portrayals of men under pressure. 107m/B/W; VHS, DVD. **C:** Eddie Albert; Jack Palance; Lee Marvin; Robert Strauss; Richard Jaeckel; Buddy Ebsen; William (Bill) Smithers; Strother Martin; Directed by Robert Aldrich; Written by James Poe; Cinematography by Joseph Biroc. **Pr:** Robert Aldrich; Robert Aldrich; United Artists. **A:** Jr. High-Adult. **P:** Entertainment. **U:** Home. **Mov-Ent:** World War Two. **Acq:** Purchase. **Dist:** Movies Unlimited.

The Attack 2013 (R) — ★★★
A provocative drama, this Israeli film tells the story of a man caught between family, ethnicity, and origin in a powerful parable to the way history can collide with present day in the Middle East, leading to tragedy. An Arab doctor named Amin Jaafari (Suliman) has his world shattered when a suicide bombing in Tel Aviv is traced back to his wife Siham (Amsalem). Is it possible that the woman he shared his life with is a terrorist? An incredibly grounded performance from Suliman carries writer/director Ziad Doueiri's adaptation of the novel by Yasmina Khadra. 102m; DVD, Blu-Ray. **C:** Ali Suliman; Reymond Amsalem; Uri Gavriel; Directed by Ziad Doueiri; Written by Ziad Doueiri; Joelle Touma; Cinematography by Tommaso Fiorilli; Music by Eric Neveux. **Pr:** Jean Brehat; Rachid Bouchareb; Canal Plus. **A:** Sr. High-Adult. **P:** Entertainment. **U:** Home. **L:** Arabic, Hebrew. **Mov-Ent:** Israel, Middle East, Terrorism. **Acq:** Purchase. **Dist:** Cohen Media Group.

Attack and Reprisal 1946
Two short films about the Japanese attack on Pearl Harbor and the bombing of Hiroshima. 52m/B/W; VHS. **Pr:** Maljack Productions Inc. **A:** Sr. High-Adult. **P:** Education. **U:** Home. **Gen-Edu:** World War Two, Japan, Nuclear Warfare. **Acq:** Purchase. **Dist:** MPI Media Group. $39.98.

Attack Carrier 1985
A film outlining naval air achievements from WWII to Vietnam. Actual footage. 50m; VHS. **Pr:** Ferde Grofe Films. **A:** Jr. High-Adult. **P:** Entertainment. **U:** Institution, Home. **Gen-Edu:** Aeronautics. **Acq:** Purchase. **Dist:** Bennett Marine Video; Military/Combat Stock Footage Library. $24.95.

Attack Choppers 19??
The saga of lethal attack helicopters. 42m; VHS. **Pr:** Simitar. **A:** Adult. **P:** Entertainment. **U:** Home. **Gen-Edu:** Firearms, Military History. **Acq:** Purchase. **Dist:** Gun Video; Fusion Video. $19.95.

Attack Copter 1985
A professional copter training film dealing with various aspects of advanced flying. 86m; VHS. **Pr:** Ferde Grofe Films. **A:** Adult. **P:** Entertainment. **U:** Institution, Home. **Gen-Edu:** Aeronautics. **Acq:** Purchase. **Dist:** Bennett Marine Video; Military/Combat Stock Footage Library. $29.95.
Indiv. Titles: 1. Evolution of Attack Helicopter 2. Aerodynamics-Rotor Blade Actions 3. Aerodynamics-Stabilizer Bar 4. Aerodynamics-Dissymmetry of Lift 5. Aerodynamics-Rotor Blade Angles.

Attack Force 2006 (R) — **Bomb!**
Even judging by the low standards set by Seagal movies, this dreck isn't worth the effort to figure out what might be going on. After Special Agent Marshall Lawson's strike team is wiped out by a super-strong, drugged-out prostie, he's determined to figure out how it happened. This leads to a military/political conspiracy to infect the water supply with a drug that turns its users ultra-violent. Even the dialogue over-dubbing is ludicrous, with someone else obviously substituting for Seagal in various scenes. 95m; DVD. **C:** Steven Seagal; David Kennedy; Danny (Daniel) Webb; Andrew Bicknell; Lisa Lovbrand; Matthew Chambers; Directed by Michael Keusch; Written by Steven Seagal; Joe Halpin; Cinematography by Sonja Rom; Music by Barry Taylor. **A:** Sr. High-Adult. **P:** Entertainment. **U:** Home. **Mov-Ent:** Conspiracies or Conspiracy Theories. **Acq:** Purchase. **Dist:** Sony Pictures Home Entertainment Inc.

Attack Force Z 1984 (Unrated) — ★★
An elite corps of Australian military is Force Z. Volunteers are chosen for a dangerous mission: find the plane that crashed somewhere in the South Pacific and rescue the defecting Japanese government official on board, all before the end of WWII and the feature. Talented cast is effectively directed in low-key adventure featuring young Gibson. 84m; VHS, DVD. **C:** Sam Neill; Chris Haywood; Mel Gibson; John Phillip Law; John Waters; Directed by Tim Burstall. **Pr:** Lee Robinson. **A:** Jr. High-Adult. **P:** Entertainment. **U:** Home. **Mov-Ent:** World War Two. **Acq:** Purchase. **Dist:** Management Company Entertainment Group (MCEG), Inc.; MNTEX Entertainment, Inc. $19.99.

Attack from Mars 1988 (Unrated) — ★★½
Retro splatterama has really gross vampire alien land outside a Burbank movie theatre in 1956, and the really weird movie patrons try to terminate it. 86m; VHS, DVD. **C:** Robert Clarke; Ann (Robin) Robinson; Directed by Mark Stock; Written by Mark Stock; David Houston. **A:** Jr. High-Adult. **P:** Entertainment. **U:** Home. **Mov-Ent:** Science Fiction. **Acq:** Purchase. **Dist:** Image Entertainment Inc.

Attack from Outer Space 1980
Explores the possibility of extraterrestrial life, particularly on the set. 90m; VHS. **A:** Family. **P:** Entertainment. **U:** Home. **Mov-Ent:** Speculation. **Acq:** Purchase. **Dist:** VCI Entertainment. $9.95.

Attack from Space 1965 (Unrated) — ★
Starman must save the world yet again, this time from an alien race known as the Spherions who appear to be invading Earth simply because it's there. 76m/B/W; DVD. **C:** Ken Utsui; Directed by Koreyoshi Akasaka; Teruo Ishii; Akira Mitsuwa; Written by Ichiro Miyagawa; Cinematography by Takashi Watanabe; Music by Michiaki Watanabe. **A:** Family. **P:** Entertainment. **U:** Home. **L:** English. **Mov-Ent. Acq:** Purchase. **Dist:** Gotham Distributing Corp. $7.98.

Attack Girls' Swim Team vs. the Undead 2007 (Unrated) — **Bomb!**
Second in a series of zombie-themed horror comedies (the others are to date unavailable in the United States). A villain convinces a local school of a virus outbreak, and they allow him to vaccinate the students—which actually turns them into flesh-eating zombies. Chlorine renders one immune to the vaccine, and thankfully the school's new lesbian leads the girls swim team on an all-out assault against them. 80m; DVD. **C:** Sasa Handa; Yuria Hidaka; Directed by Koji Kawano; Written by Satoshi Owada; Cinematography by Mitsuaki Fujimoto; Music by Hideto Takematsu. **A:** Sr. High-Adult. **P:** Entertainment. **U:** Home. **L:** English, Japanese. **Mov-Ent. Acq:** Purchase. **Dist:** $29.98.

Attack in the Pacific 1942
Official Armed Forces footage provides overview of the United States' wartime role in the Pacific, from the attack on Pearl Harbor to the battles of Midway and the Coral Sea. 52m/B/W; VHS. **Pr:** Department of War Information. **A:** Jr. High-Adult. **P:** Entertainment. **U:** Home. **Gen-Edu:** Documentary Films, World War Two. **Acq:** Purchase. **Dist:** Synergy Entertainment, Inc. $14.98.

Attack of the Beast Creatures 1985 (Unrated) — **Bomb!**
The survivors of a wrecked ocean liner are stranded on a desert island overrun by savage creatures. This makes them anxious. 82m; VHS. **C:** Robert Nolfi; Robert Langyel; Julia Rust; Lisa Pak; Directed by Michael Stanley. **Pr:** Joseph Brenner Associates. **A:** Jr. High-Adult. **P:** Entertainment. **U:** Home. **Mov-Ent:** Horror. **Acq:** Purchase. **Dist:** No Longer Available.

Attack of the Crab Monsters 1957 (Unrated) — ★½
Short and campy Corman produced-and-directed sci-fi about a group of scientists who have gone missing on a remote Pacific island while studying the aftereffects of atomic radiation. A second group travels to the island to figure out what's happened but all they seem to find are crabs—and then those scientists start getting killed off. As you can tell from the title, the crabs are behind it all! And that clicking noise they make is surprisingly creepy. 62m/B/W; DVD. **C:** Richard Garland; Pamela Duncan; Russell Johnson; Leslie Bradley; Mel Welles; Richard Cutting; Tony Miller; Ed Nelson; Directed by Roger Corman; Written by Charles B. Griffith; Cinematography by Floyd Crosby; Music by Ronald Stein. **A:** Jr. High-Adult. **P:** Entertainment. **U:** Home. **Mov-Ent:** Science. **Acq:** Purchase. **Dist:** Shout! Factory.

Attack of the 50 Foot Woman 1958 (Unrated) — ★★½
A beautiful, abused housewife has a frightening encounter with a giant alien, causing her to grow to an enormous height. Then she goes looking for hubby. Perhaps the all-time classic '50s sci fi, a truly fun movie highlighted by the sexy, 50-foot Hayes in a giant bikini. Has intriguing psychological depth and social commentary done in a suitably cheezy manner. 72m/B/W; VHS, DVD. **C:** Allison Hayes; William (Bill) Hudson; Roy Gordon; Yvette Vickers; George Douglas; Ken Terrell; Michael Ross; Frank Chase; Eileen Stevens; Otto Waldis; Directed by Nathan "Jerry" Juran; Written by Mark Hanna; Cinematography by Jacques "Jack" Marquette; Music by Ronald Stein. **Pr:** Allied Artists International. **A:** Family. **P:** Entertainment. **U:** Home. **Mov-Ent:** Science Fiction, Cult Films. **Acq:** Purchase. **Dist:** Warner Home Video, Inc. $14.98.

Attack of the 50 Ft. Woman 1993 — ★★½
Campy remake of the 1958 sci-fi cult classic features the statuesque Hannah in the title role. Nancy's a put-upon hausfrau with zero self-esteem thanks to her domineering father (Windom) and loutish hubby (Baldwin). They should have been sweet to her because after an encounter with a flying saucer Nancy starts to grow...and grow...and grow. And then she decides to get some revenge. 90m; VHS, DVD. **C:** Daryl Hannah; Daniel Baldwin; William Windom; Frances Fisher; Cristi Conaway; Paul Benedict; Lewis Arquette; Xander Berkeley; Hamilton Camp; Richard Edson; Victoria Haas; O'Neal Compton; Directed by Christopher Guest; Written by Joseph Dougherty; Music by Nicholas Pike. **Pr:** Joseph Dougherty; Debra Hill; HBO; Warner Bros. Television. **A:** Jr. High-Adult. **P:** Entertainment. **U:** Home. **Mov-Ent:** Science Fiction, Marriage, TV Movies. **Acq:** Purchase. **Dist:** Warner Home Video, Inc.

Attack of the Giant Leeches 1959 — ★
Cheapo Corman fare about giant leeches in a murky swamp who suddenly decide to make human flesh their new food supply. Perturbed inn keeper plays along by forcing his wife and lover into the murk. Leeches frolic. Sometimes tedious, sometimes chilling, always low budget and slimy. Although the special effects aren't top notch, this might be a fine choice for a late night scare/laugh. 62m/B/W; VHS, DVD, Blu-Ray. **C:** Ken Clark; Yvette Vickers; Gene Roth; Bruno VeSota; Michael Emmet; Tyler McVey; Jan Shepard; George Cisar; Dan(iel) White; Directed by Bernard L. Kowalski; Written by Leo Gordon; Cinematography by John M. Nickolaus, Jr.; Music by Alexander Laszlo. **Pr:** American International Pictures. **A:** Jr. High-Adult. **P:** Entertainment. **U:** Home. **Mov-Ent:** Science Fiction. **Acq:** Purchase. **Dist:** Rhino Entertainment Co. $14.95.

Attack of the Gryphon 2007 (PG-13) — ★
Royals from two rival kingdoms must band together to fight a wizard attempting to wipe them out with a giant monster in order to satisfy his evil wives. The low-budget special effects are evil in and of themselves. 89m; DVD, Streaming. **C:** Jonathan LaPaglia; Larry Drake; Amber Benson; Andrew Pleavin; Douglas Roberts; Directed by Andrew Prowse; Written by Sean Keller; Boaz Davidson; Tim Cox; Kenneth M. Badish; Cinematography by Viorel Sergovici, Jr.; Music by John Dickson. **A:** Jr. High-Adult. **P:** Entertainment. **U:** Home. **L:** English. **Mov-Ent. Acq:** Purchase, Rent/Lease. **Dist:** Sony Pictures Home Entertainment Inc. $14.99 9.99.

Attack of the Herbals 2011 (Unrated) — ★
A pair of slackers try to save their small village from being bulldozed, and discover a way when a mysterious crate washes ashore. They have no idea what the contents are but decide to make tea out of them and it turns out surprisingly addictive. Only when they run out of the stuff do they notice the swastika on the bottom of the crate, and predictably all hell breaks loose. 86m; DVD. **C:** Calum Booth; Steve Worsley; Richard Currie; Liam Matheson; Lee Hutcheon; Directed by David Ryan Keith; Written by Liam Matheson; David Ryan Keith; Alisdair Cook; Cinematography by David Ryan Keith; Music by Leah Kardos. **A:** Sr. High-Adult. **P:** Entertainment. **U:** Home. **L:** English. **Mov-Ent. Acq:** Purchase. **Dist:** MTI Home Video. $24.95.

Attack of the Jurassic Shark 2012 (Unrated) — ★
An oil company unleashes a prehistoric shark which quickly traps a group of college girls on an island along with a gang of art thieves. 79m; DVD. **C:** Emanuelle Carriere; Christine Emes; Celine Filion; Angela Parent; Duncan Milloy; Directed by Brett Kelly; Written by David Lloyd; Trevor Payer; Cinematography by Amber Peters; Music by Christopher Nickel. **A:** Sr. High-Adult. **P:** Entertainment. **U:** Home. **L:** English. **Mov-Ent. Acq:** Purchase. **Dist:** Tempe DVD. $19.99.

Attack of the Killer Bees 2006 (Unrated)
In 1957, an especially defensive, new breed of bees was accidentally released from a hive in Brazil. Since then they have increased in number and capability by mating with other bee species. Now broadly referred to as "killer bees," scientists, beekeepers, and exterminators as far north as the southern United States are working hard to stop these invaders from penetrating even further north. 52m; DVD. **A:** Family. **P:** Education. **U:** Institution, Home. **Mov-Ent:** Documentary Films, Animals, Bees. **Acq:** Purchase. **Dist:** National Geographic Society. $19.95.

Attack of the Killer Refrigerator 1990
Chiller featuring a group of sleazy college students having a wild party. In the process, they abuse a hapless refrigerator. Fed up, the vengeful appliance goes on a rampage of murder and destruction. Certain to make you view kitchen appliances in a new light. Planned sequels in the newfound kitchen-utility horror genre include "Refrigerator II: Brutally Defrosted" and "Bloody, Bloody Coffee Maker." 15m; VHS. **Pr:** Phoenix Films. **A:** Adult. **P:** Entertainment. **U:** Home. **Mov-Ent:** Technology. **Acq:** Purchase. **Dist:** Phoenix Learning Group.

Attack of the Killer Tomatoes 1977 (PG) — **Bomb!**
Candidate for worst film ever made, deliberate category. Horror spoof that defined "low budget" stars several thousand ordinary tomatoes that suddenly turn savage and begin attacking people. No sci-fi cliche remains untouched in this dumb parody. A few musical numbers are performed in lieu of an actual plot. Followed by "Return of the Killer Tomatoes." Originally released at 87 minutes. 87m; VHS, DVD, CC. **C:** George Wilson; Jack Riley; Rock Peace; Eric Christmas; David Miller; Sharon Taylor; Jerry Anderson; Nigel Barber; John DeBello; Directed by John DeBello; Written by Costa Dillon; John DeBello; Cinematography by John K. Culley. **Pr:** Four Square Productions. **A:** Jr. High-Adult. **P:** Entertainment. **U:** Home. **Mov-Ent:** Science Fiction, Cult Films. **Acq:** Purchase. **Dist:** Buena Vista Home Entertainment; Rhino Entertainment Co. $12.99.

Attack of the Mayan Mummy 1963 (Unrated) — **Bomb!**
A greedy doctor gets his patient to channel her former self so that she can show him where to find an ancient tomb that is filled with treasure. Good idea. 77m/B/W; VHS. **C:** Richard Webb; Nina Knight; Norman Burton; Steve Conte; Directed by Jerry Warren. **Pr:** Medallion Pictures. **A:** Jr. High-Adult. **P:** Entertainment. **U:** Home. **Mov-Ent:** Horror. **Acq:** Purchase. **Dist:** Sinister Cinema; Something Weird Video. $16.95.

Attack of the Moon Zombies 2011 (Unrated) — ★½
Another Mihm homage to 50s drive-in monster movies. Scientists on the moon discover plant life. This is considered a good thing until the plants' spores turn humans into evil plant zombies. 99m/B/W; DVD. **C:** Michael Cook; Shannon McDonough; Michael G. Kaiser; Sid Korpi; Douglas Sidney; Directed by Christopher R. Mihm; Written by Christopher R. Mihm. **A:** Jr. High-Adult. **P:** Entertainment. **U:** Home. **L:** English. **Mov-Ent. Acq:** Purchase. **Dist:** Saint Euphoria Pictures. $14.99 9.99.

Attack of the Puppet People 1958 (Unrated) — ★★
This alternative classic from the prolific Bert I. Gordon, a rival to Ed Wood Jr. in the schlock hall of fame, will not make anyone forget "The Incredible Shrinking Man." The insane dollmaker Dr. Franz (Hoyt) shrinks six people (including our heroes Agar and Kenny) to the size of Ken and Barbie. Can they escape the mad scientist? The dog? The rat? The effects are nostalgically charming. 79m/B/W; DVD. **C:** John Agar; John Hoyt; June Kenney; Sally Reynolds; Susan Gordon; Directed by Bert I. Gordon; Written by George Worthing Yates; Cinematography by Ernest Laszlo; Music by Albert Glasser. **A:** Jr. High-Adult. **P:** Entertainment. **U:** Home. **Mov-Ent:** Horror, Miniaturization. **Acq:** Purchase. **Dist:** MGM Home Entertainment.

Attack of the Robots 1966 (Unrated) — ★½
Silly spy spoof about powerful government officials who are being killed off by a mad scientist's robots. Interpol agent Lemmy Caution comes to the rescue. 88m/B/W; VHS, DVD. **TV Std:** NTSC, PAL. **C:** Eddie Constantine; Fernando Rey; Directed by Jess (Jesus) Franco; Written by Jean-Claude Carriere. **Pr:** American International Pictures. **A:** Family. **P:** Entertainment. **U:** Home. **Mov-Ent:** Technology, Science, Satire & Parody. **Acq:** Purchase. **Dist:** Sinister Cinema. $24.95.

Attack of the Sabretooth 2005 (R) — ★½
Think cheap "Jurassic Park." Niles (Bell) invests his moolah in a combo tropical paradise resort and wildlife refuge that contains cloned sabretooth tigers. Naturally they escape and maul and munch any human in reach. 88m; DVD, CC. **C:** Robert Carradine; Nicholas Bell; Billy Aaron Brown; Brian Wimmer; Stacy Haiduk; Natalie Avital; Amanda Stephens; Directed by George Miller; Written by Tom Woosley; Cinematography by Mark Melville; Music by Timothy S. (Tim) Jones. **A:** Sr. High-Adult. **P:** Entertainment. **U:** Home. **Mov-Ent:** Animals. **Acq:** Purchase. **Dist:** Lions Gate Entertainment Inc.

Attack of the 60-Foot Centerfold 1995 (R) — ★½
Angel Grace wants to be Centerfold of the Year so badly that she gets a doctor to enhance her endowments even more through a mystery formula. Only there's a little complication. Cheesy, with pretty women and no discernable acting (and a spoof of that '58 gem "Attack of the 50 Ft. Woman"). 83m; VHS, DVD. **C:** J.J. North; Tammy Parks; John Lazar; Russ Tamblyn; Tommy Kirk; Stanley Livingston; Michelle (McClellan) Bauer; George Stover; Forrest J Ackerman; Ted Monte; Jim Wynorski; Raelyn Saalman; Tim Abell; Jay Richardson; Nikki Fritz; Directed by Fred Olen Ray; Written by Steve Armogida; Cinematography by Gary Graver; Howard Wexler; Music by Jeff Walton. **A:** Adult. **P:** Entertainment. **U:** Home. **Mov-Ent. Acq:** Purchase. **Dist:** Buena Vista Home Entertainment.

Attack of the Swamp Creature 1975 (Unrated) — **Bomb!**
A deranged scientist transforms himself into a swamp critter and terrorizes a small town. 96m; VHS, DVD, Blu-Ray. **C:** Marshall Grauer; Nancy Lien; Paul Galloway; Wade Popwell; Frank Crowell; David Robertson; Doug Thomas; Directed by Don Barton; Arnold Stevens; Written by Lee Larew; Ron Kivett. **Pr:**

Aquarius Video. **A:** Sr. High-Adult. **P:** Entertainment. **U:** Home. **Mov-Ent:** Horror. **Acq:** Purchase. **Dist:** Cultra; Lions Gate Television Corp. $29.95.

Attack on Darfur 2009 (Unrated) — **Bomb!**
Western journalists staying in a Sudanese village are gathering footage and interviews on atrocities. When they learn that the brutal Janjaweed militia is heading towards the village, the journalists don't know whether to leave or stay and help. Boll goes for importance and gets pretentious drama instead. 104m; DVD. **C:** Billy Zane; Kristanna Loken; Edward Furlong; David O'Hara; Hakeem Kae-Kazim; Matt Frewer; Directed by Uwe Boll; Written by Uwe Boll; Chris Roland; Cinematography by Mathias Neumann; Music by Jessica de Rooij. **A:** Sr. High-Adult. **P:** Entertainment. **U:** Home. **Mov-Ent:** Africa, Journalism. **Acq:** Purchase. **Dist:** Peace Arch Entertainment Group.

Attack on Leningrad 2009 (PG-13) — ★½
Clunky exposition and some questionable acting doom this true story drama. In the winter of 1941, German troops cut the food and fuel supplies in an attempt to starve the people of Leningrad into submission. British journalist Kate Davis gets left behind during an evacuation and is hidden from Russian military authorities by officer Nina Tsvetkova as the siege continues and everyone struggles to survive amidst increasingly dire circumstances. 110m; DVD, Blu-Ray. **C:** Mira Sorvino; Olga Sutulova; Gabriel Byrne; Armin Mueller-Stahl; Alexander Abdulov; Vladimir Ilin; Directed by Aleksandr (Sasha) Buravsky; Written by Aleksandr (Sasha) Buravsky; Cinematography by Vladimir Klimov; Music by Yuriy Poteenko. **A:** Jr. High-Adult. **P:** Entertainment. **U:** Home. **Mov-Ent:** USSR, World War Two, Journalism. **Acq:** Purchase. **Dist:** Entertainment One US LP.

Attack Pacific! 1985
The WWII Pacific battles in actual Documentary footage, from Pearl Harbor to Hiroshima. Also with a short, "Hell for Leather." 65m; VHS. **Pr:** Ferde Grofe Films. **A:** Jr. High-Adult. **P:** Entertainment. **U:** Institution, Home. **Gen-Edu:** World War Two. **Acq:** Purchase. **Dist:** Bennett Marine Video; Military/Combat Stock Footage Library. $24.95.

Attack Squadron 1963 — ★½
Story of Japan's suicidal WWII pilots. 105m; VHS. **C:** Toshiro Mifune; Yuzo Kayama; Takashi Shimura; Yosuke Natsuki; Makoto Sato; Directed by Shue Matsubayashi; Written by Shinobu Hashimoto; Cinematography by Takao Saito; Music by Ikuma Dan. **A:** Jr. High-Adult. **P:** Entertainment. **U:** Home. **Mov-Ent:** Aeronautics, World War Two, Suicide. **Acq:** Purchase. **Dist:** No Longer Available.

Attack the Block 2011 (R) — ★★
Debut feature from Cornish is fast and funny (although the slang may puzzle Americans). South London teen hoodlums mug nurse Sam before killing an alien (the outer-space kind) who had the bad luck to crash-land in their hood. The two incidents come together when their impetuous actions result in a full-on invasion that the authorities know nothing about since they're preoccupied with the fireworks on Guy Fawkes night. 88m; Blu-Ray, On Demand, Wide. **C:** John Boyega; Jodie Whitaker; Alex Esmail; Franz Drameh; Leeon Jones; Simon Howard; Nick Frost; Luke Treadway; Jumayh Hunter; Directed by Joe Cornish; Written by Joe Cornish; Cinematography by Tom Townsend; Music by Steven Price; Felix Buxton; Simon Radcliffe. **Pr:** Nira Park; James L. Wilson; Big Talk Pictures; Optimum Releasing. **A:** Sr. High-Adult. **P:** Entertainment. **U:** Home. **L:** English. **Mov-Ent:** Action-Comedy. **Acq:** Purchase. **Dist:** Alpha Video; Sony Pictures Home Entertainment Inc.; Amazon.com Inc.

Attack the Gas Station 1999 (R) — ★★½
Four young slackers who have been successful at robbing gas stations take one over and pose as the attendants while keeping the real workers in back as hostages. They then indulge in other brilliant behavior by beating up the local gangsters, robbing the guys who deliver their takeout food, and cheesing off anyone they encounter. Eventually this ends in a comic slugfest between them, the cops, the mob, and several local Chinese restaurants. The police and organized crime are survivable but they're pretty brave taking on Chinese delivery boys. 109m; DVD, Wide. **C:** Ji-tae Yu; Jun Jeong; Yu-won Lee; Sung-jae Lee; Oh-seong Yu; Seong-jin Kang; Yeong-gyu Park; Directed by Sang-jin Kim; Written by Jeong-woo Park; Cinematography by Jeong-won Choi; Music by Mu-hyeon Son. **A:** Sr. High-Adult. **P:** Entertainment. **U:** Home. **L:** English, Korean. **Mov-Ent:** Satire & Parody. **Acq:** Purchase. **Dist:** Movies Unlimited. $29.95.

Attacking and Defending Concepts 2009 (Unrated)
Coach Randy Waldrum discusses and demonstrates concepts for soccer offense and defense using the 4-3-3 system. 78m; DVD. **A:** Family. **P:** Education. **U:** Home, Institution. **Spo-Rec:** Soccer, Athletic Instruction/Coaching. **Acq:** Purchase. **Dist:** Championship Productions. $29.99.

Attacking and Defending Out of the 4-2-3-1 2012 (Unrated)
Coach Alan Kirkup diagrams the 4-3-2-1 system, and discusses how to implement it in a soccer team. 83m; DVD. **A:** Family. **P:** Education. **U:** Home. **L:** English. **Spo-Rec:** Athletic Instruction/Coaching, Soccer, How-To. **Acq:** Purchase. **Dist:** Championship Productions. $29.99.

Attacking and Defending Set Pieces 2011 (Unrated)
Soccer coach Brandon Koons discusses offensive set pieces along with how a team can defend itself against them. 60m; DVD. **A:** Family. **P:** Education. **U:** Home, Institution. **Spo-Rec:** Soccer, Athletic Instruction/Coaching. **Acq:** Purchase. **Dist:** Championship Productions. $29.99.

Attacking Defenses with the Spread & Shred Offense 2013 (Unrated)
Coach Jeff Steinberg demonstrates variations on the spread & shred offense. 122m; DVD. **A:** Family. **P:** Education. **U:** Home. **L:** English. **Spo-Rec:** Athletic Instruction/Coaching, Volleyball, How-To. **Acq:** Purchase. **Dist:** Championship Productions. $4.99.

Attacking Defensive Back Play in the 3-4 Defense 2013 (Unrated)
Coach Donnell Leomiti presents eleven drills for increasing a football team's turnover ratio? 39m; DVD. **A:** Family. **P:** Education. **U:** Home. **L:** English. **Spo-Rec:** Athletic Instruction/Coaching, Football. **Acq:** Purchase. **Dist:** Championship Productions. $39.99.

Attacking Defensive Line Play for the 3-4 Defense 2013 (Unrated)
Coach Paul Creighton discusses building up a football team's defensive line and correcting for errors. DVD. **A:** Family. **P:** Education. **U:** Home. **L:** English. **Spo-Rec:** Athletic Instruction/Coaching, Football. **Acq:** Purchase. **Dist:** Championship Productions. $39.99.

Attacking Exercises for Tiki-Taka Soccer 2013 (Unrated)
Coach Alan Kirkup demonstrates offensive training drills for use with the Tika-Taka style of soccer. 167m; DVD. **A:** Family. **P:** Education. **U:** Home. **L:** English. **Spo-Rec:** Athletic Instruction/Coaching, Soccer. **Acq:** Purchase. **Dist:** Championship Productions. $29.99.

Attacking Exercises to Improve Soccer Technique 2012 (Unrated)
Coach Alan Kirkup demonstrates drills for improving a soccer team's offensive abilities. DVD. **A:** Family. **P:** Education. **U:** Home. **L:** English. **Spo-Rec:** Athletic Instruction/Coaching, Soccer, How-To. **Acq:** Purchase. **Dist:** Championship Productions. $29.99.

Attacking from Behind the Goal 2014 (Unrated)
Lacrosse coaches Marc Van Arsdale and Dominic Starsia discuss building an offense that can successfully attack from behind the goal. 67m; DVD. **A:** Family. **P:** Education. **U:** Home. **L:** English. **Spo-Rec:** Athletic Instruction/Coaching, Lacrosse. **Acq:** Purchase. **Dist:** Championship Productions. $39.99.

Attacking Goalkeeping: Drills, Techniques and Tactics 2014 (Unrated)
Soccer coach Chris Ducar uses game footage to highlight how being aggressive as a goalkeeper is beneficial to the team. 107m; DVD. **A:** Family. **P:** Education. **U:** Home. **L:** English. **Spo-Rec:** Athletic Instruction/Coaching, Soccer. **Acq:** Purchase. **Dist:** Championship Productions. $39.99.

Attacking in the Final Third 2005 (Unrated)
Coach 'Butch' Lauffer discusses attacking in the final third of a soccer game to exploit the fears of the opposing team's defense. 68m; DVD. **A:** Family. **P:** Education. **U:** Home, Institution. **Spo-Rec:** Soccer, Athletic Instruction/Coaching. **Acq:** Purchase. **Dist:** Championship Productions. $29.99.

Attacking Linebacker Play in the 3-4 Defense 2013 (Unrated)
Defensive Coordinator Hunter Hughes uses game footage to discuss making the best offensive use of a football team's linebackers. 82m; DVD. **A:** Family. **P:** Education. **U:** Home. **L:** English. **Spo-Rec:** Athletic Instruction/Coaching, Football. **Acq:** Purchase. **Dist:** Championship Productions. $39.99.

Attacking On-Ball Screening Offense 2008 (Unrated)
Coach Todd Kowalczyk presents the offensive system he teaches his basketball teams. 62m; DVD. **A:** Family. **P:** Education. **U:** Home, Institution. **Spo-Rec:** Basketball, Athletic Instruction/Coaching. **Acq:** Purchase. **Dist:** Championship Productions. $39.99.

Attacking Out of a Modern 3-5-2 1999 (Unrated)
Coach Mike Berticelli provides an over view of the 3-5-2 system for soccer, and methods coaches can use for training their team to utilize it. 45m; DVD. **A:** Family. **P:** Education. **U:** Home, Institution. **Spo-Rec:** Soccer, Athletic Instruction/Coaching. **Acq:** Purchase. **Dist:** Championship Productions. $29.99.

Attacking Skills for the 90's 1991
Allows athletes to focus on the mechanics and skills of the game by watching the stars in action as well as by receiving detailed instructions. Two volumes. 30m; VHS. **A:** Sr. High-Adult. **P:** Instruction. **U:** Institution, Home. **Spo-Rec:** Soccer. **Acq:** Purchase. **Dist:** Cambridge Educational. $58.00.

Attacking Soccer in the Women's Game: Skills, Decisions and Mindset 2006 (Unrated)
The NSCAA staff lectures on developing the mindset and mental abilities of female soccer players. 145m; DVD. **A:** Family. **P:** Education. **U:** Home, Institution. **Spo-Rec:** Lacrosse, Athletic Instruction/Coaching. **Acq:** Purchase. **Dist:** Championship Productions. $29.99.

Attacking the 5-3 Defense with the Wing-T 2001 (Unrated)
Coach Dennis Creehan lectures on how football teams can employ the Wing-T offense to beat the 5-3 Defense. 58m; DVD. **A:** Family. **P:** Education. **U:** Home, Institution. **Spo-Rec:** Football, Athletic Instruction/Coaching. **Acq:** Purchase. **Dist:** Championship Productions. $39.99.

Attacking the 5-2 Defense with the Wing-T 2001 (Unrated)
Coach Dennis Creehan how football teams should attack the 5-2 Defense using the Wing-T Offense. 100m; VHS. **A:** Family. **P:** Education. **U:** Home, Institution. **Spo-Rec:** Football, Athletic Instruction/Coaching. **Acq:** Purchase. **Dist:** Championship Productions. $39.99.

Attacking the 4-4 Defense with the Wing-T 2001 (Unrated)
Coach Dennis Creehan shows plays football teams using the Wing-T Offense can use against the 4-4 Defense. 93m; DVD. **A:** Family. **P:** Education. **U:** Home, Institution. **Spo-Rec:** Football, Athletic Instruction/Coaching. **Acq:** Purchase. **Dist:** Championship Productions. $39.99.

Attacking the 4-3 Defense with the Wing-T 2001 (Unrated)
Coach Dennis Creehan discusses how to attack the 4-3 Defense with the Wing-T Offense for football teams. 87m; DVD. **A:** Family. **P:** Education. **U:** Home, Institution. **Spo-Rec:** Football, Athletic Instruction/Coaching. **Acq:** Purchase. **Dist:** Championship Productions. $39.99.

Attacking the Rim with the Dribble Drive Motion Offense 2013 (Unrated)
Basketball coach Matt Bollant details the offensive system he teaches at the University of Illinois. 58m; DVD. **A:** Family. **P:** Education. **U:** Home. **L:** English. **Spo-Rec:** Athletic Instruction/Coaching, Basketball. **Acq:** Purchase. **Dist:** Championship Productions. $39.99.

The Attacking 3-Out & 4-Out Motion Offense 2014 (Unrated)
Coach John Giannini maps out the particular style of offensive play he teaches his basketball teams. 127m; DVD. **A:** Family. **P:** Education. **U:** Home. **L:** English. **Spo-Rec:** Athletic Instruction/Coaching, Basketball. **Acq:** Purchase. **Dist:** Championship Productions. $49.99.

Attacking with the Double Leg 2001 (Unrated)
Coach Tom Brands presents drills to help wrestlers increase their abilities with the Double Leg takedown and maneuvers they can use from it. 36m; DVD. **A:** Family. **P:** Education. **U:** Home, Institution. **Spo-Rec:** Athletic Instruction/Coaching. **Acq:** Purchase. **Dist:** Championship Productions. $39.99.

Attacking with the 2-on-1 Series 2011 (Unrated)
Coach Carl Fronhofer describes various wrestling techniques that can be used from the 2-on-1 series. 67m; DVD. **A:** Family. **P:** Education. **U:** Home, Institution. **Spo-Rec:** Athletic Instruction/Coaching. **Acq:** Purchase. **Dist:** Championship Productions. $39.99.

Attacking Zone Defenses 2010 (Unrated)
Coach Dave Lebo gives an on-court demonstration of various methods basketball teams can use to attack the Zone Defense. 71m; DVD. **A:** Family. **P:** Education. **U:** Home, Institution. **Spo-Rec:** Basketball, Athletic Instruction/Coaching. **Acq:** Purchase. **Dist:** Championship Productions. $39.99.

Attain Any Goal 19??
Tolly Burkan, famous for his motivational fire-walking seminars, teaches methods to accomplish any goal. 120m; VHS. **A:** Sr. High-Adult. **P:** Education. **U:** Home. **Gen-Edu:** Self-Help. **Acq:** Purchase. **Dist:** Hartley Film Foundation. $39.95.

Attempted Murder: Confrontation 199?
Presents a mediated confrontation between an attempted murder victim and his assailant. 30m; VHS. **A:** Sr. High-Adult. **P:** Entertainment. **U:** Institution. **Gen-Edu:** Sociology, Communication. **Acq:** Purchase. **Dist:** Ambrose Video Publishing, Inc. $69.95.

Attenborough's Life Stories 2013 (Unrated)
A tribute to the work of David Attenborough who has served as writer, producer, narrator, and host for many nature documentaries. 150m; DVD, Blu-Ray. **A:** Family. **P:** Entertainment. **U:** Home. **L:** English. **Gen-Edu:** Football, Sports--General. **Acq:** Purchase. **Dist:** BBC America Inc. $29.98 24.98.

Attendance: An Employer's Expectation 1993
Teaches the importance of good attendance on the job. Provides examples of the consequences of missing work. A teacher's guide with questions and activities is included. 17m; VHS. **A:** Sr. High-Adult. **P:** Professional. **U:** Institution. **Gen-Edu:** Job Training, Business, Office Practice. **Acq:** Purchase. **Dist:** Education Associates Inc. $85.00.

The Attendant 1985
This documentary explores the relationship between David Harlan, a professional caregiver for Rik Berkenpass, who is severely handicapped. Rik would be trapped and unable to lead a full life without David's help. 30m; VHS, 3/4 U. **Pr:** Richard Osborn; Jo Parente. **A:** Jr. High-Adult. **P:** Education. **U:** Institution, Home, SURA. **Gen-Edu:** Handicapped. **Acq:** Purchase, Rent/Lease, Duplication. **Dist:** Filmakers Library Inc.

The Attendant 1992
Older black man, who works as a guard in an art museum, sees a 19th-century painting that depicts slavery come to life. 8m; VHS. **C:** Directed by Isaac Julien. **A:** College-Adult. **P:** Entertainment. **U:** Institution. **Fin-Art:** Film--Avant-Garde, Art & Artists, Slavery. **Acq:** Purchase, Rent/Lease. **Dist:** Frameline. $150.00.

Attendants Flowers 19??
Provides tips for selecting bouquets, flowers, and colors for the wedding. 60m; VHS. **A:** Sr. High-Adult. **P:** Instruction. **U:** Institution. **How-Ins:** Marriage, How-To, Flowers. **Acq:** Purchase. **Dist:** Instructional Video. $29.95.

Attention Deficit Disorder: Adults 1996
Adults with Attention Deficit Disorder reveal how the disorder affected their lives and what they have found to help them. 28m; VHS. **A:** Sr. High-Adult. **P:** Education. **U:** Institution. **Hea-Sci:**

Health Education, Learning Disabilities, Patient Education. **Acq:** Purchase. **Dist:** Aquarius Health Care Media. $149.00.

Attention Deficit Disorder: Children 1996
Examines the correct diagnosis of Attention Deficit Disorder in children and effective treatments for the problem. 28m; VHS. **A:** Family. **P:** Education. **U:** Institution. **Hea-Sci:** Health Education, Learning Disabilities, Patient Education. **Acq:** Purchase. **Dist:** Aquarius Health Care Media. $149.00.

Attention-Deficit Hyperactivity Disorder 19??
Two-part psychological education series on attention-deficit hyperactivity disorder by Russell A. Barkley. Offers information on the history, etiology and prevalence of ADHD, and effective ways of managing ADHD in the home and classroom. Includes interviews with patients, parents, and teachers. Comes with teacher's guide and program manuals. 73m; VHS. **Pr:** Fanlight Productions. **A:** College-Adult. **P:** Education. **U:** Institution. **Hea-Sci:** Psychology, Medical Education, Learning Disabilities. **Acq:** Purchase, Rent/Lease. **Dist:** Fanlight Productions.

Attention Must Be Paid 1968
Funny yet provocative story of Jesus' activity in the modern world of a senior citizens' residence. Theme: the power of love is healing and enriching. 28m; VHS, 3/4 U, Special order formats. **C:** Ned Glass; George Tobias. **Pr:** Paulist Productions. **A:** Jr. High-Adult. **P:** Religious. **U:** Institution, CCTV, SURA. **Gen-Edu:** Religion. **Acq:** Purchase, Rent/Lease. **Dist:** Paulist Productions.

Attention Shoppers 1999 (R) — ★★
Latin sitcom heartthrob Carbonell angers his wife and threatens his hunk status during a K-Mart publicity appearance in Houston that's taken over by his rival, soap star Perry. 87m; VHS, DVD, CC. **C:** Nestor Carbonell; Luke Perry; Martin Mull; Kathy Najimy; Michael Lerner; Cara Buono; Lin Shaye; Casey Affleck; Directed by Philip Charles MacKenzie; Written by Nestor Carbonell. **A:** Sr. High-Adult. **P:** Entertainment. **U:** Home. **Mov-Ent:** Comedy--Screwball. **Acq:** Purchase. **Dist:** MGM Home Entertainment.

Attention to Detail, A Choral Conductor's Guide 1994
Choral conductor Dale Warland and the Dale Warland Singers demonstrate techniques to enhance performances, including phrasing, producing different choral tones, balance, dynamics, editing the composer's score, and more. ?m; VHS. **A:** Adult. **P:** Instruction. **U:** Institution. **Fin-Art:** Music--Instruction, Singing. **Acq:** Purchase. **Dist:** American Choral Catalog Ltd. $49.95.

Attention: Women at Work! 1989
A documentary which focuses on women in non-traditional jobs, such as hovercraft pilot and construction worker. 29m; VHS, 3/4 U. **Pr:** Margaret Pettigrew. **A:** Jr. High-Adult. **P:** Education. **U:** Institution, SURA. **Gen-Edu:** Women, Construction. **Acq:** Purchase, Rent/Lease. **Dist:** National Film Board of Canada; University of Washington Educational Media Collection.

The Attic 1980 (R) — ★★½
Psycho-drama about an overbearing invalid father and his insecure and unmarried daughter. The girl learns to escape her unhappy life by hiding in the attic. Not horrifying, but a clear analytical look into the game of control. 92m; VHS, DVD. **C:** Carrie Snodgress; Ray Milland; Rosemary Murphy; Ruth Cox; Frances Bay; Marjorie Eaton; Directed by George Edwards. **Pr:** Raymond M. Dryden; Philip Randall. **A:** Sr. High-Adult. **P:** Entertainment. **U:** Home. **Mov-Ent:** Mystery & Suspense. **Acq:** Purchase. **Dist:** $59.95.

The Attic 2006 (R) — ★
Not very scary horror flick that also suffers in the script and acting departments. Emma Callan (Moss) and her family move into what seems to be a perfect Victorian home. Only Emma begins to have visions of her twin, who's supposedly dead, evil, and hiding in the attic. 85m; DVD. **C:** Elisabeth (Elissabeth, Elizabeth, Liz) Moss; Jason Lewis; John Savage; Catherine Mary Stewart; Tom Malloy; Directed by Mary Lambert; Written by Tom Malloy; Cinematography by James Callanan; Music by Mario Grigorov. **A:** Sr. High-Adult. **P:** Entertainment. **U:** Home. **Mov-Ent. Acq:** Purchase. **Dist:** Allumination Filmworks.

Attic Conversion 1990
Learn all you'll need to know about converting your attic, including furring out the rafters, insulating the attic, applying and finishing drywall, floor preparation, installing skylights and much more. 36m; VHS. **Pr:** DIY Video Corporation. **A:** College-Adult. **P:** Instruction. **U:** Home. **How-Ins:** How-To, Home Improvement. **Acq:** Purchase. **Dist:** Do It Yourself, Inc./D.I.Y. Video Corp. $19.95.

The Attic Expeditions 2001 (R) — ★½
Very non-linear story about a man committed to an asylum for the murder of a girlfriend he doesn't remember. He begins to suspect the psychiatrists are implanting delusions in his mind (not that a lot of mental patients wouldn't say that). 100m; DVD, Streaming. **C:** Andras Jones; Seth Green; Jeffrey Combs; Theodore (Ted) Raimi; Wendy Robie; Directed by Jeremy Kasten; Written by Rogan Russell Marshall; Cinematography by Greg Littlewood; Michael Negrin; Music by David Reynolds. **A:** Sr. High-Adult. **P:** Entertainment. **U:** Home. **L:** English, Spanish. **Mov-Ent. Acq:** Purchase, Rent/Lease. **Dist:** DEJ Productions. $9.98 4.99.

Attic In the Blue 1992
Animated story about an ancient whaler who goes on a dangerous mission to find his lost love accompanied only by his octopus-like companion. 27m; VHS. **A:** Family. **P:** Entertainment. **U:** Home. **Chl-Juv:** Animation & Cartoons. **Acq:** Purchase. **Dist:** Facets Multimedia Inc.; Next Gen Video. $39.95.

Attic of the Wind 1967
An iconographic film portraying the "Attic of the Wind," where lost treasures such as kites and balloons are stored. 6m; VHS, 3/4 U. **Pr:** Alexander Cochran. **A:** Primary. **P:** Entertainment. **U:** Institution, SURA. **Chl-Juv:** Fantasy. **Acq:** Purchase. **Dist:** Weston Woods Studios.

The Attic: The Hiding of Anne Frank 1988 (Unrated) — ★★½
Steenburgen is wonderful in the true story of Miep Gies, the Dutch woman who hid Otto Frank, her employer, and his family from the Nazis. Unusual because it is told from Gies's perspective, rather than from the more familiar Anne Frank story. Based on Gies's book, "Anne Frank Remembered." 95m; VHS, CC. **C:** Mary Steenburgen; Paul Scofield; Huub Stapel; Eleanor Bron; Miriam Karlin; Lisa Jacobs; Ronald Pickup; Directed by John Erman; Written by William Hanley; Music by Richard Rodney Bennett. **A:** Jr. High-Adult. **P:** Entertainment. **U:** Home. **Mov-Ent:** Drama, World War Two, TV Movies. **Acq:** Purchase. **Dist:** Unknown Distributor.

Attica 1980 (Unrated) — ★★★
Tense depiction of the infamous Attica prison takeover in 1971 and the subsequent bloodbath as state troops were called in. Although edited due to the searing commentary by Nelson Rockefeller, it remains powerful and thought-provoking. Adapted from the Tom Wicker bestseller "A Time to Die." 97m; VHS. **C:** George Grizzard; Charles Durning; Anthony Zerbe; Roger E. Mosley; Directed by Marvin J. Chomsky. **Pr:** Louis Randolph. **A:** Jr. High-Adult. **P:** Entertainment. **U:** Home. **Mov-Ent:** TV Movies. **Acq:** Purchase. **Dist:** New Line Home Video. $9.98.

Attila 199?
A revival of the early Verdi opera is performed by La Scala at the Teattro Alla Scala in Milan, Italy. 118m; VHS. **C:** Samuel Ramey; Cheryl Studer; Directed by Jerome Savary; Conducted by Riccardo Muti. **A:** Jr. High-Adult. **P:** Entertainment. **U:** Home. **L:** Italian. **Fin-Art:** Opera. **Acq:** Purchase. **Dist:** Home Vision Cinema; Music Video Distributors. $39.95.

Attila 1954 (Unrated) — ★½
Silly historical costumer. Attila (Quinn) and his brother Bleda (Manni) battle for control over the Huns. Attila wants to conquer Rome next but Bleda wants to make the Romans their allies. The weakling Roman emperor (Laydu) is willing to make peace and his ambitious sister Honoria (Loren) offers to wed Attila, but their powerful mother (Regis) refuses and tells Roman general Aetius (Vidal) to prepare the legions for battle. Italian with subtitles. 87m; DVD. **C:** Anthony Quinn; Sophia Loren; Henri Vidal; Ettore Manni; Irene Papas; Christian Marquand; Claude Laydu; Colette Regis; Directed by Christian Marquand; Pietro Francisci; Written by Primo Zeglio; Ennio De Concini; Cinematography by Aldo Tonti; Music by Enzo Masetti. **A:** Jr. High-Adult. **P:** Entertainment. **U:** Home. **L:** Italian. **Mov-Ent:** Drama. **Acq:** Purchase. **Dist:** Lions Gate Entertainment Inc.

Attila 1987
A performance of the Verdi opera taped at the Arena di Verona. Subtitled in English. 111m; VHS. **C:** Evgeny Nesterenko; Maria Chiara; Silvano Carroli. **Pr:** National Video Corporation Ltd. **A:** Family. **P:** Entertainment. **U:** Home. **L:** Italian. **Fin-Art:** Opera. **Acq:** Purchase. **Dist:** Home Vision Cinema.

Attila 2001 (Unrated) — ★★½
Epic miniseries takes on the life of Attila the Hun. Early years of Attila are swiftly dealt with as his family is slaughtered and the boy is raised by his uncle—with his cousin as his rival for leadership. The adult Attila (Butler) is tough, charismatic, and bloodthirsty enough to unite the Hun tribes and challenge the domination of the Roman empire, which leads to the politically savvy Roman general Flavius Aetius (Boothe) being dispatched to get Attila on Rome's side. Lots of big battles as this part of history is treacherous indeed. 177m; VHS, DVD, Wide. **C:** Gerard Butler; Powers Boothe; Alice Krige; Simmone MacKinnon; Tim Curry; Reg Rogers; Steven Berkoff; Tommy Flanagan; Pauline Lynch; Liam Cunningham; Jolyon Baker; Sian Phillips; Jonathan Hyde; Directed by Dick Lowry; Written by Robert Cochran; Cinematography by Steven Fierberg; Music by Nick Glennie-Smith. **A:** Sr. High-Adult. **P:** Entertainment. **U:** Home. **Mov-Ent:** Biography, Military, Drama, Politics & Government. **Acq:** Purchase. **Dist:** Movies Unlimited; Alpha Video; Universal Studios Home Video. $19.98.

Attila 74: The Rape of Cyprus 1975 (Unrated)
Cacoyannis' (a native of Cyprus) only documentary takes a hard look at the cost of the Turkish invasion of Cyprus, which helped bring about the end of the military junta that had ruled Greece since 1966 at a heavy price. Greek with subtitles. 101m; VHS, DVD. **C:** Narrated by Michael Cacoyannis; Directed by Michael Cacoyannis; Cinematography by Sakis Maniatis; Music by Michalis Christodoulidis. **A:** College-Adult. **P:** Education. **U:** Institution, Home. **L:** Greek. **Gen-Edu:** History, Politics & Government, Documentary Films. **Acq:** Purchase. **Dist:** Wellspring Media.

Attitude! 19??
Find out how good and bad attitudes affect you and people around you, and learn useful attitude adjustment techniques. ?m; VHS. **A:** Adult. **P:** Professional. **U:** Institution. **L:** English. **Bus-Ind:** Communication. **Acq:** Purchase. **Dist:** Axzo Press. $98.

Attitude Factor 198?
A film designed for school bus drivers to recognize small problems before they get out of hand. 24m; VHS, 3/4 U. **Pr:** National Safety Council. **A:** College-Adult. **P:** Education. **U:** Institution. **Gen-Edu:** Driver Education. **Acq:** Rent/Lease. **Dist:** National Safety Council, California Chapter, Film Library.

Attitudes 1972
A sub-series of EBE'S "The Most Important Person" series. Suggests positive approaches for children to cope with discouraging situations. Programs available individually. 4m; VHS, 3/4 U. **Pr:** Sutherland Learning Associates. **A:** Primary. **P:** Education. **U:** Institution, SURA. **L:** English, Spanish. **Gen-Edu:** Personality. **Acq:** Purchase, Rent/Lease, Trade-in. **Dist:** Encyclopedia Britannica.

Indiv. Titles: 1. Oops, I Made a Mistake 2. I'm Lonely 3. Why Not Try 4. We Can do it 5. It's Not Much Fun Being Angry 6. Nothing Ever Seems to Work Out for Me.

Attitudes Toward Mental Illness and the Currently Used Psychiatric Therapies 1974
A brief discussion of attitudes and current therapies in psychiatry. 12m; VHS, 3/4 U, Special order formats. **Pr:** Ohio State University Health Sciences AV Center. **A:** College-Adult. **P:** Professional. **U:** Institution, SURA. **Hea-Sci:** Psychiatry. **Acq:** Purchase, Rent/Lease. **Dist:** Ohio State University.

Attitudes Toward Production 1976
How employee needs and goals have changed in recent years is explained. The need for products and services before there can be jobs is stressed. 14m; VHS, 3/4 U. **Pr:** Resources for Education and Management. **A:** Adult. **P:** Professional. **U:** Institution, CCTV. **Bus-Ind:** Management. **Acq:** Purchase. **Dist:** Resources for Education & Management, Inc.

Attitudes Toward Women in Ob/Gyn Residencies 1983
A report on how female gynecologists feel towards pregnancy and nursing. 21m; VHS, 3/4 U. **Pr:** Emory University. **A:** College-Adult. **P:** Education. **U:** Institution, CCTV, Home, SURA. **Hea-Sci:** Gynecology, Women. **Acq:** Purchase, Rent/Lease, Subscription. **Dist:** Emory Medical Television Network.

Attracting Birds to Your Backyard 1988
The right kinds of food and shelter can bring many different species of bird right to your yard for viewing enjoyment. 60m; VHS. **C:** Roger Tory Peterson. **Pr:** 3M. **A:** Family. **P:** Education. **U:** Institution, Home. **Gen-Edu:** Birds. **Acq:** Purchase. **Dist:** WNET/Thirteen Non-Broadcast. $49.95.

Attracting Birds, Volume I: Birdfeeders, Birdhouses and Birdbaths 1998
Hosts Don and Lillian Stokes show how to attract a wide range of songbirds to your property. Filled with close-ups of the most popular backyard birds, such as cardinals, bluebirds, swallows, titmice and more. 50m; VHS. **A:** Family. **P:** Instruction. **U:** Home. **How-Ins:** Birds, How-To, Wildlife. **Acq:** Purchase. **Dist:** Willow Creek Press L.L.C. $19.95.

Attracting Birds, Volume II: Hummingbirds and Other Favorite Birds 1998
Hosts Don and Lillian Stokes show you how to attract and garden for hummingbirds. They also show you how to attract other favorite birds, such as purple martins, orioles and woodpeckers. 50m; VHS. **A:** Family. **P:** Instruction. **U:** Home. **How-Ins:** Birds, How-To, Wildlife. **Acq:** Purchase. **Dist:** Willow Creek Press L.L.C. $19.95.

Attracting Butterflies to Your Backyard 19??
Introduces butterfly gardening. Complete with reference guide. 55m; VHS. **A:** Jr. High-Adult. **P:** Education. **U:** Institution. **Gen-Edu:** Insects. **Acq:** Purchase. **Dist:** Ark Media Group Ltd.

Attracting Love: Drawing Your Soulmate to You 19??
This hypnosis tape provides the right "atmosphere" to put the viewer in the proper frame of mind to encourage and attract love. Lots of streaming light and blobs of color designed to stimulate the unconscious mind. ?m; VHS. **A:** College-Adult. **P:** Instruction. **U:** Home. **How-Ins:** Human Relations. **Acq:** Purchase. **Dist:** Valley of the Sun Publishing. $19.95.

Attraction of Gravity 1975
Clearly illustrates the relationships of mass and distance to the force of gravity. 9m; VHS, 3/4 U. **Pr:** Paideia. **A:** Jr. High. **P:** Education. **U:** Institution, SURA. **L:** English, Swedish. **Hea-Sci:** Physics. **Acq:** Purchase. **Dist:** Phoenix Learning Group.

Attributes for Successful Employability 1990
Four programs allowing students to visit a number of businesses and make decisions that will affect attitudes, teamwork, dependability, and work quantity and quality. Interactive format illustrates the effects of each decision made. Programs available individually or as set. Learner's guide available at additional cost. 60m. **A:** Jr. High-Sr. High. **P:** Education. **U:** Institution. **Gen-Edu:** Job Training, Management, Occupations. **Acq:** Purchase, Rent/Lease. **Dist:** Agency for Instructional Technology. $395.00.

Indiv. Titles: 1. Dependability: You Can Depend On Me 2. Quantity & Quality: Do It Right 3. Positive Attitude: As I Choose a Better Way 4. Teamwork: Working Well With Others.

ATV Safety for Agricultural Operations 19??
Presents basic safety strategy for the agricultural use of ATVs. Covers driving techniques, maintenance checks, pre-operation checks, personal protective equipment, and common safety rules. Also illustrates methods of driving on different types of terrains and avoid hazards. 14m; VHS. **A:** Sr. High-Adult. **P:** Education. **U:** Institution. **L:** English, Spanish. **Gen-Edu:** Safety Education, Agriculture, Occupational Training. **Acq:** Purchase. **Dist:** CEV Multimedia. $95.00.

Atwood and Family 1989
Margaret Atwood, the Canadian author talks about her fiction and her life. 30m; VHS, 3/4 U. **Pr:** Michael Rubbo. **A:** Jr. High-Adult. **P:** Education. **U:** Institution, SURA. **Gen-Edu:** Bi-

ography, Literature--Modern. **Acq:** Purchase, Rent/Lease. **Dist:** National Film Board of Canada.

Atypical Infections of the Gastrointestinal Tract 1983
A discussion of the toxin producing bacteria that leads to colitis, travelers' diarrhea and herpes. 51m; VHS, 3/4 U. **Pr:** Emory University. **A:** College-Adult. **P:** Education. **U:** Institution, CCTV, Home, SURA. **Hea-Sci:** Digestive System, Diseases. **Acq:** Purchase, Rent/Lease, Subscription. **Dist:** Emory Medical Television Network.

Atypical Lymphocytes of Infectous Mononucleosis 1975
This program shows the microscopic view of a blood cell for the identification of infectious mononucleosis. 6m; VHS, 3/4 U, Special order formats. **Pr:** Ohio State University Health Sciences AV Center. **A:** College-Adult. **P:** Professional. **U:** Institution, SURA. **Hea-Sci:** Blood. **Acq:** Purchase, Rent/Lease. **Dist:** Ohio State University.

Atypical Pneumonias 1983
Mycoplasma Pneumonia and its clinical approach is discussed in this film. 57m; VHS, 3/4 U. **Pr:** Emory University. **A:** College-Adult. **P:** Professional. **U:** Institution, CCTV, CATV, BCTV, Home, SURA. **Hea-Sci:** Respiratory System. **Acq:** Purchase, Rent/Lease, Subscription. **Dist:** Emory Medical Television Network.

Au Contraire 2009 (Unrated)
Comedian Christian Finnegan stars in his first Comedy Central special. 60m; DVD. **A:** Sr. High-Adult. **P:** Entertainment. **U:** Home. **Gen-Edu:** Comedy--Performance, Television. **Acq:** Purchase. **Dist:** Comedy Central. $19.98.

Au Hasard Balthazar 1966 (Unrated) — ★★
Allegorical story from Bresson about donkey Balthazar and poor village girl Marie. Balthazar is taken from the children who love him and he's sold to a cruel master. Marie is also abused by the village men, including her jealous lover Gerard. It's supposed to be all about purity and cruelty in the world but instead it's just grim and drab. French with subtitles. 95m/B/W; DVD. **C:** Anna Wiazemsky; Francois Lafarge; Walter Green; Philippe Asselin; Directed by Robert Bresson; Written by Robert Bresson; Cinematography by Ghislan Cloquet; Music by Jean Wiener. **A:** College-Adult. **P:** Entertainment. **U:** Home. **L:** French. **Mov-Ent:** Philosophy & Ideology, Animals, Domestic Abuse. **Acq:** Purchase. **Dist:** Criterion Collection Inc.

Au Pair 1999 (Unrated) — ★★½
MBA grad Jenny Morgan learns the job she's been hired for by widowed, wealthy business exec Oliver Caldwell is that of nanny to his two bratty kids, Kate and Alex. When the kids bond with Jenny, they decide she'd make a much-better stepmom than their dad's witchy fiancee, Vivian (Sibbert), and play matchmaker when they all travel to Paris. Originally shown on the Fox Family Channel. 90m; DVD. **C:** Heidi Lenhart Seban; Gregory Harrison; Katie Volding; Jake Dinwiddie; John Rhys-Davies; Jane Sibbett; Michael Woolson; Richard Riehle; Directed by Mark Griffiths; Written by Jeffrey C. Sherman; Cheryl Seban; Cinematography by Blake T. Evans; Music by Inon Zur. **A:** Family. **P:** Entertainment. **U:** Home. **Mov-Ent. Acq:** Purchase. **Dist:** No Longer Available.

Au Pair 2: The Fairy Tale Continues 2001 (Unrated) — ★★½
Nanny Jenny and her boss Oliver are keeping their romance a secret for fear of upsetting imperious Nell, his late wife's mother, who's willing to believe the worst about Jenny. But the bigger obstacle is the would-be merger of Oliver's firm with that of Karl Sennhauser, whose greedy grown children plan to use Jenny to ruin Oliver so they can take over instead. However, Oliver's smarter, younger kids have different ideas. Originally shown on the Fox Family Channel. 93m; DVD. **C:** Gregory Harrison; Heidi Lenhart Seban; June Lockhart; Katie Volding; Jake Dinwiddie; Rachel York; Robin Dunne; Rory Johnston; Celine Massuger; Cliff Bemis; Directed by Mark Griffiths; Written by Jeffrey C. Sherman; Cheryl Seban; Cinematography by Thomas Callaway; Music by Inon Zur. **A:** Family. **P:** Entertainment. **U:** Home. **Mov-Ent. Acq:** Purchase. **Dist:** No Longer Available.

Au Pair 3: Adventure in Paradise 2009 (Unrated) — ★★
Oliver and Jenny are married with a baby and they and his children Kate and Alex go on vacation to Puerto Rico. But it's not all fun in the sun as Jake refuses to be groomed to take over the family business and both Jake and Kate would rather go off on their own than hang out with the 'rents. An eight-year gap between sequels wasn't exactly kind to the cable family comedy and the brother/sister duo were more appealing characters when they were younger. Originally shown on ABC Family. 99m; DVD. **C:** Heidi Lenhart Seban; Gregory Harrison; Jake Dinwiddie; Katie Volding; Directed by Mark Griffiths; Written by Jeffrey C. Sherman. **A:** Family. **P:** Entertainment. **U:** Home. **Mov-Ent. Acq:** Purchase. **Dist:** Gaiam Inc.

Au Pair Girls 1972 — ★★½
Four sexy young ladies leave their various homelands to embark on careers as au pair girls, making friends and love along the way. 86m; VHS, DVD, Blu-Ray. **C:** Gabrielle Drake; Astrid Frank; Nancie Wait; Me Me Lai; Richard O'Sullivan; Johnny Briggs; Ferdinand "Ferdy" Mayne; Directed by Val Guest; Written by Val Guest; David Adnopoz; Cinematography by John Wilcox; Music by Roger Webb. **Pr:** Guido Coen. **A:** Adult. **P:** Entertainment. **U:** Home. **Mov-Ent. Acq:** Purchase. **Dist:** Image Entertainment Inc.

Au Revoir les Enfants 1987 (PG) — ★★★★
During the Nazi occupation of France in the 1940s, the headmaster of a Catholic boarding school hides three Jewish boys among the other students by altering their names and identities. Two of the students, Julien (Manesse) and Jean (Fejto), form a friendship that ends tragically when Jean and the other boys are discovered and taken away by the Gestapo. Compelling and emotionally wrenching coming of age tale based on an incident from director Malle's childhood is considered to be his best film to date and quite possibly the best he will ever make. In French with English subtitles. Other 1987 movies with similar themes are "Hope and Glory" and "Empire of the Sun." 104m; VHS, DVD, Blu-Ray. **C:** Gaspard Manesse; Raphael Fejto; Francine Racette; Stanislas Carre de Malberg; Philippe Morier-Genoud; Francois Berleand; Peter Fitz; Francois Negret; Irene Jacob; Pascal Rivet; Benoit Henriet; Richard Leboeuf; Xavier Legrand; Arnaud Henriet; Jean-Sebastien Chauvin; Luc Etienne; Directed by Louis Malle; Written by Louis Malle; Cinematography by Renato Berta. **Pr:** Louis Malle; Louis Malle; Nouvelles Editions de Films; MK2; Stella; NEF. **A:** Jr. High-Adult. **P:** Entertainment. **U:** Home. **L:** English, French. **Mov-Ent:** World War Two, Judaism, Holocaust. **Awds:** British Acad. '88: Director (Malle); Cesar '88: Art Dir./Set Dec., Cinematog., Director (Malle), Film, Sound, Writing; L.A. Film Critics '87: Foreign Film; Venice Film Fest. '87: Film. **Acq:** Purchase. **Dist:** MGM Studios Inc. ; Facets Multimedia Inc.; Home Vision Cinema. $19.98.

Aubrey Beardsley 197?
The life and work of artist Aubrey Beardsley is examined in this program. 30m/B/W; VHS, 3/4 U, EJ, Q. **Pr:** WCBS New York; Camera Three Productions. **A:** Sr. High-College. **P:** Education. **U:** Institution, SURA. **Fin-Art:** Art & Artists. **Acq:** Duplication, Free Duplication. **Dist:** Camera Three Productions, Inc.; Creative Arts Television Archive.

Aucassin and Nicolette 1966
An animated fairy tale by acclaimed German animator Lotte Reiniger, involving a handsome prince and the beautiful orphan girl he is forbidden to marry. 16m; VHS. **C:** Voice(s) by Dudley Moore; Dizzy Gillespie. **Pr:** Guy Glover; Wolf Koenig. **A:** Family. **P:** Entertainment. **U:** Institution, SURA. **Gen-Edu:** Animation & Cartoons, Fairy Tales. **Acq:** Purchase, Rent/Lease. **Dist:** National Film Board of Canada.

The Audience for Theatre 1989
Examines the beginnings of theatre where the text set the stage and described the scenes; sets came into use at first to stimulate imagination, by A.D. 100, the theatre had acquired a permanent stage. The program starts with the Days of Aeschylus when plays were performed in the honor of Dionysuys; late in Euripides's career, the presentation was the main focus. 26m; VHS, 3/4 U. **Pr:** Films for the Humanities and Sciences. **A:** College. **P:** Education. **U:** Institution, CCTV, CATV, BCTV. **Fin-Art:** Theater. **Acq:** Purchase, Rent/Lease, Duplication License. **Dist:** Films for the Humanities & Sciences.

Audit Evidence 1990
The framework for accumulating audit evidence is explained and presented. 30m; VHS, 3/4 U. **Pr:** Center for Video Education Inc. **A:** Adult. **P:** Professional. **U:** Institution. **Bus-Ind:** Finance. **Acq:** Purchase, Rent/Lease. **Dist:** SmartPros Ltd.

Audit Sampling, Materiality and Risk 1989
Accountants newly assigned to auditor function will find this video helpful in giving them a refresher course on SAS 47 and SAS 39. 45m; VHS. **Pr:** James K. Loebbecke. **A:** Adult. **P:** Professional. **U:** Institution. **Bus-Ind:** Finance. **Acq:** Purchase. **Dist:** SmartPros Ltd. $395.00.

Auditing in an EDP Environment 1992
Internal controls and auditing as effected by EDP is the subject of this tape. 57m; VHS, 3/4 U. **Pr:** Center for Video Education Inc. **A:** Adult. **P:** Professional. **U:** Institution. **Bus-Ind:** Management. **Acq:** Purchase, Rent/Lease. **Dist:** SmartPros Ltd.

Audition 1981
A young woman preparing for a theatrical audition grapples with her conflicting desires for both career and family. 9m; VHS, 3/4 U, Special order formats. **Pr:** Candy Kugel. **A:** Jr. High-Adult. **P:** Education. **U:** Institution, Home, SURA. **Gen-Edu:** Performing Arts, Women. **Acq:** Purchase, Rent/Lease. **Dist:** Direct Cinema Ltd.

The Audition 1990
Drama wherein a woman auditions her one-time actress mother for a small role in her film. Explores the nuances of mother/daughter roles. 24m; VHS. **A:** College-Adult. **P:** Education. **U:** Institution. **Gen-Edu:** Women, Drama, Family. **Acq:** Purchase, Rent/Lease. **Dist:** Women Make Movies. $225.00.

Audition 1999 (Unrated) — ★★½
Director Miike successfully illustrates a middle-aged widower's worst nightmares about remarrying a younger woman. The benign first half of the film, in which businessman Aoyama (Ishibashi) is persuaded by a producer friend to stage a fake movie audition in order to find a new bride, belies the gruesome turn of events revealed later. Seven years single, Aoyama wants a traditional, submissive young girl, which he finds in one of the actresses, Asami (Shiina). Aoyama's smitten, but buddy Yoshikawa (Kunimura) is decidedly less so, sensing something a tad askew in the graceful beauty. Something definitely is amiss, as numerous flashbacks showing the girl's sadistic bent attest. Soon enough, Aoyama is on the business end of Asami's macabre doings. Based on a story by Ryu Murakami. In Japanese with subtitles. 115m; VHS, DVD, Blu-Ray. **C:** Ryo Ishibashi; Eihi Shiina; Tetsu Sawaki; Jun Kunimura; Miyuki Matsuda; Directed by Takashi Miike; Written by Daisuke Tengan; Cinematography by Hideo Yamamoto; Music by Koji Endo. **A:** College-Adult. **P:** Entertainment. **U:** Home. **L:** Japanese. **Mov-Ent. Acq:** Purchase. **Dist:** Ventura Distribution Inc.

Audition Power! A Dancer's Guide to Working in Hollywood 1992
Panel discussion aimed at budding professional dancers describes the trials and tribulations of breaking into the field. Focuses on the all-important audition process. 51m; VHS. **A:** Sr. High-Adult. **P:** Education. **U:** Institution, Home. **How-Ins:** Dance--Instruction. **Acq:** Purchase. **Dist:** Princeton Book Company Publishers; Cambridge Educational. $39.95.

Audition Techniques 19??
Provides auditioning tips for aspiring thespians looking to work in high school, community, university, and professional theatre, as well as theme parks. Covers monologues/songs, warm-ups, cold-reading, resume and photo preparation, and more. Complete with teacher's guide and selective biblio. 70m; VHS. **A:** Sr. High-Adult. **P:** Education. **U:** Institution. **Gen-Edu:** Theater. **Acq:** Purchase. **Dist:** Stagestep. $94.95.

Auditioning ????
Advice and techniques for successful auditioning in a variety of situations. Also discusses character development and "tune-up" exercises for building confidence. 43m; VHS. **A:** Adult. **P:** Instruction. **U:** Institution. **How-Ins:** Performing Arts, Theater. **Acq:** Purchase. **Dist:** Stagestep. $79.00.

Auditioning for the Actor 19??
Provides a practical approach to getting acting roles, including choosing material, evaluating personal strengths, selecting clothing, introducing yourself, and tips on handling cold readings. Includes an outline and sample resumes and photos. 45m; VHS. **A:** College-Adult. **P:** Instruction. **U:** Home. **How-Ins:** Performing Arts. **Acq:** Purchase. **Dist:** Stagestep. $118.95.

Auditions and Insights 19??
Mann provides tips on audition preparation and presentation, dealing with nerves, rejection, how to handle singing, dancing, and reading parts, how to hire an agent, going to equity and open calls, and how to avoid typecasting. 30m; VHS. **C:** Hosted by Terrence Mann. **A:** College-Adult. **P:** Instruction. **U:** Home. **How-Ins:** Theater. **Acq:** Purchase. **Dist:** Stagestep. $39.95.

The Auditory Brainstem Implant Program 1984
Outlines the House Ear Institute's new project to aid individuals who are bilaterally deafened with discontinuities of the eighth nerve due to tumors and cannot be helped by cochlear implantation. 30m; VHS, 3/4 U. **TV Std:** NTSC, PAL, SECAM. **Pr:** House Ear Institute. **A:** College-Adult. **P:** Instruction. **U:** Institution, CCTV. **Hea-Sci:** Medical Education, Ear, Deafness. **Acq:** Purchase. **Dist:** House Research Institute. $90.00.

Auditory Physiology of the External and Middle Ear 1976
This program presents the auditory function of the external and middle ear. 24m; VHS, 3/4 U, Special order formats. **Pr:** Ohio State University Health Sciences AV Center. **A:** College-Adult. **P:** Professional. **U:** Institution, SURA. **Hea-Sci:** Ear. **Acq:** Purchase, Rent/Lease. **Dist:** Ohio State University.

Auditory Physiology of the External and Middle Ear: Reconfiguration 1978
A self-instructional package about the auditory function of the external and middle ear. 26m; VHS, 3/4 U, Special order formats. **Pr:** Ohio State University Health Sciences AV Center. **A:** College-Adult. **P:** Professional. **U:** Institution, SURA. **Hea-Sci:** Ear. **Acq:** Purchase, Rent/Lease. **Dist:** Ohio State University.

Audrey Hepburn Remembered 1993
Documentary of the film star includes clips from some of her best-loved films, including "Roman Holiday," "Sabrina," "Breakfast at Tiffany's," "My Fair Lady," and others as well as interviews with her directors and co-stars. Also deals with Hepburn's tireless work for the UNICEF organization. 66m; VHS. **A:** Jr. High-Adult. **P:** Entertainment. **U:** Home. **Mov-Ent:** Documentary Films, Biography: Show Business, Biography. **Acq:** Purchase. **Dist:** MPI Media Group. $19.98.

The Audrey Hepburn Story 2000 (PG) — ★★
When you play a movie icon, expect the critical brickbats to fly. Sweet Hewitt does her best in the title role (Hepburn's her longtime idol) but it's all surface gloss. Bio covers 1935 to 1960 as Hepburn deals with family crises (dad's a two-timing Nazi sympathizer who abandons his family), war years in Nazi-occupied Holland, Hepburn's beginnings as a dancer in England and her first small roles. Then it's onto New York and the world of theatre and films. Along the way there's a little romance, a marriage to actor Mel Ferrer (McCormack), and various re-creations of some Hepburn movie roles. 133m; VHS, DVD, Wide, CC. **C:** Jennifer Love Hewitt; Eric McCormack; Frances Fisher; Peter Giles; Keir Dullea; Gabriel Macht; Marcel Jeannin; Swede Svensson; Michael J. Burg; Ryan Hollyman; Directed by Steve Robman; Written by Marsha Norman; Cinematography by Pierre Letarte; Music by Lawrence Shragge. **A:** Jr. High-Adult. **P:** Entertainment. **U:** Home. **Mov-Ent:** World War Two, Romance, Biography: Show Business. **Acq:** Purchase. **Dist:** Sony Pictures Home Entertainment Inc.

Audrey Rose 1977 (PG) — ★★
Parents of a young girl are terrified when their darling daughter is having dreadful dreams. Mysterious friend Hopkins cements their fears when he declares that his dead daughter has been reincarnated in their child. The nightmares continue suggesting that none other than Lucifer could be at work. Good cast is hampered by slow-moving take-off on "The Exorcist" with a weak staged ending. Adapted by DeFelitta from his novel. 113m; VHS, DVD, Wide. **C:** Marsha Mason; Anthony Hopkins; John Beck; John Hillerman; Susan Swift; Norman Lloyd; Directed by Robert Wise; Written by Frank De Felitta; Cinematography by Victor Kemper. **Pr:** United Artists. **A:** Sr.

High-Adult. **P:** Entertainment. **U:** Home. **Mov-Ent:** Horror, Death. **Acq:** Purchase. **Dist:** MGM Home Entertainment. $14.95.

Audrey's Life 19??
Investigates the reports of miracles and mystical phenomena surrounding Audrey Santo, a young girl who has been in a coma since the age of three. 65m; VHS. **A:** Family. **P:** Religious. **U:** Home. **Gen-Edu:** Religion, Biography. **Acq:** Purchase. **Dist:** Ignatius Press. $24.95.

Audrey's Rain 2003 (Unrated) — ★★
Audrey (Smart) is already caring for her younger, mentally challenged sister Marguerite (Wilhoite) when she must take in her orphaned niece and nephew after another sister commits suicide. No wonder Audrey is grateful for the attentions of old boyfriend Terry Lloyd (Smart's husband Gilliland). But can they overcome their troubles to take a second chance on love? Packs too much story into a too-short run time but Smart is always a pleasure to watch. 88m; DVD. **C:** Jean Smart; Richard Gilliland; Kathleen Wilhoite; Angus T. Jones; Carol Kane; Directed by Sam Pillsbury; Written by Jennifer Schwalbach Smith; Kate Smith; Cinematography by James W. Wrenn; Music by Stephen (Steve) Edwards. **A:** Jr. High-Adult. **P:** Entertainment. **U:** Home. **Mov-Ent:** Drama. **Acq:** Purchase. **Dist:** Movies Unlimited.

Audubon Zoo 1989
Captures a day in the life of Louisiana's largest zoo. Comes with a teaching guide. 30m; VHS. **Pr:** Video Tours. **A:** Family. **P:** Entertainment. **U:** Institution, CCTV, Home. **Gen-Edu:** Zoos. **Acq:** Purchase. **Dist:** VT Entertainment. $24.95.

Audubon's Animal Adventures 1996
Compiles video footage from HBO's 1996 television series on wildlife creatures throughout the world along with commentary on how to protect threatened or endangered species. 1 episode. ?m; DVD. **A:** Family. **P:** Entertainment. **U:** Home. **Gen-Edu:** Television Series, Documentary Films, Animals. **Acq:** Purchase. **Dist:** Home Box Office Inc. $24.98.

Auf der schwaeb'sche Eise'bahne 1983
A tour through Schwaben and the Schwarzwald, complete with music, singing, and dancing, plus the beautiful scenery and the humor of the Schwaben. In German only. 60m; VHS. **TV Std:** NTSC, PAL. **A:** Family. **P:** Entertainment. **U:** Home. **L:** German. **Mov-Ent:** Travel, Music--Performance, Folklore & Legends. **Acq:** Purchase, Rent/Lease. **Dist:** German Language Video Center. $37.95.

Auf Wiedersehen Pet 198?
Three bricklayers join a group of people and go to Germany to find their future and their fortunes in this funny series. Each tape contains two episodes. Originally aired on British television. 101m; VHS. **Pr:** Central Independent Television. **A:** Jr. High-Adult. **P:** Entertainment. **U:** Home. **Mov-Ent:** Television. **Acq:** Purchase. **Dist:** Video Collectibles. $24.98.
Indiv. Titles: 1. If I Were a Carpenter/Private Lives 2. The Fugitive/The Lovers.

Augie Doggie and Doggie Daddy: "A Pup and His Pop" 1989
12 episodes featuring the hilarious canines. 90m; VHS. **Pr:** Hanna-Barbera Productions. **A:** Family. **P:** Entertainment. **U:** Home. **Mov-Ent:** Animation & Cartoons, Pets, Television Series. **Acq:** Purchase. **Dist:** Turner Broadcasting System Inc. $29.95.

The Augsberg High Crotch Series: Set-ups and Finishes 2009 (Unrated)
Coach Jeff Swenson demonstrates set-up moves for wrestlers to get an Inside Step High Crotch Takedown, as well as finishing maneuvers for use after the Takedown. 51m; DVD. **A:** Family. **P:** Education. **U:** Home, Institution. **Spo-Rec:** Athletic Instruction/Coaching. **Acq:** Purchase. **Dist:** Championship Productions. $39.99.

August 1995 (PG) — ★★½
Yet another version of Chekov's "Uncle Vanya," this time transported to 1890s Wales. Hopkins (who makes his directorial debut and composed the score) stars as Ieuan Davies, a bitter drinker who manages the estate of brother-in-law Alexander Blathwaite (Phillips). Blathwaite arrives for his annual summer stay with unhappy, young second wife Helen (Burton), who's the object of desire for both Ieuan and the local doctor, Michael Lloyd (Grainger). It's a perfectedly adequate rendition but offers little that's new except a change of scenery. 93m; VHS, DVD. **C:** Anthony Hopkins; Kate Burton; Leslie Phillips; Gawn Grainger; Rhian Morgan; Hugh Lloyd; Rhoda Lewis; Menna Tussler; Directed by Anthony Hopkins; Written by Julian Mitchell; Cinematography by Robin Vidgeon; Music by Anthony Hopkins. **Pr:** Pippa Cross; June Wyndham Davies; Guy East; Steve Morrison; Majestic Films International; Samuel Goldwyn Company. **A:** Sr. High-Adult. **P:** Entertainment. **U:** Home. **Mov-Ent:** Great Britain. **Acq:** Purchase. **Dist:** Movies Unlimited; Alpha Video.

August 2008 (R) — ★½
In 2001, Tom Sterling (Hartnett) is riding the dot-com bubble as CEO of Landshark, a New York internet startup company whose services are actually created by his married brother Josh (Scott). The cracks begin to show, precipitating a cash-flow crisis Tom prefers to ignore. There's no particular urgency or surprise to the story and Tom is a hollow, unlikeable character blankly played by Hartnett. 88m; DVD. **C:** Josh Hartnett; Adam Scott; Robin Tunney; Emmanuelle Chriqui; Andre Royo; Naomie Harris; Rip Torn; Caroline Lagerfelt; David Bowie; Directed by Austin Chick; Written by Howard A. Rodman; Cinematography by Andrij Parekh; Music by Nathan Larson. **A:** Sr. High-Adult. **P:** Entertainment. **U:** Home. **Mov-Ent. Acq:** Purchase.

August 2011 (Unrated) — ★★
Gay romantic triangle set during a sweltering L.A. summer. Hunky Raoul (Gonzalez) has made a green card marriage so he can stay in the U.S. with his boyfriend Jonathan (Dugan). Despite Raoul's devotion, there's a snake in their paradise when Jonathan's ex Troy (Bartlett) shows up, trying to worm his way back into his heart and bed. Jonathan can't resist but isn't sure he can depend on Troy, and Raoul isn't giving up on his lover. 99m; DVD; Closed Captioned. **C:** Daniel Dugan; Murray Bartlett; Adrian Gonzalez; Hillary Banks; Directed by Eldar Rapaport; Written by Eldar Rapaport; Cinematography by James Adolphus. **A:** College-Adult. **P:** Entertainment. **U:** Home. **L:** English. **Mov-Ent:** Sex & Sexuality, Homosexuality. **Acq:** Purchase. **Dist:** Wolfe Video.

August in the Empire State 2006
The Republican Party held its first convention in New York City in August 2004, and this documentary explores the intersection of politics, protest, and media coverage. 100m; DVD. **A:** Sr. High-Adult. **P:** Entertainment. **U:** Home. **Gen-Edu:** Documentary Films, Political Campaigns. **Acq:** Purchase. **Dist:** Entertainment One US LP.

August: Osage County 2013 (R) — ★½
An all-star cast of undeniably talented actors fight over Oscar buzz in this blatant awards bait, a melodramatic dud that guts Tracy Letts' Pulitzer Prize-winning play of its core, leaving only the "major moments" and monologues. After years of dealing with his crazy wife (Streep), Beverly Weston (Shepard) has gone missing, leading to a family reunion from all branches of this deeply damaged tree. The cast is uniformly strong, particularly Nicholson and Martindale, but the dialogue feels forced and the plot farfetched as the characters are little more than a series of crises and revelations. 121m; DVD, Blu-Ray. **C:** Meryl Streep; Julia Roberts; Chris Cooper; Ewan McGregor; Margo Martindale; Sam Shepard; Julianne Nicholson; Juliette Lewis; Benedict Cumberbatch; Directed by John Wells; Written by Tracy Letts; Cinematography by Adriano Goldman; Music by Gustavo Santaolalla. **Pr:** George Clooney; Jean Doumanian; Grant Heslov; Harvey Weinstein; Weinstein Company L.L.C. **A:** Sr. High-Adult. **P:** Entertainment. **U:** Home. **L:** English. **Mov-Ent:** Theater, Family, Pain. **Acq:** Purchase.

August Rush 2007 (PG) — ★★
Lyla (Russell) is a classical cellist who falls for club-band musician Louis (Rhys Myers) and soon finds herself pregnant with his child. Her overbearing stage father tells her the baby has died and ships him off to an orphanage. Fast-forward 11 years and little orphan Evan (adorable Highmore) hears music in everything. He thinks if he learns how to play an instrument, his parents—who he knows are musicians—will find him. Through sheer force, a few side players, a healthy dose of appropriately sappy music, and a whole lotta far-fetched coincidences, the family is reunited. Utterly and unapologetically predictable, but it won't matter a bit if your idea of a good film is one in which you need an entire box of tissues. 113m; Blu-Ray, On Demand, Wide. **C:** Freddie Highmore; Keri Russell; Jonathan Rhys Meyers; Terrence Howard; Robin Williams; William Sadler; Leon G. Thomas, III; Jamia Simone Nash; Directed by Kristen Sheridan; Written by Nick Castle; James V. Hart; Cinematography by John Mathieson; Music by Mark Mancina; Hans Zimmer. **Pr:** Richard B. Lewis; Southpaw Entertainment; Warner Bros; CJ Entertainment; Odyssey Entertainment. **A:** Family. **P:** Entertainment. **U:** Home. **L:** English. **Mov-Ent:** Music, Adoption, Homeless. **Acq:** Purchase. **Dist:** Amazon.com Inc.; Movies Unlimited; Alpha Video.

August Wilson 1992
Interviews the author/playwright of "Two Trains Running" and "Joe Turner's Come and Gone." Also includes production excerpts. 22m; VHS. **A:** Adult. **P:** Education. **U:** Institution. **Fin-Art:** Theater. **Acq:** Purchase. **Dist:** Insight Media. $129.00.

August Wilson: The American Dream, in Black and White ????
Reviews the life and career of Pulitzer Prize-winning playwright August Wilson through archival footage and interviews with critics, fellow writers, and the artist himself. 52m; VHS. **A:** Sr. High-Adult. **P:** Education. **U:** Institution. **Gen-Edu:** Black Culture, Biography, Theater. **Acq:** Purchase, Rent/Lease. **Dist:** Films for the Humanities & Sciences. $149.00.

Augusta 1978
A portrait of an 88-year-old woman, born a daughter of a Shuswap chief in Canada. She lives today in Cariboo country of British Columbia without running water or electricity. Augusta lost her status as an Indian in 1903, when she married a white man. 17m; VHS, 3/4 U. **Pr:** John Taylor. **A:** Sr. High-Adult. **P:** Education. **U:** Institution, SURA. **Gen-Edu:** Native Americans. **Acq:** Purchase. **Dist:** Phoenix Learning Group.

Augustin 1995 — ★★
Very short comedy about aspiring actor Augustin (Sibertin-Blanc), who may just get his break when he hears about a part for a room-service waiter and prepares himself rigorously by actually getting a job in a Paris hotel. Pathetically earnest and dignified, at the actual audition he bewilders actor Lhermitte, when instead of just reading the scene, Augustin proceeds to act it out in detail. Very slight but charming thanks to a deadpan performance by Sibertin-Blanc (who's also director Fontaine's brother). French with subtitles. 61m; VHS. **C:** Jean-Chretien Sibertin-Blanc; Thierry Lhermitte; Stephanie Zhang; Nora Habib; Guy Casabonne; Directed by Anne Fontaine; Written by Anne Fontaine; Cinematography by Jean-Marie Dreujou. **A:** College-Adult. **P:** Entertainment. **U:** Home. **L:** French. **Mov-Ent. Acq:** Purchase. **Dist:** Kino on Video.

Augustine 1982
Offers instruction on specific aspects of true and mythological saints and legends. 30m; VHS. **A:** Adult. **P:** Education. **U:** Institution. **Gen-Edu:** History. **Acq:** Purchase. **Dist:** RMI Media. $69.95.

Augustine 2012 (Unrated) — ★★
A 19-year-old kitchen maid named Augustine (Soko) has a seizure that gets her shipped off to a psychiatric hospital in this smart French drama that examines how women and their sexuality were treated by the 19th-century medical community. Augustine is left partially paralyzed by her seizure, but her symptoms manifest in ways that lead neurologist Charcot (Lindon) to become convinced that it's more hysteria than physical malady. And then things get really interesting when Charcot begins to experiment in the sexual arena. French with subtitles. 102m; DVD, Blu-Ray. **C:** Soko; Vincent Lindon; Chiara Mastroianni; Olivier Rabourdin; Directed by Alice Winocour; Written by Alice Winocour; Cinematography by Georges Lechaptois; Music by Jocelyn Pook. **Pr:** Emilie Tisne; Isabelle Madalaine; Music Box Films. **A:** Adult. **P:** Entertainment. **U:** Home. **L:** French. **Mov-Ent:** France, Psychology, Sex & Sexuality. **Acq:** Purchase. **Dist:** Music Box Films.

Augustine of Hippo 1972 — ★★★
One of Rossellini's later historical epics, depicting the last years of St. Augustine and how they exemplify the growing conflicts between Church and State, Christian ethic and societal necessity. In Italian with subtitles. 120m; VHS. **C:** Directed by Roberto Rossellini. **Pr:** Roberto Rosselini. **A:** Sr. High-Adult. **P:** Entertainment. **U:** Home. **L:** Italian. **Mov-Ent:** Biography: Religious Figures, Drama, Religion. **Acq:** Purchase. **Dist:** Facets Multimedia Inc. $59.95.

August's Pie Company Tour 19??
Tours the facilities at the August Pie Company, explaining the different processes involved in the pie-making industry. Includes coverage of cooking, mixing, frying, and packaging. 25m; VHS. **A:** Jr. High-Adult. **P:** Education. **U:** Institution. **Gen-Edu:** Cooking, Food Industry. **Acq:** Purchase. **Dist:** CEV Multimedia. $79.95.

Augustus Saint-Gaudens 19??
Chronicles the life and work of the great American sculptor, Augustus Saint-Gaudens. 28m; VHS. **A:** Sr. High-Adult. **P:** Education. **U:** Home. **Gen-Edu:** Documentary Films, Biography, Art & Artists. **Acq:** Purchase. **Dist:** Direct Cinema Ltd. $29.95.

Aung San Suu Kyi ????
Retrospective of Aung San Suu Kyi, daughter of Burma's martyred first president, dissident, political prisoner, Nobel Prize winner, and favored democratic candidate. Also examines Burma's independence, volatile political climate, and economic concerns. 24m; VHS. **A:** Sr. High-Adult. **P:** Education. **U:** Institution. **Gen-Edu:** Asia, Politics & Government. **Acq:** Purchase, Rent/Lease. **Dist:** Films for the Humanities & Sciences. $129.00.

Aunque la Hormona Se Vista de Seda 1973 (Unrated) — ★
A man leaves his prospective bride at the altar three times because he gets the jitters. 87m; VHS. **C:** Alfredo Landa; Manuel Summer; Ana Belen; Directed by Vincente Escriva. **Pr:** Madera Cinevideo. **A:** Sr. High-Adult. **P:** Entertainment. **U:** Home. **Mov-Ent. Acq:** Purchase. **Dist:** Spanishmultimedia. $19.95.

Aunt Arie 1975
An independent 87-year-old woman who lives in the Blue Ridge Mountains of North Carolina talks about her childhood, marriage, and adult life. 18m; VHS, 3/4 U. **Pr:** Steve Heiser. **A:** Jr. High-College. **P:** Education. **U:** Institution, SURA. **Gen-Edu:** Women. **Acq:** Purchase, Rent/Lease, Trade-in. **Dist:** Encyclopedia Britannica.

Aunt Merriweather's Adventures in the Backyard 1992
A combination of live-action and animation has Aunt Merriweather and her nephew Robin on a backyard trip to observe nature. The two encounter ants, spiders, birds, crickets, and a rabbit in an easy-to-watch educational experience. 30m; VHS. **A:** Preschool-Primary. **P:** Entertainment. **U:** Home. **Chl-Juv. Acq:** Purchase. **Dist:** Sea Studios. $24.95.

Auntie 1973 (R) — **Bomb!**
Entertainer must dress and act like his madam aunt who has died, in order to fool her former employees in a house of prostitution. 85m; VHS. **C:** Mark Jones; Sue Longhurst; Frank Thornton; Linda Regan; Directed by Derek Ford; Written by Derek Ford; Alan Selwyn; Cinematography by Geoff Glover; Music by Terry Warr. **Pr:** Black Water Film Productions. **A:** Sr. High-Adult. **P:** Entertainment. **U:** Home. **Mov-Ent:** Comedy--Screwball, Prostitution. **Acq:** Purchase. **Dist:** No Longer Available.

Auntie Lee's Meat Pies 1992 (R) — ★½
Auntie Lee's meat pie business is booming thanks to her five beautiful nieces. They help keep their aunt supplied with the secret ingredient—gorgeous young men! Four Playboy Playmates are featured in this cannibalistic horror comedy. 100m; VHS. **C:** Karen Black; Noriyuki "Pat" Morita; Pat Paulsen; Huntz Hall; Michael Berryman; David Parry; Stephen Quadros; Ava Fabian; Teri Weigel; Directed by Joseph F. Robertson; Written by Joseph F. Robertson; Cinematography by Arledge Armenaki. **Pr:** Gerald M. Steiner; Trans World Entertainment Corp. **A:** Sr. High-Adult. **P:** Entertainment. **U:** Home. **Mov-Ent. Acq:** Purchase. **Dist:** Sony Pictures Home Entertainment Inc. $79.95.

Auntie Mame 1958 — ★★★
A young boy is brought up by his only surviving relative—flamboyant and eccentric Auntie Mame. Mame is positive that "life is a banquet and most poor suckers are starving to death." Based on the Patrick Dennis novel about his life with "Auntie Mame." Part of the "A Night at the Movies" series, this tape simulates a 1958 movie evening, with a Road Runner cartoon, "Hook, Line and Stinker," a newsreel and coming attractions for "No Time for Sergeants" and "Chase a Crooked Shadow." 161m; VHS, DVD, Wide. **C:** Rosalind Russell; Patric Knowles; Roger Smith; Peggy Cass; Forrest Tucker; Coral Browne; Directed by Morton DaCosta; Written by Betty Comden; Adolph Green; Cinematography by Harry Stradling, Sr. **A:** Family. **P:** Entertainment. **U:** Home. **Mov-Ent:** Satire & Parody. **Awds:** Golden Globes '59: Actress--Mus./Comedy (Russell). **Acq:** Purchase. **Dist:** Warner Home Video, Inc. $19.95.

The Aura 2005 (Unrated) — ★★★
To escape his bleak life in Buenos Aires, Esteban (Darin)--a quiet, reserved taxidermist—has fantasies of carrying out the perfect crime using his photographic memory even though he's plagued by epileptic seizures that at first give him great clarity (the "aura") but then cause blackouts. Despite this, Esteban seizes a chance to make his crime dream come true when he figures out that Dietrich (Rodal), who he mistakenly kills while on a hunting trip, was plotting a real heist. He's able to convince Dietrich's wife and gang members that he's also in on the gig but much like his seizures the events that follow get out of control. Tense thriller was only the second movie directed by Bielinsky, who died of a heart attack after its completion. In Spanish with subtitles. 138m; DVD. **C:** Ricardo Darin; Dolores Fonzi; Alejandro Awada; Pablo Cedron; Jorge d'Elia; Nahuel Perez; Walter Reyno; Manuel Rodal; Rafael Castejon; Directed by Fabian Bielinsky; Written by Fabian Bielinsky; Cinematography by Checco Varese; Music by Lucio Godoy. **Pr:** Pablo Bossi; Gerardo Herrero; Mariela Besuievski; Samuel Hadida; Patagonik Film Group; Tornasol Films SA; Davis Films; IFC First Take. **A:** College-Adult. **P:** Entertainment. **U:** Home. **L:** Spanish. **Mov-Ent:** Handicapped, Mystery & Suspense. **Acq:** Purchase. **Dist:** IFC Films.

Aura Reading and Healing 1980
Rosalyn Bruyere, President of the Healing Light Center in Glendale, Ca., does an aura reading on a subject picked at random from the audience. From the energy field and auric colors, she is able to figure the problem area. 23m; VHS, 3/4 U. **Pr:** David Lionel. **A:** College-Adult. **P:** Education. **U:** Institution, CCTV, CATV. **Hea-Sci:** Cults. **Acq:** Purchase, Rent/Lease. **Dist:** Education 2000, Inc. $29.95.

Aurex Jazz Festival Fusion Super Jam 198? (Unrated)
The best in the jazz world perform at this music festival. ?m; VHS. **A:** College-Adult. **P:** Entertainment. **U:** Home. **Mov-Ent:** Music--Performance, Music--Jazz. **Acq:** Purchase. **Dist:** Music Video Distributors. $139.95.

Aurora 1984 — ★★½
Single mom Aurora (Loren) will do anything for her blind son Ciro (played by Loren's son Edoardo Ponti). When she discovers that there's a possible operation that could restore his sight, Aurora decides to call up all Ciro's possible fathers and get them to finance the surgery. This plan also reunites Aurora with the one man she truly loved. Made for Italian TV. 91m; VHS. **C:** Sophia Loren; Daniel J. Travanti; Ricky Tognazzi; Philippe Noiret; Anna Strasberg; Franco Fabrizi; Directed by Maurizio Ponzi; Music by Georges Delerue. **A:** Sr. High-Adult. **P:** Entertainment. **U:** Home. **Mov-Ent:** TV Movies, Blindness. **Acq:** Purchase. **Dist:** Facets Multimedia Inc.

Aurora Borealis 2006 (R) — ★★½
Sutherland happily chews scenery as aged Ronald, whose increasingly ill health is proving too much for his wife Ruth (Fletcher) to handle. Fortunately, their slacker grandson Duncan (Jackson) gets a handyman's job at their apartment building to help out. Ruth also hires free-spirited home healthcare worker Kate (Lewis), whom Duncan immediately fancies. But Kate doesn't like to stay in one place for too long so Duncan may have to make a tough decision about where his future lies. Title refers to Ronald's belief that he can see the northern lights from his window. 110m; DVD. **C:** Joshua Jackson; Donald Sutherland; Juliette Lewis; Louise Fletcher; Directed by James C.E. Burke; Written by Brent Boyd; Cinematography by Alar Kivilo; Music by Mychael Danna. **Pr:** Scott Disaroon; Rick Bieber; Entitled Entertainment; Regent Releasing. **A:** Sr. High-Adult. **P:** Entertainment. **U:** Home. **L:** English. **Mov-Ent:** Aging. **Acq:** Purchase. **Dist:** Liberty International Entertainment.

The Aurora Encounter 1985 (PG) — ★★
Aliens surreptitiously infiltrate a small town in 1897, and spread benevolence everywhere. Family fare. 90m; VHS, DVD. **C:** Jack Elam; Peter Brown; Carol Bagdasarian; Dottie West; George "Spanky" McFarland; Directed by Jim McCullough, Sr.; Written by Jim McCullough, Jr. **Pr:** New World Pictures. **A:** Jr. High-Adult. **P:** Entertainment. **U:** Home. **L:** Spanish. **Mov-Ent:** Science Fiction. **Acq:** Purchase. **Dist:** Anchor Bay Entertainment. $14.95.

Aurora: Rivers of Light in the Sky 1994
Presents the mystery and majesty of nature's celestial light show, the Aurora Borealis, or, Northern Lights. 40m; VHS. **A:** Adult. **P:** Education. **U:** Home. **Gen-Edu.** **Acq:** Purchase. **Dist:** Astronomical Society of the Pacific. $24.95.

Auschwitz and the Allies 1982
This tape features two Aushwitz escapees telling the story of the horrors that occurred at that infamous concentration camp. 110m; VHS, 3/4 U. **Pr:** British Broadcasting Corporation. **A:** Sr. High-Adult. **P:** Education. **U:** Institution, SURA. **Gen-Edu:** World War Two, Holocaust. **Acq:** Purchase. **Dist:** Home Vision Cinema.

Auschwitz of Puget Sound 1987
An Archbishop is seen denouncing the arms race as a "global crucifixion of Christ." 30m; VHS, 3/4 U. **Pr:** Radharc Productions. **A:** Jr. High-Adult. **P:** Religious. **U:** Institution, SURA. **Gen-Edu:** Nuclear Warfare. **Acq:** Purchase, Rent/Lease. **Dist:** St. Anthony Messenger Press. $24.95.

Ausser Rand und Band am Wolfgangsee 19?? (Unrated)
A young student inherits a hotel, only to find it in a bad state of disrepair and mortgaged to the hilt. With her own ingenuity and the help of friends, she turns it into a first-class inn. In German only. 90m; VHS. **TV Std:** NTSC, PAL. **C:** Gunther Philipp; Roberto Bianco; Waltraut Haas; Jutta Speidel. **Pr:** German Language Video Center. **A:** Family. **P:** Entertainment. **U:** Home. **L:** German. **Mov-Ent.** **Acq:** Purchase, Rent/Lease. **Dist:** German Language Video Center. $41.95.

Aussie and Ted's Great Adventure 2009 (G) — ★★½
Michael Brooks returns from Australia with a dog that immediately bonds with his young daughter Laney. However, Michael later buys Laney a very special teddy bear from a friend in Chinatown. Aussie gets jealous and manages to 'lose' Ted on the streets of their San Francisco hometown. Then doggie guilt sets in and Aussie hunts to find Ted, only to have the Brooks' move out to their aunt's farm in the meantime. 89m; DVD. **C:** Dean Cain; Alyssa Shafer; Leo Howard; Kristin Eggers; Beverly D'Angelo; Emily Kuroda; Vanessa Bell Calloway; Timothy Starks; Voice(s) by James Ryan; Nick Shafer; Directed by Shuki Levy; Written by Shuki Levy; Tori Avey; Cinematography by James Mathers; Music by Shuki Levy; Gil Feldman. **A:** Family. **P:** Entertainment. **U:** Home. **Mov-Ent:** Pets, Toys. **Acq:** Purchase. **Dist:** Universal Studios Home Video.

Aussie Assault 1983
On September 26, 1983 the longest winning streak in sports history came to an end when America lost the America's Cup to the Australians. Here is the race from the victor's viewpoint of Alan Bond and the crew of "Australia II." 82m; VHS. **Pr:** Gary Holt; Bill Scholer. **A:** Family. **P:** Entertainment. **U:** Institution, CATV, BCTV, Home. **Spo-Rec:** Sports--Water. **Acq:** Purchase, Rent/Lease. **Dist:** Bennett Marine Video. $39.95.

Austenland 2013 (PG-13) — ★
Jane Hayes (Russell) is a woman obsessed with Jane Austen's "Pride and Prejudice" to the degree that she travels to a British resort built around the author's work. The idea that grown adults can act like children at Disney World but with themes from Austen's work has comedic potential but the laughless script is stunningly bad as it tries to tell an odd story of the haves and have-nots at Austenland. Made years after the Austen buzz seems to have died down, director Hess based this upon co-screenwriter Shannon Hale's 2007 book. 97m; DVD, Blu-Ray. **C:** Keri Russell; Jennifer Coolidge; Bret McKenzie; J.J. Feild; James Callis; Georgia King; Ricky Whittle; Jane Seymour; Rupert Vansittart; Directed by Jerusha Hess; Written by Jerusha Hess; Shannon Hale; Cinematography by Larry Smith; Music by Ilan Eshkeri. **Pr:** Stephenie Meyer; Sony Pictures Classics. **A:** Jr. High-Adult. **P:** Entertainment. **U:** Home. **Mov-Ent:** Literature, Comedy--Screwball, Economics. **Acq:** Purchase. **Dist:** Sony Pictures Home Entertainment Inc.

Austin Powers: International Man of Mystery 1997 (PG-13) — ★★★
Hilarious spoof of '60s spy and babe movies. Groovy '60s spy Austin Powers (Myers) discovers that his arch-enemy, Dr. Evil (Myers again) has frozen himself in order to elude capture, so the swingin' dentally challenged Brit decides to do the same. They awaken 30 years later in the same state: woefully out of touch. Dr. Evil is attempting to blackmail the British government and deal with his Gen-X son, Scott Evil (Green). Austin, on the other hand, is trying to "shag" every "groovy bird" he sees. Teamed with Vanessa (Hurley), the daughter of his former partner, they try to stop the evil machinations of...well..Evil. Myers revels in playing the fool, and he may step over the line every once in a while, but he gets plenty of mileage out of the one-joke premise. 88m; VHS, DVD, Blu-Ray, UMD, CC. **C:** Mike Myers; Elizabeth Hurley; Michael York; Seth Green; Mimi Rogers; Robert Wagner; Fabiana Udenio; Paul Dillon; Charles Napier; Will Ferrell; Mindy Sterling; Cameo(s) Tom Arnold; Carrie Fisher; Directed by Jay Roach; Written by Mike Myers; Cinematography by Peter Deming; Music by George S. Clinton. **Pr:** Suzanne Todd; Demi Moore; Jennifer Todd; Eric McLeod; Claire Rudnick Polstein; Moving Pictures Company Ltd; Eric's Boy; New Line Cinema. **A:** Jr. High-Adult. **P:** Entertainment. **U:** Home. **Mov-Ent:** International Relations, Satire & Parody, Pets. **Awds:** MTV Movie Awards '98: Dance Seq. (Mike Myers/ Londoners), Villain (Myers). **Acq:** Purchase. **Dist:** New Line Home Video.

Austin Powers 2: The Spy Who Shagged Me 1999 (PG-13) — ★★★
Old snaggle-tooth (Myers) returns and time travels back to 1969 in order to foil his look-alike nemesis, Dr. Evil, who steals Powers' mojo. Myers wisely highlights the not-so-good Dr., along with some hilarious new characters, instead of the periodically wearisome Powers. Again plot takes a back seat to the great dialogue, characters (including Rob Lowe doing a dead-on Robert Wagner and a third Myers incarnation, Fat Bastard), and kitchy eye candy. It all still works because of Myers' winking good nature. 95m; VHS, DVD, Blu-Ray, CC. **C:** Mike Myers; Heather Graham; Elizabeth Hurley; Seth Green; Robert Wagner; Rob Lowe; Verne Troyer; Kristen Johnston; Mindy Sterling; Gia Carides; Clint Howard; Michael York; Will Ferrell; Muse Watson; Charles Napier; Tim Robbins; Fred Willard; Jack Kehler; Cameo(s) Burt Bacharach; Elvis Costello; Rebecca Romijn; Woody Harrelson; Willie Nelson; Jerry Springer; Directed by Jay Roach; Written by Mike Myers; Michael McCullers; Cinematography by Ueli Steiger; Music by George S. Clinton. **Pr:** Suzanne Todd; Jennifer Todd; Demi Moore; Eric McLeod; John Lyons; Eric's Boy; New Line Cinema. **A:** Jr. High-Adult. **P:** Entertainment. **U:** Home. **Mov-Ent:** Satire & Parody, Photography. **Awds:** MTV Movie Awards '00: On-Screen Duo (Mike Myers/Verne Troyer), Villain (Myers). **Acq:** Purchase. **Dist:** New Line Home Video.

Austin Powers In Goldmember 2002 (PG-13) — ★★½
Shag-happy superspy Austin Powers is back for the third installment of the spy-spoof franchise. Austin travels back to the 70's to find his secret agent dad Nigel (Caine), hook up with new love interest and fellow spy Foxxy Cleopatra (Knowles), and rescue the world. Myers again takes on numerous roles, this time adding new villain Goldmember, a disco-clad Dutchman with a gilded prosthetic and a penchant for world domination. Dr. Evil is in good form but soft newcomer Goldmember comes up short, and Myers is running out of funny ideas. Bond studio MGM raised a stink about the title (too close to "Goldfinger") but finally saw the light and allowed the parody to continue. 94m; VHS, DVD, Blu-Ray. **C:** Mike Myers; Michael Caine; Seth Green; Beyonce Knowles; Verne Troyer; Michael York; Robert Wagner; Mindy Sterling; Fred Savage; Tommy (Tiny) Lister; Clint Howard; Nathan Lane; Cameo(s) Steven Spielberg; Gwyneth Paltrow; Tom Cruise; Kevin Spacey; Danny DeVito; John Travolta; Quincy Jones; Burt Bacharach; Britney Spears; Ozzy Osbourne; Donna D'Errico; Susanna Hoffs; Directed by Jay Roach; Written by Mike Myers; Michael McCullers; Cinematography by Peter Deming; Music by George S. Clinton. **Pr:** Suzanne Todd; Jennifer Todd; Demi Moore; Eric McLeod; John Lyons; Team Todd; Moving Pictures Company Ltd; Gratitude International; New Line Cinema. **A:** Jr. High-Adult. **P:** Entertainment. **U:** Home. **Mov-Ent.** **Acq:** Purchase. **Dist:** New Line Home Video.

Austin Stevens Snakemaster: In Search of the Giant Lizard, Monster Rattler and More! 2004
Presents highlights from the Animal Planet's television series "Snakemaster," including host Austin Stevens as he seeks out some of the most dangerous reptiles. 3 episodes. 125m; DVD. **A:** Jr. High-Adult. **P:** Entertainment. **U:** Home. **Gen-Edu:** Television Series, Animals, Documentary Films. **Acq:** Purchase. **Dist:** Sony Pictures Home Entertainment Inc. $9.95.

Austin Stevens, Snakemaster: In Search of the Giant Lizard, Monster Rattler, and More 2005
In three adventures, the wildlife photographer searches for the most lethal reptiles on the planet: Borneo's reticulated python, Australia's Perentie lizard, and Florida's eastern diamondback snake. 125m; DVD. **A:** Jr. High-Adult. **P:** Entertainment. **U:** Home. **Gen-Edu:** Documentary Films. **Acq:** Purchase. **Dist:** Sony Pictures Home Entertainment Inc.

Australia 1976
A look at life down under-the history, geography, and people of Australia. 17m; 3/4 U. **Pr:** Lyle Bebensee. **A:** Primary-Adult. **P:** Education. **U:** Institution, SURA. **Gen-Edu:** Australia. **Acq:** Purchase, Rent/Lease. **Dist:** Kinetic Film Enterprises Ltd.

Australia 1991
Features the smallist, flattest, and one of the driest continents. Looks at the vast desert outback, lush rain forest, busy cities, green farmlands, and massive western mining operations. Part of a six-part series. 25m; VHS, 3/4 U. **A:** Primary-Sr. High. **P:** Education. **U:** Institution. **Gen-Edu:** Geography, Australia. **Acq:** Purchase. **Dist:** National Geographic Society. $99.00.

Australia 2008 (PG-13) — ★★½
Luhrmann's near-three-hour epic, set in northern Australia shortly before WWII, finds English aristocrat Lady Sarah Ashley inheriting a sprawling cattle station, eyed by local barons looking to take over. So Lady Sarah joins forces with a stockman known only as The Drover to drive 2,000 head of cattle to market, only to then face the bombing of Darwin by the Japanese. Long and melodramatic all-things-Down-Under story is beautiful to watch, with astonishing photography, sweeping vistas, and easy-on-the-eyes leads in Kidman and Jackman, but is ultimately overwhelmed by its own grandiose ambitions (note the similarities between posters for "Australia" and "Gone With the Wind"). 165m; Blu-Ray, On Demand, Wide. **C:** Nicole Kidman; Hugh Jackman; David Wenham; Bryan Brown; Jack Thompson; Ben Mendelsohn; David Gulpilil; David Ngoombujarra; Yuen Wah; Barry Otto; Bruce Spence; Brandon Walters; Lillian Crombie; Directed by Baz Luhrmann; Written by Baz Luhrmann; Stuart Beattie; Ronald Harwood; Richard Flanagan; Cinematography by Mandy Walker; Music by David Hirschfelder. **Pr:** Baz Luhrmann; G. Mac Brown; Catherine Knapman; Baz Luhrmann; Bazmark; Dune Entertainment; Ingenious Media Partners; 20th Century-Fox. **A:** Jr. High-Adult. **P:** Entertainment. **U:** Home. **L:** English. **Mov-Ent:** Australia, Drama. **Acq:** Purchase. **Dist:** Fox Home Entertainment; Amazon.com Inc.; Movies Unlimited.

Australia: Down Under and Outback 1973
A look at life in Australia's primitive outback country. 25m; 3/4 U, Special order formats. **Pr:** National Geographic Society. **A:** Primary. **P:** Education. **U:** Institution, Home, SURA. **Gen-Edu:** Australia. **Acq:** Purchase, Trade-in, Duplication License. **Dist:** National Geographic Society.

Australia: Land Before Time 2005
The evolution of the continent, from deserts to rainforests, and its unique creatures. 75m; DVD. **A:** Jr. High-Adult. **P:** Entertainment. **U:** Home. **Gen-Edu:** Documentary Films, Australia. **Acq:** Purchase. **Dist:** Razor Digital.

Australia Now 1984
A look at the people and the music from the lands down under, Australia and New Zealand. 60m; VHS. **Pr:** Pom Oliver; Peter Clifton. **A:** Jr. High-Adult. **P:** Entertainment. **U:** Home. **Mov-Ent:** Music--Performance. **Acq:** Purchase. **Dist:** Music Video Distributors. $14.95.

Australia: Pace and a Race of Horses 19??
Two programs from Australia are contained on one cassette. "Pace" tell of the cycle that one horse goes through to become a winning trotter. "A Race of Horses" transforms a simple horse race into a visual poem of style and grace. 33m; VHS. **Pr:** Film Australia. **A:** Family. **P:** Entertainment. **U:** Home. **Gen-Edu:** Horses--Racing. **Acq:** Purchase. **Dist:** , On Moratorium.

Australia: Secrets of the Land Down Under 19??
Tours Australia, visiting its modern cities, various coastlines, and the outback, discussing the cultures and geography of the country. Comes with teacher's manual. 45m; VHS. **A:** Jr. High-Adult. **P:** Education. **U:** Institution. **Gen-Edu:** Australia, Cities & Towns, Geography. **Acq:** Purchase. **Dist:** Educational Video Network. $49.95.

Australia: The Timeless Land 1969
A visit to Australia's outback country, the dirty, hot heartland of the continent. 52m; 3/4 U, Special order formats. **Pr:** National Geographic Society. **A:** Primary-Jr. High. **P:** Education. **U:** Institution, Home, SURA. **Gen-Edu:** Australia. **Acq:** Purchase, Trade-in, Duplication License. **Dist:** National Geographic Society.

Australia—2nd Edition 1959
This tape depicts the many geographic, social, economic, and cultural concepts important to an understanding of this vast continent. 22m; VHS, 3/4 U; Open Captioned. **Pr:** Encyclopedia Britannica Educational Corporation. **A:** Primary-Sr. High. **P:** Education. **U:** Institution, SURA. **L:** English, Spanish. **Gen-Edu:** Australia. **Acq:** Purchase, Rent/Lease, Trade-in. **Dist:** Encyclopedia Britannica.

Australian Aborigines 19??
Outlines the life and history of the Gagudju Aborigines of Australia, discussing what their future may hold for them. Comes with teacher's manual. 60m; VHS. **A:** Jr. High-Adult. **P:** Education. **U:** Institution. **Gen-Edu:** Australia, Geography, History. **Acq:** Purchase. **Dist:** Educational Video Network. $49.95.

Australian Animals 19??
Travel to Australia where children can witness the continent's peculiar animals in their natural habitats. Examines life cycles, behaviour, defense mechanisms, and more. 25m; VHS. **Pr:** Centre Films. **A:** Primary-Adult. **P:** Education. **U:** Institution. **Gen-Edu:** Australia, Wildlife. **Acq:** Purchase. **Dist:** Clear Vue Inc. $149.95.
Indiv. Titles: 1. Fauna of Australia 2. The Kangaroos 3. The World of the Koalas 4. Reptiles 5. Crocodiles.

Australian Ark: Amazing Marsupials 1988
An examination of the pouched mammals including kangaroos, koalas, and Tasmanian devils. 79m; VHS. **A:** Family. **P:** Entertainment. **U:** Home. **Gen-Edu:** Documentary Films, Animals, Australia. **Acq:** Purchase. **Dist:** Karol Media; Sony Pictures Home Entertainment Inc. $19.95.

Australian Ark: Changing Face of Australia 1988
A look at how tourism and increasing development may affect Australia's natural wonders. 54m; VHS. **A:** Family. **P:** Entertainment. **U:** Home. **Gen-Edu:** Documentary Films, Australia, Ecology & Environment. **Acq:** Purchase. **Dist:** Karol Media; Sony Pictures Home Entertainment Inc. $19.98.

Australian Ark: Coming of Man 1988
A look at the 50,000-year-old aboriginal rites that have been practiced since the last Ice Age. 67m; VHS. **A:** Family. **P:** Entertainment. **U:** Home. **Gen-Edu:** Documentary Films, Australia, Evolution. **Acq:** Purchase. **Dist:** Karol Media; Sony Pictures Home Entertainment Inc. $19.98.

Australian Ark: Farthest West 1988
Creatures little changed since prehistoric times are visited in this video filmed in Australia's remote west. First aired on PBS. 50m; VHS. **Pr:** PBS. **A:** Family. **P:** Education. **U:** Home. **Gen-Edu:** Documentary Films, Geography, Australia. **Acq:** Purchase. **Dist:** Karol Media; Sony Pictures Home Entertainment Inc. $19.95.

Australian Ark: Green World 1988
An examination of Australia's lush jungles and rain forests and the startling creatures that have adapted to life there. 52m; VHS. **A:** Family. **P:** Entertainment. **U:** Home. **Gen-Edu:** Documentary Films, Australia, Forests & Trees. **Acq:** Purchase. **Dist:** Karol Media; Sony Pictures Home Entertainment Inc. $19.98.

Australian Ark: Land of the Birds 1988
Australia is home to some of the world's most exotic feathered denizens. Included are looks at the bowerbird, the lyrebird, and the cassowary. 59m; VHS. **A:** Family. **P:** Entertainment. **U:** Home. **Gen-Edu:** Documentary Films, Australia, Birds. **Acq:** Purchase. **Dist:** Karol Media; Sony Pictures Home Entertainment Inc. $19.98.

Australian Ark: Life and Death in the Great Barrier Reef 1988
The Great Barrier Reef is one of the most hostile environments on Earth, yet a startling array of creatures call it home. 55m; VHS. **A:** Family. **P:** Entertainment. **U:** Home. **Gen-Edu:** Documentary Films, Australia, Oceanography. **Acq:** Purchase. **Dist:** Karol Media; Sony Pictures Home Entertainment Inc. $19.98.

Australian Ark: Life in the Desert 1988
Although the oppressive daytime heat makes the desert appear to be void of life, at night it teems with mammals, birds, and reptiles. 48m; VHS. **A:** Family. **P:** Entertainment. **U:** Home. **Gen-Edu:** Documentary Films, Australia, Wildlife. **Acq:** Purchase. **Dist:** Karol Media; Sony Pictures Home Entertainment Inc. $19.98.

Australian Ark: Return to the Dreaming 1988
The ancient aboriginal concept of "dream time" is examined. 53m; VHS. **A:** Family. **P:** Entertainment. **U:** Home. **Gen-Edu:** Documentary Films, Australia, Ecology & Environment. **Acq:** Purchase. **Dist:** Karol Media; Sony Pictures Home Entertainment Inc. $19.98.

Australian Ark: Small World 1988
The highly complex, and surprisingly developed world of insects is explored. 45m; VHS. **A:** Family. **P:** Entertainment. **U:** Home. **Gen-Edu:** Documentary Films, Australia, Insects. **Acq:** Purchase. **Dist:** Karol Media; Sony Pictures Home Entertainment Inc. $19.98.

Australian Ark: Survivors 1988
Australia plays host to some of the world's most bizarre creatures, including the duckbill platypus. This edition looks at these creatures and examines how they have responded to the demands of evolution. 55m; VHS. **A:** Family. **P:** Entertainment. **U:** Home. **Gen-Edu:** Documentary Films, Australia, Ecology & Environment. **Acq:** Purchase. **Dist:** Karol Media. $19.98.

The Australian Ballet Favorites ????
Highlights and historical background of early and contemporary classics including "Giselle," "Coppelia," "Swan Lake," "Sleeping Beauty," "Spartacus," and "Songs of a Wayfarer." 126m; VHS. **A:** Adult. **P:** Entertainment. **U:** Home. **Fin-Art:** Dance--Ballet, Dance--Performance. **Acq:** Purchase. **Dist:** Stagestep. $19.95.

Australian Mammals: Life Down Under 19??
Concentrates on mammals that live in Australia, including the kangaroo, the koala, and the platypus. Includes teacher's guide. ?m; VHS. **Pr:** Children's Television Workshop. **A:** Primary-Jr. High. **P:** Education. **U:** Institution. **Chl-Juv:** Animals, Australia. **Acq:** Purchase. **Dist:** GPN Educational Media. $15.00.

Australian Opera Gala Concert 1986
Sydney Opera House presents selections ranging from Handel to Donizett and many more. 142m; VHS. **Pr:** Kultur. **A:** Family. **P:** Entertainment. **U:** Home. **Fin-Art:** Opera, Australia. **Acq:** Purchase. **Dist:** Kultur International Films Ltd., Inc. $29.95.

Australian Royal Tours Collection, 1901-1988 19??
Covers various tours by the Royal Family to Australia during the 20th century. Includes trips by King George VI and Queen Elizabeth (as Duke and Duchess of Windsor), Queen Elizabeth II in 1954, and Prince Charles and Princess Diana in 1983 and 1988. 90m; VHS. **TV Std:** NTSC, PAL. **A:** Jr. High-Adult. **P:** Education. **U:** Home. **Gen-Edu:** Great Britain, Australia, Travel. **Acq:** Purchase. **Dist:** International Historic Films Inc. $29.95.

The Australian Story 1952 (Unrated) — ★★
After a botched robbery, Connor (Lawford) and Gamble (Boone) stumble across the McGuire ranch and convince drunken Michael McGuire (Currie) that Connor is the old man's long-lost son. This becomes a problem when Connor falls in love with his 'sister' Dell (O'Hara) as they help out on a cattle drive. 84m; DVD. **C:** Maureen O'Hara; Finlay Currie; Peter Lawford; Richard Boone; Chips Rafferty; Directed by Lewis Milestone; Written by Harry Kleiner; Cinematography by Charles G. Clarke; Music by Sol Kaplan. **A:** Jr. High-Adult. **P:** Entertainment. **U:** Home. **Mov-Ent:** Australia. **Acq:** Purchase. **Dist:** VCI Entertainment.

Australia's Aborigines 19??
Looks at the unique culture of the Aborigines. 59m; VHS, 3/4 U; Closed Captioned. **A:** Primary-Adult. **P:** Education. **U:** Institution. **Gen-Edu:** Australia. **Acq:** Purchase. **Dist:** National Geographic Society. $24.20.

Australia's Animal Mysteries 1983
This documentary looks at some of Australia's unique animals, including possums that "fly," mammals that lay eggs, and a frog that broods its eggs in its stomach. 59m; 3/4 U, Special order formats. **Pr:** National Geographic Society. **A:** Family. **P:** Education. **U:** Institution, Home, SURA. **Gen-Edu:** Animals, Australia. **Acq:** Purchase, Trade-in, Duplication License. **Dist:** National Geographic Society.

Australia's Art of the Dreamtime: Quinkin Country 1989
Documents the rock paintings of the Australian aborigine and the stories behind them. 60m; VHS. **A:** Jr. High-Adult. **P:** Education. **U:** Institution, Home. **Gen-Edu:** Art & Artists, Australia. **Acq:** Purchase. **Dist:** GPN Educational Media. $49.95.

Australia's Kangaroos 2000 (Unrated)
The kangaroos of Australia have evolved over millions of years to become a true symbol of the land down under. Faced with predators both human and animal, these extraordinary creatures have developed defenses so exceptional that they now thrive in almost any environment. 58m; VHS, DVD. **A:** Family. **P:** Education. **U:** Institution, Home. **Mov-Ent:** Documentary Films, Australia, Animals. **Acq:** Purchase. **Dist:** National Geographic Society. $19.95.

Austria 1986
Follow in the footsteps of author Hans Weigl through the Austrian countryside, from the Bodensee to Neusiedlersee. In English. 55m; VHS. **TV Std:** NTSC, PAL. **C:** Hosted by Gunther Less. **A:** Family. **P:** Entertainment. **U:** Home. **Gen-Edu:** Travel. **Acq:** Purchase, Rent/Lease. **Dist:** Home Vision Cinema; German Language Video Center. $49.90.

Austria and Germany 1983
Gunther Less takes another "Journey to Adventure" as he visits Vienna and Muenchen. 50m; VHS. **TV Std:** NTSC, PAL. **Pr:** Video Explorer Inc. **A:** Family. **P:** Education. **U:** Home. **Gen-Edu:** Travel, Germany. **Acq:** Purchase. **Dist:** German Language Video Center.

Austria: Journeys Through the Salt Mines 2002
Chronicles the history of Austria from the 13th century onward with a focus on the wealthy and opulent city of Salzburg. 48m; VHS. **A:** Adult. **P:** Education. **U:** Home. **Gen-Edu:** History. **Acq:** Purchase. **Dist:** Janson Media. $24.95.

Austria: The Land of Music 1989
From Mozart's home in Salzburg to the Vienna Boys Choir, Austria has been responsible for many of history's greatest musicians. Breath-taking art and architecture are also featured. 55m; VHS. **Pr:** Applause Productions. **A:** Family. **P:** Education. **U:** Institution, Home. **Gen-Edu:** Documentary Films. **Acq:** Purchase. **Dist:** German Language Video Center. $42.00.

Austrian Bike Grand Prix '88 1988
Thrills and spills from the Austrian Grand Prix. ?m; VHS. **A:** Family. **P:** Entertainment. **U:** Home. **Spo-Rec:** Sports--General, Motorcycles. **Acq:** Purchase. **Dist:** Powersports - Powerdocs. $39.95.

Author! Author! 1982 (PG) — ★★½
Sweet, likable comedy about playwright Pacino who is about to taste success with his first big hit. Suddenly his wife walks out, leaving him to care for her four children and his own son. His views shift as he begins to worry about, among other things, who will watch the obnoxious kids on opening night. 100m; VHS, DVD. **C:** Al Pacino; Tuesday Weld; Dyan Cannon; Alan King; Andre Gregory; Directed by Arthur Hiller; Written by Israel Horovitz; Music by Dave Grusin. **Pr:** 20th Century-Fox. **A:** Jr. High-Adult. **P:** Entertainment. **U:** Home. **Mov-Ent:** Comedy-Drama. **Acq:** Purchase. **Dist:** Movies Unlimited; Fox Home Entertainment. $14.98.

Author Bank: Colin and Jacqui Hawkins 19??
Profiles husband and wife writing team Colin and Jacqui Hawkins, and introduces their work. 21m; VHS. **A:** Primary-Jr. High. **P:** Education. **U:** Institution. **Chl-Juv:** Biography, Literature--Children, Language Arts. **Acq:** Purchase. **Dist:** Boynton/Cook Publishers Inc. $49.95.

Author Bank: Dick King-Smith 1992
Children's author Dick King-Smith, known for "The Sheep Pig" and "Babe, the Gallant Pig," offers young writers advice on how to come up with writing ideas. Complete with teacher's guide. 20m; VHS. **A:** Primary. **P:** Education. **U:** Institution. **Gen-Edu:** Language Arts. **Acq:** Purchase. **Dist:** Boynton/Cook Publishers Inc. $49.95.

Author Bank: Paula Danziger 1992
Portrait sketch of writer/teacher Paula Danziger. She speaks about her writing and personal values, illustrating the process of finding ideas and putting them into story form. She compares her writing to the artworks of Charles Rennie Macintosh. Complete with teacher's guide. 20m; VHS. **A:** Primary-Jr. High. **P:** Education. **U:** Institution. **Gen-Edu:** Language Arts, Storytelling. **Acq:** Purchase. **Dist:** Boynton/Cook Publishers Inc. $49.95.

Author Bank: Shirley Hughes 1992
Children's author Shirley Hughes illustrates the parallels between her written work and real life. Viewers see the evolution of a rough idea to its finished form with sketches from the "Alfie" stories and "Trotter Street" series. Complete with teacher's guide. 20m; VHS. **A:** Primary-Jr. High. **P:** Education. **U:** Institution. **Gen-Edu:** Language Arts. **Acq:** Purchase. **Dist:** Boynton/Cook Publishers Inc. $49.95.

Author Bank: Susanna Gretz 19??
Profiles children's author Susanna Gretz and introduces her work. 21m; VHS. **A:** Primary-Jr. High. **P:** Education. **U:** Institution. **Chl-Juv:** Biography, Literature--Children, Language Arts. **Acq:** Purchase. **Dist:** Boynton/Cook Publishers Inc. $49.95.

Author-to-Author Video Series 1988
Five-part series features various authors as they discuss poetry, the short story, and fiction. Includes lecture guide and study material. 40m; VHS. **A:** Sr. High-Adult. **P:** Education. **U:** Institution. **Gen-Edu:** Literature, Language Arts. **Acq:** Purchase. **Dist:** Omnigraphics Inc. $165.00.
Indiv. Titles: 1. Contemporary Poets 2. Contemporary Short-Story Writers 3. The Fiction of Mary Lee Settle 4. First Novelists 5. The Modernist Movement in Poetry.

The Authoring Cycle: Read Better, Write Better, Reason Better 1985
An instruction series for teachers in teaching basic language skills functionally and through writing to primary level students. 30m; VHS, 3/4 U. **Pr:** Jerome Harste. **A:** Adult. **P:** Professional. **U:** Institution. **Gen-Edu:** Education, Language Arts. **Acq:** Purchase, Rent/Lease. **Dist:** Boynton/Cook Publishers Inc.
Indiv. Titles: 1. A Natural Curriculum 2. The Authoring Curriculum 3. A Classroom for Authors 4. Taking Ownership 5. Author's Circle 6. Editor's Table 7. Celebrating Authorship 8. Extending the Cycle.

Authority 1980
An in-depth study of authority by Jim McDoniel of Shreveport, La. 27m; VHS, 3/4 U. **Pr:** International Video Bible Lessons. **A:**

Family. **P:** Religious. **U:** Institution, CCTV, CATV, BCTV, Home. **Gen-Edu:** Religion. **Acq:** Purchase, Rent/Lease. **Dist:** Gospel Services, Inc.

Authority and Rebellion 1973
This specially edited version of the feature film, "The Caine Mutiny," explores the first half of the novel by Herman Wouk, and raises questions about the relationship between responsibility and rebellion. 32m; VHS, 3/4 U. **C:** Humphrey Bogart; Jose Ferrer; Fred MacMurray; Van Johnson; Orson Welles. **Pr:** Learning Corporation of America; Columbia Pictures. **A:** Sr. High-College. **P:** Education. **U:** Institution, SURA. **Gen-Edu:** Literature. **Acq:** Purchase, Rent/Lease. **Dist:** Phoenix Learning Group.

Authorized Employees 1995
Training on procedures for safely isolating, locking out and tagging all common forms of energy. Teaches safety and procedures and special situations. 14m; VHS. **A:** Adult. **P:** Professional. **U:** Institution. **Bus-Ind:** Job Training, Safety Education. **Acq:** Rent/Lease. **Dist:** National Safety Council, California Chapter, Film Library.

Authorized Personnel on Low and High Voltages 1995
Involves identifying exposed live parts, working with energized circuits, the importance of lockout procedures, and how to determine nominal voltage. 12m; VHS. **A:** Adult. **P:** Professional. **U:** Institution. **Bus-Ind:** Job Training, Safety Education, Electricity. **Acq:** Rent/Lease. **Dist:** National Safety Council, California Chapter, Film Library.

Authors Anonymous 2014 (PG-13) — ★★
A group of eccentric, unpublished writers welcome Hannah Rinaldi (Cuoco) into their crowd until she becomes a sudden success. Then jealousy and rivalries set in as they each try to find their own way to fame and fortune, but it ain't pretty. 92m; DVD, Blu-Ray. **C:** Kaley Cuoco; Chris Klein; Dennis Farina; Teri Polo; Dylan Walsh; Jonathan Bennett; Tricia Helfer; Jonathan Banks; Directed by Ellie Kanner; Written by David Congalton; Cinematography by Tobias Datum; Music by Jeff Cardoni. **A:** Jr. High-Adult. **P:** Entertainment. **U:** Home. **L:** English. **Mov-Ent:** Literature. **Acq:** Purchase. **Dist:** Screen Media Films.

Autism 1992
Examines the lives of autistic people and their families in order to shed light on the disability and the attempts to treat it. 28m; VHS. **A:** Family. **P:** Education. **U:** Institution. **Hea-Sci:** Health Education, Handicapped, Patient Education. **Acq:** Purchase. **Dist:** Aquarius Health Care Media. $149.00.

Autism: A Strange, Silent World 1991
Depicts three children of different ages with behavior patterns that are symbolic of autism. It also acquaints us with parents, teachers and therapists who try to adapt to these children. American Psychiatric Association, 1991; American Psychological Association, 1991; Association for the Care of Children's Health, 1991. 52m; VHS. **A:** College-Adult. **P:** Education. **U:** Institution. **Gen-Edu:** Psychiatry, Psychology, Documentary Films. **Acq:** Purchase, Rent/Lease. **Dist:** Filmakers Library Inc. $350.00.

Autism: A World Apart 1989
This program examines the lives of three families who have an autistic child. Although deeply loved, the child is often withdrawn and violent, and unable to communicate in any way with other family members. 28m; VHS, 3/4 U. **A:** Sr. High-Adult. **P:** Education. **U:** Institution, SURA. **Gen-Edu:** Mental Retardation, Family. **Acq:** Purchase, Rent/Lease. **Dist:** Fanlight Productions.

Autism: Breaking Through 1989
The causes, symptoms, and treatment options for autistic patients are given. 26m; VHS, 3/4 U. **Pr:** Films for the Humanities. **A:** Jr. High-Adult. **P:** Education. **U:** Institution, SURA. **Hea-Sci:** Mental Retardation, Learning Disabilities. **Acq:** Purchase, Rent/Lease. **Dist:** Films for the Humanities & Sciences. $149.00.

Autism: Childhood and Beyond 1989
The therapies currently being used to help this condition are discussed. 19m; VHS, 3/4 U. **Pr:** Films for the Humanities. **A:** Jr. High-Adult. **P:** Education. **U:** Institution, SURA. **Hea-Sci:** Mental Retardation, Learning Disabilities. **Acq:** Purchase, Rent/Lease. **Dist:** Films for the Humanities & Sciences. $149.00.

Autism: Equipment Turn-On's for Adapted Physical Education 2004 (Unrated)
Physical Education Teacher Ann Griffin discusses using equipment to entice autistic students to participate in physical education. 46m; DVD. **A:** Family. **P:** Education. **U:** Home, Institution. **Gen-Edu:** Autism, Physical Education. **Acq:** Purchase. **Dist:** Championship Productions. $34.99.

Autism: Reaching the Child Within 1985
A profile of three children with infantile autism and their families, which serves to alert viewers to the symptoms of autism and what it means to live with this lifelong developmental disability. 30m; VHS, 3/4 U. **Pr:** Friends of WHA Madison. **A:** Jr. High-Adult. **P:** Education. **U:** Institution, CCTV, CATV. **Gen-Edu:** Learning Disabilities, Children, Education. **Acq:** Purchase, Rent/Lease, Off-Air Record. **Dist:** PBS Home Video. $69.95.

Autism the Musical 2008 (Unrated)
A documentary following acting coach Elaine Hall and the families of five autistic children as they attempt to put on an original stage production. 93m; DVD. **A:** Sr. High-Adult. **P:** Education. **U:** Home. **Gen-Edu:** Documentary Films, Autism. **Acq:** Purchase. **Dist:** Docurama. $26.95.

Auto Accident: What to Do Afterward 1977
A concise list of guidelines is presented to assist the motorist in dealing with an accident situation. 11m; VHS, 3/4 U. **Pr:** William Boundey. **A:** Sr. High-College. **P:** Education. **U:** Institution, SURA. **Gen-Edu:** Consumer Education, Automobiles. **Acq:** Purchase. **Dist:** Phoenix Learning Group.

Auto Assembly Line General Repairman 1982
A 15-year employee of auto manufacturing offers his insights on the industry for those wishing to pursue such a career. 30m; VHS. **Pr:** Morris Video. **A:** Sr. High-Adult. **P:** Instruction. **U:** Home. **How-Ins:** How-To, Occupations, Automobiles. **Acq:** Purchase. **Dist:** Morris Video. $89.95.

Auto Body Repair 1985
On four tapes for trainees, body repair is demonstrated. 64m; VHS, 3/4 U. **Pr:** Bergwall Productions. **A:** Sr. High-Adult. **P:** Vocational. **U:** Institution. **Bus-Ind:** Automobiles. **Acq:** Purchase. **Dist:** Bergwall Productions, Inc.

Auto Body Repair: Basic Metal Straightening Techniques 1990
Auto body repair specialist Vern Phillips explains and demonstrates techniques for auto collision repair. 24m; VHS. **A:** Adult. **P:** Instruction. **U:** Institution. **How-Ins:** Automobiles. **Acq:** Purchase. **Dist:** RMI Media. $59.95.

Auto Body Repair: The Steck Pullrod Process 1990
Auto body repair specialist Vern Phillips explains and demonstrates the Steck Pullrod method. 13m; VHS. **A:** Adult. **P:** Instruction. **U:** Institution. **How-Ins:** Automobiles. **Acq:** Purchase. **Dist:** RMI Media. $59.95.

Auto Body Rust Repair 1988
Rusted auto bodies are repaired to look like new, with discussions on such interesting topics as plastic filler and featheredging. 13m; Open Captioned. **Pr:** Bergwall Productions. **A:** Sr. High-Adult. **P:** Instruction. **U:** Institution. **How-Ins:** Automobiles, Education. **Acq:** Purchase. **Dist:** Bergwall Productions, Inc. $179.00.
Indiv. Titles: 1. Tools and Techniques 2. Sheet Metal Patching 3. Filling and Refinishing.

Auto Body Series 1984
Series covering all aspects of automotive body repair with program lengths ranging from 12 minutes to 49 minutes. 30m; VHS, 3/4 U. **Pr:** RMI Media Productions. **A:** Sr. High-Adult. **P:** Instruction. **U:** Institution, CCTV, Home. **How-Ins:** Automobiles. **Acq:** Purchase. **Dist:** RMI Media.
Indiv. Titles: 1. Metal Finishing, Tool Identification and Minor Dent 2. Metal Finishing, Large Dent 3. Fiberglass Rust Repair 4. Repairing Door Damage Using the Door Stretcher 5. Use of the Resistance Spot Welder 6. Use of the Wire Feed Welder 7. Acrylic Lacquer Spot Repair 8. Plastics Identification and Repair 9. Front End Assembly Removal 10. Front End Assembly Installation 11. Windshield Water Leak Repair 12. Water and Dust Leak Repair 13. Outer Door Panel Replacement 14. Quarter Panel Replacement Parts One and Two 15. Setting up the Korek Frame Repair 16. Dent-Repair with Weld on Washers 17. Korek Frame Repair Equipment 18. Auto Body Safety 19. Air Conditioning Discharge and Evaluation 20. Air Conditioning Recharge System.

Auto Body Tools Explained 1982
On two tapes, auto body tools are explicated for the mechanically minded viewer. 22m; VHS, 3/4 U. **Pr:** Bergwall Productions. **A:** Sr. High-Adult. **P:** Vocational. **U:** Institution. **Bus-Ind:** Automobiles. **Acq:** Purchase. **Dist:** Bergwall Productions, Inc.

Auto Buyer Alert 1996
Presents car buying tips on when to buy, how to make trade-ins, financing, and more. 33m; VHS. **A:** Adult. **P:** Instruction. **U:** Home. **How-Ins:** Automobiles. **Acq:** Purchase. **Dist:** Tapeworm Video Distributors Inc. $14.95.

Auto Dimensions 1987
The viewer is reduced to miniature size so he can take a guided tour of a car's engine and electrical system. 45m; VHS. **Pr:** Cambridge Career Productions. **A:** Jr. High-Adult. **P:** Education. **U:** Institution, Home. **Gen-Edu:** Automobiles. **Acq:** Purchase. **Dist:** Cambridge Educational. $29.95.

Auto Focus 2002 (R) — ★★★
Paul Schrader examines the sordid life and death of "Hogan's Heroes" star Bob Crane (Kinnear). Kinnear's portrayal of Crane from the seemingly normal father and husband to the sexaholic who was found bludgeoned to death amongst his amateur pornography is startling. The trouble starts when he meets creepy pal (and possible murderer) Carpenter (Dafoe), who gets him drumming gigs in strip clubs. This easy access to women, along with his affable manner and Carpenter's array of video equipment lead to a torrent of carnal acts that the two obsessively commit to tape. Crane loses two wives (Wilson, Bello) and his wholesome image while remaining oblivious to the descent that his sex addiction is causing in his personal and professional life. The cast does a great job with difficult material, especially Kinnear and Ron Leibman as Crane's weary agent. 104m; VHS, DVD, CC. **C:** Greg Kinnear; Willem Dafoe; Rita Wilson; Maria Bello; Ron Leibman; Kurt Fuller; Ed Begley, Jr.; Michael E. Rodgers; Michael McKean; Bruce Solomon; Christopher Neiman; Lyle Kanouse; Directed by Paul Schrader; Written by Michael Gerbosi; Cinematography by Fred Murphy; Music by Angelo Badalamenti. **Pr:** Alicia Allain; Scott Alexander; Larry Karaszewski; Todd Rosken; Pat Dollard; Propaganda Films; Good Machine; Sony Pictures Classics. **A:** Sr. High-Adult. **P:** Entertainment. **U:** Home. **Mov-Ent:** Biography: Show Business, Pornography, Marriage. **Acq:** Purchase. **Dist:** Sony Pictures Home Entertainment Inc.

Auto Maintenance: Play it Safe 1979
Shows the elementary warning devices in your automobile. 19m; VHS, 3/4 U. **A:** Sr. High-College. **P:** Education. **U:** Institution, SURA. **Gen-Edu:** Safety Education. **Acq:** Purchase. **Dist:** Phoenix Learning Group.

Auto Mechanics 1988
Provides step-by-step instruction in auto mechanics, including set-up procedures, alignment techniques, and brake repair and installation. 10m; VHS, 3/4 U. **Pr:** RMI Media Productions. **A:** Sr. High-Adult. **P:** Vocational. **U:** Institution, CCTV, Home. **How-Ins:** Industrial Arts, Automobiles, Consumer Education. **Acq:** Purchase. **Dist:** RMI Media. $75.00.
Indiv. Titles: 1. John Bear Equipment Set-Up 2. Reading And Adjusting Caster & Chamber John Bear Alignment Machine 3. Read & Adjust Toe John Bear Alignment Machine 4. Checking Steering Axis And Inclination 5. Alignment and Adjustment Locations Fords Products 6. Alignment Adjustment Locations Ford Products With Strut Rod 7. Alignment Adjustment Locations Chrysler K-Car 8. Alignment Adjustment Locations General Motors 9. Mounting Rotor & Drums With Hubs Ammco Brake Lathe 10. Mounting Hubless Rotors & Drums On Ammco Brake Lathe 11. Machine Brake Drum Ammco Brake Lathe 12. Machining Disk Brake Rotor Ammco Brake Lathe 13. Mounting A Hubless Rotor On The F.M.C. Brake Lathe 14. Mounting A Rotor With A Hub On The F.M.C. Brake Lathe 15. Machining A Rotor On The F.M.C. Brake Lathe 16. Knurling A Valve Guide-UPT Equipment 17. Selecting & Dressing The Grinding Stone Of The Sioux Valve Seat Grinder 18. Grinding A Valve Seat With Sioux Valve Seat Grinder 19. Cutting A Valve Seat With A Neway Valve Seat Cutter 20. Measurement For Valve String Installed Height 21. Measuring Valve Stem Height 22. Inspecting & Pressure Testing Valve Springs 23. Checking For Head Warpage 24. Detecting Cracks On Cylinder Heads Using Magna Flux 25. Removing Valves From Cylinder Head 26. Dressing Wheel Or Stone On Sioux Valve 27. Grinding A Valve Face On Sioux Valve 28. Valve Stem, Tip Grinding & Champhering On Sioux Valve Grinder 29. Measuring Valve Guides 30. Automotive, Bend And Twist A Rod 31. F.M.C. Tire Removal And Introduction 32. F.M.C. Tire Installation, Mounting 33. Piston Knurling 34. Computerized Wheel Balance Calibration 35. Computerized Wheel Balance 36. Valve Guide Coring Setup 37. Valve Guide Coring, Drilling, Reaming & Installing 38. Piston Pin Removal-Burroughs Tool 39. Piston Pin Installation-Burroughs Tool.

Auto Mechanics 1992
Part of a series offering instruction on applied vocational mathematics. 30m; VHS. **A:** Adult. **P:** Education. **U:** Institution. **Gen-Edu:** Mathematics. **Acq:** Purchase. **Dist:** RMI Media. $149.00.

Auto Recovery 2008 (Unrated) — ★★
Some films can still be pretty good even with a low budget, or even if the plot is cliched and overdone. This is not one of them. A repo man with a checkered past has to nab a pastor's car or do 20 years in prison. Steal a car or go to jail. How does that work exactly? Isn't it usually the other way around? That's kind of like saying "People who obey the speed limit will have their drivers license taken." 113m; DVD. **C:** Pierre August; Larry Barry; Tim Bell; Shelli Boone; Tyrone Burton; Anthony Coleman; Corey Miguel Curties; Aaron A. Frazier; Leonard George, III; David Alan Graf; Brian Keith Hall; Sir Majesty; Jolin Miranda; Steven Slates; Directed by Ernest Johnson; Written by Ernest Johnson; Cinematography by Dave Bouza; Crystal Burdette; Music by Dwayne Madison; Dwight Madison. **A:** Sr. High-Adult. **P:** Entertainment. **U:** Home. **Mov-Ent:** Terrorism. **Acq:** Purchase. **Dist:** Maverick Entertainment. $16.98.

Auto Safety Series 1978
This three-part series is an in-depth study of all facets of owning and operating an automobile. Subject matter includes car care, accident situation reactions, and driving tips that every driver should know. 16m; VHS, 3/4 U. **Pr:** Greenhouse Films Productions. **A:** Sr. High-Adult. **P:** Education. **U:** Institution, SURA. **Gen-Edu:** Automobiles, Driver Education. **Acq:** Purchase. **Dist:** Phoenix Learning Group.
Indiv. Titles: 1. Auto Maintenance: Play it Safe 2. Driving Tips to Avoid Accidents 3. Auto Accident: What to Do Afterward.

Auto Shop Safety 1987
The basics of working safely in an auto shop are given. The entire series is also available as a single tape for the same cost. 10m; VHS. **Pr:** Bergwall Productions. **A:** Sr. High-Adult. **P:** Instruction. **U:** Institution. **How-Ins:** Industrial Arts, Automobiles. **Acq:** Purchase. **Dist:** Bergwall Productions, Inc. $299.00.
Indiv. Titles: 1. Proper Attitude and Dress 2. Jacking and Lifting an Automobile 3. Hand Tools and Fire Safety 4. Battery Charger and Power Tools 5. Working On the Car.

Autobahn 1981
This experiment in the art of animation which combines electronic with manual animation techniques is set to the music of Kraftwerk. 13m; VHS, 3/4 U. **Pr:** Italas and Batchelor Films. **A:** Sr. High-Adult. **P:** Education. **U:** Institution, SURA. **Fin-Art:** Art & Artists. **Acq:** Purchase. **Dist:** Phoenix Learning Group.

Autobiography of a Princess 1975 (Unrated) — ★★
A brief character study shot by Merchant-Ivory in six days. An East Indian princess, living in self-enforced exile in London, invites her father's former tutor to tea. They watch old movie footage of royal India together and dream of a happier past. 59m; VHS, DVD. **C:** James Mason; Madhur Jaffrey; Directed by James Ivory; Written by Ruth Prawer Jhabvala. **Pr:** Merchant-Ivory Productions. **A:** College-Adult. **P:** Entertainment. **U:** Home. **Mov-Ent:** India. **Acq:** Purchase. **Dist:** Home Vision Cinema. $29.95.

The Autobiography of Miss Jane Pittman 1974 — ★★★½
The history of blacks in the South is seen through the eyes of a 110-year-old former slave. From the Civil War through the Civil Rights movement, Miss Pittman relates every piece of black history, allowing the viewer to experience the injustices. Tyson is spectacular in moving, highly acclaimed drama. Received nine Emmy awards; adapted by Tracy Keenan Wynn from the novel by Ernest J. Gaines. 110m; VHS, DVD. **C:** Cicely Tyson; Odetta; Joseph Tremice; Richard Dysart; Michael Murphy; Katherine Helmond; Directed by John Korty; Written by Tracy Keenan Wynn; Cinematography by James A. Crabe; Music by Fred Karlin. **Pr:** Tomorrow Entertainment Inc. **A:** Sr. High-Adult. **P:** Entertainment. **U:** Home. **Mov-Ent:** Drama, Biography, Civil Rights. **Acq:** Purchase. **Dist:** VCI Entertainment.

AutoCAD: An Introduction 1985
This video serves as an introduction to the AutoCAD computer-assisted drafting system. 17m; VHS. **Pr:** Bergwall Productions. **A:** College-Adult. **P:** Instruction. **U:** Institution. **How-Ins:** Architecture, Education. **Acq:** Purchase. **Dist:** Bergwall Productions, Inc. $249.00.
Indiv. Titles: 1. System Orientation 2. Basic Drawing Operations 3. Support Functions 4. Completing the Drawing.

AutoCAD: Architectural Drafting 1992
Specially designed drafting software for those in the architectural profession. Features AutoCAD release 12. Four programs explore such concepts as the GUI interface, BHATCH, creating elevations, and more. Comes with study guide. ?m; VHS. **A:** Adult. **P:** Professional. **U:** Institution. **Bus-Ind:** Computers, Drawing, Architecture. **Acq:** Purchase. **Dist:** Bergwall Productions, Inc. $299.00.

AutoCAD Basics 1992
A self-study system in 104 lessons that will make you brilliant in AutoCAD, a computer aided drawing software package. Comes with study guide. Accompanying software and printed lesson sets available separately. 755m; VHS. **A:** Adult. **P:** Professional. **U:** Institution. **Bus-Ind:** Education, Computers, Drawing. **Acq:** Purchase. **Dist:** Bergwall Productions, Inc. $288.00.
Indiv. Titles: 1. AutoCAD Basics: Draw Commands 2. AutoCAD Basics: Display, Layer, and Inquiry Command 3. AutoCAD Basics: Edit Commands 4. AutoCAD Basics: Dimension, Text and Hatch Commands 5. AutoCAD Basics: View, Block and Plot Commands 6. R12 Update: Workspace Commands 7. R12 Update: FILE Interface Commands.

AutoCAD: Electronic Drafting 1986
The basics of AutoCAD are explained. 15m; VHS. **Pr:** Bergwall Productions. **A:** College-Adult. **P:** Instruction. **U:** Institution. **How-Ins:** Architecture, Education. **Acq:** Purchase. **Dist:** Bergwall Productions, Inc. $249.00.
Indiv. Titles: 1. Electronic Symbols 2. Construction of Schematic Drawings 3. Component Documentation 4. Design and Logic Diagrams.

AutoCAD Explained 1987
The AutoCAD computer-assisted drafting system is demonstrated. Also available as one tape at the same cost. 14m; VHS. **Pr:** Bergwall Productions. **A:** College-Adult. **P:** Instruction. **U:** Institution. **How-Ins:** Architecture, Education. **Acq:** Purchase. **Dist:** Bergwall Productions, Inc. $389.00.
Indiv. Titles: 1. Hardware Introduction 2. Drawing Commands 3. Edit and Inquiry Commands 4. Entity Draw Commands 5. File Utilities.

AutoCAD Explained 2 1987
The sequel to the popular how-to program explores advanced applications of AutoCAD. Also available as a single tape at the same cost. 11m; VHS. **Pr:** Bergwall Productions. **A:** College-Adult. **P:** Instruction. **U:** Institution. **How-Ins:** Architecture, Education. **Acq:** Purchase. **Dist:** Bergwall Productions, Inc. $199.00.
Indiv. Titles: 1. Associative Dimentioning 2. 3D Theory 3. 3D Drawing Construction.

AutoCAD: Mechanical Drafting 1986
Mechanical drafting using AutoCAD is demonstrated. 17m; VHS. **Pr:** Bergwall Productions. **A:** College-Adult. **P:** Instruction. **U:** Institution. **How-Ins:** Architecture, Education. **Acq:** Purchase. **Dist:** Bergwall Productions, Inc. $249.00.
Indiv. Titles: 1. Detail Drawings 2. Dimensioning Methods 3. Machining Specifications 4. Assembly Drawings.

AutoCAD Release 10: Advanced Operations 1989
More applications are demonstrated. Also available as a single tape at the same cost. 18m; VHS. **Pr:** Bergwall Productions. **A:** Sr. High-Adult. **P:** Instruction. **U:** Institution. **How-Ins:** Architecture, Education. **Acq:** Purchase. **Dist:** Bergwall Productions, Inc. $299.00.
Indiv. Titles: 1. 3D Construction Using LISP 2. LISP Programming 3. AutoSHADE 4. AutoFLIX.

AutoCAD Release 10: For the Beginner 1989
The AutoCAD computer-assisted drafting system is explained, focusing on recent revisions of the system. Also available on a single tape at the same cost. 14m; VHS. **Pr:** Bergwall Productions. **A:** College-Adult. **P:** Instruction. **U:** Institution. **How-Ins:** Architecture, Education. **Acq:** Purchase. **Dist:** Bergwall Productions, Inc. $299.00.
Indiv. Titles: 1. Viewing the Drawing 2. Creating a Drawing 3. Editing the Drawing 4. Controlling Properties.

AutoCAD: Release 11 1992
Program describes next-to-latest version of software including three dimensional drawing, TILEMODE, Xref, and Xbind. Comes with study guide. 88m; VHS. **A:** Adult. **P:** Professional. **U:** Institution. **Bus-Ind:** Business, Computers, Drawing. **Acq:** Purchase. **Dist:** Bergwall Productions, Inc. $299.00.
Indiv. Titles: 1. Drawing Made Easy 2. Working with Paper Space 3. Drawing Border Construction 4. Drawing Assembly.

Autociticas: Self-Critics 1980
An experimental video which organizes the tension between video-painting-body. 15m; VHS, 3/4 U. **Pr:** Marcelo Serrano. **A:** Jr. High-Adult. **P:** Education. **U:** Institution, SURA. **Gen-Edu:** Art & Artists, Video. **Acq:** Rent/Lease. **Dist:** Video Out Distribution.

AutoManiac: Death Cars ????
Presents the History Channel special on celebrity car-related fatalities, including actors James Dean and Jayne Mansfield as well as comedian Sam Kinison, among others. 50m; DVD. **A:** Jr. High-Adult. **P:** Entertainment. **U:** Home, CATV. **Mov-Ent:** Television Series, Documentary Films, Biography: Show Business. **Acq:** Purchase. **Dist:** A&E Television Networks L.L.C. $24.95.

Automated Assembly 1987
A video for manufacturers interested in the automation of their production, the program illustrates companies such as Tandy/ Bell and Remmele and how automated assembly has increased speed, improved quality, and decreased costs. 34m; VHS. **A:** Adult. **P:** Professional. **U:** Institution. **L:** English. **Bus-Ind:** Industry & Industrialists. **Acq:** Purchase. **Dist:** Society of Manufacturing Engineers. $228.

Automated Inspection Non-Destructive Testing 1988
Automated Inspection is profiled in this program as several companies are utilized to demonstrate dimensional inspection of parts. 30m; VHS. **A:** Adult. **U:** Institution. **L:** English. **Bus-Ind:** Industry & Industrialists. **Acq:** Purchase. **Dist:** Society of Manufacturing Engineers. $228.

Automated Material Handling 1986
This video profiles General Motors and 3M, and how they've utilized automated guided vehicles, computer-controlled conveyors, and robots in moving their products. 29m; VHS. **A:** Adult. **P:** Professional. **U:** Institution. **L:** English. **Bus-Ind:** Industry & Industrialists. **Acq:** Purchase. **Dist:** Society of Manufacturing Engineers. $228.

Automatic 1975
A satirical presentation of the never-ending conflict of man vs. machine. Presents the question: Can the machine and humanity co-exist? 4m; VHS, 3/4 U. **Pr:** Short Film Prague. **A:** Jr. High-Adult. **P:** Education. **U:** Institution, SURA. **Gen-Edu:** Satire & Parody. **Acq:** Purchase. **Dist:** Phoenix Learning Group.

Automatic 1994 (R) — ★½
Renegade RobGen Industries android Gruner saves Ashbrook from the loathsome sexual advances of the boss but kills the scum in the process. So the duo are targeted for death by company head Glover with killers, led by Kober, sent to do the mopping up. 90m; VHS, CC. **C:** Olivier Gruner; Daphne Ashbrook; John Glover; Jeff Kober; Dennis Lipscomb; Directed by John Murlowski; Written by Susan Lambert; Patrick Highsmith. **Pr:** Ken Badish; Avi Nesher; Active Entertainment. **A:** Sr. High-Adult. **P:** Entertainment. **U:** Home. **Mov-Ent:** Science Fiction. **Acq:** Purchase. **Dist:** Lions Gate Entertainment Inc.

Automatic Golf 1988
This tape claims that it will add an extra 30 to 80 yards to your golf drive. 77m; VHS, 3/4 U. **C:** Bob Mann. **Pr:** Champions on Film. **A:** Jr. High-Adult. **P:** Instruction. **U:** Institution, CCTV, Home. **Spo-Rec:** Golf. **Acq:** Purchase. **Dist:** School-Tech Inc. $19.95.

Automatic Locks 1982
The program develops the concept that new inventions are necessary when old ones no longer work. Part of the "Inventive Child" Series. 11m; VHS, 3/4 U. **Pr:** Film Polski. **A:** Primary-Jr. High. **P:** Education. **U:** Institution, SURA. **Chl-Juv:** Inventors & Inventions. **Acq:** Purchase, Rent/Lease, Trade-in. **Dist:** Encyclopedia Britannica.

Automatic Process Control 1986
In two tapes, the basics and advanced methods of automatic process control are taught. 120m; VHS, 3/4 U. **TV Std:** NTSC, PAL, SECAM. **Pr:** Instructional Society of America. **A:** Adult. **P:** Professional. **U:** Institution, CCTV. **Bus-Ind:** Engineering. **Acq:** Purchase, Rent/Lease. **Dist:** ISA -The International Society of Automation.

Automatic Sampling of Petroleum and Petroleum Products 1985
Shows the components and their functions in automatic sampling systems and explains the need for adequate mixing and sample-rate frequency to obtain a representative sample. Includes workbook. 26m; VHS. **A:** Adult. **P:** Professional. **U:** Institution. **Bus-Ind:** Job Training, Management, Industry & Industrialists. **Acq:** Purchase. **Dist:** $110.

Automatic Sprinkler Systems 1995
Discusses the care and maintenance of sprinkler systems. 30m; VHS. **A:** Adult. **P:** Professional. **U:** Institution. **Bus-Ind:** Safety Education, Management, Occupational Training. **Acq:** Rent/ Lease. **Dist:** National Safety Council, California Chapter, Film Library.

Automatic Tennis 198?
Cliff Drysdale has distilled tennis to four essentials; bounce, rotation, acceleration, and target. Tennis players can learn to hit automatically with these four steps behind them. 58m; VHS. **A:** Jr. High-Adult. **P:** Instruction. **U:** Home. **Spo-Rec:** Tennis. **Acq:** Purchase. **Dist:** ESPN Inc. $29.95.

The Automatic Transmission 1985
The operation and maintenance of the automatic transmission of an automobile is the focus of this video series. 15m; VHS. **Pr:** Bergwall Productions. **A:** Sr. High-Adult. **P:** Instruction. **U:** Institution. **How-Ins:** Automobiles, Education. **Acq:** Purchase. **Dist:** Bergwall Productions, Inc. $269.00.
Indiv. Titles: 1. Basic Parts and Principles-Part One 2. Basic Parts and Principles-Part Two 3. Power Flow of Mechanical Components-Part One 4. Power Flow of Mechanical Components-Part Two 5. Operation of Hydraulic Circuits-Part One 6. Operation of Hydraulic Circuits-Part Two.

Automatic Transmissions 1992
Details the various components and functions of automatic transmission elements such as the torque converters, clutches, pistons and servos, band and planetary gear sets. 29m; VHS. **A:** Adult. **P:** Instruction. **U:** Institution. **How-Ins:** Automobiles. **Acq:** Purchase. **Dist:** RMI Media. $95.00.

Automating the Office 1985
A series of programs that clarify modern methods of automating workplaces for maximum efficency and productivity. 30m; VHS, 3/4 U, Special order formats. **Pr:** TV Ontario. **A:** Adult. **P:** Professional. **U:** Institution, SURA. **Bus-Ind:** Business, Office Practice. **Acq:** Purchase, Rent/Lease. **Dist:** Time-Life Video and Television.
Indiv. Titles: 1. More Than a Machine 2. The Report: Decision Support Tools 3. The Revolt: Secretaries and the Changing Office 4. The Delta File: Information Storage & Retrieval 5. Routes and Relationships 6. Telephone Tag: Electronic Mail 7. Data Communications 8. The Office Network 9. Best-Laid Plans: Planning and Implementation.

Automaton Transfusion 2006 (R) — **Bomb!**
Dumb title, worse movie. It's cheap, gory zombie horror that has the advantage of at least having a short run-time. Teens in some backwater Florida burg find their town is being overrun by bloodthirsty zombies that are result of a misbegotten military experiment. 75m; DVD. **C:** Garrett Jones; Juliet Reeves; Kendra Farner; Joel Hebner; Rowan Bousaid; William Howard Bowman; Directed by Steven C. Miller; Written by Steven C. Miller; Cinematography by Jeff Dolan; Music by Jamey Scott. **A:** Sr. High-Adult. **P:** Entertainment. **U:** Home. **Mov-Ent. Acq:** Purchase. **Dist:** Allumination Filmworks.

Automatons 2006 (Unrated) — ★
Micro-budget homage to old sci-fi movies. Humans take on robots in the aftermath of yet another pointless World War. 83m/ B/W; DVD. **C:** Christine Spencer; Angus Scrimm; Brenda Cooney; Directed by James Felix McKenney; Written by James Felix McKenney; Cinematography by David W. Hale; Music by Noah De Filippis. **A:** Jr. High-Adult. **P:** Entertainment. **U:** Home. **L:** English. **Mov-Ent. Acq:** Purchase. **Dist:** Facets Multimedia Inc. $24.95.

L'Automobile 1971 (Unrated) — ★½
Longtime Roman prostitute Anna is tired of her usual routine. She buys an automobile to make herself feel normal and to give her a sense of freedom. A trip to the beach in her new car doesn't work out as Anna thought it would. Originally filmed for Italian TV as part of the "Tre Donne" miniseries. Italian with subtitles. 98m; DVD. **C:** Anna Magnani; Vittorio Caprioli; Christian Hay; Directed by Alfredo Giannetti; Written by Alfredo Giannetti; Cinematography by Pasqualino De Santis; Music by Ennio Morricone. **A:** College-Adult. **P:** Entertainment. **U:** Home. **L:** Italian. **Mov-Ent:** TV Movies, Automobiles, Prostitution. **Acq:** Purchase. **Dist:** Entertainment One US LP.

Automobile Tire Hydroplaning—What Happens 198?
This film demonstrates how and why automobile tires lose contact with wet pavements. 12m; VHS, 3/4 U. **Pr:** National Safety Council. **A:** College-Adult. **P:** Education. **U:** Institution. **Gen-Edu:** Driver Education. **Acq:** Rent/Lease. **Dist:** National Safety Council, California Chapter, Film Library.

Automobiles: BMW 2006
Looks at the history, design, and production of BMW, which was founded in 1927. 50m; DVD. **A:** Jr. High-Adult. **P:** Entertainment. **U:** Home. **Gen-Edu:** Documentary Films. **Acq:** Purchase. **Dist:** A&E Television Networks L.L.C.

Automobiles: Cadillac ????
Presents the History Channel special on the creation and evolution of the Cadillac brand automobile by General Motors and how it came to set the standard in the industry. 50m; DVD. **A:** Family. **P:** Entertainment. **U:** Home, CATV. **Mov-Ent:** Television Series, Documentary Films, Automobiles. **Acq:** Purchase. **Dist:** A&E Television Networks L.L.C. $24.95.

Automobiles: Corvette 2006
Looks at the history and design of the sport car, including a high-speed test drive. 50m; DVD. **A:** Jr. High-Adult. **P:** Entertainment. **U:** Home. **Gen-Edu:** Documentary Films. **Acq:** Purchase. **Dist:** A&E Television Networks L.L.C.

Automobiles: Model T 2006
Traces the history of the "Tin Lizzie" from its earliest production in 1908 to the late 1920s. Collectors also show off restored models. 50m; DVD. **A:** Jr. High-Adult. **P:** Entertainment. **U:** Home. **Gen-Edu:** Documentary Films, Automobiles. **Acq:** Purchase. **Dist:** A&E Television Networks L.L.C.

The Automotive Air Conditioner 1982
On three tapes, the parts and principles of automotive air conditioners are described. 40m; VHS, 3/4 U. **Pr:** Bergwall Productions. **A:** Sr. High-Adult. **P:** Vocational. **U:** Institution. **Bus-Ind:** Automobiles. **Acq:** Purchase. **Dist:** Bergwall Productions, Inc.

Automotive, Bend and Twist a Rod 1987
Offers instruction on specific aspects of automotive maintenance and repair. 5m; VHS. **A:** Adult. **P:** Instruction. **U:** Institution. **How-Ins:** Automobiles. **Acq:** Purchase. **Dist:** RMI Media. $59.95.

The Automotive Computer 1989
The evolution and uses of on-board automotive computers are examined. This series is also available as a single tape at the same cost. ?m; VHS. **Pr:** Bergwall Productions. **A:** Sr. High-Adult. **P:** Instruction. **U:** Institution. **How-Ins:** Automobiles, Industrial Arts. **Acq:** Purchase. **Dist:** Bergwall Productions, Inc. $299.00.
Indiv. Titles: 1. Explaining the Black Box 2. Input: Sensors 3. Output: Activators 4. The Computer In Action.

Automotive Computer System Operation 1991
Combines live action with animation to illustrate the functions of an automotive computer system. ?m; VHS. **A:** Sr. High-Adult. **P:** Education. **U:** Institution. **Gen-Edu:** Automobiles. **Acq:** Purchase. **Dist:** Meridian Education Corp. $95.00.

Automotive Computer System Service 1992
Explains problem sources, symptoms, tests, and repairs used to fix common computer system malfunctions. 25m; VHS. **A:** Adult. **P:** Instruction. **U:** Institution. **How-Ins:** Automobiles. **Acq:** Purchase. **Dist:** RMI Media. $95.00.

Automotive Computers Series 1990
Four-part series that furnishes information on automotive computers, discussing how they work and how to find and repair potential problems. Includes instruction on the computer's trouble codes, scanning tools, computer electrical values, and modern-type analysis systems. 100m; VHS. **A:** Sr. High-Adult. **P:** Vocational. **U:** Institution. **How-Ins:** Automobiles, Computers, Occupational Training. **Acq:** Purchase. **Dist:** Cambridge Educational. $349.95.
Indiv. Titles: 1. Automotive Computer Self-Diagnosis 2. Scanning Automotive Computer Problems 3. Automotive Computer System Operation 4. Automotive Computer System Service.

The Automotive Cooling System 1988
The construction and repair of automotive air conditioning systems is examined. 11m; VHS. **Pr:** Bergwall Productions. **A:** Sr. High-Adult. **P:** Instruction. **U:** Institution. **How-Ins:** Automobiles, Education. **Acq:** Purchase. **Dist:** Bergwall Productions, Inc. $279.00.
Indiv. Titles: 1. Basic Parts and Operations-Part One 2. Basic Parts and Operations-Part Two 3. Problems-External and Internal Leaks 4. Problems-Coolant and Air Blockage 5. Problems-Additives and Moving Parts 6. Problems-Exhaust Leaks and Unusual Conditions.

Automotive Cylinder Boring 1987
Automotive cylinder boring is performed before the video camera, including the use of the boring bar. 11m; VHS. **Pr:** Bergwall Productions. **A:** Sr. High-Adult. **P:** Instruction. **U:** Institution. **How-Ins:** Automobiles, Education. **Acq:** Purchase. **Dist:** Bergwall Productions, Inc. $149.00.
Indiv. Titles: 1. The Boring Bar 2. Boring the Cylinders 3. Honing the Cylinders.

Automotive Electronics Explained 1986
Automotive electronics are explained for the lay person. 13m; VHS. **Pr:** Bergwall Productions. **A:** Sr. High-Adult. **P:** Instruction. **U:** Institution. **How-Ins:** Automobiles. **Acq:** Purchase. **Dist:** Bergwall Productions, Inc. $349.00.
Indiv. Titles: 1. Comparing Old and New Systems 2. Basic Concepts and Equipment 3. Microprocessor Design and Usage 4. Schematics and Components 5. Troubleshooting Techniques.

Automotive Hand Tools Explained 1985
On four tapes, automotive tools are demonstrated. 46m; VHS, 3/4 U. **Pr:** Bergwall Productions. **A:** Sr. High-Adult. **P:** Vocational. **U:** Institution. **Bus-Ind:** Tools. **Acq:** Purchase. **Dist:** Bergwall Productions, Inc.

Automotive Measurement 19??
Illustrates correct procedures for using automotive measuring devices, including micrometers, dial indicators, feeler gauges, plastigauge, dial bore gauges, and straight edges. Contains demonstrations of actual measurements of various automotive parts. 30m; VHS. **A:** Sr. High-Adult. **P:** Instruction. **U:** Institution. **How-Ins:** Automobiles, Tools, How-To. **Acq:** Purchase. **Dist:** Cambridge Educational. $95.00.

Automotive Microprocessors Explained 1984
On four tapes, the uses of microprocessors in automobile engines are detailed. 54m; VHS, 3/4 U. **Pr:** Bergwall Productions. **A:** Sr. High-Adult. **P:** Vocational. **U:** Institution. **Bus-Ind:** Automobiles. **Acq:** Purchase. **Dist:** Bergwall Productions, Inc.

Automotive Pollution Control 1982
On five tapes, car pollution systems are dissected and discussed. 71m; VHS, 3/4 U. **Pr:** Bergwall Productions. **A:** Sr. High-Adult. **P:** Vocational. **U:** Institution. **Bus-Ind:** Automobiles. **Acq:** Purchase. **Dist:** Bergwall Productions, Inc.

Automotive Series 1987
A comprehensive "how-to" of automotive repair, covering basic maintenance as well as engine overhaul. 40m; VHS. **A:** Sr. High-Adult. **P:** Instruction. **U:** Institution, Home. **How-Ins:** How-To, Automobiles, Engineering. **Acq:** Purchase. **Dist:** Meridian Education Corp. $89.00.
Indiv. Titles: 1. Vehicle Maintenance & Fluid Services 2. Engine Disassembly 3. Cylinder Head Service 4. Automotive Measurement 5. Short Block Services 6. Engine Reassembly.

Automotive Shop Safety 1976
This 5-tape program shows how to remain safe and uninjured in an automotive repair garage. 50m; VHS, 3/4 U. **Pr:** Bergwall Productions. **A:** Sr. High-Adult. **P:** Vocational. **U:** Institution. **Bus-Ind:** Automobiles, Safety Education. **Acq:** Purchase. **Dist:** Bergwall Productions, Inc.

Automotive Tech Series 1987
Demonstrates various aspects of auto mechanics using a step-by-step format. Developed by automotive instructors at the College of Du Page in Glen Ellyn, Illinois. 25m; VHS, 3/4 U. **Pr:** RMI Media Productions. **A:** Sr. High-Adult. **P:** Vocational. **U:** Institution. **How-Ins:** Automobiles. **Acq:** Purchase. **Dist:** RMI Media.
Indiv. Titles: 1. Caliper Overhaul 2. Using the Disc & Drum Micrometer 3. Wheel Bearing Service 4. Rebuilding Wheel Cylinders 5. Brake Shoe Servicing: Ford Type 6. Brake Shoe Servicing: GM Type 7. Servicing Parking Brakes 8. Wheel Bearing & Seal Servicing.

Automotive Tune-Up Guide 1989
All the basics of car care are shown on this one videotape. 60m; VHS. **C:** Jay Geraghty. **Pr:** Associated Video Publishers. **A:** Sr. High-Adult. **P:** Instruction. **U:** Home. **How-Ins:** Automobiles. **Acq:** Purchase. **Dist:** Karol Media. $29.95.

Autonomous Production Groups: Responsibility Shared 1988
This program shows us how alternative forms of job sharing can generate amazing results—from entire divisions to smaller groups being run by employees. 29m; VHS, 3/4 U. **Pr:** National Educational Media Inc. **A:** College-Adult. **P:** Vocational. **U:** Institution, SURA. **Bus-Ind:** Business, Management, Industry & Industrialists. **Acq:** Purchase, Rent/Lease, Trade-in. **Dist:** Encyclopedia Britannica. $395.00.

Autonomous Working Groups: Smarter Together 1988
In this program, (filmed at a Japanese plant), skilled workers, engineers, and executives demonstrate how semi-autonomous groups share responsibility for planning, control, production, and marketing. 29m; VHS, 3/4 U. **Pr:** National Educational Media Inc. **A:** College-Family. **P:** Professional. **U:** Institution, SURA. **Bus-Ind:** Business, Management, Human Relations. **Acq:** Purchase, Rent/Lease, Trade-in. **Dist:** Encyclopedia Britannica. $395.00.

Autopsy 1973 (Unrated) — ★
A young gold-digger and a millionaire marry, and then cheat on each other, provoking blackmail and murder. 90m; VHS, DVD. **C:** Fernando Rey; Gloria Grahame; Christian Hay; Sue Lyon; Directed by Jose Maria Forque; Written by Rafael Azcona; Cinematography by Alejandro Ulloa; Music by Michel Colombier. **Pr:** O.P.C. Productions. **A:** Sr. High-Adult. **P:** Entertainment. **U:** Home. **Mov-Ent:** Mystery & Suspense. **Acq:** Purchase. **Dist:** Movies Unlimited. $26.99.

Autopsy 1975 (R) — ★½
Forensic pathologist Farmer is working at a morgue compiling statistics concerning suicides and murders staged to look like suicides. Farmer begins to go nuts when it seems a stalker is killing people around her using the fake suicide method. Then there's the fact that the pathological pathologist is also sexually repressed and everything and everyone starts to scream sex to her and things get really kinky (and gory). 100m; VHS, DVD. **C:** Mimsy Farmer; Barry Primus; Angela Goodwin; Ray Lovelock; Directed by Armando Crispino; Written by Armando Crispino; Lucio Battistrada; Cinematography by Carlo Carlini; Music by Ennio Morricone. **Pr:** Joseph Brenner Associates. **A:** College-Adult. **P:** Entertainment. **U:** Home. **Mov-Ent:** Horror, Suicide. **Acq:** Purchase. **Dist:** Anchor Bay Entertainment; MPI Media Group.

Autopsy 2008 (R) — ★★
The usual band of young adults has a car accident on a lonely road and gets taken to a mostly abandoned country hospital full of evil doctors. 89m; DVD, Streaming. **C:** Michael Bowen; Robert Patrick; Ross Kohn; Robert LaSardo; Jessica Lowndes; Ashley Schneider; Jenette Goldstein; Janine Venable; Directed by Adam Gierasch; Written by Adam Gierasch; Jace Anderson; E. L. Katz; Cinematography by Anthony B. Richmond; Music by Joseph Bishara. **A:** Sr. High-Adult. **P:** Entertainment. **U:** Home. **L:** English, Spanish. **Mov-Ent. Acq:** Purchase, Rent/Lease. **Dist:** Lions Gate Entertainment Inc. $14.98 9.99.

Autopsy: A Love Story 2002 (Unrated) — ★★½
Life is a cold, lonely place for morgue-worker Charlie, whose pushy boss has him knee-deep in the bootlegged organs business. Meanwhile, his cross, crippled girlfriend torments him. The arrival of a hot new amour at the office livens things up—even though she's dead—but the pitiful lad is thrown when her (living) twin sister shows up. 90m; VHS, DVD. **C:** Joe Estevez; Paul DeGruccio; Dina Osmussen; Ginny Harman; Wendy Crawford; Robert McClure; Jill Seitz; Greg Hanson; Mike Watkis; Keith Arbo; Ashley Smith; John Scott Mills; Directed by Guy Crawford; Written by Guy Crawford; Tamarie Hargrove. **A:** Sr. High-Adult. **P:** Entertainment. **U:** Home. **Mov-Ent:** Drug Abuse. **Acq:** Purchase. **Dist:** Movies Unlimited. $29.95.

Autopsy of a Ghost 1967 — ★½
Comedy/horror film stars Rathbone as a ghost and Mitchell as a mad scientist. Notable as Rathbone's last screen appearance. In Spanish with no subtitles. 110m; VHS. **C:** Basil Rathbone; John Carradine; Cameron Mitchell; Amadee Chabot; Directed by Ismael Rodriguez; Written by Armando Crispino; Lucio Battistrada. **A:** Sr. High-Adult. **P:** Entertainment. **U:** Home. **L:** Spanish. **Mov-Ent. Acq:** Purchase. **Dist:** Sinister Cinema. $16.95.

Autopsy Pathology Demonstration 1974
A demonstration of an autopsy. 14m; VHS, 3/4 U, Special order formats. **Pr:** Ohio State University Health Sciences AV Center. **A:** College-Adult. **P:** Professional. **U:** Institution, SURA. **Hea-Sci:** Autopsy. **Acq:** Purchase, Rent/Lease. **Dist:** Ohio State University.

Autopsy: Postmortem with Dr. Michael Baden 2008
The forensic pathologist talks about some of his most prominent cases, including President Kennedy, the Romanovs, and 9/11 first responders. 57m; DVD. **A:** Adult. **P:** Entertainment. **U:** Home. **Hea-Sci:** Medical Education, Documentary Films. **Acq:** Purchase. **Dist:** Home Box Office Inc. $19.98.

Autos of Yesteryear 1988
The Model T and Duesenburg are just a few of the cars that can be seen in this video. 30m; VHS. **Pr:** Visual Horizons. **A:** Sr. High-Adult. **P:** Education. **U:** Institution, Home. **Gen-Edu:** Automobiles. **Acq:** Purchase. **Dist:** Visual Horizons. $39.95.

Autumn Across America 198?
A film focusing on species of animal and plant life near or at the point of extinction because of man's destabilizing influence. 50m; 3/4 U, Special order formats. **Pr:** Hobel Leiterman Productions. **A:** Jr. High-Adult. **P:** Education. **U:** Institution. **Gen-Edu:** Seasons, Ecology & Environment. **Acq:** Purchase. **Dist:** The Cinema Guild.

An Autumn Afternoon 1962 — ★★★½
Ozu's final film is a beautiful expression of his talent. In postwar Tokyo, an aging widower loses his only daughter to marriage and begins a life of loneliness. A heart-wrenching tale of relationships and loss. In Japanese with English subtitles. 112m; VHS, DVD. **C:** Chishu Ryu; Shima Iwashita; Shin-Ichiro Mikami; Mariko Okada; Keiji Sada; Directed by Yasujiro Ozu; Written by Yasujiro Ozu; Cinematography by Yuuharu Atsuta; Music by Kojun Saito. **A:** College-Adult. **P:** Entertainment. **U:** Home. **L:** English, Japanese. **Mov-Ent:** Parenting. **Acq:** Purchase. **Dist:** Criterion Collection Inc. $69.95.

Autumn Born 1979 (R) — ★½
Young heiress is abducted by her guardian and imprisoned while she's taught to obey his will. Ill-fated ex-Playmate Dorothy Stratton's first film. 76m; VHS. **C:** Dorothy Stratten; Ihor Procak, Dory Jackson; Gisselle Fredette; Nate MacIntosh; Joanna McClelland Glass; Roberta Weiss; Roman Buchok; Sharon Elder; Directed by Lloyd A. Simandl; Written by Ihor Procak; Sharon Christensen; Shannon Lee; Cinematography by Lloyd A. Simandl. **Pr:** Lloyd A. Simandl; Lloyd A. Simandl; North American Pictures Ltd. **A:** Adult. **P:** Entertainment. **U:** Home. **Mov-Ent. Acq:** Purchase. **Dist:** Amazon.com Inc. $39.95.

Autumn: Frost Country 1969
Beautifully framed by Robert Frost's readings of his two most beloved poems?"The Road Not Taken" and "Reluctance." 9m; VHS, 3/4 U. **Pr:** Pyramid Film Productions. **A:** Jr. High-Sr. High. **P:** Education. **U:** Institution, SURA. **Gen-Edu:** Literature--American. **Acq:** Purchase. **Dist:** Phoenix Learning Group.

Autumn Hearts: A New Beginning 2007 (Unrated) — ★★
A notable cast in a story that's sentimental and somewhat familiar. In 1945, Jewish dissident Jakob protected youngsters Melanie and Christopher when they were all interred at a detention camp outside Paris. After 35 years, the trio is unexpectedly reunited at Melanie's (Sarandon) rural home in Quebec, where she lives unhappily with husband David (Plummer). Christopher (Byrne) has never gotten over his first love for Melanie and the strong emotional bonds of the past prove to be equally potent in the present. 100m; DVD. **C:** Susan Sarandon; Christopher Plummer; Gabriel Byrne; Max von Sydow; Roy Dupuis; Kris Holden-Ried; Dakota Goya; Regan Jewitt; Alexandre Nachi; Directed by Paolo Barzman; Written by Jefferson Lewis; Cinematography by Luc Montpellier; Music by Normand Corbeil. **A:** Sr. High-Adult. **P:** Entertainment. **U:** Home. **Mov-Ent:** Canada. **Acq:** Purchase. **Dist:** Image Entertainment Inc.

Autumn in New York 2000 (PG-13) — ★½
Start with one clunky love story with no chemistry, then mix in cheesy melodrama and a dash of creepy Freudian undertones and what do you get? This recipe for disaster about a doomed May-December romance. Middle-aged Will Keane (Gere) leads a playboy's life as the owner of one of New York's most fashionable restaurants. He falls for much younger sensitive gal Charlotte (Ryder) after finding out that he dated her mother. Unfortunately, Charlotte is afflicted with a life-threatening disease whose symptoms include saying "Wow!" a lot and fainting at overly dramatic moments. Will's life is changed, and he rushes around trying to find some medical miracle or plot device which might be able to save her. Rent "Love Story" instead. Because love means never having to say you're sorry you wasted two hours of your life on this movie. 104m; VHS, DVD, Wide, CC. **C:** Richard Gere; Winona Ryder; Anthony LaPaglia; Elaine Stritch; Vera Farmiga; Sherry Stringfield; Jill(ian) Hennessey; Directed by Joan Chen; Written by Allison Burnett; Cinematography by Changwei Gu; Music by Gabriel Yared. **A:** Jr. High-Adult. **P:** Entertainment. **U:** Home. **Mov-Ent:** Melodrama. **Acq:** Purchase. **Dist:** MGM Home Entertainment.

Autumn Landscape 1988
The last and most difficult of Palluth's "Workshop in Oils" series. Fledgling artists learn methods of depicting the colors of Fall including the creation of clouds, grasses and weeds, and tree leaves. The long brush bristle method is also explained. Accompanied by a sketch for use by beginners. 60m; VHS. **C:** Hosted by William Palluth. **Pr:** Finley-Holiday Film Corporation. **A:**

Family. **P:** Instruction. **U:** Institution, Home. **How-Ins:** How-To, Painting, Art & Artists. **Acq:** Purchase. **Dist:** Karol Media; Finley Holiday Film Corp. $24.95.

Autumn Leaves 1956 — ★★½
Crawford plays a middle-aged typist grasping at her last chance for love. She marries a younger man who's been romancing her, then finds him more and more unstable and violent. Weak story material that could turn melodramatic and tawdry, but doesn't because of Crawford's strength. 108m/B/W; VHS. **C:** Cliff Robertson; Joan Crawford; Vera Miles; Lorne Greene; Directed by Robert Aldrich; Written by Robert Blees; Lewis Meltzer; Hugo Butler; Jean Rouverol; Cinematography by Charles B(ryant) Lang, Jr. **Pr:** Columbia Pictures. **A:** Jr. High-Adult. **P:** Entertainment. **U:** Home. **Mov-Ent:** Aging, Marriage. **Awds:** Berlin Intl. Film Fest. '56: Director (Aldrich). **Acq:** Purchase. **Dist:** $9.95.

Autumn Marathon 1979 — ★★½
To say that this is one of the better Russian movies of the past three decades is sort of faint praise, given the state of Soviet cinema. Written by playwright Volodin, it's just another paint-by-number version of the philandering man who's really an OK Joe who loves his kids comedy. In Russian with English subtitles. 100m; VHS, DVD. **C:** Oleg Basilashvili; Natalia Gundareva; Marina Neyolova; Directed by Georgi Daniela; Written by Alexander Volodin. **A:** Sr. High-Adult. **P:** Entertainment. **U:** Home. **L:** Russian, English. **Mov-Ent:** Comedy-Drama, Marriage. **Acq:** Purchase. **Dist:** Kino on Video. $59.95.

Autumn Moon 1992 (Unrated) — ★★
Young Japanese tourist (Nagase) travels to Hong Kong to enjoy some sexual fun but instead he befriends a 15-year-old girl (Wai), who's afraid of her family's impending emigration to Canada. Not much happens but the Hong Kong setting is eye-catching. English and Cantonese with subtitles. 108m; VHS, DVD. **C:** Masatoshi Nagase; Li Pui Wai; Directed by Clara Law; Cinematography by Tony Leung Siu Hung. **A:** College-Adult. **P:** Entertainment. **U:** Home. **L:** Chinese. **Mov-Ent:** Drama, Adolescence. **Acq:** Purchase. **Dist:** Image Entertainment Inc.

The Autumn Rain: Crime in Japan 19??
Takes a look at the rising incidence of crimes in Japan perpetuated by and on ordinary citizens, the role of the police in society, and the growth of organized crime. Includes footage of crime prevention measures being undertaken in Japan and Japanese police patrolling the streets. 30m; VHS. **Pr:** National Film Board of Canada. **A:** Jr. High-Adult. **P:** Education. **U:** Institution. **Gen-Edu:** Japan. **Acq:** Purchase. **Dist:** National Film Board of Canada; Clear Vue Inc.

Autumn Sonata 1978 (Unrated) — ★★★
Nordic family strife as famed concert pianist Bergman is reunited with a daughter she has not seen in years. Bergman's other daughter suffers from a degenerative nerve disease and had been institutionalized until her sister brought her home. Now the three women settle old scores, and balance the needs of their family. Excellent performance by Bergman in her last feature film. 97m; VHS, DVD, Blu-Ray. **C:** Ingrid Bergman; Liv Ullmann; Halvar Bjork; Lena Nyman; Gunnar Bjornstrand; Erland Josephson; Directed by Ingmar Bergman; Written by Ingmar Bergman; Cinematography by Sven Nykvist. **Pr:** ITC Entertainment Group; Personafilm. **A:** Sr. High-Adult. **P:** Entertainment. **U:** Home. **L:** Swedish. **Mov-Ent:** Handicapped. **Awds:** Golden Globes '79: Foreign Film; Natl. Bd. of Review '78: Actress (Bergman), Director (Bergman); N.Y. Film Critics '78: Actress (Bergman); Natl. Soc. Film Critics '78: Actress (Bergman). **Acq:** Purchase. **Dist:** Movies Unlimited; Alpha Video; Criterion Collection Inc.

An Autumn Story: Mrs. Pennypacker's Package 1967
A short film about helping others, wherein a woman's lost package is sought by her neighbors. 11m; VHS, 3/4 U. **Pr:** Encyclopedia Britannica Educational Corporation. **A:** Preschool-Primary. **P:** Entertainment. **U:** Institution, SURA. **Chl-Juv.** **Acq:** Purchase, Rent/Lease, Trade-in. **Dist:** Encyclopedia Britannica.

Autumn Sun 1998 (Unrated) — ★★★
This is a love story for appreciative adults. Clara (Aleandro) is a middleaged Buenos Aires accountant whose personal ad for a Jewish gentleman caller is answered by older widower (and non-Jew) Raul Ferraro (Luppi). Still, they're attracted to each other, and since Clara needs a man to pose as her admirer for a visit from her long-absent brother, Raul agrees to the ruse and undergoes a crash course in Jewish customs. This isn't actually played for laughs but as a reflection on expanding one's horizons and taking chances. Spanish with subtitles. 103m; VHS, DVD. **C:** Norma Aleandro; Federico Luppi; Jorge Luz; Cecilia Rossetto; Directed by Eduardo Mignogna; Written by Eduardo Mignogna; Santiago Carlos Oves; Cinematography by Marcelo Camorino; Music by Edgardo Rudnitzky. **A:** College-Adult. **P:** Entertainment. **U:** Home. **L:** Spanish. **Mov-Ent:** Judaism. **Acq:** Purchase. **Dist:** Movies Unlimited.

Autumn Tale 1998 (PG) — ★★½
Middleaged, widowed winegrower Magali (Romand) is lonely now that her children are grown, so her best friend Isabelle (Riviere) secretly places a personal ad and decides to meet the respondents herself in order to find someone suitable for her friend. Isabelle decides saleman Gerald (Libolt) is a likely prospect and schemes to introduce them. Meanwhile, Rosine (Portal), the live-wire girlfriend of Magali's son Leo (Darmon), thinks that her older philosophy professor (and ex-lover), Etienne (Sandre), might be a match. Magali is simply mortified by the entire situation. The fourth film in Rohmer's "Tales of the Four Seasons." French with subtitles. 110m; VHS. **C:** Beatrice Romand; Marie Riviere; Alexia Portal; Alain Libolt; Didier Sandre; Stephane Darmon; Directed by Eric Rohmer; Written by Eric Rohmer; Cinematography by Diane Baratier; Music by Claude Marti. **Pr:** Margaret Menegoz; Les Films du Losange; La Sept Cinema; October Films. **A:** College-Adult. **P:** Entertainment. **U:** Home. **L:** French. **Mov-Ent:** Romance, Aging. **Awds:** Natl. Soc. Film Critics '99: Foreign Film. **Acq:** Purchase.

An Autumn's Tale 1987 (Unrated) — ★★
After following her less-than-admirable boyfriend from Hong Kong to New York, a gullible young woman learns that he is about to move to another city with a Chinese-American lover. In Cantonese with English subtitles. 98m; VHS, DVD. **C:** Cherie Chung; Directed by Mabel Cheung. **A:** Sr. High-Adult. **P:** Entertainment. **U:** Home. **L:** English, Chinese. **Mov-Ent:** Drama. **Acq:** Purchase. **Dist:** Facets Multimedia Inc. $39.95.

Aux Champs 1989
A childless bourgeois couple approaches two destitute families wishing to purchase a child. The families become bitter enemies after one mother accepts the offer. Finally, the son who was given up returns as an elegant young man. 52m; VHS, 3/4 U. **Pr:** Films for the Humanities and Sciences. **A:** College. **P:** Education. **U:** Institution, CCTV, CATV, BCTV. **L:** French. **Fin-Art:** Literature. **Acq:** Purchase, Rent/Lease, Duplication License. **Dist:** Films for the Humanities & Sciences.

Aux Quatre Coins de France 1974
A tour to the four corners of France: Britanny, Auvergne, the Basque country, and Alsace. For use in beginning level French classes. From the "Pays Francophones" series. 11m; VHS, 3/4 U. **Pr:** Encyclopedia Britannica Educational Corporation. **A:** Sr. High-College. **P:** Education. **U:** Institution, SURA. **L:** French. **Gen-Edu:** Language Arts. **Acq:** Purchase, Rent/Lease, Trade-in. **Dist:** Encyclopedia Britannica.

Avalanche 1978 (PG) — ★½
Disasterama as vacationers at a new winter ski resort find themselves at the mercy of a monster avalanche leaving a so-called path of terror and destruction in its wake. Talented cast is buried by weak material, producing a snow-bound adventure yawn. 91m; VHS, DVD. **C:** Rock Hudson; Mia Farrow; Robert Forster; Rick Moses; Directed by Corey Allen; Written by Corey Allen; Cinematography by Pierre William Glenn; Music by William Kraft. **Pr:** New World Pictures. **A:** Jr. High-Adult. **P:** Entertainment. **U:** Home. **Mov-Ent:** Action-Adventure, Skiing. **Acq:** Purchase. **Dist:** Movies Unlimited. $12.74.

Avalanche 1999 (PG-13) — ★½
Prototypical cheesy disaster flic. Alaskan chopper pilot Neil (Griffith) helps out Lia (Feeney), the widow of an old pal, who works for the EPA. She believes the establishment of an oil company's overland pipeline through the mountains will trigger an avalanche that could destroy the city of Juneau. Naturally, no one believes her until there's an avalanche. (Considering the movie's title, you could have guessed this.) 105m; VHS, DVD. **C:** Thomas Ian Griffith; Caroleen Feeney; R. Lee Ermey; C. Thomas Howell; John Ashton; Hilary Shepard; Directed by Steve Kroschel; Written by Steve Kroschel; Cinematography by Steve Kroschel; Richard Pepin; Music by K. Alexander (Alex) Wilkinson. **Pr:** Joseph Merhi; Richard Pepin. **A:** Jr. High-Adult. **P:** Entertainment. **U:** Home. **Mov-Ent:** Action-Adventure, Arctic Regions. **Acq:** Purchase. **Dist:** Alpha Video.

Avalanche Awareness 1988
The basics of avalanche safety for the backcountry traveller. Endorsed by the National Mountain Rescue Association and the U.S. Forest Service. 28m; VHS. **Pr:** Alliance Communications Corporation. **A:** Jr. High-Adult. **P:** Education. **U:** Institution, Home. **Gen-Edu:** Safety Education. **Acq:** Purchase. **Dist:** Pyramid Media. $29.95.

Avalanche Express 1979 (PG) — ★
Marvin is a CIA agent who uses a defector (Shaw) to lure a scientist (Schell), specializing in biological warfare, aboard a European train. Marvin wants to eliminate Schell but all plans go awry when the snow begins to fall. Ineffective thriller. Director Robson's and actor Shaw's last film—much of Shaw's dialogue was dubbed due to his death before the film's soundtrack was completed. Based on a novel by Colin Forbes. 89m; VHS, DVD. **C:** Lee Marvin; Robert Shaw; Maximilian Schell; Linda Evans; Mike Connors; Joe Namath; Horst Buchholz; David A(lexander) Hess; Directed by Mark Robson; Written by Abraham Polonsky; Cinematography by Jack Cardiff. **Pr:** Mark Robson; Mark Robson; Lorimar Productions; Fox. **A:** Jr. High-Adult. **P:** Entertainment. **U:** Home. **Mov-Ent:** Action-Adventure, Trains, Intelligence Service. **Acq:** Purchase. **Dist:** WarnerArchive.com; Warner Home Video, Inc. $19.98.

Avalon 1990 (PG) — ★★★
Powerful but quiet portrait of the break-up of the family unit as seen from the perspective of a Russian family settled in Baltimore at the close of WWII. Initally, the family is unified in their goals, ideologies, and social lives. Gradually, all of this disintegrates; members move to the suburbs and TV replaces conversation at holiday gatherings. Levinson based his film on experiences within his own family of Russian Jewish immigrants. 126m; VHS, DVD, 8 mm, Wide, CC. **C:** Armin Mueller-Stahl; Aidan Quinn; Elizabeth Perkins; Joan Plowright; Lou Jacobi; Leo Fuchs; Eve Gordon; Kevin Pollak; Israel Rubinek; Elijah Wood; Grant Gelt; Bernard Hiller; Directed by Barry Levinson; Written by Barry Levinson; Cinematography by Allen Daviau; Music by Randy Newman. **Pr:** Tri-Star Pictures; Columbia Pictures. **A:** Sr. High-Adult. **P:** Entertainment. **U:** Home. **Mov-Ent:** Comedy-Drama, Immigration. **Awds:** Writers Guild '90: Orig. Screenplay. **Acq:** Purchase. **Dist:** Facets Multimedia Inc.; Sony Pictures Home Entertainment Inc. $19.95.

The Avant-Garde in Russia, 1910-1930 198?
A tour of the largest Russian avant-garde art exhibition ever compiled. The works, from the years 1910-30, has been labeled subversive by the socialist government in Russia. 60m; VHS, 3/4 U. **A:** Sr. High-Adult. **P:** Education. **U:** Institution, SURA. **Fin-Art:** Art & Artists, USSR. **Acq:** Purchase. **Dist:** Films for the Humanities & Sciences.

Avant-Garde Program #11 1970
A collection of three short experimental films: Lynch's student film "Alphabet" (1970), a semi-animated, dark look at the ABCs; Duchamp's famous "Anemic Cinema" (1926, silent), the only true Dada film; and Mitry's "Pacific 231" (1949), an abstract film-poem dedicated to Arthur Honegger and the train of the title. 25m/B/W; VHS. **C:** Directed by David Lynch; Marcel Duchamp; Jean Mitry. **A:** Family. **P:** Entertainment. **U:** Home. **Mov-Ent:** Film--Avant-Garde. **Acq:** Purchase. **Dist:** Facets Multimedia Inc.

Avant-Garde Program #12 1962
Three famous experimental shorts: Dulac's "The Seashell and the Clergyman" (1927), a surrealist piece written by Artaud; Marker's "La Jetee" (1962), a fascinating sci-fi time travel story told completely with still images (in French with subtitles); and Vorkapich's and Florey's "Life and Death of 9413, A Hollywood Extra" (1928), a sardonic look at a would-be star abused by the system. 60m/B/W; VHS. **C:** Directed by Germaine Dulac; Chris Marker; Robert Florey; Slavko Vorkapich; Written by Antonin Artaud. **A:** Family. **P:** Entertainment. **U:** Home. **L:** English, French. **Mov-Ent:** Film--Avant-Garde. **Acq:** Purchase. **Dist:** Facets Multimedia Inc.

Avant-Garde Program #14 1929
Three experimental shorts by Ray: "Retour a la Raison" (1923), produced by exposing film stock to light without a camera; "Emak Bakia" (1927), an abstract short made by Ray tossing the camera into the air; and "Les Mysteres du Chateau du De" (1929), a narrative mood piece with an unsolved mystery at its center. Silent. 43m/B/W; Silent; VHS. **C:** Directed by Man Ray. **Pr:** Man Ray. **A:** Family. **P:** Entertainment. **U:** Home. **Mov-Ent:** Film--Avant-Garde, Silent Films. **Acq:** Purchase. **Dist:** Facets Multimedia Inc.

Avanti! 1972 (R) — ★★½
Stuffy businessman Wendell Armbruster (Lemmon) heads to Italy to claim his father's body when the old man dies while on vacation. Then he discovers dad has been visiting his mistress lo these many years. While trying to get through mountains of red tape, Wendell finds himself romancing the woman's daughter (Mills). Too long but still amusing. 144m; VHS, DVD. **C:** Jack Lemmon; Juliet Mills; Clive Revill; Edward Andrews; Gianfranco Barra; Franco Angrisano; Directed by Billy Wilder; Written by I.A.L. Diamond; Billy Wilder. **Pr:** Billy Wilder; Billy Wilder; United Artists. **A:** Sr. High-Adult. **P:** Entertainment. **U:** Home. **Mov-Ent:** Comedy--Romantic, Family, Italy. **Acq:** Purchase. **Dist:** MGM Home Entertainment. $19.98.

Ava's Magical Adventure 1994 (PG) — ★★½
Ten-year-old Eddie decides to take Ava on a little adventure. Too bad she's a 2-ton elephant he's stolen from the circus. Based on the Mark Twain story "The Stolen White Elephant." 97m; VHS, DVD. **C:** Timothy Bottoms; Georg Stanford Brown; Patrick Dempsey; Priscilla Barnes; David Lander; Kaye Ballard; Remi Ryan; Directed by Patrick Dempsey; Rocky Parker; Written by Susan D. Nimm; Music by Mark Holden. **Pr:** Steven Paul; Barry Collier; Barbara Javitz; Gary Binkow; Crystal Sky Communications. **A:** Family. **P:** Entertainment. **U:** Home. **Mov-Ent:** Circuses, Animals, Family Viewing. **Acq:** Purchase. **Dist:** Unknown Distributor.

Avatar 2009 (PG-13) — ★★★
Cameron's first directorial effort since "Titanic" is an elaborate 3-D sci-fi adventure with dazzling technique and a behind-the-scenes story more interesting than what appears onscreen. Cameron created (in collaboration) advanced motion-capture at an alleged cost of more than $200 million and four years of actual production. The plot itself is fairly standard, set in 2154 when Earth has suffered some disaster. Paraplegic ex-Marine Jake Sully (Worthington) is taken to the human outpost on Pandora where a shady corporation is trying to mine a rare mineral. Because the atmosphere is toxic, humans are mind-linked to a remote-controlled biological body called an avatar. Jake's avatar allows him to walk again and he's supposed to infiltrate the indigenous Na'vi. Too bad Jake becomes completely intrigued with their civilization and warrior Neytiri (Saldana) and is torn between duty and the exotic alien world. 163m; Blu-Ray, Wide. **C:** Sam Worthington; Zoe Saldana; Michelle Rodriguez; Sigourney Weaver; Giovanni Ribisi; Laz Alonso; Wes Studi; Stephen Lang; CCH Pounder; Joel David Moore; Directed by James Cameron; Written by James Cameron; Cinematography by Mauro Fiore; Music by James Horner. **Pr:** Jon Landau; James Cameron; Lightstorm Entertainment; Giant Studios; Dune Entertainment; Ingenious Media Partners; 20th Century-Fox. **A:** Jr. High-Adult. **P:** Entertainment. **U:** Home. **L:** English. **Mov-Ent:** Science Fiction, Space Exploration, Handicapped. **Awds:** Oscars '09: Art Dir./Set Dec., Cinematog., Visual FX; British Acad. '09: Visual FX; Golden Globes '10: Director (Cameron), Film--Drama. **Acq:** Purchase. **Dist:** Fox Home Entertainment; Movies Unlimited; Alpha Video.

Avatar: The Last Airbender - Book 2: Earth, Volume 4 2004
Appa is reunited with Aang, Katara, Sokka, and Toph and together they must stop Princess Azula from capturing the city of Ba Sing, a quest that will end in the ultimate of bending battles. 123m; DVD. **A:** Primary-Jr. High. **P:** Entertainment. **U:** Home. **Chl-Juv:** Animation & Cartoons, Action-Adventure, Fantasy. **Acq:** Purchase. **Dist:** Viacom International Inc.

Avatar: The Last Airbender: The Complete Book 2 20??
Twelve-year old Aang, must set aside his selfish endeavors and master his powers over the four elements in order to save the nations from the treacherous Princess Azula. His friends Katara, Sokka, Momo, and Appa travel with him across the Earth Kingdom in search of his Earthbending mentor who will help him face his destiny as Avatar, the Chosen One. 20 episodes. 492m; DVD. **C:** Voice(s) by Dee Bradley Baker; Mae Whitman; Zach Tyler; Jack De Sena. **A:** Primary-Jr. High. **P:** Entertainment. **U:** Home. **Chl-Juv:** Animation & Cartoons, Animation & Cartoons. **Acq:** Purchase. **Dist:** Viacom International Inc.

Avatar: The Last Airbender—Book 1: Water, Volume 1 2005
Presents the children's animated Nickelodeon television series about a 12-year-old boy named Aang who is the Avatar, a special soul capable of bringing peace to a troubled, futuristic Earth split into the four entities of the Water Tribes, the Earth Kingdom, the Fire Nation, and the Air Nomads—when he's not having cool adventures. Includes: "The Boy in the Iceberg," "The Avatar Returns," "The Southern Air Temple," and "The Warriors of Kyoshi." 4 episodes. 95m; DVD. **A:** Family. **P:** Entertainment. **U:** Home. **Chl-Juv:** Television Series, Children's Shows, Animation & Cartoons. **Acq:** Purchase. **Dist:** Paramount Pictures Corp. $16.99.

Avatar: The Last Airbender—Book 1: Water, Volume 2 2005
Presents the children's animated Nickelodeon television series about a 12-year-old boy named Aang who is the Avatar, a special soul capable of bringing peace to a troubled, futuristic Earth split into the four entities of the Water Tribes, the Earth Kingdom, the Fire Nation, and the Air Nomads—when he's not having cool adventures. Includes: "The King of Omashu," "Imprisoned," "Winter Solstice: Part 1 The Spirit World," and "Winter Solstice: Part 2 Avatar Roku." 4 episodes. 97m; DVD. **A:** Family. **P:** Entertainment. **U:** Home. **Chl-Juv:** Television Series, Children's Shows, Animation & Cartoons. **Acq:** Purchase. **Dist:** Paramount Pictures Corp. $16.99.

Avatar: The Last Airbender—Book 1: Water, Volume 3 2005
Presents the children's animated Nickelodeon television series about a 12-year-old boy named Aang who is the Avatar, a special soul capable of bringing peace to a troubled, futuristic Earth split into the four entities of the Water Tribes, the Earth Kingdom, the Fire Nation, and the Air Nomads—when he's not having cool adventures. Includes: "The Waterbending Scroll," "Jet," "The Great Divide," and "The Storm." 4 episodes. 99m; DVD. **A:** Family. **P:** Entertainment. **U:** Home. **Chl-Juv:** Television Series, Children's Shows, Animation & Cartoons. **Acq:** Purchase. **Dist:** Paramount Pictures Corp. $16.99.

Avatar: The Last Airbender—Book 1: Water, Volume 4 2005
Presents the children's animated Nickelodeon television series about a 12-year-old boy named Aang who is the Avatar, a special soul capable of bringing peace to a troubled, futuristic Earth split into the four entities of the Water Tribes, the Earth Kingdom, the Fire Nation, and the Air Nomads—when he's not having cool adventures. Includes: "The Blue Spirit," "The Fortuneteller," "Bato of the Water Tribe," and "The Deserter." 4 episodes. 99m; DVD. **A:** Family. **P:** Entertainment. **U:** Home. **Chl-Juv:** Television Series, Children's Shows, Animation & Cartoons. **Acq:** Purchase. **Dist:** Paramount Pictures Corp. $16.99.

Avatar: The Last Airbender—Book 1: Water, Volume 5 2005
Presents the children's animated Nickelodeon television series (2005-) about a 12-year-old boy named Aang who is the Avatar, a special soul capable of bringing peace to a troubled, futuristic Earth split into the four entities of the Water Tribes, the Earth Kingdom, the Fire Nation, and the Air Nomads—when he's not having cool adventures. Includes: "The Northern Air Temple," "The Waterbending Master," "The Siege of the North, Part 1," and "The Siege of the North, Part 2." 4 episodes. 99m; DVD. **A:** Family. **P:** Entertainment. **U:** Home. **Chl-Juv:** Television Series, Children's Shows, Animation & Cartoons. **Acq:** Purchase. **Dist:** Paramount Pictures Corp. $16.99.

Avatar: The Last Airbender—Book 2: Earth, Volume 1 2006
Presents the children's animated Nickelodeon television series (2005-) about a 12-year-old boy named Aang who is the Avatar, a special soul capable of bringing peace to a troubled, futuristic Earth split into the four entities of the Water Tribes, the Earth Kingdom, the Fire Nation, and the Air Nomads—when he's not having cool adventures. Includes: "The Avatar State," "The Cave of Two Lovers," "The Return to Omashu," and "The Swamp," and "Avatar Day." 5 episodes. 123m; DVD. **A:** Family. **P:** Entertainment. **U:** Home. **Chl-Juv:** Television Series, Children's Shows, Animation & Cartoons. **Acq:** Purchase. **Dist:** Paramount Pictures Corp. $16.99.

Avatar: The Last Airbender—Book 2: Earth, Volume 2 2006
Presents the children's animated Nickelodeon television series about a 12-year-old boy named Aang who is the Avatar, a special soul capable of bringing peace to a troubled, futuristic Earth split into the four entities of the Water Tribes, the Earth Kingdom, the Fire Nation, and the Air Nomads—when he's not having cool adventures. Includes: "The Blind Bandit," "Zuko Alone," "The Chase," "Bitter Work," and "The Library." 5 episodes. 120m; DVD. **A:** Family. **P:** Entertainment. **U:** Home.

Chl-Juv: Television Series, Children's Shows, Animation & Cartoons. **Acq:** Purchase. **Dist:** Paramount Pictures Corp. $16.99.

Avatar: The Last Airbender—Book 2: Earth, Volume 3 2006
Presents the children's animated Nickelodeon television series about a 12-year-old boy named Aang who is the Avatar, a special soul capable of bringing peace to a troubled, futuristic Earth split into the four entities of the Water Tribes, the Earth Kingdom, the Fire Nation, and the Air Nomads—when he's not having cool adventures. Includes: "The Desert," "The Serpent's Pass," "The Drill," "City of Walls and Secrets," and "The Tales of Ba Sing Se." 5 episodes. 120m; DVD. **A:** Family. **P:** Entertainment. **U:** Home. **Chl-Juv:** Television Series, Children's Shows, Animation & Cartoons. **Acq:** Purchase. **Dist:** Paramount Pictures Corp. $16.99.

Avatar: The Last Airbender—Book 3, Fire: Volume 1 2005
Aang has an "Awakening" on a Fire Nation warship after weeks of being unconscious and takes on the Fire Lord before his is actually ready. "The Headband" has him enrolled in Fire Nation school and dealing with bullies and strict teachers. Traveling incognito, Aang, Sokka, Katara, and Toph have to fight their instincts to help in "The Painted Lady" for fear they may be recognized. Feeling inadequate compared to his friends, Sokka gets a position as a sword master's apprentice in "Sokka's Master," and Prince Zuko, Azula, Mai and Ty Lee take a holiday at "The Beach." 123m; DVD. **C:** Dante Basco; Voice(s) by Dee Bradley Baker; Mae Whitman; Zach Tyler; Jack De Sena. **A:** Adult. **P:** Entertainment. **U:** Home. **Mov-Ent:** Animation & Cartoons, Animation & Cartoons, Action-Adventure. **Acq:** Purchase. **Dist:** Viacom International Inc.

Avatar: The Last Airbender—Book 3: Fire, Volume 2 2005
"The Avatar and the Firelord" provide the backstory of the fire nation leader. The mischievous Toph uses her earthbending powers and gets in big trouble in "The Runaway." A waterbending old woman enchants Katara in "The Puppetmster," and Aang experiences anxious hallucinations before battle in "Nightmares and Daydreams." "The Day of Black Sun" shows the start of the Allie invasion of fire nation. 123m; DVD. **C:** Voice(s) by Dee Bradley Baker; Zach Tyler; Mae Whitman; Jack De Sena; Dante Basco. **A:** Primary-Jr. High. **P:** Entertainment. **U:** Home. **Chl-Juv:** Animation & Cartoons, Anime. **Acq:** Purchase. **Dist:** Viacom International Inc.

Avatar: The Last Airbender—The Complete Book 3 Collection 2007 (Unrated)
Animated television series on Nickelodean (2005-). Season three is full of surprises for Aang (Tyler), starting with waking up trapped on an enemy ship and with a full head of black hair. Katara, Sokka, and Hakoda are also prisoners and each share the events that brought them there. Prince Zuko faces his father at home and during the visit realizes his sister Princess Azula has told everyone he killed Aang. Back in Fire Nation the crew is under cover as colonist infiltrating everyday life until they can reunite the world's four estranged nations. 14 episodes. 519m; DVD. **C:** Zach Tyler; Mae Whitman; Jack De Sena; Dee Bradley Baker. **A:** Primary-Sr. High. **P:** Entertainment. **U:** Home. **Chl-Juv:** Anime, Action-Adventure, Animation & Cartoons. **Acq:** Purchase. **Dist:** Viacom International Inc.

The Avenger 1960 — ★★½
The story of a criminal who cuts off the heads of people and mails them off makes for a shocker. Graphic violence will appeal to those who like a good mail-order gorefest and are not employed by the post office. 102m/B/W; VHS, DVD. **C:** Ingrid van Bergen; Heinz Drache; Ina Duscha; Mario Litto; Klaus Kinski; Directed by Karl Anton. **A:** College-Adult. **P:** Entertainment. **U:** Home. **L:** German. **Mov-Ent:** Horror. **Acq:** Purchase. **Dist:** Sinister Cinema. $16.95.

The Avenger 1962 — ★
This time muscleman Reeves plays Aeneas and leads the Trojans in battle against the Greeks. It's supposedly an adaptation of "The Aeneid" by Virgil. 108m; VHS, DVD. **C:** Steve Reeves; Giacomo "Jack" Rossi-Stuart; Carla Marlier; Gianni "John" Garko; Liana Orfei; Directed by Giorgio Rivalta. **Pr:** Albert Band; Medallion Pictures. **A:** Jr. High-Adult. **P:** Entertainment. **U:** Home. **Mov-Ent:** War--General. **Acq:** Purchase. **Dist:** Sinister Cinema. $19.95.

Avengers 198?
Three live performances of Avengers, a renowned and politically idealistic punk group of the late '70s. Songs include "We are the One," "Car Crash," and "Open Your Eyes." 30m; VHS. **Pr:** Target Video. **A:** College-Adult. **P:** Entertainment. **U:** Home. **Mov-Ent:** Music--Performance. **Acq:** Purchase. **Dist:** Music Video Distributors. $29.95.

The Avengers 1998 (PG-13) — ★★
Based on the culty '60s Brit TV series, this unfortunate big screen adaptation fails by choosing style over campy charm. Set in a surreal 1999 London, scientist (and leather-girl) Mrs. Emma Peel (Thurman) teams up with dapper secret agent John Steed (Fiennes) to defeat maximum baddie, Sir August de Wynter (Connery). Seems de Wynter has a machine that can manipulate the world's weather—and he's not intending to do good deeds. It's dull, the leads have no chemistry together (although they have their separate charms), and the creators have chosen to include some lesser aspects of the series, such as the boring character of Mother (Broadbent). Unforgiveably, Laurie Johnson's memorable TV theme is not used for the film's opening—replaced instead by generic music by McNeely. (Johnson's theme is heard later.) Original Steed, Patrick MacNee, does have an amusing cameo. 90m; VHS, DVD. **C:** Ralph Fiennes; Uma Thurman; Sean Connery; Jim Broadbent; Fiona Shaw; Eileen Atkins; John Wood; Eddie Izzard; Carmen Ejogo; Keeley Hawes; Cameo(s) Patrick Macnee; Directed by Jeremiah S. Chechik; Written by Don MacPherson; Cinematography by Roger Pratt; Music by Joel McNeely. **Pr:** Jerry Weintraub; Susan Ekins; Warner Bros. **A:** Jr. High-Adult. **P:** Entertainment. **U:** Home. **Mov-Ent:** **Awds:** Golden Raspberries '98: Worst Remake/Sequel. **Acq:** Purchase. **Dist:** Warner Home Video, Inc.

The Avengers 2012 (PG-13) — ★★★½
Nick Fury, the director of international peacekeeping agency SHIELD, needs a superhero team to defeat Norse god Loki and his army. He recruits Iron Man, Captain America, Thor, the Incredible Hulk, Hawkeye, and Black Widow. Perfect blend of action and humor, helped along by superhero banter and the feeling that everyone involved is having a good time. 143m; DVD, Blu-Ray. **C:** Samuel L. Jackson; Robert Downey, Jr.; Chris Evans; Mark Ruffalo; Chris Hemsworth; Scarlett Johansson; Jeremy Renner; Stellan Skarsgard; Tom Hiddleston; Clark Gregg; Cobie Smulders; Gwyneth Paltrow; Harry Dean Stanton; Voice(s) by Paul Bettany; Directed by Joss Whedon; Written by Zak Penn; Joss Whedon; Cinematography by Seamus McGarvey; Music by Alan Silvestri. **Pr:** Kevin Feige; Marvel Studios; Paramount Pictures; Walt Disney Studios. **A:** Jr. High-Adult. **P:** Entertainment. **U:** Home. **L:** English. **Mov-Ent:** Science Fiction. **Acq:** Purchase. **Dist:** Walt Disney Studios Home Entertainment.

The Avengers '64 2000
A dozen digitally remastered episodes of the cult classic spy series, including "The White Elephant," "Mandrake," "Build a Better Mousetrap," "Lobster Quadrille," and "Esprit de Corps." ?m/B/W; VHS, DVD. **A:** Adult. **P:** Entertainment. **U:** Home. **Mov-Ent:** Television Series, Mystery & Suspense. **Acq:** Purchase. **Dist:** A&E Television Networks L.L.C. $29.95.

Avengers '68: The Final Curtain Call, Sets 1 & 2 2001
Twelve digitally remastered episodes from the 1968-69 spy series in their complete, uncut, original U.K. transmission order. 312m; VHS, DVD. **A:** Adult. **P:** Entertainment. **U:** Home. **Mov-Ent:** Television Series, Action-Adventure. **Acq:** Purchase. **Dist:** A&E Television Networks L.L.C. $29.95.

The Avengers: Set '63-'64 1963
Dapper John Steed battles diabolical masterminds with a series of sexy sidekicks. ?m; VHS, DVD. **A:** Adult. **P:** Entertainment. **U:** Home. **Mov-Ent:** Television Series, Action-Adventure. **Acq:** Purchase. **Dist:** A&E Television Networks L.L.C. $229.95.

The Avengers: Set '65-'67 1965
Dapper John Steed battles diabolical masterminds with a series of sexy sidekicks. ?m; VHS, DVD. **A:** Adult. **P:** Entertainment. **U:** Home. **Mov-Ent:** Television Series, Action-Adventure. **Acq:** Purchase. **Dist:** A&E Television Networks L.L.C. $199.95.

The Avengers: Set '68 I & II 1968
Dapper John Steed battles diabolical masterminds with a series of sexy sidekicks. ?m; VHS, DVD. **A:** Adult. **P:** Entertainment. **U:** Home. **Mov-Ent:** Television Series, Action-Adventure. **Acq:** Purchase. **Dist:** A&E Television Networks L.L.C. $69.95.

The Avengers: Set '68 III & IV 1968
Dapper John Steed battles diabolical masterminds with a series of sexy sidekicks. ?m; DVD. **A:** Adult. **P:** Entertainment. **U:** Home. **Mov-Ent:** Television Series, Action-Adventure. **Acq:** Purchase. **Dist:** A&E Television Networks L.L.C. $74.95.

The Avengers: Set '68 V 1968
Dapper John Steed battles diabolical masterminds with a series of sexy sidekicks. 364m; DVD. **A:** Adult. **P:** Entertainment. **U:** Home. **Mov-Ent:** Television Series, Action-Adventure. **Acq:** Purchase. **Dist:** A&E Television Networks L.L.C. $39.95.

The Avengers: '62 Set 1962
Presents the second season of the 1961-1969 British television mystery-comedy series with the adventures of intelligence agent John Steed (Macnee) with new partner Catherine Gale (Blackman) as they encounter an array of peculiar problems and corruption. Includes: Mr. Teddy Bear is suspected of a murder executed on live television; Steed goes undercover with French assassins; and Cathy investigates a diamond-smuggling ring. 14 episodes. 728m; DVD. **C:** Patrick Macnee; Honor Blackman; Arthur Hewlett; Douglas Muir; Julie Stevens; Jon Rollason. **A:** Jr. High-Adult. **P:** Entertainment. **U:** Home. **Mov-Ent:** Television Series, Action-Adventure, Comedy-Drama. **Acq:** Purchase. **Dist:** A&E Television Networks L.L.C. $59.95.

The Avengers: '63 Set 1 1963
Presents episodes from the third season of the 1961-1969 British television mystery-comedy series with the adventures of intelligence agent John Steed (Macnee) with partner Catherine Gale (Blackman) as they encounter an array of peculiar problems and corruption. Includes: "The Undertakers," "Man With Two Shadows," "The Nutshell," "Death of a Batman," "November Five," and "The Gilded Cage." 6 episodes. 312m; DVD. **C:** Patrick Macnee; Honor Blackman; Douglas Muir; Julie Stevens; Jon Rollason. **A:** Jr. High-Adult. **P:** Entertainment. **U:** Home. **Mov-Ent:** Television Series, Action-Adventure, Comedy-Drama. **Acq:** Purchase. **Dist:** A&E Television Networks L.L.C. $44.95.

The Avengers: '63 Set 2 1963
Presents episodes from the third season of the 1961-1969 British television mystery-comedy series with the adventures of intelligence agent John Steed (Macnee) with partner Catherine Gale (Blackman) as they encounter an array of peculiar problems and corruption. Includes: "Second Sight," "The Medicine Men," "The Grandeur That Was Rome," "The Golden Fleece," "Don't Look Behind You," "Death A La Carte," and "Dressed to Kill." 7 episodes. 364m; DVD. **C:** Patrick Macnee; Honor

Blackman; Douglas Muir; Julie Stevens; Jon Rollason. **A:** Jr. High-Adult. **P:** Entertainment. **U:** Home. **Mov-Ent:** Television Series, Action-Adventure, Comedy-Drama. **Acq:** Purchase. **Dist:** A&E Television Networks L.L.C. $44.95.

The Avengers: '63 Set 3 1963
Presents episodes from the third season of the 1961-1969 British television mystery-comedy series with the adventures of intelligence agent John Steed (Macnee) with partner Catherine Gale (Blackman) as they encounter an array of peculiar problems and corruption. Includes: "Intercrime," "Immortal Clay," "Box of Tricks," "Warlock," "The Golden Eggs," and "School for Traitors." 6 episodes. 312m; DVD. **C:** Patrick Macnee; Honor Blackman; Douglas Muir; Julie Stevens; Jon Rollason. **A:** Jr. High-Adult. **P:** Entertainment. **U:** Home. **Mov-Ent:** Television Series, Action-Adventure, Comedy-Drama. **Acq:** Purchase. **Dist:** A&E Television Networks L.L.C. $44.95.

The Avengers: '63 Set 4 1963
Presents episodes from the third season of the 1961-1969 British television mystery-comedy series with the adventures of intelligence agent John Steed (Macnee) with partner Catherine Gale (Blackman) as they encounter an array of peculiar problems and corruption. Includes: "The White Dwarf," "Man in the Mirror," "A Conspiracy of Silence," "A Chorus of Frogs," "Six Hands Across the Table," "Killer Whale," and "Brief for Murder." 7 episodes. 364m; DVD. **C:** Patrick Macnee; Honor Blackman; Douglas Muir; Julie Stevens; Jon Rollason. **A:** Jr. High-Adult. **P:** Entertainment. **U:** Home. **Mov-Ent:** Television Series, Action-Adventure, Comedy-Drama. **Acq:** Purchase. **Dist:** A&E Television Networks L.L.C. $44.95.

The Avengers: '64 Set 1 1964
Presents episodes from the third season of the 1961-1969 British television mystery-comedy series with the adventures of intelligence agent John Steed (Macnee) with partner Catherine Gale (Blackman) as they encounter an array of peculiar problems and corruption. Includes: "The White Elephant," "The Little Wonders," "The Wringer," "Mandrake," "The Secrets Broker," and "The Trojan Horse." 6 episodes. 340m; DVD. **C:** Patrick Macnee; Honor Blackman; Douglas Muir; Julie Stevens; Jon Rollason. **A:** Jr. High-Adult. **P:** Entertainment. **U:** Home. **Mov-Ent:** Television Series, Action-Adventure, Comedy-Drama. **Acq:** Purchase. **Dist:** A&E Television Networks L.L.C. $44.95.

The Avengers: '64 Set 2 1964
Presents episodes from the third season of the 1961-1969 British television mystery-comedy series with the adventures of intelligence agent John Steed (Macnee) with partner Catherine Gale (Blackman) as they encounter an array of peculiar problems and corruption. Includes: "Build a Better Mousetrap," "The Outside-In Man," "The Charmers," "Concerto," "Espirit De Corps," and "Lobster Quadrille." Marked the final appearances of Blackman's character. 6 episodes. 340m; DVD. **C:** Patrick Macnee; Honor Blackman; Douglas Muir; Julie Stevens; Jon Rollason. **A:** Jr. High-Adult. **P:** Entertainment. **U:** Home. **Mov-Ent:** Television Series, Action-Adventure, Comedy-Drama. **Acq:** Purchase. **Dist:** A&E Television Networks L.L.C. $44.95.

The Avengers: '65 Set 1—Volume 1 1965
Presents episodes from the fourth season of the 1961-1969 British television mystery-comedy series with the adventures of intelligence agent John Steed (Macnee) with new partner Emma Peel (Rigg) as they encounter an array of peculiar problems and corruption. Includes: "The Town of No Return," "The Gravediggers," and "The Cybernauts." 3 episodes. 170m; DVD. **C:** Patrick Macnee; Diana Rigg; Patrick Newell. **A:** Jr. High-Adult. **P:** Entertainment. **U:** Home. **Mov-Ent:** Television Series, Action-Adventure, Comedy-Drama. **Acq:** Purchase. **Dist:** A&E Television Networks L.L.C. $24.95.

The Avengers: '65 Set 1—Volume 2 1999
Presents episodes from the fourth season of the 1961-1969 British television mystery-comedy series with the adventures of intelligence agent John Steed (Macnee) with new partner Emma Peel (Rigg) as they encounter an array of peculiar problems and corruption. Includes: "Death at Bargain Prices," "Castle De'ath," and "The Master Minds." 3 episodes. 170m; DVD. **C:** Patrick Macnee; Diana Rigg; Patrick Newell. **A:** Jr. High-Adult. **P:** Entertainment. **U:** Home. **Mov-Ent:** Television Series, Action-Adventure, Comedy-Drama. **Acq:** Purchase. **Dist:** A&E Television Networks L.L.C. $24.95.

The Avengers: '65 Set 2—Volume 3 1999
Presents episodes from the fourth season of the 1961-1969 British television mystery-comedy series with the adventures of intelligence agent John Steed (Macnee) with new partner Emma Peel (Rigg) as they encounter an array of peculiar problems and corruption. Includes: "The Murder Market," "The Surfeit H2O," and "The Hour That Never Was." 3 episodes. 170m; DVD. **C:** Patrick Macnee; Diana Rigg; Patrick Newell. **A:** Jr. High-Adult. **P:** Entertainment. **U:** Home. **Mov-Ent:** Television Series, Action-Adventure, Comedy-Drama. **Acq:** Purchase. **Dist:** A&E Television Networks L.L.C. $24.95.

The Avengers: '65 Set 2—Volume 4 1999
Presents episodes from the fourth season of the 1961-1969 British television mystery-comedy series with the adventures of intelligence agent John Steed (Macnee) with new partner Emma Peel (Rigg) as they encounter an array of peculiar problems and corruption. Includes: "Dial a Deadly Number," "Man-Eater of Surrey Green," "Two's a Crowd," and "Too Many Christmas Trees." 4 episodes. 208m; DVD. **C:** Patrick Macnee; Diana Rigg; Patrick Newell. **A:** Jr. High-Adult. **P:** Entertainment. **U:** Home. **Mov-Ent:** Television Series, Action-Adventure, Comedy-Drama. **Acq:** Purchase. **Dist:** A&E Television Networks L.L.C. $24.95.

The Avengers: '66 Set 1—Volume 1 1999
Presents episodes from the fourth season of the 1961-1969 British television mystery-comedy series with the adventures of intelligence agent John Steed (Macnee) with partner Emma Peel (Rigg) as they encounter an array of peculiar problems and corruption. Includes: "Silent Dust," "Room Without a View," and "Small Game for Big Hunters." 3 episodes. 170m; DVD. **C:** Patrick Macnee; Diana Rigg; Patrick Newell. **A:** Jr. High-Adult. **P:** Entertainment. **U:** Home. **Mov-Ent:** Television Series, Action-Adventure, Comedy-Drama. **Acq:** Purchase. **Dist:** A&E Television Networks L.L.C. $24.95.

The Avengers: '66 Set 1—Volume 2 1999
Presents episodes from the fourth season of the 1961-1969 British television mystery-comedy series with the adventures of intelligence agent John Steed (Macnee) with partner Emma Peel (Rigg) as they encounter an array of peculiar problems and corruption. Includes: "The Girl From Auntie," "The 13th Hole" and "Quick-Quick-Slow Death." 3 episodes. 170m; DVD. **C:** Patrick Macnee; Diana Rigg; Patrick Newell. **A:** Jr. High-Adult. **P:** Entertainment. **U:** Home. **Mov-Ent:** Television Series, Action-Adventure, Comedy-Drama. **Acq:** Purchase. **Dist:** A&E Television Networks L.L.C. $24.95.

The Avengers: '66 Set 2—Volume 3 1999
Presents episodes from the fourth season of the 1961-1969 British television mystery-comedy series with the adventures of intelligence agent John Steed (Macnee) with partner Emma Peel (Rigg) as they encounter an array of peculiar problems and corruption. Includes: "The Danger Makers," "A Touch of Brimstone," and "What the Butler Saw." 3 episodes. 170m; DVD. **C:** Patrick Macnee; Diana Rigg; Patrick Newell. **A:** Jr. High-Adult. **P:** Entertainment. **U:** Home. **Mov-Ent:** Television Series, Action-Adventure, Comedy-Drama. **Acq:** Purchase. **Dist:** A&E Television Networks L.L.C. $24.95.

The Avengers: '66 Set 2—Volume 4 1999
Presents episodes from the fourth season of the 1961-1969 British television mystery-comedy series with the adventures of intelligence agent John Steed (Macnee) with partner Emma Peel (Rigg) as they encounter an array of peculiar problems and corruption. Includes: "The House That Jack Built," "A Sense of History," "How to Succeed...at Murder," and "Honey for the Prince." 4 episodes. 208m; DVD. **C:** Patrick Macnee; Diana Rigg; Patrick Newell. **A:** Jr. High-Adult. **P:** Entertainment. **U:** Home. **Mov-Ent:** Television Series, Action-Adventure, Comedy-Drama. **Acq:** Purchase. **Dist:** A&E Television Networks L.L.C. $24.95.

The Avengers: '67 Set 1—Volume 1 1999
Presents episodes from the fifth season of the 1961-1969 British television mystery-comedy series with the adventures of intelligence agent John Steed (Macnee) with partner Emma Peel (Rigg) as they encounter an array of peculiar problems and corruption. Includes: "From Venus With Love," "The Fear Merchants," and "Escape in Time." 3 episodes. 170m; DVD. **C:** Patrick Macnee; Diana Rigg; Patrick Newell. **A:** Jr. High-Adult. **P:** Entertainment. **U:** Home. **Mov-Ent:** Television Series, Action-Adventure, Comedy-Drama. **Acq:** Purchase. **Dist:** A&E Television Networks L.L.C. $24.95.

The Avengers: '67 Set 1—Volume 2 1999
Presents episodes from the fifth season of the 1961-1969 British television mystery-comedy series with the adventures of intelligence agent John Steed (Macnee) with partner Emma Peel (Rigg) as they encounter an array of peculiar problems and corruption. Includes: "The See-Through Man," "The Bird Who Knew Too Much," and "The Winged Adventure." 3 episodes. 170m; DVD. **C:** Patrick Macnee; Diana Rigg; Patrick Newell. **A:** Jr. High-Adult. **P:** Entertainment. **U:** Home. **Mov-Ent:** Television Series, Action-Adventure, Comedy-Drama. **Acq:** Purchase. **Dist:** A&E Television Networks L.L.C. $24.95.

The Avengers: '67 Set 2—Volume 3 1999
Presents episodes from the fifth season of the 1961-1969 British television mystery-comedy series with the adventures of intelligence agent John Steed (Macnee) with partner Emma Peel (Rigg) as they encounter an array of peculiar problems and corruption. Includes: "The Living Dead," "The Hidden Tiger," and "The Correct Way to Kill." 3 episodes. 170m; DVD. **C:** Patrick Macnee; Diana Rigg; Patrick Newell. **A:** Jr. High-Adult. **P:** Entertainment. **U:** Home. **Mov-Ent:** Television Series, Action-Adventure, Comedy-Drama. **Acq:** Purchase. **Dist:** A&E Television Networks L.L.C. $24.95.

The Avengers: '67 Set 2—Volume 4 1999
Presents episodes from the fifth season of the 1961-1969 British television mystery-comedy series with the adventures of intelligence agent John Steed (Macnee) with partner Emma Peel (Rigg) as they encounter an array of peculiar problems and corruption. Includes: "Never Never Say Die," "Epic," and "The Superlative Seven." 3 episodes. 170m; DVD. **C:** Patrick Macnee; Diana Rigg; Patrick Newell. **A:** Jr. High-Adult. **P:** Entertainment. **U:** Home. **Mov-Ent:** Television Series, Action-Adventure, Comedy-Drama. **Acq:** Purchase. **Dist:** A&E Television Networks L.L.C. $24.95.

The Avengers: '67 Set 3—Volume 5 1999
Presents episodes from the fifth season of the 1961-1969 British television mystery-comedy series with the adventures of intelligence agent John Steed (Macnee) with partner Emma Peel (Rigg) as they encounter an array of peculiar problems and corruption. Includes: "A Funny Thing Happened on the Way to the Station," "Something Nasty in the Nursery," and "The Joker." 3 episodes. 170m; DVD. **C:** Patrick Macnee; Diana Rigg; Patrick Newell. **A:** Jr. High-Adult. **P:** Entertainment. **U:** Home. **Mov-Ent:** Television Series, Action-Adventure, Comedy-Drama. **Acq:** Purchase. **Dist:** A&E Television Networks L.L.C. $24.95.

The Avengers: '67 Set 3—Volume 6 1967
Presents episodes from the fifth season of the 1961-1969 British television mystery-comedy series with the adventures of intelligence agent John Steed (Macnee) with partner Emma Peel (Rigg) as they encounter an array of peculiar problems and corruption. Includes: "Who's Who," "Return of the Cybernauts," and "Death's Door." 3 episodes. 170m; DVD. **C:** Patrick Macnee; Diana Rigg; Patrick Newell. **A:** Jr. High-Adult. **P:** Entertainment. **U:** Home. **Mov-Ent:** Television Series, Action-Adventure, Comedy-Drama. **Acq:** Purchase. **Dist:** A&E Television Networks L.L.C. $24.95.

The Avengers: '67 Set 4—Volume 7 1999
Presents episodes from the fifth season of the 1961-1969 British television mystery-comedy series with the adventures of intelligence agent John Steed (Macnee) with partner Emma Peel (Rigg) as they encounter an array of peculiar problems and corruption. Includes: "The 50,000 Pound Breakfast," "Dead Man's Treasure," and "You Have Just Been Murdered." 3 episodes. 170m; DVD. **C:** Patrick Macnee; Diana Rigg; Patrick Newell. **A:** Jr. High-Adult. **P:** Entertainment. **U:** Home. **Mov-Ent:** Television Series, Action-Adventure, Comedy-Drama. **Acq:** Purchase. **Dist:** A&E Television Networks L.L.C. $24.95.

The Avengers: '67 Set 4—Volume 8 1967
Presents episodes from the fifth season of the 1961-1969 British television mystery-comedy series with the adventures of intelligence agent John Steed (Macnee) with partner Emma Peel (Rigg) as they encounter an array of peculiar problems and corruption. Includes: "The Positive-Negative Man," "Murdersville," "Mission Highly Improbable," and "The Forget-Me-Know." 4 episodes. 208m; DVD. **C:** Patrick Macnee; Diana Rigg; Patrick Newell. **A:** Jr. High-Adult. **P:** Entertainment. **U:** Home. **Mov-Ent:** Television Series, Action-Adventure, Comedy-Drama. **Acq:** Purchase. **Dist:** A&E Television Networks L.L.C. $24.95.

The Avengers: '68 Set 3—Volume 5 and 6 1968
Presents episodes from the sixth and final season of the 1961-1969 British television mystery-comedy series with the adventures of intelligence agent John Steed (Macnee) with new partner Tara King (Thorson) as they encounter an array of peculiar problems and corruption. Includes: "The Interrogators," "The Rotters," "Invasion of the Earthmen," "Killer," "The Morning After," and "The Curious Case of the Countless Clues." 6 episodes. 312m; DVD. **C:** Patrick Macnee; Patrick Newell; Linda Thorson. **A:** Jr. High-Adult. **P:** Entertainment. **U:** Home. **Mov-Ent:** Television Series, Action-Adventure, Comedy-Drama. **Acq:** Purchase. **Dist:** A&E Television Networks L.L.C. $39.95.

The Avengers: '68 Set 3—Volume 7 and 8 1968
Presents episodes from the sixth and final season of the 1961-1969 British television mystery-comedy series with the adventures of intelligence agent John Steed (Macnee) with new partner Tara King (Thorson) as they encounter an array of peculiar problems and corruption. Includes: "Wish You Were Here," "Stay Tuned," "Take Me to Your Leader," "Fog," "Homicide and Old Lace," "Love All," and "Get-A-Way." 7 episodes. 364m; DVD. **C:** Patrick Macnee; Linda Thorson; Patrick Newell. **A:** Jr. High-Adult. **P:** Entertainment. **U:** Home. **Mov-Ent:** Television Series, Action-Adventure, Comedy-Drama. **Acq:** Purchase. **Dist:** A&E Television Networks L.L.C. $39.95.

The Avengers: '68 Set 3—Volume 9 and 10 1968
Presents episodes from the sixth and final season of the 1961-1969 British television mystery-comedy series with the adventures of intelligence agent John Steed (Macnee) with new partner Tara King (Thorson) as they encounter an array of peculiar problems and corruption. Includes: "Thingumajig," "Pandora," "Requiem," "Take-Over," "Who Was That Man I Saw You With?," "My Wildest Dream," and "Bizarre." 7 episodes. 364m; DVD. **C:** Patrick Macnee; Linda Thorson; Patrick Newell. **A:** Jr. High-Adult. **P:** Entertainment. **U:** Home. **Mov-Ent:** Television Series, Action-Adventure, Comedy-Drama. **Acq:** Purchase. **Dist:** A&E Television Networks L.L.C. $39.95.

The Avengers: The Best of the Original Avengers 2001
Presents highlighted episodes from the 1961-1969 British television mystery-comedy series with intelligence agent John Steed (Macnee) and his adventures with all three female partners—Catherine Gale (Blackman), Emma Peel (Rigg), and Tara King (Thorson)?as they encounter an array of peculiar problems and corruption. Includes: "Mr. Teddy Bear," "Don't Look Behind You," "Death At Bargain Prices," "Too Many Christmas Trees," "Look (Stop Me If You've Heard This One)" and "All Done With Mirrors." 6 episodes. 330m; DVD. **C:** Patrick Macnee; Honor Blackman; Diana Rigg; Linda Thorson. **A:** Jr. High-Adult. **P:** Entertainment. **U:** Home. **Mov-Ent:** Television Series, Action-Adventure, Comedy-Drama. **Acq:** Purchase. **Dist:** A&E Television Networks L.L.C. $39.95.

The Avengers: The Complete Emma Peel Megaset Collector's Edition 2006
Presents episodes from the fourth and fifth seasons of the 1961-1969 British television mystery-comedy series with Emma Peel (Rigg) and her adventures with intelligence agent and partner John Steed (Macnee) as they encounter an array of peculiar problems and corruption. 51 episodes. 2913m; DVD. **C:** Patrick Macnee; Diana Rigg; Patrick Newell. **A:** Jr. High-Adult. **P:** Entertainment. **U:** Home. **Mov-Ent:** Television Series, Action-Adventure, Comedy-Drama. **Acq:** Purchase. **Dist:** A&E Television Networks L.L.C. $179.95.

The Avenging 1992 (PG) — ★★
Horse comes home from college to run the family ranch but has problems with his two resentful brothers. 100m; VHS, CC. **C:** Michael Horse; Efrem Zimbalist, Jr.; Sherry Hursey; Joseph Runningfox; Taylor Lacher; Directed by Lyman Dayton; Written

by Lyman Dayton. **Pr:** Imperial Entertainment. **A:** Jr. High-Adult. **P:** Entertainment. **U:** Home. **Mov-Ent:** Western, Native Americans. **Acq:** Purchase. **Dist:** Imperial Entertainment Corp. $89.95.

Avenging Angel 1985 (R) — **Bomb!**
Law student Molly "Angel" Stewart is back on the streets to retaliate against the men who killed the policeman who saved her from a life of prostitution. Worthless sequel to 1984's "Angel," exploiting the original's exploitative intent. Followed listlessly by "Angel III: The Final Chapter." 94m; VHS, DVD, CC. **C:** Betsy Russell; Rory Calhoun; Susan Tyrrell; Ossie Davis; Barry Pearl; Ross Hagen; Karin Mani; Robert Tessier; Directed by Robert Vincent O'Neil; Written by Joseph M. Cala; Cinematography by Peter Lyons Collister; Music by Paul Antonelli. **Pr:** New World Pictures. **A:** Sr. High-Adult. **P:** Entertainment. **U:** Home. **L:** Spanish. **Mov-Ent:** Prostitution. **Acq:** Purchase. **Dist:** Anchor Bay Entertainment. $14.95.

The Avenging Angel 1995 (Unrated) — ★★½
Unusual take on religion and western justice. Brigham Young (Heston) and his Mormon sect have established themselves in Utah—with the aid of some sharpshooting vigilantes, including Miles Utley (Berenger). When an assassination attempt is made on Young's life, Utley finds he's stumbled into an ever-widening church conspiracy that threatens to consume him. Based on the novel by Gary Stewart. 100m; DVD. **C:** Tom Berenger; Charlton Heston; James Coburn; Kevin Tighe; Jeffrey Jones; Tom Bower; Joanna Miles; Directed by Craig R. Baxley; Written by Dennis Nemec; Cinematography by Mark Irwin; Music by Gary Chang. **Pr:** Turner Network Television. **A:** Jr. High-Adult. **P:** Entertainment. **U:** Home. **Mov-Ent:** Western, Religion, TV Movies. **Acq:** Purchase. **Dist:** WarnerArchive.com. $14.98.

Avenging Angel 2007 (Unrated) — ★½
Cliches abound in this oater about a nameless preacher (Sorbo) who suffered a personal tragedy at the hands of greedy land baron Col. Cusack (Hauser) and his evil minions. The preacher turns bounty hunter before rethinking his path thanks to outcast single mother Maggie (Watros). But when Cusack turns to violence again to get rid of some pesky settlers, the preacher straps on his trusty six-shooter. 81m; DVD. **C:** Kevin Sorbo; Cynthia Watros; Wings Hauser; Nick (Nicholas) Chinlund; Richard Lee Jackson; Jim Haynie; Directed by David S. Cass, Sr.; Written by William Sims Myers; Cinematography by Maximo Munzi; Music by Joe Kraemer. **A:** Jr. High-Adult. **P:** Entertainment. **U:** Home. **Mov-Ent:** Western. **Acq:** Purchase. **Dist:** Genius.com Incorporated.

Avenging Angelo 2002 (R) — ★
The Hound thinks this flick is supposed to be a mobster comedy with some romance and, well, it's such a mess who knows what was intended, except it's not gonna revive Stallone's career. He's bodyguard Frankie Delano. He works for mob boss Angelo Allighieri (Quinn), who gets whacked. Frankie then decides Angelo's daughter Jennifer (Stowe) is in danger, so he goes to protect her. Only Jennifer was adopted and doesn't know she's a mobster's daughter and thinks Frankie is nuts—until she nearly gets whacked. Then she believes him and wants revenge. 96m; VHS, DVD. **C:** Sylvester Stallone; Madeleine Stowe; Harry Van Gorkum; Raoul Bova; Anthony Quinn; Directed by Martyn Burke; Written by Will Aldis; Steve Mackall; Cinematography by Ousama Rawi; Music by Bill Conti. **A:** Sr. High-Adult. **P:** Entertainment. **U:** Home. **Mov-Ent. Acq:** Purchase. **Dist:** Sony Pictures Home Entertainment Inc.

Avenging Conscience 1914 (Unrated) — ★★
An early eerie horror film, based on tales of Edgar Allan Poe. D.W. Griffith's first large-scale feature. Silent. 78m/B/W; Silent; VHS, DVD. **TV Std:** NTSC, PAL. **C:** Henry B. Walthall; Blanche Sweet; Directed by D.W. Griffith. **Pr:** Biograph. **A:** Family. **P:** Entertainment. **U:** Home. **Mov-Ent:** Horror, Silent Films, Classic Films. **Acq:** Purchase. **Dist:** Kino on Video; Glenn Video Vistas Ltd. $19.95.

Avenging Disco Godfather 1976 (R) — ★½
Moore parodies the "Godfather" and martial arts movies. 99m; VHS, DVD. **C:** Rudy Ray Moore; Carol Speed; Jimmy Lynch; Jeny Jones; Lady Reeds; James H. Hawthorne; Frank Finn; Julius J. Carry, III; Directed by J. Robert Wagoner; Written by J. Robert Wagoner; Cliff Roquemore; Cinematography by Arledge Armenaki; Music by Ernie Fields, Jr. **Pr:** Rudy Ray Moore; Theadore Toney; Rudy Ray Moore; UHV. **A:** College-Adult. **P:** Entertainment. **U:** Home. **Mov-Ent:** Action-Adventure, Drugs. **Acq:** Purchase. **Dist:** Xenon Pictures Inc. $29.95.

Avenging Force 1986 (R) — ★★
Okay actioner about retired CIA agent Dudikoff returning to the force to help colleague James run for political office. A group of right-wing terrorists called "Pentangle" threatens James, so Dudikoff adds his name to their wanted list. Conflict leads to a forest manhunt where the avenging force does its avenging. 104m; VHS, CC. **C:** Michael Dudikoff; Steve James; John P. Ryan; Directed by Sam Firstenberg; Written by Mercer Ellington; James Booth; Music by George S. Clinton. **Pr:** Cannon Films. **A:** Sr. High-Adult. **P:** Entertainment. **U:** Home. **Mov-Ent:** Intelligence Service, Secret Service. **Acq:** Purchase. **Dist:** Anchor Bay Entertainment. $19.95.

The Avenging Hand 1936 (Unrated) — ★½
Leaden suspense story about a hotel filled with thieves all searching for stolen loot. 56m/B/W; VHS, DVD. **C:** Noah Beery, Jr.; Kathleen Kelly; Louis Borel; James Harcourt; Charles Oliver; Reginald Long; Directed by Victor Hanbury. **Pr:** John Stafford; RKO. **A:** Family. **P:** Entertainment. **U:** Home. **Mov-Ent:** Mystery & Suspense, Hotels & Hotel Staff Training. **Acq:** Purchase. **Dist:** Sinister Cinema.

Avenging Rider 1943 (Unrated) — ★½
Brit and his sidekick Ike travel to help out Brit's friend, miner Sam Trotter. Only Trotter's been murdered and Brit unwittingly helps the killers take off with Trotter's gold. This leads to the duo being arrested for murder and escaping jail to prove their innocence. 56m/B/W; DVD. **C:** Tim Holt; Cliff Edwards; Ann Summers; Davison Clark; Norman Willis; Karl Hackett; Edward Cassidy; Directed by Sam Nelson; Written by Morton Grant; Harry Hoyt; Cinematography by J. Roy Hunt. **A:** Family. **P:** Entertainment. **U:** Home. **Mov-Ent:** Western, Miners & Mining. **Acq:** Purchase. **Dist:** WarnerArchive.com.

Avenging Shadow 1958
Mexican film about a masked hero in the tradition of Santo and Neutron. In Spanish without subtitles. ?m; VHS. **A:** Sr. High-Adult. **P:** Entertainment. **U:** Home. **L:** Spanish. **Mov-Ent:** Horror. **Acq:** Purchase. **Dist:** Something Weird Video. $20.

Avenging Shadow vs. the Black Hand 1959
Sequel to "The Avenging Shadow." ?m; VHS. **A:** Sr. High-Adult. **P:** Entertainment. **U:** Home. **L:** Spanish. **Mov-Ent:** Horror. **Acq:** Purchase. **Dist:** Something Weird Video. $20.

Avenue Montaigne 2006 (PG-13) — ★★½
Sweet provincial gamine Jessica (De France) comes to Paris and gets a job at a cafe along the titular street. The cafe is particularly busy because three major events will be happening nearby: classical pianist Jean-Francois (Dupontel) is giving a concert; popular TV actress Catherine (Lemercier) is starring onstage; and aging businessman Jacques (Brasseur) is going to auction off his extensive art collection. Each are having personal difficulties, which come to a boil over a three-day period, with Jessica providing her common-sense reactions. French with subtitles. 100m; DVD. **C:** Cecile de France; Valerie Lemercier; Albert Dupontel; Claude Brasseur; Dani; Laura Morante; Sydney Pollack; Annelise Hesme; Suzanne Flon; Directed by Daniele Thompson; Written by Daniele Thompson; Cinematography by Jean-Marc Fabre; Music by Nicola Piovani. **Pr:** Christine Gozlan; StudioCanal; TF-1 Films; Thelma Films; Radis Films Production; ThinkFilm. **A:** Sr. High-Adult. **P:** Entertainment. **U:** Home. **L:** French. **Mov-Ent:** Comedy-Drama. **Acq:** Purchase. **Dist:** ThinkFilm Company Inc.

Avenue of the Americas 1982
A documentary on the Popular Unity years in Chile which focuses on the nature and extent of U.S. government and corporate complicity in the overthrow and death of Salvador Allende. English subtitles. 82m; 3/4 U, Special order formats. **C:** Written by Charles Hormon. **Pr:** Jorge Reyes. **A:** Sr. High-Adult. **P:** Education. **U:** Institution. **L:** Spanish. **Gen-Edu:** South America, Documentary Films. **Acq:** Purchase. **Dist:** The Cinema Guild.

Avenue of the Just 1983
Recounts the experiences of ten Christians who saved Jewish lives during the Hitler years. 55m; VHS, 3/4 U. **Pr:** Anti-Defamation League of B'nai B'rith. **A:** Jr. High-Adult. **P:** Religious. **U:** Institution, CCTV, CATV, BCTV, Home. **Gen-Edu:** Documentary Films, World War Two, Judaism. **Acq:** Purchase. **Dist:** Anti-Defamation League of B'nai B'rith.

The Average Woman 1924 — ★★
Gritty journalist consults plain Jane for "Modern Woman" story and finds a major rewrite in order when he falls with a thud for Miss Jane. 52m/B/W; Silent; VHS. **C:** Pauline Garon; David Powell; Burr McIntosh; Harrison Ford; De Sacia Mooers; Directed by Christy Cabanne. **Pr:** C.C. Burr. **A:** Sr. High-Adult. **P:** Entertainment. **U:** Home. **Mov-Ent:** Drama, Journalism, Silent Films. **Acq:** Purchase. **Dist:** Grapevine Video; Glenn Video Vistas Ltd. $14.95.

Avery Johnson: Attacking Man-to-Man Defenses 2006
A presentation of attacking man-to-man defense from a defensive standpoint and then from an offensive perspective. 101m; DVD. **A:** Adult. **P:** Instruction. **U:** Institution. **Spo-Rec:** Basketball. **Acq:** Purchase. **Dist:** Championship Productions.

AVH: Alien vs. Hunter 2007 (Unrated) — **Bomb!**
All-around rip-off woofer. Reporter Lee (Katt) goes to a small town to investigate what turns out to be the crash landing of two spaceships. One contains a vicious alien spider thingy and the other the alien hunter that is trying to kill it. But those pesky human residents are in the way! 85m; DVD, Blu-Ray. **C:** William Katt; Dedee Pfeiffer; Randy Mulkey; Jennifer Couch; Jason S. Gray; Directed by Scott Harper; Written by David Michael Latt; Cinematography by Mark Atkins. **A:** Sr. High-Adult. **P:** Entertainment. **U:** Home. **Mov-Ent:** Science. **Acq:** Purchase. **Dist:** Echo Bridge Home Entertainment.

Avia: Vampire Hunter 2005 (Unrated) — ★
A mentally disturbed young woman discovers vampires are real and spends her life running about whacking them with a Samurai sword. Little known fact: apparently American vampires are allergic to Japanese steel. 90m; DVD. **C:** Rodney Jackson; Allison Valentino; Directed by Leon Hunter; Written by Leon Hunter; Cinematography by Leon Hunter. **A:** Sr. High-Adult. **P:** Entertainment. **U:** Home. **L:** English. **Mov-Ent. Acq:** Purchase. **Dist:** York Pictures Inc. $9.99.

Avianca Airbus A319 & Fokker 100 2013 (G)
Documentary following Brazilian airline Avianca on several flights as they phase out their Fokker 100 aircraft for the Airbus. 273m; Blu-Ray. **A:** Family. **P:** Entertainment. **U:** Home. **L:** English. **Gen-Edu:** Aeronautics, Documentary Films, South America. **Acq:** Purchase. **Dist:** Justplanes.com. $30.00.

Aviation Disasters 1992
Explores the causes and consequences of commercial airplane crashes. Includes interviews with personnel assigned the identification and removal of human remains, and graphic footage from crash sites. Not intended for children. 60m; VHS. **A:** Adult. **P:** Education. **U:** Home. **Gen-Edu. Acq:** Purchase. **Dist:** Jim Meyers Film Enterprises.

Aviation in the News 194?
Compilation of aviation related stories shot during WWII battles by combat cameramen. Newsreel footage has been restored and edited. Each volume of the four-tape set covers a different year of the war. ?m/B/W; VHS. **A:** Sr. High-Adult. **P:** Education. **U:** Home. **Gen-Edu:** Documentary Films, World War Two, Aeronautics. **Acq:** Purchase. **Dist:** Fusion Video. $29.98.
Indiv. Titles: 1. 1942 (72 minutes) 2. 1943 (105 minutes) 3. 1944 (112 minutes) 4. 1945 (72 minutes).

Aviation Video Quarterly, Vol. 1 1984
This program is exclusively devoted to the interests of the aviation community, covering a broad spectrum of subject matter. 120m; VHS. **Pr:** Ferde Grofe Films. **A:** Sr. High-Adult. **P:** Education. **U:** Institution, Home. **Gen-Edu:** Aeronautics. **Acq:** Purchase. **Dist:** Bennett Marine Video; Military/Combat Stock Footage Library. $29.95.
Indiv. Titles: 1. Go-Along-EZ 2. The Wing Derringer 3. Flying the Ultra-Light-P38 4. Flying the Gyrocopter with Ken Brock 5. Mountain Flying with Rocky Warren.

Aviation Video Quarterly, Vol. 2 1984
This program provides an exciting variety of aviation oriented films. 95m; VHS. **Pr:** Ferde Grofe Films. **A:** Sr. High-Adult. **P:** Education. **U:** Institution, Home. **Gen-Edu:** Armed Forces--U.S. **Acq:** Purchase. **Dist:** Bennett Marine Video; Military/Combat Stock Footage Library. $29.95.
Indiv. Titles: 1. NASA Test Flies The Long-EZ 2. Cri-Cri 3. Flying is Vari-Eze 4. Some Thoughts on Winter Flying 5. Warbirds on Parade-EAH, Oshkosk-'81.

Aviation, Vol. 1 19??
Newsreels highlight aviation history from Wright Brothers through evolution of the helicopter. Includes de Pinedo's death, the Graf Zeppelin, Lindberg's trans-Atlantic flight, and Pan American Clippers. 60m/B/W; VHS. **C:** William Hurt; Timothy Hutton; Melissa Leo; Stockard Channing; Megan Follows; Directed by Gregory Nava. **A:** Family. **P:** Entertainment. **U:** Home. **Mov-Ent:** Aeronautics. **Acq:** Purchase. **Dist:** $19.95.

Aviation Weather 1984
This program presents important information about the kinds of weather which concern every pilot. 90m; VHS. **Pr:** Ferde Grofe Films. **A:** College-Adult. **P:** Education. **U:** Institution, Home. **Gen-Edu:** Aeronautics. **Acq:** Purchase. **Dist:** Bennett Marine Video; Military/Combat Stock Footage Library. $29.95.
Indiv. Titles: 1. Advection Fog and Ground Fog 2. Upsiope Fog and Frontal Fog 3. The Cold Front 4. Ice Formation on Aircraft 5. The Warm Front.

The Aviator 1985 (PG) — ★★
Pilot Reeve, haunted by the memory of a fatal crash, tries to find a new line of work. Large sums of money persuade him to transport spoiled Arquette to Washington. When the biplane crashes in the mountain wilderness, the two fall in love between scavenging for food and fighting wild animals. From the director of "Man From Snowy River." 98m; VHS, DVD, Wide. **C:** Christopher Reeve; Rosanna Arquette; Jack Warden; Tyne Daly; Marcia Strassman; Sam Wanamaker; Scott Wilson; Directed by George Miller; Written by Marc Norman; Cinematography by David Connell; Music by Dominic Frontiere. **Pr:** United Artists. **A:** Jr. High-Adult. **P:** Entertainment. **U:** Home. **Mov-Ent:** Action-Adventure, Romance, Aeronautics. **Acq:** Purchase. **Dist:** MGM Home Entertainment. $14.95.

The Aviator 2004 (PG-13) — ★★★½
Scorsese's sweeping, rich biopic of eccentric movie producer/aviation pioneer Howard Hughes soars on many levels. The film follows Hughes from maverick producer taking Hollywood by storm in the '20s through his successes in aviation and the founding of TWA, and finally battling Pan Am and Congress in the '40s. Di Caprio, in full-on movie idol mode, captures the drive and intensity of Hughes, letting the audience see glimpses of the coming breakdown, but mostly keeping it bubbling below the surface (until a slightly over-the-top sequence about 90 minutes in). Blanchett also shines in a dazzling portrayal of Katharine Hepburn. Scorsese's eye for detail and love of Old Hollywood serve the proceedings well, providing fascinating peeks into the workings of the old studio system, the testing and building of experimetal aircraft, and the wheeling and dealing of high-stakes politics. 166m; VHS, DVD, Blu-Ray, HD-DVD. **C:** Leonardo DiCaprio; Cate Blanchett; Kate Beckinsale; John C. Reilly; Alec Baldwin; Alan Alda; Ian Holm; Danny Huston; Jude Law; Adam Scott; Matt Ross; Kelli Garner; Frances Conroy; Brent Spiner; Stanley DeSantis; Edward Herrmann; Willem Dafoe; J.C. MacKenzie; Kenneth Welsh; Amy Sloan; Kevin O'Rourke; Lisa Bronwyn Moore; Gwen Stefani; Vincent Laresca; Josie Maran; Directed by Martin Scorsese; Written by John Logan; Cinematography by Robert Richardson; Music by Howard Shore. **Pr:** Michael Mann; Sandy Climan; Graham King; Charles Evans; Forward Pass Productions; Initial Entertainment Group; Miramax. **A:** Jr. High-Adult. **P:** Entertainment. **U:** Home. **L:** English. **Mov-Ent:** Biography: Show Business. **Awds:** Oscars '04: Art Dir./Set Dec., Cinematog., Costume Des., Film Editing, Support. Actress (Blanchett); British Acad. '04: Film, Makeup, Support. Actress (Blanchett); Golden Globes '05: Actor--Drama (DiCaprio), Film--Drama, Orig. Score; Screen Actors Guild '04: Support. Actress (Blanchett). **Acq:** Purchase. **Dist:** Warner Home Video, Inc. $29.95.

The Aviator's Wife 1980 (Unrated) — ★★★
The first in Rohmer's Comedies and Proverbs series is a comedy of errors involving a post-office worker (Marlaud) who believes that his older girlfriend (Riviere) is seeing another man,

a pilot (Carriere). He enlists the aid of a young girl (Meury) to help him spy on his romantic obsession. French with subtitles. 104m; VHS, DVD. **C:** Philippe Marlaud; Marie Riviere; Anne-Laure Meury; Matthieu Carriere; Directed by Eric Rohmer; Written by Eric Rohmer; Cinematography by Bernard Lutic; Music by Jean-Louis Valero. **A:** College-Adult. **P:** Entertainment. **U:** Home. **L:** French. **Mov-Ent:** Comedy--Romantic. **Acq:** Purchase. **Dist:** Wellspring Media.

Avoid Repair Ripoffs: How to Find an Honest Mechanic 1988
People who watch this tape will know if they are being cheated when they get their car fixed. 30m; VHS. **Pr:** Cambridge Career Productions. **A:** Sr. High-Adult. **P:** Instruction. **U:** Institution, Home. **How-Ins:** Consumer Education, Automobiles. **Acq:** Purchase. **Dist:** Cambridge Educational. $29.95.

Avoiding AIDS: What You Can Do 1988
A complete explanation of the AIDS virus-how it is spread, its effect on the body, and other related topics. 45m; VHS, 3/4 U. **Pr:** Centers for Disease Control. **A:** Primary-Adult. **P:** Education. **U:** Institution. **Hea-Sci:** AIDS, Health Education. **Acq:** Purchase. **Dist:** Marshmedia. $52.95.

Avoiding Back Pain 199?
Uses testimonials from workers who have injured their backs in the workplace and demonstrations of proper techniques to educate employees on how to avoid back injuries. ?m; VHS. **A:** Sr. High-Adult. **P:** Education. **U:** Home, Institution. **Hea-Sci:** Safety Education, Back Disorders. **Acq:** Purchase. **Dist:** Aurora Pictures Inc.

Avoiding Communication Breakdown 1965
This program from the "Effective Communication" series examines topics relating to improving employee attitudes and customer relations. 26m; VHS, 3/4 U. **A:** College-Adult. **P:** Professional. **U:** Institution, SURA. **L:** English, Dutch, French, German, Portuguese, Spanish, Swedish. **Bus-Ind:** Personnel Management. **Acq:** Purchase, Rent/Lease. **Dist:** Learning Communications L.L.C.

Avoiding Decisions? 1982
Art Dodger demonstrates common decision-avoiding ploys used in business. 15m; VHS, 3/4 U. **Pr:** Seven Dimensions Films of Australia. **A:** Adult. **P:** Professional. **U:** Institution, SURA. **Bus-Ind:** Employee Counseling, Management. **Acq:** Purchase, Rent/Lease. **Dist:** Phoenix Learning Group.

Avoiding Electrical Hazards 199?
Covers personal protection, safe work procedures, working near equipment and lines, lockout/tagout, and more. 19m; VHS. **A:** Adult. **P:** Vocational. **U:** Institution. **L:** English, Spanish. **Bus-Ind:** Electricity. **Acq:** Purchase, Rent/Lease. **Dist:** Audio Graphics Training Systems. $450.00.

Avoiding Electrical Safety Hazards 1995
Looks at safe work practices concerning electricity. 19m; VHS. **A:** Adult. **P:** Professional. **U:** Institution. **L:** Spanish. **Bus-Ind:** Job Training, Safety Education, Electricity. **Acq:** Rent/Lease. **Dist:** National Safety Council, California Chapter, Film Library.

Avoiding Medication Errors 1989
Reviews common medication errors, steps in the medication process, interpreting the doctor's order, transcribing the medication order and much more. Includes a booklet. 30m; VHS. **A:** Adult. **P:** Education. **U:** Institution. **Hea-Sci:** Medical Care, Medical Education, Nursing. **Acq:** Purchase. **Dist:** Nursing Center. $36.95.

Avoiding or Surviving Law Firm Breakup 1990
Offers a review of why and how law firms breakup and suggestions for easy transitions. Examines media relations, client communication, resolving pensions, profit-sharing, and more. Complete with study guide. 50m; VHS. **A:** Adult. **P:** Professional. **U:** Institution. **Bus-Ind:** Law. **Dist:** American Law Institute - Committee on Continuing Professional Education. $95.

Avoiding Pinning Situations 1992
Wrestling dos and dont's to avoid being trapped on the mat. Moves shown include the half nelson and the head lock. 15m; VHS. **A:** Sr. High-College. **P:** Instruction. **U:** Institution, Home. **Spo-Rec:** Sports--General. **Acq:** Purchase. **Dist:** Cambridge Educational. $39.95.

Avoiding Slips and Falls 1995
Emphasizes the seriousness of injuries caused by slips and falls and offers safety tips. 18m; VHS. **A:** Adult. **P:** Professional. **U:** Institution. **Bus-Ind:** Job Training, Safety Education. **Acq:** Rent/Lease. **Dist:** National Safety Council, California Chapter, Film Library. $410.00.

Avoiding Slips, Trips and Falls 1995
Features situations which lead to slips, trips and falls and what can be done to prevent them. 14m; VHS. **A:** Adult. **P:** Professional. **U:** Institution. **L:** Spanish. **Bus-Ind:** Job Training, Safety Education. **Acq:** Purchase, Rent/Lease. **Dist:** National Safety Council, California Chapter, Film Library. $395.00.

Avoiding Slips, Trips and Falls on the Inland Waterways ?
Examines the accident danger zones experienced specifically by deck crews and offers recommendations on how to avoid high risk practices. 30m; VHS. **A:** Sr. High-Adult. **P:** Education. **U:** Home, Institution. **Bus-Ind:** Industry & Industrialists, Safety Education. **Acq:** Purchase. **Dist:** John Sabella & Associate. $295.00.

Avoiding the Negative in Sales 1987
Negative behavior can turn a client off, and the result may be declining sales. 19m; VHS, 3/4 U. **Pr:** First Financial Network. **A:** Adult. **P:** Education. **U:** Institution, Home. **Bus-Ind:** Sales Training. **Acq:** Purchase, Rent/Lease. **Dist:** 1st Financial Training Services. $250.00.

Avoiding the Research Paper Blues 19??
Follows a student as she demonstrates techniques for successfully writing a research paper. 10m; VHS. **A:** Jr. High-Sr. High. **P:** Education. **U:** Institution. **Gen-Edu:** Language Arts. **Acq:** Purchase. **Dist:** Educational Video Network. $49.95.

Avoiding the Slips: Working a Program of Inches 19??
Earnie Larsen focuses on concepts to keep moving ahead to sobriety without falling back into relapse. 33m; VHS. **A:** Adult. **P:** Education. **U:** Institution. **Hea-Sci:** Alcoholism, Self-Help. **Acq:** Purchase. **Dist:** Hazelden Publishing. $200.00.

Avoiding the Surgeon's Knife 1990
Provides an intimate portrayal of four patients, four wives, and one doctor who have illustrated that heart disease can be reversed through changes in one's lifestyle. Winner of many awards. 57m; VHS. **Pr:** Maysles Films. **A:** Jr. High-Adult. **P:** Education. **U:** Home. **Hea-Sci:** Documentary Films, Health Education, Heart. **Acq:** Purchase. **Dist:** Maysles Films, Inc.

AVT Shorthand 1978
A series of ten untitled programs providing a complete beginner's course in shorthand. ?m; 3/4 U. **Pr:** Media Systems Corporation. **A:** Sr. High-Adult. **P:** Instruction. **U:** Institution, CCTV. **How-Ins:** Office Practice. **Acq:** Purchase. **Dist:** Harcourt Brace College Publishers.

Awake 2007 (R) — ★½
Wealthy Clayton Beresford (Christensen), stricken with a heart defect, must undergo a transplant to save his life. Unfortunately, something goes wrong, and he experiences "anesthesia awareness," which means that he appears asleep but is actually awake and fully aware of everything going on during his operation. Rather than build suspense and tension from such an intense premise, the story's twists and surprises (including an absurd-even-by-horror-movie-standards plot for poor Clay to die on the operating table) pile on ad nauseum, and Christensen is expected to carry much of the movie while flat on his back. 78m; Blu-Ray, On Demand, Wide. **C:** Hayden Christensen; Jessica Alba; Terrence Howard; Lena Olin; Arliss Howard; Christopher McDonald; Fisher Stevens; Sam Robards; Georgina Chapman; Directed by Joby Harold; Written by Joby Harold; Cinematography by Russell Carpenter; Music by Graeme Revell. **Pr:** Joana Vicente; Jason Kliot; Fisher Stevens; Bob Weinstein; Fisher Stevens; MGM; Open City Films; Greenstreet. **A:** Sr. High-Adult. **P:** Entertainment. **U:** Home. **L:** English. **Mov-Ent:** Marriage, Hospitals. **Acq:** Purchase. **Dist:** Magnolia Home Entertainment; Amazon.com Inc.; Movies Unlimited.

Awake Zion 2005
Margaret Haim's documentary exploring the connections between Judaism and reggae culture. 65m; VHS, DVD. **A:** Sr. High-Adult. **P:** Education. **U:** Home, Institution. **Gen-Edu:** Judaism, Documentary Films. **Acq:** Purchase, Rent/Lease. **Dist:** The Cinema Guild. $295.00.

Awaken to Hope: Affirming Thoughts to Begin Your Day 1993
Offers 12 short mediations on positive ideas for living accompanied by soothing nature photography. Followed by "Be at Peace." 30m; VHS. **A:** Adult. **P:** Education. **U:** Home. **Gen-Edu:** Philosophy & Ideology. **Acq:** Purchase. **Dist:** Willowgreen Productions. $59.95.

The Awakening 1980 (R) — ★½
An archeologist discovers the tomb of a murderous queen, but upon opening the coffin, the mummy's spirit is transferred to his baby daughter, born at that instant. They call that bad luck. 101m; VHS, Streaming. **C:** Charlton Heston; Susannah York; Stephanie Zimbalist; Patrick Drury; Ian McDiarmid; Bruce Myers; Nadim Sawalha; Jill Townsend; Directed by Mike Newell; Written by Allan Scott; Chris Bryant; Clive Exton; Cinematography by Jack Cardiff; Music by Claude Bolling. **Pr:** Orion Pictures. **A:** Sr. High-Adult. **P:** Entertainment. **U:** Home. **Mov-Ent:** Horror, Anthropology. **Acq:** Purchase. **Dist:** Warner Home Video, Inc. $19.95.

The Awakening 1995 (Unrated) — ★½
Smalltown Sara (Geary) has had to turn the family home into a boardinghouse in order to meet expenses. Bounty hunter Flynn (Beecroft) moves in while pursuing an antiques smuggler and he and Sara join forces to find romance as well as adventure. From the Harlequin Romance Series; adapted from the Patricia Coughlin novel. 95m; DVD. **C:** Cynthia Geary; David Beecroft; Sheila McCarthy; Maurice Godin; Directed by George Bloomfield; Written by Maria Nation; Cinematography by Manfred Guthe; Music by Amin Bhatia. **A:** Jr. High-Adult. **P:** Entertainment. **U:** Home. **Mov-Ent. Acq:** Purchase. **Dist:** Movies Unlimited; Alpha Video.

The Awakening 2011 (R) — ★★
Florence Cathcart (Hall) spends her time debunking false reports of hauntings but finds herself challenged when she investigates an orphanage that reportedly has a ghostly child roaming its halls. Set in 1921 England, director Murphy's film starts with some promising themes regarding loneliness, survivor's guilt, and depression but becomes a rather generic affair as its supernatural angles work toward a twist ending that doesn't have nearly the power that its filmmakers believe it does. Hall delivers the dramatic goods and there's an interesting sense of setting but the overall production ends up more monotonous than terrifying. 107m; DVD, Blu-Ray. **C:** Rebecca Hall; Dominic West; Imelda Staunton; Isaac Hempstead-Wright; Shaun Dooley; Joseph Mawle; Directed by Nick Murphy; Written by Nick Murphy; Stephen Volk; Cinematography by Eduard Grau. **Pr:** Sarah Curtis; David M. Thompson; StudioCanal; BBC Films; Cohen Media Group. **A:** Sr. High-Adult. **P:** Entertainment. **U:** Home. **L:** English. **Mov-Ent:** Horror, Child Care, World War One. **Acq:** Purchase. **Dist:** Universal Studios Home Video.

Awakening Intuition 1989
Frances Vaughn demonstrates ways to increase intuitive faculty by concentrating on the physical, emotional, spiritual and intellectual aspects of the mind and body. 30m; VHS. **Pr:** Thinking Allowed Productions. **A:** College-Adult. **P:** Education. **U:** Home. **Gen-Edu:** New Age, Psychology, Self-Help. **Acq:** Purchase. **Dist:** Thinking Allowed Productions. $29.95.

The Awakening Land 1978 (Unrated) — ★★½
Well-acted miniseries based on Conrad Richter's trilogy follows the fortunes of the pioneering Luckett family in the Ohio Territory from 1790 through 1817. Illiterate homesteader Sayward Luckett (Montgomery) falls in love and marries frontier lawyer Portius Wheeler (Holbrook), who's rightly known as "The Solitary." It's up to Sayward to raise their children and make a go of their lives amidst various hardships and many changes. 333m; DVD. **C:** Elizabeth Montgomery; Hal Holbrook; Jane Seymour; Louise Latham; Steven Keats; Jeannette Nolan; Tony Mockus, Jr.; William H. Macy; Directed by Boris Sagal; Written by James Lee Barrett; Liam O'Brien; Cinematography by Michel Hugo; Music by Fred Karlin. **A:** Family. **P:** Entertainment. **U:** Home. **Mov-Ent:** TV Movies. **Acq:** Purchase. **Dist:** WarnerArchive.com.

Awakening of Candra 1981 (Unrated) — **Bomb!**
Based on a real 1975 incident, a young couple honeymooning in the mountains is assaulted by a lunatic fisherman. The psycho kills the husband and rapes the girl, then he brainwashes poor Candra into thinking it was all an accident. Intense subject matter should be horrifying, but falls short of the mark in this flop. 96m; VHS. **C:** Blanche Baker; Cliff DeYoung; Richard Jaeckel; Jeffrey Tambor; Paul Regina; Elizabeth Cheshire; Directed by Paul Wendkos; Cinematography by Richard C. Glouner; Music by Billy Goldenberg. **Pr:** Telefeature. **A:** Family. **P:** Entertainment. **U:** Home. **Mov-Ent:** Mystery & Suspense, Rape, TV Movies. **Acq:** Purchase. **Dist:** Unknown Distributor.

Awakening of Intelligence 19??
Examines Joseph Chilton Pearce's conclusion that intelligence is innate, not accumulated or learned. 60m; VHS. **A:** Adult. **P:** Education. **U:** Home. **Gen-Edu:** Psychology. **Acq:** Purchase. **Dist:** Mystic Fire Video. $24.95.

The Awakening of Nancy Kaye 1986
Nancy Kaye, born with spina bifida, was able to overcome limited mobility to become a respected educator with a doctorate in special education and a single mother. After being diagnosed with cancer, Nancy searched and found many of the answers to her life and spirituality that had earlier eluded her. 46m; VHS, 3/4 U. **Pr:** Ann Hershey. **A:** Sr. High-Adult. **P:** Education. **U:** Institution, Home, SURA. **Gen-Edu:** Death, Cancer, Handicapped. **Acq:** Purchase, Rent/Lease, Duplication. **Dist:** Filmakers Library Inc.

Awakening the Global Mind 199?
Haverford College philosophy professor Ashok K. Gangadean expresses that all spiritual and philosophical traditions of humanity connects to the Logos, an underlying union between all reality that is expressed through various forms in different cultures. He also discusses the attributes and misfortunes of an ego-based mind focus. 90m; DVD. **A:** Adult. **P:** Education. **U:** Home, Institution. **Gen-Edu:** Philosophy & Ideology, Psychology. **Acq:** Purchase. **Dist:** Thinking Allowed Productions. $49.95.

Awakenings 1990 (PG-13) — ★★★½
Marshall's first dramatic effort is based on the true story of Dr. Oliver Sacks, from his book of the same title. It details his experimentation with the drug L-dopa which inspired the "awakening" of a number of catatonic patients, some of whom had been "sleeping" for as long as 30 years. Occasionally oversentimental, but still providing a poignant look at both the patients—who find themselves confronted with lost opportunities and faded youth—and at Sacks, who must watch their exquisite suffering as they slip away. De Niro's performance as the youngest of the group is heart-rending, while Williams offers a subdued, moving performance as the doctor. 120m; VHS, DVD, 8 mm, CC. **C:** Robin Williams; Robert De Niro; John Heard; Julie Kavner; Penelope Ann Miller; Max von Sydow; Anne Meara; Dexter Gordon; Alice Drummond; Richard Libertini; Judith Malina; Barton Heyman; Bradley Whitford; Peter Stormare; Laura Esterman; Vincent Pastore; Vin Diesel; Directed by Penny Marshall; Written by Steven Zaillian; Music by Randy Newman. **A:** Jr. High-Adult. **P:** Entertainment. **U:** Home. **Mov-Ent:** Comedy-Drama, Human Relations, Hospitals. **Awds:** Natl. Bd. of Review '90: Actor (De Niro), Actor (Williams); Natl. Soc. Film Critics '90: Actor (De Niro). **Acq:** Purchase. **Dist:** Facets Multimedia Inc.; Sony Pictures Home Entertainment Inc. $14.95.

Awakenings of the Beast 1968 — ★
Documents the protracted sufferings of an LSD drug user who is beset with hallucinatory visions and is prone to fits of frenzied violence. Director Jose Mojica Marins (AKA Coffin Joe) steps out of his Ze do Ciaxia character in this disjointed mix of drugs and sex intercut with Mojica Marins himself on trial for his offensive movies, followed by a case study on drugs and sexual behavior. By the end of the movie, there is a point—that drugs aren't the cause of evil behavior—but it's very painful getting there. In Portugese with English subtitles. 93m/B/W; VHS, DVD, Wide. **C:** Jose Mojica Marins; Sergio Hingst; Andrea Bryan; Mario Lima; Directed by Jose Mojica Marins; Written by Jose Mojica Marins; Rubens Francisco Lucchetti; Cinematography

by Giorgio Attili. **A:** College-Adult. **P:** Entertainment. **U:** Home. **L:** Spanish. **Mov-Ent:** Drugs. **Acq:** Purchase. **Dist:** Something Weird Video; Facets Multimedia Inc. $20.00.

Awara Soup 1995
Introduces the viewer to a multi-cultural community in the back country of French Guyana where 1500 people speak 13 different languages yet live together in remarkable harmony. 71m; VHS. **A:** Sr. High-Adult. **P:** Education. **U:** Home, Institution. **Gen-Edu:** Ethnicity, Cities & Towns, Human Relations. **Acq:** Purchase. **Dist:** California Newsreel. $195.00.

Award Winning Smiles 1977
This program introduces the health professional to numerous dental aids available for home use by patients. Plaque control aids are specifically recommended. 15m; VHS, 3/4 U, EJ, Q, Special order formats. **Pr:** University of Oklahoma. **A:** College-Adult. **P:** Professional. **U:** Institution, CCTV. **Hea-Sci:** Dentistry. **Acq:** Purchase. **Dist:** University of Oklahoma.

Awareness 1969
Examples of the Gestalt Method as a learning process are given in this program. Part of the "Gestalt" series. 27m; VHS, 3/4 U. **Pr:** Aquarian Productions. **A:** College-Adult. **P:** Education. **U:** Institution, SURA. **Hea-Sci:** Psychology. **Acq:** Purchase. **Dist:** Home Vision Cinema.

Awareness Level 1995
Overviews briefly, the RCRA, SARA, and other related laws. 20m; VHS. **A:** Adult. **P:** Professional. **U:** Institution. **Bus-Ind:** Job Training, Safety Education, Management. **Acq:** Rent/Lease. **Dist:** National Safety Council, California Chapter, Film Library.

Away All Boats 1956 — ★★½
The true story of one Captain Hawks, who led a crew of misfits to victory in WWII Pacific aboard transport USS Belinda. Battle scenes are well done; look for early (and brief) appearance by young Clint Eastwood. 114m/B/W; VHS, DVD. **C:** Jeff Chandler; George Nader; Richard Boone; Julie Adams; Keith Andes; Lex Barker; Clint Eastwood; Directed by Joseph Pevney; Written by Ted Sherdeman; Cinematography by William H. Daniels; Music by Frank Skinner. **Pr:** Mark Huffam; Howard Christie. **A:** Family. **P:** Entertainment. **U:** Home. **Mov-Ent:** World War Two, Boating. **Acq:** Purchase. **Dist:** $19.95.

Away From Her 2006 (Unrated) — ★★★
Polley makes her directorial debut with this adaptation of the Alice Munro story "The Bear Who Came Over the Mountain." Grant (Pinsent) and Fiona (Christie) have been married more than 40 years when she is diagnosed with Alzheimer's. As her mental acuity deteriorates, Fiona insists on entering a nursing home, where she befriends another married patient (Murphy), while Grant struggles to cope with the changes. Gracefully aging '60s British icon Christie is well-matched by Canadian actor Pinsent in a tender story about love and loss that shouldn't be seen by cynics. 110m; DVD. **C:** Julie Christie; Gordon Pinsent; Olympia Dukakis; Michael Murphy; Wendy Crewson; Alberta Watson; Kristen Thomson; Directed by Sarah Polley; Written by Sarah Polley; Cinematography by Luc Montpellier; Music by Jonathan Goldsmith. **Pr:** Daniel Iron; Simone Urdl; Jennifer Weiss; Foundry Films; The Film Farm; Lions Gate Films. **A:** Sr. High-Adult. **P:** Entertainment. **U:** Home. **L:** English. **Mov-Ent:** Diseases, Aging, Marriage. **Awds:** Golden Globes '08: Actress--Drama (Christie); Screen Actors Guild '07: Actress (Christie). **Acq:** Purchase. **Dist:** Warner Home Video, Inc.

Away from Home 1987
This tape provides a look at life in an institution and examines the need for reforms. 29m; VHS, 3/4 U. **Pr:** RMI Media Productions. **A:** Adult. **P:** Education. **U:** Institution. **Gen-Edu:** Hospitals. **Acq:** Purchase. **Dist:** RMI Media.

Away We Go! 1996
A singing puppet named Newt takes two children on a musical journey exploring the many uses of modern transportation. Songs written by late director Jonathon Larson. 30m; VHS. **A:** Preschool-Primary. **P:** Entertainment. **U:** Home. **Chl-Juv:** Music--Children, Puppets. **Acq:** Purchase. **Dist:** Rainbow Educational Media, Inc. $14.95.

Away We Go 2009 (R) — ★★
Thirty-somethings Burt (Krasinski) and Verona (Rudolph) are a longtime unmarried couple who are expecting their first child. Uncommitted to their life in Colorado, they decide to travel around the U.S., visiting various cities to see if any appeal as the perfect place to start their family. Along the way, they have misadventures and find fresh connections with an assortment of relatives and old friends who just might help them discover "home" for the first time. The leads are appealing but the writers seem determined to showcase various domestic hells and condescending caricatures with their secondary characters. 97m; Blu-Ray, On Demand, Wide. **C:** John Krasinski; Jeff Daniels; Maggie Gyllenhaal; Melanie Lynskey; Maya Rudolph; Allison Janney; Catherine O'Hara; Jim Gaffigan; Carmen Ejogo; Josh Hamilton; Chris Messina; Paul Schneider; Directed by Sam Mendes; Written by Dave Eggers; Vendela Vida; Cinematography by Ellen Kuras; Music by Alex Murdoch. **Pr:** Edward Saxon; Marc Turtletaub; Peter Saraf; Big Beach; Neal Street Productions; Focus Features L.L.C. **A:** Sr. High-Adult. **P:** Entertainment. **U:** Home. **L:** English. **Mov-Ent:** Comedy-Drama, Family, Marriage. **Acq:** Purchase. **Dist:** Movies Unlimited; Alpha Video; Universal Studios Home Video.

Away We Go: All About Transportation 19??
Provides a history of transportation, explaining how today's technology has a profound influence on how we get around, and what's in store for the future. 20m; VHS. **Pr:** Rainbow. **A:** Primary. **P:** Education. **U:** Institution. **Gen-Edu:** Technology. **Acq:** Purchase. **Dist:** Clear Vue Inc. $89.00.

Awe-Inspiring Waves Series 2003
Four-part collection of spectacular waves from the coasts of California and Hawaii designed to help those recovering from illness, injury, or addiction find inner peace and rest. 240m; VHS. **A:** Adult. **P:** Vocational. **U:** Institution. **Hea-Sci:** Health Education, Mental Health, Occupational Training. **Acq:** Purchase. **Dist:** Aquarius Health Care Media. $300.00.

Awesome All-Star Action 200?
Presents amazing All-Star Game moments in history. 60m; DVD. **A:** Adult. **P:** Entertainment. **U:** Home. **Spo-Rec:** Baseball, Sports--General. **Acq:** Purchase. **Dist:** Baseball Direct. $19.95.

The Awesome Factor 1991
Documentary that highlights the thrills of Harley-Davidson motorcycle drag racing. Filmed on location at five different dragways in the United States. Contains footage of the Nitro-burning dragster bikes. 55m; VHS. **A:** Adult. **P:** Entertainment. **U:** Home. **Gen-Edu:** Motorcycles. **Acq:** Purchase. **Dist:** Panacom. $19.95.

Awesome! I F*in' Shot That!** 2006 (R) — ★★★
Combination of professional and fans' footage of The Beastie Boys' October 9, 2004 show at Madison Square Garden. The band encouraged fans to film the concert and send them the results. Works as both a document of the show and as an experiment in cooperation and collaboration between the artists and their fans. 90m; DVD. **C:** Directed by Adam "MCA" Yauch; Cinematography by Alexis Boling; Music by Adam "MCA" Yauch; Adam Horovitz; Mike D. **Pr:** John Doran; Adam Yauch; Oscilloscope Films; ThinkFilm. **A:** Sr. High-Adult. **P:** Entertainment. **U:** Home. **Mov-Ent:** Documentary Films, Music--Pop/Rock. **Acq:** Purchase. **Dist:** Velocity Home Entertainment; ThinkFilm Company Inc.

The Awful Dr. Orloff 1962 (Unrated) — ★
Set in a bygone era, Dr. Orloff (Vernon) is a retired prison physician who needs unblemished skin to remedy the horrible disfigurement of his daughter Melissa (Lorys), ravaged by fire. He abducts promising young women candidates with the help of his blind zombie henchman Morpho (Valle), who simply cannot be trusted with a scalpel. After several surgical mishaps, they kidnap the perfect specimen, a woman who bears an uncanny resemblance to Melissa. Unfortunately, she is engaged to suspicious police Inspector Tanner (San Martin). French version with English subtitles that includes more explicit gore is also available. 86m/B/W; DVD, Blu-Ray. **C:** Howard Vernon; Diana Lorys; Frank Wolff; Riccardo Valle; Conrado San Martin; Perla Cristal; Maria Silva; Mara Laso; Directed by Jess (Jesus) Franco; Written by Jess (Jesus) Franco; Cinematography by Godofredo Pacheco; Music by Jose Pagan; Antonio Ramirez Angel. **Pr:** Marius Lasoeur. **A:** College-Adult. **P:** Entertainment. **U:** Home. **L:** English, French. **Mov-Ent:** Horror, Surgical Transplantation. **Acq:** Purchase. **Dist:** Something Weird Video; Tapeworm Video Distributors Inc. $23.00.

The Awful Fate of Melpomenus Jones 1984 (Unrated)
A timid minister is not assertive enough to expel a guest from his home, extending an afternoon tea into a six week stay. 8m; VHS. **Pr:** National Film Board of Canada. **A:** Family. **P:** Entertainment. **U:** Institution, SURA. **Mov-Ent:** Animation & Cartoons, Children. **Acq:** Purchase. **Dist:** Center for Humanities, Inc./Guidance Associates.

Awful Nice 2014 (R) — ★
Deliberately obnoxious behavior highlights this indie comedy. Belligerently estranged brothers Jim and Dave start up their sibling rivalry once again by fighting at their dad's funeral. Then they learn they've equally inherited the family lakeside cottage in Branson, resulting in a road trip. Only the house is a disaster that they'll have to fix up in order to sell, which leads to a number of mishaps. 88m; DVD. **C:** Alex Rennie; James Pumphrey; Christopher Meloni; Brett Gelman; Keeley Hazell; Directed by Todd A. Sklar; Written by Alex Rennie; Todd A. Sklar; Cinematography by Adam Ginsberg; Music by Mark Harrison. **Pr:** Todd A. Sklar. **A:** Sr. High-Adult. **P:** Entertainment. **U:** Home. **L:** English. **Mov-Ent:** Family. **Acq:** Purchase. **Dist:** Screen Media Ventures, LLC.

The Awful Truth 1937 (Unrated) — ★★★★
Lucy (Dunne) and Jerry (Grant) Warriner are a young couple who discard their marriage made in heaven and go their separate ways in search of happiness. Meticulously sabotaging each others' new relationships, they discover they really were made for each other. Grant is at his most charming with dead-on comic timing while Dunne is brilliant as his needling ex. The scene where Dunne poses as Grant's prodigal fan-dancing sister who pays a surprise cocktail-hour visit to the family of his stuffy, upper-class girlfriend (Lamont) is among the most memorable screwball vignettes of all time. And don't miss the custody battle they have over the family dog (Asta of "The Thin Man" fame). Based on Arthur Richman's 1922 play. Preceded by 1925 and 1929 versions; remade in 1953 as "Let's Do it Again." 92m/B/W; VHS, DVD. **C:** Irene Dunne; Cary Grant; Ralph Bellamy; Alexander D'Arcy; Cecil Cunningham; Molly Lamont; Esther Dale; Joyce Compton; Robert "Tex" Allen; Robert Warwick; Mary Forbes; Directed by Leo McCarey; Written by Vina Delmar. **Pr:** Columbia Pictures. **A:** Family. **P:** Entertainment. **U:** Home. **Mov-Ent:** Comedy--Screwball, Pets, Divorce. **Awds:** Oscars '37: Director (McCarey); Natl. Film Reg. '96. **Acq:** Purchase. **Dist:** Baker and Taylor; Sony Pictures Home Entertainment Inc. $19.95.

The Awful Truth: The Best of the Awful Truth 2006
Contains highlighted episodes from the 1999-2000 cable television series with filmmaker Michael Moore as he challenges the questionable activities of politicians and businesses with his investigative reporting, protests, and satire. 6 episodes. 180m; DVD. **A:** Jr. High-Adult. **P:** Entertainment. **U:** Home. **Mov-Ent:** Television Series, Documentary Films, Politics & Government. **Acq:** Purchase. **Dist:** A&E Television Networks L.L.C. $19.95.

The Awful Truth: The Complete First Season 1999
Filmmaker and provocateur Michael Moore confronts the mayor of New York, Humana Insurance, Philip Morris, and Disneyland, among others, during his investigations of the insurance and tobacco industries as well as unfair labor practices. 300m; DVD, CC. **A:** Sr. High-Adult. **P:** Entertainment. **U:** Home. **Mov-Ent:** Television Series. **Acq:** Purchase. **Dist:** New Video Group.

The Awful Truth: The Complete Second Season 2001
Contains 12 complete and unedited episodes of filmmaker, iconoclastic, ultra-liberal rabblerouser Michael Moore, targeting corporate and political issues with his "guerrilla video" antics. 300m; VHS, DVD. **C:** Michael Moore; Directed by Michael Moore. **A:** Adult. **P:** Entertainment. **U:** Home. **Mov-Ent:** Television, Satire & Parody. **Acq:** Purchase. **Dist:** New Video Group. $39.95.

An Awfully Big Adventure 1994 (R) — ★★
Coming-of-age saga set in postwar Liverpool around a provincial reperatory company. Stage-struck 16-year-old Stella (Cates) gets work as a company apprentice, immediately getting a crush on arch, callous theatre manager Meredith Potter (a deliciously nasty Grant), who enjoys degrading everyone around him. The company's chance for success rests on a production of "Peter Pan," with visiting actor P.L. O'Hara (dashing Rickman), who immediately seduces Stella and has more than a few secrets of his own. Theatrically exaggerated; based on the novel by Beryl Bainbridge. 113m; VHS, DVD, CC. **C:** Georgina Cates; Hugh Grant; Alan Rickman; Peter Firth; Alun Armstrong; Prunella Scales; Rita Tushingham; Alan Cox; Edward Petherbridge; Nicola Pagett; Carol Drinkwater; Clive Merrison; Gerard McSorley; Directed by Mike Newell; Written by Charles Wood; Cinematography by Dick Pope; Music by Richard Hartley. **Pr:** Philip Hinchcliffe; Hilary Heath; Mark Shivas; John Sivers; Portman Productions; Fine Line Features. **A:** Sr. High-Adult. **P:** Entertainment. **U:** Home. **Mov-Ent:** Theater, Great Britain. **Acq:** Purchase. **Dist:** New Line Home Video.

Awkward Customers 1973
This program studies the awkward customer. John Cleese and Angharad Rees (of Monty Python) play the sales representatives who demonstrate the most common errors in handling awkward customers, and also show the right way to serve them. 24m; 3/4 U. **C:** John Cleese; Angharad Rees. **Pr:** Video Art Ltd. **A:** College-Adult. **P:** Instruction. **U:** Institution, SURA. **Bus-Ind:** Sales Training. **Acq:** Purchase, Rent/Lease. **Dist:** Video Arts, Inc.

Awkward Loads 1995
Offers safety suggestions for moving awkward loads while protecting your back. 12m; VHS. **A:** Adult. **P:** Professional. **U:** Institution. **Bus-Ind:** Job Training, Safety Education, Health Education. **Acq:** Rent/Lease. **Dist:** National Safety Council, California Chapter, Film Library.

Awkward Places 1995
Helpful suggestions for moving or lifting to avoid back injury. 12m; VHS. **A:** Adult. **P:** Professional. **U:** Institution. **Bus-Ind:** Job Training, Safety Education, Health Education. **Acq:** Rent/Lease. **Dist:** National Safety Council, California Chapter, Film Library.

Awkward: Season One 2011
MTV 2011-? teen comedy-drama. "Pilot": Thanks to her angst-ridden blog, teen wallflower Jenna's bizarre accident is thought to be a suicide attempt. "Jenna Lives": Clueless hunk Matty tells Jenna he's not ready for a relationship. "I Am Jenna Hamilton": Since Matty and Jenna are officially dating, she expects him to ask her to the Winter Formal, but Jake asks her instead. 12 episodes. 298m; DVD. **C:** Ashley Rickards; Beau Mirchoff; Brett Davern; Greer Grammer. **A:** Jr. High-Adult. **P:** Entertainment. **U:** Home. **Mov-Ent:** Adolescence, Comedy-Drama, Television Series. **Acq:** Purchase. **Dist:** MTV Networks Inc. $19.95.

Awkward: Season Two 2012
MTV 2011-? teen comedy-drama. "Resolutions": Jenna is given until midnight on New Year's Eve to declare that Jake is her boyfriend on her blog. "Time After Time" Jenna decides to tell Jake she loves him but being a flower girl at Ally's wedding gets in the way. "The Other Shoe": Jenna's back with Matty but he'll be working instead of going to Europe with her for the summer and Lissa wants Jake back. 12 episodes. 344m; DVD. **C:** Ashley Rickards; Beau Mirchoff; Brett Davern; Greer Grammer. **A:** Jr. High-Adult. **P:** Entertainment. **U:** Home. **Mov-Ent:** Adolescence, Comedy-Drama, Television Series. **Acq:** Purchase. **Dist:** MTV Networks Inc. $19.95.

The Ax Fight 1975
A look at the problems of Yanomamo kinship, alliance and village fission. 30m; 3/4 U. **Pr:** Timothy Asch; Napoleon Chagnon. **A:** Jr. High-College. **P:** Education. **U:** Institution, SURA. **Gen-Edu:** South America, Anthropology. **Acq:** Purchase. **Dist:** Documentary Educational Resources.

Ax Men: Season 2 2009 (Unrated)
A&E's 2008-? occupational reality series. Captures the difficult and dangerous work of four logging crews in the Pacific Northwest as they combat the elements and a bad economy. 12 episodes. 611m; DVD. **A:** Sr. High-Adult. **P:** Entertainment. **U:** Home. **Mov-Ent:** Occupations, Television Series. **Acq:** Purchase. **Dist:** A&E Television Networks L.L.C. $39.99.

Ax Men: Season One 2007 (Unrated)
History Channel series explores the logging industry by following four companies working in the Oregon forests. The loggers

are macho and crass talking but when it comes to harvesting "green gold" they stop at nothing, for any setback could destroy everyone's livelihood. 14 episodes. 670m; DVD. **A:** Sr. High-Adult. **P:** Entertainment. **U:** Home. **Mov-Ent:** History, Labor & Unions, Television Series. **Acq:** Purchase. **Dist:** A&E Television Networks L.L.C.

Axe 1974 (R) — ★½
After a group of thugs kill a man (on an embarrassingly shoddy set), they flee to the country, where they take over a farmhouse. The only residents of this farmhouse are a young girl, Lisa (Lee), and her invalid grandfather. The criminals force Lisa to cook a chicken dinner (NO!) and then generally terrorize the girl and her grandfather. Eventually, Lisa (who is actively hallucinating throughout this episode) gets the titular axe and seeks her revenge. The film is slow and boring, and the sub-amateur acting doesn't help. The only positive aspect is the suspense that mounts over the course of the movie. Having seen films like this before, and given the fact that nothing else is happening, the audience knows that Lisa is going to strike back at some time. 68m; DVD. **C:** Leslie Lee; Jack Canon; Frederick Friedel; Frank Jones; Directed by Frederick Friedel; Written by Frederick Friedel; Cinematography by Austin McKinney. **A:** Sr. High-Adult. **P:** Entertainment. **U:** Home. **Mov-Ent. Acq:** Purchase. **Dist:** Image Entertainment Inc.

Axe 2006 (Unrated) — Bomb!
Underwear acting. Babes Raven and Ashley (who spend a lot of time in their scanties) hit a desert bar after a rock-climbing expedition. After being harassed by a biker gang, they steal one of the bikes and wind up at a lonely motel with a satchel of cash. Oh, and there's an escaped con, Ivan the Axeman, on the loose as well. London has limited screen time as the bar owner in this incredibly stupid mishmash of genres. 92m; DVD. **C:** Tim Sitarz; Jason London; Joe Goodrich; Andrea Bogart; Darlena Tejeiro; Directed by Ron Wolotzky; Written by Eyal Sher; Dred Ross; Cinematography by Moshe Levin; Scott Carrithers; Music by Erik Godal; Mark Fontana. **A:** Sr. High-Adult. **P:** Entertainment. **U:** Home. **Mov-Ent. Acq:** Purchase. **Dist:** Bedford Entertainment Inc.

The Axe in the Attic 2007
Documentary exploring the diaspora of New Orleans citizens after Hurricane Katrina. 110m; VHS, DVD. **A:** Sr. High-Adult. **P:** Education. **U:** Home, Institution. **Gen-Edu:** Documentary Films, U.S. States. **Acq:** Purchase, Rent/Lease. **Dist:** The Cinema Guild. $395.00.

Axillary Approach for Block of the Brachial Plexus 1978
The anatomy of the brachial plexus is reviewed, including an analysis and clinical example of the procedure for blocking the upper arm, forearm, and hand. 8m; VHS, 3/4 U, Special order formats. **Pr:** Health Sciences Learning Resources. **A:** College-Adult. **P:** Professional. **U:** Institution, CCTV. **Hea-Sci:** Anatomy & Physiology, Medical Education. **Acq:** Purchase. **Dist:** Health Sciences Center for Educational Resources.

Axonal Peripheral Neuropathy 1978
A demonstration of the physical findings and typical presentation of a peripheral neuropathy. 10m; VHS, 3/4 U, Special order formats. **Pr:** Ohio State University Health Sciences AV Center.

A: College-Adult. **P:** Professional. **U:** Institution, SURA. **Hea-Sci:** Neurology. **Acq:** Purchase, Rent/Lease. **Dist:** Ohio State University.

Ay, Carmela! 1990 — ★★★
During the Spanish Civil War, two vaudevillians with strong anti-Franco views are captured by Franco forces and sentenced to execution. They are reprieved when a theatre-loving Lieutenant offers to spare their lives if they will entertain the troops. Clever and entertaining farce, with poignant undertones. 105m; VHS. **C:** Carmen Maura; Andres Pajares; Gabino Diego; Maurizio De Razza; Miguel Rellan; Edward Zentara; Jose Sancho; Antonio Fuentes; Directed by Carlos Saura; Written by Rafael Azcona; Cinematography by Jose Luis Alcaine. **Pr:** Prestige Pictures Releasing Corporation; IberoAmericana. **A:** Sr. High-Adult. **P:** Entertainment. **U:** Home. **L:** English, Spanish. **Mov-Ent:** Comedy-Drama, Spain, War--General. **Acq:** Purchase. **Dist:** $89.98.

Ay De Los Vencidos: Beware of the Conquered 1986
A look at the new frontiers in space from a Latin-American perspective. 2m; VHS, 3/4 U. **Pr:** Lotty Rosenfeld. **A:** Jr. High-Adult. **P:** Education. **U:** Institution, SURA. **Gen-Edu:** South America, Space Exploration. **Acq:** Rent/Lease. **Dist:** Video Out Distribution.

¡Ay Que Bonitas Piernas 1952 — ★
A Mexican musician makes his way up the charts with the help of a promoter. 101m/B/W; VHS. **C:** German Valdes; Rosita Quintana; Rosina Pagan; Nelly Montiel. **Pr:** Madera Cinevideo. **A:** Family. **P:** Entertainment. **U:** Home. **L:** Spanish. **Mov-Ent. Acq:** Purchase. **Dist:** Spanishmultimedia. $64.95.

¡AY SUDAMERICA! 1981
Documentary on the CADA's Art Action, featuring the story of six civil pilots who drop 400,000 pamphlets about the function of art and politics on Santiago. 4m; VHS, 3/4 U. **Pr:** C.A.D.A. **A:** Adult. **P:** Education. **U:** Institution. **Gen-Edu:** Human Rights, Art & Artists, Politics & Government. **Acq:** Rent/Lease. **Dist:** Video Out Distribution.

The Ayatollah in the Cathedral 1986
Former Iranian hostage Moorhead Kennedy leads this adult education series on the Christian's understanding of terrorism. In six 15-minute segments. 90m; VHS, 3/4 U. **Pr:** Episcopal Radio-TV Foundation. **A:** Jr. High-Adult. **P:** Religious. **U:** Institution, CCTV, CATV, BCTV, Home. **Gen-Edu:** Religion. **Acq:** Purchase, Rent/Lease. **Dist:** Alliance for Christian Media.

Ayurveda: The Science of Self-Healing 1990
An examination of this ancient art of healing, first practiced by Hindus more than five thousand years ago, is presented by Dr. Vasant Lad. 91m; VHS. **Pr:** Wishing Well. **A:** Sr. High-Adult. **P:** Education. **U:** Home. **How-Ins:** How-To, Health Education, Self-Help. **Acq:** Purchase. **Dist:** Tapeworm Video Distributors Inc. $29.95.

Aziz Ansari: Intimate Moments for a Sensual Evening 2010 (Unrated)
Debut stand-up performance of comedian Aziz Ansari taped for Comedy Central. 55m; DVD. **A:** Sr. High-Adult. **P:** Entertainment. **U:** Home. **Gen-Edu:** Comedy--Performance, Television. **Acq:** Purchase. **Dist:** Comedy Central. $14.98.

Aztec Basketball Academy Elite Training-Workout 1 2013 (Unrated)
Trainer Myron Epps and the Aztec staff present the first part of a workout designed to challenge basketball players both mentally and physically. 28m; DVD. **A:** Family. **P:** Education. **U:** Home. **L:** English. **Spo-Rec:** Athletic Instruction/Coaching, Basketball. **Acq:** Purchase. **Dist:** Championship Productions. $19.99.

Aztec Basketball Academy Elite Training-Workout 2 2013 (Unrated)
Basketball trainer Myron Epps follows up with the second portion of the Aztec Academy's workout session. 29m; DVD. **A:** Family. **P:** Education. **U:** Home. **L:** English. **Spo-Rec:** Athletic Instruction/Coaching, Basketball. **Acq:** Purchase. **Dist:** Championship Productions. $19.99.

Azumi 2003 (R) — ★★★
In 19th century Japan, Azumi, a young orphan girl is raised, along with other orphans, to become an assassin. Azumi (Ueto) soon becomes the best of them. When they come of age, they are cruelly tested, and the survivors are given a mission to eliminate warlords who are tearing the country apart. The action is top-notch, as expected, and the script manages to show both the beauty and brutality of the end of the Samurai era in Japan. Not all Western audience will appreciate the humor, fatalism, or meandering storytelling, but patience and attention is definitely rewarded. 128m; DVD. **C:** Shun Oguri; Yoshio Harada; Masato Ibu; Joe Odagiri; Naoto Takenaka; Aya Ueto; Hiroki Narimiya; Kenji Kohashi; Takatoshi Kaneko; Yuma Ishigaki; Yasuomi Sano; Shinji Suzuki; Eita Nagayama; Shogo Yamaguchi; Kazuki Kitamura; Kenichi Endo; Kazuya Shimizu; Ryo; Michael P. Greco; Shoichiro Masumoto; Minoru Matsumoto; Aya Okamoto; Tak Sakaguchi; Hideo Sakaki; Directed by Ryuhei Kitamura; Written by Yu Koyama; Rikiya Mizushima; Isao Kiriyama; Cinematography by Takumi Furuya; Music by Taro Iwashiro. **Pr:** Toshiaki Nakazawa; Mataichiro Yamamoto. **A:** College-Adult. **P:** Entertainment. **U:** Home. **L:** Japanese. **Mov-Ent:** Japan, Adoption, Action-Adventure. **Acq:** Purchase. **Dist:** Urban Vision Entertainment Inc.

Azumi 2 2005 (Unrated) — ★★½
Beginning directly where the first film leaves off, Azumi (Ueto) and Nagara (Ishigaki) continue their pursuit of their assigned target Masayuki Sanada (Nagasawa). He hires the Koga Ninja clan, a band of specialized assassins to take them out before they can reach him. The first film is required viewing for this one as there are no flashbacks or explanations given. Fans of "Kill Bill" should look for Chiaki Kuriyama (she played Go Go) as one of the ninja super assassins. 108m; DVD. **C:** Aya Ueto; Yuma Ishigaki; Chiaki Kuriyama; Shun Oguri; Kenichi Endo; Kai Shishido; Tak Sakaguchi; Shoichiro Masumoto; Eugene Nomura; Aki Maeda; Toshie Negishi; Toshiya Nagasawa; Kenji Takechi; Shigeru Koyama; Mikijiro Hira; Kazuki Kitamura; Reiko Takashima; Directed by Shusuke (Shu) Kaneko; Written by Yu Koyama; Yoshiaki Kawajiri; Mataichiro Yamamoto; Cinematography by Yoshitaka Sakamoto. **A:** Sr. High-Adult. **P:** Entertainment. **U:** Home. **L:** English, Japanese, Spanish. **Mov-Ent:** Martial Arts. **Acq:** Purchase. **Dist:** Urban Vision Entertainment Inc. $24.95.

B

The B-24 Trilogy 1997
Three-volume set presents the heroic saga of the men who flew B-24 bombers during the war. 180m; VHS. **A:** Adult. **P:** Education. **U:** Home. **Gen-Edu:** World War Two. **Acq:** Purchase. **Dist:** 411 Video Information. $39.95.
Indiv. Titles: 1. Target Nazi Europe 2. Bombers Over Normandy 3. Target Imperial Japan.

B-25: "One Helluva Bomber" 1988
The account of the WWII bomber plane, the Mitchell B-25, is the main subject. 50m; VHS. **A:** Family. **P:** Entertainment. **U:** Institution, Home. **Gen-Edu:** Aeronautics. **Acq:** Purchase. **Dist:** Military/Combat Stock Footage Library; Bennett Marine Video. $24.95.

B-52s: 1979-1989 1989
The popular music group performs some of their most well-known tunes, such as "Rock Lobster," "Planet Z," "Love Shack," "Roam," "Legal Tender," "The Girl from Ipanema Goes to Greenland" and more. 32m; VHS. **Pr:** Warner Bros; Warner Reprise Video. **A:** Jr. High-Adult. **P:** Entertainment. **U:** Home. **Mov-Ent:** Music Video. **Acq:** Purchase. **Dist:** Music Video Distributors. $19.98.

The B-84: Leaving Ground 1981
The filmmaker explores airport security by running his VCR through security, immigration, and even the X-ray baggage inspection machine. 20m; VHS, 3/4 U. **Pr:** Byron Black. **A:** Jr. High-Adult. **P:** Education. **U:** Institution, SURA. **Gen-Edu:** Video. **Acq:** Rent/Lease. **Dist:** Video Out Distribution.

B-A-C-K: Posture, Mechanics, Exercise 1995
Offers several health tips for the back including simple back exercises. 19m; VHS. **A:** Adult. **P:** Professional. **U:** Institution. **Bus-Ind:** Job Training, Safety Education, Health Education. **Acq:** Rent/Lease. **Dist:** National Safety Council, California Chapter, Film Library; Audio Graphics Training Systems.

B&E: A to Z—How to Get in Anywhere, Anytime 19??
A look at the difficulty of building security, designed for security professionals, police, locksmiths, and private detectives. For informational purposes only. 118m; VHS. **A:** College-Adult. **P:** Education. **U:** Institution, Home. **How-Ins:** How-To, Police Training. **Acq:** Purchase. **Dist:** Gun Video. $99.99.

B. D. Women 1994
Celebrates the history and culture of Black lesbians. Features Black women talking candidly about their sexual and racial identities. 20m; VHS. **A:** College-Adult. **P:** Education. **U:** Institution. **Gen-Edu:** Women, Homosexuality, Black Culture. **Acq:** Purchase, Rent/Lease. **Dist:** Women Make Movies. $225.00.

The B Faxtor 1997
Presents a love story/courtroom drama about an athlete framed for rape. ?m; VHS. **A:** Adult. **P:** Entertainment. **U:** Home. **Gen-Edu. Acq:** Purchase. **Dist:** Tapeworm Video Distributors Inc. $19.95.

B-Mode and Real Time Sonography Series 1 1980
A postgraduate videotape course in diagnostic radiology, featuring expert presentations relevant to the current state of the art. 60m; VHS, 3/4 U. **Pr:** University of California San Francisco. **A:** College-Adult. **P:** Professional. **U:** Institution, CCTV. **Hea-Sci:** Radiography. **Acq:** Rent/Lease. **Dist:** University of California at San Francisco.
Indiv. Titles: 1. Clinical Instrumentation 2. Complete Abdominal Scanning-Part I: Liver 3. Complete Abdominal Scanning-Part II 4. Complete Obstetrical Scanning 5. Gynecological Scanning 6. Neonatal Skull Sonography.

B. Monkey 1997 (R) — ★★
B—AKA Beatrice (Argento)--hopes she can escape her world of drugs and crime (she's a thief) with the romantic aid of schoolteacher Alan (Harris). But her past catches up with her when ex-partners Paul (Everett) and Bruno (Rhys Meyers) convince her to do one last job (she misses the rush). Based on the novel by Andrew Davies, this one is mainly cool Brit style over substance. 91m; VHS, DVD, Blu-Ray, Wide. **C:** Asia Argento; Jared Harris; Rupert Everett; Jonathan Rhys Meyers; Tim Woodward; Ian Hart; Directed by Michael Radford; Written by Michael Thomas; Chloe King; Cinematography by Ashley Rowe; Music by Jennie Muskett. **Pr:** Stephen Woolley; Scala Productions; Miramax Film Corp. **A:** Sr. High-Adult. **P:** Entertainment. **U:** Home. **Mov-Ent:** Romance, Drug Abuse. **Acq:** Purchase. **Dist:** Buena Vista Home Entertainment.

B-Movie 1980
A filmed map of Philadelphia's famed Broad Street using humor, street sounds and time-lapse photography to create a fun view of city life. 16m; 3/4 U. **Pr:** Jim Starr. **A:** Family. **P:** Education. **U:** Institution, SURA. **Gen-Edu:** Cities & Towns. **Acq:** Purchase, Rent/Lease. **Dist:** Temple University Dept. of Film and Media Arts.

B-17 Flying Fortress: A Tribute 1985
An analysis of the B-17 bomber, featuring both wartime footage and new prototype footage. 30m/B/W; VHS. **Pr:** Ferde Grofe Films. **A:** Family. **P:** Education. **U:** Institution, Home. **Gen-Edu:** Aeronautics, World War Two. **Acq:** Purchase. **Dist:** Military/Combat Stock Footage Library; Bennett Marine Video; Fast Forward. $19.95.

B-17 Flying Legend 2004 (Unrated)
Documentary on the creation and history of the B17 Flying Fortress, and efforts to preserve the few remaining operational ones. 211m; DVD. **A:** Jr. High-Adult. **P:** Entertainment. **U:** Home. **Gen-Edu:** Documentary Films, World War Two. **Acq:** Purchase. **Dist:** Janson Media. $24.95.

B-17s: The Flying Fortress 19??
A profile of the WWII Allied bombing campaign on Nazi Germany. 30m; VHS. **C:** Narrated by Edward Mulhare. **A:** Family. **P:** Education. **U:** Home. **Gen-Edu:** War--General, World War Two. **Acq:** Purchase. **Dist:** Karol Media; Fusion Video. $14.95.

Baa Baa Black Sheep: Volume 1 1976
Includes the first half of season one of the war drama television series taken from the actual life of Lt. Col. Gregory "Pappy" Boyington (Conrad), a fighter pilot during World War II, with stories about missions that he and his men performed while stationed in the Pacific. 12 episodes. 588m; DVD. **C:** Robert Conrad; Dirk Blocker; Robert Ginty; John Larroquette; Steven Richmond. **A:** Jr. High-Adult. **P:** Entertainment. **U:** Home. **Mov-Ent:** Television Series, Action-Adventure, Drama. **Acq:** Purchase. **Dist:** Universal Studios Home Video. $39.98.

Baa Baa Black Sheep: Volume 2 1977
Includes the second half of season one of the war drama television series taken from the actual life of Lt. Col. Gregory "Pappy" Boyington (Conrad), a fighter pilot during World War II, with stories about missions that he and his men performed while stationed in the Pacific. 12 episodes. 585m; DVD. **C:** Robert Conrad; Dirk Blocker; Robert Ginty; John Larroquette; Steven Richmond. **A:** Jr. High-Adult. **P:** Entertainment. **U:** Home. **Mov-Ent:** Television Series, Action-Adventure, Drama. **Acq:** Purchase. **Dist:** Universal Studios Home Video. $39.98.

Baadasssss! 2003 (R) — ★★★½
Mario Van Peebles' fictionalized biopic of his father Melvin's efforts to get his influential indie film "Sweet Sweetback's Baadasssss Song" (the forerunner of the blaxploitation genre) made. Melvin (Mario, who also directed, co-wrote, and produced) is plagued with money and health problems, union troubles and lack of studio interest. Well-made and highly entertaining film was adapted from Melvin's "making of" book. Mario honors his father's work without over-romaticizing the often-imperfect man behind it. 108m; DVD. **C:** Mario Van Peebles; Nia Long; David Alan Grier; Ossie Davis; Terry Crews; Rainn Wilson; Joy Bryant; Saul Rubinek; T.K. Carter; Paul Rodriguez; Vincent Schiavelli; Khleo Thomas; Len Lesser; Sally Struthers; Adam West; Glenn Plummer; Khalil Kain; Pamela Gordon; Joseph Culp; Karimah Westbrook; Ralph Martin; Robert Peters; Wesley Jonathan; John Singleton; Directed by Mario Van Peebles; Written by Mario Van Peebles; Dennis Haggerty; Cinematography by Robert Primes; Music by Tyler Bates. **Pr:** Bruce Wayne Gillies; Bad Aaas Cinema; MVP Filmz; Sony Pictures Classics. **A:** Sr. High-Adult. **P:** Entertainment. **U:** Home. **Mov-Ent:** Biography: Show Business, Black Culture, Documentary Films. **Acq:** Purchase. **Dist:** Sony Pictures Home Entertainment Inc. $24.96.

Baadasssss Cinema: A Bold Look at 70's Blaxpoitation Films 2003 (Unrated)
Documentary researching the rise of "blaxploitation" films in the 1970s originally filmed for the Independent Film Channel. 58m; DVD. **A:** Sr. High-Adult. **P:** Education. **U:** Home. **Gen-Edu:** Documentary Films, Film History, Black Culture. **Acq:** Purchase. **Dist:** Docurama. $24.95.

The Baader Meinhof Complex 2008 (R) — ★★
Overstuffed drama crams ten years worth of history on the notorious 1960-70s West German terrorist group, the Red Army Faction (RAF), reducing it to re-enactments (albeit with some ferocious acting) with not much explanation for those not already familiar with the history. Left-wing journalist Ulricke Meinhof (Gedeck) uses the German government's heavy-handed reaction to student demonstrations to leave behind her life as a prosaic middle-class wife and mother. Instead, she becomes involved in the political activities of Andreas Baader (Bleibtrue) and Gudrun Ensslin (Wokalek) that were transformed from idealism to nihilism and violence, including bombings, hijackings, kidnappings, jailbreaks, and assassinations. Adapted from the book by Stefan Aust. English, German, French, and Arabic with subtitles. 150m; Blu-Ray, On Demand, Wide. **C:** Martina Gedeck; Moritz Bleibtreu; Johanna Wokalek; Bruno Ganz; Nadja Uhl; Jan Josef Liefers; Stipe Erceg; Niels Bruno Schmidt; Vinzenz Kiefer; Simon Licht; Directed by Uli Edel; Written by Uli Edel; Bernd Eichinger; Cinematography by Rainer Klausmann; Music by Peter Hindertuer; Florian Tesslof. **Pr:** Bernd Eichinger; Bernd Eichinger; Constantin Film; Vitagraph. **A:** College-Adult. **P:** Entertainment. **U:** Home. **L:** German, French, Arabic, English. **Mov-Ent:** Terrorism, Germany. **Acq:** Purchase. **Dist:** MPI Media Group; Amazon.com Inc.; Movies Unlimited.

Ba'al: The Storm God 2008 (PG-13) — **Bomb!**
An archaeologist gathers four ancient amulets, designed to reawaken the storm god Ba'al, hoping their mystical properties will cure his terminal cancer. Cheapo Sci-Fi Channel movie with a lousy script and equally bad acting. 90m; DVD. **C:** Jeremy London; Lexa Doig; Michael Kopsa; Directed by Paul Ziller; Written by Paul Ziller; Andrew Black; Cinematography by Mahlon Todd Williams; Music by Pinar Toprak. **A:** Jr. High-Adult. **P:** Entertainment. **U:** Home. **Mov-Ent:** Science Fiction. **Acq:** Purchase.

Baaria 2009 (Unrated) — ★★
Old-fashioned and over-extended multi-decade saga from writer/director Tornatore that focuses on the Sicilian Torrenuova clan, who survive through Fascism, WWII, and the political chaos of postwar Italy. In the 1930s, shepherd Ciccio works for corrupt landowner Giacinto, and his trials turn his son Peppino into an ambitious Communist activist. Peppino's son Pietro will become a photographer, recording the changes around him. The title is local dialect for the Sicilian town of Bagheria where Tornatore was born. Italian with subtitles. 150m; DVD, Blu-Ray. **C:** Angela Molina; Enrico Lo Verso; Lina Sastri; Francesco Scianna; Margareth Made; Lollo Franco; Giovanni Gambino; Davide Viviani; Marco Iermano; Gaetano Aronica; Directed by Giuseppe Tornatore; Written by Giuseppe Tornatore; Cinematography by Enrico Lucidi; Music by Ennio Morricone. **Pr:** Giampaolo Letta; Mario Spedaletti; Tarak Ben Ammar; Medusa Film; Quinta Communications; Regione Siciliana; Sicilia Film Commission; Summit Entertainment. **A:** College-Adult. **P:** Entertainment. **U:** Home. **L:** Italian. **Mov-Ent:** World War Two, Italy, Politics & Government. **Acq:** Purchase. **Dist:** Image Entertainment Inc.; Movies Unlimited.

Bab El-Oued City 1994
Shortly after the bloody riots of October 1988 a young man commits an act that puts his entire district in jeopardy in this dramatic expose of Islamic fundamentalism in Algeria. Subtitled in English. 93m; VHS. **A:** Adult. **P:** Entertainment. **U:** Institution, BCTV. **L:** Arabic. **Mov-Ent:** Drama, Middle East. **Acq:** Purchase, Rent/Lease. **Dist:** Arab Film Distribution. $200.00.

Baba 1973 (Unrated) — ★★★
A poor boatman agrees to be the fall guy in a murder in exchange for the actual murderer supporting his family. But after 24 years in prison, the boatman finds all his sacrificing has been in vain. His daughter has become a prostitute and his son is working as one of the murderer's henchman. In Turkish with English subtitles. 95m; VHS. **C:** Directed by Yilmaz Guney. **A:** College-Adult. **P:** Entertainment. **U:** Home. **L:** Turkish. **Mov-Ent:** Family. **Acq:** Purchase. **Dist:** Facets Multimedia Inc. $39.95.

Baba, The Father 1973
A man takes the rap for a murder in exchange for support of his family only to find out after 24 years of hard labor the deal was in vain. 95m; VHS. **A:** Adult. **P:** Entertainment. **U:** Home. **Mov-Ent:** Middle East, Drama. **Acq:** Purchase. **Dist:** Arab Film Distribution. $39.99.

Baba Who? 1980
This documentary examines the religious leader Baba Muktananda, his followers, and their beliefs. 17m; VHS, 3/4 U. **Pr:** Shari Reich Able. **A:** Sr. High-Adult. **P:** Education. **U:** Institution, SURA. **Gen-Edu:** Religion. **Acq:** Purchase. **Dist:** Phoenix Learning Group.

Baba Yaga 1973 (Unrated) — ★
Euro-horror loosely based on the erotic comic books of Guido Crepax. Talented young Milan photog Valentina accepts a late-night ride from the oddly-named Baba Yaga and then can't get the older woman out of her life. Valentina starts having kinky nightmares and her camera seems to be cursed. She discovers that Baba Yaga is literally a witch (and an S&M-loving lesbian). Dubbed. 83m; DVD. **C:** Carroll Baker; Isabelle DeFunes; George Eastman; Ely Galleani; Directed by Corrado Farina; Written by Corrado Farina; Cinematography by Aiace Parolini; Music by Piero Umiliani. **A:** College-Adult. **P:** Entertainment. **U:** Home. **Mov-Ent:** Photography, Italy. **Acq:** Purchase. **Dist:** Blue Underground, Inc.

The Babadook 2014 (Unrated) — ★★★
Samuel (Wiseman) was born the day his father died, as he tried to get his mother Amelia (Davis) to the hospital to deliver. Naturally, this blend of grief and joy around Samuel's birthday leads to emotional turmoil, which results in a haunting of sorts in this excellent Australian boogeyman tale. Amelia and Samuel find a book they didn't know they had that tells the story of the deadly Babadook and how it's coming to get them. And then it does. Davis is fantastic in a tale that feels reminiscent of "The Shining" and "The Orphanage." 95m; DVD. **C:** Essie Davis; Noah Wiseman; Daniel Henshall; Directed by Jennifer Kent; Written by Jennifer Kent; Cinematography by Radek Kotatko; Music by Jed Kurzel. **Pr:** IFC Midnight. **A:** Sr. High-Adult. **P:** Entertainment. **U:** Home. **L:** English. **Mov-Ent:** Horror, Children, Parenting. **Acq:** Purchase.

Babalu Music! I Love Lucy's Greatest Hits 1991
A wacky collection of music from the "I Love Lucy" show including "Babalu Rap," produced by "Weird" Al Yankovic. Also includes the theme song, Lucy and Ethel's "Friendship" duet, "Cuban Pete," "Straw Hat Song," "Cheek to Cheek," "Babalu," "California Here I Come," "We're Having a Baby" and more. 52m/B/W; VHS. **C:** Lucille Ball; Desi Arnaz, Sr; William Frawley; Vivian Vance. **Pr:** CBS/Fox. **A:** Family. **P:** Entertainment. **U:** Home. **Mov-Ent:** Music Video, Television Series. **Acq:** Purchase. **Dist:** Fox Home Entertainment. $14.98.

Babar and Father Christmas 1986
More adventures of the animated French elephant created by Jean de Brunhoff. 30m/B/W; VHS. **Pr:** Crawley's Animation. **A:** Family. **P:** Entertainment. **U:** Home. **L:** English, French. **Chl-Juv:** Animation & Cartoons, Children, Christmas. **Acq:** Purchase. **Dist:** Anchor Bay Entertainment. $9.98.

Babar Comes to America 1984
Babar, Celeste, and Artur head to Hollywood to make a movie but get sidetracked several times along the way. 23m; VHS. **A:** Family. **P:** Entertainment. **U:** Home. **Chl-Juv:** Animation & Cartoons. **Acq:** Purchase. **Dist:** Facets Multimedia Inc. $14.95.

Babar: King of the Elephants 1999
Feature-length animated film based on the popular HBO chidlren's series. 78m; DVD, CC. **C:** Directed by Raymond Jafelice; Written by Raymond Jafelice; Peter Sauder. **A:** Family. **P:** Entertainment. **U:** Home. **Chl-Juv:** Animation & Cartoons, Family Viewing. **Acq:** Purchase. **Dist:** Home Box Office Inc.

Babar: Monkey Business 1991
Babar the little elephant finds himself up to his trunk in fun thanks to a mischievious simian. 30m; VHS. **Pr:** FHE. **A:** Family.

P: Entertainment. **U:** Home. **Chl-Juv**: Animation & Cartoons, Fantasy, Family Viewing. **Acq:** Purchase. **Dist:** Lions Gate Entertainment Inc. $12.95.

Babar Returns 1989
Babar tells his daughter Flora the story of how he was crowned king of the elephant herd. 49m; VHS. **Pr:** Nelvana Productions Ltd. **A:** Family. **P:** Entertainment. **U:** Home. **Chl-Juv**: Animation & Cartoons, Children. **Acq:** Purchase. **Dist:** Facets Multimedia Inc. $14.95.

Babar the Elephant Comes to America 1985
Based on Jean de Brunhoff's famous character, this animated film depicts Babar's adventures in Hollywood. 25m; VHS. **C:** Narrated by Peter Ustinov. **Pr:** Children's Video Library. **A:** Family. **P:** Entertainment. **U:** Home. **Chl-Juv**: Fantasy, Animation & Cartoons. **Acq:** Purchase. **Dist:** Lions Gate Television Corp.

Babar the Little Elephant 1987
Actor Peter Ustinov narrates Jean de Brunhoff's animated story of the wise elephant. 25m; VHS. **C:** Narrated by Peter Ustinov. **Pr:** Vestron Video. **A:** Family. **P:** Entertainment. **U:** Home. **Chl-Juv**: Children, Animation & Cartoons. **Acq:** Purchase, Rent/Lease. **Dist:** Lions Gate Television Corp. $14.98.

Babar: The Movie 1988 (G) — ★★½
The lovable Babar, king of the elephants, must devise a plan to outwit an angry hoard of attacking rhinos. Based on the characters of Jean and Laurent de Brunhoff. 75m; VHS, DVD, 8 mm. **C:** Voice(s) by Gavin Magrath; Gordon Pinsent; Sarah Polley; Chris Wiggins; Elizabeth Hanna; Directed by Alan Bunce; Written by Alan Bunce; John deKlein. **Pr:** Patrick Loubert. **A:** Family. **P:** Entertainment. **U:** Home. **Mov-Ent**: Animation & Cartoons, Family Viewing. **Acq:** Purchase. **Dist:** Image Entertainment Inc. $24.95.

Babar's Triumph 1991
Babar gathers together all his animal friends to discuss ways in which they can save their jungle. 51m; VHS. **Pr:** FHE. **A:** Family. **P:** Entertainment. **U:** Home. **Chl-Juv**: Children, Animation & Cartoons, Fantasy. **Acq:** Purchase. **Dist:** Lions Gate Entertainment Inc. $14.95.

Bab'Aziz: The Prince Who Contemplated His Soul 2006
Bab—Aziz and his daughter wander the desert telling tales and searching for a gathering of dervishes that takes place only once every 30 years. With English subtitles. Also available in 35mm as a rental. 96m; VHS. **A:** Sr. High-Adult. **P:** Entertainment. **U:** Institution, Home. **L:** Farsi, Arabic. **Mov-Ent**: Islam, Storytelling. **Acq:** Rent/Lease. **Dist:** Arab Film Distribution.

Babe! 1975 (Unrated) — ★★★½
A fine TV movie about the life of one of America's most famous woman athletes, Babe Didrickson. Adapted by Joanna Lee from Didrickson's autobiography "The Life I've Led." The movie was nominated for Outstanding Special of 1975-76 and Clark won an Emmy for her work. 120m; VHS, DVD. **C:** Susan Clark; Alex Karras; Slim Pickens; Jeannette Nolan; Ellen Geer; Ford Rainey; Directed by Buzz Kulik; Music by Jerry Goldsmith. **Pr:** MGM. **A:** Family. **P:** Entertainment. **U:** Home. **Mov-Ent**: Biography: Sports, TV Movies, Sports--Fiction: Drama. **Acq:** Purchase. **Dist:** Unknown Distributor.

The Babe 1992 (PG) — ★★½
Follows the life of legendary baseball player Babe Ruth, portrayed as a sloppy drunkard whose appetites for food, drink, and sex were as large as he was. Alvarado and McGillis do well as the Babe's first and second wives, but this is Goodman's show from start to finish. He's excellent as Ruth, and looks the part, but his fine performance can't make up for a lackluster script filled with holes. 115m; VHS, DVD, CC. **C:** John Goodman; Kelly McGillis; Trini Alvarado; Bruce Boxleitner; Peter Donat; J.C. Quinn; Richard Tyson; James Cromwell; Joe Ragno; Bernard Kates; Michael McGrady; Stephen Caffrey; Michael (Mike) Papajohn; Directed by Arthur Hiller; Written by John Fusco; Cinematography by Haskell Wexler; Music by Elmer Bernstein. **Pr:** John Fusco; Waterhorse; Finnegan-Pinchuk Co. **A:** Jr. High-Adult. **P:** Entertainment. **U:** Home. **Mov-Ent**: Baseball, Biography: Sports, Sports--Fiction: Drama. **Acq:** Purchase. **Dist:** Movies Unlimited; Alpha Video. $19.98.

Babe 1995 (G) — ★★★½
Totally charming fable has intelligent piglet Babe being raised by matriarch sheepdog Fly, and learning the art of sheep herding along with his new canine brothers. Farmer Hoggett (Cromwell), Babe's owner by virtue of a winning raffle ticket, sees that he's more than just a ham, and enters them in the world sheepdog herding championship. Whimsy that never crosses the line into treacle. Four different special effects houses were used to make the barnyard animals talk and walk. Filmed on location in Australia; based on Dick King-Smith's book "The Sheep-Pig." 91m; VHS, DVD, Blu-Ray, CC. **C:** James Cromwell; Magda Szubanski; Voice(s) by Christine Cavanaugh; Miriam Margolyes; Danny Mann; Hugo Weaving; Narrated by Roscoe Lee Browne; Directed by Chris Noonan; Written by Chris Noonan; George Miller; Cinematography by Andrew Lesnie; Music by Nigel Westlake. **Pr:** Bill Miller; George Miller; Doug Mitchell; George Miller; Kennedy Miller Productions; Universal Pictures. **A:** Family. **P:** Entertainment. **U:** Home. **Mov-Ent**: Fantasy, Family Viewing, Birds. **Awds:** Oscars '95: Visual FX; Golden Globes '96: Film--Mus./Comedy; Natl. Soc. Film Critics '95: Film. **Acq:** Purchase. **Dist:** Universal Music and Video Distribution. $22.98.

Babe: Pig in the City 1998 (PG) — ★★½
Miller takes over the director's chair for this trip. And he brings along more money, more effects, more animals, and more unsettling images, including Mickey Rooney in a creepy clown suit, than anyone who saw the original would expect. Babe returns home to a hero's welcome, but the joy doesn't last long. Farmer Hoggett (Cromwell) is injured, and with foreclosure imminent, Babe and Mrs. Hoggett (Szubanski) head out to turn Babe's fame into a little cash. Along the way, they miss their connecting flight in "the city" and are forced to stay at a hotel that caters to animals. There, they meet the aforementioned Rooney and his three chimp partners, along with various dogs and cats. Technically well-done, and sporting an imaginative story, but may be a little dark for the younger kiddies. 96m; VHS, DVD, Blu-Ray, CC. **C:** James Cromwell; Magda Szubanski; Mickey Rooney; Mary Stein; Julie Godfrey; Voice(s) by Elizabeth Daily; Danny Mann; Glenne Headly; Steven Wright; James Cosmo; Stanley Ralph Ross; Russi Taylor; Adam Goldberg; Nathan Kress; Myles Jeffrey; Narrated by Roscoe Lee Browne; Directed by George Miller; Written by Judy Morris; Mark Lamprell; Cinematography by Andrew Lesnie; Music by Nigel Westlake. **A:** Family. **P:** Entertainment. **U:** Home. **Mov-Ent**: Fantasy, Pets, Pets. **Acq:** Purchase. **Dist:** Movies Unlimited; Alpha Video.

Babe Ruth 1998
Explores the life and times of baseball player--and celebrity--Babe Ruth. 60m; DVD. **A:** Family. **P:** Entertainment. **U:** Home. **Gen-Edu**: Baseball, Biography: Sports, Documentary Films. **Acq:** Purchase. **Dist:** Home Box Office Inc. $19.98.

Babe Ruth Story 1948 — ★★
An overly sentimental biography about the famed baseball slugger. Bendix is miscast as the Bambino, but the actual film clips of the Babe are of interest. A movie to be watched during those infrequent bouts of sloppy baseball mysticism. 107m/B/W; VHS, DVD, CC. **C:** William Bendix; Claire Trevor; Charles Bickford; William Frawley; Sam Levene; Gertrude Niesen; Directed by Roy Del Ruth. **Pr:** Allied Artists International. **A:** Family. **P:** Entertainment. **U:** Home. **Mov-Ent**: Baseball, Biography: Sports, Sports--Fiction: Drama. **Acq:** Purchase. **Dist:** WarnerArchive.com. $19.98.

Babe Ruth: The Life Behind the Legend 1999
Profiles the on- and off-field life of Babe Ruth, focusing on his excellence and eccentricity. 59m; VHS. **A:** Family. **P:** Entertainment. **U:** Home. **Spo-Rec**: Baseball. **Acq:** Purchase. **Dist:** Baseball Direct. $19.95.

Babe Winkelman's Fishing Secrets 1987
Learn some inside angling tips from one of the best fishermen around. 50m; VHS. **C:** Babe Winkelman. **Pr:** Babe Winkelman. **A:** Primary-Adult. **P:** Instruction. **U:** Institution, Home. **How-Ins**: Fishing. **Acq:** Purchase. **Dist:** ESPN Inc. $19.95.
Indiv. Titles: 1. Land of the Midnight Sun: Saskatchewan Fly-In Fishing 2. Water Wolves of the North: A Northern Pike Spectacular 3. Wilderness Walleyes: The Lure of Ontario 4. "Summer Heat" Bass: No Sweat! 5. The Great Lake Erie: A Fishing Success Story 6. Trophy Time: Fall Fishing Bonanza 7. Cold Water-Hot Action: Ice Fishing Fever 8. Land of 100,000 Lakes: Manitoba Magic 9. Fishing the Canadian Shield: The Ultimate Experience 10. Bronzebacks of the North: Smallmouth Spectacular 11. Great Plains Reservoirs: Fishing Midwestern Impoundments 12. Spring Fishing: The Cure for Cabin Fever 13. Big Water Bounty: Great Lakes Fishing Made Easy 14. Family Fishing Fun: Sharing the Good Times 15. Fishing the Flow: Wonders of the River 16. Trophy Walleye Patterns: The Seminar 17. Prime Time Panfish: Thrills for Kids of All Ages.

Babel 2006 (R) — ★★★½
A father in a Moroccan village allows his two young sons to shoot his hunting rifle and an international incident is sparked. The boys innocently aim at a tourist bus, never believing the bullets could actually hit someone. They do, of course, and this one foolish act leads to complications that will encompass a Mexican nanny and her Anglo charges back in California and an angry deaf-mute teenaged girl in Tokyo. Somehow director Gonzalez Inarritu manages to tie the stories together (with a certain amount of unbelievability). Pitt and Blanchett join an impressive international cast who live up to this gritty, realistic dramatic puzzle. 142m; DVD, Blu-Ray, HD-DVD. **C:** Brad Pitt; Cate Blanchett; Gael Garcia Bernal; Adriana Barraza; Elle Fanning; Koji Yakusho; Nathan Gamble; Rinko Kikuchi; Said Tarchani; Boubker Ait El Caid; Mustapha Rachidi; Abdelkader Bara; Directed by Alejandro Gonzalez Inarritu; Written by Guillermo Arriaga; Cinematography by Rodrigo Prieto; Music by Gustavo Santaolalla. **Pr:** Steven Golin; Jon Kilik; Alejandro Gonzalez Inarritu; Zeta Films; Anonymous Content; Central Films; Paramont Vantage. **A:** Sr. High-Adult. **P:** Entertainment. **U:** Home. **L:** English, Spanish, Japanese, French. **Mov-Ent**: Africa, Mexico, Deafness. **Awds:** Oscars '06: Orig. Score; British Acad. '06: Orig. Score; Golden Globes '07: Film--Drama. **Acq:** Purchase. **Dist:** Paramount Pictures Corp.

Baberellas 2003 (R) — ★½
In this parody of old scifi nudies like "Barbarella" or "Flesh Gordon" an evil alien queen hopes to steal all of the Earth's 'sexy energy' to promote her tv show (and incidentally killing off all life in the process). Standing in her way is an all girl rock band. 80m; DVD. **C:** Shauna O'Brien; Julie K. Smith; Regina Russell; Julie Strain; Directed by Chuck Cirino; Written by Chuck Cirino; Tip McPartland; Dave Nichols; Mark Wilde; Cinematography by David Winters; Music by John Beal. **A:** Sr. High-Adult. **P:** Entertainment. **U:** Home. **L:** English. **Mov-Ent**. **Acq:** Purchase. **Dist:** Xenon Entertainment, Xenon Pictures. $24.98.

Babes in Arms 1939 (Unrated) — ★½
The children of several vaudeville performers team up to put on a show to raise money for their financially impoverished parents. Loosely adapted from the Rodgers and Hart Broadway musical of the same name; features some of their songs as well as new additions. 91m/B/W; VHS, DVD. **C:** Judy Garland; Mickey Rooney; Charles Winninger; Guy Kibbee; June Preisser; Directed by Busby Berkeley; Music by George Bassman; Richard Rodgers; Lyrics by Lorenz Hart. **Pr:** Arthur Freed; MGM. **A:** Family. **P:** Entertainment. **U:** Home. **Mov-Ent**: Musical, Romance, Dance. **Acq:** Purchase. **Dist:** Warner Home Video, Inc. $19.98.
Songs: Babes in Arms; I Cried for You; Good Morning; You Are My Lucky Star; Broadway Rhythm; Where or When; Daddy Was a Minstrel Man; I'm Just Wild About Harry; God's Country.

Babes in the Woods 1917
The story of Hansel and Gretel performed by children. ?m/B/W; Silent; VHS, 8 mm. **A:** Family. **P:** Entertainment. **U:** Home. **Mov-Ent**: Fairy Tales, Children, Family Viewing. **Acq:** Purchase. **Dist:** Glenn Video Vistas Ltd. $35.95.

Babes in Toyland 1961 — ★★
A lavish Disney production of Victor Herbert's timeless operetta, with Toyland being menaced by the evil Barnaby and his Bogeymen. Yes, Annette had a life after Mickey Mouse and before the peanut butter commercials. Somewhat charming, although the roles of the lovers seem a stretch for both Funicello and Kirk. But the flick does sport an amusing turn by Wynn. 105m; VHS, DVD, Blu-Ray. **C:** Annette Funicello; Ray Bolger; Tommy Sands; Ed Wynn; Tommy Kirk; Directed by Jack Donohue; Cinematography by Edward Colman; Music by George Bruns. **Pr:** Walt Disney Productions. **A:** Family. **P:** Entertainment. **U:** Home. **Mov-Ent**: Musical, Toys, Family Viewing. **Acq:** Purchase. **Dist:** Walt Disney Studios Home Entertainment. $14.99.

Babes in Toyland 1986 — ★½
Young girl must save Toyland from the clutches of the evil Barnaby and his monster minions. Bland TV remake of the classic doesn't approach the original. 96m; VHS. **C:** Drew Barrymore; Noriyuki "Pat" Morita; Richard Mulligan; Eileen Brennan; Keanu Reeves; Jill Schoelen; Googy Gress; Directed by Clive Donner; Written by Paul Zindel; Music by Leslie Bricusse. **Pr:** Finnegan-Pinchuk Co; Bavaria Atelier Gmbh. **A:** Family. **P:** Entertainment. **U:** Home. **Mov-Ent**: Musical, Christmas, TV Movies. **Acq:** Purchase. **Dist:** MGM Studios Inc. $9.98.

Babes of Burlesque, Vol. 1 19??
Collection of skimpily clad burlesque dancers. No real nudity; lots of G strings. ?m; VHS. **A:** Sr. High-Adult. **P:** Entertainment. **U:** Home. **Mov-Ent**: Exploitation. **Acq:** Purchase. **Dist:** Sinister Cinema. $16.95.

Babes of Burlesque, Vol. 2 19??
More classic burlesque features from the '30s and '40s. ?m; VHS. **A:** Sr. High-Adult. **P:** Entertainment. **U:** Home. **Mov-Ent**: Exploitation. **Acq:** Purchase. **Dist:** Sinister Cinema. $16.95.

Babes of Burlesque, Vol. 3 19??
More performances from those big, bad, burlesque dancers. ?m; VHS. **A:** Sr. High-Adult. **P:** Entertainment. **U:** Home. **Mov-Ent**: Exploitation. **Acq:** Purchase. **Dist:** Sinister Cinema. $16.95.

Babes of Burlesque, Vol. 4 19??
Features another collection of those hefty burlesque dancers. ?m; VHS. **A:** Sr. High-Adult. **P:** Entertainment. **U:** Home. **Mov-Ent**: Exploitation. **Acq:** Purchase. **Dist:** Sinister Cinema. $16.95.

Babes on Broadway 1941 — ★★½
Mickey and Judy put on a show to raise money for a settlement house. Nearly the best of the Garland-Rooney series, with imaginative numbers staged by Berkeley. 118m/B/W; VHS, DVD. **C:** Mickey Rooney; Judy Garland; Fay Bainter; Richard Quine; Virginia Weidler; Ray Macdonald; Busby Berkeley; Directed by Busby Berkeley; Music by George Bassman. **Pr:** MGM. **A:** Family. **P:** Entertainment. **U:** Home. **Mov-Ent**: Musical, Adoption. **Acq:** Purchase. **Dist:** Warner Home Video, Inc. $19.98.
Songs: Babes on Broadway; Anything Can Happen in New York; How About You?; Hoe Down; Chin Up! Cheerio! Carry On!; Mama Yo Quiero; F.D.R. Jones; Waiting for the Robert E. Lee.

Babette's Feast 1987 — ★★★½
A simple, moving pageant-of-life fable. Philippa (Kjer) and Martina (Federspiel) took over their late father's ministry in a small Danish coastal town. Widowed Frenchwoman Babette (Audran) has spent 14 years in their service and, after winning a lottery prize, decides she will prepare a lavish banquiet in honor of their father's 100th birthday. The religiously conservative villagers don't know what to make of such bounty—or the pleasure it brings to their senses. Adapted from a tale by Isak Dinesen. French and Danish with subtitles. 102m; VHS, DVD, Blu-Ray, Wide. **C:** Stephane Audran; Bibi Andersson; Bodil Kjer; Birgitte Federspiel; Jean-Philippe LaFont; Ebbe Rode; Jarl Kulle; Narrated by Ghita Norby; Directed by Gabriel Axel; Written by Gabriel Axel; Cinematography by Henning Kristiansen; Music by Per Norgard. **Pr:** Panorama Entertainment; Nordisk; Just Betzer. **A:** Family. **P:** Entertainment. **U:** Home. **L:** English, French, Dutch. **Mov-Ent**: Comedy-Drama, Cooking, Food Industry. **Awds:** Oscars '87: Foreign Film; British Acad. '88: Foreign Film. **Acq:** Purchase. **Dist:** MGM Studios Inc. ; Facets Multimedia Inc.; Home Vision Cinema. $19.98.

Babies 2010 (PG) — ★★★
Gets extra bones for the awww factor. Director Balmes chronicles the first year of life for four babies (one boy, three girls) born in Mongolia, Namibia, San Francisco, and Tokyo. There's crying and various bodily functions to deal with; crawling, walking and exploring; and interacting with family and caregivers. There's no narration or subtitles to bother about. 79m; Blu-Ray, On Demand, Wide. **C:** Directed by Thomas Balmes;

Cinematography by Jerome Almeras; Steeven Petitteville; Music by Bruno Coulais. **Pr:** Armandine Billot; Alain Chabat; Christine Rouxel; Canal Plus; Studio Canal; Chez Wam; Focus Features L.L.C. **A:** Family. **P:** Entertainment. **U:** Home. **L:** English. **Mov-Ent:** Documentary Films, Parenting, Africa. **Acq:** Purchase. **Dist:** Movies Unlimited; Alpha Video; Amazon.com Inc.

Babies and Their Parents: An Overview of Our Approach 1977
The focus of this series is on helping the mother to see herself as the infant's most important teacher. These programs were recorded as unstaged and unrehearsed interactions of mothers, infants, and teachers; introduces the High/Scope approach to parent-infant education. 20m/B/W; 3/4 U, EJ. **Pr:** High Scope. **A:** College-Adult. **P:** Education. **U:** Institution, CCTV, CATV, BCTV, SURA. **Gen-Edu:** Infants. **Acq:** Purchase. **Dist:** High/Scope Educational Research Foundation.
Indiv. Titles: 1. Babies Are Active Learners 2. Skills and Stages in Infancy 3. Supporting Early Learning.

Babies Are People Too 1988
Parents have to be sensitive to how they treat their young children because things children experience as youngsters can affect them for the rest of their lives. 27m; VHS, 3/4 U. **Pr:** Churchill Films. **A:** Sr. High-Adult. **P:** Education. **U:** Institution, Home, SURA. **Hea-Sci:** Children, Parenting. **Acq:** Purchase, Rent/Lease, Duplication License. **Dist:** Clear Vue Inc. $395.00.

Babies at Play 1995
Features babies engaging in different activities, from visiting the zoo to splashing around in the rain to playing at a carnival. 39m; VHS. **A:** Preschool. **P:** Entertainment. **U:** Home. **Chl-Juv:** Infants. **Acq:** Purchase. **Dist:** Warner Home Video, Inc. $14.95.
Indiv. Titles: 1. On a Fun, Rainy Day 2. In Their Favorite Places 3. Under a Blue, Blue Sky.

Babies at Risk 1989
A jarring look at the infant mortality tragedy, and how preventative prenatal care can be used to lower the statistics. 60m; VHS, 3/4 U. **Pr:** PBS. **A:** Jr. High-Adult. **P:** Education. **U:** Institution, SURA. **Hea-Sci:** Infants. **Acq:** Purchase, Rent/Lease. **Dist:** Phoenix Learning Group.

Babies: Know More Than You Think 19??
David Chamberlain Ph.D. and Suzanne Arms present scientific research that will change the way you think of babies and the learning process. 60m; VHS. **A:** Sr. High-Adult. **P:** Education. **U:** Home. **Hea-Sci:** Infants, Education. **Acq:** Purchase. **Dist:** Hartley Film Foundation. $29.95.

Babies, Tots & Toddlers 1996
A video of baby faces, this video provides children the opportunity to see other children from different cultural backgrounds they may not be exposed to on a daily basis. 30m; VHS. **A:** Family. **P:** Entertainment. **U:** Home. **L:** English. **Chl-Juv:** Children. **Acq:** Purchase. **Dist:** Tapeworm Video Distributors Inc. $9.95.

Babine 2008 (PG) — ★★½
A woman known as "The Witch" gives birth to a mentally ill child named Babine, who will spend his life being blamed for all of the villages ills. 112m; DVD, Blu-Ray. **C:** Vincent-Guillaume Otis; Luc Picard; Alexis Martin; Isabel Richer; Rene Richard Cyr; Directed by Luc Picard; Written by Fred Pellerin; Cinematography by Jerome Sabourin; Music by Serge Fiori. **A:** Primary-Adult. **P:** Entertainment. **U:** Home. **L:** English, French. **Mov-Ent. Acq:** Purchase. **Dist:** $38.99 18.05.

Baboon 1984
Examines the baboon's lifestyle and compares some of its habits to that of humans, including competitiveness, aggressiveness, sociability, and sexuality. 20m; VHS, SVS, 3/4 U. **Pr:** Peter Chermayeff. **A:** Preschool-Jr. High. **P:** Education. **U:** Institution. **Hea-Sci:** Animals. **Acq:** Purchase. **Dist:** Encyclopedia Britannica. $59.00.

Baboona 1932 (Unrated)
One in the extraordinary series on nature from the Johnsons. This adventure underwent massive and lengthy production. An aerial spectacle of thousands of miles of the African continent. Remarkable. 78m; VHS. **C:** Martin Johnson; Osa Johnson. **Pr:** Fox. **A:** Sr. High-Adult. **P:** Entertainment. **U:** Home. **Mov-Ent:** Documentary Films, Africa. **Acq:** Purchase. **Dist:** Grapevine Video. $16.95.

The Baby 1972 (PG) — ★★
Bizarre story of a social worker who resorts to swinging an ax to cut the apron strings of "baby," a retarded man-child, from his over-protective and insane (bad combination) mother and sisters. Low-budget production looks and feels like a low-budget production, but any movie featuring a grown man wandering about in diapers can't be all bad. 85m; VHS, DVD. **C:** Anjanette Comer; Ruth Roman; Marianna Hill; Suzanne Zenor; David Manzy; Michael Pataki; Erin O'Reilly; Virginia Vincent; Directed by Ted Post; Written by Abe Polsky; Cinematography by Michael D. Margulies; Music by Gerald Fried. **Pr:** Scotia International Films. **A:** Jr. High-Adult. **P:** Entertainment. **U:** Home. **Mov-Ent:** Horror. **Acq:** Purchase. **Dist:** Movies Unlimited; Image Entertainment Inc.

Baby 2000 (Unrated) — ★★
John (Carradine) and Lily (Fawcett) Malone are unsuccessful in coping with their grief over the death of their infant son and in helping their 12-year-old daughter, Larkin (Pill), to deal with her own pain. Then a baby girl is abandoned on the Malone doorstep and Lily immediately wants to keep the child—much to the others' dismay. Formulaic weepie based on the novel by Patricia MacLachlan. 93m; DVD. **C:** Farrah Fawcett; Keith Carradine; Jean Stapleton; Alison Pill; Vincent Berry; Ann

Dowd; Narrated by Glenn Close; Directed by Robert Allan Ackerman; Written by Kerry Kennedy; Patricia MacLachlan; David Manson; Cinematography by Ron Garcia; Music by Jeff Danna. **A:** Jr. High-Adult. **P:** Entertainment. **U:** Home. **Mov-Ent. Acq:** Purchase. **Dist:** WarnerArchive.com.

Baby Alive 1990
Top medical experts join Phylicia Rashad in this comprehensive step-by-step guide for prevention and treatment of life-threatening situations facing children from birth to age five years. 60m; VHS. **C:** Hosted by Phylicia Rashad. **Pr:** Twin Towers Entertainment. **A:** Sr. High-Adult. **P:** Instruction. **U:** Home. **Hea-Sci:** Child Care, Emergencies, Safety Education. **Acq:** Purchase. **Dist:** Karol Media; ACTIVIDEO; Cambridge Educational. $19.98.

The Baby and the Battleship 1956 (Unrated) — ★★½
The old baby out of (on the?) water plot. While on liberty in Italy, a sailor, after a series of complications, becomes custodian of a baby and attempts to hide the tyke aboard his battleship (hence the title). More complications ensue. Some funny moments. Great cast. 96m; VHS. **C:** John Mills; Richard Attenborough; Andre Morell; Bryan Forbes; Lisa Gastoni; Michael Hordern; Lionel Jeffries; Gordon Jackson; John Le Mesurier; Directed by Jay Lewis. **Pr:** British Lion. **A:** Jr. High-Adult. **P:** Entertainment. **U:** Home. **L:** English. **Mov-Ent:** Comedy--Screwball, Boating. **Acq:** Purchase. **Dist:** Movies Unlimited. $19.95.

Baby and Toddler Yoga 2005
Easy-to-follow yoga exercises geared for babies and young children. 143m; DVD. **A:** Preschool. **P:** Instruction. **U:** Home. **Chl-Juv:** Fitness/Exercise, Children, Yoga. **Acq:** Purchase. **Dist:** BFS Video. $19.98.

Baby Animal Fun 19??
Complete six video series featuring baby animals and how they adapt to the world around them as they mature. Children will see the animals' instinctual propensity to play and survive. 45m; VHS. **A:** Primary. **P:** Education. **U:** Institution. **Hea-Sci:** Animals. **Acq:** Purchase. **Dist:** Clear Vue Inc. $120.00.
Indiv. Titles: 1. Babies of the Forest 2. Baby Animal Fun 3. Barnyard Babies 4. Prairie Babies 5. Babies of the Home 6. Babies of the Pond.

Baby Animals 1993
Part of the 14-part First Time Science Series that uses animation to profile how baby animals learn to survive. 9m; VHS. **Pr:** Film Ideas, Inc. **A:** Preschool-Primary. **P:** Education. **U:** Institution. **Chl-Juv:** Science, Animals. **Acq:** Purchase. **Dist:** Film Ideas, Inc. $37.50.

Baby Animals at the Zoo 1993
Children's performer Mark Eskola in a video-enhanced sing-along visit to the zoo. 25m; VHS. **A:** Preschool-Primary. **P:** Entertainment. **U:** Home. **Chl-Juv:** Singing, Music--Children. **Acq:** Purchase. **Dist:** Baker and Taylor. $9.95.
Songs: Baby Animals at the Zoo; Quack-Quack, Waddle, Waddle—A Duck's Tale; Happy Birthday to Me, Happy Birthday to You; Oh, How I Love My Teddy Bear.

Baby Animals Just Want to Have Fun 1987
Features puppies, skunks, baby deer and other small creatures, along with music and dialogue to entertain and educate children. 30m; VHS. **A:** Preschool-Primary. **P:** Entertainment. **U:** Home. **Chl-Juv:** Pets, Pets, Animals. **Acq:** Purchase. **Dist:** Music for Little People. $15.98.

Baby Animals, Mammals & More 1996
A fun-filled video that introduces your child to ponies, puppies, camels, and calves, "Baby Animals, Mammals & More" is filled with music, cute critters, and lots of facts, making it visually exciting, entertaining, and educational. 30m; VHS. **A:** Family. **P:** Entertainment. **U:** Home. **L:** English. **Chl-Juv:** Children. **Acq:** Purchase. **Dist:** Tapeworm Video Distributors Inc. $12.95.

Baby Basics 1987
This video provides instruction, demonstration, and support to new and expectant parents. It is designed to be used during the last months of pregnancy and the first 12 weeks of parenthood. 120m; VHS, 3/4 U. **Pr:** VIDA Health Communications. **A:** Sr. High-Adult. **P:** Instruction. **U:** Institution, Home. **Hea-Sci:** Infants, Child Care, Parenting. **Acq:** Purchase, Rent/Lease, Duplication License. **Dist:** Karol Media; ACTIVIDEO; GPN Educational Media. $39.95.
Indiv. Titles: 1. The Newborn at Birth 2. Post-partum Care for Parents 3. First Days at Home 4. Daily Care 5. Feeding 6. Infant Health and Safety 7. Crying and Sleeping 8. Growth and Development.

Baby Blues 19??
Everything is going great for Kristen and Jason until Kristen is given reason to believe that she may be pregnant. The couple reevaluates their feelings and relationship, and must ask themselves difficult questions concerning their new predicament. 24m; VHS. **A:** Jr. High-Sr. High. **P:** Education. **U:** Institution. **Gen-Edu:** Pregnancy. **Acq:** Purchase, Rent/Lease. **Dist:** National Film Board of Canada. $200.

Baby Bonding: Creative Infant Massage 19??
Touch is the first form of language between child and parent. Massaging a newborn is a valuable way to bond. 53m; VHS. **A:** Family. **P:** Education. **U:** Home, Institution. **How-Ins:** Child Care, Massage. **Acq:** Purchase. **Dist:** School-Tech Inc. $24.95.

Baby Boom 1987 (PG) — ★★½
J.C. Wiatt (Keaton) is a hard-charging exec who becomes the reluctant mother to an orphaned baby girl (a gift from a long-lost relative). She adjusts with great difficulty to motherhood and life outside the rat race and New York City when J.C. decides she must make some radical changes to her routine. A fairly harmless collection of cliches bolstered by Keaton's usual

nervous performance as a power-suited yuppie ad queen saddled with a noncareer-enhancing baby, who moves from manic career woman to jelly-packing Vermont store-owner/mom. Shepherd serves as her new, down-home, doctor beau. To best appreciate flick, see it with a bevy of five- and six-year-olds (a good age for applauding the havoc that a baby creates). 103m; VHS, DVD, Wide, CC. **C:** Diane Keaton; Sam Shepard; Harold Ramis; Sam Wanamaker; James Spader; Pat Hingle; Mary Gross; Victoria Jackson; Paxton Whitehead; Annie Golden; Dori Brenner; Robin Bartlett; Chris Noth; Britt Leach; Directed by Charles Shyer; Written by Charles Shyer; Nancy Meyers; Cinematography by William A. Fraker; Music by Bill Conti. **Pr:** MGM Home Entertainment. **A:** Sr. High-Adult. **P:** Entertainment. **U:** Home. **Mov-Ent:** Comedy--Romantic, Parenting, Veterinary Medicine. **Acq:** Purchase. **Dist:** Facets Multimedia Inc.; MGM Home Entertainment. $14.95.

Baby Booming 1989
The transformations that take place in a pregnant woman's body are displayed. 2m; VHS, 3/4 U. **Pr:** Mary Cybulsky; John Tintori. **A:** Jr. High-Adult. **P:** Education. **U:** Institution, Home, SURA. **Hea-Sci:** Pregnancy. **Acq:** Purchase, Rent/Lease. **Dist:** Pyramid Media. $125.00.

Baby Boy 2001 (R) — ★★½
Singleton's candid look at a culture that fosters and tolerates lack of emotional maturity in young African-American males. Jody (Gibson) is a 20-year-old manchild who still lives with his mother (Johnson), has two children with two different women, no job, and cheats on his current girl, Yvette. Jody's life changes when his mother's boyfriend moves in. Melvin (Rhames), an ex-con who's been down the road Jody is heading, shows no tolerance for his attitude. Real trouble starts when Rodney (Snoop Dogg), a street thug and Yvette's ex, is released from prison and refuses to leave her house. Singleton toys with two endings, but finishes the story with the message that the means to fix the problems he's described are within reach. 129m; VHS, DVD, UMD, Wide, CC. **C:** Tyrese Gibson; Omar Gooding; Taraji P. Henson; Adrienne-Joi (AJ) Johnson; Snoop Dogg; Tamara La Seon Bass; Ving Rhames; Angell Conwell; Directed by John Singleton; Written by John Singleton; Cinematography by Charles Mills; Music by David Arnold. **Pr:** John Singleton; John Singleton; New Deal; Columbia Pictures. **A:** Sr. High-Adult. **P:** Entertainment. **U:** Home. **Mov-Ent:** Black Culture. **Acq:** Purchase. **Dist:** Sony Pictures Home Entertainment Inc.

Baby Broker 1981 (Unrated) — ★½
Dated TV melodrama finds social worker Kate Carlin (Carter) learning that a 14-year-old client has agreed to a private adoption. When the teen tries to change her mind, a greedy lawyer who's arranging the black market baby sales hands the tyke over to paying-but-unfit parents anyway. Naturally Kate's in jeopardy when she starts investigating. 94m; DVD. **C:** Lynda Carter; Harold Gould; Dean Stockwell; Sharon Farrell; Philip Sterling; Lloyd Haynes; Ed Nelson; Donna Wilkes; Directed by Burt Brinckerhoff; Written by Karen Harris; Cinematography by William Cronjager; Music by Johnny Harris. **A:** Jr. High-Adult. **P:** Entertainment. **U:** Home. **Mov-Ent:** Crime Drama. **Acq:** Purchase. **Dist:** Image Entertainment Inc.

A Baby by Caesarean 1983
An animated film about father-aided caesarian surgery. 25m; VHS, 3/4 U, Special order formats. **Pr:** Jane Treiman. **A:** Adult. **P:** Education. **U:** Institution, Home, SURA. **Hea-Sci:** Childbirth. **Acq:** Purchase, Duplication License. **Dist:** Clear Vue Inc.

Baby Clock 1988
This film takes a sensitive look at the lives of five career women who must face the issues as their biological clocks continue to tick. 30m; VHS, 3/4 U. **Pr:** Centre Productions, Inc. **A:** Sr. High-Adult. **P:** Education. **U:** Institution, SURA. **Gen-Edu:** Women. **Acq:** Purchase. **Dist:** Clear Vue Inc.

Baby Comes Home 1986
A program outlining initial infant care, from bonding to breast feeding to educational games. Part of "Parents Video Magazine." 60m; VHS, CC. **Pr:** Arnold Shapiro; Jean O'Neill. **A:** Adult. **P:** Education. **U:** Home. **Gen-Edu:** Infants. **Acq:** Purchase. **Dist:** MGM Studios Inc. $19.95.

The Baby Dance 1998 — ★★★
Well-off, middleaged Hollywood marrieds Rachel (Channing) and Richard (Reigert) Luckman have unsuccessfully tried to have a baby for years. Finally they place an adoption ad and receive a response from poor Louisiana trailer park inhabitants Wanda (Dern) and Art (Lineback) LeFauvre, who have an unwanted fifth child on the way. A meeting between the couples soon points out monetary, religious, and cultural differences that may derail their bargain. The two leading ladies carry the picture, which is based on director Anderson's Off-Broadway play. 95m; VHS, DVD, CC. **C:** Stockard Channing; Laura Dern; Peter Riegert; Richard Lineback; Directed by Jane Anderson; Written by Jane Anderson; Cinematography by Jan Kiesser; Music by Terry Allen. **Pr:** Vicky Herman; Jodie Foster; Robert Halmi, Jr.; Tony Allard; Matthew O'Connor; Egg Pictures; Pacific Motion Pictures; Showtime Networks. **A:** Sr. High-Adult. **P:** Entertainment. **U:** Home. **Mov-Ent:** Pregnancy, Poverty. **Acq:** Purchase. **Dist:** Showtime Networks Inc.

Baby Doll 1956 — ★★★
Suggestive sex at its best, revolving around the love of cotton in Mississippi. Nubile Baker is married to slow-witted Malden, who runs a cotton gin. His torching of Wallach's cotton gin begins a cycle of sexual innuendo and tension, brought to exhilarating life on screen, without a single filmed kiss. Performers and sets ooze during the steamy exhibition, which was considered highly erotic when released. Excellent performances from entire cast, with expert pacing by director Kazan. Screenplay is based on Tennessee Williams' "27 Wagons Full of Cotton." 115m/B/W;

VHS, DVD. **C:** Eli Wallach; Carroll Baker; Karl Malden; Mildred Dunnock; Rip Torn; Directed by Elia Kazan; Written by Tennessee Williams; Cinematography by Boris Kaufman. **Pr:** Warner Bros; Newtown Productions. **A:** Jr. High-Adult. **P:** Entertainment. **U:** Home. **Mov-Ent:** Marriage, Sex & Sexuality. **Awds:** Golden Globes '57: Director (Kazan). **Acq:** Purchase. **Dist:** Facets Multimedia Inc.; Warner Home Video, Inc. $19.98.

The Baby Doll Murders 1992 (R) — ★★
Someone in L.A. is killing beautiful young women and then leaving a broken baby doll at the scene of the crime. The gruesome murderer manages to elude everyone, until Detective Benz discovers a link between the victims and a pattern begins to form. He also discovers that his partner's wife is going to be the next victim unless he can stop this ruthless serial killer from striking again. 90m; VHS, CC. **C:** Jeff Kober; Melanie Smith; John Saxon; Tom (Thomas E.) Hodges; Bobby DiCicco; Directed by Paul Leder; Written by Paul Leder. **A:** Sr. High-Adult. **P:** Entertainment. **U:** Home. **Mov-Ent:** Mystery & Suspense, Sex & Sexuality. **Acq:** Purchase. **Dist:** Lions Gate Entertainment Inc. $89.98.

Baby Dolls 1978
An 18-year-old male talks of his sex change and how he imagines life as a woman in this experimental video. 21m; VHS, 3/4 U. **Pr:** Rodney Werden. **A:** College-Adult. **P:** Entertainment. **U:** Institution, SURA. **Gen-Edu:** Sex & Sexuality, Psychology, Video. **Acq:** Rent/Lease. **Dist:** Video Out Distribution.

Baby Dynamics, Vol. 1 1985
Linda Westin, the co-founder of the Baby Dynamics program demonstrates an exercise regiment that aids in developing young children's motor skills and coordination. 36m; VHS. **Pr:** Sheri Singer. **A:** Family. **P:** Instruction. **U:** Home. **Hea-Sci:** Childbirth, Fitness/Exercise. **Acq:** Purchase. **Dist:** New Line Home Video. $19.95.

Baby Dynamics, Vol. 2 198?
Physical activities for you and your baby, before and after childbirth. 36m; VHS. **A:** Family. **P:** Instruction. **U:** Home. **Hea-Sci:** Fitness/Exercise, Child Care, Infants. **Acq:** Purchase. **Dist:** New Line Home Video. $19.99.

Baby Einstein: Baby Wordsworth—First Words—Around the House 2005
Introduces toddlers to 30 common words, and their sign language equivalent, for familiar objects around the home and yard. 30m; DVD. **A:** Preschool. **P:** Entertainment. **U:** Home. **Chl-Juv:** Animation & Cartoons. **Acq:** Purchase. **Dist:** Buena Vista Home Entertainment.

Baby Eyes 1983
Non-verbal video that suggests the primitive nature of communications as it offers a look at "reality" through the eyes of a newborn baby. 3m; VHS, 3/4 U. **Pr:** Elizabeth Vander Zaag. **A:** Adult. **P:** Education. **U:** Institution. **Gen-Edu:** Childbirth, Pregnancy, Infants. **Acq:** Rent/Lease. **Dist:** Video Out Distribution.

Baby Face 1933 (Unrated) — ★★
A small town girl moves to the city when her father dies. There she gets a job at a bank and sleeps her way to the top of the business world, discarding used men left and right. The Hays Office was extremely upset with the then risque material and forced Warner to trim the first cut. 70m/B/W; VHS, DVD. **C:** Barbara Stanwyck; George Brent; Donald Cook; John Wayne; Henry Kolker; Margaret Lindsay; Douglass Dumbrille; James Murray; Directed by Alfred E. Green; Written by Gene Markey; Kathryn Scola; Cinematography by James Van Trees; Music by Leo F. Forbstein. **Pr:** Warner Bros. **A:** Jr. High-Adult. **P:** Entertainment. **U:** Home. **Mov-Ent:** Melodrama, Sex & Sexuality, Classic Films. **Awds:** Natl. Film Reg. '05. **Acq:** Purchase. **Dist:** Facets Multimedia Inc.; MGM Home Entertainment. $19.98.

Baby Face Morgan 1942 — ★★
Poor comedy about gangsters who attempt to take advantage of the FBI's preoccupation with saboteurs and spies by muscling in on an insurance firm. 60m/B/W; VHS, DVD. **C:** Mary Carlisle; Richard Cromwell; Robert Armstrong; Chick Chandler; Charles (Judel, Judells) Judels; Warren Hymer; Vince Barnett; Ralf Harolde; Directed by Arthur Dreifuss. **Pr:** Jack Schwarz; Producers Releasing Corporation. **A:** Jr. High-Adult. **P:** Entertainment. **U:** Home. **Mov-Ent:** Comedy--Black, Insurance. **Acq:** Purchase. **Dist:** Sinister Cinema. $16.95.

Baby Face Nelson 1997 (R) — ★½
Lame Depression-era gangster flick with George "Baby Face" Nelson (Howell) and his moll Helen Womack (Zane) fighting rival Al Capone (Abraham) in Chicago. Kove comes off well as gangster John Dillinger. 80m; VHS. **C:** C. Thomas Howell; Lisa Zane; F. Murray Abraham; Doug Wert; Martin Kove; Directed by Scott Levy; Written by Joseph Farrugia; Craig J. Nevius; Cinematography by Christopher Baffa; Music by Christopher Lennertz. **Pr:** Concorde Pictures. **A:** Sr. High-Adult. **P:** Entertainment. **U:** Home. **Mov-Ent:** Crime Drama. **Acq:** Purchase. **Dist:** New Horizons Picture Corp.

Baby Faces '96 1996
Contains dozens of baby faces, along with baby laughter, gurgles, and noises. Aimed at captivating the attention of children. 30m; VHS. **A:** Family. **P:** Entertainment. **U:** Home. **Gen-Edu:** Children, Child Care. **Acq:** Purchase. **Dist:** Tapeworm Video Distributors Inc. $12.95.

Baby Farm Animals 199?
Take a trip to the farm to enjoy the baby animals. Children visit the cows, horses, pigs, goats, chickens and more. 30m; VHS. **A:** Preschool-Primary. **P:** Entertainment. **U:** Institution, Home. **Chl-Juv:** Animals. **Acq:** Purchase. **Dist:** Knowledge Unlimited, Inc. $14.95.

Baby Farm: Animals and Friends 1998
Stuffed animals Teddy and Bunny help children discover the world of baby farm animals in their natural setting. 30m; VHS. **A:** Family. **P:** Entertainment. **U:** Home. **Chl-Juv:** Animals, Children. **Acq:** Purchase. **Dist:** Tapeworm Video Distributors Inc. $12.95.

The Baby Formula 2008 (Unrated) — ★½
Sentimental mockumentary with too many caricatures. Thanks to an experimental scientific procedure, married Toronto lesbians Athena (Vint) and Lilith (Fahlenbock) are able to have a baby using the DNA of both women. Now they're both pregnant and have to explain everything to their respective (and dysfunctional) families. Both actresses were actually pregnant during filming, which at least makes the awkward (and sometimes gross) situations very real (and the musical end credits very funny). 82m; DVD. **C:** Megan Fahlenbock; Rosemary Dunsmore; Roger Dunn; Angela Vint; Hal Eisen; Jessica Booker; Michael Hanrahan; Directed by Allison Reid; Brian Harper; Written by Richard Beattie; Music by Robert Carli. **A:** Sr. High-Adult. **P:** Entertainment. **U:** Home. **Mov-Ent:** Pregnancy. **Acq:** Purchase. **Dist:** Wolfe Video.

Baby Geniuses 1998 (PG) — ★½
Steals the most irritating parts of "Look Who's Talking," "Home Alone" and that creepy dancing baby and pastes them onto a lame good kids vs. evil adults plot. Turner and Lloyd are evil scientists attempting to crack the secret language of babies, which they believe holds the secrets of the universe (such as how to enjoy drooling and making in your pants). Standing in their way are nursery school operators Cattrall and MacNichol and an array of babies that spout inane dialogue thanks to an abuse of computer morphing. The effect is more disturbing than cute, and an excellent supporting cast is wasted. More interesting things can be found inside a diaper. 94m; VHS, DVD, CC. **C:** Kathleen Turner; Christopher Lloyd; Kim Cattrall; Peter MacNichol; Dom DeLuise; Ruby Dee; Kyle Howard; Leo Fitzgerald; Myles Fitzgerald; Gerry Fitzgerald; Directed by Bob (Benjamin) Clark; Written by Bob (Benjamin) Clark; Steven Paul; Francisca Matos; Robert Grasmere; Greg Michael; Cinematography by Stephen M. Katz; Music by Paul Zaza. **Pr:** Columbia Pictures. **A:** Family. **P:** Entertainment. **U:** Home. **Mov-Ent. Acq:** Purchase. **Dist:** Sony Pictures Home Entertainment Inc.

Baby Girl Scott 1987 (Unrated) — ★★½
Hurt and Lithgow play the parents of an extremely premature infant who is being kept alive by technology. They make a heartrending decision and then must battle doctors and the system to let their daughter die with dignity. 97m; VHS, Streaming. **C:** John Lithgow; Mary Beth Hurt; Linda Kelsey; Directed by John Korty. **A:** Jr. High-Adult. **P:** Entertainment. **U:** Home. **Mov-Ent:** Parenting, Infants, Death. **Acq:** Purchase. **Dist:** Amazon.com Inc.; Lions Gate Television Corp. $59.98.

A Baby Is Born—Revised 1977
Presents a photographic record of an actual hospital delivery. An epilogue, dealing with methods of birth control is not meant to be shown to elementary grades. 24m; CC, 3/4 U, Special order formats. **Pr:** Mayer and Espar. **A:** Jr. High-Adult. **P:** Education. **U:** Institution, Home, SURA. **L:** English, Spanish. **Hea-Sci:** Childbirth. **Acq:** Purchase, Rent/Lease, Trade-in, Duplication License. **Dist:** United Learning Inc.

Baby It's You 1982 (R) — ★★★
In New Jersey in the '60s, the relationship between a smart, attractive Jewish girl who yearns to be an actress and a street-smart Catholic Italian boy puzzles their family and friends. It all works due to Arquette's strong acting and Sayles' script, which explores adolescent dreams, the transition to adulthood, class differences, and the late 1960s with insight and humor. Interesting period soundtrack (Woolly Bully and, for some reason, Bruce Springsteen) helps propel the film, a commercial job which helped finance Sayles' more independent ventures. 105m; VHS, DVD, CC. **C:** Rosanna Arquette; Vincent Spano; Jack Davidson; Joanna Merlin; Nick Ferrari; Leora Dana; Robert Downey, Jr.; Tracy Pollan; Matthew Modine; Directed by John Sayles; Written by John Sayles; Cinematography by Michael Ballhaus. **Pr:** Griffin Dunne; Amy Robinson; Paramount Pictures. **A:** Sr. High-Adult. **P:** Entertainment. **U:** Home. **Mov-Ent:** Comedy-Drama, Romance, Adolescence. **Acq:** Purchase. **Dist:** Paramount Pictures Corp.; Legend Films. $79.95.

Baby, It's You 1997
Documentary of filmmaker Anne Makepeace and her husband's quest to conceive a child through medical fertility methods. Chronicles the myriad of procedures and tests, a sudden death in the family, and Makepeace's family history. 56m; VHS. **A:** Adult. **P:** Education. **U:** Home. **Gen-Edu:** Documentary Films, Women, Pregnancy. **Acq:** Purchase, Rent/Lease. **Dist:** Filmakers Library Inc. $295.

Baby Laurence: Jazz Hoofer 1981
Jazz dancer Baby Laurence is seen here in his only filmed appearance, with dancing segments and interviews. 28m; VHS. **C:** Directed by Bill Hancock. **Pr:** Bill Hancock. **A:** Sr. High-Adult. **P:** Entertainment. **U:** Home. **Mov-Ent:** Music--Jazz, Dance, Interviews. **Acq:** Purchase. **Dist:** Music Video Distributors; Rhapsody Films, Inc.; Facets Multimedia Inc. $19.95.

Baby Lock: Function & Fashion 1989
A representative from the Tacony Corporation shows how to use their sewing machine. 33m; VHS. **C:** Nancy Mix. **Pr:** Nancy's Notions Ltd. **A:** Jr. High-Adult. **P:** Instruction. **U:** Institution, Home. **How-Ins:** Sewing. **Acq:** Rent/Lease. **Dist:** Nancy's Notions Ltd.

Baby Lock Key Plate Knitter 1989
Learning to use a knitting machine is made easy with this tape. 36m; VHS. **C:** Nancy Mix. **Pr:** Nancy's Notions Ltd. **A:** Jr. High-Adult. **P:** Instruction. **U:** Institution, Home. **How-Ins:** Crafts, Sewing. **Acq:** Rent/Lease. **Dist:** Nancy's Notions Ltd.

Baby Looney Tunes—Eggs-Traordinary Adventure 2002
Includes episodes of the animated television cartoon with Looney Tunes members Taz, Sylvester, Lola, Bugs, Daffy, Tweety, and Petunia as babies who live with Granny; also includes "Flower Power" and "The Magic of Spring." 3 episodes. 80m; DVD. **A:** Preschool-Primary. **P:** Entertainment. **U:** Home. **Chl-Juv:** Television Series, Children's Shows, Animation & Cartoons. **Acq:** Purchase. **Dist:** Warner Home Video, Inc. $14.96.

Baby Looney Tunes—Volume 1: Playday Pals 2002
Includes episodes of the animated television cartoon with Looney Tunes members Taz, Sylvester, Lola, Bugs, Daffy, Tweety, and Petunia as babies who live with Granny: "Taz in Toyland," "A Secret Tweet," "Comfort Level," and "Like a Duck to Water." 4 episodes. 48m; DVD. **A:** Preschool-Primary. **P:** Entertainment. **U:** Home. **Chl-Juv:** Television Series, Children's Shows, Animation & Cartoons. **Acq:** Purchase. **Dist:** Warner Home Video, Inc. $14.97.

Baby Looney Tunes—Volume 2: Let's Play Pretend 2002
Includes episodes of the animated television cartoon with Looney Tunes members Taz, Sylvester, Lola, Bugs, Daffy, Tweety, and Petunia as babies who live with Granny: "School Daze," "Things That Go Bump in the Night," "The Creature from the Chocolate Chip," and "Card Board Box." 4 episodes. 48m; DVD. **A:** Preschool-Primary. **P:** Entertainment. **U:** Home. **Chl-Juv:** Television Series, Children's Shows, Animation & Cartoons. **Acq:** Purchase. **Dist:** Warner Home Video, Inc. $14.97.

Baby Looney Tunes—Volume 3: Puddle Olympics 2002
Includes episodes of the animated television cartoon with Looney Tunes members Taz, Sylvester, Lola, Bugs, Daffy, Tweety, and Petunia as babies who live with Granny; with "Time and Time Again," "May the Best Taz Win," "Mine!" "Sylvester the Pester," "Cat-taz-trophy," "Duck! Monster! Duck!" "The Brave Little Tweety," and "The Puddle Olympics." 8 episodes. 88m. **A:** Preschool-Primary. **P:** Entertainment. **Chl-Juv:** Television Series, Children's Shows, Animation & Cartoons. **Acq:** Purchase. **Dist:** Warner Home Video, Inc. $14.97.

Baby Looney Tunes—Volume 4: Tooth Fairy Tales 2002
Includes episodes of the animated television cartoon with Looney Tunes members Taz, Sylvester, Lola, Bugs, Daffy, Tweety, and Petunia as babies who live with Granny: with "A Lot Like Lola," "Takers Keepers," "Spinout," and "Shadow of a Doubt," 8 episodes. 88m; DVD. **A:** Preschool-Primary. **P:** Entertainment. **U:** Home. **Chl-Juv:** Television Series, Children's Shows, Animation & Cartoons. **Acq:** Purchase. **Dist:** Warner Home Video, Inc. $14.97.

Baby Love 1969 (R) — **Bomb!**
A softcore fluff-fest about a trollop seducing a doctor's family. The doctor may or may not be her father. Hayden tantalizes the doctor, the doctor's son, and the doctor's wife, as well as the neighbors, leaving only those in adjoining communities untouched. Based on the novel by Tina Chad Christian. 98m; VHS. **C:** Ann Lynn; Keith Barron; Linda Hayden; Derek Lamden; Diana Dors; Patience Collier; Directed by Alastair Reid. **Pr:** Avco Embassy. **A:** Family. **P:** Entertainment. **U:** Home. **Mov-Ent:** Comedy--Black, Sex & Sexuality, Family. **Acq:** Purchase. **Dist:** New Line Home Video. $59.95.

Baby Love 1983 (Unrated) — **Bomb!**
Nerds get revenge against the freshmen who run the local frat house. 80m; VHS. **C:** Dolly Dollar; Bea Fiedler; Jesse Katzur; Yftach Katzur; Dvora Kedar; Renate Langer; Zachi Noy; Jonathan Sagalle; Directed by Dan Wolman; Cinematography by Ilan Rosenberg. **Pr:** Noah Films Ltd. **A:** Sr. High-Adult. **P:** Entertainment. **U:** Home. **Mov-Ent. Acq:** Purchase. **Dist:** MGM Home Entertainment. $59.95.

Baby Love 1998
Uses interviews with girls from diverse social, racial and economic backgrounds to take a look at how teenage mothers see things—from love, sex and virginity to pregnancy and the reality of single motherhood. 57m; VHS. **A:** Jr. High-Adult. **P:** Education. **U:** Home. **Gen-Edu:** Documentary Films, Child Care, Pregnancy. **Acq:** Purchase. **Dist:** Direct Cinema Ltd. $24.95.

The Baby Maker 1970 (R) — ★★
A couple who cannot have children because the wife is sterile decides to hire a woman to have a child for them. However, the relationship between the husband and the surrogate progresses beyond what either of them wanted. Hershey stars as the free-love surrogate mama (just before she underwent the supreme 60s transformation into Barbara Seagull) and Bridges makes his directorial debut. Flick is interesting as a combo critique/exploitation of those wild and groovy 1960s. 109m; VHS, DVD. **C:** Barbara Hershey; Collin Wilcox-Paxton; Sam Groom; Scott Glenn; Jeannie Berlin; Directed by James Bridges; Written by James Bridges. **Pr:** National General Pictures. **A:** College-Adult. **P:** Entertainment. **U:** Home. **Mov-Ent:** Marriage, Pregnancy, Sex & Sexuality. **Acq:** Purchase. **Dist:** WarnerArchive.com. $59.95.

Baby Mama 2008 (PG-13) — ★★½
Predictable mom com starring Fey and Poehler, who got comfortable doing skits together on SNL. Single, 37-year-old

workaholic Kate Holbrook (Fey) determines she now has the time and resources to have a baby, but dang if her biological clock hasn't stopped ticking. So Kate goes the surrogacy route and chooses an unlikely candidate—South Philly good-time gal Angie (Poehler), who's unwilling to follow Kate's precise pregnancy plans when the duo wind up as roommates. Naturally, over the course of nine months and lots of preggo jokes, they bond. The leads sell the weak material and are backed up by such pros as Weaver, Kinnear, and Martin. 99m; DVD, Blu-Ray, Wide. **C:** Tina Fey; Amy Poehler; Greg Kinnear; Dax Shepard; Romany Malco; Holland Taylor; Sigourney Weaver; Maura Tierney; Steve Martin; Siobhan Fallon Hogan; Directed by Michael McCullers; Written by Michael McCullers; Cinematography by Daryn Okada; Music by Jeff Richmond. **Pr:** Lorne Michaels; John Goldwyn; Relativity Media; Universal. **A:** Jr. High-Adult. **P:** Entertainment. **U:** Home. **L:** English. **Mov-Ent:** Pregnancy. **Acq:** Purchase. **Dist:** Movies Unlimited; Alpha Video; Universal Studios Home Video.

Baby Massage 1998
Instructs how to give a complete massage to your baby. 65m; VHS. **A:** Adult. **P:** Instruction. **U:** Home. **Hea-Sci:** Infants. **Acq:** Purchase. **Dist:** 411 Video Information. $29.95.

Baby Massage and Exercise 1989
Provides step-by-step instructions for parents to massage and exercise their ba bies. 30m; VHS. **A:** Sr. High-Adult. **P:** Instruction. **U:** Home. **Hea-Sci:** Child Care, Infants, Massage. **Acq:** Purchase. **Dist:** ACTIVIDEO. $19.95.

A Baby Maybe? 1983
Follows the lives of two couples in their 30s who are trying to decide whether to have children. 29m; VHS, 3/4 U. **Pr:** KUHT-TV; PBS. **A:** Adult. **P:** Education. **U:** Institution, CCTV, Home, SURA. **Gen-Edu:** Children, Family, Parenting. **Acq:** Purchase, Rent/Lease, Duplication, Off-Air Record. **Dist:** PBS Home Video. $59.95.

Baby Monitor: Sound of Fear 1997 (R) — ★★½
Matt (Beghe) makes the mistake of falling in love with nanny Ann (Bissett), which makes his wife Carol (Tyson) go psychotic. She overhears everyhing thanks to that darn baby monitor and decides to have Ann killed in a botched kidnapping attempt. But Ann discovers the evil goings-on (because of the baby monitor, natch) and works to save the good guys. 91m; VHS, CC. **C:** Josie Bissett; Jason Beghe; Barbara Tyson; Jeffrey Noah; Vincent Gale; Gerard Plunkett; Directed by John L. Roman; Written by Edgar van Cossart. **Pr:** John L. Roman; Universal Television. **A:** Sr. High-Adult. **P:** Entertainment. **U:** Home. **Mov-Ent:** Mystery & Suspense, TV Movies. **Acq:** Purchase.

Baby of the Bride 1991 — ★★½
Follow-up to "Children of the Bride," has McClanahan settling into wedded bliss with younger husband Shackleford when she discovers she's pregnant. Not only is she unsure about wanting to be a mom again at her age but then grown—and single—daughter McNichol announces she is also pregnant. The sheer silliness of this TV fare makes it fun to watch. 93m; VHS, DVD, CC. **C:** Rue McClanahan; Ted Shackleford; Kristy McNichol; John Wesley Shipp; Anne Bobby; Conor O'Farrell; Directed by Bill Bixby; Written by Bart Baker. **Pr:** Cyrus Yavneh; Leonard Hill; Bart Baker. **A:** Jr. High-Adult. **P:** Entertainment. **U:** Home. **Mov-Ent:** Pregnancy, TV Movies. **Acq:** Purchase. **Dist:** Turner Broadcasting System Inc. $89.98.

Baby on Board 1992 (PG) — ★★
Kane plays the wife of a Mafia bookkeeper who is accidentally killed in a gangland murder. Out for revenge, she tracks her husband's killer to JFK airport with her four-year-old daughter in tow. Just as she pulls the loaded gun from her purse and takes aim, a pickpocket snatches her purse, accidentally firing the gun. Now she's on the run and she jumps into the first cab she can find, driven by Reinhold. New York City is turned upside down as mother, daughter, and cabbie try to elude the mob in this funny but predictable comedy. 90m; VHS, CC. **C:** Carol Kane; Judge Reinhold; Geza Kovacs; Errol Slue; Alex Stapley; Holly Stapley; Directed by Francis Schaeffer. **Pr:** Damian Lee. **A:** Jr. High-Adult. **P:** Entertainment. **U:** Home. **Mov-Ent:** Action-Adventure. **Acq:** Purchase. **Dist:** Unknown Distributor.

Baby on Board 2008 (R) — ★
Witless pregnancy comedy. Chicago ad exec Angela (Graham), half of a power couple along with dopey husband Curtis (O'Donnell), is confounded by her unexpected pregnancy, which she feels will derail her career. Angela goes all hormonal and you won't really care what happens over the next nine months. 94m; DVD. **C:** Heather Graham; Jerry O'Connell; Lara Flynn Boyle; John Corbett; Kate Finneran; Anthony Starke; Directed by Brian Herzlinger; Written by Russell Sealise; Cinematography by Denis Maloney; Music by Teddy Castellucci. **A:** Sr. High-Adult. **P:** Entertainment. **U:** Home. **Mov-Ent:** Marriage, Pregnancy. **Acq:** Purchase. **Dist:** Entertainment One US LP.

Baby Phases Quiz 1991
Helps parents and expectant parents address the most often asked questions about childcare, including the lastest childcare techniques and advances in child health care. 60m; VHS, 3/4 U. **A:** Adult. **P:** Education. **U:** Institution, CCTV. **Gen-Edu:** Parenting. **Acq:** Purchase, Rent/Lease. **Dist:** Maryland Public Television. $29.95.

Baby Pig Management Techniques 1981
Follows the piglet from birth through the first 24 hours. Includes farrowing techniques and post-partum pointers. 21m; VHS. **A:** College-Adult. **P:** Education. **U:** Institution. **Gen-Edu:** Agriculture, Animals. **Acq:** Purchase. **Dist:** Purdue University. $15.00.

Baby Play 1995
Incorporates "play" into the daily routine of any caretaker. 30m; VHS. **A:** Family. **P:** Instruction. **U:** Home. **Gen-Edu:** Parenting, Family. **Acq:** Purchase. **Dist:** Paragon Home Video. $19.95.

Baby Praise 1997
Presents babies and toddlers in a music-video format, including such songs as "Everything Is Beautiful" and "Jesus Loves the Little Children." 30m; VHS. **A:** Preschool. **P:** Entertainment. **U:** Home. **Chl-Juv:** Children, Music--Children. **Acq:** Purchase. **Dist:** Tapeworm Video Distributors Inc. $9.95.

Baby Proofer 1995
Points out potential household hazards that could be fatal to a child's safety. 30m; VHS. **A:** Family. **P:** Instruction. **U:** Home. **Gen-Edu:** Parenting, Safety Education. **Acq:** Purchase. **Dist:** Paragon Home Video. $14.95.

Baby Rabbit 1971
Three central city children raise a family of rabbits. Rabbits, boy, girl, and baby brother all need food, sleep, and a warm house in order to live and grow. For use in creative expression. 11m; VHS, 3/4 U, Special order formats. **Pr:** Churchill. **A:** Primary. **P:** Education. **U:** Institution, Home, SURA. **Chl-Juv:** Language Arts. **Acq:** Purchase, Duplication License. **Dist:** Clear Vue Inc.

Baby Rattlesnake 1993
Based on the Chickasaw teaching tale originally told by storyteller Te Ata. Centers on family love and forgiveness as a baby rattlesnake begs for his rattle before he is old enough to have it. Includes parental guides and activities. 20m; VHS. **Pr:** Film Ideas, Inc. **A:** Primary. **P:** Education. **U:** Institution, Home. **L:** English, Spanish. **Chl-Juv:** Native Americans, Folklore & Legends. **Acq:** Purchase. **Dist:** Film Ideas, Inc. $150.00.

The Baby Safe Home 1985
Hazard areas, and possible killing zones found in the average home are examined. Learn the basic life-saving principles that will make your dwelling safe for baby. 60m; VHS. **C:** Hosted by David Horowitz. **A:** Adult. **P:** Instruction. **U:** Home. **How-Ins:** Safety Education, Infants. **Acq:** Purchase. **Dist:** New Line Home Video; Cambridge Educational. $19.95.

Baby. . . Secret of the Lost Legend 1985 (PG) — ★★
A sportswriter and his paleontologist wife risk their lives to reunite a hatching brontosaurus with its mother in the African jungle. Although this Disney film is not lewd in any sense, beware of several scenes displaying frontal nudity and some violence. 95m; VHS, DVD, Blu-Ray. **C:** William Katt; Sean Young; Patrick McGoohan; Julian Fellowes; Directed by Bill W.L. Norton. **Pr:** Buena Vista; Touchstone Pictures. **A:** Family. **P:** Entertainment. **U:** Home. **Mov-Ent:** Fantasy, Dinosaurs. **Acq:** Purchase. **Dist:** Walt Disney Studios Home Entertainment. $79.95.

Baby See, Baby Do 1998
Contains images and sounds intended to delight infants and their caregivers. ?m; VHS. **A:** Preschool. **P:** Entertainment. **U:** Home. **Hea-Sci:** Infants. **Acq:** Purchase. **Dist:** 411 Video Information. $14.95.

Baby Shakespeare 1999
Teaches classic poetry rhythm, structure and common words in classic poetry to children ages 1 to 4 years. Hosted by Bard, the word-loving dragon, and featuring puppets, music and poems. 30m; VHS. **A:** Preschool. **P:** Education. **U:** Home. **Chl-Juv:** Children, Parenting, Education. **Acq:** Purchase. **Dist:** Instructional Video. $19.95.

The Baby-Sitters' Club 1995 (PG) — ★★½
Centering on the summer vacation of seven enterprising Connecticut 13-year-olds and their teen trials with parents, boys, and babysitting, this film is sure to hit home with a crowd that is rarely featured, pre-teen girls. Director Mayron claims, "It's the 'Mystic Pizza' of their age." Young girls and girls young at heart should enjoy this touching look at the fragile years of our youth, leaving baby dolls behind and heading towards dating. Based on the best-selling book series by Ann Martin. Fisk, who plays club leader Kristy, is the daughter of actress Sissy Spacek and director Jack Fisk. 92m; VHS, DVD, CC. **C:** Schuyler Fisk; Bre Blair; Rachael Leigh Cook; Larisa Oleynik; Tricia Joe; Stacey Linn Ramsower; Zelda Harris; Brooke Adams; Peter Horton; Bruce Davison; Ellen Burstyn; Austin O'Brien; Aaron Michael Metchik; Directed by Melanie Mayron; Written by Dalene Young; Cinematography by Willy Kurant; Music by David Michael Frank. **Pr:** Jane Startz; Peter O. Almond; Armyan Bernstein; Marc Abraham; Martin Keltz; Beacon Films; Scholastic Productions, Inc; Columbia Pictures. **A:** Primary-Adult. **P:** Entertainment. **U:** Home. **Mov-Ent:** Comedy-Drama, Adolescence. **Acq:** Purchase. **Dist:** Sony Pictures Home Entertainment Inc.

The Baby-Sitters' Club: Baby-Sitters and the Boy Sitters 1993
The baby-sitters have more business than they can handle, but when they train boys to help them out, they all experience different standards from their employers based on gender expectations. 30m; VHS, CC. **A:** Primary-Jr. High. **P:** Entertainment. **U:** Home. **Chl-Juv:** Adolescence. **Acq:** Purchase. **Dist:** Baker and Taylor. $14.95.

The Baby-Sitters' Club: Claudia and the Mystery of the Secret Passage 1993
When Claudia finds a mysterious letter in the attic's "secret passage," she and the other girls do research, including a seance, to discover what happened to the author. 30m; VHS, CC. **A:** Primary-Jr. High. **P:** Entertainment. **U:** Home. **Chl-Juv:** Adolescence, Occult Sciences, Mystery & Suspense. **Acq:** Purchase. **Dist:** Baker and Taylor. $14.95.

The Baby-Sitters' Club: Dawn Saves the Trees 1993
Dawn becomes politically active in an effort to save the trees, and wins herself the respect of the boy in whom she's interested. 30m; VHS, CC. **A:** Primary-Jr. High. **P:** Entertainment. **U:** Home. **Chl-Juv:** Adolescence, Ecology & Environment. **Acq:** Purchase. **Dist:** Baker and Taylor. $14.95.

The Baby-Sitters' Club: Jessi and the Mystery of the Stolen Secrets 1993
Club secrets are leaked and the girls try to find the culprit but their detective work only makes things worse. 30m; VHS. **A:** Family. **P:** Entertainment. **U:** Home. **Chl-Juv:** Children. **Acq:** Purchase. **Dist:** Baker and Taylor. $14.95.

The Baby-Sitters' Club Special Christmas 1991
Dawn, Stacey, Claudia, Kristy, Mary Anne, and Malory learn some valuable lessons about the true spirit of giving and friendship. 30m; VHS. **C:** Melissa Chase; Jessica Prunell; Avriel Hillman; Meghan Lahey; Nicole Leach; Megan Andrews. **Pr:** Scholastic. **A:** Family. **P:** Entertainment. **U:** Home. **Chl-Juv:** Adolescence, Christmas. **Acq:** Purchase. **Dist:** Baker and Taylor. $12.95.

The Baby-Sitters' Club: Stacey Takes a Stand 1993
Stacey's tired of living with her mom in Stoneybrook and visiting her Dad in New York City. Her friends try to help her cope. 30m; VHS, CC. **A:** Family. **P:** Entertainment. **U:** Home. **Chl-Juv:** Children. **Acq:** Purchase. **Dist:** Baker and Taylor. $14.95.

The Baby-Sitters' Club: The Baby-Sitters Remember 1993
The Baby-Sitters celebrate their friendship by reliving their favorite and funniest moments together. 30m; VHS. **A:** Family. **P:** Entertainment. **U:** Home. **Chl-Juv:** Children. **Acq:** Purchase. **Dist:** Baker and Taylor. $14.95.

Baby-Sitting Basics 1988
Find out the proper way to handle baby-sitting emergencies. 45m; VHS, 3/4 U. **Pr:** Marshfilm. **A:** Primary-Sr. High. **P:** Education. **U:** Institution. **Gen-Edu:** Emergencies, Children. **Acq:** Purchase. **Dist:** Marshmedia. $45.50.

Baby-Sitting: Taking the Basics to Work 1988
Dramatic reenactments show what proper baby-sitting procedures are. 45m; VHS, 3/4 U. **Pr:** Marshfilm. **A:** Primary-Sr. High. **P:** Instruction. **U:** Institution. **Gen-Edu:** Children, Infants. **Acq:** Purchase. **Dist:** Marshmedia. $45.50.

Baby-Sitting the Responsible Way 19??
Covers issues in responsible babysitting, including handling emergencies, keeping children on schedule, mealtime, handling behavior problems, and accident avoidance. Outlines behaviors to avoid such as talking extensively on the phone, failing to clean-up, and doing homework. Includes manual. 30m; VHS. **Pr:** Cambridge Career Productions. **A:** Jr. High-Adult. **P:** Instruction. **U:** Home, Institution. **How-Ins:** How-To. **Acq:** Purchase. **Dist:** Cambridge Educational. $49.00.

Baby Snakes: The Complete Version 1979
Concert footage of Zappa is interspersed with clay animation by Bruce Bickford. 166m; VHS. **C:** Frank Zappa; Directed by Frank Zappa. **Pr:** Frank Zappa; Frank Zappa. **A:** Sr. High-Adult. **P:** Entertainment. **U:** Home. **Mov-Ent:** Music--Performance, Animation & Cartoons. **Acq:** Purchase. **Dist:** Music Video Distributors. $79.95.

Baby Songs 1987
A series of music videos designed for toddlers; songs including "My Mommy Comes Back," "Sittin' in a High Chair" and "Shout & Whisper." 30m; VHS. **C:** Music by Hap Palmer. **Pr:** Hi-Tops Video. **A:** Preschool. **P:** Entertainment. **U:** Home. **Chl-Juv:** Music--Children. **Acq:** Purchase. **Dist:** Music for Little People. $16.98.

Baby Songs ABC, 123, Colors and Shapes 1999
Host Hap Palmer helps young viewers learn through the use of song. This volume helps children learn counting, ABCs, colors and shapes. 32m; VHS. **A:** Family. **P:** Education. **U:** Home. **Chl-Juv:** Children, Music--Children. **Acq:** Purchase. **Dist:** Anchor Bay Entertainment. $12.98.

Baby Songs Animals 2000
Host Hap Palmer helps young viewers learn through the use of song. This volume helps children learn such concepts as big and little, fast and slow and others through the exciting world of animals. 30m; VHS. **A:** Family. **P:** Education. **U:** Home. **Chl-Juv:** Children, Music--Children. **Acq:** Purchase. **Dist:** Anchor Bay Entertainment. $12.98.

Baby Songs Baby's Busy Day 1999
Host Hap Palmer helps young viewers learn through the use of song. This volume helps children learn about waking up, getting dressed and other topics. 32m; VHS. **A:** Family. **P:** Education. **U:** Home. **Chl-Juv:** Children, Music--Children. **Acq:** Purchase. **Dist:** Anchor Bay Entertainment. $12.98.

Baby Songs Christmas 1991
A charming array of holiday songs for infants. 23m; VHS. **Pr:** Hi-Tops Video. **A:** Family. **P:** Entertainment. **U:** Home. **Chl-Juv:** Music--Children, Christmas. **Acq:** Purchase. **Dist:** Golden Book Video. $12.95.

Baby Songs: Follow Along Songs 19??
Children are introduced to colors, the alphabet and musical instruments all through the use of music. ?m; VHS. **A:** Preschool-Primary. **P:** Entertainment. **U:** Home. **Chl-Juv:** Animation & Cartoons. **Acq:** Purchase. **Dist:** Golden Book Video. $12.95.

Baby Songs Presents: Follow Along Songs with Hap Palmer 1991
Palmer sings songs aimed to get children to act out the lyrics. Selections include "The Mice Go Marching," "Parade of Sticks," "Homemade Band" and others. 30m; VHS. **Pr:** Hi-Tops Video. **A:** Preschool. **P:** Entertainment. **U:** Home. **Chl-Juv**: Music--Children. **Acq:** Purchase. **Dist:** Golden Book Video. $14.95.

Baby Songs Presents: John Lithgow's Kid-Size Concert 1990
Delightful fun aimed at very young children. Songs include, "I Can Put My Clothes on By Myself," "Getting Up Time," and "What a Miracle I Am." Easy to follow songbook included. 32m; VHS. **C:** John Lithgow. **Pr:** Hi-Tops Video. **A:** Family. **P:** Entertainment. **U:** Home. **Chl-Juv**: Music--Children. **Acq:** Purchase. **Dist:** Anchor Bay Entertainment. $14.98.

Baby Songs Rock & Roll 2000
Host Hap Palmer helps young viewers learn through the use of song. This volume helps children learn to relate the lyrics of classic rock and roll songs to everyday aspects of their lives. 30m; VHS. **A:** Family. **P:** Education. **U:** Home. **Chl-Juv**: Children, Music--Children. **Acq:** Purchase. **Dist:** Anchor Bay Entertainment. $12.98.

Baby Songs: Sing Together 1992
Nine sing-along songs for the wee set. 25m; VHS. **A:** Preschool-Primary. **P:** Entertainment. **U:** Home. **Chl-Juv**: Music--Children. **Acq:** Purchase. **Dist:** Golden Book Video. $12.95.

Baby Songs: Turn on the Music 1989
In addition to the usual song-fest, this edition of Baby Songs features a claymation segment. 30m; VHS. **Pr:** Hi-Tops Video. **A:** Family. **P:** Entertainment. **U:** Home. **Chl-Juv**: Children, Singing. **Acq:** Purchase. **Dist:** Anchor Bay Entertainment. $14.98.

Baby Steps: Monitor Your Baby's Physical Development 199?
Parents learn to monitor their child's physical development and motor skills during baby's first year. ?m; VHS. **A:** Adult. **P:** Education. **U:** Home, Institution. **Gen-Edu**: Infants, Child Care. **Acq:** Purchase. **Dist:** Baker and Taylor. $19.98.

Baby, Take a Bow 1934 (PG) — ★★
Temple's first starring role. As a cheerful Pollyanna-type she helps her father, falsely accused of theft, by finding the true thief. 76m/B/W; VHS, DVD, CC. **C:** Shirley Temple; James Dunn; Claire Trevor; Alan Dinehart; Directed by Harry Lachman. **Pr:** 20th Century-Fox. **A:** Family. **P:** Entertainment. **U:** Home. **Mov-Ent**: Comedy-Drama. **Acq:** Purchase. **Dist:** Movies Unlimited.

Baby Talk 1992
Jean Smart hosts this program which answers the questions that confront new parents with practical information. Divided into ten segments including "Looking at Your Newborn," "Basic Baby Care," "Diapering," "Breast Feeding," "Bottle Feeding," "Sleep and Awake Patterns," "Personality and Development," "Crying and Colic," "Illness and Doctor Visits," and "Taking Care of Yourself." 56m; VHS. **A:** Sr. High-Adult. **P:** Education. **U:** Home. **Hea-Sci**: Parenting, Child Care, Infants. **Acq:** Purchase. **Dist:** Polymorph Films, Inc. $24.95.

Baby Talk: Videoguide for New Parents 1995
Describes all aspects of infant care in ten chapters. Comes with guidebook. 60m; VHS. **A:** Adult. **P:** Education. **U:** Home. **Gen-Edu**: Health Education, Infants, Parenting. **Acq:** Purchase. **Dist:** Cambridge Educational; Injoy Productions. $29.95.

The Baby Test 1984
Parents are told what to expect from their child at different stages of his life. 22m; VHS, 3/4 U. **Pr:** Professional Research. **A:** Sr. High-Adult. **P:** Education. **U:** Institution, CCTV, SURA. **Hea-Sci**: Infants. **Acq:** Purchase, Rent/Lease. **Dist:** Discovery Education. $295.00.

Baby, the Rain Must Fall 1964 — ★★
A rockabilly singer, paroled from prison after serving time for a knifing, returns home to his wife and daughter, but his outbursts of violence make the reunion difficult. Unsentimental with realistic performances, but script is weak (although written by Foote, based on his play, "The Traveling Lady"). Theme song was a Top 40 hit. 100m/B/W; VHS, DVD. **C:** Steve McQueen; Lee Remick; Don Murray; Directed by Robert Mulligan; Written by Horton Foote; Cinematography by Ernest Laszlo; Music by Elmer Bernstein. **Pr:** Alan J. Pakula; Columbia Pictures. **A:** Jr. High-Adult. **P:** Entertainment. **U:** Home. **Mov-Ent**: Family. **Acq:** Purchase. **Dist:** Sony Pictures Home Entertainment Inc.; Movies Unlimited. $9.95.

Baby Time 1996
This fun-filled collection of baby close-ups provides fascinating and entertaining video of infants and toddlers smiling and gurgling and just looking cute. The video is for kids of all ages and is sure to entertain you and your child. 30m; VHS. **A:** Family. **P:** Entertainment. **U:** Home. **L:** English. **Chl-Juv**: Children. **Acq:** Purchase. **Dist:** Tapeworm Video Distributors Inc. $14.95.

The Baby Video Library 1995
Offers an extensive overview of infant care for first-time parents. 288m; VHS. **A:** Family. **P:** Instruction. **U:** Institution, Home. **Gen-Edu**: Health Education, Infants, Pregnancy. **Acq:** Purchase. **Dist:** Cambridge Educational. $299.00.
Indiv. Titles: 1. Pregnancy, 1st Trimester 2. Pregnancy, 2nd Trimester 3. Pregnancy, 3rd Trimester 4. Pregnancy, 38 Weeks & Labor 5. Birth Using Anesthesia 6. Birth, Prepared Childbirth & C-Section 7. The Newborn Baby 8. Childhood, 2 Month Old 9. Childhood, 4 Month Old 10. Childhood, 6 Month Old 11. Childhood, 9 to 15 Month Old 12. Childhood, 15 to 18 Month Old.

Baby Vision, Vol. 1 1989
Video recommended for children aged 9 to 36 months. Features simple but stimulating pictures, narration and music. Volume one contains toys and animals. From New Zealand. 45m; VHS. **C:** Directed by Barron Christian. **A:** Preschool. **P:** Entertainment. **U:** Home. **Chl-Juv**: Children, Graphics. **Acq:** Purchase. **Dist:** j2 Global; Production Associates. $14.95.

Baby Vision, Vol. 2 1989
Beautiful production from New Zealand for children aged 9 to 36 months. Simple graphics of motion, plants and liquid set to simple narration and music. 45m; VHS. **C:** Directed by Barron Christian. **A:** Preschool. **P:** Entertainment. **U:** Home. **Chl-Juv**: Children, Graphics. **Acq:** Purchase. **Dist:** j2 Global. $14.95.

Babycakes 1989 — ★★½
A marshmellow romance between an overweight mortuary attendant who decides to follow her heart when she falls for a hunky ice skater. Can she make him appreciate her inner beauty instead of just her not-the-normal-beauty-standard outward appearance? (Happy ending guaranteed.) TV remake of the darker German film "Sugarbaby." 94m; VHS, DVD, CC. **C:** Ricki Lake; Craig Sheffer; Paul Benedict; Betty Buckley; John Karlen; Nada Despotovich; Directed by Paul Schneider; Written by Joyce Eliason; Cinematography by Tony Imi; Music by William Olvis. **A:** Jr. High-Adult. **P:** Entertainment. **U:** Home. **Mov-Ent**: Comedy--Romantic, TV Movies. **Acq:** Purchase. **Dist:** Turner Broadcasting System Inc. $89.98.

Babyface: Tender Lover 1989
Pop music singer Babyface sings three of his songs including "It's No Crime," "Tender Love," and "Whip Appeal." 16m; VHS. **Pr:** CBS. **A:** Jr. High-Adult. **P:** Entertainment. **U:** Home. **Mov-Ent**: Music Video, Music--Performance. **Acq:** Purchase. **Dist:** Music Video Distributors; Sony Music Entertainment Inc. $12.98.

Babyface: The Cool Collection 1994
Features clips from the album "For the Cool In You," as well as an interview with the writer/singer. 30m; VHS. **A:** Jr. High-Adult. **P:** Entertainment. **U:** Home. **Mov-Ent**: Music Video. **Acq:** Purchase. **Dist:** Sony Music Entertainment Inc.; Music Video Distributors. $14.98.
Songs: When Can I See You; Never Keeping Secrets; For the Cool In You; And Our Feelings; Rock Bottom.

Babyfever 1994 (R) — ★★½
Women gather at a baby shower and tell stories about motherhood and related topics. May be viewed as a babblefest with video accompaniment or as an overdue cinematic exploration of a fairly important aspect of life (where would we be without mom?). That said, pace of the comedy drama is less than feverish, although director Jaglom captures the essence of the stories without disturbing their flow. Foyt, Jaglom's wife and co-screenwriter, makes her acting debut. 110m; VHS, DVD. **C:** Matt Salinger; Eric Roberts; Frances Fisher; Victoria Foyt; Zack Norman; Dinah Lenney; Elaine Kagan; Directed by Henry Jaglom; Written by Victoria Foyt; Henry Jaglom; Cinematography by Hanania Baer. **Pr:** Judith Wolinsky; Jagtoria Productions; Rainbow Film Company. **A:** Sr. High-Adult. **P:** Entertainment. **U:** Home. **Mov-Ent**: Documentary Films, Women, Storytelling. **Acq:** Purchase. **Dist:** Wellspring Media.

Babylon A.D. 2008 (PG-13) — ★
See if this sounds familiar: War-torn, post-apocalyptic, bleak future finds mercenary loner who is forced into a seemingly impossible trans-global mission where he is accosted by bad guys every step of the way. Thought so. In this version, Diesel plays Toorop , the brooding ex-pat who must transport Aurora (Thierry), a young woman with a potentially lethal secret, from Russia to New York by whatever means necessary, including a snowmobile! Someone forgot to tell French co-writer/director Kassovitz that Diesel cannot carry a movie, even with a decent French cast and a few visually interesting sets. Kassovitz disowned it in the end, calling it "stupid." Who are we to disagree? 90m; Blu-Ray, Wide. **C:** Vin Diesel; Melanie Thierry; Gerard Depardieu; Charlotte Rampling; Mark Strong; Lambert Wilson; Michelle Yeoh; Jerome Le Banner; Directed by Mathieu Kassovitz; Written by Mathieu Kassovitz; Eric Besnard; Cinematography by Thierry Arbogast; Music by Atli Orvarsson. **Pr:** Ilan Goldman; StudioCanal; M6 Films; 20th Century-Fox. **A:** Jr. High-Adult. **P:** Entertainment. **U:** Home. **L:** English. **Mov-Ent**: Science Fiction, Pregnancy. **Acq:** Purchase. **Dist:** Movies Unlimited; Alpha Video; Fox Home Entertainment.

Babylon 5: Lost Tales 2007
Compiles scenes that piece together the storyline of the 1994-1998 science fiction television series set aboard a futuristic space station that is used as a neutral area for the various alien races to work out differences under President Sheridan (Boxleitner). 1 episode. 72m; DVD. **C:** Jerry Doyle; Mira Furlan; Richard Biggs; Bruce Boxleitner; Claudia Christian; Peter Jurasik; Andreas Katsulas. **A:** Jr. High-Adult. **P:** Entertainment. **U:** Home. **Mov-Ent**: Television Series, Science Fiction, Space Exploration. **Acq:** Purchase. **Dist:** Warner Home Video, Inc. $24.98.

Babylon 5: Movie Collection 2004
Presents episodes from the 1994-1998 science fiction television series set aboard a futuristic space station that is used as a neutral area for the various alien races to work out differences under President Sheridan (Boxleitner). Includes "The Gathering," "In The Beginning," "Thirdspace," "River of Souls," and "A Call to Arms." 5 episodes. 469m; DVD. **C:** Jerry Doyle; Mira Furlan; Richard Biggs; Bruce Boxleitner; Claudia Christian; Peter Jurasik; Andreas Katsulas. **A:** Jr. High-Adult. **P:** Entertainment. **U:** Home. **Mov-Ent**: Television Series, Science Fiction, Space Exploration. **Acq:** Purchase. **Dist:** Warner Home Video, Inc. $59.98.

Babylon 5: The Complete Fifth Season 1998
Presents the final season of the 1994-1998 science fiction television series set aboard a futuristic space station that is used as a neutral area for the various alien races to work out differences under President Sheridan (Boxleitner). Includes Sheridan works for peace in the Interstellar Alliance and the aging ship meets its ultimate fate—as does Sheridan. 22 episodes. 968m; DVD. **C:** Jerry Doyle; Mira Furlan; Richard Biggs; Bruce Boxleitner; Claudia Christian; Peter Jurasik; Andreas Katsulas. **A:** Jr. High-Adult. **P:** Entertainment. **U:** Home. **Mov-Ent**: Television Series, Science Fiction, Space Exploration. **Acq:** Purchase. **Dist:** Warner Home Video, Inc. $99.98.

Babylon 5: The Complete First Season 1994
Presents the debut season of the 1994-1998 science fiction television series set aboard a futuristic space station that is used as a neutral area for the various alien races to work out differences under Commander Sinclair (O'Hare). Includes the pilot in which an assassination attempt is made on the Vorlon ambassador, a "Soul Hunter" threatens the ship's occupants, two men abduct Sinclair (O'Hare), and the ship is in danger of exploding due to an Earthforce heavy cruiser. 22 episodes. 990m; DVD. **C:** Michael O'Hare; Jerry Doyle; Mira Furlan; Richard Biggs; Bruce Boxleitner; Claudia Christian; Peter Jurasik; Andreas Katsulas. **A:** Jr. High-Adult. **P:** Entertainment. **U:** Home. **Mov-Ent**: Television Series, Science Fiction, Space Exploration. **Acq:** Purchase. **Dist:** Warner Home Video, Inc. $99.98.

Babylon 5: The Complete Fourth Season 1996
Presents the fourth season of the 1994-1998 science fiction television series set aboard a futuristic space station that is used as a neutral area for the various alien races to work out differences under President Sheridan (Boxleitner). An explosion on Z'ha'dum appears to have killed Sheridan, as the Vorlons continue their deadly spree Sheridan feels he must kill one who is on the ship, after President Clark kills 10,000 innocent refugees Sheridan gears up for war, the civil war comes to an end, and a future is shown with video footage being archived of the Earth and Interstellar Alliance. 22 episodes. 966m; DVD. **C:** Jerry Doyle; Mira Furlan; Richard Biggs; Bruce Boxleitner; Claudia Christian; Peter Jurasik; Andreas Katsulas. **A:** Jr. High-Adult. **P:** Entertainment. **U:** Home. **Mov-Ent**: Television Series, Science Fiction, Space Exploration. **Acq:** Purchase. **Dist:** Warner Home Video, Inc. $99.98.

Babylon 5: The Complete Second Season 1994
Presents the second season of the 1994-1998 science fiction television series set aboard a futuristic space station that is used as a neutral area for the various alien races to work out differences under President Sheridan (Boxleitner), who replaces Commander Sinclair (O'Hare). The ship is overloaded with 25,000 Earthforce soldiers and the Minbari Lavell attacks Sheridan who kills him in self-defense though a Manbari says otherwise. 22 episodes. 960m; DVD. **C:** Jerry Doyle; Mira Furlan; Richard Biggs; Bruce Boxleitner; Claudia Christian; Peter Jurasik; Andreas Katsulas; Michael O'Hare. **A:** Jr. High-Adult. **P:** Entertainment. **U:** Home. **Mov-Ent**: Television Series, Science Fiction, Space Exploration. **Acq:** Purchase. **Dist:** Warner Home Video, Inc. $99.98.

Babylon 5: The Complete Third Season 1995
Presents the third season of the 1994-1998 science fiction television series set aboard a futuristic space station that is used as a neutral area for the various alien races to work out differences under President Sheridan (Boxleitner). Includes a three-parter: President Clark's attack forces Sheridan to withdraw from the Earth Alliance. 22 episodes. 968m; DVD. **C:** Jerry Doyle; Mira Furlan; Richard Biggs; Bruce Boxleitner; Claudia Christian; Peter Jurasik; Andreas Katsulas. **A:** Jr. High-Adult. **P:** Entertainment. **U:** Home. **Mov-Ent**: Television Series, Science Fiction, Space Exploration. **Acq:** Purchase. **Dist:** Warner Home Video, Inc. $99.98.

Babylon 5: The Gathering 1994
Presents the pilot episode ("The Gathering") of the 1994-1998 science fiction television series set aboard a futuristic space station that is used as a neutral area for the various alien races to work out differences under President Sheridan (Boxleitner). 1 episode. ?m; DVD. **C:** Jerry Doyle; Mira Furlan; Richard Biggs; Bruce Boxleitner; Claudia Christian; Peter Jurasik; Andreas Katsulas. **A:** Jr. High-Adult. **P:** Entertainment. **U:** Home. **Mov-Ent**: Television Series, Science Fiction, Space Exploration. **Acq:** Purchase. **Dist:** Warner Home Video, Inc. $99.98.

Babylon 5: The Legend of the Rangers 2002
Presents a special movie based on the 1994-1998 science fiction television series set aboard a futuristic space station that is used as a neutral area for the various alien races to work out differences under President Sheridan (Boxleitner). Set in a postwar 2264, the Interstellar Alliance and Earth encounter use a group of human and aliens known as the Rangers to combat a lethal alien race. 1 episode. 90m; DVD. **C:** Jerry Doyle; Mira Furlan; Richard Biggs; Bruce Boxleitner; Claudia Christian; Peter Jurasik; Andreas Katsulas. **A:** Jr. High-Adult. **P:** Entertainment. **U:** Home. **Mov-Ent**: Television Series, Science Fiction, Space Exploration. **Acq:** Purchase. **Dist:** Warner Home Video, Inc. $19.99.

Babylon 5, Vol. 1.1: The Gathering 1993
Pilot episode of the series finds Cdr. Jeffrey Sinclair (O'Hare) commanding the new Earth-Minbari space station Babylon 5. The station is awaiting the arrival of the fifth Ruling Council ambassador but only Minbari Delenn (Furlan) seems eager for

the last member to arrive. Maybe because serious trouble follows in his wake. 93m; VHS. **C:** Michael O'Hare; Jerry Doyle; Mira Furlan; Andreas Katsulas; Peter Jurasik; Tamlyn Tomita; Patricia Tallman; Directed by Richard Compton; Written by J. Michael Straczynski; Music by Stewart Copeland. **A:** Jr. High-Adult. **P:** Entertainment. **U:** Home. **Mov-Ent**: Science Fiction. **Acq:** Purchase. **Dist:** Warner Home Video, Inc.

Babylon 5, Vol. 1.2: Midnight on the Firing Line/ Soul Hunter 1994
In "Midnight on the Firing Line," Mollari is shocked when the Centauri colony on Ragesh 3, which his young cousin commands, is attacked and new commercial telepath Talia Winters is having difficulties with Lt. Cdt. Ivanova. An unidentified alien winds up in the station's med lab in "Soul Hunter." Turns out the creature captures the souls of the dying and Delenn is determined to kill him. 89m; VHS. **C:** Michael O'Hare; Claudia Christian; Mira Furlan; Andrea Thompson; Jerry Doyle; Richard Biggs; William Morgan Sheppard; Directed by Richard Compton; Jim Johnston; Written by J. Michael Straczynski. **A:** Jr. High-Adult. **P:** Entertainment. **U:** Home. **Mov-Ent**: Science Fiction. **Acq:** Purchase.

Babylon 5, Vol. 1.3: Born to the Purple/ Infection 1994
Londo is distracted by pretty dancer Adira Tyree, who turns out to be a blackmailing spy and Garibaldi has a security breach to deal with in "Born t the Purple." In "Infection," Dr. Franklin is delighted when his mentor, Vance Hendricks, comes aboard to study artifiacts gathered from a long-dead race. Only the artifacts seem to have a deadly power. 89m; VHS. **C:** Jerry Doyle; Michael O'Hare; Claudia Christian; Peter Jurasik; Andreas Katsulas; Fabiana Udenio; Richard Biggs; David McCallum; Directed by Richard Compton; Bruce Seth Green; Written by J. Michael Straczynski; Lawrence G. DiTillio. **A:** Jr. High-Adult. **P:** Entertainment. **U:** Home. **Mov-Ent**: Science Fiction. **Acq:** Purchase. **Dist:** Warner Home Video, Inc.

Babylon 5, Vol. 5.1: In the Beginning 1998
A prequel storyline shown as a 5th season TV series movie. In 2245, 40 years before Babylon 5 was established, Earth leaders talk to Mollari about a mysterious race called the Minbari. Mollari preaches caution but the military begins a move into Minbari space. Unfortunately, Minbari leadership takes this the wrong way and begins a war with Earth. 93m; VHS. **C:** Bruce Boxleitner; Mira Furlan; Peter Jurasik; Andreas Katsulas; Richard Biggs; Claudia Christian; Theodore Bikel; Reiner Schone; Directed by Michael Vejar; Written by J. Michael Straczynski. **A:** Jr. High-Adult. **P:** Entertainment. **U:** Home. **Mov-Ent**: Science Fiction. **Acq:** Purchase. **Dist:** Warner Home Video, Inc.

The Babymakers 2012 (R) — ★
Difficulty with getting his wife (Munn) pregnant forces Tommy (Schneider) to try and break into a sperm bank where the man believes his deposit from years ago may still contain a few good swimmers. A heist film set in a sperm bank is a recipe for bodily fluid disaster and leads Schneider and Munn are miscast in this misguided affair. But you can't really blame them. There are a few laughs here and there but the script's focus on gross-out humor is mostly shooting blanks. 93m; DVD, Blu-Ray. **C:** Paul Schneider; Olivia Munn; Kevin Heffernan; Wood Harris; Nat Faxon; Aisha Tyler; Collette Wolfe; Hayes Macarthur; Jay Chandrasekhar; Directed by Jay Chandrasekhar; Written by Peter Gaulke; Gerry Swallow; Cinematography by Frank DeMarco; Music by Ed Shearmur. **Pr:** Jason Blum; Jay Chandrasekhar; Millennium Entertainment L.L.C; Blumhouse Productions. **A:** Sr. High-Adult. **P:** Entertainment. **U:** Home. **L:** English. **Mov-Ent**: Comedy--Black, Parenting, Infants. **Acq:** Purchase. **Dist:** Millennium Entertainment L.L.C.

BabyMugs! 1994
Taps into infants' fascination with other baby's faces and expressions and provides an alternative method of entertaining the little tykes. 30m; VHS. **Pr:** Three Friends Production. **A:** Preschool. **P:** Entertainment. **U:** Home. **Chl-Juv**: Infants. **Acq:** Purchase. **Dist:** Tapeworm Video Distributors Inc. $19.95.

BabyPro: Let's Dance & Tumble 2005
Introduces young children to sports fundamentals. DVD. **A:** Preschool. **P:** Entertainment. **U:** Home. **Chl-Juv**: Children, Sports--General. **Acq:** Purchase. **Dist:** Consumer Vision. $12.98.

Baby's Day Out 1994 (PG) — ★★½
Poor man's "Home Alone" refits tired Hughes formula using little tiny baby for original spin. Adorable Baby Bink crawls his way onto the city streets, much to his frantic mother's dismay, and unwittingly outsmarts his would-be kidnappers. As in "HA I and II," the bad guys fall victim to all sorts of cataclysmic Looney Tunes violence. Small kids will get a kick out of this one. Particular problem for the moviemakers was that the nine-month old Worton twins were past the year mark by the end of the shoot, a world of difference in infantdom. Blue screens and out-of-sequence shooting were used to overcome the developmental gap. 99m; VHS, DVD, Wide, CC. **C:** Adam Worton; Jacob Worton; Joe Mantegna; Lara Flynn Boyle; Joe Pantoliano; Fred Dalton Thompson; John Neville; Brian Haley; Matthew Glave; Directed by Patrick Read Johnson; Written by John Hughes; Cinematography by Thomas Ackerman; Music by Bruce Broughton. **Pr:** John Hughes; Richard Vane; William S. Beasley; Bill Ryan; John Hughes; Hughes Entertainment; Fox. **A:** Family. **P:** Entertainment. **U:** Home. **Mov-Ent**: Comedy--Slapstick, Family Viewing. **Acq:** Purchase. **Dist:** Fox Home Entertainment. $14.98.

Baby's First Impressions Vol. 1: Shapes 1996
A video produced to help identify four shapes to nurture your child's early learning skills, "Shapes" utilizes strong, bold colors to assist in the development patterns. Soft and inspiring voices are added to help capture your child's interest. 30m; VHS. **A:** Family. **P:** Education. **U:** Home. **L:** English. **Chl-Juv**: Children. **Acq:** Purchase. **Dist:** Tapeworm Video Distributors Inc. $29.95.

Baby's First Impressions Vol. 2: Colors 1996
Utilizing all of the colors of the rainbow, this video advances your child's early learning skills. It teaches color association with everyday objects and also uses black and white patterns to assist in increasing cognitive abilities. 30m; VHS. **A:** Family. **P:** Education. **U:** Home. **L:** English. **Chl-Juv**: Children. **Acq:** Purchase. **Dist:** Tapeworm Video Distributors Inc. $29.95.

Baby's First Impressions Vol. 3: Letters 1996
"Letters"enhances your child's natural desire to learn in this adventure through ABC's. The video will cultivate your child's early learning skills by associating letters with objects. 30m; VHS. **A:** Family. **P:** Education. **U:** Home. **L:** English. **Chl-Juv**: Children. **Acq:** Purchase. **Dist:** Tapeworm Video Distributors Inc. $29.95.

Baby's First Impressions Vol. 4: Numbers 1997
Helps children 8 months to 5 years learn to count from 1-20 and do basic addition and substraction. 32m; VHS. **A:** Preschool. **P:** Education. **U:** Home. **Gen-Edu**: Infants, Children. **Acq:** Purchase. **Dist:** Small Fry Productions. $14.95.

Baby's First Impressions Vol. 5: Opposites 1997
Helps children 8 months to 5 years learn the differences between hot/cold, left/right, up/down, and more. 32m; VHS. **A:** Preschool. **P:** Education. **U:** Home. **Gen-Edu**: Infants, Children. **Acq:** Purchase. **Dist:** Small Fry Productions. $14.95.

Baby's First Impressions Vol. 6: Animals 1997
Helps children 8 months to 5 years learn about animals from all over the world. 32m; VHS. **A:** Preschool. **P:** Education. **U:** Home. **Gen-Edu**: Infants, Children, Animals. **Acq:** Purchase. **Dist:** Small Fry Productions. $14.95.

Baby's First Impressions Vol. 7: Sounds 1998
Created for viewers aged eight months to five years old, these productions feature colorful images and subjects that cater to a young child's desire to learn. Designed to stimulate and enhance a child's early learning experience. This volume features material designed to sharpen a child's listening skills as they play guessing games and distinguish sounds. 30m; VHS. **A:** Family. **P:** Education. **U:** Home. **Gen-Edu**: Children, Infants, Education. **Acq:** Purchase. **Dist:** Small Fry Productions. $14.95.

Baby's First Impressions Vol. 8: Seasons 1998
Created for viewers aged eight months to five years old, these productions feature colorful images and subjects that cater to a young child's desire to learn. Designed to stimulate and enhance a child's early learning experience. This volume explores the wonder of the four seasons, featuring holidays associated with each time of year. 30m; VHS. **A:** Family. **P:** Education. **U:** Home. **Gen-Edu**: Children, Infants, Education. **Acq:** Purchase. **Dist:** Small Fry Productions. $14.95.

Baby's First Impressions Vol. 9: Head to Toe 1998
Created for viewers aged eight months to five years old, these productions feature colorful images and subjects that cater to a young child's desire to learn. Designed to stimulate and enhance a child's early learning experience. This volume helps children learn about their own bodies and identify body parts while encouraging interactive play. 30m; VHS. **A:** Family. **P:** Education. **U:** Home. **Gen-Edu**: Children, Infants, Education. **Acq:** Purchase. **Dist:** Small Fry Productions. $14.95.

Baby's First Impressions Vol. 10: Food Fun 1998
Created for viewers aged eight months to five years old, these productions feature colorful images and subjects that cater to a young child's desire to learn. Designed to stimulate and enhance a child's early learning experience. This volume teaches the difference between fruits and vegetables as well as manners and nutrition. 30m; VHS. **A:** Family. **P:** Education. **U:** Home. **Gen-Edu**: Children, Infants, Education. **Acq:** Purchase. **Dist:** Small Fry Productions. $14.95.

Baby's First Touch: Step-by-Step Training for Infant Massage 1993
Licensed massage therapist Diane Moore demonstrates 10 to 30 minute massages for babies. Includes captioned screens and close-up shots to highlight the technique. 30m; VHS. **A:** Adult. **P:** Instruction. **U:** Home. **How-Ins**: How-To, Massage, Infants. **Acq:** Purchase. **Dist:** Instructional Video. $29.95.

Baby's First Workout: The Gerard Method 1989
This video offers a systematic program for motor skills development in a child's first year. Furthermore, the video shows parents the way to monitor their children's physical development through creative play. A special chart for recording the child's progress is included. 42m; VHS. **Pr:** HPG Home Video. **A:** Family. **P:** Education. **U:** Home. **Hea-Sci**: Fitness/Exercise, Infants. **Acq:** Purchase. **Dist:** Karol Media.

A Baby's World 1994
Three-volume series takes a look at the transformation of babies from helpless infants to a toddler's first experiences with reasoning out their behavior. Available as a boxed set or individually. ?m; VHS. **A:** College-Adult. **P:** Education. **U:** Home. **Gen-Edu**: Documentary Films, Infants. **Acq:** Purchase. **Dist:** Discovery Home Entertainment. $39.95.
Indiv. Titles: 1. A Whole New World 2. The Language of Being 3. Reason and Relationships.

The Babysitter 1980 (Unrated) — ★★
A family hires the mysterious but ingratiating Johanna (Zimbalist) as live-in help without checking on her references (who'd all checked out). The babysitter is the answer to all their problems—Mom's an alcoholic, Dad's a workaholic, and their daughter's just plain maladjusted—but once Johanna's gained their trust (or, in Dad's case, lust), she sets out to manipulate and exploit the family for her own psychotic purposes. Houseman plays the nosy neighbor who's on to her evil plan. Fair made-for-TV treatment of a common suspense plot. 96m; VHS. **C:** William Shatner; Patty Duke; Stephanie Zimbalist; Quinn Cummings; John Houseman; David Wallace; Directed by Peter Medak. **Pr:** Moonlight Productions. **A:** Sr. High-Adult. **P:** Entertainment. **U:** Home. **Mov-Ent**: Mystery & Suspense, TV Movies. **Acq:** Purchase. **Dist:** Unknown Distributor.

The Babysitter 1995 (R) — ★★½
All-American teen Jennifer (Silverstone) becomes the unexpected object of desire for family man Harry (Walsh), whose wife Dolly (Garlington) is fantasizing about having an affair with a neighbor (Segal). But then Jennifer's boyfriend (London) gets caught up in a malicious prank that turns bad for everyone involved. Based on a short story by Robert Coover. 90m; VHS, DVD, CC. **C:** Alicia Silverstone; Jeremy London; J.T. Walsh; Lee Garlington; Nicky Katt; Lois Chiles; George Segal; Directed by Guy Ferland; Written by Guy Ferland; Music by Loek Dikker. **A:** Sr. High-Adult. **P:** Entertainment. **U:** Home. **Mov-Ent**: Mystery & Suspense. **Acq:** Purchase. **Dist:** Lions Gate Entertainment Inc. $14.98.

The Babysitter Series 1980
This series is designed to teach babysitters how to deal with any possible emergency that may arise whilst they are caring for the tots. 12m; VHS, 8 mm, 3/4 U. **TV Std:** NTSC, PAL, SECAM. **Pr:** Film Communicators. **A:** Jr. High-Adult. **P:** Education. **U:** Institution, CCTV, SURA. **Gen-Edu**: Children. **Acq:** Purchase, Rent/Lease, Duplication License. **Dist:** Phoenix Learning Group. $210.00.
Indiv. Titles: 1. Handling Babysitting Emergencies 2. Planning Babysitting 3. Understanding Babysitting.

Babysitter Wanted 2008 (R) — ★½
A young college girl travels to a lonely farm for a babysitting job and quickly discovers why the other co-eds became strippers or waitresses instead of babysitters: because farmers with children are evil, evil people. 90m; DVD, Blu-Ray. **C:** Matt Dallas; Tina Houtz; Sarah Thompson; Nana Visitor; Jillian Schmitz; Directed by Jonas Barnes; Michael Manasseri; Written by Jonas Barnes; Cinematography by Alex Vendler; Music by Kurt Oldman. **A:** Sr. High-Adult. **P:** Entertainment. **U:** Home. **L:** English. **Mov-Ent. Acq:** Purchase. **Dist:** Big Screen Entertainment Group. $29.99 24.95.

The Babysitters 1985
A survey of the responsibilities and requirements of babysitters, and how they must face certain emergency problems. 24m; VHS, 3/4 U. **Pr:** BFA Educational Media; Phoenix Films. **A:** Jr. High-Adult. **P:** Education. **U:** Institution, SURA. **Gen-Edu**: Children. **Acq:** Purchase. **Dist:** Phoenix Learning Group.

The Babysitters 2007 (R) — ★½
Married men in midlife crises turn to teen girls for sex. Babysitter Shirley (Waterston) is having an affair with married dad Mike (Leguizamo), who tips her very generously. Mike tells pal Jerry (Comeau) while Shirley tells friend Melissa (Birkell), who's willing to oblige Jerry with special services. Soon Shirley is recruiting a couple of other gals into her little sex ring and things start to get dicey before director Ross completely loses control of his sexcapade. 90m; DVD. **C:** John Leguizamo; Andy Comeau; Denis O'Hare; Cynthia Nixon; Ethan Phillips; Katherine Waterston; Lauren Birkell; Louisa Krause; Halley Wegryn; Jason Dubin; Directed by David Ross; Written by David Ross; Cinematography by Michael McDonough; Music by Chad Fischer. **A:** Sr. High-Adult. **P:** Entertainment. **U:** Home. **Mov-Ent**: Prostitution. **Acq:** Purchase. **Dist:** Phase 4/kaBOOM Entertainment.

Babysitters Beware 2008 (PG) — ★★½
Seven-year-old Danny Parker is tired of being left with even the nicest babysitter while his parents go out to their endless business dinners. His friend Marco tells him if he's terrible enough, Danny will get on the 'no-sit list' and his folks will have to stay home. Then the Parkers hire former prison guard Clyde and the battle of wills is on. 70m; DVD. **C:** Trenton Rogers; Danny Trejo; Rico Rodriguez; Kate Orsini; Chris Cleveland; Brittany Renee Finamore; Luis Anthony; Dee Wallace; Taylor Negron; Directed by Douglas Horn; Written by Douglas Horn; Cinematography by Milton Santiago; Music by Nathan Lanier. **A:** Family. **P:** Entertainment. **U:** Home. **Mov-Ent. Acq:** Purchase. **Dist:** Peace Arch Entertainment Group.

Babysitting 1976
The importance of a babysitter's ability to act quickly in an emergency is stressed. 27m; VHS, 3/4 U. **Pr:** National Safety Council. **A:** College-Adult. **P:** Education. **U:** Institution. **Gen-Edu**: Occupations, Emergencies. **Acq:** Rent/Lease. **Dist:** National Safety Council, California Chapter, Film Library.

Babysitting ABCs 19??
A video produced to enlighten teens interested in starting their own babysitting service, "Babysitting ABC's" provides information on good child care skills, organization, and some basics on running your own business. 20m; VHS. **A:** Sr. High. **P:** Education. **U:** Institution. **L:** English. **Gen-Edu**: Child Care. **Acq:** Purchase. **Dist:** Meridian Education Corp. $95.

Babysitting the Responsible Way 1988
Babysitting is not a game. Learn how to cope with any problem or emergency that comes along. 30m; VHS, 3/4 U. **Pr:** Cambridge Video. **A:** Jr. High-Adult. **P:** Education. **U:** Institution, Home. **Gen-Edu**: Children, Child Care, Emergencies. **Acq:** Purchase. **Dist:** Cambridge Educational. $49.00.

Babysitting: Training for Emergencies 1988
A primer for sitters on how to handle emergencies as they may arise. 90m; VHS. **Pr:** Cambridge Career Productions. **A:** Jr. High-Adult. **P:** Education. **U:** Institution, Home. **Gen-Edu**: Children, Emergencies. **Acq:** Purchase. **Dist:** Cambridge Educational. $189.00.

Babyswim 1979
A program about babies swimming in oceans and pools with the aid of their mothers. "Babyswim" shows how much fun the water can be at any age. 13m; VHS, 3/4 U. **Pr:** John Hoskyns. **A:** Preschool-Adult. **P:** Education. **U:** Institution, Home, SURA. **Spo-Rec**: Sports--Water, Infants. **Acq:** Purchase, Duplication License. **Dist:** Bullfrog Films, Inc.

BabyVision 1995
A kaleidoscope of colors, shapes, and images of baby animals and flowers meant to stimulate babies and toddlers. 45m; VHS. **A:** Preschool. **P:** Entertainment. **U:** Home. **Chl-Juv**: Children, Child Care. **Acq:** Purchase. **Dist:** Victory Multimedia; j2 Global. $19.95.

Bacall on Bogart 19??
Lauren Bacall discusses the career of her husband, Humphrey Bogart. Includes vintage clips from some of Bogie's best films. 87m/B/W; VHS. **C:** Narrated by Lauren Bacall. **A:** Family. **P:** Education. **U:** Home. **Gen-Edu**: Performing Arts, Biography. **Acq:** Purchase. **Dist:** Instructional Video. $59.98.

Baccarat 1989
The basic rules and strategies of the game are shown, using actual sequences of play at the table. 60m; VHS. **Pr:** John Patrick Productions. **A:** College-Adult. **P:** Instruction. **U:** Home. **Spo-Rec**: Gambling. **Acq:** Purchase. **Dist:** John Patrick Entertainment, Inc. $39.95.

The Bacchantes 1963 — ★★
Poorly dubbed account of a ballerina, her life and loves. Based on the play by Euripides. 100m/B/W; VHS. **C:** Taina Elg; Pierre Brice; Alessandra Panaro; Alberto Lupo; Akim Tamiroff; Directed by Giorgio Ferroni. **A:** Sr. High-Adult. **P:** Entertainment. **U:** Home. **Mov-Ent**: Theater, Dance, Dance--Ballet. **Acq:** Purchase. **Dist:** Facets Multimedia Inc. $39.95.

Bach: All That Bach—A Celebration 1985
A diverse musical tribute to Johann Sebastian Bach, taped on the occasion of his tercentenary at the Canadian Bach 300 Festival. In HiFi Stereo. 50m; VHS. **C:** Maureen Forrester; Keith Jarrett. **Pr:** Canadian Broadcasting Corp. **A:** Jr. High-Adult. **P:** Entertainment. **U:** Home. **Fin-Art**: Music--Performance, Music--Classical. **Acq:** Purchase. **Dist:** Music Video Distributors; Video Artists International. $39.95.

Bach & Broccoli 1987
When a little orphan girl living with her bachelor uncle is placed in a foster home, the previously preoccupied uncle tries to get her back. 96m; VHS. **C:** Mahee Paiement; Directed by Andre Melancon. **Pr:** Rock Demers. **A:** Preschool-Primary. **P:** Entertainment. **U:** Home. **Chl-Juv**: Family, Canada. **Acq:** Purchase. **Dist:** Lions Gate Television Corp.; Facets Multimedia Inc. $14.98.

Bach: Brandenburg Concerto #6 19?? (Unrated)
The music of Bach is played at the Huberman Festival in Israel. ?m; VHS. **A:** Sr. High-Adult. **P:** Entertainment. **U:** Home. **Mov-Ent**: Music--Classical. **Acq:** Purchase. **Dist:** Music Video Distributors. $14.95.

Bach: Concert at Barbicon 19?? (Unrated)
Performed by the English Chamber Orchestra, this video features A-Minor concerto for violin, Partita, two cantatas and more. 86m; VHS. **A:** Sr. High-Adult. **P:** Entertainment. **U:** Home. **Mov-Ent**: Music--Classical. **Acq:** Purchase. **Dist:** Music Video Distributors. $29.95.

Bach in Auschwitz 2000
Tells the story of the "Auschwitz Orchestra," over 40 female musicians brought to the concentration camp by the Nazi SS after 1943, and their survival through music. 105m; VHS. **A:** Jr. High-Adult. **P:** Education. **U:** Home. **Gen-Edu**: World War Two, Music--Classical, Holocaust. **Acq:** Purchase. **Dist:** Wellspring Media. $19.98.

Bach: Magnificat 1984
The Berlin Philharmonic Orchestra, the RIAS Chamber choir, and various soloists perform selections from Bach. 60m; VHS. **A:** Jr. High-Adult. **P:** Entertainment. **U:** Home. **Mov-Ent**: Music Video, Music--Classical. **Acq:** Purchase. **Dist:** Music Video Distributors. $24.98.

Bach: Organ Works 19??
Various churches and monasteries in Germany form the backdrop for Wolfgang Ruebsam's performance of various selections by Bach. 54m; VHS. **A:** Sr. High-Adult. **P:** Entertainment. **U:** Home. **Fin-Art**: Music--Classical, Germany. **Acq:** Purchase. **Dist:** Music Video Distributors. $29.95.

Bach: St. John Passion 19??
The Salzburg Chamber Orchestra, conducted by Alan Hacker, performs from Venice's Felice Theater. 130m; VHS. **A:** Sr. High-Adult. **P:** Entertainment. **U:** Home. **Mov-Ent**: Music--Performance, Music Video. **Acq:** Purchase. **Dist:** Music Video Distributors; Image Entertainment Inc. $39.95.

Bachata: Music of the People 2003
Documentary on Bachata, a traditional form of music from the Dominican Republic. 60m; VHS, DVD. **A:** Sr. High-Adult. **P:** Education. **U:** Institution. **Gen-Edu**: Documentary Films, Music. **Acq:** Purchase, Rent/Lease. **Dist:** The Cinema Guild. $295.00.

The Bachelor 1993 — ★★★
Beautiful, seductive period drama about a shy and solitary physician who is forced into a new life when a family tragedy changes everything he once took for granted. Richardson and Carradine give brilliant performances in this provocative story of one man's sexual awakening. Based on a novel by Arthur Schnitzler. 105m; VHS. **C:** Keith Carradine; Miranda Richardson; Mari Torocsik; Max von Sydow; Kristin Scott Thomas; Sarah-Jane Fenton; Franco Diogene; Directed by Roberto Faenza; Written by Roberto Faenza; Ennio de Concini; Hugh Fleetwood; Music by Ennio Morricone. **A:** Sr. High-Adult. **P:** Entertainment. **U:** Home. **Mov-Ent**: Sex & Sexuality. **Acq:** Purchase. **Dist:** Unknown Distributor.

The Bachelor 1999 (PG-13) — ★★
Exec producer/star Chris O'Donnell's remake of Buster Keaton's 1925 silent comedy "Seven Chances" falls short of bringing the story to a modern audience. Well, an audience that's aware of the discovery of talkies, feminism and plot holes anyway. O'Donnell plays Jimmy, who stands to inherit a fortune from his grandfather (Ustinov) if he marries before the age of 30. Unfortunately, he receives this news immediately after his odious proposal to girlfriend Anne (Zellweger) is rejected...and of course his 30th birthday happens to be 27 hours away. Madcap antics allegedly ensue as Jimmy trolls for a wife from the pool of his ex-girlfriends and flees the husband-hunting horde who respond to a front-page ad placed by his pal Marco (Lange). 101m; VHS, DVD, CC. **C:** Chris O'Donnell; Renee Zellweger; Hal Holbrook; James Cromwell; Artie Lange; Ed Asner; Marley Shelton; Stacy Edwards; Rebecca Cross; Jennifer Esposito; Peter Ustinov; Mariah Carey; Brooke Shields; Directed by Gary Sinyor; Written by Steve Cohen; Cinematography by Simon Archer; Music by David A. Hughes; John Murphy. **Pr:** New Line Cinema. **A:** Jr. High-Adult. **P:** Entertainment. **U:** Home. **Mov-Ent. Acq:** Purchase. **Dist:** Warner Home Video, Inc.

The Bachelor and the Bobby-Soxer 1947 (Unrated) — ★★★
Playboy Grant is brought before Judge Loy for disturbing the peace and sentenced to court her teenage sister Temple. Cruel and unusual punishment? Maybe, but the wise Judge hopes that the dates will help Temple over her crush on handsome Grant. Instead, Loy and Grant fall for each other. 95m/B/W; VHS, DVD. **C:** Cary Grant; Myrna Loy; Shirley Temple; Rudy Vallee; Harry Davenport; Ray Collins; Veda Ann Borg; Directed by Irving Reis; Written by Sidney Sheldon. **Pr:** Dore Schary; RKO. **A:** Family. **P:** Entertainment. **U:** Home. **Mov-Ent**: Comedy--Screwball, Adolescence. **Awds:** Oscars '47: Orig. Screenplay. **Acq:** Purchase. **Dist:** Warner Home Video, Inc.; Turner Broadcasting System Inc. $14.98.

Bachelor Apartment 1931 (Unrated) — ★★½
Once at the leading edge of the bachelor on the loose genre, this one's hopelessly dated. The scandalous womanizing of a wealthy '30s Lothario just doesn't have the same impact on the "men just don't understand" generation. Nevertheless, as vintage if-the-walls-could-talk fluff, it's good for a giggle. 77m/B/W; VHS. **C:** Lowell Sherman; Irene Dunne; Norman Kerry; Claudia Dell; Noel Francis; Charles Coleman; Mae Murray; Ivan Lebedeff; Purnell Pratt; Kitty Kelly; Directed by Lowell Sherman; Written by John Howard Lawson; J. Walter Ruben; Cinematography by Leo Tover; Music by Max Steiner. **Pr:** RKO. **A:** Jr. High-Adult. **P:** Entertainment. **U:** Home. **Mov-Ent**: Comedy--Romantic, Romance, Men. **Acq:** Purchase. **Dist:** Turner Broadcasting System Inc.; Facets Multimedia Inc. $19.98.

Bachelor Bait 1934 (Unrated) — ★½
A marriage license clerk who's tired of just handing out licenses opens a matrimonial service for men. 75m/B/W; VHS. **C:** Stuart Erwin; Rochelle Hudson; Pert Kelton; Richard "Skeets" Gallagher; Berton Churchill; Grady Sutton; Clarence Wilson; Directed by George Stevens; Written by Glenn Tryon; Cinematography by Dave Abel; Music by Max Steiner. **Pr:** Pandro S. Berman. **A:** Family. **P:** Entertainment. **U:** Home. **Mov-Ent**: Comedy--Romantic. **Acq:** Purchase.

The Bachelor Father 1931 (Unrated) — ★★
Aging British peer Sir Basil (Smith) wants to get to know his three grown children (by three different mothers) and invites them to his country estate. He bonds the most with adventurous American Antoinette (Davies), who decides to meddle in his life as well. 84m/B/W; DVD. **C:** Sir C. Aubrey Smith; Marion Davies; Ray Milland; Nina Quartero; Ralph Forbes; Guinn "Big Boy" Williams; David Torrence; Doris Lloyd; Halliwell Hobbes; Directed by Robert Z. Leonard; Written by Laurence E. Johnson; Cinematography by Oliver Marsh. **A:** Sr. High-Adult. **P:** Entertainment. **U:** Home. **Mov-Ent**: Great Britain, Aging. **Acq:** Purchase. **Dist:** WarnerArchive.com.

Bachelor Flat 1962 — ★½
A broad, somewhat tiresome comedy. Professor Bruce Patterson (Terry-Thomas) is the unlikely lust object for numerous ladies, so he's happy to use fiancée Helen's (Holm) home when she goes out of town. Only Helen has neglected to mention her first marriage and her 17-year-old daughter, Libby (Weld), who shows up unaware of her mother's engagement and then pretends to be some juvenile delinquent after Patterson. 91m; DVD. **C:** Terry-Thomas; Tuesday Weld; Richard Beymer; Celeste Holm; Directed by Frank Tashlin; Written by Frank Tashlin; Budd Grossman; Cinematography by Daniel F. Fapp; Music by John Williams. **A:** Jr. High-Adult. **P:** Entertainment. **U:** Home. **L:** English. **Mov-Ent**: Adolescence. **Acq:** Purchase. **Dist:** Fox Home Entertainment.

Bachelor in Paradise 1961 — ★★½
Silly tale starring Hope as a writer of books to the lovelorn who decides to do firsthand research on the sexual goings-on of a suburban California community. All the married ladies find him charming (much to their husbands' disgust) and the lone single woman, Turner, isn't single by the end of the movie. 109m; VHS, DVD, CC. **C:** Bob Hope; Lana Turner; Janis Paige; Jim Hutton; Paula Prentiss; Don Porter; Virginia Grey; Agnes Moorehead; John McGiver; Directed by Jack Arnold; Written by Hal Kanter; Valentine Davies; Music by Henry Mancini. **Pr:** Ted Richmond; Metro-Goldwyn-Mayer Pictures. **A:** Jr. High-Adult. **P:** Entertainment. **U:** Home. **Mov-Ent**: Comedy--Romantic, Marriage, Sex & Sexuality. **Acq:** Purchase. **Dist:** WarnerArchive.com; MGM Home Entertainment; Facets Multimedia Inc. $19.98.

Bachelor Mother 1939 (Unrated) — ★★★
A single salesgirl causes a scandal when she finds an abandoned baby and is convinced by her boss to adopt the child. Smart, witty comedy with nice performance by Rogers. 82m/B/W; VHS, DVD. **C:** Ginger Rogers; David Niven; Charles Coburn; Directed by Garson Kanin. **Pr:** B.G. DeSylva; RKO. **A:** Family. **P:** Entertainment. **U:** Home. **Mov-Ent**: Comedy--Screwball, Parenting, Adoption. **Acq:** Purchase. **Dist:** WarnerArchive.com; Facets Multimedia Inc.; Turner Broadcasting System Inc. $19.98.

Bachelor of Hearts 1958 (Unrated) — ★½
Sophomoric British comedy set at Cambridge University, with a German exchange student whose difficulty with English brings him to date several women in one evening. Notable for horror fans as the debut of femme fright fave Barbara Steele. 94m; VHS. **C:** Hardy Kruger; Sylvia Syms; Ronald Lewis; Directed by Wolf Rilla; Written by Frederic Raphael; Leslie Bricusse. **Pr:** Rank. **A:** Jr. High-Adult. **P:** Entertainment. **U:** Home. **Mov-Ent**: Comedy--Screwball. **Acq:** Purchase. **Dist:** No Longer Available.

Bachelor Party 1984 (R) — ★★
Rick (Hank) is silly, cute, and poor. Debbie (Kitaen) is intelligent, beautiful, and rich. It must be a marriage made in heaven, because no one in their right mind would put these two together. All is basically well, except that her parents hate him and his friends dislike her. Things are calm until right before the big event, when the bride-to-be objects to Rick's traditional prenuptial partying and with good reason. Light and semi-entertaining with scattered laughs. 105m; VHS, DVD, Blu-Ray, Wide, CC. **C:** Tom Hanks; Tawny Kitaen; Adrian Zmed; George Grizzard; Robert Prescott; William Tepper; Wendie Jo Sperber; Barry Diamond; Michael Dudikoff; Deborah Harmon; John Bloom; Toni Alessandra; Monique Gabrielle; Angela Aames; Rosanne Katon; Bradford Bancroft; Directed by Neal Israel; Written by Pat Proft; Cinematography by Hal Trussel; Music by Robert Folk. **Pr:** 20th Century-Fox. **A:** Sr. High-Adult. **P:** Entertainment. **U:** Home. **Mov-Ent**: Marriage, Sex & Sexuality. **Acq:** Purchase. **Dist:** Movies Unlimited; Alpha Video; Fox Home Entertainment. $14.98.

Bachelor Party 2: The Last Temptation 2008 (Unrated) — ★
Has, of course, nothing to do with the 1984 Tom Hanks comedy. Ron (Cooke) gets engaged to wealthy Melinda (Foster). Her scheming brother Todd (Christie) is convinced that the affable Ron will be anointed heir to the family business so he takes Ron and his buds to South Beach hoping some compromising situations will lead to the wedding being called off. An excuse for a lot of topless women to be on parade and men-behaving-badly stupidity. 103m; DVD. **C:** Sara Foster; Danny A. Jacobs; Harland Williams; Emmanuelle Vaugier; Audrey Landers; Josh Cooke; Warren Christie; Greg Pitts; Maj. Mike Russell; Directed by James Ryan; Written by Jay Longino; Cinematography by Roy Wagner; Music by James Dooley. **A:** Sr. High-Adult. **P:** Entertainment. **U:** Home. **Mov-Ent. Acq:** Purchase. **Dist:** Fox Home Entertainment.

Bachelor Party in the Bungalow of the Damned 2008 (Unrated) — ★½
A wild bachelor party at a house in the Hamptons (complete with a creepy caretaker) goes awry amid the jiggle and debauchery when the gates of hell open up mid-bash, leaving some to wonder, can I get my shower present back? 90m; DVD. **C:** Trina Analee; Monique Dupree; Gregg Aaron Greenburg; Kaitlyn Gutkes; Zoe Hunter; Sean Parker; Joseph Parker; Gelu Dan Rusu; Joe Testa; Directed by Brian Thomson; Written by Brian Thomson; Cinematography by Demian Barba; Music by Brian Thomson. **A:** Sr. High-Adult. **P:** Entertainment. **U:** Home. **Mov-Ent**: Horror. **Acq:** Purchase. **Dist:** Brain Damage Films. $14.98.

Bachelor Party Vegas 2005 (R) — **Bomb!**
Things go wrong for five friends when they head to Vegas and discover their bachelor party planner is a casino thief, which leads to all sorts of misunderstandings. Unbelievably crass and unfunny comedy that should have stayed in Vegas, preferably so the master print could have been shredded by one of Siegfried & Roy's white tigers. 90m; DVD. **C:** Kal Penn; Jonathan Bennett; Donald Adeosun Faison; Charlie Talbert; Vincent Pastore; Jaime Pressly; Aaron Himelstein; Diora Baird; Lin Shaye; Graham Beckel; Daniel Stern; Steve Hytner; Kathy Griffin; Directed by Eric Bernt; Written by Eric Bernt; Cinematography by Robert Primes. **A:** Sr. High-Adult. **P:** Entertainment. **U:** Home. **Mov-Ent. Acq:** Purchase. **Dist:** Sony Pictures Home Entertainment Inc.

The Bachelor: The Best of the Bachelor 2002
Compiles highlights from the debut season in 2002 of the reality television competition series about single man Alex Michel as he must choose one of 25 women to marry while traveling to a variety of exotic locations. 170m; DVD. **A:** Jr. High-Adult. **P:** Entertainment. **U:** Home. **Mov-Ent**: Television Series, Documentary Films, Game Show. **Acq:** Purchase. **Dist:** Warner Home Video, Inc. $19.98.

Bachelorette 2012 (R) — ★
Foul-mouthed chick flicks that follow the success of "Bridesmaids" are fair game for comparisons--this falls far short. Regan (Dunst) spends the weekend organizing her friend's NYC wedding, and trying to look after the wilder, cocaine-laced members of the wedding party, Gena (Caplan) and Katie (Fisher). One misstep after another leads to an unsurprisingly chaotic wedding day. Drug abuse and casual sex are pushed to such an absurd limit that the romp loses all credibility in characters and circumstances. A mean-spirited, soulless, and dull debut for director Headland. 93m; DVD, Blu-Ray, Download. **C:** Kirsten Dunst; Isla Fisher; Lizzy Caplan; Rebel Wilson; James Marsden; Adam Scott; Kyle Bornheimer; Hayes Macarthur; Directed by Leslye Headland; Written by Leslye Headland; Cinematography by Doug Emmett; Music by Andrew Feltenstein; John Nau. **Pr:** Brice Dal Farra; Claude Dal Farra; Jessica Elbaum; Will Ferrell; Adam McKay; Lauren Munsch; BCDF Pictures; Gary Sanchez Productions; Weinstein Co. **A:** Sr. High-Adult. **P:** Entertainment. **U:** Home. **L:** English. **Mov-Ent:** Drug Abuse. **Acq:** Purchase, Off-Air Record. **Dist:** Anchor Bay Entertainment Inc.

BachelorMan 2003 (R) — ★★
Easygoing Ted Davis (DeLuise) considers himself an authority on bachelorhood. But when hot brunette Heather (Pyle) becomes his next-door neighbor, all Ted's tricks to woo her fail. Even worse, Ted realizes he's actually fallen in love. Based on the sketch comedy act of Rodney Lee Conover, who plays Ted's outspoken buddy Gordie. 90m; DVD. **C:** David DeLuise; Missi Pyle; Karen Bailey; Rodney Lee Conover; Directed by John Putch; Written by Jeffrey Hause; David Hines; Cinematography by Keith J. Duggan; Music by Steve Bauman; J. Lynn Duckett. **A:** Sr. High-Adult. **P:** Entertainment. **U:** Home. **Mov-Ent:** Comedy--Romantic. **Acq:** Purchase. **Dist:** Magnolia Home Entertainment.

Bach's Fight for Freedom 199?
Fictional child character enters into the life of world famous composer Johann Sebastian Bach. 53m; VHS. **A:** Family. **P:** Education. **U:** Home. **Gen-Edu:** Music--Classical, History. **Acq:** Purchase. **Dist:** Hal Leonard Corp. $19.95.

Back Alley Detroit 1992
Pro-choice women, doctors, and activists remember the consequences of seeking an illegal abortion in the '50s, '60s, and early '70s in Detroit. 47m; VHS. **A:** Adult. **P:** Education. **U:** Institution. **Gen-Edu:** Abortion, History--Modern. **Acq:** Purchase, Rent/Lease. **Dist:** Filmakers Library Inc. $395.00.

Back and Ergonomic Safety Procedures for Offshore Personnel ?
Outlines safe work practices required for offshore personnel to work injury-free in the oil field environment, including lifting techniques, stretching and strengthening. 40m; VHS. **A:** Sr. High-Adult. **P:** Education. **U:** Home, Institution. **Bus-Ind:** Industry & Industrialists, Safety Education. **Acq:** Purchase. **Dist:** John Sabella & Associate. $375.00.

Back at the Ranch 1988
Families from the American midwest are being forced to deal with the economic hardships of the cattle industry. 60m; VHS, 3/4 U. **Pr:** NETCHE. **A:** Jr. High-Adult. **P:** Education. **U:** Institution, CCTV, BCTV, SURA. **Gen-Edu:** Agriculture, Finance. **Acq:** Purchase, Rent/Lease, Subscription. **Dist:** NETCHE; GPN Educational Media. $29.95.

The Back Attack 1983
An orthopedic surgeon dismisses the myths surrounding back disorders. 58m; VHS, 3/4 U. **Pr:** TV Ontario. **A:** Sr. High-Adult. **P:** Education. **U:** Institution. **Hea-Sci:** Back Disorders. **Acq:** Purchase. **Dist:** Filmakers Library Inc.

Back Basics 19??
Provides information on back injuries and how to avoid them in the workplace. Covers three areas: good posture, proper lifting techniques, and exercise. Includes Leader's Guide and 25 Program Guides. 14m; VHS, 3/4 U. **A:** Adult. **P:** Education. **U:** Institution. **Bus-Ind:** Safety Education, Back Disorders. **Acq:** Purchase. **Dist:** Williams Learning Network.

The Back-Breaking Leaf 1989
Tobacco harvests are the subject of this documentary. 30m; VHS, 3/4 U. **A:** Jr. High-Adult. **P:** Education. **U:** Institution, SURA. **Bus-Ind:** Agriculture. **Acq:** Purchase, Rent/Lease. **Dist:** National Film Board of Canada.

Back Care and Safety 1995
Includes how back injuries occur and how to prevent them. Includes physiology, and basic back exercises. 15m; VHS. **A:** Adult. **P:** Professional. **U:** Institution. **L:** Spanish. **Bus-Ind:** Job Training, Safety Education, Health Education. **Acq:** Purchase, Rent/Lease. **Dist:** National Safety Council, California Chapter, Film Library.

Back-Care-Cise #4 1991
Part 4 of Back-Care-Cise Series. Centers on the neck and upper back. Features sports-injury specialist, Linda J. Nelson, as she discusses techniques and exercises to help relieve and reduce pain. Provides information on the elimination of neck and back pain, strengthening and toning weak back muscles, increased flexibility, poor posture improvement, and boosting energy. 30m; VHS. **A:** Adult. **P:** Instruction. **U:** Home. **Hea-Sci:** Sports Medicine, Back Disorders. **Acq:** Purchase. **Dist:** New & Unique Videos.

Back-Care-Cise #5 1992
Part 5 of the Back-Care-Cise Series. Concentrates on the shoulder, wrist, and elbow. Provides information from sports-injury specialist, Linda J. Nelson, as she demonstrates techniques and exercises to help reduce and relieve pain. Includes information on how to increase joint flexibility, improve poor posture, recover quickly from injury, relieve stress, and boost energy. 40m; VHS. **A:** Adult. **P:** Education. **U:** Home. **Hea-Sci:** Sports Medicine, Pain. **Acq:** Purchase. **Dist:** New & Unique Videos.

Back Care for Maritime Industry 2000
Educates production and supervisory personnel on the hows and whys of back care and safety. Offers workers a visual guide to protecting themselves and provides supervisory personnel with an idea of the costs associated with back injuries, as well as a real-world program for reducing back injury risks. ?m; VHS. **TV Std:** NTSC, PAL. **P:** Instruction. **U:** Institution, Home. **Bus-Ind:** Back Disorders, Safety Education. **Acq:** Purchase. **Dist:** John Sabella & Associate. $225.00.
Indiv. Titles: 1. Lift It Safely: A Guide for Employees 2. Minimize the Risk: The Role of Management.

Back Care in Pregnancy 1991
Demonstrates exercises for the expecting mother, along with good posture techniques and suggestions for supportive clothing. 18m; VHS. **A:** Adult. **P:** Education. **U:** Institution. **Hea-Sci:** Pregnancy, Fitness/Exercise. **Acq:** Purchase. **Dist:** Milner-Fenwick, Inc. $150.00.

Back Chat 198?
The correct procedure for office workers to bend, lift, carry and reach to avoid back injuries is demonstrated. 22m; VHS, 3/4 U. **A:** College-Adult. **P:** Education. **U:** Institution. **Bus-Ind:** Safety Education. **Acq:** Rent/Lease. **Dist:** National Safety Council, California Chapter, Film Library.

Back Combing Technique 1990
Offers instruction on specific aspects of barbering and cosmetology. 6m; VHS. **A:** Adult. **P:** Vocational. **U:** Institution. **Bus-Ind:** Cosmetology. **Acq:** Purchase. **Dist:** RMI Media. $39.95.

Back Door to Heaven 1939 (Unrated) — ★★★½
Traces the path of a young boy who is born into a poor family and the reasons for his turning to a life of crime. A grim and powerful drama with many convincing performances. 85m/B/W; VHS, DVD. **C:** Wallace Ford; Aline MacMahon; Stuart Erwin; Patricia Ellis; Kent Smith; Van Heflin; Jimmy Lydon; Directed by William K. Howard. **Pr:** Paramount Pictures. **A:** Sr. High-Adult. **P:** Entertainment. **U:** Home. **Mov-Ent. Acq:** Purchase. **Dist:** Movies Unlimited. $19.95.

Back from Eternity 1956 (Unrated) — ★★
Eleven survivors of a plane crash are stranded in a headhunter region of South America's jungle. Remake of "Five Came Back" (1939), which was also directed by Farrow. 97m/B/W; VHS. **C:** Robert Ryan; Rod Steiger; Anita Ekberg; Phyllis Kirk; Keith Andes; Gene Barry; Jon(athan) Provost; Beulah Bondi; Barbara Eden; Directed by John Farrow; Cinematography by William Mellor. **Pr:** John Farrow; Mark Huffam; John Farrow. **A:** Family. **P:** Entertainment. **U:** Home. **Mov-Ent:** Mystery & Suspense. **Acq:** Purchase. **Dist:** No Longer Available.

Back from Hell: A Tribute to Sam Kinison 2010 (Unrated)
A cast of famous comedian convene at the Comedy Store in Los Angeles to pay tribute to late stand-up artist Sam Kinison in 2010. 60m; DVD, Streaming. **A:** Sr. High-Adult. **P:** Entertainment. **U:** Home. **L:** English. **Mov-Ent:** Comedy--Performance, Television. **Acq:** Purchase, Rent/Lease. **Dist:** Comedy Partners L.P. $12.98 9.99.

Back from Light 1991
Survivors of "Near Death Experiences" have formed a support group at the University of Connecticut where members share their feelings and how their lifestyles and/or priorities changed. 28m; VHS. **A:** College-Adult. **P:** Education. **U:** Institution. **Gen-Edu:** Death, Psychology. **Acq:** Purchase, Rent/Lease. **Dist:** Filmakers Library Inc. $195.00.

The Back Game 1995
Features a lively question and answer format to teach techniques for preventing back injuries and offers information on proper lifting, and exercising and diet. 15m; VHS. **A:** Adult. **P:** Professional. **U:** Institution. **Bus-Ind:** Job Training, Safety Education, Health Education. **Acq:** Rent/Lease. **Dist:** National Safety Council, California Chapter, Film Library.

Back Home 1990 — ★★½
A family reunion movie with pure Disney sentiment. A 12-year-old English girl, who has been living in America during WWII, is reunited with her family in postwar England. 103m; VHS, DVD, CC. **C:** Hayley Carr; Hayley Mills; Jean Anderson; Rupert Frazer; Brenda Bruce; Adam Stevenson; George Clark; Directed by Piers Haggard. **A:** Family. **P:** Entertainment. **U:** Home. **Mov-Ent:** World War Two, Great Britain, TV Movies. **Acq:** Purchase. **Dist:** Walt Disney Studios Home Entertainment.

Back in Action 1981
Following patients of all ages and walks of life as they recuperate from heart attacks or surgery, the steps to take toward a return to good health are demonstrated. 21m; VHS, 3/4 U. **Pr:** Stacy Keach, Sr. **A:** Adult. **P:** Education. **U:** Institution, CCTV, BCTV. **Hea-Sci:** Heart. **Acq:** Purchase. **Dist:** Discovery Education.

Back in Action 1994 (R) — ★½
Veteran LA detective Rossi (Piper) is out to bust the ruthless drug gang who gunned down his partner. But he's got company—martial-arts expert Billy (Blanks) whose young sister has fallen prey to the same gang. So the two action junkies reluctantly team up to cause some major damage. 93m; VHS, DVD, CC. **C:** Roddy Piper; Billy Blanks; Bobbie Phillips; Matt Birman; Nigel Bennett; Damon D'Oliveira; Kai Soremekun; Directed by Paul Ziller; Steve DiMarco; Written by Karl Schiffman. **Pr:** George Flak; Shapiro Glickenhaus Entertainment Corporation. **A:** Sr. High-Adult. **P:** Entertainment. **U:** Home. **Mov-Ent:** Martial Arts, Drugs, Violence. **Acq:** Purchase. **Dist:** Universal Music and Video Distribution.

Back in Business 1990
A look at the ergonomics of back problems, including causes, symptoms, and remedies. Designed to help train workers to find ways of preventing back stress and injuries. A leader's guide and participants' workbooks are included. 16m; VHS, 3/4 U. **A:** College-Adult. **P:** Instruction. **U:** Institution. **Bus-Ind:** How-To, Safety Education, Occupational Training. **Acq:** Rent/Lease. **Dist:** Learning Communications L.L.C. $175.00.

Back in Business 1996 (R) — ★★
Joe Elkhart's (Bosworth) life is down the drain. After failing to expose a fellow police officer as corrupt, he's kicked off the force, abandoned by his friends, and divorced by his wife. Now working as a mechanic, Joe gets pulled back into the action when his ex-partner, Tony (Torry), goes undercover to bring down a major drug dealer and Joe discovers the corrupt cops that framed him are also behind the current heroin deal. 93m; VHS, Streaming, CC. **C:** Brian Bosworth; Joe Torry; Dara Tomanovich; Alan Scarfe; Brion James; Ron Glass; Directed by Philippe Mora; Written by Ed Decatur; Ash Staley; Cinematography by Walter Bal. **Pr:** Peter McAlevey; Daniel Gerst; Ted Rosenblat; Gary Winchard; PFG Entertainment; Ocean Avenue Productions. **A:** Sr. High-Adult. **P:** Entertainment. **U:** Home. **Mov-Ent:** Federal Bureau of Investigation (FBI). **Acq:** Purchase. **Dist:** Amazon.com Inc.; Sony Pictures Home Entertainment Inc.

Back in Business 2006 (Unrated) — ★
Lame Brit crime caper. Con man Will Spencer (Kemp) and his various allies plot to steal a technologically advanced space exploration device developed by Britain and sought after by a number of foreign investors. But is ex-detective Jarvis (Waterman) planning to doublecross the crew or make the scam his own? 82m; DVD. **C:** Martin Kemp; Dennis Waterman; Chris Barrie; Brian Blessed; Stefan Booth; Joanna Taylor; Directed by Chris Munro; Written by Chris Munro; Cinematography by Martin Kenzie; Music by Mark Thomas. **A:** Jr. High-Adult. **P:** Entertainment. **U:** Home. **Mov-Ent. Acq:** Purchase. **Dist:** BFS Video.

Back in Business: Disaster Recovery/Business Resumption 19??
Various strategies for overcoming loss of business due to disaster (natural or man-initiated) are covered. Includes procedures for mopping-up operations. 25m; VHS. **A:** College-Adult. **P:** Professional. **U:** Institution. **Bus-Ind:** Business, Safety Education, Emergencies. **Acq:** Purchase. **Dist:** Commonwealth Films Inc. $525.00.

Back in Shape: The Complete Back Pain Prevention Program 1986
A seven-chapter video instructing the viewer in back testing, anatomy and pain relief. 60m; VHS, CC. **Pr:** Karl/Lorimar. **A:** Sr. High-Adult. **P:** Instruction. **U:** Home. **Hea-Sci:** Back Disorders. **Acq:** Purchase. **Dist:** MGM Studios Inc. ; Warner Home Video, Inc.

Back in the Day 2005 (R) — ★★½
Reggie Cooper (Ja Rule) is living with his successful, divorced father (Esposito) in an effort to stay away from the 'hood that nearly cost him his life. But when Reggie reconnects with gangster mentor J-Bone (Rhames) it can only mean trouble because J-Bone has some scores to settle. Reggie gets involved in the murder of a local preacher (Morton), but tries to keep his part a secret after he falls for the man's daughter (Ali). Now he must choose between old loyalties and new love. Decent effort with a familiar cast doing professional work. 103m; DVD. **C:** Ja Rule; Ving Rhames; Tatyana Ali; Giancarlo Esposito; Pam Grier; Joe Morton; Tia Carrere; Frank Langella; Debbi (Deborah) Morgan; Al Sapienza; Lahmard Tate; Directed by James Hunter; Written by James Hunter; Michael Raffanello; Cinematography by Donald M. Morgan; Music by Robert Folk. **A:** Sr. High-Adult. **P:** Entertainment. **U:** Home. **Mov-Ent. Acq:** Purchase. **Dist:** Movies Unlimited; Alpha Video.

Back in the Day 2014 (R) — **Bomb!**
Dreary raunch that's a complete comic misfire. Jim Owens goes home to Indiana for his high school reunion, wanting to relive his past with some drunken partying while trying to get the girl that had the good sense to get away back then. 94m; DVD. **C:** Michael Rosenbaum; Morena Baccarin; Nick Swardson; Harland Williams; Emma Caulfield; Directed by Michael Rosenbaum; Written by Michael Rosenbaum; Cinematography by Bradley Stonesifer; Music by Rob Danson. **A:** Sr. High-Adult. **P:** Entertainment. **U:** Home. **L:** English. **Mov-Ent:** Men. **Acq:** Purchase. **Dist:** Screen Media Films.

Back in the Saddle 1941 — ★½
Autry is a ranch foreman who discovers a nearby copper mine is poisoning his cattle. Gene manages to do a lot of singing in between the fist fights. 71m/B/W; VHS. **C:** Gene Autry; Smiley Burnette; Mary Lee; Edward Norris; Directed by Lew Landers; Written by Richard Murphy; Jesse Lasky, Jr.; Cinematography by Ernest Miller. **Pr:** Republic Pictures. **A:** Family. **P:** Entertainment. **U:** Home. **Mov-Ent:** Western. **Acq:** Purchase. **Dist:** Buena Vista Home Entertainment.

Back in the USSR 1988
A candid portrait of a nation as seen through the eyes of an American family. 60m; VHS, 3/4 U. **Pr:** PBS. **A:** Jr. High-Adult. **P:** Education. **U:** Institution, SURA. **Gen-Edu:** USSR, International Relations. **Acq:** Purchase, Rent/Lease. **Dist:** PBS Home Video. $300.00.

Back in the USSR 1992 (R) — ★¹/₂
Danger follows two lovers caught up in the Moscow underworld. When young American touring Russia unwittingly gets involved with a beautiful art thief. Lots of fast-paced action in an otherwise muddled film. The first American film shot entirely on location in Moscow. 87m; VHS. **C:** Frank Whaley; Natalia (Natalya) Negoda; Roman Polanski; Claudia Robinson; Dey Young; Andrew Divoff; Brian Blessed; Ravil Isyanov; Directed by Deran Sarafian; Cinematography by Yuri Neyman. **A:** College-Adult. **P:** Entertainment. **U:** Home. **Mov-Ent:** Action-Adventure, USSR, Art & Artists. **Acq:** Purchase. **Dist:** Fox Home Entertainment. $19.98.

Back Injury Prevention Program 1993
Three educational modules discuss ways to improve back health and safety to prevent injuries and lost work time. Includes administrator's, leader's, and participant's guides as well as a back injury prevention booklet. ?m; VHS. **A:** College-Adult. **P:** Education. **U:** Institution. **Bus-Ind:** Safety Education, Back Disorders. **Acq:** Purchase. **Dist:** DuPont Sustainable Solutions. $690.00.
Indiv. Titles: 1. Introduction and Biomechanics 2. Ergonomics 3. Fitness and Review.

Back Injury Prevention/Slips and Falls Prevention 1995
Explains the two major causes of employee injuries, and how to prevent them. 12m; VHS. **A:** Adult. **P:** Professional. **U:** Institution. **L:** Spanish. **Bus-Ind:** Safety Education, Management, Occupational Training. **Acq:** Purchase, Rent/Lease. **Dist:** National Safety Council, California Chapter, Film Library. $175.00.

Back Injury Prevention Through Ergonomics 198?
This is a demonstration of how a total ergonomics program can reduce workers' on-the-job injuries. 14m; VHS, 3/4 U. **A:** College-Adult. **P:** Education. **U:** Institution. **Bus-Ind:** Safety Education. **Acq:** Rent/Lease. **Dist:** National Safety Council, California Chapter, Film Library.

Back Injury Responsibility 1995
Demonstrates a variety of safe lifting methods. 10m; VHS. **A:** Adult. **P:** Professional. **U:** Institution. **L:** Spanish. **Bus-Ind:** Job Training, Safety Education, Health Education. **Acq:** Purchase, Rent/Lease. **Dist:** National Safety Council, California Chapter, Film Library. $175.00.

Back Inside Herself 1984
This poetic film urges black women to reject imposed notions and create their own identities. 5m; VHS, 3/4 U. **Pr:** Sandra Sharp. **A:** Jr. High-Adult. **P:** Education. **U:** Institution, SURA. **Gen-Edu:** Black Culture, Women. **Acq:** Purchase, Rent/Lease. **Dist:** Women Make Movies. $125.00.

Back of Beyond 1995 (R) — ★★
Spectacular setting in the Australian outback can't make up for unfocused plot and characters with little impact. Tom (Mercutio) ran a remote desert gas station with his sister, Susan (Elmalogulou), before she was killed on his motorbike. When Connor's (Friels) car breaks down by the derelict station, he, girlfriend Charlie (Smart), and sidekick Nick (Polson) must wait while Tom tries to fix it. Only Connor is a diamond thief and patience isn't one of his virutes, especially when he notices the unhappy Charlie making friends with Tom. Mystical/supernatural elements involving ghosts and Aboriginal sites only add to the confusion. 85m; Streaming. **C:** Paul Mercurio; Colin Friels; Dee Smart; John Polson; Rebekah Elmaloglou; Bob Maza; Terry Serio; Directed by Michael Robertson; Written by Paul Leadon; A.M. Brooksbank; Richard I. Sawyer; Cinematography by Stephen Dobson; Music by Mark Moffatt; Wayne Goodwin. **Pr:** John Sexton; Beyond Films Limited; Australian Film Finance Corp. **A:** Sr. High-Adult. **P:** Entertainment. **U:** Home. **Mov-Ent:** Australia. **Acq:** Purchase. **Dist:** Lions Gate Entertainment Inc.; Lions Gate Television Corp.

Back on the Street: Teen Alcohol & Drug Abusers 1986
A speech by Jesse Jackson is just one way that an anti-drug message is delivered. Also contains a series of short interviews with six young people who have been through treatment for drug or alcohol abuse. Includes one leader's guide and one set of Blackline Masters. 26m; VHS, 3/4 U. **Pr:** United Learning Inc. **A:** Primary-Sr. High. **P:** Education. **U:** Institution, CCTV, CATV, Home, SURA. **Hea-Sci:** Drug Abuse, Alcoholism, Adolescence. **Acq:** Purchase, Rent/Lease. **Dist:** United Learning Inc.; Harcourt Religion Publishers. $95.00.

Back on Track 1988
Reporter Sue Kopen goes for a behind the scenes look at the Maryland horse racing business. 30m; VHS, 3/4 U. **Pr:** Maryland Center for Public Broadcasting. **A:** Jr. High-Adult. **P:** Education. **U:** Institution, CCTV, CATV, BCTV. **Spo-Rec:** Horses--Racing. **Acq:** Purchase. **Dist:** Maryland Public Television. $29.95.

The Back Operation 1989
A review of common back problems and remedies. Plus, a look at surgery to correct scoliosis in teenage patients. 90m; VHS, 3/4 U. **Pr:** WHYY Philadelphia. **A:** Sr. High-Adult. **P:** Education. **U:** Institution, CCTV, CATV, SURA. **Hea-Sci:** Back Disorders, Anatomy & Physiology, Surgery. **Acq:** Purchase, Duplication License, Off-Air Record. **Dist:** PBS Home Video. $79.95.

Back Pain 19??
An orthopedic surgeon explains the major causes of back pain, and offers exercises and and behavior changes which can aid in the prevention of back flare-ups. 42m; VHS. **A:** Family. **P:** Instruction. **U:** Home. **Hea-Sci:** Back Disorders, Health Education. **Acq:** Purchase. **Dist:** Cambridge Educational. $24.95.

Back Pain Patient 1984
A medical survey of back pain and its various treatments. 18m; 3/4 U. **Pr:** McMaster University. **A:** Adult. **P:** Professional. **U:** Institution, SURA. **Hea-Sci:** Back Disorders. **Acq:** Purchase, Rent/Lease. **Dist:** McMaster University.

Back Pay 1930 (Unrated) — ★¹/₂
Hester Bevins (Griffith) feels trapped by her small town and even the naive love of local boy Gerald (Withers). Offered a way out by traveling salesman Bloom (Cooley), Hester gets to the city and eventually becomes the lover of war profiteer Charles Wheeler (Love). A nostalgic visit home has Hester realizing, despite her fancy life, she does love Gerald. A rare talkie from silent screen star Griffith; she retired in 1932 after one more film. 55m/B/W; DVD. **C:** Corinne Griffith; Montagu Love; Grant Withers; Hallam Cooley; Directed by William A. Seiter; Written by Francis Edwards Faragoh; Cinematography by John Seitz. **A:** Family. **P:** Entertainment. **U:** Home. **L:** English. **Mov-Ent:** Melodrama, Blindness. **Acq:** Purchase. **Dist:** WarnerArchive.com. $19.98.

Back: Rehabilitation & Injury 1978
Back strengthening exercises to help overcome weaknesses, relieve pain, and condition muscles and tissue to prevent further stress. Part of the "Rehabilitation and Injury" series. 30m; VHS. **C:** Hosted by Ann Dugan. **Pr:** Health 'N Action. **A:** Adult. **P:** Instruction. **U:** Home. **Hea-Sci:** Fitness/Exercise. **Acq:** Purchase. **Dist:** Sony Pictures Home Entertainment Inc.

Back Road Diner 1999 (Unrated) — ★
A couple of old friends go on a road trip leaving Harlem for the backwoods. It goes well until they meet the local redneck deputies who've been told they're drug dealers because unlike all the locals they happen to be African-American. Predictably their vacation quickly goes downhill. 89m; DVD. **C:** Andre M. Carrington; Winston I. Dunlop, II; Directed by Winston I. Dunlop, II; Cinematography by Joseph Matina; Music by William Brown. **A:** Sr. High-Adult. **P:** Entertainment. **U:** Home. **L:** English. **Mov-Ent. Acq:** Purchase. **Dist:** Troma Entertainment. $19.95.

Back Roads 1981 (R) — ★★
Southern hooker meets a down-on-his-luck boxer and both head out for a better life in California, finding love along the way. Ritt road trip lacks any comedic rhythm and survives on Field and Jones working to entertain. 94m; VHS, DVD. **C:** Sally Field; Tommy Lee Jones; David Keith; Directed by Martin Ritt; Written by Gary De Vore; Cinematography by John A. Alonzo; Music by Henry Mancini. **Pr:** Ronald Sheldo. **A:** Adult. **P:** Entertainment. **U:** Home. **Mov-Ent:** Comedy-Drama, Action-Adventure, Prostitution. **Acq:** Purchase. **Dist:** Movies Unlimited; Alpha Video; Paramount Pictures Corp. $69.98.

Back Safety for Employees 1995
Features safe proper lifting of heavy articles, shoveling, etc. 15m; VHS. **A:** Adult. **P:** Professional. **U:** Institution. **L:** Spanish. **Bus-Ind:** Safety Education, Occupational Training, Construction. **Acq:** Purchase, Rent/Lease. **Dist:** National Safety Council, California Chapter, Film Library. $175.00.

Back Safety for Health Care Providers 1995
Teaches how the back works, body mechanics, and the proper method of lifting. 11m; VHS. **A:** Adult. **P:** Professional. **U:** Institution. **Bus-Ind:** Safety Education, Occupational Training, Back Disorders. **Acq:** Purchase, Rent/Lease. **Dist:** National Safety Council, California Chapter, Film Library. $175.00.

Back Safety for Inland Waterways Personnel ?
Demonstrates the proper working postures and strengthening exercises that inland water personnel should utilize in order to avoid injury. 55m; VHS. **A:** Sr. High-Adult. **P:** Education. **U:** Home, Institution. **Bus-Ind:** Industry & Industrialists, Safety Education. **Acq:** Purchase. **Dist:** John Sabella & Associate. $295.00.

Back Safety Training Kit 19??
Teaches employees the causes and prevention of back injury in the workplace. Comes with instructor's guide, employee handbooks, training log, back safety posters, lifting signs, wallet cards, certificates of training, and employee safety training records. Helps in preparation for OSHA/workers' compensation verification. 18m; VHS. **A:** Adult. **P:** Vocational. **U:** Institution. **Bus-Ind:** Job Training, Safety Education, Back Disorders. **Acq:** Purchase. **Dist:** J.J. Keller and Associates Inc. $149.00.

Back Seat 1978
A study of New York City cabdrivers, as seen through the eyes of their passengers. 30m/B/W; VHS, 3/4 U. **Pr:** Susan Milano. **A:** Sr. High-Adult. **P:** Education. **U:** Institution, SURA. **Gen-Edu:** Cities & Towns. **Acq:** Purchase. **Dist:** Media Bus, Inc.

Back Shiatsu for Lovers 19??
Presents how to eroticize your partner with a full-body back massage. 40m; VHS. **A:** Adult. **P:** Instruction. **U:** Home. **Hea-Sci:** Massage. **Acq:** Purchase. **Dist:** Acupressure Institute. $29.95.

Back Street 1941 — ★★¹/₂
Pretty Rae Stevens (Sullavan) falls in love with Walter Saxel (Boyer) but, thanks to a misunderstanding, they part company. They meet again five years later and, although Walter is married and has children, begin an affair. Over the years, Rae is to learn that the life of a mistress is a lonely one. Based on the novel by Fannie Hurst; also filmed in 1932 and 1961. 89m/B/W; DVD. **C:** Margaret Sullavan; Charles Boyer; Richard Carlson; Frank McHugh; Tim Holt; Frank Jenks; Esther Dale; Samuel S. Hinds; Directed by Robert Stevenson; Written by Bruce Manning; Felix Jackson; Cinematography by William H. Daniels; Music by Frank Skinner. **A:** Jr. High-Adult. **P:** Entertainment. **U:** Home. **Mov-Ent:** Drama. **Acq:** Purchase. **Dist:** Universal Studios Home Video. $19.98.

Back Street 1961 — ★★
The forbidden affair between a married man and a beautiful fashion designer carries on through many anxious years to a tragic end. The lavish third film version of the Fannie Hurst novel. 107m; VHS, DVD. **C:** Susan Hayward; John Gavin; Vera Miles; Directed by David Miller; Cinematography by William H. Daniels. **Pr:** Mark Huffam. **A:** Family. **P:** Entertainment. **U:** Home. **Mov-Ent:** Drama, Melodrama. **Acq:** Purchase. **Dist:** Turner Broadcasting System Inc. $14.98.

Back Talk 1978
This program demonstrates the right way to perform daily activities and prevent unnecessary strain to the back. 12m; VHS, 3/4 U. **Pr:** Professional Research. **A:** Sr. High-Adult. **P:** Education. **U:** Institution, CCTV. **Hea-Sci:** Back Disorders. **Acq:** Purchase, Rent/Lease. **Dist:** Discovery Education.

Back Talk 1988
Emphasizes proper back care for nurses and staff. Also points out the seven nursing tasks that produce the most back injuries—lifting patients, controlling patient falls, pulling patients up in bed, bedside procedures, making beds, pushing medicine carts, and twisting. Offers information on the anatomy and physiology of the back, proper body mechanics, and back-strengthening exercises. AJN Media Festival Winner. 30m; VHS. **Pr:** Hospital Corporation of America. **A:** College-Adult. **P:** Education. **U:** Institution. **Hea-Sci:** Nursing, Patient Care, Back Disorders. **Acq:** Purchase, Rent/Lease. **Dist:** AJN Video Library/Lippincott Williams & Wilkins. $285.00.

Back to Africa 1998
Tells the story of Sade, a young black woman on a spiritual quest to find the father that was compelled to leave her and her mother in New York 22 years earlier. Her journey takes her to Nigeria where she discovers herself, her roots and her true culture. 105m; VHS. **A:** Family. **P:** Entertainment. **U:** Home. **Mov-Ent:** Africa, Black Culture. **Acq:** Purchase. **Dist:** Tapeworm Video Distributors Inc. $29.95.

Back to Arafat 1991
Documentary about the Armenian genocide in which 1.5 million Armenians were killed, and the remainder driven from Turkey. The dream of three generations of Armenians to return the homeland is examined. 100m; VHS. **A:** Sr. High-Adult. **P:** Education. **U:** Home. **Gen-Edu:** Documentary Films, History. **Acq:** Purchase. **Dist:** Facets Multimedia Inc. $50.00.

Back to Ararat 1988
Examines the genocide of 1.5 million Armenians during WWI as well as currnt Turkish response to the episode and present-day Armenian communities. 100m; VHS. **C:** Directed by PeA Holmquist. **A:** College-Adult. **P:** Education. **U:** Institution. **Gen-Edu:** History--Modern, Middle East, World War One. **Acq:** Purchase, Rent/Lease. **Dist:** First Run/Icarus Films. $490.00.

Back to Back 1990 (R) — ★
A beautiful young vigilante embarks on a rampage to clear her family's name and make her town's redneck crooks pay for their crimes. Never released in theatres. 95m; VHS. **C:** Bill Paxton; Todd Field; Apollonia; Luke Askew; Ben Johnson; David Michael-Standing; Susan Anspach; Sal Landi; Directed by John Kincade; Cinematography by James L. Carter. **Pr:** Concorde Pictures. **A:** College-Adult. **P:** Entertainment. **U:** Home. **Mov-Ent. Acq:** Purchase. **Dist:** MGM Home Entertainment. $79.95.

Back to Back 1996 (R) — ★★¹/₂
Ex-cop Malone (Rooker) must team up with hitman Koji (Ishibashi), who's holding Malone's daughter hostage, to double-cross a corrupt cop and stay alive while being hunted by the Mafia. 95m; VHS, DVD, CC. **C:** Michael Rooker; Ryo Ishibashi; John Laughlin; Danielle Harris; Bobcat Goldthwait; Vincent Schiavelli; Directed by Roger Nygard; Written by Lloyd Keith; Cinematography by Mark W. Gray; Music by Walter Werzowa. **Pr:** W.K. Border; Aki Komine; Joel Soisson; Taka Ichise; Overseas Film Group; Ozla Pictures. **A:** Sr. High-Adult. **P:** Entertainment. **U:** Home. **Mov-Ent. Acq:** Purchase. **Dist:** BMG Entertainment.

Back to Back: L.A. Lakers '87-'88 Championship 1988
Important footage from the pro team's bumper year. 60m; VHS. **C:** Narrated by Chick Hearn. **Pr:** CBS/Fox. **A:** Family. **P:** Entertainment. **U:** Home. **Spo-Rec:** Basketball. **Acq:** Purchase. **Dist:** ESPN Inc. $19.98.

Back 2 Back: Toronto Blue Jays '93 1993
Chronicles the Toronto Blue Jays' 1993 season as they repeat as World Champions. Includes highlights and interviews. 60m; VHS. **A:** Family. **P:** Entertainment. **U:** Home. **Spo-Rec:** Sports--General, Baseball, Canada. **Acq:** Purchase. **Dist:** Major League Baseball Productions. $19.95.

Back to Basics for Safe Lifting 1984
A cautionary film for businesses about proper procedures for lifting heavy objects. 21m; VHS, 3/4 U. **Pr:** Bureau of Business Practice. **A:** Adult. **P:** Professional. **U:** Institution, CCTV. **Bus-Ind:** How-To, Safety Education. **Acq:** Purchase, Rent/Lease. **Dist:** Aspen Publishers, Inc. $495.00.

Back to Bataan 1945 (Unrated) — ★★¹/₂
Colonel forms guerrilla army to raid Japanese in the Philippines and to help Americans landing on Leyte. Also available in a colorized version. 95m/B/W; VHS, DVD, CC. **C:** John Wayne; Anthony Quinn; Beulah Bondi; Fely Franquelli; Richard Loo; Philip Ahn; Lawrence Tierney; Directed by Edward Dmytryk. **Pr:** RKO. **A:** Family. **P:** Entertainment. **U:** Home. **Mov-Ent:** World War Two. **Acq:** Purchase. **Dist:** Turner Broadcasting System Inc. $19.98.

Back to College with Fred Waring 1958
A nostalgic salute to college life with Fred Waring and the Pennsylvanians. Features an appearance by comedian Sterling Holloway. 25m; VHS. **C:** Conducted by Fred Waring. **Pr:** VAI. **A:** Jr. High-Adult. **P:** Entertainment. **U:** Home. **Mov-Ent:** Television Series, Singing. **Acq:** Purchase. **Dist:** Video Artists International. $19.95.

Back to Hannibal: The Return of Tom Sawyer and Huckleberry Finn 1990 (Unrated) — ★★½
Mark Twain's characters Tom Sawyer and Huckleberry Finn are reunited as adults to solve a murder mystery. Tom is a lawyer, Finn a newspaper man, and it's Becky Thatcher's husband who's been murdered. Did a freed slave really commit the crime? 92m; VHS, DVD. **C:** Raphael Sbarge; Mitchell Anderson; Megan Follows; William Windom; Ned Beatty; Paul Winfield; Directed by Paul Krasny; Music by Lee Holdridge. **A:** Family. **P:** Entertainment. **U:** Home. **Mov-Ent:** Mystery & Suspense, Family Viewing, TV Movies. **Acq:** Purchase. **Dist:** Walt Disney Studios Home Entertainment. $19.99.

Back to My Lai 1998
Segment from 60 Minutes follows a former U.S. Army helicopter crew as they return to My Lai 30 years after rescuing a handful of women and children during a massacre. 14m; VHS. **A:** Sr. High. **P:** Education. **U:** Institution. **Gen-Edu:** History, Vietnam War. **Acq:** Purchase. **Dist:** Zenger Media. $29.95.

Back to 1942 2012 (Unrated) — ★★½
In Henan Province one of China's worst famines in history struck just as war with Japan was looming. Three million people starved to death on the trek west, hoping to avoid the Japanese army and somehow find food. Their quest amounts to little as the politicians of the time prefer to ignore the masses in preference for dining with the elite, a somewhat revisionist history as those same politicians were not on good terms with the Communist Party at the time. Based more on the novel "Remembering 1942" than actual events in particular, it still portrays a decent account of the death and degradation of the time's events. 145m; DVD, Blu-Ray. **C:** Guoli Zhang; Adrien Brody; Mo Zhang; Ziwen Wang; Tim Robbins; Directed by Xiaogang Feng; Written by Zhenyun Liu; Cinematography by Yue Lu; Music by Jiping Zhao. **A:** Sr. High-Adult. **P:** Entertainment. **U:** Home. **L:** English, Chinese. **Mov-Ent. Acq:** Purchase. **Dist:** Well Go USA, Inc. $29.98 24.98.

Back to Reality 1990
The lives and problems of people who are addicted to drugs or alcohol are studied. 83m; VHS, 3/4 U. **Pr:** American Media Inc. **A:** Sr. High-Adult. **P:** Education. **U:** Institution, CCTV, Home. **Hea-Sci:** Drug Abuse, Alcoholism. **Acq:** Purchase, Rent/Lease. **Dist:** American Media, Inc. $525.00.
Indiv. Titles: 1. Back to Reality 2. Enabling: Masking Reality 3. Intervention: Facing Reality.

Back to School 1986 (PG-13) — ★★½
Dangerfield plays an obnoxious millionaire who enrolls in college to help his wimpy son, Gordon, achieve campus stardom. His motto seems to be "if you can't buy it, it can't be had." At first, his antics embarrass his shy son, but soon everyone is clamoring to be seen with the pair as Gordon develops his own self confidence. 96m; VHS, DVD, Blu-Ray, Wide, CC. **C:** Rodney Dangerfield; Keith Gordon; Robert Downey, Jr.; Sally Kellerman; Burt Young; Paxton Whitehead; Adrienne Barbeau; M. Emmet Walsh; Severn Darden; Ned Beatty; Sam Kinison; Kurt Vonnegut, Jr.; Robert Picardo; Terry Farrell; Edie McClurg; Jason Hervey; William Zabka; Directed by Alan Metter; Written by Will Aldis; Steven Kampmann; Harold Ramis; Peter Torokvei; Cinematography by Thomas Ackerman; Music by Danny Elfman. **Pr:** Orion Pictures; Paper Clip Productions. **A:** Sr. High-Adult. **P:** Entertainment. **U:** Home. **Mov-Ent:** Comedy--Screwball, Education, Family. **Acq:** Purchase. **Dist:** Movies Unlimited. $11.99.

Back to School with Franklin 2003
Franklin and his friends have fun and learn new things with their teacher Miss Koala. Also includes a read-a-along, sing-a-long, and lots of games and activities. 47m; DVD, CC. **A:** Preschool. **P:** Entertainment. **U:** Home. **Chl-Juv:** Animation & Cartoons, Children. **Acq:** Purchase. **Dist:** Universal Studios Home Video. $19.98.

Back to the Beach 1987 (PG) — ★½
Frankie and Annette return to the beach as self-parodying, middle-aged parents with rebellious kids, and the usual run of sun-bleached, lover's tiff comedy ensues. Plenty of songs and guest appearances from television past. Tries to bring back that surf, sun, and sand feel of the original "Beach Party" movies, but fails. 92m; DVD, CC. **C:** Frankie Avalon; Annette Funicello; Connie Stevens; Lori Loughlin; Tommy Hinkley; Demian Slade; John Calvin; Joe Holland; David Bowe; Paul (Pee-wee Herman) Reubens; Don Adams; Bob Denver; Alan Hale, Jr.; Tony Dow; Jerry Mathers; Dick Dale; Stevie Ray Vaughan; Edd Byrnes; Barbara Billingsley; Directed by Lyndall Hobbs; Written by James Komack; Bill W.L. Norton; Cinematography by Bruce Surtees; Music by Steve Dorff. **Pr:** Paramount Pictures. **A:** Jr. High-Adult. **P:** Entertainment. **U:** Home. **Mov-Ent:** Comedy--Romantic, Parenting. **Acq:** Purchase. **Dist:** WarnerArchive.com. $19.95.
Songs: Absolute Perfection; California Sun; Catch a Ride; Jamaica Sky; Papa-Oom-Mow-Mow; Sign of Love; Sun, Sun, Sun, Sun, Sun; Surfin' Bird; Wooly Bully.

Back to the Future 1985 (PG) — ★★★
When neighborhood mad scientist Doc Brown (Lloyd) constructs a time machine from a DeLorean, his youthful companion Marty (Fox) accidentally transports himself to 1955. There, Marty must do everything he can to bring his high-school age parents together (so he can be born), elude the local bully, and get back...to the future. Solid fast-paced entertainment is even better due to Lloyd's inspired performance as the loony Doc while Fox is perfect as the boy completely out of his element. Soundtrack features Huey Lewis and the News. Followed by two sequels. 116m; VHS, DVD, Blu-Ray, Wide, CC. **C:** Michael J. Fox; Christopher Lloyd; Lea Thompson; Crispin Glover; Wendie Jo Sperber; Marc McClure; Thomas F. Wilson; James Tolkan; Casey Siemaszko; Billy Zane; George DiCenzo; Courtney Gains; Claudia Wells; Jason Hervey; Harry Waters, Jr.; Maia Brewton; J.J. (Jeffrey Jay) Cohen; Cameo(s) Huey Lewis; Directed by Robert Zemeckis; Written by Robert Zemeckis; Bob Gale; Cinematography by Dean Cundey; Music by Alan Silvestri. **Pr:** Bob Gale; Bob Gale; Neil Canton; Steven Spielberg; Mark Huffam; Amblin Entertainment. **A:** Family. **P:** Entertainment. **U:** Home. **Mov-Ent:** Action-Adventure, Automobiles, Technology. **Awds:** Natl. Film Reg. '07. **Acq:** Purchase. **Dist:** Facets Multimedia Inc.; Time-Life Video and Television. $19.95.

Back to the Future, Part 2 1989 (PG) — ★★½
Taking up exactly where Part 1 left off, Doc Brown and Marty time-hop into the future (2015 to be exact) to save Marty's kids, then find themselves returning to 1955 to retrieve a sports almanac that causes havoc for the McFly family. Clever editing allows for Marty Part 2 to see Marty Part 1 at the school dance. Most of the cast returns, although Glover appears only in cuts from the original and Shue steps in as girlfriend Jennifer. Not up to the original, but still satisfying. Cliffhanger ending sets up Part 3, which was shot simultaneously with this. 107m; VHS, DVD, Blu-Ray, Wide, CC. **C:** Michael J. Fox; Christopher Lloyd; Lea Thompson; Thomas F. Wilson; Harry Waters, Jr.; Charles Fleischer; Joe Flaherty; Elisabeth Shue; James Tolkan; Casey Siemaszko; Jeffrey Weissman; Flea; Billy Zane; J.J. (Jeffrey Jay) Cohen; Darlene Vogel; Jason Scott Lee; Crispin Glover; Ricky Dean Logan; Elijah Wood; Directed by Robert Zemeckis; Written by Robert Zemeckis; Bob Gale; Cinematography by Dean Cundey; Music by Alan Silvestri. **Pr:** Bob Gale; Neil Canton; Steven Spielberg; Mark Huffam; Bob Gale; Amblin Entertainment. **A:** Jr. High-Adult. **P:** Entertainment. **U:** Home. **Mov-Ent:** Action-Adventure, Gambling. **Acq:** Purchase. **Dist:** Movies Unlimited; Alpha Video; Universal Studios Home Video. $19.95.

Back to the Future, Part 3 1990 (PG) — ★★★
Picks up where Part 2 climaxed a la cliffhanger. Stuck in 1955, time-traveling hero Marty frantically searches for Doc Part 1 so he can return to 1985. Instead, he finds himself in the Wild West circa 1885, trying to save Doc's life. Plot is related to earlier BTTFs, so first time viewers might be confused. For those who've seen previous incarnations, the clever interconnections are really nifty. Nearly matches the original for excitement and offers some snazzy special effects. The complete trilogy is available as a boxed set. 118m; VHS, DVD, Blu-Ray, Wide, CC. **C:** Michael J. Fox; Christopher Lloyd; Mary Steenburgen; Thomas F. Wilson; Lea Thompson; Elisabeth Shue; Matt Clark; Richard Dysart; Pat Buttram; Harry Carey, Jr.; Dub Taylor; James Tolkan; Marc McClure; Wendie Jo Sperber; J.J. (Jeffrey Jay) Cohen; Ricky Dean Logan; Jeffrey Weissman; Directed by Robert Zemeckis; Written by Robert Zemeckis; Bob Gale; Cinematography by Dean Cundey; Music by Alan Silvestri. **Pr:** Bob Gale; Bob Gale; Neil Canton; Steven Spielberg; Mark Huffam; Amblin Entertainment. **A:** Jr. High-Adult. **P:** Entertainment. **U:** Home. **Mov-Ent:** Action-Adventure, Trains. **Acq:** Purchase. **Dist:** Universal Studios Home Video; Movies Unlimited; Alpha Video. $19.95.

Back to the Secret Garden 2001 — ★★½
Well-meaning but dull sequel based on characters from the novel by Frances Hodgson Burnett. It's now the 1940s and sullen Mary has grown into the elegant Lady Mary (Lunghi), the wife of the ambassador to the U.S. Mistlethwaite has turned into a sunny English orphanage that is run by Martha (Plowright). Lady Mary arranges for Brooklyn-born orphan Lizzie (Buelle) to join their little band, and the young girl just happens to be a gardening whiz. Which is a good thing, since Mary's special garden been badly neglected once again. 100m; VHS, DVD. **C:** Camilla Belle; Cherie Lunghi; Joan Plowright; David Warner; Leigh Lawson; Florence Hoath; Directed by Michael Tuchner; Written by Joe Wiesenfeld; Cinematography by Ian Wilson. **A:** Family. **P:** Entertainment. **U:** Home. **Mov-Ent:** Adoption, Great Britain, Gardening. **Acq:** Purchase. **Dist:** Showtime Networks Inc.

Back to the Stagedoor Canteen 19??
Patriotism ran high in Hollywood during WWII. Nostalgic look at how the greatest stars and biggest names encouraged the troops and lifted morale. ?m; VHS. **A:** Jr. High-Adult. **P:** Entertainment. **U:** Home, Institution. **Gen-Edu:** World War Two. **Acq:** Purchase. **Dist:** Silver Mine Video Inc. $29.95.

Back to the Wall 1956 (Unrated) — ★★
Moreau is an adulturous wife whose web of deceit results in a suspenseful tale of murder and blackmail. 94m/B/W; VHS. **C:** Jeanne Moreau; Gerard Oury; Claire Maurier; Directed by Edouard Molinaro. **A:** Sr. High-Adult. **P:** Entertainment. **U:** Home. **L:** English, French. **Mov-Ent:** Mystery & Suspense, Marriage. **Acq:** Purchase. **Dist:** Facets Multimedia Inc. $29.95.

Back to You and Me 2005 (Unrated) — ★★½
Hallmark Channel family drama. Big city doctor Sydney Ludwick has been estranged from her widowed mom Helen ever since her dad's funeral. Needing a break, Syd decides to return home for her high school reunion and notices that her one-time boyfriend Gus is still a hunk and now a widower. His son Jake, who happens to need Syd's medical help, thinks she would also be a good choice for a stepmom. However, first Syd has to deal with her own mom issues. 85m; DVD. **C:** Rue McClanahan; Lisa Hartman Black; Dale Midkiff; Blake Woodruff; Don Harvey; Lisa Long; Barbara Niven; Larry Manetti; Directed by David S. Cass, Sr.; Written by Tom Amundsen; Cinematography by James W. Wrenn; Music by Kevin Kliesch. **A:** Jr. High-Adult. **P:** Entertainment. **U:** Home. **Mov-Ent. Acq:** Purchase. **Dist:** RHI Entertainment.

Back to You: Season 1 2008 (Unrated)
Television sitcom series on FOX (2007-2008). News anchor Chuck Darling (Grammer) returns to Pittsburgh's WURG after failing miserably in Dallas, Los Angeles, and other large markets but that doesn't make him any less big headed. But finding out a drunken tryst years ago with future co-anchor Kelly Carr (Heaton) resulted in a daughter (now 10) markably throws him off kilter. Will Chuck and Kelly admit the truth to Gracie and others? Only time will tell. The station staff car pool together in "A Night of Possibilities." Ended quickly due to the 2007 Writers' Guild strike. 17 episodes. 291m; DVD. **A:** Sr. High-Adult. **P:** Entertainment. **U:** Home. **Mov-Ent:** Television Series. **Acq:** Purchase. **Dist:** Fox Home Entertainment.

The Back Trail 1924 (Unrated) — ★★
Unusual silent western that deals with post-war problems. Due to shell shock, WWI veteran Jeff Prouty has amnesia. The cowboy is manipulated by bad guy Gentleman Harry King into believing he's a criminal and then into breaking his father's will so King can gain access to Jeff's inheritance. ?m/B/W; Silent; DVD. **C:** Jack Hoxie; Eugenia Gilbert; William Berke; Claude Payton; William (Bill, Billy) McCall; Al Hoxie; Directed by Clif-f(ord) Smith; Written by Isadore Bernstein; Cinematography by Harry Neumann. **A:** College-Adult. **P:** Entertainment. **U:** Home. **Mov-Ent:** Western, Silent Films, Veterans. **Acq:** Purchase. **Dist:** Sinister Cinema.

Back Up 1978
Two women leave the pool rooms to become domestics in a private school in this experimental video. 36m; VHS, 3/4 U. **Pr:** Margaret Dragu; Kate Craig; Western Front Video. **A:** College-Adult. **P:** Entertainment. **U:** Institution. **Fin-Art:** Video. **Acq:** Rent/Lease. **Dist:** Video Out Distribution.

The Back-Up Plan 2010 (PG-13) — ★★½
Tepid romantic comedy (that packs on the schmaltz as well) with Lopez game for various outrageous and humiliating situations (she has a funny lament about what pregnancy has done to her curves, especially her butt). Pet shop-owner Zoe (Lopez) is tired of waiting for the right man to father her child so she goes the sperm donor route. Of course just when she gets pregnant, Zoe meets frequently shirtless, cheese-making goat farmer Stan (O'Loughlin) who may be a keeper since he's willing to stick around and help her with the pregnancy. But then the realization of upcoming parenthood sinks in, causing both of them to question the suddenness of their relationship. 106m; Blu-Ray, On Demand, Wide, CC. **C:** Jennifer Lopez; Eric Christian Olsen; Danneel Harris; Melissa McCarthy; Alex O'Loughlin; Anthony Anderson; Michaela Watkins; Directed by Alan Poul; Written by Kate Angelo; Cinematography by Xavier Perez Grobet; Music by Stephen Trask. **Pr:** Todd Black; Jason Blumenthal; Steve Tisch; Escape Artists; CBS Films. **A:** Jr. High-Adult. **P:** Entertainment. **U:** Home. **L:** English. **Mov-Ent:** Pregnancy, Comedy--Romantic, Agriculture. **Acq:** Purchase. **Dist:** Sony Pictures Home Entertainment Inc.; Amazon.com Inc.; Movies Unlimited.

Back Wards to Back Streets 1980
A documentary look at the deinstitutionalization of the mentally ill. The program takes a nationwide look at both the disasters of community health care and the exception programs that provide supportive after-care for discharged mental patients. 60m; VHS, 3/4 U. **Pr:** WNET New York. **A:** College-Adult. **P:** Education. **U:** Institution, CCTV, Home. **Hea-Sci:** Psychiatry. **Acq:** Purchase, Rent/Lease. **Dist:** WNET/Thirteen Non-Broadcast; Filmakers Library Inc.

Back with a Vengeance 1995
Investigates the typical workplace killer and stresses prevention methods and screening tools when hiring. 15m; VHS. **A:** Adult. **P:** Professional. **U:** Institution. **Bus-Ind:** Job Training, Safety Education, Management. **Acq:** Rent/Lease. **Dist:** National Safety Council, California Chapter, Film Library.

Backache 1974
Examines the most frequent human ailment aside from the common cold and the headache-the backache. 14m; VHS, 3/4 U, Special order formats. **Pr:** American Medical Association. **A:** Sr. High-College. **P:** Education. **U:** Institution, SURA. **Hea-Sci:** Back Disorders. **Acq:** Purchase, Rent/Lease. **Dist:** Time-Life Video and Television.

Backache: Causes and Prevention 1977
A program that examines the causes, preventive measures and curative exercises relating to backaches. 23m; VHS, 3/4 U. **Pr:** Aims Media. **A:** Jr. High-Adult. **P:** Education. **U:** Institution, SURA. **Hea-Sci:** Back Disorders, Health Education. **Acq:** Purchase, Rent/Lease, Duplication License. **Dist:** National Safety Council, California Chapter, Film Library.

Backbeat 1994 (R) — ★★★
Backed by the beat of early Beatle tunes as rendered by some of today's top alternative musicians, the debut for director Softley explores the Fab Four's beginnings in Hamburg's underground music scene. Storyline is driven by the complications of a romantic triangle between John Lennon, Astrid Kirchherr (the photographer who came up with the band's signature look) and Stu Sutcliffe, Lennon's best friend and the original bass player for the Beatles. Hart's dead-on as Lennon, playing him a second time (check out "The Hours and Times"). Energetic and enjoyable, particularly when the Was-produced music takes center stage. 100m; VHS, DVD, Wide, CC. **C:** Stephen Dorff; Sheryl Lee; Ian Hart; Gary Bakewell; Chris O'Neill; Scot Williams; Kai Wiesinger; Jennifer Ehle; Directed by Iain Softley;

Written by Michael Thomas; Stephen Ward; Iain Softley; Cinematography by Ian Wilson; Music by Don Was. **Pr:** Stephen Woolley; Finola Dwyer; Nik Powell; Polygram; Channel 4; Royal Films International; Gramercy Pictures. **A:** Sr. High-Adult. **P:** Entertainment. **U:** Home. **Mov-Ent:** Biography: Music, Music--Pop/Rock, Germany. **Acq:** Purchase. **Dist:** Movies Unlimited; Alpha Video. $94.99.

The Backbone of Night 1980
The island of Samos is visited and the scientific findings of ancient Ionian physicists is explored. Science as a structured body was born here, but it declined amidst the Pythagorean and Platonic mysticism that followed. Part of the "Cosmos" series. 60m; VHS, 3/4 U. **C:** Dr. Carl Sagan. **Pr:** Carl Sagan Productions. **A:** Jr. High-Adult. **P:** Education. **U:** Institution, SURA. **Gen-Edu:** Science. **Acq:** Purchase, Off-Air Record. **Dist:** Home Vision Cinema.

Backcountry Skiing: Telemarking in the '80s 1984
Another colorful skiing film, this time interspersed with introductions to telemarking. 15m; VHS. **Pr:** Video Travel, Inc. **A:** Jr. High-Adult. **P:** Entertainment. **U:** Home. **Spo-Rec:** Sports--Winter. **Acq:** Purchase. **Dist:** Vivid Publisher.

Backdraft 1991 (R) — ★★½
High action story of Chicago firemen has some of the most stupendous incendiary special effects ever filmed. But then there's that plot, B-movie hokum about a mystery arsonist torching strategic parts of the community with the finesse of an expert and a brother-against-brother conflict. Straight-forward performances from most of the cast in spite of the weak storyline. Writer Widen wrote from experience—he used to be a fireman; real-life Chicago firefighters were reportedly very happy with the realistic and intense fire scenes. Forget the plot and just watch the fires. Also available in a letterboxed version. 135m; VHS, DVD, Blu-Ray, HD-DVD, Wide, CC. **C:** Kurt Russell; William Baldwin; Robert De Niro; Donald Sutherland; Jennifer Jason Leigh; Scott Glenn; Rebecca De Mornay; Jason Gedrick; J.T. Walsh; Tony Mockus, Sr.; Clint Howard; David Crosby; Directed by Ron Howard; Written by Gregory Widen; Cinematography by Mikael Salomon; Music by Hans Zimmer. **Pr:** Imagine Entertainment; Brian Grazer Production. **A:** Sr. High-Adult. **P:** Entertainment. **U:** Home. **Mov-Ent:** Action-Adventure, Fires. **Acq:** Purchase. **Dist:** Movies Unlimited; Alpha Video; Universal Studios Home Video. $19.98.

Backdraft and Smoke Explosions 19??
Uses live fire scene footage, still photography, and graphic illustrations to explain backdraft, how it occurs, what the warning signs are, and the safety precautions to take. Includes study booklet that gives a general overview of the video. Approved for fire service training. 20m; VHS. **A:** College-Adult. **P:** Instruction. **U:** Institution. **How-Ins:** Job Training. **Acq:** Purchase. **Dist:** Fire Engineering Books & Videos. $149.95.

The Backer Zone Defense 2012 (Unrated)
Coach Scott Tucker discusses the backer zone defense and how to install it on a lacrosse team. ??m; DVD. **A:** Family. **P:** Education. **U:** Home, Institution. **Spo-Rec:** Lacrosse, Athletic Instruction/Coaching. **Acq:** Purchase. **Dist:** Championship Productions. $39.99.

Backfield in Motion 1991 — ★★½
Silly but harmless comedy about a widowed mom who tries to get closer to her high-schooler son by organizing a mother-son football game. But it's the boys' football coach who really wants to get close—to mom. TV movie debut of both Arnolds (past and present). 95m; VHS, DVD, CC. **C:** Roseanne; Tom Arnold; Colleen Camp; Conchata Ferrell; Johnny Galecki; Kevin Scannell; Directed by Richard Michaels. **A:** Family. **P:** Entertainment. **U:** Home. **Mov-Ent:** Parenting, Football, Education. **Acq:** Purchase. **Dist:** Turner Broadcasting System Inc.

Backfire 198?
This film is designed to inform employees how to do their work without risking a back injury. 15m; VHS, 3/4 U, Special order formats. **Pr:** Altschul Group. **A:** College-Adult. **P:** Education. **U:** Institution. **Bus-Ind:** Safety Education. **Acq:** Rent/Lease. **Dist:** National Safety Council, California Chapter, Film Library. $420.00.

Backfire 1922 — ★★
If you're gonna rob a bank, you shouldn't let anyone hear you plan it, and if you're not gonna rob a bank, you shouldn't let anyone hear you plan one. This vintage "Lightning" Carson crime western has Carson and friend suspected of bank robbery because someone heard them planning one. The sheriff follows their every footstep as they search for the real perpetrators. 56m/B/W; Silent; VHS. **C:** Jack Hoxie; George Sowards; Lew Meehan; Florence Gilbert; Directed by Alan James. **Pr:** Sunset Productions. **A:** Sr. High-Adult. **P:** Entertainment. **U:** Home. **Mov-Ent:** Western, Silent Films. **Acq:** Purchase. **Dist:** Grapevine Video. $9.95.

Backfire 1950 (Unrated) — ★★½
Bob Corey (MacRae) has spent months in an LA veterans hospital where he and Army nurse Julie Benson (Mayo) fall in love. Bob's worried when he loses contact with buddy Steve Connolly (O'Brien) and, after his release, the cops tell him that Steve is on the lam for murdering a gambler. Bob doesn't believe them and he and Julie start investigating, which leads to a series of flashbacks narrated by different characters who don't all tell the truth. MacRae successfully moved on from his musical past to this postwar crime thriller. 91m/B/W; DVD. **C:** Gordon MacRae; Virginia Mayo; Edmond O'Brien; Dane Clark; Viveca Lindfors; Ed Begley, Sr.; Monte Blue; Richard Rober; Directed by Vincent Sherman; Written by Ben Roberts; Lawrence B. Marcus; Ivan Goff; Cinematography by Carl Guthrie; Music by Daniele Amfitheatrof. **A:** Sr. High-Adult. **P:** Entertainment. **U:** Home. **Mov-Ent:** Crime Drama, Veterans. **Acq:** Purchase. **Dist:** WarnerArchive.com.

Backfire 1988 (R) — ★★
A mysterious stranger enters the lives of a disturbed 'Nam vet and his discontented wife, setting a pattern of murder and double-cross in motion. 90m; VHS, DVD. **C:** Karen Allen; Keith Carradine; Jeff Fahey; Bernie Casey; Dinah Manoff; Dean Paul (Dino Martin Jr.) Martin; Directed by Gilbert Cates; Written by Larry Brand; Music by David Shire. **Pr:** JTC Productions. **A:** Sr. High-Adult. **P:** Entertainment. **U:** Home. **Mov-Ent:** Mystery & Suspense, Veterans. **Acq:** Purchase. **Dist:** CinemaNow Inc. $29.95.

Backfire! 1994 (PG-13) — ★½
Silly spoof finds Jeremy (Mosby) wanting to join New York City's all-female fire brigade who are trying to stop an arsonist from blowing up the city's toilets. Mitchum is the fire marshal and Ireland the mayor's charming assistant. 88m; VHS. **C:** Josh Mosby; Kathy Ireland; Robert Mitchum; Shelley Winters; Directed by A. Dean Bell. **A:** Jr. High-Adult. **P:** Entertainment. **U:** Home. **Mov-Ent:** Satire & Parody. **Acq:** Purchase. **Dist:** $92.95.

Backflash 2001 (R) — ★★
Ray (Patrick) runs a videostore and needs a little excitement in his life. He picks up pretty hitchhiker Harley (Esposito), who's just out of jail, and gets more than he's bargained for since Harley needs Ray to pretend to be her husband so she can get into a safety deposit box. But just who's conning who? 90m; VHS, DVD. **C:** Robert Patrick; Jennifer Esposito; Melissa Joan Hart; Directed by Philip Jones; Written by Philip Jones; Jennifer Farrell; Lillian Jackson; Cinematography by Maximo Munzi; Music by Valentine Leone; Carl Wurtz. **A:** Sr. High-Adult. **P:** Entertainment. **U:** Home. **Mov-Ent.** **Acq:** Purchase. **Dist:** Buena Vista Home Entertainment.

The Background of the Civil War—Revised 1981
The beginnings of the American Civil War lie buried in the differences between the North and the South. 20m; VHS, 3/4 U. **Pr:** BFA Educational Media. **A:** Preschool. **P:** Education. **U:** Institution, SURA. **Gen-Edu:** History--U.S. **Acq:** Purchase. **Dist:** Phoenix Learning Group.

The Background of the Reconstruction Period 1986
The trying times of the post-Civil War South are recounted, focusing on legislation of the Johnson and Grant administrations. 21m; VHS, 3/4 U. **A:** Jr. High-Adult. **P:** Entertainment. **U:** Institution, SURA. **Gen-Edu:** Civil War, History--U.S. **Acq:** Purchase. **Dist:** Phoenix Learning Group. $320.00.

The Background of the U.S. Constitution 1984
A dramatic study of the events that led to the drafting of the U.S. Constitution. 20m/B/W; VHS, 3/4 U. **Pr:** BFA Educational Media. **A:** Primary-Jr. High. **P:** Education. **U:** Institution, SURA. **Gen-Edu:** History--U.S., Politics & Government. **Acq:** Purchase. **Dist:** Phoenix Learning Group.

Background to Beowulf 19??
Explains some of the historical and literary traditions behind the epic Old English poem "Beowulf." Contains enhanced artwork. 25m; VHS. **A:** College-Adult. **P:** Education. **U:** Institution. **Gen-Edu:** Literature--English. **Acq:** Purchase. **Dist:** Educational Video Network. $49.95.

Background to Danger 1943 — ★★★
A suspenseful WWII actioner about American agent Raft who travels to Turkey to receive secret documents from the soon-to-be-murdered Massen. Greenstreet is the Nazi master spy who also wants the documents as do Russian spies, Lorre and Marshall. Somewhat confusing plot but fast-paced. Based on the thriller "Uncommon Danger" by Eric Ambler. This film was Warner Bros.' follow-up to "Casablanca" with Raft in the Bogie role he had turned down in that cinema classic. 80m/B/W; VHS, DVD. **C:** George Raft; Sydney Greenstreet; Peter Lorre; Brenda Marshall; Osa Massen; Turhan Bey; Kurt Katch; Directed by Raoul Walsh; Written by W.R. Burnett. **Pr:** Jerry Wald; Warner Bros. **A:** Jr. High-Adult. **P:** Entertainment. **U:** Home. **Mov-Ent.** **Acq:** Purchase. **Dist:** WarnerArchive.com; Movies Unlimited. $19.98.

Backgrounds: A Brief History of Israel and the Arab/Palestinian Conflict 1992
Examines the roots and developments of the conflict between Israel and the Arabs and Palestinians from the 13th century B.C. to the present day, including the birth of Zionism, wars, conquests, partition plans, and struggles for independence. Study guide available. 29m; VHS, Special order formats. **C:** Directed by Barbara Pfeffer. **A:** Sr. High-Adult. **P:** Education. **U:** Institution. **Gen-Edu:** Documentary Films, Israel. **Acq:** Purchase. **Dist:** First Run/Icarus Films. $190.00.

Backhoe/Loader Operations 1995
Features safety practices and operating rules for anyone who operates a backhoe. 10m; VHS. **A:** Adult. **P:** Professional. **U:** Institution. **L:** Spanish. **Bus-Ind:** Safety Education, Occupational Training, Construction. **Acq:** Purchase, Rent/Lease. **Dist:** National Safety Council, California Chapter, Film Library. $175.00.

Backhoe Safety 199?
Focusing on tractor-loading backhoes, this program examines safety procedures including pre-inspection/start-up hazards, loading and unloading trailers, safe work practices for crew and personnel working around a backhoe and more. ?m; VHS. **A:** Sr. High-Adult. **P:** Education. **U:** Home, Institution. **Bus-Ind:** Safety Education, Construction, Occupational Training. **Acq:** Purchase. **Dist:** Aurora Pictures Inc.

Backlash 1956 — ★½
Jim Slater (Widmark) and Karyl Orton (Reed) are both searching for the surivors of an Apache attack. Karyl's husband is dead but one man got away with a fortune in gold and Jim is determined to find him. 84m; DVD. **C:** Richard Widmark; Donna Reed; John McIntire; William Campbell; Barton MacLane; Directed by John Sturges; Written by Borden Chase; Cinematography by Irving Glassberg; Music by Herman Stein. **A:** Jr. High-Adult. **P:** Entertainment. **U:** Home. **L:** English. **Mov-Ent:** Western. **Acq:** Purchase. **Dist:** Universal Studios Home Video.

Backlash 1986 (R) — ★★½
An aborigine barmaid is raped. When her assailant turns up dead, she's charged with murder and winds up in the custody of two police officers on a trip across the outback. Holes in the plot undermine this interesting, although graphic, drama with racial overtones. 88m; VHS. **C:** David Argue; Gia Carides; Lydia Miller; Brian Syron; Anne Smith; Directed by Bill Bennett; Written by Bill Bennett; Music by Michael Atkinson; Michael Spicer. **Pr:** Mermaid Beach Productions. **A:** College-Adult. **P:** Entertainment. **U:** Home. **Mov-Ent:** Action-Adventure, Rape. **Acq:** Purchase. **Dist:** Management Company Entertainment Group (MCEG), Inc. $79.95.

Backlash 1999 (R) — ★★
Federal prosecutor Gina Gallagher (Needham) has gotten on the wrong side of the Colombian drug cartel. After her partner is killed, Gina works with veteran homicide detective Moe Ryan (Durning) and uncovers a government conspiracy—so maybe trusting a convict (Belushi) to protect her isn't such a bad idea. 103m; VHS, DVD, UMD, CC. **C:** Tracey Needham; Charles Durning; James Belushi; JoBeth Williams; Patrick Ersgard; Tony Plana; Henry Silva; Warren Berlinger; Directed by Joakim (Jack) Ersgard; Written by Patrick Ersgard. **A:** Sr. High-Adult. **P:** Entertainment. **U:** Home. **Mov-Ent:** Conspiracies or Conspiracy Theories, Crime Drama. **Acq:** Purchase. **Dist:** Sony Pictures Home Entertainment Inc.

Backlash: Oblivion 2 1995 (PG-13) — ★★½
Galactic supervillainess Lash stakes her claim to a rare derconium mine on the remote space outpost of Oblivion. Will cave monsters thwart her evil plan before space cowboys come to the town's rescue? 82m; VHS, DVD, CC. **C:** Andrew Divoff; Meg Foster; Isaac Hayes; Julie Newmar; Carel Struycken; George Takei; Musetta Vander; Jimmie F. Skaggs; Irwin Keyes; Maxwell Caulfield; Directed by Sam Irvin; Written by Peter David; Music by Pino Donaggio. **Pr:** Oana Paunescu; Vlad Paunescu; Charles Band; Full Moon Entertainment. **A:** Sr. High-Adult. **P:** Entertainment. **U:** Home. **Mov-Ent:** Science Fiction, Miners & Mining. **Acq:** Purchase. **Dist:** Full Moon Pictures. $89.95.

Backslash 2005 (Unrated) — ★½
Members of a group of would-be moviemakers are being killed off one by one, when they notice all the victims are fit college girls who appeared on a local website. Which is not exactly a new theme for a slasher movie. 88m; DVD. **C:** Steven J. Burge; Laura Bruner; Directed by Kevin Campbell; Written by Kevin Campbell; Cinematography by Victor Zorba. **A:** Sr. High-Adult. **P:** Entertainment. **U:** Home. **L:** English. **Mov-Ent.** **Acq:** Purchase. **Dist:** Lions Gate Home Entertainment. $19.98.

Backstab 1990 (R) — ★★½
A spellbinding tale of work, lust, and murder. Architect Brolin finds himself unable to get over the death of his wife, until a seductive and mysterious woman helps him over his grief. They spend the night together, engulfed in passion, but in the morning he wakes to find himself sleeping with the corpse of his boss. Only the first twist in this intriguing thriller. 91m; VHS, CC. **C:** James Brolin; Meg Foster; Isabelle Truchon; Directed by Jim Kaufman. **Pr:** Media. **A:** College-Adult. **P:** Entertainment. **U:** Home. **Mov-Ent:** Mystery & Suspense. **Acq:** Purchase. **Dist:** Anchor Bay Entertainment. $89.98.

Backstage 1973
A behind-the-scenes look at a theatre group (the Drexel Players) rehearsing and performing. 11m/B/W; 3/4 U. **Pr:** Ed Ozalas; Steve Lipshutz; Jim Whitters. **A:** Family. **P:** Education. **U:** Institution, SURA. **Fin-Art:** Theater. **Acq:** Purchase, Rent/Lease. **Dist:** Temple University Dept. of Film and Media Arts.

Backstage 2000 (R)
Absolutely nothing about this concert film will appeal to those who do not already embrace hip-hop music. It follows several rappers on a bus tour. As the title suggests, most of the action takes place away from the auditoriums—in hotels, corridors, buses, and bathrooms. The guys swear constantly, smoke a lot of dope, and brag about their various exploits. 87m; DVD. **C:** DMX; Method Man; Jay-Z; Redman; Ja Rule; Beanie Sigel; Directed by Chris Fiore; Cinematography by Elena "EZ" Sorre; Mark Petersson; Lenny Santiago. **A:** Sr. High-Adult. **P:** Entertainment. **U:** Home. **Mov-Ent:** Documentary Films, Music--Rap. **Acq:** Purchase. **Dist:** Buena Vista Home Entertainment.

Backstage at the Kirov 1983
A unique look at the Russian Kirov ballet company mixed with a profile of Leningrad. 83m; VHS. **C:** Galina Mezentseva; Konstantin Zaklinsky; Altyani Assylmuratova; Directed by Derek Hart. **Pr:** Dr. Armand Hammer. **A:** Sr. High-Adult. **P:** Entertainment. **U:** Home. **Fin-Art:** Performing Arts, Dance, Dance--Ballet. **Acq:** Purchase. **Dist:** Stagestep; Corinth Films Inc.; Facets Multimedia Inc. $14.95.

Backstairs 1921 — ★★
An obscure German silent film about urban degradation and familial strife. Currently only available as part of a collection. 44m/B/W; Silent; VHS, DVD. **TV Std:** NTSC, PAL. **C:** Henny Porten; Fritz Kortner; William Dieterle; Directed by Leopold Jessner. **A:** Jr. High-Family. **P:** Entertainment. **U:**

Home. **L:** German. **Mov-Ent**: Silent Films. **Acq:** Purchase, Rent/Lease. **Dist:** Grapevine Video; German Language Video Center. $39.95.

Backstairs at the White House 1979 (Unrated) — ★★★½
Drawn from Lillian Rogers Parks' 1961 novel "My Thirty Years Backstairs at the White House" and originally aired on NBC, recounts the head maid's real life as she works for eight presidents—from Taft through Eisenhower—and narrates a wide array of historical events during her 52 years of service. 540m; DVD. **C:** Olivia Cole; Leslie Uggams; Louis Gossett, Jr.; Robert Hooks; Leslie Nielsen; Cloris Leachman; Hari Rhodes; Paul Winfield; Julie Harris; Victor Buono; David Downing; Helen Carroll; Robert Vaughn; Kim Hunter; James A. Watson, Jr.; Claire Bloom; Celeste Holm; George Kennedy; Ed Flanders; Lee Grant; Larry Gates; Eileen Heckart; John Anderson; Harry (Henry) Morgan; Estelle Parsons; Jan Sterling; Barbara Barrie; Andrew Duggan; Heather Angel; Matthew "Stymie" Beard; Bibi Besch; Gerry Black; Marilyn Chris; Tom Clancy; Ann Doran; BeBe Drake; Kevin Hooks; Nancy Morgan; Harrison Page; Woodrow Parfrey; Bill Quinn; Ford Rainey; John Randolph; Noble Willingham; Dana Wynter; Ian Abercrombie; Louise Latham; Directed by Michael O'Herlihy; Written by Paul Dubov; Cinematography by Robert L. Morrison; Music by Morton Stevens. **A:** Jr. High-Adult. **P:** Entertainment. **U:** Home. **Mov-Ent**: Drama, Presidency. **Acq:** Purchase. **Dist:** Acorn Media Group Inc. $59.99.

The Backstreet Boys: A Night Out with the Backstreet Boys 1998
Long form video capturing the group live in Cologne, Germany in April '98, plus solo performances by each band member and interviews. Includes 5.1 Dolby digital surround sound and web links. ?m; DVD. **A:** Jr. High-Sr. High. **P:** Entertainment. **U:** Home. **Mov-Ent**: Music Video, Music--Pop/Rock. **Acq:** Purchase. **Dist:** BMG Entertainment. $19.98.

The Backstreet Boys: All Access 1998
Long form video capturing the beautiful harmonies, energetic dance moves, special effects, and pyrotechnics the group has become known for. ?m; DVD. **A:** Jr. High-Sr. High. **P:** Entertainment. **U:** Home. **Mov-Ent**: Music Video, Music--Pop/Rock. **Acq:** Purchase. **Dist:** BMG Entertainment. $19.98.

The Backstreet Boys: Around the World 2001
Captures the band on their promotional tour for the "Black & Blue" album including media events in Stockholm, Tokyo, Sydney, Capetown and Rio de Janeiro. Plus an exclusive video for "Shape of My Heart" that combines live performances from five venues around the world. 90m; DVD. **A:** Jr. High-Sr. High. **P:** Entertainment. **U:** Home. **Mov-Ent**: Music Video, Music--Pop/Rock. **Acq:** Purchase. **Dist:** BMG Entertainment. $24.98.

The Backstreet Boys: Homecoming: Live in Orlando 1998
Live performance from a sold out New Year's Eve show in Orlando, Florida, plus interview footage, 5.1 Dolby digital surround sound option and web links. ?m; DVD. **A:** Jr. High-Sr. High. **P:** Entertainment. **U:** Home. **Mov-Ent**: Music Video, Music--Pop/Rock. **Acq:** Purchase. **Dist:** BMG Entertainment. $19.98.

Backstreet Boys—Backstreet Stories 2002
Interviews, profiles, and behind-the-scenes footage of the boy band. 50m; DVD. **A:** Jr. High-Adult. **P:** Entertainment. **U:** Home. **Fin-Art**: Documentary Films, Biography: Music. **Acq:** Purchase. **Dist:** Music Video Distributors.

Backstreet Dreams 1990 (R) — ★★
The young parents of an autistic child find themselves torn apart due to their feelings of guilt. The father has an affair with a specialist hired to help the boy, causing further strife. Interesting story possibilities never get far. 104m; VHS, Streaming. **C:** Brooke Shields; Jason O'Malley; Sherilyn Fenn; Tony Fields; Burt Young; Anthony (Tony) Franciosa; Nick Cassavetes; Ray "Boom Boom" Mancini; Directed by Rupert Hitzig; Music by Bill Conti. **Pr:** Vidmark Entertainment. **A:** College-Adult. **P:** Entertainment. **U:** Home. **Mov-Ent**: Drama, Marriage, Adolescence. **Acq:** Purchase. **Dist:** CinemaNow Inc. $79.98.

Backstreet Justice 1993 (R) — ★★½
Pittsburgh PI Keri Finnegan (Kozlowski) is investigating a series of murders in her neighborhood when she uncovers ties to police corruption dating back 30 years. This doesn't make her popular since it involves her dead cop father and a number of old friends (and enemies). Kozlowski is appropriately feisty and the plot twists will hold your attention. 91m; VHS. **C:** Linda Kozlowski; Hector Elizondo; John Shea; Paul Sorvino; Viveca Lindfors; Tammy Grimes; Directed by Chris T. McIntyre; Written by Chris T. McIntyre. **A:** Sr. High-Adult. **P:** Entertainment. **U:** Home. **Mov-Ent**: Mystery & Suspense, Women. **Acq:** Purchase. **Dist:** Unknown Distributor.

The Backstreet Six 1980
The summer adventures of six children whose playground is the city are chronicled in this program. Also available in three separate 26-minute episodes. 80m; VHS, 3/4 U. **Pr:** Les Productions Prisma. **A:** Primary-Jr. High. **P:** Entertainment. **U:** Institution, SURA. **Chl-Juv**. **Acq:** Purchase. **Dist:** Phoenix Learning Group.

The Backstretch 1984
This tape looks at the behind the scenes workforce involved in maintenance and preparation of a racehorse. 51m; VHS. **Pr:** Oak Tree Racing Association. **A:** Adult. **P:** Education. **U:** Home. **L:** English, Spanish. **Spo-Rec**: Horses--Racing. **Acq:** Purchase. **Dist:** , On Moratorium.

The Backstretch, Part 2 1984
Another look at the home team of horse-racing-the skilled professionals responsible for a race's success. 23m; VHS. **Pr:** Mercedes Maharis Productions. **A:** Sr. High-Adult. **P:** Education. **U:** Home. **Spo-Rec**: Horses--Racing. **Acq:** Purchase. **Dist:** , On Moratorium.

Backstroke Drills 2001
Demonstrates 23 drill to help correct and enhance backstroke efficiency and speed including single arm drills, 30-degree drills, spin drill, recovery drills and turn drills. 35m; VHS. **A:** Adult. **P:** Instruction. **U:** Institution. **How-Ins**: Swimming, Sports--Water, How-To. **Acq:** Purchase. **Dist:** Championship Productions. $34.95.

Backstroke Technique 2001
Technique, drills and training tips are discusses during a backstroke workout session demonstration. 25m; VHS. **A:** Adult. **P:** Instruction. **U:** Institution. **How-Ins**: Swimming, Sports--Water, How-To. **Acq:** Purchase. **Dist:** Championship Productions. $34.95.

Backstroke Training 2001
Demonstrates proper backstroke technique and presents several basic in pool drills. Discusses dryland and weekly training plans. 38m; VHS. **A:** Adult. **P:** Instruction. **U:** Institution. **How-Ins**: Swimming, Sports--Water, How-To. **Acq:** Purchase. **Dist:** Championship Productions. $34.95.

Backtalk: A Program for Nurses 1995
Features the importance of posture in sitting or standing to ensure against back injury. Also demonstrates back-strengthening exercises. 17m; VHS. **A:** Adult. **P:** Professional. **U:** Institution. **Hea-Sci**: Health Education, Safety Education, Occupational Training. **Acq:** Rent/Lease. **Dist:** National Safety Council, California Chapter, Film Library.

Backtrack 1977
A drifter, 15 years on the road, meets up with his 15-year-old daughter and the child's mother. Responsibility is the theme throughout the program. 14m; VHS, 3/4 U. **Pr:** Ron Ellis. **A:** Jr. High-Adult. **P:** Education. **U:** Institution, SURA. **Gen-Edu**: Family, Ethics & Morals. **Acq:** Purchase. **Dist:** Phoenix Learning Group.

Backtrack 1989 (R) — ★★★
Foster co-stars in this thriller about an artist who accidentally witnesses a mob hit. The mob puts a hitman (Hopper) on her trail, and after studying her background and listening to audio tapes she recorded, he finds himself falling in love. Originally intended for a theatrical release, it hit the European screens in a different cut as "Catchfire"; Hopper restored his original version and it was released on cable TV in the U.S. 102m; VHS, DVD, CC. **C:** Dennis Hopper; Jodie Foster; Dean Stockwell; Vincent Price; John Turturro; Fred Ward; G. Anthony "Tony" Sirico; Julie Adams; Frank Gio; Sy Richardson; Helena Kallianiotes; Bob Dylan; Cameo(s) Charlie Sheen; Joe Pesci; Directed by Dennis Hopper; Written by Ann Louise Bardach; Music by Michel Colombier. **Pr:** Vestron Video. **A:** College-Adult. **P:** Entertainment. **U:** Home. **Mov-Ent**: Mystery & Suspense, Romance, TV Movies. **Acq:** Purchase, Rent/Lease. **Dist:** Lions Gate Television Corp. $19.98.

Backup Supervision 1986
For supervisors, this tape addresses the importance of, and shows how to properly train, assistant supervisors in the workplace. 20m; VHS, 3/4 U. **Pr:** Bureau of Business Practice. **A:** Adult. **P:** Professional. **U:** Institution, CCTV. **Bus-Ind**: Management, Job Training. **Acq:** Purchase, Rent/Lease. **Dist:** Aspen Publishers, Inc. $495.00.

Backwards 2012 (PG) — ★★
Standard sports drama. After 30-year-old Abi Brooks is again only chosen as an alternate for the Olympic rowing team, she decides to reevaluate her life and takes a coaching job at her Philadelphia alma mater. This also gives her the chance to renew a romance with ex-beau Geoff. Abi struggles until she discovers a couple of girls with real potential just as she gets a call from her former coach about her own Olympic chances. 89m; DVD. **C:** Sarah Megan Thomas; James Van Der Beek; Glenn Morshower; Margaret Colin; Alexandra Metz; Meredith Apfelbaum; Directed by Ben Hickernell; Written by Sarah Megan Thomas; Cinematography by Harlan Bosmajian; Music by David Torn. **A:** Jr. High-Adult. **P:** Entertainment. **U:** Home. **L:** English. **Mov-Ent**: Sports--Olympic. **Acq:** Purchase. **Dist:** Phase 4/kaBOOM Entertainment.

Backwards: The Riddle of Dyslexia 1984
A dramatized look at dyslexia's effect on the life of a grade-school student and how the problem was surmounted. 30m; VHS, 3/4 U. **Pr:** LCA/Highlight; ABC Afterschool Special. **A:** Jr. High-Sr. High. **P:** Education. **U:** Institution. **Gen-Edu**: Learning Disabilities. **Acq:** Purchase, Rent/Lease. **Dist:** Phoenix Learning Group.

Backwoods 1987 (R) — ★
Two campers wish they had never encountered a mountain man when he begins to stalk them with murder in mind. 90m; VHS, DVD. **C:** Jack O'Hara; Dick Kreusser; Brad Armacot; Directed by Dean Crow. **A:** College-Adult. **P:** Entertainment. **U:** Home. **Mov-Ent**: Horror, Camps & Camping, Wilderness Areas. **Acq:** Purchase. **Dist:** Unknown Distributor.

The Backwoods 2006 (R) — ★½
Weak, schlocky psycho-thriller. In 1978, Norman (Considine) and his unhappy wife Lucy (Ledoyen) visit Spain's Basque Country to stay at the isolated house that's being renovated by their friends Paul (Oldman) and Isabel (Sanchez-Gijon). When the guys go out hunting, they find a hut where a disfigured, feral young girl (Esteve) is chained. After freeing her, they bring her back to the house but for some reason this makes the locals very upset. English and Spanish with subtitles. 97m; DVD. **C:** Gary Oldman; Paddy Considine; Virginie Ledoyen; Aitana Sanchez-Gijon; Lluis Homar; Yaiza Esteve; Andres Gertudix; Jon Arino; Directed by Koldo Serra; Written by Koldo Serra; Jon Sagala; Cinematography by Unax Mendia; Music by Fernando Verazquez. **A:** Sr. High-Adult. **P:** Entertainment. **U:** Home. **L:** Spanish, English. **Mov-Ent**: Forests & Trees, Spain, Mystery & Suspense. **Acq:** Purchase. **Dist:** Lions Gate Entertainment Inc.

Backwoods 2008 (R) — ★
Despite the rating and subject matter, this is a remarkably tame horror show about computer programmers on a corporate wilderness retreat in Northern California. They are preyed on by religious fanatics/survivalists who are interested in the women for breeding purposes. The men are expendable. 84m; DVD. **C:** Haylie Duff; Ryan Merriman; Danny Nucci; Mark Rolston; Troy Winbush; Deborah Van Valkenburgh; Directed by Marty Weiss; Written by Anthony Jaswinski; Cinematography by James W. Wrenn; Music by Paul D'Amour. **A:** Sr. High-Adult. **P:** Entertainment. **U:** Home. **Mov-Ent**: Forests & Trees. **Acq:** Purchase. **Dist:** Genius Entertainment.

Backyard 1983
Ross McElwee turned his camera on his family and neighbors in their genteel Southern town, without embarrassment. The interdependencies and estrangement of Southern blacks and whites living together is explored. 60m; VHS, UMD. **C:** Directed by Ross McElwee. **Pr:** Ross McElwee; Ross McElwee. **A:** Jr. High-Adult. **P:** Entertainment. **U:** Home. **Mov-Ent**: Documentary Films, Black Culture. **Acq:** Purchase. **Dist:** First Run/Icarus Films.

Backyard Baseball Drills ????
Fun baseball drills one can perform in their own backyard, presented by Coach Marty Schupak. ?m; VHS. **A:** Primary-Jr. High. **P:** Instruction. **U:** Home. **Spo-Rec**: Baseball, Sports--General. **Acq:** Purchase. **Dist:** Baseball Direct. $17.95.

The Backyard Bird Watcher 1996
Features George Harrison, author and birding expert, who demonstrates how to create a wild bird sanctuary in your own backyard. Includes how to provide food and cover and where to place your birdhouses. 45m; VHS. **A:** Adult. **P:** Instruction. **U:** Home. **How-Ins**: Birds, Hobbies. **Acq:** Purchase. **Dist:** Willow Creek Press L.L.C. $19.95.

Backyard Birds 1988
Introduces the seasonal habits, territorial needs and maintenance of migratory and non-migratory birds. 15m; VHS. **A:** Preschool-Primary. **P:** Education. **U:** Institution. **Gen-Edu**: Animals, Birds. **Acq:** Purchase. **Dist:** National Geographic Society. $80.

Backyard Birds in Winter 1985
How common birds survive during the harsh winter months in New Jersey is the subject of this program. 30m; VHS, 3/4 U. **Pr:** New Jersey Network. **A:** Jr. High-Adult. **P:** Education. **U:** Institution. **Gen-Edu**: Birds. **Acq:** Purchase. **Dist:** New Jersey Network.

Backyard Bugs 1990
Ordinary bugs and the good they do for the environment is the focus of this children's education film. Includes teacher's guide. 15m; VHS, Special order formats. **Pr:** National Geographic Society. **A:** Preschool-Jr. High. **P:** Education. **U:** Institution. **Chl-Juv**: Insects, Children. **Acq:** Purchase. **Dist:** National Geographic Society. $59.95.

Backyard Coach: Basket Fundamentals 19??
This video, a first in a series, helps parents and children build strong relationships while learning basic basketball skills. Parents and children will have hours of fun learning the basketball basics. ?m; VHS. **A:** Family. **P:** Education. **U:** Home. **L:** English. **Spo-Rec**: Sports--General. **Acq:** Purchase. **Dist:** Neurology, Learning, & Behavior Center. $12.95.

Backyard Safari 1998
Series of 13 30-minute videos designed to teach preschool children through grade six basic science and natural history. 390m; VHS. **A:** Preschool-Primary. **P:** Education. **U:** Institution. **Chl-Juv**: Science. **Acq:** Purchase. **Dist:** GPN Educational Media. $467.35.

Backyard Science Series 197?
This series explores various common insects and their habitats. Programs are available as a series and/or individually. 12m; VHS, 3/4 U. **Pr:** Norman Bean. **A:** Primary. **P:** Education. **U:** Institution, SURA. **Hea-Sci**: Insects. **Acq:** Purchase. **Dist:** Phoenix Learning Group.
Indiv. Titles: 1. Ants: Backyard Science (Revised) 2. Bees: Backyard Science (Revised) 3. Beetles: Backyard Science 4. Crickets: Backyard Science 5. Snails: Backyard Science (Revised) 6. Spiders: Backyard Science (Revised).

Bacteria 1962
Demonstrates the basic characteristics of bacteria: their external and internal structures, their manner of feeding, reproductive processes, and ecological importance. 19m; VHS, 3/4 U. **Pr:** Encyclopedia Britannica Educational Corporation. **A:** Sr. High. **P:** Education. **U:** Institution, SURA. **L:** English, Spanish. **Hea-Sci**: Microbiology. **Acq:** Purchase, Rent/Lease, Trade-in. **Dist:** Encyclopedia Britannica.

Bacteria 1985
Offers a look at bacteria, its forms, structure, reproductive processes, and importance. 23m; VHS. **A:** Jr. High-Adult. **P:** Education. **U:** Institution. **Gen-Edu**: Biology. **Acq:** Purchase. **Dist:** National Geographic Society. $80.

Bacteria and Disease Control 1995
Explains how bacteria can be damaging, and how to alleviate it. 10m; VHS. **A:** Adult. **P:** Professional. **U:** Institution. **L:** Spanish. **Bus-Ind:** Safety Education, Occupational Training, Management. **Acq:** Purchase, Rent/Lease. **Dist:** National Safety Council, California Chapter, Film Library. $175.00.

Bacteria and Health 19??
Distinguishes between bacteria that could be of use to the body and bacteria that could be a threat to the body, and explains preventive measures such as careful washing and maintaining good health. Includes teaching materials. 18m. **Pr:** AIMS. **A:** Primary-Adult. **P:** Education. **U:** Institution. **Hea-Sci:** Health Education, Hygiene. **Acq:** Purchase. **Dist:** Clear Vue Inc. $295.00.

Bacteria and Viruses 1989
This program talks about how bacteria and viruses spread and how they affect the body. 20m; VHS, 3/4 U. **Pr:** Films for the Humanities. **A:** Jr. High-Adult. **P:** Education. **U:** Institution, SURA. **Hea-Sci:** Immunology, Health Education. **Acq:** Purchase, Rent/Lease. **Dist:** Films for the Humanities & Sciences. $149.00.

Bacteria: Friend and Foe 1954
Shows the importance of bacteria in everyday life and discusses techniques of modern bacteriology. 11m; VHS, 3/4 U. **Pr:** Stewart A. Koser; Encyclopedia Britannica Educational Corporation. **A:** Sr. High. **P:** Education. **U:** Institution, SURA. **Hea-Sci:** Microbiology. **Acq:** Purchase, Rent/Lease, Trade-in. **Dist:** Encyclopedia Britannica.

Bacteria: Invisible Friends and Foes 1983
Examines the role of bacteria, both beneficial and detrimental. ?m; VHS. **A:** Sr. High. **P:** Education. **U:** Institution. **Hea-Sci:** Science, Microbiology. **Acq:** Purchase. **Dist:** HRM Video; Educational Images Ltd. $175.00.

Bad Actress 2011 (Unrated) — ★★
Has-been TV actress Alyssa is now doing commercials for hubby Bernie's appliance store chain. Their daughter dies in a bizarre accident and the media attention rejuvenates Alyssa but Bernie deals with the tragedy by turning spiritual and wanting to give all their money away. Alyssa refuses to be poor so Bernie has to go and the body count starts to rise. 85m; DVD. **C:** Beth Broderick; Chris Mulkey; Whitney Able; Vincent Ventresca; Ryan Hansen; Keri Lynn Pratt; Directed by Robert Lee King; Written by David M. Barrett; Cinematography by Andrew Huebscher; Music by Frederik Wiedmann. **A:** Sr. High-Adult. **P:** Entertainment. **U:** Home. **Mov-Ent:** Mass Media. **Acq:** Purchase. **Dist:** Strand Releasing.

The Bad and the Beautiful 1952 — ★★★½
The rise and fall of a Hollywood producer. Douglas stars as the ruthless, arrogant Jonathan Shields, who alienates actress Georgia (Turner), writer James Lee Bartlow (Powell), and director Fred Amiel (Sullivan) as he pursues his career. Much speculation at the time as to who the real-life models for the insider story actually were. Winner of five Oscars, a splendid drama. 118m/B/W; VHS, DVD, CC. **C:** Kirk Douglas; Lana Turner; Dick Powell; Gloria Grahame; Barry Sullivan; Walter Pidgeon; Gilbert Roland; Leo G. Carroll; Elaine Stewart; Directed by Vincente Minnelli; Written by Charles Schnee; Cinematography by Robert L. Surtees; Music by David Raksin. **Pr:** MGM. **A:** Sr. High-Adult. **P:** Entertainment. **U:** Home. **Mov-Ent:** Classic Films. **Awds:** Oscars '52: Art Dir./Set Dec., B&W, B&W Cinematog., Costume Des. (B&W), Screenplay, Support. Actress (Grahame); Natl. Film Reg. '02. **Acq:** Purchase. **Dist:** MGM Home Entertainment; Baker and Taylor. $19.98.

Bad Ass 2009 (Unrated) — ★½
Corrado works as a hitman for Frankie who wants him to deal with elderly mob boss Vittorio. The hit goes bad when Corrado is surprised by the mobster's live-in nurse Julia. She gets blamed for the death by Vittorio's crazy son Paolo and Corrado decides to save Julia and himself by going on the lam. 84m; DVD. **C:** Johnny Messner; Tom Sizemore; Ken Kercheval; Candace Elaine; Joseph Gannascoli; Directed by Adamo P. Cultraro; Written by Adamo P. Cultraro; Cinematography by David Fox; Music by Ryan Franks. **A:** Sr. High-Adult. **P:** Entertainment. **U:** Home. **Mov-Ent. Acq:** Purchase. **Dist:** Well Go USA, Inc.

Bad Attitude 1993 (R) — ★★
Leon is a narcotics officer on a mission to restore his badge after his careless pistol work gets him booted off the force. The quick-tempered cop relentlessly pursues druglord Finque with the help of an open-minded preacher (De Veaux) and his sexy, streetwise assistant (Lim). 87m; VHS, DVD. **C:** Leon; Gina Lim; Nathaniel DeVeaux; Susan Finque; Directed by Bill Cummings. **A:** Sr. High-Adult. **P:** Entertainment. **U:** Home. **Mov-Ent. Acq:** Purchase. **Dist:** Xenon Pictures Inc. $69.95.

Bad Behavior 1992 (R) — ★★½
Unscripted character-driven drama. Gerry and Ellie McAllister are an Irish couple living in North London. He's tired of working for the local planning commission, she's bored being just a mum at home, and both are still a little uneasy living in England. When they decide to remodel the family bath, the unexpected problems lead to an emotional shakeup. Don't expect a lot of drama, the film works only if you accept the decency of the characters and the small moments of recognizable daily life. Director Blair wrote a basic script outline and had the actors improvise their dialogue, in character, over a long rehearsal period to develop their roles. 103m; VHS, DVD, CC. **C:** Stephen Rea; Sinead Cusack; Philip Jackson; Clare Higgins; Phil Daniels; Saira Todd; Directed by Les Blair; Music by John Altman. **Pr:** Sarah Curtis; October Films; Channel 4. **A:** College-Adult. **P:** Entertainment. **U:** Home. **Mov-Ent:** Comedy-Drama, Marriage. **Acq:** Purchase. **Dist:** CinemaNow Inc. $94.95.

Bad Blonde 1953 (Unrated) — ★½
Minor Brit crime melodrama would have benefited from some better acting. Giuseppe Vecchi (Valk) is the promoter of young prizefighter Johnny Flanagan (Wright), who makes the mistake of fooling around with Vecchi's hotsie, scheming wife Lorna (Payton). Lorna tells Johnny she's expecting and insists they get rid of her hubby so the lovers can be together. But Johnny can't take the guilt after doing the deed. 80m/B/W; DVD. **C:** Barbara Payton; Tony Wright; Frederick Valk; John Slater; Sidney James; Marie Burke; Directed by Reginald LeBorg; Written by Richard H. Landau; Guy Elmes; Cinematography by Walter J. (Jimmy W.) Harvey; Music by Ivor Slaney. **A:** Sr. High-Adult. **P:** Entertainment. **U:** Home. **Mov-Ent:** Boxing, Crime Drama. **Acq:** Purchase. **Dist:** VCI Entertainment.

Bad Blood 1981 (Unrated) — ★★
The true story of Stan Graham, who went on a killing spree in the New Zealand bush when his farm was foreclosed and his life ruined. 104m; VHS, DVD. **C:** Jack Thompson; Carol Burns; Dennis (Denis) Lill; Directed by Mike Newell; Written by Andrew Brown; Cinematography by Gary Hansen; Music by Richard Hartley. **Pr:** Southern Pictures. **A:** Sr. High-Adult. **P:** Entertainment. **U:** Home. **Mov-Ent. Acq:** Purchase. **Dist:** Unknown Distributor.

Bad Blood 1994 (R) — ★½
Travis Blackstone (Lamas) will use any methods to protect his brother Franklin, who's targeted for death by a ruthless drug lord. Lots of action and violence. 90m; VHS, CC. **C:** Lorenzo Lamas; Hank Cheyne; Frankie Thorn; Kimberley Kates; Joe Son; Directed by Tibor Takacs; Written by Neil Ruttenberg; Cinematography by Berhard Salzmann. **A:** Sr. High-Adult. **P:** Entertainment. **U:** Home. **Mov-Ent:** Violence. **Acq:** Purchase. **Dist:** Lions Gate Television Corp. $92.98.

Bad Boy 1939 — ★½
A country boy goes to the big city, and succumbs to urban evils and temptations, but is eventually saved by motherly love. 60m/B/W; VHS. **C:** Johnny Downs; Helen MacKellar; Rosalind Keith; Holmes Herbert; Directed by Kurt Neumann. **Pr:** Gateway Productions. **A:** Family. **P:** Entertainment. **U:** Home. **Mov-Ent. Acq:** Purchase. **Dist:** No Longer Available.

Bad Boy Bubby 1993 — ★★
Bizarre black comedy about the extremely maladjusted Bubby (Hope), who becomes a pop culture phenomena. The 35-year-old childlike Bubby has been kept a virtual prisoner by his monstrous mom, who has told him the world outside is filled with poisonous gas. Wondering how his cat survived, Bubby wraps it in plastic wrap and is puzzled when it dies. Still, this gives Bubby an idea—he wraps mom in plastic and escapes outside, where he's soon adopted by a struggling rock band that writes a cult song hit about his experiences. It's even stranger than it sounds. 114m; VHS, DVD. **C:** Nicholas Hope; Claire Benito; Carmel Johnson; Ralph Cotterill; Norman Kaye; Paul Philpot; Graham Duckett; Bridget Walters; Directed by Rolf de Heer; Written by Rolf de Heer; Music by Graham Tardif. **Pr:** Domenico Procacci; Giorgio Draskovic; Rolf de Heer; Rolf de Heer; Fandango; Bubby Pty; South Australian Film Corporation. **A:** College-Adult. **P:** Entertainment. **U:** Home. **Mov-Ent:** Comedy--Black. **Awds:** Australian Film Inst. '94: Actor (Hope), Director (de Heer), Film Editing, Orig. Screenplay. **Acq:** Purchase. **Dist:** Blue Underground, Inc.

Bad Boys 1960 (Unrated) — ★½
Hani's first feature is based on a collection of papers written by boys at a reform school. Filmed on location and acted by the inmates, the boys dramatize their own troubling stories. In Japanese with English subtitles. 90m; VHS. **C:** Directed by Susumu Hani. **A:** Sr. High-Adult. **P:** Entertainment. **U:** Home. **L:** Japanese. **Mov-Ent:** Adolescence. **Acq:** Purchase. **Dist:** Facets Multimedia Inc. $39.95.

Bad Boys 1978
A cinema verite documentary that examines how three public institutions deal with troubled youngsters: a high school (Bryant H.S.), a detention center (Spofford Juvenile Center in the South Bronx, New York City), and a maximum security prison (Brookwood Center for boys under 16). 120m/B/W; VHS, UMD, 3/4 U, Special order formats. **Pr:** Alan Raymond; Susan Raymond; Video Verite Productions. **A:** Jr. High-Adult. **P:** Education. **U:** Institution, Home, SURA. **Gen-Edu:** Adolescence. **Acq:** Purchase, Rent/Lease. **Dist:** DeepFocus Productions Film Library.

Bad Boys 1983 (R) — ★★★
When a gang member's little brother is killed in a rumble, the teen responsible (Penn, who else?) goes to a reformatory, where he quickly (though somewhat reluctantly) takes charge. Meanwhile, on the outside, his rival attacks Penn's girlfriend (Sheedy, in her feature film debut) in retaliation, is incarcerated, and ends up vying with Penn for control of the cell block. Backed into a corner by their mutual hatred and escalating peer pressure, the two are pushed over the brink into a final and shattering confrontation. Not as violent as it could be, to its credit; attempts to communicate a message. 104m; VHS, DVD, Wide. **C:** Sean Penn; Esai Morales; Reni Santoni; Jim Moody; Eric Gurry; Ally Sheedy; Clancy Brown; Directed by Rick Rosenthal; Written by Richard Dilello; Cinematography by Donald E. Thorin; Music by Bill Conti. **Pr:** EMI Media. **A:** Sr. High-Adult. **P:** Entertainment. **U:** Home. **Mov-Ent:** Crime Drama. **Acq:** Purchase. **Dist:** Lions Gate Entertainment Inc. $14.98.

Bad Boys 1995 (R) — ★★½
And you thought the old buddy-cop formula was played out. Well, Hollywood sticks with what works, and pairing the two TV personalities definitely works at the minimalist level required. Mike (Smith) and Marcus (Lawrence) are Miami cops who must track down $100 million worth of heroin stolen from their evidence room before internal affairs shuts down the precinct. The case leads them to a vicious thief and a beautiful female witness to his murderous handiwork. Plot lacks depth, but high energy and dazzling action sequences keep things moving. Loud adventure is made louder still by cranking soundtrack. Satisfying addition to the odd-couple cops genre with potential to spawn a "Lethal Weapon"-type franchise. Feature film debut for director Bay. 118m; VHS, DVD, CC. **C:** Martin Lawrence; Will Smith; Tcheky Karyo; Tea Leoni; Theresa Randle; Marg Helgenberger; Joe Pantoliano; John Salley; Nestor Serrano; Michael Imperioli; Julio Oscar Mechoso; Directed by Michael Bay; Written by Michael Barrie; Jim Mulholland; Cinematography by Howard Atherton; Music by Mark Mancina. **Pr:** Don Simpson; Jerry Bruckheimer; Bruce S. Pustin; Lucas Foster. **A:** Sr. High-Adult. **P:** Entertainment. **U:** Home. **Mov-Ent:** Drugs. **Awds:** Blockbuster '96: Male Newcomer, T. (Smith). **Acq:** Purchase. **Dist:** Sony Pictures Home Entertainment Inc.

Bad Boys 2 2003 (R) — ★★
Bombastic sequel finds Miami narcs Mike Lowrey (Smith) and Marcus Burnett (Lawrence) going after a violent network of Ecstasy dealers. The duo also has personal problems when Mike falls for Marcus' sister, Syd (Union), an undercover cop. Meanwhile, Marcus ponders whether he wants to remain partners with Mike, and whether, in classic Det. Murtaugh style, he's getting too old for this...stuff. Typical action-flick paper-thin plot doesn't stop Smith and Lawrence from clicking as a comedy-action team. Since this flick is basically the original, amped up to a ridiculous degree, your enjoyment will hinge on your opinion of that one, and your tolerance for the Bruckheimer-Bay "make-go-boom!" style. 146m; VHS, DVD, UMD. **C:** Will Smith; Martin Lawrence; Gabrielle Beauvais; Joe Pantoliano; Theresa Randle; Jordi Molla; Peter Stormare; Michael Shannon; Jon Seda; Yul Vazquez; Henry Rollins; Jason Manuel Olazabel; Otto Sanchez; Directed by Michael Bay; Written by Ron Shelton; Jerry Stahl; Cinematography by Amir M. Mokri. **Pr:** Jerry Bruckheimer; Columbia Pictures. **A:** Sr. High-Adult. **P:** Entertainment. **U:** Home. **Mov-Ent:** Drug Trafficking/Dealing. **Acq:** Purchase. **Dist:** Sony Pictures Home Entertainment Inc.

Bad Boys: Detroit Pistons '87-'88 Season 1988
Footage of the pro team's stellar season, including the Finals and Playoff games. 60m; VHS. **C:** Narrated by George Blaha. **Pr:** MGM Home Entertainment. **A:** Family. **P:** Entertainment. **U:** Home. **Spo-Rec:** Basketball. **Acq:** Purchase. **Dist:** ESPN Inc.

Bad Bunch 1976 (Unrated) — ★★
A white liberal living in Watts tries to befriend a ruthless black street gang, but is unsuccessful. 82m; VHS, DVD. **C:** Greydon Clark; Tom Johnigam; Pamela Corbett; Jacqulin Cole; Aldo Ray; Jock Mahoney; Directed by Greydon Clark. **Pr:** Greydon Clark; Greydon Clark. **A:** Sr. High-Adult. **P:** Entertainment. **U:** Home. **Mov-Ent. Acq:** Purchase. **Dist:** VCI Entertainment. $59.95.

Bad Cat 1991
Delightful animated program from the folks at ABC Kidtime. 23m; VHS. **Pr:** ABC. **A:** Family. **P:** Entertainment. **U:** Home. **Chl-Juv:** Animation & Cartoons, Family Viewing, Pets. **Acq:** Purchase. **Dist:** Anchor Bay Entertainment. $9.98.

B.A.D. Cats 1980 (Unrated) — ★
Two members of a police burglary auto detail team chase after a group of car thieves who are planning a million-dollar gold heist. 74m; VHS. **C:** Asher Brauner; Michelle Pfeiffer; Vic Morrow; Jimmie Walker; Steve Hanks; LaWanda Page; Directed by Bernard L. Kowalski. **Pr:** Aaron Spelling; Douglas S. Cramer. **A:** Jr. High-Adult. **P:** Entertainment. **U:** Home. **Mov-Ent:** Mystery & Suspense. **Acq:** Purchase. **Dist:** MGM Studios Inc. $59.95.

Bad Channels 1992 (R) — ★★
Radio goes awry when female listeners of station KDUL are shrunk and put into speciman jars by a way-out disc jockey and a visiting alien, who plans to take the women back to his planet. Mildly amusing comedy features ex-MTV VJ Quinn and score by Blue Oyster Cult. Also available with Spanish subtitles. 88m; VHS, DVD, CC. **C:** Paul Hipp; Martha Quinn; Aaron Lustig; Ian Patrick Williams; Charlie Spradling; Tim Thomerson; Sonny Carl Davis; Robert Factor; Michael Huddleston; Directed by Ted Nicolaou; Written by Jackson Barr; Cinematography by Adolfo Bartoli. **Pr:** Keith Payson; Full Moon Entertainment. **A:** Sr. High-Adult. **P:** Entertainment. **U:** Home. **Mov-Ent:** Science Fiction, Miniaturization. **Acq:** Purchase. **Dist:** Full Moon Pictures.

Bad Charleston Charlie 1973 (PG) — **Bomb!**
Dud of a gangster comedy with terrible acting. A comedy? 91m; VHS. **C:** Ross Hagen; Kelly Thordsen; John Carradine; Hoke Howell; Carmen Zapata; Directed by Ivan Nagy; Written by Ross Hagen; Ivan Nagy; Stan Kamber; Cinematography by Albert Aley; Music by Luchi De Jesus. **Pr:** International Cinemedia Center Ltd. **A:** Adult. **P:** Entertainment. **U:** Home. **Mov-Ent:** Comedy--Black. **Acq:** Purchase. **Dist:** No Longer Available.

Bad City 2006 (R) — ★★
Yes, gnomish Pendleton is playing a depraved Chicago crime lord named Julian Healy and he's scarily effective. Derek Manning (Reddick) is a tough detective with a gambling problem who is in debt to Healy, which makes investigating the murder of hooker Bridgette (McDonough) difficult. Then there's too-slick politico Frank Sullivan (McGlone) whose troublesome wife (Anglin) is also killed. 97m; DVD, Wide. **C:** Lance Reddick; Mike McGlone; Austin Pendleton; Nutsa Kukhianidze; Tim Decker; Meghan Maureen McDonough; Karin Anglin; Directed by Bruce Terris; Written by Bruce Terris; Rick Rose; Cinematography by David Blood; Music by Mark Messing. **A:** Sr.

High-Adult. **P:** Entertainment. **U:** Home. **Mov-Ent:** Crime Drama. **Acq:** Purchase. **Dist:** Movies Unlimited; Alpha Video.

Bad Company 1972 (PG) — ★★★½
Thoughtful study of two very different Civil War draft dodgers roaming the Western frontier and eventually turning to a fruitless life of crime. Both the cast and script are wonderful in an entertaining film that hasn't been given the attention it's due. 94m; DVD, Wide. **C:** Jeff Bridges; Barry Brown; Jim Davis; John Savage; Directed by Robert Benton; Written by Robert Benton; David Newman; Cinematography by Gordon Willis; Music by Harvey Schmidt. **Pr:** Paramount Pictures. **A:** Jr. High-Adult. **P:** Entertainment. **U:** Home. **Mov-Ent:** Western, Civil War, Veterans. **Acq:** Purchase. **Dist:** WarnerArchive.com; Paramount Pictures Corp. $14.95.

Bad Company 1994 (R) — ★★
Cynical thriller pits the bad against the worst. Vic Grimes (Langella) and Margaret Wells (Barkin) run a company of former secret agents who specialize in corporate dirty work. Nelson Crowe (Fishburne) is an ex-CIA agent who's their latest recruit. But maybe he's not so ex and maybe Margaret doesn't like sharing power and maybe the cold-blooded duo will get together to make some changes. Everything is stylish, including the leads, but there's a definite chill in the air. 118m; VHS, DVD, CC. **C:** Ellen Barkin; Laurence Fishburne; Frank Langella; Michael Beach; Gia Carides; David Ogden Stiers; Spalding Gray; James Hong; Daniel Hugh-Kelly; Directed by Damian Harris; Written by Ross Thomas; Cinematography by Jack N. Green; Music by Carter Burwell. **Pr:** Amedeo Ursini; Jeffrey Chernov; Touchstone Pictures. **A:** Sr. High-Adult. **P:** Entertainment. **U:** Home. **Mov-Ent:** Mystery & Suspense, Sex & Sexuality. **Acq:** Purchase. **Dist:** Buena Vista Home Entertainment.

Bad Company 1999 (Unrated) — ★★½
Delphine (Forget) is a typically dissatisfied middle-class teen suspectible to her more-worldly peers, which include the attitudinal, punked-out Olivia (Doillon). Olivia takes Delphine clubbing and she meets requisite smoldering bad boy, Laurent (Stevenin). Delphine's hormones are soon out of control and she agrees to some very questionable suggestions to prove her "love." Frank and unsettling. French with subtitles. 98m; VHS, DVD. **C:** Maud Forget; Lou Doillon; Robinson Stevenin; Maxime Mansion; Delphine Rich; Rene Berleand; Micheline Presle; Cyril Cagnat; Directed by Jean-Pierre Ameris; Written by Alain Layrac; Cinematography by Yves Vanderemeeren; Music by Lene Marlin; Giya Kanchell. **A:** Sr. High-Adult. **P:** Entertainment. **U:** Home. **L:** French. **Mov-Ent:** Adolescence, Sex & Sexuality. **Acq:** Purchase. **Dist:** Wellspring Media.

Bad Company 2002 (PG-13) — ★★
Hustler Rock discovers his twin brother was a CIA operative who has just been murdered. He gets recruited by agency honcho Hopkins to take over his bro's assignment, which involves terrorists, bombs, and New York City. Considering these elements, it's no wonder this one got delayed. Rock deserves a better movie, but he almost salvages this one, anyway...almost. He's up against a standard-issue plot that merely serves to get to the next action set piece which, this being a Bruckheimer production, are done well, but done too often. Schumacher manages to (mostly) subdue his worst instincts (see "Batman & Robin" to watch him surrender to them completely), but it doesn't really help. 111m; VHS, DVD. **C:** Chris Rock; Anthony Hopkins; Matthew Marsh; Garcelle Beauvais; Kerry Washington; Gabriel Macht; Peter Stormare; Adoni Maropis; Brooke Smith; Directed by Joel Schumacher; Written by Michael Browning; Jason Richman; Cinematography by Dariusz Wolski; Music by Trevor Rabin. **Pr:** Jerry Bruckheimer; Michael Browning; Touchstone Pictures; Buena Vista. **A:** Sr. High-Adult. **P:** Entertainment. **U:** Home. **Mov-Ent:** Intelligence Service, Terrorism. **Acq:** Purchase. **Dist:** Buena Vista Home Entertainment.

Bad Day at Black Rock 1954 (Unrated) — ★★★½
Story of a one-armed man uncovering a secret in a Western town. Wonderful performances from all concerned, especially Borgnine. Fine photography, shot using the new Cinemascope technique. Based on the novel by Howard Breslin. 81m; VHS, DVD, Wide. **C:** Spencer Tracy; Robert Ryan; Anne Francis; Dean Jagger; Walter Brennan; John Ericson; Ernest Borgnine; Lee Marvin; Directed by John Sturges; Cinematography by William Mellor; Music by Andre Previn. **Pr:** MGM. **A:** Jr. High-Adult. **P:** Entertainment. **U:** Home. **Mov-Ent:** Western. **Awds:** Cannes '55: Actor (Tracy). **Acq:** Purchase. **Dist:** MGM Home Entertainment; Facets Multimedia Inc. $19.98.

Bad Dreams 1988 (R) — ★½
The only surviving member of a suicidal religious cult from the '60s awakens in 1988 from a coma. She is pursued by the living-dead cult leader, who seeks to ensure that she lives up (so to speak) to the cult's pact. Blood begins flowing as her fellow therapy group members begin dying, but the only bad dreams you'd get from this flick would be over the money lost on the video rental. 84m; VHS, DVD, Blu-Ray, CC. **C:** Bruce Abbott; Jennifer Rubin; Richard Lynch; Harris Yulin; Dean Cameron; Elizabeth Daily; Susan Ruttan; Charles Fleischer; Sy Richardson; Directed by Andrew Fleming; Written by Andrew Fleming; Steven E. de Souza; Cinematography by Alexander Grusynski; Music by Jay Ferguson. **Pr:** Gale Anne Hurd; 20th Century-Fox. **A:** Sr. High-Adult. **P:** Entertainment. **U:** Home. **Mov-Ent:** Horror, Occult Sciences, Cults. **Acq:** Purchase. **Dist:** Movies Unlimited; Alpha Video. $89.98.

Bad Education 2004 (Unrated) — ★★★
Complicated film noir begins in 1980 Madrid where young movie director Enrique (Martinez) is seeking inspiration. It comes to him, literally, when old school friend Ignacio (Garcia Bernal) turns up and hands Enrique a story he's written about the sexual abuse he suffered at the hands of the principal of their Catholic boys' school. But something is wrong—and it's not just the fact that the wannabe actor returns demanding to play the part of transsexual prostitute Zahara (Garcia Bernal again—making quite a pretty woman) in the film, which plays out in Enrique's mind so you're watching two films at once. And if that's not confusing enough, the film has flashbacks to the boys' schooldays and a subsequent meeting in 1977. Somehow Almodovar makes it work. Spanish with subtitles. 104m; DVD. **C:** Fele Martinez; Gael Garcia Bernal; Lluis Homar; Javier Camara; Petra Martinez; Nacho Perez; Raul Garcia Forneiro; Juan Fernandez; Daniel Gimenez Cacho; Alberto Ferreiro; Francisco Boira; Directed by Pedro Almodovar; Written by Pedro Almodovar; Cinematography by Jose Luis Alcaine; Music by Alberto Iglesias. **Pr:** Agustin Almodovar; El Deseo; Sony Pictures Classics. **P:** Entertainment. **U:** Home. **L:** Spanish. **Mov-Ent:** Mystery & Suspense, Spain, Sexual Abuse. **Dist:** Sony Pictures Home Entertainment Inc. $26.96.

Bad English 198?
Bad English video concert. Enjoy such tunes as, "Best of What I Got," "When I See You Smile" "Price of Love" and more. 30m; VHS. **A:** Jr. High-Adult. **P:** Entertainment. **U:** Home. **Mov-Ent:** Music--Performance, Music Video, Interviews. **Acq:** Purchase. **Dist:** Music Video Distributors; Sony Music Entertainment Inc. $14.98.

Bad for Each Other 1953 (Unrated) — ★★
Predictable melodrama with a stiff Heston starring as a former-Korean War Army medico who is torn between helping the poor in his coal-mining hometown and becoming a society doc so he can romance an ice-cold socialite beauty (Scott). The beauty wins out for awhile until miners get trapped in a cave-in and the doc's conscience kicks in. 83m/B/W; DVD. **C:** Charlton Heston; Lizabeth Scott; Dianne Foster; Mildred Dunnock; Arthur Franz; Ray Collins; Directed by Irving Rapper; Written by Horace McCoy; Irving Wallace; Cinematography by Franz Planer; Music by Mischa Bakaleinikoff. **A:** Sr. High-Adult. **P:** Entertainment. **U:** Home. **Mov-Ent:** Miners & Mining. **Acq:** Purchase. **Dist:** Sony Pictures Home Entertainment Inc.

Bad Georgia Road 1977 (R) — ★½
A New Yorker inherits a moonshine operation from her uncle, and fights off the syndicate for its profits. 85m; VHS. **C:** Gary Lockwood; Carol Lynley; Royal Dano; John Wheeler; John Kerry; Directed by John Broderick. **Pr:** Demension Pictures. **A:** Jr. High-Adult. **P:** Entertainment. **U:** Home. **Mov-Ent:** Alcoholic Beverages. **Acq:** Purchase. **Dist:** VCI Entertainment. $49.95.

Bad Girl 1931 (Unrated) — ★★
Apparently sassy model Dorothy (Eilers) is a bad girl because she has sex with Eddie (Dunn) before marriage and gets herself into trouble. Eddie does the right thing and they get married, although he doesn't really want to be a father and isn't happy to give up his dreams to support his unexpected family. So they have to struggle to make things work amidst hard times. 90m/B/W; DVD. **C:** James Dunn; Sally Eilers; Minna Gombell; William Pawley; Frank Darien; Directed by Frank Borzage; Written by Edwin J. Burke; Cinematography by Chester Lyons. **A:** Sr. High-Adult. **P:** Entertainment. **U:** Home. **Mov-Ent:** Marriage, Pregnancy, Drama. **Acq:** Purchase. **Dist:** Fox Home Entertainment.

Bad Girl 2001
Documentary following women who make pornographic films for a market comprised of fellow women. 58m; VHS, DVD. **A:** Sr. High-Adult. **P:** Education. **U:** Institution. **Gen-Edu:** Documentary Films, Pornography. **Acq:** Purchase, Rent/Lease. **Dist:** The Cinema Guild. $295.00.

Bad Girls 1994 (R) — ★★½
Latest in the current western craze turns the tables as women take their turns being the gunslingers. Four hooker chums hastily flee town after one kills a nasty customer—only to find the bank where their cash was stashed was robbed by baddies Loggia and Russo. Wearing stylish duds and with each hair perfectly in place the beauties manage to recover their loot. Unexciting script leaves a lot to be desired, but a strong performance from Stowe makes this nearly worthwhile. Lots of off-set drama with original director Tamra Davis fired, and the actresses reportedly having a less-than-bonding experience. 99m; VHS, DVD, Wide, CC. **C:** Andie MacDowell; Madeleine Stowe; Mary Stuart Masterson; Drew Barrymore; James Russo; Dermot Mulroney; Robert Loggia; James LeGros; Nick (Nicholas) Chinlund; Will MacMillan; Jim Beaver; Directed by Jonathan Kaplan; Written by Ken Friedman; Yolande Finch; Music by Jerry Goldsmith. **Pr:** Albert S. Ruddy; Andre Morgan; Charles Finch; Lynda Obst; 20th Century-Fox. **A:** Sr. High-Adult. **P:** Entertainment. **U:** Home. **Mov-Ent:** Prostitution. **Acq:** Purchase. **Dist:** Fox Home Entertainment.

Bad Girls 1994
Martha Tucker, director of the New Museum of Contemporary Art in New York City, visits the studios of various female artists for works to include in an exhibit entitled "Bad Girls." ?m; VHS. **A:** Sr. High-Adult. **P:** Education. **U:** Institution. **Gen-Edu:** Art & Artists, Women. **Acq:** Purchase, Rent/Lease. **Dist:** Michael Blackwood Productions.

Bad Girls Do Cry 1954 (Unrated) — **Bomb!**
Unbelievably bad exploitation film. Idiotic plot with long scenes of girls stripping down to their undies. Although an American film, the voice track was dubbed in later. 59m/B/W; VHS, DVD. **C:** Bill Page; Misty Ayers; Heather English; Ben Frommer; Directed by Sid Melton. **A:** Sr. High-Adult. **P:** Entertainment. **U:** Home. **Mov-Ent. Acq:** Purchase. **Dist:** Sinister Cinema; Tapeworm Video Distributors Inc. $16.95.

Bad Girls Dormitory 1984 (R) — ★★
At the New York Female Juvenile Reformatory, suicide seems a painless and welcome escape. Utilizes standard genre identifiers, including rape, drugs, soapy showers, bad docs, and desperate young women trapped in a web of frustration and desire. Cheap and mindless titillation. 95m; VHS, DVD. **C:** Carey Zuris; Teresa Farley; Directed by Tim Kincaid. **Pr:** Cynthia DePaula. **A:** Sr. High-Adult. **P:** Entertainment. **U:** Home. **Mov-Ent:** Horror, Suicide. **Acq:** Purchase. **Dist:** Unknown Distributor.

Bad Girls from Mars 1990 (R) — **Bomb!**
"B" movie sleaze-o-rama in which everyone is murdered, either before, after, or during sex, just like in real life. When the director of the film within this film hires an actress who is, shall we say, popular, to be the heroine of his latest sci-fier, the fun, slim as it is, begins. 86m; VHS, DVD. **C:** Edy Williams; Brinke Stevens; Jay Richardson; Oliver Darrow; Dana Bentley; Jeffrey Culver; Jasae; Directed by Fred Olen Ray; Written by Mark Thomas McGee; Fred Olen Ray; Cinematography by Gary Graver; Music by Chuck Cirino. **A:** Adult. **P:** Entertainment. **U:** Home. **Mov-Ent:** Science Fiction, Violence, Exploitation. **Acq:** Purchase. **Dist:** Lions Gate Home Entertainment; CinemaNow Inc. $89.95.

Bad Girls Go to Hell 1965 (Unrated) — **Bomb!**
From the sultana of sleaze, Wishman, comes this winning entry into Joe Bob Briggs' "Sleaziest Movies in the History of the World" series. A ditsy-but-sexy housewife accidentally commits murder and what follows is a plethora of perversion involving hirsute men and gender-bending women who are hell-bent on showing her how hot it is where bad girls go. 98m/B/W; VHS, DVD. **C:** Gigi Darlene; George La Rocque; Sam Stewart; Sandee Norman; Alan Yorke; Bernard L. Sankett; Darlene Bennett; Marlene Starr; Harold Key; Directed by Doris Wishman; Written by Doris Wishman; Dawn Whitman; Cinematography by C. Davis Smith. **A:** Adult. **P:** Entertainment. **U:** Home. **Mov-Ent:** Cult Films. **Acq:** Purchase. **Dist:** Anchor Bay Entertainment. $19.98.

Bad Girls in the Movies 1986 — ★
A compilation of film clips depicting sleazy, criminal, female characters from women's prison films and other seedy subgenres. 56m; VHS. **C:** David Carradine; Gene Autry; Yvonne De Carlo. **Pr:** Lightning Video. **A:** Jr. High-Adult. **P:** Entertainment. **U:** Home. **Mov-Ent. Acq:** Purchase. **Dist:** Lions Gate Television Corp. $19.98.

Bad Guy 2001 (Unrated) — ★★½
Han-ki (Jae-hyeon Jo) is a brutal thug and a pimp who one day sees Sun-hwa (Won Seo) on a park bench and becomes obsessed with her. Forcibly kissing her, he is beaten by bystanders. Han-ki then sets her up in a sting, and blackmails her into becoming a prostitute when she is caught breaking the law. After which he watches her through a peephole. 100m; DVD. **C:** Jae-hyeon Jo; Won Seo; Yun-tae Kim; Duek-mun Choi; Yoo-jin Shin; Jung-young Kim; Directed by Kim Ki Duk; Written by Kim Ki Duk; Cinematography by Cheol-hyeon Hwang; Music by Ho-jun Park. **A:** Sr. High-Adult. **P:** Entertainment. **U:** Home. **L:** English, Korean. **Mov-Ent:** Prostitution. **Acq:** Purchase. **Dist:** Lifesize Entertainment. $29.98.

Bad Guys 1979 (Unrated) — ★★
A goulash western about the outlaw days of Hungary in the 1860s. A gang of bandits terrorizes the Transdanubian countryside. In Hungarian with English subtitles. For those seeking the Eastern European Wild West experience. 93m; VHS. **C:** Janos Derzsi; Djoko Rosic; Mari Kiss; Gyorgy Dorner; Laszlo Szabo; Miklos Benedek; Directed by Gyorgy Szomjas. **Pr:** Mafilm; Hungarofilm. **A:** Jr. High-Adult. **P:** Entertainment. **U:** Home. **L:** English, Hungarian. **Mov-Ent:** Western. **Acq:** Purchase. **Dist:** Facets Multimedia Inc. $69.95.

Bad Guys 1986 (PG) — ★
An inane comedy about two ridiculous policemen who decide to take the wrestling world by storm after being kicked off the police force. Featuring scenes with many of the world's most popular wrestlers. 86m; VHS. **C:** Adam Baldwin; Mike Jolly; Michelle Nicastro; Ruth Buzzi; James Booth; Gene LeBell; Norman Burton; Directed by Joel Silberg; Cinematography by Hanania Baer; Music by William Goldstein. **Pr:** Tomorrow Entertainment Inc. **A:** Jr. High-Adult. **P:** Entertainment. **U:** Home. **Mov-Ent:** Action-Adventure. **Acq:** Purchase. **Dist:** Lions Gate Television Corp. $79.95.

Bad Guys 2008 (Unrated) — ★½
A too-much-talk and too-little-action crime drama. Disbarred criminal attorney Zena hooks up with three former clients to make a fortune with a new designer drug. Unfortunately, the plan goes bad when Eddie gets inexplicably trigger-happy while meeting their drug connection, who works for the yakuza. 86m; DVD. **C:** Kate del Castillo; Sherman Augustus; Danny Strong; Art LaFleur; Quinton 'Rampage' Jackson; Antonio Fargas; Directed by Rick Jacobsen; Written by Timothy Cogshell; Cinematography by Brian Agnew; Music by Dan Radlauer. **A:** Sr. High-Adult. **P:** Entertainment. **U:** Home. **Mov-Ent:** Crime Drama. **Acq:** Purchase. **Dist:** Maya Entertainment.

Bad Inclination 2003 (Unrated) — ★
A fading singer takes advantage of a serial killer murdering people in her building with an architect's drawing tool to stage a comeback. 95m; DVD. **C:** Eva Robins; Elisabetta Cavallotti; Elisabetta Rocchetti; Directed by Pierfrancesco Campanella; Written by Pierfrancesco Campanella; Enzo Gallo; Gianluca Curti; Cinematography by Giovanni Ragone; Music by Alberto Antinori. **A:** Sr. High-Adult. **P:** Entertainment. **U:** Home. **L:** English. **Mov-Ent. Acq:** Purchase. **Dist:** Media Blasters Inc. $19.95.

Bad Influence 1990 (R) — ★½
A lackluster effort in the evil-doppelganger school of psychological mystery, where a befuddled young executive (Spader) is led into the seamier side of life by a mysterious stranger

(Lowe). 99m; VHS, DVD; Open Captioned. **C:** Rob Lowe; James Spader; Lisa Zane; Christian Clemenson; Kathleen Wilhoite; Directed by Curtis Hanson; Cinematography by Robert Elswit; Music by Trevor Jones. **Pr:** Epic Productions; Triumph. **A:** College-Adult. **P:** Entertainment. **U:** Home. **Mov-Ent**: Mystery & Suspense. **Acq:** Purchase. **Dist:** Sony Pictures Home Entertainment Inc. $14.95.

Bad Jim 1989 (PG) — ★½
A cowpoke buys Billy the Kid's horse and, upon riding it, becomes an incorrigible outlaw himself. First feature film for Hollywood legend Clark Gable's son. 110m; DVD. **C:** James Brolin; Richard Roundtree; John Clark Gable; Harry Carey, Jr.; Ty Hardin; Pepe Serna; Rory Calhoun; Directed by Clyde Ware. **Pr:** 21st Century Film Corporation. **A:** Jr. High-Adult. **P:** Entertainment. **U:** Home. **Mov-Ent:** Western. **Acq:** Purchase. **Dist:** MGM Home Entertainment. $79.95.

Bad Lands 1939 (Unrated) — ★★½
A small cowboy posse finds themselves trapped by a band of Apache Indians in the Arizona desert. A remake of "The Lost Patrol." 70m/B/W; VHS. **C:** Robert Barrat; Guinn "Big Boy" Williams; Douglas Walton; Andy Clyde; Addison Richards; Robert Coote; Paul Hurst; Noah Beery, Jr.; Directed by Lew Landers. **Pr:** RKO. **A:** Adult. **P:** Entertainment. **U:** Home. **Mov-Ent**: Western, Native Americans. **Acq:** Purchase. **Dist:** Turner Broadcasting System Inc. $19.98.

Bad Lieutenant 1992 (NC-17) — ★★★
Social chaos and degeneration characterize story as well as nameless loner lieutenant Keitel, who is as corrupt as they come. Assigned to a case involving a raped nun, he's confronted by his own lagging Catholic beliefs and the need for saving grace. From cult filmmaker Ferrara ("Ms. 45") and filled with violence, drugs, and grotesque sexual situations. Tense, over-the-top, urban drama is not intended for seekers of the subtle. Rent it with "Reservoir Dogs" and prepare yourself for a long tense evening of top-rated Keitel and screen-splitting violence. "R" rated version is also available at 91 minutes. 98m; VHS, DVD, CC. **C:** Harvey Keitel; Brian McElroy; Frankie Acciario; Peggy Gormley; Stella Keitel; Victor Argo; Paul Calderon; Leonard Thomas; Frankie Thorn; Zoe Tamerlis; Directed by Abel Ferrara; Written by Zoe Tamerlis; Abel Ferrara; Cinematography by Ken Kelsch; Music by Joe Delia. **Pr:** Edward R. Pressman; Mary Kane; Randall Sabusawa; Aries Films. **A:** College-Adult. **P:** Entertainment. **U:** Home. **Mov-Ent**: Crime Drama, Rape, Violence. **Awds:** Ind. Spirit '93: Actor (Keitel). **Acq:** Purchase. **Dist:** Lions Gate Television Corp.; Facets Multimedia Inc. $19.98.

Bad Lieutenant: Port of Call New Orleans 2009 (R) — ★★
Loopy director Herzog does his 'reimaging' of Abel Ferrara's 1992 guilt-ridden cult flick "Bad Lieutenant" that starred an over-the-top Harvey Keitel. This time it's Cage as New Orleans homicide detective Terence McDonaugh, who's a gambling and drug addict who hallucinates evil iguanas. He also has a beautiful drug-addicted hooker girlfriend (Mendes) and a gangland slaying (that's drug related) to investigate. It's all just secondary to watching Cage act bizarrely, which (for a change) is actually in keeping with his erratic character. 121m; DVD, Blu-Ray, Wide. **C:** Nicolas Cage; Val Kilmer; Eva Mendes; Fairuza Balk; Jennifer Coolidge; Brad Dourif; Michael Shannon; Shawn Hatosy; Denzel Whitaker; Shea Whigham; Xzibit; Tom Bower; Irma P. Hall; Vondie Curtis-Hall; Directed by Werner Herzog; Written by William M. Finkelstein; Cinematography by Peter Zeitlinger; Music by Mark Isham. **Pr:** Nicolas Cage; Randall Emmett; Alan Polsky; Gabe Polsky; Stephen Belafonte; Nicolas Cage; Millennium Films; Nu Image Films; Osiris Films; Saturn Films; First Look Pictures. **A:** Sr. High-Adult. **P:** Entertainment. **U:** Home. **L:** English. **Mov-Ent**: Drug Abuse, Gambling, Drug Trafficking/Dealing. **Acq:** Purchase. **Dist:** Movies Unlimited; Alpha Video.

Bad Love 1995 (R) — ★★½
Unlucky Eloise (Gidley) stays true to nature when she falls for loser Lenny (Sizemore), who decides the big score lies with robbing the fading movie star (O'Neill) Eloise works for. Naturally, things go badly. Slick production for anyone who likes fringe romances. 93m; VHS, DVD. **C:** Tom Sizemore; Pamela Gidley; Debi Mazar; Jennifer O'Neill; Margaux Hemingway; Richard Edson; Seymour Cassel; Joe Dallesandro; Directed by Jill Goldman; Cinematography by Gary Tieche; Music by Rick Cox. **A:** Sr. High-Adult. **P:** Entertainment. **U:** Home. **Mov-Ent**: Drama. **Acq:** Purchase.

The Bad Man 1941 (Unrated) — ★★
With a particularly ripe Mexican accent, Beery stars in a convoluted comedic western as bandit Pancho Lopez. Henry Jones (Barrymore) and his nephew Gil (Reagan) own a ranch in Mexico that's being unjustly foreclosed on by men who both think there's oil on the property. When not rustling the Jones? cattle and holding people for ransom, Pancho decides to save the ranch because Gil once saved his life. It's hard to tell who chews more scenery—Beery or Barrymore. 70m/B/W; DVD. **C:** Wallace Beery; Lionel Barrymore; Ronald Reagan; Laraine Day; Tom Conway; Henry Travers; Nydia Westman; Chill Wills; Directed by Richard Thorpe; Written by Wells Root; Cinematography by Clyde De Vinna; Music by Franz Waxman. **A:** Jr. High-Adult. **P:** Entertainment. **U:** Home. **Mov-Ent**: Mexico, Oil Industry. **Acq:** Purchase. **Dist:** WarnerArchive.com.

The Bad Man of Brimstone 1938 (Unrated) — ★½
Rascally but violent outlaw Trigger Bill (Beery) discovers his estranged son Jeffrey (O'Keefe) is a prizefighter. Trigger wants his son to go to law school and promises to reform so they—ll both be legit but Bill is tested in one final showdown by villain Blackjack McCreedy (Cabot). 89m/B/W; DVD. **C:** Wallace Beery; Dennis O'Keefe; Bruce Cabot; Virginia Bruce; Lewis Stone; Guy Kibbee; Cliff Edwards; Guinn "Big Boy" Williams; Noah Beery, Sr.; Joseph Calleia; Directed by J. Walter Ruben; Written by Richard Maibaum; Cyril Hume; Cinematography by Clyde De Vinna; Music by William Axt. **A:** Sr. High-Adult. **P:** Entertainment. **U:** Home. **Mov-Ent**: Western, Boxing. **Acq:** Purchase. **Dist:** WarnerArchive.com.

Bad Man of Deadwood 1941 — ★
A man-with-a-past joins a circus as a sharp-shooter, and is threatened with disclosure. 54m/B/W; VHS, DVD. **C:** Roy Rogers; George "Gabby" Hayes; Carol Adams; Henry (Kleinbach) Brandon; Herbert Rawlinson; Sally Payne; Wally Wales; Jay Novello; Horace Murphy; Monte Blue; Directed by Joseph Kane; Written by James R. Webb; Cinematography by William Nobles; Music by Cy Feuer. **Pr:** Republic. **A:** Family. **P:** Entertainment. **U:** Home. **Mov-Ent**: Western, Circuses. **Acq:** Purchase, Rent/Lease. **Dist:** Rex Miller Artisan Studio. $24.95.

Bad Manners 1984 (R) — ★
When an orphan is adopted by a wealthy but entirely selfish couple, a group of his orphan friends try to free him from his new home and lifestyle. 85m; VHS. **C:** Martin Mull; Karen Black; Anne DeSalvo; Murphy Dunne; Pamela Segall; Edy Williams; Susan Ruttan; Richard Deacon; Directed by Bobby Houston; Cinematography by Jan De Bont. **Pr:** New World Pictures. **A:** Sr. High-Adult. **P:** Entertainment. **U:** Home. **L:** Spanish. **Mov-Ent**: Satire & Parody. **Acq:** Purchase. **Dist:** Anchor Bay Entertainment. $19.95.

Bad Manners 1998 (R) — ★★
Pompous musicologist Matt (Rubinek) returns to Boston with his razor-tongued girlfriend Kim (Feeney) to give a lecture and check in on his old girlfriend, brittle unhappy Nancy (Bedelia), and her prissy academic husband Wes (Strathairn). It's a weekend in hell for houseguests and hosts as they play not-so-adult games of truth-or-dare. Based on Gilman's play "Ghost in the Machine." 88m; VHS, DVD, Wide. **C:** David Strathairn; Bonnie Bedelia; Saul Rubinek; Caroleen Feeney; Julie Harris; Directed by Jonathan Kaufer; Written by David Gilman; Cinematography by Denis Maloney; Music by Ira Newborn. **A:** Sr. High-Adult. **P:** Entertainment. **U:** Home. **Mov-Ent**: Marriage. **Acq:** Purchase.

Bad Man's River 1972 (Unrated) — ★★
A Mexican revolutionary leader hires a gang of outlaws to blow up an arsenal used by the Mexican Army. 92m; VHS, DVD. **C:** Lee Van Cleef; James Mason; Gina Lollobrigida; Directed by Eugenio (Gene) Martin; Written by Philip Yordan; Cinematography by Alejandro Ulloa; Music by Waldo de los Rios. **Pr:** Philip Yordan; Philip Yordan. **A:** Sr. High-Adult. **P:** Entertainment. **U:** Home. **L:** Italian, Spanish. **Mov-Ent**. **Acq:** Purchase. **Dist:** Movies Unlimited. $13.49.

Bad Meat 2011 (Unrated) — ★
Unruly teens arriving at a boot camp intended to put them back on the path to more responsible behavior have more than the usual bad camp experience when a disease causes their sadistic counselors to put on leather outfits and run around eating people. 96m; DVD, Streaming. **C:** Dave Franco; Elisabeth Harnois; Mark Pellegrino; Jessica Parker Kennedy; Monique Ganderton; Directed by Lulu Jarmen; Written by Paul Gerstenberger. **A:** Sr. High-Adult. **P:** Entertainment. **U:** Home. **L:** English. **Mov-Ent**: Horror. **Acq:** Purchase, Rent/Lease. **Dist:** Jinga Films Ltd.; Amazon.com Inc.

Bad Medicine 1985 (PG-13) — **Bomb!**
A youth who doesn't want to be a doctor is accepted by a highly questionable Latin American school of medicine. Remember that it was for medical students like these that the U.S. liberated Grenada. 97m; VHS, Streaming, CC. **C:** Steve Guttenberg; Alan Arkin; Julie Hagerty; Bill Macy; Curtis Armstrong; Julie Kavner; Joe Grifasi; Robert Romanus; Taylor Negron; Gilbert Gottfried; Directed by Harvey Miller; Written by Harvey Miller. **Pr:** Alex Winitsky; Arlene Sellers; 20th Century-Fox. **A:** Jr. High-Adult. **P:** Entertainment. **U:** Home. **Mov-Ent**: Satire & Parody, Drugs. **Acq:** Purchase. **Dist:** Fox Home Entertainment. $79.98.

Bad Medicine for Big Bucks 1993
Features archery hunters Tom Storm and Paul Brunner as they demonstrate techniques for luring big bucks into bow range. Covers rattling, grunt calling, decoying, and the use of scents. 70m; VHS. **A:** Adult. **P:** Instruction. **U:** Home. **Spo-Rec**: Hunting. **Acq:** Purchase. **Dist:** Stoney-Wolf Productions, Inc. $49.95.

Bad Men of the Border 1945 — ★½
Routine oater has Kirby posing as a bandit in order to infiltrate an outlaw band passing counterfeit money. He rounds up the bad guys and finds time to romance Armida too. 56m/B/W; VHS. **C:** Kirby Grant; Fuzzy Knight; Armida; John Eldridge; Francis McDonald; Directed by Wallace Fox; Written by Adele Buffington. **Pr:** Mark Huffam. **A:** Jr. High-Adult. **P:** Entertainment. **U:** Home. **Mov-Ent**: Western. **Acq:** Purchase. **Dist:** Movies Unlimited. $19.99.

Bad Moon 1996 (R) — ★½
Let's put it this way, the werewolf in this movie is not the only thing that bites. Shortest (mercifully) studio release in recent history is a horror (in more ways than one) film with Pare leading the pack as Ted, a photojournalist who comes back from the Amazon a different, more nocturnally hirsute man. Fleeing from the site of his nightly gore, Ted takes refuge with his loving sister Janet (Hemingway) and her son Brett (Gamble). The real hero (and best actor) is a German shepherd named Thor (Primo) who discovers that Ted's a werewolf. Dog steals the show paws down (naturally). Decent special FX. Adapted from Wayne Smith's novel "Thor." 79m; VHS, DVD, Wide, CC. **C:** Mariel Hemingway; Michael Pare; Mason Gamble; Ken Pogue; Directed by Eric Red; Written by Eric Red; Cinematography by Jan Kiesser; Music by Daniel Licht. **Pr:** James G. Robinson; Gary Barber; Morgan Creek Productions; Warner Bros. **A:** Sr. High-Adult. **P:** Entertainment. **U:** Home. **Mov-Ent**: Horror, Pets. **Acq:** Purchase. **Dist:** Warner Home Video, Inc.

The Bad Mother's Handbook 2007 (PG-13) — ★½
Self-absorbed single mom Karen (Tate) thinks she can bend anyone to her will but learns differently in this BBC family drama. She expects her teenage daughter Charlotte (Grainger) to go to college but when Charlotte becomes pregnant, Karen refuses to help. Instead, the girl turns to geeky friend Daniel (Pattinson) and her grandmother Nancy (Reid) for comfort and Karen learns some hard lessons in parenting. Adaptation of the Kate Long novel. 90m; DVD. **C:** Catherine Tate; Holliday Grainger; Anne Reid; Robert Pattinson; Steve John Shepherd; Steve Pemberton; Directed by Robin Shepperd; Written by Kate Long; Kate O'Riordan; Music by Mark Russell. **A:** Jr. High-Adult. **P:** Entertainment. **U:** Home. **Mov-Ent**: Pregnancy. **Acq:** Purchase. **Dist:** Lions Gate Entertainment Inc.

The Bad News Bears 1976 (PG) — ★★★
Family comedy about a misfit Little League team that gets whipped into shape by a cranky, sloppy, beer-drinking coach who recruits a female pitcher. O'Neal and Matthau are top-notch. Spawned two sequels and a TV series. 102m; VHS, DVD, 8 mm, Wide. **C:** Walter Matthau; Tatum O'Neal; Vic Morrow; Joyce Van Patten; Jackie Earle Haley; Chris Barnes; Erin Blunt; Gary Cavagnaro; Alfred Lutter; David Stambaugh; Brandon Cruz; Jaime Escobedo; Scott Firestone; George Gonzales; Brett Marx; David Pollock; Quinn Smith; Directed by Michael Ritchie; Written by Bill Lancaster; Cinematography by John A. Alonzo; Music by Jerry Fielding. **Pr:** Paramount Pictures. **A:** Family. **P:** Entertainment. **U:** Home. **Mov-Ent**: Comedy--Slapstick, Children, Baseball. **Awds:** Writers Guild '76: Orig. Screenplay. **Acq:** Purchase. **Dist:** Paramount Pictures Corp. $14.95.

The Bad News Bears 2005 (PG-13) — ★★
Here's some bad news: Indie darling Linklater hit a home run with his kid-friendly "School of Rock," but he couldn't squeeze any life out of this watered-down remake of the 1976 Walter Matthau classic. It's disturbing that the updated "Bears" is a million times less subversive, vulgar, and (let's face it) funny than the original, a film that was released almost thirty years ago. Isn't society supposed to be declining? Shouldn't Linklater's movie be raunchier than a film released during the Carter administration? Casting Thornton in the lead was an inspired choice, but the toothless script just forces him to do the PG version of his "Bad Santa" routine. Do yourself a favor and rent the original. 111m; DVD, UMD. **C:** Billy Bob Thornton; Greg Kinnear; Marcia Gay Harden; Tyler Patrick Jones; Sammi Kraft; Timmy Deters; Ridge Canipe; Brandon Craggs; Jeff Davies; Carter Jenkins; Jeffrey Tedmori; Troy Gentile; Carlos Estrada; Emmanuel Estrada; Kenneth "K.C." Harris; Aman Johal; Directed by Richard Linklater; Written by Glenn Ficarra; John Requa; Bill Lancaster; Cinematography by Rogier Stoffers; Music by Ed Shearmur; Randall Poster. **Pr:** J. Geyer Kosinski; Richard Linklater; Detour Filmproduction; Paramount Pictures. **A:** Jr. High-Adult. **P:** Entertainment. **U:** Home. **L:** English. **Mov-Ent**: Baseball, Sports--Fiction: Comedy, Alcoholism. **Acq:** Purchase. **Dist:** Paramount Pictures Corp.

The Bad News Bears Go to Japan 1978 (PG) — ★
The second sequel, in which the famed Little League team goes to the Little League World Series in Tokyo. Comic adventure features Curtis as a talent agent out to exploit the team's fame. 92m; VHS, DVD, Wide. **C:** Tony Curtis; Jackie Earle Haley; Tomisaburo Wakayama; George Wyner; Erin Blunt; George Gonzales; Brett Marx; David Pollock; David Stambaugh; Regis Philbin; Directed by John Berry; Written by Bill Lancaster; Cinematography by Gene Polito; Music by Paul Chihara. **Pr:** Paramount Pictures. **A:** Family. **P:** Entertainment. **U:** Home. **Mov-Ent**: Comedy--Slapstick, Baseball, Sports--Fiction: Comedy. **Acq:** Purchase. **Dist:** Paramount Pictures Corp. $19.95.

The Bad News Bears in Breaking Training 1977 (PG) — ★½
With a chance to take on the Houston Toros for a shot at the little league baseball Japanese champs, the Bears devise a way to get to Texas to play at the famed Astrodome. Disappointing sequel to "The Bad News Bears"; followed by "The Bad News Bears Go to Japan" (1978). 99m; VHS, DVD, Wide. **C:** William Devane; Clifton James; Jackie Earle Haley; Jimmy Baio; Chris Barnes; Erin Blunt; George Gonzales; Jaime Escobedo; Alfred Lutter; Brett Marx; David Pollock; Quinn Smith; David Stambaugh; Dolph Sweet; Directed by Michael Pressman; Written by Paul Brickman; Cinematography by Fred W. Koenekamp; Music by Craig Safan. **Pr:** Leonard Goldberg; Paramount Pictures. **A:** Family. **P:** Entertainment. **U:** Home. **Mov-Ent**: Comedy--Slapstick, Baseball, Sports--Fiction: Comedy. **Acq:** Purchase. **Dist:** Paramount Pictures Corp. $14.95.

Bad News Tour 1989
The cast of the relentlessly tasteless (but funny) TV show "The Young Ones" star in this spoof of heavy metal musicians and their antics as the fictitious band "Bad News" is seen preparing for an American tour. Several real heavy metal bands also appear, including Ozzy Osbourne, the Scorpions and Motorhead, to keep the joke alive. 84m; VHS. **Pr:** RHI Entertainment Inc. **A:** Adult. **P:** Entertainment. **U:** Home. **Mov-Ent**: Satire & Parody, Music Video. **Acq:** Purchase. **Dist:** Music Video Distributors; Rhino Entertainment Co. $19.95.

The Bad Pack 1998 (R) — ★½
Soldier of fortune puts together a team when he's hired to defend a town beseiged by a sadistic militia. 93m; VHS, DVD. **C:** Robert Davi; Ralph (Ralf) Moeller; Roddy Piper; Brent Huff; Larry B. Scott; Patrick Dollaghan; Marshall Teague; Directed by

Brent Huff. **A:** Sr. High-Adult. **P:** Entertainment. **U:** Home. **Mov-Ent. Acq:** Purchase. **Dist:** Lions Gate Entertainment Inc.

Bad Paper: Kiting and Check Schemes 1989
A three-part series about phony checks and the people who pass them off. 55m; VHS, 3/4 U. **C:** Narrated by Efrem Zimbalist, Jr. **Pr:** Institute for Financial Crime Prevention. **A:** Sr. High-Adult. **P:** Education. **U:** Institution. **Bus-Ind:** Finance. **Acq:** Purchase, Rent/Lease. **Dist:** Association of Certified Fraud Examiners. $585.00.
Indiv. Titles: 1. Check Schemes 2. Forgery & I.D. 3. Check Kiting.

Bad Parents 2012 (Unrated) — ★★½
Satire may get knowing nods from parents who cart their kids around to organized sports leagues. New Jersey housewife Kathy signs her younger daughter up for soccer not realizing the craziness that will ensue. The parents are obsessed with which team their girls are assigned to and how much playing time they get and they and Coach Nick are obsessed with winning, especially as the A team heads towards the state semi-finals. These adults couldn't even spell 'sportsmanship.' 100m; DVD. **C:** Janeane Garofalo; Christopher Titus; Cheri Oteri; Kristen Johnston; Michael Boatman; Rebecca Budig; Reiko Aylesworth; Bill Sage; Directed by Caytha Jentis; Written by Caytha Jentis; Cinematography by Anthony Savini; Music by James Harrell. **A:** Jr. High-Adult. **P:** Entertainment. **U:** Home. **L:** English. **Mov-Ent:** Children, Parenting, Soccer. **Acq:** Purchase. **Dist:** Gaiam International Inc.

Bad Religion: Along the Way 1992
The punk band is featured in clips from 14 different concerts. Songs include "Land of Competition," "WWIII," "Damned to be Free," and "1000 More Fools." 75m; VHS. **A:** Jr. High-Adult. **P:** Entertainment. **U:** Home. **Mov-Ent:** Music Video, Music--Pop/Rock. **Acq:** Purchase. **Dist:** Music Video Distributors. $24.95.

Bad Reputation 2005 (R) — ★★★
Chillingly disturbing portrayal of victim's revenge. Michelle, though poor, attends an affluent school on scholarship. She chooses to keep buried in a book rather than mix with the shallow class populous. One night at a party, she is drugged and gang-raped. A metamorphosis follows, as the shy, smart, attractive girl becomes an avenging assassin, swiftly wiping out all who humiliated her. Excellent character development, smart script, and bright directing make for a very satisfying retaliation tale. 90m; DVD. **C:** Angelique Hennessy; Jerad Anderson; Danielle Noble; Mark Kunzman; Kristina Conzen; Directed by Jim Hemphill; Written by Jim Hemphill; Cinematography by Forrest Allison; Music by John LeBec; Eric Choronzy. **A:** Sr. High-Adult. **P:** Entertainment. **U:** Home. **Mov-Ent. Acq:** Purchase. **Dist:** Maverick Entertainment.

Bad Ronald 1974 (Unrated) — ★★★
No, not a political biography of Ronald Reagan... Fascinating thriller about a disturbed teenager who kills a friend after being harassed repeatedly. The plot thickens after the boy's mother dies, and he is forced to hide out in a secret room when an unsuspecting family with three daughters moves into his house. The story is accurately recreated from the novel by John Holbrook Vance. 78m; VHS, DVD. **C:** Scott Jacoby; Pippa Scott; John Larch; Dabney Coleman; Kim Hunter; John Fiedler; Directed by Buzz Kulik. **Pr:** Lorimar Productions. **A:** Jr. High-Adult. **P:** Entertainment. **U:** Home. **Mov-Ent:** Mystery & Suspense, TV Movies, Adolescence. **Acq:** Purchase. **Dist:** WarnerArchive.com. $49.95.

Bad Santa 2003 (R) — ★★½
This is not your grandparents' Christmas movie. Or your kids' for that matter. Thornton is Willie Stokes, an alcoholic, vulgarian, self-loathing departmant store Santa who uses the gig to rob the store safe on Christmas Eve. His partner is sidekick/elf Marcus, the brains of the duo, who berates Willie for letting his liquor-soaked ways interfere with the job. When they set up shop in Phoenix, things get complicated when a doughy outcast kid leeches onto Willie. Sentimentality is crushed beneath the boot of bitter misanthropy as the movie swerves from tasteless to merely outrageous and back. Luckily, the commitment of the cast to their unsavory roles makes most of the comedy work. Zwigoff and the script let in a little light at the end, but not so much that it betrays what came before. Ritter is excellent in his final role, as the meek store manager. 91m; VHS, DVD, Blu-Ray. **C:** Billy Bob Thornton; Tony Cox; Lauren Graham; Brett Kelly; John Ritter; Bernie Mac; Lauren Tom; Cloris Leachman; Directed by Terry Zwigoff; Written by Glenn Ficarra; John Requa; Cinematography by Jamie Anderson; Music by David Kitay. **Pr:** Bob Weinstein; John Cameron; Sarah Aubrey; Triptych Pictures; Dimension Films. **A:** Sr. High-Adult. **P:** Entertainment. **U:** Home. **Mov-Ent:** Christmas, Alcoholism. **Acq:** Purchase. **Dist:** Buena Vista Home Entertainment.

The Bad Seed 1956 — ★★½
A mother makes the tortuous discovery that her cherubic eight-year-old daughter harbors an innate desire to kill. Based on Maxwell Anderson's powerful Broadway stage play. 129m/B/W; VHS, DVD, Blu-Ray. **C:** Patty McCormack; Nancy Kelly; Eileen Heckart; Henry Jones; Evelyn Varden; Paul Fix; Jesse White; Gage Clark; Joan Croyden; Frank Cady; William Hopper; Directed by Mervyn LeRoy; Written by John Lee Mahin; Cinematography by Harold Rosson; Music by Alex North. **Pr:** Mervyn LeRoy; Mervyn LeRoy. **A:** Jr. High-Adult. **P:** Entertainment. **U:** Home. **Mov-Ent:** Mystery & Suspense. **Awds:** Golden Globes '57: Support. Actress (Heckart). **Acq:** Purchase. **Dist:** Warner Home Video, Inc. $59.95.

The Bad Seed 1985 — ★★
TV remake of the movie with the same name. Story about a sadistic little child who kills for her own evil purposes. Acting is not up to par with previous version. 100m; VHS, DVD. **C:** Blair Brown; Lynn Redgrave; David Carradine; Richard Kiley; David Ogden Stiers; Carrie Wells; Chad Allen; Christa Denton; Anne Haney; Eve Smith; Directed by Paul Wendkos; Music by Paul Chihara. **A:** Sr. High-Adult. **P:** Entertainment. **U:** Home. **Mov-Ent:** Horror, TV Movies. **Acq:** Purchase. **Dist:** No Longer Available.

Bad Seed 2000 (R) — ★★
Mild-mannered Preston (Wilson) storms out of the house when he discovers wife Emily (Avital) is having an affair. He returns home to find her murdered—maybe by her boyfriend Jonathan (Reedus) whom Preston then tries to track down. There's another murder, both men go on the lam, and Preston turns to a hard-luck PI, Dick (Farina), for help. Too bad the film doesn't hang together better since it had the makings of a fine little thriller. 92m; VHS, DVD, Wide, CC. **C:** Luke Wilson; Norman Reedus; Dennis Farina; Mili Avital; Vincent Kartheiser; Directed by Jon Bokenkamp; Written by Jon Bokenkamp; Cinematography by Joey Forsyte; Music by Kurt Kuenne. **A:** Sr. High-Adult. **P:** Entertainment. **U:** Home. **Mov-Ent. Acq:** Purchase. **Dist:** Lions Gate Television Corp.

The Bad Sleep Well 1960 — ★★★½
Japanese variation of the 1940 Warner Bros. crime dramas. A tale about corruption in the corporate world as seen through the eyes of a rising executive. 135m/B/W; VHS, DVD. **C:** Toshiro Mifune; Masayuki Kato; Masayuki Mori; Takashi Shimura; Akira Nishimura; Directed by Akira Kurosawa; Written by Akira Kurosawa; Shinobu Hashimoto; Ryuzo Kikushima; Hideo Oguni; Cinematography by Yuzuru Aizawa; Music by Masaru Sato. **A:** College-Adult. **P:** Entertainment. **U:** Home. **L:** Japanese. **Mov-Ent. Acq:** Purchase. **Dist:** Home Vision Cinema; Sony Pictures Home Entertainment Inc.

The Bad Son 2007 (Unrated) — ★½
A Seattle serial killer targets the women who come into his life, except for his mom who protects him because she actually works for the cops and has access to confidential documents. Whenever the police get too close, Frances cries harassment but two at-odds detectives are determined to bring him to justice. 90m; DVD. **C:** Catherine Dent; Tom McBeath; Ben Cotton; Marilyn Norry; Paul Jarrett; Tegan Moss; Kimberly Warnat; Directed by Neill Fearnley; Written by Richard Leder; Cinematography by Eric Goldstein; Music by Jerry Lambert; Harry Manfredini. **A:** Sr. High-Adult. **P:** Entertainment. **U:** Home. **Mov-Ent. Acq:** Purchase. **Dist:** A&E Television Networks L.L.C.

Bad Taste 1988 (Unrated) — ★★★
A definite pleaser for the person who enjoys watching starving aliens devour the average, everyday human being. Alien fast-food manufacturers come to earth in hopes of harvesting all of mankind. The earth's fate lies in the hands of the government who must stop these rampaging creatures before the whole human race is gobbled up. Terrific make-up jobs on the aliens add the final touch to this gory, yet humorous cult horror flick. 90m; VHS, DVD, Wide. **C:** Peter Jackson; Pete O'Herne; Mike Minett; Terry Potter; Craig Smith; Doug Wren; Dean Lawrie; Peter Vere-Jones; Ken Hammon; Michael Gooch; Directed by Peter Jackson; Written by Peter Jackson; Ken Hammon; Tony Hiles; Cinematography by Peter Jackson; Music by Michelle Scullion. **A:** College-Adult. **P:** Entertainment. **U:** Home. **Mov-Ent:** Cult Films. **Acq:** Purchase. **Dist:** Facets Multimedia Inc. $19.95.

Bad Teacher 2011 (R) — ★★
Wild-living and completely inappropriate 7th-grade teacher Elizabeth (Diaz) wants to dump her job for a wealthy match and sets her sights on a rich, handsome substitute teacher (Timberlake). However, she has competition from perfectly-behaved colleague Amy (Punch). Diaz and Segel are game, but the plot tries too hard to be raunchy and funny enough to join the "hard R comedy" revival, and comes up a bit short. 92m; DVD, Blu-Ray. **C:** Cameron Diaz; Justin Timberlake; Lucy Punch; John Michael Higgins; Thomas Lennon; Jason Segel; Directed by Jake Kasdan; Written by Gene Stupnitsky; Lee Eisenberg; Cinematography by Alar Kivilo; Music by Michael Andrews. **Pr:** Columbia Pictures; Sony Pictures Home Entertainment Inc. **P:** Entertainment. **U:** Home. **L:** English. **Mov-Ent:** Physical Education, Sex & Sexuality. **Acq:** Purchase. **Dist:** Movies Unlimited; Alpha Video; Sony Pictures Home Entertainment Inc.

Bad Timing: A Sensual Obsession 1980 (Unrated) — ★★
Perverse sex drama from Brit director Roeg. Milena (Russell) is admitted to a Vienna hospital nearly dead from an overdose, making the staff suspicious and Inspector Netusil (Keitel) is called in. It seems her ex-lover, psychologist Alex (Garfunkel), can't quite account for the time they spent together before he called for help. Flashbacks depict Milena's increasingly crazy behavior and Alex's unhealthy obsession with her. 123m; DVD. **C:** Art Garfunkel; Theresa Russell; Harvey Keitel; Denholm Elliott; Directed by Nicolas Roeg; Written by Yale Udoff; Cinematography by Anthony B. Richmond; Music by Richard Hartley. **A:** College-Adult. **P:** Entertainment. **U:** Home. **Mov-Ent:** Suicide, Hospitals. **Acq:** Purchase. **Dist:** Criterion Collection Inc.

Bad Words 2013 (R) — ★★
Bateman stars and makes his directorial debut as a foul-mouthed sore loser. Disgruntled 40-year-old Guy Trilby exploits a technicality in the spelling bee regulations that allows him to compete against the 8th-grade participants. Going on to the national spelling bee in L.A., he forms an unexpected bond with charming youngster Chaitanya Chopra (Chand)--they're both dealing with daddy issues--despite Guy's worst behavior. Joyfully irresponsible and uncensored. 88m; DVD. **C:** Jason Bateman; Rohan Chand; Kathryn Hahn; Allison Janney; Philip Baker Hall; Ben Falcone; Anjul Nigam; Directed by Jason Bateman; Written by Andrew Dodge; Cinematography by Ken Seng; Music by Rolfe Kent. **Pr:** Jason Bateman; Darko Entertainment; Focus Features L.L.C. **A:** Sr. High-Adult. **P:** Entertainment. **U:** Home. **L:** English. **Mov-Ent:** Children, Men. **Acq:** Purchase.

The Badge 1990
After many failed attempts at a career, a young man finally joins the police force to appease his domineering father. 30m; VHS. **C:** Directed by Robert Spara. **A:** Sr. High-Adult. **P:** Entertainment. **U:** Home. **Mov-Ent:** Family. **Acq:** Purchase. **Dist:** The Cinema Guild. $59.95.

The Badge 2002 (R) — ★★
Small-town sheriff Darl (Thornton) must set aside his personal distate to investigate the murder of a local transsexual, who was once married to stripper Scarlett (Arquette). But the deeper Darl digs, the more the powers that be want the incident covered up. Mediocre mystery despite the name cast. 103m; VHS, DVD. **C:** Billy Bob Thornton; Patricia Arquette; Sela Ward; William Devane; Jena Malone; Tom Bower; Ray McKinnon; Julie Hagerty; Hill Harper; Directed by Robby Henson; Written by Robby Henson; Cinematography by Irek Hartowicz; Music by David Bergeaud. **A:** Sr. High-Adult. **P:** Entertainment. **U:** Home. **Mov-Ent. Acq:** Purchase. **Dist:** CinemaNow Inc.

Badge of Honor 1934 (Unrated) — ★
Playboy Bob Gordon poses as a reporter and gets a job at a newspaper after rescuing Helen, the daughter of the publisher. Gangsters and political corruption are also involved in the uninteresting plot. 62m/B/W; DVD. **C:** Buster Crabbe; Ruth Hall; Ralph Lewis; Betty Blythe; John Trent; Directed by Spencer Gordon Bennet; Written by George Morgan; Cinematography by James S. Brown, Jr. **A:** Jr. High-Adult. **P:** Entertainment. **U:** Home. **Mov-Ent:** Journalism. **Acq:** Purchase. **Dist:** Sinister Cinema.

Badge of the Assassin 1985 (Unrated) — ★★
True story of a New York assistant DA who directed a campaign to catch a pair of cop-killers from the '70s. 96m; VHS. **C:** James Woods; Yaphet Kotto; Alex Rocco; David Harris; Pam Grier; Steven Keats; Richard Bradford; Rae Dawn Chong; Directed by Mel Damski. **Pr:** Daniel H. Blatt. **A:** Jr. High-Adult. **P:** Entertainment. **U:** Home. **Mov-Ent:** TV Movies. **Acq:** Purchase. **Dist:** CinemaNow Inc. $29.95.

Badge 373 1973 (R) — ★½
In the vein of "The French Connection," a New York cop is suspended and decides to battle crime his own way. 116m; VHS, DVD, Blu-Ray, Streaming. **C:** Robert Duvall; Verna Bloom; Eddie Egan; Directed by Howard W. Koch. **Pr:** Paramount Pictures. **A:** Sr. High-Adult. **P:** Entertainment. **U:** Home. **Mov-Ent. Acq:** Purchase. **Dist:** Paramount Pictures Corp. $14.95.

Badland 2007 (R) — ★½
Overly-solemn and way too long. Marine reservist Jerry wound up with a dishonorable discharge and PTSD after a stint in Iraq. Now he's got a nothing job in a nowhere Wyoming town when his boss falsely accuses him of theft. When shrewish wife Nora nags once too often—well, Jerry takes young daughter Celia and hits the road. 165m; DVD. **C:** Jamie Draven; Vinessa Shaw; Joe Morton; Chandra West; Grace Fulton; Patrick Richards; Directed by Francesco Lucente; Written by Francesco Lucente; Cinematography by Carlo Varini; Music by Ludek Drizhal. **A:** Sr. High-Adult. **P:** Entertainment. **U:** Home. **Mov-Ent. Acq:** Purchase. **Dist:** Vanguard International Cinema, Inc.

The Badlanders 1958 (Unrated) — ★★
A western remake of the 1950 crime drama "The Asphalt Jungle." In 1898, Peter 'The Dutchman' Van Hoek (Ladd) and John McBain (Borgnine) are released from Yuma state prison. Both wind up in Prescott, Arizona where the Dutchman is unwelcome since the mining engineer was framed and sent to the pen by gold mine owner Cyril Lounsberry (Smith). McBain wants to go straight but is drawn into the Dutchman's revenge scheme. 83m; DVD. **C:** Alan Ladd; Ernest Borgnine; Kent Smith; Claire Kelly; Katy Jurado; Nehemiah Persoff; Directed by Delmer Daves; Written by Richard Collins; Cinematography by John Seitz. **A:** Jr. High-Adult. **P:** Entertainment. **U:** Home. **Mov-Ent:** Western, Miners & Mining. **Acq:** Purchase. **Dist:** WarnerArchive.com.

Badlands 1974 (PG) — ★★★½
Based loosely on the Charlie Starkweather murders of the 1950s, this impressive debut by director Malick recounts a slow-thinking, unhinged misfit's killing spree across the mid-western plains, accompanied by a starry-eyed 15-year-old schoolgirl. Sheen and Spacek are a disturbingly numb, apathetic, and icy duo. 94m; VHS, DVD, Blu-Ray. **C:** Martin Sheen; Sissy Spacek; Warren Oates; Ramon Bieri; Alan Vint; Gary Littlejohn; Charles Fitzpatrick; Howard Ragsdale; John Womack, Jr.; Dona Baldwin; Cameo(s) Terrence Malick; Directed by Terrence Malick; Written by Terrence Malick; Cinematography by Tak Fujimoto; Stevan Larner; Brian Probyn; Music by Carl Orff. **Pr:** Warner Bros. **A:** Jr. High-Adult. **P:** Entertainment. **U:** Home. **Mov-Ent:** Cult Films, Classic Films. **Awds:** Natl. Film Reg. '93. **Acq:** Purchase. **Dist:** Criterion Collection Inc.; Warner Home Video, Inc. $39.98.

Badlands: Dag the Giblets 1991
Veteran hard rock talent combines to become Badlands. Ray Gillen from Black Sabbath, Jake E. Lee who played with Ozzy Osbourne, Jeff Martin from Racer X, and Greg Chaisson form a new band with a classic hard rock sound. Songs include "The Last Time," "Winter's Call," and "Dreams in the Dark"?full-length versions—and more. Plus interviews, live performance footage, candid shots of the band on tour, and even some home video segments. 40m; VHS. **A:** Jr. High-Adult. **P:** Entertainment. **U:**

Home. **Mov-Ent**: Music--Pop/Rock. **Acq:** Purchase. **Dist:** WarnerVision; Fast Forward. $16.98.

Badman's Territory 1946 (Unrated) — ★★★
A straight-shooting marshal has to deal with such notorious outlaws as the James and Dalton boys in a territory outside of government control. 79m/B/W; VHS, DVD. **C:** Randolph Scott; Ann Richards; George "Gabby" Hayes; Steve Brodie; Directed by Tim Whelan. **Pr:** RKO. **A:** Sr. High-Adult. **P:** Entertainment. **U:** Home. **Mov-Ent**: Western. **Acq:** Purchase. **Dist:** WarnerArchive.com. $19.98.

Badminton 19??
A program in two parts in which Dr. Jim Poole of Louisiana State University helps demonstrate techniques of badminton including the serve, overhand, forehand and backhand strokes, underhand net strokes, drives around the head strokes, and footwork. 14m; VHS, 3/4 U. **Pr:** Champions on Film. **A:** Family. **P:** Instruction. **U:** Institution, CCTV, Home. **Spo-Rec**: Sports--General. **Acq:** Purchase, Rent/Lease. **Dist:** School-Tech Inc.

Badminton 1993
Vic Braden and champions Chris and Utami Kinard teach you all the necessary moves of this new Olympic sport. Includes footage of players at major events and competitions. ?m; VHS. **A:** Sr. High-Adult. **P:** Instruction. **U:** Home. **Spo-Rec**: Sports--General. **Acq:** Purchase. **Dist:** Braden Enterprises. $39.95.

Badminton By the Badminton Association of England 1981
Coach Paul Whetnail offers advice for everyone from the uncoordinated beginner to the suave expert. 90m; VHS. **Pr:** British Broadcasting Corporation. **A:** Family. **P:** Instruction. **U:** Home. **Spo-Rec**: Sports--General. **Acq:** Purchase. **Dist:** Video Collectibles; School-Tech Inc. $29.95.

Badminton: Winning Fundamentals 1990
Learn the drills that instill the fundamental skills you need to become an effective competitior. Contains actual footage so you can witness the pros in action. 30m; VHS. **A:** Sr. High-Adult. **P:** Instruction. **U:** Institution, Home. **Spo-Rec**: Sports--General. **Acq:** Purchase. **Dist:** Cambridge Educational. $39.95.

Badsville 2002
Explore L.A.'s underground clubs and bands, including the Hangmen, the Superbees, the Streetwalkin' Cheetahs, Texas Terri, and others. 84m; DVD. **A:** Sr. High-Adult. **P:** Entertainment. **U:** Home. **Fin-Art**: Documentary Films, Biography: Music. **Acq:** Purchase. **Dist:** Music Video Distributors.

Baer vs. Louis/Louis vs. Schmeling 19??
Joe Louis meets ex-champ Max Baer at Yankee Stadium on September 24, 1935. On June 19, 1936 Joe Louis fights with Max Schmeling at Yankee Stadium. 54m/B/W; VHS. **C:** Max Baer, Sr; Joe Louis. **A:** Family. **P:** Entertainment. **U:** Home. **Spo-Rec**: Boxing. **Acq:** Purchase.

Baeus 1988
A beetle helps a woman who is thinking of leaving her husband. 6m; VHS, 3/4 U. **Pr:** Lucerne Films. **A:** Family. **P:** Entertainment. **U:** Institution, SURA. **Chl-Juv**: Storytelling. **Acq:** Purchase. **Dist:** Lucerne Media. $150.00.

Baffled 1972 (Unrated) — ★★½
Nimoy is a race car driver who has visions of people in danger. He must convince an ESP expert (Hampshire) of the credibility of his vision, and then try to save the lives of the people seen with his sixth sense. A failed NBC TV pilot movie. 90m; DVD, Streaming. **C:** Leonard Nimoy; Susan Hampshire; Vera Miles; Rachel Roberts; Jewel Blanch; Christopher Benjamin; Directed by Philip Leacock; Written by Theodore Apstein; Cinematography by Ken Hodges; Music by Richard Hill. **Pr:** ATV Ltd. **A:** Jr. High-Adult. **P:** Entertainment. **U:** Home. **L:** English. **Mov-Ent**: Mystery & Suspense, Automobiles--Racing, TV Movies. **Acq:** Purchase. **Dist:** Movies Unlimited.

Bag It 2010 (Unrated)
Documentary on where disposed plastic ends up and the harm it causes (along with the environmental destruction the creation of it makes). 78m; DVD, Streaming. **A:** Jr. High-Adult. **P:** Education. **U:** Home, Institution. **L:** English. **Gen-Edu**: Documentary Films, Plastics, Ecology & Environment. **Acq:** Purchase, Rent/Lease. **Dist:** Docurama. $29.95 14.99.

The Bag Man 2014 (R) — ★
Cusack continues his remarkable descent into less than B-movie nonsense with this insipid piece masquerading as a crime drama but actually little more than a paycheck movie for its lazy stars. The king of the paycheck movies in the current century, De Niro co-stars as a legendary crime boss (of course) who hires a bag man named Jack (Cusack) to wait at a seedy motel for his arrival. While Jack wonders what the crime boss has in store for him, he meets a stunner named Rivka (Da Costa). A waste of time on every level—ridiculous, repugnant, and just plain stupid. 109m; DVD, Blu-Ray. **C:** John Cusack; Rebecca Da Costa; Robert De Niro; Dominic Purcell; Crispin Glover; Kirk "Sticky Fingaz" Jones; Directed by David Grovic; Written by David Grovic; Paul Conway; Cinematography by Steve Mason; Music by Tony Morales; Edward Rogers. **Pr:** Universal Pictures Inc. **A:** Sr. High-Adult. **P:** Entertainment. **U:** Home. **L:** English. **Mov-Ent**: Crime Drama. **Acq:** Purchase. **Dist:** Universal Studios Home Video.

Bag of Bones 2011 (Unrated) — ★★
Underwhelming A&E miniseries finds bestselling novelist Mike Noonan (Brosnan) retreating to a New England lake house to grieve the sudden death of his wife Jo (Gish). Mike starts suffering from nightmares and it becomes clear that Jo is contacting him over long-ago secrets involving the disappearance of 1930s blues singer Sara Tidwell (Rose) and a town curse. Also involved are single mom Mattie (George), who's being harassed in a custody battle over her daughter by her evil, elderly father-in-law Max (Schallert) that also has ties to the past. Based on Stephen King's 1998 novel. 170m; DVD. **C:** Pierce Brosnan; Melissa George; Annabeth Gish; Anika Noni Rose; William Schallert; Deborah Grover; Caitlin Carmichael; Matt Frewer; Jason Priestley; Directed by Mick Garris; Written by Matt Venne; Cinematography by Barry Donlevy; Music by Nicholas Pike. **A:** Sr. High-Adult. **P:** Entertainment. **U:** Home. **Mov-Ent**: TV Movies. **Acq:** Purchase. **Dist:** Sony Pictures Home Entertainment Inc.

A Bag of Hammers 2011 (Unrated) — ★★
Offbeat indie comedy (with some maudlin moments) finds L.A. slacker buds Ben (Ritter) and Alan (Sandvig) living lives of irresponsibility and scams until they befriend neglected 12-year-old Kelsey (Canterbury), who's unstable single mom Lynette (Preston) abandons him to the guys' unlikely care. Can they actually assume adult responsibilities? 85m; DVD, Blu-Ray, Wide. **C:** Jason Ritter; Jake Sandvig; Chandler Canterbury; Rebecca Hall; Carrie Preston; Todd Louiso; Gabriel Macht; Amanda Seyfried; Directed by Brian Crano; Written by Jake Sandvig; Brian Crano; Cinematography by Byron Shah; Quyen Tran; Music by Johnny Flynn. **A:** Sr. High-Adult. **P:** Entertainment. **U:** Home. **L:** English. **Mov-Ent**: Parenting, Children. **Acq:** Purchase. **Dist:** MPI Media Group.

Bagdad 1949 (Unrated) — ★★
Arabian nights story with the lovely O'Hara starring as Princess Marjan, the daughter of a sheik. She returns from England to find her father murdered and Hassan (Christian), the leader of a suspicious group known as The Black Riders, the main suspect. But then there's Turkish Pasha Al Nadim (Price) lurking sinisterly, as well. 83m; VHS. **C:** Maureen O'Hara; Paul (Christian) Hubschmid; Vincent Price; John Sutton; Jeff Corey; Frank Puglia; David Wolfe; Fritz Leiber; Directed by Charles Lamont; Cinematography by Russell Metty. **Pr:** Robert Arthur; Universal Studios. **A:** Jr. High-Adult. **P:** Entertainment. **U:** Home. **Mov-Ent**: Middle East. **Acq:** Purchase. **Dist:** Universal Music and Video Distribution.

Bagdad Cafe 1988 (PG) — ★★★
A large German woman, played by Sagebrecht, finds herself stranded in the Mojave desert after her husband dumps her on the side of the highway. She encounters a rundown cafe where she becomes involved with the off-beat residents. A hilarious story in which the strange people and the absurdity of their situations are treated kindly and not made to seem ridiculous. Spawned a short-lived TV series with Whoopi Goldberg. 91m; VHS, DVD, Wide, CC. **C:** Marianne Saegebrecht; CCH Pounder; Jack Palance; Christine Kaufmann; Monica Calhoun; Darron Flagg; Directed by Percy Adlon; Written by Percy Adlon; Eleonore Adlon; Cinematography by Bernd Heinl; Music by Bob Telson. **Pr:** Barry Shils; Percy Adlon; Percy Adlon; Eleonore Adlon; Pelemele Film GmbH; Island Pictures. **A:** Jr. High-Adult. **P:** Entertainment. **U:** Home. **Mov-Ent**: Action-Adventure. **Awds:** Cesar '89: Foreign Film. **Acq:** Purchase. **Dist:** Facets Multimedia Inc. $14.98.

Baggage Claim 2013 (PG-13) — ★
Another offensive romantic comedy that posits that all women over 30 are desperate enough to get married that they'll act stupidly in their pursuit to do so. The ridiculously named Montana Moore (Patton) is a flight attendant who decides that her biological clock is ticking to the point that she goes back through her ex-boyfriends to find the one that got away. Montana goes on a 30-day, 30,000-mile expedition to find the right beau before her younger sister's wedding. It's one of those comedies that's not just unfunny but deeply misogynistic when it's not just deadly dull. 96m; DVD, Blu-Ray. **C:** Paula Patton; Derek Luke; Taye Diggs; Boris Kodjoe; Jill Scott; Directed by David E. Talbert; Written by David E. Talbert; Cinematography by Anastas Michos; Music by Aaron Zigman. **Pr:** David E. Talbert; Steven J. Wolfe; Sneak Preview Entertainment; Fox Searchlight. **A:** Jr. High-Adult. **P:** Entertainment. **U:** Home. **L:** English. **Mov-Ent**: Comedy--Romantic, Black Culture. **Acq:** Purchase. **Dist:** Fox Home Entertainment.

Baghdad Shorts Collection Volume 1 2007 (Unrated)
A collection of 5 short films made by the students of the Independent Film and Television College of Baghdad between the end of 2004 and May of 2007. In Arabic with English subtitles. 87m; DVD. **A:** Sr. High-Adult. **P:** Education. **U:** BCTV, Institution. **L:** English, Arabic. **Gen-Edu**: Documentary Films, Middle East. **Acq:** Purchase, Rent/Lease. **Dist:** Arab Film Distribution. $300.

Baghdad Shorts Collection Volume 2 2007 (Unrated)
Follow up to the first collection of short films and documentaries by Iraqi film students. In Arabic with English subtitles. 106m; DVD. **A:** Adult. **P:** Entertainment. **U:** BCTV, Institution. **L:** English, Arabic. **Gen-Edu**: Documentary Films, Middle East. **Acq:** Purchase, Rent/Lease. **Dist:** Arab Film Distribution. $300.

Baghead 2008 (R) — ★
Four wannabe actor/writers take a weekend retreat to a woodsy cabin so they can come up with a screenplay they can star in. The two sorta couples are having relationship issues and then some peeper, wearing a bag on his head, starts peering in the windows. But no one's sure if it's just a prank or something more sinister. A mumblecore indie mash-up of genres best appreciated by those who enjoy watching the self-absorbed yammer. 84m; DVD. **C:** Ross Partridge; Greta Gerwig; Elise Muller; Steve Zissis; Directed by Mark Duplass; Jay Duplass; Written by Mark Duplass; Jay Duplass; Cinematography by Jay Duplass; Music by J. Scott Howard. **A:** Sr. High-Adult. **P:** Entertainment. **U:** Home. **Mov-Ent**: Horror. **Acq:** Purchase. **Dist:** Sony Pictures Home Entertainment Inc.

The Bagman 2002 (Unrated) — ★
A disfigured young man is murdered 'accidentally' while being hazed by his peers, and years later they start dying. The survivors begin to wonder if he's really dead in this hilariously awful re-imagining of every bad remake of "I Know What You Did Last Summer." 88m; DVD. **C:** Mikul Robins; Ron Ford; Stephanie Beaton; Directed by Beverly Beaton; Written by Beverly Beaton; Cinematography by Eric Lasher; Music by Jay Woelfel. **A:** Sr. High-Adult. **P:** Entertainment. **U:** Home. **L:** English. **Mov-Ent**. **Acq:** Purchase. **Dist:** Razor Digital. $5.99.

Bags of Life 1981
Our body cells are bounded by tough, invisible membranes which react to water by turning into the double-layered bags upon which all life depends. This program highlights recent scientific discoveries about these simple bags. 50m; VHS, 3/4 U. **Pr:** BBC Horizon. **A:** Primary-Sr. High. **P:** Education. **U:** Institution, SURA. **Hea-Sci**: Biology. **Acq:** Purchase, Rent/Lease. **Dist:** Home Vision Cinema.

Baguettes and Pain de Campagne 199?
Professor Raymond Calvel of the Ecole Francaise de Meunerie instructs viewers on the techniques of baking classic French breads in this three volume series. In this volume, he reviews two classic French breads: the baguette and Pain de Compagne. 27m; VHS. **A:** Sr. High-Adult. **P:** Instruction. **U:** Home. **How-Ins**: Cooking, Food Industry, How-To. **Acq:** Purchase. **Dist:** Culinary Institute of America. $75.00.

Bahama Passage 1942 (Unrated) — ★★½
Trite story of one lady's efforts to win the affection of a macho Bahamas stud. 83m; VHS. **C:** Madeleine Carroll; Sterling Hayden; Flora Robson; Leo G. Carroll; Dorothy Dandridge; Mary Anderson; Cecil Kellaway; Fred Kohler, Jr.; Directed by Edward H. Griffith; Written by Virginia Van Upp; Cinematography by Leo Tover. **Pr:** Paramount Pictures. **A:** Sr. High-Adult. **P:** Entertainment. **U:** Home. **Mov-Ent**: Romance, Comedy--Romantic, Classic Films. **Acq:** Purchase. **Dist:** Paramount Pictures Corp.

Bahamas: Club Med Style Diving 198?
Live the life of French luxury at the Eleuthera Club Med and explore blue holes and reefs on a diving expedition. 30m; VHS. **Pr:** Bennett Marine Video. **A:** Family. **P:** Entertainment. **U:** Home. **Spo-Rec**: Travel, Oceanography, Scuba. **Acq:** Purchase. **Dist:** Bennett Marine Video. $19.95.

The Bahamas: The Available Paradise 19??
These islands are particularly close to the U.S. An ideal destination for adventuresome boaters. This program is geared toward those who love sailing. A helpful guide for traveling procedures, both nautical and administrative. 60m; VHS. **A:** College-Adult. **P:** Entertainment. **U:** Home. **Spo-Rec**: Boating, Travel, Caribbean. **Acq:** Purchase. **Dist:** Bennett Marine Video. $39.95.

Bahamas: Treasure Cay 198?
Treasure Cay is brimming with wrecks and reefs. Explore them and the tourist facilities at Grand Abaco Island. 30m; VHS. **Pr:** Bennett Marine Video. **A:** Family. **P:** Entertainment. **U:** Home. **Spo-Rec**: Travel, Oceanography, Scuba. **Acq:** Purchase. **Dist:** Bennett Marine Video. $19.95.

The Bahamas—Abacos 19??
Cruising guide to the Abacos region of the Bahama Islands. 45m; VHS. **Pr:** Bennett Marine Video. **A:** Adult. **P:** Entertainment. **U:** Home. **Spo-Rec**: Boating, Travel, Caribbean. **Acq:** Purchase. **Dist:** Bennett Marine Video. $19.95.

The Bahamas—An Overview 19??
Provides a complete cruising guide to the Bahama Island region. 45m; VHS. **Pr:** Bennett Marine Video. **A:** Adult. **P:** Entertainment. **U:** Home. **Spo-Rec**: Boating, Travel, Caribbean. **Acq:** Purchase. **Dist:** Bennett Marine Video. $19.95.

The Bahamas—Berry Islands 19??
Provides a detailed look at the cruising opportunities found in the Berry Island region of the Bahamas. 45m; VHS. **Pr:** Bennett Marine Video. **A:** Adult. **P:** Entertainment. **U:** Home. **Spo-Rec**: Boating, Travel, Caribbean. **Acq:** Purchase. **Dist:** Bennett Marine Video. $19.95.

Bail Jumper 1989 (Unrated) — ★★
A story of love and commitment against incredible odds; some of which happen to be a swarm of locusts, a tornado, and falling meteorites. Joe and Elaine are small-time hoods escaping their dreary lives in Murky Springs Missouri by heading for that great bastion of idyllism and idealism—New York City. But even as the world starts to crumble around them, get the message that love prevails. 96m; VHS. **C:** Eszter Balint; B.J. Spalding; Tony Askin; Joie Lee; Directed by Christian Faber. **Pr:** Angelika Films. **A:** Jr. High-Adult. **P:** Entertainment. **U:** Home. **Mov-Ent**: Comedy-Drama, Romance. **Acq:** Purchase. **Dist:** Wellspring Media. $79.95.

Bail Out 1990 (R) — ★
Three bounty hunters, armed to the teeth, run a car-trashing police gauntlet so they may capture a valuable crook. 88m; VHS, DVD. **C:** David Hasselhoff; Linda Blair; John Vernon; Tom Rosales; Charlie Brill; Directed by Max Kleven. **Pr:** Vestron Pictures. **A:** Sr. High-Adult. **P:** Entertainment. **U:** Home. **Mov-Ent**: Automobiles. **Acq:** Purchase. **Dist:** Lions Gate Television Corp. $89.98.

Bail Out at 43,000 1957 (Unrated) — ★★
Movie about the lifestyles and love affairs of your average, everyday parachutist. 80m/B/W; VHS. **C:** John Payne; Karen Steele; Paul Kelly; Directed by Francis D. Lyon; Written by Paul Monash. **Pr:** United Artists Pictures. **A:** Jr. High-Adult. **P:** Entertainment. **U:** Home. **Mov-Ent**: Aeronautics. **Acq:** Purchase. **Dist:** MGM Home Entertainment.

Bailar Lambada 19??
Learn how to dance the lambada. ?m; VHS. **A:** Sr. High-Adult. **P:** Instruction. **U:** Home. **How-Ins**: Dance--Instruction. **Acq:** Purchase. **Dist:** Inspired Corp. $14.98.

A Bailar!: The Journey of a Latin Dance Company 1988
The journey of a group of Spanish club and street dancers, led by company leader Eddie Torres, is documented in this film. 30m; VHS, 3/4 U. **Pr:** Independent. **A:** Jr. High-Adult. **P:** Education. **U:** Institution. **Gen-Edu**: Dance, Hispanic Culture. **Acq:** Purchase. **Dist:** The Cinema Guild. $250.00.

Bailey House: To Live As Long As You Can 19??
Paints a portrait of the people who live at Bailey House, a 44-room residence for homeless people with AIDS, and captures the fabric of daily life, the courage, and the fears of these residents. 55m; VHS. **A:** Sr. High. **P:** Education. **U:** Institution. **Gen-Edu**: AIDS, Homeless, Medical Care. **Acq:** Purchase. **Dist:** Filmakers Library Inc. $99.

Bailey's Billion$ 2005 (G) — ★★½
Bailey (voiced by Lovitz) is a golden retriever who has been left a fortune by his late owner. Naturally, the woman's greedy nephew Caspar (Curry) and his scheming wife Dolores (Tilly) plot to get the money by kidnapping the dog. However, Bailey's guardian Theodore (Cain), a geeky animal behaviorist who can speak dog, and animal-rights activist Marge (Holden) team up to do right by him. 93m; DVD. **C:** Dean Cain; Laurie Holden; Tim Curry; Jennifer Tilly; Angela Vallee; Max Baker; Sheila McCarthy; Kenneth Welsh; Voice(s) by Jon Lovitz; Directed by David Devine; Written by Heather Conkie; Mary Walsh; Cinematography by Gavin Finney; Music by Lou Pomanti. **A:** Family. **P:** Entertainment. **U:** Home. **Mov-Ent. Acq:** Purchase. **Dist:** Echo Bridge Home Entertainment.

Bailey's Birthday 199?
Bailey, a dalmation pup, thinks that if he very good he will receive many presents on his birthday. He finds out that love if the most important gift of all. Includes storybook and teaching guide which contains information on the history and sights of New York as well. 18m; VHS. **A:** Preschool-Primary. **P:** Education. **U:** Institution, Home. **Chl-Juv**: Education, Children. **Acq:** Purchase. **Dist:** Marshmedia. $79.95.

Baise Moi 2000 (Unrated) — **Bomb!**
French porn dressed up for the arthouse crowd had critics spinning like tops to justify not calling the film what it is—exploitative trash, even if it is done by women. After Manu (Anderson) gets gang raped, she kills her boyfriend, steals his money, and hooks up with prostitute Nadine (Bach) to go on a sex and murder spree. Very, very graphic sex and violence and the literal translation of the French title is not "rape" but another four-letter word beginning with "f." Based on the novel by co-writer/director Despentes; French with subtitles. 77m; VHS, DVD. **C:** Raffaela Anderson; Karen Bach; Directed by Virginie Despentes; Coralie Trinh Thi; Written by Virginie Despentes; Coralie Trinh Thi; Cinematography by Benoit Chamaillard; Music by Varou Jan. **A:** Adult. **P:** Entertainment. **U:** Home. **L:** French. **Mov-Ent**: Rape. **Acq:** Purchase. **Dist:** Remstar Corp.

Bait 1954 — ★½
Low-budget melodrama has longtime prospector Marko (Haas) finally striking it rich. Only he doesn't want to share the wealth with young partner, Ray (Agar). Marko decides to use his comely young wife Peggy (Moore) to lure Ray into an affair so he has an excuse to kill him, but neither Peggy nor Ray cooperate as expected. 79m/B/W; DVD. **C:** Cleo Moore; John Agar; Hugo Haas; Directed by Hugo Haas; Written by Samuel W. Taylor; Cinematography by Eddie (Edward) Fitzgerald; Music by Vaclav Divina. **A:** Adult. **P:** Entertainment. **U:** Home. **L:** English. **Mov-Ent**: Miners & Mining. **Acq:** Purchase. **Dist:** Sony Pictures Home Entertainment Inc.

Bait 2000 (R) — ★★
Bait is what you use to catch bigger fish, and hopefully star Foxx can use his performance in this otherwise by-the-book action-comedy to snag bigger and better roles. Petty thief Alvin (Foxx) winds up in the clink after a botched seafood robbery. His cellmate Jaster (Pastorelli) is the double-crossing partner of prancing archvillain Bristol (Hutchinson), who has stolen $40 million in gold. Unfortunately for Alvin, Jaster winds up in the Big House in the sky before he can tell anyone where the hidden loot is stashed. Head Fed Clenteen (Morse), thinking that Alvin knows where the gold is hidden, has him unwittingly equipped with surveillance devices and springs him from the pokey. Alvin, now followed by Bristol and the feds, tries to find the stashed loot by piecing together the cryptic clues that Jaster has left him. Lots of action on a minimal (for these types of movies) budget. 119m; VHS, DVD, Wide. **C:** Jamie Foxx; Doug Hutchison; David Morse; Jamie Kennedy; Robert Pastorelli; Kimberly Elise; David Paymer; Tia Texada; Mike Epps; Nestor Serrano; Megan Dodds; Jeffrey Donovan; Kirk Acevedo; Directed by Antoine Fuqua; Written by Tom Gilroy; Jeff Nathanson; Adam Scheinman; Andrew Scheinman; Cinematography by Tobias Schliessler; Music by Mark Mancina. **A:** Sr. High-Adult. **P:** Entertainment. **U:** Home. **Mov-Ent**: Action-Comedy, Federal Bureau of Investigation (FBI). **Acq:** Purchase. **Dist:** Warner Home Video, Inc.

Bait 2002 (Unrated) — ★★½
Jack Blake does a good deed on a cold, rainy night, taking in Pam and her daughter Stephanie when their car breaks down. Their gratitude is short-lived as Jack, still anguished over his daughter's unsolved murder years before, realizes that Stephanie looks like her and holds them captive so he can use her to catch the killer. 98m; VHS, DVD. **C:** John Hurt; Sheila Hancock; Rachael Stirling; Angeline Ball; Jonathan Firth; Nicholas Farrell; Matthew Scurfield; Directed by Nicholas Renton; Written by Daniel Boyle; Cinematography by Oliver Curtis; Music by John Keane. **A:** Sr. High-Adult. **P:** Entertainment. **U:** Home. **Mov-Ent**: Crime Drama. **Acq:** Purchase. **Dist:** BFS Video. $19.98.

Bait, Bite, and Switch 1976
A young man goes to a stereo store to buy a sale tape deck, but gets talked into buying one much more expensive. With the aid of a consumer agency, the boy is able to return the expensive one for a less-expensive model. 10m; VHS, 3/4 U. **Pr:** Parthenon Pictures. **A:** College-Adult. **P:** Education. **U:** Institution, Home, SURA. **Gen-Edu**: Consumer Education. **Acq:** Purchase, Rent/Lease, Duplication License. **Dist:** Pyramid Media.

Bait Shop 2008 (PG) — ★½
Good ole boy bait shop owner Bill (Engvall) is going to lose his business to the bank unless he can come up 15,000 smackers. His one chance is to win the annual Bass Tournament, which he's lost every previous year to smug rival Hot Rod Johnson (Cyrus). 85m; DVD. **C:** Bill Engvall; Billy Ray Cyrus; Vincent Martella; Harve Presnell; Billy Joe Shaver; Directed by C.B. Harding; Written by Bear Aderhold; Tom Sullivan; Cinematography by Jamie Barber; Music by Steven R. Phillips. **A:** Family. **P:** Entertainment. **U:** Home. **Mov-Ent**: Fishing. **Acq:** Purchase. **Dist:** Lions Gate Entertainment Inc.

Baited Trap: A Tale of Meat, Torment and Murder 1986
Zany romp through the brutality of a meat-packing family. 12m; VHS. **C:** Directed by Jonathan Reiss. **A:** Adult. **P:** Entertainment. **U:** Home. **Mov-Ent. Acq:** Purchase. **Dist:** Survival Research Laboratories. $12.00.

Baja 1995 (R) — ★★
Bebe (Ringwald) hides out in Baja with her beau Alex (Logue) after a drug deal goes bad. They hold up in a sleazy motel while Bebe waits for dad, John (Bernsen), to bail her out. But instead, John persuades estranged hubby Michael (Nickles) to track down the runaways and Michael finds out that hitman Tom (Henriksen) is hunting for Alex. Must be the desert heat causing all the ensuing commotion. 92m; VHS, DVD, CC. **C:** Molly Ringwald; Lance Henriksen; Michael A. (M.A.) Nickles; Donal Logue; Corbin Bernsen; Directed by Kurt Voss; Written by Kurt Voss; Cinematography by Denis Maloney; Music by Reg Powell. **Pr:** Larry Rattner; Ehud Bleiberg; Yitzhak Ginsburg; Republic Entertainment Inc; Dream Entertainment Inc. **A:** Sr. High-Adult. **P:** Entertainment. **U:** Home. **Mov-Ent**: Drugs. **Acq:** Purchase. **Dist:** Lions Gate Entertainment Inc.

Baja Oklahoma 1987 — ★
A country barmaid has dreams of being a country singer. Songs by Willie Nelson, Emmylou Harris, and Billy Vera. 97m; VHS. **C:** Lesley Ann Warren; Peter Coyote; Swoosie Kurtz; Willie Nelson; Julia Roberts; Directed by Bobby Roth; Written by Bobby Roth; Cinematography by Michael Ballhaus. **Pr:** HBO. **A:** Jr. High-Adult. **P:** Entertainment. **U:** Home. **Mov-Ent**: Comedy--Romantic, Romance, Music--Country/Western. **Acq:** Purchase. **Dist:** Warner Home Video, Inc.; MGM Studios Inc. $19.98.

Baja Passage 19??
Presentation of 1000-mile Mexican cruise aboard the Hubba Hubba. Includes equipment tips and route planning. Featuring aerial photography. 60m; VHS. **A:** College-Adult. **P:** Entertainment. **U:** Home. **Spo-Rec**: Boating, Travel. **Acq:** Purchase. **Dist:** Bennett Marine Video. $29.95.

Baja Sportfishing 199?
Provides information on setting up a fishing trip to remote Baja, California, such as permits, border crossing, and local highways in a two-tape series. Includes live action fishing. ?m; VHS. **A:** Sr. High. **P:** Education. **U:** Home. **Gen-Edu**: Fishing, Travel. **Acq:** Purchase. **Dist:** John Sabella & Associate. $19.95.

Baja's Giants of the Deep 19??
These real life sea monsters can terrify or intrigue. The devil fish, the moray eel, the hammerhead, the whale shark are just some of the examples you will find that make the deep Sea of Cortez their home. 30m; VHS. **A:** Sr. High-Adult. **P:** Entertainment. **U:** Home. **Spo-Rec**: Scuba, Fish. **Acq:** Purchase. **Dist:** Bennett Marine Video. $24.95.

Baja's Midriff 19??
The bleak Midriff islands are the backdrop for some of the world's most exciting skiff fishing. Features both surface and bottom fishing and everywhere else squid, grouper, whales, and yellowtail might be hiding. 44m; VHS. **A:** Adult. **P:** Instruction. **U:** Home. **Spo-Rec**: Fishing. **Acq:** Purchase. **Dist:** Bennett Marine Video. $29.95.

Baka and Test: Summon the Beasts OVA 2013 (Unrated)
Two part OVA of the popular anime series about a competitive school wherein the students summon spirits to fight one another for classroom supplies. 92m; DVD, Blu-Ray. **A:** Jr. High-Adult. **P:** Entertainment. **U:** Home. **L:** English, Japanese. **Mov-Ent**: Anime, Romance. **Acq:** Purchase. **Dist:** FUNimation Entertainment. $34.98 34.98.

Baka: People of the Forest 19??
Provides an insightful look into the world of the Baka. 59m; VHS, 3/4 U; Closed Captioned. **A:** Primary-Adult. **P:** Education. **U:** Institution. **Gen-Edu**: Forests & Trees, Women, Children. **Acq:** Purchase. **Dist:** National Geographic Society. $24.20.

Bakemonogatari: Complete Set 2008 (Unrated)
Anime about a young man who used to be a vampire helping girls afflicted with various supernatural problems. 350m; Blu-Ray. **A:** Jr. High-Adult. **P:** Entertainment. **U:** Home. **L:** English, Japanese. **Mov-Ent**: Anime, Fantasy. **Acq:** Purchase. **Dist:** Aniplex. $189.98.

A Baker's Dozen: 13 European Concepts, 144 Great Ideas! 19??
Merchandising and training video. 20m; VHS. **A:** Adult. **P:** Vocational. **U:** Institution. **Bus-Ind**: Food Industry, Occupational Training. **Acq:** Purchase. **Dist:** International Dairy-Deli-Bakery Association. $100.00.

Baker's Hawk 1976 (Unrated) — ★★
A young boy befriends a red-tailed hawk and learns the meaning of family and caring. 98m; VHS, DVD. **C:** Clint Walker; Diane Baker; Burl Ives; Lee Montgomery; Alan Young; Danny Bonaduce; Directed by Lyman Dayton; Written by Dan Greer; Hal Harrison, Jr.; Cinematography by Bernie Abramson; Music by Lex de Azevedo. **Pr:** Bridgestone Production Group. **A:** Family. **P:** Entertainment. **U:** Home. **Mov-Ent. Acq:** Purchase. **Dist:** Alpha Video; Movies Unlimited; Echo Bridge Home Entertainment.

The Baker's Wife 1933 — ★★★½
There's a new baker in town, and he brings with him to the small French village an array of tantalizing breads, as well as a discontented wife. When she runs off with a shepherd, her loyal and naive husband refuses to acknowledge her infidelity; however, in his loneliness, the baker can't bake, so the townspeople scheme to bring his wife back. Panned as overly cute Marcel Pagnol peasant glorification, and hailed as a visual poem full of wit; you decide. In French with subtitles. Also available for French students without subtitles; a French script booklet is also available. 101m/B/W; VHS. **C:** Raimu; Ginette LeClerc; Charles Moulton; Charpin; Robert Vattier; Directed by Marcel Pagnol; Written by Marcel Pagnol; Cinematography by Georges Benoit; Music by Vincent Scotto. **Pr:** Hakim Brothers. **A:** Family. **P:** Entertainment. **U:** Home. **L:** English, French. **Mov-Ent**: Comedy-Drama. **Awds:** N.Y. Film Critics '40: Foreign Film. **Acq:** Purchase. **Dist:** Facets Multimedia Inc.; Tapeworm Video Distributors Inc.; Interama, Inc. $39.95.

Bakery/Grocery Clerk 1921 — ★★
A package of shorts featuring crazy comedian Larry Semon, getting tangled up in mayhem and molasses. Silent with piano score. 55m/B/W; Silent; VHS. **C:** Larry Semon; Oliver Hardy; Lucille Carlisle; Directed by Larry Semon. **Pr:** Vitagraph. **A:** Family. **P:** Entertainment. **U:** Home. **Mov-Ent**: Comedy--Slapstick, Silent Films. **Acq:** Purchase. **Dist:** $19.98.

Bakery High Notes from Europe 19??
Merchandising and training video. 25m; VHS. **A:** Adult. **P:** Vocational. **U:** Institution. **Bus-Ind**: Food Industry, Occupational Training. **Acq:** Purchase. **Dist:** International Dairy-Deli-Bakery Association. $100.00.

Bakery Merchandising 101 19??
Discusses ways for successful promotion and product appeal to help increase bakery sales. 12m; VHS. **A:** Adult. **P:** Vocational. **U:** Institution. **Bus-Ind**: Food Industry, Occupational Training. **Acq:** Purchase. **Dist:** International Dairy-Deli-Bakery Association. $50.00.

Bakery Merchandising Certificate Program 19??
Examines the benefits of suggestive selling, sampling, displays, and event merchandising. ?m; VHS. **A:** Adult. **P:** Vocational. **U:** Institution. **Bus-Ind**: Food Industry, Occupational Training. **Acq:** Purchase. **Dist:** International Dairy-Deli-Bakery Association. $160.00.

Bakhtiari Migration 1974
The fascinating anthropological study of a biennial Iranian trek between summer and winter pastures, in which half a million people and millions of sheep and goats cross the massive Zagros range. Also available in 27-minute edited version. 52m; VHS, 3/4 U. **Pr:** Anthony David Productions. **A:** Jr. High-Sr. High. **P:** Education. **U:** Institution, SURA. **Gen-Edu**: Anthropology. **Acq:** Purchase. **Dist:** Home Vision Cinema.

The Baking Deserts 1984
How desert plants and animals have adapted to extreme conditions of heat and drought. 55m; VHS, 3/4 U, Special order formats. **Pr:** British Broadcasting Corporation; Time-Life Films. **A:** Sr. High-Adult. **P:** Education. **U:** Institution, SURA. **Hea-Sci**: Geology, Natural Resources. **Acq:** Purchase, Rent/Lease. **Dist:** Time-Life Video and Television.

The Bakwet: Refugees in Their Own Land 1989
An account of the displacement of Philippine farmers which has resulted from Corazon Aquino's military offensive against the New People's Army. 33m; VHS. **Pr:** The Cinema Guild. **A:** Sr. High-Adult. **P:** Entertainment. **U:** Home. **Gen-Edu**: Documentary Films, Asia, Pacific Islands. **Acq:** Purchase, Rent/Lease. **Dist:** The Cinema Guild. $250.00.

Balablok 198?
Conflict develops between animated blocks and balls because of their physical differences. An allegory which reduces human conflict to simple forms. 8m; VHS, 3/4 U. **Pr:** National Film Board of Canada. **A:** Jr. High. **P:** Education. **U:** Institution, SURA. **Gen-Edu**: Psychology. **Acq:** Purchase, Rent/Lease, Trade-in. **Dist:** Encyclopedia Britannica.

Balalaika 1939 — ★★
Rather dull operetta about the Russian revolution with Eddy playing a Russian prince. Eddy masquerades as a member of the proletariat in order to romance Massey, who was expected to become the next Garbo. Didn't happen, though. Eddy's rendition of "Stille Nacht" ("Silent Night") is highlight of film. Based on the operetta by Eric Maschwitz, George Ponford, and Bernard Gruen. 102m/B/W; VHS, Streaming. **C:** Nelson Eddy; Ilona Massey; Charlie Ruggles; Frank Morgan; Lionel Atwill; Sir C. Aubrey Smith; Joyce Compton; Directed by Reinhold Schunzel; Written by Leon Gordon; Charles Bennett; Jacques Deval; Cinematography by Karl Freund. **Pr:** Lawrence

Weingarten; MGM; MGM/UA Entertainment Company. **A:** Jr. High-Adult. **P:** Entertainment. **U:** Home. **Mov-Ent:** Musical, USSR, Romance. **Acq:** Purchase. **Dist:** Amazon.com Inc.; MGM Home Entertainment. $19.98.

Balance in Lifting 198?
A training film that teaches health care professionals how to move or carry a patient. 18m; VHS, 3/4 U. **Pr:** National Safety Council. **A:** College-Adult. **P:** Education. **U:** Institution. **Hea-Sci:** Patient Care. **Acq:** Rent/Lease. **Dist:** National Safety Council, California Chapter, Film Library.

Balance in Nature: A First Film 1975
See how populations of mice, plant life, and foxes respond to the availability of water in the balance in nature. 9m; VHS, 3/4 U. **Pr:** Arthur D. Nelles. **A:** Primary-Jr. High. **P:** Education. **U:** Institution, SURA. **Hea-Sci:** Ecology & Environment. **Acq:** Purchase. **Dist:** Phoenix Learning Group.

Balance, Line, Strength with Clare Dunphy: Power, Grace, Strength ????
An intermediate to advanced workout using yoga, dance and Pilates inspired movements. 60m; VHS. **A:** Adult. **P:** Instruction. **U:** Home. **Hea-Sci:** Fitness/Exercise, How-To. **Acq:** Purchase. **Dist:** Body Bar Systems. $19.95.

Balance of Life and the Space Age 1963
This show considers the earth's living things in terms of their basic needs. Just as the fish needs food and oxygen to stay alive, so do astronauts in today's space explorations. 14m; VHS, 3/4 U. **Pr:** BFA Educational Media. **A:** Jr. High. **P:** Education. **U:** Institution, SURA. **Hea-Sci:** Space Exploration. **Acq:** Purchase. **Dist:** Phoenix Learning Group.

Balance of Power 1996 (R) — ★½
Martial arts master Matsumoto (Mako) prepares fighter Niko (Blanks) for a death match against a former student who's gone bad. 92m; VHS, CC. **C:** Billy Blanks; Mako; James Lew; Directed by Rick Bennet; Written by Phil Good; Rick Bennet; Cinematography by Gilles Corbeil. **A:** Sr. High-Adult. **P:** Entertainment. **U:** Home. **Mov-Ent:** Martial Arts. **Acq:** Purchase. **Dist:** Lions Gate Television Corp.

The Balance Sheet Barrier 1977
The purpose of this program is to take line managers through the balance sheet barrier. By visually linking every line of the balance sheet with an object or an event in the factory or office, the program exposes the simplicity of business finance. 30m; VHS, 8 mm, 3/4 U, Special order formats. **C:** John Cleese; Ron Scroggs. **Pr:** Video Arts Limited. **A:** College-Adult. **P:** Education. **U:** Institution, SURA. **Bus-Ind:** Business, Management, Finance. **Acq:** Purchase, Rent/Lease. **Dist:** Video Arts, Inc. $790.00.

Balanced Body Mat Exercise Program ????
Presents 20 exercises done seated or lying on your back that focus on controlled, smooth flowing movements performed in precise alignment with deep breathing. Based on Pilates techniques. 87m; VHS. **A:** Adult. **P:** Instruction. **U:** Home. **Hea-Sci:** Fitness/Exercise, Dance--Instruction. **Acq:** Purchase. **Dist:** Stagestep. $29.95.

Balanced Conditioning for Basketball 2008 (Unrated)
Coach Robert Taylor presents drills to improve basketball players' abilities as well as exercises designed to help better condition players and thusly lower injuries. 46m; DVD. **A:** Family. **P:** Education. **U:** Home, Institution. **Spo-Rec:** Basketball, Athletic Instruction/Coaching. **Acq:** Purchase. **Dist:** Championship Productions. $39.99.

Balanced-Draft Fired Heaters 1991
A two-part look at the design evolution and the components and operating procedures of balanced-draft fired heaters. A leader's guide and workbook are included. 40m; VHS, 3/4 U. **TV Std:** NTSC, PAL, SECAM. **Pr:** Gulf Publishing Co. **A:** Adult. **P:** Vocational. **U:** Institution, SURA. **Bus-Ind:** Industrial Arts, Engineering. **Acq:** Purchase. **Dist:** Gulf Publishing Co. $395.00.

Balanced Training for Soccer 2008 (Unrated)
Coach Robert Taylor presents strength and conditioning workout program designed for soccer players. 75m; DVD. **A:** Family. **P:** Education. **U:** Home, Institution. **Spo-Rec:** Soccer, Athletic Instruction/Coaching, Fitness/Exercise. **Acq:** Purchase. **Dist:** Championship Productions. $29.99.

Balanchine: Ballo Della Regina, Steadfast Tin Soldier, Elegie, Tschaikovsky Pas de Deux ????
Classic choreography by George Balanchine performed by the New York City Ballet featuring Mikhail Baryshnikov, Patricia McBride, Karin Von Aroldingen and Merrill Ashley. 51m; VHS. **A:** Adult. **P:** Entertainment. **U:** Home. **Fin-Art:** Dance--Ballet, Dance--Performance. **Acq:** Purchase. **Dist:** Stagestep. $29.95.

Balanchine Celebration—Part 1: New York City Ballet 19??
Contains select performances by the New York City Ballet of some of Balanchine's classics. Includes selections from "Apollo," "Square Dance," "Theme and Variations," "Union Jack," "Vienna Waltzes," "Walpurgisnacht Ballet," plus the complete "Scherzo a la Russe." Features guest artists from the Kirov Ballet, Pacific Northwest Ballet, and Paris Opera Ballet. 86m; VHS. **A:** Jr. High-Adult. **P:** Entertainment. **U:** Institution, Home. **Fin-Art:** Performing Arts, Dance--Ballet. **Acq:** Purchase. **Dist:** Stagestep. $29.95.

Balanchine Celebration—Part 2, New York City Ballet 19??
Includes performances of select Balanchine selections by the New York City Ballet with appearances by guest artists from the Royal Ballet, American Ballet Theatre, San Francisco Ballet, and the Dance Theatre of Harlem. 86m; VHS. **A:** Family. **P:** Entertainment. **U:** Institution, Home. **Fin-Art:** Performing Arts, Dance--Ballet. **Acq:** Purchase. **Dist:** Stagestep. $29.95.

Balanchine: Chaconne, Prodigal Son ????
Classic choreography by George Balanchine performed by the New York City Ballet featuring Mikhail Baryshnikov, Karin Von Aroldingen, Suzanne Farrell and Peter Martins. 51m; VHS. **A:** Adult. **P:** Entertainment. **U:** Home. **Fin-Art:** Dance--Ballet, Dance--Performance. **Acq:** Purchase. **Dist:** Stagestep. $29.95.

The Balanchine Essays: Arabesque ????
Principle dancer, Merrill Ashley and former dancer Suki Schorer of the New York City Ballet explain and demonstrate principles of Balanchine technique. Features excerpts from "The Nutcracker" and "Swan Lake." 45m; VHS. **A:** Adult. **P:** Instruction. **U:** Institution. **How-Ins:** Dance--Ballet, Dance--Instruction. **Acq:** Purchase. **Dist:** Stagestep. $29.95.

The Balanchine Essays: Passe and Attitude 19??
Merrill Ashley and Suki Schorer use excerpts from "Agon," "Diamonds," "Scotch Symphony," "The Nutcracker," and many more to help illustrate the passe and attitude choreographic preferences and aesthetics of the great Balanchine. 45m; VHS. **A:** Jr. High-Adult. **P:** Education. **U:** Institution, Home. **Gen-Edu:** Dance--Ballet. **Acq:** Purchase. **Dist:** Stagestep. $29.95.

The Balanchine Essays: Port de Bras and Epaulement 19??
Excerpts from "Divertimento No. 15" and "Symphony in C" help Merrill Ashley and Suki Schorer explore the aesthetic and choreographic preferences and styles of Balanchine. 43m; VHS. **A:** Jr. High-Adult. **P:** Education. **U:** Institution, Home. **Gen-Edu:** Dance--Ballet. **Acq:** Purchase. **Dist:** Stagestep. $29.95.

Balanchine: Robert Schumann's Davidsbundler-Tanze ????
The last major ballet choreographed by George Balanchine performed by the New York City Ballet featuring Suzanne Farrell, Jacques d'Ambiose, Karin von Aroldingen, Adam Luders, and Peter Martins. 51m; VHS. **A:** Adult. **P:** Entertainment. **U:** Home. **Fin-Art:** Dance--Ballet, Dance--Performance. **Acq:** Purchase. **Dist:** Stagestep. $29.95.

Balanchine: Selections from Jewels, Stravinsky Violin Concerto ????
Classic choreography by George Balanchine performed by the New York City Ballet featuring Karin Von Aroldingen, Merrill Ashley, Suzanne Farrell, Peter Martins and many others. 56m; VHS. **A:** Adult. **P:** Entertainment. **U:** Home. **Fin-Art:** Dance--Ballet, Dance--Performance. **Acq:** Purchase. **Dist:** Stagestep. $29.95.

Balanchine: The Four Temperaments, Andante from Divertimento No. 15, Tzigane ????
Classic choreography by George Balanchine performed by the New York City Ballet featuring Suzanne Farrell, Peter Martins, Merrill Ashley, and Robert Weiss. 54m; VHS. **A:** Adult. **P:** Entertainment. **U:** Home. **Fin-Art:** Dance--Ballet, Dance--Performance. **Acq:** Purchase. **Dist:** Stagestep. $29.95.

Balanchine's Chaconne and Prodigal Son 19??
Features Mikhail Baryshnikov and Karin von Aroldingen in the Balanchine/Prokofiev classic "Prodigal Son." Also Contains the Balanchine's masterpeice "Chaconne" with Suzanne Farrell and Peter Martins, two great stars of the New York City Ballet. 57m; VHS. **A:** Jr. High-Adult. **P:** Entertainment. **U:** Home. **Fin-Art:** Performing Arts, Dance--Ballet. **Acq:** Purchase. **Dist:** Stagestep. $29.95.

Balanchine's Stravinsky Violin Concerto & Jewels Selections—New York City Ballet 19??
Contains two selections from Jewels, "Emeralds" as performed with Merrill Ashley, and "Diamonds" as perfromed with Suzanne Farrell and Peter Martins. Also contains performance of "Stravinsky Violin Concerto," featuring Kay Mazzo and Peter Martins. 56m; VHS. **A:** Jr. High-Adult. **P:** Entertainment. **U:** Home. **Fin-Art:** Performing Arts, Music--Performance, Dance--Ballet. **Acq:** Purchase. **Dist:** Stagestep. $29.95.

Balanchine's Tzigane Divertimento No. 15, Four Temperaments 19??
Contains Balanchine's "Tzigane," which is considered to be one of his most enduring achievements which he made exclusively for the incomparable Suzanne Farrell. Also provides performance of Mozart's "Divertimento No. 15" by members of the New York City Ballet. 54m; VHS. **A:** Jr. High-Adult. **P:** Entertainment. **U:** Home. **Fin-Art:** Performing Arts, Dance--Ballet. **Acq:** Purchase. **Dist:** Stagestep. $29.95.

Balancing 19??
Fifth and sixth graders engage in activities such as making mobiles, making equalarm and pan balances and an array of other improvised equipment. In this silent program the children are absorbed and self-sufficient as they go about their work. 12m; 3/4 U, Special order formats. **Pr:** Dorothy Welch. **A:** College-Adult. **P:** Education. **U:** Institution, CCTV, CATV, BCTV. **Gen-Edu:** Children. **Acq:** Purchase, Rent/Lease. **Dist:** Education Development Center.

Balancing Act 1979
The human body is equipped with an elaborate set of preventive, reactive, and repair mechanisms to assist our chances of survival. 60m; VHS, 3/4 U. **A:** Sr. High-Adult. **P:** Education. **U:** Institution, SURA. **Hea-Sci:** Health Education, Anatomy & Physiology. **Acq:** Purchase. **Dist:** Home Vision Cinema.

A Balancing Act: Family and Work in the '90s 1993
Explores new workplace alternatives for people juggling career and family, such as flex-time, satellite offices, and job sharing. Also includes interviews with corporate managers who identify issues of concern to the corporation. 25m; VHS, SVS, CC, 3/4 U. **Pr:** National Film Board of Canada. **A:** Adult. **P:** Professional. **U:** Institution, CCTV. **Bus-Ind:** Business, Family, Personnel Management. **Acq:** Purchase, Rent/Lease. **Dist:** Lucerne Media. $225.00.

Balancing Act: Your Fall Prevention Program 2000
Overviews factors and conditions that increase risk of a resident fall and explains how to assess each resident for risk. 24m; VHS. **A:** Adult. **P:** Professional. **U:** Institution. **Hea-Sci:** Aging, Patient Care, Health Education. **Acq:** Purchase. **Dist:** Aquarius Health Care Media. $160.00.

Balancing Home & Career 1991
A training program showing how various people handle the issues of family and job. A leader's guide and workbook are included. 25m; VHS, 3/4 U, Special order formats. **Pr:** Crisp Publications. **A:** College-Adult. **P:** Education. **U:** Institution. **Bus-Ind:** How-To, Business, Family. **Acq:** Purchase, Rent/Lease. **Dist:** Excellence in Training Corp. $495.00.

Balancing Home and Career 1994
"Balancing Home and Career" touches upon what kind of load one might bear and teaches viewers what they can do to relieve stress in their lives and maintain balance by determining personal values and set goals and priorities. 20m; VHS. **A:** Adult. **P:** Education. **U:** Institution. **L:** English. **Gen-Edu:** Home Economics. **Acq:** Purchase. **Dist:** Meridian Education Corp. $99.

Balboa 1982 (Unrated) — **Bomb!**
Set on sun-baked Balboa Island, this is a melodramatic tale of high-class power, jealousy, and intrigue. Never-aired pilot for a TV miniseries, in the night-time soap tradition (even features Steve Kanaly from TV's "Dallas"). Special appearance by Cassandra Peterson, also known as horror hostess Elvira; and if that interests you, look for Sonny Bono, as well. 92m; VHS, DVD. **C:** Tony Curtis; Carol Lynley; Chuck Connors; Sonny Bono; Steve Kanaly; Jennifer Chase; Lupita Ferrer; Martine Beswick; Henry Jones; Cassandra Peterson; Directed by James Polakof. **Pr:** Simcom. **A:** Jr. High-Adult. **P:** Entertainment. **U:** Home. **Mov-Ent:** Melodrama, Pacific Islands. **Acq:** Purchase. **Dist:** Lions Gate Television Corp. $69.98.

The Balcony 1963 (Unrated) — ★★★
A film version of the great Jean Genet play about a surreal brothel, located in an unnamed, revolution-torn city, where its powerful patrons act out their fantasies. Scathing and rude. 87m/B/W; VHS, DVD. **C:** Peter Falk; Shelley Winters; Lee Grant; Kent Smith; Peter Brocco; Ruby Dee; Jeff Corey; Leonard Nimoy; Joyce Jameson; Directed by Joseph Strick; Written by Ben Maddow; Cinematography by George J. Folsey. **Pr:** City Films; Sterling. **A:** Sr. High-Adult. **P:** Entertainment. **U:** Home. **Mov-Ent:** Prostitution. **Acq:** Purchase. **Dist:** Mystic Fire Video. $29.95.

The Bald Eagle in New Jersey 1985
This film follows the efforts of conservationists to prevent the bald eagle's impending extinction. 30m; VHS, 3/4 U. **Pr:** New Jersey Network. **A:** Jr. High-Adult. **P:** Education. **U:** Institution. **Gen-Edu:** Birds, Ecology & Environment. **Acq:** Purchase. **Dist:** New Jersey Network.

The Bald Soprano 1999
Performance of the surreal opera by the Center for Contemporary Opera. 62m; VHS, DVD. **A:** Sr. High-Adult. **P:** Education. **U:** Institution. **Fin-Art:** Opera. **Acq:** Purchase. **Dist:** The Cinema Guild. $79.95.

Baler Safety 1995
Trains to ensure the safety of employees using this equipment. 8m; VHS. **A:** Adult. **P:** Professional. **U:** Institution. **Bus-Ind:** Safety Education, Management, Occupational Training. **Acq:** Purchase, Rent/Lease. **Dist:** National Safety Council, California Chapter, Film Library. $175.00.

Bali Beyond the Post Card 1993
Illustrates a family spanning four generations sharing an important event, the passing down of the Legong dance legacy to the youngest. Winner of the Gold Apple, National Educational Film & Video Festival, 1992; Honorable Mention, American Film & Video Festival, 1992; Athens International Film Festival, 1992; Margaret Mead Film Festival, 1991; Association for Asian Studies, 1992; Hawaii International Film Festival, 1991. 60m; VHS. **A:** Sr. High-Adult. **P:** Education. **U:** Institution. **Gen-Edu:** Documentary Films, Asia, Dance. **Acq:** Purchase, Rent/Lease. **Dist:** Filmakers Library Inc. $395.00.

Bali High 1984
Wild Indonesian and Hawaiian surf brought to you by Stephen Spaulding. Explore the waves of these secret waters and the legendary "Isle of Kong." 90m; VHS. **C:** Directed by Stephen Spaulding. **Pr:** NSI. **A:** Jr. High-Adult. **P:** Entertainment. **U:** Home. **Spo-Rec:** Sports--General. **Acq:** Purchase. **Dist:** NSI Sound & Video Inc. $59.95.

Bali, Masterpiece of the Gods 19??
Brings the splendor of Indonesia's most beautiful island into your classroom. 59m; VHS, 3/4 U; Closed Captioned. **A:** Primary-Adult. **P:** Education. **U:** Institution. **Gen-Edu.** **Acq:** Purchase. **Dist:** National Geographic Society. $24.20.

Bali: The Mask of Rangda 1974
Authentic picture of a culture as yet untouched by the West. 30m; VHS, 3/4 U, Special order formats. **Pr:** Hartley Productions. **A:** Sr. High-Adult. **P:** Education. **U:** Institution,

CCTV, Home. **Gen-Edu:** Anthropology. **Acq:** Purchase. **Dist:** Hartley Film Foundation. $39.95.

Bali: The Mystical Land ????
Overviews the life, religion, and rituals of the Balinese. 56m; VHS. **A:** Sr. High-Adult. **P:** Education. **U:** Institution. **Gen-Edu:** Geography. **Acq:** Purchase, Rent/Lease. **Dist:** Films for the Humanities & Sciences. $149.00.

A Balinese Trance Seance 1980
A seance is held to find out the cause of death of a young man. 30m; 3/4 U. **Pr:** Australian National University. **A:** Jr. High-Sr. High. **P:** Education. **U:** Institution, SURA. **Gen-Edu:** Asia, Anthropology. **Acq:** Purchase. **Dist:** Documentary Educational Resources.

Balkan Express 1983 — ★½
A crew of unlikely slobs become heroes in war-ravaged Europe. 102m; VHS. **A:** Jr. High-Adult. **P:** Entertainment. **U:** Home. **Mov-Ent:** World War Two. **Acq:** Purchase. **Dist:** Anchor Bay Entertainment. $19.95.

B.A.L.L. 19??
The band's most popular tracks from their first Shimmydisc album are performed. 60m; VHS. **A:** Jr. High-College. **P:** Entertainment. **U:** Home. **Mov-Ent:** Music Video. **Acq:** Purchase. **Dist:** Music Video Distributors. $29.95.

Ball Above All 2007
Street basketball as played on courts in Los Angeles, Chicago, Houston, Atlanta, Philadelphia, and other cities. 40m; DVD. **A:** Jr. High-Adult. **P:** Entertainment. **U:** Home. **Gen-Edu:** Documentary Films, Basketball. **Acq:** Purchase. **Dist:** Entertainment One US LP.

Ball & Chain 2004 (PG-13) — ★★½
Although raised in America, Ameet (Malhotra) and Saima (Ray) can't escape the customs of India when their respective parents arrange their marriage. They want to break their engagement, so Ameet decides that if he behaves outrageously enough, his prospective in-laws will be so dismayed that they will call things off. Only the more time Ameet and Saima spend together, the more they realize that the arrangement could actually work. 90m; DVD. **C:** Lisa Ray; Kal Penn; Purva Bedi; Suni Malhotra; Ismail Bashey; Directed by Shriaz Jafri; Written by Thomas Mortimer; Cinematography by Peter Simonite; Music by Deane Ogden. **A:** Jr. High-Adult. **P:** Entertainment. **U:** Home. **Mov-Ent:** Comedy--Romantic. **Acq:** Purchase. **Dist:** Lions Gate Entertainment Inc.

**Ball Bearing Maintenance and Failure
   Analysis** 1986
Part of a series offering instruction on installation and maintenance procedures for service life of common power transmission products. 18m; VHS. **A:** Adult. **P:** Vocational. **U:** Institution. **Gen-Edu:** Industrial Arts, Technology. **Acq:** Purchase. **Dist:** RMI Media. $132.50.

**Ball Bearing Maintenance and Failure
   Analysis** 1995
Covers what makes bearings run, and how to determine why and when they don't. 18m; VHS. **A:** Adult. **P:** Professional. **U:** Institution. **Bus-Ind:** Job Training, Management. **Acq:** Rent/Lease. **Dist:** National Safety Council, California Chapter, Film Library.

Ball Bearings 1985
Part of a series offering instruction on power transmission products, including nomenclature, applications, classification, numbering systems, and other information on components and equipment. 20m; VHS. **A:** Adult. **P:** Vocational. **U:** Institution. **Gen-Edu:** Industrial Arts, Technology. **Acq:** Purchase. **Dist:** RMI Media. $112.50.

Ball Bearings 1995
Covers the two major types of ball bearings, as well as various mounting types and housing configurations. 15m; VHS. **A:** Adult. **P:** Professional. **U:** Institution. **Bus-Ind:** Job Training, Management. **Acq:** Rent/Lease. **Dist:** National Safety Council, California Chapter, Film Library.

**Ball Control: Winning Through
   Attrition** 2005 (Unrated)
Coach Geoff Carlston discusses why he believes ball control and dominant passing are the keys to winning volleyball games. 38m; DVD. **A:** Family. **P:** Education. **U:** Home, Institution. **Spo-Rec:** Volleyball, Athletic Instruction/Coaching. **Acq:** Purchase. **Dist:** Championship Productions. $39.99.

Ball Mill Safety 1988
The various steps that must be followed to safely shut down and inspect a ball mill are outlined. 17m; VHS, 3/4 U. **Pr:** Mine Safety and Health Academy. **A:** Adult. **P:** Education. **U:** Institution. **Bus-Ind:** Safety Education, Miners & Mining. **Acq:** Purchase. **Dist:** U.S. Department of Labor, Mine Safety and Health Administration. $20.00.

Ball of Fire 1941 — ★★★
A gang moll hides out with a group of mundane professors, trying to avoid her loathsome boyfriend. The professors are busy compiling an encyclopedia and Stanwyck helps them with their section on slang in the English language. Cooper has his hands full when he falls for this damsel in distress and must fight the gangsters to keep her. Stanwyck takes a personal liking to naive Cooper and resolves to teach him more than just slang. 111m/B/W; VHS, DVD. **C:** Gary Cooper; Barbara Stanwyck; Dana Andrews; Gene Krupa; Oscar Homolka; Dan Duryea; S.Z. Sakall; Henry Travers; Directed by Howard Hawks; Written by Billy Wilder; Charles Brackett; Cinematography by Gregg Toland; Music by Alfred Newman. **Pr:** Samuel

Goldwyn. **A:** Family. **P:** Entertainment. **U:** Home. **Mov-Ent:** Comedy--Romantic, Romance. **Acq:** Purchase. **Dist:** Unknown Distributor.

Ball of Wax 2003 (Unrated) — ★½
Superstar baseball player Bret Packard (Mench) is a domination freak who plots the downfall of his teammates basically because he's a wealthy, arrogant sociopath and he can. Then manager Ingels (Morris) brings in motivational speaker Bob Tower (Tobias) to get the team back on track and Packard flips to find he's losing control of the situation. 90m; DVD, Wide. **C:** Larry Tobias; Mark Mench; Justin Smith; Traci Dinwiddie; Cullen Moss; Daniel Morris; Kevin Scanlon; Stephanie Wallace; Directed by Daniel Kraus; Written by Daniel Kraus; Cinematography by Michael Caporale; Music by Eric Bachman. **A:** Sr. High-Adult. **P:** Entertainment. **U:** Home. **Mov-Ent:** Baseball, Sports--Fiction; Drama. **Acq:** Purchase. **Dist:** Movies Unlimited.

**The Ball Screen Dribble Drive
   Offense** 2013 (Unrated)
Basketball coach Dave Clarke demonstrates combining the dribble drive offense with ball screens. 83m; DVD. **A:** Family. **P:** Education. **U:** Home. **L:** English. **Spo-Rec:** Athletic Instruction/Coaching, Basketball. **Acq:** Purchase. **Dist:** Championship Productions. $39.99.

Ball Talk: Baseball's Voices of Summer 1989
A nostalgic celebration of baseball announcers and their fondest memories of the game. 60m; VHS. **Pr:** J2 Communications. **A:** Family. **P:** Entertainment. **U:** Home. **Spo-Rec:** Baseball. **Acq:** Purchase. **Dist:** j2 Global. $29.95.

The Ballad and the Source 1983
English balladeer Walter Pardon is profiled. 16m; VHS, 3/4 U. **TV Std:** NTSC, PAL, SECAM. **Pr:** John Cohen. **A:** Jr. High-Adult. **P:** Education. **U:** Institution, SURA. **Fin-Art:** Great Britain. **Acq:** Purchase, Rent/Lease, Duplication. **Dist:** The Cinema Guild.

Ballad in Blue 1966 (Unrated) — ★★
Real life story of Ray Charles and a blind child. Tearjerker also includes some of Charles' hit songs. 89m/B/W; VHS, DVD. **C:** Ray Charles; Tom Bell; Mary Peach; Dawn Addams; Piers Bishop; Betty McDowall; Directed by Paul Henreid. **Pr:** Fox. **A:** Family. **P:** Entertainment. **U:** Home. **Mov-Ent:** Melodrama, Blindness. **Acq:** Purchase. **Dist:** Lions Gate Entertainment Inc. $39.95.
Songs: I Got a Woman; What'd I Say?.

Ballad of a Gunfighter 1964 (Unrated) — ★
A feud between two outlaws reaches the boiling point when they both fall in love with the same woman. 84m; VHS. **C:** Marty Robbins; Bob (Robert) Barron; Joyce Redd; Nestor Paiva; Laurette Luez; Directed by Bill Ward; Written by Bill Ward; Cinematography by Brydon Baker; Music by Jaime Mendoza-Nava. **Pr:** Bill Ward. **A:** Jr. High-Adult. **P:** Entertainment. **U:** Home. **Mov-Ent:** Western, Romance. **Acq:** Purchase. **Dist:** $9.99.

Ballad of a Soldier 1960 (Unrated) — ★★★½
As a reward for demolishing two German tanks, a 19-year-old Russian soldier receives a six-day pass so he can see his mother; however, he meets another woman. Well directed and photographed, while avoiding propaganda. Russian with subtitles. 88m/B/W; VHS, DVD. **C:** Vladimir Ivashov; Shanna Prokhorenko; Antonina Maximova; Nikolai Kryuchkov; Directed by Grigori Chukhraj; Written by Grigori Chukhraj; Valentin Yezhov; Cinematography by Sergei Mukhin; Music by Mikhail Ziv. **A:** College-Adult. **P:** Entertainment. **U:** Home. **L:** Russian. **Mov-Ent:** War--General. **Awds:** British Acad. '61: Film. **Acq:** Purchase. **Dist:** Criterion Collection Inc.; New Yorker Video; International Historic Films Inc.

The Ballad of Andy Crocker 1969 — ★★½
Early TV movie take on vets returning home from Vietnam. Andy (Majors) comes home to find his girlfriend has married someone else, his small business is in ruins, and his friends and family haven't a clue as to what has happened or what to expected from the disillusioned ex-soldier. 80m; VHS, DVD. **C:** Lee Majors; Joey Heatherton; Jimmy Dean; Marvin Gaye; Agnes Moorehead; Pat Hingle; Jill Haworth; Peter Haskell; Bobby Hatfield; Directed by George McCowan; Written by Stuart Margolin; Cinematography by Henry Cronjager, Jr.; Music by Billy May. **A:** Jr. High-Adult. **P:** Entertainment. **U:** Home. **Mov-Ent:** Vietnam War, Veterans. **Acq:** Purchase. **Dist:** Facets Multimedia Inc.

The Ballad of Bering Strait 2003
Documentary following the Russian-born band members of Bering Strait and their journey to Nashville to record their first country music album. 98m; VHS, DVD. **A:** Sr. High-Adult. **P:** Entertainment. **U:** Home, Institution. **Gen-Edu:** Documentary Films, Music--Country/Western. **Acq:** Purchase, Rent/Lease. **Dist:** The Cinema Guild. $295.00.

Ballad of Cable Hogue 1970 (R) — ★★★
A prospector, who had been left to die in the desert by his double-crossing partners, finds a waterhole. A surprise awaits his former friends when they visit the remote well. Not the usual violent Peckinpah horse drama, but a tongue-in-cheek comedy romance mixed with tragedy. Obviously offbeat and worth a peek. 122m; VHS, DVD. **C:** Jason Robards, Jr.; Stella Stevens; David Warner; L.Q. Jones; Strother Martin; Slim Pickens; Directed by Sam Peckinpah; Cinematography by Lucien Ballard; Music by Jerry Goldsmith. **Pr:** Warner Bros. **A:** Sr. High-Adult. **P:** Entertainment. **U:** Home. **Mov-Ent:** Miners & Mining, Romance. **Acq:** Purchase. **Dist:** Warner Home Video, Inc. $19.98.

Ballad of Gregorio Cortez 1983 (PG) — ★★★
Tragic story based on one of the most famous manhunts in Texas history. A Mexican cowhand kills a Texas sheriff in self-defense and tries to elude the law, all because of a misunderstanding of the Spanish language. Olmos turns in a fine performance as Cortez. 105m; VHS. **C:** Edward James Olmos; James Gammon; Tom Bower; Alan Vint; Barry Corbin; Rosanna Desoto; Bruce McGill; Brion James; Pepe Serna; William Sanderson; Directed by Robert M. Young; Written by Robert M. Young; Cinematography by Reynaldo Villalobos; Music by W. Michael Lewis. **Pr:** Moctesuma Esparza Productions. **A:** Jr. High-Adult. **P:** Entertainment. **U:** Home. **L:** English, Japanese. **Mov-Ent:** Western. **Acq:** Purchase. **Dist:** New Line Home Video. $14.98.

The Ballad of Jack and Rose 2005 (R) — ★★★
Absorbing story about an idealistic father and daughter living on their own like the last two hippies on earth in an abandoned commune. Rose (Belle) loves her father, Jack (Day-Lewis). A lot. Actually, she's probably in love with him. This is a touchy subject (not literally, don't worry) for Jack. Jack knows his daughter is too attached, is going to lose him one day, and may not make it on her own. After venturing into the real world for six months Jack begins dating a woman, mother to two boys, and asks her and the boys to move into the commune. Rose reacts with jealousy, trying to anger her father by seducing the sons. Writer/director Rebecca Miller, daughter of playwright Arthur Miller, sidesteps any cliches but piles on a few too many tricks at the end. 138m; DVD. **C:** Daniel Day-Lewis; Catherine Keener; Camilla Belle; Beau Bridges; Jason Lee; Jena Malone; Paul Dano; Susanna Thompson; Ryan McDonald; Directed by Rebecca Miller; Written by Rebecca Miller; Cinematography by Ellen Kuras; Music by Michael Rohatyn. **Pr:** Graham King; Jonathan Sehring; Caroline Kaplan; Lemore Syvan; Melissa Marr; Initial Entertainment Group; Elevation Pictures; IFC Films. **A:** Sr. High-Adult. **P:** Entertainment. **U:** Home. **L:** English. **Mov-Ent. Awds:** L.A. Film Critics '05: Actress (Keener). **Acq:** Purchase. **Dist:** MGM Home Entertainment. $26.98.

The Ballad of Jimmy Kerr 19??
Presents a music video with lyrics by Barry Campbell that gives tribute to a young soldier named Jimmy Kerr and others like him who volunteered to go off to war. 8m; VHS. **A:** Jr. High-Adult. **P:** Education. **U:** Home. **Gen-Edu:** War--General, Music Video. **Acq:** Purchase. **Dist:** The War Amps. $10.00.

The Ballad of Josie 1967 — ★½
Studio backlot western comedy. After managing to accidentally kill her drunken lout of a husband, perky frontier widow Josie (Day) needs a way to support herself and her son. She takes up sheep ranching--in cattle country--which makes her very unpopular with most everyone except good guy Jason Meredith (Graves). 103m; DVD. **C:** Doris Day; Peter Graves; George Kennedy; Andy Devine; William Talman; David Hartman; Directed by Andrew V. McLaglen; Written by Harold Swanton; Cinematography by Milton Krasner. **A:** Family. **P:** Entertainment. **U:** Home. **Mov-Ent.** **Acq:** Purchase. **Dist:** Universal Studios Home Video.

The Ballad of Little Jo 1993 (R) — ★★½
Inspired by a true story set during the 1866 gold rush. Easterner Josephine Monaghan is cast out of her wealthy family after she has a baby out of wedlock. Heading west, she passes herself off as a man—Little Jo'in an attempt to forestall harrassment. Solemn and overly earnest attempt by Greenwald to demystify the old west and bring a feminist viewpoint to a familiar saga. 110m; VHS, DVD, CC. **C:** Suzy Amis; Bo Hopkins; Ian McKellen; Carrie Snodgress; David Chung; Rene Auberjonois; Heather Graham; Anthony Heald; Sam Robards; Ruth Maleczech; Directed by Maggie Greenwald; Written by Maggie Greenwald; Cinematography by Declan Quinn; Music by David Mansfield. **Pr:** Fred Berner; Brenda Goodman; Barry Bernardi; John Sloss; Ira Deutchman; Polygram; Fine Line Features. **A:** Sr. High-Adult. **P:** Entertainment. **U:** Home. **Mov-Ent. Acq:** Purchase. **Dist:** Sony Pictures Home Entertainment Inc. $19.95.

The Ballad of Narayama 1958 (Unrated) — ★★★
Filmed in a style similar to traditional Kabuki plays, this is the story of a remote village near Narayama Mountain. Famine is so bad, that it has become policy that anyone reaching the age of 70 is to be carried off into the mountains by their family and left to die. 98m; DVD, Blu-Ray, Streaming. **C:** Kinuyo Tanaka; Teiji Takahashi; Yuko Mochizuki; Danko Ichikawa; Keiko Ogasawara; Directed by Keisuke Kinoshita; Written by Keisuke Kinoshita; Cinematography by Hiroshi Kusuda; Music by Chuji Kinoshita; Matsunosuke Nozawa. **A:** Jr. High-Adult. **P:** Entertainment. **U:** Home. **L:** English, Japanese. **Mov-Ent. Acq:** Purchase, Rent/Lease. **Dist:** Criterion Collection Inc. $29.95 19.95 14.99.

The Ballad of Narayama 1983 — ★★★★
Director Imamura's subtle and vastly moving story takes place a vague century ago. In compliance with village law designed to control population among the poverty-stricken peasants, a healthy 70-year-old woman must submit to solitary starvation atop a nearby mountain. We follow her as she sets into motion the final influence she will have in the lives of her children and grandchildren, a situation described with detachment and without imposing a tragic perspective. In Japanese with English subtitles. 129m; VHS, DVD. **C:** Ken Ogata; Sumiko Sakamoto; Takejo Aki; Tonpei Hidari; Shoichi Ozawa; Directed by Shohei Imamura; Written by Shohei Imamura; Cinematography by Maseo Tochizawa; Music by Shinichiro Ikebe. **Pr:** Toei Studios; Shochiku Company. **A:** College-Adult. **P:** Entertainment. **U:** Home. **L:** Japanese. **Mov-Ent:** Drama, Parenting, Aging. **Awds:** Cannes '83: Film. **Acq:** Purchase. **Dist:** AnimEigo Inc.; Facets Multimedia Inc.; Kino on Video. $59.95.

The Ballad of Paul Bunyan 1972
The good-humored, legendary American giant is pitted against a powerful lumber camp boss who likes to pick on the little guy. 30m; VHS. **C:** Directed by Arthur Rankin, Jr; Jules Bass. **Pr:** Rankin/Bass Productions. **A:** Family. **P:** Entertainment. **U:** Home. **Mov-Ent:** Comedy-Drama, Family Viewing, Folklore & Legends. **Acq:** Purchase. **Dist:** Anchor Bay Entertainment. $6.95.

The Ballad of Ramblin' Jack 2000 — ★★★
Seminal '60s folk singer "Ramblin' Jack" Elliott was born Elliott Adnopoz, son of a Jewish doctor in New York. But bitten by the bug of the romantic West, the young free spirit transformed himself into the spiritual heir of Woody Guthrie who, to a degree, paved the way for Bob Dylan. Along the way he had a wife and family, though he seldom saw them. His daughter Aiyana made this documentary about her father, so strict objectivity is not high on the list of the film's attributes. 112m; DVD. **C:** Jack Elliott; Arlo Guthrie; Kris Kristofferson; Pete Seeger; Odetta; Dave Van Ronk; Directed by Aiyana Elliott; Written by Aiyana Elliott; Dick Dahl; Music by Jack Elliott. **A:** Jr. High-Adult. **P:** Entertainment. **U:** Home. **Mov-Ent:** Documentary Films, Music. **Acq:** Purchase. **Dist:** Wellspring Media.

The Ballad of the Irish Horse 1984
This program looks at the Irish horse and its performance in a variety of competitions. 48m; VHS. **Pr:** Pan International Films. **A:** Primary-Adult. **P:** Entertainment. **U:** Home. **Spo-Rec:** Animals, Horses--Racing. **Acq:** Purchase. **Dist:** , On Moratorium.

The Ballad of the Iron Horse 1970
The dramatic story of the building of the first transcontinental railroad which in 1869 linked the two coasts. 29m; VHS, 3/4 U; Open Captioned. **Pr:** Helen Jean Rogers; John Secondari. **A:** Family. **P:** Education. **U:** Institution, SURA. **Gen-Edu.** **Acq:** Purchase, Rent/Lease. **Dist:** Phoenix Learning Group.

The Ballad of the Sad Cafe 1991 (PG-13) — ★★½
Unusual love story set in a small Southern town during the Depression. The everday lives of its townspeople are suddenly transformed when a distant relation of the town's outcast (Redgrave) unexpectedly shows up. A moving story that tries to portray both sides of love and its power to enhance and destroy simultaneously. Emotion never seems to come to life in a movie that's nice to watch, but is ultimately disappointing. Adapted from the play by Edward Albee, which was based on the critically acclaimed novella by Carson McCullers. A British/U.S. co-production. 100m; VHS, DVD, CC. **C:** Vanessa Redgrave; Keith Carradine; Cork Hubbert; Rod Steiger; Austin Pendleton; Beth Dixon; Lanny Flaherty; Mert Hatfield; Earl Hindman; Anne Pitoniak; Directed by Simon Callow; Written by Michael Hirst; Cinematography by Walter Lassally; Music by Richard Robbins. **Pr:** Ismail Merchant; Merchant-Ivory Productions. **A:** Jr. High-Adult. **P:** Entertainment. **U:** Home. **Mov-Ent:** Drama. **Acq:** Purchase. **Dist:** Sony Pictures Home Entertainment Inc.

Ballad Without End 1973
Set during the Civil War, depicts the senseless dying of two soldiers who have both turned their backs on war and their minds and spirits to the beauty of all nature and their dreamed-of joys of living. 12m; VHS, 3/4 U. **Pr:** Robert Lyons. **A:** Jr. High-Adult. **P:** Education. **U:** Institution, SURA. **Gen-Edu:** Ethics & Morals. **Acq:** Purchase. **Dist:** Phoenix Learning Group.

Ballast 2008 (Unrated) — ★★
Hammer's debut follows the misfortunes of a poor Mississippi Delta family and the little bit of hope that sustains them. Lawrence (Smith, Sr.) shot himself after his twin brother Darius OD'd. He's slowly recovering at home where he's confronted by Darius' reckless 12-year-old son James (Ross), who believes he and his ex-druggie mother Marlee (Riggs) are owed money from the small business the brothers ran. They need the cash since Marlee has just lost her job but there's a lot of bitterness on both sides to overcome. 96m; Blu-Ray, On Demand, Wide. **C:** Tarra Riggs; JimMyron Ross; Michael J. Smith, Sr.; Johnny McPhail; Directed by Lance Hammer; Written by Lance Hammer; Cinematography by Lol Crawley. **Pr:** Nina Parikh; Lance Hammer; Alluvial Film Company. **A:** Sr. High-Adult. **P:** Entertainment. **U:** Home. **L:** English. **Mov-Ent:** Black Culture, Poverty, Suicide. **Acq:** Purchase. **Dist:** Kino on Video; Amazon.com Inc.; Movies Unlimited.

Ballbuster 1989 — ★½
Cops take on gangs in an all-out high-stakes battle to win back the streets. 100m; VHS. **C:** Ivan Rogers; Bonnie Paine; W. Randolph Galvin; Bill Shirk; Brenda Banet; Directed by Eddie Beverly, Jr.; Written by Eddie Beverly, Jr. **Pr:** Ivan Rogers; Ivan Rogers. **A:** College-Adult. **P:** Entertainment. **U:** Home. **Mov-Ent.** **Acq:** Purchase. **Dist:** Xenon Pictures Inc. $39.95.

Ballerina 2006
Offers biographies of five Russian ballerinas affiliated with the Mariinsky Theatre, including both their training and performances. 77m; DVD. **A:** Jr. High-Adult. **P:** Entertainment. **U:** Home. **Mov-Ent:** Dance--Ballet, USSR, Documentary Films. **Acq:** Purchase. **Dist:** First Run Features. $77.

Ballerina, Ballerina 1994
Contains footage of the everyday life of a ballerina, covering everything from how they dress and rehearse to exercises and performances. 25m; VHS. **A:** Family. **P:** Education. **U:** Home. **Fin-Art:** Dance--Ballet, Performing Arts. **Acq:** Purchase. **Dist:** Tapeworm Video Distributors Inc. $19.95.

The Ballerinas 1987
A recreation of Parisian ballet from the middle of the 19th century to the present. 108m; VHS. **C:** Carla Fracci; Peter Ustinov; Michel Denard; Vladimir Vasiliev. **Pr:** Princeton/Dance Horizons. **A:** Jr. High-Adult. **P:** Entertainment. **U:** Institution, Home. **Fin-Art:** Dance--History, Dance--Ballet. **Acq:** Purchase. **Dist:** Stagestep; Kultur International Films Ltd., Inc.; Princeton Book Company Publishers. $39.95.

Ballet 1995
Documentary takes a look at the American Ballet Theatre, including segments on rehearsal, touring, administration, and fund raising. 170m; VHS. **A:** Sr. High-Adult. **P:** Entertainment. **U:** Home, Institution. **Gen-Edu:** Documentary Films, Dance--Ballet. **Acq:** Purchase, Rent/Lease. **Dist:** Zipporah Films. $400.00.

Ballet 201: Beyond the Basics ????
Designed for ages five to adult, this video lesson picks up from the basics in "Ballet 101" and introduces more advanced moves and center work. 45m; VHS. **A:** Family. **P:** Instruction. **U:** Home. **How-Ins:** Dance--Ballet, Dance--Instruction. **Acq:** Purchase. **Dist:** Stagestep. $19.95.

Ballet Adagio 1972
A dance production, shot in slow motion, enhancing the ease, grace, and beauty with which the Canadian artists, Anna Marie and David Holmes, execute their lifts and turns. 10m; VHS, 3/4 U, Special order formats. **C:** Anna Marie; David Holmes. **Pr:** Norman McLaren; National Film Board of Canada. **A:** Jr. High-Adult. **P:** Entertainment. **U:** Institution, Home, SURA. **Fin-Art:** Film--Avant-Garde, Dance--Ballet. **Acq:** Purchase, Rent/Lease, Duplication License. **Dist:** Pyramid Media. $195.00.

A Ballet Class for Beginners 1986
Basic ballet movements are taught by renowned dancer Dave Howard. 40m; VHS. **Pr:** American Home Video Library. **A:** Family. **P:** Instruction. **U:** Institution, Home. **How-Ins:** Dance--Ballet, Dance--Instruction. **Acq:** Purchase. **Dist:** Music Video Distributors; Princeton Book Company Publishers; Kultur International Films Ltd., Inc. $39.95.

Ballet Class: Intermediate-Advanced 1986
Former Royal Ballet soloist David Howard teaches the intermediate and advanced levels of dance movement. 56m; VHS. **C:** David Howard; Cynthia Harvey; Peter Fonesca. **Pr:** New Age Video. **A:** Sr. High-Adult. **P:** Education. **U:** Institution, Home. **How-Ins:** Dance--Ballet, Dance--Instruction. **Acq:** Purchase. **Dist:** Music Video Distributors; Princeton Book Company Publishers; Kultur International Films Ltd., Inc. $39.95.

Ballet Episodes 197?
Excerpts from ballets by James Clouser are featured in this program. 30m/B/W; VHS, 3/4 U, EJ, Q. **Pr:** WCBS New York; Camera Three Productions. **A:** Sr. High-Adult. **P:** Education. **U:** Institution, SURA. **Fin-Art:** Dance. **Acq:** Duplication, Free Duplication. **Dist:** Camera Three Productions, Inc.

Ballet Floor Barre: A Warm-Up and Conditioning Program 19??
Provides a program of exercises done on the floor which are aimed at warming up the body and strengthening the back. 45m; VHS. **A:** Jr. High-Adult. **P:** Instruction. **U:** Institution, Home. **How-Ins:** Fitness/Exercise, Dance--Ballet, Dance--Instruction. **Acq:** Purchase. **Dist:** Stagestep. $39.95.

Ballet Folklorico Nacional de Mexico 1990
The traditions of Mexican dance come together in this show of the Ballet Folklorico. 60m; VHS. **Pr:** Gessler Educational Software. **A:** Sr. High-Adult. **P:** Entertainment. **U:** Home. **L:** Spanish. **Mov-Ent:** Performing Arts, Dance, Mexico. **Acq:** Purchase. **Dist:** QUSA. $59.95.

Ballet Gold Collection ????
Four-tape set features archival footage of Russian ballet performances, as well as the Royal Ballet and American Ballet Theatre highlighting such dancers as Margot Fonteyn, Rudolf Nureyev, Vladimar Vasiliev, Mikhail Baryshnikov, Darcy Russell and many more. ?m; VHS. **A:** Adult. **P:** Entertainment. **U:** Institution, Home. **Fin-Art:** Dance--Ballet, Dance--Performance. **Acq:** Purchase. **Dist:** Stagestep. $49.95.
Indiv. Titles: 1. Glory of the Bolshoi 2. Glory of the Kirov 3. Ballet Favorites 4. Great Pas de Deux.

Ballet in Jazz 1962
American jazz as interpreted by German ballet dancers. 11m/B/W; VHS, 3/4 U. **TV Std:** NTSC, PAL, SECAM. **Pr:** Roto-Film GmbH. **A:** Jr. High-Adult. **P:** Education. **U:** Institution, SURA. **Fin-Art:** Dance--Ballet, Dance, Music--Jazz. **Acq:** Purchase, Rent/Lease, Duplication. **Dist:** The Cinema Guild.

Ballet Legends: The Kirov's Ninel Kurgapkina 19??
Kurgapkina was a prima ballerina with the Kirov from 1947-72, renowed for her impeccable technique and passionate acting. Offers highlights of some of her most important leading roles in "Le Corsaire," "Don Quixote," "Harlequinade," and "Sleeping Beauty." 40m; VHS. **A:** College-Adult. **P:** Entertainment. **U:** Home. **Fin-Art:** Dance--Ballet. **Acq:** Purchase. **Dist:** V.I.E.W. Inc./Arkadia Entertainment Corp. $29.98.

Ballet Mecanique 1924
An abstract film that creates a "dance" from the movement of non-animate objects, and uses people as inanimate objects in repeating patterns. ?m/B/W; 8 mm. **C:** Directed by Fernand Leger. **A:** Sr. High-Adult. **P:** Entertainment. **U:** Home. **Mov-Ent:** Film--Avant-Garde. **Acq:** Purchase. **Dist:** Glenn Video Vistas Ltd.

Ballet 101 1997
Introduces basic ballet warm-up exercises and technique. Based on a University of California major program. 45m; VHS. **A:** Family. **P:** Instruction. **U:** Home. **How-Ins:** Dance. **Acq:** Purchase. **Dist:** Tapeworm Video Distributors Inc. $19.95.

Ballet, Part 1: Beginning Ballet Lessons 1995
Ballet training exercises are demonstrated by dancer Melinda Cordell. 60m; VHS. **A:** Family. **P:** Instruction. **U:** Home. **How-Ins:** Dance--Instruction, Dance--Ballet. **Acq:** Purchase. **Dist:** Videoactive Co. $29.95.

Ballet Robotique 1983
Assembly line robots perform their functions to classical music. 8m; VHS, 3/4 U, Special order formats. **A:** Family. **P:** Entertainment. **U:** Institution, Home, SURA. **Gen-Edu:** Technology. **Acq:** Purchase, Rent/Lease, Duplication License. **Dist:** Pyramid Media. $295.00.

Ballet Ruse 1989
Two comedic ballets, "Yes Virginia, Another Piano Ballet" and "Forgotten Memories," are performed starring Peter Anastos. 35m; VHS. **Pr:** New Jersey Network. **A:** Jr. High-Adult. **P:** Entertainment. **U:** Home. **Fin-Art:** Dance--Ballet, Dance--Performance. **Acq:** Purchase. **Dist:** Image Entertainment Inc.; Music Video Distributors. $29.95.

Ballet Russes 2005 (Unrated) — ★★★
Documentary covering the history of the various ballet companies who have used the Ballet Russes name, from its founding by impresario Serge Daghilev in 1909 to the last performance in 1962, including its legendary choreographers, dancers, and designers. Although there's footage of various performances, the most appealing aspects are the interviews of dancers, who were in their 80s and 90s when reunited in 2000, recalling their lives on stage. 118m; DVD. **C:** Directed by Dan Geller; Dayna Goldfine; Written by Dan Geller; Dayna Goldfine; Gary Weimberg; Cinematography by Dan Geller; Music by Todd Boekelheide; David Conte. **Pr:** Robert Hawk; Douglas Blair Turnbaugh; Dan Geller; Dayna Goldfine. **P:** Entertainment. **U:** Home. **L:** English. **Mov-Ent:** Documentary Films, Dance--Ballet, Biography: Artists. **Acq:** Purchase. **Dist:** Zeitgeist Films Ltd.

Ballet Shoes 19??
The classic children's tale of three sisters living a very sheltered life with their guardian Sylvia, who is working to support all four of them. A story of hope and possibilities. From the BBC Television network. 120m; VHS, DVD. **Pr:** British Broadcasting Corporation. **A:** Family. **P:** Entertainment. **U:** Home. **Chl-Juv:** Children. **Acq:** Purchase. **Dist:** Video Collectibles; Home Vision Cinema. $29.95.

Ballet Shoes 2007 (Unrated) — ★★½
Orphans Pauline (Watson), Petrova (Paige), and Posy (Boynton) are adopted by eccentric paleontologist Great Uncle Matthew (Griffiths), who leaves their raising to his niece Sylvia (Fox) while he's off exploring. Each girl has an ambition: Pauline wants to act, Posy wants to be a ballet dancer, and Petrova wants to be an aviatrix. Times are tough in 1930s London and Sylvia is forced to take boarders. Luckily dance teacher Theo (Cohu) is able to help out with the girls' desire to raise some money. Sweet adaptation of the novel by Noel Streatfeild. 84m; DVD. **C:** Emma Watson; Yasmin Paige; Emilia Fox; Richard Griffiths; Victoria Wood; Lucy Cohu; Marc Warren; Eileen Atkins; Gemma Jones; Harriet Walter; Lucy Boynton; Directed by Sandra Goldbacher; Written by Heidi Thomas; Cinematography by Peter Greenhalgh; Music by Kevin Sargent. **A:** Family. **P:** Entertainment. **U:** Home. **Mov-Ent:** Adoption. **Acq:** Purchase. **Dist:** Entertainment One US LP.

Ballet with Edward Villella 1970
Excerpts from George Balanchine's "Jewels" and "Apollo" as well as the classic "Giselle." Villella shows ballet not just as an art form but as an arduous, highly disciplined profession. 27m; VHS, 3/4 U. **C:** Edward Villella; Patricia McBride. **Pr:** Robert Saudek; Learning Corporation of America. **A:** Sr. High-Adult. **P:** Entertainment. **U:** Institution, SURA. **Fin-Art:** Dance, Dance--Ballet. **Acq:** Purchase, Rent/Lease. **Dist:** Phoenix Learning Group.

The Ballet Workout 1987
Keep in shape using techniques of dance and ballet. Divided into two levels for those with or without ballet experience. 83m; VHS. **Pr:** Kultur Video. **A:** Family. **P:** Instruction. **U:** Home. **Hea-Sci:** Fitness/Exercise, Dance--Ballet. **Acq:** Purchase. **Dist:** Music Video Distributors; Kultur International Films Ltd., Inc.; Signals Video. $19.95.

The Ballet Workout II 1993
Melissa Lowe's follow-up the the Ballet Workout, provides the viewer with two new workouts that address the goal of achieving a lithe, supple body, an improves carriage, and the look and grace of a professional dancer. 70m; VHS. **A:** Adult. **P:** Instruction. **U:** Institution. **How-Ins:** Dance--Instruction. **Acq:** Purchase. **Dist:** Princeton Book Company Publishers. $19.95.

Balletcise: Advanced 1992
Simple ballet steps are used to stretch and tone muscles. Hosted by prima ballerina Marguerite Porter. 45m; VHS. **A:** Jr. High-Adult. **P:** Instruction. **U:** Home. **Hea-Sci:** Fitness/Exercise. **Acq:** Purchase. **Dist:** Fast Forward; Anchor Bay Entertainment. $9.98.

Balletcise: Beginners 1992
Marguerite Porter, a 22-year veteran of the Royal and Sadlers Wells Ballet Companies, teaches a fitness program using simple ballet steps. 45m; VHS. **A:** Jr. High-Adult. **P:** Instruction. **U:** Home. **Hea-Sci:** Fitness/Exercise. **Acq:** Purchase. **Dist:** Fast Forward; Anchor Bay Entertainment. $9.98.

Balletone Center Moves 2004
Graceful, easy-to-follow cardio workout with Jody Hoedstedt, based on classic ballet moves that also provide conditioning and toning to the core and lower body. 41m; DVD. **A:** Adult. **P:** Instruction. **U:** Home. **Hea-Sci:** Fitness/Exercise. **Acq:** Purchase. **Dist:** Collage Video Specialties, Inc.

Balletone Sole Synthesis 2006
Dance-inspired total-body toning workout led by Shannon Griffiths-Fable uses techniques from ballet and yoga to improve strength, balance, and flexibility. 42m; DVD. **A:** Adult. **P:** Instruction. **U:** Home. **Hea-Sci:** Fitness/Exercise. **Acq:** Purchase. **Dist:** Collage Video Specialties, Inc.

Balletone with Jody Hoegstedt 2003
Flowing, graceful workout based on ballet-style moves, including classic barrework performed without a ballet bar and a segment of similarly fluid Pilates matwork. 44m; DVD. **A:** Adult. **P:** Instruction. **U:** Home. **Hea-Sci:** Fitness/Exercise. **Acq:** Purchase. **Dist:** Collage Video Specialties, Inc.

Ballistic 1994 (R) — ★½
L.A. cop Jesse Gavin (Holden) gets in trouble when the government witness she's supposed to be protecting gets murdered. So she teams up with her ex-con father and her boyfriend to track the mobster responsible for the hit. 86m; VHS, CC. **C:** Marjean Holden; Richard Roundtree; Sam Jones; Joel Beeson; Charles Napier; Directed by Kim Bass. **A:** Sr. High-Adult. **P:** Entertainment. **U:** Home. **Mov-Ent.** **Acq:** Purchase. **Dist:** Imperial Entertainment Corp.; Image Entertainment Inc.

Ballistic: Ecks vs. Sever 2002 (R) — ★½
Awkwardly titled actioner stars Banderes as Ecks, a disillusioned former FBI manhunter mourning his dead wife. Liu is code-name Sever, a former government-trained assassin. Ecks has been rehired to track Sever for kidnapping the son of her former boss Gant (Henry), chief of the Defense Intelligence Agency. Both agents are also on the lookout for a supposedly dangerous and supremely ridiculous techno virus. Once the operatives find they have a lot in common, including a common enemy, they join forces to gun down and blow up everything in sight. Superb, if overdone stunts take top billing, while dim lighting matches equally dim plot. Neophyte director Kaos (short for Kaosayananda) cops all the moves of "The Matrix." Based on the far more entertaining video game. 95m; VHS, DVD, CC. **C:** Antonio Banderas; Lucy Liu; Gregg Henry; Ray Park; Talisa Soto; Miguel (Michael) Sandoval; Terry Chen; Sandrine Holt; Roger R. Cross; Steve Bacic; Aidan Drummond; Directed by Kaos; Written by Alan B. McElroy; Cinematography by Julio Macat; Music by Don Davis. **Pr:** Elie Samaha; Chris Lee; Franchise Pictures; Warner Bros. **A:** Sr. High-Adult. **P:** Entertainment. **U:** Home. **Mov-Ent:** Federal Bureau of Investigation (FBI), Intelligence Service. **Acq:** Purchase. **Dist:** Warner Home Video, Inc.

Ballistica 2010 (Unrated) — ★★
Stoic, action-oriented lead; eye candy in ridiculous role; solid, familiar faces as good guy backup and terrorists; fast pace (dumb plot). What more do you need for mindless entertainment? CIA field operative Sloan teams up with scientist Amanda who unwittingly developed a bomb for Russian terrorist Dragomir, who plans to set it off in L.A. 90m; DVD. **C:** Paul Logan; Martin Kove; Robert Davi; Andrew Divoff; C.B. Spencer; Directed by Gary Jones; Written by Sean Rourke; Cinematography by Mark Morris; Music by Shie Rozow. **A:** Sr. High-Adult. **P:** Entertainment. **U:** Home. **Mov-Ent:** Intelligence Service, Science, Terrorism. **Acq:** Purchase. **Dist:** The Asylum.

Balloon Animal Safari 1993
Entertainer Richard Levin demonstrates how to make a teddy bear, dachshund, snake, party hat, and pirate sword from balloons. Each project is shown twice, in wide angle and close-up views. 30m; VHS. **Pr:** Michael S. Dilley. **A:** Family. **P:** Instruction. **U:** Home. **How-Ins:** How-To, Games. **Acq:** Purchase. **Dist:** Producers Studio; Baker and Taylor. $12.95.

Balloon Farm 1997 (Unrated) — ★★½
Harvey Potter (Torn), using some magic, raises a crop of balloons on cornstalks. His drought-stricken fellow farmers see the miraculous crop as symbols of hope but grumpy farmer Wheezle (Blossom) is suspicious. And his suspcions begin to infect the rest of the community, except for spunky young Willow (Wilson). Based on Jerdine Nolen's children's book "Harvey Potter's Balloon Farm." 89m; VHS, DVD, CC. **C:** Rip Torn; Mara Wilson; Roberts Blossom; Laurie Metcalf; Neal McDonough; Frederic Lehne; Adam Wylie; Directed by William Dear; Written by Steven M. Karczynski. **A:** Family. **P:** Entertainment. **U:** Home. **Mov-Ent:** Agriculture, Magic. **Acq:** Purchase. **Dist:** Buena Vista Home Entertainment.

Balloon Safari 1981
Joan and Alan Root photograph the wildlife and landscapes of Kenya from a balloon. Then, an even greater challenge is undertaken-a hot air balloon flight over the top of Mt. Kilimanjaro. 55m; VHS, 3/4 U. **C:** Narrated by David Niven. **A:** Family. **P:** Entertainment. **U:** Institution, CCTV. **Gen-Edu:** Aeronautics, Filmmaking. **Acq:** Purchase. **Dist:** Benchmark Media.

Balloon Tree 1970
Stresses the importance of human value over precious possessions by following the adventures of a boy who runs away after getting his finger stuck in his aunt's jade carving. 10m; VHS, 3/4 U. **Pr:** Ross Lowell. **A:** Sr. High-College. **P:** Education. **U:** Institution, Home, SURA. **Gen-Edu:** Personality. **Acq:** Purchase, Rent/Lease, Duplication License. **Dist:** Pyramid Media.

The Balloonatic/One Week 1923
"The Balloonatic" (1923) features Keaton in several misadventures. In "One Week" (1920), Keaton and his new bride, Seely, receive a new home as a wedding gift—the kind you have to assemble yourself. Silent. 48m/B/W; Silent; VHS. **C:** Buster Keaton; Phyllis Haver; Sybil Seely; Directed by Buster Keaton. **Pr:** Buster Keaton Productions; Metro. **A:** Family. **P:** Entertainment. **U:** Home. **Mov-Ent:** Action-Adventure, Comedy--Romantic, Silent Films. **Acq:** Purchase. **Dist:** $17.95.

Ballooning: High on Hot Air 1987
This documentary captures the high altitude color and celebration of Albuquerque's International Balloon Fiesta. 20m; VHS, 3/4 U. **Pr:** Centre Productions, Inc. **A:** Sr. High-Adult. **P:** Education. **U:** Institution, SURA. **Gen-Edu:** Sports--General, Parades & Festivals. **Acq:** Purchase. **Dist:** Clear Vue Inc.

Balloons and Boats 1987
Two films, "Steamboat" and "Windflower," both non-narrated, are used to show two different kinds of transportation. 30m; VHS, 3/4 U. **A:** Primary. **P:** Education. **U:** Institution, SURA. **Gen-Edu.** **Acq:** Purchase, Trade-in. **Dist:** Encyclopedia Britannica. $300.00.

Ballot Measure 9 1994
Covers the 1992 Oregon political campaign for the anti-gay ballot initiative (which was defeated). Focuses on grassroots democracy and such broader issues as human rights, cultural diversity, and the American political process from various perspectives over an eight-month period. 71m; VHS. **C:** Directed by Heather MacDonald. **Pr:** David Meieran; Heather MacDonald; Oregon Tape Project. **A:** College-Adult. **P:** Education. **U:** Home. **Gen-Edu:** Documentary Films, Ethics & Morals, Politics & Government. **Awds:** Sundance '95: Aud. Award. **Acq:** Purchase. **Dist:** Wellspring Media; Zeitgeist Films Ltd. $89.98.

The Ballots Are in on Daley: The Last Boss 1996
Creates a portrait study of Chicago Mayor Richard J. Daley, one of America's most powerful and controversial urban politicians ever. 112m; VHS. **A:** College. **P:** Education. **U:** Home. **Gen-Edu:** Biography, Politics & Government. **Acq:** Purchase. **Dist:** Home Vision Cinema. $19.95.

Ballroom Dancing: Advanced 1993
Instructor Teresa Mason illustrates advanced ballroom dancing lessons and addresses the fine points of the most popular ballroom dances. 60m; VHS. **A:** Family. **P:** Instruction. **U:** Home. **How-Ins:** Dance--Instruction. **Acq:** Purchase. **Dist:** Kultur International Films Ltd., Inc. $29.95.

Ballroom Dancing Basics 2005
Six popular ballroom dance routines—waltz, fox trot, rumba, samba, meringue, and night club sway—are taught by professional dancers Tony Meredith and Melanie LaPatin. 73m; DVD. **A:** College-Adult. **P:** Entertainment. **U:** Home. **How-Ins:** Dance--Instruction, Education. **Acq:** Purchase. **Dist:** Acorn Media Group Inc. $24.99.

Ballroom Dancing: Beginning 1989
The basics of ballroom dancing are demonstrated, starting with a basic four-step and progressing to the tango, rumba and other sophisticated dances. 57m; VHS. **C:** Susan Major; Teresa Mason. **A:** Jr. High-Adult. **P:** Instruction. **U:** Home. **How-Ins:** Dance--Instruction. **Acq:** Purchase. **Dist:** Stagestep; Kultur International Films Ltd., Inc.; Fusion Video. $29.95.

Ballroom Dancing for Beginners 1988
Teaches viewers how to master the basic techniques of ballroom dancing. Includes patterns for the Fox Trot, Tango, and Rumba. 57m; DVD. **A:** Sr. High. **P:** Education. **U:** Home. **L:** English. **Gen-Edu:** Dance. **Acq:** Purchase. **Dist:** Kultur International Films Ltd., Inc. $19.98.

Ballroom Dancing: Intermediate 1991
This sequel to the top-selling "Ballroom Dancing for Beginners" offers more opportunities for mastery of the fox trot, tango, waltz, rumba, swing and cha-cha dances. Each dance is explained, demonstrated and repeated until viewers have mastered the maneuver. 48m; VHS. **C:** Hosted by Teresa Mason. **Pr:** Kultur Video. **A:** Family. **P:** Education. **U:** Home. **How-Ins:** Dance--Instruction. **Acq:** Purchase. **Dist:** Stagestep; Kultur International Films Ltd., Inc.; Fusion Video. $29.95.

Ballroom Dancing: The International Championships 1993
Six couples compete for the International Championship title for the most romantic dance form today—ballroom dancing. Contestants demonstrate their skill and grace at the Grand Prix Unitrading Ostrova 91. Includes footage of professional World Champs Donnie Burns & Gaynor Fairweather and Marcus & Karen Hilton. 60m; VHS, DVD. **A:** Adult. **P:** Entertainment. **U:** Home. **Spo-Rec:** Dance, Dance--Performance. **Acq:** Purchase. **Dist:** V.I.E.W. Inc./Arkadia Entertainment Corp. $19.98.

Ballroom Dancing: Wedding Waltz and More 19??
Professional dance instructors provide step-by-step instruction on seven different types of ballroom dancing steps, covering the wedding waltz, electric slide, new electric slide, swing, cha-cha, basic waltz, fox trot, and jitter bug. 60m; VHS. **A:** Jr. High-Adult. **P:** Instruction. **U:** Home. **How-Ins:** Dance--Instruction. **Acq:** Purchase. **Dist:** Tapeworm Video Distributors Inc. $19.95.

Balls of Fury 2007 (PG-13) — ★★½
Former child prodigy ping-pong star Randy Daytona (Fogler) finds himself fat and washed up at the ripe old age of 32. He's approached by the feds (Lopez as FBI agent) to take on a dangerous mission—infiltrate an underground ping-pong tournament run by shifty Chinese crime boss Feng (Walken), who also happens to be responsible for Randy's fathers' (Patrick) death. But Randy finds his mission has a dual purpose: avenge his father's murder, and attempt a high-stakes comeback. Of course every would-be hero needs a little help, and Randy's crackpot team includes blind restaurateur and ping-pong sage Master Wong (Hong) and his totally hot niece Maggie (Maggie Q). Some funny moments intertwine with a backdrop of Def Leppard in this ode to '80s nostalgia and martial arts, but it never fully takes off. 90m; DVD, HD-DVD, Wide. **C:** Dan Fogler; Christopher Walken; George Lopez; James Hong; Terry Crews; Robert Patrick; Diedrich Bader; Aisha Tyler; Maggie Q; Thomas Lennon; Patton Oswalt; David Koechner; Jason Scott Lee; Masi Oka; David Proval; Jenny Robertson; Toby Huss; Directed by Robert Ben Garant; Written by Thomas Lennon; Robert Ben Garant; Cinematography by Thomas Ackerman; Music by Randy Edelman. **Pr:** Thomas Lennon; Gary Barber; Roger Birnbaum; Jonathan Glickman; Thomas Lennon; Spyglass Entertainment; Intrepid Pictures; Rogue Pictures. **A:** Jr. High-Adult. **P:** Entertainment. **U:** Home. **L:** English. **Mov-Ent:** Sports--Fiction: Comedy, Federal Bureau of Investigation (FBI), Blindness. **Acq:** Purchase. **Dist:** Movies Unlimited; Alpha Video.

Balls Out: Gary the Tennis Coach 2009 (R) — ★½
Raunchy, dumb sports comedy about a loser with dreams of greatness. High school janitor Gary Houseman (Scott) decides to coach the long-neglected, losing tennis team. Soon, despite his crude behavior, his unorthodox methods actually get the team to the state championships. 93m; DVD. **C:** Seann William Scott; Randy Quaid; Leonor Varela; Deke Anderson; Justin Chon; Brent Anderson; Directed by Danny Leiner; Written by Andy Stock; Rick Stempson; Cinematography by Rogier Stoffers; Music by John Swihart. **A:** Sr. High-Adult. **P:** Entertainment. **U:** Home. **Mov-Ent:** Tennis, Sports--Fiction: Comedy. **Acq:** Purchase. **Dist:** Sony Pictures Home Entertainment Inc.

Bally Sally Cato 19??
Introduces teachers to storytelling techniques which stimulate education beyond the simple telling of a tale, but into science and math. 42m; VHS. **A:** Adult. **P:** Teacher Education. **U:** Institution. **Gen-Edu:** Storytelling. **Acq:** Purchase. **Dist:** Kaw Valley Films, Inc. $29.95.

Ballyhoo Baby 1990 — ★½
When a couple traveling cross-country pick up a young hitchhiker, the sexual tension between the three builds to a frightening climax. 30m; VHS. **C:** Directed by Paul Young. **A:** Sr. High-Adult. **P:** Entertainment. **U:** Home. **Mov-Ent:** Sex & Sexuality. **Acq:** Purchase. **Dist:** The Cinema Guild. $59.95.

Ballykissangel 1 1996
Father Peter Clifford arrives at his new parish in London with a youthful exuberance and high expectations. 300m; DVD, CC. **A:** Adult. **P:** Entertainment. **U:** Home. **Mov-Ent:** Television, Comedy-Drama. **Acq:** Purchase. **Dist:** Warner Home Video, Inc. $39.98.

Ballykissangel 2 1997
Father Peter Clifford rises to every challenge as he struggles to save parishioners' souls and not lose his own heart to the local barmaid. 400m; DVD, CC. **A:** Adult. **P:** Entertainment. **U:** Home. **Mov-Ent:** Television, Comedy-Drama. **Acq:** Purchase. **Dist:** Warner Home Video, Inc. $39.98.

Ballykissangel: Series 3 1997
Features the third season of the 1996-2001 British television dramatic comedy series about a young priest, Peter Clifford (Tompkinson), who wins over the interesting residents of the town of Ballykissangel, Ireland. Niamh (Kellegher) and Ambrose (Peter Hanly) have their baby in a car; Peter shares his feelings for Assumpta (Kirwan); Assumpta surprises Peter when she gets married; and a tragic accident causes Peter to leave forever. 11 episodes. 600m; DVD. **C:** Stephen Tompkinson; Frankie McCafferty; Joe Savino; Tina Kellegher; Dervla Kirwan; Deirdre Donnelly; Gary Whelan. **A:** Primary-Adult. **P:** Entertainment. **U:** Home. **Mov-Ent:** Television Series, Comedy-Drama, Religion. **Acq:** Purchase. **Dist:** Warner Home Video, Inc. $49.98.

Ballykissangel: Series 4 1998
Features the fourth season of the 1996-2001 British television dramatic comedy series about a new young priest, Father Aidan (Wycherley), and the interesting residents of the town of Ballykissangel, Ireland. Aidan takes over once Father Peter Clifford (Tompkinson) leaves; Sean Dillon (Cranitch) returns to the town after two decades; and Brian (Doyle) buys the pub after Assumpta's death and has Niamh (Kellegher) run it. Colin Farrell also has a supporting role. 12 episodes. 600m; DVD. **C:** Don Wycherley; Lorcan Cranitch; Frankie McCafferty; Joe Savino; Deirdre Donnelly; Tina Kellegher; Gary Whelan; Tony Doyle. **A:** Primary-Adult. **P:** Entertainment. **U:** Home. **Mov-Ent:** Television Series, Comedy-Drama, Religion. **Acq:** Purchase. **Dist:** Warner Home Video, Inc. $49.99.

Ballykissangel: Series 5 1999
Features the fifth season of the 1996-2001 British television dramatic comedy series about a new priest, Father Aidan (Wycherley), and the interesting residents of the town of Ballykissangel, Ireland. Niamh (Kellegher) decides it's time to end her marriage to Ambrose (Peter Hanly) because of her love for Sean (Cranitch); Ambrose's attempt to help others leads him to a fatal fall; Niamh considers leaving Ballykissangel and Sean behind and Brian (Doyle) sells the pub; the Dooley family moves to town; Sean and Niamh get married and leave town. Colin Farrell also has a supporting role. 12 episodes. 560m; DVD. **C:** Don Wycherley; Lorcan Cranitch; Frankie McCafferty; Joe Savino; Deirdre Donnelly; Tina Kellegher; Gary Whelan; Tony Doyle. **A:** Primary-Adult. **P:** Entertainment. **U:** Home. **Mov-Ent:** Television Series, Comedy-Drama, Religion. **Acq:** Purchase. **Dist:** Warner Home Video, Inc. $49.99.

Ballykissangel: Series 6 2001
Features the final season of the 1996-2001 British television dramatic comedy series about a new priest, Father Vincent Sheahan (Taylor), and the interesting residents of the town of Ballykissangel, Ireland. Brian vanishes though his clothes are found folded on the beach and Vincent is caught drinking and driving. 8 episodes. 560m; DVD. **C:** Lorcan Cranitch; Frankie McCafferty; Joe Savino; Deirdre Donnelly; Tina Kellegher; Gary Whelan; Robert Taylor. **A:** Primary-Adult. **P:** Entertainment. **U:** Home. **Mov-Ent:** Television Series, Comedy-Drama, Religion. **Acq:** Purchase. **Dist:** $29.98.

Balseros 2005 (Unrated)
Documentary following the 1994 exodus of 50,000 people from Cuba to America on makeshift rafts, and their yearlong detainment at the Guantanamo Naval Base. 120m; DVD. **A:** Sr. High-Adult. **P:** Education. **U:** Home. **Gen-Edu:** Documentary Films, Refugees. **Acq:** Purchase. **Dist:** Docurama. $26.95.

Balthus at the Pompidou 1984
Renowned art authority Michael Peppiatt presents key Balthus paintings, drawings, and prints that have fascinated viewers through the years. 28m; VHS, 3/4 U, Special order formats. **C:** Directed by Paul Falkenberg; George Freedland. **Pr:** Hans Namuth; George Freedland; Paul Falkenberg; George Freedland. **A:** Sr. High-Adult. **P:** Education. **U:** Institution. **Fin-Art:** Painting, Art & Artists. **Acq:** Purchase, Rent/Lease. **Dist:** Museum of Modern Art.

Baltic Deputy 1937 (Unrated) — ★★★½
An early forerunner of Soviet historic realism, where an aging intellectual deals with post-revolution Soviet life. In Russian with subtitles. 95m/B/W; VHS, DVD, 3/4 U. **TV Std:** NTSC, PAL. **C:** Nikolai Cherkassov; Boris Livanov; Marta Domasheva; Oleg Zhakov; Directed by Yosif Heifitz; Iosif Kheifits; Alexander Zarkhi; Written by Iosif Kheifits; Alexander Zarkhi; Cinematography by Edgar Shtyrtskober; Music by Nikolai Timofeyev. **Pr:** Soviet Exportfilm. **A:** Sr. High-Adult. **P:** Entertainment. **U:** Home. **L:** Russian. **Mov-Ent:** Propaganda, USSR. **Acq:** Purchase. **Dist:** International Historic Films Inc. $35.95.

The Baltic Tragedy 194?
A documentary look, compiled from newsreels, of how the Baltic nations of Latvia, Lithuania, and Estonia witnessed some of the worst battles of the Second World War. (Two cassettes.) In German with English subtitles. 148m/B/W; VHS, 3/4 U. **TV Std:** NTSC, PAL. **A:** Jr. High-Adult. **P:** Education. **U:** Institution, Home. **L:** German. **Gen-Edu:** Documentary Films, World War Two. **Acq:** Purchase. **Dist:** International Historic Films Inc.; German Language Video Center. $49.95.

Baltimore & Ohio in Transition ????
The 1940s and 1950s in eastern Ohio is the scene, where the B&O transitions from steam to diesel engines. 60m; VHS, DVD. **A:** College-Adult. **P:** Education. **U:** Home. **Gen-Edu:** Trains. **Acq:** Purchase. **Dist:** The Civil War Standard. $24.95.

Baltimore & Ohio Steam ????
Watch 267 run-by and pacing scenes of the Baltimore & Ohio (B&O) line's steam engines. 90m; VHS. **A:** College-Adult. **P:** Education. **U:** Home. **Gen-Edu:** Trains. **Acq:** Purchase. **Dist:** The Civil War Standard. $39.95.

The Baltimore Bullet 1980 (PG) — ★★
Two men make their living traveling through the country as pool hustlers, bilking would-be pool sharks. Features ten of the greatest pool players in the world. 103m; VHS. **C:** James Coburn; Omar Sharif; Bruce Boxleitner; Ronee Blakley; Jack O'Halloran; Directed by Robert Ellis Miller; Written by Robert Vincent O'Neil; John F. Brascia. **Pr:** Avco Embassy. **A:** Jr. High-Adult. **P:** Entertainment. **U:** Home. **Mov-Ent:** Action-Adventure. **Acq:** Purchase. **Dist:** New Line Home Video. $9.98.

The Baltimore Clipper 197?
Documentary on the Baltimore Clipper, one of the most significant vessels in the development of the American shipping industry. 30m; VHS, 3/4 U. **C:** Hosted by Bob Callahan. **Pr:** Maryland Center for Public Broadcasting. **A:** Family. **P:** Education. **U:** Institution, CCTV, CATV, BCTV. **Gen-Edu:** Boating. **Acq:** Purchase, Rent/Lease. **Dist:** Maryland Public Television.

Baltimore Colts: Glory Days of Yesteryear 1964, 1965, 1968, 1970 1985
A compilation of highlights from The Colts 1964, 1965, 1968, and 1970 seasons. 140m; VHS. **Pr:** NFL Films. **A:** Family. **P:** Entertainment. **U:** Home. **Spo-Rec:** Football. **Acq:** Purchase. **Dist:** NFL Films Video. $19.98.

Baltimore Orioles Legends: Cal Ripken, Jr. Collector's Edition 20??
Presents the A&E cable channel special on Baltimore Oriole shortstop Cal Ripken, Jr., best known for playing in 2,632 consecutive major league games, breaking Lou Gehrig's streak, during his time with the club from 1981-2001. 912m; DVD. **A:** Family. **P:** Entertainment. **U:** Home, CATV. **Spo-Rec:** Television Series, Documentary Films, Biography: Sports. **Acq:** Purchase. **Dist:** A&E Television Networks L.L.C. $59.95.

Baltimore Orioles: Team Highlights 1984
Highlights from the Baltimore Orioles four successful early '80s seasons. 30m; VHS. **Pr:** Major League Baseball Productions. **A:** Family. **P:** Entertainment. **U:** Institution, Home, SURA. **Spo-Rec:** Baseball. **Acq:** Purchase. **Dist:** Major League Baseball Productions, On Moratorium.
Indiv. Titles: 1. 1981: Oriole Magic 2. 1982: Something Magic Happened 3. 1983: O's What A Feeling 4. 1984: A Winning Tradition.

Baltimore Orioles: Vintage World Series Films 20??
Presents the A&E cable channel special on the Baltimore Orioles during their many successful years from 1966 to 1983, which brought them three World Series titles, three more World Series appearances, and two other American League Championship Series appearances; features clips on managers Hank Bauer, Earl Weaver, and Joe Altobelli along with players Frankie Robinson and Jim Palmer. 178m; DVD. **A:** Family. **P:** Entertainment. **U:** Home, CATV. **Spo-Rec:** Television Series, Documentary Films, Biography: Sports. **Acq:** Purchase. **Dist:** A&E Television Networks L.L.C. $19.95.

Balto 1995 (G) — ★★½
Animated adventure, based on a true story, of a half-husky, half-wolf sled dog, Balto, who faces overwhelming odds to bring life-saving medicine to Nome, Alsaka. It's 1925, there's a diptheria epidemic, and Balto is the lead team dog on the final leg of the race to get the serum to Nome in time. Balto and the rest of the team dogs became instant heroes and even journeyed to Hollywood to star in their own silent film "Balto's Race to Nome." 78m; VHS, DVD, CC. **C:** Voice(s) by Kevin Bacon; Bob Hoskins; Bridget Fonda; Jim (Jonah) Cummings; Phil Collins; Juliette Brewer; Danny Mann; Miriam Margolyes; Directed by Simon Wells; Written by Cliff Ruby; Elana Lesser; David Steven Cohen; Roger S.H. Schulman; Music by James Horner. **Pr:** Stephen Hickner; Steven Spielberg; Kathleen Kennedy; Bonne Radford; Amblin Entertainment; Universal Pictures. **A:** Family. **P:** Entertainment. **U:** Home. **Mov-Ent:** Animation & Cartoons, Pets, Arctic Regions. **Acq:** Purchase. **Dist:** Universal Music and Video Distribution. $19.98.

Balto 2: Wolf Quest 2002 (G)
Balto's daughter is ashamed of her half-canine/half-wolf heritage and sets off on her own adventures to discover her identity and come to terms with her family. 74m; DVD, CC. **C:** Voice(s) by Lacey Chabert; Maurice LaMarche; Jodi Benson; David Carradine; Mark Hamill; Directed by Phil Weinstein. **A:** Family. **P:** Entertainment. **U:** Home. **Chl-Juv:** Animation & Cartoons. **Acq:** Purchase. **Dist:** Universal Studios Home Video.

Balzac: A Life of Passion 1999 (Unrated) — ★★★
Bio of French writer Honore de Balzac (1799-1850)?a larger-then-life figure played by the larger-than-life Depardieu. He has mom problems (she never loved him) and turns to women who encourage him as his writing consumes him. There are balls and duels and all sorts of high and low society life during the Napoleonic era to enjoy. French with subtitles. 210m; VHS, DVD. **C:** Gerard Depardieu; Jeanne Moreau; Fanny Ardant; Virna Lisi; Katja Riemann; Claude Rich; Directed by Josee Dayan; Written by Didier Decoin; Cinematography by Willy Stassen; Music by Bruno Coulais. **A:** College-Adult. **P:** Entertainment. **U:** Home. **L:** French. **Mov-Ent. Acq:** Purchase. **Dist:** Wellspring Media.

Balzac and the Little Chinese Seamstress 2002 (Unrated) — ★★
Sijie dreamily adapts his own autobiographical novel depicting life in a remote Chinese mountain village in 1971. City boys Luo (Chen) and Ma (Liu) are sent to be re-educated under Mao's Cultural Revolution. The young men perform manual labor under the watchful eyes of the village chief (Wang) and both become attracted to the nameless young woman (Zhou) of the title, reading to her from a secreted cache of Western books (including Balzac, Flaubert, and Dumas) and teaching her to read and write. There is eventual separation and loss and an abrupt epilogue that shows the men 20 years later wondering whatever happened to the girl they once knew. Mandarin and French with subtitles. 111m; DVD. **C:** Liu Ye; Hongwei Wang; Ziiou Xun; Chen Kun; Wang Shuangbao; Chung Zhijun; Directed by Dai Sijie; Written by Dai Sijie; Nadine Perront; Cinematography by Jean-Marie Dreujou; Music by Wang Pujian. **Pr:** Lise Fayolle; TF-1 Films; Bac Distribution. **A:** Jr. High-Adult. **P:** Entertainment. **U:** Home. **L:** Chinese, French. **Mov-Ent:** Biography: Politics, China, Drama. **Acq:** Purchase. **Dist:** Movies Unlimited. $24.29.

Bam Bam & Celeste 2005 (Unrated) — ★★★
Margaret Cho's screenplay features herself as Celeste, a social outcast on a quest to win a makeover on "Trading Faces," a popular show filmed in New York. On the road trip from Illinois to the Big Apple with her gay hairdresser, boyfriend/buddy Bam Bam (Daniels), the pair encounter offbeat characters and situations and a showdown with their high school rivals, while discovering beauty is more than skin deep. Cheeky, loose, cry-while-you're-laughing entertainment. 85m; DVD. **C:** Margaret Cho; Bruce Daniels; Alan Cumming; Elaine Hendrix; Jane Lynch; John Cho; Wilson Cruz; Kathy Najimy; Butch Klein; Directed by Lorene Machado; Written by Margaret Cho; Cinematography by Matthew Clark; Music by Pat Irwin. **P:** Entertainment. **U:** Home. **Mov-Ent. Acq:** Purchase. **Dist:** Wolfe Video.

Bamako 2006 (Unrated) — ★★
Didactic drama that pits African debt against the International Monetary Fund (IMF) and the World Bank. A makeshift courtroom is set up in the courtyard of Mele (Maiga) and Chaka's (Traore) home in a poor section of Bamako. Because of international monetary policies, African nations are in serious debt and cannot meet their obligations to their own people while paying exorbitant interest rates. Lawyers listen to witness testimony while life goes on around them. It's important, but most Westerners will probably go "huh?" French and Bambara with subtitles. 115m; DVD. **C:** Aissa Maiga; Maimouna Helene Diarra; Tiecoura Traore; Habib Dembele; Directed by Abderrahmane Sissako; Written by Abderrahmane Sissako; Cinematography by Jacques Besse. **Pr:** Denis Freyd; Abderrahmane Sissako; Archipel 33; Chinguitty Films; Mali Images; New Yorker Films. **A:** College-Adult. **P:** Entertainment. **U:** Home. **L:** French. **Mov-Ent:** Africa, Finance. **Acq:** Purchase. **Dist:** New Yorker Video.

Bamako Sigi-kan 2002 (Unrated)
Arthur Jafa's documentary examines the evolution of democracy in Mali and the changes imposed in the city and its society as revealed by the tales of some citizens. 76m; VHS, DVD. **A:** Adult. **P:** Education. **U:** Institution. **Gen-Edu:** Africa, Politics & Government. **Acq:** Purchase. **Dist:** Third World Newsreel. $225.

Bambi 1942 (G) — ★★★★
A true Disney classic, detailing the often harsh education of a newborn deer and his friends in the forest. Proves that Disney animation was—and still is—the best to be found. Thumper still steals the show and the music is delightful, including "Let's Sing a Gay Little Spring Song," "Love is a Song," "Little April Shower," "The Thumper Song," and "Twitterpated." Stands as one of the greatest children's films of all time; a genuine perennial from generation to generation. Based very loosely on the book by Felix Salten. 69m; VHS, DVD, Blu-Ray, CC. **C:** Voice(s) by Bobby Stewart; Peter Behn; Stan Alexander; Cammie King; Donnie Dunagan; Hardie Albright; John Sutherland; Tim Davis; Sam Edwards; Sterling Holloway; Ann Gillis; Perce Pearce; Directed by David Hand; Written by Larry Morey; Music by Frank Churchill; Edward Plumb. **Pr:** Walt Disney Studios. **A:** Family. **P:** Entertainment. **U:** Home. **L:** English, French. **Mov-Ent:** Animation & Cartoons, Family Viewing, Classic Films. **Awds:** Natl. Film Reg. '11. **Acq:** Purchase. **Dist:** Walt Disney Studios Home Entertainment. $26.99.

Bambi II 2006 (G) — ★★½
The sequel might not be up to the standards of the original but it will keep the tykes occupied. Bambi's dad, the Great Prince, takes over the raising of his fawn when mom gets killed but he's having a tough time. Still, Bambi tries his best to learn despite clumsiness and teasing with some help from his pals Thumper and Flower. 72m; DVD, Blu-Ray. **C:** Voice(s) by Patrick Stewart; Alexander Gould; Brendon Baerg; Nicky Jones; Directed by Brian Pimental; Written by Alicia Kirk; Music by Bruce Broughton. **A:** Family. **P:** Entertainment. **U:** Home. **Mov-Ent:** Animals, Forests & Trees. **Acq:** Purchase. **Dist:** Buena Vista Home Entertainment.

Bambi Meets Godzilla 1969 — ★★½
A spoof on endless film credits, after which the title bout lasts about six seconds. Must be seen to be appreciated. 2m/B/W; VHS. **C:** Directed by Marv Newland; Written by Marv Newland; Cinematography by Marv Newland. **Pr:** Marv Newland. **A:** Family. **P:** Entertainment. **U:** Institution, Home, SURA. **Mov-Ent:** Animation & Cartoons, Satire & Parody, Cult Films. **Acq:** Purchase, Rent/Lease, Duplication License. **Dist:** Pyramid Media. $9.95.

Bambi Meets Godzilla and Other Weird Cartoons 1987
Bambi meets Godzilla, plus many classic animated shorts, including "Crazy Town" with Betty Boop, and Max Fleischer creations. 30m/B/W; VHS. **Pr:** Marv Newland. **A:** Sr. High-Adult. **P:** Entertainment. **U:** Home. **Mov-Ent:** Animation & Cartoons, Comedy--Black. **Acq:** Purchase. **Dist:** Rhino Entertainment Co. $9.95.

Bambinger 1989
A bond grows between a 12-year-old boy and a Jewish refugee during WWII, in this film based on a short story by Mordecai Richler. 24m; VHS, 3/4 U. **A:** Jr. High-Adult. **P:** Education. **U:** Institution, SURA. **Gen-Edu:** World War Two. **Acq:** Purchase, Rent/Lease. **Dist:** National Film Board of Canada.

Bambole 1965 (Unrated) — ★½
Silly Italian sex farce with four sixties beauties in four separate, not very interesting stories from four different directors. Italian with subtitles. 109m/B/W; DVD. **C:** Virna Lisi; Monica Vitti; Elke Sommer; Gina Lollobrigida; Nino Manfredi; Jean Sorel; Akim Tamiroff; Directed by Mauro Bolognini; Luigi Comencini; Dino Risi; Franco Rossi; Written by Rodolfo Sonego; Cinematography by Leonida Barboni; Ennio Guarnieri; Music by Armando Trovajoli. **A:** Adult. **P:** Entertainment. **U:** Home. **L:** Italian. **Mov-Ent:** Italy, Sex & Sexuality, Women. **Acq:** Purchase. **Dist:** Sony Pictures Home Entertainment Inc.

Bamboo 1992
The story of bamboo, one of the world's most versatile materials. Numerous applications make this one of the most useful products known to man. Long known in Asia for its practical uses, see how modern civilization in the East benefits from bamboo today. 58m; VHS, SVS, 3/4 U, Special order formats. **Pr:** Lucerne Media. **A:** Primary-Jr. High. **P:** Education. **U:** Institution. **Gen-Edu:** Education, Economics, Plants. **Acq:** Purchase, Rent/Lease, Duplication License. **Dist:** Lucerne Media. $350.00.

The Bamboo Blonde 1946 (Unrated) — ★★½
Wartime romance in which nightclub singer Louise (Langford) meets cute with B-29 pilot Patrick (Wade). She gives him her photograph and when he heads to Saipan, his bomber crew decides to paint Louise's picture on the nose of their plane for good luck. When the crew starts sinking Japanese ships and shooting down Zeros, the "Bamboo Blonde" becomes famous and Eddie (Edwards), the huckster club owner who employs Louise, gets rich by exploiting that fact. Told in flashbacks. 67m/B/W; DVD. **C:** Frances Langford; Ralph Edwards; Russell Wade; Iris Adrian; Jane Greer; Richard Martin; Paul Harvey; Directed by Anthony Mann. **A:** Jr. High-Adult. **P:** Entertainment. **U:** Home. **Mov-Ent:** World War Two, Aeronautics, Nightclubs. **Acq:** Purchase. **Dist:** WarnerArchive.com.

The Bamboo Saucer 1968 — ★½
Russian and American scientists race to find a U.F.O. in Red China. 103m; DVD, Blu-Ray. **C:** Dan Duryea; John Ericson; Lois Nettleton; Nan Leslie; Directed by Frank Telford; Written by Frank Telford; John P. Fulton; Cinematography by Hal Mohr; Music by Nicholas Carras; Edward Paul. **Pr:** NTA. **A:** Jr. High-Adult. **P:** Entertainment. **U:** Home. **Mov-Ent:** Science Fiction. **Acq:** Purchase. **Dist:** Olive Films. $19.98.

Bamboozled 2000 (R) — ★★½
Spike Lee aims for controversy once again as he criticizes Hollywood's portrayal of African-Americans as well as pointing the finger at the black community's complicity in the process. Fed-up black writer Pierre Delacroix (Wayans) comes up with a series idea for a fledgling TV network as a form of protest—a modern day minstrel show complete with performers in burnt

cork blackface. Fully expecting the show to fail, he hires struggling street performers Manray (Glover) and Womack (Davidson), changing their names to Mantan and Sleep 'N Eat (a reference to '30s and '40s black actors Mantan Moreland and Stepin Fetchit). The show becomes a surprise hit but also riles a militant black group, resulting in chaos in the lives of Delacroix and his assistant Sloan (Pinkett). The feel of the movie sways toward melodrama halfway through, but the wry observations of the artistic treatment of AfricanAmericans ring eerily true. Don't say it couldn't happen these days. 135m; VHS, DVD, Wide, CC. **C:** Damon Wayans; Jada Pinkett Smith; Savion Glover; Tommy Davidson; Michael Rapaport; Thomas Jefferson Byrd; Paul Mooney; Susan Batson; Mos Def; Sarah Jones; Gillian Iliana Waters; Directed by Spike Lee; Written by Spike Lee; Cinematography by Ellen Kuras; Music by Terence Blanchard. **A:** Sr. High-Adult. **P:** Entertainment. **U:** Home. **Mov-Ent**: Black Culture, Satire & Parody. **Acq:** Purchase. **Dist:** New Line Home Video.

Banacek: The 2nd Season 1973
Self-made Boston millionaire Thomas Banacek (George Peppard) recovers stolen items for insurance companies with the help of his chauffer Jay (Ralph Manza) and bibliophile/bookstore owner buddy Felix Mulholland (Murray Matheson). 8 episodes. 576m; DVD. **C:** George Peppard; Ralph Manza; Murray Matheson. **A:** Adult. **P:** Entertainment. **U:** Home. **Mov-Ent**: Drama, Mystery & Suspense. **Acq:** Purchase. **Dist:** Virgil Films & Entertainment.

Banacek: The Complete Series 1972 (Unrated)
Television dramedy series on NBC from 1972-1974. George Peppard is Thomas Banacek, a private investigator in Boston who helps break cases other area insurance investigators can't, such as missing amored car filled with gold in "Detour to Nowhere," the disappearance of a revolutionary new car prototype in "Project Phoenix," a priceless book in"Ten Thousand Dollars a Page," and a prototype engine taken from a tradeshow floor in "Rocket to Oblivion." Stephanie Powers, Margot Kidder, Michael Lerner, Brenda Vaccaro, Victoria Principal and a host of others guest star in this classic detective series. 16 episodes. 1276m; DVD. **A:** Sr. High-Adult. **P:** Entertainment. **U:** Home. **Mov-Ent**: Drama, Television Series. **Acq:** Purchase. **Dist:** Virgil Films & Entertainment.

Banacek: The First Season 1972
Includes the debut television season of the crime-fighting efforts of insurance investigator Thomas Banacek (Peppard) as he gets richly paid to locate others stolen property with the aide of smart-aleck chauffeur Jay (Manza) and bookstore owner Felix (Matheson). 8 episodes. 576m; DVD. **C:** George Peppard; Ralph Manza; Murray Matheson. **A:** Jr. High-Adult. **P:** Entertainment. **U:** Home. **Mov-Ent**: Television Series, Action-Adventure. **Acq:** Purchase. **Dist:** Virgil Films & Entertainment. $29.95.

Banana, Banana, Banana Slugs 1988
This film introduces children to an animal usually overlooked in nature studies: the slug, the shell-less snail. Youngsters on a walk in California's redwood forests share their feelings on encountering this unusual animal. 9m; VHS, 3/4 U. **Pr:** Education for Management. **A:** Primary. **P:** Education. **U:** Institution, Home, SURA. **Chl-Juv**: Science. **Acq:** Purchase, Duplication License. **Dist:** Bullfrog Films, Inc.

Banana Company 1984
A look at the working conditions of banana companies in Nicaragua. 15m; 3/4 U. **Pr:** Nicaraguan Film Institute. **A:** Sr. High-Adult. **P:** Education. **U:** Institution, SURA. **Gen-Edu**: Central America. **Acq:** Purchase. **Dist:** First Run/Icarus Films.

Banana Cop 1984 (Unrated) — ★
A spoof of Anglo-Chinese identity and detective films. An Asian Scotland Yard inspector (dressed in tweeds), investigating a killing in Chinatown, recruits his unlikely partner in Hong Kong. In Cantonese with English subtitles. 96m; VHS. **C:** George Lam; Teddy Robin Kwan; Directed by Po-Chih Leung. **A:** Sr. High-Adult. **P:** Entertainment. **U:** Home. **L:** English, Chinese. **Mov-Ent**: Comedy--Screwball. **Acq:** Purchase. **Dist:** Facets Multimedia Inc. $49.95.

Banana Fever 1975
An "invisible thing" sneaks up in the night, arranges a clump of bananas in rectangular array, and steals off with the largest proper divisor. If there are 15 bananas, 5 disappear; 12 bananas, 6 disappear. Part of "Math That Counts" series. 11m; VHS, 3/4 U. **Pr:** Davidson Films. **A:** Primary. **P:** Education. **U:** Institution, SURA. **Chl-Juv**: Mathematics. **Acq:** Purchase, Rent/Lease, Trade-in. **Dist:** Encyclopedia Britannica.

Banana Split 19??
Answers questions for people who are the product of biracial heritage and addresses the problem America faces with its definitions of race and ethnicity. The filmaker uses humor and his own experiences to bring awareness to this diffcult subject matter. 38m; VHS. **A:** Sr. High-Adult. **P:** Education. **U:** Home. **Gen-Edu**: Prejudice, Human Relations, Ethnicity. **Acq:** Purchase, Rent/Lease. **Dist:** Third World Newsreel. $175.00.

The Banana Splits and Friends 1968
Four large furry creatures, the Banana Splits, perform their slapstick antics and present cartoons. 59m; VHS. **Pr:** Hanna-Barbera Productions. **A:** Family. **P:** Entertainment. **U:** Home. **Mov-Ent**: Animation & Cartoons, Television Series, Family Viewing. **Acq:** Purchase. **Dist:** Turner Broadcasting System Inc. $19.95.

The Banana Verdict 2000
Documentary of the international banana trade. Raises issues of environmental and worker safety, labor unions, management, and business concerns. 50m; VHS. **A:** Adult. **P:** Education. **U:** Home. **Gen-Edu**: Documentary Films, Food Industry, Agriculture. **Acq:** Purchase, Rent/Lease. **Dist:** Filmakers Library Inc. $350.

Bananarama: And That's Not All. . . 1984
The harmonious female new wave trio's conglomeration of videos and performances, including "Robert DeNiro's Waiting," "Really Say Something," "Shy Boy," "Na Na Hey Hey Kiss Him Goodbye" and more. 35m; VHS. **Pr:** Polygram Music Video. **A:** Family. **P:** Entertainment. **U:** Home. **Mov-Ent**: Music--Performance, Music Video. **Acq:** Purchase. **Dist:** Music Video Distributors. $14.95.

Bananarama: The Greatest Hits Collection 1989
The singing trio's greatest video hits include "Robert De Niro's Waiting," "Cruel Summer," "Venus," "I Heard a Rumor," and more. 40m; VHS. **Pr:** Polygram Music Video. **A:** Jr. High-Adult. **P:** Entertainment. **U:** Home. **Mov-Ent**: Music Video. **Acq:** Purchase. **Dist:** Music Video Distributors. $19.98.

Bananarama: True Confessions 1989
This four clip compilation includes "Venus," "More than Physcial," "Do Not Disturb" and "Trick of the Night." 15m; VHS. **A:** Jr. High-College. **P:** Entertainment. **U:** Home. **Mov-Ent**: Music Video. **Acq:** Purchase. **Dist:** Music Video Distributors. $14.95.

Bananas 1971 (PG-13) — ★★★
Intermittently hilarious pre-"Annie Hall" Allen fare is full of the director's signature angst-ridden philosophical comedy. A frustrated product tester from New York runs off to South America, where he volunteers his support to the revolutionary force of a shaky Latin-American dictatorship and winds up the leader. Don't miss an early appearance by Stallone. Witty score contributes much. 82m; VHS, DVD, Wide. **C:** Woody Allen; Louise Lasser; Carlos Montalban; Howard Cosell; Charlotte Rae; Conrad Bain; Allen Garfield; Sylvester Stallone; Directed by Woody Allen; Written by Woody Allen; Mickey Rose; Cinematography by Andrew M. Costikyan; Music by Marvin Hamlisch. **Pr:** Jack Grossberg; United Artists; Rollins Jaffe. **A:** Jr. High-Adult. **P:** Entertainment. **U:** Home. **Mov-Ent**: Satire & Parody, South America. **Acq:** Purchase. **Dist:** MGM Home Entertainment; Facets Multimedia Inc. $14.95.

Bananas Boat 1978 (Unrated) — **Bomb!**
A captain takes a man and his daughter away from the collapsing government of their banana republic. The cast and director take a few risks but fail in this would-be comedy. 91m; VHS. **C:** Doug McClure; Hayley Mills; Lionel Jeffries; Dilys Hamlett; Warren Mitchell; Directed by Sidney Hayers. **A:** Adult. **P:** Entertainment. **U:** Home. **Mov-Ent**: Action-Adventure. **Acq:** Purchase. **Dist:** VCI Entertainment. $79.95.

A Band Called Death 2013 (Unrated) — ★★★
In much the same vein as the Oscar-winning "Searching for Sugar Man," this punk roc doc offers hope that creativity and staying true to one's personal vision will someday lead to success. In the early '70s, before The Ramones and The Sex Pistols, three brothers from Detroit were revolutionizing rock in a punk style. With the name Death, fame eluded them (and their leader refused to change it) until their demos were found decades later and a new generation gave them the artistic credit they always deserved. Fun, poignant, and inspirational, pic captures the timeless power of passionate creativity. 96m; DVD, Blu-Ray. **C:** Directed by Mark Christopher Covino; Jeff Howlett; Cinematography by Mark Christopher Covino; Music by Tim Boland; Sam Retzer. **Pr:** Mark Christopher Covino; Jeff Howlett; Drafthouse Films. **A:** Sr. High-Adult. **P:** Entertainment. **U:** Home. **L:** English. **Mov-Ent**: Documentary Films, Music. **Acq:** Purchase.

The Band Director 198?
This program features the preparations of the University of Michigan Marching Band for appearances at Disneyland, the Tournament of Roses and the Rose Bowl in Pasadena, California. 33m; 3/4 U, Special order formats. **Pr:** Michigan Media. **A:** Jr. High-Adult. **P:** Education. **U:** Institution, CCTV, CATV, BCTV. **Gen-Edu**. **Acq:** Purchase, Rent/Lease. **Dist:** Cambridge Educational.

The Band: Japan Tour '83 1983
The Band performs 22 songs including "Milk Cow Boogie," "King Harvest," "Rag Mama Rag," and "Up on Cripple Creek" live from Tokyo on a reunion tour. 120m; VHS. **A:** Jr. High-Adult. **P:** Entertainment. **U:** Home. **Mov-Ent**: Music Video, Music--Performance. **Acq:** Purchase. **Dist:** Music Video Distributors. $54.95.

Band of Angels 1957 — ★★½
Orphaned Amantha (De Carlo) learns she has African-American blood and since it's the pre-Civil War era she promptly winds up on the auction block. She becomes both the property and the mistress of mysterious New Orleans landowner Hamish Bond (Gable). Then the Civil War comes along bringing threats and revelations. De Carlo looks properly sultry but this is a weak attempt at costume drama. Based on the novel by Robert Penn Warren. 127m; VHS, DVD. **C:** Clark Gable; Yvonne De Carlo; Sidney Poitier; Efrem Zimbalist, Jr.; Rex Reason; Patric Knowles; Torin Thatcher; Andrea King; Ray Teal; Directed by Raoul Walsh; Written by John Twist; Ivan Goff; Music by Max Steiner. **Pr:** Warner Bros. **A:** Jr. High-Adult. **P:** Entertainment. **U:** Home. **Mov-Ent**: Drama, Civil War, Slavery. **Acq:** Purchase. **Dist:** Movies Unlimited; Warner Home Video, Inc. $29.99.

Band of Brothers 2001 — ★★★½
Steven Spielberg and Tom Hanks executive produced this excellent adaptation of Stephen Ambrose's epic tale of the 101 Airborne's Easy Company as they made their way from D-Day through the capture of Hitler's "Eagle's Nest" compound. Although uniformly showing the influence of "Saving Private Ryan," each episode focuses on a separate sub-theme or character while not losing sight of the big-picture depth. Some characters are given short shrift, and sometimes it's hard to tell which characters lived or died during a battle, but that's a minor quibble with such a large and, in most cases, unknown, cast. Although they're young and mostly anonymous, they do give excellent, and in some cases, breakout performances. The battle scenes are bracing, harrowing, and well-constructed, and the quiet moments serve to underscore the bond that develops between the men as they become battle tested. 600m; VHS, DVD, Blu-Ray. **C:** Eion Bailey; Jamie Bamber; Michael Cudlitz; Dale Dye; Scott Grimes; Frank John Hughes; Ron Livingston; James Madio; Neal McDonough; Rene L. Moreno; David Schwimmer; Donnie Wahlberg; Colin Hanks; Marc Warren; Damian Lewis; Kirk Acevedo; Rick Gomez; Richard Speight, Jr.; Jimmy Fallon; Ian Virgo; Thomas Hardy; Directed by David Frankel; Tom Hanks; Richard Loncraine; Phil Alden Robinson; Mikael Salomon; David Nutter; David Leland; Tony To; Written by Tom Hanks; E. Max Frye; Erik Jendresen; Bruce McKenna; Graham Yost; Stephen E. Ambrose; Erik Bork; John Orloff; Cinematography by Remi Adefarasin; Music by Michael Kamen. **A:** Sr. High-Adult. **P:** Entertainment. **U:** Home. **Mov-Ent**: World War Two, Basic Training/Boot Camp. **Acq:** Purchase. **Dist:** Movies Unlimited; Alpha Video; Home Box Office Inc.
Indiv. Titles: 1. Currahee 2. Day of Days 3. Carentan 4. Replacements 5. Crossroads 6. Bastogne 7. The Breaking Point 8. The Patrol 9. Why We Fight 10. Points.

Band of Gold 1995 — ★★★
Unflinching British miniseries follows the lives of Yorkshire prostitutes Rosie (James), Carol (Tyson), and Gina (Gemmell). They try to survive the streets of Bradford while a serial killer is targeting the local hookers. On six cassettes. 312m; VHS, DVD. **C:** Geraldine James; Cathy Tyson; Ruth Gemmell; Barbara Dickson; David Schofield; Richard Moore; Rachel Davies; Samantha Morton; Directed by Richard Standeven; Richard Laxton; Written by Kay Mellor; Cinematography by Peter Jessop; Music by Hal Lindes. **Pr:** Granada Television International Ltd. **A:** Sr. High-Adult. **P:** Entertainment. **U:** Home. **Mov-Ent**: Prostitution, Great Britain, TV Movies. **Acq:** Purchase. **Dist:** Entertainment One US LP.

Band of Outsiders 1964 (Unrated) — ★★½
A woman hires a pair of petty criminals to rip off her aunt; Godard vehicle for expousing self-reflexive comments on modern film culture. In French with English subtitles. 97m/B/W; VHS, DVD, Blu-Ray. **C:** Sami Frey; Anna Karina; Claude Brasseur; Louisa Colpeyn; Directed by Jean-Luc Godard; Written by Jean-Luc Godard; Cinematography by Raoul Coutard; Music by Michel Legrand. **Pr:** Jean-Luc Godard; Jean-Luc Godard. **A:** Sr. High-Adult. **P:** Entertainment. **U:** Home. **L:** French. **Mov-Ent**: Comedy-Drama, Film--Avant-Garde. **Acq:** Purchase. **Dist:** Hen's Tooth Video; Criterion Collection Inc.; Facets Multimedia Inc.

The Band of the Grenadier Guards: Sousa Marches 2007 (Unrated)
Britain's Band of the Grenadier Guards performs a live tribute to John Philip Sousa. Also includes archival footage of Sousa directing. 83m; DVD. **A:** Sr. High-Adult. **P:** Entertainment. **U:** Home. **Gen-Edu**: Music, Music--Performance. **Acq:** Purchase. **Dist:** Kultur International Films Ltd., Inc. $19.99.

Band of the Hand 1986 (R) — ★
A "Miami Vice" type melodrama about five convicts who are trained to become an unstoppable police unit. The first feature film by Glaser, last seen as Starsky in "Starsky & Hutch." 109m; VHS, DVD. **C:** Stephen Lang; Michael Carmine; Lauren Holly; Leon Robinson; Directed by Paul Michael Glaser; Written by Jack Baran; Leo Garen. **Pr:** Tri-Star Pictures. **A:** Sr. High-Adult. **P:** Entertainment. **U:** Home. **Mov-Ent**. **Acq:** Purchase. **Dist:** Movies Unlimited. $21.24.

Band Together at CBGB's 1986
Live performances by Rest in Pieces, Warzone, Ludichrist, Bedlam, Straight Ahead, Ed Gein's Car, and Far Back Deep at CBGB's in New York City. 120m; VHS. **A:** Jr. High-Adult. **P:** Entertainment. **U:** Home. **Mov-Ent**: Music Video. **Acq:** Purchase. **Dist:** Music Video Distributors. $29.95.

The Band Wagon 1953 — ★★★
A Hollywood song-and-dance man finds trouble when he is persuaded to star in a Broadway musical. Charisse has been called Astaire's most perfect partner, perhaps by those who haven't seen Rogers. 112m; VHS, DVD. **C:** Fred Astaire; Cyd Charisse; Oscar Levant; Nanette Fabray; Jack Buchanan; Bobby Watson; Directed by Vincente Minnelli; Written by Betty Comden; Music by Arthur Schwartz; Howard Dietz. **Pr:** Arthur Freed; MGM. **A:** Family. **P:** Entertainment. **U:** Home. **Mov-Ent**: Musical--Drama, Romance, Dance. **Awds:** Natl. Film Reg. '95. **Acq:** Purchase. **Dist:** MGM Home Entertainment; Facets Multimedia Inc. $19.98.
Songs: That's Entertainment; Dancing in the Dark; By Myself; A Shine On Your Shoes; Something to Remember You By; High and Low; I Love Louisa; New Sun in the Sky; I Guess I'll Have to Change My Plan; Louisiana Hayride; Triplets; The Girl Hunt.

The Banda Brothers: Primavera 2013 (Unrated)
Live musical performance by brothers Ramon and Tony Banda. 49m; Blu-Ray. **A:** Family. **P:** Entertainment. **U:** Home. **L:** English. **Gen-Edu**: Music--Classical, Music--Performance. **Acq:** Purchase. **Dist:** AIX Media Group Inc. $34.99.

Banda Vallarta: Banda Vallarta Show 19??
Compilation of Ezequiel Pena & the Banda Vallarta's greatest hits including "Muevelo," "Con Musica de Banda," "Charanga Constena," and more. ?m; VHS. **A:** Jr. High-Adult. **P:** Entertainment. **U:** Home. **Mov-Ent**: Music Video, Music--Performance. **Acq:** Purchase. **Dist:** Music Video Distributors. $19.95.

Bandages 1983
This video covers bandages of all types. From the EMT video: group two series. 22m; VHS, 3/4 U. **Pr:** USAAHS. **A:** Adult. **P:** Instruction. **U:** Institution, SURA. **How-Ins:** First Aid. **Acq:** Purchase. **Dist:** National Audiovisual Center. $110.00.

Bandages: Wound to the Head 1983
This video demonstrates how to bandage a head wound. From the EMT video: group two series. 8m; VHS, 3/4 U. **Pr:** USAAHS. **A:** Adult. **P:** Instruction. **U:** Institution, SURA. **How-Ins:** First Aid, Head. **Acq:** Purchase. **Dist:** National Audiovisual Center. $80.00.

Bandh Darwaza 1990 (Unrated) — ★★½
A woman who desperately wishes to have a child visits the Black Mountain and conceives with the help of a monster who resembles a western vampire (Bandh Darwaza is often referred to as the Indian Dracula). She is told that if the child is female it must be given to the mountain, and the consequences will be horrible if she refuses. Of course it's a girl, and of course she refuses. Pic veers into musical dance numbers at random moments; it was one of the last films to come out of the late 1980s/early 1990s horror boom in India. 145m; DVD. **C:** Viyajendra Ghatge; Anirudh Agarwal; Beena Banerjee; Raza Murad; Aruna Irani; Kunika; Directed by Shyam Ramsay; Tulsi Ramsay; Written by Shyam Ramsay; Dev Kishan; Cinematography by Gangu Ramsay; Music by Anand Chitragupth; Milind Chitragupth. **A:** Sr. High-Adult. **P:** Entertainment. **U:** Home. **L:** English, Hindi. **Mov-Ent:** Horror, Drama, Musical. **Acq:** Purchase. **Dist:** Mondo Macabro.

Bandidas 2006 (PG-13) — ★★½
A New York bank wants to build a railroad line to Mexico, and decide the best way will be to buy up small banks in Mexico and evict anyone that owes the banks money. Opposing them is the daughter of one of the owners of the small banks, and a peasant woman who decide to become modern day Robin Hoods. Getting in their way of course is the fact that they've never robbed banks before. Considering that the guy sent from New York to take out the banks killed their father, they have some inspiration. 92m; DVD. **C:** Penelope Cruz; Salma Hayek; Steve Zahn; Dwight Yoakam; Denis Arndt; Audra Blaser; Sam Shepard; Ismael Carlo; Gary Cervantes; Jose Maria Negri; Lenny Zundel; Directed by Joachim Ronning; Espen Sandberg; Written by Luc Besson; Robert Mark Kamen; Cinematography by Thierry Arbogast; Music by Eric Serra. **A:** Sr. High-Adult. **P:** Entertainment. **U:** Home. **L:** English, Spanish. **Mov-Ent. Acq:** Purchase. **Dist:** Fox Home Entertainment. $14.98.

Bandit King of Texas 1949 — ★★½
A varmint is swindling unsuspecting settlers in a land scheme and then robbing and murdering them when they go to visit their supposed property. Rocky and friends come to the rescue. 60m/B/W; VHS, DVD, CC. **C:** Allan "Rocky" Lane; Eddy (Eddie, Ed) Waller; Helene Stanley; Robert Bice; Harry Lauter; Jim Nolan; John Hamilton; Lane Bradford; Directed by Fred Brannon; Written by Olive Cooper. **Pr:** Gordon Kay; Republic Pictures. **A:** Family. **P:** Entertainment. **U:** Home. **Mov-Ent:** Western. **Acq:** Purchase. **Dist:** Lions Gate Entertainment Inc.; Grapevine Video. $11.95.

The Bandit of Sherwood Forest 1946 (Unrated) — ★★½
Technicolor swashbuckler with Wilde properly athletic and dashing as the true lead in this Robin Hood story. An aged Robin Hood (Hicks), now the respectable Robert of Huntington, and his namesake son Robert (Wilde) join again with the merry men to prevent usurper William of Pembroke (Daniell) from seizing the throne of England after he imprisons the young king and revokes the Magna Carta. 86m; DVD. **C:** Cornel Wilde; Henry Daniell; Anita Louise; Russell Hicks; Jill Esmond; Edgar Buchanan; George Macready; John Abbott; Lloyd Corrigan; Ray Teal; Leslie Denison; Directed by George Sherman; Henry Levin; Written by Melvin Levy; Wilfred Pettitt; Cinematography by Gaetano Antonio "Tony" Gaudio; George Meehan; William E. Snyder; Music by Hugo Friedhofer. **A:** Family. **P:** Entertainment. **U:** Home. **Mov-Ent:** Great Britain. **Acq:** Purchase. **Dist:** Sony Pictures Home Entertainment Inc.

Bandit Queen 1951 (Unrated) — ★½
Spanish girl forms a band to stop seizure of Spanish possessions by lawless Californians. 71m/B/W; VHS. **C:** Barbara Britton; Willard Parker; Phillip Reed; Jack Perrin; Directed by William Berke. **Pr:** Lippert Productions. **A:** Family. **P:** Entertainment. **U:** Home. **Mov-Ent:** Western. **Acq:** Purchase. **Dist:** Rex Miller Artisan Studio.

Bandit Queen 1994 (Unrated) — ★★
Phoolan Devi (Biswas) is a female Robin Hood in modern-day India. A lower-caste woman, Devi is sold into marriage at 11, brutalized by her husband (and many others throughout the film), and eventually winds up with an equally brutal group of hill bandits. Only this time around, Devi takes action by aiding the group in robbing, kidnapping (and murdering) the rich and higher castes. Devi surrendered to authorities in 1983 and spent 11 years in jail. Based on screenwriter Sen's biography "India's Bandit Queen: The True Story of Phoolan Devi" and Devi's diaries. In Hindi with subtitles. 119m; VHS, DVD. **C:** Seema Biswas; Nirmal Pandey; Manoj Bajpai; Raghuvir Yadav; Rajesh Vivek; Govind Namdeo; Directed by Shekhar Kapur; Written by Mala Sen; Cinematography by Ashok Mehta; Music by Nusrat Fateh Ali Khan; Roger White. **Pr:** Sundeep S. Bedi; Film Four International; Kaleidoscope; Arrow Releasing. **A:** College-Adult. **P:** Entertainment. **U:** Home. **Mov-Ent:** Biography: Law Enforcement, Women, India. **Acq:** Purchase. **Dist:** Entertainment One US LP.

Bandit Ranger 1942 (Unrated) — ★½
Rancher Clay Travers is falsely accused of murdering Texas Ranger Frank Mattison. Crooked businessman Mark Kenyon gets rustler Ed Martin to cause more trouble and Clay has to clear his name and catch the real culprits. 58m/B/W; DVD. **C:** Tim Holt; Leroy Mason; Kenneth Harlan; Joan Barclay; Cliff Edwards; Glenn Strange; Directed by Lesley Selander; Written by Bennett Cohen; Morton Grant; Cinematography by Nicholas Musuraca. **A:** Jr. High-Adult. **P:** Entertainment. **U:** Home. **Mov-Ent:** Western. **Acq:** Purchase. **Dist:** WarnerArchive.com.

Bandit Trail 1941 (Unrated) — ★½
When his rancher father is killed over a crooked bank loan, Steve is persuaded by his outlaw uncle Red Haggerty to rob the bank in question. They plan another robbery in the next town and Steve is sent ahead to get inside info. He discovers crooked saloon owner Joel Nesbitt is also planning a heist but Steve has second thoughts when he falls for Ellen, the banker's daughter, and Uncle Red feels betrayed. 59m/B/W; DVD. **C:** Tim Holt; Morris Ankrum; Lee White; Ray Whitley; Roy Barcroft; Janet Waldo; J. Merrill Holmes; Eddy (Eddie, Ed) Waller; Glenn Strange; Frank Ellis; Directed by Edward Killy; Written by Norton S. Parker; Cinematography by Harry Wild. **A:** Jr. High-Adult. **P:** Entertainment. **U:** Home. **Mov-Ent:** Western. **Acq:** Purchase. **Dist:** WarnerArchive.com.

The Bandits 1967 (PG) — ★½
Three cowboys team up with a band of Mexican outlaws to find a traitor in the midst of the Mexican revolution. 83m; VHS. **C:** Robert Conrad; Jan-Michael Vincent; Roy Jenson; Manuel Lopez Ochoa; Directed by Robert Conrad; Alfredo Zacharias. **Pr:** Lone Star Pictures International. **A:** Jr. High-Adult. **P:** Entertainment. **U:** Home. **Mov-Ent:** Western. **Acq:** Purchase. **Dist:** $19.95.

Bandits 1986 (Unrated) — ★★½
Simon Verini (Yanne), a sophisticated fence, is given the loot from a $10 million Cartier heist to exchange for cash by Mozart (Bruel) the leader of the thieves. But two of Mozart's gang want to keep the jewels instead and kidnap Verini's wife as ransom. She's killed, even after he returns the goods, and Verini is then framed for the theft and spends 10 years in prison. He's sent his daughter Marie-Sophie to a Swiss boarding school and upon his release works to both establish a relationship with her and to find those responsible for his wife's death. Director Lelouch's wife portrays the adult Marie-Sophie. In French with English subtitles. 98m; VHS. **C:** Jean Yanne; Marie-Sophie L(elouch); Patrick Bruel; Charles Gerard; Corinne Marchand; Christine Barbelivien; Directed by Claude Lelouch; Written by Pierre Uytterhoeven; Claude Lelouch. **Pr:** Claude Lelouch; Claude Lelouch. **A:** Sr. High-Adult. **P:** Entertainment. **U:** Home. **L:** English, French. **Mov-Ent:** Crime Drama. **Acq:** Purchase. **Dist:** Wellspring Media; Facets Multimedia Inc. $89.95.

Bandits 1999 (R) — ★★
Talk about your band on the run! Four young women form a prison rock-and-roll band called the Bandits. Their first gig on the outside is the policeman's ball, where they escape. They become folk heroes as they elude the police and a clandestine recording they sent to a music exec zooms up the charts. German with subtitles. 109m; VHS, DVD, Wide. **C:** Katja Riemann; Jutta Hoffmann; Jasmin Tabatabai; Nicolette Krebitz; Hannes Jaenicke; Werner Schreyer; Directed by Katja von Garnier; Written by Katja von Garnier; Uwe Wilhelm; Cinematography by Torsten Breuer. **A:** College-Adult. **P:** Entertainment. **U:** Home. **L:** German. **Mov-Ent:** Music. **Acq:** Purchase. **Dist:** Sony Pictures Home Entertainment Inc.

Bandits 2001 (PG-13) — ★★½
Willis and Thornton are Joe and Terry, quirky bank robbers known as the "sleepover bandits" for their unusual but non-violent heists. With Willis as the smirky brawn and Thornton as the neurotic brain, the two play the Butch-and-Sundance act until fate puts bored housewife Kate (Blanchett) in their path. She talks her way into their little gang, but can't decide which of the two she should fall for most. The plot then slams on the brakes, although Levinson adds enough padding to cushion the blow. Blanchett is excellent as the sultry, vulnerable Kate, but Thornton steals the show (and chomps on considerable scenery) as the omniphobic hypochondriac Terry (his fear of antique furniture is actually one of Thornton's well-documented quirks as well). 123m; VHS, DVD, Wide. **C:** Bruce Willis; Billy Bob Thornton; Cate Blanchett; Troy Garity; Bobby Slayton; Brian F. O'Byrne; Azura Skye; Stacey Travis; William Converse-Roberts; Richard Riehle; Micole Mercurio; January Jones; Directed by Barry Levinson; Written by Harley Peyton; Cinematography by Dante Spinotti; Music by Christopher Young. **Pr:** Michele Berk; Michael Birnbaum; Paula Weinstein; Ashok Amritraj; Barry Levinson; MGM; Baltimore Pictures; Hyde Park Entertainment; Spring Creek Productions; Empire Pictures; Lotus Pictures. **A:** Jr. High-Adult. **P:** Entertainment. **U:** Home. **Mov-Ent:** Runaways. **Awds:** Natl. Bd. of Review '01: Actor (Thornton). **Acq:** Purchase. **Dist:** MGM Home Entertainment.

The Bandits of Corsica 1953 (Unrated) — ★½
Swashbuckler has Greene playing identical twins who, though separated at birth, maintain a psychic connection. Mario Franchi wants to overthrow ruling despot Jonatto and bring freedom to the people of Corsica. He's hoping his gypsy brother Carlos will help him, but there's a complication when Carlos falls in love with Mario's wife Christina. Burr and Van Cleef make good in their bad guy roles. 82m/B/W; DVD. **C:** Richard Greene; Raymond Burr; Lee Van Cleef; Paula Raymond; Dona Drake; Raymond Greenleaf; Frank Puglia; Directed by Ray Nazarro; Written by Richard Schayer; Cinematography by George E. Diskant; Music by Irving Gertz. **A:** Jr. High-Adult. **P:** Entertainment. **U:** Home. **Mov-Ent. Acq:** Purchase. **Dist:** MGM Home Entertainment; Movies Unlimited.

Bandits of Orgosolo 1961 (Unrated) — ★★½
An acclaimed, patient drama about a Sardinian shepherd who shelters a band of thieves from the police. When one of the cops is killed the shepherd panics and flees into the hills for survival. Dubbed in English. 98m/B/W; VHS. **C:** Michele Cossu; Peppeddu Cuccu; Directed by Vittorio de Seta; Written by Vittorio de Seta; Vera Gherarducci; Cinematography by Vittorio de Seta; Luciano Tovoli; Music by Valentino Bucchi. **Pr:** Titanus. **A:** Jr. High-Adult. **P:** Entertainment. **U:** Home. **Mov-Ent. Acq:** Purchase. **Dist:** Facets Multimedia Inc. $24.95.

B&O/C&O Steam ????
Presents film of steam trains on the Baltimore & Ohio Railroad (B&O) and the Chesapeake & Ohio Railway (C&O) during the middle of the 1950s; includes Alleghenies and Mikados. 30m; VHS, DVD. **A:** College-Adult. **P:** Education. **U:** Home. **Gen-Edu:** Trains. **Acq:** Purchase. **Dist:** Herron Rail Video. $29.95.

B&O Lake Sub Main Line and Yard Action: 1950s to 1980 ????
The Baltimore & Ohio's busy Lake Subdivision in Ohio is the scene for footage of three decades of steam and diesel passenger and freight train runs. 60m; VHS, DVD. **A:** College-Adult. **P:** Education. **U:** Home. **Gen-Edu:** Trains. **Acq:** Purchase. **Dist:** The Civil War Standard. $24.95.

B&O Odyssey Vol. 2 2002
Railroad photographer Emery Gulash captures the 'Cincinnatian' enroute in Michigan, Pennsylvania, and West Virginia from 1965 to 1968. 60m; VHS, DVD. **A:** Family. **P:** Entertainment. **U:** Home. **Gen-Edu:** Trains. **Acq:** Purchase. **Dist:** Pentrex Media Group L.L.C. $29.95.

B&O Odyssey Volume I 2000
Historical look at the Baltimore & Ohio Railroad and their scenic routes throughout the Great States. 60m; VHS. **A:** Family. **P:** Education. **U:** Home. **Gen-Edu:** Trains. **Acq:** Purchase. **Dist:** Pentrex Media Group L.L.C. $29.95.

Bandolero! 1968 (PG) — ★★½
In Texas, Stewart and Martin are two fugitive brothers who foil a hanging, escape to Mexico, and run into trouble with their Mexican counterparts. Enjoyable all-star Western boasts beautiful cinematography and solid performances all around. 106m; VHS, DVD, CC. **C:** James Stewart; Raquel Welch; Dean Martin; George Kennedy; Will Geer; Harry Carey, Jr.; Andrew Prine; Denver Pyle; Directed by Andrew V. McLaglen; Cinematography by William Clothier; Music by Jerry Goldsmith. **Pr:** 20th Century-Fox. **A:** Family. **P:** Entertainment. **U:** Home. **Mov-Ent:** Western. **Acq:** Purchase. **Dist:** Movies Unlimited; Alpha Video; Fox Home Entertainment. $19.98.

The Band's Visit 2007 (PG-13) — ★★★
Eight members of an Egyptian police orchestra are accidentally stranded in the Israeli desert, far away from their intended destination. They end up in an Israeli town where they are anything but welcome. Through the culture clash, connections are made, and an unlikely attraction develops between band members and the beautiful restaurant owner who gives them a place to stay. Director Kolirin draws comedy out of the isolated, sad characters and their awkward situation without exploiting them. 89m; Blu-Ray, On Demand, Wide. **C:** Sasson Gabai; Ronit Elkabetz; Saleh Bakri; Shlomi Avraham; Khalifa Natour; Rubi Muscovich; Directed by Eran Kolirin; Written by Eran Kolirin; Cinematography by Shai Goldman; Music by Habib Shehadeh Hanna. **Pr:** Eilon Ratzkovsky; Ehud Bleiberg; Yossi Uzrad; Kobi Gal-Raday; Guy Jacoel; July August Production; Sophie Dulac Productions; Bleiberg Entertainment; Sony Pictures Classics. **A:** Sr. High-Adult. **P:** Entertainment. **U:** Home. **L:** English, Hebrew, Arabic. **Mov-Ent:** Music, Comedy-Drama, Israel. **Acq:** Purchase. **Dist:** Sony Pictures Home Entertainment Inc.; Amazon.com Inc.; Movies Unlimited.

Bandslam 2009 (PG) — ★★½
Awkward but pleasant teen musical. Geek introvert Will (Connell) is the new kid at New Jersey's Van Buren High School. He bonds over shared musical tastes with sullen Sam (Hudgens) and cheerleader-turned-singer Charlotte (Michalka) who want Will to manage her garage band. After a few changes and a lot of practice, Will figures they have a shot at the tri-state battle-of-the-bands competition. Music isn't terribly memorable but everyone is just so darn cute. 111m; On Demand, Wide. **C:** Alyson Michalka; Scott Porter; Vanessa Anne Hudgens; Lisa Kudrow; Ryan Donowho; Gaelen Connell; Charlie Saxton; Cameo(s) David Bowie; Directed by Todd Graff; Written by Todd Graff; Josh A. Cagan; Cinematography by Eric Steelberg; Music by Junkie XL. **Pr:** Elaine Goldsmith-Thomas; Walden Media; Summit Entertainment. **A:** Family. **P:** Entertainment. **U:** Home. **L:** English. **Mov-Ent. Acq:** Purchase. **Dist:** Summit Entertainment; Amazon.com Inc.; Movies Unlimited.

Bandwagon 1995 (Unrated) — ★★
Four unlikely twentysomething guys decide to form a band in Raleigh, NC. Tony Ridge (Holmes) is the lead singer-songwriter who's so shy he practices in a closet; chatty drummer Charlie Flagg (Hennessey) has the rehearsal space; Wynn Knapp (Corrigan) is the band's perpetually stoned guitarist; and bass player Eric Ellwood's (Parlavecchio) hot temper has him in big trouble with a local loan shark. They finally come up with a name (Circus Monkey), get a gig (a raucous frat party), and are on their way when they acquire Zen-like road manager Linus Tate (MacMillan) and a battered van. Of course, life on the road proves to be a challenge. 99m; VHS, Streaming. **C:** Kevin Corrigan; Steve Parlavecchio; Lee Holmes; Matthew Hennessey; Doug MacMillan; Lisa Keller; Directed by John Schultz; Written by John Schultz; Cinematography by Shawn Maurer; Music by Greg Kendall. **Pr:** Lakeshore Entertainment; Cinepix. **A:** Sr. High-Adult. **P:** Entertainment. **U:** Home. **Mov-Ent:** Biography: Music. **Acq:** Purchase. **Dist:** Bedford Entertainment Inc.

Banff Blastout 1988
The North American Snowboard Championships at Banff, Canada. Features footage from the mogul and half pipe events with pros Chris Karol, Ricky Fruhman, Jose Fernandes, Dave Achenbach, Bert Lamar, and Craig Kelly. 30m; VHS. **Pr:** NSI. **A:** Jr. High-Adult. **P:** Entertainment. **U:** Home. **Spo-Rec**: Sports--General, Sports--Winter. **Acq:** Purchase. **Dist:** NSI Sound & Video Inc. $19.95.

Bang 1995 (Unrated) — ★★
This $20,000 indie concerns a nameless, powerless Asian-American would-be actress (Narita) in L.A. She gets kicked out of her apartment, accosted by a homeless crazy (Greene), and sexually propositioned by a sleazy producer (Graff). Finally, she's accused of causing a public disturbance by a cop (Newland), who'll let her off in exchange for sexual favors. Instead, she grabs his gun, forces him to strip, ties him to a tree, puts on the cop's uniform, and steals his motorcycle. In uniform, she's suddenly viewed with authority and decides to take some time to see what that's like. 98m; VHS, DVD. **C:** Darling Narita; Peter Greene; Michael Newland; David Allen Graff; Eric Schrody; Michael Arturo; James Sharpe; Luis Guizar; Art Cruz; Stanley Herman; Directed by Ash; Written by Ash; Cinematography by Dave Gasperik. **Pr:** Ladd Vance; Panorama Entertainment. **A:** College-Adult. **P:** Entertainment. **U:** Home. **Mov-Ent**: Women. **Acq:** Purchase. **Dist:** Monarch Home Video.

The Bang Bang Club 2010 (Unrated) — ★½
Superficial true story of four photojournalists covering the last days of apartheid in South Africa before the country's first free elections in 1994. Unfortunately the story becomes repetitive as the four men compete for some dangerous assignment/shot, spend their downtime drinking and fooling around with some very willing women, and then go out and shoot some more pictures. 106m; DVD. **C:** Ryan Phillippe; Taylor Kitsch; Frank Rautenbach; Neels Van Jaarsveld; Malin Akerman; Directed by Steven Silver; Written by Steven Silver; Cinematography by Miroslaw Baszak; Music by Philippe Miller. **A:** Sr. High-Adult. **P:** Entertainment. **U:** Home. **Mov-Ent**: Africa, Apartheid, Photography. **Acq:** Purchase. **Dist:** Entertainment One US LP.

Bang Bang Kid 1967 (G) — ★★
A western spoof about a klutzy gunfighter defending a town from outlaws. 78m; VHS, DVD. **C:** Tom Bosley; Guy Madison; Sandra Milo; Directed by Stanley Prager. **A:** Primary. **P:** Entertainment. **U:** Home. **Mov-Ent. Acq:** Purchase. **Dist:** No Longer Available.

Bang! Bang! You're Dead! 1966 — ★½
Generally silly, occasionally dull, spy comedy. American tourist Andrew Jessel (Randall) gets caught up with spies in Marrakesh when he's given the wrong hotel room and finds it already occupied by a dead body. It's a set-up for CIA agent Kyra Stanovy (Berger), involving crime boss Mr. Casimir (Lom) and some secret documents. It leads to Andrew and Kyra going on the lam, sought by Casimir's henchmen, including Jonquil (Kinski). 92m; DVD, Blu-Ray. **C:** Tony Randall; Senta Berger; Herbert Lom; Klaus Kinski; Wilfrid Hyde-White; Terry-Thomas; John Le Mesurier; Directed by Don Sharp; Written by Peter Yeldham; Cinematography by Michael Reed; Music by Malcolm Lockyer. **A:** Jr. High-Adult. **P:** Entertainment. **U:** Home. **L:** English. **Mov-Ent**: Africa. **Acq:** Purchase. **Dist:** Olive Films.

Bang, Bang, You're Dead 2004
A troubled teen finds a way to express his thoughts and feelings with the guidance of his film teacher. 93m; DVD; Closed Captioned. **A:** Family. **P:** Entertainment. **U:** Home. **Mov-Ent**: Drama, Violence, Adolescence. **Acq:** Purchase. **Dist:** Paramount Pictures Corp. $20.00.

Bang Rajan 2000 (Unrated) — ★★★½
Kind of a Thai version of the Alamo. The small village of Bang Rajan, circa 1765, finds itself geographically in the path of a very angry Burmese army on their way to the warring city of Ayudhay. With no outside help, the community must band together in hopes of protecting their land. One of the country's most legendary battles, told with Hollywood-like epic production helped the film become Thailand's biggest box office hit ever. One-upping "Braveheart," the film arguably contains the most violent images of warfare to date. Fan Oliver Stone helped secure U.S. release. 119m; DVD. **C:** Winai Kraibutr; Bin Bunluerit; Chumphorn Thepphithak; Jaran Ngamdee; Suntharee Maila-or; Directed by Thanit Jitnukul; Written by Thanit Jitnukul; Kongkiat Khomsiri; Bunthin Thuaykaew; Patikarn Phejmunee; Suttipong Muttanavee; Cinematography by Wichian Ruangwijchayakul; Music by Chartachai Phongpraphaphan. **A:** Sr. High-Adult. **P:** Entertainment. **U:** Home. **L:** Thai. **Mov-Ent**: Action-Adventure, War--General, Asia. **Acq:** Purchase. **Dist:** Virgil Films & Entertainment.

Bang the Drum Slowly 1956 — ★★
The original TV adaptation of a Mark Harris novel about baseball. A ball player stricken by a terminal illness strikes an unlikely friendship with a teammate. Interesting role for an actor (Newman) who claims to have been driven to acting by running away from the sporting goods business. 60m/B/W; VHS, DVD. **C:** Paul Newman; George Peppard; Albert Salmi; Directed by Daniel Petrie. **Pr:** Wood Knapp Video. **A:** Family. **P:** Entertainment. **U:** Home. **Mov-Ent**: Melodrama, Diseases, Baseball. **Acq:** Purchase. **Dist:** Criterion Collection Inc. $14.99.

Bang the Drum Slowly 1973 (PG) — ★★★
The touching story of a major league catcher who discovers that he is dying of Hodgkins disease and wants to play just one more season. De Niro is the weakening baseball player and Moriarty is the friend who helps him see it through. Based on a novel by Mark Harris. 97m; VHS, DVD. **C:** Robert De Niro; Michael Moriarty; Vincent Gardenia; Phil Foster; Ann Wedgeworth; Heather MacRae; Selma Diamond; Danny Aiello; Directed by John Hancock. **Pr:** Paramount Pictures. **A:** Jr. High-Adult. **P:** Entertainment. **U:** Home. **Mov-Ent**: Melodrama, Baseball, Sports--Fiction: Drama. **Awds:** N.Y. Film Critics '73: Support. Actor (De Niro). **Acq:** Purchase. **Dist:** Paramount Pictures Corp.; Facets Multimedia Inc. $14.95.

The Banger Sisters 2002 (R) — ★★
Fast forward "Almost Famous" thirty years and you'll find Kate Hudson has turned into her real-life mother, Hawn, who plays Suzette, a middle-aged former '60s/'70s "band-aid" turned, well, not turned at all, still living the wild, free-spirit life. Her partner in rock n' roll groupie-dom, Vinnie (Sarandon), however, has grown up and uptight; now she's suburban mom Lavinia living in the 'burbs. When Suzette loses her job, she drifts back into Vinnie's life and helps her get back to her sleazy, but more honest, roots. Sanitized-for-your-protection version of groupie life rings false throughout. Characters are essentially modeled on groupie legends the Plaster Casters. Material isn't worthy of these A-listers and nostalgia appeal runs thin. Amurri is Sarandon's real-life daughter. 97m; VHS, DVD. **C:** Goldie Hawn; Susan Sarandon; Geoffrey Rush; Erika Christensen; Robin Thomas; Eva Amurri; Matthew Carey; Directed by Bob Dolman; Written by Bob Dolman; Cinematography by Karl Walter Lindenlaub; Music by Trevor Rabin. **Pr:** Mark Johnson; Elizabeth Cantillon; Gran Via; Fox Searchlight. **A:** Sr. High-Adult. **P:** Entertainment. **U:** Home. **Mov-Ent**: Sex & Sexuality, Aging, Adolescence. **Acq:** Purchase. **Dist:** Fox Home Entertainment.

Bangkok 1979
A look at modern Bangkok, the capital of Thailand, and the hundreds of temples which signify the importance of religion to the Thai people. Part of the "Southeast Asia" series. 10m; VHS, 3/4 U. **Pr:** Japanese Broadcasting Commission. **A:** Jr. High-Adult. **P:** Education. **U:** Institution, SURA. **Gen-Edu**: Asia. **Acq:** Purchase. **Dist:** Lucerne Media.

Bangkok Adrenaline 2009 (R) — ★½
Four backpackers on holiday in Thailand go gambling and end up in such massive debt to a mob boss that they can't pay him. So they kidnap a rival mob bosses daughter intending to ransom her, only to find out he'd actually prefer she end up dead. Obviously Father's Day at his house isn't celebrated much. 90m; DVD, Blu-Ray. **C:** Daniel O'Neill; Priya Suandokemai; Gwion Jacob Miles; Conan Stevens; Raimund Huber; Geoffrey Giuliano; Dom Hetrakul; Lex de Groot; Michael Ocholi; Directed by Raimund Huber; Written by Conan Stevens; Raimund Huber; Gregory T. Eismin; Cinematography by Teerawat Rujintham; Jiradeht Samnansanor; Wardhana Vuncguplou. **A:** Sr. High-Adult. **P:** Entertainment. **U:** Home. **Mov-Ent**: Action-Comedy, Martial Arts. **Acq:** Purchase. **Dist:** Image Entertainment Inc. $27.97.

Bangkok Dangerous 2000 (R) — ★★
A moderately interesting action film that inspired a horrible Hollywood remake that was somehow done by the same team of directors (you'd think they'd get it better the second time around). A deaf mute assassin who doesn't know sign language (good thing he can read) becomes a one-man army after deciding to leave the business for his girlfriend. 105m; DVD, Blu-Ray, Wide. **C:** Pawalit Mongkolpisit; Premsinee Ratanasopha; Patharawarin Timkul; Pisek Intrakanchit; Directed by Oxide Pang Chun; Danny Pang; Written by Oxide Pang Chun; Danny Pang; Cinematography by Decha Srimantra; Music by Orange Music. **A:** Sr. High-Adult. **P:** Entertainment. **U:** Home. **L:** English, Thai. **Mov-Ent**: Crime Drama, Deafness. **Acq:** Purchase. **Dist:** Movies Unlimited; Alpha Video. $9.98.

Bangkok Dangerous 2008 (R) — ★½
The Pang Brothers come to Hollywood for the remake of their 1999 Hong Kong cult classic. Hitman Joe (Cage), not deaf like the original hitman, is sent to Thailand to complete four last jobs before he can retire. Struggling with culture shock, he hires street rat Kong (Yamnarm) as an interpreter/assistant. Each kill brings him closer to ending his career, but the progressive difficulties bring him closer to ending his life. Shelved for almost two years after production, with execs hoping Cage's career would pick up enough to guarantee box-office success. Instead, Cage's tendency towards wildly inconsistent performances continues, and he's utterly awful and joyless, not to mention silly-looking in his leather jacket and lousy haircut. Awkward title likely comes from studio heads assuming a semicolon would turn off American audiences. 100m; Blu-Ray, On Demand, Wide. **C:** Nicolas Cage; Charlie Yeung; Shahkrit Yamnarm; Panward Hemmanee; James With; Dom Hetrakul; Philip Waley; Shaun Delaney; Directed by Danny Pang; Oxide Pang; Written by Jason Richman; Cinematography by Decha Srimantra; Music by Brian Tyler. **Pr:** William Sherak; Jason Shuman; Nicolas Cage; Norm Golightly; Nicolas Cage; Blue Star Entertainment; Saturn Films; IEG Virtual Studios; Lionsgate. **A:** Sr. High-Adult. **P:** Entertainment. **U:** Home. **L:** English. **Mov-Ent**: Asia, Crime Drama. **Acq:** Purchase. **Dist:** Movies Unlimited; Alpha Video; Lions Gate Entertainment Inc.

Bangkok Haunted 2001 (Unrated) — ★½
Three young women meet in a bar and tell one another ghost stories as the backdrop for this horror anthology about the consequences of love and relationships gone bad. 130m; DVD. **C:** Dawan Singha-Wee; Kalyanut Sriboonreung; Pete Thongchua; Pimsiree Pimsee; Directed by Pisut Praesangeam; Oxide Pang Chun; Written by Pisut Praesangeam; Cinematography by Piyapan Choopetch. **A:** Sr. High-Adult. **P:** Entertainment. **U:** Home. **L:** English, Spanish, Thai. **Mov-Ent. Acq:** Purchase. **Dist:** Synapse. $19.95.

Bangkok Love Story 2007 (Unrated) — ★★½
An assassin can't bring himself to kill a police informant, and is nursed back to health by his intended target. Despite the informant being married they fall in love, turning everyone they know against them. Not necessarily because they're gay, but because the relationship is a betrayal of one man's wife (who turns out to be unexpectedly homicidal) and the other's criminal boss. 104m; DVD. **C:** Rattanaballang Tohssawat; Chaiwat Thongsaeng; Wiradit Srimalai; Chutcha Rujinanon; Suchao Pongwilai; Chonprakhan Janthareuang; Uthumporn Silaphan; Rachanu Boonchuduang; Directed by Poj Arnon; Written by Poj Arnon; Cinematography by Tiwa Moeithaisong; Music by Giant Wave. **A:** Sr. High-Adult. **P:** Entertainment. **U:** Home. **L:** English, Thai. **Mov-Ent. Acq:** Purchase. **Dist:** TLA Releasing. $19.99.

Bangkok Zigzag 2001
A profile of the motorcycle taxi drivers of Bangkok, Thailand. 50m; VHS, DVD. **A:** Sr. High-Adult. **P:** Education. **U:** Institution. **Gen-Edu**: Documentary Films, Motorcycles. **Acq:** Purchase, Rent/Lease. **Dist:** The Cinema Guild. $275.00.

Bangles Greatest Hits 1990
All-woman band performs "Hero Takes A Fall," "Goin' Down to Liverpool," "Manic Monday," "If She Knew What She Wants," "Walk Like an Egyptian," "Eternal Flame," "In My Room," and "Be With You." 33m; VHS. **Pr:** CBS. **A:** Adult. **P:** Entertainment. **U:** Home. **Mov-Ent**: Music Video, Music--Performance, Music--Pop/Rock. **Acq:** Purchase. **Dist:** Music Video Distributors; Sony Music Entertainment Inc. $16.98.

Banguza Timbila 1982
Reveals a window into Mozambique's musical heritage, 10 timbila players and 15 dancers perform in a show, telling the story of Mozambique's struggle for independence. 30m; VHS, Special order formats. **A:** Family. **P:** Education. **U:** Institution. **Gen-Edu**: Dance, Africa. **Acq:** Purchase, Rent/Lease. **Dist:** First Run/Icarus Films. $280.00.

Banished 2007
Documentary covering the destruction and theft of African American homes and communities from 1860 to 1920. 84m; DVD. **A:** Sr. High-Adult. **P:** Education. **U:** Home, Institution. **Gen-Edu**: Documentary Films, Prejudice, Black Culture. **Acq:** Purchase. **Dist:** California Newsreel. $26.95.

The Banjo According to John Hartford: Ideas, Advice and Music 199?
Two-tape series features John Hartford demonstrating a variety of rolls and licks, tips for getting a good tone, phrasing, accenting, using picks, playing backup, and much more. 120m; VHS. **A:** Sr. High-Adult. **P:** Education. **U:** Home. **How-Ins**: Music--Instruction. **Acq:** Purchase. **Dist:** Hal Leonard Corp. $49.95.

The Banjo According to John Hartford: Ideas, Advice and Music: Video One 199?
John Hartford demonstrates a variety of rolls and licks, tips for getting a good tone, phrasing, accenting, using picks, playing backup, and much more. 60m; VHS. **A:** Sr. High-Adult. **P:** Education. **U:** Home. **How-Ins**: Music--Instruction. **Acq:** Purchase. **Dist:** Hal Leonard Corp. $29.95.

The Banjo According to John Hartford: Ideas, Advice and Music: Video Two 199?
John Hartford demonstrates a variety of rolls and licks, tips for getting a good tone, phrasing, accenting, using picks, playing backup, and much more. 60m; VHS. **A:** Sr. High-Adult. **P:** Education. **U:** Home. **How-Ins**: Music--Instruction. **Acq:** Purchase. **Dist:** Hal Leonard Corp. $29.95.

Banjo Hackett 1976 — ★★½
Banjo (Meredith) and his orphaned nephew (Eisenmann) travel the West in search of a rare Arabian horse that was stolen from the boy's mother before she died. Also in pursuit are a millionaire and a devious bounty hunter who will stop at nothing to capture the missing steed. Although the storyline is as rambling as the West, it's heartfelt all the same. 100m; DVD. **C:** Don Meredith; Ike Eisenmann; Carol Connors; Gloria De Haven; Jeff Corey; L.Q. Jones; Jan Murray; Dan O'Herlihy; Jennifer Warren; David Young; Richard Young; Anne Francis; Slim Pickens; Directed by Andrew V. McLaglen; Written by Ken Trevey; Cinematography by Al Francis; Music by Morton Stevens. **A:** Adult. **P:** Entertainment. **U:** Home. **Mov-Ent**: Western, Horses. **Acq:** Purchase. **Dist:** Sony Pictures Home Entertainment Inc. $19.95.

The Banjo of Eddie Adcock 199?
Accomplished banjo player documents his techniques for learning players. 75m; VHS. **A:** Sr. High-Adult. **P:** Education. **U:** Home. **How-Ins**: Music--Instruction. **Acq:** Purchase. **Dist:** Hal Leonard Corp. $29.95.

The Banjo of Ralph Stanley: From Old-Time to Bluegrass 199?
Accomplished banjo player documents his techniques for learning players. 90m; VHS. **A:** Sr. High-Adult. **P:** Education. **U:** Home. **How-Ins**: Music--Instruction. **Acq:** Purchase. **Dist:** Hal Leonard Corp. $39.95.

The Banjo of Ralph Stanley: From Old-Time to Bluegrass 1992
Features Ralph Stanley, Mike Seeger, and The Clinch Mountain Boys as they demonstrate Ralph's pioneering banjo style, including old-time clawhammer technique and three-finger bluegrass picking. 90m; VHS. **A:** Jr. High-Adult. **P:** Instruction. **U:** Home, Institution. **How-Ins**: Music--Instruction. **Acq:** Purchase. **Dist:** Homespun Tapes Ltd. $49.95.

Banjo the Woodpile Cat 1985
This children's cartoon features a country cat who visits the big city, encountering mishaps every step of the way. 29m; VHS. **Pr:** Children's Video Library. **A:** Family. **P:** Entertainment. **U:**

Home. **Chl-Juv**: Animation & Cartoons. **Acq:** Purchase. **Dist:** Fox Home Entertainment; Lions Gate Television Corp. $19.98.

The Bank 2001 (Unrated) — ★★½
Geeky mathematician/computer whiz Jim Doyle (Wenham) is offered a job by unscrupulous Centrabank CEO Simon O'Reilly (LaPaglia) to set up a computer program that will predict stock market fluctuations and increase the bank's profits. Victims of Centrabank's drive for profits are Wayne (Rodgers) and Diane (McElhinney) Davis, who are suing the bank as a cause of a family tragedy. The two stories come to overlap when O'Reilly pressures Doyle into questionable practices to resolve the various situations. 103m; VHS, DVD. **C:** David Wenham; Anthony LaPaglia; Steve Rodgers; Mandy McElhinney; Mitchell Butel; Sibylla Budd; Directed by Robert Connolly; Written by Robert Connolly; Cinematography by Tristan Milani; Music by Alan John. **A:** Sr. High-Adult. **P:** Entertainment. **U:** Home. **Mov-Ent**: Mathematics. **Acq:** Purchase. **Dist:** New Yorker Video.

Bank Alarm 1937 (Unrated) — ★½
Government agents Alan O'Connor and Bobbie Reynolds are after a gang of bank robbers who leave dead bodies behind. However, the crooks also stole a stash of counterfeit money and when they starting passing it around, the feds have another trail to follow. 61m/B/W; DVD. **C:** Conrad Nagel; Eleanor Hunt; Vince Barnett; Marlo Dwyer; Wheeler Oakman; Frank Milan; William Thorne; Directed by Louis Gasnier; Written by Griffin Jay; David S. Levy; Cinematography by Mack Stengler. **A:** Jr. High-Adult. **P:** Entertainment. **U:** Home. **Mov-Ent**: Federal Bureau of Investigation (FBI). **Acq:** Purchase. **Dist:** Sinister Cinema.

The Bank Dick 1940 (Unrated) — ★★★★
Fields wrote the screenplay (using an alias) and stars in this zany comedy about a man who accidentally trips a bank robber and winds up as a guard. Fields' last major role is a classic, a worthy end to his great career. 73m/B/W; VHS, DVD. **C:** W.C. Fields; Cora Witherspoon; Una Merkel; Evelyn Del Rio; Jack Norton; Jessie Ralph; Franklin Pangborn; Shemp Howard; Grady Sutton; Russell Hicks; Richard Purcell; Reed Hadley; Directed by Edward F. (Eddie) Cline; Written by W.C. Fields; Cinematography by Milton Krasner. **Pr:** Mark Huffam. **A:** Jr. High-Adult. **P:** Entertainment. **U:** Home. **Mov-Ent**: Comedy--Slapstick, Classic Films. **Awds:** Natl. Film Reg. '92. **Acq:** Purchase. **Dist:** Criterion Collection Inc.; Movies Unlimited; Alpha Video. $14.98.

Bank Dory 19??
A film depicting the building of one of the famous Bank dories, film footage shows the dory at work and at Captain Allen's boat building shop in Nova Scotia. 18m; VHS. **A:** Family. **P:** Education. **U:** Institution. **L:** English. **Gen-Edu**: Boating. **Acq:** Purchase. **Dist:** Northeast Historic Film. $24.95.

Bank Holiday 1938 — ★½
Contrived weepie with some comic relief provided by the subplots. Nursing Catherine Lawrence is spending an illicit weekend with her boyfriend at a seaside resort but she can't stop thinking about her last case. Ann Howard died in childbirth and Catherine is worried about how new father and widower Stephen is coping. Meanwhile, Doreen and her friend Milly are interested in the local beauty pageant and Cockney Arthur is trying to find some peace away from his rambunctious family. 86m/B/W; DVD. **C:** Margaret Lockwood; John Lodge; Hugh Williams; Wally Patch; Kathleen Harrison; Rene Ray; Merle Tottenham; Directed by Carol Reed; Written by Rodney Ackland; Roger Burford; Cinematography by Arthur Crabtree. **A:** Adult. **P:** Entertainment. **U:** Home. **L:** English. **Mov-Ent**: Comedy-Drama, Family, Great Britain. **Acq:** Purchase. **Dist:** VCI Entertainment.

The Bank Job 2007 (Unrated) — ★½
When inmate Kenny (Brad Jurjens, who is also the writer and director) gets out of prison he immediately hooks up with an old friend who intends to rob a bank. Things go bad, and to escape Kenny steals a car that incidentally has a dead body hidden in the trunk. God must really hate ex-cons. Watching this film you may think he's not very fond of the fans of action films either. 76m; DVD. **C:** Johann Urb; Brad Jurjen; Perry Caravello; Rene Escapite; Alfred Soyyar; Renee Darmiento; Nano Cabello; Directed by Brad Jurjen; Written by Brad Jurjen; Cinematography by "Mad" Marty Rockatansky; Music by Brad Jurjen. **A:** Sr. High-Adult. **P:** Entertainment. **U:** Home. **Mov-Ent. Acq:** Purchase. **Dist:** Laguna Productions; York Entertainment. $9.95.

The Bank Job 2008 (R) — ★★★
Terry (Statham) thinks his ex-lover Martine (Burrows) has recruited him to assemble a crew including his number two guy, porn king Kevin (Campbell Moore), for a straightforward cash heist. They end up involved in one of the greatest bank robberies in British history: the 1971 tunneled break in at the Baker Street branch of Lloyd's. The real-life investigation produced no arrests and recovered no loot, thus allowing writers Clement and La Frenais to construct an elaborate albeit fictionalized account that ties the crime to a conspiracy to retrieve sexually-compromising photos of a British royal from the safe deposit box of a black power operative (De Jersey). A near-perfect period heist-caper film that extracts terrific effect from the fashion and technology of the 70's. Particularly humorous are the giant walkie-talkies alleged to have played a role in the crime. 111m; DVD. **C:** Jason Statham; Saffron Burrows; Daniel Mays; David Suchet; Richard Lintern; James Faulkner; Directed by Roger Donaldson; Written by Dick Clement; Ian La Frenais; Cinematography by Michael Coulter; Music by J. Peter Robinson. **Pr:** Charles Roven; Steve Chasman; Mosaic Media Group; Relativity Media; Ominilab Media Group; Lions Gate Films. **A:** Sr. High-Adult. **P:** Entertainment. **U:** Home. **L:** English. **Mov-Ent**: Conspiracies or Conspiracy Theories, Crime Drama. **Acq:** Purchase. **Dist:** Lions Gate Entertainment Inc.

Bank on It 1992
Discusses bank services and explains how both the depositor and the bank profit, highlighting the success of a 12-year-old entrepreneur who designed shirts. 14m; VHS. **A:** Primary. **P:** Education. **U:** Institution. **Chl-Juv**: Finance. **Acq:** Purchase. **Dist:** Pyramid Media. $60.00.

Bank Robber 1993 (R) — ★★
Billy (Dempsey) is a thief who will retire after one final bank heist, if only he hadn't forgotten to break that surveillance camera. Holed up in a New York hotel he's subjected to extortion schemes and finds himself a new outlaw celebrity to newshounds. Bonet is a sweet hooker who falls in love with him. Satire on crooks and fame is too mild-mannered for its own good but not without charm. Directorial debut of Mead. Unedited NC-17 version also available. 94m; VHS, CC. **C:** Patrick Dempsey; Lisa Bonet; Olivia D'Abo; James Garde; Forest Whitaker; Judge Reinhold; Michael Jeter; Joe Alaskey; John Chappoulis; Directed by Nick Mead; Written by Nick Mead; Music by Stewart Copeland. **Pr:** Lilia Cazes; Initial Pictures; I.R.S. World Media. **A:** College-Adult. **P:** Entertainment. **U:** Home. **Mov-Ent**: Satire & Parody, Sex & Sexuality. **Acq:** Purchase. **Dist:** Lions Gate Television Corp.

Bank Secrecy Act 1987
Spotting suspicious looking transactions is one of the keys of this series. 33m; VHS, 3/4 U. **Pr:** First Financial Network. **A:** Adult. **P:** Education. **U:** Institution, Home. **Bus-Ind**: Finance. **Acq:** Purchase, Rent/Lease. **Dist:** 1st Financial Training Services. $250.00.
Indiv. Titles: 1. Update fro Frontline Employees 2. Update for Senior Management.

Bank Security: Kidnap/Extortion Call 1987
Bank workers have to know how to handle a situation which involves a threatening phone call. 15m; VHS, 3/4 U. **Pr:** First Financial Network. **A:** Adult. **P:** Education. **U:** Institution, Home. **Bus-Ind**: Finance. **Acq:** Purchase, Rent/Lease. **Dist:** 1st Financial Training Services. $275.00.

Bank Shot 1974 (Unrated) — ★★★
Hilarious comedy about a criminal who plans to rob a bank by stealing the entire building. Based on the novel by Donald Westlake, and the sequel to "The Hot Rock." 83m; VHS, DVD, CV. **C:** George C. Scott; Joanna Cassidy; Sorrell Booke; G(eorge) Wood; Clifton James; Bob Balaban; Bibi Osterwald; Directed by Gower Champion; Written by Wendell Mayes; Cinematography by Harry Stradling, Jr. **A:** Jr. High-Adult. **P:** Entertainment. **U:** Home. **Mov-Ent**: Comedy--Screwball. **Acq:** Purchase. **Dist:** Movies Unlimited. $12.74.

Bank—Customer Relations 1989
Explains contractual relationships involved in banking. 30m; VHS. **A:** Adult. **P:** Professional. **U:** Institution. **Bus-Ind**: Business, Law. **Acq:** Purchase. **Dist:** RMI Media. $99.00.

The Banker 1989 (R) — ★★
A cop, played by Forster, suspects a wealthy, highly influential banker of brutal serial killings. 90m; VHS; Open Captioned. **C:** Robert Forster; Jeff Conaway; Leif Garrett; Duncan Regehr; Shanna Reed; Deborah Richter; Richard Roundtree; Teri Weigel; E.J. Peaker; Michael Fairman; Juan Garcia; Directed by William Webb; Cinematography by John Huneck; Music by Reg Powell; Sam Winans. **Pr:** Westwind Productions. **A:** Sr. High-Adult. **P:** Entertainment. **U:** Home. **Mov-Ent**: Mystery & Suspense. **Acq:** Purchase. **Dist:** Amazon.com Inc.

Bankhead: 1905-1922 19??
A study in contrast of a former coal mining town in the Rocky Mountains (now part of Banff National Park) between its past and present selves. 20m; VHS. **Pr:** Parks Canada. **A:** Jr. High-Sr. High. **P:** Education. **U:** Institution. **Gen-Edu**: Cities & Towns, Miners & Mining, Canada. **Acq:** Purchase. **Dist:** Access The Education Station. $49.00.

Banking 1977
The differences between commercial banks and savings accounts, opening accounts, interest, and reconciling balances. 22m; VHS, 3/4 U, Special order formats. **C:** Nettie Mooselock. **Pr:** Churchill Films. **A:** Jr. High-Adult. **P:** Education. **U:** Institution, Home, SURA. **Gen-Edu**: Economics. **Acq:** Purchase, Duplication License. **Dist:** Clear Vue Inc.

Banking and the Federal Reserve System 1992
Discusses money demand, money supply, and interest rates. 60m; VHS. **A:** Adult. **P:** Education. **U:** Institution. **Gen-Edu**: Economics. **Acq:** Purchase. **Dist:** RMI Media. $89.00.

Banking on Disaster 1988
A unique and vitally important documentary about this century's worst environmental disaster-the destruction of the Amazon rain forest. 78m; VHS, 3/4 U. **A:** Family. **P:** Education. **U:** Institution, Home. **Gen-Edu**: Ecology & Environment. **Acq:** Purchase, Duplication License. **Dist:** Bullfrog Films, Inc.

Banking on Hitler 2001
Reveals the roles played by the Anglo-German banking clique during World War II; how Swiss, British, and American bankers continued to do business with Hitler even as Germany was invading Europe. 60m; VHS. **A:** College-Adult. **P:** Education. **U:** Institution. **Gen-Edu**: World War Two, Finance. **Acq:** Purchase, Rent/Lease. **Dist:** Filmakers Library Inc. $325.00.

Banking on the Brink 1983
This program looks at the changes in banking over the last 25 years and how they affect the general public. 52m; VHS, 3/4 U. **Pr:** National Broadcasting Company. **A:** Sr. High-Adult. **P:** Education. **U:** Institution, SURA. **Bus-Ind**: Finance. **Acq:** Purchase. **Dist:** Home Vision Cinema.

Banking Our Genes 19??
Outlines the ethical and legal issues associated with DNA gene banking and databanking. Explores the implications of DNA research and how this new technology can be used responsibly. 33m; VHS. **Pr:** Fanlight Productions. **A:** Sr. High-Adult. **P:** Education. **U:** Institution. **Hea-Sci**: Science, Genetics. **Acq:** Purchase, Rent/Lease. **Dist:** Fanlight Productions. $195.00.

Bankrupt 1981
This program chronicles the decline, fall, and eventual takeover of Inforex-a computer firm that crashed for lack of a second product. Part of the "Enterprise" series. 30m; VHS, 3/4 U. **C:** Hosted by Eric Sevareid. **Pr:** PBS. **A:** Jr. High-Adult. **P:** Education. **U:** Institution, SURA. **Gen-Edu**: Business. **Acq:** Purchase, Rent/Lease. **Dist:** Phoenix Learning Group.

Bankruptcy 19??
Attorney Eugene Grossman offers financial and legal information about the new personal bankruptcy laws. 100m; VHS. **A:** College-Adult. **P:** Education. **U:** Home. **Gen-Edu**: Personal Finance, Law, Consumer Education. **Acq:** Purchase. **Dist:** Instructional Video. $29.95.

Bankruptcy Law and the Lender 1980
A course on bankruptcy law, designed for attorneys, and personnel of banks, credit unions, and lender organizations. 180m; VHS, 3/4 U. **Pr:** Professional Education Systems. **A:** Adult. **P:** Professional. **U:** Institution, SURA. **Bus-Ind**: Law, Finance. **Acq:** Purchase, Rent/Lease. **Dist:** Professional Education Systems, Inc.

Banks and Their Borrowers 1984
An extensive outline of today's market for financial services. 330m; VHS, 3/4 U. **Pr:** Practicing Law Institute. **A:** Adult. **P:** Professional. **U:** Institution, SURA. **Bus-Ind**: Law. **Acq:** Purchase, Rent/Lease. **Dist:** Practising Law Institute.

Banks in Insurance 1986
For bankers, a look at the expansion of banking services into the insurance area. 90m; VHS. **Pr:** Executive Enterprises. **A:** Adult. **P:** Professional. **U:** Institution. **Bus-Ind**: Insurance. **Acq:** Purchase. **Dist:** Executive Enterprises.

Banks Should Market the Neiman-Marcus Way 1987
Since Neiman-Marcus was so successful with its marketing plan, why aren't more companies copying them? This tape explains why. 12m; VHS, 3/4 U. **Pr:** First Financial Network. **A:** Adult. **P:** Education. **U:** Institution, Home. **Bus-Ind**: Sales Training, Business. **Acq:** Purchase, Rent/Lease. **Dist:** 1st Financial Training Services. $250.00.

Banks: The Money Movers 1977
In a humorous adventure, a greedy old miser, Arthur Scrooge, is visited by the Spirit of Banking. 16m; VHS, 3/4 U. **Pr:** Greenhouse Films Productions. **A:** Jr. High-Sr. High. **P:** Education. **U:** Institution, SURA. **Gen-Edu**: Finance. **Acq:** Purchase. **Dist:** Phoenix Learning Group.

The Bannen Way 2010 (Unrated) — ★★
Slick, fast-paced, edited to feature film version of the web series. Con man Neil Bannen (co-creator Gantt) has a mobster uncle, a cop dad, and enough audacious charm to think he can maneuver out of any trouble he finds himself in. 94m; DVD. **C:** Mark Gantt; Robert Forster; Autumn Reeser; Vanessa Marcil; Michael Ironside; Michael Lerner; Brynn Thayer; Directed by Jesse Warren; Written by Mark Gantt; Jesse Warren; Cinematography by Roger Chingirian; Music by Joseph Trapanese. **A:** Sr. High-Adult. **P:** Entertainment. **U:** Home. **Mov-Ent. Acq:** Purchase. **Dist:** Sony Pictures Home Entertainment Inc.

Banner 4th of July 2013 (Unrated) — ★★½
Desiree Banner now owns a record company, but she used to be part of a music trio with her brothers Mitchell and Johnny. Desiree and Mitchell have been estranged for years until their mother's heart attack brings the siblings back to their hometown in time for the 4th of July celebration. Only it may be the community's last because the town faces bankruptcy unless they can make a land payment. From the Hallmark Channel. 85m; DVD. **C:** Brooke White; Christian Campbell; Michael Barbuto; Mercedes Ruehl; Directed by Don McBrearty; Written by Michael Vickerman; Cinematography by Peter Benison; Music by Steve London. **A:** Jr. High-Adult. **P:** Entertainment. **U:** Home. **L:** English. **Mov-Ent**: Family, Holidays, TV Movies. **Acq:** Purchase. **Dist:** Gaiam Inc.

Banner in the Sky 1990
Rudi sets out to conquer the mountain where his father lost his life in this story of courage from the book by James Ramsey Ullman. 36m; VHS, 3/4 U, EJ, Special order formats. **TV Std:** NTSC, PAL, SECAM. **Pr:** Disney Educational Productions. **A:** Primary-Sr. High. **P:** Education. **U:** Institution, CCTV, SURA. **Chl-Juv**: Mountaineering, Death. **Acq:** Purchase, Rent/Lease. **Dist:** Phoenix Learning Group. $250.00.

Banner of the Stars II—Volume 1: Hunters 2001
Features the anime television series of the sequel to "Banner of the Stars" as Jinto Lin and Lafiel try to combat the Imperial Forces; the pair go to the captured planet Lobnas but many problems ensue. 4 episodes. 100m; DVD. **A:** Jr. High-Adult. **P:** Entertainment. **U:** Home. **Mov-Ent**: Television Series, Animation & Cartoons, Anime. **Acq:** Purchase. **Dist:** Bandai Entertainment Inc. $29.98.

Banner of the Stars II—Volume 2: Prey 2001
Features the 2001 anime television series of the sequel to "Banner of the Stars" as Jinto Lin and Lafiel try to combat the Imperial Forces; the pair are on the captured planet Lobnas but

many problems ensue. 3 episodes. 75m; DVD. **A:** Jr. High-Adult. **P:** Entertainment. **U:** Home. **Mov-Ent:** Television Series, Animation & Cartoons, Anime. **Acq:** Purchase. **Dist:** Bandai Entertainment Inc. $29.98.

Banner of the Stars II—Volume 3: Return 2001
Features the anime television series of the sequel to "Banner of the Stars" as Jinto Lin and Lafiel try to combat the Imperial Forces; the pair are on the captured planet Lobnas but Jinto is caught. 3 episodes. 75m; DVD. **A:** Jr. High-Adult. **P:** Entertainment. **U:** Home. **Mov-Ent:** Television Series, Animation & Cartoons, Anime. **Acq:** Purchase. **Dist:** Bandai Entertainment Inc. $29.98.

Banner of the Stars—Volume 1: No Turning Back 2000
Features the anime television series of the sequel to "Crest of the Stars" as Jinto Lin must broker peace between the waging Mankind and Abh Empire. 5 episodes. 125m; DVD. **A:** Jr. High-Adult. **P:** Entertainment. **U:** Home. **Mov-Ent:** Television Series, Animation & Cartoons, Anime. **Acq:** Purchase. **Dist:** Bandai Entertainment Inc. $29.98.

Banner of the Stars—Volume 2: The Basroil Unleashed! 2000
Features the anime television series of the sequel to "Crest of the Stars" as Jinto Lin must broker peace between the waging Mankind and Abh Empire but ends up battling the Empire with Lafiel. 4 episodes. 100m; DVD. **A:** Jr. High-Adult. **P:** Entertainment. **U:** Home. **Mov-Ent:** Television Series, Animation & Cartoons, Anime. **Acq:** Purchase. **Dist:** Bandai Entertainment Inc. $29.98.

Banner of the Stars—Volume 3: Only the Beginning 2000
Features the anime television series of the sequel to "Crest of the Stars" as Jinto Lin must broker peace between the waging Mankind and Abh Empire; the United Mankinds have a powerful new weapon to use against the Imperial Star Forces. 4 episodes. 100m; DVD. **A:** Jr. High-Adult. **P:** Entertainment. **U:** Home. **Mov-Ent:** Television Series, Animation & Cartoons, Anime. **Acq:** Purchase. **Dist:** Bandai Entertainment Inc. $29.98.

Bannerfilm 1989
The work of designer Norman Laliberte is documented here. 10m; VHS, 3/4 U. **Pr:** Tom Daly. **A:** Jr. High-Adult. **P:** Education. **U:** Institution, SURA. **Gen-Edu:** Art & Artists. **Acq:** Purchase, Rent/Lease. **Dist:** National Film Board of Canada.

Banquo's Wagon, Program 1 1993
Multicultural series using puppets, music, and folktales to familiarize young children with the language, location, and culture of particular countries. Includes on-location footage. Complete with audiocassettes, music books, student books, and teacher's guides. 15m; VHS. **A:** Preschool-Primary. **P:** Education. **U:** Institution. **Gen-Edu:** Geography, Ethnicity. **Acq:** Purchase. **Dist:** Celestial Media. $59.95.
Indiv. Titles: 1. Puerto Rico 2. Vietnam 3. Jamaica, West Indies 4. Beijing, China 5. Teacher Training Video.

The Banshee 1991
Scottish and Irish folktale tells the story of the banshee, a female spirit which looks for a lonely soul for company. In her village, however, the citizens are happy and she is left unsuccessful in her search. Soft-colored iconographic presentation from "The Banshee," by Karen Ackerman. 7m; VHS. **A:** Preschool-Primary. **P:** Entertainment. **U:** Institution, Home. **Chl-Juv:** Folklore & Legends, Scotland, Ireland. **Acq:** Purchase. **Dist:** Facets Multimedia Inc.

Banshee 2006 (R) — ★½
Kind of a woman-in-peril/action/psycho-thriller. Pro car thief Sage (Manning), nicknamed Banshee, is always in competition with boyfriend Tony (Kelly) for the hottest cars to boost. She steals a 1966 Dodge Charger, knowing it will bring top dollar, but not knowing the ride belongs to serial killer/DJ Larch (Campbell). Larch has this little kink about recording the screams of his victims and then mixing them in with his techno sounds. Larch not only wants his car back but he wants to teach Sage a very unpleasant lesson. 95m; DVD. **C:** Taryn Manning; Christian Campbell; Morgan Kelly; Tony Calabretta; Mike Lombardi; Directed by Keri Skogland; Written by Kirsten Elms; Cinematography by David Franco; Music by Ned Bouhalassa. **A:** Sr. High-Adult. **P:** Entertainment. **U:** Home. **Mov-Ent:** Mystery & Suspense. **Acq:** Purchase. **Dist:** Image Entertainment Inc.

Banshee!!! 2008 (Unrated) — ★
Some college kids on spring break meet up with a monster that uses sound to cause them to hallucinate. Odd that the film is called 'Banshee' considering that the monster bears little resemblance to the creature from Irish myth, nor are the victims in Ireland. 86m; DVD, Streaming. **C:** Kevin Shea; Troy Walcott; Ashley Bates; Kerry McGann; Iris McQuillan-Grace; Directed by Colin Theys; Written by John Doolan; Christian Pindar; Gregory Parker; Cinematography by Matthew Wauhkonen; Andrew Gernhard; Music by Matthew Llewellyn. **A:** Sr. High-Adult. **P:** Entertainment. **U:** Home. **L:** English, Spanish. **Mov-Ent. Acq:** Purchase, Rent/Lease. **Dist:** Synthetic Cinema. $14.95 14.99.

Banshee: The Complete First Season 2013
Cinemax 2013-? crime drama. Ex-con and master thief Lucas Hood assumes the identity of the new and unknown sheriif of Banshee, Pennsylvania when the man is murdered before he can enter the rural Amish community. Lucas wants to find his former partner and lover Annie, who's now Carrie Hopewell, a mom who's married to the local DA. Complicating matters is local crime boss Kai Proctor and a vengeful New York mobster called Mr. Rabbit. 10 episodes. 600m; DVD, Blu-Ray. **C:** Antony Starr; Ivana Milicevic; Ulrich Thomsen; Frankie Faison; Matt Servitto; Ben Cross. **A:** Sr. High-Adult. **P:** Entertainment. **U:** Home. **Mov-Ent:** Crime Drama, Identity, Television Series. **Acq:** Purchase. **Dist:** HBO Home Video. $39.98.

Banzai Runner 1986 (Unrated) — ★★
A cop whose brother was killed in an exclusive desert-highway race decides to avenge by joining the race himself. 88m; VHS, DVD. **C:** Dean Stockwell; John Shepherd; Charles Dierkop; Directed by John G. Thomas; Written by Phil Harnage; Cinematography by Howard Wexler; Music by Joel Goldsmith. **A:** Jr. High-Adult. **P:** Entertainment. **U:** Home. **Mov-Ent:** Automobiles--Racing. **Acq:** Purchase. **Dist:** CinemaNow Inc. $19.95.

Baobab Play 1974
Children throw objects at each other from perches in the Baobab tree. 8m; 3/4 U. **Pr:** Laurence Marshall; John Marshall. **A:** Sr. High-Adult. **P:** Education. **U:** Institution, SURA. **Gen-Edu:** Africa, Anthropology. **Acq:** Purchase. **Dist:** Documentary Educational Resources.

Baobab: Portrait of a Tree 1983
Africa's most interesting trees, the baobabs, are presented in this program. 30m; VHS, 3/4 U. **Pr:** Joan Root. **A:** Jr. High-College. **P:** Education. **U:** Institution, CCTV. **Gen-Edu:** Africa, Forests & Trees. **Acq:** Purchase. **Dist:** Benchmark Media.

Baoh 1989 — ★½
The secret organization Doress has developed the genetically engineered parasite Baoh and implanted it in a man's brain. When he and another test subject escape, Doress will do anything to get him back. A terrible battle ensues as he discovers his powers and faces everyone sent after him in one gruesome battle after another. Many tedious "psychic battles" and incidents of torture result in copious amount of red ink being splashed all over the screen as the story lurches toward what is, more or less, the end. 50m; VHS. **A:** College-Adult. **P:** Entertainment. **U:** Home. **L:** Japanese, English. **Mov-Ent:** Animation & Cartoons, Science Fiction. **Acq:** Purchase. **Dist:** AnimEigo Inc. $24.95.

B.A.P.'s 1997 (PG-13) — ★½
Ghetto to riches story about Georgia waitresses Nisi (Berry) and Mickey (Desselle) who dream about opening their own business—a combo restaurant and hair salon. An L.A. audition offering $10,000 gets them to the sunny coast and eventually into the Beverly Hills mansion of Mr. Blakemore (Landau), where Nisi's persuaded to pose as the granddaughter of his lost love by Blakemore's money-grubbing nephew, Isaac (Fried). Everybody bonds and butler Manley (Richardson) instructs the women in taste and etiquette. Good cast is wasted and the comedy's lame when not offensive. 91m; VHS, DVD. **C:** Halle Berry; Natalie Desselle; Martin Landau; Ian Richardson; Troy Beyer; Luigi Amodeo; Jonathan Fried; A.J. (Anthony) Johnson; Directed by Robert Townsend; Written by Troy Beyer; Cinematography by Bill Dill; Music by Stanley Clarke. **Pr:** Mark Burg; Loretha Jones; Michael De Luca; Jay Stern; Island Pictures; New Line Cinema. **A:** Jr. High-Adult. **P:** Entertainment. **U:** Home. **Mov-Ent:** Black Culture. **Acq:** Purchase. **Dist:** New Line Home Video.

Baptism: Journey of Faith 197?
This series utilizes five true, dramatic stories to present different facets of the sacrament of baptism. Fr. Scannell introduces each program and explains how the experience of baptism touches and is lived out in each Christian's life. Programs are available individually. 19m; VHS, 3/4 U. **C:** Fr. Anthony Scannell. **Pr:** Franciscan Communications. **A:** Adult. **P:** Religious. **U:** Institution, SURA. **Gen-Edu. Acq:** Purchase. **Dist:** St. Anthony Messenger Press.
Indiv. Titles: 1. Baptism, Sacrament of Belonging 2. The Widow's Mite 3. Godparent Gussie 4. Water and Spirit 5. Commitment to Caring.

Baptism of Fire 1940
The complete version of this rare Nazi propaganda film, in which the Nazis attempt to prove they were totally justified in invading Poland. Narrated in English. Following the film is a compilation of Nazi newsreels. 51m/B/W; VHS. **Pr:** Third Reich. **A:** Adult. **P:** Education. **U:** Institution, Home. **L:** German. **Gen-Edu:** World War Two, Propaganda. **Acq:** Purchase. **Dist:** Festival Films. $24.95.

Baptism: Sacrament of Belonging 1970
Baptism as the sacrament of welcome into God's family and a sign of our being called from alienation of sin to oneness in God and each other is exemplified in the true story of a scarred and orphaned Mexican boy who finds a home and a family. Part of the "Baptism: Journey of Faith" series. 15m; VHS, 3/4 U. **C:** Fr. Anthony Scannell. **Pr:** Franciscan Communications. **A:** Adult. **P:** Religious. **U:** Institution, SURA. **Gen-Edu. Acq:** Purchase. **Dist:** St. Anthony Messenger Press.

Baptist Faith and Message Series 1989
Dr. Herschel Hobbs leads the way in this lengthy discussion of Christian topics. 30m; VHS. **Pr:** Broadman. **A:** Adult. **P:** Religious. **U:** Institution, CCTV. **Gen-Edu. Acq:** Purchase. **Dist:** Broadman & Holman Publishers. $130.00.

Bar-B-Q 2000 (Unrated) — **Bomb!**
A pro-ball player turned actor needs a break and heads home to have a Bar-B-Q with his girl and old homies. When word gets out the entire neighborhood shows up for the party. A lot of music and a lot of crude jokes and infantile humor make this poorly made, horribly acted film practically unwatchable. The 102-minute running time includes nearly 15 minutes of credits and what the cast and crew apparently considered humorous outtakes. 102m; DVD. **C:** Layzie Bone; John West; Chanda Watts; Lea Griggs; Directed by Amanda Moss; John West; Written by John West. **A:** Sr. High-Adult. **P:** Entertainment. **U:** Home. **Mov-Ent:** Food Industry. **Acq:** Purchase. **Dist:** York Entertainment. $19.98.

Bar Girls 1995 (R) — ★★
Mating rituals, set in L.A. wateringhole "The Girl Bar," finds usually tough cookie Loretta (Wolfe) spotting new face Rachael (D'Agostino) and deciding she likes what she sees. There's various mind games as they chart a rocky course to true love—with jealousy, possessiveness, and past romance all playing their parts. Hoffman adapted from her play and the staginess remains; film debut for director Giovanni. 95m; VHS, DVD, Wide, CC. **C:** Nancy Allison Wolfe; Liza D'Agostino; Justine Slater; Paula Sorge; Camila Griggs; Pam Raines; Directed by Marita Giovanni; Written by Lauran Hoffman; Cinematography by Michael Ferris; Music by Lenny Meyers. **Pr:** Marita Giovanni; Lauran Hoffman; Orion Pictures. **A:** College-Adult. **P:** Entertainment. **U:** Home. **Mov-Ent:** Comedy--Romantic, Women. **Acq:** Purchase. **Dist:** MGM Studios Inc.

Bar Glasses and Washtubs: Identification and Setup 1986
Offers instruction on specific aspects of cooking and food preparation. 7m; VHS. **A:** Adult. **P:** Instruction. **U:** Institution. **Gen-Edu:** Cooking. **Acq:** Purchase. **Dist:** RMI Media. $39.95.

Bar Hopping 2000 — ★
Disjointed series of vignettes about the singles scene in L.A. centered around a bar with Arnold as the bartender, narrating the action (or lack thereof). Lame. 88m; VHS, DVD, CC. **C:** Tom Arnold; Nicole Sullivan; Scott Baio; John Henson; Sally Kellerman; Kevin Nealon; Kelly Preston; Roy Thinnes; Linda Favila; Anson Downes; Directed by Steve Cohen; Written by Linda Favila; Anson Downes; Cinematography by Joe Montgomery; Music by Nick Loren. **A:** Sr. High-Adult. **P:** Entertainment. **U:** Home. **Mov-Ent. Acq:** Purchase. **Dist:** Showtime Networks Inc.

Bar-20 1943 — ★½
Stage hold-ups and jewel robberies abound in this Hopalong Cassidy western. 54m/B/W; VHS. **C:** William Boyd; Andy Clyde; Robert Mitchum; Victor Jory; George Reeves; Douglas Fowley; Directed by Lesley Selander. **Pr:** United Artists. **A:** Family. **P:** Entertainment. **U:** Home. **Mov-Ent:** Western. **Acq:** Purchase. **Dist:** Glenn Video Vistas Ltd. $19.95.

Bar Yohai 1988
A film about Shimon Bar Yohai, a mystic from the second century who wrote most of the Kabbalah text. 6m; VHS. **Pr:** R. Ascher. **A:** Primary-Adult. **P:** Education. **U:** Institution, CCTV, CATV, BCTV, Home. **Gen-Edu:** Religion, History--Ancient, Judaism. **Acq:** Purchase, Rent/Lease. **Dist:** Cornell University. $80.00.

Barabbas 1962 — ★★½
Barabbas, a thief and murderer, is freed by Pontius Pilate in place of Jesus. He is haunted by this event for the rest of his life. Excellent acting, little melodrama, lavish production make for fine viewing. Based on the novel by Lagerkvist. 144m; VHS, DVD, Wide. **C:** Anthony Quinn; Silvana Mangano; Arthur Kennedy; Jack Palance; Ernest Borgnine; Katy Jurado; Vittorio Gassman; Directed by Richard Fleischer; Written by Diego Fabbri; Christopher Fry; Ivo Perilli; Nigel Balchin; Cinematography by Aldo Tonti; Music by Mario Nascimbene. **Pr:** Dino De Laurentiis; Columbia Pictures. **A:** Family. **P:** Entertainment. **U:** Home. **Mov-Ent:** Drama. **Acq:** Purchase. **Dist:** Sony Pictures Home Entertainment Inc. $59.95.

Baraka 1993 (Unrated) — ★★★
Time-lapse photography transforms a fascinating array of scenic panoramas into a thought-provoking experience. No dialogue, but the captivating visuals, shot in 24 countries, are a feast for the eyes. Points of interest include Iguacu Falls in Argentina, Ayers Rock in Australia, the temples of Angkor Wat in Cambodia, and the Grand Canyon. Also tours Auschwitz and the streets of Calcutta, in an effort to warn the viewer of the planet's fragility. Filmed in 70mm. 96m; VHS, DVD, Blu-Ray, Wide. **C:** Directed by Ron Fricke; Written by Ron Fricke; Mark Magidson; Bob Green; Cinematography by Ron Fricke; Music by Michael Stearns. **Pr:** Samuel Goldwyn; Mark Magidson. **A:** Jr. High-Adult. **P:** Entertainment. **U:** Home. **Mov-Ent:** Film--Avant-Garde, Documentary Films. **Acq:** Purchase. **Dist:** MPI Media Group. $29.98.

Baran 2001 (PG) — ★★½
Latif (Abedini) works as a tea boy and cook on a construction site in Iran where many of the other laborers are illegal Afghan emigres. When one of his co-workers is injured, the man's young son, Baran (Bahrami), comes to take his place, although he's too frail to do the job. So Baran takes Latif's place and he must move to a more strenuous job, which he doesn't mind when he discovers that Baran is actually a girl; so Latif begins an awkward courtship while trying to keep her secret. Farsi with subtitles. 94m; VHS, DVD. **C:** Hossein Abedini; Zahra Bahrami; Mohammad Reza Naji; Hossein Rahimi; Directed by Majid Majidi; Written by Majid Majidi; Cinematography by Mohammad Davudi; Music by Ahmad Pejman. **Pr:** Majid Majidi; Fouad Nahas; Majid Majidi; Miramax Film Corp. **A:** Sr. High-Adult. **P:** Entertainment. **U:** Home. **L:** Farsi. **Mov-Ent:** Romance, Immigration, Afghanistan. **Acq:** Purchase. **Dist:** Buena Vista Home Entertainment.

Barb: Breaking the Cycle of Child Abuse 1978
Presented in this program is a case history of child abuse from the moment the police investigator arrives at the home through the mother's treatment in a group session with other parents who have abused their children. 28m; VHS, 3/4 U, Special order formats. **Pr:** National Center on Child Abuse. **A:** College-Adult. **P:** Education. **U:** Institution, SURA. **Gen-Edu:** Child Abuse. **Acq:** Purchase. **Dist:** National Audiovisual Center.

Barb Wire 1996 (R) — ★½
"Don't call me babe!" That'll be difficult when the figure in question is Anderson Lee's big-screen take on Dark Horse comic book heroine Barb Wire. Barb runs the sleazy Hammerhead Bar & Grille in Steel Harbor, the only neutral city in an America torn by a second civil war, and reluctantly agrees to aid hunky resistance leader Axel (Morrison) on a dangerous peace mission. Pambo gives Stallone a fight for the action title—fetching in high heels and black leather—with lots of fire power and a take-no-prisoners attitude. Plot's secondary to pulchritude but, unfortunately, the movie's just not a lotta fun. 98m; DVD, Wide, CC. **C:** Pamela Anderson; Temuera Morrison; Jack Noseworthy; Victoria Rowell; Xander Berkeley; Udo Kier; Steve Railsback; Clint Howard; Tony Bill; Directed by David Glenn Hogan; Written by Chuck Pfarrer; Ilene Chaiken; Cinematography by Rick Bota; Music by Michel Colombier. **Pr:** Michael Richardson; Brad Wyman; Todd Moyer; Peter Heller; Polygram Filmed Entertainment; Propaganda Films; Dark Horse Entertainment; Gramercy Pictures. **A:** Sr. High-Adult. **P:** Entertainment. **U:** Home. **Mov-Ent:** Science Fiction, War--General. **Awds:** Golden Raspberries '96: Worst New Star (Anderson). **Acq:** Purchase. **Dist:** Universal Music and Video Distribution.

Barbados, a Culture in Progress 1975
An extensive panorama of general patterns of culture of the region. 15m; VHS, 3/4 U. **Pr:** Museum of Modern Art of Latin America. **A:** Jr. High-Adult. **P:** Education. **U:** Institution, SURA. **Fin-Art:** Caribbean. **Acq:** Purchase. **Dist:** Art Museum of The Americas; Facets Multimedia Inc.

Barbara Frietchie 1924 (Unrated) — ★★½
Southern belle Barbara (Vidor) and Yankee captain William Trumbell (Lowe) are introduced by her brother Arthur (Delaney) and begin a romance. The war starts and his troops occupy the hometown of the Frietchies—Trumbell is wounded and Barbara thinks he's dying so she decides to defy the Confederacy to publicly declare her love. Adapted from Clyde Fitch's 1899 play. 103m/B/W; Silent; DVD. **C:** Florence Vidor; Edmund Lowe; Joseph Bennett; Charles Delaney; Mattie Peters; Emmett King; Louis Fitzroy; Gertrude Short; George A. Billings; Directed by Lambert Hillyer; Written by Lambert Hillyer; Agnes Christine Johnson; Cinematography by Henry Sharp. **A:** Sr. High-Adult. **P:** Entertainment. **U:** Home. **Mov-Ent:** Silent Films, Civil War. **Acq:** Purchase. **Dist:** Movies Unlimited.

Barbara Hendricks 1995
Traces the life and career of opera star Barbara Hendricks. Includes clips of her performances in Rigoletto, Der Rosenkavalier, La Boheme, and La Nozze di Figaro. 47m; VHS. **A:** Jr. High-Adult. **P:** Education. **U:** Home. **Fin-Art:** Opera, Performing Arts, Biography. **Acq:** Purchase. **Dist:** Kultur International Films Ltd., Inc. $19.95.

Barbara Hendricks: Don Pasquale 1991
Barbara Hendricks offers her rendition of her favorite character, Norina, from Donizetti's Don Pasquale. Part of the "My Favorite Opera" series. 60m; VHS. **A:** Jr. High-Adult. **P:** Entertainment. **U:** Home. **Fin-Art:** Opera, Performing Arts, Music--Performance. **Acq:** Purchase. **Dist:** Kultur International Films Ltd., Inc. $24.95.

Barbara Hepworth at the Tate 1968
A retrospective of the work of Hepworth, including early figurative pieces from the '20s, experiments in abstractions and form of the '30s and '40s, and innovative bronzes of the '60s. 12m; VHS, 3/4 U, Special order formats. **Pr:** Arts Council of Great Britain. **A:** Sr. High-Adult. **P:** Education. **U:** Institution. **Fin-Art:** Documentary Films, Sculpture, Art & Artists. **Acq:** Purchase, Rent/Lease. **Dist:** Museum of Modern Art.

Barbara Is a Vision of Loveliness 1978
The sheer beauty of the female form is conveyed through optical effects and sensitive camera work. 6m/B/W; VHS, 3/4 U. **Pr:** R. Bruce Elder. **A:** Sr. High-Adult. **P:** Entertainment. **U:** Institution, SURA. **Fin-Art:** Film--Avant-Garde. **Acq:** Purchase. **Dist:** Phoenix Learning Group.

Barbara Mandrell and the Mandrell Sisters: Best of 1980
Performance highlights from the country music variety show featuring Barbara, Louise, and Irlene Mandrell joking with each other and singing with a long list of guest artists including Johnny Cash, Alabama, Dolly Parton, Ray Charles, Kenny Rogers, and John Schneider. 180m; DVD. **C:** Barbara Mandrell; Irlene Mandrell; Louise Mandrell. **A:** Family. **P:** Entertainment. **U:** Home. **Mov-Ent:** Music--Performance, Music--Country/Western, Variety. **Acq:** Purchase. **Dist:** Time-Life Video and Television.

Barbara Morgan: Everything Is Dancing 1983
Photographer Barbara Morgan explains why movement and dance have become important elements in her photography. 18m; VHS, 3/4 U. **Pr:** Edgar B. Howard; Checkerboard Productions, Inc. **A:** Jr. High-Adult. **P:** Education. **U:** Institution, Home. **Gen-Edu:** Photography. **Acq:** Purchase, Rent/Lease. **Dist:** Museum of Modern Art. $200.00.

Barbara Murray 1978
A substitute teacher and non-drinker finds her junior high school class involved in a discussion on the use of alcohol. 15m; VHS, 3/4 U, Special order formats. **Pr:** National Institute on Alcohol Abuse. **A:** Jr. High-Adult. **P:** Education. **U:** Institution, SURA. **Hea-Sci:** Alcoholism. **Acq:** Purchase. **Dist:** National Audiovisual Center.

The Barbara Stanwyck Show: Volume 1 1960 (Unrated)
NBC 1960 anthology series. Following her illustrious movie career Ms. Stanwyck dove into television playing a new character each week alongside business veterans in dramas that ranged from murder to westerns and semi-comedic all produced at a level worthy of feature film. Includes "The Key to the Killer," "House in Order," "The Miraculous Journey of Tadpole Chan," "The Secret of Mrs. Randall," "Ironbark's Bride," "Out of the Shadows," "Night Visitor," "Size 10," "Dear Charlie," "Dragon by the Tail," "The Sisters," "Big Career," "Confession," "Along the Barbary Coast," and "Shock." 15 episodes. 390m; DVD. **C:** Barbara Stanwyck. **A:** Jr. High-Adult. **P:** Entertainment. **U:** Home. **Mov-Ent:** Drama, Television Series. **Acq:** Purchase. **Dist:** eOne Home Video. $39.99.

The Barbara Stanwyck Show: Volume 2 1960 (Unrated)
NBC 1960-? drama. Emmy-winning anthology series featuring performances by Dana Andres, Robert Culp, Buddy Ebsen, Peter Falk and more. Includes "The Golden Acres," "Adventure on Happiness Street," "High Tension," "Sign of the Zodiac," "The Choice," "Frightened Doll," "Yanqui Go Home," "Little Big Mouth," "Assassin," "The Hitch-Hiker," "Big Jake," and "A Man's Game." 312m; DVD. **C:** Hosted by Barbara Stanwyck. **A:** Family. **P:** Entertainment. **U:** Home. **Mov-Ent:** Drama, Television Series. **Acq:** Purchase. **Dist:** eOne Home Video. $29.99.

The Barbara Walters Specials 1991
ABC commemorates the 50th episode of this series with a tribute to the famous celebrity interviewer. Highlights include chats with Fidel Castro, Elizabeth Taylor, Eddie Murphy, Johnny Carson, Clint Eastwood, and many more. 120m; VHS. **C:** Barbara Walters. **Pr:** ABC. **A:** Adult. **P:** Entertainment. **U:** Home. **Mov-Ent:** Documentary Films, Interviews. **Acq:** Purchase. **Dist:** MPI Media Group. $19.98.

Barbara's Problem Dogs 1982
This tape features the one and only Barbara Woodhouse as she deals with problem dogs and their problem owners. 50m; VHS, 3/4 U. **Pr:** British Broadcasting Corporation. **A:** Family. **P:** Education. **U:** Institution, SURA. **How-Ins:** Pets. **Acq:** Purchase. **Dist:** Home Vision Cinema.

Barbarella 1968 (PG) — ★★½
Based on the popular French sci-fi comic strip drawn by Jean-Claude Forest, this cult classic details the bizarre adventures of a space nymphette (Fonda) encountering fantastic creatures and super beings. You'll see sides of Fonda you never saw before (not even in the workout videos). Notorious in its day; rather silly, dated camp now. Don't miss the elbow-sex scene. Terry Southern contributed to the script. 98m; VHS, DVD, Blu-Ray, Wide. **C:** Jane Fonda; John Phillip Law; David Hemmings; Marcel Marceau; Anita Pallenberg; Milo O'Shea; Ugo Tognazzi; Veronique Vendell; Giancarlo Cobelli; Serge Marquand; Directed by Roger Vadim; Written by Roger Vadim; Terry Southern; Vittorio Bonicelli; Claude Brule; Tudor Gates; Clement Biddle Wood; Brian Degas; Jean-Claude Forest; Cinematography by Claude Renoir; Music by Charles Fox. **Pr:** Paramount Pictures. **A:** Sr. High-Adult. **P:** Entertainment. **U:** Home. **Mov-Ent:** Fantasy, Science Fiction, Sex & Sexuality. **Acq:** Purchase. **Dist:** Fusion Video; Paramount Pictures Corp. $19.98.

The Barbarian 1921 (Unrated)
Salisbury's only known surviving film takes place in the northwoods. Some scenes show signs of decomposing. 52m/B/W; VHS. **C:** Monroe Salisbury; Jane Novak; Alan Hale, Jr. **A:** Sr. High-Adult. **P:** Entertainment. **U:** Home. **Mov-Ent:** Forests & Trees, Wilderness Areas. **Acq:** Purchase. **Dist:** Facets Multimedia Inc.; Grapevine Video. $19.95.

The Barbarian 1933 (Unrated) — ★★
Diana (Loy) travels to Cairo with her Uncle Cecil (Smith) and sharp-tongued companion Powers (Hale) to meet stuffy fiance Gerald (Denny). Arab guide Jamil (Navarro) is immediately attracted to the beauty, eventually kidnapping her and taking Diana on a desert trek to further his romantic plans after revealing to her that he's actually a prince. Pre-Code MGM production has a risque bathing scene by Loy and a questionable seduction scene common to the milieu. Based on Edgar Selwyn's racy play "The Arab." 84m/B/W; DVD. **C:** Myrna Loy; Reginald Denny; Louise Closser Hale; Sir C. Aubrey Smith; Edward Arnold; Ramon Novarro; Directed by Sam Wood; Written by Anita Loos; Elmer Harris; Cinematography by Harold Rosson; Music by Herbert Stothart. **A:** Sr. High-Adult. **P:** Entertainment. **U:** Home. **Mov-Ent. Acq:** Purchase. **Dist:** WarnerArchive.com.

Barbarian and the Geisha 1958 — ★★
The first US diplomat in Japan undergoes culture shock as well as a passionate love affair with a geisha, circa 1856. 104m; VHS, Blu-Ray, Streaming, CC. **C:** John Wayne; Eiko Ando; Sam Jaffe; So Yamamura; Directed by John Huston; Music by Hugo Friedhofer. **Pr:** 20th Century-Fox. **A:** Family. **P:** Entertainment. **U:** Home. **Mov-Ent:** Drama, Japan. **Acq:** Purchase. **Dist:** Fox Home Entertainment. $19.98.

The Barbarian Invasions 2003 (R) — ★★★
Writer/director Arcand reunites characters from his 1986 film "The Decline of the American Empire" to capture the last days of lecherous, lustful divorced academic Remy (Girard), hospitalized with terminal cancer in his fifties. Through some pleading by his ex-wife (Berryman), estranged son Sebastian (Rousseau) reconnects with his father and deftly orchestrates his twilight days. He upgrades his medical care, persuades ex lovers and colleagues to come and see him off, and sneaks him heroin to ease the physical pain. Takes a few jabs at the Canadian health care system while showing how life and death can be celebrated. Sparkling performances by all, with clever writing that avoids being overly sentimental or maudlin, well deserving of its win in Cannes. 110m; VHS, DVD. **C:** Remy Girard; Stephane Rousseau; Marie Josee Croze; Marina Hands; Dorothee Berryman; Johanne-Marie Tremblay; Dominique Michel; Louise Portal; Yves Jacques; Pierre Curzi; Directed by Denys Arcand; Written by Denys Arcand; Cinematography by Guy Dufaux; Music by Pierre Aviat. **Pr:** Denise Robert; Daniel Louis; Cinemaginaire Inc; Pyramide Productions; Miramax Film Corp. **A:** College-Adult. **P:** Entertainment. **U:** Home. **L:** French. **Mov-Ent:** Hospitals, Drug Abuse. **Awds:** Oscars '03: Foreign Film; British Acad. '03: Orig. Screenplay; Cannes '03: Actress (Croze), Screenplay; Natl. Bd. of Review '03: Foreign Film. **Acq:** Purchase. **Dist:** Miramax Film Corp.

Barbarian Queen 1985 (R) — ★
Female warriors led by beauteous babe seek revenge for the capture of their men in this sword-and-sorcery epic. Low-budget rip-off "Conan the Barbarian" is laughable. Also available in an unrated version. Followed by "Barbarian Queen 2: The Empress Strikes Back." 71m; VHS, DVD. **C:** Lana Clarkson; Frank Zagarino; Katt Shea; Dawn Dunlap; Susana Traverso; Directed by Hector Olivera; Written by Howard R. Cohen; Cinematography by Rudy Donovan; Music by Christopher Young. **Pr:** Cinema Group. **A:** Sr. High-Adult. **P:** Entertainment. **U:** Home. **Mov-Ent:** Fantasy, Occult Sciences. **Acq:** Purchase. **Dist:** Lions Gate Television Corp. $29.98.

Barbarian Queen 2: The Empress Strikes Back 1989 (R) — ★
Apparently one movie wasn't enough to tell the beautiful Princess Athalia's story. This time she fights her evil brother Ankaris. He throws her in prison, she escapes, joins a band of female rebels, and leads them into battle. No better than the first attempt. 87m; VHS, DVD. **C:** Lana Clarkson; Greg Wrangler; Rebecca Wood; Elizabeth Jaegen; Roger Cundy; Directed by Joe Finley; Written by Howard R. Cohen; Cinematography by Francisco Bojorquez; Music by Christopher Young. **A:** Sr. High-Adult. **P:** Entertainment. **U:** Home. **Mov-Ent:** Violence. **Acq:** Purchase. **Dist:** Lions Gate Television Corp. $89.98.

The Barbarians 1982
Offers instruction on specific aspects of true and mythological saints and legends. 30m; VHS. **A:** Adult. **P:** Education. **U:** Institution. **Gen-Edu:** History. **Acq:** Purchase. **Dist:** RMI Media. $69.95.

The Barbarians 1987 (R) — ★
Two bodybuilder siblings in animal skins battle wizards and warlords in this dumb-but-fun U.S./Italian co-production. 88m; VHS. **C:** David Paul; Peter Paul; Richard Lynch; Eva LaRue; Virginia Bryant; Sheeba Alahani; Michael Berryman; Directed by Ruggero Deodato; Music by Pino Donaggio. **Pr:** Cannon Films. **A:** Sr. High. **P:** Entertainment. **U:** Home. **Mov-Ent. Acq:** Purchase. **Dist:** Anchor Bay Entertainment. $19.95.

Barbarians at the Gate 1993 (R) — ★★★½
In the "greed is good" financial climate of the '80s, this movie chronicles the $25 billion battle in 1988 for RJR Nabisco, which at the time was working on developing a "smokeless cigarette." Garner is CEO F. Ross Johnson, who is confident that their "smokeless cigarette" will boost the stock's value—until he gets the test-marketing results. Unwilling to risk the product's failure, Johnson decides to buy the company and is challenged by master dealer Kravis (Pryce). Fascinating social commentary on the nastiest mega-deal in history. Based on the book by Bryan Burrough and John Helyar. 107m; VHS, DVD, CC. **C:** James Garner; Jonathan Pryce; Peter Riegert; Joanna Cassidy; Fred Dalton Thompson; Leilani Sarelle Ferrer; Matt Clark; Jeffrey DeMunn; Directed by Glenn Jordan; Written by Larry Gelbart; Cinematography by Thomas Del Ruth; Nicholas D. Knowland; Music by Richard Gibbs. **Pr:** Ray Stark; Thomas M. Hammel; Rastar Productions; HBO. **A:** Sr. High-Adult. **P:** Entertainment. **U:** Home. **Mov-Ent:** Ethics & Morals, TV Movies. **Acq:** Purchase. **Dist:** Facets Multimedia Inc.; Baker and Taylor. $92.99.

Barbarosa 1982 (PG) — ★★★
Offbeat western about an aging, legendary outlaw constantly on the lam who reluctantly befriends a naive farmboy and teaches him survival skills. Nelson and Busey are a great team, solidly directed. Lovely Rio Grande scenery. 90m; VHS, DVD. **C:** Willie Nelson; Gilbert Roland; Gary Busey; Isela Vega; Directed by Fred Schepisi; Written by William D. Wittliff; Cinematography by Ian Baker; Music by Bruce Smeaton. **Pr:** ITC Entertainment Group. **A:** Family. **P:** Entertainment. **U:** Home. **Mov-Ent:** Western. **Acq:** Purchase. **Dist:** Lions Gate Entertainment Inc. $19.95.

Barbary Coast 1935 (Unrated) — ★★★
A ruthless club owner tries to win the love of a young girl by building her into a star attraction during San Francisco's gold rush days. 90m/B/W; VHS, DVD. **C:** Edward G. Robinson; Walter Brennan; Brian Donlevy; Joel McCrea; Donald Meek; David Niven; Miriam Hopkins; Directed by Howard Hawks. **Pr:** Samuel Goldwyn. **A:** Family. **P:** Entertainment. **U:** Home. **Mov-Ent:** Action-Adventure. **Acq:** Purchase. **Dist:** Movies Unlimited. $19.99.

The Barbary Coast 1974 — ★★
A turn-of-the-century detective sleuths the streets of San Francisco in this average TV movie. 100m; VHS. **C:** William Shatner; Dennis Cole; Lynda Day George; John Vernon; Charles Aidman; Michael Ansara; Neville Brand; Bill Bixby; Directed by Bill Bixby. **A:** Family. **P:** Entertainment. **U:** Home. **Mov-Ent. Acq:** Purchase. **Dist:** MGM Studios Inc.

Barbary Coast 1975
ABC 1975-76 western comedy. Undercover government agent Jeff Cable teams up with saloon owner Cash Canover to track down criminals in the corruption-ridden city of San Francisco in the 1880s. 13 episodes. 745m; DVD. **C:** William Shatner; Doug McClure; Richard Kiel. **A:** Jr. High-Adult. **P:** Entertainment. **U:** Home. **L:** English. **Mov-Ent:** Western, Television Series, Cities & Towns. **Acq:** Purchase. **Dist:** Acorn Media Group Inc. $59.99.

Barbecue Video Cookbook: The Great Q 1994
Acclaimed chef and author, Robin Vietetta demonstrates a variety of helpful, easy techniques to cook barbecue. Robin presents actual cooking demonstrations and unique recipes to ensure great tasting meat. 50m; VHS. **Pr:** JAJ Productions. **A:** Adult. **P:** Instruction. **U:** Home. **How-Ins:** Cooking. **Acq:** Purchase. **Dist:** Tapeworm Video Distributors Inc. $14.95.

The Barber of Seville 1973
Sutherland and some of her puppet friends relate the tale of this famous opera to young people and adults. Sections of the opera are performed featuring the London Symphony Orchestra. 30m; VHS. **C:** Joan Sutherland. **Pr:** Nathan Kroll. **A:** Preschool. **P:** Entertainment. **U:** Institution, SURA. **Mov-Ent:** Opera, Puppets. **Acq:** Purchase. **Dist:** Phoenix Learning Group. $29.95.

The Barber of Seville 1976
Sills stars in this production of the comic opera. 157m; VHS. **Pr:** Paramount Pictures. **A:** Jr. High-Adult. **P:** Entertainment. **U:** Home. **Fin-Art:** Performing Arts, Opera. **Acq:** Purchase. **Dist:** Home Vision Cinema; Paramount Pictures Corp. $29.95.

The Barber of Seville 1987
A performance of the Rossini comic opera taped at the Glyndebourne Festival Opera, with the London Philharmonic. English subtitles. 156m; VHS. **C:** Maria Ewing; Robert Dean; John Rawnsley; Max-Rene Cosotti. **Pr:** National Video Corporation Ltd. **A:** Family. **P:** Entertainment. **U:** Home. **L:** Italian. **Fin-Art:** Music--Performance, Opera. **Acq:** Purchase. **Dist:** Home Vision Cinema; Music Video Distributors. $39.95.

The Barber of Seville 1990
This La Scala production of the opera features soloists Berganza, Prey, Malagu, Alva, Dora and other greats. 142m; VHS. **A:** Sr. High-Adult. **P:** Entertainment. **U:** Home. **Fin-Art:** Opera. **Acq:** Purchase. **Dist:** Music Video Distributors. $34.95.

The Barber of Seville 1991
A live performance of Rossini's opera recorded at the Metropolitan Opera. Conducted by Ralf Weikert. 161m; VHS. **C:** Kathleen Battle; Leo Nucci. **A:** Family. **P:** Entertainment. **U:** Home. **Mov-Ent:** Performing Arts, Opera. **Acq:** Purchase. **Dist:** Facets Multimedia Inc. $34.95.

The Barber Shop 1933 — ★★★
Fields portrays the bumbling, carefree barber Cornelius O'Hare, purveyor of village gossip and problem solver. Havoc begins when a gangster enters the shop and demands that Cornelius change his appearance. 21m/B/W; VHS, DVD. **C:** W.C. Fields; Elise Cavanna; Harry Watson; Dagmar Oakland; Frank Yaconelli; Directed by Arthur Ripley. **Pr:** Paramount Pictures. **A:** Family. **P:** Entertainment. **U:** Home. **Mov-Ent:** Comedy--Slapstick. **Acq:** Purchase. **Dist:** $24.98.

Barbershop 2002 (PG-13) — ★★★
Ensemble comedy looks at the unique culture found in barbershops in the black male community. Cube plays Calvin, discontented owner of a barbershop he inherited from his father. In debt, Calvin sells the shop to a loan shark, which sends all the shop's regulars reeling, as their haven will be turned into a strip club. During the shop's final day, when the film takes place, Calvin must come to grips with his mistake and recognize the value of his father's legacy. Though two lesser subplots detract from the engrossing barbershop talk, a host of interesting characters mesh with an original and entertaining story. 102m; VHS, DVD, UMD, CC. **C:** Ice Cube; Anthony Anderson; Cedric the Entertainer; Eve; Sean Patrick Thomas; Troy Garity; Michael Ealy; Leonard Earl Howze; Keith David; Lahmard Tate; Tom Wright; Jazsmin Lewis; Directed by Tim Story; Written by Mark Brown; Don D. Scott; Marshall Todd; Cinematography by Tom Priestley; Music by Terence Blanchard. **Pr:** George Tillman, Jr.; Mark Brown; Robert Teitel; Cube Vision; State Street Pictures; MGM. **A:** Jr. High-Adult. **P:** Entertainment. **U:** Home. **Mov-Ent:** Black Culture, Pregnancy. **Acq:** Purchase. **Dist:** MGM Home Entertainment.

Barbershop 2: Back in Business 2004 (PG-13) — ★★★
Calvin and the rest of the crew are back. This time around, the shop faces a community crisis in the form of franchise cutters Nappy Cutz moving in across the street, threatening to put Calvin's shop out business. Lacks the fresh charm of the first one, but the strong cast and crisp writing save the day. 106m; VHS, DVD. **C:** Ice Cube; Cedric the Entertainer; Sean Patrick Thomas; Eve; Troy Garity; Michael Ealy; Leonard Earl Howze; Harry J. Lennix; Robert Wisdom; Jazsmin Lewis; Carl Wright; Kenan Thompson; Queen Latifah; Garcelle Beauvais; Directed by Kevin Rodney Sullivan; Written by Don D. Scott; Cinematography by Tom Priestley; Music by Richard Gibbs. **Pr:** Robert Teitel; George Tillman, Jr.; Alex Gartner; State Street Pictures; Cube Vision; MGM. **A:** Jr. High-Adult. **P:** Entertainment. **U:** Home. **Mov-Ent:** Real Estate, Black Culture. **Acq:** Purchase. **Dist:** MGM Home Entertainment.

Barbie in the Nutcracker 2001 — ★★★
After a half-century of existence, Barbie finally gets her own movie. Here, she relates (and stars in) the familiar tale of "The Nutcracker." Clara (played by Barbie) is given a nutcracker as a Christmas gift. This enchanted toy leads Clara into a magical world, as she must help the Nutcracker defeat the evil Mouse King. Despite the fact that "The Nutcracker" has been performed countless times, there is a fresh quality to this production. While not matching the level of films such as "Toy Story," the computer animation is quite impressive. Clearly, the film is aimed at young girls, but the colorful animation and the well-paced story made it accessible to a wider audience. 78m; DVD, Wide. **C:** Voice(s) by Kelly Sheridan; Kirby Morrow; Tim Curry; Peter Kelamis; Directed by Owen Hurley; Written by Linda Engelsiepen; Hilary Hinkle; Rob Hudnut. **A:** Family. **P:** Entertainment. **U:** Home. **Mov-Ent:** Music--Classical, Christmas, Fairy Tales. **Acq:** Purchase. **Dist:** Lions Gate Television Corp.

Barbie in the Pink Shoes 2013 (Unrated)
The popular doll stars as a ballerina in a cartoon in which she must dance to defeat an evil Snow Queen. 75m; DVD, Blu-Ray, Streaming. **A:** Family. **P:** Entertainment. **U:** Home. **L:** English, French, Spanish. **Mov-Ent:** Animation & Cartoons, Fantasy. **Acq:** Purchase, Rent/Lease. **Dist:** Universal Studios Home Video. $26.98 29.98 14.99.

Barbra Streisand: A Happening in Central Park 1967
Songs include, "People," "Second-Hand Rose," "Cry Me a River" and "Silent Night." 60m; VHS. **C:** Barbra Streisand. **A:** Jr. High-Adult. **P:** Entertainment. **U:** Home. **Mov-Ent:** Music--Performance, Singing, Performing Arts. **Acq:** Purchase. **Dist:** Music Video Distributors. $19.98.

Barbra Streisand: Color Me Barbra 1966
Streisand's second television special. She sings "Yesterdays," "The Minute Waltz," "Where Am I Going?" and others, in various settings within an art museum. 60m; VHS. **C:** Barbra Streisand. **Pr:** CBS. **A:** Family. **P:** Entertainment. **U:** Home. **Mov-Ent:** Music--Performance, Television Series. **Acq:** Purchase. **Dist:** Music Video Distributors. $19.95.

Barbra Streisand: My Name Is Barbra 1965
This is Streisand's first television special, wherein she sings "I Am Woman," "Make Believe" and "Lover, Come Back to Me," among others, some done before a live audience. 60m/B/W; VHS. **Pr:** CBS. **A:** Family. **P:** Entertainment. **U:** Home. **Mov-Ent:** Music--Performance, Television Series. **Acq:** Purchase. **Dist:** Music Video Distributors. $19.95.

Barbra Streisand: One Voice 1986
Barbra Streisand's first live concert in over a decade was taped at her Malibu mansion in 1986. She performs a number of her standards, plus some new tunes, including "Over the Rainbow," "It's a New World," "Somewhere," "Evergreen," "People," "The Way We Were," and "Something's Coming." 68m; VHS. **C:** Barbra Streisand. **Pr:** The Streisand Foundation. **A:** Family. **P:** Entertainment. **U:** Home. **Mov-Ent:** Music--Performance, Music Video. **Acq:** Purchase. **Dist:** Music Video Distributors. $19.95.

Barbra Streisand: Putting It Together 1986
A behind-the-scenes look at the recording sessions for Streisand's popular "Broadway Album," showing her at work in the studio. The tape also includes music videos of several tracks from the album. 40m; VHS. **C:** Barbra Streisand. **Pr:** CBS/Fox. **A:** Family. **P:** Entertainment. **U:** Home. **Mov-Ent:** Music Video, Music--Performance. **Acq:** Purchase. **Dist:** Music Video Distributors. $19.95.

Barcelona ????
Film program and 500 still pictures of works from the Picasso and Miro museums in Barcelona. ?m; DVD. **A:** Sr. High-Adult. **P:** Education. **U:** Home, Institution. **Gen-Edu:** Art & Artists, Museums. **Acq:** Purchase. **Dist:** Crystal Productions. $75.00.

Barcelona 1980
A visit to the capital city of Catalonia, the gothic architecture, the moderate climate, and the music, dancing and swimming on the Costa Brava. 15m; VHS, 3/4 U. **Pr:** CEC. **A:** Jr. High-Adult. **P:** Education. **U:** Institution, SURA. **Gen-Edu:** Spain. **Acq:** Purchase. **Dist:** Lucerne Media.

Barcelona 1994 (PG-13) — ★★★
Old-fashioned talkfest about two neurotic Americans experiencing sibling rivalry in Spain. Serious Ted (Nichols) is an American sales rep, posted to Barcelona, who can't quite get into the city's pleasure-loving rhythm. This is not a problem for Ted's cousin Fred (Eigeman), an obnoxious naval officer, with whom Ted has had a rivalry dating back to their boyhood. Set in the 1980s, the two must also deal with anti-Americanism, which leads both to violence and romantic developments. Tart dialogue, thoughtful performances, and exotic locales prove enticing in low-budget sleeper that effectively mixes drama and dry comedy. Watch for Eigeman in Tom Cruise's uniform from "A Few Good Men." 102m; VHS, DVD, Wide. **C:** Taylor Nichols; Christopher Eigeman; Tushka Bergen; Mira Sorvino; Pep Munne; Francis Creighton; Thomas Gibson; Jack Gilpin; Nuria Badia; Hellena Schmied; Directed by Whit Stillman; Written by Whit Stillman; Cinematography by John Thomas; Music by Tom Judson; Mark Suozzo. **Pr:** Rosc Romero; Whit Stillman; Whit Stillman; Castle Rock Entertainment; Fine Line Features. **A:** Sr. High-Adult. **P:** Entertainment. **U:** Home. **Mov-Ent:** Comedy-Drama, Spain, Romance. **Awds:** Ind. Spirit '95: Cinematog. **Acq:** Purchase. **Dist:** New Line Home Video; Image Entertainment Inc.; Turner Broadcasting System Inc.

The Barcelona Kill 1977 (Unrated) — ★1/2
When a journalist and her boyfriend get in too deep with the Barcelona mob, their troubles begin. 86m; VHS. **C:** Linda Hayden; John Astin; Simon Andreu; Maximo Valverde; Directed by Jose Antonio De La Loma. **Pr:** Michael Klinger Productions. **A:** Adult. **P:** Entertainment. **U:** Home. **Mov-Ent:** Mystery & Suspense, Journalism, Spain. **Acq:** Purchase. **Dist:** No Longer Available.

Barclay James Harvest: Berlin—A Concert for the People 2010 (Unrated)
79m; DVD. **A:** Jr. High-Adult. **P:** Entertainment. **U:** Home. **Mov-Ent:** Music--Performance, Documentary Films, Germany. **Acq:** Purchase. **Dist:** Eagle Rock Entertainment Inc. $9.99.

Bardelys the Magnificent 1926 (Unrated) — ★★
Boastful, womanizing swashbuckler the Marquis de Bardelys (Gilbert) sets out to woo Roxalanne (Boardman) who has already rejected the advances of sinister Chatellerault (D'Arcy). Bardelys assumes the disguise of a rebel leader, gets into trouble, and winds up on the gallows thanks to his rival. A gap in the surviving print is bridged with stills and footage from the original trailer. Based on the novel by Rafael Sabatini. 90m/B/W; Silent; DVD. **C:** John Gilbert; Eleanor Boardman; Roy D'Arcy; Arthur Lubin; Lionel Belmore; Emily Fitzroy; Directed by King Vidor; Written by Dorothy Farnum; Cinematography by William H. Daniels. **A:** College-Adult. **P:** Entertainment. **U:** Home. **Mov-Ent:** Silent Films. **Acq:** Purchase. **Dist:** Flicker Alley.

Bare Essentials 1991 (PG) — ★
Made for TV yuppie Club Med nightmare in which a high-strung couple from New York find themselves marooned on a desert isle with only two other inhabitants. With no cellular telephoning ability and an absence of large-ticket consumer goods to purchase, the two turn their reluctant sights on each other, focusing on the bare essentials, as it were. Great soul-searching scenes for the inarticulate. 94m; VHS, CC. **C:** Gregory Harrison; Lisa Hartman Black; Mark Linn-Baker; Charlotte Lewis; Directed by Martha Coolidge. **Pr:** Jay Benson. **A:** Jr. High-Adult. **P:** Entertainment. **U:** Home. **Mov-Ent:** Comedy--Romantic, TV Movies. **Acq:** Purchase. **Dist:** Lions Gate Entertainment Inc. $89.98.

Bare Hunt 1963 — ★
Detective Max T. Unimportant is dragged into the underground world of prospective nude actresses in this supposedly funny "nudie." 69m/B/W; VHS. **Pr:** August Entertainment. **A:** Adult. **P:** Entertainment. **U:** Home. **Mov-Ent:** Comedy--Black. **Acq:** Purchase. **Dist:** Tapeworm Video Distributors Inc. $19.95.

Bare Knees 1928 (Unrated) — ★★
A woman causes a scandal in her family when she arrives at her sister's birthday party with bare knees, cigarettes, and other flapper items. The quintessential flapper movie. 61m/B/W; Silent; VHS, DVD. **C:** Virginia Lee Corbin; Donald Keith; Jane Winton; Johnnie Walker; Forrest Stanley; Maude Fulton; Directed by Erle C. Kenton. **Pr:** Gotham Productions. **A:** Family. **P:** Entertainment. **U:** Home. **Mov-Ent:** Silent Films. **Acq:** Purchase. **Dist:** Grapevine Video. $17.95.

Bare Knuckles 1977 (R) — ★
The adventures of a low-rent bounty hunter. 90m; VHS, DVD. **C:** Robert Viharo; Sherry Jackson; Michael Heit; Gloria Hendry; John Daniels; Directed by Don Edmonds; Cinematography by Dean Cundey. **Pr:** Don Edmonds; Don Edmonds. **A:** Sr. High-Adult. **P:** Entertainment. **U:** Home. **Mov-Ent. Acq:** Purchase. **Dist:** Unknown Distributor.

Bare Minimum 198?
In this film, a safety director and his foreman offer several recommendations for the care and proper use of safety gear. 10m; VHS, 3/4 U. **A:** College-Adult. **P:** Education. **U:** Institution. **Bus-Ind:** Safety Education. **Acq:** Rent/Lease. **Dist:** National Safety Council, California Chapter, Film Library.

Bareboat Charter Checklist 19??
Safety checklist for those taking a charter boat vacation. 25m; VHS. **A:** Adult. **P:** Instruction. **U:** Home. **Spo-Rec:** Boating. **Acq:** Purchase. **Dist:** Bennett Marine Video. $24.95.

Barefoot 2014 (PG-13) — ★
Misbegotten remake of a 2005 German comedy. Needing to convince his wealthy family he's changed, n'er-do-well Jay (Speedman) has innocent Daisy (Wood) pose as his girlfriend at his brother's New Orleans wedding. And where did they meet? In the mental ward of an L.A. hospital (he was a janitor, she was a patient). When Jay's plan doesn't work as intended, they steal his dad's vintage RV and road-trip back to Cali. Daisy's inappropriate behavior is meant to be charming but pic comes off as exploitative and rather icky. 90m; DVD, Blu-Ray. **C:** Scott Speedman; Evan Rachel Wood; J.K. Simmons; Treat Williams; Kate Burton; Directed by Andrew Fleming; Written by Stephen Zotnowski; Cinematography by Alexander Gruszynski; Music by Michael Penn. **A:** Jr. High-Adult. **P:** Entertainment. **U:** Home. **L:** English. **Mov-Ent:** Mental Health, Comedy--Romantic, Family. **Acq:** Purchase. **Dist:** Lions Gate Home Entertainment.

Barefoot Adventure 1960 (Unrated)
Californian and Hawaiian surf are featured here in the legendary Bruce Brown's third film. Includes footage of Point surf at Makaha. Music by Bud Shank. 75m; VHS, DVD. **C:** Narrated by Bruce Brown; Music by Bud Shank. **Pr:** Bruce Brown; Bruce Brown. **A:** Jr. High-Adult. **P:** Entertainment. **U:** Home. **Mov-Ent. Acq:** Purchase. **Dist:** Facets Multimedia Inc. $24.95.

Barefoot Boy 1938 (Unrated) — ★1/2
An ex-con sends his snob of a son to the farm of an old friend to learn a few life lessons, which materialize in the form of a gang of crooks and a haunted house. 63m/B/W; DVD. **C:** Jackie Moran; Marcia Mae Jones; Bradley Metcalfe; Johnnie Morris; Marilyn Knowlden; Directed by Karl Brown; Written by John Thomas "Jack" Neville; Cinematography by Gilbert Warrenton. **A:** Primary-Adult. **P:** Entertainment. **U:** Home. **L:** English. **Mov-Ent. Acq:** Purchase. **Dist:** Gotham Distributing Corp. $7.98.

The Barefoot Contessa 1954 — ★★★
The story, told in flashback, of a Spanish dancer's rise to Hollywood stardom, as witnessed by a cynical director. Shallow Hollywood self-examination. 128m; VHS, DVD. **C:** Ava Gardner; Humphrey Bogart; Edmond O'Brien; Valentina Cortese; Rossano Brazzi; Warren Stevens; Marius Goring; Directed by Joseph L. Mankiewicz; Written by Joseph L. Mankiewicz; Cinematography by Jack Cardiff. **Pr:** United Artists. **A:** Jr. High-Adult. **P:** Entertainment. **U:** Home. **Mov-Ent:** Dance. **Awds:** Oscars '54: Support. Actor (O'Brien); Golden Globes '55: Support. Actor (O'Brien). **Acq:** Purchase. **Dist:** MGM Home Entertainment; Facets Multimedia Inc.; Baker and Taylor. $19.98.

The Barefoot Doctors of Rural China 19??
Provides an unique look at how the barefoot doctors of the Chinese countryside originated. 52m; VHS, Special order formats. **Pr:** Cambridge. **A:** Adult. **P:** Education. **U:** Institution. **Gen-Edu:** Documentary Films, China, Medical Care. **Acq:** Purchase, Rent/Lease. **Dist:** Cambridge Documentary Films, Inc. $150.00.

Barefoot Doctors of Rural China 20??
Documentary showcasing the development of the "barefoot" doctors in the Chinese rural countryside in the 1970s. Also available for purchase in 16mm. 52m; VHS. **A:** Sr. High-Adult. **P:** Education. **U:** Institution. **Gen-Edu:** Medical Care, Documentary Films, China. **Acq:** Purchase, Rent/Lease. **Dist:** Cambridge Documentary Films, Inc. $165.00.

The Barefoot Executive 1971 (Unrated) — ★★
A mailroom boy who works for a national TV network finds a chimpanzee that can pick hit shows in this Disney family comedy. 92m; VHS, DVD. **C:** Kurt Russell; John Ritter; Harry (Henry) Morgan; Wally Cox; Heather North; Joe Flynn; Directed by Robert Butler; Music by Robert F. Brunner. **Pr:** Walt Disney Studios. **A:** Family. **P:** Entertainment. **U:** Home. **Mov-Ent:** Comedy--Slapstick, Animals, Family Viewing. **Acq:** Purchase. **Dist:** Walt Disney Studios Home Entertainment, On Moratorium.

Barefoot in Athens 1966 (Unrated) — ★★
TV presentation from "George Schaefer's Showcase Theatre" chronicles the last years of the philosopher Socrates who, barefoot and unkempt, an embarrassment to his wife, and a dangerous critic to the corrupt Athenian leaders, nevertheless believes that democracy and truth are all-important in his city. 76m; VHS. **C:** Peter Ustinov; Geraldine Page; Anthony Quayle; Directed by George Schaefer. **Pr:** George Schaefer; George Schaefer. **A:** Family. **P:** Entertainment. **U:** Institution, Home. **Mov-Ent:** Drama, Philosophy & Ideology, TV Movies. **Acq:** Purchase. **Dist:** Films for the Humanities & Sciences.

Barefoot in the Park 1967 — ★★★
Neil Simon's Broadway hit translates well to screen. A newly wedded bride (Fonda) tries to get her husband (Redford, reprising his Broadway role) to loosen up and be as free-spirited as she is. 106m; VHS, DVD. **C:** Robert Redford; Jane Fonda; Charles Boyer; Mildred Natwick; Herb Edelman; Mabel Albertson; Directed by Gene Saks; Written by Neil Simon; Cinematography by Joseph LaShelle; Music by Neal Hefti. **Pr:** Hal B. Wallis; Paramount Pictures. **A:** Sr. High-Adult. **P:** Entertainment. **U:** Home. **Mov-Ent:** Comedy--Romantic, Marriage. **Acq:** Purchase. **Dist:** Paramount Pictures Corp. $14.95.

Barefoot Skiing and Jumping 1981
Champion Brett Wing instructs you on all aspects of barefoot skiing, from one ski stepoffs to world record trick runs. 120m; VHS, 3/4 U. **Pr:** Double Vision. **A:** Jr. High-Adult. **P:** Instruction. **U:** Institution, SURA. **Spo-Rec:** Sports--Water. **Acq:** Purchase. **Dist:** Double Vision Prod.

Barenboim on Beethoven: The Complete Piano Sonatas 2007
Maestro Berenboim performs eight concerts in Berlin and hosts six masterclasses with up-and-coming pianists from around the world and in various stages of professional development. Saleem Abboud Ashkar (of Palestinian/Israeli background); Alessio Bax (Italy); Jonathan Biss (U.S.); David Kadouch (France); Lang Lang (China); and Shai Wosner (Israel) each work through a sonata movement he has specifically chosen for them. 1020m; DVD. **A:** Adult. **P:** Entertainment. **U:** Home, Institution. **Mov-Ent:** Music--Classical, Music--Performance, How-To. **Acq:** Purchase. **Dist:** WGBH/Boston. $149.95.

Baretta: Season One 1975
Three-disc set contains 13 episodes of the popular cop show starring Robert Blake. 612m; DVD. **A:** Adult. **P:** Entertainment. **U:** Home. **Mov-Ent:** Television, Drama, Mystery & Suspense. **Acq:** Purchase. **Dist:** Universal Studios Home Video. $39.98.

Barfly 1987 (R) — ★★★
Bukowski's semi-autobiographical screenplay is the story of a talented writer who chooses to spend his time as a lonely barfly, hiding his literary abilities behind glasses of liquor. Dunaway's character is right on target as the fellow alcoholic. 100m; VHS, DVD, 8 mm, CC. **C:** Mickey Rourke; Faye Dunaway; Alice Krige; Frank Stallone; J.C. Quinn; Jack Nance; Charles Bukowski; Pruitt Taylor Vince; Fritz Feld; Sandy Martin; Damon Hines; Directed by Barbet Schroeder; Written by Charles Bukowski; Cinematography by Robby Muller; Music by Jack Baran. **Pr:** Francis Ford Coppola; Cannon Films. **A:** Jr. High-Adult. **P:** Entertainment. **U:** Home. **Mov-Ent:** Alcoholism. **Acq:** Purchase. **Dist:** Facets Multimedia Inc.; Warner Home Video, Inc. $19.98.

The Bargain 1915 — ★½
Hart's first feature, in which he portrays a bandit desperately trying to go straight. Original titles with musical score. 50m/B/W; Silent; VHS, DVD. **C:** William S. Hart; J. Frank Burke; J. Barney Sherry; Clara Williams; Joseph J. Dowling; Roy Laidlaw; Herschel Mayall; Charles Swickard; Charles French; Directed by Reginald Barker; Written by William H. Clifford; Thomas Ince; Cinematography by Joseph August. **Pr:** Thomas H. Ince; New York Motion Picture Corporation. **A:** Family. **P:** Entertainment. **U:** Institution, Home. **Mov-Ent:** Western, Silent Films. **Awds:** Natl. Film Reg. '10. **Acq:** Purchase, Rent/Lease. **Dist:** Alpha Video. $19.95.

Baritone 1985 — ★★
Concerned Polish drama about a prominent opera singer who promises to deliver a grand concert upon returning to his small town, only to lose his voice just before the show is to start. Proof positive that the opera ain't over 'til the fat lady sings. 100m; VHS. **C:** Zbigniew Zapasiewicz; Directed by Janusz Zaorski. **Pr:** Polish. **A:** Sr. High-Adult. **P:** Entertainment. **U:** Home. **L:** Polish. **Mov-Ent. Acq:** Purchase. **Dist:** Facets Multimedia Inc. $49.95.

Barjo 1993 — ★★
In a bland and isolated French suburb lives willful housewife Fanfan (Bouchet) with her older businessman husband Charles (Bohringer) and her eccentric twin brother Barjo (Girardot). Barjo is obsessed with lists and extraterrestrials and his sister's affair with their next-door neighbor, which he likes to spy on. Her husband naturally begins to go crazy. Deadpan satire based on the novel "Confessions of a Crap Artist" by Philip K. Dick. The post-WWII American setting of the novel makes a decidedly uneasy transistion to contemporary French life. In French with English subtitles. 85m; VHS. **C:** Anne Brochet; Hippolyte Girardot; Richard Bohringer; Consuelo de Haviland; Renaud Danner; Nathalie Boutefeu; Directed by Jerome Boivin; Written by Jerome Boivin; Jacques Audiard; Music by Hugues LeBars. **Pr:** Patrick Godeau; Myriad Pictures. **A:** College-Adult. **P:** Entertainment. **U:** Home. **L:** French. **Mov-Ent:** Comedy--Black, Marriage, Satire & Parody. **Acq:** Purchase. **Dist:** Wellspring Media. $89.98.

Bark! 2002 (R) — ★½
L.A. dog walker Lucy (Morgan) begins to overly-identify with her clients when she stops speaking and begins barking and displaying other canine behavior. Her baffled husband Peter (Tergesen) consults Lucy's equally odd parents as well as a vet (Kudrow) and a shrink (D'Onofrio) and decides to have his wife committed. But when Lucy becomes catatonic in the hospital, Peter decides to take her home and learn to adapt. He's a lot more understanding than the viewer will be. 100m; VHS, DVD, On Demand. **C:** Lee Tergesen; Lisa Kudrow; Vincent D'Onofrio; Heather Morgan; Hank Azaria; Mary Jo Deschanel; Scott Wilson; Aimee Graham; Wade Andrew Williams; Directed by Kasia Adamik; Written by Heather Morgan; Cinematography by Irek Hartowicz; Music by Eric Colvin. **Pr:** Alicia Allain; Tom Reed; High Wire Films; Propaganda Films; First Look Pictures. **A:** Sr. High-Adult. **P:** Entertainment. **U:** Home. **Mov-Ent:** Pets, Marriage, Psychiatry. **Acq:** Purchase. **Dist:** Amazon.com Inc.; Alpha Video.

Barking Dogs Never Bite 2000 (Unrated) — ★★★
Black comedy involving a janitor and a stressed academic, one of which could be a serial killer specializing in small dogs. May be distressing for lovers of cute fluffy animals. Scratch that, it will be traumatizing for fluffy animal lovers. 108m; DVD. **C:** Sung-jae Lee; Doona Bae; Directed by Joon-ho Bong; Written by Joon-ho Bong; Ji-ho Song; Derek Son Tae-woong; Cinematography by Yong-kyou Cho; Yeong-gyu Jo; Music by Sung-woo Jo. **A:** Sr. High-Adult. **P:** Entertainment. **U:** Home. **L:** English, Korean, Spanish. **Mov-Ent:** Comedy--Black. **Acq:** Purchase. **Dist:** Magnolia Home Entertainment. $26.98.

Barking Plate 1982
The program demonstrates some of the steps involved in the invention of the phonograph. Part of the "Inventive Child" series. 10m; VHS, 3/4 U. **Pr:** Film Polski. **A:** Primary-Jr. High. **P:** Education. **U:** Institution, SURA. **Chl-Juv**. **Acq:** Purchase, Rent/Lease, Trade-in. **Dist:** Encyclopedia Britannica.

The Barkleys of Broadway 1949 — ★★★
The famous dancing team's last film together; they play a quarreling husband/wife showbiz team. 109m; VHS, DVD. **C:** Fred Astaire; Ginger Rogers; Gale Robbins; Oscar Levant; Jacques Francois; Billie Burke; Directed by Charles Walters; Written by Adolph Green; Betty Comden; Cinematography by Harry Stradling, Sr.; Music by Ira Gershwin; Harry Warren. **Pr:** MGM. **A:** Family. **P:** Entertainment. **U:** Home. **Mov-Ent:** Musical--Drama, Dance, Marriage. **Acq:** Purchase. **Dist:** MGM Home Entertainment. $19.98.
Songs: They Can't Take That Away From Me; The Sabre Dance; Swing Trot; Manhattan Downbeat; A Weekend in the Country; My One and Only Highland Fling; You'd Be Hard to Replace; Bouncin' the Blues; Shoes With Wings On; Piano Concerto in B-flat Minor.

Barn Again! 1990
Tells the stories of barns, one of America's most distinctive architectural forms, that have been given new life through restoration. Restoration efforts are undertaken through a program sponsored by the National Trust for Historic Preservation and "Successful Farming Magazine." 60m; VHS. **A:** Jr. High-Adult. **P:** Education. **U:** Institution, Home. **Gen-Edu:** Architecture, History--U.S. **Acq:** Purchase. **Dist:** GPN Educational Media. $23.95.

Barn Burning 1980
William Faulkner's story of the late 19th-century South. The son of a tenant farmer is torn between trying to win his father's acceptance and his aversion to his father's unrelenting and violent nature. Part of the "American Short Story II" series. 41m; VHS. **C:** Tommy Lee Jones; Diane Kagan. **Pr:** Learning in Focus, Inc. **A:** Sr. High-Adult. **P:** Education. **U:** Home. **Mov-Ent:** Literature--American. **Acq:** Purchase. **Dist:** Karol Media; Monterey Home Video. $24.95.

Barn Construction 1988
Through tours at other stables, shows the proper contruction of a barn for fire safety, durability, function, and cost. 45m; VHS. **Pr:** The Blood-Horse. **A:** College-Adult. **P:** Instruction. **U:** Institution, Home. **How-Ins:** Construction, Horses--Racing. **Acq:** Purchase. **Dist:** The Blood-Horse, Inc.

Barn of the Naked Dead 1973 (Unrated) — **Bomb!**
Prine plays a sicko who tortures women while his radioactive monster dad terrorizes the Nevada desert. Rudolph's first film, directed under the pseudonym Gerald Comier. 86m; VHS, DVD. **C:** Andrew Prine; Manuella Thiess; Sherry Alberoni; Gylian Roland; Al Cormier; Jennifer Ashley; Directed by Alan Rudolph; Written by Alan Rudolph; Roman Valenti. **A:** Adult. **P:** Entertainment. **U:** Home. **Mov-Ent:** Horror, Exploitation. **Acq:** Purchase. **Dist:** Amazon.com Inc.

The Barn Owl 1987
This rare species is caught on film performing many typical activities. 20m; VHS, 3/4 U. **Pr:** Institut fur Film und Bild. **A:** Jr. High-College. **P:** Education. **U:** Institution, SURA. **Hea-Sci:** Birds. **Acq:** Purchase, Trade-in. **Dist:** Encyclopedia Britannica. $300.00.

Barn Ventilation 1981
This tape provides information on the push, pull, center and side methods of barn ventilation. 17m; VHS, 3/4 U, EJ, Q. **Pr:** Cornell University. **A:** Sr. High-Adult. **P:** Education. **U:** Institution, CCTV, CATV, BCTV, Home. **Gen-Edu:** Animals, Agriculture. **Acq:** Purchase, Rent/Lease. **Dist:** Cornell University.

Barnabas: The RCIA Sponsor 1987
This video features personal accounts from Catholic sponsors. 30m; VHS. **Pr:** POD Evangelization Productions. **A:** Sr. High-Adult. **P:** Religious. **U:** Institution. **Gen-Edu:** Religion. **Acq:** Purchase. **Dist:** Harcourt Religion Publishers. $79.95.

Barnaby and Me 1977 (Unrated) — ★★
Australian star Barnaby the Koala Bear joins an international con-man in this romantic adventure. The mob is chasing the con-man when he meets and falls for a lovely young woman and her daughter. 90m; VHS. **C:** Sid Caesar; Juliet Mills; Sally Boyden; Directed by Norman Panama. **Pr:** Transatlantic Enterprises. **A:** Family. **P:** Entertainment. **U:** Home. **Mov-Ent:** Comedy--Romantic. **Acq:** Purchase. **Dist:** Movies Unlimited. $14.99.

Barnaby: Father Dear Father 1981
A little boy named Barnaby and his fairy godfather, Mr. J. J. O'Malley, have many adventures while trying to decide what to get Barnaby's father for Father's Day. 6m; VHS, 3/4 U. **Pr:** Halas and Batchelor Studios. **A:** Primary. **P:** Entertainment. **U:** Institution, SURA. **Chl-Juv:** Animation & Cartoons. **Acq:** Purchase. **Dist:** Phoenix Learning Group.

Barnaby: Overdue Dues Blues 1981
Barnaby's fairy godfather, Mr. O'Malley, is long overdue in paying his dues to his club, and Barnaby must help him solve his problem. 6m; VHS, 3/4 U. **Pr:** Halas and Batchelor Studios. **A:** Preschool-Primary. **P:** Entertainment. **U:** Institution, SURA. **Chl-Juv:** Animation & Cartoons. **Acq:** Purchase. **Dist:** Phoenix Learning Group.

Barnes and Barnes: Zabagabee 1984
A retrospective of the quirky music video artists, featuring their hits "Fish Heads" and "Party In My Pants." 40m; VHS. **Pr:** Barnes and Barnes. **A:** Jr. High-Adult. **P:** Entertainment. **U:** Home. **Mov-Ent:** Music Video, Documentary Films. **Acq:** Purchase. **Dist:** Music Video Distributors; Rhino Entertainment Co. $19.95.

Barney & Friends: Barney Rhymes with Mother Goose 1993
That big purple dinosaur is back with a dozen classic songs and rhymes, including "Polly Put the Kettle On" and "Little Jack Horner." 30m; VHS. **A:** Preschool. **P:** Entertainment. **U:** Home. **Chl-Juv:** Music--Children, Dinosaurs. **Acq:** Purchase. **Dist:** HIT Entertaiment/Lyons Group. $14.95.

Barney & Friends: Barney's Best Manners 1993
The big purple dinosaur and his pals have a picnic with games and songs to teach manners, including "Please and Thank-You," "Snackin' on Healthy Food," "Does Your Chewing Gum Lose Its Flavor," and for fun "Three Little Fishies." 30m; VHS. **A:** Preschool. **P:** Entertainment. **U:** Home. **Chl-Juv:** Children, Music--Children, Dinosaurs. **Acq:** Purchase. **Dist:** HIT Entertaiment/Lyons Group. $14.95.

Barney & Friends: Families Are Special 1995
Through games and songs Barney and his friends explore family values. Meanwhile, Tosha is excited by the new birth in her family. 30m; VHS. **A:** Preschool. **P:** Entertainment. **U:** Home. **Chl-Juv:** Children, Dinosaurs. **Acq:** Purchase. **Dist:** HIT Entertaiment/Lyons Group. $14.95.

Barney & the Backyard Gang: Barney Goes to School 1989
Barney and pals discover the fun of learning during a typical day in school. There's fingerpainting and other creative learning, plus a wild search for an adventurous hamster! ?m; VHS. **Pr:** Lyons Film. **A:** Preschool-Primary. **P:** Entertainment. **U:** BCTV. **Mov-Ent:** Animation & Cartoons, Education, Children. **Acq:** Purchase. **Dist:** HIT Entertaiment/Lyons Group. $14.95.

Barney & the Backyard Gang: Barney in Concert 1991
Barney the purple dinosaur and his friend Baby Bop perform fun songs that allow children to interact. 50m; VHS. **A:** Preschool-Primary. **P:** Entertainment. **U:** Home. **Chl-Juv:** Children, Music--Children, Dinosaurs. **Acq:** Purchase. **Dist:** HIT Entertaiment/Lyons Group. $14.95.

Barney & the Backyard Gang: Barney's Birthday Party 1992
The big purple dinosaur is having a birthday party, and everyone is invited. In addition to the usual birthday fun, you'll also learn about birthday customs from other parts of the world. Songs include "Barney Theme Song," "She'll Be Comin' Round the Mountain," "Happy Birthday," and "Hey, Hey, Our Friends Are Here." 30m; VHS. **A:** Preschool-Primary. **P:** Entertainment. **U:** Home. **Chl-Juv:** Children, Dinosaurs, Music--Children. **Acq:** Purchase. **Dist:** HIT Entertaiment/Lyons Group. $14.95.

Barney & the Backyard Gang: Barney's Campfire Sing-along 1989
Barney shows the Backyard Gang how much fun camping can be. Learn about woodland animals, stars, and forest safety. 47m; VHS. **A:** Preschool-Primary. **P:** Entertainment. **U:** Home. **Chl-Juv:** Children, Camps & Camping, Music--Children. **Acq:** Purchase. **Dist:** HIT Entertaiment/Lyons Group. $14.95.

Barney & the Backyard Gang: Barney's Magical Musical Adventure 1992
Barney appears when the Backyard Gang is building a sand castle to take them on an imaginary trip to a real castle. 40m; VHS. **A:** Preschool-Primary. **P:** Entertainment. **U:** Home. **Chl-Juv:** Children, Dinosaurs, Music--Children. **Acq:** Purchase. **Dist:** HIT Entertaiment/Lyons Group. $14.95.

Barney & the Backyard Gang: Rock with Barney 1991
Barney the friendly purple dinosaur sings some of his favorite songs. ?m; VHS. **A:** Preschool-Primary. **P:** Entertainment. **U:** Home. **Chl-Juv:** Children, Music--Children, Dinosaurs. **Acq:** Purchase. **Dist:** HIT Entertaiment/Lyons Group. $14.95.

Barney & the Backyard Gang: Waiting for Santa 1991
Barney and his gang travel to the North Pole to learn the real meaning of Christmas and friendship. 45m; VHS. **A:** Family. **P:** Entertainment. **U:** Home. **Chl-Juv:** Christmas. **Acq:** Purchase. **Dist:** HIT Entertaiment/Lyons Group. $14.95.

Barney Bear Cartoon Festival 1948
Four Barney Bear adventures: "The Bear That Couldn't Sleep," "The Bear and the Bean," "The Bear and the Hare" and "A Rainy Day." 32m; VHS. **C:** Directed by Rudolf Ising. **Pr:** MGM; Loew's, Inc. **A:** Family. **P:** Entertainment. **U:** Home. **Mov-Ent:** Animation & Cartoons. **Acq:** Purchase. **Dist:** MGM Home Entertainment. $14.95.

Barney: Egg-cellent Adventures 2010 (Unrated)
Live-action children's television program. It's Easter fun with Barney, Mother Goose, and friends. 42m; DVD. **A:** Preschool-Primary. **P:** Entertainment. **U:** Home. **Mov-Ent:** Family Viewing, Children's Shows. **Acq:** Purchase. **Dist:** Lions Gate Entertainment Inc. $11.98.

Barney: Fun on Wheels 2009 (Unrated)
Live-action children's television program. Barney and his friend, Pop Wheely, teach the children about many different modes of transportation. 45m; DVD. **A:** Preschool-Primary. **P:** Entertainment. **U:** Home. **Mov-Ent:** Family Viewing, Children's Shows. **Acq:** Purchase. **Dist:** Lions Gate Entertainment Inc. $11.98.

Barney: Happy, Mad, Silly, Sad 2003
Barney and his friends help preschoolers understand emotions and how to express themselves in ways that are healthy. 45m; VHS, DVD. **A:** Preschool. **P:** Entertainment. **U:** Home. **Chl-Juv:** Television, Music--Children. **Acq:** Purchase. **Dist:** HIT Entertainment Ltd. $14.95.

Barney: Hi! I'm Riff! 2008 (Unrated)
Live-action children's television program. Riff, the new dinosaur on the block, starts a special club to meet new friends. 57m; DVD. **A:** Preschool-Primary. **P:** Entertainment. **U:** Home. **Mov-Ent:** Family Viewing, Children's Shows. **Acq:** Purchase. **Dist:** Lions Gate Entertainment Inc. $11.98.

Barney: Jungle Friends 2009 (Unrated)
Live-action children's television program. Barney and the gang explore a magical rainforest, learning all about the many plants, animals, and insects that live there. 51m; DVD. **A:** Preschool-Primary. **P:** Entertainment. **U:** Home. **Mov-Ent:** Family Viewing, Children's Shows. **Acq:** Purchase. **Dist:** Lions Gate Entertainment Inc. $12.98.

Barney Kessel: Elementary Guitar 1989
Instructional video exemplifying the basics of guitar. 77m; VHS. **C:** Hosted by Barney Kessel. **Pr:** Kultur. **A:** Jr. High-Adult. **P:** Instruction. **U:** Home. **How-Ins:** How-To, Music--Instruction. **Acq:** Purchase. **Dist:** Kultur International Films Ltd., Inc.; Music Video Distributors. $29.95.

Barney: Let's Go on Vacation 2003 (Unrated)
Live-action children's television program. Join Barney and friends on a vacation that explores different cultures and highlights some important beliefs that are held worldwide. 51m; DVD. **A:** Preschool-Primary. **P:** Entertainment. **U:** Home. **Mov-Ent:** Family Viewing, Children's Shows. **Acq:** Purchase. **Dist:** Lions Gate Entertainment Inc. $11.98.

Barney, Let's Go to the Zoo 2001
Barney and his friends find out about animals at the Ft. Worth Zoo. 50m; VHS. **A:** Preschool. **P:** Entertainment. **U:** Home. **L:** Spanish. **Chl-Juv:** Animation & Cartoons, Children. **Acq:** Purchase. **Dist:** HIT Entertainment Ltd. $14.95.

Barney: Let's Pretend with Barney 2004
Sing-along, dance-along songs take kids on creative adventures as Barney and his friends pretend they're flying in an airplane and looking for lost treasure. 45m; VHS, DVD. **A:** Preschool. **P:** Entertainment. **U:** Home. **Chl-Juv:** Music--Children, Children. **Acq:** Purchase. **Dist:** HIT Entertainment Ltd. $16.99.

Barney Live in New York City 1994
The Purple dinosaur hits Radio City Music Hall for an evening of songs and general niceness. Parents may want to take something for their queasiness before viewing. 60m; VHS. **A:** Preschool. **P:** Entertainment. **U:** Home. **Chl-Juv:** Music--Performance, Music--Children, Family Viewing. **Acq:** Purchase. **Dist:** HIT Entertaiment/Lyons Group.

Barney Miller: Fan Favorites 1975 (Unrated)
ABC's 1975-82 New York precinct comedy. Captain Barney Miller keeps a team of New York detectives in line as well as a bevy of unusual suspects and criminals. Includes "Excavation," "Quarantine Parts 1 & 2," "Bus Stop," "The Election," "Werewolf," "Recluse," and "Non-Involvement." 8 episodes. 198m; DVD. **C:** Hal Linden; Max Gail; Ron Glass; Steve Landesberg. **A:** Sr. High-Adult. **P:** Entertainment. **U:** Home. **Mov-Ent:** Occupations, Television Series. **Acq:** Purchase. **Dist:** Sony Pictures Home Entertainment Inc. $14.99.

Barney Miller: The Complete Second Season 1976
Barney and his detectives take on a crazed gunman in "The Sniper," job insecurity in "The Layoff," and a marauding rodent in "You Dirty Rat." Detective Fish falls for a pickpocket's mother in "The Kid" and Wojo checks out claims of police harassment by a gay couple in "Discovery." 22 episodes. 553m; DVD. **C:** Hal Linden; Abe Vigoda; Max Gail. **A:** Adult. **P:** Entertainment. **U:** Home. **Mov-Ent:** Television Series. **Acq:** Purchase. **Dist:** Sony Pictures Home Entertainment Inc.

Barney Miller: The Complete Third Season 1976 (Unrated)
ABC 1975-82 police comedy. Steve Landesburg joins the cast this season as the phlegmatic Dietrich, and Ron Carey as the over-eager Carl Levitt. In "Quarantine" the detectives do some soul searching during a smallpox outbreak and quarantine; their loyalties are tested in "Strike" when the precinct is suddenly shut down; and a prisoner believes he is a "Werewolf." Doris Roberts guests stars in "Sex Surrogate," Fish goes undercover in drag for mugging detail in "Group Home," and Wojo's well-intentioned gift of brownies contains "Hash." 22 episodes. 553m; DVD. **C:** Hal Linden; Max Gail; Ron Glass; Steven Landsesberg; Ron Carey; Jack Soo. **A:** Jr. High-Adult. **P:** Entertainment. **U:** Home. **Mov-Ent:** Comedy-Drama, Television Series. **Acq:** Purchase. **Dist:** Sony Pictures Home Entertainment Inc. $29.95.

Barney Miller: The First Season 1974
1970s television series about a group of comedic crime fighters in New York's 12th precinct. 300m; DVD. **A:** Adult. **P:** Entertainment. **U:** Home. **Mov-Ent:** Television. **Acq:** Purchase. **Dist:** Sony Pictures Home Entertainment Inc. $34.95.

Barney: Movin' and Groovin' 2004
Using song and dance Barney and friends help reinforce key concepts and skills to children such as numbers and counting, following along, rhythm, and more. ?m; VHS, DVD. **A:** Preschool. **P:** Entertainment. **U:** Home. **Chl-Juv:** Music--Children, Children. **Acq:** Purchase. **Dist:** HIT Entertainment Ltd. $16.99.

Barney Oldfield's Race for a Life/Super-Hooper-Dyn 1920 — ★★½
In the first of two shorts on this tape from 1913, Barney chases a villain who has abducted a lovely girl. In the second film from 1925, radio-controlled Model-T Fords co-star with comic Billy Bevan. 42m/B/W; Silent; VHS. **C:** Barney Oldfield; Mack Sennett; Mabel Normand; Ford Sterling; Billy Bevan; Andy Clyde. **Pr:** Mack Sennett; Mack Sennett; Pathe. **A:** Family. **P:** Entertainment. **U:** Home. **Mov-Ent:** Comedy-Drama, Silent Films. **Acq:** Purchase. **Dist:** Glenn Video Vistas Ltd. $19.98.

Barney: Once Upon a Dino Tale 2009 (Unrated)
Live-action children's television program. Barney, Baby Bop, BJ, and Riff spend time in a world made up of familiar fairy tales. 52m; DVD. **A:** Preschool-Primary. **P:** Entertainment. **U:** Home. **Mov-Ent:** Family Viewing, Children's Shows. **Acq:** Purchase. **Dist:** Lions Gate Entertainment Inc. $11.98.

Barney: Please & Thank You 2010 (Unrated)
Live-action children's television program. Barney reminds his friends of the importance of good manners. 65m; DVD. **A:** Preschool-Primary. **P:** Entertainment. **U:** Home. **Mov-Ent:** Family Viewing, Children's Shows. **Acq:** Purchase. **Dist:** Lions Gate Entertainment Inc. $11.98.

Barney: Shake Your Dino Tail! 2007 (Unrated)
Live-action children's television program. Barney uses dance to teach the importance of exercise and good nutrition. 51m; DVD. **A:** Preschool-Primary. **P:** Entertainment. **U:** Home. **Mov-Ent:** Family Viewing, Children's Shows. **Acq:** Purchase. **Dist:** Lions Gate Entertainment Inc. $11.98.

Barney: Sharing is Caring 2009 (Unrated)
Live-action children's television program. The gang learns about the impact of generosity and sharing in friendship. 51m; DVD. **A:** Preschool-Primary. **P:** Entertainment. **U:** Home. **Mov-Ent:** Family Viewing, Children's Shows. **Acq:** Purchase. **Dist:** Lions Gate Entertainment Inc. $11.98.

Barney: Sing & Dance 2009 (Unrated)
Live-action children's television program. With 27 of Barney's favorite songs, this sing-along party travels to a farm, a campsite, and a storybook land, and includes many old friends as well as new ones. 55m; DVD. **A:** Preschool-Primary. **P:** Entertainment. **U:** Home. **Mov-Ent:** Family Viewing, Children's Shows. **Acq:** Purchase. **Dist:** Lions Gate Entertainment Inc. $11.98.

Barney: Songs from the Park 2002
Barney and his friends sing about things around them that inspire them, like ponds, picnics, playgrounds and parades. 45m; VHS, DVD. **A:** Preschool. **P:** Entertainment. **U:** Home. **Chl-Juv:** Children, Television. **Acq:** Purchase. **Dist:** HIT Entertainment Ltd. $14.95.

Barney: Super Singing Circus 2009 (Unrated)
Live-action children's television program. It's a music-filled circus with everything from a car full of clowns to a flying squirrel as Barney and all his friends have fun under the Big Top. 50m; DVD. **A:** Preschool-Primary. **P:** Entertainment. **U:** Home. **Mov-Ent:** Family Viewing, Children's Shows. **Acq:** Purchase. **Dist:** Lions Gate Entertainment Inc. $11.98.

Barney: We Love Our Family 2009 (Unrated)
Live-action children's television program. The importance of family and friends is celebrated in a collection of heartwarming moments. 40m; DVD. **A:** Preschool-Primary. **P:** Entertainment. **U:** Home. **Mov-Ent:** Family Viewing, Children's Shows. **Acq:** Purchase. **Dist:** Lions Gate Entertainment Inc. $11.98.

Barney: You Can Be Anything! 2001
Barney and his friends sing catchy songs and visit fanciful sets to learn about different careers. 46m; VHS. **A:** Preschool. **P:** Entertainment. **U:** Home. **Chl-Juv:** Animation & Cartoons, Children. **Acq:** Purchase. **Dist:** HIT Entertainment Ltd. $14.95.

Barney's Alphabet Zoo 1994
Purple dinosaur and friends take trip to imaginary zoo. 30m; VHS. **A:** Preschool. **P:** Entertainment. **U:** Home. **Chl-Juv:** Children. **Acq:** Purchase. **Dist:** HIT Entertaiment/Lyons Group. $14.95.

Barney's Beach Party 2002
Barney travels to Hawaii and teaches kids about marine life, health and safety tips for the beach, and learns to hula with the natives. 50m; VHS, DVD. **A:** Preschool. **P:** Entertainment. **U:** Home. **Chl-Juv:** Television, Children. **Acq:** Purchase. **Dist:** HIT Entertainment Ltd. $14.95.

Barney's Best Manners 2003
Barney and his friends help preschoolers understand sharing, taking turns, politeness and healthy habits. 45m; VHS, DVD. **A:** Preschool. **P:** Entertainment. **U:** Home. **Chl-Juv:** Television, Music--Children. **Acq:** Purchase. **Dist:** HIT Entertainment Ltd. $14.95.

Barney's Big Surprise! 1998
Filmed recording of the popular purple dinosaur's musical stage show. ?m; VHS. **A:** Preschool-Primary. **P:** Entertainment. **U:** Home. **Chl-Juv:** Children, Musical. **Acq:** Purchase. **Dist:** Sunburst Digital Inc. $19.99.

Barney's Christmas Star 2002
Barney and buddies celebrate holiday traditions from Christmas, Hanukkah and Kwanza. ?m; VHS, DVD. **A:** Preschool. **P:** Entertainment. **U:** Home. **Chl-Juv:** Christmas, Television. **Acq:** Purchase. **Dist:** HIT Entertainment Ltd. $14.95.

Barney's Great Adventure 1998 (G) — ★★
First the bad news: that big purple dweebosaur made a movie and your three-year-old is going to make you buy the video. Now the good news: since it's on video you can cue it up for the young-uns and run screaming from the room. You see, they don't care what you think about Barney, who looks a little like a big lug in a purple felt suit, actually. In this extravaganza of not so special effects, Barney and two little girls chase a magical egg around town and encounter a parade, a circus and other allegedly wonderful things, all while trying to convince the older Kyle that Barney is "cool." In a surprise move, the egg hatches to reveal....that new stuffed animal you're going to have to buy! 75m; VHS, DVD, CC. **C:** George Hearn; Shirley Douglas; Kyla Pratt; Trevor Morgan; Diana Rice; Renee Madeleine Le Guerrier; Voice(s) by Bob West; Julie Johnson; Directed by Steve Gomer; Written by Stephen White; Cinematography by Sandi Sissel. **Pr:** Polygram. **A:** Family. **P:** Entertainment. **U:** Home. **Mov-Ent:** Family Viewing, Parades & Festivals, Circuses. **Acq:** Purchase. **Dist:** Movies Unlimited; Alpha Video.

Barney's Halloween Party 2001
Halloween fun with Barney and his friends. 50m; VHS. **A:** Preschool. **P:** Entertainment. **U:** Home. **Chl-Juv:** Animation & Cartoons, Children. **Acq:** Purchase. **Dist:** HIT Entertainment Ltd. $14.95.

Barney's Imagination Island 1994
Tosha and Min sail with Barney and friends to Imagination Island where they meet toy inventor Professor Tinkerputt who doesn't want anyone to play with his toys. 48m; VHS. **A:** Preschool. **P:** Entertainment. **U:** Home. **Chl-Juv:** Children, Dinosaurs. **Acq:** Purchase. **Dist:** HIT Entertaiment/Lyons Group. $14.95.

Barney's Night Before Christmas 1999
Barney the big purple dinosaur entertains kids with the help of his dinosaur friends. In this release, Barney and his pals take a trip to the North Pole to visit Santa as he gets ready for Christmas. 57m; VHS. **A:** Family. **P:** Entertainment. **U:** Home. **Chl-Juv:** Children, Puppets. **Acq:** Purchase. **Dist:** HIT Entertainment Ltd. $14.95.

Barney's Rhyme Time Rhythm 2000
Barney the big purple dinosaur entertains kids with the help of his dinosaur friends. In this release, Barney and his pals take a journey to The Land of Mother Goose. 50m; VHS. **A:** Family. **P:** Entertainment. **U:** Home. **Chl-Juv:** Children, Puppets. **Acq:** Purchase. **Dist:** HIT Entertainment Ltd. $14.95.

Barney's Round and Round We Go 2002
Barney and friends talk about transportation methods on land, sea and in the air, bike safety, and lessons with rhyming, counting and shapes. 45m; VHS, DVD. **A:** Preschool. **P:** Entertainment. **U:** Home. **Chl-Juv:** Television, Children. **Acq:** Purchase. **Dist:** HIT Entertainment Ltd. $14.95.

Barney's Super Singing Circus 2000
Barney the big purple dinosaur entertains kids with the help of his dinosaur friends. In this release, Barney and pals visit the circus. 50m; VHS. **A:** Family. **P:** Entertainment. **U:** Home. **Chl-Juv:** Children, Puppets. **Acq:** Purchase. **Dist:** HIT Entertainment Ltd. $14.95.

Barney's Version 2010 (R) — ★★
Necessarily compacted adaptation of Mordecai Richler's dense 1997 satire/memoir. It follows 40 years in the life of curmudgeonly, triple-married and divorced Montreal Jew Barney Panofsky (Gimatti) and his various excesses, which could include murder. Not a sympathetic character, Barney is self-involved and obsessive, particularly with near-saintly third wife Miriam (Pike). Also watch the close relationship between Barney and his sly cop father, Izzy (well-played by Hoffmann). 132m; Blu-Ray. **C:** Paul Giamatti; Dustin Hoffman; Rosamund Pike; Minnie Driver; Rachelle Lefevre; Scott Speedman; Bruce Greenwood; Mark Addy; Saul Rubinek; Directed by Richard J. Lewis; Written by Michael Konyves; Cinematography by Guy Dufaux; Music by Pasquale Catalano. **Pr:** Robert Lantos; Serendipity Point Films; Fandango; Lyla Films; Sony Pictures Classics. **A:** College-Adult. **P:** Entertainment. **U:** Home. **L:** English. **Mov-Ent:** Judaism, Marriage, Satire & Parody. **Awds:** Golden Globes '11: Actor--Mus./Comedy (Giamatti). **Acq:** Purchase. **Dist:** Alpha Video; Sony Pictures Home Entertainment Inc.; Movies Unlimited.

Barnstormers 2006
Since 1999, David Ellis has invited more than 30 fellow artists to his hometown of Cameron, North Carolina, a farming community, to paint murals on tobacco barns and farm equipment. The artists display their creations over the years. 30m; DVD. **A:** Sr. High-Adult. **P:** Entertainment. **U:** Home. **Fin-Art:** Documentary Films, Art & Artists. **Acq:** Purchase. **Dist:** Microcinema International.

Barnum 1980
Spectacle abounds as Crawford (of recent "Phantom of the Opera" fame) stars as the showman of showmen in this performance of "Barnum" captured live at London's Victoria Palace. 113m; VHS. **C:** Michael Crawford; Eileen Battye; Sharon Benson; Christine Collier; Directed by Terry Hughes; Music by Cy Coleman. **Pr:** Joe Layton; British Broadcasting Corporation. **A:** Jr. High-Adult. **P:** Entertainment. **U:** Home. **Mov-Ent:** Musical, Biography, Theater. **Acq:** Purchase. **Dist:** Facets Multimedia Inc.; Water Bearer Films Inc. $59.95.

Barnum 1986 — ★★½
P.T. Barnum's life is focused upon in this biography about the man who helped to form "The Greatest Show On Earth." 100m; VHS, DVD. **C:** Burt Lancaster; Hanna Schygulla; Jenny Lind; John Roney; Directed by Lee Philips. **A:** Jr. High-Adult. **P:** Entertainment. **U:** Home. **Mov-Ent:** Biography, Circuses. **Acq:** Purchase. **Dist:** Movies Unlimited. $29.95.

Barnum Was Right 1929 — ★
Poor boy needs money to marry sweetheart so he tries to revive business at his old hotel by leaking a story that there's pirate treasure hidden somewhere in the building. Title refers to P.T. Barnum maxim that "there's a sucker born every minute." 45m/B/W; Silent; VHS. **C:** Glenn Tryon; Merna Kennedy; Otis Harlan; Basil Radford; Clarence Burton; Lew Kelly; Directed by Del Lord. **Pr:** Mark Huffam. **A:** Adult. **P:** Entertainment. **U:** Home. **Mov-Ent:** Hotels & Hotel Staff Training, Silent Films. **Acq:** Purchase. **Dist:** Grapevine Video. $14.95.

Barnyard 2006 (PG) — ★★
Young Otis the cow (James) is unconcerned about keeping the secret that animals can not only talk, but like to dance, sing, party, and play pranks. But when the farmer's away, Otis is given the unexpected responsibility of looking after things. Cute, but probably more enjoyable for younger kids. Some jokes click for older kids and adults, but not quite enough. 89m; DVD. **C:** Voice(s) by Kevin James; Courteney Cox; Sam Elliott; Danny Glover; Andie MacDowell; Wanda Sykes; David Koechner; Steve Oedekerk; Rob Paulsen; Dom Irrera; Maria Bamford; Laraine Newman; Maurice LaMarche; Jeff Garcia; Directed by Steve Oedekerk; Written by Steve Oedekerk; Music by John Debney. **Pr:** Steve Oedekerk; Paul Marshall; Steve Oedekerk; Nickelodeon Movies; O Entertainment; Paramount Pictures. **A:** Primary-Adult. **P:** Entertainment. **U:** Home. **L:** English. **Mov-Ent:** Animation & Cartoons, Agriculture. **Acq:** Purchase. **Dist:** Paramount Pictures Corp.

Barocco 1976 — ★★
Crook kills his lookalike and takes his place and his girlfriend. Together the duo try blackmail to get the money they need to start a new life. Self-conscious would-be film noir. French with subtitles. 102m; VHS, DVD. **C:** Gerard Depardieu; Isabelle Adjani; Marie-France Pisier; Jean-Claude Brialy; Directed by Andre Techine; Written by Andre Techine; Marilyn Goldin; Cinematography by Bruno Nuytten; Music by Philippe Sarde. **A:** College-Adult. **P:** Entertainment. **U:** Home. **L:** French. **Mov-Ent.** **Acq:** Purchase. **Dist:** Movies Unlimited.

The Baron 1988 (Unrated) — ★½
Vengeance is the name of the game when an underworld boss gets stiffed on a deal. Fast-paced no-brainer street drama. 88m; VHS, DVD. **C:** Calvin Lockhart; Charles McGregor; Joan Blondell; Richard Lynch; Marlene Clark; Directed by Philip Fently. **A:** College-Adult. **P:** Entertainment. **U:** Home. **Mov-Ent:** Action-Adventure. **Acq:** Purchase. **Dist:** Movies Unlimited. $18.99.

The Baron and the Kid 1984 — ★
A pool shark finds out that his opponent at a charity exhibition game is his long-lost son. Based on Johnny Cash's song. Made for TV. 100m; VHS, DVD, CC. **C:** Johnny Cash; Darren McGavin; June Carter Cash; Richard Roundtree; Directed by Gary Nelson; Music by Brad Fiedel. **Pr:** Telecom Entertainment. **A:** Family. **P:** Entertainment. **U:** Home. **Mov-Ent:** TV Movies. **Acq:** Purchase. **Dist:** Movies Unlimited; Alpha Video. $59.98.

Baron Munchausen 1943 — ★★★
The German film studio UFA celebrated its 25th anniversary with this lavish version of the Baron Munchausen legend, starring a cast of top-name German performers at the height of the Third Reich. Filmed in Agfacolor; available in English subtitled or dubbed versions. 120m; VHS, DVD. **C:** Hans Albers; Kathe Haack; Hermann Speelmanns; Leo Slezak; Directed by Josef von Baky. **Pr:** UFA. **A:** Sr. High-Adult. **P:** Entertainment. **U:** Home. **L:** English, German. **Mov-Ent:** Fantasy. **Acq:** Purchase. **Dist:** German Language Video Center; Tapeworm Video Distributors Inc. $59.95.

Baron of Arizona 1951 (Unrated) — ★★★
Land office clerk almost succeeds in convincing the U.S. that he owned the state of Arizona. 99m/B/W; VHS, DVD. **C:** Vincent Price; Ellen Drew; Beulah Bondi; Reed Hadley; Vladimir Sokoloff; Directed by Samuel Fuller; Written by Samuel Fuller; Cinematography by James Wong Howe. **Pr:** Lippert Productions. **A:** Family. **P:** Entertainment. **U:** Home. **Mov-Ent:** Western. **Acq:** Purchase. **Dist:** Rex Miller Artisan Studio.

The Baron: The Complete Series 1966 (Unrated)
ITC British drama series. John Mannering (Forrest) is known as The Baron, an international art and antiques dealer who works in tandem with British Intelligence and the lovely Cordelia (Lloyd) to recover priceless treasures and bring criminals to justice. 30 episodes. 1470m; DVD. **C:** Steve Forrest; Sue Lloyd. **A:** Adult. **P:** Entertainment. **U:** Home. **Mov-Ent:** Drama, Television Series. **Acq:** Purchase. **Dist:** eOne Home Video. $59.98.

The Baroness and the Butler 1938 (Unrated) — ★★
Johann (Powell) is butler to Baron Georg (Schildkraut) and his wife Katrina (Annabella), who is the daughter of the Hungarian Prime Minister. Politically active Johann becomes the opposition party leader and is elected to parliament--much to his employers' shock. Baron Georg happens to be a philanderer and it's no surprise when the Baroness and the butler find romance. Annabella's first American film. 80m/B/W; DVD. **C:** William Powell; Annabella; Joseph Schildkraut; Henry Stephenson; Nigel Bruce; J. Edward Bromberg; Directed by Walter Lang; Written by Sam Hellman; Lamar Trotti; Kathryn Scola; Cinematography by Arthur C. Miller. **A:** Adult. **P:** Entertainment. **U:** Home. **L:** English. **Mov-Ent:** Comedy--Romantic, Politics & Government. **Acq:** Purchase. **Dist:** Twentieth Century Fox Film Corp.

The Baroque ????
Overviews several Baroque artists and styles used in Spain, Holland, and France and explores the use of art in the Catholic church. 43m; VHS. **A:** Sr. High-Adult. **P:** Education. **U:** Home, Institution. **Gen-Edu:** Art & Artists, History--Renaissance. **Acq:** Purchase. **Dist:** Crystal Productions. $127.50.

Baroque Duet 1992
Opera star Kathleen Battle and jazz trumpeter Wynton Marsalis combine their talents to explore the baroque style of music of the 17th century. Originally broadcasted on PBS's Great Performances. 78m; VHS. **C:** Directed by Albert Maysles; Music by Wynton Marsalis; Kathleen Battle. **A:** Jr. High-Adult. **P:** Entertainment. **U:** Home. **Fin-Art:** Music--Classical, Music--Performance, Performing Arts. **Acq:** Purchase. **Dist:** Maysles Films, Inc.

Barracuda 1978 (R) — **Bomb!**
Lots of innocent swimmers are being eaten by crazed killer barracudas. Currently only available as part of a collection. 90m; VHS, DVD, Streaming. **C:** Wayne Crawford; Jason Evers; Roberta Leighton; Directed by Harry Kerwin. **Pr:** Republic Industries. **A:** Sr. High-Adult. **P:** Entertainment. **U:** Home. **Mov-Ent:** Horror, Poisons, Swimming. **Acq:** Purchase. **Dist:** No Longer Available.

The Barrens 2012 (R) — ★★
Standard psycho/creep fare. A family travels to the Pine Barrens to scatter their grandfather's ashes only to encounter trouble as the other campers go missing. Instead of thinking they may have gotten lost they remember the urban legends about the Jersey Devil, and Dad immediately assumes the Devil is killing people. 97m; DVD, Blu-Ray, Streaming. **C:** Shawn Ashmore; Stephen Moyer; Peter DaCunha; Erik Knudsen; Mia Kirshner; Allie MacDonald; Directed by Darren Lynn Bousman; Written by Darren Lynn Bousman; Cinematography by Joseph White; Music by Bobby Johnston. **A:** Sr. High-Adult. **P:** Entertainment. **U:** Home. **L:** English. **Mov-Ent.** **Acq:** Purchase, Rent/Lease. **Dist:** Anchor Bay Entertainment Inc. $29.99 26.98 14.99.

The Barretts of Wimpole Street 1934 — ★★★
The moving, almost disturbing, account of poetess Elizabeth Barrett, an invalid confined to her bed, with only her poetry and her dog to keep her company. She is wooed by poet Robert Browning, in whose arms she finds true happiness and a miraculous recovery. Multi-faceted drama expertly played by all. 110m/B/W; DVD. **C:** Fredric March; Norma Shearer; Charles Laughton; Maureen O'Sullivan; Katherine Alexander; Una O'Connor; Ian Wolfe; Directed by Sidney Franklin; Cinematography by William H. Daniels. **Pr:** Irving Thalberg; MGM. **A:** Jr. High-Adult. **P:** Entertainment. **U:** Home. **Mov-Ent:** Drama. **Acq:** Purchase. **Dist:** WarnerArchive.com.

Barricade 1949 (Unrated) — ★★
Massey practically twirls a mustache of evil in this odd western that's an alleged adaptation of Jack London's "The Sea Wolf." Gold mine owner Boss Kruger uses fugitives on the lam to dig for his ore, including new arrivals Bob (Clark) and Judith (Roman). They befriend lawyer Milburn (Douglas) who wants revenge on Kruger for murdering his brother, the mine's original owner. 75m; DVD. **C:** Raymond Massey; Dane Clark; Ruth Roman; Robert Douglas; Morgan Farley; Directed by Peter Godfrey; Written by William Sackheim; Cinematography by Carl Guthrie. **A:** Jr. High-Adult. **P:** Entertainment. **U:** Home. **Mov-Ent:** Western, Miners & Mining. **Acq:** Purchase. **Dist:** WarnerArchive.com.

Barricade 1966
A complete study of the Berlin Wall from its construction to its psychological impact on eastern Germany. Montage shots tell an emotional history of the notorious structure and those who have attempted to escape over it. Somewhat dated by the events of November 1989, when it was finally opened. 13m/B/W; VHS, 3/4 U. **TV Std:** NTSC, PAL. **A:** Jr. High-Adult. **P:** Education. **U:** Institution, Home. **Gen-Edu:** History--Modern, Documentary Films, Germany. **Acq:** Purchase. **Dist:** International Historic Films Inc.; German Language Video Center. $19.00.

Barrier of the Law 1954 (Unrated) — ★½
In this Italian crime drama, cop Mario Grandi (Brazzi) goes undercover to infiltrate a gang of smugglers operating between the French and Italian Riviera. His cover may be blown when young Anna (Padovani) falls in love with him. Italian with subtitles. 81m/B/W; DVD. **C:** Rossano Brazzi; Lea Padovani; Jacques Sernas; Cesare Fantoni; Directed by Piero Costa; Written by Piero Costa; Guido Malatesta; Cinematography by Augusto Tiezzi; Music by Franco D'Achiardi. **A:** Adult. **P:** Entertainment. **U:** Home. **L:** Italian. **Mov-Ent.** **Acq:** Purchase. **Dist:** Sinister Cinema.

Barriers of Solitude 1998
Historical account of San Jose, a small, rural, Mexican town. Includes interviews with and memories of its inhabitants and archival footage serving to illustrate the point that personal and public history are often very different. 52m; VHS. **A:** Adult. **P:** Education. **U:** Home. **Gen-Edu:** Documentary Films, Mexico, History. **Acq:** Purchase, Rent/Lease. **Dist:** Filmakers Library Inc. $350.

Barriers to Communicating 1979
This tape examines some of the reasons we have problems in communicating, and how effective communicators overcome them. 9m; VHS, 3/4 U. **Pr:** Resources for Education and Management. **A:** Adult. **P:** Professional. **U:** Institution, CCTV. **Bus-Ind:** Communication. **Acq:** Purchase. **Dist:** Resources for Education & Management, Inc.

Barriers to Cross-Cultural Counseling 19??
"Barriers" provides a theoretical and practical base emphasizing the importance of cultural differences in the helping process. 75m; VHS. **A:** Adult. **P:** Professional. **U:** Institution. **L:** English. **Hea-Sci:** Employee Counseling. **Acq:** Purchase. **Dist:** Microtraining Associates, Inc. $125.

Barriers to the Prevention of Ground Fall Accidents 1986
Miners talk about why they feel that ground fall accidents happen, and how they can be avoided. 22m; VHS, 3/4 U. **Pr:** Mine Safety and Health Academy. **A:** Adult. **P:** Education. **U:** Institution. **Gen-Edu:** Miners & Mining, Safety Education. **Acq:** Purchase. **Dist:** U.S. Department of Labor, Mine Safety and Health Administration. $20.00.

Barrington Levy 198? (Unrated)
Levy plays live from Manhattan Center in New York, and with guest Marcia Griffiths performs "Get Up Stand Up," "My Woman," "Teach the Youth," "Dibbi Dibbi Girl, Dumb Girl," "Collie Wood" and more. 75m; VHS. **A:** Adult. **P:** Entertainment. **U:** Home. **Mov-Ent:** Music--Performance. **Acq:** Purchase. **Dist:** Music Video Distributors. $19.95.

Barrio Wars 2002 (R) — ★½
Hip hop Latino Romeo and Juliet staged on the mean streets of L.A. Plato and Angelina are the star-crossed lovers from rival gangs sparking violence and turmoil all over the city. Nice try, but the standard no-budget acting style and a rather jarring soft-core sex scene defeats any intended purpose. But really, what's the point? Leonardo DiCaprio and Claire Danes have already done modern-day Shakespeare much better. 90m; VHS, DVD. **C:** Sevier Crespo; Luchana Gatica; Anthony Martins; Beny Mena; Chino XL; Directed by Paul Wynne; Written by Paul Wynne. **A:** Adult. **P:** Entertainment. **U:** Home. **Mov-Ent:** Hispanic Culture. **Acq:** Purchase. **Dist:** York Entertainment. $14.99.

Barry Brodzinski Five-Star Shooting Series 2006
Features basketball drills in a program designed by expert shooting instructor Barry Brodzinski; in four parts, includes creating open shots, techniques for teaching children, increasing team shooting percentage, and shooting drills. 226m; DVD. **A:** Sr. High-Adult. **P:** Instruction. **U:** Institution. **Spo-Rec:** Basketball. **Acq:** Purchase. **Dist:** Championship Productions. $149.95.

Barry Gibb: Now Voyager 1984
The prominent Mr. Gibb dives headlong into the conceptual video world with this unified production of nine songs, including "Shine Shine" and "Temptation." His exotic and musical travels with singers and dancers excel. 79m; VHS. **C:** Barry Gibb; Michael Hordern. **Pr:** Polygram Music Video. **A:** Adult. **P:** Entertainment. **U:** Home. **Mov-Ent:** Music--Performance, Music Video. **Acq:** Purchase. **Dist:** Music Video Distributors. $19.95.

Barry Goldwater: Photographs and Memories 19??
Centers on the internationally acclaimed photography of Senator Barry Goldwater while outlining his love for photography and Arizona. 30m; VHS. **A:** Family. **P:** Education. **U:** Home. **Gen-Edu:** Biography, Photography, U.S. States. **Acq:** Purchase. **Dist:** Arizona Highways Magazine. $19.95.

Barry Harris: Passing It On 1989
A portrait of the jazz pianist, as musician, teacher and self-proclaimed "inveterate be-bopper." The film focuses a great deal on his activities at his Jazz Cultural Center in the Chelsea section of Manhattan. 23m; VHS. **C:** Directed by David Chan;

Ken Freundlich. **Pr:** Kino International Corporation. **A:** Sr. High-Adult. **P:** Entertainment. **U:** Home. **Fin-Art:** Music--Jazz. **Acq:** Purchase. **Dist:** Music Video Distributors; Rhapsody Films, Inc. $19.95.

Barry Harris: Spirit of Bebop 1999
Modern jazz pianist Barry Harris shares his insights and experiences of playing, composing and teaching bebop music, plus discusses working with fellow musicians such as Charlie Parker, Thelonious Monk, Miles Davis and others. Also includes him performing live at the Village Vanguard in New York City. 55m; VHS. **A:** Adult. **P:** Education. **U:** Home, Institution. **Mov-Ent:** Music--Jazz, Music, Biography. **Acq:** Purchase. **Dist:** Rhapsody Films, Inc. $19.95.

Barry Hinson: Offensive Relocation?"Middle to Explore, Baseline to Score!" 2007 (Unrated)
Coach Hinson discusses techniques basketball teams can use to avoid getting stopped by Man-to-Man Defenses. 55m; DVD. **A:** Family. **P:** Education. **U:** Home, Institution. **Spo-Rec:** Basketball, Athletic Instruction/Coaching. **Acq:** Purchase. **Dist:** Championship Productions. $39.99.

Barry Lyndon 1975 (PG) — ★★★½
Ravishing adaptation of the classic Thackeray novel about the adventures of an Irish gambler moving from innocence to self-destructive arrogance in the aristocracy of 18th Century England. Visually opulent. Kubrick received excellent performances from all his actors, and a stunning display of history, but the end result still overwhelms. O'Neal has seldom been better. 185m; VHS, DVD, Wide. **C:** Ryan O'Neal; Marisa Berenson; Patrick Magee; Hardy Kruger; Guy Hamilton; Directed by Stanley Kubrick; Written by Stanley Kubrick; Cinematography by John Alcott. **Pr:** Warner Bros. **A:** Jr. High-Adult. **P:** Entertainment. **Mov-Ent:** Gambling, Great Britain. **Awds:** Oscars '75: Art Dir./Set Dec., Cinematog., Costume Des., Orig. Song Score and/or Adapt.; British Acad. '75: Director (Kubrick); L.A. Film Critics '75: Cinematog.; Natl. Bd. of Review '75: Director (Kubrick); Natl. Soc. Film Critics '75: Cinematog. **Acq:** Purchase. **Dist:** Warner Home Video, Inc. $29.95.

Barry Manilow: Because It's Christmas 1990
The Barrister performs a delightfully spellbinding array of holiday tunes. Selections include "Because It's Christmas," "Jingle Bells," "The Christmas Song," "We Wish you a Merry Christmas" and "Its Just Another New Years Eve." 30m; VHS. **C:** Barry Manilow. **A:** Family. **P:** Entertainment. **U:** Home. **Mov-Ent:** Music--Performance, Holidays, Christmas. **Acq:** Purchase. **Dist:** BMG Entertainment. $14.98.

Barry Manilow: First Special 1977
The emotionally charged vocalist performs his best-loved hits from the '70s. Included are "I Write the Songs" and "Mandy," plus countless others. A rare, uplifting, Emmy-winning show. 52m; VHS. **C:** Barry Manilow. **A:** Jr. High-Adult. **P:** Entertainment. **U:** Home. **Mov-Ent:** Music--Performance, Singing. **Acq:** Purchase. **Dist:** MGM Home Entertainment. $29.95.

Barry Manilow: Live on Broadway 1990 (Unrated)
Bop with that mainstream man Manilow as he performs some of his hits live. 90m; VHS. **Pr:** RCA. **A:** Family. **P:** Entertainment. **U:** Home. **Mov-Ent:** Music--Performance. **Acq:** Purchase. **Dist:** Music Video Distributors; BMG Entertainment. $19.98.

Barry Manilow: Making of 2 A.M. Paradise Cafe 19??
Barry is joined by Mel Torme, Gerry Mulligan and others in this behind the scenes look at the making of his new album "2 A.M. Paradise Cafe." 55m; VHS. **Pr:** RCA. **A:** Adult. **P:** Entertainment. **U:** Home. **Mov-Ent:** Music--Performance, Filmmaking. **Acq:** Purchase. **Dist:** Music Video Distributors; Sony Pictures Home Entertainment Inc.; BMG Entertainment. $16.95.

Barry Manilow: The Concert at Blenheim Palace 1985 (Unrated)
Manilow performs 20 songs live, including "I Write the Songs," "It's a Miracle," and "Mandy." 90m; VHS. **Pr:** Townway Productions. **A:** Jr. High-Adult. **P:** Entertainment. **U:** Home. **Mov-Ent:** Music--Performance. **Acq:** Purchase. **Dist:** Music Video Distributors. $16.95.

Barry Manilow: The Greatest Hits. . .And Then Some 1994
Live performance from showman Manilow, recorded in 1993 at Wembley Arena, features 12 songs, plus four medleys. 90m; VHS, DVD. **A:** Sr. High-Adult. **P:** Entertainment. **U:** Home. **Mov-Ent:** Music--Pop/Rock, Music--Performance. **Acq:** Purchase. **Dist:** BMG Entertainment. $19.98.
Songs: Copacabana; Can't Smile Without You; I Write the Songs; I'm Your Man; The Best of Me.

Barry McKenzie Holds His Own 1974 (Unrated) — ★★
In this sequel to "The Adventures of Barry McKenzie," we find that after a young man's aunt is mistaken for the Queen of England, two emissaries of Count Plasma of Transylvania kidnap her to use as a Plasma tourist attraction. Based on the 'Private Eye' comic strip, this crude Australian film is as disappointing as the first of the Barry McKenzie stories. 93m; VHS, DVD. **C:** Barry Humphries; Barry Crocker; Donald Pleasence; Directed by Bruce Beresford; Written by Barry Humphries; Bruce Beresford. **Pr:** Satori Entertainment Corporation. **A:** Sr. High-Adult. **P:** Entertainment. **U:** Home. **Mov-Ent:** Satire & Parody, Australia. **Acq:** Purchase. **Dist:** Unknown Distributor.

Barry Munday 2010 (R) — ★½
Self-absorbed 30-something Barry (Wilson) crudely propositions every potentially available woman he sees. At least until his private parts are permanently injured by an irate father. At this neutered moment, Barry is told by one-night stand Ginger, whom he doesn't remember, that she is pregnant. Predictably, he has his doubts about fatherhood. 99m; DVD. **C:** Patrick Wilson; Judy Greer; Chloe Sevigny; Jean Smart; Cybill Shepherd; Malcolm McDowell; Billy Dee Williams; Colin Hanks; Shea Whigham; Missi Pyle; Emily Procter; Christopher McDonald; Directed by Chris D'Arienzo; Written by Chris D'Arienzo; Cinematography by Morgan Susser; Music by Jude Christodal. **A:** Sr. High-Adult. **P:** Entertainment. **U:** Home. **Mov-Ent:** Pregnancy, Parenting. **Acq:** Purchase. **Dist:** Magnolia Home Entertainment.

Barry Youngblood "Strait Playin" ????
Step-by-step instruction of hip hop routines such as "Strait Playin," "Is It Good to You?," "Bass Train," "Slip-N-Slide," and "Another Part of Me." 60m; VHS. **A:** Adult. **P:** Instruction. **U:** Institution, Home. **How-Ins:** Dance, Dance--Instruction. **Acq:** Purchase. **Dist:** Stagestep. $40.00.

Barrymore 2011 (Unrated) — ★★½
Dramatic film based on a one man play about the life of actor John Barrymore. Old and in bad health, and no longer a leading actor, Barrymore (Christopher Plummer) has rented an old theater to rehearse for a backer's audtion of a revival of the play that made him famous. 84m; DVD, Blu-Ray, Streaming. **C:** Christopher Plummer; Directed by Erik Canuel; Written by Erik Canuel; Cinematography by Bernard Couture; Music by Michael Corriveau. **A:** Sr. High-Adult. **P:** Entertainment. **U:** Home. **L:** English. **Mov-Ent. Acq:** Purchase, Rent/Lease. **Dist:** Fox Home Entertainment. $39.98 29.99 14.99.

Barry's Scrapbook: A Window Into Art 1994
Childrens' singer and songwriter Barry Louis Polisar introduces art to young children through song and actual visits to the Baltimore Museums of Art. Accompanied with a group of children, Polisar asks questions about certain exhibits such as a Renoir and a 1500-year-old mosaic. Creates childrens' awareness for art matters such as scupltures and cartoons. 40m; VHS. **A:** Primary. **P:** Entertainment. **U:** Home. **Chl-Juv:** Art & Artists, Children. **Acq:** Purchase. **Dist:** Library Video Network. $19.95.

Bars of Hate 1936 (Unrated) — ★
District Attorney Ted Clark and pickpocket Danny come to the aid of Ann Dawson, who's trying to save the life of her wrongly convicted brother on death row. She's got a letter for the governor detailing the true criminals who are now after her. 57m/B/W; DVD. **C:** Regis Toomey; Snub Pollard; Sheila Terry; Fuzzy Knight; Gordon Griffith; Molly O'Day; Robert Warwick; Directed by Al(bert) Herman; Written by Al Martin; Cinematography by William (Bill) Hyer. **A:** Sr. High-Adult. **P:** Entertainment. **U:** Home. **Mov-Ent:** Crime Drama. **Acq:** Purchase. **Dist:** Sinister Cinema.

Bars, Punches and Drifts 198?
The specific purposes and correct uses of bars, punches and drifts are explained in this program. 60m; VHS, 3/4 U. **A:** College-Adult. **P:** Education. **U:** Institution. **Bus-Ind:** Tools. **Acq:** Rent/Lease. **Dist:** National Safety Council, California Chapter, Film Library.

Barstool Cowboy 2008 (Unrated) — ★
Boring and predictable low-budget indie. Unemployed, 30-something, self-pitying Mick is spending time on a barstool after a bad breakup when 19-year-old art student Arcy comes along. Despite the fact that she's too young to legally drink, she becomes a bar regular and she and Mick decide to spend some time together for no other reason than they're both alone. 90m; DVD. **C:** Tim Woodward; Rachel Lien; Directed by Mark Thimijan; Written by Mark Thimijan; Cinematography by Doug McMains; Music by Natalie Ileana. **A:** Sr. High-Adult. **P:** Entertainment. **U:** Home. **Mov-Ent. Acq:** Purchase. **Dist:** Celebrity Video Distribution, Inc.

Bart Cook: Choreographer 1987
Bart Cook, renowned dancer with the New York City Ballet, is seen here choreographing a dance for students from the School of the American Ballet. 30m; VHS, 3/4 U. **Pr:** Patsy Tarr; Jeff Tarr; Checkerboard Productions, Inc. **A:** Jr. High-Adult. **P:** Education. **U:** Institution, Home. **Gen-Edu:** Dance--Ballet. **Acq:** Purchase, Rent/Lease. **Dist:** Museum of Modern Art. $275.00.

Bart Got a Room 2008 (PG-13) — ★½
All-too familiar plot overdoes the fact that Hollywood, Florida high school nerd Danny (Kaplan) lives in a geriatric haven. Danny spends a fortune renting a room for the prom (after he learns ever dweebier Bart has apparently scored) with the expectation of losing his virginity. But first he has to get a date and he keeps overlooking his best friend Camille (Shawkat). Maybe he can't think of her 'that way.' Funniest thing in the movie is Macy's (Danny's divorced, dating dad) Jewish 'fro. 80m; DVD. **C:** Alia Shawkat; William H. Macy; Cheryl Hines; Ashley Benson; Jennifer Tilly; Steve Kaplan; Brandon Hardesty; Chad Jamian Williams; Directed by Brian Hecker; Written by Brian Hecker; Cinematography by Hallvard Braein; Music by Jamie Lawrence. **A:** Jr. High-Adult. **P:** Entertainment. **U:** Home. **Mov-Ent:** Hotels & Hotel Staff Training, Divorce. **Acq:** Purchase. **Dist:** Anchor Bay Entertainment.

Bartending for Fun & Profit 19??
Professional bartender Max shows the viewer bartending techniques, such as bar set-up, pouring methods, where to look for a job, and how to pour responsibly. 52m; VHS. **A:** Sr. High-Adult. **P:** Instruction. **U:** Home. **How-Ins:** Alcoholic Beverages, How-To, Job Training. **Acq:** Purchase. **Dist:** Production Associates. $19.95.

Bartleby 1969
A dramatization of the story of a man who "preferred not to." Based on Herman Melville's short story "Bartleby, the Scrivener." 28m; VHS, 3/4 U. **Pr:** Encyclopedia Britannica Educational Corporation. **A:** Sr. High-College. **P:** Education. **U:** Institution, SURA. **Gen-Edu:** Literature--American. **Acq:** Purchase, Rent/Lease, Trade-in. **Dist:** Encyclopedia Britannica.

Bartleby 1970 (Unrated) — ★★½
A new version of the classic Herman Melville short story. McEnery is Bartleby the clerk, who refuses to leave his job even after he's fired; Scofield is his frustrated boss. 79m; VHS, DVD. **C:** Paul Scofield; John McEnery; Colin Jeavons; Thorley Walters; Directed by Anthony Friedman; Written by Rodney Carr-Smith. **Pr:** British Lion. **A:** Jr. High-Adult. **P:** Entertainment. **U:** Home. **Mov-Ent:** Comedy-Drama. **Acq:** Purchase. **Dist:** White Star. $29.95.

Bartleby 2001 (PG-13) — ★★
Contempo version of Herman Melville's 1856 novella "Bartleby the Scrivener." Eccentric Bartleby (Glover) is the model of efficiency when first hired to do clerical work in a nondescript records office. But gradually Bartleby begins to refuse tasks, then to do anything at all—even firing him has no effect to the consternation of his boss (Paymer) and the bewilderment of his co-workers. 83m; VHS, DVD. **C:** Crispin Glover; David Paymer; Glenne Headly; Joe Piscopo; Maury Chaykin; Seymour Cassel; Carrie Snodgress; Dick Martin; Directed by Jonathan Parker; Written by Jonathan Parker; Catherine Di Napoli; Cinematography by Wah Ho Chan; Music by Jonathan Parker; Seth Asarnow. **Pr:** Jonathan Parker; Parker Film Co; Outrider Pictures. **A:** Sr. High-Adult. **P:** Entertainment. **U:** Home. **Mov-Ent. Acq:** Purchase. **Dist:** Wellspring Media.

Bartleby: A Discussion 1969
Author Charles Van Doren presents a commentary on Herman Melville's, "Bartleby." 28m; VHS, 3/4 U. **C:** Charles Van Doren. **Pr:** Encyclopedia Britannica Educational Corporation. **A:** Jr. High-College. **P:** Education. **U:** Institution, SURA. **Gen-Edu:** Literature--American. **Acq:** Purchase, Rent/Lease, Trade-in. **Dist:** Encyclopedia Britannica.

Bartleby the Scrivener 197?
Tale about Bartleby, a lawyer who must deal with the many facets of everyday life. Written by Herman Melville. 60m; VHS, 3/4 U. **Pr:** Maryland Center for Public Broadcasting; Center Stage. **A:** Sr. High-College. **P:** Education. **U:** Institution, CCTV, CATV, BCTV. **Gen-Edu:** Literature--American. **Acq:** Purchase, Rent/Lease. **Dist:** Maryland Public Television.

Bartok the Magnificent 1999 (G)
Bartok the bat is on his own, entertaining the Moscow crowds with his quick patter. But when one of his fans, young Prince Ivan, is kidnapped, Bartok must rescue the boy from the evil witch, Baba Yaga. 68m; VHS, DVD. **C:** Voice(s) by Hank Azaria; Kelsey Grammer; Jennifer Tilly; Tim Curry; Catherine O'Hara; Directed by Don Bluth; Gary Goldman; Written by Jay Lacopo; Music by Stephen Flaherty. **A:** Family. **P:** Entertainment. **U:** Home. **Chl-Juv:** Animation & Cartoons. **Acq:** Purchase. **Dist:** Fox Home Entertainment.

Barton Fink 1991 (R) — ★★★
This eerie comic nightmare comes laden with awards (including the Palme D'Or from Cannes) but only really works if you care about the time and place. Fink is a trendy New York playwright staying in a seedy Hollywood hotel in the 1940s, straining to write a simple B-movie script. Macabre events, both real and imagined, compound his writer's block. Superb set design from Dennis Gassner complements an unforgettable cast of grotesques. 116m; VHS, DVD. **C:** John Turturro; John Goodman; Judy Davis; Michael Lerner; John Mahoney; Tony Shalhoub; Jon Polito; Steve Buscemi; David Warrilow; Richard Portnow; Christopher Murney; Directed by Joel Coen; Written by Joel Coen; Ethan Coen; Cinematography by Roger Deakins; Music by Carter Burwell. **Pr:** Circle Films. **A:** Sr. High-Adult. **P:** Entertainment. **U:** Home. **Mov-Ent:** Comedy--Black, Filmmaking. **Awds:** Cannes '91: Actor (Turturro), Director (Coen), Film; L.A. Film Critics '91: Cinematog., Support. Actor (Lerner); N.Y. Film Critics '91: Cinematog., Support. Actress (Davis); Natl. Soc. Film Critics '91: Cinematog. **Acq:** Purchase. **Dist:** Critics' Choice Video & DVD. $19.98.

Baryshnikov at Wolf Trap 1975
The dancer performs "Coppelia," "Le Spectre de la Rosa," "Vestris" and "Don Quixote" in his American television debut and is accompanied by a number of celebrated ballerinas. 50m; VHS. **Pr:** Kultur. **A:** Family. **P:** Entertainment. **U:** Home. **Fin-Art:** Dance--Ballet. **Acq:** Purchase. **Dist:** Stagestep; Kultur International Films Ltd., Inc.; Facets Multimedia Inc. $29.95.

The Baryshnikov Collection 2012 (Unrated)
Collection focusing on Russian ballet dancer, choreographer, and actor Mikhail Baryshnikov, including his production of "Carmen," his first film, and early footage of him competing. 180m; DVD. **A:** Preschool-Adult. **P:** Entertainment. **U:** Home. **L:** English. **Gen-Edu:** Dance--Performance, Dance--Ballet, USSR. **Acq:** Purchase. **Dist:** Acorn Media Group Inc. $49.99.

Baryshnikov Dances Sinatra 1975
Baryshnikov performs Sinatra Suite, Push Comes to Shove, and The Little Ballet, choreographed by Twyla Tharp. ?m; VHS. **A:** Adult. **P:** Entertainment. **U:** Home. **Fin-Art:** Dance--Ballet, Dance--Performance. **Acq:** Purchase. **Dist:** Video Artists International. $19.95.

Baryshnikov Dances Sinatra and More. . . 1984
Twyla Tharp choreographed this Baryshnikov spectacular. Inlcudes "Push comes to Shove," "Sinatra Suite," "The Little Ballet," and "The ABC's of Ballet." 60m; VHS. **C:** Mikhail Baryshnikov; Directed by Twyla Tharp. **Pr:** Kultur. **A:** Family. **P:** Entertainment. **U:** Home. **Fin-Art:** Performing Arts, Dance--Ballet. **Acq:** Purchase. **Dist:** Kultur International Films Ltd., Inc.; Music Video Distributors; Stagestep. $19.95.

Baryshnikov: The Dancer and the Dance 1986
The history of Baryshnikov's dance career, from the Soviet Union to his defection to America. 85m; VHS. **C:** Mikhail Baryshnikov; Narrated by Shirley MacLaine. **Pr:** Princeton/Dance Horizons. **A:** Family. **P:** Education. **U:** Institution, Home. **Fin-Art**: Music--Performance, Dance--Ballet, Dance--Performance. **Acq:** Purchase. **Dist:** Music Video Distributors; Home Vision Cinema; Princeton Book Company Publishers. $19.95.

The Base 1999 (R) — ★★½
Army Intelligency officer Major John Murphy (Dacascos) is sent undercover to Fort Tilman to investigate the murder of an army operations officer. Murphy is assigned to a border patrol unit and discovers his fellow soldiers are muscling in on the Mexican/American drug trade. When he discovers who's behind the operation, Murphy's cover is blown and he's in for the fight of his life. 101m; VHS, DVD. **C:** Mark Dacascos; Tim Abell; Paula Trickey; Noah Blake; Frederick Coffin; Directed by Mark L. Lester; Written by Jeff Albert; William C. Martell; Cinematography by Jacques Haitkin; Music by Paul Zaza. **A:** Sr. High-Adult. **P:** Entertainment. **U:** Home. **Mov-Ent**. **Acq:** Purchase. **Dist:** Movies Unlimited; Alpha Video.

The Base 2: Guilty as Charged 2000 (R) — ★½
The U.S. Army sends a undercover investigator to look into mysterious deaths on one of their bases. Turns out a Colonel and his unit have gone rogue and are executing enlisted men they believe were wrongly acquitted of crimes. Might be enjoyable to diehard action fans, presuming they haven't actually joined the military and gained any knowledge of how it works. 97m; DVD. **C:** Antonio Sabato, Jr.; James Remar; Duane Davis; Yuji Okumoto; Melissa Lewis; Elijah Mahar; Emilio Rivera; Johnny Urbon; William Jones; Daron McBee; Randy Mulkey; Gary Cervantes; Robert Crow; Bob Rudd; Directed by Mark L. Lester; Written by Jeff Albert; C. Courtney Joyner; Cinematography by George Mooradian; Music by Andrew Kereztes. **A:** Sr. High-Adult. **P:** Entertainment. **U:** Home. **L:** English, French, Spanish. **Mov-Ent**. **Acq:** Purchase. **Dist:** Lions Gate Entertainment Inc. $9.98.

Base of Skull and Thin Areas 1985
The cranial fosse is examined for professionals. 26m; 3/4 U. **Pr:** McMaster University. **A:** Adult. **P:** Professional. **U:** Institution, SURA. **Hea-Sci**: Head. **Acq:** Purchase, Rent/Lease. **Dist:** McMaster University.

Base Running 1984
This program shows the proper way to lead off a base and how not to get picked off plus tips for young ball players. 60m; VHS, 8 mm, 3/4 U. **Pr:** Champions on Film. **A:** Family. **P:** Education. **U:** Institution, CCTV, Home. **Spo-Rec**: Baseball. **Acq:** Purchase, Rent/Lease. **Dist:** School-Tech Inc.

Base Stunts and Fronts for 4-3 Defense 2014 (Unrated)
Coach Pat Narduzzi presents the defensive scheme he taught while coaching football at Michigan State. 83m; DVD. **A:** Family. **P:** Education. **U:** Home. **L:** English. **Spo-Rec**: Athletic Instruction/Coaching, Football. **Acq:** Purchase. **Dist:** Championship Productions. $39.99.

Baseball 1987
Baseball professionals discuss and demonstrate the skills of hitting, pitching, and baserunning. Features former Cincinnati Reds hitting star Vada Pinson, Major League pitching coach Wes Stock, and famous base stealer Maury Wills. 60m; VHS, 3/4 U. **Pr:** RMI Media Productions. **A:** Adult. **P:** Instruction. **U:** Institution. **Spo-Rec**: Baseball. **Acq:** Purchase. **Dist:** RMI Media.
Indiv. Titles: 1. The Art of Hitting 2. The Fundamentals of Pitching 3. Maury Wills on Baserunning.

Baseball 1994
Ken Burns' follow-up to "The Civil War" is an equally epic history of the great American pastime, spanning 150 years. On nine tapes, released in a collector's edition or individually. 1080m; VHS. **C:** Narrated by John Chancellor; Directed by Ken Burns. **A:** Jr. High-Adult. **P:** Entertainment. **U:** Home. **Spo-Rec**: Documentary Films, Baseball, History--U.S. **Acq:** Purchase. **Dist:** PBS Home Video; Warner Home Video, Inc. $179.95.
Indiv. Titles: 1. Our Game 2. Something like a War 3. The Faith of 50 Million People 4. A National Heirloom 5. Shadow Ball 6. The National Pastime 7. The Capital of Baseball 8. A Whole New Ballgame 9. Home.

Baseball Bunch: Fielding 1985
Johnny Bench is joined by a number of baseball super stars as he teaches young people the basics of fielding. Guests include Ozzie Smith, Gary Carter and Craig Nettles. 60m; VHS, CC. **Pr:** Major League Baseball Productions. **A:** Primary-Sr. High. **P:** Instruction. **U:** Home. **Spo-Rec**: Sports--General, Baseball. **Acq:** Purchase. **Dist:** Warner Home Video, Inc. $14.95.

Baseball Bunch: Hitting 1985
Johnny Bench is joined by a number of baseball stars as he teaches the rudiments of hitting to young people. 60m; VHS, CC. **C:** Hosted by Johnny Bench. **Pr:** Major League Baseball Productions. **A:** Primary-Sr. High. **P:** Instruction. **U:** Home. **Spo-Rec**: Sports--General, Baseball. **Acq:** Purchase. **Dist:** Warner Home Video, Inc. $14.95.

Baseball Bunch: Pitching 1985
Johnny Bench is joined by a number of baseball's finest as he teaches the fundamentals of pitching to young people. 60m; VHS, CC. **C:** Hosted by Johnny Bench. **Pr:** Major League Baseball Productions. **A:** Primary-Sr. High. **P:** Instruction. **U:** Home. **Spo-Rec**: Sports--General, Baseball. **Acq:** Purchase. **Dist:** Warner Home Video, Inc. $14.95.

Baseball Card Collecting for Big Bucks 1992
This definitive guide to collecting baseball cards offers advice in five related areas: knowledge, planning, market strategy, negotiation, and card care. 60m; VHS. **A:** Primary-Adult. **P:** Education. **U:** Home. **Gen-Edu**: Baseball, Hobbies. **Acq:** Purchase. **Dist:** JLS Video Productions. $29.95.

Baseball Card Collector 1989
Mel Allen narrates this guide to the buying and selling of baseball cards. Also available as a "deluxe edition," half an hour longer for $29.99. 35m; VHS. **C:** Narrated by Mel Allen. **Pr:** BFV. **A:** Family. **P:** Instruction. **U:** Home. **Spo-Rec**: Baseball, Hobbies. **Acq:** Purchase. **Dist:** Karol Media. $19.99.

Baseball Classics: 1953-1955 Milwaukee Braves 200?
Four films from the early fifties ("Meet Your Braves," "The Milwaukee Story," "Home of the Braves," and "Baseball's Main Street") chronicle the early years of the Milwaukee Braves baseball team. 115m/B/W; DVD. **A:** Family. **P:** Entertainment. **U:** Home. **Spo-Rec**: Baseball, Sports--General. **Acq:** Purchase. **Dist:** Baseball Direct. $34.95.

Baseball Classics: 1957-1958-1959 Boston Red Sox 2008
Three vintage films from the 1950s of the Boston Red Sox, as well as special promotions and footage of the 1959 All-Star game. 67m; DVD. **A:** Family. **P:** Entertainment. **U:** Home. **Spo-Rec**: Baseball, Sports--General. **Acq:** Purchase. **Dist:** Baseball Direct. $34.95.

Baseball Classics: 1966 and 1971 Chicago Cubs 2008
Contains two short television spots recorded at the Cubs spring training site. 39m; DVD. **A:** Family. **P:** Entertainment. **U:** Home. **Spo-Rec**: Baseball, Sports--General. **Acq:** Purchase. **Dist:** Baseball Direct. $34.95.

Baseball Classics: 1954 St. Louis Cardinals 20?? (Unrated)
Three classic baseball films ("Lets Train with the Cardinals," "The Cardinal Tradition," and "The Game Nobody Saw") along with vintage footage of Busch Stadium. 81m; DVD. **A:** Family. **P:** Entertainment. **U:** Home. **Spo-Rec**: Baseball, Sports--General. **Acq:** Purchase. **Dist:** Baseball Direct. $34.95.

Baseball Classics: 1955 World Series, Game 5 20?? (Unrated)
A partial television broadcast of the 1955 game between the Yankees and the Brooklyn Dodgers. 90m/B/W; DVD. **A:** Family. **P:** Entertainment. **U:** Home. **Spo-Rec**: Baseball, Sports--General. **Acq:** Purchase. **Dist:** Championship Productions. $34.95.

Baseball Classics: 1956 World Series Game 3 1956
Original TV broadcast of Game 3 of the 1956 World Series between the Brooklyn Dodgers (in their last World Series as Brooklyn) and the New York Yankees. Includes the complete game, excluding innings 2 and 3, as well as all the commercials and complete pre- and post-game commentary. Viewer may choose between both television and radio play-by-play. 120m; DVD. **A:** Family. **P:** Entertainment. **U:** Home. **Spo-Rec**: Baseball. **Acq:** Purchase. **Dist:** Rare Sportsfilms, Inc. $29.95.

Baseball Classics: 1960-1961-1962 Milwaukee Braves 20?? (Unrated)
Three vintage baseball films showing highlights from the Milwaukee Braves from the early 1960s. 85m; DVD. **A:** Family. **P:** Entertainment. **U:** Home. **Spo-Rec**: Baseball, Sports--General. **Acq:** Purchase. **Dist:** Baseball Direct. $34.95.

Baseball Classics: Stars of Baseball 1945-1953 20?? (Unrated)
Six baseball instructional films made with stars from the 1945-1953 seasons, including Ted Williams, Joe DiMaggio, and others. 125m; DVD. **A:** Family. **P:** Entertainment. **U:** Home. **Spo-Rec**: Baseball, Sports--General. **Acq:** Purchase. **Dist:** Baseball Direct. $34.95.

Baseball Conditioning Drills 2003
San Diego State University Strength and Conditioning Director David Ohton discusses and demonstrates warm up and flexibility drills, plus an endurance building running program. Also shows over 20 baseball-specific agility drills. 35m; VHS. **A:** Adult. **P:** Instruction. **U:** Institution. **How-Ins**: Baseball, Sports--General, How-To. **Acq:** Purchase. **Dist:** Championship Productions. $39.95.

Baseball Drills for Confined Spaces 2011 (Unrated)
Coach Matt Walbeck demonstrates various training drills for baseball coaches who have limited space to practice. 78m; DVD. **A:** Family. **P:** Education. **U:** Home, Institution. **Spo-Rec**: Baseball, Athletic Instruction/Coaching. **Acq:** Purchase. **Dist:** Championship Productions. $39.99.

Baseball Fun and Games 1980
Bloopers, trivia tests, and other interesting ways to pass the time. 60m; VHS. **C:** Hosted by Joe Garagiola. **A:** Family. **P:** Entertainment. **U:** Home. **Spo-Rec**: Sports--General, Hobbies, Baseball. **Acq:** Purchase. **Dist:** School-Tech Inc. $29.95.

Baseball: Fun and Games 1988
A collection of bloopers and trivia questions about America's pastime. A section is included where the viewer is allowed to be the umpire. 60m; VHS. **Pr:** Cambridge Career Productions. **A:** Primary-Adult. **P:** Entertainment. **U:** Institution, Home. **Spo-Rec**: Baseball, Outtakes & Bloopers. **Acq:** Purchase. **Dist:** Cambridge Educational. $14.98.

Baseball Fundamentals Tape 2003
Professional scouts explain proper techniques for hitting, pitching, infield/outfield moves, and baserunning. 59m; VHS. **A:** Adult. **P:** Instruction. **U:** Institution. **How-Ins**: Baseball, Sports--General, How-To. **Acq:** Purchase. **Dist:** Championship Productions. $29.95.

Baseball Funnies 1988
From Ty Cobb to Dave Winfield, great plays and great blunders can be seen on this tape. 30m; VHS. **Pr:** Simitar. **A:** Family. **P:** Entertainment. **U:** Home. **Spo-Rec**: Baseball, Outtakes & Bloopers. **Acq:** Purchase. **Dist:** Karol Media; Cambridge Educational; Major League Baseball Productions. $9.95.

Baseball: Funny Side Up 1987
Funster Tug McGraw hosts this look at the wackiest, goofiest and downright oddest plays in the history of baseball. 45m; VHS. **C:** Narrated by Mel Allen; Hosted by Tug McGraw. **Pr:** Major League Baseball Productions. **A:** Family. **P:** Entertainment. **U:** Home. **Spo-Rec**: Sports--General, Baseball. **Acq:** Purchase. **Dist:** ESPN Inc.; Major League Baseball Productions; Karol Media. $19.95.

Baseball in the '80s 19??
Profiles the great players and teams of the 1980s. 65m; VHS. **A:** Family. **P:** Entertainment. **U:** Home. **Spo-Rec**: Sports--General, Baseball, History. **Acq:** Purchase. **Dist:** Major League Baseball Productions. $14.95.

Baseball in the News 1990
Series covering the years 1951 to 1967 via a collection of newsreels that were originally shown in movie theatres. Highlights include the Dodgers winning the World Series in 1955, Joe DiMaggio's last home run, Willie Mays' four homers in a single game, the beginning of the Mets, and the Baltimore Orioles' four-game sweep of the Series over L. A. in 1966. Available individually or as a set. 60m; VHS. **A:** Family. **P:** Entertainment. **U:** Home. **Spo-Rec**: Documentary Films, Baseball. **Acq:** Purchase. **Dist:** Acorn Media Group Inc. $29.95.
Indiv. Titles: 1. Vol. 1: 1951-1955 2. Vol. 2: 1956-1960 3. Vol. 3: 1961-1967.

Baseball in the '70s 19??
Chronicles the great players and teams of the 1970s. Also looks at major developments such as expansion, free agency, the designated hitter, and multi-colored double-knit uniforms. 48m; VHS. **A:** Family. **P:** Entertainment. **U:** Home. **Spo-Rec**: Sports--General, Baseball, History. **Acq:** Purchase. **Dist:** Major League Baseball Productions.

Baseball Like It Oughta Be: 1996 Cardinals 200?
Relives the trials and triumphs of the 1996 St. Louis Cardinals. ?m; VHS. **A:** Adult. **P:** Entertainment. **U:** Home. **Spo-Rec**: Baseball, Sports--General. **Acq:** Purchase. **Dist:** Baseball Direct. $19.95.

Baseball Masters: Conditioning & Baserunning 1986
Baserunning and conditioning techniques are covered by Al Kaline and University of Arizona head coach Jerry Kindall. 40m; VHS. **Pr:** Major League Baseball Productions. **A:** Primary-Adult. **P:** Instruction. **U:** Home. **Spo-Rec**: Sports--General, Baseball. **Acq:** Purchase. **Dist:** Cambridge Educational. $14.95.

Baseball Masters: Fielding 1986
Al Kaline is joined by hitting great George Kell in this guide to infield and outfield fundamentals. 40m; VHS. **Pr:** Major League Baseball Productions. **A:** Primary-Adult. **P:** Instruction. **U:** Home. **Spo-Rec**: Sports--General, Baseball. **Acq:** Purchase. **Dist:** Cambridge Educational. $14.95.

Baseball Masters: Hitting 1986
A complete guide to hitting fundamentals covering not only the technical aspects but the mental approaches as well. 40m; VHS. **Pr:** Major League Baseball Productions. **A:** Primary-Adult. **P:** Instruction. **U:** Home. **Spo-Rec**: Sports--General, Baseball. **Acq:** Purchase. **Dist:** Cambridge Educational. $14.95.

Baseball Masters: Pitching 1986
A comprehensive look at the mechanics of pitching, from proper stance to proper follow through. 40m; VHS. **Pr:** Major League Baseball Productions. **A:** Primary-Adult. **P:** Instruction. **U:** Home. **Spo-Rec**: Sports--General, Baseball. **Acq:** Purchase. **Dist:** Cambridge Educational. $14.95.

Baseball 1990: Year in Review 1990
Contains highlights, record breakers, big stories, and post season footage of the 1990 baseball season. 60m; VHS. **A:** Family. **P:** Entertainment. **U:** Home. **Spo-Rec**: Sports--General, Baseball. **Acq:** Purchase. **Dist:** Major League Baseball Productions. $9.95.

Baseball 1991: A Video Yearbook 1991
Reviews the oustanding individual and team performances, pennant races, and post-season action of the 1991 baseball season. 60m; VHS. **A:** Family. **P:** Entertainment. **U:** Home. **Spo-Rec**: Sports--General, Baseball. **Acq:** Purchase. **Dist:** Major League Baseball Productions. $9.95.

Baseball 1992: A Video Yearbook 1992
Features great moments, big stories, interviews, and post season footage from the 1992 baseball season. 60m; VHS. **A:** Family. **P:** Entertainment. **U:** Home. **Spo-Rec**: Sports--General, Baseball. **Acq:** Purchase. **Dist:** Major League Baseball Productions. $19.95.

Baseball Our Way 1988
A variety of Major League personalities cover baseball fundamentals respective to their positions. The names include manager Tommy Lasorda, catcher Steve Yeager, pitcher Don Sutton, infielder Bill Russell, outfielder Eric Davis and for hitting, Wally Joyner. 90m; VHS. **Pr:** Major League Baseball Produc-

tions. **A:** Primary-Adult. **P:** Instruction. **U:** Home. **Spo-Rec:** Sports--General, Baseball. **Acq:** Purchase. **Dist:** Cambridge Educational. $29.95.

Baseball Series 1985
This series shows the basics of pitching, hitting, and running for the baseball novice. 60m; VHS. **C:** Vada Pinson; Wes Stock; Maury Wills. **Pr:** Morris Video. **A:** Jr. High-Adult. **P:** Instruction. **U:** Home. **How-Ins:** Sports--General, Baseball. **Acq:** Purchase. **Dist:** Morris Video; Cambridge Educational. $38.00.
Indiv. Titles: 1. The Art of Hitting 2. The Science of Pitching 3. Maury Wills on Baserunning.

Baseball Skills & Drills 1984
Little League expert Dr. Bragg Stockton hosts this series on all aspects of baseball—pitching, hitting, fielding, base running, and defensive play for all positions. Included is a discussion of coaching psychology, focusing on motivating players and handling problem players. 55m; VHS. **C:** Hosted by Bragg Stockton. **Pr:** Champions on Film. **A:** Jr. High-Adult. **P:** Instruction. **U:** Institution, Home. **How-Ins:** Sports--General, How-To, Baseball. **Acq:** Purchase. **Dist:** School-Tech Inc.; Cambridge Educational. $49.00.
Indiv. Titles: 1. The Fundamentals of Pitching 2. The Fundamentals of Hitting 3. The Fundamentals of Fielding 4. The Fundamentals of Base Running 5. Defensive Skills by Position 6. Coaching Psychology - How to Handle Parents.

Baseball Strength & Conditioning 1992
Complete overview of the time-tested and up and coming techniques to prepare for action on the diamond. Stretching, weight lifting, mental focus. Includes tips on implementing a throwing program and a running program. 60m; VHS. **A:** Sr. High-Adult. **P:** Instruction. **U:** Institution, Home. **Hea-Sci:** Weight Lifting, Fitness/Exercise. **Acq:** Purchase. **Dist:** Cambridge Educational. $39.95.

Baseball Strength Training 2003
San Diego State University Strength and Training Director David Ohton demonstrate warm ups, circuit training, dumb bell training and medicine ball training beneficial to baseball players with emphasis on proper technique and safety. 39m; VHS. **A:** Adult. **P:** Instruction. **U:** Institution. **How-Ins:** Baseball, Sports--General, How-To. **Acq:** Purchase. **Dist:** Championship Productions. $39.95.

Baseball: The Now Career 1975
Television star Chuck Connors, a former ballplayer, helps tell the story of the road to the major leagues, along with several of the game's stars. 26m; VHS. **C:** Chuck Connors; Nolan Ryan; Johnny Bench; Tug McGraw. **Pr:** Major League Baseball Productions. **A:** Family. **P:** Entertainment. **U:** Institution, Home, SURA. **Spo-Rec:** Sports--General, Baseball. **Acq:** Purchase. **Dist:** Major League Baseball Productions.

Baseball the Pete Rose Way 1986
Rose demonstrates the art of playing baseball, using a group of youngsters to demonstrate his lessons. 60m; VHS, 8 mm, CC. **Pr:** Embassy Pictures. **A:** Primary-Jr. High. **P:** Instruction. **U:** Home. **Spo-Rec:** Sports--General, Baseball. **Acq:** Purchase. **Dist:** Sony Pictures Home Entertainment Inc. $14.95.

Baseball the Right Way: Fielding for Kids 1987
This film teaches kids the basics of fielding a ball and throwing with speed and accuracy. Features the fielding instructor for the New York Mets, Bud Harrelson. 30m; VHS. **C:** Hosted by Bud Harrelson. **Pr:** Rainbow. **A:** Primary-Sr. High. **P:** Instruction. **U:** Home. **Spo-Rec:** Baseball. **Acq:** Purchase. **Dist:** School-Tech Inc.; Karol Media. $14.95.

Baseball the Right Way: Hitting for Kids 1987
Helps teach children the basics of baseball, including improving their swing. Features Bill Robinson, former player and hitting coach. 30m; VHS. **C:** Hosted by Bill Robinson. **Pr:** Rainbow. **A:** Primary-Sr. High. **P:** Instruction. **U:** Home. **Spo-Rec:** Baseball. **Acq:** Purchase. **Dist:** School-Tech Inc.; Karol Media. $14.95.

Baseball the Right Way: Pitching for Kids 1987
Teaches children the basics of baseball and fundamentals of pitching. Features the pitching coach for the New York Mets, Mel Stottlemyre. 30m; VHS. **C:** Hosted by Mel Stottlemyre. **Pr:** Rainbow. **A:** Primary-Sr. High. **P:** Instruction. **U:** Home. **Spo-Rec:** Baseball. **Acq:** Purchase. **Dist:** School-Tech Inc.; Karol Media. $14.95.

Baseball: The Tenth Inning 2010 (Unrated)
Continuation/sequel of the Ken Burns documantary explores the on- and off-field issues of the late 1990s and the first decade of the 21st century, such as labor-related work stoppages, additional expansion, expanded playoffs, and the Steroids Era. Also looks at the stars and growth of the game during the era. 240m; DVD, Blu-Ray. **A:** Family. **P:** Entertainment. **U:** Home. **Spo-Rec:** Baseball, Documentary Films. **Acq:** Purchase. **Dist:** PBS Home Video. $24.95.

Baseball the Yankee Way 1964
Filmed during the last of the Yankees' golden days, when names like Mantle, Maris and Ford prowled the grounds at Yankee stadium. 45m/B/W; VHS. **Pr:** New York Yankees. **A:** Family. **P:** Entertainment. **U:** Home. **Spo-Rec:** Baseball. **Acq:** Purchase. **Dist:** Rhino Entertainment Co. $19.99.

Baseball Training Program for Kid's, Coaches and Parents 19??
Explains ways to run practices, drills and games to improve skills and generate enthusiasm and how to promote good sportsmanship. 60m; VHS. **A:** Adult. **P:** Instruction. **U:** Institution. **How-Ins:** Baseball, Sports--General, How-To. **Acq:** Purchase. **Dist:** Championship Productions. $29.95.

Baseball with Rod Carew 1986
Carew demonstrates for young people the art of hitting, using the Syberberg method of visual training. 60m; VHS. **Pr:** SyberVision Systems. **A:** Jr. High-Adult. **P:** Instruction. **U:** Home. **Spo-Rec:** Sports--General, Baseball. **Acq:** Purchase. **Dist:** SyberVision Systems, Inc.; Karol Media. $29.95.

Baseball's Funniest Bloopers 19??
Watch major leaguers fall down, run into each other, and generally play the game the way it wasn't meant to be played. 35m; VHS. **A:** Family. **P:** Entertainment. **U:** Home. **Spo-Rec:** Sports--General, Baseball, Outtakes & Bloopers. **Acq:** Purchase. **Dist:** Major League Baseball Productions. $14.95.

Baseball's Greatest Games Collector's Edition 2011 (Unrated)
Eleven-DVD set covering 10 championship games from the Major League Baseball archives, along with added footage and interviews. 1796m; DVD. **A:** Family. **P:** Entertainment. **U:** Home. **Spo-Rec:** Baseball, Sports--General. **Acq:** Purchase. **Dist:** A&E Television Networks L.L.C. $99.95.

Baseball's Greatest Games: Derek Jeter's 3000th Hit 2011 (Unrated)
Complete television broadcast of the game in which Derek Jeter made his 3000th hit; the radio play-by-play is also contained within the special features. 180m; DVD. **A:** Family. **P:** Entertainment. **U:** Home. **Spo-Rec:** Baseball, Sports--General. **Acq:** Purchase. **Dist:** A&E Television Networks L.L.C. $19.95.

Baseball's Greatest Games: 1952 World Series Game 6 Yankees vs. Dodgers 1999
Profiles Game 6 of the 1952 World Series, which featured Billy Martin's game-saving catch of Jackie Robinson's infield pop-up. 90m; VHS. **A:** Family. **P:** Entertainment. **U:** Home. **Spo-Rec:** Baseball. **Acq:** Purchase. **Dist:** Baseball Direct. $19.95.

Baseball's Greatest Games: 1978 AL East Playoff, Yankee vs. Red Sox 1999
Documents the 1978 AL east playoff game that decided the East Division champs on Bucky Dent's improbable game-winning homer. 90m; VHS. **A:** Family. **P:** Entertainment. **U:** Home. **Spo-Rec:** Baseball. **Acq:** Purchase. **Dist:** Baseball Direct. $19.95.

Baseball's Greatest Games 1985 NCLS Game 2011 (Unrated)
Complete television broadcast of the 1985 game between the St. Louis Cardinals and the Los Angeles Dodgers; special features include the radio play-by-play. 150m; DVD. **A:** Family. **P:** Entertainment. **U:** Home. **Spo-Rec:** Baseball, Sports--General. **Acq:** Purchase. **Dist:** A&E Television Networks L.L.C. $12.95.

Baseball's Greatest Games: 1986 World Game 6, Red Sox vs. Mets 1999
Documents Game 6 of the 1986 World Series, in which the New York Mets went from being one out from elimination to forcing a Game 7. This is the infamous "Bill Buckner" game. 126m; VHS. **A:** Family. **P:** Entertainment. **U:** Home. **Spo-Rec:** Baseball. **Acq:** Purchase. **Dist:** Baseball Direct. $19.95.

Baseball's Greatest Games: 1988 World Series Game 1, A's vs. Dodgers 1999
Profiles Game 1 of the 1988 World Series, in which Kirk Gibson ended the game, and changed the momentum of the series with his pinch-hit home run in the bottom of the ninth inning (his only at-bat in the entire series). 90m; VHS. **A:** Family. **P:** Entertainment. **U:** Home. **Spo-Rec:** Baseball. **Acq:** Purchase. **Dist:** Baseball Direct. $19.95.

Baseball's Greatest Games: 1991 World Series Game 7, Twins vs. Braves 1999
Profiles Game 7 of the 1991 World Series, in which Jack Morris pitched a 10-inning shutout to conclude what some say was the best World Series ever. 92m; VHS. **A:** Family. **P:** Entertainment. **U:** Home. **Spo-Rec:** Baseball. **Acq:** Purchase. **Dist:** Baseball Direct. $19.95.

Baseball's Greatest Games 1992 NCLS Game 2011 (Unrated)
Complete radio play-by-play and television broadcast of the 1992 game between the Pittsburgh Pirates and the Atlanta Braves. 157m; DVD. **A:** Family. **P:** Entertainment. **U:** Home. **Spo-Rec:** Baseball, Sports--General. **Acq:** Purchase. **Dist:** A&E Television Networks L.L.C. $12.95.

Baseball's Greatest Games 2003 NCLS Game 2011 (Unrated)
Full game broadcast and radio play-by-play of the 2003 game between the New York Yankees and the Boston Red Sox. 188m; DVD. **A:** Family. **P:** Entertainment. **U:** Home. **Spo-Rec:** Baseball, Sports--General. **Acq:** Purchase. **Dist:** A&E Television Networks L.L.C. $12.95.

Baseball's Greatest Games 2004 NCLS Game 2011 (Unrated)
Full game broadcast of the 2004 game between the Boston Red Sox and the New York Yankees; special features also include the radio broadcast. 242m; DVD. **A:** Family. **P:** Entertainment. **U:** Home. **Spo-Rec:** Baseball, Sports--General. **Acq:** Purchase. **Dist:** A&E Television Networks L.L.C. $12.95.

Baseball's Greatest Games: Wrigley Field Slugfest 2011 (Unrated)
Complete game broadcast of the 1979 game between the Philadelphia Phillies and the Chicago Cubs. 213m; DVD. **A:** Family. **P:** Entertainment. **U:** Home. **Spo-Rec:** Baseball, Sports--General. **Acq:** Purchase. **Dist:** A&E Television Networks L.L.C. $12.95.

Baseball's Greatest Hits 1990
A montage of some of baseball's greatest moments, including Bobby Thompson's, "shot heard 'round the world." Salvador Dali and Whitey Ford team up to do an advertisement for an airline. Harry Caray does his famous rendition of "Take Me Out to the Ballgame." And Willie Mays appears as himself in "Say Hey," a tribute to the baseball great by the Treniers. 30m; VHS. **A:** Family. **P:** Entertainment. **U:** Home. **Spo-Rec:** Sports--General, Baseball. **Acq:** Purchase. **Dist:** Rhino Entertainment Co.; Image Entertainment Inc. $14.95.

Baseball's Greatest Moments 19??
Footage of 20 of record breaking or famous moments in baseball, including Babe Ruth's called shot in the 1932 World Series, Pete Rose's 4,192nd hit, and Orel Hershiser's record 59th consecutive scoreless inning. 60m; VHS. **A:** Family. **P:** Entertainment. **U:** Home. **Spo-Rec:** Sports--General, Baseball. **Acq:** Purchase. **Dist:** Major League Baseball Productions; Baseball Direct. $19.95.

Baseball's Greatest Rivalries 200?
Examines great rivalries like the Dodgers-Giants, Red Sox-Yankees and Cubs-Cardinals and includes extra bonus footage. 70m; DVD. **A:** Adult. **P:** Entertainment. **U:** Home. **Spo-Rec:** Baseball, Sports--General. **Acq:** Purchase. **Dist:** Baseball Direct. $19.95.

Baseball's Hottest Stars 19??
Profiles some of the most popular players in baseball. Includes highlights and interviews. 55m; VHS. **A:** Family. **P:** Entertainment. **U:** Home. **Spo-Rec:** Sports--General, Baseball. **Acq:** Purchase. **Dist:** Major League Baseball Productions. $14.95.

Baseball's Official Ballpark Bloopers 19??
Players are caught cutting up in the dugout and messing up on the field. 35m; VHS. **A:** Family. **P:** Entertainment. **U:** Home. **Spo-Rec:** Baseball, Outtakes & Bloopers. **Acq:** Purchase. **Dist:** Major League Baseball Productions. $14.95.

Baseball's Record Breakers 19??
Profiles the players who broke some of baseball's most famous and long-standing records. 45m; VHS. **A:** Family. **P:** Entertainment. **U:** Home. **Spo-Rec:** Sports--General, Baseball. **Acq:** Purchase. **Dist:** Major League Baseball Productions. $14.95.

Based on an Untrue Story 1993 — ★★½
Campy spoof of popular "true story" TV docudramas in which powerful Satin Chau (Fairchild), a perfume mogul, loses her sense of smell. Satin leaves her mentor Varda (Cannon) to discovery herself but finds that only her two separated-at-birth sisters, Velour (Lake) and Corduroy (Jackson), hold the secrets to the past. It's hard to spoof a genre that's become a cliche but this TV movie does its best. 90m; VHS, CC. **C:** Morgan Fairchild; Dyan Cannon; Victoria Jackson; Ricki Lake; Harvey Korman; Robert Goulet; Dan Hedaya; Directed by Jim Drake. **Pr:** Paul A. Lussier. **A:** Jr. High-Adult. **P:** Entertainment. **U:** Home. **Mov-Ent:** Satire & Parody, TV Movies. **Acq:** Purchase. **Dist:** Fox Home Entertainment.

BASEketball 1998 (R) — ★★½
Dude! Three slacker buddies ("South Park"'s Parker and Stone plus Bachar) invent a new game in their driveway—a combo of basketball with baseball rules—and see it turn into big business. Parkere gets to romance Jenna Reed (Bleeth), a social worker who helps "health-challenged" kids. Stone and Parker's penchant for gross-out humor and having their characters say whatever's on their minds (no matter how offensive) mixes well with Zucker's talent for sight gags and physical humor to create an enjoyably guilty pleasure. Based on a game that Zucker invented with friends. 103m; VHS, DVD, CC. **C:** Trey Parker; Matt Stone; Yasmine Bleeth; Jenny McCarthy; Ernest Borgnine; Dian Bachar; Robert Vaughn; Bob Costas; Al Michaels; Reggie Jackson; Robert Stack; Steve Garvey; Kareem Abdul-Jabbar; Directed by David Zucker; Written by David Zucker; Robert Locash; Jeffrey Wright; Lewis Friedman; Cinematography by Steve Mason; Music by Ira Newborn. **Pr:** David Zucker; David Zucker; Gil Netter; Robert LoCash; Universal Pictures. **A:** Sr. High-Adult. **P:** Entertainment. **U:** Home. **Mov-Ent:** Sports--Fiction: Comedy, Hospitals, Cheerleaders. **Acq:** Purchase. **Dist:** Movies Unlimited; Alpha Video.

Baseline Killer 2008 (R) — ★
Yet another film based (very) loosely on the exploits of a serial killer by obsessed director Ulli Lommel. This time, the subject is Mark Goudeau, also known as the Baseline Killer, who was convicted of nine murders along with a host of sexual assaults and robberies. 90m; DVD, Streaming. **C:** Victoria Ullmann; Pia Pownall; Directed by Ulli Lommel; Written by Ulli Lommel; Cinematography by Ulli Lommel; Music by Ulli Lommel. **A:** Sr. High-Adult. **P:** Entertainment. **U:** Home. **L:** English. **Mov-Ent**. **Acq:** Purchase, Rent/Lease. **Dist:** North American Motion Pictures, LLC. $22.98 4.99.

The Basement 1989 (Unrated) — ★½
Cult horror anthology from the 80s that was thought lost. It opens with four people wandering a basement and encountering a towering figure who asks them to confess the sins they will commit in the future. Apparently their sins involve a demon, a psychopathic teacher, zombies, and a really angry snake in a pool. 79m; DVD. **C:** Dennis Driscoll; Kathleen Heidinger; David Webber; Scott Corizzi; Traci Mann; Directed by Timothy O'Rawe; Written by Timothy O'Rawe; Cinematography by Michael Raso. **A:** Sr. High-Adult. **P:** Entertainment. **U:** Home. **L:** English. **Mov-Ent**. **Acq:** Purchase. **Dist:** Alternative Distribution Alliance. $34.98.

The Basement Girl 2000
A young women finds solace in her basement, a diet of junk food, mundane routines, and television after being abandoned by her lover. 12m; VHS. **A:** Adult. **P:** Education. **U:** Institution,

BCTV. **Gen-Edu**: Women, Documentary Films. **Acq**: Purchase, Rent/Lease. **Dist**: Women Make Movies. $195.00.

Basement Jack 2009 (R) — ★
A serial killer who surprised his victims by hiding in their basements is released, and immediately travels home to pick up where he left off. Apparently the maximum sentence for wiping out several families is 10 years if you're a minor and no one thought to notify the public. 93m; DVD. **C**: Eric Peter-Kaiser; Sam Skoryna; Michele Morrow; Lynn Lowry; Directed by Michael Shelton; Written by Brian Patrick O'Toole; Cinematography by Matthew Rudenberg; Music by Alan Howarth. **A**: Sr. High-Adult. **P**: Entertainment. **U**: Home. **L**: English. **Mov-Ent**: **Acq**: Purchase. **Dist**: Brink Films. $19.95.

Baserunning and Sliding 2000
Baylor University Assistant Coach Steve Johnigan covers techniques and drills with demonstrations for proper baserunning and sliding. 45m; VHS. **A**: Adult. **P**: Instruction. **U**: Institution. **How-Ins**: Baseball, Sports--General, How-To. **Acq**: Purchase. **Dist**: Championship Productions. $29.95.

Baserunning, Stealing and Sliding 2001 (Unrated)
Coach Carol Bruggeman presents baserunning drills and discusses using an aggressive style of play in softball. 35m; DVD. **A**: Family. **P**: Education. **U**: Home, Institution. **Spo-Rec**: Softball, Athletic Instruction/Coaching. **Acq**: Purchase. **Dist**: Championship Productions. $29.99.

Baserunning Strategies and Drills 1999
Louisiana State University Coach "Turtle" Thomas discusses and demonstrates sliding, reading pick-off moves, returns, primary and secondary lead-offs, beating-out ground balls and more. 61m; VHS. **A**: Adult. **P**: Instruction. **U**: Institution. **How-Ins**: Baseball, Sports--General, How-To. **Acq**: Purchase. **Dist**: Championship Productions. $39.95.

Bases and Sauces 199?
Teaches the food service employee or kitchen staff to create healthy yet delicious bases and sauces. Part of the Techniques of Healthy Cooking Video Series. 40m; VHS. **A**: Sr. High-Adult. **P**: Instruction. **U**: Home. **How-Ins**: Cooking, Food Industry, How-To. **Acq**: Purchase. **Dist**: Culinary Institute of America. $75.00.

Bases for Several Pavement Design Methods 197?
This series covers all aspects of several pavement design methods, including design, construction, and testing. Programs available individually. 60m/B/W; VHS, 3/4 U, EJ. **Pr**: University of Arizona. **A**: Adult. **P**: Professional. **U**: Institution, CCTV, Home. **Bus-Ind**: Engineering. **Acq**: Purchase, Rent/Lease. **Dist**: University of Arizona.
Indiv. Titles: 1. Pavement Systems Definitions 2. Stresses in Elastic Masses I 3. Stresses in Elastic Masses II 4. Laboratory Test for Asphaltic Concrete 5. Basics of Flexible Pavement Designs I 6. Basics of Flexible Pavement Designs II 7. Basics of Flexible Pavement Designs III 8. Rigid Pavement Design and Methods I 9. Rigid Pavement Design and Methods II.

The Bashful Bachelor 1942 (Unrated) — ★★
Yokel joker Abner trades his delivery car for a race horse, hoping to win a big race. 78m/B/W; VHS, DVD. **C**: Chester Lauck; Norris Goff; Zasu Pitts; Grady Sutton; Louise Currie; Irving Bacon; Earle Hodgins; Benny Rubin; Directed by Malcolm St. Clair. **Pr**: RKO. **A**: Jr. High-Adult. **P**: Entertainment. **U**: Home. **Mov-Ent**: Comedy--Romantic, Horses--Racing. **Acq**: Purchase. **Dist**: Rex Miller Artisan Studio. $24.95.

Basia: Prime Time TV 1990
The lovely Polish singer performs "Until You Come Back to Me," "New Day for You," "Promises," and "Prime Time TV." 40m; VHS. **Pr**: Columbia Pictures. **A**: Jr. High-Adult. **P**: Entertainment. **U**: Home. **Mov-Ent**: Music Video, Singing. **Acq**: Purchase. **Dist**: Music Video Distributors; Sony Music Entertainment Inc. $17.98.

Basic 2003 (R) — ★★
Travolta, swallowing scenery and his fellow actors in one gulp, is DEA agent and ex-Army Ranger Tom Hardy, brought in to investigate how a training mission ended in all but two soldiers being killed. Over the objections of the base's top cop, Capt. Julia Osborne (Nielsen, sporting an inconsistent Southern accent), he interrogates both survivors and gets two completely differing accounts, "Rashomon" style. In flashback, it's learned that the platoon's commander, Sgt. West, was universally hated, and the men were killed by each other, and some kind of drug smuggling ring may have been involved. Convoluted and confusing are two words you could use for this script, but both are woefully inadequate to describe how it messes with your head, and not in that good, "Wow, that was clever" way. It seems that the actors are as confused as the audience, and decide to cover that with epidemic over-acting. 95m; VHS, DVD. **C**: John Travolta; Samuel L. Jackson; Connie Nielsen; Giovanni Ribisi; Brian Van Holt; Taye Diggs; Christian de la Fuente; Dash Mihok; Timothy Daly; Roselyn Sanchez; Harry Connick, Jr.; Directed by John McTiernan; Written by James Vanderbilt; Cinematography by Steve Mason; Music by Klaus Badelt. **Pr**: Mike Medavoy; Arnie Messer; James Vanderbilt; Michael Tadross; Intermedia Films; Phoenix Pictures; Columbia Pictures. **A**: Sr. High-Adult. **P**: Entertainment. **U**: Home. **Mov-Ent**: Drug Enforcement Agency (DEA). **Acq**: Purchase. **Dist**: Sony Pictures Home Entertainment Inc.

Basic AC Circuits 1981
Contains 15 theory and 15 laboratory sessions; examines alternating current circuits. 30m; VHS. **Pr**: Texas Instruments. **A**: Sr. High-Adult. **P**: Education. **U**: Institution, CCTV, BCTV,

SURA. **Gen-Edu**: Electricity, Education. **Acq**: Purchase, Rent/Lease, Loan. **Dist**: Wisconsin Technical College System Foundation.
Indiv. Titles: 1. Overview 2. Introduction to AC 3. AC and the Sine Wave 4. The Oscilloscope and Its Use 5. The Sine Wave and Phase 6. Resistive Circuits 7. Capacitance 8. RC Circuit Analysis 9. Induction and Transformers 10. RL Circuit Analysis 11. RC and RL Time Constants 12. RLC Circuit Analysis 13. Phasor Algebra 14. Complex RLC Circuit Analysis 15. Resonance 16-30.Laboratory Sessions.

Basic AC Electricity for HVAC, Part 1 and 2 1980
On 12 tapes, the basics of HVAC AC electrical repair and control are shown. 165m; VHS, 3/4 U. **Pr**: Bergwall Productions. **A**: Sr. High-Adult. **P**: Vocational. **U**: Institution. **Bus-Ind**: Electronics. **Acq**: Purchase. **Dist**: Bergwall Productions, Inc.

Basic Accounting for Lawyers 1982
Shows lawyers who have no background in accounting how to use it in various legal and business situations. 420m; VHS, 3/4 U. **Pr**: Practicing Law Institute. **A**: Sr. High-Adult. **P**: Education. **U**: Institution, Home. **How-Ins**: Law, Finance, How-To. **Acq**: Purchase, Rent/Lease. **Dist**: Practising Law Institute.

Basic Accounting Video Series 1988
The four parts of this tape cover all pertinent information about learning accounting. Worksheets are included. The tapes can be purchased individually or as a set. 45m; VHS. **Pr**: Cambridge Career Productions. **A**: Sr. High-Adult. **P**: Instruction. **U**: Institution, Home. **Bus-Ind**: Business, Finance, Education. **Acq**: Purchase. **Dist**: Cambridge Educational. $98.00.
Indiv. Titles: 1. The Nature of Transactions 2. Books of Entry 3. Financial Statements 4. Computerized Basic Accounting.

Basic Acrylic Painting 19??
Five-tape package in which Jerry Yarnell presents basic skills and techniques in acrylic painting. 298m; VHS. **A**: Sr. High-Adult. **P**: Instruction. **U**: Institution. **How-Ins**: Painting, Art & Artists. **Acq**: Purchase. **Dist**: Educational Video Network. $189.95.

Basic Air Conditioning 1980
On four tapes, the basics of AC repair and maintenance are shown for trainees. 55m; VHS, 3/4 U. **Pr**: Bergwall Productions. **A**: Sr. High-Adult. **P**: Vocational. **U**: Institution. **Bus-Ind**: Electronics. **Acq**: Purchase. **Dist**: Bergwall Productions, Inc.

Basic Amplifiers 1964
This video discusses the theory, construction, and operation of basic amplifiers, and explains four general methods of coupling. 30m/B/W; VHS, 3/4 U. **Pr**: U.S.A. **A**: Sr. High-Adult. **P**: Education. **U**: Institution, SURA. **Gen-Edu**: Technology. **Acq**: Purchase. **Dist**: National Audiovisual Center. $110.00.

Basic and Petroleum Geology for Non-Geologists 1984
This series upgrades engineers' understanding and comprehension of geology in the oil and gas industry. 50m; VHS, 3/4 U. **Pr**: Philips Petroleum Company. **A**: College-Adult. **P**: Education. **U**: Institution. **Hea-Sci**: Geology, Education. **Acq**: Purchase. **Dist**: Gulf Publishing Co.
Indiv. Titles: 1. Fundamentals and Rock Identification 2. Geologic Age 3. Structural Geology and Mapping 4. Landforms 5. Landforms II 6. Earth's Interior and Platetectonics 7. Sedimentary Rocks 8. Historical Geology of North America 9. Hydrocarbons and Reservoir Rocks 10. Traps 11. Reservoirs and Well Logging 12. Drilling and Completing a Well 13. Petroleum Geology.

Basic Application Techniques with West System Epoxy 19??
Outlines the correct application procedures to follow when making repairs using West System Brand Epoxy. Includes tips on cooling, bonding, and fairing on wood and composite materials. Also covers safety procedures. 20m; VHS. **Pr**: Bennett Marine Video. **A**: Adult. **P**: Instruction. **U**: Home. **How-Ins**: Boating, How-To. **Acq**: Purchase. **Dist**: Bennett Marine Video. $19.95.

Basic Art by Video 1: Painting 1984
Instructor Charles Haddock teaches the basic techniques of painting. 120m; VHS. **Pr**: Charles Haddock. **A**: Sr. High-Adult. **P**: Instruction. **U**: Home. **How-Ins**: Painting, How-To. **Acq**: Purchase. **Dist**: Instructional Video.

Basic Art by Video 2: Drawing and Design 1984
Instructor Charles Haddock teaches the basic skills needed for drawing. 120m; VHS. **Pr**: Charles Haddock. **A**: Sr. High-Adult. **P**: Instruction. **U**: Home. **How-Ins**: Drawing, How-To. **Acq**: Purchase. **Dist**: Instructional Video.

Basic Art by Video 3: Color 1984
Instructor Charles Haddock demonstrates the color techniques used by painters from the Renaissance through modern times. 120m; VHS. **Pr**: Charles Haddock. **A**: Sr. High-Adult. **P**: Instruction. **U**: Home. **How-Ins**: Painting, How-To. **Acq**: Purchase. **Dist**: Instructional Video.

Basic Attending Skills—3rd Edition 1992
Designed for the inexperienced or experienced helper who wishes to learn about interviewing, this program focuses on effective listening and nonverbal components of the interview. 150m/B/W; VHS, 3/4 U, EJ. **Pr**: Microtraining Associates. **A**: College-Adult. **P**: Instruction. **U**: Institution, SURA. **L**: English, French, Spanish, Swedish. **Bus-Ind**: Communication, Interviews, How-To. **Acq**: Purchase, Rent/Lease, Duplication License. **Dist**: Microtraining Associates, Inc.

Basic Automatic Process Control 199?
An instrument technology training program on basic automatic process control. Includes a manual. 30m; VHS. **A**: Adult. **P**:

Instruction. **U**: Institution. **Bus-Ind**: Technology, Job Training. **Acq**: Purchase. **Dist**: ISA -The International Society of Automation. $95.00.

Basic Automotive Jobs Explained 1985
Simple automotive repairs are explained. 15m; VHS. **Pr**: Bergwall Productions. **A**: Sr. High-Adult. **P**: Instruction. **U**: Institution. **How-Ins**: Automobiles, Education. **Acq**: Purchase. **Dist**: Bergwall Productions, Inc. $269.00.
Indiv. Titles: 1. Using Reference Material and Starter Replacement 2. Performing Road Service, Tie Road End and Idler Arm Replacement 3. Performing Underhood Services and Muffler Replacement 4. Changing Engine Oil, Automatic Transmission Fluid, Valve Cover Gasket, and Thermostat Replacement 5. Alternator, Battery, Shocks and Spark Plug Replacement.

Basic Banking Etiquette 1987
Bank employees are taught how to be more pleasant to their customers. 16m; VHS, 3/4 U. **Pr**: First Financial Network. **A**: Adult. **P**: Education. **U**: Institution, Home. **Bus-Ind**: Customer Service, Etiquette. **Acq**: Purchase, Rent/Lease. **Dist**: 1st Financial Training Services. $325.00.

Basic Banking Products Made Simple 1987
New bank employees will benefit most from this program which simplifies their job. 18m; VHS, 3/4 U. **Pr**: First Financial Network. **A**: Adult. **P**: Education. **U**: Institution, Home. **Bus-Ind**: Employee Counseling, Finance. **Acq**: Purchase, Rent/Lease. **Dist**: 1st Financial Training Services. $325.00.

Basic Bass Fishing 19??
Fishing aficionados can learn the basics of bass fishing from experts in the beautiful wilds of Montana and Oregon. 58m; VHS. **A**: Jr. High-Adult. **P**: Instruction. **U**: Home. **Spo-Rec**: Fishing. **Acq**: Purchase. **Dist**: ESPN Inc. $29.95.

Basic Beginning Woodworking 1991
Learn the basic techniques for building furniture successfully. Includes tips for professional appearance and safety instruction. 77m; VHS. **A**: Sr. High-Adult. **P**: Instruction. **U**: Institution, Home. **How-Ins**: How-To, Woodworking. **Acq**: Purchase. **Dist**: Silver Mine Video Inc. $29.95.

Basic Bird Hunting 1990
Champion shooter Kay Ohye takes you through a crash course on bird hunting covering all the basics in safety and the hunt. 50m; VHS. **C**: Kay Ohye. **A**: Adult. **P**: Entertainment. **U**: Home. **How-Ins**: Sports--General, How-To, Hunting. **Acq**: Purchase. **Dist**: ESPN Inc.; Fast Forward.

Basic Blackjack 1989
Blackjack strategies such as when to split and when to double down are covered in this video. 60m; VHS. **Pr**: John Patrick Productions. **A**: College-Adult. **P**: Instruction. **U**: Home. **Gen-Edu**: Gambling. **Acq**: Purchase. **Dist**: John Patrick Entertainment, Inc. $39.95.

Basic Bluegrass Rhythm Guitar 1994
Steve Kaufman covers the basics of back-up guitar, including bass walks, the Lester Flatt "G run," altered chords, complex progressions, and other techniques. 70m; VHS. **A**: Jr. High-Adult. **P**: Instruction. **U**: Home. **How-Ins**: How-To, Music--Instruction. **Acq**: Purchase. **Dist**: Homespun Tapes Ltd. $39.95.

Basic Burda: Achieving Perfect Fit 1990
Learn how to size, ease allowance, cut and fit fabric to eliminate those dreaded sewing nightmares. 70m; VHS. **A**: Sr. High-Adult. **P**: Instruction. **U**: Home. **How-Ins**: How-To, Sewing. **Acq**: Purchase. **Dist**: Victorian Video/Yarn Barn of Kansas, Inc. $24.95.

Basic Car Care 1981
Step-by-step instructions on basic car maintenance and repair procedures are given. Simple, easy-to-understand language is used. 60m; VHS, Special order formats. **C**: Ray Hill. **Pr**: Cinema Associates. **A**: Sr. High-Adult. **P**: Instruction. **U**: Institution, CCTV, BCTV, Home. **How-Ins**: Automobiles, How-To. **Acq**: Purchase. **Dist**: RMI Media.

The Basic Care Guide for Elderly Patients ????
Three-part series explains to nursing home staff how to check vital signs and other mental and physical symptoms; recognizing and handling emergency situations; and understanding the physical, emotional and social losses connected with the process of aging. 75m; VHS. **A**: Adult. **P**: Vocational. **U**: Institution. **Hea-Sci**: Mental Health, Occupational Training, Medical Education. **Acq**: Purchase. **Dist**: University of Maryland. $400.00.
Indiv. Titles: 1. Care Essentials: Vital Signs Plus 2. Recognizing and Preventing Emergencies 3. Care Means Caring.

Basic Carpentry 1990
Learn what tools are appropriate for any carpentry project you have in mind. Instruction is featured on tape measure, combination squares, level, power saws, drills, sanders, wall framing, panel application, wall-shelving installation, using air-comp ressors and more. Inlcudes a 44 page instruction booklet. 56m; VHS. **Pr**: DIY Video Corporation. **A**: Sr. High-Adult. **P**: Instruction. **U**: Home. **How-Ins**: How-To, Woodworking. **Acq**: Purchase. **Dist**: Do It Yourself, Inc./D.I.Y. Video Corp. $19.95.

The Basic Carpentry Series 1990
This six volume series reviews many facets of woodworking instruction designed for the do-it-yourself home carpenter. 30m; VHS, CC. **Pr**: Goldcrest Films and Television. **A**: Sr. High-Adult. **P**: Instruction. **U**: Home. **How-Ins**: How-To, Woodworking. **Acq**: Purchase. **Dist**: You Can Do It Videos. $34.95.
Indiv. Titles: 1. Constructing Stud Walls 2. Installing Insulation and Sheetrock 3. Principles of Paneling 4. Installing a Pre-Hung Door 5. Installing a Lockset 6. Installing a Suspended Ceiling.

Basic Cartooning 199?
Mike Artell provides easy-to-follow instruction on basic cartooning. Some of the elements covered include drawing cartoon animals from letters of the alphabet, a caterpillar and a robot drawn from four basic shapes, a prehistoric Cartoon-a-saurus, and a cool cat tiger in the jungle. He also shows how to create simple stories and flip books. Comes with workbook. ?m; VHS. **A:** Preschool-Jr. High. **P:** Instruction. **U:** Home, Institution. **How-Ins:** Drawing, Animation & Cartoons, How-To. **Acq:** Purchase. **Dist:** Video Specialties; Crystal Productions. $24.95.

Basic Chemistry for Biology Students 1993
Illustrates the nucleus of the atom, the formation of ionic and covalent bonds, the pH scale, and the major molecules (carbohydrates, lipids, proteins, and nucleic acids). 30m; VHS. **A:** Sr. High-Adult. **P:** Education. **U:** Institution. **Gen-Edu:** Chemistry. **Acq:** Purchase. **Dist:** HRM Video. $189.00.

Basic Christmas Designs: Nosegays and Centerpieces 1984
Demonstrates how to make simple holiday floral designs. 60m; VHS, 3/4 U. **Pr:** RMI Media Productions. **A:** Sr. High-Adult. **P:** Instruction. **U:** Institution, CCTV, Home. **How-Ins:** Flowers, Hobbies, How-To. **Acq:** Purchase. **Dist:** RMI Media.

Basic Clerical Skills for New Employees 1992
Basic instruction covering topics such as handling the mail and alphabetized filing. Ineffective format and poor quality production. 45m; VHS. **A:** Sr. High-Adult. **P:** Professional. **U:** Institution. **Bus-Ind:** Business, Job Training. **Acq:** Purchase. **Dist:** Cambridge Educational. $79.95.

Basic Computer Literacy 19??
Provides answers to most of the common questions associated with learning how to use a computer. 45m; VHS. **A:** Sr. High-Adult. **P:** Education. **U:** Institution. **Gen-Edu:** Computers, Education. **Acq:** Purchase. **Dist:** Educational Video Network. $39.95.

Basic Computer Terminology for Lawyers 1985
A tape of the first hour of "Introduction to Computer Law," in which computer science is outlined for the lawyer. 60m; VHS. **Pr:** Practicing Law Institute. **A:** Adult. **P:** Professional. **U:** Institution, SURA. **Bus-Ind:** Law, Computers, Education. **Acq:** Purchase. **Dist:** Practising Law Institute.

Basic Computer Terms 1976
Uses comedy to present basic terms, parts, and processes of computers today. 26m; VHS, 3/4 U. **Pr:** Sheldon Renan. **A:** Primary-Adult. **P:** Education. **U:** Institution, Home, SURA. **Gen-Edu:** Computers, Education. **Acq:** Purchase, Rent/Lease, Duplication License. **Dist:** Pyramid Media.

Basic Concepts 1981
This series teaches young children about abstract social concepts such as law, government, and employment. Spanish and Swedish versions of these titles are available. 10m; VHS, 3/4 U. **Pr:** Learning Corporation of America. **A:** Primary-Jr. High. **P:** Education. **U:** Institution, SURA. **Chl-Juv:** Human Relations, Animation & Cartoons, Education. **Acq:** Purchase, Rent/Lease. **Dist:** Phoenix Learning Group.
Indiv. Titles: 1. Why We Have Laws 2. Why People Have Special Jobs 3. Why We Conserve Energy; Why We Have Elections 4. Why We Have Taxes 5. Why We Need Doctors 6. Why We Need Each Other 7. Why We Need Reading 8. Why We Take Care of Property 9. Why We Tell The Truth 10. Why We Use Money.

Basic Concepts of the Law of Evidence 1987
A series of tapes for training law students in evidence theory. 45m; VHS, 3/4 U. **Pr:** National Institute for Trial Advocacy. **A:** Adult. **P:** Professional. **U:** Institution. **Gen-Edu:** Law, Education. **Acq:** Purchase, Rent/Lease. **Dist:** National Institute for Trial Advocacy.
Indiv. Titles: 1. Introduction 2. Basic Concepts 3. Failure of Recollection, Best Evidence Rule, Perception 4. Expert Witnesses, Cross Examinations & Impeachment 1 5. Cross Examination & Impeachment 2, Rehabilitation 1 6. Rehabilitation 2, Character as Defense 7. Hearsay 1 8. Hearsay 2 9. Hearsay 3 10. Hearsay 4 11. Burdens of Proof & Presumptions 12. Hearsay & the Right to Confrontation 1 13. Hearsay & the Right to Confrontation 2 14. The 10 Commandments of Cross Examination 15. Hearsay Update.

Basic Considerations for Peripheral Nerve Repair and Grafting 1987
Dr. Millesi introduces a new system for classifying the degrees of nerve scarring at the time of surgery, and uses this as the basis for clinical treatment. 30m; VHS. **A:** Adult. **P:** Professional. **U:** Institution. **Hea-Sci:** Medical Education, Surgery. **Acq:** Purchase. **Dist:** American Society for Surgery of the Hand. $39.95.

Basic Construction and Maintenance for Gas Distribution 1981
This program covers equipment, procedures, and steps in the construction and maintenance of a new gas service or mainline. 16m; VHS, 3/4 U. **Pr:** University of Texas Austin. **A:** College-Adult. **P:** Instruction. **U:** Institution, CCTV. **Bus-Ind:** Oil Industry, How-To. **Acq:** Purchase.

Basic Control Applications 1973
This presentation takes a practical look at what the control variables are, where they appear in the column, their relationship, and how to select the best combinations to achieve responsive control. Part of the "Control of Distillation Columns" series. 30m; 3/4 U, Special order formats. **Pr:** Instrument Society of America. **A:** College-Adult. **P:** Professional. **U:** Institution, CCTV. **Bus-Ind:** Engineering. **Acq:** Purchase. **Dist:** ISA -The International Society of Automation.

The Basic Costumer 19??
Presents an overview of all aspects of the costumer's job. Covers costume research, the taking of measurements, costume acquisition and maintenance, and various approaches to pattern making. Includes a teacher's guide with a detailed outline of the program, measurement forms, sample quiz, research source list and bibliography. 73m; VHS. **A:** College-Adult. **P:** Education. **U:** Home, Institution. **Gen-Edu:** Clothing & Dress, Theater. **Acq:** Purchase, Rent/Lease. **Dist:** Stagestep; TMW Media Group. $119.

Basic Crocheting 19??
Learn the basics of crocheting with this instructional video. ?m; VHS. **A:** Jr. High-Adult. **P:** Instruction. **U:** Home. **How-Ins:** How-To, Crafts. **Acq:** Purchase. **Dist:** Inspired Corp. $14.98.

Basic Cross Stitch Designing 1988
The process of turning a pattern or design into cross stitched art is described. 40m; VHS, 3/4 U. **C:** Sandra Filler. **Pr:** RMI Media Productions. **A:** Jr. High-Adult. **P:** Instruction. **U:** Institution, CCTV, Home. **How-Ins:** Crafts, Sewing. **Acq:** Purchase. **Dist:** RMI Media. $49.95.

Basic Cross Stitch on Linen 1989
Using different fabrics can give cross stitch pieces a unique look. 50m; VHS. **Pr:** Nancy's Notions Ltd. **A:** Jr. High-Adult. **P:** Instruction. **U:** Institution, Home. **How-Ins:** Crafts, Sewing. **Acq:** Rent/Lease. **Dist:** Nancy's Notions Ltd.; RMI Media; Victorian Video/Yarn Barn of Kansas, Inc.

Basic Cruising Skills 1988
An introduction to the world of yacht cruising. 75m; VHS. **Pr:** Bennett Marine Video. **A:** Jr. High-Adult. **P:** Instruction. **U:** Home. **How-Ins:** Boating, Sports--Water. **Acq:** Purchase. **Dist:** Bennett Marine Video. $49.95.

Basic Custom Framing for Needlework 1988
Techniques for preparing needlework projects to be framed and mounted are taught. 60m; VHS, 3/4 U. **Pr:** RMI Media Productions. **A:** Jr. High-Adult. **P:** Instruction. **U:** Institution, CCTV, Home. **How-Ins:** Crafts. **Acq:** Purchase. **Dist:** RMI Media. $49.95.

Basic Darkroom Techniques 1988
Explains the techniques used in a photographic darkroom. 30m; VHS. **Pr:** Educational Filmstrips and Video. **A:** Primary-Sr. High. **P:** Instruction. **U:** Institution, Home. **How-Ins:** Photography, How-To. **Acq:** Purchase. **Dist:** Educational Video Network. $129.99.
Indiv. Titles: 1. Developing Black and White Film 2. Negative Evaluation and Contact Printing 3. Making a Photographic Enlargement.

Basic DC Electricity for HVAC 1980
On seven tapes, the basics of electronic HVAC maintenance and repair are shown. 98m; VHS, 3/4 U. **Pr:** Bergwall Productions. **A:** Sr. High-Adult. **P:** Vocational. **U:** Institution. **Bus-Ind:** Electronics, How-To. **Acq:** Purchase. **Dist:** Bergwall Productions, Inc.

Basic Digital Math 1989
Binary numbers and math systems designed to be used with them are examined. Also available as a single tape at the same cost. 30m; VHS. **Pr:** Bergwall Productions. **A:** Sr. High-Adult. **P:** Instruction. **U:** Institution. **Gen-Edu:** Industrial Arts, Electricity. **Acq:** Purchase. **Dist:** Bergwall Productions, Inc. $359.00.
Indiv. Titles: 1. Introduction to Digital Technology 2. Identifying Number Systems 3. Using Binary Numbers 4. Introduction to Boolean Algebra 5. Basic Laws of Boolean.

Basic Drafting 1980
On four tapes, the basics of mechanical drafting are explicated. 57m; VHS, 3/4 U. **Pr:** Bergwall Productions. **A:** Sr. High-Adult. **P:** Vocational. **U:** Institution. **Bus-Ind:** Graphics, How-To. **Acq:** Purchase. **Dist:** Bergwall Productions, Inc.

Basic Drafting 2 1982
On four tapes, more basic drafting is demonstrated to the viewer. 56m; VHS, 3/4 U. **Pr:** Bergwall Productions. **A:** Sr. High-Adult. **P:** Vocational. **U:** Institution. **Bus-Ind:** Graphics, How-To. **Acq:** Purchase. **Dist:** Bergwall Productions, Inc.

Basic Drafting 3 1983
An additional 6-tape series of basic drafting techniques. 12m; VHS, 3/4 U. **Pr:** Bergwall Productions. **A:** Sr. High-Adult. **P:** Vocational. **U:** Institution. **Bus-Ind:** Graphics, How-To. **Acq:** Purchase. **Dist:** Bergwall Productions, Inc.

Basic Dressage for North America 1990
Christilot Boylen, one of the leading dressage riders in international riding, guides you through the steps necessary to produce an advanced dressage horse. 46m; VHS. **A:** Family. **P:** Entertainment. **U:** Home. **How-Ins:** How-To, Horses--Racing. **Acq:** Purchase. **Dist:** Video Collectibles. $29.95.

Basic Dysrhythmia Interpretation 1988
Saved lives may result from these programs, since they teach nurses how to correct dysrhythmias. 28m; VHS, 3/4 U. **Pr:** Hospital Satellite Network. **A:** Adult. **P:** Professional. **U:** Institution, CCTV, SURA. **Hea-Sci:** Nursing, Respiratory System. **Acq:** Purchase, Rent/Lease. **Dist:** AJN Video Library/Lippincott Williams & Wilkins. $625.00.
Indiv. Titles: 1. Normal Sinus Rhythm and Sinus Dysrhythmias 2. Atrial and Junctional Dysrhythmias 3. Ventricular Dysrhythmias and AV Blocks.

Basic Ecology 1978
Discusses delicate and complex interrelationships. 29m; VHS. **A:** Adult. **P:** Education. **U:** Institution. **Hea-Sci:** Biology. **Acq:** Purchase. **Dist:** RMI Media. $75.00.

Basic Economic Principles 1999
Introduction to economic concepts such as supply and demand, economic indicators, inflation and deflation, interest rates, money supply, and financial planning. For use with Grades 10 and up. 30m; VHS; Closed Captioned. **A:** Sr. High-College. **P:** Education. **U:** Institution. **Gen-Edu:** Economics, Finance. **Acq:** Purchase. **Dist:** Social Studies School Service; Zenger Media. $64.95.

Basic Education: Teaching the Adult 1979
This two-part series consists of college level courses of on-campus seminars and televised lessons. Covers problems characteristic of the ABE learner, needs and interests, physiological factors affecting the adult learner, interpersonal relations, and communications. Focuses on modern teaching practices in adult basic education. 30m; VHS, 3/4 U. **Pr:** Maryland State Department of Education. **A:** Adult. **P:** Teacher Education. **U:** Institution, CCTV, CATV, BCTV. **Gen-Edu:** Education. **Acq:** Purchase, Rent/Lease. **Dist:** Maryland Public Television.
Indiv. Titles: 1. Orientation to ABE 2. Characteristics of the ABE Learner 3. Can Adults Learn 4. What Is the Student/Teacher Role? 5. Success, Needs and Interests 6. Human Relations 7. Program Planning 8. A Climate for Learning 9. Goal Performances and Objectives 10. Listening and Speaking 11. Diagnosing for Reading Placement 12. Teaching Basic Reading 13. Teaching Word Recognition 14. Teaching Reading Comprehension 15. Teaching Mathematics-Basic Level 16. Intermediate Mathematics 17. Teaching Writing 18. Developing Occupational Concepts 19. Methods and Techniques 20. Selection and Use of Materials 21. Individualization of Instruction 22. Teaching Machines 23. Recruitment and Retention 24. Community Resources 25. Guiding the ABE Learner 26. Evaluation of Progress 27. Paraprofessionals and Volunteers 28. Articulation to GED 29. Learners with Problems 30. Overview.

Basic Electrical Safety on the Jobsite 1995
Features mandatory training in electrical safety and explains how to avoid specific hazards. 11m; VHS. **A:** Adult. **P:** Professional. **U:** Institution. **L:** Spanish. **Bus-Ind:** Safety Education, Occupational Training, Construction. **Acq:** Purchase, Rent/Lease. **Dist:** National Safety Council, California Chapter, Film Library. $175.00.

Basic Electricity 1985
Part of a series offering instruction on power transmission products, including nomenclature, applications, classification, numbering systems, and other information on components and equipment. 20m; VHS. **A:** Adult. **P:** Vocational. **U:** Institution. **Gen-Edu:** Industrial Arts, Technology. **Acq:** Purchase. **Dist:** RMI Media. $112.50.

Basic Electricity and AC Circuits: Laboratory Series 1984
This is the second part of a series of 15 programs of how to control AC circuit behavior in a computer system. 120m; 3/4 U. **Pr:** Texas Instruments. **A:** College-Adult. **P:** Education. **U:** Institution. **Gen-Edu:** Electricity, How-To. **Acq:** Purchase, Rent/Lease. **Dist:** SkillSoft.
Indiv. Titles: 1. Laboratory Safety 2. Oscilloscope-Calibration and Use 3. Oscilloscope-Input Coupling and Wave Form Analysis 4. Oscilloscope-Triggering 5. Resistive Circuit Analysis 6. Series RC Circuits 7. Parallel RC Circuits 8. Transformers 9. Series RL Circuits 10. Parallel RC Circuits 11. RC Time Constants 12. RL Time Constants 13. Series Resistive and Reactive Circuits 14. Parallel Resistive and Reactive Circuits 15. Resonance.

Basic Electricity and AC Circuits: Lecture Series 1984
This is the first part of a series of lectures about how to control the AC circuit behavior in a computer system. 120m; 3/4 U. **Pr:** Texas Instruments. **A:** College-Adult. **P:** Education. **U:** Institution. **Gen-Edu:** Electricity, How-To. **Acq:** Purchase, Rent/Lease. **Dist:** SkillSoft.
Indiv. Titles: 1. Introduction to Alternating Current 2. AC and the Sine Wave 3. The Oscilloscope and Its Use 4. The Sine Wave and Phase 5. Resistive Circuits 6. Capacitance 7. RC Circuit Analysis 8. Inductance and Transformers 9. RL Circuit Analysis 10. RC and RL Time Constants 11. RLC Circuit Analysis 12. Phasor Algebra 13. Complex RLC Circuit Analysis 14. Resonance.

Basic Electricity and DC Circuits: Laboratory Series 1984
This is the first of a series of 15 programs that teach beginners the basics of electricity and direct current circuits. 120m; 3/4 U. **Pr:** Texas Instruments. **A:** College-Adult. **P:** Education. **U:** Institution. **Gen-Edu:** Electricity. **Acq:** Purchase, Rent/Lease. **Dist:** SkillSoft.
Indiv. Titles: 1. Laboratory Safety 2. The Ohmmeter and Its Use 3. Interpreting the Resister Color Code 4. The Voltmeter and Its Use 5. The Ammeter and Its Use 6. Ohm's Law and Series Circuits 7. Parallel Resistance 8. Parallel Circuits and Their Analysis 9. The Mechanical Switch 10. Series-Parallel Circuits 11. Voltage Dividers with Parallel Branch Currents 12. Network Analysis with Multiple Voltage Sources 13. The Wheatstone Bridge 14. RC Time Constants 15. L/R Time Constants.

Basic Electricity and DC Circuits: Lecture Series 1984
This is the second of a series of 14 programs that teach beginners the basics of electricity and direct current circuits. 120m; 3/4 U. **Pr:** Texas Instruments. **A:** College-Adult. **P:** Education. **U:** Institution. **Gen-Edu:** Electricity. **Acq:** Purchase, Rent/Lease. **Dist:** SkillSoft.
Indiv. Titles: 1. An Introduction to Electricity 2. Voltage, Current and Resistance 3. Scientific Notation and Metric Prefixes 4.

Ohm's Law and Power 5. Series Circuits 6. Introduction to Parallel Circuits 7. Parallel Circuits Analysis 8. Parallel-Series Circuits 9. Series-Parallel Circuits 10. Voltage Dividers and Power 11. Introduction to Kirchoff's Law 12. Advanced Methods of DC Circuit Analysis 13. Capacitors and the RC Time Constant 14. Inductors and the LIR Constant.

Basic Electricity and Electronics: Alternating Current—revised 1986
On 10 tapes, the basics of alternating circuit repair and function are demonstrated. 150m; VHS, 3/4 U. **Pr:** Bergwall Productions. **A:** Sr. High-Adult. **P:** Vocational. **U:** Institution. **Bus-Ind:** Electronics, How-To. **Acq:** Purchase. **Dist:** Bergwall Productions, Inc.

Basic Electricity and Electronics: Direct Current 1976
On six tapes, the basics of manipulating direct current are shown. 120m; VHS, 3/4 U. **Pr:** Bergwall Productions. **A:** Sr. High-Adult. **P:** Vocational. **U:** Institution. **Bus-Ind:** Electronics, How-To. **Acq:** Purchase. **Dist:** Bergwall Productions, Inc.

Basic Electricity and Electronics: Reactive Circuits 1982
On seven tapes, the basics of reactive circuits are explained for electrical trainees. 107m; VHS, 3/4 U. **Pr:** Bergwall Productions. **A:** Sr. High-Adult. **P:** Vocational. **U:** Institution. **Bus-Ind:** Electronics. **Acq:** Purchase. **Dist:** Bergwall Productions, Inc.

Basic Electricity: DC Circuits 1989
Simple and complex direct current circuits are examined. Also available on one tape at the same cost. 30m; VHS. **Pr:** Bergwall Productions. **A:** Sr. High-Adult. **P:** Instruction. **U:** Institution. **How-Ins:** Industrial Arts, Electricity. **Acq:** Purchase. **Dist:** Bergwall Productions, Inc. $239.00.
Indiv. Titles: 1. Series Circuits 2. Parallel Circuits 3. Resistors and Complex Circuits.

Basic Electricity: Direct Current 1987
The basics of electricity are explained. Also available on a single tape for the same cost. 14m; VHS. **Pr:** Bergwall Productions. **A:** Sr. High-Adult. **P:** Instruction. **U:** Institution. **How-Ins:** Industrial Arts, Electricity. **Acq:** Purchase. **Dist:** Bergwall Productions, Inc. $299.00.
Indiv. Titles: 1. Electron Flow 2. Symbols, Diagrams and Circuits 3. Ammeters and Voltmeters 4. Ohm's Law in Action.

Basic Electricity for Auto Mechanics 1989
Electrical basics are explained, with special emphasis on their importance to the auto mechanic. The series is also available on one tape for the same cost. ?m; VHS. **Pr:** Bergwall Productions. **A:** Sr. High-Adult. **P:** Instruction. **U:** Institution. **How-Ins:** Automobiles, Industrial Arts. **Acq:** Purchase. **Dist:** Bergwall Productions, Inc. $359.00.
Indiv. Titles: 1. What is Electricity? 2. Measuring Electricity 3. Electricity in the Automobile 4. Test Equipment 5. Electrical Troubleshooting.

Basic Electricity for HVAC 19??
A series of programs introducing the fundamental electronic principles behind heating, ventilating, and air conditioning (HVAC). Includes a manual coordinated to the subject of each tape. 20m; VHS. **A:** Sr. High-Adult. **P:** Instruction. **U:** Institution. **Gen-Edu:** How-To, Science, Technology. **Acq:** Purchase. **Dist:** Meridian Education Corp. $65.00.
Indiv. Titles: 1. Electron World 2. Working Wires 3. Meters & Measurements 4. Inside Circuits 5. Electricity at Work.

Basic Electricity I 1995
Features flow of electricity, how it moves along a conductor, Ohm's law, the Power law, static electricity, mechanical electricity, chemically generated electricity, and more. 20m; VHS. **A:** Adult. **P:** Professional. **U:** Institution. **Bus-Ind:** Job Training, Safety Education, Electricity. **Acq:** Rent/Lease. **Dist:** National Safety Council, California Chapter, Film Library.

Basic Electricity II 1995
Features AC current, hertz and cycle, single phase current, fuses and circuit breakers, wire sizes, and how the National Electrical Code is used. 22m; VHS. **A:** Adult. **P:** Professional. **U:** Institution. **Bus-Ind:** Job Training, Safety Education, Electricity. **Acq:** Rent/Lease. **Dist:** National Safety Council, California Chapter, Film Library.

Basic Electricity in the Workplace 1995
Covers static electricity; basic electrical safety; grounding; double insulation; and more. 11m; VHS. **A:** Adult. **P:** Professional. **U:** Institution. **L:** Spanish. **Bus-Ind:** Job Training, Safety Education, Management. **Acq:** Purchase, Rent/Lease. **Dist:** National Safety Council, California Chapter, Film Library. $175.00.

Basic Electromechanical Instrument Mechanisms 19??
Each of the fundamental characteristics of four electromechanical mechanisms—the permanent-magnet moving coil, the electro-dynamometer, the moving iron vane, and the electrostatic mechanisms—is introduced through an experiment demonstrating the physical law on which the mechanism is based. 29m/B/W; 3/4 U, Special order formats. **Pr:** National Committee for Electrical Engineering. **A:** College-Adult. **P:** Education. **U:** Institution, CCTV, CATV, BCTV. **Hea-Sci:** Engineering. **Acq:** Purchase, Rent/Lease. **Dist:** Education Development Center.

Basic Electronic Counter Functions 1980
Seven basic counter functions—manual, frequency period, multiple period, ratio, multiple ratio, and scaler—are discussed to provide users of electronic counters with knowledge in choosing which functions available to them are best for a given measurement situation. 17m; VHS, 3/4 U. **Pr:** Hewlett Packard. **A:** College-Adult. **P:** Professional. **U:** Institution, CCTV, Home. **L:** English, Spanish. **Bus-Ind:** Electronics. **Acq:** Purchase. **Dist:** Hewlett-Packard Media Solutions.

Basic Electronic Test Equipment 1985
Devices for testing things on cars are demonstrated. 13m; VHS. **Pr:** Bergwall Productions. **A:** Sr. High-Adult. **P:** Instruction. **U:** Institution. **How-Ins:** Automobiles, Education. **Acq:** Purchase. **Dist:** Bergwall Productions, Inc. $199.00.
Indiv. Titles: 1. Introduction to Multimeters 2. Resistance and Continuity Measurements 3. Voltage and Current Measurements.

Basic Electronic Test Instruments 1987
Instruments for testing the functioning of electronic circuits are demonstrated and explained. 13m; VHS. **Pr:** Bergwall Productions. **A:** Sr. High-Adult. **P:** Instruction. **U:** Institution. **How-Ins:** Electronics, Education. **Acq:** Purchase. **Dist:** Bergwall Productions, Inc. $199.00.
Indiv. Titles: 1. Introduction to Multimeters 2. Resistance and Continuity Measurements 3. Voltage and Current Measurements.

Basic Engine Rebuilding 19??
Offers step-by-step instruction on how to rebuild an automotive engine. Uses a Chevy 350 V-8 to demonstrate the correct steps for tearing the engine down and then rebuilding it. Covers all areas of engine rebuilding. Comes with reproducible printed quiz and answer sheet. 20m; VHS. **A:** Sr. High-Adult. **P:** Vocational. **U:** Institution. **How-Ins:** Automobiles, Occupational Training, How-To. **Acq:** Purchase. **Dist:** Cambridge Educational. $89.95.

Basic English/ESL 1995
This two volume set is designed for native speakers of other languages who want to learn English quickly and correctly. Study guide included. 120m; VHS. **A:** Jr. High-Adult. **P:** Education. **U:** Home. **Gen-Edu:** Education, Language Arts, Study Skills. **Acq:** Purchase. **Dist:** Video Aided Instruction Inc. $79.95.

Basic Equation Solving 1980
One of the "Mathematics for Modern Living" series, a program designed for people's mathematical needs that arise in everyday living. 30m; VHS, 3/4 U, Q. **Pr:** Magna Systems. **A:** College-Adult. **P:** Education. **U:** Institution, CCTV, CATV, BCTV. **Gen-Edu:** Mathematics. **Acq:** Purchase. **Dist:** Magna Systems, Inc.

Basic Equation Solving 2 1980
One of the "Mathematics for Modern Living" series, a program designed for people's mathematical needs that arise in everyday living. 30m; VHS, 3/4 U, Q. **Pr:** Magna Systems. **A:** College-Adult. **P:** Education. **U:** Institution, CCTV, CATV, BCTV. **Gen-Edu:** Mathematics. **Acq:** Purchase. **Dist:** Magna Systems, Inc.

Basic Field Production: Lighting 1994
Teaches how to implement a variety of effective lighting strategies for a basic interview shoot, using gear that fits into the back of a van. Topics include options for balancing mixed light sources, setting exposure, and monitoring. 24m; VHS. **Pr:** Australian Film, Radio and Television School. **A:** Adult. **P:** Instruction. **U:** Institution. **Gen-Edu:** Filmmaking. **Acq:** Purchase. **Dist:** TMW Media Group. $149.00.

Basic Field Production: Sound Recording 1994
Moves step by step through an actual office interview shoot with the sound recordist demonstrating advance planning, evaluating the space, choosing the right equipment, mixing strategies, test recording, and session procedures. 32m; VHS. **Pr:** Australian Film, Radio and Television School. **A:** Adult. **P:** Instruction. **U:** Institution. **Gen-Edu:** Filmmaking. **Acq:** Purchase. **Dist:** TMW Media Group. $149.00.

Basic Film Editing 1975
Illustrates both basic techniques of cutting and examples of their application, which turn out as mini-films. 17m; VHS, 3/4 U. **Pr:** Jerry Samuelson. **A:** Sr. High-College. **P:** Instruction. **U:** Institution, Home, SURA. **How-Ins:** Filmmaking, How-To. **Acq:** Purchase, Rent/Lease, Duplication License. **Dist:** Pyramid Media.

Basic Film Photography 1976
An introduction to basic principles of photography as they apply to filmmaking. 17m; VHS, 3/4 U. **Pr:** Jerry Samuelson. **A:** Sr. High-College. **P:** Instruction. **U:** Institution, Home, SURA. **How-Ins:** Filmmaking, Photography. **Acq:** Purchase, Rent/Lease, Duplication License. **Dist:** Pyramid Media.

Basic Film Terms 1970
Precise visual examples of the most important film terms provide us with a common vocabulary for discussing films, and film technique. 14m; VHS, 3/4 U, Special order formats. **Pr:** Sheldon Renan. **A:** Jr. High-Adult. **P:** Education. **U:** Institution, Home, SURA. **L:** Swedish. **How-Ins:** Filmmaking. **Acq:** Purchase, Rent/Lease, Duplication License. **Dist:** Pyramid Media. $195.00.

Basic First Aid 1990
Demonstrates basic first aid procedures including the proper techniques for giving CPR, first aid for choking victims, the correct procedure for controlling excessive bleeding, and the steps for treating shock. ?m; VHS. **A:** Jr. High-Sr. High. **P:** Education. **U:** Institution. **Hea-Sci:** First Aid, Health Education. **Acq:** Purchase. **Dist:** Meridian Education Corp. $45.00.

Basic Fly Fishing 1990
From scenic Montana, Greg Lilly and Dave Corcoran teach you the basics of fly fishing. 58m; VHS. **C:** Greg Lilly; Dave Corcoran. **A:** Jr. High-Adult. **P:** Instruction. **U:** Home. **Spo-Rec:** Fishing. **Acq:** Purchase. **Dist:** Fast Forward; ESPN Inc. $29.95.

Basic Folk Art Painting 1989
Folk art as printed on furniture and ornaments, as well as other objects, is explained. 60m; VHS, 3/4 U. **C:** Peggy Caldwell. **Pr:** RMI Media Productions. **A:** Jr. High-Adult. **P:** Instruction. **U:** Institution, CCTV, Home. **How-Ins:** Painting, Crafts. **Acq:** Purchase. **Dist:** RMI Media. $49.95.

Basic Forklift Principles 199?
Covers types of forklifts and their use. 14m; VHS. **A:** Adult. **P:** Vocational. **U:** Institution. **Bus-Ind:** Job Training. **Acq:** Purchase, Rent/Lease. **Dist:** Audio Graphics Training Systems; National Safety Council, California Chapter, Film Library. $450.00.

Basic Gardening 1980
Basic gardening is discussed by syndicated columnist Ed Hume. Part of the "Lawn and Garden" series. 60m; VHS, 3/4 U, Special order formats. **Pr:** Cinema Associates. **A:** Jr. High-Adult. **P:** Instruction. **U:** Institution, CCTV, CATV, BCTV, Home. **How-Ins:** Gardening. **Acq:** Purchase. **Dist:** RMI Media.

Basic Gas Chromatography 19??
The essentials of gas chromatography are explained by Dr. Harold McNair. Topics include separation of gases, liquids, and solids into component parts, kinds of materials used in both packed and capillary columns, and more. Comes with study guide. 50m; VHS. **A:** Sr. High. **P:** Education. **U:** Institution. **Hea-Sci:** Chemistry. **Acq:** Purchase. **Dist:** American Chemical Society. $800.00.

Basic Genetics 19??
Uses human genetic examples to teach key genetics terms, including chromosome, dominant, recessive, homozygous, heterozygous, genotype, and phenotype. ?m; VHS. **A:** Jr. High-Adult. **P:** Education. **U:** Institution. **Hea-Sci:** Science, Genetics. **Acq:** Purchase. **Dist:** CEV Multimedia. $39.95.

Basic Geology for Technicians 1984
This series leads technicians through a practical explanation of the forces influencing the formation of hydrocarbons. 40m; VHS, 3/4 U. **TV Std:** NTSC, PAL, SECAM. **Pr:** Gulf Publishing Co. **A:** College-Adult. **P:** Professional. **U:** Institution, SURA. **Hea-Sci:** Education, Geology, Oil Industry. **Acq:** Purchase. **Dist:** Gulf Publishing Co. $400.00.
Indiv. Titles: 1. The Earth's Crust 2. Identification of Common Rocks and Minerals 3. Weathering, Erosion, and Unconformities 4. Folding and Faulting 5. Relative and Absolute Age Dating 6. The Use of Fossils and the Geological Time Scale 7. Sandstone Deposition-Dunes, Beaches, and Submarine Fans 8. Sandstone Deposition-Rivers and Deltas 9. Carbonate Rock Deposition 10. Subsurface Fluids 11. Sedimentary Rock Depositional Patterns 12. Surface and Subsurface Mapping 13. Oceanic Environment 14. Plate Tetonics 15. North American Framework.

Basic German by Video 1990
The rudiments of the German language are conveyed to the viewer through the magic of videotape. 90m; VHS. **Pr:** MSV. **A:** Jr. High-Adult. **P:** Education. **U:** Home. **Gen-Edu:** Language Arts. **Acq:** Purchase. **Dist:** German Language Video Center. $74.95.

Basic Grammar Series 1980
This series uses animation to instruct children in grammar. 8m; VHS. **A:** Primary. **P:** Education. **U:** Institution. **Chl-Juv:** Language Arts. **Acq:** Purchase, Rent/Lease. **Dist:** Clear Vue Inc. $199.00.
Indiv. Titles: 1. Nouns 2. Verbs 3. Modifiers.

The Basic Growth Foundations 1982
A look at religion's assumedly positive role in maturation. 28m; VHS, 3/4 U. **Pr:** Broadman. **A:** Adult. **P:** Religious. **U:** Institution, CCTV. **Gen-Edu:** Religion. **Acq:** Purchase. **Dist:** Broadman & Holman Publishers.

Basic Guide to Archery 19??
Teaches the basics of archery including choosing the right bow, accessory selection, tune up techniques, bow set up, and arrow selection. Hosted by PSE President Pete Shepley and top pro Terry Ragsdale. 65m; VHS. **A:** Sr. High-Adult. **P:** Instruction. **U:** Home. **Spo-Rec:** Sports--General. **Acq:** Purchase. **Dist:** Precision Shooting Equipment Inc. $15.00.

Basic Guide to Bankruptcy 19??
Outlines techniques for resolving accounting and auditing problems during bankruptcy proceedings. Also contains information on bankruptcy taxes for individuals, estates, partnerships, and corporations. Includes workbook and quizzer. 120m; VHS. **A:** College-Adult. **P:** Education. **U:** Institution, Home. **Gen-Edu:** Economics, Finance, Business. **Acq:** Purchase. **Dist:** Bisk Education. $199.00.

Basic Guide to Handguns 1990
A comprehensive look at owning and shooting a handgun. Covers buying, shooting, cleaning, marksmanship, safety and more. 60m; VHS. **A:** Sr. High-Adult. **P:** Instruction. **U:** Home. **How-Ins:** How-To, Firearms. **Acq:** Purchase. **Dist:** Gun Video. $39.95.

Basic Guide to Resume Writing & Job Interviews 1988
Learn what todays employers are looking for in a resume. This video explains the eight steps to landing a job and uncovers eleven sources for job leads. Study guide available for $8.95. 45m; VHS. **A:** Sr. High-Adult. **P:** Instruction. **U:** Home, Institution. **Gen-Edu:** Job Hunting, Interviews. **Acq:** Purchase. **Dist:** Cambridge Educational. $98.00.

Basic Guide to Shotguns 1988
Learn all about buying and using a shotgun in this video geared toward hunters from a living legend, John Satterwhite. 45m; VHS, 3/4 U. **C:** John Satterwhite. **Pr:** Champions on Film. **A:** Sr. High-Adult. **P:** Instruction. **U:** Institution, CCTV, Home. **How-Ins:** How-To, Firearms, Safety Education. **Acq:** Purchase. **Dist:** School-Tech Inc.; Gun Video. $49.95.

Basic Guitar & String Set Up 199?
Explains the parts of the electric and acoustic guitar. Demonstrates how to change strings; hold the guitar and pick; tune with an electric tuner, keyboard, and by ear; common chords, and strumming patterns. ?m; VHS. **A:** Sr. High-Adult. **P:** Instruction. **U:** Home. **How-Ins:** Music--Instruction. **Acq:** Purchase. **Dist:** Hal Leonard Corp. $7.95.

Basic Guitar Chords and Accompaniment Styles 19??
Video course for the beginning guitarist providing basic skills to play country, blues, gospel and bluegrass. 60m; VHS. **A:** Family. **P:** Entertainment. **U:** Home. **How-Ins:** Music--Instruction. **Acq:** Purchase. **Dist:** Texas Music and Video; Video Collectibles. $19.95.

Basic Guitar Set-Up and Repair 1984
Learn how to set up a guitar and make the minor repairs that frequently need to be taken care of on the instrument. 90m; VHS. **Pr:** Homespun Video. **A:** Sr. High-Adult. **P:** Instruction. **U:** Home. **How-Ins:** How-To, Music--Instruction. **Acq:** Purchase. **Dist:** Homespun Tapes Ltd. $49.95.

Basic Hand Sewing 1991
Demonstrates basic stitches, explains the uses of different needles and thread, and shows how to thread a needle. ?m; VHS. **A:** Jr. High-Sr. High. **P:** Education. **U:** Institution. **Gen-Edu:** Sewing, Home Economics. **Acq:** Purchase. **Dist:** Meridian Education Corp. $45.00.

Basic Holemaking 1995
Provides basic theory and practice of holemaking, including various drills, holemaking machines, operating parameters, and hole finishing operations. 24m; VHS. **A:** Adult. **P:** Vocational. **U:** Institution. **Bus-Ind:** Metal Work, Occupational Training. **Acq:** Purchase. **Dist:** Society of Manufacturing Engineers. $255.00.

Basic Home Repair 1990
Plenty of tips are offered for minor home repairs, such as replacing a faucet or toilet, sweating copper pipe, unclogging drains, caulking a tub, replacing light fixtures and switches, repairing lamps, replacing broken tiles, fixing leaky faucets and running tiolets, replacing shower heads and more. Includes a 44 page booklet. 56m; VHS. **Pr:** DIY Video Corporation. **A:** Sr. High-Adult. **P:** Instruction. **U:** Home. **How-Ins:** How-To, Home Improvement. **Acq:** Purchase. **Dist:** Do It Yourself, Inc./D.I.Y. Video Corp. $39.95.

Basic Horse Care 19??
Illustrates the fundamentals of caring for a horse by covering the basics of proper feeding, grooming, safety, tack selection, medication, transporting, and horse psychology. Provides expert insight from Odette Larson. 80m; VHS. **A:** Jr. High-Adult. **P:** Instruction. **U:** Institution, Home. **How-Ins:** Horses, How-To. **Acq:** Purchase. **Dist:** CEV Multimedia. $89.95.

Basic Horsemanship Series, Vol. II: Health Care 19??
Offers general knowledge on how to spot potential health problems in horses and prevent them. Also covers basic horse anatomy, a horse's medical needs, and proper nutrition. 60m; VHS. **A:** Jr. High-Adult. **P:** Instruction. **U:** Institution. **How-Ins:** Horses, How-To. **Acq:** Purchase. **Dist:** CEV Multimedia. $65.00.

Basic Horsemanship Series—Vol. I: From the Ground Up 19??
Outlines elements of safe and correct horsemanship and covers health considerations, bathing and grooming, exercise, proper care of the horse's legs, and basic riding techniques. 60m; VHS. **A:** Jr. High-Adult. **P:** Instruction. **U:** Institution. **How-Ins:** Horses, How-To. **Acq:** Purchase. **Dist:** CEV Multimedia. $65.00.

Basic Horsemanship Series—Vol. III: Mount Up 19??
Provides basic English and Western horseback riding instruction, covering techniques for walking, trotting, jogging, cantering, loping, lead changes, and picking up the proper diagonal. ?m; VHS. **A:** Jr. High-Adult. **P:** Instruction. **U:** Institution. **How-Ins:** Horses, How-To. **Acq:** Purchase. **Dist:** CEV Multimedia. $39.95.

Basic Horseshoeing Principles 1992
Basic principles for beginning horseshoers and horse owners. 25m; VHS. **TV Std:** NTSC, PAL. **A:** Adult. **P:** Instruction. **U:** Institution, Home. **Gen-Edu:** Horses. **Acq:** Purchase. **Dist:** Doug Butler Enterprises Inc.

Basic House Framing 1984
On four tapes, basic house frame construction is demonstrated. 60m; VHS, 3/4 U. **Pr:** Bergwall Productions. **A:** Sr. High-Adult. **P:** Vocational. **U:** Institution. **Bus-Ind:** Architecture, How-To. **Acq:** Purchase. **Dist:** Bergwall Productions, Inc.

Basic Housekeeping Series 1986
A series instructing the skills of custodial maintenance. 15m; VHS, 3/4 U. **Pr:** AMS Dist. **A:** Adult. **P:** Education. **U:** Institution, Home. **How-Ins:** Custodial Service, How-To. **Acq:** Purchase. **Dist:** AMS Distributors, Inc.
Indiv. Titles: 1. Introduction to Housekeeping 2. Basics of Floor Care 1 3. Basics of Floor Care 2 4. Basics of Restroom Cleaning 5. Basic Procedures in General Cleaning 6. Basics of Carpet Care 7. Custodial Safety 8. Shower & Locker Room 9. Kitchen Sanitation 10. Lawn Care 1 11. Lawn Care 2 12. Tree & Shrub Care.

Basic Immunology 1994
First of educational series that targets undergraduate, pre-med students, practicing physicians and anyone interested in the physiology of the immune system. 37m; VHS. **A:** College-Adult. **P:** Education. **U:** Institution. **Hea-Sci:** Medical Care, Medical Education. **Acq:** Purchase. **Dist:** Medical Visual Creations. $39.95.

Basic Influencing Skills, 3rd Edition ????
Demonstrates how to help clients tell their stories, reframe them, and change behavior. Central issues are family and diversity. 90m; VHS. **A:** Adult. **P:** Professional. **U:** Institution. **Hea-Sci:** Psychology, Mental Health. **Acq:** Purchase. **Dist:** Microtraining Associates, Inc. $275.00.

Basic Influencing Skills—2nd Edition 1984
The interview is presented as a process of interpersonal influence. Included is systematic instruction in dimensions of helping such as empathy, respect, concreteness, and genuineness. 150m/B/W; VHS, 3/4 U, EJ. **Pr:** Microtraining Associates. **A:** College-Adult. **P:** Instruction. **U:** Institution, SURA. **Bus-Ind:** Communication, Interviews, How-To. **Acq:** Purchase, Rent/Lease. **Dist:** Microtraining Associates, Inc.

Basic Instinct 1992 (R) — ★★½
Controversial thriller had tongues wagging months before its theatrical release. Burnt-out detective Douglas falls for beautiful, manipulative murder suspect Stone, perfectly cast as a bisexual ice queen who may or may not have done the deed. Noted for highly erotic sex scenes and an expensive (3 million bucks) script; ultimately the predictable plot is disappointing. Gay activists tried to interrupt filming because they objected to the depiction of Stone's character but only succeeded in generating more free publicity. The American release was edited to avoid an "NC-17" rating, but an uncut, unrated video version is also available. 123m; VHS, DVD, Blu-Ray, CC. **C:** Michael Douglas; Sharon Stone; George Dzundza; Jeanne Tripplehorn; Denis Arndt; Leilani Sarelle Ferrer; Bruce A. Young; Chelcie Ross; Dorothy Malone; Wayne Knight; Stephen Tobolowsky; Directed by Paul Verhoeven; Written by Joe Eszterhas; Cinematography by Jan De Bont; Music by Jerry Goldsmith. **Pr:** Alan Marshall; Tri-Star Pictures. **A:** College-Adult. **P:** Entertainment. **U:** Home. **Mov-Ent:** Mystery & Suspense, Violence. **Awds:** MTV Movie Awards '93: Female Perf. (Stone), Most Desirable Female (Stone). **Acq:** Purchase. **Dist:** Lions Gate Television Corp. $49.98.

Basic Instinct 2 2006 (R) — ★
It took 14 years for a sequel and this glossy, laughably overwrought mess is what we get? Stone tries too hard reprising her role as cold-blooded vamp Catherine Tramell, who's now living in London. After a fatal car crash, suspicious Scotland Yard detective Washburn (Thewlis) asks criminologist Michael Glass (Morrissey) to evaluate Catherine for possible criminal charges. His diagnosis is "risk addiction." Gee, doc, no kidding. Soon Michael is drawn into Catherine's possibly deadly web. Maybe this effort will become a midnight movie, just waiting to be mocked. 114m; DVD, Blu-Ray. **C:** Sharon Stone; David Morrissey; David Thewlis; Charlotte Rampling; Hugh Dancy; Flora Montgomery; Iain Robertson; Indira Varma; Anne Caillon; Stan Collymore; Heathcote Williams; Directed by Michael Caton-Jones; Written by Leora Barish; Henry Bean; Cinematography by Gyula Pados; Music by John Murphy. **Pr:** Joel B. Michaels; Mario Kassar; Andrew G. Vajna; Metro-Goldwyn-Mayer Pictures; IMF; C2/Intermedia; Sony Pictures Entertainment. **A:** Sr. High-Adult. **P:** Entertainment. **U:** Home. **L:** English. **Mov-Ent:** Crime Drama, Sex & Sexuality, Psychiatry. **Awds:** Golden Raspberries '06: Worst Actress (Stone), Worst Picture, Worst Screenplay, Worst Sequel/Prequel. **Acq:** Purchase. **Dist:** Sony Pictures Home Entertainment Inc.

Basic/Intermediate Craps 1989
A guide for the craps player on an intermediate level. 60m; VHS. **A:** College-Adult. **P:** Instruction. **U:** Home. **Gen-Edu:** Sports--General. **Acq:** Purchase. **Dist:** John Patrick Entertainment, Inc. $39.95.

Basic Jewelry 19??
Artist Paulette Werger demonstrates the jewelry-making techniques of cutting, piercing, soldering, filing, and polishing in this teaching aid for art education. 26m; VHS. **A:** Jr. High-College. **P:** Education. **U:** Institution. **Gen-Edu:** Art & Artists. **Acq:** Purchase. **Dist:** Crystal Productions. $39.95.

Basic Landscaping 19??
Shows you how to design a landscape plan, prepare and mulch new beds and plant various types of trees and shrubs. 48m; VHS. **A:** Sr. High-Adult. **P:** Instruction. **U:** Home. **How-Ins:** How-To, Landscaping. **Acq:** Purchase. **Dist:** Hometime Video Publishing Inc. $11.95.

BASIC Language Calculator, 9830A 1981
Helps the viewer calculate simple arithmetic, log and trig functions, write a simple program that utilizes the printer, edit the simple program, and use the cassette to store and load programs and data. 17m/B/W; VHS, 3/4 U. **Pr:** Hewlett Packard. **A:** College-Adult. **P:** Education. **U:** Institution, CCTV, Home. **L:** English, French, German, Italian, Portuguese, Spanish. **How-Ins:** Computers, How-To. **Acq:** Purchase. **Dist:** Hewlett-Packard Media Solutions.

Basic Law Terms 1973
Two major divisions of law, criminal and civil, are clearly defined in easily understandable terms to help explain how young people can make the law work for them. 18m; VHS, 3/4 U. **Pr:** Noel Nosseck. **A:** Sr. High-College. **P:** Education. **U:** Institution, Home, SURA. **Gen-Edu:** Law. **Acq:** Purchase, Rent/Lease, Duplication License. **Dist:** Pyramid Media.

Basic Lessons in Awareness Through Movement 1988
A four tape series for beginners and intermediates that present unique floor exercises designed to reorganize patterns of movement toward more effortless and efficient configurations. 60m; VHS. **A:** Family. **P:** Instruction. **U:** Institution. **How-Ins:** Dance--Instruction. **Acq:** Purchase. **Dist:** Princeton Book Company Publishers. $39.95.

The Basic Listening Sequence and Issues of Trauma 19??
Offers techniques on how to draw out client stories with a minimum of interference. Includes demonstration of techniques and explanation of the various skills. 26m; VHS, 3/4 U. **Pr:** Microtraining Associates. **A:** College-Adult. **P:** Instruction. **U:** Institution, SURA. **L:** English, French, Spanish, Swedish, Chinese, Danish, Dutch, German, Japanese, Norwegian. **Bus-Ind:** Communication, Human Relations. **Acq:** Purchase. **Dist:** Microtraining Associates, Inc. $75.00.

Basic Living Skills: Consumerism 1976
A series which provides practical money-saving ideas and shows how to live within means in these inflationary times. Programs are available individually. 15m; VHS, 3/4 U. **Pr:** RMI Media Productions. **A:** Sr. High-Adult. **P:** Education. **U:** Institution, CCTV, Home. **Gen-Edu:** Consumer Education, Finance. **Acq:** Purchase. **Dist:** RMI Media; Cambridge Educational.
Indiv. Titles: 1. Housing-Renting and Decoration 2. Food-Purchasing and Preparation 3. Clothing-Buying and Care 4. Home Maintenance-Simple Repairs 5. Cars-Selection and Financing.

Basic Manicure 1990
Offers instruction on specific aspects of barbering and cosmetology. 10m; VHS. **A:** Adult. **P:** Vocational. **U:** Institution. **Bus-Ind:** Cosmetology. **Acq:** Purchase. **Dist:** RMI Media. $39.95.

Basic Marksmanship: .45 Caliber Pistol 1972
A Marine training film on techniques for using the .45 caliber pistol. 14m; VHS. **Pr:** U.S. Marine Corps. **A:** Adult. **P:** Education. **U:** Institution, Home. **How-Ins:** Armed Forces--U.S., How-To. **Acq:** Purchase. **Dist:** International Historic Films Inc. $19.95.

Basic Masonry 1987
The basics of masonry construction are demonstrated. Also available on a single tape at the same cost. 13m; VHS. **Pr:** Bergwall Productions. **A:** Sr. High-Adult. **P:** Instruction. **U:** Institution. **How-Ins:** Construction, Education. **Acq:** Purchase. **Dist:** Bergwall Productions, Inc. $359.00.
Indiv. Titles: 1. Spreading Mortar 2. The Pyramid 3. Building a Corner 4. Wall Construction: Part One 5. Wall Construction: Part Two.

Basic Math: Fractions and Decimals 1989
The use of the basic math concepts of fractions and decimals are taught to a vocational audience. Also available on a single tape at the same cost. ?m; VHS. **Pr:** Bergwall Productions. **A:** Jr. High-Adult. **P:** Instruction. **U:** Institution. **How-Ins:** Mathematics, Education. **Acq:** Purchase. **Dist:** Bergwall Productions, Inc. $299.00.
Indiv. Titles: 1. Understanding Fractions 2. Adding and Subtracting Fractions 3. Multiplication and Division of Fractions 4. Decimal Numbers 5. Conversion of Fractions, Decimals and Percentages.

Basic Math: Precision Measuring Tools 1991
Six programs highlight common precision tools used by machinists and technicians with the math skills needed to operate them. 101m; VHS. **A:** Adult. **P:** Professional. **U:** Institution. **Bus-Ind:** Business, Mathematics, Tools. **Acq:** Purchase. **Dist:** Bergwall Productions, Inc. $399.00.
Indiv. Titles: 1. Using the Vernier Caliper 2. Introduction to the Outside Micrometer 3. Measuring With Bore Gauges 4. Working with Depth Gauges 5. Using Dial Indicators 6. Exploring Protractors and Gauge Blocks.

Basic Math Series 1980
This seven-program series develops basic and foundational arithmetic skills for students. Programs are available individually. 9m; VHS, 3/4 U. **Pr:** BFA Educational Media. **A:** Primary. **P:** Education. **U:** Institution, SURA. **Gen-Edu:** Mathematics, Education. **Acq:** Purchase. **Dist:** Phoenix Learning Group.
Indiv. Titles: 1. Fractions 2. Telling Time 3. Counting by Ten's and Five's 4. Adding 5. Comparing 6. Numbers and Order 7. Subtracting.

Basic Mathematical Skills: Fractions, Least Common Denominator, Addition, and Subtraction 1992
Demonstrates math problems involving fractions. 27m; VHS. **A:** Primary. **P:** Education. **U:** Institution. **Gen-Edu:** Mathematics, Education. **Acq:** Purchase. **Dist:** Video Resources. $50.00.

Basic Mathematics Skills 19??
Twenty-seven part educational series that teaches basic mathematical concepts, covering whole numbers, addition, subtraction, multiplication, division, estimating, fractions, decimals, percentages, metric system, signed numbers, variables, equations, and exponents. 575m; VHS. **A:** Primary-Adult. **P:** Education. **U:** Institution. **Gen-Edu:** Mathematics, Education. **Acq:** Purchase. **Dist:** Video Resources. $29.95.
Indiv. Titles: 1. Whole Numbers - Place Values, Addition and Subtraction, Rounding 2. Whole Numbers - Multiplication, Order of Operations 3. Whole Numbers - Division 4. Estimating 5. Factors and Multiples 6. Fractions - Equivalent Fractions, Lowest Terms, Comparing Fractions and Mixed Numbers 7.

Fractions - Multiplication and Division 8. Fractions - Least Common Denominator, Addition and Subtraction 9. Applications with Fractions 10. Decimals - Addition, Subtraction, Multiplication, and Rounding 11. Decimals - Division, Converting to Fractions 12. Ratios and Proportions 13. Applications and Proportions 14. Percent and Applications 15. Percent and Applications II 16. Comfortable with Percents 17. U.S. Customary System 18. Metric System 19. Thinking Metric 20. Perimeter and Area 21. Operations on Signed Numbers 22. Order of Operations 23. Introduction to Variables 24. Solving Equations 25. Applications of Linear Equations 26. Exponents 27. More Exponents and Introduction to Radicals.

Basic Measurements 1973
Details three categories of measurement variables to be measured, instruments used, and problems in and methods of measurement. Focuses on conventional measurements, composition measurements, and variables computed from other measurements. Part of the "Control of Distillation Columns" series. 30m; 3/4 U, Special order formats. **Pr:** Instrument Society of America. **A:** College-Adult. **P:** Professional. **U:** Institution, CCTV. **Bus-Ind:** Engineering. **Acq:** Purchase. **Dist:** ISA -The International Society of Automation.

Basic Metabolic Processes Series 1983
An overview of the digestion of food is provided in these two programs. 20m; VHS, 3/4 U, Special order formats. **Pr:** Ohio State University Health Sciences AV Center. **A:** College-Adult. **P:** Professional. **U:** Institution, SURA. **Hea-Sci:** Digestive System, Metabolism, Medical Education. **Acq:** Purchase, Rent/Lease. **Dist:** Ohio State University.
Indiv. Titles: 1. The Digestive Process 2. Metabolism.

Basic Money Management 1984
Seven ten-minute programs teach the basic principles for successful money management. 10m; VHS, 3/4 U. **Pr:** RMI Media Productions. **A:** Sr. High-Adult. **P:** Education. **U:** Institution, CCTV, Home. **How-Ins:** Personal Finance, How-To. **Acq:** Purchase. **Dist:** RMI Media.
Indiv. Titles: 1. Checking Accounts-Basic Building Blocks 2. Savings Plans-Cornerstone to Security 3. Budgets-The Why and How 4. Credit-A Personal Guide 5. Loans-How to Borrow Money 6. Investments-What, Why, When and Who 7. Net Worth-How Do You Do.

Basic Mother Sauces: Espagnole, Bechamel, and Pan Gravy 1984
Chef Paul demonstrates techniques for creating three basic mother sauces. 19m; VHS. **A:** Adult. **P:** Instruction. **U:** Institution. **Gen-Edu:** Cooking. **Acq:** Purchase. **Dist:** RMI Media. $39.95.

Basic Navigation 19??
Commander Dave Smith teaches basic boating navigation procedures, covering buoys, lights, ranges, structural charts, navigational symbols, visual fix locating, line position, dumb compass, triangulation, and depth contours. 60m; VHS. **A:** Jr. High-Adult. **P:** Instruction. **U:** Institution. **Spo-Rec:** Boating, How-To. **Acq:** Purchase. **Dist:** Instructional Video. $29.95.

Basic Navigation Rules of the Road 19??
Offers a basic introduction to the various types of navigational aids, including buoys, ranges, chart-reading, visual fix, line of position, dumb compass, triangulation, depth contours, and speed determination. 60m; VHS. **Pr:** Bennett Marine Video. **A:** Jr. High-Adult. **P:** Instruction. **U:** Home. **Spo-Rec:** Boating, How-To. **Acq:** Purchase. **Dist:** Bennett Marine Video. $29.95.

The Basic Needs Series 1979
Man's basic needs of clothing, food and shelter are discussed. Programs are available as a series or individually. 15m; VHS, 3/4 U. **Pr:** Wayne Mitchell. **A:** Primary. **P:** Education. **U:** Institution, SURA. **Gen-Edu:** Documentary Films, Human Relations, Poverty. **Acq:** Purchase. **Dist:** Phoenix Learning Group.
Indiv. Titles: 1. Clothing Around the World 2. Food Around the World 3. Shelter Around the World.

Basic Nutrition: Let's Make a Meal 1976
In the form of a game show, this program presents basic nutritional facts and fallacies. 18m; VHS, 3/4 U. **Pr:** Professional Research. **A:** Family. **P:** Education. **U:** Institution, CCTV, SURA. **Hea-Sci:** Nutrition, Health Education. **Acq:** Purchase, Rent/Lease. **Dist:** Discovery Education. $99.00.

Basic Nymph Fishing with Jim Teeny 1990
Jim Teeny helps to improve your skills in wet fly or "nymph" fishing. 50m; VHS. **C:** Jim Teeney. **A:** Adult. **P:** Entertainment. **U:** Home. **Spo-Rec:** Sports--General, Fishing. **Acq:** Purchase. **Dist:** ESPN Inc.; Fast Forward.

Basic O.R. Instrumentation 19??
Discusses and demonstrates the four main categories of operating room instrumentation: sharps, graspers, retractors, and clamps. Outlines proper care of these instruments, including cleaning methods, preventive maintenance, counting methods, and prevention of bloodborne diseases. Emphasizes safety and efficiency of surgical procedures and control costs. Includes study guide. Approved for CE credit. 28m; VHS. **A:** College-Adult. **P:** Education. **U:** Institution. **Hea-Sci:** Nursing, Medical Education, Surgery. **Acq:** Purchase, Rent/Lease. **Dist:** AJN Video Library/Lippincott Williams & Wilkins. $285.00.

Basic Oscilloscope Measurements 197?
A basic introduction to oscilloscopes for use by electronics students and technicians who want to learn how to use an oscilloscope for measuring. 23m; VHS, 3/4 U. **Pr:** Hewlett Packard. **A:** College-Adult. **P:** Professional. **U:** Institution, CCTV, Home. **L:** English, French. **How-Ins:** Electronics, How-To. **Acq:** Purchase. **Dist:** Hewlett-Packard Media Solutions.

Basic Padding Plate: Arc Weld 1978
Offers instruction on specific aspects of arc and MIG welding. 17m; VHS. **A:** Adult. **P:** Vocational. **U:** Institution. **Bus-Ind:** Welding. **Acq:** Purchase. **Dist:** RMI Media. $78.00.

Basic Parenting Skills 1990
An instructional and amusing look at the fundamentals of parenting, featuring specific techniques and skills. 50m; VHS. **Pr:** Cambridge Career Productions. **A:** College-Adult. **P:** Education. **U:** Institution, Home. **Gen-Edu:** Parenting, Children, Education. **Acq:** Purchase. **Dist:** Cambridge Educational. $89.95.

Basic Parliamentary Procedure 19??
Explains basic concepts of parliamentary procedure, stressing the importance of having orderly meetings for handling club business. Also discusses nominations, elections, and committees. 23m; VHS. **A:** Jr. High-Adult. **P:** Education. **U:** Institution. **Gen-Edu:** Education, Communication. **Acq:** Purchase. **Dist:** Educational Video Network. $89.95.

Basic Perm Wrap: SCTuration, Processing and Neutralization 1990
Offers instruction on specific aspects of barbering and cosmetology. 19m; VHS. **A:** Adult. **P:** Vocational. **U:** Institution. **Bus-Ind:** Cosmetology. **Acq:** Purchase. **Dist:** RMI Media. $59.95.

Basic Perspective Drawing 19??
Teaching aid for art education provides students with an understanding of the use of perspective in drawing. 26m; VHS. **A:** Jr. High-College. **P:** Education. **U:** Institution. **Gen-Edu:** Art & Artists, Drawing. **Acq:** Purchase. **Dist:** Crystal Productions. $24.95.

Basic Photography 1980
Bruce McKim demonstrates some useful tips on basic photography. 60m; VHS, 3/4 U, Special order formats. **Pr:** Cinema Associates. **A:** Sr. High-Adult. **P:** Instruction. **U:** Institution, CCTV, CATV, BCTV, Home. **How-Ins:** Photography, How-To. **Acq:** Purchase. **Dist:** RMI Media.

Basic Photojournalism 19??
Outlines basic techniques in photojournalism covering camera skills, equipment, and the dark room. 51m; VHS. **A:** Jr. High-Adult. **P:** Education. **U:** Institution. **Gen-Edu:** Photography, Journalism, How-To. **Acq:** Purchase. **Dist:** Educational Video Network. $129.95.

Basic Piecing and Applique 1989
Piecing materials together on the sewing machine is demonstrated. 60m; VHS. **C:** Joe Cunningham; Gwen Marston. **Pr:** Nancy's Notions Ltd. **A:** Jr. High-Adult. **P:** Instruction. **U:** Institution, Home. **How-Ins:** Sewing. **Acq:** Rent/Lease. **Dist:** Nancy's Notions Ltd.

Basic Plumbing and Pipe Fitting 1984
On five tapes, the basics of plumbing and pipe fitting are explained. 80m; VHS, 3/4 U. **Pr:** Bergwall Productions. **A:** Sr. High-Adult. **P:** Vocational. **U:** Institution. **Bus-Ind:** Home Improvement, How-To. **Acq:** Purchase. **Dist:** Bergwall Productions, Inc.

Basic Plumbing: Plastic Piping 1985
On four tapes, the fixing, cutting, and installation of plastic piping is demonstrated. 62m; VHS, 3/4 U. **Pr:** Bergwall Productions. **A:** Sr. High-Adult. **P:** Vocational. **U:** Institution. **Bus-Ind:** Home Improvement, How-To. **Acq:** Purchase. **Dist:** Bergwall Productions, Inc.

Basic Plumbing Practices—II: Copper Pipe 1994
Focuses on proper techniques for measuring, cutting, and fitting of rigid and flexible copper pipe in the plumbing industry. Covers proper preparation, soldering, cutting techniques, burr removal, scarifying, selecting and using soldering paste and solder, safety precautions, set-up, and use of a propane torch. Also discusses assembly and soldering techniques for a gate valve and the necessary preparation and usage for threaded connections as an alternative. 40m; VHS. **A:** Sr. High-Adult. **P:** Instruction. **U:** Institution. **How-Ins:** Occupational Training, Industrial Arts, How-To. **Acq:** Purchase. **Dist:** Cambridge Educational. $89.95.

Basic Plumbing Practices—III: Steel Pipe and Material Combination 1994
Demonstrates proper procedures for working with steel pipe in the plumbing industry, covering cutting, threading, burr removal, fitting, and use of teflon tape or pipe compound for watertight seals. Also discusses methods for joining together different combinations of piping (plastic, copper, or galvanized steel). 29m; VHS. **A:** Sr. High-Adult. **P:** Instruction. **U:** Institution. **How-Ins:** Occupational Training, Industrial Arts, How-To. **Acq:** Purchase. **Dist:** Cambridge Educational. $89.95.

Basic Plumbing Systems: Residential 1994
Outlines the steps involved in installing a basic residential plumbing system. Includes demonstrations of layout, hot and cold water supply lines, drain systems, vent systems, rough-in plumbing stage, stub-out stage, and plumbing fixture installation. 38m; VHS. **A:** Sr. High-Adult. **P:** Instruction. **U:** Institution. **How-Ins:** Occupational Training, Industrial Arts, How-To. **Acq:** Purchase. **Dist:** Cambridge Educational. $89.95.

Basic Principles of Boiler Combustion Control: Fuel and Other Solid Fuels 197?
This program addresses the basic control problem of maintaining the correct steam pressure while the BTU content of the fuel changes. 22m; 3/4 U, Special order formats. **Pr:** Instrument Society of America. **A:** Adult. **P:** Vocational. **U:** Institution, CCTV. **Bus-Ind:** Industrial Arts. **Acq:** Purchase. **Dist:** ISA -The International Society of Automation.

Basic Principles of Boiler Combustion Control: Gas Oil and Auxiliary Fuels 1980
Gives an operational familiarity with combustion control—its important principles and hardware. 24m; 3/4 U, Special order formats. **Pr:** Instrument Society of America. **A:** Adult. **P:** Vocational. **U:** Institution, CCTV. **Bus-Ind:** Industrial Arts. **Acq:** Purchase. **Dist:** ISA -The International Society of Automation.

Basic Principles of Continuous Gas Lift, Parts 1-4 1974
This series of gas-lift instructional programs uses a physical well model to give physical insights and explanations relative to continuous gas flow lift. 12m; VHS, 3/4 U. **Pr:** University of Texas Austin. **A:** College-Adult. **P:** Instruction. **U:** Institution, CCTV. **Bus-Ind:** Oil Industry. **Acq:** Purchase.
Indiv. Titles: 1. Natural Flow: An Introduction to Gas Lift 2. The Well: Flowing, Dead, and Unloading 3. Effect of Gas Rates and Depth of Injection on Well Performance 4. Effect of Surface Conditions on Gas-Lift Performance 5. Valve Spacing and Pressuring.

Basic Principles of Electricity 19??
A dramatic reenactment of an actual electrocution shows employees how electricity affects the body and what can be done to prevent electrical accidents and injuries. First part of the two-part series "Rules of Danger." Includes a leader's guide and 10 workbooks. 12m; VHS, 8 mm, CC, 3/4 U. **TV Std:** NTSC, PAL. **A:** College-Adult. **P:** Vocational. **U:** Institution. **Bus-Ind:** Safety Education, Electricity. **Acq:** Purchase, Rent/Lease. **Dist:** Learning Communications L.L.C. $395.00.

Basic Principles of Partnering 1994
Covers the preparation for partnering, including strengthening exercises for both males and females so that each will be powerful enough to lift his/her own weight. Instruction is also provided on back lengthening, abdominal stretching, placement, and balance. 45m; VHS. **A:** Family. **P:** Instruction. **U:** Institution. **How-Ins:** Dance--Instruction. **Acq:** Purchase. **Dist:** Princeton Book Company Publishers. $29.95.

Basic Principles of Pointe with Patricia Dickinson 1994
Pre-pointe students strengthen their feet, ankles, and calves in a series of exercises using Therabands, scarves, and bottles, progressing from the more basic to the more complex techniques pertaining to pointe. 45m; VHS. **A:** Family. **P:** Instruction. **U:** Institution. **How-Ins:** Dance--Instruction. **Acq:** Purchase. **Dist:** Princeton Book Company Publishers. $29.95.

Basic Procedures and Techniques in Microbiology Series: Calibration of the Ocular Micrometer 1979
This program demonstrates the setup and use of the ocular micrometer in microscopy. 10m; VHS, 3/4 U. **Pr:** Michigan State University. **A:** College-Adult. **P:** Education. **U:** Institution, CCTV. **Hea-Sci:** Microbiology. **Acq:** Purchase, Rent/Lease. **Dist:** Michigan State University.

Basic Procedures and Techniques in Microbiology Series: Demonstration of Aseptic Technique by Transfer of Bacterial Cultures 1979
This program demonstrates the aseptic transfer of bacterial cultures from broth to broth, broth to agar slant, agar slant to broth, and an agar slant to an agar deep. 13m; VHS, 3/4 U. **Pr:** Michigan State University. **A:** College-Adult. **P:** Education. **U:** Institution, CCTV. **Hea-Sci:** Microbiology. **Acq:** Purchase, Rent/Lease. **Dist:** Michigan State University.

Basic Procedures and Techniques in Microbiology Series: Enrichment and Differential Culture Techniques 1979
This program defines enrichment and differential media, shows examples of each class of media, and demonstrates techniques for enriching and differentiating microorganisms. 10m; VHS, 3/4 U. **Pr:** Michigan State University. **A:** College-Adult. **P:** Education. **U:** Institution, CCTV. **Hea-Sci:** Microbiology. **Acq:** Purchase, Rent/Lease. **Dist:** Michigan State University.

Basic Procedures and Techniques in Microbiology Series: Kohler Illumination 1979
This program demonstrates the setup and use of Kohler illumination in microscopy. 11m; VHS, 3/4 U. **Pr:** Michigan State University. **A:** College-Adult. **P:** Education. **U:** Institution, CCTV. **Hea-Sci:** Microbiology. **Acq:** Purchase, Rent/Lease. **Dist:** Michigan State University.

Basic Procedures and Techniques in Microbiology Series: Phase Contrast Microscopy 1979
This program reviews the concepts of amplitude, wavelength, phase, and diffraction of light waves; points out the specific parts for phase contrast optics; and demonstrates how to set up a phase-contrast microscope. 17m; VHS, 3/4 U. **Pr:** Michigan State University. **A:** College-Adult. **P:** Education. **U:** Institution, CCTV. **Hea-Sci:** Microbiology. **Acq:** Purchase, Rent/Lease. **Dist:** Michigan State University.

Basic Procedures and Techniques in Microbiology Series: Preparing and Dispensing Culture Media 1979
This program explains the properties of and necessity for culture media. The preparation and dispensing of broth and broth to which agar is added are demonstrated. 24m; VHS, 3/4 U. **Pr:** Michigan State University. **A:** College-Adult. **P:** Education. **U:** Institution, CCTV. **Hea-Sci:** Microbiology. **Acq:** Purchase, Rent/Lease. **Dist:** Michigan State University.

Basic Procedures and Techniques in Microbiology Series: Procedures for Sterilizing Microbiological Materials 1979
This program demonstrates and discusses sterilization with both moist and dry heat, chemicals, and filtration. 31m; VHS, 3/4 U. **Pr:** Michigan State University. **A:** College-Adult. **P:** Education. **U:** Institution, CCTV. **Hea-Sci:** Microbiology. **Acq:** Purchase, Rent/Lease. **Dist:** Michigan State University.

Basic Procedures and Techniques in Microbiology Series: Quantitation of Bacteria 1979
This program demonstrates both the quantitative plating method and turbidity determination method of quantitating bacteria. 34m; VHS, 3/4 U. **Pr:** Michigan State University. **A:** College-Adult. **P:** Education. **U:** Institution, CCTV. **Hea-Sci:** Microbiology. **Acq:** Purchase, Rent/Lease. **Dist:** Michigan State University.

Basic Procedures and Techniques in Microbiology Series: Streak Plate Techniques 1979
This program opens with a short discussion of streak plating and dilution, two indirect methods of separating micro-organisms. 10m; VHS, 3/4 U. **Pr:** Michigan State University. **A:** College-Adult. **P:** Education. **U:** Institution, CCTV. **Hea-Sci:** Microbiology. **Acq:** Purchase, Rent/Lease. **Dist:** Michigan State University.

Basic Procedures and Techniques in Microbiology Series: The Gram Stain Procedure 1979
This program utilizes the Kopeloff modification of the gram stain, emphasizing the four fundamental steps of the procedure. 13m; VHS, 3/4 U. **Pr:** Michigan State University. **A:** College-Adult. **P:** Education. **U:** Institution, CCTV. **Hea-Sci:** Microbiology. **Acq:** Purchase, Rent/Lease. **Dist:** Michigan State University.

Basic Procedures and Techniques in Microbiology Series: The Simple Stain 1979
This program explains and demonstrates the procedures for cleaning a glass microscope slide, preparing a smear from a growth on an agar surface, and staining with basic dye, methylene blue. 11m; VHS, 3/4 U. **Pr:** Michigan State University. **A:** College-Adult. **P:** Education. **U:** Institution, CCTV. **Hea-Sci:** Microbiology. **Acq:** Purchase, Rent/Lease. **Dist:** Michigan State University.

Basic Procedures in General Cleaning 19??
Provides an overview of cleaning procedures used in a variety of public buildings. 16m; VHS. **A:** College-Adult. **P:** Vocational. **U:** Institution. **L:** Spanish. **Bus-Ind:** Job Training, Custodial Service, Industrial Arts. **Acq:** Purchase, Rent/Lease. **Dist:** AMS Distributors, Inc.

Basic Programming 1987
Programming for computers in BASIC is presented here in a six-part series, aimed at beginners. ?m; VHS. **A:** Jr. High-Sr. High. **P:** Education. **U:** Institution. **Gen-Edu:** How-To, Computers. **Acq:** Purchase. **Dist:** Educational Images Ltd. $99.95.
Indiv. Titles: 1. All About BASIC 2. BASIC Algorithms 3. BASIC Variables 4. Branches, Loops, and Subroutines 5. BASIC Math Functions 6. BASIC Statements.

Basic Pulmonary Physiology 1 19??
Interesting basic pulmonary physiology necessary to understand pulmonary diagnostic measurements and the equipment that makes such measurements possible is shown. 50m; VHS, 3/4 U. **Pr:** Hewlett Packard. **A:** College-Adult. **P:** Education. **U:** Institution, CCTV, Home. **Bus-Ind:** Respiratory System, Medical Education. **Acq:** Purchase. **Dist:** Hewlett-Packard Media Solutions.

Basic Pulmonary Physiology 2 19??
A continuation of the Part I program which informs the viewer about the respiratory process and shows how serious pulmonary disease can exist in people who think they have no problem. 30m; VHS, 3/4 U. **Pr:** Hewlett Packard. **A:** College-Adult. **P:** Education. **U:** Institution, CCTV, Home. **Bus-Ind:** Respiratory System, Health Education. **Acq:** Purchase. **Dist:** Hewlett-Packard Media Solutions.

Basic Radio Skills: Announcing and Presentation 19??
Six announcers on talk, news and music shows provide insights into the specific requirements of their formats and into their personal approaches to gathering, organizing, and presenting material. Topics include research, scripting, scheduling, and equipment operation. 28m; VHS. **Pr:** Australian Film, Radio and Television School. **A:** College-Adult. **P:** Education. **U:** Home, Institution. **Gen-Edu. Acq:** Purchase, Rent/Lease. **Dist:** TMW Media Group. $149.

Basic Radio Skills: Editing 19??
Introduces the two basic audiotape editing techniques: splice editing and dub editing. Features graphics and overlays to make the procedures clear, and examples of music and voice edits are performed. 16m; VHS. **Pr:** Australian Film, Radio and Television School. **A:** College-Adult. **P:** Education. **U:** Home, Institution. **Gen-Edu. Acq:** Purchase, Rent/Lease. **Dist:** TMW Media Group. $119.

Basic Radio Skills: Radio News 19??
Five journalists present an in-depth view of radio news at work. Topics covered include news sources, item selection and scripting, presentation skills, telephone interviews, field reports, and more. 38m; VHS. **Pr:** Australian Film, Radio and Television School. **A:** College-Adult. **P:** Education. **U:** Home, Institution. **Gen-Edu. Acq:** Purchase, Rent/Lease. **Dist:** TMW Media Group. $149.

Basic Radio Skills: Radio Talkback 19??
Explores a wide range of styles and approaches for the live call-in show. Includes an instructional segment that examines phone operation, delay systems and call dumping. 35m; VHS. **Pr:** Australian Film, Radio and Television School. **A:** College-Adult. **P:** Education. **U:** Home, Institution. **Gen-Edu. Acq:** Purchase, Rent/Lease. **Dist:** TMW Media Group. $149.

Basic Radio Skills: Radio Writing 19??
Features writing for news and current affairs, commercial copywriting and radio comedy writing. 47m; VHS. **Pr:** Australian Film, Radio and Television School. **A:** College-Adult. **P:** Education. **U:** Home, Institution. **Gen-Edu. Acq:** Purchase, Rent/Lease. **Dist:** TMW Media Group. $47.

Basic Radio Skills: The Radio Interview 19??
Covers the basic technical requirements of the audio interview, with a strong emphasis on content and interaction: how to prepare your questions, how to get the subject to relax, how to deal with subjects who take over the interview, or respond in monosyllables, or evade questions altogether. 20m; VHS. **Pr:** Australian Film, Radio and Television School. **A:** College-Adult. **P:** Education. **U:** Home, Institution. **Gen-Edu:** Interviews. **Acq:** Purchase, Rent/Lease. **Dist:** TMW Media Group. $149.

Basic Radio Skills: The Radio Studio 19??
Introduces the hardware of the radio studio environment: the console, microphones, telephone talkback, turntables and CDs, cart players, tape recorders, cassette decks, DAT recorders and more. Emphasizes the procedures for cueing, labeling, cleaning and machine care. 31m; VHS. **Pr:** Australian Film, Radio and Television School. **A:** College-Adult. **P:** Education. **U:** Home, Institution. **Gen-Edu. Acq:** Purchase, Rent/Lease. **Dist:** TMW Media Group. $149.

Basic Reading and Writing Skills 1976
A series of humorous skits, performed by an improvisational theatre group, dramatically portrays the consequences of poor reading and writing skills. 15m; VHS, 3/4 U. **Pr:** Moctesuma Esparza Productions. **A:** Primary-Jr. High. **P:** Education. **U:** Institution, SURA. **Gen-Edu:** Communication. **Acq:** Purchase. **Dist:** Phoenix Learning Group.

Basic Reading Workshop 1989
This set of tapes shows how to teach people to read. 45m; VHS, 3/4 U. **Pr:** Literacy Volunteers of America. **A:** Sr. High-Adult. **P:** Teacher Education. **U:** Institution. **Gen-Edu:** Learning Disabilities, Voluntary Services, Language Arts. **Acq:** Purchase. **Dist:** ProLiteracy. $550.00.
Indiv. Titles: 1. Introduction 2. Language Experience Approach 3. Sight Words/Context Clues 4. Phonics/ Word Patterns 5. Assessment/Goal Setting 6. Goal Analysis/Lesson Planning.

Basic Real Estate Investing 19??
Chuck Baker, a seasoned Real Estate professional, gives his sage advice on Real Estate as an investment. 60m; VHS. **C:** Hosted by Chuck Baker. **A:** Family. **P:** Education. **U:** Institution, Home. **Gen-Edu:** Real Estate. **Acq:** Purchase. **Dist:** Blockbuster L.L.C. $19.95.

Basic Retail Selling Skills 1987
A step by-step-approach that will improve the performance of a sales team. 26m; VHS, 3/4 U. **Pr:** American Media Inc. **A:** Adult. **P:** Education. **U:** Institution, CCTV, Home. **Bus-Ind:** Sales Training. **Acq:** Purchase, Rent/Lease. **Dist:** American Media, Inc.; United Learning Inc. $425.00.

Basic Ribbon Crafts and Decorations 1989
Many ways of decorating with ribbons are explained. 60m; VHS, 3/4 U. **Pr:** RMI Media Productions. **A:** Jr. High-Adult. **P:** Instruction. **U:** Institution, CCTV, Home. **How-Ins:** Crafts. **Acq:** Purchase. **Dist:** RMI Media. $49.95.

Basic Rig Hydraulics 1978
Explains how pressure and power losses occur in the circulating system. 22m; VHS, 3/4 U. **Pr:** University of Texas Austin. **A:** College-Adult. **P:** Instruction. **U:** Institution, CCTV. **Bus-Ind:** Oil Industry. **Acq:** Purchase.

Basic Rockclimbing with John Long 1986
This video, shot on location at Yosemite, works from the ground up and covers all the fundamentals you'll need to know in order to start climbing the sheerest of cliffs. ?m; VHS. **Pr:** Champions on Film. **A:** Adult. **P:** Instruction. **U:** Home. **Spo-Rec:** Sports--General. **Acq:** Purchase. **Dist:** School-Tech Inc. $39.95.

Basic Roulette 1993
The techniques of roulette are explained in this video, including the "action number" strategy. 50m; VHS. **Pr:** John Patrick Productions. **A:** College-Adult. **P:** Instruction. **U:** Home. **How-Ins:** Gambling, How-To. **Acq:** Purchase. **Dist:** John Patrick Entertainment, Inc. $39.95.

Basic Sailing Skills 1988
An instructional tape which teaches how to sail small dinghies. 75m; VHS. **Pr:** Bennett Marine Video. **A:** Jr. High-Adult. **P:** Instruction. **U:** Home. **How-Ins:** Boating, Sports--Water. **Acq:** Purchase. **Dist:** Bennett Marine Video. $49.95.

Basic Sales 1971
Demonstrates effective sales techniques and is useful for training new sales personnel. Comprised of six modules: What is Salesmanship?; Opening the Door; Knowing the Prospect; Presenting the Story; Making It Live; and A Happy Beginning. 82m; VHS, 3/4 U. **Pr:** Resources for Education and Management. **A:** Adult. **P:** Professional. **U:** Institution, CCTV. **Bus-Ind:** Sales Training. **Acq:** Purchase. **Dist:** Resources for Education & Management, Inc.

Basic Satellite Principles ????
Introductory course covers satellite design, GEO, MEO, LEO, radio wave properties, analog and digital signals, bandwidth modulation noise, and much more. ?m; VHS. **A:** Adult. **P:** Education. **U:** Institution. **Gen-Edu:** Electronics, Engineering. **Acq:** Purchase, Rent/Lease. **Dist:** SatNews Publishers. $395.00.

Basic Schooling 19??
Offers training tips for the early stages of jumper competition and first-level dressage competition. ?m; VHS. **A:** Sr. High-Adult. **P:** Instruction. **U:** Institution. **How-Ins:** Horses, How-To. **Acq:** Purchase. **Dist:** CEV Multimedia. $39.95.

Basic Screen Printing 19??
Teaching aid for art education introduces screen printing on paper and fabric. 24m; VHS. **A:** Jr. High-College. **P:** Education. **U:** Institution. **Gen-Edu:** Art & Artists. **Acq:** Purchase. **Dist:** Crystal Productions. $39.95.

Basic Search and Rescue 1978
This methodical approach to search and rescue problems is designed for training fire fithers, industrial training, and emergency response teams. 20m; VHS, 3/4 U, Special order formats. **Pr:** Fire Fighter Films. **A:** Adult. **P:** Vocational. **U:** Institution, CCTV. **Bus-Ind:** Safety Education. **Acq:** Purchase. **Dist:** Courter Films & Associates.

Basic Secretarial Skills 1989
A video-training course for people who want to be secretaries. 61m; VHS. **Pr:** Time-Life Video. **A:** Sr. High-Adult. **P:** Instruction. **U:** Institution, SURA. **How-Ins:** Occupations, Office Practice. **Acq:** Purchase. **Dist:** Ambrose Video Publishing, Inc. $99.95.
Indiv. Titles: 1. Part of the Team 2. Getting the Job Done 3. Working with Others.

Basic Self-Defense Techniques 1993
An expert in the field of Isshinryu karate, Harold Long demonstrates 45 empty-handed self-defense techniques for men, women, and children. Slow-motion movements and close-ups allow for easy learning and understanding of street fighting, knife and club defense, and hold breaking. 50m; VHS. **A:** Jr. High-Adult. **P:** Instruction. **U:** Institution, Home. **How-Ins:** How-To, Martial Arts. **Acq:** Purchase. **Dist:** Isshin-Ryu Productions, Inc. $29.95.

Basic Self-Defense Techniques for Women 1993
Demonstrates 44 empty-handed self-defense techniques for women. Slow motion demonstrations provided by 10th degree black beltist Harold Long aided by 17-year-old 4th degree black belt Stacie Manis. 50m; VHS. **A:** Primary-Adult. **P:** Instruction. **U:** Institution, Home. **How-Ins:** How-To, Martial Arts, Women. **Acq:** Purchase. **Dist:** Isshin-Ryu Productions, Inc. $29.95.

Basic Serving Techniques: Serving 1988
Offers instruction on specific aspects of cooking and food preparation. 15m; VHS. **A:** Adult. **P:** Instruction. **U:** Institution. **Gen-Edu:** Cooking. **Acq:** Purchase. **Dist:** RMI Media. $49.95.

Basic Serving Techniques: Taking the Order 1988
Offers instruction on specific aspects of cooking and food preparation. 13m; VHS. **A:** Adult. **P:** Instruction. **U:** Institution. **Gen-Edu:** Cooking. **Acq:** Purchase. **Dist:** RMI Media. $49.95.

Basic Servo Control: Design Principles and Applications 1989
Information about the design, uses, and development of servo controlled automated systems is discussed. 30m; VHS. **Pr:** Society of Manufacturing Engineers. **A:** College-Adult. **P:** Education. **U:** Institution. **Bus-Ind:** Technology. **Acq:** Purchase. **Dist:** Society of Manufacturing Engineers. $4500.00.

Basic Sewing Skills 1967
All sorts of different stitches are demonstrated on the loom. 12m; VHS, 3/4 U. **Pr:** Bailey Films. **A:** Jr. High-Adult. **P:** Instruction. **U:** Institution, SURA. **How-Ins:** Sewing. **Acq:** Purchase. **Dist:** Phoenix Learning Group. $135.00.

Basic Shooting 1997
Presents guidelines for buying a camcorder, button basics, light and filters, microphone techniques, composition and smooth moves. 30m; VHS. **A:** Adult. **P:** Instruction. **U:** Home. **How-Ins:** Video. **Acq:** Purchase. **Dist:** Tapeworm Video Distributors Inc. $14.95.

Basic Slots 1993
Takes a look at various slot machines and provides money management tips for gamblers. 60m; VHS. **Pr:** John Patrick Productions. **A:** College-Adult. **P:** Instruction. **U:** Home. **Gen-Edu:** Gambling. **Acq:** Purchase. **Dist:** John Patrick Entertainment, Inc.

Basic Stairbuilding with Scott Schuttner 1990
All you need to know about building stairs. Winner of the American Film Institute's best video award for Home Arts/Home Improvement. Also available as a book/video set. 60m; VHS. **C:** Hosted by Scott Schuttner. **A:** Family. **P:** Instruction. **U:** Home. **How-Ins:** How-To, Home Improvement, Woodworking. **Acq:** Purchase. **Dist:** Taunton Press Inc. $29.95.

Basic Statistical Applications 1986
This video starts from statistical fundamentals and continues through analysis and interpretation. Learn to use a variety of tools and determine the causes of out-of-control operations. 71m; VHS. **A:** Adult. **P:** Professional. **U:** Institution. **L:** English. **Bus-Ind:** Industry & Industrialists. **Acq:** Purchase. **Dist:** Society of Manufacturing Engineers. $270.

Basic Stenciling Techniques 1989
Stenciling techniques on wood, fabric, and other techniques are taught by the well-known author on this subject. 45m; VHS, 3/4

U. **C:** Jeannie Serpa. **Pr:** RMI Media Productions. **A:** Jr. High-Adult. **P:** Instruction. **U:** Institution, CCTV, Home. **How-Ins:** Crafts. **Acq:** Purchase. **Dist:** RMI Media. $49.95.

Basic Steps for Better Business Writing 1988
This package of five video-cassettes, including a Leader's Guide, shows employees how to cut their writing time in half while generating written communications that sell ideas, stimulate action and reduce confusion. 265m; VHS, 3/4 U. **C:** Deanna (Dee) Booher. **Pr:** National Educational Media Inc. **A:** College-Adult. **P:** Professional. **U:** Institution, SURA. **Bus-Ind:** Business, Communication. **Acq:** Purchase, Rent/Lease, Trade-in. **Dist:** Encyclopedia Britannica. $1995.00.

Basic Steps in Plastic Product Design 1995
The nine basic steps of product design are included, and cover issues such as establishing end-use requirements, initial concept sketch, final materials selection, and more. 63m; VHS. **A:** Adult. **P:** Professional. **U:** Institution. **L:** English. **Bus-Ind:** Industry & Industrialists. **Acq:** Purchase. **Dist:** Society of Manufacturing Engineers. $495.

The Basic Steps of Baking Bread 199?
Teaches food service employees and kitchen staff how to bake high-quality breads such as baguettes, hard rolls, focaccia and more. 31m; VHS. **A:** Sr. High-Adult. **P:** Instruction. **U:** Home. **How-Ins:** Cooking, Food Industry, How-To. **Acq:** Purchase. **Dist:** Culinary Institute of America. $75.00.

Basic Stud Frame Construction 19??
Construction expert Dr. Billy Harrell uses a scale model of a stud frame building to illustrate techniques for laying out a plate, making a corner and a tee, framing, making headers, ceiling joists, and rafters. Part of the "Building Construction Video Series." 38m; VHS. **A:** Sr. High-Adult. **P:** Vocational. **U:** Institution. **How-Ins:** Construction, How-To, Occupational Training. **Acq:** Purchase. **Dist:** CEV Multimedia. $49.95.

Basic Stunts, Dismounts, and Transitions 2010 (Unrated)
Coach Mark Coleman and his team demonstrate 10 basic stunts as well as several activities for beginning cheerleaders. ??m; DVD. **A:** Family. **P:** Education. **U:** Home, Institution. **Spo-Rec:** Cheerleaders, Athletic Instruction/Coaching. **Acq:** Purchase. **Dist:** Championship Productions. $29.99.

Basic Sugar Decoration 199?
Ewald Notter of the International School of Confectionary Arts instructs viewers on the art of using sugar works to create decorative showpieces in this two part series. In this volume, he teaches the viewer how to boil sugar to prepare it for handling, and cast, pull and pour sugar into a variety of shapes. 42m; VHS. **A:** Sr. High-Adult. **P:** Instruction. **U:** Home. **How-Ins:** Cooking, Food Industry, How-To. **Acq:** Purchase. **Dist:** Culinary Institute of America. $75.00.

Basic Survival Skills: Making It Out the Door 1991
Supplies newly independent teens and young adults with useful information on laundry, bus schedules, newspapers, phone books, maps, credit cards, and more. 15m; VHS. **A:** Sr. High-College. **P:** Education. **U:** Institution. **Gen-Edu:** Home Economics, Adolescence. **Acq:** Purchase. **Dist:** Cambridge Educational. $79.00.

The Basic System: Accounting for Small Businesses 199?
Explains how to use Excel for business accounting functions, such as setting up the general ledger, internal control, accounts receivable, accounts payable, the payroll and more. 120m; VHS. **A:** Adult. **P:** Education. **U:** Institution. **Bus-Ind:** Business, Finance. **Acq:** Purchase. **Dist:** Cambridge Educational. $34.95.

Basic System One 197?
A program designed to give salespeople a better understanding of why precise planning can increase the effectiveness of their sales presentation. 15m; VHS, 3/4 U, Special order formats. **Pr:** Dartnell. **A:** College-Adult. **P:** Instruction. **U:** Institution, CCTV. **Bus-Ind:** Sales Training. **Acq:** Purchase. **Dist:** Dartnell Corp.

Basic Tactics for Field Hockey 2009 (Unrated)
Coach Tjerk Van Herwaarden details tactics and strategies for field hockey teams at the beginner level. ??m; DVD. **A:** Family. **P:** Education. **U:** Home, Institution. **Spo-Rec:** Hockey, Athletic Instruction/Coaching. **Acq:** Purchase. **Dist:** Championship Productions. $39.99.

Basic T'ai-chi Form Part 1 1997
Presents common Yang and Wu style postures that can be practiced in a small space. 63m; VHS. **A:** Adult. **P:** Instruction. **U:** Home. **Hea-Sci:** Fitness/Exercise. **Acq:** Purchase. **Dist:** Artistic Video. $34.95.

Basic T'ai-chi Form Part 2 1997
Showcases traditional T'ai-chi-Ch'uan family styles. 67m; VHS. **A:** Adult. **P:** Instruction. **U:** Home. **Hea-Sci:** Fitness/Exercise. **Acq:** Purchase. **Dist:** Artistic Video. $34.95.

Basic Tap Course ????
Danny Daniels's 12-week tap course starts with the basics through barre and across the floor exercises and ending with a routine of eight steps. 60m; VHS. **A:** Adult. **P:** Teacher Education. **U:** Institution. **How-Ins:** Dance, Dance--Instruction. **Acq:** Purchase. **Dist:** Stagestep. $99.00.

Basic Techniques in Practical Chemistry 1997
Ten-volume series provide hands on presentations and precise, analytical content that make difficult chemistry understandable for all levels. 300m; VHS. **A:** Sr. High. **P:** Instruction. **U:** Institution. **Gen-Edu:** Chemistry. **Acq:** Purchase. **Dist:** TMW Media Group. $395.00.
Indiv. Titles: 1. Determination of Melting Point 2. Recrystallization Part 1 3. Recrystallization Part 2 4. Distillation 5. Infrared

Spectroscopy 6. Weighing Samples of Analysis 7. Volumetric Techniques 8. Hydrolysis of an Ester 9. Thin Layer Chromatography 10. Gravimetric Techniques.

Basic Telecommunication Principles 1992
An introduction to the basics of telecommunications, including information on the electromagnetic spectrum, properties of waves, and amplification. Part of the "Satellite Training Series." 46m; VHS. **TV Std:** NTSC, PAL, SECAM. **C:** Hosted by Dr. Joseph Pelton; Dr. Frank Baylin. **A:** College-Adult. **P:** Professional. **U:** Institution. **Bus-Ind:** Communication, Technology. **Acq:** Purchase, Rent/Lease. **Dist:** SatNews Publishers. $395.00.

Basic Television Makeup 19??
A demonstration of makeup techniques for a young woman, older woman, and three men, providing techniques for winkled skin, baldness, beard shadow, and other special effects. 30m; VHS. **A:** College-Adult. **P:** Instruction. **U:** Home. **How-Ins:** Television, Cosmetology. **Acq:** Purchase. **Dist:** Stagestep. $148.95.

Basic Television Terms: A Video Dictionary 1977
Leonard Nimoy takes the audience through the steps of producing television from start to finish. 17m; VHS, 3/4 U, Special order formats. **C:** Hosted by Leonard Nimoy. **Pr:** Sheldon Renan. **A:** Jr. High-Adult. **P:** Education. **U:** Institution, Home, SURA. **Gen-Edu:** Television. **Acq:** Purchase, Rent/Lease, Duplication License. **Dist:** Pyramid Media. $195.00.

Basic Temperature Control of Batch Processes 199?
An instrument technology training program on the basic temperature control of batch processes. Includes a manual. 30m; VHS. **A:** Adult. **P:** Instruction. **U:** Institution. **Bus-Ind:** Technology, Job Training. **Acq:** Purchase. **Dist:** ISA -The International Society of Automation. $95.00.

Basic Textiles 1986
A comprehensive outline of the basics of textile manufacture. 50m; VHS, 3/4 U. **Pr:** North Carolina State University. **A:** Adult. **P:** Education. **U:** Institution, CCTV, Home. **Bus-Ind:** Textile Industry. **Acq:** Purchase, Rent/Lease. **Dist:** North Carolina State University.
Indiv. Titles: 1. Overview 2. Fiber Sources, Classifications 3. Textile Fiber Properties and End Uses 4. How Spun Yarns Are Made 5. How Filament Yarns Are Made and Modified 6. Typical Properties and Uses of Spun and Filament Yarns 7. Preparing Yarns for Fabric Making 8. Fabrics Formed from Yarns-Wovens 9. Fabrics Formed from Yarns-Knits and Hosiery 10. Nonconventional Fabrics 11. Dyeing & Finishing: Fabric Preparation 12. Dyestuffs & Color 13. Color Application by Dyeing 14. Color Application by Printing 15. Fabric Finishing.

Basic Thinking Skills 1988
Students are introduced to the concepts of analyzing, making inferences, and determining cause and effect relationships. 45m; VHS, 3/4 U. **Pr:** SVE. **A:** Primary-Jr. High. **P:** Education. **U:** Institution, CCTV, Home. **Gen-Edu:** Education. **Acq:** Purchase, Duplication. **Dist:** Clear Vue Inc. $129.00.

Basic 35mm Photography 1988
Explains the basic elements and techniques of 35mm photography. 30m; VHS. **Pr:** Educational Filmstrips and Video. **A:** Primary-Sr. High. **P:** Education. **U:** Institution, Home. **How-Ins:** Photography, How-To. **Acq:** Purchase. **Dist:** Educational Video Network. $219.99.
Indiv. Titles: 1. Choosing a 35mm Camera 2. Using a 35mm Reflex Camera 3. Using 35mm Single Lens Reflex Accessories 4. Photographic Lighting 5. How To Take Better Photos 6. Travel Photograph.

Basic Tole and Decorative Painting 1989
Tole means painting on tin, and painting on wood, porcelain, and fabric are also explained. 75m; VHS, 3/4 U. **C:** Peggy Caldwell. **Pr:** RMI Media Productions. **A:** Jr. High-Adult. **P:** Instruction. **U:** Institution, CCTV, Home. **How-Ins:** Painting, Crafts. **Acq:** Purchase. **Dist:** RMI Media. $49.95.

Basic Tools 19??
Veteran woodworking teacher Kenneth Bowers demonstrates the proper techniques to use when working with basic woodworking tools. 88m; VHS. **A:** Jr. High-Adult. **P:** Instruction. **U:** Institution. **How-Ins:** How-To, Woodworking, Tools. **Acq:** Purchase. **Dist:** CEV Multimedia. $49.95.

Basic Training 1971
Documentary follows a company of draftees and enlisted men through the nine weeks of the basic training cycle of the United States Army. 89m; VHS. **A:** Sr. High-Adult. **P:** Entertainment. **U:** Home, Institution. **Gen-Edu:** Documentary Films, Armed Forces--U.S. **Acq:** Purchase, Rent/Lease. **Dist:** Zipporah Films. $350.00.

Basic Training 1986 (R) — Bomb!
Three sexy ladies wiggle into the Pentagon in their efforts to clean up the government. 85m; VHS, DVD. **C:** Ann Dusenberry; Rhonda Shear; Angela Aames; Walter Gotell; Directed by Andrew Sugarman. **Pr:** Moviestore Entertainment. **A:** Sr. High-Adult. **P:** Entertainment. **U:** Home. **Mov-Ent:** Satire & Parody, Sex & Sexuality, Exploitation. **Acq:** Purchase. **Dist:** Lions Gate Television Corp. $79.98.

Basic Training of Oxen 1988
The author of "The Oxen Handbook" shows his way of training an ox. 43m; VHS. **C:** Drew Conroy. **Pr:** Doug Butler. **A:** Adult. **P:** Instruction. **U:** Institution, Home. **How-Ins:** Animals, Agriculture. **Acq:** Purchase. **Dist:** Doug Butler Enterprises Inc. $69.95.

Basic Training: School of American Ballet 1979
Professional dancers and instructors are shown giving strict ballet lessons to beginning and experienced students. 30m; VHS, 3/4 U. **Pr:** WNET New York. **A:** Sr. High-Adult. **P:** Education. **U:** Institution, CCTV, Home. **Fin-Art:** Performing Arts, Dance--Ballet, Dance. **Acq:** Purchase, Rent/Lease. **Dist:** WNET/Thirteen Non-Broadcast.

Basic Training with Ada Janklowicz 1991
Ada Janklowicz uses a motivating boot-camp instructional style to teach this intermediate level workout that combines floor aerobics with both standing and floor toning exercises. 64m; VHS. **A:** Jr. High-Adult. **P:** Instruction. **U:** Home. **Hea-Sci:** Fitness/Exercise. **Acq:** Purchase. **Dist:** Collage Video Specialties, Inc. $19.95.

Basic Training with Sherry Catlin: Faster Metabolism, Stronger Bones ????
A beginner to advanced workout designed to strengthen and define the entire body. 30m; VHS. **A:** Adult. **P:** Instruction. **U:** Home. **Hea-Sci:** Fitness/Exercise, How-To. **Acq:** Purchase. **Dist:** Body Bar Systems. $14.95.

Basic Tube Guitar Amplifier Servicing and Overhaul 199?
Amplifier expert Gerald Weber teaches the viewer how to diagnose, inspect, service and repair the tube guitar amplifier. 90m; VHS. **A:** Family. **P:** Instruction. **U:** Home. **How-Ins:** Electronics, How-To. **Acq:** Purchase. **Dist:** Hal Leonard Corp. $34.95.

Basic Upholstery Techniques 19??
Describes the five basic steps of upholstery: stripping, installing webbing, padding the frame, applying outside fabric, and sewing the cushions. Also explains how to select used furniture and what tools are needed. Follows an old sofa as it proceeds through the five steps and becomes a beautiful piece of furniture. 30m; VHS. **A:** Sr. High-Adult. **P:** Instruction. **U:** Institution. **How-Ins:** Home Improvement, Interior Decoration, How-To. **Acq:** Purchase. **Dist:** CEV Multimedia. $49.95.

Basic Watercolor Techniques 19??
Demonstrates the basic steps of watercolor painting for beginners. 20m; VHS. **A:** Sr. High-Adult. **P:** Instruction. **U:** Institution. **How-Ins:** Painting, Art & Artists. **Acq:** Purchase. **Dist:** Educational Video Network. $49.95.

Basic Weight Training 1978
An instructional sports program emphasizes basic weight training and exercises. Exercises for shoulders, arms, back, waist, and legs are included with correct breathing, warm-up and warm-down procedures, and tips for the more experienced athlete. 17m; VHS, 3/4 U. **Pr:** Champions on Film. **A:** Sr. High-College. **P:** Instruction. **U:** Institution, CCTV, Home. **Hea-Sci:** Fitness/Exercise. **Acq:** Purchase, Rent/Lease. **Dist:** School-Tech Inc.

Basic Writing Skills 1989
A set of videos that explains how to write memos, notes, and other basic writing skills. 32m; VHS. **C:** Hosted by Cicely Tyson. **Pr:** Time-Life Video. **A:** Primary-Sr. High. **P:** Education. **U:** Institution, SURA. **Gen-Edu:** How-To, Office Practice, Language Arts. **Acq:** Purchase. **Dist:** Ambrose Video Publishing, Inc. $99.95.
Indiv. Titles: 1. Words and Sentences 2. Paragraphs & Meanings 3. Letters and Memos.

Basic Yacht Maintenance 1992
Different programs geared to most types of marine structure materials. Range of projects you can learn include touch-up painting and bottom work. 90m; VHS. **A:** Adult. **P:** Instruction. **U:** Home. **How-Ins:** Boating. **Acq:** Purchase. **Dist:** Bennett Marine Video; Emily Riddell Photography. $39.95.
Indiv. Titles: 1. Wooden Boats 2. Steel Boats 3. Fiberglass Boats.

Basic Yoga for Dummies 2000
Easy-to-follow direction in performing 12 basic hatha yoga poses, which can be done in sequence for a basic workout. Led by Sara Ivanhoe. 53m; DVD. **A:** Adult. **P:** Instruction. **U:** Home. **Hea-Sci:** Fitness/Exercise, Yoga. **Acq:** Purchase. **Dist:** Collage Video Specialties, Inc.

Basically Business I 1988
Offers advice for those considering starting their own businesses. 45m; VHS. **A:** Adult. **P:** Education. **U:** Institution. **Gen-Edu:** Business. **Acq:** Purchase. **Dist:** RMI Media. $79.95.

Basically Business II 1988
Discusses market planning, financial management, customers, hiring, business image, sales, pricing, and advertising. 45m; VHS. **A:** Adult. **P:** Education. **U:** Institution. **Gen-Edu:** Business. **Acq:** Purchase. **Dist:** RMI Media. $79.95.

Basics of Adolescent Medicine or How to Succesfully Treat Teenagers 1983
How pediatricians can successfully include teenagers in their patient care groups. 60m; VHS, 3/4 U. **Pr:** Emory University. **A:** College-Adult. **P:** Education. **U:** Institution, CCTV, Home, SURA. **Hea-Sci:** Patient Care, Adolescence, Pediatrics. **Acq:** Purchase, Rent/Lease, Subscription. **Dist:** Emory Medical Television Network.

The Basics of Basic: Programming 19??
Offers instruction on specific aspects of computer software and components. 63m; VHS. **A:** Adult. **P:** Education. **U:** Institution. **Gen-Edu:** Computers. **Acq:** Purchase. **Dist:** RMI Media. $39.95.

Basics of Basketball with the NBA Pros 1990
Ball handling, rebounding, shooting, conditioning, and defense are demonstrated by top NBA stars. 30m; VHS. **Pr:** Panasonic Film Library. **A:** Family. **P:** Instruction. **U:** Home. **Spo-Rec:** Sports--General, Basketball. **Acq:** Purchase. **Dist:** Karol Media. $14.95.

Basics of Bass Fishing 1987
How, where, when and why to catch bass; for the amateur. 47m; VHS. **C:** Dr. John Davis. **Pr:** Ken Anderson Films. **A:** Jr. High-Adult. **P:** Instruction. **U:** Home. **Spo-Rec:** Sports--General, Fishing. **Acq:** Purchase. **Dist:** The Market Place. $9.95.

Basics of Big Game Fishing 19??
Learn the specialized techniques you need to successfully fish for the ocean roaming fish. The fighting chair, high-speed lures, tackle selection and boat handling are discussed. 45m; VHS. **Pr:** Bennett Marine Video. **A:** Sr. High-Adult. **P:** Instruction. **U:** Home. **Spo-Rec:** Fishing. **Acq:** Purchase. **Dist:** Bennett Marine Video. $29.95.

Basics of Cable Fault Locating 1980
The program describes cables in a communications network, examines different types of cables in use today, shows some typical cable faults, and gives directions for a six-step cable fault-locating procedure. 25m/B/W; VHS, 3/4 U. **Pr:** Hewlett Packard. **A:** College-Adult. **P:** Professional. **U:** Institution, CCTV, Home. **Bus-Ind:** Electronics. **Acq:** Purchase. **Dist:** Hewlett-Packard Media Solutions.

Basics of Cake Decorating 1988
The essentials of cake decorating, including lessons in flower-making, distinctive borders and air brush techniques. 60m; VHS. **C:** Frances Kuyper. **Pr:** Cine-Video West. **A:** Family. **P:** Instruction. **U:** Home. **How-Ins:** Cooking. **Acq:** Purchase. **Dist:** Cine-Video West.

Basics of Carpet Care 19??
Illustrates proper maintenance procedures associated with caringfor carpet and provides information on the four most popular cleaning methods: dry-foam, dry extraction, wet extraction, and the bonnet method. 22m; VHS. **A:** College-Adult. **P:** Vocational. **U:** Institution. **L:** Spanish. **Bus-Ind:** Job Training, Custodial Service, Industrial Arts. **Acq:** Purchase, Rent/Lease. **Dist:** AMS Distributors, Inc.

The Basics of Catching 2006
Matt Walbeck discusses the proper stance for catchers, footwork, and throwing, as well as additional drills. 64m; DVD. **A:** Adult. **P:** Instruction. **U:** Institution. **Spo-Rec:** Baseball. **Acq:** Purchase. **Dist:** Championship Productions.

Basics of Color 1989
An introduction to basic color theory, physics of color, and physiology of vision. 29m; VHS. **A:** Adult. **P:** Education. **U:** Institution. **Fin-Art:** Art & Artists. **Acq:** Purchase. **Dist:** RMI Media. $69.95.

Basics of Consumer Law 1986
These tapes help lawyers who are representing a business. 55m; VHS, 3/4 U. **Pr:** ABA. **A:** Adult. **P:** Professional. **U:** Institution, CCTV, Home, SURA. **Bus-Ind:** Law. **Acq:** Purchase, Rent/Lease. **Dist:** American Bar Association. $295.00.

Basics of Directing for the Stage ????
Explains and demonstrates basic aspects of the directing and rehearsal process such as reading through a script; implementing directional concepts; collaborating with actors without compromising creativity; and how and when to do blocking. 65m; VHS. **A:** Adult. **P:** Instruction. **U:** Institution. **How-Ins:** Performing Arts, Theater. **Acq:** Purchase. **Dist:** Stagestep. $149.00.

Basics of Drug Interaction 1975
Through a multi-media learning package, teaches the fundamental concepts of how drugs can be affected by other drugs. 30m; VHS, 3/4 U, CV, Special order formats. **Pr:** Professional Research. **A:** Adult. **P:** Professional. **U:** Institution, CCTV. **Hea-Sci:** Drugs, Health Education. **Acq:** Purchase, Rent/Lease. **Dist:** Discovery Education.

Basics of Floor Care, Pt. 1 19??
Demonstrates the procedures for stripping and refinishing various types of floors, including hard surface and resilient. 17m; VHS. **A:** College-Adult. **P:** Vocational. **U:** Institution. **L:** Spanish. **Bus-Ind:** Job Training, Custodial Service, Industrial Arts. **Acq:** Purchase, Rent/Lease. **Dist:** AMS Distributors, Inc.

Basics of Floor Care, Pt. 2 19??
Offers tips on how to maintain a refinished floor for years without having to perform major stripping and refinishing. 17m; VHS. **A:** College-Adult. **P:** Vocational. **U:** Institution. **L:** English, Spanish. **Bus-Ind:** Job Training, Custodial Service, Industrial Arts. **Acq:** Purchase, Rent/Lease. **Dist:** AMS Distributors, Inc.

The Basics of Gambling 1991
Learn all of the ins and outs of playing Craps, Roulette, Baccarat, Blackjack, Slots, Keno, Red Dog, Pai-Gow Poker and Study Poker. Jimmy "The Scot" Jordan also offers advice for betting on baseball, football, basketball and the track. 60m; VHS. **Pr:** UPI. **A:** College-Adult. **P:** Education. **U:** Home. **How-Ins:** How-To, Gambling. **Acq:** Purchase. **Dist:** Universal Productions International/Gaming Tapes, Inc. $9.99.

Basics of Geography 1990
Physical geography is examined and its effect on human behavior is discussed in this series. ?m; VHS. **Pr:** United Learning Inc. **A:** Primary-Jr. High. **P:** Education. **U:** Institution, CCTV, CATV, Home, SURA. **Gen-Edu:** Geography, Sociology. **Acq:** Purchase, Duplication. **Dist:** United Learning Inc. $79.95.
Indiv. Titles: 1. Places and How to Find Them 2. Water — Climate and Patterns of Living 3. Land Forms and Patterns of Living 4. Organizing by Regions.

Basics of Grinding 1995
Provides an introduction to cylindrical, internal, centerless, and surface grinding. Also discusses abrasives and relationships between grain size, bond type and pore spacing on grinding wheels. 25m; VHS. **A:** Adult. **P:** Vocational. **U:** Institution. **Bus-Ind:** Metal Work, Occupational Training. **Acq:** Purchase. **Dist:** Society of Manufacturing Engineers. $255.00.

The Basics of Home Recording ????
Explains basic techniques needed to set up and run a home multitrack studio, plus how to turn a closet into an isolation booth, create special effects, and operate a mixing board. 60m; VHS. **A:** Adult. **P:** Instruction. **U:** Home. **How-Ins:** How-To, Music--Instruction. **Acq:** Purchase. **Dist:** Calprod Pro Film/Video Production, Inc. $19.95.

The Basics of Indoor Lacrosse 2011 (Unrated)
Coach Johnny Mouradian presents a lecture on the fundamental skills needed by indoor lacrosse players. 73m; DVD. **A:** Family. **P:** Education. **U:** Home, Institution. **Spo-Rec:** Lacrosse, Athletic Instruction/Coaching. **Acq:** Purchase. **Dist:** Championship Productions. $39.99.

The Basics of Infield Play 2001
University of Miami Head Coach Jim Morris covers the mental approach to infield play, various levels of positioning on the field, and proper positioning for fielding the ball. 33m; VHS. **A:** Adult. **P:** Instruction. **U:** Institution. **How-Ins:** Baseball, Sports--General, How-To. **Acq:** Purchase. **Dist:** Championship Productions. $39.95.

Basics of Internet 19??
"The Basics of Internet" unlocks the mysteries of the Internet to let you confidently explore the information superhighway with low-tech efficiency. It teaches viewers how to get connected, navigate the net, communicate with others, and perform basic business research. ?m; VHS. **A:** Adult. **P:** Professional. **U:** Institution. **L:** English. **Bus-Ind:** Computers. **Acq:** Purchase. **Dist:** American Management Association. $129.

Basics of Interviewing 1982
Shows how lawyers can improve the first consulation sessions between lawyer and client. 120m; VHS, 3/4 U. **Pr:** Practicing Law Institute. **A:** Sr. High-Adult. **P:** Education. **U:** Institution, Home. **Gen-Edu:** Law. **Acq:** Purchase, Rent/Lease. **Dist:** Practising Law Institute.

Basics of Negotiation 1984
Presents basic principles of negotiation for lawyers by simulating negotiating sessions. 120m; VHS, 3/4 U. **Pr:** Practicing Law Institute. **A:** Sr. High-Adult. **P:** Education. **U:** Institution, Home. **Gen-Edu:** Law. **Acq:** Purchase, Rent/Lease. **Dist:** Practising Law Institute. $95.00.

The Basics of Office Procedures 19??
Takes a humorous look at the reasons why office procedures are so important and points out the basic skills needed to put together a smooth-running office environment. 15m; VHS. **A:** Sr. High-Adult. **P:** Vocational. **U:** Home. **Bus-Ind:** Business, How-To, Job Training. **Acq:** Purchase. **Dist:** Instructional Video. $79.00.

Basics of Okinawan Karate 19??
Three volumes to introduce the Okinawan Shorin-Ryu system of karate. Taught by Sensei James Coffman, 7th degree black belt champion. 60m; VHS. **C:** Hosted by James Coffman. **Pr:** Creative Image. **A:** Jr. High-Adult. **P:** Instruction. **U:** Home. **How-Ins:** Martial Arts, How-To. **Acq:** Purchase. **Dist:** ESPN Inc. $39.95.
Indiv. Titles: 1. Part I: Basics of Okinawan Karate 2. Part II: Basics of Okinawan Karate 3. Part III: Complete Workout.

Basics of Radio-Controlled Model Airplanes 1986
Professionals show how to build and fly radio-controlled airplanes. 60m; VHS, 3/4 U. **Pr:** GN Communications, Ltd; PBS. **A:** Jr. High-Adult. **P:** Instruction. **U:** Institution, CCTV, Home, SURA. **How-Ins:** How-To, Crafts, Hobbies. **Acq:** Purchase, Rent/Lease, Duplication, Off-Air Record. **Dist:** PBS Home Video. $69.96.

Basics of Restroom Cleaning 19??
Complete guide to fast, effective restroom cleaning with proven procedures and outstanding results. 16m; VHS. **A:** Adult. **P:** Vocational. **U:** Institution. **L:** Spanish. **Bus-Ind:** Job Training, Custodial Service, Industrial Arts. **Acq:** Purchase, Rent/Lease. **Dist:** AMS Distributors, Inc.

Basics of Safe Lifting 198?
Presents an overview of the back and shows how various stresses can lead to poor back health. 20m; VHS, 3/4 U. **A:** College-Adult. **P:** Education. **U:** Institution. **Bus-Ind:** Health Education, Stress. **Acq:** Rent/Lease. **Dist:** National Safety Council, California Chapter, Film Library.

Basics of Successful Investing 19??
Guides viewers through the basics of money management and financial planning. 70m; VHS. **A:** Adult. **P:** Instruction. **U:** Home. **How-Ins:** Finance. **Acq:** Purchase. **Dist:** Tapeworm Video Distributors Inc. $29.95.

The Basics of the Air Raid Offense 2007 (Unrated)
Coach Hal Mumme demonstrates drills for football teams wishing to use the Air Raid Offense, and uses game footage to discuss plays and strategy. 47m; DVD. **A:** Family. **P:** Education. **U:** Home, Institution. **Spo-Rec:** Football, Athletic Instruction/Coaching. **Acq:** Purchase. **Dist:** Championship Productions. $39.99.

The Basics of the Single Wing Offense 2006 (Unrated)
Coach Mike Rude discusses the formations and blocking rules for football teams thinking of using the Single Wing Offense. 98m; DVD. **A:** Family. **P:** Education. **U:** Home, Institution. **Spo-Rec:** Football, Athletic Instruction/Coaching. **Acq:** Purchase. **Dist:** Championship Productions. $39.99.

Basics of Transistors and ICs 1980
Reviews the basics of transistors and diodes and explains the function and make-up of integrated circuits, which have revolutionized digital electronics. 18m; VHS, 3/4 U. **Pr:** Hewlett Packard. **A:** College-Adult. **P:** Professional. **U:** Institution, CCTV, Home. **Bus-Ind:** Electronics. **Acq:** Purchase. **Dist:** Hewlett-Packard Media Solutions.

The Basics of Work Series 1983
This series offers an overview of work policies in a medical establishment. 13m; VHS, 3/4 U. **Pr:** Health Communications Network. **A:** Adult. **P:** Professional. **U:** Institution, SURA. **Hea-Sci:** Medical Education. **Acq:** Purchase, Rent/Lease, Subscription.
Indiv. Titles: 1. Your Medical Facility 2. Human Relationships 3. Understanding Human Relationships by Understanding Problems 4. The Meaning of Discipline.

Basics to Bullseyes with John Pride 1990
Practical tips on coordinating mind and body for top shooting performance. Also covers street situations and stress-handling. 36m; VHS. **A:** College-Adult. **P:** Instruction. **U:** Home. **How-Ins:** How-To, Firearms, Sports--General. **Acq:** Purchase. **Dist:** Gun Video. $39.95.

The Basics to Improve Your Memory 19??
Illustrates memory-building methods, placing emphasis on the eight memory devices: concentration, classification, association, substitution, visualization, memory pegs, observation, and linking. 54m; VHS. **A:** College-Adult. **P:** Education. **U:** Institution. **Bus-Ind:** Business, How-To, Job Training. **Acq:** Purchase. **Dist:** Cambridge Educational. $99.95.

Basil 1998 (R) — ★★½
Turn of the century English aristocrat Basil (Leto) strives for the approval of his overbearing father (Jacobi) while also trying to please the selfish woman he loves (Forlani). Based on the novel by Wilkie Collins. 113m; VHS, DVD, CC. **C:** Jared Leto; Claire Forlani; Christian Slater; Derek Jacobi; Directed by Radha Bharadwaj. **A:** Sr. High-Adult. **P:** Entertainment. **U:** Home. **Mov-Ent:** Drama, Great Britain. **Acq:** Purchase. **Dist:** Walt Disney Studios Home Entertainment.

Basil Hears a Noise 1993
In this musical adventure, Basil the bear is on a mission in an enchanted forest. He tries to find the meaning of courage and gets help from his friends, the Muppets. Includes a lyric sheet. 28m; VHS. **Pr:** Children's Television Workshop. **A:** Preschool-Primary. **P:** Entertainment. **U:** Home. **Chl-Juv:** Music--Children, Puppets. **Acq:** Purchase. **Dist:** Lions Gate Entertainment Inc.; Sesame Workshop; Baker and Taylor. $12.98.

Basil in Blunderland 1998
The Roman Catholic Archbishop of Westminster Basil Hume re-enacts a game of hide and seek from his childhood that had a profound impact on his approach to spiritual life. In this candid portrait, Cardinal Hume talks openly about prayer, life after death and his own moments of doubt and despair. 60m; VHS. **A:** Family. **P:** Education. **U:** Home. **Chl-Juv:** Family Viewing, Religion. **Acq:** Purchase. **Dist:** First Run Features. $19.95.

Basil Poledouris: His Life and Music 1997
Biography of Basil Poledouris, one of Hollywood's most successful composers of scores for TV and film. 50m; VHS. **A:** Sr. High-Adult. **P:** Education. **U:** Home, Institution. **Gen-Edu:** Biography: Artists, Documentary Films. **Acq:** Purchase, Rent/Lease. **Dist:** The Cinema Guild. $39.95.

Basileus Quartet 1982 — ★★★
The replacement for a violinist in a well-established quartet creates emotional havoc. Beautiful music, excellent and evocative photography. 118m; VHS. **C:** Pierre Malet; Hector Alterio; Omero Antonutti; Michel Vitold; Alain Cuny; Gabriele Ferzetti; Elisabeth (Lisa) Kreuzer; Directed by Fabio Carpi; Written by Fabio Carpi; Cinematography by Dante Spinotti. **Pr:** Libra Films; Cinema 5. **A:** Sr. High-Adult. **P:** Entertainment. **U:** Home. **L:** Italian. **Mov-Ent:** Music--Classical. **Acq:** Purchase. **Dist:** Tapeworm Video Distributors Inc. $29.95.

The Basket 1999 (PG) — ★★½
There's a lot going on in a small Washington community, circa 1918. Martin Conlon (Coyote) is the new teacher (he's from Boston) at the one-room schoolhouse who introduces opera and basketball into the curriculum. Then German orphans Helmut (Burke) and Brigitta (Willenborg) come to live with the local doctor and are persecuted for their nationality because of WWI. Mr. Emery (MacDonald) is especially hostile since his son was wounded in the war but Mrs. Emery (Allen) is willing to give the newcomers a chance. Helmut turns out to be a hoops natural and the team has a chance to compete in a national championship—if they can set their differences aside. 104m; VHS, DVD, Wide. **C:** Karen Allen; Peter Coyote; Robert Karl Burke; Amber Willenborg; Jock MacDonald; Eric Dane; Casey Cowan; Brian Skala; Tony Lincoln; Patrick Treadway; Ellen Travolta; Directed by Rich Cowan; Written by Rich Cowan; Frank Swoboda; Tessa Swoboda; Cinematography by Dan Heigh; Music by Don Caron. **A:** Family. **P:** Entertainment. **U:** Home. **Mov-Ent:** Basketball, Education, Prejudice. **Acq:** Purchase. **Dist:** MGM Home Entertainment.

Basket Case 1982 (Unrated) — ★★★
A gory horror film about a pair of Siamese twins—one normal, the other gruesomely deformed. The pair is surgically separated at birth, and the evil disfigured twin is tossed in the garbage. Fraternal ties being what they are, the normal brother retrieves his twin—essentially a head atop shoulders—and totes him around in a basket (he ain't heavy). Together they begin twisted

and deadly revenge, with the brother-in-a-basket in charge. Very entertaining, if you like this sort of thing. Followed by two sequels, if you just can't get enough. 89m; VHS, DVD, Blu-Ray. **C:** Kevin Van Hentenryck; Terri Susan Smith; Beverly Bonner; Robert Vogel; Diana Browne; Lloyd Pace; Bill Freeman; Joe Clarke; Ruth Neuman; Richard Pierce; Dorothy Strongin; Directed by Frank Henenlotter; Written by Frank Henenlotter; Cinematography by Bruce Torbet; Music by Gus Russo. **Pr:** Edgar Ievins. **A:** Adult. **P:** Entertainment. **U:** Home. **Mov-Ent:** Horror, Cult Films. **Acq:** Purchase. **Dist:** Movies Unlimited. $11.99.

Basket Case 2 1990 (R) — ★★½
Surgically separated teenage mutant brothers Duane and Belial are back! This time they've found happiness in a "special" family—until they're plagued by the paparazzi. Higher production values make this sequel slicker than its low-budget predecessor, but it somehow lacks the same charm. 90m; VHS, DVD, CC. **C:** Kevin Van Hentenryck; Annie Ross; Kathryn Meisle; Heather Rattray; Jason Evers; Ted (Theodore) Sorel; Matt Mitler; Ron Fazio; Leonard Jackson; Beverly Bonner; Directed by Frank Henenlotter; Written by Frank Henenlotter; Cinematography by Robert M. "Bob" Baldwin, Jr.; Music by Joe Renzetti. **Pr:** Shapiro Glickenhaus Entertainment Corporation. **A:** College-Adult. **P:** Entertainment. **U:** Home. **Mov-Ent:** Horror. **Acq:** Purchase. **Dist:** Anchor Bay Entertainment; Image Entertainment Inc.; Amsell Entertainment Inc. $9.99.

Basket Case 3: The Progeny 1992 (R) — ★★½
In this sequel to the cult horror hits "Basket Case" and "Basket Case 2," Belial is back and this time he's about to discover the perils of parenthood as the mutant Mrs. Belial delivers a litter of bouncing mini-monsters. Everything is fine until the police kidnap the little creatures and chaos breaks out as Belial goes on a shocking rampage in his newly created mechanical body. Weird special effects make this a cult favorite for fans of the truly outrageous. 90m; VHS, DVD, CC. **C:** Annie Ross; Kevin Van Hentenryck; Gil Roper; Tina Louise Hilbert; Dan Biggers; Jim O'Doherty; Jackson Faw; Jim Grimshaw; Directed by Frank Henenlotter; Written by Frank Henenlotter; Robert Martin; Cinematography by Bob Paone; Music by Joe Renzetti. **Pr:** Shapiro Glickenhaus Entertainment Corporation. **A:** College-Adult. **P:** Entertainment. **U:** Home. **Mov-Ent:** Horror, Parenting. **Acq:** Purchase. **Dist:** Amsell Entertainment Inc. $19.98.

Basketball 1987
College basketball coach Marv Harshman discusses basic offensive and defensive strategies. 58m; VHS, 3/4 U. **Pr:** RMI Media Productions. **A:** Adult. **P:** Instruction. **U:** Institution. **Spo-Rec:** Sports--General, Basketball. **Acq:** Purchase. **Dist:** RMI Media.
Indiv. Titles: 1. Men's Basketball Basics: Creating an Offense 2. Men's Basketball Basics: Defensive Play 3. Men's Basketball Basics: Offensive Drills 4. Fundamentals of Women's Basketball: Defensive Play 5. Fundamentals of Women's Basketball: Offensive Play.

The Basketball Diaries 1995 (R) — ★★
Disappointing adaptation of undeground writer/musician Jim Carroll's 1978 cult memoirs, with DiCaprio starring as the teen athlete whose life spirals into drug addiction and hustling on the New York streets. Carroll and friends Mickey (Wahlberg), Neutron (McGaw), and Pedro (Madio), form the heart of St. Vitus' hot hoopster team. But the defiant quartet really get their kicks from drugs, dares, and petty crime—leading to an ever-downward turn. The book takes place in the '60s but the film can't make up its mind what the decade is, although DiCaprio (and Wahlberg) are particularly effective in a self-conscious first effort from Kalvert. 102m; VHS, DVD. **C:** Leonardo DiCaprio; Mark Wahlberg; Patrick McGaw; James Madio; Bruno Kirby; Ernie Hudson; Lorraine Bracco; Juliette Lewis; Josh Mostel; Michael Rapaport; Michael Imperioli; James Dennis (Jim) Carroll; Directed by Scott Kalvert; Written by Bryan Goluboff; Cinematography by David Phillips; Music by Graeme Revell. **Pr:** John Bard Manulis; Liz Heller; Chris Blackwell; Dan Genetti; Island Pictures; New Line Cinema. **A:** Sr. High-Adult. **P:** Entertainment. **U:** Home. **Mov-Ent:** Drug Abuse, Basketball. **Acq:** Purchase. **Dist:** Palm Pictures. $94.99.

Basketball for All Ages with Paul Westphal 1991
Westphal demonstrates techniques for offensive moves, dribbling, passing and shooting a basketball. 25m; VHS. **Pr:** Champions on Film. **A:** Primary-Sr. High. **P:** Instruction. **U:** Home. **Spo-Rec:** Sports--General, Basketball. **Acq:** Purchase. **Dist:** School-Tech Inc. $12.95.

Basketball for Boys: Fundamentals 1959
The basics of basketball footwork, ball handling, and shooting are explained. 11m/B/W; VHS, 3/4 U. **Pr:** Bailey Films Associates. **A:** Primary-Sr. High. **P:** Instruction. **U:** Institution, SURA. **Spo-Rec:** Basketball. **Acq:** Purchase. **Dist:** Phoenix Learning Group. $110.00.

Basketball for Boys: Teamplay 1959
Both offensive and defensive team concepts are taught for prospective hoopsters. 11m/B/W; VHS, 3/4 U. **Pr:** Bailey Films Associates. **A:** Primary-Sr. High. **P:** Instruction. **U:** Institution, SURA. **Spo-Rec:** Basketball. **Acq:** Purchase. **Dist:** Phoenix Learning Group. $110.00.

Basketball Fundamentals 1972
Some of the drills and techniques used to develop the basketball player's mastery of the fundamentals are demonstrated in this three-lesson series. 30m; EJ. **Pr:** NETCHE. **A:** College-Adult. **P:** Education. **U:** Institution, CCTV, BCTV, SURA. **Spo-Rec:** Sports--General, Basketball. **Acq:** Purchase, Rent/Lease, Subscription. **Dist:** NETCHE.
Indiv. Titles: 1. Drills 2. Defense 3. Offense.

Basketball of the '90s 1990
Four of the country's top basketball coaches (Jerry Tarkanian, Tara VanDerveer, Lute Olson, and Henry Bibby) present their advice on developing winning basketball players and teams. Tapes are available individually. 60m; VHS. **A:** Jr. High-Adult. **P:** Instruction. **U:** Institution, Home. **How-Ins:** How-To, Basketball. **Acq:** Purchase. **Dist:** Cambridge Educational; Allied Video Corp. $39.95.
Indiv. Titles: 1. Developing the Big Man 2. Developing the Perimeter Player 3. The Shark on Offense 4. The Shark on Defense 5. Building a Championship Offense 6. Building a Championship Defense 7. Beginning Basketball With Bibby.

Basketball Offense 1988
The University of North Carolina coach who has produced such basketball greats as Sleepy Floyd, J.R. Reed, and Michael Jordan explains what a team must do to have a potent offense. 20m; VHS, 3/4 U. **C:** Dean Smith. **Pr:** Champions on Film. **A:** Jr. High-Adult. **P:** Instruction. **U:** Institution, CCTV, Home. **Spo-Rec:** Basketball. **Acq:** Purchase. **Dist:** School-Tech Inc. $32.50.

Basketball Series with Coach Marv Harshman 1992
These four programs deal with strategies of the game. Available individually or as a set. 60m; VHS. **A:** Jr. High-Sr. High. **P:** Instruction. **U:** Institution, Home. **Spo-Rec:** Basketball. **Acq:** Purchase. **Dist:** Cambridge Educational. $139.80.
Indiv. Titles: 1. Drills to Help Your Score 2. Fundamentals of Women's Basketball 3. Tough Defense 4. Winning Offense.

Basketball Skills 1988
Passing, shooting, dribbling, defense and other basketball basics are taught here. 20m; VHS, 3/4 U. **Pr:** Champions on Film. **A:** Jr. High-Adult. **P:** Instruction. **U:** Institution, CCTV, Home. **Spo-Rec:** Basketball. **Acq:** Purchase. **Dist:** School-Tech Inc. $32.50.

Basketball: The Don Meyer Way 2008 (Unrated)
Cameras follow Coach Don Meyer as he and his basketball team practice for a post-season game and scout the opposing team, and get highlights of how the practice drills paid off during the actual game. 240m; DVD. **A:** Family. **P:** Education. **U:** Home, Institution. **Gen-Edu:** Basketball, Athletic Instruction/Coaching. **Acq:** Purchase. **Dist:** Championship Productions. $79.99.

Basketball with U.S. Gold Medal Coach Marv Harshma 1985
Outstanding college coach Marv Harshman outlines the basic strategies of basketball. 56m; VHS. **Pr:** Morris Video. **A:** Sr. High-Adult. **P:** Instruction. **U:** Home. **Spo-Rec:** Sports--General, Basketball. **Acq:** Purchase. **Dist:** Morris Video.
Indiv. Titles: 1. A Winning Offense 2. Tough Defense 3. Drills That Get Scoreboard Results.

Basketmaking in Colonial Virginia 19??
Part of the Colonial Crafts and Trade Series. Covers the basketmaking methods of 18th-century Virginia. 29m; VHS. **A:** Jr. High-Adult. **P:** Education. **U:** Home, Institution, SURA. **Gen-Edu:** History--U.S., Crafts. **Acq:** Purchase. **Dist:** Colonial Williamsburg Foundation. $25.95.

Baskets of Gold: Preserving an African-American Tradition 1998
History of the grass basket and how it was brought to the U.S. from Western African slaves. Focuses on African-American history and tradition. 23m; VHS. **A:** Family. **P:** Education. **U:** Home. **Gen-Edu:** Africa, History--U.S., Black Culture. **Acq:** Purchase. **Dist:** Instructional Video. $34.95.

Basketweave 2006 (Unrated) — ★
Her parents murdered by a serial killer, a young girl spends 10 years locked in a brutal mental institution being fed experimental drugs. She escapes after a series of difficult-to-believe subplots come to fruition, and meets her parents' murderer who has been happily waiting in the hospital all this time. 76m; DVD. **C:** Vance Strickland; Anna Harden; Directed by Christopher Forbes; Written by Christopher Forbes; Ken Forbes; Kevin Forbes; Cinematography by Richard Kelly; Michael G. Hennessy; Music by Christopher Forbes; Ken Forbes. **A:** Sr. High-Adult. **P:** Entertainment. **U:** Home. **L:** English. **Mov-Ent. Acq:** Purchase. **Dist:** York Pictures Inc. $24.98.

Basquiat 1996 (R) — ★★★
First-time writer/director and reknowned '80s pop artist Schnabel paints a celluloid portrait of African-American artist Jean Michel Basquiat, who went from grafitti artist to overnight sensation in the mid-1980s before dying of a drug overdose at 27. Schnabel's first-hand knowledge provides details of the painters, the dealers, and the patrons of the whirlwind New York art scene of the time, using an all-star cast (no mean feat on a $3 million budget). Making the move from stage to screen, Wright is an aptly deep and elusive Basquiat and Bowie stands out in a marvelously concevied portrayal of Basquiat's pseudo-mentor, the equally sensational Warhol. Features authentic works of the artists portrayed and some very convincing Basquiat reproductions done by Schnabel. 108m; VHS, DVD, CC. **C:** Jeffrey Wright; David Bowie; Dennis Hopper; Gary Oldman; Christopher Walken; Michael Wincott; Benicio Del Toro; Parker Posey; Elina Lowensohn; Courtney Love; Claire Forlani; Willem Dafoe; Paul Bartel; Tatum O'Neal; Chuck Pfeiffer; Directed by Julian Schnabel; Written by Julian Schnabel; Cinematography by Ron Fortunato; Music by John Cale. **Pr:** Jon Kilik; Randy Ostrow; Joni Sighvatsson; Peter Brant; Joseph Allen; Michiyo Yoshizaki; Miramax Film Corp. **A:** Sr. High-Adult. **P:** Entertainment. **U:** Home. **Mov-Ent:** Art & Artists, Drug Abuse, Biography: Artists. **Awds:** Ind. Spirit '97: Support. Actor (Del Toro). **Dist:** Miramax Film Corp.

Bass as a Solo Instrument 199?
Ten contemporary bass players share their soloing techniques and how to apply them to a variety of musical styles. ?m; VHS. **A:** Sr. High-Adult. **P:** Instruction. **U:** Home. **How-Ins:** Music--Instruction. **Acq:** Purchase. **Dist:** Hal Leonard Corp. $19.95.

Bass Basics: Part I 19??
Learn stringing, rhythmic and harmonic theory, basic scales, actual bass patterns, and more. 65m; VHS. **A:** Sr. High. **P:** Education. **U:** Home. **L:** English. **Gen-Edu:** Music--Instruction. **Acq:** Purchase. **Dist:** Calprod Pro Film/Video Production, Inc. $19.98.

Bass Day 1998 199?
Celebrated bass players perform live and share playing techniques. 105m; VHS. **A:** Sr. High-Adult. **P:** Instruction. **U:** Home. **How-Ins:** Music--Instruction, Music--Performance. **Acq:** Purchase. **Dist:** Hal Leonard Corp. $24.95.

The Bass Guitar of Jack Casady 199?
Demonstrates the techniques and musical thinking of Jack's unique bass style. 80m; VHS. **A:** Sr. High-Adult. **P:** Education. **U:** Home. **How-Ins:** Music--Instruction. **Acq:** Purchase. **Dist:** Hal Leonard Corp. $39.95.

Bass Magic 1989
Learn the details of spinnerbait fishing and don't let the big one get away! 50m; VHS. **A:** Adult-Family. **P:** Entertainment. **U:** Home. **How-Ins:** Sports--General, How-To, Fishing. **Acq:** Purchase. **Dist:** Anchor Bay Entertainment. $7.99.

Bass on Titles 1977
Academy Award winner Bass translates the themes of major motion pictures into graphic animation. 32m; VHS. **Pr:** Saul Bass. **A:** Sr. High-College. **P:** Education. **U:** Institution, Home, SURA. **Mov-Ent:** Animation & Cartoons, Film History. **Acq:** Purchase, Rent/Lease, Duplication License. **Dist:** Pyramid Media.

Bass Strategies 1991
You will learn the best kept secrets from selecting your rod and reel to actually finding the bass. 30m; VHS. **C:** Dave Embry. **Pr:** Bennett Marine Video. **A:** Jr. High-Adult. **P:** Instruction. **U:** Home. **Spo-Rec:** Fishing. **Acq:** Purchase. **Dist:** Bennett Marine Video. $6.95.

Bass Tackle: How to Buy & Save 1988
This is a guide to fishing tackle, with an emphasis on looking for bargains. 92m; VHS. **Pr:** BFV. **A:** Jr. High-Adult. **P:** Instruction. **U:** Home. **How-Ins:** Fishing. **Acq:** Purchase. **Dist:** Bennett Marine Video. $29.99.

Bassin' Today 19??
Explains calendar periods and how the largemouth adapts to lakes, rivers, reservoirs, strip pits, and ponds. 73m; VHS. **A:** Adult. **P:** Instruction. **U:** Home. **Spo-Rec:** Fishing. **Acq:** Purchase. **Dist:** In-Fisherman.

The Bassoon-Piano Show 19??
Features conductor Isaiah Jackson as he demonstrates the musical sounds of the bassoon and the piano. Includes teacher's guide. 30m; VHS. **A:** Primary-Jr. High. **P:** Education. **U:** Institution. **Chl-Juv:** Education. **Acq:** Purchase. **Dist:** GPN Educational Media. $29.95.

Basstactics 1990
Ricky Clunn offers advice on locating and catching largemouth bass. 30m; VHS. **C:** Hosted by Jerry Chiappetta. **Pr:** Chiappetta Productions. **A:** Family. **P:** Instruction. **U:** Home. **How-Ins:** Sports--General, Fishing, How-To. **Acq:** Purchase. **Dist:** Karol Media. $14.95.

The Bastard 1978 — ★★½
Dashing (but alas, illegitimate) nobleman roams Europe on futile, "Roots"-like search, then settles for America during the Revolutionary War in this long-winded TV adaptation of John Jakes's equally cumbersome bestseller (part of his popular Bicentennial series). Stevens stars, along with many supporting performers merely keeping active. Followed by "The Rebels" and "The Seekers." 189m; DVD. **C:** Andrew Stevens; Tom Bosley; Kim Cattrall; Buddy Ebsen; Lorne Greene; Olivia Hussey; Cameron Mitchell; Harry (Henry) Morgan; Patricia Neal; Eleanor Parker; Donald Pleasence; William Shatner; Barry Sullivan; Noah Beery, Jr.; William Daniels; Keenan Wynn; Peter Bonerz; James Gregory; Mark Neely; Ike Eisenmann; Charles Haid; Russell Johnson; James Whitmore, Jr.; Alan Napier; Stephen Furst; Philip Baker Hall; Narrated by Raymond Burr; Directed by Lee H. Katzin; Written by Guerdon (Gordon) Trueblood; Cinematography by Michel Hugo; Music by John Addison. **Pr:** Mark Huffam. **A:** Jr. High-Adult. **P:** Entertainment. **U:** Home. **Mov-Ent:** Drama, Revolutionary War, TV Movies. **Acq:** Purchase. **Dist:** Acorn Media Group Inc. $29.98.

Bastard out of Carolina 1996 (R) — ★★
Huston's steeped-in-controversy directorial debut tells the story of young mom Anney (Leigh), who lives a hardscrabble life in Greenville, South Carolina, with an illegitimate daughter nicknamed Bone (Malone). Working as a waitress, Anney's eager to find love and succumbs to the charms of laborer Glen (Eldard), despite his nasty temper. Eleven-year-old Bone and Glen are immediately at odds and he begins to beat her, with Anney unwilling to face the truth, until a final horrific event. Based on the 1992 semiautiobiographical novel by Dorothy Allison, the film was originally made for Ted Turner's TNT network but was rejected as unsuitable because of its graphic depiction of child abuse. 97m; VHS, DVD. **C:** Jennifer Jason Leigh; Jena Malone; Ron Eldard; Glenne Headly; Lyle Lovett; Dermot Mulroney; Christina Ricci; Michael Rooker; Diana Scarwid; Susan Traylor; Grace Zabriskie; Sonny Shroyer; Directed by Anjelica Huston; Written by Anne Meredith; Cinematography by Anthony B. Richmond; Music by Van Dyke Parks. **Pr:** Gary Hoffman. **A:** Sr.

High-Adult. **P:** Entertainment. **U:** Home. **Mov-Ent:** Child Abuse, Rape, Family. **Acq:** Purchase. **Dist:** BMG Entertainment.

Bastet 2001
Uses a literary cross-curriculum to teach students about making and keeping friends, information about present day and ancient Egypt, and the science of archeology. 15m; VHS. **A:** Primary. **P:** Education. **U:** Institution. **Chl-Juv:** Language Arts, Archaeology, History--Ancient. **Acq:** Purchase. **Dist:** Marshmedia. $79.95.

Bastien, Bastienne 19?? (Unrated)
A delicately unfolding period piece which chronicles the family life of a woman, her two sons, her sister-in-law, a widow, and her son before they are forced to flee the specter of WWI. In French with English subtitles. ?m; VHS. **C:** Juliet Berto. **A:** Family. **P:** Entertainment. **U:** Home. **L:** English, French. **Mov-Ent:** Family. **Acq:** Purchase. **Dist:** Facets Multimedia Inc. $49.95.

The Bat 1926 (Unrated) — ★★★
A bat-obsessed killer stalks the halls of a spooky mansion in this early film version of the Mary Roberts Rinehart novel. 81m/B/W; Silent; VHS, DVD, Blu-Ray. **C:** Andre de Beranger; Charles Herzinger; Emily Fitzroy; Louise Fazenda; Arthur Houseman; Robert McKim; Jack Pickford; Jewel Carmen; Directed by Roland West; Written by Roland West. **Pr:** United Artists. **A:** Family. **P:** Entertainment. **U:** Home. **Mov-Ent:** Horror, Silent Films. **Acq:** Purchase. **Dist:** Sinister Cinema; Fusion Video. $16.95.

The Bat 1959 (Unrated) — ★★
A great plot centering around a murderer called the Bat, who kills hapless victims by ripping out their throats when he isn't busy searching for $1 million worth of securities stashed in the old house he is living in. Adapted from the novel by Mary Roberts Rinehart. 80m/B/W; VHS, DVD. **C:** Vincent Price; Agnes Moorehead; Gavin Gordon; John Sutton; Lenita Lane; Darla Hood; Directed by Crane Wilbur; Written by Crane Wilbur; Cinematography by Joseph Biroc; Music by Louis Forbes. **Pr:** Allied Artists International. **A:** Sr. High-Adult. **P:** Entertainment. **U:** Home. **Mov-Ent:** Horror. **Acq:** Purchase. **Dist:** Sinister Cinema. $16.95.

The Bat People 1974 (R) — ★
Less-than-gripping horror flick in which Dr. John Bech is bitten by a bat while on his honeymoon. He then becomes a sadistic bat creature, compelled to kill anyone who stumbles across his path. The gory special effects make for a great movie if you've ever been bitten by that sort of thing. 95m; VHS, DVD. **C:** Stewart Moss; Marianne McAndrew; Michael Pataki; Paul Carr; Directed by Jerry Jameson; Cinematography by Matthew F. Leonetti; Music by Artie Kane. **Pr:** American International Pictures. **A:** Sr. High-Adult. **P:** Entertainment. **U:** Home. **Mov-Ent:** Horror. **Acq:** Purchase. **Dist:** MGM Home Entertainment. $14.95.

Bat 21 1988 (R) — ★★
Hackman, an American officer, is stranded in the wilds of Vietnam alone after his plane is shot down. He must rely on himself and Glover, with whom he has radio contact, to get him out. Glover and Hackman give solid performances in this otherwise average film. 112m; VHS, DVD, CC. **C:** Gene Hackman; Danny Glover; Jerry Reed; David Marshall Grant; Clayton Rohner; Erich Anderson; Joe Dorsey; Directed by Peter Markle; Written by Marc Norman; William C. Anderson; Cinematography by Mark Irwin; Music by Christopher Young. **Pr:** Tri-Star Pictures. **A:** College-Adult. **P:** Entertainment. **U:** Home. **Mov-Ent:** Vietnam War. **Acq:** Purchase. **Dist:** Anchor Bay Entertainment. $19.98.

The Bat Whispers 1930 (Unrated) — ★★½
A masked madman is stalking the halls of a creepy mansion; eerie tale that culminates in an appeal to the audience to keep the plot under wraps. Unusually crafted film for its early era. Comic mystery based on the novel and play by Mary Roberts Rinehart and Avery Hopwood. 82m/B/W; VHS, DVD. **C:** Chester Morris; Chance Ward; Richard Tucker; Wilson Benge; DeWitt Jennings; Una Merkel; Spencer Charters; Directed by Roland West; Written by Roland West; Cinematography by Ray June; Robert Planck. **Pr:** United Artists. **A:** Jr. High-Adult. **P:** Entertainment. **U:** Home. **Mov-Ent:** Mystery & Suspense. **Acq:** Purchase. **Dist:** New Yorker Video; Rex Miller Artisan Studio.

Bat Without Wings 1980 (Unrated) — ★★
The Shaw Brothers occasionally dabbled in horror films about black magic and the supernatural, which usually weren't quite as successful. There's a reason for that. They weren't as good. A villain known as The Bat (who is supposed to be long dead) returns, and kidnaps and murders a young woman. A local swordsman volunteers to track him down and bring him to justice. And so the really bad special effects begin. 92m; DVD. **C:** Shen Chan; Feng Ku; Wah Yuen; Directed by Yuen Chor. **A:** Sr. High-Adult. **P:** Entertainment. **U:** Home. **Mov-Ent:** Martial Arts, Horror. **Acq:** Purchase. **Dist:** Image Entertainment Inc. $19.98.

Bataan 1943 — ★★½
A rugged war-time combat drama following the true story of a small platoon in the Philippines endeavoring to blow up a pivotal Japanese bridge. Also available in a colorized version. 115m/B/W; VHS, DVD. **C:** Robert Taylor; George Murphy; Thomas Mitchell; Desi Arnaz, Sr.; Lee Bowman; Lloyd Nolan; Robert Walker; Barry Nelson; Phillip Terry; Tom Dugan; Roque Espiritu; Kenneth Spencer; Alex Havier; Donald Curtis; Lynne Carver; Bud Geary; Dorothy Morris; Directed by Tay Garnett; Written by Robert D. (Robert Hardy) Andrews; Cinematography by Sidney Wagner; Music by Bronislau Kaper; Eric Zeisl. **Pr:** Irving Starr; MGM; Loew's, Inc. **A:** Family. **P:** Entertainment. **U:** Home. **Mov-Ent:** Action-Adventure, World War Two. **Acq:** Purchase. **Dist:** MGM Home Entertainment; Time-Life Video and Television. $59.95.

Bataan: The Forgotten Hell 1983
Features eyewitness accounts of the horror of the infamous death march on Bataan. 52m; VHS, 3/4 U. **Pr:** National Broadcasting Company. **A:** Sr. High-Adult. **P:** Education. **U:** Institution, SURA. **Gen-Edu:** Documentary Films, World War Two. **Acq:** Purchase. **Dist:** Home Vision Cinema.

Batch Control 1988
The many different things a person must look for when using the Batch system are explained. 45m; VHS, 3/4 U. **Pr:** Instrument Society of America. **A:** Adult. **P:** Education. **U:** Institution, CCTV. **Bus-Ind:** Technology. **Acq:** Purchase, Rent/Lease. **Dist:** ISA -The International Society of Automation. $1200.00.
Indiv. Titles: 1. Fundamentals of Batch Processes 2. Basic Temperature Control of Batch Processes 3. Temperature Control of Complex Batch Processes 4. Multivariable Control of Batch Processes.

Bates Motel: Season One 2013
A&E 2013--? family drama/horror. Prequel to "Psycho" shows Norman Bates during his teenage years. "First You Dream, Then You Die": Recent widow Norma Bates and son Norman move to White Pine Bay, Oregon where Norma buys a foreclosed motel. "Ocean View": Norma is arrested for murder and Norman puts up the motel as collateral for her bail. Norman's older half-brother Dylan offers to let Norman move in with him. "A Boy and His Dog": Norman learns taxidermy from Emma's father and Norma is worried that the bypass the town wants to build will ruin her business. 10 episodes. 435m; DVD, Blu-Ray. **C:** Vera Farmiga; Freddie Highmore; Max Thieriot; Olivia Cooke; Nestor Carbonell. **A:** Sr. High-Adult. **P:** Entertainment. **U:** Home. **L:** English. **Mov-Ent:** Drama, Family, Horror. **Acq:** Purchase. **Dist:** Universal Studios Home Video. $44.98.

Batfink: The Complete Series 2007
Features the entire late 1960s television cartoon series about Batfink—a Batman parody—who fights crime with the aide of metal wings and his bumbling sidekick Karate. 100 episodes. 510m; DVD. **A:** Family. **P:** Entertainment. **U:** Home. **Chl-Juv:** Television Series, Family, Children's Shows. **Acq:** Purchase. **Dist:** Shout! Factory. $34.98.

Bath Waters 1980
Looks at the findings of a dig under Britain's most famous Roman bath house. 50m; VHS, 3/4 U. **Pr:** British Broadcasting Corporation. **A:** Sr. High-Adult. **P:** Education. **U:** Institution, SURA. **Hea-Sci:** Documentary Films, Archaeology, Great Britain. **Acq:** Purchase. **Dist:** Home Vision Cinema.

Bathing Beauty 1944 — ★★½
This musical stars Skelton as a pop music composer with the hots for college swim teacher Williams. Rathbone is a music executive who sees the romance as a threat to Skelton's career and to his own profit margin. Full of aquatic ballet, Skelton's shtick, and wonderful original melodies. The first film in which Williams received star billing. 101m; VHS, DVD. **C:** Red Skelton; Esther Williams; Basil Rathbone; Bill Goodwin; Jean Porter; Carlos Ramirez; Donald Meek; Ethel Smith; Helen Forrest; Directed by George Sidney; Cinematography by Harry Stradling, Sr.; Music by Xavier Cugat. **Pr:** Jack Cummings; MGM. **A:** Family. **P:** Entertainment. **U:** Home. **Mov-Ent:** Musical, Romance, Classic Films. **Acq:** Purchase. **Dist:** Facets Multimedia Inc.; MGM Home Entertainment; Turner Broadcasting System Inc. $19.98.
Songs: I Cried for You; Bim, Bam, Boom; Tico-Tico; I'll Take the High Note; Loch Lomond; By the Waters of Minnetonka; Magic is the Moonlight; Trumpet Blues; Hora Staccato.

Bathrooms 19??
Shows how to design a bathroom and select products, tear out old elements and frame new elements, rough-in mechanical systems, install drywall, install cabinets and countertops, install ceramic tile and vinyl, install plumbing fixtures and update the bathroom with a "facelift." 64m; VHS. **A:** Sr. High-Adult. **P:** Instruction. **U:** Home. **How-Ins:** How-To, Home Improvement. **Acq:** Purchase. **Dist:** Hometime Video Publishing Inc. $11.95.

Bathrooms Miniseries 19??
Shows how to renovate a bathroom to meet new design standards; as well as how to rough-in the plumbing and electrical systems and install a vanity, ceramic tile and water-efficient fixtures. 75m; VHS. **A:** Sr. High-Adult. **P:** Instruction. **U:** Home. **How-Ins:** How-To, Home Improvement. **Acq:** Purchase. **Dist:** Hometime Video Publishing Inc. $11.95.

Batik as Fine Art 1992
Artist Helen Carkin demonstrates the art of Batik using parafin wax, silk cloth, and fabric dye. Includes a guide. 60m; VHS. **A:** Primary-College. **P:** Instruction. **U:** Institution, Home. **How-Ins:** How-To, Crafts. **Acq:** Purchase. **Dist:** Crystal Productions. $39.95.

Batman 1966 — ★★½
Holy television camp, Batman! Will the caped crusader win the Bat-tle against the combined forces of the Joker, the Riddler, the Penguin, and Catwoman? Will Batman and Robin save the United World Security Council from dehydration? Will the Bat genius ever figure out that Russian journalist Miss Kitka and Catwoman are one and the same? Biff! Thwack! Socko! Not to be confused with the Michael Keaton version of the Dark Knight, this is the pot-bellied Adam West Batman, teeming with Bat satire and made especially for the big screen. 104m; VHS, DVD, Wide, CC. **C:** Burt Ward; Adam West; Burgess Meredith; Cesar Romero; Frank Gorshin; Lee Meriwether; Alan Napier; Neil Hamilton; Stafford Repp; Madge Blake; Reginald Denny; Milton Frome; Directed by Leslie Martinson; Written by Lorenzo Semple, Jr.; Cinematography by Howard Schwartz; Music by Nelson Riddle. **Pr:** 20th Century-Fox. **A:** Family. **P:** Entertainment. **U:** Home. **Mov-Ent:** Cult Films. **Acq:** Purchase. **Dist:** Fox Home Entertainment. $19.98.

Batman 1967
The caped crusader and his faithful sidekick Robin battle crime in Gotham City in this collection of eight animated adventures. 60m; VHS, UMD, CC. **Pr:** Filmation Associates. **A:** Family. **P:** Entertainment. **U:** Home. **Mov-Ent:** Animation & Cartoons. **Acq:** Purchase. **Dist:** Warner Home Video, Inc. $12.95.

Batman 1989 (PG-13) — ★★★½
The blockbuster fantasy epic that renewed Hollywood's faith in media blitzing. The Caped Crusader (Keaton) is back in Gotham City, where even the criminals are afraid to walk the streets alone. There's a new breed of criminal in Gotham, led by the infamous Joker (Nicholson). Their random attacks via acid-based make-up are just the beginning. Keaton is surprisingly good as the dual personality hero though Nicholson steals the show with his campy performance. Basinger is blonde and feisty as photog Vicki Vale, who falls for mysterious millionaire Bruce Wayne (and the bat). Marvelously designed and shot. Followed by three sequels. 126m; VHS, DVD, Blu-Ray, UMD, Wide, CC. **C:** Michael Keaton; Jack Nicholson; Kim Basinger; Robert Wuhl; Tracey Walter; Billy Dee Williams; Pat Hingle; Michael Gough; Jack Palance; Jerry Hall; Directed by Tim Burton; Written by Sam Hamm; Warren Skaaren; Cinematography by Roger Pratt; Music by Danny Elfman; Prince. **Pr:** Warner. **A:** Jr. High-Adult. **P:** Entertainment. **U:** Home. **Mov-Ent:** Fantasy, Family Viewing. **Awds:** Oscars '89: Art Dir./Set Dec. **Acq:** Purchase. **Dist:** Warner Home Video, Inc. $19.98.

Batman and Robin 1997 (PG-13) — ★½
Includes lots of flash but, as usual, not much substance in this fourth adventure, which features a less angst-ridden caped crusader in the charming persona of Clooney. O'Donnell, who apparently knows a good gig when he's got one, returns as Robin. They must battle evil industrialist, Mr. Freeze (an impressively costumed Schwarzenegger), and his partner-with-the-deadly-kiss (but what a way to go!), Poison Ivy (Thurman), who have plans to freeze Gotham City. Our heroes have some additional help in the person of Batgirl (Silverstone), who's now butler Alfred's (Gough) niece (she was Commissioner Gordon's daughter in the comics). Story's simplified but the secondary characters still get lost in the crowd. Director Schumacher's already agreed to helm a fifth film, but don't hold your breath since he succeeded in doing the impossible: killing the franchise. 125m; VHS, DVD, CC. **C:** George Clooney; Chris O'Donnell; Arnold Schwarzenegger; Uma Thurman; Alicia Silverstone; Michael Gough; Pat Hingle; John Glover; Elle Macpherson; Vivica A. Fox; Vendela Thommessen; Jeep Swenson; Directed by Joel Schumacher; Written by Joel Schumacher; Akiva Goldsman; Cinematography by Stephen Goldblatt; Music by Elliot Goldenthal. **Pr:** Peter MacGregor-Scott; Benjamin Melnicker; Michael Uslan; Warner Bros. **A:** Jr. High-Adult. **P:** Entertainment. **U:** Home. **Mov-Ent:** Fantasy, Poisons, Diseases. **Awds:** Golden Raspberries '97: Worst Support. Actress (Silverstone). **Acq:** Purchase. **Dist:** Warner Home Video, Inc.

Batman and Robin, Vol. 1 1949 (Unrated)
The first movie serial appearance of the Caped Crusader with his partner, Robin. The first seven parts of fifteen part series. ?m/B/W; VHS. **Pr:** Columbia Pictures. **A:** Family. **P:** Entertainment. **U:** Home. **Mov-Ent:** Serials. **Acq:** Purchase. **Dist:** Sony Pictures Home Entertainment Inc.

Batman and Robin, Vol. 2 1949 (Unrated)
The second half of the original movie serial, containing the last eight chapters. ?m/B/W; VHS. **Pr:** Columbia Pictures. **A:** Family. **P:** Entertainment. **U:** Home. **Mov-Ent:** Serials. **Acq:** Purchase. **Dist:** Sony Pictures Home Entertainment Inc.

Batman Begins 2005 (PG-13) — ★★★
They got rid of the Bat-nipples? Joel Schumacher will be so disappointed. Fortunately for everyone else, Nolan rejects the other Bat-sequels' lame campiness and returns Batman to his gritty roots, showing us how a young Bruce Wayne (Bale) first became the Caped Crusader. After training abroad with the mysterious Ducard (Neeson) and Ra's Al Ghul (Watanabe), Wayne begins his one-man war on crime with the help of his butler Alfred (Caine), good cop Jim Gordon (Oldman), and tech-savvy Lucius Fox (Freeman). The cast is beyond stellar, and Nolan does an amazing job of making Batman's world seem almost plausible. There's a bit too much angsty pondering about the nature of fear, but you'll forget all that once you see the Lamborghini-inspired Batmobile. 141m; DVD, Blu-Ray, UMD, HD-DVD. **C:** Christian Bale; Michael Caine; Ken(saku) Watanabe; Cillian Murphy; Tom Wilkinson; Morgan Freeman; Katie Holmes; Gary Oldman; Liam Neeson; Rutger Hauer; Mark Boone, Jr.; Linus Roache; Gus Lewis; Directed by Christopher Nolan; Written by Christopher Nolan; David S. Goyer; Cinematography by Wally Pfister; Music by Hans Zimmer; James Newton Howard. **Pr:** Charles Roven; Emma Thomas; Larry J. Franco; Syncopy; Warner Bros. **A:** Jr. High-Adult. **P:** Entertainment. **U:** Home. **L:** English. **Mov-Ent:** Adoption, Cults. **Acq:** Purchase. **Dist:** Warner Home Video, Inc.

Batman Beyond: Return of the Joker 2000 (PG-13)
The Joker is back terrorizing Gotham and seeking revenge on an aging Bruce Wayne. But now new Batman Terry McGinnis is the one to take on the Clown Prince of Crime. 77m; VHS, DVD, Wide. **C:** Voice(s) by Will Friedle; Mark Hamill; Kevin Conroy; Melissa Joan Hart; Directed by Curt Geda. **A:** Jr. High-Adult. **P:** Entertainment. **U:** Home. **Chl-Juv:** Animation & Cartoons. **Acq:** Purchase. **Dist:** Warner Home Video, Inc.

Batman Beyond: School Dayz and Spellbound 2004
Presents the animated 1999-2001 television series with teenager Terry McGinnis, whose father's murder at Wayne-Powers Corporation leads him to ask for help from Bruce Wayne when he discovers his secret identity—although Wayne is now too old. Using Batman's high-tech outfit, Terry seeks revenge with Wayne as his mentor. Includes: "School Dayz" ("Dead Man's Hand," "Golem," and "The Winning Edge") and "Spellbound" ("Hooked Up," "Spellbound," and "A Touch of Curare"). 6 episodes. 124m; DVD. **C:** Voice(s) by Will Friedle; Kevin Conroy; Lauren Tom; Cree Summer; Ryan O'Donohue. **A:** Primary-Adult. **P:** Entertainment. **U:** Home. **Mov-Ent:** Television Series, Animation & Cartoons, Action-Adventure. **Acq:** Purchase. **Dist:** Warner Home Video, Inc. $12.98.

Batman Beyond: Tech Wars and Disappearing Inque 2004
Presents the animated 1999-2001 television series with teenager Terry McGinnis whose father's murder at Wayne-Powers Corporation leads him to ask for help from Bruce Wayne when he discovers his secret identity—although Wayne is now too old. Using Batman's high-tech outfit, Terry seeks revenge with Wayne as his mentor. Includes: "Tech Wars" ("Heroes," "Lost Soul," and "Splicers") and "Disappearing Inque" ("Black Out," "Disappearing Inque," and "Shriek"). 6 episodes. 126m; DVD. **C:** Voice(s) by Will Friedle; Kevin Conroy; Lauren Tom; Cree Summer; Sigurd Rachman. **A:** Primary-Adult. **P:** Entertainment. **U:** Home. **Mov-Ent:** Television Series, Animation & Cartoons, Action-Adventure. **Acq:** Purchase. **Dist:** Warner Home Video, Inc. $12.98.

Batman Beyond: The Complete First Season 1999
Presents the animated 1999-2001 television series with teenager Terry McGinnis, whose father's murder at Wayne-Powers Corporation leads him to ask for help from Bruce Wayne when he discovers his secret identity—although Wayne is now too old. Using Batman's high-tech outfit, Terry seeks revenge with Wayne as his mentor. 13 episodes. ?m; DVD. **C:** Voice(s) by Will Friedle; Kevin Conroy; Lauren Tom; Cree Summer; Ryan O'Donohue. **A:** Primary-Adult. **P:** Entertainment. **U:** Home. **Mov-Ent:** Television Series, Animation & Cartoons, Action-Adventure. **Acq:** Purchase. **Dist:** Warner Home Video, Inc. $26.99.

Batman Beyond: The Complete Second Season 1999
Presents the animated 1999-2001 television series with teenager Terry McGinnis, whose father's murder at Wayne-Powers Corporation leads him to ask for help from Bruce Wayne when he discovers his secret identity—although Wayne is now too old. Using Batman's high-tech outfit, Terry seeks revenge with Wayne as his mentor. 26 episodes. 544m; DVD. **C:** Voice(s) by Will Friedle; Kevin Conroy; Lauren Tom; Cree Summer; Ryan O'Donohue. **A:** Primary-Adult. **P:** Entertainment. **U:** Home. **Mov-Ent:** Television Series, Animation & Cartoons, Action-Adventure. **Acq:** Purchase. **Dist:** Warner Home Video, Inc. $44.98.

Batman Beyond: The Complete Third Season 2000
Presents the animated 1999-2001 television series with teenager Terry McGinnis, whose father's murder at Wayne-Powers Corporation leads him to ask for help from Bruce Wayne when he discovers his secret identity—although Wayne is now too old. Using Batman's high-tech outfit, Terry seeks revenge with Wayne as his mentor. 13 episodes. 273m; DVD. **C:** Voice(s) by Will Friedle; Kevin Conroy; Lauren Tom; Cree Summer; Ryan O'Donohue. **A:** Primary-Adult. **P:** Entertainment. **U:** Home. **Mov-Ent:** Television Series, Animation & Cartoons, Action-Adventure. **Acq:** Purchase. **Dist:** Warner Home Video, Inc. $26.99.

Batman Beyond: The Movie 1999
Presents the animated 1999-2001 television series with teenager Terry McGinnis whose father's murder at Wayne-Powers Corporation leads him to ask for help from Bruce Wayne when he discovers his secret identity—although Wayne is now too old. Using Batman's high-tech outfit, Terry seeks revenge with Wayne as his mentor. Includes: "The Pilot Movie," "Gotham Golem," "The Winning Edge," "Dead Man's Hand," and "Meltdown." 5 episodes. 132m; DVD. **C:** Voice(s) by Will Friedle; Kevin Conroy; Lauren Tom; Cree Summer; Ryan O'Donohue. **A:** Primary-Adult. **P:** Entertainment. **U:** Home. **Mov-Ent:** Television Series, Animation & Cartoons, Action-Adventure. **Acq:** Purchase. **Dist:** Warner Home Video, Inc. $26.99.

Batman Forever 1995 (PG-13) — ★★★
Holy franchise, Batman! Third-time actioner considerably lightens up Tim Burton's dark vision for a more family-oriented Caped Crusader (now played by Kilmer, who fills out lip requirement nicely). The Boy Wonder also makes a first-time appearance in the bulked-up form of O'Donnell, a street-smart Robin with revenge on his mind. Naturally, the villains still steal the show in the personas of maniacal Carrey (the Riddler) and the sartorially splendid Jones as Harvey "Two-Face" Dent. Rounding out this charismatic cast is Kidman's slinky psychologist Chase Meridian, who's eager to find the man inside the bat (and who can blame her). Lots of splashy toys for the boys and awe-inspiring sets to show you where the money went. A Gotham City gas that did $53 million at it's opening weekend boxoffice—breaking the "Jurassic Park" record, testimony to the power of aggressive marketing. 121m; VHS, DVD, CC. **C:** Val Kilmer; Tommy Lee Jones; Jim Carrey; Chris O'Donnell; Nicole Kidman; Drew Barrymore; Debi Mazar; Michael Gough; Pat Hingle; Jon Favreau; George Wallace; Don "The Dragon" Wilson; Ed Begley, Jr.; Rene Auberjonois; Joe Grifasi; Jessica Tuck; Kimberly Scott; Directed by Joel Schumacher; Written by Janet Scott Batchler; Akiva Goldsman; Lee Batchler; Cinematography by Stephen Goldblatt; Music by Elliot Goldenthal. **Pr:** Tim Burton; Peter MacGregor-Scott; Benjamin Melnicker; Michael Uslan; Warner Bros. **A:** Jr. High-Adult. **P:** Entertainment. **U:** Home. **Mov-Ent:** Fantasy, Family Viewing, Circuses. **Awds:** Blockbuster '96: Action Actress, T. (Kidman). **Acq:** Purchase. **Dist:** Warner Home Video, Inc. $19.96.

Batman: Mask of the Phantasm 1993 (PG) — ★★½
Based on the Fox TV series with the animated Batman fending off old enemy the Joker, new enemy the Phantasm, and dreaming of his lost first love. Cartoon film noir set in the 1940s but filled with '90s sarcasm. Complicated storyline with a stylish dark look may be lost on the kiddies but adults will stay awake. 77m; VHS, DVD, Wide, CC. **C:** Voice(s) by Kevin Conroy; Dana Delany; Mark Hamill; Stacy Keach; Hart Bochner; Abe Vigoda; Efrem Zimbalist, Jr.; Dick Miller; Directed by Eric Radomski; Bruce W. Timm; Written by Michael Reaves; Alan Burnett; Paul Dini; Martin Pako; Music by Shirley Walker. **Pr:** Benjamin Melnicker; Michael Uslan; Warner Bros. **A:** Jr. High-Adult. **P:** Entertainment. **U:** Home. **Mov-Ent:** Animation & Cartoons. **Acq:** Purchase. **Dist:** Warner Home Video, Inc. $19.96.

Batman: Mystery of the Batwoman 2003 (PG)
The creators of 'Batman: The Animated Series' produced this film in which Batwoman arrives in Gotham to prevent illegal arms trade being perpetrated by the Penguin. 75m; DVD, Blu-Ray, Streaming. **A:** Primary-Adult. **P:** Entertainment. **U:** Home. **L:** English. **Mov-Ent:** Animation & Cartoons, Action-Adventure. **Acq:** Purchase, Rent/Lease. **Dist:** Warner Home Video, Inc. $14.98 14.96 9.99.

Batman Returns 1992 (PG-13) — ★★½
More of the same from director Burton, with Batman more of a supporting role overshadowed by provocative villains. DeVito is the cruely misshapen Penguin who seeks to rule over Gotham City; Pfeiffer is the exotic and dangerous Catwoman—who has more than a passing purr-sonal interest in Batman; Walken is the maniacal tycoon Max Shreck. Pfeiffer fares best in her wickedly sexy role and second-skin costume (complete with bullwhip). Plot is secondary to special effects and nightmarish settings. Despite a big budget, this grandiose sequel is of the love it or leave it variety. 126m; VHS, DVD, Blu-Ray, CC. **C:** Michael Keaton; Danny DeVito; Michelle Pfeiffer; Christopher Walken; Michael Gough; Michael Murphy; Cristi Conaway; Pat Hingle; Vincent Schiavelli; Jan Hooks; Paul (Pee-wee Herman) Reubens; Andrew Bryniarski; Directed by Tim Burton; Written by Daniel Waters; Cinematography by Stefan Czapsky; Music by Danny Elfman. **Pr:** Denise Di Novi; Tim Burton; Tim Burton. **A:** Jr. High-Adult. **P:** Entertainment. **U:** Home. **Mov-Ent:** Fantasy, Christmas, Pets. **Acq:** Purchase. **Dist:** Warner Home Video, Inc. $19.98.

Batman The Animated Series: The Complete Animated Series 1992 (Unrated)
Animated 1990s adventures of the Dark Knight of Gotham City battling Clayface ("Feat of Clay"), Mr. Freeze ("Heart of Ice"), the Joker ("Trial"), Catwoman ("You Scratch My Back"), the Riddler and many other villains. 107 episodes. 2379m; DVD. **C:** Voice(s) by Kevin Conroy; Efrem Zimbalist, Jr; Bob Hastings. **A:** Primary-Jr. High. **P:** Entertainment. **U:** Home. **Chl-Juv:** Animation & Cartoons, Action-Adventure. **Acq:** Purchase. **Dist:** Warner Home Video, Inc. $107.92.

Batman: The Animated Series—Out of the Shadows 199?
Presents episodes from the 1992-1995 animated television series about the Caped Crusader as he battles crime and injustice at night while in the day living as the normal-yet-wealthy Bruce Wayne. Includes: "Two-Face Parts I and II," "It's Never Too Late," and "I've Got Batman in My Basement." 4 episodes. 88m; DVD. **C:** Voice(s) by Kevin Conroy; Efrem Zimbalist, Jr; Bob Hastings; Loren Lester. **A:** Family. **P:** Entertainment. **U:** Home. **Chl-Juv:** Television Series, Animation & Cartoons, Action-Adventure. **Acq:** Purchase. **Dist:** Warner Home Video, Inc. $19.98.

Batman: The Animated Series—Secrets of the Caped Crusader 199?
Presents the 1992-1995 animated television series about the Caped Crusader as he battles crime and injustice at night while in the day living as the normal-yet-wealthy Bruce Wayne. Includes: "Heart of Ice," "The Cat and the Claw Parts I and II," and "See No Evil." 4 episodes. 89m; DVD. **C:** Voice(s) by Kevin Conroy; Efrem Zimbalist, Jr; Bob Hastings; Loren Lester. **A:** Family. **P:** Entertainment. **U:** Home. **Chl-Juv:** Television Series, Animation & Cartoons, Action-Adventure. **Acq:** Purchase. **Dist:** Warner Home Video, Inc. $19.98.

Batman: The Animated Series—Tales of the Dark Knight 199?
Presents episodes from the 1992-1995 animated television series about the Caped Crusader as he battles crime and injustice at night while in the day living as the normal-yet-wealthy Bruce Wayne. Includes: "The Underdwellers," "P.O.V.," "Forgotten," and "Be a Clown." 4 episodes. 112m; DVD. **C:** Voice(s) by Kevin Conroy; Efrem Zimbalist, Jr; Bob Hastings; Loren Lester. **A:** Family. **P:** Entertainment. **U:** Home. **Chl-Juv:** Television Series, Animation & Cartoons, Action-Adventure. **Acq:** Purchase. **Dist:** Warner Home Video, Inc. $19.98.

Batman: The Animated Series—Volume Four 1995
Presents episodes from the 1992-1995 animated television series about the Caped Crusader as he battles crime and injustice at night while in the day living as the normal-yet-wealthy Bruce Wayne. Batman's partnership with Robin ends and Batman takes on a new sidekick Nightwing along with Batgirl. 24 episodes. 521m; DVD. **C:** Kevin Conroy; Efrem Zimbalist, Jr; Bob Hastings; Loren Lester. **A:** Family. **P:** Entertainment. **U:** Home. **Chl-Juv:** Television Series, Animation & Cartoons, Action-Adventure. **Acq:** Purchase. **Dist:** Warner Home Video, Inc. $44.98.

Batman: The Animated Series—Volume One 1992
Presents the 1992-1995 animated television series about the Caped Crusader as he battles crime and injustice at night while in the day living as the normal-yet-wealthy Bruce Wayne; includes his enemies the Penguin, Catwoman, the Joker, Poison Ivy, and others. 28 episodes. 625m; DVD. **C:** Voice(s) by Kevin Conroy; Efrem Zimbalist, Jr; Bob Hastings; Loren Lester. **A:** Family. **P:** Entertainment. **U:** Home. **Chl-Juv:** Television Series, Animation & Cartoons, Action-Adventure. **Acq:** Purchase. **Dist:** Warner Home Video, Inc. $44.98.

Batman: The Animated Series—Volume Three 1994
Presents the 1992-1995 animated television series about the Caped Crusader as he battles crime and injustice at night while in the day living as the normal-yet-wealthy Bruce Wayne; includes his battling enemies Scarface, Rupert Thorne, the Penguin, and the Joker. 29 episodes. 609m; DVD. **C:** Voice(s) by Kevin Conroy; Efrem Zimbalist, Jr; Bob Hastings; Loren Lester. **A:** Family. **P:** Entertainment. **U:** Home. **Chl-Juv:** Television Series, Animation & Cartoons, Action-Adventure. **Acq:** Purchase. **Dist:** Warner Home Video, Inc. $44.98.

Batman: The Animated Series—Volume Two 1993
Presents the 1992-1995 animated television series about the Caped Crusader as he battles crime and injustice at night while in the day living as the normal-yet-wealthy Bruce Wayne; includes his enemies the Penguin, Catwoman, the Joker, Poison Ivy, and others. 28 episodes. 624m; DVD. **C:** Voice(s) by Kevin Conroy; Efrem Zimbalist, Jr; Bob Hastings; Loren Lester. **A:** Family. **P:** Entertainment. **U:** Home. **Chl-Juv:** Television Series, Animation & Cartoons, Action-Adventure. **Acq:** Purchase. **Dist:** Warner Home Video, Inc. $44.98.

Batman: The Brave and the Bold--The Complete First Season 2008
Cartoon Network 2008-2011. An updated version of the DC Comics hero as Batman partners with fellow superheroes, including Aquaman, Green Arrow, Blue Beetle, and others to fight villains. 26 episodes. 572m; DVD. **A:** Family. **P:** Entertainment. **U:** Home. **L:** English. **Chl-Juv:** Animation & Cartoons, Television Series. **Acq:** Purchase. **Dist:** WarnerArchive.com. $26.99.

Batman: The Brave and the Bold—Volume 2 2008 (Unrated)
Cartoon Network 2008-? animated adventure. Classic superhero storylines have Batman fighting evil on other planets, under water, in alternate dimensions, and villains that create evil toys at Christmas. 4 episodes. 88m; DVD. **C:** Voice(s) by Diedrich Bader. **A:** Primary-Jr. High. **P:** Entertainment. **U:** Home. **Chl-Juv:** Animation & Cartoons, Action-Adventure, Television Series. **Acq:** Purchase. **Dist:** Warner Home Video, Inc. $14.99.

The Batman: The Complete First Season 2004
Features the animated television series from the Cartoon Network with a young Dark Knight as he first meets classic foes such as the Joker, Catwoman, Mr. Freeze, and the Riddler with a full array of fancy gizmos. 13 episodes. 276m; DVD. **C:** Voice(s) by Rino Romano; Alastair Duncan; Kevin M. Richardson; Ming Na; Tom Kenny. **A:** Primary-Adult. **P:** Entertainment. **U:** Home. **Mov-Ent:** Television Series, Animation & Cartoons, Action-Adventure. **Acq:** Purchase. **Dist:** Warner Home Video, Inc. $19.99.

The Batman: The Complete Second Season 2005
Features the animated television series from the Cartoon Network with a young Dark Knight as he first meets classic foes such as the Joker, Catwoman, Mr. Freeze, and the Riddler with a full array of fancy gizmos; also, detective Gordon (future commissioner) offers Batman an alliance. 13 episodes. 338m; DVD. **C:** Voice(s) by Rino Romano; Alastair Duncan; Kevin M. Richardson; Tom Kenny; Mitch Pileggi; Danielle Judovits. **A:** Primary-Adult. **P:** Entertainment. **U:** Home. **Mov-Ent:** Television Series, Animation & Cartoons, Action-Adventure. **Acq:** Purchase. **Dist:** Warner Home Video, Inc. $19.98.

The Batman: The Complete Third Season 2005
Features the animated television series from the Cartoon Network with a young Dark Knight as he first meets classic foes such as the Joker, Catwoman, Mr. Freeze, and the Riddler with a full array of fancy gizmos; also, Gordon's daughter Barbara takes on the role of Batgirl. 13 episodes. 273m; DVD. **C:** Voice(s) by Rino Romano; Alastair Duncan; Kevin M. Richardson; Danielle Judovits; Ming Na; Tom Kenny. **A:** Primary-Adult. **P:** Entertainment. **U:** Home. **Mov-Ent:** Television Series, Animation & Cartoons, Action-Adventure. **Acq:** Purchase. **Dist:** Warner Home Video, Inc. $19.99.

Batman: The Dark Knight Returns, Part 2 2013 (PG-13)
Second part of the animated adaptation of the Frank Miller story of the same name. 78m; DVD, Blu-Ray, Streaming. **A:** Jr. High-Adult. **P:** Entertainment. **U:** Home. **L:** English. **Mov-Ent:** Action-Adventure, Animation & Cartoons. **Acq:** Purchase, Rent/Lease. **Dist:** Warner Home Video, Inc. $24.98 19.98 14.99.

The Batman: The Man Who Would Be Bat—Season 1, Volume 2 2004
Features the animated television series from the Cartoon Network with a young Dark Knight as he first meets classic foes such as The Joker, Catwoman, Mr. Freeze, and the Riddler with a full array of fancy gizmos. Includes: "The Man Who Would Be Bat," "The Big Chill," and "The Cat and the Bat." 3 epi-

sodes. 63m; DVD. **C:** Voice(s) by Rino Romano; Alastair Duncan; Kevin M. Richardson; Ming Na; Tom Kenny. **A:** Primary-Adult. **P:** Entertainment. **U:** Home. **Mov-Ent:** Television Series, Animation & Cartoons, Action-Adventure. **Acq:** Purchase. **Dist:** Warner Home Video, Inc. $14.97.

The Batman: Training for Power—Season 1, Volume 1 2004
Features the animated television series from the Cartoon Network with a young Dark Knight as he first meets classic foes such as The Joker, Catwoman, Mr. Freeze, and the Riddler with a full array of fancy gizmos. Includes: "The Bat in the Belfry," "Traction," and "Call of the Cobblepot." 3 episodes. 63m; DVD. **C:** Voice(s) by Rino Romano; Alastair Duncan; Kevin M. Richardson; Ming Na; Tom Kenny. **A:** Primary-Adult. **P:** Entertainment. **U:** Home. **Mov-Ent:** Television Series, Animation & Cartoons, Action-Adventure. **Acq:** Purchase. **Dist:** Warner Home Video, Inc. $14.96.

Batmania 1990
Engaging documentary traces the "career" of the winged superhero Batman from the beginnings in comic books through television and the movies. 45m; VHS. **A:** Family. **P:** Entertainment. **U:** Home. **Mov-Ent. Acq:** Purchase. **Dist:** Anchor Bay Entertainment. $9.98.

The Baton 1988
A program which explains how music can draw out people's innermost feelings. 27m; VHS. **Pr:** Jewish Chautauqua Society. **A:** Primary-Adult. **P:** Education. **U:** Institution, Home. **Gen-Edu:** Documentary Films. **Acq:** Purchase, Rent/Lease. **Dist:** Alden Films. $49.95.

Baton Rouge 1988 (Unrated) — ★★
Gigolo Antonio (Banderas) gets together with psychiatrist Anao (Abril) in a scheme to seduce one of her patients, the wealthy Isabel (Maura), who suffers from terrible nightmares. They plan to kill her wealthy ex-husband and accuse her of the crime in order to get her fortune. But there's an elaborate double-cross and things go back for all concerned. The spanish trio, all veterans of director Pedro Almodovar's films, certainly know how to steam up the screen. Spanish with subtitles. 90m; VHS. **C:** Antonio Banderas; Victoria Abril; Carmen Maura; Directed by Rafael Moleon; Written by Rafael Moleon; Agustin Diaz Yanes; Cinematography by Angel Luis Fernandez. **A:** College-Adult. **P:** Entertainment. **U:** Home. **L:** Spanish. **Mov-Ent:** Sex & Sexuality, Psychiatry. **Acq:** Purchase. **Dist:** Facets Multimedia Inc.; New Yorker Video.

Batouka: 1st International Festival of Percussion 1989
Celebrates the 1988 music festival which took place in Guadeloupe. 30m; VHS. **C:** Directed by Marc Haraux; Francois Migeat. **A:** Jr. High-Adult. **P:** Entertainment. **U:** Home. **Mov-Ent:** Music--Performance, Music--Jazz, Black Culture. **Acq:** Purchase. **Dist:** Rhapsody Films, Inc.; Facets Multimedia Inc. $39.95.

Bats 1988
A demonstration by a world renowned expert on bats, the world's only flying mammal. 16m; VHS, 3/4 U. **Pr:** Paulle Clarke. **A:** Family. **P:** Education. **U:** Institution, Home, SURA. **Gen-Edu:** Documentary Films, Animals. **Acq:** Purchase, Duplication License. **Dist:** Bullfrog Films, Inc.

Bats 1999 (PG-13) — ★½
B-grade comedy/thriller proves that people with a warped vision can create something that'll suck the life right out of you. Unfortunately, they use dialogue and plot, and not the winged critters in the title. A mad scientist (Gunton) working for the military genetically engineers some extra-nasty super-intelligent bats. Mad scientists being notoriously bad at cage maintenance, they escape. They then rile up a bunch of normally docile bats, turning them into vicious killers through some type of rodent peer pressure. After several attacks on his small Texas town, Sheriff Kimsey (Phillips) summons the nearest beautiful female bat expert (Meyer) and comic relief sidekick (Leon) so the bats have someone to chase around until the finale. They decide to freeze the bats in their cave, at the risk of trudging through a lot of guano to reach the end. You'll know how they feel. 91m; VHS, DVD, Wide, CC. **C:** Lou Diamond Phillips; Dina Meyer; Bob Gunton; Leon; Carlos Jacott; Oscar Rowland; David Shawn McConnell; Marcia Dangerfield; Directed by Louis Morneau; Written by John Logan; Cinematography by George Mooradian; Music by Graeme Revell. **Pr:** Dale Pollock. **A:** Jr. High-Adult. **P:** Entertainment. **U:** Home. **Mov-Ent. Acq:** Purchase. **Dist:** Sony Pictures Home Entertainment Inc.

Bats: Human Harvest 2007 (R) — **Bomb!**
Basically an in-name-only sequel to 1999's "Bats" (well, except for the genetically mutated flying rodents). A special ops squad is sent to Chechnya to retrieve a renegade doctor (Arana). Seems the doc has turned bats into flesh-eating monsters that are now infesting the local woods. Just terrible in every possible way, including its bad CGI. 84m; DVD. **C:** Tomas Arana; Michael Jace; David Chokachi; Melissa De Sousa; Directed by Jamie Dixon; Written by Chris Denk; Cinematography by Ivo Peitchev; Music by James Bairian; Louis Castle. **A:** Sr. High-Adult. **P:** Entertainment. **U:** Home. **Mov-Ent. Acq:** Purchase. **Dist:** Sony Pictures Home Entertainment Inc.

The Bats of Carlsbad 1986
This is the video shown to visitors at world-famous Carlsbad Caverns, now available for other use. It shows the nightly flight of the bats out of the caverns, and other footage. 5m; VHS, 3/4 U. **Pr:** USDAVA. **A:** Family. **P:** Entertainment. **U:** Institution, SURA. **Gen-Edu:** Wildlife, National Parks & Reserves. **Acq:** Purchase. **Dist:** National Audiovisual Center. $55.00.

Bats: The True Story 1999
Features facts about bats from a leading government authority. Includes bat rescuers discussing how to help injured bats and designing a bat house. 42m; VHS. **A:** Family. **P:** Education. **U:** Home. **Gen-Edu:** Animals, Wildlife. **Acq:** Purchase. **Dist:** Instructional Video. $19.95.

Battenburg Lace Making—A Beginners Primer 19??
Janet Pace provides instruction on the basics of Battenburg lacemaking. She also demonstrates five different filling stitches. Comes with a full-size pattern. 38m; VHS. **Pr:** Victorian Video Productions. **A:** Jr. High-Adult. **P:** Instruction. **U:** Home, Institution. **How-Ins:** Crafts, How-To. **Acq:** Purchase. **Dist:** Victorian Video/Yarn Barn of Kansas, Inc. $29.95.

Battered 1978 (Unrated) — ★½
Wife beating and its effects on three couples are dramatized in this movie, which also tells of the agencies now available to help these women. 98m; VHS. **C:** Karen Grassle; Mike Farrell; Joan Blondell; Howard Duff; LeVar Burton; Chip Fields; Directed by Peter Werner. **Pr:** Henry Jaffe Enterprises. **A:** Adult. **P:** Entertainment. **U:** Institution, SURA. **Mov-Ent:** TV Movies, Domestic Abuse. **Acq:** Purchase, Rent/Lease. **Dist:** Phoenix Learning Group. $49.95.

Battered 1991
A documentary on the problem of domestic violence, focusing on women who have been abused by husbands or boyfriends. Includes interviews with offenders now in treatment. 56m; VHS, 3/4 U. **Pr:** HBO. **A:** Sr. High-Adult. **P:** Education. **U:** Institution, CCTV, CATV, BCTV, SURA. **Hea-Sci:** Documentary Films, Domestic Abuse, Violence. **Acq:** Purchase, Duplication. **Dist:** Ambrose Video Publishing, Inc. $99.95.

Battered Teens 1981
The story of Lisa Hutchinson, an abused teenager, who has lived with beatings for most of her 16 years. 12m; VHS, 3/4 U. **Pr:** CBS. **A:** Jr. High-Adult. **P:** Education. **U:** Institution, SURA. **Gen-Edu:** Documentary Films, Adolescence, Child Abuse. **Acq:** Purchase, Rent/Lease. **Dist:** Home Vision Cinema.

Battered Wives, Shattered Lives 1984
An analysis of this common form of domestic violence and the motivation behind it. 90m; VHS, 3/4 U. **Pr:** New Jersey Network. **A:** Jr. High-Adult. **P:** Education. **U:** Institution. **Gen-Edu:** Documentary Films, Domestic Abuse, Psychology. **Acq:** Purchase. **Dist:** New Jersey Network.

The Battered Woman 197?
Insight to the crime of wife-beating with interviews with battered women. Also a psychiatrist, lawyer, judge, and hospital administrator discuss the problem at different levels in our society. 60m; VHS, 3/4 U. **C:** Hosted by Patrick McGrath. **Pr:** Maryland Center for Public Broadcasting. **A:** Adult. **P:** Education. **U:** Institution, CCTV, CATV, BCTV. **Gen-Edu:** Documentary Films, Domestic Abuse. **Acq:** Purchase, Rent/Lease. **Dist:** PBS Home Video.

***batteries not included** 1987 (PG) — ★★½
As a real estate developer fights to demolish a New York tenement, the five remaining residents are aided by tiny metal visitors from outer space in their struggle to save their home. Each resident gains a renewed sense of life in this sentimental, wholesome family film produced by Spielberg. Cronyn and Tandy keep the schmaltz from getting out of hand. Neat little space critters. 107m; VHS, DVD. **C:** Hume Cronyn; Jessica Tandy; Frank McRae; Michael Carmine; Elizabeth Pena; Dennis Boutsikaris; James LeGros; Directed by Matthew Robbins; Written by Matthew Robbins; Brad Bird; Brent Maddock; S.S. Wilson; Cinematography by John McPherson; Music by James Horner. **Pr:** Mark Huffam; Amblin Entertainment. **A:** Family. **P:** Entertainment. **U:** Home. **Mov-Ent:** Science Fiction, Fantasy, Aging. **Acq:** Purchase. **Dist:** Alpha Video; Movies Unlimited; Universal Studios Home Video. $14.98.

Battery Changing/Refueling 1995
Offers proper methods to refuel gas, diesel and liquid propane, in electric powered trucks. 11m; VHS. **A:** Adult. **P:** Professional. **U:** Institution. **L:** Spanish. **Bus-Ind:** Job Training, Safety Education. **Acq:** Rent/Lease. **Dist:** National Safety Council, California Chapter, Film Library.

Battery Charging Safety 1995
Offers safety precautions when handling batteries on forklifts and pallet jacks. 10m; VHS. **A:** Adult. **P:** Professional. **U:** Institution. **L:** Spanish. **Bus-Ind:** Job Training, Safety Education. **Acq:** Purchase, Rent/Lease. **Dist:** National Safety Council, California Chapter, Film Library. $175.00.

Battery Load Test Using Vat 40 1988
Offers instruction on specific aspects of automotive maintenance and repair. 6m; VHS. **A:** Adult. **P:** Instruction. **U:** Institution. **How-Ins:** Automobiles. **Acq:** Purchase. **Dist:** RMI Media. $29.95.

Batting with Ted Williams: The Science of Hitting 1972
Two vintage instructional films on the fundamentals of good hitting. 53m; VHS. **A:** Adult. **P:** Instruction. **U:** Home. **Spo-Rec:** Baseball, Sports--General. **Acq:** Purchase. **Dist:** Baseball Direct. $29.95.

The Battle 19??
Reenactment that captures the sights and sounds of the first battle between the blue and the gray after a long hard winter during the Civil War. Features musical score by Mike Lynch, narrative by Bill Coleman, vocals by Susan Jacobson, and filming by Jan Kurtis. Filmed on location in Fort Stevens. 40m; VHS. **A:** Jr. High-Adult. **P:** Education. **U:** Home. **Gen-Edu:** History--U.S., Civil War. **Acq:** Purchase. **Dist:** Camelot Media. $15.00.

Battle Action 1984
Presents four 30-minute films of the most exciting combat footage in history; "The Battle for New Britain—Dec. '42," "The Battle for Leyte Gulf," "Action at Angaur," and "The Fleet That Came to Stay." 120m/B/W; VHS. **Pr:** Ferde Grofe Films. **A:** Sr. High-Adult. **P:** Education. **U:** Institution, Home. **Gen-Edu:** Documentary Films, World War Two. **Acq:** Purchase. **Dist:** Bennett Marine Video; Military/Combat Stock Footage Library. $29.95. **Indiv. Titles:** 1. The Battle of New Britain-Dec.'42 2. The Battle for Leyte Gulf 3. Action at Angaur 4. The Fleet that Came to Stay.

Battle at Bloody Beach 1961 — ★
Craig Benson (Murphy) was separated from his bride, Ruth (Michaels), when the Japanese invaded Manila. Two years later, he's still searching for her and teams up with Army Sgt. Sackler (Crosby), who's working with Filipino insurgents. Ruth, thinking Craig died, is involved with guerilla leader Julio (Rey), when Craig finds her. Catalina Island made for a cheap location for this poorly-scripted, no-budget drama. 79m/B/W; DVD. **C:** Audie Murphy; Dolores Michaels; Gary Crosby; Alejandro Rey; Directed by Herbert Coleman; Written by Richard Maibaum; Willard Willingham; Cinematography by Kenneth Peach, Sr.; Music by Henry Vars. **A:** Sr. High-Adult. **P:** Entertainment. **U:** Home. **L:** English. **Mov-Ent:** World War Two, Pacific Islands, Marriage. **Acq:** Purchase. **Dist:** Fox Home Entertainment.

The Battle at Durango: First Ever World Mountain Bike Championships 1991
The world of mountain biking explodes on this one-hour video covering six days of action at the World Mountain Biking Championships in Durango, Colorado. Events include the Cross-Country Championship, the grueling hill climb, the duel-slalom and the breathtaking downhill. 60m; VHS. **Pr:** New and Unique Videos. **A:** Jr. High-Adult. **P:** Entertainment. **U:** Home. **Spo-Rec:** Sports--General, Bicycling. **Acq:** Purchase. **Dist:** New & Unique Videos. $29.95.

Battle Beneath the Earth 1968 — ★★
The commies try to undermine democracy once again when American scientists discover a Chinese plot to invade the U.S. via a series of underground tunnels. Perhaps a tad jingoistic. 112m; VHS, DVD. **C:** Kerwin Mathews; Peter Arne; Viviane Ventura; Robert Ayres; Directed by Montgomery Tully. **Pr:** MGM. **A:** Jr. High-Adult. **P:** Entertainment. **U:** Home. **Mov-Ent:** Science Fiction, International Relations. **Acq:** Purchase. **Dist:** Warner Home Video, Inc. $59.95.

Battle Beyond the Stars 1980 (PG) — ★★½
The planet Akir must be defended against alien rapscallions in this intergalactic Corman creation. Sayles authored the screenplay and co-authored the story on which it was based. 105m; VHS, DVD, Wide. **C:** Richard Thomas; Robert Vaughn; George Peppard; Sybil Danning; Sam Jaffe; John Saxon; Darlanne Fluegel; Jeff Corey; Morgan Woodward; Marta Kristen; Ron Ross; Eric Morris; Directed by Jimmy T. Murakami; Written by John Sayles; Cinematography by Daniel Lacambre; Music by James Horner. **Pr:** Orion Pictures. **A:** Primary-Adult. **P:** Entertainment. **U:** Home. **Mov-Ent:** Science Fiction, Space Exploration. **Acq:** Purchase. **Dist:** Lions Gate Television Corp. $19.98.

Battle Beyond the Sun 1963 (Unrated) — ★★
Former Russian movie "Nebo Zowet" is Americanized. Everyone is trying to send a mission to Mars. Roger Corman was the producer, director Coppola used the pseudonym Thomas Colchart. 75m; VHS, DVD. **C:** Edd Perry; Arla Powell; Bruce Hunter; Andy Stewart; Directed by Francis Ford Coppola; Written by Nicholas Colbert; Edwin Palmer; Music by Les Baxter. **Pr:** Filmgroup. **A:** Jr. High-Adult. **P:** Entertainment. **U:** Home. **Mov-Ent:** Science Fiction, Space Exploration. **Acq:** Purchase. **Dist:** Sinister Cinema. $16.95.

Battle Circus 1953 (Unrated) — ★½
Sappy drama casts Bogart as a surgeon at a M*A*S*H unit during the Korean War. Allyson is a combat nurse who finds love amongst the harsh reality of a war zone. Bogart was badly miscast and his performance proves it. Weak script and uninspired performances don't help this depressing story. 90m/B/W; DVD. **C:** Humphrey Bogart; June Allyson; Keenan Wynn; Robert Keith; William Campbell; Perry Sheehan; Patricia Tiernan; Adele Longmire; Jonathon Cott; Ann Morrison; Helen Winston; Sarah Selby; Danny Chang; Philip Ahn; Steve Forrest; Jeff Richards; Dick Simmons; Directed by Richard Brooks; Written by Richard Brooks; Cinematography by John Alton; Music by Lennie Hayton. **Pr:** Pandro S. Berman; MGM. **A:** Sr. High-Adult. **P:** Entertainment. **U:** Home. **Mov-Ent:** Korean War, Romance. **Acq:** Purchase. **Dist:** WarnerArchive.com. $19.98.

The Battle/Contact Ambush 1965
"The Battle" describes Operation Piranha from start to finish, including the tactical and logistical aspects, climaxing in the capture of Viet Cong. "Contact Ambush" contains combat footage of an attack on a Viet Cong village by a Marine patrol. 27m; VHS. **TV Std:** NTSC, PAL. **Pr:** U.S. Government. **A:** Jr. High-Adult. **P:** Education. **U:** Institution, Home. **Gen-Edu:** Documentary Films, Vietnam War, Military History. **Acq:** Purchase. **Dist:** International Historic Films Inc. $24.95.

Battle Creek Brawl 1980 (Unrated) — ★★
Jerry Kwan (Jackie Chan) is forced to fight in a brutal martial arts competition to save the family business from a mobster. Ironically, Chan had fled the Triads (Chinese mobsters) who were sent after him by an angry ex director who wanted to make him the next Bruce Lee, only to make this film under another director who wanted to make him Bruce Lee. The irony of the real-life situation is probably the most interesting thing about the

movie. 95m; DVD, Blu-Ray. **C:** Jackie Chan; Jose Ferrer; Kristine DeBell; Mako; Ron Max; David S. Sheiner; Rosalind Chao; Lenny Montana; Pat E. Johnson; H.B. Haggerty; Chao-Li Chi; Joycelyne Lew; Directed by Robert Clouse; Written by Robert Clouse; Fred Weintraub; Cinematography by Robert C. Jessup; Music by Lalo Schifrin. **A:** Sr. High-Adult. **P:** Entertainment. **U:** Home. **Mov-Ent:** Martial Arts, Action-Comedy. **Acq:** Purchase. **Dist:** Fox Home Entertainment. $9.98.

Battle Cry 1955 — ★★★
A group of U.S. Marines train, romance, and enter battle in WWII. But it takes 'em a while to do it. Walsh's film focuses on the psychology of training men to fight, and to wait for the chance. Uris's script (from his own novel) also spends an inordinate amount of time on the love lives of the soldiers. 169m; VHS, DVD, Wide, CC. **C:** Van Heflin; Aldo Ray; Mona Freeman; Tab Hunter; Dorothy Malone; Anne Francis; James Whitmore; Raymond Massey; William Campbell; John Lupton; L.Q. Jones; Perry Lopez; Fess Parker; Jonas Applegarth; Tommy Cook; Felix Noriego; Nancy Olson; Susan Morrow; Carleton Young; Rhys Williams; Gregory Walcott; Frank Ferguson; Sarah Selby; Willis Bouchey; Directed by Raoul Walsh; Written by Leon Uris; Cinematography by Sidney Hickox; Music by Max Steiner. **Pr:** Raoul Walsh; Raoul Walsh; Warner Bros. **A:** Family. **P:** Entertainment. **U:** Home. **Mov-Ent:** Australia, World War Two. **Acq:** Purchase. **Dist:** Warner Home Video, Inc.

The Battle for Europe: The War on Land and Sea 19??
Four volume series reviewing WWII events of Europe. 60m; VHS. **A:** Jr. High-Sr. High. **P:** Education. **U:** Institution. **Gen-Edu:** World War Two, Military History. **Acq:** Purchase. **Dist:** Cambridge Educational. $39.95.
Indiv. Titles: 1. Churchill's War 2. Dunkirk 3. Waffen-SS 4. D-Day.

The Battle for Marjah 2011
Follows Bravo Company, 1st Battalion, 6th Marines as they target the Taliban stronghold of Marjah, Afghanistan. 84m; DVD, Blu-Ray. **A:** Adult. **P:** Education. **U:** Home. **Gen-Edu:** Afghanistan, Military History. **Acq:** Purchase. **Dist:** Acorn Media Group Inc. $34.99.

The Battle for Midway: Discovery of the U.S.S. Yorktown 1998
Overviews the battle at Midway using historical combat footage, recounts actions of heroism, and explains technology used in locating and photographing sunken ships. 84m; VHS, DVD; Closed Captioned. **A:** Jr. High-Sr. High. **P:** Education. **U:** Institution. **Gen-Edu:** Military History, World War Two. **Acq:** Purchase. **Dist:** Zenger Media. $14.95.

The Battle for North Africa 1985
The North African battles with footage of Rommel, Montgomery and Patton, the battles of southern Italy, and the seige of Monte Casino. 93m/B/W; VHS. **Pr:** Ferde Grofe Films. **A:** Jr. High-Adult. **P:** Education. **U:** Institution, Home. **Gen-Edu:** Documentary Films, World War Two. **Acq:** Purchase. **Dist:** Bennett Marine Video; Military/Combat Stock Footage Library. $29.95.

Battle for Our Minds 1992
Three-part series which studies the attitudes of the classical/biblical age, the Enlightenment era, and post-Christian secularism about such subjects as religion and public life, science, law and government, the nature of life, and the arts. Study guide is included. 30m; VHS. **A:** Sr. High-Adult. **P:** Religious. **U:** Institution. **Gen-Edu:** Religion, History. **Acq:** Purchase. **Dist:** Ligonier Ministries Inc. $39.00.

The Battle for Peace: Shimon Peres 1996
Documentary of Simon Peres, the leading Israeli politician campaigning for peace in the Middle East. Also features the late Prime Minister Rabin and his bid for peace. Narrated by Itzhak Perlman. 57m; VHS. **A:** Adult. **P:** Education. **U:** Home. **Gen-Edu:** Documentary Films, Middle East, War--General. **Acq:** Purchase, Rent/Lease. **Dist:** Filmakers Library Inc. $195.

The Battle for San Bruno Mountain 1993
Summarizes the 25-year history of the struggle by environmentalists over the protection of San Bruno Mountain, located two miles south of San Francisco. Covers the story of America's first use of the Endangered Species Act's Habitat Conservation Plan (HCP). Contains interviews with conservationists, developers, and local residents. 26m; VHS. **A:** Jr. High-Adult. **P:** Education. **U:** Institution. **Hea-Sci:** Documentary Films, Ecology & Environment, Wilderness Areas. **Acq:** Purchase. **Dist:** Cambridge Educational. $25.00.

Battle for Terra 2009 (PG) — ★★★
A sci-fi story with a moral and some great 3-D animation. Having ruined Earth, human survivors are seeking another planet to colonize. This leads them to peaceful Terra, where the Terrans have set aside weapons and war long ago. Rebellious teen Mala (Wood) saves the life of human pilot Jim (Wilson) and, in return, asks for his help in rescuing her father who is a prisoner. The Terrans themselves are in danger since General Hammer (Cox) wants to get rid of the pesky natives and make the planet Earthlings-only. Don't worry, it's still fun as well. 85m; Blu-Ray, Wide, CC. **C:** Voice(s) by Evan Rachel Wood; Luke Wilson; Brian Cox; James Garner; Chris Evans; Dennis Quaid; David Cross; Danny Glover; Amanda Peet; Directed by Aristomenis Tsirbas; Written by Evan Spiliotopolos; Music by Abel Korzeniowski. **Pr:** Keith Calder; Jessica Wu; Dane Allan Smith; Ryan Colucci; Snoot Entertainment; MeniThings Entertainment; Roadside Attractions. **A:** Family. **P:** Entertainment. **U:** Home. **L:** English. **Mov-Ent. Acq:** Purchase. **Dist:** Alpha Video; Lions Gate Entertainment Inc.; Movies Unlimited.

Battle for the Elephants 2013 (Unrated)
With their ivory tusks now literally worth their weight in gold, elephants are finding it harder to survive in the wild, as poachers and other criminals do whatever they can to keep their ivory supply intact. At the same time, scientists are studying the majestic animals more closely, as they have realized that elephants are among the most complex on the planet thanks to their intelligence, highly structured communal living arrangements, and ability to mourn, love, and even communicate over large distances in the wild. 50m; DVD. **A:** Family. **P:** Education, Entertainment. **U:** Home, Institution. **Mov-Ent:** Africa, Animals, Documentary Films. **Acq:** Purchase. **Dist:** $24.95.

Battle for the Falklands 1984
Documents the complete account of the dramatic battle for the Falklands. 110m; VHS. **Pr:** Thorn. **A:** Sr. High-Adult. **P:** Education. **U:** Home. **Gen-Edu:** Documentary Films, War--General, Great Britain. **Acq:** Purchase. **Dist:** MPI Media Group. $29.95.

Battle for the Planet of the Apes 1973 (G) — ★★
A tribe of human atomic bomb mutations are out to make life miserable for the peaceful ape tribe. The story is told primarily in flashback with the opening and closing sequences taking place in the year A.D. 2670. Final chapter in the five-movie simian saga. 96m; VHS, DVD, Blu-Ray, Wide, CC. **C:** Roddy McDowall; Lew Ayres; John Huston; Paul Williams; Claude Akins; Severn Darden; Natalie Trundy; Austin Stoker; Noah Keen; Michael Stearns; John Landis; Directed by J. Lee Thompson; Written by John W. Corrington; Joyce H. Corrington; Cinematography by Richard H. Kline; Music by Leonard Rosenman. **Pr:** 20th Century-Fox. **A:** Family. **P:** Entertainment. **U:** Home. **Mov-Ent:** Science Fiction. **Acq:** Purchase. **Dist:** Fox Home Entertainment; Movies Unlimited; Alpha Video. $19.98.

Battle for the Planet Series: Eight Litres a Minute 19??
Examines the high levels of air pollution which can currently be found in Mexico and Brazil. 31m; VHS. **Pr:** National Film Board of Canada. **A:** Jr. High-Adult. **P:** Education. **U:** Institution. **Gen-Edu:** Ecology & Environment. **Acq:** Purchase. **Dist:** National Film Board of Canada; Indiana University.

Battle for the Planet Series: Greening the Land 19??
Investigates the impact of deforestation on the people in Sudan and presents the case for local community control in the regeneration of deforested lands. 32m; VHS. **Pr:** National Film Board of Canada. **A:** Jr. High-Adult. **P:** Education. **U:** Institution. **Gen-Edu:** Ecology & Environment. **Acq:** Purchase. **Dist:** National Film Board of Canada; Indiana University.

Battle for the Planet Series: Kingdom of the Third Day 19??
Centers on the dumping of nuclear waste in the Irish Sea. Third part of a five-part series. 31m; VHS. **Pr:** National Film Board of Canada. **A:** Jr. High-Adult. **P:** Education. **U:** Institution. **Gen-Edu:** Ecology & Environment, Nuclear Energy, Ireland. **Acq:** Purchase. **Dist:** National Film Board of Canada; Indiana University.

Battle for the Planet Series: People Count 19??
Explores the social, political, and economic issues associated with the population growth in Kenya, the fastest growing country in the world. Part four of a five-part series. 30m; VHS. **Pr:** National Film Board of Canada. **A:** Jr. High-Adult. **P:** Education. **U:** Institution. **Gen-Edu:** Ecology & Environment, Sociology, Politics & Government. **Acq:** Purchase. **Dist:** National Film Board of Canada; Indiana University.

Battle for the Planet Series: Shifting Sands 19??
Discusses the processes associated with the desertification of northern China. Final part of a five-part series. 31m; VHS. **Pr:** National Film Board of Canada. **A:** Jr. High-Adult. **P:** Education. **U:** Institution. **Gen-Edu:** Ecology & Environment, China. **Acq:** Purchase. **Dist:** National Film Board of Canada; Indiana University.

Battle for the Skies: History of the British Royal Air Force 1918-2008 2011 (Unrated)
A documentary following the history of the British Royal Air Force. 510m/B/W; DVD. **A:** Sr. High-Adult. **P:** Education. **U:** Home. **Gen-Edu:** Documentary Films, Military History. **Acq:** Purchase. **Dist:** Acorn Media Group Inc. $24.99.

Battle for the Soul of Russia 1992
Upheaval in the former Soviet Union has resulted in a rich harvest for some 350 Western missionary groups in the country. Includes first-hand footage of how a religious revival has been spawned from chaos. 51m; VHS. **Pr:** VISN Television. **A:** Sr. High-Adult. **P:** Religious. **U:** Institution, Home. **Gen-Edu:** USSR. **Acq:** Purchase. **Dist:** Vision Video/Gateway Films. $19.95.

Battle for the Trees 19??
Examines the strategies of both sides involved in the liquidation of the public forests located along the West Coast of Canada. Includes comments from citizens, scientists, loggers, environmentalists, natives, corporations, and government officials. Emphasizes the need to balance economic concerns with environmental preservation. 57m; VHS. **Pr:** National Film Board of Canada. **A:** Jr. High-Adult. **P:** Education. **U:** Institution. **Gen-Edu:** Ecology & Environment, Canada. **Acq:** Purchase. **Dist:** National Film Board of Canada; Indiana University.

Battle for the United States 1988
This film follows the true story behind the FBI's efforts to track down communists and other subversives. 29m/B/W; VHS. **Pr:** Fireworks Pictures. **A:** Jr. High-Adult. **P:** Education. **U:** Institution, Home. **Gen-Edu:** History--U.S., Intelligence Service. **Acq:** Purchase. **Dist:** Silver Mine Video Inc. $14.95.

Battle Girls Time Paradox: Complete Collection 2013 (Unrated)
Anime featuring a young high school girl who falls through a space/time warp into an alternate history version of feudal Japan composed of attractive women. 325m; DVD, Blu-Ray. **A:** Jr. High-Adult. **P:** Entertainment. **U:** Home. **L:** English, Japanese. **Gen-Edu:** Anime, Fantasy. **Acq:** Purchase. **Dist:** Section 23. $69.98 59.98.

Battle Heater 1989 (Unrated) — ★
Two junk collectors who spend their days rummaging through landfills find a kotatsu heater (a Japanese table) with a sacred seal on it. Once they remove the seal it becomes a man-eating monster and begins devouring the tenants of the apartment building they live in. Fortunately a punk rock band lives there, and they specialize in whoopin' animated house appliances. 93m; DVD. **C:** Pappara Kawai; Yasuko Tomita; Directed by Joji Iida. **A:** Jr. High-Adult. **P:** Entertainment. **U:** Home. **L:** English, Japanese. **Mov-Ent. Acq:** Purchase. **Dist:** Navarre Corp. $19.98.

Battle Hell 1956 — ★★
The true story of how a British ship was attacked by the Chinese Peoples Liberation Army on the Yangtze River in 1949. 112m/B/W; VHS. **C:** Richard Todd; Akim Tamiroff; Keye Luke; Directed by Michael Anderson, Sr.; Written by Eric Ambler. **Pr:** Distributors Corporation of America. **A:** Jr. High-Adult. **P:** Entertainment. **U:** Home. **Mov-Ent:** Action-Adventure, War--General. **Acq:** Purchase. **Dist:** Unknown Distributor.

Battle Hell: Vietnam 1984
Takes a look at the choppers, air strikes and air troops that were involved in the Vietnam War. Also includes a captured enemy newsreel depicting ambush and assault tactics. 113m; VHS. **Pr:** Ferde Grofe Films. **A:** Sr. High-Adult. **P:** Education. **U:** Institution, Home. **Gen-Edu:** Documentary Films, Vietnam War, Armed Forces--U.S. **Acq:** Purchase. **Dist:** Military/Combat Stock Footage Library; Bennett Marine Video. $29.95.
Indiv. Titles: 1. The Sky Soldiers 2. The Black Horse Regiment 3. The Air Mobile Division 4. Know Your Enemy.

Battle Hymn 1957 (Unrated) — ★★½
After accidentally bombing an orphanage as a WWII fighter pilot, Dean Hess (Hudson) becomes a minister. He returns to the Air Force in 1950 to train Korean pilots in Seoul and winds up building a home for the local orphans. True story on which the real Hess served as technical advisor. 109m; VHS, DVD, CC. **C:** Rock Hudson; Dan Duryea; Martha Hyer; Anna Kashfi; Don DeFore; Jock Mahoney; Carl Benton Reid; Alan Hale, Jr.; Richard Loo; Philip Ahn; Directed by Douglas Sirk; Written by Charles Grayson; Vincent B. Evans; Cinematography by Russell Metty; Music by Frank Skinner. **Pr:** Ross Hunter; Universal Pictures. **A:** Jr. High-Adult. **P:** Entertainment. **U:** Home. **Mov-Ent:** Adoption, Korean War, Biography; Military. **Acq:** Purchase. **Dist:** Universal Music and Video Distribution. $14.98.

Battle in Heaven 2005 (Unrated) — ★★
Set in Mexico, Marcos (Hernandez) is a general's chauffeur whose life collapses around him when the baby he and his wife kidnapped for ransom unexpectedly dies. He seeks out Ana (Mushkadiz)?the general's daughter and a prostitute in her spare time—to ease his pain. She in turn entrusts Marcos, her driver since she was a young child, with her secret life. For some, this is cutting edge art house material that lays bare the lives of Mexico's haves and have-nots; others may view the nonprofessional actors and blandly graphic sex scenes as a big yawn. 94m; DVD. **C:** Marcos Hernandez; Anapola Mushkadiz; Berta Ruiz; David Bornstien; Rosalinda Ramirez; El Abuelo; Directed by Carlos Reygadas; Written by Carlos Reygadas; Cinematography by Diego Martinez Vignatti; Music by John Tavener; Marcha Cordobesa. **Pr:** Philippe Bober; Florence Schapiro; Lene Ingemann; Mantarraya Producciones; No Dream Cinema; Tarantula; Tartan Films. **A:** College-Adult. **P:** Entertainment. **U:** Home. **L:** Spanish. **Mov-Ent:** Crime Drama, Mexico, Sex & Sexuality. **Acq:** Purchase. **Dist:** Palisades Tartan Video. $24.99.

Battle in Seattle 2007 (R) — ★★
Dramatic (and heavily biased) reenactment of five days in 1999 when the World Trade Organization convened in Seattle and was met with tens of thousands of activists upset with the corporate entity's globalization policies and damage to the environment. Soon, however, the protests turned violent, with the police donning riot gear and the National Guard swooping in to clean up the mess. All the players get their turn: good-guy cop Dale (Harrelson) and his pregnant wife Ella (Theron), protest leader Jay (Henderson) and his angry girlfriend Lou (Rodriguez), over-zealous newswoman Jean (Nielsen), and finally, non-fictionalized Mayor Tobin (Liotta) to ineffectively calm both groups' fears. Despite writer-director Townsend's attempt for grit and realism, silly monologues and overt melodrama reek of pure Hollywood. 100m; Blu-Ray, On Demand, Wide. **C:** Andre Benjamin; Jennifer Carpenter; Michelle Rodriguez; Martin Henderson; Ray Liotta; Woody Harrelson; Charlize Theron; Connie Nielsen; Channing Tatum; Isaach de Bankole; Joshua Jackson; Rade Serbedzija; Directed by Stuart Townsend; Written by Stuart Townsend; Cinematography by Barry Ackroyd; Music by One Point Six. **Pr:** Maxime Remillard; Stuart Townsend; Kirk Shaw; Mary Aloe; Stuart Townsend; Remstar; Insight Film Studios; Proud Mary Entertainment; ThinkFilm; Redwood Palm Pictures. **A:** Sr. High-Adult. **P:** Entertainment. **U:** Home. **L:** English. **Mov-Ent:** Politics & Government. **Acq:** Purchase. **Dist:** Alpha Video; Screen Media Ventures, LLC; Movies Unlimited.

Battle Is Their Birthright 1989
A propaganda documentary on the different attitudes of the citizens of Japan, Germany, the U.S.S.R. and China who, born after WWI have "battle as their birthright." 18m; VHS, 3/4 U. **Pr:**

John Grierson. **A:** Jr. High-Adult. **P:** Education. **U:** Institution, SURA. **Gen-Edu:** World War One, Propaganda. **Acq:** Purchase, Rent/Lease. **Dist:** National Film Board of Canada.

Battle Line—The Great Battles of World War 2: Vol. 1 19??
Four programs include early WWII battles that put Britain and its allies on the defensive from Nazi aggression. 104m/B/W; VHS. **TV Std:** NTSC, PAL, SECAM. **A:** Sr. High-Adult. **P:** Education. **U:** Home, Institution. **Gen-Edu:** World War Two. **Acq:** Purchase. **Dist:** International Historic Films Inc. $19.95.
Indiv. Titles: 1. Invasion of Norway 2. Dunkirk 3. Battle of Britain 4. Invasion of Southern France.

Battle Line—The Great Battles of World War 2: Vol. 2 19??
Four programs focus on the land war in western Europe after the invasion at Normandy. 104m/B/W; VHS. **TV Std:** NTSC, PAL, SECAM. **A:** Sr. High-Adult. **P:** Education. **U:** Home, Institution. **Gen-Edu:** World War Two. **Acq:** Purchase. **Dist:** International Historic Films Inc. $19.95.
Indiv. Titles: 1. Dieppe 2. Omaha Beach 3. Breakout from Normandy 4. Bridgehead at Rhine.

Battle Line—The Great Battles of World War 2, Vol. 3 19??
Explores efforts of Allies to turn tide against Nazis from Mediterranean position. 104m; VHS. **TV Std:** NTSC, PAL, SECAM. **A:** College-Adult. **P:** Education. **U:** Home, Institution. **Gen-Edu:** World War Two. **Acq:** Purchase. **Dist:** International Historic Films Inc. $19.95.
Indiv. Titles: 1. Malta 2. Operation Torch 3. Tobruk 4. El Alamein.

Battle Line—The Great Battles of World War 2: Vol. 4 19??
Contains four programs covering difficult battles with staggering losses for the Allies that forestalled their efforts to contain the Nazis. 104m; VHS. **TV Std:** NTSC, PAL, SECAM. **A:** Sr. High-Adult. **P:** Education. **U:** Home, Institution. **Gen-Edu:** World War Two. **Acq:** Purchase. **Dist:** International Historic Films Inc. $19.95.
Indiv. Titles: 1. Crete 2. Anzio 3. Monte Cassino 4. Arnhem.

Battle Line—The Great Battles of World War 2: Vol. 5 19??
Four programs witness the final defeats of the Germans as the Allies overrun the remaining Nazi outposts in central Europe. 104m; VHS. **TV Std:** NTSC, PAL, SECAM. **A:** Sr. High-Adult. **P:** Education. **U:** Home, Institution. **Gen-Edu:** World War Two. **Acq:** Purchase. **Dist:** International Historic Films Inc. $19.95.
Indiv. Titles: 1. Stalingrad 2. Battle of the Gothic Line 3. Battle of the Bulge 4. Fall of Berlin.

Battle: Los Angeles 2011 (PG-13) — ★★
Sci-fi action for those who just want to be entertained by the loud, undemanding, and familiar. Stoic Marine Staff Sgt. Nantz (Eckhart) and his platoon are the last line of defense, first on the Santa Monica streets, and then L.A. when Earth is attacked by outer space invaders who want to colonize our planet. There's no wink-wink to the audience as the script and the actors take their mission seriously as good soldiers should amidst all the pyrotechnics. 116m; Blu-Ray, Wide, CC. **C:** Aaron Eckhart; Michelle Rodriguez; Bridget Moynahan; Ramon Rodriguez; Cory Hardrict; Michael Pena; Lucas Till; Bryce Cass; Ne-Yo; Directed by Jonathan Liebesman; Written by Christopher Bertolini; Cinematography by Lukas Ettlin; Music by Brian Tyler. **Pr:** Neal H. Moritz; Ori Marmur; Columbia Pictures; Relativity Media; Original Film; Sony Pictures Home Entertainment Inc. **A:** Jr. High-Adult. **P:** Entertainment. **U:** Home. **L:** English. **Mov-Ent:** Science Fiction. **Acq:** Purchase. **Dist:** Sony Pictures Home Entertainment Inc.; Movies Unlimited; Alpha Video.

Battle Night: The Krump Wars 2005 (Unrated)
Director David LaChapelle explores the origins of the L.A. underground dance movement called "krumping" by filming an amateur contest. 79m; DVD. **A:** Jr. High-Adult. **P:** Entertainment. **U:** Home. **Gen-Edu:** Documentary Films, Dance. **Acq:** Purchase. **Dist:** Razor Digital.

The Battle of Algiers 1966 — ★★★½
Famous, powerful, award-winning film depicting the uprisings against French Colonial rule in 1954 Algiers. A seminal documentary-style film which makes most political films seem ineffectual by comparison in its use of non-professional actors, gritty photography, realistic violence, and a boldly propagandistic sense of social outrage. 123m/B/W; VHS, DVD, Blu-Ray, 3/4 U. **TV Std:** NTSC, PAL. **C:** Yacef Saadi; Jean Martin; Brahim Haggiag; Tommaso Neri; Samia Kerbash; Fawzia el Kader; Michele Kerbash; Mohamed Ben Kassen; Directed by Gillo Pontecorvo; Written by Gillo Pontecorvo; Franco Solinas; Cinematography by Marcello Gatti; Music by Gillo Pontecorvo; Ennio Morricone. **Pr:** Antonio Musu; Yacef Saadi; Casbah Igor Films. **A:** Sr. High-Adult. **P:** Entertainment. **U:** Home. **L:** French. **Mov-Ent:** Drama, War--General, Documentary Films. **Awds:** Venice Film Fest. '66: Film. **Acq:** Purchase. **Dist:** International Historic Films Inc.; Tapeworm Video Distributors Inc. $29.95.

Battle of Antietam 1988
Historian William Brown talks about the battle that left 26,000 people dead. 60m; VHS, 3/4 U. **Pr:** Maryland Center for Public Broadcasting. **A:** Jr. High-Adult. **P:** Education. **U:** Institution, CCTV, CATV, BCTV. **Gen-Edu:** Civil War. **Acq:** Purchase. **Dist:** Maryland Public Television; Inspired Corp. $29.95.

Battle of Arnhem 1990
The story of "The Bridge too Far" is told, and film, photos and the sounds of Field Marshall Montgomery's plans are experienced. 47m; VHS. **Pr:** Films for the Humanities. **A:** Sr. High-

Adult. **P:** Education. **U:** Institution. **Gen-Edu:** Documentary Films, World War Two. **Acq:** Purchase. **Dist:** Films for the Humanities & Sciences. $149.00.

The Battle of Austerlitz 1960 (PG) — ★★
Ambitious but numbing costume drama about the events leading up to the epic battle between Napoleon and the overwhelming forces of the Czar and the Austrian Emperor at Austerlitz. Napoleon won. Film has been drastically cut from original 166 minute release. Watch director Gance's silent version, "Napoleon," for a truly epic experience. 123m; VHS. **C:** Claudia Cardinale; Martine Carol; Rossano Brazzi; Vittorio De Sica; Jean Marais; Ettore Manni; Jack Palance; Orson Welles; Directed by Abel Gance. **A:** Sr. High-Adult. **P:** Entertainment. **U:** Home. **Mov-Ent:** War--General. **Acq:** Purchase. **Dist:** Lions Gate Television Corp.; Tapeworm Video Distributors Inc. $69.95.

The Battle of Beech Hall 1982
Documents the dramatic 8-month struggle by a group of senior citizens to save their homes and preserve their cherished community. 28m; VHS, 3/4 U. **Pr:** Christopher Wilson. **A:** Sr. High-Adult. **P:** Education. **U:** Institution. **Gen-Edu:** Documentary Films, Aging, Housing. **Acq:** Purchase. **Dist:** Kinetic Film Enterprises Ltd.

The Battle of Blood Island 1960 — ★
Two G.I.s, one Christian and one Jewish, face death at the hands of the Japanese during WWII. Still, they bicker incessantly before finally pulling together to save themselves. 64m/B/W; VHS, DVD. **C:** Richard Devon; Ron Kennedy; Directed by Joel Rapp. **Pr:** Filmgroup. **A:** Jr. High-Adult. **P:** Entertainment. **U:** Home. **Mov-Ent:** World War Two. **Acq:** Purchase. **Dist:** Sinister Cinema. $16.95.

Battle of Britain 1943
Britain stands alone in her "finest hour" through a tremendous Nazi air onslaught. Part of the "Why We Fight" series. 55m/B/W; VHS. **TV Std:** NTSC, PAL. **C:** Directed by Frank Capra. **Pr:** U.S. War Department. **A:** Jr. High-Adult. **P:** Education. **U:** Home. **Gen-Edu:** Documentary Films, World War Two. **Acq:** Purchase. **Dist:** MPI Media Group; International Historic Films Inc.; Time-Life Video and Television. $19.98.

Battle of Britain 1969 (G) — ★★½
A powerful retelling of the most dramatic aerial combat battle of WWII, showing how the understaffed Royal Air Force held off the might of the German Luftwaffe. 132m; VHS, DVD, Blu-Ray, Wide, CC. **C:** Harry Andrews; Michael Caine; Laurence Olivier; Trevor Howard; Kenneth More; Christopher Plummer; Robert Shaw; Susannah York; Ralph Richardson; Curt Jurgens; Michael Redgrave; Nigel Patrick; Edward Fox; Ian McShane; Patrick Wymark; Directed by Guy Hamilton; Written by James Kennaway; Wilfred Greatorex; Cinematography by Frederick A. (Freddie) Young; Music by Malcolm Arnold; Ronald Goodwin; William Walton. **Pr:** Harry Saltzman; Benjamin Fisz; United Artists. **A:** Family. **P:** Entertainment. **U:** Home. **Mov-Ent:** Drama, Aeronautics, World War Two. **Acq:** Purchase. **Dist:** MGM Home Entertainment. $14.95.

Battle of Chalons 1982
Offers instruction on specific aspects of true and mythological saints and legends. 30m; VHS. **A:** Adult. **P:** Education. **U:** Institution. **Gen-Edu:** History. **Acq:** Purchase. **Dist:** RMI Media. $69.95.

The Battle of Chickamauga 19??
Cissell of the National Park Service discusses the Civil War Battle of Chickamauga. ?m; VHS. **A:** Jr. High-Adult. **P:** Entertainment. **U:** Home, Institution. **Gen-Edu:** Documentary Films, Civil War. **Acq:** Purchase. **Dist:** Inspired Corp. $14.98.

The Battle of Chile 1976
Two-part series documents the bloody coup to overthrow the democratically elected president of Chile, Salvador Allende, in 1973. Part 1 follows the violent tactics used by the right to weaken the government and provoke crisis; Part 2 shows the left divided over strategy while the right closes in for military seizure of power and completes the coup d'etat. 184m/B/W; VHS. **A:** Adult. **P:** Education. **U:** BCTV, Institution. **Gen-Edu:** South America, Politics & Government, Documentary Films. **Acq:** Purchase, Rent/Lease. **Dist:** First Run/Icarus Films. $490.00.

Battle of China 1944
A look at the people, culture, and industry of China, and Japan's total commitment to conquer the country during WWII, through authentic newsreel footage. 67m/B/W; VHS. **C:** Directed by Frank Capra. **Pr:** U.S. War Department. **A:** Family. **P:** Education. **U:** Home. **Gen-Edu:** Documentary Films, World War Two, China. **Acq:** Purchase. **Dist:** Alpha Video; International Historic Films Inc. $19.98.

The Battle of Culloden 1964
The Battle of Culloden in 1746 marked the end of the Jacobite rebellion against King George II. This reconstruction of the battle and its aftermath was filmed at the original site using cinema verite techniques. 70m/B/W; VHS, 3/4 U. **C:** Directed by Peter Watkins. **Pr:** Peter Watkins; Peter Watkins; BBC Horizon. **A:** Jr. High-Adult. **P:** Education. **U:** Institution, SURA. **Gen-Edu:** Documentary Films, Great Britain, History. **Acq:** Purchase, Rent/Lease. **Dist:** Home Vision Cinema.

The Battle of El Alamein 1968 — ★★
Action filled movie about the alliance of Italy and Germany in a war against the British, set in a North African desert in the year 1942. Ferroni used the pseudonym Calvin Jackson Padget. 105m; VHS, DVD. **C:** Frederick Stafford; Ettore Manni; Robert Hossein; Michael Rennie; George Hilton; Ira Furstenberg; Directed by Giorgio Ferroni. **A:** Sr. High-Adult. **P:**

Entertainment. **U:** Home. **Mov-Ent:** Action-Adventure, World War Two. **Acq:** Purchase. **Dist:** Movies Unlimited. $14.95.

Battle of Elderbush Gulch 1913 — ★★½
An ancient pioneering western short famous for innocently employing the now-established cliches of bad guy, good guy, and helpless frontier heroine. One of Gish's first films. 22m/B/W; Silent; VHS, DVD. **C:** Lillian Gish; Mae Marsh; Alfred Paget; Robert "Bobbie" Harron; Lionel Barrymore; Leslie Loveridge; Directed by D.W. Griffith; Cinematography by Billy (G.W.) Bitzer. **A:** College-Adult. **P:** Education. **U:** Home. **Mov-Ent:** Western, Silent Films. **Acq:** Purchase. **Dist:** Pyramid Media; Glenn Video Vistas Ltd. $29.95.

The Battle of Elderbush Gulch/The Musketeers of Pig Alley 1914 — ★★
Two classic Griffith two-reelers from 1914 and 1912 respectively on one tape. 33m/B/W; Silent; VHS. **C:** Lillian Gish; Mae Marsh; Harry Carey, Sr.; Directed by D.W. Griffith. **Pr:** Biograph. **A:** Family. **P:** Entertainment. **U:** Home. **Mov-Ent:** Silent Films. **Acq:** Purchase. **Dist:** $19.95.

The Battle of Gettysburg in Miniature 1988
Recreates the famous Civil War battle using 12,000 hand-painted cast-iron figures, original music, and special effects. 40m; VHS. **A:** Jr. High-Adult. **P:** Education. **U:** Home. **Gen-Edu:** Civil War, History--U.S. **Acq:** Purchase. **Dist:** GPN Educational Media. $29.95.

Battle of Greed 1935 (Unrated) — ★★
Lawyer John Storm (Keene) takes a job in a Virginia mining town and makes the acquaintance of Mark Twain (Bush) who is working as a local newspaper editor. They soon have to join forces against corrupt locals trying to jump the claims of local silver miners. Notable for being a fairly well done film given its budget, and for actor Keene's propensity for bursting into laughter with little or no provocation. 59m/B/W; DVD. **C:** Gwynne Shipman; Foxy Callahan; Tom Keene; James Bush; Jimmy Butler; Robert (Fisk) Fiske; Carl Stockdale; Ray Bennett; William Worthington; Henry Roquemore; Lloyd Ingraham; Budd Buster; Directed by Howard Higgin; Written by John Thomas "Jack" Neville; Cinematography by Paul Ivano. **A:** Jr. High-Adult. **P:** Entertainment. **U:** Home. **Mov-Ent:** Action-Adventure, Western. **Acq:** Purchase. **Dist:** Alpha Video. $11.98.

The Battle of Kharkov 1984
Shows Adolf Hitler vacationing in Finland, near Kharkov in the Spring of 1942. This Nazi newsreel preserves the story of the German Army's crushing of the Soviet Red Army in the Battle of Kharkov. In German with English subtitles. 27m/B/W; VHS, 3/4 U. **TV Std:** NTSC, PAL. **A:** Sr. High-Adult. **P:** Education. **U:** Home. **L:** German. **Mov-Ent:** Documentary Films, World War Two, Germany. **Acq:** Purchase. **Dist:** International Historic Films Inc.; German Language Video Center. $24.95.

The Battle of Khe Sanh 1969
The story of one of the most bitterly fought battles of the Vietnam War. 30m; VHS, 3/4 U. **TV Std:** NTSC, PAL. **Pr:** U.S. Government. **A:** Jr. High-Adult. **P:** Education. **U:** Institution, Home. **Gen-Edu:** Documentary Films, Vietnam War, Military History. **Acq:** Purchase. **Dist:** International Historic Films Inc. $29.95.

The Battle of Local 5668 2007
Documentary on the battle between a union and the owners of the Ravenswood Aluminum Plant in West Virginia. 54m; VHS, DVD. **A:** Sr. High-Adult. **P:** Education. **U:** Institution. **Gen-Edu:** Documentary Films, Labor & Unions. **Acq:** Purchase, Rent/Lease. **Dist:** The Cinema Guild. $295.00.

The Battle of Manassas 1968
A depiction of the events which led to the famous Civil War battle in which "Stonewall" Jackson made his stand at Bull Run, defeating the Union Army. 11m; VHS, 3/4 U, Special order formats. **A:** Jr. High-College. **P:** Education. **U:** Institution, SURA. **Gen-Edu:** Documentary Films, History--U.S., Civil War. **Acq:** Purchase. **Dist:** National Audiovisual Center.

Battle of Midway/To the Shores of Iwo Jima/Fury in the Pacific 1945
Three films that highlight some of WWII's most exciting moments. 57m; VHS. **TV Std:** NTSC, PAL. **C:** Directed by John Ford. **Pr:** U.S. Marine Corps. **A:** Sr. High-Adult. **P:** Education. **U:** Institution, Home. **Gen-Edu:** Documentary Films, World War Two, Armed Forces--U.S. **Acq:** Purchase. **Dist:** International Historic Films Inc. $35.95.

The Battle of Mortimer's Cross 1990
A re-creation of the battle in England's War of the Roses is featured in original locations and authentic medieval fashion. 80m/B/W; VHS. **Pr:** Fusion Video. **A:** Sr. High-Adult. **P:** Education. **U:** Home. **Gen-Edu:** Documentary Films, War--General, Great Britain. **Acq:** Purchase. **Dist:** Fusion Video. $29.98.

Battle of Neretva 1969 — ★★
During WWII, Yugoslav partisans are facing German and Italian troops and local Chetniks as they battle for freedom. Big budget war film lost continuity with U.S. cut. 106m; VHS, DVD, Streaming. **C:** Yul Brynner; Curt Jurgens; Orson Welles; Hardy Kruger; Franco Nero; Sergei Bondarchuk; Directed by Veljko Bulajic. **Pr:** American International Pictures. **A:** Sr. High-Adult. **P:** Entertainment. **U:** Home. **Mov-Ent:** World War Two. **Acq:** Purchase. **Dist:** Lions Gate Entertainment Inc. $39.98.

The Battle of New Market 19??
Joseph W.A. Whitehorn, a U.S. Army historian, discusses the Civil War Battle of New Market. ?m; VHS. **A:** Jr. High-Adult. **P:** Entertainment. **U:** Home, Institution. **Gen-Edu:** Documentary Films, Civil War. **Acq:** Purchase. **Dist:** Inspired Corp. $14.98.

The Battle of New Orleans 19??
Describes the victory by Andrew Jackson's forces over the British forces at New Orleans at the end of the War of 1812, which helped send Jackson straight to the Presidency of the U.S. 26m; VHS. **A:** Primary-Adult. **P:** Education. **U:** Institution. **Gen-Edu:** History--U.S., War--General, Presidency. **Acq:** Purchase. **Dist:** Educational Video Network. $49.95.

Battle of Rogue River 1954 (Unrated) — ★½
Cavalry officer Frank Archer is told to obtain a truce with the local warring tribes so Oregon can gain statehood. There's the usual group of bad guys who prefer the fighting to continue so they can control the area's mineral wealth. 71m; DVD. **C:** Richard Denning; George Montgomery; Charles Evans; Martha Hyer; Emory Parnell; John Crawford; Michael Granger; Directed by William Castle; Written by Douglas Heyes; Cinematography by Henry Freulich. **A:** Jr. High-Adult. **P:** Entertainment. **U:** Home. **Mov-Ent:** Western, Native Americans. **Acq:** Purchase. **Dist:** Sony Pictures Home Entertainment Inc.

The Battle of Russia 1944
Hitler's forces are victorious in Moscow and Leningrad but are thoroughly defeated at the battle of Stalingrad. Authentic newsreel footage. 83m/B/W; VHS. **TV Std:** NTSC, PAL. **C:** Directed by Frank Capra. **Pr:** U.S. War Department. **A:** Sr. High-Adult. **P:** Education. **U:** Home. **Gen-Edu:** Documentary Films, World War Two, History--Modern. **Acq:** Purchase, Rent/Lease. **Dist:** Synergy Entertainment, Inc.; Amazon.com Inc.; MPI Media Group. $19.98.

The Battle of San Pietro 1944
John Huston's powerful documentary about the famous battle in Italy's Liri Valley, stressing the number of losses sustained in taking this military objective. The film was almost suppressed by the U.S. government, because it was considered to be too strong for general release. 43m/B/W; VHS, 3/4 U. **TV Std:** NTSC, PAL. **C:** Narrated by John Huston; Directed by John Huston; Written by John Huston; Eric Ambler; Cinematography by John Huston; Jules Buck; Music by Dimitri Tiomkin. **Pr:** Frank Capra; U.S. Office of War Information. **A:** Jr. High-Adult. **P:** Education. **U:** Institution, Home. **Gen-Edu:** Documentary Films, World War Two, Military History. **Awds:** Natl. Film Reg. '91. **Acq:** Purchase. **Dist:** Quality Information Publishers; Synergy Entertainment, Inc.; International Historic Films Inc. $19.98.

The Battle of Shaker Heights 2003 (PG-13) — ★½
Disappointing sophomore effort from the HBO series "Project Greenlight," backed once again by producers Ben Affleck and Matt Damon. Kelly Ernswiler (LaBeouf) is bright, middle-class Midwestern teen whose hobby is military re-enactment. He becomes best friends with Bart (Henson) after "saving his life" in a mock battle. He soon develops a crush on Bart's older sister Tabby, an engaged Yale grad student, much to the dismay of his supermarket co-worker Sarah (Appleby). This only adds to Kelly's mounting problems, which include myriad family problems with ex-addict dad (Sadler) and "art" entrepreneur mom (Quinlan). LaBeouf is appealing, rising above the disjointed, uninspired mess. If there is another "Project," they should look for a director who will provide satisfying drama on the big screen as well as on the show. 85m; VHS, DVD. **C:** Shia LaBeouf; Elden (Ratliff) Henson; Amy Smart; Billy Kay; Shiri Appleby; Kathleen Quinlan; William Sadler; Ray Wise; Anson Mount; Philipp Karner; Directed by Kyle Rankin; Efram Potelle; Written by Erica Beeney; Cinematography by Thomas Ackerman; Music by Richard (Rick) Marvin. **Pr:** Chris Moore; Jeff Balis; LivePlanet; Miramax Film Corp. **A:** Jr. High-Adult. **P:** Entertainment. **U:** Home. **Mov-Ent:** Adolescence. **Acq:** Purchase. **Dist:** Miramax Film Corp.

The Battle of Stalingrad 1960
A Russian documentary which offers the Soviet view of the grueling battle for Stalingrad, which changed the course of the Second World War in the Allies' favor. Narrated in English. 90m/B/W; VHS, 3/4 U. **TV Std:** NTSC, PAL. **A:** Sr. High-Adult. **P:** Education. **U:** Institution, Home. **Gen-Edu:** Documentary Films, Propaganda, World War Two. **Acq:** Purchase, Rent/Lease. **Dist:** International Historic Films Inc.; German Language Video Center. $39.95.

Battle of the Atlantic 2006
A three-part series on U-boats versus Nazi submarines that includes eyewitness accounts and reconstructions. 150m; DVD. **A:** Sr. High-Adult. **P:** Entertainment. **U:** Home. **Gen-Edu:** Documentary Films, World War Two. **Acq:** Purchase. **Dist:** Warner Home Video, Inc.

Battle of the Big Tuna 19??
Tuna heaven at Cabo San Lucas on the West Coast should lure sportfishers to this program loaded with tips and techniques. 60m; VHS. **A:** Adult. **P:** Instruction. **U:** Home. **Spo-Rec:** Fishing. **Acq:** Purchase. **Dist:** Bennett Marine Video. $29.95.

Battle of the Blimps 1986
Airship Industries takes on Goodyear for control of the reborn blimp market. 30m; VHS, 3/4 U. **Pr:** Learning Corporation of America. **A:** Sr. High-Adult. **P:** Education. **U:** Institution, SURA. **Gen-Edu:** Business, Aeronautics. **Acq:** Purchase, Rent/Lease. **Dist:** Phoenix Learning Group. $310.00.

Battle of the Bombs 1985
A collection of excerpts from the worst films of all time. 60m; VHS. **Pr:** Impulse Entertainment. **A:** Jr. High-Adult. **P:** Entertainment. **U:** Home. **Mov-Ent:** Exploitation. **Acq:** Purchase. **Dist:** Rhino Entertainment Co. $39.95.

Battle of the Bulbs 2010 (Unrated) — ★½
In this goofy Hallmark Channel flick, Bob has been the king of Christmas decorations in the neighborhhod until Stu and his family move in across the street. They turn out to be ex-friends, still holding a 25-year-old grudge, who now pit themselves against each other to win the prize for the best holiday display. There's a couple of sappy subplots than ruin the slapstick. 88m; Streaming. **C:** Daniel Stern; Matt Frewer; Allison Hossack; Teryl Rothery; Emily Tennant; William Hutchinson; Directed by Harvey Frost; Written by W. Paul Thompson; Cinematography by Paul Mitchnick; Music by Hal Beckett. **A:** Family. **P:** Entertainment. **U:** Home. **L:** English. **Mov-Ent:** Christmas, TV Movies. **Acq:** Rent/Lease. **Dist:** Amazon.com Inc.

Battle of the Bulge 1965 — ★★
A re-creation of the famous offensive by Nazi Panzer troops on the Belgian front during 1944-45, an assault that could have changed the course of WWII. 141m; VHS, DVD, Blu-Ray, HD-DVD, Wide, CC. **C:** Henry Fonda; Robert Shaw; Robert Ryan; Dana Andrews; Telly Savalas; Ty Hardin; Pier Angeli; George Montgomery; Charles Bronson; Barbara Werle; Hans-Christian Blech; James MacArthur; Karl Otto Alberty; Directed by Ken Annakin; Written by Philip Yordan; John Melson; Cinematography by Jack Hildyard; Music by Benjamin Frankel. **Pr:** Sidney Harmon; Milton Sperling; Philip Yordan; Philip Yordan; Warner Bros. **A:** Sr. High-Adult. **P:** Entertainment. **U:** Home. **Mov-Ent:** Drama, World War Two, Tanks. **Acq:** Purchase. **Dist:** Warner Home Video, Inc. $59.95.

The Battle of the Bulge 1985
A partially re-created documentary of the famous battle, from an artilleristic point of view. 53m/B/W; VHS. **Pr:** National Broadcasting Company. **A:** Jr. High-Adult. **P:** Entertainment. **U:** Institution, Home. **Gen-Edu:** Documentary Films, World War Two. **Acq:** Purchase. **Dist:** Bennett Marine Video; Military/Combat Stock Footage Library. $24.95.

Battle of the Bullies 1985 — **Bomb!**
An unsalvageable nerd plots a high-tech revenge upon a slew of high school bullies. 45m; VHS. **C:** Manny Jacobs; Chris Barnes; Sarah Inglis. **Pr:** New World Pictures. **A:** Family. **P:** Entertainment. **U:** Home. **Mov-Ent:** Comedy--Black, Adolescence, TV Movies. **Acq:** Purchase. **Dist:** Unknown Distributor.

Battle of the Commandos 1971 (Unrated) — ★
A tough Army colonel leads a group of convicts on a dangerous mission to destroy a German-built cannon before it's used against the Allied Forces. 94m; VHS. **C:** Jack Palance; Curt Jurgens; Thomas Hunter; Robert Hunter; Directed by Umberto Lenzi. **Pr:** Commonwealth United. **A:** Sr. High-Adult. **P:** Entertainment. **U:** Home. **Mov-Ent:** World War Two. **Acq:** Purchase. **Dist:** Lions Gate Entertainment Inc. $39.98.

Battle of the Coral Sea 1959 (Unrated) — ★½
Strictly a war B-movie all the way. The crew of a submarine is captured by the Japanese while on a recon mission in the Pacific and sent to a POW camp. Three officers escape in time to provide the needed intel before the titular 1942 battle, which is not shown. 86m/B/W; DVD. **C:** Cliff Robertson; Gia Scala; Teru Shimada; L.Q. Jones; Gene Blakely; Rian Garrick; Directed by Paul Wendkos; Written by Stephen Kandel; Daniel Ullman; Cinematography by Wilfred M. Cline; Music by Ernest Gold. **A:** Sr. High-Adult. **P:** Entertainment. **U:** Home. **Mov-Ent:** World War Two. **Acq:** Purchase. **Dist:** Sony Pictures Home Entertainment Inc.

Battle of the Damned 2014 (R) — ★
Killer Asian robots, a zombie-like plague, and even Dolph Lundgren can't make for much entertainment. A city is quarantined with a military blockade when a deadly virus is accidentally released. Former commando Max Gatling is hired to rescue a wealthy man's daughter from the chaos, but when he finds Jude, she refuses to abandon a group of survivors who are using robots to battle the zombie-like plague victims. 89m; DVD, Blu-Ray. **C:** Dolph Lundgren; Melanie Zanetti; Matt Doran; David Field; Directed by Christopher Hatton; Written by Christopher Hatton; Cinematography by Roger Chingirian; Music by joe Ng. **A:** Sr. High-Adult. **P:** Entertainment. **U:** Home. **L:** English. **Mov-Ent:** Violence. **Acq:** Purchase. **Dist:** Anchor Bay Entertainment Inc.

Battle of the Eagles 1979 — ★½
Follows the true adventures of the "Partisan Squadron," the courageous airmen known as the "Knights of the Sky" during WWII in Yugoslavia. 102m; VHS, DVD. **C:** Bekim Fehmiu; George Taylor; Gloria Samara; Directed by Tom Raymonth. **Pr:** Victor Films. **A:** Family. **P:** Entertainment. **U:** Home. **Mov-Ent:** Action-Adventure, Aeronautics, World War Two. **Acq:** Purchase. **Dist:** No Longer Available.

The Battle of the Giants 1988
The total story of the unofficial rugby tournament between New Zealand and South Africa, held in South Africa. 100m; VHS. **Pr:** Trace Video. **A:** Family. **P:** Entertainment. **U:** Institution, Home, SURA. **Spo-Rec:** Sports--General. **Acq:** Purchase, Rent/Lease, Subscription. **Dist:** Reedswain Inc. $36.50.

The Battle of the Japan Sea 1970 (G) — ★★
A Japanese epic, dubbed in English, centering around the historic WWII battle between Japan and Russia. 120m; VHS. **C:** Toshiro Mifune; Tatsuya Nakadai; Yuzo Kayama; Chishu Ryu; Susumu Fujita; Mitsuko Kusabe; Directed by Seiji Maruyama; Written by Toshio Yasumi; Cinematography by Masaru Sato; Music by Hiroshi Murai. **Pr:** Tohi Productions. **A:** Jr. High-Adult. **P:** Entertainment. **U:** Home. **Mov-Ent:** Action-Adventure, World War Two, Japan. **Acq:** Purchase. **Dist:** $69.95.

Battle of the Planets, Vol. 4 1978
Features the 1978 animated television series with G-Force, a team of teenaged heroes, as they take a stand against the evil Zoltar from Planet Spectra with the aid of Chief Anderson, 7-Zark-7, Colonel Cronos, President Kane, Susan, and 1-Rover-1; the first English version of the Japanese series "Science Ninja Team Gatchaman." Includes "Ace from Outer Space" and "The Fearful Sea Anemone" along with three bonus episodes. 5 episodes. 125m; DVD. **A:** Family. **P:** Entertainment. **U:** Home. **Chl-Juv:** Television Series, Action-Adventure, Animation & Cartoons. **Acq:** Purchase. **Dist:** Rhino Entertainment Co. $19.95.

Battle of the Planets, Vol. 5 2002
Features the 1978 animated television series with G-Force, a team of teenaged heroes, as they take a stand against the evil Zoltar from Planet Spectra with the aide of Chief Anderson, 7-Zark-7, Colonel Cronos, President Kane, Susan, and 1-Rover-1—it was the first English version of the Japanese series "Science Ninja Team Gatchaman"; includes "A Demon From the Moon," and "The Big Battle of the Underground" along with three bonus episodes. 5 episodes. 125m; DVD. **C:** Voice(s) by Alan Young; Keye Luke; Ronnie Schell; Janet Waldo; Casey Kasem; Alan Dinehart. **A:** Family. **P:** Entertainment. **U:** Home. **Chl-Juv:** Television Series, Action-Adventure, Animation & Cartoons. **Acq:** Purchase. **Dist:** Rhino Entertainment Co. $19.95.

Battle of the Planets, Vol. 6 1978
Features the 1978 animated television series with G-Force, a team of teenaged heroes, as they take a stand against the evil Zoltar from Planet Spectra with the aide of Chief Anderson, 7-Zark-7, Colonel Cronos, President Kane, Susan, and 1-Rover-1; the first English version of the Japanese series "Science Ninja Team Gatchaman" includes "Space Rocket Escort," "Beast With a Sweet Tooth," "The Mysterious Red Impulse," "The Greedy Monster," and "Micro-Robots." 5 episodes. 125m; DVD. **C:** Voice(s) by Alan Young; Keye Luke; Ronnie Schell; Janet Waldo; Casey Kasem; Alan Dinehart. **A:** Family. **P:** Entertainment. **U:** Home. **Chl-Juv:** Television Series, Action-Adventure, Animation & Cartoons. **Acq:** Purchase. **Dist:** Rhino Entertainment Co. $19.95.

Battle of the Rails 1946 (Unrated) — ★★★
Docudrama based on actual events of French Resistance fighters who worked on the railways and, at great peril, stymied the Nazis efforts throughout World War II and aided the Allies during the D-Day invasion. Powerful debut feature film for French director Clement, who included real railroad workers in recreating events. In French with subtitles. 85m/B/W; DVD. **C:** Marcel Barnault; Jean Clarieux; Jean Daurand; Jacques Desagneaux; Francois Joux; Directed by Rene Clement; Written by Rene Clement. **A:** Jr. High-Adult. **P:** Entertainment. **U:** Home. **L:** French. **Mov-Ent:** France, World War Two, Documentary Films. **Acq:** Purchase. **Dist:** Facets Multimedia Inc. $29.95.

Battle of the Sexes 1928 — ★★
Real estate tycoon Judson (Hersholt) abandons his wife (Bennett) and home for money-hungry flapper Marie (Haver). Based on the novel "The Single Standard" by Daniel Carson Goodman. Griffith's remake of his own 1913 film. 88m/B/W; Silent; VHS, DVD. **C:** Jean Hersholt; Phyllis Haver; Belle Bennett; Don Alvarado; William "Billy" Bakewell; Sally O'Neil; Directed by D.W. Griffith; Written by Gerrit J. Lloyd; Cinematography by Billy (G.W.) Bitzer; Karl Struss. **A:** College-Adult. **P:** Entertainment. **U:** Home. **Mov-Ent:** Marriage, Sex & Sexuality, Real Estate. **Acq:** Purchase. **Dist:** Kino on Video.

The Battle of the Sexes 1960 (Unrated) — ★★★
Sophisticated British comedy has mild-mannered Sellers trying to prevent a business takeover by the brash American Cummings. A good supporting cast and the impeccable Sellers make this one unique. Adapted from the James Thurber short story "The Catbird Seat." 88m/B/W; VHS. **C:** Peter Sellers; Robert Morley; Constance Cummings; Jameson Clark; Ernest Thesiger; Donald Pleasence; Moultrie Kelsall; Alex Mackenzie; Roddy McMillan; Michael Goodliffe; Norman MacOwen; William Mervyn; Narrated by Sam Wanamaker; Directed by Charles Crichton; Written by Monja Danischewsky; Cinematography by Freddie Francis; Music by Stanley Black. **Pr:** Bryanston Pictures. **A:** Sr. High-Adult. **P:** Entertainment. **U:** Home. **Mov-Ent:** Comedy--Slapstick. **Acq:** Purchase.

Battle of the Titans 1999
Helps the viewer to better understand how the opportunities of globalization are threatened by economic imbalances. ?m; VHS. **A:** Adult. **P:** Education. **U:** Home, Institution. **Bus-Ind:** Business. **Acq:** Purchase. **Dist:** Learning Communications L.L.C. $695.00.

Battle of the Titans: Problems of the Global Economy 1993
Filmed in Indonesia, Venezuela, Egypt, and Nigeria, asks tough economic questions while showing the correlation between economic deprivation and political unrest in a world that is competing more and more in trade wars. 54m; VHS. **A:** Sr. High. **P:** Education. **U:** Institution. **Gen-Edu:** International Relations. **Acq:** Purchase. **Dist:** Filmakers Library Inc. $395.

Battle of the Warriors 2006 (R) — ★★½
More commonly known as 'A Battle of Wits,' this story is set in 370 B.C. in China's warring states period. The kingdom of Zhao invades the smaller (and fictional) city-state of Liang with an army 25 times their size. Enter Ge Li (Andy Lau), a Mohist philosopher who wishes to warn the citizens and find a way to stop the invaders from killing them all. The King of Liang is threatened by Ge Li's popularity however, and Li must deal with his machinations while trying to slow down or turn aside the oncoming army. 131m; DVD, Blu-Ray. **C:** Andy Lau; Sung-kee Ahn; Zhiwen Wang; Si Won Choi; Bingbing Fan; Directed by Chi Leung Cheung; Written by Chi Leung Cheung; Cinematography by Yoshitaka Sakamoto; Music by Kenji Kawai. **A:** Sr. High-Adult. **P:** Entertainment. **U:** Home. **L:** English, Mandarin Dialects, Spanish. **Mov-Ent:** War--General. **Acq:** Purchase. **Dist:** Weinstein Company L.L.C. $6.95 19.97.

Battle of the Worlds 1961 (Unrated) — ★
Typical low-budget science fiction. A scientist tries to stop an alien planet from destroying the Earth. Even an aging Rains

can't help this one. Poorly dubbed in English. 84m; VHS, DVD, CV. **C:** Claude Rains; Maya Brent; Bill Carter; Marina Orsini; Jacqueline Derval; Directed by Anthony M. Dawson. **Pr:** Ultra Films. **A:** Jr. High-Adult. **P:** Entertainment. **U:** Home. **Mov-Ent**: Science Fiction. **Acq:** Purchase. **Dist:** Sinister Cinema. $16.95.

Battle of the Year 2013 (PG-13) — ★½
After losing his wife and son, washed-up, boozing dance coach Jason (Holloway) assembles a rag-tag team of street dancers to battle their way to the world championships. Little more than a fictional re-telling of director Benson's outstanding 2007 competitive breakdancing documentary, "Planet B-Boy," mixed with the usual "Rocky"-like underdog clichés. A flashy, fun, and ultimately dumb guilty pleasure that never takes itself too seriously. "Step Up" fans, step up. 110m; DVD, Blu-Ray. **C:** Josh Holloway; Laz Alonso; Josh Peck; Caity Lotz; Chris Brown; Directed by Benson Lee; Written by Brin Hill; Chris Parker; Cinematography by Michael Barrett; Music by Christopher Lennertz. **Pr:** Screen Gems; Sony Pictures Entertainment Inc. **A:** Jr. High-Adult. **P:** Entertainment. **U:** Home. **L:** English. **Mov-Ent**: Dance, Romance. **Acq:** Purchase. **Dist:** Sony Pictures Home Entertainment Inc.

Battle of Valiant 1963 (Unrated) — ★
Thundering hordes of invading barbarians trample the splendor of ancient Rome beneath their grimy sandals. 90m; VHS. **C:** Gordon Mitchell; Ursula Davis; Massimo Serato; Directed by John Gentil. **Pr:** Empire Pictures. **A:** Jr. High-Adult. **P:** Entertainment. **U:** Home. **Mov-Ent**: Drama. **Acq:** Purchase. **Dist:** Unknown Distributor.

The Battle of Verdun 1990
Trench warfare in WWI was never as brutal as in the French defensive at Verdun, as witnessed in this video. 30m; VHS. **Pr:** Fusion Video. **A:** Sr. High-Adult. **P:** Education. **U:** Home. **Gen-Edu**: Documentary Films, World War One, France. **Acq:** Purchase. **Dist:** Fusion Video. $19.98.

The Battle of Vieques 1986
U.S. Navy control and use of Vieques, a small island of Puerto Rico is examined. Many believe the Navy's use of the island has harmed the local population. The film contains interviews with residents and government officials. 40m; VHS, 3/4 U. **TV Std:** NTSC, PAL, SECAM. **Pr:** Zydnia Nazario. **A:** Sr. High-Adult. **P:** Education. **U:** Institution, SURA. **Gen-Edu**: Documentary Films, Caribbean. **Acq:** Purchase, Rent/Lease. **Dist:** The Cinema Guild.

The Battle of Washington Monocacy 19??
Shore hosts this look at the Battle of Washington Monocacy. ?m; VHS. **C:** Hosted by Bill Shore. **A:** Jr. High-Adult. **P:** Entertainment. **U:** Home, Institution. **Gen-Edu**: Documentary Films, War--General. **Acq:** Purchase. **Dist:** Inspired Corp. $14.98.

The Battle of Waterloo: 1815 ????
Illustrates the events leading up to the Battle of Waterloo using political cartoons, maps and battle diagrams. 30m; VHS. **A:** Jr. High-Sr. High. **P:** Education. **U:** Institution. **Gen-Edu**: History--Modern, War--General. **Acq:** Purchase. **Dist:** Zenger Media. $89.95.

The Battle of Yorktown 1958
Describes the events which led to the decisive battle of the American Revolution at Yorktown. 13m; VHS, 3/4 U. **Pr:** Encyclopedia Britannica Educational Corporation. **A:** Primary-Jr. High. **P:** Education. **U:** Institution, SURA. **Gen-Edu**: Documentary Films, Revolutionary War, History--U.S. **Acq:** Purchase, Rent/Lease, Trade-in. **Dist:** Encyclopedia Britannica.

Battle of Yorktown 1981
A documentary, using Bicentennial re-enactment footage, outlining the famous battle. 30m; VHS, 3/4 U. **Pr:** BFA Educational Media. **A:** Jr. High-Adult. **P:** Education. **U:** Institution, SURA. **Gen-Edu**: Documentary Films, Revolutionary War, History--U.S. **Acq:** Purchase. **Dist:** Phoenix Learning Group.

The Battle of Yorktown: 1781 1991
An overview of the entire American Revolution, which culminated with this British defeat. Techniques used include live reenactments, art reproductions, and live-action footage of battlefield sites. 35m; VHS. **A:** Jr. High-Sr. High. **P:** Education. **U:** Institution. **Chl-Juv**: History--U.S. **Acq:** Purchase, Rent/Lease. **Dist:** Films for the Humanities & Sciences. $75.00.

Battle Over the Blackboard 1991
Deals with secular humanism and the fundamentalist backlash against it, and also delves into the selection of books in schools and libraries. 26m; VHS, 3/4 U. **Pr:** Films for the Humanities. **A:** Sr. High-Adult. **P:** Education. **U:** Institution. **Gen-Edu**: Documentary Films, Education, Religion. **Acq:** Purchase. **Dist:** Films for the Humanities & Sciences. $149.00.

Battle Planet 2008 (Unrated) — ★½
A special forces officer is sent to a desolate planet on a secret mission to capture an alien terrorist. All too quickly he learns the experimental battlesuit he was given has trapped him inside, and there's more to his mission than he has been told. 86m; DVD, Streaming. **C:** Zack (Zach) Ward; Monica May; Kevin Thompson; John Duerler; Voice(s) by Colleen Smith; Directed by Greg Aronowitz; Written by Greg Aronowitz; Cinematography by Dallas Sterling; Music by Mel Lewis. **A:** Sr. High-Adult. **P:** Entertainment. **U:** Home. **L:** English. **Mov-Ent. Acq:** Purchase, Rent/Lease. **Dist:** Echo Bridge Home Entertainment. $6.99 9.99.

Battle Queen 2020 1999 (R) — ★★
In a frozen post-apocalyptic future (eternal winter after asteroid crash), Gayle (Strain) leads the downtrodden masses in a revolution against the Elites who live above ground. She's a courtesan by day, freedom fighter by night...or is the other way around? This one is at least as good as "Battlefield Earth." It's certainly shorter and was made by people who were under no illusions about what they were doing. 80m; DVD. **C:** Julie Strain; Jeff Wincott; Directed by Daniel D'or; Written by Michael B. Druxman; William Hulkower; William D. Bostjancic; Caron Nightengale; Cinematography by Billy Brao; Music by Robert Duncan. **A:** Sr. High-Adult. **P:** Entertainment. **U:** Home. **Mov-Ent**: Science Fiction. **Acq:** Purchase. **Dist:** New Horizons Picture Corp.

Battle Royal High School 1987 — ★★
Riki Hyoudo wants to be the champion of his karate club. He has a really cool leopard mask to wear, but his enthusiasm is more than the other students can take. Meanwhile, his double in the Dark Realm crosses through the dimensional gate bringing with him a myriad of evil spirits and other things to cause the semi-possessed Riki problems. As the title suggests, there are lots of fights at high school.Riki's fascination with some of the magical powers he can temporarily use is amusing. Certain aspects of the title will be lost on those not familiar with the comic book series, but its sheer adrenaline wins some fans. 60m; VHS. **A:** Sr. High-College. **P:** Entertainment. **U:** Home. **L:** Japanese, English. **Mov-Ent**: Anime, Animals. **Acq:** Purchase. **Dist:** AnimEigo Inc.

Battle Royale 2000 (Unrated) — ★★½
Insightful condemnation of modern Japanese society and politics masquerading as a thriller. In the near future, Japan has more graduates than jobs. Each year a class of random middle school children is kidnapped and forced to murder each other one by one lest they all die. The winner gets a job, assuming they remain sane enough for it. 122m; DVD, Blu-Ray, Streaming. **C:** Tatsuya Fujiwara; Aki Maeda; Taro Yamamoto; Takeshi "Beat" Kitano; Chiaki Kuriyama; Directed by Kinji Fukasaku; Written by Kenta Fukasaku; Cinematography by Katsumi Yanagijima; Music by Masamichi Amano. **A:** Sr. High-Adult. **P:** Entertainment. **U:** Home. **L:** English, Japanese. **Mov-Ent. Acq:** Purchase, Rent/Lease. **Dist:** Anchor Bay Entertainment Inc. $39.99 19.98 5.99.

Battle Scars: An Overview of Our Defense Against Disease 19??
Learning program for young students examines how the immune system works and what defenses the human body has against disease. Part of the "Biology Studies" series. 30m; VHS. **A:** Jr. High-Adult. **P:** Education. **U:** Home, Institution. **Chl-Juv**: Science, Biology. **Acq:** Purchase. **Dist:** Educational Activities Inc. $89.00.

Battle Shock 1956 (Unrated) — ★★
Ex-GI painter is accused of murdering a cantina waitress while on his honeymoon in Mexico. Soon other women are turning up dead and he realizes he is having blackouts. Solid work all around. 88m; VHS. **C:** Ralph Meeker; Janice Rule; Paul Henreid; Rosenda Monteros; Jose Torvay; Yerye Beirut; Directed by Paul Henreid; Written by Robert J. Hill; Cinematography by Jorge Stahl, Jr.; Music by Les Baxter. **Pr:** Republic Pictures. **A:** Sr. High-Adult. **P:** Entertainment. **U:** Home. **Mov-Ent**: Mystery & Suspense, Mexico, Art & Artists. **Acq:** Purchase. **Dist:** Lions Gate Entertainment Inc. $39.95.

Battle Tank 1990
Views from the turret and a complete explanation of modern land warfare are featured. 60m/B/W; VHS. **Pr:** Fusion Video. **A:** Sr. High-Adult. **P:** Entertainment. **U:** Home. **Gen-Edu**: Documentary Films, War--General. **Acq:** Purchase. **Dist:** Fusion Video. $29.98.

Battle Zone 1952 (Unrated) — ★★½
WWII vet Danny Young (Hodiak) re-enlists to fight in Korea, and he and combat photographer Mitch Turner (McNally) volunteer to gather intel from behind enemy lines. This means putting aside their romantic rivalry since Mitch is engaged to Red Cross nurse Jeanne (Christian), whom Danny was once involved with. 81m/B/W; DVD. **C:** John Hodiak; Stephen McNally; Linda Christian; Martin Milner; Jack Larson; Directed by Lesley Selander; Written by Steve Fisher; Cinematography by Ernest Miller; Music by Marlin Skiles. **A:** Sr. High-Adult. **P:** Entertainment. **U:** Home. **L:** English. **Mov-Ent**: Korean War, Romance. **Acq:** Purchase. **Dist:** WarnerArchive.com.

Battlefield Baseball 2003 (Unrated) — ★½
Seido High School has a chance to make it to the championships, but their next opponent, Gedo High, fields a baseball team of flesh-eating zombie mutants. Technically a spoof of cliched sports films, it goes off into the Twilight Zone pretty quickly and never comes back. Ultra campy with cyborgs, zombies, random naked men, senseless death, and superhumanly powered high school baseball players. 87m; DVD. **C:** Tak Sakaguchi; Hideo Sakaki; Atsushi Ito; Directed by Yudai Yamaguchi; Written by Yudai Yamaguchi; Isao Kiriyama; Gataro Man; Ryuichi Takatsu; Music by Daisuke Yano. **A:** Sr. High-Adult. **P:** Entertainment. **U:** Home. **L:** English, Japanese. **Mov-Ent**: Baseball, Sports--Fiction: Comedy, Musical. **Acq:** Purchase. **Dist:** Subversive Cinema. $19.95.

Battlefield Britain 2005
Presents the eight-part PBS series by Peter Snow and son Dan Snow detailing specific military battles in British history covering about 2,000 years such as "The Battle of Hastings," "Battle for Wales," and "The Battle of Britain." 510m; DVD. **A:** Jr. High-Sr. High. **P:** Entertainment. **U:** Home. **Gen-Edu**: Television, War--General, Documentary Films. **Acq:** Purchase. **Dist:** Warner Home Video, Inc. $49.98.

Battlefield Detectives 2012 (Unrated)
Documentary on famous disastrous military battles in history and what the causes were behind them. 180m; DVD, Streaming. **A:** Sr. High-Adult. **P:** Entertainment. **U:** Home. **Gen-Edu**: Documentary Films, Military History. **Acq:** Purchase, Rent/Lease. **Dist:** Acorn Media Group Inc. $59.99.

Battlefield Earth 2000 (PG-13) — **Bomb!**
In the year 3000, the Earth has been decimated by 10-foot tall aliens known as Psychlos who are stripping the planet of its natural resources. Only a few humans survive, including Pepper who becomes the leader of a rebellion. Travolta plays the leader of the bad aliens and is extremely evil-lookng but in a strangely campy way. Based on a 1982 novel by Scientology founder L. Ron Hubbard. Film generated controversy for that reason and supposedly "subliminal" church messages but you'll simply be stunned into submission by how badly it blows. 117m; VHS, DVD, Wide, CC. **C:** John Travolta; Barry Pepper; Forest Whitaker; Kelly Preston; Kim Coates; Richard Tyson; Sabine Karsenti; Michael Byrne; Sean Hewitt; Michel Perron; Shaun Austin-Olsen; Marie Josee Croze; Directed by Roger Christian; Written by J. David Shapiro; Cory Mandell; Cinematography by Giles Nuttgens; Music by Elia Cmiral. **A:** Sr. High-Adult. **P:** Entertainment. **U:** Home. **Mov-Ent. Awds:** Golden Raspberries '00: Worst Actor (Travolta), Worst Director (Christian), Worst Picture, Worst Screenplay, Worst Support. Actor (Pepper), Worst Support. Actress (Preston). **Acq:** Purchase. **Dist:** Warner Home Video, Inc.

Battleforce 1978 (Unrated) — ★
Exciting battle scenes lose their power in the confusion of this mixed-up WWII film about Rommel's last days. Dubbed sequences, news-reel vignettes and surprise performances by big name stars are incomprehensibly glued together. 97m; VHS, DVD. **C:** Henry Fonda; Stacy Keach; Helmut Berger; Samantha Eggar; Giuliano Gemma; John Huston; Narrated by Orson Welles; Directed by Umberto Lenzi. **Pr:** Saxton Communications Group Ltd. **A:** Jr. High-Adult. **P:** Entertainment. **U:** Home. **Mov-Ent**: Action-Adventure, World War Two. **Acq:** Purchase. **Dist:** Time-Life Video and Television. $9.99.

Battleground 1949 — ★★★
A tightly conceived post-WWII character drama, following a platoon of American soldiers through the Battle of the Bulge. Available in a Colorized version. 118m/B/W; VHS, DVD, CC. **C:** Van Johnson; John Hodiak; James Whitmore; George Murphy; Ricardo Montalban; Marshall Thompson; Jerome Courtland; Don Taylor; Bruce Cowling; Leon Ames; Douglas Fowley; Richard Jaeckel; Scotty Beckett; Herbert Anderson; Thomas E. Breen; Denise Darcel; James Arness; Brett King; Directed by William A. Wellman; Written by Robert Pirosh; Cinematography by Paul Vogel; Music by Lennie Hayton. **Pr:** Dore Schary; MGM. **A:** Jr. High-Adult. **P:** Entertainment. **U:** Home. **Mov-Ent**: World War Two. **Awds:** Oscars '49: B&W Cinematog., Story & Screenplay; Golden Globes '50: Screenplay, Support. Actor (Whitmore). **Acq:** Purchase. **Dist:** MGM Home Entertainment. $19.98.

Battleground: ICN 197?
Captures the continuing drama of an intensive care nursery, centering on a newborn suffering from respiratory distress syndrome, one of the most common serious birth defects. 7m; 3/4 U. **Pr:** March of Dimes. **A:** Sr. High-Adult. **P:** Education. **U:** Institution, CCTV, CATV. **Hea-Sci**: Infants, Patient Care. **Acq:** Free Loan. **Dist:** March of Dimes.

Battleline Series 1962
Frontline soldiers offer their view of WWII in original combat footage. Four epsiodes on each untitled volume. 120m/B/W; VHS. **Pr:** International Historic Films Inc. **A:** Sr. High-Adult. **P:** Entertainment. **U:** Home. **Gen-Edu**: Documentary Films, World War Two. **Acq:** Purchase. **Dist:** Fusion Video; International Historic Films Inc. $24.95.

Indiv. Titles: 1. Vol. 1: Invasion of Norway, Dunkirk, Battle of Britain, Invasion of Southern France 2. Vol. 2: Dieppe, Omaha Beach, Breakout from Normandy, Bridgehead at Rhine 3. Vol. 3: Malta, Operation Torch, Tobruk, El Alamein 4. Vol. 4: Crete, Anzio, Monte Cassino, Arnhem 5. Vol. 5: Stalingrad, Battle of the Gothic Line, Battle of the Bulge, Fall of Berlin.

Battles of Chief Pontiac 1952 (Unrated) — ★★
Set in America before the Revolutionary war, a Colonial officer is attempting to broker a peace deal between Indian chief Pontiac (Lon Cheney Jr.) and the settlers. Complicating this is a Hessian mercenary company waging a campaign of extermination against the Indians. The film is unusual in that it is one of the few films of its age that portrays the Native Americans as the good guys, and white men as the evil bad guys. 72m/B/W; DVD. **C:** Lex Barker; Helen Westcott; Lon Chaney, Jr.; Berry Kroeger; Roy Roberts; Larry Chance; Katherine Warren; Ramsay Hill; Directed by Felix Feist; Written by Jack DeWitt; Cinematography by Charles Van Enger; Music by Elmer Bernstein. **A:** Sr. High-Adult. **P:** Entertainment. **U:** Home. **Mov-Ent**: Western, Native Americans. **Acq:** Purchase. **Dist:** Alpha Video. $7.98.

Battle's Poison Cloud 2006
Examines the long-lasting effects of Agent Orange as it was used in the war in Vietnam, from environmental damage to birth defects and long-term health problems. 56m; DVD. **A:** Sr. High-Adult. **P:** Entertainment. **U:** Home. **Gen-Edu**: Documentary Films. **Acq:** Purchase. **Dist:** Cinema Libre Studio.

Battles That Changed the World: Campaigns in History ???
Ten-volume set presents pivotal events in world history using computer graphics, reenactments, narration, and historian commentary. 500m; VHS. **A:** Sr. High. **P:** Education. **U:** Institution. **Gen-Edu**: History, War--General. **Acq:** Purchase. **Dist:** Social Studies School Service; Zenger Media. $59.95.

Indiv. Titles: 1. Battle of New Orleans 2. Bunker Hill 3. Franco-Prussian War 4. Gallic Wars 5. Greek-Persian Wars 6. Peasants' Revolt 7. Peloponnesian Wars 8. Punic Wars 9. Spanish Armada 10. Trojan War.

Battleship 2012 (PG-13) — ★
Yep, it's based on Hasbro's combat game. Naval officer Alex Hopper (Kitsch) and his fellow crewman aboard the USS John Paul Jones are trapped by an unknown force that's destroying the planet. They fight back. As bloated as one would expect from a summer blockbuster that attempts to turn a straightforward child's game into a Transformers-esque CGI orgy, director Berg's film is popcorn entertainment at its most formulaic. Movies like this one are not unlike watching someone else play a video game--it may look good but there's no real involvement on your part. 131m; DVD, Blu-Ray, Streaming. **C:** Taylor Kitsch; Alexander Skarsgard; Rhianna; Brooklyn Decker; Tadanobu Asano; Liam Neeson; Peter MacNichol; Directed by Peter Berg; Written by Erich Hoeber; Jon Hoeber; Cinematography by Tobias Schliessler; Music by Steve Jablonsky. **Pr:** Sarah Aubrey; Brian Goldner; Duncan Henderson; Scott Stuber; Bennett Schneir; Peter Berg; Bluegrass Films; Film 44; Universal Pictures. **A:** Jr. High-Adult. **P:** Entertainment. **U:** Home. **L:** English, French, Spanish. **Mov-Ent:** Science Fiction. **Awds:** Golden Raspberries '12: Worst Support. Actress (Rhianna). **Acq:** Purchase, Rent/Lease. **Dist:** Universal Studios Home Video. $34.98 29.98 14.99.

The Battleship Potemkin 1925 (Unrated) — ★★★★
Eisenstein's best work documents mutiny aboard the Russian battleship Potemkin in 1905 which led to a civilian uprising against the Czar in Odessa, and the resulting crackdown by troops loyal to the Czar. Beautiful cinematography, especially the use of montage sequences, changed filmmaking. In particular, a horrifying sequence depicting the slaughter of civilians on an Odessa beach by soldiers coming down the stairs leading to it is exceptional; many movies pay homage to this scene including "The Untouchables" and "Love and Death." Viewers should overlook obvious Marxist overtones and see this film for what it is: a masterpiece. 71m/B/W; Silent; VHS, DVD, Blu-Ray. **TV Std:** NTSC, PAL. **C:** Alexander Antonov; Vladimir Barsky; Grigori Alexandrov; Mikhail Gomorov; Sergei Eisenstein; I. Brobov; Beatrice Vitoldi; N. Poltavseva; Alexandr Levshin; Repnikova; Korobei; Levchenko; Directed by Grigori Alexandrov; Sergei Eisenstein; Written by Sergei Eisenstein; Nina Agadzhanova Shutko; Cinematography by Eduard Tisse. **Pr:** Goskino. **A:** Jr. High-Adult. **P:** Entertainment. **U:** Home. **Mov-Ent:** Drama, Classic Films, Silent Films. **Acq:** Purchase. **Dist:** Kino International Corp.; Image Entertainment Inc.; Lions Gate Entertainment Inc. $19.98.

Battlestar Galactica 1978 (PG) — ★★1/2
Plot episode of the sci-fi TV series which was later released in the theatres. The crew of the spaceship Galactica must battle their robot enemies in an attempt to reach Earth. Contains special effects designed by John "Star Wars" Dykstra. Individual episodes are also available. 125m; VHS, DVD, Blu-Ray. **C:** Lorne Greene; Dirk Benedict; Maren Jensen; Jane Seymour; Patrick Macnee; Terry Carter; John Colicos; Richard A. Colla; Laurette Spang; Richard Hatch; Directed by Richard A. Colla; Written by Richard A. Colla; Glen Larson; Cinematography by Ben Colman; Music by Stu Phillips. **Pr:** Glen Larson; Glen Larson. **A:** Family. **P:** Entertainment. **U:** Home. **Mov-Ent:** Science Fiction, Space Exploration. **Acq:** Purchase. **Dist:** Movies Unlimited. $14.98.

Battlestar Galactica: Blood & Chrome 2012 (Unrated)
Intended as a pilot for another prequel "Battlestar Galactica" series that the Syfy Channel didn't pick up. Young fighter pilot William Adama is assigned to Galatica during the first Cylon War. Along with his more experienced co-pilot Coker, Adama is sent on an escort mission that turns dangerous. 94m; DVD, Blu-Ray. **C:** Luke Pasqualino; Ben Cotton; Lili Bordan; John Pyper-Ferguson; Jill Teed; Directed by Jonas Pate; Written by Michael Taylor; Cinematography by Lukas Ettlin; Music by Bear McCreary. **A:** Jr. High-Adult. **P:** Entertainment. **U:** Home. **Mov-Ent:** Science Fiction, TV Movies. **Acq:** Purchase. **Dist:** Universal Studios Home Video. $29.98.

Battlestar Galactica: Gun on Ice Planet Zero 1979
Baltar attempts to get the Galactica in range of a giant pulsar cannon hidden on an icy planet. But when Adama discovers the ruse he sends Starbuck, Apollo, and a group of convicts on a mission to destroy the weapon. 96m; DVD. **C:** Lorne Greene; Richard Hatch; Dirk Benedict; Maren Jensen; John Colicos; Herbert Jefferson, Jr; Noah Hathaway; Laurette Spang; Britt Ekland; Dan O'Herlihy; Roy Thinnes; James Olson. **A:** Primary-Adult. **P:** Entertainment. **U:** Home. **Mov-Ent:** Science Fiction, Television Series. **Acq:** Purchase. **Dist:** Universal Studios Home Video.

Battlestar Galactica: Lost Planet of the Gods 1979
Commander Adama leads a group of ships to the planet Kobol, hoping to find clues to Earth's location but the Viper pilots have contracted a disease, necessitating the women to take on fighter patrol duties. And the traitor Baltar is leading the Cyclons in an attack on the Galactica. 96m; VHS. **C:** Lorne Greene; Richard Hatch; Dirk Benedict; Maren Jensen; John Colicos; Herbert Jefferson, Jr; Noah Hathaway; Laurette Spang; Terry Carter; Jane Seymour; Ed Begley, Jr; George Murdock. **Pr:** Universal Television. **A:** Primary-Adult. **P:** Entertainment. **U:** Home. **Mov-Ent:** Science Fiction, Television Series. **Acq:** Purchase. **Dist:** Universal Studios Home Video.

Battlestar Galactica: Razor 2007
A prequel TV movie with events taking place within the timeframe of season 2. Lee Adama takes control of Battlestar Pegasus and appoints Kendra Shaw as his XO. A controversial move considering her time serving with ruthless Admiral Helena Cain, which is revealed in flashbacks. 101m; DVD, Blu-Ray. **C:** Stephanie Jacobsen; Jamie Bamber; Katee Sackhoff; Michelle Forbes; Edward James Olmos; Tricia Helfer; Mary McDonnell; Directed by Felix Alcala; Written by Michael Taylor; Cinematography by Stephen McNutt; Music by Bear McCreary. **A:** Sr. High-Adult. **P:** Entertainment. **U:** Home. **Mov-Ent:** Science Fiction. **Acq:** Purchase. **Dist:** Universal Studios Home Video. $14.98.

Battlestar Galactica: Season 1 2004
Presents the debut season of the science fiction television series as Commander William Adama (Olmos) must defend his spaceship, the Battlestar Galactica, against a robot race that is bent on revenge against their former human masters; remake of the original 1970s series. 13 episodes. 713m; DVD, Blu-Ray, Wide, CC. **C:** Edward James Olmos; Mary McDonnell; Katee Sackhoff; Jamie Bamber; James Callis; Tricia Helfer. **A:** Jr. High-Adult. **P:** Entertainment. **U:** Home. **Mov-Ent:** Television Series, Science Fiction, Fantasy. **Acq:** Purchase. **Dist:** Universal Studios Home Video. $59.98.

Battlestar Galactica: Season 3 2007
Settled on New Caprica, Dr. Baltar is now president but quickly falls under the manipulations of the Cylon occupation. Col. Tigh leads a resistance movement with the help of Chief Tyrol and Samuel Anders. Upon Admiral Adama's return the colonists are led to escape. Eventually trials are held and Cylon collaborators convicted. 20 episodes. 955m; DVD, Blu-Ray. **C:** James Callis; Mary McDonnell; Michael Trucco; Jamie Bamber; Katee Sackhoff; Grace Park. **A:** Jr. High-Adult. **P:** Entertainment. **U:** Home. **Mov-Ent:** Drama, Action-Adventure, Science Fiction. **Acq:** Purchase. **Dist:** Universal Studios Home Video.

Battlestar Galactica: Season 2.0 2005
Presents the second season of the science fiction television series as Commander William Adama (Olmos) must defend his spaceship, the Battlestar Galactica, against a robot race that is bent on revenge against their former human masters; remake of the original 1970s series. 10 episodes. 438m; DVD, Blu-Ray, Wide, CC. **C:** Edward James Olmos; Mary McDonnell; Katee Sackhoff; Jamie Bamber; James Callis; Tricia Helfer. **A:** Jr. High-Adult. **P:** Entertainment. **U:** Home. **Mov-Ent:** Television Series, Science Fiction, Fantasy. **Acq:** Purchase. **Dist:** Universal Studios Home Video. $49.95.

Battlestar Galactica: Season 2.5 2006
Presents the third season of the science fiction television series (2003) as Commander William Adama (Olmos) must defend his spaceship, the Battlestar Galactica, against a robot race that is bent on revenge against their former human masters; remake of the original 1970s series. 11 episodes. 521m; DVD, Wide, CC. **C:** Edward James Olmos; Mary McDonnell; Katee Sackhoff; Jamie Bamber; James Callis; Tricia Helfer. **A:** Jr. High-Adult. **P:** Entertainment. **U:** Home. **Mov-Ent:** Television Series, Science Fiction, Fantasy. **Acq:** Purchase. **Dist:** Universal Studios Home Video.

Battlestar Galactica: Season 4.0 2007 (Unrated)
Sci Fi Network drama from 2004-2009. Galactica Commander Adama and President Laura Roslin lead a group of refugees in search of the fabled lost thirtheeth colony while Cylons diligently hunt down and attack them. Gaius Baltar aids the Cylons while Tom Zarek creates internal political conflict aboard the Battlestar. 755m; DVD, Blu-Ray. **A:** Jr. High-Adult. **P:** Entertainment. **U:** Home. **Mov-Ent:** Science Fiction, Television Series. **Acq:** Purchase. **Dist:** Universal Studios Home Video. $49.98.

Battlestar Galactica: Season 4.5 2009
SciFi Network 2004-09 drama. The final 10 episodes reveal Tigh, Anders, Foster, and Tyrol are actually Cylons; Kara questions her own humanity; Felix Gaeta organizes a mutiny; Vice President Tom Zarek makes an ambitious move; and President Roslin and Admiral Adama try tp keep the fleet together. 763m; DVD, Blu-Ray. **C:** Edward James Olmos; Mary McDonnell; Jamie Bamber; Tricia Helfer; Richard Hatch. **A:** Sr. High-Adult. **P:** Entertainment. **U:** Home. **Mov-Ent:** Science Fiction, Television Series. **Acq:** Purchase. **Dist:** Universal Studios Home Video. $39.98.

Battlestar Galactica: The Plan 2009 (Unrated) — ★★
The human-Cylon war, as seen through the eyes of the machines, opens with their destruction of Caprica. It then wanders off to show backstory on too many of the series's pivotal events in order to try and tie up some loose ends. A fans-only watch. 112m; DVD, Blu-Ray. **C:** Edward James Olmos; Tricia Helfer; Dean Stockwell; Grace Park; Michael Hogan; Michael Trucco; Callum Keith Rennie; Kate Vernon; Directed by Edward James Olmos; Written by Jane Espenson; Cinematography by Stephen McNutt; Music by Bear McCreary. **A:** Jr. High-Adult. **P:** Entertainment. **U:** Home. **Mov-Ent:** Science Fiction, Space Exploration. **Acq:** Purchase. **Dist:** Universal Studios Home Video.

The Battlin' Bucs: First 100 Years of the Pittsburgh Pirates 1986
A visual history of the much-loved Major League baseball team. 60m; VHS. **Pr:** Major League Baseball Productions. **A:** Family. **P:** Entertainment. **U:** Home. **Spo-Rec:** Sports--General, Baseball. **Acq:** Purchase. **Dist:** Major League Baseball Productions. $19.95.

Battling Brook Primary School 19??
A view of how two teachers handle a class of 86 students in an open education facility in England. 23m/B/W; 3/4 U, Special order formats. **Pr:** Education Development Center. **A:** College-Adult. **P:** Education. **U:** Institution, CCTV, CATV, BCTV. **Gen-Edu:** Documentary Films, Education, Children. **Acq:** Purchase, Rent/Lease. **Dist:** Education Development Center.

Battling Bunyon 1924 (Unrated) — ★★1/2
A wily youngster becomes a comedy boxer for profit, and eventually gets fed up and battles the champ. Silent. 71m/B/W; Silent; VHS. **C:** Chester Conklin; Wesley Barry; Mollie Malone; Jackie Fields; Paul Hurst; Frank Campeau; Johnny Relasco; Landers Stevens; Harry Mann; Pat Kemp; Directed by Paul Hurst. **Pr:** Arthur S. Kane. **A:** Family. **P:** Entertainment. **U:** Home. **Mov-Ent:** Boxing, Silent Films. **Acq:** Purchase. **Dist:** Grapevine Video. $16.95.

Battling Butler 1926 (Unrated) — ★★1/2
Rich young Keaton tries to impress a young lady by impersonating a boxer. All goes well until he has to fight the real thing. Mostly charming if uneven; one of Keaton's more unusual efforts, thought to be somewhat autobiographical. Silent. 70m/B/W; Silent; VHS, DVD, Blu-Ray. **C:** Buster Keaton; Sally O'Neil; Snitz Edwards; Francis McDonald; Mary O'Brien; Tom Wilson; Walter James; Directed by Buster Keaton; Written by Al Boasberg; Lex Neal; Charles Henry Smith; Paul Girard Smith; Cinematography by Bert Haines; Devereaux Jennings. **Pr:** Metro-Goldwyn-Mayer Pictures. **A:** Family. **P:** Entertainment. **U:** Home. **Mov-Ent:** Comedy--Romantic, Boxing, Silent Films. **Acq:** Purchase. **Dist:** Image Entertainment Inc.

Battling for Baby 1992 — ★★
It's the war of the Grandmas. New mother Katherine decides to return to work and both her mother and mother-in-law want to look after the little tyke. Silly made-for-TV fluff. 93m; VHS, DVD, CC. **C:** Courteney Cox; Suzanne Pleshette; Debbie Reynolds; John Terlesky; Doug McClure; Leigh Lawson; Mary Jo Catlett; Directed by Art Wolff; Written by Walter Lockwood; Nancy Silvers. **Pr:** Steve McGlothen; Frank Von Zerneck; Robert M. Sertner. **A:** Jr. High-Adult. **P:** Entertainment. **U:** Home. **Mov-Ent:** Parenting, TV Movies, Family. **Acq:** Purchase. **Dist:** Turner Broadcasting System Inc. $89.98.

Battling Marshal 1948 — ★1/2
Carson battles bad guys out to steal a family's gold-rich land. He foils a fake smallpox scare, thugs, and cheapo production values. 52m/B/W; VHS, DVD. **C:** Sunset Carson; Lee Roberts; Pat Gleason; Directed by Oliver Drake. **Pr:** Astor Pictures. **A:** Family. **P:** Entertainment. **U:** Home. **Mov-Ent:** Western. **Acq:** Purchase. **Dist:** Movies Unlimited; Alpha Video. $29.95.

Battling Orioles 1924 — ★★1/2
The once scrappy baseball team is now a bunch of grumpy old men, that is until Glenn whips them into shape. Silent. 58m/B/W; Silent; VHS, DVD, 8 mm. **C:** Glenn Tryon; Blanche Mehaffey; Noah Young; Directed by Ted Wilde; Fred Guiol. **A:** Family. **P:** Entertainment. **U:** Home. **Mov-Ent:** Baseball. **Acq:** Purchase. **Dist:** Grapevine Video; Glenn Video Vistas Ltd. $35.95.

Battling Outlaw 1940 — ★1/2
Billy is made sheriff of a lawless Texas town after standing up to the local gang. Then he and his friend Fuzzy set out to retrieve money stolen by the gang. 64m/B/W; VHS, DVD. **C:** Bob Steele; Al "Fuzzy" St. John; John Merton; Terry Walker; Carleton Young; Charles "Blackie" King; Charles "Slim" Whitaker; Frank LaRue; Directed by Sam Newfield; Written by Joseph O'Donnell; Cinematography by Jack Greenhalgh. **A:** Family. **P:** Entertainment. **U:** Home. **Mov-Ent. Acq:** Purchase. **Dist:** Movies Unlimited. $19.95.

Battling with Buffalo Bill 1931 — ★★
Twelve episodes of the vintage serial concerning the exploits of the legendary Indian fighter. 180m/B/W; VHS, DVD. **C:** Tom Tyler; Rex Bell; Franklyn Farnum; Lucille Browne; Francis Ford; William Desmond; Jim Thorpe; Yakima Canutt; Chief Thunderbird; Bud Osborne; Directed by Ray Taylor; Written by Ella O'Neill; George Plympton. **Pr:** Mark Huffam. **A:** Family. **P:** Entertainment. **U:** Home. **Mov-Ent:** Western, Serials. **Acq:** Purchase. **Dist:** VCI Entertainment. $29.95.

Batty World of Baseball 1981
A zany look at the lighter side of America's past time including the now mythic San Diego Chicken. 30m; VHS. **Pr:** Major League Baseball Productions. **A:** Family. **P:** Entertainment. **U:** Home. **Spo-Rec:** Sports--General, Baseball. **Acq:** Purchase. **Dist:** Sony Pictures Home Entertainment Inc. $49.95.

Bauhaus: Archive 198?
This British import features clips of "Passion of Lovers," "Stigmata Martyr," "Dark Entries" and more. 40m; VHS. **A:** Jr. High-College. **P:** Entertainment. **U:** Home. **Mov-Ent:** Music Video. **Acq:** Purchase. **Dist:** Music Video Distributors. $39.95.

Bauhaus/Chrome: Compilation 198?
A tape of live performance by the English punk band Bauhaus, and the San Francisco punk group Chrome. Songs include, "Bela Lugosi's Dead," "Telegram Sam," "Dark Entries," "Flat Fields" and more. 60m; VHS. **Pr:** Target Video. **A:** College-Adult. **P:** Entertainment. **U:** Home. **Mov-Ent:** Music--Performance. **Acq:** Purchase. **Dist:** Music Video Distributors. $39.95.

Bauhaus: Its Impact on the World of Design—1919-1923 1987
Located in Germany, the Bauhaus was the art school foremost in beautifying the technical and sometimes merciless world around it. With teachers such as Gropius, Feininger, Klee, Kandinsky, and Moholy-Nagy, the Bauhaus produced an art form to be marvelled at for generations to come. 19m; VHS, 8 mm, Special order formats. **Pr:** Applause Productions. **A:** Sr. High-Adult. **P:** Education. **U:** Institution, Home. **Gen-Edu:** Documentary Films, Art & Artists, Germany. **Acq:** Purchase, Rent/Lease. **Dist:** The Roland Collection. $89.00.

Bauhaus: Shadow of Light 1991
The British band is captured live, performing "Bela Lugosi's Dead," "Telegram Sam," "Rose Garden/Funeral of Sores," "Spirit," "She's in Parties," "Ziggy Stardust" and more. 60m; VHS. **A:** Jr. High-Adult. **P:** Entertainment. **U:** Home. **Mov-Ent:** Music--Performance, Music--Pop/Rock. **Acq:** Purchase. **Dist:** Music Video Distributors. $19.95.

Bavaria: Castles and History of the Wittelsbach Dynasty 1986
A tour of this lovely region from the Alps to the River Main and from Bayerischer Wald to the Bodensee. English dialogue. 45m; VHS. **A:** Jr. High-Adult. **P:** Entertainment. **U:** Institution, Home. **Gen-Edu:** Travel, Germany. **Acq:** Purchase. **Dist:** German Language Video Center.

Bavarian Forest 1987
A video trip through the Bayerwald, including Ratisbon and Passau. Features artisans and scenic views, including a visit to the world's largest organ in Passau. 30m; VHS. **A:** Family. **P:** Education. **U:** Home. **Gen-Edu:** Travel, Germany, Forests & Trees. **Acq:** Purchase. **Dist:** German Language Video Center. $29.95.

Bavarian Storyland 1991
A video tour of Oberbayern, from Garmisch-Partenkirchen to Oberammergau. In English. 45m; VHS. **TV Std:** NTSC, PAL. **Pr:** German Language Video Center. **A:** Family. **P:** Entertainment. **U:** Home. **Gen-Edu:** Travel, Germany. **Acq:** Purchase, Rent/Lease. **Dist:** German Language Video Center. $49.95.

The Bawdy Adventures of Tom Jones 1976 (R) — ★½
An exploitive extension of the Fielding novel about the philandering English lad, with plenty of soft-core skin and lewdness. 89m; VHS. **C:** Joan Collins; Trevor Howard; Terry-Thomas; Arthur Lowe; Murray Melvin; Directed by Cliff Owen. **Pr:** Chromebridge Ltd. **A:** Sr. High-Adult. **P:** Entertainment. **U:** Home. **Mov-Ent:** Satire & Parody, Sex & Sexuality. **Acq:** Purchase. **Dist:** $59.95.

Baxter 1989 (Unrated) — ★★½
A bull terrier lives his life with three different sets of masters. He examines all of humankind's worst faults and the viewer quickly realizes that Baxter's life depends on his refusal to obey like a good dog should. Based on the novel by Ken Greenhall. Funny, sometimes erotic, quirky comedy. In French with English subtitles. 82m; VHS, DVD. **C:** Lisa (Lise) Delamare; Jean Mercure; Jacques Spiesser; Catherine Ferran; Jean-Paul Roussillon; Sabrina Leurquin; Directed by Jerome Boivin; Written by Jerome Boivin; Jacques Audiard; Cinematography by Yves Angelo; Music by Marc Hillman; Patrick Roffe. **A:** Sr. High-Adult. **P:** Entertainment. **U:** Home. **L:** French. **Mov-Ent:** Comedy-Drama, Pets. **Acq:** Purchase. **Dist:** Lions Gate Entertainment Inc. $89.95.

The Baxter 2005 (PG-13) — ★★
Elliot Sherman (Showalter) is so CPA mega-nerd even his sweet grandmother knows he's "the Baxter," the also-ran, the nice, safe, dull guy who never gets the girl. In the opening scene he's dumped at the altar by his beautiful fiancee Caroline (Banks) when her high school flame Bradley (Theroux) reappears. You might want to feel something for Elliot, but he's so unlikable that sympathy will be hard to find. Soon it becomes apparent that Elliot's office temp Cecil (Williams), who has been right there under his nose, is the perfect woman for him. 91m; DVD. **C:** Michael Showalter; Elizabeth Banks; Michelle Williams; Justin Theroux; Zak Orth; Michael Ian Black; Catherine Lloyd Burns; Peter Dinklage; Paul Rudd; Directed by Michael Showalter; Written by Michael Showalter; Music by Theodore Shapiro; Craig (Shudder to Think) Wedren. **Pr:** Galt Niederhoffer; Daniela Taplin Lundberg; Celine Rattray; Reagan Silber; IFC Films; MGM. **A:** Jr. High-Adult. **P:** Entertainment. **U:** Home. **L:** English. **Mov-Ent:** Comedy-Drama, Comedy--Romantic. **Acq:** Purchase. **Dist:** MGM Home Entertainment.

The Bay 2012 (R) — ★★½
A la "Blair Witch Project" and "Cloverfield's" found-footage style, this horror/mockumentary pits a sleepy, fictional town in Maryland's Chesapeake Bay against some bacterial enemy that's infected the water. Over the course of 24 hours, townspeople flock to the local ER with rashes, boils, and other gross symptoms. People are dying from a flesh-eating bacteria, and the living are panicking. The town is shut down, but the government is covering something up. The story unfolds through pieced-together clips from budding journalist, Donna (Donohue)--only it's three years later that the truth of this eco-disaster is unveiled. 84m; DVD. **C:** Kristen Connolly; Kether Donohue; Christopher Denham; Stephen Kunken; Frank Deal; Nansi Aluka; Directed by Barry Levinson; Written by Michael Wallach; Cinematography by Josh Nussbaum; Music by Marcelo Zarvos. **Pr:** Jason Blum; Steven Schneider; Hydraulx; Automatik Entertainment. **A:** Sr. High-Adult. **P:** Entertainment. **U:** Home. **L:** English. **Mov-Ent:** Acq: Purchase. **Dist:** Lions Gate Home Entertainment; Roadside Attractions.

The Bay Boy 1985 (R) — ★★½
Set in the 1930s in Nova Scotia, this period piece captures the coming-of-age of a rural teenage boy. Young Sutherland's adolescent angst becomes a more difficult struggle when he witnesses a murder, and is tormented by the secret. 107m; VHS, CC. **C:** Liv Ullmann; Kiefer Sutherland; Peter Donat; Matthieu Carriere; Joe MacPherson; Isabelle Mejias; Alan Scarfe; Chris Wiggins; Leah K. Pinsent; Directed by Daniel Petrie; Music by Claude Bolling. **Pr:** ICC International Cinema. **A:** Sr. High-Adult. **P:** Entertainment. **U:** Home. **Mov-Ent:** Adolescence, Canada. **Awds:** Genie '85: Film, Support. Actor (Scarfe). **Acq:** Purchase. **Dist:** MGM Studios Inc. $79.98.

Bay City Rollers: Japan Tour, 1976 1976
The group performs "Saturday Night" and other hits from their Japan tour. 25m; VHS. **A:** Jr. High-Adult. **P:** Entertainment. **U:** Home. **Mov-Ent:** Music--Performance, Music--Pop/Rock. **Acq:** Purchase. **Dist:** Music Video Distributors. $49.95.

Bay of Dolphins/Stingray Man 19??
The grace of marine life is captured through beautiful underwater cinematography which was the hallmark of the late Jack McKenney. 46m; VHS. **A:** Jr. High-Adult. **P:** Entertainment. **U:** Home. **Spo-Rec:** Scuba. **Acq:** Purchase. **Dist:** Bennett Marine Video. $19.95.

Bay of Pigs 1972
A re-creation of the CIA supported invasion of Cuba, including actual documentary footage and re-enactments. English subtitles. 103m/B/W; VHS, 3/4 U. **TV Std:** NTSC, PAL, SECAM. **Pr:** Manuel Herrera. **A:** Jr. High-Adult. **P:** Education. **U:** Institution, SURA. **L:** English, Spanish. **Gen-Edu:** Documentary Films, Caribbean, International Relations. **Acq:** Rent/Lease. **Dist:** The Cinema Guild.

Bayern: Geschichte und Schloesser der Wittelsbacher 1986
A look at the history, architecture, and music of Bayern, from the Main River to the Alps and from the Koenigsee to the Bayrische Wald, plus a tour of the capitol city of Muenchen. In German only. 45m; VHS. **TV Std:** NTSC, PAL. **Pr:** German Language Video Center. **A:** Family. **P:** Entertainment. **U:** Home. **L:** German. **Gen-Edu:** History--Medieval, Travel, Germany. **Acq:** Purchase, Rent/Lease. **Dist:** German Language Video Center. $49.95.

Baymen 1999
Documentary about the workers who harvest shellfish from Long Island Bay. 56m; VHS, DVD. **A:** Sr. High-Adult. **P:** Education. **U:** Home, Institution. **Gen-Edu:** Documentary Films, Labor & Unions. **Acq:** Purchase, Rent/Lease. **Dist:** The Cinema Guild. $295.00.

Bayou Romance 1986 (Unrated) — ★
Painter inherits a Louisiana plantation, moves in, and falls in love with a young gypsy. 90m. **C:** Annie Potts; Michael Ansara; Barbara Horan; Paul Rossilli; Directed by Alan Myerson. **Pr:** Commworld Productions; Romance Theater. **A:** Sr. High-Adult. **P:** Entertainment. **U:** Home. **Mov-Ent:** Drama. **Acq:** Purchase. **Dist:** No Longer Available.

The Baytown Outlaws 2012 (R) — ★
Violent, cartoonish action filled with stereotypes. The dumber-than-dirt, redneck Alabama Oodie brothers are hired by Celeste to retrieve her wheelchair-bound godson Rob, who's been kidnapped by her sleazy criminal ex-husband Carlos, who wants the teen's trust fund. Getting Rob out of Carlos' Texas compound means going up against a series of violent (and weird) killers. 98m; DVD, Blu-Ray. **C:** Clayne Crawford; Daniel Cudmore; Travis Fimmel; Andre Braugher; Eva Longoria; Billy Bob Thornton; Thomas Brodie-Sangster; Paul Wesley; Directed by Barry Battles; Written by Barry Battles; Griffin Hood; Cinematography by Dave McFarland; Music by Kostas Christides; Christopher Young. **A:** Sr. High-Adult. **P:** Entertainment. **U:** Home. **L:** English. **Mov-Ent:** Family, Action-Comedy. **Acq:** Purchase. **Dist:** Phase 4/kaBOOM Entertainment.

Baywatch: Nightmare Bay 1994
Mitch manages to save the life of an underwater photographer who was attacked in a sea cave. But crazed media hype is a bigger challenge when the photographer tells her incredible story. 89m; VHS, DVD, CC. **C:** David Hasselhoff. **A:** Jr. High-Adult. **P:** Entertainment. **U:** Home. **Mov-Ent:** Mass Media. **Acq:** Purchase. **Dist:** Lions Gate Television Corp. $14.95.

Baywatch: Season 1 1989 (Unrated)
Veteran lifeguard Mitch Buchanan is in charge of the team working at Malibu Beach—a mixed group of veterans and rookies. In this season, which was on NBC, Mitch is battling his ex-wife over custody of their son; lifeguards Eddie and Shauni begin a romance; and one of the team dies after a shark attack. 20 episodes. 880m; DVD. **C:** David Hasselhoff; Billy Warlock; Erika Eleniak; Shawn Weatherly; Parker Stevenson. **A:** Jr. High-Adult. **P:** Entertainment. **U:** Home. **Mov-Ent:** Television Series, Action-Adventure. **Acq:** Purchase. **Dist:** Universal Studios Home Video.

Baywatch: Season 2 1991 (Unrated)
After being cancelled by NBC, the series moved to syndication with a mix of new and old cast members. Among those added are veteran Ben, who coordinated rescue operations, and young prankster Harvey. 20 episodes. 968m; DVD. **C:** David Hasselhoff; Billy Warlock; Erika Eleniak; Richard Jaeckel; Tom McTigue. **A:** Jr. High-Adult. **P:** Entertainment. **U:** Home. **Mov-Ent:** Television Series, Action-Adventure. **Acq:** Purchase. **Dist:** Universal Studios Home Video.

Baywatch the Movie: Forbidden Paradise 1995 (PG) — ★★½
The "Baywatch" babes and their fellow lifesaving hunks-in-trunks head off to Hawaii to study the latest search and rescue techniques from the state's premier lifeguard team. 90m; VHS. **C:** David Hasselhoff; Pamela Anderson; Alexandra Paul; Yasmine Bleeth; David Charvet; Gregory Alan-Williams; Jeremy Jackson; Directed by Douglas Schwartz. **A:** Jr. High-Adult. **P:** Entertainment. **U:** Home. **Mov-Ent:** Oceanography, TV Movies. **Acq:** Purchase. **Dist:** Lions Gate Television Corp. $92.98.

Baywatch: White Thunder at Glacier Bay 1997 (PG)
When offered a photo shoot for a sports magazine, those life-saving babes and hunks leave their sunny beaches for an Alaskan cruise. Also on board is a beautiful jewel thief with a cache of emeralds and the hit man sent to get the goods back. Naturally, both become involved with the lifeguards. Based on the syndicated TV series; contains 15 minutes of footage not shown in the TV movie. 107m; VHS. **C:** David Hasselhoff; Carmen Electra; Gena Lee Nolin; David Chokachi; Donna D'Errico. **A:** Jr. High-Adult. **P:** Entertainment. **U:** Home. **Mov-Ent:** TV Movies, Boating, Bears. **Acq:** Purchase. **Dist:** CinemaNow Inc.

Bazaar Bizarre: The Strange Case of Serial Killer Bob Berdella 2006
Novelist James Ellroy presents the case of Robert A. Berdella, who tortured, photographed, and murdered six men, leaving their dismembered bodies in plastic bags for garbage pickup. Berdella was caught in 1988 when another victim escaped. 89m; DVD. **A:** Jr. High-Adult. **P:** Entertainment. **U:** Home. **Gen-Edu:** Documentary Films. **Acq:** Purchase. **Dist:** Pathfinder Pictures.

Bazaar Spa Fabulous Abs 1996
Offers challenging abdominal floorwork with easy-to-follow aerobics. Works to flatten your stomach, and tone your abdominal muscles while the aerobics burn the fat above those muscles. 52m; VHS. **A:** Adult. **P:** Instruction. **U:** Home. **Hea-Sci:** Fitness/Exercise, How-To, Self-Help. **Acq:** Purchase. **Dist:** Collage Video Specialties, Inc. $14.95.

B.B. King and Friends: A Night of Red Hot Blues 1986
King and other blues greats such as Eric Clapton, Etta James, and the late Stevie Ray Vaughn jam at the Ebony Showcase Theatre in L.A. Includes the songs "Why I Sing the Blues," "Sky is Crying," "Take My Hand, Precious Lord," "I'd Rather Go Blind," "In the Midnight Hour," "The Thrill Is Gone," "Please Send Me Someone to Love," "When Something is Wrong with My Baby," "Something's Got a hold on Me," "Ain't Nobody's Business but My Own," "Let the Good Times Roll," and a finale. 56m; VHS. **Pr:** HBO. **A:** Family. **P:** Entertainment. **U:** Home. **Mov-Ent:** Music--Performance. **Acq:** Purchase. **Dist:** WarnerVision; Music Video Distributors; Fast Forward. $19.95.

B.B. King: Blues Master #1 19??
Features B.B. King and his band performing live and discussing subjects like bending, signature phrases, right and left hand technique, vibrato, creating a solo and more. ?m; VHS. **Pr:** DCI Music Video. **A:** Jr. High-Adult. **P:** Entertainment. **U:** Home. **Mov-Ent:** Music Video. **Acq:** Purchase. **Dist:** Music Video Distributors. $49.95.

B.B. King: Live at the Apollo 1992
Blues great King performs "When Love Comes to Town," "Sweet Sixteen," "Since I Met You Baby," and more live from the legendary Apollo Theater. 60m; VHS. **A:** Jr. High-Adult. **P:** Entertainment. **U:** Home. **Mov-Ent:** Music Video, Music--Performance, Music--Jazz. **Acq:** Purchase. **Dist:** Music Video Distributors. $19.95.

B.B. King: Live in Africa 1974
Performing live in the "Zaire '74" festival, King plays his most famous songs, including "The Thrill Is Gone," "I Like to Live the Love," "Guess Who" and "Ain't Nobody Home." 43m; VHS, DVD. **C:** B.B. King. **Pr:** GRAVITY S.A.R.L. **A:** Family. **P:** Entertainment. **U:** Home. **Mov-Ent:** Music--Performance, Black Culture. **Acq:** Purchase. **Dist:** Music Video Distributors; Facets Multimedia Inc. $19.95.

B.B. King: Memories of Greatness Live 198?
This Japanese import contains live material from the blues great. 50m; VHS. **A:** Sr. High-Adult. **P:** Entertainment. **U:** Home. **Mov-Ent:** Music--Performance. **Acq:** Purchase. **Dist:** Music Video Distributors. $59.95.

BBC Children's Favourites 19??
More of the BBC's cartoons for kids: three favourites featuring Ivor the Engine, Bagpuss and Clangers. 55m; VHS. **Pr:** British Broadcasting Corporation. **A:** Preschool-Jr. High. **P:** Entertainment. **U:** Home. **Chl-Juv:** Children, Animation & Cartoons. **Acq:** Purchase. **Dist:** Video Collectibles. $14.98.

BBC Foreign Languages Series 1984
This unusual series of 30 untitled programs introduces students to various aspects of Greek and Italian life while learning the languages. 20m; VHS, 3/4 U. **Pr:** British Broadcasting Corporation. **A:** Sr. High-Adult. **P:** Education. **U:** Institution, SURA. **Gen-Edu:** How-To, Language Arts. **Acq:** Purchase, Rent/Lease. **Dist:** Home Vision Cinema. **Indiv. Titles:** 1. Greek Language and People (10 programs) 2. Buongiorno Italia! (20 programs).

BBC History of World War II 2005
A 12-part series on how and why World War II started, from the rise of the Nazis to the reasons Japan entered the war. Includes archival footage and eyewitness accounts. 1870m; DVD. **A:** Sr. High-Adult. **P:** Entertainment. **U:** Home. **Gen-Edu:** Documentary Films, World War Two. **Acq:** Purchase. **Dist:** Warner Home Video, Inc.

B.C.: A Special Christmas 1971
The popular comic-strip gang comes to life in this festive Christmas special. 25m; VHS, CC. **C:** Voice(s) by Bob Elliott; Ray Goulding. **A:** Family. **P:** Entertainment. **U:** Home. **Chl-Juv:** Animation & Cartoons, Christmas. **Acq:** Purchase. **Dist:** Sony Pictures Home Entertainment Inc.; New Line Home Video. $14.95.

B.C. Rock 1984 (R) — ★★
A cave man learns how to defend himself and has some prehistoric fun with a tribe of female amazons. Animated. 87m; VHS. **Pr:** Almi Pictures. **A:** Sr. High-Adult. **P:** Entertainment. **U:** Home. **Mov-Ent:** Fantasy, Animation & Cartoons. **Acq:** Purchase. **Dist:** Lions Gate Television Corp. $69.98.

B.C.: The First Thanksgiving 1972
The caveman B.C. and his friends are trying to find a turkey to flavor their rock soup in this animated featurette. 25m; VHS, CC. **C:** Voice(s) by Donald E. Messick; Daws Butler; Bob Holt. **A:** Family. **P:** Entertainment. **U:** Home. **Chl-Juv:** Animation & Cartoons, Holidays. **Acq:** Purchase. **Dist:** New Line Home Video. $14.98.

BCL-A Key to Improved Productivity 1986
This program touts the usefulness of the BCL data format for numerically controlled machines. 18m; VHS, 3/4 U. **Pr:** USDLA. **A:** Adult. **P:** Professional. **U:** Institution, SURA. **Bus-Ind:** Industrial Arts. **Acq:** Purchase. **Dist:** National Audiovisual Center. $95.00.

B.D. Women 1994
Black lesbians discuss their sexual and racial identities. 20m; VHS. **A:** Adult. **P:** Education. **U:** Institution. **Gen-Edu:** Black Culture, Sex & Sexuality, Women. **Acq:** Purchase, Rent/Lease. **Dist:** Women Make Movies. $225.00.

Be a Ballerina 1994
Geared to teach young children basic ballet techniques. 35m; VHS. **Pr:** Fern Gladstone; New England Media; Tu Tu Good Productions. **A:** Preschool-Primary. **P:** Instruction. **U:** Home. **How-Ins:** Dance--Ballet, Children, Dance--Instruction. **Acq:** Purchase. **Dist:** Tapeworm Video Distributors Inc. $15.95.

Be a Better Listener 1995
Teaches students to become better listeners with the aid of graphics and song lyrics. Explains how tone of voice and body language emphasizes listening skills. Comes with teacher's guide. 15m; VHS. **A:** Primary. **P:** Education. **U:** Institution. **Chl-Juv:** Children, Education. **Acq:** Purchase. **Dist:** Sunburst Digital Inc. $95.

Be a Better Shopper 1989
Thirteen episodes for consumers on specific ways to get the most for the food dollar. Each program 30 minutes long and are available individually. 390m; VHS, 3/4 U, EJ, Q. **Pr:** Cornell University. **A:** College-Adult. **P:** Education. **U:** Institution, CCTV, CATV, BCTV, Home. **Gen-Edu:** Consumer Education. **Acq:** Purchase, Rent/Lease. **Dist:** Cornell University.
Indiv. Titles: 1. Behind Food Prices 2. Where Does All the Money Go? 3. Shopping Strategies 4. Comparison Shopping 5. Lable to Table-Part I 6. Label to Table-Part II 7. The Meat of the Matter-Part I 8. The Meat of the Matter-Part II 9. The Meat of the Matter-Part III 10. Don't Get a Lemon When What You Want is a Peach 11. Super Marketing at the Supermarket 12. Where But the Supermarket 13. The Responsible Consumer.

Be a Magician 1987
Easy to follow lessons make learning magic fun for the entire family. Includes magic wand and more. 50m; VHS. **Pr:** Family Express. **A:** Family. **P:** Entertainment. **U:** Home. **How-Ins:** Magic. **Acq:** Purchase. **Dist:** Music for Little People. $19.98.

Be a Patriot, Kill a Priest 2001
Reviews the role of the Church in the civil war in El Salvador; specifically, that many Latin American clergy were murdered for demanding—in the name of the Gospel—justice, food, and education for the poor. 26m; VHS. **A:** College-Adult. **P:** Education. **U:** Institution. **Gen-Edu:** South America, War--General, Religion. **Acq:** Purchase, Rent/Lease. **Dist:** Filmakers Library Inc. $250.00.

Be a Pro 198?
This training film helps workers develop a professional attitude toward their work. 15m; VHS, 3/4 U. **A:** College-Adult. **P:** Education. **U:** Institution. **Bus-Ind:** Personality, Job Training. **Acq:** Rent/Lease. **Dist:** National Safety Council, California Chapter, Film Library.

Be an Inventor 1994
Provides students with hands-on activities which lets them plan, design, build, and sell their inventions to the class. Teaches creativity, drawing, research, building, writing, public speaking, problem solving, and mathematics skills while involving them in science. Comes with teacher's guide and blackline masters. 20m; VHS. **A:** Primary. **P:** Education. **U:** Institution. **Chl-Juv:** Science, Education, Speech. **Acq:** Purchase. **Dist:** United Learning Inc. $95.00.

Be at Peace 1995
Presents meditations and tranquil scenes designed to help hospital patients unwind from their day and prepare for a restful night. 30m; VHS. **A:** Family. **P:** Entertainment. **U:** Institution. **Gen-Edu:** Stress, Hospitals. **Acq:** Purchase. **Dist:** Aquarius Health Care Media. $79.95.

Be at Peace: Assuring Thoughts to End Your Day 1993
Companion work to "Awaken to Hope" offers 14 meditations to help viewers unwind at the end of the day, accompanied by tranquil nature images. 30m; VHS. **A:** Adult. **P:** Education. **U:** Home. **Gen-Edu:** Philosophy & Ideology. **Acq:** Purchase. **Dist:** Willowgreen Productions. $59.95.

Be Cool 2005 (PG-13) — ★
Paging Dr. Tarantino STAT! This turgid sequel to "Get Shorty" proves that Travolta is in need of another new-career-ectomy. Jettisoning anything even mildly cool about the witty original, director Gray instead focuses on bombast and pointless cameos in the continuing adventures of Hollywood shylock Chili Palmer (Travolta). This time, Chili tries to break into the music business with the help of a widowed record producer (Thurman) and a young ingenue (Milian). Standing in their way are Russian mobsters, gangsta rap kingpins, and Vince Vaughn doing the tired white-guy-who-thinks-he's-black routine. Even The Rock as a flamboyantly gay bodyguard can't inject any life into such a flat, unfunny mess. 112m; VHS, DVD, UMD. **C:** John Travolta; Uma Thurman; Vince Vaughn; Cedric the Entertainer; Andre Benjamin; Robert Pastorelli; Christina Milian; Paul Adelstein; Debi Mazar; Gregory Alan Williams; Harvey Keitel; Dwayne "The Rock" Johnson; Danny DeVito; James Woods; Directed by F. Gary Gray; Written by Peter Steinfeld; Cinematography by Jeffrey L. Kimball; Music by John Powell. **Pr:** Danny DeVito; Michael H. Shamberg; Stacey Sher; David Nicksay; Danny DeVito; Jersey Films; Double Feature Films; MGM. **A:** Jr. High-Adult. **P:** Entertainment. **U:** Home. **L:** English. **Mov-Ent:** Music, Music--Rap. **Acq:** Purchase. **Dist:** MGM Home Entertainment.

Be Fair and Take Care 1988
See how life looks through the eyes of a disabled boy and a terminally ill girl. 45m; VHS, 3/4 U. **Pr:** Marshfilm. **A:** Primary. **P:** Education. **U:** Institution. **Gen-Edu:** Handicapped, Human Relations. **Acq:** Purchase. **Dist:** Marshmedia. $45.50.

Be Good My Children 1992
Dramatizes a Korean immigrant family in New York City. Examines conflict between a hard-working, religious mother and her two grown children, who all have different ideas about what life should be like in New York. Studies racism, sexism, and representation of Asian-Americans in mainstream media. 47m; VHS. **A:** College-Adult. **P:** Education. **U:** Institution. **Gen-Edu:** Asia, Immigration, Ethnicity. **Acq:** Purchase, Rent/Lease. **Dist:** Women Make Movies. $250.00.

Be Good, Smile Pretty 2004 (Unrated)
Documentary following Tacy Droz Tragos as she hunts down her dead father's wartime comrades in order to learn about him. 52m; DVD. **A:** Sr. High-Adult. **P:** Education. **U:** Home. **Gen-Edu:** Documentary Films, Vietnam War. **Acq:** Purchase. **Dist:** Docurama. $24.95.

Be Healthy! Be Happy! Second Edition 1983
An animated film for primary grade students which teaches good health habits. 11m; 3/4 U, Special order formats. **Pr:** Portafilm Productions. **A:** Preschool-Primary. **P:** Education. **U:** Institution, Home, SURA. **Hea-Sci:** Health Education. **Acq:** Purchase, Rent/Lease, Trade-in, Duplication License. **Dist:** United Learning Inc.

Be Here To Love Me: A Film About Townes Van Zandt 2004 (Unrated) — ★★★
Biographical documentary on the life and times of singer/songwriter Townes Van Zandt. It includes interviews with his peers and family, and unpublished clips from a film early in his career. 99m; DVD, Streaming. **C:** Directed by Margaret Brown; Cinematography by Lee Daniel; Music by Willie Nelson; Merle Haggard; Lyle Lovett; Townes Van Zandt. **Pr:** Sam Brumbaugh; Margaret Brown; Rake Films Production; Palm Pictures. **A:** Jr. High-Adult. **P:** Entertainment. **U:** Home. **L:** English. **Mov-Ent.** **Acq:** Purchase, Rent/Lease. **Dist:** Palm Pictures. $26.97 9.99.

Be Kind Rewind 2008 (PG-13) — ★★½
Simple guy Jerry (Black) lives in a trailer, works at a junkyard, and likes to hang out at Mr. Fletcher's (Glover) titular video rental store, where his buddy Mike (Def) works. After a mishap at a local power plant magnetizes Jerry, accidentally erases all of the videotapes (the store is VHS only), so Jerry and Mike enlist the talents of the very cute Alma (Diaz) from the nearby dry cleaner to help them re-enact and re-record all of the movies for rental as usual. The oddball store regulars get wise to their shenanigans and everyone wants to play a part, which makes Jerry, Mike and the video store unlikely celebrities. Black is Black and the whole thing is often silly and obvious, but entertaining nonetheless. 100m; DVD, Blu-Ray. **C:** Jack Black; Mos Def; Danny Glover; Mia Farrow; Melonie Diaz; Arjay Smith; Sigourney Weaver; Chandler Parker; Irv Gooch; Directed by Michel Gondry; Written by Michel Gondry; Cinematography by Ellen Kuras; Music by Jean-Michel Bernard. **Pr:** Michael Gondry; Julie Fong; Georges Bermann; Partizan Films; New Line Cinema. **A:** Jr. High-Adult. **P:** Entertainment. **U:** Home. **L:** English. **Mov-Ent:** Filmmaking. **Acq:** Purchase. **Dist:** New Line Home Video.

Be My Valentine 2013 (Unrated) — ★★
A typical Hallmark Channel rom com. Young Tyler Farrell looks for advice from his widowed dad, Dan, when he gets his first crush on a girl at school. But it's been a long time since romance was part of the firefighter's life--at least until he and his crew respond to a call at Kate's flower shop. Dan falls for the florist and he and Kate seem to share some mutual feelings until her ex-boyfriend comes back into town. 90m; DVD. **C:** William Baldwin; Natalie Brown; Christian Martyn; James Thomas; Directed by Graeme Campbell; Written by David Titcher; Cinematography by Peter Benison; Music by Trevor Yuile. **A:** Jr. High-Adult. **P:** Entertainment. **U:** Home. **L:** English. **Mov-Ent:** TV Movies, Comedy--Romantic. **Acq:** Purchase. **Dist:** Cinedigm Entertainment Group.

Be Prepared ?
Depicts treatment of a maritime crew member who has suffered a seizure due to lack of medication, and teaches other crew members the correct emergency actions. 10m; VHS. **A:** Sr. High-Adult. **P:** Education. **U:** Home, Institution. **Hea-Sci:** Safety Education, Health Education. **Acq:** Purchase. **Dist:** John Sabella & Associate. $125.00.

Be Prepared for Meetings 2000
Teaches the viewer techniques for leading productive business meetings, including segments on planning, organizing, starting participation, maintaining pacing, keeping on track, controlling problem participants and motivating action. Includes study guide. 24m; VHS. **A:** Sr. High-Adult. **P:** Education. **U:** Home. **Bus-Ind:** Business. **Acq:** Purchase. **Dist:** Advantage Media. $89.95.

Be Prepared for the A.C.T. 1984
A training film that aids in preparing for the ACT tests. 30m; VHS, 3/4 U, Special order formats. **Pr:** Jerry Bobrow. **A:** Adult. **P:** Education. **U:** Institution, Home, SURA. **How-Ins:** How-To, Education. **Acq:** Purchase, Duplication License. **Dist:** Clear Vue Inc.

Be Prepared for the S.A.T and P.S.A.T 1982
This program helps to prepare students for the SAT's by describing dozens of successful strategies. 30m; VHS, 3/4 U, Special order formats. **Pr:** Bobrow Test Preparation Services. **A:** Sr. High. **P:** Education. **U:** Institution, Home, SURA. **How-Ins:** How-To, Education. **Acq:** Purchase, Duplication License. **Dist:** Clear Vue Inc.

Be Prepared: Security and Your Library 1994
Security experts and library staff members discuss techniques on establishing an effective security program in the library. Contains information on setting policies, approaching patrons, personal safety, management support, law enforcement cooperation, isolated libraries, inventory control, and internal theft. Includes tip-sheet. 35m; VHS. **A:** College-Adult. **P:** Education. **U:** Institution. **Gen-Edu:** Safety Education. **Acq:** Purchase. **Dist:** Library Video Network. $130.00.

Be Prepared to Lead 1991
Psychological approach suggests that there are four leadership types that the potential leader must review in order to see which type he/she most closely resembles. 27m; VHS. **A:** Adult. **P:** Professional. **U:** Institution. **Bus-Ind:** Management. **Acq:** Purchase. **Dist:** Advantage Media. $89.95.

Be Prepared to Sell 2000
Teaches the viewer techniques for selling a product, proposal or idea using persuasive psychological methods. Includes study guide. 24m; VHS. **A:** Sr. High-Adult. **P:** Education. **U:** Home. **Bus-Ind:** Business, Sales Training. **Acq:** Purchase. **Dist:** Advantage Media. $89.95.

Be Prepared to Speak 19??
A guide, presented by Toastmasters International, to speaking in front of audiences. Covers speechwriting, presentation, and dealing with stage fright. 27m; VHS. **A:** Jr. High-Adult. **P:** Instruction. **U:** Home. **How-Ins:** How-To, Speech. **Acq:** Purchase. **Dist:** Instructional Video; Advantage Media; Cambridge Educational. $79.95.

The Be Safe, Be Smart Series 1989
Kids are made aware of dangerous situations in the home, on the street and in school, and are encouraged to think and be careful before they act. 13m; VHS, 3/4 U. **Pr:** Altschul Group. **A:** Primary-Jr. High. **P:** Education. **U:** Institution, SURA. **Chl-Juv:** Safety Education, Children. **Acq:** Purchase, Rent/Lease. **Dist:** United Learning Inc. $225.00.
Indiv. Titles: 1. Safe Home 2. Safe Neighborhood 3. Safe School.

Be Safe, Not Sorry 19??
Deli food safety training course. ?m; VHS. **A:** Adult. **P:** Vocational. **U:** Institution. **Bus-Ind:** Occupational Training, Safety Education. **Acq:** Purchase. **Dist:** International Dairy-Deli-Bakery Association. $160.00.

Be Smart, Be Safe! A Drug Education Program 1990
A program designed to introduce children to the dangers of drug abuse. A teacher's guide and skill sheets are included. 30m; VHS. **Pr:** SVE. **A:** Primary-Jr. High. **P:** Education. **U:** Institution. **Hea-Sci:** Alcoholic Beverages, Health Education, Drug Abuse. **Acq:** Purchase. **Dist:** Clear Vue Inc. $129.00.

Be the Creature: The Complete First Season 2004
Features the first season of the National Geographic television series with brothers and wildlife filmmakers Martin and Chris Kratt as they go worldwide exploring nature and wildlife such as lions, wild dogs, killer whales, and grizzly bears. 13 episodes. 624m; DVD. **A:** Family. **P:** Entertainment. **U:** Home. **Gen-Edu:** Television Series, Documentary Films, Nature. **Acq:** Purchase. **Dist:** National Geographic Society. $44.98.

Be Water Wise: Boating 1960
Safe methods for canoeing, outboard motorboating, sailing, and skiing are depicted. Marine traffic regulations, emergency measures, and courtesy codes are discussed. 21m; VHS, 3/4 U, Special order formats. **Pr:** Department of the Air Force. **A:** Sr. High-Adult. **P:** Education. **U:** Institution, SURA. **Spo-Rec:** Sports--General, Boating. **Acq:** Purchase. **Dist:** National Audiovisual Center.

Be Water Wise: Swimming 1960
This program shows how to enjoy safe swimming and points out what happens when safety rules are ignored. 25m; VHS, 3/4 U, Special order formats. **Pr:** Department of the Air Force. **A:** Jr. High-Adult. **P:** Education. **U:** Institution, SURA. **Spo-Rec:** Sports--General, Safety Education, Sports--Water. **Acq:** Purchase. **Dist:** National Audiovisual Center.

Be Well: The Later Years 1983
This series is designed to educate older people about good health habits. 24m; VHS, 3/4 U, Special order formats. **Pr:** John McDonald. **A:** Adult. **P:** Education. **U:** Institution, Home, SURA. **Hea-Sci:** Aging, Health Education. **Acq:** Purchase, Duplication License. **Dist:** Clear Vue Inc.
Indiv. Titles: 1. Health in the Later Years 2. Nutrition in the Later Years 3. Physical Fitness in the Later Years 4. Stress in the Later Years.

Be Your Best Self: Assertiveness Training 1989
This program shows teens how to improve themselves by learning constructive assertive behavior. 35m; VHS, 3/4 U. **Pr:** Sunburst Communications. **A:** Jr. High-Sr. High. **P:** Education. **U:** Institution. **Gen-Edu:** Adolescence, Personality. **Acq:** Purchase. **Dist:** Human Relations Media; Sunburst Digital Inc. $185.00.

Be Your Own Boss: Start a Business 1992
Four Chicago-area entrepreneurs offer advice on starting your own business and cover topics such as market research,

location selection, promotion, financial planning, legal requirements and more. 21m; VHS. **A:** Adult. **P:** Instruction. **U:** Institution. **How-Ins:** How-To, Business. **Acq:** Purchase. **Dist:** The Learning Seed. $89.00.

Be Your Own Plumber 1987
The potential to save thousands of dollars is as close as your VCR. This tape covers all the basic plumbing fundamentals. 60m; VHS. **Pr:** Morris Video. **A:** Sr. High-Adult. **P:** Entertainment. **U:** Home. **How-Ins:** How-To, Home Improvement. **Acq:** Purchase. **Dist:** Morris Video. $19.95.

Be Your Own Traffic Judge 198?
Seven different traffic accidents are re-enacted in this film and are analyzed to see how they could have been prevented. 10m; VHS, 3/4 U. **Pr:** National Safety Council. **A:** College-Adult. **P:** Education. **U:** Institution. **Gen-Edu:** Driver Education. **Acq:** Rent/Lease. **Dist:** National Safety Council, California Chapter, Film Library.

Be Yourself 1930 — ★★½
Thin plot contrived for Ziegfeld Follies star Brice, who stars as nightclub entertainer Fanny Field. Fanny falls for a down-and-out-boxer (Armstrong) trying to make a comeback. Brice, who was married to impresario Billy Rose at the time, sings several songs co-written by Rose, including "Cookin' Breakfast for the One I Love." 65m/B/W; VHS, DVD. **C:** Fanny Brice; Robert Armstrong; Harry Green; Gertrude Astor; G. Pat Collins; Marjorie "Babe" Kane; Directed by Thornton Freeland; Written by Thornton Freeland; Cinematography by Karl Struss; Robert Planck. **A:** Jr. High-Adult. **P:** Entertainment. **U:** Home. **Mov-Ent:** Musical, Nightclubs, Boxing. **Acq:** Purchase. **Dist:** Kino on Video.

The Beach 1980 (Unrated)
Fictional essay on the 1979 detainment, torture, and assassination of Salvadoran teachers just before the war of resistance. 14m; VHS, DVD. **A:** Adult. **P:** Education. **U:** Institution. **Gen-Edu:** Central America. **Acq:** Purchase. **Dist:** Third World Newsreel. $95.

The Beach 2000 (R) — ★★
DiCaprio's follow-up to the blockbuster "Titantic" is an uneven adaptation of the novel by Alex Garland concerning a group of hedonists trying to find paradise and destroying their ideal in the process. Cynical young journalist Richard (DiCaprio) meets the manic Daffy (Carlyle) in a Bangkok dive and is given a map to a supposedly unspoiled island off the Thai coast. Impulsively, Richard asks French acquaintances Francoise (Ledoyen) and Etienne (Canet) to accompany him and they discover an odd settlement of Euro-trash, headed by Sal (Swinton), amidst a marijuana plantation guarded by gun-wielding thugs. Paradise turns out to be less than paradisical. 120m; VHS, DVD, Wide, CC. **C:** Leonardo DiCaprio; Tilda Swinton; Virginie Ledoyen; Guillaume Canet; Robert Carlyle; Paterson Joseph; Peter Youngblood Hills; Jerry Swindall; Directed by Danny Boyle; Written by John Hodge; Cinematography by Darius Khondji; Music by Angelo Badalamenti. **Pr:** Andrew Macdonald; 20th Century-Fox. **A:** Sr. High-Adult. **P:** Entertainment. **U:** Home. **Mov-Ent:** Drug Abuse. **Acq:** Purchase. **Dist:** Fox Home Entertainment.

The Beach: A River of Sand 1966
An analysis of currents produced by waves proves that most of the pronounced net movement of sand is usually along the shore. 21m; VHS, 3/4 U; Open Captioned. **Pr:** Encyclopedia Britannica Educational Corporation. **A:** Jr. High-Sr. High. **P:** Education. **U:** Institution, SURA. **L:** English, Spanish. **Hea-Sci:** Oceanography. **Acq:** Purchase, Rent/Lease, Trade-in. **Dist:** Encyclopedia Britannica.

Beach and Sea Animals—2nd Edition 1957
Explains the characteristics, adaptations, and inter-relationships of invertebrate animals living near the beach. 11m; VHS, 3/4 U. **Pr:** Encyclopedia Britannica Educational Corporation. **A:** Primary-Jr. High. **P:** Education. **U:** Institution, SURA. **Hea-Sci:** Documentary Films, Oceanography, Wildlife. **Acq:** Purchase, Rent/Lease, Trade-in. **Dist:** Encyclopedia Britannica.

Beach Babes 2: Cave Girl Island 1995 — ★
The babes crash land on a prehistoric planet populated by horny cavemen. 78m; VHS, DVD. **C:** Sara Bellomo; Stephanie Hudson; Rodrigo Botero; Directed by David DeCoteau. **Pr:** Full Moon Entertainment. **A:** Sr. High-Adult. **P:** Entertainment. **U:** Home. **Mov-Ent. Acq:** Purchase. **Dist:** Full Moon Pictures.

Beach Babes from Beyond 1993 (R) — ★
"HOT. TAN. ALIEN." Three words that would send shivers through the body of any red-blooded American boy. And as if alien silicone isn't enough to draw a crowd, this piece of fluff also features the relatives of big name stars hoping to cash in on the family name. Typical Hollywood cheese and sleaze should be fun for those who still can't get this kind of quality entertainment on cable. 78m; VHS, CC. **C:** Joe Estevez; Don Swayze; Joey Travolta; Burt Ward; Jacqueline Stallone; Linnea Quigley; Sara Bellomo; Tamara Landry; Nicole Posey; Directed by David DeCoteau. **Pr:** Torchlight Entertainment. **A:** Adult. **P:** Entertainment. **U:** Home. **Mov-Ent. Acq:** Purchase. **Dist:** Paramount Pictures Corp.

Beach Blanket Bingo 1965 (Unrated) — ★★★
Fifth entry in the "Beach Party" series (after "Pajama Party") is by far the best and has achieved near-cult status. Both Funicello and Avalon are back, but this time a very young Evans catches Avalon's eye. Throw in a mermaid, some moondoggies, skydiving, sizzling beach parties, and plenty of nostalgic golly-gee-whiz fun and you have the classic '60s beach movie. Totally implausible, but that's half the fun when the sun-worshipping teens become involved in a kidnapping and occasionally break into song. Followed by "How to Stuff a Wild Bikini." 96m; VHS, DVD, Wide. **C:** Frankie Avalon; Annette Funicello; Linda Evans; Don Rickles; Buster Keaton; Paul Lynde; Harvey Lembeck; Deborah Walley; John Ashley; Jody McCrea; Marta Kristen; Timothy Carey; Earl Wilson; Bobbi Shaw; Brian Wilson; Directed by William Asher; Written by William Asher; Sher Townsend; Leo Townsend; Cinematography by Floyd Crosby; Music by Les Baxter. **Pr:** James H. Nicholson; Samuel Z. Arkoff; American International Pictures. **A:** Family. **P:** Entertainment. **U:** Home. **Mov-Ent:** Musical, Adolescence. **Acq:** Purchase. **Dist:** Movies Unlimited. $12.74.
Songs: Beach Blanket Bingo; The Cycle Set; Fly Boy; The Good Times; I Am My Ideal; I Think You Think; It Only Hurts When I Cry; New Love; You'll Never Change Him.

Beach Blast 1993
The boys of wrestling play doubles—Big Van Vader and Sid Vicious vs. Davey Boy Smith and Sting. Also features the NWA wrestling match between Ric Flair and Barry Windam. 120m; VHS. **A:** Jr. High-Adult. **P:** Entertainment. **U:** Home. **Spo-Rec. Acq:** Purchase. **Dist:** Turner Broadcasting System Inc. $39.98.

Beach Boys: An American Band 1985 (PG-13)
An in-depth look at the lives and music of the Beach Boys with a soundtrack that features over 40 of their songs. 103m; VHS, CC. **C:** Directed by Malcolm Leo. **Pr:** High Ridge Productions. **A:** Jr. High-Adult. **P:** Entertainment. **U:** Home. **Mov-Ent:** Documentary Films. **Acq:** Purchase. **Dist:** Music Video Distributors; Lions Gate Television Corp. $29.95.

The Beach Boys: Live in Concert 2012 (Unrated)
Live performance by the rock band taped on their 50th anniversary tour. 60m; DVD, Blu-Ray, Streaming. **A:** Primary-Adult. **P:** Entertainment. **U:** Home. **L:** English. **Gen-Edu:** Music--Performance, Music--Pop/Rock. **Acq:** Purchase. **Dist:** BlastMusic. $19.98 14.98 9.99.

Beach Girls 1982 (R) — ★
Three voluptuous coeds intend to re-educate a bookish young man and the owner of a beach house. 91m; VHS, DVD, Blu-Ray. **C:** Debra Blee; Val Kline; Jeana Tomasina; Adam Roarke; Paul Richards; Directed by Patrice Townsend; Cinematography by Michael D. Murphy. **Pr:** Crown International Pictures. **A:** College-Adult. **P:** Entertainment. **U:** Home. **Mov-Ent:** Sex & Sexuality. **Acq:** Purchase. **Dist:** Paramount Pictures Corp. $39.95.

The Beach Girls and the Monster 1965 (Unrated) — ★
Here's one on the cutting edge of genre bending: while it meticulously maintains the philosophical depth and production values of '60s beach bimbo fare, it manages to graft successfully with the heinous critter from the sea genre to produce a hybrid horror with acres o' flesh. 70m/B/W; VHS, DVD. **C:** Jon Hall; Sue Casey; Walker Edmiston; Arnold Lessing; Elaine DuPont; Dale Davis; Directed by Jon Hall; Written by Joan Gardner; Cinematography by Dale Davis; Music by Frank Sinatra, Jr. **Pr:** American International Pictures. **A:** Jr. High-Adult. **P:** Entertainment. **U:** Home. **Mov-Ent:** Horror. **Acq:** Purchase. **Dist:** Image Entertainment Inc.; Sinister Cinema. $19.98.

Beach Hotel 1992 (Unrated) — ★★
Accused of fraud, a politican escapes to a remote and semi-abandoned hotel that he owns. He summons his family to decide what to do next, hoping his friends will also assist him. But his friends refuse their aid, and even his family eventually abandons him to his fate. Spanish with subtitles. 96m; VHS, DVD. **C:** Sergio Bustamante; Pilar Pellicer; Mercedes Olea; Directed by Alfredo Joskowicz; Written by Alfredo Joskowicz; Cinematography by Rodolfo Sanchez; Music by Amparo Rubin. **A:** College-Adult. **P:** Entertainment. **U:** Home. **L:** Spanish. **Mov-Ent:** Family, Hotels & Hotel Staff Training. **Acq:** Purchase. **Dist:** Vanguard International Cinema, Inc.

Beach House 1982 (Unrated) — ★
In this boring comedy, adolescents frolic on the beach, get inebriated, and listen to rock 'n' roll. 76m; VHS. **C:** Kathy McNeil; Richard Duggan; Ileana Seidel; John Cosola; Spence Waugh; Paul W.S. Anderson; John A. Gallagher; Directed by John A. Gallagher; Written by John A. Gallagher; Marino Amaruso. **Pr:** HBO. **A:** Sr. High-Adult. **P:** Entertainment. **U:** Home. **Mov-Ent:** Adolescence. **Acq:** Purchase. **Dist:** No Longer Available.

Beach Kings 2008 (PG-13) — ★½
Thirty-year-old Cameron Day (Charvet) is a former college basketball star who couldn't stand the pressure of trying to make a pro career. A chance meeting with Mia (DeVitto) has Cam returning to sports as a pro beach volleyball player but as the pressures build again so do his own insecurities. 95m; DVD. **C:** David Charvet; Torrey DeVitto; Brody Hutzler; Kristin Cavallari; Court Young; Jaleel White; Bret Roberts; Directed by Paul Nihipali; Written by Paul Nihipali; Cinematography by David Waldman; Music by Craig Eastman. **A:** Jr. High-Adult. **P:** Entertainment. **U:** Home. **Mov-Ent:** Sports--Fiction: Drama, Volleyball. **Acq:** Purchase. **Dist:** MGM Home Entertainment.

Beach Party 1963 (Unrated) — ★★
Started the "Beach Party" series with the classic Funicello/Avalon combo. Scientist Cummings studying the mating habits of teenagers intrudes on a group of surfers, beach bums, and bikers, to his lasting regret. Typical beach party bingo, with sand, swimsuits, singing, dancing, and bare minimum in way of a plot. Followed by "Muscle Beach Party." 101m; VHS, DVD. **C:** Frankie Avalon; Annette Funicello; Harvey Lembeck; Robert Cummings; Dorothy Malone; Morey Amsterdam; Jody McCrea; John Ashley; Candy Johnson; Dolores Wells; Yvette Vickers; Eva Six; Brian Wilson; Vincent Price; Peter Falk; Dick Dale; Directed by William Asher; Written by Lou Rusoff; Cinematography by Kay Norton; Music by Les Baxter. **Pr:** Lou Rusoff; James H. Nicholson; Lou Rusoff; American International Pictures. **A:** Family. **P:** Entertainment. **U:** Home. **Mov-Ent:** Musical, Adolescence, Science. **Acq:** Purchase. **Dist:** Movies Unlimited. $11.99.
Songs: Beach Party; Don't Stop Now; Promise Me Anything; Secret Surfin' Spot; Surfin' and a-Swingin'; Treat Him Nicely.

Beach Patrol 1979 (Unrated) — ★
Lightweight ABC TV movie has pretty cop Jan Plummer transferring from the narcotics division to an L.A. police team that patrols the beaches in dune buggies. All because a drug lord has a hit out on her. Naturally, it's at her new job that Jan spots the fugitive bad guy. 75m; DVD. **C:** Christine De Lisle; Jonathan Frakes; Paul Burke; Rick Hill; Michael Gregory; Directed by Bob Kelljan; Written by Rick Edelstein; Cinematography by Archie Dalzell; Music by Barry DeVorzon. **A:** Jr. High-Adult. **P:** Entertainment. **U:** Home. **L:** English. **Mov-Ent:** Crime Drama, TV Movies. **Acq:** Purchase. **Dist:** Sony Pictures Home Entertainment Inc.

Beach Red 1967 (Unrated) — ★★★
American Marines storm an unnamed Pacific island held by the Japanese in WWII in this anti-war film. Unlike many war films from the '60s, it is somewhat gory (in other words they tried to be realistic with the combat scenes). It is also unusual in that it tells the story of each of the characters in flashback, including the Japanese soldiers, preventing them from being demonized. To increase the realism, all the actors wore full 40 pound gear during all scenes, and the director enlisted the help of the U.S. armed forces to create the film. 114m; DVD. **C:** Cornel Wilde; Rip Torn; Burr DeBenning; Patrick Wolfe; Jean Wallace; Jaime Sanchez; Dale Ishimoto; Genki Koyama; Gene Blakely; Michael Parsons; Norman Pak; Dewey Stringer; Fred Galang; Hiroshi Kiyama; Directed by Cornel Wilde; Written by Cornel Wilde; Peter Bowman; Clint Johnston; Don Peters; Cinematography by Cecil R. Cooney; Music by Ismail Darbar. **A:** Sr. High-Adult. **P:** Entertainment. **U:** Home. **L:** English, French, Spanish. **Mov-Ent:** World War Two. **Acq:** Purchase. **Dist:** MGM Home Entertainment. $14.98.

Beach Volleyball Defensive Strategies & Footwork 2009 (Unrated)
Coach Danalee Bragado-Corso shares her techniques for proper volleyball footwork training, along with some defensive strategies. 53m; DVD. **A:** Family. **P:** Education. **U:** Home, Institution. **Spo-Rec:** Volleyball, Athletic Instruction/Coaching. **Acq:** Purchase. **Dist:** Championship Productions. $34.99.

Beachcomber 1938 (Unrated) — ★★★
Comedy set in the Dutch East Indies about a shiftless beachcomber (Laughton) who falls in love with a missionary's prim sister (Lanchester), as she attempts to reform him. The real-life couple of Laughton and Lanchester are their usual pleasure to watch. Remade in 1954. Story by W. Somerset Maugham. 88m/B/W; VHS, DVD, Special order formats. **C:** Charles Laughton; Elsa Lanchester; Robert Newton; Tyrone Guthrie; Directed by Erich Pommer. **Pr:** Mayflower. **A:** Family. **P:** Entertainment. **U:** Home. **Mov-Ent:** Comedy--Romantic. **Acq:** Purchase, Rent/Lease. **Dist:** Cable Films/i2bs Online World. $19.95.

Beaches 1988 (PG-13) — ★★★½
Based on the novel by Iris Rainer Dart about two girls whose friendship survived the test of time. The friendship is renewed once more when one of the now middle-aged women learns that she is dying slowly of a fatal disease. 123m; VHS, DVD, Blu-Ray, 8 mm; Open Captioned. **C:** Bette Midler; Barbara Hershey; John Heard; Spalding Gray; Lainie Kazan; James Read; Mayim Bialik; Directed by Garry Marshall; Written by Mary Agnes Donoghue; Cinematography by Dante Spinotti; Music by Georges Delerue. **Pr:** Buena Vista. **A:** Jr. High-Adult. **P:** Entertainment. **U:** Home. **Mov-Ent:** Melodrama, Diseases, Women. **Acq:** Purchase. **Dist:** Buena Vista Home Entertainment. $19.99.

The Beaches Are Moving: The Drowning of America's Shoreline 1992
Illustrates beach evolution and examines the impact of population growth on the coastal region. 60m; VHS. **C:** Hosted by Dr. Orrin H. Pilkey. **A:** Jr. High-College. **P:** Education. **U:** Institution. **Hea-Sci:** Ecology & Environment, Geology, TV Movies. **Acq:** Purchase. **Dist:** Environmental Media. $29.95.

Bead Embroidery 19??
Valerie Campbell-Harding and Pamela Watts demonstrate techniques in bead embroidery. They cover beads for wire and thread, how to embroider buggle, seed beads, and sequins onto fabric, applying gold leaf onto beads, dyeing and painting beads, bead weaving, couching, the lazy squaw stitch, how to make beaded machine wrapped cords and tassels with beaded heads, and sewing machine usage. 60m; VHS. **Pr:** Victorian Video Productions. **A:** Jr. High-Adult. **P:** Instruction. **U:** Home, Institution. **How-Ins:** Crafts, How-To. **Acq:** Purchase. **Dist:** Victorian Video/Yarn Barn of Kansas, Inc. $39.95.

The Bead Game 1978
Thousands of beads are arranged and manipulated into shapes of real and mythical creatures. 6m; VHS, 3/4 U. **Pr:** Ishu Patel. **A:** Jr. High-Adult. **P:** Entertainment. **U:** Institution, Home. **Fin-Art:** Film--Avant-Garde. **Acq:** Purchase, Rent/Lease, Duplication License. **Dist:** Pyramid Media.

Bead Woven Necklaces: Loom-Beading Techniques 1993
Bead artist Virginia Blakelocl introduces the basics of loom-beading to loom construction. 82m; VHS. **A:** Jr. High-Adult. **P:** Instruction. **U:** Institution, Home. **How-Ins:** How-To, Hobbies. **Acq:** Purchase. **Dist:** Victorian Video/Yarn Barn of Kansas, Inc.; Baker and Taylor. $39.95.

Beada-beada with Vicki Payne and Phil Teefy 19??
Demonstrates how to make glass beads with a few simple tools. Includes a bead stringing booklet and supply list. 60m; VHS. **A:** Adult. **P:** Instruction. **U:** Home. **How-Ins:** Crafts, Hobbies, How-To. **Acq:** Purchase. **Dist:** Cutters Productions. $19.95.

Beah: A Black Woman Speaks 2003 (Unrated)
A tribute to African American actress, poet and political activist Beah Richards best known for her role in "Guess Who's Coming to Dinner" for which she was nominated for an Academy Award. 90m; DVD. **A:** Adult. **P:** Education. **U:** Institution. **Gen-Edu:** Women, Art & Artists, Film History. **Acq:** Purchase. **Dist:** Women Make Movies. $295.00.

Beaks: The Movie 1987 (R) — **Bomb!**
Two TV reporters try to figure out why birds of prey are suddenly attacking humans. Owes nothing to Hitchcock's "The Birds." 86m; VHS, DVD. **C:** Christopher Atkins; Michelle Johnson; Directed by Rene Cardona, Jr. **Pr:** Rene Cardona, Jr; Rene Cardona, Jr. **A:** Sr. High-Adult. **P:** Entertainment. **U:** Home. **Mov-Ent:** Horror, Birds. **Acq:** Purchase. **Dist:** Lions Gate Television Corp. $14.95.

The Beales of Grey Gardens 2006
A continuation of 1976's "Grey Gardens," depicting the lives of eccentric East Hampton recluses Big and Little Edie Beale. 91m; DVD. **A:** Sr. High-Adult. **P:** Entertainment. **U:** Home. **Gen-Edu:** Documentary Films, Biography. **Acq:** Purchase. **Dist:** Image Entertainment Inc.

Beam Builder, Orbital Servicing System, MIT Students in NBS 1978
A look at the beam builder, designed to make metal construction beams in the same manner as gutters are made on Earth. Silent. 30m; 3/4 U. **Pr:** National Aeronautics and Space Administration. **A:** Jr. High-Adult. **P:** Education. **U:** BCTV, SURA. **Hea-Sci:** Technology. **Acq:** Free Loan. **Dist:** NASA Lyndon B. Johnson Space Center.

Beam Pumping Units 1970
This program describes the installation, operation, and maintenance of beam pumping units. 32m; VHS, 3/4 U. **Pr:** University of Texas Austin. **A:** College-Adult. **P:** Instruction. **U:** Institution, CCTV. **Bus-Ind:** Oil Industry. **Acq:** Purchase.

Beamship Meier Chronicles 1990
This UFO documentary focuses on Eduard Meier, a Swiss everyman around whom the most well-documented UFO controversy revolves. Supposedly, alien beings from somewhere deep in the Pleiades contacted earth: Meier has photographs, film footage, tape recordings, and unique metal fragments, as well as collaborative testimony from individuals who claim to have seen the Beamships. 90m; VHS. **A:** Primary-Adult. **P:** Education. **U:** Home. **Gen-Edu:** Documentary Films, Space Exploration. **Acq:** Purchase. **Dist:** ESPN Inc. $59.95.

Beamship Metal Analysis 1990
An in-depth, scientific analysis of the metal fragments said to have been given to Eduard Meier by the Beamship aliens. The metal has such amazing qualities that top national scientists from IBM have concluded that, considering man's present technological limitations, the metal could not have been made on Earth. Well, okay. 45m; VHS. **A:** Primary-Adult. **P:** Education. **U:** Home. **Gen-Edu:** Metallurgy. **Acq:** Purchase. **Dist:** ESPN Inc. $39.95.

Beamship Movie Footage 1990
Eduard Meier offers photographic proof of alien visitation in the form of 8mm film clips, in slow motion and freeze-frame, of the Pleiadians' ships. Touch football scene is compelling. 60m; VHS. **A:** Primary-Adult. **P:** Education. **U:** Home. **Gen-Edu:** Documentary Films. **Acq:** Purchase. **Dist:** ESPN Inc. $49.95.

Bean 1997 (PG-13) — ★★★
Big screen adaptation of rubber-faced Atkinson's Mr. Bean character finds disaster-magnet hero working as a guard in London's National Gallery. When a famous painting is purchased by a museum in L.A., the Gallery's curators jump at the chance to send Bean along with the painting as an "expert," although he is nearly mute and definitely not qualified. David (MacNicol), the American curator, invites him to stay at his house, much to the dismay of his wife and children. Bean, of course, wrecks the painting, ruins David's marriage and career, and generally makes an ass out of himself. He then resourcefully (and sometimes accidentally) puts things right. Atkinson proves himself a master of the almost lost art of slapstick comedy. 92m; VHS, DVD. **C:** Rowan Atkinson; Peter MacNichol; Pamela Reed; Harris Yulin; Burt Reynolds; Larry Drake; Johnny Galecki; Richard Gant; Tom McGowan; Dakin Matthews; Peter Capaldi; Sandra Oh; Tricia Vessey; Peter Egan; Directed by Mel Smith; Written by Richard Curtis; Robin Driscoll; Cinematography by Francis Kenny; Music by Howard Goodall. **Pr:** Working Title Productions; Polygram Filmed Entertainment. **A:** Jr. High-Adult. **P:** Entertainment. **U:** Home. **Mov-Ent:** Comedy--Slapstick, Art & Artists, Great Britain. **Acq:** Purchase. **Dist:** Universal Music and Video Distribution.

Bean Sprouts 1979
This five-part series focuses on what is unique about Chinese-American children's experiences, as well as what they share in common with other children. Programs are available individually. 30m; VHS, CC, 3/4 U. **Pr:** Children's Television Project. **A:** Primary. **P:** Education. **U:** Institution, CCTV, CATV, BCTV. **Gen-Edu:** Documentary Films, Sociology, Minorities. **Acq:** Purchase. **Dist:** GPN Educational Media; Chinese for Affirmative Action. $250.00.
Indiv. Titles: 1. Try It, You'll Like It 2. Boys and Girls, Girls and Boys 3. What Can You Show Me 4. Movin' Around and Movin' Out 5. Growing Up from Here.

Beanie Lover Video 1998
This comprehensive look at the Beanie Baby craze features the history of Beanie Babies, the art of buy-sell-trade, how to spot counterfeits, a tag generations seminar and a video catalog of rare and retired Beanie Babies. Also features interviews with Beanie Baby experts and enthusiasts. 60m; VHS. **A:** Family. **P:** Education. **U:** Home. **Gen-Edu:** Hobbies, Toys. **Acq:** Purchase. **Dist:** Tapeworm Video Distributors Inc. $16.95.

Beanstalk 1994 (PG) — ★★½
Modern-day version of the fairytale finds young Jack Taylor (Daniels) scheming to make it big to help his hardworking single mom. He meets up with a wacky scientist (Kidder), who gives Jack some recently discovered seeds that naturally grow into an enormous beanstalk. And what does Jack find when he climbs the beanstalk—why an entire family of silly giants. 80m; VHS, CC. **C:** J.D. Daniels; Margot Kidder; Richard Moll; Amy Stock-Poynton; Patrick Renna; Richard Paul; David Naughton; Stuart Pankin; Cathy McAuley; Directed by Michael Davis; Written by Michael Davis; Music by Kevin Bassinson. **Pr:** Charles Band; Debra Dion; Moonbeam Entertainment. **A:** Family. **P:** Entertainment. **U:** Home. **Mov-Ent:** Fantasy, Fairy Tales, Children. **Acq:** Purchase. **Dist:** Paramount Pictures Corp.

Beany & Cecil: Matty's Funday Funnies—The Special Edition Volume 2 1959 (Unrated)
ABC's 1959-63 original animated series featuring Beany, his buddy Cecil and Captain Huffenpuff of the Leakin' Lena, sailing the seas and outsmarting dastardly villains like Dishonest John. Includes "Invasion of Earth by Robots," "Davey Cricket," "Strange Objects," "The Capture of Tear-a-long the Dotted Lion," "Cecil Meets Cecilia," "Beany and Cecil Meet Ping Pong," "Sleeping Beauty and the Beast," "Beany's Beany-Cap Copter," "Malice in Blunderland," "Here Comes the Shmoe Boat," "Ben Hare," and lots of bonus features. 200m; DVD. **C:** Voice(s) by Scatman Crothers; Jim MacGeorge; Gwen Ffrangcon Davies. **A:** Preschool-Primary. **P:** Entertainment. **U:** Home. **Chl-Juv:** Animation & Cartoons, Children's Shows. **Acq:** Purchase. **Dist:** Hen's Tooth Video. $24.95.

Beany & Cecil Series 196?
The lovable little boy Beany joins his pal Cecil the Seasick Sea Serpent in this series of adventures. Each tape includes six or seven programs. Some volumes are available in 8mm. 60m; VHS, CC. **Pr:** Bob Clampett. **A:** Family. **P:** Entertainment. **U:** Home. **Chl-Juv:** Animation & Cartoons. **Acq:** Purchase. **Dist:** Sony Pictures Home Entertainment Inc.

Beany & Cecil, Vol. 1 1962
Six 10-minute titles including "Spots Off a Leopard," "Invasion of the Earth by Robots," "Cecil Meets the Singing Dinosaur," "Little Ace from Outer Space," "Super Cecil," and "The Wildman of Wildsville." 60m; VHS, 8 mm. **Pr:** Bob Clampett. **A:** Family. **P:** Entertainment. **U:** Home. **Mov-Ent:** Animation & Cartoons, Television Series. **Acq:** Purchase. **Dist:** Magic Window Productions, Inc.; Image Entertainment Inc. $24.95.

Beany & Cecil, Vol. 2 1962
Six titles: "Davy Crickett," "Strange Objects," "A Trip to the Schmoon," "Beany's Buffalo Hunt," "Tearalong the Dotted Lion," and "Grime Doesn't Pay." 60m; VHS. **Pr:** Bob Clampett. **A:** Family. **P:** Entertainment. **U:** Home. **Mov-Ent:** Animation & Cartoons, Television Series. **Acq:** Purchase. **Dist:** Magic Window Productions, Inc. $24.95.

Beany & Cecil, Vol. 3 1962
Six titles featuring the little boy and his seasick serpent, including "The Monstrous Monster," "Tommy Hawk," "Yo Ho Ho and a Bubble of Gum," "The Seventh Voyage of Singood," "Cecil meets Cecilia," and "The Capture of Thunderbolt the Wondercolt." 60m; VHS. **Pr:** Bob Clampett. **A:** Family. **P:** Entertainment. **U:** Home. **Mov-Ent:** Animation & Cartoons, Television Series. **Acq:** Purchase. **Dist:** Magic Window Productions, Inc. $24.95.

Beany & Cecil, Vol. 4 1962
Six titles: "The Rat Race for Space," "Beany & the Boo Birds," "Meet Ping Pong," "The Greatest Schmoe on Earth," "Billy the Squid," and "The Capture of the Dreaded Three-Headed Threep." 60m; VHS, CC. **Pr:** Bob Clampett. **A:** Family. **P:** Entertainment. **U:** Home. **Mov-Ent:** Animation & Cartoons, Television Series. **Acq:** Purchase. **Dist:** Magic Window Productions, Inc. $24.95.

Beany & Cecil, Vol. 5 1962
Six 10-minute episodes: "Beany and the Jackstalk," "The Humbug," "Custard's Last Stand," "Hero by Trade," "Illegal Eagle Egg" and "Cecil Gets Careless." 60m; VHS, CC. **Pr:** Bob Clampett. **A:** Family. **P:** Entertainment. **U:** Home. **Mov-Ent:** Animation & Cartoons, Television Series. **Acq:** Purchase. **Dist:** Magic Window Productions, Inc. $24.95.

Beany & Cecil, Vol. 6 1962
Six titles including "Sleeping Beauty and the Beast," "Never Eat Quackers in Bed," "Dishonest John Meets Cowboy Starr," "Beany's Beany Cap Copter," "The Indiscreet Squeet," and "The Phantom of the Horse Opera." 60m; VHS, CC. **Pr:** Bob Clampett. **A:** Family. **P:** Entertainment. **U:** Home. **Mov-Ent:** Animation & Cartoons, Television Series. **Acq:** Purchase. **Dist:** Magic Window Productions, Inc. $24.95.

Beany & Cecil, Vol. 7 196?
Join Beany, Cecil and Captain Huffenpuff as they board the Leakin' Lena for six animated adventures. Included are "Davy Crickett's Leading Lady Bug," "Buffalo Billy," "20,000 Leaguers Under the Sea," "Malice in Blunderland," "The Dirty Birdy," and "The Attack of the Man-Eater Skeeters." 60m; VHS, CC. **Pr:** Bob Clampett. **A:** Family. **P:** Entertainment. **U:** Home. **Chl-Juv:** Animation & Cartoons, Television Series. **Acq:** Purchase. **Dist:** Magic Window Productions, Inc. $24.95.

Beany & Cecil, Vol. 8 1962
More adventures with Beany and Cecil the Sea Sick Serpent. Titles included are "Rin Tin Can," "Vild Vast Vasteland," "Invisible Man Has Butter Fingers," "Here Comes the Schmoe Boat," "Tain't Cricket, Crickett," and "Cecil Always Saves the Day." 60m; VHS, CC. **Pr:** Bob Clampett. **A:** Family. **P:** Entertainment. **U:** Home. **Mov-Ent:** Animation & Cartoons, Television Series. **Acq:** Purchase. **Dist:** Magic Window Productions, Inc. $24.95.

Beany & Cecil, Vol. 9 1962
Contains classic cartoons from the little boy and his pet sea serpent. Includes "Aint't I a Little Stinger," "The Warring 20s," "Beany and Cecil Meet the Invisible Man," "Ain't That a Cork in the Snorkel," "Makes a Sea Serpent Sore," and "So What & the Seven Whatnots." 60m; VHS, CC. **Pr:** Bob Clampett. **A:** Family. **P:** Entertainment. **U:** Home. **Mov-Ent:** Animation & Cartoons, Television Series. **Acq:** Purchase. **Dist:** Magic Window Productions, Inc. $24.95.

Beany & Cecil, Vol. 10 1962
Six episodes featuring Beany and Cecil: "Cecil's Comical Strip," "Beany's Resid-jewels," "Wot the Heck," "Dragon Train," "Ten Feet Tall and Wet" and "Dirty Pool." 60m; VHS, CC. **Pr:** Bob Clampett. **A:** Family. **P:** Entertainment. **U:** Home. **Mov-Ent:** Animation & Cartoons, Television Series. **Acq:** Purchase. **Dist:** Magic Window Productions, Inc. $24.95.

Beany & Cecil, Vol. 11 1962
Collection of classic Beany and Cecil cartoons. Includes "Thumb Fun," "Living Doll," "Beanyland," "Beany Blows His Top," "Beany Flips His Lid" and "The Fleastone Kops Kaper." 60m; VHS. **Pr:** Bob Clampett. **A:** Family. **P:** Entertainment. **U:** Home. **Mov-Ent:** Animation & Cartoons, Television Series. **Acq:** Purchase. **Dist:** Magic Window Productions, Inc. $24.95.

Beany & Cecil, Vol. 12 1962
Collection of classic Beany and Cecil cartoons. Includes "Mad Isle of Madhattan," "Hare-cules and the Golden Fleecing," "The Hammy Awards," "Cheery Cheery Beany," "Beans and Peas Corp" and "Nya Ha Ha and the Singin' Swingin' Sea Serpent." 70m; VHS. **Pr:** Bob Clampett. **A:** Family. **P:** Entertainment. **U:** Home. **Mov-Ent:** Animation & Cartoons, Television Series. **Acq:** Purchase. **Dist:** Magic Window Productions, Inc. $24.95.

Beany & Cecil, Vol. 13 1962
Collection of Beany and Cecil cartoons. Title include "There Goes a Squid," "Ben-Hare," "Hare Today, Gone Tomorrow," "Oil's Well That Ends Well," "Joy-a-Soya Bean Oil," "There's No Such Thing As a Sea Serpent," and "D.J. the D.J." 70m; VHS. **Pr:** Bob Clampett. **A:** Family. **P:** Entertainment. **U:** Home. **Mov-Ent:** Animation & Cartoons, Television Series. **Acq:** Purchase. **Dist:** Magic Window Productions, Inc. $24.95.

The Bear 1989 (PG) — ★★★
Breathtaking, effortlessly entertaining family film (from France) about an orphaned bear cub tagging after a grown Kodiak male and dealing with hunters. The narrative is essentially from the cub's point of view, with very little dialogue. A huge moneymaker in Europe; shot on location in the Dolomites and the Candian Arctic. Based on the 1917 novel "The Grizzly King" by James Oliver Curwood. 92m; VHS, DVD, Wide, CC. **C:** Jack Wallace; Tcheky Karyo; Andre Lacombe; Directed by Jean-Jacques Annaud; Written by Gerard Brach; Michael Kane; Cinematography by Philippe Rousselot; Music by Bill Conti. **Pr:** Claude Berri; Price Entertainment; Tri-Star Pictures. **A:** Jr. High-Adult. **P:** Entertainment. **U:** Home. **Mov-Ent:** Animals, Hunting, Bears. **Acq:** Purchase. **Dist:** Sony Pictures Home Entertainment Inc.; Reader's Digest Home Video; Home Vision Cinema. $14.95.

The Bear & the Fly 1985
Paula Winter's animated tale of a pesty fly that visits a temperamental bear during his dinnertime. 5m; VHS. **A:** Preschool-Primary. **P:** Entertainment. **U:** Institution. **Chl-Juv:** Animation & Cartoons, Insects, Storytelling. **Acq:** Purchase, Rent/Lease. **Dist:** Weston Woods Studios. $125.00.

The Bear and the Mouse 1966
Real animals perform a variation on the "Androcles and the Lion" story for young children. 8m; VHS, 3/4 U. **Pr:** National Film Board of Canada. **A:** Preschool-Primary. **P:** Entertainment. **U:** Institution, SURA. **Chl-Juv:** Children, Fantasy. **Acq:** Purchase, Rent/Lease. **Dist:** National Film Board of Canada.

Bear Dance 1988
Follows an Indian boy as he experiences the Bear Dance, an ageless cultural practice of the Ute Indians of Colorado. 13m; VHS, SVS, 3/4 U. **A:** Primary-Sr. High. **P:** Education. **U:** Institution. **Gen-Edu:** Native Americans. **Acq:** Purchase, Rent/Lease. **Dist:** Encyclopedia Britannica. $69.00.

Bear Dreams: Learn to Read 1992
Kool Kat tells two stories about Barefoot Bear that help teach children to read while learning about friendship. Part of the "Look and Learn" series. 30m; VHS. **A:** Preschool-Primary. **P:** Education. **U:** Home. **Chl-Juv:** Animation & Cartoons, Education, Children. **Acq:** Purchase. **Dist:** V.I.E.W. Inc./Arkadia Entertainment Corp. $14.98.

Bear Friends: Learn to Read 1992
Two stories, "Barefoot Bear and the Ice Cream Factory" and "Barefoot Bear Plays Ball," narrated by Kool Kat help children learn to read while learning about friendship and self-esteem. Part of the "Look and Learn" series. 30m; VHS. **A:** Preschool-Primary. **P:** Education. **U:** Home. **Chl-Juv:** Animation & Cartoons, Education, Language Arts. **Acq:** Purchase. **Dist:** V.I.E.W. Inc./Arkadia Entertainment Corp. $14.98.

Bear Hugs Video 1988
The Bear Hugs series teaches Christian values and virtues to children through animation. Each tape contains two stories; based on the "Bear Hugs" book series. 30m; VHS. **C:** Written by Pat Kirk; Alice Brown. **Pr:** Brownlow Publishing Co., Inc. **A:** Preschool-Primary. **P:** Religious. **U:** Home. **Chl-Juv:** Animation & Cartoons, Children. **Acq:** Purchase. **Dist:** Karol Media. $11.95.
Indiv. Titles: 1. Vol. 1: I Can Hardly Wait & Bearing Burdens 2. Vol. 2: Bearing Fruit & Bear Buddies 3. Vol. 3: Love Bears All Things & Bear Up.

Bear in the Big Blue House: A Bear for All Seasons 2003
Presents the live-action children's television series with puppets by Jim Henson Productions following the adventures of Bear and his friends Tutter, Pip and Pop, Ojo, and Treelo. Includes: "Summer Cooler," "Falling for Fall," and "All-Weather Bear." 3 episodes. 75m; DVD. **A:** Preschool-Primary. **P:** Entertainment. **U:** Home. **Chl-Juv:** Television Series, Children's Shows, Puppets. **Acq:** Purchase. **Dist:** Sony Pictures Home Entertainment Inc. $14.95.

Bear in the Big Blue House: A Berry Bear Christmas 2000
Features Bear and other characters featured on the Disney Channel series in a celebration of the holidays of Christmas, Chanukah, Kwanzaa and Winterberry. 50m; VHS. **A:** Family. **P:** Entertainment. **U:** Home. **Chl-Juv:** Fiction--Children, Puppets, Holidays. **Acq:** Purchase. **Dist:** Sony Pictures Home Entertainment Inc. $12.95.

Bear in the Big Blue House: Dance Party 2002
Presents the live-action children's television series with puppets by Jim Henson Productions following the adventures of Bear and his friends Tutter, Pip and Pop, Ojo, and Treelo. Includes: "Music to My Ears," "Dance Fever," and "I For-got Rhythm!?" 3 episodes. 75m; DVD. **A:** Preschool-Primary. **P:** Entertainment. **U:** Home. **Chl-Juv:** Television Series, Children's Shows, Puppets. **Acq:** Purchase. **Dist:** Sony Pictures Home Entertainment Inc. $19.95.

Bear in the Big Blue House: Early to Bed Early to Rise 2005
Presents the live-action children's television series with puppets by Jim Henson Productions following the adventures of Bear and his friends Tutter, Pip and Pop, Ojo, and Treelo. Includes: "A Winter's Nap," "Morning Glory," and "Go to Sleep." 3 episodes. 75m; DVD. **A:** Preschool-Primary. **P:** Entertainment. **U:** Home. **Chl-Juv:** Television Series, Children's Shows, Puppets. **Acq:** Purchase. **Dist:** Sony Pictures Home Entertainment Inc. $14.95.

Bear in the Big Blue House: Everybody's Special 2002
Presents the live-action children's television series with puppets by Jim Henson Productions following the adventures of Bear and his friends Tutter, Pip and Pop, Ojo, and Treelo. Includes: "As Different as Day and Night," "Bats Are People Too," and "The Yard Sale." 3 episodes. 75m; DVD. **A:** Preschool-Primary. **P:** Entertainment. **U:** Home. **Chl-Juv:** Television Series, Children's Shows, Puppets. **Acq:** Purchase. **Dist:** Sony Pictures Home Entertainment Inc. $19.95.

Bear in the Big Blue House: Halloween & Thanksgiving 2000
Features Bear and other characters featured on the Disney Channel series in a celebration of the holidays of Halloween and Thanksgiving. 50m; VHS. **A:** Family. **P:** Entertainment. **U:** Home. **Chl-Juv:** Fiction--Children, Puppets, Holidays. **Acq:** Purchase. **Dist:** Sony Pictures Home Entertainment Inc. $12.95.

Bear in the Big Blue House: Heroes of Woodland Valley 2003
Presents the live-action children's television series with puppets by Jim Henson Productions following the adventures of Bear and his friends Tutter, Pip and Pop, Ojo, and Treelo. Includes: Bear and his friends learn that helping others is fun and important such as removing a tree off of the library. 3 episodes. 72m; DVD. **A:** Preschool-Primary. **P:** Entertainment. **U:** Home. **Chl-Juv:** Television Series, Children's Shows, Puppets. **Acq:** Purchase. **Dist:** Sony Pictures Home Entertainment Inc. $19.95.

Bear in the Big Blue House: Party Time with Bear 2000
Contains three episdoes, each dealing with a party. ?m; DVD. **A:** Family. **P:** Education. **U:** Home. **Chl-Juv:** Puppets, Children. **Acq:** Purchase. **Dist:** Sony Pictures Home Entertainment Inc.

Bear in the Big Blue House: Potty Time with Bear 1999
Uses puppets, music, and storytelling to entertain and teach young children. In this volume, Bear and his pals Tutter and Ojo learn about toilet training. 75m; VHS, DVD. **A:** Family. **P:** Education. **U:** Home. **Chl-Juv:** Puppets, Children. **Acq:** Purchase. **Dist:** Sony Pictures Home Entertainment Inc. $12.95.

Bear in the Big Blue House: Practice Makes Perfect 2003
Presents the live-action children's television series with puppets by Jim Henson Productions following the adventures of Bear and his friends Tutter, Pip and Pop, Ojo, and Treelo. Includes: "Show Your Stuff" and "The Great Bandini" (with guest star Whoopi Goldberg). 2 episodes. 50m; DVD. **A:** Preschool-Primary. **P:** Entertainment. **U:** Home. **Chl-Juv:** Television Series, Children's Shows, Puppets. **Acq:** Purchase. **Dist:** Sony Pictures Home Entertainment Inc. $14.95.

Bear in the Big Blue House: Safe and Sound 2001
Features the "Nothing to Fear" episode of the Disney Channel children's series created by Jim Henson. 50m; VHS; Closed Captioned. **A:** Preschool. **P:** Entertainment. **U:** Home. **Chl-Juv:** Children, Animation & Cartoons. **Acq:** Purchase. **Dist:** Sony Pictures Home Entertainment Inc. $12.95.

Bear in the Big Blue House: Sense-Sational 2003
Presents the live-action children's television series with puppets by Jim Henson Productions following the adventures of Bear and his friends Tutter, Pip and Pop, Ojo, and Treelo. Includes: "Smellorama" and "The Senseless Detectives." 3 episodes. 75m; DVD. **A:** Preschool-Primary. **P:** Entertainment. **U:** Home. **Chl-Juv:** Television Series, Children's Shows, Puppets. **Acq:** Purchase. **Dist:** Sony Pictures Home Entertainment Inc. $14.95.

Bear in the Big Blue House: Shapes, Sounds & Colors 2000
Three episodes of the Disney Channel series. 75m; DVD. **A:** Family. **P:** Education. **U:** Home. **Chl-Juv:** Puppets, Children. **Acq:** Purchase. **Dist:** Sony Pictures Home Entertainment Inc.

Bear in the Big Blue House: Sharing with Friends 2001
Features the "What's Mine is Yours" episode of the Disney Channel children's series created by Jim Henson. 50m; VHS; Closed Captioned. **A:** Preschool. **P:** Entertainment. **U:** Home. **Chl-Juv:** Children, Animation & Cartoons. **Acq:** Purchase. **Dist:** Sony Pictures Home Entertainment Inc. $12.95.

Bear in the Big Blue House: Sleepy Time with Bear and Friends 2000
Presents the live-action children's television series with puppets by Jim Henson Productions following the adventures of Bear and his friends Tutter, Pip and Pop, Ojo, and Treelo. Includes: "Friends for Life" "The Big Sleep," and "To All a Good Night." 3 episodes. 73m; DVD. **A:** Preschool-Primary. **P:** Entertainment. **U:** Home. **Chl-Juv:** Television Series, Children's Shows, Puppets. **Acq:** Purchase. **Dist:** Sony Pictures Home Entertainment Inc. $14.95.

Bear in the Big Blue House: Storytelling 2000
Presents the live-action children's television series with puppets by Jim Henson Productions following the adventures of Bear and his friends Tutter, Pip and Pop, Ojo, and Treelo. Includes: "Words Words Words," "What's the Story?," and "Read My Book." 3 episodes. 75m; DVD. **A:** Preschool-Primary. **P:** Entertainment. **U:** Home. **Chl-Juv:** Television Series, Children's Shows, Puppets. **Acq:** Purchase. **Dist:** Sony Pictures Home Entertainment Inc. $14.95.

Bear in the Big Blue House: Tidy Time with Bear 2001
Presents the live-action children's television series with puppets by Jim Henson Productions following the adventures of Bear and his friends Tutter, Pip and Pop, Ojo, and Treelo. Includes: "Working Like a Bear," "Woodland House Wonderful," and "We Did it Our Way." 3 episodes. 75m; DVD. **A:** Preschool-Primary. **P:** Entertainment. **U:** Home. **Chl-Juv:** Television Series, Children's Shows, Puppets. **Acq:** Purchase. **Dist:** Sony Pictures Home Entertainment Inc. $14.95.

Bear in the Big Blue House: Visiting the Doctor with Bear 2000
Uses puppets, music and storytelling to entertain and teach young children. In this volume, Bear and his pals Tutter and Ojo learn about the doctor and how to overcome their fears. 50m; VHS. **A:** Family. **P:** Education. **U:** Home. **Chl-Juv:** Puppets, Children. **Acq:** Purchase. **Dist:** Sony Pictures Home Entertainment Inc. $12.95.

Bear in the Big Blue House: Volume 1 1998
Contains two episodes of the children's show which features an insatiably curious bear and his close friends created by the Jim Henson Company. Volume 1 contains the episodes "Home is Where the Bear Is" and "What's in the Mail Today." 50m; VHS. **A:** Family. **P:** Entertainment. **U:** Home. **Chl-Juv:** Children, Family Viewing, Puppets. **Acq:** Purchase. **Dist:** Sony Pictures Home Entertainment Inc. $12.95.

Bear in the Big Blue House: Volume 2 1998
Contains two episodes of the children's show which features an insatiably curious bear and his close friends created by the Jim Henson Company. Volume 2 contains the episodes "Friends for Life" and "The Big Little Visitor." 50m; VHS. **A:** Family. **P:** Entertainment. **U:** Home. **Chl-Juv:** Children, Family Viewing, Puppets. **Acq:** Purchase. **Dist:** Sony Pictures Home Entertainment Inc. $12.95.

Bear in the Big Blue House: Volume 3 1998
Contains two episodes of the children's show which features an insatiably curious bear and his close friends created by the Jim Henson Company. Volume 3 contains the episodes "Dancin' the Day Away" and "Listen Up." 50m; VHS. **A:** Family. **P:** Entertainment. **U:** Home. **Chl-Juv:** Children, Family Viewing, Puppets. **Acq:** Purchase. **Dist:** Sony Pictures Home Entertainment Inc. $12.95.

Bear in the Big Blue House: Volume 4 1998
Contains two episodes of the children's show which features an insatiably curious bear and his close friends created by the Jim Henson Company. Volume 4 contains the episodes "I Need a Little Help Today" and "Lost Thing." 50m; VHS. **A:** Family. **P:** Entertainment. **U:** Home. **Chl-Juv:** Children, Family Viewing, Puppets. **Acq:** Purchase. **Dist:** Sony Pictures Home Entertainment Inc. $12.95.

Bear Island 1980 (PG) — ★½
Group of secret agents cleverly disguising themselves as U.N. weather researchers converge upon Bear Island in search of a Nazi U-Boat. Looks like rain. 118m; VHS. **C:** Donald Sutherland; Richard Widmark; Barbara Parkins; Vanessa Redgrave; Christopher Lee; Lloyd Bridges; Directed by Don Sharp. **Pr:** Taft International Pictures. **A:** Jr. High-Adult. **P:** Entertainment. **U:** Home. **Mov-Ent:** Action-Adventure. **Acq:** Purchase. **Dist:** Unknown Distributor.

Bear With Us 19??
A collection of cartoons featuring bears. ?m; VHS. **A:** Family. **P:** Entertainment. **U:** Home. **Mov-Ent:** Animation & Cartoons, Animals. **Acq:** Purchase. **Dist:** Video Resources.

Bear Ye One Another's Burden. . . 1988 — ★★
In the early 50s, communist police officer Josef Heilinger (Pose) is sent to a private sanitorium for consumptives. He's forced to share a room with a young Protestant curate, Hubertus Koschenz (Mock). Their ill health is the only thing they have in common, and they deliberately seem to annoy each other, but soon their situation has them grudgingly developing a mutual respect and even friendship. German with subtitles. 118m; VHS. **C:** Jorg Pose; Manfred Mock; Susanne Luning; Dieter Knaup; Directed by Lothar Warneke; Cinematography by Peter Ziesche; Music by Gunther Fischer. **Pr:** Deutsche Film-Aktiengesellschaft. **A:** College-Adult. **P:** Entertainment. **U:** Home. **L:** German. **Mov-Ent:** Diseases, Religion, Politics & Government. **Acq:** Purchase.

Bearcats!: The Complete Television Series 1971
CBS 1971-1972 action-adventure. In 1914, mercenaries Hank Brackett and Johnny Reach travel the American Southwest in thier Stutz Bearcat automobile looking for adventure and jobs that will make them some profit. 13 episodes. 650m; DVD. **C:** Rod Taylor; Dennis Cole. **A:** Family. **P:** Entertainment. **U:** Home. **Mov-Ent:** Action-Adventure, Automobiles, Television Series. **Acq:** Purchase. **Dist:** Shout! Factory. $19.99.

BearCity 2010 (Unrated) — ★½
Rom-com featuring a group of large, hairy, gay men supporting a younger friend who comes out about his love for older, hairy men who don't fit the usual ultra-toned and fit stereotype. 99m; DVD, Blu-Ray, Streaming. **C:** Joe Conti; Brian Keane; Gerald McCullouch; Stephen Guarino; Directed by Douglas Langway; Written by Douglas Langway; Lawrence Ferber; Cinematography by Michael Hauer; Music by Kerry Muzzey. **A:** Sr. High-Adult. **P:** Entertainment. **U:** Home. **L:** English, Spanish. **Mov-Ent.** **Acq:** Purchase, Rent/Lease. **Dist:** TLA Releasing. $24.99 14.99 14.99.

Bears! 1990
Shows the magnificent beauty of grizzly bears. Illustrates what grizzlies need to survive—from food to open space; explains their seasons of sleeping, eating and raising their cubs; and explodes some myths of these animals. 13m; VHS. **Pr:** Daniel Zatz. **A:** Family. **P:** Education. **U:** Institution. **Gen-Edu:** Animals. **Acq:** Purchase, Rent/Lease. **Dist:** Bullfrog Films, Inc. $195.00.

Bears 2014 (G) — ★★½
Disney's Disneynature documentaries are experts at making wild animals humanlike, while making the kids inside all of us believe that ocean creatures and African cats all have cute names, funny quirks, and convenient three-act journeys. Co-directors Fothergill and Scholey turn their, admittedly, gorgeously cinematic gaze towards a family of bears this time, affectionately named Sky, Scout, and Amber. Their footage of the bears' trek across Alaska is jaw-droppingly beautiful and Reilly is a fine, friendly narrator, but the documentary could've benefitted from more actual wildlife information and less manufactured family drama. 78 minutesm; DVD. **C:** Narrated by John C. Reilly; Directed by Alastair Fothergill; Keith Scholey; Music by George Fenton. **Pr:** DisneyNature. **A:** Family. **P:** Entertainment. **U:** Home. **L:** English. **Mov-Ent:** Animals, Documentary Films, U.S. States. **Acq:** Purchase. **Dist:** Not Yet Released.

The Bears & I 1974 (G) — ★★
A young Vietnam vet helps Indians regain their land rights while raising three bear cubs. Beautiful photography in this Disney production. 89m; VHS, DVD. **C:** Patrick Wayne; Chief Dan George; Andrew Duggan; Michael Ansara; Directed by Bernard McEveety; Written by Jack Speirs; John Whedon; Cinematography by Ted D. Landon; Music by Buddy (Norman Dale) Baker. **Pr:** Buena Vista. **A:** Family. **P:** Entertainment. **U:** Home. **Mov-Ent:** Bears, Native Americans, Animals. **Acq:** Purchase. **Dist:** Walt Disney Studios Home Entertainment. $69.95.

Bear's Barnyard: "It's a Dog's Life" 1994
Joins a dog named Bear as he discovers the meaning of friendship through his experiences with the talking animals on a farm. 30m; VHS. **A:** Preschool-Primary. **P:** Education. **U:** Home. **Chl-Juv:** Children, Animals. **Acq:** Purchase. **Dist:** Not Yet Released.

Bear's Big Lake 1995
Bear the dog appears again, this time lost on a camping trip to the lake, but friendly forest folk help him out. 30m; VHS. **A:** Preschool-Primary. **P:** Entertainment. **U:** Home. **Chl-Juv:** Animals, Pets. **Acq:** Purchase. **Dist:** Tapeworm Video Distributors Inc.

The Bear's Christmas 1989
The Bear, a grumpy and depressed cartoon character, is uplifted by the Christmas spirit. 30m; VHS, 3/4 U. **Pr:** Don Warobey; John Taylor. **A:** Primary. **P:** Entertainment. **U:** Institution, SURA. **Chl-Juv:** Animation & Cartoons, Christmas, Family Viewing. **Acq:** Purchase, Rent/Lease. **Dist:** National Film Board of Canada.

Bears: Kings of the Wild 1982
Several varieties of bears are examined as to their life cycles, behavioral patterns, and characteristics. 23m; VHS, 3/4 U. **Pr:** Avatar Learning. **A:** Primary-Sr. High. **P:** Education. **U:** Institu-

tion, SURA. **Gen-Edu**: Documentary Films, Wildlife, Animals. **Acq:** Purchase, Rent/Lease, Trade-in. **Dist:** Encyclopedia Britannica.

Bears of the Ice 1982
Scientists study polar bears during the bears' annual migration through the town of Churchill, Manitoba. 23m; 3/4 U, Special order formats. **Pr:** National Geographic Society. **A:** Jr. High-Adult. **P:** Education. **U:** Institution, Home, SURA. **Hea-Sci**: Documentary Films, Wildlife. **Acq:** Purchase, Trade-in, Duplication License. **Dist:** National Geographic Society.

Bearskin 1983
A man makes a deal with the devil which he finds hard to live up to: he gets unending riches, but he isn't allowed to wash himself for seven years. 20m; VHS, 3/4 U, Special order formats. **Pr:** Davenport Films. **A:** Jr. High-Adult. **P:** Education. **U:** Institution, Home, SURA. **Gen-Edu**: Folklore & Legends. **Acq:** Purchase, Rent/Lease. **Dist:** Davenport Films. $60.00.

Bea's Own Good 19??
Part of a curriculum plan designed to teach elementary students the importance of rules, responsibility, and self-control through the story of Bea the honeybee of France. Includes storybook and teaching guide. 15m; VHS. **A:** Primary. **P:** Education. **U:** Institution. **Chl-Juv**: Ethics & Morals, Education. **Acq:** Purchase. **Dist:** Marshmedia. $79.95.

The Beast 1975 — ★½
Long considered taboo due to its erotic subject matter, this 1975 French film from director Borowczyk arrives in its uncensored form for the first time in 2000. Young heiress Lucy Broadhurst (Hummel) arrives at the de l'Esperance chateau, where she is to marry the young Mathurn de l'Esperance (Benedetti). After retiring to her room, Lucy finds herself dreaming of the 18th-century lady of the chateau, Romilda de l'Esperance (Lane), who according to legend, encountered a wild, sexual monster in the forest near the manor. Was this an isolated incident or does the Beast still roam the grounds? The once shocking sex scenes will be considered quite tame by today's audience, and some of them come across as quite silly. 94m; DVD, Wide. **C:** Sirpa Lane; Lisbeth Hummel; Elizabeth Kaza; Pierre Benedetti; Guy Trejan; Directed by Walerian Borowczyk; Written by Walerian Borowczyk; Cinematography by Bernard Daillencourt; Marcel Grignon. **A:** College-Adult. **P:** Entertainment. **U:** Home. **Mov-Ent**: Drama, Sex & Sexuality. **Acq:** Purchase. **Dist:** $24.95.

The Beast 1988 (R) — ★★½
Violent and cliche-driven war drama notable for its novel twist: wild Russian tank officer becomes lost in the Afghanistan wilderness while being tracked by Afghan rebels with revenge in mind. Filmed in the Israel desert and adapted by William Mastrosimone from his play. 93m; VHS, DVD, Wide, CC. **C:** George Dzundza; Jason Patric; Steven Bauer; Stephen Baldwin; Don Harvey; Kabir Bedi; Erik Avari; Haim Gerafi; Directed by Kevin Reynolds; Written by William Mastrosimone; Cinematography by Doug Milsome; Music by Mark Isham. **Pr:** A&M Films. **A:** Sr. High-Adult. **P:** Entertainment. **U:** Home. **Mov-Ent**: Tanks, War--General. **Acq:** Purchase. **Dist:** Sony Pictures Home Entertainment Inc. $89.95.

The Beast 1996 (PG-13) — ★★
Benchley once again terrorizes a small coastal community with a giant sea creature that preys on sailors and divers. When a poacher's attempts to capture the creature result in further disaster, a fishing boat captain, a Coast Guard officer, and a marine biologist set sail to to kill the critter. 116m; VHS, DVD, Blu-Ray, CC. **C:** William L. Petersen; Karen Sillas; Charles Martin Smith; Ronald Guttman; Missy (Melissa) Crider; Sterling Macer; Denis Arndt; Larry Drake; Directed by Jeff Bleckner; Written by J.B. White; Cinematography by Geoff Burton; Music by Don Davis. **Pr:** Michael Joyce; Dan Wigutow. **A:** Jr. High-Adult. **P:** Entertainment. **U:** Home. **Mov-Ent**: Oceanography, TV Movies. **Acq:** Purchase. **Dist:** Timeless Media Group.

Beast Cops 1998 — ★★★
Until the last quarter of the film, director Chan's "Beast Cops" is more of a buddy/buddy cop click than a shoot 'em up. But don't worry, once it passes that point, the cops live up to their titular name and deliver a brutal slaughter worthy of the finest and/or vilest of Hong Kong action films. The near-romantic build up makes the climax seem even all the more violent. Wong is excellent as the cop who loves the whoring and gambling that he uses to stay in touch with his mob contacts. 108m; DVD. **C:** Anthony Wong; Michael Wong; Roy Cheung; Directed by Gordon Chan; Written by Gordon Chan; Chan Hing-Kai. **A:** Sr. High-Adult. **P:** Entertainment. **U:** Home. **Mov-Ent**: Crime Drama. **Acq:** Purchase. **Dist:** Media Asia.

The Beast from Haunted Cave 1960 — ★★
Gold thieves hiding in a wilderness cabin encounter a spiderlike monster. Surprisingly good performances from Sinatra (Frank's nephew) and Carol. Produced by Gene Corman, Roger's brother. 64m/B/W; VHS, DVD, Wide. **C:** Michael Forest; Sheila Carol; Frank Wolff; Richard Sinatra; Wally Campo; Directed by Monte Hellman; Written by Charles B. Griffith; Cinematography by Andrew M. Costikyan. **Pr:** Filmgroup. **A:** Jr. High-Adult. **P:** Entertainment. **U:** Home. **Mov-Ent**: Horror. **Acq:** Purchase. **Dist:** Synapse; Sinister Cinema. $19.98.

The Beast from 20,000 Fathoms 1953 (Unrated) — ★★½
Atomic testing defrosts a giant dinosaur in the Arctic; the hungry monster proceeds onwards to its former breeding grounds, now New York City. Oft-imitated saurian-on-the-loose formula is still fun, brought to life by Ray Harryhausen special effects. Based loosely on the Ray Bradbury story "The Foghorn." 80m/B/W; VHS, DVD. **C:** Paul (Christian) Hubschmid; Paula Raymond; Cecil Kellaway; Kenneth Tobey; Donald Woods; Lee Van Cleef; Steve Brodie; Mary Hill; Jack Pennick; Ross Elliot; Directed by Eugene Lourie; Written by Eugene Lourie; Fred Freiberger; Louis Morheim; Robert Smith; Cinematography by John L. "Jack" Russell; Music by David Buttolph. **Pr:** Warner Bros. **A:** Jr. High-Adult. **P:** Entertainment. **U:** Home. **Mov-Ent**: Science Fiction. **Acq:** Purchase. **Dist:** Warner Home Video, Inc.; Facets Multimedia Inc.; Sinister Cinema. $19.95.

Beast Hunter 2011 (Unrated)
A two-disc collection of National Geographic episodes seeking to prove the existence of mythological monsters around the world. 225m; DVD. **A:** Family. **P:** Entertainment. **U:** Institution, Home. **Gen-Edu**: Documentary Films, Folklore & Legends. **Acq:** Purchase. **Dist:** National Geographic Society. $39.95.

The Beast in Space 1980 (Unrated) — ★
Pointless reimagining of Walerian Borowyczyk's film "La Bete" set in space. The crew of a ship looking for rare elements is seduced by the computer of a faraway world. It convinces them all to get naked and party, not noticing the homicidal robot running around killing the natives. 92m; DVD. **C:** Sirpa Lane; Vassili Karis; Umberto Ceriani; Maria D'Alessandro; Marina Hedman; Directed by Alfonso Brescia; Written by Alfonso Brescia; Aldo Crudo; Cinematography by Silvio Fraschetti; Music by Marcello Giombini. **A:** College-Adult. **P:** Entertainment. **U:** Home. **L:** English, Italian. **Mov-Ent**. **Acq:** Purchase. **Dist:** Severin Films. $29.98.

Beast in the Cellar 1970 (R) — ★½
Every family has something to hide, and in the case of two spinster sisters, it's their murderous inhuman brother, whom they keep chained in the cellar. Like all brothers, however, the "beast" rebels against his sisters' bossiness and escapes to terrorize their peaceful English countryside. The sisters' (Reid and Robson) performances aren't bad, but rest of effort is fairly disappointing. 85m; VHS, DVD. **C:** Beryl Reid; Flora Robson; T.P. McKenna; Directed by James Kelly. **Pr:** Graham Harris; Wrightwood. **A:** Sr. High-Adult. **P:** Entertainment. **U:** Home. **Mov-Ent**: Horror, Family. **Acq:** Purchase. **Dist:** Unknown Distributor.

Beast Machines—Transformers: The Complete Series 2006
Features 1999-2001 animated television series spin-off of the "Transformers" series about the struggle between the Maximals and Megatron and his army of Vehicons with the Maximals' home planet of Cybertron hanging in the balance. 26 episodes. 700m; DVD. **A:** Primary-Adult. **P:** Entertainment. **U:** Home. **Mov-Ent**: Television Series, Animation & Cartoons, Children's Shows. **Acq:** Purchase. **Dist:** Rhino Entertainment Co. $59.98.

The Beast Must Die 1975 (PG) — ★★
A millionaire sportsman invites a group of men and women connected with bizarre deaths or the eating of human flesh to spend the cycle of a full moon at his isolated lodge. 93m; VHS, DVD, Wide. **C:** Peter Cushing; Calvin Lockhart; Charles Gray; Anton Diffring; Marlene Clark; Ciaran Madden; Tom Chadbon; Michael Gambon; Directed by Paul Annett; Written by Michael Winder; Cinematography by Jack Hildyard; Music by Douglas Gamley. **Pr:** Max J. Rosenberg; Cinerama Releasing. **A:** Jr. High-Adult. **P:** Entertainment. **U:** Home. **Mov-Ent**: Horror. **Acq:** Purchase. **Dist:** Movies Unlimited. $9.95.

The Beast of Babylon Against the Son of Hercules 1963 (Unrated) — ★
Nippur (Gordon) probably doesn't have any filial bond to Hercules but it's a convenient hook for this dubbed Italian flick. Tyrant Balthazar (Lulli) rules Assyria, sacrificing virgins to the goddess Istar. Nippur, the rightful heir to the throne, leads a slave revolt to overthrow the bloodthirsty ruler. 98m; DVD. **C:** Gordon Scott; Genevieve Grad; Pierro Lulli; Andrea Scotti; Moira Orfei; Mario Petri; Directed by Siro Marcellini; Written by Siro Marcellini; Gian Paolo Callegari; Albert Valentin; Cinematography by Pier Ludovico Pavoni; Music by Carlo Franci. **A:** Jr. High-Adult. **P:** Entertainment. **U:** Home. **Mov-Ent**. **Acq:** Purchase. **Dist:** Sinister Cinema.

Beast of Blood 1971 (Unrated) — ★½
In this sequel to "Mad Doctor of Blood Island," an insane scientist finally captures the chlorophyll zombie, beheads him, and keeps the head alive to insult it daily. As opposed to the not-insane people who burn monsters so they can't somehow gain revenge (hint, hint). 90m; DVD. **C:** John Ashley; Eddie Garcia; Alfonso Carvajal; Bruno Punzalan; Celeste Yarnall; Liza Belmonte; Justo Paulino; Directed by Eddie Romero; Written by Eddie Romero; Beverly Miller; Music by Tito Arevalo. **A:** Sr. High-Adult. **P:** Entertainment. **U:** Home. **L:** English. **Mov-Ent**. **Acq:** Purchase. **Dist:** Gotham Distributing Corp. $7.98.

The Beast of Monsieur Racine 1974
An animated film about Monsieur Racine and the harmless-looking beast who has been stealing his prize pears, and how the two become great friends. 9m; VHS, 3/4 U. **C:** Narrated by Charles Duvall. **Pr:** Gene Deitch. **A:** Primary. **P:** Entertainment. **U:** Institution, SURA. **L:** English, French. **Chl-Juv**: Family Viewing, Human Relations, Animation & Cartoons. **Acq:** Purchase. **Dist:** Weston Woods Studios.

The Beast of Monsieur Racine and Other Stories 1974
A compilation of children's animated films, including "Rosie's Walk," "The Story About Ping" and "Charlie Needs a Cloak." Available separately from Weston Woods Studios. 32m; VHS. **Pr:** Morton Schindel. **A:** Preschool-Primary. **P:** Entertainment. **U:** Home. **Chl-Juv**: Family Viewing, Animation & Cartoons. **Acq:** Purchase, Rent/Lease. **Dist:** Facets Multimedia Inc.

Beast of Morocco 1966 — ★★
Interesting vampire film about a Morrocan vampire princess who sets her sights on seducing a noted archaeologist. Of course his girlfriend ends up being abducted by the vampire's servant. 88m; VHS, DVD. **C:** William Sylvester; Alizia Gur; Terence de Marney; Diane Clare; Edward Underdown; William Dexter; Sylvia Marriott; Directed by Frederick Goode; Written by Bruce Stewart; Cinematography by William Jordan; Music by John Shakespeare. **A:** Sr. High-Adult. **P:** Entertainment. **U:** Home. **Mov-Ent**: Horror. **Acq:** Purchase. **Dist:** Amazon.com Inc.; Sinister Cinema. $16.95.

The Beast of the City 1932 (Unrated) — ★★
Crime melodrama that ends in a violent machine-gun rubout, making you wonder just who the good guys are. Chicago police captain Jim Fitzpatrick (Huston) is obsessed with cleaning up the city but crime boss Belmonte (Hersholt) gets off because he has city and police officials on his payroll. When Jim becomes a hero foiling a bank robbery, public opinion demands he be appointed the new police commissioner and his first order is to get Belmonte by any means necessary. Harlow plays gun moll Daisy. 85m/B/W; DVD. **C:** Walter Huston; Jean Harlow; Jean Hersholt; Wallace Ford; Dorothy Peterson; Tully Marshall; Emmett Corrigan; Directed by Charles Brabin; Written by John Lee Mahin; Cinematography by Norbert Brodine. **A:** Jr. High-Adult. **P:** Entertainment. **U:** Home. **Mov-Ent**: Crime Drama. **Acq:** Purchase. **Dist:** WarnerArchive.com.

Beast of the Yellow Night 1970 (R) — **Bomb!**
A dying soldier sells his soul to Satan at the close of WWII. Years later, existing without aging, he periodically turns into a cannibal monster. Although the first half is tedious, the monster turns things around when he finally shows up. Decent gore effects. 87m; VHS, DVD. **C:** John Ashley; Mary Wilcox; Eddie Garcia; Vic Diaz; Directed by Eddie Romero. **Pr:** John Ashley; Eddie Romero; John Ashley; Eddie Romero; New World Pictures. **A:** Jr. High-Adult. **P:** Entertainment. **U:** Home. **Mov-Ent**: Horror. **Acq:** Purchase. **Dist:** VCI Entertainment; Silver Mine Video Inc. $19.95.

The Beast of Yucca Flats 1961 — **Bomb!**
A really cheap, quasi-nuclear protest film. A Russian scientist is chased by communist agents into a nuclear testing area and is caught in an atomic blast. As a result, he turns into a club-weilding monster. Voice over narration is used in lieu of dialogue as that process proved too expensive. 53m/B/W; VHS, DVD. **C:** Tor Johnson; Douglas Mellor; Larry Aten; Barbara Francis; Conrad Brooks; Anthony Cardoza; Bing Stafford; John Morrison; Directed by Coleman Francis; Written by Coleman Francis; Cinematography by John Cagle; Music by Irwin Nafshun; Al Remington. **Pr:** Anthony Cardoza; Anthony Cardoza; Crown International Pictures. **A:** Jr. High-Adult. **P:** Entertainment. **U:** Home. **Mov-Ent**: Science Fiction. **Acq:** Purchase. **Dist:** Sinister Cinema. $12.95.

The Beast Penalty Kill System 2013 (Unrated)
Coach Jack Arena demonstrates the penalty kill system he teaches his hockey teams to use to disrupt power plays. 48m; DVD. **A:** Family. **P:** Education. **U:** Home. **L:** English. **Spo-Rec**: Athletic Instruction/Coaching, Hockey. **Acq:** Purchase. **Dist:** Championship Productions. $29.99.

The Beast: Season 1 2009 (Unrated)
A&E 2009 crime drama. Patrick Swayze, in his final performances, plays Charles Barker, a veteran FBI agent who's methods are extremely unorthodox but highly effective as he trains his rookie partner agent Ellis Dove (Fimmel) in the intricacies of undercover work going up against drug lords, arms dealers, corrupt cops and assassins. Dove in addition to being trained is also being pressured to become an informant for the bureau who suspects Barker of going rogue. 13 episodes. 590m; DVD. **C:** Patrick Swayze; Travis Fimmel; Lindsay Pulsipher; Kevin J. O'Connor. **A:** Sr. High-Adult. **P:** Entertainment. **U:** Home. **Mov-Ent**: Drama, Television Series. **Acq:** Purchase. **Dist:** Sony Pictures Home Entertainment Inc. $39.99.

The Beast That Killed Women 1965 — ★★½
Colonists at a sunny Florida nudist camp have their beach party interrupted by an escaped gorilla. Director Mahon, in his first color effort, stretches this panicky moment into an hour of fleshy fun and games. 60m; VHS, DVD. **C:** Darlene Bennett; Gigi Darlene; June Roberts; Directed by Barry Mahon; Written by Barry Mahon; Cinematography by Barry Mahon. **A:** College-Adult. **P:** Entertainment. **U:** Home. **Mov-Ent**: Horror, Animals. **Acq:** Purchase. **Dist:** Something Weird Video; Tapeworm Video Distributors Inc. $24.95.

Beast Wars: Transformers, Vol. 2 2996
Presents the 1996-1999 animated television series—a spin-off of the "Transformers" series—as the kind-hearted Maximals and the vicious Predacons and Megatron continue to fight each other when Megatron is challenged by the Terrorsaur. Includes: "Fallen Comrades," "Double Jeopardy," "The Probe," "Gorilla Warfare," "A Better Mousetrap," and "Victory." 6 episodes. 150m; DVD. **A:** Primary-Adult. **P:** Entertainment. **U:** Home. **Mov-Ent**: Television Series, Animation & Cartoons, Children's Shows. **Acq:** Purchase. **Dist:** Rhino Entertainment Co. $19.95.

Beast Wars—Transformers: The Complete First Season 1996
Presents the animated television series—a spin-off of the "Transformers" series—as the kind-hearted Maximals and the vicious Predacons and Megatron continue to fight each other when Megatron is challenged by the Terrorsaur. 26 episodes. 620m; DVD. **A:** Primary-Adult. **P:** Entertainment. **U:**

Home. **Mov-Ent**: Television Series, Animation & Cartoons, Children's Shows. **Acq:** Purchase. **Dist:** Rhino Entertainment Co. $59.95.

Beast Wars—Transformers: The Complete Second Season 1997
Presents the 1996-1999 animated television series—a spin-off of the "Transformers" series—as the kind-hearted Maximals and the vicious Predacons and Megatron continue to fight each other when Megatron is challenged by the Terrorsaur. 13 episodes. 310m; DVD. **A:** Primary-Adult. **P:** Entertainment. **U:** Home. **Mov-Ent**: Television Series, Animation & Cartoons, Children's Shows. **Acq:** Purchase. **Dist:** Rhino Entertainment Co. $29.95.

Beast Wars—Transformers: The Complete Third Season 1998
Presents the 1996-1999 animated television series—a spin-off of the "Transformers" series—as the kind-hearted Maximals and the vicious Predacons and Megatron continue to fight each other when Megatron is challenged by the Terrorsaur. 26 episodes. 350m; DVD. **A:** Primary-Adult. **P:** Entertainment. **U:** Home. **Mov-Ent**: Television Series, Animation & Cartoons, Children's Shows. **Acq:** Purchase. **Dist:** Rhino Entertainment Co. $29.95.

The Beast With a Million Eyes 1956 (Unrated) — ★
Silly and very cheap Roger Corman-produced sci fi. The desert-dwelling Kelly family finds a spaceship has landed with an alien that plans to dominate earthlings with mind control. 78m/B/W; DVD. **C:** Paul Birch; Lorna Thayer; Dona Cole; Chester Conklin; Dick Sargent; Leonard Tarver; Directed by David Kramarsky; Written by Tom Filer; Cinematography by Everett Baker; Music by John Bickford. **A:** Jr. High-Adult. **P:** Entertainment. **U:** Home. **Mov-Ent**: Science Fiction. **Acq:** Purchase. **Dist:** MGM Home Entertainment.

The Beast with Five Fingers 1946 — ★★½
After a pianist mysteriously dies and leaves his fortune to his private nurse, the occupants of his villa are terrorized by a creature that turns out to be the pianist's hand which was severed by his personal secretary (Lorre). Lorre is also terrorized by hallucinations of the hand, and no matter what he does to stop it (nail it to a desk, throw it in the fire, etc.), nothing can keep the hand from carrying out its mission. A creepy thriller with inventive shots of the severed hand. 88m/B/W; DVD, Streaming. **C:** Robert Alda; Andrea King; Peter Lorre; Victor Francen; J. Carrol Naish; Charles Dingle; Directed by Robert Florey; Written by Curt Siodmak; Cinematography by Wesley Anderson; Music by Max Steiner. **Pr:** Warner Bros. **A:** Jr. High-Adult. **P:** Entertainment. **U:** Home. **Mov-Ent**: Horror. **Acq:** Purchase. **Dist:** WarnerArchive.com; Amazon.com Inc. $19.98.

The Beast Within 1982 (R) — ★★
Young woman has the misfortune of being raped by an unseen creature in a Mississippi swamp. Seventeen years later, her son conceived from that hellish union begins to act quite strange, developing a penchant for shedding his skin before turning into an insect-like critter with a cannibalistic appetite. First film to use the air "bladder" type of prosthetic make-up popularized in later, and generally better, horror films. Contains some choice cuts in photo editing: the juxtaposition of hamburger and human "dead meat" is witty. Based on Edward Levy's 1981 novel. 98m; VHS, DVD, Blu-Ray, Wide. **C:** Ronny Cox; Bibi Besch; L.Q. Jones; Paul Clemens; Don Gordon; Katherine Moffat; John Dennis Johnston; R.G. Armstrong; Logan Ramsey; Ron Soble; Meshach Taylor; Directed by Philippe Mora; Written by Tom Holland; Cinematography by Jack L. Richards; Music by Les Baxter. **Pr:** MGM Home Entertainment. **A:** Sr. High-Adult. **P:** Entertainment. **U:** Home. **Mov-Ent**: Horror, Rape, Family. **Acq:** Purchase. **Dist:** MGM Home Entertainment. $14.95.

Beast Within 2008 (R) — ★
Yet another zombie flick with a too-predictable plot (this time from Germany). Medical student Robert and his friends are whooping it up in his grandfather's country mansion when zombies (infected by diseased birds) come a-callin'. 93m; DVD. **C:** Philipp Danne; Anna Breuer; Marvin Gronen; Birthe Wolter; Alex Attimoneilli; Directed by Wolf Wolff; Written by Wolf Janke; Cinematography by Heiko Rahnenfuhrer. **A:** Sr. High-Adult. **P:** Entertainment. **U:** Home. **Mov-Ent. Acq:** Purchase. **Dist:** Lions Gate Entertainment Inc.

The Beastie Boys 1987
The rap/punk trio's video hits, including "Fight for Your Right (To Party)," "She's On It" and "No Sleep Til Brooklyn." In HiFi Stereo. 25m; VHS. **Pr:** CBS/Fox. **A:** Jr. High. **P:** Entertainment. **U:** Home. **Mov-Ent**: Music Video, Music--Performance. **Acq:** Purchase. **Dist:** Music Video Distributors. $19.95.

The Beastie Boys: The Skills to Pay the Bills 199?
Features the Beastie Boy's videos from the "Paul's Boutique" and "Check Your Head" albums, including the two latest videos "Pass the Mic" and "So What'cha Want." Home movies from the Beastie's teen years and a dopey yet charming "dream sequence" starring Beastie Mike D are also included. ?m; VHS. **A:** Jr. High-Adult. **P:** Entertainment. **U:** Home. **Mov-Ent**: Music Video, Music--Rap. **Acq:** Purchase. **Dist:** EMI/Capitol Records; Music Video Distributors. $14.98.

Beastly 2011 (PG-13) — ★★½
Modern retelling of the "Beauty and the Beast" story based on the novel by Alex Finn and intended for tween girls (and maybe some older sisters). Wealthy, handsome Kyle (Pettyfer) has a mean streak, but he humiliates the wrong classmate when witchy Kendra (Olsen) uses a spell to transform Kyle into a (somewhat) repulsive character with weird tribal tattoos, scars, and piercings. Banished to Brooklyn seclusion, his curse can only be lifted if Kyle can find someone to love him as he is. So he makes a deal with wrong side of the tracks Linda Taylor (Hudgens) who moves in and becomes his companion. 86m; Blu-Ray, On Demand, Wide, CC. **C:** Alex Pettyfer; Vanessa Anne Hudgens; Mary-Kate Olsen; Peter Krause; Neil Patrick Harris; Dakota Johnson; Directed by Daniel Barnz; Written by Daniel Barnz; Cinematography by Mandy Walker; Music by Marcelo Zarvos. **Pr:** Susan Cartonis; Storefront Pictures; CBS Films. **A:** Jr. High-Adult. **P:** Entertainment. **U:** Home. **L:** English. **Mov-Ent**: Fantasy, Handicapped. **Acq:** Purchase. **Dist:** Amazon.com Inc.; Movies Unlimited; Alpha Video.

Beastly Boyz 2006 (R) — ★
A young man worms his way into an all-gay male sports camp to avenge the death of his twin sister because her ghost just can't let it go. 75m; DVD, Streaming. **C:** Sebastian Gacki; Emrey Wright; Charlie Marsh; Andrew Butler; Dean Hrycan; Tyler Burrows; Directed by David DeCoteau; Written by David DeCoteau; David Grove; Cinematography by Todd Turner; Music by Joe Silva. **A:** Sr. High-Adult. **P:** Entertainment. **U:** Home. **L:** English. **Mov-Ent. Acq:** Purchase, Rent/Lease. **Dist:** Rapid Heart Pictures. $12.99 9.99.

Beastmaster 1982 (PG) — ★★
Adventure set in a wild and primitive world. The Beastmaster is involved in a life-and-death struggle with overwhelming forces of evil. Campy neanderthal flesh flick. 119m; VHS, DVD, Wide. **C:** Marc Singer; Tanya Roberts; Rip Torn; John Amos; Josh Milrad; Billy Jacoby; Ben Hammer; Directed by Don A. Coscarelli; Written by Don A. Coscarelli; Paul Pepperman; Cinematography by John Alcott; Music by Lee Holdridge. **Pr:** MGM Home Entertainment. **A:** Jr. High-Adult. **P:** Entertainment. **U:** Home. **Mov-Ent**: Fantasy, Animals. **Acq:** Purchase. **Dist:** Anchor Bay Entertainment.

Beastmaster 2: Through the Portal of Time 1991 (PG-13) — ★½
This time the laughs are intentional as the Beastmaster follows an evil monarch through a dimensional gate to modern-day L.A., where the shopping is better for both trendy clothes and weapons. Fun for genre fans, with a behind-the-scenes featurette on the tape. 107m; VHS, CC. **C:** Marc Singer; Kari Wuhrer; Sarah Douglas; Wings Hauser; James Avery; Robert Fieldsteel; Arthur Malet; Robert Z'Dar; Michael Berryman; Directed by Sylvio Tabet; Music by Robert Folk. **Pr:** Sylvio Tabet; New Line Cinema. **A:** Jr. High-Adult. **P:** Entertainment. **U:** Home. **Mov-Ent**: Fantasy, Animals. **Acq:** Purchase. **Dist:** Lions Gate Entertainment Inc. $9.98.

Beastmaster 3: The Eye of Braxus 1995 (PG) — ★★½
Heroic hunk Dar the Beastmaster (Singer) returns to battle evil. Lord Agon (Warner) needs to obtain a jeweled eye that will bring the demon Braxus back to life—and he'll stop at nothing, including kidnapping Dar's brother King Tal (Van Dien), to reach his terrifying goal. But Dar isn't alone—he's got the bewitching sorceress Morgana (Down), tempting warrioress Shada (Hess), and loyal advisor Seth (Todd) to help him out. 92m; VHS, CC. **C:** Marc Singer; David Warner; Lesley-Anne Down; Tony Todd; Casper Van Dien; Keith Coulouris; Sandra Hess; Patrick Kilpatrick; Directed by Gabrielle Beaumont; Written by David Wise; Cinematography by Barbara Claman; Music by Jan Hammer. **Pr:** Stu Segall; Sylvio Tabet; David Wise. **A:** Jr. High-Adult. **P:** Entertainment. **U:** Home. **Mov-Ent**: Fantasy. **Acq:** Purchase. **Dist:** Universal Music and Video Distribution.

Beasts 1983 (Unrated) — ★
A young couple's plans for a romantic weekend in the Rockies are slightly changed when the pair are savagely attacked by wild beasts. 92m; VHS. **C:** Tom Babson; Kathy Christopher; Vern Potter; Directed by Don Hawks. **Pr:** American National Enterprises. **A:** Sr. High-Adult. **P:** Entertainment. **U:** Home. **Mov-Ent**: Animals. **Acq:** Purchase. **Dist:** No Longer Available.

The Beasts Are On the Streets 1978 — ★★½
A Hanna-Barbera live-action NBC TV disaster pic that has the animals from a safari tourist park escaping after a careening truck tears off the fencing. Park rangers and cops try to recapture the beasts while some of the public decide to go big game hunting and vet Dr. McCauley tries to stop the man vs. beast panic. 98m; DVD. **C:** Carol Lynley; Dale Robinette; Billy Green Bush; Philip Michael Thomas; Casey Biggs; Directed by Peter R. Hunt; Written by Laurence Heath; Cinematography by Chuck Arnold; Music by Gerald Fried. **A:** Jr. High-Adult. **P:** Entertainment. **U:** Home. **L:** English. **Mov-Ent**: Animals, TV Movies. **Acq:** Purchase. **Dist:** WarnerArchive.com.

The Beasts of Marseilles 1957 (Unrated) — ★★
In 1943, two Brits escape from a POW camp and hide out among the refugees in the French port city of Marseilles. They're bored waiting to find a ship to take them back to England and get into trouble, including finding Dr. Martout, a friendly local who turns out to be a serial killer. (His character is based on the mass murderer Dr. Marcel Petiot.) 100m/B/W; DVD. **C:** Stephen Boyd; Tony Wright; James Robertson Justice; Anna Gaylor; Kathleen Harrison; Anton Diffring; Directed by Hugo Fregonese; Written by John Baines; Cinematography by Wilkie Cooper; Music by Antony Hopkins. **A:** Sr. High-Adult. **P:** Entertainment. **U:** Home. **Mov-Ent**: World War Two, Refugees, France. **Acq:** Purchase. **Dist:** Timeless Media Group.

Beasts of the Southern Wild 2012 (PG-13) — ★★★
This multi-award winner at the 2012 Sundance Film Festival is a daring post-Katrina tale of people living off the grid in the deep south. Six-year-old Hushpuppy (Wallis) narrates and most of the film's dream-like nature comes from the fact that it's clearly a story seen through the eyes of a child. As her father's health struggles and their house and lives are in peril, she manages to stay hopeful. Director Zeitlin's debut is stunning as it blends youth-like wonder with the true horrors of the real world into something that feels poetic, original, and mesmerizing. 93m; DVD, Blu-Ray, Wide. **C:** Quvenzhane Wallis; Dwight Henry; Jean Battiste; Lowell Landes; Directed by Benh Zeitlin; Written by Benh Zeitlin; Lucy Alibar; Cinematography by Ben Richardson; Music by Benh Zeitlin; Daniel Romer. **Pr:** Michael Gottwald; Dan Janvey; Josh Penn; Journeyman Pictures; Cinereach; Court 13; Fox Searchlight. **A:** Sr. High-Adult. **P:** Entertainment. **U:** Home. **L:** English. **Mov-Ent**: Drama, Black Culture, U.S. States. **Awds:** Ind. Spirit '13: Cinematog. **Acq:** Purchase. **Dist:** Fox Home Entertainment.

The Beat 1988 — ★
Unrealistic film about a bookish new kid who intercedes in the tension between two rival street gangs, changing their lives in his literary way. 101m; VHS. **C:** John Savage; Kara Glover; Paul Dillon; David Jacobson; William McNamara; Directed by Peter Mones; Written by Peter Mones; Music by Carter Burwell. **Pr:** Julia Phillips. **A:** Sr. High-Adult. **P:** Entertainment. **U:** Home. **Mov-Ent**: Adolescence. **Acq:** Purchase. **Dist:** Lions Gate Television Corp. $79.98.

Beat 2000 — ★★
Disappointing look at the events leading up to William S. Burroughs's shooting of his wife in Mexico in 1951. Tangled hetero- and homosexual relationships and unrequited longings between future literarati Burroughs (Sutherland), his wife (Love), Allen Ginsberg (Livingston), Lucien Carr (Reedus), and Jack Kerouac (Martinez) should've provided more spark, but the indifferent direction and poor script give the actors little to work with. 89m; VHS, DVD. **C:** Courtney Love; Kiefer Sutherland; Ron Livingston; Kyle Secor; Daniel Martinez; Sam Trammell; Directed by Gary Walkow; Written by Gary Walkow; Cinematography by Ciro Cabello; Music by Ernest Troost. **A:** Sr. High-Adult. **P:** Entertainment. **U:** Home. **Mov-Ent**: Mexico, Drug Abuse, Alcoholism. **Acq:** Purchase. **Dist:** Lions Gate Home Entertainment.

Beat Girl 1960 (Unrated) — ★★
Pouty rebellious teen Jennifer (Hill) spends her days in art school and her nights at a London beat hangout. She's jealous when daddy (Farrar) marries sexy French Nichole (Adam) and plots to break them up. When Jennifer discovers Nichole's sordid past she winds up in a burlesque club, attracting the unsavory attentions of owner Kenny (Lee). Then Kenny winds up dead. Singer Adam Faith performs and Reed has a bit as a youthful tough. 85m/B/W; VHS, DVD. **C:** Gillian Hills; David Farrar; Noelle Adam; Christopher Lee; Shirley Anne Field; Oliver Reed; Nada Beall; Adam Faith; Nigel Green; Claire Gordon; Directed by Edmond T. Greville; Written by Dail Ambler; Cinematography by Walter Lassally; Music by John Barry. **Pr:** Victoria Films. **A:** Sr. High-Adult. **P:** Entertainment. **U:** Home. **Mov-Ent**: Cult Films, Architecture. **Acq:** Purchase. **Dist:** Kino on Video; Facets Multimedia Inc.; Sinister Cinema.

The Beat Hotel 2011
Explores the importance of the Paris hotel that became known as the Beat Hotel as many American Beats, including Allen Ginsberg, William S. Burroughs, and Gregory Corso, made their home and wrote some of their best-known works in the mid to late 1950s. 82m; DVD. **A:** Jr. High-Adult. **P:** Entertainment. **U:** Home. **Mov-Ent**: Literature--American, France, Documentary Films. **Acq:** Purchase. **Dist:** First Run Features. $27.95.

The Beat My Heart Skipped 2005 (Unrated) — ★★★
In adapting James Toback's 1978 "Fingers," French director Audiard changed the place (from New York to Paris), the pace (more somber and less high-strung), and the names—but the heart of the story stayed the same. Here Thomas Seyr (Duris, in Harvey Keitel's "Johnny Fingers" role) does his dad's dirty collections work in crooked real estate schemes though it repulses him. But when his long-discarded dreams of becoming a concert pianist reemerge, the pull between his two lives proves more than he can bear. 107m; DVD. **C:** Romain Duris; Niels Arestrup; Linh Dan Pham; Emmanuelle Devos; Jonathan Zaccai; Gilles Cohen; Anton Yakovlev; Melanie Laurent; Directed by Jacques Audiard; Written by Jacques Audiard; Tonino Benaquista; Cinematography by Stephane Fontaine. **Pr:** Pascal Caucheteux; UGC; Why Not Productions; Sedif; France 3 Cinema. **A:** Sr. High-Adult. **P:** Entertainment. **U:** Home. **L:** English, French, Russian. **Mov-Ent**: Real Estate. **Awds:** British Acad. '05: Foreign Film. **Acq:** Purchase. **Dist:** Wellspring Media.

Beat of Distant Hearts 1999
Poets, singers and painters share the experiences of exile, loss and war felt by the Saharawis, a nomadic society forced to flee their homeland when Morocco was invaded in 1975. Subtitled in English. 45m; VHS. **A:** Adult. **P:** Education. **U:** Institution, BCTV. **L:** Arabic. **Gen-Edu**: Documentary Films, Middle East. **Acq:** Purchase, Rent/Lease. **Dist:** Arab Film Distribution. $150.00.

Beat of the Live Drum 1985 — ★
Guitarist/singer/songwriter Rick Springfield performs such hits as "Jessie's Girl," "Affair of the Heart" and "Love Somebody" in this concert taped in Tucson, Arizona. This tape also features three conceptual music videos from his "Tao" LP. 75m; VHS. **C:** Rick Springfield. **Pr:** Z Street Films; Famous Dog Productions. **A:** Jr. High-Adult. **P:** Entertainment. **U:** Home. **Mov-Ent**: Music--Performance, Music Video. **Acq:** Purchase. **Dist:** Sony Pictures Home Entertainment Inc. $29.95.

Beat Route: Around the World With Jools Holland 2007
A mix of music, travel, and culture with British TV host and musician Holland as he travels to Chicago, Dublin, Seville, Havana, Budapest, and Beirt. 175m; DVD. **C:** Hosted by Jools Holland. **A:** Adult. **P:** Entertainment. **U:** Home. **Gen-Edu**: Music, Travel. **Acq:** Purchase. **Dist:** Acorn Media Group Inc.; Kultur International Films Ltd. $19.99.

Beat Street 1984 (PG) — ★★½
Intended as a quick cash-in on the break dancing trend, this essentially plotless musical features kids trying to break into local show biz with their rapping and dancing skills. Features the music of Afrika Bambaata and the Soul Sonic Force, Grand Master Melle Mel and the Furious Five, and others. 106m; VHS, DVD. **C:** Rae Dawn Chong; Leon Grant; Saundra Santiago; Guy Davis; Jon Chardiet; Duane Jones; Kadeem Hardison; Directed by Stan Lathan; Written by Andrew Davis. **Pr:** Harry Belafonte; David Picker; Orion Pictures. **A:** Family. **P:** Entertainment. **U:** Home. **Mov-Ent**: Musical, Dance, Music--Pop/Rock. **Acq:** Purchase. **Dist:** Lions Gate Television Corp. $79.98.
Songs: Beat Street Breakdown; Baptize the Beat; Stranger in a Strange Land; Beat Street Strut; Us Girls; This Could Be the Night; Breakers Revenge; Tu Carino (Carmen's Theme); Frantic Situation.

Beat the Baja 1986
A history of the world's most famous off-road racing event, with footage of the 1986 race. 48m; VHS. **Pr:** Fox Hills Video. **A:** Jr. High-Adult. **P:** Entertainment. **U:** Home. **Spo-Rec**: Sports--General, Automobiles--Racing. **Acq:** Purchase. **Dist:** ESPN Inc. $24.95.

Beat the Devil 1953 (Unrated) — ★★★
Each person on a slow boat to Africa has a scheme to beat the other passengers to the uranium-rich land that they all hope to claim. An unusual black comedy which didn't fare well when released, but over the years has come to be the epitome of spy-spoofs. 89m; VHS, DVD, CC. **C:** Humphrey Bogart; Gina Lollobrigida; Peter Lorre; Robert Morley; Jennifer Jones; Edward Underdown; Ivor Barnard; Bernard Lee; Marco Tulli; Directed by John Huston; Written by John Huston; Truman Capote; Cinematography by Oswald Morris; Music by Franco Mannino. **Pr:** Columbia Pictures. **A:** Jr. High-Adult. **P:** Entertainment. **U:** Home. **Mov-Ent**: Comedy--Black, Boating. **Acq:** Purchase. **Dist:** Karol Media; Sony Pictures Home Entertainment Inc.; Critics' Choice Video & DVD. $9.95.

Beat the Heat! 1995
Reveals heat stress with a humorous touch. Explains the cause, symptoms, prevention techniques, and emergency first aid. 15m; VHS. **A:** Adult. **P:** Professional. **U:** Institution. **Bus-Ind**: Job Training, Safety Education, Health Education. **Acq:** Purchase, Rent/Lease. **Dist:** National Safety Council, California Chapter, Film Library. $195.00.

Beat the Heat! Safety Strategies for Exercise in the Heat 2002 (Unrated)
Athletic Trainer Mark Cobeley lectures on the dangers awaiting athletes exercising in extreme heat, and how to overcome them. 30m; DVD. **A:** Family. **P:** Education. **U:** Home, Institution. **Spo-Rec**: Basketball, Athletic Instruction/Coaching. **Acq:** Purchase. **Dist:** Championship Productions. $39.99.

Beat the House! 1989
A summary of essential strategies and philosophies of gambling, selected from the TV shows and videos of John Patrick. 40m; VHS. **A:** College-Adult. **P:** Instruction. **U:** Home. **Gen-Edu**: Gambling. **Acq:** Purchase. **Dist:** John Patrick Entertainment, Inc. $14.95.

Beat the Rush 1990
From the World Cup Ski Circuit comes this funny, musical and thrilling blend of action including spills and thrills! 25m; VHS. **A:** Family. **P:** Entertainment. **U:** Home. **Spo-Rec**: Skiing. **Acq:** Purchase. **Dist:** Video Collectibles. $24.95.

Beat the SAT: Math 1986
How to pass the math section of the college-entrance exam. 60m; VHS. **Pr:** Cambridge Career Productions. **A:** Sr. High. **P:** Education. **U:** Institution, Home. **How-Ins**: How-To, Education, Mathematics. **Acq:** Purchase. **Dist:** Cambridge Educational. $19.95.

Beat the SAT: Verbal 1986
How to pass the reading/writing section of the college-entrance exam. 60m; VHS. **Pr:** Cambridge Career Productions. **A:** Sr. High. **P:** Education. **U:** Institution, Home. **How-Ins**: How-To, Language Arts, Education. **Acq:** Purchase. **Dist:** Cambridge Educational. $19.95.

Beatdown 2010 (R) — ★
An MMA fighter flees the city after his brother is murdered for not paying off a debt to a gangster. He becomes involved in illegal cage-fighting while trying to figure a way out of the mess. 90m; DVD, Blu-Ray. **C:** Rudy Youngblood; Michael Bisping; Bobby Lashley; Kyle Woods; Mike Swick; Susie Abromeit; Directed by Mike Gunther; Written by Mike Gunther; Bobby Mort; Sean Patrick O'Reilly; Cinematography by Joe Passarelli; Music by Alan Derian. **A:** Sr. High-Adult. **P:** Entertainment. **U:** Home. **L:** English, Spanish. **Mov-Ent. Acq:** Purchase. **Dist:** Lions Gate Home Entertainment. $14.99 14.98.

Beating and Bleeding 1987
Profiles the heart and describes how the organ works to pump blood throughout the entire body. Part of the Bodytalk Series. 8m; VHS, SVS, 3/4 U. **Pr:** Bodytalk Programmes. **A:** Primary. **P:** Education. **U:** Institution. **Hea-Sci**: Health Education, Heart, Blood. **Acq:** Purchase. **Dist:** Encyclopedia Britannica. $89.00.

Beating Any Defense with Play Action Passing 20?? (Unrated)
Coach Kalen DeBoer demonstrates five play-action passes for football teams wishing to use this offensive style. 43m; DVD. **A:** Family. **P:** Education. **U:** Home, Institution. **Spo-Rec**: Football, Athletic Instruction/Coaching. **Acq:** Purchase. **Dist:** Championship Productions. $39.99.

Beating Breast Cancer 199?
CBS series "48 Hours" covers breast cancer treatment and early warning signs. 48m; VHS. **A:** Sr. High-Adult. **P:** Entertainment. **U:** Institution. **Gen-Edu**: Cancer, Medical Education, Women. **Acq:** Purchase. **Dist:** Ambrose Video Publishing, Inc. $99.95.

Beating the Booze Blues 1977
"Beating the Booze Blues" points out the dangers of drinking in a believable manner, through the use of songs, demonstrations, and comedy sketches performed by high school students. 25m; VHS, 3/4 U. **C:** Lawrence-Hilton Jacobs. **Pr:** John Cosgrove. **A:** Sr. High. **P:** Education. **U:** Institution, Home, SURA. **Hea-Sci**: Alcoholism. **Acq:** Purchase, Rent/Lease, Duplication License. **Dist:** Pyramid Media.

Beating the High Cost of Eating: The Shopping Tutor 1992
Information on how to make the most of one's grocery budget. Techniques include learning how to interpret advertisements, how to get all shopping completed in one trip and the differences between house brands and name brands. Suitable for home economics classes. 95m; VHS. **A:** Sr. High. **P:** Education. **U:** Institution. **Gen-Edu**: Home Economics. **Acq:** Purchase. **Dist:** Cambridge Educational. $29.95.

Beating the 3-Man Front 2009 (Unrated)
Coach Kalen DeBoer discusses techniques football teams can use to beat the 3-4 or 3-3 Stack defenses. 96m; DVD. **A:** Family. **P:** Education. **U:** Home, Institution. **Spo-Rec**: Football, Athletic Instruction/Coaching. **Acq:** Purchase. **Dist:** Championship Productions. $39.99.

Beatlemania! The Movie 1981 (Unrated) — ★
Boring look at the Fab Four. Not the real Beatles, but impersonators who do a very inadequate job. Based on the equally disappointing stage show. 86m; VHS. **C:** Mitch Weissman; Ralph Castelli; David Leon; Tom Teeley; Directed by Joseph Manduke. **A:** Jr. High-Adult. **P:** Entertainment. **U:** Home. **Mov-Ent**: Musical--Drama, Music--Performance. **Acq:** Purchase. **Dist:** Image Entertainment Inc.

The Beatles 19??
Musical anthology of the Beatles, centering on how they influenced the culture of world. 60m; VHS. **A:** Family. **P:** Entertainment. **U:** Institution, Home. **Fin-Art**: Music--Pop/Rock, History. **Acq:** Purchase. **Dist:** Educational Video Network. $49.95.

The Beatles: Alone & Together 1989
A video history of the Beatles, and their influences on the musical, sartorial, and political scenes of the past 25 years. Includes footage of each of the Beatles, plus clips from their movies. 35m; VHS. **C:** John Lennon; Paul McCartney; George Harrison; Ringo Starr. **A:** Jr. High-Adult. **P:** Entertainment. **U:** Home. **Mov-Ent**: Documentary Films, Music--Pop/Rock. **Acq:** Purchase. **Dist:** Music Video Distributors.

The Beatles Anthology 1995
Twenty-five year retrospective on the Fab Four. On eight cassettes; available separately or as a set. 600m; VHS. **A:** Jr. High-Adult. **P:** Entertainment. **U:** Home. **Mov-Ent. Acq:** Purchase. **Dist:** Turner Broadcasting System Inc.

Beatles/Comedy Featurettes 1984
Short subjects on the making of several famous comedies and Beatles features. Movies include "The Owl and the Pussycat," "Return of the Pink Panther" and more. Beatles features include "Cold Turkey," "With Respect to Mr. Lester" and "The Beatles: A Mod Odyssey." 60m; VHS. **Pr:** SF Rush Video. **A:** Adult. **P:** Entertainment. **U:** Home. **Mov-Ent**: Music--Pop/Rock. **Acq:** Purchase. **Dist:** Passport International Entertainment L.L.C.

The Beatles: Live at Budokan 1966
The Beatles' final tour, known as the "Black Suits" tour. Filmed in Tokyo, Japan. Contains "Yesterday," "Paperback Writer," "Day Tripper" and other Beatles standards. 44m; VHS. **A:** Family. **P:** Entertainment. **U:** Home. **Mov-Ent**: Music--Performance, Music--Pop/Rock. **Acq:** Purchase. **Dist:** Music Video Distributors.

Beatles Live: Ready, Steady, Go 1985
The Fab Four perform "Twist and Shout" "Roll Over Beethoven" and nine other songs in this compilation of clips from the "Ready Steady Go" series. Japanese import has the complete episode. 20m/B/W; VHS. **C:** John Lennon; Paul McCartney; Ringo Starr; George Harrison. **Pr:** Dave Clark Limited. **A:** Family. **P:** Entertainment. **U:** Home. **Mov-Ent**: Music--Performance, Music--Pop/Rock. **Acq:** Purchase. **Dist:** Music Video Distributors; Karol Media. $9.95.

The Beatles: Liverpool 2007
BBC DJ Spencer Leigh and Beatles historian Ray O'Brien explore more than 60 Beatles sites in Liverpool, including childhood homes, the Cavern Club, and those associated with the 60s scene. ?m; DVD. **A:** Jr. High-Adult. **P:** Entertainment. **U:** Home. **Fin-Art**: Documentary Films, Music--Pop/Rock. **Acq:** Purchase. **Dist:** Rykodisc Corp.

The Beatles: London 2007
Richard Porter, author and founder of the London Beatles Fan Club, plays tour guide to key Beatles sites, including EMI Studio, Abbey Road, and the musicians' London homes. ?m; DVD. **A:** Jr. High-Adult. **P:** Entertainment. **U:** Home. **Fin-Art**: Documentary Films, Music--Pop/Rock. **Acq:** Purchase. **Dist:** Rykodisc Corp.

The Beatles: The First U.S. Visit 1991
Behind the scenes and on the stage with America's most beloved British import: The Beatles. Includes the Sullivan show performances in their entirety, and features newly re-mastered recordings of the Beatles' hits of the early '60s. Songs include "I Wanna Hold Your Hand," "She Loves You," "All My Loving," "Please, Please Me," "Twist and Shout," and more. 85m/B/W; VHS, DVD. **C:** Paul McCartney; Ringo Starr; John Lennon; George Harrison; Ed Sullivan; Directed by Albert Maysles; David Maysles. **Pr:** Apple Films. **A:** Jr. High-Adult. **P:** Entertainment. **U:** Home. **Mov-Ent**: Music--Pop/Rock, Biography, History--Modern. **Acq:** Purchase. **Dist:** MPI Media Group; Baker and Taylor. $24.98.

The Beatles: The Making of a Hard Day's Night 19??
Phil Collins hosts this look at the making of the Beatles "A Hard Day's Night." Includes commentary from the Beatles, producer Walter Shenson, director Richard Lester, the writers, and the cast members. Contains never before seen backstage footage, Abbey Road studio footage, and footage of the original U.S. and European trailers. Special appearances by Roger Ebert, Peter Noone, Roger McGuinn, and Micky Dolenz. Also includes the never-before seen performance by the Beatles of "You Can't Do That." 65m; VHS, DVD. **C:** Roger Ebert; Peter Noone; Roger McGuinn; Mickey Dolenz; Richard Lester; Hosted by Phil Collins. **Pr:** MPI Media Group. **A:** Family. **P:** Entertainment. **U:** Home. **Mov-Ent**: Music--Pop/Rock, Music--Performance, Music Video. **Acq:** Purchase. **Dist:** MPI Media Group. $29.98.

The Beatles: The Mystery Trip 1992
Follows the Beatles on home movie footage over 12 months from October 1966 to September 1967. Includes clips of cast and crew filming "Magical Mystery Tour." ?m; VHS. **A:** Jr. High-Adult. **P:** Entertainment. **U:** Home. **Mov-Ent**: Music Video. **Acq:** Purchase. **Dist:** Music Video Distributors. $34.95.

The Beatles: The Ultimate DVD Collection 2000
Comprised of two features, "Help!" and "Magical Mystery Tour," as well as two documentaries, the Maysles brothers' "The First U.S. Visit" and "You Can't Do That: The Making of 'A Hard Day's Night.'" ?m; DVD. **A:** Jr. High-Adult. **P:** Entertainment. **U:** Home. **Mov-Ent**: Documentary Films, Music--Pop/Rock. **Acq:** Purchase. **Dist:** MPI Media Group. $79.99.

The Beatnicks 2000 (Unrated) — ★
Weird, frustrating drama. Would-be L.A. beat poet Nick Beat (Reedus) and his bandmate Nick Nero (Boone Jr.) find a mysterious electronic box washed up on the beach that sparks their music. While trying to get gigs, Beat falls for Nica (Bouchez), the wife of mobster/club owner Mack (Roberts), and Nero just kinda hangs out in a daze. 96m; DVD. **C:** Norman Reedus; Patrick Bauchau; Mark Boone, Jr.; Elodie Bouchez; Eric Roberts; Lisa Marie; Jon(athan) Gries; Directed by Nicholson Williams; Written by Nicholson Williams; Cinematography by Joseph Montgomery; Music by Zander Schloss. **A:** Sr. High-Adult. **P:** Entertainment. **U:** Home. **Mov-Ent**: Music. **Acq:** Purchase. **Dist:** Passion River.

The Beatniks 1960 (Unrated) — ★
Story about the dark secrets of the beat generation in which a man is promised fame and fortune by an agent, but his dreams are dashed when his friend commits murder. A big waste of time. 78m/B/W; VHS, DVD. **C:** Tony Travis; Peter Breck; Karen Kadler; Joyce Terry; Sam Edwards; Bob Wells; Directed by Paul Frees; Written by Paul Frees; Cinematography by Murray Deatley; Music by Stanley Wilson. **Pr:** Ron Miller; Barjul. **A:** Jr. High-Adult. **P:** Entertainment. **U:** Home. **Mov-Ent. Acq:** Purchase. **Dist:** Sinister Cinema; Tapeworm Video Distributors Inc. $16.95.

Beatrice 1988 (R) — ★★★½
In France during the Middle Ages, a barbaric soldier of the Hundred Years' War returns to his estate that his daughter has maintained, only to brutalize and abuse her. In French with English subtitles. 132m; VHS. **C:** Julie Delpy; Barnard Pierre Donnadieu; Nils (Niels) Tavernier; Directed by Bertrand Tavernier; Written by Colo Tavernier O'Hagan; Cinematography by Bruno de Keyzer; Music by Lili Boulanger. **Pr:** Adolphe Viezzi; Samuel Goldwyn Company. **A:** Sr. High-Adult. **P:** Entertainment. **U:** Home. **L:** French. **Mov-Ent**: Exploitation. **Awds:** Cesar '88: Costume Des. **Acq:** Purchase. **Dist:** Amazon.com Inc.

Beatrice Cenci 1969 (Unrated) — ★½
Italian historical horror, based on a true story, set in the 16th-century. Teenaged Beatrice is locked in the Cenci castle dungeon by her crazy nobleman father Francesco who also abuses her. Beatrice, her stepmother Lucrezia, obsessed servant Olimpo, and local bandit Catalano come up with a plan to kill him. However, the Vatican gets involved because they want the Cenci fortune. Italian with subtitles. 99m; DVD. **C:** Adrienne Larussa; Tomas Milian; Georges Wilson; Mavie; Pedro Sanchez; Raymond Pellegrin; Directed by Lucio Fulci; Written by Lucio Fulci; Roberto Gianviti; Cinematography by Erico Menczer; Music by Angelo Francesco Lavagnino. **A:** College-Adult. **P:** Entertainment. **U:** Home. **L:** Italian. **Mov-Ent**: Drama, Italy. **Acq:** Purchase. **Dist:** Sinister Cinema.

Beatrix Potter: A Private World 1991
Uncovers the private life of Beatrix Potter through interviews with people who knew her and dramatizations. 42m; VHS. **A:** Sr. High-Adult. **P:** Education. **U:** Institution, Home. **Gen-Edu**: Biography, Literature--Children. **Acq:** Purchase, Rent/Lease. **Dist:** Films for the Humanities & Sciences. $149.00.

Beatrix Potter: Artist, Storyteller and Countrywoman 1993 (Unrated)
A documentary on the life of English author/artist Potter and her beloved for generations books, including "The Tale of Peter Rabbit." Includes photographs of her childhood, her paintings, and the countryside which so influenced her. Based on the book by Judy Taylor. 55m; VHS. **C:** Narrated by Lynn Redgrave. **A:** College-Adult. **P:** Entertainment. **U:** Home. **Gen-Edu**: Docu-

mentary Films, Literature--Children, Biography. **Acq:** Purchase. **Dist:** Weston Woods Studios; Baker and Taylor. $39.00.

The Beatrix Potter Collection: The World of Peter Rabbit 1997
Collection of nine animated tales from the divine story teller featuring Peter Rabbit, Tom Kitten, Jemima Puddle-Duck, Mrs. Tiggy-Winkle, and Pigling Bland. 225m; DVD, Wide, CC. **A:** Family. **P:** Entertainment. **U:** Home. **Chl-Juv:** Fairy Tales, Literature--Children. **Acq:** Purchase. **Dist:** BBC Worldwide Publishing Ltd.

The Beats: An Existential Comedy 1980
Documentary explores the beat poetry movements of the late 1950s. Features poets Stuart Perkoff, Jack Hirschman, Aya, Lawrence Ferlinghetti, and Allen Ginsberg. 60m/B/W; VHS. **A:** College. **P:** Education. **U:** Institution. **Gen-Edu:** Documentary Films, Literature--American. **Acq:** Purchase. **Dist:** The Cinema Guild. $79.95.

Beats Go On: Percussion from Pleistocene to Paradiddle 1972
A history of percussion instruments, from prehistoric times to the present. 13m; VHS, 3/4 U. **Pr:** Bosustow Entertainment. **A:** Primary. **P:** Education. **U:** Institution, SURA. **Fin-Art:** Music--Performance. **Acq:** Purchase. **Dist:** Center for Humanities, Inc./Guidance Associates.

Beats, Rhymes and Life: The Travels of a Tribe Called Quest 2011 (R) — ★★★
Actor and A Tribe Called Quest mega-fan Rapaport's feature directorial debut joins the 2008 reunion tour of the troubled hip-hop legends who try to recapture the magic of the 1980s and '90s. Rapaport doesn't shy away from the drama that led up to their 1998 breakup primarily due to squabbling between leads Q-Tip and Phife Dawg. Credible and engaging for non-fans as well, includes interviews with the group and industry folks. 95m; Blu-Ray, On Demand, Wide. **C:** Q-Tip; Ali Shaheed Muhammad; Adam "MCA" Yauch; Phife Dawg; Jarobi White; Mike D; Directed by Michael Rapaport; Cinematography by Robert Benavides. **Pr:** Debra Koffler; Eric Matthies; Frank Mele; Robert Benavides; A Tribe Called Quest; Rival Pictures; Om Films; Sony Pictures Classics. **A:** Sr. High-Adult. **P:** Entertainment. **U:** Home. **Mov-Ent:** Documentary Films, Music, Biography: Music. **Acq:** Purchase. **Dist:** Sony Pictures Home Entertainment Inc.; Amazon.com Inc.

Beau Brummel 1924 (Unrated) — ★★¹/₂
The famous silent adaptation of the Clyde Fitch play about an ambitious English dandy's rise and fall. 80m/B/W; Silent; VHS, DVD. **C:** John Barrymore; Mary Astor; Willard Louis; Irene Rich; Carmel Myers; Alec B. Francis; William Humphreys; Directed by Harry Beaumont. **A:** Family. **P:** Entertainment. **U:** Home. **Mov-Ent:** Silent Films. **Acq:** Purchase. **Dist:** Televista; Grapevine Video; Glenn Video Vistas Ltd. $19.95.

Beau Brummell 1954 — ★★★
Lavish production casts Granger in the role of the rags-to-riches dandy and chief adviser to the Prince of Wales. Born into a life of poverty, George Bryan Brummel uses wit and intelligence to meet the vain Prince and ingratiate himself to the future king (George IV). He also manages to catch the eye of Taylor, who falls in love with him. Outstanding period piece cinematography, sets, and costumes. Shot on location in England's beautiful countryside, many of the interior shots are from a 15th-century mansion, Ockwell Manor, located near Windsor Castle. Remake of the 1924 silent film starring John Barrymore. Based on the play by Clyde Fitch. 113m; VHS, Streaming. **C:** Stewart Granger; Elizabeth Taylor; Peter Ustinov; Robert Morley; James Donald; James Hayter; Rosemary Harris; Paul Rogers; Noel Willman; Peter Dyneley; Charles Carson; Directed by Curtis Bernhardt; Written by Karl Tunberg; Cinematography by Oswald Morris. **Pr:** Sam Zimbalist; MGM Home Entertainment. **A:** Jr. High-Adult. **P:** Entertainment. **U:** Home. **Mov-Ent:** Drama, Great Britain. **Acq:** Purchase. **Dist:** Amazon.com Inc.; MGM Home Entertainment. $19.98.

Beau Brummell: This Charming Man 2006 (Unrated) — ★★¹/₂
Brummell (Purefoy) is a Regency dandy who changes the powders, perfumes, and foppery of male dress to one of elegance and expensive simplicity. He does a makeover on the Prince of Wales (Bonneville) and uses his royal connection to further his extravagant lifestyle. Then Beau meets the much more fascinating Lord Byron (Rhys), falls out of royal favor, and winds up in greatly-reduced circumstances. Based on Ian Kelly's biography. 79m; DVD. **C:** James Purefoy; Hugh Bonneville; Matthew Rhys; Anthony Calf; Nicholas (Nick) Rowe; Philip Davis; Zoe Telford; Directed by Philippa Lowthorpe; Written by Simon Bent; Cinematography by Graham Smith; Music by Peter Salem. **A:** Jr. High-Adult. **P:** Entertainment. **U:** Home. **Mov-Ent:** Biography, Clothing & Dress, Great Britain. **Acq:** Purchase. **Dist:** Acorn Media Group Inc.

Beau Geste 1939 — ★★★¹/₂
The classic Hollywood adventure film based on the Percival Christopher Wren novel. To protect aging Lady Patricia (Thatcher), who raised the orphaned brothers, Beau Geste (Cooper) takes the blame for a jewel theft and decides to enlist in the Foreign Legion. He's followed by his brothers John (Milland) and Digby (Preston), and all face desert wars and despicable officers, including the psychotic Sgt. Markoff (Donlevy). A rousing, much-copied epic. 114m/B/W; VHS, DVD. **C:** Gary Cooper; Ray Milland; Robert Preston; Brian Donlevy; Donald O'Connor; J. Carrol Naish; Susan Hayward; James Stephenson; Albert Dekker; Broderick Crawford; Charles T. Barton; Heather Thatcher; James Burke; G.P. (Tim) Huntley, Jr.; Harold Huber; Harvey Stephens; Stanley Andrews; Harry Woods; Arthur Aylesworth; Henry (Kleinbach) Brandon; Nestor

Paiva; George Chandler; George Regas; Directed by William A. Wellman; Written by Robert Carson; Cinematography by Theodor Sparkuhl; Louis Clyde Stouman; Archie Stout; Music by Alfred Newman. **Pr:** William A. Wellman; William A. Wellman; Paramount Pictures. **A:** Family. **P:** Entertainment. **U:** Home. **Mov-Ent:** Action-Adventure, War--General, Classic Films. **Acq:** Purchase. **Dist:** Movies Unlimited; Alpha Video. $29.95.

Beau Ideal 1931 (Unrated) — ★¹/₂
A young American man joins the French Foreign Legion in hopes of finding his captured childhood friend and rescuing him. The third film in a trilogy (along with "Beau Geste" and "Beau Sabreur"), it was such a massive financial failure at the box office that a planned remake of "Beau Geste" in 1939 almost didn't happen because it was considered too risky. It's one of the first movies with sound, which is also a nice way of saying the acting would be considered stiff and awkward even by standards in the 1950s. 82m/B/W; DVD. **C:** Ralph Forbes; Loretta Young; Irene Rich; Lester Vail; Frank McCormick; Otto Matieson; Don Alvarado; Bernard Siegel; Myrtle Stedman; Leni Stengel; Directed by Herbert Brenon; Written by Percival Christopher Wren; Paul Schofield; Elizabeth Meehan; Cinematography by J. Roy Hunt; Music by Max Steiner. **A:** Sr. High-Adult. **P:** Entertainment. **U:** Home. **Mov-Ent.** **Acq:** Purchase. **Dist:** Alpha Video.

Beau Pere 1981 — ★★★
Bittersweet satiric romp from Blier about the war zone of modern romance, wherein 14-year-old Besse pursues her 30-year-old irresponsible, widowed stepfather (Dewaere). Sharp-edged and daring. In French with subtitles. 125m; VHS, DVD. **C:** Patrick Dewaere; Nathalie Baye; Ariel Besse; Maurice Ronet; Genevieve Mnich; Maurice Risch; Macha Meril; Rose Thiery; Directed by Bertrand Blier; Written by Bertrand Blier; Cinematography by Sacha Vierny; Music by Philippe Sarde. **Pr:** Alain Sarde; New Line Cinema. **A:** Sr. High-Adult. **P:** Entertainment. **U:** Home. **L:** French. **Mov-Ent:** Sex & Sexuality, Adolescence. **Acq:** Purchase. **Dist:** Wellspring Media. $59.95.

Beau Revel 1921 (Unrated) — ★★★¹/₂
Critically acclaimed romantic drama of the silent era. A passionate dancing girl played by Vidor, one of the '20s' more prolific romantic leads and erstwhile wife of director King Vidor, is the object of romantic interest of a father and son, which leaves the threesome lovelorn, suicidal, and emotionally scarred. You might recognize Stone from his later role as Judge Hardy in the MGM "Hardy Family" series. 70m/B/W; Silent; VHS. **C:** Lewis Stone; Florence Vidor; Lloyd Hughes; Katherine Kirkham; William Conklin; Directed by John Griffith Wray. **Pr:** Thomas H. Ince; Paramount Pictures. **A:** Sr. High-Adult. **P:** Entertainment. **U:** Home. **Mov-Ent:** Drama, Silent Films. **Acq:** Purchase. **Dist:** Grapevine Video; Facets Multimedia Inc. $24.95.

Beau Travail 1998 (Unrated) — ★★¹/₂
Very loose adaptation of Melville's "Billy Budd" is set in the French Foreign Legion at an outpost near Djibouti in Africa. Second-in-command Galoup (Lavant) tries to break popular new soldier Sentain (Colin) before he can become the Commandant's favorite. Visual style and attention to the male form take precedence over the story itself, which is mostly provided in Galoup's flashback narration. French with subtitles. 89m; VHS, DVD, Wide. **C:** Denis Lavant; Michel Subor; Gregoire Colin; Directed by Claire Denis; Written by Claire Denis; Jean-Pol Fargeau; Cinematography by Agnes Godard. **A:** College-Adult. **P:** Entertainment. **U:** Home. **L:** French. **Mov-Ent.** **Acq:** Purchase. **Dist:** New Yorker Video.

Beaufort 2007 (Unrated) — ★★★¹/₂
A fascinating, intense look at the strife in the Middle East through the eyes of soldiers who have lived their entire lives under the shadow of conflict. As the 18-year Israeli occupation of the medieval Lebanese castle Beaufort comes to an end, the soldiers pray to survive random Hezbollah bombing attacks while waiting out the days until withdrawal. As the bombings increase, commander Liberti (Cohen) and his troops must hold on to hope while trying to manage the tedium of holding a castle for largely symbolic purposes. Film avoids political commentary and instead explores the minds of soldiers on the ground, to excellent effect. 125m; DVD. **C:** Oshri Cohen; Ohad Knoller; Eli Eltonyo; Gal Friedman; Nevo Kimchi; Daniel Brook; Directed by Joseph Cedar; Written by Joseph Cedar; Cinematography by Ofer Inov; Music by Ishai Adar. **Pr:** David Mandil; David Silber; United King Films; Metro Communications; Movie Plus; Kino International Corporation. **A:** Sr. High-Adult. **P:** Entertainment. **U:** Home. **L:** Hebrew. **Mov-Ent:** Middle East. **Acq:** Purchase. **Dist:** Kino on Video.

Beaumarchais the Scoundrel 1996 (Unrated) — ★★¹/₂
Adapted from an unpublished play by Sacha Guitry. Beautifully filmed romp of the social-climbing and political-spying gadfly Pierre Augustin Caron de Beaumarchais. Molinaro has simplified the fantastic life of the 18th-century dramatist, courtier, and watchmaker to Louis XV (and author of the comic masterpieces "The Barber of Seville" and "The Marriage of Figaro") but the result is still dizzying. French with subtitles. 100m; VHS, DVD. **C:** Fabrice Luchini; Jacques Weber; Michel Piccoli; Claire Nebout; Jean-Francois Balmer; Florence Thomassin; Michel Serrault; Dominique Besnehard; Jean-Claude Brialy; Murray Head; Jeff Nuttal; Jean Yanne; Manuel Blanc; Sandrine Kiberlain; Axelle Laffont; Directed by Edouard Molinaro; Written by Edouard Molinaro; Jean-Claude Brisville; Cinematography by Michael Epp; Music by Jean-Claude Petit. **A:** College-Adult. **P:** Entertainment. **U:** Home. **L:** French. **Mov-Ent:** Biography, Theater. **Acq:** Purchase. **Dist:** Amazon.com Inc.; New Yorker Video.

Beaune, Roger van der Weyden 1987
A look at van der Weyden's mural in the chapel of the Musee de l'Hotel Dieu at Beaune, which was originally built as a hospital for the poor. 14m; VHS, 8 mm, Special order formats. **C:** Directed by Jacques Berthier. **A:** Sr. High-Adult. **P:** Education. **U:** Institution, Home. **Fin-Art:** Documentary Films, Art & Artists. **Acq:** Purchase. **Dist:** The Roland Collection. $79.00.

The Beautician and the Beast 1997 (PG) — ★★
Evita meets Lucille Ball when TV's "Nanny" enters Eastern Europe whining to conquer fictional "Slovetzia" royalty. Camp comedy casts Drescher as Joy, a beautician who becomes a local hero after a fire in her beauty class and is subsequently hired by a visiting emissary to tutor the children of despotic dictator Pochenko (Dalton). Overridingly well-known caricatures, loosely based on the fairy tale "Beauty and the Beast," as well as a host of old-time, culture clash movies ("The King and I," "Sound of Music"), where the humble nanny attempts to bring joy (get it?) into the life of a man who carries the weight of the world on his shoulders. Lensed in Prague inside a Gothic, 17th-century castle. Pleasant enough, if not original, time-killer. 105m; DVD, CC. **C:** Fran Drescher; Timothy Dalton; Ian McNeice; Patrick Malahide; Lisa Jakub; Michael Lerner; Phyllis Newman; Directed by Ken Kwapis; Written by Todd Graff; Cinematography by Peter Lyons Collister; Music by Cliff Eidelman. **Pr:** Howard W. Koch, Jr.; Todd Graff; Peter Marc Jacobson; Fran Drescher; Todd Graff; Koch Company; High School Sweethearts; Paramount Pictures. **A:** Jr. High-Adult. **P:** Entertainment. **U:** Home. **Mov-Ent:** Comedy--Romantic. **Acq:** Purchase. **Dist:** WarnerArchive.com; Paramount Pictures Corp.

Beauties of the Night 1952 (Unrated) — ★★
Dreamy fantasy finds a shy music teacher (Philipe) escaping from his boring life into romantic adventures with beautiful women. But his dreams slowly turn nightmarish and he's forced to deal with reality—and real love. French with subtitles. 89m/B/W; VHS, DVD, Streaming. **C:** Gerard Philipe; Gina Lollobrigida; Martine Carol; Magali Vendeuil; Paolo Stoppa; Raymond Bussieres; Raymond Cordy; Directed by Rene Clair; Written by Rene Clair; Cinematography by Armand Thirard; Music by Georges Van Parys. **A:** College-Adult. **P:** Entertainment. **U:** Home. **L:** French. **Mov-Ent:** Fantasy, Romance, Sleep. **Acq:** Purchase. **Dist:** Amazon.com Inc.; Water Bearer Films Inc. $29.95.

Beautiful 2000 (PG-13) — ★
Field's directorial debut is a cloying beauty pageant satire that wants you to like it. REALLY wants you to like it. Unfortunately, the jokes and characters are U-G-L-Y and they ain't got no alibi. Minnie Driver is Mona, a bright girl from an abusive home who escapes her grim reality by trying to win beauty pageants. She's shown as a little ugly duckling who uses any means necessary to win her way up the escalating ladder of swimsuitability. Finally, she qualifies for the Holy Grail of beauty pageants, the Miss American Miss competition. Along the way, however, she has become a single mother, which automatically disqualifies her as a contestant. She comes up with a plan where her daughter Vanessa (Pepsi prodigy and demon-child Hallie Kate Eisenberg) is passed off as the child of her patient best friend Ruby (Adams). Mona then screeches complaints about the kid's behavior being a distraction to her goal (which is no way to treat your child, even if she is Satan's hand-puppet) while an ambitious reporter (Stefanson) tries to reveal her secret. Overly padded, and it doesn't even have a nice personality. 112m; VHS, DVD, Wide, CC. **C:** Minnie Driver; Hallie Kate Eisenberg; Joey Lauren Adams; Kathleen Turner; Leslie Stefanson; Bridgette Wilson-Sampras; Kathleen Robertson; Michael McKean; Gary Collins; Brent Briscoe; Directed by Sally Field; Written by Jon Bernstein; Cinematography by Robert Yeoman; Music by John (Gianni) Frizzell. **A:** Jr. High-Adult. **P:** Entertainment. **U:** Home. **Mov-Ent:** Satire & Parody. **Acq:** Purchase. **Dist:** Sony Pictures Home Entertainment Inc.

Beautiful 2009 (R) — ★★
Shy 14-year-old photographer Daniel is persuaded by his beautiful, manipulative, 17-year-old neighbor Suzy to help her investigate the disappearance of three teenage girls in their middle-class Australian suburb of Sunshine Hills. Suzy is convinced that the reclusive widow who lives in Number 46 is involved but getting too close to the crimes could prove dangerous. 103m; DVD, Blu-Ray. **C:** Anthony (Tony) Vorno; Tahyna Tozzi; Peta Wilson; Deborra-Lee Furness; Erick Thomson; Aaron Jeffery; Socratis Otto; Asher Keddie; Directed by Dean O'Flaherty; Written by Dean O'Flaherty; Cinematography by Kent Smith; Music by Paul Mac. **A:** Sr. High-Adult. **P:** Entertainment. **U:** Home. **Mov-Ent:** Crime Drama, Australia, Adolescence. **Acq:** Purchase. **Dist:** Entertainment One US LP.

Beautiful Arrangements 1995
Offers to open the door to the world of dried flower arranging and teaches a way to work with dried and preserved flowers. 50m; VHS. **A:** Family. **P:** Instruction. **U:** Home. **Gen-Edu:** Hobbies, Flowers. **Acq:** Purchase. **Dist:** Paragon Home Video; Education 2000, Inc. $19.95.

Beautiful Beast 1995 — ★★
Mysterious Chinese warrior woman known as Black Orchid arrives in Japan and rubs out mob boss Ishizuka. Fleeing the scene, she hides out with bartender Yoichi Fujinami, who becomes torn between helping his old pal Yaguchi and the mystery girl that he's falling in love with. Foregoes a lot of empty soft-core sex in favor of providing more action. Director Toshiharu Ikeda is no John Woo, but at least Black Orchid's trunk full of high-powered weaponry provides a little fun. 87m; DVD. **C:** Kaori Shimamura; Takanori Kikuchi; Hakuryu; Minako Ogawa; Directed by Toshiharu Ikeda; Written by Tamiya

Takehashi; Hiroshi Takehashi; Cinematography by Seizo Sengen. **A:** College-Adult. **P:** Entertainment. **U:** Home. **Mov-Ent. Acq:** Purchase.

The Beautiful Blonde from Bashful Bend 1949 — ★★½
Charming comedy-western gets better with age. Grable is the pistol packing mama mistaken for the new school teacher. Fun performances by all, especially Herbert. 77m; DVD, Streaming. **C:** Betty Grable; Cesar Romero; Rudy Vallee; Olga San Juan; Hugh Herbert; Porter Hall; Sterling Holloway; El Brendel; Directed by Preston Sturges. **Pr:** Fox. **A:** Family. **P:** Entertainment. **U:** Home. **Mov-Ent. Acq:** Purchase. **Dist:** Fox Home Entertainment.

Beautiful Boy 2010 (R) — ★★½
On the verge of separation, troubled married couple, Bill (Sheen) and Kate (Bello), are horrified by the news that their 18-year-old son Sam (Gallner) killed himself after committing a mass shooting at his college. As the media dogs them, the couple is forced to turn to each other as they attempt to cope with the consequences of the killer they brought into the world. Can they ever find happiness together again? Sheen and Bello are genuine and the concept is engaging, but it's distant and formulaic at times. 100m; DVD, Blu-Ray. **C:** Michael Sheen; Maria Bello; Kyle Gallner; Moon Bloodgood; Austin Nichols; Directed by Shawn Ku; Written by Shawn Ku; Michael Armbruster; Cinematography by Michael Fimognari; Music by Trevor Morris. **Pr:** Lee Clay; Eric Gozlan; First Point Entertainment; Braeburn Entertainment; Goldrush Entertainment; Anchor Bay Entertainment Inc. **A:** Sr. High-Adult. **P:** Entertainment. **U:** Home. **L:** English. **Mov-Ent:** Marriage, Parenting. **Acq:** Purchase. **Dist:** Movies Unlimited; Anchor Bay Entertainment.

The Beautiful Country 2004 (R) — ★★½
In 1990, 20-year-old Binh (Nguyen) lives with poverty and discrimination in Vietnam because of his mixed ancestry: his father was an American solider. Binh's dying mother sends him on an illegal journey to the U.S. in hopes of tracking down his dad in Houston. There's an extended sequence involving a Malaysian refugee camp (with Ling as a friendly prostitute) and a trip on a freighter (captained by Roth) before the young man makes it to the States and finally meets his dad (Nolte). Earnest, gentle, and sometimes harrowing (and rather too long). 137m; DVD. **C:** Nick Nolte; Tim Roth; Bai Ling; Temuera Morrison; Damien Nguyen; Nguyen Thi Huong Dung; Chau Thi Kim Xuan; Anh Thu; Khong Duc Thuan; Chapman To; Vu Tang; Nguyen Than Kien; Bui Ti Hong; John Hussey; Directed by Hans Petter Moland; Written by Larry Gross; Sabina Murray; Cinematography by Stuart Dryburgh; Music by Zbigniew Preisner. **Pr:** Peter Borgli; Terrence Malick; Edward R. Pressman; Tomas Backstrom; Sunflower; Dinamo Story; Sony Pictures Classics; SF Norge. **A:** Sr. High-Adult. **P:** Entertainment. **U:** Home. **L:** English, Chinese. **Mov-Ent:** Immigration, Asia, Action-Adventure. **Acq:** Purchase. **Dist:** Sony Pictures Home Entertainment Inc. $24.96.

Beautiful Creatures 2000 (R) — ★★
Fitful comedy/thriller follows the adventures of Petulia (Weisz) and Dorothy (Lynch), two Glasgow lasses with abusive boyfriends. Dorothy escapes a beating from her druggie boyfriend Tony (Glen), only to wind up aiding Petulia, who is being attacked in the street by drunken Brian (Mannion). Unfortunately, Brian dies and the women decides to make it look like he's been kidnapped and ask a ransom from his equally violent brother Ronnie (Roeves) so they can get out of town. Then a crooked detective (Norton) enters the scene and the women's plans turn a little complicated. 88m; VHS, DVD, Wide. **C:** Rachel Weisz; Susan Lynch; Alex Norton; Iain Glen; Maurice Roeves; Tom Mannion; Directed by Bill Eagles; Written by Simon Donald; Cinematography by James Welland; Music by Murray Gold. **Pr:** Alan J. Wands; Simon Donald; Universal Focus; DNA Films Ltd; Snakeman; United Pictures International; Arts Council of Great Britain. **A:** Sr. High-Adult. **P:** Entertainment. **U:** Home. **Mov-Ent:** Pets. **Acq:** Purchase. **Dist:** Movies Unlimited; Alpha Video.

Beautiful Creatures 2013 (PG-13) — ★★
Yet another Hollywood attempt to cultivate that "Twilight" magic in this adaptation of the young adult novel by Kami Garcia and Margaret Stohl. Wanting to flee his suffocating small Southern town, Ethan (Ehrenreich) meets the lovely Lena (Englert), who carries dark secrets into this supernatural Romeo and Juliet. She is a caster, a creature not unlike a witch, who will be drawn to the light or dark side on her impending 16th birthday. Writer/director LaGravenese elicits charming performances from his leads and talented ensemble but even he seems bored by the generic source material. 124m; DVD, Blu-Ray, Wide. **C:** Alden Ehrenreich; Alice Englert; Jeremy Irons; Emma Thompson; Emmy Rossum; Viola Davis; Thomas Mann; Kyle Gallner; Eileen Atkins; Margo Martindale; Pruitt Taylor Vince; Directed by Richard LaGravenese; Written by Richard LaGravenese; Cinematography by Philippe Rousselot; Music by Mary Ramos. **Pr:** Erwin Stoff; Broderick Johnson; Andrew A. Kosove; Warner Brothers; Alcon Entertainment. **A:** Jr. High-Adult. **P:** Entertainment. **U:** Home. **L:** English. **Mov-Ent:** Adolescence, Romance. **Acq:** Purchase. **Dist:** Not Yet Released.

Beautiful Dreamers 1992 (PG-13) — ★½
Maurice Bucke is a young Canadian physician who runs the London Insane Asylum. After a chance meeting with poet Walt Whitman, both men discover their mutual outrage for current treatment of the mentally ill. Bucke persuades Whitman to visit his asylum in order to try Whitman's theory of human compassion on the asylum's inmates. However, Bucke runs into opposition from the local townspeople, scandalized by Whitman's radical reputation. Fairly humdrum with a larger-than-life performance by Torn as Whitman. Based on Whitman's visit to Canada in 1880. 108m; VHS, Wide, CC. **C:** Rip Torn; Colm Feore; Wendel Meldrum; Sheila McCarthy; Colin Fox; Directed by John Kent Harrison; Written by John Kent Harrison. **A:** Jr. High-Adult. **P:** Entertainment. **U:** Home. **Mov-Ent:** Canada. **Acq:** Purchase. **Dist:** Facets Multimedia Inc. $9.95.

Beautiful Girls 1996 (R) — ★★★
Slow but easy-going film highlights the differences between men, women, and relationships. A 10-year high school reunion brings together buddies Tommy (Dillon), Kev (Perlich), Paul (Rapaport), Mo (Emmerich), and Willie (Hutton). They ice-fish, drink, and talk about women (about whom they haven't a clue). All are smitten by Andera (Thurman), the gorgeous visiting cousin of another friend, and Willie becomes intrigued by Marty (Portman), his precociously tantalizing 13-year-old neighbor. The guys' whining gets annoying and the women are strictly secondary characters, but O'Donnell's tirade about fake femininity is just one of many amusing examples of smart dialogue. The Afghan Whigs are featured as the bar band. 110m; VHS, DVD, CC. **C:** Matt Dillon; Timothy Hutton; Michael Rapaport; Max Perlich; Noah Emmerich; Lauren Holly; Uma Thurman; Natalie Portman; Mira Sorvino; Martha Plimpton; Rosie O'Donnell; Annabeth Gish; Pruitt Taylor Vince; Sam Robards; David Arquette; Anne Bobby; Richard Bright; Directed by Ted (Edward) Demme; Written by Scott Rosenberg; Cinematography by Adam Kimmel; Music by David A. Stewart. **Pr:** Cary Woods; Bob Weinstein; Harvey Weinstein; Cathy Konrad; Woods Entertainment; Miramax. **A:** Sr. High-Adult. **P:** Entertainment. **U:** Home. **Mov-Ent:** Comedy-Drama. **Acq:** Purchase. **Dist:** Buena Vista Home Entertainment.

Beautiful Hunter 1994 — ★★
Shion has been raised since birth to be the perfect assassin and executioner for the Magnificat crime family, a devoutly Catholic gang that do their criminal business in the vestments of priests and nuns. Blind Father Kano fully controls the life of his adopted daughter, until photographer Ito gets photos of her. The lethal yet naive heroine finds herself attracted to Ito, but Father Kano Sister Mitsuko and a squad of killers after them. Kuno looks—well, beautiful, in and out of a series of foxy outfits, but doesn't display any kind of martial arts to convince us of her master assassin status. 91m; DVD. **C:** Makiko Kuno; Koji Shimizu; Directed by Masaura Konuma. **A:** College-Adult. **P:** Entertainment. **U:** Home. **Mov-Ent. Acq:** Purchase.

Beautiful Joe 2000 (R) — ★★
Joe (Connolly) decides to hit the road for adventure and discovers it in Louisville, Kentucky when he meets Hush (Stone), an ex-stripper turned con artist. Then Joe gets in trouble when he tries to help Hush with her debt to crime boss George the Geek (Holm) and the twosome take off to Vegas with Geek's henchman (Bellows) on their trail. 98m; VHS, DVD, Wide, CC. **C:** Billy Connolly; Sharon Stone; Gil Bellows; Ian Holm; Dann Florek; Barbara Tyson; Directed by Stephen Metcalfe; Written by Stephen Metcalfe; Cinematography by Thomas Ackerman. **A:** Sr. High-Adult. **P:** Entertainment. **U:** Home. **Mov-Ent:** Comedy--Romantic. **Acq:** Purchase. **Dist:** Sony Pictures Home Entertainment Inc.

Beautiful Kate 2009 (R) — ★★★
Writer/director feature debut of actress Ward is a haunting family drama. Forty-year-old author Ned reluctantly returns to the isolated farm where he grew up to see his belligerent, terminally ill father Bruce. They've been estranged for 20 years and their rancor goes back to the death of Ned's twin sister Kate and the subsequent suicide of Ned's elder brother Cliff. However, neither has ever wanted to face why the tragedies occurred. Adapted from Newton Thornburg's novel. 90m; DVD. **C:** Ben Mendelsohn; Bryan Brown; Rachel Griffiths; Sophie Lowe; Scott O'Donnell; Josh McFarlane; Maeve Dermody; Directed by Rachel Ward; Written by Rachel Ward; Cinematography by Andrew Commis; Music by Tex Perkins; Murray Paterson. **A:** Sr. High-Adult. **P:** Entertainment. **U:** Home. **Mov-Ent:** Agriculture, Suicide, Australia. **Acq:** Purchase. **Dist:** Entertainment One US LP.

A Beautiful Life 2008 (Unrated) — ★
Cliched, predictable drama with a very annoying lead character. Abused teenaged runaway Maggie comes to L.A. and is befriended by illegal immigrant David, who works as a janitor in a strip club. They also get romantically involved, though whiny Maggie is a thorough nuisance. The two are befriended by stripper Esther and librarian Susan who try to help after David loses his job and while Maggie searches for her mother. Adaptation of Wendy Hammond's play "Jersey City." 81m; DVD. **C:** Angela Sarafyan; Jesse Garcia; Bai Ling; Debi Mazar; Dana Delaney; Jonathan LaPaglia; Rena Owen; Directed by Alejandro Chomski; Written by Deborah Calla; Wendy Hammond; Cinematography by Nancy Schreiber; Music by Ruy Folguera. **A:** Sr. High-Adult. **P:** Entertainment. **U:** Home. **Mov-Ent:** Runaways, Illegal Immigration. **Acq:** Purchase. **Dist:** Image Entertainment Inc.

A Beautiful Mind 2001 (PG-13) — ★★★½
Loose adaptation of Sylvia Nasar's 1998 bio of Nobel Prize winning mathematician John Forbes Nash Jr. An anti-social genius at Princeton University, Nash wrote his thesis on game theory at 21 and worked for the government in the 1950s before succumbing to paranoid schizophrenia, necessitating his confinement to a mental institution. (The treatment scenes are not for the faint-hearted.) His apparent recovery, after some 30 years, led to sharing a Nobel award in economics in 1994. Director Howard manages to keep the inherent sentimentality and sensationalism generally under control thanks to some powerful performances from Crowe (as Nash), Connelly (as wife Alicia), and Harris (as a sinister government official). The usual controversies swirled about the accuracy of the biopic and what was left out. Ignore the petty carping. 129m; VHS, DVD, Blu-Ray. **C:** Russell Crowe; Jennifer Connelly; Ed Harris; Paul Bettany; Christopher Plummer; Judd Hirsch; Adam Goldberg; Josh(ua) Lucas; Anthony Rapp; Austin Pendleton; Vivien Cardone; Directed by Ron Howard; Written by Akiva Goldsman; Cinematography by Roger Deakins; Music by James Horner. **Pr:** Brian Grazer; Ron Howard; Ron Howard; DreamWorks SKG; Imagine Entertainment; Universal Pictures. **A:** Sr. High-Adult. **P:** Entertainment. **U:** Home. **Mov-Ent:** Biography: Science & Medical, Science, Marriage. **Awds:** Oscars '01: Adapt. Screenplay, Director (Howard), Film, Support. Actress (Connelly); British Acad. '01: Actor (Crowe), Support. Actress (Connelly); Directors Guild '01: Director (Howard); Golden Globes '02: Actor--Drama (Crowe), Film--Drama, Screenplay, Support. Actress (Connelly); Screen Actors Guild '01: Actor (Crowe); Writers Guild '01: Adapt. Screenplay; Broadcast Film Critics '01: Actor (Crowe), Director (Howard), Film, Support. Actress (Connelly). **Acq:** Purchase. **Dist:** Movies Unlimited; Alpha Video; Universal Studios Home Video.

Beautiful Ohio 2006 (Unrated) — ★★
Coming-of-age age story about sibling rivalry, set in the 1970s. Clive Messerman (Call) is a teen math prodigy who's grown distant from his once-idolized older brother William (Davern). William is not only jealous of his parents' hopes for Clive but covets his troubled girlfriend Sandra (Trachtenberg), which leads to an unexpected revelation. Directorial debut of Lowe. 90m; DVD. **C:** Rita Wilson; William Hurt; Michelle Trachtenberg; Julianna Margulies; Thomas (Tom) McCarthy; David Call; Brett Davern; Hale Appleman; Directed by Chad Lowe; Written by Ethan Canin; Cinematography by Stephen Kazmierski; Music by Craig (Shudder to Think) Wedren. **A:** Sr. High-Adult. **P:** Entertainment. **U:** Home. **Mov-Ent:** Mathematics. **Acq:** Purchase. **Dist:** IFC Films.

Beautiful People 1999 (R) — ★★
The war in Bosnia (circa 1993) comes to London when former neighbors-turned-enemies, one a Serbian and the other a Croatian, accidentally meet on a bus and try to kill each other. This chaos leads to a variety of intersecting situations: Portia (Coleman), a doctor and daughter of a snobby Tory MP, falls for a refugee; another doctor (Farrell) counsels a pregnant refugee who wants to abort her baby, who is the product of a rape; a druggy skinhead (Nussbaum) winds up experiencing battle firsthand, and on and on and on. 107m; VHS, DVD, Wide. **C:** Charlotte Coleman; Nicholas Farrell; Danny Nussbaum; Edin Dzandzanovic; Charles Kay; Rosalind Ayres; Heather Tobias; Siobhan Redmond; Gilbert Martin; Linda Bassett; Steve Sweeney; Directed by Jasmin Dizdar; Written by Jasmin Dizdar; Cinematography by Barry Ackroyd; Music by Gary Bell. **A:** College-Adult. **P:** Entertainment. **U:** Home. **Mov-Ent:** Comedy--Black, Pregnancy, Romance. **Acq:** Purchase. **Dist:** Lions Gate Home Entertainment.

Beautiful People: The Complete First Season 2005
Newly divorced Lynn Kerr (Zuniga) agrees to move her two daughters to New York so they can begin again. Lynn wants to revive her fashion designer ambitions, Karen (DeVitto) wants to be a model, and Sophie (Foret) has a scholarship to a prestigious private school where she soon finds out she doesn't fit in with the wealthy, "beautiful people" crowd. But all three Kerrs are determined to make their dreams come true. Shown on the ABC Family channel; 16 episodes. 800m; DVD. **C:** Daphne Zuniga; Ricky Mabe; Sarah Foret; Torrey DeVitto; Jackson Rathbone. **A:** Jr. High-Adult. **P:** Entertainment. **U:** Home. **Mov-Ent:** Television Series. **Acq:** Purchase. **Dist:** Sony Pictures Home Entertainment Inc.

The Beautiful Person 2008 (Unrated) — ★★
After the death of her mother, 16-year-old Junie starts over at a high school in Paris. The pouty beauty is pursued by a number of boys and chooses the reticent Otto to discourage the rest. Junie is really only interested in her foreign language teacher Mr. Nemours whose love life is already very complicated. French with subtitles. 97m; DVD. **C:** Lea Seydoux; Louis Garrel; Gregoire Leprince-Ringuet; Esteban Carvajal-Alegria; Simon Truxillo; Agathe Benitzer; Anais Demoustier; Directed by Christophe Honore; Written by Christophe Honore; Gilles Taurand; Cinematography by Laurent Brunet; Music by Alexandre Beaupain. **A:** Sr. High-Adult. **P:** Entertainment. **U:** Home. **L:** French. **Mov-Ent. Acq:** Purchase. **Dist:** MPI Media Group.

Beautiful Piggies 1995
Follows the story of a compulsive eater and the trials of family members who love and live with her. Sidney Film Festival, 1995; Bronze Apple, National Educational Film & Video Festival, 1994; Honorable Mention, Atlanta Film & Video Festival, 1994. 28m; VHS. **A:** College-Adult. **P:** Education. **U:** Institution. **Gen-Edu:** Documentary Films, Eating Disorders, Sociology. **Acq:** Purchase, Rent/Lease. **Dist:** Filmakers Library Inc. $295.00.

The Beautiful, the Bloody and the Bare 1964 — ★
Sordid screamer in the Herschell Gordon Lewis tradition. Set in New York City in the '60s, a depraved artist kills the nude models who pose for him. ?m; VHS, DVD. **C:** Adela Rogers St. John; Marlene Denes; Debra Page; Jack Lowe; Directed by Sande N. Johnsen; Written by Sande N. Johnsen; Cinematography by Jerry Denby; Music by Steve Karmen. **A:** Sr. High-Adult. **P:** Entertainment. **U:** Home. **Mov-Ent:** Horror, Photography. **Acq:** Purchase. **Dist:** Movies Unlimited. $24.99.

Beautiful! The Total Look 1986
How to properly use make-up and pick out a wardrobe are just a few of the beauty secrets revealed here. 120m; VHS. **C:** Beverly Sassoon; Cathy Lee Crosby; Eva Gabor; Marla Gibbs. **Pr:** Cambridge Career Productions. **A:** Jr. High-Adult. **P:** In-

struction. **U:** Institution, Home. **How-Ins:** Cosmetology, Clothing & Dress. **Acq:** Purchase. **Dist:** Cambridge Educational. $39.95.

Beautiful Thing 1995 (R) — ★★★
Sweet, fairytalish, gay coming-of-age story set in a working-class southeast London housing estate. Shy teenager Jamie (Berry) lives with his barmaid mum, Sandra (Henry), and her lover, Tony (Daniels). Next-door is his best mate, the stoic Ste (Neal), who's regularly abused by his father and brother. But when things get too bad, he sleeps over with Jamie. And one night, nature hesitantly takes its course. Their tart-tongued, Mama Cass fanatic, friend Leah (Empson) starts rumors about the twosome that lead to some uneasy (but ultimately conciliatory) confrontations. Fine performances; Harvey adapted from his play. 89m; VHS, DVD, CC. **C:** Glen Berry; Scott Neal; Linda Henry; Tameka Empson; Ben Daniels; Directed by Hettie Macdonald; Written by Jonathan Harvey; Cinematography by Chris Seager. **Pr:** Tony Garnett; Bill Shapter; Channel 4; World Productions; Sony Pictures Classics. **A:** Sr. High-Adult. **P:** Entertainment. **U:** Home. **Mov-Ent:** Comedy-Drama, Adolescence. **Acq:** Purchase. **Dist:** Sony Pictures Home Entertainment Inc.

Beautiful Video Series: Tranquillity and Serenity 2002
Four-part series presents natural tranquil scenes to help achieve a state of relaxation. 240m; VHS. **A:** Adult. **P:** Professional. **U:** Institution. **Hea-Sci:** Mental Health, Health Education. **Acq:** Purchase. **Dist:** Aquarius Health Care Media. $250.00.
Indiv. Titles: 1. Islands: Relax, Restore, Renew 2. Northlands: Relax, Restore, Renew 3. Southern Springs 4. Wings, Water & Skies.

Beautiful Wave 2011 (PG-13) — ★½
Cliched, coming-of-age surfer flick. Teenager Nicole (Teegarden) is having trouble dealing with her dad's death, and her mom sends her to California to stay with her grandma. Nicole befriends some surfers and aims to learn how to ride the waves herself. She also discovers that her surfer grandpa had a favorite spot in Mexico, leading Nicole and her new buddies to take a road trip in search of it. 96m; DVD, Blu-Ray. **C:** Aimee Teegarden; Patricia Richardson; Lance Henriksen; Alicia Ziegler; Ben Milliken; Helen Slater; Directed by David Mueller; Written by David Mueller; Lynn Salt; Cinematography by Kev Robertson; Music by Edward White. **A:** Jr. High-Adult. **P:** Entertainment. **U:** Home. **L:** English. **Mov-Ent:** Sports--Water, Family. **Acq:** Purchase. **Dist:** Anchor Bay Entertainment Inc.

The Beauty Academy of Kabul 2006
In post-Taliban Afghanistan, a group of female American hairstylists open a beauty school in Kabul and deal with culture clashes and bonding with Afghani women. 74m; DVD. **A:** Sr. High-Adult. **P:** Entertainment. **U:** Home. **Gen-Edu:** Documentary Films. **Acq:** Purchase. **Dist:** New Video Group.

Beauty and the Beach 1998
Documentary of the evolution of women's swimwear and the history of women throughout, from Victorian to modern society. Issues include social and cultural values, body image, and power. 53m; VHS. **A:** Adult. **P:** Education. **U:** Home. **Gen-Edu:** Documentary Films, Women, History--U.S. **Acq:** Purchase, Rent/Lease. **Dist:** Filmakers Library Inc. $295.

Beauty and the Beast 1946 (Unrated) — ★★★★
The classic medieval fairy tale is brought to life on the big screen for the first time. Beauty takes the place of her father after he is sentenced to die by the horrible Beast and falls in love with him. Cocteau uses the story's themes and famous set-pieces to create a cohesive and captivating surreal hymn to romantic love that is still the definitive version of B&B. In French with subtitles. 90m/B/W; VHS, DVD, Blu-Ray. **C:** Jean Marais; Josette Day; Marcel Andre; Mila Parely; Nane Germon; Michel Auclair; Directed by Jean Cocteau; Written by Jean Cocteau; Cinematography by Henri Alekan; Music by Georges Auric. **Pr:** Jean Cocteau; Jean Cocteau. **A:** Sr. High-Adult. **P:** Entertainment. **U:** Home. **L:** French. **Mov-Ent:** Drama, Fairy Tales, Classic Films. **Acq:** Purchase. **Dist:** Home Vision Cinema; Criterion Collection Inc.; New Line Home Video. $19.95.

Beauty and the Beast 1980
Part of the "Classic Tales Retold" series, this version of the story features lively animation. 11m; VHS, 3/4 U. **Pr:** BFA Educational Media. **A:** Primary. **P:** Entertainment. **U:** Institution, SURA. **Chl-Juv:** Family Viewing, Fairy Tales. **Acq:** Purchase. **Dist:** Phoenix Learning Group.

Beauty and the Beast 1981
The classic tale of a gentle beauty who goes to live in the Beast's castle to save her father's life. 12m; VHS, 3/4 U, Special order formats. **Pr:** Bosustow Entertainment. **A:** Preschool-Primary. **P:** Entertainment. **U:** Institution, Home, SURA. **Chl-Juv:** Family Viewing, Fairy Tales. **Acq:** Purchase, Duplication License. **Dist:** Clear Vue Inc.

Beauty and the Beast 1983 — ★★★
From "Faerie Tale Theatre" comes the story of a Beauty who befriends a Beast and learns a lesson about physical appearance and true love. 60m; VHS, DVD, CC. **C:** Susan Sarandon; Anjelica Huston; Klaus Kinski; Stephen Elliott; Directed by Roger Vadim. **Pr:** Gaylord Productions; Platypus Productions. **A:** Family. **P:** Entertainment. **U:** Home. **Mov-Ent:** Romance, Fairy Tales, TV Movies. **Acq:** Purchase. **Dist:** Facets Multimedia Inc. $12.95.

Beauty and the Beast 1991 (G) — ★★★★
Wonderful Disney musical combines superb animation, splendid characters, and lively songs about a beautiful girl, Belle, and the fearsome and disagreeable Beast. Supporting cast includes the castle servants (a delightful bunch of household objects). Notable as the first animated feature to be nominated for the Best Picture Oscar. Destined to become a classic. The deluxe video version features a work-in-progress rough film cut, a compact disc of the soundtrack, a lithograph depicting a scene from the film, and an illustrated book. 84m; VHS, DVD, Blu-Ray, Wide. **C:** Voice(s) by Paige O'Hara; Robby Benson; Rex Everhart; Richard White; Jesse Corti; Angela Lansbury; Jerry Orbach; David Ogden Stiers; Bradley Michael Pierce; Jo Anne Worley; Kimmy Robertson; Directed by Kirk Wise; Gary Trousdale; Written by Linda Woolverton; Music by Alan Menken; Lyrics by Howard Ashman. **Pr:** Walt Disney Studios. **A:** Family. **P:** Entertainment. **U:** Home. **Mov-Ent:** Animation & Cartoons, Family Viewing, Fairy Tales. **Awds:** Oscars '91: Orig. Score, Song ("Beauty and the Beast"); Golden Globes '92: Film--Mus./Comedy; Natl. Film Reg. '02. **Acq:** Purchase. **Dist:** Walt Disney Studios Home Entertainment, On Moratorium. $24.99.
Songs: Beauty and the Beast; Belle; Something There; Be Our Guest.

Beauty and the Beast: A Dark Tale 2010 (R) — ★
The Syfy Channel goes silly, gory, and cheap for this re-imagining of the classic fairytale. Mini-skirted peasant Belle is saved from a wolf by the Beast, who's being accused of numerous bloody crimes plaguing the local village. There's an evil Count, a witch, and a CGI troll involved. 90m; DVD. **C:** Estella Warren; Victor Parascos; Rhett Giles; Vanessa Gray; Tony Bellette; Tony Thurbon; Directed by David Lister; Written by Gavin Scott; Cinematography by Nino Martinetti; Music by Garry MacDonald. **A:** Sr. High-Adult. **P:** Entertainment. **U:** Home. **Mov-Ent:** TV Movies, Fairy Tales, Forests & Trees. **Acq:** Purchase. **Dist:** Entertainment One US LP.

Beauty and the Beast: Above, Below and Beyond 1989
In the episode "To Reign in Hell," Vincent battles with his passion for Catherine and the knowledge that he must return her to the human world while "Orphans" sees the unlikely pair consummate their love. 100m; VHS. **C:** Linda Hamilton; Ron Perlman. **Pr:** Republic Pictures. **A:** Jr. High-Adult. **P:** Entertainment. **U:** Home. **Mov-Ent:** Fantasy, Romance, TV Movies. **Acq:** Purchase. **Dist:** Lions Gate Entertainment Inc. $19.98.

Beauty and the Beast, Episode 1: Once Upon a Time in New York 1987
When socialite attorney Catherine Chandler is brutally attacked in New York, Vincent, a mysterious man/beast, rescues and befriends her, taking her to his fantastical subterranean world. Pilot for the popular television series. Additional episodes are available. 48m; VHS. **C:** Ron Perlman; Linda Hamilton; Roy Dotrice; Ray Wise. **Pr:** Republic Pictures. **A:** Family. **P:** Entertainment. **U:** Home. **Mov-Ent:** Television Series, Fantasy, Romance. **Acq:** Purchase. **Dist:** Lions Gate Entertainment Inc.; Movies Unlimited. $14.98.

Beauty and the Beast, Episode 2: Terrible Savior 1987
A mysterious man/beast is sadistically slashing subway criminals, and Catherine fears the possibility that Vincent is the perpetrator. 48m; VHS. **C:** Ron Perlman; Linda Hamilton; Roy Dotrice; Dorian Harewood. **Pr:** Republic Pictures. **A:** Family. **P:** Entertainment. **U:** Home. **Mov-Ent:** Mystery & Suspense, Fantasy, TV Movies. **Acq:** Purchase. **Dist:** Lions Gate Entertainment Inc. $14.98.

Beauty and the Beast, Episode 3: Siege 1987
Catherine investigates a charming land developer who is romantically attracted to her. But he may not be the legitimate businessman he seems. 48m; VHS. **C:** Ron Perlman; Linda Hamilton; Roy Dotrice; Edward Albert. **Pr:** Republic Pictures. **A:** Family. **P:** Entertainment. **U:** Home. **Mov-Ent:** Drama, Fantasy, TV Movies. **Acq:** Purchase. **Dist:** Lions Gate Entertainment Inc. $14.98.

Beauty and the Beast, Episode 4: No Way Down 1987
Vincent is injured by a wicked gang as he is protecting Catherine above ground. He then struggles to get back to safety below as he is hunted mercilessly by the thugs. 48m; VHS. **C:** Linda Hamilton; Ron Perlman; Roy Dotrice; Chris Nash. **Pr:** Republic Pictures. **A:** Family. **P:** Entertainment. **U:** Home. **Mov-Ent:** Drama, Fantasy, TV Movies. **Acq:** Purchase. **Dist:** Lions Gate Entertainment Inc. $14.98.

Beauty and the Beast, Episode 5: Masques 1987
Catherine and an Irish peace activist are kidnapped by a man seeking revenge for his brother's death at the hands of the IRA. Seems he wants to find and kill the activist's father. Can Vincent find him first? 52m; VHS. **C:** Linda Hamilton; Ron Perlman; Roy Dotrice; Ren Woods; Jay Acovone; John McMartin; Eric Pierpoint; Caitlin (Kathleen Heaney) O'Heaney; Gerry Gibson; Directed by Alan Cooke. **Pr:** Ron Koslow; Witt/Thomas. **A:** Jr. High-Adult. **P:** Entertainment. **U:** Home. **Mov-Ent:** Drama, Ireland. **Acq:** Purchase. **Dist:** Lions Gate Entertainment Inc. $14.98.

Beauty and the Beast, Episode 6: The Beast Within 1987
Catherine investigates the mob death of a pro-union longshoreman, even though Vincent implores her to quit. She is soon kidnapped by the mob boss, a man who grew up in the world Below with Vincent, and his gang. 52m; VHS. **C:** Linda Hamilton; Ron Perlman; Roy Dotrice; Ren Woods; Jay Acovone; Asher Brauner; Michael Alldredge; Michael Pniewski; Stan Kamber; Directed by Paul Lynch. **Pr:** Ron Koslow; Witt/Thomas. **A:** Jr. High-Adult. **P:** Entertainment. **U:** Home. **Mov-Ent:** Drama, Labor & Unions, TV Movies. **Acq:** Purchase. **Dist:** Lions Gate Entertainment Inc. $14.98.

Beauty and the Beast, Episode 7: Nor Iron Bars a Cage 1987
Vincent is captured by two recognition-hungry scientists, and Catherine, with the help of an eyewitness, set out to rescue him. Too bad one of the scientists has gone insane. 52m; VHS. **C:** Linda Hamilton; Ron Perlman; Roy Dotrice; Ren Woods; Jay Acovone; Michael Ensign; Darryl Hickman; Christian Clemenson; Ellen A. Dow; Directed by Thomas J. Wright. **Pr:** Ron Koslow; Witt/Thomas. **A:** Jr. High-Adult. **P:** Entertainment. **U:** Home. **Mov-Ent:** Drama, TV Movies. **Acq:** Purchase. **Dist:** Lions Gate Entertainment Inc. $14.98.

Beauty and the Beast, Episode 8: Song of Orpheus 1987
Father is summoned to the world Above by his ex-wife in a classified ad, but when he goes up he is mistakenly put in jail for the murder of her lawyer. Catherine and Vincent try to unravel Father's mysterious past and try to reunite him with his lost love. 52m; VHS. **C:** Linda Hamilton; Ron Perlman; Roy Dotrice; Ren Woods; Jay Acovone; Diana Douglas; Robert Symonds; Paul Gleason; Directed by Peter Medak. **Pr:** Ron Koslow; Witt/Thomas. **A:** Jr. High-Adult. **P:** Entertainment. **U:** Home. **Mov-Ent:** Drama. **Acq:** Purchase. **Dist:** Lions Gate Entertainment Inc. $14.98.

Beauty and the Beast, Episode 9: Dark Spirit 1987
Catherine investigates the bizarre death of a wealthy businessman, leading to a crisis in the relationship between herself and Vincent. 49m; VHS. **C:** Linda Hamilton; Ron Perlman; Roy Dotrice; Jay Acovone. **A:** Jr. High-Adult. **P:** Entertainment. **U:** Home. **Mov-Ent:** Drama. **Acq:** Purchase. **Dist:** Lions Gate Entertainment Inc. $14.98.

Beauty and the Beast, Episode 10: A Children's Story 1987
Kipper, a boy from the Labyrinth, befriends a runaway orphan and Vincent urges Catherine to investigate the sinister Riddley Foster Home. 49m; VHS. **C:** Linda Hamilton; Ron Perlman; Roy Dotrice; Jay Acovone. **A:** Jr. High-Adult. **P:** Entertainment. **U:** Home. **Mov-Ent:** Drama. **Acq:** Purchase. **Dist:** Lions Gate Entertainment Inc. $14.98.

Beauty and the Beast, Episode 11: An Impossible Silence 1987
The deaf Laura, who lives in the Labyrinth, witnesses the murder of a police detective. Vincent and Father are torn between their desire to protect her and Catherine's need to find the culprit. 49m; VHS. **C:** Linda Hamilton; Ron Perlman; Roy Dotrice; Jay Acovone. **A:** Jr. High-Adult. **P:** Entertainment. **U:** Home. **Mov-Ent:** Drama. **Acq:** Purchase. **Dist:** Lions Gate Entertainment Inc. $14.98.

Beauty and the Beast, Episode 12: Shades of Grey 1987
Vincent and Father become trapped in a collapsing tunnel and it's up to Catherine to rescue them. 49m; VHS. **C:** Linda Hamilton; Ron Perlman; Roy Dotrice; Jay Acovone. **A:** Jr. High-Adult. **P:** Entertainment. **U:** Home. **Mov-Ent:** Drama. **Acq:** Purchase. **Dist:** Lions Gate Entertainment Inc. $14.98.

Beauty and the Beast, Episode 13: China Moon 1987
Lin Wong's true love is Henry but her grandfather arranges a marriage to Peter, the heir to a powerful Chinatown dynasty. Lin goes to Vincent seeking sanctuary but Lin and Henry are overtaken by Peter and his henchman. When Henry kills Peter in self-defense, it's up to Vincent to protect the lovers from the wrath of Peter's family. 49m; VHS. **C:** Ron Perlman; Linda Hamilton; Roy Dotrice. **A:** Jr. High-Adult. **P:** Entertainment. **U:** Home. **Mov-Ent:** Fantasy, Romance. **Acq:** Purchase. **Dist:** Lions Gate Entertainment Inc. $14.98.

Beauty and the Beast, Episode 14: Alchemist 1987
Catherine goes undercover at a club where a new designer drug is being distributed. The drug's chemical makeup contains minerals found in Vincent's subterranean world and the man/beast learns its likely creator is the exiled Paracelsus. 49m; VHS. **C:** Ron Perlman; Linda Hamilton; Roy Dotrice. **A:** Jr. High-Adult. **P:** Entertainment. **U:** Home. **Mov-Ent:** Fantasy, Romance. **Acq:** Purchase. **Dist:** Lions Gate Entertainment Inc. $14.98.

Beauty and the Beast, Episode 15: Temptation 1987
Catherine's friend Joe Maxwell is smitten by attorney Erika Salven. But Catherine is suspicious because Erika's clients include a shady businessman under investigation by the D.A.'s office. Sure enough, Joe is set up in a drug deal and Catherine seeks a dangerous confrontation with Erika. 49m; VHS. **C:** Ron Perlman; Linda Hamilton; Roy Dotrice; Jay Acovone. **A:** Jr. High-Adult. **P:** Entertainment. **U:** Home. **Mov-Ent:** Fantasy, Romance. **Acq:** Purchase. **Dist:** Lions Gate Entertainment Inc. $14.98.

Beauty and the Beast, Episode 16: Promises of Someday 1987
Catherine is suspicious of new lawyer Jeff Radler and spots him entering a tunnel in Central Park and confronting Vincent. It seems Jeff is actually Devin, Vincent's long-lost childhood friend, and that Father knows a secret about Devin that will change everyone's lives. 49m; VHS. **C:** Ron Perlman; Linda Hamilton; Roy Dotrice. **A:** Jr. High-Adult. **P:** Entertainment. **U:** Home. **Mov-Ent:** Fantasy, Romance. **Acq:** Purchase. **Dist:** Lions Gate Entertainment Inc. $14.98.

Beauty and the Beast, Episode 17: Down to a Sunless Sea 1987
Catherine's former lover, Steven, reappears and claims to be dying from cancer. Then he kidnaps her and tries to create a

fantasy life for them while Vincent searches desperately to save Catherine from danger. 48m; VHS, CC. **C:** Ron Perlman; Linda Hamilton; Roy Dotrice. **A:** Jr. High-Adult. **P:** Entertainment. **U:** Home. **Mov-Ent:** Fantasy, Romance. **Acq:** Purchase. **Dist:** Lions Gate Entertainment Inc.

Beauty and the Beast, Episode 18: Fever 1987
Mouse finds a treasure of gold and jewels in a cave and tells the family. Though Father pleads for everyone to leave it alone, Cullen gets greedy and steals some antiques which he sells to a dealer who will risk anything to get his hands on the rest of the loot. 48m; VHS, CC. **C:** Ron Perlman; Roy Dotrice; Linda Hamilton. **A:** Jr. High-Adult. **P:** Entertainment. **U:** Home. **Mov-Ent:** Fantasy, Romance. **Acq:** Purchase. **Dist:** Lions Gate Entertainment Inc.

Beauty and the Beast, Episode 19: Everything Is Everything 1987
Catherine befriends a street-wise orphan who has been banished by his gypsy community for a crime blamed on his late father. Vincent and Catherine then talk to the boy's grandfather, the King of the Gypsies, and try to help the boy prove his father's innocence so that he may rejoin the community. 48m; VHS, CC. **C:** Ron Perlman; Linda Hamilton; Roy Dotrice. **A:** Jr. High-Adult. **P:** Entertainment. **U:** Home. **Mov-Ent:** Fantasy, Romance. **Acq:** Purchase. **Dist:** Lions Gate Entertainment Inc.

Beauty and the Beast, Episode 20: To Reign in Hell 1987
When Catherine is kidnapped, Vincent discovers clues in an ancient code developed by his sworn enemy, who was banished from their community. Now Vincent must risk his own life to save Catherine's. 48m; VHS, CC. **C:** Ron Perlman; Linda Hamilton; Roy Dotrice. **A:** Jr. High-Adult. **P:** Entertainment. **U:** Home. **Mov-Ent:** Fantasy, Romance. **Acq:** Purchase. **Dist:** Lions Gate Entertainment Inc.

Beauty and the Beast, Episode 21: Ozymandias 1987
Business mogul Elliott Burch has fallen in love with Catherine and asks her to marry him—just as soon as his latest project is completed. But Burch Tower is set to be the tallest building in the world and building the foundation will destroy Vincent's world below—unless Catherine can change Elliott's mind. 48m; VHS, CC. **C:** Ron Perlman; Linda Hamilton; Edward Albert; Roy Dotrice. **A:** Jr. High-Adult. **P:** Entertainment. **U:** Home. **Mov-Ent:** Fantasy, Romance. **Acq:** Purchase. **Dist:** Lions Gate Entertainment Inc.

Beauty and the Beast, Episode 22: A Happy Life 1987
Catherine is overwhelmed on the anniversary of her mother's death when she realizes her love for Vincent will never give her what she wants most—a husband and family. So Vincent decides to set her free to live a life without him. 48m; VHS, CC. **C:** Ron Perlman; Linda Hamilton; Roy Dotrice. **A:** Jr. High-Adult. **P:** Entertainment. **U:** Home. **Mov-Ent:** Fantasy, Romance. **Acq:** Purchase. **Dist:** Lions Gate Entertainment Inc.

Beauty and the Beast: The Complete 3rd Season 1989
Catherine begins the season healthy and pregnant but now Vincent can not sense when she's in danger. A fateful case puts her life in jeopardy and Vincent arrives too late to save her. An evil drug lord steals her baby son leaving Vincent and Catherine's former flame, Elliot Burch to track down her killer and rescue the child. 12 episodes. 539m; DVD. **C:** Linda Hamilton; Ron Perlman; Stephen McHattie; Edward Albert. **A:** Adult. **P:** Entertainment. **U:** Home. **Mov-Ent:** Drama, Fairy Tales. **Acq:** Purchase. **Dist:** Paramount Pictures Corp.

Beauty and the Beast: The Complete First Season 1987
Offers the first season of the 1987-1990 drama-romance television series with wealthy assistant DA Catherine (Hamilton), who forms a special bond with Vincent (Perlman), an underground man-beast, after he saves her life. Though they cannot truly be together, Vincent aides Catherine in her cases while she assists Vincent and his underground friends. Catherine struggles as she wonders if Vincent might be guilty of attacking people in the subway; Vincent becomes blind and disoriented while caught between warring gangs and is held captive; they celebrate their one-year anniversary; and Catherine's sorrow over their relationship leads to Vincent's difficult choice. 22 episodes. 1020m; DVD. **C:** Linda Hamilton; Ron Perlman; Richard Paltlow. **A:** Jr. High-Adult. **P:** Entertainment. **U:** Home. **Mov-Ent:** Television Series, Drama, Romance. **Acq:** Purchase. **Dist:** Paramount Pictures Corp. $49.99.

Beauty and the Beast: The Complete Second Season 1988
Offers the second season of the 1987-1990 drama-romance television series with wealthy assistant DA Catherine (Hamilton), who forms a special bond with Vincent (Perlman), an underground man-beast, after he saves her life. Though they cannot truly be together, Vincent aides Catherine in her cases while she assists Vincent and his underground friends. Catherin celebrates Winterfest with the underground people; Catherine convinces a pregnant troubled young woman to live in the tunnels and she winds up falling for Vincent; and Vincent becomes ill and lashes out at Catherine. 22 episodes. 1043m; DVD. **C:** Linda Hamilton; Ron Perlman; Richard Paltlow. **A:** Jr. High-Adult. **P:** Entertainment. **U:** Home. **Mov-Ent:** Television Series, Drama, Romance. **Acq:** Purchase. **Dist:** Paramount Pictures Corp. $49.99.

Beauty and the Beast: The Complete Series 1987 (Unrated)
Television fantasy crime drama series from 1987-1990 built around the romance of mythic, noble man-beast Vincent (Perlman) and New York assistant DA Catherine (Hamilton). The two share intimate moments in his underground lair but whenever Catherine is in danger in the World Above, Vincent is there to rescue her. The final season finds Catherine murdered and her new born baby taken by a murderous drug-lord, with Vincent relentlessly pursuing her killer and his abducted child. 2654m; DVD. **A:** Sr. High-Adult. **P:** Entertainment. **U:** Home. **Mov-Ent:** Drama, Fantasy, Romance. **Acq:** Purchase. **Dist:** Paramount Pictures Corp.

Beauty and the Beast: The Enchanted Christmas 1997
A flashback to Belle's first Christmas with the Beast, when she was still his prisoner. She tries planning a special Christmas celebration but the Beast has forbidden any kind of merriment. But Belle decides to go ahead with her plans and enlists the household's help, including Mrs. Potts, Lumiere, and Cogsworth. But the evil Forte, the castle pipe organ, is determined to ruin Belle's surprise. 71m; VHS, DVD. **C:** Voice(s) by Robby Benson; Angela Lansbury; Tim Curry; Bernadette Peters; Paige O'Hara; Jerry Orbach; David Ogden Stiers; Paul (Pee-wee Herman) Reubens; Haley Joel Osment; Directed by Andy Knight; Written by Flip Kobler; Cindy Marcus; Bill Motz; Bob Roth; Music by Rachel Portman. **A:** Family. **P:** Entertainment. **U:** Home. **Chl-Juv:** Animation & Cartoons, Christmas. **Acq:** Purchase. **Dist:** Buena Vista Home Entertainment.

Beauty & the Beast: The First Season 2012
The CW 2012--? crime/fantasy. Homicide detective Catherine 'Cat' Chandler learns the identity of the man who once saved her life. Only Vincent Keller is hiding a terrible secret: as the subject of government DNA experiments, he turns into a man-beast when angered. He and Cat team up on a variety of cases while his past becomes a challenge to them both. 22 episodes. 923m; DVD. **C:** Kristin Kreuk; Jay Ryan; Austin Basis; Nina Lisandrello; Sendhil Ramamurthy. **A:** Jr. High-Adult. **P:** Entertainment. **U:** Home. **L:** English. **Mov-Ent:** Crime Drama, Fantasy, Romance. **Acq:** Purchase. **Dist:** Paramount Pictures Corp. $49.99.

Beauty and the Beast: Though Lovers Be Lost 1989 (Unrated)
The love affair of Vincent and Catherine takes a tragic turn when she is kidnapped by a crime lord. Feature-length drama from the television series. 90m; VHS, CC. **C:** Linda Hamilton; Ron Perlman; Directed by Richard Franklin; Victor Lobl. **Pr:** Republic. **A:** Jr. High-Adult. **P:** Entertainment. **U:** Home. **Mov-Ent:** Fantasy, Romance, TV Movies. **Acq:** Purchase. **Dist:** Lions Gate Entertainment Inc. $19.98.

Beauty and the Beasts: A Leopard's Story 1996 (Unrated)
The leopard and the warthog share parallel lives on the African Savanna but when the two face-off with each other, the result is predictable—the predator leopard overpowers its prey, the warthog. 56m; VHS. **A:** Family. **P:** Education. **U:** Institution, Home. **Mov-Ent:** Documentary Films, Africa, Animals. **Acq:** Purchase. **Dist:** National Geographic Society. $2.99.

Beauty and the Billfish 19??
Combination information/entertainment program stars Minda and Tracy, who go on vacation together to attempt to beat the world sailfish catch record. Viewers will learn a lot about reeling in billfish while the girls take off all their clothes. For mature audiences only, contains nudity. 45m; VHS. **A:** Adult. **P:** Entertainment. **U:** Home. **Spo-Rec:** Fishing. **Acq:** Purchase. **Dist:** Bennett Marine Video. $29.95.

Beauty and the Boss 1933 (Unrated) — ★★½
Playboy Viennese bank exec Josef von Ullrich (William) is too attracted to his pretty stenographer Olive (Doran) so he fires her and hires plain-but-efficient Susie (Marsh) instead. He thinks she won't be a distraction but when Susie gets romance on her mind, she also gets a makeover (thanks to Olive) that draws Josef's attention after all. Remade as 1934's "The Church Mouse." 66m/B/W; DVD. **C:** Marian Marsh; Warren William; Mary Doran; Charles Butterworth; Frederick Kerr; David Manners; Robert Greig; Directed by Roy Del Ruth; Written by Joseph Jackson; Cinematography by Barney McGill. **A:** Sr. High-Adult. **P:** Entertainment. **U:** Home. **Mov-Ent. Acq:** Purchase. **Dist:** WarnerArchive.com.

Beauty & the Briefcase 2010 (Unrated) — ★★½
ABC Family cable rom com. Journalist Lane Daniels (Duff) gets a chance at a Cosmo cover story after pitching a "finding love in the workplace" story to editor Kate White (Pressly). Lane gets a job as a corporate assistant at a finance company and proceeds to date as many of her male co-workers as possible. She only falls for Liam (Carmack), who doesn't work in her office, and Lane may blow her chance when Kate doesn't go for her changes. 83m; DVD. **C:** Hilary Duff; Chris Carmack; Matt Dallas; Michael McMillen; Jaime Pressly; Jennifer Coolidge; Directed by Gil Junger; Michael Horowitz; Cinematography by Greg Gardiner; Music by Danny Lux. **A:** Jr. High-Adult. **P:** Entertainment. **U:** Home. **Mov-Ent:** Comedy--Romantic, Journalism, TV Movies. **Acq:** Purchase. **Dist:** Image Entertainment Inc.

Beauty and the Devil 1950 (Unrated) — ★★
Ambitious retelling of the Faust legend finds old Faust (Simon) willing to sell his soul to the Devil, courtesy of his agent Mephistopheles (Philipe), in return for youth and beauty to pursue the beautiful woman he loves. Clair has his actors trade roles midway through as Faust makes his bargain. French with subtitles. 97m/B/W; VHS. **C:** Michel Simon; Gerard Philipe; Simone Valere; Raymond Cordy; Gaston Modot; Paolo Stoppa; Nicole Besnard; Directed by Rene Clair; Written by Rene Clair; Armand Salacrou; Cinematography by Michel Kelber; Music by Roman Vlad. **A:** College-Adult. **P:** Entertainment. **U:** Home. **L:** French. **Mov-Ent:** Fantasy, Romance, Folklore & Legends. **Acq:** Purchase. **Dist:** Water Bearer Films Inc. $29.95.

Beauty Basics for the Contemporary Black Woman 1987
The Broadway star tells black women how to make themselves up so they'll look their best. 30m; VHS, CC. **C:** Hosted by Sheryl Lee Ralph. **Pr:** Cambridge Career Productions. **A:** Jr. High-Adult. **P:** Instruction. **U:** Institution, Home. **How-Ins:** Black Culture, Cosmetology. **Acq:** Purchase. **Dist:** Cambridge Educational. $29.95.

Beauty Becomes the Beast 1979
A work of video art by Vivienne Dick. 15m; 3/4 U. **Pr:** Vivienne Dick. **A:** Adult. **P:** Entertainment. **U:** Institution, Home. **Fin-Art:** Video. **Acq:** Rent/Lease. **Dist:** Kitchen Center for Video, Music & Dance.

Beauty Becomes the Beast 1985
Many myths and fairytales are combined in this story of a woman who abandons the rational course of the brain in favor of the intuitive path of nature. 10m; VHS, 3/4 U. **Pr:** Lydia Schouten. **A:** Jr. High-Adult. **P:** Education. **U:** Institution, SURA. **Gen-Edu:** Psychology. **Acq:** Rent/Lease. **Dist:** Video Out Distribution.

Beauty for the Asking 1939 — ★
It sounds like a workable Lucille Ball vehicle—a beautician develops a bestselling skin cream—and even the title sounds like something you'd like to love Lucy in. But somehow the numerous plot implausibilities managed to get by the story's five writers, and the idea of a jilted woman making millions while being financed by her ex's wife just doesn't fly (perhaps it was an idea ahead of its time). Die-hard Lucy fans may find this interesting. 68m/B/W; VHS. **C:** Lucille Ball; Patric Knowles; Donald Woods; Frieda Inescort; Frances Mercer; Directed by Glenn Tryon. **Pr:** B.P. Fineman; RKO. **A:** Jr. High-Adult. **P:** Entertainment. **U:** Home. **Mov-Ent. Acq:** Purchase. **Dist:** Turner Broadcasting System Inc.; Facets Multimedia Inc. $19.98.

Beauty: Hair Care 19??
Offers techniques for styling and keeping all different types of hair textures and colors healthy and manageable. 45m; VHS. **A:** Sr. High-Adult. **P:** Instruction. **U:** Institution. **How-Ins:** How-To, Cosmetology. **Acq:** Purchase. **Dist:** Cambridge Educational. $39.95.

Beauty: How To Make-Up 19??
Demonstrates step-by-step make-up applications to cover flaws and emphasize favorable features. 45m; VHS. **A:** Sr. High-Adult. **P:** Instruction. **U:** Institution. **How-Ins:** How-To, Cosmetology. **Acq:** Purchase. **Dist:** Cambridge Educational. $39.95.

Beauty Knows No Pain 1971
The ordeal of trying out for the nationally known Kilgore College Rangerettes is shown. The value of the Rangerette ideal is demonstrated by the determinedness of the participants, and their hysteria when the results are posted. 25m; VHS, 3/4 U. **Pr:** Elliot Erwitt. **A:** Sr. High-College. **P:** Education. **U:** Institution, CCTV. **Gen-Edu:** Documentary Films, Women. **Acq:** Purchase. **Dist:** Benchmark Media.

Beauty: Nail Care 19??
Explains basic techniques for manicures and pedicures, addressing equipment needs, cosmetics, etc. Demonstrates linen wraps, nail tips, sculptured nails, and more. 45m; VHS. **A:** Sr. High-Adult. **P:** Education. **U:** Institution. **Gen-Edu:** Cosmetology. **Acq:** Purchase. **Dist:** Cambridge Educational. $39.95.

Beauty on the Beach 1961 (Unrated) — ★
A comedy about a mad psychologist, his bizarre experiments with women, and his eventual descent into insanity. In Italian with English subtitles. 90m; VHS. **C:** Valeria Fabrizi; Ennio Girolami; Gloria Milland; Alberto Talegalli; Lorella De Luca; Directed by Romolo Guerrieri; Written by Tito Carpi; Fabio Dipas; Carlo Moscovini; Cinematography by Mario Fioretti; Music by Carlo Savina. **A:** Jr. High-Adult. **P:** Entertainment. **U:** Home. **L:** Italian. **Mov-Ent:** Psychiatry. **Acq:** Purchase. **Dist:** No Longer Available.

Beauty Queen Butcher! 1991 (Unrated) — ★½
A group of mean girls convince a fat girl to enter a beauty pageant to humiliate her. Of course she goes crazy and starts killing everyone in sight. Kind of insulting to all concerned as it implies all "hot" women are inherently evil and cruel, and all "non-hot" women are a cruel joke away from becoming psychopathic death machines. 118m; DVD. **C:** Jim Boggess; Rhona Brody; Kathryn A. Mensik; Tammy Pescatelli; Kimberly Ann Kurtenbach; Laura Schutter; Directed by Jill Rae Zurborg; Written by Jill Rae Zurborg; Shane Partlow; Cinematography by Jeff Carney; Music by Dana P. Rowe. **A:** Sr. High-Adult. **P:** Entertainment. **U:** Home. **L:** English. **Mov-Ent. Acq:** Purchase. **Dist:** Alternative Distribution Alliance. $12.98.

The Beauty Queens 1989
A documentary series examining three women who helped shape the beauty industry. The first tape tells the history of Helena Rubinstein's rise from poverty. The second tape discusses Elizabeth Arden and her introduction of the health-farm concept. The final tape shares the life of marketing genius Estee Lauder. 60m; VHS. **Pr:** RM Arts. **A:** Jr. High-Adult. **P:** Education. **U:** Home. **Gen-Edu:** Biography, Women, Cosmetology. **Acq:** Purchase. **Dist:** Home Vision Cinema. $29.95.
Indiv. Titles: 1. Helena Rubinstein 2. Elizabeth Arden 3. Estee Lauder.

Beauty School 1993 (R) — ★
The promise of an advertising contract pits the owners of rival beauty schools against each other. 95m; VHS. **C:** Sylvia Kristel; Kevin Bernhardt; Kimberly Taylor; Jane Hamilton; Directed by Ernest G. Sauer; Written by Merrill Friedman; Music by Jonathan Hannah. **Pr:** Ernest G. Sauer; Gary P. Conner; Amy Lynn Baxter; Shapiro Glickenhaus Entertainment Corporation; Private Screenings, Inc; Imperial Entertainment. **A:** Sr. High-Adult. **P:** Entertainment. **U:** Home. **Mov-Ent**: Advertising. **Acq:** Purchase. **Dist:** Imperial Entertainment Corp. $89.95.

The Beauty Series 1987
From hair care to putting on make-up, this is a total package that will help you look good. 45m; VHS. **Pr:** Cambridge Career Productions. **A:** Sr. High-Adult. **P:** Instruction. **U:** Institution, Home. **How-Ins**: Cosmetology. **Acq:** Purchase. **Dist:** Cambridge Educational. $39.95.
Indiv. Titles: 1. Hair Care 2. Skin Care 3. Nail Care 4. How to Make-Up.

Beauty Shop 2005 (PG-13) — ★★★
Spinning off from the "Barbershop" series, familiar tale of female empowerment succeeds, thanks to Queen Latifah's classy, charismatic lead performance. Beautician Gina moves to Atlanta, landing a job working for pretentious upscale salon owner Jorge (Bacon). Frustrated with Jorge's lack of respect, Gina opens her own beauty shop in a working-class black neighborhood, gathering a group of good-natured, eccentric stylists like outspoken Ms. Josephine (Woodard) and clueless white girl Lynn (Silverstone). All of the community pride themes from the "Barbershop" movies are touched on here, but "Beauty" distinguishes itself with genuine characters. Bacon and Suvari are exceptions, choosing instead to go ridiculously broad. 105m; DVD, UMD. **C:** Queen Latifah; Alicia Silverstone; Andie MacDowell; Alfre Woodard; Mena Suvari; Della Reese; Golden Brooks; Paige Hurd; LisaRaye; Keisha Knight Pulliam; Bryce Wilson; Kevin Bacon; Djimon Hounsou; Adele Givens; Miss Laura Hayes; Little JJ; Sherri Shepherd; Kimora Lee Simmons; Sheryl Underwood; Directed by Bille Woodruff; Written by Kate Lanier; Norman Vance, Jr.; Cinematography by Theo van de Sande; Music by Christopher Young. **Pr:** David Hoberman; Robert Teitel; George Tillman, Jr.; Shakim Compere; Queen Latifah; State Street Pictures; Mandeville Films; MGM. **A:** Jr. High-Adult. **P:** Entertainment. **U:** Home. **L:** English. **Mov-Ent**: Black Culture, Women. **Acq:** Purchase. **Dist:** MGM Home Entertainment.

Beauty: Skin Care 19??
Identifies several skin types and explains how to keep them healthy and glowing. 45m; VHS. **A:** Jr. High-Sr. High. **P:** Education. **U:** Institution. **Gen-Edu**: Skin. **Acq:** Purchase. **Dist:** Cambridge Educational. $39.95.

Beauvais Cathedral: Architecture of Transcendence ????
Visual tour set to music of the Beauvais Cathedral in northern France. 10m; VHS. **A:** Sr. High-Adult. **P:** Education. **U:** Home, Institution. **Gen-Edu**: Art & Artists, Architecture. **Acq:** Purchase. **Dist:** Crystal Productions. $29.95.

The Beaver 2011 (PG-13) — ★★½
Formerly successful toy executive Walter Black's (Gibson) life is spiraling out of control as severe depression tears apart his marriage and his family. Nothing seems to help—except, of all things, a beaver hand puppet that he uses to communicate as "therapy." The title, premise, and the involvement of the controversial-at-the-time lead actor would all seem to contribute to a cinematic train wreck. Instead, director Foster (who also stars as Black's wife) has created a lovely, unexpected surprise. With a strong script that gives dignity to an emotional and psychological family drama, Gibson is charming, brave, and sincere. 91m; DVD, Blu-Ray, On Demand. **C:** Mel Gibson; Jodie Foster; Anton Yelchin; Jennifer Lawrence; Riley Thomas Stewart; Zachary Booth; Directed by Jodie Foster; Written by Kyle Killen; Cinematography by Hagen Bogdanski; Music by Marcelo Zarvos. **Pr:** Steven Golin; Keith Redmon; Ann Ruark; Participant Media; Summit Entertainment. **A:** Jr. High-Adult. **P:** Entertainment. **U:** Home. **L:** English. **Mov-Ent**: Comedy-Drama, Puppets, Mental Health. **Acq:** Purchase. **Dist:** Summit Entertainment; Amazon.com Inc.; Movies Unlimited.

The Beaver Family—2nd edition 1982
Illustrates the physical characteristics that have helped the beaver adapt to his environment and reveals the unique construction of a beaver dam. 14m; VHS, 3/4 U. **Pr:** Encyclopedia Britannica Educational Corporation. **A:** Primary. **P:** Education. **U:** Institution, SURA. **Hea-Sci**: Documentary Films, Animals. **Acq:** Purchase, Rent/Lease, Trade-in. **Dist:** Encyclopedia Britannica.

Beaver Felton: Superchops 1990
Learn the intricacies of bass playing from one of the greats. ?m; VHS. **A:** Jr. High-Adult. **P:** Instruction. **U:** Home. **How-Ins**: Music--Instruction. **Acq:** Purchase. **Dist:** Music Video Distributors. $44.95.

Beavertail Snowshoes 1990
A look at the construction of beavertail snowshoes by the Eastern Cree Indians of Mistassini Lake, Quebec. 40m; VHS, 3/4 U. **Pr:** Trust for Native American Cultures. **A:** Family. **P:** Education. **U:** Institution, Home, SURA. **Gen-Edu**: Documentary Films, Native Americans. **Acq:** Purchase, Rent/Lease. **Dist:** Trust for Native American Cultures and Crafts. $100.00.

Beavis and Butt-Head Do America 1996 (PG-13) — ★★½
Moronic MTV metalheads go on the road in search of their stolen TV and are somehow mistaken for criminal masterminds. Okay, enough about plot. If you're thinking of renting this one, you don't care about that stuff anyway. Director/writer/voice of B&B Judge is smart enough not to change our "heroes" just because they're on a bigger screen. They're still stupid, obsessed with chicks, (Yeah! Chicks are cool!) and blissfully unaware of what's happening around them. The opening sequence, a parody of 70s cop shows, is hilarious (and cool). For those who like the show, and for people who just don't admit that they do, the boys' movie debut (he said "but") doesn't suck. 82m; VHS, DVD, CC. **C:** Voice(s) by Mike Judge; Robert Stack; Cloris Leachman; Demi Moore; Eric Bogosian; Richard Linklater; Pamela Blair; Tim Guinee; David Letterman; David Spade; Bruce Willis; Toby Huss; Directed by Mike Judge; Written by Mike Judge; Joe Stillman; Music by John (Gianni) Frizzell. **Pr:** Abby Terkuhle; David Gale; Van Toffler; MTV Films; Geffen Film Company; Paramount Pictures. **A:** Jr. High-Adult. **P:** Entertainment. **U:** Home. **Mov-Ent**: Animation & Cartoons, Federal Bureau of Investigation (FBI), Adolescence. **Acq:** Purchase. **Dist:** Paramount Pictures Corp.

Beavis and Butt-head Do Christmas 1997
Features episodes from the 1993-1997 animated MTV television series with Beavis and Butt-head. Includes Christmas episodes "Huh Huh Humbug" and "It's a Miserable Life." 2 episodes. 40m; DVD. **C:** Voice(s) by Mike Judge; Tracy Grandstaff; Adam Welsh; Rottilio Michieli. **A:** Jr. High-Adult. **P:** Entertainment. **U:** Home. **Mov-Ent**: Television Series, Animation & Cartoons, Music Video. **Acq:** Purchase. **Dist:** Sony Music Entertainment Inc. $24.98.

Beavis and Butt-head: The Best-Of Series 2002
Features episodes from the 1993-1997 animated MTV television series with Beavis and Butt-head. Includes only the episodes without music videos in three parts: "Innocence Lost," "Chicks N Stuff," and "Troubled Youth." 43 episodes. 305m; DVD. **C:** Voice(s) by Mike Judge; Tracy Grandstaff; Adam Welsh; Rottilio Michieli. **A:** Jr. High-Adult. **P:** Entertainment. **U:** Home. **Mov-Ent**: Television Series, Animation & Cartoons, Music Video. **Acq:** Purchase. **Dist:** Time-Life Video and Television. $29.99.

Beavis and Butt-Head: The Final Judgment 1994
Seven episodes with the cartoon clowns, including "Manners Suck" and "The Great Cornholio." 43m; VHS. **A:** Jr. High-Adult. **P:** Entertainment. **U:** Home. **Mov-Ent**: Animation & Cartoons. **Acq:** Purchase. **Dist:** Sony Music Entertainment Inc. $14.98.

Beavis and Butt-head: The History of Beavis and Butt-head 2002
Features episodes from the 1993-1997 animated MTV television series with Beavis and Butt-head, idiotic metal-head teens who sit on the couch while making satiric comments during music videos; creator Mike Judge voices both main characters. 32 episodes. 165m; DVD. **C:** Voice(s) by Mike Judge; Tracy Grandstaff; Adam Welsh; Rottilio Michieli. **A:** Jr. High-Adult. **P:** Entertainment. **U:** Home. **Mov-Ent**: Television Series, Animation & Cartoons, Music Video. **Acq:** Purchase. **Dist:** Paramount Pictures Corp. $24.98.

Beavis and Butt-head: The Mike Judge Collection, Vol. 1 2005
Features the 1993-1997 animated MTV television series with Beavis and Butt-head, idiot metal-head teenagers who sit on the couch while making satiric comments during music videos; creator Mike Judge voices both main characters. 40 episodes. 214m; DVD. **C:** Voice(s) by Mike Judge; Tracy Grandstaff; Adam Welsh; Rottilio Michieli. **A:** Jr. High-Adult. **P:** Entertainment. **U:** Home. **Mov-Ent**: Television Series, Animation & Cartoons, Music Video. **Acq:** Purchase. **Dist:** Paramount Pictures Corp. $29.99.

Beavis and Butt-head: The Mike Judge Collection, Vol. 2 2006
Features the 1993-1997 animated MTV television series with Beavis and Butt-head, idiotic metal-head teens who sit on the couch while making satiric comments during music videos; creator Mike Judge voices both main characters. 40 episodes. 226m; DVD. **C:** Voice(s) by Mike Judge; Tracy Grandstaff; Adam Welsh; Rottilio Michieli. **A:** Jr. High-Adult. **P:** Entertainment. **U:** Home. **Mov-Ent**: Television Series, Animation & Cartoons, Music Video. **Acq:** Purchase. **Dist:** Paramount Pictures Corp. $29.99.

Beavis and Butt-head: The Mike Judge Collection, Vol. 3 2006
Features the 1993-1997 animated MTV television series with Beavis and Butt-head, idiotic metal-head teens who sit on the couch while making satiric comments during music videos; creator Mike Judge voices both main characters. 42 episodes. 257m; DVD. **C:** Voice(s) by Mike Judge; Tracy Grandstaff; Adam Welsh; Rottilio Michieli. **A:** Jr. High-Adult. **P:** Entertainment. **U:** Home. **Mov-Ent**: Television Series, Animation & Cartoons, Music Video. **Acq:** Purchase. **Dist:** Paramount Pictures Corp. $29.99.

Beavis and Butt-Head: There Goes the Neighborhood 1994
Neighbor Tom Anderson must deal with the fact that he lives next-door to the notorious duo. 45m; VHS. **A:** Jr. High-Adult. **P:** Entertainment. **U:** Home. **Mov-Ent**: Animation & Cartoons. **Acq:** Purchase. **Dist:** Music Video Distributors. $14.98.

Beavis and Butt-Head: Work Sucks! 1994
The lame-brained duo hatch even more lame-brained schemes to get rich without having to work for their money. 45m; VHS. **A:** Jr. High-Adult. **P:** Entertainment. **U:** Home. **Mov-Ent**: Animation & Cartoons. **Acq:** Purchase. **Dist:** Music Video Distributors. $14.98.

Bebe + Cece Winans! 199?
The Grammy Award-winning gospel duo sing five of their songs, including "Heaven," "Celebrate a New Life," and "Addictive Love." 30m; VHS. **A:** Jr. High-Adult. **P:** Entertainment. **U:** Home. **Mov-Ent**: Music Video, Music--Pop/Rock. **Acq:** Purchase. **Dist:** Music Video Distributors. $14.98.

Bebe's Kids 1992 (PG-13) — ★★½
When ladies' man Robin falls for the lovely Jamika, he gets some unexpected surprises when he takes her out on a first date to an amusement park—and she brings along four kids. Animated comedy takes some funny pot-shots at both black and white culture and Disneyland. The children are amusing, especially baby PeeWee, a tot with chronically dirty diapers and Tone Loc's gravelly voice. Based on characters created by the late comedian Robin Harris. The video includes the seven-minute animated short "Itsy Bitsy Spider." 74m; VHS, DVD, CC. **C:** Voice(s) by Faizon Love; Vanessa Bell Calloway; Wayne Collins; Jonell Green; Marques Houston; Tone Loc; Nell Carter; Myra J.; Directed by Bruce Smith; Written by Reginald (Reggie) Hudlin; Music by John Barnes. **Pr:** Willard Carroll; Thomas L. White; Paramount Pictures. **A:** Family. **P:** Entertainment. **U:** Home. **Mov-Ent**: Animation & Cartoons, Black Culture. **Acq:** Purchase. **Dist:** Paramount Pictures Corp. $14.95.

Beca de Gilas: Rebeca's Story 2001
Rebeca Armendariz is a 21-year-old college student committed to changing the Chicano community in Gilroy, California. Beca organized her community to vote against an antiaffirmative action initiative, Proposition 209. 20m; VHS. **A:** College-Adult. **P:** Education. **U:** Institution. **Gen-Edu**: Ethnicity, Public Affairs, Social Service. **Acq:** Purchase, Rent/Lease. **Dist:** Filmakers Library Inc. $195.00.

Because I Said So 200?
Comedian Kevin Yon uses humor to help parents of preschool children think about the discipline methods they were raised on, and possible alternatives. 22m; VHS. **A:** Sr. High-Adult. **P:** Education. **U:** Institution. **Gen-Edu**: Parenting, Education. **Acq:** Purchase. **Dist:** Universal Studios Home Video. $49.00.

Because I Said So 2007 (PG-13) — ★★
Keaton stars as Daphne, a well-intentioned but overprotective and meddling mom to three beautiful daughters. Maggie (Graham) and Mae (Perabo) are safely married and successful, but youngest chick Milly (Moore) has terrible taste in men, so Daphne places a personal ad and screens the replies. Daphne approves of architect Jason (Scott) but Milly is drawn to musician and single dad Johnny (Macht), whose own dad, Joe (Collins), strikes unexpected sparks with Daphne. Much over-the-top shtick follows but everything (and everyone) looks gorgeous. 102m; DVD, Wide. **C:** Diane Keaton; Mandy Moore; Lauren Graham; Piper Perabo; Gabriel Macht; Tom Everett Scott; Stephen Collins; Ty Panitz; Colin Ferguson; Tony Hale; Matt Champagne; Directed by Michael Lehmann; Written by Karen Leigh Hopkins; Jessie Nelson; Cinematography by Julio Macat; Music by David Kitay. **Pr:** Paul Brooks; Jessie Nelson; Gold Circle Films; Universal Pictures. **A:** Jr. High-Adult. **P:** Entertainment. **U:** Home. **L:** English. **Mov-Ent**: Comedy--Romantic. **Acq:** Purchase. **Dist:** Movies Unlimited; Alpha Video.

Because of Him 1945 (Unrated) — ★★½
Actress Kim Walker (Durbin) fakes a letter of introduction from famous thespian John Sheridan (Laughton) in order to impress Broadway producer Charles Gilbert (Ridges). It works and she's given the lead, much to the dismay of the playwright, Paul Taylor (Tone). Naturally, Kim turns out to be an opening night success and Paul comes around and realizes what a swell gal she is. Laughton is at his best as the hammy veteran performer. 88m/B/W; VHS, DVD, CC. **C:** Deanna Durbin; Franchot Tone; Charles Laughton; Stanley Ridges; Helen Broderick; Donald Meek; Directed by Richard Wallace; Written by Edmund Beloin; Cinematography by Hal Mohr; Music by Miklos Rozsa. **Pr:** Felix Jackson; Universal Pictures. **A:** Jr. High-Adult. **P:** Entertainment. **U:** Home. **Mov-Ent. Acq:** Purchase. **Dist:** Movies Unlimited; Universal Studios Home Video.

Because of That War 1997
Two of Israel's leading rock musicians, both children of Holocaust survivors, confront their horrifying legacy. 90m; VHS, DVD. **A:** Adult. **P:** Education. **U:** Home. **Gen-Edu**: Holocaust. **Acq:** Purchase. **Dist:** SISU Home Entertainment, Inc. $89.95.

Because of the Cats 1974 (Unrated) — ★½
Police inspector uncovers an evil cult within his seaside village while investigating a bizarre rape and burglary. 90m; VHS. **C:** Bryan Marshall; Alexandra Stewart; Alex Van Rooyen; Sylvia Kristel; Sebastian Graham Jones; Directed by Fons Rademakers. **Pr:** American Transcontinental Pictures. **A:** Sr. High-Adult. **P:** Entertainment. **U:** Home. **Mov-Ent**: Horror, Rape, Occult Sciences. **Acq:** Purchase. **Dist:** No Longer Available.

Because of Winn-Dixie 2005 (PG) — ★★½
Based on the popular children's book by Kate DiCamillo of the same name about a lonely young girl who adopts a stray dog. India Opal Buloni (played by Robb) is a lonely 10 year-old who's just moved to Florida with her preacher father (Daniels). Without friends, and missing her mother, who left her when she was three, Opal encounters a stray dog at the local grocery store. She adopts the dog as her own, naming him Winn-Dixie after the store. Slowly, the dog helps Opal ease her loneliness and she discovers some rare friendships in unusual places. While not perfect, the movie has more hits than misses and is helped along with a strong supporting cast, including Dave Matthews as a singing pet store clerk. 105m; DVD. **C:** Jeff Daniels; Cicely Tyson; Eva Marie Saint; Courtney Jines; Elle Fanning; AnnaSophia Robb; Dave Matthews; Nick Price; Luke Benward; Directed by Wayne Wang; Written by Joan Singleton; Cinematography by Karl Walter Lindenlaub; Music by Rachel Portman. **Pr:** Trevor Albert; Joan V. Singleton; 20th Century-Fox. **A:**

Primary-Adult. **P:** Entertainment. **U:** Home. **L:** English. **Mov-Ent:** Comedy-Drama, Pets. **Acq:** Purchase. **Dist:** Fox Home Entertainment. $29.98.

Because of You 1952 — ★★½
Parolee Christine Carroll (Young) marries Steve Kimberly (Chandler) without revealing her sordid past. Then said past bites her in the butt when her criminal associates find and involve her in another crime. Lots of tears. 95m/B/W; VHS. **C:** Loretta Young; Jeff Chandler; Alex Nicol; Frances Dee; Alexander Scourby; Lynne Roberts; Mae Clarke; Directed by Joseph Pevney; Written by Ketti Frings; Cinematography by Russell Metty; Music by Frank Skinner. **A:** Jr. High-Adult. **P:** Entertainment. **U:** Home. **Mov-Ent:** Drama, Marriage, Melodrama. **Acq:** Purchase. **Dist:** Facets Multimedia Inc.

Because of You 1995 (R) — ★★
Jose (Osorio), a Cuban-American serviceman stationed in Japan, taught the young Kyoko how to do latin dancing. When she's 21, Kyoko (Takaoka) travels to New York to see Jose again. When she does find him, she discovers Jose has AIDS and no longer remembers much of his past, including Kyoko. Terminally ill, his one wish is to be reunited with his family in Miami. Kyoko decides to drive Jose home, hoping somehow he'll come to remember her. 85m; VHS, DVD. **C:** Saki Takaoka; Carlos Osorio; Scott Whitehurst; Mauricio Bustamante; Oscar Colon; Bradford West; Angel Stephens; Directed by Ryu Murakami; Written by Ryu Murakami; Cinematography by Sarah Cawley. **Pr:** Roger Corman; Concorde Pictures. **A:** College-Adult. **P:** Entertainment. **U:** Home. **Mov-Ent:** AIDS, Dance. **Acq:** Purchase. **Dist:** New Horizons Picture Corp.

Because Somebody Cares 1982
An upbeat film about a volunteer program for the elderly that everyone enjoys. 27m; VHS, 3/4 U. **Pr:** Terra Nova Films. **A:** Adult. **P:** Education. **U:** Institution. **Gen-Edu:** Aging. **Acq:** Purchase, Rent/Lease. **Dist:** EcuFilm; Filmakers Library Inc.; New Dimension Media.

Because the Dawn 1988
A comedy set in New York City, in which vampire Marie seduces Ariel with Swing musical accompaniment. Campy and contemporary. 40m; VHS, 3/4 U. **Pr:** Amy Goldstein. **A:** Jr. High-Adult. **P:** Entertainment. **U:** Institution, SURA. **Gen-Edu:** Women, Photography. **Acq:** Purchase, Rent/Lease. **Dist:** Women Make Movies.

Because They're Young 1960 (Unrated) — ★★½
Routine teen drama. Big city high school history teacher Neil Hendry (Dick Clark in his film debut) becomes a role model for some of his juvenile delinquent kids and still finds the time to romance school secretary Joan. Naturally, Principal Dolan is opposed to Neil befriending his students. 98m/B/W; DVD. **C:** Dick Clark; Victoria Shaw; Warren Berlinger; Michael Callan; Tuesday Weld; Doug McClure; Wendell Holmes; Roberta Shore; Chris Robinson; Rudy Bond; Directed by Paul Wendkos; Written by James Gunn; Cinematography by Wilfred M. Cline; Music by John Williams. **A:** Jr. High-Adult. **P:** Entertainment. **U:** Home. **Mov-Ent:** Adolescence. **Acq:** Purchase. **Dist:** WarnerArchive.com.

Because This Is About Love: A Portrait of Gay and Lesbian Marriage 1992
Profiles gay and lesbian weddings, and examines why these couples choose to publicly commit themselves to each other. 28m; VHS. **A:** Adult. **P:** Education. **U:** Institution. **Gen-Edu:** Marriage, Homosexuality. **Acq:** Purchase. **Dist:** Filmakers Library Inc. $295.00.

Because We Are Disciples 1992
Illustrates the meaning of evangelization and its role in Christian life. Includes discussion guide. 12m; VHS. **A:** Adult. **P:** Religious. **U:** Institution, Home. **Gen-Edu:** Religion. **Acq:** Purchase. **Dist:** U.S. Catholic Conference of Catholic Bishops. $17.95.

Because Why? 1993 (Unrated) — ★★
After travelling abroad for five years, Alex (Riley) returns to Montreal with a back pack, a skateboard, and an old girlfriend's address. The address only leads to a demolished building, so Alex finds himself a new home and—longing to belong somewhere—a potentially new family and friends. 104m; VHS, DVD. **C:** Michael Riley; Martine Rochon; Doru Bandol; Heather Mathieson; Directed by Arto Paragamian; Written by Arto Paragamian; Cinematography by Andre Turpin; Music by Nana Vasconcelos. **A:** Sr. High-Adult. **P:** Entertainment. **U:** Home. **Mov-Ent. Acq:** Purchase. **Dist:** Vanguard International Cinema, Inc.

Because You Are My Friend 1978
Animated presentation introducing children to epileptic seizures, first aid, and more and stressing the importance of friendship, despite these obstacles. 5m; VHS. **A:** Preschool-Primary. **P:** Education. **U:** Institution. **Hea-Sci:** Epilepsy. **Acq:** Purchase. **Dist:** Epilepsy Foundation of America. $12.95.

Because You're Mine 1952 (Unrated) — ★★
Lanza plays an opera star who is drafted and falls in love with Morrow, his top sergeant's sister. Plenty of singing—maybe too much at times, but Lanza's fans will enjoy it nonetheless. 103m; VHS, DVD. **C:** Mario Lanza; James Whitmore; Doretta Morrow; Dean Miller; Rita (Paula) Corday; Jeff Donnell; Spring Byington; Directed by Alexander Hall. **Pr:** Joe Pasternak; MGM. **A:** Jr. High-Adult. **P:** Entertainment. **U:** Home. **Mov-Ent:** Musical. **Acq:** Purchase. **Dist:** MGM Home Entertainment. $19.98.
Songs: All the Things You Are; Because You're Mine; Be My Love; Granada; Lee-Ah-Loo; The Lord's Prayer; The Song Angels Sing; You Do Something to Me.

Becker: The 2nd Season 1999 (Unrated)
Television sitcom series on CBS from 1998-2004. Dr. Becker (Danson) helps a choking woman at the diner who becomes

obsessed with expressing her gratitude in "Point of Contact," gets advice on how to quit smoking in "Imm-Oral Fixations," gives a patient tips on how to romance Reggie in "Cyrano De-Beckerac," and "Linda Quits" after she makes a dreadful mistake on a patient's perscription. 24 episodes. 526m; DVD. **A:** Jr. High-Adult. **P:** Entertainment. **U:** Home. **Mov-Ent:** Television Series, Comedy-Drama. **Acq:** Purchase. **Dist:** Paramount Pictures Corp. $36.98.

Becker: The 3rd Season 2000 (Unrated)
CBS 1998-2004 comedy. Harvard Med graduate John Becker is dedicated to his New York practice but disgusted with life in general. When the gang gets on him about being a creature of habit John decides to change up his routine and eat at a different Chinese restaurant with disastrous results in "One Wong Move," in "What Indifference a Day Makes" he tries to convey to a high school student the pressures of operating a medical practice, and accidentally discovers Linda and Reggie are unknowingly dating the same guy in "The More You Know." 20 episodes. 520m; DVD. **C:** Ted Danson; Hattie Winston; Terry Farrell; Alex Desert. **A:** Jr. High-Adult. **P:** Entertainment. **U:** Home. **Mov-Ent:** Television Series. **Acq:** Purchase. **Dist:** Paramount Pictures Corp. $36.99.

Becket 1964 — ★★★
Adaptation of Jean Anouilh's play about the tumultuous friendship between Henry II of England and the Archbishop of Canterbury Thomas Becket. Becket views his position in the church of little relation to the sexual and emotional needs of a man, until he becomes archbishop. His growing concern for religion and his shrinking need of Henry as friend and confidant eventually cause the demise of the friendship and the resulting tragedy. Flawless acting from every cast member, and finely detailed artistic direction make up for the occasional slow moment. 148m; VHS, DVD, Blu-Ray, Wide. **C:** Richard Burton; Peter O'Toole; John Gielgud; Donald Wolfit; Directed by Peter Glenville; Written by Edward Anhalt; Cinematography by Geoffrey Unsworth. **Pr:** Paramount Pictures; Hal Wallis Productions. **A:** Family. **P:** Entertainment. **U:** Home. **Mov-Ent:** Drama. **Awds:** Oscars '64: Adapt. Screenplay; Golden Globes '65: Actor--Drama (O'Toole), Film--Drama. **Acq:** Purchase. **Dist:** MPI Media Group. $59.95.

Becky Sharp 1935 (Unrated) — ★★½
This premiere Technicolor film tells the story of Becky Sharp, a wicked woman who finally performs one good deed. 83m; VHS, DVD. **C:** Miriam Hopkins; Frances Dee; Cedric Hardwicke; Billie Burke; Nigel Bruce; Pat Nixon; Directed by Rouben Mamoulian; Cinematography by Ray Rennahan. **Pr:** RKO. **A:** Family. **P:** Entertainment. **U:** Home. **Mov-Ent:** Marriage. **Acq:** Purchase. **Dist:** Movies Unlimited; Alpha Video. $19.95.

Becoming a Celibate Lover: Promises and Pitfalls 19??
A four-part series providing help and suggestions for healthy celibate loving. Emphasis is placed on the acceptance of Jesus Christ and God into one's life and the importance of celibacy in these callings. 120m; VHS. **A:** Sr. High-Adult. **P:** Religious. **U:** Institution, Home. **Gen-Edu:** Religion, Sex & Sexuality, Self-Help. **Acq:** Purchase. **Dist:** Alba House Media Center. $29.95.

Becoming a Champion: An Athlete's Guide to Building Self-Confidence 2005 (Unrated)
Discusses how to pick a team captain, how to convey to him what you expect of him, and how they can develop leadership skills. 40m; DVD. **A:** Family. **P:** Education. **U:** Home, Institution. **How-Ins:** Sports--General, Athletic Instruction/Coaching. **Acq:** Purchase. **Dist:** Championship Productions. $39.99.

Becoming a Champion Athlete: Goal Setting for Success 2004 (Unrated)
Sports psychologist Greg Dale discusses how to properly set and meet goals in order to further ones athletic career. 29m; DVD. **A:** Family. **P:** Education. **U:** Home, Institution. **How-Ins:** Sports--General, Athletic Instruction/Coaching. **Acq:** Purchase. **Dist:** Championship Productions. $29.99.

Becoming a Champion Athlete: Making Every Practice Count! 2004 (Unrated)
Duke University Mental Training Coach Greg Dale talks about how athletes can get the most from their practice sessions. 35m; DVD. **A:** Family. **P:** Education. **U:** Home, Institution. **How-Ins:** Sports--General, Athletic Instruction/Coaching. **Acq:** Purchase. **Dist:** Championship Productions. $29.99.

Becoming a Champion Athlete: Mastering Pressure Situations! 2004 (Unrated)
Sports psychologist Greg Dale discusses playing in pressure situations, and how to deal with and learn from them. 34m; DVD. **A:** Family. **P:** Education. **U:** Home, Institution. **How-Ins:** Sports--General, Athletic Instruction/Coaching. **Acq:** Purchase. **Dist:** Championship Productions. $29.99.

Becoming a Champion Basketball Player: Creating Open Shots and Improving at the Line 2006
Features basketball drills that create better shooting chances along with greater success at the free throw line in a program designed by expert shooting instructor Barry Brodzinski. 48m; DVD. **A:** Sr. High-Adult. **P:** Instruction. **U:** Institution. **Spo-Rec:** Basketball. **Acq:** Purchase. **Dist:** Championship Productions. $39.95.

Becoming a Champion Basketball Player: Creating Open Shots and Improving the Line 2006 (Unrated)
Shooting instructor Barry Brodzinski gives pointers on how to best make shots, including foul shot drills intended to be done when players are tired to improve their ability to make shots under pressure. 48m; DVD. **A:** Family. **P:** Education. **U:** Home,

Institution. **How-Ins:** Basketball, Athletic Instruction/Coaching. **Acq:** Purchase. **Dist:** Championship Productions. $39.99.

Becoming a Champion Basketball Player: Five-Star's Individual Improvement Program 2005 (Unrated)
Coach Mike Moreau presents drills meant for basketball players in any position to improve their abilities. 73m; DVD. **A:** Family. **P:** Education. **U:** Home, Institution. **How-Ins:** Basketball, Athletic Instruction/Coaching. **Acq:** Purchase. **Dist:** Championship Productions. $39.99.

Becoming a Champion Basketball Player: Jackie Stiles' 1,000 Shots Workout Routine 2009 (Unrated)
Former WNBA player Jackie Stiles demonstrates the workout she used to increase her shooting abilities as a high school basketball player. 45m; DVD. **A:** Family. **P:** Education. **U:** Home, Institution. **Spo-Rec:** Basketball, Athletic Instruction/Coaching. **Acq:** Purchase. **Dist:** Championship Productions. $39.99.

Becoming a Champion Basketball Player: Jackie Stiles' Ball Handling Drills 2009 (Unrated)
Former WNBA Player Jackie Stiles demonstrates stationary, moving, and cone drills designed to help develop a basketball player's ball handling skills. 61m; DVD. **A:** Family. **P:** Education. **U:** Home, Institution. **Spo-Rec:** Basketball, Athletic Instruction/Coaching. **Acq:** Purchase. **Dist:** Championship Productions. $39.99.

Becoming a Champion Basketball Player: The Perimeter Player 2005 (Unrated)
Scott Adubato presents drills for, and discussion about, increasing the abilities of perimeter players in basketball. 97m; DVD. **A:** Family. **P:** Education. **U:** Home, Institution. **How-Ins:** Basketball, Athletic Instruction/Coaching. **Acq:** Purchase. **Dist:** Championship Productions. $39.99.

Becoming a Champion Basketball Player: The Point Guard 2005 (Unrated)
Basketball coach/trainer Scott Adubato discusses the abilities needed by a high-level point guard. 83m; DVD. **A:** Family. **P:** Education. **U:** Home, Institution. **How-Ins:** Basketball, Athletic Instruction/Coaching. **Acq:** Purchase. **Dist:** Championship Productions. $39.99.

Becoming a Champion Basketball Player: The Post Player 2005 (Unrated)
Basketball coach/instructor Evan Pickman introduces techniques from the Five Star camps for training post players. 95m; DVD. **A:** Family. **P:** Education. **U:** Home, Institution. **How-Ins:** Basketball, Athletic Instruction/Coaching. **Acq:** Purchase. **Dist:** Championship Productions. $39.99.

Becoming a Champion Basketball Player: The Rebounder 2005 (Unrated)
Coach David Thorpe and NBA forward Udonis Haslem give tips and drills to improve players rebound abilities. 58m; DVD. **A:** Family. **P:** Education. **U:** Home, Institution. **How-Ins:** Basketball, Athletic Instruction/Coaching. **Acq:** Purchase. **Dist:** Championship Productions. $39.99.

Becoming a Champion Basketball Player: The Scorer 2005 (Unrated)
Basketball coach/instructor Tony Bergeron presents scoring techniques from the Five Star basketball training camps. 56m; DVD. **A:** Family. **P:** Education. **U:** Home, Institution. **How-Ins:** Basketball, Athletic Instruction/Coaching. **Acq:** Purchase. **Dist:** Championship Productions. $39.99.

Becoming a Champion: Defense and Blocking 2002 (Unrated)
Coach John Dunning discusses what it takes to make a good defensive volleyball player, and presents drill for improving those attributes. 53m; DVD. **A:** Family. **P:** Education. **U:** Home, Institution. **How-Ins:** Volleyball, Athletic Instruction/Coaching. **Acq:** Purchase. **Dist:** Championship Productions. $29.99.

Becoming a Champion: Discus for Girls' Track and Field 2013 (Unrated)
Coach Carrie Lane discusses the skills necessary for becoming a discus thrower before moving on to 40 drills designed to develop those skills. 45m; DVD. **A:** Family. **P:** Education. **U:** Home. **L:** English. **Spo-Rec:** Athletic Instruction/Coaching, Sports--Track & Field, How-To. **Acq:** Purchase. **Dist:** Championship Productions. $29.99.

Becoming a Champion Diver: Skills and Drills for Success 2007 (Unrated)
Coach Jeff Huber discusses various diving concepts and presents drills designed to help divers improve their skill with them. 115m; DVD. **A:** Family. **P:** Education. **U:** Home, Institution. **Spo-Rec:** Swimming, Athletic Instruction/Coaching. **Acq:** Purchase. **Dist:** Championship Productions. $39.99.

Becoming a Champion: 800/1500M for Girls' Track and Field 2013 (Unrated)
Coach Rose Monday demonstrates more than 50 drills for training distance runners. 52m; DVD. **A:** Family. **P:** Education. **U:** Home. **L:** English. **Spo-Rec:** Athletic Instruction/Coaching, Sports--Track & Field, How-To. **Acq:** Purchase. **Dist:** Championship Productions. $29.99.

Becoming a Champion: Errors and Corrections for the Short Game 2005 (Unrated)
Tina Mickelson discusses common errors made in the short game in golf, and how to correct them. 41m; DVD. **A:** Family. **P:** Education. **U:** Home, Institution. **Gen-Edu:** Golf, Athletic Instruction/Coaching. **Acq:** Purchase. **Dist:** Championship Productions. $29.99.

Becoming a Champion: Glide & Spin Shot Put for Girls' Track and Field 2013 (Unrated)
Coach Erin Wibbels discusses her training program for rotational shot putters before introducing the drills and exercises comprising it. 39m; DVD. **A:** Family. **P:** Education. **U:** Home. **L:** English. **Spo-Rec:** Athletic Instruction/Coaching, Sports--Track & Field, How-To. **Acq:** Purchase. **Dist:** Championship Productions. $29.99.

Becoming a Champion Goalkeeper 2003 (Unrated)
Champion goalkeeper Marybeth Freeman presents tips for success at the goalkeeper position in field hockey. 48m; DVD. **A:** Family. **P:** Education. **U:** Home, Institution. **How-Ins:** Hockey, Athletic Instruction/Coaching. **Acq:** Purchase. **Dist:** Championship Productions. $39.99.

Becoming a Champion Golfer: Course Management 2006 (Unrated)
College head coach John Inman discusses club selection and the importance of learning the proper way to think on a golf course. 31m; DVD. **A:** Family. **P:** Education. **U:** Home, Institution. **How-Ins:** Golf, Athletic Instruction/Coaching. **Acq:** Purchase. **Dist:** Championship Productions. $29.99.

Becoming a Champion: High Jump for Girls' Track & Field 2013 (Unrated)
Coach Karen Gaita demonstrates various drills for training track and field students participating in the high jump. 95m; DVD. **A:** Family. **P:** Education. **U:** Home. **L:** English. **Spo-Rec:** Athletic Instruction/Coaching, Baseball, How-To. **Acq:** Purchase. **Dist:** Championship Productions. $29.99.

Becoming a Champion: Hitting 2002 (Unrated)
Coach John Dunning discusses the basics of hitting the volleyball as well as drills designed to improve skills. 57m; DVD. **A:** Family. **P:** Education. **U:** Home, Institution. **How-Ins:** Volleyball, Athletic Instruction/Coaching. **Acq:** Purchase. **Dist:** Championship Productions. $29.99.

Becoming a Champion Hockey Player: Angling, Body Checking, & Puck Protection 2007 (Unrated)
Coach Enrico Blasi talks about putting yourself between your opponent and the puck, and how to perform or take a body check. 31m; DVD. **A:** Family. **P:** Education. **U:** Home, Institution. **How-Ins:** Hockey, Athletic Instruction/Coaching. **Acq:** Purchase. **Dist:** Championship Productions. $29.99.

Becoming a Champion Hockey Player: Off-Ice Training for Faster, Stronger Hockey 2007 (Unrated)
Coach and former defenseman Matt Cady presents an exercise program for ice hockey players designed to increase their strength. 40m; DVD. **A:** Family. **P:** Education. **U:** Home, Institution. **Gen-Edu:** Hockey, Athletic Instruction/Coaching. **Acq:** Purchase. **Dist:** Championship Productions. $29.99.

Becoming a Champion Hockey Player: Offensive Essentials for Passing, Receiving, & Shooting 2007 (Unrated)
Enrico Blasi discusses passing, receiving, and shooting the puck, and presents drills for increasing a player's skill with all three. 56m; DVD. **A:** Family. **P:** Education. **U:** Home, Institution. **How-Ins:** Hockey, Athletic Instruction/Coaching. **Acq:** Purchase. **Dist:** Championship Productions. $29.99.

Becoming a Champion Hockey Player: Puck Control & Stick Handling 2007 (Unrated)
Coach Enrico Blasi presents drills designed to increase an ice hockey players' ability to control the puck and his stick. 28m; DVD. **A:** Family. **P:** Education. **U:** Home, Institution. **How-Ins:** Hockey, Athletic Instruction/Coaching. **Acq:** Purchase. **Dist:** Championship Productions. $29.99.

Becoming a Champion: How to Jump Higher! 2003 (Unrated)
Dr. Don Chu presents workout routines designed to increase an athlete's jumping abilities. 30m; DVD. **A:** Family. **P:** Education. **U:** Home, Institution. **How-Ins:** Sports--General, Athletic Instruction/Coaching. **Acq:** Purchase. **Dist:** Championship Productions. $29.99.

Becoming a Champion: How to Run Faster! 2003
Stanford University Director of Performance Enhancement Don Chu, Ph.D. presents a training plan, proper techniques, and drills to improve speed and performance. 40m; VHS, DVD. **A:** Adult. **P:** Instruction. **U:** Institution. **How-Ins:** Baseball, Sports--General, How-To. **Acq:** Purchase. **Dist:** Championship Productions. $29.95.

Becoming a Champion: Hurdles for Girls' Track & Field 2013 (Unrated)
Coach Elisha Brewer discusses the techniques needed for developing competitive young female hurdlers. 118m; DVD. **A:** Family. **P:** Education. **U:** Home. **L:** English. **Spo-Rec:** Athletic Instruction/Coaching, Sports--Track & Field, How-To. **Acq:** Purchase. **Dist:** Championship Productions. $29.99.

Becoming A Champion Infielder 2006 (Unrated)
Coach Frank Leoni describes the attributes necessary for an infielder, and also presents several drills intended to improve players. 86m; DVD. **A:** Family. **P:** Education. **U:** Home, Institution. **How-Ins:** Baseball, Athletic Instruction/Coaching. **Acq:** Purchase. **Dist:** Championship Productions. $34.99.

Becoming a Champion: Javelin for Girls' Track and Field 2013 (Unrated)
Coach Debra Farwell discusses javelin throwing mechanics before moving on to training drills. 74m; DVD. **A:** Family. **P:** Education. **U:** Home. **L:** English. **Spo-Rec:** Athletic Instruction/

Coaching, Sports--Track & Field, How-To. **Acq:** Purchase. **Dist:** Championship Productions. $29.99.

Becoming a Champion Kicker 2004 (Unrated)
Coaches Mike McCabe and Todd Sievers give techniques for placekickers who wish to improve their field goal kicking abilities. 61m; DVD. **A:** Family. **P:** Education. **U:** Home, Institution. **How-Ins:** Football, Athletic Instruction/Coaching. **Acq:** Purchase. **Dist:** Championship Productions. $39.99.

Becoming a Champion Lacrosse Player: The Face-Off 2006 (Unrated)
Coach Kevin Cassesse presents drills designed to help lacrosse players improve their in-game abilities during the face-off. 43m; DVD. **A:** Family. **P:** Education. **U:** Home, Institution. **How-Ins:** Sports--General, Athletic Instruction/Coaching. **Acq:** Purchase. **Dist:** Championship Productions. $39.99.

Becoming a Champion Lacrosse Player: The Goalie 2004 (Unrated)
Coach Tony Seaman and lacrosse player John Horrigan present drills and tips for aspiring lacrosse goalies. 41m; DVD. **A:** Family. **P:** Education. **U:** Home, Institution. **How-Ins:** Sports--General, Athletic Instruction/Coaching. **Acq:** Purchase. **Dist:** Championship Productions. $39.99.

Becoming a Champion Lacrosse Player with Gary Gait: Shooting Techniques & Drills 2007 (Unrated)
Former lacrosse player and coach Gary Gait discusses different shooting techniques and 'trick shots' for the game. 44m; DVD. **A:** Family. **P:** Education. **U:** Home, Institution. **How-Ins:** Sports--General, Athletic Instruction/Coaching. **Acq:** Purchase. **Dist:** Championship Productions. $39.99.

Becoming a Champion Lacrosse Player with Gary Gait: Stick Tricks & Dodging 2007 (Unrated)
Gary Gait discuses ways to improve one's ability to dodge and pass in the game of lacrosse. 52m; DVD. **A:** Family. **P:** Education. **U:** Home, Institution. **How-Ins:** Sports--General, Athletic Instruction/Coaching. **Acq:** Purchase. **Dist:** Championship Productions. $39.99.

Becoming a Champion Libero 2011 (Unrated)
Ex-volleyball player Sarah Drury-Petkovic demonstrates passing and defensive drills for liberos wishing to improve. 45m; DVD. **A:** Family. **P:** Education. **U:** Home, Institution. **Spo-Rec:** Volleyball, Athletic Instruction/Coaching. **Acq:** Purchase. **Dist:** Championship Productions. $39.99.

Becoming a Champion: Long Jump for Girls' Track & Field 2013 (Unrated)
Coach Heidi Yost presents drills for training and developing long jumpers. 44m; DVD. **A:** Family. **P:** Education. **U:** Home. **L:** English. **Spo-Rec:** Athletic Instruction/Coaching, Sports--Track & Field, How-To. **Acq:** Purchase. **Dist:** Championship Productions. $29.99.

Becoming a Champion Long Jumper 2002 (Unrated)
Coach Rick Attig presents drills to attain a quicker and bigger takeoff in the sport of long jumping. 50m; DVD. **A:** Family. **P:** Education. **U:** Home, Institution. **How-Ins:** Sports--Track & Field, Athletic Instruction/Coaching. **Acq:** Purchase. **Dist:** Championship Productions. $34.99.

Becoming a Champion: Off Season Strength & Conditioning for Volleyball 2012 (Unrated)
Coach Tim McClellan presents a workout program for keeping volleyball athletes in shape in the off-season. 49m; DVD. **A:** Family. **P:** Education. **U:** Home. **L:** English. **Spo-Rec:** Athletic Instruction/Coaching, Volleyball, How-To. **Acq:** Purchase. **Dist:** Championship Productions. $39.99.

Becoming a Champion Offensive Lineman 2006 (Unrated)
Coach Thomas and four of his former players present drills for improving offensive linemen. 75m; DVD. **A:** Family. **P:** Education. **U:** Home, Institution. **How-Ins:** Football, Athletic Instruction/Coaching. **Acq:** Purchase. **Dist:** Championship Productions. $39.99.

Becoming a Champion: Passing and Serving 2002 (Unrated)
Coach John Dunning presents drills to improve a volleyball players serve and passing skills. 53m; DVD. **A:** Family. **P:** Education. **U:** Home, Institution. **How-Ins:** Volleyball, Athletic Instruction/Coaching. **Acq:** Purchase. **Dist:** Championship Productions. $29.99.

Becoming a Champion: Pole Vault for Girls' Track & Field 2013 (Unrated)
Coach Caroline White demonstrates various pole vault training drills, including pool drills for safely learning mechanics. 63m; DVD. **A:** Family. **P:** Education. **U:** Home. **L:** English. **Spo-Rec:** Athletic Instruction/Coaching, Sports--Track & Field, How-To. **Acq:** Purchase. **Dist:** Championship Productions. $29.99.

Becoming a Champion Pole Vaulter 2002 (Unrated)
Coach Rick Attig discusses safety and shows drills for improving skill at the pole vault. 50m; DVD. **A:** Family. **P:** Education. **U:** Home, Institution. **How-Ins:** Sports--Track & Field, Athletic Instruction/Coaching. **Acq:** Purchase. **Dist:** Championship Productions. $34.99.

Becoming a Champion Punter 2004 (Unrated)
Coaches Mike McCabe and Freddie Capshaw teach the art of punting through various drills. 62m; DVD. **A:** Family. **P:** Education. **U:** Home, Institution. **How-Ins:** Football, Athletic Instruction/Coaching. **Acq:** Purchase. **Dist:** Championship Productions. $39.99.

Becoming a Champion Setter 2002 (Unrated)
Coach John Dunning discusses the role of the 'setter' in volleyball, and shares techniques for improving their abilities. 63m; DVD. **A:** Family. **P:** Education. **U:** Home, Institution. **How-Ins:** Volleyball, Athletic Instruction/Coaching. **Acq:** Purchase. **Dist:** Championship Productions. $29.99.

Becoming a Champion: Sprints & Relays for Girls' Track & Field 2013 (Unrated)
Coach Dana Boone demonstrates exercises and training drills for girls participating in the sprints and relay events. 41m; DVD. **A:** Family. **P:** Education. **U:** Home. **L:** English. **Spo-Rec:** Athletic Instruction/Coaching, Sports--Track & Field, How-To. **Acq:** Purchase. **Dist:** Championship Productions. $29.99.

Becoming a Champion Swimmer: Backstroke 2006 (Unrated)
Drills to improve a swimmer's backstroke from Auburn University Head men's and women's Swim Coach Richard Quick. 49m; DVD. **A:** Family. **P:** Education. **U:** Home, Institution. **How-Ins:** Swimming, Athletic Instruction/Coaching. **Acq:** Purchase. **Dist:** Championship Productions. $29.99.

Becoming a Champion Swimmer: Breaststroke 2006 (Unrated)
Techniques to improve a swimmer's breaststroke, presented by Coach Richard Quick. 59m; DVD. **A:** Family. **P:** Education. **U:** Home, Institution. **How-Ins:** Swimming, Athletic Instruction/Coaching. **Acq:** Purchase. **Dist:** Championship Productions. $29.99.

Becoming a Champion Swimmer: Butterfly 2006 (Unrated)
Richard Quick presents drills and techniques to improve a swimmer's abilities while doing the butterfly stroke. 51m; DVD. **A:** Family. **P:** Education. **U:** Home, Institution. **How-Ins:** Swimming, Athletic Instruction/Coaching. **Acq:** Purchase. **Dist:** Championship Productions. $29.99.

Becoming a Champion Swimmer: Freestyle 2006 (Unrated)
Drills to increase freestyle swimming performance by Coach Richard Quick. 65m; DVD. **A:** Family. **P:** Education. **U:** Home, Institution. **How-Ins:** Swimming, Athletic Instruction/Coaching. **Acq:** Purchase. **Dist:** Championship Productions. $29.99.

Becoming a Champion Swimmer: Starts and Turns 2006 (Unrated)
Coach Richard Quick introduces this video of drills for improving a swimmers ability to start, and improving his turns. 58m; DVD. **A:** Family. **P:** Education. **U:** Home, Institution. **How-Ins:** Swimming, Athletic Instruction/Coaching. **Acq:** Purchase. **Dist:** Championship Productions. $29.99.

Becoming a Champion Tennis Player: 33 Individual Workout Drills 2004 (Unrated)
Tennis professional and instructor Renata Marcinkowska presents a program of exercises and tips for improving one's tennis game. 40m; DVD. **A:** Family. **P:** Education. **U:** Home, Institution. **How-Ins:** Tennis, Athletic Instruction/Coaching. **Acq:** Purchase. **Dist:** Championship Productions. $29.99.

Becoming a Champion Tennis Player: Doubles Strategies and Techniques 2005 (Unrated)
Tennis instructor Bill Mountford techniques for doubles tennis players, and advice on becoming a positive teammate. 55m; DVD. **A:** Family. **P:** Education. **U:** Home, Institution. **How-Ins:** Tennis, Athletic Instruction/Coaching. **Acq:** Purchase. **Dist:** Championship Productions. $29.99.

Becoming a Champion Tennis Player: The Serve 2005 (Unrated)
Bill Mountford demonstrates drills for improving a tennis player's serve, including maintaining ones serving abilities during fatigue. 47m; DVD. **A:** Family. **P:** Education. **U:** Home, Institution. **How-Ins:** Tennis, Athletic Instruction/Coaching. **Acq:** Purchase. **Dist:** Championship Productions. $29.99.

Becoming a Champion: The Attackman 2009 (Unrated)
Coach John Danowski discusses various offensive techniques, drills, and concepts for lacrosse players. 45m; DVD. **A:** Family. **P:** Education. **U:** Home, Institution. **Spo-Rec:** Lacrosse, Athletic Instruction/Coaching. **Acq:** Purchase. **Dist:** Championship Productions. $39.99.

Becoming a Champion: The Complete Guide to the Full Swing 2005 (Unrated)
Golfer Tina Mickelson presents techniques to improve one's golf swing, including different stances for different situations. 31m; DVD. **A:** Family. **P:** Education. **U:** Home, Institution. **How-Ins:** Golf, Athletic Instruction/Coaching. **Acq:** Purchase. **Dist:** Championship Productions. $29.99.

Becoming a Champion: The Complete Guide to the Short Game 2005 (Unrated)
Professional golfer Tina Mickelson introduces drills designed to improve a golfer's short game. 30m; DVD. **A:** Family. **P:** Education. **U:** Home, Institution. **How-Ins:** Golf, Athletic Instruction/Coaching. **Acq:** Purchase. **Dist:** Championship Productions. $29.99.

Becoming a Champion: The Defenseman 2009 (Unrated)
Coach John Danowski discusses various defensive techniques, drills, and concepts for lacrosse players. 58m; DVD. **A:** Family. **P:** Education. **U:** Home, Institution. **Spo-Rec:** Lacrosse, Athletic Instruction/Coaching. **Acq:** Purchase. **Dist:** Championship Productions. $39.99.

Becoming a Champion: The Midfielder 2009 (Unrated)
Coach John Danowski discusses various techniques, drills, and concepts for midfielder lacrosse players, who do both offense and defense. 32m; DVD. **A:** Family. **P:** Education. **U:** Home, Institution. **Spo-Rec:** Lacrosse, Athletic Instruction/Coaching. **Acq:** Purchase. **Dist:** Championship Productions. $39.99.

Becoming a Champion: The Quarterback 2004 (Unrated)
Coach John Booty shows drills and techniques to improve the abilities of quarterback players. 52m; DVD. **A:** Family. **P:** Education. **U:** Home, Institution. **How-Ins:** Football, Athletic Instruction/Coaching. **Acq:** Purchase. **Dist:** Championship Productions. $39.99.

Becoming a Champion: Tips and Drills to Improve Your Full Swing 2005 (Unrated)
Drills for becoming a better and more consistent golfer presented by professional golfer Tina Mickelson. 39m; DVD. **A:** Sr. High-Adult. **P:** Education. **U:** Home. **How-Ins:** Golf, Athletic Instruction/Coaching. **Acq:** Purchase. **Dist:** Championship Productions. $29.99.

Becoming a Champion: Triple Jump for Girls' Track & Field 2013 (Unrated)
Coach Stacey Smith demonstrates drills for building up female athletes participating in the triple jump event. 48m; DVD. **A:** Family. **P:** Education. **U:** Home. **L:** English. **Spo-Rec:** Athletic Instruction/Coaching, Sports--Track & Field, How-To. **Acq:** Purchase. **Dist:** Championship Productions. $29.99.

Becoming a Champion Triple Jumper 2002 (Unrated)
Coach Rick Attig discusses the three basic concepts of the triple jump, and presents drills to help athletes improve. 40m; DVD. **A:** Family. **P:** Education. **U:** Home, Institution. **How-Ins:** Sports--Track & Field, Athletic Instruction/Coaching. **Acq:** Purchase. **Dist:** Championship Productions. $34.99.

Becoming a Champion Volleyball Player: 50 Advanced Tips to Elevate Your Game! 2005 (Unrated)
Coach John Dunning presents tips and drills for volleyball players in any position to improve their play. 56m; DVD. **A:** Family. **P:** Education. **U:** Home, Institution. **How-Ins:** Volleyball, Athletic Instruction/Coaching. **Acq:** Purchase. **Dist:** Championship Productions. $29.99.

Becoming a Champion Water Polo Goalie 2011 (Unrated)
Coach Sean Nolan presents progressive training drills and exercises for building up your water polo team's goalie. 92m; DVD. **A:** Family. **P:** Education. **U:** Home, Institution. **Spo-Rec:** Sports--Water, Athletic Instruction/Coaching. **Acq:** Purchase. **Dist:** Championship Productions. $39.99.

Becoming a Champion Water Polo Player: Defensive Techniques, Skills & Drills 2008 (Unrated)
Coach Kirk Everist details the 2 meter defensive position in water polo along with various defensive techniques. 51m; DVD. **A:** Family. **P:** Education. **U:** Home, Institution. **Spo-Rec:** Sports--Water, Athletic Instruction/Coaching. **Acq:** Purchase. **Dist:** Championship Productions. $39.99.

Becoming a Champion Water Polo Player: Offensive & Defensive Game Tactics 2008 (Unrated)
Coach Kirk Everist breaks down water polo offense and defense into five separate areas before detailing each one. 100m; DVD. **A:** Family. **P:** Education. **U:** Home, Institution. **Spo-Rec:** Sports--Water, Athletic Instruction/Coaching. **Acq:** Purchase. **Dist:** Championship Productions. $39.99.

Becoming a Champion Water Polo Player: Offensive Techniques, Skills & Drills 2008 (Unrated)
Coach Kirk Everist begins with passing and shooting drills before moving on to other offensive techniques for water polo. 127m; DVD. **A:** Family. **P:** Education. **U:** Home, Institution. **Spo-Rec:** Sports--Water, Athletic Instruction/Coaching. **Acq:** Purchase. **Dist:** Championship Productions. $39.99.

Becoming a Champion Wrestler: Breakdowns-Stopping the First Move 2006 (Unrated)
Coach John Smith covers three wrestling breakdown moves and the situations in which they are best used. 44m; DVD. **A:** Family. **P:** Education. **U:** Home, Institution. **How-Ins:** Athletic Instruction/Coaching, Anthropology. **Acq:** Purchase. **Dist:** Championship Productions. $29.99.

Becoming a Champion Wrestler: Escapes and Reversals-The Attitude to Get Away! 2005 (Unrated)
Coach Greg Strobel discusses how to escape 'riders' in wrestling, and reversing their techniques. 42m; DVD. **A:** Family. **P:** Education. **U:** Home, Institution. **How-Ins:** Athletic Instruction/Coaching, Anthropology. **Acq:** Purchase. **Dist:** Championship Productions. $29.99.

Becoming a Champion Wrestler: Fundamental Motor Skills for Wrestling 2010 (Unrated)
Coach Eric Guerrero presents various drills for wrestlers looking to expand their skill base. 40m; DVD. **A:** Family. **P:** Education. **U:** Home, Institution. **Spo-Rec:** Athletic Instruction/Coaching. **Acq:** Purchase. **Dist:** Championship Productions. $29.99.

Becoming a Champion Wrestler: Homework Drills & Skills 2007 (Unrated)
Coach Greg Strobel introduces drills for teaching and developing basic wrestling skills. 79m; DVD. **A:** Family. **P:** Education. **U:** Home, Institution. **Spo-Rec:** Athletic Instruction/Coaching. **Acq:** Purchase. **Dist:** Championship Productions. $39.99.

Becoming a Champion Wrestler: Riding and Pinning-Finding a Handle! 2005 (Unrated)
Coach Greg Strobel discusses and demonstrates various riding and pinning techniques for wrestling. 46m; DVD. **A:** Family. **P:** Education. **U:** Home, Institution. **How-Ins:** Athletic Instruction/Coaching, Anthropology. **Acq:** Purchase. **Dist:** Championship Productions. $29.99.

Becoming a Champion Wrestler: Scrambling—Scoring from a Bad Position 2006 (Unrated)
Wrestling coach John Smith discusses how to come back from a failed takedown attempt. 43m; DVD. **A:** Family. **P:** Education. **U:** Home, Institution. **How-Ins:** Athletic Instruction/Coaching, Anthropology. **Acq:** Purchase. **Dist:** Championship Productions. $29.99.

Becoming a Champion Wrestler: Skills for the Upper Weights 2011 (Unrated)
Coach Hudson Taylor demonstrates various offensive and defensive skills as well as riding and escapes for wrestlers in higher weight classes. 128m; DVD. **A:** Family. **P:** Education. **U:** Home, Institution. **Spo-Rec:** Athletic Instruction/Coaching. **Acq:** Purchase. **Dist:** Championship Productions. $49.99.

Becoming a Champion Wrestler: Stand-ups-The Art of Coming Off the Mat 2006 (Unrated)
Coach John Smith discusses how to perform a wrestling stand-up properly, and how to counter three common breakdowns used to stop it. 45m; DVD. **A:** Family. **P:** Education. **U:** Home, Institution. **How-Ins:** Athletic Instruction/Coaching, Anthropology. **Acq:** Purchase. **Dist:** Championship Productions. $29.99.

Becoming a Champion Wrestler: Takedowns-Control the Man, Control the Mat! 2005 (Unrated)
Coach Greg Strobel covers takedown techniques and counter offense against them. 70m; DVD. **A:** Family. **P:** Education. **U:** Home, Institution. **How-Ins:** Athletic Instruction/Coaching, Anthropology. **Acq:** Purchase. **Dist:** Championship Productions. $29.99.

Becoming a Champion Wrestler: Tips for Controlling the Edge of the Mat 2007 (Unrated)
Coach Chris Bono demonstrates techniques for wrestlers who find themselves having to wrestle on the edge of the mat in freestyle. 40m; DVD. **A:** Family. **P:** Education. **U:** Home, Institution. **Spo-Rec:** Athletic Instruction/Coaching. **Acq:** Purchase. **Dist:** Championship Productions. $39.99.

Becoming a Championship Diver: Striving to Reach Your Potential 2007 (Unrated)
Coach Jeff Huber discusses mental and emotional endurance for divers wishing to compete at higher levels. 58m; DVD. **A:** Family. **P:** Education. **U:** Home, Institution. **Spo-Rec:** Swimming, Athletic Instruction/Coaching. **Acq:** Purchase. **Dist:** Championship Productions. $39.99.

Becoming a Christian 1979
Interview with educator and activist Paulo Freire in which he speaks about organized religion and his personal faith. Part of the Meeting with Freire Series. 12m/B/W; VHS. **A:** Adult. **P:** Education. **U:** Institution. **Gen-Edu:** Interviews, Religion, Documentary Films. **Acq:** Purchase, Rent/Lease. **Dist:** University of Toronto. $39.00.

Becoming a Consultant 1989
Two consultants discuss how to get started in the field, find customers, and build a quality-based track record. 30m; VHS. **A:** Adult. **P:** Professional. **U:** Institution. **Bus-Ind:** Business, Management. **Acq:** Purchase. **Dist:** RMI Media. $89.95.

Becoming a Contagious Christian: Communicating Your Faith in a Style that Fits You 1995
Evangelism course that offers a practical method showing how anyone can share the gospel naturally, confidently, and effectively. Includes leader's guide, participant's guide, and 80 overhead masters. 60m; VHS. **A:** Adult. **P:** Religious. **U:** Institution, Home. **How-Ins:** Education, Religion. **Acq:** Purchase. **Dist:** Gold 'N' Honey Books. $79.99.

Becoming a Modern Nation 1981
A history of the Spanish American War and the First World War. Part of the "American History: A Bilingual Study" series. Available in English, Spanish, or bilingual versions. 60m; VHS, 3/4 U. **Pr:** Video Knowledge, Inc. **A:** Primary. **P:** Education. **U:** Institution, Home. **L:** English, Spanish. **Gen-Edu:** Documentary Films, History--U.S., War--General. **Acq:** Purchase. **Dist:** Video Knowledge, Inc.

Becoming a Professional Actor 19??
Details the necessary steps for aspiring actors to follow to help them get their first break, what to avoid, and the necessary training needed. 55m; VHS. **A:** Adult. **P:** Education. **U:** Institution. **How-Ins:** Performing Arts, How-To. **Acq:** Purchase. **Dist:** Educational Video Network. $49.95.

Becoming a Successful Actor 19??
Manager and producer Faye Nuell Mayo provides tips on avoiding pitfalls on the way to an acting career. She also interviews an agent, acting coach, personal manager, casting director, and photographer for their insights. 77m; VHS. **A:** College-Adult. **P:** Education. **U:** Home. **Gen-Edu:** Performing Arts. **Acq:** Purchase. **Dist:** Stagestep; Cambridge Educational. $24.95.

Becoming a Woman in Okrika 1991
A Nigerian village is the site of this wonderful tale about a young girl's coming of age. Narrated by a woman, a society's tradition continues to be preserved. Includes non-gratuitous topless footage. 27m; VHS. **A:** Sr. High. **P:** Education. **U:** Institution. **Chl-Juv:** Travel, Anthropology, Africa. **Acq:** Purchase, Rent/Lease. **Dist:** Filmakers Library Inc. $295.00.

Becoming American 1983
Follows the resettlement of a Laos refugee family in the United States. 59m; VHS, 3/4 U. **Pr:** Ken Waterworth Levine; Ivory Waterworth Levine. **A:** Jr. High-Adult. **P:** Education. **U:** Institution, SURA. **Gen-Edu:** Documentary Films, Immigration. **Acq:** Purchase, Rent/Lease. **Dist:** New Day Films Library.

Becoming Barbie 1993
Powerful media images from the fashion and advertising industries and commentary from Naomi Wolf, author of "Beauty Myth," are the backdrop for this sobering look at the impossible physical goals women often strive to achieve. 47m; VHS. **A:** Sr. High-Adult. **P:** Education. **U:** Home, Institution. **Gen-Edu:** Women. **Acq:** Purchase. **Dist:** Moving Images Distribution.

Becoming Colette 1992 (R) — ★★
Tedious flashbacking bio of French writer Colette, from her innocent days in the country to her (bad) marriage to writer/publisher Willy and on and on to her own growing career as a writer. She begins writing stories, using an alter-ego character, Claudine, which detail her sexual escapades. Lots of naked flesh but little passion. A postscript notes that Colette wrote "Gigi" and was the first woman to receive the French Legion of Honor. 97m; VHS, CC. **C:** Mathilda May; Klaus Maria Brandauer; Virginia Madsen; Paul Rhys; Jean-Pierre Aumont; John van Dreelen; Lucienne Hamon; Directed by Danny Huston; Written by Ruth Graham; Music by John Scott. **Pr:** Heinz Bibo; Castle Hill Productions. **A:** College-Adult. **P:** Entertainment. **U:** Home. **Mov-Ent:** Sex & Sexuality, France. **Acq:** Purchase. **Dist:** Movies Unlimited. $18.99.

Becoming God's Child 1982
Important questions relating to salvation are discussed by Dave Boyer and puppet friend, Buford the Bloodhound. 30m; VHS. **Pr:** Erik Jacobson. **A:** Primary. **P:** Religious. **U:** Institution. **Gen-Edu:** Documentary Films, Religion. **Acq:** Rent/Lease. **Dist:** Gospel Communications International.

Becoming Jane 2007 (PG) — ★★½
Jane Austen's writing has withstood the test of time, but films about the writer and her writings are still fledgling. This one's a love story—supposedly her own—and takes place before Jane (Hathaway) is, well, Jane Austen as we know her. Penniless mom and dad (Walters and Cromwell) don't take the whole writing thing seriously and expect 20-year-old Jane to choose a wealthy suitor from among those that come calling. Then Thomas Lefroy (McAvoy) shows up, dashing and pushy, and Jane—after initial annoyance—entertains the thought of shelving her writing, at least temporarily. Alas, relatives from both sides disapprove of the match. No matter, she becomes a fantastic writer whom we still read, speak of, and make films about nearly 200 years later. Pretty costumes, but with a been-there-done-that (think "Pride and Prejudice" remake) feel. Still worthwhile for Austen fans and non-fans alike. 120m; DVD, Blu-Ray. **C:** Anne Hathaway; James McAvoy; Julie Walters; James Cromwell; Laurence Fox; Maggie Smith; Ian Richardson; Anna Maxwell Martin; Joe Anderson; Helen McCrory; Leo Bill; Directed by Julian Jarrold; Written by Kevin Hood; Sarah Williams; Cinematography by Eigil Bryld; Music by Adrian Johnston. **Pr:** Graham Broadbent; Douglas Rae; Robert Bernstein; Ecosse Films; Scion Films; Blueprint Films; Octagan Films; Miramax Film Corp. **A:** Jr. High-Adult. **P:** Entertainment. **U:** Home. **L:** English. **Mov-Ent:** Drama, Women, Great Britain. **Acq:** Purchase. **Dist:** Miramax Film Corp.

Becoming More Fully Human 1990
Learn how to eliminate personal habits that can be unhealthy and change into a better person through personal awareness with Virginia Satir. 30m; VHS. **Pr:** Thinking Allowed Productions. **A:** Sr. High-Adult. **P:** Instruction. **U:** Home. **How-Ins:** How-To, Personality, Self-Help. **Acq:** Purchase. **Dist:** Thinking Allowed Productions. $29.95.

Becoming Orgasmic: A Sexual Growth Program for Women 1992
Women are told what they can do to have better, more enjoyable sex. 16m; VHS, 3/4 U. **Pr:** Focus International. **A:** Sr. High-Adult. **P:** Education. **U:** Institution. **Hea-Sci:** Sex & Sexuality. **Acq:** Purchase, Rent/Lease. **Dist:** Sinclair Institute. $725.00.
Indiv. Titles: 1. Self Discovery 2. Pleasuring 3. Sharing.

Becoming Responsible 1978
The need for freedom and the need to be responsible is seen as a thin line which teenagers have to walk. 30m; VHS. **Pr:** HRM. **A:** Jr. High-Sr. High. **P:** Education. **U:** Institution. **Gen-Edu:** Adolescence. **Acq:** Purchase. **Dist:** HRM Video. $117.00.

Becoming Skillwise 1992
Students learn the importance of social skills. 43m; VHS. **A:** Jr. High. **P:** Education. **U:** Institution. **Gen-Edu:** Sociology, Children. **Acq:** Purchase. **Dist:** United Learning Inc. $199.00.

Becoming Successful Problem Solvers 1992
Three video set, each available separately, presents situations where young people have a chance to apply their math knowledge. Each set comes with classroom activities and reproducible worksheets. 60m; VHS. **A:** Primary-Jr. High. **P:** Education.

U: Institution. **Gen-Edu**: Mathematics. **Acq:** Purchase. **Dist:** HRM Video; Human Relations Media. $175.00.

Bed and Board 1970 (Unrated) — ★★★
The fourth film in the Antoine Doinel (Leaud) cycle finds him marrying Christine (Jade) and becoming a father. The responsibilities of adulthood upset him so much that Antoine leaves his new family and begins an affair. French with subtitles. 100m; VHS, DVD. **C:** Jean-Pierre Leaud; Claude Jade; Barbara Laage; Hiroko Berghauer; Daniel Boulanger; Pierre Maguelon; Jacques Jouanneau; Jacques Rispal; Jacques Robiolles; Pierre Fabre; Billy Kearns; Daniel Ceccaldi; Daniele Girard; Claire Duhamel; Sylvana Blasi; Claude Vega; Christian de Tiliere; Annick Asty; Marianne Piketi; Guy Pierauld; Marie Dedieu; Marie Irakane; Yvon Lec; Ernest Menzer; Christophe Vesque; Directed by Francois Truffaut; Written by Francois Truffaut; Bernard Revon; Claude de Givray; Cinematography by Nestor Almendros; Music by Antoine Duhamel. **A:** Sr. High-Adult. **P:** Entertainment. **U:** Home. **L:** French. **Mov-Ent**: Comedy-Drama, Marriage, Pregnancy. **Acq:** Purchase. **Dist:** Wellspring Media.

Bed & Breakfast 1992 (PG-13) — ★★1/2
Three generations of women lead quiet lives while running a failing Nantucket bed and breakfast. When a mystery man washes up on their beach, he charms them all, but it seems that he has a past that could endanger everyone. Lightweight final role for Dewhurst, though she provides some sparks as the strong and loving matriarch. Gentle romantic comedy skims the surface, but is still enjoyable. 97m; VHS, CC. **C:** Roger Moore; Talia Shire; Colleen Dewhurst; Nina Siemaszko; Ford Rainey; Stephen (Steve) Root; Jamie Walters; Victor Slezak; Directed by Robert Ellis Miller; Written by Cindy Myers; Music by David Shire. **A:** Jr. High-Adult. **P:** Entertainment. **U:** Home. **Mov-Ent**: Comedy--Romantic, Family. **Acq:** Purchase. **Dist:** Movies Unlimited. $59.99.

Bed & Breakfast 2010 (Unrated) — ★★
Formulaic rom com. His wife leaves him and Jake Sullivan (Cain) gladly escapes to the bed and breakfast he's inherited in California's wine country. Unfortunately, Brazilian Ana (Paes) shows up with a deed to the same property, left to her by her father. Let the predictable romance ensue. 89m; DVD. **C:** Dean Cain; Juliana Paes; Julian Stone; Bill Engvall; Eric Roberts; John Savage; Julia Duffy; Directed by Marcio Garcia; Written by Leland Douglas; Cinematography by Craig Kief; Music by John Hunter. **A:** Sr. High-Adult. **P:** Entertainment. **U:** Home. **L:** English. **Mov-Ent**: Comedy--Romantic, Wine & Vinyards. **Acq:** Purchase. **Dist:** Green Apple Entertainment.

Bed and Sofa 1927 (Unrated) — ★★★1/2
Adultery, abortion, and women's rights are brought about by a housing shortage which forces a man to move in with a married friend. Famous, ground-breaking Russian silent. 73m/B/W; Silent; VHS, DVD, 3/4 U. **TV Std:** NTSC, PAL. **C:** Nikolai Batalov; Vladimar Fogel; Directed by Abram Room. **A:** Sr. High-Adult. **P:** Entertainment. **U:** Institution, Home. **Mov-Ent**: Silent Films. **Acq:** Purchase. **Dist:** International Historic Films Inc. $49.95.

Bed Bath 1993
Offers a step-by-step lesson in bathing a patient in bed. 25m; VHS, 3/4 U. **Pr:** Trainex. **A:** College-Adult. **P:** Professional. **U:** Institution. **L:** English, Spanish. **Hea-Sci**: Nursing, Patient Care. **Acq:** Purchase, Rent/Lease. **Dist:** Medcom Inc.

Bed Baths 1988
A program for nurses that covers proper patient bathing methods with emphasis on the comfort and privacy of the patient. 20m; VHS, 3/4 U. **Pr:** Altschul Group. **A:** College-Adult. **P:** Instruction. **U:** Institution, SURA. **Hea-Sci**: Nursing, Patient Care. **Acq:** Purchase, Rent/Lease. **Dist:** Lippincott Williams & Wilkins. $250.00.

Bed of Roses 1995 (PG) — ★★1/2
Wistful romance finds workaholic investment banker Lisa Walker (Masterson) receiving lavish floral tributes from an unknown admirer. When Lisa tracks her giver down, it turns out to be lovestruck widowed florist Lewis Farrell (Slater), who noticed Lisa crying through her apartment window and sent the flowers to cheer her up. Best friend Kim (Seagall) urges Lisa to go for Lewis but a problematic past has Lisa distrusting her emotions and their romantic path has a few bumps (easily overcome). Appealing leads, lots of cliches. Goldenberg's debut. 88m; VHS, DVD, Wide, CC. **C:** Christian Slater; Mary Stuart Masterson; Pamela Segall; Josh Brolin; Ally Walker; Debra Monk; Directed by Michael Goldenberg; Written by Michael Goldenberg; Cinematography by Adam Kimmel; Music by Michael Convertino. **Pr:** Allan Mindel; Denise Shaw; Joseph Hartwick; Lynn Harris; New Line Cinema. **A:** Jr. High-Adult. **P:** Entertainment. **U:** Home. **Mov-Ent**: Drama, Flowers. **Acq:** Purchase. **Dist:** New Line Home Video.

The Bed Sitting Room 1969 (Unrated) — ★
Too weird for words, episodic Brit black comedy. After the nuclear bombing of Britain, survivors living in the ruins of London try to establish some semblance of normal behavior. Despite the fact some of them seem to be mutating into objects like a chest of drawers and a bed sitting room. 90m; DVD. **C:** Rita Tushingham; Ralph Richardson; Peter Cook; Dudley Moore; Spike Milligan; Michael Hordern; Directed by Richard Lester; Written by John Antrobus; Cinematography by David Watkin; Music by Ken Thorne. **A:** Sr. High-Adult. **P:** Entertainment. **U:** Home. **Mov-Ent**: Pregnancy, Comedy--Black. **Acq:** Purchase. **Dist:** Fox Home Entertainment.

Bed-wetting: Jasper to the Rescue 1997
Offers support and solutions for bed-wetters. 11m; VHS. **A:** Primary. **P:** Education. **U:** Institution. **Gen-Edu**: Children, Animation & Cartoons. **Acq:** Purchase. **Dist:** Buena Vista Home Entertainment. $99.00.

The Bed You Sleep In 1993 (Unrated) — ★★
Ray (Blair) is a struggling lumber mill owner, living with his wife Jean (McLaughlin) in a small Oregon town. The couple are torn apart when they receive a letter from their daughter, who's away at college, accusing her father of sexual abuse. The secrets and lies of the family soon echo throughout their community. 117m; VHS, DVD, Wide. **C:** Tom Blair; Ellen McLaughlin; Kathryn Sannella; Directed by Jon Jost; Written by Jon Jost; Cinematography by Jon Jost. **A:** College-Adult. **P:** Entertainment. **U:** Home. **Mov-Ent**: Sexual Abuse. **Acq:** Purchase. **Dist:** Vanguard International Cinema, Inc.

Bedazzled 1968 (PG) — ★★★
Short-order cook Stanley Moon (Moore) is saved from suicide by the devil, here known as George Spiggot (Cook), who makes Stanley an offer: seven wishes in exchange for his soul. What Stanley wants is waitress Margaret (Bron) but each of Stanley's wishes is granted with surprising consequences. Cult comedy is a sometimes uneven, but thoroughly entertaining and funny retelling of the Faustian story. 107m; VHS, DVD, Wide. **C:** Dudley Moore; Peter Cook; Eleanor Bron; Michael Bates; Raquel Welch; Bernard Spear; Parnell McGarry; Howard Goorney; Daniele Noel; Barry Humphries; Lockwood West; Robert Russell; Michael Trubshawe; Robin Hawdon; Evelyn Moore; Charles Lloyd-Pack; Directed by Stanley Donen; Written by Dudley Moore; Peter Cook; Cinematography by Austin Dempster; Music by Dudley Moore. **Pr:** 20th Century-Fox. **A:** Jr. High-Adult. **P:** Entertainment. **U:** Home. **L:** English, Spanish. **Mov-Ent**: Comedy--Screwball, Cult Films, Suicide. **Acq:** Purchase. **Dist:** Movies Unlimited; Alpha Video; Fox Home Entertainment.

Bedazzled 2000 (PG-13) — ★★1/2
Mortals have been falling for this scam for centuries: seven wishes in exchange for your eternal soul. Once again the Devil finds a taker. Fraser plays Elliot, a nice but hopeless geek who will do anything to improve his lowly stature in life and nab the girl of his dreams (O'Connor). The Devil's (Hurley) misinterpretations of his requests result in Elliot becoming, among other things, a drug lord, an NBA star, and a much too sensitive bore. Will Elliot find a way out of his hellish obligation? Is there a lesson to be learned from his experiences? You probably know the answers. Ramis occasionally misfires, but the hits outnumber the misses. An updated remake of the Dudley Moore/Peter Cook film. 105m; VHS, DVD, Blu-Ray, Wide, CC. **C:** Brendan Fraser; Elizabeth Hurley; Frances O'Connor; Rudolf Martin; Orlando Jones; Gabriel Casseus; Miriam Shor; Brian Doyle-Murray; Directed by Harold Ramis; Written by Harold Ramis; Larry Gelbart; Peter Tolan; Cinematography by Bill Pope. **A:** Sr. High-Adult. **P:** Entertainment. **U:** Home. **Mov-Ent**: Romance. **Acq:** Purchase. **Dist:** Fox Home Entertainment.

Bedding Plant Production 1990
Presents the world of colorful bedding plants, identifying types, uses, and seed production. Part of "Greenhouse Production Series." 27m; VHS. **A:** Adult. **P:** Vocational. **U:** Institution. **Bus-Ind**: Landscaping, Plants. **Acq:** Purchase. **Dist:** American Nurseryman Publishing Co.; CEV Multimedia; San Luis Video Publishing. $95.00.

Beddy Bear 1989
A stuffed doll strives for the love of his master. Based on the story by Don Freeman. 8m; VHS. **Pr:** Live Oak Media. **A:** Family. **P:** Entertainment. **U:** Institution, SURA. **Chl-Juv**: Fantasy, Literature. **Acq:** Purchase. **Dist:** Live Oak Media. $34.95.

Bedelia 1946 (Unrated) — ★★★
Lockwood well-plays a black widow. Bedelia is living happily in Monte Carlo with hubby Charlie (Hunter) until Ben Chaney (Barnes) shows up. Posing as an artist—but really a private eye—Ben has questions about Bedelia's past. Seems she poisoned three previous husbands for the insurance money and Charlie is a good bet to be her next victim. Based on the novel by Vera Caspary. 90m/B/W; VHS. **C:** Margaret Lockwood; Ian Hunter; Barry Barnes; Anne Crawford; Beatrice Varley; Jill Esmond; Julien Mitchell; Kynaston Reeves; Louise Hampton; Written by Isadore Goldsmith; Herbert Victor; Cinematography by Frederick A. (Freddie) Young; Music by Hans May. **A:** Jr. High-Adult. **P:** Entertainment. **U:** Home. **Mov-Ent**: Marriage, Insurance. **Acq:** Purchase. **Dist:** Nostalgia Family Video/ Hollywood's Attic.

Bedevil 1993
Australian trilogy exploring characters who are haunted by the past and bewitched by memories. 90m; VHS. **A:** College-Adult. **P:** Education. **U:** Institution. **Gen-Edu**: Women, Australia. **Acq:** Purchase, Rent/Lease. **Dist:** Women Make Movies. $295.00. **Indiv. Titles:** 1. Mister Chuck 2. Choo Choo Choo Choo 3. Lovin' the Spin I'm In.

Bedevilled 1955 (Unrated) — ★1/2
Dull MGM crime drama that doesn't make a lot of sense. What it does have going for it are the Paris locations and the CinemaScope cinematography by Freddie Young. Seminarian Gregory Fitzgerald (Forrest) stops in Paris before heading to Rome to receive his ordination as a priest. He gets mixed up with cynical cabaret singer Monica (Baxter), who's killed her married lover. She's hunted by the cops and the dead man's gangster brother. Greg offers to help her out. 85m; DVD. **C:** Steve Forrest; Anne Baxter; Maurice Teynac; Simone Renant; Victor Francen; Joseph Tomelty; Directed by Mitchell Leisen; Written by Jo Eisinger; Cinematography by Frederick A. (Freddie) Young; Music by William Alwyn. **A:** Sr. High-Adult. **P:** Entertainment. **U:** Home. **Mov-Ent**: Crime Drama. **Acq:** Purchase. **Dist:** WarnerArchive.com.

Bedford Incident 1965 — ★★1/2
The U.S.S. Bedford discovers an unidentified submarine in North Atlantic waters. The Bedford's commander drives his crew to the point of exhaustion as they find themselves the center of a fateful controversy. 102m/B/W; VHS, DVD. **C:** Richard Widmark; Sidney Poitier; James MacArthur; Martin Balsam; Wally Cox; Donald Sutherland; Eric Portman; Directed by James B. Harris. **Pr:** Richard Widmark; Richard Widmark; James B. Harris; James B. Harris. **A:** Jr. High-Adult. **P:** Entertainment. **U:** Home. **Mov-Ent**: Mystery & Suspense. **Acq:** Purchase. **Dist:** Image Entertainment Inc.; Sony Pictures Home Entertainment Inc. $14.95.

Bedknobs and Broomsticks 1971 (G) — ★★1/2
A novice witch and three cockney waifs ride a magic bedstead and stop the Nazis from invading England during WWII. Celebrated for its animated art. 117m; VHS, DVD, Wide. **C:** Angela Lansbury; Roddy McDowall; David Tomlinson; Bruce Forsyth; Sam Jaffe; Directed by Robert Stevenson; Written by Don DaGradi; Bill Walsh; Cinematography by Frank V. Phillips; Music by Richard M. Sherman; Robert B. Sherman. **Pr:** Walt Disney Studios. **A:** Family. **P:** Entertainment. **U:** Home. **Mov-Ent**: Musical, World War Two, Magic. **Awds:** Oscars '71: Visual FX. **Acq:** Purchase. **Dist:** Walt Disney Studios Home Entertainment. $24.99.

Bedlam 1945 (Unrated) — ★★★
Creeper set in the famed asylum in 18th-century London. A woman, wrongfully committed, tries to stop the evil doings of the chief (Karloff) of Bedlam, and endangers herself. Fine horror film co-written by producer Lewton. 79m/B/W; VHS, DVD. **C:** Jason Robards, Sr.; Ian Wolfe; Glenn Vernon; Boris Karloff; Anna Lee; Billy House; Richard Fraser; Elizabeth Russell; Skelton Knaggs; Robert Clarke; Ellen Corby; Leyland Hodgson; Joan Newton; Directed by Mark Robson; Written by Mark Robson; Val Lewton; Cinematography by Nicholas Musuraca; Music by Roy Webb. **Pr:** RKO. **A:** Family. **P:** Entertainment. **U:** Home. **Mov-Ent**: Horror. **Acq:** Purchase. **Dist:** Facets Multimedia Inc.; Turner Broadcasting System Inc. $19.95.

Bedrock Wedlock 1989
Young Fred is on the brink of despair when his wedding plans go awry. Also includes more cartoon fun with Wally Gator, Yogi Bear, Loopy D'Loop, and more! 80m; VHS. **C:** Voice(s) by Mel Blanc; Jean Vander Pyl; Alan Reed. **Pr:** Hanna-Barbera Productions. **A:** Family. **P:** Entertainment. **U:** Home. **Mov-Ent**: Animation & Cartoons, Television Series, Family Viewing. **Acq:** Purchase. **Dist:** Turner Broadcasting System Inc. $29.95.

Bedrockin' and Rappin' 1991
Join your favorite Hanna-Barbera cartoon characters, including the Flintstones, Scooby-Doo, and Top Cat, for an exciting, unique rap session. 30m; VHS. **Pr:** Hanna-Barbera Productions. **A:** Family. **P:** Entertainment. **U:** Home. **L:** Spanish. **Mov-Ent**: Animation & Cartoons, Music--Rap. **Acq:** Purchase. **Dist:** Turner Broadcasting System Inc. $9.95.

Bedroom Eyes 1986 (R) — ★★
A successful businessman becomes a voyeur by returning nightly to a beautiful woman's window, until she is killed and he is the prime suspect. Part comic, part disappointing thriller. 90m; VHS, DVD. **C:** Kenneth Gilman; Dayle Haddon; Christine Cattall; Directed by William Fruet. **Pr:** Robert Lantos; Stephen J. Roth; Film Gallery. **A:** Sr. High-Adult. **P:** Entertainment. **U:** Home. **Mov-Ent**: Mystery & Suspense, Sex & Sexuality. **Acq:** Purchase. **Dist:** $29.95.

Bedroom Eyes 2 1989 (R) — ★★
After discovering his wife has had an affair, a stockbroker takes a lover. When she turns up dead, he and his wife become murder suspects. Provides some suspenseful moments. 85m; VHS. **C:** Wings Hauser; Kathy Shower; Linda Blair; Jane Hamilton; Jennifer Delora; Directed by Chuck Vincent. **Pr:** Anant Singh; Distant Horizon. **A:** Adult. **P:** Entertainment. **U:** Institution. **Mov-Ent**: Mystery & Suspense, Sex & Sexuality, Marriage. **Acq:** Purchase. **Dist:** CinemaNow Inc.; Image Entertainment Inc. $89.95.

The Bedroom Window 1987 (R) — ★★1/2
Guttenberg is having an illicit affair with his boss' wife (Huppert), who witnesses an assault on another woman (McGovern) from the bedroom window. To keep the affair secret Guttenberg reports the crime, but since it is secondhand, the account is flawed and he becomes a suspect. Semi-tight thriller reminiscent of Hitchcock mysteries isn't always believable, but is otherwise interesting. 113m; VHS, DVD, Wide, CC. **C:** Steve Guttenberg; Elizabeth McGovern; Isabelle Huppert; Wallace Shawn; Paul Shenar; Carl Lumbly; Frederick Coffin; Brad Greenquist; Directed by Curtis Hanson; Written by Curtis Hanson; Cinematography by Gilbert Taylor; Music by Patrick Gleeson; Michael Shrieve; Felix Mendelessohn. **Pr:** De Laurentiis Entertainment Group. **A:** Sr. High-Adult. **P:** Entertainment. **U:** Home. **Mov-Ent**: Mystery & Suspense. **Acq:** Purchase. **Dist:** Lions Gate Television Corp.; Facets Multimedia Inc. $9.99.

Bedrooms and Hallways 1998 (Unrated) — ★★1/2
Single gay Leo (McKidd) is urged to join a new agey men's therapy group where, during one of their meetings, he expresses his interest in Brendan (Purefoy), who's breaking up with longtime lover, Sally (Ehle). After Leo and Brendan get together, Leo realizes that Sally is his old high school girlfriend and there's still a certain spark between them. And things just get more complicated. Zippy if glib humor, although the film tends to lose steam at the end. 96m; VHS, DVD. **C:** Kevin McKidd; James Purefoy; Jennifer Ehle; Tom Hollander; Hugo Weaving; Simon Callow; Harriet Walter; Christopher Fulford; Julie Graham; Directed by Rose Troche; Written by Robert Farrar; Cinematography by Ashley Rowe; Music by Alfredo Troche. **A:** College-Adult. **P:** Entertainment. **U:** Home. **Mov-Ent**: Comedy--Romantic. **Acq:** Purchase. **Dist:** First Run Features.

Bedside Cardiac Output 1978
This program provides professional principles and training necessary to monitor bedside cardiac output. 33m; VHS, 3/4 U. **Pr:** Pyramid Film Productions. **A:** College-Adult. **P:** Professional. **U:** Institution, Home, SURA. **Hea-Sci:** Medical Care, Heart. **Acq:** Purchase, Rent/Lease, Duplication License. **Dist:** Pyramid Media.

Bedside Diagnosis in Cardiology 1974
A step-by-step diagnostic approach to a case of aortic regurgitation—from pulsating ear lobe and dancing tattoo to a correlation between the carotid pulse recording and the apex cardiogram and phono. 23m; 3/4 U. **Pr:** American College of Cardiology. **A:** College-Adult. **P:** Professional. **U:** Institution, CCTV. **Hea-Sci:** Documentary Films, Diagnosis. **Acq:** Purchase. **Dist:** American College of Cardiology.

Bedside Manners 1990
Using dramatizations, this tape focuses on how physician behavior affects patients. Non-verbal communication and the needs, concerns, and perceptions of patients are all covered. Practical and easily understood. 21m; VHS. **A:** College-Adult. **P:** Professional. **U:** Institution. **Hea-Sci:** Patient Care. **Acq:** Purchase. **Dist:** University of Connecticut Health Center. $130.00.

Bedside Manners 1992
Examines the changing position and work of doctors in North America. 60m; VHS. **A:** Adult. **P:** Education. **U:** Institution. **Gen-Edu:** Health Education, Sociology. **Acq:** Purchase. **Dist:** RMI Media. $89.95.

Bedside Safety 198?
Depicts several bedside accidents at a health care facility and how they could have been prevented. 13m; VHS, 3/4 U. **Pr:** National Safety Council. **A:** College-Adult. **P:** Education. **U:** Institution. **Hea-Sci:** Patient Care, Safety Education. **Acq:** Rent/Lease. **Dist:** National Safety Council, California Chapter, Film Library.

Bedtime for Bonzo 1951 (Unrated) — ★★½
A professor adopts a chimp to prove that environment, not heredity, determines a child's future. Fun, lighthearted comedy that stars a future president. Followed by "Bonzo Goes to College." 83m/B/W; VHS, DVD. **C:** Ronald Reagan; Diana Lynn; Walter Slezak; Jesse White; Bonzo the Chimp; Lucille Barkley; Herbert (Hayes) Heyes; Herb Vigran; Harry Tyler; Edward Clark; Directed by Fred de Cordova; Written by Lou Breslow; Val Burton; Cinematography by Carl Guthrie; Music by Frank Skinner. **Pr:** Mark Huffam. **A:** Family. **P:** Entertainment. **U:** Home. **Mov-Ent:** Comedy--Slapstick, Animals. **Acq:** Purchase. **Dist:** Facets Multimedia Inc. $14.95.

Bedtime for Frances 2009 (Unrated)
Animated children's television program. Based on the "Frances the Badger" storybook character, includes the full-length, animated version of "Bedtime for Frances," as well as a collection of episodes that star Frances, her sister, Gloria, and her best friend, Albert. 46m; DVD. **A:** Preschool-Primary. **P:** Entertainment. **U:** Home. **Mov-Ent:** Family Viewing, Animation & Cartoons, Children's Shows. **Acq:** Purchase. **Dist:** Lions Gate Entertainment Inc. $11.98.

Bedtime Stories 2008 (PG) — ★★½
Skeeter (Sandler) is a lowly maintenance guy at the hotel now standing on the site of the motel he and his sister (Cox) grew up in. Skeeter's lifelong dream of running it as his father (Pryce) once did seems unlikely as he toils under the loathsome hotel manager, Kendall (Pearce), a pompous dream-crusher who's double-timing his girlfriend Violet (Palmer)?the hotel owner's daughter who Skeeter has a colossal crush on. Skeeter's luck begins to change when he realizes, while caring for his sister's kids, that his wild bedtime stories of heroic daring can show up in real life. Thus he concocts tales giving him the upper hand with his boss and catching the eye of his girl. Uneven story but the outrageous special effects deliver a wholesome family comedy. 99m; Blu-Ray, Wide. **C:** Adam Sandler; Keri Russell; Guy Pearce; Courteney Cox; Teresa Palmer; Russell Brand; Lucy Lawless; Richard Griffiths; Jonathan Pryce; Aisha Tyler; Laura Ann Kesling; Madisen Beaty; Directed by Adam Shankman; Written by Tim Herlihy; Matt Lopez; Cinematography by Michael Barrett; Music by Rupert Gregson-Williams. **Pr:** Andrew Gunn; Adam Sandler; Jack Giarraputo; Adam Sandler; Happy Madison Productions; Offspring Entertainment; Conman and Izzy; Walt Disney Pictures. **A:** Family. **P:** Entertainment. **U:** Home. **L:** English. **Mov-Ent.** **Acq:** Purchase. **Dist:** Movies Unlimited; Alpha Video; Buena Vista Home Entertainment.

Bedtime Story 1963 (Unrated) — ★★
Two con artists attempt to fleece an apparently wealthy woman and each other on the French Riviera. Re-made in 1988 as "Dirty Rotten Scoundrels." One of Brando's thankfully few forays into comedy. 99m; VHS, DVD. **C:** Marlon Brando; David Niven; Shirley Jones; Dody Goodman; Marie Windsor; Directed by Ralph Levy. **Pr:** Universal Pictures. **A:** Jr. High-Adult. **P:** Entertainment. **U:** Home. **Mov-Ent:** Comedy--Screwball, France. **Acq:** Purchase. **Dist:** $14.98.

Bee Basics 1992
Presents a "Bee's-Eye View" of one of Nature's busiest and most benevolent insects. 12m; VHS, Special order formats. **A:** Primary. **P:** Education. **U:** Institution. **Gen-Edu:** Science, Insects. **Acq:** Purchase, Rent/Lease. **Dist:** Pyramid Media. $225.00.

Bee Breeding: The Search for the Perfect Honeybee 1988
A look at the work and genetic advances in bee breeding by Brother Adam, a 90-year-old English monk who stands as the world's foremost bee-breeder. 29m; VHS, 3/4 U. **A:** Family. **P:** Education. **U:** Institution, Home, SURA. **Hea-Sci:** Documentary Films, Insects, Genetics. **Acq:** Purchase, Duplication License. **Dist:** Bullfrog Films, Inc. $250.00.

The Bee Gees: Music Biography 19??
Contains 21 songs from the trio, with both live and video clips. 54m; VHS. **A:** Jr. High-Adult. **P:** Entertainment. **U:** Home. **Mov-Ent:** Music Video, Music--Pop/Rock. **Acq:** Purchase. **Dist:** Music Video Distributors. $59.95.

Bee Gees: One for All Tour, Vol. 1 1990
Part of a two-tape set in which the Brothers Gibb perform songs which span their entire career. Songs include, "Massachusetts," "How Deep Is Your Love?," "Nights on Broadway," "How Can You Mend a Broken Heart?" "Stayin Alive," "Jive Talkin" and more. 50m; VHS. **C:** Barry Gibb; Robin Gibb; Maurice Gibb. **Pr:** MPI Media Group. **A:** Jr. High-Adult. **P:** Entertainment. **U:** Home. **Mov-Ent:** Music--Performance. **Acq:** Purchase. **Dist:** Music Video Distributors; MPI Media Group. $16.95.

Bee Gees: One for All Tour, Vol. 2 1990
Part of a two-tape set in which the Brothers Gibb perform songs which span their entire career. Songs include, "Massachusetts," "How Deep Is Your Love?," "Nights on Broadway," "How Can You Mend a Broken Heart?" and many more. 50m; VHS. **C:** Barry Gibb; Takaaki Yamashita; Maurice Gibb. **Pr:** MPI Media Group. **A:** Jr. High-Adult. **P:** Entertainment. **U:** Home. **Mov-Ent:** Music--Performance. **Acq:** Purchase. **Dist:** Music Video Distributors; MPI Media Group. $16.95.

The Bee Gees: One Night Only 1997
The Bee Gees perform their first U.S. concert in almost 10 years at the MGM Grand in Las Vegas. Guest appearance by Celine Dion. 150m; DVD. **A:** Sr. High-Adult. **P:** Entertainment. **U:** Home. **Music:** Music--Performance, Music--Pop/Rock. **Acq:** Purchase. **Dist:** Acorn Media Group Inc. $19.99.

Bee Movie 2007 (PG) — ★★
A bee named Barry B. Benson (Seinfeld) finds himself on a mission when he learns that humans have been profiting off bees forever. Wanting more out of life than his job at a honey-production company can offer, Barry goes out in search of adventure and meets florist Vanessa (Zellweger), a former lawyer wannabe. A budding legal eagle himself, Barry ends up taking on the honey industry with Vanessa's help, and by recruiting all sorts of folks to further his cause (Sting and Larry King, among others). The environmental tones are sound, but the big names behind this film (Seinfeld also co-wrote and co-produced) are the only real buzz. There are bursts of cuteness and the kids will enjoy it, but the frenetic pace and endless string of one-liners tend to come off as just too much busyness. 90m; DVD, Blu-Ray. **C:** Voice(s) by Jerry Seinfeld; Renee Zellweger; Matthew Broderick; John Goodman; Patrick Warburton; Chris Rock; Kathy Bates; Barry Levinson; Oprah Winfrey; Larry Miller; Megan Mullally; Rip Torn; Michael Richards; Larry King; Ray Liotta; Sting; Directed by Simon J. Smith; Steve Hickner; Written by Jerry Seinfeld; Spike Feresten; Barry Marder; Andy Robin; Music by Rupert Gregson-Williams. **Pr:** Jerry Seinfeld; Christina Steinberg; Jerry Seinfeld; Columbus 81 Productions; DreamWorks Animation; Paramount. **A:** Family. **P:** Entertainment. **U:** Home. **L:** English. **Mov-Ent:** Insects, Animation & Cartoons, Bees. **Acq:** Purchase. **Dist:** DreamWorks Home Entertainment.

Bee Season 2005 (PG-13) — ★★★
Based on the bestselling novel by Myla Goldberg. Eleven-year-old Eliza (Cross), an average kid who lacks attention from her bright but aptly troubled parents, finds she's got a gift for spelling. Dad Saul (Gere), a religious studies professor and follower of Kabbalah mysticism, is at a loss as scientist wife Miriam (Binoche) teeters on the edge of instability. Meanwhile Eliza has fantastical visions of the words she is to spell as she wins local spelling bees and heads toward the national competition in Washington, D.C. Dad becomes obsessed with Eliza's gift, ignoring Miriam and their other child, Aaron (Minghella). Viewers who didn't read the book may be set adrift in this somewhat pretentious, but earnest film. 104m; DVD. **C:** Richard Gere; Juliette Binoche; Flora Cross; Max Minghella; Kate (Catherine) Bosworth; Directed by Scott McGehee; David Siegel; Written by Naomi Foner; Cinematography by Giles Nuttgens. **Pr:** Albert Berger; Ron Yerxa; Bona Fide; 20th Century-Fox. **A:** Jr. High-Adult. **P:** Entertainment. **U:** Home. **L:** English. **Mov-Ent:** Gifted Children, Judaism. **Acq:** Purchase. **Dist:** Fox Home Entertainment.

The Bee/The Butterflies: Beyond Beauty 197?
"The Bee" debunks the myth of bee's danger. "Butterflies-Beyond Beauty" explores courting fights, migrations, and transformation from pupa to adult. 46m; VHS, 3/4 U, Special order formats. **Pr:** Time-Life Films. **A:** Family. **P:** Education. **U:** Institution, SURA. **Gen-Edu:** Documentary Films, Insects. **Acq:** Purchase. **Dist:** Time-Life Video and Television.

Beebtots 19??
Four favorite cartoon features, with Noggin, Ivor, Glancers and Bagpuss. From British TV. 52m; VHS. **Pr:** British Broadcasting Corporation. **A:** Preschool-Jr. High. **P:** Entertainment. **U:** Home. **Mov-Ent:** Children, Animation & Cartoons. **Acq:** Purchase. **Dist:** Video Collectibles. $14.98.

Beef and the Slicing Machine 1980
Proper slicing methods for maximizing profits from roast beef, corned beef, and pastrami are demonstrated in this program. 15m; VHS, 3/4 U. **Pr:** Culinary Institute of America. **A:** College-Adult. **P:** Instruction. **U:** Institution, SURA. **How-Ins:** Cooking. **Acq:** Purchase, Rent/Lease. **Dist:** Culinary Institute of America.

Beef Carcass Evaluation 1988
Scrutinizes animal carcasses for maturing, marbling, color, and quality. Checks fat depths of special areas. Defines standards of evaluation. 31m; VHS. **A:** College-Adult. **P:** Education. **U:** Institution. **Gen-Edu:** Agriculture, Animals. **Acq:** Purchase. **Dist:** Purdue University. $15.00.

Beef Cattle Castration 19??
Presents information on basic beef cattle physiology, testicle function and reasons for castration. Emphasis is placed on health considerations and infection prevention. ?m; VHS. **A:** Jr. High-Adult. **P:** Instruction. **U:** Institution. **How-Ins:** Agriculture, Animals, Veterinary Medicine. **Acq:** Purchase. **Dist:** CEV Multimedia. $49.95.

Beef Cut Judging 19??
Points out the parts and principles associated with beef cut judging with the help of five examples of wholesale cuts classes (rounds, loins, shortloins, ribs, and oven-prepared ribs) and three retail cut classes (T-Bone, Porterhouse, and Blade steaks). Also contains the placing and showing of eight demonstration classes. 31m; VHS. **A:** Sr. High-Adult. **P:** Vocational. **U:** Institution. **Gen-Edu:** Agriculture, Food Industry. **Acq:** Purchase. **Dist:** CEV Multimedia. $59.95.

Beef Fillet Saute 1988
Offers instruction on specific aspects of cooking and food preparation. 6m; VHS. **A:** Adult. **P:** Instruction. **U:** Institution. **Gen-Edu:** Cooking. **Acq:** Purchase. **Dist:** RMI Media. $39.95.

Beef Forequarter Fabrication 19??
Reveals the processes by which beef forequarters are turned into chuck, rib, plate, brisket, and shank. Also discusses the fundamentals of beef grading, carcass ribbing, and breaking. 25m; VHS. **A:** Sr. High-Adult. **P:** Vocational. **U:** Institution. **Gen-Edu:** Food Industry, Agriculture. **Acq:** Purchase. **Dist:** CEV Multimedia. $59.95.

Beef Hindquarters Fabrication 19??
Illustrates the procedures involved in the fabrication of beef hindquarters into round, rump, sirloin, loin, flank, and subsequent cutting into closely trimmed retail cuts. Discusses the various cuts, retail yield, safety, and hygiene associated with these procedures. 21m; VHS. **A:** Sr. High-Adult. **P:** Vocational. **U:** Institution. **Gen-Edu:** Food Industry, Agriculture. **Acq:** Purchase. **Dist:** CEV Multimedia. $69.95.

Beef Judging Practice Class 19??
Part of the "Livestock Judging Video Set #2." Contains information on judging beef cattle, including footage of various views and of different breed classes such as Shorthorn Heifers, Angus Heifers, and Polled Hereford Heifers. ?m; VHS. **A:** Jr. High-Adult. **P:** Instruction. **U:** Institution. **How-Ins:** Agriculture, Animals, How-To. **Acq:** Purchase. **Dist:** CEV Multimedia. $49.95.

Beef Management Practices Video Transfer Series 19??
Series of filmstrips that have been transferred to video that teaches different aspects of beef management, including beef cattle castration, dehorning beef cattle, basic nutrition for beef cattle, identification of beef cattle, preventative health care, calving management, and equipment and facilities handling. ?m; VHS. **A:** Sr. High-Adult. **P:** Education. **U:** Institution. **Gen-Edu:** Agriculture, Food Industry, Animals. **Acq:** Purchase. **Dist:** CEV Multimedia. $19.95.

Beef Quality Grading 19??
Provides a thorough explanation of the aspects of beef quality grading while displaying all five carcass maturity scores, describing the principles of percent ossification in the top three buttons, and marbling scores ranging from PD to MdAb. Emphasis is placed on USDA Quality Grading for Prime, Choice, Select, Standard, Commercial, and Utility. 24m; VHS. **A:** Sr. High-Adult. **P:** Vocational. **U:** Institution. **Gen-Edu:** Agriculture, Food Industry. **Acq:** Purchase. **Dist:** CEV Multimedia. $59.95.

Beef Reproduction, Breeding & Calving, Part I 19??
Contains information on bull and heifer selection for reproduction, functional anatomy of the bull and cow, and footage of sperm and egg cells. Also provides quizzes with answers. 30m; VHS. **A:** Jr. High-Adult. **P:** Instruction. **U:** Institution. **How-Ins:** Agriculture, Animals, Reproduction. **Acq:** Purchase. **Dist:** CEV Multimedia. $79.95.

Beef Reproduction, Breeding & Calving, Part II 19??
Provides information on breeding beef cattle such as the estrous cycle and period, natural mating, semen collection and processing, pregnancy diagnosis, ovum development, and reproductive tracts during pregnancy. Contains quizzes with answers. 43m; VHS. **A:** Jr. High-Adult. **P:** Instruction. **U:** Institution. **How-Ins:** Agriculture, Animals, Reproduction. **Acq:** Purchase. **Dist:** CEV Multimedia. $79.95.

Beef Reproduction III 19??
Final section of the three-part series which covers reproduction in beef cattle. Presents five fetuses at various stages of development to help explain palpation, stages of calving, assistance at calving, and post-calving managemnt. 36m; VHS. **A:** Sr. High-Adult. **P:** Education. **U:** Institution. **Hea-Sci:** Agriculture, Animals, Veterinary Medicine. **Acq:** Purchase. **Dist:** CEV Multimedia. $79.95.

Beef Retail Cut Identification 19??
Teaches the different principles of beef cuts identification. Uses examples of a live steer, a skeleton, and a side of beef to illustrate the wholesale cuts and major bones. Contains footage of more than 50oneless and bone-in retail cuts and gives their accepted industry names. 41m; VHS. **A:** Sr. High-Adult. **P:**

Vocational. **U:** Institution. **Gen-Edu:** Agriculture, Food Industry. **Acq:** Purchase. **Dist:** CEV Multimedia. $59.95.

Beef Slaughter and Dressing 19??
Expert beef skinner and USDA veterinarian inspector illustrate the steps involved in the slaughter and dressing of cattle. They discuss safety, dressing yield, and USDA inspection criteria. 36m; VHS. **A:** Sr. High-Adult. **P:** Vocational. **U:** Institution. **Gen-Edu:** Agriculture, Animals, Food Industry. **Acq:** Purchase. **Dist:** CEV Multimedia. $59.95.

Beef Yield Grading 19??
Explains beef yield grading, covering the fundamentals of estimating the PYG, REA, and KPH and calculating USDA Yield Grade. Also uses five typical YG carcasses to help demonstrate advanced yield grading with instructions on adjustment of the preliminary yield grade. 21m; VHS. **A:** Sr. High-Adult. **P:** Vocational. **U:** Institution. **Gen-Edu:** Agriculture, Food Industry. **Acq:** Purchase. **Dist:** CEV Multimedia. $59.95.

Beefcake 1999 — ★★
Campy docudrama set in 1950s L.A. covers the muscle (or men's physique) magazine culture. Doting mama's boy Bob Mizer (MacIvor) found his talents as a still photographer and filmmaker, who also published Physique Pictorial, all of which featured chiseled studs. While Mizer insisted that his models were just clean-cut, all-American boys, he still fell afoul of pornography charges and operating a prostitution ring. The mock style turns harder-edged with Mizer's tribulations. To further confuse things, the film also includes present-day interviews with some of Mizer's one-time models and others familiar with the culture. 93m; VHS, DVD. **C:** Daniel MacIvor; Josh Peace; Carroll Godsman; Directed by Thom Fitzgerald; Written by Thom Fitzgerald; Cinematography by Thomas M. (Tom) Harting; Music by John Roby. **A:** College-Adult. **P:** Entertainment. **U:** Home. **Mov-Ent:** Documentary Films, Men, Photography. **Acq:** Purchase. **Dist:** Strand Releasing.

Beehive 1985
Although it sounds like a sequel to "Hairspray," this experimental film is teeming with dancing and animation. A worker bee is accidently turned into a queen bee by a drone. Beautiful and fascinating. 16m; VHS. **C:** Directed by Frank Moore; Jim Self; Written by Frank Moore; Jim Self. **A:** Family. **P:** Entertainment. **U:** Home. **Mov-Ent:** Animation & Cartoons, Insects, Dance. **Acq:** Purchase. **Dist:** Facets Multimedia Inc. $29.95.

Been Rich All My Life 2006
Describes the history of the Silver Belles, five tap dancing women who performed at the Apollo and Cotton Club in the 1930s and reunited several decades later. 80m; DVD. **A:** Primary-Adult. **P:** Entertainment. **U:** Home. **Mov-Ent:** Documentary Films, Dance, Women. **Acq:** Purchase. **Dist:** First Run Features. $24.95.

Beep Beep 1975
Two boys build a wondrous packing crate "car," but one is so unwilling to share the driver's seat that the car and perhaps the friendship end in rubble. Useful in provoking creative expression. 12m; VHS, 3/4 U. **Pr:** Churchill Films. **A:** Primary. **P:** Education. **U:** Institution, Home, SURA. **Chl-Juv:** Language Arts. **Acq:** Purchase, Duplication License. **Dist:** Clear Vue Inc.

Beer 1985 (R) — ★
A female advertising executive devises a dangerous sexist campaign for a cheap beer, and both the beer and its nickname become nationwide obsessions. Not especially amusing. 83m; VHS, DVD, Streaming, CC. **C:** Loretta Swit; Rip Torn; Dick Shawn; David Alan Grier; William Russ; Kenneth Mars; Peter Michael Goetz; Directed by Patrick Kelly; Cinematography by Bill Butler; Music by Bill Conti. **Pr:** Orion Pictures. **A:** Sr. High-Adult. **P:** Entertainment. **U:** Home. **Mov-Ent:** Comedy--Screwball, Advertising. **Acq:** Purchase. **Dist:** Unknown Distributor.

Beer and Ale: A Video Guide 1993
Surveys the brewery industry for connisseurs, covering history, terminology, and local types. 55m; VHS. **A:** Adult. **P:** Education. **U:** Institution. **Gen-Edu:** Alcoholic Beverages. **Acq:** Purchase. **Dist:** Paragon Home Video. $24.95.

Beer Drinker in a Champagne World 1992
Part of the "Upon Reflection" series, this program features Edward Villela, priemere dancer, discussing his childhood in New York City, and his book, "Prodigal Son: Dancing for Balanchine in a World of Pain and Magic." 28m; VHS. **A:** Sr. High-Adult. **P:** Education. **U:** Institution. **Gen-Edu:** Biography, Dance. **Acq:** Purchase. **Dist:** University of Washington Educational Media Collection. $15.00.

Beer for My Horses 2008 (PG-13) — ★
Country singer Toby Keith writes and stars in this dim comedy adaptation of one of his songs. Rack and Lonnie are deputies in a usually quiet small southern town. Then Rack's girlfriend is kidnapped by a drug lord whose brother has been arrested, and the duo, joined by fellow lawman Skunk, go on a rescue mission. Stick to the music career, Toby. 86m; DVD. **C:** Ted Nugent; Tom Skerritt; Claire Forlani; Greg Serano; Toby Keith; Rodney Carrington; Carlos Sanz; Barry Corbin; Willie Nelson; Gina Gershon; Directed by Mikael Salomon; Written by Toby Keith; Rodney Carrington; Cinematography by Paul Elliott; Music by Toby Keith; Jeff Cardoni. **A:** Jr. High-Adult. **P:** Entertainment. **U:** Home. **Mov-Ent. Acq:** Purchase. **Dist:** Lions Gate Entertainment Inc.

The Beer Hunter 19??
Beer expert and author Michael Jackson takes a tour of four-star breweries in Germany, Austria, Britain, Holland, and elsewhere. Learn about the different types of beer, brewing history and customs, and high-tech innovations. On three cassettes. Originally broadcast on The Discovery Channel. 180m; VHS. **A:** College-Adult. **P:** Entertainment. **U:** Home. **Gen-Edu:** Alcoholic Beverages. **Acq:** Purchase. **Dist:** Discovery Home Entertainment; Baker and Taylor. $49.95.

Beer League 2006 (R) — ★
Howard Stern sidekick Lange sticks to his booze, smokes, and broads persona as Artie DeVanzo, the head of a lousy New Jersey softball team at war with their perennial winning crosstown rivals. The deadbeat team of losers can't win a game, but that's okay, they've got beer and brawls. Except that the local law is fed up and demands the team either win or be forced to disband. Oh, the horror. If you actually know who Lange is, you know what to expect, and criticism is beside the point. Sit back and have another beer. 86m; DVD. **C:** Artie Lange; Ralph Macchio; Anthony De Sando; Seymour Cassel; Cara Buona; Jimmy Palumbo; Joe Lo Truglio; Laurie Metcalf; Directed by Frank Sebastiano; Written by Frank Sebastiano; Cinematography by David Phillips; Music by B.C. Smith. **Pr:** Anthony Mastromauro; Artie Lange; Artie Lange; Identity Films; Ckrush Entertainment; Echo Bridge Home Entertainment. **A:** Sr. High-Adult. **P:** Entertainment. **U:** Home. **L:** English. **Mov-Ent:** Sports--Fiction: Comedy, Softball. **Acq:** Purchase. **Dist:** Echo Bridge Home Entertainment.

Beer With Us 19??
Features classic beer commercials. ?m; VHS. **A:** Family. **P:** Entertainment. **U:** Home. **Mov-Ent:** Television Series, Commercials. **Acq:** Purchase. **Dist:** Video Resources.

Beerfest 2006 (R) — ★★
It's from those Broken Lizard boys, so don't go looking for sophistication. American brothers Todd and Jan Wolfhouse travel to Germany's Oktoberfest and stumble across a secret, long-standing beer competition. They also meet the arrogant German branch of the family who humiliate the brothers when they attempt to enter the contest and stand up for American males' ability to drink themselves stupid. "Strange Brew" meets "Fight Club" as this raucous comedy will probably become an instructional video to aspiring frat boys everywhere. 111m; DVD, Blu-Ray. **C:** Jay Chandrasekhar; Kevin Heffernan; Steve Lemme; Paul Soter; Erik Stolhanske; Eric Christian Olsen; Cloris Leachman; Donald Sutherland; Mo'Nique; Jurgen Prochnow; M.C. Gainey; Will Forte; Blanchard Ryan; Ralph (Ralf) Moeller; Directed by Jay Chandrasekhar; Written by Jay Chandrasekhar; Kevin Heffernan; Steve Lemme; Paul Soter; Erik Stolhanske; Cinematography by Frank DeMarco; Music by Nathan Barr. **Pr:** Bill Gerber; Richard Perello; Gerber Pictures; Legendary Pictures; Cataland Films; Broken Lizard; Warner Bros. **A:** Sr. High-Adult. **P:** Entertainment. **U:** Home. **L:** English. **Mov-Ent:** Germany. **Acq:** Purchase. **Dist:** Warner Home Video, Inc.

The Bees 1978 (PG) — **Bomb!**
Sting of a poor movie is painful. A strain of bees have ransacked South America and are threatening the rest of the world. The buzz is that no one is safe. Cheap rip-off of "The Swarm," which is saying something. 93m; VHS. **C:** John Saxon; John Carradine; Angel Tompkins; Claudio Brook; Alicia Encinas; Directed by Alfredo Zacharias. **Pr:** New World Pictures; Bee One Panorama Films. **A:** Jr. High-Adult. **P:** Entertainment. **U:** Home. **Mov-Ent:** Science Fiction, Bees. **Acq:** Purchase. **Dist:** Warner Home Video, Inc. $29.98.

Bees: Backyard Science—Revised 1978
Presents the way in which a colony of bees is formed. 13m; VHS, 3/4 U. **Pr:** Norman Bean; Marjorie Bean. **A:** Primary. **P:** Education. **U:** Institution, SURA. **Hea-Sci:** Documentary Films, Insects. **Acq:** Purchase. **Dist:** Phoenix Learning Group.

Bees in Paradise 1944 (Unrated) — ★★
Typical wartime comedy from Askey. Four airmen are forced to parachute out of their plane and they land on a tropical isle populated entirely by women. They think this is wonderful until they realize why there are no other men around. The women practice a marriage ceremony that requires the new hubby to commit suicide after the honeymoon. Arthur and his fellows try to convince the ladies that part of the ritual really isn't necessary. 72m/B/W; DVD. **C:** Arthur Askey; Peter Graves; Jean Kent; Max Bacon; Ronald Shiner; Antoinette Cellier; Joy Shelton; Beatrice Varley; Anne Shelton; Directed by Val Guest; Written by Val Guest; Marriott Edgar; Cinematography by Phil Grindrod. **A:** Jr. High-Adult. **P:** Entertainment. **U:** Home. **Mov-Ent. Acq:** Purchase. **Dist:** Movies Unlimited.

Beethoven 1936 — ★★
Startling biography of the musical genius, filled with opulent, impressionistic visuals. French with subtitles. 116m/B/W; VHS, DVD. **C:** Harry Baur; Jean-Louis Barrault; Marcel Dalio; Directed by Abel Gance; Written by Abel Gance; Cinematography by Marc Fossard; Robert Lefebvre. **A:** College-Adult. **P:** Entertainment. **U:** Home. **L:** French. **Mov-Ent:** Biography: Music. **Acq:** Purchase. **Dist:** Tapeworm Video Distributors Inc. $59.95.

Beethoven 1992 (PG) — ★★½
Adorable St. Bernard puppy escapes from dognappers and wanders into the home of the Newtons, who, over dad's objections, adopt him. Beethoven grows into a huge, slobbering dog who sorely tries dad's patience. To make matters worse, two sets of villains also wreak havoc on the Newton's lives. Evil veterinarian Dr. Varnick plots to steal Beethoven for lab experiments, and yuppie couple Brad and Brie plot to take over the family business. Enjoyable cast, particularly Grodin as dad and Chris as Beethoven enable this movie to please more than the milk and cookies set. Followed by "Beethoven's 2nd." 89m; VHS, DVD, CC. **C:** Charles Grodin; Bonnie Hunt; Dean Jones; Oliver Platt; Stanley Tucci; Nicholle Tom; Christopher Castile; Sarah Rose Karr; David Duchovny; Patricia Heaton; Laurel Cronin; Directed by Brian Levant; Written by John Hughes; Amy Holden Jones; Cinematography by Victor Kemper; Music by Randy Edelman. **Pr:** Ivan Reitman; Joe Medjuck; Michael Gross. **A:** Family. **P:** Entertainment. **U:** Home. **Mov-Ent:** Comedy--Slapstick, Pets, Family. **Acq:** Purchase. **Dist:** Facets Multimedia Inc. $14.98.

Beethoven By Barenboim 1987
A documentary series devoted to an analysis of Beethoven's life and music. 28m; VHS, 3/4 U. **C:** Narrated by Daniel Barenboim. **Pr:** Films for the Humanities and Sciences. **A:** College-Adult. **P:** Education. **U:** Institution, SURA. **Fin-Art:** Documentary Films, Music--Classical, Biography. **Acq:** Purchase. **Dist:** Films for the Humanities & Sciences. $29.98.
Indiv. Titles: 1. Beethoven, the Promethean 2. Minuet into Scherzo 3. The Appassionata 4. The Working Process 5. Beethoven and the Sonata Form 6. The Comprehensive Vision 7. Orpheus Taming the Furies 8. Amid Tears and Sorrow 9. The Eroica 10. The Symphonist 11. The Late Works 12. The Last Piano Sonata 13. The Fifth Symphony.

Beethoven 'Eroica' Symphony: Serebrier 1989
Beethoven's "Eroica," Tchaikovsky's "Symphony No. 1," and Prokofiev's "Alexander Nevsky" conducted by the renowned master, Serebrier. 134m; VHS. **C:** Conducted by Jose Serebrier. **Pr:** Kultur. **A:** Family. **P:** Entertainment. **U:** Home. **Fin-Art:** Music--Classical. **Acq:** Purchase. **Dist:** Kultur International Films Ltd., Inc. $29.95.

Beethoven: Klassix 13 19??
The life and times of the great German composer are explored in this documentary, featuring landmarks of his life—his homes in Bonn and Wien, the cemetery where he is buried, and parts of the Rheinland. 60m; VHS. **TV Std:** NTSC, PAL. **C:** Anthony Quayle; Balint Vazsonyi. **A:** Sr. High-Adult. **P:** Entertainment. **U:** Home. **Fin-Art:** Documentary Films, Music--Classical, Biography. **Acq:** Purchase. **Dist:** Music Video Distributors; German Language Video Center. $24.95.

Beethoven Lives Upstairs 1992 (Unrated) — ★★½
In 19th century Vienna 10 year-old Christoph's life is turned upside-down when the family's eccentric new tenant turns out to be composer Ludwig Van Beethoven. In time, Christoph comes to appreciate the beauty of the music and the tragedy of the composer's deafness. Features more than 25 excerpts of Beethoven's works. 52m; VHS, DVD, CC. **C:** Neil Munro; Ilya Woloshyn; Fiona Reid; Paul Soles; Sheila McCarthy; Albert Schultz; Directed by David Devine; Written by Heather Conkie. **A:** Family. **P:** Entertainment. **U:** Home. **Mov-Ent:** Music--Classical, Biography: Music. **Acq:** Purchase. **Dist:** BMG Entertainment; Music Video Distributors. $19.98.

Beethoven: Missa Solemnis 19??
Features the Berlin Philharmonic Orchestra conducted by Von Karajan with soloists Baldani, Tomowa-Sintow, Tappy and van Dam. 83m; DVD. **Pr:** Polygram Music Video. **A:** Jr. High-Adult. **P:** Entertainment. **U:** Home. **Fin-Art:** Music--Classical. **Acq:** Purchase. **Dist:** Music Video Distributors. $34.95.

Beethoven Piano Concerti 1989 (Unrated)
Pianist Murray Perahia plays Beethoven's concertos at the Royal Festival Hall along with the Academy of St. Martin-in-the-Fields, conducted by Sir Neville Mariner. The series also includes interviews of Perahia conducted by Jane Glover of the London Mozart players. 70m; VHS. **C:** Claudio Arrau; Murray Perahia. **Pr:** Home Vision. **A:** Family. **P:** Entertainment. **U:** Institution, Home. **Mov-Ent:** Music--Performance, Interviews. **Acq:** Purchase. **Dist:** Music Video Distributors; Home Vision Cinema. $29.95.
Indiv. Titles: 1. Beethoven: Piano Concertos 1 & 3 2. Beethoven: Piano Concertos 2 & 4 3. Beethoven: Piano Concerto 5.

Beethoven: Piano Concerti 3 & 4 199?
Bernstein's final conducting project for the camera. Krystian Zimerman is the featured pianist, performing with the Vienna Philharmonic Orchestra. 79m; VHS. **A:** Jr. High-Adult. **P:** Entertainment. **U:** Home. **Mov-Ent:** Music Video, Music--Performance. **Acq:** Purchase. **Dist:** Music Video Distributors. $24.95.

Beethoven: Piano Concerti 4 & 5 19??
Features pianist Claudio Arrau and both the Philadelphia Orchestra conducted by Riccardo Muti (in the fourth concerto) and the London Symphony conducted by Sir Colin Davis (in the fifth concerto). 81m; VHS. **Pr:** Polygram Music Video. **A:** Jr. High-Adult. **P:** Entertainment. **U:** Home. **Fin-Art:** Music--Classical. **Acq:** Purchase. **Dist:** Music Video Distributors. $24.95.

Beethoven: Piano Concerto No. 3 19??
Beethoven and Brahms' first Piano Concerto is heard live from Amsterdam's Concertgebouw Hall. 84m; VHS. **Pr:** Unitel. **A:** Jr. High-Adult. **P:** Entertainment. **U:** Home. **Mov-Ent:** Music Video, Music--Performance, Music--Classical. **Acq:** Purchase. **Dist:** Music Video Distributors. $24.95.

Beethoven: Piano Concerto No. 5 "Emperor" 19??
Leonard Bernstein conducts the Vienna Philharmonic Orchestra. Krystian Zimerman is the featured pianist. 45m; VHS. **A:** Jr. High-Adult. **P:** Entertainment. **U:** Home. **Mov-Ent:** Music Video, Music--Performance, Music--Classical. **Acq:** Purchase. **Dist:** Music Video Distributors. $24.95.

Beethoven, Schumann & Brahms 1985
An orchestral concert featuring short works by the three composers. Weissenberg performs Schubert's "Arabeske in C," "Kinderszenen," Beethoven's 7th Violin Sonata and Brahms' "Lieder," and is joined by Pierre Amoyal (Violin) and Teresa Berganza (Mezzo-soprano). 55m; VHS. **Pr:** Sony Video. **A:** Sr. High-Adult. **P:** Entertainment. **U:** Home. **Fin-Art:** Music--Classical. **Acq:** Purchase. **Dist:** Music Video Distributors; Kultur International Films Ltd., Inc.

Beethoven String Quartets 19??
Features music by the Guarneri Quartet. 58m. **A:** Jr. High-Adult. **P:** Entertainment. **U:** Home. **Fin-Art:** Music--Classical. **Acq:** Purchase. **Dist:** Music Video Distributors. $74.95.

Beethoven: String Quartets 9 & 11 19??
The Guarnieri Quartet performs some Beethoven. ?m; VHS. **A:** Sr. High-Adult. **P:** Entertainment. **U:** Home. **Fin-Art:** Music--Classical. **Acq:** Purchase. **Dist:** Music Video Distributors. $29.95.

Beethoven: Symphonies 1 and 8 1991
Features the Berlin Philharmonic Orchestra conducted by Herbert von Karajan. ?m; DVD. **A:** Jr. High-Adult. **P:** Entertainment. **U:** Home. **Fin-Art:** Music--Classical. **Acq:** Purchase. **Dist:** Music Video Distributors. $64.95.

Beethoven: Symphonies 2 and 3 1991
Features the Berlin Philharmonic Orchestra conducted by Herbert von Karajan. 84m. **A:** Jr. High-Adult. **P:** Entertainment. **U:** Home. **Fin-Art:** Music--Classical. **Acq:** Purchase. **Dist:** Music Video Distributors. $79.95.

Beethoven: Symphonies 4 & 7 19??
Carlos Kleiber conducts the Amsterdam Concertgebouw Orchestra. 72m; VHS. **A:** Sr. High-Adult. **P:** Entertainment. **U:** Home. **Fin-Art:** Music--Classical. **Acq:** Purchase. **Dist:** Music Video Distributors. $24.95.

Beethoven: Symphonies 5 & 6 19??
Leonard Bernstein conducts the Vienna Philharmonic Orchestra in this UNITEL feature. 102m; VHS. **A:** Sr. High-Adult. **P:** Entertainment. **U:** Home. **Fin-Art:** Music--Classical. **Acq:** Purchase. **Dist:** Music Video Distributors. $24.95.

Beethoven: Symphonies 6 and 7 19??
Features the Berlin Philharmonic Orchestra conducted by Herbert von Karajan. 73m; DVD. **A:** Jr. High. **P:** Entertainment. **U:** Home. **Fin-Art:** Music--Classical. **Acq:** Purchase. **Dist:** Music Video Distributors. $79.95.

Beethoven Symphonies: 1-9 2013 (Unrated)
Live taping of Claudio Abbado and the Berlin Philharmonic performing Beethoven's Symphonies. 413m; DVD, Blu-Ray. **A:** Family. **P:** Entertainment. **U:** Home. **L:** English, French, German, Spanish. **Gen-Edu:** Music--Classical, Music--Performance. **Acq:** Purchase. **Dist:** EuroArts Entertainment. $89.99 34.99.

Beethoven: Symphony No. 3 "Eroica" and 7 1985
Bernstein conducts two of Beethoven's greatest "heroic" symphonies, written during the most productive years of the composer's life. 97m; VHS. **A:** Family. **P:** Entertainment. **U:** Home. **Fin-Art:** Music--Classical. **Acq:** Purchase. **Dist:** Music Video Distributors; Kultur International Films Ltd., Inc.; Facets Multimedia Inc. $24.95.

Beethoven: Symphony No. 3—Eroica 1985
Conductor Jose Serebrier leads the Melbourne and Sydney Symphony Orchestras in the performance of three classical music selections: Prokofiev's "Alexander Neusky"; Tchaikovsky's "Symphony No. 1"; and Beethoven's "Symphony No. 3 (Eroica)." 134m; VHS. **A:** Jr. High-Adult. **P:** Entertainment. **U:** Home. **Fin-Art:** Performing Arts, Music--Performance, Music--Classical. **Acq:** Purchase. **Dist:** Kultur International Films Ltd., Inc. $19.95.

Beethoven: Symphony No. 5 1990
Fine production of what may the most recognizable symphony of all time. 51m; VHS. **A:** Family. **P:** Entertainment. **U:** Home. **Fin-Art:** Music--Performance, Music--Classical. **Acq:** Purchase. **Dist:** Music Video Distributors. $19.95.

Beethoven: Symphony No. 5-Concert Aid 1985
Solti conducts the gorgeous BBC Symphony Orchestra in this benefit sponsored by Oxfam which raised over $30 million in charity relief for Ethiopia and Sudan. 40m; VHS. **C:** Conducted by George Solti. **A:** Jr. High-Family. **P:** Entertainment. **U:** Home. **Fin-Art:** Music--Performance, Performing Arts. **Acq:** Purchase. **Dist:** Music Video Distributors; Kultur International Films Ltd., Inc. $19.95.

Beethoven Symphony No. 6 "Pastoral" 1992
Jean-Claude Casadesus conducts the National Orchestra of Lille in a performance of "Pastoral," a symphony that demonstrates Beethoven's love of nature. 49m; VHS. **A:** Jr. High-Adult. **P:** Entertainment. **U:** Home. **Mov-Ent:** Music Video, Music--Performance, Music--Classical. **Acq:** Purchase. **Dist:** V.I.E.W. Inc./Arkadia Entertainment Corp. $19.97.

Beethoven: Symphony No. 7/Excerpt from Symphony No. 5 19??
Ludwig's work is performed, and a discussion about the music is included as well. 90m; VHS. **C:** Conducted by Andre Previn. **A:** Sr. High-Adult. **P:** Entertainment. **U:** Home. **Fin-Art:** Music--Classical. **Acq:** Purchase. **Dist:** Music Video Distributors. $39.95.

Beethoven: Symphony No. 9 1979
Leonard Bernstein conducts the Vienna Philharmonic Orchestra in this September 1979 concert filmed at the Staatsoper, with soloists Gwyneth Jones, Hanna Schwartz, Rene Kollo, and Kurt Moll. 75m; VHS. **A:** College-Adult. **P:** Entertainment. **U:** Home. **Fin-Art:** Music--Classical, Music--Performance. **Acq:** Purchase. **Dist:** Music Video Distributors. $29.95.

Beethoven: Symphony No. 9 "Choral" 1990
Excellent production of this popular symphony. 60m; VHS, DVD. **C:** Anne McKnight; Jane Hoson; Irwin Dillon; Norman Scott. **Pr:** RCA. **A:** Sr. High-Adult. **P:** Entertainment. **U:** Home. **Fin-Art:** Music--Classical. **Acq:** Purchase. **Dist:** Music Video Distributors; BMG Entertainment; V.I.E.W. Inc./Arkadia Entertainment Corp. $24.95.

Beethoven: The Ninth Symphony 198?
The Vienna Philharmonic, conducted by Leonard Bernstein, celebrates the 200th anniversary of Beethoven's birth with the help of Gwyneth Jones, Placido Domingo, Martti Talvela, and Shirley Verrett. ?m; VHS. **A:** Adult. **P:** Entertainment. **U:** Home. **Fin-Art:** Music--Performance, Music--Classical. **Acq:** Purchase. **Dist:** Kultur International Films Ltd., Inc. $29.95.

Beethoven: Triumph Over Silence 1983
A look at Beethoven's deafness in relation to his music, and how the latter might have changed if he were permitted to hear it. 37m; VHS, 3/4 U. **Pr:** Hamid Naficy. **A:** Jr. High-Adult. **P:** Education. **U:** Institution, Home, SURA. **Gen-Edu:** Documentary Films, Deafness, Biography. **Acq:** Purchase, Rent/Lease. **Dist:** Pyramid Media.

Beethoven: Violin Concerto 19??
Famed musician Itzhak Perlman works Beethoven's compositions. ?m; VHS. **A:** Sr. High-Adult. **P:** Entertainment. **U:** Home. **Fin-Art:** Music--Classical. **Acq:** Purchase. **Dist:** Music Video Distributors. $19.95.

Beethoven's 2nd 1993 (PG) — ★★½
Sequel has awwww factor going for it as new daddy Beethoven slobbers over four adorable and appealing St. Bernard pups and his new love Missy. Same basic evil subplot as the first, with wicked kidnappers replacing evil vet. During the upheaval, the Newtons take care of the little yapping troublemakers, providing the backdrop for endless puppy mischief and exasperation on Grodin's part. Silly subplots and too many human moments tend to drag, but the kids will find the laughs (albeit stupid ones). 87m; VHS, DVD, Wide, CC. **C:** Charles Grodin; Bonnie Hunt; Nicholle Tom; Christopher Castile; Sarah Rose Karr; Debi Mazar; Christopher Penn; Ashley Hamilton; Directed by Rod Daniel; Written by Len Blum; Cinematography by Bill Butler; Music by Randy Edelman. **Pr:** Michael Gross; Joe Medjuck; Ivan Reitman; Universal Pictures. **A:** Family. **P:** Entertainment. **U:** Home. **Mov-Ent:** Comedy--Slapstick, Family, Pets. **Acq:** Purchase. **Dist:** Universal Music and Video Distribution. $14.98.

Beethoven's 3rd 2000 (PG) — ★★½
Dad Richard Newton (Reinhold) wants to take the family on vacation and, naturally, huge St. Bernard Beethoven is coming along. Suddenly, that rented luxury RV doesn't seem very big and dad's idea of fun is lame to the kids. Of course, it's not a typical vacation anyway, seems thieves Tommy (Ciccolini) and Bill (Marsh) need to retrieve a videotape that Richard has rented. Beethoven tries to protect his family while being blamed for every little mishap. A dog's life, indeed! 99m; VHS, DVD, Wide, CC. **C:** Judge Reinhold; Julia Sweeney; Joe Pichler; Michaela Gallo; Jamie Marsh; Michael Ciccolini; Frank Gorshin; Danielle Wiener; Directed by David Mickey Evans; Written by Jeff Schechter; Cinematography by John Aronson; Music by Philip Giffin. **A:** Family. **P:** Entertainment. **U:** Home. **Mov-Ent:** Pets, Family. **Acq:** Purchase. **Dist:** Movies Unlimited; Alpha Video.

Beethoven's 4th 2001 — ★½
Unruly Beethoven is sent to obedience school where he's accidentally switched with a well-behaved St. Bernard. Imagine the family's confusion. 94m; VHS, DVD, Wide. **C:** Judge Reinhold; Julia Sweeney; Joe Pichler; Michaela Gallo; Matt McCoy; Veanne Cox; Mark Lindsay Chapman; Art LaFleur; Kaleigh Krish; Natalie Marston; Directed by David Mickey Evans; Written by John Loy; Cinematography by John Aronson. **A:** Family. **P:** Entertainment. **U:** Home. **Mov-Ent:** Pets. **Acq:** Purchase. **Dist:** Movies Unlimited; Alpha Video.

Beethoven's 5th 2003 (Unrated) — ★★½
Twelve-year-old Sara (Chase) and Beethoven spend the summer with eccentric Uncle Freddy (Thomas) in the old mining town of Quicksilver. Beethoven manages to dig up an old $10 bill that apparently comes from some loot buried by a couple of crooks in the 1920s and soon everyone in town is looking for the rest of the cash. 90m; VHS, DVD. **C:** Daveigh Chase; Dave Thomas; Faith Ford; John Larroquette; Kathy Griffin; Tom Poston; Katherine Helmond; Clint Howard; Directed by Mark Griffiths; Written by Elana Lesser; Cliff Ruby; Cinematography by Christopher Baffa; Music by Adam Berry. **A:** Family. **P:** Entertainment. **U:** Home. **Mov-Ent:** Pets. **Acq:** Purchase. **Dist:** Movies Unlimited; Alpha Video.

Beethoven's Big Break 2008 (PG) — ★★½
Struggling animal trainer Eddie gets his big break as the wrangler for a movie star St. Bernard. But the dog's fame means some criminal-types have come up with a kidnapping and ransom scheme. 101m; DVD. **C:** Jonathan Silverman; Moises Arias; Rhea Perlman; Stephen Tobolowsky; Eddie Griffin; Osmar Nunez; Joey Fatone; Jennifer Finnigan; Directed by Mike Elliott; Written by Derek Rydall; Cinematography by Stephen Campbell; Music by Robert Folk. **A:** Family. **P:** Entertainment. **U:** Home. **Mov-Ent. Acq:** Purchase. **Dist:** Universal Studios Home Video.

Beethoven's Christmas Adventure 2011 (PG) — ★★½
Henry the elf accidentally takes off in Santa's toy-filled sleigh and crash lands in Beethoven's neighborhood. Santa's magic toy bag gets stolen and it's up to the St. Bernard (who now talks) and his human pal Mason to rescue Henry, retrieve the toy bag, and make sure that Christmas isn't ruined. 90m; DVD, Wide. **C:** Kyle Massey; Munro Chambers; Kim Rhodes; Robert Picardo; John O'Hurley; Curtis Armstrong; Voice(s) by Tom Arnold; Narrated by John Cleese; Directed by John Putch; Written by Daniel Altiere; Steven Altiere; Cinematography by Ross Berryman; Music by Chris Bacon. **A:** Family. **P:** Entertainment. **U:** Home. **Mov-Ent:** Christmas, Pets. **Acq:** Purchase. **Dist:** Universal Studios Home Video.

Beethoven's Nephew 1988 — ★½
A tepid pseudo-historical farce about Beethoven's strange obsession with his only nephew. Directed by erstwhile Warhol collaborator Morrissey. 103m; VHS. **C:** Wolfgang Reichmann; Ditmar Prinz; Jane Birkin; Nathalie Baye; Directed by Paul Morrissey; Written by Paul Morrissey; Matthieu Carriere. **Pr:** New World Pictures. **A:** Preschool. **P:** Entertainment. **U:** Home. **Mov-Ent:** Drama, Music--Classical. **Acq:** Purchase. **Dist:** Anchor Bay Entertainment. $9.99.

Beetle Bailey: Military Madness 1991
When that test bomb accidentally blows up in Sarge's face, you know Beetle's to blame. Find out more in this all new program, part of King Feature's "Animated Comics" series. 30m; VHS. **C:** Voice(s) by Howard Morris. **Pr:** King Features Entertainment. **A:** Family. **P:** Entertainment. **U:** Home. **L:** English, Spanish. **Mov-Ent:** Animation & Cartoons, Armed Forces--U.S. **Acq:** Purchase. **Dist:** Best Video. $9.99.

Beetle Bailey: Pranks in the Ranks 1991
Who put live ammo in the rifles during target practice? Probably Beetle. Find out for sure in this brand new comedy adventure from King Feature's "Animated Comics" series. 30m; VHS. **Pr:** King Features Entertainment. **A:** Family. **P:** Entertainment. **U:** Home. **L:** English, Spanish. **Mov-Ent:** Animation & Cartoons, Armed Forces--U.S. **Acq:** Purchase. **Dist:** Best Video. $9.99.

Beetle Bailey: Sarge's Last Stand 1991
Sarge has had it up to here, and Beetle's really in for it. A brand new adventure from the King Features "Animated Comics" series. 30m; VHS. **Pr:** King Features Entertainment. **A:** Family. **P:** Entertainment. **U:** Home. **L:** English, Spanish. **Mov-Ent:** Animation & Cartoons, Armed Forces--U.S. **Acq:** Purchase. **Dist:** Best Video. $9.99.

Beetlejuice 1988 (PG) — ★★★½
The after-life is confusing for a pair of ultra-nice novice ghosts Adam Maitland (Baldwin) and his wife Barbara (Davis), who are faced with chasing an obnoxious family of post-modern art lovers who move into their house. Then they hear of a poltergeist who promises to rid the house of all trespassers for a price. Things go from bad to impossible when the maniacal Keaton (as the demonic "Betelgeuse") works his magic. The calypso scene is priceless. A cheesy, funny, surreal farce of life after death with inventive set designs popping continual surprises. Ryder is striking as the misunderstood teen with a death complex, while O'Hara is hilarious as the yuppie art poseur. 92m; VHS, DVD, Blu-Ray, 8 mm, Wide, CC. **C:** Michael Keaton; Geena Davis; Alec Baldwin; Sylvia Sidney; Catherine O'Hara; Winona Ryder; Jeffrey Jones; Dick Cavett; Glenn Shadix; Robert Goulet; Directed by Tim Burton; Written by Michael McDowell; Warren Skaaren; Cinematography by Thomas Ackerman; Music by Danny Elfman. **A:** Adult. **P:** Entertainment. **U:** Home. **Mov-Ent:** Death. **Awds:** Oscars '88: Makeup; Natl. Soc. Film Critics '88: Actor (Keaton). **Acq:** Purchase. **Dist:** Facets Multimedia Inc.; Warner Home Video, Inc.; Time-Life Video and Television. $19.98.

Beetlejuice: The Series 1989
A cartoon series for kids based on the popular film. Each volume has three 15-minute episodes. 45m; VHS. **Pr:** Geffen Film Company. **A:** Preschool-Jr. High. **P:** Entertainment. **U:** Home. **Chl-Juv:** Children, Animation & Cartoons. **Acq:** Purchase. **Dist:** Warner Home Video, Inc. $14.95.

Beetlejuice, Vol. 1 1989
The ghost with the most is back in this animated cartoon. Episodes include: "Critter Sitters," "The Big Faceoff," and "Skeletons in the Closet." 45m; VHS. **Pr:** Nelvana Productions Ltd. **A:** Family. **P:** Entertainment. **U:** Home. **Chl-Juv:** Children, Animation & Cartoons. **Acq:** Purchase. **Dist:** Warner Home Video, Inc. $12.95.

Beetlejuice, Vol. 2 1989
The ghost with the most and his netherworld pal, Lydia shake up reality in this animated adventure. Three exciting episodes include: "Worm Welcome," "Out of My Mind," and "A Dandy Handy Man." 45m; VHS. **Pr:** Nelvana Productions Ltd. **A:** Family. **P:** Entertainment. **U:** Home. **Chl-Juv:** Children, Animation & Cartoons. **Acq:** Purchase. **Dist:** Warner Home Video, Inc. $12.95.

Beetlejuice, Vol. 3 1989
Beetlejuice and Lydia get into hilarious trouble in this animated adventure. Frightfully pleasant episodes include: "Pest of the West," "Stage Fright," and "Spooky Tree." 45m; VHS. **Pr:** Nelvana Productions Ltd. **A:** Family. **P:** Entertainment. **U:** Home. **Chl-Juv:** Children, Animation & Cartoons. **Acq:** Purchase. **Dist:** Warner Home Video, Inc. $12.95.

Beetlejuice, Vol. 5 1989
That beetle-crunching ghost with the most is back in these animated cartoons. Two spooky tales include: "Prince of the Netherworld" and "It's the Pits." 33m; VHS. **Pr:** Nelvana Productions Ltd. **A:** Family. **P:** Entertainment. **U:** Home. **Chl-Juv:** Children, Animation & Cartoons. **Acq:** Purchase. **Dist:** Warner Home Video, Inc. $12.95.

Beetlejuice, Vol. 6 1989
An animated Beetlejuice and Lydia take on the real world and the netherworld in these hilarious adventures. Episodes include: "Quit While You're a Head" and "Bad Neighbor Beetlejuice." 33m; VHS. **Pr:** Nelvana Productions Ltd. **A:** Family. **P:** Entertainment. **U:** Home. **Chl-Juv:** Children, Animation & Cartoons. **Acq:** Purchase. **Dist:** Warner Home Video, Inc. $12.95.

Beetles: Backyard Science 1967
Beetles are a common form of insect and are found almost everywhere. Examples of harmful and helpful beetles are given. 11m; VHS, 3/4 U. **Pr:** Norman Bean. **A:** Primary. **P:** Education. **U:** Institution, SURA. **Hea-Sci:** Documentary Films, Insects. **Acq:** Purchase. **Dist:** Phoenix Learning Group.

Beezbo 1985
The friendly alien Beezbo arrives on Earth with good intentions, but his ignorance of manners hampers his progress. Children will learn proper etiquette along with their alien friend. 70m; VHS, CC. **C:** Josh Williams; Melissa Clayton; Christopher Dalbec; Karen Renee; Directed by Robert C. Bailey. **Pr:** LCA. **A:** Preschool-Primary. **P:** Entertainment. **U:** Home. **L:** Spanish. **Chl-Juv:** Children, Etiquette. **Acq:** Purchase. **Dist:** Anchor Bay Entertainment; Facets Multimedia Inc. $19.95.

BEEZBO: Adventures in Learning Manners 1995
Teaches children manners, through a series of enjoyable adventures. 50m; VHS. **A:** Family. **P:** Education. **U:** Institution, Home. **Gen-Edu:** Children, Etiquette. **Acq:** Purchase. **Dist:** Cambridge Educational. $19.95.

Before and After 1995 (PG-13) — ★½
Disjointed drama depicts well-off suburban couple, Carolyn (Streep) and Ben (Neeson), who are thrown into chaos when their teenaged son Jacob (Furlong) is accused of murdering his girlfriend. Upon notification by the police that his son is the prime suspect and on the lam, Ben finds what seems to be bloody evidence in the family's car, which he destroys. The story loses steam from there. Based on the novel by Rosellen Brown, the focus is on the effect the death has on this picture book Massachusetts family. Neeson and Streep fall short of usually deliverable goods and director Schroeder takes the middle-of-the-road sentimental approach. 107m; VHS, DVD, Blu-Ray, CC. **C:** Meryl Streep; Liam Neeson; Edward Furlong; Alfred Molina; John Heard; Julia Weldon; Daniel von Bargen; Ann Magnuson; Alison Folland; Kaiulani Lee; Directed by Barbet Schroeder; Written by Ted Tally; Cinematography by Luciano Tovoli; Music by Howard Shore. **Pr:** Barbet Schroeder; Barbet Schroeder; Buena Vista. **A:** Jr. High-Adult. **P:** Entertainment. **U:** Home. **Mov-Ent:** Adolescence, Family, Law. **Acq:** Purchase. **Dist:** Buena Vista Home Entertainment.

Before and After Surgery—Revised 1987
A look for the patient at the pre- and post-operative hospital experience, designed to allay irrational fears. 15m; VHS, 3/4 U. **Pr:** Professional Research. **A:** Sr. High-Adult. **P:** Education. **U:** Institution, CCTV. **Hea-Sci:** Surgery, Patient Education. **Acq:** Purchase, Rent/Lease. **Dist:** Discovery Education.

Before and After the Pitch: Defensive Techniques for Pitchers 2006 (Unrated)
Coach Barry Davis discusses pitcher defense, and presents techniques for improving a pitchers defensive playing. 58m; DVD. **A:** Family. **P:** Education. **U:** Home, Institution. **How-Ins:** Baseball, Athletic Instruction/Coaching. **Acq:** Purchase. **Dist:** Championship Productions. $34.99.

Before and After Your Surgery—3rd edition 1984
This revised edition is designed to help diminish anxiety and promote patient cooperation before and after the hospital experience. Nursing care, medication and "recovery room" are also covered in this program. 15m; VHS, CC, 3/4 U, CV. **Pr:** Professional Research. **A:** Sr. High-Adult. **P:** Education. **U:** Institution, CCTV, SURA. **L:** English, Spanish. **Hea-Sci:** Surgery, Patient Education. **Acq:** Purchase, Rent/Lease. **Dist:** Discovery Education. $295.00.

Before I Forget 2007 (Unrated) — ★★
When his wealthy benefactor dies after 30 years of support and he doesn't get an expected inheritance, former gigolo Pierre (Nolot) struggles insouciantly to cope with age, poverty, and the increasing complications of his HIV status. He pursues sex with rent boys though he doesn't seem to take any pleasure in it, except for gossiping with his friend Georges (Pommier) about the cost, and takes an unsentimental look back on his life while writing his memoirs. French with subtitles. 108m; DVD. **C:** Jacques Nolot; Jean Pommier; Bastien d'Asnieres; Marc Rioufol; Jean-Pol Dubois; Cinematography by Josee Desaies. **A:** College-Adult. **P:** Entertainment. **U:** Home. **L:** French. **Mov-Ent:** Aging, Prostitution. **Acq:** Purchase. **Dist:** Strand Releasing.

Before I Hang 1940 — ★★★
When a doctor invents a youth serum from the blood of a murderer, he'll stop at nothing to keep his secret. Karloff himself stands the test of time, and is satisfying as the mad scientist, giving this horror flick its appeal. 60m/B/W; VHS, DVD. **C:** Boris Karloff; Evelyn Keyes; Bruce Bennett; Edward Van Sloan; Ben Taggart; Pedro de Cordoba; Wright Kramer; Bertram Marburgh; Don Beddoe; Robert (Fisk) Fiske; Directed by Nick Grinde; Written by Robert D. (Robert Hardy) Andrews; Cinematography by Benjamin (Ben H.) Kline. **A:** Family. **P:** Entertainment. **U:** Home. **Mov-Ent:** Horror. **Acq:** Purchase. **Dist:** Sony Pictures Home Entertainment Inc. $59.95.

Before I Say Goodbye 2003 (Unrated) — ★½
Political hopeful Nell's (Young) hubby faces accusations of crooked business deeds when he and his boat are blown to bits. But her desperate search for the truth might make her the next victim. A Mary Higgins Clark adaptation. 95m; VHS, DVD. **C:** Sean Young; Lloyd Bochner; Peter DeLuise; Ursula Karven; Directed by Michael Storey; Written by John Benjamin Martin; Jon Cooksey; Ali Matheson; Cinematography by David Pelletier. **A:** Jr. High-Adult. **P:** Entertainment. **U:** Home. **Mov-Ent:** Conspiracies or Conspiracy Theories, Mystery & Suspense. **Acq:** Purchase. **Dist:** Allumination Filmworks. $24.99.

Before It's Too Late 1993
Investigates modern zoos, emphasizing their focus on preservation rather than exhibition. Highlights the efforts of Australia's Perth Zoo, the Jersey Preservation Trust, and the Bronx Zoo to protect animals threatened by predators and pollution. 48m; VHS. **C:** Directed by Peter Du Cane. **Pr:** Storytellers Productions. **A:** Jr. High-Adult. **P:** Education. **U:** Institution. **Gen-Edu:** Zoos, Animals. **Acq:** Purchase, Rent/Lease. **Dist:** The Video Project. $79.00.

Before It's Too Late 1998
Features interviews and performances by the AIDS Theater Project, actors with HIV/AIDS who perform for high school and college students. Factual information on the disease is also given. 19m; VHS. **A:** Sr. High-Adult. **P:** Education. **U:** Institution. **Hea-Sci:** Health Education, AIDS, Diseases. **Acq:** Purchase. **Dist:** Aquarius Health Care Media. $125.00.

Before It's Too Late: A Film on Teenage Suicide 1985
This video teaches students how to deal with their own suicidal tendencies and help their classmates. 20m; VHS, 3/4 U, EJ, Special order formats. **TV Std:** NTSC, PAL, SECAM. **Pr:** Disney Educational Productions. **A:** Jr. High-Sr. High. **P:** Education. **U:** Institution, CCTV, SURA. **Gen-Edu:** Suicide. **Acq:** Purchase, Rent/Lease, Duplication License. **Dist:** Phoenix Learning Group. $370.00.

Before Mickey 19??
A look at the early animation of Walt Disney. 120m; VHS. **A:** Sr. High-Adult. **P:** Entertainment. **U:** Home. **Gen-Edu:** Filmmaking, Animation & Cartoons. **Acq:** Purchase. **Dist:** Direct Cinema Ltd. $39.95.

Before Midnight 2013 (R) — ★★★
Linklater, Delpy, and Hawke continue the story of Jesse and Celine that began in "Before Sunrise" and continued through "Before Sunset" in the best film of the now-trilogy. The now-married couple walks to a hotel room for a night away from their twin girls at the tail end of a Grecian vacation and the conversation swirls around their romantic past and complicated future. Linklater and his co-writer/stars not only know these characters so completely but understand how people in long-term relationships fight and love each other even in the same heated moment. It's a mesmerizing character study of romance, resentment, and hope. 108m; DVD, Blu-Ray. **C:** Julie Delpy; Ethan Hawke; Directed by Richard Linklater; Written by Julie Delpy; Ethan Hawke; Richard Linklater; Cinematography by Christos Voudouris; Music by Graham Reynolds. **Pr:** Christos V. Konstatakopoulos; Richard Linklater; Detour Filmproduction; Sony Pictures Classics. **A:** Sr. High-Adult. **P:** Entertainment. **U:** Home. **L:** English. **Mov-Ent:** Drama, Romance, Marriage. **Acq:** Purchase. **Dist:** Sony Pictures Home Entertainment Inc.

Before Morning 1933 — ★½
Police officer poses as a blackmailer to find out which of the two women in the murder victim's life are guilty. 68m/B/W; VHS. **C:** Leo Carrillo; Lora Baxter; Taylor Holmes; Blaine Cordner; Louise Prussing; Russell Hicks; Louis Jean Heydt; Jules Epailly; Constance Bertrand; Terry Carroll; Directed by Arthur Hoerl; Cinematography by Walter Strenge. **Pr:** Greenblatt. **A:** Family. **P:** Entertainment. **U:** Home. **Mov-Ent:** Mystery & Suspense. **Acq:** Purchase. **Dist:** Movies Unlimited. $18.99.

Before Night Falls 2000 (R) — ★★★
Director Schnabel takes a quantum leap in skill in his second film (after "Basquiat"). This time his tortured artist is the literally tortured late Cuban poet Reinaldo Arenas (Bardem), who falls victim to Castro's repression against both his writings and his sexuality (he's gay). Arenas gets thrown into prison, eventually gets released after confessing his "crimes," and makes his escape as part of the 1980 Mariel boatlift. Ironically, freedom offers little solace to Arenas either in Miami or his last home in New York. Spanish actor Bardem is outstanding as the poet who only seeks to be true to himself and pays a tragic price. Based on the writer's autobiography. 134m; VHS, DVD, Wide. **C:** Javier Bardem; Olivier Martinez; Andrea Di Stefano; Johnny Depp; Michael Wincott; Sean Penn; Hector Babenco; Najwa Nimri; Directed by Julian Schnabel; Written by Julian Schnabel; Lazaro Gomez Carilles; Cunningham O'Keefe; Cinematography by Xavier Perez Grobet; Guillermo Rosas; Music by Carter Burwell. **Pr:** Fine Line Features. **A:** College-Adult. **P:** Entertainment. **U:** Home. **Mov-Ent:** AIDS. **Awds:** Ind. Spirit '01: Actor (Bardem); Natl. Bd. of Review '00: Actor (Bardem); Natl. Soc. Film Critics '00: Actor (Bardem). **Acq:** Purchase. **Dist:** New Line Home Video.

Before Saturn and America in Space 1980
An examination of the development of rocket technology, beginning with the invention of the rocket by the Chinese and moving forward to the ultimate machine in Werner von Braun's Saturn V. 28m; 3/4 U, Q. **Pr:** National Aeronautics and Space Administration. **A:** Primary-Adult. **P:** Education. **U:** BCTV, SURA. **Hea-Sci:** Documentary Films, Technology, Space Exploration. **Acq:** Free Loan. **Dist:** NASA Lyndon B. Johnson Space Center. $29.99.

Before Stonewall 1984
An examination of homosexuality in America from the 1920s to the beginnings of the Gay Liberation Movement. 87m; VHS, DVD. **C:** Directed by Greta Schiller; Robert Rosenberg. **Pr:** John Scagliotti; Robert Rosenberg. **A:** Sr. High-Adult. **P:** Education. **U:** Institution, Home. **Gen-Edu:** Documentary Films, History--U.S., Homosexuality. **Acq:** Purchase. **Dist:** First Run Features.

Before Students Will Learn 19??
This teacher video lesson teaches an understanding of what motivation is and how it causes students to want to learn and ways teachers can identify voids in student motivation. Also, teachers will see the reasons behind how life's primary needs may affect students' ability to learn. 22m; VHS. **A:** Adult. **P:** Teacher Education. **U:** Institution. **L:** English. **Gen-Edu:** Education. **Acq:** Purchase. **Dist:** Master Teacher Inc. $129.95.

Before Sunrise 1994 (R) — ★★½
Light, "getting-to-know-you," romance unfolds as two 20-somethings share an unlikely 14-hour date. Gen-Xer Jesse (Hawke) and French beauty (Delpy) meet on the Eurail and he convinces her to join him in exploring Vienna and their mutual attraction before he heads back to the States in the morning. The two exchange life experiences and philosophies in the typical Linklater conversational fashion, but the film strays from the comical accounts of earlier works "Slacker" and "Dazed and Confused." Cinematographer Daniel captures the Old World with finesse, especially in the inevitable "first kiss" atop the Ferris wheel made famous in Orson Welles' "The Third Man." 101m; VHS, DVD, CC. **C:** Ethan Hawke; Julie Delpy; Directed by Richard Linklater; Written by Richard Linklater; Kim Krizan; Cinematography by Lee Daniel. **Pr:** Anne Walker-McBay; Ellen Winn Wendl; Gernot Schaffler; Wolfgang Ramml; John Sloss; Detour Filmproduction; Columbia Pictures; Castle Rock Entertainment; Filmhaus, Inc. **A:** Sr. High-Adult. **P:** Entertainment. **U:** Home. **Mov-Ent:** Drama, Trains, Cities & Towns. **Awds:** Berlin Intl. Film Fest. '94: Director (Linklater). **Acq:** Purchase. **Dist:** Sony Pictures Home Entertainment Inc. $19.95.

Before Sunset 2004 (R) — ★★★½
Sequel to Linklater's "Before Sunrise" reunites Jesse (Hawke) and Celine (Delpy), nine years after their Viennese fling, on the sidewalks of Paris. He's a writer promoting his book about their brief affair. She, a Parisian, shows up at his book signing. The two have only a few hours to catch up before Jesse has to fly back to America. In real time, they walk through Paris together, just talking. But what talking! They begin awkwardly polite and impersonal, but as the minutes slip away their questions and responses take on more urgency. Hawke and Delpy co-wrote the screenplay (with Hawke using his real-life divorce as inspiration) and there's real chemistry between them. Movie veers cleverly back and forth between them and ends ambiguously. Great date film (Sorry, guys). 80m; VHS, DVD. **C:** Ethan Hawke; Julie Delpy; Rodolphe Pauly; Directed by Richard Linklater; Written by Ethan Hawke; Julie Delpy; Richard Linklater; Cinematography by Lee Daniel; Music by Julie Delpy; Glover Gill. **Pr:** Anne Walker-McBay; Detour Filmproduction; Castle Rock Entertainment; Warner Independent Pictures. **A:** Sr. High-Adult. **P:** Entertainment. **U:** Home. **L:** English. **Mov-Ent:** Drama, France. **Acq:** Purchase. **Dist:** Warner Home Video, Inc. $27.95.

Before the Devil Knows You're Dead 2007 (R) — ★★★
At 83, director Lumet shows he still has crime chops in this grubby tragedy about a botched heist. Calculating, fleshy Andy (Hoffman) has a drug problem and a trophy wife, Gina (Tomei), while his sad-sack, skinny baby bro Hank (Hawke), who happens to be hitting the sheets with Gina, needs cash for his shrewish ex (Ryan). Andy plans a heist on their family's jewelry store but Hank manages to screw it up and things just get more complicated. Good performances by all concerned. 117m; DVD. **C:** Philip Seymour Hoffman; Ethan Hawke; Marisa Tomei; Albert Finney; Rosemary Harris; Brian F. O'Byrne; Amy Ryan; Michael Shannon; Aleksa Palladino; Directed by Sidney Lumet; Written by Kelly Masterson; Cinematography by Ron Fortunato; Music by Carter Burwell. **Pr:** Michael Cerenzie; William S. Gilmore; Brian Linse; Paul Parmar; Capitol Films; Unity Productions; Funky Buddha Group; Linsefilm; ThinkFilm. **A:** Sr. High-Adult. **P:** Entertainment. **U:** Home. **L:** English. **Mov-Ent:** Crime Drama. **Acq:** Purchase. **Dist:** Image Entertainment Inc.

Before the Fall 2004 (Unrated) — ★★
In 1942, teenager Friedrich Weimer (Riemelt) goes against his father's wishes to enter an exclusive Berlin school designed to educate future Nazi leaders. Friedrich distinguishes himself with his boxing prowess but eventually begins to question his indoctrination. German with subtitles. 110m; DVD. **C:** Tom Schilling; Max Riemelt; Michael Schenk; Jonas Jagermeyr; Leon A. Kersten; Thomas Dreschel; Directed by Dennis Gansel; Written by Dennis Gansel; Maggie Peren; Cinematography by Torsten Brewer; Music by Angelo Badalamenti; Normand Corbeil. **A:** Sr. High-Adult. **P:** Entertainment. **U:** Home. **L:** German. **Mov-Ent:** Education, Boxing. **Acq:** Purchase. **Dist:** Picture This! Home Video.

Before the Fall 2008 (Unrated) — ★
Predictable and dull wannabe apocalypse thriller. A giant meteorite is headed to apparently destroy the Earth, which has everyone freaking out except for lazy screw-up Alejandro (Clavijo). His mom is more worried that a prison escapee is on his way to kill her absent older son and insists that Alejandro must guard his kids who live out in the country. Spanish with subtitles. 96m; DVD. **C:** Victor Clavijo; Eduardo Fernandez; Mariana Cordero; Directed by F. Javier Gutierrez; Written by F. Javier Gutierrez; Juan Velarde; Cinematography by Miguel Angel Mora; Music by Antonio Meliveo. **A:** Sr. High-Adult. **P:** Entertainment. **U:** Home. **L:** Spanish. **Mov-Ent. Acq:** Purchase. **Dist:** IFC Films.

Before the Hyphen 19?? (Unrated)
Nostalgic film and narration reviews the Erie and Lackawanna railroads before and after they merged together to become the Erie-Lackawanna, showing early FT units, freights thundering down a New York mainline, the Phoebe Snow at Binghamton, and much more. 90m; DVD. **A:** Family. **P:** Education. **U:** Home. **Gen-Edu:** Trains, U.S. States. **Acq:** Purchase. **Dist:** The Civil War Standard. $24.95.

Before the Industrial Revolution 19??
Takes a look at what life in the United States was like before the Industrial Revolution. Includes teacher's manual. 17m; VHS. **A:** Jr. High-Adult. **P:** Education. **U:** Institution. **Gen-Edu:** History--U.S., Industry & Industrialists. **Acq:** Purchase. **Dist:** Educational Video Network. $49.95.

Before the Nickelodeon: The Early Cinema of Edwin S. Porter 1982
The history of filmmaking from 1896-1909, with special attention focused on Porter's classics such as "The Great Train Robbery" and "Life of an American Fireman." 60m; VHS. **Pr:** Charles Musser. **A:** Jr. High-Adult. **P:** Education. **U:** Institution, Home. **Gen-Edu:** Filmmaking, Film History. **Acq:** Purchase. **Dist:** Kino on Video.

Before the Rain 1994 (Unrated) — ★★★
War-torn Macedonia is the backdrop for Manchevski's first film (and first made in the newly declared republic of Macedonia). Powerful circular narrative joins three stories about the freedom of love and the pervasiveness of violence. "Words" finds young Macedonian monk Kiril (Colin) distracted from his spiritual duties by young Albanian Muslim Zamira (Mitevska), who takes refuge in his monastery. In "Faces," pregnant picture editor Anne (Cartlidge) is torn between her estranged husband and her lover, Aleksander (Serbedzija), a London-based war photographer who left his native Macedonia years before. "Pictures" finds Aleksandar returning to his old village—now torn by ethnic strife. In Macedonian, Albanian, and English, with subtitles. 120m; VHS, DVD. **C:** Rade Serbedzija; Katrin Cartlidge; Gregoire Colin; Labina Mitevska; Phyllida Law; Directed by Milcho Manchevski; Written by Milcho Manchevski; Cinematography by Manuel Teran; Music by Anastasia. **Pr:** Judy Counihan; Cedomir Kolar; Sam Taylor; Cat Villiers; Aim Productions; Noe Productions; Vardar Film. **A:** College-Adult. **P:** Entertainment. **U:** Home. **Mov-Ent:** Drama, War--General, Violence. **Awds:** Ind. Spirit '96: Foreign Film; Venice Film Fest. '94: Golden Lion. **Acq:** Purchase. **Dist:** Criterion Collection Inc. $94.99.

Before the Rains 2007 (PG-13) — ★★
Lavishly photographed period piece about Brits behaving badly in India. In 1937, spice baron Henry Moores (Roache) plans to build a road that will help expand his business but it needs to be completed before monsoon season. His right-man man T.K. (Bose) smooths the way but Moores is having an affair with married housemaid Sajani (Das), whose suspicious husband (Paul) beats her. When Sajani comes to Moores for help, he coldly turns her over to the loyal T.K. to deal with, causing more turmoil and eventual tragedy. 98m; DVD. **C:** Linus Roache; Rahul Bose; Nandita Das; Jennifer Ehle; Lal Paul; John Standing; Leopold Benedict; Directed by Santosh Sivan; Written by Cathy Rabin; Cinematography by Santosh Sivan; Music by Mark Kilian. **A:** Jr. High-Adult. **P:** Entertainment. **U:** Home. **Mov-Ent:** India. **Acq:** Purchase. **Dist:** Lions Gate Entertainment Inc.

Before the Revolution 1965 (Unrated) — ★★
One of Bertolucci's first films. Love and politics are mixed when the young Fabrizio, who is dabbling in communism, is also flirting with his young aunt. Striking and powerful film that has yet to lose its effect despite the times. Italian with subtitles. 115m; VHS. **C:** Francesco Barilli; Adriana Asti; Alain Midgette; Morando Morandini; Domenico Alpi; Directed by Bernardo Bertolucci; Written by Bernardo Bertolucci; Cinematography by Aldo Scavarda; Music by Ennio Morricone; Gino Paoli. **A:** Sr. High-Adult. **P:** Entertainment. **U:** Home. **L:** Italian. **Mov-Ent. Acq:** Purchase. **Dist:** New Yorker Video. $59.95.

Before the White Man: Vol. 1 19??
Part of a three-volume teaching aid for art appreciation that explores this history of the American West through art. Includes the work of Moran, Hill, Remington, and others. 22m; VHS. **A:** Jr. High-College. **P:** Education. **U:** Institution. **Gen-Edu:** Art & Artists, Western. **Acq:** Purchase. **Dist:** Crystal Productions. $29.95.

Before They Were Kings: Vol. 1 2005 (Unrated)
Taped performances from six famous African American comedians before they achieved fame, including Chris Rock, Steve Harvey, D.L. Hughley, Arsenio Hall, A.J. Jamal, and George Wallace. 72m; DVD. **A:** Sr. High-Adult. **P:** Entertainment. **U:** Home. **Mov-Ent:** Comedy--Performance, Television. **Acq:** Purchase. **Dist:** Comedy Central. $14.98.

Before They Were Kings: Vol. 2 2005 (Unrated)
A second volume of performances from famous African American comedians in their early careers, including Dave Chappelle, Martin Lawrence, Steve Harvey, Michael Colver, Keenan Wayans, and John Ridley. 71m; DVD. **A:** Sr. High-Adult. **P:** Entertainment. **U:** Home. **Gen-Edu:** Comedy--Performance, Television. **Acq:** Purchase. **Dist:** Comedy Central. $295.

Before Tomorrow Becomes Today 1987
Encourages proper planning to determine and attain life and employment goals. Discusses the types of education and training required for skilled and unskilled jobs. 9m; VHS. **A:** Adult. **P:** Professional. **U:** Institution. **Bus-Ind:** Job Hunting. **Acq:** Purchase. **Dist:** Education Associates Inc. $85.00.

The Before Tour: An Operation Preparation Video 1994
Prepares children for their first visit to the hospital, explaining admission, diagnostic procedures, surgical environment and medical personnel. 16m; VHS. **A:** Preschool-Primary. **P:** Education. **U:** Institution. **Hea-Sci:** Hospitals. **Acq:** Purchase. **Dist:** Milner-Fenwick, Inc.

Before We Ruled the Earth: Hunt or Be Hunted 2003
Looks at how primitive man dealt with bloodthirsty predators. 49m; DVD. **A:** Adult. **P:** Education. **U:** Home. **Gen-Edu:** Science, Nature, Anthropology. **Acq:** Purchase. **Dist:** Discovery Home Entertainment. $19.98.

Before We Ruled the Earth: Mastering the Beasts 2003
Looks at how primitive man dealt with the enormous creatures that shared his world. 49m; DVD. **A:** Adult. **P:** Education. **U:** Home. **Gen-Edu:** Science, Nature, Anthropology. **Acq:** Purchase. **Dist:** Discovery Home Entertainment. $19.98.

Before Winter Comes 1969 (Unrated) — ★½
Starts off as a bland military comedy before it gets a little serious. In 1945, British Major Giles Burnside is assigned to oversee a displaced persons camp in Austria where there's friction between British and Russian troops and wrangling over zoning areas. Burnside's wheeler-dealer interpreter Janovic is found to be a Russian deserter and the Soviets want him back. 103m; DVD. **C:** David Niven; Topol; John Hurt; Anna Karina; Anthony Quayle; Ori Levy; Directed by J. Lee Thompson; Written by Andrew Sinclair; Cinematography by Gilbert Taylor; Music by Ron Grainer. **A:** Jr. High-Adult. **P:** Entertainment. **U:** Home. **Mov-Ent:** Refugees. **Acq:** Purchase. **Dist:** Sony Pictures Home Entertainment Inc.

Before You Buy: How to Inspect a Used Car 1996
Helps the viewer to determine whether the car that they are about to buy is a dependable vehicle or a lemon. Produced by an ASE certified mechanic who has owned a used automobile inspection service since 1993. Also included is a checklist for reviewing used cars before purchase. ?m; VHS. **A:** Adult. **P:** Instruction. **U:** Home. **How-Ins:** Automobiles, How-To. **Acq:** Purchase. **Dist:** Tapeworm Video Distributors Inc. $14.95.

Before You Can Discipline 19??
This video contains the professional foundations that underpin a solid philosophy of discipline. Topics covered in depth include: the three variables of any discipline problem, the four relationships of students, and the four primary causes of misbehavior. 22m; VHS. **A:** Adult. **P:** Teacher Education. **U:** Institution. **L:** English. **Gen-Edu:** Education. **Acq:** Purchase. **Dist:** Master Teacher Inc. $129.95.

Before You Say Good-Bye 1998
People whose lives have been intmately touched by suicide share their stories of grief and ways someone might help a troubled person before they attempt taking their life. 30m; VHS, DVD. **A:** Adult. **P:** Professional. **U:** Institution. **Hea-Sci:** Death, Suicide, Mental Health. **Acq:** Purchase. **Dist:** Aquarius Health Care Media. $149.00.

Before You Say 'I Do' 2009 (Unrated) — ★★½
Undemanding rom com (with adorable leads) from the Hallmark Channel. George (Sutcliffe) proposes to Jane (Westfeldt) but she refuses because of her lousy first marriage to Doug (Roop)?who cheated on their wedding day. A car crash leads to George going back in time 10 years so he can stop Jane's wedding and get her to fall in love with him instead. 120m; DVD. **C:** David Sutcliffe; Jennifer Westfeldt; Lauren Holly; Jeff Roop; Brad Borbridge; Brandon Firla; John Boylan; Roger Dunn; Directed by Paul Fox; Written by Elena Krupp; Cinematography by David Makin; Music by Lawrence Shragge. **A:** Jr. High-Adult. **P:** Entertainment. **U:** Home. **Mov-Ent:** Comedy--Romantic. **Acq:** Purchase. **Dist:** Movies Unlimited.

Beg! 1994 (Unrated) — ★½
The wealthy owners of a mental institution announce possible cuts to an already-thin budget, and the staff immediately sets out to stab one another in the back. Quite literally in some cases. 108m; DVD, Streaming. **C:** Philip Pelew; Julian Bleach; Olegar Fedoro; Jeremy Wilkin; Peta Lily; Directed by Robert Golden; Written by Peta Lily; Robert Golden; David Glass; Cinematography by Chris Middleton; Music by David Pearl; Stephen Parsons. **A:** Sr. High-Adult. **P:** Entertainment. **U:** Home. **L:** English. **Mov-Ent. Acq:** Purchase, Rent/Lease. **Dist:** Troma Entertainment. $14.98 9.99.

Beggars and Noblemen 1991
While a police inspector confronts a former university professor charged with killing a young prostitute in a moment of insanity for a confession, both parties are lead to startling realizations. Subtitled in English. 92m; VHS. **A:** Adult. **P:** Entertainment. **U:** Institution, BCTV. **L:** Arabic. **Mov-Ent:** Drama, Middle East. **Acq:** Purchase, Rent/Lease. **Dist:** Arab Film Distribution. $250.00.

Beggars in Ermine 1934 (Unrated) — ★★
A handicapped, impoverished man organizes all the beggars in the world into a successful corporation. Unusual performance from Atwill. 70m/B/W; VHS, DVD. **C:** Lionel Atwill; Henry B. Walthall; Betty Furness; Jameson Thomas; James Bush; Astrid Allwyn; George "Gabby" Hayes; Directed by Phil Rosen. **Pr:** Monogram. **A:** Jr. High-Adult. **P:** Entertainment. **U:** Home. **Mov-Ent:** Poverty, Politics & Government. **Acq:** Purchase. **Dist:** Sinister Cinema. $14.95.

Beggars of Life 1928 (Unrated) — ★★
In a panic, Nancy (Brooks) kills her abusive stepfather. She disguises herself as a boy and, with fellow runaway Jim (Arlen) serving as her protector, decides to hop a train to Canada. They wind up spending the night in a hobo camp, looked after by Oklahoma Red (Beery) who aids in their escape at great cost to himself. 100m/B/W; Silent; VHS, DVD. **C:** Louise Brooks; Richard Arlen; Wallace Beery; Robert Perry; Roscoe Karns; Edgar "Blue" Washington; Directed by William A. Wellman; Written by Benjamin Glazer; Jim Tully; Cinematography by Henry W. Gerrard; Music by Karl Hajos. **A:** Jr. High-Adult. **P:** Entertainment. **U:** Home. **Mov-Ent:** Silent Films. **Acq:** Purchase. **Dist:** Grapevine Video; Nostalgia Family Video/Hollywood's Attic. $20.98.

Beggar's Opera 1954 (Unrated) — ★★
Brooks' directorial debut was this adaptation of John Gay's 18th-century comic opera. Highwayman MacHeath (Olivier), a prisoner in Newgate who's condemned to hang, regales a beggar (Griffith) with his life story and the beggar decides to write an opera about him. Olivier did his own singing (badly) while most of the other performers were dubbed. 93m; DVD. **C:** Laurence Olivier; Hugh Griffith; Stanley Holloway; Dorothy Tutin; George Devine; Mary Clare; Athene Seyler; Daphne Anderson; Directed by Peter Brooks; Written by Christopher Fry; Denis Cannan; Cinematography by Guy Green; Music by Arthur Bliss. **A:** Sr. High-Adult. **P:** Entertainment. **U:** Home. **Mov-Ent:** Musical. **Acq:** Purchase. **Dist:** WarnerArchive.com.

Beggar's Opera 1984
A production of the John Gay opera taped for British television. 138m; VHS. **C:** Roger Daltrey; Bob Hoskins; Directed by Jonathan Miller. **Pr:** British Broadcasting Corporation. **A:** Family. **P:** Entertainment. **U:** Home. **Fin-Art:** Music--Performance, Opera, Theater. **Acq:** Purchase. **Dist:** Music Video Distributors; Home Vision Cinema; Facets Multimedia Inc. $49.95.

Begin Again 2013 (R)
Gretta (Knightley) and her boyfriend Dave (Levine) come to New York to pursue their music dreams. Dave dumps Gretta after getting a big solo record contract, but her luck may change when down-on-his-luck record producer, Dan (Ruffalo), hears Gretta sing and thinks she's his second chance at success. But Gretta isn't sure what she wants from a musical career. DVD. **C:** Keira Knightley; Mark Ruffalo; Adam Levine; Hailee Steinfeld; Catherine Keener; James Corden; Mos Def; Directed by John Carney; Written by John Carney; Cinematography by Yaron Orbach; Music by Gregg Alexander. **Pr:** Weinstein Company L.L.C. **A:** Sr. High-Adult. **P:** Entertainment. **U:** Home. **L:** English. **Mov-Ent:** Singing. **Acq:** Purchase.

Begin to Sew 1987
A course in sewing basics for the complete novice. 60m; VHS. **Pr:** Nancy's Notions Ltd. **A:** Jr. High-Adult. **P:** Instruction. **U:** Institution, Home. **How-Ins:** How-To, Sewing. **Acq:** Purchase, Rent/Lease. **Dist:** Nancy's Notions Ltd.

Begin with Goodbye 1979
A series designed to help individuals and families confront change, personal loss, grief, and new beginnings. 28m; VHS, 3/4 U, Q. **C:** Hosted by Eli Wallach. **Pr:** United Methodist Communications. **A:** Family. **P:** Education. **U:** Institution, CCTV. **Gen-Edu:** Documentary Films, Religion, Family. **Acq:** Purchase, Rent/Lease. **Dist:** EcuFilm; Mass Media Ministries.
Indiv. Titles: 1. Changes 2. Turned Loose 3. Exits and Entrances 4. Mirror, Mirror on the Wall 5. A Time to Cry 6. The Death of Ivan Ilych.

Begin with the End in Mind 1972
Relates the way supervision and making proper use of visual aids and library materials improves a father's teachings in church and awakens an awareness of his need to communicate with his son. 29m; 3/4 U. **Pr:** Brigham Young University. **A:** Adult. **P:** Education. **U:** Institution, CCTV, SURA. **Gen-Edu:** Parenting. **Acq:** Purchase. **Dist:** Brigham Young University.

Beginners 2010 (Unrated) — ★★★
Oliver (McGregor) is completely shocked when his elderly father, Hal (Plummer), declares that he is gay and dating a young man named Andy (Visnjic). As if that weren't enough, he also learns that his father has terminal lung cancer. As Oliver reflects on his father's unconventional and inspirational life, he strives to take a chance with new love Anna (Laurent) despite a long string of unsuccessful relationships. Profoundly funny and tragic as it explores life's bittersweet lessons—including how well we know even those closest to us. Autobiographical story from writer/director Mills. 105m; DVD, Blu-Ray. **C:** Ewan McGregor; Christopher Plummer; Melanie Laurent; Goran Visnjic; Kai Lennox; Mary Page Keller; Keegan Boos; Directed by Mike Mills; Written by Mike Mills; Cinematography by Kasper Tuxen; Music by Roger Neill; David Palmer; Brian Reitzell. **Pr:** Leslie Urdang; Dean Vanech; Miranda De Pencier; Jay Van Hoy; Lars Knudsen; Parts&Labor; Olympus Pictures; Focus Features L.L.C. **A:** Sr. High-Adult. **P:** Entertainment. **U:** Home. **L:** English. **Mov-Ent:** Aging. **Awds:** Oscars '11: Support. Actor (Plummer); British Acad. '11: Support. Actor (Plummer); Golden Globes '12: Support. Actor (Plummer); Ind. Spirit '12: Support. Actor (Plummer); Screen Actors Guild '11: Support. Actor (Plummer). **Acq:** Purchase. **Dist:** Movies Unlimited; Universal Studios Home Video.

The Beginner's Bible: The Story of Jesus and His Miracles 1998
Tells the story of how Jesus' disciples use their account of his many miracles to show the incredible things made possible by the power of faith. 30m; VHS. **A:** Family. **P:** Entertainment. **U:** Home. **Mov-Ent:** Family Viewing, Religion. **Acq:** Purchase. **Dist:** SONY Wonder. $9.98.

The Beginner's Bible: The Story of the Good Samaritan 1998
Recounts Jesus' tale of the man who feared anyone different from his own people until he was saved by a stranger after being set upon by robbers and left for dead. 30m; VHS. **A:** Family. **P:** Entertainment. **U:** Home. **Mov-Ent:** Family Viewing, Religion. **Acq:** Purchase. **Dist:** SONY Wonder. $9.98.

Beginner's Craps 1989
The basics of craps are covered, from the standard rules to table etiquette. 60m; VHS. **Pr:** John Patrick Productions. **A:**

College-Adult. **P:** Instruction. **U:** Home. **How-Ins:** Gambling, How-To. **Acq:** Purchase. **Dist:** John Patrick Entertainment, Inc. $39.95.

A Beginner's Guide to Endings 2010 (R) — ★
In this lame black comedy three brothers discover at the reading of their father's will that the quick cash drug trials he forced them into have severely shortened their own life spans. They decide to fulfill their individual bucket lists. 92m; DVD. **C:** Scott Caan; Jason Jones; Paulo Costanzo; J.K. Simmons; Tricia Helfer; Harvey Keitel; Wendy Crewson; Directed by Jonathan Sobol; Written by Jonathan Sobol; Cinematography by Samy Inayeh. **A:** Sr. High-Adult. **P:** Entertainment. **U:** Home. **L:** English. **Mov-Ent:** Family. **Acq:** Purchase. **Dist:** Entertainment One US LP.

Beginners Guide to Inline Skating 1992
Introduction to safe in-line skating. Leanna Moore shares her skating experience, explaining basic techniques for stopping, suggested equipment, getting up from falls, and common courtesy. 30m; VHS. **Pr:** Bill Burroughs Productions. **A:** Jr. High-Adult. **P:** Instruction. **U:** Institution. **Spo-Rec:** Sports--General. **Acq:** Purchase. **Dist:** Quality Books Inc. $29.95.

Beginner's Guide to Professional Guitar 2007
Writer and instructor Max Milligan teaches basic skills, including tuning, finger exercises, chords and scales, positioning, and more. ?m; DVD. **A:** Jr. High-Adult. **P:** Instruction. **U:** Home. **How-Ins:** Documentary Films, Music--Instruction. **Acq:** Purchase. **Dist:** Rykodisc Corp.

Beginner's Luck 1984 (R) — Bomb!
A young man convinces his neighbors to engage in swinging activities, leading to predictable and raunchy situations. 85m; VHS. **C:** Sam Rush; Riley Steiner; Charles Homet; Kate Talbot; Directed by Frank Mouris. **A:** Sr. High-Adult. **P:** Entertainment. **U:** Home. **L:** Spanish. **Mov-Ent:** Exploitation, Sex & Sexuality. **Acq:** Purchase. **Dist:** Anchor Bay Entertainment. $19.95.

Beginner's Patchwork Projects 1980
Lee Maher demonstrates how to get started on a colorful patchwork project. Part of the "Crafts and Decorating" series. 60m; VHS, 3/4 U, Special order formats. **Pr:** Cinema Associates. **A:** Adult. **P:** Instruction. **U:** Institution, CCTV, CATV, BCTV, Home. **How-Ins:** How-To, Crafts. **Acq:** Purchase. **Dist:** RMI Media. $39.95.

The Beginning 1970
As a butterfly dares a man to "try his wings," viewers are inspired to try new ideas. Non-narrative. 5m; VHS, 3/4 U, Special order formats. **Pr:** C.O. Hayward. **A:** Jr. High-Adult. **P:** Education. **U:** Institution, Home, SURA. **Bus-Ind:** Employee Counseling, Meeting Openers. **Acq:** Purchase, Duplication License. **Dist:** Clear Vue Inc.

Beginning Acoustic Guitar 199?
Michael Thompson provides an introduction to guitar using a variety of chord work and techniques. ?m; VHS. **A:** Sr. High-Adult. **P:** Instruction. **U:** Home. **How-Ins:** Music--Instruction. **Acq:** Purchase. **Dist:** Hal Leonard Corp. $14.95.

Beginning Algebra 19??
Thirty-one part series that offers beginning algebra education, covering such areas as fractional operations, factoring, functions, graphs, quadratic equations, and rational exponents. 775m; VHS. **A:** Jr. High-Adult. **P:** Education. **U:** Institution, SURA. **Gen-Edu:** Mathematics, Education. **Acq:** Purchase, Duplication License. **Dist:** Video Resources. $29.95. **Indiv. Titles:** 1. Operations on Fractions 2. Operations on Real Numbers 3. Exponents, Order of Operations, and Introduction to Variables 4. Combining Like Terms 5. Solving Linear Equations 6. Applications of Linear Equations 7. Solving Linear Equations 8. Exponents 9. Operations on Polynomials 10. Factoring, Part I 11. Factoring, Part II 12. Solving Quadratic Equations by Factoring 13. Rational Expressions, Part I 14. Rational Expressions, Part II 15. Equations with Rational Expressions 16. Ratio and Proportion 17. Applications with Rational Expressions 18. Graphing Linear Equations 19. Slope and Equation of Lines 20. Functions and Graphing Inequalities 21. Systems of Equations 22. Word Problems 23. Introduction to Radicals 24. Adding and Subtracting Radicals 25. Multiplying and Dividing Radicals 26. Radical Equations and Applications 27. Systems of Linear Inequalities 28. Rational Exponents 29. Solving Quadratic Equations by Completing the Square 30. Solving Quadratic Equations by the Quadratic Formula 31. Complex Solutions of Quadratic Equations and Graphing Quadratic Equations.

Beginning American Sign Language Videocourse 1993
A 16-lesson course which features the fictional Bravo family, who include a hearing mother, deaf father, and two deaf children. Each lesson covers new vocabulary, a vist to the Bravos which dramatizes real-life situations, and practice sessions. Also includes a look at the deaf community and at the creative talent behind the project. Each tape is available separately; run times vary from 30-45 minutes. 45m; VHS, CC. **A:** Sr. High-Adult. **P:** Instruction. **U:** Institution, Home. **How-Ins:** Deafness. **Acq:** Purchase. **Dist:** Baker and Taylor. $49.95. **Indiv. Titles:** 1. Meet the Bravo Family 2. Breakfast with the Bravos 3. Where's the TV Remote? 4. Let's Go Food Shopping 5. Review Tape Lessons 1-4 6. Read Any Good Fingers Lately? 7. A School Daze 8. A School Daze...The Sequel 9. Dollar Signs 10. Review Tape Lessons 6-9 11. Playing in the Park 12. The Doctor Is In 13. Business as Unusual 14. Let's Go Clothes Shopping 15. Review Lessons 1-15 16. The People Behind the Bravo Family.

Beginning and Intermediate Drum Set Techniques 19??
Two-program study of drumming techniques. Demonstrates instrument set-up; stroke/hand technique; coordination and reading rhythms; and concepts of time, style, sound, and groove. 60m; VHS. **A:** Jr. High-Adult. **P:** Instruction. **U:** Home. **How-Ins:** How-To, Music--Instruction. **Acq:** Purchase. **Dist:** Cambridge Educational. $29.95. **Indiv. Titles:** 1. Beginning 2. Intermediate.

Beginning and Intermediate Water Skiing for Kids 1985
Two programs on one tape; the first instructs water skiing for inexperienced adults, the second details skiing for children. 75m; VHS. **Pr:** Double Vision. **A:** Family. **P:** Instruction. **U:** Home. **How-Ins:** Sports--General, How-To. **Acq:** Purchase. **Dist:** Double Vision Prod.

Beginning Archery 1981
Olympic Archery Team coach Dwight Nyquist demonstrates basic techniques for safe enjoyment of this sport. 50m; VHS, 3/4 U, Special order formats. **Pr:** Cinema Associates. **A:** Jr. High-Adult. **P:** Instruction. **U:** Institution, CCTV, CATV, BCTV, Home. **How-Ins:** Sports--General, How-To. **Acq:** Purchase. **Dist:** RMI Media; School-Tech Inc.

Beginning Bass 1 199?
Describes parts of the bass. Explains how to tune, achieve a good tone, play with fingers or a pick, right- and left-hand positioning, various bass line formats, and scales. ?m; VHS. **A:** Sr. High-Adult. **P:** Instruction. **U:** Home. **How-Ins:** Music--Instruction. **Acq:** Purchase. **Dist:** Hal Leonard Corp. $9.95.

Beginning Bass 2 199?
Geared for the beginning to intermediate bassist. Explains pentatonic scales, harmonics, chords, increasing speed, and playing in sync with a drummer. ?m; VHS. **A:** Sr. High-Adult. **P:** Instruction. **U:** Home. **How-Ins:** Music--Instruction. **Acq:** Purchase. **Dist:** Hal Leonard Corp. $9.95.

Beginning Bluegrass Banjo 1985
Peter Wernick teaches bluegrass banjo playing techniques for the beginner, including basic chords and right-hand rolls. Includes tab. 120m; VHS. **A:** Jr. High-Adult. **P:** Instruction. **U:** Home, Institution. **How-Ins:** Music--Instruction. **Acq:** Purchase. **Dist:** Homespun Tapes Ltd. $49.95.

Beginning Boardsailing Technique 1991
Provides step by step, detailed yet simple advice on how to boardsail. 30m; VHS. **Pr:** NSI. **A:** Family. **P:** Instruction. **U:** Home. **How-Ins:** Sports--General, Sports--Water, How-To. **Acq:** Purchase. **Dist:** NSI Sound & Video Inc.; Bennett Marine Video. $19.95.

Beginning Bodyboarding 1990
Bodyboarding experts Jay Reale, Keith Sasaki, and Cameron Steele guide you through the basic techniques of bodyboarding. You'll be able to master this fun sport in style and ease. 50m; VHS. **Pr:** NSI. **A:** Family. **P:** Instruction. **U:** Home. **How-Ins:** How-To, Sports--Water. **Acq:** Purchase. **Dist:** NSI Sound & Video Inc. $29.95.

Beginning Bodybuilding 19??
Demonstrates exercises that best target muscle stimulation and common errors to avoid. 35m; VHS. **A:** Adult. **P:** Instruction. **U:** Home. **Hea-Sci:** Health Education, Fitness/Exercise. **Acq:** Purchase. **Dist:** Victory Multimedia. $9.98.

Beginning Breastfeeding 1986
Mothers learn how to make the first nursing stages safe, effective and comfortable. 23m; VHS, 3/4 U. **Pr:** Alvin Fiering. **A:** Adult. **P:** Education. **U:** Institution. **Hea-Sci:** Women, Parenting, Infants. **Acq:** Purchase, Rent/Lease. **Dist:** Polymorph Films, Inc.

Beginning Breastfeeding 1987
This detailed explanation of how to be a nursing mother discusses preparing ahead, the first weeks of nursing, and how to involve the children and the family. 15m; VHS, 3/4 U. **Pr:** Milner-Fenwick. **A:** Adult. **P:** Education. **U:** Institution, CCTV. **L:** English, French, Spanish. **Hea-Sci:** Parenting, Infants, Women. **Acq:** Purchase. **Dist:** Milner-Fenwick, Inc.

The Beginning Business Series 1985
Seperates business start-up into four sections for would-be entrepreneurs. 90m; VHS. **A:** Sr. High-Adult. **P:** Professional. **U:** Institution. **Bus-Ind:** Business. **Acq:** Purchase. **Dist:** Purdue University. $36.00. **Indiv. Titles:** 1. Before You Begin—Consider 2. Securing a Loan 3. Pricing 4. Record Keeping.

Beginning Choral Music: Choral Warm-ups and Diction 19??
David Bray and the Grande Prairie Composite High School Jazz Choir demonstrate the exercises they use when warming-up for a performance. Part of a series aimed at choir directors and choir members. Supported by program guide (available separately). 29m; VHS. **C:** Narrated by Dr. Robert de Frece. **A:** Jr. High-Adult. **P:** Education. **U:** Institution. **Gen-Edu:** Music--Instruction, Singing. **Acq:** Purchase. **Dist:** Access The Education Station. $59.00.

Beginning Choral Music: Physical Preparation for Singing, Breathing, and Tone Production 19??
Elaine Quilichini and the Mount Royal Children's Choir demonstrate physical exercises that professional singers use to limber up for performances. Part of a series aimed at choir directors and choir members. Supported by program guide (available separately). 40m; VHS. **C:** Narrated by Dr. Robert de Frece. **A:**

Jr. High-Adult. **P:** Education. **U:** Institution. **Gen-Edu:** Music--Instruction, Singing. **Acq:** Purchase. **Dist:** Access The Education Station. $59.00.

Beginning Choral Music: Word Colouring and Phrasing 19??
Marilyn Kerley and the St. Theresa Junior High School Choir demonstrate how they give special treatment to certain words called "coloring" (using the voice in creative ways to get the meanings of words across). The concept of voice shading is also introduced. Part of a series aimed at choir directors and choir members. Narrated by Dr. Robert De Frece of the University of Alberta. Supported by program guide (available separately). 19m; VHS. **C:** Narrated by Dr. Robert de Frece. **A:** Jr. High-Adult. **P:** Education. **U:** Institution. **Gen-Edu:** Music--Instruction, Singing. **Acq:** Purchase. **Dist:** Access The Education Station. $59.00.

Beginning Chords and Strumming 199?
Rick Plunkett provides step-by-step demonstrations of basic, bar, and power chords, as well as other beneficial chording techniques. 30m; VHS. **A:** Sr. High-Adult. **P:** Instruction. **U:** Home. **How-Ins:** Music--Instruction. **Acq:** Purchase. **Dist:** Hal Leonard Corp. $9.95.

Beginning Co-Ed Stunts 1997 (Unrated)
The staff of the American Cheerleading Federation demonstrate over 15 stunts and dismounts for cheerleading squads with new male cheerleaders. 33m; VHS. **A:** Family. **P:** Education. **U:** Home, Institution. **Spo-Rec:** Cheerleaders, Athletic Instruction/Coaching. **Acq:** Purchase. **Dist:** Championship Productions. $39.99.

Beginning Course Videocassette 1987
Gospel principles are taught to children through short stories. Two volume set contains adaptations of 44 filmstrips. ?m; VHS. **A:** Family. **P:** Religious. **U:** Home. **Gen-Edu:** Religion. **Acq:** Purchase. **Dist:** Church of Jesus Christ of Latter-day Saints. $18.00.

A Beginning Drama Workshop for Kids! 1993
Uses the story of a kingdom whose residents have lost their imaginations to teach basic theatre warm-up techniques to children. These techniques include the mirror exercise, statue maker, and stretching imaginary clay into objects. 30m; VHS. **A:** Primary. **P:** Education. **U:** Home, Institution. **Gen-Edu:** Theater, Children. **Acq:** Purchase. **Dist:** Crystal Ball Dramatics. $20.00.

Beginning Drums 1 199?
Explains how to set up the drums, proper positioning, holding the sticks, basic grooves, plus bass and snare drum patterns. ?m; VHS. **A:** Sr. High-Adult. **P:** Instruction. **U:** Home. **How-Ins:** Music--Instruction. **Acq:** Purchase. **Dist:** Hal Leonard Corp. $9.95.

Beginning Drums 2 199?
Focuses on flams, paradiddles, fills and phrasing, snare accents, funk and shuffle grooves, and how to develop a fluid movement around the drum set. ?m; VHS. **A:** Sr. High-Adult. **P:** Instruction. **U:** Home. **How-Ins:** Music--Instruction. **Acq:** Purchase. **Dist:** Hal Leonard Corp. $9.95.

Beginning Electric Bass, Vol. 1 1988
Roly Salley teaches left- and right-hand techniques, scales, theory, and some standard country, blues, rock, and R&B bass lines. 60m; VHS. **Pr:** Homespun Video. **A:** Sr. High-Adult. **P:** Instruction. **U:** Home. **How-Ins:** How-To, Music--Instruction. **Acq:** Purchase. **Dist:** Homespun Tapes Ltd. $49.95.

Beginning Electric Bass, Vol. 2 1988
Roly Salley teaches left-hand exercises, 12-bar blues, inversions, and turnarounds, and offers tips on performing, playing with a rhythm section, and choosing equipment. 60m; VHS. **A:** Jr. High-Adult. **P:** Instruction. **U:** Home. **How-Ins:** How-To, Music--Instruction. **Acq:** Purchase. **Dist:** Homespun Tapes Ltd. $49.95.

Beginning Electric Blues Guitar 199?
Andy Aledort explains the essentials for playing a variety of blues forms. ?m; VHS. **A:** Sr. High-Adult. **P:** Instruction. **U:** Home. **How-Ins:** Music--Instruction. **Acq:** Purchase. **Dist:** Hal Leonard Corp. $14.95.

Beginning 5-String Bass 199?
Brian Emmel demonstrates basic techniques, with exercises to help build familiarity. Covers scales, chords, slap, and rhythm patterns for a variety of styles. 60m; VHS. **A:** Sr. High-Adult. **P:** Education. **U:** Home. **How-Ins:** Music--Instruction. **Acq:** Purchase. **Dist:** Hal Leonard Corp. $19.95.

Beginning Four Harness Weaving 1985
For ultimate beginners, the essentials of four-harness loom weaving are demonstrated. 86m; VHS. **Pr:** Victorian Video Productions. **A:** Jr. High-Adult. **P:** Instruction. **U:** Home. **How-Ins:** How-To, Crafts. **Acq:** Purchase. **Dist:** Victorian Video/Yarn Barn of Kansas, Inc. $49.95.

Beginning Funk Bass 199?
Session player Abe Laboriel demonstrates a variety of basic techniques. ?m; VHS. **A:** Sr. High-Adult. **P:** Instruction. **U:** Home. **How-Ins:** Music--Instruction. **Acq:** Purchase. **Dist:** Hal Leonard Corp. $14.95.

Beginning Girl's Volleyball 1990
This series of programs is intended to introduce girls to the pleasures of competitive volleyball. Learn how to develop individual skills and instill the concept of working together as a team. 90m; VHS. **A:** Jr. High-Sr. High. **P:** Instruction. **U:** Institution, Home. **Spo-Rec:** Volleyball. **Acq:** Purchase. **Dist:** Cambridge Educational. $139.95. **Indiv. Titles:** 1. Individual Skills 2. Team Tactics 3. Individual & Team Drills.

Beginning Golf for Women 1988
Donna White of the Ladies' Professional Golf Association, demonstrates the proper techniques of playing golf. 40m; VHS. **Pr:** Bridgestone Production Group. **A:** Jr. High-Adult. **P:** Instruction. **U:** Home. **How-Ins:** How-To, Sports--General, Golf. **Acq:** Purchase. **Dist:** Alpha Omega Publications Inc.; Karol Media. $14.95.

Beginning Guitar 199?
Teacher and author Will Schmid presents the basics for guitar playing using on-screen music and guitar diagrams, plus play-along trax with full band accompaniment. 60m; VHS. **A:** Sr. High-Adult. **P:** Education. **U:** Home. **How-Ins:** Music--Instruction. **Acq:** Purchase. **Dist:** Hal Leonard Corp. $19.95.

Beginning Guitar 1 199?
Describes parts of the electric and acoustic guitar. Explains how to tune, create a good tone with an amplifier, hold the pick, left- and right-hand positions, open and power chords, strumming patterns, and beginning soloing using a variety of styles. ?m; VHS. **A:** Sr. High-Adult. **P:** Instruction. **U:** Home. **How-Ins:** Music--Instruction. **Acq:** Purchase. **Dist:** Hal Leonard Corp. $9.95.

Beginning Guitar 2 199?
Geared for the beginning to intermediate player. Explains barre chords, 7th and 9th chords, funk rhythms, double stops, scales, sequences, vibrato, hammer-ons, and pull-offs using a variety of playing styles. ?m; VHS. **A:** Sr. High-Adult. **P:** Instruction. **U:** Home. **How-Ins:** Music--Instruction. **Acq:** Purchase. **Dist:** Hal Leonard Corp. $9.95.

Beginning Handbuilding 19??
Features artist Graham Sheehan as part of a five-video workshop for potters. 60m; VHS. **A:** Jr. High-College. **P:** Education. **U:** Institution. **Gen-Edu:** Art & Artists. **Acq:** Purchase. **Dist:** Crystal Productions. $39.95.

Beginning Keyboards 1 199?
Provides an introduction to note names, finger positions, scales, chords, left-hand bass, and playing with other musicians. ?m; VHS. **A:** Sr. High-Adult. **P:** Instruction. **U:** Home. **How-Ins:** Music--Instruction. **Acq:** Purchase. **Dist:** Hal Leonard Corp. $9.95.

Beginning Keyboards 2 199?
Explains the circle of fifths, chords and their progressions, simple soloing, improvising, and playing with others using a variety of musical styles. ?m; VHS. **A:** Sr. High-Adult. **P:** Instruction. **U:** Home. **How-Ins:** Music--Instruction. **Acq:** Purchase. **Dist:** Hal Leonard Corp. $9.95.

Beginning Lindy Hop ????
Explains and demonstrates basic lindy moves such as swing-out from open position, 8-count rhythm, swing-out from closed position, lindy circle, and mixing 6- and 8-count patterns. 70m; VHS. **A:** Adult. **P:** Instruction. **U:** Institution, Home. **How-Ins:** Dance, Dance--Instruction. **Acq:** Purchase. **Dist:** Stagestep. $19.95.

Beginning Metal Rhythm Guitar 199?
Nick Bowcott demonstrates a variety of techniques used for playing heavy metal styles. ?m; VHS. **A:** Sr. High-Adult. **P:** Instruction. **U:** Home. **How-Ins:** Music--Instruction. **Acq:** Purchase. **Dist:** Hal Leonard Corp. $14.95.

The Beginning of Life 1968
The evolution of a single cell into a completely formed baby is recorded. The development of the human embryo from fertilization to birth is captured. 30m; VHS, 3/4 U; Open Captioned. **Pr:** Benchmark Films. **A:** Sr. High-College. **P:** Education. **U:** Institution, CCTV. **Hea-Sci:** Embryology, Education. **Acq:** Purchase. **Dist:** Benchmark Media.

The Beginning of Life 1975
In-depth study of conception and development of the embryo. 26m; VHS, 3/4 U. **Pr:** Cine-Science; Tokyo. **A:** Sr. High-Adult. **P:** Education. **U:** Institution, Home, SURA. **Hea-Sci:** Embryology, Education. **Acq:** Purchase, Rent/Lease, Duplication License. **Dist:** Pyramid Media.

Beginning of the End 1957 (Unrated) — ★1/2
Produced the same year as "The Deadly Mantis," Gordon's effort adds to 1957's harvest of bugs on a rampage "B"-graders. Giant, radiation-spawned grasshoppers attack Chicago causing Graves to come to the rescue. Easily the best giant grasshopper movie ever made. 73m/B/W; VHS, DVD. **C:** Peggy Castle; Peter Graves; Morris Ankrum; Richard Benedict; James Seay; Thomas B(rowne). Henry; Larry J. Blake; John Close; Frank Wilcox; Directed by Bert I. Gordon; Written by Lester Gorn; Fred Freiberger; Cinematography by Jack Marta; Music by Albert Glasser. **Pr:** Bert I. Gordon; Bert I. Gordon; Republic. **A:** Primary-Adult. **P:** Entertainment. **U:** Home. **Mov-Ent:** Science Fiction. **Acq:** Purchase. **Dist:** Movies Unlimited. $17.99.

Beginning of the Food Chain: Plankton 1987
The ocean's plankton community is the subject of this film. 12m; VHS, 3/4 U. **Pr:** National Geographic Society. **A:** Primary. **P:** Education. **U:** Institution, SURA. **Hea-Sci:** Ecology & Environment, Fish. **Acq:** Purchase, Trade-in, Duplication License. **Dist:** Encyclopedia Britannica. $240.00.

Beginning Pieces 1986
A stirring exploration of the development of Sarah Guzzetti, from the age of two to five. We see her beginning the mastery of language, socialization skills, imagination, and self-awareness. 40m; VHS, 3/4 U. **Pr:** Alfred Guzzetti. **A:** Primary-Adult. **P:** Education. **U:** Institution, Home, SURA. **Gen-Edu:** Documentary Films, Psychology, Children. **Acq:** Purchase, Rent/Lease, Duplication. **Dist:** Filmakers Library Inc.

Beginning Raku 19??
Features artist Gordon Hutchins as part of a five-video workshop for potters. 60m; VHS. **A:** Jr. High-College. **P:** Education. **U:** Institution. **Gen-Edu:** Art & Artists. **Acq:** Purchase. **Dist:** Crystal Productions. $39.95.

Beginning Reading & Sign Language 1990
This video is designed for priming communications skills in hearing impaired youngsters. 90m; VHS. **Pr:** Aylmer Press. **A:** Family. **P:** Instruction. **U:** Home. **How-Ins:** How-To, Children, Communication. **Acq:** Purchase. **Dist:** Aylmer Press. $24.95.

Beginning Rhythmics 1988
Rhythmic gymnastics coaches are told how they can instruct their students. 45m; VHS, 3/4 U. **C:** Hosted by Judy Avener; Marshall Avener. **Pr:** Champions on Film. **A:** Adult. **P:** Teacher Education. **U:** Institution, CCTV, Home. **Spo-Rec:** Sports--General, Gymnastics, Women. **Acq:** Purchase. **Dist:** School-Tech Inc. $59.95.

Beginning Rock Bass 199?
Babys and Bad English bassist Ricki Phillips provides simple instruction for playing rock bass styles. ?m; VHS. **A:** Sr. High-Adult. **P:** Instruction. **U:** Home. **How-Ins:** Music--Instruction. **Acq:** Purchase. **Dist:** Hal Leonard Corp. $14.95.

Beginning Rock Drums 199?
Mike Terrana provides fundamentals for solid drumming through a series of basic rudiments. ?m; VHS. **A:** Sr. High-Adult. **P:** Instruction. **U:** Home. **How-Ins:** Music--Instruction. **Acq:** Purchase. **Dist:** Hal Leonard Corp. $14.95.

Beginning Rock Guitar 199?
Michael Thompson presents an introduction to rock guitar using simple techniques and solos. ?m; VHS. **A:** Sr. High-Adult. **P:** Instruction. **U:** Home. **How-Ins:** Music--Instruction. **Acq:** Purchase. **Dist:** Hal Leonard Corp. $14.95.

Beginning Rock Keyboard 199?
Tom Gimbel provides the basics needed to solo or play with a rock group. ?m; VHS. **A:** Sr. High-Adult. **P:** Instruction. **U:** Home. **How-Ins:** Music--Instruction. **Acq:** Purchase. **Dist:** Hal Leonard Corp. $14.95.

Beginning Rock Lead Guitar 199?
Dave Celentano teaches the viewer beginning lead guitar techniques. Includes booklet. 60m; VHS. **A:** Family. **P:** Instruction. **U:** Home. **How-Ins:** Music--Instruction. **Acq:** Purchase. **Dist:** Hal Leonard Corp. $19.95.

Beginning Rock Lead Guitar: For Electric and Acoustic Guitars 199?
Provides exercises for learning scales, hammer-ons and pull-offs, slides, vibrato, and more. Plus a lesson on transposing keys. ?m; VHS. **A:** Sr. High-Adult. **P:** Education. **U:** Home. **How-Ins:** Music--Instruction. **Acq:** Purchase. **Dist:** Hal Leonard Corp. $19.95.

Beginning Rock Rhythm Guitar 199?
Dave Celentano teaches the viewer beginning rock rhythm guitar techniques. Includes booklet. 60m; VHS. **A:** Family. **P:** Instruction. **U:** Home. **How-Ins:** Music--Instruction. **Acq:** Purchase. **Dist:** Hal Leonard Corp. $19.95.

Beginning Rock Rhythm Guitar: For Electric and Acoustic Guitars 199?
Explains anatomy of the electric guitar, string gauges, tuning, finger exercises and picking techniques. Plus a lesson about chording. ?m; VHS. **A:** Sr. High-Adult. **P:** Education. **U:** Home. **How-Ins:** Music--Instruction. **Acq:** Purchase. **Dist:** Hal Leonard Corp. $19.95.

Beginning Sax 199?
Scott Page presents the basics essential for rock-style soloing. ?m; VHS. **A:** Sr. High-Adult. **P:** Instruction. **U:** Home. **How-Ins:** Music--Instruction. **Acq:** Purchase. **Dist:** Hal Leonard Corp. $14.95.

Beginning Sewing Techniques 1988
Beginning with a pattern selection at a fabric store, this tape shows beginners how to get started or helps improve the skills of people who already know how to sew. 60m; VHS. **Pr:** Cambridge Career Productions. **A:** Jr. High-Adult. **P:** Instruction. **U:** Institution, Home. **How-Ins:** Home Economics, Sewing, Crafts. **Acq:** Purchase. **Dist:** Cambridge Educational. $49.00.

Beginning Shorthand 1988
The theory of Gregg shorthand is presented in this lengthy course. 30m; VHS, 3/4 U. **Pr:** Michigan State University. **A:** Sr. High-Adult. **P:** Instruction. **U:** Institution, CCTV. **How-Ins:** Office Practice, Occupations. **Acq:** Purchase, Rent/Lease. **Dist:** Michigan State University. $650.00.

Beginning Stunts Volume 10 2008 (Unrated)
Coach Mark Bagon and the Iowa All-Stars demonstrate 12 new stunts for cheerleaders at the beginning level. 26m; DVD. **A:** Family. **P:** Education. **U:** Home, Institution. **Spo-Rec:** Cheerleaders, Athletic Instruction/Coaching. **Acq:** Purchase. **Dist:** Championship Productions. $29.99.

Beginning Surfing 1990
Richard Chew, former World Surfing Champion, shows neophyte surfers what it's all about. Focus is on board fundamentals and technique. 60m; VHS. **Pr:** NSI. **A:** Jr. High-Adult. **P:** Instruction. **U:** Home. **Spo-Rec:** Sports--General. **Acq:** Purchase. **Dist:** NSI Sound & Video Inc. $24.95.

Beginning to Glaze and Fire 19??
Features artist Graham Sheehan as part of a five-video workshop for potters. 60m; VHS. **A:** Jr. High-College. **P:** Education. **U:** Institution. **Gen-Edu:** Art & Artists. **Acq:** Purchase. **Dist:** Crystal Productions. $39.95.

Beginning to Read and Write 1993
Demonstrates and discusses strategies for integrating a whole language approach to reading and writing into the first grade classroom. Part of the Whole Language Classroom Series. 30m; VHS. **A:** Adult. **P:** Teacher Education. **U:** Institution. **Gen-Edu:** Language Arts, Education. **Acq:** Purchase, Rent/Lease. **Dist:** Films for the Humanities & Sciences. $149.00.

Beginning to Throw on the Potter's Wheel 19??
Features artist Robin Hopper as part of a five-video workshop for potters. 60m; VHS. **A:** Jr. High-College. **P:** Education. **U:** Institution. **Gen-Edu:** Art & Artists. **Acq:** Purchase. **Dist:** Crystal Productions. $39.95.

Beginning Tole Painting 1986
Jayne Swartzwelder instructs the novice viewer in the basics of tole painting. 110m; VHS. **Pr:** WJER. **A:** Jr. High-Adult. **P:** Instruction. **U:** Institution, SURA. **How-Ins:** How-To, Painting. **Acq:** Purchase. **Dist:** WJER Video Services.

Beginning Training for Your Retriever 1993
Mike Mathiot, professional dog trainer and hunting guide, illustrates techniques for training your hunting dog including obedience, voice and whistle commands, and water retrieving. 46m; VHS. **A:** Adult. **P:** Instruction. **U:** Home. **How-Ins:** Hunting, Pets. **Acq:** Purchase. **Dist:** Stoney-Wolf Productions, Inc. $19.95.

Beginning Trumpet 199?
Michael Harris demonstrates exercises and techniques for beginners to start playing scales and simple melodies. ?m; VHS. **A:** Sr. High-Adult. **P:** Instruction. **U:** Home. **How-Ins:** Music--Instruction. **Acq:** Purchase. **Dist:** Hal Leonard Corp. $14.95.

Beginning Underwater Photography 1990
Learn all of the important techniques for successful camera photography under the sea, including what type of film to use, exposure, lighting methods and focussing. 18m; VHS. **Pr:** Bennett Marine Video. **A:** Sr. High-Adult. **P:** Instruction. **U:** Home. **How-Ins:** How-To, Photography. **Acq:** Purchase. **Dist:** Bennett Marine Video. $16.95.

Beginning Values Clarification 1977
Values clarification techniques in the classroom are gaining acceptance in the education field. This program discusses facts, concepts, and values, based on John Dewey's philosophy. 29m; 3/4 U. **Pr:** Media Five. **A:** College-Adult. **P:** Teacher Education. **U:** Institution, CCTV, SURA. **Gen-Edu:** Education, Psychology. **Acq:** Purchase. **Dist:** Home Vision Cinema.

Beginning Watercolor Painting 1984
The fundamental techniques for successful watercolor painting are demonstrated. 56m; VHS, 3/4 U. **Pr:** RMI Media Productions. **A:** Sr. High-Adult. **P:** Education. **U:** Institution, CCTV, Home. **How-Ins:** Painting, How-To. **Acq:** Purchase. **Dist:** RMI Media.

Beginning Waterskiing 198?
A video for the beginner, covering equipment options, water starts, single and double ski, safety practices, hand signals, turns and more. Also included is a special section for kids. 30m; VHS. **A:** Sr. High-Adult. **P:** Entertainment. **U:** Home. **How-Ins:** How-To, Children, Skiing. **Acq:** Purchase. **Dist:** Bennett Marine Video. $19.95.

Beginning with Bong 19??
Documentary outlining the various obstacles faced by children with functional limitations in the school environment. Offers special medical information on arthrogryposis, spina bifida, spinal cord injury, muscular dystrophy, and cerebral palsy. Winner of the British Medical Association Award, the CINE Golden Award, and the Emmy Award. 54m; VHS. **A:** Primary-Adult. **P:** Education. **U:** Institution. **Hea-Sci:** Pediatrics, Medical Care, Handicapped. **Acq:** Purchase, Rent/Lease. **Dist:** University of Maryland. $75.00.

The Beginning—Bouquets & Headpieces for the Bride 19??
Betty Ann provides all the necessary information to easily and professionally complete an entire wedding. 60m; VHS. **A:** Sr. High-Adult. **P:** Instruction. **U:** Institution. **How-Ins:** Marriage, How-To. **Acq:** Purchase. **Dist:** Instructional Video. $29.95.

Beginnings 1980
Describes the animator's personal view of the universe, as abstract landscapes evolve into strange, godlike figures. 9m; VHS, 3/4 U. **C:** Directed by Clorinda Warny; Suzanne Gervais; Lina Gagnon. **Pr:** National Film Board of Canada. **A:** College-Adult. **P:** Entertainment. **U:** Institution, SURA. **Fin-Art:** Film--Avant-Garde, Video. **Acq:** Purchase, Rent/Lease. **Dist:** National Film Board of Canada.

Beginnings: Fundamentals of Ballet Vol. I ????
Jan Miller explains basic posture and alignment, correct use of muscle energy, the action of turn-out, and how to avoid common problems of incorrect pelvic placement. 70m; VHS. **A:** Adult. **P:** Instruction. **U:** Home, Institution. **How-Ins:** Dance--Ballet, Dance--Instruction. **Acq:** Purchase. **Dist:** Stagestep. $59.95.

Beginnings: Fundamentals of Ballet Vol. II ????
Jan Miller explains proper foot alignment, weight placement and transfer, the difference between relever and elever, knee and ankle coordination, and use of the barre. 70m; VHS. **A:** Adult. **P:** Instruction. **U:** Home, Institution. **How-Ins:** Dance--Ballet, Dance--Instruction. **Acq:** Purchase. **Dist:** Stagestep. $59.95.

Beginnings: Handicapped Children Birth to Age 5 1985
Teachers, child development specialists, and other professionals offer advice and practical instruction to parents raising young children who are moderately to severely disabled. 30m;

VHS, 3/4 U. **Pr:** Maryland State Department of Education; Maryland Instructional Television; PBS. **A:** College-Adult. **P:** Instruction. **U:** Institution, CCTV, Home, SURA. **Gen-Edu:** Children, Handicapped, Parenting. **Acq:** Purchase, Rent/Lease, Duplication, Off-Air Record. **Dist:** PBS Home Video. $75.00.

Indiv. Titles: 1. Overview of Child Development 2. Neurodevelopment 3. Gross Motor Development 4. Fine Motor Development 5. Communication: Language Development 6. Communication: Disorders 7. Cognitive Development 8. Social Development 9. Interactions 10. Assessment 11. Environments 12. Special Issues.

The Beginnings of Exploration 1965
A description of the first stages in Europe's expansion; why the first explorers were anxious to discover a new sea route to India and how they accomplished their aims. 15m; VHS, 3/4 U. **Pr:** Encyclopedia Britannica Educational Corporation. **A:** Primary-Jr. High. **P:** Education. **U:** Institution, SURA. **L:** English, Spanish. **Gen-Edu:** Documentary Films, Explorers. **Acq:** Purchase, Rent/Lease, Trade-in. **Dist:** Encyclopedia Britannica.

Beginnings of Vertebrate Life 1987
Time-lapse photography shows how a newly fertilized egg changes and grows before birth. 11m; VHS, 3/4 U. **A:** Jr. High-Sr. High. **P:** Education. **U:** Institution, SURA. **Hea-Sci:** Biology. **Acq:** Purchase, Trade-in. **Dist:** Encyclopedia Britannica. $190.00.

Beginnings—A Hat 1989
Elizabeth knits a hat while the viewers follow along and learn from her example. 120m; VHS. **C:** Elizabeth Zimmerman. **Pr:** Nancy's Notions Ltd. **A:** Jr. High-Adult. **P:** Instruction. **U:** Institution, Home. **How-Ins:** Crafts. **Acq:** Rent/Lease. **Dist:** Nancy's Notions Ltd.

The Beguiled 1970 (R) — ★★★
During the Civil War a wounded Union soldier is taken in by the women at a girl's school in the South. He manages to seduce both a student and a teacher, and jealousy and revenge ensue. Decidedly weird psychological melodrama from action vets Siegel and Eastwood. 109m; VHS, DVD. **C:** Clint Eastwood; Geraldine Page; Elizabeth Hartman; Jo Ann Harris; Directed by Donald Siegel; Written by Albert (John B. Sherry) Maltz; Irene (Grimes Grice) Kamp; Cinematography by Bruce Surtees; Music by Lalo Schifrin. **Pr:** Mark Huffam. **A:** Sr. High-Adult. **P:** Entertainment. **U:** Home. **Mov-Ent:** Civil War, Education. **Acq:** Purchase. **Dist:** Movies Unlimited; Alpha Video; Universal Studios Home Video. $14.98.

Behave Yourself! 1952 (Unrated) — ★½
A married couple adopts a dog who may be the key for a million-dollar hijacking setup by a gang of hoodlums. 81m/B/W; VHS, DVD. **C:** Shelley Winters; Farley Granger; William Demarest; Lon Chaney, Jr.; Hans Conried; Elisha Cook, Jr.; Francis L. Sullivan; Directed by George Beck. **Pr:** Jerry Wald; Norman Krasna; RKO. **A:** Family. **P:** Entertainment. **U:** Home. **Mov-Ent:** Pets, Family Viewing. **Acq:** Purchase. **Dist:** Movies Unlimited. $18.99.

Behaving Badly 1989 (Unrated) — ★½
When Bridget's husband of 20 years left her for a younger woman, she didn't put up a fuss. But after five years of keeping a stiff upper lip, Bridget hasn't really moved on with her life and she decides to start over by changing her attitude and not being so accomodating. Some of the characters are little more than charicatures, which doesn't help the slow-moving story. 203m; DVD. **C:** Judi Dench; Ronald Pickup; Frances Barber; Joely Richardson; Douglas Hodge; Directed by David Tucker; Written by Catherine Heath; Moira Williams; Cinematography by Andy Watt; Music by Stephen Oliver. **A:** Adult. **P:** Entertainment. **U:** Home. **L:** English. **Mov-Ent:** Divorce. **Acq:** Purchase. **Dist:** Acorn Media Group Inc.

Behavior in Organizations 1979
This course presents analyzed research findings and behavioral science concepts. Focuses on the behavior of people in work situations, and the applications of research and concepts to the world of work. 30m; 3/4 U. **Pr:** Seneca College of Applied Arts and. **A:** College-Adult. **P:** Education. **U:** Institution, CCTV, BCTV, Home. **Bus-Ind:** Business, Management. **Acq:** Purchase. **Dist:** Seneca College of Applied Arts & Technology.

Indiv. Titles: 1. Course Overview 2. The Organization as a Social System 3. Formal and Informal Organizations 4. The Organization Environment 5. Motivation 6. Job Satisfaction 7. Effective Management 8. Leadership Styles and Power 9. Management of Change 10. Team Building and Participative Management 11. Communication at Work 12. Employee Appraisal and Counselling 13. Managing Different Employees 14. Working with Unions 15. The Future Perspective.

Behavior Modification 1979
From the "Stretch" series developed by educators to facilitate mainstreaming. The development of behavior modification is shown with specific techniques for better classroom management. 30m; VHS, 3/4 U, EJ. **Pr:** Metropolitan Cooperative Educationa. **A:** College-Adult. **P:** Teacher Education. **U:** Institution, CCTV. **Gen-Edu:** Handicapped, Education, Psychology. **Acq:** Purchase. **Dist:** American Educational Products LLC.

The Behavior of Matter 1982
Observations of chemical changes in demonstrations of experiments and illustrations of common physical phenomena are included in this program. 15m; VHS, 3/4 U. **Pr:** Encyclopedia Britannica Educational Corporation. **A:** Primary-Jr. High. **P:** Education. **U:** Institution, SURA. **Hea-Sci:** Chemistry. **Acq:** Purchase, Rent/Lease, Trade-in. **Dist:** Encyclopedia Britannica.

Behavioral Disorders/Learning Disabilities 1976
The relationship of behavioral disorders to learning disabilities is drawn through observations of the two problems. 30m; VHS, 3/4 U. **Pr:** Learning Disabilities Council. **A:** College-Adult. **P:** Education. **U:** Institution, SURA. **Gen-Edu:** Learning Disabilities, Psychology. **Acq:** Purchase. **Dist:** Home Vision Cinema.

Behavioral Interviewing With Couples 19??
Uses dramatized scenes to illustrate six basic stages of an initial marriage counseling interview. 14m; VHS. **A:** Adult. **P:** Education. **U:** Home, Institution. **Hea-Sci:** Psychology, Marriage. **Acq:** Purchase, Rent/Lease. **Dist:** Research Press. $255.00.

Behavioral Interviewing with Couples 1976
A look at the six basic stages of an interview for beginning a counseling program for married couples. 14m; VHS, 3/4 U, Special order formats. **Pr:** Behavioral Images. **A:** Adult. **P:** Professional. **U:** Institution, CCTV, Home, SURA. **Hea-Sci:** Psychology, Marriage, Interviews. **Acq:** Purchase, Rent/Lease. **Dist:** Research Press. $255.00.

Behavioral Principles for Parents: A Discrimination Program 1979
Thirty-five short vignettes of parent-child interactions including examples of positive reinforcement of both appropriate and inappropriate behaviors, punishment, time-out procedures, and extinction. 13m; VHS, 3/4 U, Special order formats. **Pr:** Norman E. Baxley. **A:** Adult. **P:** Education. **U:** Institution, CCTV, Home, SURA. **Gen-Edu:** Psychology, Parenting. **Acq:** Purchase, Rent/Lease. **Dist:** Research Press. $240.00.

Behaviorism and Whole Language: Dialogue or Debate? 19??
Documents a 1988 debate between behaviorists Alan Cohen and Joan Hyman of the University of San Francisco, and whole language advocates Ken and Yetta Goodman of the University of Arizona. Available separately, or as part of the "Whole Language Workshop" series. 105m; VHS. **A:** Adult. **P:** Teacher Education. **U:** Institution. **Gen-Edu:** Language Arts, Education. **Acq:** Purchase, Rent/Lease. **Dist:** Boynton/Cook Publishers Inc. $150.00.

Behaviors Associated with Dementia: Case Presentations 19??
Outlines the behaviors associated with dementia, including disorientation, confusion, agitation, and depression. Filmed on-location at a nursing home. Contains no narration. 28m; VHS. **A:** Adult. **P:** Education. **U:** Institution. **Hea-Sci:** Aging, Medical Care, Patient Care. **Acq:** Purchase, Rent/Lease. **Dist:** University of Maryland. $300.00.

Behavorial Principles for Parents 19??
Consists of 31 short vignettes of parent-child interactions. Shows examples of reinforcement, extinction, punishment, and time-out being used correctly and incorrectly. 13m; VHS. **A:** Adult. **P:** Education. **U:** Home, Institution. **Gen-Edu:** Children, Parenting, Psychology. **Acq:** Purchase, Rent/Lease. **Dist:** Research Press. $240.00.

Behemoth 2011 (Unrated) — ★
Part of the Syfy Channel's "Maneater" series. An earthquake reactivates a long-dormant volcano on Mount Lincoln and as scientists investigate, they find a subterranean creature has been released to cause havoc. The special effects are mostly shaky cams, steam, and monster parts since there's no budget for anything more. 90m; DVD. **C:** Ed Quinn; Pascale Hutton; William B. Davis; Ty Olsson; Cindy Busby; James Kirk; Jessica Parker Kennedy; Garry Chalk; Directed by David (W.D.) Hogan; Written by Rachelle S. Howie; Cinematography by Anthony C. Metchie; Music by Michael Neilson. **A:** Sr. High-Adult. **P:** Entertainment. **U:** Home. **Mov-Ent:** TV Movies, Science, Volcanos. **Acq:** Purchase. **Dist:** Vivendi Visual Entertainment.

Behind Bars 1979
A behind the scenes look at the first weeks of imprisonment for James Olsen. The question is asked: Is Olsen an enemy, or a victim of the society that incarcerated him? 19m; VHS, 3/4 U. **Pr:** Mediavision. **A:** Primary-Adult. **P:** Education. **U:** Institution, SURA. **Gen-Edu:** Documentary Films. **Acq:** Purchase. **Dist:** Lucerne Media.

Behind Closed Doors 1992
Presents two case histories on childhood abuse and its ramifications on the children after they reach adulthood: David grows up to beat his wife, and Margaret marries an abusive man. Includes an overview of their recovery and treatment. 46m; VHS. **A:** College-Adult. **P:** Education. **U:** Institution. **Gen-Edu:** Child Abuse, Domestic Abuse. **Acq:** Purchase, Rent/Lease. **Dist:** Filmakers Library Inc. $350.00.

Behind Closed Doors 2001
Examines underlying factors of domestic violence, child abuse, assault and suicide and how they affect emotional and physical health. 28m; VHS, DVD. **A:** Adult. **P:** Professional. **U:** Institution. **Hea-Sci:** Violence, Health Education, Nursing. **Acq:** Purchase. **Dist:** Aquarius Health Care Media. $99.00.

Behind Closed Doors: Crisis at Home 1989
Students who have had problems with anything from parental remarriage to sexual abuse, talk candidly. 30m; VHS, 3/4 U. **Pr:** HRM. **A:** Jr. High-Sr. High. **P:** Education. **U:** Institution. **Gen-Edu:** Documentary Films, Sexual Abuse, Divorce. **Acq:** Purchase. **Dist:** HRM Video. $195.00.

Behind Enemy Lines 1985 (R) — ★½
Special Forces soldier goes on a special mission to eliminate a possible Nazi spy. 83m; VHS, Blu-Ray, UMD. **C:** Hal Holbrook; Ray Sharkey; David McCallum; Tom Isbell; Anne Twomey; Robert Patrick; Directed by Sheldon Larry. **Pr:** Heron Communications. **A:** Sr. High-Adult. **P:** Entertainment. **U:** Home. **Mov-Ent:** TV Movies, World War Two. **Acq:** Purchase. **Dist:** No Longer Available.

Behind Enemy Lines 1996 (R) — ★★
Ex-Marine Mike Weston (Griffith) believes he was responsible for the death of his friend Jones (Mulkey) during assignment in Vietnam. When Weston discovers Jones is actually being hostage, he decides on a rescue mission. 89m; VHS, DVD, CC. **C:** Thomas Ian Griffith; Chris Mulkey; Courtney Gains; Directed by Mark Griffiths; Written by Andrew Osborne; Dennis Cooley; Cinematography by Blake T. Evans; Music by Arthur Kempel. **Pr:** Brad Krevoy; Orion Pictures. **A:** Sr. High-Adult. **P:** Entertainment. **U:** Home. **Mov-Ent. Acq:** Purchase. **Dist:** MGM Studios Inc.

Behind Enemy Lines 2001 (PG-13) — ★★
Balkan civil war is mere scenery, and soldiers only caricatures, in this cartoonish cat-and-mouse chase movie. Ace Navy navigator Lt. Burnett (Wilson), tired of flying peace missions, yearns for some real action. When a routine reconnaissance operation goes awry—his plane shot down over Serbian territory and his pilot ruthlessly executed—Burnett gets his wish. Crusty Admiral Reigart (Hackman) wants to rescue his flyboy, but a pesky international peace agreement gets in the way. First-time director Moore, best known for Sega promos, takes a video game approach to war. Utterly unconvincing suspense, but action sequences do their duty. Despite a clear connection to the ordeal of real-life Air Force captain Scott O'Grady, this is no true story. 106m; VHS, DVD, Wide. **C:** Owen Wilson; Gene Hackman; Joaquim de Almeida; David Keith; Gabriel Macht; Charles Malik Whitfield; Olek Krupa; Vladimir Mashkov; Marko Ogonda; Directed by John Moore; Written by David Veloz; Zak Penn; Cinematography by Brendan Galvin; Music by Don Davis. **Pr:** John Davis; Davis Entertainment Company; 20th Century-Fox. **A:** Jr. High-Adult. **P:** Entertainment. **U:** Home. **Mov-Ent. Acq:** Purchase. **Dist:** Fox Home Entertainment.

Behind Enemy Lines 2: Axis of Evil 2006 (R) — ★½
Navy SEALs are on a covert op to North Korea to take out a nuclear missile site. The mission is aborted when they are already on the ground so the soldiers decide to get it done anyway despite the bad guys hunting for them. Dumb but generally fast-paced escapist fare. 96m; DVD, Blu-Ray. **C:** Nicholas Gonzalez; Keith David; Denis Arndt; Ben Cross; Bruce McGill; Peter Coyote; Glenn Morshower; Matt Bushell; Dennis James Lee; Directed by James Dodson; Written by James Dodson; Cinematography by Lorenzo Senatore; Music by Pinar Toprak. **A:** Sr. High-Adult. **P:** Entertainment. **U:** Home. **Mov-Ent. Acq:** Purchase. **Dist:** Fox Home Entertainment.

Behind Enemy Lines 3: Colombia 2008 (R) — ★½
An in-name-only sequel that finds a team of Navy SEALS, on assignment in Colombia, falsely accused of assassinating the leaders of two opposing factions. With the U.S. government disavowing their mission, the commandoes are left to sort out the mess on their own. 94m; DVD. **C:** Joe Manganiello; Kenneth Anderson; Keith David; Channon Roe; Yancey Arias; Steven Bauer; Tim Matheson; Directed by Tim Matheson; Written by Tobias Iaconis; Cinematography by Claudio Chea; Music by Joseph Conlan. **A:** Sr. High-Adult. **P:** Entertainment. **U:** Home. **Mov-Ent:** South America. **Acq:** Purchase. **Dist:** Fox Home Entertainment.

Behind Kremlin Walls 1990
The "Prime Time Live" television show details the inner workings of the once highly classified Kremlin government building in Moscow. 80m; VHS. **C:** Hosted by Sam Donaldson; Diane Sawyer. **Pr:** ABC News. **A:** Sr. High-Adult. **P:** Education. **U:** Home. **Gen-Edu:** Documentary Films, USSR. **Acq:** Purchase. **Dist:** MPI Media Group; Knowledge Unlimited, Inc.; Cambridge Educational. $19.98.

Behind Locked Doors 1948 — ★★½
A journalist fakes mental illness to have himself committed to an asylum, where he believes a crooked judge is in hiding. A superior "B" mystery/suspense feature, with some tense moments. 61m/B/W; VHS, DVD. **C:** Lucille Bremer; Richard Carlson; Tor Johnson; Douglas Fowley; Herbert (Hayes) Heyes; Ralf Harolde; Directed by Budd Boetticher; Written by Eugene Ling; Malvin Wald; Cinematography by Guy Roe; Music by Irving Friedman. **Pr:** Eagle Lion. **A:** Jr. High-Adult. **P:** Entertainment. **U:** Home. **Mov-Ent:** Mystery & Suspense. **Acq:** Purchase. **Dist:** Movies Unlimited; Alpha Video; Kino on Video. $19.95.

Behind Nazi Guns 1944
German factory workers who made the Nazi weapons are profiled. 21m/B/W; VHS, 3/4 U. **TV Std:** NTSC, PAL. **C:** Narrated by William L. Shirer. **Pr:** U.S. Navy. **A:** Jr. High-Adult. **P:** Education. **U:** Institution, Home. **Gen-Edu:** Documentary Films, Propaganda, World War Two. **Acq:** Purchase. **Dist:** International Historic Films Inc. $22.00.

Behind Office Doors 1931 (Unrated) — ★★
Astor stars as the secretarial "power behind the throne" in this look at who really wields power in an office. Her boss takes her for granted until things go wrong. 82m/B/W; VHS, DVD. **C:** Mary Astor; Robert Ames; Ricardo Cortez; Charles Sellon; Directed by Melville Brown; Written by Carey Wilson. **Pr:** RKO. **A:** Jr. High-Adult. **P:** Entertainment. **U:** Home. **Mov-Ent. Acq:** Purchase. **Dist:** Movies Unlimited; Alpha Video. $19.95.

Behind Prison Walls 1943 — ★★
A steel tycoon and his son are sent to prison, and the son tries to convert his dad to socialism. A fun, light hearted film, the last for veteran Tully. 64m/B/W; VHS. **C:** Alan Baxter; Gertrude Michael; Tully Marshall; Edwin Maxwell; Jacqueline Dalya; Matt Willis; Directed by Steve Sekely. **Pr:** Producers Releasing

Corporation. **A:** Jr. High-Adult. **P:** Entertainment. **U:** Home. **Mov-Ent. Acq:** Purchase. **Dist:** Sinister Cinema. $16.95.

Behind Stone Walls 1932 (Unrated) — ★½
Bob Clay is prosecuted by his own D.A. father John when he takes the rap for his adulterous mother Esther who's killed her lover Jack Keene. Bob goes to prison and his girlfriend Peg works to prove his innocence while Esther's being blackmailed by Keene's butler Druggett. 58m/B/W; DVD. **C:** Edward J. Nugent; Priscilla Dean; Robert Elliott; Ann Christy; Robert Ellis; George Chesebro; Directed by Frank Strayer; Written by George B. Seitz; Cinematography by Jules Cronjager. **A:** Jr. High-Adult. **P:** Entertainment. **U:** Home. **Mov-Ent:** Crime Drama. **Acq:** Purchase. **Dist:** Sinister Cinema.

Behind That Curtain 1929 — ★½
Charlie Chan (Park) makes a brief appearance as a Scotland Yard detective in this melodrama. Wealthy Eve Mannering (Moran) marries rotter Eric Durand (Strange) and they go off to India. Soon unhappy, Eve is eager to leave Eric behind when old friend John Beetham (Baxter) assures her of his love. They travel to San Francisco with a murderous Eric in pursuit. Boris Karloff makes an appearance in his first sound picture as a nameless servant. 91m/B/W; DVD. **C:** Warner Baxter; Lois Moran; Philip Strange; Charles King; Gilbert Emery; E.L. Park; Directed by Irving Cummings; Written by Sonya Levien; Clarke Silvernail; Cinematography by Conrad Wells. **A:** Jr. High-Adult. **P:** Entertainment. **U:** Home. **Mov-Ent. Acq:** Purchase. **Dist:** Fox Home Entertainment.

Behind the Burly Q 2010
The history of burlesque in the United States is examined in its golden age, the first half of the 1900s. 98m; DVD. **A:** College-Adult. **P:** Entertainment. **U:** Home. **Mov-Ent:** Dance--History, History--U.S., Documentary Films. **Acq:** Purchase. **Dist:** First Run Features. $27.95.

Behind the Candelabra 2013 (Unrated) — ★★
Soderbergh wraps Douglas and Damon in over-the-top (even for Vegas) glitz and secrecy in looking at the last decade of entertainer Liberace's life. In 1977, 18-year-old Scott Thorsen meets the 58-year-old 'Lee" and soon becomes his companion, even appearing onstage with him. There's something both kind and unnerving about Liberace, especially after he persuades Scott to undergo plastic surgery to look more like him with the help of supremely creepy Dr. Jack Startz (Lowe). But drugs enter their lavish lifestyle, Scott becomes an addict, and eventually realizes he's going to be replaced, leading to a palimony suit. Based on Thorson's book. 120m; DVD, Blu-Ray. **C:** Michael Douglas; Matt Damon; Rob Lowe; Scott Bakula; Dan Aykroyd; Debbie Reynolds; Cheyenne Jackson; Mike O'Malley; Directed by Steven Soderbergh; Written by Richard LaGravenese; Cinematography by Steven Soderbergh; Music by Marvin Hamlisch. **A:** Sr. High-Adult. **P:** Entertainment. **U:** Home. **L:** English. **Mov-Ent:** Biography: Show Business, Drug Abuse, Homosexuality. **Acq:** Purchase. **Dist:** HBO Home Video.

Behind the Curtain: A Search for Solutions to Autism 1992
Explores new therapies for autism, and includes the perspective of the mother of an autistic son. 28m; VHS. **A:** Adult. **P:** Education. **U:** Institution. **Hea-Sci:** Documentary Films, Mental Health, Mental Retardation. **Acq:** Purchase, Rent/Lease. **Dist:** Filmakers Library Inc. $295.00.

Behind the Flag 1991
A different perspective on the Persian Gulf War, focusing on theories of the causes and consequences, as well as alternatives to the war. 20m; VHS, 3/4 U, Special order formats. **A:** College-Adult. **P:** Education. **U:** Institution, CCTV, CATV, BCTV, Home, SURA. **Gen-Edu:** Persian Gulf War, Middle East, Journalism. **Acq:** Purchase, Rent/Lease. **Dist:** The Video Project. $59.95.

Behind the Front 1926 — ★★½
Two friends tumble in and out of trouble in this comic Army film. One of the most profitable films of the late '20s. 60m/B/W; Silent; VHS. **C:** Wallace Beery; Raymond Hatton; Richard Arlen; Mary Brian; Chester Conklin; Directed by Edward Sutherland. **A:** Primary-Adult. **P:** Entertainment. **U:** Home. **Mov-Ent:** Action-Adventure, War--General, Silent Films. **Acq:** Purchase. **Dist:** Grapevine Video.

Behind the Green Lights 1935 (Unrated) — ★½
Mary, who works for ruthless criminal lawyer Raymond Cortell, switches loyalties when her policeman father is shot by one of Cortell's acquitted clients. She then takes up with detective Dave Britten to help prove Cortell is dirty and put him behind bars. 68m/B/W; DVD. **C:** Sidney Blackmer; Judith Allen; Norman Foster; Purnell Pratt; Theodore von Eltz; Directed by Christy Cabanne; Written by James Gruen; Cinematography by Ernest Miller; Jack Marta. **A:** Jr. High-Adult. **P:** Entertainment. **U:** Home. **Mov-Ent:** Law, Crime Drama. **Acq:** Purchase. **Dist:** Alpha Video; Sinister Cinema.

Behind the Line Featuring Craig Hodges 1993
Craig Hodges, an expert on three point shots for the Chicago Bulls, shows eager basketball enthusiasts how to master the dramatic and difficult three-point shot with this step-by-step program. 30m; VHS. **A:** Jr. High-Adult. **P:** Instruction. **U:** Home. **Spo-Rec:** Basketball, Sports--General. **Acq:** Purchase. **Dist:** Tapeworm Video Distributors Inc. $14.95.

Behind the Lines 1997 (R) — ★★
Focuses on the friendship between WWI soldier/poets Siegfried Sassoon (Wilby) and Wilfred Owen (Bunce), who receive a brief reprieve from the war when they're treated for shell shock at Edinburgh's Craiglockhart Hospital in 1917. Another patient is working-class soldier Billy Prior (Miller), made mute from the horrors he's witnessed. But their compassionate doctor, William Rivers (Pryce), is himself becoming increasingly unstable over the ethical concerns his work engenders. If he cures his patients, they go back to the front to fight again. The first book in Pat Barker's war trilogy. 96m; VHS, DVD, CC. **C:** Jonathan Pryce; James Wilby; Jonny Lee Miller; Stuart Bunce; Tanya Allen; John Neville; Dougray Scott; David Hayman; David Robb; Julian Fellowes; Kevin McKidd; Jeremy Child; Directed by Gilles Mackinnon; Written by Allan Scott; Cinematography by Glen MacPherson; Music by Mychael Danna. **Pr:** Allan Scott; Peter R. Simpson; Mark Shivas; Saskia Sutton; Allan Scott; Norstar Entertainment; BBC Films; Rafford Films; Artificial Eye. **A:** Sr. High-Adult. **P:** Entertainment. **U:** Home. **Mov-Ent:** World War One, Psychiatry, Scotland. **Acq:** Purchase. **Dist:** Lions Gate Television Corp.

Behind the Mask 1932 — ★½
Federal agent Jack Hart (Holt) goes undercover to infiltrate a drug smuggling syndicate headed by the mysterious Mr. X. The mastermind is really the sinister Dr. Steiner (Van Sloan), who kills his victims and stuffs their coffins with his drugs. Karloff is strictly a supporting character as chief henchman Henderson. 68m/B/W; DVD. **C:** Jack Holt; Edward Van Sloan; Constance Cummings; Boris Karloff; Directed by John Francis Dillon; Written by Jo Swerling; Cinematography by Ted Tetzlaff. **A:** Adult. **P:** Entertainment. **U:** Home. **L:** English. **Mov-Ent:** Crime Drama, Drug Trafficking/Dealing. **Acq:** Purchase. **Dist:** Turner Classic Movies (TCM).

Behind the Mask 1946 — ★★½
Lamont Cranston, better known as do-gooder "The Shadow," finds himself accused of murdering a blackmailing newspaper reporter. Based on the radio serial. 68m; VHS, DVD. **C:** Kane Richmond; Barbara Read; George Chandler; Dorothea Kent; Robert Shayne; June Clyde; Directed by Phil Karlson. **Pr:** Joe Kauffman; Monogram. **A:** Jr. High-Adult. **P:** Entertainment. **U:** Home. **Mov-Ent. Acq:** Purchase. **Dist:** MGM Home Entertainment; Grapevine Video; Anti-Defamation League of B'nai B'rith. $16.95.

Behind the Mask 1999 (Unrated) — ★★½
Mentally challenged janitor James Jones (Fox) is employed at a center run by workaholic doctor Bob Shushan (Sutherland). When the doc suffers a heart attack, it's James who saves him. Shushan takes this as a wake-up call and decides to help James find the father who abandoned him while reconnecting with his own neglected adult son, Brian (Whitford). Based on a true story. 90m; DVD. **C:** Donald Sutherland; Matthew Fox; Bradley Whitford; Mary McDonnell; Sheila Larken; Currie Graham; Lorena Gale; Ron Sauve; Directed by Tom McLoughlin; Written by Gregory Goodell; Cinematography by Arthur Albert. **A:** Jr. High-Adult. **P:** Entertainment. **U:** Home. **Mov-Ent:** Mental Retardation. **Acq:** Purchase. **Dist:** Movies Unlimited; Alpha Video.

Behind the Mask: A Fresh Approach to Fighting Prejudice 19??
In this animated short on prejudice, a "Red" meets two "Blues" and stereotypes them because they are unfamiliar. When the Blues react, all colors learn a lesson. 8m; VHS. **A:** Primary. **P:** Education. **U:** Institution. **Chl-Juv:** Animation & Cartoons, Prejudice. **Acq:** Purchase. **Dist:** Human Relations Media. $69.00.

Behind the Mask: The Rise of Leslie Vernon 2006 (R) — ★★
Hilarious satire of slasher films set in a world where killers apparently have enough fans to warrant documentary crews chasing them about to interview them. Crews composed of people who should, in theory, be smart enough to realize at some point that they might end up becoming victims because slashers are, you know, crazy. 92m; DVD, Blu-Ray, Streaming. **C:** Nathan Baesel; Robert Englund; Scott Wilson; Ben Pace; Britain Spellings; Angela Goethals; Zelda Rubenstein; Bridgett Newton; Kate Johnson; Directed by Scott Glosserman; Written by Scott Glosserman; David J. Stieve; Cinematography by Jaron Presant; Music by Gordy Haab. **A:** Sr. High-Adult. **P:** Entertainment. **U:** Home. **L:** English. **Mov-Ent. Acq:** Purchase, Rent/Lease. **Dist:** Anchor Bay Entertainment Inc. $17.99 14.98 9.99.

Behind the Planet of the Apes 1998
AMC documentary hosted by Roddy McDowall. 120m; DVD. **C:** Narrated by Roddy McDowall; Directed by Kevin Burns; David Comtois; Written by Kevin Burns; David Comtois; Brian Anthony. **A:** Jr. High-Adult. **P:** Entertainment. **U:** Home. **Gen-Edu:** Documentary Films. **Acq:** Purchase. **Dist:** Fox Home Entertainment.

Behind the Red Door 2002 (R) — ★★
Natalie (Sedgwick) hasn't spoken to her arrogant older brother Roy (Sutherland) for 10 years. A New York photographer, Natalie is tricked by her friend and agent Julia (Channing) into accepting an assignment in Boston that turns out to be for her brother's company. Roy then bullies Natalie into staying for his birthday party—later revealing to her that he's dying of AIDS. He wants to reconcile but a shaken Natalie (who blames Roy for some childhood traumas) insists she must return home. Good cast, but Sutherland's character is so secretive and obnoxious it's hard to dredge up any sympathy for him. 105m; VHS, DVD, CC. **C:** Kyra Sedgwick; Kiefer Sutherland; Stockard Channing; Jason Carter; Philip Craig; Directed by Matia Karrell; Written by Matia Karrell; C.W. Cressler; Cinematography by Robert Elswit; Music by David Fleury. **A:** Sr. High-Adult. **P:** Entertainment. **U:** Home. **Mov-Ent:** AIDS. **Acq:** Purchase. **Dist:** Showtime Networks Inc.

Behind the Rising Sun 1943 (Unrated) — ★★½
A Japanese publisher's political views clash with those of his American-educated son in 1930s Japan. Well done despite pre-war propaganda themes. 88m/B/W; VHS. **C:** Tom Neal; J. Carrol Naish; Robert Ryan; Mike Mazurki; Margo; Gloria Holden; Donald "Don" Douglas; Directed by Edward Dmytryk. **Pr:** RKO. **A:** Family. **P:** Entertainment. **U:** Home. **Mov-Ent:** Mass Media, Japan, Propaganda. **Acq:** Purchase. **Dist:** Unknown Distributor.

Behind the Scenes 197?
Juanita Hall introduces and sings songs made famous by blues singers such as Bessie Smith and Billie Holliday in this program. 30m/B/W; VHS, 3/4 U, EJ, Q. **Pr:** WCBS New York; Camera Three Productions. **A:** Sr. High-Adult. **P:** Entertainment. **U:** Institution, SURA. **Fin-Art:** Music--Performance, Music--Jazz. **Acq:** Duplication, Free Duplication. **Dist:** Camera Three Productions, Inc.; Creative Arts Television Archive.

Behind the Scenes 1981
All the behind-the-scenes action that goes on at a ballet company is described in these related programs from the "Eye on Dance" series. 30m; VHS, 3/4 U, EJ. **C:** Hosted by Celia Ipiotis. **Pr:** ARC Videodance. **A:** Family. **P:** Entertainment. **U:** Institution, CCTV, Home, SURA. **Fin-Art:** Dance--Ballet. **Acq:** Purchase. **Dist:** Eye on the Arts.
Indiv. Titles: 1. Rosemary Dunleavy, Mary Barnett and Alan Lewis 2. Alma Law, Phil Lee, and Beverly Emmons 3. Sylvia Nolan and Paul Moore 4. Leopold Allen, Brian Dube, and Raymond Serrano.

Behind the Scenes 1992
A PBS series geared to showing children the creative processes behind the visual and performing arts. Topics covered include painting, drawing, sculpture, music, dance, photography, and theatre. Hosted by magic and comedy duo Penn and Teller. Ten episodes on six cassettes. 30m; VHS. **A:** Primary-Jr. High. **P:** Entertainment. **U:** Home. **Chl-Juv:** Art & Artists. **Acq:** Purchase. **Dist:** Home Vision Cinema; GPN Educational Media; Ambrose Video Publishing, Inc. $99.95.
Indiv. Titles: 1. David Hockney: The Illusion of Depth 2. Robert Gil de Montes: Color 3. Nancy Graves: Balance 4. Carrie Mae Weems: Framing 5. Wayne Thiebaud: Line 6. Allen Toussaint: Melody 7. Max Roach: Rhythm 8. JoAnn Falletta: Texture 9. David Parsons: Pattern 10. Julie Taymor: Setting a Scene.

Behind the Scenes at the Supermarket 1958
Johnny visits the local supermarket and looks at the behind-the-scenes activities. 11m; VHS, 3/4 U. **Pr:** Josef Lesser, BFA Educational Media. **A:** Primary. **P:** Education. **U:** Institution, SURA. **L:** English, Spanish. **Chl-Juv:** Food Industry. **Acq:** Purchase. **Dist:** Phoenix Learning Group.

Behind the Scenes of Telstar 1962
The first active telecommunications satellite, Telstar, is shown in all stages of development. The first Presidential press conference to reach Europe via satellite is introduced by President Kennedy. 42m; VHS. **TV Std:** NTSC, PAL. **Pr:** National Aeronautics and Space Administration. **A:** Jr. High-Adult. **P:** Education. **U:** Institution, Home. **Gen-Edu:** Documentary Films, Communication, Space Exploration. **Acq:** Purchase. **Dist:** International Historic Films Inc. $24.95.

Behind the Scenes: The Complete Series 1992
Presents the entire 10-volume PBS television educational series that explores the processes involved in drawing, painting, theater acting, sculpture, photography, music, and dance with David Hockney, Wayne Thiebaud, Robert Gil de Montes, Carrie Mae Weems, Nancy Graves, David Parsons, Joann Falletta, Allen Touissaint, and Max Roach Taymor and hosted by Penn & Teller. 10 episodes. 280m; DVD. **C:** Penn Jillette; Teller. **A:** Family. **P:** Entertainment. **U:** Home. **Gen-Edu:** Television Series, Documentary Films, Education. **Acq:** Purchase. **Dist:** First Run Features. $59.95.

Behind the Scenes Tour of a Museum 1995
Visits Chicago's Field Museum of Natural History to reveal that modern museums do much more than provide the public with historic displays—they provide the scientific community with specimens and artifacts for research. Complete with teacher's guide. 20m; VHS. **A:** Primary-Jr. High. **P:** Education. **U:** Institution. **Gen-Edu:** Museums, Science. **Acq:** Purchase. **Dist:** United Learning Inc. $69.95.

Behind the Scenes Volume 1: Painting and Drawing 1992
How artists create their works, including the process they go through, is considered through interviews with David Hockney, Wayne Thiebaud, Robert Gil de Montes, and Matt Groening. 85m; DVD. **A:** Jr. High-Adult. **P:** Entertainment. **U:** Home. **Mov-Ent:** Art & Artists, Biography, Documentary Films. **Acq:** Purchase. **Dist:** First Run Features. $24.95.

Behind the Scenes Volume 2: Theater, Sculpture and Photography 1992
Looking at the nature of creativity of artists, the mediums of visual theater, sculpture, and photography are explored via Julia Taymor, Nancy Graves, and Carrie Mae Williams, respectively. 85m; DVD. **A:** Jr. High-Adult. **P:** Entertainment. **U:** Home. **Mov-Ent:** Art & Artists, Sculpture, Theater. **Acq:** Purchase. **Dist:** First Run Features. $24.95.

Behind the Scenes Volume 3: Music and Dance 1992 (Unrated)
Artists working in dance, classical music, and jazz demonstrate basics about their chose genre and the creative process. 110m; DVD. **A:** Family. **P:** Entertainment. **U:** Home. **Mov-Ent:** Dance, Documentary Films, Music--Classical. **Acq:** Purchase. **Dist:** Eagle Rock Entertainment Inc.; First Run Features. $24.95.

Behind the Scenes with Allen Toussaint 1999
Jazz composer and pianist Allen Toussaint demonstrstes musical composition by writing a piano melody and then completing

the song in the recording studio. And musical improvisation is demonstrated with Bobby McFerrin and saxophonist Jane Ira Bloom. 30m; VHS. **A:** Jr. High-Adult. **P:** Entertainment. **U:** Home. **Fin-Art**: Music. **Acq:** Purchase. **Dist:** First Run Features.

Behind the Scenes with Carrie Mae Weems 1999
African-American photographer Carrie Mae Weems shows how to use composition and content to create meaning in a photograph. Also includes a look at William Wegman working with his Weimeraner dogs to recreate the alphabet. 30m; VHS. **A:** Jr. High-Adult. **P:** Entertainment. **U:** Home. **Fin-Art**: Photography. **Acq:** Purchase. **Dist:** First Run Features.

Behind the Scenes with David Hockney 1998
World-famous artist David Hockney shows how artists play with perspective, illusion of depth and the vanishing point through his drawings. 30m; VHS. **A:** Sr. High-Adult. **P:** Entertainment. **U:** Home. **Fin-Art**: Art & Artists, Interviews. **Acq:** Purchase. **Dist:** First Run Features.

Behind the Scenes with David Parsons 1999
A former dancer with the Paul Taylor Dance Company, David Parsons is a choreographer for the American Ballet Theatre and the Feld Ballet. He demonstrates how he's inspired by everyday action and how movement is transformed into dance on stage. 30m; VHS. **A:** Sr. High-Adult. **P:** Entertainment. **U:** Home. **Fin-Art**: Dance--Ballet. **Acq:** Purchase. **Dist:** First Run Features.

Behind the Scenes with Eden Ryl 1982
In this lively interview, Eden shares her behavioral insight and some of her most nerve shattering personal experiences. 30m; VHS, 3/4 U. **Pr:** Ramic Productions. **A:** Adult. **P:** Education. **U:** Institution, CCTV. **Gen-Edu**: Interviews. **Acq:** Purchase, Rent/Lease. **Dist:** Ramic Productions.

Behind the Scenes with Joann Falletta 1999
Conductor Joann Falletta shows how a symphony orchestra uses layers of sound to create music and how to listen for these layers. 30m; VHS. **A:** Jr. High-Adult. **P:** Entertainment. **U:** Home. **Fin-Art**: Music. **Acq:** Purchase. **Dist:** First Run Features.

Behind the Scenes with Julie Taymor 1998
Julie Traymor, the award-winning director of the Broadway hit musical "The Lion King," turns her focus to Shakespeare's "The Tempest," using masks, puppets, and music. 30m; VHS. **A:** Sr. High-Adult. **P:** Entertainment. **U:** Home. **Fin-Art**: Theater, Interviews. **Acq:** Purchase. **Dist:** First Run Features.

Behind the Scenes with Max Roach 1999
Legendary jazz percussionist and composer Max Roach helps viewers learn about rhythm. 30m; VHS. **A:** Jr. High-Adult. **P:** Entertainment. **U:** Home. **Fin-Art**: Music--Jazz. **Acq:** Purchase. **Dist:** First Run Features.

Behind the Scenes with Nancy Graves 1999
Sculptor Nancy Graves demonstrates how to work with balance in gravity defying ways, including using a crane. Also featured is highwire daredevil Brian Dewhurst. 30m; VHS. **A:** Jr. High-Adult. **P:** Entertainment. **U:** Home. **Fin-Art**: Art & Artists. **Acq:** Purchase. **Dist:** First Run Features.

Behind the Scenes with Robert Gil de Montes 1999
Artist Robert Gil de Montes showcases his unusual use of color to create works that reflect his Mexican roots. Guest artist Marilynn Ono demonstrates the same use of color on a computer. 30m; VHS. **A:** Jr. High-Adult. **P:** Entertainment. **U:** Home. **Fin-Art**: Art & Artists. **Acq:** Purchase. **Dist:** First Run Features.

Behind the Scenes with Wayne Thiebaud 1999
Thiebaud and fellow animator Matt Groening demonstrate how lines can show movement in comic strips, while Thiebaud explains how simple lines work in art and motion pictures. 30m; VHS. **A:** Sr. High-Adult. **P:** Entertainment. **U:** Home. **Fin-Art**: Art & Artists. **Acq:** Purchase. **Dist:** First Run Features.

Behind the Screen 1916 — ★★★½
Chaplin starts out as a property man on a movie set and winds up in a pie-throwing sequence. Silent; musical soundtrack added. 20m/B/W; Silent; VHS, 3/4 U, Special order formats. **TV Std:** NTSC, PAL, SECAM. **C:** Charlie Chaplin. **Pr:** RKO. **A:** Family. **P:** Entertainment. **U:** Institution, CCTV, CATV, BCTV, Home. **Mov-Ent**: Classic Films, Silent Films. **Acq:** Purchase. **Dist:** Cable Films/i2bs Online World. $24.95.

Behind the Screens 199?
Argues that mainstream big-budget Hollywood movies have largely become vehicles for advertising and marketing due to the proliferation of product placement, fast-food chain tie-ins and toy merchandising. Special price for high schools. 40m; VHS. **A:** Sr. High-Adult. **P:** Education. **U:** Home. **Gen-Edu**: Filmmaking, Marketing, Commercials. **Acq:** Purchase. **Dist:** Media Education Foundation. $250.00.

Behind the Smile 1998
Documentary of lives and culture of young women working in the factories of Bangkok. Follows three such women, their roles, and the price they pay for Thailand's rapid industrialization. 46m; VHS. **A:** Adult. **P:** Education. **U:** Home. **Gen-Edu**: Documentary Films, Asia, Labor & Unions. **Acq:** Purchase, Rent/Lease. **Dist:** Filmakers Library Inc. $295.

Behind the Sun 2001 (PG-13) — ★★
A blood feud between two families nearly destroys them both in Salles' adaptation of Ismail Kadare's novel, which the director relocated to Brazil in 1910. The Ferreiras and the Breveses are both sugarcane planters determined to protect their honor if nothing else. Tonho Breves (Santoro) is expected to avenge the death of his older brother at the hands of the Ferreiras. Tonho's young brother (Lacerda) can't understand why the pointless violence continues and when Tonho falls in love with traveling circus performer Clara (Antonio), the boy becomes determined to see his brother safe and happy. Portuguese with subtitles. 91m; VHS, DVD. **C:** Jose Dumont; Rita Assemany; Rodrigo Santoro; Ravi Ramos Lacerda; Luiz Carlos Vasconcelos; Othon Bastos; Flavia Marco Antonio; Directed by Walter Salles; Written by Walter Salles; Karim Ainouz; Sergio Machado; Cinematography by Walter Carvalho; Music by Antonio Pinto. **Pr:** Arthur Cohn; Haut et Court; BAC Films Ltd; VideoFilmes; Dan Valley Film; Miramax Film Corp. **A:** Sr. High-Adult. **P:** Entertainment. **U:** Home. **L:** Portuguese. **Mov-Ent**: Circuses, Romance, South America. **Awds:** British Acad. '01: Foreign Film. **Acq:** Purchase. **Dist:** Buena Vista Home Entertainment.

Behind the Veil: Nuns 1984
An analogy is made between the invisibility of nuns in history, and the invisibility of women, whose achievements are minimally documented. 130m; VHS, 3/4 U. **A:** Jr. High-Adult. **P:** Education. **U:** Institution, SURA. **Gen-Edu**: Women. **Acq:** Purchase, Rent/Lease. **Dist:** National Film Board of Canada; Facets Multimedia Inc.; First Run Features. $99.95.

Behind the Wall 2008 (R) — ★½
A small community in Maine has decided to renovate a local lighthouse that's reputed to be haunted because of a 20-year-old murder case, despite the objections of an elderly priest. The pace picks up in the latter half of this low-budget horrorfest. 94m; DVD. **C:** Souleymane Sy Savane; Diana Franco-Galindo; Jody Richardson; Lindy Booth; Lawrence Dane; James Thomas; Andy Jones; Directed by Paul Schneider; Written by Anna Singer; Michael Bafaro; Cinematography by Larry Lynn. **A:** Sr. High-Adult. **P:** Entertainment. **U:** Home. **Mov-Ent**: Horror. **Acq:** Purchase. **Dist:** Monarch Home Video.

Behind the Wheel 1983
Five programs designed to make high school driver education students aware of safety hazards. Teacher's guide available. 30m; VHS. **A:** Sr. High. **P:** Education. **U:** Institution. **Gen-Edu**: Driver Education. **Acq:** Purchase. **Dist:** GPN Educational Media. $225.00.
Indiv. Titles: 1. DUI Arrest 2. Drunk Driving: Whose Responsibility? 3. The Second Collision 4. Driving Emergencies 5. Traffic Violations.

Behind the Wheel with Jackie Stewart 1986
A glimpse of the world, enjoyment and science of car racing with the famed trophy holder. 60m; VHS. **C:** Jackie Stewart. **Pr:** Karl/Lorimar. **A:** Jr. High-Adult. **P:** Instruction. **U:** Home. **Spo-Rec**: Documentary Films, Automobiles--Racing. **Acq:** Purchase. **Dist:** MGM Studios Inc. ; Warner Home Video, Inc.

Behind These Walls: Mumia Abu-jamal and the Long Struggle for Freedom 1996 (Unrated)
Documents Mumia Abu-Jamal's trial history and subsequent hearings while retelling the story of this famous case against one of the country's most controversial political prisons, a journalist and former Black Panther Party Member. Jamal was scheduled to be executed August 17, 1995 but the warrant was stayed along with an announcement from the Governor of Pennsylvania that he would sign a new death warrant as soon as legally possible. 70m; VHS. **A:** Adult. **P:** Education. **U:** Institution. **Gen-Edu**: Law, Politics & Government, Documentary Films. **Acq:** Purchase. **Dist:** Third World Newsreel. $225.

Behind Two Guns 1924 (Unrated) — ★½
A medicine show doctor and his trusty Indian sidekick help a frontier town's citizens discover who's constantly robbing the strongbox from the stagecoach. 62m/B/W; Silent; DVD. **C:** Otto Lederer; J.B. Warner; Guillermo Calles; Hazel Newman; Jim Welch; Directed by Robert North Bradbury; Written by Robert North Bradbury; Cinematography by Bert Longenecker. **A:** Jr. High-Adult. **P:** Entertainment. **U:** Home. **Mov-Ent**: Silent Films, Welding. **Acq:** Purchase. **Dist:** Movies Unlimited.

Behold a Pale Horse 1964 — ★★½
A Spanish police captain attempts to dupe Peck into believing that his mother is dying and he must visit her on her deathbed. Loyalist Spaniard Peck becomes privy to the plot against him, but goes to Spain anyway in this post Spanish Civil War film. 118m/B/W; VHS, DVD. **C:** Gregory Peck; Anthony Quinn; Omar Sharif; Mildred Dunnock; Directed by Fred Zinnemann; Written by J(ames) P(inckney) Miller; Music by Maurice Jarre. **Pr:** Columbia Pictures. **A:** Sr. High-Adult. **P:** Entertainment. **U:** Home. **Mov-Ent**: Spain. **Acq:** Purchase. **Dist:** Movies Unlimited; Alpha Video; Sony Pictures Home Entertainment Inc. $9.95.

Behold the Promised Land 1991
Combines interviews gathered on July 4, 1989 with American propaganda films of the late 1940s and early '50s to examine the effects of media and see how pro-American information is reflected in actual experience. 23m; VHS, 3/4 U. **A:** College-Adult. **P:** Entertainment. **U:** Institution. **Fin-Art**: Video, Propaganda, Interviews. **Acq:** Purchase, Rent/Lease. **Dist:** Video Data Bank.

The Beiderbecke Affair 1985 (Unrated)
British screwball mystery. Trevor (Bolam) orders a set of Bix Beiderbecke LPs from a dishy blonde door-to-door saleswoman. Upon receiving the wrong records he tries to remedy the situation causing he and girlfriend Jill (Flynn) to get caught up in a mystery of black market goods, secret parking lot meetings, and serious corruption. Enlivening the adventure are Big Al and Little Norm, a snoopy senior citizen, a town planner with an arsenal of incriminating files, and an overeager police officer. 6 episodes. 300m; DVD. **A:** Sr. High-Adult. **P:** Entertainment. **U:** Home. **Mov-Ent**: Mystery & Suspense. **Acq:** Purchase. **Dist:** Acorn Media Group Inc. $39.99.

The Beiderbecke Affair 1985
British comedy mystery series has amateur detective Jill Swinburne and Trevor Chaplin tracking down a shady sales lady and getting more than they bargained for. 312m; VHS, DVD. **A:** Adult. **P:** Entertainment. **U:** Home. **Mov-Ent**: Television, Mystery & Suspense. **Acq:** Purchase. **Dist:** Acorn Media Group Inc. $39.95.

The Beiderbecke Connection 1988
British comedy mystery series has amateur detective Jill Swinburne and Trevor Chaplin taking in a mysterious refugee with a passion for jazz music and a scheme to turn the world's currency into chaos. 200m; VHS, DVD. **A:** Adult. **P:** Entertainment. **U:** Home. **Mov-Ent**: Television, Mystery & Suspense. **Acq:** Purchase. **Dist:** Acorn Media Group Inc. $39.95.

Beijing Bicycle 2001 (PG-13) — ★★
Guei (Lin) leaves his provincial home and gets a job as a bike messenger in Beijing where most of his meager wages go to purchase his mountain bike. His bike is stolen and Guei loses his job. He finally discovers that petulant high schooler Jian (Bin), whose father wouldn't buy him a bike of his own, has purchased Geui's from a flea market and, because he can now join his friends riding after school, he refuses to let it go. Their confrontation turns violent as more and more people become involved. Chinese with subtitles. 113m; VHS, DVD. **C:** Cui Lin; Bin Li; Zhou Xun; Gao Yuanyuahn; Li Shuang; Zhao Yiwei; Pang Yan; Directed by Xiaoshuai Wang; Written by Xiaoshuai Wang; Danian Tang; Peggy Chiao; Hsiang-Ming Hsu; Cinematography by Jie Liu; Music by Wang Hsiao Feng. **Pr:** Peggy Chiao; Hsiao-Ming Hsu; Sony Pictures Classics. **A:** Sr. High-Adult. **P:** Entertainment. **U:** Home. **L:** Chinese. **Mov-Ent**: Job Hunting, China, Adolescence. **Acq:** Purchase. **Dist:** Sony Pictures Home Entertainment Inc.

The Being 1983 (R) — ★
People in Idaho are terrorized by a freak who became abnormal after radiation was disposed in the local dump. Another dull monster-created-by-nuclear-waste non-event. Of limited interest is Buzzi. However, you'd be more entertained (read: amused) by Troma's "The Toxic Avenger," which takes itself much (much!) less seriously. 82m; VHS, DVD. **C:** Ruth Buzzi; Martin Landau; Jose Ferrer; Directed by Jackie Kong. **Pr:** William Osco. **A:** Adult. **P:** Entertainment. **U:** Home. **Mov-Ent**: Horror. **Acq:** Purchase. **Dist:** Unknown Distributor.

Being a Complete Receiver 2007 (Unrated)
Coach Henry Mason lectures on what is needed to make a football team's receiver the best he can be. 88m; DVD. **A:** Family. **P:** Education. **U:** Home, Institution. **Spo-Rec**: Football, Athletic Instruction/Coaching. **Acq:** Purchase. **Dist:** Championship Productions. $39.99.

Being a Fat Child 1984
A study of the trials and tribulations of childhood obesity. 15m; VHS, 3/4 U. **Pr:** ABC 20/20. **A:** Jr. High-Adult. **P:** Education. **U:** Institution. **Gen-Edu**: Documentary Films, Human Relations, Obesity. **Acq:** Purchase, Rent/Lease. **Dist:** Phoenix Learning Group. $160.00.

Being a Friend: What Does It Mean? 1995
Children are taught how to build healthy friendships, and how to recognize constructive and destructive friendships. Includes teacher's guide. 19m; VHS. **A:** Primary. **P:** Education. **U:** Institution. **Chl-Juv**: Children, Education, Human Relations. **Acq:** Purchase. **Dist:** Sunburst Digital Inc. $149.00.

Being a Joines: A Life in the Brush Mountains 1988
The North Carolina storyteller John E. Joines talks about his life and what it means to live in the mountains. 55m; VHS, 3/4 U, Special order formats. **Pr:** Davenport Films. **A:** Jr. High-Adult. **P:** Education. **U:** Institution, Home, SURA. **Gen-Edu**: Documentary Films, Biography, Storytelling. **Acq:** Purchase, Rent/Lease. **Dist:** Davenport Films. $90.00.

Being a Leader: Man on the White Horse 1978
Shows how to develop the qualities of leadership in any vocation. 11m; VHS, 3/4 U. **Pr:** Nightingale-Conant Corp. **A:** College-Adult. **P:** Education. **U:** Institution, CCTV, CATV, BCTV, Home. **How-Ins**: Management, How-To. **Acq:** Purchase. **Dist:** Nightingale-Conant Corp.

Being a Professional Caregiver ????
Covers many life-ending topics such as accepting death, families' decision on treatment, communicating with a terminally ill patient, and minimizing family stress. 24m; VHS. **A:** Adult. **P:** Vocational. **U:** Institution. **Hea-Sci**: Death, Occupational Training, Medical Education. **Acq:** Purchase. **Dist:** University of Maryland. $150.00.

Being Abraham Maslow 1972
The only autobiographical film portrait of the psychologist whose ideas are fundamental to the human potential movement. 30m/B/W; VHS, 3/4 U. **Pr:** Leonard Zweig; Warren Bennis. **A:** Adult. **P:** Education. **U:** Institution. **Gen-Edu**: Psychology, Biography. **Acq:** Purchase. **Dist:** Filmakers Library Inc.

Being an Adult Child ????
Explains steps for dealing with a parent in the final stage of life. 24m; VHS. **A:** Adult. **P:** Vocational. **U:** Institution. **Hea-Sci**: Death, Occupational Training, Medical Education. **Acq:** Purchase. **Dist:** University of Maryland. $150.00.

Being and Vibration 199?
Picuris Pueblo Indian Joseph Rael, whose sacred name means Beautiful Painted Arrow, discusses the Tiwa language of his people, his childhood visionary experiences, and his work creating sound chambers for peace around the world. He prescribes that all physical manifestation is a result of vibrations from eternity which can lead to transformation and higher

consciousness. 90m; DVD. **A:** Adult. **P:** Education. **U:** Home, Institution. **Gen-Edu:** Philosophy & Ideology, Native Americans, Music. **Acq:** Purchase. **Dist:** Thinking Allowed Productions. $49.95.

Being at Home with Claude 1992 — ★★
Yves (Dupuis) is a 22-year-old Montreal hustler being interrogated by a nameless inspector (Godin) for the murder of his lover, Claude (Pichette). Yves has admitted his guilt but the inspector wants to reconstruct the event and determine a motive. Lots of black-and-white flashbacks as Yves dwells on his work and his psychologically love-death relationship with Claude. Rather pretentious and long-winded. Based on the play by Rene-Daniel DuBois. In French with English subtitles. 86m; VHS. **C:** Roy Dupuis; Jacques Godin; Jean-Francois Pichette; Gaston Lepage; Directed by Johanne Boisvert; Written by Jean Boudin. **A:** College-Adult. **P:** Entertainment. **U:** Home. **L:** French. **Mov-Ent:** Mystery & Suspense, Prostitution. **Awds:** Genie '92: Score. **Acq:** Purchase. **Dist:** Wellspring Media; Facets Multimedia Inc.

Being Born 197?
Bright folk-pop music and lyrics provide the background for this colorful, fast-moving montage celebrating the right to a healthy, happy start in life. 3m; 3/4 U. **Pr:** March of Dimes. **A:** Family. **P:** Education. **U:** Institution, CCTV, CATV. **Gen-Edu:** Infants, Human Rights. **Acq:** Free Loan. **Dist:** March of Dimes.

Being Different 1985
A docudrama of deformed men and women who have learned to live their lives to the fullest. 102m; VHS. **C:** Narrated by Christopher Plummer; Directed by Harry Rasky. **Pr:** Independent. **A:** Family. **P:** Entertainment. **U:** Home. **Gen-Edu:** Documentary Films, Handicapped. **Acq:** Purchase. **Dist:** Lions Gate Television Corp. $59.98.

Being Dumb. . .It's No Good 19??
Tony, an eighth grade student, is the subject of this film portrait. The program depicts the views held by Tony's parents, his teachers, school principal and peers about a "good student," as well as their expectations for Tony, both in school and in the future. 20m/B/W; 3/4 U, Special order formats. **Pr:** Education Development Center. **A:** College-Adult. **P:** Education. **U:** Institution, CCTV, CATV, BCTV. **Gen-Edu:** Documentary Films, Education, Learning Disabilities. **Acq:** Purchase, Rent/Lease. **Dist:** Education Development Center.

Being Elmo: A Puppeteer's Journey 2011 (PG) — ★★½
Entertaining, but not particularly enlightening, documentary on African-American puppeteer Kevin Clash, who provides the movement and voice for furry, red, childlike Elmo. Clash always knew he wanted to be a puppeteer, made his own puppets, and started his career on a local Baltimore-area children's TV program. His talent eventually led to his meeting Jim Henson in the mid-1980s, joining "Sesame Street," and his work as Elmo. 80m; DVD. **C:** Kevin Clash; Narrated by Whoopi Goldberg; Directed by Philip Shane; Constance Marks; Written by Philip Shane; Justin Weinstein; Cinematography by James Miller; Music by Joel Goodman. **Pr:** Constance A. Marks; Corrine LaPook; James Miller; Submarine Deluxe. **A:** Jr. High-Adult. **P:** Entertainment. **U:** Home. **L:** English. **Mov-Ent:** Documentary Films, Black Culture, Puppets. **Acq:** Purchase. **Dist:** New Video Group.

Being Erica: Season 1 2009 (Unrated)
Canadian Broadcasting Company situation comedy. Erica Strange is 32 years old, with no boyfriend, no job, and no prospects. Enter Dr. Tom, a therapist who gives her the chance to go back in time and right the wrongs of her past that she blames for her current condition. She returns to 1995, her second year in college when she joined a secret society in "What I Am Is What I Am," confronts her creative-writing professor in "The Secret of Now," and goes to 1999 when her best friend was a lesbian in "Everything She Wants." 20 episodes. ?m; DVD. **C:** Erin Karpluk; Michael Riley; Vinessa Antoine; John Boylan. **A:** Sr. High-Adult. **P:** Entertainment. **U:** Home. **Mov-Ent:** Comedy-Drama, Fantasy, Television Series. **Acq:** Purchase. **Dist:** BBC Worldwide Publishing Ltd. $39.99.

Being Flynn 2012 (R) — ★★½
Struggling writer Nick Flynn (Dano) takes a job at a homeless shelter as he searches to find meaning in his life. His mother committed suicide and his father Jonathan, a con man (De Niro), hasn't been around for 18 years. When Jonathan shows up at the shelter, the pair begin to forge a tenuous relationship. Jonathan is eccentric, unhinged, but also a writer; Nick's mother (Moore) shows up in flashbacks; and Nick is drawn to Denise (Thirlby), another lost soul looking for answers by working at the shelter. Based on Flynn's 2004 memoir, "Another Bullshit Night in Suck City." 102m; DVD. **C:** Robert De Niro; Paul Dano; Julianne Moore; Olivia Thirlby; Eddie Rouse; Steve Cirbus; Lili Taylor; Victor Rasuk; Directed by Paul Weitz; Written by Paul Weitz; Cinematography by Declan Quinn; Music by Damon Gough. **Pr:** Andrew Miano; Michael Costigan; Paul Weitz; Depth of Field; Corduroy Films; Tribeca Films; Focus Features L.L.C. **A:** Sr. High-Adult. **P:** Entertainment. **U:** Home. **L:** English. **Mov-Ent. Acq:** Purchase. **Dist:** Not Yet Released.

Being Friends 1992
Dramatization examines issues such as friendship and feeling left out. 28m; VHS. **A:** Primary. **P:** Education. **U:** Institution. **Chl-Juv:** Children, Psychology. **Acq:** Purchase. **Dist:** Rainbow Educational Media, Inc. $59.95.

Being Human 1994 (PG-13) — ★★½
Ambitious comedy drama promises more than it delivers, and shackles Williams in the process. Hector (Williams) is a regular guy continuously reincarnated throughout the milennia. He plays a caveman, a Roman slave, a Middle Ages nomad, a crew member on a 17th century new world voyage, and a modern New Yorker in separate vignettes that echo and/or extend the main themes of family, identity, and random fate. But he manages to emerge from each sketch as an unassuming everyman who never learns his lesson. One of Williams' periodic chancy ventures away from his comedic roots occasionally strikes gold, but often seems overly restrained. 122m; VHS, DVD, Wide, CC. **C:** Robin Williams; John Turturro; Anna Galiena; Vincent D'Onofrio; Hector Elizondo; Lorraine Bracco; Lindsay Crouse; Kelly Hunter; William H. Macy; Grace Mahlaba; Theresa Russell; Helen Miller; Robert Carlyle; Tony Curran; Bill Nighy; David Morrissey; Ewan McGregor; David Proval; Directed by Bill Forsyth; Written by Bill Forsyth; Cinematography by Michael Coulter; Music by Michael Gibbs. **Pr:** Robert F. Colesberry; David Puttnam; Enigma Productions; Fujisankei Comm; British Sky Broadcasting; Natwest Ventures; Warner Bros. **A:** Jr. High-Adult. **P:** Entertainment. **U:** Home. **Mov-Ent:** Comedy-Drama, Family, Philosophy & Ideology. **Acq:** Purchase. **Dist:** WarnerArchive.com.

Being Human: Season Four 2012
BBC 2008-? fantasy/horror. "Eve of the War": With Mitchell and Nina dead, Annie, young werewolf Tom, and George look after his and Nina's daughter Eve, who's in danger because of a vampire prophecy, so George must make a sacrifice to keep her safe. "Hold the Front Page": Vampire Adam comes to visit with his lover Yvonne, who's a succubus. "Making History": Annie is told to kill Eve if she wants to save the world from the Old Ones and Alex becomes a ghost despite vampire Hal's efforts. 8 episodes. 480m; DVD, Blu-Ray. **C:** Lenora Crichlow; Michael Socha; Damien Molony; Kate Bracken. **A:** Sr. High-Adult. **P:** Entertainment. **U:** Home. **Mov-Ent:** Fantasy, Horror, Occult Sciences. **Acq:** Purchase. **Dist:** BBC Worldwide Ltd. $49.98.

Being Human: Season One 2008
BBC 2008-? fantasy/horror. "Pilot": George (a werewold) and his best friend Mitchell (a vampire) try to maintain somewhat normal lives. When they decide to rent a home, they find it's already occupied by the ghost of previous tenant Annie, who died under mysterious circumstances. "Ghost Town": Annie meets another ghost who tells her she must resolve unfinished business in her life before she can cross over and George has a date with nurse Nina. "Where the Wild Things Ae": A disillusioned Mitchell joins with other vampires to make some new recruits and Annie tries haunting her former fiance, Owen. 7 episodes. 343m; DVD, Blu-Ray. **C:** Aidan Turner; Russell Tovey; Lenora Crichlow; Sinead Keenan. **A:** Sr. High-Adult. **P:** Entertainment. **U:** Home. **Mov-Ent:** Television Series, Fantasy, Horror. **Acq:** Purchase. **Dist:** BBC Worldwide Ltd. $34.98.

Being Human: Season Three 2011
BBC 2008-? fantasy/horror. "Lia": Mitchell, George, and Nina move into an abandoned B&B in Wales. Mitchell follows a dead man into limbo to rescue Annie and meets teenaged ghost Lia (Lacey Turner). "The Pack": Nina is pregnant and she and George consult older werewolf McNair (Robson Green), who has a son, Tom. "The Wolf-Shaped Bullet": Herrick (Jason Watkins) has been resurrected and wants George to kill Mitchell. Annie is lured back into limbo by Lia. 8 episodes. 460m; DVD, Blu-Ray. **C:** Aidan Turner; Russell Tovey; Lenora Crichlow; Sinead Keenan; Michael Socha. **A:** Sr. High-Adult. **P:** Education. **U:** Home. **Mov-Ent:** Fantasy, Horror, Occult Sciences. **Acq:** Purchase. **Dist:** BBC Worldwide Ltd. $49.98.

Being Human: Season Two 2010
BBC 2008-? fantasy/horror. "Cure and Contagion":After being accidentally scratched by George, Nina is infected and also becomes a werewolf. Mitchell is warned after Herrick's death causes a power struggle among the vampires. "The Looking Glass": Annie looks after a ghost baby, George moves in with single mother Sam, and Chief Constable Wilson wants Mitchell to kill a pedophile. "All God's Children": Annie gets pushed into limbo and Mitchell, George, and Nina escape Kemp's (Donald Sumpter) lab and try a quiet country life. 8 episodes. 460m; DVD, Blu-Ray. **C:** Aidan Turner; Russell Tovey; Lenora Crichlow; Sinead Keenan. **A:** Sr. High-Adult. **P:** Entertainment. **U:** Home. **How-Ins:** Fantasy, Horror, Occult Sciences. **Acq:** Purchase. **Dist:** BBC Worldwide Ltd. $49.98.

Being Human: The Complete First Season 2011
Syfy Channel 2011-? fantasy/horror. The first season of the U.S. adaptation of the BBC series follows the basic premise. In Boston, vampire Aidan and werewolf Josh move into a house already occupied by ghost Sally in "There Goes the Neighborhood." "Wouldn't It Be Nice (If We Were Human)": Josh encounters older werewolf Ray (Andreas Apergis) in the woods and learns that Ray is the one who attacked and infected him. "A Funny Thing Happened On the Way to Me Killing You": Aidan and Bishop (Mark Pellegrino) have their final confrontation, Nora learns Josh is a werwolf, and Sally develops the ability to touch. 13 episodes. 572m; DVD, Blu-Ray. **C:** Sam Witwer; Sam Huntington; Meaghan Rath; Kristen Hager. **A:** Sr. High-Adult. **P:** Education. **U:** Home. **Mov-Ent:** Fantasy, Horror, Occult Sciences. **Acq:** Purchase. **Dist:** Entertainment One US LP. $29.98.

Being John Malkovich 1999 (R) — ★★★
Very weird comedy is the debut feature for Jonze. High-strung street puppeteer Craig Schwartz (Cusack) is married to frumpy pet-store worker Lotte (an unrecognizable Diaz). Forced to take a job as an office clerk in a building on floor seven-and-a-half, Craig falls for office vixen, Maxine (Keener), but his big discovery is a sealed door that reveals a tunnel leading directly into actor John Malkovich's mind. Craig views the world through the actor's eyes for 15 minutes at a time and decides to profit on his findings. Things just get more surreal when both Lotte and Maxine get involved. 112m; VHS, DVD, Blu-Ray, HD-DVD, Wide. **C:** John Cusack; Cameron Diaz; Catherine Keener; John Malkovich; Orson Bean; Mary Kay Place; Charlie Sheen; Directed by Spike Jonze; Written by Charlie Kaufman; Cinematography by Lance Acord; Music by Carter Burwell. **Pr:** Sandy Stern; Steven Golin; Michael Kuhn; Michael Stipe; Propaganda Films; Gramercy Pictures. **A:** Sr. High-Adult. **P:** Entertainment. **U:** Home. **Mov-Ent:** Comedy--Black, Marriage. **Awds:** British Acad. '99: Orig. Screenplay; Ind. Spirit '00: First Feature, First Screenplay; L.A. Film Critics '99: Screenplay; MTV Movie Awards '00: New Filmmaker (Jonze); N.Y. Film Critics '99: Support. Actor (Malkovich), Support. Actress (Keener); Natl. Soc. Film Critics '99: Film, Screenplay. **Acq:** Purchase. **Dist:** Movies Unlimited; Alpha Video.

Being Julia 2004 (R) — ★★★
Bening triumphs in the title role as a larger-than-life stage actress suffering a midlife dip. But this delightful diva still has the deviousness to show a couple of whippersnappers what it means to be a star. Swanning about in 1938 London, Julia has a strong support system, led by her unfaithful but loving manager/husband Michael (Irons). However, she's bored and ready for a little fling with Tom (Evans), a fawning young fan with an agenda of his own, involving his ambitious actress girlfriend (Punch). When Julia discovers she's been used, she takes the opportunity not only to get revenge but as a step in revitalizing her life. Based on the novel "Theatre" by W. Somerset Maugham. 105m; DVD. **C:** Annette Bening; Jeremy Irons; Bruce Greenwood; Miriam Margolyes; Juliet Stevenson; Shaun Evans; Lucy Punch; Maury Chaykin; Sheila McCarthy; Michael Gambon; Leigh Lawson; Rosemary Harris; Rita Tushingham; Thomas Sturridge; Directed by Istvan Szabo; Written by Ronald Harwood; Cinematography by Lajos Koltai; Music by Mychael Danna. **Pr:** Robert Lantos; Serendipity Point Films; First Choice Films; Astral Media; Telefilm Canada; Sony Pictures Classics. **A:** Sr. High-Adult. **P:** Entertainment. **U:** Home. **Mov-Ent. Awds:** Golden Globes '05: Actress--Mus./Comedy (Bening). **Acq:** Purchase. **Dist:** Sony Pictures Home Entertainment Inc. $26.96.

Being Me 1975
Explores the many areas and origins of personal identity, and reveals how children perceive themselves in terms of their surroundings, family, and ethnicity. 20m; VHS, 3/4 U. **Pr:** Madeline Anderson. **A:** Primary-Jr. High. **P:** Education. **U:** Institution, SURA. **Chl-Juv:** Children. **Acq:** Purchase. **Dist:** Phoenix Learning Group.

Being Osama 2004
Documentary following six men named Osama in the wake of 9/11. 45m; VHS, DVD. **A:** Adult. **P:** Education. **U:** Home, Institution. **Gen-Edu:** Documentary Films, Prejudice. **Acq:** Purchase, Rent/Lease. **Dist:** Arab Film Distribution. $24.99.

Being Part of It All 1981
A profile of Gary and Barbara, moderately mentally handicapped, who left an institution, got married, and set up a life on their own. 24m; VHS, 3/4 U. **Pr:** Richard Burman. **A:** College-Adult. **P:** Education. **U:** Institution. **Gen-Edu:** Documentary Films, Handicapped, Marriage. **Acq:** Purchase. **Dist:** Filmakers Library Inc.

Being Real 1975
Theme: you can't be true to anyone else until you've been true to yourself. 11m; VHS, 3/4 U, Special order formats. **Pr:** Paulist Productions. **A:** Jr. High-Adult. **P:** Religious. **U:** Institution, CCTV, SURA. **Gen-Edu:** Self-Help. **Acq:** Purchase, Rent/Lease. **Dist:** Paulist Productions.

Being Responsible: Good Health 1969
Without "preaching," points out the good health practices for which boys and girls should be responsible. 12m; VHS, 3/4 U; Open Captioned. **Pr:** Kahana Films. **A:** Primary. **P:** Education. **U:** Institution, SURA. **Hea-Sci:** Children, Health Education. **Acq:** Purchase. **Dist:** Phoenix Learning Group.

Being "Smart on the Ball:" 13 Advanced Turns for Soccer Players 2006 (Unrated)
Coach Jason Vittrup gives on-field demonstrations of the skills soccer players will need to quickly decide what to do with the ball once they gain possession. 49m; DVD. **A:** Family. **P:** Education. **U:** Home, Institution. **Spo-Rec:** Soccer, Athletic Instruction/Coaching. **Acq:** Purchase. **Dist:** Championship Productions. $29.99.

Being the Perfect College Student 19??
Offers tips on how to get through everyday college life, covering registration, roommates, safe sex, homesickness, drugs, and more. 33m; VHS. **A:** Sr. High-College. **P:** Education. **U:** Institution. **Gen-Edu:** Adolescence, Education, Self-Help. **Acq:** Purchase. **Dist:** Educational Video Network. $49.95.

Being There 1979 (PG) — ★★★½
A feeble-minded gardener, whose entire knowledge of life comes from watching TV, is sent out into the real world when his employer dies. Equipped with his prize possession, his remote control unit, the gardener unwittingly enters the world of politics and is welcomed as a mysterious sage. Sellers is wonderful in this satiric treat adapted by Jerzy Kosinski from his novel. 130m; VHS, DVD, Blu-Ray, Wide, CC. **C:** Peter Sellers; Shirley MacLaine; Melvyn Douglas; Jack Warden; Richard Dysart; Richard Basehart; Directed by Hal Ashby; Written by Jerzy Kosinski; Cinematography by Caleb Deschanel; Music by Johnny Mandel. **Pr:** Andrew Braunsberg; Lorimar Productions; Natwest Ventures; Northstar Pictures. **A:** Jr. High-Adult. **P:** Entertainment. **U:** Home. **Mov-Ent:** Satire & Parody, Politics & Government. **Awds:** Oscars '79: Support. Actor (Douglas); Golden Globes '80: Actor--Mus./Comedy (Sellers), Support. Actor (Douglas); L.A. Film Critics '79: Support. Actor (Douglas); Natl. Bd. of Review '79: Actor (Sellers); N.Y. Film Critics '79: Support. Actor (Douglas); Natl. Soc. Film Critics '79:

Cinematog.; Writers Guild '79: Adapt. Screenplay. **Acq:** Purchase. **Dist:** Facets Multimedia Inc.; Baker and Taylor; Warner Home Video, Inc. $19.98.

Being Two Isn't Easy 1962 — ★★½
Director Ichikawa shows the world through the eyes of a two-year-old as a young couple struggle to raise their son. In Japanese with English subtitles. 88m; VHS. **C:** Fujiko Yamamoto; Eiji Funakoshi; Directed by Kon Ichikawa. **A:** College-Adult. **P:** Entertainment. **U:** Home. **L:** Japanese. **Mov-Ent:** Comedy-Drama, Parenting. **Acq:** Purchase. **Dist:** Home Vision Cinema; Facets Multimedia Inc. $29.95.

Being with John F. Kennedy 1983
This documentary goes behind the scenes with John F. Kennedy from his days as a senator to the assassination in Dallas. Some black and white segments. 100m; VHS, 3/4 U, Special order formats. **Pr:** Nancy Dickerson. **A:** Sr. High-Adult. **P:** Education. **U:** Institution, Home, SURA. **Gen-Edu:** Documentary Films, Presidency, Biography. **Acq:** Purchase, Rent/Lease. **Dist:** Direct Cinema Ltd.

Being Young 1985
A survey of the problems of youth in six different cultures. 27m; VHS, 3/4 U. **Pr:** United Nations. **A:** Family. **P:** Education. **U:** Institution, Home, SURA. **Gen-Edu:** Documentary Films, Children, Adolescence. **Acq:** Purchase, Rent/Lease, Trade-in. **Dist:** United Learning Inc.

Beirut Diaries 2006 (Unrated)
Documentary focusing on Nadine Zaidan, one of thousands of Lebanese citizens present in Beirut's Martyrs Square in he days after the assassination of Prime Minister Rafiq Hariri. In Arabic with English subtitles. 80m; DVD. **A:** Sr. High-Adult. **P:** Entertainment. **U:** BCTV, Institution. **L:** English, Arabic. **Gen-Edu:** Documentary Films, Middle East. **Acq:** Purchase, Rent/Lease. **Dist:** Arab Film Distribution. $300.

Beirut! Not Enough Death to Go Round 1989
Filmed shortly after the 1982 massacres at Sabra and Chatila, this documentary explores the day to day struggles of the people of war torn Beirut. 57m; VHS, 3/4 U. **Pr:** Jacques Vallee. **A:** Jr. High-Adult. **P:** Education. **U:** Institution, SURA. **Gen-Edu:** Middle East. **Acq:** Purchase, Rent/Lease. **Dist:** National Film Board of Canada.

Beirut, Palermo, Beirut 1998
Six young people face the challenge of finding employment in this parody of performance, success, acting, interview format and video technology. The purpose is to confront habitual ways of viewing situations. Subtitled in English. 17m; VHS. **A:** Adult. **P:** Education. **U:** Institution, BCTV. **L:** Arabic. **Gen-Edu:** Documentary Films, Middle East. **Acq:** Purchase, Rent/Lease. **Dist:** Arab Film Distribution. $95.00.

Beirut: The Last Home Movie 1988
Captures three months in the life of a Lebanese family living in a heavily bombed Beirut neighborhood. Examines the connections between their personal and political lives and the psychology of war. 90m; VHS. **A:** Adult. **P:** Education. **U:** Institution, BCTV. **Gen-Edu:** Middle East, War--General, Documentary Films. **Acq:** Purchase, Rent/Lease. **Dist:** Women Make Movies. $295.00.

Beit Shean 19??
A documentary about the Beit Shean Valley, its history, modern day kibbutz life, and problems of terrorism. 28m; VHS, 3/4 U, Special order formats. **TV Std:** NTSC, PAL, SECAM. **C:** Narrated by Garry Moore. **Pr:** Alden Films. **A:** Sr. High-Adult. **P:** Education. **U:** Institution, Home, SURA. **Gen-Edu:** Israel, War--General, History. **Acq:** Purchase, Rent/Lease. **Dist:** Alden Films.

Bekoidintu: Any House Is Better Than Mine 1979
Kolani, a lineage head in Northern Togo, engages in a bitter conflict with his third and youngest wife, who has left him for her lover. Questions the value of the local judiciary and if it can deal adequately with severed relationships. 35m; 3/4 U, Special order formats. **Pr:** Stichting Film en Wetenschap. **A:** College-Adult. **P:** Education. **U:** Institution, SURA. **Gen-Edu:** Documentary Films, Anthropology. **Acq:** Purchase, Rent/Lease. **Dist:** International Science Film Collection.

Bel Ami 2012 (R) — ★½
Although Pattinson is attractive in his 19th-century finery, he doesn't display the necessary charisma to put over the scheming, charm, and ruthlessness of social climbing Georges Duroy in this adaptation of Guy de Maupassants's 1885 novel. Penniless in Paris, Georges takes advantage of a meeting with a former mentor to get a newspaper job and the first of several amours who'll pave his way to money and power. 102m; DVD, Streaming. **C:** Robert Pattinson; Uma Thurman; Kristin Scott Thomas; Christina Ricci; Colm Meaney; Philip Glenister; Holliday Grainger; Directed by Declan Donnellan; Nick Ormerod; Written by Rachel Bennette; Cinematography by Stefano Falivene; Music by Rachel Portman; Lakshman Joseph De Saram. **Pr:** Uberto Pasolini; Magnolia Pictures; Redwave Films. **A:** Sr. High-Adult. **P:** Entertainment. **U:** Home. **L:** English, French. **Mov-Ent:** Marriage, Romance, Sex & Sexuality. **Acq:** Purchase, Rent/Lease. **Dist:** Sony Pictures Home Entertainment Inc. $22.99 12.99.

Bel Canto: The Tenors of the 78 Era 1998
Features the performances of great opera tenors at the dawn of the recording industry. Each episode contains interviews with the tenors' families and friends, as well as discussions with contemporary singers and music teachers. Volume One includes Caruso, Gigli and Schipa; Volume Two includes Tauber, Slezak and Schmidt; Volume Three includes Bjorling, Melchior and Rosvaenge; Volume Four includes Thill and Kozlovsky. Six hours on four videocassettes. 90m/B/W; VHS. **A:** Family. **P:** Entertainment. **U:** Home. **Fin-Art:** Opera, Performing Arts. **Acq:** Purchase. **Dist:** PBS Home Video. $99.95.

Bela Fleck and the Flecktones: Flight of the Cosmic Hippo 1991
The jazz-fusion group performs "Sinister Minster," "Frontiers," "Sunset Road," "The Flecktone Rap," "Blu-Bop," "Tell It to the Gov'nor," "Flight of the Cosmic Hippo," "The Star Spangled Banner," and "Turtle Rock." 45m; VHS. **A:** Jr. High-Adult. **P:** Entertainment. **U:** Home. **Mov-Ent:** Music Video, Music--Jazz. **Acq:** Purchase. **Dist:** Warner Reprise Video. $16.98.

Bela Fleck: Banjo Picking Styles 1984
The musician demonstrates techniques for banjo playing, including single string picking, harmonics, blues imrpovisation, Keith Tuners and more. 60m; VHS. **Pr:** Homespun Video. **A:** Sr. High-Adult. **P:** Instruction. **U:** Home. **How-Ins:** How-To, Music--Instruction. **Acq:** Purchase. **Dist:** Homespun Tapes Ltd. $49.95.

Bela Lugosi Meets a Brooklyn Gorilla 1952 (Unrated) — **Bomb!**
Two men who look like Dean Martin and Jerry Lewis (but aren't) get lost in the jungle, where they meet mad scientist Lugosi. Worse than it sounds. Real Jerry sued for unflattering imitation. 74m/B/W; VHS, DVD. **C:** Bela Lugosi; Duke Mitchell; Sammy Petrillo; Charlita; Martin Garralaga; Al Kikume; Muriel Landers; Milton Newberger; Directed by William Beaudine; Written by Tim Ryan; Cinematography by Charles Van Enger; Music by Richard Hazard. **Pr:** Realart; Jack Broder Productions. **A:** Jr. High-Adult. **P:** Entertainment. **U:** Home. **Mov-Ent. Acq:** Purchase. **Dist:** Sinister Cinema. $19.95.

Bela Lugosi Scrapbook 197?
A compilation of Lugosi appearances, outtakes, flubs, and trailers. 60m/B/W; VHS. **C:** Bela Lugosi. **Pr:** Discount Video; U-I. **A:** Family. **P:** Entertainment. **U:** Home. **Mov-Ent:** Biography: Show Business, Outtakes & Bloopers. **Acq:** Purchase. **Dist:** Rex Miller Artisan Studio. $29.95.

Bela Lugosi: The Forgotten King 1988
An examination of the horror film star's life and career including vintage interviews, clips from a large selection of his films, stills, and much more. 55m/B/W; VHS. **A:** Jr. High-Adult. **P:** Entertainment. **U:** Home. **Mov-Ent:** Documentary Films, Biography, Biography: Show Business. **Acq:** Purchase. **Dist:** Movies Unlimited; MPI Media Group. $19.98.

Belafonte Presents Fincho 1975
A docudrama shot in Nigeria concerning the problems a jungle village faces when suddenly brought into the 20th Century. 79m; VHS. **C:** Hosted by Harry Belafonte; Directed by Sarn Zebba. **Pr:** Rohauer Films. **A:** Sr. High-Adult. **P:** Education. **U:** Home. **Gen-Edu:** Documentary Films, Africa, Black Culture. **Acq:** Purchase. **Dist:** Facets Multimedia Inc. $69.95.

Belcebu 2005 (Unrated) — ★
Odd little supernatural horror comedy about a rock star selling his soul to the Devil, his junkie ex-girlfriend trying to stop them from destroying the world, and a really shy guy who mans cameras in the adult film industry. Recommended for those who like tons of fake blood and nudity. 80m; DVD, Streaming. **C:** Oscar Pastor; Diego Braguinsky; Ruben Rodriguez; Mapi Romero; Directed by Sergio Blasco; Written by Sergio Blasco; Cinematography by Cueto Lominchar; Music by Javier Giner; Juan Lizaso; Juanma Millan. **A:** College-Adult. **P:** Entertainment. **U:** Home. **L:** English, Spanish. **Mov-Ent. Acq:** Purchase, Rent/Lease. **Dist:** Troma Entertainment. $19.95 9.99.

Belfast Assassin 1984 — ★
A British anti-terrorist agent goes undercover in Ireland to find an IRA assassin who shot a British cabinet minister. 130m; VHS. **C:** Derek Thompson; Ray Lonnen; Gil Brailey; Benjamin Whitrow; Directed by Lawrence Gordon-Clark. **Pr:** Independent. **A:** Sr. High-Adult. **P:** Entertainment. **U:** Home. **Mov-Ent:** Terrorism. **Acq:** Purchase. **Dist:** Unknown Distributor.

Belfast: Black or Green 1978
Suspense story about the troubles in Ireland. Theme: we find God in loving our bitterest enemies or we don't find Him at all. 25m; VHS, 3/4 U, Special order formats. **Pr:** Paulist Productions. **A:** Jr. High-Adult. **P:** Religious. **U:** Institution, CCTV, Home. **Gen-Edu:** Ireland. **Acq:** Purchase, Rent/Lease. **Dist:** Paulist Productions.

Belfast Girls 2006 (Unrated)
Swedish director Malin Andersson explores the daily struggles and triumphs of two young women that share the legacy of Northern Ireland's thirty-year conflict. Mairead Mc Ilkenny is a Catholic who has never known a Protestant in her life while Christine Savage is a Protestant who falls in love with a Catholic boy; although they live on opposite sides of the concrete "peace walls" they have more commonalities than differences. 58m; DVD. **A:** Adult. **P:** Education. **U:** Institution. **Gen-Edu:** Ireland, Women, Religion. **Acq:** Purchase. **Dist:** Women Make Movies. $295.00.

Belfast, Maine 1999
Documentary provides a glimpse into the everyday life of a New England port city, with emphasis on the work and cultural life of the community. 248m; VHS. **A:** Sr. High-Adult. **P:** Entertainment. **U:** Home, Institution. **Gen-Edu:** Documentary Films, Cities & Towns, U.S. States. **Acq:** Purchase, Rent/Lease. **Dist:** Zipporah Films. $400.00.

Belgian Bike GP '88 1988
Exciting footage from the 1988 Belgian bike Grand Prix. ?m; VHS. **A:** Family. **P:** Entertainment. **U:** Home. **Spo-Rec:** Sports--General, Motorcycles. **Acq:** Purchase. **Dist:** Powersports - Powerdocs. $39.95.

Belgian 500 Motocross GP '88 1988
Highlights from the Belgian 500 Motocross Grand Prix of 1988. ?m; VHS. **A:** Family. **P:** Entertainment. **U:** Home. **Spo-Rec:** Sports--General, Motorcycles. **Acq:** Purchase. **Dist:** Powersports - Powerdocs. $39.95.

Belgian Motocross '89 1989
Highlights from the Belgian Motocross of 1989. ?m; VHS. **A:** Family. **P:** Entertainment. **U:** Home. **Spo-Rec:** Sports--General, Motorcycles. **Acq:** Purchase. **Dist:** Powersports - Powerdocs. $39.95.

Believe! 1982
Presents a vivid example of what any person can do who commits his or her life to the basic Biblical and social values that make for balanced success. 57m; VHS. **Pr:** Gospel Films. **A:** Sr. High-Adult. **P:** Religious. **U:** Institution. **Gen-Edu:** Bible, Ethics & Morals, Religion. **Acq:** Purchase, Rent/Lease. **Dist:** Gospel Communications International. $29.95.

Believe 1999 (PG-13) — ★★½
Teen prankster Ben Stiles (Mabe) loves to scare people. In fact, his behavior gets him kicked out of prep school and sent to live with his no-nonsense grandfather (Rubes). But the fright's on him when Ben and his friend Katherine (Cuthbert) decide to turn the abandoned Wickwire House into a haunted mansion and a ghostly figure suddenly starts making appearances. 97m; VHS, DVD. **C:** Ricky Mabe; Elisha Cuthbert; Jan Rubes; Ben Gazzara; Andrea Martin; Jayne Heitmeyer; Directed by Robert Tinnell. **A:** Jr. High-Adult. **P:** Entertainment. **U:** Home. **Mov-Ent. Acq:** Purchase. **Dist:** Movies Unlimited.

Believe 2007 (PG) — ★★½
After Adam Pendon loses his steel mill job he's recruited by salesman Mark Fuller to join Believe Industries, a multi-level marketing company promising wealth through direct sales opportunities that seems just too good to be true. Adam becomes a success pushing products and signing up new salespeople but there's trouble brewing from some ex-Believers. 80m; DVD. **C:** Larry Bagby; Lincoln Hoppe; Jeff Olson; Craig Clyde; Vanessa DeHart; Brian Clark; Britani Bateman; Steve Anderson; Ann Bosler; K. Danor Gerald; Directed by Loki Mulholland; Written by Loki Mulholland; Cinematography by Ryan Little; Music by Aaron Merrill. **A:** Jr. High-Adult. **P:** Entertainment. **U:** Home. **Mov-Ent:** Unemployment. **Acq:** Purchase. **Dist:** SunWorld Pictures.

Believe in Me 2006 (PG) — ★★
Formulaic, standard "inspiring story" sports film plays like a distaff "Hoosiers" but occasionally conjures up an interesting twist. Clay Driscoll (Donovan) moves to small-town America to discover that his new job coaching a high school boy's team has been taken from him and he's been given the girl's team instead. At first offended, he takes the young women from zeros (giggling losers) to heroes (state finals) through hard work, dedication, inspiring locker room speeches, and other well-mined sports cliches. Based on a true story (of course). 108m; DVD, Blu-Ray, Wide. **C:** Jeffrey Donovan; Samantha Mathis; Bruce Dern; Bob Gunton; Heather Matarazzo; Alicia Lagano; Directed by Robert Collector; Written by Robert Collector; Cinematography by James L. Carter; Music by David Torn. **Pr:** Caldecott Chubb; John Bard Manulis; Visionbox Pictures; ChubbCo Film Co; IFC Films. **A:** Jr. High-Adult. **P:** Entertainment. **U:** Home. **L:** English. **Mov-Ent:** Basketball, Sports--Fiction: Drama. **Acq:** Purchase. **Dist:** Movies Unlimited; Alpha Video.

The Believer 2001 — ★★
Inspired by the true story of neo-Nazi Daniel Burros and the New York Times expose that revealed he was Jewish. In Bean's version, Danny Balint (Gosling) is a ferociously intelligent former yeshiva student whose personal identity crisis has led him to a fascist movement led by Curtis Zampf (Zane) and to virulent anti-Semitism. But even while leading his own band of skinheads, Danny discovers he can't easily leave his Jewish heritage behind. 98m; VHS, DVD. **C:** Ryan Gosling; Summer Phoenix; Billy Zane; Theresa Russell; Glenn Fitzgerald; Directed by Henry Bean; Written by Henry Bean; Cinematography by Jim Denault; Music by Joel Diamond. **A:** Sr. High-Adult. **P:** Entertainment. **U:** Home. **Mov-Ent:** Judaism. **Acq:** Purchase. **Dist:** Vivendi Visual Entertainment.

Believercise 1988
An aerobic exercise program is set to Christian music. 60m; VHS. **Pr:** Bridgestone Production Group. **A:** Jr. High-Adult. **P:** Religious. **U:** Home. **Hea-Sci:** Fitness/Exercise. **Acq:** Purchase. **Dist:** Alpha Omega Publications Inc.

The Believers 1987 (R) — ★★½
Tense horror mystery set in New York city about a series of gruesome, unexplained murders. A widowed police psychologist investigating the deaths unwittingly discovers a powerful Santeria cult that believes in the sacrifice of children. Without warning he is drawn into the circle of the "Believers" and must free himself before his own son is the next sacrifice. Gripping (and grim), unrelenting horror. 114m; VHS, DVD, CC. **C:** Martin Sheen; Helen Shaver; Malick Bowens; Harris Yulin; Robert Loggia; Jimmy Smits; Richard Masur; Harley Cross; Elizabeth Wilson; Lee Richardson; Carla Pinza; Directed by John Schlesinger; Written by Mark Frost; Cinematography by Robby Muller; Music by J. Peter Robinson. **Pr:** Orion Pictures. **A:** Sr. High-Adult. **P:** Entertainment. **U:** Home. **Mov-Ent:** Horror, Occult Sciences, Cults. **Acq:** Purchase. **Dist:** Movies Unlimited; Alpha Video. $19.99.

Believers 2007 (R) — ★½
Two paramedics (Messner, Huertas) are kidnapped by a doomsday cult that believes the end is at hand so they're going to commit mass suicide. Not quite sure why a suicidal cult wants paramedics in its midst, but it's a creepy story. 101m; DVD. **C:**

Johnny Messner; Elizabeth Bogush; Daniel Benzali; Jon Huertas; John Farley; Deanna Russo; Directed by Daniel Myrick; Written by Daniel Myrick; Cinematography by Andrew Huebscher; Music by Kays Al-Atrakchi. **A:** Sr. High-Adult. **P:** Entertainment. **U:** Home. **Mov-Ent**: Cults, Suicide. **Acq:** Purchase. **Dist:** Warner Home Video, Inc.

The Believers: Stories from Jewish Havana 1994
Explores the lives of Jews living in Cuba, the importance of their religion, their struggle for food and medicine, etc. Also looks at the life of a young doctor worried about the country's children. 16m; VHS. **A:** Adult. **P:** Education. **U:** Institution. **Gen-Edu**: Judaism, Documentary Films. **Acq:** Purchase. **Dist:** PBS Home Video. $50.

Believing in Yourself 19??
Earnie Larsen talks about how to identify negative behavior patterns, what causes them, and how to overcome them. 60m; VHS. **A:** Adult. **P:** Education. **U:** Institution. **Hea-Sci**: Self-Help. **Acq:** Purchase. **Dist:** Hazelden Publishing. $39.95.

Belinda 1986
The ex-Go-Go Belinda Carlisle is seen in videos, concert appearances, rehearsals and interviews in this well-rounded musical portrait. 60m; VHS. **Pr:** MCA Entertainment; International Record Syndicate Video Inc. **A:** Family. **P:** Entertainment. **U:** Home. **Mov-Ent**: Music Video, Music--Performance, Music--Pop/Rock. **Acq:** Purchase. **Dist:** Music Video Distributors. $19.95.

Belinda 1992
Belinda Mason was a normal woman from eastern Kentucky until she was infected with the HIV virus. Today she is a national advocate for AIDS education, prevention, treatment, and human rights, speaking about the need to fight AIDS. 40m; VHS. **C:** Directed by Anne Johnson. **A:** Sr. High-Adult. **P:** Education. **U:** Institution. **Gen-Edu**: Documentary Films, AIDS. **Acq:** Purchase, Rent/Lease. **Dist:** Appalshop Films & Video. $195.00.

Belinda Carlisle: Belinda Live 1988
This presentation captures Belinda in 1988 in live performances around America. The 14 tunes she belts out are "Heaven Is a Place on Earth," "Mad About You," "We Got the Beat," "Our Lips Are Sealed," "Circle in the Sand," "I Feel Free," "Lust for Love," "I Get Weak," "Fool for Love," "World Without You," "Nobody Owns Me," "Vacation," "Love Never Dies," and "Head Over Heels." 60m; VHS, DVD. **Pr:** Virgin Music Video. **A:** Jr. High-Adult. **P:** Entertainment. **U:** Home. **Mov-Ent**: Music--Performance, Music--Pop/Rock. **Acq:** Purchase. **Dist:** Music Video Distributors; Management Company Entertainment Group (MCEG), Inc. $19.98.

Belinda Carlisle: Runaway Live 1990 (Unrated)
Belinda performs 17 songs live including, "Mad About You," "Heaven Is a Place on Earth," "Our Lips Are Sealed," "I Get Weak," and "We Got the Beat." 81m; VHS, DVD. **C:** Belinda Carlisle. **Pr:** MCA Entertainment. **A:** Jr. High-Adult. **P:** Entertainment. **U:** Home. **Mov-Ent**: Music--Performance, Music--Pop/Rock. **Acq:** Purchase. **Dist:** Music Video Distributors. $19.95.

Belinda Carlisle: Runaway Videos 1990
A collection of seven promotional videos which chronicles Carlisle's activities since leaving the Go-Go's supergroup. The songs performed on the presentation include "Mad About You" and "Summer Rain." As an extra bonus, the tape includes two videos, "Heaven Is a Place on Earth" and "I Get Weak," which feature famed actress Diane Keaton's directorial skills. 30m; VHS. **C:** Directed by Diane Keaton. **Pr:** MCA Entertainment. **A:** Jr. High-Adult. **P:** Entertainment. **U:** Home. **Mov-Ent**: Music Video, Music--Pop/Rock. **Acq:** Purchase. **Dist:** Music Video Distributors. $16.98.

Belinda Mason AIDS Interview 1988
Belinda Mason, a victim of AIDS, discusses how she contracted the virus from a blood transfusion while she was giving birth to her baby. 91m; VHS. **A:** Sr. High-Adult. **P:** Education. **U:** Institution. **Gen-Edu**: AIDS. **Acq:** Purchase. **Dist:** Geographical Studies and Research Center, Department of Geography and Planning.

Belizaire the Cajun 1986 (PG) — ★★½
19th-century Louisiana love story. White prejudice against the Cajuns is rampant and violent, but that doesn't stop sexy faith healer Assante from falling in love with the inaccessible Cajun wife (Youngs) of a rich local. Made with care on a tight budget. Worthwhile, though uneven. 103m; VHS, DVD, CC. **C:** Armand Assante; Gail Youngs; Will Patton; Stephen McHattie; Michael Schoeffling; Robert Duvall; Nancy Barrett; Directed by Glen Pitre; Written by Glen Pitre; Cinematography by Richard Bowen; Music by Michael Doucet; Howard Shore. **Pr:** Allan L. Durand; Skouras Pictures; Norstar Entertainment; Cote Blanche Ltd. **A:** Jr. High-Adult. **P:** Entertainment. **U:** Home. **Mov-Ent**. **Acq:** Purchase. **Dist:** $79.98.

Belize & Guatemala—The Legacy of the Maya 19??
Takes a look at the countries of Belize and Guatemala. Offers insight on the hidden cities of the ancient Maya, and profiles the cultures, rituals, and myths of this ancient people. Also provides a look at the descendants of the Mayans, the Tikal, Xunantunich, Altun Ha, Nimle Punit, and Copan people. 80m; VHS. **A:** Family. **P:** Education. **U:** Home. **Gen-Edu**: Central America, History, Travel. **Acq:** Purchase. **Dist:** Trailwood Films. $29.95.

Belize, British Honduras 1967
Shows the general patterns of culture of the region. 20m; VHS, 3/4 U. **Pr:** Museum of Modern Art of Latin America. **A:** Jr. High-Adult. **P:** Education. **U:** Institution, SURA. **Gen-Edu**: Documentary Films, Central America. **Acq:** Purchase. **Dist:** Art Museum of The Americas.

Belize: Cay Bokel 19??
Neat tropical fish populate this fascinating world below an island off the coast of central America. Includes tour of Turneffe Island. 30m; VHS. **A:** Sr. High-Adult. **P:** Entertainment. **U:** Home. **Spo-Rec**: Scuba, Travel. **Acq:** Purchase. **Dist:** Bennett Marine Video. $19.95.

Belize: Maruba and Ramada 19??
Dive in the waters off this much-ignored nation which combines uncrowded beaches with tropical rainforests. 30m; VHS. **A:** Sr. High-Adult. **P:** Entertainment. **U:** Home. **Spo-Rec**: Scuba, Travel. **Acq:** Purchase. **Dist:** Bennett Marine Video. $19.95.

Bell Biv Devoe: Mental Videos 1991
A compilation of four hits from Michael Bivins, Ronnie DeVoe and Ricky Bell including "Poison," "Do Me," "BBD (I Thought it Was Me)," and "When Will I See You Smile Again?" 30m; VHS. **A:** Primary-Adult. **P:** Entertainment. **U:** Home. **Mov-Ent**: Music Video, Music--Rap. **Acq:** Purchase. **Dist:** Music Video Distributors. $14.95.

Bell Biv Devoe: Word to the Mutha! 1992
The latest video hit from the rap trio includes special appearances by Bobby Brown, Johnny Gill, and Ralph Tresvant. 5m; VHS. **A:** Jr. High-Adult. **P:** Entertainment. **U:** Home. **Mov-Ent**: Music Video, Music--Rap. **Acq:** Purchase. **Dist:** Music Video Distributors. $7.98.

Bell, Book and Candle 1958 — ★★½
Gillian Holroyd (Novak) is a beautiful modern-day witch (from a family of witches) who has made up her mind to refrain from using her powers. That is until Sheperd Henderson (Stewart) moves into her building and she decides to enchant him with a love spell. But spells have a way of backfiring on those who cast them. Lanchester is romantic Aunt Queenie and Lemmon is a standout as Gillian's jazz-loving, bongo-playing brother, Nicky. 106m; VHS, DVD, Blu-Ray. **C:** James Stewart; Kim Novak; Jack Lemmon; Elsa Lanchester; Ernie Kovacs; Hermione Gingold; Janice Rule; Directed by Richard Quine; Written by Daniel Taradash; Cinematography by James Wong Howe; Music by George Duning. **Pr:** Columbia Pictures. **A:** Jr. High-Adult. **P:** Entertainment. **U:** Home. **Mov-Ent**: Family Viewing. **Acq:** Purchase. **Dist:** Sony Pictures Home Entertainment Inc.; Facets Multimedia Inc. $19.95.

Bell Diamond 1981 (Unrated)
A study by the experimental filmmaker of a Vietnam vet surviving in a bankrupt mining town. Created without a script using non-professional actors. 96m; VHS. **C:** Directed by Jon Jost. **Pr:** Jon Jost; Jon Jost. **A:** Sr. High-Adult. **P:** Entertainment. **U:** Home. **Fin-Art**: Film--Avant-Garde, Veterans, Vietnam War. **Acq:** Purchase. **Dist:** Facets Multimedia Inc.

Bell from Hell 1974 (Unrated) — ★★
A tale of insanity and revenge, wherein a young man, institutionalized since his mother's death, plots to kill his aunt and three cousins. 80m; VHS, DVD. **C:** Viveca Lindfors; Renaud Verley; Alfredo Mayo; Directed by Claudio Guerin Hill. **Pr:** Santiago Moncada Productions. **A:** Jr. High-Adult. **P:** Entertainment. **U:** Home. **L:** English, Spanish. **Mov-Ent**: Mystery & Suspense. **Acq:** Purchase. **Dist:** Movies Unlimited. $49.95.

bell hooks: Cultural Criticism and Transformation ?
Cultural critic bell hooks discusses the theories and foundations she uses and applies them to modern media, addressing the biases hidden in the messages. 66m; VHS. **A:** College-Adult. **P:** Education. **U:** Institution. **Gen-Edu**: Mass Media. **Acq:** Purchase. **Dist:** Media Education Foundation. $195.00.

The Bell Jar 1979 (R) — ★½
Based on poet Sylvia Plath's acclaimed semi-autobiographical novel, this is the story of a young woman who becomes the victim of mental illness. Not for the easily depressed and a disjointed and disappointing adaptation of Plath's work. 113m; VHS, DVD. **C:** Marilyn Hassett; Julie Harris; Barbara Barrie; Anne Bancroft; Robert Klein; Anne Jackson; Directed by Larry Peerce. **Pr:** Avco Embassy; Brandt-Todd. **A:** Sr. High-Adult. **P:** Entertainment. **U:** Home. **Mov-Ent**: Suicide. **Acq:** Purchase. **Dist:** Televista; Alpha Video. $29.98.

Bell Science: About Time 1956
The professor explains everyone's dependence on accurate clocks. 60m; VHS. **C:** Hosted by Dr. Frank Baxter. **Pr:** Bell Telephone. **A:** Primary-Sr. High. **P:** Education. **U:** Home. **Chl-Juv**: Science, Education, Clocks & Watches. **Acq:** Purchase. **Dist:** Rhino Entertainment Co. $19.98.

Bell Science: Alphabet Conspiracy 1956
Easy, fun science lessons for children originally sponsored by Bell Telephone. In this episode, narrator Dr. Frank Baxter, Hans Conreid, and Friz Freleng's animation take children through the world of language. 60m; VHS. **C:** Hans Conried; Hosted by Dr. Frank Baxter. **Pr:** Warner; Bell Telephone. **A:** Family. **P:** Education. **U:** Home. **Chl-Juv**: Animation & Cartoons, Language Arts. **Acq:** Purchase. **Dist:** Rhino Entertainment Co.; Facets Multimedia Inc. $19.95.

Bell Science: Gateway to the Mind 194?
Dr. Frank Baxter, with the help of Chuck Jones' animation, takes children through the world of the five senses. 60m; VHS. **C:** Hosted by Dr. Frank Baxter. **Pr:** Warner; Bell Telephone. **A:** Family. **P:** Education. **U:** Home. **Chl-Juv**: Animation & Cartoons, Science. **Acq:** Purchase. **Dist:** Rhino Entertainment Co. $19.95.

Bell Science: Hemo the Magnificent 1956
Super science for young people. Today the professor discusses blood and circulatory systems in humans and other animals. 60m; VHS. **C:** Hosted by Dr. Frank Baxter. **Pr:** Bell Telephone. **A:** Primary-Sr. High. **P:** Entertainment. **U:** Institution, Home. **Chl-Juv**: Science, Education, Blood. **Acq:** Purchase. **Dist:** Rhino Entertainment Co. $19.98.

Bell Science: Our Mr. Sun 1959
Join Dr. Frank Baxter, Eddie Albert and Lionel Barrymore as Father Time as they explore the mysteries of the sun. 60m; VHS. **C:** Eddie Albert; Voice(s) by Lionel Barrymore; Hosted by Dr. Frank Baxter. **Pr:** Frank Capra; Bell Telephone; UPA. **A:** Family. **P:** Education. **U:** Home. **Chl-Juv**: Animation & Cartoons, Astronomy, Science. **Acq:** Purchase. **Dist:** Rhino Entertainment Co.; Facets Multimedia Inc. $19.95.

Bell Science: Strange Case of the Cosmic Rays 194?
Atoms, radiation and other scientific mysteries are explained by Dr. Frank Baxter with the help of Shamus Culhane's ("Betty Boop") animation and Bil and Cora's marionettes. 55m; VHS. **C:** Hosted by Dr. Frank Baxter; Directed by Frank Capra; Written by Frank Capra. **Pr:** Frank Capra; Frank Capra; Bell Telephone. **A:** Family. **P:** Entertainment. **U:** Home. **Chl-Juv**: Animation & Cartoons, Science, Nuclear Energy. **Acq:** Purchase. **Dist:** Rhino Entertainment Co. $19.95.

Bell Science: Thread of Life 194?
Vintage learning series hosted by Dr. Frank Baxter. This episode features a look at the basics of life, including genes and chromosomes. 52m/B/W; VHS. **C:** Hosted by Dr. Frank Baxter; Directed by Jack Warner. **Pr:** Bell Telephone; Warner. **A:** Family. **P:** Entertainment. **U:** Home. **Chl-Juv**: Science, Genetics, Education. **Acq:** Purchase. **Dist:** Rhino Entertainment Co. $19.95.

Bell Science: Unchained Goddess 194?
Dr. Frank Baxter takes a look at our planet and its weather. 54m/B/W; VHS. **C:** Hosted by Dr. Frank Baxter; Directed by Frank Capra. **Pr:** Bell Telephone. **A:** Family. **P:** Entertainment. **U:** Home. **Chl-Juv**: Science, Meteorology. **Acq:** Purchase. **Dist:** Rhino Entertainment Co. $19.95.

Bella 2006 (PG-13) — ★★
Saccharine storytelling, appealing leads. Jose (Verastegui) is the head chef at his brother Manny's (Perez) upscale Mexican restaurant in Manhattan. Intolerant of unprofessional behavior, Manny fires waitress Nina (Blanchard) when she's late for work. Jose discovers the reason is because the unmarried young woman has just learned she's pregnant, so he leaves as well. Jose then spends the day with Nina, trying to convince her to have the baby, with his motives slowly revealed through flashbacks. 91m; DVD. **C:** Eduardo Verastegui; Tammy Blanchard; Manny Perez; Angelica Aragon; Jamie Tirelli; Ali Landry; Ramon Rodriguez; Directed by Alejandro Monteverde; Written by Patrick Million; Cinematography by Andrew Cadelago; Music by Stephen Altman. **A:** Jr. High-Adult. **P:** Entertainment. **U:** Home. **Mov-Ent**: Pregnancy. **Acq:** Purchase. **Dist:** Lions Gate Entertainment Inc.

Bella Abzug 1978
Feminist leader Bella Abzug discusses her background and her view of the American women's movement. 30m; 3/4 U. **C:** Hosted by Dr. Helen Hawkins. **Pr:** Dr. Helen Hawkins; KPBS Humanities Office. **A:** Sr. High-Adult. **P:** Education. **U:** Institution, CCTV. **Gen-Edu**: Women, Interviews. **Acq:** Purchase. **Dist:** KPBS-TV.

Bella Mafia 1997 (R) — ★★½
Over-the-top trash and that's meant in the finest possible way. This lurid melodrama, originally a two-part miniseries, concerns the Sicilian mob family, the Lucianos, who have suffered the loss of father Roberto (Farina) and three sons. Widowed matriarch Graziella (Redgrave) decides to join with her three daughters-in-law, Sophia (Kinski), Teresa (Douglas), and Moyra (Tilly), and avenge their deaths. Oh yes, there's also Sophia's secret son Luca (Marsden), a killer who turns up to insinuates himself into family life. Adapted by La Plante from her novel. 117m; VHS, CC. **C:** Vanessa Redgrave; Nastassja Kinski; Illeana Douglas; Jennifer Tilly; James Marsden; Peter Bogdanovich; Dennis Farina; Gina Philips; Directed by David Greene; Written by Lynda La Plante. **Pr:** Jack Clements; Frank Konigsberg; Konigsberg Co. Productions. **A:** Jr. High-Adult. **P:** Entertainment. **U:** Home. **Mov-Ent**: Family, Women, TV Movies. **Acq:** Purchase. **Dist:** CinemaNow Inc.

Bella Strength with Gin Miller 2005
Barbell-focused exercises for muscle development; also uses dumbbells and a step. 61m; DVD. **A:** College-Adult. **P:** Instruction. **U:** Home. **Hea-Sci**: Fitness/Exercise. **Acq:** Purchase. **Dist:** Collage Video Specialties, Inc. $14.95.

Belladonna 2008 (Unrated) — ★½
Luke is in the midst of wedding plans with his high-strung, longtime girlfriend Katherine when he becomes attracted to Amelia. As his wedding draws closer, Luke is increasingly plagued by nightmares and finally goes into therapy. Under hypnosis, his nightmares reveal a medieval town, devil worship, and a romantic triangle that turns into a reincarnation story. 93m; DVD. **C:** Katherine Kendall; Katie Jean Harding; Todd MacDonald; Indiana Avent; John Jacobs; Anne Cordiner; Katia Mazurek; Daryl Pellizzer; Directed by Annika Glac; Written by Annika Glac; Cinematography by Marcus Struzina; Music by Volmer Haas I. **A:** Sr. High-Adult. **P:** Entertainment. **U:** Home. **Mov-Ent**: Hypnosis & Hypnotists. **Acq:** Purchase. **Dist:** Osiris Entertainment.

Bellamy 1981 (Unrated) — ★
Murderous madman massacres masseuses, and Bellamy is the cop out to get him. 92m; VHS. **C:** John Stanton; Timothy Elston;

Sally Conabere; Directed by Gary Conway. **Pr:** Don Hattye. **A:** Jr. High-Adult. **P:** Entertainment. **U:** Home. **Mov-Ent:** Mystery & Suspense. **Acq:** Purchase. **Dist:** Unknown Distributor.

Bell'Antonio 1962
Italian sex farce about Antonio, a man incapable of making love to those few women who are high-born, pure, and manageable. Italian with English subtitles. 101m/B/W; VHS. **C:** Marcello Mastroianni; Claudia Cardinale. **A:** Jr. High-Adult. **P:** Entertainment. **U:** Home. **L:** English, Italian. **Mov-Ent:** Sex & Sexuality. **Acq:** Purchase. **Dist:** Kino on Video. $59.95.

Bellas de Noche 1975 — ★
A Mexican pimp gets in trouble with the mob. In Spanish. 110m; VHS. **C:** Jorge (George) Rivero; Lalo El Mimo; Rafael Inclan; Sasha Montenegro. **A:** Sr. High-Adult. **P:** Entertainment. **U:** Home. **L:** Spanish. **Mov-Ent:** Prostitution. **Acq:** Purchase. **Dist:** Spanishmultimedia. $53.95.

The Bellboy 1960 (Unrated) — ★★½
Lewis makes his directorial debut in this plotless but clever outing. He also stars as the eponymous character, a bellboy at Miami's Fountainbleau Hotel. Cameos from Berle and Winchell are highlights. 72m/B/W; VHS, DVD, Wide. **C:** Jerry Lewis; Alex Gerry; Bob Clayton; Sonny Sands; Bill Richmond; Larry Best; Maxie "Slapsie" Rosenbloom; Cameo(s) Milton Berle; Walter Winchell; Directed by Jerry Lewis; Written by Jerry Lewis; Cinematography by Haskell Boggs; Music by Walter Scharf. **Pr:** Paramount Pictures. **A:** Family. **P:** Entertainment. **U:** Home. **Mov-Ent:** Comedy--Slapstick, Cult Films. **Acq:** Purchase. **Dist:** Lions Gate Television Corp. $59.95.

The Bellboy and the Playgirls 1962 (Unrated) — **Bomb!**
Early Coppola effort adds new film footage to a 1958 German movie. Stars Playboy playmate June "The Body" Wilkinson, with other centerfolds of the time. 93m; VHS. **C:** June Wilkinson; Donald Kenney; Karin Dor; Willy Fritsch; Michael Cramer; Louise Lawson; Ann Myers; Directed by Francis Ford Coppola; Written by Francis Ford Coppola. **Pr:** Francis Ford Coppola; Francis Ford Coppola. **A:** College-Adult. **P:** Entertainment. **U:** Home. **Mov-Ent. Acq:** Purchase. **Dist:** Amazon.com Inc.

Bellcore's Transport Technologies Videotape Series 199?
Six-part telecommunication technology series that centers on various aspects of the information superhighway, covering such topics as wireless technology, loop carrier systems, digital cross-connect systems, ISDN's, HDSL technology, and fiber engineering. Comes with viewer's guides. 172m; VHS. **TV Std:** NTSC, PAL. **A:** College-Adult. **P:** Special Education. **U:** Institution. **Gen-Edu:** Technology, Communication. **Acq:** Purchase. **Dist:** Telcordia Technologies Inc. $870.00.
Indiv. Titles: 1. Wireless Communications 2. Digital Loop Carrier Systems 3. Digital Cross-Connect System 4. Integrated Services Digital Network 5. High Bit-Rate Digital Subscriber Line 6. Fiber in the Loop Engineering.

Belle 2013 (PG) — ★★½
A well-intentioned and well-staged drama that nonetheless feels flat. This period piece is based on the true story of Dido Elizabeth Belle (Mbatha-Raw), the illegitimate mixed-race daughter of a Royal Navy Admiral. Belle is raised by her great uncle Lord Mansfield (Wilkinson) and his wife (Watson) but occupies a unique place in history given the privilege allowed by her family's place in society balanced against the way she's treated for the color of her skin. With the help of those sympathetic to her cause and a little bit of love, Belle's story actually helped end slavery in England. 105m; DVD. **C:** Gugu Mbatha-Raw; Tom Wilkinson; Emily Watson; Sarah Gadon; Sam Reid; James Norton; Tom Felton; Miranda Richardson; Penelope Wilton; Directed by Amma Asante; Written by Misan Sagay; Cinematography by Ben Smithard; Music by Rachel Portman. **Pr:** Fox Searchlight. **A:** Jr. High-Adult. **P:** Entertainment. **U:** Home. **L:** English. **Mov-Ent:** Women, Slavery, Great Britain. **Acq:** Purchase.

Belle Americaine 1961 — ★★
Title refers to the Cadillac car young Parisian factory worker Dhery buys at a suspiciously bargain price. Naturally, his deal is too good to be true and trouble follows. Dubbed in English. 97m; VHS. **C:** Robert Dhery; Louis de Funes; Collette Brosset; Alfred Adam; Bernard Lavalette; Annie Ducaux; Directed by Robert Dhery; Written by Robert Dhery; Alfred Adam; Pierre Tchernia; Cinematography by Ghislan Cloquet; Music by Gerard Calvi. **A:** College-Adult. **P:** Entertainment. **U:** Home. **Mov-Ent:** Automobiles. **Acq:** Purchase. **Dist:** Facets Multimedia Inc.

Belle Case La Follette: 1859-1931 1987
A documentary on the life of the writer, speaker, mother, and political advisor, which highlights hers work as a national leader in the suffrage, peace, and progressive movements. Part of the Women's History and Literature Media series. 15m; VHS, 3/4 U. **Pr:** Jocelyn Riley. **A:** Jr. High-Adult. **P:** Education. **U:** Institution. **Gen-Edu:** Documentary Films, Biography, Women. **Acq:** Purchase, Rent/Lease. **Dist:** Her Own Words Productions. $95.00.

Belle de Jour 1967 (R) — ★★★½
Based on Joseph Kessel's novel, one of director Bunuel's best movies has all his characteristic nuances: the hypocrisy of our society; eroticism; anti-religion. Deneuve plays Severine, a chic, frigid Parisian newlywed, who decides to become a daytime prostitute, unbeknownst to her husband. Bunuel blends reality with fantasy, and the viewer is never sure which is which in this finely crafted movie. French with subtitles. 100m; VHS, DVD, Blu-Ray, Wide. **C:** Catherine Deneuve; Jean Sorel; Genevieve Page; Michel Piccoli; Francisco Rabal; Pierre Clementi; Georges Marchal; Francoise Fabian; Directed by Luis Bunuel; Written by Luis Bunuel; Jean-Claude Carriere; Cinematography by Sacha Vierny. **Pr:** Raymond Hakim. **A:** College-Adult. **P:** Entertainment. **U:** Home. **L:** French. **Mov-Ent:** Prostitution. **Acq:** Purchase. **Dist:** Buena Vista Home Entertainment.

Belle Epoque 1992 (R) — ★★★
Young army deserter Fernando (Sanz) embarks on a personal voyage of discovery when he meets Manolo (Gomez), an eccentric old man, and father to four beautiful daughters. Fernando can't believe his luck—and the sisters share his interest, resulting in an amusing round of musical beds. Bittersweet tale set amidst the anarchy and war of 1930s Spain with a terrific screenplay that tastefully handles the material without stooping to the obvious leering possibilities. In addition to Oscar, won nine Spanish Goyas, including best picture, director, actress (Gil), and screenplay. Title ironically refers to the era at the end of the 19th century before the wars of the 20th century tore Europe apart. Spanish with English subtitles or dubbed. 108m; VHS, DVD. **C:** Jorge Sanz; Fernando Fernan-Gomez; Ariadna Gil; Maribel Verdu; Penelope Cruz; Miriam Diaz-Aroca; Mary Carmen Ramirez; Michel Galabru; Gabino Diego; Directed by Fernando Trueba; Written by Rafael Azcona; Cinematography by Jose Luis Alcaine; Music by Antoine Duhamel. **Pr:** Andres Vincente Gomez; Sony Pictures Classics. **A:** College-Adult. **P:** Entertainment. **U:** Home. **L:** Spanish. **Mov-Ent:** Comedy--Romantic, Sex & Sexuality, Spain. **Awds:** Oscars '93: Foreign Film. **Acq:** Purchase. **Dist:** Sony Pictures Home Entertainment Inc. $19.95.

The Belle of Amherst 1980
Harris re-creates her Tony Award-winning portrait of Emily Dickinson. 90m; VHS. **C:** Julie Harris. **Pr:** Dove; Creative Image. **A:** Family. **P:** Entertainment. **U:** Institution, Home. **Fin-Art:** Biography, Literature--American. **Acq:** Purchase. **Dist:** Kino on Video. $59.95.

The Belle of Amherst 1988
Theatre production portrays the life of Emily Dickinson, featuring Julie Harris. 118m; VHS. **A:** Adult. **P:** Education. **U:** Institution. **Fin-Art:** Theater. **Acq:** Purchase. **Dist:** Insight Media. $119.00.

The Belle of New York 1952 (Unrated) — ★★
A turn-of-the-century bachelor falls in love with a Salvation Army missionary in this standard musical. 82m; VHS, DVD. **C:** Fred Astaire; Vera-Ellen; Marjorie Main; Keenan Wynn; Alice Pearce; Gale Robbins; Clinton Sundberg; Directed by Charles Walters. **Pr:** MGM. **A:** Family. **P:** Entertainment. **U:** Home. **Mov-Ent:** Musical--Drama, Romance, Dance. **Acq:** Purchase. **Dist:** Warner Home Video, Inc. $19.98.
Songs: Naughty But Nice; Baby Doll; Oops; I Wanna Be a Dancin' Man; Seeing's Believing; Bachelor's Dinner Song; When I'm Out With the Belle of New York; Let a Little Love Come In.

Belle of the Nineties 1934 — ★★½
West struts as a 1890s singer who gets involved with a boxer. Her trademark sexual innuendos were already being censored but such lines as "It's better to be looked over than overlooked," done in West style, get the point across. 73m/B/W; DVD. **C:** Mae West; Roger Pryor; Johnny Mack Brown; John Miljan; Katherine DeMille; Harry Woods; Edward (Ed) Gargan; Directed by Leo McCarey; Written by Mae West; Cinematography by Karl Struss; Music by Arthur Johnston. **Pr:** William LeBaron; Paramount Pictures. **A:** Jr. High-Adult. **P:** Entertainment. **U:** Home. **Mov-Ent:** Sex & Sexuality, Boxing. **Acq:** Purchase. **Dist:** Turner Broadcasting System Inc. $14.98.

Belle Starr 1979 — ★½
The career of Wild West outlaw Belle Starr is chronicled in this strange western pastiche about lawlessness and sexual agression. Wertmuller directed under the pseudonym Nathan Wich. Dubbed in English. 90m; VHS, DVD. **C:** Elsa Martinelli; George Eastman; Dan Harrison; Directed by Lina Wertmuller. **A:** Jr. High-Adult. **P:** Entertainment. **U:** Home. **Mov-Ent. Acq:** Purchase. **Dist:** Mill Creek Entertainment L.L.C. $59.95.

Belle Toujours 2006 (Unrated) — ★★★
Thirty-nine years after "Belle de Jour" comes this sequel—or perhaps more of an homage—from Manoel de Oliveira. A chance meeting after so many years places Henri Husson (Piccoli) and Severine (Ogier) at a candlelit dinner table where they discuss the past, the intervening years, and thoughts of the future. Severine, now a widow worn down by years of carrying secrets and lies, seems to care little about reliving their sexually complicated past and in fact is prepared to retire to a convent. Henri, still feeling the dart of her rejection, wants to recount the sordid history they share. In the earlier film the young Severine supported herself and her disabled husband as a daytime prostitute, a secret she meticulously kept from her husband; Henri wanted a relationship with her that never happened. Paris sparkles in this beautifully crafted work. 68m; DVD. **C:** Michel Piccoli; Bulle Ogier; Ricardo Trepa; Leonor Baldaque; Julia Buisel; Directed by Manoel de Oliveira; Written by Manoel de Oliveira; Cinematography by Sabine Lancelin. **Pr:** Miguel Caldhile; Serge Lalou; Les Films d'Ici; Filbox Producoes; New Yorker Films. **A:** College-Adult. **P:** Entertainment. **U:** Home. **L:** French. **Mov-Ent:** Aging. **Acq:** Purchase. **Dist:** New Yorker Video.

The Belles of St. Trinian's 1953 (Unrated) — ★★★
Sim is priceless in a dual role as the eccentric headmistress of a chaotic, bankrupt girls' school and her bookie twin brother who scheme the school into financial security. The first in a series of movies based on a popular British cartoon by Ronald Searles about a girls' school and its mischievous students. Followed by "Blue Murder at St. Trinian's," "The Pure Hell of St. Trinian's," and "The Great St. Trinian's Train Robbery." 86m/B/W; VHS, Streaming. **C:** Alastair Sim; Joyce Grenfell; Hermione Baddeley; George Cole; Eric Pohlmann; Renee Houston; Beryl Reid; Balbina; Jill Braidwood; Annabelle Covey; Betty Ann Davies; Diana Day; Jack Doyle; Irene Handl; Arthur Howard; Sidney James; Lloyd Lamble; Jean Langston; Belinda Lee; Vivian Martin; Andree Melly; Mary Merrall; Guy Middleton; Joan Sims; Jerry Verno; Richard Wattis; Directed by Frank Launder; Written by Frank Launder; Sidney Gilliat; Val Valentine; Cinematography by Stanley Pavey; Music by Malcolm Arnold. **Pr:** Lauder Gillist Productions. **A:** Family. **P:** Entertainment. **U:** Home. **Mov-Ent:** Education. **Acq:** Purchase. **Dist:** Amazon.com Inc.; Lions Gate Entertainment Inc. $9.98.

Belles on Their Toes 1952 (Unrated) — ★★
Somewhat less charming sequel to 1950's "Cheaper by the Dozen" is big on nostalgia. Now widowed, Lillian Gilbreth (Loy) is struggling to support her large family, having to overcome women in the workplace prejudice. Using her industrial engineering degree, Lillian finally gets a job training young engineers, but this means eldest daughter Ann (Crain) must pick up the domestic slack. Which puts a crimp in Ann's budding romance with young Dr. Bob (Hunter). Based on the memoir by Gilbreth children Frank and Ernestine. 89m; DVD. **C:** Myrna Loy; Jeanne Crain; Debra Paget; Jeffrey Hunter; Edward Arnold; Hoagy Carmichael; Barbara Bates; Robert Arthur; Martin Milner; Verna Felton; Carole Nugent; Tommy "T.V." Ivo; Jimmy Hunt; Robert Easton; Cecil Weston; Directed by Henry Levin; Written by Henry Ephron; Phoebe Ephron; Cinematography by Arthur E. Arling; Music by Cyril Mockridge. **A:** Family. **P:** Entertainment. **U:** Home. **Mov-Ent. Acq:** Purchase. **Dist:** Fox Home Entertainment.

Belle's Tales of Friendship 1999
This combination of live-action and animation features the character of Belle from the Disney movie "Beauty and the Beast" teaching her friends about the importance of working together. 70m; VHS. **A:** Family. **P:** Entertainment. **U:** Home. **Chl-Juv:** Animation & Cartoons, Children. **Acq:** Purchase. **Dist:** Buena Vista Home Entertainment. $19.99.

Bellflower 2011 (R) — ★★
A queasy, hot mess of a male fantasy with on-the-edge Woodrow (played by debut writer/director Glodell) and his equally grungy friend Aiden (Dawson) drinking too much and obsessing over sex, muscle cars, and a post-apocalyptic "Mad Max" world as well as setting things on fire with their homemade flamethrower. Woodrow falls for tough blond Milly (Wiseman) and seems to be making a play towards adulthood until she cheats on him and the situation gets violent instead. 104m; DVD, Wide. **C:** Evan Glodell; Tyler Dawson; Jessie Wiseman; Vincent Grashaw; Rebekah Brandes; Directed by Evan Glodell; Written by Evan Glodell; Cinematography by Joel Hodge; Music by Jonathan Keevil. **Pr:** Evan Glodell; Vincent Grashaw; Coatwolf Prods; Oscilloscope Films. **A:** Sr. High-Adult. **P:** Entertainment. **U:** Home. **L:** English. **Mov-Ent:** Fires. **Acq:** Purchase. **Dist:** Oscilloscope Films.

Bellhop/The Noon Whistle 1922
Two comedic shorts back to back, separately featuring the famous comics Laurel and Hardy. 46m/B/W; Silent; VHS. **C:** Stan Laurel; Oliver Hardy. **Pr:** Hal Roach. **A:** Family. **P:** Entertainment. **U:** Home. **Mov-Ent:** Comedy--Slapstick, Silent Films. **Acq:** Purchase. **Dist:** $49.95.

Bellini: La Sonnambula 1987
A feature film version of the opera about a beautiful young country girl who sleepwalks her way into a love affair and a series of chance adventures. Sung in Italian with English narration between arias. 90m/B/W; VHS. **C:** Gino Sinimberghi; Fiorello Ortis; Franca Tamantini. **Pr:** V.I.E.W. Video. **A:** Jr. High-Adult. **P:** Entertainment. **U:** Home. **L:** Italian. **Fin-Art:** Music--Performance, Opera. **Acq:** Purchase. **Dist:** Music Video Distributors; V.I.E.W. Inc./Arkadia Entertainment Corp. $39.95.

Bellini: The Feast of the Gods 1990
"The Feast of the Gods" is a work originally painted by Bellini. Two other masters, Dossi and Titian, each altered the painting in their own way. Now it's impossible to tell which parts of the work belong to which master. With the help of modern science, this documentary strives to unravel the mystery behind this masterpiece. 27m; VHS. **Pr:** National Gallery of Art. **A:** Jr. High-Adult. **P:** Education. **U:** Home. **Gen-Edu:** Documentary Films, Art & Artists, Painting. **Acq:** Purchase. **Dist:** Home Vision Cinema; Crystal Productions. $29.95.

Bellissima 1951 — ★★★
A woman living in an Italian tenement has unrealistic goals for her plain but endearing daughter when a famous director begins casting a role designed for a child. The mother's maternal fury and collision with reality highlight a poignant film. Italian with subtitles. 130m/B/W; VHS, DVD. **C:** Anna Magnani; Walter Chiari; Alessandro Blasetti; Tina Apicella; Gastone Renzelli; Directed by Luchino Visconti; Written by Luchino Visconti; Cesare Zavattini; Francesco Rosi; Suso Cecchi D'Amico; Cinematography by Piero Portalupi; Paul Ronald. **Pr:** Hobel Leiterman Productions. **A:** Family. **P:** Entertainment. **U:** Home. **L:** English, Italian. **Mov-Ent. Acq:** Purchase. **Dist:** The Cinema Guild. $49.95.

Bellissimo: Images of the Italian Cinema 1987
A panoramic film history of Italian cinema, featuring film clips, behind-the-scenes footage and interviews with the industry's leading figures. Clips from "Open City," "Divorce Italian Style," "8 1/2," and "Seven Beauties" are included. In English, and Italian with subtitles. 110m; VHS. **C:** Sophia Loren; Marcello Mastroianni; Bernardo Bertolucci; Dino De Laurentiis; Marco Ferreri; Roberto Rossellini; Vittorio De Sica; Pier Paolo Pasolini; Franco Zeffirelli; Federico Fellini; Lina Wertmuller; Monica Vitti; Giancarlo Giannini; Anna Magnani; Directed by Gianfranco Mingozzi. **Pr:** Gianfredo Mingozzi. **A:** Family. **P:** Entertainment.

U: Home. L: English, Italian. Mov-Ent: Film History. Acq: Purchase. Dist: Water Bearer Films Inc.; Facets Multimedia Inc. $29.95.

Bellman and True 1988 (R) — ★★½
Rewarding, but sometimes tedious character study of a mild mannered computer whiz who teams with a gang of bank robbers. Fine performances, especially subtle dangerous gang characters. 112m; VHS, Streaming. **C:** Bernard Hill; Kieran O'Brien; Richard Hope; Frances Tomelty; Derek Newark; John Kavanagh; Ken Bones; Directed by Richard Loncraine; Written by Desmond Lowden; Cinematography by Ken Westbury; Music by Colin Towns. **Pr:** Handmade Films. **A:** College-Adult. **P:** Entertainment. **U:** Home. **Mov-Ent.** **Acq:** Purchase. **Dist:** Image Entertainment Inc.; MGM Home Entertainment.

The Bells 1926 (Unrated) — ★★★
The mayor of an Alsatian village kills a wealthy merchant and steals his money. The murderer experiences pangs of guilt which are accentuated when a traveling mesmerist comes to town and claims to be able to discern a person's darkest secrets. Silent with music score. 67m/B/W; Silent; VHS, DVD. **C:** Lionel Barrymore; Boris Karloff; Gustav von Seyffertitz; Directed by James L. Young; Written by James L. Young; Cinematography by L. William O'Connell. **Pr:** Independent. **A:** Sr. High-Adult. **P:** Entertainment. **U:** Home. **Mov-Ent:** Horror, Silent Films. **Acq:** Purchase. **Dist:** Kino on Video; Sinister Cinema; Grapevine Video.

Bells Are Ringing 1960 — ★★★
A girl who works for a telephone answering service can't help but take an interest in the lives of the clients, especially a playwright with an inferiority complex. Based on Adolph Green and Betty Comden's Broadway musical. 126m; VHS, DVD, Wide. **C:** Judy Holliday; Dean Martin; Fred Clark; Eddie Foy, Jr.; Jean Stapleton; Directed by Vincente Minnelli; Written by Betty Comden; Adolph Green; Cinematography by Milton Krasner; Music by Andre Previn. **Pr:** MGM. **A:** Family. **P:** Entertainment. **U:** Home. **Mov-Ent:** Musical--Drama, Comedy--Romantic. **Acq:** Purchase. **Dist:** MGM Home Entertainment. $19.98.
Songs: Just in Time; The Party's Over; It's a Perfect Relationship; Do It Yourself; It's a Simple Little System; Better Than a Dream; I Met a Girl; Drop That Name; I'm Going Back.

Bells of Capistrano 1942 — ★½
The last film Autry made before serving in the Army finds the singing star wanted as a crowd-drawing attraction for two rival rodeo companies. Gene chooses the one owned by the pretty girl, which causes problems with the competition. 73m/B/W; VHS. **C:** Gene Autry; Smiley Burnette; Virginia Grey; Lucien Littlefield; Directed by William M. Morgan; Written by Lawrence Kimble; Cinematography by Reggie Lanning. **Pr:** Republic Pictures. **A:** Family. **P:** Entertainment. **U:** Home. **Mov-Ent:** Western, Rodeos. **Acq:** Purchase. **Dist:** Buena Vista Home Entertainment.
Songs: In Old Capistrano; Forgive Me; Don't Bite the Hand That's Feeding You; At Sundown.

The Bells of Chernobyl 2000
Chronicles the Chernobyl disaster through archival footage and eyewitness accounts. Details the efforts of a government cover-up and the plight of the residents of Pripyat, where the explosion occurred, and throughout Russia. 52m; VHS. **A:** Adult. **P:** Education. **U:** Home. **Gen-Edu:** Documentary Films, USSR, Nuclear Energy. **Acq:** Purchase, Rent/Lease. **Dist:** Filmakers Library Inc. $295.

Bells of Coronado 1950 — ★★
Rogers and Evans team up to expose the murderer of the owner of a profitable uranium mine. A gang of smugglers trying to trade the ore to foreign powers is thwarted. The usual thin storyline, but filled with action and riding stunts. 67m/B/W; VHS, DVD. **C:** Roy Rogers; Dale Evans; Pat Brady; Grant Withers; Directed by William Witney. **Pr:** Republic. **A:** Family. **P:** Entertainment. **U:** Home. **Mov-Ent:** Western. **Acq:** Purchase. **Dist:** Lions Gate Entertainment Inc. $9.98.

The Bells of Death 1968 (Unrated) — ★★
In this classic Shaw Brothers wuxia effort, Wei Fu (Yi Chang) is a simple woodcutter whose family is slaughtered by a trio of marauding bad guys. Wei undergoes extensive (i.e. years) martial arts training before chasing them down to exact his revenge. Along the way he performs various good deeds, including rescuing a young woman from a life of prostitution. While the tale of a kung fu fighter devoting his entire life to the revenge of wrongs on his loved ones is now cliche, this film was among the first to use that theme and inspired many later martial arts movie efforts. 110m; DVD. **C:** Yi Chang; Ping Chin; Hsin Yen Chao; Kau Lam; Directed by Feng Yueh (Yue); Written by Kang Chien Chiu; Cinematography by Hsueh Li Pao; Music by Fu-ling Wang. **A:** Sr. High-Adult. **P:** Entertainment. **U:** Home. **L:** English, Mandarin Dialects. **Mov-Ent:** Action-Adventure, Martial Arts. **Acq:** Purchase. **Dist:** Image Entertainment Inc. $19.99.

Bells of Rosarita 1945 — ★★½
Roy helps foil an evil plan to swindle Evans out of the circus she inherited. All-star western cast under the big top. 54m/B/W; VHS, DVD, 3/4 U, Special order formats. **C:** Roy Rogers; Dale Evans; George "Gabby" Hayes; Sunset Carson; Adele Mara; Grant Withers; Roy Barcroft; Addison Richards; Directed by Frank McDonald. **Pr:** Republic. **A:** Adult. **P:** Entertainment. **U:** Home. **Mov-Ent:** Western, Circuses. **Acq:** Purchase. **Dist:** Gotham Distributing Corp.; Synergy Enterprises Inc.; Rex Miller Artisan Studio. $19.95.

The Bells of St. Mary's 1945 — ★★★½
An easy-going priest finds himself in a subtle battle of wits with the Mother Superior over how the children of St. Mary's school should be raised. It's the sequel to "Going My Way." Songs include the title tune and "Aren't You Glad You're You?" Also available in a colorized version. 126m/B/W; VHS, DVD, Blu-Ray, CC. **C:** Bing Crosby; Ingrid Bergman; Henry Travers; Directed by Leo McCarey; Written by Dudley Nichols; Cinematography by George Barnes; Music by Robert Emmett Dolan; Johnny Burke; James Van Heusen. **Pr:** RKO. **A:** Family. **P:** Entertainment. **U:** Home. **Mov-Ent:** Comedy-Drama, Education. **Awds:** Oscars '45: Sound; Golden Globes '46: Actress--Drama (Bergman); N.Y. Film Critics '45: Actress (Bergman). **Acq:** Purchase. **Dist:** Lions Gate Entertainment Inc.; Ignatius Press. $39.98.

Bells of San Angelo 1947 — ★
Roy foils thieves' attempts to steal a girl's inherited ranch. 54m; VHS, DVD. **C:** Roy Rogers; Dale Evans; Directed by William Witney. **Pr:** Republic. **A:** Family. **P:** Entertainment. **U:** Home. **Mov-Ent:** Western, Horses. **Acq:** Purchase, Rent/Lease. **Dist:** Movies Unlimited; Alpha Video. $19.95.

Bells of San Fernando 1947 — ★
An Irish seaman wanders into California during early Spanish rule and confronts a cruel overseer in this lackluster Western drama. Scripted by "Cisco Kid" Renaldo. 75m/B/W; VHS, DVD. **C:** Donald Woods; Gloria Warren; Byron Foulger; Directed by Terry Morse; Written by Jack DeWitt; Duncan Renaldo. **Pr:** James Burkett; Screen Guild. **A:** Jr. High-Adult. **P:** Entertainment. **U:** Home. **Mov-Ent:** Western. **Acq:** Purchase. **Dist:** Movies Unlimited. $19.99.

Bells of San Fernando 1975
Documents the plight of Spanish settlers in California, and the guidance they receive from missionaries. 70m; VHS. **Pr:** Keep the Faith, Inc. **A:** Family. **P:** Religious. **U:** Institution, Home. **Gen-Edu:** Documentary Films, Religion, U.S. States. **Acq:** Purchase. **Dist:** Keep the Faith Inc.

Bell's Palsy 1971
A brief interview and pertinent clinical examination. 9m; VHS, 3/4 U, Special order formats. **Pr:** Ohio State University Health Sciences AV Center. **A:** College-Adult. **P:** Professional. **U:** Institution, SURA. **Hea-Sci:** Neurology, Medical Education. **Acq:** Purchase, Rent/Lease. **Dist:** Ohio State University.

Belly 1996
Documentary of Katherine Bruce Laing, a former bulimic who gained self-acceptance through belly dancing. 22m; VHS. **A:** Adult. **P:** Education. **U:** Home. **Gen-Edu:** Documentary Films, Dance--Performance, Eating Disorders. **Acq:** Purchase, Rent/Lease. **Dist:** Filmakers Library Inc. $295.

Belly 1998 (R) — ★★
Inner-city crime tale preaches against crime, violence and drugs while it visually glorifies the opulent benefits of them. Childhood pals Tommy (Simmons) and Sincere (Jones) are successful criminals who head down different paths. Sincere dreams of turning legit and moving his family to Africa. Tommy gets deeper into the drug biz until he is caught by feds and forced to bring down innocent black leader Reverend Saviour (Muhammed). Although the movie ends with a plea for change, it may itself be part of the problem. 95m; VHS, DVD. **C:** DMX; Taral Hicks; Nasir Jones; Tionne "T-Boz" Watkins; Method Man; Tyrin Turner; Hassan Johnson; Power; Louie Rankin; Rev. Benjamin F. Muhammed; Directed by Hype Williams; Written by Nasir Jones; Hype Williams; Anthony Bodden; Cinematography by Malik Hassan Sayeed; Music by Stephen Cullo. **A:** Sr. High-Adult. **P:** Entertainment. **U:** Home. **Mov-Ent:** Crime Drama, Drug Abuse. **Acq:** Purchase. **Dist:** Lions Gate Television Corp.

Belly Dance with Alicia Dhanifu 19??
Instructor Alicia Dhanifu presents a beginning level class into the world of belly dancing. Includes historical and cultural information as well as instruction on basic finger cymbal patterns, veil wrapping and removing, and a few head, shoulder, arm, and hip isolations. Also offers an introduction to some of the common Middle Eastern instruments used to accompany oriental dance. 24m; VHS. **A:** Jr. High-Adult. **P:** Instruction. **U:** Institution, Home. **How-Ins:** Dance--Instruction, Middle East. **Acq:** Purchase. **Dist:** Stagestep. $29.95.

Belly Dancing 1995
Susan Diamond provides a complete course of movements as well as a brief history of dance origins and instructions on costume design. 60m; VHS. **A:** Sr. High-Adult. **P:** Instruction. **U:** Home. **How-Ins:** Dance--Instruction. **Acq:** Purchase. **Dist:** Videoactive Co. $29.95.

Belly Dancing for Fun and Fitness with Janine Rabbitt 1995
Features belly dancing to trim and tone problem areas. 55m; VHS. **A:** Adult. **P:** Instruction. **U:** Home, Institution. **Hea-Sci:** How-To, Fitness/Exercise, Dance--Instruction. **Acq:** Purchase. **Dist:** Paragon Home Video. $19.98.

The Belly of an Architect 1991 (R) — ★★★½
A thespian feast for the larger-than-life Dennehy as blustering American architect whose personal life and health both crumble as he obsessively readies an exhibition in Rome. A multi-tiered, carefully composed tragicomedy from the ideosyncratic filmmaker Greenaway, probably his most accessible work for general audiences. 119m; VHS, DVD. **C:** Brian Dennehy; Chloe Webb; Lambert Wilson; Sergio Fantoni; Geoffrey Copleston; Marino (Martin) Mase; Directed by Peter Greenaway; Written by Peter Greenaway; Cinematography by Sacha Vierny; Music by Glenn Branca; Wim Mertens. **Pr:** Film Four International; British Screen; Hemdale Films. **A:** College-Adult. **P:** Entertainment. **U:** Home. **Mov-Ent:** Art & Artists, Architecture. **Acq:** Purchase. **Dist:** Movies Unlimited. $13.49.

Belly of the Beast 2003 (R) — ★
Actor Steven Seagal sells his soul to the devil to get a chance to do an action film with HK action director Siu-Tung Ching. Not really, but there's no other way to explain how this stinker got made AND Seagal got a sex scene in it. A retiring CIA agent is on vacation in Thailand when terrorists kidnap his daughter. Worth seeing for the stunt double who does most of Seagal's fight scenes, and the fact that they occasionally dub over Steven's voice with that of a different actor for unknown reasons. 91m; DVD. **C:** Steven Seagal; Byron Mann; Monica Lo; Tom Wu; Sara Malakul Lane; Patrick Robinson; Vincent Riotta; Norman Veeratum; Elidh MacQueen; Ching Siu Tung; Kevork Malikyan; Pongpat Wachirabunjong; Directed by Siu-Tung Ching; Written by Steven Seagal; James Townsend; Cinematography by Danny Nowak; Music by The Music Sculptors; Mark Sayer-Wade. **A:** Sr. High-Adult. **P:** Entertainment. **U:** Home. **L:** English, Thai. **Mov-Ent:** Terrorism, Martial Arts. **Acq:** Purchase. **Dist:** Sony Pictures Home Entertainment Inc. $9.95.

Bellybuttons Are Navels 1984
Two kids learn about different body parts when their grandmother reads them a story. 12m; VHS, 3/4 U. **Pr:** Focus International. **A:** Primary-Jr. High. **P:** Education. **U:** Institution. **L:** Spanish. **Gen-Edu:** Anatomy & Physiology. **Acq:** Purchase, Rent/Lease. **Dist:** Sinclair Institute. $195.00.

Bellydance Core Conditioning 2005
Twin sisters Neena and Veena present a total-body workout that combines standard exercises with bellydance moves. Includes both cardio and toning segments, all with a graceful bellydance flair. 58m; DVD. **A:** Adult. **P:** Instruction. **U:** Home. **Hea-Sci:** Fitness/Exercise. **Acq:** Purchase. **Dist:** Collage Video Specialties, Inc.

Bellydance! Fast Moves 1996
Presents beginner through intermediate movements and combinations designed to increase vitality. 40m; VHS. **A:** Adult. **P:** Instruction. **U:** Home. **How-Ins:** Dance, Fitness/Exercise. **Acq:** Purchase. **Dist:** Tapeworm Video Distributors Inc.

Bellydance Fitness for Beginners: Arms & Abs 1999
Bellydance instruction, focusing on arms and abdominals, for beginners. 30m; VHS. **A:** Adult. **P:** Instruction. **U:** Home. **Hea-Sci:** Fitness/Exercise, Dance--Instruction. **Acq:** Purchase. **Dist:** Instructional Video. $19.98.

Bellydance Fitness for Beginners: Basic Moves 1999
Bellydance instruction, focusing on basic moves, for beginners. 30m; VHS. **A:** Adult. **P:** Instruction. **U:** Home. **Hea-Sci:** Fitness/Exercise, Dance--Instruction. **Acq:** Purchase. **Dist:** Instructional Video. $19.98.

Bellydance Fitness for Beginners: Fat Burning 1999
Bellydance instruction, focusing on fat burning exercises, for beginners. 30m; VHS. **A:** Adult. **P:** Instruction. **U:** Home. **Hea-Sci:** Fitness/Exercise, Dance--Instruction. **Acq:** Purchase. **Dist:** Instructional Video. $19.98.

Bellydance Fitness for Beginners: Hips, Buns & Thighs 1999
Bellydance instruction, focusing on exercises for hips, gluteus, and thighs, for beginners. 30m; VHS. **A:** Adult. **P:** Instruction. **U:** Home. **Hea-Sci:** Fitness/Exercise, Dance--Instruction. **Acq:** Purchase. **Dist:** Instructional Video. $19.98.

Bellydance! Magical Motion 1986
Atea and friends instruct the viewer in bellydancing, best utilized both as a dance and as exercise. 60m; VHS. **Pr:** Magical Motion Enterprises. **A:** College-Adult. **P:** Instruction. **U:** Home. **How-Ins:** How-To, Dance, Fitness/Exercise. **Acq:** Purchase. **Dist:** New & Unique Videos. $29.95.

Bellydance! Slow Moves 1996
Presents beginner through intermediate movements and combinations designed to tone and reduce stress. 40m; VHS. **A:** Adult. **P:** Instruction. **U:** Home. **How-Ins:** Dance, Fitness/Exercise. **Acq:** Purchase. **Dist:** Tapeworm Video Distributors Inc.

Bellyfruit 1999 (Unrated) — ★★
Film, which refers to pregnancy, was inspired by the real-life stories of teen mothers in L.A. 14-year-old Shanika is living in a home for troubled girls when she's taken in by the charms of Damon, equally young Christina witnesses her mother (who had Christina when she was a teen) drug and party and decides to follow her example, while 16-year-old Aracely becomes pregnant by her boyfriend Oscar. Although he stands by her, Aracely's traditional Latin father kicks her out of the house. And when they have their babies, the teens lives just get more confused. 95m; VHS, DVD, Wide. **C:** Kelly Vint; Tamara La Seon Bass; Tonatzin Mondragon; T.E. Russell; Michael Pena; Bonnie Dickenson; Kimberly Scott; James Dumant; Directed by Kerri Green; Written by Kerri Green; Maria Bernhard; Suzannah Blinkoff; Janet Borrus; Cinematography by Peter Calvin. **A:** Sr. High-Adult. **P:** Entertainment. **U:** Home. **Mov-Ent:** Pregnancy, Adolescence. **Acq:** Purchase. **Dist:** Vanguard International Cinema, Inc.

Belonging: A Film About Adoption 1987
An in-depth, personal look at the adoption process through interviews with the natural mother, the adoptive parents, and the adopted child. 30m; VHS, 3/4 U. **Pr:** RMI Media Productions. **A:** Adult. **P:** Education. **U:** Institution. **Gen-Edu:** Documentary Films, Family, Adoption. **Acq:** Purchase. **Dist:** RMI Media.

The Belonging Game 1982
When a girl moves to a new town, she is forced to decide on either staying with the popular crowd or doing what she knows is right. 30m; VHS, 3/4 U. **Pr:** Daughters of St. Paul. **A:**

Primary-Jr. High. **P:** Religious. **U:** Institution, Home. **Gen-Edu:** Ethics & Morals. **Acq:** Purchase. **Dist:** Concordia Publishing House. $39.95.

Beloved 1998 (R) — ★★½
Sethe (Winfrey) is a middle-aged former slave in rural Ohio years after her emancipation from a Kentucky planation. She is haunted (literally) by the painful legacy of slavery in the form of a mud-covered feral child known as Beloved (Newton). Another reminder is Paul D (Glover), a former slave from the same Kentucky plantation, who stokes Sethe's embers. Metaphors abound as we wonder if Beloved really is the child Sethe killed years before. Oprah's pet project (she's owned the film rights for 10 years) is a faithful adaptation of Toni Morrison's Pulitzer Prize-winning novel. Unfortunately, the long-awaited feature can't fulfill the huge expectations. While performances are excellent, pic suffers from a sense of self-indulgence, which is accentuated by the three-hour running time. At times powerful and moving, but also slow and occasionally confusing. 172m; VHS, DVD, CC. **C:** Oprah Winfrey; Thandie Newton; Danny Glover; Kimberly Elise; Lisa Gay Hamilton; Beah Richards; Irma P. Hall; Albert Hall; Jason Robards, Jr.; Jude Ciccolella; Directed by Jonathan Demme; Written by Akosua Busia; Richard LaGravenese; Adam Brooks; Cinematography by Tak Fujimoto; Music by Rachel Portman. **Pr:** Edward Saxon; Jonathan Demme; Gary Goetzman; Oprah Winfrey; Ron Bozman; Oprah Winfrey; Jonathan Demme; Harpo Films; Clinica Estetico; Buena Vista. **A:** Sr. High-Adult. **P:** Entertainment. **U:** Home. **Mov-Ent:** Slavery, Black Culture. **Acq:** Purchase. **Dist:** Buena Vista Home Entertainment.

Beloved 2011 (Unrated) — ★★
Real-life mother/daughter Deneuve and Mastroianni play the same roles in Honore's romantic/musical drama that covers some 40 years. In 1964, young Madeleine (Sagnier) almost accidentally becomes a prostitute to live the good life. She marries, has a daughter, but doesn't leave her life of pleasure behind as she ages (Deneuve). Meanwhile, her daughter Vera (Mastroianni) is a commitment-phobe who makes impossible romantic choices. The characters also randomly express themselves in song in a manner similar to the director's 2007 film "Love Songs." French with subtitles. 139m; DVD. **C:** Catherine Deneuve; Chiara Mastroianni; Ludivine Sagnier; Louis Garrel; Milos Forman; Paul Schneider; Radivoje (Rasha) Bukvic; Michel Delpech; Directed by Christophe Honore; Written by Christophe Honore; Cinematography by Remy Chevrin; Music by Alexandre Beaupain. **A:** Adult. **P:** Entertainment. **U:** Home. **L:** French. **Mov-Ent:** Drama, Romance, Parenting. **Acq:** Purchase. **Dist:** IFC Films.

The Beloved Community 2006
Documentary covering the environmental destruction and fallout from chemical exposure in a Canadian oil town. 56m; DVD. **A:** Sr. High-Adult. **P:** Education. **U:** Home, Institution. **Gen-Edu:** Documentary Films, Public Health. **Acq:** Purchase. **Dist:** California Newsreel. $26.95.

Beloved Enemy 1936 (Unrated) — ★★★
A romantic tragedy set in Civil War-torn Ireland in the 1920s. A rebel leader and a proper English lady struggle to overcome the war's interference with their burgeoning relationship. 86m/B/W; VHS. **C:** David Niven; Merle Oberon; Brian Aherne; Karen Morley; Donald Crisp; Directed by H.C. Potter; Cinematography by Gregg Toland. **Pr:** United Artists. **A:** Family. **P:** Entertainment. **U:** Home. **Mov-Ent:** Drama, Ireland. **Acq:** Purchase. **Dist:** Cable Films/i2bs Online World.

Beloved/Friend 1999 — ★★
Everybody wants something (or someone) they can't have. Jaume (Pou) is a middleaged gay college prof who pines for his student David (Selvas), a cold-hearted stud who hustles to pay his tuition. In fact, the only way Jaume can get attention from David is to buy his services (although David has something of a father figure complex). Then, Jaume's best friend Pere (Gas) discovers that David has gotten his daughter, Alba (Montala), pregnant. David seems to be a catalyst for a lot of soul-searching but nothing much gets resolved. Spanish with subtitles. 90m; VHS, DVD. **C:** Jose(p) Maria Pou; David Selvas; Mario Gas; Irene Montala; Rosa Maria Sarda; Directed by Ventura Pons; Written by Josep Maria Benet i Jornet; Cinematography by Jesus Escosa; Music by Carles Cases. **A:** College-Adult. **P:** Entertainment. **U:** Home. **L:** Spanish. **Mov-Ent:** Prostitution, Pregnancy. **Acq:** Purchase. **Dist:** Strand Releasing.

The Beloved: Happiness 1990
Music video collection from the winners of the 1990 Best New Pop Artist Award. Songs are "Time After Time," "Hello," "Your Love Takes Me Higher" and "The Sun Rising." This video contains a parental advisory, indicating that some material may not be suitable for younger viewers. 30m; VHS. **Pr:** A*Vision. **A:** Jr. High-Adult. **P:** Entertainment. **U:** Home. **Mov-Ent:** Music Video, Dance. **Acq:** Purchase. **Dist:** WarnerVision; Music Video Distributors; Fast Forward. $14.98.

Beloved Infidel 1959 — ★★½
Sudsy, lavish romancer, based on the book by gossip queen Sheilah Graham, about her brief romance with novelist F. Scott Fitzgerald. Fitzgerald (a badly miscast Peck) is in Hollywood trying to write screenplays when he meets young, English, aspiring writer Graham (an equally miscast Kerr). She becomes his mistress, putting up with Fitzgerald's drinking and insults, while he interferes with her career. Story is slanted towards Graham nobly trying to rescue Fitzgerald from himself (he did actually die from a heart attack while with Graham). 123m; DVD, Blu-Ray. **C:** Gregory Peck; Deborah Kerr; Eddie Albert; Philip Ober; Herbert Rudley; John Sutton; Karin (Karen, Katharine) Booth; Directed by Henry King; Written by Sy Bartlett; Cinematography by Leon Shamroy; Music by Franz Waxman. **Pr:** Jerry Wald; 20th Century-Fox. **A:** Jr. High-Adult. **P:** Entertainment. **U:** Home. **Mov-Ent:** Drama. **Acq:** Purchase. **Dist:** Fox Home Entertainment.

Beloved Murderer! 1991
Animated film noir tale of two lesbian hit women hired to kill each other. German with subtitles. 8m/B/W; VHS. **C:** Directed by Heidi Kull. **A:** College-Adult. **P:** Entertainment. **U:** Institution. **L:** German. **Fin-Art:** Animation & Cartoons. **Acq:** Purchase, Rent/Lease. **Dist:** Frameline. $150.00.

The Beloved Rogue 1927 (Unrated) — ★★★
Crosland—who gained a reputation for innovation by directing "Don Juan" and "The Jazz Singer"?mounted this well-designed and effects-laden medieval costumer with poetic license and typical excesses of the day. Barrymore is swashbuckling poet Francois Villon, who battles verbally with Louis XI (Veidt, in his first US role). Louis banishes him after a tiff with the evil Duke of Burgundy and Villon must uncover the Dukes's plans. Crosland plays fast and loose when the facts aren't fab enough, but it's great entertainment. 98m/B/W; Silent; DVD. **C:** John Barrymore; Conrad Veidt; Lawson Butt; Marceline Day; Henry Victor; Slim Summerville; Mack Swain; Directed by Alan Crosland, Jr.; Written by Paul Bern; Cinematography by Joseph August. **A:** College-Adult. **P:** Entertainment. **U:** Home. **Mov-Ent:** Silent Films, Drama. **Acq:** Purchase. **Dist:** Kino on Video.

Beloved Strangers 2003
Profiles three caregiving situations involving Alzheimer's. Part of the Caregiver Resource Library series covering caregiving issues appropriate for use in courses for nursing, psychology, and gerontology. 25m; VHS. **A:** Adult. **P:** Vocational. **U:** Institution. **Hea-Sci:** Health Education, Medical Care, Occupational Training. **Acq:** Purchase. **Dist:** Aquarius Health Care Media. $125.00.

The Belovs 1992
Stories and conversation of a family from a rural Russian village. 60m/B/W; VHS. **A:** Adult. **P:** Education. **U:** BCTV, Institution. **Gen-Edu:** USSR, Documentary Films. **Acq:** Purchase, Rent/Lease. **Dist:** First Run/Icarus Films. $390.00.

Below 2002 (R) — ★★½
Nothing is certain in director David Twohy's creepy submarine thriller. The captain of World War II sub U.S.S. Manta has died under dubious circumstances, and the crew is already on edge when they rescue three survivors of a torpedoed British hospital ship. When one of these survivors is a woman (Williams), allegedly unlucky on a sub, tensions run even higher. With the Germans tracking the sub, strange events begin to occur, which could be vengeful actions of the captain's ghost, a saboteur, hallucinations caused by lack of oxygen or some combination of the three. As the disasters pile up, the crew becomes divided between acting captain Brice (Greenwood) and rebellious ensign O'Dell (Davis), who has the strangely outspoken Claire on his side. Characters are a bit one-dimensional, but the effects and acting are above average for a B movie. 103m; VHS, DVD, Blu-Ray. **C:** Bruce Greenwood; Matthew Davis; Olivia Williams; Holt McCallany; Scott Foley; Zach Galifianakis; Jason Flemyng; Dexter Fletcher; Nick (Nicholas) Chinlund; Andrew Howard; Christopher Fairbank; Directed by David N. Twohy; Written by David N. Twohy; Darren Aronofsky; Lucas Sussman; Cinematography by Ian Wilson; Music by Graeme Revell. **Pr:** Darren Aronofsky; Darren Aronofsky; Sue Baden-Powell; Eric Watson; Protozoa Pictures; Dimension Films. **A:** Sr. High-Adult. **P:** Entertainment. **U:** Home. **Mov-Ent:** World War Two. **Acq:** Purchase. **Dist:** Buena Vista Home Entertainment.

Below the Belt 1980 (R) — ★★
Almost interesting tale of street-smart woman from New York City who becomes part of the blue-collar "circus" of lady wrestlers. Ex-wrestling champ Burke plays herself. 98m; VHS, DVD. **C:** Regina Baff; Mildred Burke; John C. Becher; Lenny Montana; Directed by Robert Fowler. **Pr:** Aberdeen/RLF/Tom-Mi Productions. **A:** College-Adult. **P:** Entertainment. **U:** Home. **Mov-Ent.** **Acq:** Purchase. **Dist:** Tapeworm Video Distributors Inc. $59.99.

Below the Belt with Keli Roberts: Strengthen, Lengthen, Define ????
A beginner to advanced workout that targets the lower body. 30m; VHS. **A:** Adult. **P:** Instruction. **U:** Home. **Hea-Sci:** Fitness/Exercise, How-To. **Acq:** Purchase. **Dist:** Body Bar Systems. $14.95.

Below the Border 1942 — ★½
The Rough Riders go undercover to straighten out some cattle rustlers. 57m/B/W; VHS, DVD. **C:** Buck Jones; Tim McCoy; Raymond Hatton; Linda Brent; Roy Barcroft; Charles "Blackie" King; Directed by Howard Bretherton. **Pr:** Monogram. **A:** Family. **P:** Entertainment. **U:** Home. **Mov-Ent:** Western. **Acq:** Purchase, Rent/Lease. **Dist:** Alpha Video; Movies Unlimited. $9.99.

Below the Deadline 1929 (Unrated) — ★★
A man framed for embezzlement is set free and allowed to clear his name by a sympathetic detective. 79m/B/W; Silent; VHS. **C:** Frank Leigh; Barbara Worth; Arthur (L.) Rankin; Walter Merrill; Directed by J(ohn) P(aterson) McGowan. **A:** Jr. High-Adult. **P:** Entertainment. **U:** Home. **Mov-Ent:** Silent Films. **Acq:** Purchase. **Dist:** Sinister Cinema. $16.95.

Below the Ramparts 1981
Close-up shots of many mountain flowers and unique shots of the American Dipper, the Golden-Mantled Ground Squirrel, and other animals of the mountains highlight this program in the "Animals and Plants of North America" series. 15m; VHS, 3/4 U. **Pr:** Karvonen Films Ltd. **A:** Primary-Adult. **P:** Education. **U:** Institution, SURA. **Hea-Sci:** Documentary Films, Ecology & Environment, Wildlife. **Acq:** Purchase, Rent/Lease. **Dist:** Phoenix Learning Group.

Below the Rim: Little Big Men of the NBA 1994
Action-filled profiles of NBA stars, including 5-foot 3-inch Mugsy Bogues, Spud Webb, Kevin Johnson, Kenny Anderson, Bob Cousy, Nate "Tiny" Archibald, and Calvin Murphy. ?m; VHS. **A:** Family. **P:** Entertainment. **U:** Home. **Spo-Rec:** Basketball. **Acq:** Purchase. **Dist:** Fox Home Entertainment. $14.98.

Belphegor: Phantom of the Louvre 2001 (Unrated) — ★½
Gets the extra half-bone because Marceau is such a looker. Silly French horror (remake of a 1965 miniseries that was based on a pulp novel) about a sarcophagus discovered during a renovation of the museum. A demon is unleashed and poor Lisa (Marceau) becomes its unwitting host. British archeologist Glenda Spencer (Christie) tries to find out more about the mummy inside while retired police detective Verlac (Serrault) is called in to investigate the theft of items from the Egyptology wing, which is similar to an earlier unsolved case. French with subtitles. 97m; DVD. **C:** Sophie Marceau; Michel Serrault; Julie Christie; Jean-Francois Balmer; Patachou; Frederic Diefenthal; Directed by Jean-Paul Salome; Written by Daniele Thompson; Jerome Tonnerre; Jean-Paul Salome; Cinematography by Jean-Francois Robin; Music by Bruno Coulais. **A:** Sr. High-Adult. **P:** Entertainment. **U:** Home. **L:** French. **Mov-Ent:** Archaeology. **Acq:** Purchase. **Dist:** Lions Gate Entertainment Inc.

The Belstone Fox 1973 — ★★
Orphaned fox goes into hiding, and is hunted by the hound he has befriended and his former owner. 103m; VHS. **C:** Eric Porter; Rachel Roberts; Jeremy Kemp; Directed by James Hill. **Pr:** Julian Wintle. **A:** Family. **P:** Entertainment. **U:** Home. **Mov-Ent:** Animals, Hunting. **Acq:** Purchase. **Dist:** Amazon.com Inc.

Belt Drive Selection 1986
Part of a series offering instruction on selection procedures of common power transmission products for various applications. 16m; VHS. **A:** Adult. **P:** Vocational. **U:** Institution. **Gen-Edu:** Industrial Arts, Technology. **Acq:** Purchase. **Dist:** RMI Media. $132.50.

Belts and Sheaves 1985
Part of a series offering instruction on power transmission products, including nomenclature, applications, classification, numbering systems, and other information on components and equipment. 20m; VHS. **A:** Adult. **P:** Vocational. **U:** Institution. **Gen-Edu:** Industrial Arts, Technology. **Acq:** Purchase. **Dist:** RMI Media. $112.50.

Beluga Baby 1980
"Beluga Baby" is an actual filmed record of the first successful birth of a whale in captivity. The entire birth process is pictured. The calf, alive and vigorous, captures public and scientific attention and appears to be thriving. It's death poses questions for scientists and viewers. 14m; VHS, 3/4 U. **Pr:** National Film Board of Canada. **A:** Primary-Adult. **P:** Education. **U:** Institution, SURA. **Gen-Edu:** Documentary Films, Animals, Pregnancy. **Acq:** Purchase, Rent/Lease. **Dist:** Phoenix Learning Group.

Ben 1972 (PG) — ★½
Sequel to "Willard" finds police Detective Kirtland still on the hunt for a killer rat pack led by Ben, king of the rodents. Title song by young Michael Jackson hit the top of the charts. 95m; VHS. **C:** Joseph Campanella; Lee Montgomery; Arthur O'Connell; Rosemary Murphy; Meredith Baxter; Norman Alden; Paul Carr; Kaz Garas; Kenneth Tobey; Richard Van Heet; Directed by Phil Karlson; Written by Gilbert Ralston; Cinematography by Russell Metty; Music by Walter Scharf. **Pr:** BCP Productions; Cinerama Releasing. **A:** Jr. High-Adult. **P:** Entertainment. **U:** Home. **Mov-Ent:** Horror. **Awds:** Golden Globes '73: Song ("Ben"). **Acq:** Purchase. **Dist:** Unknown Distributor.

Ben 10: Alien Force Volume 2 2008 (Unrated)
Cartoon Network's animated monster-smashing adventure. Ben's date is interrupted by a shape-shifting Galvanic Mechomorph in "Pier Pressure," and his sidekick Gwen must choose between her extraterrestrial heritage and life with her Earth friends in "What Are Little Girls Made Of?" 4 episodes. 88m; DVD. **A:** Primary-Jr. High. **P:** Entertainment. **U:** Home. **Chl-Juv:** Animation & Cartoons, Action-Adventure. **Acq:** Purchase. **Dist:** Warner Home Video, Inc. $14.98.

Ben 10: Season 3 2007
Ben and Gwen meet future versions of themselves in "Ben 10,000," Ben seeks revenge on whoever is making rip-offs of his alien heroes in "Super Alien Hero Buddies," and Xylen thinks Max owns the Omnitrix in "The Visitor." 13 episodes. 299m; DVD. **C:** Voice(s) by Tara Strong; Meagan Smith; Paul Eiding; Dee Bradley Baker. **A:** Primary. **P:** Entertainment. **U:** Home. **Chl-Juv:** Animation & Cartoons, Action-Adventure, Science Fiction. **Acq:** Purchase. **Dist:** Warner Home Video, Inc.

Ben 10: Season One 2006
Ten-year-old Ben Tennyson's life changes drastically after he finds an alien watch, called the Omnitrix, in a fallen meteorite that gives him the ability to transform into ten different alien forms. As he struggles to learn how to control the Omnitrix, (which doesn't always summon the right alien hero), he's also fighting crime and holding the obnoxious Vilgax at bay. Dr. Amino creates powerful monsters out of mutated animals in "Washington B.C." Ben battles alien bounty hunters in "Hunted," a kid with power to absorb energy in "Kevin 11," and in "Tourist Trap" a meaningless prank unleashes the electrical being Megawhatt. 13 episodes. 280m; DVD. **C:** Voice(s) by Tara Strong; Paul Eiding; Meagan Smith. **A:** Adult. **P:** Entertainment. **U:** Home. **Chl-Juv:** Animation & Cartoons, Action-Adventure, Science Fiction. **Acq:** Purchase. **Dist:** Warner Home Video, Inc.

Ben 10: The Complete Season 2 2007
Ben uses his alter-alien hero forms such as Four Arms, Wildmutt, Stinkfly, Wildvine and Cannonbolt to save the day and escape madcap mishaps. An old friend of Grandpa Max hoists an evil plan in "Truth," Ben and Kevin 11 are abducted to an alien carrier in "Grudge Match," and "Dr. Animo and the Mutant Ray" return for revenge. Ben must find a way to get Ghostfreak back into the device in "Ghostfreaked Out" and what if "Gwen 10" found the omnitrix instead of Ben? 13 episodes plus a how-to-draw feature, deleted scenes, and an in-depth look at Ben's alien heroes. 292m; DVD. **A:** Preschool-Primary. **P:** Entertainment. **U:** Home. **Chl-Juv**: Animation & Cartoons, Action-Adventure, Science Fiction. **Acq:** Purchase. **Dist:** Warner Home Video, Inc.

Ben and Eddie 1990
A modern-day spiritual series built around orphan home director Ben, and Eddie, one of the orphans at the home. 45m; VHS. **A:** Primary-Sr. High. **P:** Entertainment. **U:** Home. **Mov-Ent**: Children, Religion. **Acq:** Purchase. **Dist:** Chordant Distribution Group. $14.95.

Ben and Me 1954
Amos, the mouse, befriends Benjamin Franklin and takes his own look at events leading up to the American Revolution. Also available with "Bongo" on laserdisc. 25m; VHS, 3/4 U, EJ, Special order formats. **TV Std:** NTSC, PAL, SECAM. **C:** Voice(s) by Sterling Holloway; Directed by Hamilton Luske. **Pr:** Walt Disney Studios. **A:** Primary-Jr. High. **P:** Education. **U:** Institution, CCTV, Home, SURA. **Chl-Juv**: Animation & Cartoons, Children, History--U.S. **Acq:** Purchase, Rent/Lease. **Dist:** Phoenix Learning Group. $12.99.

Ben Bailey: Road Rage & Accidental Ornithology 2011 (Unrated)
Former Cash Cab host Ben Bailey gets his chance at doing a stand-up comedy routine. 60m; DVD, Streaming. **A:** Sr. High-Adult. **P:** Entertainment. **U:** Home. **Gen-Edu**: Comedy--Performance, Performing Arts. **Acq:** Purchase, Rent/Lease. **Dist:** Comedy Central; Entertainment One US LP. $19.98.

Ben Braun: Principles of Offensive Zone Attack 2008
Coach Ben Braun discusses and demonstrates principles for beating the Zone Defense in basketball. 77m; DVD. **A:** Family. **P:** Education. **U:** Home, Institution. **Spo-Rec**: Basketball, Athletic Instruction/Coaching. **Acq:** Purchase. **Dist:** Championship Productions. $39.99.

Ben Braun: 30 Fundamental Drills for Daily Improvement 2004 (Unrated)
Coach Braun demonstrates numerous drills for basketball teams and individual players to help improve their skills. 72m; DVD. **A:** Family. **P:** Education. **U:** Home, Institution. **Spo-Rec**: Basketball, Athletic Instruction/Coaching. **Acq:** Purchase. **Dist:** Championship Productions. $39.99.

Ben Braun: Two Guard High Post Offense 2007 (Unrated)
Coach Ben Braun demonstrates drills to improve a basketball player's offensive skills, along with discussing the Motion offense. 80m; DVD. **A:** Family. **P:** Education. **U:** Home, Institution. **Spo-Rec**: Basketball, Athletic Instruction/Coaching. **Acq:** Purchase. **Dist:** Championship Productions. $39.99.

Ben Carson M.D.: World Famous Neurosurgeon 2000
The sixteenth episode in the "Black Achievers" video series chronicles the life of Ben Carson, director of pediatric neurosurgery at Johns Hopkins Hospital. 39m; VHS, DVD. **A:** Sr. High-Adult. **P:** Education. **U:** Home, Institution. **Gen-Edu**: Documentary Films, Biography: Science & Medical. **Acq:** Purchase, Rent/Lease. **Dist:** The Cinema Guild. $99.95.

Ben Crenshaw: The Art of Putting 1986
The renowned pro golfer demonstrates the nuances of putting. 44m; VHS. **C:** Ben Crenshaw. **Pr:** HPG Home Video. **A:** Jr. High-Adult. **P:** Instruction. **U:** Home. **How-Ins**: How-To, Sports--General, Golf. **Acq:** Purchase. **Dist:** ESPN Inc.; Cambridge Educational; Karol Media. $34.95.

Ben Franklin: Portrait of a Family 1976
The story of Franklin's relationship with his family before and after the Revolution. 25m; VHS, 3/4 U, EJ, Q. **Pr:** U.S. Division of Audio-Visual Arts. **A:** Jr. High-Adult. **P:** Education. **U:** Institution, SURA. **Gen-Edu**: Documentary Films, Biography, History--U.S. **Acq:** Duplication, Free Duplication. **Dist:** $19.99.

Ben Franklin's Pirate Fleet 2011 (Unrated)
Investigates the little known story that during the Revolutionary War Benjamin Franklin employed privateers to capture British sailors to use in trade for American prisoners of war. 45m; DVD. **A:** Family. **P:** Entertainment. **U:** Institution, Home. **Mov-Ent**: Documentary Films, France, History--U.S. **Acq:** Purchase. **Dist:** National Geographic Society. $19.95.

Ben-Gurion: One Place, One People 1980
Former Israeli prime minister David Ben-Gurion's main goal in life was to establish an independent Jewish state in Palestine. Part of the "Portraits of Power" series. 24m/B/W; VHS, 3/4 U. **A:** Sr. High-Adult. **P:** Education. **U:** Institution, SURA. **Gen-Edu**: Documentary Films, History--Modern, Middle East. **Acq:** Purchase, Rent/Lease. **Dist:** Phoenix Learning Group.

Ben-Hur 1926 — ★★★★
Second film version of the renowned story of Jewish and Christian divisiveness in the time of Jesus. Battle scenes and chariot races still look good, in spite of age. Problems lingered on the set and at a cost of over $4,000,000 it was the most expensive film of its time and took years to finish. A hit at the boxoffice, it still stands as the all-time silent classic. In 1931, a shortened version was released. Based on the novel by Lewis Wallace. 148m/B/W; Silent; VHS, DVD. **C:** Ramon Novarro; Francis X. Bushman; May McAvoy; Betty Bronson; Claire McDowell; Carmel Myers; Nigel de Brulier; Ferdinand P. Earle; Directed by Fred Niblo; Cinematography by Clyde De Vinna. **Pr:** MGM. **A:** Jr. High-Adult. **P:** Entertainment. **U:** Home. **Mov-Ent**: Drama, Silent Films, Classic Films. **Awds:** Natl. Film Reg. '97. **Acq:** Purchase. **Dist:** MGM Home Entertainment. $29.95.

Ben-Hur 1959 (Unrated) — ★★★★
The third film version of the Lew Wallace classic stars Heston in the role of a Palestinian Jew battling the Roman empire at the time of Christ. Won a record 11 Oscars. The breathtaking chariot race is still one of the best screen races today. Perhaps one of the greatest pictures of all time. Also available in letterbox format. 212m; VHS, DVD, Blu-Ray, Wide, CC. **C:** Charlton Heston; Jack Hawkins; Stephen Boyd; Haya Harareet; Hugh Griffith; Martha Scott; Sam Jaffe; Cathy O'Donnell; Finlay Currie; Directed by William Wyler; Written by Karl Tunberg; Cinematography by Robert L. Surtees; Music by Miklos Rozsa. **Pr:** Sam Zimbalist; MGM. **A:** Family. **P:** Entertainment. **U:** Home. **Mov-Ent**: Drama, Slavery, Judaism. **Awds:** Oscars '59: Actor (Heston), Art Dir./Set Dec., Color, Color Cinematog., Costume Des. (C), Director (Wyler), Film, Film Editing, Orig. Dramatic Score, Sound, Support. Actor (Griffith); AFI '98: Top 100; British Acad. '59: Film; Directors Guild '59: Director (Wyler); Golden Globes '60: Director (Wyler), Film--Drama, Support. Actor (Boyd); Natl. Film Reg. '04; N.Y. Film Critics '59: Film. **Acq:** Purchase. **Dist:** Baker and Taylor; Ignatius Press; MGM Home Entertainment. $29.98.

Ben Hur 2010 (Unrated) — ★★
British/Canadian miniseries plays down the religious aspects of the Lew Wallace novel and the previous film versions (but there's still chariot races). Solider Messala has been assigned by Rome to safeguard the arrival of Pontius Pilate into Jersusalem. He demands his childhood friend Judah Ben Hur inform him of any plots against the new governor's life, but when Pilate comes under attack, Judah's family suffers and he wants revenge. 180m; DVD, CC. **C:** Joseph Morgan; Stephen Campbell Moore; Hugh Bonneville; Emily VanCamp; Kristin Kreuk; Alex Kingston; Ben Cross; Ray Winstone; Directed by Steve Shill; Written by Alan Sharp; Cinematography by Ousama Rawi; Music by Rob Lane. **A:** Sr. High-Adult. **P:** Entertainment. **U:** Home. **L:** English. **Mov-Ent**: History--Ancient, TV Movies. **Acq:** Purchase. **Dist:** Sony Pictures Home Entertainment Inc.

Ben-Hur: A Race to Glory 19??
Presents the story of two best friends, Ben-Hur and Messala, and what becomes of their friendship when they are older. Includes book. 30m; VHS. **A:** Preschool-Primary. **P:** Education. **U:** Home. **Chl-Juv**: Animation & Cartoons. **Acq:** Purchase. **Dist:** Ignatius Press. $24.95.

Ben Jacobson: Fundamental Drills for Basketball Practice 2010 (Unrated)
Coach Ben Jacobson shares 14 of his favorite offensive and defensive drills for use in basketball practices. 68m; DVD. **A:** Family. **P:** Education. **U:** Home, Institution. **Spo-Rec**: Basketball, Athletic Instruction/Coaching. **Acq:** Purchase. **Dist:** Championship Productions. $39.99.

Ben Jacobson: Man-to-Man Screening Offense 2010 (Unrated)
Coach Ben Jacobson demonstrates plays designed to force the opposing basketball team's defense to move out of position, and drills to improve players' abilities to capitalize on that. 70m; DVD. **A:** Family. **P:** Education. **U:** Home, Institution. **Spo-Rec**: Basketball, Athletic Instruction/Coaching. **Acq:** Purchase. **Dist:** Championship Productions. $39.99.

Ben Nicholson: Razor Edge 1987
A portrait of the British abstractionist's life, work and influences. 54m; VHS. **Pr:** RM Arts. **A:** Jr. High-Adult. **P:** Education. **U:** Home. **Fin-Art**: Documentary Films, Biography, Art & Artists. **Acq:** Purchase. **Dist:** Home Vision Cinema. $39.95.

Ben Peterson's Favorite Moves: Rolls 2001 (Unrated)
Olympian Ben Peterson demonstrates nine different rolls wrestlers can use, and how to get to them from four different positions. 52m; DVD. **A:** Family. **P:** Education. **U:** Home, Institution. **Spo-Rec**: Athletic Instruction/Coaching. **Acq:** Purchase. **Dist:** Championship Productions. $39.99.

The Ben Stiller Show 1992
Presents the 1992-1993 sketch comedy television series starring comedian Ben Stiller with guest stars including Dennis Miller, Roseanne and Tom Arnold, Sarah Jessica Parker, Rob Morrow, and David Cassidy. 13 episodes. 299m; DVD. **C:** Ben Stiller; Andy Dick; Janeane Garofalo; Bob Odenkirk; John F. O'Donohue. **A:** Jr. High-Adult. **P:** Entertainment. **U:** Home. **Mov-Ent**: Television Series, Satire & Parody, Comedy--Slapstick. **Acq:** Purchase. **Dist:** Warner Home Video, Inc. $26.99.

Ben 10: Alien Force—Season 1, Vol.1 2008 (Unrated)
Television animated series on Cartoon Network (2008-). "Ben 10 Returns" after living a normal life for 5 years to find his missing Grandfather. The team learns more about an alien conspiracy from some crop circles in "Everybody Talks About the Weather," then Ben and Gwen wrongly trust Mike Morningstar in "All That Glitters" leaving Gwen drained of her magical powers and forced to be Mike's slave. 5 episodes. 110m; DVD. **A:** Primary. **P:** Entertainment. **U:** Home. **Chl-Juv**: Animation & Cartoons, Action-Adventure, Children's Shows. **Acq:** Purchase. **Dist:** Warner Home Video, Inc.

Ben 10: Alien Force—Volume 3 2009 (Unrated)
Cartoon Network animated sci-fi adventure series, 2005-07. Ben's new ally, Alien X has an internal debate between personalities that may cost Ben his life in "X=Ben+2," perceptions of a fearsome monster are misleading in "Be-Knighted," and menacing aliens are actually just concerned parents in "Plumber's Helper." 88m; DVD. **C:** Voice(s) by Yuri Lowenthal; Ashley Johnson; Greg Cipes. **A:** Primary. **P:** Entertainment. **U:** Home. **Chl-Juv**: Animation & Cartoons, Action-Adventure, Science Fiction. **Acq:** Purchase. **Dist:** Warner Home Video, Inc. $14.99.

Ben 10: Alien Force—Volume 5 2008 (Unrated)
Cartoon Network 2008-? animated action adventure. Ben is grounded after his parents catch him turning into Swampfire but he still manages to save mankind once again, DNAliens capture Kevin, and Grandpa Max helps battle the Null Void. Episodes 19-22. 110m; DVD. **C:** Voice(s) by Yuri Lowenthal; Dee Bradley Baker; Ashley Johnson; Greg Cipes. **A:** Primary-Jr. High. **P:** Entertainment. **U:** Home. **Chl-Juv**: Animation & Cartoons, Action-Adventure, Television Series. **Acq:** Purchase. **Dist:** Warner Home Video, Inc. $14.99.

Ben 10: Alien Force—Volume 7 2010 (Unrated)
Cartoon Network animated adventure series. "Vengence of Vilgax" has Ben pushing his powers to the max causing him to accidentally overload the Omnitrix, lose his transformations, and turn Kevin into a monster. 7 episodes. 127m; DVD. **C:** Voice(s) by Yuri Lowenthal; Greg Cipes; Dee Bradley Baker. **A:** Primary-Jr. High. **P:** Entertainment. **U:** Home. **Chl-Juv**: Animation & Cartoons, Action-Adventure, Television Series. **Acq:** Purchase. **Dist:** Warner Home Video, Inc. $14.99.

Ben Vereen: Sing Along Live with the Peter Pan Kids 19??
Children can sing along to some of the best-loved kid's songs. 30m; VHS. **A:** Preschool-Primary. **P:** Entertainment. **U:** Home. **Mov-Ent**: Music Video, Music--Children. **Acq:** Purchase. **Dist:** Inspired Corp.; Music Video Distributors. $12.98.

Ben Vereen Sing Along: Welcome to the Party 1991
Low production values spoil some good tap footage by Vereen and some others. Songs are geared towards audience participation, including "Head, Shoulders, Knees, and Toes" and "Old MacDonald"? who has a band instead of a farm. 25m; VHS. **A:** Preschool-Primary. **P:** Entertainment. **U:** Institution. **Chl-Juv**: Music--Children. **Acq:** Purchase. **Dist:** Inspired Corp. $19.98.

Ben Webster/Dexter Gordon: Top Tenors 19??
Live from London in 1969, the Ben Webster Quintet performs four selections. Plus "Those Were the Days" and "Fried Bananas" are performed by the Dexter Gordon Quartet. 49m; VHS. **A:** Jr. High-Adult. **P:** Entertainment. **U:** Home. **Mov-Ent**: Music--Performance. **Acq:** Purchase. **Dist:** Music Video Distributors. $19.95.

Ben Webster: The Brute and the Beautiful 19??
Documents Webster's evolution as a saxophonist from Kansas City in the 1920s to his last professional performance in Holland, 1972. Includes clips featuring Webster with Duke Ellington, Benny Carter, Teddy Wilson and others. 60m; VHS. **A:** Jr. High-Adult. **P:** Entertainment. **U:** Home. **Mov-Ent**: Documentary Films, Music--Jazz. **Acq:** Purchase. **Dist:** Music Video Distributors; Shanachie Entertainment. $24.95.

Ben X 2007 (Unrated) — ★★
Ben has Asperger's Syndrome, which makes social interactions difficult, so he is repeatedly bullied at his public high school. His only comfort is an online role-playing game where his alter ego Ben X can win the day. When the bullying becomes intolerable, Ben loses control and plans a way to get even with the aid of a fellow gamer he knows as Scarlite. Based on a true story; Flemish with subtitles. 93m; DVD. **C:** Greg Timmermans; Laura Verlinden; Titus De Voogdt; Maarten Claeyssens; Directed by Nic Balthazar; Written by Nic Balthazar; Cinematography by Lou Berghmans; Music by Praga Khan. **A:** College-Adult. **P:** Entertainment. **U:** Home. **L:** Flemish. **Mov-Ent**: Autism, Adolescence. **Acq:** Purchase. **Dist:** Film Movement.

Benaat Chicago: Growing Up Arab & Female in Chicago 1996
Documents the lives of Arab American teenagers living on Chicago's southwest side. 30m; VHS. **A:** Adult. **P:** Education. **U:** Home. **Gen-Edu**: Middle East, Identity, Documentary Films. **Acq:** Purchase. **Dist:** Arab Film Distribution. $29.99.

Benazir Bhutto: Walking the Tightrope 1996
Chronicles Benazir Bhutto, Prime Minister of Pakistan, the first woman to head a Muslim country. Also examines the political past of Pakistan and how Benazir is trying to help women, as they have long been victims of discrimination and violence. Zulifikar Ali Bhutto who was the first democratic leader of Pakistan, was her father. 52m; VHS. **A:** College-Adult. **P:** Education. **U:** Institution. **Gen-Edu**: Documentary Films, Prejudice, Women. **Acq:** Purchase, Rent/Lease. **Dist:** Filmakers Library Inc. $350.00.

Bench Defense 1995
Easy-to-follow step aerobics workout blended with self defense/karate moves. Helps burn fat while teaching specific techniques to use if you're attacked. 57m; VHS. **A:** Jr. High-Adult. **P:** Instruction. **U:** Home. **Hea-Sci**: Fitness/Exercise, Martial Arts. **Acq:** Purchase. **Dist:** Collage Video Specialties, Inc. $29.95.

Bench Metalwork 1988
Techniques of working with metal are demonstrated on a workbench. 13m; VHS. **Pr:** Bergwall Productions. **A:** Sr. High-Adult. **P:** Instruction. **U:** Institution. **How-Ins**: Metal Work, Education. **Acq:** Purchase. **Dist:** Bergwall Productions, Inc. $339.00.

Indiv. Titles: 1. Introduction-Tools and Processes 2. Cutting Processes 3. Files and the Filing Process 4. Bending and Shaping 5. Drilling, Reaming and Threading 6. Peening, Finishing and Assembly 7. The Forging Process.

Benchmarking Manufacturing Processes 1994
This video demonstrates the most efficient way to benchmark in a manufacturing setting, and helps improve company operations from customer service to cellular manufacturing operations. 90m; VHS. **A:** Adult. **P:** Professional. **U:** Institution. **L:** English. **Bus-Ind:** Industry & Industrialists. **Acq:** Purchase. **Dist:** Society of Manufacturing Engineers. $895.

The Benchwarmers 2006 (PG-13) — ★
Relentlessly stupid comedy with more than its share of gross-out moments. Gus (Schneider) was a bullied nerd in school, as were his two still-maladjusted pals, Richie (Spade) and Clark (Heder). Ex-bullied nerd-turned-billionaire Mel (a fun-loving Lovitz) offers a chance for sweet revenge by putting his trio of losers up against a Little League team of young terrors. Farting, vomiting, and booger jokes follow, and Reggie Jackson offers baseball advice. 81m; DVD, Blu-Ray, UMD. **C:** Rob Schneider; David Spade; Jon Heder; Jon Lovitz; Molly Sims; Craig Kilborn; Tim Meadows; Nick Swardson; Amaury Nolasco; Dennis Dugan; Erinn Bartlett; Max Prado; Brooke Langton; Lochlyn Munro; Mary Jo Catlett; Blake Clark; Terry Crews; Cameo(s) Reggie Jackson; Voice(s) by James Earl Jones; Directed by Dennis Dugan; Written by Nick Swardson; Allen Covert; Cinematography by Thomas Ackerman; Music by Waddy Wachtel. **Pr:** Adam Sandler; Jack Giarraputo; Columbia Pictures; Revolution Studios; Happy Madison Productions; Sony Pictures Entertainment. **A:** Jr. High-Adult. **P:** Entertainment. **U:** Home. **L:** English. **Mov-Ent:** Baseball, Sports--Fiction: Comedy. **Acq:** Purchase. **Dist:** Sony Pictures Home Entertainment Inc.

A Bend in the River 1987
Taking place during the Civil War, this drama focuses on the myths of war and the experiences of Union and Confederate soldiers. 25m; VHS, 3/4 U. **A:** Jr. High-Adult. **P:** Education. **U:** Institution, Home. **Gen-Edu:** Civil War. **Acq:** Rent/Lease. **Dist:** New Dimension Media. $40.00.

Bend It Like Beckham 2002 (PG-13) — ★★★
Sweet family comedy has girl power galore. Jesminder (Nagra) is the teenaged daughter of East Indian parents, living in a middle-class London suburb. They wish Jess would be more like her older sister Pinky (Panjabi), who is anticipating her traditional wedding. But what shy Jess wants is to play professional soccer—her hero is superstar player David Beckham—and she secretly joins a local team after befriending fellow player Juliette (Knightley). She impresses (and develops a crush on) her coach Joe (Rhys-Meyers) while trying to keep her activities from her disapproving parents. Of course, there has to be a big game, which will showcase Jess's talents. 112m; VHS, DVD. **C:** Parminder K. Nagra; Keira Knightley; Jonathan Rhys Meyers; Shaheen Khan; Anupam Kher; Archie Panjabi; Juliet Stevenson; Frank Harper; Shaznay Lewis; Directed by Gurinder Chadha; Written by Gurinder Chadha; Paul Mayeda Berges; Guljit Bindra; Cinematography by Jong Lin; Music by Craig Pruess. **Pr:** Deepak Nayar; Gurinder Chadha; Gurinder Chadha; Kintop Pictures; Road Movies; Roc Media; Fox Searchlight. **A:** Jr. High-Adult. **P:** Entertainment. **U:** Home. **Mov-Ent:** Sports--Fiction: Comedy, Soccer, Youth Sports. **Acq:** Purchase. **Dist:** Fox Home Entertainment.

Bend of the River 1952 (Unrated) — ★★★
A haunted, hardened guide leads a wagon train through Oregon territory, pitting himself against Indians, the wilderness and a former comrade-turned-hijacker. 91m; VHS, DVD. **C:** James Stewart; Arthur Kennedy; Rock Hudson; Harry (Henry) Morgan; Royal Dano; Directed by Anthony Mann. **Pr:** Aaron Rosenberg. **A:** Family. **P:** Entertainment. **U:** Home. **Mov-Ent:** Western, Rivers & Streams. **Acq:** Purchase. **Dist:** Movies Unlimited; Alpha Video; Universal Studios Home Video. $14.98.

Bending All the Rules 2002 (R) — ★★
Kenna (Porch) prefers to keep her personal life casual so she can concentrate on her photography career. Just when she's offered her first gallery exhibition, two men make a serious play for her affections: sweet, struggling DJ Jeff (Cooper) and confident, successful businessman Martin (Gail). Of course Kenna wants to know why she can't have it all but jealousy becomes a problem. Filmed in Tampa Bay, Florida. 86m; DVD. **C:** Colleen Porch; David Gail; Bradley Cooper; Kurt McKinney; James Martin Kelly; Ed Carine; Directed by Morgan Klein; Peter Knight; Written by Morgan Klein; Peter Knight; Cinematography by Rob Allen; Music by Martin Klein; Molly Knight Forde. **A:** Sr. High-Adult. **P:** Entertainment. **U:** Home. **Mov-Ent:** Comedy--Romantic, Photography. **Acq:** Purchase. **Dist:** Lions Gate Entertainment Inc.

Bending and Reflecting Sunlight 1971
A study of the reflection and refraction of light. Part of EBE'S "Wonder Walks" series. 7m; VHS, 3/4 U. **Pr:** Encyclopedia Britannica Educational Corporation. **A:** Primary. **P:** Education. **U:** Institution, SURA. **Hea-Sci:** Documentary Films, Physics. **Acq:** Purchase, Rent/Lease, Trade-in. **Dist:** Encyclopedia Britannica.

Bene Israel: A Family Portrait 1994
Explores the lives of Jews in India through the eyes of one family. Topics of special interest include "The State of the Community Today," "Integration," and "Today's Faith." 33m; VHS. **A:** Jr. High-Adult. **P:** Education. **U:** Institution. **Gen-Edu:** India, Judaism. **Acq:** Purchase. **Dist:** National Center for Jewish Film.

Beneath 2007 (R) — ★
Convoluted and plodding story about creepy, depressed people having visions usually followed by someone ending up dead.

Initial suspense stems from in-laws' eerie house complete with mysterious hatches, weird holes, and a monster inside the walls. Although intriguing, its eccentricities never get fully explained as the darkness and drab lead only to an anti-climatic snore. 81m; DVD. **C:** Nora Zehetner; Matthew Settle; Gabrielle Rose; Carly Pope; Don S. Davis; Jessica Amlee; Directed by Dagen Merrill; Written by Dagen Merrill; Kevin Burke; Cinematography by Mike Southon; Music by John (Gianni) Frizzell; Frederik Wiedmann. **A:** Sr. High-Adult. **P:** Entertainment. **U:** Home. **Mov-Ent:** Mystery & Suspense. **Acq:** Purchase. **Dist:** Paramount Pictures Corp.

Beneath Arizona Skies/Paradise Canyon 1935 — ★½
A package of John Wayne westerns filled with lots of rumble tumble action. 109m/B/W; VHS. **C:** John Wayne. **Pr:** Monogram. **A:** Family. **P:** Entertainment. **U:** Home. **Mov-Ent:** Western. **Acq:** Purchase. **Dist:** Lions Gate Entertainment Inc. $19.95.

Beneath Hill 60 2010 (R) — ★★½
True story about WWI Aussie soldiers. In 1916, mining engineer Oliver Woodward joins up with the Australian 1st Tunnellers to fight on the Western Front. Their mission is to secretly tunnel beneath the German lines in France and Belgium, packing the tunnels with explosives to destroy the enemy troops fighting above. 122m; DVD, Blu-Ray. **C:** Brendan Cowell; Chris Haywood; Harrison Gilbertson; Steve LeMarquand; Gyton Grantley; Anthony Hayes; Bella Heathcote; Directed by Jeremy Sims; Written by David Roach; Cinematography by Toby Oliver; Music by Cezary Skubiszewski. **A:** Sr. High-Adult. **P:** Entertainment. **U:** Home. **Mov-Ent:** World War One, Miners & Mining, France. **Acq:** Purchase. **Dist:** Entertainment One US LP.

Beneath Loch Ness 2001 (Unrated) — ★
Laughable adventure tale finds paleontologist Case Howell (Wimmer) carrying on the work of his mentor, Professor Egan, who believed that Loch Ness was a breeding ground for ancient marine reptiles. Unfortunately, the prof disappeared while conducting research at the loch. But that isn't stopping Howell from leading another expedition to find Nessie. 95m; VHS, DVD, Blu-Ray, Wide. **C:** Brian Wimmer; Patrick Bergin; Lysette Anthony; Vernon Wells; Directed by Chuck Comisky; Written by Justin Stanley; Chuck Comisky; Shane Bitterling; Cinematography by Philip Timme; Music by Richard John Baker. **A:** Jr. High-Adult. **P:** Entertainment. **U:** Home. **Mov-Ent:** Scotland. **Acq:** Purchase. **Dist:** Buena Vista Home Entertainment.

Beneath Still Waters 2005 (R) — ★½
Two boys travel to see a town one last time before it's flooded forever by a new dam, and one of them dies accidentally, unleashing a demon. Four decades later it finally decides to get busy causing trouble. Darn lazy them critters from Hell. 92m; DVD. **C:** Michael McKell; Patrick Gordon; Josep Maria Pou; Raquel Merono; Charlotte Salt; Directed by Brian Yuzna; Written by Mike Hostench; Angel Sala; Zacarias De la Riva; Cinematography by Johnny Yebra. **A:** Sr. High-Adult. **P:** Entertainment. **U:** Home. **L:** English. **Mov-Ent:** Acq: Purchase. **Dist:** Lions Gate Home Entertainment. $14.98.

Beneath the Bermuda Triangle 1998 (R) — ★★
Submarine commander Alan Deakins (Fahey) and his crew are cruising in dangerous waters when they unexpectedly enter a time portal that transports them to the future. As usual, it's ugly—a repressive, military government is in control and Deakins decides to join a rebel organization, that happens to be lead by his grandson (Fahey again). No-brain actioner. 84m; VHS. **C:** Jeff Fahey; Richard Tyson; Linda Hoffman; Jack Coleman; Directed by Scott Levy. **A:** Sr. High-Adult. **P:** Entertainment. **U:** Home. **Mov-Ent:** Science Fiction. **Acq:** Purchase.

Beneath the Blue 2010 (PG) — ★½
Tourist Craig Morrison is vacationing in the Bahamas when he falls in love with Alyssa, who's researching dolphin communications. However Navy sonar experiments are endangering the local dolphin population and the scientists want it to stop. 93m; DVD. **C:** Paul Wesley; Caitlin Wachs; David Keith; Michael Ironside; Ivana Milicevic; George Harris; Directed by Michael D. Sellers; Written by Wendell Morris; Cinematography by Lila Javan; Music by Alan Derian. **A:** Jr. High-Adult. **P:** Entertainment. **U:** Home. **Mov-Ent:** Oceanography, Science. **Acq:** Purchase. **Dist:** Inception Media Group.

Beneath the Dark 2010 (R) — ★
Paul and Adrienne are driving from Texas to L.A. for a wedding. A sleepy Paul nearly crashes their car and they pull into a creepy Mohave desert motel for the night. A nameless man is prodding a guilty Paul to reveal secrets from his frat boy past, which seem to involve the motel owner's promiscuous wife Sandy. 102m; DVD. **C:** Josh Stewart; Jamie-Lynn Sigler; Chris Browning; Angela Featherstone; Trevor Morgan; Afemo Omilami; Directed by Chad Feehan; Written by Chad Feehan; Cinematography by Jason Blount; Music by Daniel Licht. **A:** Sr. High-Adult. **P:** Entertainment. **U:** Home. **Mov-Ent:** Mystery & Suspense. **Acq:** Purchase. **Dist:** MPI Media Group.

Beneath the Darkness 2012 (R) — ★½
Quaid obviously enjoys his villainous role as a psycho mortician in a small Texas town, but the rest is simply a generic horror flick. Dysfunctional teens all seem to have recently lost a family member and start watching the creepy doings of Ely Vaughn, who likes to bury his victims alive. 96m; DVD, Blu-Ray, Wide. **C:** Dennis Quaid; Tony Oiler; Aimee Teegarden; Stephen Lunsford; Devon Werkheiser; Brett Cullen; Directed by Martin Guigui; Written by Bruce Wilkinson; Cinematography by Massimo Zeri; Music by Geoff Zanelli. **A:** Sr. High-Adult. **P:** Entertainment. **U:** Home. **Mov-Ent:** Adolescence, Horror. **Acq:** Purchase. **Dist:** Image Entertainment Inc.

Beneath the Flesh 2009 (Unrated) — ★½
Odd horror anthology mixing live action and stop-motion animation that's about overcoming one's fears. Granted, most of the fears these people have are perfectly reasonable to have, so it's not like they're just being foolish. 72m/B/W; DVD. **C:** Steve Arons; Randall Kaplan; Brandon McCluskey; Michael Whitney; Bianca Jamotte; Adair Moran; Directed by Randall Kaplan; Written by Randall Kaplan; Cinematography by Leo A. Schott, III; Music by Randall Kaplan. **A:** Sr. High-Adult. **P:** Entertainment. **U:** Home. **L:** English. **Mov-Ent:** Acq: Purchase. **Dist:** Pathfinder Pictures. $24.98.

Beneath the Harvest Sky 2014 (Unrated) — ★★
A familiar story of small town frustration and bad choices gets tender treatment in this indie drama. High school seniors Casper and Dominic have made a pact to escape their potato-farming Maine community after graduation but they take different paths to earn the money to get out. Honest Dom works the fields but Casper follows in the footsteps of his drug-dealing dad by smuggling prescription meds over the Canadian border--and that's before he finds out that his 15-year-old girlfriend is pregnant. Naturally, trouble thwarts their dreams. 116m; On Demand. **C:** Callan McAuliffe; Emory Cohen; Aidan Gillen; Zoe Levin; Sarah Sutherland; Directed by Aron Gaudet; Gita Pullapilly; Written by Aron Gaudet; Gita Pullapilly; Cinematography by Steven Capitano Calitri; Music by Dustin Hamman. **Pr:** Tribeca Film Institute. **A:** Sr. High-Adult. **P:** Entertainment. **U:** Home. **L:** English. **Mov-Ent:** Adolescence, Drug Trafficking/Dealing, Pregnancy. **Acq:** Purchase, Rent/Lease. **Dist:** Amazon.com Inc.

Beneath the Mississippi 2008 (Unrated) — Bomb!
Crappy sound and lighting and an incoherent plot doom this indie. Documentary filmmaker Elly (Shaffer) brings her camera crew to investigate an isolated island area of the Mississippi river where hundreds of people have disappeared. She hires riverman Jack (Hazell) as their guide but the closer they get to the site, the scarier things become. 95m; DVD. **C:** Ariadne Shaffer; Jon Hazell; Nick Murray; Lonnie Schuyler; Directed by Lonnie Schuyler; Written by Jon Hazell; Lonnie Schuyler; Cinematography by Ken Moehn; Music by Patrick Hazell. **A:** Primary-Adult. **P:** Entertainment. **U:** Home. **L:** English. **Mov-Ent:** Horror. **Acq:** Purchase. **Dist:** Green Apple Entertainment.

Beneath the North Atlantic 2001
In-depth look at marine life in the dark recesses of the North Atlantic Ocean features endangered and thriving species, unusual creatures, births, deaths, hunters and the hunted. ?m; VHS. **A:** Adult. **P:** Education. **U:** Home. **Hea-Sci:** Oceanography, Biology, Documentary Films. **Acq:** Purchase. **Dist:** Janson Media.

Beneath the Planet of the Apes 1970 (G) — ★★½
In the first sequel, another Earth astronaut passes through the same warp and follows the same paths as Taylor, through Ape City and to the ruins of bomb-blasted New York's subway system, where warhead-worshipping human mutants are found. The strain of sequelling shows instantly, and gets worse through the next three films; followed by "Escape from the Planet of the Apes." 108m; VHS, DVD, Blu-Ray, Wide, CC. **C:** James Franciscus; Kim Hunter; Maurice Evans; Charlton Heston; James Gregory; Natalie Trundy; Jeff Corey; Linda Harrison; Victor Buono; Paul (E.) Richards; David Watson; Thomas Gomez; Directed by Ted Post; Written by Paul Dehn; Cinematography by Milton Krasner; Music by Leonard Rosenman. **Pr:** Apjac Productions. **A:** Family. **P:** Entertainment. **U:** Home. **Mov-Ent:** Science Fiction, Nuclear Warfare. **Acq:** Purchase. **Dist:** Fusion Video. $19.98.

Beneath the Sea: The Galapagos 1991
Join the author of "Jaws," Peter Benchley, for an investigation of Darwin's favorite isles. Explore the exotic sea life on and around the Galapagos Islands. From the "Mutual of Omaha's Spirit of Adventure" series. 50m; VHS. **C:** Hosted by Peter Benchley. **A:** Family. **P:** Education. **U:** Home. **Gen-Edu:** Documentary Films, Pacific Islands, Oceanography. **Acq:** Purchase. **Dist:** MPI Media Group; Facets Multimedia Inc. $19.98.

Beneath the Skin 1983
A young woman slowly realizes that her boyfriend has destroyed his last girlfriend-piece by piece. 12m; VHS, 3/4 U. **Pr:** Cecilia Condit. **A:** Jr. High-Adult. **P:** Education. **U:** Institution, SURA. **Mov-Ent:** Mystery & Suspense, Video. **Acq:** Purchase, Rent/Lease. **Dist:** Women Make Movies. $200.00.

Beneath the Surface: Why People Buy 1992
Discusses consumer motivations for buying products. 28m; VHS. **A:** Adult. **P:** Professional. **U:** Institution. **Bus-Ind:** Business, Sales Training. **Acq:** Purchase. **Dist:** RMI Media. $99.00.

Beneath the 12-Mile Reef 1953 — ★★
Two rival groups of divers compete for sponge beds off the Florida coast. Lightweight entertainment notable for underwater photography and early Cinemascope production, as well as Moore in a bathing suit. 102m; DVD. **C:** Robert Wagner; Terry Moore; Gilbert Roland; Richard Boone; Peter Graves; J. Carrol Naish; Angela (Clark) Clarke; Directed by Robert D. Webb; Written by A(lbert) I(saac) Bezzerides; Cinematography by Edward Cronjager; Music by Bernard Herrmann. **Pr:** 20th Century-Fox. **A:** Family. **P:** Entertainment. **U:** Home. **Mov-Ent:** Action-Adventure, Scuba. **Acq:** Purchase. **Dist:** Alpha Video Distributors. $19.95.

Beneath the Valley of the Ultra-Vixens 1979 (Unrated) — ★
Sex comedy retread directed by the man with an obsession for big. Scripted by Roger Ebert, who also scripted the cult classic "Beyond the Valley of the Dolls." Explicit nudity. 90m; VHS, DVD. **C:** Francesca "Kitten" Natividad; Ann Marie; Ken Kerr; Stuart Lancaster; Steve Tracy; Henry Rowland; DeForest

Covan; Aram Katcher; Candy Samples; Robert Pearson; Directed by Russ Meyer; Written by Roger Ebert; Russ Meyer; Cinematography by Russ Meyer. **A:** Adult. **P:** Teacher Education. **U:** Home. **Mov-Ent:** Cult Films, Sex & Sexuality. **Acq:** Purchase. **Dist:** RM Films International, Inc. $89.95.

Benedict Arnold: A Question of Honor 2003 — ★★
By-the-numbers bio of Revolutionary War general turned British Loyalist, Benedict Arnold (Quinn). By 1776, Arnold was falling out of favor with Congress amidst accusations of incompetence, although he's still supported by his friend, George Washington (Grammer). But after meeting Margaret Shippen (Montgomery), the daughter of a loyalist sympathizer, the increasingly resentful Arnold, who also needs money to stave off bankruptcy, begins to sell information to the enemy and comes up with a plan to turn over West Point to the redcoats. 100m; VHS, DVD, CC. **C:** Aidan Quinn; Kelsey Grammer; Flora Montgomery; John Light; John Kavanagh; Directed by Mikael Salomon; Written by William Mastrosimone; Cinematography by Seamus Deasy; Music by David Williams. **A:** Jr. High-Adult. **P:** Entertainment. **U:** Home. **Mov-Ent:** Revolutionary War, Biography: Military. **Acq:** Purchase. **Dist:** A&E Television Networks L.L.C.

Benedita Da Silva 1990
Chronicles the 1990 re-election campaign of the first black woman Senator in Brazil, who overcame her beginnings in a Brazilian slum. 30m; VHS, 3/4 U. **A:** College-Adult. **P:** Education. **U:** Institution. **Gen-Edu:** Documentary Films, Politics & Government, Women. **Acq:** Purchase, Rent/Lease. **Dist:** The Cinema Guild; Third World Newsreel. $250.00.

Beneficent Euthanasia 1972
Drs. Maguire and Kohl argue that euthanasia is a basic human right. Dr. Reich disagrees. Part of the "Humanist Alternative" series. 30m; 3/4 U, Special order formats. **Pr:** American Humanist Association. **A:** College-Adult. **P:** Education. **U:** Institution, CCTV, CATV. **Gen-Edu:** Death. **Acq:** Purchase, Rent/Lease. **Dist:** American Humanist Association.

The Beneficiary 1997 (R) — ★★
Widow Haiduk is the primary suspect in her wealthy husband's death until she gives her inheritance to charity, thus eliminating her motive for murder. But detective Ashby, a friend of the husband, still decides to keep his eye (and maybe more) on the lady. 97m; VHS, CC. **C:** Suzy Amis; Ron Silver; Linden Ashby; Stacy Haiduk; Robert Davi; Directed by Marc Bienstock; Written by Vladimir Nemirovsky; Cinematography by Sead Muhtarevic. **A:** Sr. High-Adult. **P:** Entertainment. **U:** Home. **Mov-Ent:** Mystery & Suspense, Marriage. **Acq:** Purchase. **Dist:** MGM Studios Inc.

Benefit of the Doubt 1993 (R) — ★★
Ex-con Sutherland, released from prison after 22 years, attempts to repaint his family a la Norman Rockwell. Grown-up daughter Irving, who testified against him in her mother's murder, wants to put a crimp in those plans since daddy's new vision of family fondness frankly makes her stomach turn. Aside from the sexual shenanigans, and the haunting Monument Valley backdrop, an extended chase scene would seem to be the film's only hope of salvation. Unfortunately, it fails to deliver, since it's both implausible and boring. Based on a story by Michael Lieber. 92m; VHS, DVD, Blu-Ray, CC. **C:** Donald Sutherland; Amy Irving; Christopher McDonald; Rider Strong; Graham Greene; Theodore Bikel; Gisele Kovach; Ferdinand "Ferdy" Mayne; Directed by Jonathan Heap; Written by Jeffrey Polman; Christopher Keyser; Music by Hummie Mann. **Pr:** Brad M. Gilbert; Michael Spielberg; Bob Weinstein; Harvey Weinstein; Momument Pictures; Miramax. **A:** Sr. High-Adult. **P:** Entertainment. **U:** Home. **Mov-Ent:** Mystery & Suspense. **Acq:** Purchase. **Dist:** Echo Bridge Home Entertainment; Paramount Pictures Corp.

The Benefits of Breastfeeding 1999
Discusses health and nutritional benefits that breastfeeding provides for baby and mother. 21m; VHS. **A:** Adult. **P:** Education. **U:** Institution. **Hea-Sci:** Infants, Parenting. **Acq:** Purchase. **Dist:** Eagle Video Productions. $59.00.

The Benefits of Insects 1990
Life in the insect world is viewed by members of the Bug Club. Includes a teacher's guide. 17m; VHS, Special order formats. **Pr:** National Geographic Society. **A:** Primary. **P:** Education. **U:** Institution. **Gen-Edu:** Insects. **Acq:** Purchase. **Dist:** National Geographic Society. $69.95.

Benefits of Long-Term Meditation 1990
Rise above the ego through meditation, and enter the realm of altered states of awareness, exploring various conciousness levels, eventually achieving enlightenment. 30m; VHS. **Pr:** Thinking Allowed Productions. **A:** College-Adult. **P:** Instruction. **U:** Home. **Hea-Sci:** New Age, Self-Help, Philosophy & Ideology. **Acq:** Purchase. **Dist:** Thinking Allowed Productions. $29.95.

The Benefits of Treating Mild Hypertension 1983
How patients with hypertension can be treated by inexpensive drugs. 60m; VHS, 3/4 U. **Pr:** Emory University. **A:** College-Adult. **P:** Education. **U:** Institution, CCTV, Home, SURA. **Hea-Sci:** Hypertension. **Acq:** Purchase, Rent/Lease, Subscription. **Dist:** Emory Medical Television Network.

The Bengali Night 1988 (Unrated) — ★★
Slow-moving romantic drama was the first starring role for Grant who plays British engineer Allan, who works in Calcutta. When he becomes ill, his employer invites Allan to recuperate at his home and lets him stay on after his recovery. But when Allan and the Sens' eldest daughter Gayatri (Pathak) become romantically involved, the culture clash leads to heartbreak. Based on a true story. 111m; DVD. **C:** Hugh Grant; Shabana Azmi; Soumitra Chatterjee; John Hurt; Anne Brochet; Supriya Pathak; Directed by Nicolas Klotz; Written by Nicolas Klotz; Cinematography by Jean-Claude Carriere; Music by Emmanuel Machuel; Brij Narayan. **A:** Jr. High-Adult. **P:** Entertainment. **U:** Home. **Mov-Ent:** Drama, India. **Acq:** Purchase. **Dist:** Cinema Libre Studio.

Benign Inverted Papilloma 1972
A presentation that presents a physical examination which reveals benign inverted papilloma. 14m; VHS, 3/4 U, Special order formats. **Pr:** Ohio State University Health Sciences AV Center. **A:** College-Adult. **P:** Professional. **U:** Institution, SURA. **Hea-Sci:** Head, Medical Education. **Acq:** Purchase, Rent/Lease. **Dist:** Ohio State University.

The Beniker Gang 1983 (G) — ★★½
Five orphans, supported by the eldest who writes a syndicated advice column, work together as a family. 87m; VHS, DVD. **C:** Andrew McCarthy; Jennifer (Jennie) Dundas Lowe; Danny Pintauro; Charlie (Charles) Fields; Directed by Ken Kwapis. **Pr:** Doro Bachrach. **A:** Family. **P:** Entertainment. **U:** Home. **Mov-Ent:** Journalism, TV Movies, Adoption. **Acq:** Purchase. **Dist:** WarnerArchive.com. $59.95.

Benito Mussolini 1983
Studies the rise and fall of Mussolini and his Fascist regime in Italy. 14m/B/W; VHS, 3/4 U. **Pr:** WGBH Boston. **A:** Jr. High-Adult. **P:** Education. **U:** Institution, SURA. **Gen-Edu:** Documentary Films, Biography, Italy. **Acq:** Purchase, Rent/Lease. **Dist:** Hearst Entertainment/King Features.

Benito Perez Galdos: La Fontana de Oro 1984
Many readers of Galdos' novels find them difficult to read today. The film makes his work more accessible by bringing characters and plot to life. The political implications and historical background of Galdos' writings are analyzed as well. 60m; VHS, 3/4 U. **A:** College-Adult. **P:** Education. **U:** Institution, SURA. **L:** Spanish. **Fin-Art:** Literature, Education. **Acq:** Purchase. **Dist:** Films for the Humanities & Sciences.

Benjamin and the Miracle of Hanukah 1987
An animated Hanukah film for children, from a modern point of view. 25m; VHS. **C:** Narrated by Herschel Bernardi. **Pr:** Ergo Media. **A:** Preschool-Primary. **P:** Religious. **U:** Home. **Chl-Juv:** Judaism, Animation & Cartoons. **Acq:** Purchase. **Dist:** WNET/Thirteen Non-Broadcast; Ergo Media Inc. $29.95.

Benjamin Banneker: The Man Who Loved the Stars 1981
This docudrama provides a look at the life and work of Benjamin Banneker, a black man born in 1731 who overcame racial barriers to become an accomplished mathematician, surveyor, and astronomer. 58m; VHS, 3/4 U. **C:** Ossie Davis. **Pr:** Jochen Breitenstein. **A:** Sr. High-Adult. **P:** Education. **U:** Institution, SURA. **Gen-Edu:** Documentary Films, Biography, Science. **Acq:** Purchase. **Dist:** Phoenix Learning Group.

Benjamin Britten: In Rehearsal and Performance with Peter Pears 1962
Shows the composer/conductor rehearsing and performing Nocturne for Tenor and Seven Obbligato Instruments & Strings, Op. 60 with tenor Peter Pears and the CBC Vancouver Chamber Orchestra. ?m/B/W; VHS. **A:** Adult. **P:** Entertainment. **U:** Home. **Fin-Art:** Music--Classical, Music--Performance. **Acq:** Purchase. **Dist:** Video Artists International. $29.95.

Benjamin Britten: Peter Grimes 2012 (Unrated)
English production of the Benjamin Britten opera filmed at La Scala and updated to the modern era. 168m; DVD, Blu-Ray. **A:** Jr. High-Adult. **P:** Entertainment. **U:** Home. **L:** English, French, German, Japanese, Korean. **Gen-Edu:** Opera, Performing Arts. **Acq:** Purchase. **Dist:** Opus Arte. $39.99 29.99.

Benjamin Franklin 19??
Profiles the life of the inventor, printer, writer, scientist, editor, statesman, and diplomat. 16m; VHS. **A:** Jr. High-Sr. High. **P:** Education. **U:** Institution. **Gen-Edu:** History, Documentary Films, Biography. **Acq:** Purchase. **Dist:** Thomas S. Klise Co. $58.00.

Benjamin Franklin: Citizen of Two Worlds 1979
The story of Benjamin Franklin's eight years in Paris as America's first ambassador to France is told through paintings and memoirs of the period. 27m; VHS. **Pr:** Stanley Cohen. **A:** Jr. High-Adult. **P:** Education. **U:** Institution, SURA. **Mov-Ent:** Drama, Biography. **Acq:** Purchase. **Dist:** Phoenix Learning Group.

Benjamin Franklin: Portrait of a Family 19??
A recreation of Franklin's return to Philadelphia after the War for Indepndence. 20m; VHS. **A:** Jr. High-Adult. **P:** Education. **U:** Institution. **Gen-Edu:** Revolutionary War, Biography. **Acq:** Purchase. **Dist:** Harpers Ferry Historical Association.

Benji 1974 (G) — ★★★
In the loveable mutt's first feature-length movie, he falls in love with a female named Tiffany, and saves two young children from kidnappers. Kiddie classic that was a boxoffice hit when first released. Followed by "For the Love of Benji." 87m; VHS, DVD, Blu-Ray. **C:** Benji; Peter Breck; Christopher Connelly; Patsy Garrett; Deborah Walley; Cynthia Smith; Directed by Joe Camp; Written by Joe Camp; Cinematography by Don Reddy; Music by Euel Box. **Pr:** Joe Camp; Joe Camp; Mulberry Square Productions. **A:** Family. **P:** Entertainment. **U:** Home. **L:** English, Spanish. **Mov-Ent:** Comedy-Drama, Pets, Family Viewing. **Awds:** Golden Globes '75: Song ("I Feel Love"). **Acq:** Purchase. **Dist:** Facets Multimedia Inc.; Home Vision Cinema. $19.99.

Benji: Off the Leash! 2004 (PG) — ★★½
A generally amiable retro addition to the series that began in 1974. Colby's (Whitaker) nasty stepfather Hatchett (Kendrick) runs a puppy mill in their small Mississippi town. He plans to kill a mongrel pup, which Colby rescues and hides (and calls Puppy). Puppy (played by the latest version of Benji) befriends a smart stray named Lizard Tongue while avoiding a couple of inept dogcatchers (Newsome, Stephens) and trying to rescue his sickly mom from the mean breeder. The abuse themes (both animal and human) may scare the little ones but, of course, the dogs are cute and lovable. 97m; VHS, DVD, Blu-Ray, Wide. **C:** Nick Whitaker; Nate Bynum; Chris Kendrick; Randall Newsome; Duane Stephens; Forrest Landis; Carleton Bluford; Neal Barth; Melinda Haynes; Kathleen Camp; Jeff Olson; Lincoln Hoppe; Joey Miyashima; Scott Wilkinson; Christy Summerhays; Directed by Joe Camp; Written by Joe Camp; Cinematography by Don Reddy; Music by Anthony DiLorenzo. **Pr:** Joe Camp; Margaret Loesch; Joe Camp; Benji Returns; Mulberry Square Productions. **A:** Primary-Adult. **P:** Entertainment. **U:** Home. **Mov-Ent:** Action-Adventure, Pets. **Acq:** Purchase. **Dist:** Movies Unlimited; Alpha Video. $19.99.

Benji the Hunted 1987 (G) — ★½
The heroic canine, shipwrecked off the Oregon coast, discovers a litter of orphaned cougar cubs, and battles terrain and predators to bring them to safety. 89m; VHS, DVD, CC. **C:** Benji; Red Steagall; Frank Inn; Directed by Joe Camp; Written by Joe Camp; Music by Euel Box. **Pr:** Walt Disney Studios. **A:** Family. **P:** Entertainment. **U:** Home. **Mov-Ent:** Action-Adventure, Pets, Family Viewing. **Acq:** Purchase. **Dist:** Walt Disney Studios Home Entertainment. $19.99.

Benny & Joon 1993 (PG) — ★★½
Depending on your tolerance for cute eccentrics and whimsy this will either charm you with sweetness or send you into sugar shock. Masterson is Joon, a mentally disturbed young woman who paints and has a habit of setting fires. She lives with overprotective brother Benny (Quinn). Sam (Depp) is the outsider who charms Joon, a dyslexic loner who impersonates his heroes Charlie Chaplin and Buster Keaton with eery accuracy. Depp is particularly fine with the physical demands of his role, but the film's easy dismissal of Joon's mental illness is a serious flaw. 98m; VHS, DVD, Blu-Ray, Wide, CC. **C:** Johnny Depp; Mary Stuart Masterson; Aidan Quinn; Julianne Moore; Oliver Platt; CCH Pounder; Dan Hedaya; Joe Grifasi; William H. Macy; Eileen Ryan; Directed by Jeremiah S. Chechik; Written by Barry Berman; Cinematography by Jason Schwartzman; Music by Rachel Portman. **Pr:** Susan Arnold; Donna Roth; Metro-Goldwyn-Mayer Pictures. **A:** Jr. High-Adult. **P:** Entertainment. **U:** Home. **Mov-Ent:** Comedy--Romantic, Mental Health, Mime. **Acq:** Purchase. **Dist:** MGM Home Entertainment. $19.98.

Benny and the 'Roids: A Story about Steroid Abuse 1988
Benny can't quite compete on his high school football team, so he takes anabolic steroids, but then he starts to have side effects. This video is designed to open discussions of steroid abuse with teenagers. 25m; VHS, 3/4 U, EJ, Special order formats. **TV Std:** NTSC, PAL, SECAM. **Pr:** Disney Educational Productions. **A:** Jr. High-Sr. High. **P:** Education. **U:** Institution, CCTV, SURA. **Hea-Sci:** Drug Abuse. **Acq:** Purchase, Rent/Lease, Duplication License. **Dist:** Phoenix Learning Group. $375.00.

Benny Andrews 19??
Teaching aid for art appreciation examines the artist's collages and paintings. 28m; VHS. **A:** Jr. High-College. **P:** Education. **U:** Institution. **Gen-Edu:** Art & Artists. **Acq:** Purchase. **Dist:** Crystal Productions. $39.95.

Benny Bliss & the Disciples of Greatness 2007 (Unrated) — **Bomb!**
Stilted, stupid comedy. Benny is a crazy musician who finds enlightenment and decides to rid the world of distracting electronic gadgets that he believes are holding back human evolution. He and his band go on a cross-country road trip to spread the word and destroy the evil. Of course they drive and Benny uses a mic to reach his followers and the band plays electric guitars and has a sound system, so Benny isn't exactly a technophobe is he? 94m; DVD. **C:** Martin Guigui; Courtney Gains; Michael Hateley; Norman John Cutliff, III; Corey Britz; Yvonne Delarosa; Directed by Martin Guigui; Written by Martin Guigui; Courtney Gains; Michael Hateley; Cinematography by Massimo Zeri; Music by Cody Westheimer. **A:** Sr. High-Adult. **P:** Entertainment. **U:** Home. **Mov-Ent:** Technology. **Acq:** Purchase. **Dist:** Anthem Pictures.

Benny Carter 1982
Immortal jazz great Benny Carter performs many jazz standards like "Misty," "Cottontail," and "Take the A Train." Features accompaniment by Kenny Barron, Joe Kennedy, Ronnie Bedford, and George Duvivier. 60m; VHS. **A:** Jr. High-Adult. **P:** Entertainment. **U:** Home. **Fin-Art:** Performing Arts, Music--Performance, Music--Jazz. **Acq:** Purchase. **Dist:** Kultur International Films Ltd., Inc. $14.95.

Benny Golson/Tubby Hayes 19??
This video features the Benny Golson Orchestra performing in London in 1966, also Tubby Hayes' Big Band in London. 42m/B/W; VHS. **A:** Jr. High-Adult. **P:** Entertainment. **U:** Home. **Mov-Ent:** Music--Performance. **Acq:** Purchase. **Dist:** Music Video Distributors. $19.95.

Benny Goodman: Adventures in the Kingdom of Swing 1993
Compilation of early clips from TV and movies; includes "Clarenitis" and "Avalon." 60m; VHS. **A:** Sr. High-Adult. **P:** Entertainment. **U:** Home. **Mov-Ent:** Music Video, Music--Jazz. **Acq:** Purchase. **Dist:** Sony Music Entertainment Inc. $19.98.

Benny Goodman: At the Tivoli 19??
The famed clarinetist filmed live at the Tivoli Gardens in Copenhagen, performing his classics. Accompanying Goodman are Sven Osmussen, Pete Witte, Harry Pepe, Don Haas, Jimmy Maxwell, Harry Pepe, and Jimmy Maxwell. 50m; VHS. **A:**

College-Adult. **P:** Entertainment. **U:** Home. **Mov-Ent:** Music--Performance, Music--Jazz. **Acq:** Purchase. **Dist:** Kultur International Films Ltd., Inc.; Facets Multimedia Inc. $29.95.

Songs: Lady Be Good; I Should Care; Send in the Clowns; Airmail Special Delivery; The World is Waiting; For the Sunrise.

Benny Goodman: Live 1977 (Unrated)
The great jazz musician plays live in this Japanese import. ?m; VHS. **A:** College-Adult. **P:** Entertainment. **U:** Home. **Mov-Ent:** Music--Performance, Music--Jazz. **Acq:** Purchase. **Dist:** Music Video Distributors. $99.95.

Benny Goodman: 1980 Aurex Jazz Festival 1980
The jazz legend performs live at the well-known music fest. 48m; VHS. **A:** College-Adult. **P:** Entertainment. **U:** Home. **Mov-Ent:** Music--Performance, Music--Jazz. **Acq:** Purchase. **Dist:** Music Video Distributors. $119.95.

The Benny Goodman Story 1955 — ★★
The life and music of Swing Era bandleader Benny Goodman is recounted in this popular bio-pic. Covering Benny's career from his child prodigy days to his monumental 1938 Carnegie Hall Jazz Concert, the movie's soggy plot machinations are redeemed by a non-stop music track featuring the real Benny and an all-star lineup. 116m; VHS, DVD. **C:** Steve Allen; Donna Reed; Gene Krupa; Lionel Hampton; Kid Ory; Ben Pollack; Harry James; Stan Getz; Teddy Wilson; Martha Tilton; Directed by Valentine Davies; Music by Henry Mancini. **Pr:** Mark Huffam. **A:** Family. **P:** Entertainment. **U:** Home. **Mov-Ent:** Biography: Music, Music--Jazz. **Acq:** Purchase. **Dist:** Facets Multimedia Inc. $19.95.

Songs: Don't Be That Way; Memories of You; Sing, Sing, Sing; Slipped Disc.

The Benny Hill Show: Best of the Early Years 1955 (Unrated)
Collection of Benny's hilariously raunchy comedy, playing such classic characters as a randy surgeon, an inept fitness instructor, a befuddled countess, bumbling talk show host, and many others along with spoofs, commericial paradies, cheeky songs, and the buxum "Hills Angels." 87m; DVD. **A:** Jr. High-Adult. **P:** Entertainment. **U:** Home. **Mov-Ent:** Variety. **Acq:** Purchase. **Dist:** Lions Gate Entertainment Inc. $14.98.

The Benny Hill Show: Golden Classics 2003
Offers highlights from the 1969-1989 British comedy television series with zany Benny Hill as he performs over-the-top sketches and parodies, often with sexual overtones. 1 episode. 403m; DVD. **C:** Benny Hill; Henry McGee; Jackie Wright; Bob Todd; Sue Upton. **A:** Jr. High-Adult. **P:** Entertainment. **U:** Home. **Mov-Ent:** Television Series, Comedy--Slapstick, Great Britain. **Acq:** Purchase. **Dist:** A&E Television Networks L.L.C. $39.98.

The Benny Hill Show: The Naughty Early Years, Complete & Unadulterated, Set Five—1982-1985 2006
Offers episodes from 1982-1985 of the 1969-1989 British comedy television series with zany Benny Hill as he performs over-the-top sketches and parodies, often with sexual overtones. 9 episodes. 450m; DVD. **C:** Benny Hill; Henry McGee; Jackie Wright; Bob Todd; Sue Upton. **A:** Jr. High-Adult. **P:** Entertainment. **U:** Home. **Mov-Ent:** Television Series, Comedy--Slapstick, Great Britain. **Acq:** Purchase. **Dist:** New Video Group. $49.95.

The Benny Hill Show: The Naughty Early Years, Complete & Unadulterated, Set Four—1978-1981 2006
Offers episodes from 1978-1981 of the 1969-1989 British comedy television series with zany Benny Hill as he performs over-the-top sketches and parodies, often with sexual overtones. 10 episodes. 500m; DVD. **C:** Benny Hill; Henry McGee; Jackie Wright; Bob Todd; Sue Upton. **A:** Jr. High-Adult. **P:** Entertainment. **U:** Home. **Mov-Ent:** Television Series, Comedy--Slapstick, Great Britain. **Acq:** Purchase. **Dist:** New Video Group. $49.95.

The Benny Hill Show: The Naughty Early Years, Complete & Unadulterated, Set One—1969-1971 2004
Offers episodes from 1969-1971 of the 1969-1989 British comedy television series with zany Benny Hill as he performs over-the-top sketches and parodies, often with sexual overtones. 11 episodes. 550m; DVD. **C:** Benny Hill; Henry McGee; Jackie Wright; Bob Todd; Sue Upton. **A:** Jr. High-Adult. **P:** Entertainment. **U:** Home. **Mov-Ent:** Television Series, Comedy--Slapstick, Great Britain. **Acq:** Purchase. **Dist:** New Video Group. $49.95.

The Benny Hill Show: The Naughty Early Years, Complete & Unadulterated, Set Six—1986-1989 2006
Offers episodes from 1986-1989 of the 1969-1989 British comedy television series with zany Benny Hill as he performs over-the-top sketches and parodies, often with sexual overtones. 8 episodes. 400m; DVD. **C:** Benny Hill; Henry McGee; Jackie Wright; Bob Todd; Sue Upton. **A:** Jr. High-Adult. **P:** Entertainment. **U:** Home. **Mov-Ent:** Television Series, Comedy--Slapstick, Great Britain. **Acq:** Purchase. **Dist:** New Video Group. $49.95.

The Benny Hill Show: The Naughty Early Years, Complete & Unadulterated, Set Three—1975-1977 2005
Offers episodes from 1975-1977 of the 1969-1989 British comedy television series with zany Benny Hill as he performs over-the-top sketches and parodies, often with sexual overtones. 10 episodes. 500m; DVD. **C:** Benny Hill; Henry McGee; Jackie Wright; Bob Todd; Sue Upton. **A:** Jr. High-Adult. **P:** Entertainment. **U:** Home. **Mov-Ent:** Television Series, Comedy--Slapstick, Great Britain. **Acq:** Purchase. **Dist:** New Video Group. $49.95.

The Benny Hill Show: The Naughty Early Years, Complete & Unadulterated, Set Two'1972-1974 2004
Offers episodes from 1972-1974 of the 1969-1989 British comedy television series with zany Benny Hill as he performs over-the-top sketches and parodies, often with sexual overtones. 10 episodes. 500m; DVD. **C:** Benny Hill; Henry McGee; Jackie Wright; Bob Todd; Sue Upton. **A:** Jr. High-Adult. **P:** Entertainment. **U:** Home. **Mov-Ent:** Television Series, Comedy--Slapstick, Great Britain. **Acq:** Purchase. **Dist:** New Video Group. $49.95.

Benny Hill: The Lost Years 2005
Compilation of the outrageous comedian's previously unseen (in the United States) sketches from his British television series. 200m; DVD. **A:** College-Adult. **P:** Entertainment. **U:** Home. **Mov-Ent:** Television, Great Britain. **Acq:** Purchase. **Dist:** Warner Home Video, Inc. $19.98.

Benny Hill: The Naughty Early Years 2005
Three-volume collection of Britain's most recognizable comedian. 500m; DVD. **A:** Adult. **P:** Entertainment. **U:** Home. **Mov-Ent:** Television Series, Comedy--Screwball. **Acq:** Purchase. **Dist:** A&E Television Networks L.L.C. $49.95.

Benny's Video 1992 (Unrated) — ★½
Teen Benny (Frisch) is obsessed with the violent videos he watches and makes, including the slaughter of a pig with a bolt gun, which Benny then uses in a very unfortunate manner. Heavy-handed message movie was Hanecke's second feature. German with subtitles. 105m; DVD. **C:** Arno Frisch; Angela Winkler; Ulrich Muhe; Ingrid Strassner; Directed by Michael Haneke; Written by Michael Haneke. **A:** Sr. High-Adult. **P:** Entertainment. **U:** Home. **L:** German. **Mov-Ent:** Adolescence. **Acq:** Purchase. **Dist:** Kino on Video.

Ben's Dream and Other Stories 19??
Ben dreams of a trip around the world. Includes two other stories. 30m; VHS. **A:** Preschool-Primary. **P:** Entertainment. **U:** Home. **Chl-Juv:** Animation & Cartoons, Literature--Children. **Acq:** Purchase. **Dist:** Facets Multimedia Inc. $14.95.

Ben's Mill 1981
Ben Thresher's water-powered, wood-working mill has been operating in rural Vermont since 1948. It's one of the few such mills left in the country. Part of the "Odyssey" series. 60m; VHS, 3/4 U. **Pr:** Public Broadcasting Associates. **A:** Sr. High-College. **P:** Education. **U:** Institution, CCTV, CATV. **Gen-Edu:** Documentary Films, Agriculture. **Acq:** Purchase, Rent/Lease, Off-Air Record. **Dist:** PBS Home Video.

Benson 1979
In this spinoff from "Soap," butler Benson DuBois travels from the crazy Tate family to the disorganized household of Jessica Tate's widowed cousin Eugene Gatling—the governor. Benson has to manage the household, battle with formidable housekeeper Gretchen, and help well-meaning Governor Gatling raise his precocious daughter Katie. 597m; DVD, CC. **C:** Robert Guillaume; James Noble; Inga Swenson; Caroline McWilliams; Missy Gold. **A:** Family. **P:** Entertainment. **U:** Home. **Mov-Ent:** Television Series. **Acq:** Purchase. **Dist:** Sony Pictures Home Entertainment Inc.

Benson: The Complete First Season 1979
Jessica Tate sends her beloved butler Benson DuBois (Guillaume) to assist her widowed cousin Governor Eugene Gatling (Noble). Benson quickly finds himself managing the governor's mansion staff, butting heads with housekeeper Gretchen Kraus (Swenson), helping to raise his daughter Katie (Gold), and even advising the state leader in this "Soap" spin-off. 24 episodes. 595m; DVD. **C:** Robert Guillaume; James Noble; Inga Swenson; Missy Gold. **A:** Jr. High-Adult. **P:** Entertainment. **U:** Home. **Mov-Ent:** Family. **Acq:** Purchase. **Dist:** Sony Pictures Home Entertainment Inc.

Benson: The Complete Second Season 1980 (Unrated)
ABC television comedy series featuring Head of Household Affairs Benson DuBois as employed by widowed, unorganized Governor Eugene Gatling. In "Thick as Thieves," Benson and Kraus are hostages during a robbery. "Benson in the Hospital" shows Benson stumping medical professionals with his health symptoms; "Fool's Gold" focuses on the discovery of a treasure map which makes the governor's employees anxious to locate the treasure; a valuable statue is targeted for theft in "Masquerade." And the governor makes a hostess feel special and his daughter feel jealous in "First Lady". 24 episodes. 580m; DVD. **A:** Family. **P:** Entertainment. **U:** Home. **Mov-Ent:** Television Series. **Acq:** Purchase. **Dist:** Sony Pictures Home Entertainment Inc. $35.99.

Bent 1997 (NC-17) — ★★
Theatre director Mathias makes his film debut with Sherman's adaptation of his 1979 play. Gay playboy Max (Owen) is enjoying the nightlife in decadent Berlin—until the Nazi crackdown. Soon, Max is in a cattle car on his way to Dachau, where he passes himself off as Jewish, thinking he'll be treated better. However Horst (Bluteau), who befriended Max on the train, is openly part of the pink triangle prisoners. Still, Max gets Horst assigned to the same meaningless hard labor and the duo fall in love—without ever being allowed to touch. Good performances (with Jagger notable in a brief role as a drag star) but the lingering staginess is to the film's detriment. An R-rated version is also available. 104m; VHS, DVD. **C:** Clive Owen; Lothaire Bluteau; Ian McKellen; Brian Webber; Mick Jagger; Nikolaj Coster-Waldau; Paul Bettany; Cameo(s) Jude Law; Rupert Graves; Directed by Sean Mathias; Written by Martin Sherman; Cinematography by Yorgos Arvanitis; Music by Philip Glass. **Pr:** Dixie Linder; Hisami Kuriowa; Michael Solinger; Sarah Radclyffe; Channel Four Film; Goldwyn Entertainment Company. **A:** College-Adult. **P:** Entertainment. **U:** Home. **Mov-Ent:** Sex & Sexuality. **Acq:** Purchase. **Dist:** MGM Studios Inc.

Bent Familia 1997
Three educated women, on the brink of self-awareness and questioning their own fate, struggle to reconcile their cultural and social traditions. Subtitled in English. 105m; VHS. **A:** Adult. **P:** Education. **U:** Institution, BCTV. **L:** Arabic. **Gen-Edu:** Drama, Women. **Acq:** Purchase, Rent/Lease. **Dist:** Arab Film Distribution. $200.00.

The Bent Tree 1980
A film in sand animation based on the Yiddish folk song by Yitzhak Manger about a child's longing and a mother's responsibility. Sung in Yiddish with English narration, or available in Yiddish only. 4m; VHS, 3/4 U, Special order formats. **Pr:** Sally Heckel. **A:** Primary. **P:** Entertainment. **U:** Institution. **L:** Yiddish. **Chl-Juv:** Family Viewing, Folklore & Legends. **Acq:** Purchase. **Dist:** Ergo Media Inc.

The Benzedrine Monks of Santo Domonica 1994
Parody of the platinum selling album "Chant," features versions of "(The Theme) The Monkees," "We Will Rock You," "Losing My Religion," "Smells Like Teen Spirit," and "Da Ya Think I'm Sexy?" 30m; VHS. **A:** Sr. High-Adult. **P:** Entertainment. **U:** Home. **Mov-Ent:** Music Video, Satire & Parody. **Acq:** Purchase. **Dist:** Music Video Distributors. $12.98.

Benzene 19??
Profiles new Federal regulations regarding the handling and processing of benzene. Covers permissible exposure limits, revised spill, transfer, and handling procedures, medical surveillance for employees, MSDS on benzene, sampling and control equipment, and personal protection equipment. Includes Leader's Guide and 25 Program Guides. 17m; VHS, 3/4 U. **A:** Adult. **P:** Education. **U:** Institution. **Bus-Ind:** Safety Education, Industry & Industrialists. **Acq:** Purchase. **Dist:** Williams Learning Network.

Benzene: How to Handle It Safely 1995
Explains how to identify where benzene may be found at work, and its physical and health hazards. 11m; VHS. **A:** Adult. **P:** Professional. **U:** Institution. **Bus-Ind:** Job Training, Safety Education, Management. **Acq:** Rent/Lease. **Dist:** National Safety Council, California Chapter, Film Library.

Benzene Safety Training 1979
This program provides training in several critical areas related to benzene safety, and includes first aid procedures. 23m; VHS, 3/4 U. **Pr:** Gulf Publishing Co; International Training Company. **A:** Adult. **P:** Instruction. **U:** Institution, CCTV. **Bus-Ind:** How-To, Safety Education. **Acq:** Purchase. **Dist:** Gulf Publishing Co. $495.00.

Benzene, Toluene, & Xylene 1989
Storage and fire control of these carcinogens are shown. 28m; VHS, 3/4 U. **A:** Adult. **P:** Instruction. **U:** Institution. **How-Ins:** Fires, Safety Education, Emergencies. **Acq:** Purchase, Rent/Lease. **Dist:** Emergency Film Group. $395.00.

Benzodiazepines: Panacea or Poison? 1980
Discusses benzodiazepines, with emphasis on their role in the management of the patient with anxiety. 24m; VHS, 3/4 U. **Pr:** Health Communications Network. **A:** College-Adult. **P:** Professional. **U:** Institution, SURA. **Hea-Sci:** Drugs, Medical Education. **Acq:** Purchase, Rent/Lease, Subscription.

Beowulf 1975
A look at the Celtic-British classic epic. 38m; VHS, 3/4 U. **Pr:** Films for the Humanities and Sciences. **A:** College. **P:** Education. **U:** Institution, CCTV, CATV, BCTV. **Fin-Art:** Performing Arts, Literature--English, Literature. **Acq:** Purchase, Rent/Lease, Duplication License. **Dist:** Films for the Humanities & Sciences.

Beowulf 1998 (R) — ★½
Cheesy retelling of the dark ages Saxon saga that has seemingly time travelled to a vague post-apocalypse time. Wandering knight Beowulf (Lambert) battles beast Grendel, who comes each night to feed on those who live in the Outpost. Cult icon Mitra was one of the models for Lara Croft of "Tomb Raider" game fame. 92m; VHS, DVD, Wide. **C:** Christopher Lambert; Rhona Mitra; Oliver Cotton; Patricia Velasquez; Goetz Otto; Layla Roberts; Brent J. Lowe; Directed by Graham Baker; Written by Mark Leahy; David Chappe; Cinematography by Christopher Faloona; Music by Ben Watkins. **Pr:** Miramax Film Corp. **A:** Sr. High-Adult. **P:** Entertainment. **U:** Home. **Mov-Ent.** **Acq:** Purchase. **Dist:** Buena Vista Home Entertainment.

Beowulf 2007 (PG-13) — ★★★
Not your father's epic poem! Director Zemeckis takes the Old English classic and turns it into both a highly stylized computer-generated swordfest and a satirical take on the lit class staple. Beowulf (Winstone) battles Grendel (Glover), gets sexy with Grendel's mom (Jolie), and fights a dragon on his way to eternal heroic glory. Purists may object to the liberties taken by writers Gaiman and Avery, but they do a good job of connecting and streamlining the source material's various storylines. While still resembling a video game, Zemeckis's second attempt at the "performance capture" digital style is a dramatic improvement over his previous attempt in the lifeless "The Polar Express." 114m; Blu-Ray, On Demand, Wide. **C:** Voice(s) by Ray Winstone; Angelina Jolie; Crispin Glover; Anthony Hopkins; Robin Wright; John Malkovich; Alison Lohman; Directed by Robert Zemeckis; Written by Neil Gaiman; Roger Avary; Cinematography by Robert Presley; Music by Alan Silvestri. **Pr:** Jack

Rapke; Steve Starkey; Robert Zemeckis; Robert Zemeckis; Shangri-La Entertainment; Imagemovers; Paramount. **A:** Jr. High-Adult. **P:** Entertainment. **U:** Home. **L:** English. **Mov-Ent**: Action-Adventure, Drama, Animation & Cartoons. **Acq:** Purchase. **Dist:** Amazon.com Inc.; Movies Unlimited; Alpha Video.

Beowulf & Grendel 2006 (R) — ★★
Live-action adaptation of the 1000-year-old Scandanavian poem retells the story of Beowulf (Butler), the Norse warrior who helps his pal, Danish King Hrothgar (Skarsgard), rid his land of the murderous troll Grendel (Sigurdsson). Tries to appeal to modern audiences with flashy fighting, lots of blood, and awkward comedic attempts, but succeeds only in showing how beautiful Iceland is (that's where it was filmed). 102m; DVD, Blu-Ray. **C:** Gerard Butler; Stellan Skarsgard; Sarah Polley; Eddie Marsan; Ingvar Sigurdsson; Tony Curran; Rory McCann; Ronan Vilbert; Martin Delaney; Olafur Darri Olafsson; Mark Lewis; Elva Osk Olafsdottir; Directed by Sturla Gunnarsson; Written by Andrew Rai Berzins; Cinematography by Jan Kiesser; Music by Hilmar Orn Hilmarsson. **Pr:** Paul Stephens; Eric Jordan; Jason Piette; Michael Cowan; Sturla Gunnarrsson; Telefilm Canada; Astral Media; Harold Greenberg Fund; Icelandic Film Corp; Equinox Films. **A:** Sr. High-Adult. **P:** Entertainment. **U:** Home. **L:** English. **Mov-Ent**: Folklore & Legends, Action-Adventure, Fantasy. **Acq:** Purchase. **Dist:** Anchor Bay Entertainment.

Beowulf and the Anglo-Saxons 2007
Uses 3-D animation, location footage, archival material, and interviews to examine the Anglo-Saxon "Beowulf" manuscript and the culture that created it. ?m; DVD. **A:** Jr. High-Adult. **P:** Entertainment. **U:** Home. **Fin-Art**: Documentary Films, History. **Acq:** Purchase. **Dist:** Rykodisc Corp.

Beowulf and the Old English Tradition 1984
A journey through the beginnings of English literature, from the oral tradition to Caedmon and the only surviving epic, "Beowulf." 38m; VHS, 3/4 U. **Pr:** Stephen Mantell. **A:** Jr. High-Adult. **P:** Education. **U:** Institution, SURA. **Fin-Art**: Performing Arts, Literature--English. **Acq:** Purchase, Rent/Lease. **Dist:** Films for the Humanities & Sciences.

Berberian Sound Studio 2012 (Unrated) — ★★
An ode to '70s Giallos (Italian horror films) finds meek Brit sound engineer Gilderoy (Jones) brought to an Italian film studio to help finish a controversial genre flick. With a surreal style, director Strickland captures his protagonist as he creates the sound effects for a film filled with gore (that we brilliantly never actually see). As Gilderoy becomes more engrossed in the movie and the weird people making it, his sanity slides until the film truly goes off the rails in the final act, playing with film stocks, visual effects, and, of course, great sound design. English and Italian with subtitles. 92m; Streaming. **C:** Toby Jones; Tonia Sotiropoulou; Susanna Cappellaro; Cosimo Fusco; Directed by Peter Strickland; Written by Peter Strickland; Cinematography by Nicholas D. Knowland. **Pr:** Mary Burke; Keith Griffiths; IFC Midnight. **A:** Adult. **P:** Entertainment. **U:** Home. **L:** English, Italian. **Mov-Ent**: Italy, Horror, Mental Health. **Acq:** Purchase. **Dist:** Amazon.com Inc.

Berchtesgaden/Lake Koenigsee 1986
Travel along the Salzbergstrasse from Berchtesgaden to the Adlerhorst, then by boat across the Koenigsee and on to the Obersee. In English. 60m; VHS. **TV Std:** NTSC, PAL. **Pr:** German Language Video Center. **A:** Family. **P:** Entertainment. **U:** Home. **Gen-Edu**: Travel, Germany. **Acq:** Purchase, Rent/Lease. **Dist:** German Language Video Center. $49.95.

Bereavement 2010 (R) — ★
Formulaic torture/slasher flick. Young Martin Bristol is kidnapped by psycho sadist Graham Sutter who keeps the boy in his family's abandoned slaughterhouse as a witness to his bloody crimes. Orphaned teenager Allison Miller comes to live with her Uncle Jonathan and his family and gets curious about their reclusive neighbor, which is a big, big mistake. 107m; DVD, Blu-Ray. **C:** Alexandra Daddario; Martha Tilton; Brett Rickaby; Spencer List; John Savage; Nolan Gerard Funk; Kathryn Meisle; Peyton List; Directed by Stevan Mena; Written by Stevan Mena; Cinematography by Marco Cappetta; Music by Stevan Mena. **A:** Sr. High-Adult. **P:** Entertainment. **U:** Home. **Mov-Ent**: Child Abuse. **Acq:** Purchase. **Dist:** Anchor Bay Entertainment.

Berenice Abbott: A View of the 20th Century 19??
Filmed in Maine during her 91st and 92nd years, Abbott takes viewers on a guided tour of her century through her photography in Paris of the 1920s to small-town America of the 1950s. 60m; VHS. **A:** Family. **P:** Education. **U:** Institution. **L:** English. **Gen-Edu**: History--U.S. **Acq:** Purchase. **Dist:** Northeast Historic Film. $99.00.

The Berenstain Bears: Adventure and Fun for Everyone 2003
Presents the animated children's television series about the life of the Berenstain bears family. Includes: "Go to Camp," "The Jump Rope Contest," "Visit Fun Park," "The Slumber Party," "The Talent Show," and "The Perfect Fishing Spot." 6 episodes. 82m; DVD. **A:** Preschool-Primary. **P:** Entertainment. **U:** Home. **Chl-Juv**: Television Series, Animation & Cartoons, Children's Shows. **Acq:** Purchase. **Dist:** Sony Pictures Home Entertainment Inc. $14.94.

Berenstain Bears and the Messy Room 1982
Mamma Bear is frustrated with the children's messy rooms and turns to Papa Bear for help. "The Berenstain Bears and the Terrible Termite" is also included. 30m; VHS, CC. **A:** Family. **P:** Entertainment. **U:** Home. **Chl-Juv**: Children, Animation & Cartoons. **Acq:** Purchase. **Dist:** Random House of Canada Ltd. $14.95.

Berenstain Bears and the Missing Dinosaur Bone 1990
That famous family of bears has lost a dinosaur bone and the exhibit opens in one hour! Can they find it before it's too late? Also includes "Bears in the Night" and "The Bear Detectives." 30m; VHS, CC. **Pr:** Random House Inc. **A:** Family. **P:** Entertainment. **U:** Home. **Chl-Juv**: Family Viewing, Animation & Cartoons, Children. **Acq:** Purchase. **Dist:** Random House of Canada Ltd. $9.95.

The Berenstain Bears and the Trouble with Friends 1982
There is a new cub in Bear Country, the same age as sister and just as bossy. "The Berenstain Bears and the Coughing Catfish" is included also. 30m; VHS, CC. **A:** Family. **P:** Entertainment. **U:** Home. **Chl-Juv**: Children, Animation & Cartoons. **Acq:** Purchase. **Dist:** Random House of Canada Ltd. $14.95.

The Berenstain Bears and the Truth 1982
Brother and sister bear learn that losing Mama Bear's trust is worse than breaking her favorite lamp. "The Berenstain Bears Save the Bees" is included. 30m; VHS, CC. **A:** Family. **P:** Entertainment. **U:** Home. **Chl-Juv**: Children, Animation & Cartoons. **Acq:** Purchase. **Dist:** Random House of Canada Ltd. $14.95.

The Berenstain Bears and Too Much Birthday 1982
Papa and the cubs find out at Sister's sixth birthday that there really could be such a thing as too much birthday. 30m; VHS, CC. **A:** Family. **P:** Entertainment. **U:** Home. **Chl-Juv**: Children, Animation & Cartoons. **Acq:** Purchase. **Dist:** Random House of Canada Ltd. $14.95.

The Berenstain Bears: Bears Get a Babysitter 2004
Presents the animated children's television series about the life of the Berenstain bears family. Includes: "The Sitter," "The Baby Chipmunk," "Trouble with Grown Ups," "Family Get Together," "The Birthday Boy," and "Count Their Blessings." 6 episodes. 81m; DVD. **A:** Preschool-Primary. **P:** Entertainment. **U:** Home. **Chl-Juv**: Television Series, Animation & Cartoons, Children's Shows. **Acq:** Purchase. **Dist:** Sony Pictures Home Entertainment Inc. $19.95.

The Berenstain Bears: Bears Out and About 2005
Presents the animated children's television series about the life of the Berenstain bears family. Includes: "The Haunted Lighthouse," "That Stump Must Go," "White Water Mystery," "Summer Job," "Don't Pollute," and "Hug and Make Up." 6 episodes. 82m; DVD. **A:** Preschool-Primary. **P:** Entertainment. **U:** Home. **Chl-Juv**: Television Series, Animation & Cartoons, Children's Shows. **Acq:** Purchase. **Dist:** Sony Pictures Home Entertainment Inc. $14.94.

The Berenstain Bears: Bears Team Up! 2004
Presents the animated children's television series about the life of the Berenstain bears family. Includes: "Out for the Team," "In the Crowd," "Fly It," "Mama's New Job," "Too Small for the Team," and "Lost in a Cave." 6 episodes. 82m; DVD. **A:** Preschool-Primary. **P:** Entertainment. **U:** Home. **Chl-Juv**: Television Series, Animation & Cartoons, Children's Shows. **Acq:** Purchase. **Dist:** Sony Pictures Home Entertainment Inc. $19.95.

The Berenstain Bears' Christmas 1990
Despite Mama Bear's warning of bad weather, Papa Bear decides that this year he will find his perfect Christmas tree. Also includes "Inside Outside Upside Down" and "The Bike Lesson." 30m; VHS, CC. **Pr:** Cates Films. **A:** Family. **P:** Entertainment. **U:** Home. **Chl-Juv**: Animation & Cartoons, Christmas. **Acq:** Purchase. **Dist:** Random House of Canada Ltd. $9.95.

The Berenstain Bears Forget Their Manners 1986
Mama Bear draws up the Bear Family Politeness Plan which punishes rudeness with chores. The cubs foil the plan by being super polite, and actually enjoy it. 30m; VHS, CC. **A:** Family. **P:** Teacher Education. **U:** Home. **Chl-Juv**: Children, Animation & Cartoons. **Acq:** Purchase. **Dist:** Random House of Canada Ltd. $14.95.

The Berenstain Bears: Fun Lessons to Learn 2003
Presents the animated children's television series about the life of the Berenstain bears family Includes: "Trouble at School," "Go to School," "The Homework Hassle," "Lend a Helping Hand," "Too Much Pressure," and "The Trouble with Pets." 6 episodes. 82m; DVD. **A:** Preschool-Primary. **P:** Entertainment. **U:** Home. **Chl-Juv**: Television Series, Animation & Cartoons, Children's Shows. **Acq:** Purchase. **Dist:** Sony Pictures Home Entertainment Inc. $19.95.

Berenstain Bears Get in a Fight 1982
Brother and Sister make a mountain out of a mole hill, and Mama Bear has to act as mediator. 30m; VHS, CC. **A:** Family. **P:** Entertainment. **U:** Home. **Chl-Juv**: Children, Animation & Cartoons. **Acq:** Purchase. **Dist:** Random House of Canada Ltd. $14.95.

The Berenstain Bears Get Stage Fright 1990
Acclaimed family cartoon plus another, "The Berenstain Bears Go Bonkers Over Honkers." 30m; VHS, CC. **Pr:** Buzz Potamkin. **A:** Family. **P:** Entertainment. **U:** Home. **Chl-Juv**: Children, Animation & Cartoons. **Acq:** Purchase. **Dist:** Random House of Canada Ltd. $14.95.

The Berenstain Bears in the Dark 1982
After Brother reads Sister a scary story, she can't fall asleep. Papa comes to the rescue with his childhood night light and a reassuring talk. 30m; VHS, CC. **A:** Family. **P:** Entertainment. **U:** Home. **Mov-Ent**: Children, Animation & Cartoons. **Acq:** Purchase. **Dist:** Random House of Canada Ltd. $14.95.

The Berenstain Bears Learn About Strangers 1982
After Papa Bear talks to the cubs about strangers, Sister becomes afraid, and Brother ignores Papa's advice. 30m; VHS, CC. **A:** Family. **P:** Entertainment. **U:** Home. **Chl-Juv**: Children, Animation & Cartoons. **Acq:** Purchase. **Dist:** Random House of Canada Ltd. $14.95.

Berenstain Bears: No Girls Allowed 1990
A classic Berenstain Bears episode plus "The Berenstain Bears and the Missing Dinosaur Bone." 30m; VHS, CC. **Pr:** Buzz Potamkin. **A:** Family. **P:** Entertainment. **U:** Home. **Chl-Juv**: Children, Animation & Cartoons. **Acq:** Purchase. **Dist:** Random House of Canada Ltd. $14.95.

The Beretta 92SB-F: Military's Choice 198?
Covers all aspects of the operation and maintenance of the Beretta 92SB 9mm autoloader. 60m; VHS. **A:** Sr. High-Adult. **P:** Instruction. **U:** Home. **How-Ins**: How-To, Firearms. **Acq:** Purchase. **Dist:** Gun Video. $49.95.

Beretta's Island 1992 (R) — ★★
When Interpol operative Beretta comes out of retirement to track his friend's killer, the chase leads him back to his homeland of Sardinia, which has been overrun by drugs. 97m; VHS. **C:** Franco (Columbo) Columbu; Ken Kercheval; Elizabeth Kaitan; Van Quattro; Jo Champa; Cameo(s) Arnold Schwarzenegger; Directed by Michael Preece; Cinematography by Massimo Zeri; Music by Cliff Magness. **A:** Sr. High-Adult. **P:** Entertainment. **U:** Home. **Mov-Ent**: Drugs. **Acq:** Purchase. **Dist:** Lions Gate Television Corp. $89.98.

Berga: Soldier of Another War 2005
Story of American infantrymen captured during the Battle of the Bulge and sent to Nazi slave labor camps where most of them died. 90m; DVD, CC; Closed Captioned. **A:** Adult. **P:** Entertainment. **U:** Home. **Mov-Ent**: World War Two, Holocaust. **Acq:** Purchase. **Dist:** PBS Home Video. $19.98.

Bergkristall 1949 (Unrated)
A reformed poacher and a game warden are both after the same woman, whose heart belongs to the poacher. When one of the men is murdered, the other is suspected, and the key to the mystery is locked in the ice of the mountain. In German only. 82m/B/W; VHS. **TV Std:** NTSC, PAL. **Pr:** German Language Video Center. **A:** Jr. High-Adult. **P:** Entertainment. **U:** Home. **L:** German. **Mov-Ent**: Drama, Germany. **Acq:** Purchase, Rent/Lease. **Dist:** German Language Video Center. $33.95.

Berkeley 2005 (R) — ★½
In 1968, Ben Sweet (Nick Roth) enrolls at UC Berkeley mainly to avoid the draft and is introduced to political activism, drugs, and sex. The lead actor is the director's son and the film is based on Bobby Roth's own college days although the rambling nostalgia isn't as interesting as Roth seems to believe. 88m; DVD. **C:** Nick Roth; Henry Winkler; Sarah Carter; Laura Jordan; Bonnie Bedelia; Sebastian Tillinger; Jake Newton; Tom Morello; Directed by Bobby Roth; Written by Bobby Roth; Cinematography by Steve Burns; Music by Christopher Franke. **A:** Sr. High-Adult. **P:** Entertainment. **U:** Home. **Mov-Ent. Acq:** Purchase. **Dist:** Rivercoast Media.

Berkeley in the Sixties 1990
The rise and fall of the protest movement is remembered in this analysis by 15 campus activists who comment on their actions and on the era. 117m; VHS. **C:** Directed by Mark Kitchell. **A:** Sr. High-Adult. **P:** Entertainment. **U:** Home. **Gen-Edu**: Documentary Films, Education. **Acq:** Purchase. **Dist:** PBS Home Video; California Newsreel; First Run Features. $79.95.

Berkeley Square 1998 — ★★½
In 1902 London, three young women become nannies and grow to be friends. Tough and experienced East Ender Matty (Wilkie) goes to work for the well-bred St. Johns; country-raised Hannah (Smurfit) has an illegitimate child by her previous titled employer's son—a fact she keeps hidden from the neglectful Hutchinsons; and farm girl Lydia (Wady) is hired by the avant-garde Lamson-Scribeners, who believe in education even for servants. Naturally, the threesome become very involved in each other's lives and loves. On five cassettes. 500m; VHS, DVD. **C:** Victoria Smurfit; Tabitha Wady; Clare Wilkie; Rosemary Leach; Judy Parfitt; Directed by Leslie Manning; Richard Signy; Martin Hutchings; Richard Holthouse. **Pr:** British Broadcasting Corporation. **A:** Jr. High-Adult. **P:** Entertainment. **U:** Home. **Mov-Ent**: Romance. **Acq:** Purchase. **Dist:** Video Collectibles.

Berkshires & Hudsons of the Boston & Albany/ Railroading in the Northeast 19??
Railroad buffs will enjoy these scenes of classic steam locomotives from the New Haven, New York Central, Central Vermont, Delaware & Hudson and B & A lines. 30m/B/W; VHS. **Pr:** J.W. Deely; E.R. Blanchard. **A:** Jr. High-Adult. **P:** Entertainment. **U:** Home. **Gen-Edu**: Trains. **Acq:** Purchase. **Dist:** $19.95.

Berlin 1982
A video tour of the once and future capital of Germany, including the Wannsee, Schloss Charlottenburg, the Ku'damm, the Brandenburg Gate, and the since-removed Checkpoint Charley. 30m; VHS. **A:** Family. **P:** Education. **U:** Institution, Home. **Gen-Edu**: Travel, Germany. **Acq:** Purchase. **Dist:** German Language Video Center. $29.95.

Berlin: A Lesson in Survival 1976
The struggle of the once and future capitol of Germany to survive after WWII is depicted in this promotional German film. 25m; VHS, 3/4 U. **TV Std:** NTSC, PAL. **A:** Jr. High-Adult. **P:** Education. **U:** Institution, Home. **Gen-Edu**: Documentary Films,

Germany, World War Two. **Acq:** Purchase, Rent/Lease. **Dist:** International Historic Films Inc.; German Language Video Center. $22.00.

The Berlin Affair 1985 (R) — ★★
A sordid tale from "The Night Porter" director about a Japanese woman seducing various parties in pre-WWII Germany. 97m; VHS. **C:** Mio Takaki; Gudrun Landgrebe; Kevin McNally; Directed by Liliana Cavani; Music by Pino Donaggio. **Pr:** Cannon Films. **A:** Sr. High-Adult. **P:** Entertainment. **U:** Home. **Mov-Ent:** Mystery & Suspense. **Acq:** Purchase. **Dist:** MGM Home Entertainment. $79.95.

Berlin Airlift 1990
Discusses the Allied airlift of food and supplies to German citizens during the Soviet blockade of West Berlin in 1948. 17m; VHS, SVS, 3/4 U. **A:** Jr. High-Sr. High. **P:** Education. **U:** Institution. **Gen-Edu:** History--Modern, World War Two, Germany. **Acq:** Purchase, Rent/Lease. **Dist:** Encyclopedia Britannica. $79.00.

Berlin Alexanderplatz 1980 — ★★★½
Fassbinder's 15 1/2-hour epic follows the life, death, and resurrection of Franz Biberkof, a former transit worker who has just finished a lengthy prison term and must learn to adjust in the harsh social atmosphere of Berlin in the 1920s. Melodramatic parable with biblical overtones considered by some to be a masterpiece. Based on the novel by Alfred Doblin; originally aired as a miniseries on German TV. 930m; VHS, DVD. **C:** Gunter Lamprecht; Hanna Schygulla; Barbara Sukowa; Gottfried John; Elisabeth Trissenaar; Brigitte Mira; Karin Baal; Ivan Desny; Margit Carstensen; Directed by Rainer Werner Fassbinder; Written by Rainer Werner Fassbinder; Cinematography by Xaver Schwarzenberger; Music by Peer Raben. **Pr:** Peter Martheshmeimer; TeleCulture Films. **A:** Jr. High-Adult. **P:** Entertainment. **U:** Home. **L:** German. **Mov-Ent:** TV Movies, Germany. **Acq:** Purchase, Rent/Lease. **Dist:** Criterion Collection Inc.; MGM Home Entertainment. $400.00.

Berlin Blues 1989 (PG-13) — ★★
A nightclub singer is torn between two men. 90m; VHS, Streaming. **C:** Julia Migenes; Keith Baxter; Directed by Ricardo Franco. **A:** Adult. **P:** Entertainment. **U:** Home. **Mov-Ent:** Drama, Nightclubs. **Acq:** Purchase. **Dist:** No Longer Available.

Berlin: Capital of a United Germany 19??
Contains historical footage of the dismantling of the Berlin Wall and discusses the future of the united Germany. Comes with teacher's manual. 19m; VHS. **A:** Jr. High-Adult. **P:** Education. **U:** Institution. **Gen-Edu:** Germany, History. **Acq:** Purchase. **Dist:** Educational Video Network. $59.95.

The Berlin Conspiracy 1991 (R) — ★★
Espionage/action potboiler does an imaginative job of setting its action against the fall of the Berlin Wall and the end of the Cold War. A CIA agent forms a shaky alliance with his East German spymaster rival to prevent germ warfare technology from falling into terrorist hands. 83m; VHS. **C:** Marc Singer; Mary Crosby; Stephen Davies; Richard Leparmentier; Terence Henry; Directed by Terence H. Winkless. **Pr:** Concorde Pictures; New Horizons Pictures. **A:** Sr. High-Adult. **P:** Entertainment. **U:** Home. **Mov-Ent:** Action-Adventure, Intelligence Service. **Acq:** Purchase. **Dist:** Sony Pictures Home Entertainment Inc. $89.95.

Berlin Correspondent 1942 — ★★
Briskly-paced Fox propaganda flick stars a dashing Andrews as foreign correspondent Bill Roberts, who's smuggling info on Axis plans out of Germany in bland news reports. Nazi counter-agent Karen (Gilmore) is tasked to get close and learn who's supplying Bill with his info. Turns out to be her own father (Kalser), who gets picked up by the Gestapo, leading Karen to change her alliance and ask Bill for help. 70m/B/W; DVD. **C:** Dana Andrews; Virginia Gilmore; Erwin Kalser; Sig Rumann; Martin Kosleck; Mona Maris; Directed by Eugene Forde; Written by Jack Andrews; Steve Fisher; Cinematography by Virgil Miller; Music by Emil Newman. **A:** Sr. High-Adult. **P:** Entertainment. **U:** Home. **L:** English. **Mov-Ent:** Journalism, World War Two, Germany. **Acq:** Purchase. **Dist:** Fox Home Entertainment.

Berlin Dream 198? (Unrated)
German alternative music is featured, including bands such as Einstuerzende Neubauten, Blixa Bargeld, Matador, Sprung aus den Wolken, Mona Mur, Die Haut, Die Schlampen and more. 70m; VHS. **A:** Jr. High-Adult. **P:** Entertainment. **U:** Home. **Mov-Ent:** Music--Performance. **Acq:** Purchase. **Dist:** Music Video Distributors. $129.95.

Berlin Express 1948 (Unrated) — ★★★½
Battle of wits ensues between the Allies and the Nazis who are seeking to keep Germans divided in post-WWII Germany. Espionage and intrigue factor heavily. 86m/B/W; VHS, DVD. **C:** Robert Ryan; Merle Oberon; Paul Lukas; Charles Korvin; Directed by Jacques Tourneur. **Pr:** RKO. **A:** Family. **P:** Entertainment. **U:** Home. **Mov-Ent:** Mystery & Suspense, Trains. **Acq:** Purchase. **Dist:** WarnerArchive.com; Facets Multimedia Inc. $19.95.

Berlin Job 2012 (Unrated) — ★★
Cousins Mickey and Ray are London gangsters looking for a big payday, thanks to a cocaine shipment form the Russian mob. When the drugs go astray, the Russians give them one week to pay up, so the two set up a diamond heist in Berlin on the same day that a big soccer match between England and Germany is being held. Naturally, things don't go as planned. 109m; DVD, Blu-Ray. **C:** Frank Harper; Craig Fairbrass; Charles Dance; Jamie Foreman; Sean Pertwee; Vincent Regan; Luke Treadaway; Directed by Frank Harper; Written by Frank Harper; Urs Buehler; Cinematography by Mike Southon; Music by Tim Atack. **A:** Sr. High-Adult. **P:** Entertainment. **U:** Home. **L:** English. **Mov-Ent:** Crime Drama. **Acq:** Purchase. **Dist:** New Video Group Inc.

The Berlin Philharmoniker in Singapore 2013 (Unrated)
The Berlin Philharmonic ends its 2010 tour with a performance of Mahler's Symphony No. 1 and Rachmaninov's Symphonic Dances. 120m; DVD. **A:** Family. **P:** Entertainment. **U:** Home. **L:** English. **Mov-Ent:** Music--Classical, Music--Performance. **Acq:** Purchase. **Dist:** EuroArts Entertainment. $24.99.

Berlin: Symphony of a Great City 1927 (Unrated)
An expression of the life of a city from morning to nighttime, set to music with many wildly impressionistic camera angles, montages, etc. An important and influential documentary. Silent with musical score. 70m/B/W; Silent; VHS, DVD, 3/4 U. **TV Std:** NTSC, PAL. **C:** Directed by Walter Ruttman. **Pr:** Fox Europa. **A:** Jr. High-Adult. **P:** Entertainment. **U:** Home. **L:** German. **Mov-Ent:** Cities & Towns, Film--Avant-Garde, Germany. **Acq:** Purchase, Rent/Lease. **Dist:** Image Entertainment Inc.; Glenn Video Vistas Ltd.; International Historic Films Inc. $24.95.

Berlin: The Doomed City 1968
A chronicle of the devastation wreaked by Allied bombing of Berlin during WWII. 65m/B/W; VHS. **TV Std:** NTSC, PAL. **A:** Jr. High-Adult. **P:** Education. **U:** Institution, Home. **Gen-Edu:** Documentary Films, World War Two, Germany. **Acq:** Purchase, Rent/Lease. **Dist:** German Language Video Center. $39.95.

Berlin Tunnel 21 1981 — ★½
Based on the novel by Donald Lindquist in which five American soldiers attempt a daring Cold War rescue of a beautiful German girl. The plan is to construct a tunnel under the Berlin Wall. Better-than-average. 150m; VHS, Streaming. **C:** Richard Thomas; Jose Ferrer; Horst Buchholz; Directed by Richard Michaels. **Pr:** Filmways Pictures. **A:** Jr. High-Adult. **P:** Entertainment. **U:** Home. **Mov-Ent:** TV Movies. **Acq:** Purchase. **Dist:** No Longer Available.

The Berlin Wall 19??
Describes the 30-year history of the Berlin Wall and what it took to finally unite Germany and bring the Wall down. Comes with teacher's manual. 50m; VHS. **A:** Jr. High-Adult. **P:** Education. **U:** Institution. **Gen-Edu:** Germany, Cities & Towns, History. **Acq:** Purchase. **Dist:** Educational Video Network. $39.95.

The Berlin Wall 1990
Historical presentation of the political conditions which led to the building and eventual dismantling of the infamous structure which divided the German city into two sections: democratic and communist. 30m; VHS. **A:** Sr. High. **P:** Education. **U:** Institution. **Chl-Juv:** History--Modern, Politics & Government. **Acq:** Purchase, Rent/Lease. **Dist:** Films for the Humanities & Sciences. $75.00.

Berliner Weisse mit Schuss 1985 — ★
Berlin actor and cabaret artist Gunter Pritzman acts out comic stories that show the four sides of the personality of a Berliner. In German only. 60m; VHS. **A:** Jr. High-Adult. **P:** Entertainment. **U:** Institution, Home. **L:** German. **Mov-Ent:** Comedy--Performance, Variety, Germany. **Acq:** Purchase. **Dist:** German Language Video Center.

Berlinguer I Love You 1977 (Unrated) — **Bomb!**
Crude and disgustingly obnoxious comedy about a mama's-boy loser who is led to believe that his shrewish mother has died. When he returns home for her funeral, she is not happy to see him. Title refers to a popular politician of the era. Italian with subtitles. 95m; DVD. **C:** Roberto Benigni; Alida Valli; Carlo Monni; Directed by Giuseppe Bertolucci; Written by Roberto Benigni; Giuseppe Bertolucci; Cinematography by Renato Tafuri; Music by Frank Coletta. **A:** College-Adult. **P:** Entertainment. **U:** Home. **Mov-Ent:** Comedy--Black. **Acq:** Purchase. **Dist:** Entertainment One US LP.

Berlioz: Les Troyens 1983
Filmed at the Metropolitan Opera on October 8, 1983, this performance features Norman, Troyanos, and Domingo, while Levine conducts. 253m; VHS. **Pr:** Paramount Pictures; Metropolitan Opera. **A:** Sr. High-Adult. **P:** Entertainment. **U:** Home. **Fin-Art:** Music--Classical. **Acq:** Purchase. **Dist:** Music Video Distributors. $39.95.

Berlioz: Symphonie Fantastique 19??
Classical music is performed and discussed by the musicians. 90m; VHS, DVD, Blu-Ray. **A:** Sr. High-Adult. **P:** Entertainment. **U:** Home. **Fin-Art:** Music--Classical. **Acq:** Purchase. **Dist:** Music Video Distributors.

Berloiz the Bear 199?
From the "Reading Rainbow" series, this episode features the title book by Jan Brett. Host LeVar Burton discusses sound, music, and instruments, and visits with the Boys Choir of Harlem. Includes three book reviews by children: "The Science Book of Sound," "Georgia Music," and "An Introduction to Music Series: Brass, Strings, Woodwinds and Percussion." 30m; VHS. **A:** Primary-Jr. High. **P:** Entertainment. **U:** Home, Institution. **Chl-Juv. Acq:** Purchase. **Dist:** PBS Home Video. $33.70.

Bermuda Bound 19??
Long range cruising video features trip planning, watches, custom procedures, boat handling, and more. 40m; VHS. **A:** Adult. **P:** Instruction. **U:** Home. **Spo-Rec:** Boating. **Acq:** Purchase. **Dist:** Bennett Marine Video. $39.95.

The Bermuda Depths 1978 (Unrated) — ★½
Made-for-TV fantasy horror involving the Bermuda Triangle, a giant sea turtle, a beautiful ghostly girl who apparently sold her soul for eternal youth, a troubled young man, and a couple of scientists. It's sorta goofy and watchable at the same time. 98m; DVD. **C:** Leigh McCloskey; Connie Sellecca; Burl Ives; Carl Weathers; Julie Woodson; Ruth Attaway; Directed by Tom Kotani; Written by William Overgard; Cinematography by Jeri Sopanen; Music by Maury Laws. **A:** Family. **P:** Entertainment. **U:** Home. **Mov-Ent:** The Bermuda Triangle, TV Movies. **Acq:** Purchase. **Dist:** WarnerArchive.com.

Bermuda Overboard! 1988
Action on board the yacht "Intuition" as it races from Newport to Bermuda is seen here. 30m; VHS. **Pr:** Sea-TV. **A:** Jr. High-Adult. **P:** Entertainment. **U:** Home. **Spo-Rec:** Boating. **Acq:** Purchase. **Dist:** Bennett Marine Video. $39.95.

Bermuda Triangle 19??
Documents incidents that occured within the Bermuda Triangle. 94m; VHS. **A:** Adult. **P:** Education. **U:** Home. **Gen-Edu:** Boating, The Bermuda Triangle. **Acq:** Purchase. **Dist:** Bennett Marine Video. $29.95.

The Bermuda Triangle 1989 (Unrated) — ★★
Three middle-aged best friends, a doctor, a lawyer, and the owner of an auto repair shop, have big problems. Someone is blackmailing the doctor's daughter; the lawyer's wife and her lover have evil plans; and the shop owner is in debt up to his ears. Who can blame the guys if they join forces to pull off a "perfect crime" and solve their problems. The question is, can they pull it off? In Polish with English subtitles. 99m; VHS. **C:** Directed by Wojcik Wojciech. **Pr:** Polish. **A:** Sr. High-Adult. **P:** Entertainment. **U:** Home. **L:** English, Polish. **Mov-Ent. Acq:** Purchase. **Dist:** Facets Multimedia Inc. $14.98.

Bermuda's Depths: Those Who Dared to Dive 2000 (Unrated)
Watch William Beebe and Otis Barton negotiate new depths in deep-sea exploration from 1930 to 1934 when they used a giant steel ball, designed by Barton, as a sort of two-man research submarine. 56m; VHS, DVD. **A:** Family. **P:** Entertainment. **U:** Institution, Home. **Mov-Ent:** Documentary Films, Explorers, History. **Acq:** Purchase. **Dist:** National Geographic Society. $19.95.

Bermuda's Yellowfin Tuna 1984
This film features a world record 16 pound test catch on Bermuda's Challenger Bank, a discussion of relevant fishing techniques, and some chum-action. 30m; VHS. **Pr:** Bermuda Sportfishing. **A:** Jr. High-Adult. **P:** Entertainment. **U:** Home. **Spo-Rec:** Sports--General, Fishing. **Acq:** Purchase. **Dist:** Salt Water Sportsman.

Bernadette 1990 — ★★½
A French-made version of the legend of St. Bernadette, who endured persecution after claiming to have seen the Virgin Mary. Beautiful in its simplicity, but overly long. 120m; VHS, DVD. **C:** Sydney Penny; Roland LeSaffre; Michele Simonnet; Bernard Dheran; Arlette Didier; Directed by Jean Delannoy. **Pr:** Pathe. **A:** Preschool. **P:** Entertainment. **U:** Home. **L:** English, Spanish. **Mov-Ent:** Biography: Religious Figures, Religion. **Acq:** Purchase. **Dist:** Ignatius Press.

Bernard and Doris 2008 (Unrated) — ★★★
Doris (Sarandon) is eccentric, cynical, lonely, aging billionaire tobacco heiress Doris Duke. Bernard Lafferty (Fiennes) is her Irish, gay, alcoholic butler. They form a delightfully odd-couple partnership where the ever-more devoted Bernard protects Doris from hangers-on (and herself)?so much so that Duke made Lafferty the executor of her will (and when he died, he left everything to her trusts). Gets the bones for the Sarandon/Fiennes combo alone even if Sarandon looks waaaaay too good as the ravaged Duke. 109m; DVD, Wide. **C:** Susan Sarandon; Ralph Fiennes; James Rebhorn; Nick Rolfe; Directed by Bob Balaban; Written by Hugh Costello; Cinematography by Mauricio Rubinstein; Music by Alex Wurman. **A:** Sr. High-Adult. **P:** Entertainment. **U:** Home. **Mov-Ent:** Biography. **Acq:** Purchase. **Dist:** Alpha Video; Movies Unlimited.

Bernard and the Genie 1991 (G) — ★★½
It seems Bernard Bottle is not going to have a happy Christmas—he's been fired from his job and his girlfriend has left him. But things take a turn for the better when he discovers an antique lamp and its resident Genie. But with the Genie granting his every wish, Bernard's sudden wealth is causing some suspicions among both his greedy ex-employer and the police. Meanwhile, the Genie discovers the delights of modern-day England and poses as a department store Santa to truly fulfill a child's Christmas wish. Amusing family fare. 70m; VHS, DVD, CC. **C:** Alan Cumming; Lenny Henry; Rowan Atkinson; Directed by Paul Weiland. **A:** Family. **P:** Entertainment. **U:** Home. **Mov-Ent:** Fantasy, Family Viewing, Christmas. **Acq:** Purchase. **Dist:** Televista; Video Collectibles. $19.98.

Bernard . . . Are You Okay? 1988
In this award-winning film for children, the muppet-like character Bernard falls off a jungle gym, breaks his arm and proceeds to learn all about the emergency room, thus easing his tensions and fears of the unknown. 14m; VHS. **Pr:** Film Ideas, Inc. **A:** Preschool-Primary. **P:** Education. **U:** Institution. **Chl-Juv:** Patient Care, Puppets, Children. **Acq:** Purchase. **Dist:** Film Ideas, Inc.

Bernard Buffet: From Here to Eternity 1998
A look at the artist who devotes each of his large canvases and shows to a single theme. 56m; VHS. **A:** Adult. **P:** Education. **U:** Home. **Fin-Art:** Art & Artists. **Acq:** Purchase. **Dist:** Home Vision Cinema; Crystal Productions.

Bernard Wilets Literature Series 19??
Nine-part series that highlights nine different stories of the courage, exploration, and inspiration from nine different authors, provoking critical and creative thinking. Includes stories from Isaac Asimov, William Faulkner, Edgar Allan Poe, John Steinbeck, Guy de Maupassant, Arthur C. Clarke, Washington

Irving, and Ray Bradbury. 198m; VHS, SVS, 3/4 U. **Pr:** Bernard Wilets. **A:** Jr. High-Adult. **P:** Education. **U:** Institution. **Gen-Edu:** Literature, Education. **Acq:** Purchase, Rent/Lease. **Dist:** Encyclopedia Britannica. $720.00.
Indiv. Titles: 1. Isaac Asimov: All the Troubles of the World 2. William Faulkner: The Bear 3. Edgar Allan Poe: The Cask of Amontillado 4. John Steinbeck: The Leader of the People 5. Guy de Maupassant: The Necklace 6. Arthur C. Clarke: Rescue Party 7. Washington Irving: Rip Van Winkle 8. Ray Bradbury: The Veldt 9. Ray Bradbury: Zero Hour.

Bernard's Gang 1987
A teenage boy becomes a leader of a gang in a South African shanty town. 28m; VHS. **Pr:** New Dimension Films. **A:** Jr. High-Adult. **P:** Education. **U:** Institution. **Gen-Edu:** Apartheid, Black Culture, Africa. **Acq:** Purchase. **Dist:** New Dimension Media. $280.00.

Bernice Bobs Her Hair 1976
An ugly and shy girl's cousin revamps her into a seductress. From the director of "Chilly Scenes of Winter," part of the American Short Story Collection. Adaptation of the F. Scott Fitzgerald story. 49m; VHS. **C:** Shelley Duvall; Henry Fonda; Veronica Cartwright; Bud Cort; Directed by Joan Micklin Silver. **Pr:** Paul R. Gurian. **A:** Family. **P:** Entertainment. **U:** Home. **Mov-Ent:** TV Movies. **Acq:** Purchase. **Dist:** Monterey Home Video; Karol Media. $24.95.

Bernie 2012 (PG-13) — ★★★
Bernie Tiede (Black) is the mortician and very well-liked resident of tiny, rural Carthage, Texas. He's an all-around good guy, sings in the church choir, is friendly to all the older ladies, and comes to the aid of anyone in need. And he is one of the few who will tolerate bitter-but-wealthy widow Marjorie Nugent (MacLaine)--so much so that the pair start taking holidays together. That is, until Bernie murders Marjorie, after which he takes great pains to create the illusion that she is still quite alive. Based on a true story, this black comedy lets Black shine. 104m; DVD, Blu-Ray. **C:** Jack Black; Shirley MacLaine; Matthew McConaughey; Brady Coleman; Richard Robichaux; Rick Dial; Brandon Smith; Larry Dotson; Directed by Richard Linklater; Written by Skip Hollandsworth; Richard Linklater; Cinematography by Dick Pope; Music by Graham Reynolds. **Pr:** Liz Glotzer; David McFadzean; Dete Meserve; Judd Payne; Matt Williams; Ginger Sledge; Martin Shafer; Celine Rattray; Richard Linklater; Millenium Films; Detour Filmproduction; Collins House Productions; Horsethief Pictures; Castle Rock Entertainment. **A:** Jr. High-Adult. **P:** Entertainment. **U:** Home. **L:** English. **Mov-Ent. Acq:** Purchase. **Dist:** Not Yet Released.

The Bernie Mac Show: Season 1 2001
Features the 2001-2006 family comedy television series with comedian Bernie Mac playing the uncle to three children who he must care for while his sister is in rehab and his inexperience in raising children causes many humorous moments. 22 episodes. 506m; DVD. **C:** Bernie Mac; Kellita Smith; Camille Winbush; Jeremy Suarez; Dee Dee Davis. **A:** Family. **P:** Entertainment. **U:** Home. **Mov-Ent:** Television Series, Family. **Acq:** Purchase. **Dist:** Fox Home Entertainment. $29.98.

Bernier on Ernst 1974
Art critic Rosamond Bernier presents a portrait of surrealist painter Max Ernst. 30m; VHS, 3/4 U, EJ, Q. **Pr:** WCBS New York; Camera Three Productions. **A:** College-Adult. **P:** Education. **U:** Institution, SURA. **Fin-Art:** Documentary Films, Art & Artists. **Acq:** Duplication, Free Duplication. **Dist:** Camera Three Productions, Inc.; Creative Arts Television Archive.

Bernstein: Candide 1989
Leonard Bernstein conducts Candide at London's Barbican Centre. 147m; VHS. **C:** Jerry Hadley; Adolph Green; June Anderson; Christa Ludwig; Nicolai Gedda. **Pr:** Polygram Music Video. **A:** Jr. High-Adult. **P:** Entertainment. **U:** Home. **Mov-Ent:** Music--Performance. **Acq:** Purchase. **Dist:** Music Video Distributors. $34.95.

Bernstein Conducts Beethoven: Program 1 1981
Leonard Bernstein introduces this 11-part series which presents Beethoven's nine symphonies in chronological order, the Missa Solemnis, several overtures and pieces of incidental music. Program 1 features Symphony No. 1 and the Egmont Overture. The programs are available as a complete series or separately. 60m; VHS, 3/4 U. **C:** Leonard Bernstein; Maximilian Schell. **Pr:** PBS. **A:** Jr. High-Adult. **P:** Entertainment. **U:** Institution, SURA. **Fin-Art:** Music--Performance, Music--Classical. **Acq:** Purchase, Rent/Lease, Off-Air Record. **Dist:** Home Vision Cinema.

Bernstein Conducts Beethoven: Program 2 1981
Bernstein conducts the Symphony No. 2 and the Coriolan Overture. 60m; VHS, 3/4 U. **C:** Leonard Bernstein; Maximilian Schell. **Pr:** PBS. **A:** Jr. High-Adult. **P:** Entertainment. **U:** Institution, SURA. **Fin-Art:** Music--Performance, Music--Classical. **Acq:** Purchase, Rent/Lease, Off-Air Record. **Dist:** Home Vision Cinema.

Bernstein Conducts Beethoven: Program 3 1981
Using Beethoven's original conducting score, Bernstein conducts the Symphony No. 3, "Eroica." 60m; VHS, 3/4 U. **C:** Leonard Bernstein; Maximilian Schell. **Pr:** PBS. **A:** Jr. High-Adult. **P:** Entertainment. **U:** Institution, SURA. **Fin-Art:** Music--Performance, Music--Classical. **Acq:** Purchase, Rent/Lease, Off-Air Record. **Dist:** Home Vision Cinema.

Bernstein Conducts Beethoven: Program 4 1981
Beethoven's Symphony No. 4 and Leonore Overture No. 3 are performed and discussed in their historical context. 60m; VHS, 3/4 U. **C:** Leonard Bernstein; Maximilian Schell. **Pr:** PBS. **A:** Jr. High-Adult. **P:** Entertainment. **U:** Institution, SURA. **Fin-Art:**

Music--Performance, Music--Classical. **Acq:** Purchase, Rent/Lease, Off-Air Record. **Dist:** Home Vision Cinema.

Bernstein Conducts Beethoven: Program 5 1981
The King Stehpan Overture and the Symphony No. 5 are performed. Bernstein examines Beethoven's struggles in writing the Fifth Symphony. 60m; VHS, 3/4 U. **C:** Leonard Bernstein; Maximilian Schell. **Pr:** PBS. **A:** Jr. High-Adult. **P:** Entertainment. **U:** Institution, SURA. **Fin-Art:** Music--Performance, Music--Classical. **Acq:** Purchase, Rent/Lease, Off-Air Record. **Dist:** Home Vision Cinema.

Bernstein Conducts Beethoven: Program 6 1981
Bernstein discusses the creation and distinguishing elements of Beethoven's Sixth Symphony, the "Pastorale," and then conducts a complete performance of this masterwork. 60m; VHS, 3/4 U. **C:** Leonard Bernstein; Maximilian Schell. **Pr:** PBS. **A:** Jr. High-Adult. **P:** Entertainment. **U:** Institution, SURA. **Fin-Art:** Music--Performance, Music--Classical. **Acq:** Purchase, Rent/Lease, Off-Air Record. **Dist:** Home Vision Cinema.

Bernstein Conducts Beethoven: Program 7 1981
The Symphony No. 7 is performed on this program; Maximilian Schell demonstrates the difference in sound between contemporary musical instruments and those of Beethoven's time. 60m; VHS, 3/4 U. **C:** Leonard Bernstein; Maximilian Schell. **Pr:** PBS. **A:** Jr. High-Adult. **P:** Entertainment. **U:** Institution, SURA. **Fin-Art:** Music--Performance, Music--Classical. **Acq:** Purchase, Rent/Lease, Off-Air Record. **Dist:** Home Vision Cinema.

Bernstein Conducts Beethoven: Program 8 1981
The Symphony No. 8 and the Creatures of Prometheus Overture are performed. 60m; VHS, 3/4 U. **C:** Leonard Bernstein; Maximilian Schell. **Pr:** PBS. **A:** Jr. High-Adult. **P:** Entertainment. **U:** Institution, SURA. **Fin-Art:** Music--Performance, Music--Classical. **Acq:** Purchase, Rent/Lease, Off-Air Record. **Dist:** Home Vision Cinema.

Bernstein Conducts Beethoven: Program 9 1981
Beethoven's Symphony No. 9, "Ode to Joy," is presented, featuring the Vienna Concert Chorus. 90m; VHS, 3/4 U. **C:** Leonard Bernstein; Maximilian Schell. **Pr:** PBS. **A:** Jr. High-Adult. **P:** Entertainment. **U:** Institution, SURA. **Fin-Art:** Music--Performance, Music--Classical. **Acq:** Purchase, Rent/Lease, Off-Air Record. **Dist:** Home Vision Cinema.

Bernstein Conducts Beethoven: Program 10 1981
After a discussion of Beethoven's final days, Bernstein leads the string section of the Vienna Philharmonic in an orchestrated version of the String Quartet in C-Sharp Minor. 60m; VHS, 3/4 U. **C:** Leonard Bernstein; Maximilian Schell. **Pr:** PBS. **A:** Jr. High-Adult. **P:** Entertainment. **U:** Institution, SURA. **Fin-Art:** Music--Performance, Music--Classical. **Acq:** Purchase, Rent/Lease, Off-Air Record. **Dist:** Home Vision Cinema.

Bernstein In Berlin: Ode to Freedom,
Beethoven's Symphony No. 9 1990
The historic celebration of the fall of the Berlin Wall as led by the late conductor has been captured on video. 92m; VHS. **A:** Jr. High-Family. **P:** Entertainment. **U:** Home. **Fin-Art:** Music--Performance, Music--Classical. **Acq:** Purchase. **Dist:** Music Video Distributors. $24.95.

Bernstein on Beethoven: A Celebration in
Vienna 1970
Special tribute written, narrated, performed, and conducted by Leonard Bernstein in honor of the 200th birthday of Beethoven. Features Placido Domingo, Shirley Verrett, Gwyneth Jones, and others. 90m; VHS. **A:** Jr. High-Adult. **P:** Entertainment. **U:** Home. **Fin-Art:** Performing Arts, Music--Performance, Music--Classical. **Acq:** Purchase. **Dist:** Kultur International Films Ltd., Inc. $19.95.

Bernstein on Beethoven: A Tribute 1971
Conductor-pianist Leonard Bernstein tells of the life of Ludwig Von Beethoven and plays sections from his Piano Concerto No. 1 in C Major. 14m; VHS, 3/4 U. **C:** Leonard Bernstein. **Pr:** CBS; Amberson Productions. **A:** Jr. High-Sr. High. **P:** Entertainment. **U:** Institution, SURA. **Fin-Art:** Music--Performance, Music--Classical. **Acq:** Purchase. **Dist:** Phoenix Learning Group.

Bernstein on Beethoven: Fidelio 1971
Leonard Bernstein directs, coaches, and conducts the Vienna State Opera Company in Beethoven's only opera, "Fidelio." 43m; VHS, 3/4 U. **C:** Leonard Bernstein. **Pr:** CBS; Amberson Productions. **A:** Jr. High-Sr. High. **P:** Entertainment. **U:** Institution, SURA. **Fin-Art:** Music--Performance, Music--Classical. **Acq:** Purchase. **Dist:** Phoenix Learning Group.

Bernstein on Beethoven: Ode to Joy 1971
The Ode to Joy from Beethoven's Ninth Symphony is presented by the Vienna State Opera Chorus and Vienna Philharmonic conducted by Leonard Bernstein. 27m; VHS, 3/4 U. **C:** Leonard Bernstein. **Pr:** CBS; Amberson Productions. **A:** Jr. High-Sr. High. **P:** Entertainment. **U:** Institution, SURA. **Fin-Art:** Music--Performance, Music--Classical. **Acq:** Purchase. **Dist:** Phoenix Learning Group.

Bernstein: West Side Story 198?
Master conductor Leonard Bernstein leads Kanawa, Carreras, Troyanos and Ollman through the music of the modern opera. 89m; VHS. **C:** Conducted by Leonard Bernstein. **Pr:** British Broadcasting Corporation. **A:** Sr. High-Adult. **P:** Entertainment. **U:** Home. **Fin-Art:** Music--Performance, Opera. **Acq:** Purchase. **Dist:** Music Video Distributors. $24.95.

Berserk! 1967 (Unrated) — ★½
A seedy traveling circus is beset by a series of murders. Not heralded as one of Crawford's best pieces. 95m; VHS, DVD, Streaming. **C:** Joan Crawford; Diana Dors; Judy Geeson; Ty

Hardin; Directed by James O'Connolly. **Pr:** Herman Cohen. **A:** Jr. High-Adult. **P:** Entertainment. **U:** Home. **Mov-Ent:** Mystery & Suspense, Circuses. **Acq:** Purchase. **Dist:** Sony Pictures Home Entertainment Inc. $19.95.

Berserk: The Golden Age Arc 1--The Egg of the
King 2012 (Unrated)
The latest animated adventures of Guts, a mercenary in a feudal fantasy world haunted by past emotional scars. 77m; DVD, Blu-Ray, Streaming. **A:** Sr. High-Adult. **P:** Entertainment. **U:** Home. **L:** English, Japanese. **Gen-Edu:** Anime, Fantasy. **Acq:** Purchase, Rent/Lease. **Dist:** Viz Media L.L.C. $24.98 19.98 14.99.

Berserk - Volume 1: War Cry 1997
Presents the animated television series set in medieval times as Guts, also known as the Black Swordsman, comes to the town of Midland and fights the new evil king with the help of Griffith and his "Band of the Hawk"; includes episodes 1-5. 125m; DVD. **A:** Jr. High-Adult. **P:** Entertainment. **U:** Home. **Mov-Ent:** Television Series, Animation & Cartoons, Anime. **Acq:** Purchase. **Dist:** Movies Unlimited. $29.95.

Berserk - Volume 2: Immortal Soldier 1997
Presents the animated television series set in medieval times as Guts, also known as the Black Swordsman, comes to the town of Midland and fights the new evil king with the help of Griffith and his "Band of the Hawk"; includes episodes 6-9. 100m; DVD. **A:** Jr. High-Adult. **P:** Entertainment. **U:** Home. **Mov-Ent:** Television Series, Animation & Cartoons, Anime. **Acq:** Purchase. **Dist:** Movies Unlimited. $29.95.

Berserk - Volume 3: White Hawk 1997
Presents the animated television series set in medieval times as Guts, also known as the Black Swordsman, comes to the town of Midland and fights the new evil king with the help of Griffith and his "Band of the Hawk"; includes episodes 10-14. 100m; DVD. **A:** Jr. High-Adult. **P:** Entertainment. **U:** Home. **Mov-Ent:** Television Series, Animation & Cartoons, Anime. **Acq:** Purchase. **Dist:** Movies Unlimited. $29.95.

Berserk - Volume 4: Devil's Advocate 1997
Presents the animated television series set in medieval times as Guts, also known as the Black Swordsman, comes to the town of Midland and fights the new evil king with the help of Griffith and his "Band of the Hawk"; includes episodes 15-19. 100m; DVD. **A:** Jr. High-Adult. **P:** Entertainment. **U:** Home. **Mov-Ent:** Television Series, Animation & Cartoons, Anime. **Acq:** Purchase. **Dist:** Movies Unlimited. $29.95.

Berserk - Volume 5: Requited Desires 1997
Presents the animated television series set in medieval times as Guts, also known as the Black Swordsman, comes to the town of Midland and fights the new evil king with the help of Griffith and his "Band of the Hawk"; includes episodes 20-24. 4 episodes. 100m; DVD. **A:** Jr. High-Adult. **P:** Entertainment. **U:** Home. **Mov-Ent:** Television Series, Animation & Cartoons, Anime. **Acq:** Purchase. **Dist:** Movies Unlimited. $29.95.

Berserk - Volume 6: God's Hand 1997
Presents the animated television series set in medieval times as Guts, also known as the Black Swordsman, comes to the town of Midland and fights the new evil king with the help of Griffith and his "Band of the Hawk"; includes episodes 25-29. 4 episodes. 100m; DVD. **A:** Jr. High-Adult. **P:** Entertainment. **U:** Home. **Mov-Ent:** Television Series, Animation & Cartoons, Anime. **Acq:** Purchase. **Dist:** Movies Unlimited. $29.95.

Berserker 1987 (R) — ★
Six camping college students are attacked by a bloodthirsty psychotic out of a Nordic myth, who takes the shape of a badder-than-the-average bear. 85m; VHS. **C:** Joseph Alan Johnson; Valerie Sheldon; Greg Dawson; Directed by Jefferson (Jeff) Richard. **Pr:** American Video Group. **A:** Sr. High-Adult. **P:** Entertainment. **U:** Home. **Mov-Ent:** Horror, Bears, Adolescence. **Acq:** Purchase. **Dist:** No Longer Available.

Bert Rigby, You're a Fool 1989 (R) — ★★½
A starstruck British coal miner finds his way to Hollywood singing old showtunes, only to be rebuffed by a cynical industry. Available with Spanish subtitles. 94m; VHS, DVD, CC. **C:** Robert Lindsay; Robbie Coltrane; Jackie Gayle; Bruno Kirby; Cathryn Bradshaw; Corbin Bernsen; Anne Bancroft; Directed by Carl Reiner; Written by Carl Reiner; Cinematography by Jan De Bont; Music by Ralph Burns. **Pr:** Clear Productions; Lorimar Productions. **A:** Sr. High-Adult. **P:** Entertainment. **U:** Home. **L:** Spanish. **Mov-Ent:** Musical, Dance. **Acq:** Purchase. **Dist:** WarnerArchive.com; Music Video Distributors. $14.95.

Bert Stern: Original Mad Man 2012
A biographical portrait of Bert Stern, an iconic American photographer best known for his classic advertising work and celebrity portraits. 89m; DVD. **A:** Jr. High-Adult. **P:** Entertainment. **U:** Home. **Mov-Ent:** Biography, Artists, Photography, Advertising. **Acq:** Purchase. **Dist:** First Run Features. $27.95.

Bertagna Goaltending Series: Fundamentals of
Goaltending 2002 (Unrated)
Coach Joe Bertagna lectures on the basics required to be a successful goaltender in ice hockey. 57m; DVD. **A:** Family. **P:** Education. **U:** Home, Institution. **Spo-Rec:** Hockey, Athletic Instruction/Coaching. **Acq:** Purchase. **Dist:** Championship Productions. $29.99.

Bertagna Goaltending Series: On-Ice Drills for
Goaltenders 2002 (Unrated)
Coach Joe Bertagna presents drills for goaltenders designed to simulate a live hockey game. 47m; DVD. **A:** Family. **P:** Education. **U:** Home, Institution. **Spo-Rec:** Hockey, Athletic Instruction/Coaching. **Acq:** Purchase. **Dist:** Championship Productions. $29.99.

Bertagna Goaltending Series: The Advanced Goaltender 2002 (Unrated)
Coach Joe Bertagna details various situations that occur in hockey games, and how an experienced goaltender should react. 27m; DVD. **A:** Family. **P:** Education. **U:** Home, Institution. **Spo-Rec**: Hockey, Athletic Instruction/Coaching. **Acq:** Purchase. **Dist:** Championship Productions. $29.99.

Berthe 1989
Guy de Maupassant's story of a Parisian physician, Henri, who is determined to rehabilitate Berthe, a mentally and emotionally retarded young woman. Berthe's family succeeds in marrying her to a fortune hunter, but the consequences are disastrous for all. 52m; VHS, 3/4 U. **Pr:** Films for the Humanities and Sciences. **A:** College. **P:** Education. **U:** Institution, CCTV, CATV, BCTV. **L:** French. **Fin-Art**: Literature. **Acq:** Purchase, Rent/Lease, Duplication License. **Dist:** Films for the Humanities & Sciences.

Berti und Suleida 1991
The story of Berti, the elephant who first resents and then comes to love his little sister. In German only. 50m; VHS. **TV Std:** NTSC, PAL. **A:** Preschool-Primary. **P:** Entertainment. **U:** Home. **L:** German. **Chl-Juv**: Animation & Cartoons, Fantasy, Fairy Tales. **Acq:** Purchase, Rent/Lease. **Dist:** German Language Video Center. $29.95.

Bertolt Brecht 1989
A biographical portrait of Bertolt Brecht through his works. 55m; VHS, 3/4 U. **Pr:** Films for the Humanities and Sciences. **A:** College. **P:** Education. **U:** Institution, CCTV, CATV, BCTV. **Fin-Art**: Documentary Films, Biography, Theater. **Acq:** Purchase, Rent/Lease, Duplication License. **Dist:** Films for the Humanities & Sciences; University of Washington Educational Media Collection.

B.E.S. Bangla East Side 2004
Follows four Bangladeshi teenagers living in the Lower East Side of New York post 9/11 and how they deal with issues at home and in school as young immigrants. 45m; VHS. **A:** Adult. **P:** Education. **U:** Institution, BCTV. **Gen-Edu**: Documentary Films, Adolescence, Identity. **Acq:** Purchase, Rent/Lease. **Dist:** Third World Newsreel. $225.00.

Besame 1987 — ★★
Intrigue, espionage, and romance get mixed together in this movie. 101m; VHS. **C:** Sara Montiel; Maurice Ronet; Franco Fabrizi. **Pr:** Madera. **A:** Preschool. **P:** Entertainment. **U:** Home. **L:** Spanish. **Mov-Ent**: Romance, Mystery & Suspense. **Acq:** Purchase. **Dist:** Spanishmultimedia. $53.95.

Beshkempir the Adopted Son 1998 (Unrated) — ★★
In a rural community in the Central Asian nation of Kyrgyzstan, a young teen lives a carefree existence getting into mild mischief with his buddies. Until one day, during an argument, he suddenly discovers he was adopted, which throws his world (at least temporarily) into rebellious turmoil. Kyrgyzstani with subtitles. 81m/B/W; VHS, DVD, Wide. **C:** Mirlan Abdykalykov; Directed by Aktan Abdykalykov; Written by Aktan Abdykalykov; Avtandil Adikulov; Marat Sarulu; Cinematography by Khasan Kydyraliyev; Music by Nurlan Nishanov. **A:** College-Adult. **P:** Entertainment. **U:** Home. **Mov-Ent**: Adoption. **Acq:** Purchase. **Dist:** Wellspring Media.

Beside Still Waters, Vol. 1 1993
Video tour of the landscapes of the world with music by Don Marsh and his orhcestra, accompanied by woodwind soloist Jon Clarke. 30m; VHS. **Pr:** Ben Ryan Films. **A:** Family. **P:** Religious. **U:** Home. **Mov-Ent. Acq:** Purchase. **Dist:** Brentwood Music/Provident Music Group. $19.95.
Songs: When Morning Gilds the Skies; Like a River Glorious; Our Great Saviour; Rock of Ages; Saviour, Like a Shepherd Lead Us; Jesus Is All the World to Me; Jesus Loves Me.

Beside Still Waters, Vol. 2 1993
The splendor of natural beauty and glorious hymnal praise complement each other to form an inspirational video. 30m; VHS. **A:** Family. **P:** Religious. **U:** Home. **Mov-Ent. Acq:** Purchase. **Dist:** Brentwood Music/Provident Music Group. $19.95.
Songs: How Great Thou Art; What a Friend We Have in Jesus Medley; Sweet Hour of Prayer; I Must Tell Jesus; I'd Rather Have Jesus; Great Is Thy Faithfulness; There Is a Balm in Gilead Medley; Amazing Grace; He Lifted Me; Blessed Assurance Medley; To God Be the Glory; O, How I Love Jesus Medley; Tis So Sweet To Trust in Jesus; Just a Closer Walk With Thee; Victory in Jesus; How Firm a Foundation Medley; My Faith Has Found a Resting Place; Haven of Rest; Moment By Moment; Day By Day; God Will Take Care of You.

Besieged 1998 (R) — ★★½
Fans of Bertolucci will enjoy this airy quasi-love story, but the slow pace and meandering plot will frustrate other viewers. Shandurai (Newton) moves to Rome after her husband becomes a political prisoner in Kenya. In order to put herself through medical school, she takes a job as a maid for an eccentric British musician (Thewlis). He begins to fall for his beautiful housekeeper, but she ignores his advances. To prove his love, he begins selling off his personal belongings so he can bribe officials to release her husband. 94m; VHS, DVD, CC. **C:** David Thewlis; Thandie Newton; Claudio Santamaria; Directed by Bernardo Bertolucci; Written by Bernardo Bertolucci; Clare Peploe; Cinematography by Fabio Cianchetti; Music by Alessio Vlad. **Pr:** Fine Line Features. **A:** Sr. High-Adult. **P:** Entertainment. **U:** Home. **Mov-Ent**: Drama. **Acq:** Purchase. **Dist:** Warner Home Video, Inc.

Bessie Smith and Friends 1986
Three jazz shorts are presented on this tape: "St. Louis Blues" (1929), the only film appearance of blues singer Bessie Smith; "Bye Bye Blackbird" (1932), starring Nina Mae McKinney and the dancing Nicholas Brothers with Eubie Blake and His Orchestra; and "Boogie Woogie Dream" (1941), featuring a youthful Lena Horne, boogie woogie pianists Albert Ammons and Pete Johnson, and Teddy Wilson's Band. 39m/B/W; VHS. **C:** Bessie Smith; Eubie Blake; Nina Mae McKinney; Lena Horne; Teddy Wilson; Albert Ammons; Pete Johnson. **Pr:** The Vitaphone Corporation; Soundies Corporation. **A:** Family. **P:** Entertainment. **U:** Home. **Mov-Ent**: Music--Performance, Music--Jazz. **Acq:** Purchase. **Dist:** Music Video Distributors; African-American Images. $19.95.

The Best! 1989
A short inspirational video showing winning athletes, to get your employees into the winning attitude. 6m; VHS, 3/4 U, Special order formats. **Pr:** Dartnell. **A:** College-Adult. **P:** Education. **U:** Institution, Home. **Bus-Ind**: Business, Management, Sales Training. **Acq:** Purchase, Rent/Lease. **Dist:** Excellence in Training Corp. $275.00.

Best Boy 1979 — ★★★
The uplifting story of Philly, a 53-year-old retarded man, and his quest for independence. 104m; VHS, 8 mm. **C:** Directed by Ira Wohl. **Pr:** Ira Wohl. **A:** Family. **P:** Education. **U:** Institution, CCTV, Home, SURA. **Gen-Edu**: Documentary Films, Handicapped. **Awds:** Oscars '79: Feature Doc. **Acq:** Purchase. **Dist:** New Video Group Inc.; Tapeworm Video Distributors Inc. $29.95.

Best Breakfast 199?
Teaches viewers that people have different breakfast habits, but everyone should eat a good breakfast. 22m; VHS, CC. **A:** Jr. High-Adult. **P:** Education. **U:** Institution. **Gen-Edu**: Nutrition, Food Industry. **Acq:** Purchase. **Dist:** The Learning Seed. $89.00.

The Best Breakfast 1988
Viewers are taught how to make sure that their first meal of the day fulfills their nutrition requirements. 45m; VHS. **Pr:** Cambridge Career Productions. **A:** Jr. High-Adult. **P:** Education. **U:** Institution, Home. **Hea-Sci**: Nutrition. **Acq:** Purchase. **Dist:** Cambridge Educational. $79.00.

Best Buns on the Beach 1987 — **Bomb!**
Sexploitation movie about 10 beautiful girls in a bikini contest, that ends up with them going topless. Ridiculous plot, for mature (??) audiences. 60m; VHS. **A:** Sr. High-Adult. **P:** Entertainment. **U:** Home. **Mov-Ent. Acq:** Purchase. **Dist:** Image Entertainment Inc. $29.95.

The Best Campaign Commercials Ever 1993
Landmark political commercials, including Nixon's "Checkers" speech, Hubert Humphrey's "Agnew for VP?" commcercial and Lyndon Johnson's "Bomb" spot. 60m; VHS. **A:** Adult. **P:** Education. **U:** Institution, Home. **Gen-Edu**: Commercials, Politics & Government. **Acq:** Purchase. **Dist:** Baker and Taylor. $90.00.

The Best Campaign Commercials of 1984 1984
Senatorial, congressional, and presidential campaign commercials from Gary Hart, Ronald Reagan, Geraldine Ferraro, John Glenn, Mitch McConnell, Phil Gramm, Gordon Humphrey, and Tim Wirth. 60m; VHS. **A:** Adult. **P:** Education. **U:** Institution, Home. **Gen-Edu**: Commercials, Politics & Government. **Acq:** Purchase. **Dist:** Baker and Taylor. $90.00.

The Best Campaign Commercials of 1986 1986
Local and national campaigns featuring Bill Cobey, Fred Eckert, Richard Stallings, Bobby Scott, Tom Kean, Alan Cranston, Brock Adams, and Dan Quayle. 60m; VHS. **A:** Adult. **P:** Education. **U:** Institution, Home. **Gen-Edu**: Commercials, Politics & Government. **Acq:** Purchase. **Dist:** Baker and Taylor. $90.00.

The Best Campaign Commercials of 1988: Non-Presidential 1988
Spots from state and national campaigns featuring Pete Dawkins, Jack Danforth, Dave Durenberger, Pete Wilson, Tret Lott, Betty Hearns, Bill Clements, and Leo McCarthy. 60m; VHS. **A:** Adult. **P:** Education. **U:** Institution, Home. **Gen-Edu**: Commercials, Politics & Government. **Acq:** Purchase. **Dist:** Baker and Taylor. $90.00.

The Best Campaign Commercials of 1988: Presidential Primaries 1988
The men who would-be president, including Alexander Haig, Pete DuPont, Michael Dukakis, Paul Simon, Bruce Babbitt, Jesse Jackson, Bob Dole, Al Gore, Jack Kemp, and George Bush. 60m; VHS. **A:** Adult. **P:** Education. **U:** Institution, Home. **Gen-Edu**: Commercials, Politics & Government, Presidency. **Acq:** Purchase. **Dist:** Baker and Taylor. $90.00.

The Best Campaign Commercials of 1988: Presidential Race 1988
Campaigns from Dukakis and Bush as well as the "Get Out the Vote" spots. 60m; VHS. **A:** Adult. **P:** Education. **U:** Institution, Home. **Gen-Edu**: Commercials, Politics & Government, Presidency. **Acq:** Purchase. **Dist:** Baker and Taylor. $90.00.

The Best Campaign Commercials of 1990 1990
Candidates represented in these commercials include Dianne Feinstein, Lynn Martin, John Kerry, Neil Hartigan, Paul Simon, Jesse Helms, and Ann Richards. 60m; VHS. **A:** Adult. **P:** Education. **U:** Institution, Home. **Gen-Edu**: Commercials, Politics & Government. **Acq:** Purchase. **Dist:** Baker and Taylor. $90.00.

The Best Campaign Commercials of 1992: General Election 1992
The most notable political commericals from George Bush, Bill Clinton, and Ross Perot. 60m; VHS. **A:** Adult. **P:** Education. **U:** Institution, Home. **Gen-Edu**: Commercials, Politics & Government, Presidency. **Acq:** Purchase. **Dist:** Baker and Taylor. $90.00.

The Best Campaign Commercials of 1992: Presidential Primaries 1992
Commericals from presidential candidates Bob Kerry, Tom Harkin, Paul Tsongas, Jerry Brown, Bill Clinton, Pat Buchanan, and George Bush. 60m; VHS. **A:** Adult. **P:** Education. **U:** Institution, Home. **Gen-Edu**: Commercials, Politics & Government, Presidency. **Acq:** Purchase. **Dist:** Baker and Taylor. $90.00.

The Best Christmas Pageant Ever 1986
The meanest kids in town just decided to participate in the town's Christmas pageant and something special happens when the curtain finally goes up. 60m; VHS. **C:** Dennis Weaver; Karen Grassle. **A:** Primary-Adult. **P:** Entertainment. **U:** Home. **Mov-Ent**: Family Viewing, Family, Christmas. **Acq:** Purchase. **Dist:** Television Representatives, Inc. $19.95.

The Best Damn Fiddler From Calabogie to Kaladar 1987
The story of a man who chooses the financially unrewarding life of a bush worker, and the effects this has on his family. 49m; VHS, 3/4 U. **C:** Margot Kidder. **Pr:** Barrie Howells. **A:** Jr. High-Adult. **P:** Education. **U:** Institution, SURA. **Gen-Edu**: Family. **Acq:** Purchase, Rent/Lease. **Dist:** National Film Board of Canada.

Best Defense 198?
Shows drivers the primary causes of accidents and how to avoid them. 15m; VHS, 3/4 U. **Pr:** National Safety Council. **A:** College-Adult. **P:** Education. **U:** Institution. **Gen-Edu**: Driver Education. **Acq:** Rent/Lease. **Dist:** National Safety Council, California Chapter, Film Library.

Best Defense 1984 (R) — ★
A U.S. Army tank operator is sent to Kuwait to test a new state-of-the-art tank in a combat situation. Although the cast is popular, the movie as a whole is not funny and the story frequently is hard to follow. 94m; VHS, DVD, CC. **C:** Dudley Moore; Eddie Murphy; Kate Capshaw; George Dzundza; Helen Shaver; Directed by Willard Huyck; Written by Willard Huyck; Gloria Katz. **Pr:** Gloria Katz; Paramount Pictures. **A:** Sr. High-Adult. **P:** Entertainment. **U:** Home. **Mov-Ent**: Technology. **Acq:** Purchase. **Dist:** Paramount Pictures Corp. $14.95.

The Best Defense: How to Prevent Shoplifting 19??
A training program on detecting and preventing shoplifting. Workshop materials are available. 22m; VHS, 3/4 U, Special order formats. **Pr:** Excellence in Training Corporation. **A:** College-Adult. **P:** Instruction. **U:** Institution. **Bus-Ind**: How-To, Business, Office Practice. **Acq:** Purchase, Rent/Lease. **Dist:** Excellence in Training Corp. $550.00.

The Best Downhill Racer in the World 1982
This program captures the tension and anxiety of the skiers as they suffered through the slump that allowed the Australian Harti Weirather to win the World Cup downhill racing crown. 51m; VHS, 3/4 U. **Pr:** Lauron Productions Ltd. **A:** Family. **P:** Entertainment. **U:** Institution, CCTV, CATV. **Spo-Rec**: Sports--General, Sports--Winter. **Acq:** Purchase, Rent/Lease, Off-Air Record. **Dist:** PBS Home Video.

The Best Drill in Lacrosse: 4 v. 4 2009 (Unrated)
Coach Tony Seaman demonstrates the 4 v 4 drill, which he considers to be the best practice drill used in lacrosse. 42m; DVD. **A:** Family. **P:** Education. **U:** Home, Institution. **Spo-Rec**: Lacrosse, Athletic Instruction/Coaching. **Acq:** Purchase. **Dist:** Championship Productions. $39.99.

Best Enemies 1986 (Unrated) — ★½
An English film about a man suffering the trials of the 1960s, including Vietnam, and how it affects his relationships with his friends and wife. 96m; VHS. **C:** Sigrid Thornton; Paul Williams; Judy Morris; Brandon Burke; Directed by David Baker. **Pr:** Gilda Barrachi. **A:** Jr. High-Adult. **P:** Entertainment. **U:** Home. **Mov-Ent**: Marriage, Flowers. **Acq:** Purchase. **Dist:** No Longer Available.

Best Evidence: The Research Video 1989
The tale of JFK's assassination is raked yet again, this time to fit a theory that a secret government conspiracy altered the body's wounds to foul the autopsy. 30m; VHS. **Pr:** RHI Entertainment Inc. **A:** Adult. **P:** Education. **U:** Home. **Gen-Edu**: History--U.S., Presidency. **Acq:** Purchase. **Dist:** Rhino Entertainment Co. $14.95.

The Best Exotic Marigold Hotel 2012 (PG-13) — ★★★
Charmingly old-fashioned comedy-drama held together by a group of old pros and an--yes--exotic setting. Seven British retirees, in various financial and romantic circumstances, are enticed by advertisements for the restored Marigold Hotel and decide to move to less-expensive India. Only they find the former palace isn't quite what they were promised by its eager young owner Sonny. As they struggle to find their footing in a foreign land, they learn that change is still possible. Based on Deborah Moggach's novel "These Foolish Things." 124m; DVD, Blu-Ray. **C:** Judi Dench; Maggie Smith; Bill Nighy; Penelope Wilton; Tom Wilkinson; Celia Imrie; Ronald Pickup; Dev Patel; Tena Desae; Directed by John Madden; Written by Ol Parker; Cinematography by Ben Davis; Music by Thomas Newman. **Pr:** Graham Broadbent; Peter Czernin; Participant Media; Fox Searchlight; Blueprint Pictures. **A:** Sr. High-Adult. **P:** Entertainment. **U:** Home. **L:** English. **Mov-Ent**: Comedy-Drama, Aging, Hotels & Hotel Staff Training. **Acq:** Purchase. **Dist:** Fox Home Entertainment.

Best Foot Forward 1943 (Unrated) — ★★½
Vintage musical about a movie star who agrees to accompany a young cadet to a military ball. Based on the popular Broadway show. The film debuts of Walker, Allyson, and DeHaven. 95m; VHS, DVD. **C:** Lucille Ball; June Allyson; Tommy Dix; Nancy Walker; Virginia Weidler; Gloria De Haven; William Gaxton; Harry James; Directed by Edward Buzzell; Written by Irving Brecher; Music by George Bassman. **Pr:** MGM; Loew's, Inc. **A:** Family. **P:** Entertainment. **U:** Home. **Mov-Ent:** Musical, Romance. **Acq:** Purchase. **Dist:** MGM Home Entertainment. $19.98.
Songs: Buckle Down, Winsocki; The Three B's (Barrelhouse, Boogie Woogie, and the Blues); Alive and Kicking; Two O'Clock Jump; Ev'ry Time; Three Men on a Date; Wish I May; Shady Lady; My First Promise; You're Lucky.

Best Foot Forward: A Manners Video 1992
Manners are stressed as a very important part of growing up, not just for their own sake but because they help people get along with each other. Includes vignettes of proper and improper behavior. Comes with catalog kit. 25m; VHS. **A:** Primary-Jr. High. **P:** Education. **U:** Institution. **Gen-Edu:** Etiquette, Children. **Acq:** Purchase. **Dist:** Sunburst Digital Inc. $169.00.

The Best Foreign Spots 19??
Political campaigns on foreign shores are featured in these commercials, including Great Britain's Margaret Thatcher. 60m; VHS. **A:** Adult. **P:** Education. **U:** Institution, Home. **Gen-Edu:** Commercials, Politics & Government. **Acq:** Purchase. **Dist:** Baker and Taylor. $90.00.

Best Friends 1970
Some of the reasons young people start smoking are considered in this program, and the effects of smoking on the human body are graphically illustrated. 6m; 3/4 U, Special order formats. **Pr:** National Film Board of Canada. **A:** Jr. High-Adult. **P:** Education. **U:** Institution, Home, SURA. **Hea-Sci:** Smoking, Adolescence, Health Education. **Acq:** Purchase, Rent/Lease, Trade-in, Duplication License. **Dist:** United Learning Inc.

Best Friends 1975 (Unrated) — ★
Strange psycho-drama with a lot of odd undertones, a tragedy, and an unsatisfying fade-out ending. Jess and fiancee Kathy get his best childhood friend Pat and Pat's girlfriend Jo Ella to join them in their Winnebago on a cross-country road trip. Pat gets increasingly weirded-out about losing his best bud to marriage and turns aggressive and violent to break them up. 83m; DVD. **C:** Richard Hatch; Doug Chapin; Susanne Benton; Ann Noland; Directed by Noel Nosseck; Written by Arnold Somkin; Cinematography by Stephen M. Katz; Music by Richard Cunha. **A:** Sr. High-Adult. **P:** Entertainment. **U:** Home. **Mov-Ent. Acq:** Purchase. **Dist:** Mill Creek Entertainment L.L.C.

Best Friends 1982 (PG) — ★★
A pair of screenwriters decide to marry after years of living and working together. Story based on the lives of screenwriters Barry Levinson and Valerie Curtin. 109m; VHS, DVD. **C:** Goldie Hawn; Burt Reynolds; Jessica Tandy; Barnard Hughes; Audra Lindley; Keenan Wynn; Ron Silver; Directed by Norman Jewison; Written by Valerie Curtin; Barry Levinson; Cinematography by Jordan Cronenweth. **A:** Jr. High-Adult. **P:** Entertainment. **U:** Home. **Mov-Ent:** Marriage. **Acq:** Purchase. **Dist:** Warner Home Video, Inc. $14.95.

Best Friends 1983
A tape series for kids about all different kinds of pets! Teaches children how to handle, care for, and be responsible for the varying needs of pets. Part 1 deals with mice, dogs, turtles, rabbits, and frogs. Part 2 discusses fish, cats, guinea pigs, ponies, and birds. Fun for kids with or without pets. 25m; VHS. **Pr:** Marble Arch Productions. **A:** Family. **P:** Entertainment. **U:** Home. **Chl-Juv:** Children, Pets, Animals. **Acq:** Purchase. **Dist:** Interama, Inc.
Indiv. Titles: 1. Best Friends, Part 1 2. Best Friends, Part 2.

Best Friends 1992
Looks at the Helping Hands program with the Lexington/Bluegrass Alzheimer's Association—a day care program where Alzheimer's patients receive one-on-one care from volunteers. 14m; VHS, 3/4 U, Special order formats. **A:** Adult. **P:** Education. **U:** Institution. **Hea-Sci:** Aging, Voluntary Services. **Acq:** Purchase, Rent/Lease. **Dist:** Terra Nova Films. $95.00.

Best Friends 2005 (Unrated) — ★★
In this Lifetime cable thriller, Beth (Gallagher) doesn't realize that her longtime friend Claudia (Mink) is the source of all the sudden troubles she's having. Claudia has gone crazy, killed her own husband, and is using the secrets Beth has confided over the years to permanently get Beth out of the way so Claudia can take over her life. 90m; DVD. **C:** Megan Gallagher; Claudette Mink; Barclay Hope; Liam Ranger; Brittney Wilson; Nels Lennarson; Graham Kosakoski; Directed by Michael Scott; Written by Donna Radik; Cinematography by Adam Sliwinski; Music by Terry Frewer. **A:** Jr. High-Adult. **P:** Entertainment. **U:** Home. **L:** English. **Mov-Ent:** TV Movies. **Acq:** Purchase. **Dist:** A&E Television Networks L.L.C.

Best Horse 1979
Wendy, determined to ride her horse in an upcoming rodeo, collides head on with her mother who is determined that she find some "better" life. Their conflict teaches them not to impose their values on others and that things do not always go as planned. Based on the book by Elizabeth Van Steenwyk. 28m; VHS, 3/4 U. **Pr:** Scholastic Magazine. **A:** Primary-Adult. **P:** Entertainment. **U:** Institution, SURA. **Chl-Juv:** Human Relations. **Acq:** Purchase, Rent/Lease. **Dist:** Phoenix Learning Group.

Best in Football 1985
England's top player instructs the young in the nuances of soccer. Series available separately. 37m; VHS. **Pr:** Ormandy International. **A:** Jr. High-College. **P:** Instruction. **U:** Institution, Home, SURA. **Spo-Rec:** Sports--General, Soccer, Great Britain. **Acq:** Purchase. **Dist:** Reedswain Inc.
Indiv. Titles: 1. Accuracy in Passing 2. Handling the Ball 3. Control with the Chest 4. Tackling and Shooting 5. Goalkeeping and Defending.

Best in Show 2000 (PG-13) — ★★★
Director Christopher Guest follows the successful "Waiting for Guffman" with another faux-documentary mixing improvisation and unique characters. This time, the subject is the snooty world of show dogs and the freaky, neurotic pooch-owners hoping to claim its greatest prize: Best in Show at the Mayflower Kennel Club Dog Show. The quirky dog-lovers include Meg (Posey) and Hamilton (Hitchcock), whose kinky sex life is giving their Weimaraner angst; doting gay Shih-Tzu owners Scott (Higgins) and Stefan (McKean); and seemingly tame suburbanites Gerry (Levy) and Cookie (O'Hara). Fred Willard steals the spotlight as Buck Laughlin, a sports announcer who has no knowledge of the event he's broadcasting. Worth a rental just for the bizarre one-liners fired off by the clueless commentator on such subjects as the dogs' anatomy and edibility. 89m; VHS, DVD, Blu-Ray, Wide. **C:** Christopher Guest; Michael McKean; Parker Posey; Eugene Levy; Catherine O'Hara; Fred Willard; Michael Hitchcock; John Michael Higgins; Jennifer Coolidge; Trevor Beckwith; Bob Balaban; Ed Begley, Jr.; Patrick Cranshaw; Don Lake; Larry Miller; Directed by Christopher Guest; Written by Christopher Guest; Eugene Levy; Cinematography by Roberto Schaefer; Music by C.J. Vanston. **A:** Sr. High-Adult. **P:** Entertainment. **U:** Home. **Mov-Ent:** Satire & Parody, Pets. **Acq:** Purchase. **Dist:** Warner Home Video, Inc.

The Best Intentions 1992 (Unrated) — ★★★½
Ingmar Bergman wrote the screenplay chronicling the early years of the stormy relationship of his parents. Set in Sweden at the turn of the century, the film focuses on the class differences that divide his mother and father, while portrayal of little Bergy is limited to a bundle under his mother's maternity dress. Inspired performances and directing illuminates the emotionally complex relationship, revealing truths about the universal human condition along the way. Six-hour version was shot for TV in Europe and Japan. Director August and actress August met and married during filming. In Swedish with English subtitles. 182m; VHS, DVD. **C:** Samuel Froler; Pernilla August; Max von Sydow; Ghita Norby; Mona Malm; Lena Endre; Bjorn Kjellman; Directed by Bille August; Written by Ingmar Bergman; Cinematography by Jorgen Persson; Music by Stefan Nilsson. **A:** College-Adult. **P:** Entertainment. **U:** Home. **L:** Swedish. **Mov-Ent:** Drama, Marriage, Biography. **Awds:** Cannes '92: Actress (August), Film. **Acq:** Purchase. **Dist:** Amazon.com Inc.; Facets Multimedia Inc. $89.98.

Best Kept Secret 1984
For parents, this tape shows how to watch for the signs indicative of child abuse or mistreatment. 15m; VHS, 3/4 U. **Pr:** ABC 20/20. **A:** Adult. **P:** Education. **U:** Institution. **Gen-Edu:** Parenting, Child Abuse. **Acq:** Purchase, Rent/Lease. **Dist:** Phoenix Learning Group.

Best Kept Secrets 1988 — ★★½
A feisty woman discovers corruption and blackmail in the police department where her husband is an officer. 104m; VHS. **C:** Patty Duke; Frederic Forrest; Peter Coyote; Directed by Jerrold Freedman. **Pr:** Vidmark Entertainment. **A:** Jr. High-Adult. **P:** Entertainment. **U:** Home. **Mov-Ent. Acq:** Purchase. **Dist:** CinemaNow Inc. $79.95.

Best Laid Plans 197?
A man wants his son to be a gold medal swimming champion while the son wishes to be a medical missionary. Eventually they have a confrontation. 28m; VHS, 3/4 U. **A:** Jr. High-Adult. **P:** Religious. **U:** Institution, SURA. **Gen-Edu:** Religion. **Acq:** Purchase, Rent/Lease. **Dist:** Faith for Today.

Best Laid Plans 1999 (R) — ★★
Another contemporary noir where no one and nothing is as it seems (except the overly familiar plot). Nick (Nivola) and his bud, Bryce (Brolin), are bar hopping when Bryce picks up Lissa (Witherspoon). Later, a frantic Bryce calls Nick saying Lissa is underage and accusing him of rape. Nick offers to talk to Lissa and the story flashes back to the beginnings of an elaborate scam leading all concerned to a number of ill-considered decisions. 90m; VHS, DVD, DVD, CC. **C:** Alessandro Nivola; Josh Brolin; Reese Witherspoon; Rocky Carroll; Michael G. (Mike) Hagerty; Jamie Marsh; Directed by Mike Barker; Written by Ted Griffin; Cinematography by Ben Seresin; Music by Craig Armstrong. **Pr:** Alan Greenspan; Betsey Beers; Chris Moore; Mike Newell; Fox 2000 Pictures; 20th Century-Fox. **A:** Sr. High-Adult. **P:** Entertainment. **U:** Home. **Mov-Ent:** Crime Drama. **Acq:** Purchase. **Dist:** Fox Home Entertainment.

The Best Little Girl in the World 1981 (Unrated) — ★★★
Exceptional made-for-TV tale of an apparently perfect teenager (Leigh) suffering from anorexia. Slow starvation is her only cry for help. Fine performances from Durning and Saint. Look for Helen Hunt and Ally Sheedy as classmates. 96m; VHS. **C:** Charles Durning; Eva Marie Saint; Jennifer Jason Leigh; Melanie Mayron; Viveca Lindfors; Jason Miller; David Spielberg; Lisa Pelikan; Ally Sheedy; Helen Hunt; Directed by Sam O'Steen; Music by Billy Goldenberg. **Pr:** Aaron Spelling. **A:** Jr. High-Adult. **P:** Entertainment. **U:** Home. **Mov-Ent:** Diseases, TV Movies, Adolescence. **Acq:** Purchase. **Dist:** Amazon.com Inc.

The Best Little Whorehouse in Texas 1982 (R) — ★★
Parton is the buxom owner of The Chicken Ranch, a house of ill-repute that may be closed down unless Sheriff-boyfriend Reynolds can think of a way out. Strong performances don't quite make up for the erratically comic script. Based on the long-running Broadway musical, in turn based on a story by Larry McMurtry. 115m; VHS, DVD, Wide. **C:** Dolly Parton; Burt Reynolds; Dom DeLuise; Charles Durning; Jim Nabors; Lois Nettleton; Directed by Colin Higgins; Written by Colin Higgins; Peter Masterson; Larry L. King; Cinematography by William A. Fraker; Music by Carol Hall. **Pr:** Mark Huffam. **A:** Sr. High-Adult. **P:** Entertainment. **U:** Home. **Mov-Ent:** Musical, Sex & Sexuality, Prostitution. **Acq:** Purchase. **Dist:** Facets Multimedia Inc. $14.98.

The Best Man 1964 — ★★★½
An incisive, darkly satiric political tract, based on Gore Vidal's play, about two presidential contenders who vie for the endorsement of the aging ex-president, and trample political ethics in the process. 104m/B/W; VHS, DVD. **C:** Henry Fonda; Cliff Robertson; Lee Tracy; Margaret Leighton; Edie Adams; Kevin McCarthy; Ann Sothern; Gene Raymond; Shelley Berman; Mahalia Jackson; Directed by Franklin J. Schaffner; Written by Gore Vidal; Cinematography by Haskell Wexler. **Pr:** United Artists. **A:** Jr. High-Adult. **P:** Entertainment. **U:** Home. **Mov-Ent:** Presidency, Ethics & Morals, Satire & Parody. **Acq:** Purchase. **Dist:** MGM Home Entertainment. $19.98.

The Best Man 1997 (PG) — ★★½
It's 1899 in a small northern Italian town and beautiful Francesca (Sastre) must marry the lascivious older Edgardo Osti (Cantarelli) in order to solve her father's business problems. Francesca is revolted but does become smitten by the best man—Angelo (Abatantuono), who's returned from America, apparently with a fortune. Marriage or no, Francesca becomes obsessed with getting Angelo. Italian with subtitles. 99m; VHS, DVD, CC. **C:** Ines Sastre; Diego Abatantuono; Dario Cantarelli; Valeria (Valerie Dobson) D'Obici; Mario Erpichini; Directed by Pupi Avati; Written by Pupi Avati; Cinematography by Pasquale Rachini; Music by Riz Ortolani. **Pr:** Antonio Avati; Aurelio De Laurentiis; October Films. **A:** College-Adult. **P:** Entertainment. **U:** Home. **L:** Italian. **Mov-Ent:** Comedy--Romantic, Marriage. **Acq:** Purchase.

The Best Man 1999 (R) — ★★★
Writer/director Malcolm D. Lee, cousin of co-producer Spike Lee, makes an impressive debut in this ensemble piece that plays like a hipper "Big Chill." Novelist Harper (Diggs) heads to New York to attend the wedding of his best friend Lance (Chestnut) and the beautiful Mia (Calhoun). Unfortunately, his soon-to-be-released first novel is a thinly disguised autobiography which alludes to an affair between Harper and the bride-to-be. As other college buddies and old flames show up for the nuptials, past issues and romantic tensions come bubbling back up to the surface. The cast gives good performances across the board, with Howard as the wisecracking and womanizing Quentin standing out in particular. 120m; VHS, DVD, Blu-Ray, CC. **C:** Taye Diggs; Monica Calhoun; Morris Chestnut; Nia Long; Melissa De Sousa; Harold Perrineau, Jr.; Terrence Howard; Sanaa Lathan; Victoria Dillard; Directed by Malcolm Lee; Written by Malcolm Lee; Cinematography by Frank Prinzi; Music by Stanley Clarke. **Pr:** Spike Lee; Sam Kitt; 40 Acres and a Mule Filmworks; Universal Pictures. **A:** Sr. High-Adult. **P:** Entertainment. **U:** Home. **Mov-Ent:** Black Culture. **Acq:** Purchase. **Dist:** Movies Unlimited; Alpha Video.

Best Man Down 2012 (PG-13) — ★★
Scott and Kristin have their wedding in Phoenix, away from their cold hometown of Minneapolis. Scott's best man, hard-partying Lumpy, parties too hard and dies after the reception. So, despite Kristin's obvious frustration, the cash-strapped couple cancel their honeymoon to make funeral arrangements. They take Lumpy's body back home while discovering that Scott's oldest friend had some secrets that turn the pic down some unexpectedly serious plot paths. 89m; DVD, Blu-Ray. **C:** Justin Long; Jess Weixler; Tyler Labine; Addison Timlin; Shelley Long; Frances O'Connor; Evan Jones; Directed by Ted Koland; Written by Ted Koland; Cinematography by Seamus Tierney; Music by Mateo (Matt) Messina. **A:** Jr. High-Adult. **P:** Entertainment. **U:** Home. **L:** English. **Mov-Ent:** Marriage. **Acq:** Purchase. **Dist:** Magnolia Home Entertainment.

The Best Man Holiday 2013 (R) — ★★
Fifteen years after director Lee began his career with the African-American ensemble comedy "The Best Man," he reunites the cast in this unexpectedly decent sequel. It's a typical patchwork of subplots and misunderstandings that come with holiday movies featuring several couples in one story, but the notable star power allows one to forgive a lot of storytelling miscues. These people are simply likable, a trait too often missing in characters of modern comedy. 123m; DVD, Blu-Ray. **C:** Morris Chestnut; Taye Diggs; Regina Hall; Terrence Howard; Sanaa Lathan; Nia Long; Harold Perrineau, Jr.; Monica Calhoun; Melissa De Sousa; Eddie Cibrian; Directed by Malcolm Lee; Written by Malcolm Lee; Cinematography by Greg Gardiner; Music by Stanley Clarke. **Pr:** Malcolm Lee; Sean Daniel; Universal Pictures Inc. **A:** Sr. High-Adult. **P:** Entertainment. **U:** Home. **L:** English. **Mov-Ent:** Marriage, Comedy-Drama, Black Culture. **Acq:** Purchase. **Dist:** Universal Studios Home Video.

Best Men 1998 (R) — ★★½
There's a wedding, there's a would-be bank heist, and there's five men caught in the siege at the bank of Independence in this kooky crime comedy/drama. Jesse (Wilson) is heading straight from prison to his wedding to Hope (Barrymore) with his four tuxedo-clad buddies. Billy (Flanery) needs some cash before

the big event and persuades the boys to stop at the bank—only his withdrawal is the illegal kind. Soon Billy's dad (Ward), who happens to be the local sheriff, is trying to contain the situation when the feds show up as does the bewildered bride-to-be. 89m; VHS, DVD, Wide. **C:** Sean Patrick Flanery; Dean Cain; Luke Wilson; Andy Dick; Mitchell Whitfield; Drew Barrymore; Fred Ward; Raymond J. Barry; Brad Dourif; Art Edler Brown; Tracy Fraim; Directed by Tamra Davis; Written by Art Edler Brown; Tracy Fraim; Cinematography by James Glennon; Music by Mark Mothersbaugh. **Pr:** Brad Jenkel; Jeffrey D. Ivers; Brad Krevoy; Rank Film Distributors; Orion Pictures. **A:** Sr. High-Adult. **P:** Entertainment. **U:** Home. **Mov-Ent:** Comedy-Drama, Federal Bureau of Investigation (FBI). **Acq:** Purchase. **Dist:** MGM Studios Inc. ; MGM Home Entertainment.

The Best Mind Since Einstein 1993
Atomic bomb pioneer, Nobel prize-winning physicist, bongo player, acclaimed teacher, and all around eccentric, Richard Feynman is profiled in this BBC-produced documentary. 60m; VHS. **A:** Sr. High-Adult. **P:** Education. **U:** Home, Institution. **Hea-Sci:** Astronomy, Documentary Films. **Acq:** Purchase. **Dist:** Astronomical Society of the Pacific. $19.95.

Best Night Ever 2014 (R) — Bomb!
There are mediocre movies, bad movies, awful movies, and then there's directors/writers Friedberg and Seltzer's stab at "Hangover"-esque hilarity in its own sub-category of horrendous. Four fun-loving, female friends (Hall, Colburn, Ritchard, Flanagan) jet off to Las Vegas for a weekend bachelorette party and attempts at hilarious hi-jinks ensue. This is straight-to-video nonsense of the worst variety with performances that are flat, at best, when they're not half-asleep. The attempts at outrageous behavior only end up as embarrassing as the film sinks deeper and deeper into frat-boy humor. 90m; DVD, Blu-Ray. **C:** Desiree Hall; Samantha Colburn; Eddie Ritchard; Crista Flanagan; Directed by Jason Friedberg; Aaron Seltzer; Written by Jason Friedberg; Aaron Seltzer; Cinematography by Shawn Maurer. **Pr:** Magnet Releasing. **A:** Sr. High-Adult. **P:** Entertainment. **U:** Home. **L:** English. **Mov-Ent. Acq:** Purchase. **Dist:** Magnolia Pictures.

The Best Night of the Year 19??
Features many different farm animals, retelling the birth of Jesus. Emphasis is placed on the importance of kindness and generosity. 14m; VHS. **A:** Primary. **P:** Religious. **U:** Institution, Home. **Chl-Juv:** Animation & Cartoons, Christmas. **Acq:** Purchase. **Dist:** Twenty-Third Publications. $24.95.

The Best of 2000 2000
Multitude of steam and diesel railroad events that took place during the Millennium Year. 113m; VHS. **A:** Family. **P:** Entertainment. **U:** Home. **Gen-Edu:** Trains. **Acq:** Purchase. **Dist:** Pentrex Media Group L.L.C. $29.95.

The Best of Abbott & Costello Live 1954
A compilation of vintage live-television routines by the duo, naturally including "Who's on First," along with their other celebrated bits. 58m/B/W; VHS. **C:** Bud Abbott; Lou Costello; George Raft; Charles Laughton. **Pr:** Abbott & Costello Ent; CBS. **A:** Family. **P:** Entertainment. **U:** Home. **Mov-Ent:** Comedy--Performance, TV Movies. **Acq:** Purchase. **Dist:** Warner Home Video, Inc. $19.88.

Best of All a Dancer 1983
A portrait of a 32-year-old man with Down's Syndrome who has been performing successful, innovative dance works for eight years. 11m; VHS, 3/4 U, Special order formats. **Pr:** Richard Heus. **A:** Jr. High-Adult. **P:** Education. **U:** Institution, SURA. **Gen-Edu:** Documentary Films, Dance, Handicapped. **Acq:** Purchase, Rent/Lease. **Dist:** Direct Cinema Ltd.

The Best of American Justice: The Mob 1995
Four-cassette series covers all aspects of the Mafia, from its beginnings to federal surveillance, insiders, and informants. 250m; VHS. **A:** Jr. High-Adult. **P:** Entertainment. **U:** Home. **Gen-Edu:** Documentary Films, Intelligence Service. **Acq:** Purchase. **Dist:** A&E Television Networks L.L.C. $59.95. **Indiv. Titles:** 1. Godfathers 2. Mob Ladies 3. Defending the Mob 4. Mob Rats.

The Best of American Pickers: Mike & Frank's Picks 2013 (Unrated)
A Best of Collection from the History Channel Reality Series. Mike Wolfe and Frank Fritz select their favorite episodes from the American Pickers series. Includes samurai artifacts, pinball machines, and huge elephant heads. 315m; DVD. **A:** Family. **P:** Entertainment. **U:** Home. **Acq:** Purchase. **Dist:** A&E Television Networks L.L.C. $14.99.

The Best of American T'ai-chi 1997
Demonstrates open hand and weapons forms, two person forms, sword sparring, open-hand self defense and push hands. 75m; VHS. **A:** Adult. **P:** Instruction. **U:** Home. **Hea-Sci:** Fitness/Exercise. **Acq:** Purchase. **Dist:** Artistic Video. $29.95.

The Best of America's Funniest Home Videos 1991
Everyone's favorite Sunday night show is back! Bob Saget hosts a selection of the funniest videos sent in by the American public. Included are: the classic baby pulling out Granddad's teeth, the somersaulting bronco and much more! 35m; VHS, CC. **C:** Hosted by Bob Saget. **Pr:** ABC. **A:** Family. **P:** Entertainment. **U:** Home. **Mov-Ent:** Video, Outtakes & Bloopers, TV Movies. **Acq:** Purchase. **Dist:** Fox Home Entertainment. $14.98.

The Best of Andy Kaufman in Taxi Volume 1 2000
Features two episodes of the long-running television series "Taxi" that center on the character of Latka Gravas, played by Andy Kaufman. This volume contains the episodes "Paper

---

Marriage" and "Mama Gravas." 50m; VHS. **A:** Jr. High-Adult. **P:** Entertainment. **U:** Home. **Mov-Ent:** Television. **Acq:** Purchase. **Dist:** Paramount Pictures Corp. $9.95.

The Best of Andy Kaufman in Taxi Volume 2 2000
Features two episodes of the long-running television series "Taxi" that center on the character of Latka Gravas, played by Andy Kaufman. This volume contains the episodes "Latka the Playboy" and "Mr. Personalities." 50m; VHS. **A:** Jr. High-Adult. **P:** Entertainment. **U:** Home. **Mov-Ent:** Television. **Acq:** Purchase. **Dist:** Paramount Pictures Corp. $9.95.

The Best of Andy Kaufman in Taxi Volume 3 2000
Features two episodes of the long-running television series "Taxi" that center on the character of Latka Gravas, played by Andy Kaufman. This volume contains the episodes "Simka Returns" and "The Wedding of Latka and Simka." 50m; VHS. **A:** Jr. High-Adult. **P:** Entertainment. **U:** Home. **Mov-Ent:** Television. **Acq:** Purchase. **Dist:** Paramount Pictures Corp. $9.95.

The Best of Andy Kaufman in Taxi Volume 4 2000
Features two episodes of the long-running television series "Taxi" that center on the character of Latka Gravas, played by Andy Kaufman. This volume contains the episodes "Sceneskees from a Marriage, Parts 1 & 2." 50m; VHS. **A:** Jr. High-Adult. **P:** Entertainment. **U:** Home. **Mov-Ent:** Television. **Acq:** Purchase. **Dist:** Paramount Pictures Corp. $9.95.

The Best of Andy Williams Christmas Shows 2001 (Unrated)
Compiles highlights of ten of legendary singer Andy Williams' Christmastime specials with classic holiday music performances. 1 episode. 90m; DVD. **C:** Andy Williams. **A:** Family. **P:** Entertainment. **U:** Home. **Mov-Ent:** Television Series, Christmas, Music Video. **Acq:** Purchase. **Dist:** Kultur International Films Ltd., Inc. $19.99.

Best of Babar, Vol. 1 1985
Contains six episodes, "The Goat," "The Miniature Golf Course," "Babar Gets Sunsstroke," "The Cheese Fondue," "The Grotto," and "The Bicycle." 30m; VHS. **A:** Family. **P:** Entertainment. **U:** Home. **Chl-Juv:** Children, Animation & Cartoons. **Acq:** Purchase. **Dist:** Random House of Canada Ltd. $14.95.

Best of Babar, Vol. 2 1986
Six complete animated episodes. "The Billiard Game," "Babar Is Sewing," "The Postman," "Astronomy," "The Masked Ball," and "Babar's Theater." 30m; VHS. **A:** Family. **P:** Entertainment. **U:** Home. **Chl-Juv:** Children, Animation & Cartoons. **Acq:** Purchase. **Dist:** Random House of Canada Ltd. $14.95.

Best of Baretta 1975
Includes the series pilot that introduced the street-smart, maverick undercover cop played by Robert Blake plus two bonus episodes. 153m; DVD. **A:** Adult. **P:** Entertainment. **U:** Home. **Mov-Ent:** Television, Drama, Mystery & Suspense. **Acq:** Purchase. **Dist:** Universal Studios Home Video. $19.98.

The Best of Beakman's World 1993
The television science series that's fun for the whole family. Nutty scientist Beakman is joined by his lab assistant Josie, Lester the Rat, and a pair of penguins for his dazzling science demonstrations. 60m; VHS. **A:** Family. **P:** Entertainment. **U:** Home. **Mov-Ent:** Television Series, Science. **Acq:** Purchase. **Dist:** Sony Pictures Home Entertainment Inc.; Baker and Taylor. $14.95.

Best of Berlin Independence Days 1990
From the Berlin Fair for independent music in October, 1988 comes this collection of live performances. Bands include Young Gods, Mudhoney, Live in a Blender, PIG, Blind Idiot God, Buzzcocks, Killer Bees, Overlords and others. 40m; VHS. **A:** Jr. High-Adult. **P:** Entertainment. **U:** Home. **Mov-Ent:** Music--Performance, Music--Pop/Rock. **Acq:** Purchase. **Dist:** Music Video Distributors. $19.95.

The Best of Bermuda 1990
A 30-minute traveler's guide to the most beautiful island in the North Atlantic. 30m; VHS. **Pr:** International Video Projects. **A:** Sr. High-Adult. **P:** Education. **U:** Home. **Gen-Edu:** Travel. **Acq:** Purchase. **Dist:** International Video Projects, Inc. $19.95.

Best of Betty Boop, Vol. 1 1939 (Unrated)
Sweet Betty Boop sashays through 11 of her classic cartoon adventures in this collection of original shorts. Mastered from the original negatives. 90m; VHS. **C:** Voice(s) by Mae Questel. **Pr:** Max Fleischer Studios; Paramount Pictures. **A:** Family. **P:** Entertainment. **U:** Home. **Mov-Ent:** Animation & Cartoons. **Acq:** Purchase. **Dist:** Lions Gate Entertainment Inc. $14.98.

Best of Betty Boop, Vol. 2 1939 (Unrated)
Another collection of original cartoons starring the "Boop-Oop-a-Doop" girl, assisted by Bimbo and Koko the Clown. These black-and-white cartoons have been recolored for this release. 85m; VHS. **C:** Voice(s) by Mae Questel. **Pr:** Max Fleischer Studios. **A:** Family. **P:** Entertainment. **U:** Home. **Mov-Ent:** Animation & Cartoons. **Acq:** Purchase. **Dist:** Lions Gate Entertainment Inc. $14.98.

The Best of Black Journal 1970
A series of programs that encompass various aspects of the black experience from the fine arts to politics. 25m; VHS. **A:** Jr. High-Adult. **P:** Education. **U:** Institution, BCTV. **Gen-Edu:** Documentary Films, Minorities, Black Culture. **Acq:** Purchase, Rent/Lease. **Dist:** William Greaves Productions, Inc. $145.00. **Indiv. Titles:** 1. Developments in Black Theatre 2. African and Afro-American Art 3. Art of Earl Sweeting 4. Afro-American Dance 5. Black Cultural Achievements in the South 6. Tribute to Paul Robeson 7. Just Like You (Visual Poem) 8. Profile of Roberta Flack 9. W.E.B. Dubois Memorial Park Dedication 10. Struggle for Mozambique 11. Apartheid in South Africa 12.

Ancient Ethiopia 13. East Africa: Ends & Beginnings 14. Black Artists Discuss Economic Survival 15. The Growth of a Cooperative (Black Economics in the South) 16. The Economics of Black Music 17. Operation Bootstrap (Small Business Profile) 18. Coretta Scott King 19. An Interview with Charles Evers 20. Political Value of Black Power 21. Political Emergence of Julian Bond 22. Tribute to Dr. Martin Luther King 23. Interview with Clifford Alexander 24. Interview with Black Political Figures-Richard Hatcher and Julian Bond 25. Charles Hamilton Previews the Seventies 26. Portrait of a Jockey 27. An Interview with Arthur Ashe 28. The Black Athlete in American Sports 29. Report on Sickle Cell Anemia 30. The Events of 1968 CA Panel (Review) 31. Crisis in Medicine 32. Malcolm X University Dedication Ceremonies 33. And We Still Survive 34. Blacks in the Military 35. The Black Cop.

The Best of Blank 1987 (Unrated)
A collection of director Les Blank's favorite works, including "Blues Accordin' to Lightnin' Hopkins," "God Respects Us When We Work" and lots more. 90m; VHS. **C:** Directed by Les Blank. **Pr:** Les Blank; Les Blank. **A:** Jr. High-Adult. **P:** Entertainment. **U:** Home. **Mov-Ent:** Video. **Acq:** Purchase. **Dist:** Music Video Distributors; Flower Films. $49.95.

Best of Blondie 1981
Original footage from the group's early days combines with promotional videos to present 15 Blondie hits linked with film shot in New York locations. Songs include: "Rapture," "The Tide is High," "Heart of Glass," "Call Me," "X," "The Defender," "In the Flesh," "Picture This," and others. 60m; VHS. **C:** Deborah Harry; Jimmy Destri; Chris Stein; Nigel Harrison; Frank Infante; Clem Burke. **Pr:** Chrysalis Records. **A:** Family. **P:** Entertainment. **U:** Home. **Mov-Ent:** Music--Performance. **Acq:** Purchase. **Dist:** Music Video Distributors. $9.95.

The Best of Bob Uecker's Wacky World of Sports 1990
Join the fun as Bob Uecker hosts another hilarious sports blooperfest. 30m; VHS. **C:** Bob Uecker. **A:** Family. **P:** Entertainment. **U:** Home. **Spo-Rec:** Sports--General. **Acq:** Purchase. **Dist:** School-Tech Inc. $16.95.

Best of Bodies in Motion, Vol. 1 1988
Exercise on Hawaii's coast with ESPN's fitness host, Gilad. Volume 1 consists of an 80-minute workout for all levels. Volume 2 has a 30-minute beginner's routine and a 60-minute advanced workout. 80m; VHS. **Pr:** ESPN. **A:** Jr. High-Adult. **P:** Instruction. **U:** Home. **Hea-Sci:** Fitness/Exercise. **Acq:** Purchase. **Dist:** ESPN Inc. $39.95. **Indiv. Titles:** 1. The Best of Bodies in Motion, Volume 1 2. Bodies in Motion, Volume 2.

The Best of Bogart 1943 — ★★★
A two-cassette gift pack of the Bogie classics "The Maltese Falcon" and "Casablanca." 204m/B/W; VHS. **C:** Humphrey Bogart; Ingrid Bergman; Mary Astor; Sydney Greenstreet. **Pr:** Warner Bros. **A:** Jr. High-Adult. **P:** Entertainment. **U:** Home. **Mov-Ent:** Biography: Show Business. **Acq:** Purchase. **Dist:** MGM Home Entertainment. $39.95.

The Best of Bonanza, Vol. 1 1967
Two episodes from the classic series. "A Rose for Lotta" has Little Joe kidnapped after being lured by a sultry saloon singer. "The Underdog" sees guest star Charles Bronson play a fugitive half-breed. 100m; VHS. **C:** Michael Landon; Dan Blocker; Lorne Greene; Pernell Roberts. **Pr:** Republic Pictures. **A:** Family. **P:** Entertainment. **U:** Home. **Mov-Ent:** Western, Television Series. **Acq:** Purchase. **Dist:** Lions Gate Entertainment Inc.

The Best of Bonanza, Vol. 2 1967
Everyone's favorite family of the West in a series of rip-roarin' adventures that aim to please. Featuring "The Dark Gate," where Adam could become a victim of his friend's insanity, and "The Honor of Cochise," seeing Ben protect a Cavalry officer. 100m; VHS. **C:** Dan Blocker; Michael Landon; Lorne Greene; Pernell Roberts; Directed by Edward Ludwig. **Pr:** Republic Pictures. **A:** Family. **P:** Entertainment. **U:** Home. **Mov-Ent:** Western, Television Series. **Acq:** Purchase. **Dist:** Lions Gate Entertainment Inc.

The Best of Bonanza, Vol. 3 1967
Great western action on the Ponderosa, including "Hoss and the Leprechauns," and "The Truckee Strip." 100m; VHS. **C:** Edward Ludwig; Dan Blocker; Lorne Greene; Michael Landon. **Pr:** Republic Pictures. **A:** Family. **P:** Entertainment. **U:** Home. **Mov-Ent:** Western, Television Series. **Acq:** Purchase. **Dist:** Lions Gate Entertainment Inc.

The Best of Bonanza, Vol. 4 1967
Still more antics on the Ponderosa involving danger, fear and romance. These two shorts include "To Own the World," and "The Boss." 100m; VHS. **C:** Lorne Greene; Dan Blocker; Pernell Roberts; Michael Landon; Directed by Edward Ludwig. **Pr:** Republic Pictures. **A:** Family. **P:** Entertainment. **U:** Home. **Mov-Ent:** Western, Television Series. **Acq:** Purchase. **Dist:** Lions Gate Entertainment Inc.

The Best of Boys in Love: Award Winning Gay Short Films 2000 — ★¹/₂
The films in this collection fall into the usual traps of shorts: extreme situations and jokes played just for effect, and the skill level of those involved, whatever it may be, is frequently more apparent than their artistic intent. "Death in Venice, CA" is the most effective in evoking an atmosphere and tone of dangerous love, but goes awry in its tragic end. "Achilles" features incredible claymation, but skirts absurdity with its sexuality and anatomical details. "Karen Black Like Me" and "Dirty Baby Does Fire Island" are long jokes that don't sustain their laugh. The black-and-white "Twilight of the Gods" is well shot and occasionally touching, but occasionally contrived. 101m; DVD, Wide.

A: Sr. High-Adult. **P:** Entertainment. **U:** Home. **Mov-Ent. Acq:** Purchase. **Dist:** First Run Features. $29.95.

The Best of Broadway Musicals 1994
Compilation of musical numbers from some of Broadway's most beloved shows. Featuring rare footage from "The Ed Sullivan Show," this program highlights the live performances of Broadway legends such as Richard Burton, Julie Andrews, Carol Channing, Ethel Merman, and Celeste Holm. Showcases numbers from such timeless musicals as "Gentlemen Prefer Blondes," "My Fair Lady," "Oklahoma," "Camelot," and "West Side Story." Also includes rare interviews with legendary music composers, Rodgers and Hammerstein and Lerner and Loewe. 56m; VHS, CC. **C:** Narrated by John Raitt; Directed by Andrew Solt; Written by Andrew Solt. **A:** Jr. High-Adult. **P:** Entertainment. **U:** Home. **Mov-Ent:** Musical. **Acq:** Purchase. **Dist:** Walt Disney Studios Home Entertainment. $19.99.

Best of Bugs Bunny & Friends 1940
This collection includes classics from great cartoon stars Bugs Bunny, Daffy Duck, Tweetie Pie and Porky Pig. Includes "Duck Soup to Nuts," "A Feud There Was" and "Tweetie Pie." 53m; VHS. **C:** Directed by Isadore "Friz" Freleng; Chuck Jones; Robert McKimson. **Pr:** The Vitaphone Corporation. **A:** Family. **P:** Entertainment. **U:** Home. **Mov-Ent:** Animation & Cartoons. **Acq:** Purchase. **Dist:** MGM Home Entertainment.

Best of Candid Camera, Vol. 1 1985
A compilation of some of the best "Candid Camera" episodes. 56m; VHS. **C:** Allen Funt; Woody Allen; Angie Dickinson; Loni Anderson; Buster Keaton; Robby Benson. **Pr:** Alan Funt Productions. **A:** Family. **P:** Entertainment. **U:** Home. **Mov-Ent:** Television Series. **Acq:** Purchase. **Dist:** Lions Gate Television Corp. $59.95.

Best of Candid Camera, Vol. 2 1986
Various segments of almost inhuman and unbelievable hilarity from the television show. 57m; VHS. **C:** Allen Funt. **Pr:** Allen Funt; Allen Funt. **A:** Family. **P:** Entertainment. **U:** Home. **Mov-Ent:** Outtakes & Bloopers, Television Series. **Acq:** Purchase. **Dist:** Lions Gate Television Corp. $59.95.

The Best of Chaplin 1918
Three Chaplin comedies when he worked with Mutual. Includes "The Rink," "One A.M.," and "The Floorwalker." 60m/B/W; Silent; VHS. **C:** Charlie Chaplin; Directed by Charlie Chaplin. **Pr:** Mutual Film Corporation. **A:** Family. **P:** Entertainment. **U:** Home. **Mov-Ent:** Silent Films. **Acq:** Purchase. **Dist:** Moviecraft Home Video; Video Resources. $59.95.

The Best of Comedy Central Presents 2008 (Unrated)
Live stand-up performances of comedians taped for the Comedy Central network, including Lewis Black, Dane Cook, Jeff Dunham, Jim Gaffigan, Demetri Martin, Carlos Mencia, Brian Regan, and Mitch Hedberg. 30m; DVD. **A:** Sr. High-Adult. **P:** Entertainment. **U:** Home. **Mov-Ent:** Comedy--Performance, Television. **Acq:** Purchase. **Dist:** Comedy Central. $19.99.

The Best of Comedy Central Presents II 2008 (Unrated)
The second collection of live comic performances taped for Comedy Central, including skits by Dave Attell, Mike Birbiglia, Frank Caliendo, Zach Galifianakis, Stepehn Lynch, Patton Oswalt, Nick Swardson, and Daniel Tosh. 30m; DVD. **A:** Sr. High-Adult. **P:** Entertainment. **U:** Home. **Mov-Ent:** Comedy--Performance, Television. **Acq:** Purchase. **Dist:** Comedy Central. $19.99.

Best of Comic Relief 1986
All-star comedic array of stand-up acts was taped "live" in concert to raise money for America's homeless and released on cable television. 120m; VHS, CC. **C:** Whoopi Goldberg; Robin Williams; Billy Crystal; Carl Reiner; Harold Ramis; Martin Short; Jerry Lewis; Howie Mandel; Eugene Levy; Steve Allen; Doc Severinsen; Sid Caesar; John Candy; George Carlin. **Pr:** Comic Relief; Karl/Lorimar. **A:** Family. **P:** Entertainment. **U:** Home. **Mov-Ent:** Comedy--Performance, TV Movies. **Acq:** Purchase. **Dist:** MGM Studios Inc. ; Warner Home Video, Inc. $39.95.

Best of Comic Relief '90 1990
More than 40 stars make this two hours a real treat, and the hosts aren't so bad themselves: Whoopi Goldberg, Billy Crystal and Robin Williams. Proceeds from this event, and subsequent tape sales go to Comic Relief, Inc. to benefit the homeless in America. Stars include: Bobcat Goldthwait, Elayne Boosler, George Carlin, Louis Anderson, Dennis Miller, The Simpsons. 120m; VHS. **C:** Hosted by Whoopi Goldberg; Billy Crystal; Robin Williams. **Pr:** RHI Entertainment Inc. **A:** Sr. High-Adult. **P:** Entertainment. **U:** Home. **Mov-Ent:** Comedy--Performance. **Acq:** Purchase. **Dist:** Rhino Entertainment Co. $29.95.

The Best of Costa Rica 19??
Takes the viewer on a tour of San Jose and the countryside of Costa Rica, including visits to volcanoes, the rain forest, fishing areas, and the beaches of both the Atlantic and Pacific coasts. 30m; VHS. **A:** Family. **P:** Education. **U:** Home. **Gen-Edu:** Travel, Central America. **Acq:** Purchase. **Dist:** International Video Projects, Inc. $24.95.

The Best of Cracker Mysteries 1993 — ★★★
Coltrane stars as brilliant-but-abrasive forensic psychologist Dr. Eddie Fitzgerald. His insatiable desires for smoking, drinking, and gambling have blown apart his marriage and caused him grief at work. But Fitz's brilliant at "cracking" cases by reading clues (and people) to nail wrongdoers. In "The Mad Woman in the Attic," a murder suspect, claiming to have amnesia, may be a serial killer. "To Say I Love You," finds a loan shark gettting murdered and a recently paroled hijacker and his girlfriend being involved. And in "One Day a Lemming Will Fly," a teen suicide turns out to be murder. On three cassettes. 350m; VHS. **C:** Robbie Coltrane; Andrew Tiernan; Susan Lynch; Christopher Eccleston; Beryl Reid; Adrian Dunbar; Barbara Flynn; Geraldine Somerville; Lorcan Cranitch; Frances Tomelty; Directed by Simon Cellan Jones; Michael Winterbottom; Andy Wilson; Written by Jimmy McGovern. **Pr:** Granada Television International Ltd. **A:** Sr. High-Adult. **P:** Entertainment. **U:** Home. **Mov-Ent:** Mystery & Suspense, Psychology. **Acq:** Purchase. **Dist:** PBS Home Video; A&E Television Networks L.L.C. $59.95.

Best of Dangerous Encounters with Brady Barr 2008 (Unrated)
Four full episodes starring reptile expert Dr. Brady Barr, who studies some of the world's most dangerous wildlife in their rapidly disappearing habitats. Episodes include "Snake Bite," "Dens of Danger," "Bite Force," and "Undercover Hippo," all of which focus on Dr. Barr's work to understand what these animals need to survive in the wild before their habitats are lost. 200m; DVD. **A:** Family. **P:** Education. **U:** Institution, Home. **Mov-Ent:** Documentary Films, Animals, Nature. **Acq:** Purchase. **Dist:** National Geographic Society. $29.95.

The Best of Dark Shadows 1989
A collection of highlights from the cult classic daytime serial of the late 60s and early 70s featuring some of the show's most memorable characters. 30m; VHS. **C:** Jonathan Frid; Joan Bennett; David Selby; Lara Parker; Kate Jackson; Mitchell Ryan; Alexandra Moltke; Louis Edmonds; Mark Allen. **Pr:** Dan Curtis Productions. **A:** Family. **P:** Entertainment. **U:** Home. **Mov-Ent:** Horror, Television Series. **Acq:** Purchase. **Dist:** MPI Media Group; Tapeworm Video Distributors Inc. $9.98.

Best of Eddie Murphy 1989 (Unrated)
A compilation of Murphy's funniest bits from his three seasons on "Saturday Night Live," including appearances as Stevie Wonder, Buckwheat, Bill Cosby and Little Richard. 78m; VHS, CC. **C:** Eddie Murphy; Joe Piscopo; Robin Duke; Tim Kazurinsky; Mary Gross; Gary Kroeger; Brad Hall; Julia Louis-Dreyfus. **Pr:** Eddie Murphy Television; National Broadcasting Company. **A:** Jr. High-Adult. **P:** Entertainment. **U:** Home. **Mov-Ent:** Television Series. **Acq:** Purchase. **Dist:** Paramount Pictures Corp. $14.95.

Best of Elvis Costello and the Attractions 1985
This is a compilation of 22 conceptual music videos that brought Elvis Costello critical acclaim. Included are "Watching the Detectives," "Pump It Up," "Accidents Will Happen," "Everyday I Write the Book," "Allison," and more. 65m; VHS. **Pr:** CBS. **A:** Jr. High-Adult. **P:** Entertainment. **U:** Home. **Mov-Ent:** Music Video, Music--Performance. **Acq:** Purchase. **Dist:** Music Video Distributors. $24.95.

Best of Ernie Kovacs 1956
A compilation of some of the best moments from Ernie Kovacs' television programs that features such memorable characters as Percy Dovetonsils and the Nairobi Trio. 60m/B/W; VHS. **C:** Ernie Kovacs; Edie Adams; Ernie Hatrak; Bill Wendell; Peter Hanley. **Pr:** National Broadcasting Company. **A:** Family. **P:** Entertainment. **U:** Home. **Mov-Ent:** Television Series. **Acq:** Purchase, Rent/Lease. **Dist:** White Star. $19.95.

The Best of Everything 1959 (Unrated) — ★★★
Trashy sexist soap opera about women seeking success and love in the publishing world of N.Y.C. Several stories take place, the best being Crawford's hard-nosed editor who's having an affair with a married man. Look for Evans as a philandering playboy (he went on to become the producer of "Chinatown," among others.) Based on the novel by Rona Jaffe. 121m; VHS, DVD, CC. **C:** Hope Lange; Stephen Boyd; Suzy Parker; Diane Baker; Martha Hyer; Joan Crawford; Brian Aherne; Robert Evans; Louis Jourdan; Directed by Jean Negulesco; Written by Edith Sommer; Mann Rubin; Cinematography by William Mellor; Music by Alfred Newman. **Pr:** Jerry Wald; Fox. **A:** Sr. High-Adult. **P:** Entertainment. **U:** Home. **Mov-Ent:** Drama, Publishing, Cities & Towns. **Acq:** Purchase. **Dist:** Fox Home Entertainment.

Best of Fests for Kids 1991
Eight award-winning short videos are featured, including "Pumpkin Madness II," "Metal Dogs of India," "The Rooster," and more. 40m; VHS. **A:** Primary. **P:** Entertainment. **U:** Institution, Home. **Chl-Juv:** Animation & Cartoons, Children. **Acq:** Purchase. **Dist:** Next Gen Video. $19.95.

Best of '50s Comedy 1990
Fans of television's golden age will enjoy this collection. Features Jack Benny, Red Skelton, Milton Berle, Jimmy Durante, and Ernie Kovacs. 30m/B/W; VHS. **Pr:** Brentwood Productions. **A:** Family. **P:** Entertainment. **U:** Home. **Mov-Ent. Acq:** Purchase. **Dist:** $7.99.

The Best of Florida 19??
Travel program offers views of the attractions across the state of Florida. 60m; VHS. **A:** Family. **P:** Entertainment. **U:** Home. **Gen-Edu:** Travel. **Acq:** Purchase. **Dist:** International Video Projects, Inc. $19.95.

The Best of Ganon Baker: Best Pro Scoring Moves 2012
Trainer Ganon Baker demonstrates moves used by top NBA basketball players and shows how to incorporate them into a team's training session. 43m; DVD. **A:** Jr. High-Adult. **P:** Education. **U:** Home, Institution. **L:** English. **Gen-Edu:** Athletic Instruction/Coaching, Basketball. **Acq:** Purchase. **Dist:** Championship Productions. $39.99.

The Best of Ganon Baker: Elite Off-Season Workouts 2012
Trainer Ganon Baker demonstrates drills and workout procedures for basketball athletes wanting to remain in shape during the off-season. 86m; DVD. **A:** Jr. High-Adult. **P:** Education. **U:** Home, Institution. **L:** English. **Gen-Edu:** Athletic Instruction/Coaching, Basketball. **Acq:** Purchase. **Dist:** Championship Productions. $39.99.

The Best of Ganon Baker: Intermediate Off-Season Workouts 2012
Ganon Baker presents off-season training drills and workout programs for aspiring basketball players. 98m; DVD. **A:** Jr. High-Adult. **P:** Education. **U:** Home, Institution. **L:** English. **Gen-Edu:** Athletic Instruction/Coaching, Basketball. **Acq:** Purchase. **Dist:** Championship Productions. $39.99.

The Best of Golf in Paradise 1996
Johnny Bench presents resort destinations, celebrity bloopers, instruction, tips, and golf gadgets. 60m; VHS. **A:** Adult. **P:** Instruction. **U:** Home. **How-Ins:** Golf, How-To. **Acq:** Purchase. **Dist:** Tapeworm Video Distributors Inc. $19.95.

The Best of Grand Prix Sailing 1990
A complete compendium of all sailboat racing from all over the world with information about the smallest to the largest boats. Hosted by Gary Jobson. 40m; VHS. **C:** Hosted by Gary Jobson. **A:** Jr. High-Adult. **P:** Entertainment. **U:** Home. **Spo-Rec:** Sports--General, Sports--Water, Boating. **Acq:** Purchase. **Dist:** Bennett Marine Video; ESPN Inc.; Fast Forward. $19.95.

Best of Hard 'n' Heavy, Part 1 1991
This volume includes features on Axl Rose, Skid Row, Queensryche, Anthrax, Iron Maiden, Ozzy, Jimi Hendrix, Warrant, Great White, Rob Halford of Judas Priest, The Cult, Megadeath, Motorhead, L.A. Guns, Alice Cooper, Voivod, Steve Jones, King Diamond, Quireboys and Blackie Lawless of W.A.S.P. This video contains a parental advisory indicating that some material may be inappropriate for younger viewers. 120m; VHS. **Pr:** A*Vision. **A:** College-Adult. **P:** Entertainment. **U:** Home. **Mov-Ent:** Music--Pop/Rock. **Acq:** Purchase. **Dist:** WarnerVision. $19.98.

The Best of Hootenanny 1963
The ABC program featured folk srtists performing on college campuses. 88 perfromances, including Judy Collins, the Carter Family, the New Chrsty Minstrels, Ian & Slyvia, and many more. 270m/B/W; DVD. **A:** Adult. **P:** Entertainment. **U:** Home. **Music:** Music--Performance, Television Series. **Acq:** Purchase. **Dist:** Acorn Media Group Inc. $44.99.

The Best of It's a Miracle 2003
Collection of episodes from the series hosted by Richard Thomas that documents a multitude of inspiring and true stories. 360m; DVD. **A:** Adult. **P:** Entertainment. **U:** Home. **Mov-Ent:** Television, Documentary Films. **Acq:** Purchase. **Dist:** Questar Inc. $59.99.

The Best of Jack Hanna 2012
Sixty episodes from animal adventurer Hanna's TV shows, "Into the Wild" and "Animal Adventures." **C:** Hosted by Jack Hanna. **A:** Family. **Dist:** Acorn Media Group Inc. $29.98.

The Best of John Candy on SCTV 198?
Some of Candy's most memorable characters, including Johnny LaRue, Yosh Schmenge, and the grown up Theodore "Beaver" Cleaver, are featured on this compilation of his years on SCTV (Second City Television). 62m; VHS. **C:** John Candy; Eugene Levy; Rick Moranis; Catherine O'Hara; Harold Ramis; Martin Short. **Pr:** Patrick Whitley. **A:** Jr. High-Adult. **P:** Entertainment. **U:** Home. **Mov-Ent:** TV Movies. **Acq:** Purchase. **Dist:** Sony Pictures Home Entertainment Inc. $14.95.

Best of Judy Garland 1985 (Unrated)
Judy Garland shines brightly in this television concert that features such standards as "The Man That Got Away," "Over The Rainbow" and "Swanee." 85m/B/W; VHS. **C:** Judy Garland. **Pr:** RCA Video Productions. **A:** Family. **P:** Entertainment. **U:** Home. **Mov-Ent:** Music--Performance, TV Movies. **Acq:** Purchase. **Dist:** Sony Pictures Home Entertainment Inc., On Moratorium.

The Best of Kermit on Sesame Street 1998
Kermit the Frog has been named "Frog of the Year" and his pal Grover is on hand to host a special tribute to Kermit's most memorable moments on Sesame Street. 30m; VHS. **A:** Family. **P:** Entertainment. **U:** Home. **Chl-Juv:** Family Viewing. **Acq:** Purchase. **Dist:** SONY Wonder. $12.98.

The Best of Liquid Television 1994
Contemporary animated works from the MTV series, including four episodes of the Japanimation action series "Aeon Flux," as well as episodes of "Stick Figure Theatre" and "Smart Talk with Raisin." 45m; VHS. **A:** Sr. High-Adult. **P:** Entertainment. **U:** Home. **Mov-Ent:** Animation & Cartoons. **Acq:** Purchase. **Dist:** Sony Music Entertainment Inc. $12.98.

The Best of Lisa Ling 2005 (Unrated)
Lisa Ling is one of the best-known voices in journalism today. This compilation brings together some of her best efforts while acting as host of National Geographic Explorer and working as an investigative journalist, including a look inside America's prisons, a piece on the little-known world of female suicide bombers, repeated trips into active war zones, and an amazing journey into Nepal where she accompanied two eye surgeons who were donating their skills to restore the sight of people who lived in remote villages. 285m; DVD. **A:** Family. **P:** Education, Entertainment. **U:** Home, Institution. **Mov-Ent:** Documentary Films, War--General, Interviews. **Acq:** Purchase. **Dist:** $29.99.

The Best of Little Lulu 19??
Mischief-prone Little Lulu returns in this special collection of cartoon adventures. 60m; VHS. **Pr:** Paramount Pictures. **A:** Family. **P:** Entertainment. **U:** Home. **Mov-Ent:** Animation & Cartoons. **Acq:** Purchase. **Dist:** Lions Gate Entertainment Inc. $19.95.

The Best of Lovejoy Mysteries 1993
Four-tape series features the best adventures of irrepressible (if untrustworthy) antiques dealer Lovejoy (McShane). What he usually discovers are forgeries, dirty dealing, and other assorted mayhem. Based on the mysteries by Jonathan Gash; made for British TV. 200m; VHS. **C:** Ian McShane; Phyllis Logan; Dudley Sutton; Chris Jury. **Pr:** Emma Hayter; Allan McKeown; Tony Charles; A&E (Arts & Entertainment) Network. **A:** Sr. High-Adult. **P:** Entertainment. **U:** Home. **Mov-Ent:** Mystery & Suspense, Antiques. **Acq:** Purchase. **Dist:** A&E Television Networks L.L.C. $59.95.
Indiv. Titles: 1. Friends in High Places 2. Scotch on the Rocks 3. Love Knots 4. The Ring.

The Best of Men 2012 (Unrated) — ★★½
Inspirational true story from the BBC. German refugee, Dr. Ludwig Guttmann, arrives at Britain's Stoke Mandeville Hospital in 1944 and is appalled to find how the paralyzed soldiers are treated. After clashing with the staff, Guttmann introduces new care and programs into the rehabilitation regime, including athletics. This leads to national wheelchair competitions and the eventual founding of the Paralympic Games. 90m; DVD. **C:** Eddie Marsan; Niamh Cusack; Rob Brydon; George MacKay; Richard McCabe; Directed by Tim Whitby; Written by Lucy Gannon; Cinematography by Matt Gray; Music by Mark Russell. **A:** Jr. High-Adult. **P:** Entertainment. **U:** Home. **L:** English. **Mov-Ent:** TV Movies, Great Britain, Medical Care. **Acq:** Purchase. **Dist:** PBS Home Video.

The Best of Miami—Rev. Ed. 1995
The best restauraunts, hotels, and tourist sites for Dade County are pointed out. 30m; VHS. **TV Std:** NTSC, PAL. **Pr:** International Video Projects. **A:** Jr. High-Adult. **P:** Education. **U:** Home. **L:** English, German, Spanish. **Gen-Edu:** Travel, Cities & Towns. **Acq:** Purchase. **Dist:** International Video Projects, Inc. $19.95.

The Best of Miramar 1993
Graphics set to music; includes "Desert Vision." ?m. **A:** Adult. **P:** Entertainment. **U:** Home. **Gen-Edu:** Animation & Cartoons, Computers. **Acq:** Purchase. **Dist:** BMG Entertainment. $14.99.

The Best of Mister Ed 1961
Wilbur Post owns Mr. Ed, a horse who can talk, but only to him, which leads to many mix-ups, gags, and comedic confusion. 630m; DVD. **A:** Adult. **P:** Entertainment. **U:** Home. **Mov-Ent:** Television Series. **Acq:** Purchase. **Dist:** MGM Home Entertainment. $34.98.

Best of Monday Night Football 1990
Great moments in football history are captured in these excerpts from the Monday Night Football archives. 50m; VHS. **C:** Howard Cosell; Don Meredith; Frank Gifford. **Pr:** ABC; NFL Films. **A:** Family. **P:** Entertainment. **U:** Home. **Spo-Rec:** Sports--General, Football. **Acq:** Purchase. **Dist:** Fusion Video. $19.98.

The Best of Motives 19??
Explains how to motivate your team, give feedback and recognize performance. 50m; VHS. **A:** Adult. **P:** Professional. **U:** Institution. **Bus-Ind:** Business. **Acq:** Purchase, Rent/Lease. **Dist:** Video Arts, Inc. $870.00.
Indiv. Titles: 1. Part 1: Nobody Ever Tells Us 2. Part 2: Nobody Ever Asks Us.

The Best of MTV's 120 Minutes 1991
Ten videos from the alternative music program seen on cable television. Includes "Gone, Daddy, Gone" (Violent Femmes), "Fool's Gold" (Stone Roses), "Eye of Fatima" (Camper van Beethoven), "Mandinka" (Sinead O'Connor) and "We Care a Lot" (Faith No More). 45m; VHS. **Pr:** MTV Films. **A:** Jr. High-Adult. **P:** Entertainment. **U:** Home. **Mov-Ent:** Music Video, Music--Pop/Rock. **Acq:** Purchase. **Dist:** Rhino Entertainment Co. $14.95.

Best of Nature 19??
Five-tape series looking at some of the world's most interesting and exotic habitats. 53m; VHS. **A:** Jr. High-Adult. **P:** Education. **U:** Institution. **Gen-Edu:** Animals, Ecology & Environment. **Acq:** Purchase. **Dist:** Ark Media Group Ltd.
Indiv. Titles: 1. Amazonia: A Burning Question 2. America's Wild Horses 3. Land of the Llamas 4. Orangutans of the Rain Forest 5. Rhino on the Run.

The Best of NeoSoul 2006
The rise of NeoSoul and some of its artists, including Ashanti, Alicia Keys, India.Arie, and Jill Scott. 85m; DVD. **A:** Sr. High-Adult. **P:** Entertainment. **U:** Home. **Fin-Art:** Documentary Films, Music--Performance. **Acq:** Purchase. **Dist:** Allumination Filmworks.

The Best of New Orleans Live 19??
Features the best of the New Orleans Festivals. Guests include the Neville Brothers, B.B. King, Robert Cray, and Harry Connick. 90m; VHS. **A:** Jr. High-Adult. **P:** Entertainment. **U:** Home. **Mov-Ent:** Music Video, Music--Performance. **Acq:** Purchase. **Dist:** Music Video Distributors. $64.95.

The Best of New Wave Theatre, Vol. 1 1985
The best of the legendary late-night cable production is now available. See predominantly L.A. bands like, Surf Punks, Circle Jerks, Blasters, Suburban Lawns and more. 60m; VHS. **Pr:** Rhino Video. **A:** Sr. High-Adult. **P:** Entertainment. **U:** Home. **Mov-Ent:** Music Video. **Acq:** Purchase. **Dist:** Music Video Distributors. $19.95.

The Best of New Wave Theatre, Vol. 2 1985
The grooviest highlights from various soft-and hard-core punk bands as shown on the New Wave Theatre television program. 60m; VHS. **Pr:** Impulse Entertainment. **A:** Jr. High-Adult. **P:** Entertainment. **U:** Home. **Mov-Ent:** Music--Performance. **Acq:** Purchase. **Dist:** Music Video Distributors. $19.95.

The Best of Nightline 1990
Selected Nightline segments culled from the Reagan Years and beyond. Some segments run longer than 30 minutes. 30m; VHS. **C:** Hosted by Ted Koppel. **Pr:** ABC. **A:** Jr. High-Adult. **P:** Education. **U:** Home. **Gen-Edu:** Television. **Acq:** Purchase. **Dist:** MPI Media Group; Facets Multimedia Inc. $14.98.
Indiv. Titles: 1. The First Nightline 2. Ronald Reagan Elected President 3. Ku Klux Klan 4. John Lennon Murdered 5. Freeing of the Hostages 6. Assassination Attempt Against Pope John Paul II 7. Judge O'Conner Nominated for Supreme Court 8. Assassination of Egyptian President Anwar Sadat 9. John Belushi's Career 10. Massacre of Marines in Beirut 11. Artificial Heart 12. AIDS 13. Klaus Barbie and His Connections 14. Louis Farrakhan 15. Jesse Jackson & His Campaign 16. Geraldine Ferraro 17. Assassination of Indira Gandhi 18. Baby Fae 19. Colonel Muammmar Qaddafi 20. Flight 847 Hijacked 21. Rock Hudson Suffers from AIDS 22. South African Debate 23. Achille Lauro Hijacked 24. Qaddafi's Warning 25. Challenger Disaster 26. Marcos & Aquino 27. Chernobyl Nuclear Disaster 28. The Titanic 29. T.V. Evangelists 30. Jackie Robinson 31. Jim & Tammy Faye Bakker 32. Oliver North 33. Yasir Arafat 34. General Manuel Noriega Indicted 35. Austrian President Kurt Waldheim 36. Jimmy Swaggart 37. Ryan White 38. Town Meeting: Holy Land 39. Iranian Jetliner Shot Down by U.S. 40. Jesse Jackson Speaks to the DNC 41. State of Israel is Recognized by Palestine 42. President Reagan's Farewell Address 43. Lucille Ball Dies 44. Student Protest in China 45. Sir Laurence Olivier Dies 46. East Germany Opens Its Borders 47. U.S. Invades Panama 48. Nelson Mandela 49. Akio Morita.

Best of 1984 1984
A variety of modern trains are shown, including the SP Olympic special, the Speno Rail Grinder and the Cajon. 90m; VHS. **Pr:** Interurban Films; Pentrex Media Group L.L.C. **A:** Jr. High-Adult. **P:** Entertainment. **U:** Home. **Gen-Edu:** Trains. **Acq:** Purchase. **Dist:** Pentrex Media Group L.L.C. $49.95.

Best of 1985 1985
A synopsis of the year in railroading, with footage of the McCloud River steam, the UP Old-Timers Special and more. 120m; VHS. **Pr:** Interurban Films; Pentrex Media Group L.L.C. **A:** Jr. High-Adult. **P:** Entertainment. **U:** Home. **Gen-Edu:** Documentary Films, Trains. **Acq:** Purchase. **Dist:** Pentrex Media Group L.L.C. $59.95.

Best of 1986 1987
Provides highlights of the railroading year, including the SP 4449 to Hollywood, GP-60 demonstrations, STSF museum special, the Santa Fe 3751, and more. 120m; VHS. **Pr:** Pentrex Media Group L.L.C. **A:** Primary-Adult. **P:** Education. **U:** Home. **Gen-Edu:** Trains. **Acq:** Purchase. **Dist:** Pentrex Media Group L.L.C. $59.95.

Best of 1987 1987
The greatest train action from '87 is featured, including California's Operation Lifesaver, UP and SP Super Bowl trains, UP 3985 and 8444, a Sherman Hill Spectacular and more. 90m; VHS. **Pr:** Pentrex Media Group L.L.C. **A:** Jr. High-Adult. **P:** Education. **U:** Home. **Gen-Edu:** Trains. **Acq:** Purchase. **Dist:** Pentrex Media Group L.L.C. $59.95.

Best of 1988 1988
Features the most exciting railroading action of the year. 120m; VHS. **Pr:** Pentrex Media Group L.L.C. **A:** Jr. High-Adult. **P:** Education. **U:** Home. **Gen-Edu:** Trains. **Acq:** Purchase. **Dist:** Pentrex Media Group L.L.C. $59.95.

Best of 1989 1989
Steam and diesel railroading is the focus of this video, including highlights from the Santa Fe Warbonnets, N&W 611 and 1218, Western Allegheny and CSX-F units, the Napa Valley Wine Train and much more. 120m; VHS. **Pr:** Pentrex Media Group L.L.C. **A:** Family. **P:** Entertainment. **U:** Home. **Mov-Ent:** Trains. **Acq:** Purchase. **Dist:** Pentrex Media Group L.L.C. $49.95.

Best of 1990 1991
Highlights of railroading during the year. 120m; VHS. **Pr:** Pentrex Media Group L.L.C. **A:** Jr. High-Adult. **P:** Education. **U:** Home. **Gen-Edu:** Trains. **Acq:** Purchase. **Dist:** Pentrex Media Group L.L.C. $49.95.

Best of 1991 1991
Highlights of the railroading scene during the past year, including Southern Pacific sugar beet trains, historic Sacramento Shops, and a look at railroading in Salt Lake City and Ogden, Utah. 120m; VHS. **A:** Family. **P:** Entertainment. **U:** Home. **Gen-Edu:** Trains. **Acq:** Purchase. **Dist:** Pentrex Media Group L.L.C. $49.95.

The Best of Not Necessarily the News 1988
From the TV show, combining comedy with actual news film footage, a satirical look at political developments and other happenings. 60m; VHS. **C:** Anne Bloom; Danny Breen; Stuart Pankin. **Pr:** HBO. **A:** Adult. **P:** Entertainment. **U:** Home. **Mov-Ent:** Satire & Parody, Mass Media, TV Movies. **Acq:** Purchase. **Dist:** Time-Life Video and Television.

The Best of On the Road with Charles Kuralt 1993
Three volume set revisiting Kuralt's most memorable stops from his "On the Road" series, including colorful characters, the evolution of American traditions, and a celebration of American rites of passage. Tapes are also available individually. 60m; VHS. **C:** Hosted by Charles Kuralt. **A:** Family. **P:** Entertainment. **U:** Home. **Mov-Ent:** Television Series, Interviews. **Acq:** Purchase. **Dist:** Baker and Taylor; Facets Multimedia Inc. $49.98.
Indiv. Titles: 1. American Heritage 2. Seasons of America 3. Unforgettable People.

The Best of Orlando'Rev. Ed. 1995
Sea World and the Space Coast are some of the points of interest in the Orlando/central Florida area. Also available in German and Spanish. 30m; VHS. **TV Std:** NTSC, PAL. **Pr:** International Video Projects. **A:** Jr. High-Adult. **P:** Education. **U:** Home. **L:** English, German, Spanish. **Gen-Edu:** Travel, U.S. States, Cities & Towns. **Acq:** Purchase. **Dist:** International Video Projects, Inc. $19.95.

The Best of Pawn Stars: Greatest Stories Ever Sold 2013 (Unrated)
History Channel reality show. Captures the priceless finds and fakes brought in by slew of unusual characters for assessment and sale at the only family-run pawn shop in Las Vegas. In this "best of" collection, Chumlee dresses like an elf, Corey wears a Christmas sweater, and a man is unable to sell his Pez dispenser collection. 244m; DVD. **A:** Family. **P:** Entertainment. **U:** Home. **Acq:** Purchase. **Dist:** A&E Television Networks L.L.C. $14.98.

The Best of Person to Person 1993
Highlights of Edward R. Murrow's television interview series from the '50s, includes Frank Sinatra, John and Jackie Kennedy, Marlon Brando, Marilyn Monroe, and others. 90m/B/W; VHS. **C:** Hosted by Edward R. Murrow. **A:** Sr. High-Adult. **P:** Entertainment. **U:** Home. **Mov-Ent:** Television Series, Interviews. **Acq:** Purchase. **Dist:** Baker and Taylor. $19.98.

The Best of Peru 1989
This tape shows everything from Lake Titicaca to the cities of Machu Pichu and Lima. Also included are "The Potter of Nazca" and a short documentary on pottery making. 30m; VHS. **TV Std:** NTSC, PAL. **Pr:** International Video Projects. **A:** Jr. High-Adult. **P:** Education. **U:** Home. **L:** English, Spanish. **Gen-Edu:** Travel, South America. **Acq:** Purchase. **Dist:** International Video Projects, Inc. $19.95.

Best of Popeye 1983
Eight classic Popeye cartoons are included in this compilation. 56m; VHS. **Pr:** Max Fleischer Studios. **A:** Family. **P:** Entertainment. **U:** Home. **Mov-Ent:** Animation & Cartoons. **Acq:** Purchase. **Dist:** MGM Home Entertainment. $29.95.

The Best of Prince's Trust 19??
Features the best of Prince's Trust music festivals. ?m; VHS. **A:** Jr. High-Adult. **P:** Entertainment. **U:** Home. **Mov-Ent:** Music Video. **Acq:** Purchase. **Dist:** Music Video Distributors. $74.95.

The Best of Red Green 1995
Canadian comedy show that specializs in making fun of men—courtesy of plaid-clad host Red Green and the boys at Possum Lodge. Skits include "Handyman Corner" and "Fun with Bill." 67m; VHS. **A:** Jr. High-Adult. **P:** Entertainment. **U:** Home. **Mov-Ent:** Men. **Acq:** Purchase. **Dist:** Acorn Media Group Inc.

Best of Reggae Sunsplash, Part 1 1982
Steel Pulse, Burning Spear, Chalice, and many others rock and funk Monterey Bay to its feet. 60m; VHS. **Pr:** SVS Ent. **A:** Sr. High-Adult. **P:** Entertainment. **U:** Home. **Mov-Ent:** Music--Performance, Black Culture. **Acq:** Purchase. **Dist:** Sony Music Entertainment Inc.; Facets Multimedia Inc. $19.95.

Best of Reggae Sunsplash, Part 2 1982
Continuation of volume 1, featuring Toots & the Maytals, Deniece Williams, and many others. 60m; VHS. **C:** Music by Yellowman. **Pr:** SVS Ent. **A:** Jr. High-Adult. **P:** Entertainment. **U:** Home. **Mov-Ent:** Music--Performance. **Acq:** Purchase. **Dist:** Music Video Distributors.

The Best of Roger Rabbit 1995
Compilation of the original theatrical cartoons featuring Baby Herman and bedeviled babysitter Roger Rabbit. ?m; VHS, CC. **A:** Family. **P:** Entertainment. **U:** Home. **Chl-Juv:** Animation & Cartoons. **Acq:** Purchase. **Dist:** Walt Disney Studios Home Entertainment. $12.99.
Indiv. Titles: 1. Tummy Trouble 2. Roller Coaster Rabbit 3. Trail Mix-Up.

The Best of Rowan & Martin's Laugh-In 1 200?
Political, sexy, and slapstick comedy bits by an all-star cast. Guest appearances by John Wayne and Richard Nixon. 360m; DVD. **A:** Adult. **P:** Entertainment. **U:** Home. **Mov-Ent:** Television Series, Comedy--Performance. **Acq:** Purchase. **Dist:** Rhino Entertainment Co. $49.95.

The Best of Rowan & Martin's Laugh-In 2 200?
Political, sexy, and slapstick comedy bits by an all-star cast including Goldie Hawn and Lily Tomlin. Guest appearances by Johnny Carson and Zsa Zsa Gabor. 330m; DVD. **A:** Adult. **P:** Entertainment. **U:** Home. **Mov-Ent:** Television Series, Comedy--Performance. **Acq:** Purchase. **Dist:** Rhino Entertainment Co. $49.95.

The Best of Saturday Night Live: Candice Bergen 19??
Sketches from Bergen's several SNL appearances include "Latent Elf," "Princess Grace," "Catherine Deneuve," and "Bee Capades." Also featured is Andy Kaufman. 58m; VHS. **A:** Jr. High-Adult. **P:** Entertainment. **U:** Home. **Mov-Ent:** Television Series, Comedy--Performance. **Acq:** Purchase. **Dist:** Movies Unlimited. $14.99.

The Best of Saturday Night Live: Danny DeVito 19??
DeVito in a "Siskel & Ebert" parody, joining Dana Carvey in a "Church Chat," pumping iron with Hans and Franz, and getting into other comedic mischief. 90m; VHS. **A:** Jr. High-Adult. **P:**

Entertainment. **U:** Home. **Mov-Ent**: Television Series, Comedy--Performance. **Acq:** Purchase. **Dist:** Movies Unlimited. $14.99.

The Best of Saturday Night Live: Eddie Murphy 19??
Murphy's greatest moments and characters, including Mr. Robinson, Buckwheat, Gumby, "White Like Me" and "Lifestyles of the Relatives of the Rich and Famous." 73m; VHS. **C:** Hosted by Eddie Murphy. **A:** Jr. High-Adult. **P:** Entertainment. **U:** Home. **Mov-Ent**: Television Series, Comedy--Performance. **Acq:** Purchase. **Dist:** Anchor Bay Entertainment; Movies Unlimited. $14.99.

The Best of Saturday Night Live: Lily Tomlin 19??
Tomlin does Edith Ann, Ernestine, and Judith Beasley as well as featuring sketches by Dan Aykroyd, John Belushi, Gilda Radner, and Chevy Chase. 70m; VHS. **A:** Jr. High-Adult. **P:** Entertainment. **U:** Home. **Mov-Ent**: Television Series, Comedy--Performance. **Acq:** Purchase. **Dist:** Movies Unlimited. $14.99.

The Best of Saturday Night Live: Rosanne Arnold 19??
A parody of "Misery" features Roseanne in the Kathy Bates role, she guests on "Coffee Talk" with Madonna and Barbra Streisand, gets together with Julia Sweeney's Pat, and joins husband Tom Arnold in "After the Laughter." 86m; VHS. **A:** Jr. High-Adult. **P:** Entertainment. **U:** Home. **Mov-Ent**: Television Series, Comedy--Performance. **Acq:** Purchase. **Dist:** Movies Unlimited. $14.99.

The Best of Saturday Night Live: The Coneheads 197?
The original Not Ready for Prime Time Players bring to life that wacky alien couple Beldar and Prymaat from the planet Remulak in a series of skits taken from the television show. 77m; VHS. **C:** Dan Aykroyd; Jane Curtin; Garrett Morris; Bill Murray; John Belushi; Gilda Radner; Laraine Newman; Steve Martin; Lily Tomlin; Charles Grodin. **A:** Jr. High-Adult. **P:** Entertainment. **U:** Home. **Mov-Ent**: Television Series. **Acq:** Purchase. **Dist:** Paramount Pictures Corp. $19.95.

The Best of Saturday Night Live: The Mr. Bill Show 197?
Nineteen segments of Bill, Sluggo, and Mr. Hand, including "Mr. Bill Shapes Up" and "Mr. Bill Goes to Jail." 50m; VHS. **A:** Jr. High-Adult. **P:** Entertainment. **U:** Home. **Mov-Ent**: Television Series. **Acq:** Purchase. **Dist:** Anchor Bay Entertainment. $14.95.

The Best of Saturday Night Live: Toonces and Friends 19??
Toonces the driving cat is the featured feline as he greets Steve Martin, Linda Hamilton, Dana Carvey, and Victoria Jackson. Other guests include SCTV's Joe Flaherty and Andrea Martin. 24m; VHS. **A:** Jr. High-Adult. **P:** Entertainment. **U:** Home. **Mov-Ent**: Television Series, Comedy--Performance. **Acq:** Purchase. **Dist:** Movies Unlimited. $14.99.

The Best of "See It Now" 199?
Legendary reporter Edward R. Murrow interviews Louis Armstrong, Grandma Moses, and Korean War soldiers. Narrated by Mike Wallace. 120m; VHS. **A:** Sr. High-Adult. **P:** Entertainment. **U:** Institution. **Gen-Edu**: Journalism, History--U.S. **Acq:** Purchase. **Dist:** Ambrose Video Publishing, Inc. $49.95.

The Best of Soap: Jessica's Wonderful Life 197?
From the camp TV sitcom comes this take-off on "It's a Wonderful Life." Jessica Tate (Helmond) finds herself at the stairway to heaven, pleading with an angel (Arthur) to return to aid her very dysfunctional family. 70m; VHS. **C:** Katherine Helmond; Bea Arthur; Robert Mandan; Cathryn Damon; Richard Mulligan; Billy Crystal. **A:** Jr. High-Adult. **P:** Entertainment. **U:** Home. **Mov-Ent**: Television Series. **Acq:** Purchase. **Dist:** Lions Gate Entertainment Inc. $14.95.

The Best of Soap: Who Killed Peter? 1977
From the outrageous comedy TV series, featuring the eccentric and rich Tate family and the equally eccentric, but working-class, Campbell family. When Jessica Tate (Helmond) is convicted of murdering her tennis pro, brother-in-law Burt (Mulligan) decides to investigate. Crystal gained attention as gay son Jodie Dallas. 72m; VHS. **C:** Katherine Helmond; Richard Mulligan; Diana Canova; Robert Urich; Robert Mandan; Ted Wass; Billy Crystal; Robert Guillaume. **A:** Jr. High-Adult. **P:** Entertainment. **U:** Home. **Mov-Ent**: Television Series. **Acq:** Purchase. **Dist:** Lions Gate Entertainment Inc. $14.95.

Best of Spike Jones, Vol. 1 1955
Segments from Jones' television series, starring the City Slickers and their gut-level song parodies, including "Cocktails for Two." 51m/B/W; VHS. **Pr:** Goldberg & O'Reilly Entertainment. **A:** Family. **P:** Entertainment. **U:** Home. **Mov-Ent**: Music--Performance, Television Series. **Acq:** Purchase. **Dist:** Paramount Pictures Corp. $29.95.

Best of Spike Jones, Vol. 2 1956
More segments from Jones' popular TV show, featuring parodies of "Indian Love Call," "Stranger in Paradise," and others. 53m/B/W; VHS. **Pr:** Goldberg & O'Reilly Entertainment. **A:** Family. **P:** Entertainment. **U:** Home. **Mov-Ent**: Music--Performance, Television Series. **Acq:** Purchase. **Dist:** Paramount Pictures Corp. $29.95.

Best of Spike Jones, Vol. 3 1952
Spike and crew destroy, "Pop Goes the Weasel," "Cocktails for Two," "Bye Bye Blues" and "Running Wild." 54m/B/W; VHS. **Pr:** Paramount Pictures. **A:** Family. **P:** Entertainment. **U:** Home. **Mov-Ent**: Television Series, Variety. **Acq:** Purchase. **Dist:** Paramount Pictures Corp. $29.98.

Best of SportsCenter with Chris Berman 1992
Berman and the ESPN SportsCenter staff take a look at the big sports stories, personalities, plays, and problems of 1991. 50m; VHS. **A:** Family. **P:** Entertainment. **U:** Home. **Spo-Rec**: Sports--General. **Acq:** Purchase. **Dist:** ESPN Inc.; Fast Forward.

Best of Starrcade: 1983-1987 1988
Join Magnum T.A. for a look at the finest matches of the Starcades inluding Flair vs. Harley Race, Valentine vs. Piper and much more. 254m; VHS. **C:** Ric Flair; Greg Valentine; Roddy Piper; Ricky "The Dragon" Steamboat. **A:** Family. **P:** Entertainment. **U:** Home. **Spo-Rec**: Sports--General. **Acq:** Purchase. **Dist:** Turner Broadcasting System Inc. $39.98.

The Best of Stoney-Wolf 1993
Contains a collection of the most outstanding hunting sequences from Stoney-Wolf's hunting videos from 1984 to 1990. Features hunting footage of whitetail deer, elk, caribou, mule deer, and turkey. 90m; VHS. **A:** Adult. **P:** Entertainment. **U:** Home. **Spo-Rec**: Hunting. **Acq:** Purchase. **Dist:** Stoney-Wolf Productions, Inc. $49.95.

The Best of Taos 1992
Planning a Taos, New Mexico ski vacation? This tape highlights the best lodging, dining, shopping, exercusions, and adventures the area has to offer as well as an overview of the skiing amenities. 45m; VHS. **Pr:** World Video Projects, Inc. **A:** Family. **P:** Entertainment. **U:** Home. **Gen-Edu**: Travel, U.S. States, Skiing. **Acq:** Purchase. **Dist:** Fast Forward. $19.95.

The Best of Tennessee Tuxedo and His Tales 2006
Contains 15 classic episodes with the wisecracking penguin and his pal Chumley, who live at the Megalopolis Zoo and constantly wage war against Stanley the zookeeper for better living conditions. Their academic friend Phineas J. Wheepee, along with his 3-D blackboard, demonstrates the basic scientific principles behind their unending schemes. 135m; DVD. **C:** Voice(s) by Don Adams; Larry Storch; Jackson Beck; George S. Irving; Bradley Bolde. **A:** Primary. **P:** Entertainment. **U:** Home. **Chl-Juv**: Animation & Cartoons. **Acq:** Purchase. **Dist:** SONY Wonder.

The Best of the Andy Williams Show 2000 (Unrated)
Compiles highlights from legendary singer Andy Williams' NBC television variety program (1962-1971) with guest performances by celebrities such as Tony Bennett, Bing Crosby, Judy Garland, and the Osmonds. 1 episode. 58m; DVD. **C:** Andy Williams. **A:** Family. **P:** Entertainment. **U:** Home. **Mov-Ent**: Television Series, Variety, Music--Performance. **Acq:** Purchase. **Dist:** Image Entertainment Inc. $24.99.

Best of the Badmen 1950 (Unrated) — ★★½
A whole bunch of outlaws, although seemingly quite nice, are brought together by an ex-Union general who is being framed. Too much talk, not enough action. 84m/B/W; VHS, DVD. **C:** Robert Ryan; Claire Trevor; Jack Buetel; Robert Preston; Walter Brennan; Bruce Cabot; John Archer; Lawrence Tierney; Directed by William D. Russell. **Pr:** Herman Schlom; RKO. **A:** Family. **P:** Entertainment. **U:** Home. **Mov-Ent**: Western. **Acq:** Purchase. **Dist:** WarnerArchive.com. $19.98.

The Best of the Beat Club: Volume 1 2006
Compiles scenes from various episodes of the 1965-1972 rock music television series with performances including Deep Purple, Santana, and Humble Pie. 43m; DVD. **A:** Jr. High-Adult. **P:** Entertainment. **U:** Home. **Mov-Ent**: Television Series, Music Video, Music--Pop/Rock. **Acq:** Purchase. **Dist:** RED Distribution L.L.C. $9.98.

The Best of the Beat Club: Volume 2 2006
Compiles scenes from various episodes of the 1965-1972 rock music television series with performances including Alice Cooper, Bachman Turner Overdrive, Doobie Brothers, and Three Dog Night. 39m; DVD. **A:** Jr. High-Adult. **P:** Entertainment. **U:** Home. **Mov-Ent**: Television Series, Music Video, Music--Pop/Rock. **Acq:** Purchase. **Dist:** RED Distribution L.L.C. $9.98.

Best of the Best 1989 (PG-13) — ★½
An interracial kick-boxing team strives to win a world championship. 95m; VHS, DVD; Open Captioned. **C:** Eric Roberts; Sally Kirkland; Christopher Penn; Phillip Rhee; James Earl Jones; John P. Ryan; John Dye; David Agresta; Tom Everett; Louise Fletcher; Simon Rhee; Edward (Eddie) Bunker; Directed by Robert Radler. **Pr:** The Movie Group; SVS Ent. **A:** Sr. High-Adult. **P:** Entertainment. **U:** Home. **Mov-Ent**: Martial Arts, Boxing, Sports--Olympic. **Acq:** Purchase. **Dist:** Sony Pictures Home Entertainment Inc. $14.95.

Best of the Best 2 1993 (R) — ★½
The Coliseum is a notorious martial-arts venue owned by the champion fighter Brackus and his manager Weldon. No rules death matches are the norm and when their friend is killed Tommy and Alex set up a grudge match with Brackus. 100m; VHS, DVD, Wide, CC. **C:** Eric Roberts; Phillip Rhee; Christopher Penn; Ralph (Ralf) Moeller; Wayne Newton; Edan Gross; Sonny Landham; Meg Foster; Simon Rhee; Claire Stansfield; Betty Carvalho; Edward (Eddie) Bunker; Directed by Robert Radler; Written by John Allen Nelson; Max Strom; Music by David Michael Frank. **Pr:** Peter E. Strauss; Philip Rhee; The Movie Group. **A:** Sr. High-Adult. **P:** Entertainment. **U:** Home. **Mov-Ent**: Martial Arts. **Acq:** Purchase. **Dist:** Fox Home Entertainment. $19.98.

Best of the Best 3: No Turning Back 1995 (R) — ★★
Asian-American Tommy Lee (Rhee) discovers a band of racist vigilantes are trying to take over the rural community of Liberty, where his sister lives. But with the help of his brother-in-law Jack (McDonald), who's also the sheriff, and school teacher Margo (Gershon), Tommy is going to fight back. 102m; VHS, DVD, CC. **C:** Phillip Rhee; Gina Gershon; Christopher McDonald; Mark Rolston; Peter Simmons; Dee Wallace; Directed by Phillip Rhee; Written by Deborah Scott; Cinematography by Jerry Watson; Music by Barry Goldberg. **A:** Sr. High-Adult. **P:** Entertainment. **U:** Home. **Mov-Ent**: Martial Arts, Prejudice. **Acq:** Purchase. **Dist:** Buena Vista Home Entertainment.

Best-of-the-Best Winning Hoops: Over 55 Powerful Plays from the 1-4 High Set 2010 (Unrated)
The editors of "Winning Hoops" magazine choose what they consider the best plays to use with the 1-4 high set from their publication. 76m; DVD. **A:** Family. **P:** Education. **U:** Home, Institution. **Spo-Rec**: Basketball, Athletic Instruction/Coaching. **Acq:** Purchase. **Dist:** Championship Productions. $39.99.

Best-of-the-Best Winning Hoops: Over 30 Sizzling Team Shooting Drills 2010 (Unrated)
The editors of "Winning Hoops" choose what they consider the best drills for improving shooting skills printed in their magazine. 115m; DVD. **A:** Family. **P:** Education. **U:** Home, Institution. **Spo-Rec**: Basketball, Athletic Instruction/Coaching. **Acq:** Purchase. **Dist:** Championship Productions. $39.99.

Best-of-the-Best Winning Hoops Series: 25 Aggressive Transition & Conditioning Drills 2005
Provides 25 basketball transition drills run with several players that improve many different types of offensive and defensive skills as designed by a group of top-level college coaches. 85m; DVD. **A:** Sr. High-Adult. **P:** Instruction. **U:** Institution. **Spo-Rec**: Basketball. **Acq:** Purchase. **Dist:** Championship Productions. $39.95.

Best-of-the-Best Winning Hoops Series: Over 50 Sensational Sideline Plays 2006 (Unrated)
Demonstrates what the editors of 'Winning Hoops' magazine thought were the best of the sidelines inbound plays submitted to their magazine for basketball teams to use. 76m; DVD. **A:** Family. **P:** Education. **U:** Home, Institution. **Spo-Rec**: Basketball, Athletic Instruction/Coaching. **Acq:** Purchase. **Dist:** Championship Productions. $39.99.

Best-of-the-Best Winning Hoops Series: Over 50 Set Plays to Attack Zone Defenses 2004 (Unrated)
Demonstrates what the editors of 'Winning Hoops' magazine thought were the best of the offensive concepts submitted to their magazine for basketball teams to use to take apart the Zone Defense. 90m; DVD. **A:** Family. **P:** Education. **U:** Home, Institution. **Spo-Rec**: Basketball, Athletic Instruction/Coaching. **Acq:** Purchase. **Dist:** Championship Productions. $39.99.

Best-of-the-Best Winning Hoops Series: Over 70 Baseline & Under-the-Basket Inbounds Plays 2004 (Unrated)
Live demonstrations of 70 baseline and inbounds basketball plays chosen by the editors of "Winning Hoops." 96m; DVD. **A:** Family. **P:** Education. **U:** Home, Institution. **Spo-Rec**: Basketball, Athletic Instruction/Coaching. **Acq:** Purchase. **Dist:** Championship Productions. $39.99.

Best-of-the-Best Winning Hoops Series: Over 60 Plays to Attack Man-to-Man Defenses 2005 (Unrated)
Demonstrates what the editors of 'Winning Hoops' magazine thought were the best of the offensive concepts submitted to their magazine for basketball teams to use to take apart the Man-to-Man Defense. 110m; DVD. **A:** Family. **P:** Education. **U:** Home, Institution. **Spo-Rec**: Basketball, Athletic Instruction/Coaching. **Acq:** Purchase. **Dist:** Championship Productions. $39.99.

Best of the Best: Without Warning 1998 (R) — ★½
It's Russian mobsters, counterfeit money, and high tech gadgets this time around as LAPD martial arts consultant Tommy Lee (Rhee) goes after the gang who killed his best friend's daughter. 90m; VHS, DVD, Blu-Ray. **C:** Phillip Rhee; Ernie Hudson; Tobin Bell; Thure Riefenstein; Chris Lemmon; Jessica Collins; Directed by Phillip Rhee; Cinematography by Michael D. Margulies; Music by David Grant. **A:** Sr. High-Adult. **P:** Entertainment. **U:** Home. **Mov-Ent**: Martial Arts. **Acq:** Purchase. **Dist:** Buena Vista Home Entertainment.

The Best of the Big Laff-Off 1983 — ★
Featuring top comics delivering their most hilarious routines, emphasis is from waistlines to punchlines. It's the best, funniest and fastest-moving segments of "The Big Laff-Off." Premiers Eddie Murphy and Robin Williams. 60m; VHS. **A:** Sr. High-Adult. **P:** Entertainment. **U:** Home. **Mov-Ent**: Comedy--Performance. **Acq:** Purchase. **Dist:** MGM Studios Inc. $19.98.

The Best of the Cayman Islands—Rev. Ed. 1994
All of the best restaurants, hotels, attractions and dive facilities of the Caymans can be seen on this tape. 25m; VHS. **TV Std:** NTSC, PAL. **Pr:** International Video Projects. **A:** Jr. High-Adult. **P:** Education. **U:** Home. **Gen-Edu**: Travel, Caribbean. **Acq:** Purchase. **Dist:** International Video Projects, Inc. $19.95.

The Best of the Colbert Report 2007
In "The Daily Show" spin-off, media-savvy, truth-buster, Stephen Colbert, presents the definition for "truthiness" (Merriam-Webster's 2006 Word of the Year), interviews Florida Democratic Congressman Robert Wexler, and exhibits classic confrontations with Bill O'Reilly, Jane Fonda, and Barry Manilow. Other collection highlights are the "Green Screen Challenge" and "Stephen Colbert's Rock and Awe: Countdown

to Guitarmageddon." 160m; DVD. **C:** Stephen Colbert. **A:** Adult. **P:** Entertainment. **U:** Home. **Mov-Ent:** Television. **Acq:** Purchase. **Dist:** Comedy Central.

Best of the Cutting Edge, Vol. 1 1988
Highlights from the MTV show are presented. 60m; VHS. **Pr:** MTV Films. **A:** Sr. High-Adult. **P:** Entertainment. **U:** Home. **Mov-Ent:** Music Video. **Acq:** Purchase. **Dist:** Image Entertainment Inc. $24.95.

Best of the Cutting Edge, Vol. 2 1988
More exciting alternative bands are featured including, Iggy Pop, Run-DMC, R.E.M., Tom Waits, The Blasters and others. 60m; VHS. **Pr:** MTV Films. **A:** Sr. High-Adult. **P:** Entertainment. **U:** Home. **Mov-Ent:** Music--Performance, Music Video. **Acq:** Purchase. **Dist:** Image Entertainment Inc. $24.95.

The Best of the Dean Martin Variety Show 2007
Collects 20 epsiodes from Martin's NBC variety show, which ran from 1965-74, including songs, dances, and comedy bits. 840m; DVD. **C:** Hosted by Dean Martin. **A:** Adult. **P:** Entertainment. **U:** Home. **Mov-Ent:** Television Series. **Acq:** Purchase. **Dist:** Acorn Media Group Inc. $59.95.

The Best of the Fest: New Orleans Jazz & Heritage Festival 1988
Live material of the Neville Brothers, Stevie Ray Vaughn, Los Lobos, Rita Coolidge, Dr. John and more are shown from the New Orleans Jazz & Heritage Festival. 50m; VHS. **A:** Sr. High-Adult. **P:** Entertainment. **U:** Home. **Mov-Ent:** Music--Performance. **Acq:** Purchase. **Dist:** Music Video Distributors. $19.95.

The Best of the Festival of Claymation 198?
Will Vinton's animated pranksters Herb and Rex host this special look at the most fantastic animation the world has to offer. Included are the incomparable Dancing Raisins. 60m; VHS. **C:** Will Vinton. **Pr:** Will Vinton. **A:** Family. **P:** Entertainment. **U:** Home. **Mov-Ent:** Family Viewing, Animation & Cartoons. **Acq:** Purchase. **Dist:** Image Entertainment Inc. $59.95.

Best of the Fests for Kids 1990
A collection of film shorts for kids of all ages. Features "The Rooster," about a rooster who decides to crow at sunset, and "Travels of a Dollar Bill," where a dollar tells the story of his life to a penny and a nickel, his grandchildren. 40m; VHS. **A:** Family. **P:** Entertainment. **U:** Home. **Mov-Ent:** Animation & Cartoons. **Acq:** Purchase. **Dist:** Next Gen Video; Facets Multimedia Inc.; Tapeworm Video Distributors Inc. $19.95.

Best of the Fests, 1988 1988 (Unrated)
This volume of film shorts includes "The Mother Art," a feature documenting the history of tatooing, and "Cerridwen's Gift," a myth concerning the birth of poetry, which was painted directly on the film. 90m; VHS. **A:** Sr. High-Adult. **P:** Entertainment. **U:** Home. **Mov-Ent:** Animation & Cartoons. **Acq:** Purchase. **Dist:** Next Gen Video; Facets Multimedia Inc.; Tapeworm Video Distributors Inc. $39.95.

Best of the Fests, 1989 1989 (Unrated)
A collection of ten high-quality short films featuring "Breakfast Messages," wherein a truck-stop cook shows his interest in a customer by his arrangement of the food on her plate. 90m; VHS. **A:** Sr. High-Adult. **P:** Entertainment. **U:** Home. **Mov-Ent:** Animation & Cartoons. **Acq:** Purchase. **Dist:** Tapeworm Video Distributors Inc.; Next Gen Video; Facets Multimedia Inc. $39.95.

Best of the Fests, 1990 1991 (Unrated)
There seems to be something for everybody in this acclaimed collection of short films which includes "Macha's Curse," a feature painted directly on 35mm film, and "No Pain No Gain," a comedy where a bodybuilder shows the ropes to a beginner. 90m; VHS. **A:** Sr. High-Adult. **P:** Entertainment. **U:** Home. **Mov-Ent:** Animation & Cartoons. **Acq:** Purchase. **Dist:** Next Gen Video; Facets Multimedia Inc.; Tapeworm Video Distributors Inc. $39.95.

Best of the Fests, 1991 1991
Features four animated and seven live-action short films from festivals around the world. Includes "Six Point Nine," "Why We Fight," "Balloon Head," "Walls in the Woods," "Post No Bills," "Wanting for Bridge," "In Transit," "Harvest Town," "Stealing Attitude," "Madcap," and "Man Descending." 90m; VHS. **A:** Jr. High-Adult. **P:** Entertainment. **U:** Home. **Mov-Ent:** Animation & Cartoons. **Acq:** Purchase. **Dist:** Tapeworm Video Distributors Inc. $39.95.

The Best of the Florida Keys—Rev. Ed. 1995
In half an hour this tape covers the highlights from Key West to Key Largo. Also available in German and Spanish. 30m; VHS. **TV Std:** NTSC, PAL. **Pr:** International Video Projects. **A:** Jr. High-Adult. **P:** Education. **U:** Home. **L:** English, German, Spanish. **Gen-Edu:** Travel, U.S. States. **Acq:** Purchase. **Dist:** International Video Projects, Inc. $19.95.

The Best of the Football Follies 1985
A compilation of the humorous events that often occur on the football field. 44m; VHS, CC. **C:** Joe Namath. **Pr:** NFL Films. **A:** Family. **P:** Entertainment. **U:** Home. **Spo-Rec:** Sports--General, Football, Outtakes & Bloopers. **Acq:** Purchase. **Dist:** ESPN Inc.; NFL Films Video; School-Tech Inc. $29.95.

The Best of the Golden Age of Televison 1955
Includes scenes from "Beat the Clock," "Howdy Doody," "McHales Navy Bloopers," and rare television promos. 60m/B/W; VHS. **A:** Family. **P:** Entertainment. **U:** Home. **Mov-Ent:** Television Series. **Acq:** Purchase. **Dist:** Video Resources.

The Best of the Kids in the Hall 1993 (Unrated)
Features some of the best clips of the hot Canadian comedy ensemble "The Kids in the Hall." Executive producer Lorne Michaels is best known for producing "Saturday Night Live." 120m; VHS. **C:** Dave Foley; Bruce McCulloch; Kevin McDonald; Mark McKinney; Scott Thompson. **Pr:** Lorne Michaels; Canadian Broadcasting Corp. **A:** Sr. High-Adult. **P:** Entertainment. **U:** Home. **Mov-Ent:** Comedy--Performance, Television Series. **Acq:** Purchase. **Dist:** Sony Pictures Home Entertainment Inc. $19.95.

The Best of the Lenny Henry Show 1990
Hilarious vignettes from the zany comedian. Includes "Thriller," "By the Riverbank" and a "Mother's Revenge." 101m; VHS. **C:** Lenny Henry; Robbie Coltrane; Frank Bruno; Directed by Geoffrey Posner. **A:** Jr. High-Adult. **P:** Entertainment. **U:** Home. **Mov-Ent:** TV Movies. **Acq:** Purchase. **Dist:** Facets Multimedia Inc. $19.98.

The Best of the Little Rascals 1931
A collection of six classic "Our Gang" two reelers featuring everyone's favorite rascals—Spanky, Alfalfa, Stymie, and Buckwheat. 103m/B/W; VHS. **C:** Darla Hood; Matthew "Stymie" Beard; George "Spanky" McFarland; Carl "Alfalfa" Switzer; Directed by Fred Wolf; Charles Swenson. **Pr:** Hal Roach. **A:** Family. **P:** Entertainment. **U:** Home. **Mov-Ent:** Family Viewing, Children, Television Series. **Acq:** Purchase. **Dist:** Lions Gate Entertainment Inc. $19.98.
Indiv. Titles: 1. Dogs is Dogs 2. Anniversary Trouble 3. Three Men in a Tub 4. Helping Grandma 5. Little Papa 6. Bear Facts.

The Best of the Midwest Volume I 1998
Features footage of locomotives and trains in Missouri, Nebraska, Iowa, South Dakota and Minnesota. 67m; VHS. **A:** Family. **P:** Entertainment. **U:** Home. **Gen-Edu:** Trains. **Acq:** Purchase. **Dist:** Pentrex Media Group L.L.C. $19.95.

The Best of the Midwest Volume II 1999
This celebration of trains and railroading features trains from South Dakota, Nebraska, Minnesota, Iowa, Illinois and Wisconsin. 97m; VHS. **A:** Family. **P:** Entertainment. **U:** Home. **Gen-Edu:** Trains. **Acq:** Purchase. **Dist:** Pentrex Media Group L.L.C. $19.95.

The Best of the Midwest Volume III 2000
This celebration of trains and railroading features trains from Kansas, Missouri, Iowa, Minnesota and Wisconsin. 81m; VHS. **A:** Family. **P:** Entertainment. **U:** Home. **Gen-Edu:** Trains. **Acq:** Purchase. **Dist:** Pentrex Media Group L.L.C. $19.95.

Best of the '90 1991
The offbeat, Chicago-produced PBS series featuring the works of independent filmmakers, edited together into individual episodes. This ten-volume set covers people, places, and ideas, including money, television, education, nutrition, malls, music, war, and other topics from a variety of perspectives. 60m; VHS. **Pr:** PBS. **A:** Sr. High-Adult. **P:** Entertainment. **U:** Home. **Mov-Ent:** Filmmaking. **Acq:** Purchase. **Dist:** 90s Home Video. $22.95.
Indiv. Titles: 1. Vol. 1: Money, Money, Money 2. Vol. 2: It's Only TV 3. Vol. 3: Bar Talk 4. Vol. 4: Food: What We Eat 5. Vol. 5: World View of the USA 6. Vol. 6: Race and Racism 7. Vol. 7: Kids and Learning 8. Vol. 8: The Street 9. Vol. 9: War 10. Vol. 10: Prisons and Their Content.

Best of the Old Campaign Commercials 19??
More than three decades worth of political commercials and how media campaigning has evolved. 60m; VHS. **A:** Adult. **P:** Education. **U:** Institution, Home. **Gen-Edu:** Commercials, Politics & Government. **Acq:** Purchase. **Dist:** Baker and Taylor. $90.00.

The Best of the Real West 1995
Features the premier collector's set. 50m; VHS, DVD. **Pr:** A&E (Arts & Entertainment) Network. **A:** Family. **P:** Entertainment. **U:** Home. **Gen-Edu:** History--U.S., Western. **Acq:** Purchase. **Dist:** New Video Group. $79.95.
Indiv. Titles: 1. Wyatt Earp: Justice at the OK Corral 2. Geronimo: The Last Renegade 3. Outlaws: The Ten Most Wanted.

The Best of the Soupy Sales Show 1990
Highlights of Soupy Sales' television program, including appearances by Dick Clark and Alice Cooper. One hilarious bit involves a custard confrontation between Soupy, Frank Sinatra, Sammy Davis Jr., and Trini Lopez. 50m; VHS. **C:** Soupy Sales; Frank Sinatra; Sammy Davis, Jr; Trini Lopez; Dick Clark; Alice Cooper. **Pr:** Rhino Video. **A:** Adult. **P:** Entertainment. **U:** Home. **Mov-Ent:** Television Series. **Acq:** Purchase. **Dist:** Rhino Entertainment Co. $19.95.

The Best of Times 1986 (PG) — ★★
Slim story of two grown men who attempt to redress the failures of the past by reenacting a football game they lost in high school due to a single flubbed pass. With this cast, it should have been better. 105m; VHS, DVD, 8 mm, CC. **C:** Robin Williams; Kurt Russell; M. Emmet Walsh; Pamela Reed; Holly Palance; Donald Moffat; Margaret Whitton; Kirk Cameron; Directed by Roger Spottiswoode; Written by Ron Shelton; Cinematography by Charles F. Wheeler; Music by Arthur B. Rubinstein. **Pr:** Gordon Carroll; Mark Huffam. **A:** Jr. High-Adult. **P:** Entertainment. **U:** Home. **Mov-Ent:** Sports--Fiction: Comedy, Football, Aging. **Acq:** Purchase. **Dist:** New Line Home Video. $14.98.

The Best of Victor Borge, Acts 1 and 2 19??
The musical comedian's best routines, including "Introducing Mozart," "The Timid Page Turner," "Phonetic Punctuation," and "Rigor Mortis." 90m; VHS. **A:** Family. **P:** Entertainment. **U:** Home. **Mov-Ent:** Comedy--Performance. **Acq:** Purchase. **Dist:** Baker and Taylor. $19.99.

Best of Videophile 1992
Features interviews and video clips by Laibach, Sleep Chamber, MC 900 Ft. Jesus, Legendary Pink Dots, PTV, KMFDM, Ministry, Dharma Bums, Chemical People, Universal Congress, Pain Teens, God Bullies, Jethro Tilton, and the Hafler Trio. 90m; VHS. **A:** Jr. High-Adult. **P:** Entertainment. **U:** Home. **Mov-Ent:** Music Video, Music--Pop/Rock, Interviews. **Acq:** Purchase. **Dist:** Music Video Distributors. $19.95.

The Best of Wake, Rattle & Roll 1990
An entertaining mixture of live action and animation chronicles the adventures of Sam the boy genius and robot pal DECKS. 30m; VHS. **C:** R.J. Williams. **Pr:** Hanna-Barbera Productions. **A:** Family. **P:** Entertainment. **U:** Home. **L:** English, Spanish. **Chl-Juv:** Children, Fantasy, Animation & Cartoons. **Acq:** Purchase. **Dist:** Turner Broadcasting System Inc. $9.95.

The Best of Wave Warriors Back and Bad 1992
Features the stars of surfing, skateboarding, and snowboarding set to alternative music by such groups as Jane's Addiction, Faith No More, and Ministry. 60m; VHS. **A:** Jr. High-Adult. **P:** Entertainment. **U:** Home. **Spo-Rec:** Sports--General, Skateboarding, Music--Pop/Rock. **Acq:** Purchase. **Dist:** Music Video Distributors. $19.98.

Best of W.C. Fields 1933
Three of W.C. Field's Mack Sennett shorts are presented in their complete, uncut form: "The Dentist," "The Fatal Glass of Beer," and "The Golf Specialist." 58m/B/W; VHS. **C:** W.C. Fields; Elise Cavanna. **Pr:** Mack Sennett. **A:** Family. **P:** Entertainment. **U:** Home. **Mov-Ent:** Comedy--Screwball. **Acq:** Purchase. **Dist:** Lions Gate Entertainment Inc. $19.95.

The Best of WCW Nitro Vol. 2 2013 (PG)
Storyline and match highlights from WCW during it's 'Monday Night War' with rival WWE's wrestling program. 540m; DVD, Blu-Ray. **A:** Primary-Adult. **P:** Entertainment. **U:** Home. **L:** English. **Gen-Edu:** Sports--General. **Acq:** Purchase. **Dist:** WWE Studios. $39.95 29.98.

Best of West Coast Rock, Vol. 1 19??
This Japanese import looks at 14 bands, including The Mamas & Papas, Poco, Santana and Big Brother & The Holding Company. 60m; VHS. **A:** Sr. High-Adult. **P:** Entertainment. **U:** Home. **Mov-Ent:** Music Video. **Acq:** Purchase. **Dist:** Music Video Distributors. $59.95.

Best of West Coast Rock, Vol. 2 19??
This Japanese import features 13 songs by such bands as The Eagles, C. C.R., Canned Heat, Steve Miller and the Byrds. 60m; VHS. **A:** Sr. High-Adult. **P:** Entertainment. **U:** Home. **Mov-Ent:** Music Video. **Acq:** Purchase. **Dist:** Music Video Distributors. $59.95.

Best of West Coast Rock, Vol. 3 19??
Jefferson Airplane, Janis Joplin, The Doors, Santana and many more groups highlight this Japanese import. 60m; VHS. **A:** Sr. High-Adult. **P:** Entertainment. **U:** Home. **Mov-Ent:** Music Video. **Acq:** Purchase. **Dist:** Music Video Distributors. $59.95.

The Best of What's Left. . .Not Only..But Also 1990
A collection of some of Moore and Cook's finest sketches from their heyday on British television's "Beyond the Fringe." Includes "Bo Dudley," "Bloody Greta Garbo" and "Pete and Dud at the London Zoo." 90m/B/W; VHS. **C:** Dudley Moore; Peter Cook. **Pr:** British Broadcasting Corporation. **A:** Jr. High-Adult. **P:** Entertainment. **U:** Home. **Mov-Ent:** Television Series. **Acq:** Purchase. **Dist:** Facets Multimedia Inc. $19.98.

Best of Wrestling Gold, Vol. 3 1991
Wrestling fans will enjoy more excitement and fun featuring Hulk Hogan vs. The Outlaw and a mud match between The Shiek and Tiger Jeet Singh. 50m; VHS. **C:** Hulk Hogan. **A:** Family. **P:** Entertainment. **U:** Home. **Spo-Rec:** Sports--General. **Acq:** Purchase. **Dist:** VCI Entertainment. $19.95.

The Best of WWE at Madison Square Garden 2013 (PG)
Documentary on the relationship between the WWE wrestling promotion and Madison Square Garden in New York City. 540m; DVD, Blu-Ray. **A:** Primary-Adult. **P:** Entertainment. **U:** Home. **L:** English. **Gen-Edu:** Sports--General, Sports Documentary. **Acq:** Purchase. **Dist:** WWE Studios. $39.95 29.93.

The Best of You, the Best of Me 198?
Presents intergenerational programs that portray young and old people joining together in mutually benefitting relationships. 28m; VHS. **A:** Adult. **P:** Education. **U:** Home. **Gen-Edu:** Human Relations. **Acq:** Purchase, Rent/Lease. **Dist:** University of Pittsburgh. $100.

Best of Youth 2003 (R) — ★★★★
Sprawling modern-times epic spanning 40 years of Italy's tumultuous history through the eyes of two brothers. At close to six hours the film encapsulates the entire relationship between Nicola (Lo Cascio), an optimistic med student, wooing women worldwide before settling into a successful career as a psychiatrist, and his brother Matteo (Boni), a world-weary, brooding idealist who eventually joins the Italian police in hopes of righting the wrongs of an unfair society. History is seen with human eyes and expressed in striking passion, somehow never overindulging itself. Originally an Italian television miniseries, went on to win over the crowds and critics at Cannes. 383m; DVD. **C:** Luigi Lo Cascio; Adriana Asti; Alessio Boni; Jasmine Trinca; Sonia Bergamasco; Fabrizio Gifuni; Maya Sansa; Valentina Carnelutti; Andrea Tidona; Lidia Vitale; Camilla Filippi; Greta Cavuoti; Sara Pavoncello; Claudio Gioe; Directed by Marco Tullio Giordana; Written by Sandro Petraglia; Stefano Rulli; Cinematography by Roberto Forza. **Pr:** Angelo Barbagallo; RAI. **A:** Sr. High-Adult. **P:** Entertainment. **U:** Home. **L:** Italian. **Mov-Ent:** Italy. **Dist:** Miramax Film Corp.

The Best of Zagreb Film ? — ★★½
This collection of short animated films from Yugoslavia owes nothing to Disney. These works are more experimental and do not follow conventional cartoon plots. They're definitely not for children; in fact, one of them, "Fisheye," is a horror story that is guaranteed to generate nightmares in any small fry who watch it. These are meant for adult fans of serious animation. Contents: Be Careful What You Wish For; Big Time; Curiosity; Musical Pig; Okay!; Elegy; The Fifth One; The Wall; Paranoia; The Ceremony; The Fly; Maxicat in the Hat, Lunch and Broom; Ersatz; Diary; Mask of the Red Death; Butterflies; Last Waltz in the Old Mill; Fisheye; Mass in A Minor. 114m; DVD. **A:** Sr. High-Adult. **P:** Entertainment. **U:** Home. **Mov-Ent:** Animation & Cartoons. **Acq:** Purchase. **Dist:** Image Entertainment Inc.

The Best of Zagreb Film: Laugh at Your Own Risk and For Children Only 19??
Some of the cartoons in this collection are showing their age with light flecks and static in the soundtrack. Others are pristine, but criticisms about image quality are secondary to the imagination, inventiveness, and playful intelligence behind the films. The disc is divided into adult and children's halves. The two best are "Tower of Babel" and "The Devil's Work," though there's not a loser in the bunch. Contents: The Tower of Babel, Exciting Love Story, The Devil's Work, Of Holes and Corks, Learning to Walk, Home Is the Best, Maxicat in Tennis, Maxicat in Rope, Maxicat in Door, Cow on the Moon, Strange Bird, Octave of Fear, Little and Big, Anna Goes to Buy Some Bread, Well Done Job, Krek, Maxicat in Ball of Yarn/Maxicat in Fishing. 109m; DVD. **A:** Sr. High-Adult. **P:** Entertainment. **U:** Home. **Mov-Ent:** Animation & Cartoons. **Acq:** Purchase. **Dist:** Image Entertainment Inc.

Best Offer 1992
Kyle is a 12-year-old girl, uncertain about the opposite sex, who is forced to sell her beloved horse. At the ranch where her horse is to be sold Kyle meets Ray, a saddle-bronc rider, who fascinates her for reasons she can't quite understand. 28m; VHS. **C:** Directed by Lisa Krueger. **A:** Jr. High-Adult. **P:** Entertainment. **U:** Institution. **Mov-Ent:** Adolescence, Sex & Sexuality. **Acq:** Purchase, Rent/Lease. **Dist:** The Cinema Guild. $250.00.

The Best Offer 2013 (R) — ★½
Eccentric high-end auctioneer Virgil Oldman (Rush) is hired by reclusive Claire (Hoeks) to appraise the contents of the villa she's inherited. Virgil's been miscataloging art works so he can have failed artist Billy (Sutherland) buy them on the cheap and among his treasures is a collection of portraits of women. But Virgil becomes obsessed with Claire rather than her art, having fallen in love for the first time. 131m; DVD. **C:** Geoffrey Rush; Sylvia Hoeks; Donald Sutherland; Jim Sturgess; Directed by Giuseppe Tornatore; Written by Giuseppe Tornatore; Cinematography by Fabio Zamarion; Music by Ennio Morricone. **A:** Adult. **P:** Entertainment. **U:** Home. **L:** English. **Mov-Ent:** Art & Artists, Romance. **Acq:** Purchase. **Dist:** IFC Films.

The Best of...What's Left of...Not Only...But Also 2008 (Unrated)
Peter Cook and Dudley Moore serve up a boatload of comedy sketches. Mother Superior (Cook) shepherds an order of leaping nuns, Moore presents soul man Bo Dudley, a leprechaun and a fairy come to blows, a father tries to have "the talk" with his son, and a parody of the 'Thunderbirds' marionette shows are just some of the highlights. 173m; DVD. **C:** Dudley Moore; Peter Cook. **A:** Adult. **P:** Entertainment. **U:** Home. **Mov-Ent:** Television Series. **Acq:** Purchase. **Dist:** BBC Worldwide Publishing Ltd.

The Best Prevention 1988
Realistic shoplifting scenes are reenacted so people who work in stores can make sure that it doesn't happen to them. 19m; VHS, 3/4 U. **Pr:** American Media Inc. **A:** Adult. **P:** Education. **U:** Institution, CCTV, Home. **Bus-Ind:** Personnel Management. **Acq:** Purchase, Rent/Lease. **Dist:** American Media, Inc. $395.00.

Best Ranger: The Ultimate Armed Forces Competition 2007
Three-part series of extreme challenges held at Fort Benning, Georgia, including marksmanship, a 21-mile road march, tactical tests, land navigation and night orienteering, and a 26-obstacle course. 150m; DVD. **A:** Jr. High-Adult. **P:** Entertainment. **U:** Home. **Gen-Edu:** Documentary Films. **Acq:** Purchase. **Dist:** Image Entertainment Inc.

Best Revenge 1983 (R) — ★★
Two aging hippies engage in a Moroccan drug deal in order to free a kidnapped friend from a sleazy gangster. They get caught by the police, but escape, searching for the engineers of the frame-up. 92m; VHS. **C:** John Heard; Levon Helm; Alberta Watson; John Rhys-Davies; Moses Znaimer; Directed by John Trent; Music by Keith Emerson. **Pr:** Michael Lebowitz. **A:** Sr. High-Adult. **P:** Entertainment. **U:** Home. **Mov-Ent:** Drugs. **Acq:** Purchase. **Dist:** MGM Studios Inc. ; Warner Home Video, Inc. $59.95.

Best Secrets for Catching More Fish 19??
Homer Circle, angling editor of Sports Afield Magazine, explores techniques which will help you become better at fishing. He covers everything from backlashing to de-hooking your hand, rescuing a lost lure, and outsmarting fish. 45m; VHS. **Pr:** Bennett Marine Video. **A:** Jr. High-Adult. **P:** Instruction. **U:** Home. **Spo-Rec:** Fishing, How-To. **Acq:** Purchase. **Dist:** Bennett Marine Video. $19.95.

Best Seller 1987 (R) — ★★★
Interesting, subtext-laden thriller about a cop/bestselling author with writer's block, and the strange symbiotic relationship he

forms with a slick hired killer, who wants his own story written. Dennehy is convincing as the jaded cop, and is paired well with the psychotic Woods. 112m; VHS, DVD, Wide; Open Captioned. **C:** James Woods; Brian Dennehy; Victoria Tennant; Paul Shenar; Seymour Cassel; Allison Balson; George Coe; Anne Pitoniak; Directed by John Flynn; Written by Larry Cohen; Cinematography by Fred Murphy; Music by Jay Ferguson. **Pr:** Hemdale Films. **A:** Sr. High-Adult. **P:** Entertainment. **U:** Home. **Mov-Ent:** Mystery & Suspense. **Acq:** Purchase. **Dist:** MGM Home Entertainment. $14.98.

Best Travels in Europe 1994
Rick Steves conducts a rapid tour through western Europe, highlighting attractions in the Netherlands, Germany, Italy, France and England. 68m; VHS. **A:** Adult. **P:** Education. **U:** Home. **Gen-Edu:** Travel. **Acq:** Purchase. **Dist:** Small World Productions. $29.95.

The Best Way 1976 (Unrated) — ★★½
Two summer camp counselors discover they might be gay and desirous of each other. Miller's first film; in French with English subtitles. 85m; VHS, DVD. **C:** Patrick Dewaere; Patrick Bouchitey; Christine Pascal; Claude Pieplu; Directed by Claude Miller; Written by Claude Miller; Luc Beraud; Cinematography by Bruno Nuytten; Music by Alain Jomy. **Pr:** Specialty. **A:** Sr. High-Adult. **P:** Entertainment. **U:** Home. **L:** French. **Mov-Ent:** Comedy-Drama, Camps & Camping. **Acq:** Purchase. **Dist:** Facets Multimedia Inc. $79.95.

Best Worst Movie 2009 (Unrated) — ★★★
Documentary recounting the making of the infamous 1990 straight-to-video bomb "Troll 2" (stealing only the title from 1986's "Troll"). Also chronicles how it reached its pinnacle of popularity over 15 years after its debut with a rabid cult following who can recite every poorly-written line of this unquestionably and hilariously terrible movie. Lovingly written and directed by original "T2" child star Stephenson, who speaks candidly about the flick's absurd origins. Funny and insightful with appeal for horror geeks and anyone who's ever sat through a real stinker. 91m; On Demand, Wide. **C:** George Hardy; Claudio; Margo Prey; Jason Steadman; Darren Ewing; Directed by Michael Stevenson; Cinematography by Katie Graham; Carl Indriago; Music by Bobby Tahouri. **Pr:** Lindsay Rowles Stephenson; Brad Klopman; Michael Paul Stephenson; Jim McKeon; Magic Stone Productions; Abramorama Films. **A:** Sr. High-Adult. **P:** Entertainment. **U:** Home. **L:** English. **Mov-Ent:** Filmmaking, Documentary Films. **Acq:** Purchase. **Dist:** New Video Group; Amazon.com Inc.; Movies Unlimited.

The Best Years of Our Lives 1946 — ★★★★
Three WWII vets return home to try to pick up the threads of their lives. A film that represented a large chunk of American society and helped it readjust to the modern postwar ambience is now considered an American classic. Supporting actor Russell, an actual veteran, holds a record for winning two Oscars for a single role. In addition to his Best Supporting Actor award, Russell was given a special Oscar for bringing hope and courage to fellow veterans. Based on the novella by MacKinlay Kantor. Remade for TV as "Returning Home" in 1975. 170m/B/W; VHS, DVD, Blu-Ray. **C:** Fredric March; Myrna Loy; Teresa Wright; Dana Andrews; Virginia Mayo; Harold Russell; Hoagy Carmichael; Gladys George; Roman Bohnen; Steve Cochran; Charles Halton; Cathy O'Donnell; Ray Collins; Victor Cutler; Minna Gombell; Walter Baldwin; Dorothy Adams; Don Beddoe; Ray Teal; Howland Chamberlain; Directed by William Wyler; Written by Robert Sherwood; Cinematography by Gregg Toland; Music by Hugo Friedhofer. **Pr:** Samuel Goldwyn. **A:** Jr. High-Adult. **P:** Entertainment. **U:** Home. **Mov-Ent:** World War Two, Veterans, Classic Films. **Awds:** Oscars '46: Actor (March), Director (Wyler), Film, Film Editing, Orig. Dramatic Score, Screenplay, Support. Actor (Russell); AFI '98: Top 100; British Acad. '47: Film; Golden Globes '47: Film--Drama; Natl. Bd. of Review '46: Director (Wyler); Natl. Film Reg. '89; N.Y. Film Critics '46: Director (Wyler), Film. **Acq:** Purchase. **Dist:** Facets Multimedia Inc.; Baker and Taylor. $14.98.

The Best Years: The Complete 2nd Season 2008 (Unrated)
CanWest Global Television Network 2007-9 drama. Samantha Best (Shea) returns to Charles University for her sophomore year with new 'frenemies' and romantic conquests. Noah's dedication to his "Documentary" puts a strain on his relationship with Robyn, Del and Kat psychoanalyze their friends in "Dermabrasion," a prank war breaks out on campus in "Different Hearts," then Samantha and Rich's "Destiny" unravels at a Canadian Thanksgiving party. 8 episodes. 368m; DVD. **C:** Randall Edwards; Charity Shea. **A:** Sr. High-Adult. **P:** Entertainment. **U:** Home. **Mov-Ent:** Drama, Romance, Television Series. **Acq:** Purchase. **Dist:** eOne Home Video. $24.99.

Besuch aus heiterem Himmel 1958 (Unrated)
After wagering that he can produce a real ghost, an expatriate German industrialist buys a likely looking castle. When he moves in, the supernatural fun begins. In German only. 94m; VHS. **TV Std:** NTSC, PAL. **C:** Johannes Heester; Elma Karlowa; Oskar Sima. **Pr:** German Language Video Center. **A:** Family. **P:** Entertainment. **U:** Home. **L:** German. **Mov-Ent:** Germany. **Acq:** Purchase, Rent/Lease. **Dist:** German Language Video Center. $37.95.

The Bet 1972
Captures the various emotions of a young man who bets his wealthy friend that he can isolate himself in a single room for five years, and emerge to enjoy his winnings. 24m; VHS, 3/4 U. **Pr:** Ron Waller. **A:** Jr. High-Adult. **P:** Entertainment. **U:** Institution, Home, SURA. **Gen-Edu:** Literature--Modern. **Acq:** Purchase, Rent/Lease, Duplication License. **Dist:** Pyramid Media. $225.00.

The Bet 1984
A young man who taunts a group of derelicts on Hollywood's skid row changes his attitude after an elderly derelict befriends him. 27m; VHS, 3/4 U, Special order formats. **C:** Philip McKeon; Henry Proach; Panchito Gomez. **Pr:** Paulist Productions. **A:** Jr. High-Adult. **P:** Religious. **U:** Institution, CCTV, SURA. **Gen-Edu:** Religion. **Acq:** Purchase. **Dist:** Paulist Productions.

Bet Herut: The End of the Beginning 2005
Documentary about a socialist farming community in Israel whose founder killed his children and took his own life. 53m; VHS, DVD. **A:** Sr. High-Adult. **P:** Education. **U:** Institution. **Gen-Edu:** Documentary Films, Judaism. **Acq:** Purchase, Rent/Lease. **Dist:** The Cinema Guild. $250.00.

Bet Your Life 1995
Teaches safety with a graphic example of a dead co-worker who "bet his life" that a circuit had been turned off. 15m; VHS. **A:** Adult. **P:** Professional. **U:** Institution. **Bus-Ind:** Safety Education, Occupational Training, Electricity. **Acq:** Rent/Lease. **Dist:** National Safety Council, California Chapter, Film Library.

Bet Your Life 2004 (Unrated) — ★½
In 2004 NBC television had a reality gameshow called "Next Action Star", and the male and female winners of it would star opposite Billy Zane in an action film. This is that film. All things considered they're probably regretting the experience now. Sonny (Sean Carrigan) is a gambling addict who catches the attention of a perverse millionaire. He bets his entire fortune that Sonny can't stay alive for 24 hours, and Sonny promptly flees to Cleveland, Ohio. Obviously Cleveland must be some sort of impregnable fortress city that hates the rich. 90m; DVD. **C:** Sean Carrigan; Corrine Van Ryck de Groot; Billy Zane; Rich Pierrelouis; Amanda Tosch; Joe Gogol; Joel Nunley; Christopher J. Quinn; Alfred Thomas Catalfo; Jeanne Brauer; Shelly Marks; Directed by Louis Morneau; Written by Louis Morneau; Jeff Welch; Cinematography by David Litz; George Mooradian; Music by Tim Truman. **A:** Sr. High-Adult. **P:** Entertainment. **U:** Home. **Mov-Ent:** Drama, War--General, Drama. **Acq:** Purchase. **Dist:** $24.99.

Beta Blockers After Myocardial Infarction 1982
Presents extensive studies on the use of beta blockers to treat myocardial infarction. 30m; VHS, 3/4 U. **Pr:** Emory University. **A:** College-Adult. **P:** Professional. **U:** Institution, CCTV, Home, SURA. **Hea-Sci:** Heart, Medical Education. **Acq:** Purchase, Rent/Lease, Subscription. **Dist:** Emory Medical Television Network.

Betania: Land of Grace & Miracles 19??
Documents the miracles, healings and urgent messages to the world connected with the appearance of the Virgin Mary in Betania, Venezuela. 58m; VHS. **A:** Sr. High-Adult. **P:** Religious. **U:** Home. **Gen-Edu:** Religion. **Acq:** Purchase. **Dist:** Hartley Film Foundation. $29.95.

Beth Hart & Joe Bonamassa: Live in Amsterdam 2014 (Unrated)
Singer Beth Hart and guitarist Joe Bonamassa team up for a performance of soul covers of famous songs, filmed live in the Koninklijk Theater Carré. 120m; DVD, Blu-Ray. **A:** Jr. High-Adult. **P:** Entertainment. **U:** Home. **L:** English. **Gen-Edu:** Music--Performance, Music--Pop/Rock, Music. **Acq:** Purchase. **Dist:** J&R Adventures. $24.98 24.98.

Bethie's Really Silly Clubhouse 1994
Children's entertainer Bethie opens her clubhouse to a group of youngsters who want to learn about animals. Lots of jokes and silly songs. 30m; VHS. **A:** Preschool-Primary. **P:** Entertainment. **U:** Home. **Chl-Juv:** Music--Children. **Acq:** Purchase. **Dist:** BMG Entertainment.

Bethune 1964
A biography of Dr. Norman Bethune, who served during the Spanish Civil War and the Sino-Japanese War, pioneering the world's first mobile blood transfusion service, among other advances. 59m/B/W; VHS, 3/4 U. **Pr:** National Film Board of Canada. **A:** Sr. High-Adult. **P:** Education. **U:** Institution, SURA. **Gen-Edu:** Documentary Films, Physicians, Biography. **Acq:** Purchase, Rent/Lease. **Dist:** National Film Board of Canada.

Bethune 1977 (Unrated) — ★★½
The life story of a Canadian doctor who started a practice in Communist China. 88m; VHS. **C:** Donald Sutherland; Kate Nelligan; David Gardner; James Hong; Directed by Eric Till. **Pr:** Robert Allen. **A:** Sr. High-Adult. **P:** Entertainment. **U:** Home. **Mov-Ent:** Biography: Science & Medical, China. **Acq:** Purchase. **Dist:** No Longer Available.

Betrayal 1974 (Unrated) — ★
Psycho-thriller pits an unhappy widow against her seemingly innocent hired companion. Seems this girl has a boyfriend who has a plan to murder the lonely lady for her money. Routine and predictable. 78m; VHS, DVD. **C:** Amanda Blake; Dick Haymes; Tisha Sterling; Sam Groom; Directed by Gordon Hessler; Music by Ernest Gold. **A:** Jr. High-Adult. **P:** Entertainment. **U:** Home. **Mov-Ent:** Mystery & Suspense. **Acq:** Purchase. **Dist:** Mill Creek Entertainment L.L.C. $79.95.

Betrayal 1978 (Unrated) — ★½
Telefilm based on the book by Lucy Freeman and Julie Roy about a historic malpractice case involving a psychiatrist and one of his female patients. The doctor convinced the female patient that sex with him would serve as therapy. 95m; VHS, DVD. **C:** Lesley Ann Warren; Rip Torn; Ron Silver; Richard Masur; Stephen Elliott; John Hillerman; Peggy Ann Garner; Directed by Paul Wendkos. **Pr:** EMI Media. **A:** Sr. High-Adult. **P:** Entertainment. **U:** Home. **Mov-Ent:** Sex & Sexuality, TV Movies, Psychiatry. **Acq:** Purchase. **Dist:** Unknown Distributor.

Betrayal 1983 (R) — ★★½
An unusual adult drama, beginning at the end of a seven-year adulterous affair and working its way back in time to finally end at the start of the betrayal of a husband by his wife and his best friend. Kingsley and Irons make Pinter's adaptation of his own play work. 95m; VHS. **C:** Ben Kingsley; Patricia Hodge; Jeremy Irons; Directed by David Hugh Jones; Written by Harold Pinter. **Pr:** 20th Century-Fox. **A:** Sr. High-Adult. **P:** Entertainment. **U:** Home. **Mov-Ent:** Marriage. **Acq:** Purchase. **Dist:** $59.98.

The Betrayal 2008 (Unrated)
The award-winning story of one Laotian family and their troubles filmed over the course of 23 years. Originally recruited by the CIA to do intelligence in Vietnam, they must flee when the American forces retreat, and seek asylum in the states. 96m; VHS, DVD. **A:** Sr. High-Adult. **P:** Education. **U:** Home, Institution. **Gen-Edu:** Vietnam War, Biography. **Acq:** Purchase, Rent/Lease. **Dist:** The Cinema Guild. $395.

Betrayal at Little Bighorn: The New Explorers 1997
Analyzes possibilities of what might have actually taken place at Little Bighorn, including politics within the Seventh Cavalry, Custer being betrayed by his subordinates, and how justified the Sioux were in their attack. 45m; VHS. **A:** Jr. High-Sr. High. **P:** Education. **U:** Institution. **Gen-Edu:** History--U.S., War--General, Native Americans. **Acq:** Purchase. **Dist:** Zenger Media. $19.95.

Betrayal from the East 1944 (Unrated) — ★★
A carnival barker saves the Panama Canal from the vicious Japanese war machine in this rather silly wartime drama. 82m/B/W; VHS. **C:** Lee Tracy; Nancy Kelly; Richard Loo; Abner Biberman; Regis Toomey; Philip Ahn; Addison Richards; Victor Sen Yung; Drew Pearson; Directed by William Berke. **Pr:** Herman Schlom; RKO. **A:** Jr. High-Adult. **P:** Entertainment. **U:** Home. **Mov-Ent:** World War Two, Circuses. **Acq:** Purchase. **Dist:** Turner Broadcasting System Inc. $19.98.

The Betrayal of Democracy 1992
Sobering program reveals the influence of special interest groups on the political process. It is through these conduits that the wealthy buy power in Washington. The challenge to the American system of government is explored. Includes interviews with various Washington insiders. From the public television program "Frontline." 118m; VHS, CC. **Pr:** Washington Media Associates. **A:** Sr. High-Adult. **P:** Education. **U:** Institution, Home. **Gen-Edu:** Politics & Government. **Acq:** Purchase. **Dist:** PBS Home Video. $89.95.

Betrayal of the Dove 1992 (R) — ★★
Slater stars as a divorced woman set-up on a blind date by best friend Le Brock. Zane is the dashing doctor who sweeps Slater off her feet but things are never quite what they seem. He may not be Mr. Right and the best friend has her own hidden agenda. 93m; VHS, DVD. **C:** Helen Slater; Kelly Le Brock; Billy Zane; Alan Thicke; Harvey Korman; Stuart Pankin; David Lander; Directed by Strathford Hamilton; Written by Robby Benson. **Pr:** Ashok Amritraj. **A:** Sr. High-Adult. **P:** Entertainment. **U:** Home. **Mov-Ent:** Mystery & Suspense, Romance. **Acq:** Purchase. **Dist:** Unknown Distributor.

Betrayed 1944 (Unrated) — ★★
Efficient crime drama from director Castle. Drunken conventioneer Prescott (Elliott) is murdered in his hotel room after flashing a wad of cash around a bar. Waitress Millie (Hunter) suspects her salesman hubby Paul (Jagger), whom she married after a whirlwind romance, could be involved after he admits meeting Prescott but it could also be her old flame Fred (Mitchum). 67m/B/W; DVD. **C:** Dean Jagger; Kim Hunter; Robert Mitchum; Neil Hamilton; Lou Lubin; Milton Kibbee; Richard Elliott; Directed by William Castle; Written by Philip Yordan; Dennis J. Cooper; Cinematography by Ira Morgan; Music by Dimitri Tiomkin. **A:** Sr. High-Adult. **P:** Entertainment. **U:** Home. **Mov-Ent:** Crime Drama, Marriage. **Acq:** Purchase. **Dist:** WarnerArchive.com.

Betrayed 1954 — ★★★
Bombshell Turner and strongman Gable star in this story of WWII intrigue. Suspected of being a Nazi informer, Turner is sent back to Holland for a last chance at redemption. Her cover as a sultry nightclub performer has the Nazis drooling and ogling (can you spell h-o-t?), but her act may be blown by an informant. Can luscious Lana get out of this one intact? 107m; VHS, DVD. **C:** Clark Gable; Lana Turner; Victor Mature; Louis Calhern; O.E. Hasse; Wilfrid Hyde-White; Ian Carmichael; Niall MacGinnis; Nora Swinburne; Roland Culver; Directed by Gottfried Reinhardt; Cinematography by Frederick A. (Freddie) Young. **Pr:** MGM. **A:** Jr. High-Adult. **P:** Entertainment. **U:** Home. **Mov-Ent:** **Acq:** Purchase. **Dist:** WarnerArchive.com; Critics' Choice Video & DVD. $19.98.

Betrayed 1988 (R) — ★★
A rabid political film, dealing with an implausible FBI agent infiltrating a white supremacist organization via her love affair with a handsome farmer who turns out to be a murderous racist. Winger is memorable in her role as the FBI agent, despite the film's limitations, and admirers of Costa-Gavras's directorial work and political stances will want to see how the director botched this one. 112m; VHS, DVD, Wide, CC. **C:** Tom Berenger; Debra Winger; John Mahoney; John Heard; Albert Hall; Jeffrey DeMunn; Directed by Constantin Costa-Gavras; Written by Joe Eszterhas; Cinematography by Patrick Blossier. **Pr:** Irwin Winkler; United Artists. **A:** Sr. High-Adult. **P:** Entertainment. **U:** Home. **Mov-Ent:** Mystery & Suspense, Federal Bureau of Investigation (FBI), Prejudice. **Acq:** Purchase. **Dist:** MGM Home Entertainment. $14.95.

The Betrayed 2008 (Unrated) — ★½
When Jamie (George), the married mom of a young son, regains consciousness after a car accident, she's being held captive in an isolated warehouse. Her captor says her husband has stolen millions from a crime syndicate and if Jamie wants to keep her son safe, she must kill her husband. 99m; DVD. **C:** Melissa George; Donald Adams; Christian Campbell; Scott Heindl; Ken Tremblett; Connor Christopher Levins; Roger Vernon; Blaine Anderson; Directed by Amanda Gusack; Written by Amanda Gusack; Music by Deborah Lurie. **A:** Sr. High-Adult. **P:** Entertainment. **U:** Home. **Mov-Ent:** Crime Drama. **Acq:** Purchase. **Dist:** Fox Home Entertainment.

Betrayed: A Story of Three Women 1995 (Unrated) — ★½
The friendship of suburbanites Amanda Nelson (Baxter) and Joan Bixler (Kurtz) is destroyed when Amanda learns her lawyer husband Rob (Terry) is having an affair with his summer intern Dana (Carey), who is the widowed Joan's daughter. Lots of shouting and angst follows. 93m; DVD. **C:** Swoosie Kurtz; Meredith Baxter; Clare Carey; John Terry; John Livingston; Breckin Meyer; Bill Brochtrup; Directed by William A. Graham; Written by James Duff; Cinematography by Robert Steadman; Music by Patrick Williams. **A:** Jr. High-Adult. **P:** Entertainment. **U:** Home. **Mov-Ent:** TV Movies. **Acq:** Purchase. **Dist:** Echo Bridge Home Entertainment.

Betrayed at 17 2011 (Unrated) — ★★
Shy 17-year-old Lexi Ross (Bauer) is flattered to be dating football star Greg (Fischer-Price). It ends tragically when he secretly makes a sex tape and it goes viral thanks to his jealous ex, Carleigh (Gill). Lexi's widowed mother, Michelle (Paul), is determined to get justice. Lifetime teen drama. 88m; DVD; Closed Captioned. **C:** Alexandra Paul; Joe Penny; Katie (Katharine) Gill; Andy Fischer-Price; Amanda Bauer; Jake Thomas; Directed by Doug Campbell; Written by Christine Conradt; Cinematography by Robert Ballo; Music by Steve Gurevitch. **A:** Jr. High-Adult. **P:** Entertainment. **U:** Home. **L:** English. **Mov-Ent:** Adolescence, Suicide. **Acq:** Purchase. **Dist:** MTI Home Video.

A Betrayed Man 1936 — ★★
Extremely rare '30s independent film. 58m; DVD. **C:** Smiley Burnette. **A:** Jr. High-Adult. **P:** Entertainment. **U:** Home. **Mov-Ent:** **Acq:** Purchase. **Dist:** Alpha Video. $15.95.

The Betsy 1978 (R) — ★★
A story of romance, money, power, and mystery centering around the wealthy Hardeman family and their automobile manufacturing business. Loosely patterned after the life of Henry Ford as portrayed in the Harold Robbins' pulp-tome. Olivier is the redeeming feature. 132m; VHS, DVD. **C:** Laurence Olivier; Kathleen Beller; Robert Duvall; Lesley-Anne Down; Edward Herrmann; Tommy Lee Jones; Katharine Ross; Jane Alexander; Directed by Daniel Petrie; Written by William Bast; Walter Bernstein; Cinematography by Mario Tosi; Music by John Barry. **Pr:** Harold Robbins International Productions. **A:** Sr. High-Adult. **P:** Entertainment. **U:** Home. **Mov-Ent:** Automobiles. **Acq:** Purchase. **Dist:** Warner Home Video, Inc. $59.98.

Betsy Bubblegum's Journey to Yummi-Land 2007 (Unrated)
Animated children's television program. In this candied world, Betsy Bubblegum visits Yummi-land and meets some folks who help her learn the importance of being a good friend. 44m; DVD. **A:** Preschool-Primary. **P:** Entertainment. **U:** Home. **Mov-Ent:** Family Viewing, Animation & Cartoons, Children's Shows. **Acq:** Purchase. **Dist:** Lions Gate Entertainment Inc. $7.98.

Betsy Ross 1917 — ★★½
Historical drama of Quaker Betsey Griscom, who married John Ross, and became the legendary seamstress of the first American flag. 58m/B/W; Silent; VHS. **C:** Alice Brady; John Bowers; Kate Lester; Frank Mayo; Richard Clarke; Directed by Travers Vale; George Cowl. **A:** Jr. High-Adult. **P:** Entertainment. **U:** Home. **Mov-Ent:** Drama, History--U.S., Revolutionary War. **Acq:** Purchase. **Dist:** Grapevine Video; Facets Multimedia Inc. $19.95.

Betsy's Wedding 1990 (R) — ★★½
Betsy wants a simple wedding, but her father has other, grander ideas. Then there's the problem of paying for it, which Dad tries to take care of in a not-so-typical manner. Alda at his hilarious best. 94m; VHS, DVD, CC. **C:** Alan Alda; Joey Bishop; Madeline Kahn; Molly Ringwald; Catherine O'Hara; Joe Pesci; Ally Sheedy; Burt Young; Anthony LaPaglia; Julie Bovasso; Nicolas Coster; Bibi Besch; Dylan Walsh; Samuel L. Jackson; Frankie Faison; Directed by Alan Alda; Written by Alan Alda; Cinematography by Kelvin Pike; Music by Bruce Broughton. **Pr:** Martin Bregman; Louis Stroller; Touchstone Pictures. **A:** Sr. High-Adult. **P:** Entertainment. **U:** Home. **Mov-Ent:** Comedy--Romantic, Marriage. **Acq:** Purchase. **Dist:** Buena Vista Home Entertainment. $89.95.

Bette Davis Collection 1990
This compilation of Bette Davis' great oldies and new releases includes "Jezebel," "Dark Victory," and "Dangerous." 60m; VHS. **C:** Bette Davis. **Pr:** MGM/UA Entertainment Company. **A:** Family. **P:** Entertainment. **U:** Home. **Mov-Ent:** **Acq:** Purchase. **Dist:** MGM Home Entertainment. $19.95.

Bette Midler: Art or Bust 1984 (Unrated)
The outrageous Bette Midler performs in the concert taped at the University of Minnesota in Minneapolis. 82m; VHS. **C:** Bette Midler. **Pr:** HBO. **A:** Sr. High-Adult. **P:** Entertainment. **U:** Home. **Mov-Ent:** Music--Performance. **Acq:** Purchase. **Dist:** Lions Gate Television Corp. $59.95.

Bette Midler: Mondo Beyondo 1988
The made-for-cable-TV cabaret/stand-up shtick of the Divine Miss M. 60m; VHS, CC. **C:** Bette Midler. **Pr:** HBO. **A:** Sr. High-Adult. **P:** Entertainment. **U:** Home. **Mov-Ent:** Comedy--Performance, Music--Performance. **Acq:** Purchase. **Dist:** Music Video Distributors. $39.95.

Bette Midler Show 1976 (Unrated)
Midler, accompanied by the Harlettes, jokes, dances and belts out a medley of songs ranging from the Andrew Sisters' "Boogie Woogie Bugle Boy" to "Friends." 84m; VHS. **C:** Bette Midler. **Pr:** HBO. **A:** Family. **P:** Entertainment. **U:** Home. **Mov-Ent:** Music--Performance. **Acq:** Purchase. **Dist:** Time-Life Video and Television, On Moratorium.

Better Active Today Than Radioactive Tomorrow 1978
Young German filmmaker Nina Gladitz documents the lives of the rural German citizens who banded together to stop a nuclear plant from being built in Wyhl. 65m/B/W; VHS, 3/4 U. **Pr:** Teldok Films. **A:** Jr. High-Adult. **P:** Education. **U:** Institution, CATV, BCTV, SURA. **Gen-Edu:** Documentary Films, Nuclear Energy, Germany. **Acq:** Purchase, Rent/Lease. **Dist:** Green Mountain Post Films.

Better Babies: Raising Intellectual "Super Stars" 19??
Documents several early learning programs for children and some of the parents and children who subscribe to them. 28m; VHS. **A:** Sr. High. **P:** Education. **U:** Institution. **Gen-Edu:** Children, Education. **Acq:** Purchase. **Dist:** Filmakers Library Inc. $195.

Better Banquets: Basic Service Skills 199?
Offers training for banquet servers. Includes guide. 22m; VHS. **A:** Adult. **P:** Instruction. **U:** Institution. **Bus-Ind:** Job Training, Food Industry. **Acq:** Rent/Lease. **Dist:** American Hotel & Lodging Educational Institute. $224.95.

The Better Boat Handling Series 1992
A comprehensive guide to handling your powerboat. Covers basics of reading the instrument panel, steering, maneuvering, the effects of the elements, backing up and more. 50m; VHS. **A:** Adult. **P:** Instruction. **U:** Home. **How-Ins:** Boating. **Acq:** Purchase. **Dist:** Bennett Marine Video. $29.95.
Indiv. Titles: 1. Handling your Twin I/O 2. Handling your Single I/O 3. Handling your Twin Outboard 4. Handling your Single Outboard.

Better Business Grammar 1991
Basic tips for managers on how to get over common stumbling blocks of the English language when writing. 12m; VHS. **A:** College-Adult. **P:** Professional. **U:** Institution. **Bus-Ind:** Business, Communication. **Acq:** Purchase. **Dist:** Briefings Publishing Group; Cambridge Educational. $79.00.

Better Business Letters 1979
This series shows how to produce accurate and persuasive business letters, memos, and reports. Each program covers one of the six parts of a business letter. 30m; VHS, 3/4 U, EJ. **Pr:** Telstar Productions. **A:** College-Adult. **P:** Education. **U:** Institution, CCTV. **Gen-Edu:** Language Arts, Business, Office Practice. **Acq:** Purchase. **Dist:** SkillSoft.
Indiv. Titles: 1. Physical Form 2. Overall Organization 3. First Paragraph 4. Last Paragraph 5. Basic Point of View 6. Personal Touch.

Better Business Writing 1991
A comprehensive program designed to teach concise, accurate business writing. A leader's guide and workbook are included. 25m; VHS, 3/4 U, Special order formats. **Pr:** Crisp Publications. **A:** College-Adult. **P:** Vocational. **U:** Institution. **Bus-Ind:** How-To, Job Training, Language Arts. **Acq:** Purchase, Rent/Lease. **Dist:** Excellence in Training Corp. $495.00.

A Better Childhood Quiz 19??
Quiz format program for the entire family which covers issues associated with such things as nutrition, health, education, day-care, and child abuse. 60m; VHS. **Pr:** KERA Dallas. **A:** Family. **P:** Education. **U:** Institution, Home. **Gen-Edu:** Family Viewing, Education, Parenting. **Acq:** Purchase. **Dist:** KERA. $19.95.

Better Dayz 2002 (Unrated) — ★½
High schooler Faye (Cargle) has her head turned by smoothie drug dealer Vaughn (Odell)?until she sees him kill a rival. When Vaughn threatens Faye, she turns to her hot-headed brother Johnny (Williams) to keep her safe. Technical flaws detract from what slowly becomes a dramatic story. 101m; VHS, DVD. **C:** Erik Williams; Shantel Cargle; Rich Odell; Directed by Norman C. Linton; Written by Norman C. Linton; Cinematography by Brenden Flint. **A:** Sr. High-Adult. **P:** Entertainment. **U:** Home. **Mov-Ent:** Black Culture. **Acq:** Purchase. **Dist:** York Entertainment. $14.99.

Better Golf with Gary Player 1996
Legendary golf pro Gary Player provides tips to help improve all phases of ones golf game. ?m; VHS. **Pr:** Walt Disney Co; Buena Vista. **A:** Jr. High-Adult. **P:** Instruction. **U:** Home. **Spo-Rec:** Golf, How-To. **Acq:** Purchase. **Dist:** Buena Vista Home Entertainment. $12.99.

Better Grades in Fewer Days 1992
Two program series introducing students to a wide variety of tests, including open book, take home, standardized, and oral. Discusses their basic characteristics and how to take them. Also shares practical and useful study techniques, including note taking, cram cards, the "buddy system," and more. 30m; VHS. **A:** Jr. High-College. **P:** Instruction. **U:** Institution. **How-Ins:** How-To, Education. **Acq:** Purchase. **Dist:** Cambridge Educational. $69.95.
Indiv. Titles: 1. This Is a Test: This Is Only a Test 2. This Way to an A: Wise Study Habits.

Better Health and Healing Through Meditation 19??
A fun, interactive video that helps viewers to learn breathing exercises, meditation, the secrets of crystal energy, and color therapy. ?m; VHS. **A:** Sr. High. **P:** Education. **U:** Home. **L:** English. **Hea-Sci:** Self-Help. **Acq:** Purchase. **Dist:** Tapeworm Video Distributors Inc. $19.95.

Better Homes and Gardens How-To Series 1989
This series provides instructions for various home improvement projects. 45m; VHS. **Pr:** Meredith Video. **A:** Sr. High-Adult. **P:** Instruction. **U:** Home. **How-Ins:** How-To, Home Improvement. **Acq:** Purchase. **Dist:** Better Home & Gardens Books; Karol Media; Cambridge Educational. $19.95.
Indiv. Titles: 1. Refinishing Furniture (57 min.) 2. Foolproof Flower Beds (55 min.) 3. Preparing Your Home to Sell (45 min.) 4. Building a Deck (20 min.) 5. Cooking Made Microwave Easy (45 min.) 6. Wallpaper Like a Pro! (55 min.) 7. Making Your Kitchen Store More (23 min.) 8. Room Arranging Do's and Don'ts (25 min.) 9. Solving Landscaping Problems (45 min.) 10. Do-It-Yourself Home Repairs (60 min.).

Better Jobs Using the OOH 1990
Three high school students explore prospective careers using the Occupational Outlook Handbook. ?m; VHS. **A:** Sr. High-College. **P:** Education. **U:** Institution. **Gen-Edu:** Job Hunting, Occupations. **Acq:** Purchase. **Dist:** Meridian Education Corp. $95.00.

Better Late Than Never 1979 — ★★
Fun TV tale of senior citizens in revolt at an old-age home. Fine characters portrayed by some of the best in the business. 100m; VHS. **C:** Harold Gould; Tyne Daly; Strother Martin; Harry (Henry) Morgan; Victor Buono; George Gobel; Lou Jacobi; Donald Pleasence; Larry Storch; Directed by Richard Crenna; Music by Charles Fox. **Pr:** Ten Four Productions. **A:** Jr. High-Adult. **P:** Entertainment. **U:** Home. **Mov-Ent:** TV Movies, Aging. **Acq:** Purchase. **Dist:** $59.98.

Better Late Than Never 1983 (Unrated) — ★½
Two penniless old fools vie for the acceptance of a bratty 10-year-old millionairess, who must choose one as her guardian. Niven's last film. 95m; VHS. **C:** David Niven; Art Carney; Maggie Smith; Kimberly Partridge; Catherine Hicks; Melissa Prophet; Directed by Bryan Forbes; Music by Henry Mancini. **Pr:** 20th Century-Fox. **A:** Family. **P:** Entertainment. **U:** Home. **Mov-Ent:** Children. **Acq:** Purchase. **Dist:** $59.98.

Better Learning Habits 197?
Part of an integrated course designed for anyone who wishes to achieve better learning habits. 30m; 3/4 U. **Pr:** Telstar. **A:** College-Adult. **P:** Education. **U:** Institution. **Gen-Edu:** Education. **Acq:** Purchase, Rent/Lease. **Dist:** SkillSoft.
Indiv. Titles: 1. How to Study Better (7TS-G01) 2. How to Build the Concentration Habit (7TS-G02) 3. How to Listen and Take Notes (7TS-G03) 4. Study Schedules That Really Work (7TS-G04) 5. How to Take a Test (7TS-G05).

A Better Life 2011 (PG-13) — ★★★
Mexican-born Carlos (Bechir) dedicates his life to working hard as a gardener in order to give his teenage son Luis (Julian) more opportunities then he had. Carlos also struggles to keep Luis away from both East L.A. gangs and immigration officials. Bechir and Julian are at the heart of this earnest but not sappy story about a father's love for his child. Director Weitz capably tells of the unrelenting struggles facing hardworking illegal immigrants while refraining from getting political on the hot topic. 110m; DVD, Blu-Ray, On Demand. **C:** Demian Bechir; Jose Julian; Carlos Linares; Tom Schanley; Directed by Chris Weitz; Written by Eric Eason; Cinematography by Javier Aguirresarobe; Music by Alexandre Desplat. **Pr:** Jami Gertz; Paul Junger Witt; Stacey Lubliner; Christian McLaughlin; Depth of Field; Lime Orchard Productions; McLaughlin Films; Witt/ Thomas; Summit Entertainment. **A:** Jr. High-Adult. **P:** Entertainment. **U:** Home. **L:** English. **Mov-Ent:** **Acq:** Purchase. **Dist:** Summit Entertainment; Amazon.com Inc.; Movies Unlimited.

Better Living Through Chemistry 2014 (Unrated) — ★½
Glib indie comedy with a strange voiceover narration by Fonda, playing herself. Small town milquetoast pharmacist Douglas (Rockwell) is married to ball-busting Kara (Monaghan) and owes his job to equally interfering father-in-law Walter (Howard). His life is turned upside down as he's willingly lead on a drug- and sex-fueled trip after falling for dangerously seductive trophy wife, Elizabeth (Wilde), but the pic doesn't mesh together well enough to be more than fitfully amusing. 91m; DVD, Blu-Ray. **C:** Sam Rockwell; Olivia Wilde; Michelle Monaghan; Ray Liotta; Jane Fonda; Ken Howard; Norbert Lee Butz; Directed by Geoff Moore; David Posamentier; Written by Geoff Moore; David Posamentier; Cinematography by Tim Suhrstedt; Music by Andrew Feltenstein; John Nau. **Pr:** Samuel Goldwyn Films. **A:** Adult. **P:** Entertainment. **U:** Home. **L:** English. **Mov-Ent:** Drug Abuse, Sex & Sexuality, Marriage. **Acq:** Purchase. **Dist:** Universal Studios Home Video.

Better Luck Tomorrow 2002 (R) — ★★★
Controversial film about Asian-American teens gone wild. Overachieving students in a wealthy Orange County suburb, they outwardly conform to the stereotype of smart, well-behaved, ambitious kids. But their extracurricular activities involve drugs and criminal activities that escalate from the petty to the serious as events spin out of their control. 98m; VHS, DVD. **C:** Parry Shen; Jason J. Tobin; Roger Fan; Sung Kang; John Cho; Karin Anna Cheung; Directed by Justin Lin; Written by Justin Lin; Ernesto M. Foronda; Fabian Marquez; Cinematography by Patrice Lucien Cochet; Music by Michael J. Gonzales. **Pr:** Julie Asato; Justin Lin; Justin Lin; Ernesto M. Foronda; Hudson River Film Company; Cherry Sky Films; Day O Productions; Trailing

---

Johnson Productions; Paramount Pictures; MTV Films. **A:** Sr. High-Adult. **P:** Entertainment. **U:** Home. **Mov-Ent:** Adolescence, Drug Trafficking/Dealing. **Acq:** Purchase. **Dist:** Paramount Pictures Corp.

Better Mind the Computer—Artificial Intelligence 1983
This documentary takes a look at the startling developments and problems that have occurred since the information revolution began. 50m; VHS, 3/4 U. **Pr:** British Broadcasting Corporation. **A:** Sr. High-Adult. **P:** Education. **U:** Institution, SURA. **Bus-Ind:** Computers. **Acq:** Purchase, Rent/Lease. **Dist:** Home Vision Cinema.

Better Off Dead 1985 (PG) — ★★½
A compulsive teenager's girlfriend leaves him and he decides to end it all. After several abortive attempts, he decides instead to out-ski his ex-girlfriend's obnoxious new boyfriend. Uneven but funny. 97m; VHS, DVD, Blu-Ray. **C:** John Cusack; Curtis Armstrong; Diane Franklin; Kim Darby; David Ogden Stiers; Dan Schneider; Amanda Wyss; Taylor Negron; Vincent Schiavelli; Demian Slade; Scooter Stevens; Elizabeth Daily; Yano Ayana; Steven Williams; Directed by Savage Steve Holland; Written by Savage Steve Holland; Cinematography by Isidore Mankofsky; Music by Rupert Hine. **A:** Jr. High-Adult. **P:** Entertainment. **U:** Home. **Mov-Ent:** Skiing, Suicide. **Acq:** Purchase. **Dist:** Movies Unlimited; Alpha Video. $79.98.

Better Off Dead 1994 — ★★½
Preachy, manipulative TV movie redeemed by good performances. Kit (Winningham) is an unrepentant white-trash thief who kills a black police officer and is sentenced to death. Cutter Dubuque (Ferrell) is the ambitious black district attorney who prosecuted the case but comes to doubt the wisdom of the death penalty and slowly begins to try to help Kit. 91m; VHS. **C:** Mare Winningham; Tyra Ferrell; Kevin Tighe; Don Harvey; Directed by Neema Barnette; Written by Marlane X. Meyer; Cinematography by Ueli Steiger; Music by John Barnes. **Pr:** Rosilyn Heller; Gloria Steinem. **A:** Sr. High-Adult. **P:** Entertainment. **U:** Home. **Mov-Ent:** TV Movies, Law, Prejudice. **Acq:** Purchase. **Dist:** Turner Broadcasting System Inc.

Better Off Dead? 1984
This documentary, from the PBS series Frontline, examines the life-and-death decisions faced by hospitals, doctors, and nurses who treat severely injured newborns who are being kept alive by medical technology. 60m; VHS, 3/4 U. **Pr:** Graham Chedd; Andrew Liebman; Documentary Consortium. **A:** Sr. High-Adult. **P:** Education. **U:** Institution, SURA. **Hea-Sci:** Documentary Films, Medical Care, Infants. **Acq:** Purchase, Rent/Lease. **Dist:** Leo Media, Inc.

The Better 'Ole 1926 (Unrated) — ★½
Cockney Old Bill (Chaplin) is a WWI private with the British infantry. Bill and his mate Alfie (Ackroyd) must find the traitor in their ranks who is responsible for a French town falling to the Germans. Based on cartoon characters created by Bruce Bairnsfather, with the title referring to a foxhole. Some of the humor is blunted by the passage of time, although the visual of Chaplin and Ackroyd in a horse's costume is still amusing. 97m/ B/W; Silent; DVD. **C:** Syd Chaplin; Jack Ackroyd; Edgar Kennedy; Charles Gerrard; Theodore Lorch; Harold Goodwin; Directed by Charles Reisner; Written by Charles Reisner; Darryl F. Zanuck; Cinematography by Edwin DuPar. **A:** College-Adult. **P:** Entertainment. **U:** Home. **Mov-Ent:** Silent Films, World War One, France. **Acq:** Purchase. **Dist:** WarnerArchive.com.

Better Productivity Is Not By Chance—Dr. Robert Lorher 19??
Dr. Robert Lorher offers five factors that will improve motivational skills and productivity, and support the importance of setting reachable goals. 60m; VHS. **A:** College-Adult. **P:** Professional. **U:** Institution. **Bus-Ind:** Business, How-To, Personnel Management. **Acq:** Purchase. **Dist:** Instructional Video. $169.00.

Better Safe Than Sorry 1989
An injury prevention video which identifies common danger areas and materials--traffic, water, electrical appliances, heights, poisons, hot liquids, and substances commonly choked on--and explains how to avoid getting hurt. 14m; VHS. **A:** Family. **P:** Education. **U:** Institution. **Gen-Edu:** Safety Education. **Acq:** Purchase. **Dist:** United Learning Inc. $79.95.

The Better Sex Video Series 1992
Nudity and explicit sexual techniques are featured in this eight-volume series which offers couples demonstrating methods and fantasies to enhance sexual relationships. 628m; VHS. **Pr:** Playboy Enterprises. **A:** Adult. **P:** Instruction. **U:** Home. **How-Ins:** Sex & Sexuality, How-To, Self-Help. **Acq:** Purchase. **Dist:** Universal Music and Video Distribution.
Indiv. Titles: 1. Better Sexual Techniques 2. Advanced Sexual Techniques 3. Making Sex Fun 4. Exploring Sexual Fantasies 5. Sharing Sexual Fantasies 6. Acting Out Your Sexual Fantasies 7. Advanced Sexual Fantasies 8. You Can Last Longer.

Better Spelling 1979
This series promotes better spelling abilities through examples of correctly spelled and misspelled words, tests, and dictation. 15m; VHS, 3/4 U, EJ. **Pr:** Telstar Productions. **A:** Sr. High-Adult. **P:** Education. **U:** Institution, CCTV. **Gen-Edu:** Language Arts, Education. **Acq:** Purchase. **Dist:** SkillSoft.
Indiv. Titles: 1. Introductory Lesson I 2. Introductory Lesson II 3. The Final Consonant Rule 4. The Silent E Rule 5. Word Elements 6. Assimilative Changes 7. The Apostrophe 8. Pronunciation Difficulties 9. Tackling the Demons.

Better, Stronger 1979
Lana, a young actress, tries to break the audience of some bad habits—bad sexual habits, bad television habits. 55m; 3/4 U. **C:**

Karen Achenbach; John McNulty; Charles Ruas. **Pr:** Walsung Company. **A:** College-Adult. **P:** Education. **U:** Institution, Home. **Fin-Art:** Video, Self-Help, Television. **Acq:** Rent/Lease. **Dist:** Kitchen Center for Video, Music & Dance.

Better Than Chocolate 1999 (R) — ★★
Sweetly touching romantic comedy follows college dropout Maggie (Dwyer), who's trying to establish her own identity, which isn't so easy when she hasn't told her flighty mother, Lila (Crewson), that she's a lesbian. But now mom is getting divorced and she and Maggie's brother Paul (Mundy) are temporarily moving in, with Maggie trying to pass off her lover Kim (Cox) as just a roommate. Meanwhile, naive Lila is confiding in Maggie's transseuxual friend, singer Judy (a stellar Outerbridge), and discovering the joys of sex toys. 101m; VHS, DVD, Wide. **C:** Karyn Dwyer; Wendy Crewson; Christina Cox; Peter Outerbridge; Ann-Marie MacDonald; Kevin Mundy; Marya Delver; Jay Brazeau; Tony Nappo; Directed by Anne Wheeler; Written by Peggy Thompson; Cinematography by Gregory Middleton; Music by Graeme Coleman. **A:** Sr. High-Adult. **P:** Entertainment. **U:** Home. **Mov-Ent:** Comedy--Romantic, Sex & Sexuality, Nightclubs. **Acq:** Purchase. **Dist:** Lions Gate Home Entertainment; CinemaNow Inc.

. . .Better Than Cure 198?
This film demonstrates the need for protection from potential hazards around the office. 19m; VHS, 3/4 U. **A:** College-Adult. **P:** Education. **U:** Institution. **Bus-Ind:** Safety Education. **Acq:** Rent/Lease. **Dist:** National Safety Council, California Chapter, Film Library.

Better Than Sex 2000 (R) — ★★½
Cin (Porter) meets Josh (Wenham) at a party and takes him home for the night. When things go exceptionally well, Cin agrees to Josh's staying on until he flies home to London in a couple of days. But amidst all the sex, little things like relationships, love, and commitment begin to creep in. Voiceovers from the twosome comment on the action and what they're really feeling rather than what they're telling each other. Porter and Wenham are attractive and there's (unsurprisingly) a lot of displayed skin. 85m; VHS, DVD. **C:** David Wenham; Susie Porter; Catherine McClements; Kris McQuade; Simon Bossell; Imelda Corcoran; Directed by Jonathan Teplitzky; Written by Jonathan Teplitzky; Cinematography by Garry Phillips; Music by David Hirschfelder. **Pr:** Frank Cox; Bruno Papandrea; Fireworks Pictures; Samuel Goldwyn Films; IDP Films. **A:** Sr. High-Adult. **P:** Entertainment. **U:** Home. **Mov-Ent:** Comedy--Romantic, Sex & Sexuality. **Awds:** Australian Film Inst. '00: Director, Film, Score (Hirschfelder). **Acq:** Purchase. **Dist:** Sony Pictures Home Entertainment Inc.

A Better Tomorrow 2002
Documents the struggles a family in East Los Angeles endured trying to overcome the loss of income due to an industrial accident the husband was involved in. When the mom decides to go back to school and work part time tension in the home mounts. 30m; VHS. **A:** Adult. **P:** Vocational. **U:** Institution. **Gen-Edu:** Education, Family, Occupational Training. **Acq:** Purchase. **Dist:** Aquarius Health Care Media. $129.00.

A Better Tomorrow, Part 1 1986 (Unrated) — ★★½
Former hit men (Lung and Fat) team up to bring down the mob boss who double-crossed them and sent one to prison and the other to the streets. One of them also has to protect his younger brother, a cop, from the gang. Considered one of the best of Woo's Hong Kong efforts, there's plenty of his hallmark balletic action and an interesting story. In Cantonese with English subtitles. 95m; VHS, DVD, Wide. **C:** Chow Yun-Fat; Leslie Cheung; Ti Lung; Emily Chu; Waise Lee; John Woo; Directed by John Woo; Written by John Woo; Cinematography by Wing-Hung Wong; Music by Ka-Fai Koo. **A:** Sr. High-Adult. **P:** Entertainment. **U:** Home. **L:** Chinese. **Mov-Ent:** **Acq:** Purchase. **Dist:** Lions Gate Entertainment Inc.; Facets Multimedia Inc. $14.98.

A Better Tomorrow, Part 2 1988 — ★½
A smooth-talking gangster, who was killed in Part I, returns in Part II as the dead man's twin brother (unmentioned in Part I). He teams up with a cop and a reformed gangster to fight the forces of evil. In Cantonese with English subtitles. 100m; VHS, DVD, Wide. **C:** Chow Yun-Fat; Leslie Cheung; Directed by John Woo; Written by John Woo; Music by Joseph Koo. **A:** Sr. High-Adult. **P:** Entertainment. **U:** Home. **L:** English, Chinese. **Mov-Ent:** **Acq:** Purchase. **Dist:** Facets Multimedia Inc. $39.95.

A Better Tomorrow, Part 3 1989 — ★★
Prequel set in 1974 finds detective Mark Gor (Fat) and his cousin (Leung) seeking to escape from Saigon. Unfortunately, they both fall for the same sultry babe (Mui), who's also a gangster's moll. Mandarin with subtitles. 114m; VHS, DVD. **C:** Chow Yun-Fat; Tony Leung Ka-Fai; Anita (Yim-Fong) Mui; Directed by Tsui Hark. **A:** Sr. High-Adult. **P:** Entertainment. **U:** Home. **L:** Chinese. **Mov-Ent:** Family. **Acq:** Purchase. **Dist:** Facets Multimedia Inc.

A Better Way: Emotional Child Abuse Prevention 1988
The newest theories assert that yelling at a child after they have done something wrong can cause emotional damage, so this video tries to answer the thorny question of how to discipline a child. 24m; VHS, 8 mm, 3/4 U. **TV Std:** NTSC, PAL, SECAM. **Pr:** Azimuth Productions, Inc. **A:** College-Adult. **P:** Education. **U:** Institution, CCTV, SURA. **Gen-Edu:** Children, Communication. **Acq:** Purchase, Rent/Lease, Duplication License. **Dist:** Phoenix Learning Group. $540.00.

A Better Way to Die 2000 (R) — ★★
An ex-cop heads home to try to start a new life but is instead mistaken for a government agent who has had a contract put out on his life by a Chicago mob boss. So the cop tries to get the

feds to assist him before the wiseguys get to him first. 101m; VHS, DVD, Wide, CC. **C:** Andre Braugher; Joe Pantoliano; Natasha Henstridge; Lou Diamond Phillips; Wayne Duvall; Scott Wiper; Directed by Scott Wiper; Written by Scott Wiper. **A:** Sr. High-Adult. **P:** Entertainment. **U:** Home. **Mov-Ent:** Crime Drama, Federal Bureau of Investigation (FBI). **Acq:** Purchase. **Dist:** Sony Pictures Home Entertainment Inc.

A Better Way to Go: An Introduction to Non-Manipulative Selling 1981
An introduction to the sales training series, "The Nick Price Story of Non-Manipulative Selling." Salesman Nick learns how to communicate with his customers, build trust, and increase sales. 17m; 3/4 U, Special order formats. **Pr:** Walt Disney Training and Development. **A:** College-Adult. **P:** Professional. **U:** Institution, SURA. **Bus-Ind:** Sales Training. **Acq:** Purchase, Rent/Lease. **Dist:** Disney Educational Productions.

A Better Way to Teach Goalie Play 2006 (Unrated)
Coach Nick Pasquarello demonstrates drills for soccer coaches wishing to increase their goalies' playing skills. 106m; DVD. **A:** Family. **P:** Education. **U:** Home, Institution. **Spo-Rec:** Soccer, Athletic Instruction/Coaching. **Acq:** Purchase. **Dist:** Championship Productions. $29.99.

Better Your Best 1970
This program highlights the Marine Corps physical fitness program for high schools. 13m; VHS, 3/4 U, Special order formats. **Pr:** Department of the Navy. **A:** Sr. High-Adult. **P:** Education. **U:** Institution, SURA. **Spo-Rec:** Fitness/Exercise. **Acq:** Purchase. **Dist:** National Audiovisual Center.

Betty 1992 — ★★
Sulky, drunken Betty (Trintignant) is doing her best to destroy her bourgeois life, escaping from her marriage into adultery and debasement. She meets the concerned middle-aged widow Laure (Audran), who inexplicably takes her to her hotel room, cleans her up, and spends the remainder of the movie as Betty's sounding-board. Betty's passive personality offers little to explain her appeal to either Laure or the viewer. Based on the novel by Georges Simenon. French with subtitles. 103m; VHS, DVD. **C:** Marie Trintignant; Stephane Audran; Jean-Francoise Garreaud; Yves Lambrecht; Christiane Minazzoli; Pierre Vernier; Directed by Claude Chabrol; Written by Claude Chabrol; Music by Matthieu Chabrol. **Pr:** Marin Karmitz; MK2. **A:** Sr. High-Adult. **P:** Entertainment. **U:** Home. **L:** French, English. **Mov-Ent:** Alcoholism, Women. **Acq:** Purchase. **Dist:** New Yorker Video. $89.95.

Betty 1997 (Unrated) — ★★½
Betty Monday (Pollak) is a well-known actress undergoing a breakdown. So she leaves Hollywood for Palm Springs and tries out a "normal" life—at least by movie star standards. Offbeat comedy has the potential to pleasantly surprise. 88m; VHS, DVD. **C:** Cheryl Pollak; Holland Taylor; Udo Kier; Ron Perlman; Stephen Gregory; Directed by Richard D. (R.D.) Murphy; Written by Richard D. (R.D.) Murphy. **A:** Sr. High-Adult. **P:** Entertainment. **U:** Home. **Mov-Ent:** Psychiatry. **Acq:** Purchase. **Dist:** Vanguard International Cinema, Inc.

Betty & Coretta 2013 (Unrated) — ★★
Two powerhouse women (Blige and Bassett) in the title roles can't quite overcome the stilted docudrama nature of this Lifetime effort. Ruby Dee is the onscreen narrator who fills in the details about the lives of civil rights widows, Dr. Betty Shabazz, married to Malcolm X, and Coretta Scott King, married to Martin Luther King Jr., who are brought together after the deaths to carry on their husbands' work and activism. 120m; DVD. **C:** Mary J. Blige; Angela Bassett; Malik Yoba; Lindsay Owen Pierre; Narrated by Ruby Dee; Directed by Yves Simoneau; Written by Shem Bitterman; Ron Hutchinson; Cinematography by Guy Dufaux; Music by Terence Blanchard. **A:** Sr. High-Adult. **P:** Entertainment. **U:** Home. **L:** English. **Mov-Ent:** Black Culture, Women, Civil Rights. **Acq:** Purchase. **Dist:** A&E Television Networks L.L.C.

Betty Blowtorch and Her Amazing True Life Adventures 2006
Documentary filmmaker Anthony Scarpa followed the all-girl glam/garage rock band, formed in 1998, for two years through a series of performances until the death of their lead singer in a car accident. 108m; DVD. **A:** Sr. High-Adult. **P:** Entertainment. **U:** Home. **Fin-Art:** Documentary Films, Biography: Music. **Acq:** Purchase. **Dist:** Cinema Libre Studio.

Betty Blue 1986 (R) — ★★★
A vivid, intensely erotic film about two young French lovers and how their inordinately strong passion for each other destroys them, leading to poverty, violence, and insanity. English subtitles. From the director of "Diva." Based on the novel "37.2 Le Matin" by Philippe Djian. 121m; VHS, DVD, Blu-Ray, CC. **C:** Beatrice Dalle; Jean-Hugues Anglade; Gerard Darmon; Consuelo de Haviland; Clementine Celarie; Jacques Mathou; Vincent Lindon; Directed by Jean-Jacques Beineix; Written by Jean-Jacques Beineix; Cinematography by Jean-Francois Robin; Music by Gabriel Yared. **Pr:** Gaumont. **A:** College-Adult. **P:** Entertainment. **U:** Home. **L:** French. **Mov-Ent:** Drama. **Acq:** Purchase. **Dist:** Movies Unlimited; Alpha Video; Cinema Libre Studio. $79.98.

Betty Boop Classics 1939
A compilation of Betty Boop and her cartoon pals most fun-filled escapades. 60m; VHS. **C:** Voice(s) by Mae Questel. **Pr:** Paramount Pictures. **A:** Family. **P:** Entertainment. **U:** Home. **Mov-Ent:** Animation & Cartoons, Children. **Acq:** Purchase. **Dist:** Lions Gate Entertainment Inc. $19.98.

Betty Boop Program 193?
A compilation of five Betty Boop cartoons of the 1930s: "Betty in Blunderland," "Betty and the Little King," "Betty Boop with Henry," "Betty and Little Jimmy," and "Candid Candidate." 50m/B/W; VHS. **C:** Voice(s) by Mae Questel; Directed by Max Fleischer. **Pr:** Max Fleischer Studios. **A:** Family. **P:** Entertainment. **U:** Home. **Mov-Ent:** Animation & Cartoons. **Acq:** Purchase. **Dist:** Glenn Video Vistas Ltd.

Betty Boop Special Collector's Edition, Vol. 1 1935 (Unrated)
Betty Boop returns in this collection of vintage cartoons, presented in their original black-and-white form, with appearances by jazz stars Cab Calloway and Don Redman. 90m/B/W; VHS. **C:** Voice(s) by Louis Armstrong; Mae Questel; Directed by Dave Fleischer; Max Fleischer. **Pr:** Paramount Pictures; Max Fleischer Studios. **A:** Family. **P:** Entertainment. **U:** Home. **Mov-Ent:** Animation & Cartoons. **Acq:** Purchase. **Dist:** Lions Gate Entertainment Inc. $19.98.

Betty Boop Special Collector's Edition, Vol. 2 1937 (Unrated)
That boop-a-doop girl is back in this collection of classic cartoons that features Cab Calloway and his orchestra. 90m/B/W; VHS. **C:** Voice(s) by Mae Questel. **Pr:** Paramount Pictures; Max Fleischer Studios. **A:** Family. **P:** Entertainment. **U:** Home. **Mov-Ent:** Animation & Cartoons. **Acq:** Purchase. **Dist:** Lions Gate Entertainment Inc. $19.98.

Betty Boop, Vol. 1 193?
A compilation of seven Betty Boop cartoons: "Betty in Blunderland," "A Hunting We Will Go," "Betty Boop's Rise to Fame," "Candid Candidate," "Crazy Inventions," "Is My Palm Read?" and "More Pep." 57m/B/W; VHS. **C:** Mae Questel. **Pr:** Paramount Pictures; Max Fleischer Studios. **A:** Family. **P:** Entertainment. **U:** Institution, Home, SURA. **Mov-Ent:** Animation & Cartoons. **Acq:** Purchase. **Dist:** $5.99.

Betty Crocker Exercise and Lose Weight Series 1991
Low-impact exercises and advice on eating right from the folks at Betty Crocker. 30m; VHS. **Pr:** BFV. **A:** Sr. High-Adult. **P:** Instruction. **U:** Home. **Hea-Sci:** Fitness/Exercise, Nutrition. **Acq:** Purchase. **Dist:** Best Video. $14.99.
Indiv. Titles: 1. Stomach and Lower Body 2. Low Impact Aerobics.

The Betty Ford Story 1987 (Unrated) — ★★★
Gena Rowlands deserved her Emmy for her strong portrayal of First Lady Betty Ford in this adaptation of Ford's autobiography "The Times of My Life." Ford earns national admiration for her candid reveal of her breast cancer and subsequent treatment but she hides her addictions to alcohol and prescription drugs. After her husband (Sommer) loses his 1976 reelection bid, her family intervenes and Betty gets clean, then decides to open her own center for substance abusers. 93m; DVD. **C:** Gena Rowlands; Josef Sommer; Nan Woods; Concetta Tomei; Brian McNamara; Bradley Whitford; Daniel McDonald; Ken Tigar; Directed by David Greene; Written by Karen Hall; Cinematography by Dennis Dalzell; Music by Arthur B. Rubinstein. **A:** Jr. High-Adult. **P:** Entertainment. **U:** Home. **Mov-Ent:** Biography: Politics, Women, Presidency. **Acq:** Purchase. **Dist:** WarnerArchive.com.

Betty La Duke: An Artist's Journey from the Bronx to Timbuktu 19??
Teaching aid for art appreciation explores six decades of the artist's life, including her travels to third-world countries and the influence of Native and African American artists on her work. 30m; VHS. **A:** Jr. High-College. **P:** Education. **U:** Institution. **Gen-Edu:** Art & Artists. **Acq:** Purchase. **Dist:** Crystal Productions. $39.95.

Betty LaDuke: An Artist's Journey from the Bronx to Timbuktu 1996
Documentary chronicling the career of artist Betty LaDuke. 28m; VHS, DVD. **A:** Sr. High-Adult. **P:** Education. **U:** Home, Institution. **Gen-Edu:** Documentary Films, Biography: Artists. **Acq:** Purchase, Rent/Lease. **Dist:** The Cinema Guild. $39.95.

Betty Tells Her Story 1996
Features an exploration of beauty and self-image. 20m; VHS. **A:** Adult. **P:** Education. **U:** Institution. **Gen-Edu:** Self-Help. **Acq:** Purchase, Rent/Lease. **Dist:** New Day Films Library. $99.00.

Between 2005 (Unrated) — ★
Allegedly spooky pic with a nonsensical plot and weak acting. Chicago lawyer Nadine Roberts (Montgomery) keeps having terrifying visions of her estranged sister Diane, who vanished in Tijuana. So Nadine heads south of the border to investigate but doesn't get much cooperation even as her nightmares worsen. Then people start calling Nadine by Diane's name and there's all this ridiculous symbolism before the surprise ending that isn't at all. 86m; DVD. **C:** Poppy Montgomery; Danny Pino; Adam Kaufman; Jose Yenque; Patricia Reyes Spindola; Directed by David Ocanas; Written by Robert Nelms; Cinematography by Rob Sweeney; Music by Joel J. Richard. **A:** Jr. High-Adult. **P:** Entertainment. **U:** Home. **Mov-Ent:** Mexico. **Acq:** Purchase. **Dist:** Porchlight Home Entertainment.

Between Black and White 1993
Adult children of racially mixed couples discuss their family life, experiences with racial tensions, and searches for identity in a society that remains highly separatist. 26m; VHS. **A:** Sr. High-Adult. **P:** Education. **U:** Institution. **Gen-Edu:** Black Culture, Prejudice. **Acq:** Purchase. **Dist:** Filmakers Library Inc. $295.00.

Between Fighting Men 1932 — ★½
The orphaned daughter of a shepherd is adopted by the cowpoke who caused her father's death. The cowpoke's sons fall in love with, and compete for, the love of the girl. 62m/B/W; VHS, DVD. **C:** Ken Maynard; Ruth Hall; Josephine Dunn; Wallace MacDonald; Directed by Forrest Sheldon. **Pr:** Burt Kelly. **A:** Adult. **P:** Entertainment. **U:** Home. **Mov-Ent:** Western. **Acq:** Purchase. **Dist:** Mill Creek Entertainment L.L.C. $19.95.

Between Friends 1983 — ★★½
Two women with only their respective divorces in common, meet and become fast friends. The rapport between Burnett and Taylor makes for a touching drama. Adapted from the book "Nobody Makes Me Cry," by Shelley List, one of the producers. 105m; VHS. **C:** Elizabeth Taylor; Carol Burnett; Directed by Lou Antonio; Music by James Horner. **Pr:** Robert Cooper Films. **A:** Jr. High-Adult. **P:** Entertainment. **U:** Home. **Mov-Ent:** Divorce, TV Movies. **Acq:** Purchase. **Dist:** $69.95.

Between God, the Devil & a Winchester 1972 (Unrated) — ★
Violent western with plenty of shooting and dust. Lots of cowboys are hot on the trail of some stolen loot from a church but apparently God isn't on their side since the majority bite the dust and become a snack for the vultures. 98m; VHS, DVD. **C:** Gilbert Roland; Richard Harrison; Directed by Dario Silvester. **A:** Jr. High-Adult. **P:** Entertainment. **U:** Home. **Mov-Ent:** Western. **Acq:** Purchase. **Dist:** Alpha Video; Mill Creek Entertainment L.L.C. $49.95.

Between Heaven and Earth 1993 — ★★
Maria (Maura) is an ambitious TV journalist, prone to surreal dreams, who becomes pregnant after a one-night stand. After witnessing a violent protest, Maria becomes convinced that she can communicate with her unborn baby and that the child is unwilling to be born into such a violent world. So Maria must try to convince her baby otherwise. In French with English subtitles. 80m; VHS. **C:** Carmen Maura; Jean-Pierre Cassel; Didier Bezace; Samuel Mussen; Andre Delvaux; Directed by Marion Hansel; Written by Marion Hansel. **Pr:** Arrow Releasing. **A:** College-Adult. **P:** Entertainment. **U:** Home. **L:** French. **Mov-Ent:** Fantasy, Pregnancy. **Acq:** Purchase. **Dist:** Facets Multimedia Inc. $79.95.

Between Heaven and Hell 1956 (Unrated) — ★★★
Prejudiced Southern gentleman Wagner finds how wrong his misconceptions are, as he attempts to survive WWII on a Pacific Island. Ebsen is exceptional, making this rather simplistic story a meaningful classic. 94m; VHS, DVD. **C:** Robert Wagner; Terry Moore; Broderick Crawford; Buddy Ebsen; Robert Keith; Brad Dexter; Mark Damon; Ken Clark; Harvey Lembeck; Frank Gorshin; Scatman Crothers; Carl "Alfalfa" Switzer; L.Q. Jones; Tod Andrews; Directed by Richard Fleischer; Written by Harry Brown; Cinematography by Leo Tover; Music by Hugo Friedhofer. **Pr:** David Weisbart. **A:** Jr. High-Adult. **P:** Entertainment. **U:** Home. **Mov-Ent:** Action-Adventure, World War Two. **Acq:** Purchase. **Dist:** Movies Unlimited; Alpha Video; Fox Home Entertainment. $14.98.

Between Love & Goodbye 2008 (Unrated) — ★
French citizen Marcel marries lesbian Sarah so he can get a green card to stay in New York with lover Kyle. Marcel and Kyle are living together when Kyle offers his troubled transgendered sister April a place to crash. Jealous of Kyle and Marcel's relationship, April sets out to break them up, which Kyle refuses to believe. The two lovers are so petulant and clueless that their romantic problems are more annoying than compelling. 87m; DVD. **C:** Robert Harmon; Justin Tensen; Simon Miller; Jane Elliott; Directed by Casper Andreas; Written by Casper Andreas; Cinematography by Jon Fordham; Music by Scott Starrett. **A:** College-Adult. **P:** Entertainment. **U:** Home. **Mov-Ent.** **Acq:** Purchase. **Dist:** Wolfe Video.

Between Man and Woman 1972
A look at various marital roles people play in a husband-wife relationship, such as the "mother-son," the "daddy-doll," the "bitch-nice guy," and the "master-servant." 33m; VHS, 3/4 U, Special order formats. **C:** Everett Shostrom. **Pr:** Psychological Films. **A:** College-Adult. **P:** Education. **U:** Institution, SURA. **Hea-Sci:** Psychology, Marriage. **Acq:** Purchase. **Dist:** Psychological & Educational Films.

Between Men 1935 — ★★
A father kills a man he believes killed his son and flees. Later in life, the son meets his father. For father and son, this causes some major concern. 59m/B/W; VHS, DVD. **C:** Johnny Mack Brown; Beth Marion; William Farnum; Earl Dwire; Lloyd Ingraham; Milburn (Milt) Morante; Directed by Robert North Bradbury. **Pr:** Supreme. **A:** Family. **P:** Entertainment. **U:** Home. **Mov-Ent:** Western. **Acq:** Purchase. **Dist:** Alpha Video; Grapevine Video. $19.95.

Between Midnight and Dawn 1950 — ★½
Workmanlike crime drama. L.A. patrol car partners Dan Purvis and Rocky Barnes are the bane of gangster Ritchie Garvis, whom they put in jail. When Garvis breaks out, he's determined to eliminate the coppers. There's a minor subplot involving police dispatcher Kate, who infatuates both partners. 89m/B/W; DVD. **C:** Edmond O'Brien; Gale Storm; Donald Buka; Mark Stevens; Gale Robbins; Anthony Ross; Directed by Gordon Douglas; Written by Eugene Ling; Cinematography by George E. Diskant; Music by George Duning. **A:** Adult. **P:** Entertainment. **U:** Home. **L:** English. **Mov-Ent:** Crime Drama. **Acq:** Purchase. **Dist:** Sony Pictures Home Entertainment Inc.

Between North and South: Israel and Africa 1986
A study of Israel's flourishing agricultural, community development and technical training programs in which men and women from developing African countries are taught the skills to improve the quality of life in their homelands. 30m; VHS, 3/4 U. **Pr:** Anti-Defamation League of B'nai B'rith. **A:** Jr. High-Adult. **P:** Education. **U:** Institution, CCTV, CATV, BCTV, Home. **Gen-Edu:** Documentary Films, Africa, Technology. **Acq:** Purchase. **Dist:** Anti-Defamation League of B'nai B'rith.

Between Rock and a Hard Place 1981
Three coalminers in the Blue Ridge Mountains talk about their work and its place in their lives. 58m; 3/4 U. **Pr:** Kenneth Fink. **A:** Jr. High-Adult. **P:** Education. **U:** Institution, SURA. **Gen-Edu:** Documentary Films, Labor & Unions, Miners & Mining. **Acq:** Purchase. **Dist:** First Run/Icarus Films.

Between School-Time and Home-Time: Planning Activities for School-Age Child Care Programs 1990
Designed to observe children at play, examine the elements that support successful activities, and apply these ideas to their own programs. 28m; VHS. **A:** Adult. **P:** Instruction. **U:** Institution. **Gen-Edu:** Child Care, Children. **Acq:** Rent/Lease. **Dist:** Cornell University. $18.00.

Between Something & Nothing 2008 (Unrated) — ★★
Small-town teen Joe gets into a prestigious big-city art school but he and fellow student/best friend Jennifer are constantly struggling to pay tuition and other living expenses. Then Joe meets hustler Ramon, who suggests his new bud try the sex-for-pay route and soon Joe is using his new life as inspiration for his art. 105m; DVD. **C:** Tim Swain; Julia Frey; Gil Bar-Sera; Directed by Todd Verow; Written by Todd Verow; James Dwyer; Cinematography by Todd Verow; Music by Colin Owens. **A:** College-Adult. **P:** Entertainment. **U:** Home. **Mov-Ent:** Art & Artists, Prostitution. **Acq:** Purchase. **Dist:** Water Bearer Films Inc.

Between Strangers 2002 (R) — ★★
Three Toronto women suffer personal crises and contemplate changing their lives. Housewife Olivia (Loren) is debating whether to leave her abusive invalid husband (Postlethwaite); war photographer Natalia (Sorvino) is burned out trying to live up to her father's reputation and contemplates a career change; and cellist Catherine (Unger) is upset over her father's (McDowell) recent release from prison for a crime that has haunted her since childhood. Ponti's debut and his mom Loren's 100th film. 97m; VHS, DVD. **C:** Sophia Loren; Mira Sorvino; Deborah Kara Unger; Pete Postlethwaite; Malcolm McDowell; Klaus Maria Brandauer; Gerard Depardieu; Wendy Crewson; Andrew Tarbet; Directed by Edoardo Ponti; Written by Edoardo Ponti; Cinematography by Gregory Middleton; Music by Zbigniew Preisner. **A:** Sr. High-Adult. **P:** Entertainment. **U:** Home. **Mov-Ent.** **Acq:** Purchase. **Dist:** Movies Unlimited; Alpha Video.

Between the Darkness and the Dawn 1985 (Unrated) — ★★½
Abigail Foster lapses into a coma at 17 and doesn't awaken for 20 years. She (Montgomery) thinks like a teenager and has to not only adjust to being an adult but to everything that's changed in two decades. This includes her younger sister Ellen (Grassle) marrying Abigail's high school boyfriend David (Goodwin) and the worry that her conscious state may not be permanent. 96m; DVD. **C:** Elizabeth Montgomery; Dorothy McGuire; Karen Grassle; Michael Goodwin; James Naughton; Robin Gammell; Directed by Peter Levin; Written by N. Richard Nash; Dennis Turner; Cinematography by Philip H. Lathrop; Music by Diana Kaproff. **A:** Jr. High-Adult. **P:** Entertainment. **U:** Home. **Mov-Ent:** TV Movies, Hospitals. **Acq:** Purchase. **Dist:** WarnerArchive.com.

Between the Devil and the Deep Blue Sea 1990
Describes the oil spill of the Exxon Valdez and its consequences on Alaska's Prince William Sound. 32m; VHS. **Pr:** Landmark Films, Inc. **A:** Jr. High-Adult. **P:** Education. **U:** Institution. **Hea-Sci:** Oil Industry, Wildlife. **Acq:** Purchase. **Dist:** Landmark Media. $250.00.

Between the Light and the Dark 1987
An audio-visual poem combining the artists' digitally sampled score and lyrics with processed video images. 5m; VHS, 3/4 U. **Pr:** Scott Robinson. **A:** Jr. High-Adult. **P:** Education. **U:** Institution, SURA. **Gen-Edu:** Video. **Acq:** Rent/Lease. **Dist:** Video Out Distribution.

Between the Lines 1977 (R) — ★★★½
A witty, wonderfully realized ensemble comedy about the staff of a radical post-'60s newspaper always on the brink of folding, and its eventual sell-out. 101m; VHS, DVD. **C:** John Heard; Lindsay Crouse; Jeff Goldblum; Jill Eikenberry; Stephen Collins; Lewis J. Stadlen; Michael J. Pollard; Marilu Henner; Bruno Kirby; Directed by Joan Micklin Silver; Written by Fred Barron; Music by Michael Kamen. **Pr:** Raphael D. Silver; Midwest Film Productions. **A:** Sr. High-Adult. **P:** Entertainment. **U:** Home. **Mov-Ent:** Journalism. **Acq:** Purchase. **Dist:** MGM Home Entertainment. $69.95.

Between the Lines: Asian American Women's Poetry 2001
A montage of interviews and dramatic readings from more than 15 major Asian-Pacific American women poets addressing topics such as immigration, language, family, memory and spirituality. 60m; VHS. **A:** Adult. **P:** Education. **U:** Institution. **Gen-Edu:** Literature, Women. **Acq:** Purchase, Rent/Lease. **Dist:** Women Make Movies. $250.00.

Between the Lions: Farmer Ken's Puzzle 2005
Lionel won't let Leona play a computer game because she's not old enough in 'Farmer Ken's Puzzle.' Crow is banned from the library in 'The Fox and the Crow.' In 'Giants and Cubs' Leona is afraid of scary giants. 78m; VHS, DVD. **A:** Preschool-Primary. **P:** Education. **U:** Home. **Chl-Juv:** Television, Literature--Children. **Acq:** Purchase. **Dist:** WGBH/Boston. $12.95.

Between the Lions: Fuzzy Wuzzy, Wuzzy? 2005
Lionel is the only one not happy to join Fuzzy Wuzzy's conga line in the library; Lionel and Leona try to help a storybook shepherd boy; and the Lion family help a writer fix a story involving caps and monkeys. 78m; DVD. **A:** Primary. **P:** Entertainment. **U:** Home. **Chl-Juv:** Animation & Cartoons. **Acq:** Purchase. **Dist:** WBGU-TV.

Between the Lions: Pecos Bill Cleans Up the West 2005
A storybook tornado makes a terrible mess in the library; Lionel ties himself up in ropes and tries to escape without using magic words; and Leona keeps the whole family awake. 78m; DVD. **A:** Primary. **P:** Entertainment. **U:** Home. **Chl-Juv:** Animation & Cartoons. **Acq:** Purchase. **Dist:** WBGU-TV.

Between the Lions: Popcorn Popper 2005
A magic popcorn popper won't stop popping in 'The Popcorn Popper.' A sculptor falls in love with his statue in 'Hug, Hug, Hug!' And in 'Piggyback Piggyback' Leona wants to ride that way on her Dad's back forever. 78m; VHS, DVD. **A:** Preschool-Primary. **P:** Education. **U:** Home. **Chl-Juv:** Television, Literature--Children. **Acq:** Purchase. **Dist:** WGBH/Boston. $12.95.

Between the Lions: Season 1 2000
PBS series teaches fledgling readers phonics using puppetry, animation, live action, and music. Theo and Cleo are the lion puppet parents of Lionel and Leona and run the local library; in between helping patrons are bits with "Martha Reader and the Vowelles" singing about vowel sounds, the "Word Doctor" helping to sound out really long words, "Gawain's World" putting together words using letter knights that crash into each other, and "Arty Smartypants" shaking up compound words. Plus story sections with "Chicken Jane" and the "Adventures of Cliff Hanger." 30 episodes. 780m; DVD. **A:** Preschool-Primary. **P:** Entertainment. **U:** Home. **Chl-Juv:** Children's Shows, Education. **Acq:** Purchase. **Dist:** WGBH/Boston.

Between the Lions: Shooting Stars 2005
The Lion family tries to stay up very late in order to watch a meteor shower; they read jokes to Click the Mouse who doesn't want to laugh; and Lionel and Leona open a box marked "Do Not Open!" 78m; DVD. **A:** Primary. **P:** Entertainment. **U:** Home. **Chl-Juv:** Animation & Cartoons. **Acq:** Purchase. **Dist:** WBGU-TV.

Between the Lions: To the Ship, To the Ship! 2005
Three literacy-building episodes loaded with phonics fun. Includes 'To the Ship, to the Ship!,' 'The Hopping Hen,' and 'De Bop.' 78m; VHS, DVD. **A:** Preschool-Primary. **P:** Education. **U:** Home. **Chl-Juv:** Television, Literature--Children. **Acq:** Purchase. **Dist:** WGBH/Boston. $12.95.

Between the Starts: The Pitcher's Workout 2003
Oklahoma State University Head Coach Frank Anderson shares the day-to-day workout progression used by his pitchers, a combination of stretching, running, throwing, and rest. 24m; VHS. **A:** Adult. **P:** Instruction. **U:** Institution. **How-Ins:** Baseball, Sports--General, How-To. **Acq:** Purchase. **Dist:** Championship Productions. $39.95.

Between the Walls 1990
Features a girl who finds a mouse that lives between the walls of her house, and builds a better trap so she can remove the mouse in a sensible, sensitive way. Recognized by: Red Ribbon, American Film & Video Festival. 10m; VHS, Special order formats. **A:** Primary. **P:** Education. **U:** Institution. **Chl-Juv:** Ecology & Environment, Animals. **Acq:** Purchase, Rent/Lease. **Dist:** Bullfrog Films, Inc. $150.00.

Between the Wars 1978
This eight-part series chronicles the United States' international diplomacy between the end of WWI and Pearl Harbor and explains the events leading to America's deepening involvement in world affairs. Includes rare archival footage and historical interviews. Tapes are available individually or as a boxed set. 60m; VHS, 3/4 U. **C:** Narrated by Eric Sevareid. **Pr:** Alan Landsburg Productions. **A:** Jr. High-Adult. **P:** Education. **U:** Institution, Home. **Gen-Edu:** Documentary Films, History--U.S., International Relations. **Acq:** Purchase. **Dist:** Karol Media; Fusion Video; Home Vision Cinema. $19.99.
Indiv. Titles: 1. Versailles: The Lost Peace/Return to Isolationism 2. The First SALT Talks/Radio, Racism and Foreign Policy 3. The Great Depression and Foreign Affairs/America in the Pacific: The Clash of Two Cultures 4. F.D.R. and Hitler: The Dynamics of Power/F.D.R. and Hitler: Their Rise to Power 5. The Recognition of Russia: A Climate of Mutual Distrust/Latin America: Intervention in Our Own Back Yard 6. The Italian-Ethiopian War: Africa in World Affairs/The Spanish Civil War 7. The Phony War/F.D.R. and Churchill: The Human Partnership 8. Japan Invades China: Crisis in the Far East/War Comes to Pearl Harbor.

Between the Wars: American Literature from 1915 to 1945 19??
Examines the history of American literature during the period between WWI and WWII, 1915-45. 16m; VHS. **A:** Jr. High-Adult. **P:** Education. **U:** Institution, CCTV, SURA. **Gen-Edu:** Literature--American, History--U.S. **Acq:** Purchase. **Dist:** Thomas S. Klise Co. $58.00.

Between Truth and Lies 2006 (Unrated) — ★½
Hemingway is unconvincing as a shrink and the characters are generally unappealing in this ludicrous Lifetime movie. Dr. Claire Parker (Hemingway) encourages patient John Walters (Watton) to pursue his crush. Only she doesn't realize that it's on her teenage daughter Emily (Castle) and that he's seriously disturbed. Emily disappears sending Claire turns into action mom. 90m; DVD. **C:** Mariel Hemingway; Maggie Castle; Jonathan Watton; Ted Whittall; Morgan Kelly; Conrad Coates; Directed by John Bradshaw; Written by Paul B. Margolis; Cinematography by Russ Goozee; Music by Stacey Hersh. **A:** Jr. High-Adult. **P:** Entertainment. **U:** Home. **L:** English. **Mov-Ent:** TV Movies. **Acq:** Purchase. **Dist:** A&E Television Networks L.L.C.

Between Two Loves 1990
Adapted from the novel "Two Loves For Jenny" by Sandra Peden Miller, tells the story of a girl dedicated both to music and to her boyfriend, and the sacrifice she makes when they both enter the same music competition. 27m; VHS, 3/4 U, EJ, Special order formats. **TV Std:** NTSC, PAL, SECAM. **C:** Robert Reed; Lance Guest; Karlene Crockett; Paul Cooper; Directed by Robert Thompson. **Pr:** Martin Tahse; Disney Educational Productions. **A:** Jr. High-Sr. High. **P:** Entertainment. **U:** Institution, CCTV, SURA. **Mov-Ent.** **Acq:** Purchase, Rent/Lease. **Dist:** Phoenix Learning Group; New Kid Home Video. $39.95.

Between Two Women 1986 (Unrated) — ★★
A wife's relationship with her bossy mother-in-law is rocky until the latter has a stroke and needs care. Dewhurst won an Emmy for her portrayal of the mother-in-law. 95m; VHS. **C:** Farrah Fawcett; Michael Nouri; Colleen Dewhurst; Steven Hill; Bridgette Andersen; Danny Corkill; Directed by Jon Avnet. **Pr:** Carol Schreder; Polly Platt. **A:** Family. **P:** Entertainment. **U:** Home. **Mov-Ent:** Parenting, TV Movies, Diseases. **Acq:** Purchase. **Dist:** Warner Home Video, Inc. $19.98.

Between Two Worlds 1944 — ★½
Dreary fantasy drama. Despondent Austrian refugees Henry (Henreid) and his wife Ann (Parker) commit suicide in their London flat but awaken on a fog-shrouded cruise ship. The couple soon learns that they and their (dead) fellow passengers are awaiting judgment to either Heaven, Hell, sailing perpetually in limbo, or a second chance. Garfield overdoes his role as a cynical, blowhard reporter. Based on the play by Sutton Vane; remake of 1930's "Outward Bound." 112m/B/W; DVD. **C:** Paul Henreid; Eleanor Parker; John Garfield; Sydney Greenstreet; Faye Emerson; Edmund Gwenn; George Tobias; Sara Allgood; George Coulouris; Directed by Edward Blatt; Written by Daniel Fuchs; Cinematography by Carl Guthrie; Music by Erich Wolfgang Korngold. **A:** Sr. High-Adult. **P:** Entertainment. **U:** Home. **Mov-Ent:** Death, Boating, Suicide. **Acq:** Purchase. **Dist:** WarnerArchive.com.

Between Two Worlds 1990
Clash of cultures between "white" Canada and the Inuit Eskimo, symbolized by Joseph Idlout, an Inuit hunter who was a model hero in the 1950s in books and films. Unemployment, dependency, and high suicide rates followed the introduction of so-called civilization to the native peoples. 58m; VHS. **C:** Directed by Barry Greenwald. **A:** College-Adult. **P:** Education. **U:** Institution. **Gen-Edu:** Canada, Eskimos. **Acq:** Purchase, Rent/Lease. **Dist:** First Run/Icarus Films. $390.00.

Between Two Worlds: The Hmong Shaman in America 1985
This video takes a look at the ancient shamanic rituals and ceremonies such as animal sacrifice and trance-like healing. 26m; VHS, 3/4 U. **Pr:** Dwight Conquergood. **A:** Jr. High-Adult. **P:** Education. **U:** Institution, SURA. **Gen-Edu:** Philosophy & Ideology. **Acq:** Rent/Lease. **Dist:** Filmakers Library Inc. $295.00.

Between Us 1998
Documentary conceived and produced by breast cancer survivors interviewing other survivors and how they coped with the disease. 52m; VHS, DVD. **A:** Sr. High-Adult. **P:** Education. **U:** Institution. **Gen-Edu:** Cancer, Documentary Films. **Acq:** Purchase, Rent/Lease. **Dist:** The Cinema Guild. $275.00.

Between Wars 1974 (Unrated) — ★★
Young doctor in Australia's Medical Corps encounters conflict when he tries to introduce Freud's principles into his work. 97m; VHS. **C:** Corin Redgrave; Arthur Dignam; Judy Morris; Patricia Leehy; Gunter Meisner; Directed by Michael Thornhill. **Pr:** Satori Entertainment Corporation. **A:** Sr. High-Adult. **P:** Entertainment. **U:** Home. **Mov-Ent:** Australia. **Acq:** Purchase. **Dist:** Unknown Distributor.

Between White & Black 19??
Explores the impact society and history have on determining color in the U.S., and questions whether race can be determined on face value. Issues of personal and social identity are examined through interviews, family photos, and contemporary footage. 26m; VHS. **A:** Sr. High. **P:** Education. **U:** Institution. **Gen-Edu:** Minorities, Ethnicity. **Acq:** Purchase. **Dist:** Filmakers Library Inc. $295.

Between You and Me: Learning to Communicate 1991
Three segments teach good listening and speaking skills to students through role-playing and dramatized vignettes. 20m; VHS. **A:** Primary-Jr. High. **P:** Education. **U:** Institution. **Chl-Juv:** Communication, Children. **Acq:** Purchase. **Dist:** Sunburst Digital Inc. $149.00.

Between You and Me: Solving Conflict 19??
Provides solutions which help employees diffuse disagreements and prevent turf wars without management intervention. Stresses the importance of taking responsibility for conflict, uncovering both sides, controlling emotion, listening without arguing or being judgmental, and getting a consensus for commitment. Comes with course materials guide, exercises, and overhead masters. 23m; VHS; Closed Captioned. **A:** Adult. **P:** Instruction. **U:** Institution. **Bus-Ind:** Management, Job Training, Communication. **Acq:** Purchase, Rent/Lease, Duplication License. **Dist:** American Media, Inc. $695.00.

Between Your Legs 1999 — ★★
Provocatively titled sexual thriller. Receptionist Miranda (Abril) meets writer Javier (Bardem) at a group therapy session for sex

addicts. He's addicted to phone sex and the married Miranda likes to have sex with strangers. While they get to know each other a murder occurs and the investigation is assigned to detective Felix (Gomez), who happens to be Miranda's husband. Soon, suspicions begins to point in Javier's direction. The triangle is strong but subplots are undeveloped and the film sinks into implausibility. Spanish with subtitles. 120m; VHS, DVD. **C:** Victoria Abril; Javier Bardem; Carmelo Gomez; Juan Diego; Sergi Lopez; Javier Albala; Directed by Manuel Gomez Pereira; Written by Manuel Gomez Pereira; Joaquin Oristrell; Yolanda Garcia Serrano; Juan Luis Iborra; Cinematography by Juan Amoros; Music by Bernardo Bonezzi. **A:** Adult. **P:** Entertainment. **U:** Home. **L:** Spanish. **Mov-Ent.** **Acq:** Purchase. **Dist:** TLA Releasing.

Betye and Alison Saar: Conjure Women of the Arts 1994
Examines the personal and artistic relationship between artist Betye Saar and her daughter Alison Saar. Contains footage of both artists at work in the studio and discussion of their influences and collaboration on the installation piece "House of Gris Gris." 28m; VHS. **A:** Jr. High-Adult. **P:** Education. **U:** Institution, Home. **Fin-Art:** Art & Artists. **Acq:** Purchase. **Dist:** L & S Video; Crystal Productions. $39.95.

Beulah Land 1980 — ★½
Miniseries about 45 years in the lives of a Southern family, including the Civil War. Based on the novels "Beulah Land" and "Look Away, Beulah Land" by Lonnie Coleman. 267m; VHS, DVD. **C:** Lesley Ann Warren; Michael Sarrazin; Don Johnson; Meredith Baxter; Dorian Harewood; Eddie Albert; Hope Lange; Paul Rudd; Directed by Virgil W. Vogel; Harry Falk. **Pr:** Columbia Pictures Television. **A:** Jr. High-Adult. **P:** Entertainment. **U:** Home. **Mov-Ent:** Family, TV Movies. **Acq:** Purchase. **Dist:** Sony Pictures Home Entertainment Inc. $29.95.

Beulah Show 1952 — ★
Three episodes from the series chronicling the adventures of a black housekeeper and the family she serves. Includes "Beulah's Misunderstanding" when she erroneously believes that Mrs. Henderson is pregnant. A rare appearance by McDaniels occurs in "Beulah the Dance Teacher." Beulah tries to get her employers to reconcile after they have a fight in "Beulah Helps the Hendersons." Also featured are five racist cartoons including "Jasper's in a Jam" and "Jungle Jitters." 115m/B/W; VHS. **C:** Louise Beavers; Hattie McDaniel; Ernest Whitman; Butterfly McQueen; Arthur Q. Bryan; Ruby Dandridge. **Pr:** ABC. **A:** Family. **P:** Entertainment. **U:** Home. **Mov-Ent:** Television Series. **Acq:** Purchase. **Dist:** Shokus Video. $24.95.

Beulah "Sippie" Wallace 1989
This documentary takes a look at the life and music of blues singer/songwriter Sippie Wallace, a contemporary of Bessie Smith and Ma Rainey. 23m; VHS. **Pr:** Kino International Corporation. **A:** Jr. High-Adult. **P:** Entertainment. **U:** Home. **Mov-Ent:** Documentary Films, Music--Jazz, Biography. **Acq:** Purchase. **Dist:** Music Video Distributors. $24.95.

Bevel Machine Cutting 1983
Offers instruction on specific aspects of oxy-acetylene welding. 4m; VHS. **A:** Adult. **P:** Vocational. **U:** Institution. **Bus-Ind:** Welding. **Acq:** Purchase. **Dist:** RMI Media. $45.00.

Beveled Boxes and Containers 19??
Features making a beveled box using a standard bevel, art glass, and jewels. Details using a strip cutter, working with copper foil, and special soldering tips and techniques. 30m; VHS. **A:** Adult. **P:** Instruction. **U:** Home. **How-Ins:** Crafts, Hobbies, How-To. **Acq:** Purchase. **Dist:** Cutters Productions. $19.95.

Beverage and Food Service 199?
Teaches the food service employee or wait staff the essential skills of beverage service, tray and plate handling, and clearing. Part of the Basic Table and Wine Service Skills Series. 21m; VHS. **A:** Sr. High-Adult. **P:** Instruction. **U:** Home. **How-Ins:** Customer Service, Food Industry, How-To. **Acq:** Purchase. **Dist:** Culinary Institute of America. $75.00.

The Beverly Hillbillies 1962
The successful sitcom series, which ran from 1962-71, features Jed Clampett and his Ozark clan striking oil, getting rich, and heading for the good life in California. Two episodes per tape. 51m/B/W; VHS. **C:** Buddy Ebsen; Irene Ryan; Donna Douglas; Max Baer, Jr.; Nancy Kulp; Raymond Bailey; Phil Silvers; Cameo(s) John Wayne. **A:** Family. **P:** Entertainment. **U:** Home. **Mov-Ent:** Television Series. **Acq:** Purchase. **Dist:** Fox Home Entertainment; Movies Unlimited. $12.98.
Indiv. Titles: 1. The Clampetts Strike Oil/Getting Settled 2. The Clampetts in Washington/Jed Buys the Capitol 3. Jed Buys Central Park/The Clampetts in New York 4. The Indians are Coming/The South Rises Again 5. Flatt, Clampett and Scruggs/Cousin Roy 6. The Giant Jackrabbit/The Big Chicken 7. Jed Buys the Freeway/Jed Becomes a Banker 8. Elly's Animals/The Critter Doctor.

The Beverly Hillbillies 1993 (PG) — ★★½
Big-screen transfer of the long-running TV show may appeal to fans. Ozark mountaineer Jed Clampett discovers oil, becomes an instant billionaire, and packs his backwoods clan off to the good life in California. Minimal plot finds dim-bulb nephew Jethro and daughter Elly May looking for a bride for Jed. Not that any of it matters. Everyone does fine by their impersonations, particularly Varney as the good-hearted Jed and Leachman as stubborn Granny. Ebsen, the original Jed, reprises another of his TV roles, detective Barnaby Jones. And yes, the familiar strains of the "Ballad of Jed Clampett" by Jerry Scoggins starts this one off, too. 93m; VHS, DVD, CC. **C:** Jim Varney; Erika Eleniak; Diedrich Bader; Cloris Leachman; Dabney Coleman; Lily Tomlin; Lea Thompson; Rob Schneider; Linda Carlson; Penny Fuller; Kevin Connolly; Cameo(s) Buddy Ebsen; Zsa Zsa Gabor; Dolly Parton; Directed by Penelope Spheeris; Written by Larry Konner; Mark Rosenthal; Jim Fisher; Jim Staahl; Cinematography by Robert Brinkmann; Music by Lalo Schifrin. **Pr:** Penelope Spheeris; Penelope Spheeris; Ian Bryce. **A:** Jr. High-Adult. **P:** Entertainment. **U:** Home. **Mov-Ent:** Oil Industry. **Acq:** Purchase. **Dist:** Fox Home Entertainment. $19.98.

The Beverly Hillbillies: The Official 2nd Season 2007 (Unrated)
Television comedy series from 1962-1971. Mr. Drysdale (Bailey) helps the Clampetts institute a Possum Day, convincing the mayor to stage a parade. Granny finds out her favorite cowboy, played by Henry Gibson, is a faker and continues with her spells, bringing outrage from the local medical community, and planting crops on the front lawn. Mrs. Drysdale's dull garden party is turned into a bluegrass, punch-spiked, throwdown. Peter Whitney is lowlife mountain con man looking to get his hands on some of the Clapett fortune in a three-show arc. Ellie Mae continues to come across the craziest of critters. Watch with or without each episode's Winston cigarette opening. Extras include Irene Ryan's screen test and an informal interview with creator Paul Henning. 36 episodes. 918m; DVD. **A:** Family. **P:** Entertainment. **U:** Home. **Mov-Ent:** Television Series. **Acq:** Purchase. **Dist:** Paramount Pictures Corp.

The Beverly Hillbillies: The Official 3rd Season 1964 (Unrated)
The Clampetts, with Jed as the head of household are starting to learn the vast differences from living in the hills to living in Beverly Hills as they take advantage of their new-found wealth but keep their down-to-earth style in "Jed Becomes a Movie Mogul," "Elly in the Movies," "Double Naught Jethro," and "Gramma's Romance." 34 episodes. 868m; DVD. **A:** Family. **P:** Entertainment. **U:** Home. **Mov-Ent:** Television Series. **Acq:** Purchase. **Dist:** Paramount Pictures Corp. $49.98.

The Beverly Hillbillies, Vol. 7 1963
Features two episodes about the popular backwoods family. Includes "Jed Buys the Freeway" and "Jed Becomes a Banker." 60m/B/W; DVD. **C:** Buddy Ebsen; Irene Ryan; Donna Douglas; Max Baer, Jr; Nancy Kulp; Raymond Bailey. **A:** Family. **P:** Entertainment. **U:** Home. **Mov-Ent:** Television Series. **Acq:** Purchase. **Dist:** MPI Media Group. $12.98.

The Beverly Hillbillies, Vol. 8 1963
Elly May stirs up trouble in "Elly's Animals" and "The Critter Doctor." 60m/B/W; DVD. **C:** Buddy Ebsen; Irene Ryan; Donna Douglas; Max Baer, Jr; Nancy Kulp; Raymond Bailey. **A:** Family. **P:** Entertainment. **U:** Home. **Mov-Ent:** Television Series. **Acq:** Purchase. **Dist:** MPI Media Group. $12.98.

Beverly Hills Bodysnatchers 1989 (R) — ★½
A mad scientist and a greedy mortician plot to get rich, but their plan backfires when they bring a Mafia godfather back to life and he terrorizes Beverly Hills. 85m; VHS. **C:** Vic Tayback; Frank Gorshin; Brooke Bundy; Seth Jaffe; Art Metrano; Allison Barron; Rodney Eastman; Warren Selko; Keone Young; Directed by Jonathan Mostow. **A:** College-Adult. **P:** Entertainment. **U:** Home. **Mov-Ent.** **Acq:** Purchase. **Dist:** Image Entertainment Inc. $39.95.

Beverly Hills Brats 1989 (PG-13) — ★
A spoiled, rich Hollywood brat hires a loser to kidnap him, in order to gain his parents' attention, only to have both of them kidnapped by real crooks. 90m; VHS, DVD, CC. **C:** Martin Sheen; Burt Young; Peter Billingsley; Terry Moore; Directed by Dimitri Sotirakis; Music by Barry Goldberg. **Pr:** Heron Communications. **A:** Jr. High-Adult. **P:** Entertainment. **U:** Home. **Mov-Ent:** Family. **Acq:** Purchase. **Dist:** Lions Gate Television Corp.; Image Entertainment Inc.; Anchor Bay Entertainment. $89.95.

Beverly Hills Chihuahua 2008 (PG) — ★★
Chloe, a pampered Chihuahua living the good life in Beverly Hills, finds herself lost in Mexico with the spoiled pet-sitter during a weekend romp. Along the way Chloe must be rescued from the grips of Mexican dogfight wranglers and falls in love with Papi, a Chihuahua from the wrong side of the tracks. Light-hearted family affair with a strong Hispanic cast, as well as Barrymore as the voice of Chloe and Curtis as Chloe's wildly indulgent owner. Cute, tame, kind of lame. 86m; Blu-Ray, Wide. **C:** Nick Zano; Piper Perabo; Manolo Cardona; Jose Maria Yazpik; Voice(s) by Drew Barrymore; Salma Hayek; George Lopez; Andy Garcia; Jamie Lee Curtis; Marguerite Moreau; Michael Urie; Richard "Cheech" Marin; Paul Rodriguez; Placido Domingo; Edward James Olmos; Loretta Devine; Luis Guzman; Directed by Raja Gosnell; Written by Jeffrey Bushell; Analisa LaBianco; Cinematography by Phil Mereaux; Music by Hector Pereira. **Pr:** David Hoberman; John Jacobs; Todd Lieberman; Mandeville Films; Smart Entertainment; Walt Disney Pictures. **A:** Family. **P:** Entertainment. **U:** Home. **L:** English. **Mov-Ent:** Action-Comedy, Mexico. **Acq:** Purchase. **Dist:** Buena Vista Home Entertainment; Movies Unlimited; Alpha Video.

Beverly Hills Chihuahua 2 2010 (G) — ★½
Mediocre sequel may have some appeal for the kiddies. Chloe and Papi are married and have become proud parents. Papi's owner Sam has learned his own parents are about to lose their house and the dogs decide to enter a dog show hoping to win some prize money. That doesn't work out and they accidentally foil a bank robbery instead, which deserves a reward. 84m; DVD, Blu-Ray, Wide. **C:** Marcus Coloma; Lupe Ontiveros; Castulo Guerra; Erin Cahill; Susan Blakely; Voice(s) by George Lopez; Odette Yustman Annable; Zachary Gordon; Bridgit Mendler; Ernie Hudson; Emily Osment; Mel Ferrer; Directed by Alex Zamm; Written by Alex Zamm; Danielle Schneider; Dannah Feinglass; Cinematography by Robert Brinkmann; Music by Chris Hajian. **A:** Family. **P:** Entertainment. **U:** Home. **Mov-Ent:** Pets. **Acq:** Purchase. **Dist:** Buena Vista Home Entertainment.

Beverly Hills Chihuahua 3: Viva La Fiesta! 2012 (G) — ★★½
Papi, Chloe, and their five pups move into the Langham Hotel when owners Rachel and Sam get new jobs. Tiniest pup Rosa feels neglected and Papi thinks he's losing control of his family. As the hotel struggles, Papi and his pal Pedro try to figure out if someone is sabotaging the business. 89m; DVD, Blu-Ray. **C:** Marcus Coloma; Erin Cahill; Sebastien Roche; Frances Fisher; Voice(s) by George Lopez; Odette Annable; Kay Panabaker; Ernie Hudson; Jake Busey; Directed by Lev L. Spiro; Written by Dana Starfield; Cinematography by Greg Gardiner; Music by Hector Pereira. **A:** Family. **P:** Entertainment. **U:** Home. **L:** English. **Mov-Ent.** **Acq:** Purchase. **Dist:** Walt Disney Studios Home Entertainment.

Beverly Hills Cop 1984 (R) — ★★½
When a close friend of smooth-talking Detroit cop Axel Foley is brutally murdered, he traces the murderer to the posh streets of Beverly Hills. There he must stay on his toes to keep one step ahead of the killer and two steps ahead of the law. Better than average Murphy vehicle. 105m; VHS, DVD, 8 mm, Wide, CC. **C:** Eddie Murphy; Judge Reinhold; John Ashton; Lisa Eilbacher; Ronny Cox; Steven Berkoff; James Russo; Jonathan Banks; Stephen Elliott; Bronson Pinchot; Paul Reiser; Damon Wayans; Rick Overton; Directed by Martin Brest; Written by Danilo Bach; Cinematography by Bruce Surtees; Music by Harold Faltermeyer. **Pr:** Paramount Pictures. **A:** Sr. High-Adult. **P:** Entertainment. **U:** Home. **Mov-Ent:** Action-Adventure. **Acq:** Purchase. **Dist:** Paramount Pictures Corp. $14.95.

Beverly Hills Cop 2 1987 (R) — ★½
The highly successful sequel to the first profitable comedy, with essentially the same plot, this time deals with Foley infiltrating a band of international munitions smugglers. 103m; VHS, DVD, 8 mm, Wide, CC. **C:** Eddie Murphy; Judge Reinhold; Jurgen Prochnow; Ronny Cox; John Ashton; Brigitte Nielsen; Allen Garfield; Paul Reiser; Dean Stockwell; Chris Rock; Gil Hill; Robert Ridgely; Gilbert Gottfried; Todd Susman; Robert Pastorelli; Tommy (Tiny) Lister; Paul Guilfoyle; Hugh Hefner; Directed by Tony Scott; Written by Larry Ferguson; Warren Skaaren; Cinematography by Jeffrey L. Kimball; Music by Harold Faltermeyer. **Pr:** Paramount Pictures. **A:** Sr. High-Adult. **P:** Entertainment. **U:** Home. **Mov-Ent:** Action-Adventure. **Awds:** Golden Raspberries '87: Worst Song ("I Want Your Sex"). **Acq:** Purchase. **Dist:** Paramount Pictures Corp. $14.95.

Beverly Hills Cop 3 1994 (R) — ★½
Yes, Detroit cop Axel Foley (Murphy) just happens to find another case that takes him back to his friends on the Beverly Hills PD. This time he uncovers a criminal network fronting WonderWorld, an amusement park with a squeaky-clean image. Fast-paced action, lots of gunplay, and Eddie wisecracks his way through the slow spots. Reinhold returns as the still impossibly naive Rosewood, with Pinchot briefly reprising his role as Serge of the undeterminable accent. Critically panned boxoffice disappointment relies too heavily on formula and is another disappointing followup. 105m; VHS, DVD, Wide, CC. **C:** Eddie Murphy; Judge Reinhold; Hector Elizondo; Timothy Carhart; Stephen McHattie; Theresa Randle; John Saxon; Alan Young; Bronson Pinchot; Al Green; Gil Hill; Louis Lombardi; Directed by John Landis; Written by Steven E. de Souza; Cinematography by Mac Ahlberg; Music by Nile Rodgers. **Pr:** Robert Rehme; Mace Neufeld; Mark Lipsky; Neufeld-Rehme Productions; Paramount Pictures. **A:** Sr. High-Adult. **P:** Entertainment. **U:** Home. **Mov-Ent:** Action-Adventure. **Acq:** Purchase. **Dist:** Paramount Pictures Corp. $14.95.

Beverly Hills Family Robinson 1997 (Unrated) — ★★
Cooking show host Marsha Robinson decides to take her family on a yachting vacation in the South Seas. Naturally, they get hijacked by pirates and shipwrecked and must learn to survive on their not-quite-deserted island. And just how good is Marsha is at campfire cooking? 88m; VHS, CC. **C:** Dyan Cannon; Martin Mull; Sarah Michelle Gellar; Josh Picker; Nique Needles; Ryan O'Donohue; Directed by Troy Miller. **A:** Family. **P:** Entertainment. **U:** Home. **Mov-Ent.** **Acq:** Purchase. **Dist:** Buena Vista Home Entertainment.

Beverly Hills Madam 1986 (PG-13) — ★
In this routine plot, a stable of elite call girls struggle with their lifestyle and their madam, played by Dunaway. 97m; VHS. **C:** Faye Dunaway; Louis Jourdan; Donna Dixon; Robin Givens; Marshall Colt; Melody Anderson; Terry Farrell; Directed by Harvey Hart. **Pr:** Orion Pictures. **A:** Jr. High-Adult. **P:** Entertainment. **U:** Home. **Mov-Ent:** Prostitution, TV Movies, Sex & Sexuality. **Acq:** Purchase. **Dist:** MGM Studios Inc. $59.98.

Beverly Hills 90210 1990 (Unrated)
In the pilot episode for the immensely popular series, the world is introduced to the exciting teens who wander the halls of West Beverly High. Join Brandon and Brenda Walsh as they move from Minneapolis to Beverly Hills and experience all the trials and tribulations that come with the new zip code. Includes 25 minutes of previously unseen footage. 90m; VHS. **C:** Jason Priestley; Shannen Doherty; Jennie Garth; Brian Austin Green; Tori Spelling; Ian Ziering; Gabrielle Carteris. **Pr:** Aaron Spelling. **A:** Family. **P:** Entertainment. **U:** Home. **Mov-Ent:** Adolescence. **Acq:** Purchase. **Dist:** Movies Unlimited. $19.99.

Beverly Hills 90210: Behind the Zip Code 1992
A dull look at the popular television program with most of the clips gathered from talk and awards shows. 60m; VHS. **A:** Family. **P:** Entertainment. **U:** Home. **Mov-Ent:** Television. **Acq:** Purchase. **Dist:** Anchor Bay Entertainment; Fast Forward. $9.99.

Beverly Hills 90210: The 8th Season 1997 (Unrated)
Fox Television 1990-2000 adolescent drama. Brandon hunts down the gunman that shot Kelly in the LAX parking lot in "Forgive and Forget," "The Way We Weren't" has Kelly dealing with amnesia after suffering mild brain damage, Donna is hired by a widow who wants to contact her dead husband through a seance in "Toil and Trouble," and in "Skin Deep" Donna tries to help a co-worker with a self-mutilation problem. 30 episodes. 1195m; DVD. **C:** Jennie Garth; Ian Ziering; Tori Spelling; Jason Priestley. **A:** Jr. High-Adult. **P:** Entertainment. **U:** Home. **Mov-Ent:** Television Series, Drama, Romance. **Acq:** Purchase. **Dist:** Paramount Pictures Corp. $45.99.

Beverly Hills, 90210: The Complete 1st Season 1990 (Unrated)
In this Aaron Spelling production, the middle-class Walsh family moves from Minnesota to Beverly Hills and 16-year-old twins Brandon and Brenda are soon caught up with new friends and high school drama as Brandon hooks up with troubled blonde Kelly, Brenda falls for bad boy Dylan, and Steve, David, Andrea, and Donna all add to the clique. 1068m; DVD. **C:** Jason Priestley; Shannen Doherty; Jennie Garth; Luke Perry; Brian Austin Green; Tori Spelling; Ian Ziering; Gabrielle Carteris. **A:** Jr. High-Adult. **P:** Entertainment. **U:** Home. **Mov-Ent:** Television Series, Drama. **Acq:** Purchase. **Dist:** Paramount Pictures Corp.

Beverly Hills, 90210: The Complete 2nd Season 1991
Brenda and her older brother Brandon continue to make social and cultural adjustments after moving from Minnesota to Beverly Hills, California. Brenda has a pregnancy scare in "Beach Blanket Brandon" and Brandon gets a new job at the Beverly Hill Beach Club. Dylan is accused of burglary and it's found out he's been pawning family belonging to keep cash flowing in "Anaconda." When a black family moves into the Walsh's neighborhood it sparks a rash of racial attacks in "Ashes to Ashes." Dylan's mother returns from Hawaii after an 11-year absence in "Necessity Is a Mother." 28 episodes. 1305m; DVD. **C:** Shannen Doherty; Jason Priestley; Luke Perry; Tori Spelling; Jennie Garth; Christine Elise. **A:** Sr. High-Adult. **P:** Entertainment. **U:** Home. **Mov-Ent:** Drama, Television. **Acq:** Purchase. **Dist:** Paramount Pictures Corp.

Beverly Hills 90210: The Complete 6th Season 1995 (Unrated)
Steve talks Brandon into setting up a rave party at his parents vacant house in "Home Is Where the Tart Is" things get destructive, Kelly returns from New York City with new boyfriend Colin Robins, an artist, and Dylan is determined to avenge his father's death. Brandon's girlfriend Susan gets an award for her article about abortion in "Nancy's Choice" and reveals the story was about her, Valerie pretends to be Colin's agent and hopes he'll get off drugs. Kelly gets into using drugs too but goes into rehab in "All This and Mary Too," while the gang goes on a ski trip to Mammoth Mountain. Brandon and Susan get stranded in a blizzard on the mountain during the ski trip, and in "Ticket to Ride" they win $5,000 in the lottery but lose their ticket. 32 episodes. 1425m; DVD. **C:** Jennie Garth; Tori Spelling; Brian Austin Green; Ian Ziering; Joe E. Tata. **A:** Jr. High-Adult. **P:** Entertainment. **U:** Home. **Mov-Ent:** Drama, Television Series. **Acq:** Purchase. **Dist:** Paramount Pictures Corp. $59.98.

Beverly Hills 90210: The Complete 7th Season 1996 (Unrated)
Fox Television 1990-00 primetime soap opera. Senior year at California University, Brandon embarks on a Kelly-free existence and engrosses himself in the campus TV station, Val struggles to keep her club After Dark afloat, Donna and David continue their tempestuous relationship through mental breakdowns and stalker returns, and Steve repeatedly brings Clare heartbreak. Concludes with the two-part graduation special. 32 episodes. 1413m; DVD. **C:** Jason Priestley; Tiffani(-Amber) Thiessen; Ian Ziering; Tori Spelling; Brian Austin Green; Kathleen Robertson; Jennie Garth. **A:** Sr. High-Adult. **P:** Entertainment. **U:** Home. **Mov-Ent:** Drama, Television Series. **Acq:** Purchase. **Dist:** Paramount Pictures Corp. $59.98.

Beverly Hills Ninja 1996 (PG-13) — ★½
Farley plays Haru, a pathetically inept adopted son of a ninja, who is, nevertheless, sent to Beverly Hills on a rescue mission to break up an international counterfeiting ring. There, secondtime spoof siren Sheridan hires the "great white ninja" to follow her no-good boyfriend and becomes the object of Haru's desire. Farley's extraordinary gift for physical comedy is exploited to the hilt, and the increase in Haru's tripping and stumbling (and in one harrowing scene, stripping) usually coincides with the fumbling of the plot. Rock's talents are squandered on a poorly conceived bellboy character. Farley's first feature sans fellow SNL alumni Spade suffers for his absence. Director Duggan, who also helmed Adam Sandler's "Happy Gilmore," might want to start screening his calls. 88m; VHS, DVD, Wide, CC. **C:** Chris Farley; Nicolette Sheridan; Robin Shou; Nathaniel Parker; Chris Rock; Soon-Teck Oh; Francois Chau; Keith Cooke Hirabayashi; Directed by Dennis Dugan; Written by Mark Feldberg; Mitch Klebenoff; Cinematography by Arthur Albert; Music by George S. Clinton. **Pr:** Brad Krevoy; Brad Jenkel; Jeffrey D. Ivers; John Bertolli; Michael Rottenberg; TriStar Pictures; Motion Picture Corporation of America; Sony Pictures Home Entertainment Inc. **A:** Jr. High-Adult. **P:** Entertainment. **U:** Home. **Mov-Ent:** Martial Arts. **Acq:** Purchase. **Dist:** Sony Pictures Home Entertainment Inc.

The Beverly Hills Supper Club Fire 197?
Footage of the Beverly Hills fire illustrates evacuation techniques and methods used. This program stresses the need for building codes enforcement in life, safety matters. Commentary is discussed by field specialists. 15m; VHS, 3/4 U. **Pr:** National Fire Protection Association. **A:** Sr. High-Adult. **P:** Education. **U:** Institution, CCTV, Home. **Gen-Edu:** Fires, Safety Education. **Acq:** Purchase. **Dist:** National Fire Protection Association.

Beverly Hills Vamp 1988 (R) — ★★
A madame and her girls are really female vampires with a penchant for hot-blooded men. 88m; VHS, Streaming. **C:** Britt Ekland; Eddie Deezen; Debra Lamb; Michelle (McClellan) Bauer; Brigitte Burdine; Tim Conway, Jr.; Jillian Kesner; Tom Shell; Directed by Fred Olen Ray; Written by Ernest Farino; Cinematography by Stephen Blake; Music by Chuck Cirino. **Pr:** Vidmark Entertainment. **A:** Sr. High-Adult. **P:** Entertainment. **U:** Home. **Mov-Ent:** Prostitution. **Acq:** Purchase. **Dist:** CinemaNow Inc. $79.95.

Beverly Lewis' The Confession 2013 (Unrated) — ★★½
Hallmark Channel sequel to the 2011 family drama. After Katie (Leclerc) is shunned by her Amish community, she decides to be with her birth mother, Laura (Stringfield), in the outside world. Wealthy Laura is dying and her gambling addict husband, Dylan (Paul), discovers he won't inherit. So he hires actress Alyson (Whelan) to pose as long-lost Katie just when the real Katie shows up at their door. To complicate the identity mess, two different men, including Katie's childhood friend Daniel (Fisher), reach out to her. 88m; DVD. **C:** Katie Leclerc; Sherry Stringfield; Adrian Paul; Julia Whelan; Cameron Deane Stewart; Michael Rupnow; Directed by Michael Landon, Jr.; Written by Michael Landon, Jr.; Brian Bird; Cinematography by Dan Kneece; Music by Lee Holdridge. **A:** Jr. High-Adult. **P:** Entertainment. **U:** Home. **L:** English. **Mov-Ent:** TV Movies, Family, Amish. **Acq:** Purchase. **Dist:** Sony Pictures Home Entertainment Inc.

Beverly Lewis' The Shunning 2011 (Unrated) — ★★½
Hallmark Channel drama based on the first book in Lewis' trilogy. In the Amish community of Hickory Hollow, Pennsylvania, Katie Lapp (Panabaker) has somewhat reluctantly agreed to marry widower Bishop John Beiler (Jenkins) since her first love, Daniel (Topp), is presumed dead. An outsider, Laura Mayfield-Bennett (Stringfield), comes to the community looking for Katie's mother Rebecca (Van Natta) and this leads to a family secret being revealed that changes Katie's life forever. 88m; DVD. **C:** Danielle Panabaker; Sherry Stringfield; Sandra Van Natta; Bill Oberst, Jr.; Burgess Jenkins; David Topp; Sarah E. Chambers; Directed by Michael Landon, Jr.; Chris Easterly; Cinematography by Christo Bakalov; Music by Lee Holdridge. **A:** Jr. High-Adult. **P:** Entertainment. **U:** Home. **Mov-Ent:** TV Movies, Amish, Adoption. **Acq:** Purchase. **Dist:** Sony Pictures Home Entertainment Inc.

Beverly Sassoon—A Video Guide to Total Beauty 19??
Beverly Sassoon offers her beauty tips, including color analysis, make-up tips, fashion ideas, and hair, skin, nutrition, and exercise techniques. 120m; VHS. **A:** Sr. High-Adult. **P:** Instruction. **U:** Institution. **How-Ins:** Cosmetology, Self-Help. **Acq:** Purchase. **Dist:** Instructional Video. $29.95.

Beverly Sills in La Traviata 19??
Sills gives an outstanding performance as Violetta in La Traviata. In Italian with English subtitles. ?m; VHS. **A:** Sr. High-Adult. **P:** Entertainment. **U:** Home. **L:** Italian. **Fin-Art:** Opera, Music--Performance. **Acq:** Purchase. **Dist:** OPERA America. $29.95.

Beware 1946 — ★½
A black singer saves a college from bankruptcy and makes off with the gym teacher. The photography may be a bit harsh, but the all-black cast made this a pioneering but impressive film. 64m/B/W; VHS, DVD. **C:** Louis Jordan; Frank Wilson; Emory Richardson; Valerie Black; Milton Woods; Directed by Bud Pollard. **Pr:** Astor Pictures. **A:** Jr. High-Adult. **P:** Entertainment. **U:** Home. **Mov-Ent:** Musical--Drama, Black Culture. **Acq:** Purchase. **Dist:** Rex Miller Artisan Studio. $24.95.

Beware and Be Wise 198?
The importance of outdoor electrical safety especially around power lines is stressed. 15m; VHS, 3/4 U. **Pr:** National Safety Council. **A:** College-Adult. **P:** Education. **U:** Institution. **Gen-Edu:** Safety Education, Electricity. **Acq:** Rent/Lease. **Dist:** National Safety Council, California Chapter, Film Library.

Beware, Beware My Beauty Fair 1973
A play within a play: children work to present a school production while they are being plagued by a mysterious beast backstage. Presented by the Montreal Children's Theatre Company. 29m; VHS, 3/4 U. **Pr:** National Film Board of Canada. **A:** Primary-Jr. High. **P:** Entertainment. **U:** Institution, SURA. **Chl-Juv:** Mystery & Suspense. **Acq:** Purchase. **Dist:** Phoenix Learning Group.

Beware! Children at Play 1995 (R) — **Bomb!**
Cult leader kidnaps kids and introduces them to cannibalism. Bleech! As if this didn't sound grim enough, there's also an unrated version. 90m; DVD. **C:** Michael Robertson; Eric Tonken; Jamie Krause; Mik Cribben; Danny McClaughlin; Directed by Mik Cribben; Cinematography by Mik Cribben. **A:** Sr. High-Adult. **P:** Entertainment. **U:** Home. **Mov-Ent:** Horror, Children, Cults. **Acq:** Purchase. **Dist:** Troma Entertainment. $69.98.

Beware, My Lovely 1952 (Unrated) — ★★½
Taut chiller. Lonely widow Lupino hires a new handy-man. He's great with screen doors and storm windows, but has a problem with sharp tools. Intense and gripping with fine performances. 77m/B/W; VHS. **C:** Ida Lupino; Robert Ryan; Taylor Holmes; O.Z. Whitehead; Barbara Whiting; Dee Pollock; Directed by Harry Horner. **Pr:** RKO. **A:** Sr. High-Adult. **P:** Entertainment. **U:** Home. **Mov-Ent:** Mystery & Suspense. **Acq:** Purchase. **Dist:** Lions Gate Entertainment Inc. $19.98.

Beware of a Holy Whore 1970 — ★★
German film crew sits around a Spanish resort—complaining, drinking, and making love—as they wait for financial support from Bonn. Provocative and self-indulgently honest look at filmmaking. Filmed on location in Sorrento, Italy; German with subtitles. 103m; VHS, DVD. **C:** Lou Castel; Eddie Constantine; Hanna Schygulla; Marquard Bohm; Ulli Lommel; Margarethe von Trotta; Kurt Raab; Ingrid Caven; Werner Schroeter; Rainer Werner Fassbinder; Directed by Rainer Werner Fassbinder; Written by Rainer Werner Fassbinder; Cinematography by Michael Ballhaus; Music by Peer Raben. **Pr:** Antiteater-X Film; Nova International Film Inc. **A:** College-Adult. **P:** Entertainment. **U:** Home. **L:** German. **Mov-Ent**. **Acq:** Purchase. **Dist:** MGM Studios Inc. $79.98.

Beware of Ladies 1937 (Unrated) — ★½
Unhappily married reporter Betty White is covering the political campaign of honest George Martin who's running for District Attorney against a crooked opponent. Betty's estranged husband Freddie wants a divorce and obtains photos of Betty and George that could be considered compromising, threatening Martin's career. 62m/B/W; DVD. **C:** Donald Cook; Judith Allen; George Meeker; Russell Hopton; Goodee Montgomery; Dwight Frye; Directed by Irving Pichel; Written by L.C. Dublin; Cinematography by William Nobles. **A:** Jr. High-Adult. **P:** Entertainment. **U:** Home. **Mov-Ent:** Journalism, Political Campaigns. **Acq:** Purchase. **Dist:** Sinister Cinema.

Beware of Pity 1946 — ★★½
A crippled baroness thinks she's found true love with a military officer, but it turns out his marriage proposal grew out of pity for her, not passion. A quality but somber British-made historical drama, based on a novel by Stefan Zweig. 129m/B/W; VHS. **C:** Lilli Palmer; Albert Lieven; Cedric Hardwicke; Gladys Cooper; Ernest Thesiger; Freda Jackson; Linden Travers; Ralph Truman; Peter Cotes; Jenny Laird; Emrys Jones; Gerhard Kempinski; John Salew; Kenneth Warrington; Directed by Maurice Elvey; Written by W.P. Lipscomb; Elizabeth Barron; Margaret Steen; Cinematography by Derick Williams. **Pr:** Two Cities. **A:** Jr. High-Adult. **P:** Entertainment. **U:** Home. **Mov-Ent:** Drama. **Acq:** Purchase.

Beware! The Blob 1972 (PG) — ★★
A scientist brings home a piece of frozen blob from the North Pole; his wife accidentally revives the dormant gray mass. It begins a rampage of terror by digesting nearly everyone within its reach. A host of recognizable faces make for fun viewing. Post-Jeannie, pre-Dallas Hagman directed this exercise in zaniness. 87m; VHS, DVD. **C:** Robert Walker, Jr.; Godfrey Cambridge; Carol Lynley; Shelley Berman; Larry Hagman; Burgess Meredith; Gerrit Graham; Dick Van Patten; Gwynne Gilford; Richard Stahl; Richard Webb; Cindy Williams; Directed by Larry Hagman; Written by Jack Woods; Anthony Harris; Cinematography by Al Hamm; Music by Mort Garson. **Pr:** Jack H. Harris. **A:** Jr. High-Adult. **P:** Entertainment. **U:** Home. **Mov-Ent:** Science Fiction. **Acq:** Purchase. **Dist:** Image Entertainment Inc.

Beware the Jabberwock 1983
A young girl has to recite fine poetry to a dragon so he won't eat her. 27m; VHS, 3/4 U. **Pr:** Dan Bessie. **A:** Primary. **P:** Education. **U:** Institution, SURA. **Chl-Juv:** Fairy Tales. **Acq:** Purchase. **Dist:** Phoenix Learning Group. $300.00.

Beware the Naked Man Who Offers You His Shirt 1990
The author of "Swim With the Sharks Without Being Eaten Alive" offers insights and advice on increasing sales productivity. 54m; VHS, 3/4 U. **Pr:** KTCA St. Paul/Minneapolis; PBS. **A:** College-Adult. **P:** Education. **U:** Institution, CCTV, CATV, Home, SURA. **Bus-Ind:** Sales Training, Job Training, Business. **Acq:** Purchase, Rent/Lease, Duplication License, Off-Air Record. **Dist:** PBS Home Video. $395.00.

Beware the Rapist 1977
A dramatization of several incidents in which women ignored the fundamentals of rape protection. The film points out how each woman could have avoided the situation. 20m; VHS, 3/4 U. **Pr:** National Safety Council. **A:** College-Adult. **P:** Education. **U:** Institution. **Gen-Edu:** Rape, Safety Education. **Acq:** Rent/Lease. **Dist:** National Safety Council, California Chapter, Film Library.

Bewitched 1945 (Unrated) — ★★
Oboler's directorial debut was based on his radio play "Alter Ego." Joan (Thaxter) is about to be executed for murdering her boyfriend though she claims she's innocent. Shrink Dr. Bergson (Gwenn) knows Joan suffers from blackouts uses hypnosis on her. Flashbacks detail the crime, which was committed by Joan's sexy-but-evil alter ego, Karen. 65m/B/W; DVD. **C:** Phyllis Thaxter; Edmund Gwenn; Stephen McNally; Henry C. Daniels, Jr.; Addison Richards; Voice(s) by Audrey Trotter; Directed by Arch Oboler; Written by Arch Oboler; Cinematography by Charles Salerno, Jr.; Music by Bronislau Kaper. **A:** College-Adult. **P:** Entertainment. **U:** Home. **L:** English. **Mov-Ent:** Mystery & Suspense. **Acq:** Purchase. **Dist:** WarnerArchive.com.

Bewitched 2005 (PG-13) — ★★
Instead of an actual remake of the 1964-72 hit TV show, the Ephron sisters opted for a behind-the-scenes parody. Down-and-out actor Jack Wyatt (Ferrell) hopes his new role as Darrin will magically revive his career. Not wanting to be upstaged, he picks a nose-wiggling—and unknown—Isabel (Kidman) for Samantha the witch, not knowing that she really IS one. Since she disavowed (sort of) her witchery to live a mortal life, she accepts and sees Jack as a potential worldly mate. Once his egomania becomes evident, she can't help but revert to a little voodoo to shake things up. Great cast but tale doesn't cast a spell. 100m; DVD, UMD. **C:** Nicole Kidman; Will Ferrell; Shirley

MacLaine; Michael Caine; Jason Schwartzman; Heather Burns; Jim Turner; David Alan Grier; Steve Carell; Amy Sedaris; Richard Kind; Stephen Colbert; Kristin Chenoweth; Michael Badalucco; Carol(e) Shelley; Kate Walsh; Directed by Nora Ephron; Written by Nora Ephron; Delia Ephron; Cinematography by John Lindley; Music by George Fenton. **Pr:** Nora Ephron; Lucy Fisher; Douglas Wick; Penny Marshall; Nora Ephron; Sony Pictures Entertainment. **A:** Jr. High-Adult. **P:** Entertainment. **U:** Home. **L:** English. **Mov-Ent:** Magic. **Acq:** Purchase. **Dist:** Sony Pictures Home Entertainment Inc.

A Bewitched Christmas, Vol. 1 196?
Features two holiday episodes from the magical TV sitcom. In "Humbug Not to Be Spoken Here" Larry recruits Darrin to help him land the Mortimer Instant Soups account. But it's Christmas Eve and Samantha decides to show the miserly Mr. Mortimer just what the holiday means. "A Vision of Sugar Plums" finds Darrin and Samantha inviting the orphan Michael for the holidays. But Michael thinks the holiday is hooey and only Samantha's magic can change his mind. 51m; VHS. **C:** Elizabeth Montgomery; Dick York; David White. **A:** Family. **P:** Entertainment. **U:** Home. **Mov-Ent:** Television Series, Christmas. **Acq:** Purchase. **Dist:** Fusion Video; Sony Pictures Home Entertainment Inc. $14.95.

A Bewitched Christmas, Vol. 2 196?
Two more holiday episodes from the TV sitcom. "Santa Comes to Visit and Stays and Stays" finds Samantha and Esmerelda conjuring up Santa and his reindeer to show Tabitha's friend Sidney all about Christmas magic. In "Sisters at Heart" Tabitha wants her friend Lisa to be her sister but finds it doesn't work that way. So on Christmas Eve Tabitha uses her witchy powers to change them both into polka-dotted people so they can look alike. 51m; VHS. **C:** Elizabeth Montgomery; Alice Ghostley. **A:** Family. **P:** Entertainment. **U:** Home. **Mov-Ent:** Television Series, Christmas. **Acq:** Purchase. **Dist:** Sony Pictures Home Entertainment Inc.; Fusion Video. $14.95.

Bewitched: Cuz It's Witchcraft! 1997
Part of the TV Screen Gems series featuring the episodes "Nobody but a Frog Knows How to Live" and "Samantha's Wedding Present." 50m; VHS. **A:** Family. **P:** Entertainment. **U:** Home. **Mov-Ent:** Television Series. **Acq:** Purchase. **Dist:** Sony Pictures Home Entertainment Inc. $9.95.

Bewitched: Fan Favorites 1965 (Unrated)
ABC 1964-72 magic-filled sitcom. 9 episodes from the second season: "Alias Darrin Stephens," "A Very Special Delivery," "We're in for a Bad Spell," "My Grandson, the Warlock," "The Joker is a Card," "Take Two Aspirins and Half a Pint of Porpoise Milk," "Trick or Treat," "And Then I Wrote," and "The Very Informal Dress." 237m; DVD. **C:** Elizabeth Montgomery; Dick York; David White; Agnes Moorehead. **A:** Family. **P:** Entertainment. **U:** Home. **Mov-Ent:** Television Series. **Acq:** Purchase. **Dist:** Sony Pictures Home Entertainment Inc. $14.99.

A Bewitched Halloween 196?
Two episodes of the television comedy. In "The Witches Are Out" Darrin is asked to design a trademark for a client's Halloween candy and Samanatha persuades him to use a beautiful rather than an ugly witch. When the client doesn't agree, she tries more forceful matters to change his mind. "Trick or Treat" has Darrin insisting Samantha forgo a witches' Halloween festival in order to entertain some clients at dinner. Mother-in-law Endora is so enraged she puts a spell on Darrin that turns him into a werewolf—just as the guests arrive. 51m/ B/W; VHS. **C:** Elizabeth Montgomery; Dick York; Agnes Moorehead. **A:** Family. **P:** Entertainment. **U:** Home. **Mov-Ent:** Television Series, Holidays. **Acq:** Purchase. **Dist:** Sony Pictures Home Entertainment Inc. $14.95.

Bewitched: Meet the Stephens 1997
Part of the TV Screen Gems series featuring the episodes "I, Darrin, Take This Witch Samantha" and "And Then There Were Three." 51m/B/W; VHS. **A:** Family. **P:** Entertainment. **U:** Home. **Mov-Ent:** Television Series. **Acq:** Purchase. **Dist:** Sony Pictures Home Entertainment Inc. $9.95.

Bewitched: The Complete 7th Season 1970 (Unrated)
Televison sitcom series on ABC from 1964-1972. The season begins with an eight-show arc that has the fate of mortal Darrin and witch Samantha's marriage being decided by the Witches Council and a journey to Salem, MA brings curses, misadventures, and reincarnations. Paul Lynde as Uncle Arthur tries to keep his practical joking nature from his new girlfriend in "The House That Uncle Arthur Built." Imogene Coca is delightful as Mary, the dissatisfied Good Fairy who trades places with Samantha. 28 episodes. 672m; DVD. **A:** Family. **P:** Entertainment. **U:** Home. **Mov-Ent:** Television Series. **Acq:** Purchase. **Dist:** Sony Pictures Home Entertainment Inc. $39.95.

Bewitched: The Complete Fifth Season 1968
Features the fifth season of the 1964-1972 comedy television series about a good witch named Samantha (Montgomery) who married mortal Darrin (York) despite her mother Endora's (Moorehead) wishes, so Endora does whatever she can to cause Darrin misery. Samantha tries to lead a "normal" life—at least most of the time, except when she's in the mood to twitch her nose and make some magic. Endora tries to push an arranged marriage onto Samantha; when Endora tries to sabotage Darrin's business dealing Samantha saves the day; Tabitha begins preschool by confusing directions and turning a classmate into a butterfly; and Samantha and Darrin are expecting another baby. 30 episodes. 638m; DVD. **C:** Elizabeth Montgomery; Agnes Moorehead; David White; Dick York; George Tobias. **A:** Family. **P:** Entertainment. **U:** Home. **Mov-Ent:** Television Series, Magic, Family. **Acq:** Purchase. **Dist:** Sony Pictures Home Entertainment Inc. $39.95.

Bewitched: The Complete Fourth Season 1967
Features the fourth season of the 1964-1972 comedy television series about a good witch named Samantha (Montgomery) who married mortal Darrin (York) despite her mother Endora's (Moorehead) wishes, so Endora does whatever she can to cause Darrin misery. Samantha tries to lead a "normal" life—at least most of the time, except when she's in the mood to twitch her nose and make some magic. Samantha is given the title "Queen of All Witches"; Tabitha uses Endora's spell to make all of the toys come alive but with disastrous results; and Endora changes Darrin into a pony for Tabitha. 33 episodes. 837m; DVD. **C:** Elizabeth Montgomery; Agnes Moorehead; David White; Dick York; George Tobias. **A:** Family. **P:** Entertainment. **U:** Home. **Mov-Ent:** Television Series, Magic, Family. **Acq:** Purchase. **Dist:** Sony Pictures Home Entertainment Inc. $39.95.

Bewitched: The Complete Second Season 1965
Features the second season of the 1964-1972 comedy television series about a good witch named Samantha (Montgomery) who married mortal Darrin (York) despite her mother Endora's (Moorehead) wishes, so Endora does whatever she can to cause Darrin misery. Samantha tries to lead a "normal" life—at least most of the time, except when she's in the mood to twitch her nose and make some magic. Samantha is pregnant but Aunt Clara accidentally changes Darrin to a chimpanzee; Endora makes Darrin a little boy but Darrin uses it to his advantage; and baby Tabitha is born. 36 episodes. 967m; DVD. **C:** Elizabeth Montgomery; Agnes Moorehead; David White; Dick York; George Tobias. **A:** Family. **P:** Entertainment. **U:** Home. **Mov-Ent:** Television Series, Magic, Family. **Acq:** Purchase. **Dist:** Sony Pictures Home Entertainment Inc. $39.95.

Bewitched: The Complete Third Season 1966
Features the third season of the 1964-1972 comedy television series about a good witch named Samantha (Montgomery) who married mortal Darrin (York) despite her mother Endora's (Moorehead) wishes, so Endora does whatever she can to cause Darrin misery. Samantha tries to lead a "normal" life—at least most of the time, except when she's in the mood to twitch her nose and make some magic. Samantha discovers Tabitha has her magical powers; Aunt Clara goofs again and the whole eastern seaboard loses power; and Endora calls in Dr. Sigmund Freud to help Samantha and Darrin through a rough patch. 33 episodes. 836m; DVD. **C:** Elizabeth Montgomery; Agnes Moorehead; David White; Dick York; George Tobias. **A:** Family. **P:** Entertainment. **U:** Home. **Mov-Ent:** Television Series, Magic, Family. **Acq:** Purchase. **Dist:** Sony Pictures Home Entertainment Inc. $39.95.

Bewitched: The First Season 2005
The complete first season of the beloved '60s television classic. Four-disc set includes a making-of featurette, bloopers, and more. 917m; DVD. **A:** Family. **P:** Entertainment. **U:** Home. **Gen-Edu:** Television. **Acq:** Purchase. **Dist:** Sony Pictures Home Entertainment Inc. $29.95.

Bewitched: This Spells Trouble 1997
Part of the TV Screen Gems series featuring the episodes "Long Live the Queen" and "It's So Nice to Have a Spouse around the House." 51m/B/W; VHS. **A:** Family. **P:** Entertainment. **U:** Home. **Mov-Ent:** Television Series. **Acq:** Purchase. **Dist:** Sony Pictures Home Entertainment Inc. $9.95.

The Bewitched Tree 1988
Hans Christian Andersen's touching fable about the young fir tree who longs to leave the forest in hopes of becoming a Christmas tree. 28m; VHS, 3/4 U. **Pr:** Kevin Sullivan; Huntingwood Films. **A:** Primary-Jr. High. **P:** Entertainment. **U:** Institution, SURA. **Gen-Edu:** Folklore & Legends, Christmas. **Acq:** Purchase, Rent/Lease. **Dist:** Lucerne Media. $295.00.

Beyblade: Fierce Battle 2004 (Unrated) — ★★
Based on the anime series Beyblade (which itself was inspired by a toy), this is the story of Tyson, a young man who has just won the Beyblade championships (think of it as a cross between Pokemon and spinning tops), and is being stalked by his opponent Daichi, who insists on another battle. Eventually Daichi ends up releasing some evil spirits, and Tyson and friends are forced to confront him. If you've seen/liked "Pokemon" or "Digimon", you've pretty much got the idea. 71m; DVD. **C:** Voice(s) by Marlowe Gardiner-Heslin; Alex Hood; Daniel Desanto; David Reale; Gage Knox; Bryan LiPuma; Caitriona Murphy; Christopher Marren; Katie Griffin; Craig Lauzon; Julie Lemieux; Shannon Perreault; Jonathan Potts; Directed by Toshifumi Kawase; Written by Takao Aoki; Ken Cuperus; Shelley Hoffman; Robert Pincombe. **A:** Sr. High-Adult. **P:** Entertainment. **U:** Home. **Mov-Ent:** Animation & Cartoons, Children's Shows, Fantasy. **Acq:** Purchase. **Dist:** Miramax Film Corp.

The Beyond 1982 (R) — ★★
A young woman inherits a possessed hotel. Meanwhile, hellish zombies try to check out. Chilling Italian horror flick that Fulci directed under the alias "Louis Fuller." 88m; VHS, DVD, Wide. **C:** Katherine (Katriona) MacColl; David Warbeck; Farah Keller; Tony St. John; Al Cliver; Directed by Lucio Fulci; Written by Lucio Fulci; Dardano Sacchetti; Giorgio Mariuzzo; Cinematography by Sergio Salvati. **Pr:** Terry Levene. **A:** Jr. High-Adult. **P:** Entertainment. **U:** Home. **Mov-Ent:** Horror. **Acq:** Purchase. **Dist:** Anchor Bay Entertainment; Lions Gate Television Corp.

Beyond 2011 (PG-13) — ★½
A solid, if somewhat lackluster, thriller. When little Amy goes missing from her Alaska home, her police chief uncle puts troubled-but-effective, longtime detective John Koski on the case. When psychic Farley Connors insists on becoming involved, he becomes just one of John's suspects. 90m; DVD, Blu-Ray. **C:** Jon Voight; Julian Morris; Dermot Mulroney; Teri

Polo; Brett Baker; Skyler Shaye; Directed by Josef Rusnak; Written by Gregory Gieras; Cinematography by Eric Maddison; Music by Mario Grigorov. **A:** Jr. High-Adult. **P:** Entertainment. **U:** Home. **L:** English. **Mov-Ent:** Crime Drama. **Acq:** Purchase. **Dist:** Anchor Bay Entertainment Inc.

Beyond 2011 (PG-13) — ★½
Police detective Jon Koski (Voight) is heading toward retirement when Chief of Police Musker (Mulroney) asks him to find his niece Amy (Lesslie), who's gone missing. The case goes cold, and Koski is contacted by a psychic (Connors) who claims to have visions of the girl. Predictable thriller. 90m; DVD, Blu-Ray. **C:** Jon Voight; Julian Morris; Dermot Mulroney; Teri Polo; Ben Crowley; Brett Baker; Chloe Lesslie; Skyler Shaye; Directed by Josef Rusnak; Written by Gregory Gieras; Cinematography by Eric Maddison; Music by Mario Grigorov. **A:** Jr. High-Adult. **P:** Entertainment. **U:** Home. **L:** English. **Mov-Ent:** Crime Drama. **Acq:** Purchase. **Dist:** Anchor Bay Entertainment Inc.

Beyond 2000: The Explorers 1999
National Geographic special episode featuring a look at the future. Includes predictions from experts. 60m; VHS. **A:** Family. **P:** Education. **U:** Home. **Hea-Sci:** Science, Technology. **Acq:** Purchase. **Dist:** Instructional Video. $19.95.

Beyond a Mirage 1977
The Jewish and Arab problems in Palestine are investigated. 30m; VHS, 3/4 U. **A:** Sr. High-Adult. **P:** Education. **U:** Institution, Home. **Gen-Edu:** Documentary Films, Middle East. **Acq:** Purchase. **Dist:** International Historic Films Inc.

Beyond a Reasonable Doubt 1956 (Unrated) — ★★
In order to get a behind-the-scenes glimpse at the judicial system, a man plays the guilty party to a murder. Alas, when he tries to vindicate himself, he is the victim of his own folly. Not as interesting as it sounds on paper. 80m/B/W; VHS, DVD. **C:** Dana Andrews; Joan Fontaine; Sidney Blackmer; Philip Bourneuf; Barbara Nichols; Shepperd Strudwick; Arthur Franz; Edward Binns; Directed by Fritz Lang; Written by Douglas S. Morrow. **Pr:** RKO. **A:** Adult. **P:** Entertainment. **U:** Home. **Mov-Ent:** Mystery & Suspense, Law. **Acq:** Purchase. **Dist:** No Longer Available.

Beyond a Reasonable Doubt 2009 (PG-13) — ★
This remake of Fritz Lang's 1956 legal thriller gets an updated treatment but loses the pacing, suspense and intrigue of the original. The magnificently coifed Martin Hunter (Douglas) is a Louisiana DA suspected by newcomer TV reporter from New York, CJ Nichols (Metcalfe) of planting evidence to pad his conviction rate. To get the goods on the DA, Nichols acts the part of accused perp of an unsolved murder, thinking he'll trap Hunter while planting bogus evidence. Things don't quite work out as planned and the film never fully explores its chance to shine a light on judicial corruption, instead skimming the surface with car chases and Hunter's super-fine hairdo. 105m; Blu-Ray, On Demand, Wide. **C:** Michael Douglas; Jesse Metcalfe; Amber Tamblyn; Orlando Jones; Joel David Moore; Directed by Peter Hyams; Written by Peter Hyams; Cinematography by Peter Hyams; Music by David Shire. **Pr:** Ted Hartley; Kevin Cornish; Foresight Unlimited; RKO Pictures; Signature Pictures; Autonomous Films; Anchor Bay Entertainment Inc. **A:** Jr. High-Adult. **P:** Entertainment. **U:** Home. **L:** English. **Mov-Ent:** Journalism, Law. **Acq:** Purchase. **Dist:** Anchor Bay Entertainment; Amazon.com Inc.; Movies Unlimited.

Beyond Adolescence 19??
Discusses the relationship between the development of intelligence and adolescence in children. 60m; VHS. **A:** Adult. **P:** Education. **U:** Home. **Gen-Edu:** Children, Adolescence. **Acq:** Purchase. **Dist:** Mystic Fire Video. $24.95.

Beyond All Limits 1959 — ★½
Hotheaded Pepe (Armendariz) lives with his wife Magdalena (Felix) and young son Pepito in a Mexican fishing village. Slick American Jim Gatsby (Palance) comes along with an illegal shrimping scheme that could earn everyone some extra cash. Magdalena and Jim were once involved and Pepe's jealousy becomes a problem. Originally released in Spanish as "Flor de Mayo." 114m; DVD. **C:** Jack Palance; Pedro Armendariz, Sr.; Maria Felix; Carlos Montalban; Paul Stewart; Directed by Roberto Gavaldon; Written by Libertad Blasco Ibanez; Cinematography by Gabriel Figueroa; Music by Gustavo Cesar Carrion. **A:** Sr. High-Adult. **P:** Entertainment. **U:** Home. **Mov-Ent:** Fishing, Marriage. **Acq:** Purchase. **Dist:** VCI Entertainment.

Beyond Atlantis 1973 (PG) — Bomb!
An ancient underwater tribe is discovered when it kidnaps land-lubbin' women with which to mate. 91m; VHS, DVD. **C:** John Ashley; Patrick Wayne; George Nader; Directed by Eddie Romero; Written by Charles Johnson; Cinematography by Justo Paulino. **Pr:** John Ashley; Eddie Romero; John Ashley; Eddie Romero. **A:** Sr. High-Adult. **P:** Entertainment. **U:** Home. **Mov-Ent:** Fantasy. **Acq:** Purchase. **Dist:** VCI Entertainment. $49.95.

Beyond Barbed Wire 1997 (Unrated) — ★★★½
Heartfelt documentary tells the story of the Japanese-Americans who fought in the 442 Division. These were young men who were sent to "assembly centers" and "pioneer communities" (as our government called the concentration camps where Americans of Japanese descent were sent in 1942) and then volunteered to fight. The filmmakers use the same techniques seen in the HBO series "Band of Brothers," combining contemporary (late 1990s) interviews with the surviving veterans and archival footage of their combat action. 88m; DVD, Wide. **C:** Narrated by Noriyuki "Pat" Morita; Directed by Steve Rosen; Written by Steve Rosen; Cinematography by Steve Rosen. **A:** Sr. High-Adult. **P:** Entertainment. **U:** Home. **Mov-Ent:** Documentary Films, World War Two. **Acq:** Purchase. **Dist:** VCI Entertainment.

Beyond Beijing 1996
Documents the 1995 United Nations Fourth World Conference on Women, and the parallel Forum (NGO) in Beijing. The largest global gathering of women in recorded history demonstrates the strength of a worldwide movement to improve the status of women. 42m; VHS. **A:** College-Adult. **P:** Education. **U:** Institution. **Gen-Edu:** Women, History, Human Rights. **Acq:** Purchase, Rent/Lease. **Dist:** Women Make Movies. $225.00.

Beyond Belief 1976 (Unrated)
Footage of such phenomena as ESP, automatic writing, telekinesis, etc., featuring Geller fraudulently bending flatware (without touching it). 94m; VHS. **C:** Uri Geller. **Pr:** American International Pictures. **A:** Family. **P:** Entertainment. **U:** Home. **Mov-Ent:** Documentary Films, Occult Sciences. **Acq:** Purchase. **Dist:** VCI Entertainment. $29.95.

Beyond Belief: Season One 1997
Each week a collection of five supernatural stories are presented, some from the imaginations of staff writers, other based on real events research by Robert Tralins. Viewers are left to decipher which tales are true or false until revealed in the final minutes of the program. 313m; DVD. **C:** Narrated by James Brolin; Jonathan Frakes. **A:** Jr. High-Adult. **P:** Entertainment. **U:** Home. **Mov-Ent:** Science Fiction, Fantasy, Mystery & Suspense. **Acq:** Purchase. **Dist:** Anchor Bay Entertainment.

Beyond Bengal 1933
Graphic semi-documentary about an expedition into a forbidden Malayan jungle. ?m; VHS. **A:** Jr. High-Adult. **P:** Entertainment. **U:** Home. **Mov-Ent:** Acq: Purchase. **Dist:** Sinister Cinema. $16.95.

Beyond Betrayal 1994 (Unrated) — ★★
CBS TV movie. Joanna Matthews (Dey) escapes from her police officer husband, Bradley (Anderson), after years of abuse. She makes a new life under a new identity, but violent Brad hasn't stopped searching for her. When he finds out Joanna has a boyfriend (Boutsikaris) who's separated from his crazy wife, the cop makes sure to set him up for her murder. Can Joanna find the courage to come forward with the truth? 95m; DVD. **C:** Susan Dey; Richard Dean Anderson; Dennis Boutsikaris; Annie Corley; James Tolkan; Directed by Carl Schenkel; Written by Shelley Evans; Cinematography by John S. Bartley; Music by Christopher Franke. **A:** Jr. High-Adult. **P:** Entertainment. **U:** Home. **L:** English. **Mov-Ent:** Marriage, TV Movies. **Acq:** Purchase. **Dist:** WarnerArchive.com.

Beyond Black and White 1994
Explores bicultural heritage and racism through profiles of five women from various biracial backgrounds. Studies the influence of images of women in American media. 28m; VHS. **A:** College-Adult. **P:** Education. **U:** Institution. **Gen-Edu:** Women, Minorities. **Acq:** Purchase, Rent/Lease. **Dist:** Women Make Movies. $225.00.

Beyond Black and White: Affirmative Action in America ????
Panelists discuss the opportunities and drawbacks of affirmative action issues. 58m; VHS. **A:** Adult. **P:** Education. **U:** Institution. **Gen-Edu:** Education, Prejudice. **Acq:** Purchase, Rent/Lease. **Dist:** Films for the Humanities & Sciences. $129.00.

Beyond Blame: Challenging Violence in the Media 19??
Part of the multi-media literacy program of the same name that discusses the need for community empowerment for controlling the amount of violence seen in the media. ?m; VHS. **P:** Education. **U:** Home, Institution. **Gen-Edu:** Violence, Journalism. **Acq:** Purchase. **Dist:** Center for Media Literacy.

Beyond Blazing Boards 19??
Put your flip-flops on and head for the video store, dudes, to rent choice scenes of Balinese, Australian, Californian, and Mexican surf perfection. Watch Winton Kong, Ronnie Burns, Tommy Curren, Stuart Cadden, and Simon Law shred waves to the sounds of the Hoodoo Gurus, the Untouchables, and Tony Creed. 80m; VHS. **Pr:** NSI. **A:** Jr. High-Adult. **P:** Entertainment. **U:** Home. **Spo-Rec:** Sports--General. **Acq:** Purchase. **Dist:** NSI Sound & Video Inc. $59.95.

Beyond Borders 2003 (R) — ★¹/₂
Decades-spanning romance between an over-zealous doctor and a lovely do-gooder suffers from a too-earnest presentation and romantic cliches. Dashing doctor Nick (Owen) inspires American socialite Sarah (Jolie) to leave her stuffy British hubby (Roache) and really get involved in international aid relief rather than just writing a check. She follows the doc to Ethiopia and later to Cambodia and Checknya (film goes from 1984-1995), where the trouble-prone Nick has apparently been kidnapped. At least the film inspired Jolie personally since she became a goodwill ambassador for the United Nations High Commissioner for Refugees and adopted her son from Cambodia. 127m; VHS, DVD. **C:** Angelina Jolie; Clive Owen; Teri Polo; Linus Roache; Yorick Van Wageningen; Noah Emmerich; Kate Ashfield; Jamie Bartlett; Timothy West; Kate Trotter; Burt Kwouk; Directed by Martin Campbell; Written by Caspian Tredwell-Owen; Cinematography by Phil Meheux; Music by James Horner. **Pr:** Dan Halstead; Lloyd Phillips; Mandalay Pictures; Camelot; Paramount Pictures. **A:** Sr. High-Adult. **P:** Entertainment. **U:** Home. **Mov-Ent:** Drama, Asia, Africa. **Acq:** Purchase. **Dist:** Paramount Pictures Corp.

Beyond Borders: Arab Feminists Talk about Their Lives ????
United Nations gathering of renowned activists addresses the issues of repressive internal constraints and intrusive Western interference that women are facing in the Arab world. 50m; VHS. **A:** Sr. High-Adult. **P:** Education. **U:** Institution. **Gen-Edu:** Middle East, Women. **Acq:** Purchase, Rent/Lease. **Dist:** Films for the Humanities & Sciences. $129.00.

Beyond Borders: Ethics in International Business 1992
Focuses on cultural, legal, and economic issues faced by those doing business in foreign countries, including complying with the Foreign Corrupt Practices Act, marketing in culturally different environments, and transferring technology. 30m; VHS, Special order formats. **A:** Adult. **P:** Professional. **U:** Institution. **Bus-Ind:** Marketing, Ethics & Morals. **Acq:** Purchase, Rent/Lease. **Dist:** Learning Communications L.L.C. $595.00.

Beyond Compliance: Serving Customers with Disabilities 19??
Suggests service-oriented businesses go beyond minimum governmental regulations and do everything they can to cater to disabled customers. Enacts scenarios using disabled actors. 24m; VHS. **A:** Adult. **P:** Professional. **U:** Institution. **Bus-Ind:** Customer Service, Handicapped. **Acq:** Purchase. **Dist:** Phoenix Learning Group. $495.00.

Beyond Conviction 2006
A documentary examining Pennsylvania's mediation program between victims of violent crime and the perpetrators. 97m; VHS, DVD. **A:** Sr. High-Adult. **P:** Education. **U:** Home, Institution. **Gen-Edu:** Documentary Films, Violence. **Acq:** Purchase, Rent/Lease. **Dist:** The Cinema Guild. $295.00.

Beyond Culture Shock 1987
Employees transferred abroad often wonder if a good job is worth having to move to a foreign land. 30m; VHS, 3/4 U. **A:** Adult. **P:** Education. **U:** Institution, SURA. **Bus-Ind:** Business, Travel. **Acq:** Purchase, Trade-in. **Dist:** Encyclopedia Britannica. $500.00.

Beyond Darkness 1992 (R) — ★¹/₂
When Peter and his family move into their New England home they are immediately beset by some unknown terror. With the help of Father George, Peter learns his house was built upon the graves of 20 witches burned for heresy. The witches have decided to seek revenge by kidnapping Peter's young son and sacrificing him to an evil demon. Can Peter destroy the evil spirits before they destroy his son? 111m; VHS, CC. **C:** Gene Le Brock; David Brandon; Barbara Bingham; Michael Stephenson; Stephen Brown; Directed by Claudio Fragasso. **A:** Sr. High-Adult. **P:** Entertainment. **U:** Home. **Mov-Ent:** Horror, Family. **Acq:** Purchase. **Dist:** Imperial Entertainment Corp. $89.95.

Beyond Death's Door 1999
Interviews with grief counselors and personal testimonies provide an understanding of the processes of grief and mourning. 30m; VHS. **A:** Adult. **P:** Professional. **U:** Institution. **Hea-Sci:** Death, Health Education, Mental Health. **Acq:** Purchase. **Dist:** Aquarius Health Care Media. $99.00.

Beyond Desire 1994 (R) — ★★¹/₂
Elvis Ray (Forsythe) is released after 14 years in prison and gets picked up by corvette-driving prison groupie and Las Vegas prostitute Rita (Wuhrer) but more than sex is on both their minds. 87m; VHS, Streaming, CC. **C:** William Forsythe; Kari Wuhrer; Leo Rossi; Sharon Farrell; Directed by Dominique Othenin-Girard; Written by Dale Trevillion; Cinematography by Sven Kirsten; Music by Mark Holden. **A:** Sr. High-Adult. **P:** Entertainment. **U:** Home. **Mov-Ent:** Prostitution. **Acq:** Purchase. **Dist:** Lions Gate Television Corp.

Beyond Deterrence 1983
This documentary takes a look at the exotic high tech weapons that President Reagan has ordered his military scientists to perfect. 50m; VHS, 3/4 U. **Pr:** British Broadcasting Corporation. **A:** Sr. High-Adult. **P:** Education. **U:** Institution, SURA. **Gen-Edu:** Documentary Films, Technology, Armed Forces--U.S. **Acq:** Purchase, Rent/Lease. **Dist:** Home Vision Cinema.

Beyond Diagnosis: Our Journeys with Breast Cancer 1999
Shows the painful and hopeful sides of breast cancer patients by following the story of Barb and David, a couple dealing with the diagnosis and treatment of her breast cancer. 30m; VHS, DVD. **A:** Jr. High-Adult. **P:** Education. **U:** Home. **Hea-Sci:** Cancer, Patient Education. **Acq:** Purchase. **Dist:** Aquarius Health Care Media. $150.00.

Beyond Dream's Door 1988 (Unrated) — ★
A young, All-American college student's childhood nightmares come back to haunt him, making dreams a horrifying reality. 86m; VHS, DVD. **C:** Nick Baldasare; Rick Kesler; Susan Pinsky; Norm Singer; Directed by Jay Woelfel. **Pr:** Panorama Entertainment. **A:** Sr. High-Adult. **P:** Entertainment. **U:** Home. **Mov-Ent:** Horror, Occult Sciences. **Acq:** Purchase. **Dist:** Movies Unlimited.

Beyond Erotica 1974 (Unrated) — ★
After being cut out of his father's will, a sadistic young man takes out his rage on his mother and a peasant girl. 90m; VHS, DVD. **C:** David Hemmings; Alida Valli; Andrea Rau; Directed by Jose Maria Forque. **A:** College-Adult. **P:** Entertainment. **U:** Home. **Mov-Ent:** Mystery & Suspense, Violence, Sex & Sexuality. **Acq:** Purchase. **Dist:** Televista. $59.95.

Beyond Evil 1980 (R) — Bomb!
Relatively dim-witted newlywed couple moves into an old island mansion despite rumors that the house is haunted. Sure enough, wife George becomes possessed by the vengeful spirit of a woman murdered 200 years earlier, and a reign of pointless terror begins. Poor rip-off of hybrid Amityville/Exorcist paranormality. 98m; VHS, DVD. **C:** John Saxon; Lynda Day George; Michael Dante; Mario Milano; Directed by Herb Freed; Written by Herb Freed; Music by Pino Donaggio. **Pr:** David Baughn; Herb Freed. **A:** Sr. High-Adult. **P:** Entertainment. **U:** Home. **Mov-Ent:** Horror, Occult Sciences. **Acq:** Purchase. **Dist:** Movies Unlimited. $49.95.

Beyond Excellence: The Super Achievers 1989
This tape features profiles of five different people who have raised businesses up with their own intelligence and hard work. 90m; VHS, 8 mm, 3/4 U, Special order formats. **Pr:** Video Arts Limited. **A:** College-Adult. **P:** Education. **U:** Institution, SURA. **Bus-Ind:** Business, Management. **Acq:** Purchase, Rent/Lease. **Dist:** Video Arts, Inc. $310.00.

Beyond Eyruv 2006
Documentary about a young man leaving behind his traditional Hasidic Jewish community for a secular life with his grandparents in New York. 72m; VHS, DVD. **A:** Sr. High-Adult. **P:** Education. **U:** Institution. **Gen-Edu:** Documentary Films, Judaism. **Acq:** Purchase, Rent/Lease. **Dist:** The Cinema Guild. $295.00.

Beyond Fear 1975 (Unrated) — ★★¹/₂
Compelling drama about a man forced to aid a gang in robbery while they hold his wife and son captive. 92m; VHS. **C:** Michael Boquet; Michel Constantin; Marilu Tolo; Paul Crauchet; Michel Creton; Moustache; Jean-Pierre Darras; Directed by Yannick Andrei; Written by Yannick Andrei; Cinematography by Pierre Petit; Music by Alain Goraguer. **A:** Adult. **P:** Entertainment. **U:** Home. **Mov-Ent:** Acq: Purchase. **Dist:** No Longer Available.

Beyond Fear 1993 (R) — ★★¹/₂
Tipper Taylor (Lesseos) is a wilderness tour guide who's also a martial arts expert. This is going to come in handy when her tour group is stalked by two men who are after a videotape innocently filmed by someone in Tipper's group. It seems the tape shows the men committing a murder. 84m; VHS, DVD. **C:** Mimi Lesseos; Directed by Robert F. Lyons; Written by Mimi Lesseos; Robert F. Lyons; Cinematography by Bodo Holst; Music by Miriam Cutler. **A:** Sr. High-Adult. **P:** Entertainment. **U:** Home. **Mov-Ent:** Wilderness Areas. **Acq:** Purchase. **Dist:** Monarch Home Video. $89.95.

Beyond Forgiveness 1994 (R) — ★★¹/₂
Basic maverick cop goes after his brother's killers and winds up involved in an international black market in transplantable human organs. 95m; VHS, CC. **C:** Thomas Ian Griffith; Rutger Hauer; John Rhys-Davies; Directed by Bob Misiorowski; Written by Charles Cohen. **Pr:** Nu Image Films. **A:** Sr. High-Adult. **P:** Entertainment. **U:** Home. **Mov-Ent:** Acq: Purchase. **Dist:** Lions Gate Entertainment Inc.

Beyond Gay: Politics of Pride 2009 (Unrated)
Filmmaker Ken Coolen travels the world attending Gay Pride parades and conducts interviews with the locals. 85m; DVD, Blu-Ray, Streaming. **A:** Jr. High-Adult. **P:** Education. **U:** Home. **L:** English. **Gen-Edu:** Documentary Films, Homosexuality. **Acq:** Purchase, Rent/Lease. **Dist:** Gravitas Ventures L.L.C.; Passion River. $29.95 19.99 9.99.

Beyond Good and Evil 2003 (Unrated)
Scrutinizes the negative impact of media violence and its influence on children when their fantasy and reality collide following the 9/11 tragedy in which political leaders turned international relations into a fight between good and evil. 37m; VHS, DVD. **A:** Adult. **P:** Education. **U:** Institution. **Gen-Edu:** World Affairs, U.S. States, Violence. **Acq:** Purchase. **Dist:** Third World Newsreel. $175.

Beyond Goodwill 1992
Documents the efforts of Soviet and American citizens joining forces to implement constructive solutions to environmental destruction and poverty. 58m; VHS. **A:** Jr. High-Adult. **P:** Education. **U:** Institution, Home. **Gen-Edu:** Documentary Films, Ecology & Environment. **Acq:** Purchase, Rent/Lease. **Dist:** The Video Project. $85.00.

Beyond Hate 1991
Bill Moyers hosts this grim but fascinating look at hatred around the world, its possible origins, its destructive potential and why it may be a necessary component of the human psyche. 90m; VHS, CC. **C:** Elie Wiesel; Vaclav Havel; Jimmy Carter; Li Lu; Nelson Mandela; Hosted by Bill Moyers. **Pr:** Catherine Tatge; Public Affairs Television; WNET; WTTW. **A:** Jr. High-Adult. **P:** Education. **U:** Home. **Gen-Edu:** Documentary Films, Sociology, Human Relations. **Acq:** Purchase. **Dist:** Facets Multimedia Inc.; PBS Home Video; Mystic Fire Video. $39.95.

Beyond Hate Trilogy 1992
Three-part program hosted by Bill Moyers discusses how attitudes of hate differ culturally, conflict resolution strategies and thoughts from Nobel Prize-winning peace activist and author, Elie Wiesel. 149m; VHS; Closed Captioned. **A:** Jr. High-Sr. High. **P:** Education. **U:** Institution. **Gen-Edu:** Prejudice, Identity. **Acq:** Purchase. **Dist:** Zenger Media. $256.00.
Indiv. Titles: 1. Learning to Hate 2. The Heart of Hatred 3. Facing Hate.

Beyond Hate with Bill Moyers ????
Two part series explores the origins and dimensions of hate through the eyes of world leaders, human rights activists, Arabs and Israelis, high school students, youth gang members, and an American white supremacist group. 91m; VHS. **A:** Sr. High-Adult. **P:** Education. **U:** Institution. **Gen-Edu:** Prejudice, Violence, Ethnicity. **Acq:** Purchase. **Dist:** Films for the Humanities & Sciences. $159.00.
Indiv. Titles: 1. The Heart of Hatred 2. Learning to Hate.

Beyond Hatred 2007 (Unrated)
Through an examination of the 2002 murder of Francois Chenu in Rheims, France, topics such as homophobia, hate crimes, and forgiveness are considered. 85m; DVD. **A:** Sr. High-Adult.

P: Entertainment. U: Home. Mov-Ent: Homosexuality, France, Documentary Films. Acq: Purchase. Dist: $24.95.

Beyond Honor 2005 (Unrated) — ★★
Egyptian-American medical student Sahira tries to be a modern woman but her father Mohammad is a strict Muslim who dominates the family. When he discovers that Sahira has a boyfriend and is no longer a virgin, he enacts a brutal punishment for her dishonoring their family. 101m; DVD. C: Jason Smith; Ruth Osuna; Wadie Andrawis; Laurel Melegrano; Ryan Izay; Directed by Varun Khanna; Written by Varun Khanna; Cinematography by Dinesh Kampani; Music by David Mann. A: Sr. High-Adult. P: Entertainment. U: Home. Mov-Ent: Islam. Acq: Purchase. Dist: Celebrity Video Distribution, Inc.

Beyond Imagining: Margaret Anderson & the Little Review 1991
Profiles Margaret Anderson, bold literary visionary, and her overlooked but profound influence on American literature. 30m; VHS. A: College-Adult. P: Education. U: Institution. Gen-Edu: Women, Literature--American. Acq: Purchase, Rent/Lease. Dist: Women Make Movies. $250.00.

Beyond Impossible 1991
A motivational message focusing on achieving one's potential. 9m; VHS, 3/4 U, Special order formats. Pr: Busby Worldwide, Inc. A: College-Adult. P: Professional. U: Institution. Bus-Ind: Business, Management, Self-Help. Acq: Purchase, Rent/Lease. Dist: Excellence in Training Corp. $320.00.

Beyond Innocence 1987 (Unrated) — ★
A 17-year-old lusts after a mature married woman. Ostensibly based on Raymond Radiguet's "Devil in the Flesh." 87m; VHS. C: Keith Smith; Katia Caballero; John Morris; Directed by Scott Murray; Cinematography by Andrzej Bartkowiak. Pr: Westernworld Film Dist. A: Sr. High-Adult. P: Entertainment. U: Home. Mov-Ent: Adolescence. Acq: Purchase. Dist: No Longer Available.

Beyond Intolerance: Bridging the Gap Between Imposition and Acceptance ????
Subject matter designed for use in first year Intercultural Development courses. 62m; VHS. A: Adult. P: Professional. U: Institution. Hea-Sci: Psychology, Mental Health. Acq: Purchase. Dist: Microtraining Associates, Inc. $95.00.

Beyond JFK: The Question of Conspiracy 1992
Oliver Stone fans and everyone else searching for more answers about President Kennedy's assassination will relish this offering. The program is composed chiefly of interviews with the cast of "JFK" and other key personalities, including eyewitnesses, of the crime. 90m; VHS. A: Adult. P: Entertainment. U: Home. Gen-Edu: Documentary Films, Presidency. Acq: Purchase. Dist: Warner Home Video, Inc. $19.98.

Beyond Justice 1992 (PG-13) — ★★
High action-adventure with the prolific Hauer starring as an ex-CIA agent who is hired to rescue the kidnapped son of a beautiful executive. 113m; VHS, DVD, CC. C: Rutger Hauer; Carol Alt; Omar Sharif; Elliott Gould; Kabir Bedi; David Flosi; Brett Halsey; Peter Sands; Directed by Duccio Tessari; Written by Sergio Donati; Luigi Montefiore; Cinematography by Giorgio Di Battista; Music by Ennio Morricone. A: Jr. High-Adult. P: Entertainment. U: Home. Mov-Ent. Acq: Purchase. Dist: CinemaNow Inc. $9.99.

Beyond Justice 2001 (Unrated) — ★★
New Zealand TV thriller with a modicum of action. Private detectives John Lawless (Smith) and Jodie Keane (Dotchin) are hired by widow Lana Vitale (Rubin) to investigate her husband's suspicious death. Lana's not exactly grieving since she's all too willing to get up close and personal with Lawless. Meanwhile, Jodie follows some clues that lead her to a porno ring. 95m; VHS, DVD. C: Kevin Smith; Jennifer Rubin; Angela Dotchin; Bruce Hopkins; Dean O'Gorman; Directed by Geoffrey Cawthorn; Written by Gavin Strawhan. A: Sr. High-Adult. P: Entertainment. U: Home. Mov-Ent: Pornography. Acq: Purchase. Dist: New Horizons Picture Corp.

Beyond Land's End 1985
Examines the composition, origin, and changeability of the sea floor. 30m; VHS. A: Adult. P: Education. U: Institution. Hea-Sci: Oceanography. Acq: Purchase. Dist: RMI Media. $75.00.

Beyond LSD: A Film for Concerned Adults and Teenagers 1968
The communication gap between two generations: teenagers and those over 30. The teenagers' use of LSD and other drugs is only one of the symptoms of this communication gap. 25m; VHS, 3/4 U. A: Sr. High-College. P: Education. U: Institution, SURA. Hea-Sci: Documentary Films, Drug Abuse, Communication. Acq: Purchase. Dist: Phoenix Learning Group.

Beyond Nutrition: Eating for Health ????
Explains how everyday eating habits can effect long term health, slow or stop tumor growth, reduce risks of heart disease, prevent macular degeneration, and slow aging. 22m; VHS. A: Adult. P: Professional. U: Institution, CCTV. Hea-Sci: Nutrition, Fitness/Exercise. Acq: Purchase. Dist: The Learning Seed. $89.00.

Beyond Obsession 1982 — ★★
The strange relationship between a political prisioner, his daughter, and her obsession with a mysterious American is provocatively explored. 116m; VHS, DVD. C: Marcello Mastroianni; Elenora Giorgi; Tom Berenger; Michel Piccoli; Directed by Liliana Cavani; Written by Liliana Cavani. A: College-Adult. P: Entertainment. U: Home. Mov-Ent: Politics & Government. Acq: Purchase. Dist: Facets Multimedia Inc. $19.95.

Beyond Policy Limits 1986
A look at some of the situations that arise between attorneys and insurance company representatives. 50m; VHS, 3/4 U. Pr: ABA. A: Adult. P: Professional. U: Institution, CCTV, Home, SURA. Bus-Ind: Law. Acq: Purchase, Rent/Lease. Dist: American Bar Association. $295.00.

Beyond Protection 1996
Personal trainer, kinesiologist and martial artist Vanessa Friedman conducts an aerobic workout mixed with self defense techniques. 35m; VHS. A: Adult. P: Instruction. U: Home. Hea-Sci: Fitness/Exercise, Martial Arts. Acq: Purchase. Dist: Tapeworm Video Distributors Inc. $19.95.

Beyond Rangoon 1995 (R) — ★★½
Sisters Laura (Arquette) and Andy (McDormand) Bowman travel to Burma to unwind, only to have political unrest and a repressive regime spoil the holiday. Dr. Laura (yeah, right) loses her passport and must flee from trigger-happy soldiers with a political dissident (Ko, a real-life exiled Burmese activist) who befriends her. The search for her passport soon becomes a imperiled trek of survival and self-discovery. Tense, well-crafted action sequences hint at a potential for excitement and intrigue; too bad Arquette isn't the least bit convincing. Filmed in Malaysia. 100m; VHS, DVD, CC. C: Patricia Arquette; Frances McDormand; Spalding Gray; U Aung Ko; Victor Slezak; Directed by John Boorman; Written by Alex Lasker; Bill Rubenstein; Cinematography by John Seale; Music by Hans Zimmer. Pr: Barry Spikings; Eric Pleskow; John Boorman; Sean Ryerson; John Boorman; Castle Rock Entertainment. A: College-Adult. P: Entertainment. U: Home. Mov-Ent: Action-Adventure, Asia, Politics & Government. Acq: Purchase. Dist: Warner Home Video, Inc.

Beyond Rape: A Sensitive Response 1986
Police officers and health care workers are shown the proper degree of sensitivity they must employ when dealing with a rape victim. 25m; VHS, 3/4 U. Pr: Fairview Audio-Visuals. A: Adult. P: Professional. U: Institution, CCTV. Gen-Edu: Rape. Acq: Purchase, Rent/Lease. Dist: Kinetic Film Enterprises Ltd.; Medcom Inc. $295.00.

Beyond Rape: Seeking an End to Sexual Assault 1984
A look at preventing rape through precaution and an understanding of the motivations behind sexual violence. 28m; VHS, 3/4 U. Pr: Christine LeBeau; Washington State Department of Social. A: Sr. High-Adult. P: Education. U: Institution. Gen-Edu: Documentary Films, Rape, Safety Education. Acq: Purchase, Rent/Lease. Dist: Phoenix Learning Group.

Beyond Re-Animator 2003 (R) — ★★
Mad scientist Herbert West (Combs) has been in a maximum security prison for 15 years but has continued his experiments (this time on the rats in his cell). When idealistic young Howard Phillips (Barry) becomes the new prison doctor, he wants to aid West with his re-animation experiments. Of course, things still don't work out as planned and zombie mayhem ensues in this schlocky-but-fun third adventure. 95m; DVD. C: Jeffrey Combs; Jason Barry; Simon Andreu; Elsa Pataky; Directed by Brian Yuzna; Written by Jose Manuel Gomez; Cinematography by Andreu Rebes; Music by Xavier Capellas. A: Sr. High-Adult. P: Entertainment. U: Home. Mov-Ent: Journalism. Acq: Purchase. Dist: Lions Gate Home Entertainment; CinemaNow Inc.

Beyond Reality: Season One 1991
Laura Wingate (Belafonte) is a parapsychologist whose teaching duties at a private university are constantly disrupted by calls to investigate paranormal activities. Clinical psychologist, J.J. Stillman (Marotte) is her traditionally trained partner; together their expert curiosity uncovers the fascinating and seemingly plausible world of the yet explained. 22 episodes. 517m; DVD. C: Shari Belafonte; Carl Marotte. A: Sr. High-Adult. P: Entertainment. U: Home. Mov-Ent: Science Fiction, Mystery & Suspense, Drama. Acq: Purchase. Dist: Mill Creek Entertainment L.L.C.

Beyond Reason 1977 (Unrated) — ★
A psychologist uses unorthodox methods by treating the criminally insane with dignity and respect. 88m; VHS. C: Telly Savalas; Laura Johnson; Diana Muldaur; Marvin Laird; Priscilla Barnes; Directed by Telly Savalas; Cinematography by John A. Alonzo. Pr: Howard W. Koch, Jr. A: Sr. High-Adult. P: Entertainment. U: Home. Mov-Ent: Psychiatry. Acq: Purchase. Dist: No Longer Available.

Beyond Reasonable Doubt 1980 (Unrated) — ★★½
Chilling true-life murder mystery which shattered the peaceful quiet of a small New Zealand town and eventually divided the country. An innocent farmer (Hargreaves) was convicted of a grisly double murder based on evidence planted by a local cop (Hemmings, in a superb role). It wasn't until Yallop's book questioned the facts of the case that it was reopened. Yallop also wrote the screenplay. 127m; VHS. C: David Hemmings; John Hargreaves; Martyn Sanderson; Grant Tilly; Diana Rowan; Ian Watkin; Directed by John Laing; Written by David Yallop. Pr: Satori Entertainment Corporation. A: Sr. High-Adult. P: Entertainment. U: Home. Mov-Ent. Acq: Purchase. Dist: No Longer Available.

Beyond Redemption 1999 (R) — ★★
A serial killer goes after highly respected targets, crucifying his victims, and Detective Smith is in charge of catching the bad guy. It all hinges on faith—and whose is stronger. 97m; VHS, DVD. C: Andrew McCarthy; Michael Ironside; Jayne Heitmeyer; Suzy Joachim; Directed by Chris Angel. A: Sr. High-Adult. P: Entertainment. U: Home. Mov-Ent. Acq: Purchase. Dist: Movies Unlimited.

Beyond Routine 19??
Joffrey Ballet dancers deconstruct a theatre dance production number to demonstrate the elements involved. "Happy Feet" from the ballet "A Shoestring Revue" is used as the example. 40m; VHS. A: Adult. P: Instruction. U: Institution. How-Ins: Dance--Instruction. Acq: Purchase. Dist: Stagestep. $49.95.

Beyond Secretary 1993
Tips for successful administrative assistants. 162m; VHS. A: Sr. High-Adult. P: Professional. U: Institution. Bus-Ind: Business, Job Training. Acq: Purchase. Dist: Cambridge Educational. $149.95.

Beyond Sherwood Forest 2009 (Unrated) — ★
Apparently what's beyond Sherwood Forrest is the realm of stupid. Syfy cable version of the Robin Hood story has Robin (Dunne), the Merry Men, and Maid Marian (Durance) battling druids and some lame CGI dragon while Malcolm (Sands), the Sheriff of Nottingham, ineffectually hunts them down as usual. 93m; DVD, Blu-Ray. C: Robin Dunne; Erica Durance; Julian Sands; Richard de Klerk; David Richmond-Peck; David Palffy; Robert Lawrenson; Directed by Peter DeLuise; Written by Chase Parker; Music by Darren Fung. A: Jr. High-Adult. P: Entertainment. U: Home. Mov-Ent: Science Fiction. Acq: Purchase. Dist: Anchor Bay Entertainment.

Beyond Silence 1996 (PG-13) — ★★
Lara (Trieb/Testud), the daughter of deaf parents, has been their guide to the outside world since childhood. When her Aunt Clarissa (Canonica) gives her a clarinet, it opens Lara's life to music and gives her the courage to move beyond the limits of her family. German with subtitles. 109m; VHS, DVD, CC. C: Sylvie Testud; Tatjana Trieb; Howie Seago; Emmanuelle Laborit; Sibylle Canonica; Directed by Caroline Link; Written by Caroline Link; Cinematography by Gernot Roll; Music by Niki Reiser. Pr: Miramax Film Corp. A: Sr. High-Adult. P: Entertainment. U: Home. L: German. Mov-Ent: Deafness, Parenting. Acq: Purchase. Dist: Buena Vista Home Entertainment.

Beyond Start-Up: Management Lessons for Growing Companies 1989
Don't settle for being a small company—find out what it takes to expand your business. 150m; VHS, 3/4 U. Pr: Video Arts. A: Adult. P: Instruction. U: Institution, SURA. Bus-Ind: Business, Management, How-To. Acq: Purchase, Rent/Lease. Dist: Video Arts, Inc. $395.00.

Beyond Survival: Impact of Third World Development on U.S.A. Agriculture 1989
Shows how the economic development of third world countries affects farming communities in the U.S. Stresses 4-H Youth Exchange program as example of brotherhood and friendship between nations. Features an actual 1985 exchange between Indiana and Togo in West Africa. 28m; VHS. A: Adult. P: Education. U: Institution. Gen-Edu: Agriculture, Poverty, Human Relations. Acq: Purchase. Dist: Purdue University. $15.00.

Beyond Suspicion 2000 — ★½
John C. Nolan Jr. (Goldblum) is an insurance bigshot, who stops by the neighborhood liquor store and gets caught up in an armed robbery. The store clerk, Auggie Rose (Coates), gets killed and Nolan feels responsible. He learns Auggie is fresh out of prison and is expecting to meet his prison pen pal, Lucy (Heche). John meets Lucy instead and doesn't correct her assumption that he's Auggie. In fact, John decides to just give up his old life and take up with Lucy. Film's got an intriguing premise that never develops. 108m; VHS, DVD, Wide, CC. C: Jeff Goldblum; Anne Heche; Timothy Olyphant; Nancy Travis; Richard T. Jones; Kim Coates; Joe Santos; Jack Kehler; Nick (Nicholas) Chinlund; Directed by Matthew Tabak; Written by Matthew Tabak; Cinematography by Adam Kimmel; Music by Don Harper; Mark Mancina. A: Sr. High-Adult. P: Entertainment. U: Home. Mov-Ent: Insurance. Acq: Purchase. Dist: Fox Home Entertainment.

Beyond the Barriers 1998
Follows a group of disabled adventurers as they climb rocks in Utah, sail in British Colombia, body-board waves and scuba dive to deliver the message that the disabled can only be handicapped if they give up. 47m; VHS. A: Family. P: Education. U: Institution. Hea-Sci: Health Education, Handicapped. Acq: Purchase. Dist: Aquarius Health Care Media. $90.00.

Beyond the Bars: Zoos and Zoo Animals 1988
Young viewers are provided with a look inside the Philadelphia Zoo. 18m; VHS. Pr: Rainbow. A: Primary. P: Education. U: Institution. Hea-Sci: Animals, Zoos. Acq: Purchase. Dist: Rainbow Educational Media, Inc.; Clear Vue Inc. $89.00.

Beyond the Bermuda Triangle 1975 (Unrated) — ★½
Unfortunate and flat TV flick. Businessman MacMurray, now retired, doesn't have enough to do. He begins an investigation of the mysterious geometric island area when his friends and fiancee disappear. Silly. 78m; VHS, DVD. C: Fred MacMurray; Sam Groom; Donna Mills; Suzanne Reed; Dana Plato; Woody Woodbury; Directed by William A. Graham. Pr: Playboy Enterprises. A: Jr. High-Adult. P: Entertainment. U: Home. Mov-Ent: Mystery & Suspense, TV Movies. Acq: Purchase. Dist: East West.

Beyond the Black Rainbow 2010 (R) — ★½
Elena (Eva Bourne) attempts to escape from the drug hazed utopia that promises happiness to the inhabitants of the future. 110m; DVD, Blu-Ray, Streaming. C: Michael Rogers; Eva Bourne; Scott Hylands; Rondel Reynoldson; Marilyn Norry; Directed by Panos Cosmatos; Written by Panos Cosmatos; Cinematography by Norm Li; Music by Jeremy Schmidt. A: Sr. High-Adult. P: Entertainment. U: Home. L: English, Spanish.

Mov-Ent. **Acq:** Purchase, Rent/Lease. **Dist:** Magnolia Home Entertainment. $16.98 14.98 9.99.

Beyond the Blackboard 2011 (Unrated) — ★★½
Inspirational Hallmark Hall of Fame presentation based on Stacey Bess' memoir "Don't Love Nobody." A Salt Lake City wife, mom, and teacher, Stacey can only find a job trying to educate homeless kids in a rundown facility. Naturally, she rises to the occasion, badgering the administration for basic supplies even as she connects with her often-troubled students. 95m; DVD. **C:** Emily VanCamp; Steve Talley; Treat Williams; Timothy Busfield; Liam McKanna; Paola Nicole Andino; Julio Oscar Mechoso; Nicki Aycox; Directed by Jeff Bleckner; Written by Camille Thomasson; Cinematography by Eric Van Haren Noman; Music by Jeff Beal. **A:** Family. **P:** Entertainment. **U:** Home. **Mov-Ent:** Homeless, Pregnancy. **Acq:** Purchase. **Dist:** Hallmark Hall of Fame.

Beyond the Blue Horizon 1942 (Unrated) — ★★½
A young woman is trapped in a remote jungle after her parents are killed by rampaging elephants. Eventually rescued, Tama (Lamour) expects an inheritance when she goes to San Francisco but her other relatives are doubtful of her claims. So until Tama can prove her identity, she joins a circus and falls for lion tamer Jakra (Denning). 76m; DVD. **C:** Dorothy Lamour; Richard Denning; Jack Haley; Walter Abel; Helen Gilbert; Patricia Morison; Directed by Alfred Santell; Written by Frank Butler; Cinematography by Charles P. Boyle; William Mellor. **A:** Jr. High-Adult. **P:** Entertainment. **U:** Home. **Mov-Ent:** Circuses, Adoption. **Acq:** Purchase. **Dist:** Movies Unlimited.

Beyond the Borderline 1996
Profiles five women suffering from Borderline Personality Disorder, and shares the gains they have made in personal functioning after six years of treatment. 54m; VHS. **A:** College-Adult. **P:** Education. **U:** Institution. **Gen-Edu:** Documentary Films, Personality, Psychiatry. **Acq:** Purchase, Rent/Lease. **Dist:** Filmakers Library Inc. $250.00.

Beyond the Bounds 1994
Olympic medalist Jackie Joyner-Kersee conducts a fitness workout for intermediate exercisers. 50m; VHS. **A:** Adult. **P:** Instruction. **U:** Home. **Hea-Sci:** Fitness/Exercise. **Acq:** Purchase. **Dist:** BMG Entertainment. $19.98.

Beyond the Call 1996 (R) — ★★½
Connecticut housewife Pam O'Brien (Spacek) learns from the paper that her high-school sweetheart Russell Cates (Strathairn) is on death row in South Carolina for killing a cop and his execution has been scheduled within weeks. Pam writes Russell and then hears from his sister Fran (Wright), who urges Pam to visit her brother and get him to apply for a clemency hearing. Husband Keith (Howard) becomes angry and alarmed as Pam gets more involved with Russell and his case, which hinges on Russell's Vietnam experiences and post-traumatic shock syndrome. 101m; VHS, DVD, CC. **C:** David Strathairn; Sissy Spacek; Arliss Howard; Janet Wright; Directed by Tony Bill; Written by Doug Magee; Cinematography by Jean Lepine; Music by George S. Clinton. **Pr:** Helen Buck Bartlett; Tony Bill; Robert Christiansen; Rick Rosenberg; Tony Bill; Doug Magee; Hallmark Entertainment; Showtime. **A:** Sr. High-Adult. **P:** Entertainment. **U:** Home. **Mov-Ent:** TV Movies. **Acq:** Purchase. **Dist:** Echo Bridge Home Entertainment.

Beyond the Call of Duty 1992 (R) — ★½
Renegade U.S. Army Commander Len Jordan (Vincent) is after a particularly deadly Vietcong enemy. Aided by the head of a special forces naval unit he tracks his quarry through the notorious Mekong River Delta. But Jordan's mission may be hindered, both personally and professionally, by a beautiful American journalist after a hot story. 92m; VHS, DVD. **C:** Jan-Michael Vincent; Eb Lottimer; Jillian McWhirter; Directed by Cirio H. Santiago. **Pr:** Roger Corman; Concorde Pictures. **A:** Sr. High-Adult. **P:** Entertainment. **U:** Home. **Mov-Ent:** Vietnam War, Rivers & Streams. **Acq:** Purchase. **Dist:** New Horizons Picture Corp. $89.98.

Beyond the Carribean 1936 — ★★
Bizarre jungle thriller featuring voodoo and native crucifixion. 56m/B/W; VHS. **C:** Andre Roosevelt. **A:** Jr. High-Adult. **P:** Entertainment. **U:** Home. **Mov-Ent. Acq:** Purchase. **Dist:** Sinister Cinema. $16.95.

Beyond the Clouds 1995 (Unrated) — ★★½
A wandering film director (Malkovich) muses on four stories of life and obsession, including unconsummated relationships, romantic triangles, and even violence. Based on sketches from Antonioni's book "That Bowling Alley on the Tiber." English, French, and Italian with subtitles. 109m; DVD, Wide. **C:** John Malkovich; Marcello Mastroianni; Sophie Marceau; Fanny Ardant; Vincent Perez; Jean Reno; Jeanne Moreau; Irene Jacob; Peter Weller; Chiara Caselli; Ines Sastre; Kim Rossi-Stuart; Directed by Michelangelo Antonioni; Wim Wenders; Written by Michelangelo Antonioni; Wim Wenders; Tonino Guerra; Cinematography by Robby Muller; Alfio Contini; Music by Van Morrison; Lucio Dalla; Laurent Petitgand. **A:** College-Adult. **P:** Entertainment. **U:** Home. **L:** English, French, Italian. **Mov-Ent:** Drama, Italy, Filmmaking. **Acq:** Purchase. **Dist:** Olive Films.

Beyond the Curtain of Space 1953
Sci-fi adventure that marked the debut of Rocky Jones and his space rangers. ?m; VHS. **C:** Richard Crane; Sally Mansfield. **A:** Family. **P:** Entertainment. **U:** Home. **Mov-Ent:** Science Fiction, Television Series. **Acq:** Purchase. **Dist:** Sinister Cinema. $16.95.

Beyond the Da Vinci Code 2005
Scrutinizes the evidence in support and against the ideas at the root of Christianity that is proposed in the bestselling book. 90m; DVD. **A:** Adult. **P:** Education. **U:** Home. **Gen-Edu:** Documentary Films. **Acq:** Purchase. **Dist:** A&E Television Networks L.L.C. $19.95.

Beyond the Darkness: Buio Omega 1979 (Unrated) — ★½
A housekeeper offs his employer's girlfriend out of jealousy and aids him in finding (and subsequently murdering) replacements. 94m; DVD, Blu-Ray. **C:** Kieran Canter; Sam Modesto; Cinzia Monreale; Franca Stoppi; Directed by Joe D'Amato; Written by Ottavio Fabbri; Giacomo Guerrini; Cinematography by Joe D'Amato. **A:** Sr. High-Adult. **P:** Entertainment. **U:** Home. **L:** English, Italian. **Mov-Ent. Acq:** Purchase. **Dist:** Media Blasters Inc. $24.99 20.98.

Beyond the Door 1975 (R) — **Bomb!**
San Francisco woman finds herself pregnant with a demonic child. One of the first "Exorcist" ripoffs; skip this one and go right to the sequel, "Beyond the Door 2." In Italian; dubbed. 97m; VHS, DVD, CC. **C:** Juliet Mills; Richard Johnson; David Colin, Jr.; Directed by Ovidio G. Assonitis; Richard Barrett; Written by Ovidio G. Assonitis; Richard Barrett. **Pr:** Avido Assonnitis. **A:** Sr. High-Adult. **P:** Entertainment. **U:** Home. **Mov-Ent:** Horror. **Acq:** Purchase. **Dist:** Movies Unlimited; Sony Pictures Home Entertainment Inc. $18.99.

Beyond the Door 3 1991 (R) — **Bomb!**
Fool American students in Yugoslavia board a hellish locomotive which speeds them toward a satanic ritual. Demonic disaster-movie stuff (with poor miniatures) isn't as effective as the on-location filming; Serbian scenery and crazed peasants impart an eerie pagan aura. What this has to do with earlier "Beyond the Door" movies only the marketing boys can say. Some dialogue in Serbo-Croat with English subtitles. 94m; VHS, DVD, CC. **C:** Mary Kohnert; Sarah Conway Ciminera; William Geiger; Renee Rancourt; Alex Vitale; Victoria Zinny; Savina Gersak; Bo Svenson; Directed by Jeff Kwitny. **Pr:** RCA. **A:** College-Adult. **P:** Entertainment. **U:** Home. **L:** Serbo-Croatian, English. **Mov-Ent:** Horror, Occult Sciences. **Acq:** Purchase. **Dist:** Media Blasters Inc. $89.95.

Beyond the Dream 1991
Illustrates the lives of German, Irish, and Italian Catholic immigrants in America from the mid-1800s thru the early 1900s. Narrated by Monsignor John Tracy Ellis. Includes study guide. 58m; VHS. **A:** Sr. High-Adult. **P:** Religious. **U:** Institution, Home. **Gen-Edu:** Religion, Immigration, History. **Acq:** Purchase. **Dist:** U.S. Catholic Conference of Catholic Bishops. $29.95.

Beyond the Dunwich Horror 2008 (R) — ★½
Kenneth (Reed) goes home to Dunwich when he hears his brother has been put in an asylum. Relying on a reporter and a local eccentric, he sets out to find what's happened. 104m; DVD. **C:** Jason McCormick; Jeff Dylan Graham; Sarah Nicklin; Lynn Lowry; Ruth Sullivan; Directed by Richard Griffin; Written by Richard Griffin; Cinematography by Ricardo Rebelo; Music by Tony Milano; Daniel Hildreth. **A:** Sr. High-Adult. **P:** Entertainment. **U:** Home. **L:** English. **Mov-Ent. Acq:** Purchase. **Dist:** Alternative Distribution Alliance; Scorpion Releasing. $19.98.

Beyond the Forest 1949 (Unrated) — ★½
Camp diva Davis, in her last role for Warner Bros., really turns on the histrionics as a big-city gal married to a small-town guy (Cotten) and bored out of her mind. Although the most memorable line, "What a dump," has become larger-than-life, the film itself is rather small and muddled (interestingly, Vidor directed "The Fountainhead" the same year.) A trashy melodrama full of ennui, envy, unwanted pregnancy, and murder, it's definitely high on camp and low on art. 96m/B/W; VHS. **C:** Bette Davis; Joseph Cotten; David Brian; Ruth Roman; Minor Watson; Regis Toomey; Directed by King Vidor; Cinematography by Robert Burks; Music by Max Steiner. **Pr:** Warner Bros. **A:** Jr. High-Adult. **P:** Entertainment. **U:** Home. **Mov-Ent:** Classic Films. **Acq:** Purchase. **Dist:** MGM Home Entertainment; Facets Multimedia Inc. $19.95.

Beyond the Fringe 1964
Only filmed performance of the British comic revue troupe of Alan Bennett, Peter Cook, Dudley Moore, and Jonathan Miller, filmed at their gala farewell in London. 116m/B/W; DVD, CC. **A:** Adult. **P:** Entertainment. **U:** Home. **Mov-Ent:** Comedy--Performance. **Acq:** Purchase. **Dist:** BBC Worldwide Ltd.; Acorn Media Group Inc. $24.98.

Beyond the Front Page 1994
Series of ten journalism workshops visits a metropolitan daily newspaper for a behind-the-scenes look at meeting deadlines, double-checking facts, and getting to the bottom of a story. Complete with teacher's guide. 25m; VHS. **A:** Sr. High. **P:** Education. **U:** Institution. **Gen-Edu:** Journalism. **Acq:** Purchase. **Dist:** GPN Educational Media.

Beyond the Gates of Splendor 2005
Looks at the changes to the lives of Ecuador's Waodani Indians after missionaries started visiting the tribe beginning in 1956. 96m; DVD. **A:** Jr. High-Adult. **P:** Entertainment. **U:** Home. **Gen-Edu:** Documentary Films. **Acq:** Purchase. **Dist:** Fox Home Entertainment.

Beyond the Hills 2013 (Unrated) — ★★½
Award-winning director Mungiu examines the tug-of-war between two friends who represent secular life and religious faith in this accomplished drama. Best friends Alina and Voichita are heading down different paths. The former wants her closest partner to return with her from Romania to Germany but the latter is being pulled into a world of faith at an Orthodox convent. When reasoning with Alina fails, Voichita becomes convinced that she is possessed and seeks to exorcise that which keeps her from faith with drastic results. Mungiu's film is deliberate and slow but his excellent skill with actors and willingness to tackle complex themes is admirable. 150m; DVD. **C:** Cosmina Straton; Cristina Flutur; Directed by Cristian Mungiu; Written by Cristian Mungiu; Cinematography by Oleg Mutu. **Pr:** Cristian Mungiu; Mobra Films; Sundance Selects. **A:** Adult. **P:** Entertainment. **U:** Home. **L:** Romanian. **Mov-Ent:** Religion, Exorcism & Exorcists. **Acq:** Purchase. **Dist:** IFC Films.

Beyond the Law 1930 (Unrated) — ★
Basic early talkie western. Dan Wright (Frazer) and his partner Jack-Knife (Chandler) are sent to help ranchers who are being targeted by rustlers. 60m/B/W; DVD. **C:** Robert Frazer; Lane Chandler; Louise Lorraine; Charles "Blackie" King; William Walling; Edward Lynch; Directed by J(ohn) P(aterson) McGowan; Written by George Arthur Durlam; Cinematography by Harry Neumann. **A:** Jr. High-Adult. **P:** Entertainment. **U:** Home. **Mov-Ent:** Western. **Acq:** Purchase. **Dist:** Sinister Cinema.

Beyond the Law 1968 (Unrated) — ★★
Spaghetti western with Van Cleef as the too smart bad guy. He becomes sheriff, picks up the stack of silver at the depot, and disappears. Humorous and clever, with fine location photography. 91m; VHS, DVD. **C:** Lee Van Cleef; Antonio (Tony) Sabato; Lionel Stander; Bud Spencer; Gordon Mitchell; Ann Smyrner; Directed by Giorgio Stegani. **Pr:** Imperial Entertainment. **A:** Sr. High-Adult. **P:** Entertainment. **U:** Home. **L:** Italian. **Mov-Ent. Acq:** Purchase. **Dist:** Imperial Entertainment Corp. $19.95.

Beyond the Law 1992 (R) — ★½
Ex-undercover cop Danny Saxon (Sheen) is recruited by the FBI to infiltrate a biker gang involved in drugs and gun smuggling. But Saxon finds himself drawn too close into the unconventional biker lifestyle and into an uneasy friendship with leader Blood (Madsen). Clumsy and exploitative. 101m; VHS, DVD. **C:** Charlie Sheen; Michael Madsen; Linda Fiorentino; Courtney B. Vance; Leon Rippy; Rip Torn; Michael Berry; Directed by Larry Ferguson; Written by Larry Ferguson; Cinematography by Robert M. Stevens; Music by John D'Andrea; Cory Lerios. **Pr:** John Fiedler; Mark Tarlov; Ronna B. Wallace; Richard N. Gladstein; Polar Entertainment. **A:** Sr. High-Adult. **P:** Entertainment. **U:** Home. **Mov-Ent:** Motorcycles. **Acq:** Purchase. **Dist:** Lions Gate Television Corp. $92.98.

Beyond the Limit 1983 (R) — ★★½
The story of an intense and darkly ominous love triangle which takes place in the South American coastal city of Corrientes. Based on Graham Greene's novel "The Honorary Consul." 103m; VHS. **C:** Michael Caine; Richard Gere; Bob Hoskins; Elpidia Carrillo; Directed by John MacKenzie; Written by Christopher Hampton; Cinematography by Phil Meheux. **Pr:** Norma Heyman. **A:** Sr. High-Adult. **P:** Entertainment. **U:** Home. **Mov-Ent. Acq:** Purchase. **Dist:** Paramount Pictures Corp. $59.95.

Beyond the Limits 1983
This program teaches inexperienced drivers what to do in a situation beyond one's driving experience. 13m; VHS, 8 mm, 3/4 U. **TV Std:** NTSC, PAL, SECAM. **Pr:** Film Communicators. **A:** Sr. High-Adult. **P:** Education. **U:** Institution, CCTV, SURA. **Gen-Edu:** Automobiles. **Acq:** Purchase, Rent/Lease, Duplication License. **Dist:** Phoenix Learning Group. $295.00.

Beyond the Looking Glass: Self-Esteem and Body Image 199?
High school couselors help teens understand that each person is lovable, worthwhile, unique, and connected. Stresses the importance of rejecting negative feelings about oneself. 189m; VHS. **A:** Jr. High-Sr. High. **P:** Education. **U:** Institution. **Hea-Sci:** Health Education, Education, Adolescence. **Dist:** Human Relations Media. $189.

Beyond the Mat 1999 (R)
Behind-the-scenes look at the World Wrestling Federation, including WWF head Vince McMahon, and some of its most popular stars, such as The Rock, Chyna, Mankind, and others. An unrated version is also available. 103m; DVD, CC. **C:** Directed by Barry W. Blaustein; Cinematography by Michael Grady; Music by Nathan Barr. **A:** Sr. High-Adult. **P:** Entertainment. **U:** Home. **Spo-Rec:** Documentary Films. **Acq:** Purchase. **Dist:** Universal Studios Home Video.

Beyond the Milky Way 1981
Focuses upon astronomical discoveries given birth to by technological advances. Galaxies smashing into each other, mysterious black holes, and clouds of primeval material are some of the spectacular images seen. 57m; VHS, 3/4 U, Special order formats. **Pr:** WGBH Boston; British Broadcasting Corporation. **A:** Jr. High-Sr. High. **P:** Education. **U:** Institution, SURA. **Hea-Sci:** Astronomy, Technology. **Acq:** Purchase, Rent/Lease. **Dist:** Time-Life Video and Television.

Beyond the Mind's Eye 1992
Computer animation and beautiful music combine for a surreal trip to another dimension. Features animation from the movie "Lawnmower Man." 45m; VHS, DVD. **C:** Music by Jan Hammer. **A:** Jr. High-Adult. **P:** Entertainment. **U:** Home. **Fin-Art:** Animation & Cartoons. **Acq:** Purchase. **Dist:** BMG Entertainment; Baker and Taylor; Fusion Video. $19.98.

Beyond the Mirage 1987
Examines the relationship between Jews and Arabs in Israel. 25m; VHS. **C:** Narrated by Lorne Greene. **Pr:** Alden Films. **A:** Jr. High-Adult. **P:** Education. **U:** Institution, Home, SURA. **Gen-Edu:** Documentary Films, Middle East. **Acq:** Purchase, Rent/Lease. **Dist:** Alden Films. $50.00.

Beyond the Missile Crisis 1983
This documentary takes an in depth look at the political and social changes occurring inside West Germany. 49m; VHS, 3/4 U. **Pr:** National Broadcasting Company. **A:** Sr. High-Adult. **P:**

Entertainment. **U:** Institution, SURA. **Gen-Edu:** Documentary Films, Germany, Sociology. **Acq:** Purchase, Rent/Lease. **Dist:** Home Vision Cinema.

Beyond the Moon—Revised 1970
An imaginary trip through the solar system introduces the viewer to the planets, asteroids, and some planetary satellites. 11m; VHS, 3/4 U. **Pr:** Dr. Douglass Productions. **A:** Jr. High. **P:** Education. **U:** Institution, SURA. **Hea-Sci:** Astronomy, Education. **Acq:** Purchase. **Dist:** Phoenix Learning Group.

Beyond the Movie: Alexander 2004 (Unrated)
Undefeated in battle, Alexander the Great created one of the largest empires of the ancient world and is considered one of history's greatest military leaders. Discover the man behind the legend and learn what drove him to become such a fierce opponent, how he inspired his men to unquestioning loyalty, and of the possible scenarios that could explain his death. 60m; DVD. **A:** Family. **P:** Education. **U:** Institution, Home. **Mov-Ent:** Documentary Films, Folklore & Legends. **Acq:** Purchase. **Dist:** National Geographic Society. $24.95.

Beyond the Movie: Troy 2004
Takes an inside look at the making of the blockbuster movie starring Brad Pitt. 60m; VHS, DVD. **A:** Adult. **P:** Entertainment. **U:** Home. **Mov-Ent:** Filmmaking, Documentary Films. **Acq:** Purchase. **Dist:** National Geographic Society. $24.95.

Beyond the Neonatal Intensive Care Unit 19??
Psychology and social work film from the University of Calgary Learning Commons. ?m; VHS. **A:** Adult. **P:** Professional. **U:** Institution. **Gen-Edu:** Psychology, Social Service. **Acq:** Purchase. **Dist:** University of Calgary Library, Visual Resources Centre.

Beyond the Next Mountain 1987 (PG) — ★
A missionary in China attempts to convert all those he meets. Thin plot and marginal acting will likely make viewers fall asleep. 97m; VHS, DVD, Streaming. **C:** Alberto Isaac; Jon Lormer; Bennett Ohta; Richard Lineback; Edward Ashley; Barry Foster; Directed by James F. Collier; Rolf Forsberg. **Pr:** United Enterprises Ltd. **A:** Family. **P:** Religious. **U:** Home. **Mov-Ent:** China. **Acq:** Purchase. **Dist:** Unknown Distributor.

Beyond the Numbers: Professional Interview Techniques 19??
Self-study course designed to help individuals conduct professional interviews. Covers different situations and includes three hidden camera interviews for critiquing. Also explains the five major question types: introductory, informational, closing, assessment, and admission-seeking. Includes a workbook and 20-question examination. Can be used to obtain a certificate of completion for 20 hours of CPE credit. 50m; VHS. **A:** Adult. **P:** Professional. **U:** Institution. **Bus-Ind:** Business, Interviews, Communication. **Acq:** Purchase. **Dist:** Association of Certified Fraud Examiners. $199.00.

Beyond the Ocean, Beneath a Leaf 1982
Profile of photographer Kjell Sandved and his underwater close-ups and time-lapse photography. 29m; VHS, SVS, 3/4 U. **A:** Jr. High-Sr. High. **P:** Education. **U:** Institution. **Gen-Edu:** Photography. **Acq:** Purchase, Rent/Lease. **Dist:** Encyclopedia Britannica. $59.00.

Beyond the Open Door 19??
Demonstrates how supervisors and managers can handle employment equity issues as they affect women, aboriginal people, visible minorities, and the physically disabled. Guide available separately. 30m; VHS. **A:** Adult. **P:** Education. **U:** Institution. **Bus-Ind:** Business, Personnel Management, Employee Counseling. **Acq:** Purchase. **Dist:** Access The Education Station. $159.00.

Beyond the Poseidon Adventure 1979 (PG) — ★
A sequel to the 1972 film in which salvage teams and ruthless looting vandals compete for access to the sunken ocean liner. Sinking ships should be abandoned. 115m; DVD. **C:** Michael Caine; Sally Field; Telly Savalas; Peter Boyle; Jack Warden; Slim Pickens; Shirley Knight; Shirley Jones; Karl Malden; Mark Harmon; Directed by Irwin Allen; Cinematography by Joseph Biroc. **Pr:** Irwin Allen; Irwin Allen. **A:** Jr. High-Adult. **P:** Entertainment. **U:** Home. **Mov-Ent:** Action-Adventure, Boating. **Acq:** Purchase. **Dist:** Warner Home Video, Inc. $19.98.

Beyond the Post-Modern Mind 1989
Theories on the breakdown in the moral fiber of society that has led to widespread alienation and social discontent throughout the world. 30m; VHS. **Pr:** Thinking Allowed Productions. **A:** College-Adult. **P:** Education. **U:** Home. **Gen-Edu:** Philosophy & Ideology, Human Relations, Sociology. **Acq:** Purchase. **Dist:** Thinking Allowed Productions. $29.95.

Beyond the Ring of Fire 1996
Chronicles the ten-year journey of brothers Lawrence and Lorne Blair as they travel through the 13,000 islands of Indonesia, visiting many of their native peoples and experiencing their customs. ?m; VHS. **A:** Jr. High. **P:** Entertainment. **U:** Home. **Gen-Edu:** Travel, Asia. **Acq:** Purchase. **Dist:** Mystic Fire Video. $19.95.

Beyond the Rockies 1932 — ★★½
Keene and a group of cowboys battle cattle rustlers in this action-packed sagebrush saga. Solid script with good direction by Allen. 55m/B/W; VHS, DVD. **C:** Tom Keene; Rochelle Hudson; Ernie Adams; Julian Rivero; Hank Bell; Tom London; Directed by Fred Allen; Written by John P. McCarthy. **Pr:** Harry Joe Brown; Selznick Pictures. **A:** Jr. High-Adult. **P:** Entertainment. **U:** Home. **Mov-Ent:** Western. **Acq:** Purchase. **Dist:** Sinister Cinema. $19.99.

Beyond the Rocks 1922 (Unrated) — ★★½
Sam Wood's 1922 silent film stars icons Rudolph Valentino and Gloria Swanson, and was until recently thought to have been lost forever. One surviving print was found in a Dutch archive, which has been given an impressive restoration and a new sound track. Zany rescues abound: Lord Bracondale (Valentino) rescues Theadora Fitzgerald (Swanson) after her rowboat capsizes off the British coast, and again later in the Swiss Alps after a mountaineering accident. Well worth seeing for the craft involved in creating early film. 81m/B/W; Silent; DVD. **C:** Gloria Swanson; Rudolph Valentino; Edythe Chapman; Alec B. Francis; Gertrude Astor; Mabel van Buren; June Elvidge; Robert Bolder; Helen Dunbar; Raymond Blathwayt; F.R. Butler; Directed by Sam Wood; Written by Jack Cunningham; Cinematography by Alfred Gilks. **Pr:** Jesse L. Lasky; Paramount. **A:** Jr. High-Adult. **P:** Entertainment. **U:** Home. **L:** English. **Mov-Ent:** Silent Films, Marriage, Drama. **Acq:** Purchase. **Dist:** Movies Unlimited.

Beyond the Sea 2004 (PG-13) — ★★
Energetic if superficial biography of Bobby Darin is the personal labor of love for director/star/producer Spacey—even if he's technically too old for the role (Darin died at 37 in 1973). His conceit is showcasing the older Darin in his own fantasy autobiography, beginning with his childhood self (Ullrich) and advancing confidently as Darin finds success crooning at the Copa, becomes a teen idol with the ditty "Splish Splash," and falls in love with teenaged golden girl actress Sandra Dee (Bosworth). This being showbiz, things eventually take a downward spiral for the insecure Darin as his smooth style becomes irrelevant in the hippie sixties before he attempts the inevitable comeback. It's Spacey's show (and he supplies his own more-than-adequate vocals) but supporting actors Hoskins, Blethyn, Aaron, and Goodman all run with their screen time. Title is taken from a 1960 Darin hit. 121m; VHS, DVD. **C:** Kevin Spacey; Kate (Catherine) Bosworth; John Goodman; Bob Hoskins; Brenda Blethyn; Greta Scacchi; Caroline Aaron; Peter Cincotti; William Ullrich; Tayfun Bademsoy; Directed by Kevin Spacey; Written by Kevin Spacey; Lewis Colick; Cinematography by Eduardo Serra; Music by Christopher Slaski. **Pr:** Andy Paterson; Kevin Spacey; Jan Fantl; Arthur E. Friedman; Kevin Spacey; Trigger Street; Archer Street; QI Quality Intl; Lions Gate Films. **A:** Jr. High-Adult. **P:** Entertainment. **U:** Home. **L:** English. **Mov-Ent:** Biography: Music, Biography: Show Business. **Dist:** CinemaNow Inc. $27.98.

Beyond the Sexual Revolution 1972
Helen Cotton (exectuve director of Family Forum and author) and Dr. Francoeur, tell how the "sexual revolution is constantly changing our lifestyles and our approach to morality." Part of the "Humanist Alternative" series. 30m; 3/4 U, Special order formats. **Pr:** American Humanist Association. **A:** College-Adult. **P:** Education. **U:** Institution, CCTV, CATV. **Gen-Edu:** Sex & Sexuality, Ethics & Morals. **Acq:** Purchase, Rent/Lease. **Dist:** American Humanist Association.

Beyond the Silhouette 1990 (Unrated) — ★
It starts out as another sleazy video sex thriller, as the lawyer heroine discovers her sensuality and poses a lot in her underclothes. Then in the third act it become a hyper-paranoid political-conspiracy assassination-o-rama. Pretty weird junk. 90m; VHS. **C:** Tracy Scoggins; Marc Singer; Brion James; Directed by Lloyd A. Simandl. **A:** College-Adult. **P:** Entertainment. **U:** Home. **Mov-Ent:** Mystery & Suspense, Sex & Sexuality, Law. **Acq:** Purchase. **Dist:** Unknown Distributor.

Beyond the Stacks: Finding Fun in the Library 1992
A young girl tours her library and learns the variety of resources available, including books, videos, CDs, newspapers, magazines, and more. 11m; VHS. **A:** Primary-Jr. High. **P:** Education. **U:** Institution. **Chl-Juv:** Education. **Acq:** Purchase. **Dist:** Baker and Taylor.

Beyond the Stars 1989 (Unrated) — ★
A sci-fi adventure directed by the author of "Cocoon," wherein a whiz-kid investigates the NASA cover-up of a deadly accident that occurred on the moon during the Apollo 11 landing. Unfortunately, the interesting cast can't make up for the script. 94m; VHS, DVD. **C:** Martin Sheen; Christian Slater; Olivia D'Abo; F. Murray Abraham; Robert Foxworth; Sharon Stone; Directed by David Saperstein. **Pr:** Moviestore Entertainment; Five Star Ent. **A:** Jr. High-Adult. **P:** Entertainment. **U:** Home. **Mov-Ent:** Science Fiction, The Moon. **Acq:** Purchase. **Dist:** Lions Gate Television Corp. $89.95.

Beyond the Stars: A Space Story 1981
When a little boy wonders whether people live on stars, he is given a factual introduction to the sun and planets, and a science fiction trip beyond the solar system. 12m; VHS, 3/4 U. **Pr:** Polestar. **A:** Primary. **P:** Education. **U:** Institution, SURA. **Hea-Sci:** Astronomy, Education. **Acq:** Purchase, Rent/Lease. **Dist:** Phoenix Learning Group.

Beyond the Time Barrier 1960 (Unrated) — ★★½
Air Force test pilot gets more than he bargained for when his high speed plane carries him into the future. There he sees the ravages of an upcoming plague, to which he must return. 75m/B/W; VHS, DVD. **C:** Robert Clarke; Darlene Tompkins; Arianne Arden; Vladimir Sokoloff; Directed by Edgar G. Ulmer. **Pr:** American International Pictures. **A:** Jr. High-Adult. **P:** Entertainment. **U:** Home. **Mov-Ent:** Science Fiction, Aeronautics. **Acq:** Purchase. **Dist:** Sinister Cinema. $16.95.

Beyond the Trail 1926 — ★★★
One of Bill Patton's most entertaining and funny films. In this comedic Western adventure he must face Black Mike and his gang and rescue Mary from their clutches. 50m; VHS. **C:** Bill(y) (William Patten) Patton; Sheldon Lewis; Stuart Holmes; Eric Wayne; Janet Dawn; Clara Horton; James F. Fulton; Directed by Al(bert) Herman. **Pr:** Chesterfield Motion Picture Corporation. **A:** Family. **P:** Entertainment. **U:** Home. **Mov-Ent:** Classic Films. **Acq:** Purchase. **Dist:** Grapevine Video. $12.95.

Beyond the Training Room 199?
Hazardous waste workers are introduced to the health and safety hazards associated with their work. Illustrates how to handle potentially dangerous situations. Complete with trainer and participant manuals. 18m; VHS; Signed. **A:** Adult. **P:** Instruction. **U:** Institution. **Bus-Ind:** Safety Education. **Dist:** Learning Communications L.L.C. $495.

Beyond the Valley of the Dolls 1970 (NC-17) — ★★½
Sleazy, spirited non-sequel to "Valley of the Dolls." Meyer ("Faster, Pussycat! Kill! Kill!") directed this Hollywood parody ("BVD," as it came to be known) about an all-girl rock combo and their search for stardom. Labeled the first "exploitation horror camp musical"?how can you pass that up? Screenplay by film critic Ebert, from an original story by Ebert and Meyer. Mondo trasho. 109m; VHS, DVD. **C:** Dolly Reed; Cynthia Myers; Marcia McBroom; John Lazar; Michael Blodgett; David Gurian; Erica Gavin; Edy Williams; Phyllis E. Davis; Harrison Page; Duncan McLeod; James Iglehart; Charles Napier; Haji; Pam Grier; Directed by Russ Meyer; Written by Roger Ebert; Cinematography by Fred W. Koenekamp; Music by The Strawberry Alarm Clock; Stu Phillips. **A:** Adult. **P:** Entertainment. **U:** Home. **Mov-Ent:** Satire & Parody, Exploitation, Music--Pop/Rock. **Acq:** Purchase. **Dist:** Baker and Taylor. $19.98.

Beyond the Veil: Are Iranian Women Rebelling? ????
Female Islamic scholars discuss the veil in terms of Islamic religious tradition and social benefits, while professional Islamic women approach the issue of Islam's right to subjugate women by trying to control who they are and how they think with a government-enforced dress code. 22m; VHS. **A:** Sr. High-Adult. **P:** Education. **U:** Institution. **Gen-Edu:** Middle East, Women. **Acq:** Purchase, Rent/Lease. **Dist:** Films for the Humanities & Sciences. $129.00.

Beyond the Veil: The Born Again Muslims 1998
Documentary on the views of Muslims about Islam and modernization. Features liberal Islamists who accept Western ways, as well as traditionalists from Iran who shun Western beliefs. Part of a three-tape set. 52m; VHS. **A:** Adult. **P:** Education. **U:** Home. **Gen-Edu:** Documentary Films, Islam, Religion. **Acq:** Purchase, Rent/Lease. **Dist:** Filmakers Library Inc. $350.

Beyond the Veil: The Holy Warriors 1998
Documentary on the views of Muslims who believe they can preserve their traditions from Western influence only through violence. Part of a three-tape set. 52m; VHS. **A:** Adult. **P:** Education. **U:** Home. **Gen-Edu:** Documentary Films, Islam, Religion. **Acq:** Purchase, Rent/Lease. **Dist:** Filmakers Library Inc. $350.

Beyond the Veil: The New Cold War? 1998
Documentary looking at the conflicting relations between Muslim and Western cultures and suggests solutions. Part of a three-tape set. 52m; VHS. **A:** Adult. **P:** Education. **U:** Home. **Gen-Edu:** Documentary Films, Islam, Religion. **Acq:** Purchase, Rent/Lease. **Dist:** Filmakers Library Inc. $350.

Beyond the Wall of Sleep 2006 (R) — ★
Ponderous, repetitive (and loose) adaptation of a Lovecraft story. In 1908, in New York's Catskill Mountains, deformed Joe Slaader (Sanderson) is confined to the Ulster County Asylum after murdering his family. But with Joe's arrival come sinister forces that seemingly infect the inmates and they begin to take over the madhouse. 84m; DVD, CC. **C:** William Sanderson; Tom Savini; Rick Dial; Fountain Yount; Directed by Barrett J. Leigh; Tom Maurer; Written by Barrett J. Leigh; Tom Maurer; Cinematography by Bill Burton; Music by Kaveh Cohen. **A:** Sr. High-Adult. **P:** Entertainment. **U:** Home. **Mov-Ent. Acq:** Purchase. **Dist:** Lions Gate Entertainment Inc.

Beyond the Walls 1984 (R) — ★★½
The opposing factions of a hellish Israeli prison unite to beat the system. Brutal with good characterizations. Available in both subtitled and dubbed versions. 104m; VHS. **C:** Arnon Zadok; Muhamad (Mohammed) Bakri; Directed by Uri Barbash; Written by Benny Barbash. **Pr:** April Films. **A:** Jr. High-Adult. **P:** Entertainment. **U:** Home. **L:** Hebrew. **Mov-Ent. Awds:** Venice Film Fest. '85: Film. **Acq:** Purchase. **Dist:** Warner Home Video, Inc. $79.95.

Beyond the Walls 2012 (Unrated) — ★★
During a drunken evening out at a Brussels bar, Paulo meets Albanian bartender Ilir. When Paulo becomes homeless, he shows up at Ilir's who reluctantly allows him to stay. After Ilir suddenly lands in prison for drug possession, weak-willed Paulo drifts into another relationship. Ilir and Paulo have a reunion when Ilir gets out of prison but it's not a happy ending. French with subtitles. 98m; DVD. **C:** Matila Malliarakis; Guillaume Gouix; David Salles; Directed by David Lambert; Written by David Lambert; Cinematography by Matthieu Poirot Delpech; Music by Flonja Kodheli. **A:** Adult. **P:** Entertainment. **U:** Home. **L:** French. **Mov-Ent:** Homosexuality, Drama. **Acq:** Purchase. **Dist:** Strand Releasing.

Beyond the Wild Blue: History of the U.S. Air Force 1998
Documentary combines archival film and interviews to depict the history of the United States Air Force. Detailed descriptions of planes and the pilots who flew them, as well as missile development. Traces the history from World War II through to Desert Storm. Five hours on five videocassettes. 60m; VHS. **A:**

Sr. High-Adult. **P:** Education. **U:** Home. **Gen-Edu:** History, Military History. **Acq:** Purchase. **Dist:** PBS Home Video. $99.99.

Beyond Therapy 1986 (R) — ★½
A satire on modern psychotherapy, from the play by Christopher Durang, about a confused, crazily neurotic couple and their respective, and not any saner, analysts. Unfortunately, comes off as disjointed and confused. 93m; VHS, DVD, CC. **C:** Jeff Goldblum; Tom Conti; Julie Hagerty; Glenda Jackson; Christopher Guest; Directed by Robert Altman; Written by Robert Altman. **Pr:** New World Pictures. **A:** Sr. High-Adult. **P:** Entertainment. **U:** Home. **L:** Spanish. **Mov-Ent:** Satire & Parody, Psychiatry. **Acq:** Purchase. **Dist:** Anchor Bay Entertainment. $19.95.

Beyond Tomorrow 1940 (Unrated) — ★★
Young romance is guided from the spirit world during the Christmas season, as two "ghosts" come back to help young lovers. 84m/B/W; VHS, DVD. **C:** Richard Carlson; Sir C. Aubrey Smith; Jean Parker; Charles Winninger; Harry Carey, Sr.; Maria Ouspenskaya; Rod La Rocque; Directed by Edward Sutherland; Written by Adele Comandini; Cinematography by Lester White. **Pr:** RKO. **A:** Family. **P:** Entertainment. **U:** Home. **Mov-Ent:** Comedy--Romantic, Fantasy, Death. **Acq:** Purchase. **Dist:** Sinister Cinema; VCI Entertainment. $16.95.

Beyond Tradition: Contemporary Indian Art and Its Evolution 1990
More than 300 examples of prehistoric and historic Indian art created from 9000 B.C. to the early 1980s, representing the work of more than 125 known Native American artists. Based on the book of the same name. 45m; VHS. **A:** Jr. High-Adult. **P:** Entertainment. **U:** Home, Institution. **Gen-Edu:** Documentary Films, Native Americans, Art & Artists. **Acq:** Purchase. **Dist:** GPN Educational Media; Home Vision Cinema; Crystal Productions. $29.95.

Beyond Utopia: Changing Attitudes in American Architecture 1984
Examines the work and theories of Peter Eisenman, Frank Gehry, Michael Graves, and Robert Venturi and Denise Scott Brown, American architects in the vanguard of post-modernism. 58m; VHS, 3/4 U, Special order formats. **Pr:** Blackwood Productions. **A:** Adult. **P:** Education. **U:** Institution, SURA. **Gen-Edu:** Architecture. **Acq:** Purchase, Rent/Lease. **Dist:** Michael Blackwood Productions.

Beyond Victory 1931 (Unrated) — ★★
Flashbacks reveal the battle experiences of American soldiers fighting for control of a French village during WWI. 70m/B/W; DVD. **C:** William Boyd; Lew Cody; James Gleason; Zasu Pitts; Marion Shilling; Russell Gleason; Theodore von Eltz; Directed by John S. Robertson; Written by James Gleason; Horace Jackson; Cinematography by Norbert Beaudine. **A:** Sr. High-Adult. **P:** Entertainment. **U:** Home. **Mov-Ent:** World War One, France. **Acq:** Purchase. **Dist:** Movies Unlimited.

Beyond Voluntary Control 2000
Modern dance, Emily Dickinson poetry and interviews with a Parkinson's patient explore the psychological and emotional effects of physical confinement. 30m; VHS. **A:** Adult. **P:** Education. **U:** Institution. **Gen-Edu:** Psychology, Mental Health. **Acq:** Purchase, Rent/Lease. **Dist:** Women Make Movies. $250.00.

Beyond Words 1974
Dr. Harrison examines non-verbal communication within the contexts of interpersonal communication and cross-cultural communications. 40m; 3/4 U, EJ. **Pr:** NETCHE. **A:** College-Adult. **P:** Education. **U:** Institution, CCTV, BCTV, SURA. **Gen-Edu:** Communication. **Acq:** Purchase, Rent/Lease, Subscription. **Dist:** NETCHE.
Indiv. Titles: 1. Interpersonal Communications 2. Cross-Cultural Communication.

Beyond Words: Animal Communication 1984
Studies animal communication in the honeybee, humpback whale, wolf and other animals. 15m; VHS. **A:** Primary. **P:** Education. **U:** Institution. **Gen-Edu:** Animals, Communication. **Acq:** Purchase. **Dist:** National Geographic Society. $70.

BF V: The Fifth Annual Best of the Fests 1993
14 shorts from film festivals. 90m; VHS. **C:** F. Murray Abraham; Emily Lloyd. **A:** Adult. **P:** Entertainment. **U:** Home. **Gen-Edu:** Fairs & Expositions, Film--Avant-Garde. **Acq:** Purchase. **Dist:** Next Gen Video. $19.95.

B.F. Skinner and Behavior Change: Research, Practice, and Promise 1975
A distinguished group of participants join Dr. Skinner in facing the issues and controversies generated by behavioral psychology. 45m; 3/4 U. **C:** B.F. Skinner. **Pr:** Philip Blake. **A:** College-Adult. **P:** Education. **U:** Institution, CCTV, Home, SURA. **Hea-Sci:** Psychology. **Acq:** Purchase. **Dist:** Research Press. $495.00.

B.F. Skinner: Education 1972
This two part film explores the education process, from behavior to ethics. 50m; VHS, 3/4 U, Special order formats. **Pr:** Educational Films. **A:** College-Adult. **P:** Professional. **U:** Institution, SURA. **Hea-Sci:** Psychology, Education. **Acq:** Purchase. **Dist:** Psychological & Educational Films.

B.F. Skinner on Counseling 1972
B.F. Skinner gives advice to counselors on the patient-client relationship and explains his belief that the feelings of the client are not the key to changing behavior. 25m; VHS, Special order formats. **A:** Adult. **P:** Professional. **U:** Institution. **Hea-Sci:** Psychology, Psychiatry. **Acq:** Purchase, Rent/Lease. **Dist:** Psychological & Educational Films. $300.00.

The B.F.G.?Big Friendly Giant 1990
Animated tale, adapted from the book by Roald Dahl, finds young orphan Sophie making friends with the 25-foot-tall B.F.G., a fairy prince whose job is to catch dreams and blow the good ones into the minds of sleeping children. But lately, ugly, bad, bigger giants (who like to eat children) are stopping him. 95m; DVD. **C:** Voice(s) by David Jason; Amanda Root; Angela Thorne; Don Henderson; Frank Thornton; Directed by Brian Cosgrove; Written by John Hambley; Music by Keith Hopwood; Malcolm Rowe. **Pr:** Thames Television. **A:** Preschool-Primary. **P:** Entertainment. **U:** Home. **Chl-Juv:** Animation & Cartoons, Fantasy. **Acq:** Purchase. **Dist:** A&E Television Networks L.L.C. $24.98.

B.F.'s Daughter 1948 (Unrated) — ★½
Uneasy (and now-dated) satire loosely based on the John P. Marquand novel and set in the 1930s. Independent Polly, daughter of wealthy industrialist B.F. Fulton, marries lefty-leaning economics professor Thomas Brett. When her hubby's career isn't a great success, Polly uses her father's money and influence to help Thomas prosper (unbeknownst to him) but marital strains persist. 107m/B/W; DVD. **C:** Van Heflin; Barbara Stanwyck; Charles Coburn; Richard Hart; Keenan Wynn; Margaret Lindsay; Spring Byington; Directed by Robert Z. Leonard; Written by Luther Davis; Cinematography by Joseph Ruttenberg; Music by Bronislau Kaper. **A:** Sr. High-Adult. **P:** Entertainment. **U:** Home. **Mov-Ent:** Satire & Parody. **Acq:** Purchase. **Dist:** WarnerArchive.com.

Bhaji on the Beach 1994 (R) — ★★½
Amusing comedy-drama about a group of Indian women who organize a bus outing from Birmingham to the seaside resort town of Blackpool. They range from sari-clad elders to feminist Gen Xers and a couple of teenagers looking for romance. There's bonding and gossiping and secrets galore before the story is tidily wrapped up. 100m; VHS, DVD, CC. **C:** Kim Vithana; Jimmi Harkishin; Sarita Khajuria; Mo Sesay; Lalita Ahmed; Shaheen Khan; Zohra Sehgal; Directed by Gurinder Chadha; Written by Meera Syal; Gurinder Chadha; Cinematography by John Kenway; Music by John Altman; Craig Pruess. **Pr:** Nadine Marsh-Edwards; First Look Pictures; Film Four International. **A:** College-Adult. **P:** Entertainment. **U:** Home. **Mov-Ent:** Comedy-Drama, Women, Ethnicity. **Acq:** Purchase. **Dist:** Film4 Library.

Bhangra Jig 19??
Examines how young Asian people in Scotland celebrate desire and self-pride through dance and music. 4m; VHS. **A:** College-Adult. **P:** Education. **U:** Institution. **Gen-Edu:** Asia, Dance, Music. **Acq:** Purchase, Rent/Lease. **Dist:** Women Make Movies. $150.00.

The Bharvad Predicament 1987
Outlines the causes of the conflict between the local, landholding farmers and the Bharvad cattle herdsmen in Dhrangadhra, located in northern India. Illustrates how the region is in a particularly dry season and the main battle is over the use of land and water. Also explains how the farmers appear to have the support of the government. Emphasis is placed on how geography, natural resources, and governmental policies affects the survival of certain ethnic groups and cultures. 50m; VHS. **A:** Adult. **P:** Education. **U:** Institution, Home. **Gen-Edu:** Documentary Films, India, Agriculture. **Acq:** Purchase, Rent/Lease. **Dist:** Documentary Educational Resources. $245.00.

Bhavai: Folk Theater of Gujarat 1994
Explores the history, development, and present status of the Bhavai form of Sanskrit theatre as practiced by the Taragala community. 23m; VHS. **A:** Adult. **P:** Education. **U:** Institution. **Fin-Art:** Theater. **Acq:** Purchase. **Dist:** Insight Media. $199.00.

Bhowani Junction 1956 — ★★
A half-Indian, half-English woman is torn between her country and the British officer she loves in post-colonial India. Great cinematography. Based on a book by John Masters. 110m; VHS, DVD, Wide. **C:** Ava Gardner; Stewart Granger; Bill Travers; Abraham Sofaer; Francis Matthews; Marne Maitland; Peter Illing; Edward Chapman; Freda Jackson; Lionel Jeffries; Directed by George Cukor; Written by Ivan Moffat; Cinematography by Frederick A. (Freddie) Young; Music by Miklos Rozsa. **Pr:** MGM. **A:** Jr. High-Adult. **P:** Entertainment. **U:** Home. **Mov-Ent:** Drama, India, Romance. **Acq:** Purchase. **Dist:** WarnerArchive.com. $19.98.

Bhutan: Buddha-Kings of Dragon Country 1999
Examines the early history of Bhutan as an outpost of Tibetan monasteries, the struggle for power between secular and religious powers and its modern changes. 35m; VHS. **A:** Jr. High-Adult. **P:** Education. **U:** Home, Institution. **Gen-Edu:** Education, Geography, Asia. **Acq:** Purchase. **Dist:** Thomas S. Klise Co. $64.00.

Bhutan: People of the Thunder Dragon 1987
A look at Bhutan, a country trying to modernize while keeping its culture and values intact. 27m; VHS, 3/4 U. **Pr:** United Nations Development Program. **A:** Jr. High-Adult. **P:** Education. **U:** Institution. **Gen-Edu:** Documentary Films, Asia. **Acq:** Rent/Lease. **Dist:** New Dimension Media. $40.00.

Bhutan—Himalayan Cultural Diary 1999
Examines the culture and challenges of Bhutan, the easternmost country astride the Himalayan mountains. 55m; VHS. **A:** Jr. High-Adult. **P:** Education. **U:** Home, Institution. **Gen-Edu:** Education, Geography, Asia. **Acq:** Purchase. **Dist:** Thomas S. Klise Co. $64.00.

Bhutto 2010
Biography of Benazir Bhutto, who served as prime minister of Pakistan and was the first woman ever elected as the leader of a Muslim country. 111m; DVD. **A:** Sr. High-Adult. **P:** Entertainment. **U:** Home. **Mov-Ent:** Biography: Politics, Documentary Films, Asia. **Acq:** Purchase. **Dist:** First Run Features. $27.95.

Biba 197?
Biba, a woman who has lived through many wars in the Middle East, is the subject of this documentary on life in a small Israeli farming community. 60m; VHS, 3/4 U, Special order formats. **TV Std:** NTSC, PAL, SECAM. **Pr:** Alden Films. **A:** Sr. High-Adult. **P:** Education. **U:** Institution, Home, SURA. **Gen-Edu:** Israel, War--General, Documentary Films. **Acq:** Purchase, Rent/Lease. **Dist:** Alden Films. $50.00.

The Bible 1966 — ★
Bloated, even by religious epic standards, Huston's drama covers the first 22 chapters of Genesis. So you get the Creation, Adam and Eve, Noah and the ark, the flood, the Tower of Babel, and Abraham, among other would-be spectacles. 174m; VHS, DVD, Blu-Ray, Wide. **C:** Michael Parks; Ulla Bergryd; Richard Harris; Stephen Boyd; George C. Scott; Ava Gardner; Peter O'Toole; Franco Nero; John Huston; Narrated by John Huston; Directed by John Huston; Written by Christopher Fry; Vittorio Bonicelli; Cinematography by Giuseppe Rotunno; Music by Toshiro Mayuzumi. **Pr:** Dino De Laurentiis. **A:** Primary-Adult. **P:** Entertainment. **U:** Home. **Mov-Ent. Acq:** Purchase. **Dist:** Fox Home Entertainment.

The Bible: A Literary Heritage 1970
Dramatized examples of literary forms found in the Bible. Concluding sequences show the Bible's influence on Western art and culture. 27m; VHS, 3/4 U. **C:** Donald Pleasence. **Pr:** Learning Corporation of America. **A:** Sr. High-College. **P:** Education. **U:** Institution, SURA. **L:** English, Spanish. **Gen-Edu:** Bible, Literature, Education. **Acq:** Purchase, Rent/Lease. **Dist:** Phoenix Learning Group.

The Bible and Archeology 1979
A series of six untitled programs making up an in-depth study of archeological discoveries as they relate to the Bible. Programs are available individually. 27m; VHS, 3/4 U. **C:** Narrated by Dr. Jack Lewis. **Pr:** International Video Bible Lessons. **A:** Jr. High-Adult. **P:** Religious. **U:** Institution, CCTV, CATV, BCTV, Home. **Gen-Edu:** Bible, Archaeology. **Acq:** Purchase, Rent/Lease. **Dist:** Gospel Services, Inc.

The Bible and Gun Club 1996 — ★★
Foul-mouthed look at the wasted lives of five middle age traveling salesmen who sell, you guessed it, bibles and guns. There's a turf war between the Anaheim, CA and the Las Vegas branches of the club, there's a sales convention, the salesmen try to sell their goods to the real-life denizens of a poor trailer park, there's a porn shoot. There's a number of shoot-outs and to say the least, the salesmen are not politically correct—they're racist, sexist losers. It's depressing and disturbing and highlighted by some spot-on acting. Harris' debut feature. 87m/B/W; VHS. **C:** Andy Kallok; Don Yanan; Julian Ott; Al Schuerman; Robert Blumenthal; Directed by Daniel J. Harris; Written by Daniel J. Harris; Cinematography by Alex Vendler; Music by Shawn Patterson. **Pr:** Ariel Perets; Pierre Sevigny; Daniel J. Harris; Big in Vegas Pictures; Umagumma Entertainment. **A:** College-Adult. **P:** Entertainment. **U:** Home. **Mov-Ent:** Men. **Acq:** Purchase. **Dist:** Not Yet Released.

The Bible and Literature: A Personal View from Northrop Frye 1982
Renowned literary scholar Northrop Frye studies the Bible as a literary work, concentrating on the aspects of narrative, imagery, and the nature of revelation. Programs are available individually. 30m; VHS, 3/4 U. **Pr:** University of Toronto. **A:** College-Adult. **P:** Education. **U:** Institution, CCTV. **Gen-Edu:** Literature, Bible. **Acq:** Purchase, Rent/Lease. **Dist:** University of Toronto.
Indiv. Titles: 1. Introduction: An Approach 2. The Shape of the Bible 3. Images of Paradise: Trees and Water 4. Parody and Manifest Demonic: Trees and Water 5. Sexual Imagery: Bride and Bridegroom 6. The Great Whore and the Forgiven Harlot 7. - 8. Pastoral and Agricultural Imagery: Parts One and Two 9. The World of Angels 10. Leviathan, Dragons and the Anti-Christ 11. The Hero from Across the Sea 12. The Double Mirror: Exodus and the Gospel 13. The Metaphor of Kingship 14. King, Priest and Prophet 15. The Question of Primogeniture 16. Genesis: In the Beginning 17. Genesis: Creation of the Sexes 18. Exodus: A Revolutionary Heritage 19. Law: Ordering a Society 20. Wisdom: The Proverb 21. Wisdom: Playing Before God 22. Ecclesiastes: Vanity of Vanities 23. Job: A Test 24. Job: The Question of Tragedy 25. Job: Restored Humanity 26. The Language of Proclamation: Style and Rhythm in the Bible 27. The Gospel: Rewriting the Commandments 28. Revelation: Removing the Veil 29. Revelation: After the Ego Disappears 30. Conclusion: The Language of Love.

The Bible and Science 1979
A series of six untitled programs making up an in-depth study of science and how it relates to the Bible. Programs are available individually. 27m; VHS, 3/4 U. **C:** Narrated by Dr. Virgil Trout. **Pr:** International Video Bible Lessons. **A:** Jr. High-Adult. **P:** Religious. **U:** Institution, CCTV, CATV, BCTV, Home. **Gen-Edu:** Bible, Science. **Acq:** Purchase, Rent/Lease. **Dist:** Gospel Services, Inc.

The Bible as Literature, Part 1 1973
Examines some of the literary masterpieces in the Old Testament, including the story of the Creation, Noah's Ark, and the Ten Commandments. 27m; VHS, 3/4 U. **Pr:** Fred Denbeaux; Encyclopedia Britannica Educational Corporation. **A:** Sr. High-College. **P:** Education. **U:** Institution, SURA. **Gen-Edu:** Bible, Literature. **Acq:** Purchase, Rent/Lease, Trade-in. **Dist:** Encyclopedia Britannica.

The Bible as Literature, Part 2 1974
Examines the Old Testament as a source of history, lyric, poetry, and protest literature. 24m; VHS, 3/4 U. **Pr:** Fred Denbeaux; Encyclopedia Britannica Educational Corporation. **A:** Sr. High-College. **P:** Education. **U:** Institution, SURA. **Gen-Edu:** Bible, History, Literature. **Acq:** Purchase, Rent/Lease, Trade-in. **Dist:** Encyclopedia Britannica.

Bible Geography 1979
A series of ten untitled programs making up an in-depth study of the geography of the Bible lands. Programs are available individually. 27m; VHS, 3/4 U. **C:** Narrated by Don DeLukie. **Pr:** International Video Bible Lessons. **A:** Jr. High-Adult. **P:** Religious. **U:** Institution, CCTV, CATV, BCTV, Home. **Gen-Edu:** Documentary Films, Geography, Bible. **Acq:** Purchase, Rent/Lease. **Dist:** Gospel Services, Inc.

Bible Plays: Volume 1 ???? (Unrated)
Animated children's religious television series with play director Donovan as he instructs his theater class with their biblical plays and in life. Four segments: "David and Goliath," "Jonah and the Whale," "Daniel and the Lions' Den," and "Samson and Delilah." ??m; DVD. **A:** Family. **P:** Education. **U:** Institution, Home. **Mov-Ent:** Religion, Children, Children's Shows. **Acq:** Purchase. **Dist:** Bridgestone Multimedia Group Inc. $10.36.

Bible Plays: Volume 2 ???? (Unrated)
Animated children's religious television series with play director Donovan as he instructs his theater class with their biblical plays and in life. Four segments: "Noah's Ark," "The Battle of Jericho," "Shadrach, Meshach, Abednego," and "The Good Samaritan." ??m; DVD. **A:** Family. **P:** Education. **U:** Institution, Home. **Mov-Ent:** Religion, Children, Children's Shows. **Acq:** Purchase. **Dist:** Bridgestone Multimedia Group Inc. $10.36.

The Bible: Search for Truth ????
Stunning photography and 3-D computer-animated re-enactments provide background of the actual people, places, and events of the Bible. Also discusses the connections between Holy Scripture and ancient civilizations. 50m; VHS. **A:** Family. **P:** Religious. **U:** Home, Institution. **Gen-Edu:** Religion, History--Ancient. **Acq:** Purchase. **Dist:** Ignatius Press. $14.95.

Bible Stories for Children 1985
Easy to follow stories from the Old and New Testaments are presented. 100m; VHS. **A:** Primary-Jr. High. **P:** Religious. **U:** Institution, Home. **Chl-Juv:** Bible. **Acq:** Purchase. **Dist:** Church of Jesus Christ of Latter-day Saints. $8.00.
Indiv. Titles: 1. Volume 1 (Creation through King David) 2. Volume 2 (King Solomon through Christ's Ministry) 3. Volume 3 (Ministry of Christ, Ministry of Paul).

Bible Stories on Video 1982
Each one of these tapes contains four Bible stories adapted to a filmstrip format, then transferred to video. 40m; VHS, 3/4 U. **Pr:** CPH. **A:** Family. **P:** Religious. **U:** Institution, Home. **Gen-Edu.** **Acq:** Purchase. **Dist:** Concordia Publishing House. $14.95.
Indiv. Titles: 1. Children of the Bible 2. Bible Story Time: Old Testament Stories 3. Bible Story Time: New Testament Stories 4. Stories About Joseph.

Bible Stories Told in Sign Language 1988
Lou Fant signs seven stories based on Bible legends. 30m; VHS, 3/4 U; Signed. **Pr:** Joyce Media. **A:** Family. **P:** Education. **U:** Institution, Home. **Gen-Edu:** Religion, Bible, Storytelling. **Acq:** Purchase. **Dist:** Joyce Media Inc. $69.00.
Indiv. Titles: 1. Noah 2. David and Goliath 3. Moses 4. Abraham and Isaac 5. Joseph, Part I 6. Joseph, Part II 7. The Christmas Story.

The Bible Unearthed: The Making of a Religion 2006 (Unrated)
Explores the Bible's origins by looking at archaeological digs in Egypt, Jordan, and Israel. 208m; DVD. **A:** Jr. High-Adult. **P:** Entertainment. **U:** Home. **Mov-Ent:** Bible, Documentary Films, Religion. **Acq:** Purchase. **Dist:** First Run Features; Eagle Rock Entertainment Inc. $29.95.

The Bible: What's It All About? 1987
The Bible is explained for junior high school students. 90m; VHS, 3/4 U. **Pr:** Franciscan Communications. **A:** Jr. High. **P:** Religious. **U:** Institution, SURA. **Gen-Edu:** Bible. **Acq:** Purchase, Rent/Lease. **Dist:** St. Anthony Messenger Press. $100.00.
Indiv. Titles: 1. Where Did It Come From?/Who Wrote It?/Did It Really Happen Like That? 2. What Is the Old Testament?/What Is the New Testament?/How Does It Help Me Get Closer to God?.

Biblical Disasters 2005
Are biblical accounts of floods, famine, epidemics, and destruction fact or fiction? Archeologists and biblical scholars examine evidence to support their positions. 100m; DVD. **A:** Jr. High-Adult. **P:** Entertainment. **U:** Home. **Gen-Edu:** Documentary Films, Bible. **Acq:** Purchase. **Dist:** A&E Television Networks L.L.C.

Biblical Insight on Child Development 1989
Mrs. Yearick explains how children develop, according to the Bible. 45m; VHS. **Pr:** Bob Jones University. **A:** Sr. High-Adult. **P:** Religious. **U:** Institution, SURA. **Gen-Edu:** Children. **Acq:** Purchase. **Dist:** Bob Jones University; Golden Book Video. $24.95.

The Biblical Pattern of Child Discipline 1989
A look at how the Bible says to and not to raise children. 160m; VHS. **Pr:** Bob Jones University. **A:** Family. **P:** Education. **U:** Institution, SURA. **Gen-Edu:** Parenting. **Acq:** Purchase. **Dist:** Bob Jones University. $39.95.

The Biblical Perspective on Health and Grooming 1989
A religious look at grooming, physical appearance, dieting, and exercise. 48m; VHS. **Pr:** Bob Jones University. **A:** Family. **P:** Religious. **U:** Institution, SURA. **Hea-Sci:** Fitness/Exercise. **Acq:** Purchase. **Dist:** Bob Jones University. $24.95.

The Biblical Role of Women 1985
A program comparing the current roles of women and their ancient Biblical counterparts. 29m; VHS, 3/4 U. **Pr:** Bob Jones University. **A:** Sr. High-Adult. **P:** Religious. **U:** Institution, SURA. **Gen-Edu:** Documentary Films, Religion, Women. **Acq:** Purchase. **Dist:** Bob Jones University.

The Biblical View of God, Jesus and the Holy Spirit 1979
A series of three lessons making up an in-depth study on what the Bible says about God, Jesus, and the Holy Spirit. Programs are available individually. 27m; VHS, 3/4 U. **C:** Narrated by Dr. Hugo McCord. **Pr:** International Video Bible Lessons. **A:** Jr. High-Adult. **P:** Religious. **U:** Institution, CCTV, CATV, BCTV, Home. **Gen-Edu:** Bible. **Acq:** Purchase, Rent/Lease. **Dist:** Gospel Services, Inc.
Indiv. Titles: 1. Biblical View of God 2. Biblical View of Jesus 3. Biblical View of the Holy Spirit.

Bicentennial Man 1999 (PG) — ★★★½
Robin Williams is Andrew, a domestic robot of the near-future. When he's purchased by the Martin family, they notice that he's different than most robots. He exhibits compassion, as well as other human qualities. Led by Sir, the father (Niell) they help to further Andrew's growth. As time goes on, Andrew continues to develop past his programming, and eventually seeks his freedom and the pursuit of a more human form. The first hour deals mostly with a very leisurely character development, with some amusing moments. The problems occur when the film turns to the serious questions of immortality, defining humanity, and the rights of artificial entities. Director Columbus opts for sentiment and empty platitudes instead of exploring the questions the film raises. 131m; VHS, DVD, Wide, CC. **C:** Robin Williams; Embeth Davidtz; Sam Neill; Wendy Crewson; Hallie Kate Eisenberg; Oliver Platt; Stephen (Steve) Root; Lynne Thigpen; Bradley Whitford; Kiersten Warren; John Michael Higgins; George D. Wallace; Directed by Chris Columbus; Written by Nicholas Kazan; Cinematography by Phil Meheux; Music by James Horner. **Pr:** Touchstone Pictures; Columbia Pictures; 1492 Pictures; Buena Vista. **A:** Jr. High-Adult. **P:** Entertainment. **U:** Home. **Mov-Ent:** Science Fiction, Technology. **Acq:** Purchase. **Dist:** Buena Vista Home Entertainment.

Bickford Shmeckler's Cool Ideas 2006 (R) — ★★
Bickford (Fugit) is a loner college student who spends his time filing a notebook with his revelatory philosophical theories and ideas. At a party, Sarah (Wilde) steals the book, sending Bick on a wild journey to get it back, finding out in the process that it has taken on a popularity of its own among the campus "intelligensia." Mixes more big ideas than you'd expect into your basic raunchy college romp. 80m; DVD. **C:** Patrick Fugit; Olivia Wilde; John Cho; Matthew Lillard; Cheryl Hines; Directed by Scott Lew; Written by Scott Lew; Cinematography by Lowell Peterson; Music by John Swihart. **A:** Sr. High-Adult. **P:** Entertainment. **U:** Home. **Mov-Ent:** Philosophy & Ideology. **Acq:** Purchase. **Dist:** Screen Media Ventures, LLC.

Biculturalism and Acculturation Among Latinos 1992
Discusses the struggle Latinos face between their heritage vs. modern American society. Dispels common misperceptions and beliefs concerning the unique culture. 28m; VHS. **Pr:** KLRN Austin. **A:** Jr. High-Sr. High. **P:** Education. **U:** Institution. **Gen-Edu:** Hispanic Culture, Human Relations, Sociology. **Acq:** Purchase, Rent/Lease. **Dist:** Films for the Humanities & Sciences. $149.00.

Bicycle Compliance Test 1976
More than 20 test methods under the Bicycle Safety Standard, issued by the U.S. Consumer Product Safety Commission, are demonstrated. Included are tests for both frame strength and braking performance. 45m; VHS, 3/4 U, Special order formats. **Pr:** Office of Public Affairs Civil Service. **A:** Adult. **P:** Education. **U:** Institution, SURA. **Spo-Rec:** Sports--General, Bicycling. **Acq:** Purchase. **Dist:** National Audiovisual Center.

Bicycle Dancin' 1985
Learn how to pull your favorite stunts on bikes, and pick up some safety tips, too! 16m; VHS, 3/4 U, Special order formats. **Pr:** Harvey Edwards. **A:** Primary-Sr. High. **P:** Instruction. **U:** Institution, Home. **How-Ins:** Bicycling, Safety Education. **Acq:** Purchase, Rent/Lease. **Dist:** Edwards Films. $32.50.

Bicycle Racing U.S.A. 1985
A marathon viewing experience for those who love speed bike racing. 30m; VHS. **Pr:** Video Travel, Inc. **A:** Jr. High-Adult. **P:** Entertainment. **U:** Home. **Spo-Rec:** Sports--General, Bicycling. **Acq:** Purchase. **Dist:** Vivid Publisher; Edwards Films.

Bicycle Repair Made Easy 1989
This tape shows a few basic repair and maintenance techniques for bike owners. 30m; VHS. **Pr:** Increase. **A:** Jr. High-Adult. **P:** Instruction. **U:** Home. **How-Ins:** Bicycling. **Acq:** Purchase. **Dist:** Silver Mine Video Inc. $29.95.

Bicycle Safety & General Maintenance 1988
Cycling is a good way to get your exercise in, but only if it is done safely. 25m; VHS, 3/4 U. **Pr:** Champions on Film. **A:** Primary-Adult. **P:** Instruction. **U:** Institution, CCTV, Home. **Spo-Rec:** Bicycling. **Acq:** Purchase. **Dist:** School-Tech Inc. $18.95.

Bicycle Safety Camp 1990
Sam Sprocket teaches kids ages 6-12 to wear a helmet with pride and other tips on bicycle safety in this musical video. 25m; VHS. **A:** Primary-Jr. High. **P:** Instruction. **U:** Home. **Chl-Juv:** Bicycling, Safety Education, Children. **Acq:** Purchase. **Dist:** ACTIVIDEO; Tapeworm Video Distributors Inc.; Karol Media. $14.95.

Bicycle Safety: You Can Prevent an Accident 1975
Lloyd Haynes presents information on all phases of safe bicycling. 19m; VHS, 3/4 U. **Pr:** Lee Stanley. **A:** Primary-Jr. High. **P:** Education. **U:** Institution, Home, SURA. **Spo-Rec:** Sports--General, Bicycling. **Acq:** Purchase, Rent/Lease, Duplication License. **Dist:** Pyramid Media. $195.00.

The Bicycle Thief 1948 (Unrated) — ★★★★
A world classic and indisputable masterpiece about an Italian workman who finds a job, only to have the bike he needs for work stolen; he and his son search Rome for it. A simple story that seems to contain the whole of human experience, and the masterpiece of Italian neo-realism. Based on the book by Luigi Bartolini. In Italian with English subtitles. 90m/B/W; VHS, DVD. **C:** Lamberto Maggiorani; Lianella Carell; Enzo Staiola; Elena Altieri; Vittorio Antonucci; Gino Saltamerenda; Fausto Guerzoni; Directed by Vittorio De Sica; Written by Vittorio De Sica; Cesare Zavattini; Cinematography by Carlo Montuori; Music by Alessandro Cicognini. **Pr:** PDS-ENIC. **A:** Family. **P:** Entertainment. **U:** Home. **L:** English, Italian. **Mov-Ent:** Classic Films, Italy, Bicycling. **Awds:** Oscars '49: Foreign Film; British Acad. '49: Film; Golden Globes '50: Foreign Film; Natl. Bd. of Review '49: Director (De Sica); N.Y. Film Critics '49: Foreign Film. **Acq:** Purchase. **Dist:** Facets Multimedia Inc.; Tapeworm Video Distributors Inc. $69.95.

Bicycling Videos 1987
A series for bicycle mavens, which instruct on repair and journeying. 60m; VHS. **Pr:** Do It Yourself Inc. **A:** Sr. High-Adult. **P:** Instruction. **U:** Institution, Home. **Spo-Rec:** Sports--General, Bicycling. **Acq:** Purchase. **Dist:** Karol Media; Do It Yourself, Inc./D.I.Y. Video Corp. $19.95.
Indiv. Titles: 1. Anybody's Bike Video (Bike Repair) 2. Bike Tripping.

Bidder 70 2013 (Unrated)
Examines the civil disobediance efforts of Tim DeChristopher who won the right to drill on 22,000 previously untouched acres in Utah at a federal auction in 2008. Because he bid without intending to use these rights, he was given a federal prison term but brought issues of climate justice to the fore. 73m; DVD. **A:** Sr. High-Adult. **P:** Entertainment. **U:** Home. **Mov-Ent:** Miners & Mining, Documentary Films, U.S. States. **Acq:** Purchase. **Dist:** First Run Features. $24.95.

Bidding for Office-Who Should Pay for Elections? NewsMatters 1998
Explains basic facts about issue ads, soft money, lobbyists, and PACs. 19m; VHS. **A:** Jr. High-Sr. High. **P:** Education. **U:** Institution. **Gen-Edu:** Politics & Government, U.S. States. **Acq:** Purchase. **Dist:** Zenger Media. $99.00.

Bidu Sayao in Opera and Song 1990
An unforgettable performance from the Voice of Firestone telecasts in 1951-52. Sayao performs selections from Manon, Madama Butterfly, Gianni Schicchi, and many popular songs. 45m; VHS. **Pr:** Video Artists International. **A:** Family. **P:** Entertainment. **U:** Home. **Fin-Art:** Performing Arts, Music--Classical, Opera. **Acq:** Purchase. **Dist:** Music Video Distributors; Video Artists International; Corinth Films Inc. $29.95.

Bienvenidos a Costa Rica 19??
Takes a tour of the country of Costa Rica, including the capital of San Jose, the city of Cartago, and the Irazu Volcano. Narrated in simple Spanish. Comes with teacher's manual. 11m; VHS. **A:** Jr. High-Adult. **P:** Education. **U:** Institution. **L:** Spanish. **Gen-Edu:** Central America, Travel, Hispanic Culture. **Acq:** Purchase. **Dist:** Educational Video Network. $29.95.

Biff Baker U.S.A.: Earliest Episodes 1952
Two episodes of the adventure series in which Biff becomes involved with espionage behind the Iron Curtain: "Alpine Assignment" and "Grey Market." 55m/B/W; VHS. **C:** Alan Hale, Jr; Randy Stuart; Lee Marvin; Charles Bronson; Rex Evans. **A:** Family. **P:** Entertainment. **U:** Home. **Mov-Ent:** Television Series. **Acq:** Purchase. **Dist:** Moviecraft Home Video. $19.95.

Biff Baker U.S.A., Vol. 2 1952
One episode, "Saigon Incident" finds Biff and his wife Lois in Vietnam, while the other, "Mona Lisa" is set in Paris. 55m/B/W; VHS. **C:** Alan Hale, Jr; Randy Stuart; Alan Napier; Maurice Marsac. **A:** Family. **P:** Entertainment. **U:** Home. **Mov-Ent:** Television Series. **Acq:** Purchase. **Dist:** Moviecraft Home Video. $19.95.

Big 1988 (PG) — ★★★½
13-year-old Josh makes a wish at a carnival fortune-teller to be "big." When he wakes up the next morning he finds that he suddenly won't fit into his clothes and his mother doesn't recognize him. Until he finds a cure, he must learn to live in the adult world—complete with job (in a toy firm), Manhattan apartment, and romance. Perkins is wonderful as a cynical fellow employee who warms to the new guy's naivete, while Hanks is totally believable as the little boy inside a man's body. Marshall directs with authority and the whole thing clicks from the beginning. 98m; VHS, DVD, Blu-Ray; Open Captioned. **C:** Tom Hanks; Elizabeth Perkins; John Heard; Robert Loggia; Jared Rushton; David Moscow; Jon Lovitz; Mercedes Ruehl; Directed by Penny Marshall; Written by Gary Ross; Cinematography by Michael Ballhaus; Music by Howard Shore. **Pr:** 20th Century-Fox; Gracie Films. **A:** Jr. High-Adult. **P:** Entertainment. **U:** Home. **Mov-Ent:** Comedy-Drama, Fantasy, Toys. **Awds:**

Golden Globes '89: Actor--Mus./Comedy (Hanks); L.A. Film Critics '88: Actor (Hanks). **Acq:** Purchase. **Dist:** Home Vision Cinema. $19.98.

The Big A 1987
Cartoonist Don Arioli hosts this ten series program instructing children in the process of looking at, talking about, and creating art. Children work with Arioli in his studio, explore museums and galleries, and meet with artists. Teacher's guide available. 15m; VHS, CC. **A:** Primary. **P:** Education. **U:** Institution. **Gen-Edu:** Art & Artists, Children. **Acq:** Purchase. **Dist:** GPN Educational Media. $199.50.
Indiv. Titles: 1. Telling a Story in Art 2. Getting Ideas 3. Exploring Ideas 4. Tools and Materials 5. Teamwork 6. Lines, Shapes, Colors and Textures 7. Putting It Together 8. What Does It Mean? 9. I Like It Because... 10. Different Ways of Seeing.

The Big Alligator River 1979 (Unrated) — **Bomb!**
A tourist resort in Africa is attacked by a giant croc the local natives worship as a god. The croc eats a few of them, and they take that as a sign to unleash Hell. And that's pretty much what it would feel like sitting through this stinker. 89m; DVD. **C:** Claudio Cassinelli; Mel Ferrer; Romano Puppo; Richard Johnson; Barbara Bach; Silvia Collatina; George Eastman; Directed by Sergio Martino; Written by Sergio Martino; Cesare Frugoni; Ernesto Gastaldi; Mara Maryl; Cinematography by Giancarlo Ferrando; Music by Stelvio Cipriani. **A:** Sr. High-Adult. **P:** Entertainment. **U:** Home. **L:** English, Italian. **Mov-Ent**. **Acq:** Purchase. **Dist:** Mya Communication. $19.98.

Big and Hairy 1998 — ★½
When Picasso Dewlap and his family move from Chicago to a small town, the kid has trouble making friends (no wonder with that name). Then he joins the school basketball team. However, Picasso sucks. But after he meets a teen bigfoot (nicknamed Ed) who just happens to be a natural at hoops, Picasso and his hairy friend become team heroes. Based on the book by Brian Daly. 94m; VHS, DVD, CC. **C:** Richard Thomas; Donnelly Rhodes; Robert Karl Burke; Trevor Jones; Chilton Crane; Directed by Philip Spink; Cinematography by Peter Benison; Music by Daryl Bennett; Jim Guttridge. **A:** Family. **P:** Entertainment. **U:** Home. **Mov-Ent:** Basketball, Sports--Fiction: Comedy, Education. **Acq:** Purchase. **Dist:** Showtime Networks Inc.

Big and Little Number: Scientific Notation 1980
One of the "Mathematics for Modern Living" series, a program designed for people's mathematical needs that arise in everyday living. 30m; VHS, 3/4 U, Q. **Pr:** Magna Systems. **A:** College-Adult. **P:** Instruction. **U:** Institution, CCTV, CATV, BCTV. **Gen-Edu:** Mathematics, How-To. **Acq:** Purchase. **Dist:** Magna Systems, Inc.

The Big Attack/Combat Sergeant 1958
Two episodes of early television war series include "Big Slim" from the series "The Big Attack" and "All Faces East" from the series "Combat Sergeant." 55m; VHS. **C:** Jim Hutton. **A:** Family. **P:** Entertainment. **U:** Home. **Mov-Ent:** Television Series. **Acq:** Purchase. **Dist:** Moviecraft Home Video. $19.95.

Big Audio Dynamite: BAD 1 & 2 199?
Features 11 hits from Big Audio Dynamite's two albums. Includes "Contact" and "Sightsee M.C.!" 53m; VHS. **A:** Jr. High-Adult. **P:** Entertainment. **U:** Home. **Mov-Ent:** Music Video, Music--Pop/Rock. **Acq:** Purchase. **Dist:** Sony Music Entertainment Inc.; Music Video Distributors. $19.95.

Big Bad John 1990 (PG-13) — ★½
Some good ol' boys ride around in trucks as they get into a variety of shootouts. The soundtrack includes music by Willie Nelson, The Charlie Daniels Band, and others. 91m; VHS, DVD. **C:** Jimmy Dean; Ned Beatty; Jack Elam; Bo Hopkins; Romy Windsor; Doug English; John Dennis Johnston; Anne Lockhart; Jeffery Osterhage; Jerry Potter; Red Steagall; Directed by Burt Kennedy; Written by Joseph Berry; Cinematography by Ken Lamkin; Music by Ken Sutherland. **Pr:** Red Steagall; Red Steagall; Red River Film Company. **A:** Preschool. **P:** Entertainment. **U:** Home. **Mov-Ent**. **Acq:** Purchase. **Dist:** Image Entertainment Inc.

Big Bad Love 2002 (R) — ★★
Howard's ambitious directorial debut is an adaptation of the short stories of Larry Brown. Vietnam vet and would-be writer Leon Barlow's (Howard), obsession with writing about his constant melancholy and getting his stories published alienates him from everything around him, especially his family, which includes his terminally ill daughter. He seems to get away with his behavior through his wry wit and some past misfortunes. Howard gives in to his most poetic and literary impulses, which results in some breathtaking scenes alongside some annoyingly self-indulgent ones. Not surprisingly, film is uneven, with some quality performances lifting the proceedings. 111m; VHS, DVD. **C:** Arliss Howard; Debra Winger; Paul LeMat; Angie Dickinson; Rosanna Arquette; Michael Parks; Voice(s) by Sigourney Weaver; Directed by Arliss Howard; Written by Arliss Howard; Jim Howard; Cinematography by Dr. Paul Ryan; Music by Tom Waits. **A:** Sr. High-Adult. **P:** Entertainment. **U:** Home. **Mov-Ent**. **Acq:** Purchase. **Dist:** MGM Home Entertainment.

Big Bad Mama 1974 (R) — ★★½
Tough and sexy machine-gun toting mother moves her two nubile daughters out of Texas during the Depression, and they all turn to robbing banks as a means of support while creating sharp testosterone increases among the local men. "Wild Palm" Dickinson has notable nude scene with Captain Kirk. "Big Bad Mama 2" arrived some 13 years later. 83m; VHS, DVD. **C:** Angie Dickinson; William Shatner; Tom Skerritt; Susan Sennett; Robbie Lee; Sally Kirkland; Noble Willingham; Royal Dano; Dick Miller; Joan Prather; Tom Signorelli; Directed by Steve Carver; Written by William W. Norton, Sr.; Frances Doel; Cinematography by Bruce Logan; Music by David Grisman. **Pr:** Roger Corman; New World Pictures. **A:** Sr. High-Adult. **P:** Entertainment. **U:** Home. **Mov-Ent:** Action-Adventure. **Acq:** Purchase. **Dist:** Alpha Video; Movies Unlimited.

Big Bad Mama 2 1987 (R) — ★½
Belated Depression-era sequel to the 1974 Roger Corman gangster film, where the pistol-packin' matriarch battles a crooked politician with the help of her two daughters. 85m; VHS, DVD. **C:** Angie Dickinson; Robert Culp; Danielle Brisebois; Julie McCullough; Bruce Glover; Jeff Yagher; Jacque Lynn Colton; Ebbe Roe Smith; Charles Cyphers; Directed by Jim Wynorski; Written by Jim Wynorski; R.J. Robertson; Cinematography by Robert New; Music by Chuck Cirino. **Pr:** Roger Corman; Concorde Pictures. **A:** Preschool. **P:** Entertainment. **U:** Home. **Mov-Ent**. **Acq:** Purchase. **Dist:** MGM Home Entertainment. $14.95.

The Big Bad Swim 2006 (Unrated) — ★★½
Needing some stress relief from work and marital problems, Amy (Brewster) decides to join an adult swim class held at a local community center. In a mixed and quirky group, Amy befriends Jordan (Weixler), a croupier and part-time stripper who has the hots for their hunky-but-insecure instructor Noah (Branson). Sharp comedy that focuses on characters rather than situations. 93m; DVD. **C:** Paget Brewster; Joanna Adler; Jeff Branson; Jess Weixler; Grant Aleksander; Raviv (Ricky) Ullman; Avi Setton; Todd Sussman; Michael Mosley; Directed by Ishai Setton; Written by Daniel Schechter; Cinematography by Josh Silfen; Music by Chad Kelly. **A:** Sr. High-Adult. **P:** Entertainment. **U:** Home. **Mov-Ent:** Swimming. **Acq:** Purchase. **Dist:** Echo Bridge Home Entertainment.

The Big Bad Wolf 1990
The Three Little Pigs join Little Red Riding Hood in thwarting the Big, Bad Wolf. 9m; VHS, 3/4 U, EJ, Special order formats. **TV Std:** NTSC, PAL, SECAM. **Pr:** Disney Educational Productions. **A:** Preschool-Primary. **P:** Entertainment. **U:** Institution, CCTV, SURA. **Chl-Juv:** Animation & Cartoons, Fairy Tales. **Acq:** Purchase, Rent/Lease. **Dist:** Phoenix Learning Group. $150.00.

Big Bad Wolf 2006 (R) — ★½
A kid steals the key to his father's cabin so he and his friends can get drunk and make out. Unfortunately the cabin is in the territory of a sleazy, wisecracking wolfman who enjoys offing strangers a little too much. 96m; DVD, Streaming. **C:** Trevor Duke-Moretz; Richard Tyson; Christopher Shyer; Clinton Howard; David Naughton; Kimberly J. Brown; Sarah Aldrich; Directed by Lance Dreesen; Written by Lance Dreesen; Cinematography by Stephen Crawford; Music by Dana Niu. **A:** Sr. High-Adult. **P:** Entertainment. **U:** Home. **L:** English. **Mov-Ent**. **Acq:** Purchase, Rent/Lease. **Dist:** Screen Media. $14.98 9.99.

Big Bad Wolves 2013 (Unrated) — ★★½
This tense Israeli thriller earns its twists and turns through character-driven plotting. A man named Gidi (Grad) suffers the unimaginable pain of having a kidnapped, mutilated, and murdered daughter. The main suspect, Dror (Keinan), is questioned but released. Gidi takes matters into his own hands, kidnapping Dror, and the majority of the film takes place in Gidi's basement with cop Miki (Ashkenazi), who was once an ally and is now also a hostage. Hebrew with subtitles. 110m; DVD, Blu-Ray. **C:** Lior Ashkenazi; Tzahi Grad; Rotem Keinan; Dov Glickman; Directed by Aharon Keshales; Navot Papushado; Written by Aharon Keshales; Navot Papushado; Cinematography by Giora Bejach; Music by Frank Ilfman. **Pr:** Magnet Releasing. **A:** Sr. High-Adult. **P:** Entertainment. **U:** Home. **L:** Hebrew. **Mov-Ent:** Crime Drama, Comedy--Black, Mystery & Suspense. **Acq:** Purchase. **Dist:** Magnolia Pictures.

Big Bag of $ 2009 (Unrated) — ★½
In this modern attempt at film noir, five people (and members of the audience) have their lives sent into a spiral of destruction and misery by an unclaimed bag of cash. The main moral seems to be that if you're poor, you're always one step away from murdering other people for money if you ever get the chance. 85m; DVD. **C:** Shonelle Blake; Anthony Clark; Rodney C. Cummings; Lisa Dewitt; Scott F. Evans; Eddie Goines; Lanre Idewu; Trisha Mann; Brian Marshall; Elise Matturi; Kenny McClain; Michael David Ricks; Nadirah Shakirah; Rico Simonini; Solari; Treallis; Calvin Walton; Directed by Scott F. Evans; Written by Scott F. Evans; Cinematography by Scott F. Evans; Music by Angela Burris; Stewart Hollins; Ovaciir. **A:** Sr. High-Adult. **P:** Entertainment. **U:** Home. **Mov-Ent**. **Acq:** Purchase. **Dist:** Maverick Entertainment. $16.98.

Big Band Ballroom Bash 199?
Twenty world-class competitive ballroom dancers jitterbug, foxtrot, and swing to the music of big band legends performed by the Artie Shaw Orchestra. Taped live at the grand ballroom at Boston's Sheraton Hotel & Towers. 90m; VHS. **C:** Hosted by Juliet Prowse; Bobby Short. **A:** Family. **P:** Entertainment. **U:** Home. **Mov-Ent:** Dance--Performance. **Acq:** Purchase. **Dist:** Signals Video. $19.95.

Big Bands at Disneyland 1984
The swinging big band sounds of Lionel Hampton, Woody Herman, and Cab Calloway are captured in these three concerts taped at Disneyland. 180m; VHS. **C:** Peter Marshall; Lionel Hampton; Woody Herman; Cab Calloway. **Pr:** Walt Disney Productions. **A:** Family. **P:** Entertainment. **U:** Home. **Mov-Ent:** Music--Performance, Music--Jazz. **Acq:** Purchase. **Dist:** Walt Disney Studios Home Entertainment, On Moratorium.

Big Bands, Vol. 107 1985
Concert footage from 1955 with Guy Lombardo and His Royal Canadians. Includes "St. Louis Blues," "Toot Toot Tootsie," "Now Is the Hour" and "Auld Lang Syne." 55m; VHS. **Pr:** Vitaphone et al. **A:** Family. **P:** Entertainment. **U:** Home. **Mov-Ent:** Music--Performance. **Acq:** Purchase. **Dist:** Music Video Distributors. $14.95.

The Big Bang 1979
A commonly accepted theory of creation is that a cosmic fireball exploded at the center of the universe some 20 billion years ago. 29m; VHS, 3/4 U. **Pr:** OECA. **A:** Sr. High-College. **P:** Education. **U:** Institution, SURA. **Hea-Sci:** Astronomy. **Acq:** Purchase. **Dist:** Home Vision Cinema.

The Big Bang 1990
The why's and the how's of sex, God, and the universe are probed for you here by filmmaker Toback. He queries the famous as well as the common and gets answers to our most perplexing issues. Full of wit and provocation. 81m; VHS. **C:** Darryl Dawkins; Don Simpson; Elaine Kaufman; Jose Torres; Directed by James Toback. **A:** Sr. High-Adult. **P:** Entertainment. **U:** Home. **Gen-Edu:** Documentary Films, Interviews, Sex & Sexuality. **Acq:** Purchase. **Dist:** Wellspring Media. $79.95.

The Big Bang 1994
Discusses the discovery and evolution of the "big bang" theory and current theories pertaining to the events that led to the beginning of the universe. 30m; VHS. **A:** Adult. **P:** Education. **U:** Institution. **Hea-Sci:** Astronomy. **Acq:** Purchase. **Dist:** RMI Media. $89.95.

The Big Bang 2011 (R) — ★
A Russian boxer hires L.A. PI Ned Cruz (Banderas) to find his girlfriend Lexie (Guillory)?and the millions of dollars worth of diamonds she's hiding. The job seems simple at first, but it isn't long before witnesses start turning up dead. Cruz becomes obsessed with finding Lexie, especially when the path leads him to two powerful men in the New Mexico desert plotting to destroy the world. Sounds thrilling, but without Banderas it's a complete bust. 101m; DVD, Blu-Ray. **C:** Antonio Banderas; Sam Elliot; Sienna Guillory; Jimmi Simpson; Autumn Reeser; James Van Der Beek; Thomas Kretschmann; Snoop Dogg; William Fichtner; Delroy Lindo; Robert Maillet; Directed by Tony Krantz; Written by Erik Jendresen; Cinematography by Shelly Johnson; Music by Johnny Marr. **Pr:** Tony Krantz; Erik Jendresen; Richard Rionda Del Castro; Big Bang Production; Flame Ventures; North by Northwest Entertainment; Anchor Bay Entertainment Inc. **A:** Sr. High-Adult. **P:** Entertainment. **U:** Home. **L:** English. **Mov-Ent:** Mystery & Suspense, Physics. **Acq:** Purchase. **Dist:** Anchor Bay Entertainment; Movies Unlimited.

The Big Bang and Other Creation Myths 1981
Animation and an original music score are used to portray a variety of creation myths and folktales from around the world. 11m; VHS, 3/4 U, Special order formats. **Pr:** Faith Hubley Productions. **A:** Sr. High-Adult. **P:** Education. **U:** Institution, Home, SURA. **Gen-Edu:** Folklore & Legends, Animation & Cartoons. **Acq:** Purchase, Rent/Lease, Duplication License. **Dist:** Pyramid Media. $195.00.

The Big Bang Theory: The Complete Fifth Season 2011 (Unrated)
Sheldon is miffed when mom comes to visit and won't cook for him because she's too busy attending physics lectures in "The Rhinitis Revelation," Sheldon goes to great lengths to meet his hero, Dr. Stephen Hawking in "The Hawking Excitation," and the gang puts together a wedding on the fly for Howard and Bernadette before Howard goes on his space mission in "The Countdown Reflection." 24 episodes. 498m; DVD, Blu-Ray. **A:** Sr. High-Adult. **P:** Entertainment. **U:** Home. **Mov-Ent:** Comedy--Screwball, Television Series, Scientists. **Acq:** Purchase. **Dist:** $19.73.

The Big Bang Theory: The Complete First Season 2007 (Unrated)
Television comedy series on CBS from 2007. Leonard (Galecki) and Sheldon (Parsons) are two alpha geeks at the top of their intellectual game as university physicists but when it comes to girls they are idiot savants. Fortunately fate steps in bringing a pretty new tenant to live in the apartment across the hall and an opportunity to further their education far beyond the classroom. Sheldon's obsessive-compulsive neurosis along with Leonard's hard fallen crush on Penny (Cuoco) keeps the comedy commencing. Sara Gilbert guest stars as geekette Leslie, and Laurie Metcalf plays Sheldon's fundamentalist mother. 17 episodes. 355m; DVD, Blu-Ray. **C:** Johnny Galecki; Jim Parsons; Kaley Cuoco; Simon Helberg. **A:** Sr. High-Adult. **P:** Entertainment. **U:** Home. **Mov-Ent:** Television Series. **Acq:** Purchase. **Dist:** Warner Home Video, Inc.

The Big Bang Theory: The Complete Fourth Season 2010
CBS 2007- comedy. Wolowitz enlists the help of George Takei in order to win back Bernadette, and Raj and Sheldon argue over office space in "The Hot Troll Deviation," the guys enter a costume competition as members of the Justice League and convince Penny's new boyfriend to join them in "The Justice League Recombination," in the "The Benefactor Factor," Sheldon forces Leonard to sweeten up a wealthy benefactor. 24 episodes. 529m; DVD, Blu-Ray. **C:** Johnny Galecki; Jim Parsons; Kaley Cuoco; Simon Helberg; Kunal Nayyar. **A:** Jr. High-Adult. **P:** Entertainment. **U:** Home. **Mov-Ent:** Television Series, Scientists. **Acq:** Purchase. **Dist:** Warner Home Video, Inc. $19.99.

The Big Bang Theory: The Complete Second Season 2008 (Unrated)
CBS situation comedy. The geeks and hot chick continue to influence each other in comedic and endearing ways. Sheldon turns Penny on to online gaming in "The Barbarian Sublimation" and she becomes seriously addicted. Fifteen minutes of fame goes to Raj's head in "The Griffin Equivalency" after he is

featured in a People magazine article. A female grad student becomes enamored with Sheldon in "The Cooper-Nowitzki Theorem," and when Leonard steals Howard's new lady in "The Lizard-Spock Expansion" their friendship is threatened. Highlights this season include the classic 'Rock, Paper, Scissors, Lizard, Spock' game, an over-caffeinated business venture, and a ground breaking Christmas gift exchange. 23 episodes. 481m; DVD, Blu-Ray. **C:** Jim Parsons; Johnny Galecki; Kaley Cuoco; Simon Helberg; Kunal Nayyar. **A:** Jr. High-Adult. **P:** Entertainment. **U:** Home. **Mov-Ent:** Television Series. **Acq:** Purchase. **Dist:** Warner Home Video, Inc. $44.99.

The Big Bang Theory: The Complete Sixth Season 2012 (Unrated)
CBS television series. "The Date Night Variable" has Raj accompanying Sheldon and Amy's date, as well as Leonard and Penny's date. In "The Decoupling Fluctuation", Penny is considering breaking up with Leonard. "The Higgs Boson Observation" features Sheldon desperate to revisit his old childhood research in hopes of winning a Nobel Prize. Howard returns to Earth from the Space Station in "The Re-Entry Minimization". The gang attends a Halloween party in "The Holographic Excitation" and Sheldon plays an online word game with Stephen Hawking in "The Extract Obliteration". 24 episodes. 660m; DVD, Blu-Ray. **A:** Family. **P:** Entertainment. **U:** Home. **Acq:** Purchase. **Dist:** $44.98.

The Big Bang Theory: The Complete Third Season 2009
CBS 2007-? comedy. Sheldon tries to alter Penny's habits while Howard and Raj try to meet girls at a Goth club in "The Gothowitz Deviation," Leonard tries to learn about football from Sheldon to impress Penny's friends while Raj and Howard's friendship is tested in a kite war in "The Cornhusker Vortex," and Penny needs Sheldon's help when she separates her shoulder in the bathtub, while the rest of the gang accidently gets stoned while waiting for a meteor shower in the desert in "The Adhesive Duck Deficiency." 23 episodes. 529m; DVD, Blu-Ray. **C:** Johnny Galecki; Jim Parsons; Kaley Cuoco; Simon Helberg; Kunal Nayyar. **A:** Jr. High-Adult. **P:** Entertainment. **U:** Home. **Mov-Ent:** Television Series, Scientists. **Acq:** Purchase. **Dist:** Warner Home Video, Inc. $44.98.

Big Bass Patterns 19??
Covers presentation patterns, location keys, and rod and reel selections. 50m; VHS. **A:** Adult. **P:** Instruction. **U:** Home. **Spo-Rec:** Fishing. **Acq:** Purchase. **Dist:** In-Fisherman.

Big Bear 1998 — ★★½
In the 1880s, Cheif Big Bear (Tootoosis) refuses to surrender Cree ancestral lands to settlers for fear of the many broken promises made by the government. So Canadian army troops surround the Cree in order to starve them into submission. Cree warriors decide to stage an attack against the settlers that only brings the troops down on them. 190m; VHS, DVD. **C:** Tantoo Cardinal; Gordon Tootoosis; Ken Charlette; Directed by Gil Cardinal. **A:** Jr. High-Adult. **P:** Entertainment. **U:** Home. **Mov-Ent:** Native Americans, Canada. **Acq:** Purchase. **Dist:** BFS Video.

Big Ben: Ben Webster in Europe 1967
The tenor sax master musician, who played with Duke Ellington and others in the 1930s and '40s, performs such songs as "Perdido," "My Romance," and "You'd Be So Nice to Come Home To," as well as discussing his life and music. 31m/B/W; VHS. **C:** Directed by Johan van der Keuken. **A:** Sr. High-Adult. **P:** Entertainment. **U:** Home. **Fin-Art:** Documentary Films, Music--Jazz, Black Culture. **Acq:** Purchase. **Dist:** Rhapsody Films, Inc.; Music Video Distributors. $24.95.

Big Bend Encounter 1986
This is a film of the wildlife in Big Bend National Park in Texas, as shown in that park to visitors, and newly available outside of Texas. 12m; VHS, 3/4 U. **Pr:** USDAVA. **A:** Family. **P:** Entertainment. **U:** Institution, SURA. **Gen-Edu:** Wildlife, National Parks & Reserves. **Acq:** Purchase. **Dist:** National Audiovisual Center. $95.00.

Big Bend National Park, Texas 1986
The river and its surrounding scenery are surveyed for the armchair tourist. 30m; VHS. **Pr:** National Park Service. **A:** Family. **P:** Education. **U:** Home. **Gen-Edu:** Travel, U.S. States, National Parks & Reserves. **Acq:** Purchase. **Dist:** Finley Holiday Film Corp. $24.95.

Big Bend Portrait 19??
Shows the various flora and fauna found in the Chihuahuan Desert in Big Bend National Park. 20m; VHS. **A:** Family. **P:** Entertainment. **U:** Home, Institution. **Gen-Edu:** National Parks & Reserves, Wildlife, Travel. **Acq:** Purchase. **Dist:** Harpers Ferry Historical Association. $17.95.

Big Benefits from the Little I.C. Troubleshooters 197?
Shows how considerable time and money can be saved in servicing electronic devices. 14m/B/W; VHS, 3/4 U. **Pr:** Hewlett Packard. **A:** College-Adult. **P:** Education. **U:** Institution, CCTV, Home. **L:** English, French, German, Italian, Portuguese, Spanish, Swedish. **Bus-Ind:** Electronics. **Acq:** Purchase. **Dist:** Hewlett-Packard Media Solutions.

The Big Bet 1985 (R) — ★★
High school sex comedy about a guy who is challenged by the school bully to get the gorgeous new girl into bed. Energetic romp is for adults. 90m; VHS, DVD. **C:** Sylvia Kristel; Kimberly Evenson; Ron Thomas; Directed by Bert I. Gordon. **A:** Sr. High-Adult. **P:** Entertainment. **U:** Home. **Mov-Ent:** Sex & Sexuality, Adolescence. **Acq:** Purchase. **Dist:** Movies Unlimited.

The Big Bird Cage 1972 (R) — ★★
Prison spoof sequel to "The Big Doll House." Horny females incarcerated in a rural jail decide to defy their homosexual guards and plan an escape. They are aided by revolutionaries led by a Brooklynese expatriate and his lover. 93m; VHS, DVD. **C:** Pam Grier; Sid Haig; Anitra Ford; Candice Roman; Teda Bracci; Carol Speed; Karen McKevic; Vic Diaz; Directed by Jack Hill; Written by Jack Hill; Cinematography by Felipe Sacdalan; Music by William Allen Castleman; William Loose. **Pr:** New World Pictures. **A:** College-Adult. **P:** Entertainment. **U:** Home. **Mov-Ent:** Prison Breaks. **Acq:** Purchase. **Dist:** Warner Home Video, Inc. $39.98.

Big Bird Gets Lost 1997
Part of the "Kids Guide to Life" series that teaches children how to be safe and make smart decisions. 40m; DVD, CC. **A:** Preschool. **P:** Education. **U:** Home. **Chl-Juv:** Safety Education, Children. **Acq:** Purchase. **Dist:** Sesame Workshop. $12.98.

Big Bird in China 1987
Big Bird is guided through China by a six-year-old in search of the legendary phoenix. Along the way, they visit Chinese schools, children, watch a T'ai Ch'i demonstration, and learn Chinese words, traditions, and culture. 75m; VHS, CC. **Pr:** Children's Television Workshop. **A:** Family. **P:** Entertainment. **U:** Home. **Chl-Juv:** Children, China. **Acq:** Purchase. **Dist:** Knowledge Unlimited, Inc. $24.95.

Big Bird in Japan 1991
Big Bird and his pal Barkley the Dog lose their way while visiting Tokyo. As they wander about, they meet all sorts of interesting people, including a young girl who could be the legendary Bamboo Princess. Includes four new songs. 60m; VHS, CC. **Pr:** Children's Television Workshop. **A:** Family. **P:** Entertainment. **U:** Home. **Chl-Juv:** Family Viewing, Music--Children, Japan. **Acq:** Purchase. **Dist:** Random House of Canada Ltd. $14.95.

Big Black: Live Video 19??
The guitar guerillas, led by Albini, rip through "Like Being Trapped in a Twisted Metal Wreckage and Learning to Love It" plus others. 50m; VHS. **A:** Jr. High-College. **P:** Entertainment. **U:** Home. **Mov-Ent:** Music--Performance. **Acq:** Purchase. **Dist:** Music Video Distributors. $24.95.

Big Black: Pigpile 1987
Big Black performs live from the Hammersmith Clarendon in London. Video comes with a 7-inch vinyl record of "Mary Jane Girls in My House." 65m; VHS. **A:** Jr. High-Adult. **P:** Entertainment. **U:** Home. **Mov-Ent:** Music Video, Music--Pop/Rock. **Acq:** Purchase. **Dist:** Music Video Distributors. $14.95.

Big Black: The Last Blast 19??
The band's final outing from Georgetown Steamplant in Seattle. Includes "Cables," "Dead Billy," "Kerosene" and more. 45m; VHS. **A:** Jr. High-College. **P:** Entertainment. **U:** Home. **Mov-Ent:** Music--Performance. **Acq:** Purchase. **Dist:** Music Video Distributors. $24.95.

Big Blind Spot 1988
This tape advises professional drivers on techniques in dealing with blind spots in backing up, etc. 10m; VHS, 3/4 U. **Pr:** National Safety Council. **A:** Adult. **P:** Education. **U:** Institution, SURA. **Bus-Ind:** Documentary Films, Safety Education, Driver Education. **Acq:** Purchase, Rent/Lease. **Dist:** National Safety Council.

The Big Blue 1988 (PG) — ★½
Vapid, semi-true tale about competing free-divers, who descend deep into the big blue without the aid of any kind of breathing apparatus. Arquette is the ditz who makes them come up for air. 122m; VHS, DVD, Wide, CC. **C:** Rosanna Arquette; Jean Reno; Jean-Marc Barr; Paul Shenar; Sergio Castellitto; Marc Duret; Griffin Dunne; Directed by Luc Besson; Written by Luc Besson; Cinematography by Carlo Varini; Music by Bill Conti. **Pr:** Weintraub Entertainment; Gaumont Productions. **A:** Jr. High-Adult. **P:** Entertainment. **U:** Home. **Mov-Ent:** Scuba, Sports--Fiction: Drama, Oceanography. **Awds:** Cesar '89: Score, Sound. **Acq:** Purchase. **Dist:** Sony Pictures Home Entertainment Inc. $19.95.

Big Blue 2003
Features long narrated, fully-edited footage of Conrail locomotives and trains on the tracks in and around New York State from 1990 to 1999. 60m; VHS. **A:** Family. **P:** Entertainment. **U:** Home. **Gen-Edu:** Trains. **Acq:** Purchase. **Dist:** EMPAC Publications. $14.95.

Big Blue Conrail 2003
Collection of railway footage shot by a New York State Rail Fan from 1990 to 1999. ?m; VHS. **A:** Family. **P:** Entertainment. **U:** Home. **Gen-Edu:** Trains. **Acq:** Purchase. **Dist:** EMPAC Publications. $14.95.

Big Blue Marble Presents 1974
Two segments from the award winning series "The Big Blue Marble": "My Seventeenth Summer" and "Flying For Fun." 60m; VHS. **A:** Family. **P:** Entertainment. **U:** Home. **Chl-Juv:** Family Viewing, Children, Education. **Acq:** Purchase. **Dist:** Sony Pictures Home Entertainment Inc.

Big Bluff 1955 (Unrated) — ★★
Disappointing result from an interesting premise; fatally ill woman finds love, but when she surprisingly recovers, her new husband decides to help her back along the path to death. Uneven and melodramatic. 70m/B/W; VHS, DVD. **C:** John Bromfield; Martha Vickers; Robert Hutton; Rosemary Bowe; Directed by W. Lee Wilder. **A:** Sr. High-Adult. **P:** Entertainment. **U:** Home. **Mov-Ent:** Melodrama. **Acq:** Purchase. **Dist:** Alpha Video; Sinister Cinema. $19.99.

Big Boats L'il Boats: Adventures with My Uncle Bill 1995
Features a trip on an authentic steamboat and a ride on a commuter ferry. Also seen are tug boats, seaplanes, freight liners, etc. 28m; VHS. **A:** Preschool-Primary. **P:** Entertainment. **U:** Home, Institution. **Chl-Juv:** Boating, Action-Adventure. **Acq:** Purchase. **Dist:** Paragon Home Video. $14.95.

The Big Boodle 1957 (Unrated) — ★½
Unremarkable crime drama, although Flynn puts some effort into his role as Havana casino croupier Ned Sherwood. Ned gets into trouble when he's passed some phony pesos and is accused of being a counterfeiter. This puts him on the wrong side of both the crooks and the cops, who both think he knows more than he does. 84m/B/W; DVD. **C:** Errol Flynn; Rosanna Rory; Gia Scala; Pedro Armendariz, Sr.; Jacques Aubuchon; Sandro Giglio; Charles Todd; Directed by Richard Wilson; Written by Jo Eisinger; Cinematography by Lee Garmes; Music by Raul Lavista. **A:** Jr. High-Adult. **P:** Entertainment. **U:** Home. **Mov-Ent:** Crime Drama, Gambling. **Acq:** Purchase. **Dist:** Alpha Video.

Big Boss 1977 (R) — ★½
A hoodlum climbs to the top of a crime syndicate. An Italian film previously titled "Mr. Scarface." 90m; DVD. **C:** Jack Palance; Edmund Purdom; Al Cliver; Harry Baer; Gisela Hahn; Directed by Fernando Di Leo. **Pr:** Maverick Pictures. **A:** Sr. High-Adult. **P:** Entertainment. **U:** Home. **Mov-Ent. Acq:** Purchase. **Dist:** Movies Unlimited. $13.49.

The Big Bounce 1969 (R) — ★★
First adaptation of Elmore Leonard's first crime novel after years of westerns is also Ryan O'Neal's first shot at leading man status. O'Neal shows his inexperience as well as glimpes of the boxoffice star he would become as Jack Ryan (not the CIA guy), a drifter who gets mixed up with dangerous woman Nancy (Taylor-Young, also very early in her career) and her plot to swindle her married lover, who happens to be his boss. Doesn't have the spark of Leonard's later crime capers, and the flat direction, disappointing finale, and overwhelming music don't help. But the obvious chemistry between O'Neal and Taylor-Young heats up the screen. 102m; DVD. **C:** Ryan O'Neal; Leigh Taylor-Young; Van Heflin; Lee Grant; James Daly; Robert Webber; Cindy Eilbacher; Noam Pitlik; Directed by Alex March; Written by Robert Dozier; Cinematography by Howard Schwartz; Music by Michael Curb. **Pr:** Warner Bros; Seven Arts Pictures. **A:** Sr. High-Adult. **P:** Entertainment. **U:** Home. **Mov-Ent. Acq:** Purchase. **Dist:** Warner Home Video, Inc.

The Big Bounce 2004 (PG-13) — ★★
Second adaptation of Elmore Leonard's first crime novel. Owen Wilson plays Jack Ryan, a small time hood who gets mixed up with Ray Ritchie, a crooked developer. Meanwhile, Ritchie's mistress Nancy (Foster) wants Ryan to steal $200,000 from Ritchie. Of course, double-crosses and deceptions ensue. Tends to meander about and lose focus, but it's somewhat enjoyable if you don't think too hard. Disappointing, considering the solid cast and the source material. 89m; DVD. **C:** Owen Wilson; Morgan Freeman; Gary Sinise; Vinnie Jones; Sara Foster; Willie Nelson; Bebe Neuwirth; Charlie Sheen; Harry Dean Stanton; Andrew Wilson; Steve Jones; Anahit Minasyan; Directed by George Armitage; Written by Sebastian Gutierrez; Cinematography by Jeffrey L. Kimball; Music by George S. Clinton. **Pr:** Steve Bing; Jorge Saralegui; Shangri-La Entertainment; Warner Bros. **A:** Jr. High-Adult. **P:** Entertainment. **U:** Home. **Mov-Ent:** Real Estate. **Acq:** Purchase. **Dist:** Warner Home Video, Inc.

Big Boy 1930 (Unrated) — ★½
Based on Jolson's stage hit with Al in blackface in the minstrel tradition. Wisecracking Kentucky stablehand Gus turns jockey to ride the Bedford's horse Big Boy to victory in the Kentucky Derby despite gamblers trying to get him fired. There's a coda where Al comes out (as himself) telling the audience a Jolson film needs to end with a song so he does 'Tomorrow's Another Day.' 68m/B/W; DVD. **C:** Al Jolson; Claudia Dell; Lloyd Hughes; Louise Closser Hale; Eddie (Edward) Phillips; Colin Campbell; Lew Harvey; Franklin Batie; Directed by Alan Crosland; Written by William K. Wells; Perry Vekroff; Cinematography by Hal Mohr. **A:** Sr. High-Adult. **P:** Entertainment. **U:** Home. **Mov-Ent:** Horses, Horses--Racing. **Acq:** Purchase. **Dist:** WarnerArchive.com.

Big Boy Rides Again 1935 (Unrated) — ★
Tom Duncan (Williams) returns home at his estranged father's request only to discover he's been murdered. Tom thinks it was his father's shady partner Tap Smiley (Mckee) but things gets complicated because Tap's daughter Nancy (Bergen) is sweet on Tom. There are scenes and plots that go nowhere, making for a disjointed effort. 57m/B/W; DVD. **C:** Guinn "Big Boy" Williams; Charles French; Lafe (Lafayette) McKee; Victor Potel; William Gould; Bud Osborne; Frank Ellis; Louis Vincenot; Constance Bergen; Directed by Albert Herman; Written by William L. Nolte; Cinematography by Harry Forbes. **A:** Family. **P:** Entertainment. **U:** Home. **L:** English. **Mov-Ent:** Western. **Acq:** Purchase. **Dist:** Gotham Distributing Corp.; VCI Entertainment. $7.98.

Big Boys Don't Cry 1993
A sensitive dramatization of one teenager's struggle with the sexual abuse he suffered at the hands of his uncle. When he realizes his younger brother is his uncle's latest victim, he tells his parents and together they confront the problem. 45m; VHS. **A:** Jr. High-Sr. High. **P:** Education. **U:** Home. **Chl-Juv:** Sexual Abuse, Children. **Acq:** Purchase. **Dist:** Clear Vue Inc. $275.00.

The Big Brass Ring 1999 (R) — ★★½
Murky political drama based on an unproduced screenplay by Orson Welles. Ambitious William Blake Pellarin (Hurt) is a

candidate for governor of Missouri but his ultimate goal is the presidency. However, an ugly scandal threatens his campaign, thanks to the appearance of Dr. Kimball Mennaker (Hawthorne), who's a little too close to the Pellarin family and knows about some skeletons even William isn't aware of. 104m; VHS, DVD, CC. **C:** William Hurt; Nigel Hawthorne; Miranda Richardson; Irene Jacob; Jefferson Mays; Ewan Stewart; Ron Livingston; Gregg Henry; Directed by George Hickenlooper; Written by George Hickenlooper; F.X. Feeney; Cinematography by Kramer Morgenthau; Music by Thomas Morse. **A:** Sr. High-Adult. **P:** Entertainment. **U:** Home. **Mov-Ent**: Politics & Government, Political Campaigns. **Acq:** Purchase. **Dist:** Sony Pictures Home Entertainment Inc.

The Big Brawl 1980 (R) — ★½
Chicago gangster recruits a martial arts expert to fight in a free-for-all match in Texas. 95m; VHS, DVD. **C:** Jackie Chan; Jose Ferrer; Mako; Rosalind Chao; Lenny Montana; Directed by Robert Clouse; Written by Robert Clouse; Music by Lalo Schifrin. **Pr:** Warner Bros; Golden Harvest. **A:** Sr. High-Adult. **P:** Entertainment. **U:** Home. **Mov-Ent**: Martial Arts. **Acq:** Purchase. **Dist:** Warner Home Video, Inc. $19.98.

The Big Broadcast of 1938 1938 — ★½
Fields is the owner of an ocean liner which he enters in a race. Supposedly, the ship can convert the electricity from radio broadcasts into power for the propellers. No, it doesn't make sense, as it's just an excuse for various radio stars to show off their routines in the ship's entertainment room. Hope, in his first feature, gets to sing his Oscar-winning signature tune "Thanks for the Memories." 94m/B/W; VHS, DVD. **C:** W.C. Fields; Martha Raye; Dorothy Lamour; Shirley Ross; Russell Hicks; Bob Hope; Ben Blue; Leif Erickson; Directed by Mitchell Leisen; Written by Walter DeLeon; Francis Martin; Cinematography by Harry Fischbeck; Music by Boris Morros; Ralph Rainger; Leo Robin. **Pr:** Harlan Thompson; Paramount Pictures. **A:** Family. **P:** Entertainment. **U:** Home. **Mov-Ent**: Musical, Boating. **Awds:** Oscars '38: Song ("Thanks for the Memories"). **Acq:** Purchase. **Dist:** Universal Music and Video Distribution. $14.98.

Big Brother 3 2003
Offers the third season of the reality television contest with 12 contestants who live together for three months while their actions are recorded—every week the contestants vote out one of the houseguests; the eventual winner receives $500,000. Also includes a special musical performance by Sheryl Crow. 32 episodes. 360m; DVD. **A:** Jr. High-Adult. **P:** Entertainment. **U:** Home. **Mov-Ent**: Television Series, Game Show. **Acq:** Purchase. **Dist:** Ventura Distribution Inc. $69.95.

Big Brother 4 2004
Offers the fourth season of the reality television contest with 12 contestants who live together for three months while their actions are recorded—every week the contestants vote out one of the houseguests; the eventual winner receives $500,000. Also includes the new feature "X-Factor" as former lovers are brought into the house. 32 episodes. 360m; DVD. **A:** Jr. High-Adult. **P:** Entertainment. **U:** Home. **Mov-Ent**: Television Series, Game Show. **Acq:** Purchase. **Dist:** Ventura Distribution Inc. $69.95.

Big Brother and the Holding Company: Ball and Chain 1967
A rare glimpse of the 1960s rock group rehearsing and recording in the studio prior to the Monterey Pop Festival appearance that made them famous. Songs include "Ball and Chain," "Down on Me," and "The Coo-Coo." 30m/B/W. **Pr:** Big Brother and the Holding Company. **A:** Family. **P:** Entertainment. **U:** Home. **Mov-Ent**: Music--Performance, Music--Pop/Rock. **Acq:** Purchase. **Dist:** Music Video Distributors; Rhino Entertainment Co. $14.95.

Big Brother Blues: A Story About Birth 1992
Informative dramatization wherein Josh gradually accepts the birth of his future sibling. He discusses with his mother the impact that the baby will have on their lives, as well as prenatal development, physical effects of pregnancy and birth, prenatal testing, and chromosomal abnormalities. Complete with guide. 31m; VHS. **A:** Primary-Jr. High. **P:** Education. **U:** Institution. **Gen-Edu**: Family, Pregnancy, Childbirth. **Acq:** Purchase, Rent/Lease. **Dist:** Phoenix Learning Group. $375.00.

Big Brother Trouble 2000 (G) — ★★½
Mitch (Suchenek) has always lived in the shadow of his big brother Sean (Hart), who's the star of the soccer team. But it's Mitch to the rescue when Sean is kidnapped to insure that his team loses the City Championship game. 88m; VHS, DVD. **C:** Michael Suchenek; Shad Hart; Lindsay Brooke; Mario Lopez; Bo Hopkins; Dick Van Patten; Directed by Ralph Portillo; Written by Jeff Nimoy; Seth Walther; Cinematography by John Huneck; Music by Steven Stern. **A:** Family. **P:** Entertainment. **U:** Home. **Mov-Ent**: Soccer. **Acq:** Purchase. **Dist:** Monarch Home Video.

Big Brown Eyes 1936 (Unrated) — ★★
Wisecracking hotel manicurist Eve (Bennett) is in love with detective Danny Barr (Grant). When Eve loses her job, she suddenly gets a new one working as a reporter and goes off to scope out a murder, which gets her in hot water. There's a lot of screwball complications, and the convoluted plot (which also involves a jewel heist) never does make much sense. 77m/B/W; DVD. **C:** Cary Grant; Joan Bennett; Walter Pidgeon; Lloyd Nolan; Alan Baxter; Marjorie Gateson; Isabel Jewell; Douglas Fowley; Henry (Kleinbach) Brandon; Directed by Raoul Walsh; Written by Raoul Walsh; Bert Hanlon; Cinematography by George T. Clemens. **A:** Jr. High-Adult. **P:** Entertainment. **U:** Home. **Mov-Ent**: Journalism, Comedy--Screwball. **Acq:** Purchase. **Dist:** Alpha Video; Movies Unlimited.

Big Bucks in Potbellied Pigs 1991
Learn all you ever need to know about the care, breeding and marketing of all your potbellied pigs. 50m; VHS. **A:** Sr. High-Adult. **P:** Instruction. **U:** Home. **Gen-Edu**: Documentary Films, Pets. **Acq:** Purchase. **Dist:** Tapeworm Video Distributors Inc. $19.95.

Big Bully 1995 (PG) — ★★
David Leary (Moranis) is an aspiring novelist who moves back to the town where he was picked on as a kid. His son immediately starts bullying a smaller child, whose father happens to be Roscoe "Fang" Bigger (Arnold), David's former tormentor. The timid hen-pecked Roscoe's sadistic streak is awakened with the reappearance of his old prey, leading to a barrage of wet willies and indian burns. The slapstick quickly escalates to danger before all is tied up in a syrupy sweet ending. With Moranis playing the nerdy bespectacled underdog and Arnold playing the loud obnoxious guy (although that might not be acting), it may be time to call the typecasting cops. Don Knotts (looking very un-Barney-like) makes an appearance as the high school principal. 93m; VHS, DVD. **C:** Tom Arnold; Rick Moranis; Julianne Phillips; Don Knotts; Carol Kane; Jeffrey Tambor; Curtis Armstrong; Faith Prince; Tony Pierce; Blake Bashoff; Directed by Steve Miner; Written by Mark Steven Johnson; Cinematography by Daryn Okada; Music by David Newman. **Pr:** James G. Robinson; Lee Rich; Gary Foster; Gary Barber; Dylan Sellers; Morgan Creek Productions; Warner Bros. **A:** Primary-Adult. **P:** Entertainment. **U:** Home. **Mov-Ent**: Adolescence, Education. **Awds:** Golden Raspberries '96: Worst Actor (Arnold). **Acq:** Purchase. **Dist:** Warner Home Video, Inc.

The Big Bus 1976 (PG) — ★★
The wild adventures of the world's first nuclear-powered bus as it makes its maiden voyage from New York to Denver. Clumsy disaster-movie parody. 88m; VHS, DVD. **C:** Joseph Bologna; Stockard Channing; Ned Beatty; Ruth Gordon; Larry Hagman; John Beck; Jose Ferrer; Lynn Redgrave; Sally Kellerman; Stuart Margolin; Richard Mulligan; Howard Hesseman; Richard B. Shull; Directed by James Frawley; Written by Fred Freeman; Lawrence J. Cohen; Cinematography by Harry Stradling, Jr.; Music by David Shire. **Pr:** Lawrence J. Cohen; Fred Freeman. **A:** Jr. High-Adult. **P:** Entertainment. **U:** Home. **Mov-Ent**: Action-Adventure, Satire & Parody. **Acq:** Purchase. **Dist:** WarnerArchive.com. $49.95.

Big Business 1988 (PG) — ★★
Strained high-concept comedy about two sets of identical twins, each played by Tomlin and Midler, mismatched at birth by a near-sighted country nurse. The city set of twins intends to buy out the factory where the country set of twins work. So the country twins march up to the big city to stop the sale and destruction of their beloved home. Both set of twins stay in the Plaza Hotel and zany consequences ensue. Essentially a one-joke outing with some funny moments, but talented comediennes Midler and Tomlin are somewhat wasted. Great technical effects. 98m; VHS, DVD, 8 mm, CC. **C:** Bette Midler; Lily Tomlin; Fred Ward; Edward Herrmann; Michele Placido; Barry Primus; Michael Gross; Mary Gross; Daniel Gerroll; Roy Brocksmith; Directed by Jim Abrahams; Cinematography by Dean Cundey. **Pr:** Buena Vista; Touchstone Pictures. **A:** Jr. High-Adult. **P:** Entertainment. **U:** Home. **Mov-Ent**: Comedy--Screwball. **Acq:** Purchase. **Dist:** Buena Vista Home Entertainment. $89.95.

Big Business Girl 1931 — ★★
Less than remarkable comedy starring Young as a corporate climber who must dodge her boss' advances and save her troubled marriage when her jazz singer husband is called away to perform in Paris. Based on a story by Patricia Reilly and Harold N. Swanson. 72m/B/W; VHS. **C:** Loretta Young; Frank Albertson; Ricardo Cortez; Joan Blondell; Dorothy Christy; Directed by William A. Seiter; Written by Robert Lord. **Pr:** Warner Bros. **A:** Jr. High-Adult. **P:** Entertainment. **U:** Home. **Mov-Ent**: Music--Jazz, Marriage. **Acq:** Purchase. **Dist:** MGM Home Entertainment. $19.98.

The Big Bust Out 1973 (R) — **Bomb!**
Several female convicts escape from prison only to be sold into slavery and face additional torture. Nothing redeeming about this exploitative film. 75m; VHS. **C:** Vonetta McGee; Monica Taylor; Linda Fox; Karen Carter; Gordon Mitchell; Directed by Karen Carter. **Pr:** Richard Jackson. **A:** Sr. High-Adult. **P:** Entertainment. **U:** Home. **Mov-Ent**: Slavery. **Acq:** Purchase. **Dist:** Unknown Distributor.

The Big Buy—Tom DeLay's Stolen Congress 2006 (Unrated)
Documentary on a Texas District Attorney's investigation of Congressman Tom DeLay. 60m; DVD. **A:** Sr. High-Adult. **P:** Education. **U:** Home. **Gen-Edu**: Politics & Government, Conspiracies or Conspiracy Theories, Documentary Films. **Acq:** Purchase. **Dist:** Disinformation. $19.95.

Big Calibre 1935 — ★
A rancher is inches away from being lynched for his dad's murder before he is found to be innocent. 59m/B/W; VHS, DVD. **C:** Bob Steele; Bill Quinn; Earl Dwire; Peggy Campbell; John Elliott; Georgia O'Dell; Directed by Robert North Bradbury. **Pr:** Commodore. **A:** Family. **P:** Entertainment. **U:** Home. **Mov-Ent**: Western. **Acq:** Purchase. **Dist:** Alpha Video. $12.95.

The Big Caper 1957 (Unrated) — ★★
Gambler Frank Harber (Calhoun) gets into debt with the mob and persuades boss Flood (Gregory) to fund the heist of a small town bank that handles the payroll for a nearby army base. Flood sends Frank and his own moll Kay (Costa) to pose as a married couple to scope out the situation. Mistrust among the thieves may doom their plans and it doesn't help when Frank and Kay fall in love and want to go straight. 85m/B/W; DVD. **C:** Rory Calhoun; James Gregory; Mary Costa; Robert H. Harris; Corey Allen; Paul Picerni; Roxanne Arlen; Directed by Robert Stevens; Written by Martin Berkeley; Cinematography by Lionel Lindon; Music by Albert Glasser. **A:** Jr. High-Adult. **P:** Entertainment. **U:** Home. **Mov-Ent**: Crime Drama. **Acq:** Purchase. **Dist:** MGM Home Entertainment.

The Big Cat 1949 (Unrated) — ★★
Mountain valley in Utah is ravaged by a cougar, while two ranchers fuss and feud. Big cat, bickering, help make okay adventure. 75m; VHS, DVD. **C:** Lon (Bud) McCallister; Peggy Ann Garner; Preston Foster; Forrest Tucker; Directed by Phil Karlson; Cinematography by William Howard Greene. **Pr:** Eagle Lion. **A:** Family. **P:** Entertainment. **U:** Institution, Home. **Mov-Ent**: Western, Pets. **Acq:** Purchase, Rent/Lease. **Dist:** Alpha Video; Movies Unlimited. $19.95.

The Big Catfish Connection 19??
Covers pre-spawn staging locations, rigging right, summer hot spots, and how to find wintering holes. 44m; VHS. **A:** Adult. **P:** Instruction. **U:** Home. **Spo-Rec**: Fishing. **Acq:** Purchase. **Dist:** In-Fisherman.

The Big Catfish Connection II 19??
Provides information on night cats, high-water cats, bobber cats, and light-line cats. 57m; VHS. **A:** Adult. **P:** Instruction. **U:** Home. **Spo-Rec**: Fishing. **Acq:** Purchase. **Dist:** In-Fisherman.

The Big Cats 1974
Meet jaguars, lions, and cougars-the fierce hunters are both threatened and studied by man. 52m; 3/4 U, Special order formats. **Pr:** National Geographic Society. **A:** Primary-Adult. **P:** Education. **U:** Institution, Home, SURA. **Hea-Sci**: Documentary Films, Wildlife, Pets. **Acq:** Purchase, Trade-in, Duplication License. **Dist:** National Geographic Society.

Big Cats and How They Came to Be 1989
This film takes a lively, animated account of the evolution of the genus "Panthera" which includes lions, tigers, jaguars, and leopards. 9m; VHS, 3/4 U. **Pr:** Smithsonian Institution. **A:** Jr. High-Adult. **P:** Entertainment. **U:** Institution, Home, SURA. **Gen-Edu**: Documentary Films, Wildlife, Pets. **Acq:** Purchase, Rent/Lease, Duplication License. **Dist:** Pyramid Media. $195.00.

The Big Cats: Endangered Predators 1979
Provides a look at the big cats in their natural environment and presents some of their characteristics and distinctive and social patterns. 22m; VHS, 3/4 U. **Pr:** Alan P. Sloan; Avatar Learning. **A:** Primary-Sr. High. **P:** Education. **U:** Institution, SURA. **Hea-Sci**: Documentary Films, Wildlife, Pets. **Acq:** Purchase, Rent/Lease, Trade-in. **Dist:** Encyclopedia Britannica.

Big Cats of the Big Top 1986
Footage of the Ringling Bros. and Barnum & Bailey Circus 115th edition's famous tamed cat acts. 30m; VHS. **Pr:** Patty Matlen. **A:** Family. **P:** Entertainment. **U:** Home. **Mov-Ent**: Documentary Films, Circuses, Animals. **Acq:** Purchase. **Dist:** Lions Gate Television Corp. $14.95.

Big Changes, Big Choices: Middle School Survival Series 199?
Twelve-part series featuring Michael Pritchard as he teaches and counsels middle school students. Titles are: The Three R's of Growing Up, You and Your Values, Enhancing Self-Esteem, Setting and Achieving Goals, Dealing With Pressures, Handling Emotions, Preventing Conflicts & Violence, Saying No to Alcohol & Drugs, Speaking of Sex, Friendship, Getting Along with Parents, and Respecting Others. Each video runs 30 minutes and purchased separately costs $69.95. 30m; VHS. **A:** Jr. High-Adult. **P:** Education. **U:** Home, Institution. **Chl-Juv**: Children, Education, Communication. **Acq:** Purchase. **Dist:** ElkindSweet Communications Inc. $699.95.
Indiv. Titles: 1. The Three R's of Growing Up 2. Who Am I? 3. Enhancing Self-Esteem 4. Setting & Achieving Goals 5. Dealing With Pressures 6. Handling Emotions 7. Preventing & Resolving Conflicts 8. Saying "No" to Alcohol & Other Drugs 9. The Question of Sex 10. Friendship 11. Working It Out With Parents 12. Respecting Others.

Big Chase 1954 — ★
A rookie cop chases down a mob of payroll thieves in this early action film. 60m/B/W; VHS, DVD. **C:** Glenn Langan; Adele Jergens; Douglas Kennedy; Jim Davis; Jack Daly; Phil Arnold; Wheaton Chambers; Lon Chaney, Jr.; Directed by Arthur Hilton; Written by Fred Freiberger. **Pr:** Robert L. Lippert, Jr.; Lippert Productions. **A:** Family. **P:** Entertainment. **U:** Home. **Mov-Ent**. **Acq:** Purchase. **Dist:** VCI Entertainment. $14.99.

The Big Chill 1983 (R) — ★★★½
Seven former '60s radicals, now coming upon middle age and middle-class affluence, reunite following an eighth friend's suicide and use the occasion to re-examine their past relationships and commitments. A beautifully acted, immensely enjoyable ballad to both the counter-culture and its Yuppie descendants. Great period music. Kevin Costner is the dead man whose scenes never made it to the big screen. 108m; VHS, DVD, 8 mm, Wide. **C:** Tom Berenger; Glenn Close; Jeff Goldblum; William Hurt; Kevin Kline; Mary Kay Place; Meg Tilly; JoBeth Williams; Directed by Lawrence Kasdan; Written by Lawrence Kasdan; Barbara Benedek; Cinematography by John Bailey. **A:** College-Adult. **P:** Entertainment. **U:** Home. **Mov-Ent**: Comedy-Drama, Suicide. **Awds:** Writers Guild '83: Orig. Screenplay. **Acq:** Purchase. **Dist:** Sony Pictures Home Entertainment Inc.; Criterion Collection Inc. $14.95.

The Big Circus 1959 (Unrated) — ★★½
Hank Twirling's (Mature) circus is failing and to get a bank loan he must put up with the presence of bank officer Sherman (Buttons) and Helen (Fleming), the publicist that Sherman hires

to drum up business. But Hank has bigger problems since a saboteur is at work—letting the lions loose, starting a fire, and even causing a deadly train wreck. Fairly typical circus story featured many of the famous acts of the day. 108m; DVD. **C:** Victor Mature; Red Buttons; Rhonda Fleming; Gilbert Roland; Kathryn Grant; Vincent Price; Peter Lorre; David Nelson; Joseph M. Newman; Directed by Joseph M. Newman; Written by Irwin Allen; Charles Bennett; Irving Wallace. **A:** Jr. High-Adult. **P:** Entertainment. **U:** Home. **Mov-Ent**: Circuses. **Acq:** Purchase. **Dist:** WarnerArchive.com.

Big City 1937 (Unrated) — ★½
Thoroughly ridiculous plot made palatable by Tracy's leading role. Joe works for an independent taxi company in New York that's battling with a corrupt rival firm. When the other firm's garage is bombed, Joe's pregnant, Russian immigrant wife Anna is railroaded and the D.A. orders her deported and aboard a ship in record time. So a frantic Joe takes his case to the city's ex-boxer Mayor and there's a race to the harbor to get his missus back. 80m/B/W; DVD. **C:** Spencer Tracy; Luise Rainer; Charley Grapewin; Paul Harvey; Janet Beecher; Eddie Quillan; Victor Varconi; William Demarest; Directed by Frank Borzage; Written by Hugo Butler; Dore Schary; Cinematography by Joseph Ruttenberg; Music by William Axt. **A:** Sr. High-Adult. **P:** Entertainment. **U:** Home. **Mov-Ent**: Pregnancy. **Acq:** Purchase. **Dist:** WarnerArchive.com.

The Big City 1963 (Unrated) — ★★
When debts threaten to overwhelm the Mazumdar family, Arati does the unthinkable and gets a job as a saleswoman. She soon begins to realize she not only likes to work but enjoys the freedom and respect her job brings. Bengali with subtitles. 131m/B/W; VHS, Blu-Ray. **C:** Anil Chatterjee; Madhabi Mukherjee; Vicky Redwood; Haren Chatterjee; Directed by Satyajit Ray; Written by Satyajit Ray; Cinematography by Subrata Mitra; Music by Satyajit Ray. **A:** College-Adult. **P:** Entertainment. **U:** Home. **Mov-Ent**: Women, India. **Acq:** Purchase. **Dist:** Sony Pictures Home Entertainment Inc.

Big City Blues 1989
A musical documentary that takes a new look at an old American musical form—the blues. Filmed in Chicago and featuring Son Seals, Jim Brewer, Queen Sylvia Embry, and Billy Branch. 28m; VHS. **C:** Directed by St. Claire Bourne. **Pr:** St. Claire Bourne. **A:** Jr. High-Adult. **P:** Entertainment. **U:** Home. **Gen-Edu**: Documentary Films, Music--Jazz, Black Culture. **Acq:** Purchase. **Dist:** Music Video Distributors; Rhapsody Films, Inc.; Facets Multimedia Inc. $24.95.

Big City Blues 1999 (R) — ★★
One long night in the lives of hit men Connor (Reynolds) and Hudson (Forsythe) as they get mixed up with the plans of a hooker (Cates). 94m; VHS, DVD. **C:** Burt Reynolds; William Forsythe; Georgina Cates; Giancarlo Esposito; Roger Floyd; Balthazar Getty; Arye Gross; Donovan Leitch; Roxana Zal; Amy Lyndon; Jad Mager; Directed by Clive Fleury; Written by Clive Fleury; Cinematography by David Bridges; Music by Tomas San Miguel. **A:** Sr. High-Adult. **P:** Entertainment. **U:** Home. **Mov-Ent**: Prostitution. **Acq:** Purchase. **Dist:** Movies Unlimited; Alpha Video.

The Big Clock 1948 (Unrated) — ★★★
George Stroud (Milland) is the editor of the successful Crimeways magazine, owned by tyrannical publisher Earl Janoth (Laughton). Forced to miss a vacation with his wife Georgette (O'Sullivan), George winds up spending time with lovely Pauline (Johnson), whom he inadvertently discovers is the boss' mistress. Pauline's murdered and George is quick to realize all the clues are deliberately pointed in his direction. Classic crime melodrama adapted from Kenneth Fearing's novel. Remade as "No Way Out" (1987). 95m/B/W; VHS, DVD, CC. **C:** Ray Milland; Charles Laughton; Maureen O'Sullivan; George Macready; Rita Johnson; Dan Tobin; Elsa Lanchester; Harry (Henry) Morgan; Directed by John Farrow; Written by Jonathan Latimer; Cinematography by John Seitz; Music by Victor Young. **Pr:** Richard Maibaum; Paramount Pictures. **A:** Sr. High-Adult. **P:** Entertainment. **U:** Home. **Mov-Ent**: Publishing. **Acq:** Purchase. **Dist:** Movies Unlimited; Alpha Video; Universal Studios Home Video.

Big Combo 1955 — ★★★
A gangster's ex-girlfriend helps a cop to smash a crime syndicate. Focuses on the relationship between Wilde's cop and the gangster Conte in an effective film noir, with some scenes of torture that were ahead of their time. 87m/B/W; DVD, Blu-Ray. **C:** Cornel Wilde; Richard Conte; Jean Wallace; Brian Donlevy; Earl Holliman; Lee Van Cleef; Helen Walker; Directed by Joseph H. Lewis; Written by Philip Yordan; Cinematography by John Alton; Music by David Raksin. **Pr:** Allied Artists International. **A:** Sr. High-Adult. **P:** Entertainment. **U:** Home. **Mov-Ent**. **Acq:** Purchase. **Dist:** Olive Films; Movies Unlimited.

The Big Comfy Couch: Are You Ready for School? 1998
Loonette and Molly entertain children and stress important themes, including sharing and cooperation. 25m; VHS. **A:** Preschool-Primary. **P:** Entertainment. **U:** Home. **Chl-Juv**: Children. **Acq:** Purchase. **Dist:** Tapeworm Video Distributors Inc. $12.99.

The Big Comfy Couch: Be Nice, Snicklefritz! 1998
Loonette and Molly entertain children and stress important themes, including sharing and cooperation. 25m; VHS. **A:** Preschool-Primary. **P:** Entertainment. **U:** Home. **Chl-Juv**: Children. **Acq:** Purchase. **Dist:** Tapeworm Video Distributors Inc. $12.99.

The Big Comfy Couch: Dustbunny Dreams 1998
Loonette and Molly entertain children and stress important themes, including sharing and cooperation. 25m; VHS. **A:** Preschool-Primary. **P:** Entertainment. **U:** Home. **Chl-Juv**: Children. **Acq:** Purchase. **Dist:** Tapeworm Video Distributors Inc. $12.99.

The Big Comfy Couch: With a Wiggle and a Giggle 1998
Loonette and Molly entertain children with 20 favorite songs, including "Clock Rug Stretch", "Thumbs Up", and "Shake Your Fanny Dance.". 30m; VHS. **A:** Preschool-Primary. **P:** Entertainment. **U:** Home. **Chl-Juv**: Children. **Acq:** Purchase. **Dist:** Tapeworm Video Distributors Inc. $12.99.

The Big Country 1958 (R) — ★★½
Ex-sea captain Peck heads west to marry fiance Baker and live on her father's (Bickford) ranch. Peck immediately clashes with ranch foreman Heston and finds out there's a vicious feud with neighbor Ives. Then Peck decides he and Baker aren't meant to be and he falls for schoolmarm Simmons instead. It's too long but if you like sprawling western sagas, this one has its moments. 168m; VHS, DVD, Wide. **C:** Gregory Peck; Charlton Heston; Burl Ives; Jean Simmons; Carroll Baker; Chuck Connors; Charles Bickford; Directed by William Wyler; Written by Jessamyn West; Robert Wyler; James R. Webb; Sy Bartlett; Robert Wilder; Cinematography by Franz Planer; Music by Jerome Moross. **Pr:** Anthony Worldwide Productions. **A:** Sr. High-Adult. **P:** Entertainment. **U:** Home. **Mov-Ent**: Western, Romance. **Awds:** Oscars '58: Support. Actor (Ives); Golden Globes '59: Support. Actor (Ives). **Acq:** Purchase. **Dist:** MGM Home Entertainment; Baker and Taylor. $29.98.

Big Country Live 1984 (Unrated)
A concert taped in Scotland on New Year's Eve 1984. Big Country performs "Wonderland," "Fields of Fire," and "In a Big Country." 75m; VHS. **Pr:** Aubrey Powell. **A:** Sr. High-Adult. **P:** Entertainment. **U:** Home. **Mov-Ent**: Music--Performance. **Acq:** Purchase. **Dist:** Music Video Distributors. $14.95.

Big Country: Live in New York 198?
This Japanese import features the band playing "Remembrance Day," "I Walk the Hill," "Steeltown," "The Teacher," "One Great Thing," "Fields of Fire" and more. 55m; VHS. **A:** Jr. High-College. **P:** Entertainment. **U:** Home. **Mov-Ent**: Music--Performance. **Acq:** Purchase. **Dist:** Music Video Distributors. $79.95.

The Big Crimewave 1986 (Unrated) — ★★
A cast of unknowns in a comedy about a loner who takes a bus to Kansas City (Kansas City?) to become a screenwriter, with comic adventures along the way. A feast of jabs at genre films. 80m; VHS. **C:** John Paizs; Eva Covacs; Darrel Baran; Directed by John Paizs. **A:** Jr. High-Adult. **P:** Entertainment. **U:** Home. **Mov-Ent**: Canada. **Acq:** Purchase. **Dist:** No Longer Available.

Big Daddy 1999 (PG-13) — ★★
Critic-proof film for Sandler's fans—the rest won't find anything to tempt them. He's 32-year-old slacker law-school grad Sonny Koufax, who's got a big Peter Pan complex, since he's incapable of assuming any adult responsibility. However, he does want to impress women, so he decides to go for the "awww" factor by becoming the guardian of his travelling-in-China roommate Kevin's (Stewart) heretofore unknown son, five-year-old Julian (Sprouse). He teaches the kid a number of disgusting traits and winds up bonding with the tyke (they have the same emotional IQ—how hard can it be?). 95m; VHS, DVD, UMD, CC. **C:** Adam Sandler; Cole Sprouse; Dylan Sprouse; Joey Lauren Adams; Jon Stewart; Leslie Mann; Josh Mostel; Rob Schneider; Kristy Swanson; Joseph Bologna; Steve Buscemi; Directed by Dennis Dugan; Written by Adam Sandler; Steve Franks; Tim Herlihy; Cinematography by Theo van de Sande; Music by Teddy Castellucci. **Pr:** Columbia Pictures; Sony Pictures Home Entertainment Inc. **A:** Jr. High-Adult. **P:** Entertainment. **U:** Home. **Mov-Ent**: Parenting, Adoption, Law. **Awds:** MTV Movie Awards '00: Comedic Perf. (Sandler); Golden Raspberries '99: Worst Actor (Sandler). **Acq:** Purchase. **Dist:** Sony Pictures Home Entertainment Inc.

Big Daddy Kane: Chocolate City 1991
Five videos from rapper Big Daddy Kane. Includes "Cause I Can Do It Right," "I Get The Job Done," "All of Me," "It's Hard Being The Kane," and "Taste of Chocolate." Strong language and adult situations, so parental guidance is recommended. 30m; VHS. **C:** Big Daddy Kane; Directed by Lionel C. Martin. **A:** College-Adult. **P:** Entertainment. **U:** Home. **Mov-Ent**: Music Video, Music--Rap. **Acq:** Purchase. **Dist:** Music Video Distributors. $16.98.

The Big Day 1999 (R) — ★★
Sara (Margulies) is supposed to be getting married. She shows up at the church but groom John (Sergei) is a no-show after his knucklehead brother Zack (Rohner) confesses to an indiscretion that leaves John with big doubts about the marriage thing. So the family starts to panic and the wedding party tries to find the groom and it's chaos everywhere you go. 88m; VHS, DVD. **C:** Julianna Margulies; Ivan Sergei; Clayton Rohner; Dixie Carter; Kevin Tighe; Adrian Pasdar; Kathleen York; Andrew Buckley; Nancy Banks; Directed by Ian McCrudden; Written by Andrew Buckley; Nancy Banks; Cinematography by Tony Cucchiari. **A:** Sr. High-Adult. **P:** Entertainment. **U:** Home. **Mov-Ent**: Comedy--Romantic. **Acq:** Purchase. **Dist:** Monarch Home Video.

Big Deadly Game 1954 — ★½
A vacationing American gets caught up in a complicated espionage plot by helping a mysterious wartime buddy. 63m/B/W; VHS, DVD. **C:** Lloyd Bridges; Simone Silva; Finlay Currie; Directed by Daniel Birt; Written by Daniel Birt; Robert Dunbar; Cinematography by Walter J. (Jimmy W.) Harvey; Music by Michael Krein. **Pr:** Lippert Productions. **A:** Family. **P:** Entertainment. **U:** Home. **Mov-Ent**: Mystery & Suspense. **Acq:** Purchase. **Dist:** Unknown Distributor.

Big Deal on Madonna Street 1958 (Unrated) — ★★★½
Peppe (Gassman) is a bungling thief who leads a band of equally inept crooks who plan to make themselves very rich when they attempt to rob a jewelry store on Madonna Street. Their elaborate plans cause numerous (and hilarious) disasters. Italian with subtitles. Remade in 1984 as "Crackers." 90m/B/W; VHS, DVD. **C:** Marcello Mastroianni; Vittorio Gassman; Claudia Cardinale; Renato Salvatori; Memmo Carotenuto; Toto; Rosanna Rory; Directed by Mario Monicelli; Written by Mario Monicelli; Furio Scarpelli; Suso Cecchi D'Amico; Cinematography by Gianni Di Venanzo; Music by Pierro Umiliani. **Pr:** United Motion Picture Organizations. **A:** Family. **P:** Entertainment. **U:** Home. **L:** English, Italian. **Mov-Ent**: Satire & Parody. **Acq:** Purchase, Rent/Lease. **Dist:** Tapeworm Video Distributors Inc. $29.95.

The Big Dig 1974
Records some of the events in a season of excavation at Tel Gezer in Israel, as an international team of archeologists probes through strata of earth to uncover traces of an ancient civilization. 22m; VHS, 3/4 U. **Pr:** Televisual Productions Ltd. **A:** Jr. High-College. **P:** Education. **U:** Institution, SURA. **Gen-Edu**: Documentary Films, Archaeology. **Acq:** Purchase, Rent/Lease, Trade-in. **Dist:** Encyclopedia Britannica.

The Big Dinner Table 1978
The four basic food groups are explored in this simple overview of worldwide food habits, from the "Nutrition Education" series. 13m; 3/4 U, Special order formats. **Pr:** Wexler Film Productions. **A:** Primary. **P:** Education. **U:** Institution, Home, SURA. **L:** English, Spanish. **Hea-Sci**: Documentary Films, Nutrition. **Acq:** Purchase, Rent/Lease, Trade-in, Duplication License. **Dist:** United Learning Inc.

Big Dipper 1986
Addresses the dangers of using smokeless tobacco. Includes interviews with teenagers and health professionals as well as shocking images of the effects of tobacco on the mouth. 19m; VHS, 3/4 U. **A:** Jr. High-Sr. High. **P:** Education. **U:** Institution. **Gen-Edu**: Health Education. **Acq:** Purchase, Rent/Lease. **Dist:** Intervision. $195.00.

The Big Dis 1989 (Unrated) — ★★
An interracial comedy about a young black soldier on a weekend pass who's looking for a willing sexual partner. His confidence is shattered when 12 possibilities turn him down. Feature debut of Eriksen and O'Brien. 88m/B/W; VHS, DVD. **C:** Gordon Eriksen; Heather Johnston; James Haig; Kevin Haig; Monica Sparrow; Directed by Gordon Eriksen; John O'Brien; Written by Gordon Eriksen; John O'Brien; Cinematography by John O'Brien. **A:** College-Adult. **P:** Entertainment. **U:** Home. **Mov-Ent**: Sex & Sexuality, Black Culture. **Acq:** Purchase. **Dist:** Facets Multimedia Inc.; First Run Features. $59.95.

The Big Dis 1990
A young black soldier searches for a date while on a weekend pass but things don't turn out quite as he expected. 88m/B/W; VHS. **A:** Adult. **P:** Entertainment. **U:** Home. **Mov-Ent**: Drama, Romance. **Acq:** Purchase. **Dist:** First Run Features. $19.95.

The Big Ditch: The Panama Canal 2001
Short film reporting on the U.S. turnover of the Panama Canal to the government of Panama and the repercussions this event will have on Latin America. 16m; VHS. **A:** Sr. High-Adult. **P:** Education. **U:** Institution. **Gen-Edu**: History--Modern. **Acq:** Purchase, Rent/Lease. **Dist:** Filmakers Library Inc. $150.00.

Big Dogs, Little Dogs 2005
A look at dogs of all sizes, from teacup poodles to massive mastiffs, including breed origins, behavior patterns, training, and the pet industry. 100m; DVD. **A:** Family. **P:** Entertainment. **U:** Home. **Gen-Edu**: Documentary Films, Pets. **Acq:** Purchase. **Dist:** A&E Television Networks L.L.C.

The Big Doll House 1971 (R) — ★★
Roger Corman-produced prison drama about a group of tormented female convicts who decide to break out. Features vintage Grier, and a caliber of women's-prison sleaziness that isn't equalled in today's films. 93m; VHS, DVD. **C:** Judy (Judith) Brown; Roberta Collins; Pam Grier; Brooke Mills; Pat(ricia) Woodell; Sid Haig; Christiane Schmidtmer; Kathryn Loder; Jerry Frank; Charles Davis; Directed by Jack Hill; Written by Don Spencer; Cinematography by Fred Conde; Music by Les Baxter; Hall Daniels. **Pr:** Jane Schaffer; New World Pictures. **A:** Sr. High-Adult. **P:** Entertainment. **U:** Home. **Mov-Ent**: Prison Breaks. **Acq:** Purchase. **Dist:** New Line Home Video. $24.98.

The Big Easy 1987 (R) — ★★★½
A terrific thriller. Slick New Orleans detective Remy McSwain (Quaid, oozing charm and a cornball accent) uncovers a heroin-based mob war while romancing uptight assistant DA Anne Osborne (Barkin, all banked fire) who's investigating corruption on the police force. An easy, Cajun-flavored mystery, a fast-moving action-comedy, a very sexy romance, and a serious exploration of the dynamics of corruption. 101m; VHS, DVD, CC. **C:** Dennis Quaid; Ellen Barkin; Ned Beatty; John Goodman; Ebbe Roe Smith; Charles Ludlam; Lisa Jane Persky; Tom O'Brien; Grace Zabriskie; Marc Lawrence; Directed by Jim McBride; Written by Daniel Petrie, Jr.; Cinematography by Affonso Beato; Music by Brad Fiedel. **Pr:** New Century; Vista. **A:** Sr. High-Adult. **P:** Entertainment. **U:** Home. **Mov-Ent**: Mystery & Suspense. **Awds:** Ind. Spirit '88: Actor (Quaid). **Acq:** Purchase. **Dist:** Facets Multimedia Inc. $14.99.

The Big Easy: The Complete Second Season 1987 (Unrated)
USA Network's gritty crime drama set in the Latin Quarter of New Orleans. Tony Crane plays Remy McSwain, a cop who will commit a crime to solve one, as he investigates a series of gang

killings, and begins a relationship with attorney Anne Osborne while charges have been filed against him in a police corruption sting. 13 episodes. 570m; DVD. **C:** Tony Crane; Barry Corbin; Susan Walters; Leslie Bibb. **A:** Adult. **P:** Entertainment. **U:** Home. **Mov-Ent:** Drama, Television Series. **Acq:** Purchase. **Dist:** MPI Media Group. $29.98.

Big Easy to Big Empty: The Untold Story of the Drowning of New Orleans 2007 (Unrated)
A documentary following New Orleans since the events of Hurricane Katrina. Producer Matt Pascarella and reporter Greg Palast were nearly charged with violating antiterror laws during its filming. 30m; DVD. **A:** Sr. High-Adult. **P:** Education. **U:** Home. **Gen-Edu:** Documentary Films, Conspiracies or Conspiracy Theories. **Acq:** Purchase. **Dist:** Disinformation. $14.95.

Big Eden 2000 (PG-13) — ★★½
Sweet-natured gay romance says you can go home again. Henry Hart (Gross) is an artist, living in New York, who returns to the small Montana town of Big Eden when his grandfather Sam (Coe) has a stroke. Henry has never admitted to anyone in his hometown that he's gay although it's pretty clear to his quirky neighbors, including the guys who hang out at the post office/general store, which is run by shy Native American Pike Dexter (Schweig), who will display some hidden talents on Henry's behalf. Henry is thrilled to discover his first crush, Dean (DeKay), is also back in town but he's looking for love in the wrong person. A happy ending is a comforting thing. 118m; VHS, DVD. **C:** Arye Gross; Eric Schweig; George Coe; Tim DeKay; Louise Fletcher; Nan Martin; O'Neal Compton; Corinne Bohrer; Veanne Cox; Directed by Thomas Bezucha; Written by Thomas Bezucha; Cinematography by Rob Sweeney; Music by Joseph Conlan. **A:** Sr. High-Adult. **P:** Entertainment. **U:** Home. **Mov-Ent:** Food Industry, Romance, Comedy-Drama. **Acq:** Purchase. **Dist:** Wolfe Video.

The Big Empty 1998 (Unrated) — ★★★
Lloyd Matthews (writer McManus) is a private eye who's burned out on divorce work when he's hired by a suspicious wife (Goldwasser) to find the truth about her too-good-to-be true husband (Bryan). Comparisons to Coppola's "The Conversation" are not out of place. This one's a solid sleeper. 93m; VHS, DVD. **C:** James McManus; Pablo Bryant; Ellen Goldwasser; H.M. Wynant; Directed by Jack Perez; Written by James McManus; Cinematography by Shawn Maurer; Music by Jean-Michel Michenaud. **A:** Sr. High-Adult. **P:** Entertainment. **U:** Home. **Mov-Ent. Acq:** Purchase. **Dist:** Vanguard International Cinema, Inc.

The Big Empty 2004 (R) — ★★
Struggling actor John Person (Favreau) accepts an offer to deliver a suitcase to a cowboy in a desert town for $25,000. Along the way he meets a wacky band of characters, including a bartender (Hannah) and her nympho daughter (Cook), and space aliens. Solid cast who seem to be enjoying themselves, quirky and original story, and a great soundtrack add up to an entertaining time-waster. 94m; VHS, DVD. **C:** Jon Favreau; Bud Cort; Daryl Hannah; Jon(athan) Gries; Kelsey Grammer; Rachael Leigh Cook; Joey Lauren Adams; Adam Beach; Melora Walters; Sean Bean; Danny Trejo; Gary Farmer; Brent Briscoe; Directed by Steve Anderson; Written by Steve Anderson; Cinematography by Chris Manley; Music by Brian Tyler. **A:** Sr. High-Adult. **P:** Entertainment. **U:** Home. **Mov-Ent. Acq:** Purchase. **Dist:** Lions Gate Home Entertainment. $26.98.

The Big Fall 1996 (R) — ★★
L.A. private investigator Blaize Rybeck (Howell) is hired by mystery babe Emma (Ward) to find her brother, Kenny, a pilot. Blaize meets some of Kenny's thrill-seeking friends at the airfield and draws the suspicious interest of FBI agent Wilcox (Applegate). Seems Kenny was mixed up in some shady dealings that get both his sister and her nosy P.I. into trouble. 94m; VHS, DVD. **C:** C. Thomas Howell; Sophie Ward; Jeff Kober; Justin Lazard; Titus Welliver; William Applegate, Jr.; Directed by C. Thomas Howell; Written by William Applegate, Jr.; Cinematography by Jurgen Baum. **Pr:** Joseph Mehri; Richard Pepin. **A:** Sr. High-Adult. **P:** Entertainment. **U:** Home. **Mov-Ent:** Mystery & Suspense. **Acq:** Purchase. **Dist:** Movies Unlimited.

Big Fan 2009 (R) — ★★½
Uncomfortably odd film about an isolated man who has nothing in his life but his obsession with the New York Giants. Bottom-rung Paul (Oswalt) listens to sports radio all day and offers call-in diatribes to his favorite radio show at night. He and loser pal Sal (Corrigan) can't afford tickets so they watch the Giants on TV from the Meadowlands parking lot. A chance encounter with linebacker Quantrell Bishop (Hamm) leads to a string of bad events. 86m; DVD. **C:** Patton Oswalt; Kevin Corrigan; Jonathan Hamm; Gino Cafarelli; Matt Servitto; Marcia Jean Kurtz; Michael Rapaport; Directed by Robert Siegel; Written by Robert Siegel; Cinematography by Michael Simmonds; Music by Philip Watts. **A:** Sr. High-Adult. **P:** Entertainment. **U:** Home. **Mov-Ent:** Football. **Acq:** Purchase. **Dist:** Vivendi Visual Entertainment.

Big Fat Liar 2002 (PG) — ★★
The boy who cried wolf goes to Hollywood in search of Marty Wolf (Giamatti), the unscrupulous movie producer who stole his short story. As nobody believes his far-out tale of being ripped off by Hollywood, notorious liar Jason Shepherd (Muniz) also makes sure to bring along a witness to his pursuit, in the form of his friend Kaylee (Bynes). Pulling an array of inspired pranks, the teens zestfully set about dismantling the sanity of Wolf, to the delight, and sometimes with the aid of, some of his many enemies. Talented small-screen star Muniz and his co-star Bynes make this a likeable, though not especially inspired, broad comedy with Giamatti mugging up a storm. Their romp through Universal Studios, especially, lets you know who's really behind this mostly entertaining movie for the pre-teen set. 87m; VHS, DVD, Blu-Ray. **C:** Frankie Muniz; Paul Giamatti; Amanda Bynes; Amanda Detmer; Donald Adeosun Faison; Lee Majors; Sandra Oh; Russell Hornsby; Christine Tucci; Sean O'Bryan; Amy Hill; Michael Bryan French; Directed by Shawn Levy; Written by Dan Schneider; Cinematography by Jonathan Brown. **Pr:** Mike Tollin; Brian Robbins; Tollin/Robbins Productions; Mediastream Film; Universal Pictures. **A:** Primary-Adult. **P:** Entertainment. **U:** Home. **Mov-Ent:** Adolescence. **Acq:** Purchase. **Dist:** Movies Unlimited; Alpha Video.

Big Fears/Little Risks 19??
Features two programs discussing the environment and health risks. Part I explores chemicals in the environment and Part II covers the popular assumptions of chemicals, cancer, and pollution. 44m; VHS. **A:** Sr. High-Adult. **P:** Education. **U:** Institution. **Gen-Edu:** Ecology & Environment, Cancer. **Acq:** Purchase. **Dist:** Cornell University. $18.00.

Big Fella 1937 — ★★½
Musical drama starring Robeson as Joe, a Marseilles dockworker (a familiar film occupation for the actor), who's asked by the police to help find a young boy (Grant) missing from an ocean liner. When Joe locates the boy, he discovers the child ran away from his wealthy family and doesn't want to return. Joe takes the boy to his cafe singer girlfriend, Miranda (Welch), and the two become his surrogate parents. Loose adapatation of the 1929 novel, "Banjo," by Claude McKay. 73m/B/W; VHS, DVD. **C:** Paul Robeson; Elisabeth Welch; Eldon Grant; Directed by J. Elder Wills; Written by Ingram D'Abbes; Fenn Sherie; Cinematography by Cyril Bristow; Music by Eric Ansell. **A:** Sr. High-Adult. **P:** Entertainment. **U:** Home. **Mov-Ent:** Musical--Drama, France, Parenting. **Acq:** Purchase. **Dist:** Kino on Video.
Songs: Lazin'; Roll Up Sailorman; You Didn't Ought to Do Such Things; All God's Chillun Got a Robe; My Curly Headed Baby; River Steals My Folks from Me.

Big Fights, Vol. 1: Muhammad Ali's Greatest Fights 1991
The Greatest is featured in highlights from bouts with Sonny Liston, Archie Moore, Floyd Patterson, Ken Norton, Joe Frazier and Leon Spinks. ?m; VHS. **Pr:** RCA. **A:** Sr. High-Adult. **P:** Entertainment. **U:** Home. **Spo-Rec:** Sports--General, Boxing. **Acq:** Purchase. **Dist:** Sony Pictures Home Entertainment Inc.

Big Fights, Vol. 2: Heavyweight Champions' Greatest Fights 1991
Some of boxing's all-time greats are featured at their best, including Jack Johnson, Jack Dempsey, Gene Tunney and Joe Louis. ?m; VHS. **Pr:** RCA. **A:** Sr. High-Adult. **P:** Entertainment. **U:** Home. **Spo-Rec:** Sports--General, Boxing. **Acq:** Purchase. **Dist:** Sony Pictures Home Entertainment Inc.

Big Fights, Vol. 3: Sugar Ray Robinson's Greatest Fights 1991
The great pugilist if featured in his bouts with Jake "Raging Bull" LaMotta, Carmen Basilio and many more. ?m; VHS. **Pr:** RCA. **A:** Sr. High-Adult. **P:** Entertainment. **U:** Home. **Spo-Rec:** Sports--General, Boxing. **Acq:** Purchase. **Dist:** Sony Pictures Home Entertainment Inc.

Big Fish 2003 (PG-13) — ★★★
This is right up Burton's alley, as it's about a great storyteller prone to out-sized flights of fancy. Ed Bloom (Finney) is a man on his deathbed hoping to reconcile with the son (Crudup) he's alienated with the yarns he's spun about his life. When Will, who's become a journalist as a form of rebellion, returns and asks one last time for the truth, Ed again begins the familiar tall tale. This is where we learn of Ed's version of his courtship of wife Sandra, his battle with a huge catfish, his adventures with a giant in the circus, the Korean War, and an idyllic town where the residents seem content to walk around barefoot and happy. Burton is in his element with the flashback/yarn portion, but handles the delicate drama of the father-son scenes with aplomb as well. Cast is uniformly excellent, with Finney making the most of a largely sedentary role. 125m; DVD, Blu-Ray. **C:** Ewan McGregor; Albert Finney; Billy Crudup; Jessica Lange; Alison Lohman; Helena Bonham Carter; Robert Guillaume; Steve Buscemi; Danny DeVito; Marion Cotillard; David Denman; Missi Pyle; Matthew McGrory; Loudon Wainwright, III; Directed by Tim Burton; Written by John August; Cinematography by Philippe Rousselot; Music by Danny Elfman. **Pr:** Richard D. Zanuck; Bruce Cohen; Dan Jinks; Columbia Pictures. **A:** Jr. High-Adult. **P:** Entertainment. **U:** Home. **Mov-Ent:** Circuses, Marriage, Fishing. **Acq:** Purchase. **Dist:** Sony Pictures Home Entertainment Inc.

Big Fish Down Under 1988
A series of programs about fishing in and around Australia. ?m; VHS. **C:** Hosted by Malcolm Florence. **Pr:** Bennett Marine Video. **A:** Family. **P:** Education. **U:** Home. **Spo-Rec:** Sports--General, Fishing. **Acq:** Purchase. **Dist:** Bennett Marine Video; Karol Media. $24.95.
Indiv. Titles: 1. Beginnings 2. Of Tigers, Sails and Crocodiles 3. Black Marlin: The Ultimate 4. The Ribbons 5. Sailfish: A Young Man's Challenge 6. Beyond the Edge: Professionals at Play 7. Island Holiday 8. Giant Blacks & Great Whites: Parts 1 & 2 9. Giant Blacks & Great Whites: Parts 3 & 4 10. Great Whites of Dangerous Reef 11. Away From It All 12. Wild Time in Paradise 13. The Great Reef Exploration: Part 1 14. The Great Reef Exploration: Part 2 15. Barramundi Fever.

Big Fish Only 19??
Al Lindner and friends demonstrate how to catch prize-winning fish. 56m; VHS. **A:** Adult. **P:** Instruction. **U:** Home. **Spo-Rec:** Fishing. **Acq:** Purchase. **Dist:** In-Fisherman.

Big Fish Ontario 19??
Explains locations and techniques for successful fishing in Ontario. 55m; VHS. **A:** Adult. **P:** Instruction. **U:** Home. **Spo-Rec:** Fishing. **Acq:** Purchase. **Dist:** In-Fisherman.

The Big Fix 1978 (PG) — ★★★
Private investigator Moses Wine finds himself in an ironic situation: searching for a fugitive alongside whom he'd protested in the 60s. Based on a Roger Simon novel. 108m; VHS. **C:** Richard Dreyfuss; Susan Anspach; Bonnie Bedelia; John Lithgow; F. Murray Abraham; Fritz Weaver; Mandy Patinkin; Directed by Jeremy Paul Kagan; Music by Bill Conti. **Pr:** Mark Huffam. **A:** Jr. High-Adult. **P:** Entertainment. **U:** Home. **Mov-Ent:** Mystery & Suspense. **Acq:** Purchase. **Dist:** $59.95.

Big Foot 1972 (Unrated) — **Bomb!**
Even genre devotees will be disappointed with this one. Sasquatch, who has procreation on his mind, searches rather half-heartedly for a human mate. A horror flick that forgot to include the horror. 92m; VHS. **C:** Chris Mitchum; Joi Lansing; John Carradine; John Mitchum; Directed by Bob Slatzer. **Pr:** American Gemini Productions. **A:** Sr. High-Adult. **P:** Entertainment. **U:** Home. **Mov-Ent:** Horror. **Acq:** Purchase. **Dist:** No Longer Available.

The Big Gag 1987 (R) — ★
An international group of comedians travel the world and pull gags on people. Lame. 84m; VHS. **C:** Yehuda Barkan; Cyril Green; Caroline Langford; Directed by Yehuda Barkan. **A:** Sr. High-Adult. **P:** Entertainment. **U:** Home. **Mov-Ent. Acq:** Purchase. **Dist:** Amazon.com Inc. $79.95.

The Big Game 1972 (Unrated) — ★½
It's about espionage not big game hunting but it's dull in any case. Prof. Handley (Milland) designs a mind control device for the U.S. military to brainwash soldiers into becoming fighting machines. For safety's sake, the contraption is being moved via a fishing boat but the bad guys know where it's headed and plan to steal it. 90m; DVD. **C:** Stephen Boyd; Cameron Mitchell; Ray Milland; France Nuyen; John Stacy; Brendon Boone; Michael Kirner; Directed by Robert Day; Written by Robert Day; Stanley Norman; Ralph Anders; Cinematography by Mario Fioretti; Music by Francesco De Masi. **A:** Jr. High-Adult. **P:** Entertainment. **U:** Home. **Mov-Ent:** Boating, Science. **Acq:** Purchase. **Dist:** VCI Entertainment.

The Big Game 1982
Examines the rivalry between two high school basketball teams from the point of view of the community, the coaches, and the players. 60m; VHS. **C:** Directed by E.J. Vaughn. **A:** Sr. High-Adult. **P:** Education. **U:** Institution. **Gen-Edu:** Basketball, Documentary Films, Sports--General. **Acq:** Purchase, Rent/Lease, Duplication. **Dist:** First Run/Icarus Films. $390.00.

Big Game America 1968
Pro football's fascinating first 50 years. Don Meredith wired for sound in his last game as a Cowboy is also included. 51m; VHS, Special order formats. **C:** Narrated by Burt Lancaster. **Pr:** NFL Films. **A:** Family. **P:** Entertainment. **U:** Institution, CCTV, CATV, BCTV, Home. **Spo-Rec:** Sports--General, Documentary Films, Football. **Acq:** Purchase, Rent/Lease. **Dist:** NFL Films Video. $19.98.

Big Game Fishing Techniques 19??
Covers the life cycle of the blue marlin. Watch a smorgasbord of fishing equipment unfold as experts offer their two cents about applying technology to the rod and reel. 30m; VHS. **A:** Adult. **P:** Instruction. **U:** Home. **Spo-Rec:** Fishing. **Acq:** Purchase. **Dist:** Bennett Marine Video. $29.95.

Big Game Video Cookbook 1993
Tim Manion demonstrates techniques for cooking wild game including venison, moose, elk, and antelope. ?m; VHS. **A:** Adult. **P:** Instruction. **U:** Home. **How-Ins:** Cooking, Wildlife, How-To. **Acq:** Purchase. **Dist:** Stoney-Wolf Productions, Inc. $29.95.

Big Girls Don't Cry. . . They Get Even 1992 (PG) — ★½
A teenage girl decides to run away from home after she's driven crazy by her eccentric new stepfamily. Comic confusion ensues as various family members set out to find her. Hackneyed script and annoying characters hinder this comedy. 98m; VHS, DVD, CC. **C:** Hillary Wolf; Griffin Dunne; Margaret Whitton; David Strathairn; Ben Savage; Adrienne Shelly; Patricia Kalember; Directed by Joan Micklin Silver. **A:** Jr. High-Adult. **P:** Entertainment. **U:** Home. **Mov-Ent:** Comedy-Drama, Family, Parenting. **Acq:** Purchase. **Dist:** Sony Pictures Home Entertainment Inc.; New Line Home Video.

The Big Green 1995 (PG) — ★½
British teacher Anna Montgomery (D'Abo) blows into a small Texas town determined to give the deprived kiddies a boost of self-esteem. With help from the town sheriff (Guttenberg), Anna organizes a soccer team that's supposed to give the kids a reason to live. Problems abound when the star player disappears just before the face-off with the biggest, nastiest team in the league. Sound familiar? This is the soccer version of "The Bad News Bears," "The Little Giants," and "The Mighty Ducks." The formula is less successful in this case, but some mildly amusing moments and a few fresh performances from the kids offer minor bright spots in this tired scenario. 100m; VHS, DVD, CC. **C:** Olivia D'Abo; Steve Guttenberg; Jay O. Sanders; John Terry; Chauncey Leopardi; Patrick Renna; Billy L. Sullivan; Yareli Arizmendi; Bug Hall; Directed by Holly Goldberg Sloan; Written by Holly Goldberg Sloan; Cinematography by Ralf Bode; Music by Randy Edelman. **Pr:** Roger Birnbaum; Dennis Bishop; Walt Disney Pictures; Caravan Pictures; Buena Vista. **A:** Family. **P:** Entertainment. **U:** Home. **Mov-Ent:** Family Viewing, Sports--Fiction: Comedy, Soccer. **Acq:** Purchase. **Dist:** Buena Vista Home Entertainment. $19.99.

The Big Gundown 1966 — ★★
Spaghetti western that's fast-paced but familiar. Texas bounty hunter Jonathan Corbett is given a temporary lawman's badge after he's hired by tycoon Brokston to hunt down Mexican Cuchillo Sanchez who's accused of raping and murdering a young white girl. Sanchez proves to be a wily adversary as he runs for the border, but Corbett eventually gets his man only to find out he's innocent. 95m; DVD, Blu-Ray. **C:** Lee Van Cleef; Tomas Milian; Walter Barnes; Luisa Rivelli; Directed by Sergio Sollima; Written by Sergio Sollima; Sergio Donati; Cinematography by Carlo Carlini; Music by Ennio Morricone. **A:** Adult. **P:** Entertainment. **U:** Home. **L:** English. **Mov-Ent**: Western. **Acq:** Purchase. **Dist:** Grindhouse Releasing.

The Big Gusher 1951 — ★½
Oil-field roughnecks Kenny and Hank buy a supposedly worthless piece of property on the chance there's oil to be found. They rent equipment from shady businessman Jim Tolman but only have 60 days to strike oil or the property lease reverts to Tolman. 68m/B/W; DVD. **C:** Wayne Morris; Preston Foster; Emmett Vogan; Paul E. Burns; Directed by Lew Landers; Written by Daniel Ullman; Music by William P. Whitley. **A:** Adult. **P:** Entertainment. **U:** Home. **L:** English. **Mov-Ent**: Action-Adventure, Oil Industry. **Acq:** Purchase. **Dist:** Sony Pictures Home Entertainment Inc.

A Big Hand for the Little Lady 1966 — ★★½
Fonda and Woodward, playing two West-headed country bumpkins, get involved in a card game in Laredo against high rollers Robards and McCarthy. Fonda risks their savings, finds himself stuck with a losing hand, and has a bit of heart trouble; that's where the little lady comes in. Fine performances and a nifty twist ending don't entirely compensate for the overly padded script (which evolved from Carroll's 48-minute TV play). 95m; DVD. **C:** Henry Fonda; Joanne Woodward; Jason Robards, Jr.; Charles Bickford; Burgess Meredith; Kevin McCarthy; Directed by Fielder Cook; Written by Sidney Carroll; Cinematography by Lee Garmes; Music by David Raksin. **Pr:** Warner Bros. **A:** Sr. High-Adult. **P:** Entertainment. **U:** Home. **Mov-Ent**: Western. **Acq:** Purchase. **Dist:** WarnerArchive.com; Facets Multimedia Inc. $59.95.

The Big Hangover 1950 — ★★
Odd story about a man whose allergy to alcohol makes him drunk at the most inopportune moments. Johnson stars as the attorney with the peculiar problem and Taylor plays the boss' daughter who helps him overcome the allergy. Good supporting cast can't help this otherwise boring and predictable film. 82m/B/W; VHS, DVD. **C:** Van Johnson; Elizabeth Taylor; Percy Waram; Fay Holden; Leon Ames; Edgar Buchanan; Selena Royle; Gene Lockhart; Directed by Norman Krasna; Written by Norman Krasna; Cinematography by George J. Folsey. **Pr:** Norman Krasna; Norman Krasna; MGM. **A:** Sr. High-Adult. **P:** Entertainment. **U:** Home. **Mov-Ent**: Alcoholism. **Acq:** Purchase. **Dist:** WarnerArchive.com; MGM Home Entertainment. $19.98.

Big Hearted Herbert 1934 (Unrated) — ★½
Brief family comedy has self-made businessman Herbert (Kibbee), who's also a boorish stingy grouch, constantly haranguing his family until his patient wife Elizabeth (MacMahon) has enough and decides to teach him a much-needed lesson. Remade as 1940's "Father Is a Prince." 60m/B/W; DVD. **C:** Guy Kibbee; Aline MacMahon; Patricia Ellis; Phillip Reed; Trent Durkin; Jay Ward; Henry O'Neill; Nella Walker; Marjorie Gateson; Robert Barrat; Helen Lowell; Directed by William Keighley; Written by Lillie Hayward; Ben Markson; Cinematography by Arthur L. Todd. **A:** Sr. High-Adult. **P:** Entertainment. **U:** Home. **Mov-Ent. Acq:** Purchase. **Dist:** WarnerArchive.com.

The Big Heat 1953 (Unrated) — ★★★½
When detective Ford's wife (played by Jocelyn Brando, sister of Marlon) is killed in an explosion meant for him, he pursues the gangsters behind it and uncovers a police scandal. His appetite is whetted after this discovery and he pursues the criminals even more vigorously with the help of gangster moll Gloria Grahame. Definitive film noir. 90m/B/W; VHS, DVD. **C:** Glenn Ford; Lee Marvin; Gloria Grahame; Jocelyn Brando; Alexander Scourby; Carolyn Jones; Directed by Fritz Lang; Written by Sydney (Sidney) Boehm; Cinematography by Charles B(ryant) Lang, Jr. **Pr:** Robert Arthur; Columbia Pictures. **A:** Family. **P:** Entertainment. **U:** Home. **Mov-Ent**: Mystery & Suspense. **Awds:** Natl. Film Reg. '11. **Acq:** Purchase. **Dist:** Sony Pictures Home Entertainment Inc. $59.95.

Big Henry and the Polka Dot Kid 1977
A young orphan wins his battle to save the life of an old blind dog by convincing his uncle that there are values far more important than just being practical. 51m; VHS, 3/4 U. **C:** Ned Beatty; Estelle Parsons; Christopher Barnes. **Pr:** Linda Gottlieb; Learning Corporation of America. **A:** Family. **P:** Entertainment. **U:** Institution, SURA. **L:** English, Spanish. **Gen-Edu**: Pets. **Acq:** Purchase, Rent/Lease. **Dist:** Phoenix Learning Group.

The Big Hit 1998 (R) — ★★½
Combustible mixture of extravagent stunts, cartoon violence, hip-hop soundtrack, and a colorful cast serve up an intermittently funny look at organized crime. When not executing their skills as ruthless hitmen, Melvin, Cisco, Vince, and Crunch (Wahlberg, Phillips, Sabato, Jr., and Woodbine) are regular working Joes with regular problems. For Melvin, financial and female problems force him to partner with Cisco in the kidnapping of a Chinese heiress. Said heiress turns out to be the goddaughter of their own crime boss. Much hilarity ensues. Phillips brings gusto to his flamboyant homeboy character and Wahlberg is his equal as the sappy gun for hire with a heart of gold. Big plot holes and fickle storyline, but bigger laughs make you not care so much. American directorial debut of Hong Kong import Che-Kirk Wong. 91m; VHS, DVD, Blu-Ray, UMD, Wide, CC. **C:** Mark Wahlberg; Lou Diamond Phillips; Bokeem Woodbine; Antonio Sabato, Jr.; Christina Applegate; Avery Brooks; China Chow; Lainie Kazan; Elliott Gould; Lela Rochon; Sab Shimono; Directed by Kirk Wong; Written by Ben Ramsey; Cinematography by Danny Nowak; Music by Graeme Revell. **Pr:** Warren Zide; Wesley Snipes; Amen Ra; Lion Rock; TriStar Pictures. **A:** Sr. High-Adult. **P:** Entertainment. **U:** Home. **Mov-Ent**: Cooking. **Acq:** Purchase. **Dist:** Sony Pictures Home Entertainment Inc.

'Big Horse' Short Yardage Offense 2007 (Unrated)
Coach Lew Johnston demonstrates this mix of the no-Huddle Offense and Wing-T Offense for football teams. 54m; DVD. **A:** Family. **P:** Education. **U:** Home, Institution. **Spo-Rec**: Football, Athletic Instruction/Coaching. **Acq:** Purchase. **Dist:** Championship Productions. $39.99.

The Big House 1930 — ★★★
Prison melodrama at its best follows top con Beery as he plans a big breakout—and is betrayed. Life in the pen is depicted as brutal and futile, with sadistic guards and a hapless warden. Spawned numerous imitators. 80m/B/W; VHS, DVD. **C:** Wallace Beery; Chester Morris; Robert Montgomery; Lewis Stone; Leila Hyams; George F. Marion, Sr.; Karl (Daen) Dane; DeWitt Jennings; Directed by George W. Hill; Written by Frances Marion. **Pr:** MGM. **A:** Jr. High-Adult. **P:** Entertainment. **U:** Home. **Mov-Ent**: Prison Breaks, Violence. **Acq:** Purchase. **Dist:** WarnerArchive.com. $19.98.

Big House, U.S.A. 1955 (Unrated) — ★★
In this brutal crime drama, Jerry Barber (Meeker) lands in the big house, convicted of extortion after a kidnapping gone wrong. He buried most of the ransom money, and his cellmates come up with an escape plan to get the dough, but the FBI is ready to take 'em down. 82m/B/W; DVD. **C:** Ralph Meeker; Broderick Crawford; Reed Hadley; William Talman; Lon Chaney, Jr.; Charles Bronson; Directed by Howard W. Koch; Written by John C. Higgins; Cinematography by Gordon Avil; Music by Paul Dunlap. **A:** Sr. High-Adult. **P:** Entertainment. **U:** Home. **L:** English. **Mov-Ent**: Crime Drama, Federal Bureau of Investigation (FBI), Prison Breaks. **Acq:** Purchase. **Dist:** MGM Home Entertainment.

The Big Hurt 1987 (R) — ★½
A reporter investigating a bizarre double murder discovers a secret government agency involved in torture and mind-control. 90m; VHS. **C:** David Bradshaw; Lian Lunson; Simon Chilvers; Nick Waters; Directed by Barry Peak. **A:** Adult. **P:** Entertainment. **U:** Home. **Mov-Ent**: Mystery & Suspense, Journalism, Politics & Government. **Acq:** Purchase. **Dist:** No Longer Available.

The Big I Am 2010 (R) — ★
Inexperience behind (and some in front of) the camera dooms this derivative British gangster flick. Small time London crook Mickey Skinner unexpectedly saves human trafficker/crime boss Don Barber from death at the hands of rival Frankie Stubbs. To find out who betrayed him, Barber wants to lay low so he makes bungler Mickey the temporary head of his organization. 106m; DVD. **C:** Leo Gregory; Vincent Regan; Philip Davis; Beatrice Rosen; Robert Fucilla; Michael Madsen; Steven Berkoff; Directed by Nic Auerbach; Written by Tim Cummingham; Cinematography by Shane Daly; Music by James Radford. **A:** Sr. High-Adult. **P:** Entertainment. **U:** Home. **Mov-Ent**: Crime Drama. **Acq:** Purchase. **Dist:** Entertainment One US LP.

The Big If—Interferon 1981
The new wonder drug Interferon may prove to be a cure for cancer and viruses. Clinical tests are now being conducted to determine its effectiveness, as seen in this program. 50m; VHS, 3/4 U. **Pr:** BBC Horizon. **A:** Jr. High-Adult. **P:** Education. **U:** Institution, SURA. **Hea-Sci**: Drugs, Medical Education. **Acq:** Purchase, Rent/Lease. **Dist:** Home Vision Cinema.

Big Jake 1971 (PG) — ★★
An aging Texas cattle man who has outlived his time swings into action when outlaws kidnap his grandson and wound his son. He returns to his estranged family to help them in the search for Little Jake. O'Hara is once again paired up with Wayne and the chemistry is still there. 90m; VHS, DVD, Wide, CC. **C:** John Wayne; Richard Boone; Maureen O'Hara; Patrick Wayne; Chris Mitchum; Bobby Vinton; John Agar; Harry Carey, Jr.; Directed by George Sherman; Cinematography by William Clothier; Music by Elmer Bernstein. **Pr:** Batjac Productions; Cinema Center. **A:** Family. **P:** Entertainment. **U:** Home. **Mov-Ent**: Western. **Acq:** Purchase. **Dist:** Movies Unlimited; Alpha Video; Paramount Pictures Corp. $19.98.

Big Jim 1954
Cora makes a brief visit to her adult son Jim which, at his insistence, turns into a longer stay. Then Jim begins wondering what his mother's mysterious business is really about. 30m; VHS. **C:** Loretta Young; Bobby Driscoll; Directed by Richard Morris. **A:** Family. **P:** Entertainment. **U:** Home. **Mov-Ent**: Family, Television Series. **Acq:** Purchase. **Dist:** Facets Multimedia Inc.; Rhino Entertainment Co. $14.95.

Big Jim McLain 1952 (Unrated) — ★★
Wayne and Arness are federal agents working on behalf of the House Un-American Activities Committee to eliminate communist terrorism in Hawaii. And there's a suspicious psychiatrist, too: Wayne falls for a babe whose boss is a shrink who doesn't quite seem on the level. Definitely not a highpoint in the Duke's career. 90m; VHS, DVD, CC. **C:** John Wayne; Nancy Olson; James Arness; Veda Ann Borg; Directed by Edward Ludwig; Cinematography by Archie Stout. **Pr:** Warner Bros. **A:** Family. **P:** Entertainment. **U:** Home. **Mov-Ent**: Psychiatry. **Acq:** Purchase. **Dist:** Warner Home Video, Inc.; Facets Multimedia Inc. $19.98.

The Big Kahuna 2000 (R) — ★★½
Spacey produced and stars as Larry, a loudly cynical industrial lubricants salesman at a convention in Kansas. He's there with Phil (DeVito), his burned-out collegue who's going through a divorce and looking for spirituality; and Bob (Facinelli), a newlywed, devout Christian research engineer who's new to the company. They spend the night in a hospitality suite waiting for a potential client—the Big Kahuna—and discussing how work, religion, ethics, and personal life coexist. Adapted from Rueff's play "Hospitality Suite" and it feels like it. The dialogue and setting is very stagey, but the performances are excellent, especially DeVito's. 90m; VHS, DVD, Wide, CC. **C:** Kevin Spacey; Danny DeVito; Peter Facinelli; Directed by John Swanbeck; Written by Roger Rueff; Cinematography by Anastas Michos; Music by Christopher Young. **A:** Sr. High-Adult. **P:** Entertainment. **U:** Home. **Mov-Ent**: Hotels & Hotel Staff Training, Philosophy & Ideology. **Acq:** Purchase. **Dist:** Movies Unlimited; Alpha Video.

Big Kids Baseball Cards 1988
Strategies on buying and collecting baseball cards. Includes hints on speculating on tomorrow's stars, and tips from card shark Alan "Mr. Mint" Rosen. 30m; VHS. **C:** Narrated by Bill Pucko. **A:** Family. **P:** Entertainment. **U:** Home. **Spo-Rec**: Hobbies, Baseball. **Acq:** Purchase. **Dist:** ESPN Inc. $19.95.

The Big Knife 1955 (Unrated) — ★★★
Palance plays a Hollywood superstar who refuses to renew his studio contract, which enrages studio boss Steiger. It seems Steiger knows a very damaging secret about the star and is willing to go to any lengths to have Palance re-sign or wind up destroying himself. A ruthless, emotional look at fame and power, with excellent performances by all. Based on the play by Clifford Odets. 113m/B/W; DVD. **C:** Jack Palance; Rod Steiger; Ida Lupino; Shelley Winters; Wendell Corey; Jean Hagen; Ilka Chase; Everett Sloane; Wesley Addy; Paul Langton; Directed by Robert Aldrich; Cinematography by Ernest Laszlo. **Pr:** United Artists. **A:** Sr. High-Adult. **P:** Entertainment. **U:** Home. **Mov-Ent. Acq:** Purchase. **Dist:** Facets Multimedia Inc. $34.98.

Big Leaguer 1953 (Unrated) — ★★
Fictionalized sports saga about New York Giants baseball player-turned-scout Hans Lobert (Robinson). It's set at the team's Florida training camp where Lobert is eyeballing the current prospects--from a Cuban hopeful to a player who isn't sure he even likes the game. 71m/B/W; DVD. **C:** Edward G. Robinson; Vera-Ellen; Richard Jaeckel; Jeff Richards; John McKee; Lalo Rios; Bill Crandall; Directed by Robert Aldrich; Written by Herbert Baker; Cinematography by William Mellor; Music by Alberto Colombo. **A:** Jr. High-Adult. **P:** Entertainment. **U:** Home. **L:** English. **Mov-Ent**: Biography: Sports, Baseball. **Acq:** Purchase. **Dist:** WarnerArchive.com.

The Big Lebowski 1997 (R) — ★★★½
Jeff Lebowski (Bridges), a stuck-in-the-'70s stoner who insists on being called "the Dude" and loves to go bowling, is mistaken for a wheelchair-bound millionaire of the same name, and suffers at the hands of thugs who are after money owed by the rich Lebowski's slutty wife. Dude is drawn into kidnapping, the attempted scamming of payoff money, and more bowling. While this may seem like plot-a-plenty, it's mainly a showcase for the Coen brothers' unique texturing of style and quirky-but-deep characters. Goodman is loud and funny as a quick-to-anger Vietnam vet. Turturro steals his scenes as a pervert rival bowler. The showpiece is an amazing musical-bowling-fantasy sequence that would've made Busby Berkeley proud. 117m; VHS, DVD, Blu-Ray, HD-DVD. **C:** Jeff Bridges; John Goodman; Steve Buscemi; Julianne Moore; Peter Stormare; David Huddleston; Philip Seymour Hoffman; Flea; Leon Russom; Sam Elliott; John Turturro; David Thewlis; Ben Gazzara; Tara Reid; Jack Kehler; Richard Gant; Dom Irrera; Jon Polito; Directed by Joel Coen; Written by Joel Coen; Ethan Coen; Cinematography by Roger Deakins; Music by Carter Burwell. **Pr:** Ethan Coen; Ethan Coen; Working Title Productions; Polygram Filmed Entertainment. **A:** Sr. High-Adult. **P:** Entertainment. **U:** Home. **Mov-Ent**: Action-Adventure, Bowling, Handicapped. **Acq:** Purchase. **Dist:** Universal Studios Home Video.

The Big Lever 1982
The staunchly Republican mountain jurisdiction of Leslie County, Kentucky is the scene of this look at grassroots politics. 53m; VHS, 3/4 U. **Pr:** Frances Morton. **A:** Sr. High-Adult. **P:** Education. **U:** Institution, Home. **Gen-Edu**: Documentary Films, Politics & Government. **Acq:** Purchase. **Dist:** Appalshop Films & Video.

The Big Lift 1950 — ★★½
Two G.I.'s assigned to the Berlin airlift ally themselves in counter-intelligence when they discover that their mutual girlfriend is a spy. 119m/B/W; VHS, DVD. **C:** Montgomery Clift; Paul Douglas; Cornell Borchers; Bruni Lobel; O.E. Hasse; Directed by George Seaton. **Pr:** 20th Century-Fox. **A:** Family. **P:** Entertainment. **U:** Home. **Mov-Ent**: World War Two. **Acq:** Purchase, Rent/Lease. **Dist:** Movies Unlimited; Alpha Video. $19.95.

Big Long Man and Mountain Lion 1993
Native American tale as told by Rafe Martin that depicts a time when people and animals were able to talk to each other. 15m; VHS. **Pr:** Film Ideas, Inc. **A:** Family. **P:** Education. **U:** Institution, Home. **Gen-Edu**: Native Americans, Folklore & Legends. **Acq:** Purchase. **Dist:** Film Ideas, Inc. $110.00.

Big Love: The Complete Fifth Season 2011
HBO 2006-2011 drama. "Winter": After winning the election, Bill reveals he's a polygamist and everyone has to deal with the fallout. "The Oath": Bill tries to fight anti-polygamy sentiment before his swearing-in ceremony while Nicki has problems with both Margene and Barb. "Where Men and Mountains Meet":

Barb wants to join a reform-minded church, Margene wants to volunteer abroad, and Nicki fears being abandoned as Bill may be going to jail. 10 episodes. 600m; DVD. **C:** Bill Paxton; Jeanne Tripplehorn; Chloe Sevigny; Ginnifer Goodwin. **A:** Adult. **P:** Entertainment. **U:** Home. **L:** English. **Mov-Ent:** Family, Marriage, Television Series. **Acq:** Purchase. **Dist:** HBO Home Video. $39.98.

Big Love: The Complete First Season 2006 (Unrated)
Bill is a suburban Salt Lake City Mormon who goes against his church's present-day teachings by still practicing polygamy. Bill has three wives—Barb, Nicki, and Margene—seven children, and three adjoining households. Not to mention a lot of stress. And all of Bill's complications aren't just on the homefront. 12 episodes. 693m; DVD, Wide, CC. **C:** Bill Paxton; Jeanne Tripplehorn; Chloe Sevigny; Ginnifer Goodwin; Harry Dean Stanton. **A:** College-Adult. **P:** Entertainment. **U:** Home. **Mov-Ent:** Television Series, Drama. **Acq:** Purchase. **Dist:** Home Box Office Inc.

Big Love: The Complete Fourth Season 2010
HBO 2006-2011 drama. "The Greater Good": Bill wants to run for a vacant Utah State Senate seat instead of taking Nicki's advice to become Juniper Creek's next prophet. "Strange Bedfellows": Bill tries to repair his relationship with Nicki when they go to DC so Bill can get the endorsement of Congressman Clark Paley (Perry King). "End of Days": The election is days away but Bill's campaign may be in trouble. 9 episodes. 517m; DVD. **C:** Bill Paxton; Jeanne Tripplehorn; Chloe Sevigny; Ginnifer Goodwin. **A:** Adult. **P:** Entertainment. **U:** Home. **L:** English. **Mov-Ent:** Family, Marriage, Television Series. **Acq:** Purchase. **Dist:** HBO Home Video. $39.98.

Big Love: The Complete Second Season 2007
Closet polygamist Bill Henrickson confronts many crisis this season: discovering who outed his wife, Barbara, at the Mother of the Year ceremony; investigating his brother-in-law's poisoning; negotiating a deal to buy a gaming company; and working possible wife No. 4 into the fray, a Serbian waitress named Ana ("Holy Spirit Sucker Punch"). Viewers also get three prequel peeks into the Henricksons' lives: Nicki's post-partum depression after the birth of her first son, Margene's first impression ("Meet the Baby-Sitter"), and how the three wives coerce Bill to move to the suburbs. 720m; DVD, Wide, CC. **C:** Bill Paxton; Jeanne Tripplehorn; Branka Katic; Ginnifer Goodwin; Chloe Sevigny. **A:** Adult. **P:** Entertainment. **U:** Home. **Mov-Ent:** Drama, Television. **Acq:** Purchase. **Dist:** Home Box Office Inc.

Big Love: The Complete Third Season 2009
HBO 2006-2011 drama. "Block Party": Bill wants to diversify his businesses and proposes working with Native American partners to open a Mormon-friendly casino. "On Trial": Nicki struggles with her devotion to her father as Roman (Harry Dean Stanton) goes on trial and Bill tries to get Alby (Matt Ross) to break ranks. "Come, Ye Saints": The family goes on a road trip to the Joseph Smith shrine, but Bill's faith is tested by family revelations. 10 episodes. 600m; DVD. **C:** Bill Paxton; Jeanne Tripplehorn; Chloe Sevigny; Ginnifer Goodwin. **A:** Adult. **P:** Entertainment. **U:** Home. **L:** English. **Mov-Ent:** Family, Marriage, Television Series. **Acq:** Purchase. **Dist:** HBO Home Video. $39.98.

Big Mama 2000
Documentary showcasing age discrimination in the case of a grandmother trying to raise her grandson in south central Los Angeles. 35m; VHS, DVD. **A:** Sr. High-Adult. **P:** Entertainment. **U:** Home, Institution. **Mov-Ent:** Aging, Documentary Films. **Acq:** Purchase. **Dist:** California Newsreel. $26.95.

The Big Man: Crossing the Line 1991 (R) — ★★★
Neeson shines as a down on his luck Scottish miner who loses his job during a union strike. Desperate for cash and unable to resolve his bitterness at being unable to support his family, he's enticed by a Glasgow hood to fight in an illegal bare-knuckled boxing match. What follows is an overlong and extremely brutal fight. Good performances from a talented cast overcome a rather preachy script that doesn't disguise its contempt for the Thatcher government, but also allows a glimpse into the tough times that many Brits suffered during the '80s. Based on the novel by William McIlvanney. 93m; VHS, DVD. **C:** Liam Neeson; Joanne Whalley; Ian Bannen; Billy Connolly; Hugh Grant; Maurice Roeves; Rob Affleck; Directed by David Leland; Written by Don MacPherson; Music by Ennio Morricone. **Pr:** Palace Productions; Scottish Television. **A:** Sr. High-Adult. **P:** Entertainment. **U:** Home. **Mov-Ent:** Boxing, Miners & Mining, Scotland. **Acq:** Purchase. **Dist:** Sony Pictures Home Entertainment Inc. $89.95.

Big Man Japan 2007 (PG-13) — ★½
Weird mockumentary about a Japanese superhero with bad press. Everyman Daisato works for the Defense Department where he is routinely turned humungous, thanks to a burst of electricity, so he can battle a variety of monsters that plague Tokyo. Since they regularly destroy the city, this doesn't make the citizens too happy. Japanese with subtitles. 113m; DVD. **C:** Riki Takeuchi; Ryunosuke Kamiki; Itsuji Itao; Hitoshi Matsumoto; Ua; Directed by Hitoshi Matsumoto; Written by Hitoshi Matsumoto; Mitsuyoshi Yakasu; Cinematography by Hideo Yamamoto; Music by Towa Tei. **A:** Sr. High-Adult. **P:** Entertainment. **U:** Home. **L:** Japanese. **Mov-Ent. Acq:** Purchase. **Dist:** Magnolia Home Entertainment.

Big Man on Campus 1989 (PG-13) — ★
A modern-day Quasimodo makes his home in an affluent university's belltower. Of course he falls in love with one of the pretty young co-eds and races out of his tower only to be captured by the psychology department. Really, really bad. 102m; VHS. **C:** Tom Skerritt; Corey Parker; Allan Katz; Cindy Williams; Melora Hardin; Jessica Harper; Gerrit Graham; Directed by Jeremy Paul Kagan; Written by Allan Katz; Cinematography by Bojan Bazelli; Music by Joseph Vitarelli. **Pr:** Vestron Pictures. **A:** Jr. High-Adult. **P:** Entertainment. **U:** Home. **Mov-Ent. Acq:** Purchase. **Dist:** $33.96.

Big Meat Eater 1985 (Unrated) — ★★
A musical gore-comedy about extraterrestrials using radioactive butcher's discards for ship fuel. Deliberate camp that is so bad its funny! 81m; VHS, DVD. **C:** George Dawson; Big Miller; Andrew Gillies; Stephen Dimopoulos; Georgina Hegedos; Ida Carnevali; Sharon Wahl; Directed by Chris Windsor; Written by Chris Windsor; Phil Savath; Laurence Keane; Cinematography by Doug McKay. **Pr:** Laurence Keane; New Line Cinema. **A:** Sr. High-Adult. **P:** Entertainment. **U:** Home. **Mov-Ent:** Canada. **Acq:** Purchase. **Dist:** Movies Unlimited. $49.95.

Big Miracle 2012 (PG) — ★★½
Based on true events, this big fish story avoids the pitfalls of sentimentality and provides a quality family movie. Small town Alaska newsman Adam (Krakowski) teams up with ex-girlfriend and Greenpeace volunteer Rachel (Barrymore) to save a family of endangered whales that are slowly being trapped by ice in the Arctic Circle. Once the story is picked up by the national media, volunteers show up to help. The do-gooders, including a slick oilman (Danson) and an Inuit leader (Pingayak), are mostly there to further their own personal agendas however. Based on Tom Rose's book "Freeing the Whales: How the Media Created the World's Greatest Non-Event." 107m; DVD, Blu-Ray. **C:** John Krasinski; Drew Barrymore; Kristen Bell; Dermot Mulroney; Tim Blake Nelson; Ted Danson; Vinessa Shaw; Stephen (Steve) Root; Michael Gaston; Rob Riggle; James LeGros; John Pingayak; Kathy Baker; Directed by Ken Kwapis; Written by Jack Amiel; Michael Begler; Cinematography by John Bailey; Music by Cliff Eidelman. **Pr:** Tim Bevan; Liza Chasin; Eric Fellner; Steven Golin; Michael Sugar; Anonymous Content; Working Title Films; Universal Pictures. **A:** Family. **P:** Entertainment. **U:** Home. **L:** English. **Mov-Ent:** Action-Adventure, Whales, Journalism. **Acq:** Purchase. **Dist:** Universal Studios Home Video.

Big Mo 1973 (G) — ★★
True story of the friendship that developed between Cincinnati Royals basketball stars Maurice Stokes and Jack Twyman after a strange paralysis hit Stokes. 110m; VHS. **C:** Bernie Casey; Bo Svenson; Stephanie Edwards; Janet MacLachlan; Directed by Daniel Mann. **Pr:** National General Pictures. **A:** Family. **P:** Entertainment. **U:** Home. **Mov-Ent:** Biography: Sports, Basketball, Sports--Fiction: Drama. **Acq:** Purchase. **Dist:** $69.95.

Big Momma's House 2000 (PG-13) — ★★
FBI agent Lawrence is sent to Georgia to protect single mom Long and her son from her escaped con ex. Since he's a master of disguise, Lawrence passes himself off as her grandma, who's known as "Big Momma." Lawrence, like his pal Eddie Murphy, has plenty of experience with costumes, disquises, and multiple roles. So it's kind of disappointing that this isn't a better movie. Sporadic laughs are too often mined from toilet humor, and the plot doesn't allow for many quiet moments, which Lawrence needs to balance out the slapstick. 98m; VHS, DVD, Wide, CC. **C:** Martin Lawrence; Nia Long; Paul Giamatti; Terrence Howard; Anthony Anderson; Carl Wright; Ella Mitchell; Jascha Washington; Starletta DuPois; Cedric the Entertainer; Directed by Raja Gosnell; Written by Darryl Quarles; Don Rhymer; Cinematography by Michael D. O'Shea; Music by Richard Gibbs. **Pr:** 20th Century-Fox. **A:** Sr. High-Adult. **P:** Entertainment. **U:** Home. **Mov-Ent:** Federal Bureau of Investigation (FBI). **Acq:** Purchase. **Dist:** Fox Home Entertainment.

Big Momma's House 2 2006 (PG-13) — ★★
Hey, if you liked seeing Lawrence in a fat suit and a dress the first time, you'll probably think the sequel is okay. The plot, such as it is, has FBI agent Malcolm Turner's alter ego Hattie Mae Pierce posing as a nanny to investigate Tom Fuller (Moses), a computer expert who has created a worm that threatens national security. Long returns too, this time as Turner's suspicious pregnant missus. Be warned: the sight of Momma running along the beach in cornrows and a bright yellow bathing suit may scar the psyche for life. 98m; DVD, CC. **C:** Martin Lawrence; Nia Long; Emily Procter; Mark Moses; Kat Dennings; Chloe Grace Moretz; Marisol Nichols; Josh Flitter; Dan Lauria; Zachary Levi; Preston Shores; Trevor Shores; Lisa Arrindell Anderson; Directed by John Whitesell; Written by Don Rhymer; Cinematography by Mark Irwin; Music by George S. Clinton. **Pr:** David T. Friendly; Michael Green; Deep River; Runteldat Entertainment; 20th Century-Fox. **A:** Jr. High-Adult. **P:** Entertainment. **U:** Home. **L:** English. **Mov-Ent:** Federal Bureau of Investigation (FBI), Computers. **Dist:** Fox Home Entertainment.

Big Mommas: Like Father, Like Son 2011 (PG-13) — ★
FBI agent Malcolm Turner (AKA Big Momma) and his teenage stepson Trent (AKA Charmaine) go undercover at an all-girls performing arts school to catch a killer after Trent witnesses a murder. With a complete lack of imagination from both cast and crew, jokes fall flat as either offensive, unforgivably humorless, or (most frequently) both. A tired and uninspired portrayal that pokes fun at black women, and the idea of black women having power. Lawrence would do best to hang up the fat suit and the franchise. 107m; Blu-Ray, On Demand, Wide. **C:** Martin Lawrence; Brandon T. Jackson; Faizon Love; Portia Doubleday; Jessica Lucas; Michelle Ang; Emily Rios; Ken Jeong; Directed by John Whitesell; Written by Matthew Fogel; Cinematography by Anthony B. Richmond; Music by David Newman. **Pr:** David T. Friendly; Michael Green; The Collective; Friendly Films; New Regency Pictures; Regency Enterprises; Runteldat Entertainment; 20th Century-Fox. **A:** Jr. High-Adult. **P:** Entertainment. **U:** Home. **L:** English. **Mov-Ent:** Black Culture, Federal Bureau of Investigation (FBI). **Acq:** Purchase. **Dist:** Fox Home Entertainment; Amazon.com Inc.; Movies Unlimited.

The Big Money Mixup 1988
Five children find $75,000 in cash that has fallen out of an armored truck. 35m; VHS. **Pr:** Bridgestone Production Group. **A:** Family. **P:** Religious. **U:** Home. **Gen-Edu:** Children. **Acq:** Purchase. **Dist:** Alpha Omega Publications Inc. $59.95.

The Big Monster Mash 19??
A collection of trailers and clips from classic horror movies including "The Birds," "Psycho," "The Tingler," and "White Zombie." 60m; VHS. **A:** Jr. High-Adult. **P:** Entertainment. **U:** Home. **Mov-Ent:** Horror, Outtakes & Bloopers. **Acq:** Purchase. **Dist:** Video Resources.

Big Mouth 1967 — ★
A dopey fisherman gets ahold of a treasure map and is pursued by cops and gangsters. Standard Lewis fare, with the requisite infantile histrionics; must be French to appreciate. 107m; VHS. **C:** Jerry Lewis; Jeannine Riley; Harold J. Stone; Charlie Callas; Buddy Lester; Susan Bay; Directed by Jerry Lewis; Written by Jerry Lewis; Music by Harry Betts. **Pr:** Jerry Lewis; Jerry Lewis. **A:** Family. **P:** Entertainment. **U:** Home. **Mov-Ent:** Comedy--Slapstick. **Acq:** Purchase. **Dist:** Sony Pictures Home Entertainment Inc. $49.98.

Big Mouth Bassin' 1990
Tactics and techniques for landing largemouth bass are presented here. 30m; VHS. **Pr:** MNTEX Ent. **A:** Family. **P:** Instruction. **U:** Home. **How-Ins:** Sports--General, Fishing, How-To. **Acq:** Purchase. **Dist:** MNTEX Entertainment, Inc.; Karol Media. $14.95.

Big News 1929 (Unrated) — ★★
Based on the play "For Two Cents" by George S. Brooks, this early talkie uses sound to great advantage. Fired for going after a gangster who's a big advertiser (Hardy), reporter Armstrong nevertheless keeps after the crook. When the intrepid reporter pushes too far, murder enters the picture. 75m/B/W; VHS, DVD. **C:** Robert Armstrong; Carole Lombard; Tom Kennedy; Warner Richmond; Wade Boteler; Sam Hardy; Lew Ayres; Directed by Gregory La Cava. **Pr:** Pathe. **A:** Jr. High-Adult. **P:** Entertainment. **U:** Home. **Mov-Ent:** Mystery & Suspense, Journalism. **Acq:** Purchase. **Dist:** Alpha Video. $18.99.

The Big Night 1951 (Unrated) — ★★
Coming of age drama has 17-year-old George (Barrymore) watching as his nice guy dad (Foster) is beaten by thugish sports writer Al Judge (St. John). The naive teen takes his dad's gun and goes to get revenge by trying to track Judge down in the seedier parts of town. It's a long night before George confronts his foe, with some unexpected consequences. 76m/B/W; DVD. **C:** John Drew (Blythe) Barrymore, Jr.; Howard St. John; Preston Foster; Philip Bourneuf; Joan Lorring; Dorothy Comingore; Directed by Joseph Losey; Written by Joseph Losey; Stanley Ellin; Cinematography by Hal Mohr; Music by Lyn Murray. **A:** Sr. High-Adult. **P:** Entertainment. **U:** Home. **L:** English. **Mov-Ent:** Adolescence, Drama. **Acq:** Purchase. **Dist:** MGM Home Entertainment.

Big Night 1995 (R) — ★★½
Set in '50s New Jersey, film provides an Old World/New World look at Italian brothers Primo (Shalhoub) and Secondo (Tucci) Pilaggi and their elegant but failing restaurant. Primo is the perfectionist chef who hates compromise while Secondo wants to Americanize the place in an effort to make it a success. (He knows the customer is always right even if they can't appreciate Primo's exquisitely authentic Italian dishes). In order to get attention, Secondo arranges a special night in honor of jazz great Louis Prima, with Primo out to cook the feast of a lifetime—if they can pull it off. Another food film guaranteed to make you hungry. 109m; VHS, DVD, CC. **C:** Tony Shalhoub; Stanley Tucci; Ian Holm; Minnie Driver; Campbell Scott; Isabella Rossellini; Marc Anthony; Allison Janney; Dina Spybey; Directed by Stanley Tucci; Campbell Scott; Written by Stanley Tucci; Joseph Tropiano; Cinematography by Ken Kelsch. **Pr:** Jonathan Filley; Keith Samples; Rysher Entertainment. **A:** Sr. High-Adult. **P:** Entertainment. **U:** Home. **Mov-Ent:** Comedy-Drama, Food Industry. **Awds:** Ind. Spirit '97: First Screenplay; Natl. Soc. Film Critics '96: Support. Actor (Shalhoub); Sundance '96: Screenplay. **Acq:** Purchase. **Dist:** Sony Pictures Home Entertainment Inc.

Big Nothing 2006 (Unrated) — ★½
Now there's a title just leaving itself wide open. Well, it's more like "little nothing" anyway. Struggling writer Charlie (Schwimmer) takes a job at a call center. Co-worker Gus (Pegg) persuades Charlie to join him in blackmailing a preacher who likes kiddie-porn websites. They pick up a third partner in blonde babe Josie (Eve). 86m; DVD, Wide. **C:** David Schwimmer; Simon Pegg; Alice Eve; Mimi Rogers; Natascha (Natasha) McElhone; Jon Polito; Billy Asher; Mitchell Mullen; Directed by Jean-Baptiste Andrea; Written by Jean-Baptiste Andrea; Cinematography by Richard Greatrex; Music by Alan Anton. **A:** Sr. High-Adult. **P:** Entertainment. **U:** Home. **Mov-Ent. Acq:** Purchase. **Dist:** Movies Unlimited; Alpha Video.

The Big One 1998 (PG-13) — ★★
Moore once again takes his populist, CEO-baiting act on the road in search of corporate evil-doers, this time on Random House's dime. Documentary lovingly follows Moore on his 1996 book promo tour, as he highlights plant closings, verbally spars with Nike boss Phil Knight, plays pranks on his "handlers," and mugs for his adoring fans. His style is still the same as in "Roger & Me," but since he's joined the celebrity ranks, Moore isn't going to sneak up on anybody. To his credit, he doesn't try, but to his discredit, he ends up haranguing the very working people he claims to be standing up for, mostly exasperated receptionists and secretaries. Corporate greed and apathy are still

squarely in Moore's crosshairs, but this time his own ego prevents him from getting a clear shot at his target. 90m; VHS, DVD, CC. **C:** Narrated by Michael Moore; Directed by Michael Moore. **Pr:** Miramax Film Corp. **A:** Sr. High-Adult. **P:** Entertainment. **U:** Home. **Mov-Ent:** Documentary Films. **Acq:** Purchase. **Dist:** Buena Vista Home Entertainment.

The Big Parade 1925 — ★★★★
Wonderful WWI silent, considered to be one of the best war flicks of all time. Gilbert and Adoree are exceptional as lovers torn apart by the conflict. Interesting and thoughtful picture of the trauma and trouble brought to men and their loved ones in wartime. Battle scenes are compelling and intense; Vidor's masterpiece. 141m/B/W; Silent; DVD, Blu-Ray. **C:** John Gilbert; Renee Adoree; Hobart Bosworth; Claire McDowell; Claire Adams; Karl (Daen) Dane; Robert Ober; Tom (Thomas E.) O'Brien; Rosita Marstini; Directed by King Vidor; Written by Harry Behn; Cinematography by John Arnold; Music by William Axt; David Mendoza. **Pr:** Irving Thalberg; MGM. **A:** Sr. High-Adult. **P:** Entertainment. **U:** Home. **Mov-Ent:** Drama, World War One, Silent Films. **Awds:** Natl. Film Reg. '92. **Acq:** Purchase. **Dist:** Warner Home Video, Inc. $29.95.

The Big Picture 1989 (PG-13) — ★★½
A hilarious, overlooked comedy by and starring a variety of Second City/National Lampoon alumni, about a young filmmaker who is contracted by a big studio, only to see his vision trampled by formula-minded producers, crazed agents, hungry starlets, and every other variety of Hollywood predator. 95m; VHS, DVD, CC. **C:** Kevin Bacon; Jennifer Jason Leigh; Martin Short; Michael McKean; Emily Longstreth; J.T. Walsh; Eddie Albert; Richard Belzer; John Cleese; June Lockhart; Stephen Collins; Roddy McDowall; Kim Miyori; Teri Hatcher; Dan Schneider; Jason Gould; Tracy Brooks Swope; Directed by Christopher Guest; Written by Michael McKean; Christopher Guest; Michael Varhol; Music by David Nichtern. **A:** Jr. High-Adult. **P:** Entertainment. **U:** Home. **Mov-Ent:** Satire & Parody. **Acq:** Purchase. **Dist:** Sony Pictures Home Entertainment Inc. $89.95.

The Big Picture 2010 (Unrated) — ★★½
A successful lawyer fears his life is over after murdering his wife's lover, so he does what comes naturally: he steals the identity of the man he's killed and assumes his life. 115m; DVD, Blu-Ray, Streaming. **C:** Romain Duris; Marina Fois; Niels Arestup; Branka Katic; Catherine Deneuve; Directed by Eric Lartigau; Written by Eric Lartigau; Laurent de Bartillat; Cinematography by Laurent Dailland; Music by Sacha Galperine; Evgueni Galperine. **A:** Sr. High-Adult. **P:** Entertainment. **U:** Home. **L:** English, French. **Mov-Ent. Acq:** Purchase, Rent/Lease. **Dist:** MPI Media Group. $29.98 24.98 14.99.

The Big Picture: Rethinking Dyslexia 2012 (Unrated)
Documentary following a dyslexic teen as he tries out for college, along with interviews with dyslexics who have become successful in their careers. 52m; DVD, Streaming. **A:** Jr. High-Adult. **P:** Education. **U:** Home. **L:** English. **Gen-Edu:** Documentary Films, Learning Disabilities, Interviews. **Acq:** Purchase, Rent/Lease. **Dist:** Janson Media. $29.95 9.99.

The Big Picture: Sales Environment 1992
Explains the differences between sales clerks and professional sales consultants. 28m; VHS. **A:** Adult. **P:** Professional. **U:** Institution. **Bus-Ind:** Business, Sales Training. **Acq:** Purchase. **Dist:** RMI Media. $99.00.

Big Picture—The Fight for Vietnam 196?
This program explains various aspects of the army's mission in Vietnam. 30m/B/W; VHS, 3/4 U. **A:** Sr. High-Adult. **P:** Education. **U:** Institution, Home. **Gen-Edu:** Documentary Films, Vietnam War. **Acq:** Purchase. **Dist:** International Historic Films Inc.

The Big Plane Trip 1994
Live-action program for children featuring different aspects of the airline industry. Covers pilot training, the control tower, the staff of an aircraft, the cockpit, and flying. Also provides mini tour of Switzerland, including toy museum, chocolate factory, medieval castle, alpine train, and miniature Swiss village. 45m; VHS. **A:** Preschool-Jr. High. **P:** Education. **U:** Home, Institution. **Chl-Juv:** Aeronautics, Children. **Acq:** Purchase. **Dist:** Tapeworm Video Distributors Inc. $12.95.

The Big Push 1975 (PG) — ★½
Motley bunch of Alaskan lumberjacks get together to save a poor widow's logging camp from a pair of greedy mill owners. 98m; VHS, DVD. **C:** Joseph Cotten; Claude Akins; Cesar Romero; Tab Hunter; Roosevelt "Rosie" Grier; Leon Ames; Stubby Kaye; Patricia Medina; Directed by Tay Garnett. **Pr:** Chuck D. Kean. **A:** Primary-Adult. **P:** Entertainment. **U:** Home. **Mov-Ent:** Action-Adventure, Arctic Regions, Philanthropy. **Acq:** Purchase. **Dist:** Unknown Distributor.

Big Red 1962 (Unrated) — ★★½
Set amid the spectacular beauty of Canada's Quebec Province, an orphan boy protects a dog which later saves him from a mountain lion. 89m; VHS, DVD. **C:** Walter Pidgeon; Gilles Payant; Directed by Norman Tokar; Written by Louis Pelletier; Cinematography by Edward Colman; Music by Oliver Wallace; Richard M. Sherman; Robert B. Sherman. **Pr:** Buena Vista. **A:** Family. **P:** Entertainment. **U:** Home. **Mov-Ent:** Pets, Adoption, Canada. **Acq:** Purchase. **Dist:** Walt Disney Studios Home Entertainment. $69.95.

Big Red 1993
Fire safety education program for kids looks at the job of a firefighter. Introduces preparation, tools, and fire trucks. 25m; VHS. **A:** Preschool-Primary. **P:** Education. **U:** Home, Institution. **Chl-Juv:** Safety Education, Fires. **Acq:** Purchase. **Dist:** Tapeworm Video Distributors Inc. $19.95.

The Big Red One 1980 (PG) — ★★★½
Fuller's harrowing, intense semi-autobiographical account of the U.S. Army's famous First Infantry Division in WWII, the "Big Red One." A rifle squad composed of four very young men, led by the grizzled Marvin, cut a fiery path of conquest from the landing in North Africa to the liberation of the concentration camp at Falkenau, Czechoslovakia. In part a tale of lost innocence, the film scores highest by bringing the raw terror of war down to the individual level. New restored version adds about 47 minutes and sports an "R" rating. 113m; VHS, DVD, Blu-Ray. **C:** Lee Marvin; Robert Carradine; Mark Hamill; Stephane Audran; Bobby DiCicco; Perry Lang; Kelly Ward; Siegfried Rauch; Serge Marquand; Charles Macaulay; Alain Doutey; Maurice Marsac; Colin Gilbert; Joseph Clark; Ken Campbell; Doug Werner; Marthe Villalonga; Directed by Samuel Fuller; Written by Samuel Fuller; Cinematography by Adam Greenberg; Music by Dana Kaproff. **Pr:** Gene Corman; Lorimar Productions. **A:** Sr. High-Adult. **P:** Entertainment. **U:** Home. **Mov-Ent:** Drama, World War Two, Biography: Military. **Acq:** Purchase. **Dist:** Warner Home Video, Inc. $19.98.

The Big Red Scare of 1919-1920 ????
Overviews social tensions after World War I, labor strikes, the Bolshevik Revolution's effect on the U.S., and responses to wartime patriotism. 10m; VHS. **A:** Adult. **P:** Education. **U:** Institution. **Gen-Edu:** History--U.S., Labor & Unions. **Acq:** Purchase. **Dist:** Zenger Media. $30.00.

Big Red Valentine/King Clifford 2003 (Unrated)
Animated children's television program. Clifford the Big Red Dog is the star of this animated collection of episodes set in an enchanted land of kings and treasure. 30m; DVD. **A:** Preschool-Primary. **P:** Entertainment. **U:** Home. **Mov-Ent:** Family Viewing, Animation & Cartoons, Children's Shows. **Acq:** Purchase. **Dist:** Lions Gate Entertainment Inc. $11.98.

Big Rigs: Close Up and Very Personal 1993
A look at 18-wheelers and other big trucks performing a variety of tasks. Kids will get a driver's eye view, which is impressive, but the video is wordless and the background music is a detracting drone. 30m; VHS. **A:** Preschool. **P:** Entertainment. **U:** Home. **Chl-Juv. Acq:** Purchase. **Dist:** Stage Fright Productions. $14.95.

The Big Scam 1979 — ★★½
Criminal mastermind Niven recruits ex-con Jordan to pull off a massive bank heist. 102m; DVD. **C:** Richard Jordan; David Niven; Oliver Tobias; Elke Sommer; Gloria Grahame; Hugh Griffith; Richard Johnson; Joss Ackland; Alfred Molina; Directed by Ralph Thomas; Written by Guy Elmes; Cinematography by John Coquillon; Music by Stanley Myers. **A:** Adult. **P:** Entertainment. **U:** Home. **Mov-Ent:** Action-Adventure, Great Britain. **Acq:** Purchase. **Dist:** Alpha Video; Movies Unlimited. $9.95.

Big Score 1983 (R) — ★
When a policeman is falsely accused and dismissed from the Chicago Police Department, he goes after the men who really stole the money from a drug bust. Script was originally intended to be a Dirty Harry flick; too bad it wasn't. 88m; VHS, DVD. **C:** Fred Williamson; John Saxon; Richard Roundtree; Nancy Wilson; Ed Lauter; Ron Dean; D'Urville Martin; Michael Dante; Joe Spinell; Directed by Fred Williamson; Cinematography by Joao Fernandes. **Pr:** Almi Pictures. **A:** Sr. High-Adult. **P:** Entertainment. **U:** Home. **Mov-Ent. Acq:** Purchase. **Dist:** Movies Unlimited; Alpha Video. $69.95.

Big Screen Sweethearts 1989
Have a ball with the Flintstones, Scooby Doo, Precious Pupp, and other Hanna-Barbera favorites in these romance-filled cartoons. 80m; VHS. **Pr:** Hanna-Barbera Productions. **A:** Family. **P:** Entertainment. **U:** Home. **Mov-Ent:** Animation & Cartoons, Romance, Television Series. **Acq:** Purchase. **Dist:** Turner Broadcasting System Inc. $29.95.

The Big Sell 1990
A look at the strategies and tactics used to market alcohol. 30m; VHS, Special order formats. **Pr:** Illinois Feature Project. **A:** Jr. High-Adult. **P:** Education. **U:** Institution. **Gen-Edu:** Documentary Films, Advertising, Alcoholic Beverages. **Acq:** Purchase. **Dist:** Pyramid Media. $325.00.

The Big Sellout 2006
Documentary using economic science to dispute modern economic theories, and showcasing the people whose lives are affected negatively by them. In English and Spanish with English subtitles. 94m; DVD. **A:** Sr. High-Adult. **P:** Education. **U:** Institution. **L:** English, Spanish. **Gen-Edu:** Economics, Documentary Films. **Acq:** Purchase. **Dist:** California Newsreel. $49.95.

The Big Shakedown 1934 (Unrated) — ★½
Overdone melodrama. Druggist Jimmy Morrell (Farrell) is going broke when gangster Dutch Barnes Cortez) gets him counterfeiting brand name drugs. Only Jimmy's deal endangers his pregnant wife Norma (Davis). 61m/B/W; DVD. **C:** Charles Farrell; Ricardo Cortez; Bette Davis; Glenda Farrell; Allen Jenkins; Directed by John Francis Dillon; Written by Rian James; Niven Busch; Cinematography by Sidney Hickox. **A:** Sr. High-Adult. **P:** Entertainment. **U:** Home. **L:** English. **Mov-Ent:** Crime Drama, Pregnancy. **Acq:** Purchase. **Dist:** WarnerArchive.com.

Big Shot: Confessions of a Campus Bookie 2002 (R) — ★★½
Based on the true story of Brooklyn-born Benny Silman (Krumholtz) who undergoes culture shock when he begins attending Arizona State University. He takes frequent trips to Vegas and is soon running his own campus bookmaking operation but wants more. Then Benny meets hoops star Stevin Smith (Kittles) who isn't adverse to making some money on the side. So Benny hooks up with a big-time Vegas gambler (Turturro) to shave points in ASU games. 83m; VHS, DVD. **C:** David Krumholtz; Nicholas Turturro; Jennifer (Jenny) Morrison; Tory Kittles; Carmine D. Giovinazzo; Alex Rocco; James LeGros; Directed by Ernest R. Dickerson; Written by Jason Keller; Cinematography by Steven Bernstein; Music by Reinhold Heil; Johnny Klimek. **A:** Sr. High-Adult. **P:** Entertainment. **U:** Home. **Mov-Ent:** Gambling, Basketball. **Acq:** Purchase. **Dist:** Fox Home Entertainment.

Big Shots 1987 (PG-13) — ★
Two kids, one naive and white, the other black and streetwise, search for a stolen watch. 91m; VHS, DVD, CC. **C:** Ricky Busker; Darius McCrary; Robert Joy; Paul Winfield; Robert Prosky; Jerzy Skolimowski; Directed by Robert Mandel; Written by Joe Eszterhas; Music by Bruce Broughton. **Pr:** Joe Medjuck; Michael Gross; Ivan Reitman. **A:** Jr. High-Adult. **P:** Entertainment. **U:** Home. **Mov-Ent. Acq:** Purchase. **Dist:** Warner Home Video, Inc. $19.98.

Big Shot's Funeral 2001 (PG) — ★
American director Don Tyler (Sutherland) is on location in Beijing when he suffers a serious health crisis and winds up in the hospital. He tells cameraman YoYo (Ge) that should he die, he wants a blow-out funeral, which YoYo promises to arrange. Since he has no money, YoYo auctions off advertising and sponsorships for the funeral but then Don begins to improve. Would-be comedy has very few laughs. English and Manderin with subtitles. 100m; VHS, DVD. **C:** Donald Sutherland; Ge You; Rosamund Kwan; Da(nniel) Ying; Paul Mazursky; Directed by Feng Xiao Gang; Written by Feng Xiao Gang; Cinematography by Li Zhang; Music by San Bao. **A:** Jr. High-Adult. **P:** Entertainment. **U:** Home. **L:** Chinese, English. **Mov-Ent. Acq:** Purchase. **Dist:** Sony Pictures Home Entertainment Inc.

Big Show 1937 — ★★
A western adventure about the making of a western adventure. Autry jangles spurs aplenty in duel role. 54m/B/W; VHS, DVD. **C:** Gene Autry; Smiley Burnette; Directed by Mack V. Wright. **Pr:** Republic; Gene Autry Productions. **A:** Family. **P:** Entertainment. **U:** Home. **Mov-Ent:** Western, Filmmaking. **Acq:** Purchase. **Dist:** Alpha Video. $19.95.

The Big Six ????
Ride in the cab and the caboose of the former Western Maryland Shay #6 as it carries freight between Cass and Durbine, West Virginia. 48m; VHS. **A:** College-Adult. **P:** Education. **U:** Home. **Gen-Edu:** Trains. **Acq:** Purchase. **Dist:** The Civil War Standard. $19.95.

The Big Six 19??
Nautical adventure based on the stories of Arthur Ransome. 90m; VHS. **A:** Family. **P:** Entertainment. **U:** Home. **Chl-Juv:** Boating. **Acq:** Purchase. **Dist:** Janson Media. $24.95.

Big Six 2005
Lance Armstrong in the Tour de France. DVD. **A:** Adult. **P:** Entertainment. **U:** Home. **Spo-Rec:** Bicycling, Sports--General. **Acq:** Purchase. **Dist:** Front Row Entertainment. $14.99.

The Big Sky 1952 — ★★★
It's 1830, and a rowdy band of fur trappers embark upon a back breaking expedition up the uncharted Missouri River. Based on the A.B. Guthrie Jr. novel, it's an effortlessly enjoyable and level-headed Hawksian American myth, with a streak of gentle gallows humor. Also available colorized. 122m; VHS, CC. **C:** Kirk Douglas; Dewey Martin; Arthur Hunnicutt; Elizabeth Threatt; Buddy Baer; Steven Geray; Jim Davis; Directed by Howard Hawks. **Pr:** RKO. **A:** Family. **P:** Entertainment. **U:** Home. **Mov-Ent:** Western, Rivers & Streams. **Acq:** Purchase. **Dist:** Facets Multimedia Inc.; Turner Broadcasting System Inc. $14.98.

The Big Sleep 1946 (Unrated) — ★★★★
Private eye Philip Marlowe, hired to protect a young woman from her own indiscretions, falls in love with her older sister while uncovering murders galore. A dense, chaotic thriller that succeeded in defining and setting a standard for its genre. The very best Raymond Chandler on film combining a witty script with great performances, especially from Bogart and Bacall. 114m/B/W; VHS, DVD. **C:** Humphrey Bogart; Lauren Bacall; John Ridgely; Martha Vickers; Louis Jean Heydt; Regis Toomey; Peggy Knudsen; Dorothy Malone; Bob Steele; Elisha Cook, Jr.; Directed by Howard Hawks; Written by William Faulkner; Jules Furthman; Leigh Brackett; Cinematography by Sidney Hickox; Music by Max Steiner. **Pr:** Warner Bros. **A:** Jr. High-Adult. **P:** Entertainment. **U:** Home. **Mov-Ent:** Mystery & Suspense, Classic Films. **Awds:** Natl. Film Reg. '97. **Acq:** Purchase. **Dist:** MGM Home Entertainment; Time-Life Video and Television. $19.98.

The Big Sleep 1978 (R) — ★★
A tired remake of the Raymond Chandler potboiler about exhausted Los Angeles private dick Marlowe and his problems in protecting a wild young heiress from her own decadence and mob connections. Mitchum appears to need a rest. 99m; VHS, DVD. **C:** Robert Mitchum; Sarah Miles; Richard Boone; Candy Clark; Edward Fox; Joan Collins; John Mills; James Stewart; Oliver Reed; Harry Andrews; James Donald; Colin Blakely; Richard Todd; Directed by Michael Winner; Written by Michael Winner. **Pr:** United Artists; ITC Entertainment Group. **A:** College-Adult. **P:** Entertainment. **U:** Home. **Mov-Ent:** Mystery & Suspense. **Acq:** Purchase. **Dist:** Sony Pictures Home Entertainment Inc. $19.98.

The Big Slice 1990 (R) — ★½
Two would-be crime novelists want to improve their fiction. One masquerades as a cop, the other as a crook, and they infiltrate the underworld from both ends. Clever comedy premise, but vaudeville-level jokes fall flat. 86m; VHS, DVD. **C:** Casey

Siemaszko; Leslie Hope; Justin Louis; Heather Locklear; Kenneth Welsh; Nicholas (Nick) Campbell; Henry Ramer; Directed by John Bradshaw; Written by John Bradshaw; Music by Mychael Danna; Jeff Danna. **Pr:** SC Entertainment Corporation. **A:** Sr. High-Adult. **P:** Entertainment. **U:** Home. **Mov-Ent:** Action-Adventure. **Acq:** Purchase. **Dist:** Unknown Distributor.

The Big Snit 1987
An animated film which compares a domestic quarrel with the conflict of global nuclear war. 10m; VHS, 3/4 U. **Pr:** Richard Condie; Michael Scott. **A:** Jr. High-Adult. **P:** Education. **U:** Institution, SURA. **Mov-Ent:** Animation & Cartoons, Nuclear Warfare. **Acq:** Purchase, Rent/Lease. **Dist:** National Film Board of Canada.

The Big Sombrero 1949 (Unrated) — ★★½
Autry takes a stand against the marriage between an unsuspecting, wealthy Mexican girl and the fortune-seeking bridegroom who wants her land. 77m; VHS, DVD. **C:** Gene Autry; Elena Verdugo; Steve (Stephen) Dunne; George Lewis; Directed by Frank McDonald. **Pr:** Columbia Pictures. **A:** Family. **P:** Entertainment. **U:** Home. **Mov-Ent:** Western, Romance. **Acq:** Purchase. **Dist:** Lions Gate Entertainment Inc.; Movies Unlimited. $39.98.

The Big Squeeze 1996 (R) — ★★½
Married bartender Tanya (Boyle) is displeased to find out her born-again hubby Henry (Bercovici) has been holding out a large wad of cash from an insurance settlement, apparently about to donate it to a local Spanish mission. Enter Benny (Dobson), a cocky con man willing to help Tanya get her share of the dough for his own cut; sweet bartender Jesse (Nucci), who's secretly in love in Tanya; and fellow barmaid Cece (Dispina), who catches Benny's wandering eye. All get caught up in the frantic double-dealing. 100m; VHS, DVD. **C:** Lara Flynn Boyle; Peter Dobson; Luca Bercovici; Danny Nucci; Teresa Dispina; Sam Vlahos; Valente Rodriguez; Directed by Marcus De Leon; Written by Marcus De Leon; Cinematography by Jacques Haitkin; Music by Mark Mothersbaugh. **Pr:** Zane Levitt; Mark Yellen; Liz McDermott; Zeta Entertainment; First Look Pictures. **A:** Sr. High-Adult. **P:** Entertainment. **U:** Home. **Mov-Ent:** Insurance, Marriage, Religion. **Acq:** Purchase. **Dist:** BMG Entertainment.

Big Stakes 1922 — ★
Extremely rare Western feature that has a Texas cowboy falling for a Mexican senorita. Plenty of action as complications ensue. 61m/B/W; Silent; VHS. **C:** H.B. Warner; Elinor Fair; Les Bates; Directed by Clifford S. Elfelt; Written by Frank Howard Clark. **A:** Jr. High-Adult. **P:** Entertainment. **U:** Home. **Mov-Ent:** Western, Silent Films. **Acq:** Purchase. **Dist:** Glenn Video Vistas Ltd.

The Big Stampede 1932 — ★★
Twenty-five-year-old Wayne stars in this action-packed Western that was a remake of "Land Beyond the Law" from Ken Maynard's silent. Based on a story by Marion Jackson. 63m/B/W; VHS, DVD, CC. **C:** John Wayne; Noah Beery, Sr.; Luis Alberni; Berton Churchill; Paul Hurst; Lafe (Lafayette) McKee; Frank Ellis; Hank Bell; Directed by Tenny Wright; Written by Kurt Kempler. **Pr:** Warner Bros. **A:** Jr. High-Adult. **P:** Entertainment. **U:** Home. **Mov-Ent:** Western. **Acq:** Purchase. **Dist:** MGM Home Entertainment; Grapevine Video. $19.98.

Big Stan 2007 (R) — ★★
Surprisingly funny prison comedy from Schneider (who also directs) as long as you don't expect too much. Con man Stan (Schneider) gets convicted of fraud but the judge postpones his sentence for six months. Naturally worried about how he'll survive in the joint, the weakling enlists martial arts guru The Master (a deadpan Carradine) to teach him defensive skills. Stan's transformation leads to his becoming a leader among the inmates, much to the displeasure of crooked warden Gasque (Wilson). 105m; DVD. **C:** Rob Schneider; Scott Wilson; David Carradine; Jennifer (Jenny) Morrison; M. Emmet Walsh; Richard Kind; Henry Gibson; Sally Kirkland; Dan Haggerty; Marcia Wallace; Kevin Gage; Bob Sapp; Directed by Rob Schneider; Written by Josh Lieb; Cinematography by Victor Hammer; Music by John Hunter. **A:** Sr. High-Adult. **P:** Entertainment. **U:** Home. **Mov-Ent:** Martial Arts. **Acq:** Purchase. **Dist:** Warner Home Video, Inc.

Big Star: Nothing Can Hurt Me 2013 (PG-13) — ★★★
Big Star may be the most popular band that most people have never heard of. They founded a style of alternative pop music that inspired The Replacements (who even wrote a hit song about their frontman, Alex Chilton), R.E.M., The Flaming Lips, and many more. But they never really became the household name that so many music insiders thought they could and should be. DeNicola and Mori's very enjoyable documentary runs a little long (nearly two hours) but captures the adoration of a band who made it big without ever really making it famous. 113m; DVD, Blu-Ray. **C:** Directed by Drew DeNicola; Olivia Mori; Cinematography by Drew DeNicola. **Pr:** Olivia Mori; Danielle McCarthy. **A:** Jr. High-Adult. **P:** Entertainment. **U:** Home. **L:** English. **Mov-Ent:** Documentary Films, Music. **Acq:** Purchase. **Dist:** Magnolia Pictures.

Big Steal 1949 (Unrated) — ★★★
An Army officer recovers a missing payroll and captures the thieves after a tumultuous chase through Mexico. 72m/B/W; VHS, DVD. **C:** Robert Mitchum; William Bendix; Jane Greer; Ramon Novarro; Patric Knowles; Don Alvarado; John Qualen; Directed by Donald Siegel; Written by Daniel Mainwaring; Gerald Drayson Adams; Cinematography by Harry Wild; Music by Leigh Harline. **Pr:** RKO. **A:** Family. **P:** Entertainment. **U:** Home. **Mov-Ent:** Mexico. **Acq:** Purchase. **Dist:** Movies Unlimited.

Big Steam's Last Stand: Winter on Jinpeng Pass 19??
Highlights double-headed steam locomotives from China's Jitong Railway pulling freight and passenger trains over Jingpeng Pass, tours shops at Shenyang, captures an engine overhaul at Deban, visits the CTC room at Shangdian, and provides a cab view from a QJ-Class 2-10-2. 120m; DVD. **A:** Family. **P:** Education. **U:** Home. **L:** English. **Gen-Edu:** Trains, U.S. States. **Acq:** Purchase. **Dist:** Anchor Videos; The Civil War Standard. $35.95.

The Big Stick 1991
Analyzes the activist foreign policy the U.S. had toward Latin America in the early part of the 19th century. 30m; VHS. **A:** Adult. **P:** Education. **U:** Institution. **Gen-Edu:** History--U.S. **Acq:** Purchase. **Dist:** RMI Media. $99.00.

Big Store 1941 (Unrated) — ★★½
Late Marx Brothers in which they are detectives in a large metropolitan department store, foiling a hostile takeover and preventing a murder. Their last MGM effort, with some good moments between the Tony Martin song numbers which include "If It's You" and the immortal "Tenement Symphony." Groucho also leads the "Sing While You Sell" number. 96m/B/W; VHS, DVD. **C:** Groucho Marx; Harpo Marx; Chico Marx; Tony Martin; Margaret Dumont; Virginia Grey; Virginia O'Brien; Douglass Dumbrille; Marion Martin; Henry Armetta; Directed by Charles Reisner; Written by Hal Fimberg; Ray Golden; Sid Kuller; Cinematography by Charles Lawton, Jr.; Music by George Bassman. **Pr:** MGM. **A:** Family. **P:** Entertainment. **U:** Home. **Mov-Ent:** Comedy--Slapstick. **Acq:** Purchase. **Dist:** MGM Home Entertainment. $19.95.

Big Street 1942 (Unrated) — ★★½
A timid busboy, in love with a disinterested nightclub singer, gets to prove his devotion when she is crippled in a fall. Based on a Damon Runyon story, "Little Pinks." 88m/B/W; VHS, DVD. **C:** Henry Fonda; Lucille Ball; Agnes Moorehead; Louise Beavers; Barton MacLane; Eugene Pallette; Ozzie Nelson; Directed by Irving Reis. **Pr:** RKO. **A:** Jr. High-Adult. **P:** Entertainment. **U:** Home. **Mov-Ent:** Drama, Handicapped. **Acq:** Purchase. **Dist:** Turner Broadcasting System Inc. $19.95.

Big Sur 2013 (R) — ★★
Polish's unstructured narrative, based on the 1962 autobiographical novel by Jack Kerouac (featuring his literary alter-ego Jack Duluoz). In 1960, an alcohol-ravaged Kerouac still can't deal with the public attention brought on by the success of his novel "On the Road." Writer Lawrence Ferlinghetti offers Jack his remote cabin at Big Sur for a getaway, but the writer is soon lonely and heads to San Francisco to carouse with friends, bringing them back to the cabin to party. These include Neal Casady and his mistress, Billie, with whom Kerouac is soon involved although his personal demons continue to sabotage his life. 100m; DVD. **C:** Jean-Marc Barr; Josh(ua) Lucas; Kate (Catherine) Bosworth; Radha Mitchell; Anthony Edwards; Balthazar Getty; Henry Thomas; Patrick Fischler; Directed by Michael Polish; Written by Michael Polish; Cinematography by M. David Mullen; Music by Aaron Dessner; Bryce Dessner. **A:** Sr. High-Adult. **P:** Entertainment. **U:** Home. **L:** English. **Mov-Ent:** Alcoholism, Literature--American, Biography. **Acq:** Purchase. **Dist:** ARC Entertainment, LLC.

Big Sur: Wild California 2010 (Unrated)
Explore all aspects of Big Sur through the eyes of its native animals, the condor, the sea otter, and the mountain lion. 50m; DVD, Blu-Ray. **A:** Family. **P:** Education. **U:** Institution, Home. **Hea-Sci:** Documentary Films, Science, Wildlife. **Acq:** Purchase. **Dist:** National Geographic Society. $24.95.

The Big Sweat 1990 (Unrated) — ★
Maybe you've heard this one before: a man who has been framed by the mob escapes from prison and heads for Mexico. But first, he's got to get past the mobsters and police who are hot on his trail. And maybe you've seen some of it before: some of the same stock footage appears in Lommel's "Cold Heat." Not surprisingly, this one bypassed theatres and went straight to video. 85m; VHS. **C:** Robert Z'Dar; Steve Molone; Kevin McBride; William Roebuck; Cheri Caspari; David Rushing; Joanne Watkins; Ken Letner; Directed by Ulli Lommel; Written by Max Bolt; Music by John Massari. **Pr:** American International Pictures. **A:** College-Adult. **P:** Entertainment. **U:** Home. **Mov-Ent.** **Acq:** Purchase. **Dist:** Unknown Distributor.

The Big Switch 1970 (R) — ★½
Gambler is framed for murder and becomes embroiled in a plot to reinstate an old gangster kingpin. 68m; VHS. **C:** Sebastian Breaks; Virginia Wetherell; Erika Raffael; Directed by Pete Walker. **Pr:** Peter Walker. **A:** College-Adult. **P:** Entertainment. **U:** Home. **Mov-Ent:** Mystery & Suspense. **Acq:** Purchase. **Dist:** No Longer Available.

The Big Tease 1999 (R) — ★★
Gay Glasgow hairdresser Crawford Mackenzie (Ferguson) thinks he's being asked to compete in the prestigious World Freestyle Hairdressing Championship being held in Los Angeles. So he heads to Hollywood and discovers he's just been asked to observe. Blithely self-confident, Crawford simply decides he will not only find a way to enter but he will defeat his snippy Swedish rival, Stig (Rasche). Good-natured, campy fluff. 86m; VHS, DVD, Wide, CC. **C:** Kevin Allen; Craig Ferguson; Frances Fisher; Chris Langham; Mary McCormack; Donal Logue; Larry Miller; David Rasche; Charles Napier; David Hasselhoff; Cathy Lee Crosby; Bruce Jenner; Isabella Aitken; Directed by Kevin Allen; Written by Craig Ferguson; Sacha Gervasi; Cinematography by Seamus McGarvey; Music by Mark Thomas. **Pr:** Warner Bros. **A:** Sr. High-Adult. **P:** Entertainment. **U:** Home. **Mov-Ent:** Satire & Parody. **Acq:** Purchase. **Dist:** Warner Home Video, Inc.

The Big Thicket: Crossroads in the Texas Forest 1986
A portrait of a dense wilderness area of Southeast Texas and how the progress of the 20th century has changed it and the few people who live there. 28m; VHS, 3/4 U. **Pr:** Paul Yeager. **A:** Sr. High-Adult. **P:** Education. **U:** Institution, Home. **Gen-Edu:** Wilderness Areas, U.S. States. **Acq:** Purchase. **Dist:** Houston Public Television.

The Big Throws System 2013 (Unrated)
Coaches Brian Forrester and Mike Hambrick demonstrate their training system for shot put and discus throwers. 74m; DVD. **A:** Family. **P:** Education. **U:** Home. **L:** English. **Spo-Rec:** Athletic Instruction/Coaching, Sports--Track & Field, How-To. **Acq:** Purchase. **Dist:** Championship Productions. $39.99.

Big Top Pee-wee 1988 (PG) — ★★
Pee-wee's second feature film following the success of "Pee-wee's Big Adventure." This time Pee-wee owns a farm, has a girlfriend (!) and lives the good life until a weird storm blows a traveling circus onto his property. Cute, but not the manic hilarity the first one was. 86m; VHS, DVD, 8 mm, CC. **C:** Paul (Pee-wee Herman) Reubens; Kris Kristofferson; Susan Tyrrell; Penelope Ann Miller; Directed by Randal Kleiser; Written by Paul (Pee-wee Herman) Reubens; Cinematography by Steven Poster; Music by Danny Elfman. **Pr:** Paramount Pictures. **A:** Jr. High-Adult. **P:** Entertainment. **U:** Home. **Mov-Ent:** Fantasy, Children, Romance. **Acq:** Purchase. **Dist:** $14.95.

Big Town 1947 (Unrated) — ★
A newspaper is saved by a new editor who brings integrity to the once scandalous paper. The editor and his reporters also solve a series of murders. Some action, but weak dialogue and direction hold it back. Based on the radio program of the same name. 59m/B/W; VHS. **C:** Phillip Reed; Hillary Brooke; Robert Lowery; Byron Barr; Veda Ann Borg; Nana Bryant; Charles Arnt; John Dehner; Directed by William C. Thomas; Written by Daniel Mainwaring; Maxwell Shane; Cinematography by Fred H. Jackman, Jr.; Music by Darrell Calker. **Pr:** William Pine; William C. Thomas; William C. Thomas; Paramount Pictures. **A:** Jr. High-Adult. **P:** Entertainment. **U:** Home. **Mov-Ent:** Journalism. **Acq:** Purchase. **Dist:** Sinister Cinema. $16.95.

Big Town 1987 (R) — ★★½
A farmboy, lucky with dice, hits Chicago to claim his fortune where he meets floozies, criminals, and other streetlife. Standard '50s period underworld drama is elevated by exceptional cast's fine ensemble work. Look for Lane's strip number. 109m; VHS, DVD. **C:** Matt Dillon; Diane Lane; Tommy Lee Jones; Bruce Dern; Tom Skerritt; Lee Grant; Suzy Amis; David Marshall Grant; Don Francks; Del Close; Cherry Jones; David James Elliot; Don Lake; Diego Matamoros; Gary Farmer; Sarah Polley; Lolita Davidovich; Directed by Ben Bolt; Harold Becker; Written by Robert Roy Pool; Cinematography by Ralf Bode; Music by Michael Melvoin. **A:** Sr. High-Adult. **P:** Entertainment. **U:** Home. **Mov-Ent:** Gambling, Adolescence. **Acq:** Purchase. **Dist:** Lions Gate Television Corp. $89.98.

Big Town After Dark 1947 — ★★
Daring journalists search for the bottom-line story on a gang of criminals. They find themselves caught behind the firing lines when the sun goes down. Slightly better than average thriller based on the radio show "Big Town." 69m/B/W; VHS, DVD. **C:** Phillip Reed; Hillary Brooke; Richard Travis; Ann Gillis; Vince Barnett; Joseph (Joe) Sawyer; Robert Kent; Charles Arnt; Directed by William C. Thomas; Cinematography by Ellis W. Carter; Music by Darrell Calker. **Pr:** Paramount Pictures. **A:** Sr. High-Adult. **P:** Entertainment. **U:** Home. **Mov-Ent:** Mystery & Suspense, Journalism. **Acq:** Purchase. **Dist:** Sinister Cinema; Rex Miller Artisan Studio. $16.95.

The Big Trail 1930 — ★★★
This pioneering effort in widescreen cinematography was Wayne's first feature film. A wagon train on the Oregon trail encounters Indians, buffalo, tough terrain, and romantic problems. 110m/B/W; DVD, Beta, Blu-Ray. **C:** John Wayne; Marguerite Churchill; El Brendel; Tully Marshall; Tyrone Power, Sr.; Ward Bond; Helen Parrish; Directed by Raoul Walsh. **Pr:** Fox. **A:** Family. **P:** Entertainment. **U:** Home. **Mov-Ent:** Western, Classic Films. **Awds:** Natl. Film Reg. '06. **Acq:** Purchase. **Dist:** Twentieth Century Fox Film Corp.; Movies Unlimited. $19.98.

Big Train: Seasons 1 & 2 1998
Comedy sketch show makes light of office antics, a shy cop, desperate pop stars, a duck in danger, hens ready to battle, a bewildered Transport Minister, and the highly popular World Stare Out championships. 346m; DVD. **C:** Kevin Eldon; Simon Pegg; Julia Davis; Catherine Tate; Mark Heap. **A:** Adult. **P:** Entertainment. **U:** Home. **Mov-Ent.** **Acq:** Purchase. **Dist:** Warner Home Video, Inc.

Big Trees 1952 (Unrated) — ★★★
A ruthless lumberman attempts a takeover of the California Redwood Timberlands that are owned by a group of peaceful homesteaders. 89m; VHS, DVD, 3/4 U, Special order formats. **C:** Kirk Douglas; Patrice Wymore; Eve Miller; Alan Hale, Jr.; Edgar Buchanan; Directed by Felix Feist. **A:** Family. **P:** Entertainment. **U:** Home. **Mov-Ent:** Forests & Trees. **Acq:** Purchase. **Dist:** Gotham Distributing Corp. $19.95.

Big Trouble 1986 (R) — ★★
An insurance broker endeavors to send his three sons to Yale by conspiring with a crazy couple in a fraud scheme that goes awry in every possible manner. Look for the cameo by screenwriter Bergman as Warren Bogle. 93m; VHS, DVD. **C:** Alan Arkin; Peter Falk; Beverly D'Angelo; Charles Durning; Robert Stack; Paul Dooley; Valerie Curtin; Richard Libertini; Cameo(s) Andrew Bergman; Directed by John Cassavetes; Written by Andrew Bergman; Cinematography by Bill Butler; Music by Bill Conti. **Pr:** John Cassavetes; John Cassavetes; Columbia Pic-

tures. **A:** Sr. High-Adult. **P:** Entertainment. **U:** Home. **Mov-Ent:** Insurance. **Acq:** Purchase. **Dist:** Sony Pictures Home Entertainment Inc. $19.95.

Big Trouble 2002 (PG-13) — ★★
Fast-paced ensemble comedy based on the novel by Dave Barry packs a metric ton of narrative, not to mention characters, into a mere 84 minutes, most of which involve the clash of various characters tracking down a nuclear bomb in Miami. Suburban Anna (Russo) is trapped in a loveless marriage with unscrupulous businessman Arthur Herk (Tucci) who wants to buy a nuclear bomb, thus getting involved with some undesirable characters, most notably two hit men (Farina and Kehler). The plot kicks off when Matt (Foster), the son of divorced journalist Allen decides to snipe the Herk's daughter Jenny (Deschanel) with a high-powered squirt gun on the same night the hit men visit. Of the strong cast, Allen and Foster are the stand-outs. Cartoony, heavy-handed direction buries satire for which Barry is known. 84m; VHS, DVD. **C:** Tim Allen; Rene Russo; Stanley Tucci; Tom Sizemore; Johnny Knoxville; Dennis Farina; Jack Kehler; Janeane Garofalo; Patrick Warburton; Ben Foster; Zooey Deschanel; Dwight "Heavy D" Myers; Omar Epps; Jason Lee; Andy Richter; Sofia Vergara; Directed by Barry Sonnenfeld; Written by Robert Ramsey; Matthew Stone; Cinematography by Greg Gardiner; Music by James Newton Howard. **Pr:** Barry Sonnenfeld; Barry Sonnenfeld; Tom Jacobson; Barry Josephson; Touchstone Pictures. **A:** Jr. High-Adult. **P:** Entertainment. **U:** Home. **Mov-Ent:** Family, Federal Bureau of Investigation (FBI). **Acq:** Purchase. **Dist:** Buena Vista Home Entertainment.

Big Trouble in Little China 1986 (PG-13) — ★★1/2
A trucker plunges beneath the streets of San Francisco's Chinatown to battle an army of spirits. An uproarious comic-book-film parody with plenty of action and a keen sense of sophomoric sarcasm. 99m; VHS, DVD, UMD, Wide, CC. **C:** Kurt Russell; Suzee Pai; Dennis Dun; Kim Cattrall; James Hong; Victor Wong; Kate Burton; Directed by John Carpenter; Written by David Weinstein; Gary Goldman; W.D. Richter; Cinematography by Dean Cundey; Music by John Carpenter; Alan Howarth. **Pr:** Larry J. Franco; 20th Century-Fox. **A:** Jr. High-Adult. **P:** Entertainment. **U:** Home. **Mov-Ent:** Satire & Parody, Martial Arts. **Acq:** Purchase. **Dist:** Fox Home Entertainment. $14.98.

The Big Turnaround 1988 (Unrated) — ★1/2
Drug-dealing punks push their goods into Mexico via a lowly southwest town but local do-gooders led by a struggling doctor (Cranston, whose father, Joseph, serves as director and producer) and a priest (Borgnine) boldly unite to save the day in this misguided effort. 98m; VHS, DVD. **C:** Mindi Miller; Michael J. Reynolds; Robert Axelrod; Robert V. Barron; Ernest Borgnine; Bryan Cranston; Luis Latino; Rick Le Fever; Ruben Castillo; Al Fleming; Stu Weltman; Directed by Joseph L. Cranston; Written by Luis Johnston; Cinematography by Karen Grossman; Music by Jasmin Larkin. **A:** Jr. High-Adult. **P:** Entertainment. **U:** Home. **Mov-Ent:** Crime Drama, Drug Trafficking/Dealing, Action-Adventure. **Acq:** Purchase. **Dist:** Movies Unlimited. $14.95.

The Big Valley: Season One 1965
Widowed matriarch Victoria Barkley (Stanwyck, who earned an Emmy for the role) keeps the 1870 California cattle ranch, gold mines, citrus groves, and logging camps running with her eldest son Jarrod (Long), lawyer Nick (Breck), family entrepreneur Eugene (Briles), and the shamefully spoiled Audra (Evans). The dramatic arc of season one comes when the bastard son of the departed Tom Barkley appears to knock the family off their pillar in the community. Heath (Majors), determined to get his rightful inheritance, struggles to be accepted. Most scenarios follow a fairly predictable path: someone's got a grudge against the Barkleys, a friend is found untrustworthy, Audra falls for the wrong guy, and people are given the chance to redeem themselves from past wrongs. 30 episodes on five discs. 1530m; DVD. **C:** Barbara Stanwyck; Richard Long; Peter Breck; Lee Majors; Linda Evans; Charles Briles. **A:** Jr. High-Adult. **P:** Entertainment. **U:** Home. **Mov-Ent:** Western, Drama, Television Series. **Acq:** Purchase. **Dist:** Fox Home Entertainment.

The Big Valley: Season Two, Volume 1 1966
The heritage of Barkley's illegitimate son Heath is revealed in "The Lost Treasure" when a con man and mud-slinging politician come to town falsely accusing. Colleen Dewhurst appears as the outlaw Annie Morton in "A Day of Terror" and holds Victoria and Audra hostage. A pre-"Brady Bunch" Eve Plumb is a little girl trapped in a well in "Hide the Children," which deals with the intolerance toward gypsies. A band of bumbling brothers have trouble with a train station safe in "The Great Safe Robbery." 15 episodes on three discs. 771m; DVD. **C:** Barbara Stanwyck; Lee Majors; Linda Evans. **A:** Jr. High-Adult. **P:** Entertainment. **U:** Home. **Mov-Ent:** Western, Drama, Television Series. **Acq:** Purchase. **Dist:** Fox Home Entertainment.

Big Walleye Presentations 19??
Covers live bait, soft plastics, rod selection, rigging methods, spinners, and drift socks. 70m; VHS. **A:** Adult. **P:** Instruction. **U:** Home. **Spo-Rec:** Fishing. **Acq:** Purchase. **Dist:** In-Fisherman.

Big Water Catfish 19??
Offers tips on anchoring and setting lines and hints on finding the best places to fish. ?m; VHS. **A:** Adult. **P:** Instruction. **U:** Home. **Spo-Rec:** Fishing. **Acq:** Purchase. **Dist:** In-Fisherman.

The Big Wedding 2013 (R) — ★
Abrasively awful even by the standards of this subgenre of bad wedding comedies, director/writer Zackham's film only serves to prove the truth that a spectacular cast means nothing if the script wastes their talent. Don and Ellie Griffin (De Niro & Keaton) are forced to pretend to be a happy couple to keep their adopted son's family happy at the wedding. Sarandon, Heigl, Williams, Topher Grace, and Seyfried get sucked into a script that feels created by a computer program that started with the keyword "contrived." 89m; DVD, Blu-Ray. **C:** Robert De Niro; Diane Keaton; Ben Barnes; Amanda Seyfried; Susan Sarandon; Robin Williams; Katherine Heigl; Topher Grace; Marc Blucas; Christine Ebersole; Directed by Justin Zackham; Written by Justin Zackham; Cinematography by Jonathan Brown; Music by Nathan Barr. **Pr:** Clay Pecorin; Richard Salvatore; Anthony G. Katagas; Harry J. Ufland; Justin Zackham; Two Ton Films; Millenium Films; Lionsgate. **A:** Sr. High-Adult. **P:** Entertainment. **U:** Home. **L:** English. **Mov-Ent:** Divorce, Family, Adoption. **Acq:** Purchase. **Dist:** Lions Gate Home Entertainment.

Big Wednesday 1978 (PG) — ★★1/2
Three California surfers from the early '60s get back together after the Vietnam war to reminisce about the good old days and take on the big wave. 120m; VHS, DVD, Wide. **C:** Jan-Michael Vincent; Gary Busey; William Katt; Lee Purcell; Patti D'Arbanville; Directed by John Milius; Written by John Milius; Music by Basil Poledouris. **A:** Sr. High-Adult. **P:** Entertainment. **U:** Home. **Mov-Ent:** Comedy-Drama. **Acq:** Purchase. **Dist:** Warner Home Video, Inc. $59.95.

The Big Wet 1993
A look at the tropical monsoon season in the Kakadu region of Australia and the natural rhythms of growth and decline. 60m; VHS. **A:** Jr. High-Adult. **P:** Entertainment. **U:** Home. **Gen-Edu:** Australia. **Acq:** Purchase. **Dist:** Discovery Home Entertainment; Baker and Taylor. $19.95.

The Big Wheel 1949 (Unrated) — ★★1/2
Old story retold fairly well. Rooney is young son determined to travel in his father's tracks as a race car driver, even when dad buys the farm on the oval. Good acting and direction keep this a cut above average. 92m/B/W; VHS, DVD. **C:** Mickey Rooney; Thomas Mitchell; Spring Byington; Mary Hatcher; Allen Jenkins; Michael O'Shea; Directed by Edward Ludwig. **A:** Sr. High-Adult. **P:** Entertainment. **U:** Home. **Mov-Ent:** Automobiles--Racing, Parenting. **Acq:** Purchase. **Dist:** Grapevine Video; Facets Multimedia Inc.

The Big White 2005 (R) — ★1/2
A waste of talent in a lame comedy. Alaska travel agent Paul Barnell (Williams) has money problems. Then he finds a frozen body in a dumpster. Paul hopes to pass the body off as his estranged brother Raymond (Harrelson) and collect the life insurance, but agent Ted (Ribisi) is suspicious. Add in Paul's troubled wife Margaret (Hunter), the sudden return of Raymond, and a couple of wannabe kidnapper/hitmen (Nelson, Brown) and Paul's got more complications than he can handle. 105m; DVD. **C:** Robin Williams; Holly Hunter; Woody Harrelson; Tim Blake Nelson; Giovanni Ribisi; W. Earl Brown; Alison Lohman; Directed by Mark Mylod; Written by Collin Friesen; Cinematography by James Gleason; Music by Mark Mothersbaugh. **A:** Sr. High-Adult. **P:** Entertainment. **U:** Home. **Mov-Ent:** Insurance, Action-Adventure. **Acq:** Purchase. **Dist:** Echo Bridge Home Entertainment.

Big World 1984
Patriarchal "ideals" are examined in this philosophical video. 18m; VHS, 3/4 U. **Pr:** Edward Mowbray. **A:** Jr. High-Adult. **P:** Education. **U:** Institution, SURA. **Gen-Edu:** Philosophy & Ideology, Video. **Acq:** Rent/Lease. **Dist:** Video Out Distribution.

The Big Year 2011 (PG) — ★★1/2
Quirky comedy explores the offbeat world of competitive bird-watching (or "birding" as they very seriously call it). Champion birder Bostick (Wilson) neglects his wife while trying to fend off his competition. Right on his tail-feathers are stuffy CEO Stu (Martin) and goofy loser Brad (Black). The trio jet off to beautifully photographed locales in their quest to spot the most birds in one year, with alliances and friendships shifting. More pleasantly whimsical than laugh-out-loud funny, it's a family-friendly change of pace. Based on Mark Obmascik's 1998 book "The Big Year: A Tale of Man, Nature, and Fowl Obsession." 100m; DVD. **C:** Steve Martin; Jack Black; Owen Wilson; Rashida Jones; Anjelica Huston; Rosamund Pike; JoBeth Williams; Brian Dennehy; Dianne Wiest; Jim Parsons; Joel McHale; Kevin Pollak; Directed by David Frankel; Written by Howard Franklin; Cinematography by Lawrence Sher; Music by Theodore Shapiro. **Pr:** Stuart Cornfeld; Carol Fenelon; Curtis Hanson; Karen Rosenfelt; Ben Stiller; Deuce Three; Fox 2000 Pictures; Red Hour Films; Sunswept Entertainment; 20th Century-Fox. **A:** Primary-Adult. **P:** Entertainment. **U:** Home. **L:** English. **Mov-Ent:** Birds. **Acq:** Purchase. **Dist:** Fox Home Entertainment.

Big Zapper 1973 (Unrated) — ★1/2
Violent P.I. Marlowe and masochistic assistant Rock work together in this British comic strip film. 94m; VHS. **C:** Linda Marlowe; Gary Hope; Sean Hewitt; Richard Monette; Penny Irving; Directed by Lindsay Shonteff. **A:** College-Adult. **P:** Entertainment. **U:** Home. **Mov-Ent:** Action-Adventure. **Acq:** Purchase.

The Bigamist 1953 — ★1/2
Have you heard the one about the traveling salesman in this movie? He has one wife in Los Angeles, another in San Francisco, and they inevitably find out about each other. A maudlin soap opera with a do-it-yourself ending, only shows why bigamy was done better as farce in the later "Micki and Maude." 79m/B/W; DVD. **C:** Edmond O'Brien; Joan Fontaine; Ida Lupino; Edmund Gwenn; Jane Darwell; Kenneth Tobey; Directed by Ida Lupino; Written by Collier Young; Cinematography by George E. Diskant; Music by Leith Stevens. **Pr:** Filmakers Inc. **A:** Jr. High-Adult. **P:** Entertainment. **U:** Home. **Mov-Ent:** Drama. **Acq:** Purchase. **Dist:** Movies Unlimited; Alpha Video. $19.98.

Bigfoot 1970 (Unrated) — ★
Some bikers go hiking and find a Bigfoot partially buried in a grave. Something then beats everyone unconscious and steals the women-folk. The lesson here being let sleeping Bigfoots lie and watch out for Bigfoot's minions (yes, apparently he has furry minions). 84m; DVD. **C:** John Carradine; John Mitchum; James Craig; Christopher Mitchum; Joi Lansing; Judith Jordan; Directed by Robert F. Slatzer; Written by Robert F. Slatzer; James Gordon White; Cinematography by Wilson S. Hong; Music by Richard A. Podolor. **A:** Jr. High-Adult. **P:** Entertainment. **U:** Home. **L:** English. **Mov-Ent. Acq:** Purchase. **Dist:** Cheezy Flicks Entertainment, Inc. $12.95.

Bigfoot 1995
Involves the investigation into the world's most scrutinized mythical beast. 50m; VHS. **Pr:** A&E (Arts & Entertainment) Network. **A:** Family. **P:** Entertainment. **U:** Home. **Gen-Edu. Acq:** Purchase. **Dist:** New Video Group. $19.95.

Bigfoot and Wildboy, Vol. 1 1977
Bigfoot, Wildboy, the lost child he raised from infancy, and their friend Cindy set out on a number of adventures. 72m; VHS. **C:** Ray Young; Joseph Butcher; Yvonne Regalado; Monica Ramirez. **A:** Family. **P:** Entertainment. **U:** Home. **Mov-Ent:** Television Series, Fantasy. **Acq:** Purchase. **Dist:** New Line Home Video. $9.95.

Bigfoot and Wildboy, Vol. 2 1978
Contains the episodes "Outlaw Bigfoot," "Eye of the Mummy," and "Birth of the Titan." 72m; VHS. **C:** Ray Young; Joseph Butcher; Yvonne Regalado; Monica Ramirez. **A:** Family. **P:** Entertainment. **U:** Home. **Mov-Ent:** Television Series, Fantasy. **Acq:** Purchase. **Dist:** Crystal Clarity. $9.95.

Bigfoot in Action 1988
All the thrills that the giant tractor Bigfoot has provided to folks of all ages are here to excite you. 30m; VHS. **Pr:** Mediacast Television. **A:** Family. **P:** Entertainment. **U:** Home. **Spo-Rec:** Sports--General, Automobiles--Racing. **Acq:** Purchase. **Dist:** MNTEX Entertainment, Inc. $14.95.

Bigfoot: The Lost Coast Tapes 2012 (R) — ★1/2
Found footage mockumentary about an attempted comeback by an investigative journalist attempting to expose hoaxes and frauds. His first target is a hunter who claims to have the world's first real Sasquatch corpse. 87m; DVD, Blu-Ray, Streaming. **C:** Drew Rausch; Rich McDonald; Ashley Wood; Noah Weisberg; Frank Ashmore; Directed by Corey Grant; Written by Brian Kelsey; Bryan O'Cain; Cinematography by Richard J. Vialet; Music by Eddie Booze. **A:** Sr. High-Adult. **P:** Entertainment. **U:** Home. **L:** English. **Mov-Ent. Acq:** Purchase, Rent/Lease. **Dist:** XLrator Media. $20.99 14.99 3.99.

Bigfoot: The Unforgettable Encounter 1994 (PG) — ★★1/2
Young boy heads off into the woods, comes face to face with Bigfoot, and sets off a media frenzy and a band of ruthless bounty hunters determined to capture his hairy friend. 89m; VHS, DVD, CC. **C:** Zachery Ty Bryan; Matt McCoy; Barbara Willis Sweete; Clint Howard; Rance Howard; David Rasche; Directed by Corey Michael Eubanks; Written by Corey Michael Eubanks; Music by Shimon Arama. **A:** Primary-Adult. **P:** Entertainment. **U:** Home. **Mov-Ent:** Action-Adventure, Family Viewing, Mass Media. **Acq:** Purchase. **Dist:** Lions Gate Entertainment Inc.

Bigger, Faster, Stronger 1974
A tape about power weight training to produce bigger, faster, stronger athletes. Features championship high school, college, and professional athletes. Shows that success comes only to those who make a real commitment. 24m; 3/4 U. **Pr:** Brigham Young University. **A:** Jr. High-Adult. **P:** Education. **U:** Institution, CCTV, SURA. **Spo-Rec:** Fitness/Exercise. **Acq:** Purchase. **Dist:** Brigham Young University.

A Bigger Splash 1974
A film documenting that recreates the life of artist David Hockney in London during the 1970's, drawing its title from one of Hockney's trademark paintings of a California swimming pool. Hockney and his former lover Peter Schlesinger play themselves, as do many of the subjects of Hockney's paintings of the time. 105m; DVD. **C:** Directed by Jack Hazan; Written by Jack Hazan; David Mingay; Music by Patrick Gowers. **A:** College-Adult. **P:** Entertainment. **U:** Home. **Fin-Art:** Documentary Films, Biography, Art & Artists. **Acq:** Purchase. **Dist:** First Run Features. $24.95.

Bigger Stronger Faster 2008 (PG-13) — ★★1/2
Director Bell grew up in the mid 1980s, an era of steroid-enhanced wrestlers and bodybuilding actors, and his commentary on how America's obsession with winning might be destroying it is filled with ambivalence towards the fate of juiced athletes, including his two brothers. Much time is spent attempting to debunk the dangers of steroids, and the rest is devoted to the idea that the ideal of winning at any cost is the real danger. 107m; DVD. **C:** Chris Bell; Directed by Chris Bell; Written by Chris Bell; Alexander Buono; Tamsin Rawady; Cinematography by Alexander Buono; Music by Dave Porter. **A:** Jr. High-Adult. **P:** Education. **U:** Home. **L:** English, Spanish. **Gen-Edu:** Documentary Films, Sports Documentary, Drug Abuse. **Acq:** Purchase. **Dist:** Magnolia Home Entertainment. $26.98.

Bigger Than Life 1956 (Unrated) — ★★★
Exceptional cast comes through in this well made drama. Teacher Mason, hooked on drugs, destroys himself and his family. Worthwhile and compelling. Fine performances from supporting actors; Mason is superb. 95m; VHS. **C:** James

Mason; Barbara Rush; Walter Matthau; Robert F. Simon; Roland Winters; Christopher Olsen; Directed by Nicholas Ray; Written by Cyril Hume; Richard Maibaum; Cinematography by Joe MacDonald; Music by David Raksin. **Pr:** Fox. **A:** Sr. High-Adult. **P:** Entertainment. **U:** Home. **Mov-Ent**: Melodrama, Drugs, Family. **Acq:** Purchase. **Dist:** Criterion Collection Inc.

Bigger Than the Sky 2005 (PG-13) — ★★1/2
Recently-dumped Peter (Thomas), stuck in a lousy dead-end job, decides he needs something new. He tries out for the community theatre and finds what he's looking for through company regulars Michael (Corbett) and Grace (Smart). A very mild romantic comedy that almost works. Anyone involve in small theatre will relish in the details. Features Patty Duke playing mother to her real-life son, Sean Astin. 106m; VHS, DVD. **C:** Marcus Thomas; John Corbett; Amy Smart; Sean Astin; Clare Higgins; Patty Duke; Allan Corduner; Matt Salinger; Greg Germann; Directed by Al Corley; Written by Rodney Vaccaro; Cinematography by Christine Gentet; Music by Rob Cairns. **A:** Sr. High-Adult. **P:** Entertainment. **U:** Home. **Mov-Ent**: Comedy--Romantic. **Acq:** Purchase. **Dist:** MGM Home Entertainment. $19.95.

Bigger Than This Manhattan 1999
Children ages 6 to 15 share their feelings about the difficulties, fears, and loneliness of having a parent with HIV/AIDS. 15m; VHS. **A:** Adult. **P:** Professional. **U:** Institution. **Hea-Sci**: AIDS, Health Education, Children. **Acq:** Purchase. **Dist:** Aquarius Health Care Media. $149.00.

The Biggest Bears! 19??
Narrated by an adventurous five-year-old who tells of the animals he learned about when he moved to Alaska. Habitat, food, behaviors, and adult-young relationships of the grizzly bear become the focal points of this presentation. 22m; VHS. **A:** Family. **P:** Entertainment. **U:** Home. **Chl-Juv**: Animals, Wildlife. **Acq:** Purchase. **Dist:** Bullfrog Films, Inc. $14.95.

The Biggest Bundle of Them All 1968 — ★1/2
An inept group of criminals kidnap aged mobster Cesare Celli only to discover he's broke and can't pay the ransom. He offers to cut them in on a heist, but their inexperience causes problems in this hit-or-miss crime comedy. At least Raquel Welch appears in a bikini. 105m; DVD. **C:** Vittorio De Sica; Raquel Welch; Robert Wagner; Godfrey Cambridge; Davy Kaye; Francesco Mule; Edward G. Robinson; Directed by Ken Annakin; Written by Sy Salkowitz; Cinematography by Piero Portalupi; Music by Riz Ortolani. **A:** Sr. High-Adult. **P:** Entertainment. **U:** Home. **L:** English. **Mov-Ent**: Italy. **Acq:** Purchase. **Dist:** WarnerArchive.com.

The Biggest Fan 2002 (Unrated) — ★1/2
Silly teen romance about a fan and a boy band. Shy high school sophomore Debbie (Amariah) is the number one fan of Dream Street. Disappointed at missing their local concert, Debbie wakes up the next morning to a huge shock—she finds lead singer Chris Trousdale (playing himself) passed out in her room! Loopy from cold medicine, Chris missed the concert and stumbled around until he found a convenient place to crash. Debbie agrees to hide the dreamboat, who needs a timeout from all that squealing and screaming, but what if her parents find out? 95m; DVD. **C:** Marissa Tait; Richard Moll; Noriyuki "Pat" Morita; Michael Meyer; Kaila Amariah; Chris Trousdale; Morgan Brittany; Leslie Easterbrook; Jesse McCartney; Shanelle Workman; Cindy Williams; Directed by Michael Criscione; Written by Michael Criscione; LeeAnn Kemp; Liz Sinclair; Cinematography by Wes Llewellyn. **A:** Jr. High-Adult. **P:** Entertainment. **U:** Home. **Mov-Ent**. **Acq:** Purchase. **Dist:** Movies Unlimited.

The Biggest Jewish City in the World 1976
Historical footage and on-camera interviews explore Jewish immigrant experiences at the turn of the century in New York City's Lower East Side. 60m; VHS. **Pr:** Thames Television. **A:** College-Adult. **P:** Education. **U:** Institution, Home. **Gen-Edu**: Documentary Films, Judaism, Immigration. **Acq:** Purchase. **Dist:** National Center for Jewish Film. $98.00.

Biggest Loser: Boot Camp 2008 (Unrated)
A six-week training course based on the hit TV show. In order to lose weight and improve health, trainer Bob Harper guides viewers through three levels focusing on cardio, conditioning, strength training, and muscle definition. 55m; DVD. **A:** Jr. High-Adult. **P:** Instruction. **U:** Home. **Hea-Sci**: Fitness/Exercise. **Dist:** Lions Gate Entertainment Inc. $11.98.

The Biggest Loser: Cardio Max 2007 (Unrated)
A six- to eight-week program consisting of three progressively intense levels of cardio workouts. Fitness experts Bob Harper, Kim Lyons, and Jillian Michaels lead routines designed to achieve more weight loss and gain strength in less time. 50m; DVD. **A:** Jr. High-Adult. **P:** Instruction. **U:** Home. **Hea-Sci**: Fitness/Exercise, Heart. **Dist:** Lions Gate Entertainment Inc. $11.98.

The Biggest Loser: Last Chance Workout 2009 (Unrated)
Fitness expert Jillian Michaels leads three workouts using a combination of training methods intended to make fat loss happen faster. 61m; DVD. **A:** Jr. High-Adult. **P:** Instruction. **U:** Home. **Hea-Sci**: Fitness/Exercise. **Dist:** Lions Gate Entertainment Inc. $11.98.

The Biggest Loser: Power Sculpt 2007
Three strength training workouts designed to achieve more in less time. Fitness experts Jillian Michaels, Kim Lyons, and Bob Harper all conduct routines in this six- to eight-week program using techniques that include weight training and Bob's "boot camp" moves. 50m; DVD. **A:** Jr. High-Adult. **P:** Instruction. **U:** Home. **Hea-Sci**: Fitness/Exercise. **Dist:** Lions Gate Entertainment Inc. $11.98.

The Biggest Loser: The Workout 2005
Six customizable workouts featuring trainer Bob Harper and contestants from the first two seasons of the NBC show The Biggest Loser. 100m; DVD. **A:** College-Adult. **P:** Instruction. **U:** Home. **Hea-Sci**: Fitness/Exercise. **Acq:** Purchase. **Dist:** Lions Gate Home Entertainment. $14.98.

The Biggest Loser: 30-Day Jump Start 2009 (Unrated)
Bob Harper from TV's "The Biggest Loser" offers diet advice and motivation along with this 30-day weight loss program. Includes five, 10-minute routines to shed fat and improve muscle tone. 55m; DVD. **A:** Jr. High-Adult. **P:** Instruction. **U:** Home. **Hea-Sci**: Fitness/Exercise. **Dist:** Lions Gate Entertainment Inc. $11.98.

Biggest Loser: 2 2006 (Unrated)
"The Biggest Loser" trainers Bob Harper and Kim Lyons, plus contestants from seasons two and three, offer advice on topics including exercise, cooking, and how to lose more weight in less time. Includes different routines for men and women. 90m; DVD. **A:** Jr. High-Adult. **P:** Instruction. **U:** Home. **Hea-Sci**: Fitness/Exercise. **Dist:** Lions Gate Entertainment Inc. $11.98.

Biggest Loser: Weight Loss Yoga 2008 (Unrated)
Over six to eight weeks, "The Biggest Loser" trainer, Bob Harper, leads past show participants through three progressive levels of yoga routines that improve balance, strength, and metabolism, as well as increase lean muscle mass. 55m; DVD. **A:** Jr. High-Adult. **P:** Instruction. **U:** Home. **Hea-Sci**: Fitness/Exercise, Yoga. **Dist:** Lions Gate Entertainment Inc. $11.98.

The Biggest Winner—How to Win by Losing: Shape Up—Backside 2005
Exercise routines geared toward toning the gluteus maximus, back, hamstrings, and bicep muscle groups; hosted by instructor Jillian Michaels. 60m; DVD. **A:** College-Adult. **P:** Instruction. **U:** Home. **Hea-Sci**: Fitness/Exercise. **Acq:** Purchase. **Dist:** Genius Entertainment. $16.99.

The Biggest Winner—How to Win by Losing: Shape Up—Front 2005
Exercise routines geared toward toning the abdominal, thigh, shoulder, triceps, chest, and hip muscle groups; hosted by instructor Jillian Michaels. 60m; DVD. **A:** College-Adult. **P:** Instruction. **U:** Home. **Hea-Sci**: Fitness/Exercise. **Acq:** Purchase. **Dist:** Genius Entertainment. $16.99.

Biggles 1985 (PG) — ★★
Time-travel fantasy in which a young businessman from present-day New York City is inexplicably transferred into the identity of a 1917 WWI flying ace. He suddenly finds himself aboard a fighter plane over Europe during WWI. 100m; VHS, DVD, CC. **C:** Neil Dickson; Alex Hyde-White; Peter Cushing; Directed by John Hough. **Pr:** New World Pictures. **A:** Jr. High-Adult. **P:** Entertainment. **U:** Home. **Mov-Ent**: Fantasy, World War One, Aeronautics. **Acq:** Purchase. **Dist:** Anchor Bay Entertainment. $19.95.

Bighorn 1970
A study of Canadian bighorn mountain sheep, from birth to mating time. 11m; VHS, 3/4 U. **Pr:** National Film Board of Canada. **A:** Jr. High-Adult. **P:** Education. **U:** Institution, SURA. **Hea-Sci**: Documentary Films, Wildlife. **Acq:** Purchase, Rent/Lease. **Dist:** National Film Board of Canada.

The Bighorn Canyon Experience 1979
Things to see and do while visiting Bighorn Canyon are noted, amidst the telling of the history of the area. 18m; VHS, 3/4 U, Special order formats. **Pr:** Division of Audiovisual Arts. **A:** Family. **P:** Education. **U:** Institution, SURA. **Spo-Rec**: Documentary Films, Travel, History--U.S. **Acq:** Purchase. **Dist:** National Audiovisual Center.

Bighorn Sheep: Their Story 1990
A look at the life cycle of the bighorn sheep of the Rocky Mountains. 60m; VHS. **Pr:** Stoney Wolf Video Productions. **A:** Family. **P:** Education. **U:** Home. **Gen-Edu**: Documentary Films, Wildlife. **Acq:** Purchase. **Dist:** Karol Media. $29.95.

Bighorn: With John Denver 1975
Share with John Denver the sights and sounds of the wilds of the Rockies. 52m; VHS. **C:** John Denver. **Pr:** Learning Corporation of America. **A:** Preschool. **P:** Entertainment. **U:** Institution, SURA. **Mov-Ent**: Animals. **Acq:** Purchase, Rent/Lease. **Dist:** Phoenix Learning Group.

The Bike 1970
Two boys use another boy's bike without permission and break it. Raises questions about property and responsibility for one's actions. Part of "Values For Grades K-3" series. 13m; VHS, 3/4 U, Special order formats. **Pr:** Churchill Films. **A:** Primary. **P:** Education. **U:** Institution, Home, SURA. **Chl-Juv**: Ethics & Morals, Children. **Acq:** Purchase, Duplication License. **Dist:** Clear Vue Inc.

Bike Experience '87 1987
Experience motorcycle racing at it's finest. ?m; VHS. **A:** Family. **P:** Entertainment. **U:** Home. **Spo-Rec**: Sports--General, Motorcycles. **Acq:** Purchase. **Dist:** Powersports - Powerdocs. $39.95.

Bike GP Compilation '86 1986
The biggest moments from world-wide Grand Prix motorcycle competition in 1986. ?m; VHS. **A:** Family. **P:** Entertainment. **U:** Home. **Spo-Rec**: Sports--General, Motorcycles. **Acq:** Purchase. **Dist:** Powersports - Powerdocs. $39.95.

Bike Safety: Making the Right Moves 1976
Live action photography and a miniature street model demonstrates many aspects of careful, courteous bicycle driving. 15m; VHS, 3/4 U. **Pr:** Encyclopedia Britannica Educational Corporation. **A:** Family. **P:** Education. **U:** Institution, SURA. **Spo-Rec**: Sports--General, Bicycling. **Acq:** Purchase, Rent/Lease, Trade-in. **Dist:** Encyclopedia Britannica.

Bike Safety Quiz 1977
One of the most complete and up-to-date bike safety programs available, this question and answer format covers traffic rules, riding techniques, and good reasons for safety. 21m; VHS, 3/4 U. **Pr:** American Educational Films. **A:** Preschool-Adult. **P:** Education. **U:** Institution, SURA. **Spo-Rec**: Sports--General, Bicycling. **Acq:** Purchase. **Dist:** Capital Communications.

Bike Season Review '88 1988
Exciting compilation review of the Grand Prix season of 1988. ?m; VHS. **A:** Family. **P:** Entertainment. **U:** Home. **Spo-Rec**: Sports--General, Motorcycles. **Acq:** Purchase. **Dist:** Powersports - Powerdocs. $39.95.

The Bike: Technique and Training for Triathletes 2005 (Unrated)
Swimming coach and former triathlete Clark Campbell discusses training for the bicycle portion of the triathlon. 29m; DVD. **A:** Family. **P:** Education. **U:** Home, Institution. **How-Ins**: Sports--General, Athletic Instruction/Coaching. **Acq:** Purchase. **Dist:** Championship Productions. $39.99.

Bike Tripping 19??
Offers hints on planning, packing, and preparing both the bike and rider for any length of bike trip. Also covers the many kinds of bikes available and the basics of learning to ride safely. 60m; VHS. **A:** Adult. **P:** Instruction. **U:** Home. **Spo-Rec**: Bicycling. **Acq:** Purchase. **Dist:** SI Video Sales Group. $12.95.

Bike Week Daytona 1995
Visits Daytona Beach, Florida during its annual Bike Week. Experiences ten days of the sights and sounds of one of the largest gathering of bikers in the country. 60m; VHS. **A:** Jr. High-Adult. **P:** Entertainment. **U:** Home. **Gen-Edu**: Documentary Films, Motorcycles. **Acq:** Purchase. **Dist:** Tapeworm Video Distributors Inc.

Bike-Wise: To Be Sure 198?
Everything you need to know about bicycles from how to equip it to the rules of the road is explained. 14m; VHS, 3/4 U. **Pr:** National Safety Council. **A:** Family. **P:** Education. **U:** Institution. **Spo-Rec**: Sports--General, Bicycling, Safety Education. **Acq:** Rent/Lease. **Dist:** National Safety Council, California Chapter, Film Library.

Biker Boyz 2003 (PG-13) — ★★1/2
Kid (Luke) is the hotshot teenager biker who challenges Smoke (Fishburne) the long-time reigning "King of Cali." Often referred to as "The Fast and the Furious" on motorcycles, but doesn't achieve the same level of entertainment. Soap opera subplots and cliched dialogue don't help. Then again, "Furious" had the same problems and managed to make a boatload of cash. The actors, however, do a good job with a so-so script, and Luke is fast becoming an actor worth noticing. 111m; VHS, DVD. **C:** Laurence Fishburne; Derek Luke; Orlando Jones; Djimon Hounsou; Lisa Bonet; Brendan Fehr; Larenz Tate; Kid Rock; Rick Gonzalez; Meagan Good; Salli Richardson-Whitfield; Vanessa Bell Calloway; Eriq La Salle; Titus Welliver; Kadeem Hardison; Terrence Howard; Tyson Beckford; Directed by Reggie Rock Bythewood; Written by Reggie Rock Bythewood; Craig Ferandez; Cinematography by Greg Gardiner; Music by Camara Kambon. **Pr:** Erwin Stoff; Stephanie Allain; Gina Price-Bythewood; DreamWorks SKG. **A:** Jr. High-Adult. **P:** Entertainment. **U:** Home. **Mov-Ent**: Black Culture, Motorcycles. **Acq:** Purchase. **Dist:** DreamWorks Home Entertainment.

Biker Mice from Mars: The Adventure Begins 1993
The first three episodes of the syndicated animated television series. Throttle, Modo, and Vinnie, human-sized mice from Mars, work to right wrongs on planet earth—with lots of pop-culture references thrown in. 65m; VHS. **Pr:** Marvel Productions. **A:** Primary-Jr. High. **P:** Entertainment. **U:** Home. **Chl-Juv**: Animation & Cartoons. **Acq:** Purchase. **Dist:** Fusion Video. $19.99.

Bikers, Blondes, and Blood 1993
A montage of the sleaze genre's greatest moments including a clip from Jayne Mansfield's "Single Room Furnished." Suitable for dorm keggers, frat parties or any other venue where the audience has supplementary amusements available. Some clips in black and white. 90m/B/W; VHS. **Pr:** Johnny Legend. **A:** College-Adult. **P:** Entertainment. **U:** Home. **Mov-Ent**. **Acq:** Purchase. **Dist:** Something Weird Video; Tapeworm Video Distributors Inc. $23.00.

Biking 1987
These tapes describe bike travel and basic bike repairs. 40m; VHS, 3/4 U. **Pr:** RMI Media Productions. **A:** Adult. **P:** Instruction. **U:** Institution. **Spo-Rec**: Sports--General, Bicycling. **Acq:** Purchase. **Dist:** RMI Media.
Indiv. Titles: 1. Anybody's Bike Video (Bike Repair) 2. Bike Tripping 3. Bicycle Maintenance and Repair.

Bikini Beach 1964 (Unrated) — ★★1/2
Surfing teenagers of the "Beach Party" series follow up "Muscle Beach Party" with a third fling at the beach and welcome a visitor, British recording star "Potato Bug" (Avalon in a campy dual role). But, golly gee, wealthy Wynn wants to turn their sandy, surfin' shores into a retirement community. What to do? Sing a few songs, dance in your bathing suits, and have fun. Classic early '60s nostalgia is better than the first two efforts;

followed by "Pajama Party." 100m; VHS, DVD. **C:** Annette Funicello; Frankie Avalon; Martha Hyer; Harvey Lembeck; Don Rickles; Stevie Wonder; John Ashley; Keenan Wynn; Jody McCrea; Candy Johnson; Danielle Aubry; Meredith MacRae; Dolores Wells; Donna Loren; Timothy Carey; Boris Karloff; Directed by William Asher; Written by William Asher; Leo Townsend; Robert Dillon; Cinematography by Floyd Crosby; Music by Les Baxter. **Pr:** Samuel Z. Arkoff; Alta Vista; American International Pictures. **A:** Family. **P:** Entertainment. **U:** Home. **Mov-Ent:** Musical, Adolescence. **Acq:** Purchase. **Dist:** Movies Unlimited. $12.74.
Songs: Because You're You; Love's a Secret Weapon; Bikini Drag.

Bikini Bistro 1994 (R) — ★
A boring vegetarian cafe gets turned into a gourmet restaurant but, faced with an eviction notice, the female owners decide to increase business by waitressing in bikinis. Also available in an unrated version at 84 minutes. 80m; VHS, DVD. **C:** Marilyn Chambers; Amy Lynn Baxter; Joan Gerardi; Isabelle Fortea; John Altamura; Joseph Pallister; Directed by Ernest G. Sauer; Written by Matt Unger. **Pr:** Arrow Releasing. **A:** Sr. High-Adult. **P:** Entertainment. **U:** Home. **Mov-Ent:** Food Industry. **Acq:** Purchase. **Dist:** Image Entertainment Inc.

Bikini Bloodbath 2006 (Unrated) — ★
Parody of 80s slasher movies where a group of teenage girls hold a slumber party after graduation while a serial-killing chef is on the loose. Standing between them and death is their lesbian gym teacher Miss Johnson (Rochon). 73m; DVD, Streaming. **C:** Robert Cosgrove, Jr.; Russ Russo; Debbie Rochon; Sheri Lynn; Leah Ford; Directed by Jonathan Gorman; Thomas Edward Seymour; Written by Jonathan Gorman; Thomas Edward Seymour; Cinematography by Mike Anderson; Music by Tim Kulig. **A:** Sr. High-Adult. **P:** Entertainment. **U:** Home. **L:** English. **Mov-Ent. Acq:** Purchase, Rent/Lease. **Dist:** Brightly Entertainment. $7.95 9.99.

Bikini Bloodbath Carwash 2008 (Unrated) — ★¹/₂
College girls in need of money hold a carwash, little suspecting that a killer chef is about to be resurrected from the dead as a zombie and begin harrassing them. Fortunately their house matron is Miss Johnson (Rochon), the seemingly indestructible woman who helped kill him the first time. 72m; DVD. **C:** Thomas Edward Seymour; Russ Russo; Robert Cosgrove, Jr.; Debbie Rochon; Sheri Lynn; Directed by Thomas Edward Seymour; Jonathan Gorman; Written by Thomas Edward Seymour; Jonathan Gorman; Cinematography by Mike Anderson. **A:** Sr. High-Adult. **P:** Entertainment. **U:** Home. **L:** English. **Mov-Ent. Acq:** Purchase. **Dist:** Brightly Entertainment. $9.95 9.99.

Bikini Bloodbath Christmas 2009 (Unrated) — ★
Miss Johnson (Rochon) returns to battle the evil zombie chef who likes killing the girls she loves so much. Apparently the filmmakers think one of the advantages of being a lesbian is immortality considering that she was killed in the previous films of this trilogy. 71m; DVD, Streaming. **C:** Lloyd Kaufman; Matt Ford; Thomas Edward Seymour; Jonathan Gorman; Debbie Rochon; Sheri Lynn; Directed by Thomas Edward Seymour; Jonathan Gorman; Written by Thomas Edward Seymour; Jonathan Gorman; Cinematography by Mike Anderson; Music by Glen Gabriel. **A:** Sr. High-Adult. **P:** Entertainment. **U:** Home. **L:** English. **Mov-Ent. Acq:** Purchase, Rent/Lease. **Dist:** Brightly Entertainment. $14.95 12.95.

The Bikini Car Wash Company 1990 (R) — Bomb!
Babes in bikinis in Los Angeles. A young man is running his uncle's carwash when he meets a business major who persuades him to let her take over the business for a cut of the profits. She decides that a good gimmick would be to dress all the female employees in the tiniest bikinis possible. The story is of course secondary to the amount of flesh on display. Also available in an unrated version. 87m; VHS, DVD, CC. **C:** Joe Dusic; Neriah Napaul; Sara Suzanne Brown; Kristie Ducati; Directed by Ed Hansen. **A:** Sr. High-Adult. **P:** Entertainment. **U:** Home. **Mov-Ent. Acq:** Purchase. **Dist:** Imperial Entertainment Corp. $89.95.

The Bikini Car Wash Company 2 1992 (R) — ★
Entrepreneur Melissa and the other lovely ladies of the Bikini Car Wash Co. find themselves a big success, so much so that a greedy businessman wants to buy them out. In order to get money to fight the takeover, the ladies take to the airwaves of a cable-access station. Their new business adventure involves selling sexy lingerie which means the flesh quotient is as great as ever. An unrated version is also available. 94m; VHS, DVD, CC. **C:** Kristie Ducati; Sara Suzanne Brown; Neriah Napaul; Rikki Brando; Greg Raye; Larry De Russy; Directed by Gary Orona; Written by Bart B. Gustis; Music by Michael Smith. **Pr:** Alan B. Bursteen; New City Releasing. **A:** Sr. High-Adult. **P:** Entertainment. **U:** Home. **Mov-Ent. Acq:** Purchase. **Dist:** Imperial Entertainment Corp. $89.95.

Bikini Drive-In 1994 (R) — ★¹/₂
Babe (Rhey) inherits grandad's decrepit drive-in, which is wanted by a mall mogul, but she refuses to sell. So to raise some cash, Rhey stages a B-movie marathon with in-person, bikini-clad scream queens. 85m; VHS, DVD. **C:** Ashlie Rhey; Richard Gabai; Ross Hagen; Sara Bellomo; Steve Barkett; Conrad Brooks; Directed by Fred Olen Ray. **A:** Sr. High-Adult. **P:** Entertainment. **U:** Home. **Mov-Ent. Acq:** Purchase. **Dist:** AFA Entertainment.

Bikini House Calls 1996 — ★
The students of Bikini Med School love anatomy as much as they love to party. In fact, combining both activities is their idea of a perfect time. 87m; VHS, DVD. **C:** Thomas Draper; Sean Abbananto; Kim (Kimberly Dawn) Dawson; Tamara Landry; Directed by Michael Paul Girard; Written by Michael Paul

Girard; Cinematography by Denis Maloney; Music by Miriam Cutler. **A:** Sr. High-Adult. **P:** Entertainment. **U:** Home. **Mov-Ent:** Sex & Sexuality. **Acq:** Purchase. **Dist:** Vista Street Entertainment.

Bikini Island 1991 (R) — ★
Beautiful swimsuit models gather on a remote tropical island for a big photo shoot, each vying to be the next cover girl of the hottest swimsuit magazine. Before long, scantily clad lovelies are turning up dead and full out madness ensues. Will the mystery be solved before they run out of models, or will the magazine have no choice but to grace its cover with a bikinied cadaver? Low-budget trash that has few, if any, redeeming qualities. 85m; VHS. **C:** Holly Floria; Alicia Anne; Jackson Robinson; Shannon Stiles; Cyndi Pass; Sherry Johnson; Directed by Anthony Markes; Written by Emerson Bixby; Music by Marc David Decker. **Pr:** Curb Entertainment; Esquire Films. **A:** College-Adult. **P:** Entertainment. **U:** Home. **Mov-Ent:** Mystery & Suspense, Photography. **Acq:** Purchase. **Dist:** Unknown Distributor.

Bikini Med School 1998 — ★
So how do med students get rid of all that nasty tension? Why they party, of course! And practice playing doctor with all the nubile lovelies they can. 87m; VHS, DVD. **C:** Kim (Kimberly Dawn) Dawson; Tamara Landry; Thomas Draper; Sean Abbananto; Directed by Michael Paul Girard; Written by Michael Paul Girard; Cinematography by Denis Maloney; Music by Miriam Cutler. **A:** Sr. High-Adult. **P:** Entertainment. **U:** Home. **Mov-Ent:** Sex & Sexuality. **Acq:** Purchase. **Dist:** Vista Street Entertainment.

Bikini Story 1985
An examination of the history of scanty swimwear upon its 40th birthday, with lots of semi-nude models. 40m; VHS. **C:** Directed by Jef Rademakers. **Pr:** Dutch Dream. **A:** Jr. High-Adult. **P:** Entertainment. **U:** Home. **Mov-Ent:** Sex & Sexuality. **Acq:** Purchase. **Dist:** Lions Gate Television Corp. $69.98.

Bikini Summer 1991 (Unrated) — ★¹/₂
Laughs, music, and skin are the order of the day as two nutty guys and a few beautiful girls form an unlikely friendship on the beach. Konop was Julia Robert's "Pretty Woman" body double. Sort of the '90s version of the old '60s Frankie and Annette beach parties. 90m; VHS, DVD. **C:** David Millbern; Melinda Armstrong; Jason Clow; Shelley Michelle; Alex Smith; Kent Lipham; Kelly Konop; Carmen Santa Maria; Directed by Robert Veze; Written by Robert Veze; Nick Stone; Music by John Gonzalez. **Pr:** Contact Film. **A:** College-Adult. **P:** Entertainment. **U:** Home. **Mov-Ent. Acq:** Purchase. **Dist:** $29.95.

Bikini Summer 2 1992 (R) — ★
An eccentric family decides to stage a bikini contest to raise money to help the homeless. 94m; VHS, DVD, On Demand. **C:** Jeff Conaway; Jessica Hahn; Melinda Armstrong; Avalon Anders; Directed by Jeff Conaway; Music by Jim Halfpenny. **A:** Sr. High-Adult. **P:** Entertainment. **U:** Home. **Mov-Ent. Acq:** Purchase. **Dist:** Amazon.com Inc.; Echo Bridge Home Entertainment. $19.95.

Bikini Summer 3: South Beach Heat 1997 (R) — ★
Babes in bikinis frolic on Miami's fashionable South Beach for the chance to become the spokesmodel for Mermaid Body Splash. 84m; VHS, DVD. **C:** Heather-Elizabeth Parkhurst; Tiffany Turner; Directed by Ken Blakey. **A:** College-Adult. **P:** Entertainment. **U:** Home. **Mov-Ent. Acq:** Purchase. **Dist:** Echo Bridge Home Entertainment.

The Bikinians 1975
A program that focuses on the people of the Marshall Islands, who were moved from their homes to new, U.S. Government-built homes to make room for atomic bomb tests. 29m; VHS, 3/4 U. **Pr:** WGTV Athens. **A:** Sr. High-Adult. **P:** Education. **U:** Institution, CCTV, Home. **Gen-Edu:** Documentary Films, International Relations. **Acq:** Purchase, Rent/Lease. **Dist:** WNET/Thirteen Non-Broadcast.

Biko: Breaking the Silence 1988
This film traces Steve Biko's role in the Black Consciousness movement in South Africa. Biko, who was allegedly murdered by the government, played a unique and powerful role in opposing apartheid. 52m; VHS, Special order formats. **Pr:** Ollie Maruma. **A:** Jr. High-Adult. **P:** Education. **U:** Institution, Home, SURA. **Gen-Edu:** Documentary Films, Apartheid, Africa. **Acq:** Purchase, Rent/Lease, Duplication. **Dist:** Filmakers Library Inc. $195.00.

Bilal's Dream 1990
Combines rap, music, and real-life scenarios to help young viewers make decisions on smoking. Written by students at the Alice Deal Junior High School. 12m; VHS, 3/4 U. **A:** Primary-Sr. High. **P:** Education. **U:** Institution. **Gen-Edu:** Adolescence, Smoking. **Acq:** Purchase, Rent/Lease. **Dist:** Durrin Productions Inc. $200.00.

Biliary Atresia 1982
This program looks at the latest approach to management of biliary atresia in babies. 47m; VHS, 3/4 U. **Pr:** Emory University. **A:** College-Adult. **P:** Professional. **U:** Institution, CCTV, Home, SURA. **Hea-Sci:** Digestive System, Infants, Medical Education. **Acq:** Purchase, Rent/Lease, Subscription. **Dist:** Emory Medical Television Network.

Bilingual Americans 1980
This video explores the "melting pot that never happened" in America and the bilingual-bicultural nature of American society. 25m; VHS, 3/4 U. **Pr:** Video Knowledge, Inc. **A:** Jr. High-Adult. **P:** Education. **U:** Institution, Home. **Gen-Edu:** Documentary Films, Minorities, History--U.S. **Acq:** Purchase. **Dist:** Video Knowledge, Inc.

Bilingual Baby Volume 1: French ????
Multi-ethnic children, familiar objects and happy music present an introduction of more than 60 words and phrases. ?m; VHS. **A:** Preschool. **P:** Education. **U:** Home. **Chl-Juv:** Language Arts, Infants. **Acq:** Purchase. **Dist:** Small Fry Productions. $16.95.

Bilingual Baby Volume 2: Spanish ????
Multi-ethnic children, familiar objects and happy music present an introduction of more than 60 words and phrases. ?m; VHS. **A:** Preschool. **P:** Education. **U:** Home. **Chl-Juv:** Language Arts, Infants. **Acq:** Purchase. **Dist:** Small Fry Productions. $16.95.

Bilingual Baby Volume 3: German ????
Multi-ethnic children, familiar objects and happy music present an introduction of more than 60 words and phrases. ?m; VHS. **A:** Preschool. **P:** Education. **U:** Home. **Chl-Juv:** Language Arts, Infants. **Acq:** Purchase. **Dist:** Small Fry Productions. $16.95.

Bilingual Baby Volume 4: Italian ????
Multi-ethnic children, familiar objects and happy music present an introduction of more than 60 words and phrases. ?m; VHS. **A:** Preschool. **P:** Education. **U:** Home. **Chl-Juv:** Language Arts, Infants. **Acq:** Purchase. **Dist:** Small Fry Productions. $16.95.

Bilingual Baby Volume 5: Japanese ????
Multi-ethnic children, familiar objects and happy music present an introduction of more than 60 words and phrases. ?m; VHS. **A:** Preschool. **P:** Education. **U:** Home. **Chl-Juv:** Language Arts, Infants. **Acq:** Purchase. **Dist:** Small Fry Productions. $16.95.

Bilingual Baby Volume 6: Russian ????
Multi-ethnic children, familiar objects and happy music present an introduction of more than 60 words and phrases. ?m; VHS. **A:** Preschool. **P:** Education. **U:** Home. **Chl-Juv:** Language Arts, Infants. **Acq:** Purchase. **Dist:** Small Fry Productions. $16.95.

Bilingual Baby Volume 7: English ????
Multi-ethnic children, familiar objects and happy music present an introduction of more than 60 words and phrases. ?m; VHS. **A:** Preschool. **P:** Education. **U:** Home. **Chl-Juv:** Language Arts, Infants. **Acq:** Purchase. **Dist:** Small Fry Productions. $16.95.

Bilingual Baby Volume 8: Portuguese ????
Multi-ethnic children, familiar objects and happy music present an introduction of more than 60 words and phrases. ?m; VHS. **A:** Preschool. **P:** Education. **U:** Home. **Chl-Juv:** Language Arts, Infants. **Acq:** Purchase. **Dist:** Small Fry Productions. $16.95.

Bilingual Baby Volume 9: Dutch ????
Multi-ethnic children, familiar objects and happy music present an introduction of more than 60 words and phrases. ?m; VHS. **A:** Preschool. **P:** Education. **U:** Home. **Chl-Juv:** Language Arts, Infants. **Acq:** Purchase. **Dist:** Small Fry Productions. $16.95.

Bilingual Baby Volume 10: Swedish ????
Multi-ethnic children, familiar objects and happy music present an introduction of more than 60 words and phrases. ?m; VHS. **A:** Preschool. **P:** Education. **U:** Home. **Chl-Juv:** Language Arts, Infants. **Acq:** Purchase. **Dist:** Small Fry Productions. $16.95.

Bilingual Baby Volume 11: Greek ????
Multi-ethnic children, familiar objects and happy music present an introduction of more than 60 words and phrases. ?m; VHS. **A:** Preschool. **P:** Education. **U:** Home. **Chl-Juv:** Language Arts, Infants. **Acq:** Purchase. **Dist:** Small Fry Productions. $16.95.

Bilingual Baby Volume 12: Hebrew ????
Multi-ethnic children, familiar objects and happy music present an introduction of more than 60 words and phrases. ?m; VHS. **A:** Preschool. **P:** Education. **U:** Home. **Chl-Juv:** Language Arts, Infants. **Acq:** Purchase. **Dist:** Small Fry Productions. $16.95.

Bilingual Education Meeting 1975
This program shows the problems of lacking bilingual education. 30m; 3/4 U. **Pr:** Chinese for Affirmative Action. **A:** Adult. **P:** Education. **U:** Institution, CCTV. **Gen-Edu:** Documentary Films, Education. **Acq:** Loan. **Dist:** Chinese for Affirmative Action.

Bilingualism 1973
A view of management's handling of the problem of the bilingual, bicultural nature of Quebec society in a major Canadian corporation. From the "Corporation" series. 29m/B/W; VHS, 3/4 U. **Pr:** National Film Board of Canada. **A:** Sr. High-Adult. **P:** Education. **U:** Institution, SURA. **Gen-Edu:** Documentary Films, Business. **Acq:** Purchase, Rent/Lease. **Dist:** National Film Board of Canada.

Bilitis 1977 (R) — ★¹/₂
A young girl from a private girls' school is initiated into the pleasures of sex and the unexpected demands of love. One of director Hamilton's exploitative meditations on nudity. 95m; VHS, DVD. **TV Std:** NTSC, PAL. **C:** Patti D'Arbanville; Bernard Giraudeau; Mona Kristensen; Directed by David Hamilton. **Pr:** Sylvio Tabet; Jacques Nahum; Topar. **A:** Adult. **P:** Entertainment. **U:** Home. **Mov-Ent:** Sex & Sexuality. **Acq:** Purchase. **Dist:** Movies Unlimited. $19.99.

Bill 1981 (Unrated) — ★★★
Based on a true story about a mentally retarded man who sets out to live independently after 44 years in an institution. Rooney gives an affecting performance as Bill and Quaid is strong as the filmmaker who befriends him. Awarded Emmys for Rooney's performance and the well written script. Followed by "Bill: On His Own." 97m; VHS, DVD. **C:** Mickey Rooney; Dennis Quaid; Largo Woodruff; Harry Goz; Directed by Anthony Page. **Pr:** Alan Landsburg Productions. **A:** Jr. High-Adult. **P:** Entertainment. **U:** Home. **Mov-Ent:** Mental Retardation, TV Movies. **Acq:** Purchase. **Dist:** Navarre Corp. $59.95.

Bill and Suzi: New Parents 19??
Bill and Suzi discuss with Dr. Brazelton, a renowned pediatrician, how becoming parents for the first time affects a couple's life together. During the child's checkup the couple discuss their

feelings about her; they talk about the pleasures she brings, the difficulties she causes, and the adjustments they've made in their own lives. 13m/B/W; 3/4 U, Special order formats. **Pr:** Education Development Center. **A:** Sr. High-Adult. **P:** Education. **U:** Institution, CCTV, CATV, BCTV. **Gen-Edu:** Documentary Films, Parenting. **Acq:** Purchase, Rent/Lease. **Dist:** Education Development Center.

Bill & Ted's Bogus Journey 1991 (PG) — ★★
Big-budget sequel to B & T's first movie has better special effects but about the same quota of laughs. Slain by lookalike robot duplicates from the future, the airhead heroes pass through heaven and hell before tricking the Grim Reaper into bringing them back for a second duel with their heinous terminators. Most excellent closing-credit montage. Non-fans still won't think much of it. 98m; VHS, DVD, Wide, CC. **C:** Keanu Reeves; Alex Winter; William Sadler; Joss Ackland; Pam Grier; George Carlin; Amy Stock-Poynton; Hal Landon, Jr.; Annette Azcuy; Sarah Trigger; Taj Mahal; Chelcie Ross; Roy Brocksmith; William Shatner; Directed by Peter Hewitt; Written by Chris Matheson; Edward Solomon; Cinematography by Oliver Wood; Music by David Newman. **Pr:** Nelson Entertainment; Interscope Comm. **A:** Jr. High-Adult. **P:** Entertainment. **U:** Home. **Mov-Ent:** Death. **Acq:** Purchase. **Dist:** MGM Studios Inc. $14.98.

Bill & Ted's Excellent Adventure 1989 (PG) — ★★½
Excellent premise: when the entire future of the world rests on whether or not two '80s dudes pass their history final, Rufus comes to the rescue in his time-travelling telephone booth. Bill and Ted share an adventure through time as they meet and get to know some of history's most important figures. Lightweight but fun. 105m; VHS, DVD, Blu-Ray, UMD, Wide, CC. **C:** Keanu Reeves; Alex Winter; George Carlin; Bernie Casey; Dan Shor; Robert V. Barron; Amy Stock-Poynton; Ted Steedman; Terry Camillieri; Rod Loomis; Al Leong; Tony Camilieri; Directed by Stephen Herek; Written by Chris Matheson; Edward Solomon; Cinematography by Tim Suhrstedt; Music by David Newman. **Pr:** Nelson Entertainment; Interscope Comm. **A:** Jr. High-Adult. **P:** Entertainment. **U:** Home. **Mov-Ent:** Fantasy. **Acq:** Purchase. **Dist:** Sony Pictures Home Entertainment Inc.; New Line Home Video. $14.95.

Bill Bellamy: Booty Call 1994
MTV VJ Bellamy focuses on life in the nineties, including how to survive a carjacking and a young man's efforts to get a late-night date. 30m; VHS, CC. **A:** Sr. High-Adult. **P:** Entertainment. **U:** Home. **Mov-Ent:** Comedy--Performance. **Acq:** Purchase. **Dist:** Paramount Pictures Corp. $12.95.

Bill Bruford: Bruford and the Beat 1985
Bruford, former drummer for King Crimson and Yes, discusses drumming and music, with an analysis of his work on King Crimson's "Discipline" recording. Guest appearances by Steve Howe and Robert Fripp. 30m; VHS. **TV Std:** NTSC, PAL. **Pr:** Axis Video. **A:** Sr. High-Adult. **P:** Instruction. **U:** Home. **Fin-Art:** Music--Performance, Music--Pop/Rock. **Acq:** Purchase. **Dist:** Music Video Distributors. $39.95.

Bill Bryson: Notes From a Small Island 1999
Three-tape series covering modern life in Great Britain from author Bill Bryson. 180m; VHS. **A:** Adult. **P:** Education. **U:** Home. **Gen-Edu:** Travel, Great Britain. **Acq:** Purchase. **Dist:** Instructional Video. $39.95.

Bill Burr: Let It Go 2010 (Unrated)
Bill Burr gives a live comedy performance at the Fillmore Auditorium in San Francisco. 65m; DVD, Streaming. **A:** Sr. High-Adult. **P:** Entertainment. **U:** Home. **Gen-Edu:** Comedy--Performance, Performing Arts. **Acq:** Purchase, Rent/Lease. **Dist:** Comedy Central; Image Entertainment Inc. $14.98.

Bill Burr: Why Do I Do This? 2008 (Unrated)
Stand-up performance by comedian Bill Burr, focusing on his usual subjects of relationships and social commentary. 55m; DVD. **A:** Sr. High-Adult. **P:** Entertainment. **U:** Home. **Gen-Edu:** Comedy--Performance, Television. **Acq:** Purchase. **Dist:** Image Entertainment Inc. $14.98.

Bill Cartwright's Dominate the Paint! Post Drills 2012
NBA coach Bill Cartwright presents drills for building up a basketball team's post players. 74m; DVD. **A:** Jr. High-Adult. **P:** Education. **U:** Home, Institution. **L:** English. **Gen-Edu:** Athletic Instruction/Coaching, Basketball, Education. **Acq:** Purchase. **Dist:** Championship Productions. $39.99.

Bill Cartwright's Dominate the Paint! Post Moves & Fundamentals 2012
NBA coach Bill Cartwright discusses the post player position and how to improve a team's players. 62m; DVD. **A:** Jr. High-Adult. **P:** Education. **U:** Home, Institution. **L:** English. **Gen-Edu:** Athletic Instruction/Coaching, Basketball. **Acq:** Purchase. **Dist:** Championship Productions. $39.99.

Bill Cayton's Greatest Knockouts 19??
A four-volume set covering 21 knockouts over 80 years by some of the greatest boxers in the profession, including Muhammad Ali, Joe Louis, Sugar Ray Robinson, Rocky Marciano, Floyd Patterson, Mike Tyson, Jack Johnson, and others. 45m; VHS. **A:** Family. **P:** Entertainment. **U:** Home. **Spo-Rec:** Boxing. **Acq:** Purchase. **Dist:** Anchor Bay Entertainment; Fast Forward. $9.99.

Bill Cosby: 49 1989
The veteran comedian ponders his life and his experiences. Recorded live at the Chicago Theater. 60m; VHS, 8 mm. **C:** Bill Cosby. **Pr:** Century III Teleproductions. **A:** Jr. High-Adult. **P:** Entertainment. **U:** Institution, Home. **Mov-Ent:** Comedy--Performance. **Acq:** Purchase. **Dist:** Karol Media.

Bill Cosby, Himself 1981 (PG)
Cosby shares his hilarious observations on marriage, drugs, alcohol, dentists, child-bearing and child-rearing in this performance. Recorded at Toronto's Hamilton Place Performing Arts Center. 104m; VHS, CC. **C:** Bill Cosby; Directed by Bill Cosby. **Pr:** 20th Century-Fox. **A:** Family. **P:** Entertainment. **U:** Home. **Mov-Ent:** Comedy--Performance, Children, Marriage. **Acq:** Purchase. **Dist:** Fox Home Entertainment. $19.98.

Bill Cosby on Prejudice 1972
In one long, jolting monologue, Bill Cosby, portraying America's composite bigot, systematically disowns the human race. The film compels viewers to examine their own prejudices. 24m; VHS, 3/4 U, Special order formats. **C:** Bill Cosby. **Pr:** Bill Cosby; Bill Cosby. **A:** Sr. High-Adult. **P:** Education. **U:** Institution, Home, SURA. **L:** English, German. **Gen-Edu:** Human Relations, Comedy--Performance. **Acq:** Purchase, Rent/Lease, Duplication License. **Dist:** Pyramid Media. $395.00.

The Bill Cosby Show: Season 2 1970 (Unrated)
NBC 1969-71 comedy. Chet Kincaid (Cosby) is a gym teacher at Richard Allen Holmes High School in Los Angeles who gets into realistic predicaments with humorous flair. Chet's TV goes out right before the big game in "The Sesame Street Rumble," helps an immigrant gain citizenship in "Viva Ortega," fights to save a threatened tree in "Power to the Trees," and volunteers to take seven boys on a camping trip in "The March of the Antelopes." 26 episodes. 660m; DVD. **C:** Bill Cosby. **A:** Family. **P:** Entertainment. **U:** Home. **Mov-Ent:** Television Series. **Acq:** Purchase. **Dist:** Shout! Factory. $39.99.

Bill Cosby Teaches Reading 19??
Set of three videos tackling reading skills problem areas, including comprehension, vocabulary, and rate. 31m; VHS. **C:** Hosted by Bill Cosby. **Pr:** Ambrose Video. **A:** Jr. High-Adult. **P:** Education. **U:** Institution. **Gen-Edu:** Literature, Education. **Acq:** Purchase. **Dist:** Clear Vue Inc. $275.00.

Bill Cosby's Picturepages: All About Animals 1985
Bill Cosby hosts this special for children ages 3-6, teaching them all about different animals. Includes two activity books. 30m; VHS. **C:** Bill Cosby. **Pr:** Bill Cosby; Bill Cosby; Walt Disney Educational Media. **A:** Preschool-Primary. **P:** Education. **U:** Institution, Home. **Chl-Juv:** Children, Animals, Education. **Acq:** Purchase. **Dist:** Disney Educational Productions. $9.98.

Bill Cosby's Picturepages: Clear Thinking 1985
Bill Cosby hosts this special for preschool aged children discussing the differences between up and down, top and bottom, and open and closed. With Picturepages, fun and learning go hand in hand. 55m; VHS. **C:** Bill Cosby. **Pr:** Bill Cosby; Bill Cosby; Walt Disney Educational Media. **A:** Preschool-Primary. **P:** Education. **U:** Institution, Home. **Chl-Juv:** Children, Education. **Acq:** Purchase. **Dist:** Disney Educational Productions. $19.95.

Bill Cosby's Picturepages: Numbers 1985
Four episodes of brand new songs, stories, and activities emphasizing numbers hosted by Bill Cosby. A Picturepages workbook is available. 55m; VHS. **C:** Bill Cosby. **Pr:** Bill Cosby; Bill Cosby; Walt Disney Educational Media. **A:** Preschool-Primary. **P:** Education. **U:** Institution, Home. **Chl-Juv:** Children, Education. **Acq:** Purchase. **Dist:** Disney Educational Productions; Facets Multimedia Inc. $19.95.

Bill Cosby's Picturepages: Reading Readiness 1985
Bill Cosby's educational series for ages 3-6 continues. This time Bill shows how much fun reading can be while teaching the necessary skills in preparation for learning how to read. 30m; VHS. **C:** Bill Cosby. **Pr:** Walt Disney Educational Media. **A:** Preschool-Primary. **P:** Education. **U:** Institution, Home. **Chl-Juv:** Children, Education. **Acq:** Purchase. **Dist:** Disney Educational Productions. $9.95.

Bill Cosby's Picturepages: Shapes and Colors 1985
Bill Cosby hosts this educational video for children ages 3-6. Lessons turn into games about the different shapes and colors in the world. Includes two activity books. 30m; VHS. **C:** Bill Cosby. **Pr:** Bill Cosby; Bill Cosby; Walt Disney Educational Media. **A:** Preschool-Primary. **P:** Education. **U:** Institution, Home. **Chl-Juv:** Children, Education. **Acq:** Purchase. **Dist:** Disney Educational Productions. $9.98.

Bill Cosby's Picturepages: Sights and Sounds 1985
Bill Cosby hosts this educational video for children ages 3-6. The different sights we see and the sounds they make are the lessons taught through fun. Includes two activity books. 30m; VHS. **C:** Bill Cosby. **Pr:** Bill Cosby; Bill Cosby; Walt Disney Educational Media. **A:** Preschool-Primary. **P:** Education. **U:** Institution, Home. **Chl-Juv:** Children, Education. **Acq:** Purchase. **Dist:** Disney Educational Productions. $9.98.

Bill Cosby's Picturepages: Words & Letters 1985
Bill Cosby teaches a series of mini lessons titled "Match the Rhyming Words," "Make a New Word," and "Not the Same Object." Recommended by the National Education Association. A special workbook is also available. 56m; VHS. **C:** Bill Cosby. **Pr:** Bill Cosby; Bill Cosby; Walt Disney Educational Media. **A:** Preschool-Primary. **P:** Education. **U:** Institution, Home. **Chl-Juv:** Children, Education. **Acq:** Purchase. **Dist:** Disney Educational Productions; Facets Multimedia Inc. $19.95.

Bill Cracks Down 1937 (Unrated) — ★½
Disappointed in his wastrel son, William Reardon makes a proviso in his will that Bill must work at the family steel mill for a year under the supervision of manager Tons Walker before he can inherit. The situation gets more complicated when Bill starts eyeing Ton's sweetheart Susan and Tons falls for Bill's gal Elaine. 61m/B/W; DVD. **C:** Grant Withers; Ranny Weeks; Beatrice Roberts; Judith Allen; Pierre Watkins; Directed by William Nigh; Written by Dorrell McGowan; Stuart E. McGowan; Cinematography by William Nobles. **A:** Jr. High-Adult. **P:** Entertainment. **U:** Home. **Mov-Ent**. **Acq:** Purchase. **Dist:** Sinister Cinema.

Bill Cunningham New York 2010 (Unrated) — ★★½
Octogenarian Bill Cunningham is a New York Times fashion photographer who's obsessed with how people dress: those he sees on the street, at various society functions, and at runway shows. Director Richard Press, cinematographer Tony Cenicola, and producer Philip Gefter followed the dedicated, modest Cunningham around for two years as he offers insights about his work, while friends and colleagues tell their own stories. 84m; DVD, Blu-Ray. **C:** Directed by Richard Press; Cinematography by Richard Press; Tony Cenicola. **Pr:** Philip Gefter; New York Times; First Thought Films; Zeitgeist Films Ltd. **A:** Sr. High-Adult. **P:** Entertainment. **U:** Home. **L:** English. **Mov-Ent:** Documentary Films, Clothing & Dress, Photography. **Acq:** Purchase. **Dist:** Zeitgeist Films Ltd.

The Bill Dana Show 196?
"Hello. My name Jose Jimenez." If those words bring back a nostalgic smile you'll enjoy these ten episodes from the 1963-65 TV series. Dana stars as the hapless New York City bellman with a desire to succeed but the unfortunate habit of destroying everything he touches. With his friend Byron Glick (Adams), Jose goes from one disaster to the next. Tapes are available separately. ?m; VHS. **C:** Bill Dana; Don Adams; Jonathan Harris; Gary Crosby. **A:** Family. **P:** Entertainment. **U:** Home. **Mov-Ent:** Television Series. **Acq:** Purchase. **Dist:** Facets Multimedia Inc. $14.95.

Bill Dellinger's Champion Track and Field 19??
In this 17-part series, Bill Dellinger teaches techniques for each event to competitors at every level. 20m; VHS. **C:** Bill Dellinger. **A:** Jr. High-Adult. **P:** Instruction. **U:** Home, Institution. **L:** English, Spanish, German, French. **Spo-Rec:** Sports--General. **Acq:** Purchase. **Dist:** Cambridge Educational. $29.95.
Indiv. Titles: 1. Long/Triple Jump Technique 2. Pole Vault Technique 3. Discus Technique 4. Javelin Technique 5. Hammer Technique 6. Distance Technique 7. Hurdle Technique 8. Shot Put Technique 9. Sprint Technique 10. Relay Technique 11. High Jump Technique 12. 400/Intermediate Hurdle Conditioning 13. Distance Conditioning 14. Pole Vault Conditioning 15. Weight Events Conditioning 16. Sprint Conditioning 17. Jump Conditioning.

Bill Dellinger's Conditioning the 400 Meter Runner & Intermediate Hurdler 1982
Specific methods of conditioning are examined for maximum speed, strength, flexibility and endurance. 20m; VHS. **Pr:** Westwood Communications. **A:** Family. **P:** Entertainment. **U:** Home. **Spo-Rec:** Sports--General, Sports--Track & Field. **Acq:** Purchase. **Dist:** School-Tech Inc. $39.95.

Bill Dellinger's Discus Technique 1982
Comprehensive examination of the sport from throwing technique to special practice drills. 20m; VHS. **Pr:** Westwood Communications. **A:** Family. **P:** Instruction. **U:** Home. **Spo-Rec:** Sports--General, Sports--Track & Field. **Acq:** Purchase. **Dist:** School-Tech Inc. $39.95.

Bill Dellinger's Distance Conditioning 1982
No one is more qualified than winning coach Bill Dellinger to discuss the physical conditioning for maximum distance running performance. 20m; VHS. **C:** Hosted by Bill Dellinger. **Pr:** Westwood Communications. **A:** Family. **P:** Instruction. **U:** Home. **Spo-Rec:** Sports--General, Sports--Track & Field. **Acq:** Purchase. **Dist:** School-Tech Inc. $39.95.

Bill Dellinger's Distance Technique 1982
Coach Dellinger offers advice for improving distance running, helping to put the finishing touches on any race. 20m; VHS. **C:** Hosted by Bill Dellinger. **Pr:** Westwood Communications. **A:** Family. **P:** Instruction. **U:** Home. **Spo-Rec:** Sports--General, Sports--Track & Field. **Acq:** Purchase. **Dist:** School-Tech Inc. $39.95.

Bill Dellinger's Hammer Technique 1982
Detailed techniques and conditioning programs covering all track and field events for optimum athletic development and efficiency. 20m; VHS. **Pr:** Westwood Communications. **A:** Jr. High-Adult. **P:** Instruction. **U:** Home. **Hea-Sci:** Sports--General, Fitness/Exercise. **Acq:** Purchase, Rent/Lease. **Dist:** School-Tech Inc. $39.95.
Indiv. Titles: 1. Distance Conditioning 2. Distance Technique 3. Jump Conditioning 4. High Jump Technique 5. Triple Jump/Long Jump Technique 6. Pole Vault Conditioning 7. Pole Vault Technique 8. Weight Events Conditioning 9. Discus Technique 10. Shot Put Technique 11. Javelin Technique 12. Hammer Technique 13. Sprint Conditioning 14. 400 Meters/Intermediate Hurdle Conditioning 15. Sprint Technique 16. Hurdle Technique 17. Relay Technique.

Bill Dellinger's High Jump Technique 1982
Dennis Whitby presents information designed to improve and perfect high jumping skills. 20m; VHS. **Pr:** Westwood Communications. **A:** Family. **P:** Entertainment. **U:** Home. **Spo-Rec:** Sports--General, Sports--Track & Field. **Acq:** Purchase. **Dist:** School-Tech Inc. $29.95.

Bill Dellinger's Hurdle Techniques 1982
Slow-motion photography is just one method used to detail proper hurdling techniques. 20m; VHS. **Pr:** Westwood Commu-

nications. **A:** Family. **P:** Entertainment. **U:** Home. **Spo-Rec:** Sports--General, Sports--Track & Field. **Acq:** Purchase. **Dist:** School-Tech Inc. $39.95.

Bill Dellinger's Javelin Technique 1982
Complete guide to improving the techniques for javelin throwing including methods for proper training. 20m; VHS. **Pr:** Westwood Communications. **A:** Family. **P:** Instruction. **U:** Home. **Spo-Rec:** Sports--General, Sports--Track & Field. **Acq:** Purchase. **Dist:** School-Tech Inc. $39.95.

Bill Dellinger's Jump Conditioning 1982
A guide to developing the explosiveness needed to succeed in the high, triple and long jumps. 20m; VHS. **C:** Hosted by Bill Dellinger. **Pr:** Westwood Communications. **A:** Family. **P:** Instruction. **U:** Home. **Spo-Rec:** Sports--General, Sports--Track & Field. **Acq:** Purchase. **Dist:** School-Tech Inc. $39.95.

Bill Dellinger's Long/Triple Jump Techniques 1982
A comprehensive look at the form, technique and drills necessary to improve jumping height. 20m; VHS. **Pr:** Westwood Communications. **A:** Family. **P:** Entertainment. **U:** Home. **Spo-Rec:** Sports--General, Sports--Track & Field. **Acq:** Purchase. **Dist:** School-Tech Inc. $39.95.

Bill Dellinger's Pole Vault Conditioning 1982
The delicate mix of speed, strength and agility needed for successful pole vaulting is examined. 20m; VHS. **Pr:** Westwood Communications. **A:** Family. **P:** Entertainment. **U:** Home. **Spo-Rec:** Sports--General, Sports--Track & Field. **Acq:** Purchase. **Dist:** School-Tech Inc. $39.95.

Bill Dellinger's Pole Vault Technique 1984
Dennis Whitby guides you through each phase of pole vaulting motion and method. 20m; VHS. **Pr:** Westwood Communications. **A:** Family. **P:** Entertainment. **U:** Home. **Spo-Rec:** Sports--General, Sports--Track & Field. **Acq:** Purchase. **Dist:** School-Tech Inc. $39.95.

Bill Dellinger's Relay Techniques 1982
Emphasis is placed on the exchange as a means of improving times in the 400-meter and mile relays. 20m; VHS. **Pr:** Westwood Communications. **A:** Family. **P:** Instruction. **U:** Home. **Spo-Rec:** Sports--General, Sports--Track & Field. **Acq:** Purchase. **Dist:** School-Tech Inc. $39.95.

Bill Dellinger's Shot Put Technique 1982
Everything you need to know, from proper motion to follow-through, to improve distance. 20m; VHS. **Pr:** Westwood Communications. **A:** Family. **P:** Instruction. **U:** Home. **Spo-Rec:** Sports--General, Sports--Track & Field. **Acq:** Purchase. **Dist:** School-Tech Inc. $39.95.

Bill Dellinger's Sprint Conditioning 1982
Dennis Whitby offers advice on improving times in the 100 and 200 meter runs. 20m; VHS. **Pr:** Westwood Communications. **A:** Family. **P:** Entertainment. **U:** Home. **How-Ins:** Sports--General, How-To, Sports--Track & Field. **Acq:** Purchase. **Dist:** School-Tech Inc. $39.95.

Bill Dellinger's Sprint Technique 1982
Advice on form and stride designed to improve times. 20m; VHS. **Pr:** Westwood Communications. **A:** Preschool. **P:** Instruction. **U:** Home. **Spo-Rec:** Sports--General. **Acq:** Purchase. **Dist:** School-Tech Inc. $39.95.

Bill Dellinger's Weight Events Conditioning 1982
Coach Ray Burton examines training methods most effective for improving distance throwing. 20m; VHS. **Pr:** Westwood Communications. **A:** Family. **P:** Instruction. **U:** Home. **Spo-Rec:** Sports--General, Sports--Track & Field. **Acq:** Purchase. **Dist:** School-Tech Inc. $39.95.

Bill Dickens Bass Instruction Series 1990
The bass player for the Ramsey Lewis Trio demonstrates picking, soloing and chording. On two cassettes. ?m; VHS. **A:** Jr. High-Adult. **P:** Instruction. **U:** Home. **How-Ins:** Music--Instruction. **Acq:** Purchase. **Dist:** Music Video Distributors. $49.95.

Bill Elliot: Racing into History 1988
An overview of Elliot's career from his beginnings in 1976 to his 1988 Winston Cup Championship season. Includes interviews with Elliot, his family and his crew. 45m; VHS. **C:** Hosted by Benny Parsons. **A:** Jr. High-Adult. **P:** Entertainment. **U:** Home. **Spo-Rec:** Sports--General, Documentary Films, Biography. **Acq:** Purchase. **Dist:** ESPN Inc.; Fast Forward. $9.95.

Bill Engvall: 15 Inches Off Cool 2007 (Unrated)
Performance by comedian Bill Engvall in the Paramount Theatre in Austin, Texas. Also behind-the-scenes footage on his special on the Comedy Central network. 61m; DVD. **A:** Sr. High-Adult. **P:** Entertainment. **U:** Home. **Mov-Ent:** Comedy--Performance, Television. **Acq:** Purchase. **Dist:** Comedy Central; Warner Home Video, Inc. $19.95.

Bill Engvall: A Decade of Laughs 2004 (Unrated)
Collection of five of Bill Engvall's most well-known videos, including a music video with Travis Tritt. 16m; DVD. **A:** Sr. High-Adult. **P:** Entertainment. **U:** Home. **Mov-Ent:** Television. **Acq:** Purchase. **Dist:** Comedy Central. $9.98.

Bill Engvall: Aged and Confused 2009 (Unrated)
Taped live performance of comedian Bill Engvall's 2009 comedy album. 68m; DVD. **A:** Sr. High-Adult. **P:** Entertainment. **U:** Home. **Gen-Edu:** Comedy--Performance, Television. **Acq:** Purchase. **Dist:** Warner Home Video, Inc. $16.95.

Bill Engvall: Here's Your Sign Live 2004 (Unrated)
Stand-up routine of comedian Bill Engvall on how to survive family life. 72m; DVD. **A:** Sr. High-Adult. **P:** Entertainment. **U:** Home. **Mov-Ent:** Comedy--Performance, Television. **Acq:** Purchase. **Dist:** Comedy Central; Image Entertainment Inc. $14.99.

Bill Engvall's New All Stars of Country Comedy Volumes 1 and 2 2004 (Unrated)
Live performances by Bill Engvall and other country-themed comedians, including Gary Mule Deer, Henry Cho, Steve Hall & Shotgun Red, Etta Ray, Steve McGrew, and Jeff Foxworthy. 123m; DVD. **A:** Sr. High-Adult. **P:** Entertainment. **U:** Home. **Mov-Ent:** Comedy--Performance, Television. **Acq:** Purchase. **Dist:** Comedy Central. $21.99.

Bill Evans 1962
Features a performance of Bill Evans and Trio (Chuck Israelson, Paul Montian.) 28m/B/W; VHS, 3/4 U. **A:** Jr. High-Adult. **P:** Entertainment. **U:** Home. **Mov-Ent:** Music--Performance. **Acq:** Purchase. **Dist:** Camera Three Productions, Inc.

Bill Evans: Live at the Maintenance Shop, 1979 1979
Nine songs, with Marc Johnson on bass and Jo Barbara on drums. Includes Evans' last trio recordings for television. 60m; VHS. **A:** Jr. High-Adult. **P:** Entertainment. **U:** Home. **Mov-Ent:** Music--Performance, Music--Jazz. **Acq:** Purchase. **Dist:** Music Video Distributors. $64.95.

Bill Evans on the Creative Process 1966
A session of talk and music with pianist Bill Evans. 20m/B/W; VHS. **Pr:** Helen Keane. **A:** Family. **P:** Entertainment. **U:** Home. **Mov-Ent:** Music--Jazz, Interviews. **Acq:** Purchase. **Dist:** Music Video Distributors; Facets Multimedia Inc. $24.95.

Bill Evans Trio 1993
Live jazz performance from the late 1970s. 60m; VHS. **Pr:** Iowa Public Television. **A:** Adult. **P:** Entertainment. **U:** Home. **Fin-Art:** Music--Performance, Music--Jazz. **Acq:** Purchase. **Dist:** Shanachie Entertainment. $24.95.

Bill Evans: Universal Mind 1966
The noted jazz pianist performs and discusses with host Steve Allen the meaning of jazz. 45m/B/W; VHS. **C:** Hosted by Steve Allen. **A:** Family. **P:** Education. **U:** Home. **Mov-Ent:** Music--Performance, Music--Jazz, Television Series. **Acq:** Purchase. **Dist:** Facets Multimedia Inc. $29.95.

Bill Frieder's Quick Time Drills 1988
Basketball drills that improve both the performance of the team and the individual are explained. 24m; VHS, 3/4 U. **C:** Johnny Orr; Bill Frieder. **Pr:** Champions on Film. **A:** Jr. High-Adult. **P:** Instruction. **U:** Institution, CCTV, Home. **Spo-Rec:** Basketball. **Acq:** Purchase. **Dist:** School-Tech Inc. $19.95.

Bill Harley: Who Made this Mess 1992
A new entry in the kidvid market, Harley will make children laugh with his funny songs, voices, and faces. 55m; VHS. **A:** Preschool-Primary. **P:** Entertainment. **U:** Home. **Mov-Ent:** Music Video, Music--Children. **Acq:** Purchase. **Dist:** Music Video Distributors. $14.95.

Bill Harmon's Video Guide to Cruising the British Virgin Islands 19??
Travel and boating guide for the British Virgin Islands. Includes information on trip planning and preparation, navigation, charters, cruising destinations, shoreside facilities, services, secluded harbors and beaches, the best diving/snorkeling destinations, popular moorings, and little-known spots. 70m; VHS. **Pr:** Bennett Marine Video. **A:** Family. **P:** Education. **U:** Home. **Spo-Rec:** Boating, Travel, Caribbean. **Acq:** Purchase. **Dist:** Bennett Marine Video. $29.95.

Bill Harmon's Video Guide to U.S. Virgin Islands of St. Thomas and St. John 19??
Boating guide to the Caribbean islands of St. Thomas and St. John. Includes information on trip preparation, navigation charts, charters, shopping, restaurants, and all shoreside facilities. Also provides facts on all the popular destinations as well as little-known fun spots which are local favorites. 70m; VHS. **Pr:** Bennett Marine Video. **A:** Family. **P:** Education. **U:** Home. **Spo-Rec:** Boating, Travel, Caribbean. **Acq:** Purchase. **Dist:** Bennett Marine Video. $29.95.

Bill Johnson's Olympic Gold Workout 1989
The U.S. Gold Medal winner provides skiers with a pre-ski exercise program designed to loosen the body before hitting the slopes. 60m; VHS. **Pr:** Morris Video. **A:** Sr. High-Adult. **P:** Entertainment. **U:** Home. **Spo-Rec:** Sports--General, Skiing. **Acq:** Purchase. **Dist:** Morris Video. $29.95.

Bill Loosely's Heat Pump 1976
Bill Loosely explains how to set up a heat pump which will pump heat into one's house from the ground below. This simple process provides a return in heat six times greater than the energy required and is very economical in these energy-con days. 10m; VHS, 3/4 U. **Pr:** National Film Board of Canada. **A:** Jr. High-Adult. **P:** Instruction. **U:** Institution, Home, SURA. **How-Ins:** Energy, Inventors & Inventions, How-To. **Acq:** Purchase, Duplication License. **Dist:** Bullfrog Films, Inc.

Bill Maher: But I'm Not Wrong 2010
Live, stand-up comedy performance from Maher in Raleigh, North Carolina that covers his usual controversial topics: politics, racism, religion, drugs, and more. 80m; DVD. **C:** Bill Maher. **A:** Adult. **P:** Entertainment. **U:** Home. **Mov-Ent:** Comedy--Performance. **Acq:** Purchase. **Dist:** Home Box Office Inc. $19.99.

Bill Maher: New Rules 2006
A collection of segments from Maher's HBO series "Real Time with Bill Maher." 45m; DVD. **C:** Bill Maher. **A:** Adult. **P:** Entertainment. **U:** Home. **Mov-Ent:** Television Series. **Acq:** Purchase. **Dist:** Home Box Office Inc. $19.99.

Bill Maher: The Decider 2007
Live, stand-up performance by Maher includes such topics as President Bush, Iraq, immigration, and others. 60m; DVD. **C:** Bill Maher. **A:** Adult. **P:** Entertainment. **U:** Home. **Mov-Ent:** Comedy--Performance. **Acq:** Purchase. **Dist:** Home Box Office Inc. $19.99.

Bill Maher: Victory Begins at Home 2003
Maher's Tony-nominated one-man Broadway show takes on his favorite topics: sex, politics, religion, and war. 60m; DVD. **C:** Bill Maher. **A:** Adult. **P:** Entertainment. **U:** Home. **Mov-Ent:** Comedy--Performance. **Acq:** Purchase. **Dist:** Home Box Office Inc. $19.99.

Bill Moyers: A World of Ideas II--Great Thinkers 2012
16 conversations on American life culled from interviews done throughout Moyers' career. Guests include David Puttnam, Noam Chomsky, Jonas Salk, Cornel West, and others. 516m; DVD. **C:** Hosted by Bill Moyers. **A:** Adult. **P:** Education, Entertainment. **U:** Home. **Gen-Edu:** Interviews, Philosophy & Ideology. **Acq:** Purchase. **Dist:** Acorn Media Group Inc. $59.99.

Bill Moyers: A World of Ideas--Writers 2011
Interviews of literary figures culled from Moyers' career from the 1980s to 2010. Guests include Toni Morrison, Nadine Gordimer, Tom Wolfe, Isaac Asimov, and others. 637m; DVD. **C:** Hosted by Bill Moyers. **A:** Adult. **P:** Education, Entertainment. **U:** Home. **Gen-Edu:** Interviews. **Acq:** Purchase. **Dist:** Acorn Media Group Inc. $79.99.

Bill Moyers: Amazing Grace 2012
Moyers looks at the history of the hymn, written by English clergyman John Newton and published as a poem in 1779. Includes 24 various renditions of the composition. 80m; DVD. **C:** Hosted by Bill Moyers. **A:** Adult. **P:** Religious. **U:** Home. **Gen-Edu:** Music, Religion. **Acq:** Purchase. **Dist:** Acorn Media Group Inc. $29.99.

Bill Moyers: Becoming American--The Chinese Experience 2013
Moyers uses personal narratives and interviews with historians to look at Chinese immigration in California from the gold rush to the present day. 263m; DVD. **C:** Hosted by Bill Moyers. **A:** Adult. **P:** Education, Entertainment. **U:** Home. **Gen-Edu:** China, Immigration, U.S. States. **Acq:** Purchase. **Dist:** Acorn Media Group Inc. $49.99.

Bill Moyers: Beyond Hate 1991
Mpyers talks with philosophers, historians, authors, and activists about the roots of hatred and how it shapes our lives. 150m; DVD. **C:** Hosted by Bill Moyers. **A:** Adult. **P:** Education, Entertainment. **U:** Home. **Gen-Edu:** Philosophy & Ideology. **Acq:** Purchase. **Dist:** Acorn Media Group Inc. $34.99.

Bill Moyers: Capitol Crimes 2012
Moyers looks at the Jack Abramoff lobbying scandal and Washington politics. A bonus disc, "Buying the War," examines the media's part in the 2003 Iraqi invasion. 196m; DVD. **C:** Hosted by Bill Moyers. **A:** Adult. **P:** Education. **U:** Home. **Gen-Edu:** Politics & Government, Mass Media. **Acq:** Purchase. **Dist:** Acorn Media Group Inc. $49.99.

Bill Moyers: Circle of Recovery 1991
The struggle of seven African-American men to beat their various addictions and become role models for others in their community. The program examines the societal assumption that blacks cannot shake chemical addiction and return to lives of fulfillment. A leaflet, "How to Find a Circle of Recovery," is included with the video. 60m; VHS. **C:** Bill Moyers. **Pr:** PBS. **A:** Family. **P:** Education. **U:** Home. **Gen-Edu:** Alcoholism, Drug Abuse, Black Culture. **Acq:** Purchase. **Dist:** Mystic Fire Video. $29.95.

Bill Moyers: Facing Evil 1988
An insightful program which uses personal testimony from scholars, artists and philosophers to explore the relationship between good and evil. The viewer is challenged to explore the source of this conflict and find innovative methods of ending violence. 90m; VHS, CC, 3/4 U. **C:** Hosted by Bill Moyers. **Pr:** Public Affairs Television; KERA Dallas. **A:** Jr. High-Adult. **P:** Education. **U:** Institution, Home, SURA. **Gen-Edu:** Violence, Philosophy & Ideology. **Acq:** Purchase, Rent/Lease. **Dist:** PBS Home Video. $79.95.

Bill Moyers: Facing Hate 1991
Moyers and Auschwitz survivor and Nobel Peace Prize winner Elie Wiesel explore the temptation, madness and self-destructive nature of hate on a world-wide scale. 60m; VHS. **C:** Hosted by Bill Moyers. **Pr:** WNET 13 Educational Broadcasting Company. **A:** Jr. High-Adult. **P:** Education. **U:** Home. **Gen-Edu:** Documentary Films, Sociology. **Acq:** Purchase. **Dist:** Mystic Fire Video; Baker and Taylor. $29.95.

Bill Moyers: Genesis--A Living Conversation 2010
Moyers focuses on each of the 10 biblical stories from the book of Genesis, including creation, the fall of man, the flood, and more. 560m; DVD. **C:** Hosted by Bill Moyers. **A:** Adult. **P:** Education, Entertainment, Religious. **U:** Home. **Gen-Edu:** Bible. **Acq:** Purchase. **Dist:** Acorn Media Group Inc. $79.99.

Bill Moyers: God and Politics 1989
Bill Moyers explores the impact of individual faith on society, looking at not only what happened, but why. 70m; VHS, CC, 3/4 U. **C:** Hosted by Bill Moyers. **Pr:** Public Affairs Television; WNET. **A:** Jr. High-Adult. **P:** Education. **U:** Institution, SURA. **Gen-Edu:** Philosophy & Ideology, Politics & Government, Religion. **Acq:** Purchase, Rent/Lease. **Dist:** PBS Home Video. $79.95.
Indiv. Titles: 1. The Kingdom Divided 2. The Battle for the Bible 3. On Earth As It Is In Heaven.

Bill Moyers: God & Politics 2011
Explores the role of Christianity in the American political system, including how organized religion influences politics. 325m; DVD. **C:** Hosted by Bill Moyers. **A:** Adult. **P:** Education, Religious, Entertainment. **U:** Home. **Gen-Edu:** Politics & Government, Religion. **Acq:** Purchase. **Dist:** Acorn Media Group Inc. $49.99.

Bill Moyers: Hate On Trial 19??
Contains exclusive footage of courtroom testimony in a case involving the trial of leaders of the White Aryan Resistance charged in the beating death of a black student in Portland, OR. 158m; VHS, CC. **C:** Hosted by Bill Moyers; Directed by Catherine Tatge; Dominique Lasseur. **Pr:** International Cultural Programming Inc; Public Affairs Television. **A:** Jr. High-Adult. **P:** Education. **U:** Institution. **Gen-Edu:** Human Relations, Public Affairs, Politics & Government. **Acq:** Purchase. **Dist:** Mystic Fire Video. $49.95.

Bill Moyers: Healing and the Mind 1993
A five-part series has Bill Moyers probing alternative medicine and the therapeutic connection between body and mind. The series includes a trip to China to explore accupuncture, massage, Tai Chi, and other therapies. Other episodes cover psychological research and psychoneuroimmunology (PNI), meditation, patient/doctor sensitivity, and psychological healing. Moyers is joined by Dr. David Eisenberg of Harvard Medical School who is also a student of Chinese medicine and acts as a guide. Originally broadcast on PBS. 198m; VHS. **C:** Hosted by Bill Moyers. **Pr:** David Grubin Productions; Public Affairs Television. **A:** Jr. High-Adult. **P:** Education. **U:** Institution, Home. **Gen-Edu:** Documentary Films, Medical Care, New Age. **Acq:** Purchase. **Dist:** Ambrose Video Publishing, Inc. $29.95.
Indiv. Titles: 1. The Mystery of Chi 2. The Mind Body Connection 3. Healing from Within 4. The Art of Healing 5. Wounded Healers.

Bill Moyers: In Search of the Constitution 1987
Using interviews with those who interpret and teach the Constitution, Bill Moyers presents a look at our nation's most important document. 60m; VHS, 3/4 U. **C:** Hosted by Bill Moyers. **Pr:** Public Affairs Television. **A:** Jr. High-Adult. **P:** Education. **U:** Institution, CCTV, CATV, SURA. **Gen-Edu:** Politics & Government, Public Affairs, Law. **Acq:** Purchase, Duplication License, Off-Air Record. **Dist:** PBS Home Video. $59.95.
Indiv. Titles: 1. In the Beginning 2. Mr. Justice Blackmun 3. Mortimer Adler: Teaching the Constitution 4. Mr. Justice Brennan 5. Ronald Dworkin: The Changing Story 6. God and the Constitution 7. Strictly Speaking: Attorney General Edwin Meese & Judge Robert Bork 8. Justice Sandra Day O'Connor 9. For the People 10. 1987 v. The Constitution 11. Justice Lewis F. Powell, Jr.

Bill Moyers' International Hour 1975
Bill Moyers' series about worldwide public affairs features interviews with many well-known personalities which present international information to the American audience. 60m; VHS, 3/4 U. **C:** Hosted by Bill Moyers. **Pr:** WNET New York. **A:** Sr. High-Adult. **P:** Education. **U:** Institution, CCTV, Home. **Gen-Edu:** Documentary Films, Public Affairs. **Acq:** Purchase, Rent/Lease. **Dist:** WNET/Thirteen Non-Broadcast.
Indiv. Titles: 1. A Conversation with Henry Kissinger 2. A Conversation with Helmut Schmidt 3. Reflections on the News 4. A Conversation with Robert McNamara 5. American Foreign Policy: Where Are We Going? 6. Reflections on the News: What Course for Britain? 7. Middle East: The Search for Peace 8. A Conversation with Huw Wheldon 9. Earthwatch from Nairobi 10. Reflections on the News 11. Jamaica: The Other Caribbean 12. Vietnam and the Aftermath: A Conversation with Clarke Clifford 13. Our Changing World: Two Views 14. Los Campesinos, The Farmer of Mexico.

Bill Moyers: Joseph Campbell and the Power of Myth 1987
This highly acclaimed PBS series of interviews features Joseph Campbell, scholar, mythologist, and author of many books, including "The Hero With a Thousand Faces." He discusses many of the important themes, concepts, and images recurrent throughout every culture. The laserdisc edition is interactive (CAV). 60m; VHS. **C:** Joseph Campbell; Bill Moyers. **Pr:** Catherine Tatge; Apostrophe S Productions; Public Affairs Television. **A:** Sr. High-Adult. **P:** Education. **U:** Home. **Gen-Edu:** Documentary Films, Anthropology, Religion. **Acq:** Purchase. **Dist:** Mystic Fire Video. $29.95.
Indiv. Titles: 1. The Hero's Adventure 2. The Message of the Myth 3. The First Storytellers 4. Sacrifice and Bliss 5. Love and the Goddess 6. Masks of Eternity.

Bill Moyers' Journal 1979
A collection of filmed reports and interviews on a variety of subjects dealing with current events. Many programs feature talks with well-known, important personalities including Ronald Reagan, Jerry Brown, and Andrew Young. 60m; VHS, 3/4 U. **C:** Hosted by Bill Moyers. **Pr:** WNET New York. **A:** Sr. High-Adult. **P:** Education. **U:** Institution, CCTV, Home. **Gen-Edu:** Documentary Films, Public Affairs. **Acq:** Purchase, Rent/Lease. **Dist:** WNET/Thirteen Non-Broadcast.
Indiv. Titles: 1. Harvest 2. Carter and Country 3. James Earl Jones: No Easy Walk to Freedom 4. Man at Large: Poet Robert Bly 5. Mind at Large: Adler on Aristotle 6. The People of Nes Ammin 7. Andrew Young Remembers Martin Luther King 8. At the Edge of History: A Conversation with William Irwin Thompson 9. Democracy in America: A Conversation with Henry Steele Commager 10. Looking for India 11. How to Get a Job 12. The Sleuth of Oxford: Hugh Trevor-Roper 13. Women Inside 14. Levittown (30 minutes) 15. Inventing America: Garry Wills 16. John Graves: The Head Varmint of Hard Scrabble 17. A Discussion of Religion in Modern Society 18. A Conversation with Jerry Brown 19. A Conversation with Ronald Reagan 20. A Conversation with Leon Higgenbotham.

Bill Moyers' Journal: 1980 Season 1980
A series of in-depth conversations, personal documentaries, and multi-segment journals delving into political issues. Programs are available individually. 60m; VHS, 3/4 U. **C:** Hosted by Bill Moyers. **Pr:** NET. **A:** Jr. High-Adult. **P:** Education. **U:** Institution, CCTV, Home. **Gen-Edu:** Documentary Films, Politics & Government, Public Affairs. **Acq:** Purchase, Rent/Lease. **Dist:** WNET/Thirteen Non-Broadcast.
Indiv. Titles: 1. Barry Commoner and the Politics of Energy 2. Big Business: Doing Well or Doing Good 3. Black Agenda for the '80s 4. Conversation With Judge Frank M. Johnson, Jr 5. Conversation With Max Lerner, Parts I & II 6. Detroit Model, The 7. It Isn't Working 8. Many Worlds of Carlos Fuentes, The 9. Money and Politics 10. MX Debate, The 11. Our Times 12. Texas Notebook, A 13. Trillion Dollars for Defense, A 14. Voices on Iran, Parts I & II 15. What's a Party For? 16. Who's Choosing Our President 17. Within Our Power 18. World of David Rockefeller, The.

Bill Moyers' Journal: Why Work? Part 1 1976
Bill Moyers explores the labor world, which he terms "a supreme moment of creation." 60m; VHS, 3/4 U. **C:** Hosted by Bill Moyers. **Pr:** WNET New York. **A:** Sr. High-Adult. **P:** Education. **U:** Institution, CCTV, Home. **Gen-Edu:** Documentary Films, Occupations. **Acq:** Purchase, Rent/Lease. **Dist:** WNET/Thirteen Non-Broadcast.

Bill Moyers' Journal: Why Work? Part 2 1976
The second and final part of the series in which Bill Moyers looks at the intriguing world of labor. 60m; VHS, 3/4 U. **C:** Hosted by Bill Moyers. **Pr:** WNET New York. **A:** Sr. High-Adult. **P:** Education. **U:** Institution, CCTV, Home. **Gen-Edu:** Documentary Films, Occupations. **Acq:** Purchase, Rent/Lease. **Dist:** WNET/Thirteen Non-Broadcast.

Bill Moyers On Addiction: Close to Home 2012
Five episode series on substance abuse and its consequences both personally and in society. 304m; DVD. **C:** Hosted by Bill Moyers. **A:** Adult. **P:** Education. **U:** Home. **Gen-Edu:** Alcoholism, Drug Abuse. **Acq:** Purchase. **Dist:** Acorn Media Group Inc. $49.99.

Bill Moyers: On Faith & Reason 2010
Moyers sits down with 12 noted writers and thinkers to discuss how their beliefs influenced their lives and work. Guests include Salman Rushdie, Margaret Atwood, Sire John Houghton, Mary Gordon, and others. 394m; DVD. **C:** Hosted by Bill Moyers. **A:** Adult. **P:** Education, Entertainment. **U:** Home. **Gen-Edu:** Interviews, Philosophy & Ideology. **Acq:** Purchase. **Dist:** Acorn Media Group Inc. $59.99.

Bill Moyers: On Our Own Terms 2000
A four-part series on how modern culture faces death as Moyers interviews dozens of the terminally ill as well as doctors and hospital workers. 348m; DVD. **C:** Hosted by Bill Moyers. **A:** Adult. **P:** Education. **U:** Home. **Gen-Edu:** Death, Interviews. **Acq:** Purchase. **Dist:** Acorn Media Group Inc. $49.99.

Bill Moyers: On the Hudson--America's First River 2002
Moyers explores the history of the Hudson River, which played a critical role in America's development until it was nearly destroyed by pollution. He looks at the river's ecology and the efforts to save it. 230m; DVD. **A:** Family. **P:** Entertainment. **U:** Home. **Gen-Edu:** Rivers & Streams, History--U.S. **Acq:** Purchase. **Dist:** Acorn Media Group Inc. $39.99.

Bill Moyers: Spirit and Nature 1991
"Spirit and Nature" is a fascinating and timely documentary about the connection between religion and the environment. Six speakers are featured from an internatonally attended conference at Middlebury College in Vermont. The speakers are: The Dalai Lama; Native American Elder Audrey Shenandoah; Islamic Studies professor Sevyed Hossein Nasr from George Washington University; Protestant theologian Sallie McFague from Vanderbilt Divinity School; Rabbi Ishmar Schorsch from the Jewish Theological Seminary of America; and professor of social ethics Ronald Engel, from Chicago University. Each speaker discusses current attitudes toward the environment, as well as modified philosophies toward nature for a more sympathetic and productive environment. 58m; VHS, CC, 3/4 U. **C:** Hosted by Bill Moyers. **Pr:** Public Affairs Television. **A:** Jr. High-Adult. **P:** Education. **U:** Institution, CCTV, CATV, Home. **Gen-Edu:** Ecology & Environment, Religion, Philosophy & Ideology. **Acq:** Purchase, Duplication License, Off-Air Record. **Dist:** PBS Home Video; Mystic Fire Video. $29.95.

Bill Moyers: Sports for Sale 1991
Bill Moyers hosts this 90-minute documentary on college sports, followed by a 30-minute panel discussion with members of the Knight Commission on Intercollegiate Athletics. 120m; VHS, 3/4 U. **C:** Hosted by Bill Moyers. **Pr:** Public Affairs Television. **A:** Jr. High-Adult. **P:** Education. **U:** Institution, CCTV, CATV, SURA. **Gen-Edu:** Documentary Films, Sports--General, Ethics & Morals. **Acq:** Purchase, Rent/Lease, Duplication License, Off-Air Record. **Dist:** PBS Home Video. $89.95.

Bill Moyers: The Arab World 1991
A five-part series, originally aired on PBS, in which Moyers explores Arab history, mores and religion with scholars, writers and other authorities on the Arab World. Many Western misconceptions about Arabs come to light, as well as a multi-dimensional portrait of this mysterious land. Available as individual tapes, or a complete set. 140m; VHS. **C:** Hosted by Bill Moyers. **Pr:** PBS. **A:** Jr. High-Adult. **P:** Education. **U:** Institution, CCTV, CATV, Home. **Gen-Edu:** Documentary Films, Islam, Religion. **Acq:** Purchase, Duplication License, Off-Air Record. **Dist:** PBS Home Video. $79.95.
Indiv. Titles: 1. The Arabs: Who The Are, Who The Are Not 2. The Historic Memory 3. The Image of God 4. The Bonds of Pride 5. Arabs and the West.

Bill Moyers: The Language of Life 1995
Eight-part series with Moyers showcasing the work of 18 contemporary poets, including Robert Bly, Adrienne Rich, and Gary Snyder. 447m; DVD. **C:** Hosted by Bill Moyers. **A:** Adult. **P:** Education, Entertainment. **U:** Home. **Gen-Edu:** Literature. **Acq:** Purchase. **Dist:** Acorn Media Group Inc. $59.99.

Bill Moyers: The Power of the Word 1989
Bill Moyers talks with modern poets about their craft in this six-part series. 60m; VHS, 3/4 U. **C:** James Autry; Quincy Troupe; Joy Harjo; Mary Tallmountain; Gerald Stern; Li-Young Lee; Stanley Kunitz; Sharon Olds; William Stafford; W.S. Mernin; Galway Kwnell; Robert Bly; Octavio Paz; Hosted by Bill Moyers. **Pr:** PBS. **A:** Jr. High-Adult. **P:** Education. **U:** Institution, CCTV, Home, SURA. **Gen-Edu:** Language Arts, Literature--Modern, Interviews. **Acq:** Purchase, Rent/Lease. **Dist:** PBS Home Video. $59.95.
Indiv. Titles: 1. Simple Acts of Life, The 2. Living Language, The 3. Ancestral Voices 4. Voices of Memory 5. Dancing on the Edge of the Road 6. Where the Soul Lives.

Bill Moyers: The Public Mind 1989
Bill Moyers examines the formation of public opinion in this four-part series. The focus is on the use of images in the mass media. 60m; VHS, CC, 3/4 U. **C:** Hosted by Bill Moyers. **Pr:** Alvin H. Perlmutter; Public Affairs Television. **A:** Jr. High-Adult. **P:** Education. **U:** Institution, CCTV, CATV. **Gen-Edu:** Public Affairs, Interviews, Journalism. **Acq:** Purchase, Duplication License, Off-Air Record. **Dist:** PBS Home Video. $59.95.
Indiv. Titles: 1. Consuming Images 2. Leading Questions 3. Illusion of News 4. Truth About Lies, The.

Bill Moyers: The Wisdom of Faith with Huston Smith 2011
A series of conversations with comparative religion professor Huston Smith on the world's largest religions: Hinduism, Buddhism, Confucianism, Christianity, Judaism, and Islam. 276m; DVD. **C:** Hosted by Bill Moyers. **A:** Adult. **P:** Education, Religious, Entertainment. **U:** Home. **Gen-Edu:** Religion. **Acq:** Purchase. **Dist:** Acorn Media Group Inc. $49.99.

Bill Moyers' Walk Through the 20th Century 1985
Bill Moyers, one of America's most respected journalists, hosts this series which explores the events and personalities that shaped the 20th century. 58m; VHS, CC, 3/4 U. **C:** Narrated by Bill Moyers. **Pr:** The Corporation for Entertainment and Learning. **A:** Jr. High-Adult. **P:** Education. **U:** Institution, CCTV, CATV. **Gen-Edu:** Documentary Films, Sociology, Public Affairs. **Acq:** Purchase, Rent/Lease, Off-Air Record. **Dist:** PBS Home Video; Image Entertainment Inc. $29.95.
Indiv. Titles: 1. America on the Road 2. Arming of the Earth, The 3. Change, Change 4. Come to the Fairs 5. Democrat and the Dictator, The 6. Helping Hand, The 7. I.I. Rabi: Man of the Century 8. Image Makers, The 9. Marshall, Texas; Marshall, Texas 10. Out of the Depths - The Miners' Story 11. Postwar Hopes, Cold War Fears 12. Presidents and Politics with Richard Strout 13. Reel World of News, The 14. Second American Revolution Part I, The 15. Second American Revolution Part II, The 16. 30-Second President, The 17. TR and His Times 18. Twenties, The 19. World War II: The Propaganda Battle.

Bill Moyers' World of Ideas, Vol. 1: The National Soul 1989
The philosophical journalist interviews writers, artists, thinkers, scientists, and historians. In "Volume 1: The National Soul," Moyers speaks with E. L. Doctorow, Barbara Tuchman, Willard Gaylin, Elaine Pagels, F. Forrester Church, T. Berry Brazelton, the Native American novelists Louise Erdrich and Michael Dorris, and the African American Pulitzer Prize-winning playwright August Wilson, as he tries to discover what makes Americans, American. 92m; VHS. **C:** Hosted by Bill Moyers. **Pr:** PBS. **A:** Family. **P:** Education. **U:** Institution, CCTV, Home, SURA. **Gen-Edu:** Documentary Films, Children, Interviews. **Acq:** Purchase, Rent/Lease, Duplication. **Dist:** PBS Home Video; Mystic Fire Video. $29.95.
Indiv. Titles: 1. Chinua Achebe 2. Isaac Asimov, Parts 1 & 2 3. Mary Catherine Bateson 4. Robert Bellah 5. Peter Berger 6. Sissela Bok 7. T. Berry Brazelton, Parts I & II 8. James MacGregor Burns 9. Noam Chomsky, Parts I & II 10. Henry Steele Commager 11. E. L. Doctorow 12. Peter Drucker 13. Louise Erdrich & Michael Dorris 14. Northrup Frye 15. Carlos Fuentes 16. Willard Gaylin 17. Mary Ann Glendon 18. Vartan Gregorian 19. Joseph Heller 20. Michael Josephson 21. Leon Kass, Parts I & II 22. Sara Lightfoot 23. John Lukacs 24. Arturo Madrid 25. Jessica Tuchman Mathews 26. Forrest McDonald 27. Martha C. Nussbaum 28. Elaine Pagels, Parts I & II 29. David Putnam, Parts I & II 30. John Searle 31. Maxine Singer 32. Summing Up 33. Barbara Tuchman 34. Derek Walcott 35. Steven Weinberg 36. August Wilson 37. William Julius Wilson 38. Tom Wolfe, Parts I & II 39. Sheldon Wolin 40. Anne Wortham, Parts I & II 41. Chen Ning Yang.

Bill Moyers' World of Ideas, Vol. 2: Crisis of Democracy 1989
The philosophical journalist interviews writers, artists, thinkers, scientists, and historians. In "Vol. 2: Crisis of Democracy," Moyers speaks with Sheldon Wolin, Joseph Heller, Henry Steele Commager, Sessela Bok, John Lukacs, Tom Wolfe, and Noam Chomsky. 80m; VHS. **C:** Hosted by Bill Moyers. **Pr:** PBS. **A:** Sr. High-Adult. **P:** Education. **U:** Institution, Home. **Gen-Edu:** Documentary Films, Interviews, Philosophy & Ideology. **Acq:** Purchase. **Dist:** PBS Home Video; Mystic Fire Video. $29.95.

Indiv. Titles: 1. American Story with Richard Rodriguez, An, Parts I & II 2. Broken Cord with Louise Erdrich and Michael Dorris, The 3. Changing Agendas with Gro Harlem Brundtland 4. Concern for Community with Ernie Cortes, A, Parts I & II 5. Confucian Life in America with Tu Wei-ming, A 6. Conquering America with Bharati Mukherjee 7. Ethics and Work with Joanne Ciulla 8. Fame with Leo Braudy 9. Food for Thought with M. F. K. Fisher 10. Hope for the Long Run with Cornel West 11. Inventing the Future with Robert Lucky, Parts I & II 12. Invitation to Education with Mike Rose 13. Islamic Mind with Seyyed Hossein Nasr, the 14. Justice with Michael Sandel 15. Labor's Future with Gus Tyler 16. Mind for Music with Peter Sellars, Parts I & II 17. Mind of Patricia Churchland, The 18. Money with Jacob Needleman 19. Mortal Choices with Ruth Macklin, Part I/Public Policy, Private Choices with Ruth Macklin, Part II 20. On Being a White African with Nadine Gordimer 21. Peace Dividend with Seymore Melman, The 22. Quarks and the Universe with Murray Gell-Mann 23. Science and Gender with Evelyn Fox Keller 24. Science of Hope with Jonas Salk, The 25. Spiritual Democracy with Steven Rockefeller 26. State of the World with Lester Brown, The 27. Stories of Maxine Hong Kingston, Parts I & II 28. Thoughts on Capitalism with Louis Kelso 29. Witness to History with William Shirer, Parts I & II 30. Words and Music with Jeannette Halen 31. Writer's Work with Toni Morrison, Parts I & II.

Bill Moyers' World of Ideas, Vol. 3: Dissolving Boundaries 1989

The philosophical journalist interviews writers, artists, thinkers, scientists, and historians. In "Vol. 3: Dissolving Boundaries," Moyers speaks with Robert Bellah, Jessica Tuchman Mathews, Isaac Asimov, Mary Catherine Bateson, the Chinese Nobel laureate Chen Ning Yang, and West African novelist Chinua Achebe. 89m; VHS. **C:** Hosted by Bill Moyers. **Pr:** PBS. **A:** Sr. High-Adult. **P:** Education. **U:** Institution, Home. **Gen-Edu:** Documentary Films, Philosophy & Ideology, Interviews. **Acq:** Purchase. **Dist:** PBS Home Video; Mystic Fire Video. $29.95.

Bill Moyers: Your Mythic Journey 1991

A PBS special hosted by Bill Moyers that examines human potential to explore our personal lives and create order where chaos often exists. Sam Keen, a spiritualist who studied with Joseph Campbell and Robert Bly, and was a former editor of "Psychology Today," is Moyer's guest. He encourages viewers to question the stories they have been living out in their lives, and understand that they could tell different stories and change what have perhaps been destructive or less-than-fulfilling patterns. 58m; VHS, CC. **C:** Hosted by Bill Moyers; Directed by Betsy McCarthy. **Pr:** Public Affairs Television. **A:** College-Adult. **P:** Entertainment. **U:** Home. **Gen-Edu:** Documentary Films, Psychology, Self-Help. **Acq:** Purchase. **Dist:** Facets Multimedia Inc.; PBS Home Video; Home Vision Cinema. $29.95.

Bill Nye the Science Guy: Dinosaurs—Those Big Boneheads 1994

Bill Nye takes a look at dinosaurs and what has been discovered about their lifestyles. In another episode, Bill Nye explains how the Earth's surface and its inner mantle differ. 46m; VHS. **A:** Primary-Jr. High. **P:** Education. **U:** Home. **Chl-Juv:** Science, Dinosaurs. **Acq:** Purchase. **Dist:** Walt Disney Studios Home Entertainment. $12.99.

Bill Nye the Science Guy: Human Body—The Inside Scoop 1994

Bill Nye explains how the amazing epidermal system works in an episode titled "Skin." In "Blood/Circulation," Bill takes us on a tour of the human body's arterial highways, pointing out the sights along the way. 46m; VHS. **A:** Primary-Jr. High. **P:** Entertainment. **U:** Home. **Chl-Juv:** Science, Biology. **Acq:** Purchase. **Dist:** Walt Disney Studios Home Entertainment. $12.99.

Bill Nye the Science Guy: Outer Space—Way Out There 1994

Bill Nye takes everyone on a journey through the solar system and shows how the elements of outer space affect us here on planet earth. 44m; VHS. **A:** Primary-Jr. High. **P:** Education. **U:** Home. **Chl-Juv:** Science. **Acq:** Purchase. **Dist:** Walt Disney Studios Home Entertainment. $12.99.

Bill Nye the Science Guy: Powerful Forces—All Pumped Up! 199?

Part of the "Bill Nye the Science Guy" series. Bill explains the different types of external forces which affect motion. He uses examples of a Jai Alai game, a race between a fly and a RV, and a pinball game to help illustrate different types of motion and force. 46m; VHS. **A:** Primary-Jr. High. **P:** Education. **U:** Home. **Chl-Juv:** Science, Physics. **Acq:** Purchase. **Dist:** Walt Disney Studios Home Entertainment.

Bill Nye the Science Guy: Reptiles & Insects—Leapin' Lizards! 199?

Part of the "Bill Nye the Science Guy" series. Bill takes the viewer out into the field and explores the world of reptiles and insects. Includes footage and information on poisonous snakes, lizards, bees, beetles, crickets, ants, and caterpillars. 46m; VHS. **A:** Primary-Jr. High. **P:** Education. **U:** Home. **Chl-Juv:** Science, Animals, Insects. **Acq:** Purchase. **Dist:** Walt Disney Studios Home Entertainment.

Bill Nye the Science Guy Sampler V ????

Classroom Edition features 10 full-length shows with scientist Bill Nye and his high-energy hijinks that promote that fun of science. 260m; VHS; Closed Captioned. **A:** Primary-Sr. High. **P:** Education. **U:** Institution. **Chl-Juv:** Science, Television. **Acq:** Purchase. **Dist:** Disney Educational Productions. $199.00.
Indiv. Titles: 1. Atoms 2. Motion 3. Fossils 4. Fluids 5. Storms 6. Farming 7. Life Cycles 8. Probability 9. Time.

Bill O'Brien: Quarterback Technique and Empty Passing Game 2013 (Unrated)

Football coach Bill O'Brien discusses improving a quarterback's throwing arm. 64m; DVD. **A:** Family. **P:** Education. **U:** Home. **L:** English. **Spo-Rec:** Athletic Instruction/Coaching, Football. **Acq:** Purchase. **Dist:** Championship Productions. $29.99.

A Bill of Divorcement 1932 (Unrated) — ★★½

Hepburn's screen debut, as the daughter of a shell-shocked WWI vet, who requires her care after her mother decides to divorce him. Creaky early talker. 76m/B/W; VHS, CC. **C:** John Barrymore; Katharine Hepburn; Billie Burke; Henry Stephenson; David Manners; Paul Cavanagh; Elizabeth Patterson; Directed by George Cukor; Music by Max Steiner. **Pr:** David O. Selznick; RKO. **A:** Jr. High-Adult. **P:** Entertainment. **U:** Home. **Mov-Ent:** Divorce, Veterans. **Acq:** Purchase. **Dist:** Fox Home Entertainment. $39.98.

Bill of Materials/Maintaining Product Service 1991

Offers instruction on specific aspects of construction. 20m; VHS. **A:** Adult. **P:** Vocational. **U:** Institution. **Bus-Ind:** Construction. **Acq:** Purchase. **Dist:** RMI Media. $86.00.

The Bill of Rights 19??

A 10-part series which looks at the historic and contemporary significance of the first 10 amendments to the Constitution of the United States. Examines search-and-seizure laws, privacy rights, freedom of religion, freedom of the press, and others. On two cassettes with free study guide. 90m; VHS. **A:** Jr. High-Adult. **P:** Education. **U:** Home. **Gen-Edu:** History--U.S. **Acq:** Purchase. **Dist:** PBS Home Video. $39.95.

The Bill of Rights: A Living Document 1997

Animation, period art, question frames, and commentary by historians examines personal liberty from Magna Carta forward. Recommended for Grades 7-12. 24m; VHS. **A:** Jr. High-Sr. High. **P:** Education. **U:** Institution. **Gen-Edu:** Politics & Government. **Acq:** Purchase. **Dist:** Social Studies School Service; Zenger Media. $79.95.

Bill of Rights, Bill of Responsibilities: Bill Maher 1995

Comedian Bill Maher provides an explanation of the Bill of Rights for the MTV generation. Appropriate for Grades 9-12. 26m; VHS. **A:** Sr. High. **P:** Education. **U:** Institution. **Gen-Edu:** Politics & Government. **Acq:** Purchase. **Dist:** Social Studies School Service; Zenger Media. $79.95.

The Bill of Rights in Action 19??

Three program series exploring contemporary issues and the interpretation of the Bill of Rights. Includes background legal text and discussion questions. 30m; VHS. **A:** Jr. High-Sr. High. **P:** Education. **U:** Institution. **Gen-Edu:** Law, Politics & Government. **Acq:** Purchase. **Dist:** Cambridge Educational. $90.00.
Indiv. Titles: 1. The Right to Privacy 2. Equal Protection 3. First Amendment.

Bill: On His Own 1983 — ★★★

Rooney is again exceptional in this sequel to the Emmy-winning TV movie "Bill." After 44 years in an institution, a mentally retarded man copes more and more successfully with the outside world. Fine supporting cast and direction control the melodramatic potential. 100m; VHS, DVD. **C:** Mickey Rooney; Helen Hunt; Teresa Wright; Dennis Quaid; Largo Woodruff; Paul Leiber; Harry Goz; Directed by Anthony Page. **A:** Jr. High-Adult. **P:** Entertainment. **U:** Home. **Mov-Ent:** TV Movies, Mental Retardation. **Acq:** Purchase. **Dist:** Navarre Corp. $59.95.

Bill Parrot 1988

Outlines the story of a Bill Parrot and how he rose from mailroom clerk to writing, producing, and directing films. Part of The Achievers Series. 13m; VHS, SVS, 3/4 U. **Pr:** Turner Broadcasting. **A:** Jr. High-Adult. **P:** Education. **U:** Institution. **Gen-Edu:** Filmmaking, Black Culture. **Acq:** Purchase. **Dist:** Encyclopedia Britannica. $59.00.

Bill Rodgers: Running for Fun and Fitness 1985

Marathon winner Rodgers lends advice on everything from attire to proper running technique. 47m; VHS. **Pr:** Congress Video. **A:** Jr. High-Adult. **P:** Instruction. **U:** Home. **Hea-Sci:** Fitness/Exercise, Sports--Track & Field. **Acq:** Purchase. **Dist:** School-Tech Inc.; Cambridge Educational. $19.95.

Bill Self: "Basic" and "Motion" 3-Out 2-In Zone Offenses 2005

Coach Bill Self presents several Zone Offense techniques and plays for basketball teams to employ. 70m; DVD. **A:** Family. **P:** Education. **U:** Home, Institution. **Spo-Rec:** Basketball, Athletic Instruction/Coaching. **Acq:** Purchase. **Dist:** Championship Productions. $39.99.

Bill Self: Team Defense 2003

Provides basketball instruction and drills on various team-related defensive techniques by Bill Self, University of Kansas' head coach. 75m; VHS. **A:** Sr. High-Adult. **P:** Instruction. **U:** Institution. **Spo-Rec:** Basketball. **Acq:** Purchase. **Dist:** Championship Productions. $34.95.

Bill Self's Guide to Better Basketball Practice 2002

Presents 15 offensive and defensive drills by University of Illinois coach Bill Self during team practices. 38m; DVD. **A:** Sr. High-Adult. **P:** Instruction. **U:** Institution. **Spo-Rec:** Basketball. **Acq:** Purchase. **Dist:** Championship Productions. $39.95.

Bill T. Jones: Dancing to the Promised Land 1994

Interviews with African-American modern dance choreographer Jones as he works on his production of "Last Supper at Uncle Tom's Cabin/The Promised Land." 60m; VHS, DVD. **A:** College-Adult. **P:** Entertainment. **U:** Home. **Fin-Art:** Dance--Performance, Black Culture. **Acq:** Purchase. **Dist:** V.I.E.W. Inc./Arkadia Entertainment Corp. $29.98.

Bill Withers: Still Bill 2009 (Unrated)

Biographical documentary on the life of soul artist Bill Withers. 78m; DVD, Streaming. **A:** Jr. High-Adult. **P:** Education. **U:** Home, Institution. **L:** English. **Gen-Edu:** Divorce, Biography: Music. **Acq:** Purchase, Rent/Lease. **Dist:** Docurama. $29.95 14.99.

Bill Wyman: Digital Dreams 1983

A surrealistic journey into the life of Rolling Stones bassist Bill Wyman from his electronic childhood to his adult obsession with computers. 70m; VHS. **C:** Bill Wyman; Astrid Wyman; James Coburn. **Pr:** Bill Wyman; Bill Wyman. **A:** Jr. High-Adult. **P:** Entertainment. **U:** Home. **Mov-Ent:** Music Video, Music--Performance, Animation & Cartoons. **Acq:** Purchase. **Dist:** Music Video Distributors. $14.95.

Billboard Dad 1998 (G) — ★★½

The Olsen twins decide it's time for their dad to remarry so they paint a personal ad on a billboard advertising his availability. Eventually, their Dad meets Brooke, who's a winner except for her bratty son who's the girls' rival. But nothing will stop the twins if it means making Dad happy. 90m; VHS, DVD, Streaming. **C:** Ashley (Fuller) Olsen; Mary-Kate Olsen; Tom Amandes; Jessica Tuck; Sam Selatta; Carl Banks; Directed by Alan Metter; Written by Maria Jacquemetton; Cinematography by Mauro Fiore; Music by David Michael Frank. **A:** Family. **P:** Entertainment. **U:** Home. **Mov-Ent:** Family. **Acq:** Purchase. **Dist:** Amazon.com Inc.

Billboards 1994

The celebrated Joffery Ballet dances to the music of Prince in a performance recorded at State University in New York in 1993. 75m; VHS. **A:** Sr. High-Adult. **P:** Entertainment. **U:** Home. **Fin-Art:** Dance--Ballet, Dance--Performance. **Acq:** Purchase. **Dist:** Warner Reprise Video; Stagestep. $24.98.

Billiard Basics 1989

A comprehensive guide toward the mastery of billiards. 30m; VHS. **A:** Family. **P:** Instruction. **U:** Home. **How-Ins:** Sports--General, How-To. **Acq:** Purchase. **Dist:** MNTEX Entertainment, Inc.

Billiards for All Age Groups 1990

Pool legend Willie Mosconi demonstrates proper hand position and strategies for making those near-impossible shots. 25m; VHS. **Pr:** Champions on Film. **A:** Family. **P:** Instruction. **U:** Home. **How-Ins:** How-To. **Acq:** Purchase. **Dist:** School-Tech Inc. $12.95.

Billie 1965 (Unrated) — ★½

Duke stars as a tomboy athlete who puts the boys' track team to shame. Some amusing but very predictable situations, plus a few songs from Miss Duke. Based on Ronald Alexander's play "Time Out for Ginger." 86m; VHS, DVD, Wide. **C:** Patty Duke; Jim Backus; Jane Greer; Warren Berlinger; Billy DeWolfe; Charles Lane; Dick Sargent; Susan Seaforth Hayes; Ted Bessell; Richard Deacon; Directed by Don Weis; Written by Ronald Alexander. **Pr:** United Artists. **A:** Family. **P:** Entertainment. **U:** Home. **Mov-Ent:** Sports--Track & Field, Sports--Fiction: Comedy. **Acq:** Purchase. **Dist:** MGM Home Entertainment. $19.98.

Billie Holiday: A Tribute 1962

Features John Butler and Carmen de Lavallade performing modern dance interpretations to several Holiday recordings. Songs include "Guess Who's Coming to Town," "Gee Baby, Ain't I Good to You?" and "I Didn't Know What Time It Was." 28m/B/W; VHS, 3/4 U. **A:** Jr. High-Adult. **P:** Entertainment. **U:** Home. **Fin-Art:** Dance--Performance. **Acq:** Purchase. **Dist:** Camera Three Productions, Inc.

Billie Holiday: The Many Faces of Billie Holiday 19??

Includes 25 songs from the incomparable Lady Day, including "God Bless the Child," "Miss Brown to You," "St. Louis Blues," "They Can't Take That Away From Me," "Strange Fruit," "My Man," and "On the Sunny Side of the Street." 59m; VHS. **A:** College-Adult. **P:** Entertainment. **U:** Home. **Mov-Ent:** Music--Jazz. **Acq:** Purchase. **Dist:** Music Video Distributors. $29.95.

Billion Dollar Brain 1967 (Unrated) — ★★

The third of five films based on the Harry Palmer spy novels by Len Deighton, this one has Michael Caine repeating his performance as British agent Harry Palmer, now a down-on-his-luck private investigator. Forced back into the espionage game, he is sent to deliver a package to an old friend, only to find him now working for a rabid right-wing Texas oil billionaire who has made a super computer running a spy ring dedicated to perpetuating the cold war and destroying the Soviet Union. Confusing and full of triple crosses, it is fairly close to the source material. 111m; DVD. **C:** Michael Caine; Karl Malden; Ed Begley, Jr.; Oscar Homolka; Francoise Dorleac; Guy Doleman; Vladek Sheybal; Mark Elwes; John Brandon; Tony Harwood; Milo Sperber; Directed by Ken Russell; Written by Len Deighton; John McGrath; Cinematography by Billy Williams; Music by Richard Rodney Bennett. **A:** Sr. High-Adult. **P:** Entertainment. **U:** Home. **L:** English, French. **Mov-Ent:** Technology. **Acq:** Purchase. **Dist:** MGM Home Entertainment. $14.98.

The Billion Dollar Bubble 1981

The true story of the Equity Funding Corporation of America, which became a financial giant in 1973 through the use of computer fraud. This giant corporation was built on a base of forged bank certificates and doctored computer tapes. 60m; VHS, 3/4 U. **Pr:** BBC Horizon. **A:** Jr. High-Adult. **P:** Education. **U:** Institution; SURA. **Gen-Edu:** Documentary Films, Business. **Acq:** Purchase, Rent/Lease. **Dist:** Home Vision Cinema.

Billion Dollar Day 1986
An inside look at three different currency traders, who use almost two billion dollars a day. 30m; VHS, 3/4 U. **Pr:** Learning Corporation of America. **A:** Sr. High-Adult. **P:** Education. **U:** Institution, SURA. **Gen-Edu:** Business, Finance. **Acq:** Purchase, Rent/Lease. **Dist:** Phoenix Learning Group. $310.00.

The Billion Dollar Hobo 1978 (G) — ★½
Poor, unsuspecting heir of a multimillion dollar fortune must duplicate his benefactor's experience as a hobo during the Depression in order to collect his inheritance. Slow-moving family stuff. 96m; VHS, DVD. **C:** Tim Conway; Will Geer; Eric Weston; Sydney Lassick; Directed by Stuart E. McGowan. **Pr:** Samuel Goldwyn Home Entertainment. **A:** Family. **P:** Entertainment. **U:** Home. **Mov-Ent:** Homeless, Family Viewing. **Acq:** Purchase. **Dist:** Movies Unlimited; Alpha Video; MGM Home Entertainment. $59.98.

A Billion for Boris 1990 (Unrated) — ★★½
Boris' TV gives a sneak preview of the future and Boris plans to make some money off of it. Zany comedy in the vein of "Let It Ride." 89m; VHS, DVD. **C:** Lee Grant; Tim Kazurinsky; Directed by Alex Grasshof; Written by Mary Rogers. **A:** Jr. High-Adult. **P:** Entertainment. **U:** Home. **Mov-Ent:** Gambling. **Acq:** Purchase. **Dist:** Imperial Entertainment Corp. $79.95.

Billionaire Boys Club 1987 — ★★½
Chilling look at greed in the '80s. Nelson plays Joe Hunt, who gets together with a group of rich, preppie friends to manipulate investments in the commodities markets. When a slick con man (Silver) gets in their way he's murdered to keep their schemes intact. Based on a true story and adapted from the book by Sue Horton. The video version is considerably pared down from the original TV broadcast. 94m; VHS, DVD. **C:** Judd Nelson; Frederic Lehne; Brian McNamara; Raphael Sbarge; John Stockwell; Barry Tubb; Stan Shaw; Jill Schoelen; Ron Silver; James Sloyan; James Karen; Dale Dye; Directed by Marvin J. Chomsky. **A:** Sr. High-Adult. **P:** Entertainment. **U:** Home. **Mov-Ent:** Crime Drama, TV Movies. **Acq:** Purchase. **Dist:** A&E Television Networks L.L.C. $79.98.

Billy, a Teenage Apostle of Courage 1990
Billy Foreman narrates his own story of his battle against cancer. 14m; VHS, 3/4 U. **Pr:** Centre Productions, Inc. **A:** Jr. High-Sr. High. **P:** Education. **U:** Institution, SURA. **Gen-Edu:** Cancer, Adolescence. **Acq:** Purchase, Rent/Lease. **Dist:** Clear Vue Inc. $230.00.

Billy Bathgate 1991 (R) — ★★½
Uneven but well acted drama set in 1935 New York. A streetwise young man decides getting ahead during the Depression means gaining the attention of mobster Dutch Schultz and joining his gang. As Billy becomes the confidant of the racketeer he learns the criminal life is filled with suspicion and violence; in order to stay alive he must rely on every trick he's learned. Willis has a small role as a rival mobster who gets fitted for cement overshoes. Kidman does well as Dutch's girlfriend with Hill fine as the gang's number man. Based on the novel by E.L. Doctorow. 107m; VHS, DVD, Blu-Ray, Wide, CC. **C:** Dustin Hoffman; Nicole Kidman; Loren Dean; Bruce Willis; Steven Hill; Steve Buscemi; Stanley Tucci; Tim Jerome; Billy Jaye; Katharine Houghton; Mike Starr; John A. Costelloe; Moira Kelly; Directed by Robert Benton; Written by Tom Stoppard; Cinematography by Nestor Almendros; Music by Mark Isham. **A:** Sr. High-Adult. **P:** Entertainment. **U:** Home. **Mov-Ent:** Crime Drama. **Acq:** Purchase. **Dist:** Buena Vista Home Entertainment. $92.95.

Billy Bragg Goes to Moscow & Norton, Virginia Too 1990
Essentially a two-part video presenting two Bragg concerts. The first is Bragg in Virginia in 1986 playing a benefit for striking coal miners. The second is in the Soviet Union in 1989. The Virginia concert includes "Help Save the Youth of America," "A New England," "There Is Power in a Union," "A Miner's Life Is Like a Sailor's," "The Times They Are Changing," "The Price I Pay," "Great Leap Forwards," "Tank Park Salute," and "Which Side Are You On." The Moscow concert includes "To Have and Have Not," "Ever Fallen in Love," "Between the Wars," "Train Train," "Heard It Through the Grapevine," "Garage Land," "I Wanna Be a Cosmonaut," "Get Up Stand Up," "The World Turned Upside Down," "Help Save the Youth of America," "A New England," and "Think Again." 110m; VHS. **Pr:** Elektra Entertainment. **A:** Adult. **P:** Entertainment. **U:** Home. **Mov-Ent:** Music--Performance. **Acq:** Purchase. **Dist:** Music Video Distributors. $19.98.

Billy Budd 19??
The English National Opera performs Benjamin Britten's opera, Billy Budd. 151m; VHS. **A:** Adult. **P:** Entertainment. **U:** Home. **Gen-Edu:** Opera. **Acq:** Purchase. **Dist:** Music Video Distributors. $149.95.

Billy Budd 198?
Herman Melville's classic about injustice on a British man-of-war comes to the stage as an opera. Performed by the English National Opera and conducted by David Atherton. 156m; VHS. **C:** Thomas Allen; Philip Langridge; Richard Van Allan; Neil Howlett; Conducted by David Atherton. **Pr:** RM Arts; British Broadcasting Corporation. **A:** Jr. High-Adult. **P:** Entertainment. **U:** Home. **Fin-Art:** Opera, Literature--American. **Acq:** Purchase. **Dist:** Home Vision Cinema. $39.95.

Billy Budd 1962 — ★★★
The classic Melville good-evil allegory adapted to film, dealing with a British warship in the late 1700s, and its struggle between evil master-at-arms and innocent shipmate. Stamp's screen debut as the naive Billy who is tried for the murder of the sadistic first mate. Well directed and acted. 123m/B/W; VHS, DVD; Open Captioned. **C:** Terence Stamp; Peter Ustinov; Robert Ryan; Melvyn Douglas; Paul Rogers; John Neville; Ronald Lewis; David McCallum; John Meillon; Directed by Peter Ustinov; Written by Peter Ustinov; Robert Rossen; Cinematography by Robert Krasker. **Pr:** Anglo-Allied Productions. **A:** Family. **P:** Entertainment. **U:** Home. **Mov-Ent:** Action-Adventure, Boating. **Acq:** Purchase. **Dist:** Movies Unlimited; Warner Home Video, Inc. $59.98.

Billy Bunny's Animal Song 1993
The muppet characters—Billy Bunny, Cecil, Percival, Edgar Bear, the Termite, and the Porcupine—share eight songs with on-screen lyrics to which children can sing and dance. Hosted by Kermit the Frog. 30m; VHS, CC. **A:** Family. **P:** Entertainment. **U:** Home. **Chl-Juv:** Puppets, Music--Children. **Acq:** Purchase. **Dist:** Buena Vista Home Entertainment; Baker and Taylor. $12.99.

Billy Casper's Golf for Juniors 1992
Veteran player Casper instructs young golfers on everything they need to know to play the game of golf. ?m; VHS. **A:** Jr. High. **P:** Instruction. **U:** Home. **How-Ins:** Golf, How-To. **Acq:** Purchase. **Dist:** Sony Pictures Home Entertainment Inc.; Fast Forward. $19.95.

Billy Connolly: The Pick of Billy Connolly 1991 (Unrated)
More hilarious antics from Billy Connolly. 45m; VHS. **C:** Billy Connolly. **A:** Adult. **P:** Entertainment. **U:** Home. **Mov-Ent:** Comedy--Performance. **Acq:** Purchase. **Dist:** Polymorph Films, Inc. $39.95.

Billy Crystal: A Comic's Line 1983
Comedian Billy Crystal performs a one-man show, highlighting spoofs, of rock videos and other stand-up comics. 59m; VHS. **C:** Billy Crystal. **Pr:** R.J.M.B. Productions. **A:** Jr. High-Adult. **P:** Entertainment. **U:** Home. **Mov-Ent:** Comedy--Performance. **Acq:** Purchase. **Dist:** Paramount Pictures Corp. $19.95.

Billy Crystal: Don't Get Me Started 1986
Crystal hosts a comedy television special featuring his standard routines from "Saturday Night Live" and numerous guest stars. 60m; VHS. **C:** Billy Crystal; Sammy Davis, Jr; Eugene Levy; Christopher Guest; Rob Reiner. **Pr:** Vestron Video. **A:** Jr. High-Adult. **P:** Entertainment. **U:** Home. **Mov-Ent:** TV Movies. **Acq:** Purchase. **Dist:** Lions Gate Television Corp. $14.98.

Billy Crystal: Midnight Train to Moscow 1989 (Unrated)
Recorded live at Moscow's Pushkin Theatre, Crystal travels to Russia, his ancestral home, and shows that comedy is an international language. A breakthrough in Glasnost. 72m; VHS, CC. **C:** Billy Crystal; Directed by Paul Flaherty. **Pr:** HBO. **A:** Jr. High-Adult. **P:** Entertainment. **U:** Home. **Mov-Ent:** Comedy--Performance, USSR. **Acq:** Purchase. **Dist:** Warner Home Video, Inc. $19.98.

Billy Dean: Video Hits 1993
The top male country star of 1992 with some of his hits, including "Only Here for a Little While," "Somewhere in My Broken Heart," "Billy the Kid," and "Only the Wind." 23m; VHS. **A:** Jr. High-Adult. **P:** Entertainment. **U:** Home. **Mov-Ent:** Music Video, Music--Country/Western. **Acq:** Purchase. **Dist:** Music Video Distributors. $12.98.

Billy Donovan: Competitive Drills for Player Development 2008
Billy Donovan presents five competitive points based drills that he believes are the keys to his basketball teams' successes. 70m; DVD. **A:** Family. **P:** Education. **U:** Home, Institution. **Spo-Rec:** Basketball, Athletic Instruction/Coaching. **Acq:** Purchase. **Dist:** Championship Productions. $39.99.

Billy Donovan: Drills for Shooting and Defending the 3-Point Shot 2009
Coach Billy Donovan presents techniques for defending and setting up the three-point shot. 62m; DVD. **A:** Family. **P:** Education. **U:** Home, Institution. **Spo-Rec:** Basketball, Athletic Instruction/Coaching. **Acq:** Purchase. **Dist:** Championship Productions. $39.99.

Billy Donovan: Individual Skill Development Within Your Offense 2005
Instructions on how to play basketball. Focuses on offensive skills. 70m; DVD. **A:** Adult. **P:** Instruction. **U:** Home. **Spo-Rec:** Basketball, Sports--General, How-To. **Acq:** Purchase. **Dist:** Championship Productions. $39.95.

Billy Donovan: Mastering the Full-Court Match-Up Press 2004
Presents basketball pressure defense drills by Billy Donovan, the head coach at the University of Florida. 60m; DVD. **A:** Sr. High-Adult. **P:** Instruction. **U:** Institution. **Spo-Rec:** Basketball. **Acq:** Purchase. **Dist:** Championship Productions. $39.95.

Billy Donovan: The Spread "Pick and Roll Offense" 2007
Coach Billy Donovan discusses the Pick and Roll Offense in basketball, and how to beat the common methods used to defend against it. 62m; DVD. **A:** Family. **P:** Education. **U:** Home, Institution. **Spo-Rec:** Basketball, Athletic Instruction/Coaching. **Acq:** Purchase. **Dist:** Championship Productions. $39.99.

Billy Donovan: The Unstoppable Transition Game 2006
Billy Donovan shares drills and concepts meant to increase a basketball team's possibility to win a transition game. 61m; DVD. **A:** Family. **P:** Education. **U:** Home, Institution. **Spo-Rec:** Basketball, Athletic Instruction/Coaching. **Acq:** Purchase. **Dist:** Championship Productions. $39.99.

Billy Donovan: 10 Aggressive Transition & Conditioning Drills 2004
Coach Billy Donovan gives an on-court demonstration of ten offensive drills intended to improve a basketball team's offensive abilities. 60m; DVD. **A:** Family. **P:** Education. **U:** Home, Institution. **Spo-Rec:** Basketball, Athletic Instruction/Coaching. **Acq:** Purchase. **Dist:** Championship Productions. $39.99.

Billy Donovan's Father and Son Workout 2012
University of Florida's head coach Billy Donovan presents a basketball workout for parents to use to improve their child's basketball skills. 71m; DVD. **A:** Jr. High-Adult. **P:** Education. **U:** Home, Institution. **L:** English. **Gen-Edu:** Athletic Instruction/Coaching, Basketball, Education. **Acq:** Purchase. **Dist:** Championship Productions. $29.99.

Billy Donovan's Shooting Technique and Workout Drills 2012
University of Florida's head coach Billy Donovan presents drills and techniques for improving a basketball team's shooting skills. 73m; DVD. **A:** Jr. High-Adult. **P:** Education. **U:** Home, Institution. **L:** English. **Gen-Edu:** Athletic Instruction/Coaching, Basketball, Education. **Acq:** Purchase. **Dist:** Championship Productions. $29.99.

Billy Eckstine/Dizzy Gillespie Be-Bop Big Bands 1993
Eckstine's "Rhythm in a Riff" and Gillespie's "Jivin' in Bebop" feature various artists. Songs include "Taps Miller," "Lonesome Lover Blues," "I Waited for You," and others. 60m; VHS. **A:** Jr. High-Adult. **P:** Entertainment. **U:** Home. **Mov-Ent:** Music Video, Music--Performance. **Acq:** Purchase. **Dist:** Music Video Distributors. $24.95.

Billy Elliot 2000 (R) — ★★★
Eleven-year-old Billy (Bell) is trying to survive in a Durham County town during the 1984 miners' strike that is affecting his family. His widowed dad (Lewis) wants Billy to take boxing lessons but the boy is more interested in the ballet class taught at the same gym by hard-living Mrs. Wilkinson (Walters), whose daughter Debbie (Blackwell) taunts Billy into trying to dance. Billy's natural talent is so great that Mrs. Wilkinson encourages him to audition for the Royal Ballet School in London. Of course, when his dad finds out what's been going on, there's trouble. The unfortunate rating is due to language but the film has all-around appeal and some fine performances. Stage director Daldry makes his film debut as does Bell. 111m; VHS, DVD, Wide. **C:** Jamie Bell; Julie Walters; Gary Lewis; Jamie Driven; Nicola Blackwell; Jean Heywood; Stuart Wells; Adam Cooper; Directed by Stephen Daldry; Written by Lee Hall; Cinematography by Brian Tufano; Music by Stephen Warbeck. **Pr:** Universal Pictures. **A:** Sr. High-Adult. **P:** Entertainment. **U:** Home. **Mov-Ent:** Dance, Great Britain, Miners & Mining. **Awds:** British Acad. '00: Actor (Bell), Film, Support. Actress (Walters). **Acq:** Purchase. **Dist:** Movies Unlimited; Alpha Video.

Billy Galvin 1986 (PG) — ★★½
A bullheaded ironworker tries to straighten out the turbulent relationship he has with his rebellious son. 95m; VHS, Streaming. **C:** Karl Malden; Lenny Von Dohlen; Joyce Van Patten; Toni Kalem; Keith Szarabajka; Alan North; Paul Guilfoyle; Barton Heyman; Directed by John Gray; Written by John Gray; Music by Joel Rosenbaum. **Pr:** Vestron Pictures. **A:** Jr. High-Adult. **P:** Entertainment. **U:** Home. **Mov-Ent. Acq:** Purchase. **Dist:** Lions Gate Entertainment Inc. $79.95.

Billy Gillispie: 'In Your Face' Pressure Defense Drills 2007
Coach Billy Gillispie presents his philosophy (and some drills) on defense for the game of basketball. 72m; DVD. **A:** Family. **P:** Education. **U:** Home, Institution. **Spo-Rec:** Basketball, Athletic Instruction/Coaching. **Acq:** Purchase. **Dist:** Championship Productions. $39.99.

Billy Graham: Are You a Follower of Christ? 1987
Internationally renowned evangelist Billy Graham appeals to an audience at the '87 Urbana conference on the importance of acknowledging one's sins and other religious issues. 40m; VHS. **Pr:** TwentyOneHundred Productions. **A:** College-Adult. **P:** Religious. **U:** Institution, Home. **Gen-Edu:** Religion. **Acq:** Purchase. **Dist:** InterVarsity Video. $14.95.

Billy Graham: God's Ambassador 2006
Authorized biography of the spiritual leader, from his early life and first ministry to his worldwide evangelical mission. 120m; DVD. **A:** Sr. High-Adult. **P:** Entertainment. **U:** Home. **Gen-Edu:** Documentary Films, Biography: Religious Figures. **Acq:** Purchase. **Dist:** Fox Home Entertainment.

Billy Graham: How to Get into the Kingdom of Heaven 1990
Qouting passages from Luke 14: 16-23, Dr. Graham expounds on why people refuse to accept God's invitation to salvation. 49m; VHS. **C:** Billy Graham. **Pr:** Billy Graham; Billy Graham. **A:** Family. **P:** Religious. **U:** Home. **Gen-Edu:** Philosophy & Ideology. **Acq:** Purchase. **Dist:** Lions Gate Entertainment Inc. $29.98.

Billy Graham: The New Birth 1990
Dr. Graham discusses God's acceptance of us and the importance of our trust in Him to change our lives. We learn how God loves us for who we are. 49m; VHS. **C:** Billy Graham. **Pr:** Billy Graham; Billy Graham. **A:** Family. **P:** Religious. **U:** Home. **Gen-Edu:** Philosophy & Ideology. **Acq:** Purchase. **Dist:** Lions Gate Entertainment Inc. $29.98.

Billy Graham: The Road To Armageddon 1990
Dr. Graham discusses the coming of Armageddon and the necessity of living our lives for Christ in these turbulent times. He also discusses contemporary society. 47m; VHS. **C:** Billy

Graham. **Pr:** Billy Graham; Billy Graham. **A:** Family. **P:** Religious. **U:** Home. **Gen-Edu:** Philosophy & Ideology. **Acq:** Purchase. **Dist:** Lions Gate Entertainment Inc. $29.98.

Billy Graham: The Secret of Happiness 1990
Dr. Graham uses the "Sermon on the Mount" to illustrate how true happiness can be attained. 50m; VHS. **C:** Billy Graham. **Pr:** Billy Graham; Billy Graham. **A:** Family. **P:** Religious. **U:** Home. **Gen-Edu:** Philosophy & Ideology. **Acq:** Purchase. **Dist:** Lions Gate Entertainment Inc. $29.95.

Billy Idol: Shock to the System 1993
The making of Idol's cyberpunk album "Shock to the System"; includes the video title cut and the unreleased version of "Heroin." ?m; VHS. **A:** Sr. High-Adult. **P:** Entertainment. **U:** Home. **Mov-Ent:** Music Video. **Acq:** Purchase. **Dist:** Music Video Distributors. $9.98.

Billy Idol: The Charmed Life Videos 1990
The snarling singer is featured in videos for "Cradle of Love," and the uncensored versions of "L.A. Woman" and "Hot in the City." 15m; VHS. **A:** Jr. High-College. **P:** Entertainment. **U:** Home. **Mov-Ent:** Music Video. **Acq:** Purchase. **Dist:** Music Video Distributors. $12.98.

Billy Idol: Vital Idol 1987
Video clips of Billy Idol's hit songs, including "Rebel Yell," "White Wedding" and "Dancing with Myself." In HiFi Stereo. 50m; VHS. **Pr:** Chrysalis Records. **A:** Family. **P:** Entertainment. **U:** Home. **Mov-Ent:** Music Video. **Acq:** Purchase. **Dist:** Music Video Distributors; Lions Gate Television Corp. $19.95.

Billy Jack 1971 (PG) — ★★
On an Arizona Indian reservation, a half-breed ex-Green Beret with pugnacious martial arts skills (Laughlin) stands between a rural town and a school for runaways. Laughlin stars with his real-life wife Taylor. Features the then-hit song "One Tin Soldier," sung by Coven. The movie and its marketing by Laughlin inspired a "Billy Jack" cult phenomenon. A Spanish-dubbed version of this film is also available. Followed by a sequel in 1974, "Trail of Billy Jack," which bombed. 112m; VHS, DVD. **C:** Tom Laughlin; Delores Taylor; Clark Howat; Bert Freed; Julie Webb; Victor Izay; Teresa Kelly; Lynn Baker; Stan Rice; Howard Hesseman; Directed by Tom Laughlin; Written by Tom Laughlin; Delores Taylor; Cinematography by Fred W. Koenekamp; John Stephens; Music by Mundell Lowe. **Pr:** Warner Bros; National Student Film Corporation. **A:** Sr. High-Adult. **P:** Entertainment. **U:** Home. **L:** English, Spanish. **Mov-Ent:** Native Americans, Cult Films, Veterans. **Acq:** Purchase. **Dist:** Warner Home Video, Inc. $14.95.

Billy Jack Goes to Washington 1977 (Unrated) — ★½
Unlike the other Billy Jack movies, this one was never theatrically released, which is probably good, as it's such a transparent rip-off of "Mr. Smith Goes to Washington." Pardoned for the trumped-up charges that sent him to prison previously, he is appointed to the U.S. Senate (wait, what?) to 'attract young voters,' and to convince the locals to get a nuke plant built. And then he finds out his predecessor is dead under odd circumstances. Of course you saw this part coming. 155m; DVD. **C:** Tom Laughlin; Directed by Tom Laughlin; Written by Tom Laughlin; Sidney Buchman; Lewis R. Foster; Delores Taylor; Cinematography by Jack Marta; Music by Elmer Bernstein. **A:** Sr. High-Adult. **P:** Entertainment. **U:** Home. **Mov-Ent:** Politics & Government. **Acq:** Purchase. **Dist:** Image Entertainment Inc.; Ventura Distribution Inc. $29.98.

Billy Joe Royal 1990
The down home Country artist performs "Tell It Like It Is," "Till I Can't Take It Anymore," "A Ring Where a Ring Used to Be," "Love Has No Right," "I'll Pin a Note On Your Pillow," and "Out of Sight and On My Mind." Includes exclusive interviews. 30m; VHS. **Pr:** A*Vision. **A:** Jr. High-Adult. **P:** Entertainment. **U:** Home. **Mov-Ent:** Music Video, Music--Country/Western. **Acq:** Purchase. **Dist:** WarnerVision; Music Video Distributors; Fast Forward. $14.98.

Billy Joe Walker, Jr.: Studio Recording/Composing 1990
Receive some down-home country music lessons from one of the best in the business. ?m; VHS. **A:** Jr. High-Adult. **P:** Instruction. **U:** Home. **How-Ins:** Music--Instruction. **Acq:** Purchase. **Dist:** Music Video Distributors. $49.95.

Billy Joel: A Matter of Trust 1991 (Unrated)
Documentary of Billy Joel interacting with the Russian people during his groundbreaking 1987 tour. The changes which shocked the world were already in place when Joel toured, and in numerous instances the "new revolution" can be seen in the faces and actions of the Russians who reacted to the first rock 'n' roll tour by an American. 83m; VHS. **C:** Billy Joel. **Pr:** Sony Video. **A:** Family. **P:** Education. **U:** Home. **Mov-Ent:** Documentary Films, USSR, Human Relations. **Acq:** Purchase. **Dist:** Sony Music Entertainment Inc.

Billy Joel: Eye of the Storm 1990
Four songs from Joel: "We Didn't Start the Fire," "I Go to Extremes," "Leningrad" and "The Downeaster Alexa." 25m; VHS. **C:** Billy Joel. **A:** Family. **P:** Entertainment. **U:** Home. **Mov-Ent:** Music Video, Music--Pop/Rock. **Acq:** Purchase. **Dist:** Sony Music Entertainment Inc. $16.99.

Billy Joel Live at Yankee Stadium 1990
Billy Joel returns to his home turf to perform his newer songs and his greatest hits. Taped on June 22 and 23, 1990. Also included are interviews and behind the scenes footage. Songs include "Scenes from an Italian Restaurant," "Piano Man," "We Didn't Start the Fire," "A Matter of Trust" and "Pressure." 85m; VHS. **C:** Billy Joel. **Pr:** CMV. **A:** Jr. High-Adult. **P:** Entertainment. **U:** Home. **Mov-Ent:** Music--Performance. **Acq:** Purchase. **Dist:** Music Video Distributors; Sony Music Entertainment Inc. $19.98.

Billy Joel Live from Leningrad, USSR 1991
Selections from Billy Joel's groundbreaking rock 'n' roll tour of the Soviet Union in 1987. Essentially a video record of the Joel's "In Concert" album released after the tour, the video does include a previously unreleased version of Dylan's "The Times, They Are a-Changin'." Also featured are "Angry Young Man," "Allentown," "Goodnight Saigon," "A Matter of Trust," "Back in the USSR," "Uptown Girl," "Big Shot," "Baby Grand," and "Big Man on Mulberry Street." 60m; VHS. **C:** Billy Joel. **Pr:** Sony Video. **A:** Family. **P:** Entertainment. **U:** Home. **Mov-Ent:** Music--Pop/Rock, Human Relations, USSR. **Acq:** Purchase. **Dist:** Sony Music Entertainment Inc.

Billy Joel Live from Long Island 1983 (Unrated)
A recording of Joel's dynamic New Year's Eve performance at Nassau Coliseum. Classic tunes showcased include "Piano Man," "Allentown," "You May Be Right," and "Still Rock and Roll to Me." In VHS stereo and Beta Hi-Fi. 80m; VHS. **Pr:** CBS/Fox. **A:** Family. **P:** Entertainment. **U:** Home. **Mov-Ent:** Music--Performance, Music--Pop/Rock. **Acq:** Purchase. **Dist:** Music Video Distributors. $29.95.

Billy Joel: Shades of Grey 1993
From the PBS television special about how the popular singer/songwriter developed his newest release "River of Dreams." 80m; VHS. **A:** Sr. High-Adult. **P:** Entertainment. **U:** Home. **Mov-Ent:** Music Video, Music--Pop/Rock. **Acq:** Purchase. **Dist:** Sony Music Entertainment Inc.; Music Video Distributors. $19.98.
Songs: The River of Dreams; Two Thousand Years; Lullabye (Goodnight, My Angel); All About Soul; Shameless.

Billy Joel: Stormfront 1989
Joel sings "The Downeaster 'Alexa,'" "We Didn't Start the Fire," "Leningrad," "I Go To Extremes," and a live version of "The Downeaster 'Alexa.'" 24m; VHS. **C:** Music by Billy Joel. **Pr:** CBS. **A:** Jr. High-Adult. **P:** Entertainment. **U:** Home. **Mov-Ent:** Music--Performance, Music--Pop/Rock. **Acq:** Purchase. **Dist:** Music Video Distributors. $16.98.

Billy Joel: The Video Album, Vol. 1 1986
Joel's most popular songs and videos are collected on this tape, including "Pressure," "The Night Is Still Young," "Honesty," and a visualization of "Piano Man," created especially for this program. 40m; VHS. **Pr:** Marble Arch Productions. **A:** Family. **P:** Entertainment. **U:** Home. **Mov-Ent:** Music Video, Music--Performance, Music--Pop/Rock. **Acq:** Purchase. **Dist:** Music Video Distributors. $14.95.

Billy Joel: The Video Album, Vol. 2 1986
An album of Joel's more recent video hits, including "Uptown Girl," "Big Shot," "Still Rock and Roll" and "You're Only Human." 50m; VHS. **A:** Family. **P:** Entertainment. **U:** Home. **Mov-Ent:** Music Video, Music--Performance, Music--Pop/Rock. **Acq:** Purchase. **Dist:** Music Video Distributors. $14.95.

Billy Jonas: Bangin' and Sangin' 2000
"Industrial re-percussionist" Billy Jonas uses his unique blend of instruments made from found and recycled objects to perform original songs and family favorites for kids of all ages. VHS. **A:** Family. **P:** Entertainment. **U:** Home. **Mov-Ent:** Music--Children, Music--Performance. **Acq:** Purchase. **Dist:** Ivy Classics Video. $19.99.

Billy Kidd's Ski Racing 1986
Kidd instructs the viewer in optimum speed skiing skills. 27m; VHS. **Pr:** Tom Tatum. **A:** Jr. High-Adult. **P:** Instruction. **U:** Home. **Spo-Rec:** Sports--General, Sports--Winter. **Acq:** Purchase. **Dist:** ESPN Inc. $19.95.

Billy Liar 1963 (Unrated) — ★★★
A young Englishman dreams of escaping from his working class family and dead-end job as an undertaker's assistant. Parallels James Thurber's story, "The Secret Life of Walter Mitty." 94m/B/W; VHS, DVD, Wide. **C:** Tom Courtenay; Julie Christie; Finlay Currie; Directed by John Schlesinger; Written by Willis Hall; Keith Waterhouse; Cinematography by Denys Coop; Music by Richard Rodney Bennett. **Pr:** Continental. **A:** Sr. High-Adult. **P:** Entertainment. **U:** Home. **Mov-Ent:** Comedy-Drama, Family. **Acq:** Purchase. **Dist:** Lions Gate Entertainment Inc. $9.98.

Billy Madison 1994 (PG-13) — ★½
Wealthy slacker Billy (Sandler) must prove to Dad he is capable of running the family hotel business by undertaking the obvious challenge of repeating grades 1-12 in six months. Ponder a few bodily function gags, and you'll have exhausted the humor in this lame attempt at creating a feature-length movie out of what would barely pass as a Saturday Night Live sketch. For only the most diehard fans of Sandler's silly shtick. 90m; VHS, DVD, HD-DVD, CC. **C:** Adam Sandler; Darren McGavin; Bridgette Wilson-Sampras; Bradley Whitford; Josh Mostel; Norm MacDonald; Mark Beltzman; Larry Hankin; Theresa Merritt; Chris Farley; Steve Buscemi; Directed by Tamra Davis; Written by Adam Sandler; Cinematography by Victor Hammer; Music by Randy Edelman. **Pr:** Robert Simonds; Fitch Cady; Universal Pictures. **A:** Jr. High-Adult. **P:** Entertainment. **U:** Home. **Mov-Ent:** Education, Hotels & Hotel Staff Training. **Acq:** Purchase. **Dist:** Universal Music and Video Distribution. $19.98.

Billy Ocean: In London 1985
Ocean in concert at the Hammersmith Odeon in London, performing "Lover Boy," "Caribbean Queen," and others. In HiFi Stereo. 55m; VHS. **Pr:** Music Vision. **A:** Family. **P:** Entertainment. **U:** Home. **Mov-Ent:** Music--Performance. **Acq:** Purchase. **Dist:** Music Video Distributors; Sony Pictures Home Entertainment Inc. $14.95.

Billy Ocean: Tear Down These Hits 1988
Billy performs "Get Outta My Dreams, Get Into My Car," "Caribbean Queen," "When the Going Gets Tough," "Loverboy" and more. 35m; VHS. **C:** Music by Billy Ocean. **A:** Adult. **P:** Entertainment. **U:** Home. **Mov-Ent:** Music--Performance, Music Video, Performing Arts. **Acq:** Purchase. **Dist:** Music Video Distributors; Sony Pictures Home Entertainment Inc. $14.95.

Billy: Portrait of a Street Kid 1977 (Unrated) — ★★
A ghetto youngster tries to pry himself up and out of his bleak surroundings through education, but complications arise when he gets his girlfriend pregnant. 96m; VHS. **C:** LeVar Burton; Tina Andrews; Ossie Davis; Michael Constantine; Directed by Steven Gethers. **Pr:** Mark Carliner Productions. **A:** Sr. High-Adult. **P:** Entertainment. **U:** Home. **Mov-Ent:** TV Movies, Pregnancy, Homeless. **Acq:** Purchase. **Dist:** $34.95.

Billy Ray Cyrus 1992
The latest of the hot country hunks performs his hit "Achy Breaky Heart" as well as "Could've Been Me" and other songs. The video also features behind-the-scenes profile footage. 90m; VHS. **A:** Family. **P:** Entertainment. **U:** Home. **Mov-Ent:** Music Video, Music--Country/Western. **Acq:** Purchase. **Dist:** Music Video Distributors. $12.95.

Billy Ray Cyrus: The Video Collection 1993
Seven video cuts from the country heartthrob, most from his "Some Gave All" album. 30m; VHS. **A:** Jr. High-Adult. **P:** Entertainment. **U:** Home. **Mov-Ent:** Music Video, Music--Country/Western. **Acq:** Purchase. **Dist:** Music Video Distributors. $14.95.
Songs: In the Heart of a Woman; These Boots Are Made for Walking; She's Not Crying Anymore; Where'm I Gonna Live; Could've Been Me; Achy Breaky Heart; Some Gave All.

Billy Rose's Jumbo 1962 — ★★★
Better-than-average update of the circus picture. Durante and Raye are terrific, as are the Rodgers and Hart songs. Fun, with lively production numbers in the inimitable Berkeley style. 125m; DVD, Blu-Ray, Wide. **C:** Doris Day; Stephen Boyd; Jimmy Durante; Martha Raye; Dean Jagger; Directed by Charles Walters; Written by Sidney Sheldon; Cinematography by William H. Daniels. **Pr:** MGM. **A:** Family. **P:** Entertainment. **U:** Home. **Mov-Ent:** Musical, Romance, Circuses. **Acq:** Purchase. **Dist:** WarnerArchive.com. $19.98.
Songs: Over and Over Again; Circus on Parade; Why Can't I?; This Can't Be Love; The Most Beautiful Girl in the World; My Romance; Little Girl Blue; What is a Circus; Sawdust, Spangles and Dreams.

Billy Sheehan - Bass Secrets 1990
Play along with bass great Billy Sheehan as he demonstrates many of the original bass techniques developed in his spectacular career. ?m; VHS. **C:** Billy Sheehan; Hosted by Wolf Marshall. **A:** Jr. High-Adult. **P:** Instruction. **U:** Home. **How-Ins:** Music--Instruction. **Acq:** Purchase. **Dist:** Music Video Distributors. $24.95.

Billy Sheehan on Bass 1990
Sheehan talks about his personal influences and career as a bassist, then explains the basics of both left and right-handed technique. 83m; VHS. **C:** Billy Sheehan; Hosted by Wolf Marshall. **Pr:** DCI Music Video. **A:** Sr. High-Adult. **P:** Instruction. **U:** Home. **How-Ins:** Music--Instruction. **Acq:** Purchase. **Dist:** Music Video Distributors. $24.95.

Billy the Kid 1930 (Unrated) — ★★
Early talkie plays fast and loose with the facts but it was filmed on location, which gives it some authenticity. During the Lincoln County, New Mexico homesteader war, Billy the Kid (Brown) vows revenge on the men who murdered his boss. Sheriff Pat Garrett (Beery) captures Billy but he escapes jail and Garrett must hunt the young outlaw down again. 95m/B/W; DVD. **C:** Johnny Mack Brown; Wallace Beery; Kay Johnson; Karl (Daen) Dane; Wyndham Standing; James A. Marcus; Directed by King Vidor; Written by Wanda Tuchock; Charles MacArthur; Cinematography by Gordon Avil. **A:** Sr. High-Adult. **P:** Entertainment. **U:** Home. **L:** English. **Mov-Ent:** Western. **Acq:** Purchase. **Dist:** WarnerArchive.com.

Billy the Kid 1941 — ★★½
Billy Bonney joins up with a group of outlaws in a Southwest town where he bumps into his old friend Jim Sherwood, now the marshal. Attempting to change his ways, he falls back into the life of a bandit when an outlaw friend is murdered. Although an entertaining western, the story bears no resemblance to the actual last days of Billy the Kid. Based on a story by Howard Emmett Rogers and Bradbury Foote, suggested by the book "The Saga of Billy the Kid" by Walter Noble Burns. 94m; VHS, DVD, CC. **C:** Robert Taylor; Brian Donlevy; Ian Hunter; Mary Howard; Gene Lockhart; Lon Chaney, Jr.; Guinn "Big Boy" Williams; Cy Kendall; Henry O'Neill; Ted Adams; Frank Puglia; Mitchell Lewis; Dick Curtis; Grant Withers; Joe Yule; Eddie Dunn; Kermit Maynard; Chill Wills; Olive Blakeney; Carl Pitti; Directed by David Miller; Written by Gene Fowler, Sr.; Cinematography by William V. Skall; Leonard Smith; Music by David Snell. **Pr:** MGM. **A:** Jr. High-Adult. **P:** Entertainment. **U:** Home. **Mov-Ent:** Western. **Acq:** Purchase. **Dist:** WarnerArchive.com. $19.98.

Billy the Kid in Santa Fe 1941 (Unrated) — ★½
Steele's last outing as the outlaw finds Billy busting out of jail to clear his name of a murder he didn't commit. He and pals Jeff and Fuzzy travel to Santa Fe where Billy is determined to get a confession from the real killer. 61m/B/W; DVD. **C:** Bob Steele; Al "Fuzzy" St. John; Rex Lease; Dave O'Brien; Marin Sais; Dennis Moore; Karl Hackett; Directed by Sam Newfield; Written by Joseph O'Donnell; Cinematography by Jack Greenhalgh. **A:**

Family. **P:** Entertainment. **U:** Home. **Mov-Ent:** Western. **Acq:** Purchase. **Dist:** Movies Unlimited.

Billy the Kid in Texas 1940 — ★½
The famed outlaw takes on trouble and makes sure the Texans never forget that he has been there. 52m/B/W; VHS, DVD. **C:** Bob Steele; Al "Fuzzy" St. John; Carleton Young; John Merton; Directed by Sam Newfield; Written by Joseph O'Donnell; Cinematography by Jack Greenhalgh; Music by Lew Porter. **Pr:** Sigmund Neufeld; Producers Releasing Corporation. **A:** Family. **P:** Entertainment. **U:** Home. **Mov-Ent:** Western. **Acq:** Purchase. **Dist:** Mill Creek Entertainment L.L.C.; Sinister Cinema. $19.95.

Billy the Kid Outlawed 1940 (Unrated) — ★½
Billy, Fuzzy, and Jeff are branded outlaws when they come to the aid of ranchers who are being killed by a gang trying to take over Lincoln County. 52m/B/W; DVD. **C:** Bob Steele; Carleton Young; Louise Currie; Al "Fuzzy" St. John; Joe McGuinn; Ted Adams; Kenne Duncan; Hal Price; Walter McGrail; Directed by Sam Newfield; Written by Oliver Drake; Cinematography by Jack Greenhalgh. **A:** Jr. High-Adult. **P:** Entertainment. **U:** Home. **Mov-Ent:** Western. **Acq:** Purchase. **Dist:** Alpha Video.

Billy the Kid Returns 1938 — ★½
While trying to clean up a town of its criminal element, Rogers is mistaken for the legendary Billy. Complications ensue. 60m/B/W; VHS, DVD, 3/4 U, Special order formats. **C:** Roy Rogers; George "Gabby" Hayes; Smiley Burnette; Lynne Roberts; Directed by Joseph Kane. **Pr:** Republic. **A:** Family. **P:** Entertainment. **U:** Home. **Mov-Ent:** Western. **Acq:** Purchase. **Dist:** Synergy Enterprises Inc. $19.95.

Billy the Kid Trapped 1942 — ★½
Billy and his partner are rescued from hanging by an outlaw band. 59m/B/W; VHS, DVD. **C:** Buster Crabbe; Al "Fuzzy" St. John; Malcolm "Bud" McTaggart; Anne Jeffreys; Glenn Strange; Directed by Sam Newfield. **Pr:** Sigmund Neufeld. **A:** Adult. **P:** Entertainment. **U:** Home. **Mov-Ent:** Western. **Acq:** Purchase. **Dist:** Rex Miller Artisan Studio. $19.95.

Billy the Kid Versus Dracula 1966 (Unrated) — ★★
The title says it all. Dracula travels to the Old West, anxious to put the bite on a pretty lady ranch owner. Her fiance, the legendary outlaw Billy the Kid, steps in to save his girl from becoming a vampire herself. A Carradine camp classic. 95m; VHS, DVD. **C:** Chuck Courtney; John Carradine; Melinda Plowman; Walter Janovitz; Harry Carey, Jr.; Roy Barcroft; Virginia Christine; Bing (Neil) Russell; Olive Carey; William Challee; William Forrest; Directed by William Beaudine; Written by Carl K. Hittleman; Cinematography by Lothrop Worth; Music by Raoul Kraushaar. **Pr:** Carroll Case; Circle Films; Embassy Pictures. **A:** Sr. High-Adult. **P:** Entertainment. **U:** Home. **Mov-Ent:** Cult Films. **Acq:** Purchase. **Dist:** Movies Unlimited; Alpha Video; Cheezy Flicks Entertainment, Inc. $19.95.

Billy the Kid Wanted 1941 (Unrated) — ★½
Crabbe took over Producers Releasing Corporation's 'Billy the Kid' series from Bob Steele, keeping St. John as his comic sidekick Fuzzy. Billy, Fuzzy, and Jeff help out the homesteaders of Paradise Valley who are being swindled by a crooked land developer. 62m/B/W; DVD. **C:** Buster Crabbe; Dave O'Brien; Glenn Strange; Al "Fuzzy" St. John; Charles "Blackie" King; Slim Whitaker; Directed by Sam Newfield; Written by Fred Myton; Cinematography by Jack Greenhalgh. **A:** Jr. High-Adult. **P:** Entertainment. **U:** Home. **Mov-Ent:** Western. **Acq:** Purchase. **Dist:** Mill Creek Entertainment L.L.C.

Billy the Kid—A Video Travel Guide 19??
Follow in the footsteps of the legendary Billy the Kid via your living room. Includes footage of Billy the Kid Country such as Las Vegas, New Mexico, Mesilla, Lincoln, and Fort Sumner. 40m; VHS. **TV Std:** NTSC, PAL. **A:** Adult. **P:** Education. **U:** Home. **Gen-Edu:** Travel, History--U.S., Western. **Acq:** Purchase. **Dist:** Old Army Press. $24.95.

Billy the Kid's Gun Justice 1940 (Unrated) — ★½
Billy, Fuzzy, and Jeff discover Cobb Allen is involved in shady land deals that are forcing ranchers off their property. 59m/B/W; DVD. **C:** Bob Steele; Carleton Young; Al Ferguson; Al "Fuzzy" St. John; Charles "Blackie" King; Rex Lease; Louise Currie; Forrest Taylor; Edward Peil, Sr.; Kenne Duncan; Directed by Sam Newfield; Written by Tom Gibson; Cinematography by Jack Greenhalgh. **A:** Jr. High-Adult. **P:** Entertainment. **U:** Home. **Mov-Ent:** Western. **Acq:** Purchase. **Dist:** Mill Creek Entertainment L.L.C.

Billy the Kid's Range War 1941 (Unrated) — ★½
Billy is hired as a stagecoach driver and is framed for murder by outlaws trying to sabotage the stage line by having one of the bad guys impersonate Billy. 60m/B/W; DVD. **C:** Bob Steele; Carleton Young; Ted Adams; Al "Fuzzy" St. John; Joan Barclay; Rex Lease; Milton Kibbee; Karl Hackett; Directed by Sam Newfield; Written by William Lively; Cinematography by Jack Greenhalgh. **A:** Jr. High-Adult. **P:** Entertainment. **U:** Home. **Mov-Ent:** Western. **Acq:** Purchase. **Dist:** Mill Creek Entertainment L.L.C.

Billy the Kid's Smoking Guns 1942 (Unrated) — ★½
Billy, Fuzzy, and Jeff arrive in town to find land grabbers driving off the local ranchers. Wait until they discover who the gang's murderous leader is. 61m/B/W; DVD. **C:** Buster Crabbe; Al "Fuzzy" St. John; Dave O'Brien; Milton Kibbee; John Merton; Directed by Sam Newfield; Written by Milton Raison; George Wallace Sayre; Cinematography by Jack Greenhalgh. **A:** Family. **P:** Entertainment. **U:** Home. **Mov-Ent:** Western. **Acq:** Purchase. **Dist:** Alpha Video.

Billy Tubbs: Full-Court Pressure Man-to-Man 2005
Offers on-court instruction for basketball teams by Billy Tubbs, head coach at Lamar University, for applying a defensive pressure system. 70m; DVD. **A:** Sr. High-Adult. **P:** Instruction. **U:** Institution. **Spo-Rec:** Basketball. **Acq:** Purchase. **Dist:** Championship Productions. $39.95.

Billy Two Hats 1974 (PG) — ★★½
Grizzled Scottish bandit Deans (Peck) teams up with young half-breed Billy (Arnaz Jr.) to pull off a robbery that results in an accidental death and Billy's capture. Deans is shot while breaking the kid out of jail and must rely on Billy to get them through, while being pursued by the law. It ain't happy. Mainly notable as the first western shot in Israel. 139m; VHS, DVD. **C:** Gregory Peck; Desi Arnaz, Jr.; Jack Warden; Sian Barbara Allen; David Huddleston; Directed by Ted Kotcheff; Written by Alan Sharp; Cinematography by Brian West; Music by John Scott. **Pr:** Norman Jewison; Patrick Palmer. **A:** Jr. High-Adult. **P:** Entertainment. **U:** Home. **Mov-Ent:** Western, Native Americans. **Acq:** Purchase. **Dist:** MGM Home Entertainment.

Billy ze Kick 1985 (Unrated)
When his own neighborhood is terrorized by a murderer, a bumbling cop learns that the nighttime stories he has been telling his daughter about a strange killer have come true. An original and provocative film, filled with strange characters and surrealism. In French with English subtitles. 87m; VHS. **C:** Francis Perrin; Dominque Lavanant; Michael (Michel) Lonsdale; Yves Robert; Zabou; Directed by Gerard Mordillat. **Pr:** FR3. **A:** College-Adult. **P:** Entertainment. **U:** Home. **L:** English, French. **Mov-Ent:** Mystery & Suspense, Comedy-Drama. **Acq:** Purchase. **Dist:** Facets Multimedia Inc. $49.95.

Billy's Boot Camp Elite 2005
Three-disc set of cardio, upper-body, and lower-body workouts in Billy Blanks' classic Tae Bo style. Includes high-energy kickboxing-inspired sequences standing and floor exercises, and dumbbell routines. 98m; DVD. **A:** Adult. **P:** Instruction. **U:** Home. **Hea-Sci:** Fitness/Exercise. **Acq:** Purchase. **Dist:** Collage Video Specialties, Inc.

Billy's Boot Camp Elite with Bands 2005
Four-part series of Tae Bo-based workouts with Billy Blanks, based on the use of rubber resistance bands. Workouts include a combination of fat burning and total-body muscle toning, upper and lower body toning, abs, and an eight-minute "quickie" workout. 121m; DVD. **A:** Adult. **P:** Instruction. **U:** Home. **Hea-Sci:** Fitness/Exercise. **Acq:** Purchase. **Dist:** Collage Video Specialties, Inc.

Billy's Holiday 1995 (R) — ★★½
Excessively offbeat Australian musical lacks the highly polished look of Hollywood's best, but given the setting and subject matter, it is probably not meant to have it. The subject is Billy Apples (Cullen), hangdog hardware owner by day, hangdog jazz musician at night. His audiences regularly fall asleep, but Kate (McQuade), owner of the beauty shop down the street, still loves him. Then one night, Billy magically receives the ability to sing just like his idol, Billie Holiday. The main attractions are the likeably middle-aged stars and a soundtrack filled with big band tunes. 92m; DVD, Wide. **C:** Max Cullen; Kris McQuade; Tina Bursill; Drew Forsythe; Genevieve Lemon; Richard Roxburgh; Rachel Coopes; Directed by Richard Wherrett; Written by Denis Whitburn; Cinematography by Roger Lanser. **Pr:** Miramax Film Corp. **A:** Sr. High-Adult. **P:** Entertainment. **U:** Home. **Mov-Ent:** Musical, Music--Jazz. **Acq:** Purchase. **Dist:** Anchor Bay Entertainment.

Billy's Hollywood Screen Kiss 1998 (R) — ★★½
Very gay Billy (Hayes) is an aspiring arts photographer in L.A. who's looking for romance. He thinks he's got a hot prospect in handsome-if-sexually-confused Gabriel (Rowe), a waiter/model. Billy's latest project is recreating great film romantic scenes with drag queens and he hires Gabriel to play the male lover. But it looks as if Billy is going to get his heart broken if he expects Gabriel to carry the role over into real life. Amusing feature debut for director O'Haver and a standout performance from the witty Hayes. 92m; VHS, DVD. **C:** Sean P. Hayes; Brad Rowe; Richard Ganoung; Meredith Scott Lynn; Paul Bartel; Armando Valdes-Kennedy; Directed by Tommy O'Haver; Written by Tommy O'Haver; Cinematography by Mark Mervis; Music by Alan Ari Lazar. **Pr:** David Mosley; Revolutionary Eye; Trimark Pictures. **A:** College-Adult. **P:** Entertainment. **U:** Home. **Mov-Ent:** Comedy--Romantic, Photography. **Acq:** Purchase. **Dist:** Lions Gate Home Entertainment; CinemaNow Inc.

Billy's Mime 1975
Parable of a daydreaming boy and his relationship with the inner Jesus. Theme: Jesus lives within us; one must be true to his inner self. 15m; VHS, 3/4 U, Special order formats. **Pr:** Paulist Productions. **A:** Primary. **P:** Religious. **U:** Institution, CCTV, SURA. **Chl-Juv:** Religion. **Acq:** Purchase, Rent/Lease. **Dist:** Paulist Productions.

Biloxi Blues 1988 (PG-13) — ★★½
Eugene Morris Jerome has been drafted and sent to boot camp in Biloxi, Mississippi where he encounters a troubled drill sergeant, hostile recruits, and a skillful prostitute. Walken is the drill sergeant from hell. Some good laughs from the ever-wry Broderick. A sequel to Neil Simon's "Brighton Beach Memoirs" and adapted by Simon from his play. Followed by "Broadway Bound." 105m; VHS, DVD. **C:** Matthew Broderick; Christopher Walken; Casey Siemaszko; Matt Mulhern; Corey Parker; Penelope Ann Miller; Michael Dolan; Park Overall; Directed by Mike Nichols; Written by Neil Simon; Cinematography by Bill Butler; Music by Georges Delerue. **Pr:** Mark Huffam. **A:** Jr. High-Adult. **P:** Entertainment. **U:** Home. **Mov-Ent:** Basic Training/Boot Camp. **Acq:** Purchase. **Dist:** Alpha Video; Movies Unlimited; Universal Studios Home Video. $14.95.

Biltmore Estate 1991
Visit the beautiful Biltmore House in the Blue Ridge Mountains. The home built by George Washington Vanderbilt remains the largest private residence in the United States. ?m; VHS. **A:** Jr. High-Adult. **P:** Education. **U:** Home. **Gen-Edu:** Travel. **Acq:** Purchase. **Dist:** VT Entertainment. $24.95.

Bim/Dream of the Wild Horses 1952
Two famous French shorts, the first of which is dubbed into English. 110m/B/W; VHS. **A:** Sr. High-Adult. **P:** Entertainment. **U:** Home. **Mov-Ent:** Film--Avant-Garde. **Acq:** Purchase, Rent/Lease. **Dist:** Glenn Video Vistas Ltd.

Bim the Little Donkey 1952
A little boy will stop at nothing to retrieve his cherished pet donkey from the rich family which now owns him. Dubbed into English from French. 30m/B/W; VHS. **A:** Family. **P:** Entertainment. **U:** Home. **Chl-Juv:** Children, Pets. **Acq:** Purchase. **Dist:** New Line Home Video. $14.95.

Bimini Code 1984 (Unrated) — ★
Two female adventurers accept a dangerous mission where they wind up on Bimini Island in a showdown with the mysterious Madame X. 95m; VHS. **C:** Vickie Benson; Krista Richardson; Frank Alexander; Rosanna Simanaitis; Directed by Barry Clark. **Pr:** American National Enterprises. **A:** Sr. High-Adult. **P:** Entertainment. **U:** Home. **Mov-Ent.** **Acq:** Purchase. **Dist:** No Longer Available.

Binary Nature of Digital Circuits 1980
Binary digits (bits) are introduced covering the operation of the pure binary and Binary Coded Decimal (BCD) systems. 18m; VHS, 3/4 U. **Pr:** Hewlett Packard. **A:** College-Adult. **P:** Professional. **U:** Institution, CCTV, Home. **Gen-Edu:** Electronics. **Acq:** Purchase. **Dist:** Hewlett-Packard Media Solutions.

A Bing Crosby Christmas 19??
Features a compilation of highlights from Bing Crosby's annual Christmas special, including appearances from celebrities such as Fred Astaire, Jackie Gleason, Michael Landon and more. 60m; VHS. **A:** Family. **P:** Entertainment. **U:** Home. **Mov-Ent:** Christmas. **Acq:** Purchase. **Dist:** Ignatius Press. $19.95.

Bing Crosby: The Magic of Bing Crosby, Part 1 19??
Rosemary Clooney, Dean Martin, and Louis Armstrong are just a few of the performers who join Crosby in some of his best-loved hits. Songs include "White Christmas," "I Left My Heart in San Francisco," and "Don't Fence Me In." 55m; VHS. **A:** Jr. High-Adult. **P:** Entertainment. **U:** Home. **Mov-Ent:** Music Video. **Acq:** Purchase. **Dist:** WarnerVision; Music Video Distributors; Fast Forward. $19.98.

Binge 1987
The underlying reasons for eating disorders are explored in this video. 28m; VHS, 3/4 U. **Pr:** Lynn Hershman. **A:** Jr. High-Adult. **P:** Education. **U:** Institution, SURA. **Gen-Edu:** Eating Disorders. **Acq:** Rent/Lease. **Dist:** Video Out Distribution.

Binge Drinking Blowout 1998
Uses real stories to depict the tragic consequences of binge drinking to young people. 28m; VHS. **A:** Jr. High-Adult. **P:** Education. **U:** Institution. **Hea-Sci:** Health Education, Alcoholism, Children. **Acq:** Purchase. **Dist:** Aquarius Health Care Media. $149.00.

Binge Drinking Blowout: The Extreme Dangers of Alcohol Use 1999
An ER physician tells how quick and massive alcohol ingestion can destroy the body. Explains extreme consequences such as blackouts, date rape, violence, asphyxiation, car accidents, and death. 28m; VHS. **A:** Sr. High. **P:** Education. **U:** Institution. **Gen-Edu:** Alcoholism, Health Education. **Acq:** Purchase. **Dist:** Zenger Media. $149.00.

Bingo 1991 (PG) — ★★½
Mediocre spoof of hero-dog movies. The heroic title mutt roams from Denver to Green Bay in search of his absent-minded master, with numerous absurd adventures en route. Some cute moments, but sometimes Bingo is just lame-o. Good family fare. 90m; VHS, DVD, CC. **C:** Cindy Williams; David Rasche; Robert J. Steinmiller, Jr.; David French; Kurt Fuller; Joe Guzaldo; Glenn Shadix; Directed by Matthew Robbins; Written by Jim Strain; Music by Richard Gibbs. **Pr:** Tri-Star Pictures. **A:** Jr. High-Adult. **P:** Entertainment. **U:** Home. **Mov-Ent:** Action-Adventure, Pets, Family Viewing. **Acq:** Purchase. **Dist:** Sony Pictures Home Entertainment Inc. $14.95.

Bingo Long Traveling All-Stars & Motor Kings 1976 (PG) — ★★★
Set in 1939, this film follows the comedic adventures of a lively group of black ball players who have defected from the old Negro National League. The All-Stars travel the country challenging local white teams. 111m; VHS, DVD, Wide. **C:** Billy Dee Williams; James Earl Jones; Richard Pryor; Stan Shaw; Directed by John Badham; Written by Matthew Robbins; Hal Barwood; Cinematography by Bill Butler; Music by William Goldstein. **Pr:** Mark Huffam. **A:** Family. **P:** Entertainment. **U:** Home. **Mov-Ent:** Sports--Fiction: Comedy, Baseball, Black Culture. **Acq:** Purchase. **Dist:** Facets Multimedia Inc. $14.98.

Bingo: You Betcha! 1992
Looks at the game of bingo, played by an estimated 35 million Americans each week, examining both the fun of the game and the problem of some players with compulsive gambling. 28m; VHS. **C:** Directed by Susan Wehling. **A:** Adult. **P:** Education. **U:** Institution. **Gen-Edu:** Gambling. **Acq:** Purchase, Rent/Lease. **Dist:** The Cinema Guild. $250.00.

Bingoboys: How To Dance—The Extended Dance Version 1991
Princessa and Two Deadly Elements team up to produce this incredible extended version of the dance hit "How To

Dance." 6m; VHS. **Pr:** A*Vision. **A:** Sr. High-Adult. **P:** Entertainment. **U:** Home. **Mov-Ent:** Music Video, Dance. **Acq:** Purchase. **Dist:** Music Video Distributors; WarnerVision; Fast Forward. $9.98.

Bintou in Paris 1995
Fictionalized account details the realities of excision, the practice of female genital mutilation, within African culture. 17m; VHS. **A:** College. **P:** Education. **U:** Institution. **Gen-Edu:** Anthropology, Documentary Films, Africa. **Acq:** Purchase, Rent/Lease. **Dist:** Documentary Educational Resources. $145.

Bintu & Her New African Rice 1998
Features the story of Bintu and other indigent West African farmers who have benefitted from a new strain of rice developed by scientists. 27m; VHS. **A:** Adult. **P:** Education. **U:** Home. **Hea-Sci:** Food Industry, Agriculture, Africa. **Acq:** Purchase. **Dist:** Instructional Video. $24.95.

Bio Bio: Lost River of the Mapuche 1992
Travel through the Andes Mountains as canoeists and kayakers tackle one of the most challenging white-water rivers in the world. 48m; VHS. **Pr:** ESPN. **A:** Family. **P:** Entertainment. **U:** Home. **Spo-Rec:** Sports--General. **Acq:** Purchase. **Dist:** Fast Forward.

Bio-dead 2009 (R) — ★
Low-budget sci fi horror. After a bio-terrorist attack kills millions in Southern California, a corporation is contracted to send out a hazmat team to check for survivors and decontaminate the area. Only their safe zone turns out to be a refuge for the genetically mutated who have turned to cannibalism to survive. 84m; DVD. **C:** Matthew Norton; Tony Williams; Jacob Gentry; Derek Long; Rick Hall; Directed by Stephen J. Hadden; Written by Stephen J. Hadden; Cinematography by Manfred Drews; Music by Kevin Rosen-Quan. **A:** Sr. High-Adult. **P:** Entertainment. **U:** Home. **Mov-Ent:** Science Fiction, Terrorism. **Acq:** Purchase. **Dist:** Entertainment One US LP.

The Bio-Diversity Story 19??
Discusses the devastating loss of species that is presently occurring and endangering an ever-growing number of organisms. Contains field visits with scientists who are in the process of researching the problem and looking for viable solutions. Comes with teacher's guide and five blackline masters. 17m; VHS. **A:** Jr. High-Adult. **P:** Education. **U:** Institution, SURA. **Hea-Sci:** Ecology & Environment, Biology, Science. **Acq:** Purchase. **Dist:** San Luis Video Publishing. $89.95.

Bio-Dome 1996 (PG-13) — ★
Pauly Shore in a hermetically sealed environment separated from the rest of society? Great! Where do I sign? Unfortunately, it's only a movie, and a typically useless one, at that. Shore brings his lame schtick to a scientifically created "perfect environment" that he and his college (yeah, right) buddy Doyle (Baldwin) mistake for a mall and eventually destroy. In Bloom's not-too-auspicious directorial debut, bodily function jokes found in Jim Carrey's wastebasket masquerade as a script, while the supporting cast wanders aimlessly, perhaps pondering a switch in agents. 94m; VHS, DVD, Wide, CC. **C:** Pauly Shore; Stephen Baldwin; William Atherton; Henry Gibson; Joey Lauren Adams; Teresa Hill; Kylie Minogue; Jack Black; Kevin West; Denise Dowse; Dara Tomanovich; Kyle Gass; Rose McGowan; Taylor Negron; Phil LaMarr; Directed by Jason Bloom; Written by Scott Marcano; Kip Koenig; Cinematography by Phedon Papamichael; Music by Andrew Gross. **Pr:** Brad Krevoy; Brad Jenkel; Michael Rotenberg; Jason Blumenthal; Adam Leff; Mitchell Peck; Metro-Goldwyn-Mayer Pictures; MGM Home Entertainment. **A:** Jr. High-Adult. **P:** Entertainment. **U:** Home. **Mov-Ent. Awds:** Golden Raspberries '96: Worst Actor (Shore). **Acq:** Purchase. **Dist:** MGM Home Entertainment.

Bio Hazard 1985 (R) — ★
A toxic monster needs human flesh to survive and consequently goes on a rampage. 84m; VHS, DVD. **C:** Angelique Pettyjohn; Carroll Borland; Richard Hench; Aldo Ray; Directed by Fred Olen Ray. **A:** Adult. **P:** Entertainment. **U:** Home. **Mov-Ent:** Horror. **Acq:** Purchase. **Dist:** MNTEX Entertainment, Inc. $39.98.

Bio Sci II Elementary 19??
Short movies and color pictures illustrate this "visual encycolpedia of the biological world." The interactive disc offers 50 activities that allow young students to discover food chains, mammals, biomes, leaves, and many other fundamentals of biology. Includes worksheets, posters, and image directory. Dual audio tracking in English and Spanish. ?m. **Pr:** Videodiscovery, Inc. **A:** Primary. **P:** Entertainment. **U:** Institution. **Hea-Sci:** Science, Biology. **Acq:** Purchase. **Dist:** Clear Vue Inc. $395.00.

Bio-Science Series 197?
This series covers various aspects of biology such as the behavior and interaction of ants, bees, spiders, etc., and the birth and life of various organisms. Programs available individually. 12m; 3/4 U, Special order formats. **Pr:** National Geographic Society. **A:** Jr. High-Adult. **P:** Education. **U:** Institution, Home, SURA. **Hea-Sci:** Documentary Films, Biology. **Acq:** Purchase, Trade-in, Duplication License. **Dist:** National Geographic Society.
Indiv. Titles: 1. Ants: Hunters and Gardeners 2. Life Cycle of the Honeybee 3. Pond-Life Food Web 4. Chick Embryology 5. Spiders: Aggression and Mating 6. Carnivorous Plants 7. Protists: Threshold of Life 8. Life Cycle of the Silk Moth 9. Secret Life of a Trout River 10. Plankton.

Bio-Social Systems of Occupational Behavior 1979
This program focuses upon the research methodology used by occupational behavior theorists for the purpose of understanding behavior and justifying the organizational effect of purposeful activity on behavior. 52m; VHS, 3/4 U. **Pr:** American Occupational Therapy Association. **A:** College-Adult. **P:** Education. **U:** Institution, CCTV. **Hea-Sci:** Documentary Films, Occupational Therapy. **Acq:** Purchase, Rent/Lease, Subscription. **Dist:** American Occupational Therapy Association.

The Biochemedical Revolution 1976
The decades ahead will see the use of drugs to increase learning ability, to expand or delete memory, to alter skin tones, and to prevent senility. Explores this type of abuse and the tragic by-product of a pill happy society—drug abuse. 17m; 3/4 U, Special order formats. **Pr:** Hobel Leiterman Productions. **A:** Sr. High-Adult. **P:** Education. **U:** Institution. **L:** English, Spanish. **Hea-Sci:** Documentary Films, Drugs. **Acq:** Purchase. **Dist:** The Cinema Guild.

Biochemical Laboratory Safety 19??
Provides overview of biochemical laboratory safety. Covers contamination avoidance, handling of contaminated materials, handling of laboratory equipment and glassware, hazardous chemical labeling, MSDSs, and the importance of cleanliness. Includes Leader's Guide and 25 Program Guides. 15m; VHS, 3/4 U. **A:** Adult. **P:** Education. **U:** Institution. **Bus-Ind:** Safety Education, Industry & Industrialists. **Acq:** Purchase. **Dist:** Williams Learning Network.

Biochemistry Explained 1986
On seven tapes, the basics of biochemistry are taught for students. 105m; VHS, 3/4 U. **Pr:** Bergwall Productions. **A:** Sr. High-Adult. **P:** Education. **U:** Institution. **Hea-Sci:** Chemistry, Science, Biology. **Acq:** Purchase. **Dist:** Bergwall Productions, Inc.

Biodiversity! Exploring the Web of Life 19??
Teaching aid for environmental education explores the biodiversity of the earth and features interviews with experts in the field. Includes a teacher's guide. 30m; VHS. **A:** Jr. High-Sr. High. **P:** Education. **U:** Institution. **Chl-Juv:** Animals, Ecology & Environment. **Acq:** Purchase. **Dist:** Environmental Media. $24.95.

Biodiversity for Forests and Farms 1996
Documents the complex relationships between plants and animals and the benefits of maintaining an ecological balance. Useful for land-use planners, agriculturists, forest owners, rural land owners and environmental educators. 28m; VHS. **A:** Jr. High-Adult. **P:** Education. **U:** Home. **Gen-Edu:** Ecology & Environment, Wildlife, Agriculture. **Acq:** Purchase. **Dist:** Cornell University. $24.95.

Biodiversity: The Variety of Life 1991
Suggests reserves to protect existing life forms on three biodiverse levels—ecosystems, species, and genes. Maps, photos, scenic footage, and print screens document the Cascade Mountains of the Pacific Northwest, but the material used is valid for similar regions. Teacher's guide included. 43m; VHS. **C:** Narrated by Mitch Friedman. **Pr:** Dal Neitzel. **A:** Jr. High-Adult. **P:** Education. **U:** Institution. **Hea-Sci:** Ecology & Environment, Science. **Acq:** Purchase, Rent/Lease. **Dist:** Bullfrog Films, Inc. $150.00.

Bioelectricity: The Shocking Truth 19??
Discusses how cells in the human body contain electrical impulses that send messages throughout the body. Contains activities allowing students to make wet-cell batteries and simulate living cells. Includes teacher's guide. ?m; VHS. **Pr:** Children's Television Workshop. **A:** Primary-Jr. High. **P:** Education. **U:** Institution. **Chl-Juv:** Biology, Animals. **Acq:** Purchase. **Dist:** GPN Educational Media. $15.00.

Biofeedback 1980
This program examines the process of biofeedback taking as an example electromyographic recording from the muscles of the forehead in a case of headache induced by tension and teeth grinding. 24m; 3/4 U. **Pr:** McMaster University. **A:** Adult. **P:** Professional. **U:** Institution, SURA. **Hea-Sci:** Neurology, Medical Education. **Acq:** Purchase, Rent/Lease. **Dist:** McMaster University.

Biofeedback and Self-Control 1989
George Fuller von Bozzay discusses the roles of biofeedback in medical treatments, personal growth and relaxation. 30m; VHS. **Pr:** Thinking Allowed Productions. **A:** College-Adult. **P:** Education. **U:** Home. **Gen-Edu:** Psychology, Self-Help, Personality. **Acq:** Purchase. **Dist:** Thinking Allowed Productions. $29.95.

Biofeedback: Listening to Your Head 198?
Scientists' claim that eventually man can have conscious control over respiration rate, heartbeat, digestion and even our emotions through the use of biofeedback is examined. 19m; 3/4 U, Special order formats. **Pr:** Hobel Leiterman Productions. **A:** College-Adult. **P:** Education. **U:** Institution. **Hea-Sci:** Psychology, Medical Education. **Acq:** Purchase. **Dist:** The Cinema Guild.

Biofeedback: The Yoga of the West 1975
Dr. Elmer Green and his colleagues at the Menninger Foundation believe man can overcome pain by using his mind. Several tests confirm this. 40m; VHS, 3/4 U, Special order formats. **Pr:** Hartley Productions. **A:** Sr. High-Adult. **P:** Education. **U:** Institution, CCTV, Home. **Hea-Sci:** Psychology, Health Education. **Acq:** Purchase. **Dist:** Hartley Film Foundation. $39.95.

Biogas from the Sea 1987
A presentation by scientists of the conversion of excess marine algae from the Venice Lagoon into biogas. 30m; VHS, 3/4 U. **Pr:** Hans-Ernst Weitzel. **A:** Family. **P:** Education. **U:** Institution, Home, SURA. **Hea-Sci:** Ecology & Environment. **Acq:** Purchase, Duplication License. **Dist:** Bullfrog Films, Inc.

Biogas in Fiji 1981
In Fiji, methane gas is produced from pig manure and used as odorless cooking fuel and to run small motors. This video demonstrates its even greater potential. 6m; VHS, 3/4 U. **Pr:** United Nations. **A:** College-Adult. **P:** Education. **U:** Institution, Home, SURA. **Gen-Edu:** Documentary Films, Energy, Ecology & Environment. **Acq:** Purchase, Duplication License. **Dist:** Bullfrog Films, Inc.

Biography: Aaron Spelling ????
Presents the A&E cable channel special on television show producer Aaron Spelling from his humble beginnings to the creation of many popular shows including "The Love Boat," "Fantasy Island," "Dynasty," "Twin Peaks," and "Beverly Hills 90210." 50m; DVD. **A:** Jr. High-Adult. **P:** Entertainment. **U:** Home, CATV. **Mov-Ent:** Television Series, Documentary Films, Biography: Show Business. **Acq:** Purchase. **Dist:** A&E Television Networks L.L.C. $24.95.

Biography: Abraham Lincoln ????
A&E Biography combines interviews, still photography, live-action footage, reenactments, period art, and other documentary material to present historical figures and their achievements. Recommended for Grades 6-12. 45m; VHS. **A:** Jr. High-Sr. High. **P:** Education. **U:** Home, Institution. **Gen-Edu:** Biography, Presidency, History--U.S. **Acq:** Purchase. **Dist:** Social Studies School Service; Zenger Media. $14.95.

Biography: Adam and Eve ????
Presents the A&E cable channel special on Biblical figures Adam and Eve, who were the first humans according to Genesis, created by God; includes interviews with experts, location footage, rare paintings, and artifacts. 50m; DVD. **A:** Family. **P:** Entertainment. **U:** Home, CATV. **Mov-Ent:** Television Series, Documentary Films, Religion. **Acq:** Purchase. **Dist:** A&E Television Networks L.L.C. $24.95.

Biography: Adam & Eve 2005
Combines interviews, artifacts, paintings, and location footage to explore the biblical creation legend from Genesis. 50m; DVD. **A:** Jr. High-Adult. **P:** Entertainment. **U:** Home. **Gen-Edu:** Documentary Films. **Acq:** Purchase. **Dist:** A&E Television Networks L.L.C.

Biography: Admiral Chester Nimitz: Thunder of the Pacific 2006
See how Nimitz took command of the navy after the devastating attack on Pearl Harbor, regrouping and fighting until the Japanese surrender. 50m; DVD. **A:** Jr. High-Adult. **P:** Entertainment. **U:** Home. **Gen-Edu:** Documentary Films, Biography: Military. **Acq:** Purchase. **Dist:** A&E Television Networks L.L.C.

Biography: Adolf Eichmann: Hitler's Master of Death 2006
Interviews, rare photos, and film of Eichmann's 1962 trial highlight the life of the man charged with carrying out Hitler's "Final Solution" until Simon Wisenthal's 15-year hunt brought him to justice. 50m; DVD. **A:** Jr. High-Adult. **P:** Entertainment. **U:** Home. **Gen-Edu:** Documentary Films. **Acq:** Purchase. **Dist:** A&E Television Networks L.L.C.

Biography: Al Capone: Scarface 2005
Follows the life of the notorious Chicago gangster from his immigrant neighborhood to his downfall at the hands of tax accountants. 50m; DVD. **A:** Jr. High-Adult. **P:** Entertainment. **U:** Home. **Gen-Edu:** Documentary Films. **Acq:** Purchase. **Dist:** A&E Television Networks L.L.C.

Biography: Al Pacino ????
Presents the A&E cable channel special on actor Al Pacino, who has starred in numerous successful movies including the "Godfather" trilogy and "Scarface" along with receiving the Academy Award for best actor in 1992's "Scent of a Woman"; includes interviews and rare clips. 50m; DVD. **A:** Jr. High-Adult. **P:** Entertainment. **U:** Home, CATV. **Mov-Ent:** Television Series, Documentary Films, Biography: Show Business. **Acq:** Purchase. **Dist:** A&E Television Networks L.L.C. $24.95.

Biography: Al Qaeda 2006
Profiles the history and formation of the terrorist group, founded by Osama Bin Laden in the 1980s. 50m; DVD. **A:** Jr. High-Adult. **P:** Entertainment. **U:** Home. **Gen-Edu:** Documentary Films, Terrorism. **Acq:** Purchase. **Dist:** A&E Television Networks L.L.C.

Biography: Alan Jackson ????
Presents the A&E cable channel special on country singer Alan Jackson, whose 1989 album "Here in the Real World" launched his enduring career. Recounts how singer Glen Campbell helped discover the star; includes footage, photos, and interviews. 50m; DVD. **A:** Jr. High-Adult. **P:** Entertainment. **U:** Home, CATV. **Mov-Ent:** Television Series, Documentary Films, Biography: Music. **Acq:** Purchase. **Dist:** A&E Television Networks L.L.C. $24.95.

Biography: Albert Einstein 2005
A portrait of the legendary thinker, including interviews with colleagues and friends as well as scientists. 50m; DVD. **A:** Jr. High-Adult. **P:** Entertainment. **U:** Home. **Gen-Edu:** Documentary Films. **Acq:** Purchase. **Dist:** A&E Television Networks L.L.C.

Biography: Alexander Graham Bell ????
A&E Biography combines interviews, still photography, live-action footage, reenactments, period art, and other documentary material to present historical figures and their achievements. Recommended for Grades 6-12. 45m; VHS. **A:** Jr. High-Sr. High. **P:** Education. **U:** Home, Institution. **Gen-Edu:** Biography, Scientists, Inventors & Inventions. **Acq:** Purchase. **Dist:** Social Studies School Service; Zenger Media. $14.95.

Biography: All the Presidents' Kids ????
Presents the A&E cable channel special on the children of former U.S. presidents over the course of history; includes interviews with former Secret Service agents, historians, Gerald Ford's son Steven Ford, and Ronald Reagan's son Michael Reagan. 100m; DVD. **A:** Family. **P:** Entertainment. **U:** Home, CATV. **Mov-Ent:** Television Series, Documentary Films, History--U.S. **Acq:** Purchase. **Dist:** A&E Television Networks L.L.C. $29.95.

Biography: Amelia Earhart ????
A&E Biography combines interviews, still photography, live-action footage, reenactments, period art, and other documentary material to present historical figures and their achievements. Recommended for Grades 6-12. 45m; VHS. **A:** Jr. High-Sr. High. **P:** Education. **U:** Home, Institution. **Gen-Edu:** Biography, History--Modern. **Acq:** Purchase. **Dist:** Social Studies School Service; Zenger Media. $14.95.

Biography: Amelia Earhart 2005
The tomboyish daredevil pilot made aviation history by smashing numerous records. But what happened on that final flight? Includes archival footage and interviews. 50m; DVD. **A:** Jr. High-Adult. **P:** Entertainment. **U:** Home. **Gen-Edu:** Documentary Films. **Acq:** Purchase. **Dist:** A&E Television Networks L.L.C.

Biography: Anastasia: Her True Story 2005
Born in 1901, she was the youngest daughter of Tsar Nicholas and Alexandra. Did this Romanov princess survive the massacre of her family in 1918? Historians use recent forensic findings to explore her true fate. Includes interviews and rare home movies. 50m; DVD. **A:** Jr. High-Adult. **P:** Entertainment. **U:** Home. **Gen-Edu:** Documentary Films. **Acq:** Purchase. **Dist:** A&E Television Networks L.L.C.

Biography: Andrew Carnegie ????
A&E Biography combines interviews, still photography, live-action footage, reenactments, period art, and other documentary material to present historical figures and their achievements. Recommended for Grades 6-12. 45m; VHS. **A:** Jr. High-Sr. High. **P:** Education. **U:** Home, Institution. **Gen-Edu:** Biography, History, Business. **Acq:** Purchase. **Dist:** Social Studies School Service; Zenger Media. $14.95.

Biography: Andrew Cunanan ????
Presents the A&E cable channel special on murderer Andrew Cunanan, known for his killing spree in 1997 which included among the victims Italian fashion designer Gianni Versace in Miami Beach, Florida; he later committed suicide. Includes interviews with former friends and associates as well as crime scene and news footage. 50m; DVD. **A:** Sr. High-Adult. **P:** Entertainment. **U:** Home, CATV. **Mov-Ent:** Television Series, Documentary Films, Biography. **Acq:** Purchase. **Dist:** A&E Television Networks L.L.C. $24.95.

Biography: Andrew Jackson ????
A&E Biography combines interviews, still photography, live-action footage, reenactments, period art, and other documentary material to present historical figures and their achievements. Recommended for Grades 6-12. 45m; VHS. **A:** Jr. High-Sr. High. **P:** Education. **U:** Home, Institution. **Gen-Edu:** Biography, Presidency, History--U.S. **Acq:** Purchase. **Dist:** Social Studies School Service; Zenger Media. $14.95.

Biography: Andy Griffith: Hollywood's Homespun Hero ????
Presents the A&E cable channel special on actor Andy Griffith, known for his folksy television series roles on "The Andy Griffith Show" (as Sheriff Andy Taylor from 1960-1968) and "Matlock" (as lawyer Benjamin Matlock from 1986-1995). 50m; DVD. **A:** Family. **P:** Entertainment. **U:** Home, CATV. **Mov-Ent:** Television Series, Documentary Films, Biography: Show Business. **Acq:** Purchase. **Dist:** A&E Television Networks L.L.C. $24.95.

Biography: Andy Kaufman 1999
Presents the A&E cable channel special on actor and stand-up comedian Andy Kaufman, who was best known for his role as dippy-yet-lovable Latka on the television series "Taxi" (1978-1983) but was also notorious for his bizarre behavior during his performances as well as his brief encounter with wrestling; includes interviews with family, friends, and actor Jim Carrey, who played Kaufman in the 1999 biographical film "Man on the Moon." 50m; DVD. **A:** Jr. High-Adult. **P:** Entertainment. **U:** Home, CATV. **Mov-Ent:** Television Series, Documentary Films, Biography: Show Business. **Acq:** Purchase. **Dist:** A&E Television Networks L.L.C. $24.95.

Biography: Andy Williams ????
Presents the A&E cable channel special on singer and actor Andy Williams, who had 29 Top 40 pop hits from 1956 to 1972 while hosting his popular self-titled variety show from 1962-1967; also endured the trial of his ex-wife for killing her boyfriend. Includes digitally-remastered episodes of his show along with an interview with Williams himself. 100m; DVD. **C:** Andy Williams. **A:** Jr. High-Adult. **P:** Entertainment. **U:** Home, CATV. **Mov-Ent:** Television Series, Documentary Films, Biography: Show Business. **Acq:** Purchase. **Dist:** A&E Television Networks L.L.C. $29.95.

Biography: Angelina Jolie 2006
Looks at the life of the actress from her 1997 Emmy-award winning performance in "Gia" to her work as a U.N. goodwill ambassador and into her personal life. 50m; DVD. **A:** Jr. High-Adult. **P:** Entertainment. **U:** Home. **Fin-Art:** Documentary Films, Biography: Show Business. **Acq:** Purchase. **Dist:** A&E Television Networks L.L.C.

Biography: Anna Nicole Smith 2007
Presents the A&E cable channel special on the complex life and early death of celebrity Anna Nicole Smith, who had been a model, Playboy Playmate, reality TV star, and spokeswoman before she became tabloid fodder. 50m; DVD. **A:** Jr. High-Adult. **P:** Entertainment. **U:** Home, CATV. **Mov-Ent:** Television Series, Documentary Films, Biography: Show Business. **Acq:** Purchase. **Dist:** A&E Television Networks L.L.C. $24.95.

Biography: Anne Rice—Vampires, Witches and Bestsellers 2006
Profile of best-selling author Rice's life and 30-year career, including interviews with the writer and her family. 50m; DVD. **A:** Jr. High-Adult. **P:** Entertainment. **U:** Home. **Gen-Edu:** Documentary Films, Biography. **Acq:** Purchase. **Dist:** A&E Television Networks L.L.C.

Biography: Antonio Banderas: Hollywood Conquistador ????
Presents the A&E cable channel special on actor Antonio Banderas from his roots in Spain to his box office success in dozens of movies including "The Mask of Zorro" and his marriage to actress Melanie Griffith. 50m; DVD. **A:** Family. **P:** Entertainment. **U:** Home, CATV. **Mov-Ent:** Television Series, Documentary Films, Biography: Show Business. **Acq:** Purchase. **Dist:** A&E Television Networks L.L.C. $24.95.

Biography: Anwar Sadat ????
Presents the A&E cable channel special on Egyptian president Anwar Sadat, who served from 1970 to his assassination in 1981 by Muslim extremists and whose role in the 1978 Camp David Accords led to his winning the Nobel Peace Prize along with Israeli Prime Minister Menachem Begin. Includes interviews with world leaders, political insiders, and scholars along with video footage. 50m; DVD. **A:** Family. **P:** Entertainment. **U:** Home, CATV. **Mov-Ent:** Television Series, Documentary Films, Politics & Government. **Acq:** Purchase. **Dist:** A&E Television Networks L.L.C. $24.95.

Biography: Ariel Sharon 2006
Looks at the life of the military commander who became the controversial prime minister of Israel, from his leadership in the 1967 and 1973 Arab-Israeli wars to his decisions about the West Bank and the Palestinians. 50m; DVD. **A:** Jr. High-Adult. **P:** Entertainment. **U:** Home. **Gen-Edu:** Documentary Films, Biography: Military. **Acq:** Purchase. **Dist:** A&E Television Networks L.L.C.

Biography: Arnold Schwarzenegger 2005
Presents the A&E cable channel special on the life of Arnold Schwarzenegger, elected governor of California in 2003, and husband to Kennedy family member and TV reporter Maria Shriver. The Austrian began as a bodybuilder, winning Mr. Universe five times, and rose to fame in the 1977 documentary "Pumping Iron" which led to his legendary acting career in action movies including "Conan the Barbarian," "The Terminator" trilogy, "Total Recall," and "True Lies." He also managed to show a softer and comedic side with "Kindergarten Cop" and "Jingle All the Way." Includes family and friend interviews and clips. 50m; DVD. **A:** Jr. High-Adult. **P:** Entertainment. **U:** Home, CATV. **Mov-Ent:** Television Series, Documentary Films, Biography: Show Business. **Acq:** Purchase. **Dist:** A&E Television Networks L.L.C. $24.95.

Biography: Arthur Shawcross ????
Presents the A&E cable channel special on serial killer Arthur Shawcross, who was jailed in New York for only 15 years for the deaths of two children; upon his release in 1987, he began another killing spree in 1988 before his 1990 capture, which garnered national media attention. 50m; DVD. **A:** Sr. High-Adult. **P:** Entertainment. **U:** Home, CATV. **Mov-Ent:** Television Series, Documentary Films, Biography. **Acq:** Purchase. **Dist:** A&E Television Networks L.L.C. $24.95.

Biography: Attila the Hun ????
A&E Biography combines interviews, still photography, live-action footage, reenactments, period art, and other documentary material to present historical figures and their achievements. Recommended for Grades 6-12. 45m; VHS. **A:** Jr. High-Sr. High. **P:** Education. **U:** Home, Institution. **Gen-Edu:** Biography, History. **Acq:** Purchase. **Dist:** Social Studies School Service; Zenger Media. $14.95.

Biography: Attila: The Scourge of God ????
Presents the A&E cable channel special on the 5th century barbarian ruler Attila the Hun, who conquered the mighty Roman Empire though during his quest it has been estimated that he lost some 200,000 men; includes reenactments. 50m; DVD. **A:** Family. **P:** Entertainment. **U:** Home, CATV. **Mov-Ent:** Television Series, Documentary Films, History--Ancient. **Acq:** Purchase. **Dist:** A&E Television Networks L.L.C. $24.95.

Biography: Audrey Hepburn: The Fairest Lady ????
Presents the A&E cable channel special on the life of actress Audrey Hepburn from her best known movie roles in "Breakfast at Tiffany's," "My Fair Lady," and "Sabrina" to her humanitarian efforts. 50m; DVD. **A:** Family. **P:** Entertainment. **U:** Home, CATV. **Mov-Ent:** Television Series, Documentary Films, Biography: Show Business. **Acq:** Purchase. **Dist:** A&E Television Networks L.L.C. $24.95.

Biography: Ayatollah Khomeini: Holy Terror 2006
Profiles the life of the radical Islamic leader, including the seizing of the U.S. embassy in Tehran and the 444 day hostage crisis. 50m; DVD. **A:** Jr. High-Adult. **P:** Entertainment. **U:** Home. **Gen-Edu:** Documentary Films, Biography: Religious Figures. **Acq:** Purchase. **Dist:** A&E Television Networks L.L.C.

Biography: Babe Ruth ????
A&E Biography combines interviews, still photography, live-action footage, reenactments, period art, and other documentary material to present historical figures and their achievements. Recommended for Grades 6-12. 45m; VHS. **A:** Jr. High-Sr. High. **P:** Education. **U:** Home, Institution. **Gen-Edu:** Biography, History--Modern. **Acq:** Purchase. **Dist:** Social Studies School Service; Zenger Media. $14.95.

Biography: Background for Inspiration 1986
A guide to various biographical information sources, including indexes. 16m; VHS. **A:** Sr. High-College. **P:** Instruction. **U:** Institution. **Gen-Edu:** How-To, Information Science. **Acq:** Purchase. **Dist:** Meridian Education Corp. $62.00.

Biography: Barack Obama 2007
Presents the A&E cable channel special on the life of politician Barack Obama, including his time as the first African American editor of the "Harvard Law Review" and his impressive victories for his Illinois Senate seat, along with his ongoing run to become the Democratic nominee for the 2008 U.S. presidential election. 50m; DVD. **A:** Family. **P:** Entertainment. **U:** Home, CATV. **Mov-Ent:** Television Series, Documentary Films, Biography: Politics. **Acq:** Purchase. **Dist:** A&E Television Networks L.L.C. $24.95.

Biography: Barbara Bush: First Mom ????
Presents the A&E cable channel special on former First Lady and presidential mother Barbara Bush, including her campaign against illiteracy, her troubled relationship with Nancy Reagan, and her bouts with depression; includes interviews with family such as her husband George H.W. Bush and son George W. Bush and friends as well as photos and film clips. 50m; DVD. **A:** Family. **P:** Entertainment. **U:** Home, CATV. **Mov-Ent:** Television Series, Documentary Films, Presidency. **Acq:** Purchase. **Dist:** A&E Television Networks L.L.C. $24.95.

Biography: Barbara Walters: A Driving Force ????
Presents the A&E cable channel special on journalist and broadcast legend Barbara Walters, who is known for her intriguing and often emotional interviews of newsmakers and celebrities on her show "The Barbara Walters Special" as well as on ABC television's "20/20"; includes an interview with Walters as well as with family and friends. 100m; DVD. **A:** Family. **P:** Entertainment. **U:** Home, CATV. **Mov-Ent:** Television Series, Documentary Films, Biography: Show Business. **Acq:** Purchase. **Dist:** A&E Television Networks L.L.C. $29.95.

Biography: Batman ????
Presents the A&E cable channel special on the 1966-1968 television series "Batman," based on the comic book and starring Adam West in the lead role and Burt Ward as Robin; though it only aired for three seasons it had a massive cult following. Includes interviews with cast and creators as well as clips from the show. 50m; DVD. **A:** Family. **P:** Entertainment. **U:** Home, CATV. **Mov-Ent:** Television Series, Documentary Films, Television. **Acq:** Purchase. **Dist:** A&E Television Networks L.L.C. $24.95.

Biography: Beast of the Bastille—Guy Georges ????
Presents the A&E cable channel special on serial killer Guy Georges, who murdered at least seven women from 1991 to 1997 all near the French Revolutionary prison thus earning him his nickname of the "Beast of Bastille"; includes trial footage. 50m; DVD. **A:** Sr. High-Adult. **P:** Entertainment. **U:** Home, CATV. **Mov-Ent:** Television Series, Documentary Films, Biography. **Acq:** Purchase. **Dist:** A&E Television Networks L.L.C. $24.95.

Biography: Beast of Ukraine ????
Presents the A&E cable channel special on Ukrainian mass murder Andrei Chikatilo, who was convicted of the heinous killings of 53 women and children in that country from 1978 to 1990 and was executed in 1994; includes interviews with experts and archival materials. 50m; DVD. **A:** Sr. High-Adult. **P:** Entertainment. **U:** Home, CATV. **Mov-Ent:** Television Series, Documentary Films, Biography. **Acq:** Purchase. **Dist:** A&E Television Networks L.L.C. $24.95.

Biography: Beethoven—The Sound and the Fury 2000
This installment from the A&E series "Biography" examines the life of composer Ludwig van Beethoven 50m; VHS. **A:** Jr. High-Adult. **P:** Education. **U:** Home. **Gen-Edu:** Biography, Music--Classical. **Acq:** Purchase. **Dist:** A&E Television Networks L.L.C. $14.95.

Biography: Ben & Jerry ????
Presents the A&E cable channel special on popular ice cream manufacturer Ben & Jerry—s, which was launched in 1977 in Burlington, Vermont, by childhood friends Ben Cohen and Jerry Greenfield and is known for using catchy flavor names as well as their philanthropy; includes interviews with Cohen and Greenfield. 50m; DVD. **A:** Family. **P:** Entertainment. **U:** Home, CATV. **Mov-Ent:** Television Series, Documentary Films, Business. **Acq:** Purchase. **Dist:** A&E Television Networks L.L.C. $24.95.

Biography: Benedict Arnold ????
A&E Biography combines interviews, still photography, live-action footage, reenactments, period art, and other documentary material to present historical figures and their achievements. Recommended for Grades 6-12. 45m; VHS. **A:** Jr. High-Sr. High. **P:** Education. **U:** Home, Institution. **Gen-Edu:** Biography, History--U.S. **Acq:** Purchase. **Dist:** Social Studies School Service; Zenger Media. $14.95.

Biography: Benjamin Franklin ????
A&E Biography combines interviews, still photography, live-action footage, reenactments, period art, and other documentary material to present historical figures and their achievements. Recommended for Grades 6-12. 45m; VHS. **A:** Jr. High-Sr. High. **P:** Education. **U:** Home, Institution. **Gen-Edu:** Biography, History--U.S. **Acq:** Purchase. **Dist:** Social Studies School Service; Zenger Media. $14.95.

Biography: Benjamin Franklin 2006
Biographers and historians explore the life of this remarkable figure: scientist, diplomat, writer, inventor, and Founding Father. 100m; DVD. **A:** Jr. High-Adult. **P:** Entertainment. **U:** Home. **Gen-Edu:** Documentary Films, Biography: Politics. **Acq:** Purchase. **Dist:** A&E Television Networks L.L.C.

Biography: Bernie Mac 20??
Presents the A&E cable channel special on stand-up comedian and actor Bernie Mac, who began on the stage in Chicago's comedy clubs before starring in several movies which led to his popular self-titled "The Bernie Mac Show" television series from 2001-2006; profiles the personal challenges he faced as a child and the various jobs he held before finding success. 50m; DVD. **A:** Jr. High-Adult. **P:** Entertainment. **U:** Home, CATV. **Mov-Ent:** Television Series, Documentary Films, Biography: Show Business. **Acq:** Purchase. **Dist:** A&E Television Networks L.L.C. $24.95.

Biography: Bette Davis: If Looks Could Kill ????
Presents the A&E cable channel special on legendary actress Bette Davis (1908-1989) who began her career in the early 1930s and continued acting until her death; covers the ups and downs of both her career and her personal life. 50m; DVD. **A:** Jr. High-Adult. **P:** Entertainment. **U:** Home, CATV. **Mov-Ent:** Television Series, Documentary Films, Biography: Show Business. **Acq:** Purchase. **Dist:** A&E Television Networks L.L.C. $24.95.

Biography: Betty Boop: The Queen of Cartoons 2005
She came to life at Fleischer Animation Studio and remains a pop-culture icon 70 years later. Richard Fleischer, son of animator William, explores the history of the racy character and the studio's battles with censorship. 50m; DVD. **A:** Jr. High-Adult. **P:** Entertainment. **U:** Home. **Fin-Art:** Documentary Films. **Acq:** Purchase. **Dist:** A&E Television Networks L.L.C.

Biography: Betty Ford: One Day at a Time ????
Presents the A&E cable channel special on former First Lady Betty Ford, who became as well known for being former President Gerald Ford's wife as she was for her struggles with alcohol, which later led to the creation of the Betty Ford Center for substance abuse treatment; includes interviews with President Ford and other family members along with family photos, home movies, and news footage. 50m; DVD. **A:** Jr. High-Adult. **P:** Entertainment. **U:** Home, CATV. **Mov-Ent:** Television Series, Documentary Films, Presidency. **Acq:** Purchase. **Dist:** A&E Television Networks L.L.C. $24.95.

Biography: Betty Grable: Behind The Pin-Up ????
Presents the A&E cable channel special on actress Betty Grable (1916-1973), who starred in over 100 films and was the box office queen during the 1940s but is perhaps best remembered for the 1943 pin-up poster taken that made her popular among American GIs fighting in World War II; includes interviews with friends such as Debbie Reynolds and Carol Burnett as well as rare outtakes and film footage. 50m; DVD. **A:** Jr. High-Adult. **P:** Entertainment. **U:** Home, CATV. **Mov-Ent:** Television Series, Documentary Films, Biography: Show Business. **Acq:** Purchase. **Dist:** A&E Television Networks L.L.C. $24.95.

Biography: Bill Clinton 1996
A&E Biography combines interviews, still photography, live-action footage, reenactments, period art, and other documentary material to present historical figures and their achievements. Recommended for Grades 6-12. 45m; VHS. **A:** Jr. High-Sr. High. **P:** Education. **U:** Home, Institution. **Gen-Edu:** Biography, Presidency, History--U.S. **Acq:** Purchase. **Dist:** Social Studies School Service; Zenger Media. $14.95.

Biography: Bill Gates 1998
A&E Biography combines interviews, still photography, live-action footage, reenactments, period art, and other documentary material to present historical figures and their achievements. Recommended for Grades 6-12. 45m; VHS. **A:** Jr. High-Sr. High. **P:** Education. **U:** Home, Institution. **Gen-Edu:** Biography, History, Business. **Acq:** Purchase. **Dist:** Social Studies School Service; Zenger Media. $14.95.

Biography: Billy Graham: A Personal Crusade ????
Presents the A&E cable channel special on popular Christian evangelist Billy Graham, most known for counseling several U.S. presidents; includes interviews with Gerald Ford and George Bush. 50m; DVD. **A:** Family. **P:** Entertainment. **U:** Home, CATV. **Mov-Ent:** Television Series, Documentary Films, Biography: Religious Figures. **Acq:** Purchase. **Dist:** A&E Television Networks L.L.C. $24.95.

Biography: Biography Home Videos 2006
Presents the A&E cable channel special with celebrities given the camera to create "home videos" of their lives, including Fred Willard, Tony Hawk, Deborah Gibson, Chevy Chase, Danny Bonaduce, Winona Judd, and Rocco DiSpirito. 50m; DVD. **A:** Jr. High-Adult. **P:** Entertainment. **U:** Home, CATV. **Mov-Ent:** Television Series, Documentary Films, Biography: Show Business. **Acq:** Purchase. **Dist:** A&E Television Networks L.L.C. $24.95.

Biography: Blake Edwards ????
Presents the A&E cable channel special on director Blake Edwards, known for such classics as the "Pink Panther" movies

and "10" with Bo Derek and his wife, actress Julie Andrews, who also appeared in "Victor/Victoria"; though his focus had been on comedy his dark movie in 1962 on the destructiveness of alcoholism, "Days of Wine and Roses," garnered several Oscar nominations. Includes interviews with colleagues and critics as well as film clips. 50m; DVD. **A:** Jr. High-Adult. **P:** Entertainment. **U:** Home, CATV. **Mov-Ent:** Television Series, Documentary Films, Biography: Show Business. **Acq:** Purchase. **Dist:** A&E Television Networks L.L.C. $24.95.

Biography: Bloomingdales ????
Presents the A&E cable channel special on brothers Lyman and Joseph Bloomingdale, who started the now-famous and upscale Bloomingdale's store in New York City in 1872 as a dry-goods shop; also profiles subsequent generations. Includes interviews with former executives, insiders, and observers. 50m; DVD. **A:** Jr. High-Adult. **P:** Entertainment. **U:** Home, CATV. **Mov-Ent:** Television Series, Documentary Films, Business. **Acq:** Purchase. **Dist:** A&E Television Networks L.L.C. $24.95.

Biography: Bob Dylan 2005
Looks at the life of the singer/songwriter from Hibbing, Minnesota, and his journey from folkie to rock 'n' roll cultural icon. 100m; DVD. **A:** Jr. High-Adult. **P:** Entertainment. **U:** Home. **Fin-Art:** Documentary Films, Biography: Music. **Acq:** Purchase. **Dist:** A&E Television Networks L.L.C.

Biography: Bob Hope 2003
Presents the A&E cable channel special on legendary actor, comedian, and entertainer Bob Hope, who starred in numerous movies, television and radio shows, and on Broadway along with his United Service Organizations (USO) tours that traveled worldwide performing to U.S. military troops; includes family and friend interviews (Hope also appears), photographs, and video clips. 86m; DVD. **A:** Family. **P:** Entertainment. **U:** Home, CATV. **Mov-Ent:** Television Series, Documentary Films, Biography: Show Business. **Acq:** Purchase. **Dist:** A&E Television Networks L.L.C. $24.95.

Biography: Bobby Fischer ????
Presents the A&E cable channel special on American chess champion Bobby Fischer, who is best known for defeating Russian Boris Spassky in 1972; however, he became a recluse and later made controversial anti-American and anti-Semitic statements. Includes interviews and archival footage (note: produced prior to his death in January 2008). 50m; DVD. **A:** Jr. High-Adult. **P:** Entertainment. **U:** Home, CATV. **Mov-Ent:** Television Series, Documentary Films, Chess. **Acq:** Purchase. **Dist:** A&E Television Networks L.L.C. $24.95.

Biography: Bonnie and Clyde: The Story of Love & Death ????
Presents the A&E cable channel special on the infamous crime duo of Bonnie Parker and Clyde Barrow, whose spree of robberies and murders during the early 1930s was well documented by the press and followed by the country; includes interviews with John Neal Phillips (biographer) and Marie Barrow (Clyde's sister) as well as newsreel footage and period accounts. 50m; DVD. **A:** Jr. High-Adult. **P:** Entertainment. **U:** Home, CATV. **Mov-Ent:** Television Series, Documentary Films, Biography. **Acq:** Purchase. **Dist:** A&E Television Networks L.L.C. $24.95.

Biography: Boris Karloff: The Gentle Monster 2007
Presents the A&E cable channel special on actor Boris Karloff, whose most notable films include the lead in "Frankenstein" and "How the Grinch Stole Christmas"; features interviews, behind-the-scenes footage, and private photographs. 50m; DVD. **A:** Family. **P:** Entertainment. **U:** Home, CATV. **Mov-Ent:** Television Series, Documentary Films, Biography: Show Business. **Acq:** Purchase. **Dist:** A&E Television Networks L.L.C. $24.95.

Biography: Boris Yeltsin ????
Presents the A&E cable channel special on Boris Yeltsin, who became Russia's first post-Communist president in 1991 until his retirement in 1999; Yeltsin oversaw the transition of the country's economic and social systems. Includes interviews with his former bodyguard, political colleagues, and Russian citizens. 50m; DVD. **A:** Family. **P:** Entertainment. **U:** Home, CATV. **Mov-Ent:** Television Series, Documentary Films, Asia. **Acq:** Purchase. **Dist:** A&E Television Networks L.L.C. $24.95.

Biography: Brian Wilson—A Beach Boy's Tale 1999
This program from A&E's popular "Biography" series examines the life of musician Brian Wilson, the founder of the Beach Boys. 100m; VHS. **A:** Jr. High-Adult. **P:** Entertainment. **U:** Home. **Gen-Edu:** Biography, Documentary Films, Music--Pop/Rock. **Acq:** Purchase. **Dist:** A&E Television Networks L.L.C. $14.95.

Biography: Brigham Young ????
A&E Biography combines interviews, still photography, live-action footage, reenactments, period art, and other documentary material to present historical figures and their achievements. Recommended for Grades 6-12. 45m; VHS. **A:** Jr. High-Sr. High. **P:** Education. **U:** Home, Institution. **Gen-Edu:** Biography, History--U.S. **Acq:** Purchase. **Dist:** Zenger Media; Social Studies School Service. $14.95.

Biography: Brigitte Bardot 19??
A look at the life and career of France's famous "sex kitten," whose provocative image launched a new film era. 50m; VHS. **A:** Sr. High-Adult. **P:** Entertainment. **U:** Home. **Mov-Ent:** Biography, Biography: Show Business. **Acq:** Purchase. **Dist:** A&E Television Networks L.L.C.; New Video Group. $19.95.

Biography: Brooks and Dunn ????
Presents the A&E cable channel special profiling country music duo Brooks and Dunn (Leon Eric "Kix" Brooks and Ronnie Gene Dunn), who debuted in 1991 with the album "Brand New Man," which immediately was a success and led to the pair receiving the most consecutive Country Music Association awards. 50m; DVD. **A:** Jr. High-Adult. **P:** Entertainment. **U:** Home, CATV. **Mov-Ent:** Television Series, Documentary Films, Biography: Music. **Acq:** Purchase. **Dist:** A&E Television Networks L.L.C. $24.95.

Biography: Bruce Lee: Immortal Dragon 1997
Revisits moments of Mr. Lee's life through archival footage and interviews with friends and family. 50m; VHS. **A:** Adult. **P:** Education. **U:** Home. **Gen-Edu:** Biography, Martial Arts. **Acq:** Purchase. **Dist:** 411 Video Information. $19.95.

Biography: Buck Owens: Acting Naturally 2001
Presents the A&E cable channel special on country music legend Buck Owens, who had several chart-topping hits with musical partner Don Rich during the 1960s, including "I've Got a Tiger By the Tail," "Together Again," and "Act Naturally," which led to his co-hosting (1969-1986) of the popular "Hee Haw" television series with Roy Clark. (Note: Show appeared five years prior to Owens' death in 2006.) 50m; DVD. **A:** Jr. High-Adult. **P:** Entertainment. **U:** Home, CATV. **Mov-Ent:** Television Series, Documentary Films, Biography: Music. **Acq:** Purchase. **Dist:** A&E Television Networks L.L.C. $24.95.

Biography: Buddy Holly: Rave On ????
Presents the A&E cable channel special on singer Buddy Holly, who made an enormous impact on the rock and roll scene in the late 1950s with such hits as "That'll Be the Day" and "Peggy Sue" before his death in 1959 at the age of 22 in an infamous airplane crash that also included singers Ritchie Valens and J.P. "The Big Bopper" Richardson; includes photos, footage, performance clips, and interviews with family and friends, such as Holly's widow. 50m; DVD. **A:** Jr. High-Adult. **P:** Entertainment. **U:** Home, CATV. **Mov-Ent:** Television Series, Documentary Films, Biography: Music. **Acq:** Purchase. **Dist:** A&E Television Networks L.L.C. $24.95.

Biography: Buffalo Bill: Showman of the West 2006
Discover the man behind the western legend and see how Cody—and his Wild West show—shaped perceptions of the frontier. 50m; DVD. **A:** Jr. High-Adult. **P:** Entertainment. **U:** Home. **Gen-Edu:** Documentary Films, Biography. **Acq:** Purchase. **Dist:** A&E Television Networks L.L.C.

Biography: Bugsy Siegel ????
Presents the A&E cable channel special on American mobster and playboy Benjamin "Bugsy" Siegel, who was known for his ruthless activities in gambling and narcotics smuggling, his extramarital romance with Virginia Hill, and the founding of the popular Flamingo Hotel and Casino in Las Vegas; he was murdered inside Hill's mansion in 1966 while she was out of the country. Includes interviews with acquaintances and enemies as well as footage. 50m; DVD. **A:** Sr. High-Adult. **P:** Entertainment. **U:** Home, CATV. **Mov-Ent:** Television Series, Documentary Films, Biography. **Acq:** Purchase. **Dist:** A&E Television Networks L.L.C. $24.95.

Biography: Buster Keaton ????
Presents the A&E cable channel special on actor Buster Keaton, a comedic legend in silent films of the 1920s whose career and personal life went awry by the 1930s; however, he rebounded in the 1950s with major movies of "Around the World in 80 Days" and Charlie Chaplin's "Limelight." 50m; DVD. **A:** Family. **P:** Entertainment. **U:** Home, CATV. **Mov-Ent:** Television Series, Documentary Films, Biography: Show Business. **Acq:** Purchase. **Dist:** A&E Television Networks L.L.C. $24.95.

Biography: Butch Cassidy and the Sundance Kid ????
Presents the A&E cable channel special on Butch Cassidy and the Sundance Kid, outlaw partners of the old American west in the late 19th century; includes interviews with historians, rare photos, and period accounts. 50m; DVD. **A:** Family. **P:** Entertainment. **U:** Home, CATV. **Mov-Ent:** Television Series, Documentary Films, Biography. **Acq:** Purchase. **Dist:** A&E Television Networks L.L.C. $24.95.

Biography: Calamity Jane ????
Presents the A&E cable channel special on legendary American frontierswoman Calamity Jane (1852-1903), who was known for dressing as a man to be hired for typically male work and for being an expert rider and markswoman; her companion was Wild Bill Hickok who was killed in 1876. Examines the known facts of her life as compared to embellishments made since her death. 50m; DVD. **A:** Family. **P:** Entertainment. **U:** Home, CATV. **Mov-Ent:** Television Series, Documentary Films, Women. **Acq:** Purchase. **Dist:** A&E Television Networks L.L.C. $24.95.

Biography: Calvin Klein: A Stylish Obsession ????
Presents the A&E cable channel special on fashion designer Calvin Klein, known for his popular jeans and underwear though his personal life had troubles; includes interviews with Klein, his wife, and his daughter along with associates Anna Wintour of "Vogue" and Liz Tiberis of "Harper Bazaar." 50m; DVD. **A:** Jr. High-Adult. **P:** Entertainment. **U:** Home, CATV. **Mov-Ent:** Television Series, Documentary Films, Clothing & Dress. **Acq:** Purchase. **Dist:** A&E Television Networks L.L.C. $24.95.

Biography: Cameron Diaz 2007
Presents the A&E cable channel special on actress Cameron Diaz, who has starred in several successful films such as the "Charlie's Angels" set, and has provided the voice of Princess Fiona in the "Shrek" series. 50m; DVD. **A:** Family. **P:** Entertain-

ment. **U:** Home, CATV. **Mov-Ent:** Television Series, Documentary Films, Biography: Show Business. **Acq:** Purchase. **Dist:** A&E Television Networks L.L.C. $24.95.

Biography: Captain Bligh ????
A&E Biography combines interviews, still photography, live-action footage, reenactments, period art, and other documentary material to present historical figures and their achievements. Recommended for Grades 6-12. 45m; VHS. **A:** Jr. High-Sr. High. **P:** Education. **U:** Home, Institution. **Gen-Edu:** Biography, History. **Acq:** Purchase. **Dist:** Social Studies School Service; Zenger Media. $14.95.

Biography: Carl Sagan: A Cosmic Celebrity ????
Presents the A&E cable channel special on astronomer, author, and television personality Carl Sagan, who became a household name after his 1980 public television series "Cosmos"; he was able to witness and have a role in the filming of his 1985 book "Contact" prior to his 1996 death; includes interviews with colleagues and family. 50m; DVD. **A:** Family. **P:** Entertainment. **U:** Home, CATV. **Mov-Ent:** Television Series, Documentary Films, Biography: Show Business. **Acq:** Purchase. **Dist:** A&E Television Networks L.L.C. $24.95.

Biography: Carol Burnett 2005
A biography of the legendary comedienne, including early TV guest-star appearances, her own variety program, and Burnett's work on Broadway. 50m; DVD. **A:** Jr. High-Adult. **P:** Entertainment. **U:** Home. **Fin-Art:** Documentary Films, Biography: Show Business. **Acq:** Purchase. **Dist:** A&E Television Networks L.L.C.

Biography: Carole Lombard: Hollywood's Profane Angel ????
Presents the A&E cable channel special on actress Carole Lombard, who was able to continue her movie career when silent films ended and "talkies" took over; profiles her marriage to actor Clark Gable and the sorrow following her death in 1942 in an airplane crash as the World War II activist sought to aide the cause by promoting U.S. war bonds. 50m; DVD. **A:** Jr. High-Adult. **P:** Entertainment. **U:** Home, CATV. **Mov-Ent:** Television Series, Documentary Films, Biography: Show Business. **Acq:** Purchase. **Dist:** A&E Television Networks L.L.C. $24.95.

Biography: Carolyn Jones: Morticia and More 2002
Presents the A&E cable channel special on actress Carolyn Jones, best known for her role on the television series "The Addams Family" as wife Morticia though she experienced enormous success on Broadway and in film. 50m; DVD. **A:** Family. **P:** Entertainment. **U:** Home, CATV. **Mov-Ent:** Television Series, Documentary Films, Biography: Show Business. **Acq:** Purchase. **Dist:** A&E Television Networks L.L.C. $24.95.

Biography: Cary Grant—Hollywood's Leading Man 1999
This program from A&E's popular "Biography" series examines the life of film actor Cary Grant. 50m; VHS. **A:** Jr. High-Adult. **P:** Entertainment. **U:** Home. **Gen-Edu:** Biography, Documentary Films, Biography: Show Business. **Acq:** Purchase. **Dist:** A&E Television Networks L.L.C. $14.95.

Biography: Casanova: World's Greatest Lover 2006
Explores the life of the 18th-century Venetian diplomat, writer, and criminal, from his sexual escapades to his association with King Louis XV of France. 50m; DVD. **A:** Jr. High-Adult. **P:** Entertainment. **U:** Home. **Gen-Edu:** Documentary Films, Biography. **Acq:** Purchase. **Dist:** A&E Television Networks L.L.C.

Biography: Catherine the Great 2006
See how a minor German princess become the Empress of Russia during a 1762 bloodless coup and how Catherine ruled her adopted country for 34 years. 50m; DVD. **A:** Jr. High-Adult. **P:** Entertainment. **U:** Home. **Gen-Edu:** Documentary Films, Biography: Royalty. **Acq:** Purchase. **Dist:** A&E Television Networks L.L.C.

Biography: Ceausescu: The Unrepentant Tyrant 2007
Biography of the communist dictator who ruled Romania for 24 years until his execution in 1989. 50m; DVD. **A:** Jr. High-Adult. **P:** Entertainment. **U:** Home. **Gen-Edu:** Documentary Films, Biography: Politics. **Acq:** Purchase. **Dist:** A&E Television Networks L.L.C.

Biography: Charles & Anne Lindbergh: Alone Together 2006
Looks at the life of the first couple of aviation, from the tragedy of their son's kidnapping and murder through Lindbergh's reactionary views on World War II, which diminished his hero status. 50m; DVD. **A:** Jr. High-Adult. **P:** Entertainment. **U:** Home. **Gen-Edu:** Documentary Films, Biography. **Acq:** Purchase. **Dist:** A&E Television Networks L.L.C.

Biography: Charles Atlas: Modern Day Hercules 1999
Presents the A&E cable channel special on bodybuilder Charles Atlas, known for his successful mail-order exercise guides that he began distributing in the late 1920s. 50m; DVD. **A:** Family. **P:** Entertainment. **U:** Home, CATV. **Mov-Ent:** Television Series, Documentary Films, Biography: Sports. **Acq:** Purchase. **Dist:** A&E Television Networks L.L.C. $24.95.

Biography: Charles Darwin ????
A&E Biography combines interviews, still photography, live-action footage, reenactments, period art, and other documentary material to present historical figures and their achievements. Recommended for Grades 6-12. 45m; VHS. **A:** Jr. High-Sr. High. **P:** Education. **U:** Home, Institution. **Gen-Edu:**

Biography, Scientists, Inventors & Inventions. **Acq:** Purchase. **Dist:** Social Studies School Service; Zenger Media. $14.95.

Biography: Charles Kuralt: A Life on the Road ????
Presents the A&E cable channel special on journalist Charles Kuralt, best known for his work on the CBS show "On the Road"; includes interviews with colleague Walter Cronkite as well as clips. 50m; DVD. **A:** Jr. High-Adult. **P:** Entertainment. **U:** Home, CATV. **Mov-Ent:** Television Series, Documentary Films, Journalism. **Acq:** Purchase. **Dist:** A&E Television Networks L.L.C. $24.95.

Biography: Charles Manson: Journey Into Evil ????
Presents the A&E cable channel special on mass murderer and cult leader Charles Manson, who led his so-called family to the horrific killings of seven people in southern California in 1969 including pregnant actress Sharon Tate, the wife of director Roman Polanski; Features a prison interview with Manson and "family" members Lynette "Squeaky" Fromme, Patricia Krenwinkel, and Leslie Van Houten. 50m; DVD. **A:** Sr. High-Adult. **P:** Entertainment. **U:** Home, CATV. **Mov-Ent:** Television Series, Documentary Films, Biography. **Acq:** Purchase. **Dist:** A&E Television Networks L.L.C. $19.95.

Biography: Charles Whitman ????
Presents the A&E cable channel special on mass murderer Charles Whitman, who in 1966 murdered his mother and wife before going to the top of the University of Texas clock tower, where he used a massive amount of ammunition to kill 14 people and wound 31 people; includes interviews. 50m; DVD. **A:** Sr. High-Adult. **P:** Entertainment. **U:** Home, CATV. **Mov-Ent:** Television Series, Documentary Films, Biography. **Acq:** Purchase. **Dist:** A&E Television Networks L.L.C. $24.95.

Biography: Che Guevara ????
A&E Biography combines interviews, still photography, live-action footage, reenactments, period art, and other documentary material to present historical figures and their achievements. Recommended for Grades 6-12. 45m; VHS. **A:** Jr. High-Sr. High. **P:** Education. **U:** Home, Institution. **Gen-Edu:** Biography, History--Modern. **Acq:** Purchase. **Dist:** Social Studies School Service; Zenger Media. $14.95.

Biography: Cheryl Tiegs: An American Beauty ????
Presents the A&E cable channel special on American supermodel Cheryl Tiegs, covering her life as a model, make-up spokeswoman, and clothes manufacturer, along with her personal struggles as a mother and a four-time divorcee; includes interviews with family, friends, and colleagues. 50m; DVD. **A:** Jr. High-Adult. **P:** Entertainment. **U:** Home, CATV. **Mov-Ent:** Television Series, Documentary Films, Biography: Show Business. **Acq:** Purchase. **Dist:** A&E Television Networks L.L.C. $24.95.

Biography: Chiang Kai-Shek ????
A&E Biography combines interviews, still photography, live-action footage, reenactments, period art, and other documentary material to present historical figures and their achievements. Recommended for Grades 6-12. 45m; VHS. **A:** Jr. High-Sr. High. **P:** Education. **U:** Home, Institution. **Gen-Edu:** Biography, History--Modern. **Acq:** Purchase. **Dist:** Social Studies School Service; Zenger Media. $14.95.

Biography: Chris Farley: Reckless Laughter ????
Presents the A&E cable channel special on comedian and actor Chris Farley, whose talents led him to the cast of "Saturday Night Live" as well as movie roles; a drug overdose led to his untimely death in 1997 at the age of 33. Includes interviews with family and friends, such as Al Franken, Rob Schneider, and Tom Arnold. 50m; DVD. **A:** Jr. High-Adult. **P:** Entertainment. **U:** Home, CATV. **Mov-Ent:** Television Series, Documentary Films, Biography: Show Business. **Acq:** Purchase. **Dist:** A&E Television Networks L.L.C. $24.95.

Biography: Christopher Columbus ????
A&E Biography combines interviews, still photography, live-action footage, reenactments, period art, and other documentary material to present historical figures and their achievements. Recommended for Grades 6-12. 45m; VHS. **A:** Jr. High-Sr. High. **P:** Education. **U:** Home, Institution. **Gen-Edu:** Biography, History. **Acq:** Purchase. **Dist:** Social Studies School Service; Zenger Media. $14.95.

Biography: Christopher Columbus: Explorer of the New World 2005
Interviews with historians as well as period accounts and artifacts cover the explorer's journey to the New World and the problems his reputation later suffered. 50m; DVD. **A:** Jr. High-Adult. **P:** Entertainment. **U:** Home. **Gen-Edu:** Documentary Films, Explorers. **Acq:** Purchase. **Dist:** A&E Television Networks L.L.C.

Biography: Christopher Reeve: Triumph, Tragedy, and Courage ????
Presents the A&E cable channel special on actor and activist Christopher Reeve, who rose to fame in the 1978 movie "Superman" and its two sequels; his life was threatened by a 1995 equestrian accident that left him paralyzed and caused him to become an advocate for spinal injury research with his wife Dana Reeve via the Christopher Reeve Foundation. Includes film clips and family and friend interviews. 50m; DVD. **A:** Family. **P:** Entertainment. **U:** Home, CATV. **Mov-Ent:** Television Series, Documentary Films, Biography: Show Business. **Acq:** Purchase. **Dist:** A&E Television Networks L.L.C. $24.95.

Biography: Chuck Norris ????
Presents the A&E cable channel special on actor Chuck Norris, who utilized his martial arts skills in numerous movies and in the

popular television series "Walker, Texas Ranger"; includes interviews with family, co-stars, and friends. 50m; DVD. **A:** Family. **P:** Entertainment. **U:** Home, CATV. **Mov-Ent:** Television Series, Documentary Films, Biography: Show Business. **Acq:** Purchase. **Dist:** A&E Television Networks L.L.C. $24.95.

Biography: Clara Bow: Hollywood's Silent Sexpot 2002
Presents the A&E cable channel special on actress Clara Bow, who experienced great success in the silent era of film for her seductive roles though her career plummeted once movies included the actors' voices; features interviews, fan letters, and newspaper accounts of her active social life. 50m; DVD. **A:** Jr. High-Adult. **P:** Entertainment. **U:** Home, CATV. **Mov-Ent:** Television Series, Documentary Films, Biography: Show Business. **Acq:** Purchase. **Dist:** A&E Television Networks L.L.C. $24.95.

Biography: Clark Gable ????
Presents the A&E cable channel special on actor Clark Gable, a popular leading man whose best known role was as Rhett Butler in "Gone With the Wind" who also suffered personal tragedy when his wife, actress Carole Lombard, died in an airplane crash in 1942, spurring him to serve in the Army during World War II. 50m; DVD. **A:** Family. **P:** Entertainment. **U:** Home, CATV. **Mov-Ent:** Television Series, Documentary Films, Biography: Show Business. **Acq:** Purchase. **Dist:** A&E Television Networks L.L.C. $24.95.

Biography: Cleopatra: Destiny's Queen 2007
Presents the A&E cable channel special on the ancient Egyptian queen Cleopatra, utilizing dramatizations and computer animation to recount the events of her life along with expert interviews, unique footage, and privately-held photographs. 50m; DVD. **A:** Jr. High-Adult. **P:** Entertainment. **U:** Home, CATV. **Mov-Ent:** Television Series, Documentary Films, History--Ancient. **Acq:** Purchase. **Dist:** A&E Television Networks L.L.C. $24.95.

Biography: Clint Eastwood 2005
Looks at the life and career of the actor, director, producer, and musician. Includes home movies and highlights from Eastwood's films. 100m; DVD. **A:** Jr. High-Adult. **P:** Entertainment. **U:** Home. **Fin-Art:** Documentary Films, Biography: Show Business. **Acq:** Purchase. **Dist:** A&E Television Networks L.L.C.

Biography: Colonel Sanders ????
A&E Biography combines interviews, still photography, live-action footage, reenactments, period art, and other documentary material to present historical figures and their achievements. Recommended for Grades 6-12. 45m; VHS. **A:** Jr. High-Sr. High. **P:** Education. **U:** Home, Institution. **Gen-Edu:** Biography, History, Business. **Acq:** Purchase. **Dist:** Social Studies School Service; Zenger Media. $14.95.

Biography: Condoleezza Rice 200?
Presents the A&E cable channel special on Condoleezza Rice, who was selected by President George W. Bush as the first female to hold the National Security Advisor position (from 2001-2005, before becoming Secretary of State); includes interviews with colleagues. 50m; DVD. **A:** Family. **P:** Entertainment. **U:** Home, CATV. **Mov-Ent:** Television Series, Documentary Films, Biography: Politics. **Acq:** Purchase. **Dist:** A&E Television Networks L.L.C. $24.95.

Biography: Confucius ????
A&E Biography combines interviews, still photography, live-action footage, reenactments, period art, and other documentary material to present historical figures and their achievements. Recommended for Grades 6-12. 45m; VHS. **A:** Jr. High-Sr. High. **P:** Education. **U:** Home, Institution. **Gen-Edu:** Biography, History. **Acq:** Purchase. **Dist:** Zenger Media; Social Studies School Service. $14.95.

Biography: Conrad Hilton ????
Presents the A&E cable channel special on hotel empire founder Conrad Hilton (1887-1979), who began his billion-dollar hotel chain in Texas at the age of 31 and whose personal life included three marriages (his second wife was actress Zsa Zsa Gabor); features interviews with family and friends. 50m; DVD. **A:** Jr. High-Adult. **P:** Entertainment. **U:** Home, CATV. **Mov-Ent:** Television Series, Documentary Films, Hotels & Hotel Staff Training. **Acq:** Purchase. **Dist:** A&E Television Networks L.L.C. $24.95.

Biography: Constantine: The Christian Emperor 2006
Explores the life of the ruler and his 20-year struggle to control a fractured Roman Empire as well as his conversion to Christianity. 50m; DVD. **A:** Jr. High-Adult. **P:** Entertainment. **U:** Home. **Gen-Edu:** Documentary Films, Biography: Royalty. **Acq:** Purchase. **Dist:** A&E Television Networks L.L.C.

Biography: Crazy Horse ????
A&E Biography combines interviews, still photography, live-action footage, reenactments, period art, and other documentary material to present historical figures and their achievements. Recommended for Grades 6-12. 45m; VHS. **A:** Jr. High-Sr. High. **P:** Education. **U:** Home, Institution. **Gen-Edu:** Biography, History--U.S. **Acq:** Purchase. **Dist:** Social Studies School Service; Zenger Media. $14.95.

Biography: Cybill Shepherd ????
Presents the A&E cable channel special on actress Cybill Shepherd, who began as a beauty queen and received critical praise in her debut in the movie "The Last Picture Show" as well as the television series "Moonlighting" with co-star Bruce Willis (1985-1989) and her self-titled series from 1995-1998. On-set feuds and her off-screen activism and rebellious behavior made her a tabloid target. Includes interviews with family, friends, and

colleagues as well as clips. 50m; DVD. **A:** Jr. High-Adult. **P:** Entertainment. **U:** Home, CATV. **Mov-Ent:** Television Series, Documentary Films, Biography: Show Business. **Acq:** Purchase. **Dist:** A&E Television Networks L.L.C. $24.95.

Biography: Da Vinci ????
Examines the life and masterpieces of the great artist. 50m; VHS. **A:** Sr. High-Adult. **P:** Education. **U:** Home, Institution. **Gen-Edu:** Art & Artists, Biography. **Acq:** Purchase. **Dist:** Crystal Productions. $14.95.

Biography: Dalai Lama 1997
A&E Biography combines interviews, still photography, live-action footage, reenactments, period art, and other documentary material to present historical figures and their achievements. Recommended for Grades 6-12. 45m; VHS. **A:** Jr. High-Sr. High. **P:** Education. **U:** Home, Institution. **Gen-Edu:** Biography, History--Modern. **Acq:** Purchase. **Dist:** Social Studies School Service; Zenger Media. $14.95.

Biography: Daniel Boone ????
A&E Biography combines interviews, still photography, live-action footage, reenactments, period art, and other documentary material to present historical figures and their achievements. Recommended for Grades 6-12. 45m; VHS. **A:** Jr. High-Sr. High. **P:** Education. **U:** Home, Institution. **Gen-Edu:** Biography, History--U.S. **Acq:** Purchase. **Dist:** Social Studies School Service; Zenger Media. $14.95.

Biography: Danielle Steel ????
Presents the A&E cable channel special on romantic fiction author Danielle Steel, who has written around 70 novels—many of which have been adapted for film and television—and is worth about $600 million; intensely personal, her life has been difficult with multiple miscarriages, troubled marriages, and the suicide death of her son. 50m; DVD. **A:** Jr. High-Adult. **P:** Entertainment. **U:** Home, CATV. **Mov-Ent:** Television Series, Documentary Films, Biography. **Acq:** Purchase. **Dist:** A&E Television Networks L.L.C. $24.95.

Biography: Danny Bonaduce, Tabloids' Bad Boy ????
Presents the A&E cable channel special on actor and radio personality Danny Bonaduce, from his days as a child star in "The Partridge Family" through troubles with drug addiction and other personal struggles to his efforts to turn his life around with his career as a radio host; includes interviews with Bonaduce along with his friends and family. 50m; DVD. **A:** Jr. High-Adult. **P:** Entertainment. **U:** Home, CATV. **Mov-Ent:** Television Series, Documentary Films, Biography: Show Business. **Acq:** Purchase. **Dist:** A&E Television Networks L.L.C. $24.95.

Biography: Darryl F. Zanuck: 20th Century Filmmaker ????
Presents the A&E cable channel special on movie producer and writer Darryl F. Zanuck, whose work began during the silent movies days and continued through to the full sound era in the 1930s; Zanuck worked as Jack L. Warner's second hand at Warner Bros. until he decided to branch out in 1933 to co-found 20th Century Pictures. Includes interviews with his children and colleagues, such as Alice Faye and Robert Wagner. 50m; DVD. **A:** Family. **P:** Entertainment. **U:** Home, CATV. **Mov-Ent:** Television Series, Documentary Films, Biography: Show Business. **Acq:** Purchase. **Dist:** A&E Television Networks L.L.C. $24.95.

Biography: Dave Chappelle 20??
Presents the A&E cable channel special on popular comedian and television actor Dave Chappelle, who caused a stir in the industry when he refused a television deal worth about $50 million; includes interviews and footage. 50m; DVD. **A:** Jr. High-Adult. **P:** Entertainment. **U:** Home, CATV. **Mov-Ent:** Television Series, Documentary Films, Biography: Show Business. **Acq:** Purchase. **Dist:** A&E Television Networks L.L.C. $24.95.

Biography: Dave Thomas ????
Presents the A&E cable channel special on fast food chain founder and philanthropist Dave Thomas, who started his popular Wendy's hamburger restaurant in 1969 after leaving the KFC franchise; he served as its well-known spokesperson in 1989. 50m; DVD. **A:** Jr. High-Adult. **P:** Entertainment. **U:** Home, CATV. **Mov-Ent:** Television Series, Documentary Films, Biography. **Acq:** Purchase. **Dist:** A&E Television Networks L.L.C. $24.95.

Biography: David and Goliath 2006
Through the use of artifacts, location footage, and scholarly opinions, see how Old Testament hero David goes from shepherd boy and slayer of Philistine giant Goliath, to the 40-year ruler of Jerusalem. 50m; DVD. **A:** Jr. High-Adult. **P:** Entertainment. **U:** Home. **Gen-Edu:** Documentary Films, Bible. **Acq:** Purchase. **Dist:** A&E Television Networks L.L.C.

Biography: David Ben-Gurion ????
Presents the A&E cable channel special on Israel's first Prime Minister and Defense Minister David Ben-Gurion, who served his country from 1949 to 1963 (aside from a brief retirement) after his fundamental role in its formation; includes interviews and archival footage. 50m; DVD. **A:** Family. **P:** Entertainment. **U:** Home, CATV. **Mov-Ent:** Television Series, Documentary Films, Politics & Government. **Acq:** Purchase. **Dist:** A&E Television Networks L.L.C. $24.95.

Biography: David Berkowitz: Son of Sam ????
Presents the A&E cable channel special on serial killer David Berkowitz, better known as the "Son of Sam," who terrorized New York City from 1976 to 1977; includes interviews with reporters, detectives, prosecutors, an FBI profiler, victims' families, and Berkowitz. While serving his jail time, he converted to Christianity and became a minister. 50m; DVD. **A:** Sr. High-Adult. **P:** Entertainment. **U:** Home, CATV. **Mov-Ent:** Television

Series, Documentary Films, Biography. **Acq:** Purchase. **Dist:** A&E Television Networks L.L.C. $24.95.

Biography: David Bowie ????
Presents the A&E cable channel special on singer and actor David Bowie, whose unusual style of music and dramatic flair (such as taking on "alter egos" like "Ziggy Stardust" and "Thin White Duke") have translated into a successful career spanning five decades; includes rare archival footage from BBC along with interviews. 100m; DVD. **A:** Jr. High-Adult. **P:** Entertainment. **U:** Home, CATV. **Mov-Ent:** Television Series, Documentary Films, Biography: Music. **Acq:** Purchase. **Dist:** A&E Television Networks L.L.C. $29.95.

Biography: David Copperfield ????
Presents the A&E cable channel special on illusionist David Copperfield, most known for his spectacular and often large-scale magical tricks; includes interviews and performances. 50m; DVD. **A:** Family. **P:** Entertainment. **U:** Home, CATV. **Mov-Ent:** Television Series, Documentary Films, Biography: Show Business. **Acq:** Purchase. **Dist:** A&E Television Networks L.L.C. $24.95.

Biography: Davy Crockett ????
A&E Biography combines interviews, still photography, live-action footage, reenactments, period art, and other documentary material to present historical figures and their achievements. Recommended for Grades 6-12. 45m; VHS. **A:** Jr. High-Sr. High. **P:** Education. **U:** Home, Institution. **Gen-Edu:** Biography, History--U.S. **Acq:** Purchase. **Dist:** Social Studies School Service; Zenger Media. $14.95.

Biography: Dean Martin: Everybody Loves Somebody 2005
Looks at the 50-year career of Martin—from his partnership with Jerry Lewis to his "Rat Pack" days and his solo career. 50m; DVD. **A:** Jr. High-Adult. **P:** Entertainment. **U:** Home. **Gen-Edu:** Documentary Films, Biography: Show Business. **Acq:** Purchase. **Dist:** A&E Television Networks L.L.C.

Biography: Dian Fossey ????
Presents the A&E cable channel special on primatologist Dian Fossey, who became well known for her extensive and revolutionary work with the behavior of mountain gorillas in Rwanda beginning in the 1960s through her death in 1985, presumably by poachers; the film "Gorillas in the Mist" starring Sigourney Weaver was based on Fossey's book. Includes interviews. 50m; DVD. **A:** Family. **P:** Entertainment. **U:** Home, CATV. **Mov-Ent:** Television Series, Documentary Films, Animals. **Acq:** Purchase. **Dist:** A&E Television Networks L.L.C. $24.95.

Biography: Diane Keaton: On Her Own 2006
Presents the A&E cable channel special on actress Diane Keaton, who has starred in many movies such as the "Godfather" trilogy and "Annie Hall," which earned her the Academy Award for best actress. 50m; DVD. **A:** Family. **P:** Entertainment. **U:** Home, CATV. **Mov-Ent:** Television Series, Documentary Films, Biography: Show Business. **Acq:** Purchase. **Dist:** A&E Television Networks L.L.C. $24.95.

Biography: Diego Rivera ????
Presents the A&E cable channel special on Mexican artist Diego Rivera (1886-1957) who was known for his large-scale public frescoes as well as his controversial political views and troubled relationship with painter Frida Kahlo (who he married twice); includes interviews with scholars and others along with displays of his work. 50m; DVD. **A:** Jr. High-Adult. **P:** Entertainment. **U:** Home, CATV. **Mov-Ent:** Television Series, Documentary Films, Biography: Artists. **Acq:** Purchase. **Dist:** A&E Television Networks L.L.C. $24.95.

Biography: Donald Trump: Deal Maker ????
Presents the A&E cable channel special on businessman and real estate developer Donald Trump, including his successes in the 1980s and the downfall and revival he experienced in the 1990s; includes interviews. 50m; DVD. **A:** Family. **P:** Entertainment. **U:** Home, CATV. **Mov-Ent:** Television Series, Documentary Films, Biography: Show Business. **Acq:** Purchase. **Dist:** A&E Television Networks L.L.C. $24.95.

Biography: Donald Trump: Master of the Deal ????
Presents the A&E cable channel special on businessman and real estate developer Donald Trump, focusing on his turnaround from bankruptcy in 1990 and divorce from first wife Ivanka; includes interviews. 50m; DVD. **A:** Family. **P:** Entertainment. **U:** Home, CATV. **Mov-Ent:** Television Series, Documentary Films, Biography: Show Business. **Acq:** Purchase. **Dist:** A&E Television Networks L.L.C. $24.95.

Biography: Donna Karan 20??
Presents the A&E cable channel special on popular American fashion designer Donna Karan, who entered the industry via a job with Anne Klein and started her own company in 1985; includes interviews with Karan, family, and friends. 50m; DVD. **A:** Family. **P:** Entertainment. **U:** Home, CATV. **Mov-Ent:** Television Series, Documentary Films, Biography: Artists. **Acq:** Purchase. **Dist:** A&E Television Networks L.L.C. $24.95.

Biography: Doris Day ????
Presents the A&E cable channel special on singer and actress Doris Day, who starred in such movie classics as "Pillow Talk" and won an Oscar for the song "Que Sera, Sera" from Alfred Hitchhock's "The Man Who Knew Too Much"; in her personal life, she often struggled, including a nervous breakdown following the death of her third husband in 1968 who as her business manager, she discovered, had squandered her entire savings. 50m; DVD. **A:** Family. **P:** Entertainment. **U:** Home, CATV.

Mov-Ent: Television Series, Documentary Films, Biography: Show Business. **Acq:** Purchase. **Dist:** A&E Television Networks L.L.C. $24.95.

Biography: Dorothy Stratten ????
Presents the A&E cable channel special on model and actress Dorothy Stratten, who went from being an unknown to 1980's "Playboy Playmate of the Year" at the age of 20; her husband Paul Snider—who had launched her career—murdered her and killed himself in August of the same year, allegedly due to her affair with director Peter Bogdanovich, in whose movie "They All Laughed" she was the co-star. Includes interviews with Bogdanovich, Hugh Hefner, Muriel Hemingway, and Stratten's sister Louise. 50m; DVD. **A:** Jr. High-Adult. **P:** Entertainment. **U:** Home, CATV. **Mov-Ent:** Television Series, Documentary Films, Biography: Show Business. **Acq:** Purchase. **Dist:** A&E Television Networks L.L.C. $24.95.

Biography: Douglas MacArthur ????
A&E Biography combines interviews, still photography, live-action footage, reenactments, period art, and other documentary material to present historical figures and their achievements. Recommended for Grades 6-12. 45m; VHS. **A:** Jr. High-Sr. High. **P:** Education. **U:** Home, Institution. **Gen-Edu:** Biography, History--Modern. **Acq:** Purchase. **Dist:** Social Studies School Service; Zenger Media. $14.95.

Biography: Dow & Jones ????
A&E Biography combines interviews, still photography, live-action footage, reenactments, period art, and other documentary material to present historical figures and their achievements. Recommended for Grades 6-12. 45m; VHS. **A:** Jr. High-Sr. High. **P:** Education. **U:** Home, Institution. **Gen-Edu:** Biography, History, Business. **Acq:** Purchase. **Dist:** Social Studies School Service; Zenger Media. $14.95.

Biography: Dwight D. Eisenhower ????
A&E Biography combines interviews, still photography, live-action footage, reenactments, period art, and other documentary material to present historical figures and their achievements. Recommended for Grades 6-12. 45m; VHS. **A:** Jr. High-Sr. High. **P:** Education. **U:** Home, Institution. **Gen-Edu:** Biography, Presidency, History--U.S. **Acq:** Purchase. **Dist:** Social Studies School Service; Zenger Media. $14.95.

Biography: Dwight D. Eisenhower: Commander-in-Chief 2005
Follows the life of Eisenhower from his Kansas boyhood to his time as Supreme Allied Commander in World War II and his presidency. 100m; DVD. **A:** Jr. High-Adult. **P:** Entertainment. **U:** Home. **Gen-Edu:** Documentary Films, Biography: Politics. **Acq:** Purchase. **Dist:** A&E Television Networks L.L.C.

Biography: Dwight Eisenhower: Commander-In-Chief ????
Presents the A&E cable channel special on President Dwight Eisenhower, covering his time as a military commander to his service as president with interviews from politicians, news anchors, and family members; includes recordings of Eisenhower himself. 50m; DVD. **A:** Jr. High-Adult. **P:** Entertainment. **U:** Home, CATV. **Mov-Ent:** Television Series, Documentary Films, Presidency. **Acq:** Purchase. **Dist:** A&E Television Networks L.L.C. $24.95.

Biography: Eclipsed by Death: The Life of River Phoenix ????
Presents the A&E cable channel special on young actor River Phoenix, whose success in movies such as "Stand By Me" and "My Own Private Idaho" was overshadowed by his tragic drug-induced death at the age of 23. 50m; DVD. **A:** Jr. High-Adult. **P:** Entertainment. **U:** Home, CATV. **Mov-Ent:** Television Series, Documentary Films, Biography: Show Business. **Acq:** Purchase. **Dist:** A&E Television Networks L.L.C. $24.95.

Biography: Ed Gein ????
Presents the A&E cable channel special on American serial killer Ed Gein, who was infamous for his necrophiliac behavior at his remote Wisconsin farm; Gein was the basis for such horror movies as Alfred Hitchcock's 1960 "Psycho" and Jonathan Demme's 1991 "Silence of the Lambs." Includes interviews with police and former neighbors as well as film clips. 50m; DVD. **A:** Family. **P:** Entertainment. **U:** Home, CATV. **Mov-Ent:** Television Series, Documentary Films, Biography. **Acq:** Purchase. **Dist:** A&E Television Networks L.L.C. $24.95.

Biography: Edith Head ????
Presents the A&E cable channel special on costume designer Edith Head, who worked in the movie industry from the 1920s until her death in 1981; she was responsible for the costumes in more than 1,100 films as well as dressing many high-profile actresses of the era. Includes interviews as well as rare childhood photographs and her original sketches. 50m; DVD. **A:** Family. **P:** Entertainment. **U:** Home, CATV. **Mov-Ent:** Television Series, Documentary Films, Biography: Show Business. **Acq:** Purchase. **Dist:** A&E Television Networks L.L.C. $24.95.

Biography: Edward R. Murrow: Voice of America 2006
Examines Murrow's life from his beginnings on radio (and his World War II broadcasts) to his TV career. Includes clips from his work. 50m; DVD. **A:** Jr. High-Adult. **P:** Entertainment. **U:** Home. **Gen-Edu:** Documentary Films, Biography. **Acq:** Purchase. **Dist:** A&E Television Networks L.L.C.

Biography: Eleanor Roosevelt: A Restless Spirit 2005
Looks at the public and private lives of First Lady Eleanor Roosevelt. 50m; DVD. **A:** Jr. High-Adult. **P:** Entertainment. **U:** Home. **Gen-Edu:** Documentary Films, Women. **Acq:** Purchase. **Dist:** A&E Television Networks L.L.C.

Biography: Eliot Ness: Untouchable ????
Presents the A&E cable channel special on federal agent Eliot Ness, known for leading a group of officers nicknamed "The Untouchables" that battled against Chicago gangster Al Capone from 1929 to 1932; though Ness' group was considered to have nabbed Capone, he was actually charged with tax evasion. He co-authored a book on his experiences which later led to a popular television series and the 1987 movie starring Kevin Costner. However, his legacy was marred by his troubles with alcoholism. Includes interviews with biographer Paul Heimel as well as friends and family. 50m; DVD. **A:** Jr. High-Adult. **P:** Entertainment. **U:** Home, CATV. **Mov-Ent**: Television Series, Documentary Films, Biography: Law Enforcement. **Acq:** Purchase. **Dist:** A&E Television Networks L.L.C. $24.95.

Biography: Elizabeth I ????
A&E Biography combines interviews, still photography, live-action footage, reenactments, period art, and other documentary material to present historical figures and their achievements. Recommended for Grades 6-12. 45m; VHS. **A:** Jr. High-Sr. High. **P:** Education. **U:** Home, Institution. **Gen-Edu**: Biography, History. **Acq:** Purchase. **Dist:** Social Studies School Service; Zenger Media. $14.95.

Biography: Elizabeth Montgomery: A Touch of Magic 1999
Presents the A&E cable channel special on actress Elizabeth Montgomery, made famous by her role as Samantha on the television series "Bewitched," which she helped to create; also traces her life back to her appearance on her father Robert Montgomery's television show when she was only five years old. 50m; DVD. **A:** Family. **P:** Entertainment. **U:** Home, CATV. **Mov-Ent**: Television Series, Documentary Films, Biography: Show Business. **Acq:** Purchase. **Dist:** A&E Television Networks L.L.C. $24.95.

Biography: Elizabeth Taylor 199?
A look at the movie goddess from her movie debut, through her Oscar-winning performance and other roles, her eight marriages, and brushes with death. 50m; VHS. **Pr:** A&E (Arts & Entertainment) Network. **A:** Sr. High-Adult. **P:** Entertainment. **U:** Home. **Mov-Ent**: Biography, Biography: Show Business. **Acq:** Purchase. **Dist:** A&E Television Networks L.L.C.; New Video Group. $19.95.

Biography: Ella Fitzgerald—Forever Ella 2000
This installment from the A&E series "Biography" examines the life of singer Ella Fitzgerald. 100m; VHS. **A:** Jr. High-Adult. **P:** Education. **U:** Home. **Gen-Edu**: Biography, Music. **Acq:** Purchase. **Dist:** A&E Television Networks L.L.C. $14.95.

Biography: Elton John 20??
Presents the A&E cable channel special on legendary rock and pop musician Elton John, who used his piano skills and flamboyant costumes to become one of the most successful concert performers in history; his first album was released in 1969 and he continues to produce music including that of the Broadway spectacle "The Lion King" (he received an Oscar for his song "Can You Feel the Love Tonight" from the 1994 movie); includes highlights from his "Red Piano Show" playing in Las Vegas since 2003. 100m; DVD. **A:** Jr. High-Adult. **P:** Entertainment. **U:** Home, CATV. **Mov-Ent**: Television Series, Documentary Films, Biography: Music. **Acq:** Purchase. **Dist:** A&E Television Networks L.L.C. $29.95.

Biography: Emeril Lagasse: Bam! ????
Presents the A&E cable channel special on chef Emeril Lagasse, best known for his Food Network shows highlighting his Cajun cuisine and energetic personality; includes interviews. 50m; DVD. **A:** Family. **P:** Entertainment. **U:** Home, CATV. **Mov-Ent**: Television Series, Documentary Films, Biography: Show Business. **Acq:** Purchase. **Dist:** A&E Television Networks L.L.C. $24.95.

Biography: Emperor Hirohito ????
A&E Biography combines interviews, still photography, live-action footage, reenactments, period art, and other documentary material to present historical figures and their achievements. Recommended for Grades 6-12. 45m; VHS. **A:** Jr. High-Sr. High. **P:** Education. **U:** Home, Institution. **Gen-Edu**: Biography, History--Modern. **Acq:** Purchase. **Dist:** Social Studies School Service; Zenger Media. $14.95.

Biography: Ernest Shackleton: Looking South ????
Presents the A&E cable channel special on the life of British explorer Ernest Shackleton, recounting his legendary expedition to the Antarctic (named Endurance) from 1914 to 1916 when he successfully returned with all 27 members of his crew despite the destruction of the ship; includes photos taken by Frank Hurley along with interviews of scholars, archivists, and family. 50m; DVD. **A:** Jr. High-Adult. **P:** Entertainment. **U:** Home, CATV. **Mov-Ent**: Television Series, Documentary Films, Folklore & Legends. **Acq:** Purchase. **Dist:** A&E Television Networks L.L.C. $24.95.

Biography: Eugene O'Neill: A Haunted Life 2006
Presents the A&E cable channel special on American playwright Eugene O'Neill, whose most successful work, "Long Day's Journey into Night," won him posthumous acclaim; profiles the struggles he endured with troubled family members as well as with his three marriages and his children. Includes interviews with his grandchildren, among others. 100m; DVD. **A:** Jr. High-Adult. **P:** Entertainment. **U:** Home, CATV. **Mov-Ent**: Television Series, Documentary Films, Biography. **Acq:** Purchase. **Dist:** A&E Television Networks L.L.C. $29.95.

Biography: Eva Braun: Love and Death 2007
Home movies highlight the private life of the woman who loved Adolf Hitler and died with him in a German bunker. 50m; DVD. **A:** Jr. High-Adult. **P:** Entertainment. **U:** Home. **Gen-Edu**: Documentary Films, Biography: Politics. **Acq:** Purchase. **Dist:** A&E Television Networks L.L.C.

Biography: Evita ????
A&E Biography combines interviews, still photography, live-action footage, reenactments, period art, and other documentary material to present historical figures and their achievements. Recommended for Grades 6-12. 45m; VHS. **A:** Jr. High-Sr. High. **P:** Education. **U:** Home, Institution. **Gen-Edu**: Biography, History--Modern. **Acq:** Purchase. **Dist:** Zenger Media; Social Studies School Service. $14.95.

Biography: Farrah Fawcett: America's Angel ????
Presents the A&E cable channel special on actress Farrah Fawcett, best known for her television series role on "Charlie's Angels"; she struggled for success afterwards and encountered many personal crises including the end of her marriage to fellow television star Lee Majors and later the break-up of a long-term relationship with actor Ryan O'Neal. 50m; DVD. **A:** Family. **P:** Entertainment. **U:** Home, CATV. **Mov-Ent**: Television Series, Documentary Films, Biography: Show Business. **Acq:** Purchase. **Dist:** A&E Television Networks L.L.C. $24.95.

Biography: FDR: Years of Crisis ????
Presents the A&E cable channel special on the life and struggles of President Franklin D. Roosevelt, who overcame his inability to walk after suffering from polio to build his political career as governor of New York then to four terms as president; includes interviews, footage, and excerpts of his nominating speech from the 1928 Democratic convention. 50m; DVD. **A:** Family. **P:** Entertainment. **U:** Home, CATV. **Mov-Ent**: Television Series, Documentary Films, Politics & Government. **Acq:** Purchase. **Dist:** A&E Television Networks L.L.C. $24.95.

Biography: FDR—War Years ????
A&E Biography combines interviews, still photography, live-action footage, reenactments, period art, and other documentary material to present historical figures and their achievements. Recommended for Grades 6-12. 45m; VHS. **A:** Jr. High-Sr. High. **P:** Education. **U:** Home, Institution. **Gen-Edu**: Biography, Presidency, History--U.S. **Acq:** Purchase. **Dist:** Social Studies School Service; Zenger Media. $14.95.

Biography: FDR—Year of Crisis ????
A&E Biography combines interviews, still photography, live-action footage, reenactments, period art, and other documentary material to present historical figures and their achievements. Recommended for Grades 6-12. 45m; VHS. **A:** Jr. High-Sr. High. **P:** Education. **U:** Home, Institution. **Gen-Edu**: Biography, Presidency, History--U.S. **Acq:** Purchase. **Dist:** Social Studies School Service; Zenger Media. $14.95.

Biography: Federico Fellini ????
Presents the A&E cable channel special on famed director Federico Fellini, whose cinematic success included many Oscar nominations leading to an eventual lifetime achievement award; his most prominent work was the 1960 film "La Dolce Vita." 50m; DVD. **A:** Family. **P:** Entertainment. **U:** Home, CATV. **Mov-Ent**: Television Series, Documentary Films, Biography: Show Business. **Acq:** Purchase. **Dist:** A&E Television Networks L.L.C. $24.95.

Biography: Fidel Castro 1996
A&E Biography combines interviews, still photography, live-action footage, reenactments, period art, and other documentary material to present historical figures and their achievements. Recommended for Grades 6-12. 45m; VHS. **A:** Jr. High-Sr. High. **P:** Education. **U:** Home, Institution. **Gen-Edu**: Biography, History--Modern. **Acq:** Purchase. **Dist:** Social Studies School Service; Zenger Media. $14.95.

Biography: Final Days: The Fame and Fate of Marilyn Monroe & Princess Diana 20??
Presents the A&E cable channel special on the tragically-short lives of actress Marilyn Monroe and Princess Diana. 50m; DVD. **A:** Family. **P:** Entertainment. **U:** Home, CATV. **Mov-Ent**: Television Series, Documentary Films, Biography: Show Business. **Acq:** Purchase. **Dist:** A&E Television Networks L.L.C. $24.95.

Biography: Flash Gordon: Journey to Greatness ????
Presents the A&E cable channel special on the creation of comic-book hero Flash Gordon by cartoonist Alex Raymond in 1934; follows the character's transition to radio and television. Includes an interview with Steve Holland, who starred in the 1950s television series. 50m; DVD. **A:** Family. **P:** Entertainment. **U:** Home, CATV. **Mov-Ent**: Television Series, Documentary Films, Television. **Acq:** Purchase. **Dist:** A&E Television Networks L.L.C. $24.95.

Biography: Frank Serpico: Honor Bound 2006
Looks at the career of the controversial New York City detective who was penalized (and nearly killed) for publicly exposing corruption on the force. 50m; DVD. **A:** Jr. High-Adult. **P:** Entertainment. **U:** Home. **Gen-Edu**: Documentary Films, Biography: Law Enforcement. **Acq:** Purchase. **Dist:** A&E Television Networks L.L.C.

Biography: Fred Gwynne ????
Presents the A&E cable channel special on actor Fred Gwynne, best known as father Herman Munster on "The Munsters" (1964-1966) and Officer Francis Muldoon in "Car 54, Where Are You?" (1961-1963); Gwynn also appeared in several movies. 50m; DVD. **A:** Family. **P:** Entertainment. **U:** Home, CATV. **Mov-Ent**: Television Series, Documentary Films, Biography: Show Business. **Acq:** Purchase. **Dist:** A&E Television Networks L.L.C. $24.95.

Biography: Fred Rogers ????
Presents the A&E cable channel special on children's television star Fred Rogers and his PBS series "Mr. Rogers' Neighborhood"; Rogers also served as producer and writer for the iconic show which taped from 1968 to 2001 but still airs. 50m; DVD. **A:** Family. **P:** Entertainment. **U:** Home, CATV. **Mov-Ent**: Television Series, Documentary Films, Biography: Show Business. **Acq:** Purchase. **Dist:** A&E Television Networks L.L.C. $24.95.

Biography: Frederick Douglass ????
A&E Biography combines interviews, still photography, live-action footage, reenactments, period art, and other documentary material to present historical figures and their achievements. Recommended for Grades 6-12. 45m; VHS. **A:** Jr. High-Sr. High. **P:** Education. **U:** Home, Institution. **Gen-Edu**: Biography, History--U.S. **Acq:** Purchase. **Dist:** Social Studies School Service; Zenger Media. $14.95.

Biography: Frida Kahlo ????
Presents the A&E cable channel special on Mexican artist Frida Kahlo (1907-1954), who overcame serious injuries from a bus accident to produce self-portraits reflecting her suffering; also chronicles her troubled relationship with husband and muralist Diego Rivera. Features interviews with other artists and displays of her collections. 50m; DVD. **A:** Jr. High-Adult. **P:** Entertainment. **U:** Home, CATV. **Mov-Ent**: Television Series, Documentary Films, Biography: Artists. **Acq:** Purchase. **Dist:** A&E Television Networks L.L.C. $24.95.

Biography: Gallo Brothers ????
Presents the A&E cable channel special on American winemakers Ernest and Julio Gallo who co-founded E & J Gallo Winery (later Gallo Family Vineyards) and how despite their need for privacy they made numerous appearances in marketing campaigns; discusses their relationship with their other brother, Joseph, who was excluded from the family business. 50m; DVD. **A:** Jr. High-Adult. **P:** Entertainment. **U:** Home, CATV. **Mov-Ent**: Television Series, Documentary Films, Alcoholic Beverages. **Acq:** Purchase. **Dist:** A&E Television Networks L.L.C. $24.95.

Biography: General Douglas MacArthur: Return of a Legend ????
Presents the A&E cable channel special on General Douglas MacArthur, who served as a powerful force during both World War II and the Korean War; follows his early life as the son of an officer to his time at West Point. Includes interviews with his comrades, family, and friends as well as rare footage. 50m; DVD. **A:** Family. **P:** Entertainment. **U:** Home, CATV. **Mov-Ent**: Television Series, Documentary Films, Biography: Military. **Acq:** Purchase. **Dist:** A&E Television Networks L.L.C. $24.95.

Biography: General George Patton: A Genius for War ????
Presents the A&E cable channel special on legendary World War II commander George Patton, who led campaigns in Sicily, France, and Germany; includes interviews. 100m; DVD. **A:** Family. **P:** Entertainment. **U:** Home, CATV. **Mov-Ent**: Television Series, Documentary Films, Biography: Military. **Acq:** Purchase. **Dist:** A&E Television Networks L.L.C. $29.95.

Biography: General George Patton: A Genius for War 2004
Presents the A&E cable channel special on General George S. Patton, whose World War II success against the Nazis was marred by his brash behavior with his men, which led in part to his removal from command. 50m; DVD. **A:** Jr. High-Adult. **P:** Entertainment. **U:** Home, CATV. **Mov-Ent**: Television Series, Documentary Films, Military History. **Acq:** Purchase. **Dist:** A&E Television Networks L.L.C. $24.95.

Biography: Genghis Khan ????
A&E Biography combines interviews, still photography, live-action footage, reenactments, period art, and other documentary material to present historical figures and their achievements. Recommended for Grades 6-12. 45m; VHS. **A:** Jr. High-Sr. High. **P:** Education. **U:** Home, Institution. **Gen-Edu**: Biography, History. **Acq:** Purchase. **Dist:** Social Studies School Service; Zenger Media. $14.95.

Biography: Genghis Khan: Terror and Conquest 1995
Presents the A&E cable channel special on the brilliant-yet-savage 13th century Mongolian ruler Genghis Khan, whose empire spanned Asia, the Middle East, and Europe. 50m; DVD. **A:** Jr. High-Adult. **P:** Entertainment. **U:** Home, CATV. **Mov-Ent**: Television Series, Documentary Films, Biography: Military. **Acq:** Purchase. **Dist:** A&E Television Networks L.L.C. $24.95.

Biography: George A. Custer ????
A&E Biography combines interviews, still photography, live-action footage, reenactments, period art, and other documentary material to present historical figures and their achievements. Recommended for Grades 6-12. 45m; VHS. **A:** Jr. High-Sr. High. **P:** Education. **U:** Home, Institution. **Gen-Edu**: Biography, History--U.S. **Acq:** Purchase. **Dist:** Social Studies School Service; Zenger Media. $14.95.

Biography: George Armstrong Custer: America's Golden Cavalier ????
Presents the A&E cable channel special on General George A. Custer, known as a Union major general during the American Civil War and later as a commander in the Indian Wars, where he died during the 1876 battle of "Little Bighorn"; includes period accounts and artifacts, such as Custer's journals and letters. 100m; DVD. **A:** Family. **P:** Entertainment. **U:** Home, CATV. **Mov-Ent**: Television Series, Documentary Films, Military History. **Acq:** Purchase. **Dist:** A&E Television Networks L.L.C. $29.95.

Biography: George Bush 1992
A&E Biography combines interviews, still photography, live-action footage, reenactments, period art, and other documentary material to present historical figures and their achievements. Recommended for Grades 6-12. 45m; VHS. **A:** Jr. High-Sr. High. **P:** Education. **U:** Home, Institution. **Gen-Edu:** Biography, Presidency, History--U.S. **Acq:** Purchase. **Dist:** Social Studies School Service; Zenger Media. $14.95.

Biography: George C. Marshall ????
A&E Biography combines interviews, still photography, live-action footage, reenactments, period art, and other documentary material to present historical figures and their achievements. Recommended for Grades 6-12. 45m; VHS. **A:** Jr. High-Sr. High. **P:** Education. **U:** Home, Institution. **Gen-Edu:** Biography, History--Modern. **Acq:** Purchase. **Dist:** Social Studies School Service; Zenger Media. $14.95.

Biography: George C. Scott: Power & Glory ????
Presents the A&E cable channel special on actor George C. Scott, which showcases his role in the movie "Patton" for which he won an Oscar that he purposefully rebuffed; his personal life was troubled as witnessed by his five marriages. 50m; DVD. **A:** Family. **P:** Entertainment. **U:** Home, CATV. **Mov-Ent:** Television Series, Documentary Films, Biography: Show Business. **Acq:** Purchase. **Dist:** A&E Television Networks L.L.C. $24.95.

Biography: George Custer: Showdown at Little Big Horn 2007
Examines the life of the ill-fated army commander, from his actions during the Civil War to his career as an Indian fighter and his last battle. 50m; DVD. **A:** Jr. High-Adult. **P:** Entertainment. **U:** Home. **Gen-Edu:** Documentary Films, History--U.S. **Acq:** Purchase. **Dist:** A&E Television Networks L.L.C.

Biography: George Jones ????
Presents the A&E cable channel special on country music singer George Jones, who has produced the most Top 40 hits in country music history earning him the nickname of the "Rolls Royce of Country Singers." Jones has battled alcohol and drug addiction along with a stormy relationship with ex-wife and country singer Tammy Wynette; includes home videos, concert footage, and private photographs. 50m; DVD. **A:** Jr. High-Adult. **P:** Entertainment. **U:** Home, CATV. **Mov-Ent:** Television Series, Documentary Films, Biography: Music. **Acq:** Purchase. **Dist:** A&E Television Networks L.L.C. $24.95.

Biography: George Lucas: Creating an Empire ????
Presents the A&E cable channel special on director, writer, and producer George Lucas, who was responsible for all six "Star Wars" movies and used his technical skills to found the groundbreaking special-effects company Industrial, Light, and Magic; includes interviews and clips. 100m; DVD. **A:** Family. **P:** Entertainment. **U:** Home, CATV. **Mov-Ent:** Television Series, Documentary Films, Biography: Show Business. **Acq:** Purchase. **Dist:** A&E Television Networks L.L.C. $29.95.

Biography: George Patton ????
A&E Biography combines interviews, still photography, live-action footage, reenactments, period art, and other documentary material to present historical figures and their achievements. Recommended for Grades 6-12. 45m; VHS. **A:** Jr. High-Sr. High. **P:** Education. **U:** Home, Institution. **Gen-Edu:** Biography, History--Modern. **Acq:** Purchase. **Dist:** Social Studies School Service; Zenger Media. $14.95.

Biography: George Reeves: The Perils of a Superhero ????
Presents the A&E cable channel special on actor George Reeves and his prominent role in the television series "Superman" in 1951; complications from a romantic triangle have been speculated as the cause of his death in 1959 though it was ruled a suicide. 50m; DVD. **A:** Jr. High-Adult. **P:** Entertainment. **U:** Home, CATV. **Mov-Ent:** Television Series, Documentary Films, Biography: Show Business. **Acq:** Purchase. **Dist:** A&E Television Networks L.L.C. $24.95.

Biography: George W. Bush ????
Presents the A&E cable channel special on President George W. Bush that covers his childhood, his ownership of the Texas Rangers, his time as governor of Texas, and the presidential campaign; includes interviews with confidantes, colleagues, and family including former President George H.W. Bush along with private photos and behind-the-scenes footage. 50m; DVD. **A:** Family. **P:** Entertainment. **U:** Home, CATV. **Mov-Ent:** Television Series, Documentary Films, History--U.S. **Acq:** Purchase. **Dist:** A&E Television Networks L.L.C. $24.95.

Biography: George Washington ????
A&E Biography combines interviews, still photography, live-action footage, reenactments, period art, and other documentary material to present historical figures and their achievements. Recommended for Grades 6-12. 45m; VHS. **A:** Jr. High-Sr. High. **P:** Education. **U:** Home, Institution. **Gen-Edu:** Biography, Presidency, History--U.S. **Acq:** Purchase. **Dist:** Social Studies School Service; Zenger Media. $14.95.

Biography: George Washington: American Revolutionary 2006
Extensive archival material highlights the life and career of the revolutionary who went from serving in a British regiment to leading a new nation. 50m; DVD. **A:** Jr. High-Adult. **P:** Entertainment. **U:** Home. **Gen-Edu:** Documentary Films, History--U.S. **Acq:** Purchase. **Dist:** A&E Television Networks L.L.C.

Biography: Gerald Ford: Healing the Presidency ????
Presents the A&E cable channel special on former President Gerald Ford, who took over the office after Richard Nixon's resignation and helped to rebuild the office in the wake of the Watergate scandal; includes interviews with aides, Cabinet members, and family. 50m; DVD. **A:** Family. **P:** Entertainment. **U:** Home, CATV. **Mov-Ent:** Television Series, Documentary Films, Biography: Politics. **Acq:** Purchase. **Dist:** A&E Television Networks L.L.C. $19.96.

Biography: Geronimo 2007
Explores the life and legacy of the Apache warrior who fought a 10-year battle with the army rather than settle on a reservation. 50m; DVD. **A:** Jr. High-Adult. **P:** Entertainment. **U:** Home. **Gen-Edu:** Documentary Films, Native Americans. **Acq:** Purchase. **Dist:** A&E Television Networks L.L.C.

Biography: Giorgio Armani: Deconstructing Fashion 2006
Presents the A&E cable channel special on Italian fashion designer Giorgio Armani, who became known when his suits were featured in the popular 1980 film "American Gigilo"; includes interviews, presents many of his designs, and behind-the-scenes footage. 50m; DVD. **A:** Jr. High-Adult. **P:** Entertainment. **U:** Home, CATV. **Mov-Ent:** Television Series, Documentary Films, Biography. **Acq:** Purchase. **Dist:** A&E Television Networks L.L.C. $24.95.

Biography: Gloria Vanderbilt: An Heir of Style ????
Presents the A&E cable channel special on fashion designer and socialite Gloria Vanderbilt, who was born into wealth as the daughter of railroad heir Reginald Claypoole Vanderbilt, but his early death led to a custody dispute between her mother and aunt; despite her success with her designer clothing line, she struggled with three failed marriages and the presumed suicide of her son, who jumped from her penthouse as she watched. Vanderbilt is also the mother of CNN anchor Anderson Cooper. Includes interviews with Vanderbilt, family, and friends. 50m; DVD. **A:** Jr. High-Adult. **P:** Entertainment. **U:** Home, CATV. **Mov-Ent:** Television Series, Documentary Films, Biography: Artists. **Acq:** Purchase. **Dist:** A&E Television Networks L.L.C. $24.95.

Biography: Grace Kelly: Hollywood Princess 1999
Presents the A&E cable channel special on actress Grace Kelly, who shined in movies such as "High Noon," "Rear Window," and "The Country Girl" (for which she won the Oscar for best actress) but gave up on her career when she married Prince Rainier III of Monaco and became Princess Grace until her death at age 52 due to an automobile accident. 50m; DVD. **A:** Family. **P:** Entertainment. **U:** Home, CATV. **Mov-Ent:** Television Series, Documentary Films, Biography: Show Business. **Acq:** Purchase. **Dist:** A&E Television Networks L.L.C. $24.95.

Biography: Greta Garbo: The Mysterious Lady ????
Presents the A&E cable channel special on the life of actress Greta Garbo, who starred in silent films and continued her career once talkies arrived; intensely private, she was nearly as well-known for her reclusive behavior off-screen as she was for her work on-screen. 50m; DVD. **A:** Family. **P:** Entertainment. **U:** Home, CATV. **Mov-Ent:** Television Series, Documentary Films, Biography: Show Business. **Acq:** Purchase. **Dist:** A&E Television Networks L.L.C. $24.95.

Biography: Hank Williams, Jr. ????
Presents the A&E cable channel special on country music singer Hank Williams Jr., best known for his theme song for "Monday Night Football" ("Are You Ready for Some Football?") though he began performing at the age of 8; follows the personal troubles he encountered, including the death of his famous father (Hank Williams) when he was 3 years old and his depression and suicide attempts as a young man along as well as the serious injuries he sustained from a hiking accident. He overcame those adversities to top the charts in the 1980s, winning the Country Music Association's Entertainer of the Year Award along with several Grammys. 50m; DVD. **A:** Jr. High-Adult. **P:** Entertainment. **U:** Home, CATV. **Mov-Ent:** Television Series, Documentary Films, Biography: Music. **Acq:** Purchase. **Dist:** A&E Television Networks L.L.C. $24.95.

Biography: Hap Arnold: The Sky Warrior ????
Presents the A&E cable channel special on aviator Henry Harley "Hap" Arnold, who was known as the "father" of the U.S. Air Force; includes interviews with family and friends as well as newsreel and archival footage. 50m; DVD. **A:** Family. **P:** Entertainment. **U:** Home, CATV. **Mov-Ent:** Television Series, Documentary Films, Military History. **Acq:** Purchase. **Dist:** A&E Television Networks L.L.C. $24.95.

Biography: Harlem Globetrotters: America's Court Jesters 2005
They started playing basketball in Chicago in 1927 and continue to serve as worldwide goodwill ambassadors. Includes interviews and footage of past and present players. 50m; DVD. **A:** Jr. High-Adult. **P:** Entertainment. **U:** Home. **Gen-Edu:** Documentary Films, Biography: Sports. **Acq:** Purchase. **Dist:** A&E Television Networks L.L.C.

Biography: Harley-Davidson ????
Presents the A&E cable channel special on American motorcycle maker Harley-Davidson Motor Company, created in 1901 by friends William S. Harley and Arthur Davidson in Milwaukee, Wisconsin. 50m; DVD. **A:** Jr. High-Adult. **P:** Entertainment. **U:** Home, CATV. **Mov-Ent:** Television Series, Documentary Films, Motorcycles. **Acq:** Purchase. **Dist:** A&E Television Networks L.L.C. $24.95.

Biography: Harold Shipman 20??
Presents the A&E cable channel special on serial killer Harold Shipman, an English doctor believed to have murdered 215 patients via lethal injection, with the majority of those being female; his crimes possibly began in the late 1970s but came to light in 1998 after being named a sole beneficiary of an elderly woman he had been treating. Shipman committed suicide in his jail cell in 2004. 50m; DVD. **A:** Sr. High-Adult. **P:** Entertainment. **U:** Home, CATV. **Mov-Ent:** Television Series, Documentary Films, Biography. **Acq:** Purchase. **Dist:** A&E Television Networks L.L.C. $24.95.

Biography: Harrison Ford ????
Presents the A&E cable channel special on actor Harrison Ford from his late start in the movie business to his box office successes in "American Graffiti," "Star Wars," "Indiana Jones," "The Fugitive," and as Jack Ryan in "Patriot Games" and "Clear and Present Danger." 100m; DVD. **A:** Family. **P:** Entertainment. **U:** Home, CATV. **Mov-Ent:** Television Series, Documentary Films, Biography: Show Business. **Acq:** Purchase. **Dist:** A&E Television Networks L.L.C. $29.95.

Biography: Harry S Truman ????
A&E Biography combines interviews, still photography, live-action footage, reenactments, period art, and other documentary material to present historical figures and their achievements. Recommended for Grades 6-12. 45m; VHS. **A:** Jr. High-Sr. High. **P:** Education. **U:** Home, Institution. **Gen-Edu:** Biography, Presidency, History--U.S. **Acq:** Purchase. **Dist:** Zenger Media; Social Studies School Service. $14.95.

Biography: Hatfields & McCoys: An American Feud ????
Presents the A&E cable channel special on the clash between the Hatfield and McCoy families, who lived on the Kentucky and West Virginia border in the late 1800s and whose fighting resulted in about a dozen deaths; includes interviews with historians and descendents. 50m; DVD. **A:** Sr. High-Adult. **P:** Entertainment. **U:** Home, CATV. **Mov-Ent:** Television Series, Documentary Films, History--U.S. **Acq:** Purchase. **Dist:** A&E Television Networks L.L.C. $24.95.

Biography: Helen Gurley Brown ????
Presents the A&E cable channel special on author, publisher, and businesswoman Helen Gurley Brown, known for such books as "Sex and the Single Girl" and for her successful run as editor-in-chief of "Cosmopolitan" magazine from the mid-1960s to the mid-1990s, where she continues to serve as an editor; includes interviews with Judith Krantz, Gloria Steinem, Liz Smith, and Burt Reynolds, among others. 50m; DVD. **A:** Sr. High-Adult. **P:** Entertainment. **U:** Home, CATV. **Mov-Ent:** Television Series, Documentary Films, Women. **Acq:** Purchase. **Dist:** A&E Television Networks L.L.C. $24.95.

Biography: Helen Thomas: The First Lady of the Press ????
Presents the A&E cable channel special on White House journalist Helen Thomas, who has covered U.S. presidents since Kennedy and has served as the United Press International's (UPI) bureau chief since 1974; includes interviews with Thomas along with colleagues Sam Donaldson, Judy Woodruff, George Stephanopoulos, and Pierre Salinger. 50m; DVD. **A:** Jr. High-Adult. **P:** Entertainment. **U:** Home, CATV. **Mov-Ent:** Television Series, Documentary Films, Politics & Government. **Acq:** Purchase. **Dist:** A&E Television Networks L.L.C. $24.95.

Biography: Henri de Toulouse-Lautrec ????
Presents the A&E cable channel special on the short life of French painter Henri de Toulouse-Lautrec, from his early gift for art to accidents suffered as a child that caused his legs to not grow properly to his sudden death from alcoholism; includes interviews with historians. 50m; DVD. **A:** Jr. High-Adult. **P:** Entertainment. **U:** Home, CATV. **Mov-Ent:** Television Series, Documentary Films, Biography: Artists. **Acq:** Purchase. **Dist:** A&E Television Networks L.L.C. $24.95.

Biography: Henry Ford ????
A&E Biography combines interviews, still photography, live-action footage, reenactments, period art, and other documentary material to present historical figures and their achievements. Recommended for Grades 6-12. 45m; VHS. **A:** Jr. High-Sr. High. **P:** Education. **U:** Home, Institution. **Gen-Edu:** Biography, History, Business. **Acq:** Purchase. **Dist:** Social Studies School Service; Zenger Media. $14.95.

Biography: Henry Hill: Goodfella ????
Presents the A&E cable channel special on former gangster Henry Hill, who became an FBI informant and whose life was documented in the 1986 Nicholas Pileggi book "Wiseguy," which was turned into the popular 1990 Martin Scorsese film "Goodfellas" starring Ray Liotta as Hill; includes an interview with Hill. 50m; DVD. **A:** Sr. High-Adult. **P:** Entertainment. **U:** Home, CATV. **Mov-Ent:** Television Series, Documentary Films, Biography. **Acq:** Purchase. **Dist:** A&E Television Networks L.L.C. $24.95.

Biography: Henry VIII ????
A&E Biography combines interviews, still photography, live-action footage, reenactments, period art, and other documentary material to present historical figures and their achievements. Recommended for Grades 6-12. 45m; VHS. **A:** Jr. High-Sr. High. **P:** Education. **U:** Home, Institution. **Gen-Edu:** Biography, History. **Acq:** Purchase. **Dist:** Social Studies School Service; Zenger Media. $14.95.

Biography: Hercules: Power of the Gods ????
Presents the A&E cable channel special on mythological figure Hercules, son of the god Zeus and mortal woman Alcmene, while examining his fabled twelve labors. 50m; DVD. **A:** Family. **P:** Entertainment. **U:** Home, CATV. **Mov-Ent:** Television Series, Documentary Films. **Acq:** Purchase. **Dist:** A&E Television Networks L.L.C. $24.95.

Biography: H.G. Wells: Time Traveler 2006
Presents the A&E cable channel special on English author H.G. Wells (1866-1946), who was best known for his science fiction tales such as "The Time Machine," "The Invisible Man," and "The War of the Worlds," but who also wrote history and political commentary. 50m; DVD. **A:** Jr. High-Adult. **P:** Entertainment. **U:** Home, CATV. **Mov-Ent:** Television Series, Documentary Films, Biography. **Acq:** Purchase. **Dist:** A&E Television Networks L.L.C. $24.95.

Biography: Hillary R. Clinton 1994
A&E Biography combines interviews, still photography, live-action footage, reenactments, period art, and other documentary material to present historical figures and their achievements. Recommended for Grades 6-12. 45m; VHS. **A:** Jr. High-Sr. High. **P:** Education. **U:** Home, Institution. **Gen-Edu:** Biography, History--Modern. **Acq:** Purchase. **Dist:** Social Studies School Service; Zenger Media. $14.95.

Biography: Ho Chi Minh ????
A&E Biography combines interviews, still photography, live-action footage, reenactments, period art, and other documentary material to present historical figures and their achievements. Recommended for Grades 6-12. 45m; VHS. **A:** Jr. High-Sr. High. **P:** Education. **U:** Home, Institution. **Gen-Edu:** Biography, History--Modern. **Acq:** Purchase. **Dist:** Social Studies School Service; Zenger Media. $14.95.

Biography: Howard Hughes 19??
A look at the life of enigmatic American tycoon Hughes, from aviator, inventor, and Hollywood producer, to eccentric recluse. 50m; VHS. **Pr:** A&E (Arts & Entertainment) Network. **A:** Sr. High-Adult. **P:** Entertainment. **U:** Home. **Gen-Edu:** Biography, Business. **Acq:** Purchase. **Dist:** A&E Television Networks L.L.C.; New Video Group. $19.95.

Biography: Howard Schultz and Starbucks ????
Presents the A&E cable channel special on Howard Schultz, who purchased the popular Seattle-based coffee chain Starbucks in 1987 from its original owners and since has put the company on the worldwide map; traces his life from his roots growing up in a poor Brooklyn neighborhood. 50m; DVD. **A:** Jr. High-Adult. **P:** Entertainment. **U:** Home, CATV. **Mov-Ent:** Television Series, Documentary Films, Food Industry. **Acq:** Purchase. **Dist:** A&E Television Networks L.L.C. $24.95.

Biography: Howard Stern 20??
Presents the A&E cable channel special on radio "shock jock" Howard Stern, known for his outrageous antics on his morning show that was also previously televised; features his high-priced move to the fledgling Sirius satellite radio. Includes interviews and footage. 50m; DVD. **A:** Jr. High-Adult. **P:** Entertainment. **U:** Home, CATV. **Mov-Ent:** Television Series, Documentary Films, Biography: Show Business. **Acq:** Purchase. **Dist:** A&E Television Networks L.L.C. $24.95.

Biography: Huey Long ????
A&E Biography combines interviews, still photography, live-action footage, reenactments, period art, and other documentary material to present historical figures and their achievements. Recommended for Grades 6-12. 45m; VHS. **A:** Jr. High-Sr. High. **P:** Education. **U:** Home, Institution. **Gen-Edu:** Biography, History--Modern. **Acq:** Purchase. **Dist:** Social Studies School Service; Zenger Media. $14.95.

Biography: Hugh Hefner: American Playboy ????
Presents the A&E cable channel special on "Playboy" creator Hugh Hefner, including his journey to success along with personal struggles such as the break-up of his first marriage and the effects of a stroke; includes interviews with Camille Paglia, Ray Bradbury, his daughter, and his ex-wife. 50m; DVD. **A:** Jr. High-Adult. **P:** Entertainment. **U:** Home, CATV. **Mov-Ent:** Television Series, Documentary Films, Biography: Show Business. **Acq:** Purchase. **Dist:** A&E Television Networks L.L.C. $24.95.

Biography: Humphrey Bogart 2006
Profiles the actor from his 1899 birth into a blue-blood Manhattan family to a movie career specializing in tough guys and loners. 50m; DVD. **A:** Jr. High-Adult. **P:** Entertainment. **U:** Home. **Fin-Art:** Documentary Films, Biography: Show Business. **Acq:** Purchase. **Dist:** A&E Television Networks L.L.C.

Biography: Ian Fleming ????
Presents the A&E cable channel special on British author Ian Fleming, best known for creating the James Bond character along with writing the children's book "Chitty Chitty Bang Bang"; profiles his various occupations (banker, reporter, intelligence officer, among others) prior to finishing his first novel at 43. 50m; DVD. **A:** Jr. High-Adult. **P:** Entertainment. **U:** Home, CATV. **Mov-Ent:** Television Series, Documentary Films, Biography. **Acq:** Purchase. **Dist:** A&E Television Networks L.L.C. $24.95.

Biography: Irving Berlin—An American Song 2000
This installment from the A&E series "Biography" examines the life of composer Irving Berlin. 100m; VHS. **A:** Jr. High-Adult. **P:** Education. **U:** Home. **Gen-Edu:** Biography, Music. **Acq:** Purchase. **Dist:** A&E Television Networks L.L.C. $14.95.

Biography: Ivan the Terrible ????
A&E Biography combines interviews, still photography, live-action footage, reenactments, period art, and other documentary material to present historical figures and their achievements. Recommended for Grades 6-12. 45m; VHS. **A:** Jr. High-Sr. High. **P:** Education. **U:** Home, Institution. **Gen-Edu:** Biography, History. **Acq:** Purchase. **Dist:** Social Studies School Service; Zenger Media. $14.95.

Biography: J. Edgar Hoover 199?
From the A&E television series "Biography" comes this look at the controversial, longtime FBI director. Includes interviews with Julian Bond, Kathleen Cleaver, and several FBI agents. 50m; VHS. **Pr:** A&E (Arts & Entertainment) Network. **A:** Jr. High-Adult. **P:** Entertainment. **U:** Home. **Gen-Edu:** Documentary Films, Biography, History--U.S. **Acq:** Purchase. **Dist:** A&E Television Networks L.L.C.; New Video Group. $19.95.

Biography: J. Pierpont Morgan: Emperor of Wall Street ????
Presents the A&E cable channel special on American banker J. Pierpont Morgan (aka J.P. Morgan), who entered banking during the late 1850s and built a phenomenally successful business; Morgan was also responsible for providing significant financial aid to the U.S. government. Includes rare footage and interviews with biographers and historians. 50m; DVD. **A:** Jr. High-Adult. **P:** Entertainment. **U:** Home, CATV. **Mov-Ent:** Television Series, Documentary Films, Finance. **Acq:** Purchase. **Dist:** A&E Television Networks L.L.C. $24.95.

Biography: Jack Ruby 20??
Presents the A&E cable channel special on assassin Jack Ruby, who shot and killed President John F. Kennedy's alleged assassin Lee Harvey Oswald in 1963 on live television as Oswald was being transferred from his jail cell; includes footage of the event and interviews with Ruby's brother Earl and others. 50m; DVD. **A:** Sr. High-Adult. **P:** Entertainment. **U:** Home, CATV. **Mov-Ent:** Television Series, Documentary Films, Biography. **Acq:** Purchase. **Dist:** A&E Television Networks L.L.C. $24.95.

Biography: Jackie Robinson 199?
Looks at the Baseball Hall of Famer from his college and professional athlete career to his civil rights activity in both sports and the military. 50m; VHS. **A:** Family. **P:** Entertainment. **U:** Home. **Spo-Rec:** Biography, Baseball, Black Culture. **Acq:** Purchase. **Dist:** A&E Television Networks L.L.C.; New Video Group. $19.95.

Biography: Jackson Pollock ????
Presents the A&E cable channel special on abstract expressionist artist Jackson Pollock, whose began using his famous "drip paintings" technique in the late 1940s; however, he suffered from alcoholism and his life ended tragically in a 1956 automobile crash. Includes interviews with family and friends. 50m; DVD. **A:** Family. **P:** Entertainment. **U:** Home, CATV. **Mov-Ent:** Television Series, Documentary Films, Biography: Artists. **Acq:** Purchase. **Dist:** A&E Television Networks L.L.C. $24.95.

Biography: Jacqueline Kennedy Onassis 19??
Focuses on the very private widow of President John F. Kennedy and Greek tycoon Aristotle Onassis. Features interviews with Dan Rather, Mike Wallace, Phil Donahue, William F. Buckley, and Maya Angelou. 60m; VHS. **C:** Hosted by Peter Graves. **Pr:** A&E (Arts & Entertainment) Network. **A:** Jr. High-Adult. **P:** Entertainment. **U:** Home. **Gen-Edu:** Documentary Films, Biography, Women. **Acq:** Purchase. **Dist:** A&E Television Networks L.L.C.; New Video Group. $19.95.

Biography: Jacques Chirac ????
Presents the A&E cable channel special on former French president Jacques Chirac from his entrance into public service to scandals while in office along with his stance against the Iraq war; includes interviews and archival footage. 50m; DVD. **A:** Family. **P:** Entertainment. **U:** Home, CATV. **Mov-Ent:** Television Series, Documentary Films, Biography: Politics. **Acq:** Purchase. **Dist:** A&E Television Networks L.L.C. $24.95.

Biography: James Dean 2005
Profiles the legendary actor who defined rebellion in the 1950s, despite his brief career and death at age 24. 100m; DVD. **A:** Jr. High-Adult. **P:** Entertainment. **U:** Home. **Fin-Art:** Documentary Films, Biography: Show Business. **Acq:** Purchase. **Dist:** A&E Television Networks L.L.C.

Biography: James Garner: Hollywood Maverick ????
Presents the A&E cable channel special on actor James Garner, who began his long and varied career in television as "Maverick" and later in "The Rockford Files" along with dozens of films. 50m; DVD. **A:** Family. **P:** Entertainment. **U:** Home, CATV. **Mov-Ent:** Television Series, Documentary Films, Biography: Show Business. **Acq:** Purchase. **Dist:** A&E Television Networks L.L.C. $24.95.

Biography: Jan & Dean: The Other Beach Boys 2002
Presents the A&E cable channel special on singers Jan Berry and Dean Torrance, known as Jan & Dean, whose California-surfer sound in the late 1950s and early 1960s predated the Beach Boys; includes interviews and concert footage. 50m; DVD. **A:** Family. **P:** Entertainment. **U:** Home, CATV. **Mov-Ent:** Television Series, Documentary Films, Biography: Show Business. **Acq:** Purchase. **Dist:** A&E Television Networks L.L.C. $24.95.

Biography: Jane Austen 2006
Biography of the novelist whose six works about life in Georgian England are appreciated to the present day and frequently adapted for films and television. 50m; DVD. **A:** Jr. High-Adult. **P:** Entertainment. **U:** Home. **Gen-Edu:** Documentary Films, Biography. **Acq:** Purchase. **Dist:** A&E Television Networks L.L.C.

Biography: Janet Leigh ????
Presents the A&E cable channel special on actress Janet Leigh, a horror film legend for her role in the movie "Psycho"; includes interviews with former husband, actor Tony Curtis, and daughter, actress Jamie Lee Curtis. 50m; DVD. **A:** Jr. High-Adult. **P:** Entertainment. **U:** Home, CATV. **Mov-Ent:** Television Series, Documentary Films, Biography: Show Business. **Acq:** Purchase. **Dist:** A&E Television Networks L.L.C. $24.95.

Biography: J.C. Penney: Main Street Millionaire ????
Presents the A&E cable channel special on retail executive J.C. Penney, who established his popular chain stores in the early 1900s though he faced financial devastation only to rebound using his faith; includes interviews with his daughters along with video clips and photos. 50m; DVD. **A:** Jr. High-Adult. **P:** Entertainment. **U:** Home, CATV. **Mov-Ent:** Television Series, Documentary Films, Biography. **Acq:** Purchase. **Dist:** A&E Television Networks L.L.C. $24.95.

Biography: Jeff Bridges: Building Bridges ????
Presents the A&E cable channel special on actor Jeff Bridges, son of actor Lloyd Bridges and brother of actor Beau Bridges, who has starred in several successful films such as "Against All Odds," "Starman," "Tucker: The Man and His Dream," and "The Big Lebowski" and has founded the charitable organization End Hunger Network; includes interviews and home movies. 50m; DVD. **A:** Family. **P:** Entertainment. **U:** Home, CATV. **Mov-Ent:** Television Series, Documentary Films, Biography: Show Business. **Acq:** Purchase. **Dist:** A&E Television Networks L.L.C. $24.95.

Biography: Jeffrey Archer 20??
Presents the A&E cable channel special on Jeffrey Archer, a popular British author and former politician in the Conservative party who faced disgrace after a perjury charge in 2000 for a libel suit he had won in the late 1980s. 50m; DVD. **A:** Jr. High-Adult. **P:** Entertainment. **U:** Home, CATV. **Mov-Ent:** Television Series, Documentary Films, Biography: Politics. **Acq:** Purchase. **Dist:** A&E Television Networks L.L.C. $24.95.

Biography: Jeffrey Dahmer: The Monster Within ????
Presents the A&E cable channel special on serial killer Jeffrey Dahmer, who confessed to the murders and cannibalization of 17 men and boys from 1978 to 1991; includes interviews with psychologists, police, and his parents along with crime scene photos. 50m; DVD. **A:** Sr. High-Adult. **P:** Entertainment. **U:** Home, CATV. **Mov-Ent:** Television Series, Documentary Films, Biography. **Acq:** Purchase. **Dist:** A&E Television Networks L.L.C. $24.95.

Biography: Jeopardy! 20??
Presents the A&E cable channel special on the popular television game show "Jeopardy" hosted by Alex Trebek, including the longest and most successful contestant run by Ken Jennings; includes interviews with former contestants. 50m; DVD. **A:** Family. **P:** Entertainment. **U:** Home, CATV. **Mov-Ent:** Television Series, Documentary Films, Biography: Show Business. **Acq:** Purchase. **Dist:** A&E Television Networks L.L.C. $24.95.

Biography: Jerry Lewis ????
Presents the A&E cable channel special on legendary comedian and performer Jerry Lewis, from his early movie success to his time with Dean Martin along with his charitable work as the spokesman for the Muscular Dystrophy Association; includes interviews with Lewis, friends, and family as well as movie clips. 100m; DVD. **A:** Family. **P:** Entertainment. **U:** Home, CATV. **Mov-Ent:** Television Series, Documentary Films, Biography: Show Business. **Acq:** Purchase. **Dist:** A&E Television Networks L.L.C. $29.95.

Biography: Jesse Jackson 1995
A&E Biography combines interviews, still photography, live-action footage, reenactments, period art, and other documentary material to present historical figures and their achievements. Recommended for Grades 6-12. 45m; VHS. **A:** Jr. High-Sr. High. **P:** Education. **U:** Home, Institution. **Gen-Edu:** Biography, History--Modern. **Acq:** Purchase. **Dist:** Social Studies School Service; Zenger Media. $14.95.

Biography: Jessica Lange: On Her Own Terms ????
Presents the A&E cable channel special on actress Jessica Lange, who has starred in numerous movies such as "Tootsie," "The Postman Always Rings Twice," and "Blue Sky"; includes interviews of family and friends along with photographs and clips. 50m; DVD. **A:** Family. **P:** Entertainment. **U:** Home, CATV. **Mov-Ent:** Television Series, Documentary Films, Biography: Show Business. **Acq:** Purchase. **Dist:** A&E Television Networks L.L.C. $24.95.

Biography: JFK: A Personal Story 1997
Revisits moments of JFK's life and presidency through archival footage and interviews with journalists, celebrities, and White House aides. 100m; VHS. **A:** Adult. **P:** Education. **U:** Home. **Gen-Edu:** Biography, Presidency. **Acq:** Purchase. **Dist:** 411 Video Information. $19.95.

Biography: Jim Jones: Journey into Madness ????
Presents the A&E cable channel special on mass murderer and religious figure Jim Jones, who in 1978 was responsible the murder-suicides of 911 followers in the Jonestown, Guyana, community he established; includes footage and possible evidence that the victims did not commit suicide as was initially speculated. 50m; DVD. **A:** Sr. High-Adult. **P:** Entertainment. **U:** Home, CATV. **Mov-Ent:** Television Series, Documentary Films, Suicide. **Acq:** Purchase. **Dist:** A&E Television Networks L.L.C. $24.95.

Biography: Jimmy Carter 1995
A&E Biography combines interviews, still photography, live-action footage, reenactments, period art, and other documentary material to present historical figures and their achievements. Recommended for Grades 6-12. 45m; VHS. **A:** Jr. High-Sr. High. **P:** Education. **U:** Home, Institution. **Gen-Edu:** Biography, Presidency, History--U.S. **Acq:** Purchase. **Dist:** Social Studies School Service; Zenger Media. $14.95.

Biography: Jimmy Connors ????
Presents the A&E cable channel special on American tennis champion Jimmy Connors, known for his aggressive and animated style of play; includes footage of memorable matches and interviews with his competitors. 50m; DVD. **A:** Family. **P:** Entertainment. **U:** Home, CATV. **Mov-Ent**: Television Series, Documentary Films, Tennis. **Acq:** Purchase. **Dist:** A&E Television Networks L.L.C. $24.95.

Biography: Jimmy Doolittle: King of the Sky 2007
Looks at the life of the army pilot who helped develop more reliable aeronautical designs and equipment. Covers his heroics in World War II, including the first air attack on the Japanese mainland. 50m; DVD. **A:** Jr. High-Adult. **P:** Entertainment. **U:** Home. **Gen-Edu**: Documentary Films, Biography: Military. **Acq:** Purchase. **Dist:** A&E Television Networks L.L.C.

Biography: Jimmy Hoffa: The Man Behind the Mystery ????
Presents the A&E cable channel special on U.S. labor leader Jimmy Hoffa and discusses his ties to organized crime that tarnished his reputation, put him under scrutiny from President John F. Kennedy's administration, and possibly led to his unresolved disappearance in 1975; includes interviews with FBI agents, Kennedy's press secretary, a former suspect in Hoffa's disappearance, and Hoffa's son and daughter. 50m; DVD. **A:** Family. **P:** Entertainment. **U:** Home, CATV. **Mov-Ent**: Television Series, Documentary Films, Biography. **Acq:** Purchase. **Dist:** A&E Television Networks L.L.C. $24.95.

Biography: Jimmy Swaggart: Fire and Brimstone ????
Presents the A&E cable channel special on controversial television evangelist Jimmy Swaggart, who had built an enormous following since his early religious beginnings as an 8-year-old speaking in tongues and predicting the future; however, his immense popularity suffered after two involvements with prostitutes were publicized; includes interviews with colleagues including Tammy Faye Bakker and Reverend Jerry Falwell. 50m; DVD. **A:** Family. **P:** Entertainment. **U:** Home, CATV. **Mov-Ent**: Television Series, Documentary Films, Religion. **Acq:** Purchase. **Dist:** A&E Television Networks L.L.C. $24.95.

Biography: Joan of Arc ????
A&E Biography combines interviews, still photography, live-action footage, reenactments, period art, and other documentary material to present historical figures and their achievements. Recommended for Grades 6-12. 45m; VHS. **A:** Jr. High-Sr. High. **P:** Education. **U:** Home, Institution. **Gen-Edu**: Biography, History. **Acq:** Purchase. **Dist:** Social Studies School Service; Zenger Media. $14.95.

Biography: Joe Bonanno: The Last Godfather ????
Presents the A&E cable channel special on American organized crime boss, Joe Bonanno, who began his infamous Mafia Commission in 1931 and in 1983 authored a memoir; includes interviews with law enforcement and members of the crime family, an interview with Bonanno, archival footage, and news accounts. 50m; DVD. **A:** Sr. High-Adult. **P:** Entertainment. **U:** Home, CATV. **Mov-Ent**: Television Series, Documentary Films, Biography. **Acq:** Purchase. **Dist:** A&E Television Networks L.L.C. $24.95.

Biography: Joe DiMaggio 19??
A look at a baseball legend, from his 56-game hitting streak to his brief marriage to Marily Monroe. Includes interviews with Mickey Mantle, Art Buchwald, Ralph Nader, and Marvin Hamlisch. 60m; VHS. **Pr:** A&E (Arts & Entertainment) Network. **A:** Jr. High-Adult. **P:** Entertainment. **U:** Home. **Spo-Rec**: Documentary Films, Biography, Baseball. **Acq:** Purchase. **Dist:** A&E Television Networks L.L.C.; New Video Group. $19.95.

Biography: John and Abigail Adams: Love and Liberty 2005
Explores the life of the couple through their marriage, the American Revolution, and John's term as the nation's second president. Includes interviews with descendants, politicians, and biographers. 50m; DVD. **A:** Jr. High-Adult. **P:** Entertainment. **U:** Home. **Gen-Edu**: Documentary Films. **Acq:** Purchase. **Dist:** A&E Television Networks L.L.C.

Biography: John Dillinger ????
Presents the A&E cable channel special on American criminal John Dillinger, who was notorious for his violent bank robberies and numerous jail escapes during the 1920s and 1930s until he was shot to death by FBI agents in 1934; includes archival footage and photos. 50m; DVD. **A:** Sr. High-Adult. **P:** Entertainment. **U:** Home, CATV. **Mov-Ent**: Television Series, Documentary Films, Biography. **Acq:** Purchase. **Dist:** A&E Television Networks L.L.C. $24.95.

Biography: John F. Kennedy, Jr.: Child of a Dream ????
Presents the A&E cable channel special on John F. Kennedy, Jr., from his early life during his father's presidency and assassination to the tragic airplane crash he piloted that took his life; includes interviews with friends, Kennedy family experts, White House photographer Cecil Staughton, reporter Helen Thomas, and former Kennedy administration press secretary Pierre Salinger. 50m; DVD. **A:** Family. **P:** Entertainment. **U:** Home, CATV. **Mov-Ent**: Television Series, Documentary Films, Politics & Government. **Acq:** Purchase. **Dist:** A&E Television Networks L.L.C. $24.95.

Biography: John J. Pershing: The Iron General ????
Presents the A&E cable channel special on John J. Pershing, who served as the commander of the American armies during World War I after a military career that began as a frontier fighter against the Indians and a tragic person life with the loss of his wife and three daughters. 50m; DVD. **A:** Jr. High-Adult. **P:** Entertainment. **U:** Home, CATV. **Mov-Ent**: Television Series, Documentary Films, World War One. **Acq:** Purchase. **Dist:** A&E Television Networks L.L.C. $24.95.

Biography: John Kerry 20??
Presents the A&E cable channel special on U.S. Senator John Kerry, from his early family life to his time at Yale then his service in the Vietnam War through his unsuccessful bid for the presidency in 2004 as the Democratic nominee; includes interviews. 50m; DVD. **A:** Family. **P:** Entertainment. **U:** Home, CATV. **Mov-Ent**: Television Series, Documentary Films, Politics & Government. **Acq:** Purchase. **Dist:** A&E Television Networks L.L.C. $24.95.

Biography: John McCain: American Maverick ????
Presents the A&E cable channel special on U.S. politician and former POW John McCain, who overcame his five-year imprisonment by the Vietnamese during the war to become Arizona's U.S. senator in 1986; covers his survival of the 1989 "Keating Five" scandal; includes interviews with McCain and his colleagues. 50m; DVD. **A:** Family. **P:** Entertainment. **U:** Home, CATV. **Mov-Ent**: Television Series, Documentary Films, Politics & Government. **Acq:** Purchase. **Dist:** A&E Television Networks L.L.C. $19.96.

Biography: John Paul Jones ????
A&E Biography combines interviews, still photography, live-action footage, reenactments, period art, and other documentary material to present historical figures and their achievements. Recommended for Grades 6-12. 45m; VHS. **A:** Jr. High-Sr. High. **P:** Education. **U:** Home, Institution. **Gen-Edu**: Biography, History--U.S. **Acq:** Purchase. **Dist:** Social Studies School Service; Zenger Media. $14.95.

Biography: John Ritter: In Good Company 2002
Presents the A&E cable channel special on comedic actor John Ritter, best known for his role in the television sitcom "Three's Company" (1976-1984) as well as movies such as "Problem Child" and "Sling Blade," and who voiced Clifford on the PBS animated television series "Clifford the Big Red Dog"; includes clips and interviews (show aired a year before his death in September 2003). 50m; DVD. **A:** Family. **P:** Entertainment. **U:** Home, CATV. **Mov-Ent**: Television Series, Documentary Films, Biography: Show Business. **Acq:** Purchase. **Dist:** A&E Television Networks L.L.C. $24.95.

Biography: John Stamos 2004
Presents the A&E cable channel special on actor John Stamos, who gained popularity as Uncle Jesse on the long-running ABC television sitcom "Full House" (1987-1995); includes family and friend interviews, photographs, and clips. 50m; DVD. **A:** Family. **P:** Entertainment. **U:** Home, CATV. **Mov-Ent**: Television Series, Documentary Films, Biography: Show Business. **Acq:** Purchase. **Dist:** A&E Television Networks L.L.C. $24.95.

Biography: John Wayne: American Legend 1987
Presents the A&E cable channel special on iconic actor John "The Duke" Wayne, who starred in about 250 movies, mostly westerns, including "The Alamo" and "True Grit," for which he won an Academy Award for best actor; includes interviews. 50m; DVD. **A:** Family. **P:** Entertainment. **U:** Home, CATV. **Mov-Ent**: Television Series, Documentary Films, Biography: Show Business. **Acq:** Purchase. **Dist:** A&E Television Networks L.L.C. $24.95.

Biography: John Wayne Gacy: A Monster in Disguise ????
Presents the A&E cable channel special on serial killer John Wayne Gacy, who raped and murdered 33 boys and young men and buried most of them in the crawl space under his suburban Chicago home before his arrest in 1978; he was executed via lethal injection in 1994. Includes interviews and archival materials. 50m; DVD. **A:** Sr. High-Adult. **P:** Entertainment. **U:** Home, CATV. **Mov-Ent**: Television Series, Documentary Films, Biography. **Acq:** Purchase. **Dist:** A&E Television Networks L.L.C. $24.95.

Biography: John Wilkes Booth ????
A&E Biography combines interviews, still photography, live-action footage, reenactments, period art, and other documentary material to present historical figures and their achievements. Recommended for Grades 6-12. 45m; VHS. **A:** Jr. High-Sr. High. **P:** Education. **U:** Home, Institution. **Gen-Edu**: Biography, History--U.S. **Acq:** Purchase. **Dist:** Social Studies School Service; Zenger Media. $14.95.

Biography: Johnnie Cochran: The Best Defense ????
Presents the A&E cable channel special on lawyer Johnnie Cochran, who is best known as O.J. Simpson's defense lawyer in his 1995 murder trial. Also covers Cochran's career as a prosecutor as well as a defense lawyer for Sean "Diddy" Combs and Rosa Parks; includes interviews with Combs and F. Lee Bailey. 50m; DVD. **A:** Jr. High-Adult. **P:** Entertainment. **U:** Home, CATV. **Mov-Ent**: Television Series, Documentary Films, Biography: Show Business. **Acq:** Purchase. **Dist:** A&E Television Networks L.L.C. $24.95.

Biography: Johnny Cash 2005
Looks at the life and career of the country music legend, from his birth in 1932 through his career renaissance in the 1990s. Includes performance footage and interviews. 50m; DVD. **A:** Jr. High-Adult. **P:** Entertainment. **U:** Home. **Fin-Art**: Documentary Films, Biography: Music. **Acq:** Purchase. **Dist:** A&E Television Networks L.L.C.

Biography: Johnny Depp 2006
A look at the life and career of the actor who went from teen TV idol to being known for his eccentric film choices. 50m; DVD. **A:** Jr. High-Adult. **P:** Entertainment. **U:** Home. **Fin-Art**: Documentary Films, Biography: Show Business. **Acq:** Purchase. **Dist:** A&E Television Networks L.L.C.

Biography: Jonathan Harris: Never Fear, Smith Is Here ????
Presents the A&E cable channel special on actor Johnathan Harris, who starred as a kooky Dr. Smith in the futuristic television series "Lost in Space" (1965-1968) and later voiced in many animated cartoons; includes interviews, photographs, and clips. 50m; DVD. **A:** Family. **P:** Entertainment. **U:** Home, CATV. **Mov-Ent**: Television Series, Documentary Films, Biography: Show Business. **Acq:** Purchase. **Dist:** A&E Television Networks L.L.C. $24.95.

Biography: Joseph McCarthy ????
A&E Biography combines interviews, still photography, live-action footage, reenactments, period art, and other documentary material to present historical figures and their achievements. Recommended for Grades 6-12. 45m; VHS. **A:** Jr. High-Sr. High. **P:** Education. **U:** Home, Institution. **Gen-Edu**: Biography, History--Modern. **Acq:** Purchase. **Dist:** Social Studies School Service; Zenger Media. $14.95.

Biography: Joseph Stalin ????
A&E Biography combines interviews, still photography, live-action footage, reenactments, period art, and other documentary material to present historical figures and their achievements. Recommended for Grades 6-12. 45m; VHS. **A:** Jr. High-Sr. High. **P:** Education. **U:** Home, Institution. **Gen-Edu**: Biography, History--Modern. **Acq:** Purchase. **Dist:** Social Studies School Service; Zenger Media. $14.95.

Biography: Joseph "The Rat" Valachi ????
Presents the A&E cable channel special on former mobster Joseph Valachi, known for validating the existence of the Mafia during 1963 congressional committee testimony; includes interviews with experts and law enforcement along with footage of his testimony. 50m; DVD. **A:** Sr. High-Adult. **P:** Entertainment. **U:** Home, CATV. **Mov-Ent**: Television Series, Documentary Films, Biography. **Acq:** Purchase. **Dist:** A&E Television Networks L.L.C. $24.95.

Biography: Josip Broz Tito 2006
Examines the life and career of the totalitarian dictator, who defied both East and West to rule Yugoslavia for more than 40 years. 50m; DVD. **A:** Jr. High-Adult. **P:** Entertainment. **U:** Home. **Gen-Edu**: Documentary Films, Biography: Politics. **Acq:** Purchase. **Dist:** A&E Television Networks L.L.C.

Biography: Julia Child 2005
Traces the life of French cooking expert and renowned TV chef Child from her childhood through her career. 50m; DVD. **A:** Jr. High-Adult. **P:** Entertainment. **U:** Home. **Gen-Edu**: Documentary Films, Biography. **Acq:** Purchase. **Dist:** A&E Television Networks L.L.C.

Biography: Julius Caesar: Master of the Roman World 2006
The life and legacy of the Roman ruler, from his military conquests to his murder. 50m; DVD. **A:** Jr. High-Adult. **P:** Entertainment. **U:** Home. **Gen-Edu**: Documentary Films, History--Ancient. **Acq:** Purchase. **Dist:** A&E Television Networks L.L.C.

Biography: J.W. Marriott: Host to the World ????
Presents the A&E cable channel special on businessman John Willard Marriott, founder of the highly-successful hotel and restaurant chain Marriott Corp.; includes interviews with sons J.W. Marriott, Jr. and Richard Marriott, granddaughter Debbie Harrison, and his friend Rev. Billy Graham. 50m; DVD. **A:** Jr. High-Adult. **P:** Entertainment. **U:** Home, CATV. **Mov-Ent**: Television Series, Documentary Films, Hotels & Hotel Staff Training. **Acq:** Purchase. **Dist:** A&E Television Networks L.L.C. $24.95.

Biography: Katharine Graham: Pillar of the Post 2006
Presents the A&E cable channel special on the life of Katharine Graham, who served as the powerful and influential publisher of the "Washington Post" from 1963 to 1993. She assumed the position at the company owned by her father when the former publisher, her husband Philip Graham, committed suicide. 50m; DVD. **A:** Jr. High-Adult. **P:** Entertainment. **U:** Home, CATV. **Mov-Ent**: Television Series, Documentary Films, Women. **Acq:** Purchase. **Dist:** A&E Television Networks L.L.C. $24.95.

Biography: Katharine Hepburn: On Her Own Terms 2005
Presents the A&E cable channel special on legendary actress Katharine Hepburn, who starred in movies for six decades including "Little Women," "Philadelphia Story," "Guess Who's Coming to Dinner," and "On Golden Pond" and also received four Academy Awards during her career; includes home movies, film outtakes, and interviews with friends and family. 50m; DVD. **A:** Family. **P:** Entertainment. **U:** Home, CATV. **Mov-Ent**: Television Series, Documentary Films, Biography: Show Business. **Acq:** Purchase. **Dist:** A&E Television Networks L.L.C. $24.95.

Biography: Kathie Lee Gifford: Having It All 1999
Presents the A&E cable channel special on entertainer Kathie Lee Gifford, best known as the former co-host of "Live with Regis and Kathie Lee" with Regis Philbin as well as a singer and Vegas performer; includes the troubles she encountered when it was discovered that her clothing line was produced by overseas sweatshops though without her knowledge. Includes interviews with Philbin and Helen Gurley Brown, among others. 50m; DVD. **A:** Family. **P:** Entertainment. **U:** Home, CATV.

Mov-Ent: Television Series, Documentary Films, Biography: Show Business. **Acq:** Purchase. **Dist:** A&E Television Networks L.L.C. $24.95.

Biography: Keanu Reeves ????
Presents the A&E cable channel special on actor Keanu Reeves, who appeared in the goofy flick "Bill and Ted's Excellent Adventure" before later becoming an action-movie hero in "Speed" and "The Matrix" trilogy; includes clips and interviews with family and friends. 50m; DVD. **A:** Jr. High-Adult. **P:** Entertainment. **U:** Home, CATV. **Mov-Ent:** Television Series, Documentary Films, Biography: Show Business. **Acq:** Purchase. **Dist:** A&E Television Networks L.L.C. $24.95.

Biography: Kevin Costner 2006
Presents the A&E cable channel special on actor and director Kevin Costner, whose career has experienced great success, such as the film "Dances with Wolves" (which won the best picture and director awards for him), as well as several notable box office disappointments. 50m; DVD. **A:** Family. **P:** Entertainment. **U:** Home, CATV. **Mov-Ent:** Television Series, Documentary Films, Biography: Show Business. **Acq:** Purchase. **Dist:** A&E Television Networks L.L.C. $24.95.

Biography: Kevin Spacey ????
Presents the A&E cable channel special on actor Kevin Spacey, who won the Academy Award for his roles in "Unusual Suspects" and "American Beauty" as well as a Tony for the play "Lost in Yonkers"; includes interviews, photographs, and file footage. 50m; DVD. **A:** Family. **P:** Entertainment. **U:** Home, CATV. **Mov-Ent:** Television Series, Documentary Films, Biography: Show Business. **Acq:** Purchase. **Dist:** A&E Television Networks L.L.C. $24.95.

Biography: Kim Jong Il ????
Presents the A&E cable channel special on North Korean dictator Kim Jong-il, who succeeded his father Kim Il-sung, the founder of Democratic People's Republic of Korea, in 1994 though not officially until 1997; traces his early life through his rise in his father's regime to his unusual fondness for American action films. Includes interviews with experts. 50m; DVD. **A:** Jr. High-Adult. **P:** Entertainment. **U:** Home, CATV. **Mov-Ent:** Television Series, Documentary Films, Politics & Government. **Acq:** Purchase. **Dist:** A&E Television Networks L.L.C. $24.95.

Biography: King Arthur ????
A&E Biography combines interviews, still photography, live-action footage, reenactments, period art, and other documentary material to present historical figures and their achievements. Recommended for Grades 6-12. 45m; VHS. **A:** Jr. High-Sr. High. **P:** Education. **U:** Home, Institution. **Gen-Edu:** Biography, History. **Acq:** Purchase. **Dist:** Social Studies School Service; Zenger Media. $14.95.

Biography: Lance Armstrong: Racing for His Life 2005
The story of cyclist Armstrong's comeback from his 1996 cancer diagnosis and treatment to his multiple wins at the Tour de France. 50m; DVD. **A:** Jr. High-Adult. **P:** Entertainment. **U:** Home. **Gen-Edu:** Documentary Films, Biography: Sports. **Acq:** Purchase. **Dist:** A&E Television Networks L.L.C.

Biography: Larry Flynt: Fighting Dirty 2006
The life and career of "Hustler" founder Flynt, including his landmark Supreme Court case over First Amendment rights. Includes interviews. 50m; DVD. **A:** Jr. High-Adult. **P:** Entertainment. **U:** Home. **Gen-Edu:** Documentary Films, Biography. **Acq:** Purchase. **Dist:** A&E Television Networks L.L.C.

Biography: Larry Hagman 2004
Presents the A&E cable channel special on actor Larry Hagman, best known for his role of J.R. Ewing on the television drama "Dallas" (1978-1991) though his acting career began in the late 1950s; includes interviews and clips. 50m; DVD. **A:** Jr. High-Adult. **P:** Entertainment. **U:** Home, CATV. **Mov-Ent:** Television Series, Documentary Films, Biography: Show Business. **Acq:** Purchase. **Dist:** A&E Television Networks L.L.C. $24.95.

Biography: Laura Bush ????
Presents the A&E cable channel special on the life of First Lady Laura Bush; includes interviews with her and husband President George W. Bush. 50m; DVD. **A:** Family. **P:** Entertainment. **U:** Home, CATV. **Mov-Ent:** Television Series, Documentary Films, History--U.S. **Acq:** Purchase. **Dist:** A&E Television Networks L.L.C. $24.95.

Biography: LeAnn Rimes ????
Presents the A&E cable channel special on country singer LeAnn Rimes, who was an overnight sensation at the age of 13 with the album "Blue" and continues to be successful in the industry as she also pursuing an acting career; profiles her problematic relationship with her father/manager along with her marriage to a backup dancer; includes interviews, footage, and photographs. 50m; DVD. **A:** Jr. High-Adult. **P:** Entertainment. **U:** Home, CATV. **Mov-Ent:** Television Series, Documentary Films, Biography: Music. **Acq:** Purchase. **Dist:** A&E Television Networks L.L.C. $24.95.

Biography: Lech Walesa ????
Presents the A&E cable channel special on Lech Walesa, the former president of Poland who founded the labor union Solidarity in 1980 at a time when such groups were illegal; he also received the Nobel Peace Prize in 1983. Includes interviews with family, friends, and colleagues along with video footage. 50m; DVD. **A:** Family. **P:** Entertainment. **U:** Home, CATV. **Mov-Ent:** Television Series, Documentary Films, Biography: Politics. **Acq:** Purchase. **Dist:** A&E Television Networks L.L.C. $24.95.

Biography: Leif Ericson: Voyages of a Viking ????
Presents the A&E cable channel special on Norwegian explorer Leif Ericson, son of Eric the Red, who is believed to have discovered portions of North America some 500 years prior to Christopher Columbus; provides evidence to support this claim by archeologist Anne Ingstad. Includes interviews with scholars as well as a tour of the site. 50m; DVD. **A:** Family. **P:** Entertainment. **U:** Home, CATV. **Mov-Ent:** Television Series, Documentary Films, Biography. **Acq:** Purchase. **Dist:** A&E Television Networks L.L.C. $24.95.

Biography: Leona Helmsley: Queen of the Palace ????
Presents the A&E cable channel special on hotelier Leona Helmsley, known as "the Queen of Mean" for her business manner and alleged mistreatment of employees; she served prison time for tax evasion in the late 1980s; includes interviews with biographers, lawyers, Helmsley, and her husband Harry Helmsley (note: recorded prior to her death in 2007). 50m; DVD. **A:** Jr. High-Adult. **P:** Entertainment. **U:** Home, CATV. **Mov-Ent:** Television Series, Documentary Films, Hotels & Hotel Staff Training. **Acq:** Purchase. **Dist:** A&E Television Networks L.L.C. $24.95.

Biography: Leonardo da Vinci: Renaissance Master ????
Presents the A&E cable channel special on Italian artist and scientist Leonardo da Vinci; includes an examination of journals, notes, and sketches. Features interviews with biographers and art historians. 50m; DVD. **A:** Jr. High-Adult. **P:** Entertainment. **U:** Home, CATV. **Mov-Ent:** Television Series, Documentary Films, Biography: Artists. **Acq:** Purchase. **Dist:** A&E Television Networks L.L.C. $24.95.

Biography: Lewis & Clark ????
A&E Biography combines interviews, still photography, live-action footage, reenactments, period art, and other documentary material to present historical figures and their achievements. Recommended for Grades 6-12. 45m; VHS. **A:** Jr. High-Sr. High. **P:** Education. **U:** Home, Institution. **Gen-Edu:** Biography, History--U.S. **Acq:** Purchase. **Dist:** Social Studies School Service; Zenger Media. $14.95.

Biography: Lewis & Clark—Explorers of the New Frontier 2000
This installment from the A&E series "Biography" examines the lives of American explorers Meriwether Lewis and William Clark. 50m; VHS. **A:** Jr. High-Adult. **P:** Education. **U:** Home. **Gen-Edu:** Biography, History--U.S. **Acq:** Purchase. **Dist:** A&E Television Networks L.L.C. $14.95.

Biography: Liza Minnelli 2004
Presents the A&E cable channel special on legendary actress, singer, and performer Liza Minnelli, from her childhood with her famous parents (actress Judy Garland and director Vincente Minnelli) to her successful career, including Tony and Grammy awards along with an Oscar for best actress in the 1972 film "Cabaret"; also profiles her personal struggles with addiction and four failed marriages. Includes interviews with family and friends, such as Martin Scorsese, Beyonce Knowles, Robert De Niro, Goldie Hawn, and Mia Farrow. 100m; DVD. **A:** Family. **P:** Entertainment. **U:** Home, CATV. **Mov-Ent:** Television Series, Documentary Films, Biography: Show Business. **Acq:** Purchase. **Dist:** A&E Television Networks L.L.C. $29.95.

Biography: Lizzie Borden: A Woman Accused ????
Presents the A&E cable channel special on alleged murderer Lizzie Borden, who was accused but acquitted of the horrific 1892 killings of her father and stepmother with an axe; includes period accounts, police reports, and crime-scene photos. 50m; DVD. **A:** Sr. High-Adult. **P:** Entertainment. **U:** Home, CATV. **Mov-Ent:** Television Series, Documentary Films, Biography. **Acq:** Purchase. **Dist:** A&E Television Networks L.L.C. $24.95.

Biography: Lloyd Bridges: Lights, Camera, Family 1999
Presents the A&E cable channel special on actor Lloyd Bridges (1913-1988), who had roles in more than 150 films, including the popular "Airplane!" parodies, as well as numerous television series such as "Sea Hunt" (1957-1961); he is also the father of actors Beau and Jeff Bridges. Includes home movies, family interviews, and film clips. 50m; DVD. **A:** Jr. High-Adult. **P:** Entertainment. **U:** Home, CATV. **Mov-Ent:** Television Series, Documentary Films, Biography: Show Business. **Acq:** Purchase. **Dist:** A&E Television Networks L.L.C. $24.95.

Biography: Loretta Lynn: True Story of the Coal Miner's Daughter 2005
Presents the A&E cable channel special on country music legend Loretta Lynn, who famously escaped the hard life in a coal-miners' town to become one of Nashville's most celebrated singers, with 57 Top 20 country songs; includes interviews, concert footage, and photographs. 50m; DVD. **A:** Jr. High-Adult. **P:** Entertainment. **U:** Home, CATV. **Mov-Ent:** Television Series, Documentary Films, Biography: Music. **Acq:** Purchase. **Dist:** A&E Television Networks L.L.C. $24.95.

Biography: Louis B. Mayer ????
Presents the A&E cable channel special on Louis B. Mayer, one of the founders of film studio Metro-Goldwyn-Mayer (MGM) in 1924 after beginning his career by creating movie cinemas; includes interviews. 50m; DVD. **A:** Jr. High-Adult. **P:** Entertainment. **U:** Home, CATV. **Mov-Ent:** Television Series, Documentary Films, Filmmaking. **Acq:** Purchase. **Dist:** A&E Television Networks L.L.C. $24.95.

Biography: Louis Lepke ????
Presents the A&E cable channel special on American gangster Louis Lepke (aka Louis Lepke Buchalter), whose violent narcotics syndicate and murderous operation during the 1930s led to his execution in 1944; includes interviews with biographers, reporters, and friends along with archival footage and period accounts. 50m; DVD. **A:** Sr. High-Adult. **P:** Entertainment. **U:** Home, CATV. **Mov-Ent:** Television Series, Documentary Films, Biography. **Acq:** Purchase. **Dist:** A&E Television Networks L.L.C. $24.95.

Biography: Lowell Thomas: Man about the World ????
Presents the A&E cable channel special on broadcaster and filmmaker Lowell Thomas, known for his radio newscasts along with popular newsreels beginning in the 1930s along with his earlier coverage of British militaryman and writer T.E. Lawrence (the impetus of the 1962 movie "Lawrence of Arabia") with whom he spent several weeks in the desert. 50m; DVD. **A:** Family. **P:** Entertainment. **U:** Home, CATV. **Mov-Ent:** Television Series, Documentary Films, Biography: Show Business. **Acq:** Purchase. **Dist:** A&E Television Networks L.L.C. $24.95.

Biography: Lucky Luciano: Chairman of the Mob ????
Presents the A&E cable channel special on Italian-American gangster Charles "Lucky" Luciano, who was known for using a businesslike approach to running his infamous Murders, Inc.; he was able to negotiate his release from prison by assisting the government during World War II with the condition that he reside in his native Italy for the remainder of his life. Includes interviews and archival footage. 50m; DVD. **A:** Sr. High-Adult. **P:** Entertainment. **U:** Home, CATV. **Mov-Ent:** Television Series, Documentary Films, Biography. **Acq:** Purchase. **Dist:** A&E Television Networks L.L.C. $24.95.

Biography: Lucrezia Borgia: Pretty Poison 2007
The illegitimate daughter of the man who became Pope Alexander VI was married three times to further her father's political ambitions. But how did the eventual Duchess of Ferrara become a byword for depravity and what are the facts behind her infamy? 50m; DVD. **A:** Jr. High-Adult. **P:** Entertainment. **U:** Home. **Gen-Edu:** Documentary Films, Biography: Politics. **Acq:** Purchase. **Dist:** A&E Television Networks L.L.C.

Biography: Lynda Carter ????
Presents the A&E cable channel special on actress Lynda Carter, best known for her work in the television series "Wonder Woman" (1975-1979) though she was also a singer; includes family and friend interviews, video clips, and photographs. 50m; DVD. **A:** Family. **P:** Entertainment. **U:** Home, CATV. **Mov-Ent:** Television Series, Documentary Films, Biography: Show Business. **Acq:** Purchase. **Dist:** A&E Television Networks L.L.C. $24.95.

Biography: Lyndon B. Johnson ????
A&E Biography combines interviews, still photography, live-action footage, reenactments, period art, and other documentary material to present historical figures and their achievements. Recommended for Grades 6-12. 45m; VHS. **A:** Jr. High-Sr. High. **P:** Education. **U:** Home, Institution. **Gen-Edu:** Biography, Presidency, History--U.S. **Acq:** Purchase. **Dist:** Social Studies School Service; Zenger Media. $14.95.

Biography: Ma Barker: Crime Family Values ????
Presents the A&E cable channel special on alleged criminal Kate "Ma" Barker, who was suspected of leading the ruthless Barker-Karpis Gang with her four sons during the 1930s and was killed by the FBI during a shootout; however, her actual involvement has since been disputed as a cover-up by the FBI for her death. Includes interviews with witnesses and family. 50m; DVD. **A:** Sr. High-Adult. **P:** Entertainment. **U:** Home, CATV. **Mov-Ent:** Television Series, Documentary Films, Biography. **Acq:** Purchase. **Dist:** A&E Television Networks L.L.C. $24.95.

Biography: Mahatma Gandhi ????
A&E Biography combines interviews, still photography, live-action footage, reenactments, period art, and other documentary material to present historical figures and their achievements. Recommended for Grades 6-12. 45m; VHS. **A:** Jr. High-Sr. High. **P:** Education. **U:** Home, Institution. **Gen-Edu:** Biography, History--Modern. **Acq:** Purchase. **Dist:** Social Studies School Service; Zenger Media. $14.95.

Biography: Mahatma Gandhi-Pilgrim of Peace 1997
Photos, news footage, historian insights, and interviews with the Dalai Lama and Ghandi's grandson provide insight into the life of a man who defeated an empire without firing a single shot. 50m; VHS. **A:** Sr. High. **P:** Education. **U:** Institution. **Gen-Edu:** Biography, India, History. **Acq:** Purchase. **Dist:** Social Studies School Service; Zenger Media. $14.95.

Biography: Malcolm X ????
A&E Biography combines interviews, still photography, live-action footage, reenactments, period art, and other documentary material to present historical figures and their achievements. Recommended for Grades 6-12. 45m; VHS. **A:** Jr. High-Sr. High. **P:** Education. **U:** Home, Institution. **Gen-Edu:** Biography, History--Modern. **Acq:** Purchase. **Dist:** Social Studies School Service; Zenger Media. $14.95.

Biography: Manuel Noriega: The Rise and Fall of Panama's Strongman 2006
Looks at the life of the Panamanian dictator, from his rise to power to his involvement in the drug trade, which lead to his arrest, trial, and imprisonment in Miami. 50m; DVD. **A:** Jr. High-Adult. **P:** Entertainment. **U:** Home. **Gen-Edu:** Documentary Films, Biography: Politics. **Acq:** Purchase. **Dist:** A&E Television Networks L.L.C.

Biography: Mao Tse Tung: China's Peasant Emperor 2006
Looks at the life of a farmer's son turned radical social reformer and dictator from the viewpoints of those who idolized China's ruler to those who suffered through the Cultural Revolution. 50m; DVD. **A:** Jr. High-Adult. **P:** Entertainment. **U:** Home. **Gen-Edu:** Documentary Films, Biography: Politics. **Acq:** Purchase. **Dist:** A&E Television Networks L.L.C.

Biography: Marco Polo ????
A&E Biography combines interviews, still photography, live-action footage, reenactments, period art, and other documentary material to present historical figures and their achievements. Recommended for Grades 6-12. 45m; VHS. **A:** Jr. High-Sr. High. **P:** Education. **U:** Home, Institution. **Gen-Edu:** Biography, History. **Acq:** Purchase. **Dist:** Social Studies School Service; Zenger Media. $14.95.

Biography: Marconi ????
A&E Biography combines interviews, still photography, live-action footage, reenactments, period art, and other documentary material to present historical figures and their achievements. Recommended for Grades 6-12. 45m; VHS. **A:** Jr. High-Sr. High. **P:** Education. **U:** Home, Institution. **Gen-Edu:** Biography, Scientists, Inventors & Inventions. **Acq:** Purchase. **Dist:** Zenger Media; Social Studies School Service. $14.95.

Biography: Marie Antionette ????
A&E Biography combines interviews, still photography, live-action footage, reenactments, period art, and other documentary material to present historical figures and their achievements. Recommended for Grades 6-12. 45m; VHS. **A:** Jr. High-Sr. High. **P:** Education. **U:** Home, Institution. **Gen-Edu:** Biography, History. **Acq:** Purchase. **Dist:** Social Studies School Service; Zenger Media. $14.95.

Biography: Marilyn Monroe: The Mortal Goddess 2004
Presents the A&E cable channel special on legendary actress Marilyn Monroe, who was as well known for her sexy on-screen roles as she was for her many off-screen relationships and marriages; includes interviews, home movies, and clips. 100m; DVD. **A:** Jr. High-Adult. **P:** Entertainment. **U:** Home, CATV. **Mov-Ent:** Television Series, Documentary Films, Biography: Show Business. **Acq:** Purchase. **Dist:** A&E Television Networks L.L.C. $29.95.

Biography: Marjorie Merriweather Post ????
Presents the A&E cable channel special on socialite, business-woman, and philanthropist Marjorie Merriweather Post, who took over her father Charles William Post's company upon his death when she was 27 and later helped to transform it into General Mills; she is also known for her four failed marriages, including one to financier E.F. Hutton, and for her lavish lifestyle. 50m; DVD. **A:** Jr. High-Adult. **P:** Entertainment. **U:** Home, CATV. **Mov-Ent:** Television Series, Documentary Films, Biography. **Acq:** Purchase. **Dist:** A&E Television Networks L.L.C. $24.95.

Biography: Marquis de Sade: The Depraved Aristocrat 2007
Donatien Alphonse Francois celebrated sexual deviancy in writings that landed him in prison for much of his life. Learn how the name of this nobleman became synonymous with sexual cruelty. 50m; DVD. **A:** Jr. High-Adult. **P:** Entertainment. **U:** Home. **Gen-Edu:** Documentary Films, Biography. **Acq:** Purchase. **Dist:** A&E Television Networks L.L.C.

Biography: Martin Luther King, Jr.-The Man and the Dream 1997
Documentary of Dr. King's life with location footage, interviews, and excerpts from his speeches. Exposes the struggle for civil rights and the conflict between his public and private personas. Recommended for Grades 7-12. 50m/B/W; VHS. **A:** Jr. High-Sr. High. **P:** Education. **U:** Institution, Home. **Gen-Edu:** History-- U.S., Biography, Black Culture. **Acq:** Purchase. **Dist:** Social Studies School Service; Zenger Media. $14.95.

Biography: Mary-Kate and Ashley Olsen ????
Presents the A&E cable channel special on actress twins Mary-Kate and Ashley Olsen, whose careers began in their shared television role of the cutesy youngest daughter Michelle Tanner on "Full House" (1987-1995) that later morphed into the creation of a billion-dollar entertainment company; includes family and friend interviews, video clips, and photographs. 50m; DVD. **A:** Family. **P:** Entertainment. **U:** Home, CATV. **Mov-Ent:** Television Series, Documentary Films, Biography: Show Business. **Acq:** Purchase. **Dist:** A&E Television Networks L.L.C. $24.95.

Biography: Mary Kay Letourneau: Out of Bounds ????
Presents the A&E cable channel special on former teacher Mary Kay Letourneau, who was convicted of statutory rape charges after her involvement with a 13-year-old student in 1997; the couple married after she served seven years in prison and she had two children with the student. Includes interviews with Letourneau, her former husband, former colleagues, psychiatrists, and a biographer. 50m; DVD. **A:** Sr. High-Adult. **P:** Entertainment. **U:** Home, CATV. **Mov-Ent:** Television Series, Documentary Films, Biography. **Acq:** Purchase. **Dist:** A&E Television Networks L.L.C. $24.95.

Biography: Mary Magdalene: The Hidden Apostle ????
Presents the A&E cable channel special on Mary Magdalene, a close female disciple of Jesus of Nazareth, and examines their relationship, including the myth that she was a prostitute; includes interviews with scholars and presents rare art, ancient texts, and research. 50m; DVD. **A:** Family. **P:** Entertainment. **U:**

Home, CATV. **Mov-Ent:** Television Series, Documentary Films, Religion. **Acq:** Purchase. **Dist:** A&E Television Networks L.L.C. $24.95.

Biography: Mary of Nazareth ????
Presents the A&E cable channel special on biblical figure Mary of Nazareth, the virgin mother of Jesus, including her marriage to Joseph and her witnessing the crucifixion of her son; includes interviews with biblical experts and historians. 50m; DVD. **A:** Family. **P:** Entertainment. **U:** Home, CATV. **Mov-Ent:** Television Series, Documentary Films, Religion. **Acq:** Purchase. **Dist:** A&E Television Networks L.L.C. $24.95.

Biography: Mata Hari: The Seductive Spy 2006
The dancer turned World War I spy was executed by a French firing squad, but did she deserve her fate? 50m; DVD. **A:** Jr. High-Adult. **P:** Entertainment. **U:** Home. **Gen-Edu:** Documentary Films, Biography. **Acq:** Purchase. **Dist:** A&E Television Networks L.L.C.

Biography: Matthew Broderick: Center Stage 2001
Presents the A&E cable channel special on stage and movie actor Matthew Broderick, who first received acclaim in the teenage-flick "Ferris Bueller's Day Off" and later in the Broadway play "The Producers." 50m; DVD. **A:** Family. **P:** Entertainment. **U:** Home, CATV. **Mov-Ent:** Television Series, Documentary Films, Biography: Show Business. **Acq:** Purchase. **Dist:** A&E Television Networks L.L.C. $24.95.

Biography: Mayflower Madam: The Sydney Biddle Barrows Story ????
Presents the A&E cable channel special on Sydney Biddle Barrows, who despite coming from a privileged upbringing as well as being a Mayflower descendent founded a "high-class" escort service in the late 1970s that was disbanded in the mid-1980s, after she pled guilty to prostitution charges; includes interviews with Barrows and friends. 50m; DVD. **A:** Jr. High-Adult. **P:** Entertainment. **U:** Home, CATV. **Mov-Ent:** Television Series, Documentary Films, Prostitution. **Acq:** Purchase. **Dist:** A&E Television Networks L.L.C. $24.95.

Biography: Meet the Royals: The Trouble with Harry 20??
Presents the A&E cable channel special on the life of Prince Harry—son of Prince Charles and the late Princess Diana— through his troubled teenaged years. Features interviews with classmates, family friends, and royal "watcher" Andrew Morton; hosted by Davy Jones of the Monkees. 50m; DVD. **A:** Jr. High-Adult. **P:** Entertainment. **U:** Home, CATV. **Mov-Ent:** Television Series, Documentary Films, Biography: Royalty. **Acq:** Purchase. **Dist:** A&E Television Networks L.L.C. $24.95.

Biography: Melvin Purvis: The Man Who Got Dillinger 2007
Looks at the ultimately unhappy fate of the FBI agent whose public exploits lead to a rift with boss J. Edgar Hoover and his being forced from the agency he helped to make famous. 50m; DVD. **A:** Jr. High-Adult. **P:** Entertainment. **U:** Home. **Gen-Edu:** Documentary Films, Biography: Law Enforcement. **Acq:** Purchase. **Dist:** A&E Television Networks L.L.C.

Biography: Michelangelo ????
Examines the life and masterpieces of the great artist. 50m; VHS. **A:** Sr. High-Adult. **P:** Education. **U:** Home, Institution. **Gen-Edu:** Art & Artists, Biography. **Acq:** Purchase. **Dist:** Crystal Productions. $14.95.

Biography: Michelangelo: Artist and Man ????
Presents the A&E cable channel special on Italian artist Michelangelo, best known for his marble sculpture "David" and the ceiling of the Sistine Chapel; includes interviews with art historians, museum curators, and Renaissance experts. 50m; DVD. **A:** Jr. High-Adult. **P:** Entertainment. **U:** Home, CATV. **Mov-Ent:** Television Series, Documentary Films, Biography: Artists. **Acq:** Purchase. **Dist:** A&E Television Networks L.L.C. $24.95.

Biography: Mike Tyson: Fallen Champ ????
Presents the A&E cable channel special on boxer Mike Tyson, who was as well known for his boxing success as his numerous troubles out of the ring, including his abusive of his former wife, actress Robin Givens, as well as being found guilty of rape in 1992; includes interviews with childhood friends, members of his "camp," and sports journalists. 50m; DVD. **A:** Jr. High-Adult. **P:** Entertainment. **U:** Home, CATV. **Mov-Ent:** Television Series, Documentary Films, Biography: Sports. **Acq:** Purchase. **Dist:** A&E Television Networks L.L.C. $24.95.

Biography: Mike Wallace: TV's Grand Inquisitor ????
Presents the A&E cable channel special on broadcast journalist Mike Wallace, who has appeared as co-host of "60 Minutes" since 1968, where he developed a tough-nosed interview approach; follows his early career in radio broadcast and his move into the then-new television medium. Includes interviews with colleagues, family, and friends as well as video clips. 50m; DVD. **A:** Jr. High-Adult. **P:** Entertainment. **U:** Home, CATV. **Mov-Ent:** Television Series, Documentary Films, Journalism. **Acq:** Purchase. **Dist:** A&E Television Networks L.L.C. $24.95.

Biography: Milton Hershey ????
A&E Biography combines interviews, still photography, live-action footage, reenactments, period art, and other documentary material to present historical figures and their achievements. Recommended for Grades 6-12. 45m; VHS. **A:** Jr. High-Sr. High. **P:** Education. **U:** Home, Institution. **Gen-Edu:** Biography, History, Business. **Acq:** Purchase. **Dist:** Social Studies School Service; Zenger Media. $14.95.

Biography: Mitzi Gaynor: Hollywood's Cockeyed Optimist 2002
Presents the A&E cable channel special on actress Mitzi Gaynor, who was well-known for her role in the movie "South Pacific" but later became a Vegas star as she had trouble getting cinematic work; also highlights her personal life from her involvement with Howard Hughes to her long marriage to Jack Bean. 50m; DVD. **A:** Family. **P:** Entertainment. **U:** Home, CATV. **Mov-Ent:** Television Series, Documentary Films, Biography: Show Business. **Acq:** Purchase. **Dist:** A&E Television Networks L.L.C. $24.95.

Biography: Molly Brown: An American Legend ????
Presents the A&E cable channel special on American philanthropist, socialite, and social reformer Molly Brown, who became known for her courage during the sinking of the Titanic during 1912; she also lobbied for women's rights; includes period accounts. 50m; DVD. **A:** Family. **P:** Entertainment. **U:** Home, CATV. **Mov-Ent:** Television Series, Documentary Films, Women. **Acq:** Purchase. **Dist:** A&E Television Networks L.L.C. $24.95.

Biography: Montgomery Clift: The Hidden Star 1999
Presents the A&E cable channel special on actor Montgomery Clift, who appeared in several popular movies including "A Place in the Sun," "From Here to Eternity," "The Misfits," and "Judgment at Nuremberg" though his career was overshadowed by his personal dilemmas including addiction and sexuality issues; includes phone conversations between him and his mother (per recordings made by his brother) as well as clips and interviews. 50m; DVD. **A:** Jr. High-Adult. **P:** Entertainment. **U:** Home, CATV. **Mov-Ent:** Television Series, Documentary Films, Biography: Show Business. **Acq:** Purchase. **Dist:** A&E Television Networks L.L.C. $24.95.

Biography: Morgan Fairchild ????
Presents the A&E cable channel special on actress and activist Morgan Fairchild, who was known for her villainous roles on such television dramas as "Dallas" and "Falcon Crest"; in her personal life, she has been active in environmental, health, and women's issues. 50m; DVD. **A:** Family. **P:** Entertainment. **U:** Home, CATV. **Mov-Ent:** Television Series, Documentary Films, Biography: Show Business. **Acq:** Purchase. **Dist:** A&E Television Networks L.L.C. $24.95.

Biography: Moses ????
Presents the A&E cable channel special on biblical figure Moses, a Hebrew liberator and prophet who parted the Red Sea to save his people and was given the Ten Commandments by God; includes interviews with biblical experts as well as location footage, rare paintings, and artifacts. 100m; DVD. **A:** Family. **P:** Entertainment. **U:** Home, CATV. **Mov-Ent:** Television Series, Documentary Films, Religion. **Acq:** Purchase. **Dist:** A&E Television Networks L.L.C. $24.95.

Biography: Mother Teresa: A Life of Devotion ????
Presents the A&E cable channel special on religious figure and humanitarian Mother Teresa, who as a nun in Calcutta, India, worked extensively with orphans, the poor, and the dying, though the missionary she founded extended its work into 25 countries; in 1979 she won the Nobel Peace Prize. Includes interviews with world leaders and those who had known her as well as video footage. 50m; DVD. **A:** Family. **P:** Entertainment. **U:** Home, CATV. **Mov-Ent:** Television Series, Documentary Films, Religion. **Acq:** Purchase. **Dist:** A&E Television Networks L.L.C. $24.95.

Biography: Mozart 2004
Presents the A&E cable channel special on classical composer genius Wolfgang Amadeus Mozart, who struggled against his overbearing father and endured a downward spiral involving gambling and living beyond his means, leading to an early death at the age of 35; includes modern performances of his compositions. 50m; DVD. **A:** Jr. High-Adult. **P:** Entertainment. **U:** Home, CATV. **Mov-Ent:** Television Series, Documentary Films, Biography: Music. **Acq:** Purchase. **Dist:** A&E Television Networks L.L.C. $24.95.

Biography: Muhammad 2006
Theologians and historians look at the life of a merchant who founded a religion after receiving revelations from the angel Gabriel, and how Islam has been viewed through the ages. 50m; DVD. **A:** Jr. High-Adult. **P:** Entertainment. **U:** Home. **Gen-Edu:** Documentary Films, Biography: Religious Figures. **Acq:** Purchase. **Dist:** A&E Television Networks L.L.C.

Biography: Mussolini ????
A&E Biography combines interviews, still photography, live-action footage, reenactments, period art, and other documentary material to present historical figures and their achievements. Recommended for Grades 6-12. 45m; VHS. **A:** Jr. High-Sr. High. **P:** Education. **U:** Home, Institution. **Gen-Edu:** Biography, History--Modern. **Acq:** Purchase. **Dist:** Zenger Media; Social Studies School Service. $14.95.

Biography: Nancy Reagan: President's Leading Lady ????
Presents the A&E cable channel special on former First Lady Nancy Reagan, featuring her commitment to her husband Ronald Reagan during his presidency, her role in the administration, and how the actors first met in Hollywood; includes interviews with family, friends, and former White House staff members as well as video footage. 50m; DVD. **A:** Family. **P:** Entertainment. **U:** Home, CATV. **Mov-Ent:** Television Series, Documentary Films, Biography: Politics. **Acq:** Purchase. **Dist:** A&E Television Networks L.L.C. $24.95.

Biography: Napoleon Bonaparte—The Glory of France 2000
This installment from the A&E series "Biography" examines the life of French leader Napoleon Bonaparte. 50m; VHS. **A:** Jr. High-Adult. **P:** Education. **U:** Home. **Gen-Edu:** Biography, History. **Acq:** Purchase. **Dist:** A&E Television Networks L.L.C. $14.95.

Biography: Natalie Wood 2003
Presents the A&E cable channel special on actress Natalie Wood, who starred at the age of 9 in the classic "A Miracle on 34th Street" and at 17 years old in "Rebel Without a Cause." Her career continued as an adult with "Splendor in the Grass" and "West Side Story" until she accidentally drowned at age 43 while boating with her husband, Robert Wagner; includes behind-the-scenes footage and interviews with her two daughters, among others. 50m; DVD. **A:** Jr. High-Adult. **P:** Entertainment. **U:** Home, CATV. **Mov-Ent:** Television Series, Documentary Films, Biography: Show Business. **Acq:** Purchase. **Dist:** A&E Television Networks L.L.C. $24.95.

Biography: Neil Sedaka: The Show Goes On ????
Presents the A&E cable channel special on legendary pop singer, pianist, and songwriter Neil Sedaka, who had hits during the 1960s such as "Breaking Up Is Hard to Do" and "Calendar Girl" with Howard Greenfield; Sedaka also wrote for singer Connie Francis ("Stupid Cupid"); however, his career suffered when the so-called "British Invasion" took hold in the States. Includes photographs, interviews, and performance clips. 50m; DVD. **A:** Jr. High-Adult. **P:** Entertainment. **U:** Home, CATV. **Mov-Ent:** Television Series, Documentary Films, Biography: Music. **Acq:** Purchase. **Dist:** A&E Television Networks L.L.C. $24.95.

Biography: Neiman Marcus: Last of the Merchant Kings ????
Presents the A&E cable channel special on Dallas, Texas-based retail store Neiman Marcus, which was founded in 1907 by sister and brother Carrie Neiman and Herbert Marcus; includes interviews with family and historians as well as family photos and archival footage. 50m; DVD. **A:** Jr. High-Adult. **P:** Entertainment. **U:** Home, CATV. **Mov-Ent:** Television Series, Documentary Films, Business. **Acq:** Purchase. **Dist:** A&E Television Networks L.L.C. $24.95.

Biography: Nelson Mandela 1996
A&E Biography combines interviews, still photography, live-action footage, reenactments, period art, and other documentary material to present historical figures and their achievements. Recommended for Grades 6-12. 45m; VHS. **A:** Jr. High-Sr. High. **P:** Education. **U:** Home, Institution. **Gen-Edu:** Biography, History--Modern. **Acq:** Purchase. **Dist:** Social Studies School Service; Zenger Media. $14.95.

Biography: Nelson Rockefeller: Passionate Millionaire 2006
Looks at the life of the businessman, philanthropist, politician, and eventual vice president of the United States. 50m; DVD. **A:** Jr. High-Adult. **P:** Entertainment. **U:** Home. **Gen-Edu:** Documentary Films, Biography: Politics. **Acq:** Purchase. **Dist:** A&E Television Networks L.L.C.

Biography: Norman Rockwell ????
Examines the life and masterpieces of the great artist. 50m; VHS. **A:** Sr. High-Adult. **P:** Education. **U:** Home, Institution. **Gen-Edu:** Art & Artists, Biography. **Acq:** Purchase. **Dist:** Crystal Productions. $14.95.

Biography: Norman Vincent Peale: The Power of Positive Preaching ????
Presents the A&E cable channel special on Protestant preacher and author Dr. Norman Vincent Peale (1898-1993), most notable for his book "The Power of Positive Thinking," which fostered the a philosophy held popular with business executives to U.S. presidents and became the basis for the "self-help" movement in America; includes photographs and footage. 50m; DVD. **A:** Jr. High-Adult. **P:** Entertainment. **U:** Home, CATV. **Mov-Ent:** Television Series, Documentary Films, Biography. **Acq:** Purchase. **Dist:** A&E Television Networks L.L.C. $24.95.

Biography: Nostradamus: Prophet of Doom 2006
The medieval physician's legacy lies with the prophetic visions he wrote about in 900 poems. Did he predict some of history's most terrible events, including the end of the world? 50m; DVD. **A:** Jr. High-Adult. **P:** Entertainment. **U:** Home. **Gen-Edu:** Documentary Films, Biography. **Acq:** Purchase. **Dist:** A&E Television Networks L.L.C.

A Biography of Lilith 1997
Updates the creation myth through a story of the first woman and the first feminist. Contemplates Judaism and patriarchal history. 35m; VHS. **A:** College-Adult. **P:** Education. **U:** Institution. **Gen-Edu:** Women, Judaism. **Acq:** Purchase, Rent/Lease. **Dist:** Women Make Movies. $195.00.

Biography of the Unborn 1987
Find out what's going on during the development of a fertilized egg. 17m; VHS, 3/4 U. **A:** Jr. High-College. **P:** Education. **U:** Institution, SURA. **Hea-Sci:** Biology, Pregnancy. **Acq:** Purchase, Trade-in. **Dist:** Encyclopedia Britannica. $250.00.

Biography: Onassis Dynasty ????
Presents the A&E cable channel special on the Onassis family of Greece, beginning with patriarch Aristotle Onassis, who gained wealth through the construction of oil supertankers and caused controversy by marrying Jacqueline Kennedy, the widow of President John Kennedy; also covers the tragic deaths of his children, Alexander and Christina, as well as troubles that granddaughter Athina has had with her father, Thierry Roussell, in battling over the estate. 50m; DVD. **A:** Jr. High-Adult. **P:**

Entertainment. **U:** Home, CATV. **Mov-Ent:** Television Series, Documentary Films, Family. **Acq:** Purchase. **Dist:** A&E Television Networks L.L.C. $24.95.

Biography: Oscar Wilde: Wit's End 2005
Presents the A&E cable channel special on Irish writer Oscar Wilde (1854-1900), known for his vibrant works in poetry, novels, essays, plays, and children's stories as well as his scandalous personal life. 50m; DVD. **A:** Jr. High-Adult. **P:** Entertainment. **U:** Home, CATV. **Mov-Ent:** Television Series, Documentary Films, Biography. **Acq:** Purchase. **Dist:** A&E Television Networks L.L.C. $24.95.

Biography: Pablo Picasso'A Primitive Soul 2000
This installment from the A&E series "Biography" examines the life of painter Pablo Picasso. 100m; VHS. **A:** Jr. High-Adult. **P:** Education. **U:** Home. **Gen-Edu:** Biography, Art & Artists. **Acq:** Purchase. **Dist:** A&E Television Networks L.L.C. $14.95.

Biography: Pamela Anderson 2007
Profiles the life and career of the bombshell blonde, from her TV days to her activism for PETA and AIDS awareness and her tabloid scandals. 50m; DVD. **A:** Jr. High-Adult. **P:** Entertainment. **U:** Home. **Fin-Art:** Documentary Films, Biography: Show Business. **Acq:** Purchase. **Dist:** A&E Television Networks L.L.C.

Biography: Pancho Villa: Outlaw Hero 2006
Looks at the life of the outlaw who became a general during the Mexican revolution and the governor of Chihuahua. 50m; DVD. **A:** Jr. High-Adult. **P:** Entertainment. **U:** Home. **Gen-Edu:** Documentary Films, Biography. **Acq:** Purchase. **Dist:** A&E Television Networks L.L.C.

Biography: Paris Hilton 20??
Presents the A&E cable channel special on socialite Paris Hilton, best known for her exploits as a party-hopping heiress to the Hilton hotel empire as well as her forays into acting, singing, and modeling. Includes interviews and video footage. 50m; DVD. **A:** Jr. High-Adult. **P:** Entertainment. **U:** Home, CATV. **Mov-Ent:** Television Series, Documentary Films, Biography: Show Business. **Acq:** Purchase. **Dist:** A&E Television Networks L.L.C. $24.95.

Biography: Pat Tillman 20??
Presents the A&E cable channel special on football star and military man Pat Tillman, best known for leaving a successful NFL career behind to join the Army Rangers after the September 11 terrorist attacks; his death in the line of duty in 2004 not only saddened his family and the country, but also involved controversy and an alleged military cover-up. Includes interviews with family and friends, video clips, and coverage of the government's investigation into his death. 50m; DVD. **A:** Jr. High-Adult. **P:** Entertainment. **U:** Home, CATV. **Mov-Ent:** Television Series, Documentary Films, Biography: Sports. **Acq:** Purchase. **Dist:** A&E Television Networks L.L.C. $24.95.

Biography: Patricia Heaton ????
Presents the A&E cable channel special on television actress Patricia Heaton, best known for her role as the wife in Ray Romano's comedy "Everybody Loves Raymond"; includes interviews with family, friends, and her co-star Romano. 50m; DVD. **A:** Family. **P:** Entertainment. **U:** Home, CATV. **Mov-Ent:** Television Series, Documentary Films, Biography: Show Business. **Acq:** Purchase. **Dist:** A&E Television Networks L.L.C. $24.95.

Biography: Patrick Henry ????
A&E Biography combines interviews, still photography, live-action footage, reenactments, period art, and other documentary material to present historical figures and their achievements. Recommended for Grades 6-12. 45m; VHS. **A:** Jr. High-Sr. High. **P:** Education. **U:** Home, Institution. **Gen-Edu:** Biography, History--U.S. **Acq:** Purchase. **Dist:** Social Studies School Service; Zenger Media. $14.95.

Biography: Patrick Henry: Voice of Liberty 2007
Looks at the life of the founding father and legendary orator of "Give me liberty or give me death." 50m; DVD. **A:** Jr. High-Adult. **P:** Entertainment. **U:** Home. **Gen-Edu:** Documentary Films, History--U.S. **Acq:** Purchase. **Dist:** A&E Television Networks L.L.C.

Biography: Patrick Stewart: Make It So ????
Presents the A&E cable channel special on actor Patrick Stewart, whose career and life were transformed by the role of Captain Jean-Luc Picard on the television series "Star Trek: Next Generation" (1987-1994) even though he had been a member of the Royal Shakespeare Company for 20 years; he has also appeared in the movies "X-Men" and HBO's "Lion in Winter." Includes private footage, interviews with family and friends, and clips. 50m; DVD. **A:** Family. **P:** Entertainment. **U:** Home, CATV. **Mov-Ent:** Television Series, Documentary Films, Biography: Show Business. **Acq:** Purchase. **Dist:** A&E Television Networks L.L.C. $24.95.

Biography: Patrick Swayze: All the Right Moves 2000
Presents the A&E cable channel special on actor Patrick Swayze, who began his career after an injury forced him to give up his pursuit of dancing; best known for his roles in the unexpected movie hit "Dirty Dancing" as well as mega-success "Ghost"; includes dancing footage, film clips, and interviews of family and friends. 50m; DVD. **A:** Jr. High-Adult. **P:** Entertainment. **U:** Home, CATV. **Mov-Ent:** Television Series, Documentary Films, Biography: Show Business. **Acq:** Purchase. **Dist:** A&E Television Networks L.L.C. $24.95.

Biography: Patty Duke ????
Presents the A&E cable channel special on actress Patty Duke, who first made her name in show business portraying Helen

Keller in the 1962 film "The Miracle Worker" which won her a best supporting actress Oscar at the age of 16; thereafter, she starred in her self-titled television series. Her long and varied career continued despite being given the diagnosis of manic depression in 1982. Includes interviews with family and friends. 50m; DVD. **A:** Family. **P:** Entertainment. **U:** Home, CATV. **Mov-Ent:** Television Series, Documentary Films, Biography: Show Business. **Acq:** Purchase. **Dist:** A&E Television Networks L.L.C. $24.95.

Biography: Paul ????
Presents the A&E cable channel special on biblical figure Paul, an apostle who converted to Christianity to spread the word of Jesus and suffered for his preachings; includes interviews with biblical experts. 50m; DVD. **A:** Family. **P:** Entertainment. **U:** Home, CATV. **Mov-Ent:** Television Series, Documentary Films, Religion. **Acq:** Purchase. **Dist:** A&E Television Networks L.L.C. $24.95.

Biography: Paul Newman—Hollywood's Charming Rebel 1999
This program from A&E's popular "Biography" series examines the life of film actor Paul Newman. 50m; VHS. **A:** Jr. High-Adult. **P:** Entertainment. **U:** Home. **Gen-Edu:** Biography, Documentary Films, Biography: Show Business. **Acq:** Purchase. **Dist:** A&E Television Networks L.L.C. $14.95.

Biography: Paul Revere ????
A&E Biography combines interviews, still photography, live-action footage, reenactments, period art, and other documentary material to present historical figures and their achievements. Recommended for Grades 6-12. 45m; VHS. **A:** Jr. High-Sr. High. **P:** Education. **U:** Home, Institution. **Gen-Edu:** Biography, History--U.S. **Acq:** Purchase. **Dist:** Social Studies School Service; Zenger Media. $14.95.

Biography: Pervez Musharraf 20??
Presents the A&E cable channel special on Pervez Musharraf, who assumed power in Pakistan after a 1999 coup d'etat and became president in 2001; includes interviews with political insiders and diplomats along with footage and photos. 50m; DVD. **A:** Family. **P:** Entertainment. **U:** Home, CATV. **Mov-Ent:** Television Series, Documentary Films, Biography: Military. **Acq:** Purchase. **Dist:** A&E Television Networks L.L.C. $24.95.

Biography: Peter Graves: Mission Accomplished 2006
Presents the A&E cable channel special on actor Peter Graves (born Peter Aurness), who starred in the television show "Mission: Impossible" as Mr. Phelps from 1967-1973 as well as pilot Capt. Clarence Oveur in the movie parodies "Airplane!" and "Airplane II: The Sequel"; Graves also hosted the A&E "Biography" show from 1994-2005. 50m; DVD. **A:** Family. **P:** Entertainment. **U:** Home, CATV. **Gen-Edu:** Television Series, Documentary Films, Biography: Show Business. **Acq:** Purchase. **Dist:** A&E Television Networks L.L.C. $24.95.

Biography: Peter the Great: The Tyrant Reformer 2006
Archival material and scholarly research examine the contradictory life of the Russian ruler who was both tyrant and reformer during his 1696-1725 reign. 50m; DVD. **A:** Jr. High-Adult. **P:** Entertainment. **U:** Home. **Gen-Edu:** Documentary Films, Biography: Royalty. **Acq:** Purchase. **Dist:** A&E Television Networks L.L.C.

Biography: Phil Silvers: Top Banana 2006
Presents the A&E cable channel special on actor Phil Silvers, who received two Tonys for his Broadway show "Top Banana" and starred as Sgt. Ernest G. Bilko in television series "The Phil Silvers Show" (1955-1959); despite his successes, off-screen he was troubled by a gambling addiction as well as depression. Includes interviews with family and friends and video clips. 50m; DVD. **A:** Family. **P:** Entertainment. **U:** Home, CATV. **Mov-Ent:** Television Series, Documentary Films, Biography: Show Business. **Acq:** Purchase. **Dist:** A&E Television Networks L.L.C. $24.95.

Biography: Pocahontas ????
A&E Biography combines interviews, still photography, live-action footage, reenactments, period art, and other documentary material to present historical figures and their achievements. Recommended for Grades 6-12. 45m; VHS. **A:** Jr. High-Sr. High. **P:** Education. **U:** Home, Institution. **Gen-Edu:** Biography, History--U.S. **Acq:** Purchase. **Dist:** Zenger Media; Social Studies School Service. $14.95.

Biography: Pol Pot: Secret Killer 2006
Looks at the Cambodian dictator from his radical days in France in the 1950s to his control of the Khmer Rouge, who were responsible for the deaths of millions of Cambodians. 50m; DVD. **A:** Jr. High-Adult. **P:** Entertainment. **U:** Home. **Gen-Edu:** Documentary Films, Biography: Politics. **Acq:** Purchase. **Dist:** A&E Television Networks L.L.C.

Biography: Ponce De Leon ????
A&E Biography combines interviews, still photography, live-action footage, reenactments, period art, and other documentary material to present historical figures and their achievements. Recommended for Grades 6-12. 45m; VHS. **A:** Jr. High-Sr. High. **P:** Education. **U:** Home, Institution. **Gen-Edu:** Biography, History. **Acq:** Purchase. **Dist:** Social Studies School Service; Zenger Media. $14.95.

Biography: Pontius Pilate ????
Presents the A&E cable channel special on biblical figure Pontius Pilate, who was the judge responsible for sending Jesus to his crucifixion; examines his actual role and whether he was forced into his decision. Includes interviews with biblical scholars. 50m; DVD. **A:** Family. **P:** Entertainment. **U:** Home,

CATV. **Mov-Ent**: Television Series, Documentary Films, Religion. **Acq**: Purchase. **Dist**: A&E Television Networks L.L.C. $24.95.

Biography: Pretty Boy Floyd ????
Presents the A&E cable channel special on 1920s and 1930s outlaw Charles Arthur "Pretty Boy" Floyd, known as an American "Robin Hood" who was killed by the FBI in 1934; includes interviews with historians and family along with footage and period accounts. 50m; DVD. **A**: Sr. High-Adult. **P**: Entertainment. **U**: Home, CATV. **Mov-Ent**: Television Series, Documentary Films, Biography. **Acq**: Purchase. **Dist**: A&E Television Networks L.L.C. $24.95.

Biography: Priscilla Presley: Keeper of a Dream ????
Presents the A&E cable channel special on actress, author, and producer Priscilla Presley, who for years was only known as the wife of Elvis. After his death she created an enormous empire by converting Graceland, Elvis' estate, into a tourist destination and homage to "The King." Includes footage of Priscilla and Elvis together, photographs, and family and friend interviews. 50m; DVD. **A**: Family. **P**: Entertainment. **U**: Home, CATV. **Mov-Ent**: Television Series, Documentary Films, Biography: Show Business. **Acq**: Purchase. **Dist**: A&E Television Networks L.L.C. $24.95.

Biography: P.T. Barnum ????
A&E Biography combines interviews, still photography, live-action footage, reenactments, period art, and other documentary material to present historical figures and their achievements. Recommended for Grades 6-12. 45m; VHS. **A**: Jr. High-Sr. High. **P**: Education. **U**: Home, Institution. **Gen-Edu**: Biography, History, Business. **Acq**: Purchase. **Dist**: Social Studies School Service; Zenger Media. $14.95.

Biography: Pulitzer ????
A&E Biography combines interviews, still photography, live-action footage, reenactments, period art, and other documentary material to present historical figures and their achievements. Recommended for Grades 6-12. 45m; VHS. **A**: Jr. High-Sr. High. **P**: Education. **U**: Home, Institution. **Gen-Edu**: Biography, History, Business. **Acq**: Purchase. **Dist**: Zenger Media; Social Studies School Service. $14.95.

Biography: Randy Travis: Keeping the Tradition ????
Presents the A&E cable channel special on country singing legend Randy Travis, who struggled to start his career but his 1985 debut was the beginning of many successful hits and albums, as well as some acting roles; includes interviews, concert footage, and film clips. 50m; DVD. **A**: Jr. High-Adult. **P**: Entertainment. **U**: Home, CATV. **Mov-Ent**: Television Series, Documentary Films, Biography: Music. **Acq**: Purchase. **Dist**: A&E Television Networks L.L.C. $24.95.

Biography: Rasputin: The Mad Monk 2005
Presents the A&E cable channel special on Grigori (or Gregory) Rasputin, nicknamed the "mad monk," the often unruly peasant was considered a mystic by Russia's Czar Nicholas II and Empress Alexandra, who brought him into their inner circle in 1905 after Rasputin "saved" the couple's son from hemophilia. His prominence led to his assassination in 1916 by a group of bitter aristocrats. Includes photos and period accounts. 50m; DVD. **A**: Jr. High-Adult. **P**: Entertainment. **U**: Home, CATV. **Mov-Ent**: Television Series, Documentary Films, Biography: Religious Figures. **Acq**: Purchase. **Dist**: A&E Television Networks L.L.C. $24.95.

Biography: Ray Kroc ????
A&E Biography combines interviews, still photography, live-action footage, reenactments, period art, and other documentary material to present historical figures and their achievements. Recommended for Grades 6-12. 45m; VHS. **A**: Jr. High-Sr. High. **P**: Education. **U**: Home, Institution. **Gen-Edu**: Biography, History, Business. **Acq**: Purchase. **Dist**: Social Studies School Service; Zenger Media. $14.95.

Biography: Ray Liotta: Hollywood Goodfella ????
Presents the A&E cable channel special on actor Ray Liotta, well-known for his roles in movies such as "Goodfellas," "Something Wild," and "Unlawful Entry" though his career began on the soap opera "Another World." 50m; DVD. **A**: Jr. High-Adult. **P**: Entertainment. **U**: Home, CATV. **Mov-Ent**: Television Series, Documentary Films, Biography: Show Business. **Acq**: Purchase. **Dist**: A&E Television Networks L.L.C. $24.95.

Biography: Ray Romano ????
Presents the A&E cable channel special on comedian and actor Ray Romano, who began his career as a stand-up comedian before launching into stardom as the lovable-yet-frustrating sportswriter husband in "Everybody Loves Raymond" from 1996-2005 as well as the lead voice in the animated movies "Ice Age" and "Ice Age 2: The Meltdown"; includes video clips and family and friend interviews. 50m; DVD. **A**: Family. **P**: Entertainment. **U**: Home, CATV. **Mov-Ent**: Television Series, Documentary Films, Biography: Show Business. **Acq**: Purchase. **Dist**: A&E Television Networks L.L.C. $24.95.

Biography: Red Baron: Master of the Air ????
Presents the A&E cable channel special on Baron Manfred von Richthofen, a German flying ace during World War I who was dubbed by the English as "The Red Baron"; includes interviews with military and aviation historians and footage. 50m; DVD. **A**: Family. **P**: Entertainment. **U**: Home, CATV. **Mov-Ent**: Television Series, Documentary Films, Biography: Military. **Acq**: Purchase. **Dist**: A&E Television Networks L.L.C. $24.95.

Biography: Regis Philbin ????
Presents the A&E cable channel special on entertainer and television personality Regis Philbin; features the professional

---

challenges he faced until his morning show was nationally syndicated in 1988 as well as personal struggles with a disabled child and his divorce from his first wife. Includes interviews and video footage. 50m; DVD. **A**: Family. **P**: Entertainment. **U**: Home, CATV. **Mov-Ent**: Television Series, Documentary Films, Biography: Show Business. **Acq**: Purchase. **Dist**: A&E Television Networks L.L.C. $24.95.

Biography: R.H. Macy ????
Presents the A&E cable channel cable channel special on American businessman Rowland Hussey Macy (aka R.H. Macy), who founded his popular department store in New York City in 1858 after failing at several other ventures; includes interviews with industry experts and rare photographs. 50m; DVD. **A**: Jr. High-Adult. **P**: Entertainment. **U**: Home, CATV. **Mov-Ent**: Television Series, Documentary Films, Biography. **Acq**: Purchase. **Dist**: A&E Television Networks L.L.C. $24.95.

Biography: Richard Branson: The Top of the World ????
Presents the A&E cable channel special on music industry mogul Richard Branson, who formed Virgin Records in 1973, which has since morphed into mega-corporation Virgin Group; in the mid-1980s, he launched a Virgin-Atlantic Airways and showed his daredevil side by crossing oceans in a hot-air balloon. Includes interviews with family and friends. 50m; DVD. **A**: Jr. High-Adult. **P**: Entertainment. **U**: Home, CATV. **Mov-Ent**: Television Series, Documentary Films, Business. **Dist**: A&E Television Networks L.L.C. $24.95.

Biography: Richard Harris ????
Presents the A&E cable channel special on actor Richard Harris, who became well known as King Arthur in 1967's "Camelot;" his career faded until the 1990s, when he appeared in "Patriot Games" and "Unforgiven," and in the early 2000s he played the role of Albus Dumbledore in the first two "Harry Potter" movies. Includes coverage of his early music career, interviews, film clips, and archival materials. 50m; DVD. **A**: Jr. High-Adult. **P**: Entertainment. **U**: Home, CATV. **Mov-Ent**: Television Series, Documentary Films, Biography: Show Business. **Acq**: Purchase. **Dist**: A&E Television Networks L.L.C. $24.95.

Biography: Richard Nixon ????
A&E Biography combines interviews, still photography, live-action footage, reenactments, period art, and other documentary material to present historical figures and their achievements. Recommended for Grades 6-12. 100m; VHS. **A**: Jr. High-Sr. High. **P**: Education. **U**: Home, Institution. **Gen-Edu**: Biography, Presidency, History--U.S. **Acq**: Purchase. **Dist**: Social Studies School Service; Zenger Media. $14.95.

Biography: Richard Pryor: Comic on the Edge 1999
Presents the A&E cable channel special on comedian and actor Richard Pryor, who was well known for his movie roles and his uproarious stand-up albums; includes his struggle with cocaine addiction, which led to a horrific incident in which he was seriously injured after accidentally setting himself on fire in 1980, along with his relationship troubles and battle with multiple sclerosis. Features interviews with friends, colleagues, and one of his several children from his six marriages, daughter Rain. 50m; DVD. **A**: Jr. High-Adult. **P**: Entertainment. **U**: Home, CATV. **Mov-Ent**: Television Series, Documentary Films, Biography: Show Business. **Acq**: Purchase. **Dist**: A&E Television Networks L.L.C. $24.95.

Biography: Richard Speck: Natural Born Killer ????
Presents the A&E cable channel special on mass murderer Richard Speck, who entered a Chicago townhouse in 1966 where he held eight female nurses hostage in 1966 before raping and killing them; includes interviews with childhood acquaintances and the trial prosecutor. 50m; DVD. **A**: Sr. High-Adult. **P**: Entertainment. **U**: Home, CATV. **Mov-Ent**: Television Series, Documentary Films, Biography. **Acq**: Purchase. **Dist**: A&E Television Networks L.L.C. $24.95.

Biography: Richard the Lionheart ????
A&E Biography combines interviews, still photography, live-action footage, reenactments, period art, and other documentary material to present historical figures and their achievements. Recommended for Grades 6-12. 45m; VHS. **A**: Jr. High-Sr. High. **P**: Education. **U**: Home, Institution. **Gen-Edu**: Biography, History. **Acq**: Purchase. **Dist**: Social Studies School Service; Zenger Media. $14.95.

Biography: Rick Springfield: Behind the Image 2005
Behind-the-scenes look at the 30-year career of the pop/rock star and actor. 50m; DVD. **A**: Jr. High-Adult. **P**: Entertainment. **U**: Home. **Fin-Art**: Documentary Films, Biography: Show Business. **Acq**: Purchase. **Dist**: A&E Television Networks L.L.C.

Biography: Robert Blake: Dark Passage 20??
Presents the A&E cable channel special on actor Robert Blake who starred as a tough-guy detective in the television series "Baretta" (1975-1978) as well as the lead actor in Richard Brooks' 1967 film "In Cold Blood" though all of his achievements became overshadowed by the charges that he shot and killed his wife Bonnie Lee Bakley in 2001. Despite his "not guilty" verdict in 2005, later that year Bakley's children won a wrongful death civil suit against Blake. Includes interviews and film clips. 50m; DVD. **A**: Jr. High-Adult. **P**: Entertainment. **U**: Home, CATV. **Mov-Ent**: Television Series, Documentary Films, Biography: Show Business. **Acq**: Purchase. **Dist**: A&E Television Networks L.L.C. $24.95.

Biography: Robert E. Lee ????
A&E Biography combines interviews, still photography, live-action footage, reenactments, period art, and other documen-

---

tary material to present historical figures and their achievements. Recommended for Grades 6-12. 45m; VHS. **A**: Jr. High-Sr. High. **P**: Education. **U**: Home, Institution. **Gen-Edu**: Biography, History--U.S. **Acq**: Purchase. **Dist**: Social Studies School Service; Zenger Media. $14.95.

Biography: Robert F. Kennedy ????
Presents the A&E cable channel special on former U.S. Senator Robert F. Kennedy, whose assassination during his 1968 presidential run came five years after his brother John F. Kennedy was killed; follows his early life including his troubled relationship with father Joseph Kennedy as well as his involvement in JFK's campaigns and as Attorney General in his administration. Includes interviews with family and friends, rare photos, and archival footage. 50m; DVD. **A**: Family. **P**: Entertainment. **U**: Home, CATV. **Mov-Ent**: Television Series, Documentary Films, Politics & Government. **Acq**: Purchase. **Dist**: A&E Television Networks L.L.C. $24.95.

Biography: Robert Maxwell ????
Presents the A&E cable channel special on troubled media mogul Robert Maxwell, who grew up in poverty in the Czech Republic and later escaped from a concentration camp in Nazi Germany; his holdings eventually became Maxwell Communication Corporation in 1980 and also included Mirror Group Newspapers in 1984. However, after his unexplained drowning death in 1991 it was discovered he had taken money from two of his companies along with employee pension funds. 50m; DVD. **A**: Jr. High-Adult. **P**: Entertainment. **U**: Home, CATV. **Mov-Ent**: Television Series, Documentary Films, Business. **Acq**: Purchase. **Dist**: A&E Television Networks L.L.C. $24.95.

Biography: Robert Wagner: Hollywood's Prince Charming 1999
Presents the A&E cable channel special on actor Robert Wagner, who starred in many movies but experienced his greatest success as a television actor in "Switch" (1975-1978) and, in particular, "Hart to Hart" (1979-1983) until appearing in the "Austin Powers" trilogy in the late 1990s and early 2000s as Number Two. He struggled in his personal life through divorces and the tragic accidental drowning death of his wife, actress Natalie Wood, in 1981, though he remarried in 1991 to actress Jill St. John. Includes family photographs, film clips, and interviews. 50m; DVD. **A**: Jr. High-Adult. **P**: Entertainment. **U**: Home, CATV. **Mov-Ent**: Television Series, Documentary Films, Biography: Show Business. **Acq**: Purchase. **Dist**: A&E Television Networks L.L.C. $24.95.

Biography: Robin Hood: Outlaw of the Forest ????
Presents the A&E cable channel special on legendary English hero Robin Hood and his band of Merry Men, purported to have "robbed from the rich and given to the poor"; includes interviews with historians who discuss whether he was myth or fact as well as showing how the legacy has been portrayed in stories and films. 50m; DVD. **A**: Family. **P**: Entertainment. **U**: Home, CATV. **Mov-Ent**: Television Series, Documentary Films, Folklore & Legends. **Acq**: Purchase. **Dist**: A&E Television Networks L.L.C. $24.95.

Biography: Rock Hudson: Acting the Part 1999
Presents the A&E cable channel special on actor Rock Hudson, who starred in numerous films during his career often as a "heartthrob," though his death in 1985 from AIDS revealed his hidden life as a homosexual that shocked many outside of the Hollywood community; includes home movies, photographs, and interviews. 50m; DVD. **A**: Jr. High-Adult. **P**: Entertainment. **U**: Home, CATV. **Mov-Ent**: Television Series, Documentary Films, Biography: Show Business. **Acq**: Purchase. **Dist**: A&E Television Networks L.L.C. $24.95.

Biography: Ron Popeil: America's Inventor 20??
Presents the A&E cable channel special on consumer product inventor and marketer Ron Popeil, who is known for his company Ronco and for the catchy phrases he has used in infomercials for his products, such as the Veg-O-Matic and Showtime Rotissiere; despite his successes, Popeil faced financial troubles in the late 1980s but went on to recover his company, which he sold in 2005 while continuing as an inventor and marketer. 50m; DVD. **A**: Jr. High-Adult. **P**: Entertainment. **U**: Home, CATV. **Mov-Ent**: Television Series, Documentary Films, Biography: Show Business. **Acq**: Purchase. **Dist**: A&E Television Networks L.L.C. $24.95.

Biography: Ronald Reagan 1991
A&E Biography combines interviews, still photography, live-action footage, reenactments, period art, and other documentary material to present historical figures and their achievements. Recommended for Grades 6-12. 45m; VHS. **A**: Jr. High-Sr. High. **P**: Education. **U**: Home, Institution. **Gen-Edu**: Biography, Presidency, History--U.S. **Acq**: Purchase. **Dist**: Social Studies School Service; Zenger Media. $14.95.

Biography: Roy Cohn: Joe McCarthy's Right-Hand Man ????
Presents the A&E cable channel special on American lawyer Roy Cohn, known for assisting Senator Joseph McCarthy in the 1950s during the infamous hearings targeting supposed Communists within the U.S. government; includes interviews with William Safire, William F. Buckley, Jr., Jules Feiffer, Bill Fugazy, Liz Smith, and Ben Bradlee along with video footage. 50m; DVD. **A**: Family. **P**: Entertainment. **U**: Home, CATV. **Mov-Ent**: Television Series, Documentary Films, Biography: Politics. **Acq**: Purchase. **Dist**: A&E Television Networks L.L.C. $24.95.

Biography: Roy Rogers 2005
Presents the A&E cable channel special on the legendary cowboy actor Roy Rogers, who was immensely popular in the numerous movies he starred in during the 1940s and 1950s; includes home movies, film outtakes, clips, and inter-

views. 50m; DVD. **A:** Family. **P:** Entertainment. **U:** Home, CATV. **Mov-Ent:** Television Series, Documentary Films, Biography: Show Business. **Acq:** Purchase. **Dist:** A&E Television Networks L.L.C. $24.95.

Biography: Rudolph Valentino: The Great Lover ????
Presents the A&E cable channel special on Italian actor Rudolph Valentino, known as a sex symbol for movie roles in the early 1920s until his death from blood poisoning in 1926 at the age of 31; includes interviews, movie clips, and period accounts. 50m; DVD. **A:** Jr. High-Adult. **P:** Entertainment. **U:** Home, CATV. **Mov-Ent:** Television Series, Documentary Films, Biography: Show Business. **Acq:** Purchase. **Dist:** A&E Television Networks L.L.C. $24.95.

Biography: Rudy Giuliani 20??
Presents the A&E cable channel special on former New York City mayor Rudy Giuliani, covering his service as a federal prosecutor to the challenges he faced as mayor including the tragedies of the September 11 terrorist attacks on the city; interviewed by reporter Harry Smith. 50m; DVD. **A:** Family. **P:** Entertainment. **U:** Home, CATV. **Mov-Ent:** Television Series, Documentary Films, Politics & Government. **Acq:** Purchase. **Dist:** A&E Television Networks L.L.C. $24.95.

Biography: Russell Crowe 2006
Presents the A&E cable channel special on actor Russell Crowe, who has starred in such movie successes as "L.A. Confidential" and "Gladiator," for which he won an Academy Award for best actor; includes interviews and film clips. 50m; DVD. **A:** Jr. High-Adult. **P:** Entertainment. **U:** Home, CATV. **Mov-Ent:** Television Series, Documentary Films, Biography: Show Business. **Acq:** Purchase. **Dist:** A&E Television Networks L.L.C. $24.95.

Biography: Russell Simmons ????
Presents the A&E cable channel special on Russell Simmons, who broke into the rap and hip-hop music industry as a manager at the age of 22 by getting rapper Kurtis Blow his first contract and later worked with Run-DMC; he then formed the record label Def Jam with such acts as Public Enemy, LL Cool J, and the Beastie Boys, and went on to create his own apparel line (Phat Farm), produce TV shows and movies, and head his own non-profit foundation. Includes interviews and footage. 50m; DVD. **A:** Jr. High-Adult. **P:** Entertainment. **U:** Home, CATV. **Mov-Ent:** Television Series, Documentary Films, Biography: Music. **Acq:** Purchase. **Dist:** A&E Television Networks L.L.C. $24.95.

Biography: St. Francis of Assisi ????
Presents the A&E cable channel special on Italian Christian mystic St. Francis of Assisi, who after becoming a prisoner of war renounced his family's wealth to found the religious order the Franciscans; includes interviews with scholars, historic artwork, and rare documents. 50m; DVD. **A:** Family. **P:** Entertainment. **U:** Home, CATV. **Mov-Ent:** Television Series, Documentary Films, Religion. **Acq:** Purchase. **Dist:** A&E Television Networks L.L.C. $24.95.

Biography: St. Patrick: Man, Myth & Magic ????
Presents the A&E cable channel special on Ireland's most well-known saint, St. Patrick, who some have claimed brought Christianity to that country in the 5th century; includes interviews with religious scholars as well as excerpts from his "Confession." 50m; DVD. **A:** Family. **P:** Entertainment. **U:** Home, CATV. **Mov-Ent:** Television Series, Documentary Films, Bible. **Acq:** Purchase. **Dist:** A&E Television Networks L.L.C. $24.95.

Biography: Sal Mineo 1999
Presents the A&E cable channel special on actor and singer Sal Mineo, best known for his roles in the James Dean film "Rebel Without a Cause" in 1955 and with Paul Newman in "Exodus" in 1961, both of which garnered him Oscar nominations for best supporting actor; however, his career faded by the late 1960s though he continued to work in the industry until he was murdered in 1976 by a robber. Features interviews with friends, family, and co-stars along with family photos and film clips. 50m; DVD. **A:** Jr. High-Adult. **P:** Entertainment. **U:** Home, CATV. **Mov-Ent:** Television Series, Documentary Films, Biography: Show Business. **Acq:** Purchase. **Dist:** A&E Television Networks L.L.C. $24.95.

Biography: Sally Field ????
Presents the A&E cable channel special on acclaimed actress Sally Field, whose career began in television with "Gidget" and "The Flying Nun" and later in movies such as "Smokey and the Bandit" and "Forrest Gump"; includes footage, photos, and interviews with family and friends. 50m; DVD. **A:** Family. **P:** Entertainment. **U:** Home, CATV. **Mov-Ent:** Television Series, Documentary Films, Biography: Show Business. **Acq:** Purchase. **Dist:** A&E Television Networks L.L.C. $24.95.

Biography: Sally Hemings: Redefining History 2006
Examines the long-rumored relationship between Thomas Jefferson and his slave, Sally Hemings. In 1998, DNA studies confirmed that Jefferson may have fathered all of Sally's five children, and descendents of both families speak out. 50m; DVD. **A:** Jr. High-Adult. **P:** Entertainment. **U:** Home. **Gen-Edu:** Documentary Films, History--U.S. **Acq:** Purchase. **Dist:** A&E Television Networks L.L.C.

Biography: Salvador Dali ????
Presents the A&E cable channel special on 20th century Spanish surrealist artist Salvador Dali; includes interviews with family and friends. 50m; DVD. **A:** Family. **P:** Entertainment. **U:**

Home, CATV. **Mov-Ent:** Television Series, Documentary Films, Biography: Artists. **Acq:** Purchase. **Dist:** A&E Television Networks L.L.C. $24.95.

Biography: Sam Walton: Bargain Billionaire ????
Presents the A&E cable channel special on Sam Walton, best known for co-founding popular discount retailer Wal-Mart in 1962; includes interviews with associates, family, former board member Hillary Rodham Clinton, and ex-CEO David Glass. 50m; DVD. **A:** Family. **P:** Entertainment. **U:** Home, CATV. **Mov-Ent:** Television Series, Documentary Films, Biography. **Acq:** Purchase. **Dist:** A&E Television Networks L.L.C. $24.95.

Biography: Sammy "The Bull" Gravano: Giving Up the Mob ????
Presents the A&E cable channel special on mobster Salvatore "Sammy the Bull" Gravano, who worked under John Gotti during the 1980s; however, his 1991 arrest by the FBI caused him to turn on Gotti in return for a reduced sentence, earning him the nickname "The King Rat." Includes interviews with biographer Peter Maas, victims' relatives, and prosecutors. 50m; DVD. **A:** Sr. High-Adult. **P:** Entertainment. **U:** Home, CATV. **Mov-Ent:** Television Series, Documentary Films, Biography. **Acq:** Purchase. **Dist:** A&E Television Networks L.L.C. $24.95.

Biography: Samson & Delilah ????
Presents the A&E cable channel special on biblical figures Samson and Delilah, recounting their love story and her betrayal through location footage, paintings, and artifacts; includes interviews with biblical scholars. 50m; DVD. **A:** Family. **P:** Entertainment. **U:** Home, CATV. **Mov-Ent:** Television Series, Documentary Films, Religion. **Acq:** Purchase. **Dist:** A&E Television Networks L.L.C. $24.95.

Biography: Samuel Goldwyn ????
Presents the A&E cable channel special on Polish-American film producer Samuel Goldwyn, who began his career in the early 20th century and had numerous movie successes, such as "The Best Years of Our Lives," "Greed," and "Wuthering Heights"; his Goldwyn Co. merged into Metro-Goldwyn-Mayer (MGM). Includes interviews with historians and industry experts. 50m; DVD. **A:** Jr. High-Adult. **P:** Entertainment. **U:** Home, CATV. **Mov-Ent:** Television Series, Documentary Films, Filmmaking. **Acq:** Purchase. **Dist:** A&E Television Networks L.L.C. $24.95.

Biography: Sandra Bullock 2007
Presents the A&E cable channel special on actress Sandra Bullock, who has starred in such successful movies as "Speed" and "Miss Congeniality." 50m; DVD. **A:** Family. **P:** Entertainment. **U:** Home, CATV. **Mov-Ent:** Television Series, Documentary Films, Biography: Show Business. **Acq:** Purchase. **Dist:** A&E Television Networks L.L.C. $24.95.

Biography: Sandra Day O'Connor ????
Presents the A&E cable channel special on former U.S. Supreme Court Justice Sandra Day O'Connor, who became the first woman appointed in the court's history in 1981 by President Ronald Reagan; includes interviews with Justice O'Connor along with her family, friends, and colleagues. 50m; DVD. **A:** Family. **P:** Entertainment. **U:** Home, CATV. **Mov-Ent:** Television Series, Documentary Films, Biography. **Acq:** Purchase. **Dist:** A&E Television Networks L.L.C. $24.95.

Biography: Santa Claus 2005
Examines the history and legends behind the beloved figure, from his religious roots to his transformation into a secular holiday icon. 50m; DVD. **A:** Jr. High-Adult. **P:** Entertainment. **U:** Home. **Gen-Edu:** Documentary Films, Biography. **Acq:** Purchase. **Dist:** A&E Television Networks L.L.C.

Biography: Satan: Prince of Darkness 2007
Presents the A&E cable channel special on Satan, from his Biblical beginnings to modern-day tales; includes documentary "Hell: The Devil's Domain." 141m; DVD. **A:** Jr. High-Adult. **P:** Entertainment. **U:** Home, CATV. **Mov-Ent:** Television Series, Documentary Films, Biography: Religious Figures. **Acq:** Purchase. **Dist:** A&E Television Networks L.L.C. $9.95.

Biography: Saturday Night Live 1987
Goes behind the scenes to follow the cast and crew through an entire week of production as they prepare for the November 10, 2001, show featuring Gwyneth Paltrow as the host. Viewers are privy to the Monday morning pitch session, makeup tests, dress rehearsals, and the iconic "Live from New York, it's Saturday Night!" opening. Favorite SNL moments are shared by creator Lorne Michaels, writers Anne Beatts and Tom Schiller, and former stars Chevy Chase, Al Franken, Molly Shannon, Joe Piscopo, and Adam Sandler. 100m; DVD. **A:** Sr. High-Adult. **P:** Entertainment. **U:** Home. **L:** English. **Gen-Edu:** Biography, Interviews. **Acq:** Purchase. **Dist:** A&E Television Networks L.L.C. $24.95.

Biography: Saturday Night Live 2003
Presents the A&E cable channel special on the NBC television sketch comedy series "Saturday Night Live," which began in 1976 under Lorne Michaels. Shows the cast and crew as they prepare for the November 10, 2001, show hosted by actress Gwyneth Paltrow; includes interviews with past stars such as Chevy Chase, Al Franken, Molly Shannon, Joe Piscopo, and Adam Sandler as well as unaired video clips and skits. 50m; DVD. **A:** Family. **P:** Entertainment. **U:** Home, CATV. **Mov-Ent:** Television Series, Documentary Films, Biography: Show Business. **Acq:** Purchase. **Dist:** A&E Television Networks L.L.C. $24.95.

Biography: Sears ????
Presents the A&E cable channel special on mass merchandiser Sears, Roebuck and Company, founded in 1893 by Richard

Sears and Alvah Roebuck; includes interviews with corporate executives and the heirs of Sears and Roebuck. 50m; DVD. **A:** Jr. High-Adult. **P:** Entertainment. **U:** Home, CATV. **Mov-Ent:** Television Series, Documentary Films, Biography. **Acq:** Purchase. **Dist:** A&E Television Networks L.L.C. $24.95.

Biography: Sharon Tate: Murdered Innocence ????
Presents the A&E cable channel special on the 1969 murder of popular actress Sharon Tate by members of Charles Manson's so-called "family"; at the time, the Hollywood-beloved Tate was eight months pregnant and married to director Roman Polanski. Features a 1984 interview with Polanski along with friends Sheilah Wells, Julie Christie, Jacqueline Bissett, and Mia Farrow. 50m; DVD. **A:** Jr. High-Adult. **P:** Entertainment. **U:** Home, CATV. **Mov-Ent:** Television Series, Documentary Films, Biography: Show Business. **Acq:** Purchase. **Dist:** A&E Television Networks L.L.C. $24.95.

Biography: Sherlock Holmes: The Great Detective 2006
Traces the origins of Arthur Conan Doyle's famed literary character from his first print appearance in 1887 to his enduring popularity today. 50m; DVD. **A:** Jr. High-Adult. **P:** Entertainment. **U:** Home. **Gen-Edu:** Documentary Films, Biography. **Acq:** Purchase. **Dist:** A&E Television Networks L.L.C.

Biography: Shirley Muldowney ????
Presents the A&E cable channel special on professional drag racer Shirley Muldowney, known as the first female racer on the National Hot Rod Association circuit who won 18 national championships since her debut in the early 1970s despite enduring many serious injuries. 50m; DVD. **A:** Family. **P:** Entertainment. **U:** Home, CATV. **Mov-Ent:** Television Series, Documentary Films, Biography: Sports. **Acq:** Purchase. **Dist:** A&E Television Networks L.L.C. $24.95.

Biography: Shirley Temple Black 19??
From movie child star of the '30s to U.S. ambassador—a look at the life of Temple Black. Features interviews with John Agar, Dick Moore, Cesar Romero, and biographer Anne Edwards. 50m; VHS. **Pr:** A&E (Arts & Entertainment) Network. **A:** Jr. High-Adult. **P:** Entertainment. **U:** Home. **Gen-Edu:** Documentary Films, Biography, Biography: Show Business. **Acq:** Purchase. **Dist:** A&E Television Networks L.L.C.; New Video Group. $19.95.

Biography: Shirley Temple—The Biggest Little Star 1999
This program from A&E's popular "Biography" series examines the life of child star Shirley Temple. 100m; VHS. **A:** Jr. High-Adult. **P:** Entertainment. **U:** Home. **Gen-Edu:** Biography, Documentary Films, Biography: Show Business. **Acq:** Purchase. **Dist:** A&E Television Networks L.L.C. $14.95.

Biography: Sidney Sheldon: Storyteller 2000
Presents the A&E cable channel special on novelist, playwright, and screenwriter Sidney Sheldon (1917-2007), who authored 16 novels after the age of 50, including "Rage of Angels" and "Master of the Game" (both became television miniseries), which have sold more than 280 million copies; he first wrote many screenplays and produced television series hits such as "The Patty Duke Show," "I Dream of Jeannie," and "Hart to Hart." 50m; DVD. **A:** Jr. High-Adult. **P:** Entertainment. **U:** Home, CATV. **Mov-Ent:** Television Series, Documentary Films, Biography. **Acq:** Purchase. **Dist:** A&E Television Networks L.L.C. $24.95.

Biography: Siegfried & Roy 20??
Presents the A&E cable channel special on magicians Siegfried and Roy, best known for their popular Las Vegas shows featuring white tigers, and the near-fatal attack on Roy by one of the tigers in 2003; covers their early lives in Germany to the beginnings of their act. 50m; DVD. **A:** Jr. High-Adult. **P:** Entertainment. **U:** Home, CATV. **Mov-Ent:** Television Series, Documentary Films, Biography: Show Business. **Acq:** Purchase. **Dist:** A&E Television Networks L.L.C. $24.95.

Biography: Sigmund Freud ????
A&E Biography combines interviews, still photography, live-action footage, reenactments, period art, and other documentary material to present historical figures and their achievements. Recommended for Grades 6-12. 45m; VHS. **A:** Jr. High-Sr. High. **P:** Education. **U:** Home, Institution. **Gen-Edu:** Biography, Scientists, Inventors & Inventions. **Acq:** Purchase. **Dist:** Social Studies School Service; Zenger Media. $14.95.

Biography: Silvio Berlusconi 20??
Presents the A&E cable channel special on Italian prime minister Silvio Berlusconi, who created his own party "Forza Italia" in 1993 after founding Fininvest group, which included media, publishing, finance, and sports holdings; however, his administration has been plagued by controversy. 50m; DVD. **A:** Jr. High-Adult. **P:** Entertainment. **U:** Home, CATV. **Mov-Ent:** Television Series, Documentary Films, Politics & Government. **Acq:** Purchase. **Dist:** A&E Television Networks L.L.C. $24.95.

Biography: Simon Cowell ????
Presents the A&E cable channel special on music producer and executive Simon Cowell, best known for his role as the sharp-tongued judge on the television reality series "American Idol"; includes interviews with co-stars Paula Abdul, Randy Jackson, and Ryan Seacrest as well as video clips. 50m; DVD. **A:** Family. **P:** Entertainment. **U:** Home, CATV. **Mov-Ent:** Television Series, Documentary Films, Biography: Show Business. **Acq:** Purchase. **Dist:** A&E Television Networks L.L.C. $24.95.

Biography: Sir Isaac Newton ????
A&E Biography combines interviews, still photography, live-action footage, reenactments, period art, and other documen-

tary material to present historical figures and their achievements. Recommended for Grades 6-12. 45m; VHS. **A:** Jr. High-Sr. High. **P:** Education. **U:** Home, Institution. **Gen-Edu:** Biography, Scientists, Inventors & Inventions. **Acq:** Purchase. **Dist:** Social Studies School Service; Zenger Media. $14.95.

Biography: Sitting Bull ????
A&E Biography combines interviews, still photography, live-action footage, reenactments, period art, and other documentary material to present historical figures and their achievements. Recommended for Grades 6-12. 45m; VHS. **A:** Jr. High-Sr. High. **P:** Education. **U:** Home, Institution. **Gen-Edu:** Biography, History--U.S. **Acq:** Purchase. **Dist:** Social Studies School Service; Zenger Media. $14.95.

Biography: Solomon ????
Presents the A&E cable channel special on biblical figure Solomon, who was king of the ancient Hebrews (from 967-927 B.C.) and known for his wisdom and for constructing Jerusalem's First Temple of the Lord though his relationship with God was allegedly filled with strife; includes interviews with biblical scholars. 50m; DVD. **A:** Family. **P:** Entertainment. **U:** Home, CATV. **Mov-Ent:** Television Series, Documentary Films, Religion. **Acq:** Purchase. **Dist:** A&E Television Networks L.L.C. $24.95.

Biography: Solomon & Sheba ????
Presents the A&E cable channel special on the biblical figures Solomon and Sheba, retelling their love story through location footage, paintings, and artifacts; includes interviews with experts. 50m; DVD. **A:** Family. **P:** Entertainment. **U:** Home, CATV. **Mov-Ent:** Television Series, Documentary Films, Religion. **Acq:** Purchase. **Dist:** A&E Television Networks L.L.C. $24.95.

Biography: Sonja Henie: Fire on Ice ????
Presents the A&E cable channel special on Norwegian champion figure skater Sonja Henie, best known for winning three consecutive gold medals at the Winter Olympics (1928, 1932, and 1936) as well as 10 world figure skating championships; later, she became a movie star in Hollywood. Features interviews with friends and costars, such as actor Roddy McDowall and actress Ann Miller, along with video clips. 50m; DVD. **A:** Family. **P:** Entertainment. **U:** Home, CATV. **Mov-Ent:** Television Series, Documentary Films, Skating. **Acq:** Purchase. **Dist:** A&E Television Networks L.L.C. $24.95.

Biography: Sonny Bono: Pop Songs and Politics ????
Presents the A&E cable channel special on entertainer, musician, and politician Sonny Bono, who rose to fame in the late 1960s as part of a musical duo with then-wife Cher, recording hits such as "I Got You, Babe" and "The Beat Goes On" and starring in the popular 1970s television variety show "The Sonny and Cher Show." He later entered politics, first as mayor of Palm Springs, California, then in 1994 he was elected to California's House of Representatives, where he served until his death from a skiing accident in January 1998. 50m; DVD. **A:** Jr. High-Adult. **P:** Entertainment. **U:** Home, CATV. **Mov-Ent:** Television Series, Documentary Films, Biography: Show Business. **Acq:** Purchase. **Dist:** A&E Television Networks L.L.C. $24.95.

Biography: Sophia Loren: Actress Italian Style ????
Presents the A&E cable channel special on Italian actress Sophia Loren, known for her seductive roles in many films beginning in the 1950s as well as the scandal that brewed after her marriage to producer Carlo Ponti in 1957; Loren won the 1961 Oscar for best actress in "Two Women." Includes interviews with biographers, still photographs, and rare movie footage. 50m; DVD. **A:** Jr. High-Adult. **P:** Entertainment. **U:** Home, CATV. **Mov-Ent:** Television Series, Documentary Films, Biography: Show Business. **Acq:** Purchase. **Dist:** A&E Television Networks L.L.C. $24.95.

Biography: South African Strangler ????
Presents the A&E cable channel special on South African Moses Sithole, who was convicted of the rape and murder of 38 people from 1994 to 1995 in a spree known as the "ABC Murders" because of their locations—Atteridgeville, Boksburg, and Cleveland (a suburb of Johannesburg). 50m; DVD. **A:** Sr. High-Adult. **P:** Entertainment. **U:** Home, CATV. **Mov-Ent:** Television Series, Documentary Films, Biography. **Acq:** Purchase. **Dist:** A&E Television Networks L.L.C. $24.95.

Biography: Stan Lee: ComiX-Man ????
Presents the A&E cable channel special on writer, artist, and editor Stan Lee, best known for co-creating (with Jack Kirby) the Spider-Man character as well as the Fantastic Four, the X-Men, Hulk, and others; Lee was also the CEO of Marvel Comics (later Marvel Entertainment Group); includes an interview with Lee and presents some of his original art from classic comics. 50m; DVD. **A:** Family. **P:** Entertainment. **U:** Home, CATV. **Mov-Ent:** Television Series, Documentary Films, Biography: Artists. **Acq:** Purchase. **Dist:** A&E Television Networks L.L.C. $24.95.

Biography: Stanford White ????
Presents the A&E cable channel special on American architect Stanford White, best known for designing for the rich and famous of the day during the late 19th and early 20th centuries; however, his life was cut short in 1906 when millionaire Harry K. Thaw fatally shot him on the roof of the Madison Square Garden in New York City—a structure that White had designed about 15 years prior—for having an affair with his wife, actress Evelyn Nesbit. 50m; DVD. **A:** Jr. High-Adult. **P:** Entertainment. **U:** Home, CATV. **Mov-Ent:** Television Series, Documentary Films, Biography. **Acq:** Purchase. **Dist:** A&E Television Networks L.L.C. $24.95.

Biography: Stanley & Livingstone ????
A&E Biography combines interviews, still photography, live-action footage, reenactments, period art, and other documentary material to present historical figures and their achievements. Recommended for Grades 6-12. 45m; VHS. **A:** Jr. High-Sr. High. **P:** Education. **U:** Home, Institution. **Gen-Edu:** Biography, History. **Acq:** Purchase. **Dist:** Social Studies School Service; Zenger Media. $14.95.

Biography: Steve Allen: Hi-Ho, Steverino! 2006
Presents the A&E cable channel special on entertainer Steve Allen (1921-2000), who was the first host of "The Tonight Show" (1953-1957) and hosted several other comedy shows during his long career, authored about 40 books, and wrote around 4,000 songs; includes interviews with friends such as Tim Conway and Eydie Gorme along with his wife Jayne Meadows, footage, and concert clips. 50m; DVD. **A:** Jr. High-Adult. **P:** Entertainment. **U:** Home, CATV. **Mov-Ent:** Television Series, Documentary Films, Biography: Show Business. **Acq:** Purchase. **Dist:** A&E Television Networks L.L.C. $24.95.

Biography: Steve Rubell: Lord of the Disco ????
Presents the A&E cable channel special on Steve Rubell, best known for co-founding the popular and infamous New York City disco nightclub Studio 54 in the late 1970s, though he was charged with tax evasion and served 13 months in jail; includes interviews with friends and relatives along with behind-the-scene photos. 50m; DVD. **A:** Jr. High-Adult. **P:** Entertainment. **U:** Home, CATV. **Mov-Ent:** Television Series, Documentary Films, Business. **Acq:** Purchase. **Dist:** A&E Television Networks L.L.C. $24.95.

Biography: Steven Seagal ????
Presents the A&E cable channel special on action-movie actor and martial arts master Steven Seagal, who starred in a string of blockbuster movies beginning in the late 1980s such as "Above the Law," "Hard to Kill," "Under Siege," and "On Deadly Ground." 50m; DVD. **A:** Jr. High-Adult. **P:** Entertainment. **U:** Home, CATV. **Mov-Ent:** Television Series, Documentary Films, Biography: Show Business. **Acq:** Purchase. **Dist:** A&E Television Networks L.L.C. $24.95.

Biography: Stonewall Jackson ????
A&E Biography combines interviews, still photography, live-action footage, reenactments, period art, and other documentary material to present historical figures and their achievements. Recommended for Grades 6-12. 45m; VHS. **A:** Jr. High-Sr. High. **P:** Education. **U:** Home, Institution. **Gen-Edu:** Biography, History--U.S. **Acq:** Purchase. **Dist:** Social Studies School Service; Zenger Media. $14.95.

Biography: Strom Thurmond 20??
Presents the A&E cable channel special on former U.S. senator Strom Thurmond, whose controversial career began in 1946 as South Carolina's governor; in 1954 he began his senatorial service that ran until his death in 2003, making him the oldest and longest serving senator in U.S. history; though known for his ardent stance against the civil rights movement, it was disclosed after he died that he had fathered a child in 1925 with an African American maid. Includes interviews with family, friends, and colleagues. 50m; DVD. **A:** Family. **P:** Entertainment. **U:** Home, CATV. **Mov-Ent:** Television Series, Documentary Films, Biography: Politics. **Acq:** Purchase. **Dist:** A&E Television Networks L.L.C. $24.95.

Biography: Susan B. Anthony ????
A&E Biography combines interviews, still photography, live-action footage, reenactments, period art, and other documentary material to present historical figures and their achievements. Recommended for Grades 6-12. 45m; VHS. **A:** Jr. High-Sr. High. **P:** Education. **U:** Home, Institution. **Gen-Edu:** Biography, History--U.S. **Acq:** Purchase. **Dist:** Social Studies School Service; Zenger Media. $14.95.

Biography: Tammy Faye: Faith and Flamboyance ????
Presents the A&E cable channel special on Tammy Faye Bakker, as she was known during her days in the 1980s as a television evangelist with then-husband Jim Bakker; after scandals led to the end of their show and marriage, she married his best friend, Roe Messner. Includes interviews and footage (program was produced prior to her death in 2007). 50m; DVD. **A:** Jr. High-Adult. **P:** Entertainment. **U:** Home, CATV. **Mov-Ent:** Television Series, Documentary Films, Biography: Show Business. **Acq:** Purchase. **Dist:** A&E Television Networks L.L.C. $24.95.

Biography: Ted Bundy 2007
Examines the crimes of the serial killer, executed in Florida in 1989, whose four-year spree left at least 26 victims dead and possibly many more. 50m; DVD. **A:** Jr. High-Adult. **P:** Entertainment. **U:** Home. **Gen-Edu:** Documentary Films, Biography: Law Enforcement. **Acq:** Purchase. **Dist:** A&E Television Networks L.L.C.

Biography: Telly Savalas: Who Loves Ya, Baby? ????
Presents the A&E cable channel special on actor Telly Savalas, who began his career in film but became popular as detective Theo Kojak in the 1973-1978 television series "Kojak"; includes clips and interviews with family and friends. 50m; DVD. **A:** Jr. High-Adult. **P:** Entertainment. **U:** Home, CATV. **Mov-Ent:** Television Series, Documentary Films, Biography: Show Business. **Acq:** Purchase. **Dist:** A&E Television Networks L.L.C. $24.95.

Biography: The Apostles ????
Presents the A&E cable channel special on the biblical 12 disciples selected by Jesus to spread his message and teachings; includes interviews with scholars. 50m; DVD. **A:** Family. **P:** Entertainment. **U:** Home, CATV. **Mov-Ent:** Television Series, Documentary Films, Religion. **Acq:** Purchase. **Dist:** A&E Television Networks L.L.C. $24.95.

Biography: The Astors: High Society ????
Presents the A&E cable channel special on the Astor family, the American family known for their riches, philanthropy, and troubled lives; they originated with fur magnate and financier John Jacob Astor in the late 18th and early 19th centuries and also included John Jacob Astor IV, who perished aboard the Titanic in 1912. 50m; DVD. **A:** Jr. High-Adult. **P:** Entertainment. **U:** Home, CATV. **Mov-Ent:** Television Series, Documentary Films, Biography. **Acq:** Purchase. **Dist:** A&E Television Networks L.L.C. $24.95.

Biography: The Barrymores 2000
Presents the A&E cable channel special on the successful-yet-tumultuous lives of the Barrymore family, which has included several prominent actors in the past 150 years beginning with Maurice Barrymore to modern-day actress Drew Barrymore; includes video clips and interviews with friends and family. 100m; DVD. **A:** Family. **P:** Entertainment. **U:** Home, CATV. **Mov-Ent:** Television Series, Documentary Films. **Acq:** Purchase. **Dist:** A&E Television Networks L.L.C. $29.95.

Biography: The Bee Gees: This Is Where I Came In 2000
Presents the A&E cable channel special on the pop/disco music band The Bee Gees, comprised of brothers Maurice, Robin, and Barry Gibb, as they rose to fame during the 1970s but fell quickly as disco was shunned in the early 1980s; they suffered in their personal lives when youngest brother and solo artist Andy Gibb died in 1988 at the age of 30 while they were in the midst of releasing a new album (which contained a tribute to him); their final album was released in 2001 ("This Is Where I Came In") as Maurice died two years later (this is not included in this DVD). Includes concert footage and interviews with the trio. 100m; DVD. **A:** Jr. High-Adult. **P:** Entertainment. **U:** Home, CATV. **Mov-Ent:** Television Series, Documentary Films, Biography: Music. **Acq:** Purchase. **Dist:** A&E Television Networks L.L.C. $29.95.

Biography: The Bronte Sisters 2006
Biographers and literary critics examine the lives of writers Anne, Charlotte, and Emily Bronte and the parallels between their own lives and those of their enduring characters. 50m; DVD. **A:** Jr. High-Adult. **P:** Entertainment. **U:** Home. **Gen-Edu:** Documentary Films, Biography. **Acq:** Purchase. **Dist:** A&E Television Networks L.L.C.

Biography: The Complete Churchill 1991
Spans the life of Great Britain's legendary statesman, Winston Churchill, from his birth to his death in 1965 at the age of 90. Covers his years as Prime Minister during WWII, the Yalta Conference in 1945, and his years out of politics. Includes newsreels, photographs, and interviews. Available as a four-volume boxed set. 240m; VHS. **C:** Narrated by Martin Gilbert; Written by Martin Gilbert. **Pr:** British Broadcasting Corporation; Australian Broadcasting Corporation; A&E (Arts & Entertainment) Network. **A:** Sr. High-Adult. **P:** Entertainment. **U:** Home. **Gen-Edu:** Biography, Great Britain, World War Two. **Acq:** Purchase. **Dist:** A&E Television Networks L.L.C.; PBS Home Video; Video Collectibles. $59.95.

Indiv. Titles: 1. Maverick Politician 2. To Conquer or Die 3. The Beginning of the End 4. Never Despair.

Biography: The Conquerors: Andrew Jackson: Conqueror of Florida ????
Presents the History Channel special on General Andrew Jackson's controversial role in the ceding of Florida from Spain to the United States in 1819 when he countered President James Monroe's direct orders; includes interviews with historians and footage of historic sites. 50m; DVD. **A:** Family. **P:** Entertainment. **U:** Home, CATV. **Mov-Ent:** Television Series, Documentary Films, Politics & Government. **Acq:** Purchase. **Dist:** A&E Television Networks L.L.C. $24.95.

Biography: The Earp Brothers: Lawmen of the West 2006
Looks at the controversial lives of legendary gunslingers and lawmen Virgil, Morgan, James, Newton, Warren, and Wyatt Earp. 50m; DVD. **A:** Jr. High-Adult. **P:** Entertainment. **U:** Home. **Gen-Edu:** Documentary Films, Biography: Law Enforcement. **Acq:** Purchase. **Dist:** A&E Television Networks L.L.C.

Biography: The Extraordinary Voyages of Jules Verne 2006
Presents the A&E cable channel special on 19th century French author Jules Verne, who wrote many science fiction classics such as "From the Earth to the Moon," "20,000 Leagues Under the Sea," and "Journey to the Center of the Earth"; features an interview with Verne's great-grandson. 50m; DVD. **A:** Family. **P:** Entertainment. **U:** Home, CATV. **Mov-Ent:** Television Series, Documentary Films, Biography. **Acq:** Purchase. **Dist:** A&E Television Networks L.L.C. $24.95.

Biography: The Fabulous World of Faberge ????
Presents the A&E cable channel special on Russian jeweler Peter Carl Faberge, who began creating exquisitely-adorned Easter eggs covered with precious jewels during the late 19th century for Russia's royalty; his creations also included more typical fine jewelry and tableware; includes interviews with family descendants and historians. 50m; DVD. **A:** Jr. High-Adult. **P:** Entertainment. **U:** Home, CATV. **Mov-Ent:** Television Series, Documentary Films, USSR. **Acq:** Purchase. **Dist:** A&E Television Networks L.L.C. $24.95.

Biography: The Gabors: Fame, Fortune and Romance ????
Presents the A&E cable channel special on the lives of the Gabor sisters (Zsa Zsa, Magda, and Eva) from their privileged beginnings in Hungary to wealth and fame in the United States; includes interviews and footage. 50m; DVD. **A:** Family. **P:** Entertainment. **U:** Home, CATV. **Mov-Ent**: Television Series, Documentary Films, Biography: Show Business. **Acq:** Purchase. **Dist:** A&E Television Networks L.L.C. $24.95.

Biography: The Gambinos ????
Presents the A&E cable channel special on the New York City's Gambino crime family, founded by Carlo Gambino during the 1920s; at one time, the family numbered about 1,000 members, although it has been reduced to about 200 members of late. Includes interviews and footage. 100m; DVD. **A:** Sr. High-Adult. **P:** Entertainment. **U:** Home, CATV. **Mov-Ent**: Television Series, Documentary Films, Biography. **Acq:** Purchase. **Dist:** A&E Television Networks L.L.C. $29.95.

Biography: The Gettys: A Tragedy of Riches ????
Presents the A&E cable channel special on the influential Getty family, whose involvement in the oil industry began with patriarch George Franklin Getty in the 19th century and continued with his son, J. Paul Getty (1892-1976), who thrived in the early 20th century with his Getty Oil Company; though successful, the family endured many troubles including disputes between family members. Includes interviews with three generations of Gettys, family, friends, and associates as well as news footage. 50m; DVD. **A:** Jr. High-Adult. **P:** Entertainment. **U:** Home, CATV. **Mov-Ent**: Television Series, Documentary Films, Oil Industry. **Acq:** Purchase. **Dist:** A&E Television Networks L.L.C. $24.95.

Biography: The Google Boys 2006
Discover how Stanford grad students Larry Page and Sergey Brin went from a university research project to a multi-billion dollar worldwide corporation with the world's most popular Internet search engine. 50m; DVD. **A:** Jr. High-Adult. **P:** Entertainment. **U:** Home. **Gen-Edu**: Documentary Films, Biography. **Acq:** Purchase. **Dist:** A&E Television Networks L.L.C.

Biography: The Green River Killer 20??
Presents the A&E cable channel special on serial killer Gary Ridgway, known as the "Green River Killer" who murdered 49 women from 1982 to 2001 in the northwestern Washington area; includes interviews with law enforcement. 50m; DVD. **A:** Sr. High-Adult. **P:** Entertainment. **U:** Home, CATV. **Mov-Ent**: Television Series, Documentary Films, Biography. **Acq:** Purchase. **Dist:** A&E Television Networks L.L.C. $24.95.

Biography: The Grimaldi Dynasty ????
Presents the A&E cable channel special on Monaco's ruling family, the Grimaldis, in particular Prince Rainier III and wife Grace Kelly, who had been a popular Hollywood actress at the time they were married (1956); features their three children—Princess Caroline, Princess Stephanie, and Prince Albert—and the struggles they have had due to the intense media coverage of their lives since they were teenagers. 50m; DVD. **A:** Jr. High-Adult. **P:** Entertainment. **U:** Home, CATV. **Mov-Ent**: Television Series, Documentary Films, Biography: Royalty. **Acq:** Purchase. **Dist:** A&E Television Networks L.L.C. $24.95.

Biography: The Hilton Family ????
Presents the A&E cable channel special on the four generations of the hotel empire family, the Hiltons, from patriarch Conrad Hilton to socialite Paris Hilton, and the various personal troubles as well as their continued business successes. 50m; DVD. **A:** Jr. High-Adult. **P:** Entertainment. **U:** Home, CATV. **Mov-Ent**: Television Series, Documentary Films, Hotels & Hotel Staff Training. **Acq:** Purchase. **Dist:** A&E Television Networks L.L.C. $24.95.

Biography: The Home Depot 2006
Profiles the retail giant founded by Arthur Blank and Bernie Marcus, from the opening of their first Atlanta store in 1979 to its multi-national, multi-billion dollar present. 50m; DVD. **A:** Jr. High-Adult. **P:** Entertainment. **U:** Home. **Gen-Edu**: Documentary Films, Biography. **Acq:** Purchase. **Dist:** A&E Television Networks L.L.C.

Biography: The Hunchback of Notre Dame ????
Presents the A&E cable channel special on the fictional character Quasimodo, created by French author Victor Hugo in his 1831 novel "Notre Dame de Paris," or later "The Hunchback of Notre Dame"; examines his evolution into television and film. Includes interviews with experts, archival materials, and film clips. 50m; DVD. **A:** Family. **P:** Entertainment. **U:** Home, CATV. **Mov-Ent**: Television Series, Documentary Films, Literature. **Acq:** Purchase. **Dist:** A&E Television Networks L.L.C. $24.95.

Biography: The James Gang: Outlaw Brothers ????
Presents the A&E cable channel special on the Jesse James gang, who robbed banks and trains during the 19th century in the Old West; includes interviews with experts and archival photos. 50m; DVD. **A:** Sr. High-Adult. **P:** Entertainment. **U:** Home, CATV. **Mov-Ent**: Television Series, Documentary Films, Biography. **Acq:** Purchase. **Dist:** A&E Television Networks L.L.C. $24.95.

Biography: The Kellogg Brothers ????
Presents the A&E cable channel special on brothers John Harvey Kellogg and Will Keith Kellogg, best known for developing the first flaked cereal in the late 1890s, though their successful partnership later turned sour, leading to a hostile family dispute; includes interviews with family historians. 50m; DVD. **A:** Jr. High-Adult. **P:** Entertainment. **U:** Home, CATV. **Mov-Ent**: Television Series, Documentary Films, Food Industry. **Acq:** Purchase. **Dist:** A&E Television Networks L.L.C. $24.95.

Biography: The Lost Generation 2001
Presents the A&E cable channel special on the lives of several American authors—F. Scott Fitzgerald, John Dos Passos, Archibald MacLeish, Ezra Pound, Gertrude Stein and Ernest Hemingway—who left the United States during the 1920s and spent time working on their craft in Europe; includes interviews. 100m; DVD. **A:** Jr. High-Adult. **P:** Entertainment. **U:** Home, CATV. **Mov-Ent**: Television Series, Documentary Films, Biography. **Acq:** Purchase. **Dist:** A&E Television Networks L.L.C. $29.95.

Biography: The Marshall Fields: A Chicago Tradition ????
Presents the A&E cable channel special on the history of the Chicago-based Marshall Fields department stores and its founder Marshall Field, who established it in the 19th century; also profiles his family, who continued to run the business and, despite their successes, had also suffered various tragedies. Features an interview with Marshall Field V, news accounts, and video footage. 50m; DVD. **A:** Jr. High-Adult. **P:** Entertainment. **U:** Home, CATV. **Mov-Ent**: Television Series, Documentary Films, Business. **Acq:** Purchase. **Dist:** A&E Television Networks L.L.C. $24.95.

Biography: The Mystery of Edgar Allan Poe 2004
Presents the A&E cable channel special on American poet and writer Edgar Allan Poe (1809-1849), who created such dark and haunting poems and stories as "The Raven," "The Telltale Heart," and "The Pit and the Pendulum"; his life mimicked his writings as his addictions, depression, and troubled relationships culminated in his early death at the age of 40. 50m; DVD. **A:** Jr. High-Adult. **P:** Entertainment. **U:** Home, CATV. **Mov-Ent**: Television Series, Documentary Films, Biography. **Acq:** Purchase. **Dist:** A&E Television Networks L.L.C. $24.95.

Biography: The Osmonds: Pure and Simple 1999
Presents the A&E cable channel special on the singing family the Osmonds from their beginnings on "The Andy Williams Show" and in the 1970s with Donny and Marie's television show; revisits their return to the national spotlight in the 1990s; includes interviews with family members and performance clips. 50m; DVD. **A:** Family. **P:** Entertainment. **U:** Home, CATV. **Mov-Ent**: Television Series, Documentary Films, Biography: Music. **Acq:** Purchase. **Dist:** A&E Television Networks L.L.C. $24.95.

Biography: The Phantom: Comic Strip Crusader ????
Presents the A&E cable channel special on the comic strip "The Phantom," created in 1936 by Lee Falk, and follows the fictional character's transition into 1996 film starring Billy Zane; includes interviews with Zane and others. 50m; DVD. **A:** Family. **P:** Entertainment. **U:** Home, CATV. **Mov-Ent**: Television Series, Documentary Films, Fiction. **Acq:** Purchase. **Dist:** A&E Television Networks L.L.C. $24.95.

Biography: The Popes: The Legacy of Peter ????
Presents the A&E cable channel special on the papacy beginning with the selection of Peter II as the first Pope after the crucifixion of Christ through Pope John Paul II; includes interviews with biblical scholars and historians. 100m; DVD. **A:** Family. **P:** Entertainment. **U:** Home, CATV. **Mov-Ent**: Television Series, Documentary Films, Religion. **Acq:** Purchase. **Dist:** A&E Television Networks L.L.C. $24.95.

Biography: The Post-Impressionists: Van Gogh & Gauguin ????
Presents the A&E cable channel special on post-impressionist artists Vincent Van Gogh and Paul Gauguin and the brief—yet productive and intense—time they spent working together during 1888 in France; includes interviews with art historians. 100m; DVD. **A:** Jr. High-Adult. **P:** Entertainment. **U:** Home, CATV. **Mov-Ent**: Television Series, Documentary Films, Biography: Artists. **Acq:** Purchase. **Dist:** A&E Television Networks L.L.C. $29.95.

Biography: The Princesses of Monaco ????
Presents the A&E cable channel special focused on Monaco's Princess Caroline and Princess Stephanie, the daughters of Prince Ranier and Princess Grace (Kelly); details the devastation of their mother's death in 1982 from a car accident, scandals they have endured, and how they often clash with one another. 50m; DVD. **A:** Family. **P:** Entertainment. **U:** Home, CATV. **Mov-Ent**: Television Series, Documentary Films, Biography: Royalty. **Acq:** Purchase. **Dist:** A&E Television Networks L.L.C. $24.95.

Biography: The Redgraves ????
Presents the A&E cable channel special on the acting family the Redgraves of England; patriarch Roy Redgrave first entered the craft in 1900 in the theater and went on to silent film acting. His life was troubled and he moved—and married—often. Acting members of the family tree include his son Michael along with granddaughters Lynn and Vanessa and grandson Corin, whose daughter Jemma is also an actress. 50m; DVD. **A:** Jr. High-Adult. **P:** Entertainment. **U:** Home, CATV. **Mov-Ent**: Television Series, Documentary Films, Biography: Show Business. **Acq:** Purchase. **Dist:** A&E Television Networks L.L.C. $24.95.

Biography: The Rockefellers ????
A&E Biography combines interviews, still photography, live-action footage, reenactments, period art, and other documentary material to present historical figures and their achievements. Recommended for Grades 6-12. 45m; VHS. **A:** Jr. High-Sr. High. **P:** Education. **U:** Home, Institution. **Gen-Edu**: Biography, History, Business. **Acq:** Purchase. **Dist:** Social Studies School Service; Zenger Media. $14.95.

Biography: The Tiffanys: The Mark of Excellence 2006
Examines the legacy of "fancy goods" merchant Louis Comfort Tiffany and that of his son Charles. 50m; DVD. **A:** Jr. High-Adult. **P:** Entertainment. **U:** Home. **Gen-Edu**: Documentary Films, Biography. **Acq:** Purchase. **Dist:** A&E Television Networks L.L.C.

Biography: The Vanderbilts ????
A&E Biography combines interviews, still photography, live-action footage, reenactments, period art, and other documentary material to present historical figures and their achievements. Recommended for Grades 6-12. 45m; VHS. **A:** Jr. High-Sr. High. **P:** Education. **U:** Home, Institution. **Gen-Edu**: Biography, History, Business. **Acq:** Purchase. **Dist:** Social Studies School Service; Zenger Media. $14.95.

Biography: Theodore J. Kaczynski: The Unabomber ????
Presents the A&E cable channel special on American domestic terrorist Ted Kaczynski, who began his violent and fatal attacks in 1978 via the postal system using bombs—three deaths and 29 injured; he was given the nickname "The Unabomber" for targeting universities and airlines. In 1994 he began circulating his anti-technology "manifesto" publication, which caused his brother to alert authorities and led to Kaczynski's capture in 1996 in a remote area of Montana. Includes interviews with FBI agents, a college roommate, and a childhood neighbor. 50m; DVD. **A:** Family. **P:** Entertainment. **U:** Home, CATV. **Mov-Ent**: Television Series, Documentary Films, Biography. **Acq:** Purchase. **Dist:** A&E Television Networks L.L.C. $24.95.

Biography: Theodore Roosevelt ????
A&E Biography combines interviews, still photography, live-action footage, reenactments, period art, and other documentary material to present historical figures and their achievements. Recommended for Grades 6-12. 45m; VHS. **A:** Jr. High-Sr. High. **P:** Education. **U:** Home, Institution. **Gen-Edu**: Biography, Presidency, History--U.S. **Acq:** Purchase. **Dist:** Social Studies School Service; Zenger Media. $14.95.

Biography: Thomas A. Edison ????
A&E Biography combines interviews, still photography, live-action footage, reenactments, period art, and other documentary material to present historical figures and their achievements. Recommended for Grades 6-12. 45m; VHS. **A:** Jr. High-Sr. High. **P:** Education. **U:** Home, Institution. **Gen-Edu**: Biography, Scientists, Inventors & Inventions. **Acq:** Purchase. **Dist:** Social Studies School Service; Zenger Media. $14.95.

Biography: Thomas Edison: Father of Invention 2006
Biography of the inventor takes the viewer from Edison's midwestern childhood to the unhappy consequences of fame on his personal life. 50m; DVD. **A:** Jr. High-Adult. **P:** Entertainment. **U:** Home. **Gen-Edu**: Documentary Films, Biography. **Acq:** Purchase. **Dist:** A&E Television Networks L.L.C.

Biography: Thomas Jefferson ????
A&E Biography combines interviews, still photography, live-action footage, reenactments, period art, and other documentary material to present historical figures and their achievements. Recommended for Grades 6-12. 45m; VHS. **A:** Jr. High-Sr. High. **P:** Education. **U:** Home, Institution. **Gen-Edu**: Biography, Presidency, History--U.S. **Acq:** Purchase. **Dist:** Social Studies School Service; Zenger Media. $14.95.

Biography: Thurgood Marshall ????
A&E Biography combines interviews, still photography, live-action footage, reenactments, period art, and other documentary material to present historical figures and their achievements. Recommended for Grades 6-12. 45m; VHS. **A:** Jr. High-Sr. High. **P:** Education. **U:** Home, Institution. **Gen-Edu**: Biography, History--Modern. **Acq:** Purchase. **Dist:** Social Studies School Service; Zenger Media. $14.95.

Biography: Tim LaHaye ????
Presents the A&E cable channel special on minister and author Tim LaHaye (1926-), who is best known for being the co-author (with Jerry B. Jenkins) of the bestselling "Left Behind" fictional apocalyptic series as well as a powerful member of the conservative Christian Right political operative. 50m; DVD. **A:** Jr. High-Adult. **P:** Entertainment. **U:** Home, CATV. **Mov-Ent**: Television Series, Documentary Films, Biography. **Acq:** Purchase. **Dist:** A&E Television Networks L.L.C. $24.95.

Biography: Tim Robbins ????
Presents the A&E cable channel special on actor, director, and activist Tim Robbins, who has starred in a variety of films such as "Bull Durham," "The Shawshank Redemption," and "Mystic River" in 2004, for which he won the Oscar for best supporting actor, along with being nominated for the Academy Award for best director in 1996 for "Dead Man Walking" (for which his longtime partner, Susan Sarandon, won the Oscar for best actress); though protective of their children's privacy, the couple has been extremely active in displaying their political views. Includes home videos, film clips, and interviews with family and friends. 50m; DVD. **A:** Family. **P:** Entertainment. **U:** Home, CATV. **Mov-Ent**: Television Series, Documentary Films, Biography: Show Business. **Acq:** Purchase. **Dist:** A&E Television Networks L.L.C. $24.95.

Biography: Toby Keith 20??
Presents the A&E cable channel special on country singer Toby Keith, who is best known for his patriotic and controversial 2002 single "Courtesy of the Red, White and Blue (The Angry American)" which led to his winning "Entertainer of the Year" from the Country Music Association; he switched from a professional football career to music and in 1993 his debut album was certified platinum, followed by other successful albums. 50m;

DVD. **A:** Jr. High-Adult. **P:** Entertainment. **U:** Home, CATV. **Mov-Ent**: Television Series, Documentary Films, Biography: Music. **Acq:** Purchase. **Dist:** A&E Television Networks L.L.C. $24.95.

Biography: Tokyo Rose: Victim of Propaganda 2000
Presents the A&E cable channel special on Iva Toguri, an American who was one of more than 20 women known infamously as "Tokyo Rose" during World War II for broadcasting Japanese propaganda designed to squash Allied morale. Toguri's visit to Japan came during the Pearl Harbor attack, which forced her to remain in the country; despite the arduous circumstances, she was jailed for six years in the United States, though pardoned by President Gerald Ford in January 1977. 50m; DVD. **A:** Jr. High-Adult. **P:** Entertainment. **U:** Home, CATV. **Mov-Ent:** Television Series, Documentary Films, World War Two. **Acq:** Purchase. **Dist:** A&E Television Networks L.L.C. $24.95.

Biography: Tom Hanks: The Luckiest Man in the World 2007
Presents the A&E cable channel special on actor, director, and producer Tom Hanks, who began in the television series "Bosom Buddies" but has since appeared in numerous films such as "Splash," "Big," "Sleepless in Seattle," and "Apollo 13" as well as winning the Academy Award for best actor for "Philadelphia" and "Forrest Gump"; his interest in the U.S. space program led to his HBO miniseries "From the Earth to the Moon" for which he won the Emmy for best director. Includes private photographs and interviews with friends and family. 50m; DVD. **A:** Family. **P:** Entertainment. **U:** Home, CATV. **Mov-Ent**: Television Series, Documentary Films, Biography: Show Business. **Acq:** Purchase. **Dist:** A&E Television Networks L.L.C. $24.95.

Biography: Tom Selleck ????
Presents the A&E cable channel special on actor Tom Selleck, best known for his television series "Magnum P.I." (1980-1988), though he had moderate film success with "Three Men and a Baby"; includes his early appearances on the soap opera "The Young and the Restless" along with his popular recurring role as Monica's love interest on "Friends." Includes rare clips and interviews with family and friends. 50m; DVD. **A:** Family. **P:** Entertainment. **U:** Home, CATV. **Mov-Ent**: Television Series, Documentary Films, Biography: Show Business. **Acq:** Purchase. **Dist:** A&E Television Networks L.L.C. $24.95.

Biography: Tony Randall 1999
Presents the A&E cable channel special on legendary actor Tony Randall, who starred as the tidy Felix in "The Odd Couple" (1970-1975) with Jack Klugman as the sloppy Oscar; features his humble beginnings in Tulsa, Oklahoma, to the new family he started in his 70s. 50m; DVD. **A:** Family. **P:** Entertainment. **U:** Home, CATV. **Mov-Ent**: Television Series, Documentary Films, Biography: Show Business. **Acq:** Purchase. **Dist:** A&E Television Networks L.L.C. $24.95.

Biography: Tony Robbins: The Secret of His Success 2005
Presents the A&E cable channel special on motivational speaker Tony Robbins, who achieved fame through his infomercials and seminars; includes interviews, photographs, and footage. 50m; DVD. **A:** Jr. High-Adult. **P:** Entertainment. **U:** Home, CATV. **Mov-Ent**: Television Series, Documentary Films, Biography. **Acq:** Purchase. **Dist:** A&E Television Networks L.L.C. $24.95.

Biography: Travis Tritt ????
Presents the A&E cable channel special on country music singer Travis Tritt, who began his career in 1989 and had several hit singles, including "Can I Trust You With My Heart" and "Foolish Pride," and later joined the cast of the Grand Ole Opry. 50m; DVD. **A:** Jr. High-Adult. **P:** Entertainment. **U:** Home, CATV. **Mov-Ent**: Television Series, Documentary Films, Biography: Music. **Acq:** Purchase. **Dist:** A&E Television Networks L.L.C. $24.95.

Biography: Truman Capote 2005
Chronicles the life of the southern-born author whose flamboyant personality and success gained him entrance to New York society. Also discusses Capote's work, including "In Cold Blood" and "Breakfast at Tiffany's." 50m; DVD. **A:** Jr. High-Adult. **P:** Entertainment. **U:** Home. **Fin-Art**: Documentary Films, Sports--Winter. **Acq:** Purchase. **Dist:** A&E Television Networks L.L.C.

Biography: TV Game Shows ????
Presents the A&E cable channel special on various television game shows over the past several decades; includes interviews, clips, and commentary. 100m; DVD. **A:** Family. **P:** Entertainment. **U:** Home, CATV. **Mov-Ent**: Television Series, Documentary Films, Biography: Show Business. **Acq:** Purchase. **Dist:** A&E Television Networks L.L.C. $29.95.

Biography: TV-ography: All My Children 2003
Presents the A&E cable channel special on the popular television soap opera drama "All My Children" with behind-the-scenes coverage since the show's inception in 1970. 50m; DVD. **A:** Jr. High-Adult. **P:** Entertainment. **U:** Home, CATV. **Mov-Ent**: Television Series, Documentary Films, Biography: Show Business. **Acq:** Purchase. **Dist:** A&E Television Networks L.L.C. $24.95.

Biography: Van Gogh ????
Examines the life and masterpieces of the great artist. 50m; VHS. **A:** Sr. High-Adult. **P:** Education. **U:** Home, Institution. **Gen-Edu**: Art & Artists, Biography. **Acq:** Purchase. **Dist:** Crystal Productions. $14.95.

Biography: Vera Wang ????
Presents the A&E cable channel special on fashion designer Vera Wang, who gained acclaim for her celebrity wedding gowns; profiles her career from fashion editor at "Vogue" magazine to working at Ralph Lauren. Features interviews with family, friends, and clients such as actress Charlize Theron, along with Wang herself. 50m; DVD. **A:** Family. **P:** Entertainment. **U:** Home, CATV. **Mov-Ent**: Television Series, Documentary Films, Biography: Show Business. **Acq:** Purchase. **Dist:** A&E Television Networks L.L.C. $24.95.

Biography: Vincent Price: The Versatile Villain ????
Presents the A&E cable channel special on actor Vincent Price, who made a career primarily playing the bad guy in his over 100 movies and hundreds of television appearances that spanned six decades, including "House of Wax," "The Fly," "Tales of Terror," and "Edward Scissorhands"; includes his early life spent in a privileged family and features an interview with his daughter, who describes the struggles of his off-screen life. 50m; DVD. **A:** Family. **P:** Entertainment. **U:** Home, CATV. **Mov-Ent**: Television Series, Documentary Films, Biography: Show Business. **Acq:** Purchase. **Dist:** A&E Television Networks L.L.C. $24.95.

Biography: Vincent Van Gogh: A Stroke of Genius ????
Presents the A&E cable channel special on 19th century Dutch artist Vincent Van Gogh, who was best known for his "Starry Night" painting and for his emotional struggles as a tormented artist, including an episode that led to him cutting off his ear; includes an interview with biographer Cliff Edwards. 50m; DVD. **A:** Jr. High-Adult. **P:** Entertainment. **U:** Home, CATV. **Mov-Ent**: Television Series, Documentary Films, Biography: Artists. **Acq:** Purchase. **Dist:** A&E Television Networks L.L.C. $24.95.

Biography: Vladimir Lenin ????
A&E Biography combines interviews, still photography, live-action footage, reenactments, period art, and other documentary material to present historical figures and their achievements. Recommended for Grades 6-12. 45m; VHS. **A:** Jr. High-Sr. High. **P:** Education. **U:** Home, Institution. **Gen-Edu**: Biography, History--Modern. **Acq:** Purchase. **Dist:** Social Studies School Service; Zenger Media. $14.95.

Biography: Walter Cronkite: Eyewitness to History ????
Presents the A&E cable channel special on legendary broadcast journalist Walter Cronkite from his time as a reporter during World War II to anchor of CBS News' "Evening News"; includes interviews and video footage. 100m; DVD. **A:** Family. **P:** Entertainment. **U:** Home, CATV. **Mov-Ent**: Television Series, Documentary Films, Biography: Show Business. **Acq:** Purchase. **Dist:** A&E Television Networks L.L.C. $29.95.

Biography: Warhol ????
Examines the life and masterpieces of the great artist. 50m; VHS. **A:** Sr. High-Adult. **P:** Education. **U:** Home, Institution. **Gen-Edu**: Art & Artists, Biography. **Acq:** Purchase. **Dist:** Crystal Productions. $14.95.

Biography: Wayne Gretzky: The Great One ????
Presents the A&E cable channel special on legendary National Hockey League player Wayne Gretzky, who was nicknamed "The Great One" and became the league's all-time leading scorer as well as a nine-time MVP; includes interviews and footage. 50m; DVD. **A:** Family. **P:** Entertainment. **U:** Home, CATV. **Mov-Ent**: Television Series, Documentary Films, Biography: Sports. **Acq:** Purchase. **Dist:** A&E Television Networks L.L.C. $24.95.

Biography: Wayne Newton: King of Las Vegas ????
Presents the A&E cable channel special on singer and entertainer Wayne Newton, who had the 1963 hit "Danke Schoen" and has spent four decades performing some 30,000 solo shows in Las Vegas, earning him the title of "Mr. Las Vegas"; also profiles his personal turmoil in the 1980s from a divorce and financial difficulties; includes interviews and performance clips. 50m; DVD. **A:** Jr. High-Adult. **P:** Entertainment. **U:** Home, CATV. **Mov-Ent**: Television Series, Documentary Films, Biography: Music. **Acq:** Purchase. **Dist:** A&E Television Networks L.L.C. $24.95.

Biography: Whoopi Goldberg 20??
Presents the A&E cable channel special on comedienne and actress Whoopi Goldberg, who overcame early personal struggles to achieve box office success with "Ghost" and "The Color Purple" along with her popular stand-up act; includes interviews with Whoopi as well as good friends and comedians Robin Williams and Billy Crystal. 50m; DVD. **A:** Family. **P:** Entertainment. **U:** Home, CATV. **Mov-Ent**: Television Series, Documentary Films, Biography: Show Business. **Acq:** Purchase. **Dist:** A&E Television Networks L.L.C. $24.95.

Biography: Wilbur & Orville Wright ????
A&E Biography combines interviews, still photography, live-action footage, reenactments, period art, and other documentary material to present historical figures and their achievements. Recommended for Grades 6-12. 45m; VHS. **A:** Jr. High-Sr. High. **P:** Education. **U:** Home, Institution. **Gen-Edu**: Biography, Scientists, Inventors & Inventions. **Acq:** Purchase. **Dist:** Social Studies School Service; Zenger Media. $14.95.

Biography: Will Smith 2007
Presents the A&E cable channel special on singer and actor Will Smith, who began his career as a rap artist with hits such as "Parents Just Don't Understand" (for which he won the first Grammy in the rap category), which launched his television series "The Fresh Prince of Bel-Air" (1990-1996) and blockbuster movies such as "Independence Day," "Men in Black" and "Men in Black II" along with "Ali" and "The Pursuit and Happyness," both of which brought him Academy Award nominations for best actor. Includes archival clips of Smith on TV specials and dance shows as well as interviews with family and friends. 50m; DVD. **A:** Family. **P:** Entertainment. **U:** Home, CATV. **Mov-Ent**: Television Series, Documentary Films, Biography: Show Business. **Acq:** Purchase. **Dist:** A&E Television Networks L.L.C. $24.95.

Biography: William S. Paley: The Eye of CBS ????
Presents the A&E cable channel special on television executive William S. Paley, who transformed the Columbia Broadcast System (CBS) radio network in the late 1920s into a major player in the industry. Includes interviews with Walter Cronkite, Henry Kissinger, and executive Frank Stanton. 50m; DVD. **A:** Family. **P:** Entertainment. **U:** Home, CATV. **Mov-Ent**: Television Series, Documentary Films, Biography: Show Business. **Acq:** Purchase. **Dist:** A&E Television Networks L.L.C. $24.95.

Biography: William Shakespeare 1996
Program pieces together clues to the writer's life, from his youth in Stratford-on-Avon, to his marriage, work as playwright and actor, and death at 52. Includes dramatic readings and location footage. 50m; VHS. **A:** Jr. High-Adult. **P:** Entertainment. **U:** Home, Institution. **Gen-Edu**: Biography, Great Britain. **Acq:** Purchase. **Dist:** A&E Television Networks L.L.C.

Biography: William Shakespeare-A Life in Drama 1996
Provides a thorough investigation of how the man's life shaped the poet's work. For Grades 7 and up. 50m; VHS. **A:** Jr. High-Sr. High. **P:** Education. **U:** Institution, Home. **Gen-Edu**: Theater, Literature, Biography. **Acq:** Purchase. **Dist:** Social Studies School Service; Zenger Media. $14.95.

Biography: William Shatner 20??
Presents the A&E cable channel special on actor William Shatner, most known for his role as Captain James T. Kirk of the "Star Trek" franchise (television series from 1966-1969 and five Star Trek movies from 1979-1991), "T.J. Hooker" (1982-1986), and "Boston Legal" (2004-); includes interviews with his many co-stars including Leonard Nimoy and James Spader along with his daughters Lisabeth and Leslie and wife Elizabeth, among others. 50m; DVD. **A:** Jr. High-Adult. **P:** Entertainment. **U:** Home, CATV. **Mov-Ent**: Television Series, Documentary Films, Biography: Show Business. **Acq:** Purchase. **Dist:** A&E Television Networks L.L.C. $24.95.

Biography: Witness James Baldwin 2006
Throughout the 1950s and 60s, Baldwin was influential in the Civil Rights movement as the voice of Black America. Friends and colleagues look at his legacy and his writings. 50m; DVD. **A:** Jr. High-Adult. **P:** Entertainment. **U:** Home. **Gen-Edu**: Documentary Films, Biography. **Acq:** Purchase. **Dist:** A&E Television Networks L.L.C.

Biography: Wolfgang Puck: Recipe for Success ????
Presents the A&E cable channel special on Austrian-American celebrity chef and restaurateur Wolfgang Puck, who became known for serving his California cuisine creations to the Hollywood crowd beginning in the mid-1970s, which launched several international establishments; includes interviews with colleagues, patrons, family, and friends. 50m; DVD. **A:** Jr. High-Adult. **P:** Entertainment. **U:** Home, CATV. **Mov-Ent**: Television Series, Documentary Films, Food Industry. **Acq:** Purchase. **Dist:** A&E Television Networks L.L.C. $24.95.

Biography: Woodrow Wilson ????
A&E Biography combines interviews, still photography, live-action footage, reenactments, period art, and other documentary material to present historical figures and their achievements. Recommended for Grades 6-12. 45m; VHS. **A:** Jr. High-Sr. High. **P:** Education. **U:** Home, Institution. **Gen-Edu**: Biography, Presidency, History--U.S. **Acq:** Purchase. **Dist:** Social Studies School Service; Zenger Media. $14.95.

Biography: Yitzhak Rabin 1996
Profiles the life of the late Israeli Prime Minister Yitzhak Rabin. Contains rare film footage and interviews with Rabin's longtime friends and associates. 50m; VHS. **Pr:** A&E (Arts & Entertainment) Network. **A:** Jr. High-Adult. **P:** Education. **U:** Home. **Gen-Edu**: Documentary Films, Biography, Middle East. **Acq:** Purchase. **Dist:** A&E Television Networks L.L.C. $19.95.

Biography: Yvonne DeCarlo ????
Presents the A&E cable channel special on actress Yvonne DeCarlo, who starred in films such as "The Ten Commandments" and "Band of Angels" but is better known for her television series role as Mrs. Munster in "The Munsters." 50m; DVD. **A:** Family. **P:** Entertainment. **U:** Home, CATV. **Mov-Ent**: Television Series, Documentary Films, Biography: Show Business. **Acq:** Purchase. **Dist:** A&E Television Networks L.L.C. $24.95.

Biography: Zorro: Mark of the Z ????
Presents the A&E cable channel special on the fictional character Zorro, created in 1919 by pulp writer Johnston McCulley, who has since appeared in numerous comic strips, television series, and films and served as the inspiration for Bob Kane's "Batman." 50m; DVD. **A:** Family. **P:** Entertainment. **U:** Home, CATV. **Mov-Ent**: Television Series, Documentary Films, Fiction. **Acq:** Purchase. **Dist:** A&E Television Networks L.L.C. $24.95.

Biohazard: The Alien Force 1995 (R) — ★½
Reptilian mutant, the result of a genetic experiment gone awry, must be hunted down before it can reproduce. Sounds like a rip-off of "Species." 88m; VHS, DVD. **C:** Steve Zurk; Chris Mitchum; Susan Fronsoe; Tom Ferguson; Patrick Moran; John

Maynard; Directed by Steve Latshaw. **A:** Sr. High-Adult. **P:** Entertainment. **U:** Home. **Mov-Ent:** Science Fiction, Genetics. **Acq:** Purchase. **Dist:** CinemaNow Inc. $92.99.

Biological and Abiological Catalysis in Organic Synthesis 1992
Discusses the advances in the field of chemical engineering in the area of synthesizing organic compounds with special emphasis on Abiological Catalysis for Synthetic Efficiency, Asymetric Catalysis, Catalytic Antibodies, and Organic Synthesis using Enzymes. Presented in the format of a panel discussion of industry experts. 210m; VHS. **A:** Adult. **P:** Professional. **U:** Institution. **Hea-Sci:** Chemistry, Industry & Industrialists, Engineering. **Acq:** Purchase. **Dist:** American Chemical Society. $2200.00.

Biological and Spiritual Growth 199?
Joseph Chilton Pearce suggests that children are robbed of optimal development because modern birth techniques and the government system of education have created new challenges in child-raising. His advice to parents is to seek the spiritual nature of love within them. 30m; DVD. **A:** Adult. **P:** Education. **U:** Home, Institution. **Gen-Edu:** Philosophy & Ideology, Parenting, Psychology. **Acq:** Purchase. **Dist:** Thinking Allowed Productions. $29.95.

Biological Cycle Part 5 1980
This experimental video shows that humans will not become robots. 8m; VHS, 3/4 U. **Pr:** Kou Nakajima. **A:** College-Adult. **P:** Entertainment. **U:** Institution. **Fin-Art:** Video. **Acq:** Rent/Lease. **Dist:** Video Out Distribution.

Biological Hazards 1995
Centers on how infection can occur, and how workers can protect themselves from exposure. 13m; VHS. **A:** Adult. **P:** Professional. **U:** Institution. **Bus-Ind:** Safety Education, Occupational Training. **Acq:** Purchase, Rent/Lease. **Dist:** National Safety Council, California Chapter, Film Library. $395.00.

Biological Membranes: Chemical Constituents 1979
One of the most common phospholipids, lecithin, is used as an example to demonstrate the lipid's fundamental chemical structure and resultant physical properties. 11m; 3/4 U, Special order formats. **Pr:** Institut fur den Wissenschaftlichen. **A:** College-Adult. **P:** Education. **U:** Institution, SURA. **Hea-Sci:** Biology, Chemistry. **Acq:** Purchase, Rent/Lease. **Dist:** International Science Film Collection.

Biological Membranes: Fundamental Properties 1979
The cell and the cell membrane are discussed, as well as the membrane's functions. 13m; 3/4 U, Special order formats. **Pr:** Institut fur den Wissenschaftlichen. **A:** College-Adult. **P:** Education. **U:** Institution, SURA. **Hea-Sci:** Biology. **Acq:** Purchase, Rent/Lease. **Dist:** International Science Film Collection.

Biological Membranes: Physical Models; Monolayer, Bilayer and Liposomes 1979
This program documents that the physical properties of water and the interface activity of emphipathic molecules encourage the organization of special structures, demonstrated through the hydrophobe-hydrophile behavior of phospholipids. 17m; 3/4 U, Special order formats. **Pr:** Institut fur den Wissenschaftlichen. **A:** College-Adult. **P:** Education. **U:** Institution, SURA. **Hea-Sci:** Biology. **Acq:** Purchase, Rent/Lease. **Dist:** International Science Film Collection.

Biological Psychokinesis 1989
Marilyn Schlitz, a noted parapsychologist, discusses the ability to control other people's actions through a mental influence called biological psychokinesis. 30m; VHS. **Pr:** Thinking Allowed Productions. **A:** College-Adult. **P:** Education. **U:** Home. **Gen-Edu:** Psychology, New Age. **Acq:** Purchase. **Dist:** Thinking Allowed Productions. $29.95.

Biological Resources 1985
Examines man's reliance on the sea as a food source. 30m; VHS. **A:** Adult. **P:** Education. **U:** Institution. **Hea-Sci:** Oceanography. **Acq:** Purchase. **Dist:** RMI Media. $75.00.

Biological Rhythms: Studies in Chronobiology 1977
A discussion of chronobiology, the study of internal rhythms: their source, function, and how they can be changed. 22m; VHS, 3/4 U. **Pr:** Encyclopedia Britannica Educational Corporation. **A:** Jr. High-Sr. High. **P:** Education. **U:** Institution, SURA. **Hea-Sci:** Biology. **Acq:** Purchase, Rent/Lease, Trade-in. **Dist:** Encyclopedia Britannica.

Biologists At Work 19??
Two part video covers the history of the study of biology, including the work of pioneers like Darwin, Mendel, and Pasteur. The second half features interviews with present day scientists and discusses the impact that their work will have on the future. 34m; VHS. **A:** Sr. High-College. **P:** Education. **U:** Institution. **Hea-Sci:** Biology, Science. **Acq:** Purchase. **Dist:** Human Relations Media. $129.00.

Biology, Brain, and Behavior Series 1993
Eleven-part series covers the interrelated domains of biology, physiology of the brain and behavior. 328m; VHS, SVS, 3/4 U. **A:** College-Adult. **P:** Education. **U:** Institution. **Hea-Sci:** Biology, Diseases, Pain. **Acq:** Purchase. **Dist:** Encyclopedia Britannica. $1475.00.
Indiv. Titles: 1. Seasonal Affective Disorder 2. Easing the Pain 3. Stress 4. A Conflict of Interest 5. Pathfinding in the Brain 6. Living with Tourettes 7. Questions About Behavior 8. Hearing the Call 9. The Brain (a video workbook) 10. Analysis of Behavior (a video workbook) 11. Social Primates (a video workbook).

Biology Concepts through Discovery 1993
Two part program features interesting footage, lucid diagrams, and charts to explain how life recreates itself. Asexual Reproduction covers mitosis, types of asexual reproduction, and reproduction of viruses. Sexual Reproduction covers meiosis and sexual reproduction in plants and animals. 68m; VHS. **A:** Primary-Sr. High. **P:** Education. **U:** Institution. **Hea-Sci:** Sex & Sexuality, Biology. **Acq:** Purchase. **Dist:** Educational Activities Inc. $158.00.

Biology Concepts through Discovery: Cellular Respiration 1991
Part of the "Biology Concepts through Discovery" series. Illustrates the processes of respiration and provides easy-to-duplicate experiments which show how energy provided by respiration is used by life. ?m; VHS. **A:** Jr. High-Adult. **P:** Education. **U:** Institution. **Hea-Sci:** Science, Biology. **Acq:** Purchase. **Dist:** Cambridge Educational. $79.00.

Biology Concepts through Discovery: Ecology 1991
Part of the "Biology Concepts through Discovery" series. Examines different types of ecosystems, explaining the relationships between organisms, biomes, food chains and webs, nature's cycles, and ecological succession. ?m; VHS. **A:** Jr. High-Adult. **P:** Education. **U:** Institution. **Hea-Sci:** Science, Biology, Ecology & Environment. **Acq:** Purchase. **Dist:** Cambridge Educational. $79.00.

Biology Concepts through Discovery: Excretion 1991
Part of the "Biology Concepts through Discovery" series. Examines the processes of excretion associated with the lungs, kidneys, and skin. ?m; VHS. **A:** Jr. High-Adult. **P:** Education. **U:** Institution. **Hea-Sci:** Science, Biology. **Acq:** Purchase. **Dist:** Cambridge Educational. $79.00.

Biology Concepts through Discovery: Photosynthesis 1991
Part of the "Biology Concepts through Discovery" series. Explains the processes involved in photosynthesis, illustrating how the basic elements combine to produce food and water. ?m; VHS. **A:** Jr. High-Adult. **P:** Education. **U:** Institution. **Hea-Sci:** Science, Biology. **Acq:** Purchase. **Dist:** Cambridge Educational. $79.00.

Biology Concepts through Discovery: Pollution 1991
Part of the "Biology Concepts through Discovery" series. Explores different types and causes of pollution, including acid rain, the greenhouse effect, ozone depletion, water pollution, the effects of chemical and hazardous waste, and renewable and nonrenewable resources. ?m; VHS. **A:** Jr. High-Adult. **P:** Education. **U:** Institution. **Hea-Sci:** Science, Biology, Ecology & Environment. **Acq:** Purchase. **Dist:** Cambridge Educational. $79.00.

Biology: Exploring the Living World 1979
Provides an overview of the life sciences. Recommended for showing at the beginning of a course of study in biology. 17m; VHS, 3/4 U. **Pr:** Encyclopedia Britannica Educational Corporation. **A:** Jr. High-Sr. High. **P:** Education. **U:** Institution, SURA. **Hea-Sci:** Biology. **Acq:** Purchase, Rent/Lease, Trade-in. **Dist:** Encyclopedia Britannica.

Biology Fieldwork 1 19??
Learning program for young students helps them see how to complete the practical fieldwork needed to investigate a local ecosystem and how to use the data. Part of the "Biology Studies" series. 35m; VHS. **A:** Jr. High-Adult. **P:** Education. **U:** Home, Institution. **Chl-Juv:** Science, Biology, Ecology & Environment. **Acq:** Purchase. **Dist:** Educational Activities Inc. $89.00.

Biology Fieldwork 2: Investigating Marine Ecosystems 19??
Learning program for young students helps them see how to complete the practical fieldwork needed to investigate a local ecosystem and how to use the data. In this second installment, students explore a rocky shore. Part of the "Biology Studies" series. 35m; VHS. **A:** Jr. High-Adult. **P:** Education. **U:** Home, Institution. **Chl-Juv:** Science, Biology, Ecology & Environment. **Acq:** Purchase. **Dist:** Educational Activities Inc. $89.00.

Biology Form and Function 1991
Two programs investigate biological organisms, reveal the similarities between animals, and relate the valuable research made possible by the invertebrates. Tapes available separately. 24m; VHS. **A:** Jr. High-Sr. High. **P:** Education. **U:** Institution. **Hea-Sci:** Biology, Anatomy & Physiology, Science. **Acq:** Purchase. **Dist:** Encyclopedia Britannica. $325.00.

Biology Live Series 19??
Series of 12 videos, narrated by a middle school teacher, use high resolution animation and live-action photography to introduce students to various fields of study in biology. Times vary and each video can be purchased separately. ?m; VHS. **A:** Primary-Jr. High. **P:** Education. **U:** Institution. **Hea-Sci:** Science, Biology. **Acq:** Purchase. **Dist:** Human Relations Media. $1328.00.
Indiv. Titles: 1. Algae 2. Bacteria 3. The Cell 4. The Chemistry of Organisms 5. Fungi 6. How Organisms are Grouped 7. Plants: Angiosperms 8. Plants: Gymnosperms 9. Protozoa 10. Seedless Plants 11. Viruses 12. What is Life?.

The Biology of. . . 1988
The biology of microscopic and other, larger animals is explained. 18m; VHS, 3/4 U. **Pr:** BioMedia Associates. **A:** Sr. High-Adult. **P:** Education. **U:** Institution, Home. **Hea-Sci:** Biology. **Acq:** Purchase. **Dist:** Lucerne Media. $2020.00.
Indiv. Titles: 1. Bacteria 2. Protozoans 3. Fungi 4. Algae 5. Cnidaria (Coelenterates) 6. Flatworms 7. Annelids 8. Mollusks 9. Echinoderms 10. Arthropods.

The Biology of Annelids 19??
Teaching aid for biology education offers video observations of the ecology, feeding, anatomy, and physiology of earthworms. 12m; VHS. **A:** Sr. High. **P:** Education. **U:** Institution. **Chl-Juv:** Biology. **Acq:** Purchase. **Dist:** Environmental Media. $45.

The Biology of Arthropods 19??
Teaching aid for biology education offers video observations of arthropods, including millipedes, centipedes, arachnids, crustaceans, and insects. 15m; VHS. **A:** Sr. High. **P:** Education. **U:** Institution. **Chl-Juv:** Biology. **Acq:** Purchase. **Dist:** Environmental Media. $45.

The Biology of Behavior 1990
Part of a series offering instruction on the study of human behavior. 30m; VHS. **A:** Adult. **P:** Education. **U:** Institution. **Gen-Edu:** Psychology. **Acq:** Purchase. **Dist:** RMI Media. $89.95.

The Biology of Ciliates 19??
Teaching aid for biology education offers video observations of ciliates, including paramecium, vorticella, and stentor. 16m; VHS. **A:** Sr. High. **P:** Education. **U:** Institution. **Chl-Juv:** Biology. **Acq:** Purchase. **Dist:** Environmental Media. $55.

The Biology of Cnidarians 19??
Teaching aid for biology education offers video observations of the hydrozoan, scyphozoan, and anthozoan classes of cnidarians. 16m; VHS. **A:** Sr. High. **P:** Education. **U:** Institution. **Chl-Juv:** Biology. **Acq:** Purchase. **Dist:** Environmental Media. $55.

The Biology of Echinoderms 19??
Teaching aid for biology education offers video observations of echinoderms, including sea stars, sand dollars, and sea cucumbers. 11m; VHS. **A:** Sr. High. **P:** Education. **U:** Institution. **Chl-Juv:** Biology. **Acq:** Purchase. **Dist:** Environmental Media. $45.

The Biology of Flagellates and Amoebas 19??
Teaching aid for biology education offers video observations of flagellated and amoebid protists. 16m; VHS. **A:** Sr. High. **P:** Education. **U:** Institution. **Chl-Juv:** Biology. **Acq:** Purchase. **Dist:** Environmental Media. $55.

The Biology of Flatworms 19??
Teaching aid for biology education offers video observations of flatworms, including their structure, feeding behavior, and regeneration. 12m; VHS. **A:** Sr. High. **P:** Education. **U:** Institution. **Chl-Juv:** Biology. **Acq:** Purchase. **Dist:** Environmental Media. $45.

The Biology of Human Sexuality: Reproduction, Birth Control and Development 1988
An exploration of human sexuality on a scientific level, including sexual physiology, male and female reproductive organs, the production of hormones, erogenous zones, and popular birth control methods. 44m. **A:** Jr. High-Sr. High. **P:** Education. **U:** Institution, SURA. **Gen-Edu:** Education, Sex & Sexuality. **Acq:** Purchase. **Dist:** Center for Humanities, Inc./Guidance Associates.

The Biology of Imaging the Hidden World 19??
Teaching aid for biology education offers instruction on the use of microscopes. Includes segments on videomicroscopy and macrovideography. 14m; VHS. **A:** Sr. High. **P:** Education. **U:** Institution. **Chl-Juv:** Biology. **Acq:** Purchase. **Dist:** Environmental Media. $45.

The Biology of Molluscs 19??
Teaching aid for biology education offers video observations of chitons and gastropods, including snails, squid, and bivalves. 12m; VHS. **A:** Sr. High. **P:** Education. **U:** Institution. **Chl-Juv:** Biology. **Acq:** Purchase. **Dist:** Environmental Media. $45.

The Biology of Nematodes, Rotifers, Bryozoans, and "Minor Phyla" 19??
Teaching aid for biology education offers video observations of organisms, including human parasites. 16m; VHS. **A:** Sr. High. **P:** Education. **U:** Institution. **Chl-Juv:** Biology. **Acq:** Purchase. **Dist:** Environmental Media. $55.

The Biology of Plants 19??
Teaching aid for biology education offers video observations of photosynthesis and the evolution of plants from water to land. 15m; VHS. **A:** Sr. High. **P:** Education. **U:** Institution. **Chl-Juv:** Biology. **Acq:** Purchase. **Dist:** Environmental Media. $55.

The Biology of Prenatal Development 2006 (Unrated)
In this documentary, National Geographic takes perhaps the most detailed look ever at the prenatal development of the human baby, tracking it from conception through all 38 weeks of the pregnancy, with a strong emphasis on the first trimester. Using the most advanced images possible from six different types of medical imaging, viewers get to see rare shots of the living human embryo and fetus. 42m; DVD. **A:** Family. **P:** Education, Entertainment. **U:** Home, Institution. **Mov-Ent:** Documentary Films, Biology, Science. **Acq:** Purchase. **Dist:** $10.49.

The Biology of Water 1991
Four-part series which delves into the fascinating world of water, a substance that is essential to all forms of life on this planet. Program explores the physical and chemical properties

of water and stresses our dependence on it. Programs are available separately. Comes with catalog kit, blackline masters, and teacher's guide. 20m; VHS. **A:** Jr. High-Sr. High. **P:** Education. **U:** Institution. **Gen-Edu:** Ecology & Environment, Biology, Natural Resources. **Acq:** Purchase. **Dist:** United Learning Inc. $265.00.
Indiv. Titles: 1. Water: A Miraculous Substance 2. The Ocean Realm: Saltwater Ecology 3. The River of Life: Hydrologic Cycle and Water Pollution 4. Mud and Salt: The World of the Estuary.

Biomechanics of Hand Movement 1979
Mechanical principles which must be learned to restore balance to a partially paralyzed hand are illustrated. 60m; VHS, 3/4 U. **Pr:** American Society for Surgery of the Hand. **A:** College-Adult. **P:** Professional. **U:** Institution, CCTV, SURA. **Hea-Sci:** Surgery, Medical Education. **Acq:** Purchase. **Dist:** American Society for Surgery of the Hand.

The Biomechanics of Internal Fixation 1974
Designed for orthopedic surgeons, this program defines the complete process of the surgical treatment of fractures. Internal and external fixation principles are discussed. Biochemical reactions of the healing function of the bone in relation to the procedures used are also analyzed. 13m; VHS, 3/4 U. **Pr:** Springer-Verlag. **A:** College-Adult. **P:** Professional. **U:** Institution, CCTV. **Hea-Sci:** Surgery, Bones, Medical Education. **Acq:** Purchase. **Dist:** Springer-Verlag New York Inc.

BioMedia: Imagining the Hidden World—Microscopy & Videomicroscopy 1993
Covers microscope use. Takes a look at videomicroscopy and macrovideography. 14m; VHS. **A:** Jr. High-College. **P:** Education. **U:** Institution. **Hea-Sci:** Biology. **Acq:** Purchase. **Dist:** Environmental Media. $59.95.

BioMedia: The Annelids 1993
Detailed study of the earthworm, including its ecology, feeding, anatomy, and physiology. 12m; VHS. **A:** Jr. High-College. **P:** Education. **U:** Institution. **Hea-Sci:** Biology. **Acq:** Purchase. **Dist:** Environmental Media. $59.95.

BioMedia: The Arthropods 1993
Studies millipedes, centipedes, arachnids, crustaceans, and insects. 15m; VHS. **A:** Jr. High-College. **P:** Education. **U:** Institution. **Hea-Sci:** Biology. **Acq:** Purchase. **Dist:** Environmental Media. $59.95.

BioMedia: The Coelenterates 1993
Studies the structure, feeding behavior, and ecology of various marine hydroids, including hydra, obelia, physalia, Portuguese man-of-war, and more. 12m; VHS. **A:** Jr. High-College. **P:** Education. **U:** Institution. **Hea-Sci:** Biology. **Acq:** Purchase. **Dist:** Environmental Media. $59.95.

BioMedia: The Echinoderms 1993
Studies sea stars, basket stars, brittle stars, sand dollars, sea urchins, and sea cucumbers. 11m; VHS. **A:** Jr. High-College. **P:** Education. **U:** Institution. **Hea-Sci:** Biology. **Acq:** Purchase. **Dist:** Environmental Media. $59.95.

BioMedia: The Flatworms 1993
Looks at a wide variety of flatworms, including planaria, trematodes, and more. Examines their structure, feeding behavior, regeneration, and life stages. 12m; VHS. **A:** Jr. High-College. **P:** Education. **U:** Institution. **Hea-Sci:** Biology. **Acq:** Purchase. **Dist:** Environmental Media. $59.95.

BioMedia: The Micro-Life Resource, Part 1 1993
Studies bacteria, cyanobacteria, micro-life kingdoms, flagellates, euglena, termite symbionts, volvox, amoebas and heliozoans. 26m; VHS. **A:** Jr. High-College. **P:** Education. **U:** Institution. **Hea-Sci:** Biology. **Acq:** Purchase. **Dist:** Environmental Media. $59.95.

BioMedia: The Micro-Life Resource, Part 2 1993
Studies ciliates, the ecological niches of ciliates, paramecia, vorticella, giant ciliates, micro-algae, and water molds. 26m; VHS. **A:** Jr. High-College. **P:** Education. **U:** Institution. **Hea-Sci:** Biology. **Acq:** Purchase. **Dist:** Environmental Media. $59.95.

BioMedia: The Molluscs 1993
Studies chitons, gastropids, squid, and octopi. 12m; VHS. **A:** Jr. High-College. **P:** Education. **U:** Institution. **Hea-Sci:** Biology. **Acq:** Purchase. **Dist:** Environmental Media. $59.95.

Biomes Series 1989
This series examines in depth each type of biome on earth. 12m; VHS, 8 mm, 3/4 U. **TV Std:** NTSC, PAL, SECAM. **Pr:** Partridge Films, Ltd; Coronet Films. **A:** Jr. High-Sr. High. **P:** Education. **U:** Institution, CCTV, SURA. **Gen-Edu:** Ecology & Environment. **Acq:** Purchase, Rent/Lease, Duplication License. **Dist:** Phoenix Learning Group. $250.00.
Indiv. Titles: 1. Introduction 2. Coniferous Forest 3. Desert 4. Grassland 5. Temperate Deciduous Forest 6. Tropical Rain Forest 7. Tundra.

Bionic Ninja 1985 (Unrated) — ★
In one of the most confusing and obscure ninja films of all time, a CIA agent must personally take on and defeat a horde of KGB-sponsored ninjas (Russian ninjas?) to get back a stolen scientific discovery. Despite the name there are no cyborgs, or anything to do with bionics. It's actually several other ninja films with the same or similar actors spliced together into a bizarre mish-mash with new footage. 91m; VHS. **C:** Mike Abbott; Directed by Godfrey Ho; Written by Godfrey Ho; Cinematography by Raymond Chang; Music by Stephen Tsang. **A:** Sr. High-Adult. **P:** Entertainment. **U:** Home. **Mov-Ent:** Intelligence Service, Martial Arts, Action-Adventure. **Acq:** Purchase. **Dist:** Alpha Video Distributors. $4.98.

The Bionic Woman 1975 (Unrated) — ★★
Sky-diving accident leaves tennis pro Jaimie Somers crippled and near death. Her bionic buddy, Steve Austin, gets his friends to rebuild her and make her better than she was before. Pilot for the TV series. 96m; VHS, DVD. **C:** Lindsay Wagner; Lee Majors; Richard Anderson; Alan Oppenheimer; Directed by Richard (Dick) Moder. **Pr:** Mark Huffam. **A:** Family. **P:** Entertainment. **U:** Home. **Mov-Ent:** Technology. **Acq:** Purchase. **Dist:** Universal Studios Home Video. $39.95.

Bionic Woman: Volume 1 2007
Remake series. Jamie Sommers is in a terrible accident and undergoes surgery to reconstruct her (without her knowledge) with bionics by the Berkut Group. While coping with difficulties adjusting to super-strength plus moral and money obligations to Berkut, Jamie eventually resigns to join their crusade against world criminals all while keeping as normal a family life as she can for her younger sister. 8 episodes. 338m; DVD. **C:** Michelle Ryan; Miguel Ferrer; Molly Price; Will Yun Lee; Lucy Kate Hale. **A:** Sr. High-Adult. **P:** Entertainment. **U:** Home. **Mov-Ent:** Drama, Action-Adventure, Science Fiction. **Acq:** Purchase. **Dist:** Universal Studios Home Video.

Bionicle 3: Web of Shadows 2005 (PG) — ★★
In this third animated toy commercial, the Toa return to the city of Metra Nui on a rescue mission, only to find it overrun by giant spider like fiends whose paralyzing webs transform their victims. Quickly subdued, the Toa are transformed into the Toa Hardika, odd mismatched-looking machines with new powers that will hopefully give them a chance of completing their mission. 76m; DVD. **C:** Brian Drummond; Scott McNeil; Voice(s) by Kathleen Barr; Paul Dobson; Brian Drummond; Alessandro Juliani; Scott McNeil; Trevor Devall; Christopher Gaze; Tabitha St. Germain; French Tickner; Directed by David Molina; Terry Shakespeare; Written by Henry Gilroy; Bob Thompson; Bret Matthews; Music by Nathan Furst. **A:** Primary-Adult. **P:** Entertainment. **U:** Home. **Mov-Ent. Acq:** Purchase. **Dist:** Buena Vista Home Entertainment; Walt Disney Studios Home Entertainment. $19.99.

Bionics: Man or Machine? 197?
In working to overcome physical limitations, mankind has devised machinery to extend the power of our sight and hearing, mobility, and body parts. 24m; VHS, 3/4 U. **Pr:** Alan P. Sloan. **A:** Jr. High-Sr. High. **P:** Education. **U:** Institution, SURA. **Hea-Sci:** Documentary Films, Biology, Technology. **Acq:** Purchase, Rent/Lease, Trade-in. **Dist:** Encyclopedia Britannica.

Bioscope 1987
This series presents concepts such as the web of life, adaptation, the food chain, life cycles, and interdependence. It features locations from the Amazon to the Arctic and living beings from algae to great whales. The series also explores the viewer's own place in the biosphere. The programs are available individually. 10m; VHS, 3/4 U. **Pr:** Mississippi Authority for Education. **A:** Primary-Jr. High. **P:** Education. **U:** Institution, SURA. **Gen-Edu:** Video, Philosophy & Ideology, Documentary Films. **Acq:** Purchase, Rent/Lease, Duplication License. **Dist:** National Film Board of Canada.
Indiv. Titles: 1. Bioscope: The Life Sciences 2. Cells 3. The World of Living Things 4. Where Plants and Animals Live 5. Adaptation 6. The Natural Balance 7. Endangered Species 8. Frontiers in the Biosphere.

The Biosphere 19??
An overview of the biosphere includes topics such as the age of the earth, oxygen, CO2, nitrogen, amino acids, the greenhouse effect and more. 38m; VHS. **A:** Sr. High-College. **P:** Education. **U:** Institution. **Hea-Sci:** Science, Ecology & Environment. **Acq:** Purchase. **Dist:** Human Relations Media. $129.00.

Biosynthesis of Steroids 19??
The principal steps in the biosynthesis of steroid molecules from a common precursor, mevalonic acid, are illustrated. The successive sequences depict the formation of squalene, its polycyclization, and the intramolecular rearrangements leading to lanosterol, a cholesterol precursor. The role of the "isoprene units" in the building of the steroid typical molecular structure is depicted, and the so-called "isoprene rule" is illustrated in this silent computer-generated videotape. 6m/B/W; 3/4 U, Special order formats. **Pr:** Joel de Rosnay. **A:** College-Adult. **P:** Education. **U:** Institution, CCTV, CATV, BCTV. **Hea-Sci:** Biology. **Acq:** Purchase, Rent/Lease. **Dist:** Education Development Center.

Biotech in Your Backyard 1993
Blends scientific ability with homeowner know-how. Sheds light for novices on a newly emerging field. 120m; VHS. **A:** College-Adult. **P:** Education. **U:** Institution. **Hea-Sci:** Agriculture, Technology, Plants. **Acq:** Purchase. **Dist:** Purdue University. $20.00.

Biotechnology 1991
Explores genetic engineering and genetic alteration of the rapeseed plant to create a new food plant. Looks at biotechnology in agriculture. Received the Red Ribbon, American Films & Video Festival. 60m; VHS, Special order formats. **A:** Jr. High-Sr. High. **P:** Education. **U:** Institution. **Gen-Edu:** Ecology & Environment, Agriculture, Biology. **Acq:** Purchase, Rent/Lease. **Dist:** Bullfrog Films, Inc. $250.00.

Biotechnology 1995
Discusses, by the scientists themselves, their methods and the moral and ethical questions involved in the science of genetics and the business of biotechnology. 28m; VHS, 3/4 U; Closed Captioned. **A:** Jr. High-Adult. **P:** Education. **U:** Institution. **Gen-Edu:** Science, Genetics. **Acq:** Purchase. **Dist:** National Geographic Society. $99.00.

Biotechnology: Science Tool for the Future 19??
Explains biotechnology by showing how it can be used to enhance science. Also includes information on genetic engineering, recombinant DNA technology, embryo transfer, and tissue culture. 13m; VHS. **A:** Sr. High-Adult. **P:** Education. **U:** Institution. **Hea-Sci:** Science, Biology, Genetics. **Acq:** Purchase. **Dist:** CEV Multimedia. $49.95.

Biotechnology: You Be the Judge 1991
Three products of the biotechnological revolution are presented: Porcine somatotropin, Bacillus thuringiensis, and Renin. 18m; VHS. **A:** Sr. High-Adult. **P:** Education. **U:** Institution. **Hea-Sci:** Agriculture, Technology. **Acq:** Purchase. **Dist:** Purdue University. $15.00.

The Biovideo Series 1987
A series for students of all levels which graphically explains living biological systems. 30m; VHS, Special order formats. **Pr:** Carolina Biological Supply Company. **A:** Jr. High-Adult. **P:** Education. **U:** Institution, Home. **Hea-Sci:** Biology, Wildlife. **Acq:** Purchase. **Dist:** Carolina Biological Supply Co.
Indiv. Titles: 1. Locomotion 2. Animal Senses 3. Introduction to Invertebrates 4. The Evidence for Evolution 5. Sexual Reproduction in Animals 6. Introduction to Photosynthesis.

Bioy Casares: Cavar un foso 1989
Realism is contrasted with fantasy, hallucination with experience, and the peace of rural life with the hustle and bustle of city life. 60m; VHS, 3/4 U. **Pr:** Films for the Humanities and Sciences. **A:** College. **P:** Education. **U:** Institution, CCTV, CATV, BCTV. **L:** Spanish. **Fin-Art:** Literature, Fantasy. **Acq:** Purchase, Rent/Lease, Duplication License. **Dist:** Films for the Humanities & Sciences.

Biozombie 1998 (Unrated) — ★★½
Playing as a mixture of "Mallrats" and "Dawn of the Dead," this Hong Kong import is aimed squarely at a Generation-X audience. The film introduces us to Woody (Jordan Chan) and Bee (Sam Lee), two slackers who work at a video store. While on an errand to pick up their boss's car, they hit a strange pedestrian and take him back to the mall. This stranger turns out to be a zombie, and he soon infects several others. With the mall locked up for the night, Woody and Bee must take it upon themselves to protect the few humans remaining...while doing the least amount of work possible. The film turns into a true rollercoaster ride, as we start with the comedic opening, then move into the action-horror, and finally, a very nihilistic ending. 94m; DVD. **C:** Jordan Chan; Sam Lee; Directed by Wilson (Wai-Shun) Yip. **A:** Sr. High-Adult. **P:** Entertainment. **U:** Home. **Mov-Ent. Acq:** Purchase. **Dist:** Movies Unlimited.

Bip as a Skater 1975
Bip, mime Marceau's "silent alter ego," learns to ice skate-on illusionary ice. Part of EBE'S "The Art of Silence: Pantomimes with Marcel Marceau" series. 8m; VHS, 3/4 U. **C:** Marcel Marceau. **Pr:** Encyclopedia Britannica Educational Corporation. **A:** Jr. High-College. **P:** Education. **U:** Institution, SURA. **Fin-Art:** Performing Arts, Mime. **Acq:** Purchase, Rent/Lease, Trade-in. **Dist:** Encyclopedia Britannica.

Bip as a Soldier 1975
In this pantomime, Marceau demostrates through Bip that playing soldier can be fun...until the war is really there. Part of EBE'S "The Art of Silence: Pantomimes with Marcel Marceau" series. 17m; VHS, 3/4 U. **C:** Marcel Marceau. **Pr:** Encyclopedia Britannica Educational Corporation. **A:** Jr. High-College. **P:** Education. **U:** Institution, SURA. **Fin-Art:** Performing Arts, Mime. **Acq:** Purchase, Rent/Lease, Trade-in. **Dist:** Encyclopedia Britannica.

Bip at a Society Party 1975
In this Bip pantomime, Marceau portrays several amusing society characters. Part of EBE'S "The Art of Silence: Pantomimes with Marcel Marceau" series. 14m; VHS, 3/4 U. **C:** Marcel Marceau. **Pr:** Encyclopedia Britannica Educational Corporation. **A:** Jr. High-College. **P:** Education. **U:** Institution, SURA. **Fin-Art:** Performing Arts, Mime. **Acq:** Purchase, Rent/Lease, Trade-in. **Dist:** Encyclopedia Britannica.

Bip Hunts Butterflies 1975
A tragicomic pantomime about the fragility of life. Part of EBE's "The Art of Silence; Pantomimes with Marcel Marceau" series. 10m; VHS, 3/4 U. **C:** Marcel Marceau. **Pr:** Encyclopedia Britannica Educational Corporation. **A:** Jr. High-College. **P:** Education. **U:** Institution, SURA. **Fin-Art:** Performing Arts, Mime. **Acq:** Purchase, Rent/Lease, Trade-in. **Dist:** Encyclopedia Britannica.

The Birch Interval 1978 (PG) — ★★
A chronicle of a young Amish girl growing up and experiencing adult passions and fears when she visits her kin in their isolated Pennsylvania community. 104m; VHS. **C:** Eddie Albert; Rip Torn; Ann Wedgeworth; Directed by Delbert Mann; Written by Joanna Crawford. **Pr:** Robert B. Radnitz. **A:** Jr. High-Adult. **P:** Entertainment. **U:** Home. **Mov-Ent:** Religion, Family, Amish. **Acq:** Purchase. **Dist:** Unknown Distributor.

Bird 1988 (R) — ★★★
The richly textured, though sadly one-sided biography of jazz sax great Charlie Parker, from his rise to stardom to his premature death via extended heroin use. A remarkably assured, deeply imagined film from Eastwood that never really shows the Bird's genius of creation. The soundtrack features Parker's own solos re-mastered from original recordings. 160m; VHS, DVD, Wide, CC. **C:** Forest Whitaker; Diane Venora; Michael Zelniker; Samuel E. Wright; Keith David; Michael McGuire; James Handy; Damon Whitaker; Morgan Nagler; Peter Crook; Directed by Clint Eastwood; Written by Joel Oliansky; Cinematography by Jack N. Green; Music by Lennie Niehaus. **Pr:** Malpaso Productions. **A:** Preschool. **P:** Entertainment. **U:** Home. **Mov-Ent:** Music--Jazz, Drugs, Biography: Music. **Awds:** Oscars '88: Sound; Cannes '88: Actor (Whitaker); Golden Globes '89: Director (Eastwood); N.Y. Film Critics '88:

Support. Actress (Venora). **Acq:** Purchase. **Dist:** Music Video Distributors; Facets Multimedia Inc.; Warner Home Video, Inc. $19.98.

Bird Brain 1976
Examines the migration of birds, answering questions: how and why? From "Nova." 27m; VHS, 3/4 U, Special order formats. **Pr:** British Broadcasting Corporation; Time-Life Films. **A:** Sr. High-College. **P:** Education. **U:** Institution, SURA. **Gen-Edu:** Documentary Films, Birds. **Acq:** Purchase, Rent/Lease. **Dist:** Time-Life Video and Television.

Bird by Bird with Annie 2009 (Unrated)
Documentary on writer Anne Lamott (best known for her book "Bird By Bird") filmed over the course of a year of her life as she travels giving public lectures and readings. 54m; DVD. **A:** Sr. High-Adult. **P:** Education. **U:** Home. **Gen-Edu:** Biography, Documentary Films. **Acq:** Purchase. **Dist:** Docurama. $29.95.

The Bird Can't Fly 2007 (Unrated) — ★½
Melody returns to her desolate South African diamond mining hometown for the funeral of her long-estranged daughter June. She discovers she has an eccentric 10-year-old grandson River, but her bonding efforts are thwarted by his father Scoop. The town is gradually being reclaimed by sandstorms, which delay Melody's departure and allow her the time to uncover some family secrets. 89m; DVD. **C:** Barbara Hershey; Yusuf Davids; Tony Kgoroge; John Kani; Directed by Threes Anna; Written by Threes Anna; Cinematography by Guido Van Gennep; Music by Mark Killian; Paul Hepker. **A:** Sr. High-Adult. **P:** Entertainment. **U:** Home. **Mov-Ent:** Miners & Mining. **Acq:** Purchase. **Dist:** Vanguard International Cinema, Inc.

Bird Care Video 1991
Demonstrates techniques for proper health care for caged birds, including physical exams, immediate care of injuries, and other concerns. For the avian vetrinarian and knowledgable bird owner. 61m; VHS. **A:** Adult. **P:** Instruction. **U:** Home, Institution. **How-Ins:** Birds, Pets, Veterinary Medicine. **Acq:** Purchase. **Dist:** LAM Productions. $39.95.

Bird Homes 1957
Looks at different kinds of bird homes, the habitats in which they can be found, and the types of materials used in nest building. 11m; VHS, 3/4 U. **Pr:** Encyclopedia Britannica Educational Corporation. **A:** Primary. **P:** Education. **U:** Institution, SURA. **L:** English, Spanish. **Hea-Sci:** Documentary Films, Birds. **Acq:** Purchase, Rent/Lease, Trade-in. **Dist:** Encyclopedia Britannica.

The Bird Man 1987
A man who survived a Nazi death camp talks about his past from his aviary in Israel. 12m; VHS. **C:** Eitan Porat. **Pr:** Alden Films. **A:** Jr. High-Adult. **P:** Education. **U:** Institution, Home. **Gen-Edu:** Documentary Films, Holocaust, Judaism. **Acq:** Purchase, Rent/Lease. **Dist:** Alden Films. $50.00.

Bird of Paradise 1932 (Unrated) — ★★½
An exotic South Seas romance in which an adventurer is cast onto a remote Polynesian island when his yacht haphazardly sails into a coral reef. There he becomes enamored of an exotic island girl, and nature seems to disapprove. 80m/B/W; VHS, DVD, Blu-Ray, 8 mm, 3/4 U, Special order formats. **C:** Joel McCrea; Dolores Del Rio; Lon Chaney, Jr.; Directed by King Vidor; Music by Max Steiner. **Pr:** RKO. **A:** Family. **P:** Entertainment. **U:** Home. **Mov-Ent:** Drama. **Acq:** Purchase. **Dist:** Kino International Corp.; Gotham Distributing Corp.; Rex Miller Artisan Studio. $19.95.

Bird of Paradise 1951 — ★½
Technicolor remake of the 1932 pic is mildly amusing for its strange casting. Frenchman Andre Laurence (Jourdan) accompanies his friend Tenga (Hunter) back to his Polynesian island and falls for Tenga's sister, Kalua (Paget). This breaks native customs (the best parts of the film) and when the local volcano erupts, Kalua vows to throw herself in to appease the gods. 100m; DVD. **C:** Louis Jourdan; Debra Paget; Jeff Chandler; Everett Sloane; Maurice Schwartz; Jack Elam; Directed by Delmer Daves; Written by Delmer Daves; Cinematography by Winton C. Hoch; Music by Daniele Amfitheatrof. **A:** Sr. High-Adult. **P:** Entertainment. **U:** Home. **L:** English. **Mov-Ent:** Romance, Volcanos. **Acq:** Purchase. **Dist:** Fox Home Entertainment.

Bird of Prey 1995 (R) — ★★½
Nick Milev (Milushev) has just been released from a Bulgarian prison for attacking Jonathan Griffith (Chamberlain), the drugs-and-arms dealer who was responsible for the death of Milev's policeman father. But Milev still wants revenge, though matters get complicated by Kily (Tilly), Griffith's naive daughter, with whom he falls in love. Plot's so-so but characters make up for some of the routiness. Filmed on location in Sofia, Bulgaria. 102m; VHS, DVD, CC. **C:** Boyan Milushev; Jennifer Tilly; Richard Chamberlain; Lenny Von Dohlen; Robert Carradine; Lesley Ann Warren; Directed by Temistocles Lopez; Written by Boyan Milushev; Cinematography by David Knaus. **A:** Sr. High-Adult. **P:** Entertainment. **U:** Home. **Mov-Ent:** Mystery & Suspense. **Acq:** Purchase. **Dist:** Unknown Distributor.

A Bird of Prey: Red-Tailed Hawk 1972
A unique look at the endangered red-tailed hawk shows how it is equipped for its environment and why it and other birds of prey must be preserved. 14m; VHS, 3/4 U. **Pr:** Encyclopedia Britannica Educational Corporation. **A:** Jr. High-Family. **P:** Education. **U:** Institution, SURA. **Hea-Sci:** Documentary Films, Birds. **Acq:** Purchase, Rent/Lease, Trade-in. **Dist:** Encyclopedia Britannica.

Bird on a Wire 1990 (PG-13) — ★★
Disappointing action-comedy finds Gibson forced to emerge from a prolonged period under the Witness Protection Program, whereupon he and ex-girlfriend Hawn are pursued by old enemies. Too little action and too little comedy add up to surprisingly dull outing, considering the cast. 110m; VHS, DVD, Wide, CC. **C:** Mel Gibson; Goldie Hawn; David Carradine; Bill Duke; Stephen Tobolowsky; Clyde Kusatsu; Joan Severance; Harry Caesar; John Pyper-Ferguson; Jeff Corey; Directed by John Badham; Written by David Seltzer; Cinematography by Robert Primes; Music by Hans Zimmer. **Pr:** Mark Huffam. **A:** Jr. High-Adult. **P:** Entertainment. **U:** Home. **Mov-Ent:** Action-Adventure, Federal Bureau of Investigation (FBI). **Acq:** Purchase. **Dist:** Alpha Video; Movies Unlimited. $19.98.

The Bird That Beat the U.S. Navy 1981
This program looks at the Lay San Albatross, which is more commonly known as the Gooney bird. 25m; VHS, 3/4 U. **Pr:** British Broadcasting Corporation. **A:** Jr. High-Adult. **P:** Education. **U:** Institution, SURA. **Hea-Sci:** Documentary Films, Birds. **Acq:** Purchase. **Dist:** Home Vision Cinema.

Bird Watching 1989
Bird watching guru Leonard Rue III offers tips on sighting and identifying some of the over 650 species of birds in North America. 30m; VHS. **A:** Family. **P:** Entertainment. **U:** Home. **Gen-Edu:** Documentary Films, Birds, Hobbies. **Acq:** Purchase. **Dist:** Karol Media; MNTEX Entertainment, Inc. $14.95.

The Bird Who Is a Clown 1972
A study of the blue-footed booby, which nests in an inactive volcano and has a comical courtship ritual. 9m; VHS, 3/4 U. **Pr:** Encyclopedia Britannica Educational Corporation. **A:** Primary. **P:** Education. **U:** Institution, SURA. **Chl-Juv:** Documentary Films, Birds. **Acq:** Purchase, Rent/Lease, Trade-in. **Dist:** Encyclopedia Britannica.

The Bird with the Crystal Plumage 1970 (PG) — ★★½
An American writer living in Rome witnesses a murder. He becomes involved in the mystery when the alleged murderer is cleared because the woman believed to be his next victim is shown to be a psychopathic murderer. Vintage Argento mayhem. 98m; VHS, DVD, Blu-Ray. **C:** Tony Musante; Suzy Kendall; Eva Renzi; Enrico Maria Salerno; Mario Adorf; Renato Romano; Reggie Nalder; Werner Peters; Umberto Raho; Dario Argento; Directed by Dario Argento; Written by Dario Argento; Cinematography by Vittorio Storaro; Music by Ennio Morricone. **Pr:** Salvatore Argento; UMC Pictures. **A:** Jr. High-Adult. **P:** Entertainment. **U:** Home. **Mov-Ent:** Mystery & Suspense. **Acq:** Purchase. **Dist:** VCI Entertainment. $19.95.

The Birdcage 1995 (R) — ★★★
Somewhat overlong but well-played remake of "La Cage aux Folles" features Williams suppressing his usual manic schtick to portray Armand, the subdued half of a longtime gay couple living in Miami. His partner is the ever-hysterical-but-loving drag queen Albert (Lane), whose presence provides a distinct challenge when Armand's son Val (Futterman) announces his engagement to the daughter of family values, right-wing senator Kevin Keeley (Hackman). When the Senator and family arrive for dinner, Armand tries to play it straight while Albert opts for a matronly mom impersonation (think Barbara Bush). Highlights include Armand's initial attempts to teach Albert to be butch (walk like John Wayne) and Hackman congoing in drag. 120m; VHS, DVD, Blu-Ray, CC. **C:** Robin Williams; Nathan Lane; Gene Hackman; Dianne Wiest; Hank Azaria; Dan Futterman; Christine Baranski; Calista Flockhart; Tom McGowan; Directed by Mike Nichols; Written by Elaine May; Cinematography by Emmanuel Lubezki; Music by Mark Mothersbaugh; Jonathan Tunick. **Pr:** Mike Nichols; Neil Machlis; Marcello Danon; Mike Nichols; United Artists. **A:** Sr. High-Adult. **P:** Entertainment. **U:** Home. **Mov-Ent:** Politics & Government. **Awds:** Screen Actors Guild '96: Cast. **Acq:** Purchase. **Dist:** MGM Home Entertainment.

A Birder's Guide to Everything 2014 (PG-13) — ★★½
Sweet coming of age pic has shy, 15-year-old bird watcher David Portnoy (Smit-McPhee) still having trouble coping with his mother's death and even more trouble with his dad's (Le Gross) upcoming remarriage. Out birding, David spots what he thinks is a Labrador duck, a wild breed that's supposedly extinct. So instead of being his dad's best man, David takes off on a duck-hunting adventure with three fellow teen birders and with the help of bird expert Lawrence Konrad (Kingsley). 86m; DVD, Blu-Ray. **C:** Kodi Smit-McPhee; Ben Kingsley; Katie Chang; Michael Chen; Alex Wolff; James LeGros; Directed by Rob Meyer; Written by Rob Meyer; Luke Matheny; Cinematography by Tom Richmond; Music by Jeremy Turner. **A:** Jr. High-Adult. **P:** Entertainment. **U:** Home. **L:** English. **Mov-Ent:** Adolescence, Birds, Family. **Acq:** Purchase. **Dist:** Screen Media Films.

Birdies & Bloopers 1990
Gary McCord of CBS Sports hosts this film of fantastic moments, unbelievable shots, and comedy; coverage starts in the 1930s, and continues to the beginning of 1990. 30m; VHS. **C:** Jack Nicklaus; Lee Trevino; Arnold Palmer; Nancy Lopez; Hosted by Gary McCord. **A:** Family. **P:** Entertainment. **U:** Home. **Spo-Rec:** Golf, Outtakes & Bloopers. **Acq:** Purchase. **Dist:** Karol Media. $9.95.

Birding Hotspots: A Personal Tour of Fabulous Birding Locations 1998
Bird watching experts Don and Lillian Stokes take you on a tour of America's premier birding hotspots. They impart such valuable information as which trails to take, which birds to look for and how to see the area in the best way. They also offer fascinating facts about the lives of the birds you will see. 50m; VHS. **A:** Family. **P:** Instruction. **U:** Home. **How-Ins:** Birds, Wildlife. **Acq:** Purchase. **Dist:** Willow Creek Press L.L.C. $19.95.

Birdman & Galaxy Trio 1967
Birdman, a former secret agent, bestowed with powerful wings, has joined forces with the Galaxy Trio. 60m; VHS. **Pr:** Hanna-Barbera Productions. **A:** Preschool-Primary. **P:** Entertainment. **U:** Home. **Chl-Juv:** Family Viewing, Animation & Cartoons. **Acq:** Purchase. **Dist:** Turner Broadcasting System Inc. $24.95.

Birdman and the Galaxy Trio: The Complete Series 1967
Vintage collection features Birdman using his power of the sun to combat criminal mastermind Vulturo and Dr. Millenium, plus the Galaxy Trio (Gravity Girl, Vapor Man, and Meteor Man) serving their own version of justice across the cosmos. 20 episodes. 420m; DVD. **C:** Voice(s) by Keith Andes; Donald E. Messick; John Stephenson; Ted Cassidy; Virginia Eiler. **A:** Primary-Jr. High. **P:** Entertainment. **U:** Home. **Chl-Juv:** Animation & Cartoons, Action-Adventure, Television Series. **Acq:** Purchase. **Dist:** Warner Home Video, Inc.

Birdman of Alcatraz 1962 — ★★★
Robert Stroud, convicted of two murders and sentenced to life imprisonment on the Island, becomes an internationally accepted authority on birds. Lovingly told, with stunning performance from Lancaster, and exceptionally fine work from the supporting cast. The confinement of Stroud's prison cell makes the film seem claustrophobic and tedious at times, just as the imprisonment must have been. Ritter played Stroud's mother, who never stops trying to get him out of prison. 143m/B/W; VHS, DVD, Wide. **C:** Burt Lancaster; Karl Malden; Thelma Ritter; Betty Field; Neville Brand; Edmond O'Brien; Hugh Marlowe; Telly Savalas; Directed by John Frankenheimer; Written by Guy Trosper; Cinematography by Burnett Guffey; Robert Krasker; Music by Elmer Bernstein. **Pr:** United Artists. **A:** Jr. High-Adult. **P:** Entertainment. **U:** Home. **Mov-Ent:** Birds. **Awds:** British Acad. '62: Actor (Lancaster). **Acq:** Purchase. **Dist:** Sony Pictures Home Entertainment Inc.; Facets Multimedia Inc. $19.98.

The Birds 1963 (PG-13) — ★★★½
Hitchcock attempted to top the success of "Psycho" with this terrifying tale of Man versus Nature, in which Nature alights, one by one, on the trees of Bodega Bay to stage a bloody act of revenge upon the civilized world. Only Hitchcock can twist the harmless into the horrific while avoiding the ridiculous; this is perhaps his most brutal film, and one of the cinema's purest, horrifying portraits of apocalypse. Based on a short story by Daphne Du Maurier; screenplay by novelist Evan Hunter (aka Ed McBain). 120m; VHS, DVD, Blu-Ray. **C:** Rod Taylor; Tippi Hedren; Jessica Tandy; Veronica Cartwright; Suzanne Pleshette; Ethel Griffies; Charles McGraw; Ruth McDevitt; Lonny (Lonnie) Chapman; Joe Mantell; Morgan Brittany; Alfred Hitchcock; Directed by Alfred Hitchcock; Written by Evan Hunter; Cinematography by Robert Burks; Music by Bernard Herrmann. **Pr:** Mark Huffam. **A:** Jr. High-Adult. **P:** Entertainment. **U:** Home. **Mov-Ent:** Horror, Birds. **Acq:** Purchase. **Dist:** Movies Unlimited; Alpha Video; Universal Studios Home Video. $19.95.

Birds 1978
A look at the mating habits and food gathering of the different kinds of birds. 12m; 3/4 U, Special order formats. **Pr:** National Geographic Society. **A:** Primary-Jr. High. **P:** Education. **U:** Institution, Home, SURA. **Hea-Sci:** Documentary Films, Birds. **Acq:** Purchase, Trade-in, Duplication License. **Dist:** National Geographic Society. $14.95.

The Birds 2: Land's End 1994 (R) — **Bomb!**
Unfortunate rip-off of the Hitchcock fright classic. Killer seagulls begin attacking the inhabitants of east coast Gull Island. Seems they're tired of being oil slick victims. Hedren's the town shopkeeper in a role that's nothing like the one she played in the original. Definitely for the birds—even the director refuses to acknowledge it by officially using the film industry pseudonym "Alan Smithee." Made for TV. 87m; VHS, CC. **C:** Brad Johnson; Chelsea Field; Tippi Hedren; James Naughton; Jan Rubes; Megan Gallagher; Directed by Rick Rosenthal; Written by Jim Wheat; Ken Wheat. **A:** Jr. High-Adult. **P:** Entertainment. **U:** Home. **Mov-Ent:** Horror, Birds, TV Movies. **Acq:** Purchase.

Birds: A First Film 1984
The characteristics that point up the differences between birds and mammals are seen in this tape. 12m; VHS, 3/4 U. **Pr:** BFA Educational Media. **A:** Primary. **P:** Education. **U:** Institution, SURA. **Gen-Edu:** Birds. **Acq:** Purchase. **Dist:** Phoenix Learning Group.

Birds & the Bees 1956 (Unrated) — ★★
A millionaire falls in love with an alluring card shark, and then calls it all off when he learns of her profession, only to fall in love with her again when she disguises herself. A remake—and poor shade—of Preston Sturge's 1941 classic "The Lady Eve." 94m; VHS, Streaming. **C:** Mitzi Gaynor; David Niven; George Gobel; Reginald Gardiner; Hans Conried; Directed by Norman Taurog; Written by Sidney Sheldon. **Pr:** Paramount Pictures. **A:** Family. **P:** Entertainment. **U:** Home. **Mov-Ent:** Comedy--Romantic, Gambling. **Acq:** Purchase. **Dist:** $19.95.

Birds Are Interesting 1950
Physical characteristics (bills, feet, wings) of three categories of birds are presented: swimming and wading birds, birds of prey, and perching birds. 11m; VHS, 3/4 U. **Pr:** Encyclopedia Britannica Educational Corporation. **A:** Primary. **P:** Education. **U:** Institution, SURA. **Hea-Sci:** Documentary Films, Birds. **Acq:** Purchase, Rent/Lease, Trade-in. **Dist:** Encyclopedia Britannica.

Birds, Birds, Birds 1994
Reveals the characteristic behaviors and plumage of birds throughout the world; suggests methods to attract birds for

serious enthusiasts. 42m; VHS. **A:** Primary-Adult. **P:** Education. **U:** Institution. **Gen-Edu:** Birds. **Acq:** Purchase. **Dist:** Quality Books Inc. $29.95.

Birds Do It 1966 (Unrated) — ★

Incredibly dopey comedy with Cape Kennedy janitor Melvin Byrd (Sales) in charge of keeping dust from ruining another nuclear missile project. When Melvin is unexpectedly exposed to an experiment, it gives him the ability to fly and—even sillier—makes him irresistible to women. Hunter plays a dual role as a military good guy and a lookalike spy. 88m; DVD. **C:** Soupy Sales; Tab Hunter; Arthur O'Connell; Beverly Adams; Edward Andrews; Doris Dowling; Directed by Andrew Marton; Written by Art Arthur; Arnie Kogen; Cinematography by Howard Winner; Music by Samuel Matlovsky. **A:** Family. **P:** Entertainment. **U:** Home. **Mov-Ent. Acq:** Purchase. **Dist:** Sony Pictures Home Entertainment Inc.

Birds for All Seasons 1988

The behavioral patterns of different types of birds are studied. 60m; VHS, 3/4 U. **Pr:** British Broadcasting Corporation; RKO. **A:** Jr. High-College. **P:** Education. **U:** Institution, Home, SURA. **Hea-Sci:** Birds. **Acq:** Purchase, Rent/Lease, Duplication License. **Dist:** Clear Vue Inc. $435.00.
Indiv. Titles: 1. Birds at the Ends of the Earth 2. Birds of the Everlasting Heat 3. Birds of the Lands of Four Seasons.

Birds: How They Live, Where They Live: A First Film on Bird Ecology 1967

This show presents an overview of the traits all birds have in common. It also explains how different birds have adapted to their particular environments. 11m; VHS, 3/4 U. **Pr:** BFA Educational Media. **A:** Primary. **P:** Education. **U:** Institution, SURA. **Hea-Sci:** Documentary Films, Birds. **Acq:** Purchase. **Dist:** Phoenix Learning Group.

Birds in the City: A First Film 1970

Many birds are adapted to life in the city. Features examples of birds that can be seen in that environment. 11m; VHS, 3/4 U. **Pr:** Arthur D. Nelles. **A:** Primary. **P:** Education. **U:** Institution, SURA. **L:** English, French. **Hea-Sci:** Documentary Films, Birds. **Acq:** Purchase. **Dist:** Phoenix Learning Group.

Birds in Winter 1959

Describes the migration of birds and discusses how birds adjust to colder temperatures. 11m; VHS, 3/4 U. **Pr:** Encyclopedia Britannica Educational Corporation. **A:** Primary. **P:** Education. **U:** Institution, SURA. **Hea-Sci:** Documentary Films, Birds. **Acq:** Purchase, Rent/Lease, Trade-in. **Dist:** Encyclopedia Britannica.

Birds of a Feather 1988

A profile of several African birds, notably the prolific Quelea. Shot by Oscar-winner Simon Trevor. 55m; VHS, 3/4 U. **Pr:** Simon Trevor. **A:** Primary-Adult. **P:** Education. **U:** Institution, CCTV. **Gen-Edu:** Documentary Films, Birds, Africa. **Acq:** Purchase. **Dist:** Benchmark Media.

Birds of America 2008 (R) — ★★

College prof Morrie Tanager (Perry) and his wife Betty (Graham) lead a highly controlled life in reaction to Morrie's family history of mental instability. Just as it seems that Morrie will achieve his dreams of tenure, he's forced back into caretaker mode by his depressed, homeless brother Jay (Foster) and his promiscuous, booze-swilling sister Ida (Goodwin), who both move in. Betty's tolerance is fraying and Morrie has to decide how he's going to live his life. 85m; DVD, Wide. **C:** Matthew Perry; Lauren Graham; Ben Foster; Ginnifer Goodwin; Gary Wilmes; Hilary Swank; Zoe Kravitz; Directed by Craig Lucas; Written by Elyse Friedman; Cinematography by Yaron Orbach; Music by Ahrin Mishan. **A:** Sr. High-Adult. **P:** Entertainment. **U:** Home. **Mov-Ent. Acq:** Purchase. **Dist:** Movies Unlimited; Alpha Video.

Birds of Prey 1972 (Unrated) — ★★

Action film pits an ex-WWII army pilot against a group of kidnapping thieves in an airborne chopper chase. 81m; VHS, DVD. **C:** David Janssen; Ralph Meeker; Elayne Heilveil; Directed by William A. Graham; Cinematography by Jordan Cronenweth. **Pr:** Tomorrow Entertainment Inc. **A:** Jr. High-Adult. **P:** Entertainment. **U:** Home. **Mov-Ent:** Aeronautics, Veterans, TV Movies. **Acq:** Purchase. **Dist:** Unknown Distributor.

Birds of Prey 1985 (Unrated) — ★

A tough urban cop stalks a breed of cold, ruthless assassins in a large city. In HiFi. 90m; VHS. **Pr:** New World Pictures. **A:** Sr. High-Adult. **P:** Entertainment. **U:** Home. **Mov-Ent. Acq:** Purchase. **Dist:** Anchor Bay Entertainment; Wild Life Unlimited Foundation, Inc. $19.95.

Birds of the Backyard 1987

George Harrison hosts a look at common backyard birds and offers advice on creating a backyard bird sanctuary with the latest feeders and the best foods. 60m; VHS. **C:** Hosted by George Harrison. **Pr:** Eyelevel. **A:** Family. **P:** Education. **U:** Home. **Gen-Edu:** Documentary Films, Birds. **Acq:** Purchase. **Dist:** Karol Media; Reader's Digest Home Video. $29.95.

Birds of the Everglades 1996

Takes a look at the many kinds of birds that call the Florida Everglades home. Features more than 50 kinds of birds, including four endangered species, as they nest and feed. 30m; VHS. **A:** Primary. **P:** Education. **U:** Home. **Gen-Edu:** Birds. **Acq:** Purchase. **Dist:** Ivy Classics Video. $39.95.

Birds of the Sandy Beach: An Introduction to Ecology 1965

Answers the question: How do so many kinds of birds live and survive on a single sandy beach? 10m; VHS, 3/4 U. **Pr:** BFA Educational Media. **A:** Jr. High. **P:** Education. **U:** Institution, SURA. **Hea-Sci:** Documentary Films, Birds. **Acq:** Purchase. **Dist:** Phoenix Learning Group.

Birds of the Sun God/In-Flight Movie 19??

David Attenborough narrates these two episodes of wildlife adventure. "Birds of the Sun God" looks at the amazing hummingbird. "In-Flight Movie" shows what it might be like to fly like a bird. 59m; VHS. **C:** Narrated by David Attenborough. **Pr:** British Broadcasting Corporation. **A:** Jr. High-Adult. **P:** Education. **U:** Home. **Gen-Edu:** Documentary Films, Wildlife, Birds. **Acq:** Purchase. **Dist:** Home Vision Cinema. $24.95.

Birds of the World 19??

A look at the variety and beauty of our fine feathered friends. Sales benefit the Royal Society for the Protection of Birds. Tapes are available individually or as a set. 30m; VHS, DVD. **C:** Hosted by David Attenborough; Jeremy Irons. **A:** Family. **P:** Education. **U:** Home. **Gen-Edu:** Birds. **Acq:** Purchase. **Dist:** Signals Video. $19.95.
Indiv. Titles: 1. Eagles: The Majestic Hunter 2. The Masterbuilders 3. Feathered Athletes 4. A Little Owl's Story 5. Seabirds.

Birdsnest Soup 1956

Documents the collection, sale, processing, cooking and consumption of edible birdsnests. 24m/B/W; VHS. **A:** Adult. **P:** Education. **U:** Institution. **Gen-Edu:** Cooking, Documentary Films. **Acq:** Rent/Lease. **Dist:** Cornell University. $20.00.

Birdsong 2012 (Unrated) — ★★

BBC adaptation of Sebastian Faulks' 1993 novel, which is set between 1910 and 1916. In this romantic melodrama, Englishman Stephen Wraysford (Redmayne) takes a job working for Rene Azaire (Lafitte) in his French textile factory. Stephen falls in love with Rene's young, unhappy second wife, Isabelle (Poesy). The story flash-forwards to Stephen's serving in WWI in the same area, where his physical wounds are less devastating than the emotional ones shown in flashback. 165m; DVD, Blu-Ray. **C:** Eddie Redmayne; Clemence Poesy; Joseph Mawle; Laurent Lafitte; Matthew Goode; Richard Madden; Marie Josee Croze; Anthony Andrews; Directed by Philip Martin; Written by Abi Morgan; Cinematography by Julian Court; Music by Nicholas Hooper. **A:** Sr. High-Adult. **P:** Entertainment. **U:** Home. **L:** English. **Mov-Ent:** France, Romance, World War One. **Acq:** Purchase. **Dist:** PBS Home Video.

Birdy 1984 (R) — ★★★½

An adaptation of the William Wharton novel about two Philadelphia youths, one with normal interests, the other obsessed with birds, and their eventual involvement in the Vietnam War, wrecking one physically and the other mentally. A hypnotic, evocative film, with a compelling Peter Gabriel soundtrack. 120m; VHS, DVD, CC. **C:** Matthew Modine; Nicolas Cage; John Harkins; Sandy Baron; Karen Young; Bruno Kirby; Directed by Alan Parker; Written by Jack Behr; Sandy Kroopf; Music by Peter Gabriel. **Pr:** Tri-Star Pictures. **A:** Sr. High-Adult. **P:** Entertainment. **U:** Home. **Mov-Ent:** Vietnam War, Veterans. **Awds:** Cannes '85: Grand Jury Prize. **Acq:** Purchase. **Dist:** Sony Pictures Home Entertainment Inc. $79.95.

Birgit Nilsson 1961

From the "Bell Telephone Hour" comes this performance by the renowned Swedish soprano. Arias include "In Questa Reggia," "Pace Pace Mio Dio" and "Vieni t'affreta." Also performed are Wagner's "Elizabeth's Prayer" and the "Immolation Scene." 45m; VHS. **C:** Birgit Nilsson. **Pr:** Henry Jaffe Enterprises. **A:** College-Adult. **P:** Entertainment. **U:** Home. **Fin-Art:** Performing Arts, Opera. **Acq:** Purchase. **Dist:** Facets Multimedia Inc.; Kultur International Films Ltd., Inc.; Video Artists International. $29.95.

Birgitt Haas Must Be Killed 1983 — ★★½

A ruthless secret agent (Noiret) plots to murder a German female terrorist and make it appear that her boyfriend was the killer. Never quite hits the mark, despite novel premise and strong cast. 105m; VHS. **C:** Philippe Noiret; Jean Rochefort; Elisabeth (Lisa) Kreuzer; Directed by Laurent Heynemann. **Pr:** Laurent Heynemann; Aida Bure; George Bure; Laurent Heynemann. **A:** Sr. High-Adult. **P:** Entertainment. **U:** Home. **Mov-Ent:** Mystery & Suspense. **Acq:** Purchase. **Dist:** German Language Video Center. $39.95.

Birth 1988

Animated program depicting the woman's generative organs. Includes detailed descriptions and illustrations of the three stages of labor. 15m; VHS, 3/4 U. **Pr:** Milner-Fenwick. **A:** Adult. **P:** Education. **U:** Institution, CCTV. **L:** English, French, Spanish. **Hea-Sci:** Documentary Films, Childbirth. **Acq:** Purchase. **Dist:** Milner-Fenwick, Inc.

Birth 2004 (R) — ★★

Creepy psychological thriller finds widowed Anna (Kidman) finally making a commitment to marry Joseph (Huston) ten years after her husband Sean's death. That is until a strange 10-year-old, also named Sean (Bright), turns up insisting that Anna cannot remarry because he is her spouse. Sean is impervious to any suggestion otherwise and his very insistence comes to convince the emotionally fragile woman. None of this goes over well with Anna's imperious mother (Bacall) or the rest of her family, let alone her frustrated fiance. Various explanations are offered and director Glazer elegantly camouflages plot holes. Kidman, with her severe pixie haircut, somewhat resembles Mia Farrow in "Rosemary's Baby," but one thing you can be certain of is here, the devil didn't do it. 100m; DVD. **C:** Nicole Kidman; Cameron Bright; Danny Huston; Lauren Bacall; Arliss Howard; Alison Elliot; Anne Heche; Peter Stormare; Ted Levine; Cara Seymour; Zoe Caldwell; Milo Addica; Directed by Jonathan Glazer; Written by Milo Addica; Jonathan Glazer; Jean-Claude Carriere; Cinematography by Harris Savides; Music by Alexandre Desplat. **Pr:** Jean-Louis Piel; Nick Morris; Lizzie Gower; New Line Cinema. **A:** Sr. High-Adult. **P:** Enter-

tainment. **U:** Home. **Mov-Ent:** Mystery & Suspense. **Acq:** Purchase. **Dist:** Warner Home Video, Inc. $27.95.

The Birth and Death of Mountains 1961

Although mountains appear permanent, ice, wind, and especially water, are constantly wearing down the rock and carrying fragments away. 13m; VHS, 3/4 U. **Pr:** BFA Educational Media. **A:** Jr. High-Sr. High. **P:** Education. **U:** Institution, SURA. **L:** English, French. **Hea-Sci:** Documentary Films, Geology. **Acq:** Purchase. **Dist:** Phoenix Learning Group.

A Birth Class: Focus on Labor and Delivery 1991

Certified childbirth experts offer comprehensive instruction on childbirthing, focusing on the primary concerns of pregnant women, from nutritional needs to pain management. 120m; VHS. **A:** Sr. High-Adult. **P:** Instruction. **U:** Institution, Home. **Hea-Sci:** Pregnancy, Childbirth, Health Education. **Acq:** Purchase. **Dist:** Cambridge Educational; Injoy Productions. $39.95.

Birth Control 1994

An introduction to birth control methods, debunking myths and explaining more reliable techniques. 30m; VHS. **A:** Jr. High. **P:** Education. **U:** Institution. **Gen-Edu:** Adolescence, Sex & Sexuality, Birth Control. **Acq:** Purchase. **Dist:** Library Video Inc. $39.95.

Birth Control for Teens 1993

Exhaustively documents a wide range of birth control methods as well as long term procedures. 24m; VHS. **A:** Jr. High-Sr. High. **P:** Education. **U:** Institution. **Gen-Edu:** Birth Control, Adolescence. **Acq:** Purchase. **Dist:** Clear Vue Inc. $295.00.

The Birth Control Movie 1970

This tape is a sensitive and tasteful presentation of reproductive and birth control information. 24m; 3/4 U, Special order formats. **Pr:** Planned Parenthood. **A:** Jr. High-Sr. High. **P:** Education. **U:** Institution, Home, SURA. **Hea-Sci:** Birth Control. **Acq:** Purchase, Rent/Lease, Duplication License, Off-Air Record. **Dist:** United Learning Inc.

Birth Control: Myths and Methods—Revised 1991

Thorough discussion of birth control available, including sterilization and natural family planning. Popular birth control myths are debunked by doctors. ?m; VHS, Special order formats. **Pr:** Churchill Films. **A:** Jr. High-Sr. High. **P:** Education. **U:** Institution. **Hea-Sci:** Birth Control, Education. **Acq:** Purchase, Rent/Lease. **Dist:** Clear Vue Inc. $365.00.

Birth Control: The Choices 1976

Presents the uses, limitations, and side effects of the methods of birth control, as well as tubal ligation, vasectomy, and abortion. 25m; VHS, 3/4 U, EJ, Q, Special order formats. **Pr:** Churchill. **A:** Sr. High-Adult. **P:** Education. **U:** Institution, Home, SURA. **L:** Spanish. **Hea-Sci:** Birth Control. **Acq:** Purchase, Duplication License. **Dist:** Clear Vue Inc.

Birth Control: Your Responsibility, Your Choice 1990

This tape stresses the importance of a woman's individuality in her choice of contraception. Among the forms described are the pill, diaphragm, sponge, condoms, spermicides and fertility awareness. 14m; VHS, 3/4 U. **Pr:** Professional Research. **A:** Sr. High-Adult. **P:** Education. **U:** Institution, CCTV, SURA. **L:** English, Spanish. **Hea-Sci:** Birth Control. **Acq:** Purchase, Rent/Lease. **Dist:** Discovery Education. $295.00.

Birth Defects 1989

Septal defects, heart valves, and abnormal connections of aortic and pulmonary arteries in babies are outlined. 19m; VHS, 3/4 U. **Pr:** University of Nebraska. **A:** Sr. High-Adult. **P:** Education. **U:** Institution, SURA. **Hea-Sci:** Birth Defects, Documentary Films, Circulatory System. **Acq:** Purchase, Rent/Lease. **Dist:** Films for the Humanities & Sciences. $149.00.

Birth Defects: Cause and Prevention 1990

Overviews the five most common types of birth defects: malformations present at birth, inborn errors of metabolism, blood disorders, chromosomal abnormalities, and perinatal damage. Presents information on prevention and stresses good prenatal care. ?m; VHS. **A:** Sr. High-Adult. **P:** Education. **U:** Home. **Hea-Sci:** Health Education, Pregnancy, Birth Defects. **Acq:** Purchase. **Dist:** Meridian Education Corp. $45.00.

Birth Defects: Too Late to Change 1988

A videotape which tells the story of a pregnant teenager who didn't care forherself during pregnancy and wound up with a child who had defects. 45m; VHS, 3/4 U. **Pr:** Marshfilm. **A:** Jr. High-Adult. **P:** Education. **U:** Institution. **Hea-Sci:** Birth Defects, Parenting. **Acq:** Purchase. **Dist:** Marshmedia. $45.50.

Birth: How Life Begins 1978

Portrays the entire birth cycle from conception to birth to postnatal care. Spotlights changes in attitudes about childbirth. 23m; VHS, SVS, 3/4 U. **Pr:** Avatar Learning. **A:** Primary-Sr. High. **P:** Education. **U:** Institution. **Hea-Sci:** Reproduction, Childbirth. **Acq:** Purchase. **Dist:** Encyclopedia Britannica. $69.00.

Birth: How Life Begins 1981

This film investigates the new attitudes about childbirth. A look at natural childbirth as an alternative birth technique is also included. 23m; VHS, 3/4 U. **Pr:** Avatar Learning. **A:** Primary-Sr. High. **P:** Education. **U:** Institution, SURA. **Hea-Sci:** Documentary Films, Childbirth. **Acq:** Purchase, Rent/Lease, Trade-in. **Dist:** Encyclopedia Britannica.

Birth in the Squatting Position 1982

Brazilian obstetricians Dr. Moyses and Claudio Paciornik demonstrate the traditional form of childbirth. 10m; VHS, 3/4 U. **Pr:**

CPP Pesquisas. **A:** Adult. **P:** Education. **U:** Institution. **Hea-Sci**: Documentary Films, Childbirth. **Acq:** Purchase, Rent/Lease. **Dist:** Polymorph Films, Inc.

Birth of a Bugeye 1988
Filmed over seven years, rough oak and pine planks are transformed into a beautiful boat. 30m; VHS, 3/4 U. **Pr:** Maryland Center for Public Broadcasting. **A:** Jr. High-Adult. **P:** Education. **U:** Institution, CCTV, CATV, BCTV. **Gen-Edu**: Boating, Woodworking. **Acq:** Purchase. **Dist:** Maryland Public Television. $29.95.

Birth of a Democracy 1991
A survey of Cameroonians from various social and economic backgrounds reveals the difficulties this African country has encountered in trying to change from a totalitarian state to a democracy. 25m; VHS. **C:** Directed by Bassek Ba Kobhio. **A:** Sr. High-Adult. **P:** Education. **U:** Institution. **Gen-Edu**: Politics & Government, Africa, Documentary Films. **Acq:** Purchase, Rent/Lease, Duplication. **Dist:** First Run/Icarus Films. $190.00.

Birth of a Family 1978
Demonstrates preparation for childbirth for couples or single women. The relationship between careful preparation and actual delivery is made obvious to the viewer. 24m; CC, 3/4 U, Special order formats. **Pr:** Catfish Productions. **A:** College-Adult. **P:** Education. **U:** Institution, Home, SURA. **Hea-Sci**: Documentary Films, Childbirth. **Acq:** Purchase, Rent/Lease, Trade-in, Duplication License. **Dist:** United Learning Inc.

Birth of a Foal: Red Wing and Rain Drop 1983
Earl Tobler, D.V.M., induces birth in a 17-year-old Appaloosa, Red Wing, and discusses this controversial procedure. The foal, Rain Drop, makes his debut and takes his first steps. 20m; VHS. **Pr:** Mercedes Maharis Productions. **A:** Jr. High-Adult. **P:** Education. **U:** Home. **Gen-Edu**: Documentary Films, Animals. **Acq:** Purchase. **Dist:** , On Moratorium.

The Birth of a Forest 1993
Examines the evolutionary process of a forest from its beginnings as a seed bed. Discusses humus, decomposers, deciduous trees, evergreen, chlorophyll, as well as climate, soil types, seed dispersal, and the role of plants and animals in a healthy forest. Complete with interactive video instructional quiz and teacher's guide. 15m; VHS. **A:** Primary-Jr. High. **P:** Education. **U:** Institution. **Gen-Edu**: Forests & Trees. **Acq:** Purchase. **Dist:** United Learning Inc. $79.95.

Birth of a God: The Dalai Lama ????
Two-part series documents the intricate antecedents and history of the Dalai Lama, from the year 700 to today. Scholars use commentary, reenactments, maps, artwork, and scenes of monastic and rural life to present a timeline within the context of Tibetan, Mongolian and Chinese history. 90m; VHS. **A:** Sr. High-Adult. **P:** Education. **U:** Institution. **Gen-Edu**: Buddhism, Religion. **Acq:** Purchase. **Dist:** Films for the Humanities & Sciences. $265.00.
Indiv. Titles: 1. Tibetan Buddhism: Politics, Power, and the Birth of the Dalai Lama 2. The Dalai Lama and the Rituals of Reincarnation.

The Birth of a Language 1987
The development of human language is explored in this fascinating film, which looks at the differences between human and animal communication and the relationship between language and thought. 60m; VHS, 3/4 U. **Pr:** Paul Jay. **A:** Jr. High-Adult. **P:** Education. **U:** Institution, SURA. **Gen-Edu**: Documentary Films, Language Arts. **Acq:** Purchase, Rent/Lease. **Dist:** Direct Cinema Ltd. $250.00.

Birth of a Legend 1984
A documentary showing the on and off antics of Miss Pickford and Mr. Fairbanks when they reigned as King and Queen of the silver screen in 1926. 25m/B/W; VHS. **C:** Mary Pickford; Douglas Fairbanks, Sr. **Pr:** Matty Kemp; Mary Pickford Company. **A:** Family. **P:** Entertainment. **U:** Home. **Mov-Ent**: Documentary Films, Film History, Biography: Show Business. **Acq:** Purchase. **Dist:** $19.95.

The Birth of a Nation ????
Presents D.W. Griffith's 1915 film showing an extremely flawed and racist view of the Civil War and Reconstruction. It is strongly suggested that students are properly prepared before viewing this controversial program. 190m; VHS, DVD. **A:** Sr. High. **P:** Education. **U:** Institution. **Gen-Edu**: Prejudice, Identity. **Acq:** Purchase. **Dist:** Zenger Media. $24.95.

The Birth of a Nation 1915 — ★★★★
Lavish Civil War epic in which Griffith virtually invented the basics of film grammar. Gish and Walthall have some of the most moving scenes ever filmed and the masterful battle choreography brought the art of cinematography to new heights. Griffith's positive attitude toward the KKK notwithstanding, this was the first feature length silent, and it brought credibility to an entire industry. Based on the play "The Clansman" and the book "The Leopard's Spots" by Thomas Dixon, it is still a rouser, and of great historical interest. Silent with music score. Also available in a 124-minute version. 175m/B/W; Silent; VHS, DVD. **TV Std:** NTSC, PAL. **C:** Lillian Gish; Mae Marsh; Henry B. Walthall; Ralph Lewis; Robert "Bobbie" Harron; George Siegmann; Joseph Henabery; Spottiswoode Aitken; George Beranger; Mary Alden; Josephine Crowell; Elmer Clifton; Walter Long; Howard Gaye; Miriam Cooper; John Ford; Sam De Grasse; Maxfield Stanley; Donald Crisp; Raoul Walsh; Erich von Stroheim; Eugene Pallette; Wallace Reid; Directed by D.W. Griffith; Written by D.W. Griffith; Frank E. Woods; Cinematography by Billy (G.W.) Bitzer; Music by D.W. Griffith. **Pr:** D.W. Griffith; D.W. Griffith; Epoch. **A:** Family. **P:** Entertainment. **U:** Home. **Mov-Ent**: Drama, Classic Films, Silent Films. **Awds:** AFI '98: Top 100; Natl. Film Reg. '92. **Acq:** Purchase. **Dist:** Lions Gate Entertainment Inc.; Critics' Choice Video & DVD; Glenn Video Vistas Ltd. $39.95.

Birth of a Nation: 4/29/1992 19??
Offers a look at the L.A. uprising within minutes of the Rodney King verdict. Uses hand-held camera footage, along with hip-hop and rap music, to follow the events as they are happening on the streets of L.A. 45m; VHS, 3/4 U, Special order formats. **A:** College-Adult. **P:** Education. **U:** Institution. **Gen-Edu**: Documentary Films, Violence. **Acq:** Purchase, Rent/Lease. **Dist:** Third World Newsreel. $225.00.

Birth of a Nation: Thirteen Colonies 1980
This film focuses on the various groups that settled in America, with special attention to the characteristics, motivations and ideals of the new settlers. 25m; VHS, 3/4 U. **Pr:** Video Knowledge, Inc. **A:** Primary-Adult. **P:** Education. **U:** Institution, SURA. **Gen-Edu**: Documentary Films, History--U.S., Immigration. **Acq:** Purchase. **Dist:** Video Knowledge, Inc.

Birth of a Viewliner ????
Take a ride on and get first-hand views of Amtrak's custom-built Viewliner sleeper/diner cars. 60m; VHS. **A:** College-Adult. **P:** Education. **U:** Home. **Gen-Edu**: Trains. **Acq:** Purchase. **Dist:** The Civil War Standard. $24.95.

Birth of an Empire 1994
Examines the life of Genghis Khan and his quest for land and power that defined the Mongolian Empire. Part of the Mongols: Storm from the East Series. 50m; VHS. **A:** Sr. High-Adult. **P:** Education. **U:** Institution. **Gen-Edu**: History--Medieval, Military History, Asia. **Acq:** Purchase, Rent/Lease. **Dist:** Films for the Humanities & Sciences. $149.00.

Birth of Civilization 2008 (Unrated)
From caveman to modern man, National Geographic travels through time exploring the history of civilization. The journey begins 15,000 years ago at the Ice Age and along the way explores humanity's milestones to learn how and why we've come so far. 90m; DVD. **A:** Family. **P:** Education. **U:** Institution, Home. **Mov-Ent**: Documentary Films, Evolution, Anthropology. **Acq:** Purchase. **Dist:** National Geographic Society. $24.95.

The Birth of Europe: Coal, Blood, & Iron 1991
Coal was one of the principle engines to drive the Industrial Revolution. Program traces discovery of its properties, the formation of coke for smelting iron that greatly influenced industry, and the effects of "progress" on the rural way of life. Comes with guide. 54m; VHS. **Pr:** BBC Bristol Natural History Unit. **A:** Jr. High-Adult. **P:** Education. **U:** Institution. **Gen-Edu**: Natural Resources, History--Enlightenment. **Acq:** Purchase, Rent/Lease. **Dist:** Phoenix Learning Group. $250.00.

Birth of Modern Dance: Denishawn 19??
Combines dramatizations with rare footage to explain the history of the Denishawn Dance Company, one of the most influential modern dance companies in America. 40m; VHS. **A:** Jr. High-Adult. **P:** Education. **U:** Institution. **Gen-Edu**: Documentary Films, Performing Arts, Dance--History. **Acq:** Purchase. **Dist:** Educational Video Network. $69.95.

Birth of Modern Theatre: Chekhov—Uncle Vanya 198?
Chekhov's masterpiece of comedy and tragedy is analyzed through stop-action photography. 47m/B/W; VHS, 3/4 U. **C:** Laurence Olivier; Michael Redgrave. **A:** College-Adult. **P:** Education. **U:** Institution, SURA. **Gen-Edu**: Theater. **Acq:** Purchase, Rent/Lease. **Dist:** Films for the Humanities & Sciences.

Birth of Renaissance Art: Giotto to Masaccio 19??
Explores the work of such Renaissance artists as Brunnelleschi, Donatello, and Giotto. 58m; VHS. **A:** Sr. High-Adult. **P:** Education. **U:** Institution. **Gen-Edu**: History--Renaissance, Art & Artists. **Acq:** Purchase. **Dist:** Educational Video Network. $59.95.

The Birth of Soviet Cinema 1972
Directors Eisenstein, Pudovkin and Dovzhenko are linked to bring forth sequences of their brilliant masterpieces. 49m; VHS. **Pr:** Mosfilm. **A:** Sr. High-Adult. **P:** Education. **U:** Institution, SURA. **Mov-Ent**: Film History. **Acq:** Purchase, Rent/Lease. **Dist:** Films for the Humanities & Sciences.

The Birth of Sybling 1996
Experimental documentary uses computer animation of ancient religious art to tell the story of Sybling, the archetypal child who is abused by her father and silenced by the state. Created by a collaboration between artist Liz MacDougall and a group of female survivors of sexual abuse and trauma. 20m; VHS. **A:** Sr. High-Adult. **P:** Education. **U:** Home, Institution. **Gen-Edu**: Child Abuse, Animation & Cartoons. **Acq:** Purchase. **Dist:** Moving Images Distribution.

The Birth of the Bees 1986
A complete examination for the high school student on the habits, lifestyle and organization of the bee. 54m; VHS, Special order formats. **Pr:** Oxford Scientific Films, Ltd. **A:** Jr. High-Adult. **P:** Education. **U:** Institution, Home. **Hea-Sci**: Documentary Films, Insects. **Acq:** Purchase. **Dist:** Carolina Biological Supply Co.

Birth of the Big Mamoo 1978
A lyric fantasy about the conception, evolution, and birth of the Little Big Mamoo. 6m; VHS, 3/4 U. **Pr:** Jody Silver. **A:** Primary. **P:** Entertainment. **U:** Institution, SURA. **Chl-Juv**: Documentary Films, Fantasy. **Acq:** Purchase. **Dist:** Phoenix Learning Group.

Birth of the Blues 1941 (Unrated) — ★★½
Songman Crosby starts a band in New Orleans in the midst of the jazz boom. Help from partner Martin and real-life trombonist Teagarden, with comic relief from Eddie "Rochester" Anderson, make for a fun-filled story. Plot is riddled with some unbelievable gangster scenes, but the music and laughs will keep you amused. In B&W with color segments. 76m/B/W; VHS, DVD, CC. **C:** Bing Crosby; Mary Martin; Brian Donlevy; Eddie Anderson; J. Carrol Naish; Cecil Kellaway; Warren Hymer; Horace McMahon; Carolyn Lee; Jack Teagarden; Directed by Victor Schertzinger; Written by Harry Tugend; Walter DeLeon; Cinematography by William Mellor; Music by Robert Emmett Dolan. **Pr:** B.G. DeSylva; Paramount Pictures. **A:** Family. **P:** Entertainment. **U:** Home. **Mov-Ent**: Musical, Nightclubs, Music--Jazz. **Acq:** Purchase. **Dist:** Universal Music and Video Distribution. $14.98.
Songs: St. Louis Blues; St. James Infirmary; Melancholy Baby; Birth of the Blues.

The Birth of the Bomber 1997
Portrays the story of the Allies' development and deployment of the great flying weapons. 60m; VHS. **A:** Adult. **P:** Education. **U:** Home. **Gen-Edu**: World War Two. **Acq:** Purchase. **Dist:** 411 Video Information. $19.95.

Birth of the Living Dead 2013
Explores how then-novice filmmaker George A. Romero got his now-classic low-budget horror picture, "Night of the Living Dead," made in 1968. 76m; DVD. **A:** Jr. High-Adult. **P:** Entertainment. **U:** Home. **Mov-Ent**: Biography: Show Business, Documentary Films. **Acq:** Purchase. **Dist:** First Run Features. $24.95.

Birth of the Nation: The Thirteen Colonies 1989
The courageous settlers that founded our nation, their hopes, motivations, and ideals are the focus of this video on colonial America. ?m; VHS. **A:** Jr. High-Adult. **P:** Education. **U:** Institution, Home. **Gen-Edu**: History--U.S. **Acq:** Purchase. **Dist:** Knowledge Unlimited, Inc. $32.95.

Birth of the Renaissance: Giotto to Masaccio 1991
Documentary filmed on location in Florence, Siena, Pisa, Mantua and Padua traces early masterworks from the Renaissance period which developed in these cities. Artists and architects featured include Alberti, Brunelleschi, Donatello, Michelozza, Martini, Lorenzetti, Luca della Robbia, Giotto and Masaccio. 58m; VHS. **Pr:** Rizzoli Films. **A:** Jr. High-Adult. **P:** Education. **U:** Home. **Fin-Art**: Documentary Films, Art & Artists, History--Renaissance. **Acq:** Purchase. **Dist:** Facets Multimedia Inc. $39.95.

The Birth of Your Baby 197?
This program shows what to expect from admission through discharge, including labor and delivery room procedures and post-delivery care. 14m; VHS, 3/4 U, CV. **Pr:** Professional Research. **A:** Sr. High-Adult. **P:** Education. **U:** Institution, CCTV. **Hea-Sci**: Documentary Films, Childbirth. **Acq:** Purchase, Rent/Lease. **Dist:** Discovery Education.

The Birth of Your Baby—Revised 1987
An overview for mothers-to-be of the process of childbirth in a hospital environment. 14m; VHS, 3/4 U. **Pr:** Professional Research. **A:** Adult. **P:** Education. **U:** Institution, CCTV. **L:** English, Spanish. **Hea-Sci**: Documentary Films, Childbirth. **Acq:** Purchase, Rent/Lease. **Dist:** Discovery Education. $295.00.

Birth Stories 1995
Documentary reveals women's attitudes toward pregnancy and childbirth through interviews and personal stories. Includes black and white footage of actual births. 30m; VHS. **A:** College. **P:** Education. **U:** Institution. **Hea-Sci**: Documentary Films, Childbirth, Pregnancy. **Acq:** Purchase, Rent/Lease. **Dist:** The Cinema Guild. $250.

Birth with R.J. Laing 1977
Psychiatrist R.J. Laing reappraises Western childbirth procedures and raises questions about the immediate and long term effects of them. 57m; VHS, 3/4 U. **Pr:** Helen Brew; Media Insights Ltd. **A:** Sr. High-Adult. **P:** Education. **U:** Institution, SURA. **Hea-Sci**: Documentary Films, Childbirth. **Acq:** Purchase. **Dist:** Home Vision Cinema.

Birthday 19??
A portrait of a dedicated and caring doctor whose major goal of her career is the improvement of medical care for women having babies in hospitals. She is dedicated to bringing the emotional fulfillment and warmth associated with home births to the hospital; she also wants to introduce the Le Boyer method of birth to her hospital. 28m; 3/4 U, Special order formats. **Pr:** Nancy Porter. **A:** College-Adult. **P:** Education. **U:** Institution, CCTV, CATV, BCTV. **Gen-Edu**: Documentary Films, Women, Childbirth. **Acq:** Purchase, Rent/Lease. **Dist:** Education Development Center.

The Birthday 1977
This program, set in the context of Philadelphia's July 4th Bicentennial celebration, presents the complex imagery that is America. Contrasts are drawn between the order of the American Dream and the reality. 41m/B/W; 3/4 U. **Pr:** Edwin Moses. **A:** Jr. High-Adult. **P:** Education. **U:** Institution, SURA. **Gen-Edu**: Documentary Films, Sociology, U.S. States. **Acq:** Purchase, Rent/Lease. **Dist:** Temple University Dept. of Film and Media Arts.

Birthday Boy 1985 — ★★
A cable comedy about a buffoonish salesman's 30th birthday, on which he takes an ill-fated business trip. Written by Belushi. 33m; VHS. **C:** James Belushi; Directed by Claude Conrad; Written by James Belushi. **Pr:** Vestron Video. **A:** Jr. High-Adult. **P:** Entertainment. **U:** Home. **Mov-Ent**: TV Movies. **Acq:** Purchase. **Dist:** Lions Gate Television Corp. $29.98.

Birthday Girl 2002 (R) — ★★
Love story cum actioner stars Chaplin as a timid London bank clerk, John, and Kidman as Nadia, his mysterious and sexy online Russian mail-order bride with a secret. Nadia doesn't

speak English, but the two begin to speak the international language anyway. Afraid, intrigued, then tickled with his Soviet missus who brings some color into his dull, drab life, John hardly has time to wallow in his newfound bliss when he's beset by Russian baddies (Frenchmen Kassovitz and Cassel) claiming to be Nadia's relatives, who show up on his doorstep one day. Kidman shows her range, however, and reportedly learned Russian for the film. Decent turn from the Butterworth clan, who also produced the hip debut film "Mojo." 93m; VHS, DVD, CC. **C:** Nicole Kidman; Ben Chaplin; Vincent Cassel; Mathieu Kassovitz; Kate Evans; Directed by Jez Butterworth; Written by Jez Butterworth; Tom Butterworth; Cinematography by Oliver Stapleton; Music by Stephen Warbeck. **Pr:** Eric Abraham; Stephen Butterworth; Diana Phillips; Portobello Pictures; FilmFour; Mirage Enterprises; Miramax Film Corp. **A:** Sr. High-Adult. **P:** Entertainment. **U:** Home. **Mov-Ent:** Comedy--Romantic, Great Britain. **Acq:** Purchase. **Dist:** Buena Vista Home Entertainment.

Birthday Party: Pleasure Heads Must Burn 19?? (Unrated)
Live performance includes "Dead Joe," "Nick the Stripper," "Wild World," "She's Hit" and more. ?m; VHS. **A:** Jr. High-College. **P:** Entertainment. **U:** Home. **Mov-Ent:** Music--Performance. **Acq:** Purchase. **Dist:** Music Video Distributors. $24.95.

The Birthmark 1965
Nathaniel Hawthorne's short story deals with a scientist who tampers with one of nature's finest creations-his wife. Part of the "American Story Classics" series. 29m/B/W; VHS, Special order formats. **A:** Sr. High-College. **P:** Education. **U:** Institution, CCTV, CATV, BCTV. **Gen-Edu:** Documentary Films, Literature--American. **Acq:** Purchase, Rent/Lease. **Dist:** Film Ideas, Inc. $110.00.

Birthwrite: Growing Up Hispanic 1989
Cheech Marin hosts this documentary which focuses on the achievements of Hispanic-American writers. 57m; VHS, 3/4 U. **C:** Hosted by Richard "Cheech" Marin. **Pr:** Jesus Salvador Trevino. **A:** Jr. High-Adult. **P:** Education. **U:** Institution. **Gen-Edu:** Literature, Documentary Films, Hispanic Culture. **Acq:** Purchase. **Dist:** The Cinema Guild. $295.00.

Bisha—The Awesome Fire Test 19??
Documentary of three Bedouins who choose to undergo the Bisha, a traditional ceremony for revealing truth by putting a white-hot iron pan to their tongues. If they are scorched, they are deemed to by lying; if not, they are seen as innocent. 52m; VHS. **A:** Adult. **P:** Education. **U:** Home. **Gen-Edu:** Documentary Films, Anthropology, Middle East. **Acq:** Purchase, Rent/Lease. **Dist:** Filmakers Library Inc. $350.

The Bishop Murder Case 1930 (Unrated) — ★★½
Amateur sleuth Philo Vance (Rathbone) consults with New York D.A. Markham (Geldart) when college student Joseph Cochrane Robin is killed with an arrow on the grounds of scientist Bertrand Dillard's (Francis) home. A note on the body refers to the nursey rhyme "Cock Robin" and Vance has a lot of suspects to sort through. Rathbone is in one of the better adaptations of the S.S. Van Dine mysteries although this early talkie is still static in execution. 88m/B/W; DVD. **C:** Basil Rathbone; Alec B. Francis; Leila Hyams; Roland Young; Clarence Geldart; James Donlan; Directed by Nick Grinde; Written by Lenore Coffee; Cinematography by Roy F. Overbaugh. **A:** Adult. **P:** Entertainment. **U:** Home. **L:** English. **Mov-Ent:** Mystery & Suspense. **Acq:** Purchase. **Dist:** WarnerArchive.com.

Bishop Sheen on Angels 19??
Bishop Fulton Sheen shares his perspective on the existence of angels, from guardian angels to archangels. 30m; VHS. **A:** Family. **P:** Religious. **U:** Home. **Gen-Edu:** Religion. **Acq:** Purchase. **Dist:** Ignatius Press. $19.95.

Bishop Sheen's Irish Wit and Wisdom 19??
Bishop Fulton Sheen offers witty insights into the Irish psychology and sense of humor. 90m; VHS. **A:** Family. **P:** Religious. **U:** Home. **Gen-Edu:** Religion, Ireland. **Acq:** Purchase. **Dist:** Ignatius Press. $19.95.

The Bishop's Wife 1947 — ★★★
Episcopalian biship Henry (Niven) is praying to find the money to build a new church but his faith is shaky and his marriage to Julia (Young) even more so. But his prayers are answered (although Henry doesn't know it) in the form of angel Dudley (Grant), who's sent down to earth at Christmas to help work things out. Excellent performances by the cast make this an entertaining outing. Based on the novel by Robert Nathan. 109m/B/W; VHS, DVD, Blu-Ray. **C:** Cary Grant; Loretta Young; David Niven; Monty Woolley; Elsa Lanchester; James Gleason; Gladys Cooper; Regis Toomey; Directed by Henry Koster; Written by Leonardo Bercovici; Robert Sherwood; Cinematography by Gregg Toland; Music by Hugo Friedhofer. **Pr:** RKO; Samuel Goldwyn Productions. **A:** Family. **P:** Entertainment. **U:** Home. **Mov-Ent:** Fantasy, Comedy-Drama, Christmas. **Awds:** Oscars '47: Sound. **Acq:** Purchase. **Dist:** Facets Multimedia Inc. $14.98.

Bisk GAAP Guide 19??
Provides a current, comprehensive overview of all GAAP. Covers current assets and liabilities, fixed assets and long-term liabilities, intangibles and R&D, stockholders' equity method, cash flow statements, deferred taxes, leases and pensions, business combinations, and foreign operations. Comes with textbook and quizzer. Can be used for Accounting CPE credit hours. 360m; VHS. **A:** College-Adult. **P:** Instruction. **U:** Institution, Home. **Bus-Ind:** Economics, Personal Finance, Finance. **Acq:** Purchase. **Dist:** Bisk Education. $249.00.

Bisk GAAS Guide 19??
Provides a clear overview of auditing standards, the code of professional conduct, and standards for taxes, compilations, and MAS work. Includes workbook and quizzer. 180m; VHS. **A:** College-Adult. **P:** Education. **U:** Institution, Home. **Gen-Edu:** Economics, Finance. **Acq:** Purchase. **Dist:** Bisk Education. $199.00.

Bismarck 1940
The story of Bismarck's unification of the German states into the Kaiserreich during the war of 1870-71. In German only. 118m/B/W; VHS. **TV Std:** NTSC, PAL. **C:** Paul Hartmann; Walter Frank; Lil Dagover; Otto Gebuehr. **Pr:** German Language Video Center. **A:** Jr. High-Adult. **P:** Entertainment. **U:** Home. **L:** German. **Mov-Ent:** History--Modern, War--General, Germany. **Acq:** Purchase, Rent/Lease. **Dist:** German Language Video Center. $42.95.

Bismarck: Germany From Blood and Iron 1976
Focuses on the dynamic Otto von Bismarck, as he engineers the events which achieved the unification of Germany. 30m; VHS, 3/4 U. **C:** Directed by John Irvin. **Pr:** Learning Corporation of America. **A:** Jr. High-Adult. **P:** Education. **U:** Institution, SURA. **Gen-Edu:** Documentary Films, Germany. **Acq:** Purchase, Rent/Lease. **Dist:** Phoenix Learning Group.

A Bit of a Do: The Complete Collection 1989 (Unrated)
Independent Television (ITV) 1989 crime drama. The working-class Simcocks and the middle-class Rodenhursts are forever linked following a shotgun wedding causing comedic class collisions at every family function from christening to funeral. 13 episodes. 658m; DVD. **C:** David Jason; Gwen Taylor; Nicola Pagett; Stephanie Cole. **A:** Sr. High-Adult. **P:** Entertainment. **U:** Home. **Mov-Ent:** Drama, Television Series. **Acq:** Purchase. **Dist:** Acorn Media Group Inc. $59.99.

A Bit of Fry and Laurie 1987
More than 40 comedy sketches from the British team of Fry and Laurie, known for their television work in the series "Jeeves and Wooster." 89m; VHS. **Pr:** British Broadcasting Corporation. **A:** Sr. High-Adult. **P:** Entertainment. **U:** Home. **Mov-Ent:** Comedy--Performance. **Acq:** Purchase. **Dist:** Video Collectibles. $19.98.

A Bit of Fry and Laurie: Season 3 1987
British comedy team Hugh Laurie and Stephen Fry are back with their absurd hijinks and oddball sketches, highlights being "From Here to Just Over There," "Tahitian Kitchen," "The Red Hat of Patferrick," and "The Model Advert." 173m; DVD. **C:** Hugh Laurie; Stephen Fry. **A:** Adult. **P:** Entertainment. **U:** Home. **Mov-Ent:** Comedy--Screwball. **Acq:** Purchase. **Dist:** BBC Worldwide Publishing Ltd.

A Bit of Fry and Laurie: Season 4 1987
Fry and Laurie parody "A Wonderful Life," replacing the Jimmy Stewart character with one modeled after Fox network's Rupert Murdoch. Comedy sketch guests include Jane Duvitski ("Waiting for God"), Imelda Staunton ("Harry Potter"), Richard Daws ("Jeeves and Wooster"), and Phyllida Law (Emma Thompson's mum). 207m; DVD. **C:** Hugh Laurie; Stephen Fry. **A:** Adult. **P:** Entertainment. **U:** Home. **Mov-Ent:** Comedy--Screwball. **Acq:** Purchase. **Dist:** BBC Worldwide Publishing Ltd.

A Bit of Matter and a Little Bit More 19??
In this video program the viewer will see "A Bit of Matter and a Little Bit More," and "Exchange in Three Parts." Both are forms of video art. ?m; 3/4 U. **Pr:** Lawrence Weiner. **A:** Adult. **P:** Entertainment. **U:** Institution, Home. **Fin-Art:** Documentary Films, Video. **Acq:** Rent/Lease. **Dist:** Kitchen Center for Video, Music & Dance.

The Bitch 1978 (R) — **Bomb!**
High-camp follies are the rule in this lustful continuation of "The Stud" as it follows the erotic adventures of a beautiful divorcee playing sex games for high stakes on the international playgrounds of high society. A collaborative effort by the sisters Collins: written by Jackie, with sister Joan well cast in the title role. 90m; VHS, DVD. **C:** Joan Collins; Kenneth Haigh; Michael Coby; Ian Hendry; Carolyn Seymour; Sue Lloyd; John Ratzenberger; Directed by Gerry O'Hara. **Pr:** Brent Walker Film Productions. **A:** College-Adult. **P:** Entertainment. **U:** Home. **Mov-Ent:** Sex & Sexuality. **Acq:** Purchase. **Dist:** Movies Unlimited.

Bite of the Black Widow 1994
Analyzes the habits of the black widow. Uses animation to trace the movement of venom through a the nervous system as it causes pain and even death. 20m; VHS, CC. **A:** Sr. High-Adult. **P:** Education. **U:** Institution. **Gen-Edu:** Insects. **Acq:** Purchase. **Dist:** National Geographic Society. $80.

Bite the Bullet 1975 (PG) — ★★★½
Moralistic western tells of a grueling 600-mile horse race where the participants reluctantly develop respect for one another. Unheralded upon release and shot in convincing epic style by Harry Stradling, Jr. Excellent cast. 131m; VHS, DVD, Wide. **C:** Gene Hackman; James Coburn; Candice Bergen; Dabney Coleman; Jan-Michael Vincent; Ben Johnson; Ian Bannen; Paul Stewart; Sally Kirkland; Mario Arteaga; Directed by Richard Brooks; Written by Richard Brooks; Cinematography by Harry Stradling, Jr.; Music by Alex North. **Pr:** Richard Brooks. **A:** Sr. High-Adult. **P:** Entertainment. **U:** Home. **Mov-Ent:** Western, Horses--Racing. **Acq:** Purchase. **Dist:** Sony Pictures Home Entertainment Inc. $12.95.

Biting the Bullet 1991
A look at the economic implications of the military build-down in the U.S. and ways of coping with lost defense dollars. 28m; VHS, 3/4 U, Special order formats. **C:** Hosted by Ned Beatty. **A:** Sr. High-Adult. **P:** Education. **U:** Institution, CCTV, CATV, BCTV, Home, SURA. **Gen-Edu:** Economics, Business. **Acq:** Purchase, Rent/Lease. **Dist:** The Video Project. $75.00.

Bits and Bytes: Basics 199?
Presents DOS and Macintosh computer basic information including turning on the computer, entering, saving, printing, ROM, RAM, and selecting hardware. 30m; VHS. **A:** Sr. High-Adult. **P:** Entertainment. **U:** Institution. **Gen-Edu:** Computers. **Acq:** Purchase. **Dist:** Ambrose Video Publishing, Inc. $69.95.

Bits and Bytes: Files 199?
An introduction to databases, record files, and relational databases. 30m; VHS. **A:** Sr. High-Adult. **P:** Entertainment. **U:** Institution. **Gen-Edu:** Computers. **Acq:** Purchase. **Dist:** Ambrose Video Publishing, Inc. $69.95.

Bits and Bytes: Messages 199?
Presents information on file transfer programs, local area networks, E-mail, parallel and serial ports, modems, baud rate, bulletin boards, and on-line information. 30m; VHS. **A:** Sr. High-Adult. **P:** Entertainment. **U:** Institution. **Gen-Edu:** Computers. **Acq:** Purchase. **Dist:** Ambrose Video Publishing, Inc. $69.95.

Bits and Bytes: Numbers 199?
Explores spreadsheet applications, for Lotus and Excel. 30m; VHS. **A:** Sr. High-Adult. **P:** Entertainment. **U:** Institution. **Gen-Edu:** Computers. **Acq:** Purchase. **Dist:** Ambrose Video Publishing, Inc. $69.95.

Bits and Bytes: Words 199?
Offers training in basic word-processing principles for WordPerfect and Windows. 30m; VHS. **A:** Sr. High-Adult. **P:** Entertainment. **U:** Institution. **Gen-Edu:** Computers. **Acq:** Purchase. **Dist:** Ambrose Video Publishing, Inc. $69.95.

Bitten: The Complete First Season 2014
Syfy Channel 2014--? horror/fantasy. Elena Michaels, the only known living female werewolf, leaves her Stonehaven pack behind in order to lead a normal life in Toronto. But a series of murders committed by rogue werewolves means she must return and discover why they're targeting her pack. 13 episodes. 572m; DVD, Blu-Ray. **C:** Laura Vandervoort; Greyston Holt; Paul Greene; Greg Bryk. **A:** Sr. High-Adult. **P:** Entertainment. **U:** Home. **L:** English. **Mov-Ent:** Fantasy, Horror, Television Series. **Acq:** Purchase. **Dist:** Entertainment One Ltd. $39.98.

The Bitter Berry 1988
The inspirational poetry of Bryron Herbert Reece is woven together with details of his life as an American poet, farmer and teacher. 28m; VHS. **Pr:** Film Ideas, Inc. **A:** Primary-Sr. High. **P:** Education. **U:** Institution. **Gen-Edu:** Documentary Films, Biography, History--U.S. **Acq:** Purchase. **Dist:** Film Ideas, Inc. $110.00.

Bitter Cane 1983
The horrors of life in Haiti are examined from the 1804 revolution to the ascension of Baby Doc Duvalier. Contains interviews with U.S. and Haitian businessmen, land owners, peasants, and merchants. 75m; VHS, 3/4 U. **TV Std:** NTSC, PAL, SECAM. **Pr:** Haiti Films. **A:** Jr. High-Adult. **P:** Education. **U:** Institution, SURA. **Gen-Edu:** Documentary Films, Caribbean, History. **Acq:** Purchase, Rent/Lease. **Dist:** The Cinema Guild.

Bitter Feast 2010 (Unrated) — ★
Horror comedy with unpleasant characters that's neither very funny nor very scary (but kinda gross). Ambitious chef Peter Grey has his career destroyed when nasty food blogger Franks runs a scathing review. He kidnaps the blogger, whisks him off to his isolated home, and gives Franks some seemingly simple food challenges. Only Grey retaliates with severe punishment for less-than-perfect results. 104m; DVD. **C:** James LeGros; Joshua Leonard; Megan Hilty; Mario Batali; Amy Seimetz; Larry Fessenden; John Speredakos; Directed by Joe Maggio; Written by Joe Maggio; Cinematography by Michael McDonough; Music by Jeff Grace. **A:** Sr. High-Adult. **P:** Entertainment. **U:** Home. **Mov-Ent:** Food Industry. **Acq:** Purchase. **Dist:** MPI Media Group.

Bitter Harvest 1981 (Unrated) — ★★★
Emmy-nominated TV movie concerning a dairy farmer frantically trying to discover what is mysteriously killing off his herd. Howard is excellent as the farmer battling the bureaucracy to find the truth. Based on a true story. 98m; DVD. **C:** Ron Howard; Art Carney; Tarah Nutter; Richard Dysart; Barry Corbin; Jim Haynie; David Knell; Directed by Roger Young. **Pr:** Charles Fries Productions. **A:** Jr. High-Adult. **P:** Entertainment. **U:** Home. **Mov-Ent:** TV Movies, Agriculture. **Acq:** Purchase. **Dist:** MGM Home Entertainment. $14.95.

Bitter Harvest 1993 (R) — ★★
Rubin and Kensit are the femme fatales who turn their considerable wiles on the innocent Baldwin. He's more than happy to be their lover but does he want to be their victim as well? 98m; VHS, CC. **C:** Stephen Baldwin; Patsy Kensit; Jennifer Rubin; Adam Baldwin; M. Emmet Walsh; Directed by Duane Clark; Written by Randall Fontana; Cinematography by Remi Adefarasin. **Pr:** Steven Paul; Gary Binkow; Barry Collier; Crystal Sky Communications; Prism Entertainment. **A:** College-Adult. **P:** Entertainment. **U:** Home. **Mov-Ent:** Mystery & Suspense, Sex & Sexuality. **Acq:** Purchase. **Dist:** Unknown Distributor.

Bitter Is the Wind 1980
This segment of the "Vikings!" series looks at how the Norwegian Vikings, who controlled Northern England and Ireland, tried to seize Southern England in 937 AD. 29m; VHS, 3/4 U. **Pr:** KCTA Minneapolis. **A:** Jr. High-Adult. **P:** Education. **U:** Institu-

tion, CCTV, CATV. **Gen-Edu**: Documentary Films, History, Scandinavia. **Acq**: Purchase, Rent/Lease, Off-Air Record. **Dist**: PBS Home Video.

Bitter Melons 1971
This program is about the Gwi San and all of their adventures. 30m; 3/4 U. **Pr**: Laurence Marshall; John Marshall. **A**: Sr. High-Adult. **P**: Education. **U**: Institution, SURA. **Gen-Edu**: Documentary Films, Africa, Anthropology. **Acq**: Purchase. **Dist**: Documentary Educational Resources.

A Bitter Message of Hopeless Grief 1988
Survival Research Lab's machines act out torment and exasperating scenarios in a fictional world. 13m; VHS. **C**: Directed by Jonathan Reiss. **A**: Sr. High-Adult. **P**: Entertainment. **U**: Home. **Mov-Ent**: Documentary Films. **Acq**: Purchase. **Dist**: Survival Research Laboratories. $18.00.

Bitter Moon 1992 (R) — ★★
Polanski effort looks promising, but ultimately disappoints. Bored British couple (Grant and Scott Thomas) meet up with sexual deviants (Coyote and Seigner, aka Mrs. Polanski) on a cruise and learn that passion and cruelty often share the same path to destruction. Masquerades as high class art, but whenever substance is lacking expect a silly, kinky sex scene. Needless to say, there isn't much substance, so erotic mischief abounds. Scott Thomas manages to hold her own, but Coyote is almost embarrassingly over the top. Based on the Pascal Bruckner novel "Lunes de Fiel." 139m; VHS, DVD, Wide. **C**: Peter Coyote; Emmanuelle Seigner; Hugh Grant; Kristin Scott Thomas; Stockard Channing; Victor Banerjee; Sophie Patel; Directed by Roman Polanski; Written by Roman Polanski; Gerard Brach; John Brownjohn; Cinematography by Tonino Delli Colli; Music by Vangelis. **Pr**: Roman Polanski; Roman Polanski; Fine Line Features. **A**: College-Adult. **P**: Entertainment. **U**: Home. **Mov-Ent**: Mystery & Suspense, Boating. **Acq**: Purchase. **Dist**: Sony Pictures Home Entertainment Inc.

Bitter Paradise: The Sell-Out of East Timor 1996
Documentary examines the 1975 invasion of Portuguese East Timor by Indonesia and the subsequent failure of Western nations to condemn the attack or withdraw support of the corrupt military regime. 56m; VHS. **A**: College. **P**: Education. **U**: Institution. **Gen-Edu**: Documentary Films, Human Rights. **Acq**: Purchase, Rent/Lease. **Dist**: The Cinema Guild. $295.

Bitter Rice 1949 (Unrated) — ★★★
Mangano became a star with her sultry performance about survival in postwar Italy. She scrapes by, working in the rice fields of the Po Valley, loved by the down-to-earth Vallone, who provides her with little excitement. Gassman is the rotten-to-the-core thief who meets up with Mangano while he's running from the police. He mistreats her, she steals his money and betrays her friends, and both destroy each other. In Italian with English subtitles. 96m; VHS, DVD, Streaming. **C**: Silvana Mangano; Vittorio Gassman; Raf Vallone; Doris Dowling; Directed by Guiseppe de Santis; Written by Guiseppe de Santis; Carlo Lizzani; Gianni Puccini; Cinematography by Otello Martelli; Music by Goffredo Petrassi. **Pr**: Dino De Laurentiis. **A**: College-Adult. **P**: Entertainment. **U**: Home. **L**: Italian. **Mov-Ent**: Sex & Sexuality. **Acq**: Purchase. **Dist**: Facets Multimedia Inc.; Amazon.com Inc. $29.95.

Bitter Sugar 1996 (Unrated) — ★★★
Young, idealistic communist Gustavo (Lavan) is a Havana university student who still believes that the Castro regime can make things better. His rock musician brother Bobby (Villanueva) is a radical, defying government policies, and his psychiatrist father Tomas (Gutierrez) makes more money playing piano at a tourist hotel than in his practice. But Gustavo's eyes are opened, not only by his family situtation, but when he falls in love with cynical dancer Yolanda (Vilan), who longs to escape to Miami. Serious politics bolstered by excellent performances and sharp cinematography. Spanish with subtitles. 102m/B/W; VHS, DVD. **C**: Rene Lavan; Mayte Vilan; Miguel Gutierrez; Larry Villanueva; Directed by Leon Ichaso; Written by Leon Ichaso; Orestes Matacena; Cinematography by Claudio Chea; Music by Manuel Tejada. **Pr**: Jaime Pina; Leon Ichaso; Leon Ichaso; First Look Pictures. **A**: College-Adult. **P**: Entertainment. **U**: Home. **L**: Spanish. **Mov-Ent**: Drama, Politics & Government. **Acq**: Purchase. **Dist**: New Yorker Video.

Bitter Sweet 1933 (Unrated) — ★★½
Tragic tale of a woman who finally marries the man she loves, only to find that he is a compulsive gambler. Written by Coward, adapted from his operetta. 76m/B/W; VHS, DVD. **C**: Anna Neagle; Fernand Gravey; Esme Percy; Clifford Heatherley; Hugh Williams; Directed by Herbert Wilcox; Written by Noel Coward. **Pr**: Herbert Wilcox; Herbert Wilcox. **A**: Jr. High-Family. **P**: Entertainment. **U**: Home. **Mov-Ent**: Drama, Gambling. **Acq**: Purchase. **Dist**: Movies Unlimited; MGM Home Entertainment. $19.95.

Bitter Sweet 1940 (Unrated) — ★★
The second version of the Noel Coward operetta, about young romance in 1875 Vienna. Creaky and overrated, but the lush Technicolor and Coward standards help to compensate. 94m; VHS, DVD. **C**: Jeanette MacDonald; Nelson Eddy; George Sanders; Felix Bressart; Ian Hunter; Sig Rumann; Herman Bing; Fay Holden; Curt Bois; Edward Ashley; Directed by W.S. Van Dyke; Written by Lesser Samuels; Noel Coward. **Pr**: MGM. **A**: Jr. High-Family. **P**: Entertainment. **U**: Home. **Mov-Ent**: Musical, Romance, Gambling. **Acq**: Purchase. **Dist**: WarnerArchive.com. $19.98.
Songs: Ziguener; I'll See You Again.

Bitter Sweet 1998 (R) — ★★
Everhart spends four years in the big house after being tricked by her boyfriend into participating in a robbery. All she wants when she gets out is to get revenge on the lowlife and she gets the opportunity when approached by cop Russo, who's looking to bring down her ex-beau's gangster boss (Roberts). 96m; VHS, DVD. **C**: Angie Everhart; James Russo; Eric Roberts; Brian Wimmer; Directed by Luca Bercovici. **A**: Sr. High-Adult. **P**: Entertainment. **U**: Home. **Mov-Ent**: Crime Drama. **Acq**: Purchase.

Bitter/Sweet 2009 (Unrated) — ★★
Coffee expert Brian leaves his fiancee Amanda behind when he's sent to Thailand by his overbearing boss Calvert Jones to make a big purchase. The antipathy between Brian and exec Ticha, who escorts him to her family's plantation, not unexpectedly turns romantic. However, Brian gets a dual shock when both Jones and Amanda turn up. Thai/U.S. co-production. 105m; DVD. **C**: Kip Pardue; James Brolin; Napakpapha Nakrasitte; Laura Sorenson; Spencer Garrett; Kalorin Nemayothin; Directed by Jeff Hare; Written by Jeff Hare; Cinematography by Sayombhu Mukdeeprom; Pongnarin Jonghawklang. **A**: Sr. High-Adult. **P**: Entertainment. **U**: Home. **Mov-Ent**: Asia, Drama. **Acq**: Purchase. **Dist**: Vanguard International Cinema, Inc.

The Bitter Tea of General Yen 1933 — ★★★
Stanwyck arrives in Shanghai to marry a missionary (Gordon) during the threatening days of China's civil war. Unexpectedly swept into the arms of an infamous warlord (Asher), she becomes fascinated, although his attempts to seduce her fail. She even remains with him while his enemies close in. Exotic and poetic, if melodramatic by today's standards. The interracial aspects were considered very daring for their time. Adapted from the book by Grace Zaring Stone. 89m/B/W; DVD. **C**: Barbara Stanwyck; Nils Asther; Gavin Gordon; Walter Connolly; Lucien Littlefield; Toshia Mori; Richard Loo; Clara Blandick; Directed by Frank Capra; Written by Edward Paramore. **Pr**: Walter Wanger. **A**: Sr. High-Adult. **P**: Entertainment. **U**: Home. **Mov-Ent**: Drama, China, War--General. **Acq**: Purchase. **Dist**: Sony Pictures Home Entertainment Inc. $19.95.

The Bitter Tears of Petra von Kant 1972 — ★★½
Dark German story of lesbian love, the fashion world, obsession and anger. Claustrophobic settings and slow pace may frustrate some viewers. In German with English subtitles. 124m; VHS, DVD. **C**: Margit Carstensen; Hanna Schygulla; Irm Hermann; Eva Mattes; Directed by Rainer Werner Fassbinder; Written by Rainer Werner Fassbinder; Cinematography by Michael Ballhaus. **A**: College-Adult. **P**: Entertainment. **U**: Home. **L**: German. **Mov-Ent**: Drama, Clothing & Dress. **Acq**: Purchase. **Dist**: New Yorker Video; Facets Multimedia Inc. $79.95.

Bitter Vengeance 1994 (R) — ★★
Security guard Jack Westford (Greenwood) pulls off a bank heist with his lover Isabella (Hocking) and plans to frame his wife Annie (Madsen) for the crime. Only Annie finds out and sets out to get them before the police get her. 90m; VHS, CC. **C**: Virginia Madsen; Bruce Greenwood; Kristen Dalton; Eddie Velez; Gordon Jump; Carlos Gomez; Tim Russ; Directed by Stuart Cooper; Written by Pablo F. Fenjves; Music by David Michael Frank. **Pr**: Christopher Griffin; Wilshire Court Productions. **A**: College-Adult. **P**: Entertainment. **U**: Home. **Mov-Ent**: Mystery & Suspense, TV Movies. **Acq**: Purchase. **Dist**: Paramount Pictures Corp.

Bitter Victory 1958 (Unrated) — ★★
Bitter psychological war drama. British Army officers Captain Leith (Burton) and Major Brand (Jurgens) are assigned to execute a commando raid on the Libyan stronghold of General Rommel and obtain some important papers. Brand learns that Leith was once involved with Brand's wife Jane (Roman) and his hatred grows when Leith also exposes his cowardice so the mission doesn't go smoothly. 97m/B/W; DVD. **C**: Richard Burton; Curt Jurgens; Ruth Roman; Raymond Pellegrin; Anthony Bushnell; Christopher Lee; Alfred Burke; Directed by Nicholas Ray; Written by Nicholas Ray; Gavin Lambert; Rene Hardy; Cinematography by Michel Kelber; Music by Maurice Leroux. **A**: Sr. High-Adult. **P**: Entertainment. **U**: Home. **Mov-Ent**: World War Two, Middle East. **Acq**: Purchase. **Dist**: Sony Pictures Home Entertainment Inc.

Bitter Wind 1963
The story of an American Indian boy whose family is destroyed by alcoholism. For all ages and races (wherever alcohol may become a problem). With Navajo soundtrack. 30m; 3/4 U. **Pr**: Brigham Young University. **A**: Primary-Adult. **P**: Education. **U**: Institution, CCTV, SURA. **Hea-Sci**: Documentary Films, Alcoholism, Native Americans. **Acq**: Purchase. **Dist**: Brigham Young University.

Bittersweet Love 1976 (PG) — ★½
Two young people fall in love and marry, only to have the bride's mother and the groom's father confess a 30-year-old affair, disclosing that the two newlyweds are actually half-siblings. 92m; VHS. **C**: Lana Turner; Robert Lansing; Celeste Holm; Robert Alda; Meredith Baxter; Directed by David Miller. **Pr**: Avco Embassy. **A**: Jr. High-Adult. **P**: Entertainment. **U**: Home. **Mov-Ent**: Melodrama, Romance. **Acq**: Purchase. **Dist**: Unknown Distributor.

Bittersweet Survival 1982 (Unrated)
Southeast Asian refugees are re-settled in the United States following the Vietnam War to a mixed reception. This film follows their struggles from local fishermen in Monterey, California to conflicts with the black community in Philadelphia. 30m; VHS, DVD. **A**: Adult. **P**: Education. **U**: Institution. **Gen-Edu**: Vietnam War, Immigration, Asia. **Acq**: Purchase. **Dist**: Third World Newsreel. $175.

Bituminous Coal Queens of Pennsylvania 2006
Actress Sarah Rush travels back to her small coal-mining community and takes an affectionate look at the town's beauty pageant, which she won at age 16. 89m; DVD. **A**: Jr. High-Adult. **P**: Entertainment. **U**: Home. **Gen-Edu**: Documentary Films, Biography. **Acq**: Purchase. **Dist**: Genius Entertainment.

Biutiful 2010 (R) — ★★½
Title is a misspelling by the young daughter of Barcelona crook Uxbal (Bardem), whose shady dealings involve trafficking Chinese sweatshop workers and Senegalese drug dealers. Uxbal is dedicated to protecting and sacrificing for his children, but he's forced to re-evaluate his life when he learns that he's dying from cancer. Bardem shines as the dark, conflicted protagonist—but cannot overcome the profound bleakness and misery of Uxbal's road to redemption. Spanish and Mandarin with subtitles. 147m; Blu-Ray, On Demand, Wide. **C**: Javier Bardem; Maricel Alvarez; Eduardo Fernandez; Diaryatou Daff; Taisheng ("Cheng Tai Shen") Cheng; Hanaa Bouchaib; Guillermo Estrella; Directed by Alejandro Gonzalez Inarritu; Written by Armando Bo; Nicolas Giabone; Alejandro Gonzalez Inarritu; Cinematography by Rodrigo Pireto; Music by Gustavo Santaolalla. **Pr**: Jon Kilik; Alejandro Gonzalez Inarritu; Alejandro Gonzalez Inarritu; Fernando Bovaira; Mod Producciones; Menage Atroz; Ikiru Films; Focus Features L.L.C; Universal Pictures; Liddell Entertainment; Roadside Attractions. **A**: College-Adult. **P**: Entertainment. **U**: Home. **L**: Spanish, Mandarin Dialects. **Mov-Ent**: Crime Drama. **Acq**: Purchase. **Dist**: Amazon.com Inc.; Movies Unlimited; Alpha Video.

Bix 1990 — ★★
Based on the brief life of legendary Jazz Age cornetist Leon Bix Beiderbecke, who died at age 28. Story unfolds in flashbacks, through friend Joe Venuti memories of the dissipated genius and the music he created with Hoagy Carmichael, Pee Wee Russell, Paul Whiteman, and others. 100m; VHS. **C**: Bryant Weeks; Emile Levisetti; Mark Collver; Sally Groth; Directed by Pupi Avati; Written by Pupi Avati; Antonio Avati; Lino Patruno. **Pr**: Antonio Avati; DUEA Film. **A**: College-Adult. **P**: Entertainment. **U**: Home. **Mov-Ent**: Biography: Music, Music--Jazz. **Acq**: Purchase. **Dist**: Rhapsody Films, Inc. $59.95.

Bix: Ain't None of Them Play Like Him Yet 1994
Examines the life of '20s jazz cornetist Bix Beiderbecke. Includes photographs, archival footage, and interviews with musicians Hoagy Carmichael, Charlie Davis, and Artie Shaw. ?m; VHS. **A**: College-Adult. **P**: Entertainment. **U**: Home. **Gen-Edu**: Biography, Music--Jazz. **Acq**: Purchase. **Dist**: Music Video Distributors; Universal Music and Video Distribution. $19.95.

Bizarre 1987 (Unrated) — ★
When a wife escapes her perverse, psychologically threatening marriage, she finds her husband still haunts her literally and figuratively, and plots psychological revenge. Dubbed. 93m; VHS, DVD. **C**: Florence Guerin; Luciano Bartoli; Robert Egon Spechtenhauser; Stefano Sabelli; Directed by Giuliana Gamba. **Pr**: Metrofilm. **A**: Sr. High-Adult. **P**: Entertainment. **U**: Home. **Mov-Ent**: Mystery & Suspense. **Acq**: Purchase. **Dist**: No Longer Available.

Bizarre Bizarre 1939 (Unrated) — ★★★
A mystery writer is accused of murder and disappears, only to return in disguise to try to clear his name. Along the way, a number of French comedians are introduced with a revue of comedy-farce sketches that include slapstick, burlesque, black humor, and comedy of the absurd. In French with English subtitles. 90m/B/W; VHS, DVD. **C**: Louis Jouvet; Michel Simon; Francoise Rosay; Jean-Pierre Aumont; Nadine Vogel; Henri Guisol; Jenny Burnay; Directed by Marcel Carne; Written by Jacques Prevert; Cinematography by Eugen Shufftan; Music by Maurice Jaubert. **A**: Sr. High-Adult. **P**: Entertainment. **U**: Home. **L**: French. **Mov-Ent**: Comedy--Black. **Acq**: Purchase. **Dist**: Glenn Video Vistas Ltd. $24.95.

Bizarre Expeditions 1935
Consists of two films produced by the Dodge Corporation "East of Bombay," and "Wheels Across India," to hype their vehicles. Two world explorers travel to remote areas of India and Burma in a Dodge truck and car to film exotic events, rituals and cultures. 60m/B/W; VHS. **A**: Family. **P**: Entertainment. **U**: Home. **Gen-Edu**: Automobiles. **Acq**: Purchase. **Dist**: Moviecraft Home Video. $19.95.

Bizarre Foods with Andrew Zimmern: Collection 2 2007 (Unrated)
Travel Channel documentary series (2007-). Andrew Zimmern samples the world's most exotic cuisine: rotten shark meat, wild boar brains, from China to Minnesota. This season he also visits Russia, Iceland, Bolivia, and Chile. 9 episodes. 392m; DVD. **A**: Family. **P**: Entertainment. **U**: Home. **Mov-Ent**: Cooking, Travel, Television Series. **Acq**: Purchase. **Dist**: Image Entertainment Inc.

Bizarre Music Television 1985
A motley collection of strange and pointless videos, with wrestlers, kazoos, fish heads and more. 60m; VHS. **Pr**: Impulse Entertainment. **A**: Jr. High-Adult. **P**: Entertainment. **U**: Home. **Mov-Ent**: Music Video, TV Movies. **Acq**: Purchase. **Dist**: Music Video Distributors; Rhino Entertainment Co. $29.95.

Bizarre Rituals 1: Dances Sacred and Profane 1990 (Unrated)
Some weird and shocking practices are found right here in the U.S., from New York S&M clubs to the insanity of the New Orleans Mardi Gras festival. Who knew!? 83m; VHS. **Pr**: MPI Media Group. **A**: College-Adult. **P**: Entertainment. **U**: Home. **Mov-Ent**: Documentary Films, Exploitation. **Acq**: Purchase. **Dist**: MPI Media Group. $79.95.

Bizarre Rituals 2: Voodoo in Haiti 1990
The secret religions of Haiti are explored, and the influences from Africa's darkest forces are seen. Cock fights and animal mutilations and sacrifices are also included. 50m; VHS. **Pr**: MPI Media Group. **A**: College-Adult. **P**: Entertainment. **U**: Home.

Gen-Edu: Documentary Films, Africa, Religion. **Acq:** Purchase. **Dist:** MPI Media Group. $59.95.

Bizarre Sports and Incredible Feats 1986
Glimpses of cockroach racing, dog skiing, elephant soccer and greased-log walking, among other odd happenings. 30m; VHS. **Pr:** Scanline Productions. **A:** Family. **P:** Entertainment. **U:** Home. **Spo-Rec**: Sports--General. **Acq:** Purchase. **Dist:** Cambridge Educational. $9.95.

Bizet Concert 1988
Features the great Montserrat Caballe in an all-Bizet concert, including the cantata Clovis and Clotilda, L'Arlesiene Suite No. 1, and the Symphony in C Major. 95m; VHS. **A:** Family. **P:** Entertainment. **U:** Home. **Fin-Art**: Music--Performance, Music--Classical. **Acq:** Purchase. **Dist:** Kultur International Films Ltd., Inc. $19.95.

Bizet: L'Arlesienne 1988
This Japanese import features the music of Bizet recorded live at the Soisson Church on September 17, 1988 with featured guests Montserrat Caballe and Cabaret Casadesus. 80m; VHS. **A:** Sr. High-Adult. **P:** Entertainment. **U:** Home. **Fin-Art**: Music--Classical. **Acq:** Purchase. **Dist:** Music Video Distributors. $69.95.

B.L. Stryker: The Complete 1st Season 1989
Former New Orleans detective B.L. Stryker returns to his native Palm Beach to work as a private investigator. 5 episodes. 414m; DVD. **C:** Burt Reynolds; Ossie Davis. **A:** Adult. **P:** Entertainment. **U:** Home. **Mov-Ent**: Drama. **Acq:** Purchase. **Dist:** Virgil Films & Entertainment.

B.L. Stryker: The Complete Series 1989 (Unrated)
Television drama series on ABC (1989-1990). Burt Reynolds is B.L. Stryker, a former New Orleans detective who becomes a private investigator in Florida purely by circumstance. Includes episodes from the two season run: "The Dancer's Touch," "Carolann," "Blind Chess," "Auntie Sue," "Blues for Buder," "The King of Jazz," "Die Laughing," "Winner Takes All," "Grand Theft Hotel," "High Rise," "Plates," and "Night Train." 12 episodes. 1128m; DVD. **A:** Sr. High-Adult. **P:** Entertainment. **U:** Home. **Mov-Ent**: Drama, Television Series. **Acq:** Purchase. **Dist:** Virgil Films & Entertainment.

The Black Abbot 1963 — ★★
A mysterious black-hooded figure is seen entering a ruined Abbey tower that leads to a country house with buried treasure. Based on an Edgar Wallace story. 95m; VHS, DVD. **C:** Joachim Fuchsberger; Dieter Borsche; Gritt Bottcher; Eva Scholtz; Franz Gottlieb; Directed by Franz Gottlieb. **A:** Sr. High-Adult. **P:** Entertainment. **U:** Home. **Mov-Ent**: Mystery & Suspense. **Acq:** Purchase. **Dist:** Sinister Cinema. $16.95.

Black Adder Goes Forth 1989
Edmund Blackadder finds himself a British Army Captain on the Western Front in 1917. Six episodes from the popular British television sitcom on available on two cassettes. 180m; VHS, CC. **C:** Rowan Atkinson; Hugh Laurie. **Pr:** British Broadcasting Corporation. **A:** Jr. High-Adult. **P:** Entertainment. **U:** Home. **Mov-Ent**: TV Movies. **Acq:** Purchase. **Dist:** Signals Video; Critics' Choice Video & DVD; Fusion Video. $39.95.

Black Adder I, Part 1 1990
The scheming, cowardly Edmund Blackadder finds himself stuck in the Dark Ages in the reign of Richard III. Three episodes from the popular BBC series. 100m; VHS. **C:** Rowan Atkinson; Peter Cook. **A:** Jr. High-Adult. **P:** Entertainment. **U:** Home. **Mov-Ent**: TV Movies. **Acq:** Purchase. **Dist:** Facets Multimedia Inc. $19.98.
Indiv. Titles: 1. The Foretelling 2. Born to Be King 3. The Archbishop.

Black Adder I, Part 2 1990
Three more episodes from the popular British series as Edmund once again continues his sniveling ways. 96m; VHS. **C:** Rowan Atkinson; Peter Cook. **A:** Jr. High-Adult. **P:** Entertainment. **U:** Home. **Mov-Ent**: TV Movies. **Acq:** Purchase. **Dist:** Facets Multimedia Inc. $19.98.
Indiv. Titles: 1. The Queen of Spain's Beard 2. Witchsmeller Pursuivant 3. The Black Seal.

Black Adder II 1989
The sniveling Edmund Blackadder winds up in the court of Queen Elizabeth I. Six episodes of the British comedy series are available on two cassettes. 180m; VHS, CC. **C:** Rowan Atkinson. **A:** Jr. High-Adult. **P:** Entertainment. **U:** Home. **Mov-Ent**: TV Movies. **Acq:** Purchase. **Dist:** Signals Video; Critics' Choice Video & DVD; Fusion Video. $39.95.

Black Adder III 1989
Aristocrat-turned-butler Edmund Blackadder finds himself in the 18th century working for the dim-witted Prince Regent. Six episodes of the British comedy series are available on two cassettes. 180m; VHS, CC. **C:** Rowan Atkinson; Hugh Laurie. **Pr:** British Broadcasting Corporation. **A:** Jr. High-Adult. **P:** Entertainment. **U:** Home. **Mov-Ent**: TV Movies. **Acq:** Purchase. **Dist:** Signals Video; Home Vision Cinema; Fusion Video. $39.95.

Black Adder's Christmas Carol 199?
The classic Dickens tale of good cheer is turned upside down. Ebenezer Blackadder is a good-hearted soul prepared to give his last farthing to the poor. Then the Ghost of Christmas Past shows him his loathesome ancestors and his equally unhappy future. 43m; VHS. **C:** Rowan Atkinson; Robbie Coltrane; Miranda Richardson; Tony Robinson. **A:** Jr. High-Adult. **P:** Entertainment. **U:** Home. **Mov-Ent**: Christmas, TV Movies. **Acq:** Purchase. **Dist:** Signals Video; Facets Multimedia Inc.; Fusion Video. $14.98.

Black America and the Education Crisis ????
Syndicated columnist Juan Williams moderates a town meeting to discuss why black children score lower on standardized tests, how to improve academic performance, and Ebonics. 45m; VHS. **A:** Adult. **P:** Teacher Education. **U:** Institution. **Gen-Edu**: Education, Children. **Acq:** Purchase, Rent/Lease. **Dist:** Films for the Humanities & Sciences. $129.00.

Black America Series 1990
Various black people who have made important contributions to their race are profiled. 32m; VHS, 3/4 U. **Pr:** Centre Productions, Inc. **A:** Sr. High-Adult. **P:** Education. **U:** Institution, SURA. **Gen-Edu**: Black Culture, History--U.S. **Acq:** Purchase, Rent/Lease. **Dist:** Clear Vue Inc. $1470.00.
Indiv. Titles: 1. The Civil Rights Movement 2. The New South 3. The North, or the End of Illusions 4. Breaking Free.

Black American Conservatives 1992
Black conservative leaders support community-based entrepreneurship, proven through history to be highly effective, in place of less effective governmental aid. 58m; VHS. **A:** Sr. High-Adult. **P:** Education. **U:** Home, Institution. **Gen-Edu**: Business, Politics & Government, Black Culture. **Acq:** Purchase. **Dist:** PBS Home Video. $59.95.

Black Americans 1989
Black Americans who have made notable achievements in their fields are given brief biographies in these two programs. 20m; VHS, 3/4 U. **Pr:** SVE. **A:** Primary-Jr. High. **P:** Education. **U:** Institution, CCTV, Home. **Gen-Edu**: Black Culture. **Acq:** Purchase, Duplication. **Dist:** Clear Vue Inc. $99.00.
Indiv. Titles: 1. Political Leaders, Educators, Scientists 2. Artists, Entertainers, Athletes.

Black Americans and the Military 19??
Chronicles the history of African-Americans in the U.S. military. 29m; VHS. **A:** Jr. High-Adult. **P:** Education. **U:** Institution. **Gen-Edu**: Black Culture, History--U.S., Military History. **Acq:** Purchase. **Dist:** Educational Video Network. $39.95.

Black Americans: Artists, Entertainers and Athletes 19??
An inspirational overview of contributions by outstanding black Amreicans including Leontyne Price, Henry O. Tanner and Althea Gibson. 20m; VHS. **A:** Jr. High-Sr. High. **P:** Education. **U:** Home. **Gen-Edu**: Documentary Films, Black Culture, Sports--General. **Acq:** Purchase. **Dist:** African-American Images. $100.00.

The Black Americans of Achievement Video Collection 1992
A 12-volume series profiling notable African Americans of the 20th century. Tapes are available individually or as a boxed-set. 30m; VHS. **A:** Family. **P:** Education. **U:** Home, SURA. **Gen-Edu**: Black Culture, Biography. **Acq:** Purchase. **Dist:** Library Video Inc.; Baker and Taylor; Facets Multimedia Inc. $39.95.
Indiv. Titles: 1. Booker T. Washington 2. Colin Powell 3. Dr. Martin Luther King, Jr. 4. Frederick Douglas 5. George Washington Carver 6. Harriet Tubman 7. Jackie Robinson 8. Jesse Jackson 9. Madam C.J. Walker 10. Malcolm X 11. Sojourner Truth 12. Thurgood Marshall.

The Black Americans of Achievement Video Collection II 1994
Series presents 12 new profiles on influential African Americans. Contains biographical material, interviews with experts, archival footage, and period music. Available individually or as a set. 30m; VHS, CC. **Pr:** Schlessinger Video Productions. **A:** Jr. High-Adult. **P:** Education. **U:** Institution, Home. **Gen-Edu**: Black Culture, Biography. **Acq:** Purchase. **Dist:** Library Video Inc. $39.95.
Indiv. Titles: 1. Muhammad Ali 2. James Baldwin 3. Mary Mcleod Bethune 4. W.E.B. Du Bois 5. Marcus Garvey 6. Matthew Henson 7. Langston Hughes 8. Elijah Muhammad 9. Jesse Owens 10. Alice Walker 11. A History of the Civil Rights Movement 12. A History of Slavery in America.

Black Americans: Political Leaders, Educators and Scientists 19??
An overview of the contributions made by several notable black Americans, including Thurgood Marshall and Shirley Chisholm. 20m; VHS. **A:** Preschool-Jr. High. **P:** Education. **U:** Institution, Home, SURA. **Gen-Edu**: Black Culture, History, Politics & Government. **Acq:** Purchase. **Dist:** African-American Images. $100.00.

Black and Blue 1987
Archival material, news clips, and documentary footage reveal how one community in Philadelphia struggled with the issue of biased police violence against people of color. 58m; VHS, 3/4 U. **A:** Sr. High-Adult. **P:** Education. **U:** Institution. **Gen-Edu**: Civil Rights, Prejudice. **Acq:** Purchase, Rent/Lease. **Dist:** Third World Newsreel. $225.00.

Black & Tan/St. Louis Blues 1929
Two early jazz two-reelers are combined on this tape: "Black and Tan" is the first film appearance of Duke Ellington's Orchestra, featuring Cootie Williams and Johnny Hodges. "St. Louis Blues" is the only surviving film made by legendary blues singer Bessie Smith. She is backed by the Hall Johnson Choir, members of the Fletcher Henderson band directed by James P. Johnson, and dancer Jimmy Mordecai. 36m/B/W; VHS. **C:** Duke Ellington; Fredi Washington; Bessie Smith; Hall Johnson. **Pr:** Dudley Murphy; RKO. **A:** Jr. High-Adult. **P:** Entertainment. **U:** Home. **Mov-Ent**: Music--Performance, Music--Jazz. **Acq:** Purchase. **Dist:** $17.95.

The Black and the Green 1983
Five African-Americans travel to Belfast, Northern Ireland looking for the common elements in the struggle of Irish nationalists and blacks groups in America and the issues of human rights, social change, and religion. 45m; VHS. **C:** Directed by St. Claire Bourne. **A:** College-Adult. **P:** Education. **U:** Institution. **Gen-Edu**: Black Culture, Ireland, Human Rights. **Acq:** Purchase, Rent/Lease. **Dist:** First Run/Icarus Films. $375.00.

Black and White 1994 (Unrated)
Chronicles the incredible friendship of two men, one black, the other white, during the 1940s in America. We follow them from childhood to adulthood and witness their maturation in a country that will change along with them. ?m; VHS. **C:** Nick Furris; Kim Delgado; Directed by Stephen Vittoria; Written by Stephen Vittoria. **Pr:** Nicholas J. Furris; Blue Line Cinema. **A:** Sr. High-Adult. **P:** Entertainment. **U:** Home. **Mov-Ent**: Men, Korean War. **Acq:** Purchase. **Dist:** Tapeworm Video Distributors Inc. $29.95.

Black and White 1999 (R) — ★★★
Director Toback attempts to investigate white kids' facsination with black hip-hop culture by creating an intriguing combination of pseudo-documentary and urban melodrama, with cameos and performances by professional celebrities alongside professional actors. In the more effective part of the film, Shields is a documentary filmmaker asking rich white kids why they're into hip-hop. This section also includes Robert Downey as her gay husband hitting on Mike Tyson (playing himself in one of the film's strongest scenes). The part that doesn't work as well is the more conventional storyline (which seems added to satisfy studio executives looking for straight narrative) involving an undercover cop (Stiller) bribing college basketball star Dean (Houston) to throw a game in an attempt to get at Dean's best friend Rich (Power), a drug kingpin turned rap mogul. While the parts don't add up to an entirely satisfying whole, the journey is worth the interesting ride. 98m; VHS, DVD, Wide. **C:** Scott Caan; Robert Downey, Jr.; Stacy Edwards; Gaby Hoffman; Jared Leto; Marla Maples; Joe Pantoliano; Brooke Shields; Power; Claudia Schiffer; William Lee Scott; Ben Stiller; Eddie Kaye Thomas; Elijah Wood; Mike Tyson; James Toback; Allan Houston; Kidada Jones; Bijou Phillips; Raekwon; Directed by James Toback; Written by James Toback; Cinematography by David Ferrara. **Pr:** Screen Gems. **A:** Sr. High-Adult. **P:** Entertainment. **U:** Home. **Mov-Ent**: Basketball, Black Culture. **Acq:** Purchase. **Dist:** Sony Pictures Home Entertainment Inc.

Black & White 1999 (R) — ★★1/2
Rookie cop Chris O'Brien (Cochrane) is partnered with tough veteran female officer Nora Hugosian (Gershon), who's known for both her sexiness and her ruthless style. The two begin an affair while searching for a serial killer. And then the rookie comes across some evidence that seems to implicate his partner in the crimes. 97m; VHS, DVD, Wide, CC. **C:** Gina Gershon; Rory Cochrane; Ron Silver; Alison Eastwood; Marshall Bell; Directed by Yuri Zeltser; Written by Yuri Zeltser; Leon Zeltser; Cinematography by Phil Parmet. **A:** Sr. High-Adult. **P:** Entertainment. **U:** Home. **Mov-Ent**: Sex & Sexuality. **Acq:** Purchase. **Dist:** Sony Pictures Home Entertainment Inc.

Black and White 2006 (Unrated)
Mani Bruce Mitchell and photographer Rebecca Swan sensitively present the subject of intersex individuals, also referred to as hermaphrodites. Mitchell was labeled "male" at birth but later investigative surgery showed ovaries, so her gender was reassigned as "female." Tells her story since 2005 through artistic mediums. 17m; DVD. **A:** Adult. **P:** Education. **U:** Institution. **Gen-Edu**: Sex & Sexuality, Identity. **Acq:** Purchase. **Dist:** Women Make Movies. $195.00.

Black and White As Day and Night 1978 — ★★
A man's talent for the game of chess becomes a destructive obsession. In German with English subtitles. 103m; VHS. **C:** Bruno Ganz; Rene Deltgen; Ljuba Tadic; Gila von Weitershausen; Directed by Wolfgang Petersen; Written by Jochen Wedegartner; Karl Heinz Willschrei; Cinematography by Jorg-Michael Baldenius; Music by Klaus Doldinger. **A:** Sr. High-Adult. **P:** Entertainment. **U:** Home. **L:** German. **Mov-Ent**: Mystery & Suspense, Chess. **Acq:** Purchase. **Dist:** Sinister Cinema. $16.95.

Black and White in Color 1976 (PG) — ★★★
Award-winning satire about a French soldier at an African outpost, who, upon hearing the news of the beginning of WWI, takes it upon himself to attack a neighboring German fort. Calamity ensues. In French, with English subtitles. 100m; VHS, DVD. **C:** Jean Carmet; Jacques Dufilho; Catherine Rouvel; Jacques Spiesser; Dora Doll; Jacques Perrin; Directed by Jean-Jacques Annaud; Written by Georges Conchon; Jean-Jacques Annaud; Music by Pierre Bachelet. **Pr:** Arthur Cohn. **A:** Sr. High-Adult. **P:** Entertainment. **U:** Home. **L:** French. **Mov-Ent**: Satire & Parody. **Awds:** Oscars '76: Foreign Film. **Acq:** Purchase. **Dist:** MGM Studios Inc. ; Warner Home Video, Inc. $39.98.

Black and White in Colour 2000
Documentary featuring Gypsy diva Vera Bila, a cabaret singer who tours Europe and must fight discrimination from within her own country and abroad. Subtitled. 58m; VHS. **A:** Adult. **P:** Education. **U:** Home. **Gen-Edu**: Documentary Films, Ethnicity, Smoking. **Acq:** Purchase, Rent/Lease. **Dist:** Filmakers Library Inc. $295.

Black and White Photography: Creating the Image 19??
Master photographers from three diverse locations offer tips on hwo to shoot professional black and white photographs, as well as how they create fascinating and unusual images. 50m; VHS.

A: Jr. High-Adult. **P:** Instruction. **U:** Institution, Home. **How-Ins:** Photography, How-To. **Acq:** Purchase. **Dist:** Crystal Productions. $19.95.

Black and White: "Unless We. . .Live Together" 1973
Martin Luther King's words set the tone for this examination of black-white relations over the years. 16m; VHS, 3/4 U. **Pr:** Jesse Sandler. **A:** Jr. High-Sr. High. **P:** Education. **U:** Institution, SURA. **Gen-Edu:** Documentary Films, Civil Rights. **Acq:** Purchase. **Dist:** Capital Communications.

Black and White: Uptight 1969
Prejudice is the issue in this probing show. The social and economic differences that exist between blacks and whites are examined. Narration by Robert Culp. 35m; VHS, 3/4 U. **C:** Narrated by Robert Culp. **Pr:** Avanti Films. **A:** Jr. High-Sr. High. **P:** Education. **U:** Institution, SURA. **Gen-Edu:** Documentary Films, Minorities, Prejudice. **Acq:** Purchase. **Dist:** Phoenix Learning Group.

Black Angel 1946 (Unrated) — ★★★
Catherine Bennett (Vincent) tries to clear the name of estranged husband Kirk (Phillips), who's accused of murdering his lover, blackmailing chanteuse Mavis Marlowe (Dowling). Catherine enlists the aid of Mavis' husband, drunken songwriter Martin Blair (Duryea), whom she suspects actually did the deed. Another suspect is sleazy nightclub owner Marko (Lorre), where the duo get a job to check things out. Blair falls for Catherine and goes on another bender when she rejects him, as Kirk's execution day draws ever closer. Atmospheric noir is based on the novel by Cornell Woolrich. 80m/B/W; VHS, DVD. **C:** June Vincent; Dan Duryea; Peter Lorre; Broderick Crawford; John Phillips; Constance Dowling; Wallace Ford; Hobart Cavanaugh; Freddie (Fred) Steele; Directed by Roy William Neill; Written by Roy Chanslor; Cinematography by Paul Ivano; Music by Frank Skinner. **Pr:** Roy William Neill; Roy William Neill; Universal International. **A:** Sr. High-Adult. **P:** Entertainment. **U:** Home. **Mov-Ent:** Nightclubs, Alcoholism. **Acq:** Purchase. **Dist:** Movies Unlimited; Alpha Video.

Black Arrow 1948 (Unrated) — ★★★
Original adventure film of the famous Robert Louis Stevenson novel. Upon return from 16th century's War of the Roses, a young man must avenge his father's murder by following a trail of clues in the form of black arrows. Well made and fun. 76m/B/W; VHS, DVD. **C:** Louis Hayward; Janet Blair; George Macready; Edgar Buchanan; Paul Cavanagh; Directed by Gordon Douglas. **Pr:** Walt Disney Studios. **A:** Jr. High-Adult. **P:** Entertainment. **U:** Home. **Mov-Ent:** Action-Adventure. **Acq:** Purchase. **Dist:** Walt Disney Studios Home Entertainment. $69.95.

The Black Arrow 1984 (Unrated) — ★★
Exiled bowman returns to England to avenge the injustices of a villainous nobleman. Cable version of the Robert Louis Stevenson medieval romp is not as well done as the 1948 adaptation. 93m; VHS. **C:** Oliver Reed; Benedict Taylor; Georgia Slowe; Stephan Chase; Donald Pleasence; Directed by John Hough. **Pr:** Walt Disney Studios. **A:** Family. **P:** Entertainment. **U:** Home. **Mov-Ent:** Action-Adventure, TV Movies, Family Viewing. **Acq:** Purchase. **Dist:** Walt Disney Studios Home Entertainment. $69.95.

Black Athena 1991
Presents Prof. Martin Bernal's studied argument that ancient Greece, which introduced democracy, philosophy, and drama, was not a pure Aryan civilization, but had African origins as evidenced in Greek mythology. Includes commentary by eminent scholars who charge Bernal with using evidence selectively and uncritically. 52m; VHS. **Pr:** Bandung File, Channel 4. **A:** College-Adult. **P:** Education. **U:** Institution. **Gen-Edu:** History--Ancient, Africa, Philosophy & Ideology. **Acq:** Purchase, Rent/Lease. **Dist:** California Newsreel. $195.00.

The Black Athlete 1979
The changing role of blacks in sports is reviewed. Footage of early black athletes such as Jack Johnson, Joe Louis, and Jackie Robinson is included with interviews of O. J. Simpson, Harry Edwards, Muhammed Ali, Arthur Ashe, and others. 58m; VHS, 3/4 U. **C:** Narrated by James Michener. **Pr:** Cappy Productions. **A:** Family. **P:** Education. **U:** Institution, Home, SURA. **Spo-Rec:** Sports--General, Black Culture. **Acq:** Purchase, Rent/Lease, Duplication License. **Dist:** Pyramid Media; Facets Multimedia Inc.; African-American Images.

Black Atlantic: On the Orixas Route 2001
Documentary exploring how African-born slaves brought their own traditions, religion, song, and dance to Brazil; and when freed, returned to Africa where they, in turn, brought Brazilian culture to Africa. 55m; VHS. **A:** College-Adult. **P:** Education. **U:** Institution. **Gen-Edu:** Slavery, South America, Africa. **Acq:** Purchase, Rent/Lease. **Dist:** Filmakers Library Inc. $350.00.

The Black Balloon 2009 (PG-13) — ★★½
All Thomas wants is a normal adolescence. But when he and his oddball family, including his autistic brother, Charlie, move to a new neighborhood, his vulnerabilities and familial eccentricities are exposed, specifically to Jackie, the object of his kept affections. It isn't until swimming class and mandated mouth-to-mouth practice, that their mutual feelings are exposed. Effective Aussie effort is touching without resorting to melodrama. 97m; DVD. **C:** Luke Ford; Toni Collette; Erik Thomson; Rhys Wakefield; Gemma Ward; Directed by Elissa Down; Written by Elissa Down; Jimmy Jack. **Pr:** NeoClassics Films. **A:** Jr. High-Adult. **P:** Entertainment. **U:** Home. **L:** English. **Mov-Ent:** Comedy-Drama, Adolescence, Autism. **Acq:** Purchase. **Dist:** Focus Media Group.

Black Bandit 1938 (Unrated) — ★½
Don Ramsay (Baker) runs away from home at a young age and becomes the notorious 'Black Bandit' while his identical twin Bob becomes a respectable lawman. No one seems to know the two are twins and Bob eventually gets thrown in jail for Don's crimes and must finally bring his brother to justice. 60m/B/W; DVD. **C:** Bob Baker; Hal Taliaferro; Jack Rockwell; Forrest Taylor; Directed by George Waggner; Written by George Waggner; Cinematography by Gus Peterson. **A:** Family. **P:** Entertainment. **U:** Home. **L:** English. **Mov-Ent:** Western, Action-Adventure. **Acq:** Purchase. **Dist:** VCI Entertainment.

Black Bass Mania 19??
Bass fishing champion and guide Freddie Grant demonstrates some of the most high-tech fishing techniques used for catching black bass. 60m; VHS. **Pr:** Bennett Marine Video. **A:** Jr. High-Adult. **P:** Instruction. **U:** Home. **Spo-Rec:** Fishing, How-To. **Acq:** Purchase. **Dist:** Bennett Marine Video. $19.95.

Black Bears: The First Year 1990
Researchers radio tag a sow and monitor the activity of her and her five young cubs during the first year of their lives. 30m; VHS. **A:** Preschool-Primary. **P:** Education. **U:** Home, Institution. **Chl-Juv:** Animals, Wilderness Areas. **Acq:** Purchase. **Dist:** Wild Life Unlimited Foundation, Inc. $14.95.

Black Beauty 1946 (Unrated) — ★★
In this adaptation of Anna Sewell's familiar novel, a young girl develops a kindred relationship with an extraordinary horse. 74m/B/W; VHS. **C:** Mona Freeman; Richard Denning; Evelyn Ankers; Directed by Max Nosseck. **Pr:** 20th Century-Fox. **A:** Family. **P:** Entertainment. **U:** Home. **Mov-Ent:** Horses, Family Viewing. **Acq:** Purchase. **Dist:** Anchor Bay Entertainment. $9.99.

Black Beauty 1971 (G) — ★★
International remake of the classic horse story by Anna Sewell. 105m; VHS, DVD. **C:** Mark Lester; Walter Slezak; Directed by James Hill; Cinematography by Chris Menges; Music by Lionel Bart. **Pr:** Tigon British Film Production. **A:** Family. **P:** Entertainment. **U:** Home. **Mov-Ent:** Children, Horses. **Acq:** Purchase. **Dist:** Facets Multimedia Inc.; Paramount Pictures Corp. $14.95.

Black Beauty 1994 (G) — ★★★
Remake of the classic Anna Sewell children's novel about an oft-sold horse whose life has its shares of ups and downs. Timeless tale still brings children and adults to tears. Six-year-old quarterhorse named Justin gives a nuanced portrayal as the Black Beauty, recalling Olivier in "Hamlet." Directorial debut of "Secret Garden" screenwriter Thompson. 88m; VHS, DVD, Blu-Ray, CC. **C:** Andrew Knott; Sean Bean; David Thewlis; Jim Carter; Alun Armstrong; Eleanor Bron; Peter Cook; Peter Davison; John McEnery; Nicholas Jones; Directed by Caroline Thompson; Written by Caroline Thompson; Cinematography by Alex Thomson. **Pr:** Robert Shapiro; Peter MacGregor-Scott; Warner. **A:** Family. **P:** Entertainment. **U:** Home. **Mov-Ent:** Horses, Children, Classic Films. **Acq:** Purchase. **Dist:** Warner Home Video, Inc. $24.96.

The Black Belly of the Tarantula 1971 (Unrated) — ★★
Inspector Tellini (Giannini) investigates a series of murders where the victims are first paralyzed with wasp venom before being cut open while they're still alive. And the connection between the victims seems to be a beauty spa. Italian with subtitles. 89m; DVD. **C:** Giancarlo Giannini; Claudine Auger; Barbara Bouchet; Stefania Sandrelli; Barbara Bach; Rossella Falk; Directed by Paolo Cavara; Written by Marcello Danon; Lucille Laks; Cinematography by Marcello Gatti; Music by Ennio Morricone. **A:** Sr. High-Adult. **P:** Entertainment. **U:** Home. **L:** Italian. **Mov-Ent. Acq:** Purchase. **Dist:** Blue Underground, Inc.

Black Belt 1992 (R) — ★
A private detective is hired to protect a rock star from a fanatic Vietnam vet. 80m; VHS, DVD, CC. **C:** Don "The Dragon" Wilson; Richard Beymer; Alan Blumenfeld; Matthias Hues; Directed by Charles Philip Moore; Written by Charles Philip Moore. **Pr:** Roger Corman; Mike Elliott. **A:** Sr. High-Adult. **P:** Entertainment. **U:** Home. **Mov-Ent:** Martial Arts. **Acq:** Purchase. **Dist:** $89.98.

Black Belt 2007 (Unrated) — ★½
Set in Japan in the 1930s, presents a Karate dojo being dismantled by the Japanese military. The master dies before choosing a successor, and his top three students must face both the military and each other as they try to live up to the standards they believe in, and inherit their master's school. Unfortunately their philosophies are quite different, and a clash is inevitable. The main actors are all accomplished Karate practitioners, and the presentation of martial arts is far more realistic than recent wire fu efforts. 95m; DVD. **C:** Tatsuya Naka; Akihito Yagi; Yuji Suzuki; Directed by Shunich Nagasaki; Written by Joji Iida; Cinematography by Masato Kaneko; Music by Naoki Sato. **A:** Sr. High-Adult. **P:** Entertainment. **U:** Home. **L:** English, Japanese. **Mov-Ent:** Martial Arts. **Acq:** Purchase. **Dist:** Media Blasters Inc. $19.95.

Black Belt Jones 1974 (R) — ★
Martial arts expert fights the mob to save a school of self-defense in Los Angeles' Watts district. 87m; VHS, DVD. **C:** Jim Kelly; Gloria Hendry; Scatman Crothers; Directed by Robert Clouse. **Pr:** Warner Bros; Golden Harvest. **A:** Sr. High-Adult. **P:** Entertainment. **U:** Home. **Mov-Ent:** Martial Arts. **Acq:** Purchase. **Dist:** $14.95.

Black Belt Karate for Seniors 1998
72-year-old karate black belt Vic Katz teaches his techniques for relieving stress, muscle tension and weight gain often associated with aging. The martial arts moves also teach basic self-defense. 30m; VHS. **A:** Adult. **P:** Instruction. **U:** Home. **Spo-Rec:** Aging, Martial Arts. **Acq:** Purchase. **Dist:** Tapeworm Video Distributors Inc. $14.95.

Black Belt Series 1986
A pair of instructional programs that demonstrate various Tai Chi exercises for optimum fitness and health as practiced by the Chinese for centuries. 90m; VHS. **Pr:** Karl/Lorimar; Rainboe Publications. **A:** Family. **P:** Instruction. **U:** Home. **Hea-Sci:** How-To, Martial Arts, Fitness/Exercise. **Acq:** Purchase. **Dist:** MGM Studios Inc. ; Warner Home Video, Inc. $29.95.
Indiv. Titles: 1. Tai Chi Chuan 2. Instructional Karate.

Black Bikers from Hell 1970 (R) — ★½
Black gang-members infiltrate and wreak havoc on their rivals. Who can stop these brutal young men? Cast with real bikers and biker chicks. 87m; VHS. **C:** John King, III; Des Roberts; Linda Jackson; James Whitworth; James Young-El; Clancy Syrko; Beverly Gardner; Directed by Laurence Merrick; Written by Laurence Merrick. **Pr:** Merrick International. **A:** College-Adult. **P:** Entertainment. **U:** Home. **Mov-Ent:** Action-Adventure, Violence, Motorcycles. **Acq:** Purchase. **Dist:** Tapeworm Video Distributors Inc.; JEF Films, Inc. $59.95.

The Black Bird 1926 (Unrated) — ★★
Director Browning and star Chaney teamed up for an atmospheric silent crime drama. In London's notorious Limehouse district, the crippled Bishop, who runs the local mission, tries to help the desperate inhabitants while his notorious brother, The Black Bird, preys on their weaknesses. The criminal becomes infatuated with chanteuse Fifi (Adoree), but he has a rival and his jealousy may expose an unsettling secret. 86m/B/W; Silent; DVD. **C:** Lon Chaney, Sr.; Owen Moore; Renee Adoree; Doris Lloyd; Directed by Tod Browning; Written by Tod Browning; Cinematography by Percy Hilburn. **A:** Sr. High-Adult. **P:** Entertainment. **U:** Home. **L:** English. **Mov-Ent:** Crime Drama, Silent Films. **Acq:** Purchase. **Dist:** WarnerArchive.com.

Black Bird 1975 (PG) — ★★
In this satiric "sequel" to "The Maltese Falcon," detective Sam Spade, Jr. searches for the mysterious black falcon statuette that caused his father such trouble. Features appearances by Elisha Cook Jr. and Lee Patrick, who starred in the 1941 classic "The Maltese Falcon" with Humphrey Bogart. 98m; VHS. **C:** George Segal; Stephane Audran; Lionel Stander; Lee Patrick; Elisha Cook, Jr.; Connie Kreski; Directed by David Giler. **Pr:** Columbia Pictures. **A:** Jr. High-Adult. **P:** Entertainment. **U:** Home. **Mov-Ent:** Satire & Parody, Mystery & Suspense. **Acq:** Purchase. **Dist:** $9.95.

Black Body 1992
A single, bound male nude, with text and special effects is used to express the humanity underlying typical definitions of black identity. 7m; VHS, 3/4 U. **A:** College-Adult. **P:** Education. **U:** Institution. **Gen-Edu:** Black Culture. **Acq:** Purchase, Rent/Lease. **Dist:** Third World Newsreel. $150.00.

Black, Bold and Beautiful 1999
African-American women discuss the social messages of hair-styles and society's perception of beauty. 40m; VHS. **A:** Adult. **P:** Education. **U:** Institution, BCTV. **Gen-Edu:** Women, Black Culture. **Acq:** Purchase, Rent/Lease. **Dist:** Women Make Movies. $250.00.

Black Book 2006 (R) — ★★★½
Wow—Verhoeven directs his first film in his native Netherlands in 20 years and comes up with an unsentimental WWII thriller with a compelling lead performance by van Houten. In 1944, Jewish Rachel has been hiding out in the country until she joins a Dutch resistance unit. After some cosmetic changes, and now renamed Ellis, she's assigned to bed Gestapo chief Ludwig Muentze (Koch) and ferret out some Nazi secrets. What Rachel/Ellis doesn't mean to do is fall in love. The story twists and turns (eventually ending up in Israel in 1956) but is definitely worth the journey. English, Dutch, German, and Hebrew with subtitles. 145m; DVD, Blu-Ray. **C:** Sebastian Koch; Thom Hoffman; Halina Reijn; Derek de Lint; Carice van Houten; Waldemar Kobus; Christian Berkel; Peter Blok; Directed by Paul Verhoeven; Written by Paul Verhoeven; Gerard Soeteman; Cinematography by Karl Walter Lindenlaub; Music by Anne Dudley. **Pr:** San Fu Maltha; Jens Meurer; Teun Hilte; Jos van der Linden; Fu Works; Sony Pictures Classics. **A:** College-Adult. **P:** Entertainment. **U:** Home. **L:** English, Dutch, German, Hebrew. **Mov-Ent:** Judaism, Sex & Sexuality. **Acq:** Purchase. **Dist:** Sony Pictures Home Entertainment Inc.

Black Books: The Complete 1st Series 2000
Irishman Bernard Black runs a second-hand bookstore in London, and despite being in an alcoholic stupor, abusing customers, and pawning off tasks to his assistant Manny, he somehow gets himself embroiled in escapades mostly initiated by his New Age next-door-shopkeeper Fran that range from the violent to the utterly ludicrous. 6 episodes. 313m; DVD. **C:** Bill Bailey; Dylan Moran; Tamsin Greig. **A:** Adult. **P:** Entertainment. **U:** Home. **Mov-Ent:** Television. **Acq:** Purchase. **Dist:** BBC Worldwide Publishing Ltd.

Black Books: The Complete 2nd Series 2001
Manny attempts to morph the second-hand store into an upscale chain bookshop. Fran goes through extreme mental derangement while trying to find a job. Bernard is beside himself in how to ask a customer for a date. 6 episodes. 144m; DVD. **C:** Bill Bailey; Tamsin Greig; Dylan Moran. **A:** Adult. **P:** Entertainment. **U:** Home. **Mov-Ent:** Television. **Acq:** Purchase. **Dist:** BBC Worldwide Publishing Ltd.

Black Box Affair 1966 (Unrated) — ★½
An American secret agent must find a black box lost in a B-52 plane crash before it falls into the wrong hands. 95m; VHS. **C:** Craig Hill; Teresa Gimpera; Luis Martin; Jorge (George) Rigaud;

Directed by James B. Harris. **Pr:** Silvio Battistini. **A:** Sr. High-Adult. **P:** Entertainment. **U:** Home. **Mov-Ent:** Mystery & Suspense, Aeronautics. **Acq:** Purchase. **Dist:** No Longer Available.

Black Box Electric Fishing Technology 19??
Teaches techniques associated with the use of the "Black Box," a piece of electrical equipment used for fishing. Covers trolling, mooching, jigging, and tuning. 55m; VHS. **Pr:** Bennett Marine Video. **A:** Jr. High-Adult. **P:** Instruction. **U:** Home. **Spo-Rec:** How-To, Fishing, Technology. **Acq:** Purchase. **Dist:** Bennett Marine Video. $19.95.

Black Box: Video Dreams 1991 1991
The newest videos from the popular dance band. Includes "Strike It Up," "Ride on Time," "I Don't Know Anybody Else," and three more. 45m; VHS. **Pr:** VPI. **A:** Jr. High-Adult. **P:** Entertainment. **U:** Home. **Mov-Ent:** Music Video. **Acq:** Purchase. **Dist:** BMG Entertainment. $14.98.

Black Brigade 1969 (Unrated) — ★★
Pryor and Williams star in this low budget movie as leaders of an all-black outfit assigned to a suicide mission behind Nazi lines during WWII. Their force wreaks havoc and earns them the respect of military higher-ups. Lots of action and climactic finish. 90m; VHS, DVD. **C:** Stephen Boyd; Robert Hooks; Susan Oliver; Roosevelt "Rosie" Grier; Moses Gunn; Richard Pryor; Billy Dee Williams; Directed by George McCowan; Written by Aaron Spelling; Music by Fred Steiner. **A:** Sr. High-Adult. **P:** Entertainment. **U:** Home. **Mov-Ent:** World War Two, Black Culture. **Acq:** Purchase. **Dist:** Movies Unlimited; Alpha Video.

Black Cadillac 2003 (Unrated) — ★★
A night of partying goes awry when a bum car strands three buddies in the frigid, lonely mountains. Their luck seems to change after a deputy sheriff rescues them, but relief turns to terror as they find a mysterious black Cadillac on their tail. Effective entry in the "mysterious spooky car" genre. 92m; VHS, DVD. **C:** Randy Quaid; Kiersten Warren; Shane Johnson; Josh Hammond; Jason Dohring; Adam Vernier; Directed by John Murlowski; Written by John Murlowski; Will Aldis; Cinematography by S. Douglas Smith; Music by Chris Bell. **A:** Sr. High-Adult. **P:** Entertainment. **U:** Home. **Mov-Ent:** Arctic Regions, Mystery & Suspense. **Acq:** Purchase. **Dist:** Movies Unlimited; Alpha Video. $24.98.

Black Caesar 1973 (R) — ★★
A small-time hood climbs the ladder to be the head of a Harlem crime syndicate. Music by James Brown. Followed by the sequel "Hell Up in Harlem." 92m; VHS, DVD, Wide. **C:** Fred Williamson; Julius W. Harris; Val Avery; Art Lund; Gloria Hendry; James Dixon; Directed by Larry Cohen; Written by Larry Cohen; Cinematography by Fenton Hamilton; James Signorelli; Music by James Brown. **Pr:** Filmways Pictures. **A:** Sr. High-Adult. **P:** Entertainment. **U:** Home. **Mov-Ent. Acq:** Purchase. **Dist:** MGM Studios Inc. $9.98.

The Black Camel 1931 (Unrated) — ★★
In the 2nd Charlie Chan mystery, set (and filmed) in Honolulu, the detective (Oland) investigates the murder of movie starlet Sheila Fane. Lugosi plays a psychic. Based on the Earl Derr Bigger's novel. 71m/B/W; DVD. **C:** Warner Oland; Bela Lugosi; Robert Young; Victor Varconi; J.M. Kerrigan; Marjorie White; Sally Eilers; Dorothy Revier; Dwight Frye; Directed by Hamilton McFadden; Written by Barry Connors; Philip Klein; Cinematography by Joseph August; Daniel B. Clark; Music by Samuel Kaylin. **A:** Family. **P:** Entertainment. **U:** Home. **Mov-Ent:** Mystery & Suspense. **Acq:** Purchase. **Dist:** Fox Home Entertainment.

The Black Castle 1952 (Unrated) — ★★
MacNally plays an 18th-century Austrian count whose guests tend to disappear after a visit. This happens to two of Greene's friends and he decides to investigate. Uninspired and melodramatic, not enough horror. Karloff doesn't have enough to do. 81m/B/W; VHS, DVD, CC. **C:** Richard Greene; Boris Karloff; Stephen McNally; Rita (Paula) Corday; Lon Chaney Jr.; John Hoyt; Directed by Nathan "Jerry" Juran. **Pr:** Mark Huffam. **A:** Jr. High-Adult. **P:** Entertainment. **U:** Home. **Mov-Ent:** Horror. **Acq:** Purchase. **Dist:** Universal Studios Home Video. $14.98.

The Black Cat 1934
An American couple on honeymoon in Austria become entangled in a "death-feud" between two strange men. Designed to be used as a springboard for identifying elements of horror used in Poe's work plus films and literature of the same genre. 66m/B/W; VHS. **A:** Sr. High. **P:** Education. **U:** Institution. **Gen-Edu:** Mystery & Suspense, Literature, Language Arts. **Acq:** Purchase. **Dist:** Zenger Media. $14.98.

The Black Cat 1934 (Unrated) — ★★★½
The first of the Boris and Bela pairings stands up well years after release. Polished and taut, with fine sets and interesting acting. Confrontation between architect and devil worshipper acts as plot, with strange twists. Worth a look. 65m/B/W; VHS, DVD. **C:** Boris Karloff; Bela Lugosi; David Manners; Julie Bishop; Lucille Lund; Henry Armetta; Egon Brecher; Albert Conti; Harry Cording; John Carradine; Directed by Edgar G. Ulmer; Written by Edgar G. Ulmer; Peter Ruric; Cinematography by John Mescall; Music by Heinz Roemheld. **Pr:** Mark Huffam. **A:** Jr. High-Adult. **P:** Entertainment. **U:** Home. **Mov-Ent:** Horror, Classic Films, Pets. **Acq:** Purchase. **Dist:** Alpha Video; Movies Unlimited; Universal Studios Home Video. $9.95.

The Black Cat 1941 (Unrated) — ★★½
Wealthy Henrietta Winslow (Loftus) has left her estate to her greedy grandchildren but only after her faithful housekeeper Abigail (Sondergaard) and all her beloved cats die. Naturally, strange and murderous events begin occurring. Not to be confused with the 1934 classic horror film of the same title. 71m/B/W; VHS, DVD. **C:** Basil Rathbone; Hugh Herbert; Gale

Sondergaard; Broderick Crawford; Bela Lugosi; Gladys Cooper; Anne Gwynne; Cecilia Loftus; Claire Dodd; John Eldridge; Alan Ladd; Directed by Albert Rogell; Written by Robert Lees; Frederic Rinaldo; Eric Taylor; Robert Neville; Cinematography by Stanley Cortez. **Pr:** Burt Kelly; Universal International. **A:** Jr. High-Adult. **P:** Entertainment. **U:** Home. **Mov-Ent:** Horror, Pets. **Acq:** Purchase. **Dist:** Universal Studios Home Video.

The Black Cat 1981 (Unrated) — **Bomb!**
Spaghetti splatter-meister Fulci, best known for his unabashed ripoffs "Zombie" and "Gates of Hell," tones down the gore this time in a vaguely Poe-ish tale of a medium with some marbles loose (Magee) whose kitty provides the temporary habitat for spirits its master calls up. The dreary English village setting and the downright myopic camera work add up to an oppressive viewing experience. 92m; VHS, DVD, Wide. **C:** Patrick Magee; Mimsy Farmer; David Warbeck; Al Cliver; Dagmar Lassander; Geoffrey Copleston; Daniela Dorio; Directed by Lucio Fulci; Written by Lucio Fulci; Biagio Proietti; Cinematography by Sergio Salvati; Music by Pino Donaggio. **Pr:** World Northal. **A:** College-Adult. **P:** Entertainment. **U:** Home. **Mov-Ent:** Horror, Mystery & Suspense, Occult Sciences. **Acq:** Purchase. **Dist:** Anchor Bay Entertainment; Rhino Entertainment Co.

Black Cat 1990 (Unrated) — ★½
Filmmakers find lots of action in a haunted house. Chock full of references to the works of spaghetti horror dons Mario Bava and Dario Argento. 120m; VHS. **C:** Caroline Munro; Brett Halsey; Directed by Luigi Cozzi; Written by Luigi Cozzi. **A:** College-Adult. **P:** Entertainment. **U:** Home. **Mov-Ent:** Horror, Filmmaking, Pets. **Acq:** Purchase. **Dist:** Sony Pictures Home Entertainment Inc.

Black Cat Run 1998 (R) — ★★
Race car driver's girlfriend is abducted and then he gets involved with a psycho deputy. Lots of action. 88m; VHS, DVD. **C:** Patrick Muldoon; Amelia Heinle; Russell Means; Kevin J. O'Connor; Peter Greene; Jake Busey; Directed by D.J. Caruso; Written by Frank Darabont; Douglas Venturelli; Cinematography by Bing Sokolsky; Music by Jeff Rona. **A:** Sr. High-Adult. **P:** Entertainment. **U:** Home. **Mov-Ent:** Automobiles. **Acq:** Purchase. **Dist:** Movies Unlimited; Alpha Video.

Black Cat, White Cat 1998 (Unrated) — ★★★
Emir Kusturica's rambling tale of scheming Gypsies who live on the banks of the Danube river is a mixture of slapstick humor, folk tales and music. The cheesily dressed and mostly nonprofessional actors light up a plot involving a cargo of fuel, an arranged marriage, and a corpse on ice. Non-political (and much lighter) follow-up to Kusturica's Palme d'Or winning "Underground." Serbo-Croatian and Romany with subtitles. 129m; VHS. **C:** Bajram Severdzan; Florijan Ajdini; Salija Ibraimova; Branka Katic; Zabit Memedov; Sabri Sulejman; Jasar Destani; Srdan Todorovic; Ljubica Adzovic; Miki (Predrag) Manojlovic; Directed by Emir Kusturica; Written by Gordan Mihic; Cinematography by Thierry Arbogast; Music by D. Nele Karajilic; Vajislav Aralica; Dejo Sparavalo. **Pr:** October Films. **A:** College-Adult. **P:** Entertainment. **U:** Home. **Mov-Ent:** Comedy--Slapstick, Folklore & Legends. **Acq:** Purchase.

Black Catholics: People of Hope 1987
Black activity in the Catholic church is followed. 28m; VHS, 3/4 U. **Pr:** Real to Reel Productions. **A:** Jr. High-Adult. **P:** Religious. **U:** Institution, SURA. **Gen-Edu:** Black Culture. **Acq:** Purchase, Rent/Lease. **Dist:** St. Anthony Messenger Press. $19.95.

The Black Cauldron 1985 (PG) — ★★½
Disney's 25th full-length animated movie follows the adventures of pig-keeper Taran, who discovers his psychic pig Hen Wen is the key to keeping a magical cauldron out of the hands of the evil Horned King. Based on the "Chronicles of Prydain" novels by Lloyd Alexander. 82m; VHS, DVD, Wide, CC. **C:** Voice(s) by Grant Bardsley; Susan Sheridan; John Hurt; Freddie Jones; Nigel Hawthorne; John Byner; Arthur Malet; Narrated by John Huston; Directed by Ted Berman; Richard Rich; Written by Ted Berman; Richard Rich; Music by Elmer Bernstein. **Pr:** Joe Hale; Walt Disney Pictures. **A:** Family. **P:** Entertainment. **U:** Home. **Mov-Ent:** Animation & Cartoons, Fantasy, Magic. **Acq:** Purchase. **Dist:** Walt Disney Studios Home Entertainment.

Black Celebration: A Rebellion Against the Commodity 1988
Tony Cokes juxtaposes re-edited broadcast and archival footage with quotations in the form of text and voice-overs to provide a provocative look at the urban Black riots of the 1960s. 17m; VHS, 3/4 U. **A:** College-Adult. **P:** Entertainment. **U:** Institution. **Fin-Art:** Video, Black Culture. **Acq:** Purchase, Rent/Lease. **Dist:** Video Data Bank.

Black Christmas 1975 (R) — ★★½
A college sorority is besieged by an axe-murderer over the holidays. 98m; VHS, DVD, Blu-Ray. **C:** Olivia Hussey; Keir Dullea; Margot Kidder; John Saxon; Andrea Martin; Art Hindle; Directed by Bob (Benjamin) Clark; Written by Roy Moore; Cinematography by Reginald Morris; Music by Carl Zittrer. **Pr:** Ambassador. **A:** Sr. High-Adult. **P:** Entertainment. **U:** Home. **Mov-Ent:** Horror, Christmas, Canada. **Acq:** Purchase. **Dist:** Entertainment One US LP. $19.98.

Black Christmas 2006 (R) — ★
The 1974 original was an early entry in the slasher/dead teen genre. This weak remake, which takes itself way too seriously, ups the gore and adds lurid flashbacks for the killer, but so what? Sorority sisters (you may recognize a couple of faces) are stuck in their Alpha Kappa house at Christmas because of a blizzard, but the psycho killer (who lived in the sorority house when it was his family home) manages to escape the loony bin and hide out in the attic. He then terrorizes the gals before offing them, using handy holiday decorations for the most part. After seeing what he does with a cookie cutter, you may never eat

Christmas cookies again. Writer/director Morgan deserves coal in his stocking. 84m; DVD, HD-DVD. **C:** Michelle Trachtenberg; Lacey Chabert; Mary Elizabeth Winstead; Andrea Martin; Katie Cassidy; Robert Mann; Oliver Hudson; Crystal Lowe; Kristen Cloke; Jessica Harmon; Dean Friss; Directed by Glen Morgan; Written by Glen Morgan; Cinematography by Robert McLachlan; Music by Shirley Walker. **Pr:** Marty Adelstein; Dawn Parouse; Hard Eight Pictures; 2929 Productions; Copper Heart Entertainment; Dimension Films. **A:** Sr. High-Adult. **P:** Entertainment. **U:** Home. **L:** English. **Mov-Ent:** Horror, Christmas. **Acq:** Purchase. **Dist:** Weinstein Company L.L.C.

Black Circle Boys 1997 (R) — ★½
Depressed high schooler Kyle (Bairstow) is still trying to fit in at his new school. He makes the mistake of getting involved with the "Black Circle Boys"?a clique of losers involved with drugs and the occult that's led by Shane (Mabius). The Boys enjoy malicious pranks and Kyle begins to have qualms about his participation but Shane doesn't want to let him go. Murky script gets increasingly silly as pic progresses. 100m; VHS, DVD. **C:** Scott Bairstow; Eric Mabius; Heath Lourwood; Chad Lindberg; Tara Subkoff; Dee Wallace; Donnie Wahlberg; John Doe; Directed by Matthew Carnahan; Written by Matthew Carnahan; Cinematography by Geary McLeod. **A:** Sr. High-Adult. **P:** Entertainment. **U:** Home. **Mov-Ent:** Drug Abuse, Occult Sciences. **Acq:** Purchase. **Dist:** Movies Unlimited; Alpha Video.

Black Cloud 2004 (PG-13) — ★★½
Schroder debuts as a writer/director in this formulaic but appealing drama about a Native American boxer. Black Cloud (Sparks) is an angry, out-of-control young boxer whose life outside the ring is marred by an alcoholic father, a dead mother, self-hatred, and racism. All he's got in his corner is his world-wise trainer Bud (Means) and his girlfriend Sammi (Jones). Black Cloud struggles with adversity in and out of the ring, but ultimately he's his own worst enemy. The story is strictly seen-it-before, but the strong performances (especially Sparks) balance out the predictability. 95m; DVD. **C:** Eddie Spears; Russell Means; Wayne Knight; Peter Greene; Julia Jones; Rick Schroder; Nathaniel Arcand; Tim McGraw; Branscombe Richmond; Directed by Rick Schroder; Written by Rick Schroder; Cinematography by Steve Gainer; Music by John E. Nordstrom. **A:** Jr. High-Adult. **P:** Entertainment. **U:** Home. **L:** English. **Mov-Ent:** Boxing, Native Americans, Sports--Fiction: Drama. **Acq:** Purchase. **Dist:** New Line Home Video.

Black Cobra 1983 (R) — **Bomb!**
A lesbian exacts revenge for her lover's snake-bite murder by trapping the guilty party with his own snakes. 97m; VHS, DVD. **C:** Laura Gemser; Jack Palance; Directed by Joe D'Amato. **Pr:** Joe D'Amato; Joe D'Amato. **A:** Sr. High-Adult. **P:** Entertainment. **U:** Home. **Mov-Ent:** Mystery & Suspense, Animals. **Acq:** Purchase. **Dist:** Movies Unlimited. $14.99.

The Black Cobra 1987 (R) — **Bomb!**
After photographing a psychopath in the process of killing someone, a beautiful photographer seeks the help of a tough police sergeant to protect her. The leader of the Black Cobras gang gives chase. 90m; VHS, DVD. **C:** Fred Williamson; Bruno Bilotta; Eva Grimaldi; Directed by Stelvio Massi. **Pr:** Trans World Entertainment Corp. **A:** Sr. High-Adult. **P:** Entertainment. **U:** Home. **Mov-Ent. Acq:** Purchase. **Dist:** Movies Unlimited. $8.99.

Black Cobra 2 1989 (R) — ★★
A mismatched team of investigators tracks a notorious terrorist. They find him holding a school full of children as hostage. 95m; VHS, DVD. **C:** Fred Williamson; Nicholas Hammond; Emma Hoagland; Najid Jadali; Directed by Stelvio Massi; Cinematography by Guglielmo Mancori; Music by Aldo Salvi. **A:** College-Adult. **P:** Entertainment. **U:** Home. **Mov-Ent:** Terrorism. **Acq:** Purchase. **Dist:** Movies Unlimited. $13.49.

Black Cobra 3: The Manila Connection 1990 (R) — ★½
Interpol turns to police lieutenant Robert Malone (Williamson) when a team of high-tech weapons thieves threatens the world. Malone attacks like a cyclone on the terrorists' jungle haven. They won't know what hit 'em! 92m; VHS, DVD. **C:** Fred Williamson; Forry Smith; Debra Ward; Directed by Don Edwards. **A:** Adult. **P:** Entertainment. **U:** Home. **Mov-Ent:** Terrorism, Technology. **Acq:** Purchase. **Dist:** Movies Unlimited. $14.95.

The Black Coin 1936
A 15-episode adventure serial about a cursed silver piece from the Middle Ages and the ill luck that has followed its possessors through the years. 316m/B/W; VHS. **C:** Ralph Graves; Ruth Mix; Dave O'Brien; Matthew Betz; Robert Frazer; Yakima Canutt; Directed by Al(bert) Herman. **Pr:** Stage and Screen. **A:** Family. **P:** Entertainment. **U:** Home. **Mov-Ent:** Serials. **Acq:** Purchase. **Dist:** Alpha Video. $39.95.
Indiv. Titles: 1. Dangerous Men 2. The Mystery Ship 3. The Fatal Plunge 4. Monsters of the Deep 5. Wolves of the Night 6. Shark's Fang 7. Midnight Menace 8. Flames of Death 9. Smuggler's Lair 10. Flaming Guns 11. Wheels of Death 12. The Crash 13. Danger Ahead 14. Hidden Peril 15. The Phantom Treasure.

Black Communities after the Civil War ????
Focuses on the migration of former slaves and black farmers to Tulsa, Oklahoma, during the 1920s. 17m; VHS. **A:** Sr. High-Adult. **P:** Education. **U:** Institution. **Gen-Edu:** Slavery, History--U.S., Black Culture. **Acq:** Purchase. **Dist:** Films for the Humanities & Sciences. $89.95.

Black Crowes: Who Killed That Bird Out On Your Window Sill. . .The Movie 1992
This look at the unpredictable Southern rockers includes interviews, television appearances, and concert footage from the

Monsters of Rock show held in Moscow in 1991 as well as their music. Songs include "Jealous Again," "She Talks to Angels," and "Remedy." 83m; VHS. **A:** Sr. High-Adult. **P:** Entertainment. **U:** Home. **Mov-Ent**: Music--Pop/Rock, Music--Performance. **Acq:** Purchase. **Dist:** Warner Reprise Video. $19.98.

The Black Dahlia 2006 (R) — ★★
Adaptation of James Ellroy's novel about the lurid unsolved murder features director De Palma's feverish eye for noir. Great-looking, over-stuffed, and ultimately unsatisfying production has Hollywood wannabe Elizabeth Short's (Kirshner) mutilated body discovered in a vacant lot in LA in 1947. Detective Lee Blanchard (Eckhart) becomes obsessed with the case—to the detriment of his life with blonde babe lover, Kay Lake (Johansson). Meanwhile, Lee's callow partner Buck (Hartnett) is investigating wealthy brunette Madeleine's (Swank) involvement with Short, which leads him to her lunatic clan. Fedoras, red lipstick, and cigarette smoke abound, but the glam hides plenty of dirt and corruption. 121m; DVD, Blu-Ray, Wide. **C:** Josh Hartnett; Scarlett Johansson; Aaron Eckhart; Hilary Swank; Mike Starr; Fiona Shaw; John Kavanagh; Rachel Miner; Mia Kirshner; Troy Evans; Gregg Henry; Rose McGowan; Jemima Rooper; William Finley; Kevin Dunn; Ian McNeice; Pepe Serna; Patrick Fischler; Directed by Brian De Palma; Written by Josh Friedman; Cinematography by Vilmos Zsigmond; Music by Mark Isham. **Pr:** Art Linson; Avi Lerner; Moshe Diamant; Rudy Cohen; Millenium Films; Signature Pictures; Universal Pictures. **A:** Sr. High-Adult. **P:** Entertainment. **U:** Home. **L:** English. **Mov-Ent**. **Acq:** Purchase. **Dist:** Movies Unlimited; Alpha Video; Universal Studios Home Video.

The Black Dakotas 1954 (Unrated) — ★½
President Lincoln wants a peace treaty with the Sioux so the soldiers can be used to fight the Confederates. He sends an emissary with a lot of gold to sweeten the deal but the man is waylaid by southerner Brock Marsh. Stagecoach driver Mike and his girlfriend Ruth try to stop Marsh from causing more trouble. 65m; DVD. **C:** Gary Merrill; Wanda Hendrix; John Bromfield; Noah Beery, Jr.; John War Eagle; Jay Silverheels; Howard Wendell; Robert F. Simon; Directed by Ray Nazarro; Written by Ray Buffum; DeVallon Scott; Cinematography by Ellis W. Carter; Music by Mischa Bakaleinikoff. **A:** Jr. High-Adult. **P:** Entertainment. **U:** Home. **Mov-Ent**: Western, Civil War, Native Americans. **Acq:** Purchase. **Dist:** Movies Unlimited.

Black Dawn 1980
The story of the Haitian revolution and the formation of the world's first independent black republic is re-created through an animated folktale accompanied by traditional paintings and songs. Available in English, French, and Creole dialect versions. 20m; VHS, 3/4 U, EJ. **Pr:** Robin Lloyd; Doreen Kraft. **A:** Primary-Adult. **P:** Education. **U:** Institution, SURA. **L:** English, French. **Gen-Edu**: Documentary Films, Caribbean, Folklore & Legends. **Acq:** Purchase, Rent/Lease. **Dist:** First Run/Icarus Films. $215.00.

Black Dawn 2005 (R) — ★½
Former CIA agent Jonathon Cold (Seagal) is working for himself now, and takes an assignment springing a terrorist from jail so he can infiltrate his group before they detonate a nuclear bomb in downtown LA. Seagal unfortunately is an action star past his prime using a stunt double that looks nothing like him to film all his fight scenes. 96m; DVD. **C:** Steven Seagal; Tamara Davies; John Pyper-Ferguson; Julian Stone; Nicholas Davidoff; Warren DeRosa; Don Franklin; Timothy Carhart; Eddie Velez; Matt Salinger; Ryan Bollman; Roman Varshavsky; Noa Hegesh; David St. James; Angela Gots; Directed by Alexander Grusynski; Written by Darren O. Campbell; Martin Wheeler; Cinematography by Bruce McCleery; Music by David Wurst; Eric Wurst. **A:** Sr. High-Adult. **P:** Entertainment. **U:** Home. **Mov-Ent**: Action-Adventure, Intelligence Service, Terrorism. **Acq:** Purchase. **Dist:** Sony Pictures Home Entertainment Inc. $14.94.

Black Day Blue Night 1995 (R) — ★★
Rinda (Forbes) and Hallie (Sara) take a road trip from Utah to Phoenix and pick up the handsome Dodge (Bellows). Turns out he's being pursued by cop John Quinn (Walsh) as a suspect in a murder/robbery. Women-in-peril-who-help-themselves type story. 99m; VHS, Streaming, CC. **C:** Michelle Forbes; Mia Sara; Gil Bellows; J.T. Walsh; Tim Guinee; John Beck; Directed by J.S. Cardone; Written by J.S. Cardone; Cinematography by Michael Cardone; Music by Johnny Lee Schell; Joe Sublett. **Pr:** Scott Einbinder; Carol Kottenbrook; David Korda; Willi Baer; Capella Films; Sandstorm Films. **A:** Sr. High-Adult. **P:** Entertainment. **U:** Home. **Mov-Ent**: Mystery & Suspense, Women. **Acq:** Purchase. **Dist:** Lions Gate Entertainment Inc.

The Black Death 2000
Reenactments portrays the religious, social and economic effects of the European pandemic. 15m; VHS; Closed Captioned. **A:** Jr. High-Sr. High. **P:** Education. **U:** Institution. **Gen-Edu**: History--Medieval. **Acq:** Purchase. **Dist:** Zenger Media. $95.00.

Black Death 2010 (R) — ★★
Effective historical horror. In 1348, knight Ulric and his band of mercenaries accompany novice monk Osmund to an English village that is suspected of following pagan practices. Though the bubonic plague ravages the rest of the country, this village remains untouched and Ulrich is charged with capturing the leaders of a heretical cult. 101m; DVD, Blu-Ray, Streaming. **C:** Sean Bean; Eddie Redmayne; John Lynch; Carice van Houten; Tim (McInnerny) McInnery; Andy Nyman; Kimberly Nixon; Johnny Harris; David Warner; Directed by Chris Smith; Written by Dario Poloni; Cinematography by Sebastian Edscmid; Music by Christian Henson. **A:** Sr. High-Adult. **P:** Entertainment. **U:** Home. **Mov-Ent**: Religion, Death, Great Britain. **Acq:** Purchase, Rent/Lease. **Dist:** Magnolia Home Entertainment. $19.98 14.98 9.99.

Black Delta Religion 1974
The evolution from traditional rural to sanctified urban services in the Mississippi Delta, is examined. 15m/B/W; VHS, 3/4 U. **Pr:** Center for Southern Folklore. **A:** Family. **P:** Entertainment. **U:** Institution, Home, SURA. **Gen-Edu**: Documentary Films, Religion. **Acq:** Purchase. **Dist:** Center for Southern Folklore.

Black Demons 1991 (Unrated) — ★½
College students traveling in Brazil stop at a plantation when their car breaks down. While listening to a tape of a Voodoo ritual they made in the previous town, they suddenly find themselves besieged by the zombies of the slaves who died there in what was an obviously less politically correct time. 88m; DVD. **C:** Keith Van Hoven; Joe Balogh; Philip Murray; Sonia Curtis; Juliana Texeira; Maria Alves; Directed by Umberto Lenzi; Written by Umberto Lenzi; Olga Pehar; Cinematography by Maurizio Dell'Orco; Music by Franco Micalizzi. **A:** Sr. High-Adult. **P:** Entertainment. **U:** Home. **L:** English. **Mov-Ent**. **Acq:** Purchase. **Dist:** Media Blasters Inc. $20.98.

Black Devil Doll from Hell 1984 (Unrated) — ★
This shot-on-video movie deals with a nasty little voodoo doll that likes to kill its owners. 70m; VHS. **C:** Shirley Jones; Rickey Roach; Marie Sainvilvs; Directed by Chester Turner. **Pr:** Chester T. Turner. **A:** Jr. High-Adult. **P:** Entertainment. **U:** Home. **Mov-Ent**: Horror. **Acq:** Purchase. **Dist:** No Longer Available.

The Black Devils of Kali 1955 (Unrated) — ★
Adventurers in the Indian jungle discover a lost race of idol-worshipping primitives. Racist garbage produced near the end of Republic Pictures' existence. Based on a novel by Emillio Salgari. 72m/B/W; VHS, DVD. **C:** Lex Barker; Jane Maxwell; Luigi Tosi; Paul Muller; Directed by Ralph Murphy. **Pr:** Republic. **A:** Jr. High-Adult. **P:** Entertainment. **U:** Home. **Mov-Ent**: India. **Acq:** Purchase. **Dist:** Sinister Cinema. $16.95.

Black Diamond Rush 19??
Thanks to epic conditions worldwide, this is considered one of the "best ski videos ever produced." Warren Miller and his cameras follow the world's best skiers and snowboarders around the world. ?m; VHS. **A:** Family. **P:** Entertainment. **U:** Home. **L:** English. **Spo-Rec**: Skiing. **Acq:** Purchase. **Dist:** Warren Miller Entertainment.

Black Diamond Skiing 1989
A training video by SyberVision for the advanced skier. This program can increase skills and confidence by the use of repeated motion. 60m; VHS. **C:** Jens Husted; Chris Ryman. **Pr:** SyberVision Systems. **A:** Jr. High-Adult. **P:** Instruction. **U:** Home. **Spo-Rec**: Sports--General, Skiing. **Acq:** Purchase. **Dist:** SyberVision Systems, Inc.; Karol Media. $49.95.

Black Diamonds Through the Dunes 1999
This celebration of trains and railroading features locomotives powering coal through the sand dunes and windmills of Nebraska. 85m; VHS. **A:** Family. **P:** Entertainment. **U:** Home. **Gen-Edu**: Trains. **Acq:** Purchase. **Dist:** Pentrex Media Group L.L.C. $29.95.

Black Dog 1998 (PG-13) — ★
Not since the '70s heyday of CBs and C.W. McCall have 18-wheelers been so lovingly portrayed. Too bad the rest of the characters weren't given the same attention. Swayze (resurrecting his sensitive butt-kicker persona from "Roadhouse") plays disgraced trucker Jack Crews, recently released from prison after a vehicular manslaughter rap. With no driver's license and an overdue mortgage, he agrees to an "off the books" run for his shady boss (Beckel). The cargo turns out to be guns, which attracts the attention of the FBI, ATF, and a scuzzy band of hijackers led by the Bible-quoting Red (Meatloaf). Of course, the paint-by-numbers plot puts Jack's family in harm's way, and gives him a soulful, country-croonin' ally (Travis). Avoid this mutt like three-day-old roadkill unless you're a big-rig fetishist. 88m; VHS, DVD, CC. **C:** Patrick Swayze; Randy Travis; Meat Loaf Aday; Gabriel Casseus; Graham Beckel; Stephen Tobolowsky; Charles S. Dutton; Brian Vincent; Brenda Strong; Erin Broderick; Directed by Kevin Hooks; Written by William Mickelberry; Dan Vining; Cinematography by Buzz Feitshans, IV; Music by George S. Clinton. **Pr:** Universal Pictures. **A:** Jr. High-Adult. **P:** Entertainment. **U:** Home. **Mov-Ent**: Federal Bureau of Investigation (FBI). **Acq:** Purchase. **Dist:** Movies Unlimited; Alpha Video.

The Black Doll 1938 (Unrated) — ★½
Shady mine owner Nicholas Rood is murdered as revenge for killing his business partner. While local officials have things utterly confused, Rood's daughter's fiance, who happens to be a private detective, eventually pieces the clues together. Low-caliber installment of the "Crime Club" series. 66m/B/W; VHS, DVD. **C:** Donald Woods; Nan Grey; Edgar Kennedy; Doris Lloyd; Directed by Otis Garrett; Written by Otis Buckley. **A:** Adult. **P:** Entertainment. **U:** Home. **Mov-Ent**: Mystery & Suspense. **Acq:** Purchase. **Dist:** Nostalgia Family Video/ Hollywood's Attic. $19.99.

The Black Donnellys: The Complete Series 2007
The Donnellys are four working-class Irish-American brothers living in Hell's Kitchen who always protect each other. Desperate to stay in college, Tommy still gets pulled into his brothers' problems when the Italians try to take over Irish territory. Neighborhood pal Joey Ice Cream spins out his tale of the Donnellys' exploits to the cops who are investigating a series of crimes. 13 episodes. 559m; DVD. **C:** Jonathan Tucker; Tom Guiry; Keith Nobbs; Olivia Wilde; Michael Stahl-David; Billy Lush; Kate Mulgrew; Kirk Acevedo. **A:** Sr. High-Adult. **P:** Entertainment. **U:** Home. **Mov-Ent**: Television Series, Crime Drama. **Acq:** Purchase. **Dist:** Universal Studios Home Video.

The Black Dragons 1942 — ★
Weird and fairly stupid war drama involving sabotage by the Japanese. Lugosi is the plastic surgeon who deftly cuts and pastes Japanese face parts to permit agents to pass as Americans. Also available colorized. 62m/B/W; VHS, DVD, 3/4 U, Special order formats. **C:** Bela Lugosi; Joan Barclay; George Pembroke; Clayton Moore; Directed by William Nigh. **Pr:** Monogram. **A:** Family. **P:** Entertainment. **U:** Institution, Home. **Mov-Ent**: Surgery--Plastic. **Acq:** Purchase. **Dist:** Sinister Cinema; Cable Films/i2bs Online World; Rex Miller Artisan Studio. $19.95.

Black Dynamite 2009 (R) — ★★½
Sly, satiric homage to 1970s blaxploitation films that finds heroic Black Dynamite (White) fighting all the way to Honky House (AKA Richard M. Nixon's White House) to avenge his brother's murder and prevent the destruction of his 'hood by The Man. The film looks and sounds deliberately garish with grainy film stock, a funk soundtrack, gratuitous female nudity, and a swaggering, jive-talking hero who carries a .44 Magnum and wields a mean nunchuck. These are all pluses since director/ writer Sanders and writers White and Minns are complimentary to the genre rather than smug. 90m; DVD. **C:** Michael Jai White; Byron Keith Minns; Kym E. Whitley; Obba Babatunde; Kevin Chapman; Tommy Davidson; Salli Richardson-Whitfield; Arsenio Hall; Cedric Yarbrough; Mykelti Williamson; Bokeem Woodbine; James McManus; Nicole Sullivan; Directed by Scott Sanders; Written by Michael Jai White; Byron Keith Minns; Scott Sanders; Cinematography by Shawn Maurer; Music by Adrian Younge. **Pr:** Jon Steingart; Jenny Weiner Steingart; Ars Nova; Harbor Entertainment; Sony Pictures Home Entertainment Inc. **A:** Sr. High-Adult. **P:** Entertainment. **U:** Home. **L:** English. **Mov-Ent**: Black Culture, Adoption, Presidency. **Acq:** Purchase. **Dist:** Sony Pictures Home Entertainment Inc.

Black Dynamite: Season One 2011
Adult Swim 2011--? animated action comedy based on the 2009 film. Set in the 1970s, it's a satire on Blaxploitation movies with streetwise Black Dynamite and his crew--Bullhorn, Honey Bee, and Cream Corn--taking on Dr. Wu and his ninjas as well as getting involved in various outrageous adventures. 11 episodes. 288m; DVD, Blu-Ray. **A:** Adult. **P:** Entertainment. **U:** Home. **L:** English. **Mov-Ent**: Animation & Cartoons, Black Culture, Television Series. **Acq:** Purchase. **Dist:** Warner Home Video, Inc. $29.98.

Black Eagle 1988 (R) — ★★
Pre-Glasnost, anti-Soviet tale of two high-kicking spies. CIA and KGB agents race to recover innovative equipment in the Mediterranean. 93m; VHS, DVD. **C:** Bruce Doran; Jean-Claude Van Damme; Sho Kosugi; Directed by Eric Karson; Written by Shimon Arama; Music by Terry Plumeri. **A:** College-Adult. **P:** Entertainment. **U:** Home. **Mov-Ent**: Martial Arts. **Acq:** Purchase. **Dist:** Movies Unlimited. $22.49.

Black Easter: The Assassination of Abraham Lincoln 1992
Documentary investigating the murder of Abraham Lincoln. Questions the probability of a conspiracy stemming from the Civil War and the likelihood that John Wilkes Booth was a Confederate agent. 50m; VHS. **A:** Jr. High-Adult. **P:** Education. **U:** Institution. **Gen-Edu**: Documentary Films, Presidency, Civil War. **Acq:** Purchase. **Dist:** Baker and Taylor. $29.95.

Black Eliminator 1978 (Unrated) — ★
A black cop struggles to stop a maniacal secret agent who plans to destroy the world. 84m; VHS, DVD. **C:** Jim Kelly; George Lazenby; Harold Sakata; Bob Minor; Patch MacKenzie; Aldo Ray; Directed by Al Adamson. **A:** Sr. High. **P:** Entertainment. **U:** Home. **Mov-Ent**. **Acq:** Purchase. **Dist:** Movies Unlimited. $17.99.

Black Excellence: The Entrepreneurs 19??
Features successful African-Americans, such as Oprah Winfrey, who talk about how they fought the odds to become successful. 35m; VHS. **A:** College-Adult. **P:** Education. **U:** Institution. **Bus-Ind**: Black Culture, Business. **Acq:** Purchase. **Dist:** Educational Video Network. $59.95.

Black Expo Gospel Explosion #4 1991
A choir competition pitting six choirs for a cash prize and a professional recording contract. ?m; VHS. **A:** Jr. High-Adult. **P:** Entertainment. **U:** Home. **Mov-Ent**: Music Video, Religion. **Acq:** Purchase. **Dist:** BMG Entertainment; Music Video Distributors. $14.98.

Black Eye 1974 (Unrated) — ★★
Williamson goes in for some self-deprecating humor as Shep Stone, an ex-cop turned not-too-successful private eye, whose biggest case turns out to be the murder victim he finds in his own apartment. This leads Stone to a drug ring, a porn operation, a religious cult, a runaway girl, and more corpses littering the environs of Venice, California. 98m; DVD. **C:** Fred Williamson; Rosemary Forsyth; Teresa Graves; Floy Dean; Richard Anderson; Richard X. Slattery; Cyril Delevanti; Directed by Jack Arnold; Written by Mark Haggard; Cinematography by Ralph Woolsey; Music by Mort Garson. **A:** Jr. High-Adult. **P:** Entertainment. **U:** Home. **Mov-Ent**: Black Culture. **Acq:** Purchase. **Dist:** WarnerArchive.com.

Black Eyes 1939 — ★½
A lowly waiter, working in a Moscow restaurant, manages to overhear a number of stock tips from the wealthy patrons and makes a tidy pile of rubles to improve his daughter's life. The daughter already thinks he's a successful businessman and is disillusioned when she discovers dad's true profession. All comes out right in the end. 72m/B/W; VHS. **C:** Otto Kruger;

Mary Maguire; Walter Rilla; George L. Baxt; Marie Wright; Directed by Herbert Brenon. **Pr:** Walter C. Mycroft; Associated British Corporation. **A:** Jr. High-Adult. **P:** Entertainment. **U:** Home. **Mov-Ent:** Melodrama. **Acq:** Purchase.

Black Flag: Live in San Francisco 198?
Hardcore antics by one of the best alternative bands around. 53m; VHS, DVD. **A:** Jr. High-College. **P:** Entertainment. **U:** Home. **Mov-Ent:** Music--Performance. **Acq:** Purchase. **Dist:** Music Video Distributors. $29.95.

Black Flag: Six Pack 198?
This British import features the band playing "Black Coffee," "Rat's Eye" and more. 55m; VHS. **A:** Jr. High-College. **P:** Entertainment. **U:** Home. **Mov-Ent:** Music Video. **Acq:** Purchase. **Dist:** Music Video Distributors. $29.95.

Black Force 1975 (Unrated) — ★★
Brothers who fight crime with violent actions, are called for assistance in the recovery of an African artifact. Originally known as "Force Four." 82m; VHS. **C:** Malachi Lee; Warhawk Tanzania; Owen Watson; Judie Soriano; Directed by Michael Fink. **A:** College-Adult. **P:** Entertainment. **U:** Home. **Mov-Ent:** Violence, Anthropology, Africa. **Acq:** Purchase. **Dist:** Amazon.com Inc.

Black Force 2 1978 (R) — ★★
The brothers are back on the scene in another violent, cartilage-shattering adventure. 90m; VHS. **C:** Terry Carter; James B. Sikking; Gwen Mitchell; Directed by Edward Lakso. **Pr:** Platinum Pictures. **A:** College-Adult. **P:** Entertainment. **U:** Home. **Mov-Ent:** Violence, Death. **Acq:** Purchase. **Dist:** No Longer Available.

Black Forest Family Celebrates Christmas 1969
In this film a modern German family prepares a traditional Christmas celebration. Unnarrated. 14m; 3/4 U, Special order formats. **Pr:** International Film Foundation. **A:** Primary-Adult. **P:** Education. **U:** Institution, SURA. **Gen-Edu:** Family Viewing, Christmas. **Acq:** Purchase, Rent/Lease. **Dist:** International Film Foundation.

The Black Fox 1962
Disturbing documentary of the life and legacy of Adolf Hitler. Most interesting because his life is placed in the context of German mythology and literature. 89m/B/W; VHS. **TV Std:** NTSC, PAL. **C:** Narrated by Marlene Dietrich. **A:** College-Adult. **P:** Education. **U:** Home. **Gen-Edu:** Documentary Films, History--Modern, War--General. **Awds:** Oscars '62: Feature Doc. **Acq:** Purchase, Rent/Lease. **Dist:** German Language Video Center; White Star.

Black Fox: Blood Horse 1994 — ★★½
Alan Johnson (Reeve) and Britt (Todd) try to maintain an uneasy peace with the local Kiowas until evil Ralph Holtz (Wiggins) tries to stir things up and have some vigilantes attack the tribe. The second episode in the three-part series. 90m; VHS, CC. **C:** Christopher Reeve; Raoul Trujillo; Tony Todd; Chris Wiggins; Directed by Steven Hilliard Stern; Cinematography by Frank Tidy; Eric N. Robertson. **A:** Jr. High-Adult. **P:** Entertainment. **U:** Home. **Mov-Ent:** Western, Native Americans. **Acq:** Purchase. **Dist:** Unknown Distributor.

Black Fox: Good Men and Bad 1994 — ★★½
Britt (Todd) accepts a job as a federal marshall while Alan (Reeve) goes after desperado Carl Glenn (Fox) and his gang. During a stagecoach robbery, the outlaws take Hallie (Rowan) hostage, thinking she's the wife of a tycoon and Alan manages to use her to get to Glenn. The third episode in the sagebrush series. 90m; VHS, DVD, CC. **C:** Christopher Reeve; David Fox; Tony Todd; Kim Coates; Kelly Rowan; Directed by Steven Hilliard Stern; Cinematography by Frank Tidy; Music by Eric N. Robertson. **A:** Jr. High-Adult. **P:** Entertainment. **U:** Home. **Mov-Ent:** Western. **Acq:** Purchase. **Dist:** Unknown Distributor.

Black Fox: The Price of Peace 1994 — ★★½
Former plantation owner Alan Johnson (Reeve) and childhood friend Britt (Todd), whom he frees from slavery, try to forge a new life in 1860s Texas. But there's trouble when abusive bigot Ralph Holtz (Wiggins) threatens the peace between settlers and Indians when he goes after his wife delores (Holtz) who left him for a Kiowa warrior, Running Dog (Trujillo). Based on the novel by Matt Braun; made for TV. 90m; VHS, DVD, CC. **C:** Christopher Reeve; Raoul Trujillo; Tony Todd; Chris Wiggins; Cynthia (Cyndy, Cindy) Preston; Directed by Steven Hilliard Stern; Cinematography by Frank Tidy; Music by Eric N. Robertson. **A:** Jr. High-Adult. **P:** Entertainment. **U:** Home. **Mov-Ent:** Western, Slavery, TV Movies. **Acq:** Purchase. **Dist:** Unknown Distributor.

Black Friday 1940 (Unrated) — ★★½
Karloff is a surgeon who saves the life of his college professor friend (Ridges) by transplanting part of the brain of a gangster (involved in the same car crash) into the man's body. This results in a Jekyll/Hyde complex with the gangster's evil portion taking over and seeking revenge on rival mobster Lugosi. Horror stars Karloff and Lugosi never have any scenes together. 70m/B/W; VHS, DVD, CC. **C:** Boris Karloff; Stanley Ridges; Bela Lugosi; Anne Nagel; Anne Gwynne; Paul Fix; Virginia Brissac; James Craig; Directed by Arthur Lubin; Written by Curt Siodmak; Eric Taylor; Cinematography by Elwood "Woody" Bredell. **Pr:** Burt Kelly; Universal Pictures. **A:** Jr. High-Adult. **P:** Entertainment. **U:** Home. **Mov-Ent:** Horror, Surgical Transplantation. **Acq:** Purchase. **Dist:** Universal Music and Video Distribution. $14.98.

Black Fury 1935 (Unrated) — ★★★
A coal miner's efforts to protest working conditions earn him a beating by the company goons who also kill his friend. He draws national attention to this brutal plight of the workers when he barricades himself inside the mine. Muni's carefully detailed performance adds authenticity to this powerful drama, but it proved too depressing to command a big boxoffice. 95m/B/W; VHS, DVD. **C:** Paul Muni; Barton MacLane; Henry O'Neill; John Qualen; J. Carrol Naish; Directed by Michael Curtiz. **Pr:** Warner Bros. **A:** Family. **P:** Entertainment. **U:** Home. **Mov-Ent:** Labor & Unions, Miners & Mining. **Acq:** Purchase. **Dist:** WarnerArchive.com; Movies Unlimited; Alpha Video. $59.95.

The Black Gate 1995 (Unrated) — ★
Psychic investigator Scott Griffin's (Rector) vacation to a seemingly pleasant cliff-top inn is interrupted by horrific visions that lead him to an ancient object of great evil that could wreak havoc on Earth unless he can destroy it. More frightening than the lame ghost story are the poor visual effects. 81m; VHS, DVD. **C:** Jeff Rector; George Philip Saunders; Rebecca Kyler Downs; Red Montgomery; Brian Carlton; Directed by William Mesa; Written by John G. Jones; Victoria Parker; Cinematography by William Mesa. **A:** Sr. High-Adult. **P:** Entertainment. **U:** Home. **Mov-Ent:** Mystery & Suspense. **Acq:** Purchase. **Dist:** Lions Gate Television Corp. $26.98.

Black Gestapo 1975 (R) — **Bomb!**
Black-exploitation film about a vigilante army taking over a Los Angeles ghetto, first to help residents, but later to abuse them. Extremely violent. 89m; VHS, DVD. **C:** Rod Perry; Charles Robinson; Phil Hoover; Ed(ward) Cross; Angela Brent; Wes Bishop; Lee Frost; Charles Howerton; Uschi Digart; Directed by Lee Frost; Written by Wes Bishop; Lee Frost; Cinematography by Derek Scott. **A:** Sr. High-Adult. **P:** Entertainment. **U:** Home. **Mov-Ent. Acq:** Purchase. **Dist:** Movies Unlimited; Alpha Video. $59.95.

Black Girl 1966 (Unrated) — ★★★★
The first feature-length film by Senegal's Ousmane Sembene tells the tragic, inevitable story of a young Senegalese maid's forced exile when her white employers want to use her as a servant at their home in the south of France. The film that is most often cited as marking the birth of the African cinema, it remains one of the most powerfully disturbing depictions of the dehumanizing power of racism in the history of cinema. Chilling and unforgettable. 65m/B/W; DVD. **C:** Robert Fontaine; Anne-Marie Jelinek; Therese N'Bissine Diop; Momar Nar Sene; Directed by Ousmane Sembene; Written by Ousmane Sembene; Cinematography by Christian Lacoste. **A:** Jr. High-Adult. **P:** Entertainment. **U:** Home. **L:** French. **Mov-Ent:** Women, France, Slavery. **Acq:** Purchase. **Dist:** New Yorker Video.

Black Glove 1954 (Unrated) — ★
A trumpet star defends himself against charges of murdering a Spanish singer by tracking down the real killer. 84m/B/W; VHS, DVD. **C:** Alex Nicol; John Salew; Arthur Lane; Eleanor Summerfield; Paul Carpenter; Geoffrey Keen; Martin Boddey; Fred Johnson; Directed by Terence Fisher; Written by Ernest Borneman; Cinematography by Walter J. (Jimmy W.) Harvey. **Pr:** Lippert Productions. **A:** Family. **P:** Entertainment. **U:** Home. **Mov-Ent:** Mystery & Suspense, Nightclubs. **Acq:** Purchase. **Dist:** Unknown Distributor.

Black God, White Devil 1964 — ★★
Another Brazilan socio-political commentary by Rocha, an oft-incendiary filmmaker whose left-leaning works are steeped in mysticism, obscure folklore, and powerful images. An impoverished man transforms from a religious zealot to a bandit, his tale underscored by conflict between poor masses and wealthy landowners. Portuguese with subtitles. 102m; VHS. **C:** Yona Magalhaes; Geraldo Del Rey; Othon Bastos; Mauricio Do Valle; Lidio Silva; Directed by Glauce Rocha; Written by Glauce Rocha; Cinematography by Waldemar Lima. **A:** College-Adult. **P:** Entertainment. **U:** Home. **L:** English, Portuguese. **Mov-Ent. Acq:** Purchase. **Dist:** Facets Multimedia Inc. $79.95.

Black Godfather 1974 (R) — ★
The grueling story of a hood clawing his way to the top of a drug-selling mob. Features an all-black cast. 90m; VHS, DVD. **C:** Rod Perry; Damu King; Don Chastain; Jimmy Witherspoon; Diane Summerfield; Directed by John Evans; Written by John Evans; Cinematography by Jack Steely. **Pr:** Cinemation Industries. **A:** Sr. High-Adult. **P:** Entertainment. **U:** Home. **Mov-Ent:** Black Culture. **Acq:** Purchase. **Dist:** Movies Unlimited. $13.49.

Black Gold 1936 — ★★
Oil field suspense thriller by "B" movie king Hopton. 57m/B/W; VHS, DVD. **C:** Frankie Darro; Leroy Mason; Directed by Russell Hopton. **A:** Sr. High-Adult. **P:** Entertainment. **U:** Home. **Mov-Ent:** Mystiery & Suspense, Oil Industry. **Acq:** Purchase. **Dist:** Sinister Cinema. $16.95.

Black Gold 1962 (Unrated) — ★★
Pilot Frank McCandless (Carey) trades in his biplane for a chance at wildcatting for oil in 1920s Oklahoma. Ruthless oil baron Chick Carrington (Aikens) doesn't take kindly to competition. 98m/B/W; DVD. **C:** Phil Carey; Claude Akins; Diane McBain; James Best; Fay Spain; Dub Taylor; Iron Eyes Cody; Directed by Leslie Martinson; Written by Bob Duncan; Wanda Duncan; Cinematography by Harold E. Stine; Music by Howard Jackson. **A:** Jr. High-Adult. **P:** Entertainment. **U:** Home. **L:** English. **Mov-Ent:** Oil Industry, Action-Adventure. **Acq:** Purchase. **Dist:** WarnerArchive.com.

Black Gold 2006
Documentary showing the unjust and cruel conditions coffee farmers endure to keep prices low. 77m; DVD. **A:** Sr. High-Adult. **P:** Education. **U:** Home, Institution. **Gen-Edu:** Documentary Films, Economics. **Acq:** Purchase. **Dist:** California Newsreel. $26.95.

Black Gunn 1972 (R) — ★½
Early blaxploitation flick filled with car chases (one in a white Rolls Royce), fights, and explosions. L.A. nightclub owner Gunn (Brown) wants revenge on mobster Capelli (Landau) who order his brother Scott (Jefferson) killed. Of course, Scott was involved in ripping off a mobbed-up bookie joint to fund his militant activities but Gunn isn't cutting anyone any slack. 96m; DVD. **C:** Jim Brown; Martin Landau; Brenda Sykes; Bruce Glover; Luciana Paluzzi; Herbert Jefferson, Jr.; Bernie Casey; Gary Conway; Stephen McNally; Keefe Brasselle; Vida Blue; Directed by Robert Hartford-Davis; Written by Franklin Coen; Cinematography by Richard H. Kline; Music by Tony Osborne. **A:** Sr. High-Adult. **P:** Entertainment. **U:** Home. **Mov-Ent:** Black Culture. **Acq:** Purchase. **Dist:** Sony Pictures Home Entertainment Inc.

Black Hair and Black Eyed 1995
Explores the lives of young Korean-American women and the sources from where they derive their identity. Raises questions about the assimilation of this culture and promotes thought. 9m; VHS. **A:** Sr. High. **P:** Education. **U:** Home. **Gen-Edu:** Sociology. **Acq:** Rent/Lease. **Dist:** Frameline. $40.

The Black Hand 1950 (Unrated) — ★★★
Kelly plays well against character in this atmospheric turn-of-the-century thriller. The evil society of the Black Hand murders his father, and he seeks revenge. Well-made drama. 93m/B/W; VHS. **C:** Gene Kelly; J. Carrol Naish; Teresa Celli; Marc Lawrence; Frank Puglia; Directed by Richard Thorpe; Cinematography by Paul Vogel. **Pr:** MGM. **A:** Jr. High-Adult. **P:** Entertainment. **U:** Home. **Mov-Ent:** Mystery & Suspense. **Acq:** Purchase. **Dist:** No Longer Available.

Black Hand 1973 (Unrated) — ★½
Unemployed Italian immigrant is drawn into a web of murder and betrayal after he is attacked by an Irish gang. 90m; VHS. **C:** Lionel Stander; Michele Placido; Rosanna Fratello; Directed by Antonio Racciopi; Cinematography by Riccardo (Pallton) Pallottini; Music by Carlo Rustichelli. **Pr:** Stiletto Productions. **A:** Sr. High-Adult. **P:** Entertainment. **U:** Home. **Mov-Ent. Acq:** Purchase. **Dist:** No Longer Available.

Black Harvest 1992
Story of a mixed-race farm owner and his warring aboriginal workers in Papua New Guinea. Interesting view of a little-seen culture. Sequel to "First Contact." 90m; VHS. **A:** Sr. High-Adult. **P:** Education. **U:** Institution. **Gen-Edu:** Australia, Agriculture, War--General. **Acq:** Purchase. **Dist:** Direct Cinema Ltd.; Filmakers Library Inc. $195.00.

Black Hawk Down 2001 (R) — ★★★½
Producer Bruckheimer and director Scott faithfully and superbly re-create the Battle of Mogadishu of October, 1993. U.S. Army Rangers and Delta Force units are sent to apprehend Somali warlord Muhammad Farah Aidid's top staff in an Aidid-controlled section of the city. When two Black Hawk helicopters are shot down, the focus of the mission changes to rescue and defense. The usual introduction of the troops is dispensed with fairly quickly, in favor of background on the Somalian situation, and details of the impending operation. No-frills setup works perfectly with the following action, which is fierce, intense, and non-stop. Once the fighting begins, Scott's brilliance with visuals really kicks in, but nothing that happens, no matter how gruesome, seems forced or exploitative. Fine ensemble cast is nominally led by Hartnett, but no one disappoints. Based on the book by Mark Bowden. 143m; VHS, DVD, Blu-Ray, UMD, Wide. **C:** Josh Hartnett; Eric Bana; Ewan McGregor; Tom Sizemore; William Fichtner; Sam Shepard; Gabriel Casseus; Kim Coates; Hugh Dancy; Ron Eldard; Ioan Gruffudd; Tom Guiry; Charlie Hofheimer; Danny Hoch; Jason Isaacs; Zeljko Ivanek; Glenn Morshower; Jeremy Piven; Brendan Sexton, III; Johnny Strong; Richard Tyson; Brian Van Holt; Steven Ford; Gregory Sporleder; Carmine D. Giovinazzo; Chris Beetem; George Harris; Ewen Bremner; Boyd Kestner; Nikolaj Coster-Waldau; Ian Virgo; Thomas Hardy; Tac Fitzgerald; Matthew Marsden; Orlando Bloom; Kent Linville; Enrique Murciano; Michael Roof; Treva Etienne; Ty Burrell; Directed by Ridley Scott; Written by Ken Nolan; Cinematography by Slawomir Idziak; Music by Hans Zimmer. **Pr:** Jerry Bruckheimer; Ridley Scott; Ridley Scott; Scott Free; Revolution Studios; Columbia Pictures. **A:** Sr. High-Adult. **P:** Entertainment. **U:** Home. **Mov-Ent:** Africa. **Awds:** Oscars '01: Film Editing, Sound. **Acq:** Purchase. **Dist:** Sony Pictures Home Entertainment Inc.

Black Heat 1976 (R) — ★½
'Kicks' Carter (Brown) is a detective in L.A. attempting to stop a gang from using an all women's hotel as a prostitution ring. Possibly because he's supposed to be the film's hero, but equally possibly because his girlfriend of the moment happens to live there. Even as bad exploitation films go this one is pretty pointless, except for genre enthusiasts who like formulaic brutality. 90m; DVD. **C:** Timothy Brown; Russ Tamblyn; Geoffrey Land; Regina Carrol; Tanya Boyd; Al Richardson; Jana Bellan; Darlene Anders; Neal Furst; J.C. Wells; Directed by Al Adamson; Written by John D'Amato; Sheldon Lee; Bud Donnelly; Cinematography by Gary Graver; Music by Paul Lewinson. **A:** Sr. High-Adult. **P:** Entertainment. **U:** Home. **Mov-Ent:** Rape, Crime Drama. **Acq:** Purchase. **Dist:** Independent International Pictures. $7.98.

Black Heaven 2010 (Unrated) — ★½
Gaspard and his sweet girlfriend Marion are vacationing in Marseilles when they find a cell phone and try to track down the owner. This leads to vamp Audrey who easily seduces Gaspard and draws him into the virtual reality game she plays obsessively. As it turns out, the players are a suicide club who really want to find out if there's life after death. French with subtitles. 105m; DVD, Blu-Ray. **C:** Gregoire Leprince-Ringuet; Pauline Etienne; Louise Bourgoin; Melvil Poupaud; Pierre Niney; Ali Marhyar; Directed by Gilles Marchand; Written by Gilles Marchand; Dominik Moll; Cinematography by Celine Bozon; Music by Anthony Gonzalez; Emmanuel d'Orlando. **A:** College-Adult. **P:** Entertainment. **U:** Home. **L:** French. **Mov-Ent:** France, Suicide. **Acq:** Purchase. **Dist:** MPI Media Group.

Black Hephaistos - Exploring Culture and Science in African Iron Working 19??
Social sciences film from the University of Calgary Learning Commons. ?m; VHS. **A:** Adult. **P:** Education. **U:** Institution. **Gen-Edu:** Sociology, Anthropology, Documentary Films. **Acq:** Purchase. **Dist:** University of Calgary Library, Visual Resources Centre.

Black Heritage Holidays 19??
Introduces two celebrations of the African American culture, Kwanzaa and the freedom celebration known as Juneteenth. Comes with teacher's guide. 25m; VHS. **A:** Primary. **P:** Education. **U:** Institution. **Gen-Edu:** Black Culture, Holidays. **Acq:** Purchase. **Dist:** Clear Vue Inc. $59.00.

Black High School Girls 1968
Indiana students discuss their lives, families, schools, peers, and related topics. 29m; 3/4 U, Q. **Pr:** Martha Stuart Communications. **A:** Jr. High-Sr. High. **P:** Education. **U:** Institution, CCTV, CATV, BCTV, Home. **Gen-Edu:** Documentary Films, Human Relations. **Acq:** Purchase, Rent/Lease. **Dist:** Communication for Change, Inc.

Black Hills 1948 — ★
Dull oater with Dean and his sidekick Ates out to avenge the murder of a struggling ranch owner. 60m/B/W; VHS, DVD. **C:** Eddie Dean; Roscoe Ates; Shirley Patterson; Terry Frost; Nina Bara; William "Bill" Fawcett; Directed by Ray Taylor. **Pr:** Eagle Lion. **A:** Jr. High-Adult. **P:** Entertainment. **U:** Home. **Mov-Ent:** Western. **Acq:** Purchase. **Dist:** Movies Unlimited. $19.99.

The Black Hills Passion Play 1992
Features a behind-the-scenes look at the well-known Oberammergau production staged regularly in Black Hills, South Dakota. 39m; VHS. **A:** Family. **P:** Education. **U:** Home, Institution. **Gen-Edu:** Documentary Films, Religion, Theater. **Acq:** Purchase. **Dist:** Panacom. $29.95.

The Black Hills: Who Owns the Land 1989
Do these lands in South Dakota belong to the United States government or to the Indians? This program examines the historical record. 60m; VHS, 3/4 U. **Pr:** NETCHE. **A:** Jr. High-Adult. **P:** Education. **U:** Institution, CCTV, BCTV, SURA. **Gen-Edu:** Law, History--U.S., Native Americans. **Acq:** Purchase, Rent/Lease, Subscription. **Dist:** NETCHE. $140.00.
Indiv. Titles: 1. The Treaty of 1868 2. Black Hills Claim.

Black History: A Three-Part Series 19??
Part One, "Black Africa: The Beginnings," traces early African history; Part Two, "The Africans: Slaves in a New World," covers slavery; Part Three, "After the Civil War," traces emancipation to the struggle for civil rights. 47m; VHS. **A:** Jr. High-Sr. High. **P:** Education. **U:** Institution. **Gen-Edu:** History, Black Culture, Civil Rights. **Acq:** Purchase. **Dist:** Thomas S. Klise Co. $128.00.

Black History: Lost, Stolen or Strayed 1968
Bill Cosby is narrator of this eye-opening show which reviews the black contribution to the development of the United States. 54m; VHS, 3/4 U. **C:** Narrated by Bill Cosby. **Pr:** CBS News. **A:** Jr. High-Sr. High. **P:** Education. **U:** Institution, SURA. **Gen-Edu:** Documentary Films, History--U.S., Minorities. **Acq:** Purchase. **Dist:** Phoenix Learning Group; Facets Multimedia Inc.; African-American Images. $19.95.

Black History Series 19??
Seven-part series centering on seven people who helped African-Americans gain independence and freedom. 404m; VHS. **A:** Jr. High-Adult. **P:** Education. **U:** Institution. **Gen-Edu:** History, Black Culture. **Acq:** Purchase. **Dist:** Cambridge Educational. $149.95.
Indiv. Titles: 1. An Amazing Grace 2. Gordon Parks' Visions 3. Malcolm X: El Hajj Malik El Shabazz 4. The Jackie Robinson Story 5. Black History: Lost, Stolen or Strayed 6. The Joe Louis Story.

Black History: The Classics 1996
Includes Cry the Beloved Country, Native Son, and Go Tell It On the Mountain in this collection of three of the most important novels that became fims. ?m; VHS. **A:** Jr. High. **P:** Entertainment. **U:** Home. **Gen-Edu:** History--Modern, Documentary Films, Minorities. **Acq:** Purchase. **Dist:** Monterey Home Video.

The Black Hole 1979 (G) — ★½
A high-tech, computerized Disney space adventure dealing with a mad genius who attempts to pilot his craft directly into a black hole. Except for the top quality special effects, a pretty creaky vehicle. 97m; VHS, DVD. **C:** Maximilian Schell; Anthony Perkins; Ernest Borgnine; Yvette Mimieux; Joseph Bottoms; Robert Forster; Directed by Gary Nelson; Written by Gerry Day; Cinematography by Frank V. Phillips; Music by John Barry. **Pr:** Walt Disney. **A:** Family. **P:** Entertainment. **U:** Home. **Mov-Ent:** Science Fiction, Technology, Space Exploration. **Acq:** Purchase. **Dist:** Walt Disney Studios Home Entertainment, On Moratorium.

Black Holes 1999
Heather Couper and Nigel Henbest explain the astronomical "naked singularities" known as black holes using computer animation. Also available with a hardcover book at an additional price. 52m; VHS. **A:** Jr. High-Adult. **P:** Education. **U:** Home. **Gen-Edu:** Astronomy, Physics, Science. **Acq:** Purchase. **Dist:** Astronomical Society of the Pacific. $19.95.

The Black Holes of Gravity 1981
A study of black holes, which are formed by stars which collapse inward under the weight of their own gravity. A void like a whirlpool is formed, sucking all light and neighboring debris within. 55m; VHS, 3/4 U. **Pr:** BBC Horizon. **A:** Jr. High-Adult. **P:** Education. **U:** Institution, SURA. **Hea-Sci:** Documentary Films, Astronomy. **Acq:** Purchase, Rent/Lease. **Dist:** Home Vision Cinema.

Black Horizon 2001 (R) — ★½
No matter what it's called, this flick is still a less-than-exciting space opera. A Russian space station is falling apart and an international team is sent aboard a space shuttle to rescue the inhabitants. While there, the station is struck by a meteor that knocks out all communication and causes an oxygen leak, which threatens the team and crew. And on Earth, a government agent discovers that some people don't want the team to ever return. 92m; VHS, DVD. **C:** Ice-T; Hannes Jaenicke; Michael Dudikoff; Yvette Nipar; Richard Gabai; Alex Veadov; Art Hindle; Larry Poindexter; Andrew Stevens; Directed by Fred Olen Ray; Written by Steve Latshaw; Cinematography by Theo Angell. **A:** Sr. High-Adult. **P:** Entertainment. **U:** Home. **Mov-Ent:** Space Exploration. **Acq:** Purchase. **Dist:** Lions Gate Television Corp.

The Black House 2000 (Unrated) — ★★
Insurance fraud is a problem in Japan, if this film is any indication. After her husband dies, a widow pesters her insurance company to pay up. An agent goes to meet her and discovers that the widow has already remarried a very odd man and her son has hanged himself. The loving parents are most interested as to when they will begin receiving insurance payments for the boy's death as well. So the insurance company has the agent meet with a psychiatrist at a strip club (of course) as a prelude to his investigation of what will be a very odd couple. 117m; DVD. **C:** Machiko Washio; Daikichi Sugawara; Katsunobu Ito; Kenichi Katsura; Chikako Yuri; Toshie Kobayashi; Asako Kobayashi; Directed by Ataru Oikawa; Written by Ataru Oikawa; Kei Oishi; Takamasa Sato; Cinematography by Tokushu Kikomura; Music by John Lissauer; Masako Miyoshi. **A:** Sr. High-Adult. **P:** Entertainment. **U:** Home. **L:** English, Japanese. **Mov-Ent:** Mystery & Suspense, Comedy--Black, Insurance. **Acq:** Purchase. **Dist:** Movies Unlimited; Alpha Video. $29.99.

Black House 2007 (Unrated) — ★★
A Korean remake of a Japanese film of the same name, about an insurance agent investigating what may be a fraudulent claim. Jeon (Hwang Jeon-min) believes his client may have faked his son's suicide for insurance money, and believes he may be out to kill his wife as well. The Korean version drops much of the black humor of the Japanese original, and relies more on gore than story to provide frights (it's often compared to Hollywood remakes of successful Asian horror films). 103m; DVD. **C:** Shin-il Kang; Jeong-min Hwang; Seo-hyeong Kim; Seon Yu; Jeong-min Hwang; Yusuke Iseya; Kumiko Aso; Akira Terao; Fumiyo Kohinata; Hiroyuki Miyasako; Hidetoshi Nishijima; Susumu Terajima; Ryo; Tetsuji Tamayama; Hideji Otaki; Tatsuya Mihashi; Kanako Higuchi; Mayumi Sada; Jun Kaname; Mitsuhiro Oikawa; Toshiaki Karasawa; Directed by Terra Shin; Kazuaki Kiriya; Written by Yusuke Kishi; Young-jong Lee; Sung-ho Kim; Kazuaki Kiriya; Dai Sato; Shotaru Suga; Tatsuo Yoshida; Cinematography by Ju-young Choi; Kazuaki Kiriya; Music by Seung-hyun Choi; Shiroh Sagisu. **A:** Sr. High-Adult. **P:** Entertainment. **U:** Home. **L:** English, Korean. **Mov-Ent:** Horror, Mystery & Suspense, Insurance. **Acq:** Purchase. **Dist:** Genius Entertainment. $24.95.

Black Ice 1980
This program is about a group of sailing enthusiasts who have adapted the principles of the sport to winter conditions, resulting in the exciting sport of iceboat racing. 11m; VHS, 3/4 U. **Pr:** National Film Board of Canada. **A:** Jr. High-Adult. **P:** Education. **U:** Institution, SURA. **Spo-Rec:** Sports--General, Sports--Winter. **Acq:** Purchase, Rent/Lease, Trade-in. **Dist:** Encyclopedia Britannica.

Black Ice 1992 (R) — ★★
After an affair with a popular politician ends violently, Vanessa (Pacula) realizes her boss set up his death—and she's next in line. She finds the nearest taxi and offers the driver plenty of cash if he can quickly get her out of the country. It's going to be the ride of her life. Also available in an unrated version. 90m; VHS, CC. **C:** Michael Nouri; Michael Ironside; Joanna Pacula; Directed by Neill Fearnley; Music by Amin Bhatia. **Pr:** Vonnie Von Helmot; Robert Vince; Saban Entertainment; Prism Entertainment; Entertainment Securities Ltd. **A:** Sr. High-Adult. **P:** Entertainment. **U:** Home. **Mov-Ent:** Mystery & Suspense, Politics & Government. **Acq:** Purchase. **Dist:** Unknown Distributor.

Black Indians: An American Story ????
Documentary examines the issue of racial identity among Native and African Americans and the coalescence of these two groups in American history. Narrated by James Earl Jones. 60m; VHS. **A:** Family. **P:** Education. **U:** Home. **Gen-Edu:** Black Culture, History--U.S., Native Americans. **Acq:** Purchase. **Dist:** Rich-Heape Films. $24.95.

Black Irish 2007 (R) — ★★½
Familiar family drama buoyed by strong performances. Teenager Cole McKay (Angarano) is a promising high school baseball pitcher growing up in South Boston. His dad Desmond (Gleeson) is an unemployed drinker, his mother Margaret (Leo) holds to the illusion that they are a decent Catholic family, and his older sister Kathleen (Van Camp) is unmarried and pregnant. But the biggest problem for Cole is violent elder brother Terry (Guiry), who's drifted into drugs and crime and wants to drag Cole down with him. 95m; DVD, CC. **C:** Michael Angarano; Brendan Gleeson; Tom Guiry; Melissa Leo; Emily Van Camp; Michael Rispoli; Francis Capra; Finn Curtin; Directed by Brad Gann; Written by Brad Gann; Cinematography by Michael Fimognari; Music by John (Gianni) Frizzell. **A:** Sr. High-Adult. **P:** Entertainment. **U:** Home. **Mov-Ent:** Pregnancy, Adolescence. **Acq:** Purchase. **Dist:** Echo Bridge Home Entertainment.

Black Is My Color: The African American Experience 1992
In an attempt to teach children to appreciate black culture and the cultural, scientific and political contributions of its people, a multi-cultural group of children discusses what it means to be black in America. Elaborated upon with film clips, photographs and commentary, topics discussed include slavery; the Abolitionists; the Civil War; Reconstruction and Segregation; and Civil Rights. Comes with teacher's guide. 15m; VHS. **Pr:** Rainbow. **A:** Primary. **P:** Education. **U:** Institution. **Gen-Edu:** Black Culture, History--U.S., Education. **Acq:** Purchase. **Dist:** Rainbow Educational Media, Inc.; Clear Vue Inc. $89.00.

Black Is...Black Ain't 1995
Filmmaker Marlon Riggs examines the diversity of black culture and the danger of African American stereotypes of "blackness." 87m; VHS. **A:** Sr. High-Adult. **P:** Education. **U:** Home, Institution. **Gen-Edu:** Black Culture. **Acq:** Purchase. **Dist:** California Newsreel. $195.00.

Black Jack 1979 (Unrated) — ★½
In brutal, 18th-century Yorkshire, young Tolly is kidnapped by criminal Black Jack, who's just survived a hanging. Black Jack becomes a highwayman, allowing the secondary story of Belle, who's being sent to Bedlam because of her supposed mental illness, to intersect. Belle and Tolly then become part of a travelling carnival, but Loach's low-budget adventure is hampered by his non-actors performances and thick accents. Adapted from the Leon Gardfield children's book. 109m; DVD, Blu-Ray. **C:** Jean Franval; Stephen Hirst; Louise Cooper; Andrew Bennett; Directed by Ken Loach; Written by Ken Loach; Cinematography by Chris Menges; Music by Bob Pegg. **A:** Family. **P:** Entertainment. **U:** Home. **L:** English. **Mov-Ent:** Children, Great Britain. **Acq:** Purchase. **Dist:** Cohen Media Group.

Black Jazz & Blues 19??
Three classic jazz/blues shorts, "St. Louis Blues" (1929), "Symphony in Black" (1935), and "Caldonia" (1945). Features Bessie Smith, Duke Ellington, Lewis Jordan, and Billie Holiday. 44m/B/W; VHS. **Pr:** RKO. **A:** Family. **P:** Entertainment. **U:** Home. **Mov-Ent:** Music--Performance, Music--Jazz, Black Culture. **Acq:** Purchase. **Dist:** Music Video Distributors; Facets Multimedia Inc. $19.95.

Black Jesus 1968 — ★★
Lalubi (Strode) is an African leader using passive resistance to save his people from a dictatorial regime that's supported by European colonialism. When he's betrayed by a follower, Lalubi's imprisoned and tortured, along with a thief who gains a greater understanding after contact with the leader. Film is a thinly disguised depiction of Zaire and its history. 100m; VHS, DVD. **C:** Woody Strode; Jean Servais; Directed by Valerio Zurlini. **A:** College-Adult. **P:** Entertainment. **U:** Home. **Mov-Ent:** Africa, Politics & Government. **Acq:** Purchase. **Dist:** Ivy Classics Video.

Black Journal 1977
A series of current-interest interviews with the common theme of black presence in a white world. 30m; VHS, 3/4 U. **C:** Tony Brown. **Pr:** WNET New York. **A:** Sr. High-Adult. **P:** Education. **U:** Institution, CCTV, Home. **Gen-Edu:** Documentary Films, Minorities, Black Culture. **Acq:** Purchase, Rent/Lease. **Dist:** WNET/Thirteen Non-Broadcast.
Indiv. Titles: 1. The New Power: Black Vote 2. War in Africa 3. Colored Girls or Black Women? 4. Benign Neglect 5. Does Busing Work? 6. What is a Black Leader? 7. Are Black Colleges Finished 8. What Happened to the Revolution? 9. Language in Black and White 10. The New Warrior: Can Benjamin Hooks Save the NAACP? 11. A Visit with Alex Haley 12. The Black Presence: A Matter of Legitimacy.

The Black King 1932 — ★½
Prejudiced propaganda based on the life of Marcus Garvey, black leader of the '20s, who advocated black superiority and a return to Africa. A black con man takes advantage of fellow blacks by organizing a phony back-to-Africa movement, enriching himself in the process. When one man's girlfriend deserts him for the bogus leader, the jilted one blows the whistle. 70m/B/W; VHS, DVD. **C:** A.B. Comethiere; Vivianne Baber; Knolly Mitchell; Dan Michaels; Mike Jackson; Directed by Bud Pollard. **Pr:** Southland. **A:** Jr. High-Adult. **P:** Entertainment. **U:** Home. **Mov-Ent:** Comedy-Drama, Black Culture, Propaganda. **Acq:** Purchase. **Dist:** Facets Multimedia Inc.; Baker and Taylor. $24.95.

Black Kites 1996
Based on journals of Bosnian visual artist Alma Hajric who was forced into a basement shelter to survive the siege of Sarajevo. Explores artistry, imagination, and the resiliency of the human psyche. 26m; VHS. **A:** College-Adult. **P:** Education. **U:** Institution. **Gen-Edu:** Women, Human Rights. **Acq:** Purchase, Rent/Lease. **Dist:** Women Make Movies. $225.00.

The Black Klansman 1966 (Unrated) — ★
A black man masquerades as a white extremist in order to infiltrate the KKK and avenge his daughter's murder. In the interest of racial harmony, he seduces the Klan leader's daughter. As bad as it sounds. 88m/B/W; VHS, DVD. **C:** Richard Gilden; Rima Kutner; Harry Lovejoy; Directed by Ted V. Mikels. **A:** Sr. High-Adult. **P:** Entertainment. **U:** Home. **Mov-Ent.** **Acq:** Purchase. **Dist:** Movies Unlimited; Alpha Video. $39.95.

Black Knight 2001 (PG-13) — ★
The utterly unoriginal title should be a clue. Another remake of "A Connecticut Yankee in King Arthur's Court," and a particularly bad and formulaic one at that. Lazy, selfish Jamal (Lawrence) is transported from his minimum-wage job at theme park Medieval World to 14th century England, the real medieval world, where

some life lessons await. Obvious fish-out-of-water jokes ensue, as Jamal seeks to make sense of his new surroundings, knock boots with Nubian maidens and lead a revolution against an evil king. The film's few decent gags are swallowed by lots of inane humor, a tired script and Lawrence's desperate mugging. Ironically, the story's moral message about giving up selfishness for a cause is lost on its star, who acts as if he's the only person on screen. Ye olde bore. 95m; VHS, DVD, Blu-Ray, Wide. **C:** Martin Lawrence; Tom Wilkinson; Vincent Regan; Marsha Thomason; Kevin Conway; Daryl (Chill) Mitchell; Jeannette Weegar; Michael Burgess; Isabell Monk; Helen Carey; Directed by Gil Junger; Written by Darryl Quarles; Peter Gaulke; Gerry Swallow; Cinematography by Ueli Steiger; Music by Randy Edelman. **Pr:** Arnon Milchan; Paul Schiff; Darryl J. Quarles; Michael Green; Regency Enterprises; New Regency Pictures; Runteldat Entertainment; 20th Century-Fox. **A:** Jr. High-Adult. **P:** Entertainment. **U:** Home. **Mov-Ent:** Black Culture. **Acq:** Purchase. **Dist:** Fox Home Entertainment.

Black Label Society: Boozed, Boozed & Broken-Boned 2003 (Unrated)
A concert film of hard guitar rock band Black Label Society recorded in September 2002 at Harpos in Detroit. 120m; DVD. **A:** Sr. High-Adult. **P:** Entertainment. **U:** Home. **Mov-Ent:** Music--Performance, Documentary Films, Music--Pop/Rock. **Acq:** Purchase. **Dist:** Eagle Rock Entertainment Inc. $9.99.

Black Label Society: Doom Troopin'—The European Invasion 2006 (Unrated)
A concert film of hard rock band Black Label Society shot at stops on their European tour during 2005. 222m; DVD, Blu-Ray. **A:** Sr. High-Adult. **P:** Entertainment. **U:** Home. **Mov-Ent:** Music--Performance, Documentary Films, Music--Pop/Rock. **Acq:** Purchase. **Dist:** Eagle Rock Entertainment Inc. $19.98 19.98.

The Black Lash 1952 — ★
Two lawmen go undercover to break a silver hijacking gang. 55m/B/W; VHS. **C:** Lash LaRue; Al "Fuzzy" St. John; Peggy Stewart; Kermit Maynard; Directed by Ron Ormond. **Pr:** Western Adventure Productions. **A:** Family. **P:** Entertainment. **U:** Home. **Mov-Ent:** Western. **Acq:** Purchase. **Dist:** Grapevine Video. $19.95.

The Black Legion 1937 — ★★★
Social drama isn't as dated as we'd like to think. Auto worker Frank Taylor (Bogart) is angry at being passed over for an expected promotion that goes to a Polish immigrant. So he's easy pickings for a Klan-like secret society that practices hatred and Frank gets in deep, eventually losing his family. His best pal, Ed (Foran), tries to get Frank out but only tragedy follows. Very grim and one of Bogart's early unsympathetic starring roles. 83m/B/W; VHS, DVD. **C:** Humphrey Bogart; Dick Foran; Erin O'Brien-Moore; Helen Flint; Ann Sheridan; Henry (Kleinbach) Brandon; Robert Barrat; Joseph (Joe) Sawyer; Addison Richards; Samuel S. Hinds; John Litel; Eddie Acuff; Directed by Archie Mayo; Written by Abem Finkel; William Wister Haines; Cinematography by George Barnes; Music by Bernhard Kaun. **Pr:** Robert Lord; Warner Bros. **A:** Sr. High-Adult. **P:** Entertainment. **U:** Home. **Mov-Ent:** Crime Drama. **Acq:** Purchase. **Dist:** Movies Unlimited.

Black Lemons 1970 (Unrated) — ★
While in prison, a convict is stalked by the Mafia because of what he knows. He eventually spills the beans to the cops, putting himself in unavoidable jeopardy. 93m; VHS, DVD. **C:** Peter Carsten; Antonio (Tony) Sabato; Florinda Bolkan; Directed by Camillo Bazzoni. **A:** Sr. High-Adult. **P:** Entertainment. **U:** Home. **Mov-Ent. Acq:** Purchase. **Dist:** Alternative Distribution Alliance.

Black Like Me 1964 — ★½
Based on John Howard Griffin's successful book about how Griffin turned his skin black with a drug and traveled the South to experience prejudice firsthand. Neither the production nor the direction enhance the material. 107m/B/W; VHS, DVD. **C:** James Whitmore; Roscoe Lee Browne; Will Geer; Walter Mason; John Marriott; Clifton James; Dan Priest; Directed by Carl Lerner; Written by Carl Lerner; Gerda Lerner; Cinematography by Victor Lukens; Henry Mueller; Music by Meyer Kupferman. **Pr:** Alan Enterprises. **A:** Family. **P:** Entertainment. **U:** Home. **Mov-Ent:** Black Culture. **Acq:** Purchase. **Dist:** VCI Entertainment; Facets Multimedia Inc.; African-American Images. $19.95.

Black Like Who? 199?
Documentary of filmmaker Debbi Reynolds and her struggle for racial identity after being raised and educated in an all-white atmosphere. Features interviews with other black students struggling with the same issue. 30m; VHS. **A:** Adult. **P:** Education. **U:** Home. **Gen-Edu:** Documentary Films, Black Culture, Ethnicity. **Acq:** Purchase, Rent/Lease. **Dist:** Filmakers Library Inc. $295.

Black Limousine 2010 (R) — ★½
Down-on-his-luck Jack (Arquette) takes a job as a driver for a Hollywood limo service. A divorced, recovering alcoholic, Jack is trying to be a good dad and regain his former career as a film composer. Flick takes a turn for the surreal since director Colpaert likes to delve into Jack's mind but Arquette is convincing in a dramatic role. 101m; DVD. **C:** David Arquette; Bijou Phillips; Nicholas Bishop; Lin Shaye; Patrick Fabian; Vivica A. Fox; Directed by Carl Colpaert; Written by Carl Colpaert; Cinematography by Sero Mutarevic; Music by Carlos Durango. **A:** Sr. High-Adult. **P:** Entertainment. **U:** Home. **L:** English. **Mov-Ent:** Drama. **Acq:** Purchase. **Dist:** Anchor Bay Entertainment Inc.

Black Listed 2003 (R) — ★½
Fed-up lawyer Alan Chambers (Townsend) compiles a list of a dozen thugs who have escaped doing time thanks to legal loopholes. It's just a way to vent his anger, until some friends take the list and turn vigilante, dragging Alan into the mess. 94m; DVD. **C:** Robert Townsend; Harry J. Lennix; Vanessa Williams; Calvin Levels; Eugene "Porky" Lee; Dick Anthony Williams; Richard Lawson; Victoria Rowell; Dwight "Heavy D" Myers; Directed by Robert Townsend; Written by Robert Townsend; Cinematography by Charles Mills. **A:** Sr. High-Adult. **P:** Entertainment. **U:** Home. **Mov-Ent:** Black Culture. **Acq:** Purchase. **Dist:** York Entertainment.

Black Literature 1971
These programs illustrate the fact that black literature includes a dynamic and forceful body of work by writers with a wide variety of experiences and styles. 30m; EJ. **Pr:** NETCHE. **A:** College-Adult. **P:** Education. **U:** Institution, CCTV, BCTV, SURA. **Gen-Edu:** Documentary Films, Literature, Black Culture. **Acq:** Purchase, Rent/Lease, Subscription. **Dist:** NETCHE. **Indiv. Titles:** 1. Children 2. History 3. Teaching.

Black Lizard 1968 (Unrated) — ★★
A camp spectacle set in the Japanese underworld. The Lizard is the glamorous queen of Tokyo crime who plots to steal a famous diamond by first kidnapping the owner's daughter. Complications arise when she falls for a detective. The Lizard is played by female impersonator Maruyama. Mishima, who wrote the original drama and the screenplay, has a cameo as an embalmed corpse. Style is all. In Japanese with English subtitles. 112m; VHS. **C:** Akihiro Maruyama; Isao Kimura; Yukio Mishima; Kikko Matsuoka; Directed by Kinji Fukasaku; Written by Yukio Mishima. **A:** Adult. **P:** Entertainment. **U:** Home. **L:** Japanese. **Mov-Ent. Acq:** Purchase. **Dist:** $79.95.

Black Magic 1949 — ★★½
Cagliostro the magician becomes involved in a plot to supply a double for Marie Antoinette. 105m/B/W; DVD. **C:** Orson Welles; Akim Tamiroff; Nancy Guild; Raymond Burr; Directed by Gregory Ratoff; Written by Charles Bennett. **Pr:** Edward Small; United Artists. **A:** Family. **P:** Entertainment. **U:** Home. **Mov-Ent. Acq:** Purchase. **Dist:** Hen's Tooth Video. $12.95.

Black Magic 1988
The sport of "Double-Dutch" jump-roping is explained and demonstrated by a group of young inner-city girls. The group won a trip to London, and share their experiences with the viewer. 60m; VHS, CC, 3/4 U. **Pr:** PBS. **A:** Family. **P:** Education. **U:** Institution, CCTV, Home, SURA. **Gen-Edu:** Documentary Films, Children, Sociology. **Acq:** Purchase, Rent/Lease, Duplication, Off-Air Record. **Dist:** PBS Home Video. $49.95.

Black Magic 1992 (PG-13) — ★★½
Insomniac Alex, haunted by the nightly appearances of his dead cousin Ross, goes to Ross's hometown to see if he can find a way to make the apparition disappear. On the way, he runs into his cousin's ex-girlfriend Lilian and falls in love. Problem is, Lilian's a witch, maybe. Lightweight cable fare. 94m; VHS, CC. **C:** Rachel Ward; Judge Reinhold; Brion James; Anthony LaPaglia; Directed by Daniel Taplitz; Written by Daniel Taplitz. **Pr:** Harvey Frand; MTE, Inc. **A:** Jr. High-Adult. **P:** Entertainment. **U:** Home. **Mov-Ent:** Death, TV Movies. **Acq:** Purchase. **Dist:** $89.98.

Black Magic 2006 (R) — ★★
The first of two horror flicks by the Shaw Brothers, who were better known for martial arts films. Shan Jianmi (Feng Ku) is an evil sorcerer who terrorizes people with his powers. For the right price he makes love spells for the wealthy or the depraved. But this backfires and draws attention to him because so many different people ask for love spells that it ends up creating a mess (especially after Shan decides he wants one of the women for himself). But along with love spells, Shan can also kill with his magic, so taking him out won't be easy for his would-be assassins. 93m; DVD. **C:** Lung Ti; Lieh Lo; Ni Tien; Lily Li; Feng Ku; Ping Chen; Wen Chung Ku; Wei Tu Lin; Hua Yueh; Directed by Meng Hua No; Written by Kuang Ni; Cinematography by Hui-chi Tsao; Music by Yung-Yu Chen. **A:** Sr. High-Adult. **P:** Entertainment. **U:** Home. **Mov-Ent:** Horror. **Acq:** Purchase. **Dist:** Image Entertainment Inc. $14.99.

Black Magic M-66 19?? (Unrated)
In this animated adventure two prototype robot assassins are inadvertantly activated. Their program is to stalk and kill their creator's daughter. In Japanese with English subtitles. 105m; VHS. **A:** Sr. High-Adult. **P:** Entertainment. **U:** Home. **L:** Japanese. **Mov-Ent:** Animation & Cartoons. **Acq:** Purchase. **Dist:** Tapeworm Video Distributors Inc. $34.95.

Black Magic Terror 1979 (Unrated) — ★
Jilted by her lover, the old queen of black magic has everybody under her spell. Trouble starts, however, when she turns her back on one of her subjects. 85m; VHS, DVD. **C:** Suzanna; W.D. Mochtar; Alan Nuary; Directed by L. Sudjio. **Pr:** World Northal. **A:** Sr. High-Adult. **P:** Entertainment. **U:** Home. **Mov-Ent:** Horror, Magic, Occult Sciences. **Acq:** Purchase. **Dist:** Unknown Distributor.

Black Magic Woman 1991 (R) — **Bomb!**
An art gallery owner has an affair with a beautiful and exotic woman but starts to get cold feet when he's plagued by inexplicable phenomena. Seems that black magic woman has put a voodoo spell on him. Listless companion to director Warren's "Blood Spell" that gives away the ending, has a wretched script, and poor acting. 91m; VHS, CC. **C:** Mark Hamill; Amanda Wyss; Apollonia; Abadah Viera; Larry Hankin; Victor Rivers; Bonnie Ebson; Directed by Deryn Warren; Written by Gerry Daly; Music by Randy Miller. **Pr:** Vidmark Entertainment. **A:** College-Adult. **P:** Entertainment. **U:** Home. **L:** Spanish. **Mov-Ent:** Mystery & Suspense, Occult Sciences, Art & Artists. **Acq:** Purchase. **Dist:** CinemaNow Inc. $89.95.

The Black Marble 1979 (PG) — ★★★
A beautiful policewoman is paired with a policeman who drinks too much, is divorced, and is ready to retire. Surrounded by urban craziness and corruption, they eventually fall in love. Based on the Joseph Wambaugh novel. 110m; VHS, DVD. **C:** Paula Prentiss; Harry Dean Stanton; Robert Foxworth; James Woods; Michael Dudikoff; Barbara Babcock; John Hancock; Judy Landers; Anne Ramsey; Christopher Lloyd; Directed by Harold Becker; Music by Maurice Jarre. **Pr:** Frank Capra, Jr. **A:** Jr. High-Adult. **P:** Entertainment. **U:** Home. **Mov-Ent:** Drama. **Acq:** Purchase. **Dist:** New Line Home Video. $9.98.

Black Market Babies 1945 — ★½
Two-bit hood Eddie Condon uses drunk sawbones Jordon to help him operate a private maternity clinic that sells unwanted babies to childless couples. When a prepaid baby is stillborn, Eddie steals his sister-in-law's newborn but the baby switch leads to murder. Monogram's low-down expose based on a 1944 "Woman's Home Companion" article. 71m/B/W; DVD. **C:** Kane Richmond; Ralph Morgan; George Meeker; Teala Loring; Marjorie Hoshelle; Jayne Hazard; Addison Richards; Directed by William Beaudine; Written by George Wallace Sayre; Cinematography by Harry Neumann. **A:** Adult. **P:** Entertainment. **U:** Home. **L:** English. **Mov-Ent:** Crime Drama. **Acq:** Purchase. **Dist:** WarnerArchive.com.

Black Market Rustlers 1943 — ★½
The Range Busters are at it again. This time they break up a cattle rustling syndicate. 60m/B/W; VHS. **C:** Ray Corrigan; Dennis Moore; Max Terhune; Directed by S. Roy Luby. **Pr:** Monogram. **A:** Family. **P:** Entertainment. **U:** Home. **Mov-Ent:** Western. **Acq:** Purchase. **Dist:** Rex Miller Artisan Studio. $19.95.

Black Marlin: The Ultimate 19??
Contains spectacular tag and release action with giant Black Marlin as well as footage of the underwater environment of this species. 52m; VHS. **Pr:** Bennett Marine Video. **A:** Jr. High-Adult. **P:** Entertainment. **U:** Home. **Spo-Rec:** Fishing. **Acq:** Purchase. **Dist:** Bennett Marine Video. $24.95.

Black Mask 1996 (R) — ★★½
Hong Kong action star Jet Li (second only to Jackie Chan in Hong Kong boxoffice success) is Tsui, a mild-mannered librarian who used to be a member of a secret, biogenetically enhanced squad of super soldiers known as the "701 Squad." These commandos, who feel no fear or pain, are out to take over Hong Kong's underworld, and are killing the crime lords in grisly fashion. Tsui, aided by his detective buddy and dressed a lot like Kato from the "Green Hornet," goes into action to stop his ex-mates. Action may be a little bloody for those not used to the Hong Kong style, but Jet Li is an exciting performer who should break out big with this one after his impressive Stateside debut in "Lethal Weapon 4." Re-dubbed from the 1996 Hong Kong release. 95m; VHS, DVD, Wide. **C:** Jet Li; Karen Mok; Francoise Yip; Lau Ching Wan; Directed by Daniel Lee; Written by Tsui Hark; Teddy Chen; Cinematography by Cheung Tung Leung; Music by Ben Vaughn; Teddy Robin. **Pr:** Artisan Pictures, Inc. **A:** Sr. High-Adult. **P:** Entertainment. **U:** Home. **Mov-Ent:** Martial Arts, China. **Acq:** Purchase. **Dist:** Lions Gate Television Corp.

Black Mask 2: City of Masks 2002 (R) — ★½
The Black Mask (Andy On) is consulting the world's leading geneticists seeking a cure for his inability to feel pain (a condition many would probably prefer). But the people he's asking for help are getting killed one by one, and he soon discovers it's being done by a group of mutant pro wrestlers whose superpowers were created by the same super computer that made him. Far more comic book-like than the original, it will appeal to fans of that genre. 101m; DVD. **C:** Tobin Bell; Tyler Mane; Andrew Bryniarski; Scott Adkins; Sean Marquette; Oris Erhuero; Michael Bailey Smith; Traci Lords; Andy On; Silvio Simac; John Polito; Teresa Herrera; Rob van Dam; Robert Allan Mukes; Terence Yin; Directed by Tsui Hark; Written by Tsui Hark; Julien Carbon; Laurent Cortiaud; Charles Cain; Jeff Black; Cinematography by Wing-Hung Wong; William Yim; Music by J.M. Logan. **A:** Sr. High-Adult. **P:** Entertainment. **U:** Home. **L:** English, French, Korean, Polish, Spanish, Thai. **Mov-Ent:** Technology, Science Fiction, Martial Arts. **Acq:** Purchase. **Dist:** Sony Pictures Home Entertainment Inc. $9.95.

Black Men: An Endangered Species 19??
Explores the cultural issues associated with the separation of young black men from their communities during their prime years when careers and families are started. 60m; VHS. **Pr:** KERA Dallas. **A:** Jr. High-Adult. **P:** Education. **U:** Institution. **Gen-Edu:** Documentary Films, Sociology, Black Culture. **Acq:** Purchase. **Dist:** KERA. $39.95.

Black Men: Uncertain Futures 1991
Explores the plight and future of the black urban male in America. Includes discussions with young black men, the media's portrayals of black men, and an examination of problems and solutions offered by experts. 60m; VHS, 3/4 U. **C:** Hosted by Noah Nelson. **A:** Sr. High-Adult. **P:** Education. **U:** Institution, CCTV. **Gen-Edu:** Documentary Films, Black Culture, Men. **Acq:** Purchase, Rent/Lease. **Dist:** Maryland Public Television. $29.95.

Black Moon 1934 (Unrated) — ★½
Odd horror story. Juanita (Burgess) becomes obsessed with West Indian voodoo rituals and her shocked husband Stephen (Holt) follows her back to her native island where she participates in sacrificial ceremonies. He has to take drastic action when the situation goes out of control. 68m/B/W; DVD. **C:** Jack Holt; Dorothy Burgess; Fay Wray; Arnold Korff; Lumsden Hare; Directed by Roy William Neill; Written by Wells Root; Cinematography by Joseph August. **A:** Sr. High-Adult. **P:** Entertain-

ment. **U:** Home. **L:** English. **Mov-Ent**. **Acq:** Purchase. **Dist:** Sony Pictures Home Entertainment Inc.

Black Moon 1975 — ★★
A little gil escapes the harsh reality of a nebulous war between men and women by retreating into a surreal world where she lives with a strange family and a unicorn. Malle's visually stunning but incoherent experiment is definitely not for those fond of linear plotting. 100m; DVD, Blu-Ray. **C:** Cathryn Harrison; Joe Dallesandro; Alexandra Stewart; Therese Giehse; Directed by Louis Malle; Written by Louis Malle; Joyce Bunuel; Ghislain Uhry; Cinematography by Sven Nykvist; Music by Diego Masson. **A:** College-Adult. **P:** Entertainment. **U:** Home. **Mov-Ent**. **Acq:** Purchase. **Dist:** Criterion Collection Inc.

Black Moon Rising 1986 (R) — ★½
Based on an idea by John Carpenter dealing with the theft of a new jet-powered car and its involvement in an FBI investigation. Solid performances and steady action enhance this routine effort. 100m; VHS, DVD, Wide, CC. **C:** Tommy Lee Jones; Linda Hamilton; Richard Jaeckel; Robert Vaughn; Directed by Harley Cokliss; Written by John Carpenter; Cinematography by Misha (Mikhail) Suslov; Music by Lalo Schifrin. **Pr:** New World Pictures. **A:** Sr. High-Adult. **P:** Entertainment. **U:** Home. **L:** Spanish. **Mov-Ent**: Action-Adventure, Automobiles, Federal Bureau of Investigation (FBI). **Acq:** Purchase. **Dist:** Anchor Bay Entertainment. $19.95.

Black Mother, Black Daughter 1984
This is an examination of the lives of black women in a predominantly white area. 29m; VHS, 3/4 U, Special order formats. **Pr:** Shelagh Mackenzie. **A:** Sr. High-Adult. **P:** Education. **U:** Institution, SURA. **Gen-Edu**: Documentary Films, Black Culture, Women. **Acq:** Purchase, Rent/Lease. **Dist:** National Film Board of Canada. $250.00.

Black Music in America: From Then Till Now 1971
The history of the black contribution to American music. Includes performances by Louis Armstrong, Mahalia Jackson, Duke Ellington, Count Basie, Nina Simone, and Bessie Smith. 28m; VHS. **Pr:** Learning Corporation of America. **A:** College-Adult. **P:** Education. **U:** Institution, SURA. **Mov-Ent**: Music--Jazz. **Acq:** Purchase, Rent/Lease. **Dist:** Phoenix Learning Group.

Black Music in America: The Seventies 1979
From Diana Ross and Motown to Donna Summer and disco, this musical excursion includes clips of over 75 groups showing the growth and influence of black music and performers in the 1970s. 32m; VHS. **C:** Narrated by Isaac Hayes; Dionne Warwick. **Pr:** Black Music Association. **A:** Preschool. **P:** Entertainment. **U:** Institution, SURA. **Mov-Ent**: Music--Performance, Variety. **Acq:** Purchase, Rent/Lease. **Dist:** Phoenix Learning Group.

Black Narcissus 1947 — ★★★½
A group of Anglican nuns attempting to found a hospital and school in the Himalayas confront native distrust and human frailties amid beautiful scenery. Adapted from the novel by Rumer Godden. Stunning cinematography. Crucial scenes were cut from the American release by censors. 101m; VHS, DVD, Blu-Ray. **C:** Deborah Kerr; David Farrar; Sabu; Jean Simmons; Kathleen Byron; Flora Robson; Esmond Knight; Jenny Laird; Judith Furse; May Hallatt; Nancy Roberts, RN; Directed by Michael Powell; Emeric Pressburger; Written by Michael Powell; Emeric Pressburger; Cinematography by Jack Cardiff; Music by Brian Easdale. **Pr:** Mark Huffam. **A:** Jr. High-Adult. **P:** Entertainment. **U:** Home. **Mov-Ent**: India, Education. **Awds:** Oscars '47: Art Dir./Set Dec., Color, Color Cinematog.; N.Y. Film Critics '47: Actress (Kerr). **Acq:** Purchase. **Dist:** Movies Unlimited; Alpha Video; Criterion Collection Inc. $29.95.

Black Nations/Queer Nations? 1995
Experimental documentary chronicles the 1995 conference on lesbian and gay sexuality in the African diaspora. Brings together the highlights of the conference of experts who debate the economic, political and social situations of lesbians, gay men, bisexual and transgendered people. 59m; VHS. **A:** Sr. High-Adult. **P:** Education. **U:** Home. **Gen-Edu**: Africa, Homosexuality, Documentary Films. **Acq:** Purchase, Rent/Lease. **Dist:** Third World Newsreel. $125.00.

Black Nativity 2013 (PG) — ★½
Good intentions notwithstanding, this adaptation of the Langston Hughes musical from adventurous director Lemmons is a drastic misfire. Poorly cast, awkwardly paced, and dramatically inert, it's the kind of TV movie special that one expects to see on basic cable during the holiday season. Troubled teen Langston, who has been raised by his single mother, travels to New York City to stay with his grandparents, one of whom is a preacher, over the holiday season. It's a coming-of-age piece about a teen who learns about family and religion, but it never connects with the viewer through dialogue, character, or song. 93m; DVD, Blu-Ray. **C:** Forest Whitaker; Angela Bassett; Jennifer Hudson; Tyrese Gibson; Jacob Latimore; Mary J. Blige; Nasir Jones; Vondie Curtis-Hall; Directed by Kasi Lemmons; Written by Kasi Lemmons; Cinematography by Anastas Michos; Music by Laura Karpman. **Pr:** William Horberg; T.D. Jakes; Galt Niederhoffer; Celine Rattray; Trudie Styler; Fox Searchlight. **A:** Family. **P:** Entertainment. **U:** Home. **L:** English. **Mov-Ent**: Black Culture, Music--Gospel, Religion. **Acq:** Purchase.

Black Oak Conspiracy 1977 (R) — ★★
Based on a true story, this film deals with a mining company conspiracy discovered by an inquisitive stuntman. 92m; VHS. **C:** Jesse Vint; Karen Carlson; Albert Salmi; Seymour Cassel; Robert F. Lyons; Directed by Bob Kelljan. **Pr:** Jesse Vint; Tom Clark; Jesse Vint. **A:** Sr. High-Adult. **P:** Entertainment. **U:** Home. **Mov-Ent**. **Acq:** Purchase. **Dist:** New Line Home Video. $59.98.

Black Olympians 1904-1984: Athletics. . .in America 1986
A mini-history of the role of the black athlete in the Olympic Games, including Jesse Owens, the Mexico City '68 salute and more. 28m; VHS, 3/4 U. **Pr:** California Afro-American Museum. **A:** Jr. High-Adult. **P:** Education. **U:** Institution, Home, SURA. **Gen-Edu**: Sports--General, Minorities, Black Culture. **Acq:** Purchase. **Dist:** Clear Vue Inc.

Black Ops 2007 (R) — ★½
A WWII battleship is recommissioned and deployed to the Persian Gulf. When the ship falls into radio silence after a distress call, a Marine task force is sent in and finds most of the crew slaughtered. At first, they suspect terrorists but it turns out something else on the ship is responsible and it's so ridiculous, your jaw will drop open in disbelief. Henriksen does his usual professional job and Randolph is eye candy in a tiny tank top and a shower scene. 90m; DVD, Wide. **C:** Lance Henriksen; James Russo; Katherine Randolph; Gary Stretch; Jim Hanks; D.C. Douglas; Grant Mathis; Directed by Roel Reine; Written by Roel Reine; Ethan Wiley; Cinematography by Roel Reine; Music by Joseph Bauer. **A:** Sr. High-Adult. **P:** Entertainment. **U:** Home. **Mov-Ent**: Boating. **Acq:** Purchase. **Dist:** Movies Unlimited; Alpha Video.

Black Orchid 1959 (Unrated) — ★★½
A businessman and a crook's widow fall in love and try to persuade their children it can work out. 96m/B/W; VHS, DVD. **C:** Sophia Loren; Anthony Quinn; Ina Balin; Peter Mark Richman; Jimmy Baird; Directed by Martin Ritt; Written by Joseph Stefano; Cinematography by Robert Burks. **Pr:** Paramount Pictures. **A:** Jr. High-Adult. **P:** Entertainment. **U:** Home. **Mov-Ent**: Drama, Family. **Acq:** Purchase. **Dist:** Paramount Pictures Corp. $14.95.

Black Orpheus 1958 — ★★★½
The legend of Orpheus and Eurydice unfolds against the colorful background of the carnival in Rio de Janeiro. In the black section of the city, Orfeo (Mello) is a street-car conductor and Eurydice (Dawn), a country girl fleeing from a stranger sworn to kill her. The man has followed her to Rio and disguised himself as the figure of Death. Dancing, incredible music, and black magic add to the beauty of this film. Based on the play "Orfeu da Conceica" by De Moraes. In Portuguese with English subtitles or dubbed. 103m; VHS, DVD, Blu-Ray. **C:** Breno Mello; Marpessa Dawn; Lea Garcia; Fausto Guerzoni; Lourdes De Oliveira; Adhemar Da Silva; Alexandro Constantino; Waldetar De Souza; Directed by Marcel Camus; Written by Vinicius De Moraes; Jacques Viot; Cinematography by Jean (Yves, Georges) Bourgoin; Music by Antonio Carlos Jobim; Luis Bonfa. **Pr:** Lopert Pictures. **A:** College-Adult. **P:** Entertainment. **U:** Home. **L:** Portuguese. **Mov-Ent**: Folklore & Legends, Dance, Circuses. **Awds:** Oscars '59: Foreign Film; Cannes '59: Film; Golden Globes '60: Foreign Film. **Acq:** Purchase. **Dist:** Facets Multimedia Inc.; Home Vision Cinema; Tapeworm Video Distributors Inc.

Black Out 1996 (R) — ★½
John Grey (Bosworth), who's suffering from amnesia after a car crash, becomes desperate to remember his life after his wife (DuBois) is murdered. 98m; VHS. **C:** Brian Bosworth; Brad Dourif; Claire Yarlett; Marta DuBois; Directed by Allan Goldstein. **A:** Sr. High-Adult. **P:** Entertainment. **U:** Home. **Mov-Ent**. **Acq:** Purchase. **Dist:** CinemaNow Inc.

Black P. Stone Nation 1971
"The Black Stone Rangers" is a former gang from Chicago that has redirected its energies to urban renewal for the black community. 29m; 3/4 U, Q. **Pr:** Martha Stuart Communications. **A:** Jr. High-Sr. High. **P:** Education. **U:** Institution, CCTV, CATV, BCTV, Home. **Gen-Edu**. **Acq:** Purchase, Rent/Lease. **Dist:** Communication for Change, Inc.

Black Panther 1968 (Unrated)
Features a prison interview with Black Panther Party Chairman Huey P. Newton, footage of the assault against L.A. police chapter headquarter aftermath, demonstrations to free Huey, co-founder Bobby Seale recites the party's Ten-Point Platform. Original title was "Off the Pig." 15m/B/W; VHS, DVD. **A:** Adult. **P:** Education. **U:** Institution. **Gen-Edu**: Black Culture, History, U.S. States. **Acq:** Purchase. **Dist:** Third World Newsreel. $125.

Black Panther 1977 (Unrated) — ★½
True story of psycho-killer Donald Neilson, who murdered heiress Lesley Whittle in England in the 1970s. 90m; VHS. **C:** Donald (Don) Sumpter; Debbie Farrington; Directed by Ian Merrick; Written by Michael Armstrong. **Pr:** Alpha Films. **A:** Sr. High-Adult. **P:** Entertainment. **U:** Home. **Mov-Ent**: Mystery & Suspense, Great Britain. **Acq:** Purchase. **Dist:** Lions Gate Television Corp. $69.95.

Black Panther/San Francisco State: On Strike 1969
Contains two separate titles on one videocassette. "Black Panther" traces the development of the Black Panther organization and the efforts of its leaders. "San Francisco State: On Strike" chronicles the protests of students demanding an ethnic studies program at the university in 1968-69. 34m; VHS. **A:** Sr. High-Adult. **P:** Education. **U:** Home, Institution. **Gen-Edu**: History--Modern, Black Culture, Ethnicity. **Acq:** Purchase. **Dist:** California Newsreel. $195.00.

Black Panthers: Huey Newton/Black Panther Newsreel 1968
A film focusing on the "Free Huey Newton" rally in California; a separate video features an interview with Newton from Alameda County Jail, plus the Panther 10-point plan presented by Bobby Seale. 53m/B/W; VHS, 3/4 U. **TV Std:** NTSC, PAL. **Pr:** Black Panthers. **A:** College-Adult. **P:** Education. **U:** Institution, Home. **Gen-Edu**: Propaganda, Black Culture, Minorities. **Acq:** Purchase. **Dist:** International Historic Films Inc.; Facets Multimedia Inc. $39.95.

Black Patch 1957 (Unrated) — ★★
New Mexico marshal Clay Morgan (Montgomery) is nicknamed "Black Patch" because he lost an eye in the Civil War. When his old friend Hank Danner (Gordon) arrives in town, so does trouble, since Danner is married to Morgan's ex-love Helen (Brewster). Danner is also accused of bank robbery so Morgan tosses him in jail and he winds up dead after an escape. Now would-be gunslinger Carl (Pittman) thinks he should avenge his friend Danner's death. 82m/B/W; DVD. **C:** George Montgomery; Diane Brewster; Tom Pittman; Leo Gordon; House Peters, Jr.; Sebastian Cabot; Strother Martin; Directed by Allen Miner; Written by Leo Gordon; Cinematography by Edward Colman; Music by Jerry Goldsmith. **A:** Jr. High-Adult. **P:** Entertainment. **U:** Home. **Mov-Ent**: Western. **Acq:** Purchase. **Dist:** Movies Unlimited.

Black Paths of Leadership ????
Considers the social, political, and economic issues behind the civil rights movement as displayed by three leaders with varying agendas, Booker T. Washington, W.E.B. Du Bois, and Marcus Garvey. 28m; VHS. **A:** Jr. High-Sr. High. **P:** Education. **U:** Institution. **Gen-Edu**: Civil Rights, Black Culture, History--U.S. **Acq:** Purchase. **Dist:** Zenger Media. $59.95.

Black Paths of Leadership 1986
Profiles of three important black leaders in American history: Booker T. Washington, W.E.B. DuBois and Marcus Garvey. 28m; VHS, 3/4 U. **Pr:** California Afro-American Museum; Tellens Inc. **A:** Jr. High-Sr. High. **P:** Education. **U:** Institution, Home, SURA. **Gen-Edu**: Documentary Films, Civil Rights, Minorities. **Acq:** Purchase. **Dist:** Clear Vue Inc.

The Black Pearl 1988
Ramon discovers a huge black pearl while diving off the coast of California. Based on a book written by Scott O'Dell. 37m; VHS. **Pr:** Random House Inc. **A:** Primary-Jr. High. **P:** Entertainment. **U:** Institution. **Gen-Edu**: Literature. **Acq:** Purchase, Subscription. **Dist:** African-American Images. $69.95.

The Black Pearls of Polynesia 1991
Explorer Christine Doddwell travels to the tropical islands of Melanesia and Polynesia in search of the black pearl, one of the rarest treasures of the sea. She also discovers the far-reaching effects of Western civilization on island cultures and the environment. 60m; VHS, CC. **Pr:** WGBH Boston. **A:** Sr. High-Adult. **P:** Education. **U:** Institution, Home. **Gen-Edu**: Documentary Films, Pacific Islands, Ecology & Environment. **Acq:** Purchase. **Dist:** Mystic Fire Video. $24.95.

Black People Get AIDS Too 1988
The myth that AIDS is a white male disease is explored in this video. Available in two different versions. 20m; VHS, 3/4 U. **Pr:** Multicultural Prevention Resource Center. **A:** Jr. High-Adult. **P:** Education. **U:** Institution, Home, SURA. **Hea-Sci**: Black Culture, AIDS. **Acq:** Purchase, Rent/Lease, Duplication License. **Dist:** Clear Vue Inc. $295.00.

Black Peter 1963 (Unrated) — ★★½
Director Forman's first feature offers a glimpse into the struggles of a young Czech man as he copes with an oppressive father, a menial grocery store job, and first-love jitters. In Czech, with subtitles. 85m/B/W; VHS, DVD. **C:** Ladislav Jakim; Jan Vostrcil; Vladimir Pucholt; Pavla Martinkova; Pavel Sedlacek; Directed by Milos Forman; Written by Milos Forman; Jaroslav Papousek; Cinematography by Jan Nemecek; Music by Jiri Slitr. **A:** Sr. High-Adult. **P:** Entertainment. **U:** Home. **L:** Czech. **Mov-Ent**: Comedy--Romantic, Melodrama. **Acq:** Purchase. **Dist:** Facets Multimedia Inc. $29.99.

The Black Pirate 1926 — ★★★
A shipwrecked mariner vows revenge on the pirates who destroyed his father's ship. Quintessential Fairbanks, this film features astounding athletic feats and exciting swordplay. Silent film with music score. Also available in color. 122m/B/W; Silent; VHS, DVD. **TV Std:** NTSC, PAL. **C:** Douglas Fairbanks, Sr.; Donald Crisp; Billie Dove; Directed by Albert Parker; Written by Douglas Fairbanks, Sr.; Jack Cunningham; Cinematography by Henry Sharp; Music by Mortimer Wilson. **Pr:** Douglas Fairbanks; Elton Corporation. **A:** Family. **P:** Entertainment. **U:** Home. **Mov-Ent**: Silent Films, Classic Films. **Awds:** Natl. Film Reg. '93. **Acq:** Purchase. **Dist:** Kino on Video; Lions Gate Entertainment Inc.; Grapevine Video. $19.95.

Black Pit of Dr. M 1947 — ★
The ghost of a doctor who has been unjustly executed for murder seeks revenge on employees of an insane asylum. The horror is not just confined to the asylum. 90m/B/W; VHS, DVD. **C:** Gaston Santos; Rafael Bertrand; Mapita Cortes; Directed by Fernando Mendez; Written by Ramon Obon. **Pr:** Madera. **A:** Sr. High-Adult. **P:** Entertainment. **U:** Home. **L:** Spanish. **Mov-Ent**: Horror. **Acq:** Purchase. **Dist:** Spanishmultimedia; Something Weird Video. $39.95.

Black Plays in White Theater 197?
The attitude of white people towards plays written by black authors is discussed in this program. 30m/B/W; VHS, 3/4 U, EJ, Q. **Pr:** WCBS New York; Camera Three Productions. **A:** Sr. High-Adult. **P:** Education. **U:** Institution, SURA. **Fin-Art**: Documentary Films, Theater, Minorities. **Acq:** Duplication, Free Duplication. **Dist:** Camera Three Productions, Inc.; Creative Arts Television Archive.

Black Point 2001 (R) — ★★
John Hawkins (Caruso) is a former Naval captain, down on his luck and living in the harbor town of Black Point. When he meets Natalie (Haskell), he thinks she's the woman of his dreams. He's wrong. 107m; VHS, DVD, CC. **C:** David Caruso; Susan Haskell; Thomas Ian Griffith; Gordon Tootoosis; Alex Bruhanski; Directed by David Mackay; Written by Thomas Ian Griffith; Greg Mellott; Cinematography by Stephen McNutt; Music by Terry Frewer. **A:** Sr. High-Adult. **P:** Entertainment. **U:** Home. **Mov-Ent.** **Acq:** Purchase. **Dist:** Lions Gate Television Corp.

The Black Policeman: Writing. . .Black Exemplars 1973
Profile of Bill Baldwin, a Washington D.C. policeman, a man who loves his job. During riots, Baldwin worked night and day to save the city, and was then the victim of prejudice. The honest way he dealt with his problem is examined. 16m; VHS, 3/4 U. **C:** Hosted by Dennis Weaver. **Pr:** Jesse Sandler. **A:** Jr. High-Sr. High. **P:** Education. **U:** Institution, SURA. **Gen-Edu:** Documentary Films, Black Culture, Civil Rights. **Acq:** Purchase. **Dist:** Capital Communications.

Black Pond 2011 (Unrated) — ★★
Brit black comedy indie. Tom Thompson is out walking his dog, Boy, by Black Pond when he meets and befriends eccentric loner, Blake. When Boy suddenly dies, the dysfunctional family decides to bury him (illegally) by the pond. This is only the first such burial as Blake also dies suddenly at the Thompson's dinner table. When malicious, possibly fraudulent, therapist Eric spreads the story to the tabloids, the Thompsons are labelled murderers. 83m; DVD. **C:** Chris Langham; Simon Amstell; Amanda Hardingue; Helen Cripps; Anna O'Grady; Colin Hurley; Will Sharpe; Directed by Will Sharpe; Tom Kingsley; Written by Will Sharpe; Cinematography by Simon Walton; Music by Ralegh Long. **A:** Sr. High-Adult. **P:** Entertainment. **U:** Home. **L:** English. **Mov-Ent:** Comedy--Black, Family. **Acq:** Purchase. **Dist:** Entertainment One US LP; Acorn Media Group Inc.

Black Power in America: Myth or Reality? 1988
Focuses on some of the changes in society since the 1960s Civil Rights movement by looking at contemporary education and successful individuals who have achieved power and influence. 58m; VHS. **C:** Directed by William Greaves. **A:** Sr. High-Adult. **P:** Education. **U:** Institution. **Gen-Edu:** Documentary Films, Black Culture. **Acq:** Purchase. **Dist:** Facets Multimedia Inc.; William Greaves Productions, Inc. $129.95.

The Black Power Mixtape 1967-1975 2011
Swedish television journalists documented the Black Power Movement of the 1960s and '70s and highlighted key figures, including Angela Davis, Stokely Carmichael, Huey P. Newton, and Bobby Seale. 96m; DVD. **A:** Sr. High-Adult. **P:** Entertainment. **U:** Home. **Gen-Edu:** Documentary Films, Black Culture, Civil Rights. **Acq:** Purchase. **Dist:** MPI Media Group. $24.98.

Black Power, White Backlash—1966 ????
News correspondent Mike Wallace and leaders of the "Black Power" movement discuss economic power, fair housing, non-violence, and the tensions in Cicero, Illinois, the Selma of the North. 68m; VHS. **A:** Sr. High-Adult. **P:** Education. **U:** Institution. **Gen-Edu:** Civil Rights, Black Culture, History--U.S. **Acq:** Purchase. **Dist:** Films for the Humanities & Sciences. $89.95.

The Black Press: Soldiers Without Swords 1998
Chronicles the history of the black press and its central role in the construction of modern African American identity. 86m; VHS. **A:** Sr. High-Adult. **P:** Education. **U:** Home, Institution. **Gen-Edu:** Black Culture, Journalism, History. **Acq:** Purchase. **Dist:** California Newsreel. $195.00.

Black Rain 1988 — ★★★
Erstwhile Ozu assistant Imamura directs this powerful portrait of a post-Hiroshima family five years after the bombing. Tanaka plays a young woman who, having been caught in a shower of black rain (radioactive fallout) on an ill-timed visit to Hiroshima, returns to her village to find herself ostracized by her peers and no longer considered marriage-worthy. Winner of numerous awards (including five Japanese Academy Awards). In Japanese with English subtitles. 123m/B/W; VHS, DVD. **C:** Kazuo Kitamura; Yoshiko Tanaka; Etsuko Ichihara; Shoichi Ozawa; Norihei Miki; Keisuke Ishida; Directed by Shohei Imamura; Written by Shohei Imamura; Toshiro Ishido; Cinematography by Takashi Kawamata; Music by Toru Takemitsu. **A:** Sr. High-Adult. **P:** Entertainment. **U:** Home. **L:** Japanese. **Mov-Ent:** World War Two, Japan, Nuclear Warfare. **Acq:** Purchase. **Dist:** Wellspring Media; Facets Multimedia Inc. $79.95.

Black Rain 1989 (R) — ★★½
Douglas portrays a ruthless American cop chasing a Japanese murder suspect through gang-controlled Tokyo. Loads of action and stunning visuals from the man who brought you "Blade Runner." 125m; VHS, DVD, Blu-Ray, HD-DVD, 8 mm, Wide. **C:** Michael Douglas; Andy Garcia; Kate Capshaw; Ken Takakura; Yusaku Matsuda; John Spencer; Shigeru Koyama; Stephen (Steve) Root; Directed by Ridley Scott; Written by Craig Bolotin; Warren Lewis; Cinematography by Jan De Bont; Music by Hans Zimmer. **Pr:** Paramount Pictures. **A:** Sr. High-Adult. **P:** Entertainment. **U:** Home. **Mov-Ent:** Crime Drama, Japan. **Acq:** Purchase. **Dist:** Paramount Pictures Corp. $14.95.

Black Rainbow 1991 (R) — ★★★
Surprisingly good thriller that's relatively unknown, haunted by a menacing mood. Robards and Arquette are a father/daughter duo who perform clairvoyance scams at carnival sideshows. Suddenly, without warning, Arquette's former cons become real: she sees murder victims—before their demise. Quirky sleeper filmed on location in North Carolina. 103m; VHS, DVD, CC. **C:** Rosanna Arquette; Jason Robards, Jr.; Tom Hulce; Ron Rosenthal; John Bennes; Linda Pierce; Mark Joy; Directed by Mike Hodges; Written by Mike Hodges. **Pr:** Miramax Film Corp; Goldcrest Films. **A:** College-Adult. **P:** Entertainment. **U:** Home. **Mov-Ent:** Mystery & Suspense. **Acq:** Purchase. **Dist:** Anchor Bay Entertainment. $19.98.

Black Rat 2010 (Unrated) — ★½
Six classmates receive an e-mail asking them back to their school from a former peer who committed suicide due to their hazing. Despite logic and common sense telling them otherwise, they show up at the appointed place, and are promptly assaulted by a girl in a rat mask screaming about revenge. 76m; DVD. **C:** Hiroya Matsumoto; Directed by Kenta Fukasaku; Written by Futoshi Fujita; Cinematography by Hiroaki Yuasa; Music by Hikaru Yoshida. **A:** Sr. High-Adult. **P:** Entertainment. **U:** Home. **L:** English, Japanese. **Mov-Ent.** **Acq:** Purchase. **Dist:** Media Blasters Inc. $16.98.

The Black Raven 1943 — ★½
An action film that combines several plots into one. The Black Raven is an inn that sees more excitement than any other—not the least of which is murder! 64m/B/W; VHS, DVD, Blu-Ray. **C:** George Zucco; Wanda McKay; Glenn Strange; I. Stanford Jolley; Directed by Sam Newfield; Written by Fred Myton; Cinematography by Robert E. Cline. **Pr:** PRC. **A:** Adult. **P:** Entertainment. **U:** Home. **Mov-Ent:** Mystery & Suspense. **Acq:** Purchase. **Dist:** Sinister Cinema; Rex Miller Artisan Studio. $16.95.

Black Robe 1991 (R) — ★★★½
In 1634 young Jesuit priest Father Laforgue (Bluteau) journeys across the North American wilderness to bring the word of God to Canada's Huron Indians. The winter journey is brutal and perilous and he begins to question his mission after seeing the strength of the Indian's native ways. Stunning cinematography, a good script, and fine acting combine to make this superb. Portrays the Indians in a realistic manner, the only flaw being that Beresford portrays the white culture with very few redeeming qualities and as the only reason for the Indian's downfall. Moore adapted his own novel for the screen. 101m; VHS, DVD, Blu-Ray, Wide. **C:** Lothaire Bluteau; Aden Young; Sandrine Holt; August Schellenberg; Tantoo Cardinal; Billy Two Rivers; Lawrence Bayne; Harrison Liu; Marthe Tungeon; Directed by Bruce Beresford; Written by Brian Moore; Cinematography by Peter James; Music by Georges Delerue. **Pr:** Samuel Goldwyn Home Entertainment. **A:** College-Adult. **P:** Entertainment. **U:** Home. **Mov-Ent:** Drama, Native Americans, Canada. **Awds:** Australian Film Inst. '92: Cinematog.; Genie '91: Director (Beresford), Film. **Acq:** Purchase. **Dist:** MGM Home Entertainment. $94.95.

Black Rock 2012 (R) — ★★
Three gal pals (Aselton, Bosworth, and Bell) reunite at an old camping spot on a secluded island, only to be interrupted by three male veterans out hunting. When a romantic encounter goes horribly wrong, the hunters start stalking the girls. Actress/writer/director Aselton never succumbs to gender stereotypes and gives a strong performance herself but the film is a miss. But she does deserve credit for tackling a completely different genre than fans of her mumblecore films would expect but this thriller misses the tension. 83m; DVD, Blu-Ray. **C:** Katie (Kathryn) Aselton; Kate (Catherine) Bosworth; Lake Bell; Jay Paulson; Will Bouvier; Anselm Richardson; Directed by Katie (Kathryn) Aselton; Written by Mark Duplass; Cinematography by Hillary Spera; Music by Ben Lovett. **Pr:** LD Entertainment. **A:** Sr. High-Adult. **P:** Entertainment. **U:** Home. **L:** English. **Mov-Ent:** Horror, Hunting, Women. **Acq:** Purchase. **Dist:** Lions Gate Home Entertainment.

The Black Room 1935 (Unrated) — ★★★
As an evil count lures victims into his castle of terror, the count's twin brother returns to fulfill an ancient prophecy. Karloff is wonderful in his dual role as the twin brothers. 70m/B/W; DVD. **C:** Boris Karloff; Marian Marsh; Robert "Tex" Allen; Katherine DeMille; John Buckler; Thurston Hall; Directed by Roy William Neill; Written by Henry Myers; Arthur Strawn; Cinematography by Allen Siegler. **A:** Family. **P:** Entertainment. **U:** Home. **Mov-Ent:** Horror. **Acq:** Purchase. **Dist:** Sony Pictures Home Entertainment Inc. $9.95.

The Black Room 1982 (R) — ★
Couples are lured to a mysterious mansion where a brother and his sister promise to satisfy their sexual desires. Not much to recommend unless you're a fan of the vampire as psychology test case. 90m; VHS, DVD. **C:** Linnea Quigley; Stephen Knight; Cassandra Gaviola; Jim Stathis; Directed by Norman Thaddeus Vane. **Pr:** Butler/Cronin Productions. **A:** Sr. High-Adult. **P:** Entertainment. **U:** Home. **Mov-Ent:** Horror, Sex & Sexuality. **Acq:** Purchase. **Dist:** Lions Gate Television Corp. $69.95.

The Black Rose 1950 (Unrated) — ★★½
Technicolor action, set in the 13th century, as English Saxon Walter of Gurnie (Power) seeks to restore his fortunes by traveling in a caravan to the wilds of Cathay. Welles is the bizarre and brutal Tartan general Bayan, and pretty (and young) French actress Aubrey looks out of place as runaway concubine, Maryam, so the romance between her and Walter is sketchy at best. Based on the novel by Thomas B. Costain. 120m; DVD. **C:** Tyrone Power; Orson Welles; Cecile Aubry; Jack Hawkins; Finlay Currie; Herbert Lom; Michael Rennie; Robert (Bobby) Blake; Directed by Henry Hathaway; Written by Talbot Jennings; Cinematography by Jack Cardiff; Music by Richard Addinsell. **A:** Family. **P:** Entertainment. **U:** Home. **Mov-Ent.** **Acq:** Purchase. **Dist:** Fox Home Entertainment.

Black Roses 1988 (R) — ★
A disgusting band of rockers shows up in a small town, and the local kids start turning into monsters. Coincidence? 90m; VHS, DVD. **C:** Carmine Appice; Sal Viviano; Carla Ferrigno; Julie Adams; Ken Swofford; John Martin; Directed by John Fasano. **Pr:** Shapiro Glickenhaus Entertainment Corporation. **A:** Adult. **P:** Entertainment. **U:** Home. **Mov-Ent:** Horror. **Acq:** Purchase. **Dist:** Synapse. $79.95.

Black Russians 2001 (Unrated)
Feature length documentary interviews a poet, film producer, reggae artist, businessman and others ages 10 to 65 who are all Afro-Russians, born and raised in Soviet Union to chronicle current ideologies shaping international events involving race and communism along with rare footage of black soviet leaders, Paul Robeson, Kwame Nkruma, and Angela Davis. 116m; VHS, DVD. **A:** Adult. **P:** Education. **U:** Institution. **Gen-Edu:** USSR, Black Culture, Documentary Films. **Acq:** Purchase. **Dist:** Third World Newsreel. $300.

Black Sabbath 1964 (Unrated) — ★★★
An omnibus horror film with three parts, climaxing with Karloff as a Wurdalak, a vampire who must kill those he loves. 99m; VHS, DVD, Blu-Ray, Wide. **C:** Boris Karloff; Jacqueline Pierreux; Michele Mercier; Lidia Alfonsi; Susy Andersen; Mark Damon; Rika Dialina; Glauco Onorato; Massimo Righi; Directed by Mario Bava; Written by Mario Bava; Marcello Fondato; Alberto Bevilacqua; Cinematography by Ubaldo Terzano; Music by Les Baxter. **Pr:** American International Pictures. **A:** Primary-Adult. **P:** Entertainment. **U:** Home. **Mov-Ent:** Horror. **Acq:** Purchase. **Dist:** Sinister Cinema. $16.95.

Black Sabbath Live: Never Say Die 1984
Heavy metal superstar, Ozzy Osbourne, as a member of Black Sabbath, performs such hits as "War Pigs," "Never Say Die," and "Paranoid." This live performance is from 1978. 60m; VHS. **Pr:** VCL. **A:** Sr. High-Adult. **P:** Entertainment. **U:** Home. **Mov-Ent:** Music--Performance, Music--Pop/Rock. **Acq:** Purchase. **Dist:** Music Video Distributors. $19.95.

Black Sabbath: Live 1978 1978
Live show featuring Ozzy Osbourne. Songs include "Symptom of the Universe," "Snow Blind," "War Pigs," and "Paranoid." 60m; VHS. **A:** Jr. High-Adult. **P:** Entertainment. **U:** Home. **Mov-Ent:** Music Video, Music--Performance, Music--Pop/Rock. **Acq:** Purchase. **Dist:** Music Video Distributors. $49.95.

Black Sabbath: The Black Sabbath Story, Vol. 1, 1970-1978 1992
A retrospective of the band's first eight years with interviews and footage from the BBC's television program "Top of the Pops." Songs include "N.I.B.," "Paranoid," and "Children of the Grave." 58m; VHS. **A:** Sr. High-Adult. **P:** Entertainment. **U:** Home. **Mov-Ent:** Music Video, Music--Pop/Rock, Interviews. **Acq:** Purchase. **Dist:** Music Video Distributors. $19.98.

Black Sabbath: The Black Sabbath Story, Vol. 2, 1978-1992 1992
Video clips, interviews, and live performances from Black Sabbath, following the departure of Ozzy Osbourne. Tracks include "A Hard Road," "Die Young," "Neon Knights," "Trashed," "No Stranger to Love," "Feels Good to Me," and more. 90m; VHS. **A:** Jr. High-Adult. **P:** Entertainment. **U:** Home. **Mov-Ent:** Music Video, Music--Pop/Rock. **Acq:** Purchase. **Dist:** Warner Reprise Video; Music Video Distributors. $19.95.

Black Samson 1974 — **Bomb!**
A lion-owning bartender, who likes to beat Mafiosi with a staff, decides to clean the drugs out of his neighborhood in this blaxploitation classic (in the sense you just don't see films like this anymore). 87m; DVD. **C:** Rockne Tarkington; William (Bill) Smith; Titos Vandis; Carol Speed; Directed by Charles Bail; Written by Warren Hamilton, Jr.; Cinematography by Henning Schellerup; Music by Allen Toussaint. **A:** Sr. High-Adult. **P:** Entertainment. **U:** Home. **Mov-Ent:** Crime Drama. **Acq:** Purchase. **Dist:** Warner Home Video, Inc. $14.99.

Black Samurai 1977 (R) — ★
When his girlfriend is held hostage, a martial arts warrior will stop at nothing to destroy the organization that abducted her. 84m; VHS, DVD. **C:** Jim Kelly; Marilyn Joi; Biff Yeager; Bill Roy; Roberto Contreras; Directed by Al Adamson; Written by B. Readick; Cinematography by Louis Horvath. **Pr:** Continental Film Group. **A:** College-Adult. **P:** Entertainment. **U:** Home. **Mov-Ent:** Martial Arts. **Acq:** Subscription. **Dist:** Movies Unlimited. $16.99.

The Black Scorpion 1957 (Unrated) — ★½
Two geologists in Mexico unearth a nest of giant scorpions living in a dead volcano. Eventually one of the oversized arachnids escapes to wreak havoc on Mexico City. 85m/B/W; VHS, DVD. **C:** Richard Denning; Mara Corday; Carlos Rivas; Directed by Edward Ludwig; Written by Robert Blees. **Pr:** Warner Bros. **A:** Jr. High-Adult. **P:** Entertainment. **U:** Home. **Mov-Ent:** Horror, Mexico. **Acq:** Purchase. **Dist:** Warner Home Video, Inc. $19.98.

Black Scorpion 1995 (R) — ★★½
Darcy Walker (Severance) is an ex-cop-turned-superhero (the scorpion is her symbol), who dons a mask and fetching (and tight) black vinyl to fight crime and avenge her dad's death. She's got the prerequisite sidekick—an ex-chop shop operator (Morris)?and a supervillain—the asthmatic Breathtaker (Siemaszko) who threatens to annihilate the city with toxic gas. Campy, schlock fun. 92m; VHS, DVD. **C:** Joan Severance; Garrett Morris; Casey Siemaszko; Rick Rossovich; Directed by Jonathan Winfrey; Written by Craig J. Nevius; Cinematography by Geoffrey George; Music by Kevin Kiner. **Pr:** Roger Corman; Concorde Pictures; Showtime. **A:** Sr. High-Adult. **P:** Entertainment. **U:** Home. **Mov-Ent:** Science Fiction, Women, TV Movies. **Acq:** Purchase. **Dist:** Buena Vista Home Entertainment.

Black Scorpion 2: Ground Zero 1996 (R) — ★★
Fetching crimefighter Darcy Walker (Severance) returns to battle villains Gangster Prankster (Jackson) and AfterShock

(Rose), who are set on destroying the City of Angels by earthquake. 85m; VHS, DVD. **C:** Joan Severance; Whip Hubley; Stoney Jackson; Sherrie Rose; Garrett Morris; Laura Elena Harring; Directed by Jonathan Winfrey; Written by Craig J. Nevius; Cinematography by Mark Kohl; Music by Kevin Kiner. **A:** Sr. High-Adult. **P:** Entertainment. **U:** Home. **Mov-Ent:** Earthquakes, TV Movies. **Acq:** Purchase.

Black Shadows on a Silver Screen 19??
Highlights the contributions of African Americans to early films. Features many early film clips. 57m/B/W; VHS. **A:** Jr. High-Adult. **P:** Education. **U:** Home. **Gen-Edu:** Documentary Films, Black Culture, Filmmaking. **Acq:** Purchase. **Dist:** Facets Multimedia Inc.; African-American Images. $29.95.

Black Shampoo 1976 (Unrated) — **Bomb!**
A black hairdresser on the Sunset Strip fights the mob with a chainsaw. 90m; VHS, DVD. **C:** John Daniels; Tanya Boyd; Joe Ortiz; Directed by Greydon Clark. **Pr:** Alvin L. Fast; Dimension Films. **A:** Sr. High-Adult. **P:** Entertainment. **U:** Home. **Mov-Ent:** Exploitation. **Acq:** Purchase. **Dist:** VCI Entertainment. $59.95.

Black Sheep 1996 (PG-13) — ★1/2
Isn't there a five-day waiting period for remakes? The previously viewed copies of "Tommy Boy" hadn't even hit the sale bin before Spade and Farley went in search of more property to destroy. The twist here? Spade is assigned to keep the oafish brother (not son) of a gubernatorial candidate (not auto parts dealer) out of trouble until after the election (not so he can save the family business). In an effort to provide humor, plot points, and character development, Farley falls out of, off of or onto every prop in sight while Spade smirks. 87m; DVD, Blu-Ray, CC. **C:** Chris Farley; David Spade; Tim Matheson; Christine Ebersole; Gary Busey; Grant Heslov; Timothy Carhart; Bruce McGill; Fred Wolf; Directed by Penelope Spheeris; Written by Fred Wolf; Cinematography by Daryn Okada; Music by William Ross. **Pr:** Lorne Michaels; Robert K. Weiss; C.O. Erickson; Paramount Pictures. **A:** Jr. High-Adult. **P:** Entertainment. **U:** Home. **Mov-Ent:** Travel, Politics & Government. **Acq:** Purchase. **Dist:** Paramount Pictures Corp.

Black Sheep 1999
Raised in a white family but having dark skin, Lou Glover tells her story of being a lesbian, a police officer, and recently discovered Aboriginal woman. 26m; VHS. **A:** Adult. **P:** Education. **U:** Institution, BCTV. **Gen-Edu:** Women, Documentary Films. **Acq:** Purchase, Rent/Lease. **Dist:** Women Make Movies. $195.00.

Black Sheep 2006 (Unrated) — ★★
Cheery gorefest. Henry (Meister) returns to the family farm in rural New Zealand, hoping to cure his aversion to sheep and get a buyout from older brother Angus (Feeney). Only Angus has been doing some genetic experimenting on the woolies that turns the placid creatures into blood-thirsty killers! 87m; DVD. **C:** Nathan Meister; Peter Feeney; Tandi Wright; Oliver Driver; Danielle Mason; Tammy Davis; Directed by Jonathan King; Written by Jonathan King; Cinematography by Richard Buck; Music by Victoria Kelly. **A:** Sr. High-Adult. **P:** Entertainment. **U:** Home. **Mov-Ent. Acq:** Purchase. **Dist:** Genius.com Incorporated.

Black Sheep Boy/Decodings 1995
The voyeuristic "Black Sheep Boy" offers a look at the sexual thrill provided by festishizing youth. The B&W "Decodings" (1988, 15 minutes) offers footage from the '40s and '50s in an allegorical search for identity. 37m; VHS. **C:** Directed by Michael Wallin. **A:** College-Adult. **P:** Entertainment. **U:** Home. **Fin-Art:** Film--Avant-Garde. **Acq:** Purchase. **Dist:** Water Bearer Films Inc.

The Black Shield of Falworth 1954 — ★1/2
Typically silly '50s Technicolor swashbuckler with Curtis (and his New York accent) as Myles, the son of a disgraced knight, who's out to thwart a conspiracy against King Henry IV (Keith) and win the hand of fair maiden, Lady Anne (Leigh, Curtis' wife at the time). Loosely based on the Howard Pyle novel, "Men of Iron." 98m; VHS, DVD, Blu-Ray. **C:** Tony Curtis; Janet Leigh; Ian Keith; David Farrar; Barbara Rush; Herbert Marshall; Dan O'Herlihy; Rhys Williams; Torin Thatcher; Patrick O'Neal; Craig Hill; Directed by Rudolph Mate; Written by Oscar Brodney; Cinematography by Irving Glassberg; Music by Joseph Gershenson. **A:** Family. **P:** Entertainment. **U:** Home. **Mov-Ent. Acq:** Purchase. **Dist:** Universal Studios Home Video.

The Black Ships 1970
Commodore Perry's 1853 "opening of Asia" seen through the Japanese documents of the times. 8m; VHS, 3/4 U. **Pr:** Charles Eames; Ray Eames. **A:** College-Adult. **P:** Entertainment. **U:** Institution, Home, SURA. **Gen-Edu:** Documentary Films, Japan. **Acq:** Purchase, Rent/Lease, Duplication License. **Dist:** Pyramid Media.

Black Sister's Revenge 1976 — ★★
Poorly selected video title mars this intelligent drama about a young black woman's struggle to adjust to the big city after growing up in the deep South. 100m; VHS, DVD. **C:** Jerri Hayes; Ernest Williams, II; Charles D. Brook, III; Eddie Allen; Directed by Jamaa Fanaka; Written by Jamaa Fanaka. **Pr:** Jamaa Fanaka; Jamaa Fanaka. **A:** Sr. High-Adult. **P:** Entertainment. **U:** Home. **Mov-Ent:** Black Culture. **Acq:** Purchase. **Dist:** Movies Unlimited; Alpha Video. $59.95.

The Black Six 1974 (R) — ★
Six black Vietnam veterans are out to punish the white gang who killed the brother of one of the black men. 91m; VHS, DVD. **C:** Gene Washington; Carl Eller; Lem Barney; Mercury Morris; Joe "Mean Joe" Greene; Willie Lanier; Rosalind Miles; John Isenbarger; Ben Davidson; Maury Wills; Mikel Angel; Fred Scott; Directed by Matt Cimber; Written by George Theakos; Cinematography by William Swenning; Music by David Moscoe. **Pr:** Cinemation Industries. **A:** Sr. High-Adult. **P:** Entertainment. **U:** Home. **Mov-Ent:** Vietnam War, Veterans. **Acq:** Purchase. **Dist:** Movies Unlimited. $49.90.

The Black Sleep 1956 (Unrated) — ★
Mad scientist Dr. Cadman (Rathbone) invents a drug that causes a deathlike trance and uses it to perform brain surgery on unwilling patients. Needing an assistant, Cadman frames Dr. Ramsay (Rudley) for murder and uses the drug to rescue him from the gallows. Then some of Cadman's experiments get loose and want revenge. Over-the-top hokum that wastes a who's who of horror, including Lugosi (in nearly his last role) as a mute butler. 82m/B/W; VHS, DVD. **C:** Basil Rathbone; Herbert Rudley; Akim Tamiroff; Lon Chaney, Jr.; John Carradine; Bela Lugosi; Tor Johnson; Patricia Blake; Directed by Reginald LeBorg; Written by John C. Higgins; Cinematography by Gordon Avil; Music by Les Baxter. **A:** Jr. High-Adult. **P:** Entertainment. **U:** Home. **Mov-Ent. Acq:** Purchase. **Dist:** MGM Home Entertainment.

Black Snake Moan 2007 (R) — ★★
Over-heated stew finds Jackson playing grizzled blues musician/farmer Lazarus, who's turned to religion to help him cope with his wife running off. So he's the one man ready to tackle the sex demons of abused white trash Rae (tiny Ricci in barely-there attire), even if it means chaining her inside his shack until she can control that nympho itch. Part sermon, part exploitation, wholly dull. 115m; DVD, Blu-Ray, HD-DVD. **C:** Samuel L. Jackson; Christina Ricci; Justin Timberlake; S. Epatha Merkerson; John Cothran, Jr.; Kim Richards; David Banner; Directed by Craig Brewer; Written by Craig Brewer; Cinematography by Amy Vincent; Music by Scott Bomar. **Pr:** John Singleton; Stephanie Allain; New Deal Productions; Southern Cross the Dog Productions; Paramont Vantage. **A:** Sr. High-Adult. **P:** Entertainment. **U:** Home. **L:** English. **Mov-Ent:** Music. **Acq:** Purchase. **Dist:** Paramount Pictures Corp.

Black Snow 1989 (Unrated) — ★1/2
The mob is off on a violent search for 50 million bucks in cocaine. 90m; VHS. **C:** Jane Badler; Peter Sherayko; Julia Montgomery; Randy Brooks; Directed by Frank Patterson. **A:** Sr. High-Adult. **P:** Entertainment. **U:** Home. **Mov-Ent:** Drugs. **Acq:** Purchase. **Dist:** No Longer Available.

The Black Soldier 1968
Narrated by Bill Cosby, this show illustrates the history of black American participation in America's armed forces. 26m/B/W; VHS, 3/4 U. **C:** Narrated by Bill Cosby. **Pr:** CBS News. **A:** Jr. High-Sr. High. **P:** Education. **U:** Institution, SURA. **Gen-Edu:** Documentary Films, Black Culture, Minorities. **Acq:** Purchase. **Dist:** Phoenix Learning Group.

The Black Stallion 1979 (PG) — ★★★
A young boy and a wild Arabian Stallion are the only survivors of a shipwreck, and they develop a deep affection for each other. When rescued, they begin training for an important race. Exceptionally beautiful first half. Rooney plays a horse trainer, again. Great for adults and kids. 120m; VHS, DVD, Blu-Ray, Wide, CC. **C:** Kelly Reno; Mickey Rooney; Teri Garr; Clarence Muse; Hoyt Axton; Directed by Carroll Ballard; Written by William D. Wittliff; Melissa Mathison; Jeanne Rosenberg; Cinematography by Caleb Deschanel; Music by Carmine Coppola. **Pr:** Francis Ford Coppola. **A:** Family. **P:** Entertainment. **U:** Home. **Mov-Ent:** Horses, Horses--Racing. **Awds:** Oscars '79: Sound FX Editing; L.A. Film Critics '79: Cinematog.; Natl. Film Reg. '02; Natl. Soc. Film Critics '79: Cinematog. **Acq:** Purchase. **Dist:** MGM Home Entertainment; Time-Life Video and Television; Home Vision Cinema. $19.98.

The Black Stallion Returns 1983 (PG) — ★★1/2
Sequel to "The Black Stallion" follows the adventures of young Alec as he travels to the Sahara to search for his beautiful horse, which was stolen by an Arab chieftain. Unfortunately lacks much of the charm that was present in the first film. Adapted from the stories by Walt Farley. 103m; VHS, DVD, CC. **C:** Kelly Reno; Teri Garr; Vincent Spano; Angelo Infanti; Directed by Robert Dalva; Cinematography by Carlo Di Palma; Music by Georges Delerue. **Pr:** Zoetrope Studios. **A:** Family. **P:** Entertainment. **U:** Home. **Mov-Ent:** Horses. **Acq:** Purchase. **Dist:** Movies Unlimited; MGM Home Entertainment. $19.98.

Black Starlet 1974 (R) — ★1/2
A girl from the projects of Chicago travels to Hollywood in search of fame. She winds her way through a world of sleaze and drugs in order to make it to the top. 90m; VHS. **C:** Juanita Brown; Eric Mason; Rockne Tarkington; Damu King; Diane Holden; Directed by Chris Munger. **A:** Sr. High-Adult. **P:** Entertainment. **U:** Home. **Mov-Ent:** Sex & Sexuality, Drugs. **Acq:** Purchase. **Dist:** Unknown Distributor.

Black Studies 1980
A series which discusses the native origins and roots of black Americans. Programs are available individually. 60m/B/W; VHS, 3/4 U, EJ. **Pr:** University of Arizona. **A:** College-Adult. **P:** Education. **U:** Institution, CCTV, Home. **Gen-Edu:** Documentary Films, Genealogy, Black Culture. **Acq:** Purchase, Rent/Lease. **Dist:** University of Arizona.
Indiv. Titles: 1. Mini-Lectures 2. Learning About the Gambia 3. Learning About the Cameroon 4. Beginning Black American Genealogy 5. Black Americans in Arizona.

Black Studies: Then and Now 1992
A series of four videos which present an overview of African-American history. Subjects include role models, the history of African-Americans during slavery and the Civil War, and the origins and celebration of Kwanzaa and other holidays. Designed for grades 4-6. 60m; VHS. **A:** Primary. **P:** Education. **U:** Institution. **Gen-Edu:** Black Culture. **Acq:** Purchase. **Dist:** Clear Vue Inc.; Baker and Taylor. $305.00.

Black Sugar: Slavery from an African Perspective ????
An old man tells his grandson the horrors of his people being taken from their homes and families to be sold as slaves in the New World. 26m; VHS. **A:** Sr. High-Adult. **P:** Education. **U:** Institution. **Gen-Edu:** Africa, History, Slavery. **Acq:** Purchase, Rent/Lease. **Dist:** Films for the Humanities & Sciences. $149.00.

Black Sunday 1960 (Unrated) — ★★★
In 1630, witch Asa (Steele) who also happens to be a vampire, is executed along with her lover Juvato (Dominici) by her own brother. Two hundred years later, they are accidentally resurrected and in revenge, Asa goes after her descendents, including her look-alike, Katia. A must see for horror fans; firsts for Steele as star and Bava as director. 83m/B/W; VHS, DVD, Blu-Ray. **C:** Barbara Steele; John Richardson; Ivo Garrani; Andrea Checchi; Arturo Dominici; Antonio Pierfederici; Tino Bianchi; Clara Bindi; Enrico Olivieri; Germana Dominici; Directed by Mario Bava; Written by Mario Bava; Ennio de Concini; Mario Serandrei; Cinematography by Mario Bava; Ubaldo Terzano; Music by Les Baxter. **Pr:** American International Pictures. **A:** Jr. High-Adult. **P:** Entertainment. **U:** Home. **Mov-Ent:** Horror. **Acq:** Purchase. **Dist:** Sinister Cinema; Movies Unlimited; Something Weird Video. $19.98.

Black Sunday 1977 (R) — ★★1/2
An Arab terrorist group, with the help of a disgruntled Vietnam vet, plots to steal the Goodyear Blimp and load it with explosives. Their intent is to explode it over a Miami Super Bowl game to assassinate the U.S. president and to kill all the fans. Based on Thomas Harris' novel. 143m; VHS, DVD. **C:** Robert Shaw; Bruce Dern; Marthe Keller; Fritz Weaver; Steven Keats; Michael V. Gazzo; William Daniels; Clyde Kusatsu; Directed by John Frankenheimer; Written by Ernest Lehman; Cinematography by John A. Alonzo; Music by John Williams. **Pr:** Robert Evans; Paramount Pictures. **A:** Sr. High-Adult. **P:** Entertainment. **U:** Home. **Mov-Ent:** Mystery & Suspense, Federal Bureau of Investigation (FBI), Terrorism. **Acq:** Purchase. **Dist:** Paramount Pictures Corp. $24.95.

Black Sunday: Highlights of Super Bowl XVII 1984
Highlights from SuperBowl XVIII include playoffs for each of the nine teams that qualified; also included in the program is "NFL 83," a summary of the NFL 1983 Season. 46m; VHS, Special order formats. **Pr:** NFL Films. **A:** Family. **P:** Entertainment. **U:** Institution, CCTV, CATV, BCTV, Home. **Spo-Rec:** Sports--General, Documentary Films, Football. **Acq:** Purchase. **Dist:** NFL Films Video.

The Black Swan 1942 (Unrated) — ★★★
Swashbuckling pirate film, based on the novel by Rafael Sabatini, stars Power as James Waring, compatriot of notorious buccanneer Henry Morgan (Cregar). Morgan is pardoned and sent to Jamaica as its new governor—if he can prevent his from associates from continuing their criminal ways. He enlists Waring to help him fight the renegades; meanwhile Waring falls in love with former governor's daughter Margaret (O'Hara). Lots of derring do. 85m; VHS, DVD, Blu-Ray, CC. **C:** Tyrone Power; Maureen O'Hara; Laird Cregar; Thomas Mitchell; George Sanders; Anthony Quinn; George Zucco; Edward Ashley; Fortunio Bonanova; Directed by Henry King; Written by Ben Hecht; Seton I. Miller; Cinematography by Leon Shamroy; Music by Alfred Newman. **Pr:** Robert Bassler; 20th Century-Fox. **A:** Jr. High-Adult. **P:** Entertainment. **U:** Home. **Mov-Ent. Awds:** Oscars '42: Color Cinematog. **Acq:** Purchase. **Dist:** Fox Home Entertainment. $19.98.

Black Swan 2010 (R) — ★★★1/2
Harrowing tale has New York ballerina Nina (Portman) desperate to dance the lead role in the company's new production of "Swan Lake." She has an unexpected rival in newcomer Lily (Kunis), and is fighting against her own fears and paranoia. Portman does an excellent job showing Nina's descent into madness. It is a compelling and disturbing journey. Not exactly easy to watch, but well worth it for the performances. 108m; DVD, Blu-Ray. **C:** Natalie Portman; Mila Kunis; Vincent Cassel; Barbara Hershey; Winona Ryder; Janet Montgomery; Directed by Darren Aronofsky; Written by Mark Heyman; Cinematography by Matthew Libatique; Music by Clint Mansell. **Pr:** Fox Searchlight. **A:** Sr. High-Adult. **P:** Entertainment. **U:** Home. **L:** English. **Mov-Ent:** Dance--Ballet. **Awds:** Oscars '10: Actress (Portman); British Acad. '10: Actress (Portman); Golden Globes '11: Actress--Drama (Portman); Ind. Spirit '11: Actress (Portman), Cinematog., Director (Aronofsky), Film; Screen Actors Guild '10: Actress (Portman). **Acq:** Purchase. **Dist:** Movies Unlimited; Alpha Video; Fox Home Entertainment.

Black Swarm 2007 (Unrated) — ★
Cartoonish CGI wasps made for a very non-scary SciFi Channel creature feature. The sting of genetically engineered wasps creates mindless human drones of the folks of Black Stone. The wasps intend to use human innards for breeding purposes and even scientist Eli Giles (Englund) knows this is wrong. So he teams up with exterminator Devin Hall (Roberts) and sheriff Jane Kozik (Allen) to swat the flying pests permanently. 89m; DVD. **C:** Sebastien Roberts; Sarah Allen; Robert Englund; Jayne Heitmeyer; Rebecca Windheim; Robert Higden; Directed by David Winning; Written by Todd Samovitz; Ethlie Ann Vare; Cinematography by Daniel Vincelette; Music by Mario Sevigny. **A:** Sr. High-Adult. **P:** Entertainment. **U:** Home. **Mov-Ent:** Insects, Science. **Acq:** Purchase. **Dist:** Genius.com Incorporated.

Black Terrorist 1985 (Unrated) — ★★
Terrorists take over a ranch and slay the inhabitants. They keep a young boy alive and the mother tries to rescue him. 81m; VHS. **C:** Allan Granville; Vera Jones; Directed by Neil

Hetherington. **A:** Adult. **P:** Entertainment. **U:** Home. **Mov-Ent**: Terrorism, Africa. **Acq:** Purchase. **Dist:** No Longer Available.

Black Theater: Interviews 1978
Two-volume set presents a series of interviews with actors, producers, and directors who work to develop black theatre, including Ossie Davis, Rudy Dee, and Lloyd Richards. 60m; VHS. **A:** Adult. **P:** Education. **U:** Institution. **Fin-Art**: Theater. **Acq:** Purchase. **Dist:** Insight Media. $249.00.

Black Theatre: The Making of a Movement 1978
Documentary look at black theatre born from the Civil Rights activism of the 50s, 60s, and 70s. Ossie Davis, James Earl Jones, Amiri Baraka, Ntozake Shange and other artists recall the successes and failures of black theatre. Spotlights major institutions and events, such as the Urban Arts Corp, National Black Theatre, New Lafayette Theatre, and the Negro Ensemble Company. 113m; VHS. **Pr:** Woody King, Jr. **A:** Sr. High-Adult. **P:** Education. **U:** Institution. **Gen-Edu**: Documentary Films, Black Culture, Theater. **Acq:** Purchase, Rent/Lease. **Dist:** California Newsreel. $195.00.

Black Thumb 1970
A black man tends the garden behind a suburban home which he owns. A white salesman assumes he is a hired handyman. 7m; VHS, 3/4 U. **Pr:** Holt Rhinehart and Winston. **A:** Sr. High. **P:** Education. **U:** Institution, SURA. **Gen-Edu**: Minorities. **Acq:** Purchase. **Dist:** Phoenix Learning Group.

Black Thunder 1998 (R) — ★½
An Air Force stealth jet, nicknamed "Black Thunder," is hijacked by a Libyan agent during testing. A top gun, Vince Connors (Dudikoff), is paired with hotdog pilot Rick Jannick (Hudson) to retrieve the jet. A standard actioner. 85m; VHS, DVD. **C:** Michael Dudikoff; Gary Hudson; Richard Norton; Rob Madrid; Nancy Valen; Michael Cavanaugh; Robert Miranda; Frederic Forrest; Directed by Rick Jacobson; Written by William C. Martell; Cinematography by Michael G. Wojciechowski; Music by Michael Clark. **Pr:** Ashok Amritraj; Andrew Stevens; Concorde Pictures. **A:** Sr. High-Adult. **P:** Entertainment. **U:** Home. **Mov-Ent**: Aeronautics, Middle East. **Acq:** Purchase. **Dist:** New Horizons Picture Corp.

Black Tide 1958 (Unrated) — ★★
Suspicions arise that a drowning may have actually been a murder. 69m; VHS. **C:** John Ireland; Derek Bond; Leslie Dwyer; Maureen Connell; Sheldon Lawrence; Jack Taylor; Joy Webster; Cameron Hall; Arthur Lowe; John Horsley; Directed by C.M. Pennington-Richards; Written by Brock Williams; Cinematography by Geoffrey Faithfull; Music by Stanley Black. **Pr:** Monty Berman. **A:** Sr. High-Adult. **P:** Entertainment. **U:** Home. **Mov-Ent**: Mystery & Suspense. **Acq:** Purchase. **Dist:** Sinister Cinema. $16.95.

Black Tide 1979
Part of public television's "Nova" series. 58m; VHS, 3/4 U, Special order formats. **Pr:** WGBH Boston. **A:** Adult. **P:** Education. **U:** Institution, SURA. **Hea-Sci**: Documentary Films, Science. **Acq:** Purchase, Rent/Lease. **Dist:** Time-Life Video and Television.

Black Tight Killers 1966 (Unrated) — ★★★
Imagine a Japanese Matt Helm movie with an Elvis impersonator in the lead. That's essentially what's going on in this gonzo adventure/comedy from the mid-'60s. Hondo (Kobayashi) is a combat photographer just back from Vietnam. He and his stewardess girlfriend (Matsubara) become involved with various gangsters in a fast-moving plot filled with such bizarre devices as Ninja chewing gum bullets. 84m; DVD, Wide. **C:** Akira Kobayashi; Chieko Matsubara; Directed by Yasuharu Hasebe. **A:** Sr. High-Adult. **P:** Entertainment. **U:** Home. **Mov-Ent**: Action-Adventure. **Acq:** Purchase. **Dist:** Image Entertainment Inc. $24.99.

Black Tights 1960 — ★★½
Chevalier introduces four stories told in dance by Roland Petit's Ballet de Paris company: "The Diamond Crusher," "Cyrano de Bergerac," "A Merry Mourning," and "Carmen." A keeper for dance fans. Shearer's Roxanne in "Cyrano" was her last performance before retirement. 120m; VHS, DVD, Wide. **C:** Cyd Charisse; Zizi Jeanmaire; Moira Shearer; Dirk Sanders; Roland Petit; Narrated by Maurice Chevalier; Directed by Terence Young. **Pr:** Talam Films. **A:** Family. **P:** Entertainment. **U:** Home. **Mov-Ent**: Musical, Dance--Ballet. **Acq:** Purchase. **Dist:** Video Artists International; Music Video Distributors. $24.95.

Black to the Promised Land 1992
Takes a look at the lives of 11 African-American teenagers from Bedford-Stuyvesant, Brooklyn to Kibbutz Lehavot Habashan, Israel. The teenagers are taken by their Jewish teacher to work for three months on the Israeli kibbutz. Challenges to stereotypes are felt by both the Israelis and the African-American teenagers. 95m; VHS, Special order formats. **C:** Directed by Madeleine Ali. **A:** Sr. High-Adult. **P:** Education. **U:** Institution. **Gen-Edu**: Documentary Films, Black Culture, Judaism. **Acq:** Purchase, Rent/Lease. **Dist:** First Run/Icarus Films. $490.00.

Black Torment 1964 (Unrated) — ★½
A newly married Lord returns to the family manor only to be told he already returned a while back and has been running about killing people. Safe to say, it's probably not the honeymoon he was expecting. 115m; DVD. **C:** Norman Bird; John Turner; Peter Arne; Heather Sears; Ann Lynn; Directed by Robert Hartford-Davis; Written by Derek Ford; Donald Ford; Cinematography by Peter Newbrook; Music by Robert Richards. **A:** Sr. High-Adult. **P:** Entertainment. **U:** Home. **L:** English. **Mov-Ent**. **Acq:** Purchase. **Dist:** Redemption. $19.95.

The Black Tower 1985
Scotland Yard Commander Adam Dalgliesh can't even go on vacation without encountering a series of bizarre deaths and blackmail. Based on the mystery by P.D. James. 300m; DVD. **C:** Roy Marsden; Pauline Collins; Maurice Denham; John Franklyn-Robbins; Martin Jarvis; Rachel Kempson; Art Malik; Richard Heffer; Directed by Ronald Wilson; Written by William Humble; Music by Richard Harvey. **A:** Jr. High-Adult. **P:** Entertainment. **U:** Home. **Mov-Ent**: Mystery & Suspense, Great Britain. **Acq:** Purchase. **Dist:** Entertainment One US LP.

Black Triangle: Eastern Europe 1992
Examines an area where Poland, Czechoslovakia and Germany meet, called the black triangle which is the result of a major pollution problem. 52m; VHS. **A:** College-Adult. **P:** Education. **U:** Institution. **Gen-Edu**: Documentary Films, Politics & Government, Ecology & Environment. **Acq:** Purchase, Rent/Lease. **Dist:** Filmakers Library Inc. $350.00.

The Black Tulip 1988
A moving look at the personal costs of the Soviet Union's invasion of Afghanistan. Through interviews with soldiers, the viewer relives many of the same painful memories that confronted American veterans of the Vietnam War. The film concludes with an interview with a mother whose son was killed during the war. 27m; VHS, 3/4 U. **Pr:** Bruce E. Lane. **A:** Jr. High-Adult. **P:** Education. **U:** Institution, SURA. **Gen-Edu**: Documentary Films, USSR, History--Modern. **Acq:** Purchase, Rent/Lease. **Dist:** The Video Project; Facets Multimedia Inc. $45.00.

The Black Tulip 1991
Alexandre Dumas' classic tale is told here as a man grows the world's first black tulip, only to have it stolen by an evil man with plans to gain power from the devil. 50m; VHS. **A:** Preschool-Primary. **P:** Entertainment. **U:** Home. **Chl-Juv**: Animation & Cartoons, Storytelling. **Acq:** Purchase. **Dist:** Anchor Bay Entertainment. $12.95.

Black Uhuru and Steel Pulse: Tribute to Bob Marley 1989
The two reggae bands pay homage to the father of their music. 60m; VHS. **A:** Jr. High-Adult. **P:** Entertainment. **U:** Home. **Mov-Ent**: Music--Performance. **Acq:** Purchase. **Dist:** Music Video Distributors.

Black Uhuru: Tear It Up Live 1981
Prominant reggae band Black Uhuru caught live at the Rainbow Theatre in London. 48m; VHS. **Pr:** Island Visual Arts. **A:** Jr. High-Adult. **P:** Entertainment. **U:** Home. **Mov-Ent**: Music--Performance. **Acq:** Purchase. **Dist:** Music Video Distributors. $16.95.

The Black Unicorn: Dudley Randall and the Broadside Press 1996
Documentary examines the life and career of African American poet Dudley Randall, including his establishment of Broadside Press in 1965. 54m; VHS. **A:** College. **P:** Education. **U:** Institution. **Gen-Edu**: Documentary Films, Black Culture, Literature. **Acq:** Purchase, Rent/Lease. **Dist:** The Cinema Guild. $275.

A Black Veil for Lisa 1968 (Unrated) — ★★
A man attempts to exact revenge upon his unfaithful wife, but things go horribly awry. 87m; VHS. **C:** John Mills; Luciana Paluzzi; Robert Hoffman; Directed by Massimo Dallamano. **Pr:** Commonwealth United. **A:** College-Adult. **P:** Entertainment. **U:** Home. **Mov-Ent**: Mystery & Suspense, Marriage. **Acq:** Purchase. **Dist:** Lions Gate Entertainment Inc.

Black Venus 1983 (R) — **Bomb!**
A soft-core epic, starring the former Miss Bahamas, Josephine Jacqueline Jones, about the 18th-century French aristocracy. Laughably based upon the stories of Balzac. European film dubbed in English. 80m; VHS, DVD. **C:** Josephine Jacqueline Jones; Emiliano Redondo; Jose Antonio Ceinos; Monique Gabrielle; Florence Guerin; Helga Line; Mandy Rice-Davies; Directed by Claude Mulot; Written by Gregorio Garcia Segura; Harry Alan Towers; Cinematography by Jacques Assuerus; Julio Burgos. **Pr:** Film Accounting Service; Playboy Enterprises. **A:** College-Adult. **P:** Entertainment. **U:** Home. **Mov-Ent**. **Acq:** Purchase. **Dist:** MGM Home Entertainment. $79.95.

Black Warriors of the Seminole 1996
Tells the story of the alliance formed between Florida's Seminole indians and southern African Americans that still exists today. 30m; VHS. **A:** Jr. High. **P:** Education. **U:** Institution. **Gen-Edu**: History--U.S., Native Americans. **Acq:** Purchase. **Dist:** Ivy Classics Video. $49.95.

Black Water 1990
Sao Braz is a traditional maritime community in Bahia, Brazil. Dependent on fishing, the community has been badly affected by water pollution from local factories and mills. 28m; VHS. **C:** Directed by Allen Moore; Charlotte Cerf. **A:** College-Adult. **P:** Education. **U:** Institution. **Gen-Edu**: Ecology & Environment, South America. **Acq:** Purchase, Rent/Lease. **Dist:** First Run/Icarus Films. $280.00.

Black Water 1994 — ★★½
Tennessee fishing trip turns into a nightmare for an innocent man accused of murder. Based on the novel "Minnie" by Hans Werner Kettenbach. 105m; VHS, CC. **C:** Julian Sands; Stacey Dash; Ned Beatty; Ed Lauter; Denise Crosby; William McNamara; Rod Steiger; Directed by Nicolas Gessner; Written by Nicolas Gessner; Laird Koenig; Music by Gabriel Yared. **Pr:** Bernard Lang; Peter-Christian Fueter; Jurg Staubli; Roger Weil; Condor Productions; Academy Entertainment. **A:** Sr. High-Adult. **P:** Entertainment. **U:** Home. **Mov-Ent**: Mystery & Suspense, Fishing. **Acq:** Purchase. **Dist:** No Longer Available.

Black Water 2007 (R) — ★
You'll root for the crocs to get this trio of whiners as quickly as possible in this remarkably dull creature feature. Lee (Dermody) joins her sister Grace (Glenn) and brother-in-law Adam (Rodoreda) on an ill-fated boating trip into a northern Australian mangrove swamp. A croc eats their guide and the three hustle up a tree while they try to figure out how to get back into their boat without becoming dinner. 89m; DVD, CC. **C:** Ben Oxenbould; Diana Glenn; Maeve Dermody; Andy Rodoreda; Directed by Andrew Traucki; David Nerlick; Written by Andrew Traucki; David Nerlick; Cinematography by John Biggins; Music by Rafael May. **A:** Sr. High-Adult. **P:** Entertainment. **U:** Home. **Mov-Ent**: Australia. **Acq:** Purchase. **Dist:** Sony Pictures Home Entertainment Inc.

Black Water Gold 1969 (Unrated) — ★★½
TV movie about a search for sunken Spanish gold. 75m; VHS, DVD. **C:** Ricardo Montalban; Keir Dullea; Lana Wood; Bradford Dillman; France Nuyen; Directed by Alan Landsburg. **Pr:** Metromedia Producers Corporation. **A:** Jr. High-Adult. **P:** Entertainment. **U:** Home. **Mov-Ent**: TV Movies. **Acq:** Purchase. **Dist:** Movies Unlimited. $18.99.

Black Waters 1982
A look at the conflict surrounding the US government's intention to use the Black Hills of South Dakota as "national sacrifice area" for uranium mining. 28m; VHS, 3/4 U. **Pr:** Talli Nauman. **A:** Sr. High-Adult. **P:** Education. **U:** Institution, CATV, BCTV, SURA. **Gen-Edu**: Documentary Films, Nuclear Energy. **Acq:** Purchase, Rent/Lease. **Dist:** Green Mountain Post Films.

The Black Waters of Echo's Pond 2010 (R) — ★
Silly horror flick has nine college students vacationing at an old home on a Maine island (Patrick is the crusty caretaker). While playing an old board game, they release a demon that possesses each student and releases their innermost ugliest impulses that also prove deadly. The students are all bland horror fodder with too much time wasted establishing the relationships between them. Get to the gore already! 92m; DVD, Blu-Ray. **C:** Robert Patrick; Danielle Harris; James Duval; Mircea Monroe; Walker Howard; Sean Lawlor; Elise Avellan; Electra Avellan; M.D. Walton; Nick Mennell; Directed by Gabriel Bologna; Written by Gabriel Bologna; Sean Clark; Michael Berenson; Cinematography by Massimo Zeri; Music by Harry Manfredini. **Pr:** Jason Loughridge; Raymond J. Markovich; Parallel Media; Project 8 Films. **A:** Sr. High-Adult. **P:** Entertainment. **U:** Home. **L:** English. **Mov-Ent**: Games. **Acq:** Purchase. **Dist:** Not Yet Released.

Black Wheels 2006
Looks at the history of African-American participants in motor racing, from stock cars in the 1920s to present day NASCAR races. 48m; DVD. **A:** Jr. High-Adult. **P:** Entertainment. **U:** Home. **Gen-Edu**: Documentary Films, Automobiles--Racing. **Acq:** Purchase. **Dist:** Razor Digital.

Black, White, and Angry ????
NBC News program examines many issues between blacks and whites, at work, in their communities, and what the futures holds in how they relate to each other. 77m; VHS. **A:** Adult. **P:** Education. **U:** Institution. **Gen-Edu**: Education, Ethnicity. **Acq:** Purchase, Rent/Lease. **Dist:** Films for the Humanities & Sciences. $129.00.

The Black Widow 1947 — ★★
A fortune-teller plots to steal scientific secrets and take over the world. Serial in 13 episodes. 164m/B/W; VHS. **C:** Bruce Edwards; Carol Forman; Anthony Warde; Directed by Spencer Gordon Bennet. **Pr:** Republic. **A:** Family. **P:** Entertainment. **U:** Institution, Home. **Mov-Ent**: Serials. **Acq:** Purchase. **Dist:** Lions Gate Entertainment Inc. $19.98.

Black Widow 1954 (Unrated) — ★★
Rogers gets cast against type as heartless Broadway diva Lottie, who's mixed-up in the death of secretive aspiring writer Nanny (Garner). But since the gal died in the apartment of producer Peter (Heflin), he's suspect numero uno, according to Detective Bruce (Raft). And that doesn't make Peter's actress wife Iris (Tierney) too happy. 95m; DVD. **C:** Ginger Rogers; Van Heflin; Gene Tierney; George Raft; Peggy Ann Garner; Reginald Gardiner; Virginia Leith; Otto Kruger; Cathleen Nesbitt; Skip Homeier; Directed by Nunnally Johnson; Written by Nunnally Johnson; Cinematography by Charles G. Clarke; Music by Leigh Harline. **A:** Jr. High-Adult. **P:** Entertainment. **U:** Home. **Mov-Ent**. **Acq:** Purchase. **Dist:** Fox Home Entertainment.

Black Widow 1987 (R) — ★★★
A federal agent pursues a beautiful murderess who marries rich men and then kills them, making the deaths look natural. The agent herself becomes involved in the final seduction. The two women are enticing and the locations picturesque. 101m; VHS, DVD, CC. **C:** Debra Winger; Theresa Russell; Sami Frey; Nicol Williamson; Terry O'Quinn; Dennis Hopper; D.W. Moffett; Lois Smith; Mary Woronov; Rutanya Alda; James Hong; Diane Ladd; Cameo(s) David Mamet; Directed by Bob Rafelson; Written by Ronald Bass; Cinematography by Conrad L. Hall; Music by Michael Small. **Pr:** 20th Century-Fox. **A:** Sr. High-Adult. **P:** Entertainment. **U:** Home. **Mov-Ent**: Mystery & Suspense, Federal Bureau of Investigation (FBI). **Acq:** Purchase. **Dist:** Movies Unlimited; Alpha Video. $19.98.

The Black Widow 2005 (Unrated) — ★★
Upon the death of her lover, Eleanora (Colagrande) visits his eccentric estate known as the Rubber House, to discover more about this mysterious man. The caretaker (Defoe) is more than willing to help her discover a few secrets she herself has been hiding. Amateur attempts all around make for a directionless, awkwardly spoken tale. Dafoe might want to consider different writing partners. 99m; DVD. **C:** Giada Colagrande; Willem

Dafoe; Seymour Cassel; Claudio Botosso; Directed by Giada Colagrande; Written by Giada Colagrande; Willem Dafoe; Cinematography by Ken Kelsch; Music by Gyorgy Ligeti. **P:** Entertainment. **U:** Home. **Mov-Ent**. **Acq:** Purchase. **Dist:** Movies Unlimited; Alpha Video.

Black Widow Murders: The Blanche Taylor Moore Story 1993 (Unrated) — ★½
Montgomery does what she can with the title role but this true crime, made-for-TV movie is predictable fare. Blanche is a smalltown North Carolina, churchgoing serial killer. Her father was an abusive alcoholic, which left Blanche hiding the hatred she feels towards men. She poisons dad, an ex-boyfriend, her first husband, and goes after her fiance before anyone gets suspicious. Adapted from "Preacher's Girl: The Life and Crimes of Blanche Taylor Moore" by Jim Schultze. 92m; DVD. **C:** Elizabeth Montgomery; David Clennon; John M. Jackson; Grace Zabriskie; Bruce McGill; Mark Rolston; Directed by Alan Metzger; Written by Judith Paige Mitchell; Cinematography by Geoffrey Erb; Music by David Michael Frank. **A:** Jr. High-Adult. **P:** Entertainment. **U:** Home. **Mov-Ent**: TV Movies. **Acq:** Purchase. **Dist:** WarnerArchive.com.

The Black Windmill 1974 (PG) — ★★½
An English spy is caught between his service and the kidnapping of his family by rival spies. 102m; VHS. **C:** Michael Caine; Donald Pleasence; Delphine Seyrig; Clive Revill; Janet Suzman; John Vernon; Directed by Donald Siegel. **Pr:** Mark Huffam. **A:** Jr. High-Adult. **P:** Entertainment. **U:** Home. **Mov-Ent**: Mystery & Suspense, Great Britain, Family. **Acq:** Purchase. **Dist:** $59.95.

Black Winter 1975
Washington's army retreats after the loss of Long Island and New York. Part of "Decades of Decision" series. 22m; 3/4 U, Special order formats. **Pr:** National Geographic Society. **A:** Primary. **P:** Education. **U:** Institution, Home, SURA. **Gen-Edu**: Documentary Films, History--U.S., Revolutionary War. **Acq:** Purchase, Trade-in, Duplication License. **Dist:** National Geographic Society.

Black Women of Brazil 1986
Examines the ways Black women have coped with racism, while validating their lives through their own music and religion. 25m; VHS. **A:** College-Adult. **P:** Education. **U:** Institution. **Gen-Edu**: Women, Black Culture, Minorities. **Acq:** Purchase, Rent/Lease. **Dist:** Women Make Movies. $225.00.

Black Women On: The Light, Dark Thang 1999
African-American women discuss the politics of color within their community and how being too light or too dark has influenced their life and relationships from childhood through their adult years. 52m; VHS. **A:** Adult. **P:** Education. **U:** Institution, BCTV. **Gen-Edu**: Women, Black Culture. **Acq:** Purchase, Rent/Lease. **Dist:** Women Make Movies. $250.00.

Black Women on the Move 1991
Interviews with black women who are established in or are entering careers are used to initiate discussion about career planning and personal development. The women recount goals and challenges. 30m; VHS. **A:** Sr. High-Adult. **P:** Education. **U:** Institution. **Gen-Edu**: Women, Black Culture. **Acq:** Purchase. **Dist:** CDE Press. $20.00.

Black Women, Sexual Politics and the Revolution 1992 (Unrated)
Investigates how African American women cope with poverty, abortion, battering, and insufficient health care and discusses the fact that much of their activism and struggle is overlooked or ignored completely. 30m; VHS. **A:** Adult. **P:** Education. **U:** Institution. **Gen-Edu**: Women, Black Culture. **Acq:** Purchase. **Dist:** Third World Newsreel. $175.

Black Women Writers 1990
Writers such as Angela Davis, Alice Walker, Michelle Wallace, Mtosake Shange, and Maya Angelou explain critical judgments, stating that their success is due to the focus of their critism being placed on black males. 28m; VHS. **Pr:** Films for the Humanities. **A:** Sr. High-Adult. **P:** Education. **U:** Institution. **Gen-Edu**: Documentary Films, Women, Literature. **Acq:** Purchase. **Dist:** Films for the Humanities & Sciences. $149.00.

Black Zoo 1963 (Unrated) — ★½
Over-the-top, teeth-nashing acting from Gough as crazy Brit Michael Conrad, who owns a private zoo and is a member of an animal-worshiping cult. He's trained his big cats to attack anyone who annoys or betrays him, including his unhappy wife Edna (Cooper), who happens to have her own traveling monkey show. 88m; DVD. **C:** Michael Gough; Jeanne Cooper; Jerome Cowan; Rod Lauren; Virginia Grey; Elisha Cook, Jr.; Directed by Robert Gordon; Written by Aben Kandel; Cinematography by Floyd Crosby; Music by Paul Dunlap. **A:** Jr. High-Adult. **P:** Entertainment. **U:** Home. **Mov-Ent**: Zoos, Cults. **Acq:** Purchase. **Dist:** WarnerArchive.com.

Blackbeard 2006 (Unrated) — ★½
Angus Macfayden stars as pirate Edward "Blackbeard" Teach in this miniseries made for the Hallmark channel. Not much in the way of any form of historical accuracy, or a large budget. More of a comic-book version of Blackbeard's life, geared towards those with a serious pirate fetish. 180m; DVD, Blu-Ray. **C:** Angus MacFadyen; Mark Umbers; Richard Chamberlain; Stacy Keach; Rachel Ward; Anthony Green; Danny Midwinter; Patrick Regis; Alan Shearman; Dom Hetrakul; Nicholas Farrell; Nigel Terry; Steven Elder; Paul Brightwell; Kevin Connor; Bill Fellows; Jessica Chastain; Jasper Britton; Jake Curran; Robert Willox; Niko Nicotera; Christopher Clyde-Green; Wendy Mae Brown; Andrew Smith; Stuart Lounton; Ken Forge; Marion Valtas; Written by Bryce Zabel; Cinematography by Alan Caso; Music by Elia Cmiral. **A:** Sr. High-Adult. **P:** Entertainment. **U:** Home. **Mov-Ent**: Action-Adventure. **Acq:** Purchase. **Dist:** Echo Bridge Home Entertainment. $14.99.

Blackbeard the Pirate 1952 (Unrated) — ★★
The 18th-century buccaneer is given the full-blooded, Hollywood treatment. 99m; VHS, DVD. **C:** Robert Newton; Linda Darnell; Keith Andes; William Bendix; Richard Egan; Directed by Raoul Walsh. **Pr:** RKO. **A:** Family. **P:** Entertainment. **U:** Home. **Mov-Ent**. **Acq:** Purchase. **Dist:** Turner Broadcasting System Inc. $19.98.

Blackbeard's Ghost 1967 — ★★
Disney comedy in which the famed 18th-century pirate's spirit (Ustinov) is summoned to wreak havoc in order to prevent an old family home from being turned into a casino. 107m; VHS, DVD. **C:** Peter Ustinov; Dean Jones; Suzanne Pleshette; Elsa Lanchester; Richard Deacon; Joby Baker; Elliott Reid; Michael Conrad; Kelly Thordsen; Directed by Robert Stevenson; Written by Bill Walsh; Don DaGradi; Cinematography by Edward Colman; Music by Robert F. Brunner. **Pr:** Walt Disney Studios. **A:** Family. **P:** Entertainment. **U:** Home. **Mov-Ent**: Occult Sciences, Family Viewing. **Acq:** Purchase. **Dist:** Walt Disney Studios Home Entertainment. $14.99.

Blackbelt 2: Fatal Force 1993 (R) — ★½
A man seeks to avenge his brother's murder by going after his killers. 83m; VHS, DVD. **C:** Blake Bahner; Roxanne Baird; Michael Vlastas; Directed by Joe Mari Avellana. **Pr:** Roger Corman; Cirio H. Santiago; Concorde Pictures. **A:** Sr. High-Adult. **P:** Entertainment. **U:** Home. **Mov-Ent**: Martial Arts. **Acq:** Purchase. **Dist:** New Horizons Picture Corp. $89.98.

Blackberries in the Dark 1988
A sensitive dramatization which provides food for thought about death and the grieving process. Based on the children's book by Mavis Jukes. 26m; VHS, 3/4 U, EJ, Special order formats. **TV Std:** NTSC, PAL, SECAM. **Pr:** Disney Educational Productions. **A:** Primary-Jr. High. **P:** Education. **U:** Institution, CCTV, SURA. **Chl-Juv**: Death, Children. **Acq:** Purchase, Rent/Lease. **Dist:** Phoenix Learning Group. $79.00.

Blackberry Subway Jam 1987
Based on the Robert Munsch story, "Jonathan Cleaned Up-Then He Heard A Sound," this animated film focuses on a boy's first experience with the nightmare of bureaucracy. 9m; VHS, 3/4 U. **Pr:** Douglas McDonald. **A:** Primary. **P:** Education. **U:** Institution, SURA. **Chl-Juv**: Children, Fairy Tales, Documentary Films. **Acq:** Purchase, Rent/Lease. **Dist:** National Film Board of Canada.

Blackbird: The Movie 19??
A look at the once top-secret SR-71 Blackbird surveillance aircraft and the men who fly it. 45m; VHS. **A:** Jr. High-Adult. **P:** Education. **U:** Home. **Gen-Edu**: Military History, Documentary Films. **Acq:** Purchase. **Dist:** WNET/Thirteen Non-Broadcast. $39.95.

Blackboard Jungle 1955 — ★★★½
Well-remembered urban drama about an idealistic teacher in a slum area who fights doggedly to connect with his unruly students. Bill Hailey's "Rock Around the Clock" over the opening credits was the first use of rock music in a mainstream feature film. Based on Evan Hunter novel. 101m/B/W; VHS, DVD, CC. **C:** Glenn Ford; Anne Francis; Louis Calhern; Sidney Poitier; Vic Morrow; Richard Kiley; Margaret (Maggie) Hayes; John Hoyt; Warner Anderson; Paul Mazursky; Jamie Farr; Richard Deacon; Emile Meyer; Directed by Richard Brooks; Written by Richard Brooks; Cinematography by Russell Harlan; Music by Charles Wolcott. **Pr:** MGM. **A:** Jr. High-Adult. **P:** Entertainment. **U:** Home. **Mov-Ent**: Adolescence. **Acq:** Purchase. **Dist:** MGM Home Entertainment. $19.95.

Blackboards 2000
Film following the plight of a group of nomadic teachers in the Kurdistan mountain range in Iran. With English subtitles. 85m; DVD. **A:** Family. **P:** Entertainment. **U:** Home. **L:** Kurdish. **Mov-Ent**: Drama, Middle East. **Acq:** Purchase. **Dist:** Baseball Direct. $19.99.

Blackenstein 1973 (R) — **Bomb!**
Doctor into nouveau experimentation restores a man's arms and legs. But a jealous assistant gives our man a bogus injection, causing him to become "Blackenstein," a large African American with chip on hulking shoulder who enjoys killing people and otherwise causing big trouble. Ripe blaxploitation. 87m; VHS, DVD. **TV Std:** NTSC, PAL. **C:** John Hart; Ivory Stone; Andrea King; Liz Renay; Joe DeSue; Roosevelt Jackson; Nick Bolin; Directed by William A. Levey; Written by Frank R. Saletri; Cinematography by Robert Caramico; Music by Cardella Demilo; Lou Frohman. **Pr:** Prestige Pictures Releasing Corporation. **A:** Adult. **P:** Entertainment. **U:** Home. **Mov-Ent**: Horror, Exploitation. **Acq:** Purchase. **Dist:** Movies Unlimited. $19.95.

Blackfish 2013 (PG-13) — ★★★
Director Cowperthaite made waves, no pun intended, at the 2013 Sundance Film Festival with this documentary about Tilikum, a notoriously aggressive killer whale who ended up killing three people, including one of the most notable whale trainers in the world. Of course, Cowperthaite's film questions whether or not animals so large, intelligent, and sometimes fierce should even be kept in captivity in the first place. She traces Tilikum's outburst back to his capture in 1983 off the coast of Iceland and notes how he was kept in dark tanks for hours. The director clearly has an agenda but makes a good argument. Documentarian Gabriela Cowperthwaite's nightmarish exposé, shedding a dark light on the harsh conditions of Sea World's whale shows. From former park employee detailing their rushed and incompetent training, to graphic accounts of a whale's suppressed killer instinct, the proof gets nasty, leading to a fatal 2010 attack against a beloved trainer. Cowperthwaite isn't just saying these animals are abused, she's also saying they are wanting to abuse. Appropriately disturbing and intelligent, this whale show is definitely not for the kiddies. 83m; DVD, Blu-Ray. **C:** Directed by Gabriela Cowperthwaite; Written by Gabriela Cowperthwaite; Eli B. Despres; Cinematography by Jonathan Ingalls; Chris Towey; Music by Jeff Beal. **Pr:** Manuel Oteyza; Gabriela Cowperthwaite; Manny O Productiona; Magnolia Pictures. **A:** Jr. High-Adult. **P:** Entertainment. **U:** Home. **Mov-Ent**: Documentary Films, Fish, Animals. **Acq:** Purchase. **Dist:** Magnolia Pictures.

Blackfly 1991
Sing along with a north woodsman as he bemoans the infestation of the Great Outdoors by these pesky insects. Animated. 6m; VHS. **C:** Directed by Christopher Hinton. **Pr:** Bill Pettigrew. **A:** Jr. High-Adult. **P:** Education. **U:** Institution. **Fin-Art**: Animation & Cartoons, Insects. **Acq:** Purchase, Rent/Lease. **Dist:** National Film Board of Canada. $150.00.

Blackheart 1998 (R) — ★★
A pair of con artists have their scam down—the seductive Annette (Alonso) picks up wealthy men, then Ray (Grieco) steps in, roughs them up, and takes their cash. Things get messy when they learn of a young woman (Loewi) who has yet to learn of an enormous inheritance, and Ray steps into the role of seducer. Although the film runs out of steam in the last 20 minutes, Grieco and Loewi are likeable in the lead roles. 95m; VHS, DVD. **C:** Maria Conchita Alonso; Richard Grieco; Fiona Loewi; Christopher Plummer; Directed by Dominic Shiach; Written by Brock Simpson; Brad Simpson; Cinematography by Ousama Rawi. **A:** Sr. High-Adult. **P:** Entertainment. **U:** Home. **Mov-Ent**. **Acq:** Purchase. **Dist:** Image Entertainment Inc.

The Blackheath Poisonings 1992 (Unrated) — ★★½
The Collards and the Vandervents are toy-making families who share more than a profession—they share Albert Villa in the London suburb of Blackheath in 1894. Unhappy adults, an illicit affair, a scheming stranger—everyone has something to hide. But when a gruesome murder is committed the ensuing police inquiry will rattle both families skeletons. Based on the novel by Julian Symons. 150m; VHS, DVD. **C:** Christine Kavanagh; Ian McNeice; Zoe Wanamaker; Judy Parfitt; James Faulkner; Christien Anholt; Julia St. John; Nicholas Woodeson; Ronald Fraser; Donald (Don) Sumpter; Directed by Stuart Orme; Written by Simon Raven; Cinematography by Dick Pope; Music by Colin Towns. **A:** Jr. High-Adult. **P:** Entertainment. **U:** Home. **Mov-Ent**: Family. **Acq:** Purchase. **Dist:** WGBH/Boston.

Blackhills, Badlands & Lakes 1991
The beauty and splendor of Devil's Tower National Monument, the Blackhills and Badlands National Park, Wind Cave National Monument, Mount Rushmore and much more is experienced here. 60m; VHS. **TV Std:** NTSC, PAL, SECAM. **Pr:** Panacom Productions. **A:** Family. **P:** Entertainment. **U:** Home. **Gen-Edu**: National Parks & Reserves. **Acq:** Purchase. **Dist:** Panacom. $29.95.

Blacking Up: Hip-Hop's Mix of Race and Identity 2010 (Unrated)
Documentary on the embracing of hip-hop music by white youth and how it relates to racial identity. DVD, Streaming. **A:** Sr. High-Adult. **P:** Entertainment. **U:** Home, Institution. **L:** English. **Mov-Ent**: Documentary Films, Music--Rap. **Acq:** Purchase, Rent/Lease. **Dist:** California Newsreel. $24.95 24.95 99.00 195.00.

Blackjack 1978 (R) — ★★
Las Vegas is the scene for action and excitement as the mob puts the hit on tough guy William Smith! 104m; VHS. **C:** William (Bill) Smith; Tony Burton; Paris Earl; Damu King; Diane Summerfield; Angela May; Directed by John Evans. **A:** Sr. High-Adult. **P:** Entertainment. **U:** Home. **Mov-Ent**. **Acq:** Purchase. **Dist:** Tapeworm Video Distributors Inc.

Blackjack 1997 (R) — ★★½
Former U.S. Marshal Jack Devlin (Lundgren), who has a pathological fear of the color white, becomes the bodyguard of a young supermodel (Haskin) who's the target of a psycho killer (Mackenzie). To highlight Devlin's phobia, Woo sets one of his big action scenes in a dairy flooded with milk. 113m; VHS, DVD, CC. **C:** Dolph Lundgren; Kam Heskin; Saul Rubinek; Fred Williamson; Phillip MacKenzie; Kate Vernon; Padraigin Murphy; Directed by John Woo; Written by Peter Lance; Cinematography by Bill Wong; Music by Micky Erbe. **Pr:** John Ryan; John Woo; Terence Chang; John Woo. **A:** Sr. High-Adult. **P:** Entertainment. **U:** Home. **Mov-Ent**. **Acq:** Purchase. **Dist:** Buena Vista Home Entertainment.

Blacklight 1998 — ★★
Clairvoyant Sharon Avery (Welch) tried to help the police with a boy's abduction but it was too late and the child was found dead. In despair, Sharon gets into an auto accident and loses both her sight and, apparently, her gift. She later tries to drown herself, but suddenly sees images of another child kidnapping. Inspector Frank Shumann (Ironside) is reluctant to accept her help until a little girl is found murdered. Now Sharon is on a collison course with a child killer. 91m; VHS. **C:** Tahnee Welch; Michael Ironside; Currie Graham; Anne Marie Loder; Lori Hallier; Walter Mills; Billy Morton; Directed by Michael Storey; Cinematography by Michael Storey; Music by Ken Harrison. **A:** Sr. High-Adult. **P:** Entertainment. **U:** Home. **Mov-Ent**: Mystery & Suspense, Blindness, Suicide. **Acq:** Purchase.

Blackmail 1929 (Unrated) — ★★★
This first sound film for Great Britain and director Hitchcock features an early visualization of some typical Hitchcockian themes. The story follows the police investigation of a murder, and a detective's attempts to keep his girlfriend from being

involved. Look for Hitchcock's screen cameo. Made as a silent, this was reworked to become a talkie. 86m/B/W; VHS, DVD, 3/4 U, Special order formats. **C:** Anny Ondra; John Longden; Sara Allgood; Charles Paton; Cyril Ritchard; Donald Calthrop; Hannah Jones; Percy Parsons; Johnny Butt; Harvey Braban; Phyllis Monkman; Alfred Hitchcock; Directed by Alfred Hitchcock; Written by Charles Bennett; Benn W. Levy; Alfred Hitchcock; Garnett Weston; Cinematography by Jack Cox. **Pr:** Wardour; British International Pictures. **A:** Family. **P:** Entertainment. **U:** Home. **Mov-Ent**: Mystery & Suspense. **Acq:** Purchase. **Dist:** Synergy Entertainment, Inc.; Karol Media; Sinister Cinema. $9.98.

Blackmail 1991 (R) — ★★★
Familiar story is given new life in this suspenseful movie. Blakely is a lonely woman who succumbs to Midkiff's attentions. She doesn't suspect that he's conning her with the help of his lover, Toussaint. Engaging thriller adapted from a short story by Bill Crenshaw. 87m; VHS, CC. **C:** Susan Blakely; Dale Midkiff; Beth Toussaint; John Saxon; Mac Davis; Directed by Ruben Preuss. **Pr:** Ruben Preuss; Pacific Motion Pictures; Barry Weitz Films, Inc. **A:** Sr. High-Adult. **P:** Entertainment. **U:** Home. **Mov-Ent**: Mystery & Suspense. **Acq:** Purchase. **Dist:** Paramount Pictures Corp.

Blackmale 1999 (R) — ★½
Small-time hustlers Jimmy (Woodbine) and Luther (Pierce) bet everything on a fixed fight and lose big. Now they owe $100,000 to a loan shark. So they decide to blackmail a doctor (Rees) with an incriminating videotape and discover that their would-be mark is more dangerous than they could have imagined. 89m; VHS, DVD, Wide. **C:** Bokeem Woodbine; Justin Pierce; Roger Rees; Sascha Knopf; Erik Todd Dellums; Directed by George Baluzy; Mike Baluzy. **A:** Sr. High-Adult. **P:** Entertainment. **U:** Home. **Mov-Ent. Acq:** Purchase. **Dist:** Alpha Video; Allumination Filmworks.

Blackout 1950 (Unrated) — ★½
Blind man recovers his sight and finds that the brother of his girlfriend, once thought dead, is actually alive and well and running a smuggling ring. Routine. 73m/B/W; VHS, DVD. **C:** Maxwell Reed; Dinah Sheridan; Patric Doonan; Eric Pohlmann; Directed by Robert S. Baker. **Pr:** Eros Films. **A:** Jr. High-Adult. **P:** Entertainment. **U:** Home. **Mov-Ent**: Blindness. **Acq:** Purchase. **Dist:** VCI Entertainment. $16.95.

Blackout 1954 (Unrated) — ★★
A drunken private eye is offered a murder case, and is subsequently framed for the crime. 87m/B/W; VHS, DVD. **C:** Dane Clark; Belinda Lee; Betty Ann Davies; Eleanor Summerfield; Andrew Osborn; Harold Lang; Jill Melford; Alfie Bass; Directed by Terence Fisher; Written by Richard H. Landau; Cinematography by Walter J. (Jimmy W.) Harvey; Music by Ivor Slaney. **Pr:** Lippert Productions. **A:** Family. **P:** Entertainment. **U:** Home. **Mov-Ent**: Mystery & Suspense, Alcoholism. **Acq:** Purchase. **Dist:** VCI Entertainment. $89.98.

Blackout 1978 (R) — ★★
Four killers terrorize an office building during the 1977 New York electrical blackout. Soon the police enter, confront them, and the fun starts. Comic touches provide some relief from the violence here. 86m; VHS, DVD. **C:** Jim Mitchum; Robert Carradine; Ray Milland; June Allyson; Jean-Pierre Aumont; Belinda J. Montgomery; Directed by Eddy Matalon; Written by Joseph Stefano. **Pr:** Nicole M. Boisvert; Eddy Matalon. **A:** Jr. High-Adult. **P:** Entertainment. **U:** Home. **Mov-Ent**: Action-Adventure. **Acq:** Purchase. **Dist:** New Line Home Video. $59.95.

Blackout 1985 (Unrated) — ★★½
Cable thriller in which an aging police chief suspects a disfigured amnesiac is responsible for past killings, in spite of the fact that he now leads a subdued family life. 99m; VHS. **C:** Richard Widmark; Keith Carradine; Kathleen Quinlan; Michael Beck; Gerald Hiken; Directed by Douglas Hickox; Written by David Ambrose. **Pr:** HBO; Peregrine Productions. **A:** Sr. High-Adult. **P:** Entertainment. **U:** Home. **Mov-Ent**: Mystery & Suspense, TV Movies. **Acq:** Purchase. **Dist:** Unknown Distributor.

Blackout 1988 (R) — ★★
Strange memories from childhood come back to her as a woman fights for her life. 91m; VHS. **C:** Carol Lynley; Gail O'Grady; Michael Keys Hall; Joseph Gian; Joanna Miles; Directed by Doug Adams; Cinematography by Arledge Armenaki. **Pr:** Joseph Stefano; Doug Adams. **A:** College-Adult. **P:** Entertainment. **U:** Home. **Mov-Ent**: Horror. **Acq:** Purchase. **Dist:** No Longer Available.

The Blackout 1997 (R) — ★
Movie star Matty (Modine) has multiple addictions he indulges on a trip home to Miami. He proposes to pregnant girlfriend Annie (Dalle) but when he learns she's had an abortion, Matty goes on a binge and suffers a blackout. 18 months later in New York, Matty has kicked his addictions and found Susan (Schiffer) but his nightmares compel him back to Miami and the possibility that he committed murder. Sleazy and the symbolism is heavy-handed. 100m; VHS, DVD, Wide, CC. **C:** Matthew Modine; Beatrice Dalle; Claudia Schiffer; Dennis Hopper; Sarah Lassez; Directed by Abel Ferrara; Written by Abel Ferrara; Chris Zois; Marla Hanson; Cinematography by Ken Kelsch; Music by Joe Delia. **Pr:** Trimark Pictures. **A:** Sr. High-Adult. **P:** Entertainment. **U:** Home. **Mov-Ent**: Drug Abuse. **Acq:** Purchase. **Dist:** Sony Pictures Home Entertainment Inc.

Blackout 2007 (R) — ★½
A psycho-thriller unfairly marketed as a horror flick. Three troubled strangers are trapped in an elevator in a nearly-deserted building because of a blackout. Naturally, one of the three turns out to be a killer. Lots of flashbacks set up the clues as to who and why. Too short to wear out its welcome but not as intense as you might expect. 74m; DVD. **C:** Amber Tamblyn; Aidan Gillen; Katie Stuart; Armie Hammer; Directed by Rigoberto Castaneda; Written by Ed Dougherty; Cinematography by Alejandro Martinez; Music by Reinhold Heil; Johnny Klimek. **A:** Sr. High-Adult. **P:** Entertainment. **U:** Home. **Mov-Ent**: Mystery & Suspense. **Acq:** Purchase. **Dist:** Image Entertainment Inc.

Blackpool's Trams ????
Covers the electric tramway in Blackpool, England—the country's first—with footage of rides and equipment. 120m; VHS, DVD. **A:** College-Adult. **P:** Education. **U:** Home. **Gen-Edu**: Trains. **Acq:** Purchase. **Dist:** The Civil War Standard. $35.95.

Blackrock 1997 — ★★
Cliched though dramatic saga, inspired by a true story, and adapted by Enright from his play. Uncommunicative teenager Jared (Breuls) throws a bash upon the return to town of his best surfing bud Ricko (Lyndon). The party gets out of control and Jared witnesses a group of his mates beating and raping Tracey (Novakovitch), who's discovered dead the next morning. Her death attracts rabid media attention and divides the community while Jared is filled with guilt for doing nothing to stop the act. But his conflicts increase when he realizes the extent of Ricko's involvement and he tries to decide where his loyalties lie. 100m; VHS, DVD. **C:** Laurence Breuls; Simon Lyndon; Linda Cropper; Rebecca Smart; David Field; Chris Haywood; Boyana Novakovitch; Directed by Steven Vidler; Written by Nick Enright; Cinematography by Martin McGrath; George Greenough; Music by Steve Kilbey. **Pr:** David Elfick; Australian Film Finance Corp; Palm Beach Pictures; Polygram Filmed Entertainment. **A:** Sr. High-Adult. **P:** Entertainment. **U:** Home. **Mov-Ent**: Crime Drama, Rape, Australia. **Acq:** Purchase. **Dist:** Vanguard International Cinema, Inc.

Blacks and Jews 1997
Collaborative effort by Jewish and African American filmmakers attempts to find the causes and heal the misunderstandings and mistrust that has developed between the two groups since the waning of the civil rights movement. 85m; VHS. **A:** Sr. High-Adult. **P:** Education. **U:** Home, Institution. **Gen-Edu**: Black Culture, Civil Rights, Judaism. **Acq:** Purchase. **Dist:** California Newsreel. $195.00.

Blacks and the Constitution 1987
A look at how the rights of blacks have changed in this country from slavery times to the present, with respect to the Constitution. 60m; VHS, 3/4 U. **Pr:** PBS. **A:** Jr. High-Adult. **P:** Education. **U:** Institution, CCTV, CATV. **Gen-Edu**: Documentary Films, Minorities, Black Culture. **Acq:** Purchase, Rent/Lease. **Dist:** PBS Home Video. $59.95.

Blacks and the Movies 1977
Presents an interview with film critic Donald Bogle. 30m; 3/4 U, EJ. **Pr:** NETCHE. **A:** College-Adult. **P:** Education. **U:** Institution, CCTV, BCTV, SURA. **Fin-Art**: Documentary Films, Black Culture, Film History. **Acq:** Purchase, Rent/Lease, Subscription. **Dist:** NETCHE.

Blacks, Blues, Black 1967
Angelou develops and demonstrates history, heritage, and habits of blacks and how their mores and values have been preserved and assimilated into society. 57m; VHS, 3/4 U. **C:** Maya Angelou. **Pr:** KQED San Francisco. **A:** Family. **P:** Education. **U:** Institution, CCTV, CATV. **Gen-Edu**: Documentary Films, Sociology, Black Culture. **Acq:** Purchase, Rent/Lease, Off-Air Record. **Dist:** PBS Home Video.
Indiv. Titles: 1. African Cultural Carry-over Positive 2. Negative Cultural Carry-over 3. Positive Aspects in Teaching African History 4. Black Music in Passage 5. Negative Aspects in Teaching African History 6. Aspirations in Black American Youth in Education 7. Avoiding Useless or NonApplicable Education 8. Black Art and Black Literature 9. Violence in Black American Life 10. Summary.

Blacks Britannica 1978
Provides an analysis of the racial and economic oppression of blacks within modern British society using the context of British history and economic post-war crises. Also offers a look at the growing politicization of blacks in England. 58m; VHS. **C:** Directed by David Koff. **A:** College-Adult. **P:** Education. **U:** Home. **Gen-Edu**: Black Culture, Prejudice, Great Britain. **Acq:** Purchase. **Dist:** Facets Multimedia Inc. $39.95.

The Blacksmith 1979
A village blacksmith discusses his trade and provides an historical review of the blacksmith's role from colonial times to the 20th Century. 10m; VHS, 3/4 U. **Pr:** Encyclopedia Britannica Educational Corporation; Silver Dollar City Inc. **A:** Primary-Jr. High. **P:** Education. **U:** Institution, SURA. **Gen-Edu**: Documentary Films, Animals. **Acq:** Purchase, Rent/Lease, Trade-in. **Dist:** Encyclopedia Britannica.

The Blacksmith/The Cops 1922
"The Blacksmith" is a burlesque of Longfellow's famous poem "The Village Blacksmith." In "Cops" Buster tries a new business venture to win his girl's hand. Chaos ensues. Silent comedy at its most adroit. 38m/B/W; Silent; VHS. **C:** Buster Keaton; Virginia Fox. **Pr:** Comique Film Company. **A:** Family. **P:** Entertainment. **U:** Home. **Mov-Ent**: Silent Films. **Acq:** Purchase. **Dist:** $19.95.

Blacksnake! 1973 (R) — **Bomb!**
Overheated sex and race tale, set in 1835, finds a British lord travelling to a Caribbean island in search of his brother. What he finds is his sadistic sister-in-law and her evil overseer using violence to keep the slaves in line. 83m; VHS. **C:** Anouska (Anoushka) Hempel; David Warbeck; Percy Herbert; David Prowse; Milton McCollin; Directed by Russ Meyer; Written by Russ Meyer; Leonard Neubauer; Cinematography by Arthur Ornitz; Music by William Loose; Al Teeter. **A:** College-Adult. **P:** Entertainment. **U:** Home. **Mov-Ent**: Slavery. **Acq:** Purchase. **Dist:** RM Films International, Inc. $89.95.

Blackthorn 2011 (R) — ★★½
Old-fashioned, understated western takes on the mythology of Butch Cassidy. This version presumes that Butch was not killed in Bolivia in 1908, instead he's been living under the name James Blackthorn (Shepard), raising horses on his ranch. But in 1927, homesickness pushes the world-weary Blackthorn to decide to return to the States. He runs into trouble—and one last adventure—thanks to Eduardo (Noreiga), who's stolen money from the wrong man. Flashbacks to his younger days (so the Sundance Kid and Etta Place can make an appearance) and betrayal follow. English and Spanish with subtitles. 98m; DVD, On Demand. **C:** Sam Shepard; Eduardo Noreiga; Stephen Rea; Magaly Solier; Nikolaj Coster-Waldau; Padraic Delaney; Dominique McElligott; Directed by Mateo Gil; Written by Miguel Barros; Cinematography by Juan Ruiz Anchia; Music by Lucio Godoy. **Pr:** Ibon Cormenzana; Andres Santana; Quickfire Films; Arcadia Motion Pictures; Aiete-Ariane Films; Magnolia Pictures. **A:** Sr. High-Adult. **P:** Entertainment. **U:** Home. **L:** Spanish, English. **Mov-Ent**: Western, South America, Aging. **Acq:** Purchase. **Dist:** Magnolia Home Entertainment.

Blackwater Trail 1995 (R) — ★★
Novelist Matt Curran (Nelson) travels from L.A. to Michelton, Australia, to attend the funeral of his best friend Andy, a cop who supposedly committed suicide. But Andy's sister (and Matt's former lover) Cathy (Smart) thinks he was murdered because of a case involving a serial killer. Matt decides to snoop around and finds out the killer likes to leave behind body parts and biblical quotations. Contrived plotting but some good performances and some spectacular scenery. 100m; VHS, CC. **C:** Judd Nelson; Dee Smart; Peter Phelps; Mark Lee; Brett Climo; Directed by Ian Barry; Written by Andrew Russell; Cinematography by John Stokes; Music by Stephen Rae. **Pr:** John Sexton; Chris Brown; Australian Film Finance Corp; Portman Productions. **A:** Sr. High-Adult. **P:** Entertainment. **U:** Home. **Mov-Ent**: Mystery & Suspense, Australia, Bible. **Acq:** Purchase. **Dist:** Warner Home Video, Inc.

Blackwater Valley Exorcism 2006 (R) — ★
A daughter becomes possessed and the family calls a priest for an exorcism. Unfortunately he's not the most innocent of priests, and they aren't the most well-intentioned of families. Honestly you may end up rooting for the Devil. 90m; DVD, Streaming. **C:** Cameron Daddo; James Russo; Jeffrey Combs; Randy Colton; Del Zamora; Kristin Erickson; Directed by Ethan Wiley; Written by Ellary Eddy; Cinematography by Roel Reine; Music by Joseph Bauer. **A:** Sr. High-Adult. **P:** Entertainment. **U:** Home. **L:** English, Spanish. **Mov-Ent. Acq:** Purchase, Rent/Lease. **Dist:** Lions Gate Home Entertainment. $14.98 9.99.

Blackwell's Island 1939 — ★★
Crime programmer from Warner Bros. stars Garfield as crusading reporter Tim Haydon and is based on a true incident from 1934. Haydon goes undercover to expose corruption at New York's notorious Blackwell's Island penitentiary. The weak warden (Bates) looks the other way as mob boss Bull Bransom (Fields) runs the show. When Bull gets suspicious of the new inmate, Haydon's in real trouble. 71m/B/W; DVD. **C:** John Garfield; Stanley Fields; Rosemary Lane; Dick Purcell; Victor Jory; Granville Bates; Directed by William McGann; Written by Crane Wilbur; Cinematography by Sidney Hickox. **A:** Adult. **P:** Entertainment. **U:** Home. **L:** English. **Mov-Ent**: Crime Drama, Journalism. **Acq:** Purchase. **Dist:** WarnerArchive.com.

Blackwood 1978
One of Canada's greatest contemporary printmakers, David Blackwood, presents his work inspired by memories of life in Wesleyville, Newfoundland. 28m; VHS, 3/4 U. **Pr:** Tom Daly. **A:** Jr. High-Adult. **P:** Education. **U:** Institution, SURA. **Fin-Art**: Documentary Films, Art & Artists. **Acq:** Purchase. **Dist:** Phoenix Learning Group.

Blackwoods 2002 (R) — **Bomb!**
It's just like a M. Night Shyamalan movie... only much, much worse. Uwe Boll, Germany's answer to Ed Wood, directs this pointless thriller that apes every third-act twist cliche in the book. Matt (Muldoon) and Dawn (Tracy) drive up to the "Blackwoods" to visit Dawn's hillbilly family, but after checking into a creepy motel (staffed by Clint Howard, no less), Dawn disappears and crazy axe-wielding psychos start attacking Matt. It's all leading up to one big twist that's telegraphed further than a ten-meter cattle prod. Honestly, if you can't figure out the whole movie in the first five minutes, you should put down the airplane glue and move your trailer away from the power lines. 90m; VHS, DVD. **C:** Patrick Muldoon; Keegan Connor Tracy; Michael Pare; Clint Howard; Will Sanderson; Matthew (Matt) Walker; Anthony Harrison; Janet Wright; Sean Campbell; Ben Derrick; Directed by Uwe Boll; Written by Robert Dean Klein; Uwe Boll; Cinematography by Mathias Neumann; Music by Reinhard Besser. **A:** Sr. High-Adult. **P:** Entertainment. **U:** Home. **L:** English. **Mov-Ent**: Mystery & Suspense, Forests & Trees. **Acq:** Purchase. **Dist:** Velocity Home Entertainment.

Blacula 1972 (PG) — ★★
The African Prince Mamuwalde stalks the streets of Los Angeles trying to satisfy his insatiable desire for blood. Mildly successful melding of blaxploitation and horror that spawned a sequel, "Scream, Blacula, Scream." 92m; VHS, DVD. **C:** William Marshall; Thalmus Rasulala; Denise Nicholas; Vonetta McGee; Gordon Pinsent; Emily Yancy; Charles Macaulay; Ted Harris; Elisha Cook, Jr.; Lance Taylor; Directed by William Crain; Written by Raymond Koenig; Joan Torres; Cinematography by John Stevens; Music by Gene Page. **Pr:** American International Pictures. **A:** Sr. High-Adult. **P:** Entertainment. **U:** Home. **Mov-Ent**: Horror. **Acq:** Purchase. **Dist:** MGM Studios Inc. $9.98.

Blade 1972 (PG) — ★★
An honest cop challenges a dirty cover-up in killer-stalked New York. 79m; VHS. **C:** Steve Landesberg; John Schuck; Kathryn Walker; Directed by Ernest Pintoff. **Pr:** Heritage Enterprises Productions. **A:** Jr. High-Adult. **P:** Entertainment. **U:** Home. **Mov-Ent. Acq:** Purchase. **Dist:** $59.95.

Blade 1998 (R) — ★★
Action-packed gore-fest that provides for high-octane escapist entertainment, with some eye-catching visuals and a pulsating techno soundtrack. Blade (Snipes) is a half-vampire/half-human, who's intent on preventing evil, ambitious Deacon Frost (Dorff) from unleashing a vampire apocalypse upon humanity so he can take over. Helping out Blade are his grizzled mentor, vampire hunter Abraham Whistler (Kristofferson), and Dr. Karen Janson (Wright), who's searching for a cure for vampirism. Adapted from the Marvel comic book character. 91m; VHS, DVD, Blu-Ray, UMD, CC. **C:** Wesley Snipes; Stephen Dorff; Kris Kristofferson; N'Bushe Wright; Donal Logue; Udo Kier; Traci Lords; Tim Guinee; Arly Jover; Sanaa Lathan; Directed by Stephen Norrington; Written by David S. Goyer; Cinematography by Theo van de Sande; Music by Mark Isham. **Pr:** Peter Frankfurt; Wesley Snipes; Robert Engleman; Lynn Harris; Stan Lee; Avi Arad; Joseph Calimari; Wesley Snipes; Amen Ra; Imaginary Forces; New Line Cinema. **A:** Sr. High-Adult. **P:** Entertainment. **U:** Home. **Mov-Ent:** Horror, Black Culture. **Awds:** MTV Movie Awards '99: Villain (Dorff). **Acq:** Purchase. **Dist:** New Line Home Video.

Blade 2 2002 (R) — ★★
Sequel takes the more, more, more approach—more vampires, more battles, more gore. Half-vampire, half-human daywalker Blade (Snipes at his coolest) first rescues mentor Whistler (Kristofferson) from the vamps who have been holding him prisoner. Then, he's offered a truce by vampire overload Damaskinos (Kretschmann) who needs Blade to hunt an even more deadly enemy. The rat-like Reapers feed on both humans and vampires and their bite turns their victims into insatiable bloodsuckers themselves. Of course, as Blade goes a-huntin', he discovers the situation isn't as clear-cut as it seems. 116m; VHS, DVD, Blu-Ray. **C:** Wesley Snipes; Kris Kristofferson; Ron Perlman; Leonor Varela; Norman Reedus; Thomas Kretschmann; Luke Goss; Matt Schulze; Donnie Yen; Danny John Jules; Daz Crawford; Karel Roden; Tony Curran; Santiago Segura; Marit Velle Kile; Directed by Guillermo del Toro; Written by David S. Goyer; Cinematography by Gabriel Beristain; Music by Marco Beltrami; Danny Saber. **Pr:** Peter Frankfurt; Wesley Snipes; Patrick Palmer; Wesley Snipes; Amen Ra; Imaginary Forces; New Line Cinema. **A:** Sr. High-Adult. **P:** Entertainment. **U:** Home. **Mov-Ent. Acq:** Purchase. **Dist:** New Line Home Video.

Blade Boxer 1997 — ★
Police detectives go undercover to expose an illegal fight ring that has its combatants battling to the death, and equipped with deadly steel talons. 91m; VHS, DVD. **C:** Kevin King; Todd McKee; Andrew Martino; Cass Magda; Dana Plato; Directed by Bruce Reisman. **A:** Sr. High-Adult. **P:** Entertainment. **U:** Home. **Mov-Ent:** Boxing. **Acq:** Purchase. **Dist:** Bedford Entertainment Inc.

Blade: House of Chthon 2006
Pilot for the brief Spike TV series finds daywalker Blade teaming up with revenge-minded Krista Starr to defeat the vampire overlord Marcus. Seems the sect of vampires from the ancient House of Chthon is out to create a vaccine that will make super-vampires that are immune to the usual weaknesses and Blade is out to stop them. Based on the Marvel comic character. 89m; DVD, CC. **C:** Kirk Jones; Neil Jackson; Jill Wagner; Directed by Peter O'Fallon; Written by David S. Goyer; Geoff Jones. **A:** Sr. High-Adult. **P:** Entertainment. **U:** Home. **Mov-Ent:** Television Series. **Acq:** Purchase. **Dist:** New Line Home Video.

Blade in Hong Kong 1985 — ★★½
Investigator travels to Hong Kong, finds trouble and romance in the underbelly of the city. Pilot for un-sold series. 100m; VHS. **C:** Terry Lester; Keye Luke; Mike (Michael) Preston; Jean-Marie Hon; Leslie Nielsen; Nancy Kwan; Anthony Newley; Ellen Regan; Directed by Reza Badiyi. **A:** Adult. **P:** Entertainment. **U:** Home. **Mov-Ent. Acq:** Purchase. **Dist:** No Longer Available.

A Blade in the Dark 1983 (Unrated) — ★★
A young man composing a score for a horror film moves into a secluded villa and is inspired and haunted by the mysterious murder he witnesses. 104m; VHS, DVD, Wide. **C:** Andrea Occhipinti; Anny Papa; Michele (Michael) Soavi; Fabiola Toledo; Valeria Cavalli; Lara Naszinsky; Directed by Lamberto Bava; Written by Dardano Sacchetti; Cinematography by Gianlorenzo Battaglia; Music by Guido de Angelis; Maurizio de Angelis. **A:** Sr. High-Adult. **P:** Entertainment. **U:** Home. **Mov-Ent:** Horror, Italy. **Acq:** Purchase. **Dist:** Lions Gate Television Corp. $69.98.

Blade Master 1984 (PG) — ★½
In this sequel to "Ator the Fighting Eagle," O'Keeffe as Ator is back as the Blade Master. Ator defends his people and his family name in a battle against the "Geometric Nucleus": a primitive bomb. His quest leads him and his small band of men to the castle of knowledge. D'Amato used the pseudonym David Hills. 92m; VHS. **C:** Miles O'Keeffe; Lisa Foster; Directed by Joe D'Amato. **Pr:** Chris Trainor. **A:** Jr. High-Adult. **P:** Entertainment. **U:** Home. **Mov-Ent:** Birds. **Acq:** Purchase. **Dist:** No Longer Available.

Blade of the Ripper 1970 (Unrated) — **Bomb!**
A madman armed with a razor slashes his way through the lovelies of the international jet set. 90m; VHS, DVD. **TV Std:** NTSC, PAL. **C:** George Hilton; Edwige Fenech; Alberto De Mendoza; Ivan Rassimov; Directed by Sergio Martino; Written by Ernesto Gastaldi; Eduardo Brochero. **Pr:** Regal Video. **A:** Adult. **P:** Entertainment. **U:** Home. **Mov-Ent:** Horror. **Acq:** Purchase. **Dist:** Unknown Distributor.

Blade Runner 1982 (R) — ★★★½
Los Angeles, the 21st century. World-weary cop tracks down a handful of renegade "replicants" (synthetically produced human slaves who, with only days left of life, search madly for some way to extend their prescribed lifetimes). Moody, beautifully photographed, dark thriller with sets from an architect's dream. Based on "Do Androids Dream of Electric Sheep" by Philip K. Dick. Director's cut, released at 117 minutes, removes Ford's narration and the last scene of the film, which Scott considered too "up," and inserts several short scenes, including a dream sequence. 122m; VHS, DVD, Blu-Ray, HD-DVD, 8 mm, Wide. **C:** Harrison Ford; Rutger Hauer; Sean Young; Daryl Hannah; M. Emmet Walsh; Edward James Olmos; Joe Turkel; Brion James; Joanna Cassidy; William Sanderson; James Hong; Directed by Ridley Scott; Written by Hampton Fancher; David Peoples; Cinematography by Jordan Cronenweth; Music by Vangelis. **Pr:** Michael Deeley. **A:** Sr. High-Adult. **P:** Entertainment. **U:** Home. **Mov-Ent:** Science Fiction, Technology, Cult Films. **Awds:** L.A. Film Critics '82: Cinematog.; Natl. Film Reg. '93. **Acq:** Purchase. **Dist:** Sony Pictures Home Entertainment Inc.; Warner Home Video, Inc. $9.95.

Blade: The Series: House of Chthon 2006
The House of Chthon is an ancient evil sect of vampires led by overlord Marcus, whose prime objective is to create a vaccine that will develop a super new breed of vampire immune to their generational weaknesses. Blade is the sword-wielding hero who takes daily injections of a special serum to keep his bloodsucking tendencies in check, but when the ruthless and beautiful Krista Starr shows up seeking revenge for her brother's murder, he is forced to accommodate her and infiltrate the sect's secret lair. 30 episodes. 88m; DVD. **C:** Kirk "Sticky Fingaz" Jones; Jill Wagner; Neil Jackson; Jessica Gower. **A:** Sr. High-Adult. **P:** Entertainment. **U:** Home. **Mov-Ent:** Action-Adventure, Fantasy, Science Fiction. **Acq:** Purchase. **Dist:** New Line Home Video.

Blade: The Series—The Complete Series 2006
Picking up where the theatrical installment "Blade: Trinity" left off, Kirk "Sticky Fingaz" Jones steps into the role of Blade, leader of the hunt for House of Chthon bloodsuckers whose leader Marcus Van Sciver is working on a serum that will empower vampires against their only weaknesses, sunlight and garlic. Army vet Krista Star, who lost her humanity to Van Sciver, is there to aid Blade in the sword and martial arts battles. 13 episodes. 583m; DVD. **C:** Kirk "Sticky Fingaz" Jones; Jill Wagner. **A:** Adult. **P:** Entertainment. **U:** Home. **Mov-Ent:** Drama, Action-Adventure. **Acq:** Purchase. **Dist:** New Line Home Video.

Blade: Trinity 2004 (R) — ★★
The last of the "Blade" trilogy (at least with the stoic Snipes), bloody actioner sticks to what it does best, this time with writer Goyer also taking on directing chores. Bitchy bloodsucker Danica (a gleeful Posey), who leads the Vampire Nation, decides to wake up Dracula, aka Drake (Purcell)?whose blood will allow them to walk in the daylight. Blade is busy doing his slaying thing when he gets involved—along with a couple of mouthy youngsters, dishy Abigail (Biel), who happens to be Whistler's (Kristofferson) daughter, and wisecracking recovered vamp Hannibal King (Reynolds). There is, of course, a final mano a mano battle between Blade and Drac, uh, Drake. The ending also leaves wiggle room for the younger actors to continue the bloodletting. 105m; VHS, DVD, Blu-Ray. **C:** Wesley Snipes; Kris Kristofferson; Jessica Biel; Ryan Reynolds; Parker Posey; Dominic Purcell; John Michael Higgins; James Remar; Eric Bogosian; Patton Oswalt; Callum Keith Rennie; Natasha Lyonne; Mark Berry; Francoise Yip; Christopher Heyerdahl; Paul Anthony; Directed by David S. Goyer; Written by David S. Goyer; Cinematography by Gabriel Beristain; Music by RZA; Ramin Djawadi. **Pr:** Peter Frankfurt; Wesley Snipes; Lynn Harris; Wesley Snipes; Amen Ra; New Line Cinema. **A:** Sr. High-Adult. **P:** Entertainment. **U:** Home. **Mov-Ent:** Fantasy, Horror, Federal Bureau of Investigation (FBI). **Dist:** New Line Home Video. $29.95.

Blades 1989 (R) — ★
Another junk heap from Troma, dealing with the efforts of three golfers who try to stop a maniacal power mower that's been grinding duffers with regularity. 101m; VHS, DVD. **C:** Robert North; Jeremy Whelan; Victoria Scott; Jon McBride; Directed by Thomas R. Rondinella; Written by William R. Pace; Cinematography by James Hayman; Music by John Hodian. **Pr:** John P. Finegan. **A:** Preschool. **P:** Entertainment. **U:** Home. **Mov-Ent:** Horror, Golf, Technology. **Acq:** Purchase. **Dist:** Movies Unlimited. $14.99.

Blades of Courage 1988 (Unrated) — ★★
Biography of Olympic skater Lori Larouche. Choreographed by Debbi Wilkes. 98m; VHS. **C:** Lynn Nightingale; Christianne Hirt; Colm Feore; Rosemary Dunsmore; Directed by Randy Bradshaw. **Pr:** Academy Entertainment. **A:** Family. **P:** Entertainment. **U:** Home. **Mov-Ent:** Sports--Olympic, TV Movies, Biography. **Acq:** Purchase. **Dist:** Unknown Distributor.

Blades of Glory 2007 (PG-13) — ★★½
Lumpy Ferrell gets a mullet and stuffs himself into spandex and sparkles to play bad boy ice skater Chazz Michael Michaels, whose rival is wispy blonde peacock Jimmy MacElroy (Heder). After the two are banned from singles competition for public brawling, a loophole allows them to compete as the first male/male pairs skating team, much to the disgust of oh-so-close brother/sister skating champs, the Van Waldenbergs (real-life spouses Arnett and Poehler). The jokes are obvious, which doesn't necessarily mean they aren't funny. 93m; DVD, Blu-Ray, HD-DVD. **C:** Will Ferrell; Jon Heder; Amy Poehler; Will Arnett; Jenna Fischer; Craig T. Nelson; William Fichtner; Nick Swardson; Directed by Will Speck; Josh Gordon; Written by Jeff Cox; Craig Cox; John Altschuler; Dave Krinsky; Cinematography by Stefan Czapsky; Music by Theodore Shapiro. **Pr:** Ben Stiller; Stuart Cornfeld; John Jacobs; DreamWorks SKG; Red Hour; Smart Entertainment; Paramount. **A:** Jr. High-Adult. **P:** Entertainment. **U:** Home. **L:** English. **Mov-Ent:** Sports--Olympic, Men, Skating. **Acq:** Purchase. **Dist:** DreamWorks Home Entertainment.

Blaine Taylor: 14 Options for the Transition Game 2007 (Unrated)
Coach Blaine Taylor gives an on-court demonstration of full court offensive techniques for basketball teams to employ. 70m; DVD. **A:** Family. **P:** Education. **U:** Home, Institution. **Spo-Rec:** Basketball, Athletic Instruction/Coaching. **Acq:** Purchase. **Dist:** Championship Productions. $39.99.

Blaine Taylor: Scoring Against Pressure Defense and Trapping 2008
Coach Blaine Taylor demonstrates how to beat pressure defenses and trapping for basketball players. 71m; DVD. **A:** Family. **P:** Education. **U:** Home, Institution. **Spo-Rec:** Basketball, Athletic Instruction/Coaching. **Acq:** Purchase. **Dist:** Championship Productions. $39.99.

The Blair Witch Project 1999 (R) — ★★
A Sundance Film Festival favorite, this low-budget horror film turned out to be the most successful indie ever, thanks to heavy (and savvy) market promotion. In 1994, a three-person film crew heads into the Black Hills region of Maryland to document a local legend about a demonic apparition. They vanish, but a year later their film footage is found and this amateurish, black and white footage makes up what the audience sees. Largely improvisational, the film manages a palpable sense of dread and claustrophobia, while being (deliberately) technically crude. However, the herky-jerky camera movements made a number of viewers physically sick and an equal number found the would-be theatrics boring. 87m; VHS, DVD, Blu-Ray. **C:** Michael Williams; Heather Donahue; Joshua Leonard; Directed by Eduardo Sanchez; Daniel Myrick; Written by Eduardo Sanchez; Daniel Myrick; Cinematography by Neal Fredericks; Music by Tony Cora. **Pr:** Artisan Pictures, Inc. **A:** Sr. High-Adult. **P:** Entertainment. **U:** Home. **Mov-Ent:** Horror, Filmmaking, Folklore & Legends. **Awds:** Golden Raspberries '99: Worst Actress (Donahue). **Acq:** Purchase. **Dist:** Lions Gate Television Corp.

Blaise Pascal 1971 — ★★★½
Another of Rossellini's later historical portraits, detailing the life and times of the 17th-century philosopher, seen as a man whose scientific ideas conflicted with his own religious beliefs. Italian with subtitles. 131m; VHS, DVD. **C:** Pierre Arditti; Giuseppe Addobati; Christian de Sica; Rita Forzano; Directed by Roberto Rossellini; Written by Roberto Rossellini; Cinematography by Mario Fioretti; Music by Mario Nascimbene. **Pr:** Roberto Rosselini. **A:** Sr. High-Adult. **P:** Entertainment. **U:** Home. **L:** Italian. **Mov-Ent:** Drama, TV Movies, Philosophy & Ideology. **Acq:** Purchase. **Dist:** Criterion Collection Inc. $79.95.

Blake Ball 1989
This program explores the world of poet/painter William Blake, using the game of baseball as a metaphor. 16m; VHS, 3/4 U, Special order formats. **Pr:** Emily Hubley. **A:** Sr. High-Adult. **P:** Education. **U:** Institution, Home, SURA. **Gen-Edu:** Documentary Films, Literature--English. **Acq:** Purchase, Rent/Lease, Duplication License. **Dist:** Pyramid Media. $225.00.

Blake Island/Puget Sound Guide 19??
Provides the lowdown on sailboat vacationing in this primiere desrination in the Pacific Northwest and surrounding camp sites. 30m; VHS. **A:** College-Adult. **P:** Entertainment. **U:** Home. **Spo-Rec:** Boating, Travel. **Acq:** Purchase. **Dist:** Bennett Marine Video. $19.95.

Blake of Scotland Yard 1936 — ★★½
Blake, the former Scotland Yard inspector, battles against a villain who has constructed a murderous death ray. Condensed version of the 15 episode serial (originally at 180 minutes). 70m/B/W; VHS, DVD. **C:** Ralph Byrd; Herbert Rawlinson; Joan Barclay; Lloyd Hughes; Directed by Robert F. "Bob" Hill. **Pr:** Victory. **A:** Family. **P:** Entertainment. **U:** Home. **Mov-Ent:** Science Fiction, Serials. **Acq:** Purchase. **Dist:** Rex Miller Artisan Studio; Sinister Cinema. $24.95.

Blake's Seven 1978
Freedom-fighter Blake and his crew battle against a totalitarian super-power in this futuristic space adventure series from Great Britain. Created by Terry Nation of "Doctor Who" fame. Each volume contains two episodes and is available individually. 105m; VHS. **C:** Gareth Thomas; Sally Knyvette; Paul Darrow; Michael Keating; David Jackson; Jan Chappell; Directed by Michael E. Briant; Vere Lorrimer. **Pr:** David Maloney; British Broadcasting Corporation. **A:** Family. **P:** Entertainment. **U:** Home. **Mov-Ent:** Television Series, Science Fiction. **Acq:** Purchase. **Dist:** Video Collectibles; Movies Unlimited; Fusion Video. $24.98.

Indiv. Titles: 1. The Way Back/Space Fall 2. Cygnus Alpha/Time Squad 3. The Web/Seek-Locate-Destroy 4. Mission to Destiny/Duel 5. Project Avalon/Breakdown 6. Bounty/Deliverance 7. Orac/Redemption 8. Shadow/Weapon 9. Horizon/Pressure Point 10. Trial/Killer 11. Hostage/Countdown 12. Voice from the Past/Gambit 13. The Keeper/Star One 14. Aftermath/Powerplay 15. Volcano/Dawn of the Gods 16. The Harvest of Kairos/City at the Edge of the World 17. Children of Auron/Rumors of Death 18. Sarcophagus/Ultraworld 19. Moloch/Death-Watch 20. Terminal/Rescue 21. Power/Traitor

22. Stardrive/Animals 23. Headhunter/Assassin 24. Games/Sand 25. Gold/Orbit 26. Warlord/Blake.

The Blame Game: Are We a Country of Victims? 1994
John Stossel examines the tendency to blame our misfortunes on anyone but ourselves and how this victimization affects public policy and the workplace. Features improbable lawsuits and the weaknesses of Social Security and laws. 50m; VHS. **Pr:** ABC News. **A:** College-Adult. **P:** Education. **U:** Home, Institution. **Gen-Edu:** Journalism, Sociology. **Acq:** Purchase. **Dist:** MPI Media Group. $19.98.

Blame It on Fidel 2006 (Unrated) — ★★½
Amusing and tender film told from the point of view of nine-year-old Anna (Kervel), who becomes increasingly upset when her bourgeois parents, Fernando (Accorsi) and Marie (Depardieu, daughter of Gerard), suddenly decide to devote their time and money to various political/activist causes (it's 1970 in Paris). She and her younger brother are moved from their comfortable home to a shabby apartment and are left in the care of oddball political refugees. Anna doesn't take well to all these changes and is confused about what she hears and is told to believe. Writer/director Gavras is the daughter of political filmmaker Costas-Gavras. French with subtitles. 100m; DVD. **C:** Julie Depardieu; Stefano Accorsi; Olivier Perrier; Nina Kremer; Benjamin Feuillet; Martine Chevallier; Marie Kremer; Marie-Noelle Bordeaux; Directed by Julie Gavras; Written by Julie Gavras; Cinematography by Nathalie Durant; Music by Armand Amar. **A:** Sr. High-Adult. **P:** Entertainment. **U:** Home. **L:** French. **Mov-Ent:** Politics & Government. **Acq:** Purchase. **Dist:** Entertainment One US LP.

Blame It on Rio 1984 (R) — ★★
A middle-aged man has a ridiculous fling with his best friend's daughter while on vacation with them in Rio de Janeiro. Caine and Johnson are amusing, but the script is somewhat weak. Remake of the French film "One Wild Moment." 90m; VHS, DVD, Wide. **C:** Michael Caine; Joseph Bologna; Demi Moore; Michelle Johnson; Valerie Harper; Directed by Stanley Donen; Written by Charlie Peters; Larry Gelbart; Cinematography by Reynaldo Villalobos; Music by Kenneth Wannberg. **Pr:** Sherwood Productions; 20th Century-Fox. **A:** Sr. High-Adult. **P:** Entertainment. **U:** Home. **Mov-Ent:** Comedy--Romantic, Ethics & Morals. **Acq:** Purchase. **Dist:** Lions Gate Television Corp. $29.95.

Blame It on the Bellboy 1992 (PG-13) — ★★½
Wild farce set in Venice about a hotel bellboy who confuses three similarly named visitors—sending the wrong ones to meet corporate bigwigs, date women, or even kill. The brisk pace loses it towards the end and devolves into chase scenes. 79m; VHS, DVD, CC. **C:** Dudley Moore; Bryan Brown; Richard Griffiths; Andreas Katsulas; Patsy Kensit; Alison Steadman; Bronson Pinchot; Lindsay Anderson; Penelope Wilton; Directed by Mark Herman; Written by Mark Herman; Music by Trevor Jones. **A:** Jr. High-Adult. **P:** Entertainment. **U:** Home. **Mov-Ent:** Comedy--Screwball, Italy, Hotels & Hotel Staff Training. **Acq:** Purchase. **Dist:** Movies Unlimited; Alpha Video. $94.95.

Blame It on the Night 1984 (PG-13) — ★★
A rock star gets to take care of the military cadet son he never knew after the boy's mother suddenly dies. Mick Jagger helped write the story. 85m; VHS, DVD, Streaming. **C:** Nick Mancuso; Byron Thames; Leslie Ackerman; Billy Preston; Merry Clayton; Directed by Gene Taft. **Pr:** Tri-Star Pictures. **A:** Jr. High-Adult. **P:** Entertainment. **U:** Home. **Mov-Ent:** Musical, Music--Pop/Rock. **Acq:** Purchase. **Dist:** Sony Pictures Home Entertainment Inc.; Alpha Video. $79.98.

Blanche Fury 1948 — ★★½
Governess Blanche (Hobson) marries her wealthy widowed cousin but the man she truly desires is the illegitimate Philip Thorn (Granger), who manages the estate for her husband. So Blanche decides to get rid of the man she doesn't love. Based on England's 19th-century Rush murder and adapted from the novel by Joseph Shearing. 95m; VHS, Streaming. **C:** Valerie Hobson; Stewart Granger; Walter Fitzgerald; Michael Gough; Maurice Denham; Sybilla Binder; Directed by Marc Allegret; Written by Hugh Mills; Cinematography by Guy Green; Geoffrey Unsworth; Music by Clifton Parker. **Pr:** Anthony Havelock-Allan; Universal Studios. **A:** Jr. High-Adult. **P:** Entertainment. **U:** Home. **Mov-Ent:** Marriage. **Acq:** Purchase. **Dist:** Facets Multimedia Inc.

Blanche Thebom in Opera and Song 195?
A selection of arias from "Il Trovatore," "Samson et Dalila" and others. 30m; VHS. **Pr:** VAI. **A:** Jr. High-Adult. **P:** Entertainment. **U:** Home. **Fin-Art:** Opera, Music--Performance. **Acq:** Purchase. **Dist:** Music Video Distributors; Video Artists International; Facets Multimedia Inc. $19.95.

The Blancheville Monster 1963 (Unrated) — ★½
A young woman returns to the family mansion upon hearing of her father's death and that her brother has fired the staff, only to find her father alive, disfigured, and obsessed with killing her. 90m/B/W; DVD. **C:** Gerard Tichy; Leo Anchoriz; Vanni Materassi; Paco Moran; Ombretta Colli; Helga Line; Iran Eory; Directed by Alberto De Martino; Written by Bruno Corbucci; Sergio Corbucci; Giovanni Grimaldi; Natividad Zaro; Cinematography by Alejandro Ulloa; Music by Carlo Franci; Giuseppe Piccillo. **A:** Jr. High-Adult. **P:** Entertainment. **U:** Home. **L:** English. **Mov-Ent. Acq:** Purchase. **Dist:** Gotham Distributing Corp. $7.98.

Blancmange: Live at the Hacienda 1982
Performance by one of the forerunners of the '80s electronic music movement filmed in Manchester. 55m; VHS. **A:** Sr. High-Adult. **P:** Entertainment. **U:** Home. **Mov-Ent:** Music--Performance, Music--Pop/Rock. **Acq:** Purchase. **Dist:** Music Video Distributors. $29.95.
Songs: Can't Explain; I Would; I've Seen the World; Kind; Running Thin; Feel Me; Cruel; Wasted; Waves; Gods Kitchen; Living on the Ceiling; Sad Day.

A Blank Buffet 1986
A collection of fine films from director Les Blank. 69m; VHS. **C:** Directed by Les Blank. **Pr:** Les Blank; Les Blank. **A:** Jr. High-Adult. **P:** Entertainment. **U:** Home. **Mov-Ent. Acq:** Purchase. **Dist:** Flower Films. $39.95.

Blank Check 1993 (PG) — ★
Parents may want to verify the whereabouts of their checkbooks after this one. Eleven-year-old Preston receives a blank check from a mobster on the run, cashes it for a million bucks, and goes on a spending orgy under an assumed name. Where are his parents? Apparently they don't have a problem with a shadowy benefactor taking their son under his wing. Sound familiar? And who thought it would be a good idea to have the little twerp mooning after a comely bank teller? Formula aside, this blatant rip-off of "Home Alone" tries to throw in an ending moral but probably won't fool the kids either. 93m; VHS, DVD, CC. **C:** Brian Bonsall; Miguel Ferrer; Michael Lerner; Tone Loc; Ric(k) Ducommun; Karen Duffy; Directed by Rupert Wainwright; Written by Colby Carr; Blake Snyder; Music by Nicholas Pike. **Pr:** Craig Baumgarten; Gary Adelson; Buena Vista. **A:** Jr. High-Adult. **P:** Entertainment. **U:** Home. **Mov-Ent. Acq:** Purchase. **Dist:** Walt Disney Studios Home Entertainment.

Blank Page 198?
This training film stresses the importance of individual contributions to an organization. 24m; VHS, 3/4 U. **A:** College-Adult. **P:** Education. **U:** Institution. **Bus-Ind:** Meeting Openers, Job Training. **Acq:** Rent/Lease. **Dist:** National Safety Council, California Chapter, Film Library.

The Blank Point: What Is Transsexualism? 1991
An examination of the phenomena of transsexualism, people who identify with the opposite sex and undergo surgery to change their gender. 58m; VHS. **C:** Directed by Xiao-Yen Wang. **Pr:** Andrew Martin. **A:** Sr. High-Adult. **P:** Education. **U:** Institution. **Gen-Edu:** Documentary Films, Sex & Sexuality. **Acq:** Purchase, Rent/Lease. **Dist:** The Cinema Guild. $350.00.

Blankman 1994 (PG-13) — ★★
Self-appointed superhero (Wayans), who makes up in creativity what he lacks in superpowers, fights crime in his underwear and a cape made from his grandmother's bathrobe. Life is simple, until an ambitious TV reporter (Givens) finds out about him. Silly one-joke premise is carried a little too far; didn't similar "Meteor Man" crash? Gifted comedian Wayans tries, but can't make this guy fly. 96m; VHS, DVD, Wide, CC. **C:** Damon Wayans; Robin Givens; David Alan Grier; Jason Alexander; Jon Polito; Nick(y) Corello; Directed by Mike Binder; Written by Damon Wayans; J.F. Lawton; Cinematography by Newton Thomas (Tom) Sigel; Music by Miles Goodman. **Pr:** Eric Gold; C.O. Erickson; Damon Wayans; Damon Wayans; Wife N' Kids; Columbia Pictures. **A:** Jr. High-Adult. **P:** Entertainment. **U:** Home. **Mov-Ent:** Mass Media, Handicapped. **Acq:** Purchase. **Dist:** Sony Pictures Home Entertainment Inc.

Blas Elias: Drumming Instruction 19??
Elias, the drummer from the band Slaughter, demonstrates the rudiments of heavy metal drumming. Includes a performance from the band. 60m; VHS. **A:** Jr. High-Adult. **P:** Instruction. **U:** Home. **How-Ins:** How-To, Music--Instruction. **Acq:** Purchase. **Dist:** Music Video Distributors. $49.95.

Blast 1996 — ★★
Terrorists take a group of spectators hostage at the Atlanta Summer Olympics. 98m; VHS. **C:** Linden Ashby; Andrew Divoff; Rutger Hauer; Tim Thomerson; Directed by Albert Pyun. **A:** Sr. High-Adult. **P:** Entertainment. **U:** Home. **Mov-Ent:** Terrorism, Sports--Olympic. **Acq:** Purchase. **Dist:** Warner Home Video, Inc.

Blast 2004 (R) — ★★½
Mercenaries try to detonate an electromagnetic bomb over the U.S using an oil rig. A tug boat captain (Griffin) teams with an FBI agent and computer expert in order to foil the plan. Griffin is surprisingly effective as an action hero, and the proceedings, while not breaking any new ground, provide the requisite excitement and wisecracks in the "Die Hard/Under Siege" mode. 91m; DVD, Wide. **C:** Eddie Griffin; Vinnie Jones; Breckin Meyer; Vivica A. Fox; Tommy (Tiny) Lister; Anthony Hickox; Directed by Anthony Hickox; Written by Steven E. de Souza; Cinematography by Giulio Biccari; Music by Danny Saber. **A:** Sr. High-Adult. **P:** Entertainment. **U:** Home. **Mov-Ent:** Terrorism, Boating, Federal Bureau of Investigation (FBI). **Acq:** Purchase. **Dist:** Movies Unlimited; Alpha Video. $24.98.

Blast! 2008 (Unrated)
Documentary following NASA scientists as they attempt to launch a new form of telescope on a high altitude balloon. 74m; DVD, Streaming. **A:** Preschool-Adult. **P:** Education. **U:** Home, Institution. **L:** English. **Gen-Edu:** Documentary Films, Space Exploration. **Acq:** Purchase, Rent/Lease. **Dist:** Docurama. $29.95 14.99.

Blast Away the Pounds: Indoor Walk 2005
Three separate cardio routines simulate the effects of a one-mile walk. 50m; DVD. **A:** College-Adult. **P:** Instruction. **U:** Home. **Hea-Sci:** Fitness/Exercise. **Acq:** Purchase. **Dist:** CinemaNow Inc. $14.98.

Blast 'Em 1992
A documentary look at the world of the paparazzi and the celebrities they stalk in order to capture that one money-making photograph. Features the antics of agressive photographer Victor Malafronte and such celebrities as Madonna, John Kennedy Jr., Marla Maples, and Robert De Niro. 103m; VHS. **A:** College-Adult. **P:** Entertainment. **U:** Home. **Gen-Edu:** Documentary Films, Photography, Biography: Show Business. **Acq:** Purchase. **Dist:** Facets Multimedia Inc. $89.95.

Blast from the Past 1998 (PG-13) — ★★½
Mistaking a plane crash in his yard for an atomic bomb blast, paranoid scientist Calvin (Walken) and his pregnant wife Helen (Spacek) lock themselves in their bomb shelter. Fearful of radioactive fallout, they raise their son Adam (Fraser) in the shelter on a diet of canned goods, Perry Como music, and ballroom dancing. After 35 years, Adam is sent out for supplies and to find a nice, non-mutant wife. Plot degenerates into by-the-book romantic comedy mush after he meets cute with Eve (Silverstone), a thoroughly modern woman with a low opinion of modern men. 106m; VHS, DVD, CC. **C:** Brendan Fraser; Alicia Silverstone; Christopher Walken; Sissy Spacek; Dave Foley; Joey Slotnick; Dale Raoul; Scott Thomson; Nathan Fillion; Donovan Scott; Directed by Hugh Wilson; Written by Hugh Wilson; Bill Kelly; Cinematography by Jose Luis Alcaine; Music by Steve Dorff. **Pr:** New Line Cinema. **A:** Jr. High-Adult. **P:** Entertainment. **U:** Home. **Mov-Ent:** Comedy--Romantic, Cuban Missile Crisis. **Acq:** Purchase. **Dist:** Warner Home Video, Inc.

Blast of Silence 1961 (Unrated) — ★★
Hard-boiled crime. Frank Bono (Baron) comes to Manhattan at Christmas for a contract hit for the mob. He follows his target and decides on the best place to make his shot, just waiting for the right time. When Frank makes a mistake and tries to get out of the contract, he realizes that he'll be next on the hit parade. 77m/B/W; DVD. **C:** Allen Baron; Peter Clune; Larry Tucker; Molly McCarthy; Narrated by Lionel Stander; Directed by Allen Baron; Written by Allen Baron; Music by Meyer Kupferman. **A:** Sr. High-Adult. **P:** Entertainment. **U:** Home. **Mov-Ent:** Crime Drama, Christmas. **Acq:** Purchase. **Dist:** Criterion Collection Inc.

Blast-Off Girls 1967 (Unrated) — ★
A scuzzball promoter sets out to avenge himself for being blacklisted by the rock 'n' roll industry. He discovers a fresh group, but without corporate backing he can only pay them with groovy clothes and mini-skirted girls. Trouble ensues when they unexpectedly hit the charts and want real money. 83m; VHS, DVD, Wide. **C:** Ray Sager; Dan Conway; Harland "Colonel" Sanders; Directed by Herschell Gordon Lewis; Written by Herschell Gordon Lewis. **A:** College-Adult. **P:** Entertainment. **U:** Home. **Mov-Ent:** Drugs. **Acq:** Purchase. **Dist:** Movies Unlimited; Something Weird Video. $19.99.

Blastfighter 1985 (R) — **Bomb!**
After local hoodlums kill his daughter, an ex-con cop goes on a spree of violence and revenge. Director Bava uses the pseudonym "John Old, Jr.," as his father Mario Bava occasionally credited himself as John Old. Italian film shot in Atlanta. 93m; VHS. **C:** Michael Sopkiw; Valerie Blake; George Eastman; Directed by Lamberto Bava. **Pr:** Medusa. **A:** Sr. High-Adult. **P:** Entertainment. **U:** Home. **Mov-Ent. Acq:** Purchase. **Dist:** Lions Gate Television Corp. $69.95.

Blat 19?? (Unrated) — ★½
A gangster of Italian-Russian descent tries to pull a sting on merry old England's financial world in this comedy. Made for British television. 90m; VHS. **C:** Robert Hardy; Adrienne Corri; Alfred Molina. **Pr:** British Broadcasting Corporation. **A:** Sr. High-Adult. **P:** Entertainment. **U:** Home. **Mov-Ent:** Comedy-Drama, TV Movies. **Acq:** Purchase. **Dist:** Facets Multimedia Inc.; Video Collectibles. $49.95.

Blaze 1989 (R) — ★★½
The true story of Louisiana governor Earl Long who became involved with a stripper, Blaze Starr, causing a political scandal of major proportions. Robust, good-humored bio-pic featuring a fine character turn by Newman. 117m; VHS, DVD, Blu-Ray, CC. **C:** Paul Newman; Lolita Davidovich; Jerry Hardin; Robert Wuhl; Gailard Sartain; Jeffrey DeMunn; Richard Jenkins; Garland Bunting; Directed by Ron Shelton; Written by Ron Shelton; Cinematography by Haskell Wexler. **Pr:** Touchstone Pictures. **A:** College-Adult. **P:** Entertainment. **U:** Home. **Mov-Ent:** Biography: Politics, Politics & Government. **Acq:** Purchase. **Dist:** Buena Vista Home Entertainment. $89.95.

Blaze Glory 1968 — ★★
"Old West" hero falls victim to satire. Sight gags, exaggeration of stereotypes, and pixillation (a form of stop-action animation in which people move like cartoon characters) contribute minimally to the frontier humor. 10m; VHS. **Pr:** Chuck Menville; Len Janson. **A:** Family. **P:** Entertainment. **U:** Institution, Home, SURA. **Mov-Ent:** Satire & Parody. **Acq:** Purchase, Rent/Lease, Duplication License. **Dist:** Pyramid Media.

Blaze Starr Goes Nudist 1963 (Unrated) — ★
The enormously "gifted" soft-porn star of the '60s joins a nudist camp. Wacky exploits ensue. 80m; VHS, DVD. **C:** Blaze Starr; Russ Martine; Gene Berk; Directed by Doris Wishman. **A:** College-Adult. **P:** Entertainment. **U:** Home. **Mov-Ent:** Sex & Sexuality, Camps & Camping. **Acq:** Purchase. **Dist:** Wellspring Media. $39.95.

Blazin' BMX: The 1987 ABA Grand Nationals 1987
A look at the non-stop action of the BMX championships in 1987. 60m; VHS. **Pr:** Vision Street Wear. **A:** Jr. High-Adult. **P:** Entertainment. **U:** Home. **Spo-Rec:** Bicycling, Sports--General. **Acq:** Purchase. **Dist:** ESPN Inc. $29.95.

Blazing Across the Pecos 1948 — ★½
The Durango Kid (Starrett) is after Pecos Flats mayor Ace Brockaway (Wilson), who's secretly selling guns to the local Indian tribe so they'll attack the supply wagons of his business

rivals. 54m/B/W; VHS, DVD. **C:** Charles Starrett; Smiley Burnette; Charles C. Wilson; Chief Thundercloud; Directed by Ray Nazarro. **Pr:** Columbia Pictures. **A:** Family. **P:** Entertainment. **U:** Home. **Mov-Ent:** Western. **Acq:** Purchase. **Dist:** Sony Pictures Home Entertainment Inc.

Blazing Boards 1985
A good surf film set in the usual choice spots of Hawaii, Australia, California, Mexico, etc. Features Cheyne Horan, Mark Richards, Tommy Curren, Tom Carroll, Shaun Thomson, Derek Hynd, and Martin Potter. Check out the especially trendy mid-'80s soundtrack that includes INXS, Men Without Hats, and other pop fare. 94m; VHS. **C:** Martin Potter; Cheyne Horan; Tom Carroll; Mark Richards; Tommy Curren. **Pr:** NSI. **A:** Jr. High-Adult. **P:** Entertainment. **U:** Home. **Spo-Rec:** Sports--General. **Acq:** Purchase. **Dist:** NSI Sound & Video Inc. $59.95.

Blazing Frontier 1943 (Unrated) — ★½
Crooked land agents team up with crooked railroad detectives to cheat settlers out of their property. Billy and sidekick Fuzzy investigate. The last in Producers Releasing Corporation's 'Billy the Kid' series; Crabbe and St. John next went on to PRC's 'Billy Carson' series. 59m/B/W; DVD. **C:** Buster Crabbe; Al "Fuzzy" St. John; Marjorie Manners; Milton Kibbee; I. Stanford Jolley; Frank S. Hagney; Kermit Maynard; George Chesebro; Frank Ellis; Directed by Sam Newfield; Written by Patricia Harper; Cinematography by Robert E. Cline. **A:** Jr. High-Adult. **P:** Entertainment. **U:** Home. **Mov-Ent:** Western. **Acq:** Purchase. **Dist:** Mill Creek Entertainment L.L.C.

Blazing Guns 1935 (Unrated) — ★
Threadbare western from Willis Kent Productions. Good guy Bob Grady is knocked-out by outlaw Slug Raton who steals his clothes, gun, and horse. The Sheriff thinks Grady is the criminal and arrests him but he is saved from hanging by Betty Lou Rickard whose family Grady helped. This gives him the chance to go after Slug and his gang. 55m/B/W; DVD. **C:** Reb Russell; Frank McCarroll; Marion Shilling; Lafe (Lafayette) McKee; Joseph Girard; Slim Whitaker; Directed by Ray Heinz; Written by Forbes Parkhill; Cinematography by James Diamond. **A:** Jr. High-Adult. **P:** Entertainment. **U:** Home. **Mov-Ent:** Western. **Acq:** Purchase. **Dist:** Sinister Cinema.

Blazing Saddles 1974 (R) — ★★★½
Wild, wacky spoof by Brooks of every cliche in the western film genre. Little is Black Bart, a convict offered a reprieve if he will become a sheriff and clean up a nasty frontier town; the previous recipients of this honor have all swiftly ended up in shallow graves. A crazy, silly film with a cast full of lovable loonies including comedy greats Wilder, Kahn, and Korman. Watch for the Count Basie Orchestra. A group writing effort, based on an original story by Bergman. Was the most-viewed movie in its first year of release on HBO cable. 90m; VHS, DVD, Blu-Ray, HD-DVD. **C:** Cleavon Little; Harvey Korman; Madeline Kahn; Gene Wilder; Mel Brooks; John Hillerman; Alex Karras; Dom DeLuise; Liam Dunn; Slim Pickens; David Huddleston; Burton Gilliam; Count Basie; Directed by Mel Brooks; Written by Mel Brooks; Norman Steinberg; Andrew Bergman; Richard Pryor; Alan Uger; Cinematography by Joseph Biroc; Music by John Morris. **A:** College-Adult. **P:** Entertainment. **U:** Home. **Mov-Ent:** Cult Films, Horses. **Awds:** Natl. Film Reg. '06; Writers Guild '74: Orig. Screenplay. **Acq:** Purchase. **Dist:** Warner Home Video, Inc. $14.95.

Blazing Stewardesses 1975 (R) — **Bomb!**
The Hound salutes the distributor for truth in advertising, as they stamped this as one of the world's worst videos. Lusty, busty stewardesses relax at a western guest ranch under siege from hooded riders and the aging gags of the Ritz Brothers. 95m; VHS, DVD. **C:** Yvonne De Carlo; Robert "Bob" Livingston; Donald (Don "Red") Barry; Regina Carrol; Connie Hoffman; Cameo(s) Harry Ritz; Jimmy Ritz; Directed by Al Adamson. **Pr:** Al Adamson; Al Adamson. **A:** Sr. High-Adult. **P:** Entertainment. **U:** Home. **Mov-Ent. Acq:** Purchase. **Dist:** Unknown Distributor.

Bleach or Dye Techniques 199?
Janet Pray provides instructional information on bleaching and dyeing techniques used for cotton and silk. She teaches about the tools and materials needed, bleach methods for cottons, wet and dry fabric techniques, vertical floral designs, brush, squeeze bottle, and stencil techniques, Procion color water fiber reactive dye techniques, and resist methods. Includes supply list and examples of various garments that have been bleached and/or dyed. 90m; VHS. **Pr:** Victorian Video Productions. **A:** Jr. High-Adult. **P:** Instruction. **U:** Home, Institution. **How-Ins:** Crafts, How-To. **Acq:** Purchase. **Dist:** Victorian Video/Yarn Barn of Kansas, Inc. $39.95.

Bleach the Movie 4: Hell Verse 2010 (Unrated) — ★★
The fourth sequel to the long running anime and manga series finds Ichigo and his friends attempting to put down a jailbreak from Hell. 94m; DVD, Blu-Ray, Streaming. **C:** Voice(s) by Johnny Yong Bosch; Michelle Ruff; Travis Willington; Derek Prince; Wally Wingert; Directed by Noriyuki Abe; Written by Natsuko Takahashi; Ookubo Masahiro; Cinematography by Toshiyuki Fukushima; Music by Shiroh Sagisu. **A:** Sr. High-Adult. **P:** Entertainment. **U:** Home. **L:** English, Japanese. **Mov-Ent. Acq:** Purchase, Rent/Lease. **Dist:** Viz Media L.L.C. $24.98 19.98 9.99.

Bleading Lady 2010 (Unrated) — **Bomb!**
Slasher/showbiz horror crapola. Movie buff Donald Cardini works as a driver for low-budget films. His latest middle-of-nowhere location is the Forest Grove Lodge for a horror flick starring his favorite scream queen Riversa Red. Don takes it upon himself to protect her from a stalker but when his volatile temper gets him fired, Don decides to make the cast and crew part of his own deadly horror show. 75m; DVD. **C:** Dan Ellis; Sindy Faraguna; Nathan Durec; Nick Windebank; Mike LI; Paige Farbacher; Directed by Ryan Nicholson; Written by Ryan Nicholson; Cinematography by Jay Gavin; Music by Gianni Rossi. **A:** Sr. High-Adult. **P:** Entertainment. **U:** Home. **Mov-Ent. Acq:** Purchase. **Dist:** Breaking Glass Pictures.

Bleak House 1985 — ★★½
Miniseries adaptation of the Charles Dickens tome about an interminable lawsuit and the decadent, criminal ruling class of 19th-century England. 391m; VHS, DVD, CC. **C:** Denholm Elliott; Diana Rigg; Philip Franks; Peter Vaughan; T.P. McKenna; Directed by Ross Devenish; Music by Geoffrey Burgon. **Pr:** British Broadcasting Corporation. **A:** Sr. High-Adult. **P:** Entertainment. **U:** Home. **Mov-Ent:** TV Movies, Law. **Acq:** Purchase. **Dist:** Signals Video; Video Collectibles; Home Vision Cinema. $29.98.

Bleak House 2005 (Unrated) — ★★½
Charles Dickens' serialized novel gets the BBC treatment in all its extended suffering. A long court case involving a disputed inheritance hides many secrets and many protagonists, including a fiendish lawyer, an icy aristocratic beauty, two innocents, and an illegitimate child, as well as obsession, madness, and murder. 510m; DVD, Blu-Ray, Wide. **C:** Gillian Anderson; Charles Dance; Denis Lawson; Patrick Kennedy; Anna Maxwell Martin; Timothy West; Nathaniel Parker; Carey Mulligan; Tom Georgeson; Directed by Justin Chadwick; Susanna White; Written by Andrew Davies; Cinematography by Kieran McGuigan; Music by John Lunn. **A:** Jr. High-Adult. **P:** Entertainment. **U:** Home. **Mov-Ent:** Law. **Acq:** Purchase. **Dist:** Movies Unlimited; Alpha Video; Warner Home Video, Inc.

Bleak Moments 1971 — ★★
Bored secretary Sylvia (Raitt) tries to work her flirtatious charms on a repressed teacher (Allan) and an eccentric musician (Bradwell) in order to escape the pressures of caring for a mentally retarded sister. 110m; VHS, DVD. **C:** Anne Raitt; Eric Allen; Mike Bradwell; Joolia Cappleman; Directed by Mike Leigh; Written by Mike Leigh; Cinematography by Bahram Manocheri; Music by Mike Bradwell. **A:** Sr. High-Adult. **P:** Entertainment. **U:** Home. **Mov-Ent:** Comedy-Drama. **Acq:** Purchase. **Dist:** Water Bearer Films Inc.

Blechschaden—das Dorf der schwarzen Schafe 1984
A hit-and-run accident leads to wrongful arrest, blackmail, and murder. Another film from "Das Boot" director Wolfgang Petersen. In German only. 106m; VHS. **TV Std:** NTSC, PAL. **C:** Directed by Wolfgang Petersen. **Pr:** German Language Video Center. **A:** Jr. High-Adult. **P:** Entertainment. **U:** Home. **L:** German. **Mov-Ent:** Mystery & Suspense. **Acq:** Purchase, Rent/Lease. **Dist:** German Language Video Center. $33.95.

The Bledisloe Cup 1988
The best and most exciting Bledisloe Cup matches are now available on tape. 100m; VHS. **Pr:** Trace Video. **A:** Family. **P:** Entertainment. **U:** Institution, Home, SURA. **Spo-Rec:** Sports--General. **Acq:** Purchase, Rent/Lease, Subscription. **Dist:** Reedswain Inc. $285.00.

Indiv. Titles: 1. Third Test-1978 2. First Test-1982 3. Second Test-1982 4. Third Test-1982 5. Cup Match-1985 6. First Test-1986 7. Third Test-1986.

Bleeders 1997 (R) — **Bomb!**
John Struass (Dupuis), suffering from a hereditary blood disease, travels to a remote Atlantic island to research his ancestors and discovers the descendants are a grotesque clan of incestuous malformed creatures, who only emerge from their catacombs to satisfy their need for human blood and flesh. 89m; VHS, DVD. **C:** Rutger Hauer; Roy Dupuis; Jackie Burroughs; Kristen Lehman; Joanna Noyes; John Dunn-Hill; Lisa Bronwyn Moore; Directed by Peter Svatek; Written by Dan O'Bannon; Charles Adair; Ronald Shusett; Cinematography by Barry Gravelle; Music by Alan Reeves. **A:** Sr. High-Adult. **P:** Entertainment. **U:** Home. **Mov-Ent:** Horror, Blood. **Acq:** Purchase. **Dist:** Movies Unlimited.

The Bleeding 2009 (R) — ★
Shawn Black (Matthias) comes home to find his family dead, his brother is a vampire, and he himself is some sort of "chosen one" who will save the world from evil. He could reject the power of bad movie cliches but alas he does not. 83m; DVD, Streaming. **C:** Michael Madsen; Vinnie Jones; Armand Assante; William McNamara; Michael Matthias; Directed by Charlie Picerni; Written by Lance Lane; Cinematography by Tom Priestley, Jr.; Music by Justin Caine Burnett. **A:** Sr. High-Adult. **P:** Entertainment. **U:** Home. **L:** English. **Mov-Ent. Acq:** Purchase, Rent/Lease. **Dist:** Starz Entertainment; Anchor Bay Entertainment Inc. $9.98 14.99.

Bleeding Hearts 1994 — ★★½
A liberal white professor falls in love with the teenaged black student he's tutoring and then becomes aware of the vast differences between them. Their problems increase when the young woman becomes pregnant. 95m; VHS, DVD. **C:** Gregory Hines; Mark Evan Jacobs; Ranjit (Chaudry) Chowdhry; Elliott Gould; Robert Levine; Peter Riegert; Lorraine Toussaint; Directed by Gregory Hines. **A:** Jr. High-Adult. **P:** Entertainment. **U:** Home. **Mov-Ent:** Drama, Adolescence, Pregnancy. **Acq:** Purchase. **Dist:** York Entertainment.

Bleeding: What To Do 1973
Animation, models and re-enactments are used to illustrate effective first-aid techniques. 16m; VHS, 3/4 U. **Pr:** Yehuda Tarma; Pyramid Film Productions. **A:** Jr. High-Adult. **P:** Education. **U:** Institution, Home, SURA. **L:** English, Spanish. **How-Ins:** How-To, First Aid, Emergencies. **Acq:** Purchase, Rent/Lease, Duplication License. **Dist:** Pyramid Media. $195.00.

Blended 2014 (PG-13) — ★
Sandler and Barrymore continue to scrape the bottom of the comedy barrel in their third collaboration, a film that is slightly better than recent Happy Madison disasters, but that's like saying the flu is slightly better than pneumonia. Both suck. Jim Friedman (Sandler) and Lauren Reynolds (Barrymore) go on a bad blind date and then inexplicably end up at a family resort in Africa--yes, this is another film that exists purely to give Sandler a vacation. Cultural insensitivities, bodily humor, and more of the same nonsense; salvaged somewhat by Barrymore's unflappable charm. 117m; DVD. **C:** Adam Sandler; Drew Barrymore; Bella Thorne; Emma Fuhrmann; Alyvia Alyn Lind; Braxton Beckham; Kyle Red Silverstein; Terry Crews; Kevin Nealon; Jessica Lowe; Directed by Frank Coraci; Written by Ivan Menchell; Clare Sera; Cinematography by Julio Macat; Music by Rupert Gregson-Williams. **Pr:** Adam Sandler; Warner Brothers. **A:** Jr. High-Adult. **P:** Entertainment. **U:** Home. **L:** English. **Mov-Ent:** Family, Parenting, Africa. **Acq:** Purchase.

Blended Families 19??
Addresses the concerns parents and children may have regarding blended families and new lifestyle changes. Presents practical solutions to assist in handling the challenges faced by step or blended families. 30m; VHS. **A:** Family. **P:** Education. **U:** Home, Institution. **Gen-Edu:** Family. **Acq:** Purchase. **Dist:** Alliance for Children and Families. $95.00.

Blended Families: Yours, Mine, Ours 1991
Dick Van Patten narrates this guide to adjusting to new blended families. Stresses that the process takes time and offers possible solutions to common problems. 30m; VHS. **A:** Sr. High-Adult. **P:** Education. **U:** Institution. **Gen-Edu:** Divorce, Marriage, Family. **Acq:** Purchase. **Dist:** United Learning Inc.; Alliance for Children and Families. $95.00.

Bless Me, Ultima 2013 (PG-13) — ★★
Director Franklin plays with issues of religion, divinity, and faith in this adaptation of Rudolfo Anaya's novel. A healer known as Ultima (Colon) comes to young boy Antonio's (Ganalon) small New Mexico town in the early '40s, just as the world was succumbing to the changes brought on by WWII. The new perspectives on life that Ultima gives Antonio have a deep impact upon him. Essentially a coming-of-age story, it's rather blandly presented given its magical themes. The 1972 classic book has caused much debate since its publication in 1972 due to the intense adult topics that occur within a child's life. 106m; DVD. **C:** Luke Ganalon; Miriam Colon; Benito Martinez; Dolores Heredia; Castulo Guerra; Directed by Carl Franklin; Written by Carl Franklin; Cinematography by Paula Huidobro; Music by Mark Kilian. **Pr:** Jesse Beaton; Gran Via; Monarch Pictures; Arenas Entertainment. **A:** Jr. High-Adult. **P:** Entertainment. **U:** Home. **L:** English, Spanish. **Mov-Ent:** Religion, World War Two, Medical Care. **Acq:** Purchase. **Dist:** Sony Pictures Home Entertainment Inc.

Bless the Beasts and Children 1971 (PG) — ★★½
A group of six teenage boys at a summer camp attempt to save a herd of buffalo from slaughter at a national preserve. Treacly Kramer backwater. Based on the novel by Glendon Swarthout. 109m; VHS, Streaming. **C:** Billy Mumy; Barry Robins; Miles Chapin; Darel Glaser; Bob Kramer; Ken Swofford; Jesse White; Directed by Stanley Kramer; Music by Perry Botkin. **Pr:** Stanley Kramer; Stanley Kramer; Columbia Pictures. **A:** Jr. High-Adult. **P:** Entertainment. **U:** Home. **Mov-Ent:** Animals. **Acq:** Purchase. **Dist:** Sony Pictures Home Entertainment Inc. $14.95.

Bless the Child 2000 (R) — ★
Basinger doesn't even attempt to hide her boredom as Maggie, aunt and caretaker to a six-year-old with supernatural powers. Everyone drops the ball in this failed ripoff of "The ExorOmen's Baby's Sixth Sense." Satanist and self-help guru Stark (Sewell) wants to recruit the gifted tyke to work for the Devil, while Maggie gets an occult-expert FBI agent (Smits, perhaps making a mortgage payment) and a bunch of exposition cameos on her side. This movie's idea of thrills is showing kids getting kidnapped and later turning up dead. Not exactly the feel-good movie of the year. 110m; VHS, DVD, Wide, CC. **C:** Kim Basinger; Jimmy Smits; Rufus Sewell; Holliston Coleman; Christina Ricci; Michael Gaston; Lumi Cavazos; Angela Bettis; Ian Holm; Eugene Lipinski; Anne Betancourt; Dimitra Arlys; Directed by Chuck Russell; Written by Thomas (Tom) Rickman; Clifford Green; Ellen Green; Cinematography by Peter Menzies, Jr.; Music by Christopher Young. **Pr:** Paramount Pictures. **A:** Sr. High-Adult. **P:** Entertainment. **U:** Home. **Mov-Ent:** Occult Sciences, Federal Bureau of Investigation (FBI), Horror. **Acq:** Purchase. **Dist:** Paramount Pictures Corp.

Blessed Be 1982
A group of exceptional children with learning disabilities are filmed in both lively and pastoral sequences. 8m; VHS, 3/4 U, Special order formats. **Pr:** Paulist Productions. **A:** Jr. High-Sr. High. **P:** Religious. **U:** Institution, CCTV, SURA. **Gen-Edu:** Children, Learning Disabilities. **Acq:** Purchase. **Dist:** Paulist Productions.

Blessed Event 1932 — ★★★
Fast-moving, entertaining film about a Broadway gossip columnist with a poison pen. Tracy has the role of a lifetime as a Walter Winchell prototype who thinks no one is exempt from his juicy column. Powell makes film debut as a crooner after a brief career as a band singer. Based on a play by Manuel Seff and Forrest Wilson. 77m/B/W; VHS, DVD, CC. **C:** Lee Tracy; Mary Brian; Dick Powell; Allen Jenkins; Ruth Donnelly; Emma Dunn; Walter Miller; Tom Dugan; Isabel Jewell; Directed by Roy Del Ruth; Written by Howard J. Green. **Pr:** Warner Bros. **A:** Sr. High-Adult. **P:** Entertainment. **U:** Home. **Mov-Ent:** Journalism. **Acq:** Purchase. **Dist:** WarnerArchive.com; MGM Home Entertainment. $19.98.

Blessed is the Match 2008 (Unrated)
Documentary following the life of Hannah Senesh, a Jewish volunteer who parachuted into Hungary on a mission to rescue other Jews during WWII. 85m/B/W; DVD. **A:** Sr. High-Adult. **P:** Education. **U:** Home. **Mov-Ent:** Documentary Films, Biography. **Acq:** Purchase. **Dist:** Docurama. $26.95.

Blessed Mother Katherine Drexel 19??
Examines the life of Mother Katherine Drexel, who was born into one of Philadelphia's richest families but gave up her wealth to found the order of Sisters of the Blessed Sacrament. 60m; VHS. **A:** Family. **P:** Religious. **U:** Home. **Gen-Edu:** Religion, Biography. **Acq:** Purchase. **Dist:** Ignatius Press. $19.95.

Blessed! We Still Believe 2 200?
Documentary following two diehard Red Sox fans through a World Series victory. 110m; DVD. **A:** Family. **P:** Entertainment. **U:** Home. **Spo-Rec:** Baseball, Documentary Films. **Acq:** Purchase. **Dist:** Baseball Direct. $19.95.

The Blessing 19??
Examines five elements of blessing and explains how to put them into practice. Based on Gary Smalley and John Trent's best-selling book. 60m; VHS. **A:** Adult. **P:** Religious. **U:** Home. **Gen-Edu:** Religion. **Acq:** Purchase. **Dist:** Ignatius Press. $19.95.

Blessing 1994 (Unrated) — ★★
It's an unhappy time down on the Wisconsin dairy farm in this tale of family life. Embittered patriarch Jack (Griffis) can barely make a go of it and takes his frustrations out by beating his cows and climbing to the top of the silo. Despairing wife Arlene (Glynn) enters newspaper lotteries and collects religious statues while daughter Randi (Griffis) keeps delaying leaving the farm because of a nagging sense of responsibility. Claustrophobic atmosphere. 94m; VHS. **C:** Guy Griffis; Carlin Glynn; Melora Griffis; Gareth Williams; Clovis Siemon; Directed by Paul Zehrer; Written by Paul Zehrer; Cinematography by Stephen Kazmierski; Music by Joseph S. DeBeasi. **Pr:** Melissa Powell; Paul Zehrer. **A:** Sr. High-Adult. **P:** Entertainment. **U:** Home. **Mov-Ent:** Agriculture, Poverty. **Acq:** Purchase. **Dist:** Leo Films.

Blessings of Liberty 1986
This video documents the framing of the Constitution, with footage from many national parks, monuments, and historic sites. 16m; VHS, 3/4 U. **Pr:** Shirley Wilt; USDAVA. **A:** Family. **P:** Education. **U:** Institution, SURA. **Gen-Edu:** History--U.S., National Parks & Reserves. **Acq:** Purchase. **Dist:** National Audiovisual Center. $19.99.

The Bletchley Circle 2013 (Unrated) — ★★
In this Brit miniseries, four women who worked as codebreakers at top-secret Bletchley Park find postwar Britain doesn't offer the same challenges. At least until housewife and mother Susan plays an intellectual game to find a pattern in the unsolved murders of young women found around London.. As she becomes more obsessed, Susan calls on her friends Millie, Lucy, and Jean to really track down the murderer but it leads to danger as they run across a serial killer. 135m; DVD, Blu-Ray. **C:** Anna Maxwell Martin; Rachael Stirling; Julie Graham; Sophie Rundle; Mark Dexter; Michael Gould; Steven Robertson; Directed by Andy de Emmony; Written by Guy Burt; Cinematography by John Pardue; Music by Nick Green. **A:** Sr. High-Adult. **P:** Entertainment. **U:** Home. **L:** English. **Mov-Ent:** Crime Drama, Women. **Acq:** Purchase. **Dist:** PBS Video.

The Bletchley Circle: Season Two 2014
Two separate stories fill out the ITV crime/mystery series. "Blood On Their Hands": In 1953, Alice Merren, another former code breaker, is faced execution after being convicted of murdering her lover. Jean is convinced she's innocent and rounds up her friends to investigate, but this time Susan is reluctant to get involved. "Uncustomed Goods": Since Susan and her family have left England, when Millie gets into trouble over black market dealings, Jean and Lucy are joined by Alice to help bring down a criminal family profiteering from sex trafficking and stolen goods. 240m; DVD, Blu-Ray. **C:** Rachael Stirling; Julie Graham; Sophie Rundle; Hattie Morahan; Anna Maxwell Martin. **A:** Sr. High-Adult. **P:** Entertainment. **U:** Home. **L:** English. **Mov-Ent:** Crime Drama, Great Britain, Mystery & Suspense. **Acq:** Purchase. **Dist:** PBS Home Video. $29.99.

BLEVE 197?
Boiling liquid expanding vapor explosions are explained in vivid color footage. 19m; VHS, 3/4 U. **Pr:** National Fire Protection Association. **A:** Sr. High-Adult. **P:** Education. **U:** Institution, CCTV, Home. **L:** English, French. **Bus-Ind:** Fires, Science. **Acq:** Purchase. **Dist:** National Fire Protection Association.

Blind 1986
Documentary shows the educational programs and daily life of students from kindergarten through the twelfth grade at the Alabama School for the Blind. 132m; VHS. **A:** Sr. High-Adult. **P:** Entertainment. **U:** Home, Institution. **Gen-Edu:** Documentary Films, Blindness, Education. **Acq:** Purchase, Rent/Lease. **Dist:** Zipporah Films. $350.00.

Blind 2014 (Unrated) — ★★★
Writer Vogt makes his directorial debut with this excellent, mind-bending tale of a woman who may be going crazy as she is going blind. Ingrid (Petersen) has lost her sight as an adult and begins to lose track of her memories and perception of the real world. Writer/director Vogt also introduces us to people around Ingrid, a lonely neighbor and a woman who may be sleeping with Ingrid's husband, only to then force us to question what is real and what is in Ingrid's imagination. The result is a brilliant narrative trick; a film that forces us to question not just what we think but what we see. 96m; DVD. **C:** Ellen Dorrit Petersen; Henrik Rafaelsen; Vera Vitali; Marius Kolbenstvedt; Directed by Eskil Vogt; Written by Eskil Vogt; Cinematography by Thimios Bakatakis; Music by Henk Hofstede. **A:** Adult. **P:** Entertainment. **U:** Home. **L:** Norwegian. **Mov-Ent:** Blindness, Mental Health, Women. **Acq:** Purchase.

Blind Ambition 1979 (Unrated) — ★★½
Miniseries docudrama traces the career of John Dean, special counsel to President Richard M. Nixon. Focuses on his fractured personal life and touches on virtually all of the Watergate headlines. 95m; VHS. **C:** Martin Sheen; Rip Torn; Theresa Russell; Michael Callan; William Daniels; Ed Flanders; Christopher Guest; James Karen; Kip Niven; Gerald S. O'Loughlin; Alan Oppenheimer; Lawrence Pressman; John Randolph; Peter Mark Richman; William Schallert; William Windom; Directed by George Schaefer; Written by Stanley R. Greenberg; Cinematography by Edward R. Brown; Music by Walter Scharf. **A:** Preschool. **P:** Entertainment. **U:** Institution, SURA. **Mov-Ent:** Documentary Films, Biography: Politics, TV Movies. **Acq:** Purchase, Rent/Lease. **Dist:** Time-Life Video and Television.

Blind Corner 1963 (Unrated) — ★½
Routine British potboiler. Blind pop composer Paul Gregory (Sylvester) is targeted for death by his greedy wife Anne (Shelley) who persuades her lover (Davlon) to do the deed so they can inherit Paul's money. However, Paul is aware of much more than they imagine. 80m/B/W; DVD. **C:** William Sylvester; Barbara Shelley; Alex Davion; Mark Eden; Elizabeth Shepherd; Directed by Lance Comfort; Written by James Kelly; Peter Miller; Cinematography by Basil Emmott; Music by Peter Hart; Brian Fahey. **A:** Jr. High-Adult. **P:** Entertainment. **U:** Home. **Mov-Ent:** Blindness, Crime Drama. **Acq:** Purchase. **Dist:** Movies Unlimited.

Blind Country 1989
Erika Beckman and Mike Kelley present a collaborative effort based on H.G. Wells' short story "The Country of the Blind." In this version, a naked, blind man is led through a realm of the senses by guiding female figures. 20m; VHS, 3/4 U. **A:** College-Adult. **P:** Entertainment. **U:** Institution. **Fin-Art:** Video. **Acq:** Purchase, Rent/Lease. **Dist:** Video Data Bank.

Blind Date 1984 (R) — ★½
Blind man agrees to have a visual computer implanted in his brain in order to help the police track down a psychopathic killer. Violent scenes may be disturbing to some. 100m; VHS, DVD. **C:** Joseph Bottoms; Kirstie Alley; Keir Dullea; James Daughton; Lana Clarkson; Marina Sirtis; Directed by Nico Mastorakis; Written by Nico Mastorakis. **Pr:** Wescom Productions; New Line Cinema. **A:** Sr. High-Adult. **P:** Entertainment. **U:** Home. **Mov-Ent:** Mystery & Suspense, Blindness. **Acq:** Purchase. **Dist:** Lions Gate Television Corp. $79.95.

Blind Date 1987 (PG-13) — ★★
A blind date between a workaholic yuppie and a beautiful blonde starts off well, but when she drinks too much at dinner, things get out of hand. In addition to embarrassing her date and destroying the restaurant, she has a jealous ex-boyfriend who must be dealt with. 95m; VHS, DVD, Blu-Ray, Wide, CC. **C:** Kim Basinger; Bruce Willis; John Larroquette; William Daniels; George Coe; Mark Blum; Phil Hartman; Stephanie Faracy; Alice Hirson; Graham Stark; Sab Shimono; Directed by Blake Edwards; Written by Dale Launer; Cinematography by Harry Stradling, Jr.; Music by Henry Mancini. **Pr:** Tony Adams; Tri-Star Pictures. **A:** Jr. High-Adult. **P:** Entertainment. **U:** Home. **Mov-Ent:** Comedy--Romantic. **Acq:** Purchase. **Dist:** Sony Pictures Home Entertainment Inc. $14.95.

Blind Date 2008 (Unrated) — ★★
The games couples play. Estranged married couple Don (Tucci) and Janna (Clarkson) place personal ads for specific role-playing dates as they struggle to reconnect in the wake of their young daughter's tragic death. Loose but loyal interpretation of a film by Dutch director Theo van Gogh, who was murdered by a Muslim extremist in 2004. Tucci's version is not as developed as the original and is a thinly veiled attempt at an homage. Shot on a single set, it would have fared better as a play but instead is an awkward mix of tragedy, comedy, and romance. 80m; On Demand, Wide. **C:** Stanley Tucci; Patricia Clarkson; Directed by Stanley Tucci; Written by Stanley Tucci; David Schechter; Cinematography by Thomas Kist; Music by Evan Lurie. **Pr:** Gijs van de Westelaken; Bruce Weiss; Ironworks Productions; Column Productions; Variance Films. **A:** Sr. High-Adult. **P:** Entertainment. **U:** Home. **L:** English. **Mov-Ent.** **Acq:** Purchase. **Dist:** Image Entertainment Inc.; Amazon.com Inc.; Movies Unlimited.

Blind Dating 2006 (PG-13) — ★½
Danny (Pine) is a young blind man, trying to decide if he should have experimental surgery that might allow him to see. Since he has no romantic experience, his sleazy brother (Kaye) has been setting him up on a series of really bad—uh—blind dates. But Danny falls for his doctor's receptionist Leeza (Jay), an Indian woman who is in an arranged engagement. But neither can quite forget about the other. 95m; DVD. **C:** Chris Pine; Eddie Kaye Thomas; Jane Seymour; Anjali Jay; Directed by James Keach; Written by Christopher Theo; Cinematography by Julio Macat; Music by Hector Pereira. **A:** Jr. High-Adult. **P:** Entertainment. **U:** Home. **Mov-Ent:** Blindness, Comedy--Romantic. **Acq:** Purchase. **Dist:** Fox Home Entertainment.

Blind Enough to See 1993
Looks at the the most effective ways managers can interview disabled candidates for company positions. Information presented is in conformance with Americans with Disabilities Act regulations. 25m; VHS. **A:** College-Adult. **P:** Professional. **U:** Institution. **Bus-Ind:** Interviews, Handicapped, Business. **Acq:** Purchase. **Dist:** Ken Blanchard Co. $695.00.

Blind Eye 2006 (R) — ★½
Volatile cop Nick Browning (Oliver) gets a call from his ex-wife when their daughter goes missing. Nick returns to his hometown, hoping to use his personal connections to get in on the investigation. When days pass without any leads, Nick realizes that something stinks and if he wants to find his daughter alive, his now-former friends are going down. 96m; DVD. **C:** Nick Mancuso; Roddy Piper; Levi Oliver; Tara Goudreau; Simone Randall; Phil Babcock; Shaun Hood; Joel Hookey; Directed by Mark McNabb; Written by Virginia Carraway; Charlie Fitzgerald; Cinematography by Paul Dunlop; Music by Iain Kelso. **A:** Sr. High-Adult. **P:** Entertainment. **U:** Home. **Mov-Ent.** **Acq:** Purchase. **Dist:** Bedford Entertainment Inc.

Blind Faith 1989 (R) — ★
Action and adventure take a turn for the horrific when several men find themselves in captivity. ?m; VHS. **C:** Eric Gunn; Kevin Yon; Lynne Browne; Directed by Dean Wilson; Written by Dean Wilson. **Pr:** American Ent. Productions. **A:** Adult. **P:** Entertainment. **U:** Home. **Mov-Ent:** Horror. **Acq:** Purchase.

Blind Faith 1998 (R) — ★★½
In 1957, John Williams (Vance) is a struggling new lawyer, living with elder sibling Charles (Dutton) and his family in a Bronx neighborhood. The first black NYPD sergeant, Charles has an uneasy relationship with his eldest son, Charlie (Whitt). The family's shocked when Charlie's accused of murdering a white boy during a robbery attempt, especially when he confesses. John thinks the cops beat the confession out of the boy and becomes determined to defend him but he gradually becomes suspicious of the story Charlie is telling him. 122m; VHS, DVD, CC. **C:** Courtney B. Vance; Charles S. Dutton; Garland Whitt; Kadeem Hardison; Lonette McKee; Karen Glave; Dan Lett; Directed by Ernest R. Dickerson; Written by Frank Military; Cinematography by Rodney Charters; Music by Ron Carter. **Pr:** Mace Neufeld; Robert Rehme; Showtime Networks. **A:** Sr. High-Adult. **P:** Entertainment. **U:** Home. **Mov-Ent:** Black Culture, Law. **Acq:** Purchase. **Dist:** Showtime Networks Inc.

Blind Faith: London Hyde Park 1969 1969
Features rock band Blind Faith's concert performance on June 7, 1969, before 100,000 fans at London's Hyde Park. Includes Eric Clapton, Steve Winwood, Rick Grech, and Ginger Baker. 73m; DVD. **A:** Jr. High-Adult. **P:** Entertainment. **U:** Home. **Mov-Ent:** Music--Pop/Rock, Music--Performance. **Acq:** Purchase. **Dist:** Sony Music Entertainment Inc. $19.98.

Blind Fear 1989 (R) — ★½
A blind woman is stalked by three killers in an abandoned country inn. 98m; VHS, DVD. **C:** Shelley Hack; Jack Langedijk; Kim Coates; Jan Rubes; Heidi von Palleske; Directed by Tom Berry; Written by Sergio D. Altieri. **Pr:** Lace Entertainment; Allegro Films. **A:** Sr. High-Adult. **P:** Entertainment. **U:** Home. **Mov-Ent:** Mystery & Suspense, Blindness. **Acq:** Purchase. **Dist:** Movies Unlimited. $29.95.

Blind Fools 1940 — ★½
A scathing indictment of children neglected by ambitious parents. 66m/B/W; VHS. **C:** Herbert Rawlinson; Claire Whitney; Russell Hicks; Miriam Battista; Vinton (Hayworth) Haworth; Wesley Barry; Robert Emmett Keane; Directed by John Varley; Written by Arthur Hoerl; Ivan Abramson; Cinematography by William J. Miller. **A:** Family. **P:** Entertainment. **U:** Home. **Mov-Ent:** Child Abuse, Parenting. **Acq:** Purchase. **Dist:** No Longer Available.

Blind Fury 1990 (R) — ★★½
A blind Vietnam vet enlists the aid of a Zen master and a sharpshooter to tackle the Mafia. Hauer works well in the lead, but unfortunately, the movie doesn't. 86m; VHS, DVD, CC. **C:** Rutger Hauer; Terry O'Quinn; Brandon Call; Lisa Blount; Randall "Tex" Cobb; Noble Willingham; Meg Foster; Sho Kosugi; Nick Cassavetes; Charles Cooper; Rick Overton; Directed by Phillip Noyce; Written by Charles Robert Carner; Cinematography by Don Burgess; Music by J. Peter Robinson. **Pr:** Tri-Star Pictures. **A:** College-Adult. **P:** Entertainment. **U:** Home. **Mov-Ent:** Martial Arts, Blindness. **Acq:** Purchase. **Dist:** Facets Multimedia Inc.; Sony Pictures Home Entertainment Inc. $14.95.

Blind Heat 2000 (R) — ★★
Unfaithful hubby Jeffrey Scott (Sapienza) takes wife Adriana (Alonso) on a business trip to Mexico where she gets kidnapped. Rather than pay the ransom, Scott hires negotiator Paul Burke (Fahey) to get his wife back by force. Meanwhile, kidnapper Victor (Peck) falls for Adriana and doesn't want to kill her when their plot turns sour. 95m; VHS, DVD. **C:** Maria Conchita Alonso; Jeff Fahey; J. Eddie Peck; Al Sapienza; Directed by Adolfo Martinez Solares; Written by Adolfo Martinez Solares; Jeff O'Brien; Cinematography by Keith Holland. **A:** Sr. High-Adult. **P:** Entertainment. **U:** Home. **Mov-Ent.** **Acq:** Purchase. **Dist:** Monarch Home Video.

Blind Horizon 2004 (R) — ★★½
A head wound gives Frank Cavanaugh (Kilmer) a case of amnesia but he can't shake ominous flashbacks of a presidential assassination attempt—especially when he hears the president is about to visit. But trying to convince a local New Mexico sheriff (Shepard) of the imminent danger isn't so easy since he's distracted by his reelection bid. And Frank can't be sure that his fiancee Chloe (Campbell) is really who she claims to be. Subplots are overdone and memory loss is nothing new. It works well enough, though. Faye Dunaway gets a slick bit part. 99m; VHS, DVD. **C:** Amy Smart; Gil Bellows; Giancarlo Esposito; Faye Dunaway; Directed by Michael Haussman; Written by F. Paul Benz; Steve Tomlin; Cinematography by Max Malkin. **A:** Sr. High-Adult. **P:** Entertainment. **U:** Home. **Mov-Ent:** Mystery & Suspense, Conspiracies or Conspiracy Theories. **Acq:** Purchase. **Dist:** Lions Gate Home Entertainment; CinemaNow Inc. $19.98.

Blind Husbands 1919 (Unrated) — ★★★½
An Austrian officer is attracted to the pretty wife of a dull surgeon. Controversial in its day, this lurid, sumptuous melo-

drama instigated many stubborn Hollywood myths, including the stereotype of the brusque, jodhpur-clad Prussian officer. This was von Stroheim's first outing as director. 98m/B/W; Silent; VHS, DVD. **TV Std:** NTSC, PAL. **C:** Erich von Stroheim; Fay Wray; Directed by Erich von Stroheim. **Pr:** Mark Huffam. **A:** Adult. **P:** Entertainment. **U:** Home. **Mov-Ent:** Drama, Silent Films, Classic Films. **Acq:** Purchase. **Dist:** Glenn Video Vistas Ltd. $24.95.

Blind Justice 1986 (Unrated) — ★★
An innocent man is identified as a rapist, and the accusation ruins his life. 94m; VHS. **C:** Tim Matheson; Lisa Eichhorn; Mimi Kuzyk; Philip Charles MacKenzie; Tom Atkins; Directed by Rod Holcomb; Music by Miles Goodman. **Pr:** CBS. **A:** Jr. High-Adult. **P:** Entertainment. **U:** Home. **Mov-Ent:** Mystery & Suspense, TV Movies, Rape. **Acq:** Purchase. **Dist:** $59.98.

Blind Justice 1994 (R) — ★★½
Gunfighter gets blinded in battle and rides into a small town where he's nursed back to health by an attractive lady doctor. While he recovers, he learns the town is trying to protect a cache of government silver from being stolen by bandits. 85m; VHS, DVD, Wide. **C:** Armand Assante; Elisabeth Shue; Robert Davi; Adam Baldwin; Jack Black; Directed by Richard Spence; Written by Daniel Knauf; Cinematography by Jack Conroy; Music by Richard Gibbs. **A:** Sr. High-Adult. **P:** Entertainment. **U:** Home. **Mov-Ent:** Western, TV Movies, Blindness. **Acq:** Purchase. **Dist:** Home Box Office Inc.

Blind Love 1979
This program, based on a true story, deals with a wife's anxiety over the possibility that her blind husband will regain his sight and be disappointed in her appearance. 25m; 3/4 U. **Pr:** Brigham Young University. **A:** Jr. High-Adult. **P:** Education. **U:** Institution, CCTV, SURA. **Gen-Edu:** Blindness, Human Relations. **Acq:** Purchase. **Dist:** Encyclopedia Britannica.

Blind Man's Bluff 19??
Accident prevention training program that offers an interactive program that trains employees on how to spot possible hazards before they happen. Covers bad housekeeping, unsafe working practices, lack of safety protection, and breaking safety rules. Comes with leader's guide and 25 program guides. 19m; VHS. **A:** Adult. **P:** Education. **U:** Institution. **L:** English, Spanish. **Bus-Ind:** Safety Education, Job Training. **Acq:** Purchase. **Dist:** Williams Learning Network. $495.00.

Blind Man's Bluff 1991 (PG-13) — ★★
A blind professor is accused of murdering his neighbor, but as he tries to solve the mystery, evidence points to his ex-girlfriend who may have framed him for the murder. Surprisingly suspenseful cable movie is hampered by a stock Hollywood ending. 86m; VHS, CC. **C:** Robert Urich; Lisa Eilbacher; Patricia Clarkson; Ken Pogue; Ron Perlman; Directed by James Quinn; Written by Joel Gross; Music by Richard Bellis. **Pr:** Tom Rowe; Robert Urich; Robert Urich; Wilshire Court Productions; Pacific Motion Pictures. **A:** Jr. High-Adult. **P:** Entertainment. **U:** Home. **Mov-Ent:** Mystery & Suspense, Blindness, TV Movies. **Acq:** Purchase. **Dist:** Paramount Pictures Corp.

Blind Rage 1978 (R) — ★
When the United States government transports $15 million to the Philippines, five blind kung fu masters want a piece of the action. 81m; VHS. **C:** D'Urville Martin; Leo Fong; Tony Ferrer; Dick Adair; Darnell Garcia; Leila Hermosa; Fred Williamson; Directed by Efren C. Pinon. **Pr:** MGM; Cannon Films. **A:** Sr. High-Adult. **P:** Entertainment. **U:** Home. **Mov-Ent:** Martial Arts. **Acq:** Purchase. **Dist:** MGM Home Entertainment. $59.95.

Blind Revenge 2010 (Unrated) — ★½
Uneven, melodramatic thriller. Arrogant author Sir Paul (Conti) has become reclusive since being blinded and badly scarred in an accident. He hires a live-in assistant, Jane (Hannah), to help him work on his memoirs but it's apparent that she has a malevolent agenda of her own. 88m; DVD. **C:** Tom Conti; Daryl Hannah; Miriam Margolyes; Simon MacCorkindale; Directed by Raoul Ruiz; Written by Gilbert Adair; Cinematography by Ricardo Aronovich; Music by Stephen Mark Barchan. **A:** Sr. High-Adult. **P:** Entertainment. **U:** Home. **L:** English. **Mov-Ent:** Blindness, Mystery & Suspense. **Acq:** Purchase. **Dist:** Cinema Epoch.

Blind Side 1993 (R) — ★½
DeMornay and Silver are a married couple whose Mexican vacation turns into trouble when they get into a hit-and-run accident which they don't report. Back home, they're frightened by the sudden appearance of Hauer, who's also just back from Mexico. They think he's after blackmail but he's really just a run-of-the-mill psycho intrigued by DeMornay, who at least keeps her character in control. Silver and Hauer have a great time chewing scenery. Also available in a 98-minute unrated version. 92m; VHS, DVD. **C:** Rebecca De Mornay; Ron Silver; Rutger Hauer; Directed by Geoff Murphy; Written by John Carlen. **A:** Sr. High-Adult. **P:** Entertainment. **U:** Home. **Mov-Ent:** Mystery & Suspense, TV Movies. **Acq:** Purchase. **Dist:** Home Box Office Inc. $79.99.

The Blind Side 2009 (PG-13) — ★★
Although based on the true story of NFL football player Michael Oher (Aaron), this feel-good sports tale is dominated by Bullock's portrayal of Leigh Anne Tuohy. She is the sassy Memphis belle in charge of the family that takes the disadvantaged young Michael off of the streets. She charms and wisecracks her way past her amiable husband (McGraw), her snooty friends and every other obstacle in her crusade to help Michael fulfill his potential. The not-so-subtle story is heartwarming, but a bit over the top. Based on the book by Michael Lewis. 128m; Blu-Ray, On Demand, Wide. **C:** Sandra Bullock; Tim McGraw; Quinton Aaron; Kathy Bates; Ray McKinnon; Jae Head; Lily Collins; Directed by John Lee Hancock; Written by John Lee Hancock; Cinematography by Alar Kivilo; Music by Carter Burwell. **Pr:** Gil Netter; Broderick Johnson; Andrew A. Kosove; Alcon Entertainment; Zucker/Netter Productions; Warner Bros. **A:** Jr. High-Adult. **P:** Entertainment. **U:** Home. **L:** English. **Mov-Ent:** Black Culture, Sports--Fiction: Drama, Biography: Sports. **Awds:** Oscars '09: Actress (Bullock); Golden Globes '10: Actress--Drama (Bullock); Screen Actors Guild '09: Actress (Bullock). **Acq:** Purchase. **Dist:** Warner Home Video, Inc.; Amazon.com Inc.; Movies Unlimited.

Blind Spot 1993 — ★★½
Okay family drama which works because of the performances and not the script. Woodward stars as Nell Harrington, a take-charge U.S. Representative long married to Simon (Weaver). Her troubled, pregnant daughter Phoebe (Linney) is married to Nell's aide Charlie (Diamond). Charlie is killed and Phoebe injured in a car crash but the real tragedy is when Nell discovers what caused the accident—drugs—and that her daughter is a cocaine addict. Lots of suffering. 99m; VHS, CC. **C:** Joanne Woodward; Laura Linney; Fritz Weaver; Reed Edward Diamond; Cynthia Martells; Patti Yasutake; Patti D'Arbanville; Directed by Michael Toshiyuki Uno; Written by Nina Shengold; Music by Patrick Williams. **Pr:** Andrew Gottlieb; Robert Halmi, Jr.; Richard Welsh; RHI Entertainment Inc; Signboard Hill Productions, Inc; Hallmark Hall of Fame. **A:** Jr. High-Adult. **P:** Entertainment. **U:** Home. **Mov-Ent:** Drug Abuse, TV Movies, Melodrama. **Acq:** Purchase. **Dist:** Lions Gate Entertainment Inc. $14.98.

Blind Spot: Murder by Women 2000
Six women murderers share intimate details of their upbringing, anger, and acts of violence that took a life. Provides an in-depth look at throw-away children, out-of-control adults, prison life, and the emotional, psychological and spiritual consequences of murder. 55m; VHS. **A:** Adult. **P:** Education. **U:** Institution. **Gen-Edu:** Violence, Women. **Acq:** Purchase, Rent/Lease. **Dist:** Women Make Movies. $275.00.

Blind Sunday 1976
A boy, astounded by a blind girl's ability to adjust, blindfolds himself for a day in order to understand her way of life. 31m; VHS, 3/4 U, Special order formats. **Pr:** Daniel Wilson Productions. **A:** Family. **P:** Entertainment. **U:** Institution, SURA. **Gen-Edu:** Blindness, Human Relations. **Acq:** Purchase, Rent/Lease. **Dist:** Time-Life Video and Television.

Blind Trust 2006 (Unrated) — ★★
In this Lifetime crime drama, insurance adjuster Cassie Stewart (Capshaw) gets convicted of murder despite having top criminal attorney L.G. Mennick (Hindle) working the case pro bono. Cassie goes on the lam to figure out the set-up and it's no surprise who the killer is. Now she has to prove it. 90m; DVD. **C:** Jessica Capshaw; Art Hindle; Chad Willett; Robin Wilcock; Sean Tucker; Directed by Louis Bolduc; Written by Tom Gates; Cinematography by John Ashmore. **A:** Jr. High-Adult. **P:** Entertainment. **U:** Home. **L:** English. **Mov-Ent:** Crime Drama, TV Movies. **Acq:** Purchase. **Dist:** A&E Television Networks L.L.C.

Blind Vengeance 1990 (R) — ★★½
A man whose son was murdered by white supremacists decides to take his own special revenge when they are acquited by the local jury. But this isn't your usual bloodbath; instead, he plays psychological games with the men, waiting for them to break. 93m; VHS. **C:** Gerald McRaney; Marg Helgenberger; Thalmus Rasulala; Lane Smith; Don Hood; Grand L. Bush; Directed by Lee Philips; Written by Henri Simoun; Curt Allen. **Pr:** Albert J. Salzer. **A:** Sr. High-Adult. **P:** Entertainment. **U:** Home. **Mov-Ent:** Prejudice, TV Movies. **Acq:** Purchase. **Dist:** $79.95.

Blind Vision 1991 (Unrated) — ★½
Von Dohlen stars as William Dalton, a mail clerk who is in love with his beautiful neighbor Leanne (Shelton). Suffering from extreme shyness, Dalton can only spy on her through a telephoto lens. Things start to get complicated for him when one of Leanne's boyfriends turns up dead outside her apartment. Soon afterwards, their landlady and a local police detective uncover a shocking sexual secret that forces Dalton into a deadly game of obsession and desire. 92m; VHS, CC. **C:** Lenny Von Dohlen; Deborah Shelton; Ned Beatty; Robert Vaughn; Louise Fletcher; Directed by Shuki Levy. **Pr:** Saban Entertainment. **A:** Sr. High-Adult. **P:** Entertainment. **U:** Home. **Mov-Ent:** Mystery & Suspense, Sex & Sexuality. **Acq:** Purchase. **Dist:** $89.95.

Blind Witness 1989 — ★★½
Routine story about a blind woman who's the only witness to her husband's murder during a robbery. 92m; VHS, DVD, CC. **C:** Victoria Principal; Paul LeMat; Stephen Macht; Matt Clark; Tim Choate; Directed by Richard A. Colla; Music by Robert Alcivar. **A:** Jr. High-Adult. **P:** Entertainment. **U:** Home. **Mov-Ent:** Mystery & Suspense, Blindness, TV Movies. **Acq:** Purchase. **Dist:** Trinity Films. $89.95.

Blind Woman's Curse 1970 (Unrated) — ★★
Akemi (Meiko Kaji, of "Lady Snowblood" fame) is a Yakuza, and head of a group of deadly swordswomen. Attempting to kill the leader of a rival clan she blinds his daughter when the girl throws herself in front of her father. The young blind girl and her freakishly deformed henchman devote themselves to destroying Akemi by any means necessary. 85m; DVD, Wide. **C:** Meiko Kaji; Makoto Sato; Toru Abe; Hideo Sunazuka; Ryohei Uchida; Hoki Tokuda; Yoshi Kato; Shiro Otsuji; Yoko Takagi; Directed by Teru Ishii; Written by Teru Ishii; Chusei Sone; Cinematography by Shigeru Kiazumi; Music by Hajime Kaburagi. **A:** Sr. High-Adult. **P:** Entertainment. **U:** Home. **L:** English, Japanese. **Mov-Ent:** Crime Drama. **Acq:** Purchase. **Dist:** Movies Unlimited; Alpha Video. $19.95.

Blinded by the Light 1982 (Unrated) — ★★
Young woman tries to save her brother from attachment to a quasi-religious cult, The Light of Salvation. Real-life brother and sister McNichol team up in this drama, one of the earlier examinations of cult behavior. 90m; VHS. **C:** Kristy McNichol; Jimmy (James Vincent) McNichol; Anne Jackson; Michael McGuire; Directed by John A. Alonzo. **A:** Preschool. **P:** Entertainment. **U:** Institution, SURA. **Mov-Ent:** Cults, TV Movies. **Acq:** Purchase, Rent/Lease. **Dist:** Time-Life Video and Television.

Blindfold: Acts of Obsession 1994 (R) — ★★
Madeline's (Doherty) marriage is boring so she consults therapist Jennings (Nelson). He suggests a number of sexual fantasies Madeline plays out with hubby Woods only to have murder enter the picture. Then Madeline's older sister Chris (Alfonso) is assigned to investigate and lets out lots of family secrets. Shannen in the buff, murder, infidelity, deception, and sex. An unrated version is also available. 93m; VHS. **C:** Shannen Doherty; Judd Nelson; Michael Woods; Kristian Alfonso; Shell Danielson; Drew Snyder; Directed by Lawrence L. Simeone; Written by Lawrence L. Simeone; Music by Shuki Levy. **Pr:** Ronnie Hadar; Lance H. Robbins; Libra Films. **A:** College-Adult. **P:** Entertainment. **U:** Home. **Mov-Ent:** Mystery & Suspense, Sex & Sexuality, Marriage. **Acq:** Purchase. **Dist:** WarnerVision. $92.95.

Blindness 2008 (R) — ★½
An entire city's population is suddenly struck blind, degraded to lost souls wandering the streets, filthy, ruined, and dying. The only ones not affected by the epidemic are the inmates quarantined at prison, who descend into sheer madness from hunger, and an oppressive leader (Bernal) who wields a gun and newly-discovered sense of dictatorship. Much to her confusion, the local eye doctor's wife (Moore) also retains her vision, as well as her sense of order. The relentless allegorical suffering and way-too-artsy effects make it almost impossible to lay off the fast-forward button. Adapted from the novel by Jose Saramago. 118m; Blu-Ray, Wide. **C:** Julianne Moore; Mark Ruffalo; Danny Glover; Gael Garcia Bernal; Alice Braga; Maury Chaykin; Don McKellar; Directed by Fernando Meirelles; Written by Don McKellar; Cinematography by Cesar Charlone; Music by Marcus Antonio Guimaraes. **Pr:** Niv Fichman; Andrea Barata Ribeiro; Sonoko Sakai; Rhombus Media; O2 Filmes; Bee Vine Pictures; Miramax Film Corp. **A:** Sr. High-Adult. **P:** Entertainment. **U:** Home. **L:** English. **Mov-Ent:** Blindness. **Acq:** Purchase. **Dist:** Miramax Film Corp.; Movies Unlimited.

Blindness: A Family Matter 1986
A look at blindness rehabilitation centers and ways that the blind can carry on a normal life. 23m; VHS, 3/4 U. **Pr:** Cinemakers, Inc. **A:** Jr. High-Adult. **P:** Education. **U:** Institution, SURA. **Hea-Sci:** Blindness. **Acq:** Purchase. **Dist:** Phoenix Learning Group. $195.00.

Blindness: Five Points of View 1980
A documentary dealing with five blindness victims, the causes of blindness, and the link between blindness and aging. From the "Nova" series. 60m; VHS, 3/4 U, Special order formats. **Pr:** WGBH Boston. **A:** Sr. High-Adult. **P:** Education. **U:** Institution, SURA. **Hea-Sci:** Documentary Films, Blindness. **Acq:** Purchase, Rent/Lease. **Dist:** Time-Life Video and Television.

Blindside 1988 (R) — ★★
A surveillance hobbyist who owns a motel spies on his tenants until a murder involves him in a big-scale drug war. 98m; VHS. **C:** Harvey Keitel; Lori Hallier; Lolita Davidovich; Alan Fawcett; Michael Rudder; Directed by Paul Lynch. **Pr:** Peter Simpson. **A:** Sr. High-Adult. **P:** Entertainment. **U:** Home. **Mov-Ent:** Mystery & Suspense, Drugs. **Acq:** Purchase. **Dist:** New Line Home Video. $14.98.

Blindsided 1993 (PG-13) — ★★½
A former police officer temporarily loses his sight when he plays the middle man in a bank robbery. Sight improving, he falls for a woman who draws him into another crime. 93m; VHS. **C:** Jeff Fahey; Mia Sara; Rudy Ramos; Jack Kehler; Ben Gazzara; Directed by Thomas Michael Donnelly. **A:** Jr. High-Adult. **P:** Entertainment. **U:** Home. **Mov-Ent:** Mystery & Suspense. **Acq:** Purchase. **Dist:** Universal Music and Video Distribution. $89.98.

Bling Bling 2002
An up-and-coming rapper gets his first record deal only to find out the company is a front for running drugs, when he tries to break the deal he ends up running for his life. 84m; VHS, DVD. **A:** Adult. **P:** Entertainment. **U:** Home. **Mov-Ent:** Action-Adventure, Drama. **Acq:** Purchase. **Dist:** York Entertainment. $14.99.

The Bling Ring 2011 (Unrated) — ★★
Lifetime movie inspired by a true story. Zack goes to an L.A. school for troubled teens where he's befriended by risk-taker Natalie. She learns when the homes of celebrities are empty and the two break in and steal personal items like clothes and jewelry. Their friends find out and join in and their exploits are posted online, leading to attention from the media and the cops. 88m; DVD. **C:** Austin Butler; Yin Chang; Tom Irwin; Sebastian Sozzi; Jennifer Grey; Wendy Makkena; Directed by Michael Lembeck; Written by Shelley Evans; Cinematography by Ousama Rawi; Music by Lawrence Shragge. **A:** Jr. High-Adult. **P:** Entertainment. **U:** Home. **Mov-Ent:** TV Movies, Mass Media. **Acq:** Purchase. **Dist:** A&E Television Networks L.L.C.

The Bling Ring 2013 (R) — ★★★
Coppola returns to the spoiled hills of Hollywood with this excellent true crime story about the TMZ generation. In an era when a celebrity's every move is tracked by the paparazzi and the most red carpet-friendly of them amass so much wealth and property that they don't even notice when it's gone, Coppola's film dares to not demonize the kids who chose to steal from their

favorite celebs but to almost ask, "Can you blame them?" With a stunning degree of directorial confidence, this dramedy takes a unique approach to a story that could have been little more than a moral message. 90m; DVD, Blu-Ray. **C:** Emma Watson; Israel Broussard; Katie Chang; Claire Julien; Taissa Farmiga; Gavin Rossdale; Leslie Mann; Cameo(s) Paris Hilton; Directed by Sofia Coppola; Written by Sofia Coppola; Cinematography by Harris Savides; Music by Brian Reitzell. **Pr:** Roman Coppola; Youree Henley; Sofia Coppola; American Zoetrope; Nala Films; A24. **A:** Sr. High-Adult. **P:** Entertainment. **U:** Home. **L:** English. **Mov-Ent:** Adolescence, Crime Drama. **Acq:** Purchase. **Dist:** Lions Gate Home Entertainment.

Blink 1993 (R) — ★★½
Recent corneal transplants allow blind musician Emma (Stowe) to regain her sight, but until they "settle" what she sees may not register in her mind immediately, a phenomenon the script dubs "retroactive vision." This poses a problem for Chicago cop Quinn when he falls for Emma—the only one who can recognize a sadistic killer. Average thriller has been done better before, but adds two attractive leads, enough suspense, and a unique twist to the typical woman-in-jeopardy tale to keep things interesting. The distorted images in Stowe's blurry vision were created by computer. Stowe also learned fiddle for her place as the fictional member of the real-life Irish-American band, The Drovers. 106m; VHS, DVD, Wide, CC. **C:** Madeleine Stowe; Aidan Quinn; Laurie Metcalf; James Remar; Bruce A. Young; Peter Friedman; Paul Dillon; Michael Kirkpatrick; Directed by Michael Apted; Written by Dana Stevens; Cinematography by Dante Spinotti; Music by Brad Fiedel. **Pr:** David Blocker; Robert Shaye; New Line Cinema. **A:** Sr. High-Adult. **P:** Entertainment. **U:** Home. **Mov-Ent:** Crime Drama, Blindness. **Acq:** Purchase. **Dist:** New Line Home Video. $19.95.

Blink of an Eye 1992 (R) — ★½
Special agent Sam Browning (Pare) must use his psychic powers and military skills against the terrorists who have kidnapped the CIA director's daughter. 90m; VHS, CC. **C:** Michael Pare; Janis Lee; Uri Gavriel; Amos Lavi; Sasson Gabai; Jack Widerker; Directed by Bob Misiorowski; Written by Edward Kovach; Cinematography by David Gurfinkel; Music by Vladimir Horunzhy. **Pr:** Jacob Kotzky. **A:** Sr. High-Adult. **P:** Entertainment. **U:** Home. **Mov-Ent:** Terrorism, Intelligence Service. **Acq:** Purchase. **Dist:** CinemaNow Inc. $89.95.

Bliss 1985 (R) — ★★★½
A savage, surreal Australian comedy about an advertising executive who dies suddenly for a few minutes, and upon his awakening he finds the world maniacally, bizarrely changed. Based on the Peter Carey novel, and one of the most inspired absurdist films of the decade. 112m; VHS. **C:** Barry Otto; Lynette Curran; Helen Jones; Directed by Ray Lawrence; Written by Peter Carey. **Pr:** Jay Lawrence. **A:** College-Adult. **P:** Entertainment. **U:** Home. **L:** Spanish. **Mov-Ent:** Comedy--Black, Advertising, Death. **Awds:** Australian Film Inst. '85: Film. **Acq:** Purchase. **Dist:** Anchor Bay Entertainment. $19.95.

Bliss 1996 (R) — ★½
Creepy feature-length sex-ed lecture delves deeply into sexual problems in modern society. So deeply, in fact, that it could've been called "Ouch, You're on my Hair." Clueless yuppies Joseph (Sheffer) and Maria's (Lee) sexual dysfunctions lead her to seek aid from unconventional therapist Baltazar (Stamp), who does things like compare women to violins (hint: they're not really the same. Unless you REALLY like wood). Joseph has his doubts, but soon becomes a chanting tantric goofball. Too clinical to be sexy, but too sexy to be used as an Army training film. 103m; VHS, DVD, CC. **C:** Sheryl Lee; Craig Sheffer; Terence Stamp; Casey Siemaszko; Spalding Gray; Leigh Taylor-Young; Lois Chiles; Blu Mankuma; Directed by Lance Young; Written by Lance Young; Cinematography by Mike Molloy; Music by Jan A.P. Kaczmarek. **Pr:** Allyn Stewart; Matthew O'Connor; Triumph Films; Stewart Pictures; Sony Pictures Home Entertainment Inc. **A:** College-Adult. **P:** Entertainment. **U:** Home. **Mov-Ent:** Marriage, Sex & Sexuality, Psychiatry. **Acq:** Purchase. **Dist:** Sony Pictures Home Entertainment Inc.

Bliss 2007 (Unrated) — ★★
When 17-year-old Meryem is found unconscious, it's assumed she has been raped and, to protect the village's honor, she's condemned to death. But Cemal, the young man who's supposed to kill her, can't go through with it and instead the twosome run away together. Turkish with subtitles. 105m; DVD. **C:** Ozgu Namal; Murat Han; Talat Bulut; Directed by Abdullah Oguz; Written by Abdullah Oguz; Cinematography by Mirsad Herovic. **A:** Adult. **P:** Entertainment. **U:** Home. **L:** Turkish. **Mov-Ent:** Drama, Rape. **Acq:** Purchase. **Dist:** Arab Film Distribution.

Bliss: Checkmate Ballet 1990
A one act ballet presented by the Sadler's Wells Royal Ballet. One in a series of Masterpieces of British Ballet. 45m; VHS. **C:** Directed by Ninette de Valois. **Pr:** Video Artists International. **A:** Family. **P:** Entertainment. **U:** Home. **Fin-Art:** Performing Arts, Dance--Ballet, Dance--Performance. **Acq:** Purchase. **Dist:** Music Video Distributors; Video Artists International; Facets Multimedia Inc. $29.95.

The Bliss of Mrs. Blossom 1968 (Unrated) — ★★★
Three's a crowd in this light-hearted romp through the machinations of a brassiere manufacturer (Attenborough) and his neglected wife (MacLaine). Mrs. Blossom finds sewing machine repairman Booth so appetizing that she hides him in the attic of the Blossom home. He reads books and redecorates, until, several plot twists later, Attenborough discovers the truth. Witty and wise, with fine supporting cast and excellent pacing. 93m; DVD, CC. **C:** Shirley MacLaine; Richard Attenborough; James Booth; Freddie Jones; John Cleese; Directed by Joseph McGrath. **A:** Jr. High-Adult. **P:** Entertainment. **U:** Home. **Mov-Ent:** Comedy--Screwball, Marriage. **Acq:** Purchase. **Dist:** Paramount Pictures Corp.; Movies Unlimited. $14.95.

Bliss: The Complete First Season 2005
Presents the eight-episode first season from the female-oriented Oxygen cable channel about women exploring their sexuality. 184m; DVD. **A:** College-Adult. **P:** Entertainment. **U:** Home. **Mov-Ent:** Television, Sex & Sexuality, Women. **Acq:** Purchase. **Dist:** Bedford Entertainment Inc. $24.95.

Blissymbolics 1987
A story of how a thirteen-year-old developed a computer program to help severely disabled people who cannot communicate. 8m; VHS, 3/4 U. **Pr:** Paulle Clarke. **A:** Family. **P:** Education. **U:** Institution, Home, SURA. **Gen-Edu:** Documentary Films, Handicapped, Gifted Children. **Acq:** Purchase, Duplication License. **Dist:** Bullfrog Films, Inc.

Blithe Spirit 1945 (Unrated) — ★★★½
Charming and funny adaptation of Coward's famed stage play. A man re-marries and finds his long-dead wife is unhappy enough about it to come back and haunt him. Clever supporting cast, with Rutherford exceptional as the medium. Received Oscar for its Special Effects. 96m; VHS, DVD. **C:** Rex Harrison; Constance Cummings; Kay Hammond; Margaret Rutherford; Hugh Wakefield; Joyce Carey; Jacqueline Clarke; Directed by David Lean; Written by Noel Coward; Anthony Havelock-Allan; Cinematography by Ronald Neame; Music by Richard Addinsell. **Pr:** Cineguild. **A:** Adult. **P:** Entertainment. **U:** Home. **Mov-Ent:** Fantasy, Death. **Acq:** Purchase. **Dist:** Facets Multimedia Inc.; MGM Home Entertainment. $14.95.

Blitz 1985 (R) — ★½
A German car designer's pet project, a car that runs without gas, is halted by the influence of an Arab conglomerate. He nevertheless tries to complete it, and is hunted down. 104m; VHS, DVD. **C:** Jurgen Prochnow; Senta Berger; William Conrad; Agnes Soral; Directed by Michael Verhoeven; Written by Michael Verhoeven; Cinematography by Jacques Steyn; Music by Michael Landau. **Pr:** Mario Krebs. **A:** Jr. High-Adult. **P:** Entertainment. **U:** Home. **Mov-Ent:** Mystery & Suspense, Automobiles. **Acq:** Purchase. **Dist:** CinemaNow Inc.; Anchor Bay Entertainment. $79.95.

Blitz 2011 (R) — ★★
East London detective Tom Brant (Statham), a violence-prone loner, is teamed with gay, by-the-book Porter Nash (Considine) to find a serial killer targeting cops. Naturally, the killer likes to taunt the police, including using tabloid sleaze Dunphy (Morrissey). Tries to do a bit too much, but the cast is fine and the pace is quick even if the story is familiar. Based on novel by Ken Bruen. 97m; DVD, Blu-Ray. **C:** Jason Statham; Paddy Considine; Aidan Gillen; David Morrissey; Zawe Ashton; Mark Rylance; Nicky Henson; Directed by Elliott Lester; Written by Nathan Parker; Cinematography by Rob Hardy; Music by Ilan Eshkeri. **A:** Sr. High-Adult. **P:** Entertainment. **U:** Home. **Mov-Ent.** **Acq:** Purchase. **Dist:** Millennium Entertainment L.L.C.

Blitzkreig 1990
Original archive material highlights this documentary on WWII. 80m/B/W; VHS. **TV Std:** NTSC, PAL. **Pr:** PAV. **A:** Jr. High-Adult. **P:** Education. **U:** Home. **Gen-Edu:** Documentary Films, History--Modern, War--General. **Acq:** Purchase, Rent/Lease. **Dist:** German Language Video Center.

Blitzkrieg Bop 1999
Features interviews and performances from punk rock luminaries Blondie, the Ramones and the Dead Boys in 1977, the heyday of the punk rock movement. 52m; VHS. **A:** Sr. High-Adult. **P:** Entertainment. **U:** Home. **Mov-Ent:** Music--Pop/Rock, Music--Performance, Interviews. **Acq:** Purchase. **Dist:** Ivy Classics Video. $29.95.

Blitzstein's Cradle 197?
Excerpts from Marc Blitzstein's "The Cradle Will Rock" are performed in this program. 30m/B/W; VHS, 3/4 U, EJ, Q. **Pr:** WCBS New York; Camera Three Productions. **A:** Sr. High-Adult. **P:** Entertainment. **U:** Institution, SURA. **Fin-Art:** Performing Arts, Opera. **Acq:** Duplication, Free Duplication. **Dist:** Camera Three Productions, Inc.; Creative Arts Television Archive.

Blizzard of AAHHH's: A True Story 1988
A look at the known and unknown heroes of the ski world. Features cliff-jumper Scot Schmidt, extreme skier Glen Plake, and precision skier Mike Hattrup. This movie contains some of the best ski action ever filmed from the premier extreme/steep skiing destinations in the world. 75m; VHS. **Pr:** Greg Stump Productions; NSI. **A:** Family. **P:** Entertainment. **U:** Home. **Spo-Rec:** Sports--General, Sports--Winter, Skiing. **Acq:** Purchase. **Dist:** Greg Stump Productions; Fast Forward. $39.95.

Blizzard's Wonderful Wooden Toys 1988
British woodworker and TV host Richard Blizzard demonstrates seven wooden toys and models. Projects range from novice to expert, and the tape comes with an instruction booklet with complete plans. 108m; VHS. **Pr:** BBC Enterprises Ltd. **A:** Jr. High-Adult. **P:** Instruction. **U:** Home. **How-Ins:** Crafts, Woodworking, How-To. **Acq:** Purchase. **Dist:** Home Vision Cinema. $24.95.

The Blob 1958 — ★★½
Sci-fi thriller about a small town's fight against a slimy jello invader from space. Slightly rebellious McQueen (in his first starring role) redeems himself when he saves the town with quick action. Low-budget, horror/teen-fantasy became a camp classic. Other names considered included "The Glob," "The Glob that Girdled the Globe," "The Meteorite Monster," "The Molten Meteorite," and "The Night of the Creeping Dead." Followed by a worthless sequel in 1972, "Son of Blob," and a worthwhile remake in 1988. 83m; DVD, Blu-Ray. **C:** Steve McQueen; Aneta Corsaut; Olin Howlin; Earl Rowe; Alden "Steve" Chase; John Benson; Vincent Barbi; Directed by Irvin S. Yeaworth, Jr.; Written by Kay Linaker; Theodore Simonson; Cinematography by Thomas E. Spalding; Music by Burt Bacharach; Hal David; Ralph Carmichael. **Pr:** Jack H. Harris; Paramount Pictures. **A:** Family. **P:** Entertainment. **U:** Home. **Mov-Ent:** Science Fiction, Cult Films. **Acq:** Purchase. **Dist:** Criterion Collection Inc. $19.95.

The Blob 1988 (R) — ★★★
A hi-tech remake of the 1958 camp classic about a small town beset by a fast-growing, man-eating mound of glop shot into space by scientists, irradiated into an unnatural being, and then returned to earth. Well-developed characters make this an excellent tribute to the first film. 92m; VHS, DVD, CC. **C:** Kevin Dillon; Candy Clark; Joe Seneca; Shawnee Smith; Donovan Leitch; Jeffrey DeMunn; Ricky Paull Goldin; Del Close; Directed by Chuck Russell; Written by Chuck Russell; Frank Darabont; Cinematography by Mark Irwin. **Pr:** Tri-Star Pictures. **A:** Sr. High-Adult. **P:** Entertainment. **U:** Home. **Mov-Ent:** Science Fiction. **Acq:** Purchase. **Dist:** Sony Pictures Home Entertainment Inc. $89.95.

Bloc Party: God Bless Bloc Party 2006
2005 performances by Bloc Party at L.A.'s El Ray Theater and a festival in Belfort, France. Includes backstage footage and interviews. 60m; DVD. **A:** Jr. High-Adult. **P:** Entertainment. **U:** Home. **Fin-Art:** Documentary Films, Music--Performance. **Acq:** Purchase. **Dist:** Music Video Distributors.

Block-heads 1938 (Unrated) — ★★★
Twenty years after the end of WWI, soldier Stan is found, still in his foxhole, and brought back to America, where he moves in with old pal Ollie. Also includes a 1934 Charley Chase short "I'll Take Vanilla." 75m/B/W; VHS, DVD. **C:** Stan Laurel; Oliver Hardy; Billy Gilbert; Patricia Ellis; James Finlayson; Charley Chase; Directed by John Blystone. **Pr:** Hal Roach; MGM. **A:** Family. **P:** Entertainment. **U:** Home. **Mov-Ent:** Comedy--Slapstick, Classic Films. **Acq:** Purchase. **Dist:** $19.95.

Blockhouse 1973 (Unrated) — **Bomb!**
Four men are entombed in a subterranean stronghold for six years after the D-Day invasion of Normandy. Encourages claustrophobic feeling in viewer. Based on Jean Paul Cleberts' novel "Le Blockhaus." 88m; VHS, DVD. **C:** Peter Sellers; Charles Aznavour; Per Oscarsson; Peter Vaughan; Leon Lissek; Alfred Lynch; Jeremy Kemp; Directed by Clive Rees. **Pr:** Anthony Rufus Isaacs; Edgar M. Bronfman, Jr. **A:** Jr. High-Adult. **P:** Entertainment. **U:** Home. **Mov-Ent:** World War Two. **Acq:** Purchase. **Dist:** Unknown Distributor.

Blocking a Scene: Basic Staging with Actors 1990
Tips for the novice director, featuring the elements of blocking, script analysis, creating an effective floor plan, and collaborating with actors. 70m; VHS. **A:** College-Adult. **P:** Instruction. **U:** Home. **How-Ins:** Theater. **Acq:** Purchase. **Dist:** Stagestep. $148.95.

Blocking Schemes for the Inside Zone Running Game 2005 (Unrated)
Coaches Curt Newsome and Ulrick Edmonds detail the offensive scheme they teach their football team. 48m; DVD. **A:** Family. **P:** Education. **U:** Home, Institution. **Spo-Rec:** Football, Athletic Instruction/Coaching. **Acq:** Purchase. **Dist:** Championship Productions. $39.99.

Blocks 1982
Early childhood educators examine the importance of playing with building blocks for children and their potential educational capabilities. 17m; VHS, 3/4 U. **Pr:** Steve Campus Productions. **A:** Adult. **P:** Teacher Education. **U:** Institution, CCTV, Home. **Gen-Edu:** Documentary Films, Education. **Acq:** Purchase, Rent/Lease. **Dist:** Campus Film Distributors Corp.

The Blonde 1992 (Unrated) — ★★
Tommasso (Rubini) is driving through the Milan streets when he knocks down a young blonde woman (Kinski). She loses her memory (apparently due to shock) and Tommasso agrees to help her—soon falling in love. One day her memory returns and Christina remembers she's involved with a drug dealer and other shady characters. She leaves Tommasso to protect him but he's got other ideas. Italian with subtitles. 100m; VHS, DVD. **C:** Sergio Rubini; Nastassja Kinski; Ennio Fantastichini; Umberto Raho; Veronica Lazar; Giacomo Piperno; Directed by Sergio Rubini; Written by Sergio Rubini; Filippo Ascione; Umberto Marino; Cinematography by Alessio Gelsini Torresi; Music by Jurgen Knieper. **A:** College-Adult. **P:** Entertainment. **U:** Home. **L:** Italian. **Mov-Ent:** Drama, Drug Trafficking/Dealing. **Acq:** Purchase. **Dist:** Vanguard International Cinema, Inc.

Blonde 2001 (Unrated) — ★★½
Montgomery may not be as curvy as the real Marilyn Monroe, but she does well in this routine biopic about the bombshell who suffered from life-long problems with self-esteem and men. Based on the novel by Joyce Carol Oates, the miniseries covers Marilyn from her disturbing childhood/teenage Norma Jean Baker years to her transformation into a screen goddess, although it ends before her death. 240m; DVD. **C:** Poppy Montgomery; Skye McCole Bartusiak; Patricia Richardson; Ann-Margret; Kirstie Alley; Eric Bogosian; Wallace Shawn; Patrick Dempsey; Jensen Ackles; Titus Welliver; Griffin Dunne; Richard Roxburgh; Directed by Joyce Chopra; Written by Joyce Eliason; Cinematography by James Glennon; Music by Patrick Williams. **A:** Jr. High-Adult. **P:** Entertainment. **U:** Home. **Mov-Ent:** Biography: Show Business. **Acq:** Purchase. **Dist:** Allumination Filmworks.

Blonde Ambition 2007 (PG-13) — ★½
Simpson plays a clueless blonde (how's that for typecasting?) in this would-be comedy that at least has a couple of supporting

performances to save it. Naive Katie heads to NY to see her boyfriend, discovers him cheating, but bucks up when she suddenly gets a job working for a bigshot CEO (Larry Miller) and begins dating Ben (a befuddled Wilson) from the mailroom. The job is a set-up by a couple of sleazy co-workers (Penelope Ann Miller, Dick) looking for a corporate takeover and the blonde must save the day. 93m; DVD. **C:** Jessica Simpson; Luke Wilson; Larry Miller; Penelope Ann Miller; Andy Dick; Rachael Leigh Cook; Drew Fuller; Willie Nelson; Directed by Scott Marshall; Written by John Cohen; Cinematography by Mark Irwin. **A:** Jr. High-Adult. **P:** Entertainment. **U:** Home. **Mov-Ent.** **Acq:** Purchase. **Dist:** Sony Pictures Home Entertainment Inc.

Blonde and Blonder 2007 (PG-13) — ★
The distaff "Dumb and Dumber" with lots of pink. Dee (Anderson) and Dawn (Richards) witness a mob hit done by pro Kat (Vaugier) and associate Kit (Ory) and then, somehow, get mistaken for the hired killers. They are offered a contract to take out Chinese gangster Mr. Wong (Mann), naturally believing that "take out" means something much less lethal, thus leading to more comic misadventure. Both blondes are getting too old to play ditzy dames even when they're in on the joke. 95m; DVD, Wide. **C:** Pamela Anderson; Denise Richards; Byron Mann; Emmanuelle Vaugier; Meaghan Ory; John Farley; Kevin Farley; Directed by Dean Hamilton; Written by Dean Hamilton; Rolfe Kanefsky; Gerry Anderson; Cinematography by C. Kim Miles; Music by William Goodrum. **A:** Jr. High-Adult. **P:** Entertainment. **U:** Home. **Mov-Ent.** **Acq:** Purchase. **Dist:** Alpha Video; Movies Unlimited.

Blonde Blackmailer 1958 — ★
Boring story about an innocent man who serves time for the murder of a female blackmailer. When he's released, he searches for the real killer. 69m/B/W; VHS. **C:** Richard Arlen; Susan Shaw; Vincent Ball; Constance Leigh; Directed by Charles Deane; Written by Charles Deane. **A:** Jr. High-Adult. **P:** Entertainment. **U:** Home. **Mov-Ent:** Mystery & Suspense. **Acq:** Purchase. **Dist:** Rex Miller Artisan Studio.

Blonde Comet 1941 (Unrated) — ★
Betsy Blake (Vale) is a famous female European race car driver who decides to try her hand at racing in America. She soon runs into a rival in the form of Jim Flynn (Kent), a racer trying to invent a new form of carburetor. The usual evil bad guy attempts to foil his inventing efforts and their budding romance. Despite Vale playing a female driver long before women drivers were allowed, don't expect her to portray a feminist—this was made in the 40s after all. 65m/B/W; DVD. **C:** Virginia Vale; Robert Kent; Barney Oldfield; Vince Barnett; William (Bill) Halligan; Joey Ray; Red Knight; Diane Hughes; Directed by William Beaudine; Written by Phillip Juergens; Robin Daniels; Cinematography by Jack Greenhalgh; Music by Andrew Keresztes. **A:** Sr. High-Adult. **P:** Entertainment. **U:** Home. **L:** English, French, Spanish. **Mov-Ent:** Sports--Fiction: Drama, Drama, Inventors & Inventions. **Acq:** Purchase. **Dist:** Alpha Video Distributors. $7.98.

Blonde Crazy 1931 (Unrated) — ★★½
A charming grifter hooks up with a gorgeous blonde as he works the territory of a big wheel criminal. Escapist fare, with fun performances from Cagney and Blondell. 81m/B/W; VHS. **C:** James Cagney; Joan Blondell; Louis Calhern; Ray Milland; Nat Pendleton; Directed by Roy Del Ruth. **Pr:** MGM. **A:** Jr. High-Adult. **P:** Entertainment. **U:** Home. **Mov-Ent:** Comedy--Romantic. **Acq:** Purchase. **Dist:** MGM Home Entertainment. $19.98.

Blonde for a Day 1946 (Unrated) — ★½
Private eye Michael Shayne (Beaumont) is on the case for a newspaper reporter who finds herself in trouble when she writes articles attacking the police department for failing to solve a string of murders. She's got info about a gambling ring and the crooks are none too happy about it. Shayne's got to help the reporter and bring the crooks to justice. 68m/B/W; DVD. **C:** Hugh Beaumont; Kathryn Adams; Cy Kendall; Marjorie Hoshelle; Richard Fraser; Directed by Sam Newfield; Written by Brett Halliday; Fred Myton; Cinematography by Jack Greenhalgh. **Pr:** Sigmund Neufeld. **A:** Jr. High-Adult. **P:** Entertainment. **U:** Home. **Mov-Ent:** Journalism. **Acq:** Purchase. **Dist:** Nostalgia Collectibles.

Blonde Ice 1948 — ★★
Cheap and fun B-movie noir. Psycho San Francisco society columnist Claire (Brooks) turns out to be a femme who's very fatale to the men she gets involved with. She just loves to see her name in the scandal rags and is even willing to frame new boyfriend Les (Paige) if it means headlines. 74m/B/W; DVD. **C:** Leslie Brooks; Robert Paige; Walter Sande; John Holland; Emory Parnell; Directed by Jack Bernhard; Written by Kenneth Gamet; Cinematography by George Robinson; Music by Irving Gertz. **A:** Sr. High-Adult. **P:** Entertainment. **U:** Home. **Mov-Ent.** **Acq:** Purchase. **Dist:** VCI Entertainment.

Blonde in Black Leather 1977 (Unrated) — ★½
A bored Italian housewife takes up with a leather-clad lady biker, and together they cavort about. 88m; VHS. **C:** Claudia Cardinale; Monica Vitti; Directed by Carlo Di Palma. **Pr:** Franco Cristaldi. **A:** Sr. High-Adult. **P:** Entertainment. **U:** Home. **Mov-Ent.** **Acq:** Purchase. **Dist:** New Line Home Video. $59.95.

Blonde Savage 1947 — ★
Charting African territories, an adventurer encounters a white jungle queen swinging amongst the vines. Essentially a cheap, distaff "Tarzan." 62m/B/W; VHS, DVD. **C:** Leif Erickson; Gale Sherwood; Veda Ann Borg; Douglass Dumbrille; Frank Jenks; Matt Willis; Ernest Whitman; Directed by Steve Sekely. **Pr:** Eagle Lion. **A:** Primary-Adult. **P:** Entertainment. **U:** Home. **Mov-Ent.** **Acq:** Purchase. **Dist:** Sinister Cinema. $16.95.

Blonde Venus 1932 (Unrated) — ★★★½
A German cafe singer marries an Englishman, but their marriage hits the skids when he contracts radiation poisoning and she gets a nightclub job to pay the bills. Sternberg's and Dietrich's fourth film together, and characteristically beautiful, though terribly strange. Dietrich's cabaret number "Hot Voodoo," in a gorilla suit and blonde afro, attains new heights in early Hollywood surrealism. 94m/B/W; VHS, DVD. **C:** Marlene Dietrich; Herbert Marshall; Cary Grant; Dickie Moore; Hattie McDaniel; Sidney Toler; Directed by Josef von Sternberg. **Pr:** Paramount Pictures. **A:** Family. **P:** Entertainment. **U:** Home. **Mov-Ent:** Musical--Drama, Marriage. **Acq:** Purchase. **Dist:** Movies Unlimited; Alpha Video; Universal Studios Home Video. $14.98.

The Blondes 2003 (Unrated)
Albertina Carri lost her parents when she was three years old during Argentina's military rule, for her second feature film she returns to Buenos Aires to uncover facts and mysteries about their life, disappearance, and death. 89m; DVD. **A:** Adult. **P:** Education. **U:** Institution. **L:** Spanish. **Gen-Edu:** South America, War--General, Family. **Acq:** Purchase. **Dist:** Women Make Movies. $295.00.

Blondes at Work 1938 (Unrated) — ★½
Torchy scoops her rival newshounds because boyfriend detective Steve McBride and his cop assistant Gahagan can't keep their traps shut. Now Torchy wants the low-down on murdered department store tycoon Martin Spencer, especially when his friend Maitland Greer is arrested and put on trial for the crime. Fourth entry in the series. 63m/B/W; DVD. **C:** Glenda Farrell; Barton MacLane; Tom Kennedy; Don Briggs; Robert Middlemass; Frank Shannon; Kenneth Harlan; Rosella Town; Betty Compson; Directed by Frank McDonald; Written by Albert DeMond; Cinematography by Warren Lynch. **A:** Jr. High-Adult. **P:** Entertainment. **U:** Home. **Mov-Ent:** Journalism. **Acq:** Purchase. **Dist:** WarnerArchive.com.

Blondes Have More Guns 1995 (R) — ★★
Very dumb detective Harry Bates (McGaharin) is investigating a chainsaw murder and falls for the mysterious Montana (Key), who's possibly a serial killer, or maybe it's her half-sister, Dakota (Lusiak). Spoof of "Basic Instinct" and others of that ilk, done in the usual Troma fashion. 90m; VHS, DVD. **C:** Michael McGahern; Elizabeth Key; Gloria Lusiak; Richard Neil; Bonnie Buttner; Romana Lisa; Andre Brazeau; Directed by George Merriweather; Written by George Merriweather; Dan Goodman; Mary Guthrie; Cinematography by Maximo Munzi; Music by Joe Renzetti. **Pr:** Troma Team. **A:** Sr. High-Adult. **P:** Entertainment. **U:** Home. **Mov-Ent.** **Acq:** Purchase. **Dist:** Troma Entertainment. $69.98.

Blondie 1938 — ★★½
Chic Young's famous comic strip debuted on the big screen with Singleton in the title role, Lake as the bumbling Dagwood, and Simms as Baby Dumpling (son Alexander, when he grows up). The couple are about to celebrate their 5th wedding anniversary when Dagwood loses his job and Blondie suspects him of infidelity. The series eventually contained 28 films. 68m/B/W; VHS, DVD. **C:** Penny Singleton; Arthur Lake; Larry Simms; Gene Lockhart; Ann Doran; Jonathan Hale; Gordon Oliver; Stanley Andrews; Dorothy Moore; Directed by Frank Strayer; Written by Richard Flournoy; Cinematography by Henry Freulich. **Pr:** Frank Sparks; Columbia Pictures. **A:** Family. **P:** Entertainment. **U:** Home. **Mov-Ent:** Marriage. **Acq:** Purchase. **Dist:** Movies Unlimited. $19.99.

Blondie Brings Up Baby 1939 — ★★
Baby Dumpling is enrolled in school but on his first day he plays hooky to find Daisy who's been caught by the dogcatcher. But Blondie and Dagwood think the tyke has been kidnapped! 67m/B/W; VHS, DVD. **C:** Penny Singleton; Arthur Lake; Larry Simms; Jonathan Hale; Danny Mummert; Fay Helm; Peggy Ann Garner; Irving Bacon; Directed by Frank Strayer; Written by Richard Flournoy; Gladys Lehman; Cinematography by Henry Freulich. **A:** Family. **P:** Entertainment. **U:** Home. **Mov-Ent:** Family, Pets. **Acq:** Purchase. **Dist:** Movies Unlimited.

Blondie: Eat to the Beat 1980
The multi-million seller platinum album, "Eat to the Beat," taped on location and in a studio. The program contains 12 songs, including the hit singles "Dreaming" and "The Hardest Part." 60m; VHS. **Pr:** Warner Bros. **A:** Family. **P:** Entertainment. **U:** Home. **Mov-Ent:** Music--Performance. **Acq:** Purchase. **Dist:** Music Video Distributors; Warner Home Video, Inc. $14.95.

Blondie for Victory 1942 — ★½
As her personal contribution to the war effort, Blondie joins the Housewives of America who perform various home front duties. Only their husbands aren't very happy since they're left home tending to the kids and the household chores. 68m/B/W; VHS. **C:** Penny Singleton; Arthur Lake; Larry Simms; Jonathan Hale; Danny Mummert; Stuart Erwin; Irving Bacon; Directed by Frank Strayer; Written by Connie Lee; Karen De Wolf; Cinematography by Henry Freulich. **A:** Family. **P:** Entertainment. **U:** Home. **Mov-Ent:** Family. **Acq:** Purchase. **Dist:** Movies Unlimited.

Blondie Goes Latin 1942 — ★★
Mr. Dithers invites the Bumsteads on a South American cruise and Dagwood winds up the drummer in the shipboard band while Singleton gets to show off her Broadway background in some musical numbers. 70m/B/W; VHS, DVD. **C:** Penny Singleton; Arthur Lake; Jonathan Hale; Larry Simms; Ruth Terry; Tito Guizar; Danny Mummert; Irving Bacon; Directed by Frank Strayer; Written by Richard Flournoy; Karen De Wolf; Cinematography by Henry Freulich. **A:** Family. **P:** Entertainment. **U:** Home. **Mov-Ent:** Family, Boating. **Acq:** Purchase. **Dist:** Movies Unlimited.

Blondie Goes to College 1942 — ★★
Actually both Bumsteads enroll but decide to pass themselves off as single, which leads to complications. Blondie draws the attentions of the school's top athlete while Dagwood's joins the rowing team and turns the head of a pretty coed. 68m/B/W; VHS, DVD. **C:** Penny Singleton; Arthur Lake; Larry Simms; Jonathan Hale; Danny Mummert; Janet Blair; Larry Parks; Lloyd Bridges; Directed by Frank Strayer; Written by Lou Breslow; Cinematography by Henry Freulich. **A:** Family. **P:** Entertainment. **U:** Home. **Mov-Ent:** Family. **Acq:** Purchase. **Dist:** Movies Unlimited.

Blondie Has Trouble 1940 — ★★½
Mr. Dithers has a property he just can't sell because of rumors that the house is haunted. So he offers to let the Bumsteads stay in it to prove that the rumors are false. The Bumsteads also find the creepy mansion comes complete with two equally creepy servants. 6th film in the series. 70m/B/W; VHS, DVD. **C:** Penny Singleton; Arthur Lake; Larry Simms; Danny Mummert; Jonathan Hale; Arthur Hohl; Esther Dale; Irving Bacon; Directed by Frank Strayer; Written by Richard Flournoy; Cinematography by Henry Freulich; Music by Leigh Harline. **Pr:** Robert Sparks. **A:** Family. **P:** Entertainment. **U:** Home. **Mov-Ent:** Family. **Acq:** Purchase. **Dist:** Movies Unlimited. $19.99.

Blondie Hits the Jackpot 1949 — ★½
Dagwood is fired for the umpteenth time after he makes a mistake in a construction deal and tries frantically to get his job back. Meanwhile, Blondie wins the big prize on a radio quiz show. The 26th film in the series. 66m/B/W; VHS. **C:** Penny Singleton; Arthur Lake; Larry Simms; Marjorie Ann Mutchie; Jerome Cowan; Lloyd Corrigan; Danny Mummert; James Flavin; Directed by Edward L. Bernds; Written by Jack Henley; Cinematography by Vincent Farrar; Music by Mischa Bakaleinikoff. **Pr:** Ted Richmond; Columbia Pictures. **A:** Family. **P:** Entertainment. **U:** Home. **Mov-Ent:** Marriage. **Acq:** Purchase. **Dist:** Movies Unlimited. $19.99.

Blondie in Society 1941 — ★½
A weak entry (the ninth) in the comedic series. Dagwood brings home a pedigreed Great Dane and Blondie decides to enter the pooch in the local dog show. Then an important client of Dagwood's decides he wants the dog. 77m/B/W; VHS, DVD. **C:** Penny Singleton; Arthur Lake; Larry Simms; William Frawley; Edgar Kennedy; Jonathan Hale; Danny Mummert; Chick Chandler; Directed by Frank Strayer; Written by Karen De Wolf; Cinematography by Henry Freulich. **Pr:** Robert Sparks; Columbia Pictures. **A:** Family. **P:** Entertainment. **U:** Home. **Mov-Ent:** Marriage, Pets. **Acq:** Purchase. **Dist:** Movies Unlimited. $19.99.

Blondie Johnson 1933 — ★★
After suffering the loss of her family through poverty, smart cookie Blondie is determined to use her brains to get ahead. She takes up professionally with racketeer Danny and climbs the criminal ladder to success. There's ultimately a "crime doesn't pay" ending. 67m/B/W; DVD. **C:** Joan Blondell; Chester Morris; Claire Dodd; Arthur Vinton; Allen Jenkins; Mae Busch; Sterling Holloway; Earle Foxe; Directed by Ray Enright; Written by Earl Baldwin; Cinematography by Gaetano Antonio "Tony" Gaudio. **A:** Sr. High-Adult. **P:** Entertainment. **U:** Home. **Mov-Ent:** Crime Drama, Poverty. **Acq:** Purchase. **Dist:** WarnerArchive.com.

Blondie Knows Best 1946 — ★½
Dagwood impersonates his boss, Mr. Dithers, and causes all sorts of problems. Howard, one of the Three Stooges, has a cameo as a myopic process-server. The 18th film in the series. 66m/B/W; VHS. **C:** Penny Singleton; Arthur Lake; Larry Simms; Marjorie Ann Mutchie; Jonathan Hale; Steven Geray; Jerome Cowan; Danny Mummert; Cameo(s) Shemp Howard; Directed by Abby Berlin; Written by Edward L. Bernds; Al Martin. **Pr:** Burt Kelly; Columbia Pictures. **A:** Family. **P:** Entertainment. **U:** Home. **Mov-Ent:** Marriage. **Acq:** Purchase. **Dist:** Movies Unlimited. $19.99.

Blondie Live! 1983
This tape features the group Blondie's last concert. Among the tunes performed are "Heart of Glass," "Call Me" and "Rapture." 55m; VHS. **Pr:** MCA Entertainment. **A:** Family. **P:** Entertainment. **U:** Home. **Mov-Ent:** Music Video, Music--Performance. **Acq:** Purchase. **Dist:** Music Video Distributors. $19.95.

Blondie Meets the Boss 1939 — ★★
Dagwood goes on a fishing trip and manages to get into trouble with Blondie when a photograph puts him in a comprising pose with another woman. Then, Blondie winds up at the office doing Dagwood's job (whatever that may be). Second in the series. 75m/B/W; VHS, DVD. **C:** Penny Singleton; Arthur Lake; Larry Simms; Jonathan Hale; Dorothy Moore; Don Beddoe; Stanley Brown; Danny Mummert; Irving Bacon; Directed by Frank Strayer; Written by Richard Flournoy; Cinematography by Henry Freulich. **A:** Family. **P:** Entertainment. **U:** Home. **Mov-Ent:** Family, Photography. **Acq:** Purchase. **Dist:** Movies Unlimited.

Blondie On a Budget 1940 — ★★
Dagwood wins 200 bucks in a contest and enlists the aid of ex-girlfriend Joan (Hayworth) to buy Blondie the fur coat she's been wanting. But Blondie wants to use the money to get Dagwood into a fishing club and misinterprets the situation. 68m/B/W; VHS, DVD. **C:** Penny Singleton; Arthur Lake; Larry Simms; Rita Hayworth; Danny Mummert; Don Beddoe; Fay Helm; John Qualen; Irving Bacon; Directed by Frank Strayer; Written by Richard Flournoy; Cinematography by Henry Freulich. **A:** Family. **P:** Entertainment. **U:** Home. **Mov-Ent:** Family. **Acq:** Purchase. **Dist:** Movies Unlimited.

Blondie Plays Cupid 1940 — ★★
The Bumsteads are traveling to visit relatives in the country when they happen across a young couple (Ford and Walters) trying to elope. So Blondie decides to help the youngsters out. 68m/B/W; VHS, DVD. **C:** Penny Singleton; Arthur Lake; Larry Simms; Jonathan Hale; Glenn Ford; Luana Walters; Danny Mummert; Irving Bacon; Directed by Frank Strayer; Written by Richard Flournoy; Karen De Wolf; Cinematography by Henry Freulich. **A:** Family. **P:** Entertainment. **U:** Home. **Mov-Ent**: Family, Marriage. **Acq:** Purchase. **Dist:** Movies Unlimited.

Blondie Takes a Vacation 1939 — ★★½
Third in the series of fluff films adapted from Chic Young's comic strip. After the Bumstead family is snubbed at a snobby mountain resort they move to a friendlier nearby hotel where they try to help out the owners who are in danger of losing their investment. Baby Dumpling does his bit by unleashing a skunk in the ventilation system of the competing hotel. 68m/B/W; VHS, DVD. **C:** Penny Singleton; Arthur Lake; Larry Simms; Danny Mummert; Donald Meek; Donald MacBride; Thomas Ross; Robert Wilcox; Irving Bacon; Directed by Frank Strayer; Written by Richard Flournoy; Cinematography by Henry Freulich. **Pr:** Robert Sparks. **A:** Family. **P:** Entertainment. **U:** Home. **Mov-Ent**: Family, Hotels & Hotel Staff Training. **Acq:** Purchase. **Dist:** Movies Unlimited. $19.99.

Blondie's Blessed Event 1942 — ★★½
Cookie is born, causing even more chaos in the Bumstead household. Meanwhile, Dagwood gets into trouble at work when he hires a cynical playwright to write an important speech for him. 11th entry in series. 69m/B/W; VHS. **C:** Penny Singleton; Arthur Lake; Larry Simms; Norma Jean Wayne; Jonathan Hale; Danny Mummert; Hans Conried; Irving Bacon; Stanley Brown; Mary Wickes; Paul Harvey; Arthur O'Connell; Directed by Frank Strayer; Written by Richard Flournoy; Karen De Wolf; Connie Lee; Cinematography by Henry Freulich. **Pr:** Robert Sparks. **A:** Family. **P:** Entertainment. **U:** Home. **Mov-Ent**: Parenting, Family. **Acq:** Purchase. **Dist:** Movies Unlimited. $19.99.

Blood 1977
The following formed elements of the peripheral blood are demonstrated in a Wright's stain preparation: the erythrocyte, the granulocytes, agranulocytes, and the thrombocytes or platelets. Part of "Microanatomy Laboratory Orientation" series. 9m; VHS, 3/4 U, EJ, Q, Special order formats. **Pr:** University of Oklahoma. **A:** College. **P:** Professional. **U:** Institution, CCTV. **Hea-Sci**: Documentary Films, Blood. **Acq:** Purchase. **Dist:** University of Oklahoma.

Blood 2009 (Unrated) — ★
Detective Hoshino (Kanji Tsuda) has been demoted to cold cases and decides to tackle the murder of a local maid before it reaches the statute of limitations. Arriving at the murder site he arrests what he assumes is a cannibal lunatic only to find that his perp is a vampire under the spell of the mansion's owner. Japanese with subtitles. 85m; DVD. **C:** Aya Sugimoto; Kanji Tsuda; Jun Kaname; Directed by Ten Shimoyama; Written by Shigenori Takechi; Cinematography by Gen Kobayashi; Music by Kiyoshi Yoshikawa. **A:** Adult. **P:** Entertainment. **U:** Home. **L:** Japanese. **Mov-Ent**: Horror. **Acq:** Purchase. **Dist:** Retromedia Entertainment Inc.

Blood Alley 1955 — ★★
A seasoned Merchant Marine captain takes on a cargo of refugee Chinese to smuggle through enemy territory. Middling, mid-career Wayne vehicle. 115m; VHS, DVD, Wide, CC. **C:** John Wayne; Lauren Bacall; Paul Fix; Joy Kim; Berry Kroeger; Mike Mazurki; Anita Ekberg; Directed by William A. Wellman; Cinematography by William Clothier. **Pr:** Batjac Productions. **A:** Adult. **P:** Entertainment. **U:** Home. **Mov-Ent**. **Acq:** Purchase. **Dist:** Facets Multimedia Inc.; Warner Home Video, Inc. $19.98.

Blood and Black Lace 1964 (Unrated) — ★
Beautiful models are being brutally murdered and an inspector is assigned to the case, but not before more gruesome killings occur. Bava is, as usual, violent and suspenseful. Horror fans will enjoy this flick. 90m; VHS, DVD, Wide. **C:** Cameron Mitchell; Eva Bartok; Mary Arden; Dante DiPaolo; Arianna Gorini; Lea Krugher; Harriet Medin; Giuliano Raffaelli; Thomas Reiner; Frank Ressel; Massimo Righi; Directed by Mario Bava; Written by Mario Bava; Marcello Fondato; Joe Barilla; Cinematography by Ubaldo Terzano; Music by Carlo Rustichelli. **Pr:** Allied Artists International. **A:** Sr. High-Adult. **P:** Entertainment. **U:** Home. **Mov-Ent**: Horror. **Acq:** Purchase. **Dist:** Movies Unlimited. $25.49.

Blood and Bone 2009 (R) — ★½
Generic low-budget actioner with ex-con Isaiah Bone (White) getting involved in underground fighting (opposite real Mixed Martial Arts fighters) while falling for a mobster's girlfriend (Belegrin). There's at least a couple of good villains in supporting cast Sands and Walker. 94m; DVD. **C:** Michael Jai White; Michelle Belegrin; Julian Sands; Eamonn Walker; Dante Basco; Nona Gaye; Bob Sapp; Directed by Ben Ramsey; Written by Michael Andrews; Cinematography by Roy Wagner. **A:** Sr. High-Adult. **P:** Entertainment. **U:** Home. **Mov-Ent**: Bowling. **Acq:** Purchase. **Dist:** Sony Pictures Home Entertainment Inc.

Blood and Bones 2004 (Unrated) — ★★½
Brutal character study of Joon-pyong Kim, a Korean immigrant to Japan who has been abused, and goes on to abuse, assault, and rape virtually every living thing he meets in return. Rising to ownership of a factory by harsh means, he swiftly graduates to loan sharking. Not for the faint of heart. 144m; DVD. **C:** Takeshi "Beat" Kitano; Hirofumi Arai; Tomoko Tabata; Joe Odagiri; Kyoka Suzuki; Yutaka Matsushige; Mari Hamada; Yuko Nakamura; Kazuki Kitamura; Shuuji Kashiwabara; Susumu Terajima; Atsushi Ito; Miako Tadano; Mami Nakamura; Directed by Yoichi Sai; Written by Yoichi Sai; Sogil Yan; Wui Sin Chong; Cinematography by Takashi Hamada; Music by Taro Iwashiro. **A:** Sr. High-Adult. **P:** Entertainment. **U:** Home. **L:** English, Japanese. **Mov-Ent**: Crime Drama. **Acq:** Purchase. **Dist:** Kino on Video. $29.95.

Blood & Chocolate 2007 (PG-13) — ★½
Interspecies dating. American Vivian (Bruckner) works in a Bucharest chocolate shop when not turning furry at the full moon. She falls for cute human artist Aiden (Dancy), who's obsessed with werewolves, but has a problem since she's betrothed to hot pack leader Gabriel (Martinez). What's a shape-shifting gal to do? Tame story from von Garnier based on the edgier teen novel by Annette Curtis Klause; the pic's ending goes for conventional romance as does the schmaltzy music. Special effects are minimal. 96m; DVD, Blu-Ray. **C:** Agnes Bruckner; Olivier Martinez; Hugh Dancy; Bryan Dick; Katja Riemann; Directed by Katja von Garnier; Written by Ehren Kruger; Christopher Landon; Cinematography by Brendan Galvin; Music by Johnny Klimek; Reinhold Heil. **Pr:** Richard Wright; Tom Rosenberg; Hawk Koch; Wolfgang Esenwein; Lakeshore Entertainment; Berrick Filmproduktion; MGM. **A:** Jr. High-Adult. **P:** Entertainment. **U:** Home. **L:** English. **Mov-Ent**. **Acq:** Purchase. **Dist:** Sony Pictures Home Entertainment Inc.

Blood & Concrete: A Love Story 1991 (R) — ★★
Bizarre, violent and stylish film-noir spoof, definitely not for all tastes. The innocent hero gets drawn into a maelstrom of intrigue over a killer aphrodisiac drug. Beals, an addicted punk rocker, gets to perform a few songs. 97m; VHS, DVD, Streaming, Wide. **C:** Billy Zane; Jennifer Beals; Darren McGavin; James LeGros; Nicholas Worth; Mark Pellegrino; Harry Shearer; Billy Bastiani; Directed by Jeff Reiner; Written by Jeff Reiner; Richard LaBrie; Cinematography by Declan Quinn; Music by Vinnie Golia. **Pr:** I.R.S. World Media. **A:** College-Adult-Sr. High. **P:** Entertainment. **U:** Home. **Mov-Ent**: Drug Abuse. **Acq:** Purchase. **Dist:** Sony Pictures Home Entertainment Inc.; IRS Media Inc. $89.95.

Blood & Donuts 1995 (R) — ★★
Hungry vampire Boya (Currie) is looking for a rat snack when he stumbles across an all-night donut shop where pretty cashier Molly (Clarkson) and friendly cabbie Earl (Louis) seek his help with a local crime boss. Mild horror mixed with comedy and limited gore. 89m; VHS, Streaming, CC. **C:** Gordon Currie; Justin Louis; Helene Clarkson; Fiona Reid; Frank Moore; Cameo(s) David Cronenberg; Directed by Holly Dale; Written by Andrew Rai Berzins; Cinematography by Paul Sarossy. **Pr:** Steven Hoban; Colin Brunton; Malofilm Communications. **A:** Sr. High-Adult. **P:** Entertainment. **U:** Home. **Mov-Ent**. **Acq:** Purchase. **Dist:** Lions Gate Television Corp.

Blood and Guns 1979 (R) — ★½
Romance, revenge, and action abound in post-revolutionary Mexico. 96m; VHS. **C:** Orson Welles; Tomas Milian; John Steiner; Directed by Giulio Petroni. **Pr:** Four Star Entertainment. **A:** Jr. High-Adult. **P:** Entertainment. **U:** Home. **Mov-Ent**: Romance. **Acq:** Purchase.

Blood and Honey: Ancient Tales from a Promised Land 19??
British actor Tony Robinson is on location in the Holy Land, where he acquaints viewers with these timeless Biblical tales of love, betrayal, and faith. Each tape contains two 15-minute stories, and is available as a series or individually. 30m; VHS. **A:** Family. **P:** Religious. **U:** Institution. **Gen-Edu**: Bible, Religion. **Acq:** Purchase. **Dist:** EcuFilm. $24.95.
Indiv. Titles: 1. Joshua Smashes Jerico/Joshua in Trouble Valley 2. Deborah and the Headbanger/Gideon Gets His Woolly Wet 3. Gideon's Exploding Pickle Pots/Samson Gets Knotted 4. Samson Gets A Haircut/Samuel and the Spooky Godbox 5. Saul Rips Up His Camel/David Gets a Good Gig 6. David and the Hairy Man Mountain/Saul Goes Bonkers 7. Saul Bumps Into a Witch/David Gets to Number One.

Blood & Iron: The Story of the German War Machine 1996
Three-part series which explores the history of the powerful German War Machine and the Nazis during the first part of the 20th Century. 180m/B/W; VHS. **A:** Jr. High-Adult. **P:** Education. **U:** Home. **Gen-Edu**: Military History, Germany, World War One. **Acq:** Purchase. **Dist:** MPI Media Group. $79.98.
Indiv. Titles: 1. Episode One: The Great War Comes 2. Episode Two: Fatal Alliances 3. Episode Three: From Nuremberg to NATO.

Blood and Nerve Supply to the Lower Extremity 1985
The entitled physiological situation is described in detail. 20m; 3/4 U. **Pr:** McMaster University. **A:** Adult. **P:** Professional. **U:** Institution, SURA. **Hea-Sci**: Anatomy & Physiology, Medical Education. **Acq:** Purchase, Rent/Lease. **Dist:** McMaster University.

Blood and Nerve Supply to the Upper Limb 1984
The supply of blood to nerves is described in medical detail. 18m; 3/4 U. **Pr:** McMaster University. **A:** Adult. **P:** Professional. **U:** Institution, SURA. **Hea-Sci**: Anatomy & Physiology, Medical Education. **Acq:** Purchase, Rent/Lease. **Dist:** McMaster University.

Blood and Oil: The Middle East in World War I 2006 (Unrated) — ★★½
Crammed with facts, this complex, yet bland historical documentary revisits the downfall of the Ottoman Empire in 1919 after World War I by exploring the theory that the Treaty of Versailles and the Western world sparked the discord that has festered within the Middle East region as the political powers set up the new map—including Iraq, Syria, Palestine, Jordan, Saudi Arabia, and Turkey—for its own economic purposes. 112m; DVD. **C:** Narrated by Marty Callaghan; Directed by Marty Callaghan; Written by Marty Callaghan. **A:** Jr. High-Adult. **P:** Entertainment. **U:** Home. **Mov-Ent**: World War One, Middle East, Documentary Films. **Acq:** Purchase. **Dist:** Inecom Entertainment Co. $24.95.

Blood & Orchids 1986 (Unrated)
CBS 1986 mystery drama mini-series. Four young Hawaiian men find white girl Hester Murdoch (Stowe) naked and nearly beaten to death on the beach. Fighting their fear of being accused of the crime they take her to the hospital. Hester's mother uses her political influence to find out who is responsible for the crime but when she discovers who's to blame she fears a scandal and forces her daughter to blame the men who rescued her however, detective Curt Maddox (Kristofferson) is determined to get to the truth. 200m; DVD. **C:** Kris Kristofferson; Madeleine Stowe; Jane Alexander; Jose Ferrer. **A:** Sr. High-Adult. **P:** Entertainment. **U:** Home. **Mov-Ent**: Mystery & Suspense, Drama. **Acq:** Purchase. **Dist:** Warner Home Video, Inc. $19.99.

Blood and Orchids 1986 (Unrated) — ★★
Miniseries covers racism and lies in 1937 Hawaii. Hester (Stowe), the wife of naval officer Lloyd Murdoch (Russ), is beaten and raped by her lover (Salinger). She's found by four young Hawaiian men who take her to the hospital but flee, fearing they'll be accused of the crime. Hester's autocratic, plantation-owning mother (Alexander) insists Hester lie and the four are, indeed, arrested and put on trial. However, police captain Maddox (Kristofferson) thinks something stinks. Based on a true story; Katkov scripted from his novel. 200m; DVD. **C:** Kris Kristofferson; Jane Alexander; Madeleine Stowe; William Russ; Sean Young; Jose Ferrer; Matt Salinger; James Saito; Susan Blakely; David Clennon; Richard Dysart; George Coe; Directed by Jerry Thorpe; Written by Norman Katkov; Cinematography by Charles G. Arnold; Music by Mark Snow. **A:** Jr. High-Adult. **P:** Entertainment. **U:** Home. **Mov-Ent**: Prejudice, TV Movies. **Acq:** Purchase. **Dist:** WarnerArchive.com.

Blood and Roses 1961 (Unrated) — ★★
A girl who is obsessed with her family's vampire background becomes possessed by a vampire and commits numerous murders. The photography is good, but the plot is hazy and only effective in certain parts. Based on the story "Carmilla" by Sheridan Le Fanu. Later remade as "The Vampire Lovers" and "The Blood-Spattered Bride." 74m; VHS, Streaming, CC. **C:** Mel Ferrer; Elsa Martinelli; Annette (Stroyberg) Vadim; Marc Allegret; Jacques-Rene Chauffard; Serge Marquand; Gabriella Farinon; Alberto Bonucci; Nathalie Le Foret; Directed by Roger Vadim; Written by Roger Vadim; Claude Martin; Roger Vailand; Claude Brule; Cinematography by Claude Renoir; Music by Jean Prodromides. **A:** Jr. High-Adult. **P:** Entertainment. **U:** Home. **Mov-Ent**: Horror. **Acq:** Purchase. **Dist:** Paramount Pictures Corp.

Blood and Sand 1922 (Unrated) — ★★½
Vintage romance based on Vicente Blasco Ibanez's novel about the tragic rise and fall of a matador, and the women in his life. The film that made Valentino a star. Remade in 1941. Silent. 87m/B/W; Silent; VHS, DVD, 3/4 U, Special order formats. **TV Std:** NTSC, PAL, SECAM. **C:** Rudolph Valentino; Nita Naldi; Lila Lee; Walter Long; Directed by Fred Niblo; Written by June Mathis; Cinematography by Alvin Wyckoff. **Pr:** Paramount Pictures. **A:** Family. **P:** Entertainment. **U:** Institution, CCTV, CATV, BCTV, Home. **Mov-Ent**: Drama, Silent Films, Classic Films. **Acq:** Purchase. **Dist:** Gotham Distributing Corp.; Grapevine Video; Lions Gate Entertainment Inc. $19.95.

Blood and Sand 1941 — ★★★
Director Mamoulian "painted" this picture in the new technicolor technique, which makes it a veritable explosion of color and spectacle. Power is the matador who becomes famous and then falls when he is torn between two women, forsaking his first love, bullfighting. Based on the novel "Sangre y Arena" by Vicente Blasco Ibanez. This movie catapulted Hayworth to stardom, primarily for her dancing, but also for her sexiness and seductiveness (and of course, her acting). Remake of the 1922 silent classic; remade again in 1989. 123m; VHS, DVD, Blu-Ray. **C:** Tyrone Power; Linda Darnell; Rita Hayworth; Alla Nazimova; Anthony Quinn; J. Carrol Naish; John Carradine; George Reeves; Directed by Rouben Mamoulian; Written by Jo Swerling; Cinematography by Ernest Palmer; Ray Rennahan; Music by Alfred Newman. **Pr:** Fox. **A:** Jr. High-Adult. **P:** Entertainment. **U:** Home. **Mov-Ent**: Action-Adventure, Sex & Sexuality, Spain. **Awds:** Oscars '41: Color Cinematog. **Acq:** Purchase. **Dist:** Wellspring Media. $19.98.

Blood and Sand 1989 (R) — ★★
A bullfighter on the verge of super-stardom risks it all when he falls under the spell of a sexy, seductive woman. Will she destroy his one opportunity for fame? Interesting for people who actually enjoy watching the "sport" of bullfighting. Originally made in 1922 and remade in 1941. 96m; VHS, DVD. **C:** Christopher Rydell; Sharon Stone; Ana Torrent; Jose-Luis De Villalonga; Simon Andreu; Directed by Javier Elorrieta; Written by Rafael Azcona; Ricardo Franco; Thomas Fucci; Cinematography by Antonio Rios; Music by Jesus Gluck. **Pr:** Jose Frade. **A:** College-Adult. **P:** Entertainment. **U:** Home. **Mov-Ent**: Drama. **Acq:** Purchase. **Dist:** CinemaNow Inc. $89.95.

Blood and Sand/Son of the Sheik 1926
A double feature containing two abridged versions; in "Blood and Sand," an idolized matador meets another woman just before his wedding; in "Son of the Sheik," a man believes he has been betrayed by a dancing girl, and he abducts her to seek revenge. Silent. 56m/B/W; Silent; VHS. **C:** Rudolph Valentino; Lila Lee; Vilma Banky. **Pr:** Famous Players Lasky Corporation;

United Artists. **A:** Family. **P:** Entertainment. **U:** Home. **Mov-Ent:** Drama, Silent Films. **Acq:** Purchase. **Dist:** $29.98.

Blood and Steel 1925 — ★★
The railroad tycoon's daughter and the construction foreman wind up together on an exciting train ride. Silent. ?m/B/W; Silent; VHS, 8 mm. **C:** Helen Holmes; William Desmond; Directed by J(ohn) P(aterson) McGowan; Written by George Plympton; Cinematography by Roland Price. **A:** Family. **P:** Entertainment. **U:** Home. **Mov-Ent:** Trains. **Acq:** Purchase. **Dist:** Glenn Video Vistas Ltd. $55.95.

Blood and Urine Monitoring 1988
A definition of why diabetics have to be careful of how much sugar gets into their body. 10m; VHS, 3/4 U. **Pr:** Professional Research. **A:** Jr. High-Adult. **P:** Education. **U:** Institution, CCTV. **Hea-Sci:** Diabetes. **Acq:** Purchase, Rent/Lease. **Dist:** Discovery Education. $295.00.

Blood & Wine 1996 (R) — ★★½
Miami wine merchant Alex (Nicholson) gets involved with terminally ill safecracker Victor (Caine) to steal a necklace worth a cool million. Meanwhile he must deal with his crumbling marriage to Suzanne (Davis) and the bitter relationship with his stepson Jason (Dorff), who has eyes for both the necklace and his Cuban mistress (Lopez). Characterizations and strong performances (particularly by Nicholson and Caine) haul the sometimes lumbering plot to its violent conclusion. Promoted as the third part of a "dysfunctional family trilogy" with "Five Easy Pieces" and "The King of Marvin's Gardens." Seventh time Nicholson has worked with director Rafelson. 100m; VHS, DVD. **C:** Jack Nicholson; Michael Caine; Judy Davis; Stephen Dorff; Jennifer Lopez; Harold Perrineau, Jr.; Directed by Bob Rafelson; Written by Nick Villiars; Allison Cross; Cinematography by Newton Thomas (Tom) Sigel; Music by Stephen Cohen. **Pr:** Jeremy Thomas; Chris Auty; Bernie Williams; Recorded Pictures Company; Majestic Films International; Fox Searchlight. **A:** Sr. High-Adult. **P:** Entertainment. **U:** Home. **Mov-Ent:** Crime Drama, Family. **Acq:** Purchase. **Dist:** Fox Home Entertainment.

Blood Angels 2005 (R) — ★
Ashley (Baruc) left her bad home life to hang with her big sis—who, it ends up, is part of a group of half-vampire, half-human gal pals. The girls fill their human blood quota by tempting men to a club run by their oppressive master, Mr. Jones (Lamas), who won't give them full vampire powers, so they decide to use Ashley to give him the boot. 98m; VHS, DVD, Wide. **C:** Lorenzo Lamas; Siri Baruc; Sonya Salomaa; Crystal Lowe; Leah Cairns; Fiona Scott; Lisa Marie Caruk; Monica Delain; Written by Lisa Morton; Brett Thompson; Cinematography by David Pelletier. **A:** Sr. High-Adult. **P:** Entertainment. **U:** Home. **Mov-Ent. Acq:** Purchase. **Dist:** Movies Unlimited; Alpha Video. $9.99.

Blood at Sundown 1988 (Unrated) — ★½
Routine oater where man returns home after the Civil War to find his wife kidnapped by a group of Mexican outlaws who have also taken over his village. 92m; VHS. **C:** Giuliano Gemma; Hally Hamond; Nieves Navarro; Antonio Casas; Fernando (Fernand) Sancho; Pajarito; George Martin; Directed by Duccio Tessari. **A:** Adult. **P:** Entertainment. **U:** Home. **Mov-Ent:** Western, Civil War. **Acq:** Purchase. **Dist:** Imperial Entertainment Corp. $19.95.

Blood Beach 1981 (R) — **Bomb!**
A group of teenagers are devoured by menacing sand, which keeps people from getting to the water by swallowing them whole. Weak parody with some humorous moments; more silly than scary. 92m; VHS. **C:** David Huffman; Marianna Hill; John Saxon; Burt Young; Otis Young; Pamela McMyler; Bobby Bass; Darrell Fetty; Stefan Gierasch; Harriet Medin; Lynn(e) Marta; Mary Jo Catlett; Directed by Jeffrey Bloom; Written by Jeffrey Bloom; Cinematography by Steven Poster; Music by Gil Melle. **Pr:** Shaw Beckerman Productions. **A:** Sr. High-Adult. **P:** Entertainment. **U:** Home. **Mov-Ent. Acq:** Purchase. **Dist:** No Longer Available.

Blood Beast Terror 1967 (Unrated) — ★½
An entomologist transforms his own daughter into a Deathshead Moth and she proceeds to terrorize and drink innocent victims' blood. 81m; VHS, DVD, Blu-Ray, Wide. **C:** Peter Cushing; Robert Flemyng; Wanda Ventham; Vanessa Howard; Directed by Vernon Sewell; Written by Peter Bryan; Cinematography by Stanley Long; Music by Paul Ferris. **Pr:** Arnold L. Miller. **A:** Jr. High-Adult. **P:** Entertainment. **U:** Home. **Mov-Ent:** Horror. **Acq:** Purchase. **Dist:** Monterey Home Video. $39.95.

Blood Billz 2003 (R) — ★
Neicy (Morris) returns to her old neighborhood only to be confronted by an old gangster trying to collect on an old debt. Trying to fix the problem on her own, her boyfriend eventually has to be drawn in to save her. 83m; DVD. **C:** Krystal Morris; Lewis Powell; Directed by Cetre Pegues; Written by Cetre Pegues; Cinematography by Sean Simmons. **A:** Sr. High-Adult. **P:** Entertainment. **U:** Home. **Mov-Ent. Acq:** Purchase. **Dist:** York Entertainment; Mill Creek Entertainment L.L.C. $12.98.

Blood Bride 1980 (Unrated) — ★½
A lonely young woman finally finds happiness with her new husband but her world comes crashing about her with soul-mangling ferocity when she discovers he is actually a blood-thirsty maniac. 90m; VHS. **C:** Ellen Barber; Philip English; Directed by Robert J. Avrech. **A:** Adult. **P:** Entertainment. **U:** Home. **Mov-Ent:** Horror. **Acq:** Purchase. **Dist:** Unknown Distributor.

Blood Brothers 1974 (R) — ★★
A young man who dreams of becoming a lawyer is disturbed when he discovers that his family has mafia ties. 148m; VHS. **C:** Claudia Cardinale; Franco Nero; Lina Polito; Directed by Pasquale Squitieri. **A:** Adult. **P:** Entertainment. **U:** Home. **Mov-Ent:** Law. **Acq:** Purchase. **Dist:** No Longer Available.

Blood Brothers 1977
James Grizzly Adams, who lives in the mountains of the American wilderness, relives the story of how he met his Indian blood brother, Nakuma. Beautiful scenery. 50m; VHS. **C:** Dan Haggerty; Denver Pyle; Don Shanks. **A:** Family. **P:** Entertainment. **U:** Home. **Mov-Ent:** Wilderness Areas. **Acq:** Purchase. **Dist:** Management Company Entertainment Group (MCEG), Inc. $14.98.

Blood Brothers 1993 — ★★
Darryl has always looked up to older brother Sylvester. And then one day he witnesses a gang murder and Sylvester is one of the killers. The District Attorney senses Darryl knows more than he's saying and the gang bangers want to shut him up permanently, so each brother must look to his conscience and decide how best to be his brother's keeper. 91m; DVD. **C:** Clark Johnson; Richard Chevolleau; Mia Korf; Richard Yearwood; Ron White; Amir Williams; Ndehru Roberts; Timothy Stickney; Bill Nunn; Directed by Bruce Pittman; Written by Paris Qualles; Music by Harold Wheeler. **Pr:** Julian Marks; Gerald W. Abrams; Hearst Entertainment Productions, Inc; Power Pictures. **A:** Sr. High-Adult. **P:** Entertainment. **U:** Home. **Mov-Ent:** Black Culture, Family. **Acq:** Purchase.

Blood Brothers 2007 (R) — ★★
Largely told in flashback, this sketchy underworld drama depicts three childhood buddies climbing the crime ladder in 1930s Shanghai. Feng (Wu) is the romantic, Gang (Liu) the muscle, and Gang's younger brother Hu (Yang) serves as backup. Through several coincidences, the trio begins working for kingpin Boss Hong (Sun). But eventually Kang makes his own bid for power. John Woo serves as a producer, which seems only right since director Tan was inspired by Woo's 1990 pic, "A Bullet in the Head." Chinese with subtitles. 95m; DVD. **C:** Daniel Wu; Ye Liu; Tony Yang; Honglei Sun; Qi Shu; Xiaolu "Lulu" Li; Chang Chen; Directed by Alexi Tan; Written by Tony Chan; Alexi Tan; Dan Jiang; Cinematography by Michel Taburiaux; Music by Daniel Belardinelli. **A:** Sr. High-Adult. **P:** Entertainment. **U:** Home. **L:** Chinese. **Mov-Ent:** China, Crime Drama, Nightclubs. **Acq:** Purchase. **Dist:** Movies Unlimited; Alpha Video.

Blood Brothers: Bruce Springsteen & the E Street Band 1996
Documentary on the 1995 reunion of the E Street Band. 85m; DVD. **A:** Sr. High-Adult. **P:** Entertainment. **U:** Home. **Gen-Edu:** Documentary Films, Music. **Acq:** Purchase. **Dist:** Backstreets Records Catalog. $15.00.

Blood Brothers: The Joey DiPaolo Story 19??
An 11-year-old Brooklyn boy who contracted AIDS from a blood transfusion confronts his community's negative reaction to him. 30m; VHS. **A:** Sr. High-Adult. **P:** Entertainment. **U:** Institution. **Gen-Edu:** Documentary Films, AIDS. **Acq:** Purchase. **Dist:** Ambrose Video Publishing, Inc. $69.95.

Blood-C: Complete Collection 2011 (Unrated)
Set in the same world as "Blood: The Last Vampire," this anime focuses on a young schoolgirl secretly being raised to kill monsters. 300m; DVD, Blu-Ray. **A:** Sr. High-Adult. **P:** Entertainment. **U:** Home. **L:** English, Japanese. **Gen-Edu:** Anime, Horror. **Acq:** Purchase. **Dist:** FUNimation Entertainment. $69.98 69.98.

Blood Clan 1991 (R) — ★½
Based on the true story of Katy Bane, daughter of notorious Scottish cult leader, Sawney Bane, in whose lair were found the remains of over 1000 killed and cannibalized followers. When found, Bane's entire family was sentenced to death with the exception of Katy, who left to make a new start in Canada. When a rash of mysterious deaths break out in Katy's new home, she must defend herself from rumors that her father's murderous cult is resurfacing. 91m; VHS. **C:** Gordon Pinsent; Michelle Little; Robert Wisden; Directed by Charles Wilkinson. **Pr:** Monarch Entertainment. **A:** Sr. High-Adult. **P:** Entertainment. **U:** Home. **Mov-Ent:** Cults, Scotland, Canada. **Acq:** Purchase. **Dist:** Wellspring Media. $29.95.

Blood Creek 2009 (R) — ★½
Splatter horror with some good visuals and really stupid plot elements. In 1936, Nazi occultist Richard Wirth (Fassbinder) travels to a West Virginia farmhouse owned by German immigrants to examine a rune stone's demonic abilities. Decades pass and EMT worker Evan Marshall (Cavill) is shocked when his missing brother Victor (Purcell) suddenly turns up horribly scarred, claiming he was held hostage at the same farmhouse and they must stop what is happening there. Which involves Wirth. 90m; DVD. **C:** Dominic Purcell; Henry Cavill; Michael Fassbender; Emma Booth; Rainer Winkelvoss; Directed by Joel Schumacher; Written by David Kajganich; Cinematography by Darko Suvak; Music by David Buckley. **A:** Sr. High-Adult. **P:** Entertainment. **U:** Home. **Mov-Ent:** Occult Sciences. **Acq:** Purchase. **Dist:** Lions Gate Entertainment Inc.

Blood Crime 2002 — ★½
No-brainer B movie. Seattle cop Daniel Pruitt (Schaech) and his wife Jessica (Lackey) take a camping trip into Oregon. While he's away, she gets attacked in the woods. When Jessica identifies her attacker, her husband beats him. Later, she changes her mind about who her assailant is but by then it's too late—the man, who turns out to be the no-good son of Sheriff McKenna (Caan)?has died. 128m; VHS, DVD. **C:** James Caan; Johnathon Schaech; Elizabeth Lackey; David Field; Directed by William A. Graham; Written by Preston A. Whitmore, II; Mark Lawrence Miller; Cinematography by Robert Steadman; Music by Chris Boardman. **A:** Sr. High-Adult. **P:** Entertainment. **U:** Home. **Mov-Ent:** Forests & Trees. **Acq:** Purchase. **Dist:** Sony Pictures Home Entertainment Inc.

Blood Cult 1985 (R) — ★
A bizarre series of murder-mutilations take place on a small midwestern campus. Contains graphic violence that is not for the squeamish. This film was created especially for the home video market. 89m; VHS, DVD. **C:** Chuck Ellis; Julie Andelman; Jim Vance; Joe Hardt; Directed by Christopher Lewis; Music by Rod Slane. **Pr:** Linda Lewis. **A:** Adult. **P:** Entertainment. **U:** Home. **Mov-Ent:** Horror. **Acq:** Purchase. **Dist:** VCI Entertainment. $24.95.

Blood Debts 1983 (Unrated) — ★★
A father is out for revenge after he saves his daughter from some hunters who raped her and also killed her boyfriend. 91m; VHS. **C:** Richard Harrison; Mike Manty; Jim Gaines; Anne Jackson; Anne Milhench; Directed by Teddy Page. **A:** Adult. **P:** Entertainment. **U:** Home. **Mov-Ent:** Action-Adventure, Violence, Rape. **Acq:** Purchase. **Dist:** No Longer Available.

Blood Diamond 2006 (R) — ★★½
Flawed, well-intentioned adventure-drama takes place in 1999, during the horrors of civil war in Sierra Leone. Rebels raid a village, committing mass murder and forcing the boys to become child soldiers while the men are slave labor in the diamond mines. These so-called "conflict stones" are then used to buy more weapons. Solomon Vandy (Hounsou) unearths and hides a valuable pink diamond in order to ransom his family after he escapes. But Vandy's find comes to the attention of Afrikaner smuggler Danny Archer (DiCaprio), who is looking to use the diamond to his own advantage. American journalist Maddy (Connelly) happens to be around to prick Danny's nearly non-existent conscience. The actors do well and the story is harrowing but director Zwick has a tendency to be a scold. 143m; DVD, Blu-Ray, HD-DVD. **C:** Leonardo DiCaprio; Djimon Hounsou; Jennifer Connelly; Arnold Vosloo; Kagiso Kuypers; Michael Sheen; Jimi Mistry; Stephen Collins; David Harewood; Anthony Coleman; Benu Mabhena; Basil Wallace; Directed by Edward Zwick; Written by Charles Leavitt; Cinematography by Eduardo Serra; Music by James Newton Howard. **Pr:** Paula Weinstein; Edward Zwick; Marshall Herskovitz; Graham King; Edward Zwick; Virtual Studios; Spring Creek Productions; Bedford Falls; Warner Bros. **A:** Sr. High-Adult. **P:** Entertainment. **U:** Home. **L:** English. **Mov-Ent:** Action-Adventure, Africa, Miners & Mining. **Acq:** Purchase. **Dist:** Warner Home Video, Inc.

Blood Diner 1987 (Unrated) — **Bomb!**
Two spirit-possessed, diner-owning brothers kill countless young girls for demonic rituals, and serve their corpses as gourmet food in their restaurant. Some funny moments mixed in with the requisite gore. Cult potential. Currently sold only as part of a collection. 88m; VHS, DVD. **C:** Rick Burks; Carl Crew; Roger Dauer; Lisa Guggenheim; Roxanne Cybelle; Cynthia Baker; Directed by Jackie Kong; Written by Michael Sonye; Cinematography by Jurg Walther; Music by Don Preston. **Pr:** Lightning Pictures. **A:** Sr. High-Adult. **P:** Entertainment. **U:** Home. **Mov-Ent:** Horror, Occult Sciences. **Acq:** Purchase. **Dist:** Lionsgate; Lions Gate Television Corp. $19.98.

Blood Done Sign My Name 2010 (PG-13) — ★★½
Straightforward, old-fashioned storytelling about a racially charged murder that happened in 1970 in Oxford, North Carolina. Black Vietnam vet Henry Marrow (Sanford) returns to a hometown virtually unchanged by the civil rights movement. Racial violence explodes after his murder when his white killers are acquitted by an all-white jury. The parallel story is that of liberal white Methodist minister Vernon Tyson (Schroder), who has been trying to foster more racial harmony, and his 10-year-old son Tim (Griffith), a witness to some of the events. The adult Tim Tyson wrote the nonfiction book on which the movie is based. 128m; DVD. **C:** Rick Schroder; Nate Parker; Afemo Omilami; Gattlin Griffith; Lela Rochon; Nick Searcy; Cullen Moss; Darrin Dewitt Henson; Omar Benson Miller; Donna Biscoe; A.C Sanford; Directed by Jeb Stuart; Written by Jeb Stuart; Cinematography by Steve Mason; David Parker; Music by John Leftwich. **Pr:** Mari Stuart; Mel Efros; Jeb Stuart; Robert K. Steel; Jeb Stuart; Real Folk; Paladin. **A:** Jr. High-Adult. **P:** Entertainment. **U:** Home. **L:** English. **Mov-Ent:** Black Culture, Civil Rights, Prejudice. **Acq:** Purchase. **Dist:** Image Entertainment Inc.

Blood Feast 1963 (Unrated) — ★
The first of Lewis' gore-fests, in which a demented caterer butchers hapless young women to splice them together in order to bring back an Egyptian goddess. Dated, campy, and gross; reportedly shot in four days (it shows). 70m; VHS, DVD, Blu-Ray. **C:** Connie Mason; William Kerwin; Mal Arnold; Scott H. Hall; Lyn Bolton; Toni Calvert; Gene Courtier; Ashlyn Martin; Jerome Eden; David Friedman; Directed by Herschell Gordon Lewis; Written by Allison Louise Downe; Cinematography by Herschell Gordon Lewis; Music by Herschell Gordon Lewis. **Pr:** Herschell Gordon Lewis; Herschell Gordon Lewis. **A:** Adult. **P:** Entertainment. **U:** Home. **Mov-Ent:** Horror, Cult Films. **Acq:** Purchase. **Dist:** Facets Multimedia Inc.; Something Weird Video. $29.95.

Blood Feud 1979 (R) — ★★
In Italy preceding Europe's entry into WWII, a young widow is in mourning over the brutal murder of her husband by the Sicilian Mafia. In the meantime she must contend with the rivalry between Mastroianni as a lawyer and Giannini as a small-time crook both vying for her affections. Dubbed. 112m; DVD, Streaming. **C:** Sophia Loren; Marcello Mastroianni; Giancarlo Giannini; Directed by Lina Wertmuller; Written by Lina Wertmuller; Cinematography by Tonino Delli Colli; Music by

Nando De Luca. **Pr:** AFD. **A:** Sr. High-Adult. **P:** Entertainment. **U:** Home. **L:** Italian. **Mov-Ent:** Drama, Italy. **Acq:** Purchase. **Dist:** Amazon.com Inc.; Movies Unlimited. $59.95.

Blood for a Silver Dollar 1966 (Unrated) — ★½
Action-filled western, littered with murder, revenge and romance. 98m; VHS, DVD. **C:** Montgomery Wood; Evelyn Stewart; Pierre Cressoy; Directed by Giorgio Ferroni; Music by Gianni Ferrio. **Pr:** Italian/French Co-production. **A:** Family. **P:** Entertainment. **U:** Home. **Mov-Ent:** Romance. **Acq:** Purchase. **Dist:** Movies Unlimited; Alpha Video. $24.95.

Blood for Blood 1995 (R) — ★½
Cop must take up the martial arts skills he learned in childhood in order to protect his family from assassination. 93m; VHS, CC. **C:** Lorenzo Lamas; James Lew; Mako; Eric Pierpoint; James Shigeta; James Callahan; Directed by John Weidner; Music by Joel Goldsmith. **Pr:** Alan Amiel; LIVE Entertainment. **A:** Sr. High-Adult. **P:** Entertainment. **U:** Home. **Mov-Ent:** Martial Arts, Family. **Acq:** Purchase. **Dist:** Lions Gate Television Corp.

Blood Freak 1972 (Unrated) — **Bomb!**
An absolutely insane anti-drug, Christian splatter film. A Floridian biker is introduced to drugs by a young woman and eventually turns into a poultry-monster who drinks the blood of junkies. Narrated by a chain smoker who has a coughing fit. Don't miss it. 86m; VHS, DVD. **C:** Steve Hawkes; Dana Cullivan; Randy Grinter, Jr.; Tina Anderson; Heather Hughes; Directed by Steve Hawkes; Brad Grinter. **A:** Sr. High-Adult. **P:** Entertainment. **U:** Home. **Mov-Ent:** Horror, Drug Abuse, Birds. **Acq:** Purchase. **Dist:** Movies Unlimited. $17.99.

Blood Frenzy 1987 (Unrated) — ★
Psychologist's patients take a therapeutic trip to the desert. The sun and heat take their toll, and everyone gets violent. This kind of therapy we don't need, and the movie's a waste, as well. Made for video. Loring was Wednesday on TV's "The Addams Family." 90m; VHS. **C:** John Montero; Lisa Loring; Hank Garrett; Wendy MacDonald; Directed by Hal Freeman. **A:** Adult. **P:** Entertainment. **U:** Home. **Mov-Ent:** Mystery & Suspense, Psychiatry. **Acq:** Purchase. **Dist:** No Longer Available.

Blood from the Mummy's Tomb 1971 — ★★½
The immortal spirit of Tera, Egyptian queen of evil, haunts Margaret (Leon), the daughter of an archaeologist who discovered her tomb. As a long-prophesied conjunction of stars begins to occur, Margaret finds herself enthralled by Tera's power and finds herself becoming possessed by Tera's spirit. This adaptation of Bram Stoker's "The Jewel of Seven Stars" begins well, with a wonderfully mysterious and moody first half, but it loses steam in the somewhat muddled (and tedious) second half. Coulouris (without the old age makeup) looks exactly like his Thatcher character in "Citizen Kane," 30 years earlier, but sadly is given not much to do other than roll his eyes and scream. Leon is a likable heroine but that wig and false eyelashes have got to go! Remade in post-"Omen" fashion as "The Awakening." 94m; VHS, DVD, Wide. **C:** Andrew Keir; Valerie Leon; James Villiers; Hugh Burden; George Coulouris; Mark Edwards; Directed by Seth Holt; Written by Christopher Wicking; Cinematography by Arthur Grant; Music by Tristram Cary. **A:** Sr. High-Adult. **P:** Entertainment. **U:** Home. **Mov-Ent:** Horror, Archaeology. **Acq:** Purchase. **Dist:** Anchor Bay Entertainment.

Blood Games 1990 (R) — **Bomb!**
Buxom baseball team bats 1000 against the home team and the winning babes find out just how poor losers can be. Diamonds aren't always a girl's best friend. 90m; VHS, CC. **C:** Gregory Cummings; Laura Albert; Shelly Abblett; Luke Shay; Ross Hagen; Directed by Tanya Rosenberg. **Pr:** Epic Productions. **A:** Adult. **P:** Entertainment. **U:** Home. **Mov-Ent:** Horror, Baseball, Exploitation. **Acq:** Purchase. **Dist:** Sony Pictures Home Entertainment Inc. $79.95.

Blood Gases: Interpretation 1986
The interpretation of blood gas results are explained. 28m; VHS, 3/4 U. **Pr:** Fairview Audio-Visuals. **A:** Sr. High-College. **P:** Education. **U:** Institution, CCTV. **Hea-Sci:** Blood. **Acq:** Purchase, Rent/Lease. **Dist:** Kinetic Film Enterprises Ltd.; Medcom Inc. $295.00.

Blood Gnome 2002 (R) — ★
Evil, hungry gnomes attack patrons of the local dominatrix, with a crime scene photographer as the sole spectator to the carnage. Grisly and made on the cheap, and looks it. 87m; VHS, DVD. **C:** Vincent Bilancio; Stephanie Beaton; Julie Strain; Massimo Avidano; Melissa Pursley; Directed by John Lechago; Written by John Lechago. **A:** Sr. High-Adult. **P:** Entertainment. **U:** Home. **Mov-Ent:** Horror, Photography. **Acq:** Purchase. **Dist:** Movies Unlimited. $24.99.

Blood, Grace and Tears 1973
A woman is called by God to help the derelicts on skid row. She prevents their exploitation by the local blood bank. Shows that God can be most fully experienced by helping those most in need. 28m; VHS, 3/4 U, Special order formats. **C:** Michael Learned; Tom Nardini. **Pr:** Paulist Productions. **A:** Jr. High-Adult. **P:** Religious. **U:** Institution, CCTV, SURA. **Gen-Edu:** Documentary Films, Religion. **Acq:** Purchase, Rent/Lease. **Dist:** Paulist Productions.

Blood, Guts, Bullets and Octane 1999 (R) — ★★
Used-car salesmen Sid (Carnahan) and Bob (Leis) are trying to keep their failing business afloat when a broker offers then a quarter million to let a 1963 Pontiac Le Mans convertible (burgundy) stay on their lot for 48 hours. The FBI are after the car and its owners, who've left a bloody cross-country trail. And the motor-mouth duo decide to renege on the deal. Desperate lowlifes and vicious crime winds up looking very familiar. 87m; VHS, DVD, CC. **C:** Joe Carnahan; Dan Leis; Ken Rudolph; James Salter; Dan Harlan; Directed by Joe Carnahan; Written by Joe Carnahan; Cinematography by John A. Jimenez; Music by Mark Priolo; Martin Burke. **Pr:** Lions Gate Films. **A:** Sr. High-Adult. **P:** Entertainment. **U:** Home. **Mov-Ent:** Crime Drama, Automobiles, Federal Bureau of Investigation (FBI). **Acq:** Purchase. **Dist:** Movies Unlimited; Alpha Video.

Blood Hook 1986 (Unrated) — ★½
A self-parodying teenage-slasher film about kids running into a backwoods fishing tournament while on vacation, complete with ghouls, cannibalism and grotesquerie. 85m; VHS, DVD. **C:** Mark Jacobs; Lisa Todd; Patrick Danz; Directed by Jim Mallon. **Pr:** Golden Chargers Productions. **A:** Sr. High-Adult. **P:** Entertainment. **U:** Home. **Mov-Ent. Acq:** Purchase. **Dist:** Paramount Pictures Corp. $14.95.

Blood In . . . Blood Out: Bound by Honor 1993 (R) — ★½
Three-hour epic about Chicano gang culture focuses on three buddies whose lives evolve into a drug-addicted artist, a narc, and a prison regular. Written by acclaimed poet Baca, the film touches on issues such as poverty, racism, drugs, and violence as they pertain to Hispanic life. Unfortunately, the extreme violence (shootings, stabbings, and garrotings) completely overwhelms the rest of the story. Based on a story by Ross Thomas. 180m; VHS, DVD, Wide, CC. **C:** Damian Chapa; Jesse Borrego; Benjamin Bratt; Enrique Castillo; Victor Rivers; Delroy Lindo; Tom Towler; Thomas F. Wilson; Directed by Taylor Hackford; Written by Floyd Mutrux; Jimmy Santiago Baca; Jeremy Iacone; Cinematography by Gabriel Beristain; Music by Bill Conti. **Pr:** Taylor Hackford; Jerry Gershwin; Stratton Leopold; Taylor Hackford; Jimmy Santiago Baca; Hollywood Pictures; Buena Vista. **A:** Sr. High-Adult. **P:** Entertainment. **U:** Home. **Mov-Ent:** Crime Drama, Drugs, Violence. **Acq:** Purchase. **Dist:** Buena Vista Home Entertainment. $96.03.

Blood in the Face 1991
A chilling documentary look at violent, fanatic groups, including the Ku Klux Klan and the American Nazi Party. The filmmakers dispense with narration to let the participants speak for themselves. They show a gathering of the American Nazi Party at Cohoctah, Michigan, whose members look forward to a coming race war, and of the Aryan Nation's white supremacy platform. Unfortunately, as this documentary shows, it is impossible to dismiss this fringe society. 78m; DVD. **C:** Directed by Kevin Rafferty; Anne Bohlen; James Ridgeway. **Pr:** First Run Features. **A:** College-Adult. **P:** Education. **U:** Home. **Gen-Edu:** Documentary Films, Sociology, Black Culture. **Acq:** Purchase. **Dist:** Facets Multimedia Inc.; First Run Features. $29.95.

Blood Island 1968 — ★★
A couple inherits an old house on a remote New England island where the woman grew up. They discover that this old house needs more than a paint job to make it livable; seems there's something evil in them there walls. Based on an H.P. Lovecraft story. Greene, who's best known for later directing "Godspell," and the solid cast fail to animate the inert script. 100m; VHS, DVD. **C:** Gig Young; Carol Lynley; Oliver Reed; Flora Robson; Directed by David Greene. **Pr:** Seven Arts Pictures; Warner Bros. **A:** Jr. High-Adult. **P:** Entertainment. **U:** Home. **Mov-Ent:** Horror. **Acq:** Purchase. **Dist:** Warner Home Video, Inc. $29.98.

The Blood Knot 1964
Presents scenes from Athol Fugard's play featuring J.D. Cannon and James Earl Jones. 28m/B/W; VHS. **A:** Adult. **P:** Education. **U:** Institution. **Fin-Art:** Theater. **Acq:** Purchase. **Dist:** Insight Media. $139.00.

Blood Lake 1987 (Unrated) — **Bomb!**
A psychotic killer stalks teenagers, to the detriment of all. 90m; VHS. **A:** Adult. **P:** Entertainment. **U:** Home. **Mov-Ent:** Horror. **Acq:** Purchase. **Dist:** VCI Entertainment. $19.95.

Blood Legacy 1973 (R) — ★★
Four heirs must survive a night in a lonely country estate to collect their money; what do you think happens? Average treatment of the haunted house theme. 77m; VHS, DVD. **C:** John Carradine; John Russell; Faith Domergue; Merry Anders; Richard (Dick) Davalos; Jeff Morrow; Roy Engle; Directed by Carl Monson; Written by Eric Norden; Cinematography by Jack Beckett. **Pr:** ASW Films Inc. **A:** College-Adult. **P:** Entertainment. **U:** Home. **Mov-Ent:** Horror. **Acq:** Purchase. **Dist:** Movies Unlimited; Alpha Video. $14.95.

Blood Mania 1970 (R) — ★
A retired surgeon's daughter decides to murder her father to collect her inheritance prematurely, but soon learns that crime doesn't pay as well as medicine. Low-budget, low-interest flick. 90m; VHS, DVD. **C:** Peter Carpenter; Maria de Aragon; Alex Rocco; Directed by Robert Vincent O'Neil. **Pr:** Crown International Pictures. **A:** Sr. High-Adult. **P:** Entertainment. **U:** Home. **Mov-Ent:** Horror. **Acq:** Purchase. **Dist:** Movies Unlimited. $12.74.

Blood Memory: The Legend of Beanie Short 1992
Oral history of the Civil War is kept alive in Turkey Neck Bend, Kentucky as is the legend of outlaw Beanie Short. A deserter from the Confederate Army, Short terrorized the small Southern community before being gunned down by Union vigilantes. Nothing was written about Short's exploits for more than 100 years but his legend persisted due to local storytellers. 56m; VHS. **C:** Directed by Robby Henson. **A:** College-Adult. **P:** Education. **U:** Institution. **Gen-Edu:** Storytelling, Civil War. **Acq:** Purchase, Rent/Lease. **Dist:** The Cinema Guild. $350.00.

Blood Money 1980 (PG) — ★½
A dying ex-criminal returns to Australia to redeem his name and die with dignity. 64m; VHS. **C:** Bryan Brown; John Flaus; Chrissie James; Directed by Christopher Fitchett. **A:** Adult. **P:** Entertainment. **U:** Home. **Mov-Ent:** Violence. **Acq:** Purchase. **Dist:** No Longer Available.

Blood Money 1998 (R) — ★★
Five dead bodies, $4 million, and one eye-witness, stripper Candy (Petty), are what remains of a drug deal gone south. Now, Detective Connor (Ironside) must protect his witness from Mob reprisals. 95m; VHS, DVD. **C:** Michael Ironside; Lori Petty; Currie Graham; Directed by Michael Ironside. **A:** Sr. High-Adult. **P:** Entertainment. **U:** Home. **Mov-Ent:** Crime Drama. **Acq:** Purchase. **Dist:** Movies Unlimited; Alpha Video.

Blood Money 1999 (R) — ★★
Tony Restrelli (Bloom) is the legit member of a mob family who made his money in the stock market. Now his financial knowledge is needed by his family to fend off would-be interlopers—and he can also avenge his brother's murder. 95m; VHS, DVD. **C:** Brian Bloom; Alan Arkin; Alicia Coppola; Jennifer Gatti; Bruce Kirby; Jonathan Scarfe; Gregory Sierra; Leonard Stone; Directed by Aaron Lipstadt. **A:** Sr. High-Adult. **P:** Entertainment. **U:** Home. **Mov-Ent:** Family. **Acq:** Purchase. **Dist:** Paramount Pictures Corp.

Blood Money: The Story of Clinton and Nadine 1988 (Unrated) — ★★½
A confusing action/thriller with a good cast. Garcia is a small-time exotic bird smuggler whose gun-running brother has been murdered. He uses high-class hooker Barkin to get close to his brother's contacts, who turn out to be running guns to the Nicaraguan contras and involved in a dangerous government conspiracy. 95m; VHS, DVD. **C:** Andy Garcia; Ellen Barkin; Morgan Freeman; Directed by Jerry Schatzberg. **Pr:** ITC Entertainment Group. **A:** Sr. High-Adult. **P:** Entertainment. **U:** Home. **Mov-Ent:** Prostitution, TV Movies, Politics & Government. **Acq:** Purchase. **Dist:** Facets Multimedia Inc. $79.95.

Blood Monkey 2007 (Unrated) — ★
Six American grad students arrive in Africa (Thailand substituted) to study apes with Professor Hamilton (Abraham). But his studies mean investigating local rumors of a tribe of killer chimpanzees. When the students witness the carnage first-hand, they want out but neither the professor nor the chimps are willing to let them go. Not much monkey action since the budget apparently didn't stretch too far. 90m; DVD. **C:** F. Murray Abraham; Amy Manson; Matt Reeves; Freishia Bomanbehram; Sebastian Armesto; Matt Ryan; Laura Aikman; Directed by Robert Young; Written by George LaVoo; Gary Dauberman; Cinematography by Choochart Nantitanyatada; Music by Charles Olins; Mark Ryder. **A:** Jr. High-Adult. **P:** Entertainment. **U:** Home. **Mov-Ent:** Africa. **Acq:** Purchase. **Dist:** Genius.com Incorporated.

Blood Night: The Legend of Mary Hatchet 2009 (R) — ★
Teen slasher with victims portrayed by actors too old to pass for teenagers and more nudity than usual. Blood Night, celebrated by the local teens, is the anniversary of the death of a local axe murderess. After Mary Mattock butchers her parents, she's sent to an insane asylum where nasty things happen to her. She's killed after another bloody rampage and now 'Mary Hatchet' is a Long Island legend. On this Blood Night it looks like Mary has been resurrected and is ready to kill again. 85m; DVD. **C:** Danielle Harris; Bill Moseley; Nate Dushku; Samantha Facchi; Billy Magnussen; Anthony Marks; Alissa Dean; Directed by Frank Sabatella; Written by Elke Blasi; Cinematography by Christopher Walters; Jarin Blaschke; Music by Victor Bruno. **A:** Sr. High-Adult. **P:** Entertainment. **U:** Home. **Mov-Ent. Acq:** Purchase. **Dist:** Lions Gate Entertainment Inc.

The Blood of a Poet 1930 — ★★½
Cocteau's first film, a practically formless piece of poetic cinema, detailing all manner of surreal events occurring in the instant a chimney falls. In French with English subtitles. 55m/B/W; VHS, DVD. **C:** Enrique Rivero; Feral Benga; Jean Desbordes; Directed by Jean Cocteau; Written by Jean Cocteau; Cinematography by Georges Perinal; Music by Georges Auric. **Pr:** Vicomte de Noailles. **A:** Adult. **P:** Entertainment. **U:** Home. **L:** English, French. **Mov-Ent:** Fantasy, Film--Avant-Garde, Classic Films. **Acq:** Purchase. **Dist:** Home Vision Cinema; Tapeworm Video Distributors Inc. $19.95.

Blood of Dracula 1957 (Unrated) — ★½
They don't make 1950s rock 'n' roll girls' school vampire movies like this anymore, for which we may be grateful. Hypnotism, an amulet, and a greasepaint makeup job turn a shy female student into a bloodsucker. 71m/B/W; VHS, DVD. **C:** Sandra Harrison; Louise Lewis; Gail Ganley; Jerry Blaine; Heather Ames; Malcolm Atterbury; Richard Devon; Thomas B(rowne). Henry; Don Devlin; Edna Holland; Directed by Herbert L. Strock; Written by Aben Kandel; Cinematography by Monroe Askins; Music by Paul Dunlap. **Pr:** Herman Cohen; American International Pictures. **A:** Jr. High-Adult. **P:** Entertainment. **U:** Home. **Mov-Ent:** Horror, Hypnosis & Hypnotists. **Acq:** Purchase. **Dist:** Lions Gate Entertainment Inc., On Moratorium. $9.95.

Blood of Dracula's Castle 1969 (Unrated) — ★★
Couple inherits an allegedly deserted castle, but upon moving in discover Mr. and Mrs. Dracula have settled there. The vampires keep young women chained in the dungeon for continual blood supply. Also present are a hunchback and a werewolf. Awesome Adamson production is highlighted by the presence of the gorgeous Volante. Early cinematography effort by the renowned Laszlo Kovacs. 84m; VHS, DVD. **C:** John Carradine; Alexander D'Arcy; Paula Raymond; Ray Young; Vicki Volante; Robert Dix; John Cardos; Ken Osborne; Directed by Jean Hewitt; Al Adamson; Written by Rex Carlton; Cinematography by Laszlo Kovacs. **Pr:** Al Adamson; Al Adamson; Paragon. **A:** Jr. High-Adult. **P:** Entertainment. **U:** Home. **Mov-Ent:** Horror. **Acq:** Purchase. **Dist:** Amazon.com Inc.

Blood of Ghastly Horror 1972 (Unrated) — **Bomb!**
A young man thinks he has a new lease on life when he is the happy recipient of a brain transplant, but his dreams are destroyed when he evolves into a rampaging killer. This movie is so awful it hides behind numerous but rather creative aliases. 87m; VHS, DVD. **C:** John Carradine; Kent Taylor; Tommy Kirk; Regina Carrol; Roy Morton; Tracey Robbins; Directed by Al Adamson; Written by Chris Martino; Dick Poston; Cinematography by Vilmos Zsigmond. **Pr:** Al Adamson; Al Adamson; Hemisphere Productions. **A:** College-Adult. **P:** Entertainment. **U:** Home. **Mov-Ent:** Horror. **Acq:** Purchase. **Dist:** Movies Unlimited. $14.95.

The Blood of Heroes 1989 (R) — ★★
A post-apocalyptic action flick detailing the adventures of a battered team of "juggers," warriors who challenge small village teams to a brutal sport (involving dogs' heads on sticks) that's a cross between jousting and football. 97m; VHS, DVD, CC. **C:** Rutger Hauer; Joan Chen; Vincent D'Onofrio; Anna (Katerina) Katarina; Directed by David Peoples; Written by David Peoples; Cinematography by David Eggby; Music by Todd Boekelheide. **Pr:** Kings Road Entertainment. **A:** College-Adult. **P:** Entertainment. **U:** Home. **Mov-Ent:** Science Fiction. **Acq:** Purchase. **Dist:** Movies Unlimited; Alpha Video. $89.99.

Blood of Jesus 1941 (Unrated) — ★★
A sinful husband accidentally shoots his newly baptized wife, causing an uproar in their rural town. Williams later starred as Andy on the "Amos 'n' Andy" TV series. 50m; VHS, DVD. **C:** Spencer Williams, Jr.; Cathryn Caviness; Directed by Spencer Williams, Jr.; Written by Spencer Williams, Jr. **A:** Sr. High-Adult. **P:** Entertainment. **U:** Home. **Mov-Ent:** Melodrama, Marriage, Religion. **Awds:** Natl. Film Reg. '91. **Acq:** Purchase. **Dist:** Baker and Taylor; Facets Multimedia Inc. $34.95.

The Blood of Kings: A New Interpretation of Maya Art 1986
Through computer animation and onscreen commentary, a brief introduction to Mayan culture and art is given. 10m; VHS, 3/4 U. **Pr:** William Howze; Kimbell Art Museum, Fort Worth. **A:** Jr. High-Adult. **P:** Education. **U:** Institution, Home. **Gen-Edu:** Art & Artists, History--Ancient, Central America. **Acq:** Purchase, Rent/Lease. **Dist:** Museum of Modern Art. $200.00.

The Blood of My Brothers 2006
Personal look at the cost of war from an Iraqi perspective as a family mourns the death of their eldest son, who was killed by American forces. 84m; DVD. **A:** Jr. High-Adult. **P:** Entertainment. **U:** Home. **Gen-Edu:** Documentary Films, Persian Gulf War. **Acq:** Purchase. **Dist:** Entertainment One US LP.

The Blood of Others 1984 — ★
A driveling adaptation of the Simone de Beauvoir novel about a young French woman at the outbreak of WWII torn between her absent boyfriend in the Resistance and a kind, wealthy German. Made for French TV, it stars Jodie Foster and Michael Ontkean as the Gallic pair. 130m; VHS. **C:** Jodie Foster; Sam Neill; Michael Ontkean; Stephane Audran; Lambert Wilson; John Vernon; Kate Reid; Jean-Pierre Aumont; Directed by Claude Chabrol; Written by Brian Moore. **Pr:** Cine-Simone Inc; Superchannel; A2 Television France/Film A2. **A:** Jr. High-Adult. **P:** Entertainment. **U:** Home. **Mov-Ent:** Drama, World War Two, TV Movies. **Acq:** Purchase. **Dist:** No Longer Available.

Blood of the Dragon 1971 (R) — ★★½
This film has martial-arts expert Wang Yu killing everyone he meets. One scene has him fighting 100 men at the same time. 96m; VHS, DVD. **C:** Yu Wang; Lung Fei; Chiao Chiao; Yau Tin; Tin Miu; Yuen Yee; Directed by Pao Shu Kao; Written by Pao Shu Kao; Hong Ngai; Cinematography by Fang Chi Kuo. **A:** College-Adult. **P:** Entertainment. **U:** Home. **Mov-Ent:** Martial Arts. **Acq:** Purchase. **Dist:** BFS Video.

Blood of the Dragon Peril/Revenge of the Dragon 1981 — ★½
Two oriental action masterworks, together on one tape for the first time. 172m; VHS. **Pr:** HAL. **A:** Jr. High-Adult. **P:** Entertainment. **U:** Home. **Mov-Ent:** Martial Arts. **Acq:** Purchase. **Dist:** Anchor Bay Entertainment. $7.00.

Blood of the Hunter 1994 (PG-13) — ★★½
Psycho-killer holds postman's wife captive in a remote cabin in the Canadian wilderness. Turns out hubby and psycho share a mysterious past. 92m; VHS. **C:** Michael Biehn; Alexandra Vandernoot; Gabriel Arcand; Directed by Gilles Carle. **A:** Sr. High-Adult. **P:** Entertainment. **U:** Home. **Mov-Ent:** Wilderness Areas, Canada. **Acq:** Purchase. **Dist:** CinemaNow Inc.; Facets Multimedia Inc. $92.99.

Blood of the Vampire 1958 (Unrated) — ★½
A Transylvanian doctor is executed for being a vampire and his hunchbacked assistant brings him back to life. 84m; VHS, DVD. **C:** Donald Wolfit; Vincent Ball; Barbara Shelley; Victor Maddern; Directed by Henry Cass; Written by Jimmy Sangster. **Pr:** Mark Huffam. **A:** Jr. High-Adult. **P:** Entertainment. **U:** Home. **Mov-Ent:** Horror, Death. **Acq:** Purchase. **Dist:** MPI Media Group. $59.95.

The Blood of Yingzhou District 2006
Academy Award-winning short documentary on the hidden AIDS epidemic in China. 40m; VHS, DVD. **A:** Sr. High-Adult. **P:** Entertainment. **U:** Home, Institution. **Gen-Edu:** Documentary Films, China, AIDS. **Acq:** Purchase, Rent/Lease. **Dist:** The Cinema Guild. $295.00.

The Blood on Satan's Claw 1971 (Unrated) — ★★★
Graphic tale centering on the Devil himself. Townspeople in an English village circa 1670 find the spirit of Satan taking over their children, who begin to practice witchcraft. Well made with lots of attention to period details. Not for the faint-hearted. 90m; VHS. **C:** Patrick Wymark; Linda Hayden; Barry Andrews; Michele Dotrice; James Hayter; Avice Landon; Simon Williams; Tamara Ustinov; Directed by Piers Haggard; Cinematography by Dick Bush. **Pr:** Tigon British Film Production; Cannon Films. **A:** Sr. High-Adult. **P:** Entertainment. **U:** Home. **Mov-Ent:** Horror, Occult Sciences. **Acq:** Purchase. **Dist:** MGM Home Entertainment; Facets Multimedia Inc. $14.95.

Blood on the Badge 1992 (Unrated) — ★½
Illegal arms have been stolen from a military arsenal and fall into the hands of Libyan Nationalists who begin a terrorist campaign. Detective Neal Farrow is assigned to stop them. 92m; VHS. **C:** Ramon Estevez; David Harrod; Rocky Patterson; Desiree Laforge; Dean Nolen; Melissa Deleon; Todd Everett; Directed by Bret McCormick. **A:** Sr. High-Adult. **P:** Entertainment. **U:** Home. **Mov-Ent:** Terrorism. **Acq:** Purchase. **Dist:** No Longer Available.

Blood on the Cats III. . .For a Few Pussies More 198?
Video compilation featuring the Milkshakes, Sharks, The Jazz Butcher, Meteors, Alien Sex Fiend and more. 55m; VHS. **A:** Jr. High-Adult. **P:** Entertainment. **U:** Home. **Mov-Ent:** Music Video. **Acq:** Purchase. **Dist:** Music Video Distributors. $29.95.

Blood on the Moon 1948 (Unrated) — ★★½
Well-acted film about a cowboy's involvement in a friend's underhanded schemes. Based on a Luke Short novel, this dark film revolves around a western land dispute between cattlemen and homesteaders. 88m/B/W; VHS. **C:** Robert Mitchum; Robert Preston; Walter Brennan; Barbara Bel Geddes; Directed by Robert Wise. **Pr:** United Artists. **A:** Family. **P:** Entertainment. **U:** Home. **Mov-Ent:** Western, Romance. **Acq:** Purchase. **Dist:** Turner Broadcasting System Inc. $19.95.

Blood on the Mountain 1988 (Unrated) — ★
After escaping from prison, Jim plots revenge against his accomplice, only to kill an innocent man instead. 71m; VHS. **C:** Stracker Edwards; Tim Jones; Paula Preston; Cliff Turknett; Rich Jury; Directed by Donald W. Thompson. **Pr:** Heartland Productions. **A:** Family. **P:** Religious. **U:** Home. **Mov-Ent. Acq:** Purchase. **Dist:** Russ Doughten Films Inc.

Blood on the Sun 1945 (Unrated) — ★★½
Newspaperman in Japan uncovers plans for world dominance as propaganda, violence, and intrigue combine in this action-adventure. Also available colorized. 98m/B/W; VHS, DVD. **C:** James Cagney; Sylvia Sidney; Robert Armstrong; Wallace Ford; Directed by Frank Lloyd; Written by Lester Cole; Nathaniel Curtis; Frank Melford; Cinematography by Theodor Sparkuhl; Music by Miklos Rozsa. **Pr:** United Artists. **A:** Family. **P:** Entertainment. **U:** Home. **Mov-Ent:** Mystery & Suspense, World War Two, Propaganda. **Acq:** Purchase. **Dist:** Lions Gate Entertainment Inc. $19.95.

The Blood Oranges 1997 (R) — ★½
Pretentious film is set in the anything-goes '70s in a tropical backwater village. Bohemian marrieds Cyril (Dance) and Fiona (Lee) believe in fulfilling every sexual fantasy but their latest exchange of marital partners comes with unexpected complications. Fiona is attracted to photographer Hugh (Lane), who resists her charms for more deviant behavior, while Hugh's wife Catherine (Robins) is easily seduced by Cyril's courtship. Dialogue is laughable and the acting equally overblown. Based on the novel by John Hawkes. 93m; VHS, DVD. **C:** Charles Dance; Sheryl Lee; Colin Lane; Laila Robins; Rachael Bella; Directed by Philip Haas; Written by Belinda Haas; Philip Haas; Cinematography by Bernard Zitzermann; Music by Angelo Badalamenti. **Pr:** Trimark Pictures. **A:** College-Adult. **P:** Entertainment. **U:** Home. **Mov-Ent:** Sex & Sexuality, Marriage. **Acq:** Purchase. **Dist:** CinemaNow Inc.

Blood Orgy of the She-Devils 1974 (PG) — **Bomb!**
Exploitative gore nonsense about female demons, beautiful witches, and satanic worship. Some movies waste all their creative efforts on their titles. 73m; VHS, DVD. **C:** Lila Zaborin; Tom Pace; Leslie McRae; Ray Myles; Victor Izay; William Bagdad; Directed by Ted V. Mikels; Written by Ted V. Mikels; Cinematography by Anthony Salinas. **Pr:** T.V. Mikels Film Productions. **A:** Jr. High-Adult. **P:** Entertainment. **U:** Home. **Mov-Ent:** Horror, Occult Sciences. **Acq:** Purchase. **Dist:** Movies Unlimited. $12.75.

Blood Out 2010 (R) — ★
Small-town sheriff Michael Spencer sets aside his badge to go undercover as an urban gangsta when big city detectives don't pursue his brother's murder. That's because there are bad cops and a crime boss involved (although not much Kilmer or Jackson despite their billing). 89m; DVD. **C:** Luke Goss; AnnaLynne McCord; Vinnie Jones; 50 Cent; Val Kilmer; Ryan Donowho; Tamer Hassan; Ed Quinn; Directed by Jason Hewitt; Written by Jason Hewitt; Cinematography by Christian Herrera; Music by Jermaine Stegall. **A:** Sr. High-Adult. **P:** Entertainment. **U:** Home. **Mov-Ent. Acq:** Purchase. **Dist:** Lions Gate Entertainment Inc.

Blood Pledge 2009 (Unrated) — ★★
The fifth film in Korea's Whispering Corridors series is, as usual, set in an all girls' school for overachievers with malicious students and staff. Eon-joo (Jang Kyeong-ah) is found dead, an apparent suicide, and her younger sister is determined to find out why. Apparently there was a suicide pact between her and three other girls who are still alive, implying they may have been responsible for her demise. The usual ghost is not far behind. 88m; DVD. **C:** Son Eun-seo; Song Min-jeong; Oh Yeon-seo; Yoo Shin-ae; Directed by Jong-yong Lee; Written by Jong-yong Lee. **A:** Sr. High-Adult. **P:** Entertainment. **U:** Home. **L:** English, Korean. **Mov-Ent:** Horror, Education, Suicide. **Acq:** Purchase. **Dist:** Media Blasters Inc. $19.99.

Blood Pressure 1985
Blood pressure and measuring equipment are explained and demonstrated. 25m; VHS, 3/4 U. **Pr:** Trainex. **A:** College-Adult. **P:** Professional. **U:** Institution. **L:** English, Spanish. **Hea-Sci:** Nursing, Circulatory System, How-To. **Acq:** Purchase, Rent/Lease. **Dist:** Medcom Inc.

Blood Pressure Measurement in Children/Adolescents 1982
This program demonstrates how to obtain accurate blood pressure measurements in children and adolescents. 27m; VHS, 3/4 U. **Pr:** Emory University. **A:** College-Adult. **P:** Professional. **U:** Institution, CCTV, Home, SURA. **How-Ins:** Medical Education, Pediatrics, How-To. **Acq:** Purchase, Rent/Lease, Subscription. **Dist:** Emory Medical Television Network.

Blood Rage 1987 (R) — **Bomb!**
A maniacal twin goes on a murderous rampage through his brother's neighborhood. AKA "Nightmare at Shadow Woods." Only for die-hard "Mary Hartman" fans. 87m; VHS, DVD. **C:** Louise Lasser; Mike Soper; Directed by John Grissmer; Music by Richard Einhorn. **Pr:** Marianne Kanter. **A:** Sr. High-Adult. **P:** Entertainment. **U:** Home. **Mov-Ent:** Horror. **Acq:** Purchase. **Dist:** Unknown Distributor.

Blood Rain 2005 (Unrated) — ★★
Set in 1808 during Korea's Joseon dynasty, a local shaman collapses and seems to be possessed by the spirit of Lord Kang, a commissioner executed years ago for treason and practicing Catholicism. One by one all the informants in Kang's case begin dying, and investigator Won-kyu (Seung-won Cha) is sent to find out if there is a ghost at work, or simple human revenge. Not quite a detective mystery and not quite a slasher film. 115m; DVD. **C:** Seung-won Cha; Ji-na Choi; Seong Ji; Hyeon-kyeong Oh; Yong-woo Park; Ho-jin Jeon; Directed by Dae-seung Kim; Written by Seong-jae Kim; Won-jae Lee; Cinematography by Yeong-hwon Choi; Music by Yeong-wook Jo; Ji-Soo Lee. **A:** Sr. High-Adult. **P:** Entertainment. **U:** Home. **L:** English, Korean. **Mov-Ent:** Mystery & Suspense. **Acq:** Purchase. **Dist:** Pathfinder Pictures. $24.98.

Blood Red 1988 (R) — ★½
In 1895 Northern California, an Italian immigrant and his family give bloody battle to a powerful industrialist who wants their land in wine-growing country. Watch for the scenes involving veteran Roberts and his then-newcomer sister, pretty woman Julia. 91m; VHS, Streaming, 8 mm. **C:** Eric Roberts; Dennis Hopper; Giancarlo Giannini; Burt Young; Carlin Glynn; Lara Harris; Susan Anspach; Julia Roberts; Elias Koteas; Frank Campanella; Aldo Ray; Horton Foote, Jr.; Directed by Peter Masterson; Written by Ron Cutler. **Pr:** Kettledrum Productions; Hemdale Films. **A:** Sr. High-Adult. **P:** Entertainment. **U:** Home. **Mov-Ent:** Family, Immigration. **Acq:** Purchase. **Dist:** MGM Home Entertainment; Sony Pictures Home Entertainment Inc. $14.95.

Blood Relations 1979
Jonathan Miller examines the ways in which philosophers and scientists have looked at blood over the years, then shows how the process of scientific discovery has led to our better understanding of blood. 60m; VHS, 3/4 U. **A:** College-Adult. **P:** Education. **U:** Institution, SURA. **Hea-Sci:** Documentary Films, Blood. **Acq:** Purchase. **Dist:** Home Vision Cinema.

Blood Relations 1987 (R) — ★½
A woman is introduced to her fiance's family only to find out that they, as well as her fiance, are murdering, perverted weirdos competing for an inheritance. 88m; VHS, DVD. **C:** Jan Rubes; Ray Walston; Lydie Denier; Kevin Hicks; Lynne Adams; Sam Malkin; Steven Saylor; Carrie Leigh; Directed by Graeme Campbell. **Pr:** SC Entertainment Corporation. **A:** Sr. High-Adult. **P:** Entertainment. **U:** Home. **Mov-Ent:** Mystery & Suspense, Canada. **Acq:** Purchase. **Dist:** New Line Home Video. $19.98.

Blood Relatives 1977 — ★
Langlois admits she saw her brother kill her cousin, with whom he had been carrying on an incestuous relationship. But the discovery of the dead girl's diary by police inspector Sutherland reveals many more layers of intrigue than were initially evident. Based on a novel by Ed McBain. The French actors have been dubbed into English. 94m; VHS. **C:** Lisa Langlois; Donald Sutherland; Stephane Audran; David Hemmings; Donald Pleasence; Laurent Malet; Micheline Lanctot; Aude Landry; Directed by Claude Chabrol; Written by Claude Chabrol. **A:** College-Adult. **P:** Entertainment. **U:** Home. **Mov-Ent:** Mystery & Suspense. **Acq:** Purchase. **Dist:** Unknown Distributor.

Blood Relic 2005 (R) — ★½
Pilot Hank Campbell (Christian) is possessed by a mysterious talisman, commits mass murder on a naval base, and winds up in the loony bin for 22 years. Upon his release, he heads back to the scene of the crime and discovers history buff Harry (Drago) is turning the base into a museum with the help of a bunch of handy young people (handy for slaughtering that is). Anyway, mayhem is likely since Campbell is determined to find his talisman again. 86m; DVD. **C:** John Christian; Billy Drago; Jennifer Grant; Debbie Rochon; Joshua Park; Kelly Ray; Directed by J. Christian Ingvordsen; Written by J. Christian Ingvordsen; Matt Howe; Cinematography by Matt Howe; Music by Timo Elliston. **A:** Sr. High-Adult. **P:** Entertainment. **U:** Home. **Mov-Ent:** Horror. **Acq:** Purchase. **Dist:** Bedford Entertainment Inc.

Blood Ring 1993 (Unrated) — ★½
When Sue's boxer husband goes missing she enlists old friend Max to help find him. They uncover a gambling ring run by drug lords where the kickboxing matches are to the death. Naturally, Max decides to use his expert kickboxing skills to get a violent revenge. 90m; VHS. **C:** Dale "Apollo" Cook; Andrea Lamatsch; Don Nakaya Neilsen; Steve Tartalia; Directed by Irvin Johnson;

Written by Ron Davies. **Pr:** Davian International. **A:** Sr. High-Adult. **P:** Entertainment. **U:** Home. **Mov-Ent:** Martial Arts. **Acq:** Purchase. **Dist:** Unknown Distributor.

Blood: River of Life, Mirror of Health 1986
A look at blood, what it does, and how it can tell us if we're healthy or not. 30m; VHS. **Pr:** HRM. **A:** Sr. High-College. **P:** Education. **U:** Institution. **Hea-Sci:** Blood. **Acq:** Purchase. **Dist:** HRM Video; Educational Images Ltd. $145.00.

Blood Salvage 1990 (R) — ★
A crazy junkman kidnaps beautiful girls, selling their organs to the highest bidder. He meets his match when a potential target refuses to become a victim in spite of her wheelchair. Interesting plot twists keep this Grade B thriller above average. 90m; VHS. **C:** Danny Nelson; Lori Birdsong; John Saxon; Ray Walston; Christian Hesler; Ralph Pruitt Vaughn; Laura Whyte; Evander Holyfield; Directed by Tucker Johnson; Written by Tucker Johnson; Ken Sanders; Cinematography by Michael Karp. **Pr:** Magnum. **A:** Adult. **P:** Entertainment. **U:** Home. **Mov-Ent:** Horror. **Acq:** Purchase. **Dist:** Turner Broadcasting System Inc.

Blood Screams 1988 (R) — **Bomb!**
Nosy people drop in on an old town in Mexico and attempt to uncover the secrets hidden there, but bizarre entities throw out the unwelcome mat and terrorize them. Lots of blood and screaming. 75m; VHS. **C:** Ran Sands; James Garnett; Ralph Navarro; Mario Almada; Alfredo Gutierrez; Stacey Shaffer; Russ Tamblyn; Isela Vega; Directed by Glenn Gebhard. **A:** Adult. **P:** Entertainment. **U:** Home. **Mov-Ent:** Horror. **Acq:** Purchase. **Dist:** Warner Home Video, Inc. $19.98.

Blood Simple 1985 (R) — ★★★1/2
A jealous husband hires a sleazy private eye to murder his adulterous wife and her lover. A dark, intricate, morbid morality tale that deviates imaginatively from the standard murder mystery thriller. First film scripted by the Coen brothers. 96m; VHS, DVD, Blu-Ray, Wide, CC. **C:** John Getz; M. Emmet Walsh; Dan Hedaya; Frances McDormand; Samm-Art Williams; Van Brooks; Lauren Bivens; Holly Hunter; Directed by Joel Coen; Written by Joel Coen; Ethan Coen; Cinematography by Barry Sonnenfeld; Music by Carter Burwell. **Pr:** River Road Productions. **A:** Sr. High-Adult. **P:** Entertainment. **U:** Home. **Mov-Ent:** Mystery & Suspense, Cult Films. **Awds:** Ind. Spirit '86: Actor (Walsh), Director (Coen); Sundance '85: Grand Jury Prize. **Acq:** Purchase. **Dist:** Movies Unlimited; Alpha Video; MGM Home Entertainment. $14.98.

Blood Sisters 1986 (R) — **Bomb!**
Sorority babes intend to spend a giggle-strewn night in a haunted house but end up decapitated, butchered, and cannibalized. 85m; VHS, DVD. **C:** Amy Brentano; Marla MacHart; Brigete Cossu; Randy Mooers; Directed by Roberta Findlay. **A:** Adult. **P:** Entertainment. **U:** Home. **Mov-Ent:** Horror. **Acq:** Purchase. **Dist:** Sony Pictures Home Entertainment Inc. $14.95.

Blood Song 1982 (Unrated) — ★
A patient (yester-decade teen throb Frankie Avalon) escapes into the night from a mental institution after murdering an attendant. He takes his only possession with him, a carved wooden flute. A young woman sees him burying his latest victim, and now he's on a hunt to play his "blood song" for her. Pretty bad, but fun to see Avalon play a less-than-squeaky-clean role. 90m; VHS, DVD. **C:** Frankie Avalon; Donna Wilkes; Richard Jaeckel; Dane Clark; Antoinette Bower; Lenny Montana; Directed by Alan J. Levi; Written by Lenny Montana. **A:** Adult. **P:** Entertainment. **U:** Home. **Mov-Ent:** Horror. **Acq:** Purchase. **Dist:** Movies Unlimited.

The Blood Spattered Bride 1972 (Unrated) — ★
Newlywed couple honeymoons in a remote castle in southern Spain. They are visited by a mysterious young woman who begins to influence the bride in the ways of lesbian bloodsucking. O.K. '70s Euro-eroti-horror based on Sheridan Le Fanu's "Carmilla." 101m; VHS, DVD. **C:** Simon Andreu; Maribel Martin; Alexandra Bastedo; Dean Selmier; Rosa Ma Rodriguez; Montserrat Julio; Angel Lombarte; Directed by Vicente Aranda; Written by Vicente Aranda; Cinematography by Fernando Arribas. **Pr:** Europix Consolidated. **A:** College-Adult. **P:** Entertainment. **U:** Home. **Mov-Ent:** Horror. **Acq:** Purchase. **Dist:** Anchor Bay Entertainment.

Blood Stained Tradewind 1990 (Unrated) — ★1/2
Shing (Fong) and Hong (Lee) are brothers raised by a Triad Gang leader. When he decides Shing will be the new leader and refuses, he is tossed out, forced to go on the straight and narrow. Hong takes over and he and Shing are immediately accused by rivals of stealing from the gang. Blood and fists fly for the immediate future. 94m; DVD. **C:** Alex Fong; Shui-Fan Fung; Waise Lee; Carrie Ng; Fong Pao; Directed by Yuen Tat Chor; Written by Philip Cheng. **A:** Sr. High-Adult. **P:** Entertainment. **U:** Home. **L:** English, Cantonese, Mandarin Dialects. **Mov-Ent:** Crime Drama, Martial Arts. **Acq:** Purchase. **Dist:** Image Entertainment Inc. $14.99.

Blood Sugar Regulation and Diabetes 1989
Demonstrates the control of blood sugar and diabetes taking into account diet, working pattern, and lifestyle. 30m; VHS, SVS, 3/4 U. **Pr:** British Broadcasting Corporation. **A:** Jr. High-Sr. High. **P:** Education. **U:** Institution. **Hea-Sci:** Diabetes, Nutrition, Health Education. **Acq:** Purchase. **Dist:** Encyclopedia Britannica. $89.00.

Blood Surf 2000 (R) — ★
A filmmaker and her crew travel to Australia to do a documentary on the extreme sport of blood surfing where thrillseekers try to out surf sharks to shore. Only the sharks aren't the problem—a giant salt-water crocodile gets to the participants first. Very silly; your enjoyment will depend on your tolerance for the fake croc. 88m; VHS, DVD, Wide. **C:** Matt Borlenghi; Duncan Regehr; Kate Fischer; Taryn Reif; Joel West; Dax Miller; Directed by James D.R. Hickox; Written by Sam Bernard; Robert L. Levy; Cinematography by Christopher Pearson; Music by Jim Manzie. **A:** Sr. High-Adult. **P:** Entertainment. **U:** Home. **Mov-Ent:** Australia. **Acq:** Purchase. **Dist:** CinemaNow Inc.

Blood Sweat and Tears: 1973 BST 1992
Blood Sweat and Tears performs live from Stockholm in 1973. Songs include "God Bless the Child," "And When I Die," "Sorry Not to Have Left You," "Back Up Against the Wall," and others. 76m; VHS. **A:** Jr. High-Adult. **P:** Entertainment. **U:** Home. **Mov-Ent:** Music Video, Music--Performance. **Acq:** Purchase. **Dist:** Music Video Distributors. $64.95.

The Blood System: A Liquid of Life 1989
A program that takes the viewer through the entire circulatory system and explains it along the way. 45m; VHS, 3/4 U. **Pr:** Marshfilm. **A:** Jr. High. **P:** Education. **U:** Institution. **Hea-Sci:** Circulatory System, Blood, Health Education. **Acq:** Purchase. **Dist:** Marshmedia. $47.50.

Blood Tests: Native American Gamble ????
Cultural connections are investigated using blood typing and DNA matching. 50m; VHS. **A:** Sr. High-Adult. **P:** Education. **U:** Institution. **Gen-Edu:** Native Americans, History--U.S. **Acq:** Purchase, Rent/Lease. **Dist:** Films for the Humanities & Sciences. $149.00.

Blood: The Last Vampire 2009 (R) — ★1/2
Tedious live-action adaptation of a 2001 anime flick that's heavy on the gore. Saya (Jeon) is a 400-year-old samurai, who looks like a 16-year-old schoolgirl (complete with kinky uniform) who is charged with hunting down the vampires and demons who plague Japan. She is ordered by a secret organization to protect the students at an American military base where her cover is blown when she must rescue general's daughter Alice (Miller) from a vampire attack. Then it all comes down to the ultimate battle between Saya and super-vamp Onigen (Koyuki). 91m; Blu-Ray, On Demand, Wide. **C:** Koyuki; Liam Cunningham; Larry Lamb; Ji-hyun Jeon; Allison Miller; Costanza Balduzzi; Yasuaka Kurata; Directed by Chris Nahon; Written by Chris Chow; Yasuaka Kurata; Cinematography by Hang-Seng Poon; Music by Clint Mansell. **A:** Sr. High-Adult. **P:** Entertainment. **U:** Home. **L:** English. **Mov-Ent:** Japan. **Acq:** Purchase. **Dist:** Sony Pictures Home Entertainment Inc.; Amazon.com Inc.; Movies Unlimited.

Blood: The Microscopic Miracle—2nd Edition 1982
Describes the circulation of the blood, its composition, and its function in supporting cell processes. Also explains blood typing and the test for the Rh factor. 22m; VHS, 3/4 U. **Pr:** George E. Wakerlin; Encyclopedia Britannica Educational Corporation. **A:** Sr. High. **P:** Education. **U:** Institution, SURA. **L:** English, Spanish. **Hea-Sci:** Documentary Films, Blood, Circulatory System. **Acq:** Purchase, Rent/Lease, Trade-in. **Dist:** Encyclopedia Britannica.

Blood: The Vital Humor 1990
The nation's blood supply and transfusion policies are examined. 26m; VHS. **Pr:** Films for the Humanities. **A:** Sr. High-Adult. **P:** Education. **U:** Home. **Hea-Sci:** Documentary Films, Blood, Health Education. **Acq:** Purchase. **Dist:** Films for the Humanities & Sciences. $149.00.

Blood Thirst 1965 — ★★
Obscure horror film about a woman who stays young by indulging in ritual killings and strange experiments. 73m/B/W; VHS, DVD. **C:** Robert Winston; Yvonne Nielson; Vic Diaz; Directed by Newton Arnold. **A:** Sr. High-Adult. **P:** Entertainment. **U:** Home. **Mov-Ent:** Horror. **Acq:** Purchase. **Dist:** Sinister Cinema. $16.95.

Blood Tide 1982 (R) — ★
A disgusting, flesh-eating monster disrupts a couple's vacation in the Greek isles. Beautiful scenery, good cast, bad movie. 82m; VHS, DVD. **C:** James Earl Jones; Jose Ferrer; Directed by Richard Jeffries; Written by Nico Mastorakis. **Pr:** 21st Century Film Corporation. **A:** College-Adult. **P:** Entertainment. **U:** Home. **Mov-Ent:** Horror. **Acq:** Purchase. **Dist:** Movies Unlimited. $13.49.

Blood Ties 1987 (Unrated) — ★1/2
An American naval engineer in Sicily gets involved with the Mob in order to save his father's life. 98m; VHS. **C:** Brad Davis; Tony LoBianco; Vincent Spano; Barbara DeRossi; Maria Conchita Alonso; Directed by Giacomo Battiato. **A:** Jr. High-Adult. **P:** Entertainment. **U:** Home. **Mov-Ent:** Family. **Acq:** Purchase. **Dist:** No Longer Available.

Blood Ties 1992 — ★★1/2
Reporter Harry Martin belongs to an unusual family—modern-day vampires (who prefer to be known as Carpathian-Americans). But they have an age-old problem with a band of fanatical vampire hunters. This time around you'll root for the bloodsuckers. 90m; VHS, DVD. **C:** Harley Venton; Patrick Bauchau; Kim Johnston-Ulrich; Michelle Johnson; Jason London; Bo Hopkins; Grace Zabriskie; Salvator Xuereb; Directed by Jim McBride; Written by Richard Shapiro. **Pr:** Esther Shapiro; Richard Shapiro. **A:** Sr. High-Adult. **P:** Entertainment. **U:** Home. **Mov-Ent:** TV Movies, Family. **Acq:** Purchase.

Blood Ties 2013 (R) — ★1/2
Dragged-out, hackneyed crime drama, which Canet remade from 2008's "Les Liens du Sang" in which he co-starred. In 1974, 50-year-old Chris (Owen) is released from prison. His younger brother Frank (Crudup)--a Brooklyn cop--is willing to give him a second chance. Before long the career criminal is flirting with his old life--and the much-younger Natalie (Kunis)--while all Frank's sibling resentments surface. 127m; DVD, Blu-Ray. **C:** Clive Owen; Billy Crudup; Marion Cotillard; Mila Kunis; Zoe Saldana; James Caan; Lili Taylor; Matthias Schoenaerts; Noah Emmerich; Directed by Guillaume Canet; Written by Guillaume Canet; James Gray; Cinematography by Christophe Offenstein. **Pr:** Guillaume Canet; Roadside Attractions. **A:** Sr. High-Adult. **P:** Entertainment. **U:** Home. **L:** English. **Mov-Ent:** Crime Drama, Family. **Acq:** Purchase. **Dist:** Lions Gate Home Entertainment.

Blood Ties: The Complete Season 1 2006 (Unrated)
Lifetime Television 2006-8 fantasy horror drama. Ex-cop turned private eye Vicki Nelson witnesses a murder that leads to her become crime-solving partners with a 480-year old vampire. While locating a client's brother Vicki gets caught up in some voodoo in "Bad Ju Ju," runs into some supernatural occurrences while tracking down a deadbeat dad in "Gifted," and the disappearance of a homeless woman uncovers a dangerous and powerful creature in "Heart of Ice." 12 episodes. 615m; DVD. **C:** Dylan Neal; Kyle Schmid; Christina Cox; Gina Holden. **A:** Sr. High-Adult. **P:** Entertainment. **U:** Home. **Mov-Ent:** Drama, Fantasy, Television Series. **Acq:** Purchase. **Dist:** Eagle Rock Entertainment Inc. $26.99.

Blood Ties: The Complete Season 2 2008 (Unrated)
Lifetime Television 2006-? fantasy horror drama. Vicky Nelson and Henry Fitzroy are challenged by an unending array of occult adversaries. Henry is confronted by Christina, the vampire that first possessed him 480 years ago and turned him into a vampire. 20 episodes. 405m; DVD. **C:** Christina Cox; Dylan Neal; Kyle Schmid; Gina Holden. **A:** Sr. High-Adult. **P:** Entertainment. **U:** Home. **Mov-Ent:** Television Series, Horror, Fantasy. **Acq:** Purchase. **Dist:** Eagle Rock Entertainment Inc. $26.99.

Blood Tracks 1986 (Unrated) — ★1/2
A woman kills her abusive husband, then hides out in the mountains with her kids until they turn into cannibalistic savages. Years later, people show up to shoot a music video. Blood runs in buckets. 82m. **C:** Jeff Harding; Michael Fitzpatrick; Naomi Kaneda; Angelo Infanti; Directed by Mike Jackson. **Pr:** George Zecevic; Smart Egg Pictures. **A:** Sr. High-Adult. **P:** Entertainment. **U:** Home. **Mov-Ent:** Horror. **Acq:** Purchase. **Dist:** No Longer Available.

Blood Trails 2006 (R) — ★1/2
After a one-night stand with unstable bike cop Chris (Price), bike messenger Anne (Palmer) takes off with boyfriend Michael (Frederick) for a weekend of mountain biking. Guess who appears to stalk Anne? Basically a chase on two wheels and not particularly frightening. 87m; DVD. **C:** Rebecca Palmer; Ben Price; Tom Frederick; Directed by Robert Krause; Written by Robert Krause; Florian Puchert; Cinematography by Ralf Noack; Music by Ben Bartlett. **A:** Sr. High-Adult. **P:** Entertainment. **U:** Home. **Mov-Ent:** Forests & Trees, Bicycling. **Acq:** Purchase. **Dist:** Lions Gate Entertainment Inc.

Blood Vows: The Story of a Mafia Wife 1987 — ★★
TV's Laura Ingalls (Gilbert) leaps from the prairie to modern-day mafia in this warped Cinderella story. She meets the man of her dreams, whom she slowly finds is her worst nightmare as she becomes trapped within the confines of her new-found "family." TV soaper is way over the top in terms of melodrama. 100m; VHS, Streaming. **C:** Melissa Gilbert; Joe Penny; Eileen Brennan; Talia Shire; Anthony (Tony) Franciosa; Directed by Paul Wendkos; Music by William Goldstein. **Pr:** Fries Entertainment. **A:** Sr. High-Adult. **P:** Entertainment. **U:** Home. **Mov-Ent:** Crime Drama, TV Movies. **Acq:** Purchase. **Dist:** Amazon.com Inc. $39.95.

Blood Voyage 1977 (R) — **Bomb!**
A crewman aboard a pleasure yacht must find out who is killing off his passengers one by one. 80m; VHS. **C:** Jonathon Lippe; Laurie Rose; Midori; Mara Modair; Directed by Frank Mitchell. **Pr:** Gene Levy. **A:** Sr. High-Adult. **P:** Entertainment. **U:** Home. **Mov-Ent:** Horror, Boating. **Acq:** Purchase. **Dist:** Unknown Distributor.

Blood Warriors 1993 — ★1/2
An ex-Marine finds out a old buddy is leading a private army of mercenaries. When he refuses to join up their friendship turns violent. 93m; VHS, CC. **C:** David Bradley; Frank Zagarino; Directed by Sam Firstenberg; Written by David Bradley. **A:** Sr. High-Adult. **P:** Entertainment. **U:** Home. **Mov-Ent:** Martial Arts. **Acq:** Purchase. **Dist:** Image Entertainment Inc.; Imperial Entertainment Corp. $94.95.

Blood Wedding 1981 (Unrated) — ★★★
A wonderfully passionate dance film from Saura and choreographed by Gades, based on the play by famed author Federico Garcia Lorca. A young bride (Hoyos) runs off with her married lover (Gades) on her wedding day and her jilted husband (Jimenez) comes after them. The film is set-up at a dress rehearsal where the dancers, led by Gades, perform upon a bare stage. If you like flamenco, there are two more: "Carmen" and "El Amor Brujo." Spanish with subtitles. 71m; VHS, DVD. **C:** Antonio Gades; Cristina Hoyos; Marisol; Carmen Villena; Juan Antonio Jimenez; Directed by Carlos Saura; Written by Antonio Gades; Carlos Saura; Cinematography by Teodoro Escamilla; Music by Emilio De Diego. **Pr:** Carlos Saura; Carlos Saura. **A:** Jr. High-Adult. **P:** Entertainment. **U:** Home. **L:** Spanish. **Mov-Ent:** Dance, Marriage, Documentary Films. **Acq:** Purchase. **Dist:** Criterion Collection Inc.; Corinth Films Inc. $24.95.

Blood Work 2002 (R) — ★★1/2
Retired FBI profiler Terry McCaleb (Eastwood) has just had a heart transplant. But, while undergoing checkups, he's brought back to track a serial killer who apparently murdered the woman who became his donor. Clint can still do the loner detective to a T, the question is, should he? The evidence her points to "probably not." It's not that he's not good at it, it's that there's

really nothing more he can do WITH it. The killer is easy to spot from a mile away, and thankfully McCaleb does, which leaves the how and when of catching him (in the gender-nonspecific sense) as the only suspense. Well done, but ultimately forgettable. Based on the novel by Michael Connelly. 111m; VHS, DVD, Blu-Ray. **C:** Clint Eastwood; Anjelica Huston; Jeff Daniels; Wanda De Jesus; Paul Rodriguez; Tina Lifford; Dylan Walsh; Gerry Becker; Alix Koromzay; Mason Lucero; Rick Hoffman; Directed by Clint Eastwood; Written by Brian Helgeland; Cinematography by Tom Stern; Music by Lennie Niehaus. **Pr:** Clint Eastwood; Clint Eastwood; Malpaso Productions; Warner Bros. **A:** Sr. High-Adult. **P:** Entertainment. **U:** Home. **Mov-Ent**: Federal Bureau of Investigation (FBI), Boating, Surgical Transplantation. **Acq:** Purchase. **Dist:** Warner Home Video, Inc.

Bloodbath 1976 (Unrated) — ★★
Drugs, sex and terrorism—Hopper is typecast as an American degenerate who, along with his expatriate friends, is persecuted by local religious cults who need sacrifices. 89m; VHS, DVD. **C:** Dennis Hopper; Carroll Baker; Richard Todd; Faith Brook; Win Wells; Directed by Silvio Narizzano. **A:** Adult. **P:** Entertainment. **U:** Home. **Mov-Ent**: Violence, Drugs, Sex & Sexuality. **Acq:** Purchase. **Dist:** No Longer Available.

Bloodbath 1998 — ★
Detectives Tony Martin and Maggie Donovan are investigating a series of murders whose victims are all starlets. As they dig into the world of underground filmmaking, they find a literal bloodbath involving a group of movie-happy vampires. 90m; VHS. **C:** Susannah Devereux; Kathryn Cleasby; Anthony Martini; Jan Bryant; Charles Currier; Dana Fredsti; Directed by Dan Speaker; Anne Kimberly; Written by Dana Fredsti; Cinematography by Joseph Raymond Garcia. **A:** Sr. High-Adult. **P:** Entertainment. **U:** Home. **Mov-Ent**: Sex & Sexuality. **Acq:** Purchase. **Dist:** Vista Street Entertainment.

Bloodbath at the House of Death 1985 (Unrated) — ★★
Price and his compatriots fight a team of mad scientists in this parody of popular horror films. Fun to see Price spoofing his own genre; die-hard horror camp fans will be satisfied. Best line: "Wanna fork?" 92m; VHS. **C:** Kenny Everett; Pamela Stephenson; Vincent Price; Gareth Hunt; Sheila Steafel; John Fortune; Cleo Rocos; Graham Stark; Directed by Ray Cameron; Written by Ray Cameron; Barry Cryer; Cinematography by Brian West; Dusty Miller; Music by Mark London; Mike Moran. **Pr:** Ray Cameron; EMI Media. **A:** Family. **P:** Entertainment. **U:** Home. **Mov-Ent. Acq:** Purchase. **Dist:** No Longer Available.

Bloodbath in Psycho Town 1989 (R) — ★
A film crew is marked for death by a hooded man when it enters a remote little village. 87m; VHS, DVD. **C:** Ron Arragon; Donna Baltron; Dave Elliott; Directed by Allessandro DeGaetano; Written by Allessandro DeGaetano. **A:** College-Adult. **P:** Entertainment. **U:** Home. **Mov-Ent**: Horror, Filmmaking. **Acq:** Purchase. **Dist:** Movies Unlimited.

Bloodbeat 1985 (Unrated) — ★
A supernatural being terrorizes a family as they gather at their country home to celebrate Christmas. 84m; VHS. **C:** Helen Benton; Terry Brown; Claudia Peyton; Directed by Fabrice A. Zaphiratos. **Pr:** Trans World Entertainment Corp. **A:** Sr. High-Adult. **P:** Entertainment. **U:** Home. **Mov-Ent**: Horror, Christmas. **Acq:** Purchase. **Dist:** No Longer Available.

Bloodborne Compliance 1995
Looks at how to comply with OSHA 1910.1030. Covers various procedures. 25m; VHS. **A:** Adult. **P:** Professional. **U:** Institution. **Bus-Ind**: Job Training, Safety Education, Health Education. **Acq:** Rent/Lease. **Dist:** National Safety Council, California Chapter, Film Library.

Bloodborne Pathogens 1990
Outlines new government standards for determining safety levels in terms of pathogens transmitted by blood. Examples include Hepatitis B, Hepatitis C, Syphilis, Malaria, and HIV. Talk show format includes officials from the Occupational Safety and Health Administration, and notable medical professionals. 25m; VHS. **A:** Adult. **P:** Professional. **U:** Institution. **Bus-Ind**: Business, Safety Education, Diseases. **Acq:** Purchase. **Dist:** Bergwall Productions, Inc. $99.00.

Bloodborne Pathogens and Other Traveling Germs ????
Explains how to avoid transmission of pathogens such as those carried by blood and other body fluids while in a school setting. Also discusses how germs travel from person to person. Appropriate for grades K-6. 10m; VHS; Closed Captioned. **A:** Primary. **P:** Education. **U:** Institution. **Chl-Juv**: Hygiene, Health Education, Blood. **Acq:** Purchase. **Dist:** Marshmedia. $69.95.

Bloodborne Pathogens Compliance Training Program 19??
Provides information designed to help school staffs meet basic OSHA requirements. Comes with manual and trainer's guide. 25m; VHS. **A:** Adult. **P:** Vocational. **U:** Institution. **Bus-Ind**: Job Training, Safety Education, Health Education. **Acq:** Purchase, Rent/Lease. **Dist:** AMS Distributors, Inc.

Bloodborne Pathogens for Non-Healthcare Workers 1995
Explains how HIV and Hepatitis B viruses can be transmitted through blood or body fluids contaminated with blood products. Emphasizes how Knowledge can reduce the risk of exposure. 12m; VHS. **A:** Adult. **P:** Professional. **U:** Institution. **Bus-Ind**: Job Training, Safety Education, Health Education. **Acq:** Purchase, Rent/Lease. **Dist:** National Safety Council, California Chapter, Film Library. $175.00.

Bloodborne Pathogens: Hotel/Motel Service 1995
Designed specifically for the Hotel/Motel/Restaurant environment. Explains the law, who is at risk, engineering controls, safe work practices, personal hygiene, and protective measures. Applies to people trained in first aid. 17m; VHS. **A:** Adult. **P:** Professional. **U:** Institution. **L:** Spanish. **Bus-Ind**: Job Training, Safety Education, Health Education. **Acq:** Purchase, Rent/Lease. **Dist:** National Safety Council, California Chapter, Film Library. $175.00.

Bloodborne Pathogens in Industry: What Employees Must Know 19??
Helps meet the training requirements under OSHA's Bloodborne Pathogens Standard (1910.1030) while concentrating on worker exposure control concerns. Covers such topics as bloodborne diseases, workplace transmission, sanitary issues, reducing risk to exposure, safe work practices, personal protective equipment, housekeeping, and HBV vaccinations. Comes with instructor's guide, employee handbooks, training log, wallet cards, sample biohazard sign and tag, and industrial bloodborne pathogens awareness posters. 18m; VHS. **A:** Adult. **P:** Vocational. **U:** Institution. **Bus-Ind**: Job Training, Safety Education, Industry & Industrialists. **Acq:** Purchase. **Dist:** J.J. Keller and Associates Inc. $149.00.

Bloodborne Pathogens in the Workplace Healthcare Facilities 1995
Focuses on the two greatest threats to employees—HIV and Hepatitis B. Covers modes of transmission; exposure control plan; emergency procedures; and the labeling of all potentially infectious materials. 20m; VHS. **A:** Adult. **P:** Professional. **U:** Institution. **Bus-Ind**: Management, Occupational Training. **Acq:** Purchase, Rent/Lease. **Dist:** National Safety Council, California Chapter, Film Library. $395.00.

Bloodborne Pathogens in the Workplace: Larger Industrial Facilities 1995
Contains information on the two greatest threats to employees: HIV and Hepatitis B. Includes modes of transmission, exposure control plan, emergency procedures, workplace controls, housekeeping procedures, and labeling of all potentially infectious materials. 20m; VHS. **A:** Adult. **P:** Professional. **U:** Institution. **Bus-Ind**: Job Training, Safety Education, Health Education. **Acq:** Purchase, Rent/Lease. **Dist:** National Safety Council, California Chapter, Film Library. $395.00.
Indiv. Titles: 1. Bloodborne Pathogens in the Workplace: Smaller Industrial, Commercial Facilities 2. Bloodborne Pathogens in the Workplace: First Responders 3. Bloodborne Pathogens in the Workplace: Healthcare Facilities.

Bloodborne Pathogens: Manufacturing 1995
Designed specifically for manufacturing facilities. Explains the law, who is at risk, engineering controls, safe work practices, personal hygiene, and protective measures. Applies to anyone who is trained in first aid. 17m; VHS. **A:** Adult. **P:** Professional. **U:** Institution. **Bus-Ind**: Job Training, Safety Education, Health Education. **Acq:** Purchase, Rent/Lease. **Dist:** National Safety Council, California Chapter, Film Library. $175.00.

Bloodborne Pathogens Series 1992
Gives instruction to help hospitals comply with the training requirements of OSHA's Bloodborne Pathogens Act. Each tape explains the obligations of the law, modes of disease transmission, precautions required by the law, biohazard labeling and requirements for exposure reporting. Also available individually for $210.00. 9m; VHS, 3/4 U. **A:** College-Adult. **P:** Instruction. **U:** Institution. **Hea-Sci**: Medical Education. **Acq:** Purchase. **Dist:** Medfilms Inc.; ERI Safety Videos; United Learning Inc. $490.00.
Indiv. Titles: 1. For Healthcare Facilities 2. For First Responders 3. For Industrial Facilities 4. For Light Industrial Facilities.

Bloodborne Pathogens Standard 1992
Training program includes details of how to comply with federal Bloodborne Pathogens Standard. To be used to instruct personnel on how to prevent spread of disease (including HIV and HBV) in the workplace. Comes with compliance manual, trainer's guide and supplementary materials. Also available in Spanish. ?m; VHS, 3/4 U. **A:** Adult. **P:** Instruction. **U:** Institution. **L:** English, Spanish. **How-Ins**: Occupational Training, Safety Education, Blood. **Acq:** Purchase. **Dist:** AMS Distributors, Inc.

Bloodborne Pathogens: What You Need to Know 19??
Helps meet requirements under OSHA's Bloodborne Pathogens Standard (1910.1030) for healthcare industry. Covers such topics as Bloodborne Pathogens requirements, infection control, protective equipment and clothing, infectious waste disposal, exposure determination, methods of compliance, and safe work practices. Comes with instructor's guide, employee handbooks, training log, wallet cards, and sample biohazard sign and tag. 15m; VHS. **A:** Adult. **P:** Vocational. **U:** Institution. **Bus-Ind**: Job Training, Safety Education, Health Education. **Acq:** Purchase. **Dist:** J.J. Keller and Associates Inc. $149.00.

Bloodbrothers 1978 (R) — ★★½
Portrayal of working-class Italian men's lives—if that's possible without the benefit of Italian writers, producers, or director. Still, lots of cussing and general intensity, as Gere's character struggles between staying in the family construction business and doing what he wants to do'work with children. Re-cut for TV and re-titled "A Father's Love." 120m; VHS, DVD. **C:** Richard Gere; Paul Sorvino; Tony LoBianco; Kenneth McMillan; Marilu Henner; Danny Aiello; Lelia Goldoni; Yvonne Wilder; Directed by Robert Mulligan; Cinematography by Robert L. Surtees; Music by Elmer Bernstein. **Pr:** Kings Road Productions. **A:** Adult. **P:** Entertainment. **U:** Home. **Mov-Ent**: Family. **Acq:** Purchase. **Dist:** WarnerArchive.com. $19.98.

Bloodfight 1989 — ★
Exciting kick-boxing and martial arts tournament turns sour when champ offends the sense of honor of the master. Now the champ must battle the master, and only one will remain standing! 96m; VHS, DVD. **C:** Bolo Yeung; Yasuka Kurata; Simon Yam; Ken-ming Lum; Christina Lawson; Directed by Shuji Goto; Written by Sawaguchi Yoshiaki; Cinematography by Murano Nobuaki; Music by Oguchi Yuji. **Pr:** Imperial Entertainment. **A:** College-Adult. **P:** Entertainment. **U:** Home. **Mov-Ent**: Martial Arts. **Acq:** Purchase. **Dist:** Imperial Entertainment Corp.; BFS Video. $19.95.

Bloodfist 1989 (R) — ★★
A kickboxer tears through Manila searching for his brother's killer. A Roger Corman production. 85m; VHS, DVD. **C:** Don "The Dragon" Wilson; Rob Kaman; Billy Blanks; Kris Aguilar; Riley Bowman; Michael Shaner; Joe Mari Avellana; Marilyn Bautista; Directed by Terence H. Winkless; Written by Robert King; Cinematography by Ricardo Jacques Gale; Music by Sasha Matson. **Pr:** Roger Corman; Concorde Pictures. **A:** Sr. High-Adult. **P:** Entertainment. **U:** Home. **Mov-Ent**: Martial Arts. **Acq:** Purchase. **Dist:** MGM Home Entertainment. $14.95.

Bloodfist 2 1990 (R) — ★★½
Six of the world's toughest martial artists find themselves kidnapped and forced to do the bidding of the evil Su. The mysterious recluse stages a series of incredible fights between the experts and his own army of drugged warriors. 85m; VHS, DVD, CC. **C:** Don "The Dragon" Wilson; Maurice Smith; James Warring; Timothy Baker; Richard (Rick) Hill; Rina Reyes; Kris Aguilar; Joe Mari Avellana; Directed by Andy Blumenthal; Written by Catherine Cyran; Cinematography by Bruce Dorfman; Music by Nigel Holton. **Pr:** Roger Corman; Concorde Pictures. **A:** Sr. High-Adult. **P:** Entertainment. **U:** Home. **Mov-Ent**: Martial Arts, Violence. **Acq:** Purchase. **Dist:** MGM Home Entertainment. $14.95.

Bloodfist 3: Forced to Fight 1992 (R) — ★½
Just as long as nobody's forced to watch, real-life world champion kickboxer Wilson thrashes his way through another showdown-at-the-arena plot. Better-than-average fight choreography. 90m; VHS, DVD. **C:** Don "The Dragon" Wilson; Richard Roundtree; Laura Stockman; Richard Paul; Rick Dean; Peter "Sugarfoot" Cunningham; Directed by Oley Sassone; Written by Allison Burnett; Cinematography by Rick Bota; Music by Nigel Holton. **Pr:** New Horizons Pictures. **A:** Sr. High-Adult. **P:** Entertainment. **U:** Home. **Mov-Ent**: Martial Arts. **Acq:** Purchase. **Dist:** New Horizons Picture Corp. $89.98.

Bloodfist 4: Die Trying 1992 (R) — ★½
To rescue his daughter, a fighter must do battle with the FBI, the CIA, and an international arms cartel. 86m; VHS, DVD. **C:** Don "The Dragon" Wilson; Catya (Cat) Sassoon; Amanda Wyss; James Tolkan; Liz Torres; Directed by Paul Ziller. **A:** Sr. High-Adult. **P:** Entertainment. **U:** Home. **Mov-Ent**: Martial Arts. **Acq:** Purchase. **Dist:** New Horizons Picture Corp.

Bloodfist 5: Human Target 1993 (R) — ★½
When undercover FBI agent Jim Roth (Wilson) attempts to unravel an international arms deal he's found out and left for dead. He comes to with no memory only to find himself caught between the arms dealers and the FBI, who think he's turned double-agent. Both sides want Roth dead. 84m; VHS, DVD. **C:** Don "The Dragon" Wilson; Denice Duff; Yuji Okumoto; Don Stark; Danny Lopez; Steve James; Michael Yama; Directed by Jeff Yonis; Written by Jeff Yonis; Cinematography by Michael G. Wojciechowski; Music by David Wurst; Eric Wurst. **Pr:** Roger Corman. **A:** Sr. High-Adult. **P:** Entertainment. **U:** Home. **Mov-Ent**: Martial Arts, Federal Bureau of Investigation (FBI). **Acq:** Purchase. **Dist:** New Horizons Picture Corp.

Bloodfist 6: Ground Zero 1994 (R) — ★½
Nick Corrigan (Wilson) must battle terrorists who have a nuclear missile aimed at New York City. 86m; VHS, DVD. **C:** Don "The Dragon" Wilson; Cat Sasson; Steve Garvey; Directed by Rick Jacobson; Written by Brendan Broderick; Rob Kerchner; Cinematography by Michael Gallagher; Music by John Graham. **A:** Sr. High-Adult. **P:** Entertainment. **U:** Home. **Mov-Ent**: Martial Arts, Terrorism, Nuclear Warfare. **Acq:** Purchase. **Dist:** New Horizons Picture Corp.

Bloodfist 7: Manhunt 1995 (R) — ★★
Martial arts expert Jim Trudell is accused by corrupt cops of murder and is forced on the run while he tries to prove his innocence. 95m; VHS, DVD. **C:** Don "The Dragon" Wilson; Jonathan Penner; Jillian McWhirter; Stephen Davies; Cyril O'Reilly; Eb Lottimer; Steven Williams; Directed by Jonathan Winfrey; Written by Brendan Broderick; Rob Kerchner; Cinematography by Michael Gallagher; Music by Elliot Anders; Mike Elliot. **A:** Sr. High-Adult. **P:** Entertainment. **U:** Home. **Mov-Ent**: Martial Arts. **Acq:** Purchase. **Dist:** New Horizons Picture Corp.

Bloodfist 8: Hard Way Out 1996 (R) — ★
Widowed teacher Rick Cowan (Wilson) turns out to have a lurid past when he and teen son Chris (White) are targeted for death. Dull dad is ex-CIA and someone is afraid their dirty secrets will get out if he's not eliminated. 78m; VHS, DVD. **C:** Don "The Dragon" Wilson; John Patrick White; Warren Burton; Richard Farrell; Directed by Barry Samson; Written by Alex Simon; Cinematography by John Aronson; Music by John Faulkner. **Pr:** Mary Ann Fisher; Roger Corman. **A:** Sr. High-Adult. **P:** Entertainment. **U:** Home. **Mov-Ent**: Martial Arts, Intelligence Service. **Acq:** Purchase. **Dist:** New Horizons Picture Corp.

Bloodhounds 1996 (R) — ★★
Detective Nikki Cruz (Harnos), who's skilled in the martial arts, reluctantly agrees to team up with writer Harrison Coyle (Bernsen), whose specialty is criminal cases, to catch escaped serial killer, Charles Veasey (Baltz). 86m; VHS, CC. **C:** Corbin Bernsen; Christina Harnos; Kirk Baltz; Gina Mastrogiacomo;

James Pickens, Jr.; Marcus Flanagan; Directed by Michael Katleman; Written by Pablo F. Fenjves; Cinematography by Fernando Arguelles. **Pr:** Wilshire Court Productions. **A:** Sr. High-Adult. **P:** Entertainment. **U:** Home. **Mov-Ent:** Mystery & Suspense, TV Movies. **Acq:** Purchase. **Dist:** Paramount Pictures Corp.

Bloodhounds 2 1996 (PG-13) — ★★
True-crime writer Harrison Coyle (Bersen) teams up with PI Nikki Cruz (Peeples) to nab serial killer Matthew Standing (Tracey), who hunts down convicted rapists he thinks haven't been punished enough. Turns out the killer is also a fan of Coyle's and begins contacting him about them writing a book together. 89m; VHS, CC. **C:** Corbin Bernsen; Nia Peeples; Ian Tracey; Amy Yasbeck; Jim Byrnes; Suki Kaiser; Tom Cavanagh; Directed by Stuart Cooper; Written by Pablo F. Fenjves; Cinematography by Curtis Petersen; Music by Charles Bernstein. **Pr:** Wilshire Court Productions. **A:** Sr. High-Adult. **P:** Entertainment. **U:** Home. **Mov-Ent:** Mystery & Suspense, TV Movies. **Acq:** Purchase. **Dist:** Paramount Pictures Corp.

Bloodhounds of Broadway 1952 (Unrated) — ★★½
New York bookie Numbers Foster (Brady) heads out of town to avoid a criminal investigation and winds up in backwoods Georgia where he meets talented Tessie (Gaynor), who convinces Numbers to take her back up north with him. She finds success on Broadway and finally persuades the bookie to turn himself in. Based on a story by Damon Runyon. 90m; DVD. **C:** Mitzi Gaynor; Scott Brady; Mitzie Green; Marguerite Chapman; Michael O'Shea; Wally Vernon; Directed by Harmon Jones; Written by Sy Gomberg; Cinematography by Edward Cronjager; Music by Lionel Newman. **A:** Jr. High-Adult. **P:** Entertainment. **U:** Home. **Mov-Ent. Acq:** Purchase. **Dist:** MGM Home Entertainment.

Bloodhounds of Broadway 1989 (PG) — ★★½
A musical tribute to Damon Runyon, detailing the cliched adventures of an assortment of jazz-age crooks, flappers, chanteuses, and losers. 90m; VHS, DVD, Wide, CC. **C:** Madonna; Rutger Hauer; Randy Quaid; Matt Dillon; Jennifer Grey; Julie Hagerty; Esai Morales; Anita Morris; Josef Sommer; William S. Burroughs; Ethan Phillips; Stephen McHattie; Dinah Manoff; Googy Gress; Tony Azito; Tony Longo; Madeleine Potter; Directed by Howard Brookner; Written by Howard Brookner; Colman DeKay; Cinematography by Elliot Davis; Music by Jonathan Sheffer. **A:** Jr. High-Adult. **P:** Entertainment. **U:** Home. **Mov-Ent. Acq:** Purchase. **Dist:** Sony Pictures Home Entertainment Inc. $19.95.

Bloodknot 1995 (R) — ★★
The Reaves' are devastated when their son Martin is killed in a military accident. So they're an easy target when Kaye (Vernon) shows up, claiming to be Martin's girlfriend. Mom Evelyn (Kidder) and brother Tom (Dempsey) are only too eager to welcome Kaye into the family but it wouldn't be a thriller if devious Kaye didn't have some deadly ulterior motives. 98m; VHS, CC. **C:** Patrick Dempsey; Kate Vernon; Margot Kidder; Craig Sheffer; Directed by Jorge Montesi; Written by Randy Kornfield; Cinematography by Philip Linzey; Music by Ian Thomas. **Pr:** T.A. Baird; Lewis B. Chesler; David M. Perlmutter; Showtime Networks. **A:** Sr. High-Adult. **P:** Entertainment. **U:** Home. **Mov-Ent:** Mystery & Suspense, Family, TV Movies. **Acq:** Purchase. **Dist:** Paramount Pictures Corp.

Bloodlines 2005 (Unrated) — ★★½
Policewoman Justine Hopkin (Pierson) finds her mother's dead body just after her dad James (McNally) is released from prison (he was in on a murder rap). She believes he's innocent and now has to prove it. 137m; DVD. **C:** Kevin McNally; Robert Pugh; Kieran O'Brien; Jan Francis; Emma Pierson; Max Beesley; Directed by Philip Martin; Written by Mike Cullen; Cinematography by Julian Court; Music by Nicholas Hooper. **A:** Sr. High-Adult. **P:** Entertainment. **U:** Home. **Mov-Ent. Acq:** Purchase. **Dist:** Entertainment One US LP.

Bloodlines 2008 (Unrated)
Features the confrontation between two women with ties to the Holocaust. Bettina Goering is the grandniece of Herman Goering, a top military commander of Hitler's regime, who has attempted to put her family's dark legacy behind her while Ruth Rich, a daughter of Holocaust survivors, is a painter who has not resolved the anger over her parents' suffering and brother's death. Includes Ruth's paintings and archival photos. 52m; DVD. **A:** Adult. **P:** Education. **U:** Institution. **Gen-Edu:** Holocaust, Women. **Acq:** Purchase. **Dist:** Women Make Movies. $295.00.

Bloodlines and Bridges: The African Connection 1986
Follows Marian Crawford, an American orphan, who travels to Africa in search of her family's past. 30m; VHS, 3/4 U. **Pr:** WTVS-TV Detroit; PBS. **A:** Jr. High-Adult. **P:** Education. **U:** Institution, CCTV, Home, SURA. **Gen-Edu:** Documentary Films, Black Culture, Africa. **Acq:** Purchase, Rent/Lease, Duplication, Off-Air Record. **Dist:** PBS Home Video. $49.95.

Bloodlink 1986 (R) — ★½
A well-to-do doctor has a recurring nightmare about killing an elderly woman. This prompts him to explore his past, discovering that he was separated at birth from a twin brother. Naturally, only by searching frantically for his long-lost sibling can the good doctor hope to solve the mystery of the recurring nightmare. A somnolent tale indeed. 98m; VHS. **C:** Michael Moriarty; Penelope Milford; Geraldine Fitzgerald; Cameron Mitchell; Sarah Langenfeld; Directed by Alberto De Martino. **Pr:** Albert De Martino. **A:** College-Adult. **P:** Entertainment. **U:** Home. **Mov-Ent:** Horror. **Acq:** Purchase. **Dist:** Anchor Bay Entertainment. $24.95.

Bloodlust 1959 (Unrated) — ★
More teenagers fall prey to yet another mad scientist, who stores their dead bodies in glass tanks. Low-budget ripoff of "The Most Dangerous Game" and other such films. A must for Mike Brady (Robert Reed) fans though. 89m/B/W; VHS, DVD. **C:** Wilton Graff; June Kenney; Robert Reed; Lilyan Chauvin; Directed by Ralph Brooke; Written by Ralph Brooke. **Pr:** Crown International Pictures. **A:** College-Adult. **P:** Entertainment. **U:** Home. **Mov-Ent:** Horror, Technology. **Acq:** Purchase. **Dist:** Sinister Cinema. $16.95.

Bloodlust: Subspecies 3 1993 (R) — ★½
Equally gory followup to "Bloodstone: Subspecies 2." Sadistic vampire Radu is still battling for Michelle's soul, this time against Michelle's sister Becky, aided by his disgusting Mummy and the demonic Subspecies. Castle Vladislas is awash is blood and Becky discovers more than Michelle's fate is at risk. 83m; VHS, DVD, Blu-Ray, CC. **C:** Anders (Tofting) Hove; Kevin Blair Spirtas; Denice Duff; Pamela Gordon; Ion Haiduc; Michael DellaFemina; Directed by Ted Nicolaou; Written by Ted Nicolaou. **Pr:** Vlad Paunescu; Oana Paunescu; Charles Band; Full Moon Entertainment. **A:** Sr. High-Adult. **P:** Entertainment. **U:** Home. **Mov-Ent:** Horror. **Acq:** Purchase. **Dist:** Echo Bridge Home Entertainment; Full Moon Pictures.

Bloodmatch 1991 (R) — ★
A whodunit, martial-arts-style: the "sleuth" kidnaps all the suspects in a corruption case and kickboxes each to death until somebody confesses. Not exactly Agatha Christie, and artsy camera moves fail to exploit the fancy footwork. 85m; VHS, CC. **C:** Thom Mathews; Michel Qissi; Benny "The Jet" Urquidez; Marianne Taylor; Hope Marie Carlton; Dale Jacoby; Thunder Wolf; Vincent Klyn; Peter "Sugarfoot" Cunningham; Hector Pena; Directed by Albert Pyun; Written by K. Mannah; Music by Tony Riparetti. **Pr:** Power Pictures. **A:** College-Adult. **P:** Entertainment. **U:** Home. **L:** English, Spanish. **Mov-Ent:** Martial Arts. **Acq:** Purchase. **Dist:** $19.98.

Bloodmoon 1990 — **Bomb!**
The setting is Australia but the sleazy story's all too familiar: an insane killer employs knives and other sharp objects to prevent sex-crazed students from getting past third base. 104m; VHS, DVD. **C:** Leon Lissek; Christine Amor; Ian Patrick Williams; Helen Thomson; Hazel Howson; Craig Cronin; Anya Molina; Directed by Alec Mills; Written by Richard Brennan; Music by Brian May. **Pr:** Stanley O'Toole. **A:** College-Adult. **P:** Entertainment. **U:** Home. **Mov-Ent:** Horror. **Acq:** Purchase. **Dist:** Lions Gate Television Corp. $14.98.

Bloodmoon 1997 — ★½
A New York serial killer is quite a specialist—he only kills fighters, and he kills with his bare hands. So it's up to Ken O'Hara (Daniels), who specializes in tracking murderers, to find this guy before he kills again. A good display of martial arts skills keep this one interesting. 105m; VHS, DVD. **C:** Gary Daniels; Chuck Jeffreys; Darren Shahlavi; Nina Repeta; Frank Gorshin; Jeffrey Pillars; Joe Hess; Directed by Tony Leung Siu Hung; Written by Keith W. Strandberg; Cinematography by Derek M.K. Wan; Music by Richard Yuen. **Pr:** Ng See Yuen; Keith W. Strandberg; Seasonal Film Productions. **A:** Sr. High-Adult. **P:** Entertainment. **U:** Home. **Mov-Ent. Acq:** Purchase. **Dist:** BMG Entertainment.

Bloodmyth 2009 (Unrated) — ★½
Indie Brit horror with a familiar plot, but there's at least a twist to the killer's motivation. Five corporate types are forced into a team-building exercise designed by survival expert Ray. They and their two trainers have to spend a week in a woodsy campsite in Kent, but the situation goes downhill when a psycho starts picking them off. 96m; DVD. **C:** Natalie Clayton; Shelley Halstead; Ben Shockley; Keith Eyles; James Payton; Ian Attfield; Jane Gull; Henry Dunn; John Rackham; Directed by John Rackham; Written by John Rackham; Cinematography by John Rackham; Music by Maria Long. **A:** Sr. High-Adult. **P:** Entertainment. **U:** Home. **Mov-Ent. Acq:** Purchase. **Dist:** Movies Unlimited.

BloodRayne 2006 (R) — **Bomb!**
There are moments in this painful period vampire "epic" where you honestly have to wonder if director Uwe Boll was aware that the camera was rolling. Whatever the excuse, Boll's latest video game movie proves that even sex, gore, and violence can be boring in the hands of the right director. Rayne (Loken) is a half-vampire, half-human warrior who's out to stop her illegitimate father, Kagin (Kingsley), the king of vampires, from... sigh, bored yet? You will be. Even the cast looks half-asleep. (Madsen and Kingsley take "phoning it in" to a new and scary level.) But nothing beats the barely rehearsed fight scenes. A community theatre production of "Braveheart" would have more convincing stage combat. 95m; DVD. **C:** Kristanna Loken; Michael Madsen; Matthew Davis; Michelle Rodriguez; Ben Kingsley; Will Sanderson; Udo Kier; Meat Loaf Aday; Michael Pare; Billy Zane; Geraldine Chaplin; Directed by Uwe Boll; Written by Guinevere Turner; Cinematography by Mathias Neumann; Music by Henning Lohner. **Pr:** Shawn Williamson; Daniel Clarke; Boll KG Prods; Herold Prods; Pitchback Pictures; Romar Entertainment. **A:** Sr. High-Adult. **P:** Entertainment. **U:** Home. **L:** English. **Mov-Ent:** Horror, Fantasy, USSR. **Acq:** Purchase. **Dist:** Movies Unlimited; Alpha Video.

BloodRayne 2: Deliverance 2007 (R) — **Bomb!**
Probably the worst vampire western ever made, and that's saying something. After the first "BloodRayne" bombed, Boll somehow got financing to produce this direct-to-DVD sequel. Set in the Old West, the "plot" revolves around vampire Billy the Kid (played by Scut Farkus from "A Christmas Story"), and his plans to use the railroad to help his cowboy vamp posse to take over America. (Seriously.) Enter the sexually-ambiguous warrior-woman Rayne (Malthe), a half-human/half-vampire, who fights in the name of justice with her fangs and bare midriff. Unfortunately, vampire John Ford doesn't show up to punish Boll for his crimes against the western. 95m; DVD. **C:** Natassia Malthe; Zack (Zach) Ward; Brendan Fletcher; Michael Pare; Christopher Coppola; Michael Eklund; Directed by Uwe Boll; Written by Christopher Donaldson; Neil Every; Music by Jessica de Rooij. **A:** Sr. High-Adult. **P:** Entertainment. **U:** Home. **Mov-Ent. Acq:** Purchase. **Dist:** Vivendi Visual Entertainment.

Bloodrayne: The Third Reich 2011 (R) — **Bomb!**
Boll uses nudity and some soft-core sex in an attempt to hold the viewers' attention in his latest adaptation of the vampire babe videogame. In 1943, dhampir Rayne (Malthe) teams up with resistance fighters to prevent Commandant Ekart Brand (Pare) from making it to Berlin. She accidentally turned him during some fighting and Brand and evil Nazi Dr. Mangler (Howard) used his infected blood to create a serum that could make Hitler immortal. 79m; DVD, Blu-Ray. **C:** Natassia Malthe; Brendan Fletcher; Michael Pare; Clint Howard; Willam Belli; Annett Culp; Directed by Uwe Boll; Written by Michael Nachoff; Cinematography by Mathias Neumann; Music by Jessica de Rooij. **A:** Sr. High-Adult. **P:** Entertainment. **U:** Home. **Mov-Ent:** World War Two. **Acq:** Purchase. **Dist:** Peace Arch Entertainment Group.

The Bloods of 'Nam 1987
This documentary follows the lives of black soldiers who fought against discrimination in the army and disillusionment when they returned home. 58m; VHS, 3/4 U. **Pr:** PBS. **A:** Jr. High-Adult. **P:** Education. **U:** Institution, SURA. **Gen-Edu:** Documentary Films, Vietnam War. **Acq:** Purchase, Rent/Lease. **Dist:** PBS Home Video. $300.00.

BloodSisters 1995
Handelman's unflinching portrait of San Francisco's lesbian S/M community. 75m; VHS. **C:** Directed by Michelle Handelman. **A:** Adult. **P:** Entertainment. **U:** Home. **Gen-Edu:** Documentary Films, Sex & Sexuality. **Acq:** Purchase. **Dist:** Water Bearer Films Inc.

Bloodspell 1987 (R) — ★
A student with an evil power unleashes it on those who cross his path. 87m; VHS, DVD. **C:** Anthony Jenkins; Aaron Teich; Alexandra Kennedy; John Reno; Directed by Deryn Warren. **Pr:** Forum Home Video. **A:** Sr. High-Adult. **P:** Entertainment. **U:** Home. **Mov-Ent:** Horror, Occult Sciences. **Acq:** Purchase. **Dist:** Management Company Entertainment Group (MCEG), Inc. $79.98.

Bloodsport 1988 (R) — ★½
American soldier Van Damme endeavors to win the deadly Kumite, an outlawed martial arts competition in Hong Kong. Lots of kick-boxing action and the sound of bones cracking. 92m; VHS, DVD, CC. **C:** Jean-Claude Van Damme; Leah Ayres; Roy Chiao; Donald Gibb; Bolo Yeung; Norman Burton; Forest Whitaker; Directed by Newton Arnold; Written by Christopher Cosby. **A:** Adult. **P:** Entertainment. **U:** Home. **Mov-Ent:** Martial Arts. **Acq:** Purchase. **Dist:** Warner Home Video, Inc.; Time-Life Video and Television. $19.98.

Bloodsport 2: The Next Kumite 1995 (R) — ★½
Old-fashioned kickfest has Alex (Bernhardt) stealing antiquities in Thailand. He's left to take the fall by his partner in the theft of an ancient sword belonging to powerful businessman Leung (Morita) and is sent to a prison where sadistic head guard Demon (Han) takes an instant dislike to him. Alex learns about a sacred fighting competition, the Kumite, from wise prison sage Sun (Hong) and naturally, once Alex manages to get into the contest, his opponent is—you guessed it—Demon. 87m; VHS. **C:** Daniel Bernhardt; Ong Soo Han; Noriyuki "Pat" Morita; James Hong; Directed by Alan Mehrez. **A:** Sr. High-Adult. **P:** Entertainment. **U:** Home. **Mov-Ent:** Martial Arts, Asia. **Acq:** Purchase. **Dist:** Lions Gate Entertainment Inc.

Bloodsport 3 1997 — ★½
Alex (Bernhardt) must avenge the death of his mentor (Hong) and regain the Kumite sword. 92m; VHS. **C:** Daniel Bernhardt; John Rhys-Davies; James Hong; Noriyuki "Pat" Morita; Directed by Alan Mehrez; Written by James Williams; Music by Stephen (Steve) Edwards. **A:** Sr. High-Adult. **P:** Entertainment. **U:** Home. **Mov-Ent:** Martial Arts. **Acq:** Purchase. **Dist:** Lions Gate Entertainment Inc.

Bloodsport 4: The Dark Kumite 1998 (R) — ★
Undercover agent infiltrates a prison to find out why prisoners are disappearing and ends up forced to participate in a to-the-death tournament. Enjoyable if a steady dose of kicks to the head is your idea of intricate plotting. 100m; VHS, DVD. **C:** Daniel Bernhardt; Ivan Ivanov; Lisa Stothard; Elvis Restaino; Directed by Elvis Restaino; Written by George Saunders; Music by Alex Wurman. **A:** Sr. High-Adult. **P:** Entertainment. **U:** Home. **Mov-Ent:** Martial Arts. **Acq:** Purchase. **Dist:** Bedford Entertainment Inc.

The Bloodstained Shadow 1978 — ★★
Stefano (Capolicchio) decides to visit his priest brother Paolo (Hill), who lives on the island of Murano near Venice. He meets the mysterious Sandra (Casini) on his journey and then witnesses a midnight murder upon his arrival. More deaths follow as Paolo and Stefano investigate. Italian with subtitles. 109m; DVD. **C:** Lino Capolicchio; Craig Hill; Stefania Casini; Massimo Serato; Juliette Mayniel; Directed by Antonio Bido; Written by Antonio Bido; Marisa Andalo; Domenico Malan; Cinematography by Mario Vulpiani; Music by Stelvio Cipriani. **A:** Sr. High-Adult. **P:** Entertainment. **U:** Home. **L:** Italian. **Mov-Ent. Acq:** Purchase. **Dist:** Anchor Bay Entertainment.

Bloodstalkers 1976 (Unrated) — **Bomb!**
Two vacationers in Florida meet up with a band of slaughtering, swamp-based lunatics. 91m; VHS, DVD. **C:** Kenny (Ken) Miller;

Celea Ann Cole; Jerry Albert; Directed by Robert W. Morgan. **Pr:** Ben Morse. **A:** Sr. High-Adult. **P:** Entertainment. **U:** Home. **Mov-Ent:** Horror. **Acq:** Purchase. **Dist:** Infinity Entertainment Group. $39.95.

Bloodstone 1988 (PG-13) — ★★
A couple honeymooning in the Middle East unexpectedly become involved in a jewel heist when they discover a valuable ruby amongst their luggage. Non-stop action and humor. 90m; VHS, DVD. **C:** Charlie Brill; Christopher Neame; Jack Kehler; Brett Stimely; Anna Nicholas; Directed by Dwight Little; Written by Nico Mastorakis; Curt Allen. **Pr:** Omega Pictures. **A:** Jr. High-Adult. **P:** Entertainment. **U:** Home. **Mov-Ent:** Action-Adventure, Middle East. **Acq:** Purchase. **Dist:** Management Company Entertainment Group (MCEG), Inc. $79.98.

Bloodstone: Subspecies 2 1992 (R) — ★½
A gory sequel to "Subspecies" finds Radu the vampire pursuing the luscious Michelle. Radu gets some help from his ghoulish mother and yucky demonic spawn. Filmed on location in Romania. 107m; VHS, DVD, Blu-Ray, CC. **C:** Anders (Tofting) Hove; Denice Duff; Kevin Blair Spirtas; Michael Denish; Pamela Gordon; Ion Haiduc; Directed by Ted Nicolaou; Written by Ted Nicolaou. **Pr:** Vlad Paunescu; Oana Paunescu; Charles Band; Full Moon Entertainment. **A:** Sr. High-Adult. **P:** Entertainment. **U:** Home. **Mov-Ent:** Horror. **Acq:** Purchase. **Dist:** Echo Bridge Home Entertainment; Full Moon Pictures.

Bloodstorm: Subspecies 4 1998 (R) — ★½
Master vampire Radu Vladislas (Hove) has awakened with an agenda. He wants to reclaim his vast wealth and recapture fledgling vamp, Michelle (Duff). Meanwhile, Radu hangs around with former protege, Ash (Morris), and Michelle is taken in by a creepy doctor (Dinvale) who's after the bloodstone. If you liked the first three, this is just more of the same. 90m; VHS, DVD. **C:** Anders (Tofting) Hove; Denice Duff; Jonathan Morris; Mihai Dinvale; Floriella Grappini; Directed by Ted Nicolaou; Written by Ted Nicolaou; Cinematography by Adolfo Bartoli; Music by Richard Kosinski. **Pr:** Full Moon Entertainment. **A:** Sr. High-Adult. **P:** Entertainment. **U:** Home. **Mov-Ent:** Horror. **Acq:** Purchase. **Dist:** Full Moon Pictures.

Bloodstream 2000 (Unrated) — Bomb!
Convoluted plot first involves a worker who smuggles a mystery vial out of a genetics lab and then gets murdered. Now we switch to Pamela (Mills), who's come to hear her sister sing at open-mic night, only sis has gone missing. And it turns out she's been taken by a serial killer but...oh, who cares. Low-budget crap. ?m; VHS. **C:** Meredith Mills; Eric Bunton; Joe Decker; Joey Day; Directed by Dennis Devine; Steve Jarvis; Written by Dennis Devine; Steve Jarvis; Cinematography by Dennis Devine; Music by Jonathan Price. **A:** Sr. High-Adult. **P:** Entertainment. **U:** Home. **Mov-Ent:** **Acq:** Purchase. **Dist:** Unknown Productions Inc.

The Bloodsuckers 1970 (Unrated) — ★★
British horror tale set on a Greek Island. An Oxford don is seduced into an ancient vampire cult. Director Michael Burrowes replaces Hartford-Davis in the credits due to a dispute over post-production editing. 90m; VHS, DVD. **C:** Patrick Macnee; Peter Cushing; Patrick Mower; Edward Woodward; Alex Davion; Imogen Hassall; Madeline Hinde; Johnny Sekka; Directed by Robert Hartford-Davis; Written by Julian More; Cinematography by Desmond Dickinson. **Pr:** Graham Harris; Chevron. **A:** Adult. **P:** Entertainment. **U:** Home. **Mov-Ent:** Horror. **Acq:** Purchase. **Dist:** Sinister Cinema. $19.98.

Bloodsuckers from Outer Space 1983 (Unrated) — Bomb!
Via an alien invasion, Texas farmers becoming bloodsucking zombies. 80m; VHS, DVD. **C:** Thom Meyer; Laura Ellis; Billie Keller; Kim Braden; Directed by Glenn Coburn. **Pr:** Gary Boyd Latham. **A:** Jr. High-Adult. **P:** Entertainment. **U:** Home. **Mov-Ent:** Horror, Agriculture. **Acq:** Purchase. **Dist:** Media Blasters Inc.; Warner Home Video, Inc. $19.98.

Bloodsucking Freaks 1975 (R) — Bomb!
Virtually plotless Troma gagfest full of torture, cannibalistic dwarfs, and similar debaucheries, all played out on a Soho Grand Guignol stage (horror shows that allegedly contained real torture and death). Features "The Caged Sexoids," if that tells you anything (a cage of naked cannibal women tended by a dwarf). Not to mention the woman who has her brain sucked out through a straw. Filmed in "Ghoulovision" and originally rated X. Intolerable for most. 89m; VHS, DVD. **C:** Seamus O'Brian; Niles McMaster; Viju Krem; Alan Dellay; Dan Fauci; Directed by Joel M. Reed; Written by Joel M. Reed; Cinematography by Gerry Toll; Music by Michael Sahl. **Pr:** Joel Reed. **A:** Sr. High-Adult. **P:** Entertainment. **U:** Home. **Mov-Ent:** Horror, Cult Films. **Acq:** Purchase. **Dist:** Troma Entertainment; Movies Unlimited. $59.98.

Bloodsucking Pharoahs of Pittsburgh 1990 (R) — Bomb!
Pittsburgh is plagued by crazed cannibals who think eternal life is in Pennsylvania. Two detectives on the case are mystified. 89m; VHS, DVD, CC. **C:** Jake Dengel; Joe Sharkey; Suzanne Fletcher; Beverly Penberthy; Shawn Elliott; Pat Logan; Jane Hamilton; Directed by Dean Tschetter; Alan Smithee; Written by Dean Tschetter; Cinematography by Peter Reniers; Music by Michael Melvoin. **Pr:** Paramount Pictures. **A:** Jr. High-Adult. **P:** Entertainment. **U:** Home. **Mov-Ent:** Horror. **Acq:** Purchase. **Dist:** Paramount Pictures Corp.; Facets Multimedia Inc. $79.95.

Bloodworth 2010 (R) — ★★
Southern-fried family drama. After walking out on his family 40 years ago to pursue his music career, E.F. Bloodworth walks back into his Tennessee hometown. His ex-wife Julia is suffering from dementia and his three sons have grown up bitter and

angry. Only Bloodworth's grandson Fleming is willing to give the old man a chance, probably because E.F. is sympathetic to Fleming falling in love with Raven Lee, the daughter of the local prostitute. 105m; DVD. **C:** Kris Kristofferson; Frances Conroy; Dwight Yoakam; Val Kilmer; W. Earl Brown; Reece Thompson; Hilary Duff; Sheila Kelley; Barry Corbin; Hilarie Burton; Directed by Shane Dax Taylor; Written by W. Earl Brown; Cinematography by Tim Orr; Music by Patrick Warren; Randy Scruggs. **A:** Sr. High-Adult. **P:** Entertainment. **U:** Home. **Mov-Ent:** **Acq:** Purchase. **Dist:** Sony Pictures Home Entertainment Inc.

Bloody Avenger 1980 — ★
A trio of detectives search for a murderer in the streets of Philadelphia. 100m; VHS. **C:** Jack Palance; George Eastman; Jenny Tamburi; Directed by Al (Alfonso Brescia) Bradley. **A:** Sr. High-Adult. **P:** Entertainment. **U:** Home. **Mov-Ent:** Mystery & Suspense. **Acq:** Purchase. **Dist:** CinemaNow Inc. $59.95.

Bloody Beach 2000 (Unrated) — ★½
A group of teens from an Internet chat site decide to say goodbye to anonymity and meet at the beach for vacation, and sure enough a banned ex-member begins killing them off. Horror films aren't a staple of Korean cinema, so while this is probably new to Koreans it is an example of an old school American slasher film. 85m; DVD. **C:** Hyun-Jung Kim; Dong-Kun Yang; Seung-chae Lee; Jeong-jin Lee; Hyun-kyoon Lee; Tae-seong Jin; Se-eun Lee; Directed by In Soo Kim; Written by Seung-jae Baek; Jin-soo Noh; Mi-young Park; Hae-won Shim; Kwang-soo Son; Cinematography by Yoon-soo Kim; Music by Jun-Seok Bang; Young-ook Cho. **A:** Sr. High-Adult. **P:** Entertainment. **U:** Home. **L:** English, Korean. **Mov-Ent:** Horror, Mystery & Suspense. **Acq:** Purchase. **Dist:** Pathfinder Pictures. $24.98.

Bloody Birthday 1980 (R) — ★½
Three youngsters, bound together by their eerie birth during an eclipse (you know what that means), kill everyone around them that ever gave them problems. Typical "and the fun continues" ending; standard fare. 92m; VHS, DVD. **C:** Susan Strasberg; Jose Ferrer; Lori Lethin; Melinda Cordell; Joe Penny; Ellen Geer; Julie Brown; Michael Dudikoff; Billy Jacoby; Elizabeth Hoy; Andy Freeman; Directed by Ed(ward) Hunt; Written by Ed(ward) Hunt; Barry Pearson. **A:** Sr. High-Adult. **P:** Entertainment. **U:** Home. **Mov-Ent:** Horror. **Acq:** Purchase. **Dist:** Movies Unlimited. $16.99.

The Bloody Brood 1959 (Unrated) — Bomb!
Really bad flick about a drug-dealing beatnik gang who commit nasty crimes, like feeding messenger boys hamburgers filled with ground glass. Yuck. 80m; VHS, DVD. **C:** Jack Betts; Barbara Lord; Peter Falk; Robert Christie; Directed by Julian Hoffman. **Pr:** Julian Hoffman; Allied Artists International. **A:** Sr. High-Adult. **P:** Entertainment. **U:** Home. **Mov-Ent:** Exploitation, Drugs, Canada. **Acq:** Purchase. **Dist:** Sinister Cinema; Tapeworm Video Distributors Inc. $16.95.

Bloody Island 1999
Historical look at the race riots in East St. Louis, Illinois in 1917. Blacks were migrated to northern cities and hired to replace striking white workers in the town which fueled the riot and features the ensuing trials and repercussions to the black community. 42m; VHS. **A:** Adult. **P:** Education. **U:** Home. **Gen-Edu:** Documentary Films, Black Culture, Civil Rights. **Acq:** Purchase, Rent/Lease. **Dist:** Filmakers Library Inc. $295.

Bloody Korea: The Real Story 1994
Combines battle footage, interviews with combat vets, and insight from four Congressional Medal of Honor recipients to help tell the story of what happened during the Korean War. 60m; VHS. **A:** Jr. High-Adult. **P:** Education. **U:** Home. **Gen-Edu:** Korean War, Documentary Films, Military History. **Acq:** Purchase. **Dist:** Tapeworm Video Distributors Inc. $19.95.

Bloody Mama 1970 (R) — ★★½
Corman's violent, trashy story of the infamous Barker Gang of the 30s, led by the bloodthirsty and sex-crazed Ma Barker (Winters, can't you just picture it?) and backed by her four perverted sons. De Niro is the space cadet sibling, Walden the homosexual ex-con, Stroud the sadistic mama lover, and Kimbrough the lady killer. They're joined by Walden's prison lover, Dern, who also has a thing for Ma Barker. Winters is a riot in this perverse stew of crime, violence, and, of course, sentimental blood bonding (the family that slays together, stays together). First of the Corman-produced (and sometimes directed) mama movies, followed by "Big Bad Mama" and "Crazy Mama." 90m; VHS, DVD. **C:** Shelley Winters; Robert De Niro; Don Stroud; Pat Hingle; Bruce Dern; Diane Varsi; Robert Walden; Clinton Kimbrough; Scatman Crothers; Pamela Dunlap; Michael Fox; Stacy Harris; Directed by Roger Corman; Written by Robert Thom; Cinematography by John A. Alonzo; Music by Don Randi. **Pr:** American International Pictures. **A:** College-Adult. **P:** Entertainment. **U:** Home. **Mov-Ent:** **Acq:** Purchase. **Dist:** MGM Home Entertainment. $69.95.

Bloody Moon 1983 (Unrated) — Bomb!
Tourists are being brutally attacked and murdered during a small Spanish village's Festival of the Moon. 84m; VHS, DVD. **C:** Olivia Pascal; Christopher Brugger; Ann-Beate Engelke; Antonia Garcia; Nadja Gerganoff; Corinna Gillwald; Jasmin Losensky; Maria Rubio; Alexander Waechter; Directed by Jess (Jesus) Franco; Written by Jess (Jesus) Franco; Rayo Casablanca; Cinematography by Juan Soler. **Pr:** Wolf C Hartwig. **A:** Sr. High-Adult. **P:** Entertainment. **U:** Home. **Mov-Ent:** Horror. **Acq:** Purchase. **Dist:** Unknown Distributor.

Bloody Murder 1999 (R) — Bomb!
Stupid teen campers in peril from maniac movie. This time the creepoid wears a hockey mask (sound familiar?) and has a chainsaw in place of his left arm. Ick. 90m; VHS, DVD, CC. **C:** Michael Stone; Jessica Morris; Peter Guillemette; Patrick

Cavanaugh; Christelle Ford; Tracy Pacheco; Justin Martin; Directed by Ralph Portillo; Written by John R. Stevenson; Cinematography by Keith Holland; Music by Steven Stern. **A:** Sr. High-Adult. **P:** Entertainment. **U:** Home. **Mov-Ent:** Camps & Camping. **Acq:** Purchase. **Dist:** Lions Gate Television Corp.

Bloody Murder 2 2003 (R) — Bomb!
The sequel is no improvement over the first stinker, which was your basic teen slasher flick. Trevor Moorehorse returns after five years to slaughter a new batch of camp counselors at Camp Placid Pines. 85m; VHS, DVD. **C:** Katy Woodruff; Kelly Gunning; Amanda Magarian; Lane Anderson; Benjamin Schneider; Directed by Robert Spera; Cinematography by David Trulli; Music by Steven Stern. **A:** Sr. High-Adult. **P:** Entertainment. **U:** Home. **Mov-Ent:** Camps & Camping. **Acq:** Purchase. **Dist:** Lions Gate Television Corp.

Bloody New Year 1987 (R) — ★
Corpses stalk the living as a group of teens happen upon an impromptu New Year's Eve party on a deserted island. Auld acquaintance shouldn't be forgot, just this flick. 90m; VHS, DVD. **C:** Suzy Aitchison; Nikki Brooks; Colin Haeywood; Mark Powley; Catherine Roman; Julian Ronnie; Directed by Norman J. Warren; Written by Frazer Pearce; Cinematography by John Shann; Music by Nick Magnus. **Pr:** Academy. **A:** Sr. High-Adult. **P:** Entertainment. **U:** Home. **Mov-Ent:** Horror, Death. **Acq:** Purchase. **Dist:** Unknown Distributor.

The Bloody Pit of Horror 1965 (Unrated) — ★½
While wife Jayne Mansfield was in Italy filming "Primitive Love," bodybuilder Hargitay starred in this sado-horror epic. He owns a castle that is visited by a group of models for a special shoot. While in the dungeon, Hargitay becomes possessed by the castle's former owner, a sadist, and begins torturing the models. Supposedly based on the writings of the Marquis de Sade. 87m/ B/W; VHS, DVD, Wide. **C:** Mickey Hargitay; Louise Barrett; Walter Brandi; Moa Thai; Ralph Zucker; Albert Gordon; Directed by Max (Massimo Pupillo) Hunter; Written by Romano Migliorini; Roberto Natale; Cinematography by Luciano Trasatti; Music by Gino Peguri. **A:** College-Adult. **P:** Entertainment. **U:** Home. **Mov-Ent:** Horror. **Acq:** Purchase. **Dist:** Sinister Cinema. $19.98.

Bloody Proof 1999 (Unrated) — ★★★
A serial killer is stalking well-to-do women in Mexico. Detective Ibarra (Bauer) is assigned to the case. Rookie tabloid reporter Estela (Arizmendi) finds an important clue. The resolution of the stereotypical premise runs true to form, but the characters are treated seriously and the film is stylishly made with a few moments of abrupt, shocking violence. 99m; VHS, DVD. **C:** Steven Bauer; Yareli Arizmendi; Olivia Hussey; Directed by Gabriel Beristain; Written by M. Francesconi; Tim Hoy; Cinematography by Andres Leon Becker; Music by Eduardo Gamboa. **A:** Sr. High-Adult. **P:** Entertainment. **U:** Home. **Mov-Ent:** Mexico, Journalism. **Acq:** Purchase. **Dist:** Vanguard International Cinema, Inc.

Bloody Schemes 198?
The African slave trade is chronicled in this film. From the voyage of John Hawkins to the establishment of towns and forts along Africa's coasts, to full-scale trading, the film documents the vital nature of imposed labor on European and American economies. 18m; 3/4 U, Special order formats. **Pr:** Hobel Leiterman Productions. **A:** Jr. High-Adult. **P:** Education. **U:** Institution. **Gen-Edu:** Documentary Films, Slavery. **Acq:** Purchase. **Dist:** The Cinema Guild.

Bloody Shenandoah 19??
Combines battle reenactments, archival photographs, and interviews with Civil War scholars to closely examine the battle staged by Ulysses S. Grant and Robert E. Lee. 50m; VHS. **C:** Narrated by Burgess Meredith. **A:** Jr. High-Sr. High. **P:** Education. **U:** Institution. **Gen-Edu:** Civil War, History--U.S. **Acq:** Purchase. **Dist:** Cambridge Educational. $29.95.

Bloody Sunday 2001 (R) — ★★★
Docudrama covers the January 30, 1972 civil rights march through Derry, Northern Ireland to protest the policy of British internment without trial. Although the majority of the marchers are Catholic, they are led by the area's Protestant MP Ivan Cooper (Nesbitt), who believes the situation can be handled peacefully. Maj. Gen. Robert Ford (Piggott-Smith) reiterates that the British Army has banned all such marches and that participants are subject to arrest. As the march splinters into factions, the Army fires on the crowd—27 civilians are wounded and 14 died. The re-creation of the event by director Greengrass is stunning at the very least. "Sunday Bloody Sunday" was eulogized in a song by U2. 110m; DVD. **C:** James Nesbitt; Tim Pigott-Smith; Nicholas Farrell; Gerard McSorley; Kathy Kiera Clarke; Allan Gildea; Gerard Crossan; Mary Moulds; Carmel McCallion; Declan Duddy; Simon Mann; Directed by Paul Greengrass; Written by Paul Greengrass; Cinematography by Ivan Strasburg; Music by Dominic Muldowney. **Pr:** Mark Redhead; Granada International Productions Ltd; Hell's Kitchen; Irish Film Board; Portman Film; Paramount Classics. **A:** Sr. High-Adult. **P:** Entertainment. **U:** Home. **Mov-Ent:** Ireland, Civil Rights. **Awds:** Berlin Intl. Film Fest. '02: Film. **Acq:** Purchase. **Dist:** WarnerArchive.com.

Bloody Trail 1972 (Unrated) — ★
A Union soldier who chooses the recently pummeled South as the venue for postwar R-and-R is, for some reason, pursued by Confederates. And his good ol' boy pursuers don't have a sudden change of heart when he teams up with a former slave. Lots of violence and nudity; little plot and entertainment. 91m; VHS. **C:** Paul Harper; Rance Howard; John Mitchum; Directed by Richard Robinson. **Pr:** Richard Robinson. **A:** Adult. **P:** Entertainment. **U:** Home. **Mov-Ent:** Western, Civil War. **Acq:** Purchase. **Dist:** No Longer Available.

The Bloody Vampire 1962 — ★½
Atmospheric and chilling Mexican vampire film. Sequel to "Invasion of the Vampires." ?m; VHS. **C:** Carlos Agosti; Erna Martha Bauman; Directed by Miguel Morayta. **A:** Sr. High-Adult. **P:** Entertainment. **U:** Home. **Mov-Ent:** Horror. **Acq:** Purchase. **Dist:** Sinister Cinema. $16.95.

Bloody Wednesday 1987 (Unrated) — ★★½
It's sanity check-out time when a hotel caretaker is driven mad by tormentors...or is he driving himself mad? What is it about vacant hotels that make men lose their minds? If you can remove "The Shining" from yours, this flick's worthwhile. 89m; VHS, DVD. **C:** Raymond Elmendorf; Pamela Baker; Navarre Perry; Directed by Mark Gilhuis; Written by Philip Yordan; Music by Albert Sendrey. **Pr:** Visto International. **A:** College-Adult. **P:** Entertainment. **U:** Home. **Mov-Ent:** Horror, Hotels & Hotel Staff Training. **Acq:** Purchase. **Dist:** Unknown Distributor.

Bloom 2003 (R) — ★★
Rookie director Walsh's drab take of James Joyce's revered 1922 "Ulysses" lays out the events of Leopold Bloom's (Rea) daylong journey on June 16th, 1904 in Dublin as he deals with his wife Molly's (Ball) affair and serves as young poet Stephen's (O'Conor) mentor. 108m; VHS, DVD. **C:** Stephen Rea; Angeline Ball; Hugh O'Conor; Neili Conroy; Eoin McCarthy; Britta Smith; Paul Ronan; Alan Devlin; Alvaro Lucchesi; Maria Hayden; Mark Huberman; Kenneth McDonnell; Andrew McGibney; Dan Colley; Des Braiden; Donncha Crowley; Howard Jones; Russell Smith; Jimmy Keogh; Donal O'Kelly; Phelim Drew; Ronan Wilmot; Sarah Jane Drummey; Dearbhla Molloy; Jenny Maher; Ruaidhri Finnegan; Eoin MacDonagh; Peter Gaynor; Rachael Pilkington; Jamie Baker; Maria Lennon; Steve Simmonds; Colman Hanley; Conor Delaney; Charlie Bonner; Alexander Downes; Eamon Rohan; Luke Hayden; Julie Hale; Caoileann Murphy; Ciaran O'Brien; Dermot Moore; Maurice Shanahan; Seamus Walsh; Adam Fox Clarke; Directed by Sean Walsh; Written by James Joyce; Cinematography by Ciaran Tanham; Music by David Kahne. **A:** Sr. High-Adult. **P:** Entertainment. **U:** Home. **Mov-Ent:** Marriage, Drama, Action-Adventure. **Acq:** Purchase. **Dist:** Bedford Entertainment Inc. $24.99.

Bloomington 2010 (Unrated) — ★★
A former child actress, 18-year-old Jackie decides to go to college in Bloomington, Indiana to escape her pushy California family. She's finding it tough to fit in since everyone just wants to talk about her old successful TV show. Jackie soon succumbs to the charms of manipulative psychology prof Catherine Stark but school gossip spreads. With a chance to resume her acting career, what will Jackie choose to do? 83m; DVD. **C:** Sarah Stouffer; Allison McAtee; Katherine Ann McGregor; Ray Zupp; J. Blakemore; Erika Heidewald; Chelasea Rogers; Directed by Fernanda Cardoso; Written by Fernanda Cardoso; Cinematography by George Feucht; Music by Jermaine Stegall. **A:** Sr. High-Adult. **P:** Entertainment. **U:** Home. **Mov-Ent:** Drama. **Acq:** Purchase. **Dist:** Wolfe Video.

The Blooms of Banjeli: Technology and Gender in African Ironmaking 19??
Documents the interrelationship of traditional ironsmelting in Togo and the rituals surrounding it. Guide available. 29m; VHS. **TV Std:** NTSC, PAL. **Pr:** Carlyn Saltman; Candice Gaucher; Eugenia Herbert. **A:** Sr. High-Adult. **P:** Education. **U:** Institution. **Gen-Edu:** Metal Work, Africa, Anthropology. **Acq:** Purchase, Rent/Lease. **Dist:** Documentary Educational Resources. $195.00.

Bloomsday 1992
Documentary on Bloomsday, a celebration by James Joyce enthusiasts who annually recreate the odyssey of Leopold Bloom. 52m; VHS, DVD. **A:** Sr. High-Adult. **P:** Education. **U:** Institution. **Gen-Edu:** Documentary Films, Performing Arts. **Acq:** Purchase, Rent/Lease. **Dist:** The Cinema Guild. $295.00.

Bloopers #1 19??
A compilation of bloopers from classic Warner Bros. films of 1936 and 1937, followed by outtakes from CBS television programs and "Laugh-In." 58m/B/W; VHS. **Pr:** CBS; Warner Bros. **A:** Family. **P:** Entertainment. **U:** Institution, Home, SURA. **Mov-Ent:** Outtakes & Bloopers. **Acq:** Purchase. **Dist:** $37.00.

Bloqueo: Looking at the U.S. Embargo against Cuba 2005
Documentary about the U.S. blockade of Cuba, and how it has altered the island's government. 45m; VHS, DVD. **A:** Sr. High-Adult. **P:** Education. **U:** Institution. **Gen-Edu:** Documentary Films, Politics & Government. **Acq:** Purchase, Rent/Lease. **Dist:** The Cinema Guild. $295.00.

Blossom in Virgo 1978
A program that chronicles the home delivery of a baby in a peaceful country setting, amidst family and friends. 13m; VHS, 3/4 U. **Pr:** Michael Day. **A:** College-Adult. **P:** Education. **U:** Institution, SURA. **Gen-Edu:** Documentary Films, Childbirth. **Acq:** Purchase. **Dist:** Phoenix Learning Group.

Blossom: The Complete 1st & 2nd Seasons 1991 (Unrated)
NBC family sitcom television series (1991-1995). Fifteen-year-old Blossom Russo (Bialik) is the only girl in a house full of men after her mother abandons the family to pursue a singing career in Paris. Her session musician father Nick, recovering addict oldest brother Anthony, and jock brother Joey do their best to put together the pieces and watch out for each other. Six LeMeure is Blossom's best friend, a permanent fixture at the Russo house and gifted in the art of mischief. Blossom feels left out in "I Ain't Got No Buddy" when Six starts hanging around a new girl at school and the kids try to hide the divorce papers from their dad. 37 episodes. 840m; DVD. **A:** Family. **P:** Entertainment. **U:** Home. **Mov-Ent:** Comedy-Drama, Family, Television Series. **Acq:** Purchase. **Dist:** Shout! Factory. $49.99.

Blossoms in the Dust 1941 — ★★
The true story of Edna Gladney is told as she starts the Texas Children's Home and Aid Society of Fort Worth. Major league Garson tear-jerker. 100m/B/W; VHS, DVD, CC. **C:** Greer Garson; Walter Pidgeon; Felix Bressart; Marsha Hunt; Fay Holden; Samuel S. Hinds; Kathleen Howard; Directed by Mervyn LeRoy. **Pr:** MGM. **A:** Jr. High-Adult. **P:** Entertainment. **U:** Home. **Mov-Ent:** Melodrama, Adoption, Biography. **Acq:** Purchase. **Dist:** Warner Home Video, Inc. $19.98.

Blossoms of Fire 2000 (Unrated)
Gosling and Osborne attempt to set the record straight in their documentary about the Zapotec people of Juchitan, Mexico, and their supposedly matriarchal society after a series of sensationalistic articles in the popular press focus unwanted attention on the community. Narrated by Gosling in English and in Spanish and Zapotec by Sylvia Mullally Aguirre. 74m; DVD. **A:** College-Adult. **P:** Entertainment. **U:** Home. **L:** English, Spanish. **Gen-Edu:** Documentary Films, Mexico, Women. **Dist:** New Yorker Video.

Blossoms on Broadway 1937 (Unrated) — ★★
Musical-comedy pre-World War II goofiness. A young conwoman (Ross) tries to bilk a mine owner out of his fortune, only he turns out to be as short on funds as everyone else. She's got a love interest, of course, but he turns out to be a detective. 88m/B/W; VHS. **C:** Edward Arnold; Shirley Ross; John Trent; William Frawley; Directed by Richard Wallace; Written by Theodore Reeves. **A:** Jr. High-Adult. **P:** Entertainment. **U:** Home. **Mov-Ent:** Musical. **Acq:** Purchase. **Dist:** Nostalgia Family Video/Hollywood's Attic. $19.99.

The Blot 1921 — ★★
A story about a poorly paid professor and his family, whose lifestyle contrasts with that of an affluent neighbor, a butcher. 55m/B/W; Silent; VHS, DVD. **C:** Louis Calhern; Claire Windsor; Directed by Lois Weber. **Pr:** Lois Weber; Lois Weber. **A:** Sr. High-Adult. **P:** Entertainment. **U:** Home. **Mov-Ent:** Silent Films, Family. **Acq:** Purchase. **Dist:** Grapevine Video; Glenn Video Vistas Ltd. $19.95.

Blow 2001 (R) — ★★½
Memorable, visually stunning, true story of cocaine entrepreneur George Jung features, at its best, stellar performances (especially from Reubens, Cruz, and Depp), and at its worst, a "Goodfellas" meets "Traffic" familiarity. Epic follows Jung (Depp) from his humble New England beginnings through his California surfer-bum days, to his rise and fall as America's biggest cocaine pipeline of the '70s and '80s without judging him or his lifestyle, although it does tend to sympathize with his family issues with mom, dad, and his own child. 124m; VHS, DVD, Wide. **C:** Johnny Depp; Penelope Cruz; Jordi Molla; Franka Potente; Rachel Griffiths; Ray Liotta; Ethan Suplee; Paul (Pee-wee Herman) Reubens; Max Perlich; Clifford Curtis; Miguel (Michael) Sandoval; Kevin Gage; Jesse James; Dan Ferro; Emma Roberts; Bobcat Goldthwait; Jaime King; Directed by Ted (Edward) Demme; Written by David McKenna; Nick Cassavetes; Cinematography by Ellen Kuras; Music by Graeme Revell. **Pr:** Ted Demme; Joel Stiller; Denis Leary; Apostle Pictures; Spanky Pictures; New Line Cinema. **A:** Sr. High-Adult. **P:** Entertainment. **U:** Home. **Mov-Ent:** Drug Abuse, Drug Trafficking/Dealing, Biography. **Acq:** Purchase. **Dist:** New Line Home Video.

Blow Dry 2000 (R) — ★★
Comedic possibilities and family healing ensue when the National British Hairdressing Championships come to a sleepy English town. An odd assortment of Brits and Yanks populate this familiar tale, and even dependable Rickman can't save the film, whose destination is obvious from even the newspaper ads—take "The Full Monty," replace strippers with hairdressers and, voila: "Blow Dry." Written by Simon Beaufoy, author of (you guessed it) "The Full Monty." Director Breathnach fared better with his previous film, the Irish comedy "I Went Down." 91m; VHS, DVD, Wide. **C:** Alan Rickman; Natasha Richardson; Rachel Griffiths; Rachael Leigh Cook; Josh Hartnett; Bill Nighy; Warren Clarke; Rosemary Harris; Hugh Bonneville; Peter McDonald; Heidi Klum; Michael McElhatton; Directed by Paddy Breathnach; Written by Simon Beaufoy; Cinematography by Cian de Buitlear; Music by Patrick Doyle. **Pr:** Ruth Jackson; William Horberg; David Rubin; Intermedia Films; Mirage Enterprises; West Eleven Films; Miramax Film Corp. **A:** Sr. High-Adult. **P:** Entertainment. **U:** Home. **Mov-Ent:** Romance. **Acq:** Purchase. **Dist:** Buena Vista Home Entertainment.

Blow Drying and Curling Iron Techniques 1990
Offers instruction on specific aspects of barbering and cosmetology. 8m; VHS. **A:** Adult. **P:** Vocational. **U:** Institution. **Bus-Ind:** Cosmetology. **Acq:** Purchase. **Dist:** RMI Media. $39.95.

Blow Monkeys: Digging Your Video 1986
The British band's video collection, including "Digging Your Scene," "Wicked Ways," "Forbidden Fruit," and "Don't Be Scared of Me." 18m; VHS. **Pr:** RCA Video Productions. **A:** Family. **P:** Entertainment. **U:** Home. **Mov-Ent:** Music Video, Music--Performance, Music--Pop/Rock. **Acq:** Purchase. **Dist:** Music Video Distributors; Sony Pictures Home Entertainment Inc. $14.95.

Blow Monkeys: Video LP 1990
Recorded live at Camden Palace in London, this 1985 excursion includes "The Man from Russia," "He's Shedding His Skin," "Forbidden Fruit," "Get it On" and more. 58m; VHS. **A:** Jr. High-College. **P:** Entertainment. **U:** Home. **Mov-Ent:** Music--Performance. **Acq:** Purchase. **Dist:** Music Video Distributors.

Blow Out 1981 (R) — ★★★
When a prominent governor and presidential candidate is killed in a car crash, a sound effects engineer becomes involved in political intrigue as he tries to expose a conspiracy with the evidence he has gathered. An intricate mystery and homage to Antonioni's "Blow-Up." 108m; VHS, DVD, Blu-Ray, Wide. **C:** John Travolta; Nancy Allen; John Lithgow; Dennis Franz; Directed by Brian De Palma; Written by Brian De Palma; Cinematography by Vilmos Zsigmond; Music by Pino Donaggio. **Pr:** Filmways Pictures. **A:** Sr. High-Adult. **P:** Entertainment. **U:** Home. **Mov-Ent:** Mystery & Suspense, Prostitution. **Acq:** Purchase. **Dist:** Warner Home Video, Inc., On Moratorium.

Blow-Up 1966 (Unrated) — ★★★½
A young London photographer takes some pictures of a couple in the park and finds out he may have recorded evidence of a murder. Though marred by badly dated 1960s modishness, this is Antonioni's most accessible film, a sophisticated treatise on perception and the film-consumer-as-voyeur, brilliantly assembled and wrought. 111m; VHS, DVD, Wide. **C:** David Hemmings; Vanessa Redgrave; Sarah Miles; Jane Birkin; Veruschka; Peter Bowles; John Castle; Gillian Hills; Julian Chagrin; Harry Hutchinson; The Yardbirds; Directed by Michelangelo Antonioni; Written by Michelangelo Antonioni; Tonino Guerra; Cinematography by Carlo Di Palma; Music by Herbie Hancock. **Pr:** Carlo Ponti. **A:** Jr. High-Adult. **P:** Entertainment. **U:** Home. **Mov-Ent:** Mystery & Suspense, Cult Films, Classic Films. **Awds:** Cannes '67: Film; Natl. Soc. Film Critics '66: Director (Antonioni), Film. **Acq:** Purchase. **Dist:** Facets Multimedia Inc.; MGM Home Entertainment. $19.98.

Blow Up or Blow Down? 198?
A demonstration of how and why a boiler can overheat as a result of low water. 12m; VHS, 3/4 U. **Pr:** National Safety Council. **A:** College-Adult. **P:** Education. **U:** Institution. **Gen-Edu:** Documentary Films, Fires. **Acq:** Rent/Lease. **Dist:** National Safety Council, California Chapter, Film Library.

Blowback 1999 (R) — ★★
Police officer Don Morell (Van Peebles) witnesses the execution of serial killer Claude Whitman (Remar)?or does he? Former jury members are being murdered and Morell finds cryptic bible messages at the scenes—a Whitman hallmark. So has the killer come back from the grave or has someone conspired to keep Whitman alive for their own purposes? 93m; VHS, DVD. **C:** Mario Van Peebles; James Remar; Stephen Caffrey; David Groh; Directed by Mark L. Lester; Written by Jeffrey Goldenberg; Bob Held; Randall Frakes; Cinematography by Jacques Haitkin; Music by Sean Callery. **A:** Sr. High-Adult. **P:** Entertainment. **U:** Home. **Mov-Ent.** **Acq:** Purchase. **Dist:** Movies Unlimited.

Blowin' Smoke 1999 (R) — ★★
Goofball stoner Freak (Zahn) lives his life (in his parents' basement) as the ultimate slacker. His best bud (besides the pot) is the equally unambitious Dave (Hamilton), who does at least have a job. Dave also has an ex-girlfriend who wants to see him again, a sweet high schooler who has a crush on him, and a family who wishes he would do something with his life. Well, at least Dave has Freak to turn to in times of stress. Based on the novel by co-writer Galvin. 88m; VHS, DVD. **C:** Steve Zahn; Josh Hamilton; Heather McComb; Arabella Field; David Kinney; Directed by Paul Todisco; Written by Paul Todisco; Michael M.B. Galvin; Peter Speakman; Cinematography by Douglas W. Shannon; Music by Pete Snell. **A:** Sr. High-Adult. **P:** Entertainment. **U:** Home. **Mov-Ent:** Drug Abuse. **Acq:** Purchase. **Dist:** Movies Unlimited; Alpha Video.

Blowing the Whistle on Pat Robertson 1988
The former "700 Club" producer reveals some inside dirt about the televangelist who ran for president in 1988. 60m; VHS, 3/4 U. **C:** Gerard Straub. **Pr:** American Humanist Association. **A:** Sr. High-Adult. **P:** Education. **U:** Institution, CCTV, CATV. **Gen-Edu:** Documentary Films, Religion, Ethics & Morals. **Acq:** Purchase. **Dist:** American Humanist Association. $49.95.

Blowing Wild 1953 — ★½
Filmed in Mexico, this Quinn-Stanwyck-Cooper love triangle, set in the early thirties, speaks of lust and vengeance, rashness and greed. Stanwyck, married to oil tycoon Quinn, lusts after one-time lover wildcatter Cooper. 92m/B/W; DVD, Blu-Ray. **C:** Gary Cooper; Barbara Stanwyck; Anthony Quinn; Ruth Roman; Ward Bond; Directed by Hugo Fregonese; Written by Philip Yordan. **A:** Jr. High-Adult. **P:** Entertainment. **U:** Home. **Mov-Ent:** Action-Adventure, Romance, Oil Industry. **Acq:** Purchase. **Dist:** Olive Films; Lions Gate Entertainment Inc. $19.98.

The Blown-Around Room/God's Rules For Me 1988
Two religious stories for children are featured on the same videocassette. 25m; VHS, 3/4 U, Special order formats. **TV Std:** NTSC, PAL. **Pr:** Daughters of St. Paul. **A:** Preschool-Primary. **P:** Religious. **U:** Institution, CCTV, CATV, BCTV, Home. **L:** English, Spanish. **Chl-Juv:** Documentary Films. **Acq:** Purchase. **Dist:** Pauline Books and Media; Ignatius Press. $12.95.

Blown Away 1990 (R) — ★
A mafia wife goes up against her husband in order to retrieve her kidnapped child. 92m; VHS. **C:** Loni Anderson; John Heard; James Naughton; Directed by Michael Miller. **Pr:** Academy. **A:** Sr. High-Adult. **P:** Entertainment. **U:** Home. **Mov-Ent.** **Acq:** Purchase. **Dist:** Movies Unlimited. $49.99.

Blown Away 1993 (R) — ★½
Haim and Feldman are brothers working at a ski resort where Haim falls for rich teenager Eggert. She's a young femme fatale who manages to get Haim all hot and bothered but she's actually using the unsuspecting dupe in a murder plot. Also available in an unrated version at 93 minutes. 91m; VHS, DVD, CC. **C:** Nicole Eggert; Corey Haim; Corey Feldman; Jean

LeClerc; Kathleen Robertson; Gary Farmer; Directed by Brenton Spencer; Written by Robert Cooper; Music by Paul Zaza. **Pr:** Peter R. Simpson. **A:** Sr. High-Adult. **P:** Entertainment. **U:** Home. **Mov-Ent:** Mystery & Suspense, Sex & Sexuality. **Acq:** Purchase. **Dist:** Lions Gate Television Corp. $89.98.

Blown Away 1994 (R) — ★★
Boston Irish bomb-squad cop Jimmy Dove (Bridges) is after former compatriot Ryan Gaerity (Jones), an Irish radical who's taken his bombing expertise onto Jimmy's new turf. Meanwhile, Jimmy wants to keep his unsavory past from unsuspecting wife Amis. Real life dad Lloyd plays Jeff's uncle. While Jones seems adequately obsessed with making things go boom and Bridges significantly concerned that they don't, thriller moves on predictable path toward explosive climax. Special effects create the suspense, as everyday objects become lethal in Gaerity's knowledgeable hands. The final explosion was more than even the special effects coordinator desired—windows were unintentionally blown out in nearby buildings. 121m; VHS, DVD, Wide, CC. **C:** Jeff Bridges; Tommy Lee Jones; Suzy Amis; Lloyd Bridges; Forest Whitaker; Directed by Stephen Hopkins; Written by Joe Batteer; John Rice; Cinematography by Gregory McClatchy; Music by Alan Silvestri. **Pr:** John Watson; Pen Densham; Richard B. Lewis; Lloyd H. Segan; Trilogy Entertainment Group; MGM Home Entertainment. **A:** Sr. High-Adult. **P:** Entertainment. **U:** Home. **Mov-Ent:** Action-Adventure, Terrorism, Ireland. **Acq:** Purchase. **Dist:** MGM Home Entertainment. $19.98.

Blowout Preventer Controls 1975
This program explains how accumulators work to prevent well blowouts. 28m; VHS, 3/4 U. **Pr:** University of Texas Austin. **A:** College-Adult. **P:** Instruction. **U:** Institution, CCTV. **Bus-Ind:** Oil Industry. **Acq:** Purchase.

Blowout Prevention and Well Control 1984
This series demonstrates to drilling well site operations personnel a variety of training situations. Available using metric or non-metric units. A workbook is included. 15m; VHS, 3/4 U. **TV Std:** NTSC, PAL, SECAM. **Pr:** Gulf Publishing Co; Canadian Association of Oilwell Drillers. **A:** College-Adult. **P:** Professional. **U:** Institution, SURA. **Bus-Ind:** How-To, Oil Industry. **Acq:** Purchase. **Dist:** Gulf Publishing Co. $4550.00.
Indiv. Titles: 1. Introduction 2. Causes of Kicks and Blowouts 3. Equipment 4. Kicks While Drilling 5. Kicks While Tripping 6. Kicks While Out of the Hole 7. Fluid Displacement and Trip Records 8. Proper Training and Hole Fill Procedure 9. Drillers Method of Well Control 10. Low Choke Method.

Blowpipes and Bulldozers 1989
Contains the story of a Swiss man who has lived with the Penan, a tribe of rainforest nomads in Borneo, and adapted his lifestyle to theirs. His goal is to make the plight of the tribe known to the outside world before it is too late. Received recognition for: Best Film on Environmental Impact, Medikinale International, Parma; Best Anthropological Film, Festival dei Popoli, Italy; Prize for Ecology & Development, Okomedia, Germany; Best Screenplay, International Ecological Film Festival, Kranj, Yugoslavia. 60m; VHS, Special order formats. **A:** Sr. High-Adult. **P:** Education. **U:** Institution. **Gen-Edu:** Ecology & Environment, Anthropology, Sociology. **Acq:** Purchase, Rent/Lease. **Dist:** Bullfrog Films, Inc. $250.00.

Blowpipes and Bulldozers 1989
This program tells the story of the Penan, a tribe of nomads from Borneo who are losing their homes because too many trees are being cut down. 60m; VHS, 3/4 U. **Pr:** Gala Films. **A:** Sr. High-Adult. **P:** Education. **U:** Institution, Home, SURA. **Hea-Sci:** Ecology & Environment, Anthropology. **Acq:** Purchase, Rent/Lease. **Dist:** Bullfrog Films, Inc. $350.00.

BLS: Complete and Concise Renewal 1996
Features the risk factors associated with a heart attack (smoking, cholesterol control, and diet). 30m; VHS. **A:** Adult. **P:** Education. **U:** Home, Institution. **Hea-Sci:** Health Education, Medical Education, Heart. **Acq:** Purchase, Rent/Lease. **Dist:** AJN Video Library/Lippincott Williams & Wilkins. $250.00.

Blubberella 2011 (R) — **Bomb!**
Boll's intentionally comic spoof is an all-around turkey--and not one served on rye. Large and in charge, half-vampire, half-human Blubberella loves eating, perfecting her cotton candy recipe, and killing Nazis, and not necessarily in that order. She hooks up with some resistance fighters and goes after her nemesis, a commandant who's also a day-walking bloodsucker. 87m; DVD. **C:** Lindsay Hollister; Michael Pare; Clint Howard; Brendan Fletcher; William H. Bellis; Annett Culp; Directed by Uwe Boll; Written by Uwe Boll; Michael Christopher; Cinematography by Mathias Neumann; Music by Jessica de Rooij. **A:** Sr. High-Adult. **P:** Entertainment. **U:** Home. **Mov-Ent:** Food Industry. **Acq:** Purchase. **Dist:** Phase 4/kaBOOM Entertainment.

Blue 1968 (Unrated) — ★
A dull western about an American boy (Stamp) raised by Mexicans who doesn't trust another living soul until he finds himself face to face with his former gang, led by his adoptive father (Montalban). 113m; VHS, DVD, CC. **C:** Terence Stamp; Joanna Pettet; Karl Malden; Ricardo Montalban; Joe De Santis; Sally Kirkland; Directed by Silvio Narizzano; Written by Ronald M. Cohen; Music by Manos Hadjidakis. **A:** Jr. High-Adult. **P:** Entertainment. **U:** Home. **Mov-Ent:** Western. **Acq:** Purchase. **Dist:** Paramount Pictures Corp.

Blue 1993 (R) — ★★
Meditation/memoir of director Jarman's deteriorating AIDS condition consists of narration and a soundtrack set against an unvaried blue screen. Jarman ponders the associations with the color blue (sky, ocean, blindness, heaven, eternity) and his own physical problems, alternately expressed with dreamy vagueness or incendiary contempt. Limited in appeal, depending highly on boredom tolerance and ability to suspend visual expectations. 76m; VHS, DVD. **C:** Narrated by John Quentin; Nigel Terry; Tilda Swinton; Derek Jarman; Directed by Derek Jarman; Written by Derek Jarman; Music by Simon Fisher Turner. **Pr:** James Mackay; Takashi Asai; Channel 4. **A:** College-Adult. **P:** Entertainment. **U:** Home. **Mov-Ent:** Philosophy & Ideology, AIDS. **Acq:** Purchase. **Dist:** Zeitgeist Films Ltd. $24.95.

Blue: A Tlingit Odyssey 1991
Features four brothers who set out on a sea journey in search of Blue encountering marvelous creatures along the way. 60m; VHS. **A:** Family. **P:** Entertainment. **U:** Institution. **Gen-Edu:** Fiction. **Acq:** Purchase, Rent/Lease. **Dist:** Cornell University. $24.95.

The Blue and the Gray 1982 — ★★
Epic miniseries about love and hate inflamed by the Civil War. Keach plays a Pinkerton's secret service agent in this loosely based historical romance. Available in uncut and 295-minute versions. 381m; VHS, DVD. **C:** Gregory Peck; Lloyd Bridges; Colleen Dewhurst; Stacy Keach; John Hammond; Sterling Hayden; Warren Oates; Directed by Andrew V. McLaglen; Music by Bruce Broughton. **Pr:** Hugh Benson; Harry Thomason. **A:** Jr. High-Adult. **P:** Entertainment. **U:** Home. **Mov-Ent:** Action-Adventure, Romance, Civil War. **Acq:** Purchase. **Dist:** Sony Pictures Home Entertainment Inc.; Facets Multimedia Inc. $34.95.

Blue and White 1991
Documentary tracing the hard times of five Soviet Jewish Refuseniks and their families when they emigrate from the U.S.S.R. to Israel. The problems encountered in the "Promised Land" make the journey bittersweet, and fraught with uncertainty. 60m; VHS. **C:** Directed by Lauryn Axelrod. **A:** Family. **P:** Education. **U:** Institution, Home. **Gen-Edu:** Judaism, USSR. **Acq:** Purchase, Rent/Lease. **Dist:** The Cinema Guild. $350.00.

The Blue Angel 1930 (Unrated) — ★★★★
Tale of a man stripped of his dignity. A film classic filled with sensuality and decay, which made Dietrich a European star and led to her discovery in Hollywood. When a repressed professor (Jannings) goes to a nightclub hoping to catch some of his students in the wrong, he's taken by Lola, the sultry singer portrayed by Dietrich. After spending the night with her, losing his job, and then marrying her, he goes on tour with the troupe, peddling indiscreet photos of his wife. Versions were shot in both German and English, with the German version sporting English subtitles. 90m/B/W; VHS, DVD, Blu-Ray, 8 mm, 3/4 U, Special order formats. **C:** Marlene Dietrich; Emil Jannings; Kurt Gerron; Rosa Valetti; Hans Albers; Directed by Josef von Sternberg; Written by Robert Liebmann; Carl Zuckmayer; Karl Vollmoller; Cinematography by Gunther Rittau; Music by Frederick "Friedrich" Hollander. **Pr:** Paramount Pictures; Korda. **A:** Sr. High-Adult. **P:** Entertainment. **U:** Home. **L:** English, German. **Mov-Ent:** Nightclubs, Germany, Sex & Sexuality. **Acq:** Purchase. **Dist:** Synergy Entertainment, Inc.; Facets Multimedia Inc.; VCX Ltd. $24.95.
Songs: Falling in Love Again; They Call Me Wicked Lola.

The Blue Angel 1988
Stage production of Roland Petit's ballet about a dancer at the famous Blue Angel cabaret. 78m; VHS. **C:** Roland Petit; Dominique Khalfouni. **Pr:** Kultur Video. **A:** Sr. High-Adult. **P:** Entertainment. **U:** Home. **Fin-Art:** Dance--Ballet. **Acq:** Purchase. **Dist:** Music Video Distributors; Kultur International Films Ltd., Inc.; Corinth Films Inc. $29.95.

The Blue Angels: Around the World at the Speed of Sound 1994
Fly with the U.S. Navy's crack flight team on their European tour, enjoy the thrill of going Mach I in an F-14 Hornet, and learn the history of the Blue Angels through archival footage and interviews with pilots and crew. 100m; VHS. **C:** Hosted by Dennis Quaid. **A:** Jr. High-Adult. **P:** Entertainment. **U:** Home. **Gen-Edu:** Aeronautics, Armed Forces--U.S. **Acq:** Purchase. **Dist:** A&E Television Networks L.L.C.; New Video Group. $29.95.

The Blue Apron 1985
Construction paper animation is used to tell the story of industrial pollution that turns into an evil monster. 7m; VHS, 3/4 U. **Pr:** Kratky Films. **A:** Jr. High-Adult. **P:** Education. **U:** Institution, SURA. **Gen-Edu:** Film--Avant-Garde. **Acq:** Purchase. **Dist:** Phoenix Learning Group. $120.00.

The Blue Bird 1940 (G) — ★★★
A weird, dark fantasy about two children who search for the blue bird of happiness in various fantasy lands, but find it eventually at home. Overlooked and impressively fatalistic. 98m; VHS, DVD, CC. **C:** Shirley Temple; Gale Sondergaard; John Russell; Eddie Collins; Nigel Bruce; Jessie Ralph; Spring Byington; Sybil Jason; Directed by Walter Lang; Cinematography by Arthur C. Miller. **Pr:** 20th Century-Fox. **A:** Family. **P:** Entertainment. **U:** Home. **Mov-Ent:** Fantasy, Birds. **Acq:** Purchase. **Dist:** Fox Home Entertainment. $14.98.

Blue Blazes Rawden 1918 — ★★
Hart plays a lumberjack who gains control of a local saloon after shooting its villainous proprietor. 65m/B/W; Silent; VHS, DVD. **C:** William S. Hart; Robert McKim; Maud(e) (Ford) George; Jack Hoxie; Directed by William S. Hart. **A:** Family. **P:** Entertainment. **U:** Home. **Mov-Ent. Acq:** Purchase. **Dist:** Alpha Video; Sinister Cinema. $18.95.

Blue Blood 1973 (Unrated) — ★
A demonic butler inflicts nightmares upon a family to gain possession of its mansion. 90m; VHS. **C:** Oliver Reed; Derek Jacobi; Fiona Lewis; Directed by Andrew Sinclair. **Pr:** Andrew Sinclair; Andrew Sinclair. **A:** Sr. High-Adult. **P:** Entertainment. **U:** Home. **Mov-Ent:** Horror. **Acq:** Purchase. **Dist:** Unknown Distributor.

Blue Blood 2007 (Unrated) — ★½
Predictable thriller with Scheider channeling Columbo. Trophy husband Davis (Sage) resides in the Hamptons while his wealthy lawyer wife Janice (Beck) works in the city. Davis is fooling around with real estate agent Hadley (Misner) and the two decide to bump off the missus, although Hadley is the one who must do the actual work. Only their plan is botched, which brings in suspicious PI Linus (Scheider). 74m; DVD. **C:** Bill Sage; Roy Scheider; Ronald Guttman; Susan Misner; Noelle Beck; Brian McQuillan; Directed by Benjamin Cummings; Orson Cummings; Written by Benjamin Cummings; Orson Cummings; Cinematography by Bryan Pryzpek; Music by Michael Tremante. **A:** Sr. High-Adult. **P:** Entertainment. **U:** Home. **Mov-Ent. Acq:** Purchase. **Dist:** Entertainment One US LP.

Blue Bloods: The First Season 2010
CBS 2010- family drama. "Pilot": Frank Reagan is New York's police commissioner, a job once held by his retired father Henry. Eldest son Danny is a detective, daughter Erin is a D.A., and youngest son Jamie forgoes his law degree to become a rookie beat cop. "Dedication": Frank is wounded in a shooting as Danny bends the rules to figure out who did it. "To Tell the Truth": Danny is warned not to testify against a gang leader accused of murder and his wife Linda is kidnapped to make sure he understands. 22 episodes. 945m; DVD. **C:** Tom Selleck; Donnie Wahlberg; Bridget Moynahan; Will Estes; Len Cariou; Amy Carlson; Jennifer Esposito. **A:** Jr. High-Adult. **P:** Entertainment. **U:** Home. **Mov-Ent:** Television Series, Family, Drama. **Acq:** Purchase. **Dist:** Paramount Pictures Corp. $39.98.

Blue Bloods: The Second Season 2011
CBS 2010- family drama. "Friendly Fire": Danny shoots a cop and must face an Internal Affairs Investigation. "Women with Guns": A female TV journalist, who's a close friend of Frank's, is attacked but she refuses to say what story she's working on. "Mother's Day": Frank learns the city may be the target of a biological weapon but he and Mayor Poole disagree on whether to inform the public. 22 episodes. 926m; DVD. **C:** Tom Selleck; Donnie Wahlberg; Bridget Moynahan; Will Estes; Len Cariou; Amy Carlson; Jennifer Esposito. **A:** Jr. High-Adult. **P:** Entertainment. **U:** Home. **Mov-Ent:** Television Series, Drama, Family. **Acq:** Purchase. **Dist:** Paramount Pictures Corp. $55.98.

The Blue Butterfly 2004 (PG) — ★★
Based on a true story. Pete Carlton (Donato) is 10 and dying. His one wish is to capture the rare blue morpho butterfly. World-weary entomologist Alan Osborne (Hurt) is persuaded by Pete's mother, Teresa (Bussieres), to let them accompany his expedition into the rain forest of Costa Rica. Beautiful scenery but an overly-sappy saga. 97m; DVD. **C:** William Hurt; Marc Donato; Pascale Bussieres; Steve Adams; Directed by Lea Pool; Written by Pete McCormack; Cinematography by Michel Arcand; Music by Stephen Endelman. **A:** Jr. High-Adult. **P:** Entertainment. **U:** Home. **Mov-Ent:** Nature, Diseases. **Acq:** Purchase. **Dist:** Monterey Home Video.

Blue Canadian Rockies 1952 — ★½
Autry's employer sends him to Canada to discourage his daughter from marrying a fortune hunter. The daughter has turned the place into a dude ranch and wild game preserve. When Autry arrives, he encounters some mysterious killings. 58m/B/W; VHS, DVD. **C:** Gene Autry; Pat Buttram; Ross Ford; Tom London; Directed by George Archainbaud. **Pr:** BLA. **A:** Family. **P:** Entertainment. **U:** Home. **Mov-Ent:** Western. **Acq:** Purchase. **Dist:** $39.95.

Blue Car 2003 (R) — ★★★½
Impressive directorial debut by Moncrieff tells the story of troubled teen Meg (Bruckner) and her sad, beaten-down English teacher Mr. Auster (Strathairn). Meg's life has been turned upside down with the divorce of her parents. Her mother is distant and overworked, and her sister (Arnold, in an excellent performance) is self-destructive. When she finds solace in poetry, Auster recognizes and encourages her talent, which leads to an awkwardly closer relationship, skulkingly engineered by the teacher. Excellent script and direction, as well as stellar performances by Bruckner and Strathairn, allow the film to explore the situation without exploiting or judging. The characters are well-rounded and real, as is the dialogue, which makes the unfolding events that much more disturbing. 96m; VHS, DVD. **C:** Agnes Bruckner; David Strathairn; Margaret Colin; Regan Arnold; Frances Fisher; A.J. Buckley; Sarah Beuhler; Directed by Karen Moncrieff; Written by Karen Moncrieff; Cinematography by Rob Sweeney; Music by Stuart Spencer-Nash. **Pr:** Peter J. Oppenheimer; Amy Sommers; David Waters; Miramax Film Corp. **A:** Sr. High-Adult. **P:** Entertainment. **U:** Home. **Mov-Ent:** Adolescence, Divorce. **Acq:** Purchase. **Dist:** Buena Vista Home Entertainment.

Blue Chips 1994 (PG-13) — ★★½
Nolte does Bobby Knight in this saga of Western U basketball coach Pete Bell, suffering through his first losing season. What follows is a tug of war between rich alumni who want to win at any cost and his ethics as he recruits for a new season. Larger than life hoopster O'Neal's film debut. McDonnell and Woodard are merely afterthoughts, but look for cameos from many real life b-ballers, including Dick Vitale and Larry Bird. Average script is bolstered by exciting game footage, shot during real games for authenticity. 108m; VHS, DVD, Wide, CC. **C:** Nick Nolte; Shaquille O'Neal; Mary McDonnell; Ed O'Neill; J.T. Walsh; Alfre Woodard; Cameo(s) Larry Bird; Bobby Knight; Rick Pitino; Directed by William Friedkin; Written by Ron Shelton; Music by Nile Rodgers; Jeff Beck; Jed Leiber. **Pr:** Michele Rappaport; Ron Shelton; Wolfgang Glattes; Ron Shelton; Paramount Pictures. **A:** Jr. High-Adult. **P:** Entertainment. **U:** Home. **Mov-Ent:**

Basketball, Sports--Fiction: Drama, Ethics & Morals. **Acq:** Purchase. **Dist:** Paramount Pictures Corp.

Blue City 1986 (R) — ★¹/₂
A young man returns to his Florida hometown to find his father murdered, and subsequently vows to solve and avenge the matter. Based on a Ross MacDonald thriller. 83m; VHS, DVD, CC. **C:** Judd Nelson; Ally Sheedy; Paul Winfield; Anita Morris; David Caruso; Julie Carmen; Scott Wilson; Directed by Michelle Manning; Written by Walter Hill; Lukas Heller; Music by Ry Cooder. **Pr:** Paramount Pictures. **A:** Sr. High-Adult. **P:** Entertainment. **U:** Home. **Mov-Ent:** Mystery & Suspense. **Acq:** Purchase. **Dist:** Legend Films. $14.95.

Blue Collar 1978 (R) — ★★★
Funnyman Pryor (in one of his best film roles) offers most of the laughs in this very serious drama of how three Detroit auto assembly workers (Pryor, Kotto, and Keitel), feeling the strain of family life and inflation, hatch a plan to rob their corrupt union office only to stumble into a bigger crime that later costs them dearly. Schrader makes his directorial debut in this searing study of the working class and the robbing of the human spirit, which is made memorable by the strong performances of its three leads. Filmed entirely in Detroit and Kalamazoo, Michigan. 114m; VHS, DVD. **C:** Richard Pryor; Harvey Keitel; Yaphet Kotto; Ed Begley, Jr.; Lane Smith; Cliff DeYoung; Directed by Paul Schrader; Written by Paul Schrader; Leonard Schrader; Cinematography by Bobby Byrne; Music by Jack Nitzsche. **Pr:** Mark Huffam. **A:** Sr. High-Adult. **P:** Entertainment. **U:** Home. **Mov-Ent:** Labor & Unions, Black Culture, Family. **Acq:** Purchase. **Dist:** Facets Multimedia Inc. $14.98.

Blue Collar and Buddha 1987
A group of Laotian refugees who built a Buddhist temple on a small farmstead on the outskirts of a blue-collar town are the focus for this documentary. 58m; VHS, 3/4 U. **Pr:** Kati Johnston. **A:** Jr. High-Adult. **P:** Education. **U:** Institution, SURA. **Gen-Edu:** Buddhism, Human Relations, Immigration. **Acq:** Rent/Lease. **Dist:** Filmakers Library Inc.; Video Out Distribution. $295.00.

Blue Collar Comedy Tour: One for the Road 2006
Comedians Jeff Foxworthy, Larry the Cable Guy, Ron White, and Bill Engvall appear onstage at the Warner Theater in Washington, D.C., for their final performance together. 108m; DVD. **A:** Sr. High-Adult. **P:** Entertainment. **U:** Home. **Mov-Ent:** Comedy--Performance. **Acq:** Purchase. **Dist:** Paramount Pictures Corp.

Blue Collar Comedy Tour Rides Again 2004
Presents the comedy stylings of Jeff Foxworthy, Larry the Cable Guy, Bill Engvall and Ron White on stage in Denver, Colorado. 106m; DVD; Closed Captioned. **A:** Adult. **P:** Entertainment. **U:** Home. **Mov-Ent:** Comedy--Performance. **Acq:** Purchase. **Dist:** Paramount Pictures Corp. $19.99.

Blue Collar Comedy Tour, The Movie 2007 (PG-13)
Mix of behind-the-scenes documentary and live performance footage of Jeff Foxworthy and his fellow comedians on tour performing. 106m; DVD. **A:** Sr. High-Adult. **P:** Entertainment. **U:** Home. **Mov-Ent:** Comedy--Performance, Television, Documentary Films. **Acq:** Purchase. **Dist:** Comedy Central; Warner Home Video, Inc. $12.98.

Blue-Collar Dogs 2011 (Unrated)
While dogs have worked closely with humans for thousands of years, today's working dogs are taking on many new and challenging tasks, including helping to diagnose diseases based on smell, finding victims of earthquakes and other natural disasters, sniffing out drug stashes, and apprehending criminals. Episodes include —Canine MD,? —Border Hounds,? and —New York Police.? 135m; DVD. **A:** Family. **P:** Education. **U:** Institution, Home. **Mov-Ent:** Documentary Films, Pets. **Acq:** Purchase. **Dist:** National Geographic Society. $19.95.

Blue Collar Women 1986
A mini-documentary about a New Orleans program placing women in high-paying blue collar jobs traditionally reserved for men, predominantly construction work. 6m; VHS, SVS, 3/4 U, EJ, Special order formats. **Pr:** New Orleans Video Access Center. **A:** Jr. High-Adult. **P:** Education. **U:** Institution, CCTV, CATV, SURA. **Gen-Edu:** Documentary Films, Occupations, Women. **Acq:** Purchase, Rent/Lease. **Dist:** New Orleans Video Access Center.

Blue Country 1977 (PG) — ★★¹/₂
A joyful romantic comedy about a pair of free souls who leave their stagnant lives behind to seek out a more idyllic existence. Subtitled in English. 104m; VHS. **C:** Brigitte Fossey; Jacques Serres; Ginette Garcin; Armand Meffre; Ginette Mathieu; Roger Crouzet; Directed by Jean-Charles Tacchella; Written by Jean-Charles Tacchella; Cinematography by Edmond Sechan; Music by Gerard Anfosso. **Pr:** Alain Poire. **A:** Sr. High-Adult. **P:** Entertainment. **U:** Home. **L:** French. **Mov-Ent:** Comedy--Romantic. **Acq:** Purchase. **Dist:** Sony Pictures Home Entertainment Inc. $59.95.

Blue Crush 2002 (PG-13) — ★★★
Director John Stockwell brings back the beach/surfing genre with a story about board riding women who would kick Gidget's narrow behind. Surfer girl Anne Marie (Bosworth) moves to Hawaii, determined to win the traditionally all-male Rip Masters competition. Aided by fellow surfers Eden (Rodriguez) and Lena (Lake), she tries to mentally recover from a near-fatal accident in time for the meet. Unfortunately, the distraction of new boyfriend Matt (Davis) may cause her dreams to wipe out. Both the ripped bodies and the surfing action seem a little enhanced by science, but both are very visually stimulating. 104m; VHS, DVD, Blu-Ray. **C:** Kate (Catherine) Bosworth; Michelle Rodriguez; Matthew Davis; Sanoe Lake; Mika Boorem; Faizon Love; Chris Taloa; Kala Alexander; Directed by John Stockwell;

Written by John Stockwell; Elizabeth Weiss; Cinematography by David Hennings; Music by Paul Haslinger. **Pr:** Karen Kehela; Brian Grazer; Imagine Entertainment; Universal Pictures. **A:** Jr. High-Adult. **P:** Entertainment. **U:** Home. **Mov-Ent:** Romance, Hotels & Hotel Staff Training. **Acq:** Purchase. **Dist:** Movies Unlimited; Alpha Video; Universal Studios Home Video.

Blue Crush 2 2011 (PG-13) — ★
Underwhelming in-name-only sequel offers revealing swimwear and some other attractive scenery but a yawn of a plot. Bratty rich girl Dana leaves Malibu to follow her recently deceased mother's surfing diary along the same South African beaches. She makes friends with fellow surfer Pushy, gets a hot boyfriend in Tim, and has an unexplained rivalry with surf pro Tara. There's also an inexplicable poaching subplot that goes nowhere. 113m; DVD, Blu-Ray. **C:** Sasha Jackson; Sharni Vinson; Elizabeth Mathis; Ben Milliken; Gideon Emery; Chris Fisher; Directed by Mike Elliott; Written by Randall McCormick; Cinematography by Trevor Michael Brown; Music by J. Peter Robinson. **A:** Jr. High-Adult. **P:** Entertainment. **U:** Home. **Mov-Ent:** Africa. **Acq:** Purchase. **Dist:** Universal Studios Home Video.

The Blue Dahlia 1946 — ★★★¹/₂
Classic film noir finds Navy vet Johnny Morrison (Ladd) returning home to discover his wife Helen (Dowling) has been keeping the home fires burning with Eddie Harwood (Da Silva), owner of the Blue Dahlia nightclub. After a nasty fight, Johnny takes off and is picked up by sultry blonde Joyce (Lake). The next day Johnny discovers he's wanted by the cops for the murder of his wife and decides to hide out until he can find the real killer, with Joyce's help. Very stylish and fast-paced with excellent performances; Chandler's first original screenplay. 100m/B/W; DVD. **C:** Alan Ladd; Veronica Lake; William Bendix; Howard da Silva; Doris Dowling; Tom Powers; Hugh Beaumont; Howard Freeman; Don Costello; Directed by George Marshall; Written by Raymond Chandler; Cinematography by Lionel Lindon; Music by Victor Young. **Pr:** John Houseman; Paramount Pictures. **A:** Jr. High-Adult. **P:** Entertainment. **U:** Home. **Mov-Ent:** Romance. **Acq:** Purchase. **Dist:** Universal Studios Home Video. $14.98.

The Blue Dashiki: Jeffrey and His City Neighbors 196?
The adventures of a young black boy who wants to earn money to buy the dashiki he has seen in a local African import shop. 14m; VHS, 3/4 U; Open Captioned. **Pr:** Encyclopedia Britannica Educational Corporation; Roach Van Allen. **A:** Primary. **P:** Entertainment. **U:** Institution, SURA. **Chl-Juv:** Children. **Acq:** Purchase, Rent/Lease, Trade-in. **Dist:** Encyclopedia Britannica.

Blue De Ville 1986 (PG) — ★★
Two young women buy a '59 Cadillac and journey from St. Louis to New Mexico, having adventures on the way. The rambling, free-spirited movie was a pilot for a prospective series that never set sail—but when "Thelma & Louise" hit big this superficially similar item was hauled out on video. 96m; VHS, CC. **C:** Jennifer Runyon; Kimberly Pistone; Mark Thomas Miller; Alan Autry; Robert Prescott; Directed by Jim Johnston. **Pr:** Vidmark Entertainment. **A:** Jr. High-Adult. **P:** Entertainment. **U:** Home. **Mov-Ent:** Women. **Acq:** Purchase. **Dist:** CinemaNow Inc. $89.98.

Blue Demon 1963 — ★
Blue Demon, the masked wrestler, goes up against a werewolf in his first movie. In Spanish without subtitles. ?m/B/W; VHS. **A:** Sr. High-Adult. **P:** Entertainment. **U:** Home. **L:** Spanish. **Mov-Ent:** Horror. **Acq:** Purchase. **Dist:** Something Weird Video. $20.

Blue Desert 1991 (R) — ★★★
Cox is strong in her performance as Lisa Roberts, a comic book artist who leaves New York City for small town Arizona life after surviving a traumatic rape. Once there, she's befriended by Sheffer and Sweeney, a local cop. Battersby does a good job of keeping the suspense level high (in his directorial debut) as Cox finds that there's danger in small towns, too. Fine performances keep this slightly above average. 98m; VHS, DVD. **C:** D.B. Sweeney; Courteney Cox; Craig Sheffer; Philip Baker Hall; Sandy Ward; Directed by Bradley Battersby; Written by Bradley Battersby; Arthur Collis; Music by Jerry Goldsmith. **Pr:** Joel Soisson; Michael S. Murphy. **A:** Sr. High-Adult. **P:** Entertainment. **U:** Home. **Mov-Ent:** Mystery & Suspense, Rape. **Acq:** Purchase. **Dist:** Unknown Distributor.

Blue-Eyed 1995
Offers viewers a chance to watch a workshop with ethnic diversity trainer Jane Elliot. 86m; VHS. **A:** Sr. High-Adult. **P:** Education. **U:** Home, Institution. **Gen-Edu:** Ethnicity, Prejudice. **Acq:** Purchase. **Dist:** California Newsreel. $295.00.

Blue-Eyed Butcher 2012 (Unrated) — ★¹/₂
Lifetime true crime drama. In 2003, the body of Jeffrey Wright is found buried in his suburban backyard. He was stabbed 193 times by his wife Susan, whose defense is that their seemingly perfect life was a cover for his abuse. Prosecutor Kelly Siegler thinks Susan is just a sociopath using her good looks to try to get away with murder. 89m; DVD. **C:** Sara Paxton; Lisa Edelstein; Justin Bruening; Michael Gross; Directed by Stephen Kay; Written by Michael J. Murray; Jamie Pachino; Cinematography by Jamie Barber; Music by Tree Adams. **A:** Sr. High-Adult. **P:** Entertainment. **U:** Home. **L:** English. **Mov-Ent:** Crime Drama, TV Movies. **Acq:** Purchase. **Dist:** Sony Pictures Home Entertainment Inc.

Blue Eyes 2009 (Unrated) — ★★
On his last day before his compulsory retirement, alcoholic, bitter, and racist immigration chief Marshall humiliates legal Brazilian immigrant Nonato, leading to a tragedy for which Marshall is imprisoned. After his release, and terminally ill, Marshall travels to Brazil in an effort to find and make amends

to Nonato's daughter. 110m; DVD. **C:** David Rasche; Cristina Lago; Frank Grillo; Erica Gimpel; Directed by Jose Joffily; Written by Melanie Dimantas; Paulo Halm; Cinematography by Nonato Estrela; Music by Jacques Morelenbaum. **A:** College-Adult. **P:** Entertainment. **U:** Home. **Mov-Ent:** South America, Prejudice, Immigration. **Acq:** Purchase. **Dist:** Maya Entertainment.

The Blue Eyes of Yonta 1991
Makes the disillusionment of the revolutionary generation of Africa its primary focus, and offers a glimmer of hope for the future. 90m; VHS. **A:** Sr. High-Adult. **P:** Entertainment. **U:** Home, Institution. **Gen-Edu:** Africa, Fiction, Politics & Government. **Acq:** Purchase. **Dist:** California Newsreel. $195.00.

Blue Fin 1978 (PG) — ★★
When their tuna boat is shipwrecked, and the crew disabled, a young boy and his father learn lessons of love and courage as the son tries to save the ship. 93m; VHS, DVD. **C:** Hardy Kruger; Greg Rowe; Directed by Carl Schultz; Cinematography by Geoff Burton. **Pr:** South Australian Film Corporation. **A:** Family. **P:** Entertainment. **U:** Home. **Mov-Ent:** Action-Adventure. **Acq:** Purchase. **Dist:** Unknown Distributor.

Blue Fire Lady 1978 (Unrated) — ★★
The heartwarming story of a young girl and her love of horses which endures even her father's disapproval. Good family fare. 96m; VHS, DVD. **C:** Cathryn Harrison; Mark Holden; Peter Cummins; Marion Edward; Anne Sutherland; Garry Waddell; John Wood; John Ewart; Directed by Ross Dimsey; Cinematography by Vincent Monton; Music by Mike Brady. **Pr:** Antony I. Ginanne. **A:** Family. **P:** Entertainment. **U:** Home. **Mov-Ent:** Children, Horses. **Acq:** Purchase. **Dist:** Movies Unlimited. $19.95.

Blue Flame 1993 (R) — ★★
Vigilante cop is hired to track down two humanoid aliens who have escaped captivity in futuristic L.A. They evade him by time-traveling through alternate realities, infiltrating the cop's mind, and using his fantasies against him. 88m; VHS, DVD, CC. **C:** Brian Wimmer; Ian Buchanan; Kerri Green; Cecilia Peck; Jad Mager; Directed by Cassian Elwes; Written by Cassian Elwes. **Pr:** Stephan Bataillard; David Niven, Jr. **A:** Sr. High-Adult. **P:** Entertainment. **U:** Home. **Mov-Ent:** Science Fiction. **Acq:** Purchase. **Dist:** Sony Pictures Home Entertainment Inc.

The Blue Frontier 19??
Two programs offering exceptional photography of the blue deep, featuring the endangered species the manatee and humpback whales. 30m; VHS. **Pr:** Bennett Marine Video. **A:** Primary-Adult. **P:** Education. **U:** Institution, Home. **Gen-Edu:** Oceanography. **Acq:** Purchase. **Dist:** Clear Vue Inc. $20.00. **Indiv. Titles:** 1. The Vanishing Mermaids 2. To Save a Whale.

The Blue Frontier, Vol. 1: Gigi's Legacy 198?
Extraordinary viewing for the whole family. This first volume in a series of spectacular videos exalting the glory of the earth's oceans. "Gigi's Legacy" tell the tale of a baby gray whale in captivity and what happens as she is released a year after her birth. 30m; VHS. **A:** Family. **P:** Entertainment. **U:** Home. **Gen-Edu:** Documentary Films, Oceanography. **Acq:** Purchase. **Dist:** Bennett Marine Video. $19.95.

The Blue Frontier, Vol. 2: Underseas Eden 198?
An exploration of the Phillipines's Sulu Sea and its reefs, their fragile eco-structure and the mounting danger to that structure. 30m; VHS. **C:** Hosted by Leslie Nielsen. **Pr:** Bennett Marine Video. **A:** Family. **P:** Entertainment. **U:** Home. **Gen-Edu:** Oceanography, Ecology & Environment, Fish. **Acq:** Purchase. **Dist:** Bennett Marine Video. $19.95.

The Blue Frontier, Vol. 3: To Save a Whale 198?
Co-produced by Seaworld USA, this volume in the ocean-oriented series deplores the atrocities inflicted on the ocean's whales, the results being near decimation. See how a few people make a difference to the world in this inspired story. 30m; VHS. **A:** Jr. High-Adult. **P:** Entertainment. **U:** Home. **Gen-Edu:** Documentary Films, Oceanography. **Acq:** Purchase. **Dist:** Bennett Marine Video; Karol Media. $19.95.

The Blue Frontier, Vol. 4: Sea of Many Moods 198?
Visit the Sea of Cortez, off the coasts of Mexico and California. Find beautiful ocean fishes and plant life unique to this temperate area. 30m; VHS. **C:** Hosted by Leslie Nielsen. **Pr:** Bennett Marine Video. **A:** Family. **P:** Entertainment. **U:** Home. **Gen-Edu:** Oceanography, Ecology & Environment, Fish. **Acq:** Purchase. **Dist:** Bennett Marine Video. $19.95.

The Blue Frontier, Vol. 5: King of the Sea 198?
Ditch all of your preconceived notions regarding the notorious killer whale. This video reveals the truth behind the myths that perpetuate incomprehension of the great creatures. 30m; VHS. **A:** Jr. High-Adult. **P:** Entertainment. **U:** Home. **Gen-Edu:** Documentary Films, Oceanography. **Acq:** Purchase. **Dist:** Bennett Marine Video. $19.95.

The Blue Frontier, Vol. 6: Nature's Playground 198?
Dennis Connor, world famous America's Cup winning sailor, joins host Nielsen for a look at the wet world so many people adore. Get a taste of all kinds of water activities, both in the water and on-shore. 30m; VHS. **C:** Hosted by Leslie Nielsen. **Pr:** Bennett Marine Video. **A:** Family. **P:** Entertainment. **U:** Home. **Gen-Edu:** Oceanography, Fishing, Boating. **Acq:** Purchase. **Dist:** Bennett Marine Video. $19.95.

The Blue Frontier, Vol. 7: Aquaspace Adventure 198?
How do divers explore the ocean depths? This informative tape will recount the hisory and development of this fascinating

endeavor. From the beginning to the present technology, oceanic exploration has come a long way. 30m; VHS. **A:** Jr. High-Adult. **P:** Entertainment. **U:** Home. **Gen-Edu:** Documentary Films, Oceanography. **Acq:** Purchase. **Dist:** Bennett Marine Video. $19.95.

The Blue Frontier, Vol. 8: Shark Shark Shark 198?
Ever tried to glorify the shark? Well, a look at this video will make it easy. A close and indepth examination of the shark in its habitat, performing its habits. This informative film carries with it the intention of setting straight the ill-learned fallacies about the world of this incredible creature. 30m; VHS. **A:** Family. **P:** Entertainment. **U:** Home. **Gen-Edu:** Documentary Films, Oceanography. **Acq:** Purchase. **Dist:** Bennett Marine Video. $19.95.

The Blue Frontier, Vol. 9: Clown or Criminal 198?
According to the average person, sea otters are wonderful, harmless amusement. According to shellfishermen, they are profit eaters. This installation is an interesting look at how the sea otter has beat all the odds against him by populated increasingly every year. 30m; VHS. **A:** Jr. High-Adult. **P:** Entertainment. **U:** Home. **Gen-Edu:** Documentary Films, Oceanography. **Acq:** Purchase. **Dist:** Bennett Marine Video. $19.95.

The Blue Frontier, Vol. 10: Antarctic Adventure 198?
An adventure on the coldest continent. Penguins frolic where no man can live without the aid of technology. 30m; VHS. **C:** Hosted by Leslie Nielsen. **Pr:** Bennett Marine Video. **A:** Family. **P:** Entertainment. **U:** Home. **Gen-Edu:** Oceanography, Antarctic Regions, Science. **Acq:** Purchase. **Dist:** Bennett Marine Video. $19.95.

The Blue Frontier, Vol. 11: Vanishing Mermaids 198?
The ugly manatee becomes beautiful in the water, swimming gracefully and causing legends of mermaids. Visit this vanishing species. 30m; VHS. **C:** Hosted by Leslie Nielsen. **Pr:** Bennett Marine Video. **A:** Family. **P:** Entertainment. **U:** Home. **Gen-Edu:** Oceanography, Ecology & Environment, Animals. **Acq:** Purchase. **Dist:** Bennett Marine Video. $19.95.

The Blue Frontier, Vol. 12: Rescuers 198?
An intimate account of a collective effort in California to look after the sea and the creatures in it. A few good people decided that it had to be done...even if by them alone. 30m; VHS. **A:** Jr. High-Adult. **P:** Entertainment. **U:** Home. **Gen-Edu:** Documentary Films, Oceanography. **Acq:** Purchase. **Dist:** Bennett Marine Video. $19.95.

The Blue Frontier, Vol. 13: Tails From the Nursery 198?
A delightful look at the breeding ground employed by Sea World. By the hands of mankind, some good is actually coming to the world's oceans through this ingenious and unsurpassed project to repopulate the creatures closest to extinction. 30m; VHS. **A:** Family. **P:** Entertainment. **U:** Home. **Gen-Edu:** Documentary Films, Oceanography. **Acq:** Purchase. **Dist:** Bennett Marine Video. $19.95.

The Blue Gardenia 1953 — ★★★1/2
Seminal but rarely seen film noir. Norah Larkin (Baxter) wakes up one morning in the apartment of womanizing lout Harry Prebble (Burr). He's dead and she's labeled "The Blue Gardenia" murderess by newspaper columnist Casey Mayo (Conte). Required viewing for fans of vintage mysteries. 88m/B/W; DVD. **C:** Anne Baxter; Richard Conte; Ann Sothern; Raymond Burr; George Reeves; Nat King Cole; Jeff Donnell; Richard Erdman; Ray Walker; Ruth Storey; Directed by Fritz Lang; Written by Charles Hoffman; Cinematography by Nicholas Musuraca; Music by Raoul Kraushaar. **A:** Jr. High-Adult. **P:** Entertainment. **U:** Home. **Mov-Ent:** Journalism, Photography. **Acq:** Purchase. **Dist:** Image Entertainment Inc.

Blue Hawaii 1962 (PG) — ★★
A soldier, returning to his Hawaiian home, defies his parents by taking a job with a tourist agency. Presley sings "Can't Help Falling in Love." For Elvis fans. 101m; VHS, DVD. **C:** Elvis Presley; Angela Lansbury; Joan Blackman; Roland Winters; Iris Adrian; John Archer; Steve Brodie; Pam(ela) Austin; Directed by Norman Taurog; Written by Hal Kanter. **Pr:** Paramount Pictures; Hal Wallis Productions. **A:** Family. **P:** Entertainment. **U:** Home. **L:** English, Spanish. **Mov-Ent:** Musical--Drama, Romance, Pacific Islands. **Acq:** Purchase. **Dist:** Music Video Distributors. $14.98.

Blue Heaven 1984 — ★
A couple struggles through problems with their marriage and alcohol abuse. 100m; VHS. **C:** Leslie Denniston; James Eckhouse; Directed by Kathleen Dowdey. **Pr:** Five Point. **A:** Jr. High-Adult. **P:** Entertainment. **U:** Home. **Mov-Ent:** Marriage, Alcoholism. **Acq:** Purchase. **Dist:** Lions Gate Television Corp. $69.95.

Blue Helmets: The Story of United Nations Peacekeeping 1990
Incorporates archival and newsreel footage into an examination of the aims and history of U.N. peacekeeping operations around the world. 88m; VHS. **C:** Narrated by Jesse Jackson; Directed by Steven Fischler; Joel Sucher. **A:** College-Adult. **P:** Education. **U:** Institution. **Gen-Edu:** United Nations, International Relations. **Acq:** Purchase, Rent/Lease. **Dist:** First Run/Icarus Films. $490.00.

Blue Highway 199?
See Herbie Fletcher launch his jet-powered craft off some of the biggest waves seen on the North Shore of Hawaii. 25m; VHS. **A:** Sr. High-Adult. **P:** Entertainment. **U:** Home. **Gen-Edu:** Sports--Water. **Acq:** Purchase. **Dist:** Bennett Marine Video. $24.95.

Blue Hill Avenue 2001 (R) — ★★
Four childhood friends in 1970's Boston are taken under the wing of a drug dealer and taught to be gangsters. One of them, Tristan (Payne) eventually decides he has had enough and makes the inevitable betrayal of his master before the equally inevitable ensuing bloodbath. Nothing new, but still well done. 120m; DVD. **C:** Allen Payne; Angelle Brooks; Michael "Bear" Taliferro; William L. Johnson; Aaron Spears; Andrew Divoff; Richard Lawson; Marlon Young; Dee Freeman; Anthony Sherwood; Gail Fulton Ross; Veronica Redd; Clarence Williams, III; William Forsythe; Myquan Jackson; Latamara Smith; William Butler; Pooch Hall; Chris Thornton; William Springfield; Martin Roach; David Julian Hirsh; Anthony Nuncio; Nichole McLean; Linette Robinson; Kenny Robinson; Nadia-Leigh Nascimento; Directed by Craig Ross, Jr.; Written by Craig Ross, Jr.; Cinematography by Carl F. Bartels; Music by William L. Johnson; Aaron Spears; Cruel Timothy; Jan Poperans. **A:** Sr. High-Adult. **P:** Entertainment. **U:** Home. **L:** English, Spanish. **Mov-Ent:** Crime Drama. **Acq:** Purchase. **Dist:** Lions Gate Entertainment Inc. $9.98.

The Blue Hotel 1977 (G)
Stephen Crane's story dealing with chance and whether or not it has a logic of its own. From the "American Short Story" collection. 55m; VHS. **C:** David Warner; James Keach; Lisa Pelikan; John Bottoms. **Pr:** Ozzie Brown. **A:** Sr. High-College. **P:** Entertainment. **U:** Home. **Mov-Ent:** Literature--American. **Acq:** Purchase. **Dist:** Monterey Home Video; Karol Media. $24.95.

The Blue Hour 1991 — ★★
Theo is a Berlin hustler whose business is so good he can pick his clients. Marie, his next-door neighbor, lives with her boyfriend Paul until he just walks out one day. Marie is shattered and refuses to leave her apartment until Theo takes an interest in her plight. Just when it seems that the improbable couple could find true love, Paul comes back. In German with English subtitles. 87m; VHS, DVD. **C:** Andreas Herder; Dina Leipzig; Cyrill Rey-Coquais; Directed by Marcel Gisler. **A:** College-Adult. **P:** Entertainment. **U:** Home. **L:** German. **Mov-Ent:** Drama, Prostitution. **Acq:** Purchase. **Dist:** Water Bearer Films Inc.; Facets Multimedia Inc. $39.95.

Blue Ice 1992 (R) — ★★1/2
Harry Anders (Caine) is an ex-spy with an eye for the ladies and a loyalty to his friends. When his friends start winding up dead, Harry decides to investigate—a very dangerous decision, especially when a mysterious woman (Young) takes an interest. 96m; VHS, DVD, CC. **C:** Michael Caine; Sean Young; Ian Bannen; Bob Hoskins; Directed by Russell Mulcahy; Written by Ron Hutchinson; Music by Michael Kamen. **Pr:** Martin Bregman; Michael Caine; Gary Levinsohn; Michael Caine; M&M Film Productions, Ltd. **A:** Sr. High-Adult. **P:** Entertainment. **U:** Home. **Mov-Ent:** Mystery & Suspense, TV Movies. **Acq:** Purchase. **Dist:** Home Box Office Inc.

Blue Iguana 1988 (R) — ★★
An inept bounty hunter travels south of the border to recover millions from a crooked South American bank, and meets up with sexy women, murderous thugs, and corruption. 88m; VHS, DVD, CC. **C:** Dylan McDermott; Jessica Harper; James Russo; Dean Stockwell; Pamela Gidley; Tovah Feldshuh; Directed by John Lafia. **Pr:** Polygram; Propaganda Films. **A:** Jr. High-Adult. **P:** Entertainment. **U:** Home. **Mov-Ent:** Action-Adventure. **Acq:** Purchase. **Dist:** Paramount Pictures Corp. $89.95.

Blue in the Face 1995 (R) — ★★1/2
Wang and Auster's immediate follow-up to "Smoke," shot in five days, recycles the same Brooklyn cigar shop setting and contains a dozen fast-paced, loosely scripted or wholly improvised scenes that they couldn't cram into "Smoke," led by Reed's deadpan riff on eyewear, New York, and smoking. The action again centers around Auggie (Keitel), the shop manager, who hangs out with the mostly eccentric, and sometimes famous clientele. Jarmusch idly waxes philosophic on smoking technique, while puffing on what he claims is his last. Scenes are woven together with videotaped interviews from actual Brooklyn residents, creating a tribute to life in the borough with a documentary feel. Improv lovers will enjoy watching what sometimes seems more like outtakes than finished performances. 83m; VHS, DVD, CC. **C:** Harvey Keitel; Lou Reed; Michael J. Fox; Roseanne; Jim Jarmusch; Lily Tomlin; Mel Gorham; Jared Harris; Giancarlo Esposito; Victor Argo; Madonna; Keith David; Mira Sorvino; Malik Yoba; Michael Badalucco; Jose Zuniga; Stephen Gevedon; John Lurie; Sharif Rashed; RuPaul Charles; Directed by Wayne Wang; Paul Auster; Written by Wayne Wang; Paul Auster. **Pr:** Greg Johnson; Peter Newman; Diana Philips; Bob Weinstein; Harvey Weinstein; Harvey Keitel; Harvey Keitel; Miramax. **A:** Sr. High-Adult. **P:** Entertainment. **U:** Home. **Mov-Ent:** Smoking, Cities & Towns, Marriage. **Acq:** Purchase. **Dist:** Buena Vista Home Entertainment.

Blue is the Warmest Color 2013 (NC-17) — ★★★
Based on the French graphic novel "Blue Angel," this Palme d'Or winner tells the love story between French teen Adele (Exarchopoulos) and slightly older art student Emma (Seydoux), whose lives are turned upside down when they enter into a heated romance. Rarely has a film more completely captured the arc of an entire relationship--from the minute their eyes meet to its bitter end. Both actresses are remarkably honest and pure, always seeming fully in the moment and capturing something about love and romance through their genuine performances that most movies don't get anywhere near. French with subtitles. 179m; DVD, Blu-Ray. **C:** Lea Seydoux; Adele Exarchopoulos; Directed by Abdellatif Kechiche; Written by Abdellatif Kechiche; Ghalia Lacroix; Cinematography by Sofian El Fani. **Pr:** Abdellatif Kechiche; Brahim Chioua; Vincent Maraval; Wild Bunch; IFC Films. **A:** Adult. **P:** Entertainment. **U:** Home. **L:** French. **Mov-Ent:** France, Romance, Sex & Sexuality. **Awds:** Ind. Spirit '14: Foreign Film. **Acq:** Purchase. **Dist:** Criterion Collection Inc.

Blue Jasmine 2013 (PG-13) — ★★★
Maturing like a fine wine, Woody Allen returns to San Francisco after 40 years and brings along Blanchett to cover for him. Serious in tone, but bright and human at heart, finds fallen New York socialite Jasmine (Blanchett) heading West after losing her husband and their entire fortune. In search for a renewed life, the neurotic heroine goes from popping pills to dating diplomats. Blanchett's take on a femme Allen perfectly balances his fix for desperation with courage. Allen somehow stays relevant and Blanchett just hitting her prime here. 98m; DVD, Blu-Ray. **C:** Cate Blanchett; Sally Hawkins; Alec Baldwin; Bobby Cannavale; Max Casella; Tammy Blanchard; Louis CK; Peter Sarsgaard; Andrew Silverstein; Directed by Woody Allen; Written by Woody Allen; Cinematography by Javier Aguirresarobe. **Pr:** Letty Aronson; Stephen Tenenbaum; Edward Walson; Perdido; Sony Pictures Classics. **A:** Sr. High-Adult. **P:** Entertainment. **U:** Home. **L:** English. **Mov-Ent:** Comedy-Drama. **Awds:** Oscars '13: Actress (Blanchett); British Acad. '13: Actress (Blanchett); Golden Globes '14: Actress--Drama (Blanchett); Ind. Spirit '14: Actress (Blanchett); Screen Actors Guild '13: Actress (Blanchett). **Acq:** Purchase. **Dist:** Sony Pictures Home Entertainment Inc.

Blue Jeans 1978 (Unrated) — ★★1/2
A young French boy experiences sexual awakening and humiliation in a British school. In French with English subtitles. 80m; VHS. **C:** Gilles Budin; Michel Gibet; Daniel Very; Thierry Dolon; Directed by Hugues des Roziers; Written by Hugues des Roziers; Cinematography by Jacques Assuerus; Music by David MacNeil. **A:** Sr. High-Adult. **P:** Entertainment. **U:** Home. **L:** French. **Mov-Ent:** Sex & Sexuality, Great Britain, Education. **Acq:** Purchase. **Dist:** Facets Multimedia Inc. $29.95.

Blue Jeans and Dynamite 1976 (Unrated) — ★★
A stuntman is hired to lift the "Golden Mask of the Duct Tomb" and is followed on land, water, and air. Great chase scenes and action-filled finale. 90m; VHS. **C:** Robert Vaughn; Simon Andreu; Katia Kristine; Directed by Gordon Hessler; Written by Jose Maesso; Ricardo Ferrer; Cinematography by Julio Bragado; Music by Adolfo Waitzman. **A:** Adult. **P:** Entertainment. **U:** Home. **Mov-Ent. Acq:** Purchase. **Dist:** Movies Unlimited. $19.99.

Blue Juice 1995 (R) — ★★1/2
Early work from several young actors who've gone on to bigger things. Billed as Britain's first surf picture, this comedy follows the escapades of nearly 30 JC (Pertwee), a local hero of the Cornish surfing community who can't commit to his more practical girlfriend, Chloe (Zeta-Jones). Then some of JC's London buddies, Dean (McGregor), Josh (Mackintosh), and Terry (Gunn), show up for a sort of last hurrah against the boredom of acting like adults. 90m; VHS, DVD. **C:** Sean Pertwee; Catherine Zeta-Jones; Ewan McGregor; Steven Mackintosh; Peter Gunn; Heathcote Williams; Directed by Carl Prechezer; Written by Carl Prechezer; Peter Salmi; Cinematography by Richard Greatrex; Music by Simon Davison. **A:** Sr. High-Adult. **P:** Entertainment. **U:** Home. **Mov-Ent:** Sports--Fiction: Comedy. **Acq:** Purchase. **Dist:** Lions Gate Home Entertainment.

The Blue Kite 1993 — ★★★
Fifteen years of political and cultural upheaval in China is shown through the eyes of young troublemaker Tietou, who certainly earns his nickname of "Iron Head" after his 1954 birth. Soon his father is sent to a labor reform camp and his mother remarries—only to be faced with more struggles as the years go by. The kite is Tietou's cherished toy, which keeps getting lost or destroyed but is always being rebuilt, offering one token of hope. Chinese with subtitles. 138m; VHS, DVD. **C:** Liping Lu; Zhang Wenyao; Pu Quanxin; Directed by Tian Zhuangzhuang; Written by Xiao Mao; Cinematography by Yong Hou; Music by Yoshihide Otomo. **A:** College-Adult. **P:** Entertainment. **U:** Home. **L:** Chinese. **Mov-Ent:** Family, China, Children. **Acq:** Purchase. **Dist:** Kino on Video. $79.95.

The Blue Knight 1975 (Unrated) — ★★1/2
Kennedy brings energy and care to this basically standard story. Policeman waiting for retirement searches for his partner's killer. Unexceptional treatment made palatable by actors. 72m; VHS. **C:** George Kennedy; Alex Rocco; Glynn Turman; Verna Bloom; Michael Margotta; Directed by J. Lee Thompson; Cinematography by Richard L. Rawlings. **Pr:** Lorimar Productions. **A:** Adult. **P:** Entertainment. **U:** Home. **Mov-Ent:** TV Movies. **Acq:** Purchase. **Dist:** Lions Gate Television Corp. $49.95.

The Blue Lagoon 1980 (R) — **Bomb!**
Useless remake of 1949 film of the same name. An adolescent boy and girl marooned on a desert isle discover love (read: sex) without the restraints of society. Not too explicit, but nonetheless intellectually offensive. Gorgeous photography of island paradise is wasted on this Shields vehicle. 105m; VHS, DVD, Blu-Ray. **C:** Brooke Shields; Christopher Atkins; Leo McKern; William Daniels; Directed by Randal Kleiser; Written by Douglas Day Stewart; Cinematography by Nestor Almendros; Music by Basil Poledouris. **Pr:** Randal Kleiser; Randal Kleiser; Columbia Pictures. **A:** Sr. High-Adult. **P:** Entertainment. **U:** Home. **Mov-Ent:** Sex & Sexuality. **Awds:** Golden Raspberries '80: Worst Actress (Shields). **Acq:** Purchase. **Dist:** Sony Pictures Home Entertainment Inc. $84.95.

Blue Lagoon: The Awakening 2012 (Unrated) — ★★
Lifetime remake of the 1980 pic finds teens Emma (Evans) and Dean (Thwaites) on a high school field trip in the Caribbean (it was filmed in Hawaii). Their small boat gets caught in a storm and they're stranded on a desert island where they have to survive with minimal clothing in a beautiful location. This one has several slo-mo montages and is sweetly romantic rather than sexually provocative. Atkins, who starred opposite Brooke Shields in the original, pops up as a teacher, Mr. Christiansen. 89m; DVD. **C:** Indiana Evans; Brenton Thwaites; Denise Richards; Frank John Hughes; Patrick St. Esprit; Christopher Atkins; Directed by Mikael Salomon; Written by Matt Heller; Heather Rutman; Cinematography by Denis Lenoir; Music by Tree Adams. **A:** Jr. High-Adult. **P:** Entertainment. **U:** Home. **L:** English. **Mov-Ent**: TV Movies, Adolescence, Romance. **Acq:** Purchase. **Dist:** Sony Pictures Home Entertainment Inc.

The Blue Lamp 1949 (Unrated) — ★★★
Action-adventure fans familiar with the hoary plot where a cop must avenge the wrongful death of his partner will appreciate this suspenseful British detective effort. It's one of the very first in the genre to explore buddy cop revenge in a very British sort of way. Also sports a concluding chase scene which has stood the test of time. Led to the long-running British TV series "Dixon of Dock Green." 84m/B/W; VHS, Streaming. **C:** Dirk Bogarde; Jimmy Hanley; Jack Warner; Bernard Lee; Robert Flemyng; Patric Doonan; Bruce Seton; Frederick Piper; Betty Ann Davies; Peggy Evans; Directed by Basil Dearden. **Pr:** GFD. **A:** Sr. High-Adult. **P:** Entertainment. **U:** Home. **Mov-Ent**: Action-Adventure. **Awds:** British Acad. '50: Film. **Acq:** Purchase. **Dist:** Facets Multimedia Inc. $29.95.

The Blue Light 1932 (Unrated) — ★★★
Fairy-tale love story, based on an Italian fable about a mysterious woman, thought to be a witch, and a painter. Riefenstahl's first film which brought her to the attention of Adolf Hitler, who requested she make films glorifying the Nazi Party. In German with English subtitles. 77m/B/W; VHS, DVD. **C:** Leni Riefenstahl; Matthias Wieman; Max Holsboer; Directed by Leni Riefenstahl; Written by Leni Riefenstahl; Bela Balazs; Cinematography by Hans Schneeberger; Music by Giuseppe Becce. **Pr:** Leni Riefenstahl; Leni Riefenstahl. **A:** Family. **P:** Entertainment. **U:** Home. **L:** English, German. **Mov-Ent**: Drama, Romance, Art & Artists. **Acq:** Purchase. **Dist:** Pathfinder Pictures; Facets Multimedia Inc.; German Language Video Center. $19.95.

The Blue Lightning 1986 (Unrated) — ★★½
Investigator Elliott travels to Australia to retrieve the priceless Blue Lightening gem. He must fight the crime lord in his Aussie encampment. Nice scenery, but unexceptional TV story. 95m; VHS. **C:** Sam Elliott; Rebecca Gilling; Robert Culp; John Meillon; Robert Coleby; Max Phipps; Directed by Lee Philips. **A:** Jr. High-Adult. **P:** Entertainment. **U:** Home. **Mov-Ent**: TV Movies, Australia. **Acq:** Purchase. **Dist:** Amazon.com Inc. $39.95.

Blue Like Jazz 2012 (PG-13) — ★★
This well-intentioned adaptation of Donald Miller tackles the incredibly complex issue of how teenagers from faith-heavy upbringings handle life at a liberal arts college. Don (Allman) is an incoming freshman whose understanding of religion falls apart after his youth pastor sleeps with his mother. Instead of going to a religious school, he heads for the hippie teachings of the Northwest. The characters are cliché and the story doesn't play so well on film. 108m; DVD, Blu-Ray, Wide; Closed Captioned. **C:** Marshall Allman; Claire Holt; Tania Raymonde; Justin Welborn; Eric Lange; Jason Marsden; Directed by Steve Taylor; Written by Steve Taylor; Ben Pearson; Cinematography by Ben Pearson; Music by Danny Seim. **Pr:** Coke Sams; Steve Taylor; J. Clarke Gallivan; Steve Taylor; RuckusFilm; Roadside Attractions. **A:** Sr. High-Adult. **P:** Entertainment. **U:** Home. **L:** English. **Mov-Ent**: Comedy-Drama, Education, Religion. **Acq:** Purchase. **Dist:** Miramax Film Corp.

The Blue Max 1966 — ★★½
During WWI a young German, fresh out of aviation training school, competes for the coveted "Blue Max" flying award with other members of a squadron of seasoned flyers from aristocratic backgrounds. Based on a novel by Jack D. Hunter. 155m; VHS, DVD, Blu-Ray, Wide. **C:** George Peppard; James Mason; Ursula Andress; Jeremy Kemp; Karl Michael Vogler; Anton Diffring; Harry Towb; Peter Woodthorpe; Derek Newark; Derren Nesbitt; Loni von Friedl; Directed by John Guillermin; Written by Ben Barzman; Basilio Franchina; David Pursall; Jack Seddon; Gerald Hanley; Cinematography by Douglas Slocombe; Music by Jerry Goldsmith. **Pr:** Christian Ferry; Elmo Williams; 20th Century-Fox. **A:** Family. **P:** Entertainment. **U:** Home. **L:** English, Spanish. **Mov-Ent**: World War One, Aeronautics. **Acq:** Purchase. **Dist:** Movies Unlimited; Alpha Video; Fox Home Entertainment. $29.98.

The Blue Men 198?
An unusual tragedy brings a family uneasily together. Based on the story by Joy Williams. 60m; VHS. **C:** Estelle Parsons. **A:** Jr. High-Adult. **P:** Entertainment. **U:** Home. **Mov-Ent**: Family. **Acq:** Purchase. **Dist:** Monterey Home Video. $24.95.

Blue Money 1984 (Unrated) — ★★
A wild, comedic caper film about a cab-driving nightclub impressionist who absconds with a briefcase packed with cash and is pursued by everyone, even the I.R.A. 82m; VHS. **C:** Tim Curry; Dabby Bishop; Billy Connolly; Frances Tomelty; Directed by Colin Bucksey. **Pr:** London Weekend Television. **A:** Family. **P:** Entertainment. **U:** Home. **Mov-Ent**: TV Movies. **Acq:** Purchase. **Dist:** No Longer Available.

Blue Monkey 1987 (R) — ★
A mysterious alien plant impregnates a man, who gives birth to a huge, man-eating insect larva. It subsequently grows up into a giant bug, and roams around a quarantined hospital looking for patients to eat. What made you think it had anything to do with monkeys? 97m; VHS. **C:** Steve Railsback; Susan Anspach; Gwynyth Walsh; John Vernon; Joe Flaherty; Directed by William Fruet. **Pr:** Sandy Howard; Martin Walters. **A:** Sr. High-Adult. **P:** Entertainment. **U:** Home. **Mov-Ent**: Science Fiction, Fantasy. **Acq:** Purchase. **Dist:** Sony Pictures Home Entertainment Inc. $79.95.

Blue Moon 1983
Allegorical in structure, this video juxtaposes a prostitute servicing a client with a film producer visiting an old friend and guiltily offering him money for sex. 14m; VHS, 3/4 U. **Pr:** Rodney Werden. **A:** Jr. High-Adult. **P:** Education. **U:** Institution, SURA. **Gen-Edu**: Video. **Acq:** Rent/Lease. **Dist:** Video Out Distribution.

Blue Moon 2000 (PG-13) — ★★½
Marrieds Gazzara and Moreno take a trip to the Catskills and wish on the blue moon which, according to legend, will grant them a wish. Of course, exactly how that wish will come true may not be exactly as the couple would hope. 90m; VHS, DVD. **C:** Ben Gazzara; Rita Moreno; Alanna Ubach; Brian Vincent; Heather Matarazzo; Vincent Pastore; Burt Young; Victor Argo; Lillo Brancato; Directed by John A. Gallagher; Written by John A. Gallagher; Steve Carducci; Cinematography by Craig DiBona; Music by Stephen Endelman. **A:** Jr. High-Adult. **P:** Entertainment. **U:** Home. **Mov-Ent**: Marriage, Aging. **Acq:** Purchase. **Dist:** Wellspring Media.

Blue Movies 1988 (R) — **Bomb!**
A couple of jerks try their hand at making porn films with predictable results. 92m; VHS. **C:** Larry Linville; Lucinda Crosby; Steve Levitt; Darien Mathias; Larry Poindexter; Christopher Stone; Don Calfa; Russell Johnson; Directed by Paul Koval; Ed Fitzgerald; Written by Paul Koval; Ed Fitzgerald. **Pr:** Academy Entertainment. **A:** Sr. High-Adult. **P:** Entertainment. **U:** Home. **Mov-Ent**: Sex & Sexuality, Exploitation. **Acq:** Purchase. **Dist:** Unknown Distributor.

Blue Murder at St. Trinian's 1956 (Unrated) — ★★★
The second of the madcap British comedy series (based on cartoons by Ronald Searle) about an incredibly ferocious pack of schoolgirls. This time they travel to the European continent and make life miserable for a jewel thief. Highlight: fantasy sequence in ancient Rome showing the girls thrown to the lions—and scaring the lions. 86m/B/W; VHS, DVD, Streaming. **C:** Joyce Grenfell; Terry-Thomas; George Cole; Alastair Sim; Lionel Jeffries; Thorley Walters; Directed by Frank Launder; Music by Malcolm Arnold. **Pr:** British Lion. **A:** Jr. High-Adult. **P:** Entertainment. **U:** Home. **Mov-Ent**: Comedy--Screwball. **Acq:** Purchase, Rent/Lease. **Dist:** Fusion Video; Nostalgia Family Video/Hollywood's Attic. $19.99 9.99.

Blue Murder: Complete Collection 2009
ITV crime drama 2003-2009. DCI Janine Lewis heads a team that investigates gruesome crimes in Manchester. She's also a divorced single mom trying to cope with four kids as well as her partner, DI Richard Mayne, who's a former flame. 19 episodes. 1170m; DVD, CC. **C:** Caroline Quentin; Ian Kelsey. **A:** Sr. High-Adult. **P:** Entertainment. **U:** Home. **Mov-Ent**: Crime Drama, Great Britain, Television Series. **Acq:** Purchase. **Dist:** Acorn Media Group Inc. $99.99.

Blue Murder: Set 1 2003
Caroline Quentin is Manchester police detective Janine Lewis, who doggedly solves cases on the streets and crisis at home with her four children and recently divorced status. Plots link together seemingly unrelated threads and draw emotional parallels with domestic situations. Cases include murders connected with homemade porn, racial unrest, incest, and a dead hooker connected to the hit and run of a schoolgirl. 6 episodes. 414m; DVD. **C:** Caroline Quentin; David Schofield; Ian Kelsey. **A:** Adult. **P:** Entertainment. **U:** Home. **Mov-Ent**: Drama. **Acq:** Purchase. **Dist:** Acorn Media Group Inc.

Blue Murder: Set 2 2006
Single mom of four kids and detective to boot, Janine Lewis deals with a strangled member of a dysfunctional family in "The Spartacus Thing," the discovery of a child's body in a drainage tunnel in "Make Believe," the drive-by shooting of beat cop "Steady Eddie," and four college friends that are "In Deep" after the body of a small-time crook and drug dealer surfaces. 4 episodes. 275m; DVD. **C:** Caroline Quentin; Ian Kelsey. **A:** Adult. **P:** Entertainment. **U:** Home. **Mov-Ent**: Drama, Mystery & Suspense. **Acq:** Purchase. **Dist:** Acorn Media Group Inc.

Blue on Ice 1974
An action study of the Navy bobsled team at Lake Placid, New York, before and during the two and four-man North American Bobsled Championship. 20m; VHS, 3/4 U, Special order formats. **Pr:** Department of the Navy. **A:** Family. **P:** Entertainment. **U:** Institution, SURA. **Spo-Rec**: Sports--General, Sports--Winter. **Acq:** Purchase. **Dist:** National Audiovisual Center.

Blue Oyster Cult: Live '76 19??
Features a live performance from Maryland's Capitol Center, 1976. Songs include "Stairway to the Stars," "Bach's Boogie," "Born to be Wild," and "Summer of Love." ?m; VHS, DVD. **A:** Jr. High-Adult. **P:** Entertainment. **U:** Home. **Mov-Ent**: Music Video, Music--Performance, Music--Pop/Rock. **Acq:** Purchase. **Dist:** Music Video Distributors. $64.95.

Blue Planet 1972
An examination of America's role in space exploration. 10m; 3/4 U, Q. **C:** Narrated by Burgess Meredith. **Pr:** National Aeronautics and Space Administration. **A:** Primary-Adult. **P:** Education. **U:** BCTV, SURA. **Hea-Sci**: Documentary Films, Space Exploration, Technology. **Acq:** Free Loan. **Dist:** NASA Lyndon B. Johnson Space Center.

Blue Planet 1993
Amazing images from space remind earth dwellers of the immensity of the universe and the fragility of the globe. 41m; Blu-Ray, HD-DVD. **A:** Family. **P:** Entertainment. **U:** Home. **Gen-Edu**: Ecology & Environment, Space Exploration. **Acq:** Purchase. **Dist:** Baker and Taylor; Finley Holiday Film Corp. $39.95.

The Blue Planet: Seas of Life 2002
Remarkable eight-episode BBC series. "Ocean World" looks at the ecological diversity of the planet's oceans; "Frozen Seas" examines the extreme conditions of the Arctic and Antarctic Circle; "Open Ocean" looks at currents; "The Deep" examines the creatures who live in the abyssal plain; "Seasonal Seas" looks at the annual blooming of plankton; "Coral Seas" explores the miles-long reefs of living coral; "Tidal Seas" looks at the life forms that live in tidal pools; and "Coasts" captures an orca whale on the hunt—and its seal pup victim. On four discs. 392m; DVD, Blu-Ray. **C:** Narrated by David Attenborough. **A:** Family. **P:** Entertainment. **U:** Home. **Gen-Edu**: Documentary Films, Oceanography. **Acq:** Purchase. **Dist:** Warner Home Video, Inc.

The Blue Puttees 19??
Examines the Royal Newfoundland Regiment, which was raised "from scratch" in a matter of months in 1915 and became one of the most formidable fighting units of World War I. 120m; VHS. **A:** Jr. High-Adult. **P:** Education. **U:** Home. **Gen-Edu**: War--General, World War One, Canada. **Acq:** Purchase. **Dist:** The War Amps. $14.00.

The Blue Revolution Series 1990
The National Education Association endorses this 16 volume series dealing with many aspects of life under the sea, and how man will affect the future of this world. 25m; VHS. **Pr:** Films for the Humanities. **A:** Sr. High-Adult. **P:** Education. **U:** Institution. **Hea-Sci**: Documentary Films, Oceanography, Biology. **Acq:** Purchase. **Dist:** Films for the Humanities & Sciences. $149.00.

Blue Ribbon Grooming 19??
Grooming any animal for a show is all important. This video shows the step by step process to help your animal look his best and win that ribbon. 60m; VHS. **A:** Family. **P:** Instruction. **U:** Home. **How-Ins**: How-To, Horses. **Acq:** Purchase. **Dist:** Morris Video. $29.95.

Blue Ribbon Trout 1993
Discusses trout fishing providing footage on some of the most famous trout streams in the country. Features helpful tips in flyfishing for the beginner as well as a few new ideas for the more experienced fisherman. 60m; VHS. **A:** Adult. **P:** Instruction. **U:** Home. **Spo-Rec**: Fishing. **Acq:** Purchase. **Dist:** Stoney-Wolf Productions, Inc. $39.95.

Blue Ribbon Veggies 1990
Ed Hume, master gardener, demonstrates simple yet effective ways to improve each and every member of your garden. 55m; VHS. **Pr:** Morris Video. **A:** Sr. High-Adult. **P:** Instruction. **U:** Home. **How-Ins**: How-To, Gardening. **Acq:** Purchase. **Dist:** Morris Video. $14.95.

Blue Ridge Fall 1999 (R) — ★★
In the small town of Jefferson Creek, North Carolina, Danny (Facinelli) is the star high school quarterback who can do no wrong. He's befriended simple-minded Aaron (Eastman), who is driven to violent desperation by his abusive father. Danny enlists his buddies to cover up Aaron's crime but their plans quickly go wrong and things just get more desperate for them all. 99m; VHS, DVD, Wide. **C:** Peter Facinelli; Rodney Eastman; Will Estes; Jay R. Ferguson; Tom Arnold; Amy Irving; Chris Isaak; Brent Jennings; Heather Stephens; Garvin Funches; Directed by James Rowe; Written by James Rowe; Cinematography by Chris Walling; Music by Greg Edmonson. **A:** Sr. High-Adult. **P:** Entertainment. **U:** Home. **Mov-Ent**: Crime Drama, Education, Football. **Acq:** Purchase. **Dist:** Image Entertainment Inc.

Blue Ridge Steam: The Norfolk & Western 19??
Classic train footage. Norfolk & Western steam engines travel over Blue Ridge Summit, Christiansburg Grade, and along the Shenandoah Line to Hagerstown, Maryland featuring Y6b Class 2-8-8-2, A Class 2-6-6-4, Z Class 2-6-6-2, and K Class 4-8-2 engines plus a J Class 4-8-4 hauling the Powhattan Arrow. 102m; DVD. **A:** Family. **P:** Education. **U:** Home. **L:** English. **Gen-Edu**: Trains, U.S. States. **Acq:** Purchase. **Dist:** The Civil War Standard; WB Video Productions. $39.95.

Blue River 1995 (PG-13) — ★★½
Flashbacks highlight this saga of a troubled family. Successful doctor Edward Sellers (McDonough) is dismayed when his derelict older brother Lawrence (O'Connell), whom he hasn't seen in 15 years, suddenly appears on his doorstep. A gifted teenager, Lawrence once built his world around science and logic after their father deserted the family but his only purpose turns out to be getting even with everyone he feels has betrayed him. Young Edward (Stahl) tried to be the "good" son, while Mom (Dey) retreated into religion and an affair with self-righteously nasty school principal Henry Howland (Elliott). TV adaptation of the novel by Ethan Canin. 90m; VHS, DVD. **C:** Jerry O'Connell; Nick Stahl; Susan Dey; Sam Elliott; Neal McDonough; Jean Marie Barnwell; Patrick Renna; Directed by Larry Elikann; Written by Maria Nation; Cinematography by Eric Van Haren Noman; Music by Lawrence Shragge. **Pr:** Brent Shields; Richard Welsh; Signboard Hill Productions, Inc. **A:** Jr. High-Adult. **P:** Entertainment. **U:** Home. **Mov-Ent**: TV Movies. **Acq:** Purchase. **Dist:** Echo Bridge Home Entertainment.

Blue Ruin 2013 (R) — ★★★
Director/writer Saulnier's vengeance thriller features sudden outbursts of violence, dark humor, and clockwork precision. Blair stars as a vagrant who is forced into action when the man who murdered his parents is released from prison. Before he can even consider his actions, the victim has taken his vengeance and set into motion a new cycle of violence. The film hums along at a perfect pace, finding a great balance between tension and realism, never losing sight of its largely silent character and his fight to protect what he thinks is right. 92m; DVD. **C:** Macon Blair; Amy Hargreaves; Derin Ratray; Kevin Kolack; Eve Plumb; Directed by Jeremy Saulnier; Written by Jeremy Saulnier; Cinematography by Jeremy Saulnier; Music by Brooke Blair; Will Blair. **Pr:** Picturehouse Entertainment. **A:** Sr. High-Adult. **P:** Entertainment. **U:** Home. **L:** English. **Mov-Ent:** Violence, Family. **Acq:** Purchase.

Blue Seduction 2009 (Unrated) — ★½
A one-hit music wonder in the 1980s, Mikey Taylor lived the booze, drugs and sex life until he met Joyce, who sobered him up and married him. Twenty years later, Mikey is a music composer who hires sultry Matty McPherson as his demo singer and new protege. She also turns out to be his biggest (psycho) fan and is soon leading Mikey down that old decadent path. 91m; DVD. **C:** Billy Zane; Estella Warren; Jane Wheeler; Bernard Robichaud; Directed by Timothy Bond; Written by Jackie Giroux; Cinematography by Philip Hurn; Music by David Wade; Richard Wade. **A:** Sr. High-Adult. **P:** Entertainment. **U:** Home. **Mov-Ent:** Music. **Acq:** Purchase. **Dist:** Anchor Bay Entertainment.

Blue Skies 1946 — ★★★
Former dancer turned radio personality Astaire flashes back to his friendship with singer Crosby and the gal (Caulfield) that came between them. Flimsy plot is just an excuse for some 20 Irving Berlin songs and Astaire's split-screen dance number, "Puttin' on the Ritz." 104m; VHS, DVD, CC. **C:** Fred Astaire; Bing Crosby; Joan Caulfield; Billy DeWolfe; Olga San Juan; Frank Faylen; Directed by Stuart Heisler; Written by Arthur Sheekman; Cinematography by Charles B(ryant) Lang, Jr. **Pr:** Sol C. Siegel; Paramount Pictures. **A:** Family. **P:** Entertainment. **U:** Home. **Mov-Ent:** Musical, Romance. **Acq:** Purchase. **Dist:** Universal Music and Video Distribution. $19.98.
Songs: All By Myself; Always; Any Bonds Today?; Blue Skies; A Couple of Song and Dance Men; Everybody Step; Getting Nowhere; Heat Wave; I'll See You in C-U-B-A; I've Got My Captain Working for Me Now; The Little Things in Life; Not for All th Rice in China; A Pretty Girl Is Like a Melody; Puttin' On th Ritz; Russian Lullaby; Serenade to an Old-Fashioned Girl; This Is the Army, Mr. Jones; White Christmas; You'd Be Surprised; You Keep Coming Back Like a Song.

Blue Skies Again 1983 (PG) — ★½
Spunky young woman determined to play major league baseball locks horns with the chauvinistic owner and the gruff manager of her favorite team. 91m; VHS. **C:** Robyn Barto; Harry Hamlin; Mimi Rogers; Kenneth McMillan; Dana Elcar; Andy Garcia; Directed by Richard Michaels. **Pr:** Lantana Productions. **A:** Jr. High-Adult. **P:** Entertainment. **U:** Home. **Mov-Ent:** Sports--Fiction: Comedy, Baseball. **Acq:** Purchase. **Dist:** Warner Home Video, Inc. $69.95.

Blue Sky 1991 (PG-13) — ★★★
Carly Marshall (Lange) is an irrepressible beauty, long married to adoring but uptight military scientist Hank (Jones). Things are barely in control when they're stationed in Hawaii but after Hank's transfer to a backwater base in Alabama, Carly's emotional mood swings go wildly out of control. Hell truly breaks loose when Carly attracts the attention of the camp's commander (Boothe), who's only too willing to take advantage. Set in 1962, a nuclear radiation subplot (Hank's new project) proves a minor distraction. Exceptional performance by Lange with Jones providing a quiet counterpoint as a man still deeply in love with his disturbed wife. Director Richardson's final film. Release date was delayed to 1994 due to studio Orion's financial problems. 101m; VHS, DVD, Wide, CC. **C:** Jessica Lange; Tommy Lee Jones; Powers Boothe; Carrie Snodgress; Amy Locane; Chris O'Donnell; Mitchell Ryan; Dale Dye; Richard Jones; Directed by Tony Richardson; Written by Arlene Sarner; Jerry Leichtling; Rama Laurie Stagner; Cinematography by Steve Yaconelli; Music by Jack Nitzsche. **Pr:** Robert H. Solo; Orion Pictures. **A:** Sr. High-Adult. **P:** Entertainment. **U:** Home. **Mov-Ent:** Marriage, Mental Health, Armed Forces--U.S. **Awds:** Oscars '94: Actress (Lange); Golden Globes '95: Actress--Drama (Lange); L.A. Film Critics '94: Actress (Lange). **Acq:** Purchase. **Dist:** MGM Studios Inc.

The Blue Sky Awards Music Videos: A Clean Air Celebration 1993 (Unrated)
A number of musical artists grouped together to perform a benefit concert for the American Lung Association, and clean air initiatives and research. Includes performances by Midnight Oil, Rickie Lee Jones, Talking Heads, The Greatful Dead, Fishbone, and Jeffrey Osborne. Sponsored by MPI and the American Lung Association. 65m; VHS. **A:** Jr. High-Adult. **P:** Entertainment. **U:** Home. **Mov-Ent:** Music--Performance. **Acq:** Purchase. **Dist:** MPI Media Group; American Lung Association. $19.98.

Blue Sky Laws: State Regulation of Securities 1985
For legal professionals, this is an analysis of blue sky regulation of public and private offerings, including securities commissioner policies. 330m; VHS, 3/4 U. **Pr:** Practicing Law Institute. **A:** Adult. **P:** Professional. **U:** Institution, Home. **Gen-Edu:** Law. **Acq:** Purchase, Rent/Lease. **Dist:** Practising Law Institute.

Blue Smoke 2007 (Unrated) — ★★½
After her family's pizzeria is destroyed by fire when she's 11, Reena grows up to become an arson investigator. A neighborhood reunion leads her to romance with carpenter Bo, but Reena soon discovers that fire is following her. Seems an arsonist is targeting everything—and everyone—she holds dear. Lifetime original movie based on the novel by Nora Roberts. 90m; DVD. **C:** Alicia Witt; Matthew Settle; Scott Bakula; Talia Shire; John Reardon; Eric Keenleyside; Chris Fassbender; Ben Ayres; Directed by David Carson; Written by Ronni Kern; Cinematography by Nikos Evdemon; Music by Chris P. Bacon; Stuart M. Thomas. **A:** Jr. High-Adult. **P:** Entertainment. **U:** Home. **Mov-Ent:** Drama, Fires, Mystery & Suspense. **Acq:** Purchase. **Dist:** Warner Home Video, Inc.

Blue Snake 1989
This strangely innovative futuristic ballet is performed. 58m; VHS, 3/4 U. **Pr:** Rhombus Media; National Film Board of Canada. **A:** Jr. High-Adult. **P:** Education. **U:** Institution, Home, SURA. **Fin-Art:** Dance--Ballet. **Acq:** Purchase, Rent/Lease. **Dist:** Bullfrog Films, Inc. $285.00.

Blue Spring 2001 (Unrated) — ★★½
Social commentary on violence in the Japanese school system. A school that's used as a dumping ground for rejects, quickly becomes a training ground for the Yakuza. Two friends compete to be the leader of the school, and when one wins, the other quickly grows frustrated and begins a bloody war. 83m; DVD. **C:** Ryuhei Matsuda; Hirofumi Arai; Sosuke Takaoka; Yusuke Oshiba; Yuta Yamazaki; Shugo Oshinari; Eita; Onimaru; Mame Yamada; Directed by Toshiaki Toyoda; Written by Toshiaki Toyoda; Taiyo Matsumoto; Cinematography by Norimichi Kasamatsu; Music by Richiro Manabe. **A:** Jr. High-Adult. **P:** Entertainment. **U:** Home. **L:** English, Japanese. **Mov-Ent:** Education. **Acq:** Purchase. **Dist:** Movies Unlimited. $24.95.

Blue State 2007 (R) — ★
Fervently liberal John (Meyer) drunkenly proclaims that he'll move to Canada if Dubya is elected POTUS and then feels he must follow through. He finds a green card marriage website and decides to travel to Winnipeg. Needing someone to share the driving, John meets secretive Chloe (Paquin), who has her own reasons for leaving the country. Tends toward one-sided diatribes and its views on Canadians vs. Americans are stereotypical and condescending. 99m; DVD. **C:** Breckin Meyer; Anna Paquin; Richard Blackburn; Adriana O'Neill; Joyce Krenz; Directed by Marshall Lewy; Written by Marshall Lewy; Cinematography by Phil Parmet; Music by Nathan Johnson. **A:** Sr. High-Adult. **P:** Entertainment. **U:** Home. **Mov-Ent:** Canada. **Acq:** Purchase. **Dist:** Fox Home Entertainment.

Blue Steel 1934 — ★★
A young Wayne saves a town from financial ruin by leading the citizens to a gold strike. 59m/B/W; VHS, DVD, 3/4 U, Special order formats. **C:** John Wayne; George "Gabby" Hayes; Directed by Robert North Bradbury. **Pr:** Monogram. **A:** Family. **P:** Entertainment. **U:** Institution, Home. **Mov-Ent:** Western. **Acq:** Purchase. **Dist:** Facets Multimedia Inc.; Sony Pictures Home Entertainment Inc.; Lions Gate Entertainment Inc. $9.95.

Blue Steel 1990 (R) — ★★
Director Bigelow's much-heralded, proto-feminist cop thriller. A serious female rookie's gun falls into the hands of a Wall Street psycho who begins a killing spree. Action film made silly with over-anxious sub-text and patriarchy-directed rage. 102m; VHS, DVD, 8 mm, CC. **C:** Jamie Lee Curtis; Ron Silver; Clancy Brown; Louise Fletcher; Philip Bosco; Elizabeth Pena; Tom Sizemore; Directed by Kathryn Bigelow; Written by Kathryn Bigelow; Eric Red; Music by Brad Fiedel. **Pr:** Lightning Pictures; Precision Films. **A:** College-Adult. **P:** Entertainment. **U:** Home. **Mov-Ent:** Mystery & Suspense. **Acq:** Purchase. **Dist:** MGM Home Entertainment. $14.95.

Blue Streak 1999 (PG-13) — ★★
Only hardcore Martin Lawrence fans will enjoy this formulaic buddy-cop-with-a-twist action comedy. Lawrence plays jewel thief Miles Logan, who hides a gem from his latest heist at a construction site just before he's caught. Three years later and out of jail, Logan tries to retrieve his diamond only to discover the site is now a police station. While impersonating a detective in order to sneak in and grab the stash, he accidentally catches an escaping felon and is forced to continue the charade. He's saddled with rookie partner Carlson (Wilson) and begins using his criminal knowledge to catch other crooks, including his old crony Tulley (Chappelle). Lawrence gives a good effort but all of his frantic mugging can't save the lame material he's forced to work with, making this feel like a poor man's "Beverly Hills Cop." 94m; VHS, DVD, Wide, CC. **C:** Martin Lawrence; Luke Wilson; Peter Greene; Dave Chappelle; William Forsythe; Graham Beckel; Tamala Jones; Nicole Ari Parker; Robert Miranda; Olek Krupa; Anne Marie Howard; Directed by Les Mayfield; Written by Stephen Carpenter; Michael Berry; John Blumenthal; Cinematography by David Eggby. **Pr:** Columbia Pictures. **A:** Sr. High-Adult. **P:** Entertainment. **U:** Home. **Mov-Ent.** **Acq:** Purchase. **Dist:** Sony Pictures Home Entertainment Inc.

Blue Suede Shoes: A Rockabilly Session with Carl Perkins and Friends 1990
Many of Rock's renowned performers get together for an all-out jam session. Features the talents of George Harrison, Ringo Starr, Eric Clapton, Dave Edmunds, Rosanne Cash, Slim Jim Phantom, Lee Rocker, Earl Slick, and the creator of the song "Blue Suede Shoes," Carl Perkins. 57m; VHS. **C:** Music by George Harrison; Ringo Starr; Eric Clapton; Carl Perkins; Dave Edmunds; Rosanne Cash. **A:** Adult. **P:** Entertainment. **U:** Home. **Mov-Ent:** Music--Performance. **Acq:** Purchase. **Dist:** Music Video Distributors. $19.95.

Blue Sunshine 1978 (R) — ★★½
A certain brand of L.S.D. called Blue Sunshine starts to make its victims go insane. 94m; VHS, DVD. **C:** Zalman King; Deborah Winters; Mark Goddard; Robert Walden; Charles Siebert; Ann Cooper; Ray Young; Alice Ghostley; Richard Crystal; Bill Adler; Stefan Gierasch; Brion James; Directed by Jeff Lieberman; Written by Jeff Lieberman; Music by Charles Gross. **Pr:** Excel Video. **A:** Adult. **P:** Entertainment. **U:** Home. **Mov-Ent:** Horror, Drugs. **Acq:** Purchase. **Dist:** Movies Unlimited; Alpha Video. $69.95.

Blue Thunder 1983 (R) — ★★½
Police helicopter pilot Scheider is chosen to test an experimental high-tech chopper that can see through walls, record a whisper, and level a city block. Seems anti-terrorist supercopter is needed to ensure security during 1984 Olympics. Bothered by Vietnam flashbacks, Scheider then battles wacky McDowell in the skies over L.A. High-techy police drama with satisfying aerial combat scenes nearly crashes with story line. 110m; VHS, DVD, Wide, CC. **C:** Roy Scheider; Daniel Stern; Malcolm McDowell; Candy Clark; Warren Oates; Directed by John Badham; Written by Dan O'Bannon; Don Jakoby; Cinematography by John A. Alonzo. **Pr:** Gordon Carroll. **A:** Sr. High-Adult. **P:** Entertainment. **U:** Home. **Mov-Ent:** Action-Adventure, Aeronautics. **Acq:** Purchase. **Dist:** Sony Pictures Home Entertainment Inc. $12.95.

Blue Tiger 1994 (R) — ★★
Gina Hayes (Madsen) is shopping with her young son when a masked gunman enters the store and opens fire. When Gina realizes her son has been killed she becomes obsessed with finding the assailant. Her one clue—a blue tiger tattoo. 88m; VHS, DVD, CC. **C:** Virginia Madsen; Toru Nakamura; Harry Dean Stanton; Ryo Ishibashi; Directed by Norberto Barba; Written by Joel Soisson. **Pr:** Michael Leahy; Aki Komine; Taka Ichise; W.K. Border; Joel Soisson; Neo Motion Pictures; First Look Pictures; Ozla Pictures. **A:** Sr. High-Adult. **P:** Entertainment. **U:** Home. **Mov-Ent.** **Acq:** Purchase. **Dist:** Sony Pictures Home Entertainment Inc.

The Blue Tooth Virgin 2009 (R) — ★½
Insider Hollywood talkfest. Struggling screenwriter Sam (Peck) is working on his latest pretentious and unproduced screenplay (the title of the movie itself). He gives it to his friend David (Johnson), a successful magazine editor, to read. David thinks it's terrible and Sam can't stand the slightest hint of criticism, with their rift eventually affecting Sam's personal life. 80m; DVD. **C:** Austin Peck; Lauren Stamile; Bryce Johnson; Tom Gilroy; Roma Maffia; Amber Benson; Karen Black; Directed by Russell Brown; Written by Russell Brown; Cinematography by Marco Fargnoli; Music by Karen Black. **Pr:** Roni Deitz; Russell Brown; The Simon; Regent Releasing. **A:** Sr. High-Adult. **P:** Entertainment. **U:** Home. **L:** English. **Mov-Ent.** **Acq:** Purchase. **Dist:** Entertainment One US LP; Movies Unlimited; Alpha Video.

Blue Tornado 1990 (PG-13) — ★
An eerie bright light, emitted from a mountain, makes supersonic jets disappear into thin air. A beautiful researcher and a cocky pilot set out to solve the mystery. Better-than-average aerial sequences don't make up for goofy story and ludicrous dialogue. 96m; VHS. **C:** Dirk Benedict; Patsy Kensit; Ted McGinley; David Warner; Directed by Tony B. Dobb. **Pr:** Giovanni Di Clemente. **A:** Sr. High-Adult. **P:** Entertainment. **U:** Home. **Mov-Ent:** Mystery & Suspense, Aeronautics. **Acq:** Purchase. **Dist:** CinemaNow Inc. $89.95.

The Blue Tree 1979
The innovative and ground-breaking Abstract and Cubist art of Chicago artist Rudolp Weisenborn are featured. 34m; VHS, 3/4 U, Special order formats. **Pr:** Film Communications Group. **A:** Sr. High-Adult. **P:** Education. **U:** Institution, Home. **Fin-Art:** Documentary Films, Art & Artists, Painting. **Acq:** Purchase, Rent/Lease. **Dist:** Phoenix Learning Group. $150.00.

Blue Valentine 2010 (R) — ★★
Cianfrance's flick traces the frustration, anger, and dissolution of the marriage of Dean (Gosling) and Cindy (Williams) while offering flashbacks to happier times. They are a 'normal' couple—young, romantic and optimistic at first but Dean lacks ambition and likes to drink and Cindy turns sulky over their limited life and has trust issues that crop up. The story may hit too close for some while others will find the duo merely tiresome. Viewers of the NC17-rated version should not get too hot and bothered—it's for one semi-consensual sex scene that's more emotionally violent than anything else. 120m; Blu-Ray, On Demand, Wide. **C:** Ryan Gosling; Michelle Williams; Mike Vogel; John Doman; Ben Shenkman; Faith Wladyka; Jen Jones; Maryann Plunkett; Directed by Derek Cianfrance; Written by Derek Cianfrance; Joey Curtis; Cami Delavigne; Cinematography by Andrij Parekh; Music by Grizzly Bear. **Pr:** Lynette Howell; Alex Orlovsky; Jamie Patricof; Hunting Lane Films; Silverwood Films; Weinstein Co. **A:** Sr. High-Adult. **P:** Entertainment. **U:** Home. **L:** English. **Mov-Ent:** Drama, Divorce. **Acq:** Purchase. **Dist:** Amazon.com Inc.; Movies Unlimited; Alpha Video.

Blue Valley Songbird 1999 (Unrated) — ★★½
Leanne Taylor (Parton) ran away to Nashville to find singing success but is still struggling for national recognition after 15 years, thanks to her controlling manager-boyfriend Hank (Terry). When Leanne becomes interested in new band guitarist Bobby (Dean), he tells her she has the talent to become a star but Hank is holding her back and Leanne needs to make some changes. 91m; DVD. **C:** Dolly Parton; John Terry; Billy Dean; Beth Grant; Kimberley Kates; Directed by Richard A. Colla; Written by Ken Carter, Jr.; Annette Heywood-Carter; Cinematography by Rob Draper; Music by Velton Ray Bunch. **A:** Jr.

High-Adult. **P:** Entertainment. **U:** Home. **Mov-Ent:** TV Movies. **Acq:** Purchase. **Dist:** Echo Bridge Home Entertainment.

Blue Velvet 1986 (R) — ★★★
Disturbing, unique exploration of the dark side of American suburbia, involving an innocent college youth who discovers a severed ear in an empty lot, and is thrust into a turmoil of depravity, murder, and sexual deviance. Brutal, grotesque, and unmistakably Lynch; an immaculately made, fiercely imagined film that is unlike any other. Mood is enhanced by the Badalamenti soundtrack. Graced by splashes of Lynchian humor, most notably the movie's lumber theme. Hopper is riveting as the chief sadistic nutcase and Twin Peaks' MacLachlan is a study in loss of innocence. 121m; VHS, DVD, Blu-Ray, Wide, CC. **C:** Kyle MacLachlan; Isabella Rossellini; Dennis Hopper; Laura Dern; Hope Lange; Jack Nance; Dean Stockwell; George Dickerson; Brad Dourif; Priscilla Pointer; Angelo Badalamenti; Directed by David Lynch; Written by David Lynch; Cinematography by Frederick Elmes; Music by Angelo Badalamenti. **Pr:** De Laurentiis Entertainment Group. **A:** College-Adult. **P:** Entertainment. **U:** Home. **Mov-Ent:** Mystery & Suspense, Cult Films. **Awds:** Ind. Spirit '87: Actress (Rossellini); L.A. Film Critics '86: Director (Lynch), Support. Actor (Hopper); Montreal World Film Fest. '86: Support. Actor (Hopper); Natl. Soc. Film Critics '86: Cinematog., Director (Lynch), Film, Support. Actor (Hopper). **Acq:** Purchase. **Dist:** Warner Home Video, Inc. $19.98.

Blue Vinyl: The World's First Toxic Comedy 2005 (Unrated)
Documentary following filmmaker Judith Helfrand as she tries to discover the truth about the possible toxic side effects of PVC vinyl siding after her parents decide to re-side their house with it. 98m; DVD. **A:** Sr. High-Adult. **P:** Education. **U:** Home. **Gen-Edu:** Documentary Films, Ecology & Environment. **Acq:** Purchase. **Dist:** Docurama. $26.95.

Blue Water Hunters 19??
Exciting program featuring scuba daredevils who dive amidst sharks in the South Pacific. 58m; VHS. **C:** Narrated by Peter Fonda. **A:** Jr. High-Adult. **P:** Entertainment. **U:** Home. **Spo-Rec:** Scuba. **Acq:** Purchase. **Dist:** Bennett Marine Video; Pal Productions. $24.95.

Blue Water Odyssey 1988
The story of a family of five who spent a few years circumnavigating the globe. 97m; VHS. **C:** Bob Driscoll. **Pr:** Bennett Marine Video. **A:** Family. **P:** Entertainment. **U:** Home. **Gen-Edu:** Biography, Boating. **Acq:** Purchase. **Dist:** Bennett Marine Video. $49.95.

Blue Water—Great Naval Traditions 19??
An exploration of America's and Britain's naval traditions. 50m; VHS. **A:** Adult. **P:** Entertainment. **U:** Home. **Gen-Edu:** Military History, Armed Forces--U.S. **Acq:** Purchase. **Dist:** Acorn Media Group Inc. $19.95.

Blue, White and Perfect 1942 (Unrated) — ★★½
Shayne (Nolan) promises his marriage-minded girlfriend Merle (Hughes) that he'll leave the PI business behind and get a steady wartime job. Only the shamus soon finds himself mixed-up in the smuggling of industrial diamonds that has Shayne taking an ocean liner to Hawaii and discovering espionage and Nazis aboard ship. 74m/B/W; DVD. **C:** Lloyd Nolan; Mary Beth Hughes; George Reeves; Steven Geray; Helen Reynolds; Henry Victor; Curt Bois; Mae Marsh; Arthur Loft; Directed by Herbert I. Leeds; Written by Samuel G. Engel; Cinematography by Glen MacWilliams. **A:** Jr. High-Adult. **P:** Entertainment. **U:** Home. **Mov-Ent:** Mystery & Suspense, Boating, Drug Trafficking/Dealing. **Acq:** Purchase. **Dist:** Fox Home Entertainment.

The Blue Yonder 1986 (Unrated) — ★½
In this made-for-video feature, a young boy travels back in time to meet the grandfather he never knew, risking historical integrity. 89m; VHS, CC. **C:** Art Carney; Peter Coyote; Huckleberry Fox; Directed by Mark Rosman. **Pr:** Walt Disney Studios. **A:** Family. **P:** Entertainment. **U:** Home. **Mov-Ent:** Drama, Family, Family Viewing. **Acq:** Purchase. **Dist:** Walt Disney Studios Home Entertainment. $69.95.

Bluebeard 1944 (Unrated) — ★★½
Tormented painter with a psychopathic urge to strangle his models is the basis for this effective, low-budget film. One of Carradine's best vehicles. 73m/B/W; VHS, DVD, 3/4 U, Special order formats. **C:** John Carradine; Jean Parker; Nils Asther; Directed by Edgar G. Ulmer; Written by Pierre Gendron; Cinematography by Jock Feindel. **Pr:** PRC. **A:** Adult. **P:** Entertainment. **U:** Home. **Mov-Ent:** Horror, Art & Artists. **Acq:** Purchase. **Dist:** Sinister Cinema; Synergy Enterprises Inc. $19.95.

Bluebeard 1963 — ★★★
French biography of Henri-Desire Landru, who seduced and murdered 11 women and was subsequently beheaded. Dubbed into English. 108m; VHS. **C:** Charles Denner; Danielle Darrieux; Michele Morgan; Hildegarde Knef; Stephane Audran; Directed by Claude Chabrol. **Pr:** Joseph E. Levine. **A:** Jr. High-Adult. **P:** Entertainment. **U:** Home. **Mov-Ent:** Biography: Law Enforcement. **Acq:** Purchase. **Dist:** New Line Home Video.

Bluebeard 1972 (R) — ★½
Lady killer Burton knocks off series of beautiful wives in soporific remake of the infamous story. 128m; VHS, DVD, Wide. **C:** Richard Burton; Raquel Welch; Joey Heatherton; Nathalie Delon; Virna Lisi; Sybil Danning; Directed by Edward Dmytryk; Written by Edward Dmytryk; Ennio de Concini; Maria Pia Fusco; Cinematography by Gabor Pogany; Music by Ennio Morricone. **Pr:** Cinerama Releasing. **A:** College-Adult. **P:** Entertainment. **U:** Home. **Mov-Ent. Acq:** Purchase. **Dist:** Lions Gate Television Corp. $59.95.

Bluebeard 2009 (Unrated) — ★★
In the 1950s, Catherine insists on reading the Charles Perrault folktale of the murderous Bluebeard to her sister and as she does the viewer sees it come alive onscreen. In the story, impoverished teenaged sisters Anne and Marie-Catherine have no dowries but that doesn't matter to local squire Bluebeard (probably because his previous wives were never seen again). Marie-Catherine agrees to the marriage and he has one rule: don't open the forbidden room while he is away. Of course, she can't resist. Breillat always adds a feminist twist to her pictures and this stylized fantasy is no exception. French with subtitles. 80m; On Demand, Wide. **C:** Dominique Thomas; Lola Creton; Daphne Baiwir; Marilou Lopes-Benites; Lola Giovannetti; Farida Khelfa; Isabella Lapouge; Directed by Catherine Breillat; Written by Catherine Breillat; Cinematography by Vilko Filac. **Pr:** Jean-Francois Lepetit; Sylvette Frydman; Flach Films; CB Films; Arte France; Strand Releasing. **A:** Sr. High-Adult. **P:** Entertainment. **U:** Home. **L:** French. **Mov-Ent:** Folklore & Legends. **Acq:** Purchase. **Dist:** Strand Releasing; Amazon.com Inc.; Movies Unlimited.

Bluebeard's Castle 1992
Sylvia Sass and Kolos Kovats perform in Bartok's one act opera. Sir Georg Solti conducts the London Philharmonic Orchestra. 58m; VHS. **A:** Jr. High-Adult. **P:** Entertainment. **U:** Home. **Mov-Ent:** Music Video, Music--Performance. **Acq:** Purchase. **Dist:** Music Video Distributors; Home Vision Cinema. $24.95.

Bluebeard's Eighth Wife 1938 — ★★
Problematic comedy set on the French Riviera about a spoiled millionaire (Cooper) who's been married seven times and wants to go for eight with Colbert, the daughter of a destitute aristocrat. Good for a few laughs, but Coop seemed out of place in his role. Based on the play by Alfred Savoir, American version by Charlton Andrews. 86m/B/W; VHS, DVD, CC. **C:** Claudette Colbert; Gary Cooper; David Niven; Edward Everett Horton; Elizabeth Patterson; Herman Bing; William Hymer; Franklin Pangborn; Directed by Ernst Lubitsch; Written by Charles Brackett; Billy Wilder; Cinematography by Leo Tover; Music by Werner R. Heymann; Frederick "Friedrich" Hollander. **Pr:** Ernst Lubitsch; Ernst Lubitsch; Paramount Pictures. **A:** Sr. High-Adult. **P:** Entertainment. **U:** Home. **Mov-Ent:** Comedy--Romantic, Marriage, France. **Acq:** Purchase. **Dist:** Universal Studios Home Video. $14.98.

Blueberries for Sal 1967
An iconographic film in which a little girl and a little bear find themselves paired with the wrong mothers while picking blueberries. 9m; VHS, 3/4 U. **Pr:** Morton Schindel. **A:** Preschool-Primary. **P:** Entertainment. **U:** Institution, SURA. **Chl-Juv:** Family Viewing, Fantasy. **Acq:** Purchase. **Dist:** Weston Woods Studios.

Blueberry Hill 1988 (R) — ★½
While her mother struggles with the grief over husband's death, a young girl in a small town learns about life, music, and her late father from a jazz singer. Good soundtrack. 93m; VHS, Streaming. **C:** Jennifer Rubin; Carrie Snodgress; Margaret Avery; Directed by Strathford Hamilton. **Pr:** MGM Home Entertainment. **A:** Sr. High-Adult. **P:** Entertainment. **U:** Home. **Mov-Ent:** Comedy-Drama, Music--Jazz. **Acq:** Purchase. **Dist:** $79.98.

Bluebirds Up Close 19??
National Audubon presentation introducing the beauty of native U.S. bluebirds. 50m; VHS. **A:** Jr. High-Adult. **P:** Education. **U:** Institution. **Gen-Edu:** Birds. **Acq:** Purchase. **Dist:** Ark Media Group Ltd.

Bluefish Blitz 19??
Enjoy watching anglers bag bluefish by the bushel as they head out into waist-deep surf. 60m; VHS. **A:** Adult. **P:** Instruction. **U:** Home. **Spo-Rec:** Fishing. **Acq:** Purchase. **Dist:** Bennett Marine Video. $29.95.

Bluefish on Light Tackle 1984
Add drama and expertise to your bluefishing after viewing this videos proven methods for locating and catching blues using several different types of gear. 60m; VHS. **Pr:** 3M Leisure Time Productions. **A:** Family. **P:** Instruction. **U:** Home. **Spo-Rec:** Sports--General, Fishing. **Acq:** Purchase. **Dist:** Bennett Marine Video. $19.95.

Bluegrass Banjo Don Reno Style 1996
Offers Reno-style banjo lessons. Teaches traditional bluegrass breakdowns with chord-based solos, percussive techniques and single-string runs. Includes tab. 60m; VHS. **A:** Adult. **P:** Instruction. **U:** Home. **How-Ins:** Music--Instruction, How-To. **Acq:** Purchase. **Dist:** Homespun Tapes Ltd. $39.95.

The Bluegrass Banjo of Sonny Osborne 199?
Informal conversational sessions, detailed instruction, historical reminiscences, and insightful advice from the legendary bluegrass player. 90m; VHS. **A:** Sr. High-Adult. **P:** Education. **U:** Home. **How-Ins:** Music--Instruction. **Acq:** Purchase. **Dist:** Hal Leonard Corp. $39.95.

The Bluegrass Banjo of Sonny Osborne 1996
Detailed instruction is given, as well as historical reminiscenses and insightful advice. Teaches walk-downs, unusual endings, pedal steel-like licks, back-ups, chordal harmonies, and chiming. Includes tab. 90m; VHS. **A:** Adult. **P:** Instruction. **U:** Home. **How-Ins:** Music--Instruction, How-To. **Acq:** Purchase. **Dist:** Homespun Tapes Ltd. $49.95.

Bluegrass Banjo: Tune and Techniques 1991
Banjo king Tony Trischka and other banjo greats demonstrate how to get distinct sounds, covering such techniques as rools, chokes and slides, timing and speed problems, syncopation, improvisation, intros and endings, chord inversions, back up techniques and much more. 90m; VHS. **Pr:** Homespun Video. **A:** Sr. High-Adult. **P:** Instruction. **U:** Home. **How-Ins:** How-To, Music--Instruction. **Acq:** Purchase. **Dist:** Homespun Tapes Ltd. $49.95.

Bluegrass Banjo'Level One 1980
Ten programs which teach the beginner how to play bluegrass banjo by developing picking techniques and mastering traditional songs. 30m; VHS, 3/4 U, Special order formats. **Pr:** The Owl. **A:** Sr. High-Adult. **P:** Education. **U:** Institution, CCTV, CATV, BCTV. **Fin-Art:** How-To. **Acq:** Purchase, Rent/Lease, Duplication License, Off-Air Record. **Dist:** Inspired Corp.

Bluegrass Bass 1990
Ed Marsh teaches the basic skills needed to play the upright bass. ?m; VHS. **C:** Ed Marsh. **A:** Family. **P:** Entertainment. **U:** Home. **How-Ins:** How-To, Music--Instruction. **Acq:** Purchase. **Dist:** Texas Music and Video; Music Video Distributors. $29.95.

Bluegrass, Blackmarket 1994
Award-winning documentary which outlines the issues faced by the depressed rural areas in Kentucky due to little or no job availability which is forcing unemployed individuals to turn to the income potential available in the cultivation of marijuana. Includes comments from DEA agent, Task Force soldiers, a marijuana grower, Owsley County's Commonwealth Attorney, and a small town newspaper editor. 29m; VHS, 3/4 U. **A:** Adult. **P:** Education. **U:** Institution, SURA. **Gen-Edu:** Documentary Films, Economics, Poverty. **Acq:** Purchase, Rent/Lease. **Dist:** Appalshop Films & Video. $200.00.

Bluegrass Fiddle: A Private Lesson with Richard Greene 199?
Classically trained bluegrass virtuoso shares musical ideas, exercises, and instrumental examples. 85m; VHS. **A:** Sr. High-Adult. **P:** Education. **U:** Home. **How-Ins:** Music--Instruction. **Acq:** Purchase. **Dist:** Hal Leonard Corp. $29.95.

Bluegrass Fiddle Classics 1991
Kenny Kosek shows how to improve fiddle playing by demonstrating proper technique for bowing, fingering, licks, tricks of the trade, and much more. 90m; VHS. **Pr:** Homespun Video. **A:** Sr. High-Adult. **P:** Instruction. **U:** Home. **How-Ins:** How-To, Music--Instruction. **Acq:** Purchase. **Dist:** Homespun Tapes Ltd. $49.95.

Bluegrass Guitar: Building Powerful Solos 199?
David Grier analyzes and demonstrates his technique using original arrangements. Intended for the intermediate player. 75m; VHS. **A:** Sr. High-Adult. **P:** Education. **U:** Home. **How-Ins:** Music--Instruction. **Acq:** Purchase. **Dist:** Hal Leonard Corp. $39.95.

Bluegrass Jam Session 19??
Joe Carr and Alan Munde perform 15 songs for you to practice with. ?m; VHS. **C:** Alan Munde; Joe Carr. **A:** Jr. High-Adult. **P:** Entertainment. **U:** Home. **How-Ins:** Music--Instruction. **Acq:** Purchase. **Dist:** Music Video Distributors; Texas Music and Video. $29.95.

Bluegrass Mandolin 1996
Teaches the basics of bluegrass picking, dominant mandolin styles, cross-picking, rhythm chops, and left-hand fretting. Includes music and tab. 102m; VHS. **A:** Adult. **P:** Instruction. **U:** Home. **How-Ins:** Music--Instruction, How-To. **Acq:** Purchase. **Dist:** Homespun Tapes Ltd. $39.95.

The Bluegrass Mandolin of Ronnie McCoury 199?
Accomplished mandolin player documents his techniques for learning players using original repertoire. 80m; VHS. **A:** Sr. High-Adult. **P:** Education. **U:** Home. **How-Ins:** Music--Instruction. **Acq:** Purchase. **Dist:** Hal Leonard Corp. $39.95.

Bluegrass Summit Performance 1996
Features powerful music and high emotions. Features a tribute to Don Stover. 60m; VHS. **A:** Family. **P:** Entertainment. **U:** Home. **Mov-Ent:** Music--Performance. **Acq:** Purchase. **Dist:** Homespun Tapes Ltd. $24.95.

Blueprint for a Productive Baseball Practice 2011 (Unrated)
Coach Gary Gilmore presents an entire practice session of his Coastal Carolina University baseball team. 72m; DVD. **A:** Family. **P:** Education. **U:** Home, Institution. **Spo-Rec:** Baseball, Athletic Instruction/Coaching. **Acq:** Purchase. **Dist:** Championship Productions. $39.99.

Blueprint for Life 1992
Footage of a developing fetus provides a background for a presentation of how teratogens, harmful environmental substances, drugs and alcohol can endanger a forming fetus. 30m; VHS. **A:** Adult. **P:** Teacher Education. **U:** Institution. **Gen-Edu:** Child Care, Children. **Acq:** Purchase. **Dist:** RMI Media. $99.00.

A Blueprint for Murder 1953 (Unrated) — ★★½
Low-budget but well-done noir thriller. Whitney "Cam" Cameron (Cotten) becomes suspicious of his brother's attractive widow Lynne (Peters) when his young niece dies under strange circumstances (as did his brother). An autopsy reveals poisoning and Cam is convinced that Lynne wants to become the sole inheritor to her husband's estate and is going after her stepson next. Cam chases after Lynne, who's off on an ocean voyage, in order to prove she's a cold-blooded killer despite his attraction to her. 77m/B/W; DVD. **C:** Joseph Cotten; Jean Peters; Freddy Ridgeway; Gary Merrill; Catherine McLeod; Jack Kruschen; Barney (Bernard) Phillips; Directed by Andrew L. Stone; Written by Andrew L. Stone; Cinematography by Leo Tover; Music by Lionel Newman. **A:** Jr. High-Adult. **P:** Entertainment. **U:** Home. **Mov-Ent:** Boating. **Acq:** Purchase. **Dist:** Fox Home Entertainment.

Blueprint for Space: Science Fiction to Science Fact 19??
Astronaut Alan Shephard hosts this look at spaceflight, discussing it's history and what's in store for it's future. Combines footage of rare paintings, historical footage, and computer animation. 60m; VHS. **Pr:** Finley-Holiday Film Corporation. **A:** Family. **P:** Education. **U:** Home. **Gen-Edu:** Space Exploration. **Acq:** Purchase. **Dist:** Finley Holiday Film Corp. $24.95.

A Blueprint for Thinking 1992
Five-part series in which Dr. Sproul examines the basic elements of a worldview (epistemology, metaphysics, theology, anthropology, and ethics) and argues for the Christian worldview. Study guide is included. 30m; VHS. **A:** Adult. **P:** Religious. **U:** Institution. **Gen-Edu:** Religion, Philosophy & Ideology. **Acq:** Purchase. **Dist:** Ligonier Ministries Inc. $59.00.

Blueprint Reading Basics 1984
This series covers the most technically difficult chapters of the book Blueprint Reading. 40m; VHS, 3/4 U. **TV Std:** NTSC, PAL, SECAM. **Pr:** Gulf Publishing Co. **A:** Adult. **P:** Professional. **U:** Institution, SURA. **Bus-Ind:** How-To, Engineering, Industry & Industrialists. **Acq:** Purchase. **Dist:** Gulf Publishing Co. $325.00.
Indiv. Titles: 1. Dimensioning 2. Math Review and Math Shortcuts 3. Plant Coordinate Systems 4. Reading Drawings 5. Piping Drawings-Terms and Equipment 6. Piping Drawings-Valves, Flangers, and Pipe 7. Piping Drawings-Fittings and Orthographic Projections 8. Piping Drawings-Detail Dimensioning and Symbology 9. Pipe Fabrication Drawings.

Blueprint Reading for Metal Fabricators and Welders 1985
These five tapes show how to read mechanical blueprints for professional purposes. 75m; VHS, 3/4 U. **Pr:** Bergwall Productions. **A:** Sr. High-Adult. **P:** Vocational. **U:** Institution. **Bus-Ind:** Welding, Industrial Arts. **Acq:** Purchase. **Dist:** Bergwall Productions, Inc.

Blueprint Reading Skills 19??
Concise training program which offers instruction on how to read blueprints. Covers principles of orthographic projection, the alphabet of lines and planes, title block and notes/drawings, and metric drawings. 81m; VHS. **A:** College-Adult. **P:** Professional. **U:** Institution, Home. **Bus-Ind:** Architecture, Education, How-To. **Acq:** Rent/Lease. **Dist:** American Institute of Architects.

The Blueprint: Technique and Training for Triathletes 2005 (Unrated)
Clark Campbell discusses training schedules and programs for aspiring triathletes. 32m; DVD. **A:** Family. **P:** Education. **U:** Home, Institution. **How-Ins:** Sports--General, Athletic Instruction/Coaching. **Acq:** Purchase. **Dist:** Championship Productions. $39.99.

Blueprints in the Bloodstream 1978
Part of public television's "Nova" series. 57m; VHS, 3/4 U, Special order formats. **Pr:** British Broadcasting Corporation; WGBH Boston. **A:** College-Adult. **P:** Education. **U:** Institution, SURA. **Hea-Sci:** Documentary Films, Biology. **Acq:** Purchase, Rent/Lease. **Dist:** Time-Life Video and Television.

Blueprints: Planning a Building 1992
Discusses various aspects of plot plans, utilities location, and roles of support technicians. 14m; VHS. **A:** Adult. **P:** Vocational. **U:** Institution. **Bus-Ind:** Construction. **Acq:** Purchase. **Dist:** RMI Media. $59.00.

The Blues 19??
Bessie Smith, Big Bill Broonzy, Sonny Boy Williamson, T-Bone Walker, Sonny Terry and others are featured here. 57m/B/W; VHS. **A:** Jr. High-Adult. **P:** Entertainment. **U:** Home. **Mov-Ent:** Music--Performance. **Acq:** Purchase. **Dist:** Music Video Distributors. $19.95.

Blues 2008 (Unrated) — ★★
Urban thugs Chile and Head rob a convenience store and are spotted by a couple of cops. One calls for backup while the other chases the crooks straight into Pop Boudreaux's blues club. It becomes a hostage situation with manipulative Head trying to push follower Chile into escalating the violence while Pop tries to defuse the dangerous situation. 85m; DVD. **C:** Henry Sanders; Ty Hodges; Steve Connell; Marcus Folmar; Peter Gail; Ari Graynor; Sydney Tamiia Poitier; Keith Ewell; Directed by Brandon Sonnier; Written by Brandon Sonnier; Cinematography by Graham Futerfas; Music by Chris(topher) Westlake. **A:** Sr. High-Adult. **P:** Entertainment. **U:** Home. **Mov-Ent:** Crime Drama, Black Culture, Nightclubs. **Acq:** Purchase. **Dist:** Music Video Distributors.

The Blues Accordin' to Lightnin' Hopkins 1967
In his own words and music, bluesman Lightnin' Hopkins reveals his inspiration for the blues. A companion piece to the film "The Sun's Gonna Shine." 31m; VHS, 3/4 U. **C:** Directed by Les Blank. **Pr:** Les Blank; Les Blank. **A:** Primary-Adult. **P:** Education. **U:** Institution, Home. **Fin-Art:** Documentary Films, Music--Performance, Black Culture. **Acq:** Purchase. **Dist:** Music Video Distributors; Flower Films; Facets Multimedia Inc. $49.95.

Blues Alive 1983
Albert King, Junior Wells and Buddy Guy join John Mayall in a concert celebration of their blues roots. Also appearing are ex-Rolling Stone Mick Taylor and Fleetwood Mac's John McVie. 92m; VHS. **Pr:** Monarch Entertainment. **A:** Family. **P:** Entertainment. **U:** Home. **Mov-Ent:** Music--Performance. **Acq:** Purchase. **Dist:** BMG Entertainment; Music Video Distributors; Sony Pictures Home Entertainment Inc. $14.98.

Blues Alive 1990
The best of the blues from Memphis to Chicago. Includes songs and interviews with Buddy Guy, Ruth Brown, Booker T. Laury, Albert Collins, Don McMinn, Charles Brown, Ruby Wilson, Joyce Cobb, Junior Wells, Anson Funderburgh and the Rockets with Sam Myers, and Otis Rush. 71m; VHS. **C:** Directed by Jeff Jackson. **Pr:** Jeff Jackson. **A:** Jr. High-Adult. **P:** Entertainment. **U:** Home. **Mov-Ent:** Music Video, Interviews. **Acq:** Purchase. **Dist:** BMG Entertainment. $14.98.

Blues Alive 1993
From Chicago and Memphis, live performances by Albert Collins, Charles Brown, Buddy Guy, Ruth Brown, Joyce Cobb and Ruby Wilson, Junior Wells, and John Cephus and Phil Wiggins. 54m; VHS. **A:** Sr. High-Adult. **P:** Entertainment. **U:** Home. **Mov-Ent:** Music--Performance. **Acq:** Purchase. **Dist:** BMG Entertainment; Music Video Distributors. $16.98.

Blues and Rock Techniques for Hammond Organ 199?
David Cohen teaches keyboard players the techniques to play the powerful organ sound used in blues and rock music. Includes music. 82m; VHS. **A:** Family. **P:** Instruction. **U:** Home. **How-Ins:** Music--Instruction. **Acq:** Purchase. **Dist:** Hal Leonard Corp. $29.95.

The Blues Bag: Expanding Your Repertoire and Guitar Technique 199?
Two-tape series taught by Happy Traum. Explains bass runs, turnarounds, boogie-woogie bass lines, damping, improvising, and other advanced techniques using blues standards. 120m; VHS. **A:** Sr. High-Adult. **P:** Education. **U:** Home. **How-Ins:** Music--Instruction. **Acq:** Purchase. **Dist:** Hal Leonard Corp. $49.95.

The Blues Bag: Expanding Your Repertoire and Guitar Technique, Vol. 1 1992
Happy Traum examines 12-bar and 16-bar blues forms in classic tunes, and provides instruction in bass runs, turnarounds, boogie-woogie, bass lines, damping, and improvising. 120m; VHS. **A:** Jr. High-Adult. **P:** Instruction. **U:** Home. **How-Ins:** Music--Instruction. **Acq:** Purchase. **Dist:** Homespun Tapes Ltd. $79.95.

The Blues Bag: Expanding Your Repertoire and Guitar Technique, Vol. 2 1992
Happy Traum teaches chord progressions, neck positions, solo techniques, and styles of great players. 60m; VHS. **A:** Jr. High-Adult. **P:** Instruction. **U:** Home. **How-Ins:** How-To, Music--Instruction. **Acq:** Purchase. **Dist:** Homespun Tapes Ltd. $49.95.

The Blues Bag: Video One 199?
Series taught by Happy Traum. Explains bass runs, turnarounds, boogie-woogie bass lines, damping, and improvising using blues standards. 60m; VHS. **A:** Sr. High-Adult. **P:** Education. **U:** Home. **How-Ins:** Music--Instruction. **Acq:** Purchase. **Dist:** Hal Leonard Corp. $29.95.

The Blues Bag: Video Two 199?
Taught by Happy Traum. Explains advanced playing techniques using blues standards. 60m; VHS. **A:** Sr. High-Adult. **P:** Education. **U:** Home. **How-Ins:** Music--Instruction. **Acq:** Purchase. **Dist:** Hal Leonard Corp. $29.95.

Blue's Big Musical Movie 2000
Everybody wants Steve's help as Blue and her friends put together a backyard Music Show. Steve wishes he were better at finding clues and Blue's new friend Periwinkle tries to get Steve to watch her magic tricks, but there's so much to do! They have to make costumes, rehearse, build the stage, get the snacks ready, and find a singing partner for Blue. With gentle musical lessons, and Ray Charles voicing the character of G-Clef, this disc is a sure to be a hit with the kiddies. Parents may need to be prepared for perpetual viewing. 78m; DVD. **C:** Voice(s) by Ray Charles; Steven Burns. **A:** Primary. **P:** Entertainment. **U:** Home. **Chl-Juv:** Family Viewing, Music--Children, Animation & Cartoons. **Acq:** Purchase. **Dist:** Paramount Pictures Corp. $24.99.

Blue's Big News: Read All About It! 2001
Two episodes of the Nickelodeon show for preschoolers. 50m; VHS; Closed Captioned. **A:** Preschool. **P:** Entertainment. **U:** Home. **Chl-Juv:** Children, Animation & Cartoons. **Acq:** Purchase. **Dist:** Paramount Pictures Corp. $9.95.

Blue's Big News: The Baby's Here! 2001
Two episodes of the Nickelodeon show for preschoolers. 51m; VHS; Closed Captioned. **A:** Preschool. **P:** Entertainment. **U:** Home. **Chl-Juv:** Children, Animation & Cartoons. **Acq:** Purchase. **Dist:** Paramount Pictures Corp. $9.95.

Blue's Birthday 1998
From the Nickelodeon network show "Blue's Clues," this program invites viewers to help with the party arrangements for Blue's birthday and to discover Blue's clues to help host Steve figure out what the dog wants for her birthday. 38m; VHS. **A:** Primary. **P:** Entertainment. **U:** Home. **Chl-Juv:** Family Viewing, Animation & Cartoons, Education. **Acq:** Purchase. **Dist:** Library Video Network. $9.95.

The Blues Brothers 1980 (R) — ★★★
As an excuse to run rampant on the city of Chicago, Jake (Belushi) and Elwood (Aykroyd) Blues attempt to raise $5,000 for their childhood orphanage by putting their old band back together. Good music, quotable dialogue, lots of wrecked cars, plenty of cameos. A classic. 133m; VHS, DVD, Blu-Ray. **C:** John Belushi; Dan Aykroyd; James Brown; Cab Calloway; Ray Charles; Henry Gibson; Aretha Franklin; Carrie Fisher; John Candy; Kathleen Freeman; Steven Williams; Charles Napier; Stephen Bishop; Murphy Dunne; Cameo(s) Frank Oz; Steven Spielberg; Twiggy; Paul (Pee-wee Herman) Reubens; Steve Lawrence; John Lee Hooker; John Landis; Chaka Khan; Directed by John Landis; Written by Dan Aykroyd; John Landis; Cinematography by Stephen M. Katz; Music by Ira Newborn; Elmer Bernstein. **Pr:** Robert K. Weiss. **A:** Sr. High-Adult. **P:** Entertainment. **U:** Home. **Mov-Ent:** Musical, Automobiles, Music--Pop/Rock. **Acq:** Purchase. **Dist:** Universal Studios Home Video; Movies Unlimited; Alpha Video. $19.95.

Blues Brothers 2000 1998 (PG-13) — ★★
Eighteen years after the original caper, Landis, Aykroyd, and most of the original cast return to the scene of the crime. Jake's died but Elwood's (Aykroyd) still around. He gets the band back together, recruits a Blues cousin (Goodman), a half-foster-brother (Morton), and an orphan (Bonifant) in need of mentoring, and heads for a battle of the bands between New Orleans and Chicago. The music, performed by the original Blues Brothers Band as well as a rock and blues all-star lineup, is the highlight. As for the rest of the flick, watch the original instead. Did Aykroyd learn nothing from "Caddyshack 2"? 123m; VHS, DVD, DVD, CC. **C:** Dan Aykroyd; John Goodman; Joe Morton; Evan Bonifant; Nia Peeples; Kathleen Freeman; Frank Oz; Steve Lawrence; Aretha Franklin; B.B. King; James Brown; Erykah Badu; Darrell Hammond; Paul Shaffer; Murphy Dunne; Directed by John Landis; Written by Dan Aykroyd; John Landis; Cinematography by David Herrington; Music by Paul Shaffer. **Pr:** John Landis; Dan Aykroyd; Leslie Belzberg; Dan Aykroyd; John Landis; Universal Studios. **A:** Jr. High-Adult. **P:** Entertainment. **U:** Home. **Mov-Ent:** Musical, Music--Pop/Rock, Adoption. **Acq:** Purchase. **Dist:** Alpha Video; Movies Unlimited.

Blues Busters 1950 (Unrated) — ★★½
Another entry in the "Bowery Boys" series. When Sach emerges from a tonsillectomy with the velvety voice of a crooner, Slip cashes in by turning Louie's Sweet Shop into a nightclub, the better to showcase his buddy's talents. Sach's singing voice provided by John Lorenz. 68m/B/W; VHS. **C:** Leo Gorcey; Huntz Hall; Adele Jergens; Gabriel Dell; Craig Stevens; Phyllis Coates; Bernard Gorcey; David Gorcey; Directed by William Beaudine. **Pr:** Monogram. **A:** Family. **P:** Entertainment. **U:** Home. **Mov-Ent:** Comedy-Drama, Singing. **Acq:** Purchase. **Dist:** Warner Home Video, Inc. $14.98.

Blues by the Book 1993
Features Roy Book Binder as he provides instruction on the blues and ragtime styles of guitar playing and his own hillbilly country blues. He teaches several classic blues songs along with their variations, chord shapes, picking patterns, endings, runs, and slides. Includes music and tab book. 75m; VHS. **A:** Jr. High-Adult. **P:** Instruction. **U:** Home, Institution. **How-Ins:** Music--Instruction. **Acq:** Purchase. **Dist:** Homespun Tapes Ltd. $49.95.

Blue's Clues: ABC's and 123's 1999
Contains two episodes of the popular children's program "Blue's Clues" in which real-life host Steve invites young viewers into his computer-animated home to help him find clues and solve puzzles that dog Blue leaves. These two programs help children to explore the worlds of math and pre-reading, as they count, add, subtract and sound out words. 50m; VHS. **A:** Family. **P:** Education. **U:** Home. **Chl-Juv:** Family Viewing, Animation & Cartoons, Education. **Acq:** Purchase. **Dist:** Paramount Pictures Corp. $9.95.

Blue's Clues: All Kinds of Signs 2001
Two episodes of the Nickelodeon show for preschoolers: "Signs," and "Geography." 52m; VHS; Closed Captioned. **A:** Preschool. **P:** Entertainment. **U:** Home. **Chl-Juv:** Children, Animation & Cartoons. **Acq:** Purchase. **Dist:** Paramount Pictures Corp. $9.95.

Blue's Clues: Arts and Crafts 1998
Animated puppy "Blue" and live action host Steve invite youngsters to learn through solving clues in "Adventures in Art" and "What Does Blue Want to Make?". 50m; VHS. **A:** Preschool-Primary. **P:** Education. **U:** Home. **Chl-Juv:** Children, Education. **Acq:** Purchase. **Dist:** Paramount Pictures Corp. $9.95.

Blue's Clues: Big Band 2003
Blue and her friends sing songs, play instruments, hum tunes and create their own band in Blue's Big Band and Bedtime Business. 51m; VHS, DVD. **A:** Preschool. **P:** Entertainment. **U:** Home. **Chl-Juv:** Animation & Cartoons, Television. **Acq:** Purchase. **Dist:** Paramount Pictures Corp. $9.99.

Blue's Clues: Blue Takes You to School 2003
Blue tells about schooltime and education in two new episodes. DVD includes bonus episodes "Blue's ABC's" and "Math" plus Blue's School Search Game and more. 50m; DVD. **A:** Preschool. **P:** Education. **U:** Home. **Chl-Juv:** Animation & Cartoons, Television. **Acq:** Purchase. **Dist:** Paramount Pictures Corp. $9.95.

Blue's Clues: Blue's Big Holiday 2001
Two holiday episodes of the Nickelodeon show for preschoolers. 50m; VHS; Closed Captioned. **A:** Preschool. **P:** Entertainment. **U:** Home. **Chl-Juv:** Children, Animation & Cartoons. **Acq:** Purchase. **Dist:** Paramount Pictures Corp. $9.95.

Blue's Clues: Blue's Big Pajama Party 1999
Young viewers help host Steve figure out what his animated doggy pal Blue is trying to tell him in this popular series from Nickelodeon. In this episode, Blue tries to tell Steve what she would like to do before she goes to bed. 50m; VHS. **A:** Family. **P:** Entertainment. **U:** Home. **Chl-Juv:** Animation & Cartoons, Fiction--Children. **Acq:** Purchase. **Dist:** Paramount Pictures Corp. $9.95.

Blue's Clues: Blue's Discoveries 1999
Young viewers help host Steve figure out what his animated doggy pal Blue is trying to tell him in this popular series from Nickelodeon. This volume contains episodes dealing with sci-

ence and recycling. 50m; VHS. **A:** Family. **P:** Entertainment. **U:** Home. **Chl-Juv:** Animation & Cartoons, Fiction--Children. **Acq:** Purchase. **Dist:** Paramount Pictures Corp. $9.95.

Blue's Clues: Blue's First Holiday 2003
Includes four holiday episodes featuring Blue, Joe, Steve and the gang. 100m; VHS, DVD. **A:** Preschool. **P:** Entertainment. **U:** Home. **Chl-Juv:** Animation & Cartoons, Television, Holidays. **Acq:** Purchase. **Dist:** Paramount Pictures Corp. $12.95.

Blue's Clues: Blue's Safari 1999
Young viewers help host Steve figure out what his animated doggy pal Blue is trying to tell him in this popular series from Nickelodeon. This volume contains episodes dealing with exploring the wild and learning about animals. 50m; VHS. **A:** Family. **P:** Entertainment. **U:** Home. **Chl-Juv:** Animation & Cartoons, Fiction--Children. **Acq:** Purchase. **Dist:** Paramount Pictures Corp. $9.95.

Blue's Clues: Bluestock 2005
Blue's backyard celebration includes musical selections by They Might Be Giants, India Arie, Toni Braxton and Macy Gray. 102m; VHS, DVD. **A:** Preschool. **P:** Entertainment. **U:** Home. **Chl-Juv:** Television, Animation & Cartoons. **Acq:** Purchase. **Dist:** Paramount Pictures Corp. $16.99.

Blue's Clues: Classic Blues 2004
Blue and Steve play "pretend school" and make up rhymes. Includes Blue's Poetry Class Game and Oobi-The Friend Who's Always with You! 99m; DVD. **A:** Preschool. **P:** Entertainment. **U:** Home. **Chl-Juv:** Television, Animation & Cartoons. **Acq:** Purchase. **Dist:** Arab Film Distribution. $9.95.

Blue's Clues: Get to Know Joe 2002
Contains two Blue's Clues specials: Meet Joe and It's Joe Time! a total of four episodes from the Nick Jr. program. 96m; DVD. **A:** Preschool. **P:** Entertainment. **U:** Home. **Chl-Juv:** Animation & Cartoons, Television. **Acq:** Purchase. **Dist:** Paramount Pictures Corp. $19.99.

Blue's Clues: Magenta Comes Over 2000
Young viewers help host Steve figure out what his animated doggy pal Blue is trying to tell him in this popular series from Nickelodeon. In this volume, Blue's friend Magenta comes over to visit. 50m; VHS. **A:** Family. **P:** Entertainment. **U:** Home. **Chl-Juv:** Animation & Cartoons, Fiction--Children. **Acq:** Purchase. **Dist:** Paramount Pictures Corp. $9.95.

Blue's Clues: Meet Joe! 2002
Steve's brother, Joe is the new host of the show, bringing with him new games and play patterns. 51m; VHS. **A:** Preschool. **P:** Entertainment. **U:** Home. **Chl-Juv:** Animation & Cartoons, Television. **Acq:** Purchase. **Dist:** Paramount Pictures Corp. $9.95.

Blue's Clues: Playtime with Periwinkle 2001
Two episodes of the Nickelodeon show for preschoolers. 50m; VHS; Closed Captioned. **A:** Preschool. **P:** Entertainment. **U:** Home. **Chl-Juv:** Children, Animation & Cartoons. **Acq:** Purchase. **Dist:** Paramount Pictures Corp. $9.95.

Blue's Clues: Reading With Blue 2002
Blue and friends teach preschoolers about the joys of reading in two fun-filled episodes. Uses the interactive participation from preschoolers technique developed by Nick Jr. 51m; VHS; Closed Captioned. **A:** Preschool. **P:** Entertainment. **U:** Home. **Chl-Juv:** Animation & Cartoons, Television. **Acq:** Purchase. **Dist:** Paramount Pictures Corp. $9.95.

Blue's Clues: Rhythm and Blue 1999
Contains two episodes of the popular children's program "Blue's Clues" in which real-life host Steve invites young viewers into his computer-animated home to help him find clues and solve puzzles that dog Blue leaves. These two programs encourage pre-schoolers to discover music as they sing songs, listen for melodies, clap out beats and remember rhythms. 50m; VHS. **A:** Family. **P:** Education. **U:** Home. **Chl-Juv:** Family Viewing, Animation & Cartoons, Education. **Acq:** Purchase. **Dist:** Paramount Pictures Corp. $9.95.

Blue's Clues: Shapes & Colors 2003
Blue and her friends learn about the magic of color and shapes that are around them everyday. 50m; VHS, DVD. **A:** Preschool. **P:** Entertainment. **U:** Home. **Chl-Juv:** Animation & Cartoons, Television. **Acq:** Purchase. **Dist:** Paramount Pictures Corp. $9.95.

Blue's Clues: Stop, Look and Listen 2000
Young viewers help host Steve figure out what his animated doggy pal Blue is trying to tell him in this popular series from Nickelodeon. This volume contains the episodes "What Did Blue See?" and "What's That Sound?". 50m; VHS. **A:** Family. **P:** Entertainment. **U:** Home. **Chl-Juv:** Animation & Cartoons, Fiction--Children. **Acq:** Purchase. **Dist:** Paramount Pictures Corp. $9.95.

Blue's Clues: Story Time 1998
Animated puppy "Blue" and live action host Steve invite youngsters to learn through solving clues in "What's Blue's Favorite Story?" and "What Story Does Blue Want to Play?". 50m; VHS. **A:** Preschool-Primary. **P:** Education. **U:** Home. **Chl-Juv:** Children, Education. **Acq:** Purchase. **Dist:** Paramount Pictures Corp. $9.95.

Blues for a Red Planet 1980
The planet Mars is explored through actual photographs from Mariner and Viking probes, special effects, and elaborate model-making. Part of the "Cosmos" series. 60m; VHS, 3/4 U. **C:** Dr. Carl Sagan. **Pr:** Carl Sagan Productions. **A:** Jr. High-Adult. **P:** Education. **U:** Institution, SURA. **Hea-Sci:** Documentary Films, Astronomy. **Acq:** Purchase, Off-Air Record. **Dist:** Home Vision Cinema.

Blues Guitar Jammin' 199?
Five full songs to play along with feature on-screen notes and tab. 25m; VHS. **A:** Sr. High-Adult. **P:** Education. **U:** Home. **How-Ins:** Music--Instruction. **Acq:** Purchase. **Dist:** Hal Leonard Corp. $14.95.

Blues Guitar Legends II: Featuring the Styles of Blind Boy Fuller, Mississippi John Hurt, and Big Bill Broonzy 199?
Blues playing techniques intended for the intermediate-level guitarist. ?m; VHS. **A:** Sr. High-Adult. **P:** Education. **U:** Home. **How-Ins:** Music--Instruction. **Acq:** Purchase. **Dist:** Hal Leonard Corp. $19.95.

Blues Guitar Legends: In the Styles of Lightnin' Hopkins & Blind Blake 199?
Blues playing techniques intended for the intermediate-level guitarist. ?m; VHS. **A:** Sr. High-Adult. **P:** Education. **U:** Home. **How-Ins:** Music--Instruction. **Acq:** Purchase. **Dist:** Hal Leonard Corp. $19.95.

The Blues Guitar of Keb' Mo': Basic Techniques for the Contemporary Player 199?
Grammy-winning singer-songwriter teaches the basics of fingerpicking technique and traditional country blues. 75m; VHS. **A:** Sr. High-Adult. **P:** Education. **U:** Home. **How-Ins:** Music--Instruction. **Acq:** Purchase. **Dist:** Hal Leonard Corp. $29.95.

Blues Harmonica 19??
Instructor John Sebastian offers step-by-step demonstrations for blues, rock, and country tunes on the harmonica. Includes tips on instrument holding, techniques for vibrato, note-bending, "wah-wahs," tonguing, rhythm playing, and train effects. Also defines "straight" scale and "cross-harp" blues scale. 80m; VHS. **A:** Jr. High-Adult. **P:** Instruction. **U:** Institution, Home. **How-Ins:** How-To, Music--Instruction. **Acq:** Purchase. **Dist:** Cambridge Educational. $49.95.

Blues Harmonica Made Easy 19??
Learning to play blues harmonica can be easy with this video. ?m; VHS. **A:** Sr. High-Adult. **P:** Instruction. **U:** Home. **How-Ins:** Music--Instruction. **Acq:** Purchase. **Dist:** Inspired Corp. $14.98.

Blues in the Night 1941 (Unrated) — ★★
Unusually downbeat story about struggling musicians. Jigger (Whorf) forms a jazz/blues group with pals Nickie (Kazan), Peppi (Halop), Leo (Carson), and Leo's wife Ginger (Lane), who's their singer. They're not making any dough touring so they accept the offer of gangster Del Davis (Nolan) to play at his New Jersey roadhouse, where they're also introduced to hard-boiled dame Kay (Field), who immediately causes trouble. Whorf and Kazan later became better-known as directors. Harold Arlen and Johnny Mercer wrote the Oscar-nominated title song. 89m/B/W; DVD. **C:** Richard Whorf; Priscilla Lane; Betty Field; Elia Kazan; Jack Carson; Lloyd Nolan; Billy Halop; Wallace Ford; Peter Whitney; Howard de Silva; Directed by Richard Whorf; Anatole Litvak; Written by Elia Kazan; Robert Rossen; Cinematography by Ernest Haller; Music by Heinz Roemheld. **A:** Sr. High-Adult. **P:** Entertainment. **U:** Home. **Mov-Ent:** Music--Jazz. **Acq:** Purchase. **Dist:** Warner Home Video, Inc.

Blues Like Showers of Rain 197?
The history of Country Blues is examined with photographs and field recordings. Featuring Lightnin' Hopkins, Otis Spann, Little Brother Montgomery, Willie Thomas, Sunnyland Slim, Robert Lockwood, Speckled Red, and others. 30m/B/W; VHS, 3/4 U. **C:** Directed by John Jeremy. **Pr:** Paul Oliver. **A:** Sr. High-Adult. **P:** Entertainment. **U:** Institution, Home. **Mov-Ent:** Music--Performance, Black Culture. **Acq:** Purchase. **Dist:** Music Video Distributors; Rhapsody Films, Inc.; Facets Multimedia Inc. $24.95.

Blues Masters, Vol. 1 19??
The history, personalities, and evolution of the blues, featuring Son House, Leadbelly, Bessie Smith, Mamie Smith, Roy Milton and His Orchestra, Jimmy Rushing, Ethel Waters, and Big Bill Broonzy. Includes archival recording footage and photographs. 51m; VHS, DVD. **A:** Sr. High-Adult. **P:** Entertainment. **U:** Home. **Mov-Ent:** Music--Performance. **Acq:** Purchase. **Dist:** Facets Multimedia Inc. $19.98.

Blues Masters, Vol. 2 19??
More from some legendary blues performers, including Ida Cox, Billie Holiday, Big Mama Thornton, Muddy Waters, Joe Turner, Joe Williams, Buddy Guy, Jimmy Witherspoon, and B.B. King. Includes archival performance footage and photographs. 51m; VHS. **A:** Sr. High-Adult. **P:** Entertainment. **U:** Home. **Mov-Ent:** Music--Performance. **Acq:** Purchase. **Dist:** Facets Multimedia Inc. $19.98.

Blues Piano, Vol. 1: Beginning Blues Piano 1988
David Cohen provides easy-to-follow instruction for beginning blues piano enthusiasts. 60m; VHS. **A:** Sr. High-Adult. **P:** Instruction. **U:** Home. **How-Ins:** How-To, Music--Instruction. **Acq:** Purchase. **Dist:** Homespun Tapes Ltd. $49.95.

Blues Piano, Vol. 2: Learning Blues Piano 1988
David Cohen covers blues techniques and theories for the intermediate blues pianist. 60m; VHS. **A:** Sr. High-Adult. **P:** Instruction. **U:** Home. **How-Ins:** How-To, Music--Instruction. **Acq:** Purchase. **Dist:** Homespun Tapes Ltd. $49.95.

Blues Piano, Vol. 3: Expanding Your Technique 1991
David Cohen expands his piano lessons beyond the typical 12-bar blues pattern progressions and offers students advanced study in melodies, bass lines and chord progressions, theory, chord inversions, improvisation, rhythm patterns, and other techniques. 85m; VHS. **Pr:** Homespun Video. **A:** Sr. High-Adult. **P:** Instruction. **U:** Home. **How-Ins:** How-To, Music--Instruction. **Acq:** Purchase. **Dist:** Homespun Tapes Ltd. $49.95.

Blues Rock Guitar Soloing 199?
Session player Matt Gurman teaches various techniques used for soloing in the style of various contemporary artists. ?m; VHS. **A:** Sr. High-Adult. **P:** Instruction. **U:** Home. **How-Ins:** Music--Instruction. **Acq:** Purchase. **Dist:** Hal Leonard Corp. $14.95.

The Blues/Rock Piano of Johnnie Johnson: Sessions with a Keyboard Legend 199?
Performance and discussion of Johnnie's history and playing styles. 60m; VHS. **A:** Sr. High-Adult. **P:** Education. **U:** Home. **How-Ins:** Music--Instruction, Music--Jazz, Music--Pop/Rock. **Acq:** Purchase. **Dist:** Hal Leonard Corp. $39.95.

Blue's Room: It's a Hug Day! 2005
Collection of four episodes of Nick Jr.'s "Blue's Room." DVD includes two bonus episodes. 98m; VHS, DVD. **A:** Preschool. **P:** Entertainment. **U:** Home. **Chl-Juv:** Children's Shows. **Acq:** Purchase. **Dist:** Paramount Pictures Corp. $16.99.

Blues/Roots Guitar: Intermediate Level Fingerpicking 199?
Performer Steve James details five pieces in various blues styles. 80m; VHS. **A:** Sr. High-Adult. **P:** Education. **U:** Home. **How-Ins:** Music--Instruction. **Acq:** Purchase. **Dist:** Hal Leonard Corp. $29.95.

Bluesland: A Portrait in American Music 1994
A visual history of the blues, the music that influence jazz, R & B, and rock 'n' roll. Rare, vintage, and contemporary performances from Bessie Smith, B.B. King, Leadbelly, Muddy Waters, Son House, and others. Part of the "Masters of American Music" series. 90m; VHS. **Pr:** Toby Byron Multiprises. **A:** Sr. High-Adult. **P:** Entertainment. **U:** Home. **Mov-Ent:** Documentary Films. **Acq:** Purchase. **Dist:** BMG Entertainment. $29.98.

Bluetoes the Christmas Elf 1988
Bluetoes is an elf who's just too clumsy to help Santa on Christmas eve. Yet soon fate will conspire to give the little fella the break he deserves. This in turn will allow him to earn the nickname "Bluetoes." 27m; VHS. **Pr:** Lacewood Productions. **A:** Family. **P:** Entertainment. **U:** Home. **Chl-Juv:** Animation & Cartoons, Family Viewing, Christmas. **Acq:** Purchase. **Dist:** Facets Multimedia Inc. $14.95.

Bluewater Fishing Tips 19??
Sportsfishing captain James Marsh teaches advanced anglers techniques for catching big game fish. 60m; VHS. **A:** Family. **P:** Instruction. **U:** Home. **Spo-Rec:** Fishing. **Acq:** Purchase. **Dist:** Bennett Marine Video. $29.95.

Bluffing It 1987 — ★★
TV movie about an older man who has been disguising his illiteracy for years. 120m; VHS. **C:** Dennis Weaver; Janet Carroll; Michelle Little; Robert Sean Leonard; Cleavant Derricks; Victoria Wauchope; Directed by James Sadwith; Music by Brad Fiedel. **Pr:** Ohlmeyer Communications Company. **A:** Jr. High-Adult. **P:** Entertainment. **U:** Home. **Mov-Ent:** TV Movies, Learning Disabilities, Education. **Acq:** Purchase. **Dist:** No Longer Available.

The Blum Affair 1948 — ★★
In post-WWI Germany, a Jewish man is framed for the murder of an accountant and uncovers in his capture and prosecution a rat's nest of corruption and anti-Semitism. In German with English subtitles. 109m/B/W; VHS, DVD. **C:** Hans-Christian Blech; Gisela Trowe; Kurt Ehrhardt; Paul Bildt; Klaus Becker; Directed by Erich Engel. **Pr:** West German. **A:** Family. **P:** Entertainment. **U:** Home. **L:** English, German. **Mov-Ent:** Judaism. **Acq:** Purchase. **Dist:** DEFA Film Library; German Language Video Center. $24.95.

Blume in Love 1973 (R) — ★★★
An ironic comedy/drama about a man who falls hopelessly in love with his ex-wife who divorced him for cheating on her while they were married. 115m; VHS, DVD. **C:** George Segal; Susan Anspach; Kris Kristofferson; Shelley Winters; Marsha Mason; Directed by Paul Mazursky; Written by Paul Mazursky; Cinematography by Bruce Surtees; Music by Bill Conti. **Pr:** Warner Bros. **A:** Adult. **P:** Entertainment. **U:** Home. **Mov-Ent:** Comedy-Drama, Romance, Marriage. **Acq:** Purchase. **Dist:** Warner Home Video, Inc. $19.98.

Blunt Trauma to the Heart 1986
A lecture for health professionals about various coronary traumas. 25m; VHS, 3/4 U. **A:** Adult. **P:** Professional. **U:** Institution, CCTV, Home, SURA. **Hea-Sci:** Heart, Medical Education. **Acq:** Purchase, Rent/Lease, Subscription. **Dist:** Emory Medical Television Network.

Blush 1995 (Unrated) — ★★
Shanghai prostitutes and friends Quiyi (Ji) and Xiao (Saifei) are stripped of their vocation by the communist takeover in 1949. Quiyi manages to take refuge with her favorite customer, wealthy Lao Pu (Zhiwen), while Xiao is re-educated and becomes a worker in a silk factory. Eventually thrown out of the house by Lao's disapproving mother, Quiyi learns to make her own way. Xiao meets Lao after his family has lost their money and winds up marrying him, unhappily since Lao continually pines for Quiyi. Based on the novel by Su Tong; Cantonese with subtitles. 119m; VHS. **C:** Wang Ji; Saifei He; Zhiwen Wang; Wang Rouli; Directed by Li Shaohong; Written by Li Shaohong; Ni Zhen; Cinematography by Zeng Nianping; Music by Guo Wenjing. **A:** College-Adult. **P:** Entertainment. **U:** Home. **L:** Chinese. **Mov-Ent:** Drama, Prostitution, China. **Acq:** Purchase. **Dist:** First Run Features.

Bly and Woodman on Men and Women 1993
Six programs feature men's movement guru Robery Bly and women's issues expert Marion Woodman exploring the dynamics of relationships in various workshops. 57m; VHS. **A:** Adult. **P:** Education. **U:** Institution. **Gen-Edu:** Communication, Men, Women. **Acq:** Purchase. **Dist:** Applewood c/o Deringer. $149.75.

BMX Bandits 1983 (Unrated) — ★★
Three adventurous Aussie teens put their BMX skills to the test when they witness a crime and are pursued by the criminals. Much big air. 92m; VHS, DVD. **C:** Nicole Kidman; David Argue; John Ley; Angelo D'Angelo; Directed by Brian Trenchard-Smith; Written by Patrick Edgeworth. **Pr:** Imperial Entertainment. **A:** Family. **P:** Entertainment. **U:** Home. **Mov-Ent:** Bicycling, Adolescence. **Acq:** Purchase. **Dist:** Mill Creek Entertainment L.L.C. $79.95.

BMX Freestyle 19??
The latest BMX stunts are presented, with a feature on skateboard action. 30m; VHS. **A:** Primary-Adult. **P:** Entertainment. **U:** Home. **Spo-Rec:** Sports--General, Bicycling. **Acq:** Purchase. **Dist:** ESPN Inc. $14.95.

BMX: Win With the Pros 198?
Professional BMX bikers share their hints for getting ahead. Includes tips on the best way to ride a course, how to choose a bike, and how to fall. Also includes skateboarding demos. 60m; VHS. **A:** Jr. High-Adult. **P:** Entertainment. **U:** Home. **Spo-Rec:** Bicycling. **Acq:** Purchase. **Dist:** ESPN Inc. $29.95.

BMX X-Tremes 1987
An overview of the wacky world of BMX bicycling-stunts, gravity-defying action and spoke mania. 60m; VHS. **Pr:** Twin Towers Entertainment. **A:** Family. **P:** Entertainment. **U:** Home. **Spo-Rec:** Sports--General. **Acq:** Purchase. **Dist:** ESPN Inc. $29.95.

BNFS's Land of Enchantment 19??
Classic train footage captures freight action, intermodals, dramatic "meets," and Amtrak run-throughs along Burlington Northern Santa Fe's New Mexico Main with its backdrop of high plains and red cliffs. 58m; DVD. **A:** Family. **P:** Education. **U:** Home. **L:** English. **Gen-Edu:** Trains, U.S. States. **Acq:** Purchase. **Dist:** WB Video Productions; The Civil War Standard. $24.95.

BNSF: Burlington Northern and Santa Fe ????
Features over 80 diesel trains including C44-9Ws, SD70s, and SD75Ms at locations such as Cajon Pass, Barstow, Needles Subdivision, and Steven's Pass in California. 120m; VHS. **A:** College-Adult. **P:** Education. **U:** Home. **Gen-Edu:** Trains. **Acq:** Purchase. **Dist:** The Civil War Standard. $26.95.

BNSF's Trinchera Pass 19??
Classic train footage featuring Burlington Northern Santa Fe coal and manifest trains traveling the Twin Peaks sub between Trinidad, Colorado and Texline, Texas then on toward New Mexico. 90m; DVD. **A:** Family. **P:** Education. **U:** Home. **L:** English. **Gen-Edu:** Trains, U.S. States. **Acq:** Purchase. **Dist:** Highball Productions; The Civil War Standard. $35.95.

The Bo 19??
A lesson in using this martial-arts weapon from James Coffman, 7th-degree black belt champion. 45m; VHS. **Pr:** Creative Image. **A:** Jr. High-Adult. **P:** Instruction. **U:** Home. **How-Ins:** Martial Arts, How-To. **Acq:** Purchase. **Dist:** ESPN Inc. $39.95.

Bo Burnham: Words Words Words 2010 (Unrated)
Live performance by comedian Bo Burnham, who got his start posting pun-based songs on Youtube. 63m; DVD. **A:** Sr. High-Adult. **P:** Entertainment. **U:** Home. **Gen-Edu:** Comedy--Performance, Television. **Acq:** Purchase. **Dist:** Comedy Central. $14.98.

Bo Diddley and the All Star Jam Show 1992
The legendary rocker joins many of his friends to play live at the Irvine Meadows Ampitheater in 1985. Songs include "I'm a Man," "Bo Diddley," "Bo Put the Rock in Rock 'n' Roll," "Who Do You Love," "Bo Diddley's a Gun Slinger," and "Hey Bo Diddley." 55m; VHS. **Pr:** Polygram Music Video. **A:** Sr. High-Adult. **P:** Entertainment. **U:** Home. **Mov-Ent:** Music--Performance, Music--Pop/Rock, Black Culture. **Acq:** Purchase. **Dist:** Music Video Distributors; Facets Multimedia Inc. $19.95.

Bo Schembechler's Michigan Wolverines 2008 (Unrated)
Tribute film about longtime University of Michigan football coach Bo Schembechler with interviews by many of his contemporaries. 66m; DVD. **A:** Family. **P:** Entertainment. **U:** Home. **Spo-Rec:** Football, Sports--General. **Acq:** Purchase. **Dist:** A&E Television Networks L.L.C. $24.95.

Boa 2002 (R) — ★★
A prehistoric snake, 100 feet in length, makes a reappearance beneath a maximum security prison located in Antarctic. Warden Ryan (Wasson) calls for a rescue team, which includes paleontologists Robert (Cain) and his wife Jessica (Lackey). A handful of survivors try to make it from the prison to the plane but that's one hungry snake. 95m; VHS, DVD. **C:** Dean Cain; Elizabeth Lackey; Grand L. Bush; Craig Wasson; Mark A. Sheppard; Directed by Phillip J. Roth; Written by Phillip J. Roth; Terry Neish; Cinematography by Todd Barron; Music by Rich McHugh. **A:** Sr. High-Adult. **P:** Entertainment. **U:** Home. **Mov-Ent:** Arctic Regions. **Acq:** Purchase. **Dist:** Sony Pictures Home Entertainment Inc.

Boa vs. Python 2004 (R) — ★
A hunter imports a gigantic mutant python for a paid hunt for rich dilettantes outside Philly, and inevitably it runs amok. The FBI is called in since they obviously have giant-monster herding under their jurisdiction, and they 'borrow' a giant technologically enhanced snake from a local mad scientist to fight monster with monster. 92m; DVD, Streaming. **C:** David Hewlett; Jaime Bergman; Kirk B.R. Woller; Adamo Palladino; Angel Boris Reed; Directed by David Flores; Written by Chase Parker; Sam Wells; Cinematography by Lorenzo Senatore; Music by Jamie Christopherson. **A:** Sr. High-Adult. **P:** Entertainment. **U:** Home. **L:** Chinese, English, French, Georgian, Japanese, Portuguese, Spanish, Thai. **Mov-Ent. Acq:** Purchase, Rent/Lease. **Dist:** Sony Pictures Home Entertainment Inc. $9.99 7.99.

Board and Care 1979
A sensitive drama focusing on the desires of a retarded teenage boy and girl. 27m; VHS, 3/4 U. **Pr:** Ron Ellis. **A:** Jr. High-Adult. **P:** Education. **U:** Institution, Home, SURA. **Gen-Edu:** Documentary Films, Mental Retardation. **Acq:** Purchase, Rent/Lease, Duplication License. **Dist:** Pyramid Media. $225.00.

Board Development: Program 1 19??
An emergency meeting of the Centre for Volunteer Action Serving Hamford deals with an apparent show of favoritism by a member of the Board for a friend who is awarded a contract. May be a helpful guide for other not-for-profit organizations intending to avoid similar situations. Learning manual and leader guide available separately. Also includes two comic routines, "Not Just Another Training Film" and "Wide World of Meetings." 29m; VHS. **A:** College-Adult. **P:** Education. **U:** Institution. **Gen-Edu:** Voluntary Services, Management. **Acq:** Purchase. **Dist:** Access The Education Station. $199.00.

Board Development: Program 2 19??
Details the events surrounding a weekend retreat taken by a volunteer board as a strategy session. While trying to hammer out agreements, personality conflicts emerge. Could be helpful for real volunteer boards that face similar situations. Learner manual and leader guide available separately. Includes two comic routines, "Organizations Promoting Themselves" and "Committees, Committees, Committees." 29m; VHS. **A:** College-Adult. **P:** Education. **U:** Institution. **Gen-Edu:** Voluntary Services, Management. **Acq:** Purchase. **Dist:** Access The Education Station. $199.00.

Board Development: Program 3 19??
A lawyer who is a member of a volunteer board has a dream in which a court tries an ex-member who was responsible for a failed fundraiser. Highlights the maneuvers that accompany this potential scenario for real members of volunteer committees. Learner manual and leader guide available separately. Includes two comic routines, "Policy Anonymous" and "Planning." 29m; VHS. **A:** College-Adult. **P:** Education. **U:** Institution. **Gen-Edu:** Voluntary Services, Management. **Acq:** Purchase. **Dist:** Access The Education Station. $199.00.

Board Development: Program 4 19??
The funeral of a board member becomes the occasion for reflection by the others on the various problems tackled throughout the previous year. Learner manual and leader guide available separately. Includes two comic routines, "Recruitment Meeting of an Organization" and "Happy Trails." 29m; VHS. **A:** College-Adult. **P:** Education. **U:** Institution. **Gen-Edu:** Voluntary Services, Management. **Acq:** Purchase. **Dist:** Access The Education Station. $199.00.

Board-Staff Relations for the Human Services 1979
Seventeen short vignettes, each portraying a kind of interpersonal situation which might typically be encountered by a member of the board of directors of a human service agency. 25m; VHS, 3/4 U. **Pr:** University of Washington Press. **A:** College-Adult. **P:** Professional. **U:** Institution. **Bus-Ind:** Management. **Acq:** Purchase, Rent/Lease. **Dist:** University of Washington Educational Media Collection.

The Boarded Window 1978
Based on the classic horror story by Ambrose Bierce. Told in flashback sequences. 18m; VHS, 3/4 U; Open Captioned. **Pr:** Alan Beattie. **A:** Sr. High-College. **P:** Education. **U:** Institution, CCTV, SURA. **Mov-Ent:** Literature--American, Horror. **Acq:** Purchase. **Dist:** Phoenix Learning Group.

Boarding 199?
This compilation of the hottest boardsport action features segments on snowboarding, surfing, windsurfing, skateboarding and wakeboarding. Soundtrack features such artists as Foo Fighters, Megadeth, Skeleton Key, Supergrass and John Hiatt. ?m; VHS. **A:** Family. **P:** Entertainment. **U:** Home. **Spo-Rec:** Sports--General. **Acq:** Purchase. **Dist:** Tapeworm Video Distributors Inc. $19.95.

Boarding Gate 2007 (R) — ★★
It's not a good movie by any means but there's super-confident Argento in black undies, stiletto heels, and holding a gun to keep your interest. Bad girl Sandra used to be involved in a kinky sex and business relationship with shady American financier Miles (a menacing Madsen). She's now working for a shady import firm run by dragon lady Sue (Lin) and her husband Lester (Ng) and doing drug smuggling on the side for some quick cash. Sandra's also doing Lester and when he finds out about the drug deals, he pressures her into a murder-for-hire of Miles and a quick exit to Hong Kong. Why do these plans never go as expected? English, French and Chinese with subtitles. 93m; DVD. **C:** Asia Argento; Michael Madsen; Joana Preiss; Alex Descas; Kim Gordon; Kelly Lin; Carl Ng; Directed by Olivier Assayas; Written by Olivier Assayas; Cinematography by Yorick Le Saux; Music by Brian Eno. **A:** Sr. High-Adult. **P:** Entertainment. **U:** Home. **L:** French, Chinese. **Mov-Ent:** Drug Trafficking/Dealing. **Acq:** Purchase. **Dist:** Magnolia Home Entertainment.

Boarding House 1983 (R) — ★
Residents of a boardinghouse discover sinister doings in the basement. It does not occur to any of them to move to another house. 90m; VHS, DVD. **C:** Hank Adly; Kalassu; Alexandra Day; Directed by John Wintergate. **Pr:** Blustarr Films. **A:** College-Adult. **P:** Entertainment. **U:** Home. **Mov-Ent:** Horror. **Acq:** Purchase. **Dist:** Mill Creek Entertainment L.L.C.

Boarding School 19??
School is in session for those wanting to better understand the techniques of snowboarding. Shot on location at Whistler Mountain in British Columbia. Explains the relationship between body action and board movement. ?m; VHS. **A:** Sr. High-Adult. **P:** Instruction. **U:** Home. **How-Ins:** Sports--General, How-To. **Acq:** Purchase. **Dist:** Tapeworm Video Distributors Inc. $19.95.

Boarding School 1983 (R) — ★★
Basic teen sex comedy about students at a proper Swiss boarding school for girls who devise a plan to seduce the boys at a nearby school by posing as prostitutes. Kinski stars as the American girl who masterminds the caper. 100m; VHS, DVD. **C:** Nastassja Kinski; Directed by Andre Farwagi. **Pr:** Atlantic Releasing. **A:** Sr. High-Adult. **P:** Entertainment. **U:** Home. **Mov-Ent:** Sex & Sexuality, Education. **Acq:** Purchase. **Dist:** Lions Gate Television Corp. $69.95.

Boardinghouse Blues 1948 (Unrated) — ★★
A showbiz musical centered around a boarding house with tenant troubles. It's an excuse for popular black entertainers of the day to perform, including Lucky Millinder, Bull Moose Jackson, Una Mae Carlisle, and Stumpy and Stumpy. 90m; VHS, DVD. **C:** Dusty Fletcher; Moms (Jackie) Mabley; Directed by Josh Binney. **A:** Family. **P:** Entertainment. **U:** Home. **Mov-Ent:** Musical, Black Culture. **Acq:** Purchase. **Dist:** Facets Multimedia Inc.; Rex Miller Artisan Studio. $34.95.

Boardsailing 1: Learning the Basics 1990
Comprehensive look at sailboarding basics. 60m; VHS. **Pr:** ESPN. **A:** Sr. High-Adult. **P:** Instruction. **U:** Home. **Spo-Rec:** Sports--Water. **Acq:** Purchase. **Dist:** ESPN Inc.; Fast Forward. $29.95.

Boardsailing 2: The Short Board 1990
After mastering the basics of sailboarding, learn how to ride the short board, used for higher speed winds. 40m; VHS. **Pr:** ESPN. **A:** Sr. High-Adult. **P:** Instruction. **U:** Home. **Spo-Rec:** Sports--Water. **Acq:** Purchase. **Dist:** ESPN Inc.

Boardsailing . . . Maui High Performance 1991
Boardsailing, filmed as if you were there in the wind and waves! Shot at Hookipa Beach, Maui. 30m; VHS. **Pr:** NSI. **A:** Family. **P:** Entertainment. **U:** Home. **How-Ins:** Sports--General, Sports--Water, How-To. **Acq:** Purchase. **Dist:** Bennett Marine Video; NSI Sound & Video Inc. $19.95.

Boardsailing . . . Pushing the Limits 1991
See champions Robbie Nash, Matt Swizer, Mike Waltze, and more maxing out thier boardsailing expertise. Big waves, fast winds, and skilled riders make this an enjoyable video. Also includes a history on boardsailing from its origin to its present state. 30m; VHS. **Pr:** NSI. **A:** Sr. High-Adult. **P:** Entertainment. **U:** Home. **Spo-Rec:** Sports--General, Sports--Water. **Acq:** Purchase. **Dist:** Bennett Marine Video; NSI Sound & Video Inc. $19.95.

Boardsailing with Mike Waltze 199?
Mike Waltze, a pioneer of performance windsurfing, teaches you all you need to know to go from amateur to ace. 35m; VHS. **A:** Sr. High-Adult. **P:** Instruction. **U:** Home. **Spo-Rec:** Sports--Water. **Acq:** Purchase. **Dist:** Bennett Marine Video. $19.95.

Boardsailing Year, Vol. 1: 1986 Year in Review 1987
Spectacular photography and an upbeat score highlight the best boardsailing action from around the world. 105m; VHS. **Pr:** Solo Sports. **A:** Family. **P:** Entertainment. **U:** Home. **Spo-Rec:** Sports--General, Sports--Water. **Acq:** Purchase. **Dist:** ESPN Inc.; NSI Sound & Video Inc. $29.95.

Boardwalk 1979 (Unrated) — ★1/2
Manipulative drama has elderly diner owner David Rosen (Strasberg) and his ailing wife Becky (Gordon) living in a rapidly-declining Coney Island neighborhood. Gang leader Strut (Delgado) demands protection money from the local merchants but David won't pay. Escalating threats, violence, and family problems dominate. 98m; DVD, Blu-Ray. **C:** Lee Strasberg; Ruth Gordon; Janet Leigh; Kim Delgado; Eddie Barth; Joe Silver; Directed by Stephen Verona; Written by Stephen Verona; Leigh Chapman; Cinematography by Billy Williams. **A:** Adult. **P:** Entertainment. **U:** Home. **L:** English. **Mov-Ent:** Aging, Family. **Acq:** Purchase. **Dist:** Movies Unlimited.

The Boardwalk Club 1992
An elderly married couple have a longtime dispute about where to spend their retirement years. Sadie wants to go to Florida, while Max wants to remain in their New York home. 27m; VHS. **C:** Directed by Craig Shapiro. **A:** Sr. High-Adult. **P:** Entertainment. **U:** Home, Institution. **Mov-Ent:** Aging, Marriage. **Acq:** Purchase. **Dist:** The Cinema Guild. $59.95.

Boardwalk Empire: The Complete First Season 2010
HBO 2010- crime drama. "Boardwalk Empire": In 1920, Atlantic City treasurer Enoch 'Nucky' Thompson publicly supports Prohibition while privately running a bootlegging syndicate. He has to deal with the Feds and rivals, including Arnold Rothstein, Lucky Luciano, and Al Capone. "Anastasia": Nucky sends right-hand man Jimmy to Chicago to work for Al Capone and his boss, Johnny Torrio. "A Return to Normalcy": Nucky worries about how the elction will affect Atlantic City and many ponder their futures. 12 episodes. 733m; DVD, Blu-Ray. **C:** Steve

Buscemi; Michael Pitt; Shea Whigham; Michael Shannon; Kelly Macdonald; Michael K(enneth) Williams; Stephen Graham; Gretchen Mol. **A:** Adult. **P:** Entertainment. **U:** Home. **Mov-Ent**: Television Series, Crime Drama. **Acq:** Purchase. **Dist:** HBO Home Video. $59.99.

Boardwalk Empire: The Complete Second Season 2011
HBO 2010- crime drama. In "21," Nucky has problems with his organization, his brother Eli, and Jimmy. And Black bootlegger Chalky White gets into trouble with the KKK. "A Dangerous Maid": The Commodore is using his Coast Guard connections to disrupt liquor shipments so Nucky calls in apolitical favor. "Two Boats and a Lifeguard": When Nucky's father dies, he decides to take the body to Ireland for burial. 12 episodes. 720m; DVD, Blu-Ray. **C:** Steve Buscemi; Michael Pitt; Shea Whigham; Dabney Coleman; Kelly Macdonald; Michael K(enneth) Williams; Michael Shannon. **A:** Adult. **P:** Entertainment. **U:** Home. **Mov-Ent**: Crime Drama, Television Series. **Acq:** Purchase. **Dist:** HBO Home Video. $59.99.

Boardwalk Empire: The Complete Third Season 2012 (Unrated)
HBO 2010- crime drama. "Resolution" introduces the viewers to a new character, Gyp Rosetti. In "Spaghetti & Coffee", Eli is released from jail and re-entry proves difficult. "Bone for Tuna" has Nucky receiving an award from the Catholic church. Mickey ignores Nucky's mandates which upsets Eli and leads to horrible consequences in "Blue Bell Boy", and an attempt is made on Gyp's life in "You'd Be Surprised." 12 episodes. 733m; DVD, Blu-Ray. **A:** College-Adult. **P:** Entertainment. **U:** Home. **Acq:** Purchase. **Dist:** HBO Films. $79.98.

Boat Handling for the Sportfisherman 19??
Many an angler has struck paydirt only to lose the initiative to improper boat handling. Now you don't have to be left in the wake. Drive your boat to catch more fish. Clear instruction from an expert including graphics. 30m; VHS. **A:** Adult. **P:** Instruction. **U:** Home. **Spo-Rec**: Fishing. **Acq:** Purchase. **Dist:** Bennett Marine Video. $29.95.

Boat Handling Techniques for Fishermen 1992
Drop anchor, maneuver through strong winds, follow that tough catch, figure out your craft's optimum trolling speed. Learn the best speeds for your preferred bait. 40m; VHS. **A:** Adult. **P:** Instruction. **U:** Home. **How-Ins**: Boating. **Acq:** Purchase. **Dist:** Bennett Marine Video. $29.95.

Boat Insurance Made Easy 19??
Get the best insurance coverage for your money. Divided into four parts: Boat Insurance, Boating Liability, Fringe Benefits and Pricing. 20m; VHS. **A:** Adult. **P:** Instruction. **U:** Home. **Spo-Rec**: Boating, Insurance. **Acq:** Purchase. **Dist:** Bennett Marine Video. $16.95.

The Boat Is Full 1981 — ★★★
A group of refugees pose as a family in order to escape from Nazi Germany as they seek asylum in Switzerland. Available in German with English subtitles or dubbed into English. 104m; VHS, DVD. **C:** Tina Engel; Curt Bois; Renate Steiger; Mathias Gnaedinger; Hans Diehl; Martin Walz; Gerd David; Directed by Markus Imhoof; Written by Markus Imhoof; Cinematography by Hans Liechti. **Pr:** George Reinhart. **A:** Sr. High-Adult. **P:** Entertainment. **U:** Home. **L:** English, German. **Mov-Ent**: World War Two. **Awds:** Berlin Intl. Film Fest. '81: Director (Imhoof). **Acq:** Purchase. **Dist:** First Run Features; German Language Video Center; Simon Wiesenthal Center. $34.95.

Boat Maintenance 1988
Avoid costly boat mechanic fees by learning how to do small jobs yourself. 100m; VHS. **Pr:** Bennett Marine Video. **A:** Sr. High-Adult. **P:** Instruction. **U:** Home. **How-Ins**: Sports--General, Boating. **Acq:** Purchase. **Dist:** Bennett Marine Video. $49.95.

Boat Moving, Bottompainting and Cribbing 19??
Discusses weight distribution, pressure points, using jack stands and cribbing the boat. 90m; VHS. **A:** Sr. High-Adult. **P:** Instruction. **U:** Home, Institution. **How-Ins**: How-To, Boating. **Acq:** Purchase. **Dist:** Bennett Marine Video. $39.95.

The Boat That Jack Sailed 1973
These corrective and remedial reading programs are designed to reinforce basic reading skills. Children first see the story while listening to accompanying words. The story is then played back. 11m; VHS, 3/4 U. **Pr:** BFA Educational Media. **A:** Primary. **P:** Education. **U:** Institution, SURA. **Chl-Juv**: Language Arts. **Acq:** Purchase. **Dist:** Phoenix Learning Group.

Boat Trip 2003 (R) — **Bomb!**
Isn't it about time for Gooding, Jr. to give back his Oscar? Or at least fire his agent? In this pathetic attempt at comedy, he's Jerry, a lovesick guy distraught over a failed relationship. To the rescue comes his buddy Nick (Sanz), a loud-mouth skirt chaser who suggests a singles cruise. When Nick insults the travel agent, they're sent on a gay cruise, where Jerry falls for the ship's choreographer Gabrielle (Sanchez) and must pretend to be gay to win her. Yep, it's as crappy as it sounds. Gooding, Jr. tries hard, but he can't bail out this floater, which is aimed straight at the rocks of a cliche-ridden and spectacularly unfunny script and direction that wouldn't make the cut on a third-rate sitcom. 95m; VHS, DVD, UMD, CC. **C:** Cuba Gooding, Jr.; Horatio Sanz; Roselyn Sanchez; Vivica A. Fox; Maurice Godin; Roger Moore; Lin Shaye; Victoria Silvstedt; Richard Roundtree; Will Ferrell; Artie Lange; Bob Gunton; Jennifer Gareis; Directed by Mort Nathan; Written by Mort Nathan; William Bigelow; Cinematography by Shawn Maurer; Music by Robert Folk. **Pr:** Brad Krevoy; Andrew Sugerman; Gerhard Schmidt; Frank Huebner; Motion Picture Corporation of America; ApolloProMedia; Gemini Film Productions; International West Pictures; Artisan Entertainment. **A:** Sr. High-Adult. **P:** Entertainment. **U:** Home. **Mov-Ent**: Boating. **Acq:** Purchase. **Dist:** Lions Gate Television Corp.

The Boater's Video 1988
A course which reviews the safety aspects of boating. 55m; VHS. **Pr:** Bennett Marine Video. **A:** Primary-Adult. **P:** Instruction. **U:** Home. **How-Ins**: Sports--General, Safety Education, Boating. **Acq:** Purchase. **Dist:** Bennett Marine Video. $39.95.

Boating: Basic Navigation/Rules of the Road 1984
Commander Dave Smith demonstrates the basics of boating from navigation aids to determining boat speed. 60m; VHS, 3/4 U. **Pr:** RMI Media Productions. **A:** Family. **P:** Education. **U:** Institution, CCTV, Home. **How-Ins**: Boating, How-To. **Acq:** Purchase. **Dist:** Bennett Marine Video; RMI Media. $29.95.

Boating Basics 19??
A complete guide to boating for new boaters. Includes information on navigation, equipment, safety and more. 75m; VHS. **A:** Family. **P:** Instruction. **U:** Home. **Spo-Rec**: Sports--Water, Boating. **Acq:** Purchase. **Dist:** Bennett Marine Video. $24.95.

Boating: Cold Water Survivial 1983
This program explains what all boaters should know about hypothermia and cold water survival techniques. 60m; VHS. **Pr:** Video Travel, Inc. **A:** Family. **P:** Education. **U:** Home. **Spo-Rec**: Sports--General, Safety Education, Boating. **Acq:** Purchase. **Dist:** Bennett Marine Video; Vivid Publisher; RMI Media. $29.95.

Boating: Electronic Aids 1984
An overview of the current electronic equipment available for boaters is presented. 60m; VHS, 3/4 U. **Pr:** RMI Media Productions. **A:** Sr. High-Adult. **P:** Education. **U:** Institution, CCTV, Home. **Spo-Rec**: Boating, Electronics. **Acq:** Purchase. **Dist:** RMI Media.

Boating Safety 19??
Presents basic information on boating safety. 25m; VHS. **Pr:** Bennett Marine Video. **A:** Jr. High-Adult. **P:** Instruction. **U:** Home. **Spo-Rec**: Boating, How-To, Safety Education. **Acq:** Purchase. **Dist:** Bennett Marine Video. $19.95.

Boating Safety 1963
These two programs discuss the courteous and safe operation of boats near swimming and fishing areas and the correct utilization of safety equipment found on a pleasure craft. Programs are available individually. 18m; VHS, 3/4 U, Special order formats. **Pr:** U.S. Coast Guard. **A:** Family. **P:** Education. **U:** Institution, SURA. **Spo-Rec**: Sports--General, Boating. **Acq:** Purchase. **Dist:** National Audiovisual Center.

Boating Safety: Courtesy Afloat 198?
The courteous and safe operation of boats in swimming and fishing areas are demonstrated. 22m; VHS, 3/4 U. **Pr:** National Safety Council. **A:** College-Adult. **P:** Education. **U:** Institution. **Spo-Rec**: Sports--General, Boating, Safety Education. **Acq:** Rent/Lease. **Dist:** National Safety Council, California Chapter, Film Library.

Boating Safety: Safety Equipment 198?
The various types of life preservers and anchors available for boats are presented. 16m; VHS, 3/4 U. **Pr:** National Safety Council. **A:** College-Adult. **P:** Instruction. **U:** Institution. **Spo-Rec**: Sports--General, Boating, Safety Education. **Acq:** Rent/Lease. **Dist:** National Safety Council, California Chapter, Film Library.

Boating Series 1985
Various aspects of boating maintenance and maneuvering are described in this series. 58m; VHS. **C:** Dave Smith. **Pr:** Morris Video. **A:** Sr. High-Adult. **P:** Instruction. **U:** Home. **How-Ins**: Sports--General, Boating. **Acq:** Purchase. **Dist:** Morris Video; Bennett Marine Video.
Indiv. Titles: 1. Boating: Basic Navigation, Rules of the Road 2. Cold Water Survival 3. Boating Tech 4. Small Boat Engine Maintenance.

Boating Tech-Electronics That Perform 1988
The newest electronic equipment for boating is demonstrated and explained. 60m; VHS. **C:** Dave Smith; John Ford; Dan Asplund. **Pr:** Bennett Marine Video. **A:** Jr. High-Adult. **P:** Education. **U:** Home. **How-Ins**: Electronics, Boating. **Acq:** Purchase. **Dist:** Bennett Marine Video. $39.95.

Boating Technology—Electronics That Perform 19??
Commander Dave Smith demonstrates the latest electronic boating equipment, including radios, CB's, autopilots, loran, loran chart plotter, and radar. 60m; VHS. **A:** Family. **P:** Instruction. **U:** Institution. **Spo-Rec**: Boating, How-To, Technology. **Acq:** Purchase. **Dist:** Instructional Video. $29.95.

The Boatniks 1970 (G) — ★★½
An accident-prone Coast Guard ensign finds himself in charge of the "Times Square" of waterways: Newport Harbor. Adding to his already "titanic" problems is a gang of ocean-going jewel thieves who won't give up the ship! 99m; VHS, DVD. **C:** Robert Morse; Stefanie Powers; Phil Silvers; Norman Fell; Wally Cox; Don Ameche; Kelly Thordsen; Directed by Norman Tokar; Music by Robert F. Brunner. **Pr:** Ron Miller. **A:** Family. **P:** Entertainment. **U:** Home. **Mov-Ent**: Boating. **Acq:** Purchase. **Dist:** Walt Disney Studios Home Entertainment. $69.95.

Boats and Ships—3rd Edition 1982
A variety of boats and ships are discussed using simple nautical terms, and the functions of the crew and harbor personnel are examined. 14m; VHS, 3/4 U. **Pr:** Encyclopedia Britannica Educational Corporation. **A:** Primary. **P:** Education. **U:** Institution, SURA. **Gen-Edu**: Documentary Films, Boating. **Acq:** Purchase, Rent/Lease, Trade-in. **Dist:** Encyclopedia Britannica.

Bob & Carol & Ted & Alice 1969 (R) — ★★½
Two California couples have attended a trendy therapy session and, in an attempt to be more in touch with sexuality, resort to applauding one another's extramarital affairs and swinging. Wacky and well-written, this is a farce on free love and psycho-speak. Mazursky's directorial debut. 104m; VHS, DVD. **C:** Natalie Wood; Robert Culp; Dyan Cannon; Elliott Gould; Directed by Paul Mazursky; Written by Paul Mazursky; Larry Tucker; Cinematography by Charles B(ryant) Lang, Jr.; Music by Quincy Jones. **Pr:** Columbia Pictures. **A:** Sr. High-Adult. **P:** Entertainment. **U:** Home. **Mov-Ent**: Satire & Parody, Sex & Sexuality. **Awds:** N.Y. Film Critics '69: Screenplay, Support. Actress (Cannon); Natl. Soc. Film Critics '69: Screenplay; Writers Guild '69: Orig. Screenplay. **Acq:** Purchase. **Dist:** Image Entertainment Inc.; Movies Unlimited. $9.95.

Bob and Margaret Volume 1 1999
Animated series features the misadventures of Bob, a frustrated dentist, and Margaret, his chiropodist wife. This volume features the episodes "A Night In," and "Discomfort of Strangers." 44m; VHS. **A:** Jr. High-Adult. **P:** Entertainment. **U:** Home. **Mov-Ent**: Animation & Cartoons. **Acq:** Purchase. **Dist:** Paramount Pictures Corp. $14.95.

Bob and Margaret Volume 2 1999
Animated series features the misadventures of Bob, a frustrated dentist, and Margaret, his chiropodist wife. This volume features the episodes "Friends for Dinner," and "Blood, Sweat and Tears." 44m; VHS. **A:** Jr. High-Adult. **P:** Entertainment. **U:** Home. **Mov-Ent**: Animation & Cartoons. **Acq:** Purchase. **Dist:** Paramount Pictures Corp. $14.95.

Bob and Margaret Volume 3 1999
Animated series features the misadventures of Bob, a frustrated dentist, and Margaret, his chiropodist wife. This volume features the episodes "The Tale of Two Dentists," and "The Dental Convention." 44m; VHS. **A:** Jr. High-Adult. **P:** Entertainment. **U:** Home. **Mov-Ent**: Animation & Cartoons. **Acq:** Purchase. **Dist:** Paramount Pictures Corp. $14.95.

Bob Anderson's Stretching For Better Golf 1990
This video offers golfers a stretching program designed to prevent injuries and lower their scores. Since the stretches are done on the course, they will not require additional time and will even help relax golfers between holes. 40m; VHS. **A:** Jr. High-Adult. **P:** Entertainment. **U:** Home. **Hea-Sci**: Fitness/Exercise, Sports--General, Golf. **Acq:** Purchase. **Dist:** Stretching Inc. $19.95.

Bob Campbell's The Art of Hitting Slow-Pitch Softball 1992
Can the concepts of hitting baseballs be applied to hitting the softball? Learn the fundamentals on this instructional program. 45m; VHS. **A:** Jr. High-Sr. High. **P:** Instruction. **U:** Institution, Home. **Spo-Rec**: Baseball. **Acq:** Purchase. **Dist:** Cambridge Educational. $29.95.

The Bob Cummings Show 1958
Contains two episodes with commercials: "Bob Restores Male Supremacy" and "Bob Frees Schultzy." 60m; VHS. **TV Std:** NTSC, PAL. **C:** Robert Cummings; Rosemary DeCamp; Dwayne Hickman; Ann B. Davis. **A:** Family. **P:** Entertainment. **U:** Home. **Mov-Ent**: Television Series. **Acq:** Purchase. **Dist:** Moviecraft Home Video. $19.95.

The Bob Cummings Show "Love That Bob" Vol. 2 1955
Two episodes, "The Sheik" and "Bob and Schultzy Reunite" including original Winston cigarette commercials. 60m/B/W; VHS. **C:** Robert Cummings; Nancy Kulp; Joi Lansing; Barbara Nichols; Rosemary DeCamp; Dwayne Hickman; Ann B. Davis. **A:** Family. **P:** Entertainment. **U:** Home. **Mov-Ent**: Television Series. **Acq:** Purchase. **Dist:** Moviecraft Home Video. $19.95.

The Bob Cummings Show "Love That Bob", Vol. 3 1958
Contains two classic episodes: "Bob and the Dumb Blonde" and "Bob Judges a Beauty Contest." 60m; VHS. **C:** Robert Cummings; Nancy Kulp; Rosemary DeCamp; Dick Wesson; Barbara Nichols; Peter Lawford. **A:** Family. **P:** Entertainment. **U:** Home. **Mov-Ent**: Television Series. **Acq:** Purchase. **Dist:** Moviecraft Home Video. $19.95.

The Bob Cummings Show "Love That Bob" Vol. 4 1958
Contains two classic episodes: "Bob Helps Anna Maria" and "Bob Goes Birdwatching." Includes original commercials. 60m; VHS. **C:** Robert Cummings; Anna Maria Alberghetti; Nancy Kulp; Charles Coburn. **A:** Family. **P:** Entertainment. **U:** Home. **Mov-Ent**: Television Series. **Acq:** Purchase. **Dist:** Moviecraft Home Video. $19.95.

The Bob Cummings Show "Love That Bob" Vol. 5 1958
Contains two classic episodes featuring Cummings playing his own dad in "Grandpa's Christmas Visit" and "Grandpa's Old Buddy." Includes original commercials. 60m; VHS. **C:** Robert Cummings; Rosemary DeCamp; Andy Clyde; Nancy Kulp. **A:** Family. **P:** Entertainment. **U:** Home. **Mov-Ent**: Television Series. **Acq:** Purchase. **Dist:** Moviecraft Home Video. $19.95.

Bob Dylan: 30th Anniversary Concert Celebration 2014 (Unrated)
Taping of the 1992 concert event to celebrate the 30th anniversary of Bob Dylan's first Columbia Records album. 220m; DVD, Blu-Ray, Streaming. **A:** Jr. High-Adult. **P:** Entertainment. **U:** Home. **L:** English, French, German, Italian, Spanish. **Gen-Edu**: Music--Performance, Music--Pop/Rock. **Acq:** Purchase, Rent/Lease. **Dist:** Sony BMG Music Entertainment. $24.98 21.98 15.99.

Bob Dylan: The 30th Anniversary Concert Celebration 1993
"Bobfest" took place October 16, 1992 at Madison Square Garden in New York and lasted more than four hours. Performers included Eric Clapton, Eddie Vedder, Chrissie Hynde, George Harrison, Roger McGuinn, John Mellencamp, Willie Nelson, Tom Petty, Stevie Wonder, Neil Young, and others. This two-cassette version features 31 songs and includes a video montage of Dylan's career. 190m; VHS. **A:** Sr. High-Adult. **P:** Entertainment. **U:** Home. **Mov-Ent:** Music--Performance. **Acq:** Purchase. **Dist:** Sony Pictures Home Entertainment Inc. $34.98.
Songs: All Along the Watchtower; Like a Rolling Stone; Leopard-Skin Pill-Box Hat; Blowin' in the Wind; Boots of Spanish Leather; Gotta Serve Somebody; Foot of Pride; Masters of War; The Times They Are A-Changin'; It Ain't Me Babe; What Was It You Wanted; I'll Be Your Baby Tonight; Highway 61 Revisited; Seven Days; Just Like a Woman; When the Ship Comes In; War; Just Like Tom Thumb's Blues; I Shall Be Released; Love Minus Zero, No Limit; Don't Think Twice, It's All Right; Emotionally Yours; When I Paint My Masterpiece; You Ain't Goin' Nowhere; Absolutely Sweet Marie; License to Kill; Rainy Day Women #12 & 35; Mr. Tambourine Man; It's Alright, Ma (I'm Only Bleeding); My Back Pages; Knockin' On Heaven's Door.

Bob Dylan, Tom Petty & the Heartbreakers: Hard to Handle 1986
Dylan and Tom Petty and the Heartbreakers are captured in concert by director Gillian Armstrong. Features hits from both bands. 60m; VHS. **C:** Bob Dylan; Tom Petty; Directed by Gillian Armstrong. **Pr:** CBS/Fox. **A:** Family. **P:** Entertainment. **U:** Home. **Mov-Ent:** Music--Performance. **Acq:** Purchase. **Dist:** Home Box Office Inc. $19.98.

Bob Dylan—Unplugged 19??
Contains the Nov. 17, 1994 performance of Bob Dylan as filmed at Sony Studios for MTV "Unplugged" series. Classic songs include "Knockin' On Heaven's Door," "Love Minus Zero," "Desolation Row," "All Along the Watchtower," "Like A Rolling Stone," and John Brown, which has never before been seen on a Dylan release. ?m; VHS. **A:** Family. **P:** Entertainment. **U:** Home. **Mov-Ent:** Music--Pop/Rock, Music--Performance. **Acq:** Purchase. **Dist:** Music Video Distributors. $17.29.

Bob Evans The Donut Man: The Best Present of All 1992
The very first Christmas is dramatized and features Christmas favorites such as "Joy to the World," "Gentle Mary, Humble Mary," "O Come All ye Faithful," and more. ?m; VHS. **A:** Preschool-Jr. High. **P:** Entertainment. **U:** Home. **Chl-Juv:** Christmas, Music--Children. **Acq:** Purchase. **Dist:** Chordant Distribution Group; Music Video Distributors. $14.98.

Bob Funk 2009 (R) — ★½
Overly-earnest comedy. Mrs. Funk (Zabriskie) demotes eldest son Bob (Campbell) to the family futon company's janitor because his booze and broads lifestyle interferes with his work. She then hires ad exec Ms. Thorne (Cook) and depressed Bob suddenly gets a spark of interest in turning his life around. 90m; DVD. **C:** Michael Leydon Campbell; Rachael Leigh Cook; Grace Zabriskie; Amy Ryan; Edward Jemison; Stephen (Steve) Root; Robert Canada; Lucy Davis; Directed by Craig Carlisle; Written by Craig Carlisle; Cinematography by Lisa Wiegand; Music by Tim Montijo. **A:** Sr. High-Adult. **P:** Entertainment. **U:** Home. **Mov-Ent:** Alcoholism. **Acq:** Purchase. **Dist:** Magnolia Home Entertainment.

Bob Hope 1951
1951 TV special with Bob Hope and Dorothy MacGuire entertaining the troops in Korea. 60m/B/W; VHS. **C:** Bob Hope. **A:** Family. **P:** Entertainment. **U:** Home. **Mov-Ent:** Comedy--Performance, Variety, Television Series. **Acq:** Purchase. **Dist:** Karol Media. $9.95.

Bob Hope Chevy Show 1 1957
Two complete programs that were originally telecast on November 11, 1956 and March 10, 1957. Bob and his guest do spoofs of "Playhouse 90" and the Elvis Presley craze. Julie London, Perry Como, and Rosemary Clooney sing their current hits. All original commercials are included. 120m/B/W; VHS. **C:** Bob Hope; Joan Davis; Julie London; Perry Como; Rosemary Clooney; Lana Turner; Wally Cox. **Pr:** National Broadcasting Company. **A:** Family. **P:** Entertainment. **U:** Home. **Mov-Ent:** Variety, Television Series. **Acq:** Purchase. **Dist:** Shokus Video. $24.95.

Bob Hope Chevy Show 2 1957 — ★★
Bob Hope and a stellar array of guest stars present songs and comedy routines in these two complete programs, originally telecast on January 25, 1957 and April 5, 1957. All original commercials are included. 120m/B/W; VHS. **C:** Bob Hope; Eddie Fisher; Betty Grable; Harry James; Dan Rowan; Frank Sinatra; Natalie Wood; Janis Paige. **Pr:** National Broadcasting Company. **A:** Family. **P:** Entertainment. **U:** Home. **Mov-Ent:** Variety, Television Series. **Acq:** Purchase. **Dist:** Shokus Video. $24.95.

Bob Hope Chevy Show 3 1956 — ★★
Complete with those amazing car commercials of yesteryear, two classic Hope shows fill this tape. Includes a comedy routine of Bob having a meeting with TV executives from May 15, 1956 and a spoof of "I Love Lucy" from October 21, 1956. 120m/B/W; VHS. **C:** Bob Hope; Vic Damone; Leo Durocher; Desi Arnaz, Sr. **Pr:** National Broadcasting Company. **A:** Family. **P:** Entertainment. **U:** Home. **Mov-Ent:** Variety, Television Series. **Acq:** Purchase. **Dist:** Shokus Video. $24.95.

Bob Hope Comedy Hour 1950
Hope's 3rd appearance on TV, filmed in 1950. His guests include Marilyn Maxwell and Les Brown and his orchestra. See the youthful Hope in great form. 60m/B/W; VHS. **C:** Marilyn Maxwell; Bob Hope. **Pr:** National Broadcasting Company. **A:** Family. **P:** Entertainment. **U:** Home. **Mov-Ent:** Comedy--Performance, Variety. **Acq:** Purchase. **Dist:** Moviecraft Home Video. $19.95.

Bob Hope Remembers World War II 1994
Hope and wife Delores reminisce about his USO shows and early career, along with other celebrities. 52m; VHS. **A:** Adult. **P:** Entertainment. **U:** Home. **Mov-Ent:** Documentary Films, World War Two. **Acq:** Purchase. **Dist:** Kultur International Films Ltd., Inc. $49.95.

Bob Hope: The Road to Laughter 2003
Features more than 90 clips from Hope's movie career. 99m; DVD. **A:** Jr. High-Adult. **P:** Entertainment. **U:** Home. **Fin-Art:** Documentary Films, Biography: Show Business. **Acq:** Purchase. **Dist:** Virgil Films & Entertainment.

Bob Hope: The Ultimate Collection 2007
Highlight's from the entertainer's 50-year career, including TV moments, outtakes, movie shorts, Christmas specials, troop tours, and more. 481m; DVD. **C:** Bob Hope. **A:** Adult. **P:** Entertainment. **U:** Home. **Mov-Ent:** Comedy--Performance. **Acq:** Purchase. **Dist:** Acorn Media Group Inc. $39.97.

Bob Hope's Entertaining the Troops: The Vietnam Years 1998
Nine-tape set includes Bob Hope's television specials from his USO tours of Vietnam, 1964-1972. During these tours, Hope also visited U.S. bases in Guam, Okinawa, the Philippines, Korea, Thailand, and Wake Island, as well as holding shows aboard the USS Ticonderoga, Bennington, Franklin Delano Roosevelt, Hancock, Ranger, Coral Sea, and New Jersey. 540m; VHS. **A:** Family. **P:** Entertainment. **U:** Home. **Gen-Edu:** Vietnam War. **Acq:** Purchase. **Dist:** Guthy-Renker Direct Releases.

Bob Hope's Laughing with the Presidents 1998
Contains Bob Hope's last television special for NBC, in which the comedian looks back on his visits to the White House. ?m; VHS. **A:** Adult. **P:** Entertainment. **U:** Home. **Mov-Ent:** Presidency. **Acq:** Purchase. **Dist:** Guthy-Renker Direct Releases. $19.95.

Bob Hope's Unrehearsed Antics of the Stars 1998
Contains outtakes and bloopers from comedian Bob Hope's television specials. Stars featured include George Burns, Sammy Davis Jr., Tom Selleck, and others. ?m; VHS. **A:** Adult. **P:** Entertainment. **U:** Home. **Mov-Ent:** Outtakes & Bloopers. **Acq:** Purchase. **Dist:** Guthy-Renker Direct Releases. $19.95.

Bob Huggins: Cut & Fill Motion Offense 2008
Bob Huggins presents an on-floor demonstration of the Cut and Fill Motion Offense for basketball. 74m; DVD. **A:** Family. **P:** Education. **U:** Home, Institution. **Spo-Rec:** Basketball, Athletic Instruction/Coaching. **Acq:** Purchase. **Dist:** Championship Productions. $39.99.

Bob Huggins: Intense Practice Drills 2006
Offers a variety of offensive and defensive high-level basketball drills from Kansas State University's head coach Bob Huggins. 68m; DVD. **A:** Sr. High-Adult. **P:** Instruction. **U:** Institution. **Spo-Rec:** Basketball. **Acq:** Purchase. **Dist:** Championship Productions. $39.95.

Bob Huggins: Open Post Motion Offense 2004
Coach Bob Huggins demonstrates and discusses techniques for using the Open Post Motion Offense in basketball. 66m; DVD. **A:** Family. **P:** Education. **U:** Home, Institution. **Spo-Rec:** Basketball, Athletic Instruction/Coaching. **Acq:** Purchase. **Dist:** Championship Productions. $39.99.

Bob Huggins: Smothering Pressure Defense - Dominating the Box 2006
Features basketball drills designed to increase a team's defensive intensity by Bob Huggins, Kansas State University's head coach. 88m; DVD. **A:** Sr. High-Adult. **P:** Instruction. **U:** Institution. **Spo-Rec:** Basketball. **Acq:** Purchase. **Dist:** Championship Productions. $39.95.

Bob Huggins: 10 Strategies for Guarding Your Opponent's Best Plays 2007
Coach Bob Huggins discusses his views on defense in the game of basketball, as well as several defensive drills. 65m; DVD. **A:** Family. **P:** Education. **U:** Home, Institution. **Spo-Rec:** Basketball, Athletic Instruction/Coaching. **Acq:** Purchase. **Dist:** Championship Productions. $39.99.

Bob Huggins: The 'Dive and Fill' Zone Offense 2007
Coach Bob Huggins presents techniques for using his preferred version of the Zone Offense. 65m; VHS. **A:** Family. **P:** Education. **U:** Home, Institution. **Spo-Rec:** Basketball, Athletic Instruction/Coaching. **Acq:** Purchase. **Dist:** Championship Productions. $39.99.

Bob Huggins: The Evolution of Pressure Defense 2004
Features basketball drills focused on defensive pressure by Bob Huggins, former head coach at the University of Cincinnati. 73m; VHS, DVD. **A:** Sr. High-Adult. **P:** Instruction. **U:** Institution. **Spo-Rec:** Basketball. **Acq:** Purchase. **Dist:** Championship Productions. $39.95.

Bob Huggins: The Pressure 1-1-3 Zone Defense 2005
Instructions on how to play basketball. College coach Bob Huggins explains the 1-1-3 zone defense. 70m; DVD. **A:** Adult. **P:** Instruction. **U:** Home. **Spo-Rec:** Basketball, Sports--General, How-To. **Acq:** Purchase. **Dist:** Championship Productions. $39.95.

Bob Hurley: Building a Multiple Defensive System 2011 (Unrated)
Coach Bob Hurley discusses how basketball teams should not rely on a single defensive system, and change their defense to match their opponent's abilities. 72m; DVD. **A:** Family. **P:** Education. **U:** Home, Institution. **Spo-Rec:** Basketball, Athletic Instruction/Coaching. **Acq:** Purchase. **Dist:** Championship Productions. $39.99.

Bob Hurley: Developing Perimeter Players 2011 (Unrated)
Coach Bob Hurley demonstrates warm-up exercises and drills for increasing the skills of a basketball team's perimeter players. 85m; DVD. **A:** Family. **P:** Education. **U:** Home, Institution. **Spo-Rec:** Basketball, Athletic Instruction/Coaching. **Acq:** Purchase. **Dist:** Championship Productions. $39.99.

Bob Hurley: Motion and Zone Offenses 2011 (Unrated)
Coach Bob Hurley discusses two common basketball offensive systems and how to make best use of them. 77m; DVD. **A:** Family. **P:** Education. **U:** Home, Institution. **Spo-Rec:** Basketball, Athletic Instruction/Coaching. **Acq:** Purchase. **Dist:** Championship Productions. $39.99.

Bob Hurley: Practice Planning & Program Development 2011 (Unrated)
Coach Bob Hurley discusses building a successful high school basketball program. 150m; DVD. **A:** Family. **P:** Education. **U:** Home, Institution. **Spo-Rec:** Basketball, Athletic Instruction/Coaching. **Acq:** Purchase. **Dist:** Championship Productions. $39.99.

Bob James Live 1988
The pianist/composer/arranger/producer plays some of his best jazz, R & B and pop songs at this live outdoor concert at the 1985 Queen Mary Jazz Festival. 56m; VHS. **Pr:** V.I.E.W. Video. **A:** Jr. High-Adult. **P:** Entertainment. **U:** Institution, Home, SURA. **Mov-Ent:** Music--Performance, Music--Jazz. **Acq:** Purchase. **Dist:** Moonbeam Publications Inc.; V.I.E.W. Inc./Arkadia Entertainment Corp.; Music Video Distributors. $29.95.

Bob Knight: Advanced Tactics & Techniques for Man-to-Man Defense 2011 (Unrated)
Coach Bob Knight gives a thorough discussion of the man-to-man defense, and how to use it to stop offensive systems popular in basketball. 152m; DVD. **A:** Family. **P:** Education. **U:** Home, Institution. **Spo-Rec:** Basketball, Athletic Instruction/Coaching. **Acq:** Purchase. **Dist:** Championship Productions. $99.99.

Bob Knight: Advanced Tactics & Techniques for Man-to-Man Offense 2011 (Unrated)
Coach Bob Knight gives an in-depth presentation and discussion of basketball's man-to-man offense. 205m; DVD. **A:** Family. **P:** Education. **U:** Home, Institution. **Spo-Rec:** Basketball, Athletic Instruction/Coaching. **Acq:** Purchase. **Dist:** Championship Productions. $99.99.

Bob Knight: Encyclopedia of Zone Offense 2010 (Unrated)
Coach Knight gives an in-depth presentation on how to pick apart a basketball team using the zone defense. 251m; DVD. **A:** Family. **P:** Education. **U:** Home, Institution. **Spo-Rec:** Basketball, Athletic Instruction/Coaching. **Acq:** Purchase. **Dist:** Championship Productions. $119.99.

Bob Knight: Essential Drills for Building a Championship Program 2011 (Unrated)
Coach Bob Knight uses game footage and drills to explain the philosophy and skills he believes are necessary for a championship basketball team. 201m; DVD. **A:** Family. **P:** Education. **U:** Home, Institution. **Spo-Rec:** Basketball, Athletic Instruction/Coaching. **Acq:** Purchase. **Dist:** Championship Productions. $99.99.

Bob Knight: Spacing to Win 2010 (Unrated)
Coach Bob Knight discusses using spacing both offensively and defensively in basketball. 244m; DVD. **A:** Family. **P:** Education. **U:** Home, Institution. **Spo-Rec:** Basketball, Athletic Instruction/Coaching. **Acq:** Purchase. **Dist:** Championship Productions. $79.99.

The Bob Knowlton Story: Understanding the Importance of Communication and Situational Leadership 1995
Discusses the importance of communication within leadership. Includes leader's guide. 23m; VHS. **A:** Adult. **P:** Instruction. **U:** Institution. **Bus-Ind:** Management. **Dist:** American Media, Inc. $595.

Bob le Flambeur 1955 — ★★★
Aging Bob (Duchesne) is a down-on-his-luck gambler who visits the Deauville Casino with his friend Roger (Garret), who just happens to know croupier Jean (Cerval). Informed that the casino safe is bursting with cash, Bob decides to have a final fling by robbing the casino. Low-budget, bittersweet crime comedy. French with subtitles. 97m/B/W; VHS, DVD. **C:** Roger Duchesne; Isabel Corey; Daniel Cauchy; Howard Vernon; Gerard Buhr; Guy Decomble; Directed by Jean-Pierre Melville; Written by Jean-Pierre Melville; Auguste Le Breton; Cinematography by Henri Decae; Music by Jean Boyer; Eddie Barclay. **Pr:**

Jean-Pierre Melville; Jean-Pierre Melville. **A:** Sr. High-Adult. **P:** Entertainment. **U:** Home. **L:** French. **Mov-Ent:** Gambling. **Acq:** Purchase. **Dist:** Sony Pictures Home Entertainment Inc.; Ingram Entertainment Inc.

Bob Mann's Instant Karate 1987
Biomechanical researcher Bob Mann teaches the fundamentals of karate for young and old. 42m; VHS. **Pr:** Morris Video. **A:** Sr. High-Adult. **P:** Instruction. **U:** Home. **Spo-Rec:** Martial Arts. **Acq:** Purchase. **Dist:** Morris Video.

Bob Mann's Isometric Stretch 1987
Bob Mann teaches how to use isometric stretching for over all body health in simple, 15-minute programs. 26m; VHS. **Pr:** Morris Video. **A:** Sr. High-Adult. **P:** Instruction. **U:** Home. **Hea-Sci:** Fitness/Exercise. **Acq:** Purchase. **Dist:** Morris Video. $14.95.

Bob Mann's Weight Training at Home: Simplified 1988
Bob Mann and guest Carla Dunlap offer advice on maximizing weight lifting benefits. 30m; VHS. **Pr:** Morris Video. **A:** Sr. High-Adult. **P:** Entertainment. **U:** Home. **Hea-Sci:** Fitness/Exercise, Weight Lifting. **Acq:** Purchase. **Dist:** Morris Video. $12.95.

Bob Marley and the Wailers 1980
In this 1980 performance from Santa Barbara, the reggae band performs "Jamming," "I Shot the Sheriff," "Africa Unite" and many more. In addition, Marley is interviewed. 59m; VHS. **Pr:** Island Visual Arts. **A:** Jr. High-Adult. **P:** Entertainment. **U:** Home. **Mov-Ent:** Music--Performance. **Acq:** Purchase. **Dist:** Sony Pictures Home Entertainment Inc. $19.95.

Bob Marley and the Wailers: Live at the Rainbow 1977 (Unrated)
Marley and his group are seen in a performance taped at the height of their popularity. Songs include "Exodus" and "Get Up Stand Up." Taped at London's Rainbow Theatre. 72m; VHS. **Pr:** Island Records, Inc. **A:** Jr. High-Adult. **P:** Entertainment. **U:** Home. **Mov-Ent:** Music--Performance. **Acq:** Purchase. **Dist:** Music Video Distributors; Sony Pictures Home Entertainment Inc. $19.95.

Bob Marley and the Wailers: Time Will Tell 1991
A documentary of Marley's life and music, told in his own words, from his birth in the ghettos of Jamaica, to the 1963 formation of the Wailers, and the burgeoning popularity of reggae. 90m; VHS. **C:** Bob Marley. **Pr:** New Visions. **A:** Jr. High-Adult. **P:** Entertainment. **U:** Home. **Mov-Ent:** Documentary Films, Music--Reggae, Biography: Music. **Acq:** Purchase. **Dist:** Music Video Distributors; A&E Television Networks L.L.C.; New Video Group. $19.95.

Bob Marley: Catch a Fire 2006 (Unrated)
Looks at the recording of reggae star Bob Marley's classic album "Catch a Fire." 60m; DVD. **A:** Sr. High-Adult. **P:** Entertainment. **U:** Home. **Mov-Ent:** Music--Performance, Documentary Films, Music--Reggae. **Acq:** Purchase. **Dist:** Eagle Rock Entertainment Inc. $11.98.

Bob Marley: Legend 1984
This rockumentary looks at the life and music of Marley and features 13 of his songs. 55m; VHS. **Pr:** Don Letts. **A:** Jr. High-Adult. **P:** Entertainment. **U:** Home. **Mov-Ent:** Music--Performance, Black Culture. **Acq:** Purchase. **Dist:** Music Video Distributors; Sony Pictures Home Entertainment Inc.; Facets Multimedia Inc. $19.95.

The Bob Marley Story: Caribbean Nights 1988
This excellent, award-winning presentation shows Marley's performances from the very beginning of his career to the very end and includes the songs "Stir it Up," "Lively Up Yourself" and "Redemption Song." 90m; VHS. **C:** Bob Marley. **Pr:** Island Visual Arts. **A:** Jr. High-Adult. **P:** Entertainment. **U:** Home. **Mov-Ent:** Documentary Films, Music--Performance, Biography. **Acq:** Purchase. **Dist:** Facets Multimedia Inc.; Music Video Distributors. $19.95.

Bob McKillop: Building Your Offense with a Purpose 2010 (Unrated)
Coach McKillop discusses his beliefs on how to properly teach basketball team's offense, as well as presenting some drills. 86m; DVD. **A:** Family. **P:** Education. **U:** Home. **Spo-Rec:** Basketball, Athletic Instruction/Coaching. **Acq:** Purchase. **Dist:** Championship Productions. $39.99.

Bob MCKillop: Drills to Build Your Offensive Imagination 2013 (Unrated)
Basketball coach Bob McKillop gives an on-court demonstration of the offensive techniques he teaches at Davidson college. 64m; DVD. **A:** Family. **P:** Entertainment. **U:** Home. **L:** English. **Spo-Rec:** Athletic Instruction/Coaching, Basketball. **Acq:** Purchase. **Dist:** Championship Productions. $39.99.

Bob Munden: Fastest Gun Who Ever Lived 1990
A look at Guiness record holder Bob Munden, showing feats of skill with a six-shooter. Includes a how-to section. 70m; VHS. **A:** Sr. High-Adult. **P:** Entertainment. **U:** Home. **Gen-Edu:** Documentary Films, Firearms, Sports--General. **Acq:** Purchase. **Dist:** Gun Video. $49.95.

The Bob Newhart Show Christmas 197?
Bob invites his group therapy patients home during the holidays in "His Busiest Season." Bob wants to spend a quiet Christmas with Emily in "I'm Dreaming of a Slight Christmas" but everything goes wrong. 50m; VHS. **C:** Bob Newhart; Suzanne Pleshette; Marcia Wallace; Bill Daily; Peter Bonerz. **A:** Jr. High-Adult. **P:** Entertainment. **U:** Home. **Mov-Ent:** Television Series, Christmas. **Acq:** Purchase. **Dist:** Movies Unlimited. $14.99.

The Bob Newhart Show Special Release, Vol. 1: Bob's Wacky Patients 197?
Mr. Carlin is slapped with a paternity suit in "Carlin's New Suit" but doesn't mind when his accuser turns out to be beautiful. Then Mr. Carlin's marital advice to fellow patient Mr. Peterson causes him to fire Bob in "Who Was That Masked Man?" 50m; VHS. **C:** Bob Newhart; Suzanne Pleshette; Marcia Wallace; Bill Daily; Peter Bonerz; Jack Riley; Loni Anderson. **A:** Jr. High-Adult. **P:** Entertainment. **U:** Home. **Mov-Ent:** Television Series. **Acq:** Purchase. **Dist:** Movies Unlimited. $14.99.

The Bob Newhart Show: The Complete First Season 1972
Newhart stars as Dr. Robert Hartley, a Chicago psychologist married to teacher Emily. Bob is plagued by crazies at work and at home, including best friend/dentist Jerry, receptionist Carol, exasperating patient Mr. Carlin, and ubiquitous neighbor Howard. 24 episodes. 657m; DVD, CC. **C:** Bob Newhart; Suzanne Pleshette; Marcia Wallace; Bill Daily; Peter Bonerz; Jack Carlin. **A:** Family. **P:** Entertainment. **U:** Home. **Mov-Ent:** Television Series. **Acq:** Purchase. **Dist:** Fox Home Entertainment.

The Bob Newhart Show: The Complete Fourth Season 1975
Carol suddenly marries and Bob and Emily switch roles to stave off a midlife crisis, although there's jealousy brewing when Emily gets a promotion. And a booze-soaked Thanksgiving dinner proves to be a memorable event. 24 episodes. 624m; DVD, CC. **C:** Bob Newhart; Suzanne Pleshette; Marcia Wallace; Bill Daily; Peter Bonerz; Jack Carlin. **A:** Family. **P:** Entertainment. **U:** Home. **Mov-Ent:** Television Series. **Acq:** Purchase. **Dist:** Fox Home Entertainment.

The Bob Newhart Show: The Complete Second Season 1972
Offers the second season of the classic television comedy about psychiatrist Bob Hartley's life and work; Bob and wife Emily seek counseling while Bob feels inferior to Emily's dad. 645m; DVD. **A:** Family. **P:** Entertainment. **U:** Home. **Mov-Ent:** Television. **Acq:** Purchase. **Dist:** Fox Home Entertainment. $29.98.

The Bob Newhart Show: The Complete Third Season 1974
Bob's own neuroses begin to affect both his professional and personal lives so Emily suggests he get some help. He's also appalled when his younger sister (Pat Finley) falls in love with Howard and moves in across the hall. 24 episodes. 632m; DVD, CC. **C:** Bob Newhart; Suzanne Pleshette; Marcia Wallace; Bill Daily; Jack Carlin; Peter Bonerz. **A:** Family. **P:** Entertainment. **U:** Home. **Mov-Ent:** Television Series. **Acq:** Purchase. **Dist:** Fox Home Entertainment.

The Bob Newhart Show, Vol. 1 1972
The premiere episode of the comedy series, "Fly the Friendly Skies," finds psychologist Bob Harley leading his Fear of Flying workshop on a flight to New York and finding that wife Emily may be his latest patient. Bob addresses Emily's students on vocation day in "Tracy Grammar School, I'll Lick You Yet." 50m; VHS. **C:** Bob Newhart; Suzanne Pleshette; Marcia Wallace; Bill Daily; Peter Bonerz. **A:** Jr. High-Adult. **P:** Entertainment. **U:** Home. **Mov-Ent:** Television Series. **Acq:** Purchase. **Dist:** Movies Unlimited. $14.99.

The Bob Newhart Show, Vol. 2 197?
Bob tries to offer advice to secretary Carol and her new boyfriend and winds up ruining their romance in "Come Live With Me." In "Goodnight, Nancy" Bob's in trouble when his former college girlfriend and her husband pay a visit. 50m; VHS. **C:** Bob Newhart; Suzanne Pleshette; Marcia Wallace; Bill Daily; Peter Bonerz. **A:** Jr. High-Adult. **P:** Entertainment. **U:** Home. **Mov-Ent:** Television Series. **Acq:** Purchase. **Dist:** Movies Unlimited. $14.99.

The Bob Newhart Show, Vol. 3 197?
Bob wants to watch Monday night football but wife Emily wants to spend some quality time together in "Don't Go to Bed Mad." Bob's neighbor Howard thinks his son doesn't like him because he's not a sports fan in "Father Knows Worst." 50m; VHS. **C:** Bob Newhart; Suzanne Pleshette; Marcia Wallace; Bill Daily; Peter Bonerz. **A:** Jr. High-Adult. **P:** Entertainment. **U:** Home. **Mov-Ent:** Television Series. **Acq:** Purchase. **Dist:** Movies Unlimited. $14.99.

Bob Rizzo's Dance New York: Jazz 19??
Bob Rizzo teaches three jazz routines for beginner through advanced dancers. 50m; VHS. **A:** Adult. **P:** Instruction. **U:** Institution. **How-Ins:** Dance--Instruction. **Acq:** Purchase. **Dist:** Stagestep. $39.95.

Bob Rizzo's Dance New York: Lyrical 19??
Ray Leeper teaches three lyrical routines for beginner through advanced dancers. 45m; VHS. **A:** Adult. **P:** Instruction. **U:** Institution. **How-Ins:** Dance--Instruction. **Acq:** Purchase. **Dist:** Stagestep. $39.95.

Bob Rizzo's Dance New York: Tap 19??
Alan Onickel teaches three tap routines for beginner through advanced dancers. 45m; VHS. **A:** Adult. **P:** Instruction. **U:** Institution. **How-Ins:** Dance--Instruction. **Acq:** Purchase. **Dist:** Stagestep. $39.95.

Bob Rizzo's Dance Tricks ????
Demonstrates a variety of specialty steps, from simple to spectacular, that can be used in jazz style choreography. 50m; VHS. **A:** Adult. **P:** Instruction. **U:** Institution. **How-Ins:** Dance, Dance--Instruction. **Acq:** Purchase. **Dist:** Stagestep. $39.95.

Bob Rizzo's 50 Turns and Jumps 1994
Teaches over 50 turns and jump variations for beginning through advanced dancers, beginning with the basics and progressing to the more challenging. 60m; VHS. **A:** Family. **P:** Instruction. **U:** Institution. **How-Ins:** Dance--Instruction. **Acq:** Purchase. **Dist:** Princeton Book Company Publishers. $39.95.

Bob Rizzo's Jazz Class for Kids with the Riz-Biz Kids 1993
This video is geared towards ages 9-16 and has been specially designed for the beginner as well as the intermediate and advanced students. Includes jazz barre, floor stretches and progressions, presented in a clear and concise format. 55m; VHS. **A:** Family. **P:** Instruction. **U:** Institution. **How-Ins:** Dance--Instruction. **Acq:** Purchase. **Dist:** Princeton Book Company Publishers. $29.95.

Bob Roberts 1992 (R) — ★★★
Excellent pseudo-documentary satire about a 1990 Pennsylvania senatorial race between Robbins' titular right-wing folk singer/entrepreneur versus Brickley Paiste's (Vidal) aging liberal incumbent. Roberts seems like a gee-whiz kinda guy but he'll stop at nothing to get elected and he knows a lot about political dirty tricks and, even more important, manipulating the media to get what he wants. Robbins directorial debut turned out to be very timely in view of the 1992 Clinton/Bush presidential campaign. Features a number of cameos. Line to remember: "Vote first. Ask questions later." 105m; VHS, DVD, CC. **C:** Tim Robbins; Giancarlo Esposito; Ray Wise; Rebecca Jenkins; Harry J. Lennix; John Ottavino; Robert Stanton; Alan Rickman; Gore Vidal; Brian Murray; Anita Gillette; David Strathairn; Susan Sarandon; James Spader; John Cusack; Fred Ward; Pamela Reed; Jack Black; Tom Atkins; Helen Hunt; Peter Gallagher; Lynne Thigpen; Bingo O'Malley; Kathleen Chalfant; Matthew Faber; Matt McGrath; Jeremy Piven; Steve Pink; Fisher Stevens; Bob Balaban; Allan Nicholls; June Stein; Adam Simon; Ned Bellamy; Robert Hegyes; Lee Arenberg; Natalie Strong; Merilee Dale; Directed by Tim Robbins; Written by Tim Robbins; Cinematography by Jean Lepine; Music by David Robbins. **Pr:** Forrest Murray; Paramount Pictures; Miramax. **A:** Sr. High-Adult. **P:** Entertainment. **U:** Home. **Mov-Ent:** Politics & Government, Satire & Parody. **Acq:** Purchase. **Dist:** Baker and Taylor; Lions Gate Television Corp. $19.98.

Bob Saget: That Ain't Right 2007 (Unrated)
Taped performance of comedian Bob Saget's stand up act. 55m; DVD. **A:** Sr. High-Adult. **P:** Entertainment. **U:** Home. **Gen-Edu:** Comedy--Performance, Television. **Acq:** Purchase. **Dist:** Home Box Office Inc. $19.98.

Bob Soto's Diving in the Cayman Islands 19??
Guide on how to book a dive trip by a professional dive operator. Gives beginners the specifics. Good for vacations from economy to first class. 60m; VHS. **A:** Sr. High-Adult. **P:** Entertainment. **U:** Home. **Spo-Rec:** Scuba, Travel. **Acq:** Purchase. **Dist:** Bennett Marine Video. $24.95.

Bob the Builder: A Christmas to Remember 2003
Full-length animated holiday tale with Bob, Wendy and their crew of construction machines plus a guest appearance by Elton John. 50m; VHS, DVD. **A:** Preschool. **P:** Entertainment. **U:** Home. **Chl-Juv:** Holidays, Animation & Cartoons. **Acq:** Purchase. **Dist:** HIT Entertainment Ltd. $14.95.

Bob the Builder: Bob Save the Day! 2002
Bob and his friends get themselves into some hilarious predicaments in 'Bob Saves the Porcupines,' 'Scary Spud,' 'Runaway Roley,' and 'Dizzy's Bird Watch.' 50m; VHS, DVD. **A:** Preschool. **P:** Entertainment. **U:** Home. **Chl-Juv:** Animation & Cartoons, Television. **Acq:** Purchase. **Dist:** HIT Entertainment Ltd. $14.99.

Bob the Builder: Bob's Favorite Adventures 2006 (Unrated)
Animated children's television program. "Ballroom Bob," "Bob's Auntie," "Forget-Me-Knot Bob," and "Bob's Pizza" are the four episodes in this collection of the popular children's cartoon. 39m; DVD. **A:** Preschool-Primary. **P:** Entertainment. **U:** Home. **Mov-Ent:** Family Viewing, Animation & Cartoons, Children's Shows. **Acq:** Purchase. **Dist:** Lions Gate Entertainment Inc. $7.98.

Bob the Builder: Bob's Top Team 2007 (Unrated)
Animated children's television program. Bob is reminded how valuable his Can-Do Crew is when they successfully finish many different projects. 45m; DVD. **A:** Preschool-Primary. **P:** Entertainment. **U:** Home. **Mov-Ent:** Family Viewing, Animation & Cartoons, Children's Shows. **Acq:** Purchase. **Dist:** Lions Gate Entertainment Inc. $11.98.

Bob the Builder: Bob's White Christmas 2001
Five holiday-themed episodes featuring Bob, Wendy, and their crew of fun-loving machines. ?m; VHS. **A:** Preschool. **P:** Entertainment. **U:** Home. **Chl-Juv:** Animation & Cartoons, Children. **Acq:** Purchase. **Dist:** HIT Entertainment Ltd. $14.99.

Bob the Builder: Build it and They Will Come 2007 (Unrated)
Animated children's television program. Bob the Builder and his team teach the principles of hard work and perseverance as they complete building projects in their community. 85m; DVD. **A:** Preschool-Primary. **P:** Entertainment. **U:** Home. **Mov-Ent:** Family Viewing, Animation & Cartoons, Children's Shows. **Acq:** Purchase. **Dist:** Lions Gate Entertainment Inc. $7.98.

Bob the Builder: Building Bobland Bay 2008 (Unrated)
From the children's animated series, Bob the Builder and his Can-Do Crew build a town along the waterfront with the help of some exciting new machines. 45m; DVD. **A:** Preschool-Primary.

P: Entertainment. U: Home. Mov-Ent: Family Viewing, Animation & Cartoons, Children's Shows. Acq: Purchase. Dist: Lions Gate Entertainment Inc. $11.98.

Bob the Builder: Building Friendships 2003
Four animated stories with Bob and his friends that promote a positive "can-do" spirit, problem-solving, and teamwork. Includes Mr. Beasley's New Friends, Trix and the Otters, Bob and the Badgers and Hamish's New Home. 45m; VHS, DVD. A: Preschool. P: Entertainment. U: Home. Chl-Juv: Animation & Cartoons, Television. Acq: Purchase. Dist: HIT Entertainment Ltd. $14.95.

Bob the Builder: Built for Fun With Truck 2009 (Unrated)
Learn about teamwork and friendship with Bob and his friends in these five animated episodes of the popular children's program. 46m; DVD. A: Preschool-Primary. P: Entertainment. U: Home. Mov-Ent: Family Viewing, Animation & Cartoons, Children's Shows. Acq: Purchase. Dist: Lions Gate Entertainment Inc. $11.98.

Bob the Builder: Built to be Wild 2006 (Unrated)
Animated children's television program. In a new musical special, Bob and his crew find adventure and new friends in the Wild West. 56m; DVD. A: Preschool-Primary. P: Entertainment. U: Home. Mov-Ent: Family Viewing, Animation & Cartoons, Children's Shows. Acq: Purchase. Dist: Lions Gate Entertainment Inc. $7.98.

Bob the Builder: Busy Bob & Silly Spud 2002
Four episodes featuring Bob, Wendy, and their crew of fun-loving machines making sure the mischief-making scarecrow doesn't get too out of control. 45m; VHS. A: Preschool. P: Entertainment. U: Home. Chl-Juv: Animation & Cartoons, Children. Acq: Purchase. Dist: HIT Entertainment Ltd. $14.99.

Bob the Builder: Call in the Crew 2009 (Unrated)
Building adventures that focus on teamwork in five exciting cartoon episodes of TVs popular children's show. 46m; DVD. A: Preschool-Primary. P: Entertainment. U: Home. Mov-Ent: Family Viewing, Animation & Cartoons, Children's Shows. Acq: Purchase. Dist: Lions Gate Entertainment Inc. $11.98.

Bob the Builder: Can We Fix It? 2001
Four episodes featuring Bob, Wendy, and their crew of fun-loving machines: "Bob's Barnraising," "Mucky Muck," "Wendy Plays Golf," and "Magnetic Lofty." 45m; VHS. A: Preschool. P: Entertainment. U: Home. Chl-Juv: Animation & Cartoons, Children. Acq: Purchase. Dist: HIT Entertainment Ltd. $14.99.

Bob the Builder: Celebrate With Bob 2007 (Unrated)
Animated children's television program. A dance contest, a surprise party, a messy office, and a broken computer are all on the day's schedule for Bob and his friends in the Can-Do Crew. 45m; DVD. A: Preschool-Primary. P: Entertainment. U: Home. Mov-Ent: Family Viewing, Animation & Cartoons, Children's Shows. Acq: Purchase. Dist: Lions Gate Entertainment Inc. $7.98.

Bob the Builder: Dig! Lift! Haul! 2004
Includes five animated Bob stories: Scruffy's Big Dig, Bob's Boots, Mr. Beasley's Do-It-Yourself Disaster, Spud Lends a Hand and Dizzy's Crazy Paving. 45m; VHS, DVD. A: Preschool. P: Entertainment. U: Home. Chl-Juv: Animation & Cartoons, Children. Acq: Purchase. Dist: HIT Entertainment Ltd. $16.99.

Bob the Builder: Digging for Treasure 2006 (Unrated)
Three episodes of TV's animated "Bob the Builder" revolving around the common theme of finding buried treasure. 50m; DVD. A: Preschool-Primary. P: Entertainment. U: Home. Mov-Ent: Family Viewing, Animation & Cartoons, Children's Shows. Acq: Purchase. Dist: Lions Gate Entertainment Inc. $7.98.

Bob the Builder: Dizzy's Favorite Adventures 2005 (Unrated)
Animated children's television program. Four episodes, including the brand new, "Bob the Photographer," all focusing on Can-Do Crew member, Dizzy. 35m; DVD. A: Preschool-Primary. P: Entertainment. U: Home. Mov-Ent: Family Viewing, Animation & Cartoons, Children's Shows. Acq: Purchase. Dist: Lions Gate Entertainment Inc. $7.98.

Bob the Builder: Getting the Job Done! 2007 (Unrated)
Animated children's television program. This five-episode DVD features Bob the Builder cartoons that all center around the theme of overcoming obstacles in order to complete a task. 120m; DVD. A: Preschool-Primary. P: Entertainment. U: Home. Mov-Ent: Family Viewing, Animation & Cartoons, Children's Shows. Acq: Purchase. Dist: Lions Gate Entertainment Inc. $11.98.

Bob the Builder: Heavy Duty Diggers 2010 (Unrated)
Watch Bob and his Can-Do Crew at their new home in Harbor Town. The animated show appears in CGI animation for the first time. 46m; DVD. A: Preschool-Primary. P: Entertainment. U: Home. Mov-Ent: Family Viewing, Animation & Cartoons, Children's Shows. Acq: Purchase. Dist: Lions Gate Entertainment Inc. $11.98.

Bob the Builder: Help is on the Way! 2006 (Unrated)
Animated children's television program. In four episodes, Bob and his crew learn about giving, asking for, and receiving help at work and at play. 50m; DVD. A: Preschool-Primary. P: Entertainment. U: Home. Mov-Ent: Family Viewing, Animation & Cartoons, Children's Shows. Acq: Purchase. Dist: Lions Gate Entertainment Inc. $7.98.

Bob the Builder: Hold on to Your Hats! 2007 (Unrated)
These episodes of the popular children's cartoon finds Spud worried he's about to be replaced, the introduction of a new team member, and the building of an eco-home. 40m; DVD. A: Preschool-Primary. P: Entertainment. U: Home. Mov-Ent: Family Viewing, Animation & Cartoons, Children's Shows. Acq: Purchase. Dist: Lions Gate Entertainment Inc. $7.98.

Bob the Builder: Let's Build the Beach 2008 (Unrated)
Animated children's television program. Meet two new team members and find out if Bob and the gang finish the Bobland Bay Promenade in time for the grand opening. 46m; DVD. A: Preschool-Primary. P: Entertainment. U: Home. Mov-Ent: Family Viewing, Animation & Cartoons, Children's Shows. Acq: Purchase. Dist: Lions Gate Entertainment Inc. $11.98.

Bob the Builder: Lofty's Favorite Adventures 2005 (Unrated)
Animated children's television program. A four-episode collection starring Bob the Builder and his talking machine Lofty, including the never-before-seen episode "Lofty's Jungle Fun." 35m; DVD. A: Preschool-Primary. P: Entertainment. U: Home. Mov-Ent: Family Viewing, Animation & Cartoons, Children's Shows. Acq: Purchase. Dist: Lions Gate Entertainment Inc. $7.98.

Bob the Builder: Muck's Favorite Adventures 2006 (Unrated)
This four-episode DVD features the animated adventures of Bob the Builder and his construction crew, with special focus on Muck. Includes the new episode, "Racing Muck." 35m; DVD. A: Preschool-Primary. P: Entertainment. U: Home. Mov-Ent: Family Viewing, Animation & Cartoons, Children's Shows. Acq: Purchase. Dist: Lions Gate Entertainment Inc. $7.98.

Bob the Builder: New to the Crew 2007 (Unrated)
Animated children's television program. With so much work to do, Bob calls in new crew members Scrambler, Benny, Sumsy, and Packer. These talking, cartoon machines teach kids the fun to be had in hard work. 45m; DVD. A: Preschool-Primary. P: Entertainment. U: Home. Mov-Ent: Family Viewing. Acq: Purchase. Dist: Lions Gate Entertainment Inc. $7.98.

Bob the Builder: On Site—Houses & Playgrounds 2008 (Unrated)
Animated children's television program. Building houses and playgrounds are the topics in this edition. 60m; DVD. A: Preschool-Primary. P: Entertainment. U: Home. Mov-Ent: Family Viewing, Animation & Cartoons, Children's Shows. Acq: Purchase. Dist: Lions Gate Entertainment Inc. $11.98.

Bob the Builder: On Site—Roads & Bridges 2008 (Unrated)
Animated children's television program. Reality and animation combine as Bob and his crew watch the real-life construction of roads and bridges. 60m; DVD. A: Preschool-Primary. P: Entertainment. U: Home. Mov-Ent: Family Viewing, Animation & Cartoons, Children's Shows. Acq: Purchase. Dist: Lions Gate Entertainment Inc. $11.98.

Bob the Builder: On Site—Skyscrapers 2009 (Unrated)
A mix of animation and live action has Bob the Builder and members of his crew teaching about building skyscrapers. 60m; DVD. A: Preschool-Primary. P: Entertainment. U: Home. Mov-Ent: Family Viewing, Animation & Cartoons, Children's Shows. Acq: Purchase. Dist: Lions Gate Entertainment Inc. $11.98.

Bob the Builder: Pets in a Pickle 2001
Four episodes featuring Bob, Wendy, and their crew of fun-loving machines: "Pilchard in a Pickle," "Farmer Pickles' Pigpen," "Pilchard Goes Fishing," and "Roley's Tortoise." 45m; VHS. A: Preschool. P: Entertainment. U: Home. Chl-Juv: Animation & Cartoons, Children. Acq: Purchase. Dist: HIT Entertainment Ltd. $14.99.

Bob the Builder: Race to the Finish 2009 (Unrated)
Animated children's television program. A new sports stadium is the latest challenge for Bob, Wendy, and the rest of the Can-Do Crew. 60m; DVD. A: Preschool-Primary. P: Entertainment. U: Home. Mov-Ent: Family Viewing, Animation & Cartoons, Children's Shows. Acq: Purchase. Dist: Lions Gate Entertainment Inc. $11.98.

Bob the Builder: Roley's Favorite Adventures 2006 (Unrated)
Animated children's television program. Roley the steam-roller stars in this four-episode collection of the popular children's show "Bob the Builder." Episodes include "Roley to the Rescue," "Mr. Beasley's Noisy Pipes," "Roley's Tortoise," and "Runaway Roley." 35m; DVD. A: Preschool-Primary. P: Entertainment. U: Home. Mov-Ent: Family Viewing, Animation & Cartoons, Children's Shows. Acq: Purchase. Dist: Lions Gate Entertainment Inc. $7.98.

Bob the Builder: Scoop's Favorite Adventures 2006 (Unrated)
Animated children's television program. Scoop, the talking front-loader, is featured in this collection of episodes from "Bob the Builder." Included are "Scoop Saves the Day," "Scoop's in Charge," "Scoop Has Some Fun," and the never-before-seen episode, "Mr. Elli's Art Exhibition." 35m; DVD. A: Preschool-Primary. P: Entertainment. U: Home. Mov-Ent: Family Viewing, Animation & Cartoons, Children's Shows. Acq: Purchase. Dist: Lions Gate Entertainment Inc. $7.98.

Bob the Builder: Scrambler to the Rescue! 2007 (Unrated)
Animated children's television program. Bob and his animated machines are delayed by a heavy snowfall and need Scrambler to save the day. 50m; DVD. A: Preschool-Primary. P: Entertainment. U: Home. Mov-Ent: Family Viewing, Animation & Cartoons, Children's Shows. Acq: Purchase. Dist: Lions Gate Entertainment Inc. $11.98.

Bob the Builder: Snowed Under 2007 (Unrated)
Animated children's television program. Bob and his construction crew of talking machinery step in at the last minute to help build the courses for the Bobblesberg Winter Games. 50m; DVD. A: Preschool-Primary. P: Entertainment. U: Home. Mov-Ent: Family Viewing, Animation & Cartoons, Children's Shows. Acq: Purchase. Dist: Lions Gate Entertainment Inc. $7.98.

Bob the Builder: Teamwork 2003
Four animated stories with Bob and his friends that promote a positive "can-do" spirit, problem-solving, and teamwork. Includes Pilchard's Pet, Snowman Scoop, Lofty's Long Load, and Dizzy the Sheepdog. 45m; VHS, DVD. A: Preschool. P: Entertainment. U: Home. Chl-Juv: Animation & Cartoons, Television. Acq: Purchase. Dist: HIT Entertainment Ltd. $14.99.

Bob the Builder: The Best of Bob the Builder 2010 (Unrated)
Animated children's television program. Ten episodes celebrating ten years of animated construction adventures with Bob and all his friends. 140m; DVD. A: Preschool-Primary. P: Entertainment. U: Home. Mov-Ent: Family Viewing, Animation & Cartoons, Children's Shows. Acq: Purchase. Dist: Lions Gate Entertainment Inc. $11.98.

Bob the Builder: The Big Game 2001
Four episodes featuring Bob, Wendy, and their crew of fun-loving machines work on a building project, compete a road, wallpaper a guesthouse, pave a tennis court, and prep the soccer field for the Big Game. 45m; VHS. A: Preschool. P: Entertainment. U: Home. Chl-Juv: Animation & Cartoons, Children. Acq: Purchase. Dist: HIT Entertainment Ltd. $14.99.

Bob the Builder: The Knights of Fix-A-Lot 2003
Bob and his friends work together to restore an ancient castle and learn about some history in the process. 45m; VHS, DVD. A: Preschool. P: Entertainment. U: Home. Chl-Juv: Animation & Cartoons, Television. Acq: Purchase. Dist: HIT Entertainment Ltd. $14.99.

Bob the Builder: The Live Show! 2007 (Unrated)
A live stage show that brings to life characters from popular children's show "Bob the Builder." Watch as the crew turns a junkyard into a bandstand. 70m; DVD. A: Preschool-Primary. P: Entertainment. U: Home. Mov-Ent: Family Viewing, Animation & Cartoons, Children's Shows. Acq: Purchase. Dist: Lions Gate Entertainment Inc. $7.98.

Bob the Builder: Three Musketrucks 2008 (Unrated)
Animated children's television program. Meet the Three Musketrucks, Packer, Scrambler, and Dodger, in this episode of children's cartoon favorite, "Bob the Builder." 45m; DVD. A: Preschool-Primary. P: Entertainment. U: Home. Mov-Ent: Family Viewing, Animation & Cartoons, Children's Shows. Acq: Purchase. Dist: Lions Gate Entertainment Inc. $11.98.

Bob the Builder: To the Rescue! 2001
Four episodes featuring Bob, Wendy, and their crew of fun-loving machines: "Clocktower Bob," "Scoop Saves the Day," "Muck Gets Stuck," and "Lofty to the Rescue." 45m; VHS. A: Preschool. P: Entertainment. U: Home. Chl-Juv: Animation & Cartoons, Children. Acq: Purchase. Dist: HIT Entertainment Ltd. $14.99.

Bob the Builder: Tool Power! 2003
Animated stories with Bob, Wendy and their crew of construction machines. Includes Inspector Spud, Travis' Trailer, Wendy's Moving Company, Speedy Skip, and Mr. Bentley's Trains. 45m; VHS, DVD. A: Preschool. P: Entertainment. U: Home. Chl-Juv: Television, Animation & Cartoons. Acq: Purchase. Dist: HIT Entertainment Ltd. $14.95.

Bob the Builder: Truck Teamwork 2009 (Unrated)
Animated children's television program. The topic is cooperation in these five animated adventures starring Bob the Builder and his crew of talking machines. 57m; DVD. A: Preschool-Primary. P: Entertainment. U: Home. Mov-Ent: Family Viewing, Animation & Cartoons, Children's Shows. Acq: Purchase. Dist: Lions Gate Entertainment Inc. $11.98.

Bob the Builder: When Bob Became a Builder 2007 (Unrated)
An episode of the popular children's cartoon where the Can-Do Crew learns how their friend Bob became a builder. 50m; DVD. A: Preschool-Primary. P: Entertainment. U: Home. Mov-Ent: Family Viewing, Animation & Cartoons, Children's Shows. Acq: Purchase. Dist: Lions Gate Entertainment Inc. $7.98.

Bob the Builder: X-Treme Adventures 2007 (Unrated)
Animated children's television program. Watch builder, Bob, and his construction crew as they prepare for a storm. 46m; DVD. A: Preschool-Primary. P: Entertainment. U: Home. Mov-Ent: Family Viewing, Animation & Cartoons, Children's Shows. Acq: Purchase. Dist: Lions Gate Entertainment Inc. $11.98.

Bob the Builder: Yes We Can! 2006 (Unrated)
Four episodes of the animated television series "Bob the Builder." Included episodes are, "Bob the Farmer," "Roley's Important Job," "Travis's Busy Day," and "Lofty the Artist." 120m; DVD. A: Preschool-Primary. P: Entertainment. U:

Home. **Mov-Ent**: Family Viewing, Animation & Cartoons, Children's Shows. **Acq:** Purchase. **Dist:** Lions Gate Entertainment Inc. $7.98.

Bob the Butler 2005 (PG) — ★½
Harmless fluff stars the usually obnoxious Green as perennial loser Bob Tree, who can't keep a job. His latest career attempt is attending butler school. His first placement is with neurotic Anne (Shields), who fired him when he was Bob the babysitter. Still, the single mom is desperate and hires Bob to look after her house and two exasperating children (Buechner, Smith), who decide the butler is better than mom's current boyfriend. 90m; DVD. **C:** Tom Green; Brooke Shields; Benjamin Smith; Simon Callow; Genevieve Buechner; Rob LeBelle; Directed by Gary Sinyor; Written by Gary Sinyor; Jane Walker Wood; Steven Manners; Cinematography by Jason Lehel; Music by David A. Hughes. **A:** Family. **P:** Entertainment. **U:** Home. **Mov-Ent. Acq:** Purchase. **Dist:** Movies Unlimited; Alpha Video.

Bob Toski Teaches You Golf 1984
Divided into separate lessons, demonstrates the proper way to play golf. 40m; VHS. **Pr:** Golf Digest. **A:** Jr. High-Adult. **P:** Instruction. **U:** Home. **Spo-Rec**: Sports--General, Golf. **Acq:** Purchase. **Dist:** Golf Digest. $59.95.

The Bob Wieland Story 1988
This is the true story of Bob Wieland who lost his legs in Vietnam. After his return home, he walked across the nation on his hands. 45m; VHS. **Pr:** Bridgestone Production Group. **A:** Primary-Adult. **P:** Religious. **U:** Home. **Gen-Edu**: Documentary Films, Handicapped, Veterans. **Acq:** Purchase. **Dist:** Alpha Omega Publications Inc.

Bob Wilber: A Tribute to Sidney Bechet 1982
Features jazz tribute to Sidnet Bechet performed by saxophonist Bob Wilber and the six-piece Smithsonian Jazz Repertory Ensemble. Includes the Dixieland hits "Lady Be Good," "China Boy," and "Summertime." 60m; VHS. **A:** Family. **P:** Entertainment. **U:** Home. **Fin-Art**: Music--Performance, Music--Jazz. **Acq:** Purchase. **Dist:** Kultur International Films Ltd., Inc. $29.95.

Bob Wills: Fiddlin' Man 19??
Historical performances of Bob Willis and his band, The Texas Playboys. 61m; VHS, DVD. **A:** Family. **P:** Entertainment. **U:** Home. **Mov-Ent**: Music--Performance, Music. **Acq:** Purchase. **Dist:** V.I.E.W. Inc./Arkadia Entertainment Corp. $19.98.

The Bobath Approach 19??
Five-part series discusses neurodevelopmental approach to assessment and treatment planning. Each tape also available individually. 210m; VHS. **A:** Adult. **P:** Education. **U:** Institution. **Hea-Sci**: Handicapped, Medical Care, Patient Care. **Acq:** Purchase, Rent/Lease. **Dist:** University of Maryland. $700.00.
Indiv. Titles: 1. The Basics of Bobath: An Interview 2. Berta Bobath: Assessment and Treatment Planning—A Child with Cerebral Palsy 3. Berta Bobath: Assessment and Treatment Planning—An Adult with Hemiplegia 4. Dr. Karel Bobath: The Neurophysiological Basis of the Bobath Approach to Treatment, Parts I and II.

Bobbie Jo and the Outlaw 1976 (R) — ★½
Wonderwoman Carter is a bored carhop who yearns to be a country singer. She becomes involved with Marjoe, who fancies himself as a contemporary Billy the Kid. Together, they do their Bonnie and Clyde thing, to a significantly lesser dramatic effect than the original, though a glut of violence keeps the bodies dropping. 89m; VHS, DVD. **C:** Lynda Carter; Marjoe Gortner; Jesse Vint; Directed by Mark L. Lester. **Pr:** American International Pictures. **A:** College-Adult. **P:** Entertainment. **U:** Home. **Mov-Ent. Acq:** Purchase. **Dist:** MGM Home Entertainment. $69.98.

Bobbie's Girl 2002 (Unrated) — ★★
Meandering drama long on theatrics and short on sense. American Bailey (Peters) and her lover, Englishwoman Bobbie (Ward) run a pub in a seaside town near Dublin, assisted by Bailey's brother David (Silverman). Bobbie is diagnosed with breast cancer at the same time she learns that her estranged brother and his wife have died and their 10-year-old son, Alan (Sangster), is orphaned into Bobbie's care. Bobbie and Alan are naturally struggling to cope with their situations while eccentrics (they're both ex-actors) Bailey and David try to provide encouragement. 100m; VHS, DVD. **C:** Bernadette Peters; Rachel Ward; Jonathan Silverman; Thomas Brodie-Sangster; Directed by Jeremy Paul Kagan; Written by Samuel Bernstein; Cinematography by Ciaran Tanham; Music by Bruce Broughton. **A:** Jr. High-Adult. **P:** Entertainment. **U:** Home. **Mov-Ent**: Ireland, Parenting, Cancer. **Acq:** Purchase. **Dist:** Showtime Networks Inc.

Bobbikins 1959 — **Bomb!**
Insufferably cute, one-joke Brit comedy. Ben Barnaby (Bygraves) gets out of the Navy and tries to resurrect his showbiz career without any luck. So toddler son Bobbikins (who only talks to Ben) gives dad some advice and then some stock tips, leading to the family's sudden wealth. Having money adversely affects Ben so the tyke decides they need to be poor again. 89m/B/W; DVD. **C:** Max Bygraves; Shirley Jones; Billie Whitelaw; Barbara Shelley; Lionel Jeffries; Directed by Robert Day; Written by Oscar Brodney; Cinematography by Geoffrey Faithfull; Music by Philip Green. **A:** Family. **P:** Entertainment. **U:** Home. **L:** English. **Mov-Ent**: Children, Parenting. **Acq:** Purchase. **Dist:** Fox Home Entertainment.

Bobbin Lace 1989
This video provides helpful instructions in the art of bobbin-lacemaking. 109m; VHS. **C:** Doris Southard. **A:** Jr. High-Adult. **P:** Instruction. **U:** Home. **How-Ins**: How-To, Crafts, Sewing. **Acq:** Purchase. **Dist:** Victorian Video/Yarn Barn of Kansas, Inc. $39.95.

Bobby 2006 (R) — ★★½
Writer-director Emilio Estevez uses a star-studded cast to compare turbulent events of the '60s with modern problems, with mixed results. This homage to Robert F. Kennedy uses multiple storylines and characters that revolve around L.A.'s Ambassador Hotel on the day leading up to RFK's assassination. Estevez liberally sprinkles the stories of no less than twenty-two characters surrounding the imminent tragedy, including the hotel beautician (Stone), her cheating husband (Macy) and a couple soon to be married (Lohan, Wood). The characters aren't allowed to achieve much depth, and the performances are hit and miss. The impact of the assassination drives home the trivialities of the characters and reinforces the loss of RFK, who only appears in archival footage. 119m; DVD, Wide. **C:** Anthony Hopkins; Harry Belafonte; William H. Macy; Sharon Stone; Christian Slater; Freddy Rodriguez; Laurence Fishburne; Demi Moore; Martin Sheen; Helen Hunt; Lindsay Lohan; Elijah Wood; Nick Cannon; Heather Graham; Ashton Kutcher; Shia LaBeouf; Brian Geraghty; Joshua Jackson; David Krumholtz; Emilio Estevez; Mary Elizabeth Winstead; Jacob Vargas; Joy Bryant; Svetlana Metkina; Directed by Emilio Estevez; Written by Emilio Estevez; Cinematography by Michael Barrett; Music by Mark Isham. **Pr:** Michel Litvak; Edward Bass; Holly Wiersma; Bold Films. **A:** Sr. High-Adult. **P:** Entertainment. **U:** Home. **L:** English. **Mov-Ent**: Political Campaigns, Biography: Politics, Hotels & Hotel Staff Training. **Acq:** Purchase. **Dist:** Movies Unlimited; Alpha Video.

Bobby and the Midnites 1984
Grateful Dead-head Bob Weir and friends (Bobby Cochran, Alphonso Johnson, Dave Garland and Billy Cobham) are captured here in a 1984 concert filmed in Switzerland. 60m; VHS. **A:** Jr. High-Adult. **P:** Entertainment. **U:** Home. **Mov-Ent**: Music--Pop/Rock, Music--Performance. **Acq:** Purchase. **Dist:** Facets Multimedia Inc. $19.98.
Songs: Festival; Josephine; Youngblood; I Found Love.

Bobby Brown: His Prerogative 1990
Bobby Brown performs some songs from his hit album such as, "Don't Be Cruel," "My Prerogative," "Roni," and "Every Little Step." 60m; VHS. **A:** Primary-Adult. **P:** Entertainment. **U:** Home. **Mov-Ent**: Music--Performance, Music Video. **Acq:** Purchase. **Dist:** Music Video Distributors. $19.95.

Bobby Brown: Humpin' Around 1992
An extended dance remix video of Brown's hit "Humpin' Around." Also features behind-the-scenes footage of the making of the video. 15m; VHS. **A:** Jr. High-Adult. **P:** Entertainment. **U:** Home. **Mov-Ent**: Music Video, Music--Pop/Rock. **Acq:** Purchase. **Dist:** Music Video Distributors. $9.95.

Bobby Caldwell: Live in Tokyo 1991 1991
"All of Nothing at All," "This Heart of Mine," and "Stuck on You" are three of the 11 songs featured. 55m; VHS. **A:** Jr. High-Adult. **P:** Entertainment. **U:** Home. **Mov-Ent**: Music--Performance. **Acq:** Purchase. **Dist:** Music Video Distributors. $54.95.

Bobby Charlton's Soccer 1991
The British soccer instructor gives a quick demonstration of discipline, dress, ball control, passing and more. 30m; VHS. **Pr:** Morris Video. **A:** Primary-Sr. High. **P:** Instruction. **U:** Home. **Hea-Sci**: Sports--General, Soccer. **Acq:** Purchase. **Dist:** Morris Video. $9.99.
Indiv. Titles: 1. Level 1 2. Level 2.

Bobby Cremins: The 10 Trends of Successful Basketball 2006
Highlights 10 different offensive and defensive basketball systems, strategies, and techniques as outlined by Bobby Cremins, former head coach at Georgia Tech. ?m; DVD. **A:** Sr. High-Adult. **P:** Instruction. **U:** Institution. **Spo-Rec**: Basketball. **Acq:** Purchase. **Dist:** Championship Productions. $39.95.

Bobby Darin: Mack Is Back! 2000
TV special that Bobby Darin taped nine months before his death in 1973. 71m; DVD. **C:** Bobby Darin. **A:** Jr. High-Adult. **P:** Entertainment. **U:** Home. **Mov-Ent**: Music--Performance. **Acq:** Purchase. **Dist:** Questar Inc.

Bobby Darin: The Darin Invasion 1970
Darin's remarkable talent is showcased in his first and only TV special. Joined by guests Linda Ronstadt and George Burns, he performs "If I Were a Carpenter" and other hits. 60m; VHS, DVD. **C:** Bobby Darin; Linda Ronstadt; George Burns. **A:** Jr. High-Adult. **P:** Entertainment. **U:** Institution, Home, SURA. **Mov-Ent**: Music--Performance, Singing, TV Movies. **Acq:** Purchase. **Dist:** V.I.E.W. Inc./Arkadia Entertainment Corp.; Music Video Distributors; Moonbeam Publications Inc. $19.95.

Bobby Deerfield 1977 (PG) — ★★
Cold-blooded Grand Prix driver comes face to face with death each time he races, but finally learns the meaning of life when he falls in love with a critically ill woman. Even with race cars, soap opera stalls. 124m; VHS, DVD. **C:** Al Pacino; Marthe Keller; Anny (Annie Legras) Duperey; Romolo Valli; Directed by Sydney Pollack; Written by Alvin Sargent; Cinematography by Henri Decae; Music by Dave Grusin. **A:** Jr. High-Adult. **P:** Entertainment. **U:** Home. **Mov-Ent**: Automobiles--Racing, Diseases. **Acq:** Purchase. **Dist:** Sony Pictures Home Entertainment Inc. $14.95.

Bobby Gonzalez: Rules for Attacking Zone Defense 2007
Gonzalez presents 11 rules for attacking zone defense, especially attacking gaps on the dribble. 64m; DVD. **A:** Adult. **P:** Instruction. **U:** Institution. **Spo-Rec**: Basketball. **Acq:** Purchase. **Dist:** Championship Productions.

Bobby Gonzalez: Year Round Individual Improvement Drills 2007
Pre-season workouts to improve conditioning and mental attitude, including footwork and other drills. 37m; DVD. **A:** Adult. **P:** Instruction. **U:** Institution. **Spo-Rec**: Basketball. **Acq:** Purchase. **Dist:** Championship Productions.

Bobby Jones Comedy All Stars: Volume 1 2008 (Unrated)
Dr. Bobby Jones, host of the only nationally syndicated black gospel TV show hosts and performs in this collection of stand-up comedy performances also featuring Trina Jeffrie, Jonathan Slocumb, Ron Baker, Jr., LaVance Lining, Andrew Ford, and CoCo. 58m; DVD. **A:** Primary-Adult. **P:** Entertainment. **U:** Home. **Mov-Ent**: Religion, Comedy--Performance. **Acq:** Purchase. **Dist:** Lions Gate Entertainment Inc. $11.98.

Bobby Jones Comedy All Stars: Volume 2 2008 (Unrated)
The second edition of family-friendly, stand-up comedy featuring TVs Dr. Bobby Jones as well as performances by Vyck Cooley, Ron G., Broderick Rice, Small Fire, Jonathan Slocumb, and Trina "Sister Cantaloupe" Jeffrie. 78m; DVD. **A:** Primary-Adult. **P:** Entertainment. **U:** Home. **Mov-Ent**: Religion, Comedy--Performance. **Acq:** Purchase. **Dist:** Lions Gate Entertainment Inc. $11.98.

Bobby Jones: How I Play Golf, Limited Collector's Edition 1987
Historic instructional shorts starring one of golf's legends. This two-tape presentation includes an approved biography of the golf champion. Includes an accompanying booklet on the golfing great. 180m/B/W; VHS. **Pr:** SyberVision Systems. **A:** Sr. High-Adult. **P:** Instruction. **U:** Home. **Spo-Rec**: Sports--General, Golf. **Acq:** Purchase. **Dist:** SyberVision Systems, Inc. $245.00.

Bobby Jones Instructional Series, Vol. 1: Full Swing 1988
This volume demonstrates golfing pre-swing fundamentals, proper backswing position, backswing energy in the downswing, hand and foot role and how to hook, slice and stop the ball at will. 60m; VHS. **A:** Sr. High-Adult. **P:** Instruction. **U:** Home. **Spo-Rec**: Sports--General, Golf. **Acq:** Purchase. **Dist:** SyberVision Systems, Inc. $69.95.

Bobby Jones Instructional Series, Vol. 2: From Tee to Green 1988
Jones shows the basics of golf in an easy-to-understand approach. 60m; VHS. **C:** Hosted by Bobby Jones. **A:** Sr. High-Adult. **P:** Instruction. **U:** Home. **Spo-Rec**: Sports--General, Golf. **Acq:** Purchase. **Dist:** SyberVision Systems, Inc. $69.95.

Bobby Jones: Stroke of Genius 2004 (PG) — ★★½
Bloated homage to the late great golfer of the title starring a red-hot post-"Passion" Caviezel. Practically a natural, Jones, who still reigns as the only golfer to win all four major tournaments in a single calendar year, had to overcome a number of personal demons to become one of the greatest golfers in the world. An extremely moral man, Jones suffered from depression and sported a legendary temper that he battled in order to work his way to the top of golf world of the 1920s. After his Grand Slam coup, Jones was diagnosed with a spinal disorder and retired from golf at 28 to practice law and spend more time with wife Mary (Forlani). Historically faithful and elegant, with a fine performance by its star, but is hindered by sub-par script, formulaic plot, and undeveloped supports. 126m; DVD. **C:** James (Jim) Caviezel; Claire Forlani; Jeremy Northam; Malcolm McDowell; Connie Ray; Brett Rice; Dan Albright; Larry Thompson; Paul Freeman; John Curran; Aidan Quinn; Alistair Begg; Kenny Alfonso; Tom Arcuragi; Devon Gearhart; Thomas Lewis; Hilton McRae; Directed by Rowdy Herrington; Written by Rowdy Herrington; Tony Depaul; Bill Pryor; Cinematography by Tom Stern; Music by James Horner. **Pr:** Kim Dawson; Tim Moore; John Shepherd; Dean River Prods; Film Foundry. **A:** Primary-Adult. **P:** Entertainment. **U:** Home. **L:** English. **Mov-Ent**: Biography: Sports, Golf, Sports--Fiction: Drama. **Acq:** Purchase. **Dist:** Sony Pictures Home Entertainment Inc.

Bobby Lutz: 18 Full and Half Court Quick Scoring Plays 2009 (Unrated)
Coach Bobby Lutz demonstrates methods basketball teams can use to score from out of bounds, early in the game, or in half-court sets. 61m; DVD. **A:** Family. **P:** Education. **U:** Home, Institution. **Spo-Rec**: Basketball, Athletic Instruction/Coaching. **Acq:** Purchase. **Dist:** Championship Productions. $39.99.

Bobby Lutz: 4-Out 1-In Offense Sets and Plays 2006
Coach Bobby Lutz discusses and demonstrates plays for the 4-Out 1-In basketball offense. 72m; DVD. **A:** Family. **P:** Education. **U:** Home, Institution. **Spo-Rec**: Basketball, Athletic Instruction/Coaching. **Acq:** Purchase. **Dist:** Championship Productions. $39.99.

Bobby Lutz: Game Ready Practice Drills 2009 (Unrated)
Coach Bobby Lutz presents 10 competitive drills for basketball teams to use during their practices. 67m; DVD. **A:** Family. **P:** Education. **U:** Home, Institution. **Spo-Rec**: Basketball, Athletic Instruction/Coaching. **Acq:** Purchase. **Dist:** Championship Productions. $39.99.

Bobby Lutz: Getting Great Shots for Your Best Players 2006
Coach Bobby Lutz presents drills for getting players into position to make shots, as well as how to counter opponents attempting to prevent them. 82m; DVD. **A:** Family. **P:** Education. **U:** Home, Institution. **Spo-Rec:** Basketball, Athletic Instruction/Coaching. **Acq:** Purchase. **Dist:** Championship Productions. $39.99.

Bobby McFerrin: Spontaneous Inventions 1987
A performance by jazz vocal stylist McFerrin taped at The Aquarius Theater in Hollywood in 1986. Songs include "Scrapple from the Apple," "Honeysuckle Rose," "Bwee-Dop," "Cara Mia," "Fascinating Rhythm," "Itsy Bitsy Spider," "Thinkin' About Your Body," "Drive," "Opportunity," "I Got the Feelin'," "Walkin'," "Blackbird," and "Menana Igauna." 60m; VHS. **C:** Bobby McFerrin. **Pr:** HBO. **A:** Jr. High-Adult. **P:** Entertainment. **U:** Home. **Mov-Ent:** Music--Performance, Music--Jazz. **Acq:** Purchase. **Dist:** Music Video Distributors; Fast Forward. $19.95.

Bobby Rahal Explains Indy Car Racing 1987
The famed racecar driver explains his techniques for championship on the track. 30m; VHS. **Pr:** Twin Towers Entertainment. **A:** Jr. High-Adult. **P:** Instruction. **U:** Home. **How-Ins:** Sports--General, How-To, Automobiles--Racing. **Acq:** Purchase. **Dist:** Karol Media. $19.98.

Bobby Seale 1969 (Unrated)
Prison interview with Black Panther Party Chairman Bobby Seale, following his trial for conspiracy, finds him discussing his treatment as a political prisoner and his connections with the Black Liberation and anti-war movements. 15m/B/W; VHS, DVD. **A:** Adult. **P:** Education. **U:** Institution. **Gen-Edu:** Black Culture, Politics & Government. **Acq:** Purchase. **Dist:** Third World Newsreel. $125.

Bobby Short & Friends 1986
Suave pianist and vocal stylist Short performs his favorite show tunes in this program taped live at New York's Cafe Carlyle. There are also guest appearances by Jack Lemmon, Lucie Arnaz, and Tony Bennett. 60m; VHS. **C:** Bobby Short; Jack Lemmon; Lucie Arnaz. **Pr:** MGM Home Entertainment. **A:** Family. **P:** Entertainment. **U:** Home. **Mov-Ent:** Music--Performance, Music--Jazz. **Acq:** Purchase. **Dist:** Music Video Distributors; MGM Home Entertainment. $29.95.

Bobby Short at the Cafe Carlyle 1979
New York's most popular saloon singer performs in the heart of the city. Recorded in Hi-Fi Stereo. 65m; VHS, DVD. **Pr:** Lealou Productions. **A:** Family. **P:** Entertainment. **U:** Home. **Mov-Ent:** Music--Performance. **Acq:** Purchase. **Dist:** Music Video Distributors; V.I.E.W. Inc./Arkadia Entertainment Corp.; Moonbeam Publications Inc. $29.95.

Bobby Wadkins on Trouble Spots 1989
Pro Wadkins shares his technique for golf's basic fundamentals. He gives advice on club using, hitting height, and much more. 20m; VHS. **C:** Hosted by Bobby Wadkins. **A:** Adult-Family. **P:** Entertainment. **U:** Home. **Spo-Rec:** Golf. **Acq:** Purchase. **Dist:** Anchor Bay Entertainment. $9.99.

Bobby Z 2007 (R) — ★★
Lots of action and limited acting required. Con Tim Kearney (Walker) agrees to DEA agent Tad Grusza's (Fishburne) plan to pass himself off as missing surfer/drug dealer Bobby Z in order to get paroled. Seems drug lords are holding Grusza's partner hostage and they'll trade for Bobby. Things go wrong and Kearney goes on the lam with Bobby's ex-lover (Wilde) and his young son (Villareal). Based on "The Death and Life of Bobby Z" by Don Winslow. 97m; DVD. **C:** Paul Walker; Laurence Fishburne; Olivia Wilde; Joaquim Almeida; J.R. Villarreal; Jason Lewis; Jacob Vargas; Jason Flemyng; Keith Carradine; Chuck Liddell; Directed by John Herzfeld; Written by Bob Krakower; Allen Lawrence; Music by Timothy S. (Tim) Jones. **A:** Sr. High-Adult. **P:** Entertainment. **U:** Home. **Mov-Ent:** Drug Trafficking/Dealing. **Acq:** Purchase. **Dist:** Sony Pictures Home Entertainment Inc.

Bobby's World: Fish Tales and Generics Under Construction 1995
Two episodes from the Fox Kids Network Bobby's World animated television series. In the first, "Fish Tales," Bobby shows everyone how they can use their imagination to overcome boredom on a camping trip in Canada. In the second, "Generics Under Construction," Bobby saves the day when a photographer shows up to take a family portrait but a construction crew has made a mess of the house. 50m; VHS, CC. **A:** Family. **P:** Entertainment. **U:** Home. **Mov-Ent:** Animation & Cartoons, Children. **Acq:** Purchase. **Dist:** Fox Home Entertainment. $9.98.

Bobby's World, Vol. 1 1994
Kid's sing-along created by Howie Mandel. Complete with audiocassette. 45m; VHS. **A:** Preschool-Primary. **P:** Entertainment. **U:** Home. **Chl-Juv:** Animation & Cartoons, Music--Children. **Acq:** Purchase. **Dist:** Fox Home Entertainment. $12.98.

Bobby's World, Vol. 2 1994
Kid's sing-along created by Howie Mandel. Complete with audiocassette. 45m; VHS. **A:** Preschool-Primary. **P:** Entertainment. **U:** Home. **Chl-Juv:** Animation & Cartoons, Music--Children. **Acq:** Purchase. **Dist:** Fox Home Entertainment. $12.98.

Bobby's World, Vol. 3 1994
Kid's sing-along created by Howie Mandel. Complete with audiocassette. 45m; VHS. **A:** Preschool-Primary. **P:** Entertainment. **U:** Home. **Chl-Juv:** Animation & Cartoons, Music--Children. **Acq:** Purchase. **Dist:** Fox Home Entertainment. $12.98.

Bobcat! 1987
When young, bobcats are pretty much helpless and harmless, but by the time they grow up they're fierce hunters who tear their prey to pieces. 9m; VHS, 3/4 U. **A:** Primary-Jr. High. **P:** Education. **U:** Institution, SURA. **Hea-Sci:** Animals. **Acq:** Purchase, Trade-in. **Dist:** Encyclopedia Britannica. $170.00.

The Bobo 1967 — ★½
Lousy bullfighter tries to lure a gorgeous woman into romance. Filmed in Spain and Italy. 103m; VHS, DVD, Wide. **C:** Peter Sellers; Britt Ekland; Rossano Brazzi; Adolfo Celi; Directed by Robert Parrish; Written by David R. Schwartz. **Pr:** Gina Productions. **A:** Sr. High-Adult. **P:** Entertainment. **U:** Home. **Mov-Ent:** Comedy--Romantic. **Acq:** Purchase. **Dist:** WarnerArchive.com; Facets Multimedia Inc. $19.98.

Bob's Birthday 1994
Animated program which tells the story of Bob on his 40th birthday. He reflects on the meaning of life as he approaches middle age, including thoughts on diet, nutrition, sex and sexuality, career options, children, self-concept, and relationships with family and friends. 12m; VHS. **A:** Sr. High-Adult. **P:** Education. **U:** Institution, Home. **Gen-Edu:** Animation & Cartoons, Aging, Health Education. **Acq:** Purchase, Rent/Lease. **Dist:** National Film Board of Canada. $150.00.

The BOC Challenge 1986-87 19??
Follows the stories of 25 competitors as they compete in the 1986-87 BOC Challenge race through the Southern Ocean. Emphasis is placed on how they survived the treacherous course. 55m; VHS. **Pr:** Bennett Marine Video. **A:** Jr. High-Adult. **P:** Entertainment. **U:** Home. **Spo-Rec:** Boating, Sports--General, Sports--Water. **Acq:** Purchase. **Dist:** Bennett Marine Video. $39.95.

BOC Knockdown Challenge 1990-91 1992
Around the world racing at its most thrilling. Watch Don McIntyre survive the grueling BOC Challenge single-handedly. 105m; VHS. **A:** Family. **P:** Entertainment. **U:** Home. **Spo-Rec:** Boating. **Acq:** Purchase. **Dist:** Bennett Marine Video. $39.95.

Boca 1994 (R) — ★★
American journalist J.J. (Chong) arrives in Rio during Carnival to investigate a story about random killings throughout the Brazilian streets. She gets stonewalled asking questions, until she meets an up-from-poverty crimelord named Boca De Ouro (Meira). Now, our noisy journalist may learn too much to keep her alive. Filmed in Rio de Janiero. 92m; VHS, CC. **C:** Rae Dawn Chong; Martin Kemp; Tarcisio Meira; Martin Sheen; Directed by Sandra Werneck; Walter Avancini; Written by Ed Silverstein. **Pr:** Zalman King. **A:** College-Adult. **P:** Entertainment. **U:** Home. **Mov-Ent:** Journalism, South America, Circuses. **Acq:** Purchase. **Dist:** Lions Gate Entertainment Inc.

Boccaccio '70 1962 — ★★
Three short bawdy/comedy/pageant-of-life films inspired by "The Decameron," each pertaining to ironically twisted sexual politics in middle class life. A fourth story, "Renzo and Luciana," by Mario Monicelli, has been cut. Dubbed. 145m; VHS, DVD, Blu-Ray. **C:** Anita Ekberg; Romy Schneider; Tomas Milian; Sophia Loren; Peppino de Filippo; Luigi Gillianni; Directed by Vittorio De Sica; Luchino Visconti; Federico Fellini; Written by Luchino Visconti; Federico Fellini; Tullio Pinelli; Ennio Flaiano; Cesare Zavattini; Cinematography by Otello Martelli; Giuseppe Rotunno; Music by Nino Rota; Armando Trovajoli. **Pr:** 20th Century-Fox; Cineriz. **A:** Sr. High-Adult. **P:** Entertainment. **U:** Home. **Mov-Ent:** Sex & Sexuality. **Acq:** Rent/Lease. **Dist:** Facets Multimedia Inc.; Kino on Video.

Boccaccio: Tales from the Decameron 1989
Shadow puppets enact six late medieval/early Renaissance tales by Giovanni Boccaccio. 71m; VHS, 3/4 U. **Pr:** Films for the Humanities and Sciences. **A:** Primary-Sr. High. **P:** Education. **U:** Institution, CCTV, CATV, BCTV. **Fin-Art:** Literature--English. **Acq:** Purchase, Rent/Lease, Duplication License. **Dist:** Films for the Humanities & Sciences.

Bodacious Space Pirates: Collection 1 2012 (Unrated)
A young high school girl learns her father is an infamous space pirate, and that due to certain events she is now expected to take over his family business as captain of his ship. 325m; Blu-Ray. **A:** Jr. High-Adult. **P:** Entertainment. **U:** Home. **L:** English, Spanish. **Gen-Edu:** Anime, Science Fiction. **Acq:** Purchase. **Dist:** Sentai Filmworks. $69.98.

Bodacious Space Pirates: Collection 2 2012 (Unrated)
The space pirates must unite to confront a mysterious foe that is destroying them one by one. 325m; Blu-Ray. **A:** Jr. High-Adult. **P:** Entertainment. **U:** Home. **L:** English, Japanese. **Gen-Edu:** Anime, Science Fiction. **Acq:** Purchase. **Dist:** Section 23. $69.98.

Bodhisattva Way of Peace: Lay Buddhism in Japan 1977
This program integrates Buddhist concepts of peace into the Japanese, American and Indian cultures. 28m; VHS, 3/4 U. **Pr:** Hartley Film Foundation. **A:** Sr. High-Adult. **P:** Education. **U:** Institution, CCTV, Home. **Gen-Edu:** Documentary Films, Philosophy & Ideology, Buddhism. **Acq:** Purchase. **Dist:** Hartley Film Foundation; EcuFilm.

Bodies 1982
Designed for use in sex education sessions, this is a fast, frenetic portrayal of a group of young people undressing and cavorting in the nude. 10m; VHS, 3/4 U. **Pr:** Professional Research. **A:** College-Adult. **P:** Education. **U:** Institution, CCTV. **Hea-Sci:** Documentary Films, Sex & Sexuality. **Acq:** Purchase, Rent/Lease. **Dist:** Discovery Education.

Bodies, Rest & Motion 1993 (R) — ★★
Stagnant 20-something movie in which four young people basically do nothing in the sun-baked town of Enfield, Arizona. Similar to the movie "Singles," but without the Seattle grunge scene. The title's reference to Newton is fitting: "A body in rest or motion remains in that state unless acted upon by an outside force." Appealing cast is wasted in listless film that's content to just drift along. Based on the play by Roger Hedden. 94m; VHS, DVD, CC. **C:** Phoebe Cates; Bridget Fonda; Tim Roth; Eric Stoltz; Scott Frederick; Scott Johnson; Alicia Witt; Rich Wheeler; Peter Fonda; Directed by Michael Steinberg; Written by Roger Hedden; Cinematography by Bernd Heinl; Music by Michael Convertino. **A:** Sr. High-Adult. **P:** Entertainment. **U:** Home. **Mov-Ent. Acq:** Purchase. **Dist:** New Line Home Video; Baker and Taylor. $95.95.

Bodily Functions 1995
Presents notions of black lesbians dealing with blackness, gender, and lesbianism. 14m; VHS. **A:** Adult. **P:** Education. **U:** Institution. **Gen-Edu:** Sociology, Black Culture, Homosexuality. **Acq:** Purchase, Rent/Lease. **Dist:** Third World Newsreel. $175.00.

Bodily Harm 1995 (R) — ★★
By-the-numbers neo-noir features Fiorentino as Vegas detective Rita Cates, who's investigating the murders of two women with ties to ex-cop Sam McKeon (Baldwin), not incidentally Rita's former lover. She rekindles their lust but then begins to have second thoughts about Sam's innocence. Unconvincing despite the expert cast. 91m; VHS. **C:** Linda Fiorentino; Daniel Baldwin; Gregg Henry; Bill Smitrovich; Troy Evans; Joe Regalbuto; Millie Perkins; Todd Susman; Shannon Kenny; Directed by James (Momel) Lemmo; Written by James (Momel) Lemmo; Joseph Whaley; Ronda Barendse; Music by Robert Sprayberry. **Pr:** Bruce Cohn Curtis; Rysher Entertainment. **A:** Sr. High-Adult. **P:** Entertainment. **U:** Home. **Mov-Ent:** Mystery & Suspense, Sex & Sexuality. **Acq:** Purchase. **Dist:** WarnerVision. $92.95.

The Body 2001 (PG-13) — ★
Would-be religious thriller with wooden acting, laughable dialog, and clunky plot. In modern-day Jerusalem, Israeli archeologist Sharon Golban (Williams) checks out a tomb discovered beneath a shop and finds the skeleton of a crucified man. Could it be the remains of Jesus? When word reaches the Vatican, Cardinal Pesci (Wood) dispatches Father Matt Gutierrez (Banderas) to deal with the provocative situation. 108m; VHS, DVD, Wide. **C:** Antonio Banderas; Olivia Williams; John Wood; John Shrapnel; Derek Jacobi; Jason Flemyng; Makram Khoury; Vernon Dobtcheff; Ian McNeice; Directed by Jonas McCord; Written by Jonas McCord; Cinematography by Vilmos Zsigmond; Music by Serge Colbert. **Pr:** Rudy Cohen; Helkon Media AG; Green Moon Productions; Avalanche Releasing. **A:** Jr. High-Adult. **P:** Entertainment. **U:** Home. **Mov-Ent:** Archaeology, Religion. **Acq:** Purchase. **Dist:** Sony Pictures Home Entertainment Inc.

Body Addicts 19??
Gives insight into those addicted to exercise, and some of the ramifications that high exercise levels may have on people's lives. 28m; VHS. **A:** Sr. High. **P:** Education. **U:** Institution. **Gen-Edu:** Sports--General. **Acq:** Purchase. **Dist:** Filmakers Library Inc. $295.

The Body Against Disease 1980
Discusses the body's immune system, explains how it attacks organisms, and why it fails in some cases such as cancer or multiple sclerosis. ?m; VHS. **A:** Sr. High. **P:** Education. **U:** Institution. **Hea-Sci:** Science, Diseases, Biology. **Acq:** Purchase. **Dist:** HRM Video. $175.00.

Body and Soul 1924 (Unrated) — ★★
The first screen appearance of Robeson has him cast in a dual role as a conniving preacher and his good brother. The preacher preys on the heroine, making her life a misery. Objections by censors to the preacher's character caused him to be redeemed and become worthy of the heroine's love. 102m/B/W; Silent; VHS, DVD. **C:** Paul Robeson; Julia Theresa Russell; Mercedes Gilbert; Directed by Oscar Micheaux. **A:** College-Adult. **P:** Entertainment. **U:** Home. **Mov-Ent:** Religion, Black Culture, Silent Films. **Acq:** Purchase. **Dist:** Criterion Collection Inc.; Facets Multimedia Inc.

Body and Soul 1947 — ★★★½
Charlie Davis (Garfield) is a Jewish boxer whose parents want him to quit the ring and get an education. Instead, he rises quickly to the top, thanks in part to gangster "protector" Roberts (Goff). After becoming a champ, Charlie starts the inevitable downward slide. One-time pro-welterweight Lee plays boxing rival Ben. A vintage '40s boxing film that defines the genre. Remade in 1981 with Leon Isaac Kennedy. 104m/B/W; VHS, DVD, Blu-Ray. **C:** John Garfield; Lilli Palmer; Hazel Brooks; Anne Revere; William Conrad; Canada Lee; Joseph Pevney; Lloyd Goff; Directed by Robert Rossen; Written by Abraham Polonsky; Cinematography by James Wong Howe; Music by Hugo Friedhofer. **Pr:** United Artists. **A:** Jr. High-Adult. **P:** Entertainment. **U:** Home. **Mov-Ent:** Boxing, Classic Films, Sports--Fiction: Drama. **Awds:** Oscars '47: Film Editing. **Acq:** Purchase. **Dist:** Lions Gate Entertainment Inc. $14.98.

Body & Soul 1981 (R) — ★★½
Interesting remake of 1947 gem about a boxer who loses his perspective in the world of fame, fast cars, and women. 109m; VHS, DVD. **C:** Leon Isaac Kennedy; Jayne Kennedy; Peter Lawford; Muhammad Ali; Perry Lang; Directed by George Bowers. **Pr:** Cannon Films. **A:** Sr. High-Adult. **P:** Entertainment. **U:** Home. **Mov-Ent:** Boxing, Sports--Fiction: Drama. **Acq:** Purchase. **Dist:** MGM Home Entertainment. $14.95.

Body & Soul 1993 — ★★★
After spending 16 years as a cloistered nun in a Welsh convent, with vows of poverty, celibacy, and obedience, Anna Gibson (Scott Thomas) must return to the outside world. Following her brother's suicide, Anna is forced to deal with his pregnant widow (Redman) and two children and her family's failing Yorkshire mill. Anna suffers a crisis of faith as both the secular and the religious exert their strong influences and she's drawn as well to two very different men—younger Hal (Mavers), the mill's supervisor, and divorced bank manager Daniel Stern (Bowe). Based on the 1991 novel by Marcelle Bernstein; British TV miniseries. 312m; VHS, DVD. **C:** Kristin Scott Thomas; Amanda Redman; Gary Mavers; Anthony Valentine; Sandra Voe; John Bowe; Dorothy Tutin; Patrick Allen; Directed by Moira Armstrong; Written by Paul Hines; Cinematography by Peter Middleton; Music by Jim Parker. **A:** Sr. High-Adult. **P:** Entertainment. **U:** Home. **Mov-Ent:** TV Movies, Family, Suicide. **Acq:** Purchase. **Dist:** Questar Inc.

Body and Soul 1998 (R) — ★★
Cliched remake of the familiar boxing saga that finds ambitious boxer Mancini and his manager Chiklis heading for a potential championship bout in Reno. Mancini might still have the boxing moves but he's certainly no amateur and his professionalism is actually a deterrent. 95m; VHS, DVD, CC. **C:** Ray "Boom Boom" Mancini; Michael Chiklis; Rod Steiger; Joe Mantegna; Jennifer Beals; Tahnee Welch; Directed by Sam Henry Kass; Written by Sam Henry Kass; Cinematography by Arturo Smith; Music by David Waters. **A:** Sr. High-Adult. **P:** Entertainment. **U:** Home. **Mov-Ent:** Boxing. **Acq:** Purchase. **Dist:** MGM Home Entertainment.

Body and Soul: Body, Part 1 1968
Harry Reasoner examines the black American's contribution to sports in America. He interviews key athletes such as Harry Edwards, leader of those who threatened Olympic Games boycott. 24m; VHS, 3/4 U. **Pr:** CBS News. **A:** Jr. High-Sr. High. **P:** Education. **U:** Institution, SURA. **Gen-Edu:** Documentary Films, Sports--General, Black Culture. **Acq:** Purchase. **Dist:** Phoenix Learning Group.

Body & Soul Series 2000
Twenty-part series explaining new discoveries in alternative and complimentary medicine that would be a great resource for universities, public libraries and hospitals. 27m; VHS, DVD. **A:** Adult. **P:** Vocational. **U:** Institution. **Hea-Sci:** Health Education, Medical Care. **Acq:** Purchase. **Dist:** Aquarius Health Care Media. $999.00.

Body and Soul: Soul, Part 2 1968
Soul music is discussed in detail by singer Ray Charles. 28m; VHS, 3/4 U. **C:** Ray Charles; Mahalia Jackson; Billie Holiday; Aretha Franklin. **Pr:** CBS News. **A:** Jr. High-Sr. High. **P:** Education. **U:** Institution, SURA. **Gen-Edu:** Documentary Films. **Acq:** Purchase. **Dist:** Phoenix Learning Group.

Body Armor 1996 (R) — ★½
Special agent Conway (McColm) is recruited by an ex-girlfriend (Schofield) to find a missing scientist. This leads our hero to nutball virologist Dr. Krago (Perlman) who's using germ warfare for personal gain. For the action junkie (who doesn't mind a little eye candy as well). 95m; VHS, DVD. **C:** Matt McColm; Ron Perlman; Annabel Schofield; Carol Alt; Clint Howard; Morgan Brittany; Shauna O'Brien; Directed by Jack Gill; Written by Jack Gill; Cinematography by Robert Hayes; Music by Mark Holden. **A:** Sr. High-Adult. **P:** Entertainment. **U:** Home. **Mov-Ent. Acq:** Purchase.

Body Armour 2007 (Unrated) — ★½
Maybe it was a good excuse for the actors to enjoy the Spanish sunshine, because it's not much of a movie. Secret Service agent John's (Schweiger) career is ruined when the presidential nominee he's guarding gets blown up by a car bomb. Three years later, ex-agent John reluctantly accepts a bodyguard job in Barcelona and learns his client is the man responsible—international assassin Maxwell (Palminteri) who's turned on his associates and become a government witness. They want him dead (and so does John). 90m; DVD. **C:** Til Schweiger; Chazz Palminteri; Lluis Homar; Gustavo Salmeron; Cristina Brondo; Directed by Gerry Lively; Written by Ken Lamplugh; John Weidner; Cinematography by Christof Wahl; Music by Jose Mora. **A:** Sr. High-Adult. **P:** Entertainment. **U:** Home. **Mov-Ent. Acq:** Purchase. **Dist:** Image Entertainment Inc.

The Body Atlas 199?
13 part series that explores various aspects of the human body. The most important nine months of our lifetime. 25m; VHS. **A:** Sr. High-Adult. **P:** Entertainment. **U:** Institution. **Gen-Edu:** Medical Education, Anatomy & Physiology. **Acq:** Purchase. **Dist:** Ambrose Video Publishing, Inc. $99.95.
Indiv. Titles: 1. In the Womb 2. Glands and Hormones 3. Muscle and Bone 4. Breath of Life 5. Skin 6. The Food Machine 7. Taste and Smell 8. Visual Reality 9. Defense and Repair 10. Sex 11. The Human Pump 12. Now Hear This 13. The Brain.

Body Awareness: Vols. 1&2 19??
Two volume series with host Bob Klein teaching the first few movements of "Yang short form," a series of slow, relaxing, animal-like movements. 60m; VHS. **A:** Sr. High-Adult. **P:** Instruction. **U:** Home. **Hea-Sci:** Martial Arts, Fitness/Exercise. **Acq:** Purchase. **Dist:** Education 2000, Inc. $29.95.

Body Bags 1993 (R) — ★★½
Three gory, though humorous, stories hosted by horrormeister Carpenter as your friendly local coroner. "The Gas Station" finds the young female overnight attendent menaced by a psycho. "Hair" is about a balding yuppie who'll do anything for a full head of hair. Then he meets the sinister Dr. Lock and his magical new-hair growth treatment. The grisly "Eye" concerns a ballplayer who loses the aforementioned appendage and finds that his transplanted eyeball, taken from an executed serial killer, is subject to ghastly visions. Several fellow horror directors have cameos. 95m; VHS, DVD, Blu-Ray, CC. **C:** Alex Datcher; Robert Carradine; Stacy Keach; David Warner; Mark Hamill; Twiggy; John Agar; Deborah Harry; Sheena Easton; David Naughton; John Carpenter; Cameo(s) Wes Craven; Sam Raimi; Roger Corman; Tobe Hooper; Directed by Tobe Hooper; John Carpenter; Written by Billy Brown; Dan Angel; Music by John Carpenter; Jim Lang. **Pr:** John Carpenter; Sandy King; John Carpenter; Daniel M. Angel; Showtime. **A:** Sr. High-Adult. **P:** Entertainment. **U:** Home. **Mov-Ent:** Eye, TV Movies. **Acq:** Purchase. **Dist:** Lions Gate Entertainment Inc.

Body Bar Basics with Sherry Catlin: Learn Basic Skills ????
A beginner workout focusing on fundamental fitness skills. 30m; VHS. **A:** Adult. **P:** Instruction. **U:** Home. **Hea-Sci:** Fitness/Exercise, How-To. **Acq:** Purchase. **Dist:** Body Bar Systems. $14.95.

Body Bar Challenge with Keli Roberts: Strength, Definition, Muscle Fiber ????
A beginner to advanced workout using high intensity training to help develop strength. 60m; VHS. **A:** Adult. **P:** Instruction. **U:** Home. **Hea-Sci:** Fitness/Exercise, How-To. **Acq:** Purchase. **Dist:** Body Bar Systems. $19.95.

Body Bar: Ready, Set, Superset 2005
Features basic and advanced toning routines performed with a body bar and a step bench. 52m; DVD. **A:** College-Adult. **P:** Instruction. **U:** Home. **Hea-Sci:** Fitness/Exercise. **Acq:** Purchase. **Dist:** Collage Video Specialties, Inc. $19.95.

Body Bar Strength and Conditioning 2000
Sherry Catlin and Keli Roberts present three complete toning workouts (two for advanced exercisers, one for intermediate) using a body bar device and a step. 146m; DVD. **A:** Adult. **P:** Instruction. **U:** Home. **Hea-Sci:** Fitness/Exercise. **Acq:** Purchase. **Dist:** Collage Video Specialties, Inc.

Body Beat 1988 (PG) — ★★
Wild jazz and rock dancers are integrated into a previously classical ballet academy. While the students become fast friends, the teachers break off into two rival factions. 90m; VHS. **C:** Tony Fields; Galyn Gorg; Scott Grossman; Eliska Krupka; Virgil Frye; Steve La Chance; Leonora Leal; Julie Newmar; Paula Nichols; Serge Rodnunsky; Directed by Ted Mather; Written by Ted Mather; Cinematography by Dennis Peters; Music by Guido de Angelis; Maurizio de Angelis. **Pr:** RAI; Vidmark Entertainment. **A:** Primary-Adult. **P:** Entertainment. **U:** SURA. **Mov-Ent:** Musical, Dance--Ballet. **Acq:** Purchase. **Dist:** CinemaNow Inc. $29.95.

The Body Beautiful 1991
Explores the relationship between a white mother who undergoes a radical mastectomy and her Black daughter who embarks on a modeling career. Reveals the profound effects of body image and the strain of racial and sexual identity on their charged, intensely loving bond. 23m; VHS. **A:** College-Adult. **P:** Education. **U:** Institution. **Gen-Edu:** Women, Ethnicity, Family. **Acq:** Purchase, Rent/Lease. **Dist:** Women Make Movies. $295.00.

The Body Beneath 1970 (Unrated) — **Bomb!**
A living-dead ghoul survives on the blood of innocents and is still preying on victims today. 85m; VHS, DVD. **C:** Gavin Reed; Jackie Skarvellis; Susan Heard; Colin Gordon; Directed by Andy Milligan. **Pr:** Cinemedia Films. **A:** Jr. High-Adult. **P:** Entertainment. **U:** Home. **Mov-Ent:** Horror. **Acq:** Purchase. **Dist:** Movies Unlimited. $12.74.

Body Building, Body Breaking 1988
The facts about the use of anabolic steroids by over-zealous body builders are discussed. Some of the major risks include heart attack, liver tumors and permanent sterility. Acne, balding and extreme personality changes are some of the lesser side effects. 14m; VHS, 3/4 U. **Pr:** MTI. **A:** Jr. High-Adult. **P:** Education. **U:** Institution, SURA. **Hea-Sci:** Documentary Films, Fitness/Exercise, Drugs. **Acq:** Purchase, Rent/Lease. **Dist:** Phoenix Learning Group. $160.00.

Body Business 1984
Dr. Ken Cooper discusses the non-verbal signals revealed at business lunches and office meetings. 34m; 3/4 U, Special order formats. **Pr:** Salenger Educational Media; Program Source. **A:** College-Adult. **P:** Education. **U:** Institution, SURA. **Gen-Edu:** Communication, Business. **Acq:** Purchase, Rent/Lease. **Dist:** Program Source; Home Vision Cinema.

Body by Jake: Backs to Basics Awesome Abba Dabbas 1994
Features two 15-minute abdominal workouts. 30m; VHS. **A:** Adult. **P:** Instruction. **U:** Home. **How-Ins:** How-To. **Acq:** Purchase. **Dist:** Warner Home Video, Inc. $14.95.

Body by Jake: The Back to Basics Lower Body Workout 1994
Jake shows how to tone the calves, thighs, and buttocks. 57m; VHS. **A:** Adult. **P:** Instruction. **U:** Home. **How-Ins:** How-To. **Acq:** Purchase. **Dist:** Warner Home Video, Inc. $14.95.

Body by Jake: The Back to Basics Total Body Workout 1994
Jake guides viewers through a series of 30-second toning exercises and 60-second cardio-vascular moves. 54m; VHS. **A:** Adult. **P:** Instruction. **U:** Home. **How-Ins:** How-To. **Acq:** Purchase. **Dist:** Warner Home Video, Inc. $14.95.

Body Chemistry 1990 (R) — ★
A married sexual-behavior researcher starts up a passionate affair with his lab partner. When he tries to end the relationship, his female associate becomes psychotic. You've seen it all before in "Fatal Attraction." And you'll see it again in "Body Chemistry 2." 84m; VHS, DVD. **C:** Marc Singer; Mary Crosby; Lisa Pescia; Joseph Campanella; David Kagen; Directed by Kristine Peterson; Written by Jackson Barr; Thom Babbes; Cinematography by Phedon Papamichael; Music by Terry Plumeri. **Pr:** Pacific Trust. **A:** Sr. High-Adult. **P:** Entertainment. **U:** Home. **Mov-Ent:** Mystery & Suspense, Sex & Sexuality, Marriage. **Acq:** Purchase. **Dist:** Sony Pictures Home Entertainment Inc. $19.95.

Body Chemistry 2: Voice of a Stranger 1991 (R) — ★½
An ex-cop (Harrison) obsessed with violent sex gets involved with a talk-radio psychologist (Pescia) whose advice could prove deadly in this erotic sequel. 84m; VHS, DVD, CC. **C:** Gregory Harrison; Lisa Pescia; Morton Downey, Jr.; Robin Riker; Jeremy Piven; John Landis; Directed by Adam Simon; Written by Jackson Barr; Christopher Wooden; Cinematography by Richard Michalak; Music by Nigel Holton. **Pr:** Concorde Pictures; New Horizons Pictures. **A:** Sr. High-Adult. **P:** Entertainment. **U:** Home. **Mov-Ent:** Mystery & Suspense, Sex & Sexuality, Psychiatry. **Acq:** Purchase. **Dist:** Sony Pictures Home Entertainment Inc. $19.95.

Body Chemistry 3: Point of Seduction 1993 (R) — ★★
TV producer Alan Clay (Stevens) finds himself caught in a business and sexual triangle when he okays the making of a movie about the life of a TV sex therapist (Shattuck). Seems the lady's lovers have a nasty habit of getting murdered which doesn't prevent Clay from getting personally involved. His actress wife (Fairchild), who wants to star in the movie, is not pleased. Lives up to its title. 90m; VHS, DVD. **C:** Andrew Stevens; Morgan Fairchild; Shari Shattuck; Directed by Jim Wynorski; Written by Jackson Barr; Cinematography by Don E. Fauntleroy; Music by Chuck Cirino. **A:** College-Adult. **P:** Entertainment. **U:** Home. **Mov-Ent:** Mystery & Suspense, Sex & Sexuality, Filmmaking. **Acq:** Purchase.

Body Chemistry 4: Full Exposure 1995 (R) — ★½
When sex psychologist Claire Archer (Tweed) is accused of murder she hires Simon Mitchell (Poindexter), the best criminal defense attorney around. But Simon becomes just a little too closely involved with his possibly psycho client and it could cost him not only his career and marriage but his life. Also available unrated. 89m; VHS, DVD. **C:** Shannon Tweed; Larry Poindexter; Andrew Stevens; Chick Vennera; Larry Manetti; Stella Stevens; Directed by Jim Wynorski; Written by Karen Kelly; Cinematography by Zoran Hochstatter; Music by Paul Di Franco. **Pr:** Andrew Stevens; Roger Corman; Andrew Stevens; Concorde Pictures; Sunset Films. **A:** College-Adult. **P:** Entertainment. **U:** Home. **Mov-Ent:** Law. **Acq:** Purchase. **Dist:** New Horizons Picture Corp.

Body Count 1987 (Unrated) — ★½
A weird and wealthy family will stop at nothing, including murder and cannibalism, to enhance their fortune. Rather than bodies, count the minutes 'til the movie's over. 90m; VHS, Streaming. **C:** Marilyn Hassett; Dick Sargent; Steven Ford; Greg Mullavey; Thomas Ryan; Bernie (Bernard) White; Directed by Paul Leder. **Pr:** Paul Leder; Paul Leder. **A:** Adult. **P:** Entertainment. **U:** Home. **Mov-Ent:** Horror, Family. **Acq:** Purchase. **Dist:** Millennium Entertainment L.L.C. $79.98.

Body Count 1995 (R) — ★½
Professional killer Makoto (Chiba) and his partner Sybil (Nielsen) seek revenge on the New Orleans cops who set them up. Opposing them are special crime unit partners, Eddie Cook (Davi) and Vinnie Rizzo (Bauer). Lots of shootouts and macho bravado. 93m; VHS, DVD. **C:** Sonny Chiba; Brigitte Nielsen; Robert Davi; Steven Bauer; Jan-Michael Vincent; Talun Hsu; Directed by Talun Hsu; Written by Henry Madden; Cinematography by Blake T. Evans; Music by Don Peake. **A:** Sr. High-Adult. **P:** Entertainment. **U:** Home. **Mov-Ent. Acq:** Purchase. **Dist:** Lions Gate Entertainment Inc.

Body Count 1997 (R) — ★★
Fiorentino and Caruso are reteamed (after "Jade") in a crime saga about a heist gone bad. There is no honor among thieves as driver Hobbs (Caruso) learns when he plans a job with some unreliable associates at the Boston Museum of Fine Arts and things go very wrong. The gang decide to drive to Miami in order to sell their ill-gotten gains, squabbling all the way. Then mystery woman Natalie (Fiorentino) comes aboard, to cause more friction between the gun-happy boys. 84m; VHS, DVD. **C:** David Caruso; Linda Fiorentino; John Leguizamo; Ving Rhames; Donnie Wahlberg; Forest Whitaker; Directed by Robert Patton-Spruill; Written by Theodore Witcher; Cinematography by Charles Mills; Music by Curt Sobel. **Pr:** Mark Burg; Doug McHenry; George Jackson; Island Pictures. **A:** Sr. High-Adult. **P:** Entertainment. **U:** Home. **Mov-Ent:** Crime Drama. **Acq:** Purchase.

Body Count 1997 (R) — ★★
Daniel (Theroux) takes fiancee Suzanne (Milano) home to meet his wealthy family and they just happen to be out of the line of immediate mayhem when a gang of thieves (led by Ice-T) break in to steal the family art collection. Now, they're playing a very serious game of hide-and-seek in order to stay alive—only the situations isn't as clear as it seems. 88m; VHS, DVD, CC. **C:** Ice-T; Alyssa Milano; Justin Theroux; Tommy (Tiny) Lister; Jeannette O'Connor; Nicholas Walker; Eric Saiet; Marta Kristen; Ron Harper; Robert Pine; Richard Danielson; Directed by Kurt Voss; Written by David Diamond; Cinematography by Denis Maloney; Music by Joseph Williams. **Pr:** Paul Hertzberg; Lisa M. Hansen; Cinetel Films. **A:** Sr. High-Adult. **P:** Entertainment. **U:** Home. **Mov-Ent. Acq:** Purchase. **Dist:** Lions Gate Television Corp.

Body Defenses Against Disease 1937
Provides viewers with rare glimpses of disease-causing organisms, the action of antibodies on disease-causing germs, and emphasizes the importance of immunization against disease. 14m/B/W; VHS, 3/4 U. **Pr:** Encyclopedia Britannica Educational Corporation. **A:** Jr. High-Adult. **P:** Education. **U:** Institution, SURA. **Hea-Sci:** Documentary Films, Immunology. **Acq:** Purchase, Rent/Lease, Trade-in. **Dist:** Encyclopedia Britannica.

Body Defenses Against the Outside World 1979
This program describes dangers in the environment and the body's principal defenses against them: the skin, mucous membrane, bone structure, the five senses, and the autonomic nervous system. 13m; VHS, 3/4 U, Special order formats. **Pr:** Churchill. **A:** Primary. **P:** Education. **U:** Institution, Home, SURA. **Hea-Sci:** Documentary Films, Anatomy & Physiology. **Acq:** Purchase, Duplication License. **Dist:** Clear Vue Inc.

Body Double 1984 (R) — ★★★
A voyeuristic unemployed actor peeps on a neighbor's nightly disrobing and sees more than he wants to. A grisly murder leads him into an obsessive quest through the world of pornographic films. 114m; VHS, DVD, Blu-Ray, Wide, CC. **C:** Craig Wasson; Melanie Griffith; Gregg Henry; Deborah Shelton; Guy Boyd; Dennis Franz; David Haskell; Rebecca Stanley; Barbara Crampton; Mindi Miller; Directed by Brian De Palma; Written by Brian De Palma; Robert J. Avrech; Cinematography by Stephen Burum; Music by Pino Donaggio. **A:** Sr. High-Adult. **P:** Entertainment. **U:** Home. **Mov-Ent:** Mystery & Suspense, Sex & Sexuality, Pornography. **Awds:** Natl. Soc. Film Critics '84: Support. Actress (Griffith). **Acq:** Purchase. **Dist:** Sony Pictures Home Entertainment Inc. $14.95.

Body Dynamics 19??
An aerobic exercise program that includes stretching, and exercises designed for specific parts of the body. 60m; VHS. **C:** Kris Clark. **A:** Family. **P:** Instruction. **U:** Home. **Hea-Sci:** Fitness/Exercise. **Acq:** Purchase. **Dist:** Cambridge Educational. $39.95.

Body Electric Forty & Fabulous Workout 1992
A non-impact aerobic workout that features a warm-up and cool down as well as exercises for the chest, arms, legs and rear end. 40m; VHS. **C:** Hosted by Margaret Richard. **A:** Jr. High-Adult. **P:** Instruction. **U:** Home. **Hea-Sci:** Fitness/Exercise. **Acq:** Purchase. **Dist:** Brentwood Music/Provident Music Group. $19.99.

The Body Electric Workout 19??
Richard hosts this workout from the PBS series. ?m; VHS. **A:** Jr. High-Adult. **P:** Instruction. **U:** Home. **Hea-Sci:** Fitness/Exercise. **Acq:** Purchase. **Dist:** Inspired Corp. $19.98.

The Body Fights Disease 1980
This program shows how skin and mucous membranes impede germs, illustrates the action of white cells, macrophages, and lymphocytes, and discusses immunization and antibiotics. Contains extensive animation. 13m; VHS, 3/4 U, Special order formats. **Pr:** Churchill. **A:** Primary-Jr. High. **P:** Education. **U:** Institution, Home, SURA. **Hea-Sci:** Documentary Films, Anatomy & Physiology, Diseases. **Acq:** Purchase, Duplication License. **Dist:** Clear Vue Inc. $99.95.

Body Fluid 1987
An evocative video performance of the "real tinsel" of our society beneath the surface tinsel of how it is portrayed. 22m; VHS, 3/4 U. **Pr:** Paul Wong. **A:** Jr. High-Adult. **P:** Education. **U:** Institution, SURA. **Gen-Edu:** Video, Dance--Performance. **Acq:** Rent/Lease. **Dist:** Video Out Distribution.

Body for Life for Women Workout 2005
A workout created specifically for women and based on the Body for Life program. DVD. **A:** College-Adult. **P:** Instruction. **U:** Home. **Hea-Sci:** Fitness/Exercise. **Acq:** Purchase. **Dist:** Rodale Inc. $19.95.

Body Guards Vs. Convicts 19??
Features no-holds barred boxing matches from Alcatraz between body guards and convicts. Hosted by Ray "Boom Boom" Mancini. 120m; VHS. **A:** Sr. High-Adult. **P:** Entertainment. **U:** Home. **Spo-Rec:** Boxing. **Acq:** Purchase. **Dist:** Production Associates. $19.95.

Body Heat 1981 (R) — ★★★½
During a Florida heat wave, a none-too-bright lawyer becomes involved in a steamy love affair with a mysterious woman and then in a plot to kill her husband. Hurt and Turner (in her film debut) became stars under Kasdan's direction (the three would reunite for "The Accidental Tourist"). Hot love scenes supplement a twisting mystery with a suprise ending. Rourke's arsonist and Danson's soft shoe shouldn't be missed. 113m; VHS, DVD, Blu-Ray. **C:** William Hurt; Kathleen Turner; Richard Crenna; Ted Danson; Mickey Rourke; J.A. Preston; Kim Zimmer; Jane Hallaren; Directed by Lawrence Kasdan; Written by Lawrence Kasdan; Cinematography by Richard H. Kline; Music by John Barry. **Pr:** Ladd Company. **A:** Adult. **P:** Entertainment. **U:** Home. **Mov-Ent:** Mystery & Suspense. **Acq:** Purchase. **Dist:** Warner Home Video, Inc. $19.98.

The Body Image Trap: Taking Control of How You See Your Body 19??
Discusses problems young people face regarding their self-image and common traps they fall prey to such as anorexia, bulimia, and steroid use. 30m; VHS. **A:** Jr. High-Sr. High. **P:** Education. **U:** Institution. **Hea-Sci:** Adolescence, Health Education. **Acq:** Purchase. **Dist:** Hazelden Publishing. $179.00.

The Body in Question Series 1979
An understanding of biological mechanisms is presented in an intellectual and entertaining account of the history and philosophy of the human body. 60m; VHS, 3/4 U. **A:** Sr. High-Adult. **P:** Education. **U:** Institution, SURA. **Hea-Sci:** Documentary Films, Anatomy & Physiology. **Acq:** Purchase. **Dist:** Home Vision Cinema.
Indiv. Titles: 1. Naming the Parts 2. Try a Little Tenderness 3. Sleight of Hand 4. Native Medicine 5. How Do You Feel? 6. Balancing Act 7. Breathless 8. Blood Relations 9. Heart of the Matter 10. Brute Machine 11. Heads and Tails 12. Shaping the Future 13. Perishable Goods.

The Body in the Library 1984 — ★½
A Miss Marple mystery, based on Agatha Christie's 1942 novel, involving the septuagenarian detective investigating the murder of a young woman in a wealthy British mansion. 155m; VHS, DVD, CC. **C:** Joan Hickson; Gwen Watford; Valentine Dyall; Moray Watson; Frederick Jaeger; Raymond Francis; Directed by Silvio Narizzano; Written by T.R. Bowen; Cinematography by John Walker; Music by Alan Blaikley. **Pr:** British Broadcasting Corporation. **A:** Jr. High-Adult. **P:** Entertainment. **U:** Home. **Mov-Ent:** Mystery & Suspense. **Acq:** Purchase. **Dist:** Home Vision Cinema; Video Collectibles. $29.98.

Body Language 1992 (R) — ★★
A successful businesswoman, with a man problem, hires a super secretary with answers to all life's questions—and a deadly agenda all her own. 93m; VHS, CC. **C:** Heather Locklear; Linda Purl; Edward Albert; James Acheson; Directed by Arthur Allan Seidelman; Written by Dan Gurskis; Brian Ross; Cinematography by Hanania Baer. **Pr:** Robert Rolsky; Wilshire Court Productions; Mi Saamy Productions. **A:** Sr. High-Adult. **P:** Entertainment. **U:** Home. **Mov-Ent:** Mystery & Suspense. **Acq:** Purchase. **Dist:** Paramount Pictures Corp.

Body Language 1993
Analyzes the vocabulary of body language, including gesture, eye contact, facial expression, posture, and position and zones of personal space. 25m; VHS. **A:** Jr. High-Sr. High. **P:** Education. **U:** Institution. **Gen-Edu:** Communication. **Acq:** Purchase. **Dist:** The Learning Seed. $89.00.

Body Language 1995 (R) — ★★½
Criminal defense attorney Gavin St. Claire (Berenger) falls for a topless dancer (Schanz), which leads him into all sorts of trouble, including murder. 95m; VHS, DVD, CC. **C:** Tom Berenger; Heidi Schanz; Nancy Travis; Directed by George Case. **A:** Sr. High-Adult. **P:** Entertainment. **U:** Home. **Mov-Ent:** Mystery & Suspense, Law, Sex & Sexuality. **Acq:** Purchase. **Dist:** Movies Unlimited; Alpha Video.

Body Language: An Introduction to Non-Verbal Communication 1994
Eye contact, facial expressions, posture, and personal space zones are discussed. 25m; VHS. **A:** Jr. High. **P:** Education. **U:** Institution. **Gen-Edu:** Communication. **Acq:** Purchase. **Dist:** The Learning Seed. $89.00.

The Body Language of the Race Horse 1989
Chris McCarron and Bonnie Ledbetter show horse owners the subtle indications of a racehorse's disposition. 60m; VHS. **Pr:** Harris Videos and Books. **A:** College-Adult. **P:** Instruction. **U:** Home. **Spo-Rec:** Horses--Racing, Gambling. **Acq:** Purchase. **Dist:** ESPN Inc. $49.95.

Body Language: The Silent Communicator 198?
Everybody communicates through body language even if they are not aware of it. This program teaches how to read other people's body language, and how to control your own. Includes a reference guide and audio cassette. 40m; VHS. **A:** Jr. High-Adult. **P:** Education. **U:** Home. **Gen-Edu:** Communication, Self-Help. **Acq:** Purchase. **Dist:** ESPN Inc. $49.95.

Body Mechanics and Transfer Techniques 1976
The program states the principles of correct body alignment, identifies the proper body mechanics to be used when lifting or moving any object, and demonstrates the correct way to turn or move a patient in bed and in a wheelchair. 30m; VHS, 3/4 U. **Pr:** Fairview General Hospital. **A:** Adult. **P:** Professional. **U:** Institution, CCTV. **Hea-Sci:** Patient Care, How-To. **Acq:** Purchase, Rent/Lease. **Dist:** Kinetic Film Enterprises Ltd.; Medcom Inc.

Body Mechanics: You and Your Neck and Back 1988
The viewer is instructed in proper lifting, bending, reaching, carrying, pushing and pulling procedures to avoid undue stress and possible serious injury to muscles, joints and bones. 16m; VHS, 3/4 U. **Pr:** Altschul Group. **A:** Jr. High-Adult. **P:** Education. **U:** Institution, SURA. **Hea-Sci:** Health Education, Safety Education, Back Disorders. **Acq:** Purchase, Rent/Lease. **Dist:** Discovery Education. $295.00.

Body Melt 1993 — ★★½
When a crazed doctor unleashes an experimental drug on an unsuspecting town, the residents begin to literally melt away. 82m; VHS, DVD. **C:** Gerard Kennedy; Andrew Daddo; Ian Smith; Vincent (Vince Gill) Gil; Regina Gaigalas; Directed by Philip Brophy; Written by Philip Brophy; Rod Bishop; Music by Philip Brophy. **Pr:** Daniel Scharf; Rod Bishop; Beyond Films Limited; Dumb Films Production; Prism Entertainment. **A:** College-Adult. **P:** Entertainment. **U:** Home. **Mov-Ent:** Science Fiction, Horror. **Acq:** Purchase. **Dist:** Movies Unlimited. $17.99.

Body, Mind and Spirit 1982
This program follows four people as they enter a holistic health center where western medical technology is combined with psychotherapeutic techniques. 40m; VHS, 3/4 U, Special order formats. **Pr:** Hartley Productions. **A:** College-Adult. **P:** Education. **U:** Institution, CCTV, Home. **Hea-Sci:** Documentary Films, Psychology, Cults. **Acq:** Purchase. **Dist:** Hartley Film Foundation.

Body Mind Exercises 1997
Dr. Jean Houston lectures about developing mindfulness, expanding intellect, and invigorating our imagination. 42m; VHS. **A:** Adult. **P:** Education. **U:** Home. **Hea-Sci:** Religion, Documentary Films. **Acq:** Purchase. **Dist:** Mystic Fire Video. $19.95.

Body Movement 1972
A sub-series of EBE'S "The Most Important Person" series. Deals with the young child's motor development, motor skills, and coordination. Programs available individually. 4m; VHS, 3/4 U. **Pr:** Sutherland Learning Associates. **A:** Primary. **P:** Education. **U:** Institution, SURA. **Spo-Rec:** Fitness/Exercise. **Acq:** Purchase, Rent/Lease, Trade-in. **Dist:** Encyclopedia Britannica.
Indiv. Titles: 1. Watch Your Balance 2. It Takes Muscles 3. Follow the Leader 4. How Big is Big 5. Joints Let You Bend 6. Put Your Hands on the Top of Your Head.

Body Moves 1990 (PG-13) — ★★
Romantic entanglements heat up the competition when two couples enter a steamy dance contest. Not apt to move you. 98m; VHS. **C:** Kirk Rivera; Steve Messina; Dianne Granger; Linsley Allen; Philip Spruce; Nicole Kolman; Susan Gardner; Directed by Gerry Lively; Written by Daniel Steel. **Pr:** Filmirage. **A:** Sr. High-Adult. **P:** Entertainment. **U:** Home. **Mov-Ent:** Musical--Drama, Romance, Dance. **Acq:** Purchase. **Dist:** Movies Unlimited. $71.99.

The Body of a Poet: A Tribute to Audre Lorde 1995
Tribute to the life and work of Audre Lorde, Black lesbian poet and political activist. Imaginary biopic which centers on the efforts of a group of young lesbians of color. 29m; VHS. **A:** College-Adult. **P:** Education. **U:** Institution. **Gen-Edu:** Women, Homosexuality, Minorities. **Acq:** Purchase, Rent/Lease. **Dist:** Women Make Movies. $250.00.

Body of Evidence 1992 (R) — **Bomb!**
Bad movie with pretensions takes "Basic Instinct" a step further. Instead of an ice pick and sex, sex itself is used as the weapon in a murder trial featuring Madonna as the defendant, Dafoe as her lawyer, and Mantegna as the prosecutor. The plot is, of course, secondary to the S&M sex scenes with Dafoe which feature hot wax and broken glass. Madonna's lack of performance is the least of the film's problems since everyone seems to have forgotten any acting talent they possess. Director Edel fails to direct—the film even looks bad. "Body" was the subject of another NC-17 ratings flap but this film shouldn't be seen by anybody. An unrated version is also available. 99m; VHS, DVD, Wide, CC. **C:** Madonna; Willem Dafoe; Joe Mantegna; Anne Archer; Michael Forest; Charles Hallahan; Mark Rolston; Richard Riehle; Julianne Moore; Frank Langella; Jurgen Prochnow; Stan Shaw; Directed by Uli Edel; Written by Brad Mirman; Cinematography by Doug Milsome; Music by Graeme Revell. **Pr:** Bernd Eichinger; Herman Weigel; Dino De Laurentiis; Metro-Goldwyn-Mayer Pictures. **A:** College-Adult. **P:** Entertainment. **U:** Home. **Mov-Ent. Awds:** Golden Raspberries '93: Worst Actress (Madonna). **Acq:** Purchase. **Dist:** MGM Home Entertainment. $14.95.

Body of Influence 1993 (R) — ★★
A Beverly Hills psychiatrist gets overly involved with a beautiful female patient. But she not only wants his love—she wants his life. Also available in an unrated version. 96m; VHS, DVD, CC. **C:** Nick Cassavetes; Shannon Whirry; Sandahl Bergman; Don Swayze; Anna Karin; Catherine Parks; Diana Barton; Richard Roundtree; Directed by Andrew Garroni; Written by David Schreiber. **Pr:** Axis Films International. **A:** Sr. High-Adult. **P:** Entertainment. **U:** Home. **Mov-Ent:** Mystery & Suspense, Psychiatry. **Acq:** Purchase. **Dist:** Unknown Distributor.

Body of Influence 2 1996 (R) — ★
Shrink Dr. Benson (Anderson) finds he's using his couch for more than professional purposes with his latest patient, Leza (Fisher), whose seductive charms prove more than the doc can handle. The unrated version is 94 minutes. 88m; VHS, DVD. **C:** Daniel Anderson; Jodie Fisher; Steve Poletti; Jonathan Goldstein; Pat Brennan; Directed by Brian J. Smith; Written by Brian J. Smith; Cinematography by Azusa Ohno; Music by Ron Sures. **A:** College-Adult. **P:** Entertainment. **U:** Home. **Mov-Ent:** Psychiatry, Sex & Sexuality. **Acq:** Purchase.

Body of Lies 2008 (R) — ★★½
Crowe packed on the pounds and sports a southern-fried accent in another collaboration with director Scott, this time as veteran CIA operative Ed Hoffman, the stateside handler of field agent Roger Ferris (DiCaprio), who's hot on the trail of a terrorist leader in Jordan and plans to infiltrate his network. But Hoffman seems to have his own agenda, leaving Ferris to wonder whom he can trust. Fraught with formulaic post-9/11, Middle Eastern terrorist v. American spy genre cliches (satellite images, chases/explosions in the local bazaar, frantic yelling into cell phones), and elements of suspense feel manufactured by heavy doses of convoluted double-crosses. Crowe's convincing portrayal of amorality, however, props up what is an otherwise pointless rehash of the evening news. Based on the 2007 novel by David Ignatius. 129m; Blu-Ray, On Demand, Wide. **C:** Leonardo DiCaprio; Russell Crowe; Mark Strong; Carice van Houten; Golshifteh Farahani; Vince Colosimo; Michael Gaston; Oscar Isaac; Simon McBurney; Alon Aboutboul; Directed by Ridley Scott; Written by William Monahan; Cinematography by Alexander Witt; Music by Marc Streitenfeld. **Pr:** Ridley Scott; Donald DeLine; Scott Free; Ridley Scott; Warner Bros. **A:** Sr. High-Adult. **P:** Entertainment. **U:** Home. **L:** English. **Mov-Ent:** Middle East, Intelligence Service, Terrorism. **Acq:** Purchase. **Dist:** Movies Unlimited; Alpha Video; Warner Home Video, Inc.

The Body of Myth 199?
Scholar and author J. Nigro Sansonese divulges the common ancestry between Greeks and Hindus and primal traditions of all ancestral lineage involving trance states recorded and coded in myth. He eludes that in these myths are coded instructions for esoteric practices to achieve deeper body awareness. 90m; DVD. **A:** Adult. **P:** Education. **U:** Home, Institution. **Gen-Edu:** Philosophy & Ideology, Folklore & Legends. **Acq:** Purchase. **Dist:** Thinking Allowed Productions. $49.95.

Body of Proof: The Complete Final Season 2013
ABC 2011-2013 medical drama. "Abducted": Big changes are in store for Megan Hunt after she returns to works months after the murder of Peter Dunlop. She's now working with former flame, Det. Tommy Sullivan, and his partner, Adam Lucas. Their first case hits close to home as Megan's daughter Lacey (Mary Mouser) is abducted by a killer during an investigation into the murders of several young war vets. "Fallen Angel": Kate, who's working on her political campaign, has a tryst with mysterious foreigner Sergei (Ivan Sergei) that involves her in the murder of a teenaged Russian prostitute. 13 episodes. 560m; DVD. **C:** Dana Delaney; Jeri Ryan; Mark Valley; Elyes Gabel; Geoffrey Arend. **A:** Jr. High-Adult. **P:** Entertainment. **U:** Home. **Mov-Ent:** Crime Drama, Television Series, Physicians. **Acq:** Purchase. **Dist:** Buena Vista Home Entertainment. $39.99.

Body of Proof: The Complete First Season 2011
ABC 2011- crime drama. "Pilot": Megan Hunt was a brilliant, arrogant neurosurgeon who neglected her family for her work until a car accident ended her career. Now a medical examiner in Philadelphia, Megan's uncoventional methods and attitude put her at odds with the police and her colleagues. "Talking Heads": Megan's daughter Lacey (Mary Mouser) films her at work as part of a social studies project while the team work on a murder investigation. "Society Hill": Megan accepts her mother Joan's (Joanna Cassidy) invitation to a social event in order to confront the prime suspect in a magazine editor's murder. 9 episodes. 387m; DVD. **C:** Dana Delany; Jeri Ryan; John Carroll Lynch; Sonja Sohn; Nicholas Bishop. **A:** Jr. High-Adult. **P:** Entertainment. **U:** Home. **Mov-Ent:** Crime Drama, Television Series, Physicians. **Acq:** Purchase. **Dist:** Buena Vista Home Entertainment. $29.99.

Body of Proof: The Complete Second Season 2011
ABC 2011- crime drama. "Hunting Party:' Wealthy tycoon Martin Loeb's much-younger wife is shot and there's multiple suspects. "Sympathy for the Devil": Megan's mother, Judge Joan Hunt (Joanna Cassidy), is up or re-election but finding an alleged child killer innocent may cost her, especially when the killer is found murdered. "Mind Games": Megan helped send a serial killer (Peter Stormare) to prison but a new case fits his M.O. Is it a copycat or did Megan make a mistake? The outcome will change her life. 20 episodes. 860m; DVD. **C:** Dana Delany; Jeri Ryan; John Carroll Lynch; Sonja Sohn; Nicholas Bishop. **A:** Jr. High-Adult. **P:** Entertainment. **U:** Home. **Mov-Ent:** Crime Drama, Physicians, Television Series. **Acq:** Purchase. **Dist:** Buena Vista Home Entertainment. $39.99.

Body of War: The True Story of an Anti-War Hero 2008 (G)
Documentary following Thomas Young, a paralyzed Iraqi war veteran who was permanently disabled his first week in Iraq, and the events leading up to the war. 87m; DVD. **A:** Family. **P:** Education. **U:** Home. **Gen-Edu:** Documentary Films, War--General. **Acq:** Purchase. **Dist:** Docurama. $26.95.

Body Parts 1991 (R) — ★★
A crime psychologist loses his arm in an auto accident and receives a transplant from an executed murderer. Does the limb have an evil will of its own? Poorly paced horror goes off the deep end in gore with its third act. Based on the novel "Choice Cuts" by French writers Pierre Boileau and Thomas Narcejac, whose work inspired some of the greatest suspense films. 88m; VHS, DVD, Wide, CC. **C:** Jeff Fahey; Kim Delaney; Lindsay Duncan; Peter Murnik; Brad Dourif; Zakes Mokae; James Kidnie; Paul Ben-Victor; Directed by Eric Red; Written by Eric Red; Norman Snider; Patricia Herskovic; Cinematography by Theo van de Sande; Music by Loek Dikker. **Pr:** Paramount Pictures. **A:** Sr. High-Adult. **P:** Entertainment. **U:** Home. **Mov-Ent:** Horror. **Acq:** Purchase. **Dist:** Paramount Pictures Corp. $14.95.

Body Parts 1994 (Unrated) — ★
For fans of the demented dismemberer niche. Body Parts, a sleazy skin club, loses some of its star talent when the strippers start turning up in cameo video appearances. Seems there's a psycho killer on the loose who videotapes the dismemberment of his stripper-victims. The police decide they've got to meet this guy when he sends them a sample of his work. 90m; VHS, DVD. **C:** Clement von Franckenstein; Dick Monda; Johnny Mandel; Teri Marlow; Directed by Michael Paul Girard; Written by Michael Paul Girard; Music by Miriam Cutler. **Pr:** Frank Mancuso, Jr. **A:** Adult. **P:** Entertainment. **U:** Home. **Mov-Ent:** Mystery & Suspense. **Acq:** Purchase. **Dist:** Movies Unlimited. $9.99.

The Body Parts Business 19??
Documentary look at the black market trade for human organs as the transplant community sees a shortage of organs. 62m; VHS. **A:** Jr. High-Adult. **P:** Education. **U:** Institution. **Gen-Edu:** Medical Education. **Acq:** Purchase, Rent/Lease. **Dist:** National Film Board of Canada. $99.

Body Plans 1990
Illustrates the biological body patterns of sea creatures focusing on the diversity of sea life. 24m; VHS, SVS, 3/4 U. **Pr:** British Broadcasting Corporation. **A:** Jr. High-Sr. High. **P:** Education. **U:** Institution. **Hea-Sci:** Biology, Animals, Oceanography. **Acq:** Purchase. **Dist:** Encyclopedia Britannica. $89.00.

Body Rock 1984 (PG-13) — **Bomb!**
Brooklyn breakdancer Lamas deserts his buddies to work at a chic Manhattan nightclub. Watching Lamas as the emcee/breakdancing fool is a hoot. 93m; VHS, DVD. **C:** Lorenzo Lamas; Vicki Frederick; Cameron Dye; Michelle Nicastro; Ray Sharkey; Grace Zabriskie; Carole Ita White; Directed by Marcelo Epstein. **Pr:** New World Pictures. **A:** Sr. High-Adult. **P:** Entertainment. **U:** Home. **L:** Spanish. **Mov-Ent:** Musical--Drama, Dance. **Acq:** Purchase. **Dist:** Unknown Distributor.
Songs: Body Rock; Team Work; Why Do You Want to Break My Heart?; One Thing Leads to Another; Let Your Body Rock; Vanishing Point; Sharpshooter; The Jungle; Deliver; The Closest to Love.

Body Sculpt: The Video 1992
Body Sculpt of New York is an anti-drug/dropout prevention program designed to educate youngsters about the dangers of drug abuse and showing postive alternatives. A study/discussion guide is included. 35m; VHS. **C:** Directed by Derek Leid. **A:** Primary-Sr. High. **P:** Education. **U:** Institution. **Gen-Edu:** Drug Abuse, Education. **Acq:** Purchase, Rent/Lease. **Dist:** The Cinema Guild. $250.00.

The Body Shop 1972 (Unrated) — **Bomb!**
Unorthodox love story in which a man decides to patch up his relationship with his dead wife by piecing together her dismembered body. For lovers only. Under "Doctor Gore" title the film includes an intro by horror director Herschell Gordon Lewis. 91m; VHS, DVD. **C:** Pat Patterson; Jenny Driggers; Roy Mehaffey; Linda Faile; Candy Furr; Directed by Pat Patterson. **A:** Sr. High-Adult. **P:** Entertainment. **U:** Home. **Mov-Ent:** Horror. **Acq:** Purchase. **Dist:** Unknown Distributor.

Body Shop 1986
A film for all ages, that instructs necessary proper eating and exercise habits by comparing the body to a clean-running car engine. 12m; VHS, SVS, 3/4 U, EJ, Special order formats. **Pr:** New Orleans Video Access Center. **A:** Family. **P:** Education. **U:** Institution, CCTV, CATV, SURA. **Hea-Sci:** Fitness/Exercise. **Acq:** Purchase, Rent/Lease. **Dist:** New Orleans Video Access Center.

Body Shot 1993 (R) — ★★½
Celebrity shutterbug Mickey Dane (Patrick) is fingered in the murder of a rock star after it turns out he did a kinky layout for a look-alike. When police find out he had an obsession for the dead woman, he employs his photographic expertise in the search for the real killer. Effective tension-builder with fast-paced chases through the seamy side of Los Angeles. 98m; VHS, DVD. **C:** Robert Patrick; Michelle Johnson; Ray Wise; Jonathan Banks; Kim Miyori; Kenneth Tobey; Charles Napier; Directed by Dimitri Logothetis; Written by Robert Strauss; Cinematography by Nicholas Josef von Sternberg; Music by Cliff Magness. **A:** Sr. High-Adult. **P:** Entertainment. **U:** Home. **Mov-Ent:** Mystery & Suspense, Photography. **Acq:** Purchase. **Dist:** Movies Unlimited. $14.99.

Body Shots 1999 (R) — ★½
An ensemble cast of twentysomethings explores sex and dating while traversing L.A.'s nightlife. Eight friends come to reflect on their hedonistic lifestyles when Sara (Reid) accuses macho football player Michael (O'Connell) of date rape. During the ultimate "he said/she said" battle, wafer-thin declarations on love in the '90s are made by characters who are as appealing as root canal surgery. 102m; VHS, DVD, Wide. **C:** Sean Patrick Flanery; Jerry O'Connell; Amanda Peet; Tara Reid; Ron Livingston; Emily Procter; Brad Rowe; Sybil Temchen; Directed by Michael Cristofer; Written by David McKenna; Cinematography by Rodrigo Garcia; Music by Mark Isham. **Pr:** New Line Cinema. **A:** Sr. High-Adult. **P:** Entertainment. **U:** Home. **Mov-Ent:** Sex & Sexuality, Rape, Nightclubs. **Acq:** Purchase. **Dist:** New Line Home Video.

Body Slam 1987 (PG) — ★½
A small-time talent monger hits it big with a rock and roll/professional wrestling tour. Piper's debut; contains some violence and strong language. 100m; VHS, DVD. **C:** Roddy Piper; Capt. Lou Albano; Dirk Benedict; Tanya Roberts; Billy Barty; Charles Nelson Reilly; John Astin; Wild Samoan; Tonga Kid; Barry J. Gordon; Directed by Hal Needham; Written by Steven H. Burkow; Music by John D'Andrea. **Pr:** Musifilm Productions; Hemdale Films. **A:** Jr. High-College. **P:** Entertainment. **U:** Home. **Mov-Ent:** Sports--Fiction: Comedy. **Acq:** Purchase. **Dist:** MGM Home Entertainment. $19.98.

The Body Snatcher 1945 (Unrated) — ★★★½
Based on Robert Louis Stevenson's story about a grave robber who supplies corpses to research scientists. Set in Edinburgh in the 19th century, this Lewton production is superior. One of Karloff's best vehicles. 77m/B/W; VHS, DVD. **C:** Edith Atwater; Russell Wade; Rita (Paula) Corday; Boris Karloff; Bela Lugosi; Henry Daniell; Sharyn Moffett; Donna Lee; Directed by Robert Wise; Written by Philip MacDonald; Val Lewton; Cinematography by Robert De Grasse. **Pr:** Val Lewton; Val Lewton; RKO. **A:** Family. **P:** Entertainment. **U:** Home. **Mov-Ent:** Horror. **Acq:** Purchase. **Dist:** Turner Broadcasting System Inc. $19.95.

Body Snatcher from Hell 1969 (Unrated) — ★½
An airliner passes through a mysterious cloud and crashes in a desert. One by one, the passengers are turned into vampires. Some interesting special effects. 84m; VHS. **C:** Hideo Ko; Teruo Yoshida; Tomomi Sato; Eizo Kitamura; Masay Takahashi; Cathy Horlan; Kazuo Kato; Yuko Kusunoki; Directed by Hajime Sato. **Pr:** Shochiku Company. **A:** Jr. High-Adult. **P:** Entertainment. **U:** Home. **L:** Japanese. **Mov-Ent:** Horror. **Acq:** Purchase. **Dist:** Sinister Cinema. $16.95.

Body Snatchers 1993 (R) — ★★
Yet another version of "Invasion of the Body Snatchers." An innocent family arrive at an Army base which turns out to be infested with pod people. This time around the heroine is angst-ridden teenager Marti (Anwar) and the pods have something to do with a mysterious toxic spill. The 1978 remake was well done; this so-so version takes advantage of the advances in special effects (particularly in Anwar's bathtub scene) and sound technology but is slow-paced with few jolts of terror. 87m; VHS, DVD, Wide, CC. **C:** Gabrielle Anwar; Meg Tilly; Terry Kinney; Forest Whitaker; Billy Wirth; R. Lee Ermey; Reilly Murphy; Directed by Abel Ferrara; Written by Stuart Gordon; Dennis Paoli; Nicholas St. John; Cinematography by Bojan Bazelli; Music by Joe Delia. **Pr:** Robert H. Solo; Warner Bros. **A:** Sr. High-Adult. **P:** Entertainment. **U:** Home. **Mov-Ent:** Science Fiction, Adolescence. **Acq:** Purchase. **Dist:** Warner Home Video, Inc.

Body Song Oceans of Joy 1996
Contains gentle swaying motions, breathtaking ocean scenery and haunting music. Designed to relax and invigorate your body. Uses large arm movements to raise your heart rate. 66m; VHS. **A:** Adult. **P:** Instruction. **U:** Home. **Hea-Sci:** Fitness/Exercise, How-To, Self-Help. **Acq:** Purchase. **Dist:** Collage Video Specialties, Inc. $19.95.

The Body Speaks 1975
Two short theatrical pieces are performed by Jerzy Grotowski's Polish Laboratory Theatre in this program. 30m; VHS, 3/4 U, EJ, Q. **Pr:** WCBS New York; Camera Three Productions. **A:** Sr. High-Adult. **P:** Education. **U:** Institution, SURA. **Fin-Art:** Theater. **Acq:** Duplication, Free Duplication. **Dist:** Camera Three Productions, Inc.; Creative Arts Television Archive.

Body Strokes 1995 (Unrated) — ★
Blocked artist Leo Kessler (Johnston) is aroused by the wild fantasies of his beautiful models Beth (Knittle) and Claire (Weber). But it's just fantasy and it also helps get Leo's marriage back on track when manager/wife Karen (Beck) gets jealous. Also available unrated. 99m; VHS, DVD. **C:** Bobby Johnston; Dixie Beck; Kristen Knittle; Catherine Weber; Directed by Edward Holzman; Written by April Moskowitz; Cinematography by Kim Haun; Music by Richard Bronskill. **A:** College-Adult. **P:** Entertainment. **U:** Home. **Mov-Ent:** Art & Artists, Marriage. **Acq:** Purchase. **Dist:** $92.95.

Body Substance Isolation 19??
Offers instruction on body substance isolation that helps comply with OSHA's Bloodborne Pathogen Standard. Explains what body substance isolation is, as well as offers a five-step plan for implementing the procedure. Also discusses patient and staff protective measures to help in infection control. Winner of First Place Award at the American Journal of Nursing Media Festival. 8m; VHS. **A:** College-Adult. **P:** Education. **U:** Institution. **Hea-Sci:** Medical Education, Infection, Diagnosis. **Acq:** Purchase. **Dist:** Medfilms Inc. $195.00.

Body Systems 1986
A series for children outlining the body's basic functions; essentially a filmstrip series copied onto tape. 50m; VHS, 3/4 U. **Pr:** Marshfilm. **A:** Primary. **P:** Education. **U:** Institution. **Chl-Juv:** Documentary Films, Metabolism. **Acq:** Purchase. **Dist:** Marshmedia.
Indiv. Titles: 1. Digestive: The Disappearing Dinner 2. Respiratory: A Puff of Air 3. Bones & Muscles: A Team to Depend On 4. The Heart: A Mighty Pump.

A Body to Die For: The Aaron Henry Story 199?
A high school football star takes steroids and as a result, suffers many health problems such as: two heart attacks, bleeding kidneys, kidney stones, rage, depression, and an attempted suicide. 30m; VHS. **A:** Sr. High-Adult. **P:** Entertainment. **U:** Institution. **Gen-Edu:** Documentary Films, Drugs, Suicide. **Acq:** Purchase. **Dist:** Ambrose Video Publishing, Inc. $99.95.

Body Trouble 1992 (R) — ★½
After being attacked by sharks while vacationing in the Caribbean, a man washes ashore in Miami and then somehow makes his way to New York City. There he meets Vera Vin Rouge and her friends Cinnamon, Spice, Paprika, and Johnny Zero, a gangster. Zero decides he doesn't like the man, so he chases him back to the Caribbean. Supposedly this all happens in only one day. Hmmm... 98m; VHS, DVD. **C:** Dick Van Patten; Priscilla Barnes; Frank Gorshin; James Hong; Marty Rackham; Michael Unger; Jonathan Soloman; Brit Helfer; Leigh Clark; Patricia Cardell; Richie Barathy; Directed by Bill Milling; Written by Bill Milling. **Pr:** Bob Zimmerman; Tom Gioulos; Alpha Pictures International. **A:** Sr. High-Adult. **P:** Entertainment. **U:** Home. **Mov-Ent:** Action-Adventure. **Acq:** Purchase. **Dist:** Unknown Distributor.

Body Trust: Undieting Your Way to Health and Happiness 1993
Learn to live a healthy life without the use of restrictive diets and grueling exercise. Offers alternative ways you can accomplish fitness, health and happiness. 60m; VHS. **Pr:** Production West. **A:** Adult. **P:** Instruction. **U:** Home. **Hea-Sci:** Health Education. **Acq:** Purchase. **Dist:** Tapeworm Video Distributors Inc. $24.95.

The Body Vanished 1939 (Unrated) — ★★
Murder mystery featuring a corpse that disappears from the scene of the crime. 46m/B/W; VHS, DVD. **C:** Anthony Hulme; Ernest Sefton; C. Denier Warren; Directed by Walter Tennyson. **A:** Sr. High-Adult. **P:** Entertainment. **U:** Home. **Mov-Ent:** Mystery & Suspense. **Acq:** Purchase. **Dist:** Sinister Cinema. $16.95.

Body Waves 1992 (R) — ★½
Beach comedy starring Calvert as a teenager who bets his father that he can raise money on his own. In typical teen movie

fashion, he invents a sex cream that drives boys and girls wild. Brain candy featuring lots of skimpy bikinis. 80m; VHS, CC. **C:** Bill Calvert; Leah Lail; Larry Linville; Dick Miller; Jim Wise; Directed by P.J. Pesce. **Pr:** Roger Corman; Mike Elliott. **A:** Sr. High-Adult. **P:** Entertainment. **U:** Home. **Mov-Ent:** Sex & Sexuality. **Acq:** Purchase. **Dist:** $89.98.

Body without Soul 1996
Examines the adult video industry in eastern Europe. In Czech with subtitles. 90m; VHS, DVD. **A:** Adult. **P:** Education. **U:** Institution, Home. **L:** Czech. **Gen-Edu:** Pornography. **Acq:** Purchase. **Dist:** Water Bearer Films Inc. $39.95.

Bodyboarding's Hottest Maneuvers 1991
Keith Sasaki, Jay Reale, and Cameron Steele teach you spinners, tubes, drop knees, floaters, aerials and other swift bodyboard stunts. 30m; VHS. **Pr:** NSI. **A:** Jr. High-Adult. **P:** Entertainment. **U:** Home. **Spo-Rec:** Sports--General, Sports--Water. **Acq:** Purchase. **Dist:** NSI Sound & Video Inc. $19.95.

Bodyguard 1948 (Unrated) — ★★
Hot-tempered L.A. homicide detective Mike Carter (Tierney) quits the force and reluctantly takes a job as a bodyguard for wealthy Eugenia Dysen (Risdon), the owner of a local meat packing plant whose life has been threatened. Carter's case turns complicated when he's framed for the murder of his former supervisor who had a shady involvement in an allegedly accidental death at the Dysen plant. 62m/B/W; DVD. **C:** Lawrence Tierney; Priscilla Lane; Elisabeth Risdon; Phillip Reed; June Clayworth; Steve Brodie; Frank Fenton; Charles Cane; Directed by Richard Fleischer; Written by Fred Niblo, Jr.; Harry Essex; Cinematography by Robert De Grasse. **A:** Sr. High-Adult. **P:** Entertainment. **U:** Home. **Mov-Ent. Acq:** Purchase. **Dist:** WarnerArchive.com.

The Bodyguard 1976 (R) — ★½
The Yakuza, Japan's mafia, and New York's big crime families face off in this martial arts extravaganza. 89m; VHS, DVD. **C:** Sonny Chiba; Aaron Banks; Bill Louie; Judy Lee; Etsuko (Sue) Shihomi; Directed by Maurice Sarli. **Pr:** Terry Levene. **A:** Adult. **P:** Entertainment. **U:** Home. **Mov-Ent:** Martial Arts. **Acq:** Purchase. **Dist:** BFS Video.

The Bodyguard 1992 (R) — ★★
Buttoned-down, ex-Secret Service agent turned private bodyguard reluctantly takes on a wildly successful singer/actress as a client. Houston, in her acting debut as the over-indulged diva, doesn't have to stretch too far but acquits herself well. Costner has really bad hair day but easily portrays the tightly wound Frank. Critically trashed, a boxoffice smash, and too long. Originally scripted by producer Kasdan over a decade ago, with Steve McQueen in mind. Predictable romantic melodrama is kept moving by the occasional sharp dialog and a few action pieces. Songs include the smash hit "I Will Always Love You," written and originally performed by Dolly Parton. 130m; VHS, DVD, CC. **C:** Kevin Costner; Whitney Houston; Gary Kemp; Bill Cobbs; Ralph Waite; Tomas Arana; Michele Lamar Richards; Mike Starr; Christopher Birt; DeVaughn Nixon; Charles Keating; Robert Wuhl; Cameo(s) Debbie Reynolds; Directed by Mick Jackson; Written by Lawrence Kasdan; Cinematography by Andrew Dunn; Music by Alan Silvestri. **Pr:** Jim Wilson; Kevin Costner; Kevin Costner; Lawrence Kasdan; Lawrence Kasdan; TIG Productions. **A:** Sr. High-Adult. **P:** Entertainment. **U:** Home. **Mov-Ent:** Biography: Show Business. **Awds:** MTV Movie Awards '93: Song ("I Will Always Love You"). **Acq:** Purchase. **Dist:** Baker and Taylor; Warner Home Video, Inc. $19.98.

The Bodyguard 2004 (Unrated) — ★½
Wong Kom (Pechtai Wongkamlao) is a bodyguard who is fired after his client dies. Realizing the people who murdered his client will now want to murder his son to prevent him from inheriting the family business, he places the boy in hiding while he tries to sort things out. Thai humor doesn't translate well to other nationalities, and unless you have a fairly thorough knowledge of their society, it won't make sense. Unfortunately for this film, the comedy takes precedence over the action, so many audiences will be left scratching their heads. 100m; DVD. **C:** Petchthai Wongkamlao; Pumwaree Yodkamol; Directed by Petchthai Wongkamlao; Written by Petchthai Wongkamlao; Cinematography by Nattawut Kittikhun; Music by Hip-Pro. **A:** Sr. High-Adult. **P:** Entertainment. **U:** Home. **L:** English, Spanish, Thai. **Mov-Ent:** Action-Comedy, Martial Arts. **Acq:** Purchase. **Dist:** Magnolia Home Entertainment. $14.98.

The Bodyguard 2 2007 (Unrated) — ★★
In this prequel to the first film, Khumlao (Pechtai Wongkumlao) is an anti-terrorist agent posing as a singer to catch the criminal owners of a record label. Like the first film it has cameos or uses much of the crew from 'Ong-Bak'. Unlike the first one, they tried to make the humor more accessible to a non-Thai audience. 95m; DVD. **C:** Petchthai Wongkamlao; Jacqueline Apitananon; Sushin Kuan-Saghuan; Surachai Sombutchareon; Janet Khiew; Directed by Petchthai Wongkamlao; Written by Petchthai Wongkamlao; Cinematography by Jiradech Samneeyongsana; Music by Lullaby Music Production. **A:** Sr. High-Adult. **P:** Entertainment. **U:** Home. **L:** English, Spanish, Thai. **Mov-Ent:** Action-Comedy, Martial Arts. **Acq:** Purchase. **Dist:** Magnolia Home Entertainment. $14.98.

The Bodyguard from Beijing 1994 (Unrated) — ★★½
Beijing bodyguard John Chang (Li) is hired to protect pampered rich girl Michelle (Chung), who's the witness to a murder. And John also has to deal with the revenge plans of an ex-soldier whose brother John has killed. Cantonese with subtitles. 90m; VHS, DVD. **C:** Jet Li; Christy Chung; Kent Cheng; Collin Chou; Directed by Corey Yuen; Written by Gordon Chan; Kin-Chung Chan; Cinematography by Tom Lau. **A:** Sr. High-Adult. **P:** Entertainment. **U:** Home. **L:** Chinese. **Mov-Ent:** Action-Adventure. **Acq:** Purchase. **Dist:** Buena Vista Home Entertainment.

Bodyshaping 1989
Former Ms. Olympia Everson, star of ESPN's "Bodyshaping," shows you the most effective methods of slimming down and shaping up. 50m; VHS. **C:** Hosted by Cory (Corinna) Everson. **Pr:** ESPN. **A:** Sr. High-Adult. **P:** Instruction. **U:** Home. **Hea-Sci:** Fitness/Exercise. **Acq:** Purchase. **Dist:** ESPN Inc.; Fast Forward. $29.95.

BodyShaping: Circuit Training with Weights 199?
ESPN BodyShaping instructors show men and women how to use exercise machines for a circuit training workout. 55m; VHS. **A:** Jr. High-Adult. **P:** Instruction. **U:** Home. **Hea-Sci:** Fitness/Exercise. **Acq:** Purchase. **Dist:** Fast Forward; ESPN Inc.

BodyShaping: For Slender Thighs, Hips & Stomach 1989
The next step in bodyshaping is working on hips and thighs. Cory shows you how. 50m; VHS. **C:** Hosted by Cory (Corinna) Everson. **Pr:** ESPN. **A:** Sr. High-Adult. **P:** Instruction. **U:** Home. **Hea-Sci:** Fitness/Exercise. **Acq:** Purchase. **Dist:** ESPN Inc.; Fast Forward.

BodyShaping: Home Gym & Workout Video Set 1989
Bodybuilder Everson hosts this video designed to be used with the Bodyshaping Home Gym. One two, one two, everybody together now. 50m; VHS. **C:** Hosted by Cory (Corinna) Everson. **Pr:** ESPN. **A:** Sr. High-Adult. **P:** Instruction. **U:** Home. **Hea-Sci:** Fitness/Exercise. **Acq:** Purchase. **Dist:** ESPN Inc.; Fast Forward.

BodyShaping: One-on-One Personal Training Workout with Weights 199?
Men and women learn to use weight training machines and free-weights for a personalized workout program that will tone, shape and define stomachs, legs, chests and arms. 55m; VHS. **A:** Jr. High-Adult. **P:** Instruction. **U:** Home. **Hea-Sci:** Fitness/Exercise, Weight Lifting. **Acq:** Purchase. **Dist:** Fast Forward; ESPN Inc.

Bodytalk 1988
Young viewers are given a simple idea as to how various body parts function. 8m; VHS, 3/4 U. **Pr:** Bodytalk Programmes. **A:** Primary-Jr. High. **P:** Education. **U:** Institution, SURA. **Hea-Sci:** Health Education. **Acq:** Purchase, Trade-in. **Dist:** Encyclopedia Britannica. $372.00.
Indiv. Titles: 1. In and Out 2. Breathing and Talking 3. Beating and Bleeding 4. Running, Jumping and Standing Still 5. Sensing, Thinking and Feeling 6. Skin and Hair 7. Growing Up 8. Growing Old.

The Bodywatch Series 1988
This series provides information on stress management, nutrition, exercise and other important health issues. 30m; VHS, 3/4 U. **Pr:** WGBH Boston. **A:** Jr. High-Adult. **P:** Education. **U:** Institution, SURA. **Hea-Sci:** Fitness/Exercise, Health Education, Drug Abuse. **Acq:** Purchase, Rent/Lease. **Dist:** Phoenix Learning Group. $80.00.
Indiv. Titles: 1. An Ancient Form of Care 2. Are Your Hormones Getting the Best of You? 3. Back on Track 4. Beating the Depression Blues 5. Beyond Calcium 6. Beautiful Dreamers 7. Breast Cancer 8. Building Better Babies 9. A Chemical Called Cocaine 10. Corralling Your Cravings 11. The Daycare Dilemma 12. Designer Bodies 13. Doctors Are People, Too 14. Eating for Fitness 15. Fat Stuff 16. Fighting Fat 17. Good Intentions: Bad Diets for Kids 18. Good Shot 19. A Hair-Raising Experience 20. Having Babies After 30 21. Headaches 22. Heart Help 23. Hidden Family Agendas 24. Hyperactivity 25. I.Q. 26. Kidsports 27. The Knowing Nose 28. Mastering Pain 29. Music and Health 30. The New Sensible Workout 31. Nobody Ever Died of Middle Age 32. No Butts 33. The Savvy Patient 34. Secrets of Longevity 35. Sexually-Transmitted Diseases 36. Skin Deep 37. Starting and Sticking With Exercise 38. Stifle That Sneeze 39. Stress to Your Advantage 40. The Ten Most-Asked Questions About Food 41. Tough Times for Teens 42. Treading Lightly 43. Twin Reflections 44. Well-Conceived 45. The Whole Truth Diet 46. Why Am I So Tired? 47. Will To Be Well.

Bodywork 1999 (R) — ★★
Virgil Guppy (Matheson) buys a second-hand Jaguar that gives him nothing but trouble, especially when he finds a dead prostitute in the trunk of the car. Virgil goes on the run and hides out with a young woman (Coleman) who's a professional car thief. British crime caper finally has too many twists for its own good. The Winslet who plays Virgil's girlfriend is the sister of actress Kate. 93m; VHS, DVD. **C:** Hans Matheson; Charlotte Coleman; Clive Russell; Beth Winslet; Directed by Gareth Rhys Jones; Written by Gareth Rhys Jones; Cinematography by Thomas Wuthvich; Music by Dusan Kojic; Srdjan Kurpjel. **A:** Sr. High-Adult. **P:** Entertainment. **U:** Home. **Mov-Ent:** Crime Drama. **Acq:** Purchase. **Dist:** Alpha Video; Lions Gate Entertainment Inc.

Boeheim on Basketball 1990
Syracuse University Basketball Coach Jim Boeheim highlights the fundamental skills that can help a young player of today develop the abilities and knowledge necessary to become a star of the future. 45m; VHS. **Pr:** Champions on Film. **A:** Jr. High-College. **P:** Instruction. **U:** Home. **Spo-Rec:** Basketball. **Acq:** Purchase. **Dist:** School-Tech Inc. $29.95.

Boeing Boeing 1965 (Unrated) — ★★½
A dated but still amusing sex farce about a bachelor newspaperman (Curtis) in Paris, his three stewardess girlfriends, and the elaborate plots he resorts to in trying to keep them from finding out about each other. When the new Boeing jet makes air travel faster all Curtis' schemes may come crashing down. Ritter is fun as the exasperated housekeeper and Lewis amazingly subdued as Curtis' business rival. 102m; VHS, DVD, Blu-Ray, CC. **C:** Tony Curtis; Jerry Lewis; Dany Saval; Christiane Schmidtmer; Suzanna Leigh; Thelma Ritter; Directed by John Rich; Written by Edward Anhalt. **Pr:** Hal B. Wallis; Paramount Pictures. **A:** Jr. High-Adult. **P:** Entertainment. **U:** Home. **Mov-Ent:** Comedy--Screwball, Sex & Sexuality, Journalism. **Acq:** Purchase. **Dist:** Olive Films; Paramount Pictures Corp. $14.95.

Boeing vs. the World 1981
A look at how Boeing is dealing with competition from a new consortium of European government-backed firms. Part of the "Enterprise" series. 30m; VHS, 3/4 U. **C:** Hosted by Eric Sevareid. **Pr:** PBS. **A:** Jr. High-Adult. **P:** Education. **U:** Institution, SURA. **Gen-Edu:** Sports--General, Business. **Acq:** Purchase, Rent/Lease. **Dist:** Phoenix Learning Group.

Boesman & Lena 2000 (Unrated) — ★★½
Adaptation of the apartheid-era play by Athol Fugard follows the travails of downtrodden couple, Boesman (Glover) and Lena (Bassett). Their shanty town home in Cape Town has been bulldozed by the government so they take to the dusty road with their meager belongings, constantly bickering about their plight. The couple construct a makeshift abode for the night, which attracts the attention of an old man (Jonah) even lower on the economic ladder, whom Lena allows to stay to Boesman's displeasure. Performances are outstanding. Last film for director Berry. 86m; VHS, DVD, Wide. **C:** Danny Glover; Angela Bassett; Willie Jonah; Directed by John Berry; Written by John Berry; Cinematography by Alain Choquart; Music by Wally Badarou. **A:** College-Adult. **P:** Entertainment. **U:** Home. **Mov-Ent:** Apartheid, Africa, Black Culture. **Acq:** Purchase. **Dist:** Kino on Video.

Boffo! Tinseltown's Bombs and Blockbusters 2005 (Unrated)
Clips and interviews provide insight into the moviemaking process and the often thin line between blockbuster success and mega-flop. 75m; DVD, CC. **A:** Jr. High-Adult. **P:** Entertainment. **U:** Home. **Mov-Ent:** Documentary Films, Film History. **Acq:** Purchase. **Dist:** Home Box Office Inc.

Bog 1984 (PG) — ★
Boggy beast from the Arctic north awakens to eat people. Scientists mount an anti-monster offensive. 90m; VHS, DVD. **C:** Gloria De Haven; Marshall Thompson; Leo Gordon; Aldo Ray; Glen Voros; Ed Clark; Carol Terry; Directed by Don Keeslar; Written by Carl Kitt; Cinematography by Jack Willoughby; Music by Bill (William) Walker. **Pr:** Independent. **A:** Jr. High-Adult. **P:** Entertainment. **U:** Home. **Mov-Ent:** Science Fiction, Arctic Regions. **Acq:** Purchase. **Dist:** Unknown Distributor.

Bog Ecology 1987
Examines the development of the bog wetland and the various plants and animals that live in a bog. 30m; VHS, 3/4 U. **Pr:** Educational Images. **A:** Jr. High-Sr. High. **P:** Education. **U:** Institution. **Hea-Sci:** Documentary Films, Ecology & Environment, Biology. **Acq:** Purchase. **Dist:** Educational Images Ltd.

Boggy Creek II 1983 (PG) — ★½
The continuing saga of the eight-foot-tall, 300 pound monster from Texarkana. Third in a series of low-budget movies including "The Legend of Boggy Creek" and "Return to Boggy Creek." 93m; VHS, DVD. **C:** Charles B. Pierce; Cindy Butler; Serene Hedin; Directed by Charles B. Pierce; Written by Charles B. Pierce. **Pr:** Howco International Pictures. **A:** Sr. High-Adult. **P:** Entertainment. **U:** Home. **Mov-Ent:** Horror. **Acq:** Purchase. **Dist:** Amazon.com Inc. $59.95.

Bogie: The Last Hero 1980 — ★½
Biography of Humphrey Bogart, populated by almost-lookalikes who can almost act. 100m; VHS. **C:** Kevin J. O'Connor; Kathryn Harrold; Ann Wedgeworth; Patricia Barry; Alfred Ryder; Donald May; Richard Dysart; Arthur Franz; Directed by Vincent Sherman; Music by Charles Bernstein. **Pr:** CBS; Carles Fries Productions. **A:** Family. **P:** Entertainment. **U:** Home. **Mov-Ent:** TV Movies, Biography: Show Business. **Acq:** Purchase. **Dist:** Amazon.com Inc. $14.95.

Bogota: One Day 1978
This look at Columbia's capital city contrasts the rich and the poor, and profiles a group of street children. 90m; VHS, 3/4 U. **Pr:** WGBH Boston. **A:** College-Adult. **P:** Education. **U:** Institution, CCTV, CATV. **Gen-Edu:** Documentary Films, South America, Sociology. **Acq:** Purchase, Rent/Lease, Off-Air Record. **Dist:** PBS Home Video.

Bogus 1996 (PG) — ★★
Aptly named fantasy-comedy has orphan Albert (Osment) sent to foster aunt Harriet (Goldberg) after his magician's assistant mom (Travis) dies in a car accident. He brings along an imaginary friend, the eponymous Bogus (Depardieu) to ease the transition. Harriet is your typical workaholic easterner and isn't too thrilled with the arrangement. Goldberg and Depardieu are fine, but predictability drains most of the magic. 112m; VHS, DVD, CC. **C:** Whoopi Goldberg; Gerard Depardieu; Haley Joel Osment; Nancy Travis; Andrea Martin; Denis Mercier; Ute Lemper; Sheryl Lee Ralph; Al Waxman; Fiona Reid; Don Francks; Directed by Norman Jewison; Written by Alvin Sargent; Cinematography by David Watkin; Music by Marc Shaiman. **Pr:** Arnon Milchan; New Regency Pictures; Warner Bros. **A:** Primary-Adult. **P:** Entertainment. **U:** Home. **Mov-Ent:** Comedy-Drama, Magic, Adoption. **Acq:** Purchase. **Dist:** Warner Home Video, Inc.

The Bogus Witch Project 2000 (R) — ★
In the long and ignoble history of cheap parodies, this is surely one of the cheapest. It's a series of short films—sketches and blackouts, really—that use the premise of the original "Blair Witch" film to poke fun at the movie biz. Here's the preface to one: "In August 1999, three out-of-work actors disappeared in

the woods near Sherman Oaks, California, while looking for Blair Underwood to give him a script. Twenty-four hours later, their footage was found and turned into a vehicle for shameless self-promotion." The episode starring Pauly Shore is the weakest of the weak. Funnier bits appear between spoofs. 85m; DVD. **C:** Pauly Shore; Michael Ian Black; Directed by Victor Kargan; Music by Carvin Knowles. **A:** Sr. High-Adult. **P:** Entertainment. **U:** Home. **Mov-Ent:** Satire & Parody. **Acq:** Purchase. **Dist:** Lions Gate Home Entertainment. $24.99.

Bohachi Bushido: Code of the Forgotten Eight 1973 (Unrated) — ★½
Written by Kazuo Koike, this is one of the author's more over-the-top series. Shiro (Tetsuro Tamba) is an assassin tired of living. Prevented from committing suicide by the Bohashi clan, they nurse him back to health and ask only that he dispose of their enemies in return for protecting him from the authorities that have pursued him all of his life. But the Bohashi are a clan of soulless monsters charged with filling Edo's brothels, which they do through kidnapping, slavery, and torture. 81m; DVD. **C:** Tetsuro Tamba; Directed by Teru Ishii; Written by Kazuo Koike; San Kaji; Goseki Kojima; Cinematography by Jubei Suzuki; Music by Hajime Kaburagi. **A:** Sr. High-Adult. **P:** Entertainment. **U:** Home. **L:** English, Japanese. **Mov-Ent:** Exploitation. **Acq:** Purchase. **Dist:** Discotek Media. $29.95.

Bohemian Girl 1936 (Unrated) — ★★★
The last of Laurel and Hardy's comic operettas finds them as guardians of a young orphan (Hood, famous for her roles in the Our Gang comedies), whom no one realizes is actually a kidnapped princess. 74m/B/W; VHS, DVD. **C:** Stan Laurel; Oliver Hardy; Mae Busch; Darla Hood; Julie Bishop; Thelma Todd; James Finlayson; Directed by James W. Horne. **Pr:** Hal Roach; MGM. **A:** Family. **P:** Entertainment. **U:** Institution, Home. **Mov-Ent:** Comedy--Slapstick, Children. **Acq:** Purchase. **Dist:** Nostalgia Family Video/Hollywood's Attic. $19.95.

Boiler Control for Energy Efficiency: An Overview 1978
An introduction to boiler control, beginning with what a boiler is and how the operator can enhance its energy efficiency. 20m; 3/4 U, Special order formats. **Pr:** Instrument Society of America. **A:** Adult. **P:** Vocational. **U:** Institution, CCTV. **Bus-Ind:** Industrial Arts. **Acq:** Purchase. **Dist:** ISA -The International Society of Automation.

Boiler Control Series 1978
Filmed on location in major industrial plants, shows boiler operators how to maintain safety and minimize pollutants. Animation is utilized to illustrate combustion and steam output dynamics. Programs are available individually. 23m; 3/4 U, Special order formats. **Pr:** Instrument Society of America. **A:** Adult. **P:** Vocational. **U:** Institution, CCTV. **Bus-Ind:** Engineering, Industrial Arts. **Acq:** Purchase. **Dist:** ISA -The International Society of Automation.
Indiv. Titles: 1. Boiler Control for Energy Efficiency: An Overview 2. Boiler Feedwater Control: Basic Principles 3. Basic Principles of Boiler Combustion Control: Gas, Oil and Auxiliary Fuels 4. Basic Principles of Boiler Combustion Control: Coal and Other Solid Fuels 5. Principles of Boiler Safety Systems.

Boiler Design and Construction 199?
An instrument technology training program on boiler design and construction. Includes a manual. 30m; VHS. **A:** Adult. **P:** Instruction. **U:** Institution. **Bus-Ind:** Technology, Job Training. **Acq:** Purchase. **Dist:** ISA -The International Society of Automation. $95.00.

Boiler Feedwater and Steam—Controlling for Safety and Efficiency 199?
An instrument technology training program on boiler feedwater and steam. Includes a manual. 30m; VHS. **A:** Adult. **P:** Instruction. **U:** Institution. **Bus-Ind:** Technology, Job Training. **Acq:** Purchase. **Dist:** ISA -The International Society of Automation. $95.00.

Boiler Feedwater Control Basic Principles 1978
This presentation offers step-by-step explanations of the various watertube boiler feedwater control systems as well as explaining the concepts of shrink and swell. Part of the "Boiler Control" series. 18m; 3/4 U, Special order formats. **Pr:** Instrument Society of America. **A:** Adult. **P:** Vocational. **U:** Institution, CCTV. **Bus-Ind:** Engineering, Industrial Arts. **Acq:** Purchase. **Dist:** ISA -The International Society of Automation.

Boiler Fuel and Air-Conditioning for Safety and Efficiency 199?
An instrument technology training program on boiler fuel and air-conditioning safety and efficiency. Includes a manual. 30m; VHS. **A:** Adult. **P:** Instruction. **U:** Institution. **Bus-Ind:** Technology, Job Training. **Acq:** Purchase. **Dist:** ISA -The International Society of Automation. $95.00.

Boiler Operations 199?
An instrument technology training program on boiler operations. Includes a manual. 30m; VHS. **A:** Adult. **P:** Instruction. **U:** Institution. **Bus-Ind:** Technology, Job Training. **Acq:** Purchase. **Dist:** ISA -The International Society of Automation. $95.00.

Boiler Room 2000 (R) — ★★★
Basic plot about a greedy naive young man caught up in a situation that's out of his control gets the high testosterone treament. Seth (Ribisi) jumps at the chance to become a trainee at an up-and-coming brokerage firm filled with macho twentysomethings greedy for success. But what Seth eventually discovers is that the firm he's allied himself with runs an illegal stock-trading operation that's under investigation. Well-cast and stylish, with Affleck effective in a small role as the firm's strutting recruiter. 120m; VHS, DVD, Blu-Ray, Wide. **C:** Giovanni Ribisi; Vin Diesel; Nicky Katt; Nia Long; Scott Caan; Ron Rifkin; Jamie Kennedy; Taylor Nichols; Tom Everett Scott; Ben Affleck; Jon Abrahams; Kirk Acevedo; Directed by Ben Younger; Written by Ben Younger; Cinematography by Enrique Chediak. **Pr:** Jennifer Todd; Suzanne Todd; New Line Cinema. **A:** Sr. High-Adult. **P:** Entertainment. **U:** Home. **Mov-Ent:** Dropouts, Ethics & Morals. **Acq:** Purchase. **Dist:** Warner Home Video, Inc.

Boiling Point 1932 — ★½
Lawman proves once again that justice always triumphs. 67m/B/W; VHS, DVD. **C:** Hoot Gibson; Helen Foster; Wheeler Oakman; Skeeter Bill Robbins; Billy Bletcher; Lafe (Lafayette) McKee; Charles Bailey; George "Gabby" Hayes; Directed by George Melford; Written by Donald W. Lee; Cinematography by Tom Galligan; Harry Neumann. **Pr:** Allied Artists International. **A:** Family. **P:** Entertainment. **U:** Home. **Mov-Ent:** Western. **Acq:** Purchase. **Dist:** Alpha Video. $19.95.

Boiling Point 1990 (Unrated) — ★★
Masaki (Ono) is a young, inarticulate, misfit, loser gas-station attendent who even lets down his local baseball team when he tries to play ball. Then he makes the mistake of slugging a yakuza member, so he heads to Okinawa to buy a gun to defend himself and meets up with the ultimate Mr. Cool—Uehara (Kitano). Uehara is such a bad ass even the yakuza don't want anything to do with him, so who better than the master to teach Masaki how to survive. The Japanese title refers to a baseball score, which somehow seems more apt. Japanese with subtitles. 98m; VHS, DVD, Wide. **C:** Takeshi "Beat" Kitano; Masahiko Ono; Hisashi Igawa; Directed by Takeshi "Beat" Kitano; Cinematography by Katsumi Yanagishima. **A:** Sr. High-Adult. **P:** Entertainment. **U:** Home. **L:** Japanese. **Mov-Ent. Acq:** Purchase. **Dist:** Wellspring Media.

Boiling Point 1993 (R) — ★★½
Darkly flavored action drama delves into the personalities of its two main characters before setting up a final confrontation. Treasury agent Jimmy Mercer (Snipes) is trying to solve his partner's murder, relentlessly pursuing the murderers in cold and methodical fashion. Sleazy Red Diamond (Hopper), just out of prison, owes the mob and has one week to pay them back. Lawman and crook both come home to women, (Davidovich and Perrine) graduates of the Hollywood school of female martyrdom, selflessly supportive of their men. Grim but cliched. Adapted from the Gerald Petievich novel "Money Men." 93m; VHS, DVD, Wide. **C:** Wesley Snipes; Dennis Hopper; Lolita Davidovich; Viggo Mortensen; Dan Hedaya; Valerie Perrine; Seymour Cassel; Jonathan Banks; Tony LoBianco; Christine Elise; James Tolkan; Paul Gleason; Directed by James B. Harris; Written by James B. Harris; Cinematography by King Baggot; Music by Cory Lerios; John D'Andrea. **Pr:** Leonardo de la Fuente; Mark Frydman; Warner Bros. **A:** College-Adult. **P:** Entertainment. **U:** Home. **Mov-Ent:** Crime Drama, Secret Service, Prostitution. **Acq:** Purchase. **Dist:** Warner Home Video, Inc. $19.98.

Bojangles 2001 (Unrated) — ★★½
Made-for-cable biopic of Bill "Bojangles" Robinson is strictly a by-the-numbers affair from the beginning at the funeral to the various characters who turn and address the camera to explain what they thought of the contradictory man. Gregory Hines does his usual excellent job in the lead, and the film looks very good. 101m; VHS, DVD. **C:** Gregory Hines; Peter Riegert; Kimberly Elise; Savion Glover; Maria Ricossa; Directed by Joseph Sargent; Written by Richard Wesley; Robert P. Johnson; Cinematography by Donald M. Morgan; Music by Terence Blanchard. **A:** Jr. High-Adult. **P:** Entertainment. **U:** Home. **Mov-Ent:** Biography: Show Business, Dance. **Acq:** Purchase. **Dist:** Showtime Networks Inc.

Bol D'Or 1988
Highlights from the 1988 bike race known world-wide. ?m; VHS. **A:** Family. **P:** Entertainment. **U:** Home. **Spo-Rec:** Sports--General, Motorcycles. **Acq:** Purchase. **Dist:** Powersports - Powerdocs. $39.95.

The Bold Caballero 1936 — ★½
Rebel chieftain Zorro overthrows oppressive Spanish rule in the days of early California. 69m/B/W; VHS, DVD. **C:** Robert "Bob" Livingston; Heather Angel; Sig Rumann; Robert Warwick; Directed by Wells Root. **Pr:** Republic. **A:** Family. **P:** Entertainment. **U:** Home. **Mov-Ent. Acq:** Purchase. **Dist:** Rex Miller Artisan Studio. $19.95.

Bold Steps 1987
A history of the National Ballet of Canada, featuring footage of its most auspicious performances. In HiFi Stereo. 81m; VHS. **Pr:** Canadian Broadcasting Corp. **A:** Family. **P:** Entertainment. **U:** Home. **Fin-Art:** Documentary Films, Dance. **Acq:** Purchase. **Dist:** Corinth Films Inc.; Home Vision Cinema; Music Video Distributors. $39.95.

The Boldest Job in the West 1971 — ★
Italian western about bankrobbers who meet to divide their spoils. Problem is, the guys with the loot don't show. Dubbed in English. 200m; VHS. **C:** Mark Edwards; Frank Sancho; Carmen Sevilla; Directed by Jose Antonio De La Loma. **Pr:** Joseph Loman. **A:** Jr. High-Adult. **P:** Entertainment. **U:** Home. **L:** Spanish. **Mov-Ent. Acq:** Purchase. **Dist:** No Longer Available.

Boldt Decision: Impacts and Implementation 1976
A discussion of the court ruling by U.S. Judge George Boldt who ruled that treaty Indians in Washington are entitled to half the harvestable catch of salmon and steelhead. 60m; 3/4 U. **Pr:** Washington Sea Grant Presentation. **A:** Sr. High-Adult. **P:** Education. **U:** Institution. **Gen-Edu:** Documentary Films, Native Americans, Law. **Acq:** Rent/Lease. **Dist:** University of Washington Educational Media Collection.

Boldt Decision: Update 1976
A look at the impact of the court ruling by U.S. Judge George Boldt that treaty Indians in Washington are entitled to half the harvestable catch of salmon and steelhead. 60m; 3/4 U. **Pr:** Washington Sea Grant Presentation. **A:** Sr. High-Adult. **P:** Education. **U:** Institution. **Gen-Edu:** Documentary Films, Native Americans, Law. **Acq:** Rent/Lease. **Dist:** University of Washington Educational Media Collection.

The Bolero 1973
Zubin Mehta conducts the Los Angeles Philharmonic Orchestra in a performance of "Bolero" by Ravel. 26m; VHS, 3/4 U, Special order formats. **C:** Conducted by Zubin Mehta. **Pr:** Alan Miller. **A:** Jr. High-Adult. **P:** Entertainment. **U:** Institution, Home, SURA. **L:** Danish. **Fin-Art:** Music--Classical, Opera. **Acq:** Purchase, Rent/Lease, Duplication License. **Dist:** Pyramid Media. $395.00.

Bolero 1982 — ★★½
Beginning in 1936, this international epic traces the lives of four families across three continents and five decades, highlighting the music and dance that is central to their lives. 173m; VHS, DVD. **C:** James Caan; Geraldine Chaplin; Robert Hossein; Nicole Garcia; Jacques Villeret; Directed by Claude Lelouch; Written by Claude Lelouch. **Pr:** Films 13; TF-1 Films. **A:** Sr. High-Adult. **P:** Entertainment. **U:** Home. **Mov-Ent:** Family. **Acq:** Purchase. **Dist:** $19.95.

Bolero 1984 (R) — **Bomb!**
What sounds like a wet dream come true is really just a good snooze: Bo Derek plays a beautiful young woman who goes on a trip around the world in hopes of losing her virginity; in Spain, she meets a bullfighter who's willing to oblige. Too bad Bo cannot act as good as she looks. 106m; VHS, DVD. **C:** Bo Derek; George Kennedy; Andrea Occhipinti; Anna (Ana Garcia) Obregon; Olivia D'Abo; Directed by John Derek; Written by John Derek; Music by Peter Bernstein; Elmer Bernstein. **Pr:** Golan-Globus Productions; Cannon Films. **A:** College-Adult. **P:** Entertainment. **U:** Home. **Mov-Ent:** Drama. **Awds:** Golden Raspberries '84: Worst Actress (Derek), Worst Director (Derek), Worst New Star (D'Abo), Worst Picture, Worst Screenplay. **Acq:** Purchase. **Dist:** Lions Gate Television Corp. $19.95.

Bolero 1994
Presents a vituosic and sensuous love duet juxtaposed against the mechanical rotation of a giant clock work. Video also includes a rendition of Pictures At an Exhibition, also by Lubovitch. 66m; VHS. **A:** Family. **P:** Entertainment. **U:** Home. **Fin-Art:** Dance--Performance. **Acq:** Purchase. **Dist:** Princeton Book Company Publishers. $34.95.

Bollywood Burn 2007
Dance workout video by Hemalayaa Behl using traditional Indian dance as a form of exercise. 47m; DVD. **A:** Sr. High-Adult. **P:** Instruction. **U:** Home. **Hea-Sci:** Fitness/Exercise, Dance. **Acq:** Purchase. **Dist:** Acorn Media Group Inc. $14.99.

The Bollywood Dance Workout with Hemalayaa 2007
Hemalayaa Behl's workout video consisting of a mixture of yoga and Indian dance moves. 50m; DVD. **A:** Sr. High-Adult. **P:** Instruction. **U:** Home. **Hea-Sci:** Fitness/Exercise, Dance, Yoga. **Acq:** Purchase. **Dist:** Acorn Media Group Inc. $14.99.

Bollywood Hero 2009 (Unrated) — ★½
Kattan parodies himself and his acting career. Frustrated by his lack of leading roles, he impulsively agrees to travel to India to star in a Bollywood production for a brother-sister team who are trying to revive their father's film studio. The dance numbers are bright but Kattan's character is a whiner and the story lacks surprises. 168m; DVD. **C:** Chris Kattan; Pooja Kumar; Julian Sands; Ali Fazal; Rachna Shah; Neha Dhupia; Cameo(s) Maya Rudolph; Keanu Reeves; Directed by Bill Bennett; Ted Skillman; Written by Laurie Parres; Benjamin Brand; Cinematography by Tobias Hochstein; Music by David Bergeaud; Niels Bye Nielsen. **A:** Jr. High-Adult. **P:** Entertainment. **U:** Home. **Mov-Ent:** India. **Acq:** Purchase. **Dist:** Anchor Bay Entertainment.

Bologna: Two Leaning Towers 197?
The priority given by the progressive city government of Bologna toward preserving the best of the classic architecture of the city is examined. From the "In the Name of the Cities" series. 30m; VHS, 3/4 U. **Pr:** University of Toronto. **A:** Sr. High-Adult. **P:** Education. **U:** Institution, CCTV. **Gen-Edu:** Documentary Films, Italy, Architecture. **Acq:** Purchase, Rent/Lease. **Dist:** University of Toronto.

Bolshevik Victory 1971
Follows the Bolsheviks' preparation for and subsequent attack on the Winter Palace in 1917. Also examines the consequences of this event. 20m/B/W; VHS, 3/4 U. **Pr:** Granada and Novosti Productions. **A:** Sr. High-College. **P:** Education. **U:** Institution, SURA. **Gen-Edu:** Documentary Films, USSR, Politics & Government. **Acq:** Purchase. **Dist:** Home Vision Cinema.

The Bolshoi at the Bolshoi 1989
A breezy, refreshing performance by the world's most renowned ballet. Recorded during the 1989-90 season, this is the first ballet series ever produced, recorded and mastered in D-2 digital technology. ?m; VHS. **A:** Family. **P:** Entertainment. **U:** Home. **Fin-Art:** Performing Arts, Dance--Ballet. **Acq:** Purchase. **Dist:** Image Entertainment Inc. $39.95.
Indiv. Titles: 1. Swan Lake 2. Romeo & Juliet 3. The Nutcracker 4. The Sleeping Beauty 5. Raymonda 6. The Stone Flower 7. Ivan the Terrible 8. Giselle 9. Legend of Love.

The Bolshoi Ballet 1967
The world-famous dancers of the Bolshoi Ballet are featured in excerpts from eight works, including Ravel's "Bolero" and "La Valse," Prokofiev's "Stone Flower," music by Paganini and

Rachmaninoff and "Bolshoi Ballet '67." 95m; VHS, DVD. **C:** Raissa Struhkova; Maya Samokhvalova; Vladimir Vasiliev; Ekaterina Maximova; Natalia Bessmertnova. **Pr:** Kultur. **A:** Family. **P:** Entertainment. **U:** Home. **Fin-Art:** Performing Arts, Dance. **Acq:** Purchase. **Dist:** Music Video Distributors; Kultur International Films Ltd., Inc.; Facets Multimedia Inc. $19.95.

Bolshoi Ballet: Giselle 1956
The 1956 production of "Giselle" at London's Covent Garden is presented, along with "Walpurgisnacht" from Gounod's "Faust" and several other selections. Music is by the Orchestra of the Royal Opera House, Covent Garden and The Bournemouth Symphony Orchestra. This was the first post-war appearance of the Bolshoi Ballet in the West. 95m; VHS. **C:** Galina Ulanova; Nikol Fadeyechev. **Pr:** Video Artists International. **A:** Family. **P:** Entertainment. **U:** Home. **Fin-Art:** Dance--Ballet. **Acq:** Purchase. **Dist:** Video Artists International. $49.95.

Bolshoi Ballet: Les Sylphides 1984
A live Bolshoi performance of this famed Chopin ballet. Recorded in Hi-Fi. 34m; VHS, 8 mm. **C:** Natalia Bessmertnova; Alexander Bogatyrev; Galina Kozlova; Irina Kholina. **Pr:** Russian Television. **A:** Family. **P:** Entertainment. **U:** Institution, Home, SURA. **Fin-Art:** Music--Performance, Performing Arts, Dance. **Acq:** Purchase. **Dist:** V.I.E.W. Inc./Arkadia Entertainment Corp.; Moonbeam Publications Inc.; Stagestep. $59.95.

BOLSHOI: Between Fame and Drill 2000
Documentary profiling the Moscow Academy for Choreography, one of seven state schools for ballet. 50m; VHS, DVD. **A:** Sr. High-Adult. **P:** Education. **U:** Institution. **Gen-Edu:** Documentary Films, Performing Arts, Quality Control. **Acq:** Purchase. **Dist:** The Cinema Guild. $295.00.

Bolshoi Prokofiev Gala 1991
The Bolshoi Ballet, including stars Ludmilla Semenyaka, Alexander Vetrov, and Natalya Archipova, perform excerpts from three great ballets, including Romeo and Juliet, Ivan the Terrible, and Stone Flower, set to the music of Prokofiev. 170m; VHS. **A:** Family. **P:** Entertainment. **U:** Home. **Fin-Art:** Dance--Performance, Dance--Ballet. **Acq:** Purchase. **Dist:** Kultur International Films Ltd., Inc. $29.95.

Bolshoi Soloists 19??
Features classical Russian ballet performances from the Russian Bolchoi Ballet, set to the music of Tchaikovsky, Adam, Gershwin, and Albinoni. 37m; VHS. **A:** Family. **P:** Entertainment. **U:** Home, Institution. **Fin-Art:** Performing Arts, Dance--Ballet, Dance--Performance. **Acq:** Purchase. **Dist:** Instructional Video. $29.95.

Bolshoi Soloists Classique 1990
A special program of solos set to the music of Tchaikovsky. 42m; VHS. **Pr:** V.I.E.W. **A:** Family. **P:** Entertainment. **U:** Institution, Home, SURA. **Fin-Art:** Dance--Ballet. **Acq:** Purchase. **Dist:** V.I.E.W. Inc./Arkadia Entertainment Corp.; Music Video Distributors; Moonbeam Publications Inc. $39.95.

Bolshoi's Cinderella 1961
The Bolshoi Ballet performs Prokofiev's ballet of Cinderella recorded in 1961. 81m; VHS, 3/4 U. **TV Std:** NTSC, PAL. **Pr:** Gorky Film Studio. **A:** Family. **P:** Entertainment. **U:** Institution, Home. **Fin-Art:** Performing Arts, Dance--Ballet, Fairy Tales. **Acq:** Purchase. **Dist:** International Historic Films Inc. $39.95.

Bolt 2008 (PG) — ★★★½
On his hit action TV series, German Shepherd Bolt (voiced by Travolta) has superpowers to crush his arch enemy, Dr. Calico, and save his owner, Penny (voiced by Cyrus). However, having spent his entire life on the studio lot, he doesn't realize that he's just another canine actor, and not a superhero. A series of accidents leaves Bolt homeless on the streets of New York, while Penny is back in Hollywood. Convinced that the evil Dr. Calico has kidnapped his owner, Bolt, along with his two new friends, the reluctant alley cat Mittens and overeager hamster Rhino, sets out for a journey across the country to save the day. The first Disney animated feature to come out since Pixar guru John Lasseter traded teams. He wisely blends smart jokes with Disney's classic animated storytelling traditions, rather than trying to one-up his former employer's spastic cool factor. 96m; Blu-Ray, On Demand, Wide. **C:** Malcolm McDowell; James Lipton; Greg Germann; Voice(s) by John Travolta; Susie Essman; Mark Walton; Miley Cyrus; Directed by Chris Williams; Byron Howard; Written by Chris Williams; Dan Fogelman; Music by John Powell. **Pr:** Clark Spencer; Walt Disney Animation Studios; Walt Disney Pictures. **A:** Family. **P:** Entertainment. **U:** Home. **L:** English. **Mov-Ent:** Animation & Cartoons, Pets, Pets. **Acq:** Purchase. **Dist:** Amazon.com Inc.; Movies Unlimited; Alpha Video.

Bolt from the Blue 1980
A look at Viking ships, the weapon that allowed the Vikings to reign over the seas of Europe for centuries. 29m; VHS, 3/4 U. **Pr:** KTCA St. Paul/Minneapolis. **A:** Jr. High-Sr. High. **P:** Education. **U:** Institution, CCTV, CATV. **Gen-Edu:** Documentary Films, History--Ancient, Boating. **Acq:** Purchase, Rent/Lease, Off-Air Record. **Dist:** PBS Home Video.

Boltneck 1998 (Unrated) — ★½
When school outcast Karl becomes the victim of a hazing by jocks, nerdy Frank Stein (get it?) decides to try an experiment in re-animating the dead. But unknown to Frank, the brain he's used (which he stole from his father's lab—how convenient) is that of a mass killer and the new Karl has developed quite an attitude. 92m; VHS, DVD. **C:** Justin Walker; Ryan Reynolds; Christine Lakin; Bianca Lawson; Kenny Blank; Judge Reinhold; Shelley Duvall; Charles Fleischer; Matthew Lawrence; Richard Moll; Directed by Mitch Marcus; Written by Dave Payne; Music by Roger Neill. **A:** Sr. High-Adult. **P:** Entertainment. **U:** Home. **Mov-Ent. Acq:** Purchase.

Bomb at 10:10 1967 (Unrated) — ★★
An American pilot escapes from a German POW camp and plots to assassinate a camp commandant. 87m; VHS. **C:** George Montgomery; Rada Popovic; Peter Banicevic; Directed by Charles Damic. **Pr:** Ika Povic. **A:** Sr. High-Adult. **P:** Entertainment. **U:** Home. **Mov-Ent:** Action-Adventure, World War Two. **Acq:** Purchase. **Dist:** Unknown Distributor.

A Bomb for a Dictator 1957 (Unrated) — ★½
A South American dictator is returning from a trip to France and rebels intend to blow up his private plane. However, he changes his plans and takes a commercial flight, which means either the rebels kill innocent passengers or face severe reprisals if the dictator lives. French with subtitles. 90m/B/W; DVD. **C:** Pierre Fresnay; Michel Auclair; Gregoire Aslan; Tilda Thamar; Directed by Alex Joffe; Written by Alex Joffe; Jean Levitte; Cinematography by Leonce-Henri Burel; Music by Paul Misraki. **A:** College-Adult. **P:** Entertainment. **U:** Home. **L:** French. **Mov-Ent:** South America. **Acq:** Purchase. **Dist:** Sinister Cinema.

Bomb It 2008 (Unrated)
Documentary on graffiti artists and styles from Tokyo, Berlin, Sao Paulo, Barcelona, Capetown, and New York. 93m; DVD. **A:** Sr. High-Adult. **P:** Education. **U:** Home. **Gen-Edu:** Documentary Films, Art & Artists. **Acq:** Purchase. **Dist:** Docurama. $26.95.

The Bomb Shelter 1980
A tour of an abandoned nuclear bomb shelter built under an old New Hampshire house in the early 1960s. 10m; VHS, 3/4 U, Q. **Pr:** Tobe Carey. **A:** Jr. High-Adult. **P:** Education. **U:** Institution, CCTV, CATV, BCTV, Home. **Gen-Edu:** Documentary Films, Nuclear Warfare. **Acq:** Purchase, Rent/Lease. **Dist:** Media Bus, Inc.

Bomb Squad 1997 (Unrated) — ★★
Suicidal terrorist has a nuclear bomb small enough to fit into a suitcase and has decided to make Chicago his target. The Feds have 24-hours to find and defuse it. 91m; VHS, DVD. **C:** Anthony Michael Hall; Michael Ironside; Tony LoBianco; Directed by Serge Rodnunsky; Written by Serge Rodnunsky. **A:** Sr. High-Adult. **P:** Entertainment. **U:** Home. **Mov-Ent:** Nuclear Warfare, Terrorism, Intelligence Service. **Acq:** Purchase. **Dist:** Leo Films.

Bomb the System 2005 (R) — **Bomb!**
A trio of young artists conduct nightly "bombings" in New York City, covering available spaces with their graffiti signatures. In sync with the subculture, their paint is always stolen, although they do pay for their drugs. One of the outlaws is continually nagged by his mother to take the art scholarship he was offered in San Francisco, but he's deaf to her pleadings. There are run-ins with the law, some girlfriend situations and self-righteous speeches thrown into the mix but one never feels much sympathy toward the rebel-with-a-cause premise because truly they're just low-life druggie vandals. 93m; DVD, Wide. **C:** Mark Webber; Gano Grills; Jade Yorker; Jaclyn DeSantis; Joey Dedio; Stephan Buchanana; Bonz Malone; Donna Mitchell; Al Sapienza; Kumar Pallana; Directed by Adam Bhala Lough; Written by Adam Bhala Lough; Cinematography by Ben Kutchins; Music by El-P. **Pr:** Ben Rekhi; Sol Tryon. **A:** Sr. High-Adult. **P:** Entertainment. **U:** Home. **L:** English. **Mov-Ent:** Adolescence. **Acq:** Purchase. **Dist:** Movies Unlimited.

Bomb Threat Strategy 1995
Details bomb threats; what to look for; search procedures; assessing the threat; when to evacuate; and evacuation procedures. Covers preventative measures to take against bomb threats. 15m; VHS. **A:** Adult. **P:** Education. **U:** Institution. **Gen-Edu:** Safety Education, Violence, Terrorism. **Acq:** Purchase, Rent/Lease. **Dist:** National Safety Council, California Chapter, Film Library. $195.00.

Bomba and the Hidden City 1950 — ★½
In this mishmash of a plot, Bomba witnesses the assassination of the ruler of a tribal kingdom. Zita, the rightful heir, loses her memory from trauma and is raised in secret (as Leah) until evil ruler Hassan wants to marry the girl. Bomba, who's her friend, wants to put things right. 4th in the series. 71m/B/W; DVD. **C:** John(ny) Sheffield; Sue England; Paul Guilfoyle; Smoki Whitfield; Directed by Ford Beebe; Written by Carroll Young; Cinematography by William Sickner. **A:** Family. **P:** Entertainment. **U:** Home. **L:** English. **Mov-Ent:** Action-Adventure, Africa. **Acq:** Purchase. **Dist:** WarnerArchive.com.

Bomba and the Jungle Girl 1952 — ★½
Orphaned Bomba wants to know more about his parents, which leads him to the tribe they were working with. The chief and his daughter act very suspiciously and he's secretly told they're usurpers and killed both the tribe's true chieftain and his parents! Bomba gets help finding where their bodies are buried and retrieving his dad's diary, which will reveal the truth. 8th in the series. 70m/B/W; DVD. **C:** John(ny) Sheffield; Martin Wilkins; Suzette Harbin; Walter Sande; Karen Sharpe; Leonard Mudie; Directed by Ford Beebe; Written by Ford Beebe; Cinematography by Harry Neumann; Music by Raoul Kraushaar. **A:** Family. **P:** Entertainment. **U:** Home. **L:** English. **Mov-Ent:** Action-Adventure, Africa. **Acq:** Purchase. **Dist:** WarnerArchive.com.

Bomba on Panther Island 1949 — ★½
Bomba (who's not on an island) is tracking a man-eating black panther when he's sidetracked by developer Robert Maitland and his sister, Judy, who are starting a farm. 2nd in the Monogram series. 70m/B/W; DVD. **C:** John(ny) Sheffield; Allene Roberts; Harry Lewis; Charles Irwin; Smoki Whitfield; Directed by Ford Beebe; Written by Ford Beebe; Cinematography by William Sickner. **A:** Family. **P:** Entertainment. **U:** Home. **L:** English. **Mov-Ent:** Action-Adventure, Africa. **Acq:** Purchase. **Dist:** WarnerArchive.com.

Bomba, the Jungle Boy 1949 — ★★
Monogram Pictures 12-pic jungle adventure series starring a teenaged Sheffield (who had outgrown his role in the "Tarzan" films), based on the books by the pseudonymous Roy Rockwood. Bomba was raised by a now-deceased naturalist in the African jungle. George Harland and his daughter Pat have come to photgraph the wildlife when Pat gets lost. Bomba finds her and then must return her to her father while surving locust swarms,dangerous animals, and other adventures. 70m/B/W; DVD. **C:** John(ny) Sheffield; Peggy Ann Garner; Onslow Stevens; Charles Irwin; Smoki Whitfield; Directed by Ford Beebe; Written by Jack DeWitt; Cinematography by William Sickner. **A:** Family. **P:** Entertainment. **U:** Home. **L:** English. **Mov-Ent:** Action-Adventure, Africa. **Acq:** Purchase. **Dist:** WarnerArchive.com.

Bombardier 1943 (Unrated) — ★★½
A group of cadet bombardiers discover the realities of war on raids over Japan during WWII. Also available colorized. 99m/B/W; VHS, DVD. **C:** Pat O'Brien; Randolph Scott; Robert Ryan; Eddie Albert; Anne Shirley; Barton MacLane; Directed by Richard Wallace. **Pr:** Robert Fellows; RKO. **A:** Family. **P:** Entertainment. **U:** Home. **Mov-Ent:** Action-Adventure, World War Two, Aeronautics. **Acq:** Purchase. **Dist:** WarnerArchive.com. $14.98.

Bombay Calling 2006 (Unrated)
Examines the youth culture in India through the lives of eager young outsourcing firm executives, their ambition, unusual office hours, and time at all-night discos partying with income their parents could never have dreamed of earning. 71m; DVD. **A:** Adult. **P:** Education. **U:** Institution. **Gen-Edu:** India. **Acq:** Purchase. **Dist:** Third World Newsreel. $225.

Bombay Mail 1934 (Unrated) — ★½
A great example of a Universal Studio B movie, set on the train from Calcutta to Bombay and offering a multiple murder mystery with appearances of all the usual exotic suspects, from Indian mystics to eccentric scientists to larger than life opera singers, all with witty and adroit dialogue. 70m/B/W; DVD. **C:** Edmund Lowe; Shirley Grey; Onslow Stevens; Ralph Forbes; John Davidson; Directed by Edwin L. Marin; Written by Tom Reed; Lawrence G. Blochman; Cinematography by Charles Stumar; Music by Heinz Roemheld. **A:** Jr. High-Adult. **P:** Entertainment. **U:** Home. **Mov-Ent:** India, Trains. **Acq:** Purchase. **Dist:** Nostalgia Collectibles.

Bombay: Our City 1985
Tells the daily battle for survival of the four million slum dwellers of Bombay who make up half the city's population. 57m; VHS. **C:** Directed by Anand Patwardhan. **A:** College-Adult. **P:** Education. **U:** Institution. **Gen-Edu:** India, Poverty. **Acq:** Purchase, Rent/Lease. **Dist:** First Run/Icarus Films. $390.00.

Bombay Talkie 1970 (PG) — ★★½
A bored British writer (Kendal) heads to India to gather "experiences" and becomes involved with an Indian movie actor (Kapoor). Early clash-of-cultures film from Merchant Ivory has it's dull spots; the behind-the-scenes look at the Indian film industry is more interesting than the romance. 110m; VHS, DVD. **C:** Jennifer Kendal; Shashi Kapoor; Zia Mohyeddin; Aparna Sen; Directed by James Ivory; Written by Ruth Prawer Jhabvala. **Pr:** Ismail Merchant; Merchant-Ivory Productions. **A:** Jr. High-Adult. **P:** Entertainment. **U:** Home. **Mov-Ent:** Drama, Filmmaking. **Acq:** Purchase. **Dist:** New Line Home Video. $29.95.

Bombed! 1997
Details the many legal, medical, and emotional troubles that accompany teens who drink. Includes a Teacher's Resource Book with student worksheets and assignments. 28m; VHS. **A:** Jr. High-Sr. High. **P:** Education. **U:** Institution. **Gen-Edu:** Alcoholic Beverages, Alcoholism, Medical Education. **Acq:** Purchase. **Dist:** HRM Video. $189.00.

Bomber 2009 (Unrated) — ★★
Bittersweet family drama. Lazy son Ross becomes the unwilling chauffeur for his aged parents' long-planned road trip to Germany where WWII vet Alistar wants to see the village on which he dropped bombs during his first RAF mission. However, Alistar is an exasperating curmudgeon and when he finds no resolution, his wife Valerie is finally fed-up and Ross must reluctantly play marriage counselor. 84m; DVD. **C:** Benjamin Whitrow; Shane Taylor; Eileen Nicholas; Directed by Paul Cotter; Written by Paul Cotter; Cinematography by Rick Siegel; Music by Stephen Coates. **A:** Sr. High-Adult. **P:** Entertainment. **U:** Home. **Mov-Ent:** Germany, Aging. **Acq:** Purchase. **Dist:** Film Movement.

Bombers & Bombing 2006
Covers the role of Germany's Luftwaffe from 1939 to 1945 and its combat operations and bombing missions. ?m; DVD. **A:** Jr. High-Adult. **P:** Entertainment. **U:** Home. **Gen-Edu:** Documentary Films, World War Two. **Acq:** Purchase. **Dist:** Rykodisc Corp.

Bombers B-52 1957 (Unrated) — ★★
Chuck Brennan (Malden) has worked 20 years as a ground-crew chief for the Air Force and his daughter Lois (Wood) is encouraging him to retire. While Chuck decides, he tries to discourage the budding romance between Lois and commanding officer Jim Herlihy (Zimbalist), whom he distrusts. Predictable plot is all a backdrop for the showcase of various planes, especially the B-52 Superfortress. 106m; DVD. **C:** Natalie Wood; Karl Malden; Efrem Zimbalist, Jr.; Marsha Hunt; Don Kelly; Nelson Leigh; Directed by Gordon Douglas; Written by Irving Wallace; Cinematography by William Clothier; Music by Leonard Rosenman. **A:** Jr. High-Adult. **P:** Entertainment. **U:** Home. **Mov-Ent:** Aeronautics. **Acq:** Purchase. **Dist:** Warner Home Video, Inc.

Bombing L.A. 1990
A look at the young graffiti artists of Los Angeles, their work, their methods and their individual styles. Interviews are also held with people who are angered by their work. 40m; VHS. **Pr:** The Cinema Guild. **A:** Jr. High-Adult. **P:** Education. **U:** Institution, Home. **Gen-Edu:** Documentary Films, Art & Artists. **Acq:** Purchase, Rent/Lease. **Dist:** The Cinema Guild. $295.00.

The Bombing of West Philly 1987
The true story of the 1983 bombing of the headquarters of MOVE, a violent black urban cult. 58m; VHS, 3/4 U. **Pr:** PBS. **A:** Jr. High-Adult. **P:** Education. **U:** Institution, SURA. **Gen-Edu:** Documentary Films. **Acq:** Purchase, Rent/Lease. **Dist:** PBS Home Video. $150.00.

Bombs Aren't Cool! 1986
Introduces young people to the perils of nuclear war. 6m; VHS. **A:** Jr. High-Sr. High. **P:** Education. **U:** Institution. **Gen-Edu:** War--General, Nuclear Warfare. **Acq:** Purchase, Rent/Lease. **Dist:** First Run/Icarus Films. $75.00.

Bombs Away 1985
This rather dated movie depicts one child, Wai Lan, and her fears of nuclear war, leading her to join a peace march in Vancouver. 18m; VHS, 3/4 U. **Pr:** Lucerne Films. **A:** Jr. High-Adult. **P:** Education. **U:** Institution, SURA. **Gen-Edu:** Nuclear Warfare, Children. **Acq:** Purchase, Rent/Lease. **Dist:** National Film Board of Canada. $300.00.

Bombs Away! 1986 (Unrated) — ★
An atomic bomb is mistakenly shipped to a seedy war surplus store in Seattle, and causes much chicanery. 90m; VHS. **C:** Michael Huddleston; Pat McCormick; Directed by Bruce Wilson. **Pr:** Bill Fay; Bruce Wilson. **A:** Jr. High-Adult. **P:** Entertainment. **U:** Home. **Mov-Ent:** Nuclear Warfare. **Acq:** Purchase. **Dist:** Sony Pictures Home Entertainment Inc.; New Line Home Video. $14.95.

Bombs Will Break the Rainbow 1983
This tape introduces the Children's Campaign for Nuclear Disarmament. 17m; VHS, 3/4 U. **Pr:** Zahm-Hurwitz. **A:** Primary-Adult. **P:** Education. **U:** Institution, SURA. **Gen-Edu:** Documentary Films, Nuclear Warfare. **Acq:** Purchase. **Dist:** Home Vision Cinema.

Bombshell 1933 (Unrated) — ★★★
Wry insightful comedy into the Hollywood of the 1930s. Harlow plays a naive young actress manipulated by her adoring press agent. He thwarts her plans until she finally notices and begins to fall in love with him. Brilliant satire with Harlow turning in perhaps the best performance of her short career. 96m/B/W; VHS, DVD. **C:** Jean Harlow; Lee Tracy; Pat O'Brien; Una Merkel; Sir C. Aubrey Smith; Franchot Tone; Directed by Victor Fleming. **Pr:** MGM/UA Entertainment Company. **A:** Jr. High-Adult. **P:** Entertainment. **U:** Home. **Mov-Ent:** Comedy--Romantic. **Acq:** Purchase. **Dist:** WarnerArchive.com; Baker and Taylor; Facets Multimedia Inc. $19.98.

Bombshell 1997 (R) — ★★
Scientist Buck Hogan (Thomas) discovers a deadly flaw in the world's first cancer-killing drug, which he publicly reveals, much to the dismay of the manufacturer's head honcho Donald (James). But then Hogan and his girlfriend Angeline (Amick) are abducted by a terrorist group, and Buck's implanted with a device that will kill him unless he does as they say. 95m; VHS, Streaming. **C:** Henry Thomas; Frank Whaley; Madchen Amick; Brion James; Pamela Gidley; Shawnee Smith; Martin Hewitt; Michael Jace; Directed by Paul Wynne; Written by Paul Wynne. **Pr:** Trimark Pictures. **A:** Sr. High-Adult. **P:** Entertainment. **U:** Home. **Mov-Ent:** Science Fiction, Science, Terrorism. **Acq:** Purchase. **Dist:** CinemaNow Inc.

BombThreat ????
Teaches the proper procedures for reducing the incidence and impact of bomb threats. Also discusses anthrax scares, safe locations, recognizing a potential bomb, searching for secondary devices, hazmat teams, and reoccupying the building. 25m; VHS. **A:** Adult. **P:** Education. **U:** Institution. **Gen-Edu:** Safety Education, Police Training. **Acq:** Purchase. **Dist:** Emergency Film Group.

Bon Appetit Cooking Video Series 1987
A four-part gourmet chef's instructional series shows you how to prepare fabulous food without spending hours in the kitchen. Chef Mark Peel (of L.A.'s Spago restaurant) and Susan Arnell demonstrate useful cooking techniques. Yum! 60m; VHS, CC. **C:** Mark Peel; Susan Arnell. **Pr:** Warner. **A:** Jr. High-Adult. **P:** Instruction. **U:** Home. **How-Ins:** How-To, Cooking. **Acq:** Purchase. **Dist:** Karol Media.
Indiv. Titles: 1. Easy Entertaining 2. Festive Desserts 3. Light & Fresh Cooking 4. Weeknight Inspirations.

Bon Cop Bad Cop 2006 (Unrated) — ★★
A Canadian bilingual buddy cop movie that plays on the cultural differences between English and French-speakers. Quebec maverick David Bouchard (Huard) is paired with by-the-book Ontario detective Martin Ward (Feore) when a body is deliberately left straddling the border of the two provinces. The investigation soon involves a serial killer targeting the hockey community, and the bickering duo learns to work together and realizes what they have in common (they're both divorced but devoted dads). It's contrived and unsubtle but director Canuel seems to be clear that's the way he wanted it. 116m; DVD. **C:** Patrick Huard; Colm Feore; Lucie Laurier; Sarain Boylan; Pierre Lebeau; Sarah-Jeanne Labrosse; Louis-Jose Houde; Sylvain Marcel; Rick Mercer; Patrice Belanger; Directed by Erik Canuel; Written by Kevin Tierney; Cinematography by Bruce Chun; Music by Michael Corriveau. **A:** Sr. High-Adult. **P:** Entertainment. **U:** Home. **L:** English, French. **Mov-Ent:** Hockey, Action-Comedy. **Acq:** Purchase. **Dist:** BFS Video.

Bon Jovi: Access All Areas 1990
Bon Jovi performs their hit tunes, including music from "New Jersey" and "Slippery when Wet." Interviews and behind the scenes footage is included. 90m; VHS. **Pr:** Polygram Music Video. **A:** Jr. High-Adult. **P:** Entertainment. **U:** Home. **Mov-Ent:** Music Video. **Acq:** Purchase. **Dist:** Music Video Distributors; Baker and Taylor. $19.95.

Bon Jovi: Breakout 1984
The popular band performs its greatest hits in videos and concerts, including "Silent Night," "In & Out of Love," "Only Lonely," "She Don't Know Me," and "Runaway." 23m; VHS, 8 mm. **Pr:** Polygram Music Video. **A:** Family. **P:** Entertainment. **U:** Home. **Mov-Ent:** Music--Performance, Music Video. **Acq:** Purchase. **Dist:** Music Video Distributors. $14.95.

Bon Jovi: Cross Road the Video 1994
A "best of" collection that also features two new tracks. 80m; VHS. **A:** Sr. High-Adult. **P:** Entertainment. **U:** Home. **Mov-Ent:** Music--Pop/Rock, Music Video. **Acq:** Purchase. **Dist:** Music Video Distributors. $19.95.
Songs: Always; Dry County; Blaze of Glory; Livin' On a Prayer; Keep the Faith; Bad Medicine; Wanted Dead or Alive; Lay Your Hands On Me; Bad Name; In These Arms; In & Out of Love; Miracle.

Bon Jovi: Keep the Faith, an Evening with Bon Jovi 1992
MTV's "Unplugged" acoustic series strikes again with this release, which includes material not included on the televised program. Songs include "Love for Sale," "Lay Your Hands on Me," "Blaze of Glory," "Bed of Roses," "Living on a Prayer," "Bad Medicine," "Keep the Faith," and more. 90m; VHS. **A:** Sr. High-Adult. **P:** Entertainment. **U:** Home. **Mov-Ent:** Music--Performance, Music--Pop/Rock. **Acq:** Purchase. **Dist:** Music Video Distributors. $19.95.

Bon Jovi: Lost Highway Concert 2007
Presents the 2007 live concert by rock band Bon Jovi for their "Lost Highway" album with performances of 15 songs; includes backstage footage and interviews with the band. 84m; DVD. **A:** Jr. High-Adult. **P:** Entertainment. **U:** Home, CATV. **Mov-Ent:** Television Series, Documentary Films, Music--Pop/Rock. **Acq:** Purchase. **Dist:** A&E Television Networks L.L.C. $24.95.

Bon Jovi: New Jersey—The Videos 1989
The boys from the Garden State perform their hits "Bad Medicine," "Lay Your Hands on Me," "Blood on Blood" and more. 60m; VHS. **Pr:** Polygram Music Video. **A:** Jr. High-Adult. **P:** Entertainment. **U:** Home. **Mov-Ent:** Music Video. **Acq:** Purchase. **Dist:** Music Video Distributors. $19.98.

Bon Jovi: Slippery When Wet 1988
Video collection includes "Livin' on a Prayer," "You Give Love a Bad Name," "Wanted Dead or Alive," "Wild in the Streets," and "Never Say Goodbye." 30m; VHS. **Pr:** Sony Video. **A:** Jr. High-Adult. **P:** Entertainment. **U:** Home. **Mov-Ent:** Music Video. **Acq:** Purchase. **Dist:** Music Video Distributors. $19.98.

Bon Jovi: The Interview Sessions 1990
No music, but rare footage and interviews from all over the world make this a Bon Jovi collectors item. 60m; VHS. **A:** Jr. High-Adult. **P:** Entertainment. **U:** Home. **Mov-Ent:** Music Video, Interviews. **Acq:** Purchase. **Dist:** Music Video Distributors. $19.95.

Bon Jovi: Tokyo Road 198? (Unrated)
Shot live in Tokyo on April 1, 1985, the band performs "Little Song," "Breakout," "Only You" and 10 others. 80m; VHS. **A:** Jr. High-Adult. **P:** Entertainment. **U:** Home. **Mov-Ent:** Music--Performance, Music--Pop/Rock. **Acq:** Purchase. **Dist:** Music Video Distributors. $119.95.

Bon Voyage 19??
A colorful travelogue that tours Israel to a background of catchy songs. 24m; VHS, 3/4 U, Special order formats. **TV Std:** NTSC, PAL, SECAM. **Pr:** Alden Films. **A:** Sr. High-Adult. **P:** Entertainment. **U:** Institution, Home, SURA. **Gen-Edu:** Israel, Travel. **Acq:** Purchase, Rent/Lease. **Dist:** Alden Films. $50.00.

Bon Voyage! 1962 — ★½
A family's long-awaited European "dream" vacation turns into a series of comic misadventures in this very Disney, very family, very predictable comedy. 131m; VHS, DVD. **C:** Fred MacMurray; Jane Wyman; Deborah Walley; Michael Callan; Tommy Kirk; Jessie Royce Landis; Directed by James Neilson. **Pr:** Walt Disney Studios. **A:** Family. **P:** Entertainment. **U:** Home. **Mov-Ent:** Travel, Children, Family Viewing. **Acq:** Purchase. **Dist:** Walt Disney Studios Home Entertainment. $69.95.

Bon Voyage 2003 (PG-13) — ★★★
Successful comedy-adventure mixes romance, espionage, murder, and melodrama amid the chaos of the Nazi occupation of France. In the role of a lifetime, Adjani is Viviane, an amoral movie star who's seeing government minister Beaufort (Depardieu) but gets humble former flame Frederic (Derangere) to do her bidding, including disposing of the body of a blackmailer (Vaude). Fred gets busted with the body, takes the rap, and winds up in jail only to escape with the help of resourceful criminal Raoul (Attal). Coyote does a turn as a spy posing as a journalist who also has a thing for the tres popular Viviane. The lives of all the characters intersect with interesting results in this not completely original but engaging and well-made romp. 114m; DVD. **C:** Isabelle Adjani; Gerard Depardieu; Virginie Ledoyen; Yvan Attal; Peter Coyote; Aurore Clement; Xavier De Guillebon; Edith Scob; Michel Vuillermoz; Gregori Derangere; Jean-Marc Stehle; Nicolas Pignon; Directed by Jean-Paul Rappeneau; Written by Jean-Paul Rappeneau; Gilles Marchand; Patrick Modiano; Cinematography by Thierry Arbogast; Music by Gabriel Yared. **Pr:** Michael Petin; Laurent Petin; France 2 Cinema; France 3 Cinema; Canal Plus; ARP. **A:** Jr. High-Adult. **P:** Entertainment. **U:** Home. **L:** French. **Mov-Ent:** Action-Adventure, Comedy-Drama, World War Two. **Acq:** Purchase. **Dist:** Columbia House Video Library.

Bon Voyage, Charlie Brown 1980 (G) — ★★½
The "Peanuts" comic strip gang are exchange students in Europe, led by Charlie Brown, Linus, Peppermint Patty, Marcie, and the irrepressible beagle, Snoopy. How can you go wrong with the "little round-headed kid" and his pals? 76m; VHS. **C:** Voice(s) by Arrin Skelley; Laura Planting; Casey Carlson; David Anderson; Annalisa Bartolin; Scott Beads; Directed by Bill Melendez; Lee Mendelson; Written by Charles M. Schulz; Music by Ed Bogas. **Pr:** Bill Melendez Productions. **A:** Family. **P:** Entertainment. **U:** Home. **Chl-Juv:** Animation & Cartoons, TV Movies. **Acq:** Purchase. **Dist:** Paramount Pictures Corp. $14.95.

Bon Voyage: Tips for a Safe Vacation 1993
Focuses on crime prevention with Portland Police Officer Henry Groepper offering tips on how vacationers can protect themselves while they are away and what steps they should take to protect their home before they leave. 10m; VHS. **A:** College-Adult. **P:** Education. **U:** Institution. **Gen-Edu:** Safety Education. **Acq:** Purchase. **Dist:** New Media Magic. $15.00.

Bonaire: A Diver's Paradise 19??
A guide to this popular tourist destination, especially geared toward divers. Includes choice photography by Jerry Schnabel. 60m; VHS. **A:** Sr. High-Adult. **P:** Entertainment. **U:** Home. **Spo-Rec:** Scuba, Travel. **Acq:** Purchase. **Dist:** Bennett Marine Video. $29.95.

Bonaire: Miami to Sunset 19??
This former Dutch colony blends old world sophistication with tropical warmth. Highlights one of the world's best shore dives. Ideal for planning dive vacations. 30m; VHS. **A:** Sr. High-Adult. **P:** Entertainment. **U:** Home. **Spo-Rec:** Scuba, Travel. **Acq:** Purchase. **Dist:** Bennett Marine Video. $19.95.

Bonanno: A Godfather's Story 1999 — ★★
Old-fashioned storytelling seems to fit the story of an old-fashioned New York mobster—Joseph Bonanno (Landau)?thought to be the inspiration for Mario Puzo's Don Vito Corleone. The elderly Bonanno reflects on his life and how he got into criminal activity back in the Prohibition days, drawing the attention of boss Salvatore Maranzano (Olmos). From there it's just a matter of time as Joe works his way up through the ranks. Based on the autobiography of Joseph Bonanno and the book written by his son Bill. 139m; VHS, DVD, CC. **C:** Martin Landau; Bruce Ramsay; Costas Mandylor; Edward James Olmos; Tony Nardi; Zachary Bennett; Philip Bosco; Claudia Ferri; Robert Loggia; Patti LuPone; Directed by Michel Poulette; Written by Thomas Michael Donnelly; Cinematography by Serge Ladouceur; Music by Richard Gregoire. **Pr:** Showtime Networks. **A:** Sr. High-Adult. **P:** Entertainment. **U:** Home. **Mov-Ent:** Crime Drama, Biography: Law Enforcement. **Acq:** Purchase. **Dist:** Lions Gate Television Corp.

Bonanza 1964
This western series about the Cartwright clan and their Ponderosa ranch ran on TV from 1959-73, second only to "Gunsmoke." In "The Pure Truth," Hoss escapes from jail after being unjustly accused of robbing the bank. An eccentric recluse comes to his aid. Additional episodes are available. 50m; VHS, DVD. **C:** Lorne Greene; Pernell Roberts; Dan Blocker; Michael Landon; Glenda Farrell. **Pr:** Republic Pictures. **A:** Family. **P:** Entertainment. **U:** Home. **Mov-Ent:** Television Series, Western. **Acq:** Purchase. **Dist:** Movies Unlimited; Lions Gate Entertainment Inc. $14.98.

Bonanza: The Return 1993 (PG) — ★½
In 1905, the children of various members of the Cartwright clan work to see the Ponderosa is safe from an unscrupulous businessman. Lame update of the classic family western series. 96m; VHS, CC. **C:** Michael Landon, Jr.; Dirk Blocker; Emily Warfield; Alistair MacDougall; Brian Leckner; Dean Stockwell; Ben Johnson; Richard Roundtree; Linda Gray; Jack Elam; Directed by Jerry Jameson; Written by Michael McGreevey; Cinematography by Haskell Boggs. **A:** Family. **P:** Entertainment. **U:** Home. **Mov-Ent:** Western, Family. **Acq:** Purchase. **Dist:** CinemaNow Inc. $92.95.

Bonanza Town 1951 — ★½
Steve Ramsey (Starrett), aka The Durango Kid, and sidekick Smiley (Burnette) are hired to locate the loot stolen in a Dodge City hold-up. Marked money leads our heroes to Bonanza Town, where the Kid tracks down outlaws and corrupt officials. 56m/B/W; VHS, DVD. **C:** Charles Starrett; Smiley Burnette; Myron Healey; Fred F. Sears; Directed by Fred F. Sears; Cinematography by Henry Freulich. **Pr:** Columbia Pictures. **A:** Family. **P:** Entertainment. **U:** Home. **Mov-Ent:** Western. **Acq:** Purchase. **Dist:** Sony Pictures Home Entertainment Inc.

Bonanza, Vol. 2 1964
Episode: "Bullet for a Bride." Little Joe is determined to marry the girl he accidentally blinds in a shooting incident. His Pa can't change his mind, until he gets yet another shock. 50m; VHS, DVD. **C:** Lorne Greene; Dan Blocker; Pernell Roberts; Michael Landon; Marlyn Mason; Denver Pyle. **Pr:** Republic Pictures. **A:** Family. **P:** Entertainment. **U:** Home. **Mov-Ent:** Western, Television Series. **Acq:** Purchase. **Dist:** Lions Gate Entertainment Inc. $14.98.

Bonanza, Vol. 3 1964
Episode: "The Cheating Game." Adam's romantic hopes get lost when the lovely widow he's courting is trapped in a stock swindle. Can he open her eyes to the misdeeds of her dead husband's best friend without losing her love? 50m; VHS, DVD.

C: Lorne Greene; Pernell Roberts; Michael Landon; Dan Blocker; Leslie Browne; Lee Henry; Peter Breck. **Pr:** Republic Pictures. **A:** Family. **P:** Entertainment. **U:** Home. **Mov-Ent**: Western, Television Series. **Acq:** Purchase. **Dist:** Lions Gate Entertainment Inc. $14.98.

Bonanza, Vol. 4 1965
Episode: "The Trap." Little Joe's accidental shooting of his old girlfriend's husband has the entire town speculating whether it was a real accident or not. Even the girlfriend is sure he did it to get her back. He then winds up in jail and things really get confused. Will Pa and the other boys be able to keep Joe from the hangman's noose? 50m; VHS, DVD. **C:** Lorne Greene; Pernell Roberts; Dan Blocker; Michael Landon; Joan Freeman; Steve Cochran. **Pr:** Republic Pictures. **A:** Family. **P:** Entertainment. **U:** Home. **Mov-Ent**: Western, Television Series. **Acq:** Purchase. **Dist:** Lions Gate Entertainment Inc. $14.98.

Bonanza, Vol. 5 1965
Episode: "Enter Mark Twain." Reporter Samuel Clemens arrives in Virginia City to put a stop to local corruption. 50m; VHS, DVD, CC. **C:** Lorne Greene; Pernell Roberts; Dan Blocker; Michael Landon; Howard Duff. **Pr:** National Broadcasting Company. **A:** Family. **P:** Entertainment. **U:** Home. **Mov-Ent**: Western, Television Series. **Acq:** Purchase. **Dist:** Lions Gate Entertainment Inc. $14.99.

Bonanza, Vol. 6 1961
Episode: "Silent Thunder." Little Joe falls for a deaf girl to whom he has taught sign language. 50m; VHS, CC. **C:** Lorne Greene; Pernell Roberts; Dan Blocker; Michael Landon; Stella Stevens; Kenneth MacKenna; Albert Salmi. **Pr:** National Broadcasting Company. **A:** Family. **P:** Entertainment. **U:** Home. **Mov-Ent**: Western, Television Series. **Acq:** Purchase. **Dist:** Lions Gate Entertainment Inc. $14.99.

Bonanza, Vol. 7 1962
Episode: "The Crucible." Adam is ambushed by a ruthless outlaw and left to die in the desert. 50m; VHS, CC. **C:** Lorne Greene; Pernell Roberts; Dan Blocker; Michael Landon; Lee Marvin. **Pr:** National Broadcasting Company. **A:** Family. **P:** Entertainment. **U:** Home. **Mov-Ent**: Western, Television Series. **Acq:** Purchase. **Dist:** Lions Gate Entertainment Inc. $14.99.

Bonanza, Vol. 8 1963
Episode: "Any Friend of Walter's." Hoss is shot and taken prisoner by a crusty old prospector. 50m; VHS, CC. **C:** Lorne Greene; Pernell Roberts; Dan Blocker; Michael Landon; Arthur Hunnicutt. **Pr:** National Broadcasting Company. **A:** Family. **P:** Entertainment. **U:** Home. **Mov-Ent**: Western, Television Series. **Acq:** Purchase. **Dist:** Lions Gate Entertainment Inc. $14.99.

Bond Instruction Books on Video 1989
How to use the Bond machine is explained, from the basics to advanced techniques. 40m; VHS. **Pr:** Nancy's Notions Ltd. **A:** Jr. High-Adult. **P:** Instruction. **U:** Institution, Home. **How-Ins**: Sewing, Crafts. **Acq:** Rent/Lease. **Dist:** Nancy's Notions Ltd.

The Bond of Breastfeeding 1978
A clear, concise look at the pros and cons of breastfeeding, intending to provide the new mother with enough information to make the decision on whether or not to breastfeed. 20m; 3/4 U, Special order formats. **Pr:** Julian Aston. **A:** College-Adult. **P:** Education. **U:** Institution, Home, SURA. **Hea-Sci**: Documentary Films, Parenting. **Acq:** Purchase, Rent/Lease, Trade-in, Duplication License. **Dist:** United Learning Inc.

Bond of Fear 1956 (Unrated) — ★½
Routine British programmer. John Sewell (Walsh) is packing up the car, caravan, wife and kids for a trip across the Channel to the south of France. Too bad they have an unexpected guest hiding out: escaped killer Terence Dewar (Colicos) who insists the Sewells take him to the port of Dover despite road blocks, hikers needing assistance, and other complications. 66m/B/W; DVD. **C:** Anthony Pavey; Marily Baker; Dermot Walsh; John Colicos; Jane Barrett; Alan MacNaughton; Jameson Clark; Directed by Henry Cass; John Gilling; Written by John Gilling; Norman Hudis; Cinematography by Monty Berman; Music by Stanley Black. **A:** Jr. High-Adult. **P:** Entertainment. **U:** Home. **Mov-Ent**: Crime Drama. **Acq:** Purchase. **Dist:** VCI Entertainment.

Bond of Silence 2010 (Unrated) — ★★
Lifetime drama loosely based on a true story. Neighbor Bob McIntosh (Cubitt) tries to quiet a wild teen New Year's Eve party (the parents aren't home) and winds up dead. The teens refuse to talk but Bob's shattered wife Katy (Raver) is determined to get to the truth and finally the guilt gets to one young man. 98m; DVD. **C:** Kim Raver; Greg Grunberg; Charlie McDermott; David Cubitt; Haley Ramm; Rebecca Jenkins; Calum Worthy; Directed by Peter Werner; Written by Brian D. Young; Edithe Swensen; Teena Booth; Cinematography by Attila Szalay; Music by Richard (Rick) Marvin. **A:** Jr. High-Adult. **P:** Entertainment. **U:** Home. **Mov-Ent. Acq:** Purchase. **Dist:** Sony Pictures Home Entertainment Inc.

Bonded by Blood 2009 (Unrated) — ★★
Brit gangster pic based on a true crime. In December 1995, drug dealers Patrick Tate, Tony Tucker, and Craig Rolfe are found murdered. A flashback to 1993 sets up the story as accused killer Darren Nicholls meets Tate in prison. Nicholls would team with ex-cons Mickey Steele and Jack Whomes and the six would partner up but a falling out between Tate and Steele leads to trouble. 96m; DVD. **C:** Vincent Regan; Dave Legano; Tamer Hassan; Adam Deacon; Terry Stone; Neil Maskell; Directed by Sacha Bennett; Written by Sacha Bennett; Graeme Muir; Cinematography by Ali Asad; Music by Jason Kaye; Phillip Ryan. **A:** Sr. High-Adult. **P:** Entertainment. **U:** Home. **Mov-Ent**: Drug Trafficking/Dealing, Nightclubs. **Acq:** Purchase. **Dist:** Movies Unlimited.

Bonding and Grounding of Flammable Liquid Transfers 1995
Teaches proper bonding and grounding of containers to reduce static electricity explosions. 10m; VHS. **A:** Adult. **P:** Professional. **U:** Institution. **L:** Spanish. **Bus-Ind**: Safety Education, Occupational Training. **Acq:** Purchase, Rent/Lease. **Dist:** National Safety Council, California Chapter, Film Library. $175.00.

Bonding and Grounding of Flammable Liquids 1995
Features how bonding and grounding of flammables is important to reduce the exposure to explosions and fires. 10m; VHS. **A:** Adult. **P:** Professional. **U:** Institution. **L:** Spanish. **Bus-Ind**: Safety Education, Occupational Training. **Acq:** Purchase, Rent/Lease. **Dist:** National Safety Council, California Chapter, Film Library. $175.00.

The Bonding Birth Experience 1977
Depicts a shared childbirth experience and the parent's early attachment. For high school, adult, and professional use. 23m; VHS, 3/4 U, Special order formats. **Pr:** Courter Films. **A:** Sr. High-Adult. **P:** Education. **U:** Institution, CCTV, Home. **Hea-Sci**: Documentary Films, Childbirth, Parenting. **Acq:** Purchase. **Dist:** Parenting Pictures.

Bonds 1981
Securities expert Roma Sinn explains bonds in this program: types of bonds, the bond terminology and basic market principles that affect their value. 55m; VHS, 3/4 U, Special order formats. **Pr:** Cinema Associates. **A:** College-Adult. **P:** Education. **U:** Institution, CCTV, CATV, BCTV, Home. **Gen-Edu**: Finance. **Acq:** Purchase. **Dist:** RMI Media; Morris Video. $24.95.

Bonds: Types, Terminology & Principles 19??
Provides information on bonds, including the different types available, terminology, basic market principles, and how to be a knowledgeable creditor. 59m; VHS. **A:** College-Adult. **P:** Education. **U:** Institution. **Gen-Edu**: Finance, Economics. **Acq:** Purchase. **Dist:** Instructional Video. $29.95.

Bone 1977
A typical long bone is demonstrated in both dry ground and decalcified sections. 9m; 3/4 U. **Pr:** University of Oklahoma. **A:** College-Adult. **P:** Education. **U:** Institution. **Hea-Sci**: Documentary Films, Bones. **Acq:** Purchase. **Dist:** University of Oklahoma.

Bone Building Workout with Coach Hammer 1992
This dumbbell toning exercise program is specifically designed to help prevent osteoporosis. Contains two workouts: a long, carefully instructed program and a second segment to use after you've learned the proper technique. 50m; VHS. **A:** Jr. High-Adult. **P:** Instruction. **U:** Home. **Hea-Sci**: Fitness/Exercise. **Acq:** Purchase. **Dist:** Collage Video Specialties, Inc. $19.95.

The Bone Collector 1999 (R) — ★★½
Lincoln Rhyme (Washington) is a brilliant NYPD detective and forensics expert who was left a quadriplegic after an on-the-job accident. His suicidal thoughts are distracted by the work of a serial killer with a gruesome MO and the admirable work of hotshot young policewoman, Amelia Donoghy (Jolie). Amelia soon becomes Rhyme's surrogate investigator. The situation comes to a climax in Rhyme's apartment as he lies helpless. Thriller turns out to be predictable but Washington, as usual, turns in a fine performance. Based on the 1997 novel by Jeffrey Deaver. 118m; VHS, DVD, Blu-Ray, HD-DVD, CC. **C:** Denzel Washington; Angelina Jolie; Queen Latifah; Ed O'Neill; Michael Rooker; Mike McGlone; Leland Orser; Luis Guzman; John Benjamin Hickey; Bobby Cannavale; Directed by Phillip Noyce; Written by Jeremy Iacone; Cinematography by Dean Semler; Music by Craig Armstrong. **Pr:** Martin Bregman; Michael S. Bregman; Louis Stroller; Universal Pictures; Columbia Pictures; Universal Studios. **A:** Sr. High-Adult. **P:** Entertainment. **U:** Home. **Mov-Ent**: Handicapped. **Acq:** Purchase. **Dist:** Movies Unlimited; Alpha Video.

Bone Daddy 1997 (R) — ★★
Former chief medical examiner William Palmer (Hauer) turns his experiences into a best-selling novel and excites the rage of a psychopathic killer. The surgical killer, who's nicknamed "Bone Daddy" because he likes to extract the bones of his victims, is busy at work and Palmer teams up with a reluctant detective (Williams) to track the looney down. 90m; VHS, DVD, CC. **C:** Rutger Hauer; Barbara Williams; R.H. Thomson; Joseph Kell; Robin Gammell; Daniel Kash; Christopher Kelk; Directed by Mario Azzopardi; Written by Thomas Szollosi; Cinematography by Danny Nowak; Music by Christophe Beck. **A:** Sr. High-Adult. **P:** Entertainment. **U:** Home. **Mov-Ent**: Horror, Mystery & Suspense. **Acq:** Purchase. **Dist:** Echo Bridge Home Entertainment.

Bone Diseases Affecting the Facial Nerve 1976
Rare conditions that can affect the temporal bone and facial nerve and cause hearing loss are explored. 56m; VHS, 3/4 U. **Pr:** House Ear Institute. **A:** Adult. **P:** Professional. **U:** Institution, CCTV. **Hea-Sci**: Documentary Films, Ear. **Acq:** Purchase, Rent/Lease. **Dist:** House Research Institute.

Bone Dry 2007 (R) — ★★
Eddie (Goss) finds himself knocked out and left in the middle of the desert by a man named Jimmy (Hendriksen). Jimmy informs Eddie via walkie-talkie that he needs to head north, and should he go in any other direction a sniper rifle will put an end to him, and his wife and children will follow him into the ground quickly after. What follows is not pretty to watch. 100m; DVD. **C:** Lance Henriksen; Tommy (Tiny) Lister; Dee Wallace; Luke Goss; Directed by Brett Hart; Written by Brett Hart; Cinematography by John Darbonne; Kevin G. Ellis; Music by Scott Glasgow. **A:** Sr. High-Adult. **P:** Entertainment. **U:** Home. **L:** English, Spanish. **Mov-Ent. Acq:** Purchase. **Dist:** Allumination Filmworks. $9.98.

Bone Eater 2007 (Unrated) — ★
Native Americans are protesting at a construction site that's disturbing an ancient burial ground. The workers hit a pile of bones that assembles itself into the legendary Bone Eater, which promptly destroys the crew. Sheriff Evans (Boxleitner) shows up to investigate—more people disappear—corporate greed—blah, blah, blah. It's good for a chuckle (the Bone Eater figure certainly isn't scary) but that's probably not what director Wynorski intended. 90m; DVD. **C:** Bruce Boxleitner; Clara Bryant; James Storm; Gil Gerard; Veronica Hamel; Adoni Maropis; Michael Horse; Roark Critchlow; Walter Koenig; William Katt; Tom Schmid; Directed by Jim Wynorski; Written by Jim Wynorski; Music by Chuck Cirino. **A:** Sr. High-Adult. **P:** Entertainment. **U:** Home. **Mov-Ent**: Native Americans, Folklore & Legends. **Acq:** Purchase. **Dist:** Lions Gate Entertainment Inc.

Bone Marrow Transplantation: An Update & Overview 1987
A thorough discussion of marrow transplants of the three major types-allogeneic, syngeneic and autologous. 59m; VHS, 3/4 U. **Pr:** Emory University. **A:** Adult. **P:** Professional. **U:** Institution, CCTV, Home, SURA. **Hea-Sci**: Documentary Films, Bones. **Acq:** Purchase, Rent/Lease, Subscription. **Dist:** Emory Medical Television Network.

Bone Marrows & Spinal Taps: A Child's View 1986
The painful and frightening process of bone surgery for children is shown, plus ways in which professionals can intervene to ease the patient. 12m; VHS, 3/4 U. **Pr:** Dr. Susan M. Jay; Dr. Charles Elliott. **A:** Adult. **P:** Professional. **U:** Institution, SURA. **Hea-Sci**: Documentary Films, Children, Surgery. **Acq:** Purchase, Rent/Lease. **Dist:** Leo Media, Inc.
Indiv. Titles: 1. Danielle 2. Ronald.

The Bone Yard 1990 (R) — ★
A weird mortuary is the setting for strange goings on when a murder is investigated. 98m; VHS, DVD. **C:** Ed Nelson; Deborah Rose; Norman Fell; Jim Eustermann; Denise Young; Willie Stratford, Jr.; Phyllis Diller; Directed by James Cummins; Written by James Cummins; Cinematography by Irl Dixon; Music by Kathleen Ann Porter; John Lee Whitener. **Pr:** Prism Entertainment. **A:** College-Adult. **P:** Entertainment. **U:** Home. **Mov-Ent**: Death. **Acq:** Purchase. **Dist:** Amazon.com Inc. $19.95.

Bonekickers 2008 (Unrated)
BBC 2008 dramatic mystery series. In the ancient city of Bath a team of archaeologists led by Dr. Gilliam Magwilde (Graham) uncover historical artifacts that are linked to actual European history and provide reenactments to provide clearer understanding. In "Army of God" medieval Middle Eastern coins are found where a parking lot is being made, "Warriors" has the team unearthing remains in the Bristol Channel thought to be 18th century slaves, and in "The Cradle of Civilisation" an Iraqi archaeologist arrives to take possession of a Babylonian relic that was looted during the Iraq War. 6 episodes. 344m; DVD. **C:** Adrian Lester; Hugh Bonneville; Julie Graham; Michael Maloney. **A:** Jr. High-Adult. **P:** Entertainment. **U:** Home. **Mov-Ent**: Archaeology, History, Television Series. **Acq:** Purchase. **Dist:** Acorn Media Group Inc. $39.99.

Bones 19??
This silent program presents children assembling skeletons of a chicken, raccoons, and a horse. They also make a replica of a human skeleton out of classroom supplies. In both films, the children are absorbed and self-sufficient as they go about their work. 14m; 3/4 U, Special order formats. **Pr:** Dorothy Welch. **A:** College-Adult. **P:** Education. **U:** Institution, CCTV, CATV, BCTV. **Gen-Edu**: Documentary Films, Bones, Education. **Acq:** Purchase, Rent/Lease. **Dist:** Education Development Center.

Bones 2001 (R) — ★★½
Combining the best of blaxploitation and horror elements, Dickerson smartly reveals the story of benevolent pimp Jimmy Bones'(Snoop Dogg) disappearance and subsequent resurrection 22 years later as a vengeful spirit. When an entreprenuerial buppie (Kain) decides to open a dance hall in Jimmy's former digs, walls begin oozing, animals become abundant and mean, and old secrets are revealed, much to the chagrin of the kid's rich father (Davis), and a cop (Weiss). Grier shines as a neighborhood psychic, and Snoop adds miles of style and presence, keeping this one a notch above the standard-issue haunted house fare. 94m; VHS, DVD, Wide. **C:** Snoop Dogg; Pam Grier; Michael T. Weiss; Clifton Powell; Ricky Harris; Bianca Lawson; Khalil Kain; Katharine Isabelle; Merwin Mondesir; Sean Amsing; Directed by Ernest R. Dickerson; Written by Adam Simon; Cinematography by Flavio Martinez Labiano; Music by Elia Cmiral. **A:** Sr. High-Adult. **P:** Entertainment. **U:** Home. **Mov-Ent**: Horror. **Acq:** Purchase. **Dist:** New Line Home Video.

Bones and Ligaments 1988
The elements of a horse's leg are completely described. 40m; VHS. **Pr:** Doug Butler. **A:** College-Adult. **P:** Professional. **U:** Institution, Home. **Hea-Sci**: Veterinary Medicine, Animals. **Acq:** Purchase. **Dist:** Doug Butler Enterprises Inc. $69.95.

Bones and Muscles: A Team to Depend On 1988
Animated sequences demonstrate how bones and muscles work together to help people move. 45m; VHS, 3/4 U. **Pr:** Marshfilm. **A:** Primary. **P:** Education. **U:** Institution. **Hea-Sci**: Bones, Muscles, Health Education. **Acq:** Purchase. **Dist:** Marshmedia. $45.50.

The Bones and Muscles Get Rhythm 1990
Part of the Wonders of Life Series which combines live action with animation to explain how different systems of the body

work. Sixth grader Alex and his various animated body systems help to explain how the bones, muscles, tendons, ligaments, and brain all work together while attending a school dance. Listed on the Science Books and Film's Best Science AV List. 11m; VHS, Special order formats. **Pr:** Disney Educational Productions. **A:** Primary. **P:** Education. **U:** Institution, CCTV, SURA. **Chl-Juv**: Science, Anatomy & Physiology, Bones. **Acq:** Purchase, Rent/Lease, Duplication License. **Dist:** Phoenix Learning Group. $250.00.

The Bones Brigade 4: Public Domain 1989
Fourth in the series of THE most sought after skate flicks. A rad combo of color and black and white footage makes the drama for skate fans way intense. Some of the best skating in the world from boardmasters Hawk, Caballero, Guerrero, Harris, Mountain, McGill, Barbee, Mullen, Powell, and Peralta. 60m; VHS. **C:** Tony Hawk; Victor Barbee; Stacy Peralta. **Pr:** NSI. **A:** Jr. High-Adult. **P:** Entertainment. **U:** Home. **Spo-Rec**: Sports--General. **Acq:** Purchase. **Dist:** NSI Sound & Video Inc. $34.95.

The Bones Brigade Video Show 1984
Classic, vintage, ultimate skateboarding at its finest. 35m; VHS. **Pr:** Champions on Film. **A:** Jr. High-Adult. **P:** Entertainment. **U:** Home. **Spo-Rec**: Sports--General. **Acq:** Purchase. **Dist:** School-Tech Inc. $34.95.

Bones in Action 1989
The skeletal system is explained through use of X-rays and models. 15m; VHS, 3/4 U, Special order formats. **Pr:** Perennial Education Inc. **A:** Jr. High-Adult. **P:** Education. **U:** Institution, Home, SURA. **Hea-Sci**: Bones. **Acq:** Purchase, Rent/Lease, Trade-in. **Dist:** United Learning Inc. $235.00.

Bones of Contention: Native American Archaeology ????
Native American archaeology provides a background for discussions of alternate perspectives between scientists, historians, museum curators, and Native American groups. 49m; VHS. **A:** Sr. High-Adult. **P:** Education. **U:** Institution. **Gen-Edu**: Native Americans, History--U.S., Archaeology. **Acq:** Purchase, Rent/Lease. **Dist:** Films for the Humanities & Sciences. $129.00.

Bones of Turkana 2012 (Unrated)
In this documentary, famed paleoanthropologist Richard Leakey and his family spend time in Kenya's Turkana Basin to make new discoveries that will enhance what we know about human evolution. In addition, they take the time to show how all the qualities that make us humans can be traced back to origins in Africa, home to the most important fossil discoveries through the years. Includes music by Paul Simon and the Kenya Boys Choir. 45m; DVD. **A:** Family. **P:** Education, Entertainment. **U:** Home, Institution. **Mov-Ent**: Documentary Films, Anthropology, Science. **Acq:** Purchase. **Dist:** $13.97.

Bones: The Complete Eighth Season 2012
Fox 2005--? crime drama. "The Future in the Past": Bones is on the run with Christina after being framed for murder by Christopher Pelant, but the team searches for the real killer. "The Diamond in the Rough": Booth and Brennan go undercover when a dance contestant is murdered before a competition. "The Secret in the Siege": The team realizes a series of murders are tied to FBI agents close to Booth as Pelant (Andrew Leeds) returns. 26 episodes. 1041m; DVD. **C:** Emily Deschanel; David Boreanaz; Michaela Conlin; T.J. Thyne; Tamara Taylor; John Francis Daley. **A:** Jr. High-Adult. **P:** Entertainment. **U:** Home. **L:** English. **Mov-Ent**: Crime Drama, Television Series. **Acq:** Purchase. **Dist:** Fox Home Entertainment. $59.98.

Bones: The Complete Fifth Season 2010 (Unrated)
Fox Television 2005-? forensic science mystery series. In "The Plain in the Prodigy," Bones and Booth investigate an Amish piano prodigy's murder. A skeleton emerges in the overflow after a flood in the subway that derails a train in "The Bones on a Blue Line." The team uncovers clues in the stash of a hoarder in order to solve the mystery of his death in "The Beginning in the End." 22 episodes. 997m; DVD, Blu-Ray. **C:** Emily Deschanel; David Boreanaz; Michaela Conlin; T.J. Thyne; Tamara Taylor; John Francis Daley. **A:** Sr. High-Adult. **P:** Entertainment. **U:** Home. **Mov-Ent**: Television Series, Federal Bureau of Investigation (FBI), Mystery & Suspense. **Acq:** Purchase. **Dist:** 20th Century Fox Home Entertainment. $22.57.

Bones: The Complete First Season 2005 (Unrated)
FBI agent Seeley Booth reluctantly works with forensic anthropologist Dr. Temperance "Bones" Brennan and her scientific team from the Jeffersonian Institution to solve crimes. While Bones is socially awkward and cerebral, Booth is charming and visceral, but both have traumatic pasts that make them sympathetic to each other and their victims. Inspired by the work of writer/anthropologist Kathy Reichs. 22 episodes. 946m; DVD. **C:** David Boreanaz; Emily Deschanel. **A:** Jr. High-Adult. **P:** Entertainment. **U:** Home. **Mov-Ent**: Television Series, Mystery & Suspense, Federal Bureau of Investigation (FBI). **Acq:** Purchase. **Dist:** Fox Home Entertainment.

Bones: The Complete Fourth Season 2008 (Unrated)
Fox Television 2005-? forensic science mystery series. Several interns make their way through the Jeffersonian to fill the void of Zack Addy, now incarcerated after admitting to being an apprentice to the serial killer Gormogon. An artist's skull is found in a crushed car in "The Skull in the Sculpture" leaving the team to decipher if he purposely made himself part of his art or foul play was involved. On a flight to China Bones and Booth must solve the mystery of "The Passenger in the Oven" before their flight lands. In the finale "The Critic in the Cabernet," as they work on remains in a wine barrel Temperance admits to Seeley she would like to have a child and asks for his 'assistance.' 21 episodes. 964m; DVD, Blu-Ray. **C:** Emily Deschanel; David Boreanaz; T.J. Thyne; John Francis Daley. **A:** Sr. High-Adult. **P:** Entertainment. **U:** Home. **Mov-Ent**: Television Series, Federal Bureau of Investigation (FBI), Mystery & Suspense. **Acq:** Purchase. **Dist:** Fox Home Entertainment. $59.99.

Bones: The Complete Second Season 2006
Brennan continues her forensic anthropology work, assisting FBI agent Booth on cases and clashing with Camilla Saroyan, who has taken over as the team's boss at the Jeffersonian. When Booth gets into trouble and is suspended, Brennan falls for his FBI buddy Tim Sullivan (Eddie McClintock). Meanwhile, Hodgins convinces Angela to date and their romance gets serious while Zack agrees to go to Iraq. Brennan's father (Ryan O'Neal) also reappears and she learns more about his shady past. 946m; DVD. **C:** David Boreanaz; Emily Deschanel; Tamara Taylor; Eric Millegan; Michaela Conlin; T.J. Thyne. **A:** Jr. High-Adult. **P:** Entertainment. **U:** Home. **Mov-Ent**: Television Series, Federal Bureau of Investigation (FBI), Science. **Acq:** Purchase. **Dist:** Fox Home Entertainment.

Bones: The Complete Seventh Season 2012 (Unrated)
Fox Television 2005-? forensic science mystery series. A chopped-up corpse is found in several boxes in the mail, and a local Ship 'n' Print employee is missing in "The Male in the Mail." Hodgins tries to identify a blue substance which killed animals scavenging a corpse, and motives abound in "The Don't in the Do." A Hollywood studio boss is found dead on set of an action movie based on a book by Bones in "The Suit on the Set." 13 episodes. 567m; DVD, Blu-Ray. **C:** Emily Deschanel; David Boreanaz; Michaela Conlin; T.J. Thyne; Tamara Taylor; John Francis Daley. **A:** Sr. High-Adult. **P:** Entertainment. **U:** Home. **Mov-Ent**: Television Series, Federal Bureau of Investigation (FBI), Mystery & Suspense. **Acq:** Purchase. **Dist:** 20th Century Fox Home Entertainment. $33.99.

Bones: The Complete Sixth Season 2011 (Unrated)
Fox Television 2005-? forensic science mystery series. A skull and decomposing hands are found in a dumpster and the team must solve the crime and find the rest of the victim's remains in "The Body and the Bounty." The team investigates a murder at a socialite's home in "The Body in the Bag." A young deaf girl is found on the streets covered in blood and holding a knife, and the team needs to figure out if she's responsible for a recent murder in "The Signs in the Silence." 23 episodes. 1000m; DVD, Blu-Ray. **C:** Emily Deschanel; David Boreanaz; Michaela Conlin; T.J. Thyne; Tamara Taylor; John Francis Daley. **A:** Sr. High-Adult. **P:** Entertainment. **U:** Home. **Mov-Ent**: Television Series, Federal Bureau of Investigation (FBI), Mystery & Suspense. **Acq:** Purchase. **Dist:** 20th Century Fox Home Entertainment. $19.90.

Bones: The Complete Third Season 2005 (Unrated)
Fox Network's shortened season (due to the writers' strike) for the forensic crime drama opens with "The Widow's Son in the Windshield" which introduces the cannibalistic Gormogon serial killer that appears again in "The Knight on the Grid," while "The Secret of the Soil" introduces 22-year old psychotherapist Dr. Sweets who is assigned to counsel Bones and Booth, because there is concern after Booth arrested Bones' father. Sentimental standout is"The Santa in the Slush" as Bones cuts a deal to have Christmas brought to her father and brother in jail. 19 episodes. 655m; DVD. **C:** Emily Deschanel; David Boreanaz. **A:** Adult. **P:** Entertainment. **U:** Home. **Mov-Ent**: Drama, Television Series, Mystery & Suspense. **Acq:** Purchase. **Dist:** Fox Home Entertainment. $59.98.

Boneshop of the Heart 1991
Explores a rich vein of visual expression and American individuality through incisive portraits of five contemporary southern folk artists, four of whom are African-American. Takes a look at the art forms of "Tin Man" Charlie Lucas, Vollis Simpson, Thornton Dial, Bessie Harvey, and "Sandman" Lonnie Bradley Holley, discussing how their art forms challenge traditional distinctions between fine and folk art. 53m; DVD, 3/4 U, Special order formats. **TV Std:** NTSC, PAL, SECAM. **A:** Sr. High-Adult. **P:** Education. **U:** Institution. **Gen-Edu**: Folklore & Legends, Art & Artists. **Acq:** Purchase, Rent/Lease. **Dist:** Microcinema International. $295.00.

Boney 1982
An improvisational performance delivered into the camera while walking through Soho on a spring afternoon. Part of the "New TV" series. 7m; VHS, 3/4 U. **Pr:** Maxi Cohen; Joel Gold. **A:** Sr. High-Adult. **P:** Entertainment. **U:** Institution, SURA. **Gen-Edu**: Performing Arts, Video. **Acq:** Purchase, Rent/Lease. **Dist:** Maxi Cohen Film & Video Productions.

The Boney Skull 1974
The external aspects of the human skull are examined, identified, and clinically related. 34m/B/W; 3/4 U. **Pr:** New Jersey Medical School. **A:** College-Adult. **P:** Education. **U:** Institution, CCTV. **Hea-Sci**: Head, Medical Education. **Acq:** Purchase. **Dist:** New Jersey Medical School.

The Bonfire of the Vanities 1990 (R) — ★½
If you liked Tom Wolfe's viciously satirical novel, chances are you won't like this version. If you didn't read the book, you probably still won't like it. Miscast and stripped of the book's gutsy look inside its characters, the film's sole attribute is Vilmos Zsigmond's photography. Hanks is all wrong as wealthy Wall Street trader Sherman McCoy who, lost in the back streets of the Bronx, panics and accidentally kills a young black kid. Willis' drunken journalist/narrator, Griffith's mistress, and Freeman's righteous judge are all awkward and thinly written. If you're still awake, look for F. Murray Abraham's cameo as the Bronx D.A. 126m; VHS, DVD, Blu-Ray, 8 mm, Wide. **C:** Tom Hanks; Melanie Griffith; Bruce Willis; Morgan Freeman; Alan King; Kim Cattrall; Saul Rubinek; Clifton James; Donald Moffat; Richard Libertini; Andre Gregory; Robert Stephens; Cameo(s) F. Murray Abraham; Directed by Brian De Palma; Written by Michael Cristofer; Cinematography by Vilmos Zsigmond; Music by Dave Grusin. **Pr:** Peter Guber; Jon Peters; Warner Bros. **A:** College-Adult. **P:** Entertainment. **U:** Home. **Mov-Ent**: Satire & Parody. **Acq:** Purchase. **Dist:** Warner Home Video, Inc.; Facets Multimedia Inc. $19.98.

Bong and Donnell 1996
Follows the life of Bong and Donnell from third grade until senior year in high school. Bong is physically handicapped, his best friend is not. Focuses on the normal activities they do together, in spite of Bong's handicap. 56m; VHS. **A:** Adult. **P:** Education. **U:** Institution. **Hea-Sci**: Handicapped, Adolescence. **Acq:** Purchase, Rent/Lease. **Dist:** University of Maryland. $400.00.

Bongo 1947 — ★★
Originally a part of the Disney cartoon anthology "Fun and Fancy Free." Follows the adventures of a circus bear who flees the big time for the wonders of the forests. Also available with "Ben and Me" on laserdisc. 36m; VHS. **C:** Bill Roberts; Hamilton Luske; Narrated by Dinah Shore; Directed by Jack Kinney. **Pr:** Walt Disney Studios. **A:** Family. **P:** Entertainment. **U:** Home. **Mov-Ent**: Animation & Cartoons, Circuses, Family Viewing. **Acq:** Purchase. **Dist:** Walt Disney Studios Home Entertainment; Buena Vista Home Entertainment. $12.99.

Bongwater 1998 (R) — ★★
David (Wilson) is a Portland pot dealer and aspiring artist who becomes roommates with Serena (Witt), although mixed signals prevents anything closer even if David is definitely lovesick. Thanks to a misunderstanding, Serena heads to New York, a bong ignites the house where David was living—burning it to the ground—and he is forced to rely on the kindness of his fellow pot buddies while Serena has her own problems in the Big Apple. However, you won't really care except Wilson is appealing in a goofy doper sort of way. 98m; VHS, DVD. **C:** Luke Wilson; Alicia Witt; Amy Locane; Brittany Murphy; Jack Black; Andy Dick; Jeremy Sisto; Jamie Kennedy; Scott Caan; Patricia Wettig; Directed by Richard Sears; Written by Nora MacCoby; Eric Weiss; Cinematography by Richard Crudo; Music by Mark Mothersbaugh; Josh Mancell. **A:** Sr. High-Adult. **P:** Entertainment. **U:** Home. **Mov-Ent**: Comedy-Drama, Drug Abuse. **Acq:** Purchase. **Dist:** Image Entertainment Inc.

Bonhoeffer 2004
Documents the moral courage of Dietrich Bonhoeffer, a German theologian who spoke out against the German church supporting Hitler over the Jews and joined the plot to eliminate him. 90m; DVD. **A:** Adult. **P:** Education. **U:** Home. **Gen-Edu**: Documentary Films, History--Modern, Germany. **Acq:** Purchase. **Dist:** First Run/Icarus Films. $29.95.

Bonhoeffer: A Life of Challenge 1979
The life and witness of Bonhoeffer, the German theologian who asked the question "Who is Christ?," are profiled through his writings and interviews with his associates. 28m; VHS, Special order formats. **A:** Sr. High-Adult. **P:** Religious. **U:** Institution. **Gen-Edu**: Philosophy & Ideology, Religion. **Acq:** Rent/Lease. **Dist:** EcuFilm.

Boning a Chicken: Whole 1986
Offers instruction on specific aspects of cooking and food preparation. 11m; VHS. **A:** Adult. **P:** Instruction. **U:** Institution. **Gen-Edu**: Cooking. **Acq:** Purchase. **Dist:** RMI Media. $49.95.

Boning a Leg of Veal 1988
Everything having to do with the preparation of veal is explained. 18m; VHS, 3/4 U. **C:** Italo Peduzzi. **Pr:** Culinary Institute of America. **A:** Sr. High-Adult. **P:** Instruction. **U:** Institution, SURA. **How-Ins**: How-To, Cooking. **Acq:** Purchase, Rent/Lease. **Dist:** Culinary Institute of America. $100.00.

Boning Chicken Breast 1984
Chef Paul demonstrates the procedure for de-boning chicken breast. 10m; VHS. **A:** Adult. **P:** Instruction. **U:** Institution. **Gen-Edu**: Cooking. **Acq:** Purchase. **Dist:** RMI Media. $39.95.

Bonjour Les Amis! 199?
Animated three-volume program that features Moustache, France's most lovable cat, as he uses his many adventures to teach the French language to children. 150m; VHS. **A:** Primary. **P:** Education. **U:** Home. **Chl-Juv**: Language Arts, Children, Animation & Cartoons. **Acq:** Purchase. **Dist:** Monterey Home Video. $54.95.
Indiv. Titles: 1. Bonjour les Amis!, Vol. One 2. Bonjour les Amis!, Vol. Two 3. Bonjour les Amis!, Vol. Three.

Bonjour Monsieur Shlomi 2003 (Unrated) — ★★★
Light-hearted human comedy about sixteen-year-old, Shlomi, a mildly slow-witted Jewish boy juggling school, love, and the family circus at home. Willing to put his own interests aside, Shlomi dedicates most of his life to caring for his senile grandfather, cooking elaborate meals for the family, and falling behind in school. His secret joys come from poetry, snooping through his older brother's explicit diary, and daydreaming about the girl next door. A surprisingly warm Israeli film that manages to avoid the usual melodramatic pitfalls of most American coming-of-age flicks. 94m; DVD. **C:** Esti Zakheim; Aya Koren; Assi Cohen; Oshri Cohen; Arie Elias; Yigal Naor; Albert Illouz; Jonathan Rozen; Rotem Abuhav; Rotem Zisman; Nisso Keavia; Aya Steinovitz; Directed by Shemi Zarhin; Written by Shemi Zarhin; Cinematography by Itzik Portal; Music by Jonathan Bar-Girora. **P:** Entertainment. **U:** Home. **L:** Hebrew. **Mov-Ent**: Comedy-Drama, Family, Israel. **Acq:** Purchase. **Dist:** Strand Releasing. $24.99.

Bonjour Shalom 1991
Explores the lives of a community of Hassidic Jews as they attempt to preserve their traditions in a French-speaking

Montreal community. 53m; VHS. **A:** Jr. High-Adult. **P:** Education. **U:** Institution. **Gen-Edu:** Judaism. **Acq:** Purchase. **Dist:** National Center for Jewish Film.

Bonjour Tristesse 1957 (Unrated) — ★★★
An amoral French girl (Seberg) conspires to break up her playboy father's (Niven) upcoming marriage to her stuffy godmother (Kerr) in order to maintain her decadent freedom. Preminger attempted, unsuccessfully, to use this soaper to catapult Seberg to stardom. Based on the novel by Francoise Sagan. 94m/B/W; VHS, DVD, Blu-Ray. **C:** Deborah Kerr; David Niven; Jean Seberg; Mylene Demongeot; Geoffrey Horne; Walter Chiari; Jean Kent; Directed by Otto Preminger; Written by Arthur Laurents; Cinematography by Georges Perinal. **Pr:** Otto Preminger; Otto Preminger. **A:** Jr. High-Adult. **P:** Entertainment. **U:** Home. **Mov-Ent:** Melodrama, Sex & Sexuality. **Acq:** Purchase. **Dist:** Sony Pictures Home Entertainment Inc.

Bonnard 1990
A close up of the artist and his unique style is seen at the Paris Centre Pompidou. 49m; VHS. **Pr:** Home Vision. **A:** Sr. High-Adult. **P:** Entertainment. **U:** Home. **Fin-Art:** Documentary Films, Art & Artists. **Acq:** Purchase. **Dist:** Home Vision Cinema. $39.95.

Bonnet Carpet Care 19??
Demonstrates the procedures for the bonnet carpet cleaning method. 15m; VHS. **A:** College-Adult. **P:** Vocational. **U:** Institution. **L:** Spanish. **Bus-Ind:** Job Training, Custodial Service, Industrial Arts. **Acq:** Purchase, Rent/Lease. **Dist:** AMS Distributors, Inc.

Bonneville 2006 (PG) — ★★
On a mission to spread the ashes of a dead husband, three middle-aged women hit the open road in a 1966 Bonneville, driving from Idaho to California. Along the way they laugh about the good old days, cry about car trouble, and connect all the dots required of a formulaic road trip flick. Bates, Lange, and Allen are excellent, but ultimately wasted on a script that's lacking surprise and running on fumes from the start. 93m; DVD. **C:** Jessica Lange; Kathy Bates; Joan Allen; Christine Baranski; Victor Rasuk; Tom Amandes; Tom Wopat; Tom Skerritt; Directed by Christopher Rowley; Written by Daniel Davis; Cinematography by Jeffrey L. Kimball; Music by Jeff Cardoni. **Pr:** John Kilker; Robert May; Drop of Water Prods; SenArt Films. **A:** Jr. High-Adult. **P:** Entertainment. **U:** Home. **L:** English. **Mov-Ent. Acq:** Purchase. **Dist:** Fox Home Entertainment.

Bonnie & Clyde 1967 — ★★★½
Based on the biographies of the violent careers of Bonnie Parker (Dunaway) and Clyde Barrow (Beatty), who roamed the Southwest robbing banks. In the Depression era, when any job, even an illegal one, was cherished, money, greed, and power created an unending cycle of violence and fury. Highly controversial and influential, with pronounced bloodshed (particularly the pairs balletic and bullet-ridden end) that spurred mainstream cinematic proliferation. Established Dunaway as a star; produced by Beatty in one of his best performances. 111m; VHS, DVD, Blu-Ray, CC. **C:** Warren Beatty; Faye Dunaway; Michael J. Pollard; Gene Hackman; Estelle Parsons; Denver Pyle; Gene Wilder; Dub Taylor; Evans Evans; Directed by Arthur Penn; Written by David Newman; Robert Benton; Cinematography by Burnett Guffey; Music by Charles Strouse. **Pr:** Warner Bros. **A:** Jr. High-Adult. **P:** Entertainment. **U:** Home. **Mov-Ent:** Biography: Law Enforcement, Cult Films, Classic Films. **Awds:** Oscars '67: Cinematog., Support. Actress (Parsons); AFI '98: Top 100; Natl. Film Reg. '92; N.Y. Film Critics '67: Screenplay; Natl. Soc. Film Critics '67: Screenplay, Support. Actor (Hackman); Writers Guild '67: Orig. Screenplay. **Acq:** Purchase. **Dist:** Baker and Taylor; Warner Home Video, Inc. $19.98.

Bonnie & Clyde 2013 (Unrated) — ★★
A somewhat conventional biopic of the Depression era crime spree of Bonnie Parker (Grainger) and Clyde Barrow (Hirsch) where the more interesting aspect of the cable drama is the manhunt conducted by Texas Ranger Frank Hamer (Hurt). Grainger plays Parker as a young woman so relentless about getting out of rural Texas and being famous that a newspaper/newsreel life of crime is a viable option as she pushes petty crook Clyde to bolder acts. 174m; DVD, Blu-Ray. **C:** Holliday Grainger; Emile Hirsch; William Hurt; Sarah Hyland; Lane Garrison; Elizabeth Reaser; Holly Hunter; Directed by Bruce Beresford; Written by Joe Batteer; John Rice; Cinematography by Francis Kenny; Music by John Debney. **A:** Sr. High-Adult. **P:** Entertainment. **U:** Home. **L:** English. **Mov-Ent:** TV Movies, Biography: Law Enforcement, Crime Drama. **Acq:** Purchase. **Dist:** Sony Pictures Home Entertainment Inc.

Bonnie and Clyde vs. Dracula 2008 (Unrated) — ★½
Awkward combo of crime and horror comedy worth seeing for scream queen Shepis. Bonnie and Clyde need a place to hide out after a botched robbery and find the secluded mansion of Dr. Loveless. Hanging out in the doc's cellar is longtime guest Dracula, who really wants some fresh blood. 90m; DVD. **C:** Tiffany Shepis; Trent Haaga; Allen Lowman; Russell Friend; Jennifer Friend; T. Max Graham; F. Martin Glenn; Directed by Timothy Friend; Written by Timothy Friend; Cinematography by Todd Norris; Music by Joseph Allen. **A:** Sr. High-Adult. **P:** Entertainment. **U:** Home. **Mov-Ent. Acq:** Purchase. **Dist:** Indican Pictures.

Bonnie Prince Charlie 1948 — ★★½
Historical epic opening in 1745 and romanticizing the title pretender to the British throne, who united Scottish clans in a doomed campaign against King George. Talky and rather slow-moving except for stirring battle scenes. A notorious boxoffice flop in its native Britain, where the original running time was 140 minutes. 114m; VHS, CC. **C:** David Niven; Margaret Leighton; Judy Campbell; Jack Hawkins; Morland Graham; Finlay Currie; Elwyn Brook-Jones; John Laurie; Directed by Anthony Kimmins. **Pr:** British Lion. **A:** Jr. High-Adult. **P:** Entertainment. **U:** Home. **Mov-Ent:** Drama, Great Britain, Biography: Royalty. **Acq:** Purchase. **Dist:** Lions Gate Entertainment Inc. $19.95.

Bonnie Raitt: The Video Collection 199?
The Grammy Award-winning singer presents seven videos from her "Nick of Time" and "Luck of the Draw" albums, including her hit "Something to Talk About." 30m; VHS. **C:** Music by Bonnie Raitt. **A:** Jr. High-Adult. **P:** Entertainment. **U:** Home. **Mov-Ent:** Music Video, Music--Pop/Rock. **Acq:** Purchase. **Dist:** Henninger Capitol; Music Video Distributors. $19.95.

Bonnie Scotland 1935 (Unrated) — ★★½
Laurel & Hardy accidentally join an India-bound Scottish regiment. Laughs aplenty. 81m/B/W; VHS, DVD. **C:** Stan Laurel; Oliver Hardy; James Finlayson; Daphne Pollard; June Lang; Directed by James W. Horne. **Pr:** Hal Roach; MGM. **A:** Family. **P:** Entertainment. **U:** Home. **Mov-Ent:** Comedy--Slapstick, Scotland. **Acq:** Purchase. **Dist:** MGM Home Entertainment. $19.98.

Bonnie's Kids 1973 (R) — ★½
Two sisters become involved in murder, sex, and stolen money. 107m; VHS, DVD. **C:** Tiffany Bolling; Robin Mattson; Scott Brady; Alex Rocco; Directed by Arthur Marks. **Pr:** General Film Corporation. **A:** Adult. **P:** Entertainment. **U:** Home. **Mov-Ent:** Crime Drama. **Acq:** Purchase. **Dist:** No Longer Available.

Bonsoir Mes Amis: Goodnight My Friends 19??
Fiddler Ben Guillemette and singer Lionel Bouthot bring old-fashioned New England country dance up-to-date and into your living room. These self-taught musicians learned to play to make people dance to their blend of Franco-American, Irish and Western Swing music. 46m; VHS. **A:** Family. **P:** Education. **U:** Institution. **L:** English. **Gen-Edu. Acq:** Purchase. **Dist:** Northeast Historic Film. $29.95.

Bontoc Eulogy 1995
Documentary about the natives displayed in the Philippine Village exhibit at the 1904 St. Louis World's Fair. 60m/B/W; VHS, DVD. **A:** Sr. High-Adult. **P:** Education. **U:** Home, Institution. **Gen-Edu:** Fairs & Expositions, Documentary Films. **Acq:** Purchase, Rent/Lease. **Dist:** The Cinema Guild. $295.00.

Bony Pelvis and Male Pelvis Viscera 1986
Both male and female pelvises are examined in detail. 26m; 3/4 U. **Pr:** McMaster University. **A:** Adult. **P:** Professional. **U:** Institution, SURA. **Hea-Sci:** Anatomy & Physiology, Medical Education, Bones. **Acq:** Purchase, Rent/Lease. **Dist:** McMaster University.

Boo! 2005 (Unrated) — ★★
Five college students decide to check out the abandoned Santa Mira Hospital on Halloween to see if rumors about it being haunted are true. They discover a vengeful spirit that wants to make sure no one gets out alive. Low-budget but inventive and sufficiently creepy for a dark and stormy night. 100m; DVD. **C:** Dee Wallace; Trish Coren; M. Steven Felty; Josh Holt; Jilon Ghai; Nicole Rayburn; Michael Samluk; Dig Wayne; Directed by Anthony C. Ferrante; Written by Anthony C. Ferrante; Cinematography by Carl F. Bartels. **A:** Sr. High-Adult. **P:** Entertainment. **U:** Home. **Mov-Ent:** Halloween, Hospitals. **Acq:** Purchase. **Dist:** Ventura Distribution Inc.

Boo-Busters 1993
The Goof Troup discover a haunted house that's home to a Dixieland band of ghosts in "Hallow-Weenies." Chip 'n' Dale head off to jolly old England in "Ghost of a Chance" and find a prankish spook. 44m; VHS. **A:** Family. **P:** Entertainment. **U:** Home. **Chl-Juv:** Animation & Cartoons. **Acq:** Purchase. **Dist:** Walt Disney Studios Home Entertainment. $12.99.

Boo Hoo 1987
An unusual portrait film about a retired cemetery superintendent. 18m; VHS, 3/4 U. **Pr:** Rex Tasker; Ian McLaren. **A:** Jr. High-Adult. **P:** Education. **U:** Institution, SURA. **Gen-Edu:** Death, Occupations. **Acq:** Purchase, Rent/Lease. **Dist:** National Film Board of Canada.

The Boob 1926 (Unrated) — ★★
Farmhand Peter (Arthur) is in love with sweet Amy (Olmstead) who has fallen for the dubious charms of city slicker Harry (D'Algy). Peter is suspicious that Harry is a bootlegger so he becomes a revenue agent. He meets Jane (Crawford), a fellow agent, at Harry's club and she wonders if Peter is working the same undercover case she is—albeit for personal reasons. 64m/B/W; Silent; DVD. **C:** Gertrude (Olmstead) Olmsted; George K. Arthur; Joan Crawford; Charles Murray; Directed by William A. Wellman; Written by Katherine Hilliker; H. H. Caldwell; Cinematography by William H. Daniels. **A:** Sr. High-Adult. **P:** Entertainment. **U:** Home. **Mov-Ent:** Silent Films, Nightclubs. **Acq:** Purchase. **Dist:** WarnerArchive.com.

Boobah: Comfy Armchair 2004
Boobahs gallop, bounce, and spin. The Storypeople get an armchair, a skipping rope and a record player. 60m; VHS, DVD; Closed Captioned. **A:** Preschool. **P:** Entertainment. **U:** Home. **Chl-Juv:** Children, Television. **Acq:** Purchase. **Dist:** Paramount Pictures Corp. $16.99.

Boobah: Snowman 2004
Boobahs march to a magical beat and do a dizzy In and Out dance. The Storypeople find snowballs. 60m; VHS, DVD; Closed Captioned. **A:** Preschool. **P:** Entertainment. **U:** Home. **Chl-Juv:** Animation & Cartoons, Television. **Acq:** Purchase. **Dist:** Paramount Pictures Corp. $16.99.

Boobah: Squeaky Socks 2004
Boobahs hop, jump, and move their feet. The Storypeople get squeaky socks, a pot of paint and a hammock. 60m; VHS, DVD; Closed Captioned. **A:** Preschool. **P:** Entertainment. **U:** Home. **Chl-Juv:** Children, Television. **Acq:** Purchase. **Dist:** Paramount Pictures Corp. $16.99.

The Boogey Man 1980 (R) — ★★
Through the reflection in a mirror, a girl witnesses her brother murder their mother's lover. Twenty years later this memory still haunts her; the mirror is now broken, revealing its special powers. Who will be next? Murder menagerie; see footage from this flick mirrored in "The Boogey Man 2." 93m; VHS, DVD, Wide. **C:** John Carradine; Suzanna Love; Ron James; Directed by Ulli Lommel; Written by Suzanna Love; Ulli Lommel; Cinematography by Jochen Breitenstein; David Sperling; Music by Tim Krog. **Pr:** Jerry Gross. **A:** College-Adult. **P:** Entertainment. **U:** Home. **Mov-Ent:** Horror. **Acq:** Purchase. **Dist:** Movies Unlimited. $19.99.

Boogey Man 2 1983 (Unrated) — **Bomb!**
The story continues; same footage, new director but with Lommel, the director of the original "Boogey Man," co-writing the script and appearing in the film. 90m; VHS, DVD. **TV Std:** NTSC, PAL. **C:** John Carradine; Suzanna Love; Shannah Hall; Ulli Lommel; Sholto Von Douglas; Directed by Bruce Starr. **Pr:** Ulli Lommel; David DuBay; Ulli Lommel. **A:** Adult. **P:** Entertainment. **U:** Home. **Mov-Ent:** Horror. **Acq:** Purchase. **Dist:** VCX Ltd. $29.95.

Boogeyman 2005 (PG-13) — ★½
Weak horror flick about monsters in the closet. Tim (Watson) returns to his hometown for his mother's (Lawless) funeral and revisits the childhood home where his father was apparently sucked into young Tim's bedroom closet by the boogeyman and killed. Naturally, Tim has an aversion to closets. He wants to prove the boogeyman is all in his imagination like his shrink says; the boogeyman has other ideas. 86m; DVD, UMD. **C:** Barry Watson; Emily Deschanel; Skye McCole Bartusiak; Lucy Lawless; Philip Gordon; Aaron Murphy; Robyn Malcolm; Victoria (Tory) Mussett; Andrew Glover; Charles Mesure; Jennifer Rucker; Directed by Stephen Kay; Cinematography by Bobby Bukowski; Music by Joseph LoDuca. **Pr:** Sam Raimi; Robert Tapert; Sony Pictures Entertainment; Ghost House Pictures. **A:** Jr. High-Adult. **P:** Entertainment. **U:** Home. **L:** English. **Mov-Ent:** Mystery & Suspense, Horror. **Acq:** Purchase. **Dist:** Sony Pictures Home Entertainment Inc. $28.95.

Boogeyman 2 2007 (Unrated) — ★½
When Laura (Savre) and her brother (Cohen) were children, they watched their father get slaughtered by the boogeyman. Naturally, this caused a lot of trauma, so Laura decides to check herself into a local mental hospital in hopes of getting past her continuing fear. But when patients start dying, it becomes clear the creature is trolling the hospital for his next victims. 93m; DVD, CC. **C:** Tobin Bell; Renee O'Connor; Danielle Savre; Matt Cohen; Directed by Jeff Betancourt; Written by Brian Sieve; Cinematography by Nelson Cragg. **A:** Sr. High-Adult. **P:** Entertainment. **U:** Home. **Mov-Ent. Acq:** Purchase. **Dist:** Sony Pictures Home Entertainment Inc.

Boogeyman 3 2008 (Unrated) — ★½
College sophomore Sarah Morris (Cahill) witnesses the alleged suicide of friend Audrey (Sanderson), who was terrified that the boogeyman was after her. Sarah tries to convince the other dorm inhabitants that evil does exist but they all think she's crazy until they become the next victims. A cut above most DTV horror sequels since the predictable plot does offer some scares. 92m; DVD. **C:** Mimi Michaels; Matt Rippy; Kate Maberly; Erin Cahill; Chuck Hittinger; Nikki Sanderson; Directed by Gary Jones; Written by Brian Sieve; Cinematography by Lorenzo Senatore; Music by Joseph LoDuca. **A:** Sr. High-Adult. **P:** Entertainment. **U:** Home. **Mov-Ent:** Horror, Suicide. **Acq:** Purchase. **Dist:** Sony Pictures Home Entertainment Inc.

Boogie Boy 1998 (R) — ★½
Recently released from prison, Jesse (Dacascos) gets involved as muscle for a drug deal involving his ex-cellmate, the drug-addicted Larry (Woolvett), in order to get some quick cash. Naturally, the deal goes sour and they wind up on the lam. 110m; VHS, DVD. **C:** Mark Dacascos; Emily Lloyd; Jaimz Woolvett; Traci Lords; Frederic Forrest; Joan Jett; Ben Browder; James Lew; Linnea Quigley; Directed by Craig Hamann; Written by Craig Hamann; Music by Tim Truman. **A:** Sr. High-Adult. **P:** Entertainment. **U:** Home. **Mov-Ent:** Drugs. **Acq:** Purchase. **Dist:** Movies Unlimited.

Boogie Down Productions: Edutainment 1990
Rapper KRS-ONE is featured in a video that is educational, plus other material from the three other Boogie Down Productions artists is presented along with interviews and live footage. ?m; VHS. **A:** Family. **P:** Entertainment. **U:** Home. **Mov-Ent:** Music Video, Music--Rap. **Acq:** Purchase. **Dist:** Music Video Distributors. $16.98.

Boogie Down Productions Live 1990 (Unrated)
A collection of funky songs from the popular band. 70m; VHS, CV. **A:** Jr. High-Adult. **P:** Entertainment. **U:** Home. **Mov-Ent:** Music--Performance. **Acq:** Purchase. **Dist:** Music Video Distributors; BMG Entertainment. $19.98.

Boogie in Blue: Harry "The Hipster" Gibson 1992
An informal look at Harry "The Hipster" Gibson, a hit of the 1940s jazz scene with his boogie-woogie piano playing and eccentricities, who later fell into obscurity. His novelty songs included "4F Ferdinand the Frantic Freak," "Stop That Dancing Up There," and "Who Put the Benzedrine in Mrs. Murphy's Ovaltine?" 40m; VHS. **A:** Sr. High-Adult. **P:** Entertainment. **U:** Home. **Gen-Edu:** Documentary Films, Music--Jazz, Biography. **Acq:** Purchase. **Dist:** Rhapsody Films, Inc. $24.95.

The Boogie Man Will Get You 1942 (Unrated) — ★★½
Crazy scientist Nathaniel Billings (Karloff) has been working on creating a race of supermen in his basement. He sells his home to Bill (Parks) and Winnie (Donnell), who are turning the place into a bed and breakfast, thinking that he can use their guests as fresh subjects. Lorre plays multiple roles, including a fellow nutcase. Karloff was unavailable to reprise his role in the film version of "Arsenic and Old Lace" so he did this similar comedy instead. 66m/B/W; VHS, DVD. **C:** Boris Karloff; Peter Lorre; Maxie "Slapsie" Rosenbloom; Larry Parks; Jeff Donnell; Maude Eburne; Directed by Lew Landers; Written by Edwin Blum; Cinematography by Henry Freulich. **A:** Jr. High-Adult. **P:** Entertainment. **U:** Home. **Mov-Ent. Acq:** Purchase. **Dist:** Sony Pictures Home Entertainment Inc.

Boogie Nights 1997 (R) — ★★★½
Epic tale covering the rise and fall of porn star Eddie Adams (Wahlberg). The protege of director Jack Horner (Reynolds), 17-year-old Eddie jumps in a hot tub at an industry bash, christens himself Dirk Diggler, and goes on to become the toast of the adult entertainment industry. Brilliantly spanning the decadent disco-era 70s and the excess of the 80s, 27-year-old writer/director Anderson boldly delves into fresh, albeit dangerous, territory most successfully in this lengthy sophomore outing. What Tarantino did for Travolta, Anderson does here for Reynolds, who plays the past-his-prime but touchingly ambitious auteur with a dream to make a legitimately legendary skin flick. Wahlberg proves himself a serious and seriously good actor in his turn, surrounded by equally fine performances of the ensemble cast. Details such as wardrobe, bits of dialogue, and music are deftly used, avoiding parody. Nonstop disco and early 80s music, often with a message, and energetic camera work make you shake your booty. 155m; VHS, DVD, CC. **C:** Mark Wahlberg; Burt Reynolds; Julianne Moore; Don Cheadle; William H. Macy; Heather Graham; John C. Reilly; Luis Guzman; Philip Seymour Hoffman; Alfred Molina; Philip Baker Hall; Robert Ridgely; Joanna Gleason; Thomas Jane; Ricky Jay; Nicole Ari Parker; Melora Walters; Michael Jace; Nina Hartley; John Doe; Laurel Holloman; Robert Downey; Michael Penn; Directed by Paul Thomas Anderson; Written by Paul Thomas Anderson; Cinematography by Robert Elswit; Music by Michael Penn. **Pr:** New Line Cinema. **A:** College-Adult. **P:** Entertainment. **U:** Home. **Mov-Ent:** Comedy-Drama, Pornography, Drug Abuse. **Awds:** Golden Globes '98: Support. Actor (Reynolds); L.A. Film Critics '97: Support. Actor (Reynolds), Support. Actress (Moore); MTV Movie Awards '98: Breakthrough Perf. (Graham); N.Y. Film Critics '97: Support. Actor (Reynolds); Natl. Soc. Film Critics '97: Support. Actor (Reynolds), Support. Actress (Moore). **Acq:** Purchase. **Dist:** Warner Home Video, Inc.

Boogie Vision 1977 (Unrated) — ★
An aspiring filmmaker cons his girlfriend's Dad into producing his crappy science fiction film. Similar to the earlier "Groove Tube," it's a collection of skits spoofing 70's television tied together loosely by a thin plot. Except it's just not nearly as good. 84m; DVD. **C:** Michael Laibson; Marlene Selsman; Bert Belant; Directed by James Bryan; Written by James Bryan. **A:** Sr. High-Adult. **P:** Entertainment. **U:** Home. **Mov-Ent:** Satire & Parody, Comedy--Screwball, Filmmaking. **Acq:** Purchase. **Dist:** Media Blasters Inc. $19.99.

Boogie Woogie 2009 (R) — ★½
Flat spoof on the absurdity of the contemporary British art scene. London dealer Art Spindle is desperate to buy a Mondrian, titled "Boogie-Woogie," from its ailing owner Alfred Rhinegold, but he's being played against rival bidders. One bidder, Bob Maclestone, is having an affair with Art's ambitious employee Beth, who wants to open her own gallery and betrayal (by nearly every character) is a must. 90m; DVD. **C:** Danny Huston; Heather Graham; Christopher Lee; Joanna Lumley; Stellan Skarsgard; Gillian Anderson; Jaime Winstone; Alan Cumming; Amanda Seyfried; Simon McBurney; Jack Huston; Directed by Duncan Ward; Written by Danny Moynihan; Cinematography by John Mathieson; Music by Janus Podrazik; Nigel Stone. **A:** Sr. High-Adult. **P:** Entertainment. **U:** Home. **Mov-Ent:** Comedy--Black, Art & Artists. **Acq:** Purchase. **Dist:** IFC Films.

Boogie Woogie Piano: Rock-a-Boogie Piano Lessons in All the Hot Styles from Mr. Rocket 88 199?
Mitch Woods demonstrates the fundamentals of various boogie woogie patterns from basic to advanced, shows left- and right-hand fingerings in detail, and provides a booklet of notated musical examples. ?m; VHS. **A:** Sr. High-Adult. **P:** Instruction. **U:** Home. **How-Ins:** Music--Instruction, Music--Jazz, Music--Performance. **Acq:** Purchase. **Dist:** Hal Leonard Corp. $19.95.

Boogiepop and Others 2000 (Unrated) — ★½
Five young girls at the Shinyo academy try to piece together a mystery involving the appearance of a new street drug, the disappearance of some of their classmates, and an urban legend named Boogiepop who may be a personification of death itself. Originally a novel, then manga, with an anime series ("Boogiepop Phantom") as a sequel. Campy effects don't help, but it serves to set up the non-linear sequel. Deviates somewhat from the source material, but most audiences outside of Japan won't notice. 198m; DVD. **C:** Asumi Miwa; Tetsu Sawaki; Hassei Takano; Yukihiro Hotaru; Sayaka Yoshino; Maya Kurosu; Daijiro Kawaoka; Ayana Sakai; Mami Shimizu; Kai Hirohashi; Hideyuki Kasahara; Takako Baba; Erika Kuroishi; Kasumi Minagawa; Kaori Sakagami; Takeru Shibaki; Yasufumi Terawaki; Keiko Unno; Osamu Yagibashi; Ryoko Yasuda; Directed by Ryu Kaneda; Written by Sadayuki Murai; Kouhei Kadono; Cinematography by Satoshi Maeda; Music by Yuki

Kajiura. **A:** Jr. High-Adult. **P:** Entertainment. **U:** Home. **L:** English, Japanese. **Mov-Ent:** Fantasy. **Acq:** Purchase. **Dist:** The Right Stuf Inc. $29.95.

The Book Bird—Rev. Ed. 1994
This series with John Robbins is designed to stimulate a child's imagination through captivating illustrations and powerful narrations. Well known, old time favorite books are explored. Primarily for grade four. In 16 untitled programs. 15m; 3/4 U, Q. **Pr:** Children's Television International. **A:** Primary. **P:** Education. **U:** Institution, CCTV, CATV, BCTV, Home. **Gen-Edu:** Language Arts, Children. **Acq:** Purchase, Rent/Lease. **Dist:** Children's Television International.

Book 'M Danno 1995
A 1940s style private investigator reports on hazards found in many workplaces. Humorous takeoff. 14m; VHS. **A:** Adult. **P:** Professional. **U:** Institution. **Bus-Ind:** Job Training, Safety Education. **Acq:** Purchase. **Dist:** National Safety Council, California Chapter, Film Library. $175.00.

The Book of Acts 1980
A series of 28 untitled programs on the Book of Acts from the New Testament. Programs are available individually. 27m; VHS, 3/4 U. **C:** Roy Lanier, Jr. **Pr:** International Video Bible Lessons. **A:** Jr. High-Adult. **P:** Religious. **U:** Institution, CCTV, CATV, BCTV, Home. **Gen-Edu:** Documentary Films, Bible. **Acq:** Purchase, Rent/Lease. **Dist:** Gospel Services, Inc.

The Book of Co-Creation 19??
Presents ideas from Barbara Marx Hubbard's book "The Revelation: A Message of Hope for the New Millenium," including humanity's "birth from self-centeredness" to that of "being whole and God-centered." 90m; VHS. **A:** Sr. High-Adult. **P:** Entertainment. **U:** Home. **Gen-Edu:** New Age, Philosophy & Ideology. **Acq:** Purchase. **Dist:** Hartley Film Foundation. $29.95.

The Book of Colossians 1980
A series of eight untitled programs, which comprise an in-depth study of the Book of Colossians as found in the New Testament. Programs are available individually. 27m; VHS, 3/4 U. **C:** Edward C. Wharton. **Pr:** International Video Bible Lessons. **A:** Jr. High-Adult. **P:** Religious. **U:** Institution, CCTV, CATV, BCTV, Home. **Gen-Edu:** Documentary Films, Bible. **Acq:** Purchase, Rent/Lease. **Dist:** Gospel Services, Inc.

The Book of Daniel 1981
An in-depth study of Daniel taught by Jim McGuiggan of Sunset School of Preaching. 27m; VHS, 3/4 U. **Pr:** International Video Bible Lessons. **A:** Family. **P:** Religious. **U:** Institution, CCTV, CATV, BCTV, Home. **Gen-Edu:** Documentary Films, Religion, Bible. **Acq:** Purchase, Rent/Lease. **Dist:** Gospel Services, Inc.

The Book of Daniel: The Complete Series 2006
Rev. Daniel Webster (Quinn) is an Episcopalian priest with a Vicodin habit, a penchant for talking to Jesus (who literally appears to him), and family issues. His father (Rebhorn) is having an affair with a fellow bishop (Burstyn), his wife Judith (Thompson) is too fond of her martinis, and the Webster children are equally mixed up. Due to controversy (and low ratings), NBC pulled the show after 4 episodes. All 8 produced episodes are included. 344m; DVD, Wide. **C:** Aidan Quinn; Susanna Thompson; James Rebhorn; Ellen Burstyn; Christian Campbell; Alison Pill; Garret Dillahunt. **A:** Sr. High-Adult. **P:** Entertainment. **U:** Home. **Mov-Ent:** Television Series, Religion. **Acq:** Purchase. **Dist:** Universal Studios Home Video.

The Book of Deuteronomy 1981
An in-depth study of Deuteronomy taught by Clyde Woods of Freed-Hardeman College. 27m; VHS, 3/4 U. **Pr:** International Video Bible Lessons. **A:** Family. **P:** Religious. **U:** Institution, CCTV, CATV, BCTV, Home. **Gen-Edu:** Documentary Films, Bible. **Acq:** Purchase, Rent/Lease. **Dist:** Gospel Services, Inc.

The Book of Eli 2010 (R) — ★★½
Star/producer Washington plays Eli, a wanderer in a post-apocalyptic desert landscape who guards a mysterious book he believes will redeem mankind. In his divinely inspired trek westward, Eli shoots and slices through thieves, murderers and cannibals. Eventually, he crosses paths with Carnegie (Oldman), a warlord in a small town who covets the book and its power. Caught between the two are Carnegie's minions Claudia (Beals) and her daughter Solara (Kunis). The religious themes and surprise ending earned both scorn and praise for the Hughes brothers. This effort marks the siblings' return to filmmaking after a ten-year hiatus. 117m; Blu-Ray, Wide. **C:** Denzel Washington; Gary Oldman; Mila Kunis; Ray Stevenson; Jennifer Beals; Malcolm McDowell; Michael Gambon; Directed by Allen Hughes; Albert Hughes; Written by Gary Whitta; Anthony Peckham; Cinematography by Don Burgess; Music by Atticus Ross; Leopold Ross; Claudia Sarne. **Pr:** Broderick Johnson; Andrew A. Kosove; Joel Silver; David Valdes; Denzel Washington; Denzel Washington; Alcon Entertainment; Silver Pictures; Warner Bros. **A:** Sr. High-Adult. **P:** Entertainment. **U:** Home. **L:** English. **Mov-Ent:** Science Fiction. **Acq:** Purchase. **Dist:** Warner Home Video, Inc.; Movies Unlimited; Alpha Video.

The Book of Ephesians 1981
An in-depth study of Ephesians taught by Avon Malone of Harding University." 27m; VHS, 3/4 U. **Pr:** International Video Bible Lessons. **A:** Family. **P:** Religious. **U:** Institution, CCTV, CATV, BCTV, Home. **Gen-Edu:** Documentary Films, Religion, Bible. **Acq:** Purchase, Rent/Lease. **Dist:** Gospel Services, Inc.

The Book of Exodus 1981
An in-depth study of Exodus taught by Clyde Woods of Freed-Hardeman College. 27m; VHS, 3/4 U. **Pr:** International Video Bible Lessons. **A:** Family. **P:** Religious. **U:** Institution, CCTV, CATV, BCTV, Home. **Gen-Edu:** Documentary Films, Bible. **Acq:** Purchase, Rent/Lease. **Dist:** Gospel Services, Inc.

The Book of Ezekiel 1981
An in-depth study of Ezekiel taught by Jim McGuiggan of Sunset School of Preaching. 27m; VHS, 3/4 U. **Pr:** International Video Bible Lessons. **A:** Family. **P:** Religious. **U:** Institution, CCTV, CATV, BCTV, Home. **Gen-Edu:** Documentary Films, Religion, Bible. **Acq:** Purchase, Rent/Lease. **Dist:** Gospel Services, Inc.

Book of Ezekiel 1999 (Unrated)
Ancestral writings from enslaved poet Ezekiel gives young flautist Freeda Breedlove the courage to confront her tradition-bound mother. 20m; VHS, DVD. **A:** Adult. **P:** Education. **U:** Institution. **Gen-Edu:** Women, Family. **Acq:** Purchase. **Dist:** Third World Newsreel. $175.

The Book of Galatians 1980
A series of 20 untitled programs that comprise an in-depth study of the Book of Galatians as found in the New Testament. Programs are available individually. 27m; VHS, 3/4 U. **C:** Edward C. Wharton. **Pr:** International Video Bible Lessons. **A:** Jr. High-Adult. **P:** Religious. **U:** Institution, CCTV, CATV, BCTV, Home. **Gen-Edu:** Documentary Films, Bible. **Acq:** Purchase, Rent/Lease. **Dist:** Gospel Services, Inc.

The Book of Genesis 1981
An in-depth study of Genesis taught by John Willis of Abilene Christian University. 27m; VHS, 3/4 U. **Pr:** International Video Bible Lessons. **A:** Family. **P:** Religious. **U:** Institution, CCTV, CATV, BCTV, Home. **Gen-Edu:** Documentary Films, Bible. **Acq:** Purchase, Rent/Lease. **Dist:** Gospel Services, Inc.

Book of Habakuk-Malachi 1981
An in-depth study of Habakuk-Malachi taught by Furman Kearly of Abilene Christian University. 27m; VHS, 3/4 U. **Pr:** International Video Bible Lessons. **A:** Family. **P:** Religious. **U:** Institution, CCTV, CATV, BCTV, Home. **Gen-Edu:** Documentary Films, Religion, Bible. **Acq:** Purchase, Rent/Lease. **Dist:** Gospel Services, Inc.

The Book of Hebrews 1981
An in-depth study of Hebrews taught by Neil Lightfoot of Abilene Christian University. 27m; VHS, 3/4 U. **Pr:** International Video Bible Lessons. **A:** Family. **P:** Religious. **U:** Institution, CCTV, CATV, BCTV, Home. **Gen-Edu:** Documentary Films, Religion, Bible. **Acq:** Purchase, Rent/Lease. **Dist:** Gospel Services, Inc.

The Book of Hosea-Nahum 1981
An in-depth study of Hosea-Nahum taught by Furman Kearly of Abilene Christian University. 27m; VHS, 3/4 U. **Pr:** International Video Bible Lessons. **A:** Family. **P:** Religious. **U:** Institution, CCTV, CATV, BCTV, Home. **Gen-Edu:** Documentary Films, Religion, Bible. **Acq:** Purchase, Rent/Lease. **Dist:** Gospel Services, Inc.

The Book of I Corinthians 1984
Bill Smith expounds upon this New Testament book in a series of 13 lectures. 27m; VHS, 3/4 U. **Pr:** International Video Bible Lessons. **A:** Family. **P:** Religious. **U:** Institution, CCTV, CATV, Home. **Gen-Edu:** Documentary Films, Bible. **Acq:** Purchase, Rent/Lease. **Dist:** Gospel Services, Inc.

The Book of I, II, III John 1980
A series of 25 untitled programs making up an in-depth study of the Books of I, II, and III John as found in the New Testament. Programs are available individually. 27m; VHS, 3/4 U. **C:** Narrated by Edward P. Meyers. **Pr:** International Video Bible Lessons. **A:** Jr. High-Adult. **P:** Religious. **U:** Institution, CCTV, CATV, BCTV, Home. **Gen-Edu:** Documentary Films, Bible. **Acq:** Purchase, Rent/Lease. **Dist:** Gospel Services, Inc.

The Book of I, II Peter 1985
Carroll Osburn meticulously analyzes this Biblical book. 27m; VHS, 3/4 U. **Pr:** International Video Bible Lessons. **A:** Family. **P:** Religious. **U:** Institution, CCTV, CATV, Home. **Gen-Edu:** Documentary Films, Bible. **Acq:** Purchase, Rent/Lease. **Dist:** Gospel Services, Inc.

The Book of I Kings II—Esther 1981
An in-depth study of I Kings II-Esther taught by John Willis of Abilene Christian University. 27m; VHS, 3/4 U. **Pr:** International Video Bible Lessons. **A:** Family. **P:** Religious. **U:** Institution, CCTV, CATV, BCTV, Home. **Gen-Edu:** Documentary Films, Religion, Bible. **Acq:** Purchase, Rent/Lease. **Dist:** Gospel Services, Inc.

The Book of I Samuel—I Kings II 1981
An in-depth study of I Samuel-I Kings II taught by John Willis of Abilene Christian University. 27m; VHS, 3/4 U. **Pr:** International Video Bible Lessons. **A:** Family. **P:** Religious. **U:** Institution, CCTV, CATV, BCTV, Home. **Gen-Edu:** Documentary Films, Religion, Bible. **Acq:** Purchase, Rent/Lease. **Dist:** Gospel Services, Inc.

The Book of I Timothy 1981
An in-depth study of I Timothy taught by Avon Malone of Harding University. 27m; VHS, 3/4 U. **Pr:** International Video Bible Lessons. **A:** Family. **P:** Religious. **U:** Institution, CCTV, CATV, BCTV, Home. **Gen-Edu:** Documentary Films, Religion, Bible. **Acq:** Purchase, Rent/Lease. **Dist:** Gospel Services, Inc.

The Book of II Corinthians 1985
James Woodroof, expert New Testamentarian, examines in exhaustive detail the Biblical book. 27m; VHS, 3/4 U. **Pr:** International Video Bible Lessons. **A:** Family. **P:** Religious. **U:** Institution, CCTV, CATV, Home. **Gen-Edu:** Documentary Films, Bible. **Acq:** Purchase, Rent/Lease. **Dist:** Gospel Services, Inc.

The Book of II Timothy and Titus 1981
An in-depth study of II Timothy and Titus taught by Avon Malone of Harding University. 27m; VHS, 3/4 U. **Pr:** International Video Bible Lessons. **A:** Family. **P:** Religious. **U:** Institution, CCTV,

CATV, BCTV, Home. **Gen-Edu**: Documentary Films, Religion, Bible. **Acq:** Purchase, Rent/Lease. **Dist:** Gospel Services, Inc.

The Book of Isaiah 1985
A look at this Biblical book by Jim McGuiggan in 26 lessons. 27m; VHS, 3/4 U. **Pr:** International Video Bible Lessons. **A:** Family. **P:** Religious. **U:** Institution, CCTV, CATV, Home. **Gen-Edu**: Documentary Films, Bible. **Acq:** Purchase, Rent/Lease. **Dist:** Gospel Services, Inc.

The Book of James 1980
A series of 18 untitled programs that comprise an in-depth study of the Book of James as found in the New Testament. Programs are available individually. 27m; VHS, 3/4 U. **C:** J.J. Turner. **Pr:** International Video Bible Lessons. **A:** Jr. High-Adult. **P:** Religious. **U:** Institution, CCTV, CATV, BCTV, Home. **Gen-Edu**: Documentary Films, Bible. **Acq:** Purchase, Rent/Lease. **Dist:** Gospel Services, Inc.

The Book of Job 1981
An in-depth study of Job taught by Jim Young of White's Ferry Road School of Biblical Studies. 27m; VHS, 3/4 U. **Pr:** International Video Bible Lessons. **A:** Family. **P:** Religious. **U:** Institution, CCTV, CATV, BCTV, Home. **Gen-Edu**: Documentary Films, Religion, Bible. **Acq:** Purchase, Rent/Lease. **Dist:** Gospel Services, Inc.

The Book of John 1982
An in-depth study of the Gospel of John, taught by Dr. Frank Pack of Malibu, California. 27m; VHS, 3/4 U. **Pr:** International Video Bible Lessons. **A:** Family. **P:** Religious. **U:** Institution, CCTV, CATV, BCTV, Home. **Gen-Edu**: Documentary Films, Bible, Religion. **Acq:** Purchase, Rent/Lease. **Dist:** Gospel Services, Inc.

The Book of Joshua 1981
An in-depth study of Joshua taught by Norman Gipson, instructor at Bear Valley School of Preaching, Denver, Co. 27m; VHS, 3/4 U. **Pr:** International Video Bible Lessons. **A:** Family. **P:** Religious. **U:** Institution, CCTV, CATV, BCTV, Home. **Gen-Edu**: Documentary Films, Religion, Bible. **Acq:** Purchase, Rent/Lease. **Dist:** Gospel Services, Inc.

The Book of Jude 1981
An in-depth study of Jude taught by J. J. Turner of Garden Grove, California. 27m; VHS, 3/4 U. **Pr:** International Video Bible Lessons. **A:** Family. **P:** Religious. **U:** Institution, CCTV, CATV, BCTV, Home. **Gen-Edu**: Documentary Films, Religion, Bible. **Acq:** Purchase, Rent/Lease. **Dist:** Gospel Services, Inc.

The Book of Judges 1981
An in-depth study of Judges taught by Albert Lemmons of Nashville, Tenn. 27m; VHS, 3/4 U. **Pr:** International Video Bible Lessons. **A:** Family. **P:** Religious. **U:** Institution, CCTV, CATV, BCTV, Home. **Gen-Edu**: Documentary Films, Bible. **Acq:** Purchase, Rent/Lease. **Dist:** Gospel Services, Inc.

The Book of Laughs 1988
The bond between two sisters is captured in this filmed record of their recollections. 42m; VHS, 3/4 U. **Pr:** Roberta Cantow. **A:** Primary-Adult. **P:** Education. **U:** Institution, Home, SURA. **Gen-Edu**: Psychology, Family. **Acq:** Purchase, Rent/Lease, Duplication. **Dist:** Filmakers Library Inc.

The Book of Leviticus 1981
An in-depth study of Leviticus taught by Clyde Woods of Freed-Hardeman College. 27m; VHS, 3/4 U. **Pr:** International Video Bible Lessons. **A:** Family. **P:** Religious. **U:** Institution, CCTV, CATV, BCTV, Home. **Gen-Edu**: Documentary Films, Bible. **Acq:** Purchase, Rent/Lease. **Dist:** Gospel Services, Inc.

Book of Love 1991 (PG-13) — ★★
"Zany" hijinks as a teenager struggles with friendship, girls, and those all-important hormones when he moves to a new neighborhood in the mid-'50s. Average rehash of every '50s movie and TV show cliche in existence. Surprise! There's a classic rock 'n' roll soundtrack. Adapted by Kotzwinkle from his novel "Jack in the Box." 88m; VHS, DVD, 8 mm, CC. **C:** Chris Young; Keith Coogan; Aeryk Egan; Josie Bissett; Tricia Leigh Fisher; Danny Nucci; Michael McKean; John Cameron Mitchell; Lewis Arquette; Directed by Robert Shaye; Written by William Kotzwinkle; Music by Stanley Clarke. **Pr:** Robert Shaye; Rachel Talalay; Robert Shaye; New Line Cinema. **A:** Jr. High-Adult. **P:** Entertainment. **U:** Home. **Mov-Ent**: Adolescence. **Acq:** Purchase. **Dist:** Sony Pictures Home Entertainment Inc. $19.95.

Book of Love 2004 (R) — ★½
David (Baker) and Elaine's (O'Connor) childless marriage hits a lull, so the couple befriends 15-year-old Chet (Smith) to fill the void. Life for the happy wanna-be-family gets muddled up when David discovers that Chet and Elaine had a creepy and very illegal affair. 85m; VHS, DVD. **C:** Frances O'Connor; Simon Baker; Gregory Edward Smith; Bryce Dallas Howard; Joanna Adler; Ari Graynor; Directed by Alan Brown; Written by Alan Brown; Cinematography by William Rexer. **A:** Sr. High-Adult. **P:** Entertainment. **U:** Home. **Mov-Ent**: Marriage. **Acq:** Purchase. **Dist:** Virgil Films & Entertainment. $26.97.

The Book of Luke 1983
An in-depth study of the Book of Luke, taught by Neale Pryor. 27m; VHS, 3/4 U. **Pr:** International Video Bible Lessons. **A:** Family. **P:** Religious. **U:** Institution, CCTV, CATV, BCTV, Home. **Gen-Edu**: Documentary Films, Bible, Religion. **Acq:** Purchase, Rent/Lease. **Dist:** Gospel Services, Inc.

The Book of Mark 1982
A detailed study of the Book of Mark, taught by Dr. Rubel Shelly of Nashville, Tennessee. 27m; VHS, 3/4 U. **Pr:** International Video Bible Lessons. **A:** Family. **P:** Religious. **U:** Institution, CCTV, CATV, BCTV, Home. **Gen-Edu**: Documentary Films, Bible, Religion. **Acq:** Purchase, Rent/Lease. **Dist:** Gospel Services, Inc.

The Book of Matthew 1983
The Book of Matthew is studied in this series by Bill Smith, of the WFR School of Biblical Studies. 27m; VHS, 3/4 U. **Pr:** International Video Bible Lessons. **A:** Family. **P:** Religious. **U:** Institution, CCTV, CATV, BCTV, Home. **Gen-Edu**: Documentary Films, Bible, Religion. **Acq:** Purchase, Rent/Lease. **Dist:** Gospel Services, Inc.

Book of Mormon Reader 19??
Designed for second grade level, 25 stories from the Book of Mormon are presented here. ?m; VHS. **A:** Primary. **P:** Religious. **U:** Institution, Home. **Gen-Edu**: Religion. **Acq:** Purchase. **Dist:** Church of Jesus Christ of Latter-day Saints. $8.00.

The Book of Numbers 1981
An in-depth study of Numbers taught by Clyde Woods of Freed-Handeman College. 27m; VHS, 3/4 U. **Pr:** International Video Bible Lessons. **A:** Family. **P:** Religious. **U:** Institution, CCTV, CATV, Home. **Gen-Edu**: Documentary Films, Bible. **Acq:** Purchase, Rent/Lease. **Dist:** Gospel Services, Inc.

The Book of Oneself 19??
Krishnamurti, Pupul Jayakar, and Achyut Patwardhan discuss the nature of what is seen and the instrument which sees. ?m; VHS. **A:** Adult. **P:** Education. **U:** Home. **Gen-Edu**: Religion. **Acq:** Purchase. **Dist:** Krishnamurti Foundation of America. $19.95.

The Book of Philemon 1982
An in-depth study of Philemon taught by Calvin Warpula, minister, of West Monroe, La. 27m; VHS, 3/4 U. **Pr:** International Video Bible Lessons. **A:** Family. **P:** Religious. **U:** Institution, CCTV, CATV, BCTV, Home. **Gen-Edu**: Documentary Films, Religion, Bible. **Acq:** Purchase, Rent/Lease. **Dist:** Gospel Services, Inc.

The Book of Philippians 1979
A series of 13 untitled programs that make up an in-depth study of the Book of Philippians as found in the New Testament. Programs are available individually. 27m; VHS, 3/4 U. **C:** Avon Malone. **Pr:** International Video Bible Lessons. **A:** Jr. High-Adult. **P:** Religious. **U:** Institution, CCTV, CATV, BCTV, Home. **Gen-Edu**: Documentary Films, Bible. **Acq:** Purchase, Rent/Lease. **Dist:** Gospel Services, Inc.

The Book of Psalms 1981
An in-depth study of Psalms taught by Tony Ash of the Institute of Christian Studies. 27m; VHS, 3/4 U. **Pr:** International Video Bible Lessons. **A:** Family. **P:** Religious. **U:** Institution, CCTV, CATV, BCTV, Home. **Gen-Edu**: Documentary Films, Religion, Bible. **Acq:** Purchase, Rent/Lease. **Dist:** Gospel Services, Inc.

The Book of Revelation 1980
An in-depth study of Revelation taught by Jim McGuiggan of the Sunset School of Preaching. 27m; VHS, 3/4 U. **Pr:** International Video Bible Lessons. **A:** Family. **P:** Religious. **U:** Institution, CCTV, CATV, BCTV, Home. **Gen-Edu**: Documentary Films, Religion, Bible. **Acq:** Purchase, Rent/Lease. **Dist:** Gospel Services, Inc.

The Book of Romans 1983
The Book of Romans is taught in-depth by Bill Smith, of the WFR School of Biblical Studies. 27m; VHS, 3/4 U. **Pr:** International Video Bible Lessons. **A:** Family. **P:** Religious. **U:** Institution, CCTV, CATV, BCTV, Home. **Gen-Edu**: Documentary Films, Bible, Religion. **Acq:** Purchase, Rent/Lease. **Dist:** Gospel Services, Inc.

The Book of Romans 1985
A study of the Book of Romans by Jim McGuiggan in 29 programs. 27m; VHS, 3/4 U. **Pr:** International Video Bible Lessons. **A:** Family. **P:** Religious. **U:** Institution, CCTV, CATV, Home. **Gen-Edu**: Documentary Films, Bible. **Acq:** Purchase, Rent/Lease. **Dist:** Gospel Services, Inc.

The Book of Ruth 1981
An in-depth study of Ruth taught by Albert Lemmons of Nashville, Tenn. 27m; VHS, 3/4 U. **Pr:** International Video Bible Lessons. **A:** Family. **P:** Religious. **U:** Institution, CCTV, CATV, BCTV, Home. **Gen-Edu**: Documentary Films, Religion, Bible. **Acq:** Purchase, Rent/Lease. **Dist:** Gospel Services, Inc.

Book of Shadows: Blair Witch 2 2000 (R) — ★½
Thankfully, they've gotten rid of the shaky-cam (which shook more than a few viewers' stomachs), that's one plus for this sequel that finds five followers of the Blair Witch myth heading back into the woods. Unfortunately, they've also gotten rid of the scares produced by mysterious offscreen witchy shenanigans and replaced them with buckets of fake blood. This group is led by Jeff (Donovan), a townie who's decided to cash in on the Blair Witch craze by organizing tours of the sites made famous in the first movie. Grad students Tristen (Skyler) and Stephen (Turner), practicing Wiccan Erica (Leerhsen) and goth-chick Kim (Director), have fun skewering the movie and its internet movement while partying on the first night. The next day they realize they've lost five hours of their lives. They try to discover what happened, and if it has anything to do with another tour group getting disemboweled. Disappointing fictional debut from documentary director Berlinger, who filmed the truly horrific (and true) "Paradise Lost: The Child Murders at Robin Hood Hills." The townspeople of Burkittsville, Maryland were so fed up with the first film that the second was filmed elsewhere. 90m; VHS, DVD, Wide. **C:** Jeffrey Donovan; Kim Director; Tristen Skylar; Stephen Barker Turner; Erica Leerhsen; Directed by Joe Berlinger; Written by Joe Berlinger; Dick Beebe; Cinematography by Nancy Schreiber; Music by Carter Burwell. **A:** Sr. High-Adult. **P:** Entertainment. **U:** Home. **Mov-Ent**: Horror. **Awds:** Golden Raspberries '00: Worst Remake/Sequel. **Acq:** Purchase. **Dist:** Lions Gate Television Corp.

The Book of Stars 1999 (Unrated) — ★★½
Penny (Masterson) is the older sister and only support for teenaged Mary (Malone), who suffers from cystic fibrosis. Penny is a jaded, pill-popping hooker while Mary, however, refuses to give up her optomistic outlook on life. With the aid of cantankerous neighbor Professor (Lindo) and a couple of new friends, Mary is determined to change Penny's views as well. Manages to skirt the subject's inherent sentimentality with some winning performances. 98m; VHS, DVD. **C:** Mary Stuart Masterson; Jena Malone; Karl Geary; D.B. Sweeney; Delroy Lindo; Directed by Michael Miner; Written by Tasca Shadix; Cinematography by Jim Whitaker; Music by Richard Gibbs. **A:** Jr. High-Adult. **P:** Entertainment. **U:** Home. **Mov-Ent**: Diseases, Prostitution. **Acq:** Purchase. **Dist:** Wellspring Media.

The Book on Bunting 2002
University of Miami Head Coach Jim Morris explains various bunts used to steal a run and also the sacrifice bunt. Discusses how to implement bunting drills into practices. 45m; VHS. **A:** Adult. **P:** Instruction. **U:** Institution. **How-Ins**: Baseball, Sports--General, How-To. **Acq:** Purchase. **Dist:** Championship Productions. $39.95.

The Book Thief 2013 (PG-13) — ★½
Markus Zusak's young adult novel gets a frustrating adaptation in this tonally imbalanced melodrama about a girl's coming-of-age in World War II Germany. The naturally talented Nélisse plays Liesel, an orphan who moves to a small German town with new parents (Watson & Rush) just before the start of WWII. After Liesel's new family grows by an illegal one--when they offer sanctuary to a Jew in their basement--Liesel learns a lesson or two about kindness and the importance of hope. The cast is uniformly strong but TV director Percival can't find an ounce of realism, which makes it less emotional. English and German with subtitles. 131m; DVD, Blu-Ray. **C:** Sophie Nelisse; Geoffrey Rush; Emily Watson; Roger Allam; Nico Liersch; Directed by Brian Percival; Written by Michael Petroni; Cinematography by Florian Ballhaus; Music by John Williams. **Pr:** Ken Blancato; Karen Rosenfelt; Twentieth Century Fox Film Corp; Fox 2000 Pictures. **A:** Jr. High-Adult. **P:** Entertainment. **U:** Home. **L:** English, German. **Mov-Ent**: Holocaust, World War Two, Germany. **Acq:** Purchase. **Dist:** Fox Home Entertainment.

Booker 198?
The story of the life of Booker T. Washington, his struggles and his victories, are chronicled in this multi-award winner. 40m; VHS, 3/4 U, EJ, Special order formats. **TV Std:** NTSC, PAL, SECAM. **C:** LeVar Burton; Shelley Duvall. **Pr:** Disney Educational Productions. **A:** Primary-Sr. High. **P:** Education. **U:** Institution, CCTV, SURA. **Gen-Edu**: Biography. **Acq:** Purchase, Rent/Lease. **Dist:** Phoenix Learning Group. $250.00.

Booker T. Washington 1967
Chronicles the early years of Booker T. Washington. 11m; VHS, 3/4 U. **Pr:** Vignette Films Productions. **A:** Jr. High-Sr. High. **P:** Education. **U:** Institution, SURA. **Gen-Edu**: Documentary Films, Biography, Black Culture. **Acq:** Purchase. **Dist:** Phoenix Learning Group.

Booker T. Washington: Life and the Legacy 1982
A docudrama about the life and times and controversial ideas of Booker T. Washington. 30m; VHS. **C:** Maurice Woods; Al Freeman, Jr.; Narrated by Gil Noble. **Pr:** WGP; U.S. Government. **A:** Jr. High-Adult. **P:** Education. **U:** Institution, BCTV. **Gen-Edu**: Documentary Films, History--U.S., Biography. **Acq:** Purchase, Rent/Lease. **Dist:** Harpers Ferry Historical Association; William Greaves Productions, Inc.; Knowledge Unlimited, Inc. $24.99.

Booker T. Washington's Tuskegee America 1981
A biography of Washington-his life, career and achievements. 25m; VHS, 3/4 U. **C:** Hosted by Hugh Downs. **Pr:** Comco Productions. **A:** Jr. High-Sr. High. **P:** Education. **U:** Institution, SURA. **Gen-Edu**: Documentary Films, Biography, Minorities. **Acq:** Purchase, Rent/Lease, Duplication License. **Dist:** African-American Images; Clear Vue Inc. $70.00.

Bookies 2003 (R) — ★★
Thinking they can strike it rich the easy way, three college pals set up shop as bookies. Naturally, their hot streak abruptly ends when the local syndicate takes issue with the amateurs cutting into their cash flow. 90m; VHS, DVD. **C:** Nick Stahl; Lukas Haas; Johnny Galecki; Rachael Leigh Cook; David Proval; Zuri Williams; Directed by Mark Illsley; Written by Michael Bacall; Cinematography by Brendan Galvin; Music by Christopher Tyng; Giuseppe Cristiano. **A:** Sr. High-Adult. **P:** Entertainment. **U:** Home. **Mov-Ent**: Gambling. **Acq:** Purchase. **Dist:** MGM Home Entertainment. $25.99.

Bookkeeping: Occupations and Opportunities 1969
The history of bookkeeping is traced from the early Babylonians, Egyptians, and Romans, through modern times. The importance of keeping accurate records is demonstrated. 15m; VHS, 3/4 U. **Pr:** John Paul Jones. **A:** Jr. High-Sr. High. **P:** Education. **U:** Institution, SURA. **L:** English, Spanish. **Gen-Edu**: Documentary Films, Office Practice. **Acq:** Purchase. **Dist:** Phoenix Learning Group.

Books from Cover to Cover 1988
Host John Robbins introduces children to books by telling them the first part of a story and then inviting them to read the rest of the book for themselves. 15m; VHS, 3/4 U. **C:** Hosted by John Robbins. **A:** Primary. **P:** Education. **U:** Institution, CCTV, CATV. **Gen-Edu**: Fiction--Children, Language Arts, Literature. **Acq:** Purchase, Duplication License, Off-Air Record. **Dist:** PBS Home Video. $25.00.

Indiv. Titles: 1. Back Yard Angel 2. Be a Perfect Person in Just Three Days! 3. Bella Arabella 4. Cabin Faced West, The 5. Case of the Elevator Duck, The/Warton & the Castaways 6. Different Dragons 7. 4B Goes Wild 8. Going Home 9. Green Book, The 10. If You Didn't Have Me 11. Kid in the Red Jacket, The 12. Little Riders, The 13. Rich Mitch 14. Search for Grissi, The 15. Top Secret 16. Trouble with Tuck, The.

Books in the Blood 1999
Documentary about Des and Maureen Kenny, who founded one of the world's most famous bookstores and art galleries. 52m; VHS, DVD. **A:** Sr. High-Adult. **P:** Education. **U:** Institution. **Gen-Edu**: Documentary Films, Biography. **Acq:** Purchase, Rent/Lease. **Dist:** The Cinema Guild. $295.00.

Books of Entry 1989
Presents basic instruction for setup, formatting and maintaining a complete set of accounting books. 30m; VHS. **A:** Adult. **P:** Education. **U:** Institution. **Bus-Ind**: Business, Finance. **Acq:** Purchase. **Dist:** RMI Media. $98.00.

The Books of I and II Corinthians 1983
This detailed study of the Books of I-II Corinthians is taught by Avon Malone of Harding University. 27m; VHS, 3/4 U. **Pr:** International Video Bible Lessons. **A:** Family. **P:** Religious. **U:** Institution, CCTV, CATV, BCTV, Home. **Gen-Edu**: Documentary Films, Bible, Religion. **Acq:** Purchase, Rent/Lease. **Dist:** Gospel Services, Inc.

The Books of I and II Peter 1982
An in-depth study of I and II Peter taught by Carroll Osborn of Memphis, Tenn. 27m; VHS, 3/4 U. **Pr:** International Video Bible Lessons. **A:** Family. **P:** Religious. **U:** Institution, CCTV, CATV, BCTV, Home. **Gen-Edu**: Documentary Films, Religion, Bible. **Acq:** Purchase, Rent/Lease. **Dist:** Gospel Services, Inc.

The Books of I and II Thessalonians 1982
A detailed study of the Books of I-II Thessalonians, taught by Avon Malone of Harding University. 27m; VHS, 3/4 U. **Pr:** International Video Bible Lessons. **A:** Family. **P:** Religious. **U:** Institution, CCTV, CATV, BCTV, Home. **Gen-Edu**: Documentary Films, Bible, Religion. **Acq:** Purchase, Rent/Lease. **Dist:** Gospel Services, Inc.

The Books of Isaiah, Jeremiah, Lamentations 1983
An extensive study of the Books of Isaiah, Jeremiah and Lamentations, taught by Jim McGuiggan. 27m; VHS, 3/4 U. **Pr:** International Video Bible Lessons. **A:** Family. **P:** Religious. **U:** Institution, CCTV, CATV, BCTV, Home. **Gen-Edu**: Documentary Films, Bible, Religion. **Acq:** Purchase, Rent/Lease. **Dist:** Gospel Services, Inc.

Books Talk Back 1986
A look at how books are made, from cutting down the tree to the finished product. Proper care for books is also covered. A teacher's guide is included. ?m; VHS. **A:** Preschool-Primary. **P:** Education. **U:** Institution. **Gen-Edu**: How-To, Education, Children. **Acq:** Purchase. **Dist:** Meridian Education Corp. $62.00.

Books Tell Their Story 1986
An introduction to books, describing how the alphabet, printing, and paper were developed. Includes a teacher's guide. ?m; VHS. **A:** Preschool-Primary. **P:** Education. **U:** Institution. **Gen-Edu**: Documentary Films, Information Science, Communication. **Acq:** Purchase. **Dist:** Meridian Education Corp. $62.00.

Books Under Fire 1983
This program looks at both sides of the book banning controversy. 56m; VHS, 3/4 U. **Pr:** Bennett/Watts. **A:** Jr. High-Adult. **P:** Education. **U:** Institution, SURA. **Gen-Edu**: Documentary Films, Censorship. **Acq:** Purchase. **Dist:** Home Vision Cinema.

Booky's Crush 2009 (G) — ★★½
In Depression-era Toronto, 11-year-old Booky Thomson develops a crush on new classmate Georgie, whom she tutors in spelling. When a school dance is announced, Booky wonders how she can get Georgie to ask her to go. Based on Bernice Thurman Hunter's novels. 89m; DVD. **C:** Rachel Marcus; Connor Price; Megan Fellows; Sarah White; Stuart Hughes; Dylan Everett; Marc Bendavid; Directed by Peter Moss; Written by Tracey Forbes; Cinematography by Norayr Kasper; Music by Robert Carli. **A:** Family. **P:** Entertainment. **U:** Home. **Mov-Ent**: TV Movies. **Acq:** Purchase. **Dist:** Peace Arch Entertainment Group.

Boom! 1968 (PG) — ★½
Laughable adaptation of the Williams' play "The Milk Train Doesn't Stop Here Anymore" was a Hollywood star disaster. Flora Goforth (Taylor) is a dying millionairess living in isolated glory on an island near Sardinia. Chris Flanders (Burton) is a wandering poet, nicknamed the "Angel of Death," who shows up and becomes Flora's confidante. Does have pretty scenery. 113m; VHS, CC. **C:** Elizabeth Taylor; Richard Burton; Noel Coward; Joanna Shimkus; Michael Dunn; Romolo Valli; Directed by Joseph Losey; Written by Tennessee Williams; Cinematography by Douglas Slocombe; Music by John Barry. **Pr:** Universal Pictures. **A:** Sr. High-Adult. **P:** Entertainment. **U:** Home. **Mov-Ent. Acq:** Purchase.

Boom and Bust 1986
Chronicles the history of South Dakota, focusing on the buffalo boom days during the late 1800s, and the events that eventually led to the decade of the Great Depression. 20m; VHS, 3/4 U. **Pr:** Centre Productions, Inc. **A:** Sr. High-Adult. **P:** Education. **U:** Institution, SURA. **Gen-Edu**: Documentary Films, History--U.S., U.S. States. **Acq:** Purchase. **Dist:** Clear Vue Inc.

Boom! Bang! Whap! Doink! John Madden on Football 1988
The typically outspoken, overweight ex-Raider coach makes football easy to understand. 60m; VHS. **C:** Joe Namath; Johnny Unitas; Joe Montana; Hosted by John Madden. **Pr:** NFL Films. **A:** Family. **P:** Entertainment. **U:** Institution, Home. **Spo-Rec**: Football. **Acq:** Purchase. **Dist:** NFL Films Video; Cambridge Educational. $19.95.

Boom in the Moon 1946 (Unrated) — **Bomb!**
Keaton fares poorly in this sci-fi comedy. He's trapped on a space ship to the moon. Poor production, with uneven direction and acting. 83m; VHS. **C:** Buster Keaton; Angel Garasa; Virginia Serret; Fernando Soto Mantequilla; Luis Barreiro; Directed by Jaime Salvador. **A:** Family. **P:** Entertainment. **U:** Home. **Mov-Ent**: Science Fiction. **Acq:** Purchase. **Dist:** Movies Unlimited. $18.99.

Boom or Bust: Mining and the Opening of the American West 1994
Combines live-action footage from western ghost towns with historical photographs of early mining communities to help explain how the mining boom helped the development of the American West. Comes with teacher's guide and blackline masters. 20m; VHS. **A:** Primary-Adult. **P:** Education. **U:** Institution. **Gen-Edu**: History--U.S., Western, Miners & Mining. **Acq:** Purchase. **Dist:** United Learning Inc. $89.95.

Boom: The Sound of Eviction 2002 (Unrated)
Interviews with dot-com executives, real estate developers, and San Francisco Mayor Willie Brown, presents the ironies and contradictions of the "New Economy" as the dot-com boom brought instant wealth to many and sudden falls as well. 96m; DVD. **A:** Adult. **P:** Education. **U:** Institution. **Gen-Edu**: Economics, Technology. **Acq:** Purchase. **Dist:** Third World Newsreel. $250.

Boom Town 1940 — ★★½
A lively vintage comedy/drama/romance about two oil-drilling buddies competing amid romantic mix-ups and fortunes gained and lost. 120m/B/W; VHS, DVD, CC. **C:** Clark Gable; Spencer Tracy; Claudette Colbert; Hedy Lamarr; Frank Morgan; Lionel Atwill; Chill Wills; Curt Bois; Directed by Jack Conway; Written by John Lee Mahin; Cinematography by Harold Rosson; Elwood "Woody" Bredell; Music by Franz Waxman. **Pr:** MGM. **A:** Adult. **P:** Entertainment. **U:** Home. **Mov-Ent**: Comedy--Romantic, Oil Industry. **Acq:** Purchase. **Dist:** MGM Home Entertainment. $19.98.

Boom Varietal 2011 (Unrated)
Considers the history and popularity of the Malbec grape, which thrived after being introduced in Argentina and was used in wines that became globally popular. 72m; DVD. **A:** Jr. High-Adult. **P:** Entertainment. **U:** Home. **Mov-Ent**: Wine & Vinyards, Documentary Films, South America. **Acq:** Purchase. **Dist:** First Run Features. $24.95.

Boomerang 1947 (Unrated) — ★★★
Film noir based on actual events features the murder of a Connecticut clergyman and the quick arrest of vagrant John Waldron (Kennedy). Prosecuting attorney Henry Harvey (Andrews) is told by his political bosses to get an equally quick conviction to stem public outrage. The evidence seems overwhelming but Harvey begins his own investigation and suddenly switches to the defense to prove Waldron's innocence in dramatic courtroom style. Kazan filmed on location in Bridgeport, CT in a successful semi-documentary style that heightened the tension. 88m/B/W; VHS, DVD, CC. **C:** Dana Andrews; Arthur Kennedy; Lee J. Cobb; Jane Wyatt; Cara Williams; Sam Levene; Ed Begley, Sr.; Karl Malden; Taylor Holmes; Robert Keith; Directed by Elia Kazan; Written by Richard Murphy; Cinematography by Norbert Brodine; Music by David Buttolph. **Pr:** Louis de Rochemont. **A:** Sr. High-Adult. **P:** Entertainment. **U:** Home. **Mov-Ent**: Mystery & Suspense, Law. **Acq:** Purchase. **Dist:** Fox Home Entertainment. $19.98.

Boomerang 1976 — ★½
A father rescues his wrongly convicted son from prison. Dubbed. 101m; VHS, CC. **C:** Alain Delon; Carla Gravina; Dora Doll; Directed by Jose Giovanni. **Pr:** Alain Delon; Alain Delon. **A:** Jr. High-Adult. **P:** Entertainment. **U:** Home. **Mov-Ent. Acq:** Purchase. **Dist:** $59.95.

Boomerang 1992 (R) — ★★
Successful, womanizing marketing exec for a cosmetics company (Murphy) meets his match when he falls for a colleague (Givens) who is as vain and sexually predatory as he is. She treats him the way he treats women (as a sex object), and he's shocked into the arms of a nice girl (Berry). Although it's refreshing to see this sexual role reversal, the typical Murphy-style humor is in play with sexist jokes and a couple of vulgar female characters. Grier and Lawrence are great as Murphy's best friends. Blaustein and Sheffield are the same guys who wrote Murphy's "Coming to America." 118m; VHS, DVD, Wide, CC. **C:** Eddie Murphy; Halle Berry; Robin Givens; David Alan Grier; Martin Lawrence; Grace Jones; Geoffrey Holder; Eartha Kitt; Chris Rock; Tisha Campbell; John Witherspoon; Melvin Van Peebles; Directed by Reginald (Reggie) Hudlin; Written by Barry W. Blaustein; David Sheffield. **Pr:** Brian Grazer; Warrington Hudlin; Paramount Pictures. **A:** Sr. High-Adult. **P:** Entertainment. **U:** Home. **Mov-Ent**: Comedy--Romantic. **Acq:** Purchase. **Dist:** Paramount Pictures Corp. $14.95.

Boomerang Kids: Adult Children Living at Home 1990
Offers suggestions for coping with the changing relationships adult children and their parents experience when the children postpone leaving the nest, or return after divorce or other hardship. ?m; VHS. **A:** Sr. High-Adult. **P:** Education. **U:** Institution. **Gen-Edu**: Family, Parenting. **Acq:** Purchase. **Dist:** Meridian Education Corp. $45.00.

Boomsville 1969
Without narration, Robert Verrall's fast-paced animation traces step-by-step the process by which man took a virgin land and made it a frantic, congested "Boomsville." 10m; VHS, 3/4 U. **Pr:** Learning Corporation of America; National Film Board of Canada. **A:** Primary-Jr. High. **P:** Education. **U:** Institution, SURA. **Gen-Edu**: Cities & Towns, Animation & Cartoons. **Acq:** Purchase, Rent/Lease. **Dist:** Phoenix Learning Group.

Boomtown: Season 1 2002
This NBC series looked at crime from multiple angles: the uniformed officers, the investigating detectives, EMTs, the district attorneys office, and news reporters, as well as what happened to the characters in their off-duty hours. 18 episodes. 810m; DVD. **C:** Donnie Wahlberg; Jason Gedrick; Neal McDonough; Mykelti Williamson; Gary Basaraba. **A:** Jr. High-Adult. **P:** Entertainment. **U:** Home. **Mov-Ent**: Television Series. **Acq:** Purchase. **Dist:** Lions Gate Television Corp.

Boondock Saints 1999 (R) — ★★
Two Boston Irish-Catholic brothers, Connor (Flanery) and Murphy (Reedus) McManus, turn into unlikely local heroes after the self-defense killings of some Russian mobsters who were threatening to close down their local pub. They turn vigilante, believing they're doing God's work to rid the world of evil, which leads to more slaughter. Investigating the crimes is gay FBI agent Paul Smecker (Dafoe), who is shown reconstructing the carnage in a series of flashbacks. Stylish cult debut for writer-director Duffy is uneven but entertaining. 110m; VHS, DVD, Blu-Ray, UMD. **C:** Sean Patrick Flanery; Norman Reedus; Willem Dafoe; David Della Rocco; Carlo Rota; Billy Connolly; David Ferry; Brian Mahoney; Ron Jeremy; Directed by Troy Duffy; Written by Troy Duffy; Cinematography by Adam Kane; Music by Jeff Danna. **A:** Sr. High-Adult. **P:** Entertainment. **U:** Home. **Mov-Ent**: Federal Bureau of Investigation (FBI). **Acq:** Purchase. **Dist:** Fox Home Entertainment.

The Boondock Saints II: All Saints Day 2009 (R) — ★½
In this second installment, Flanery and Reedus return as twin brothers Connor and Murphy, forced out of exile when they are linked to a priest's murder. Even lower-grade Tarantino rip-off than the first, this one takes racist, homophobic jokes and impossible violence to a new level of absurdity. While writer/director Duffy's 10 years between films did improve his cinematography, it didn't hone his creativity—he overcompensates what is lacking by blasting metal and techno music. If not for the original's cult status, the Boston boys and their vigilante justice would have never been reunited. 118m; Blu-Ray, On Demand, Wide, CC. **C:** Sean Patrick Flanery; Norman Reedus; Billy Connolly; Clifton (Gonzalez) Collins, Jr.; Julie Benz; Peter Fonda; Judd Nelson; Directed by Troy Duffy; Written by Troy Duffy; Taylor Duffy; Cinematography by Miroslaw Baszak; Music by Jeff Danna. **Pr:** Don Carmody; Chris Binker; Stage Six Films; Apparition. **A:** Sr. High-Adult. **P:** Entertainment. **U:** Home. **L:** English. **Mov-Ent**: Crime Drama. **Acq:** Purchase. **Dist:** Sony Pictures Home Entertainment Inc.; Amazon.com Inc.; Movies Unlimited.

The Boondocks: The Complete First Season - Uncut and Uncensored 2005
Animated adaptation of Aaron McGruder's political comic strip as 10-year-old African-American Huey, his younger brother Riley, and their caustic granddad relocate to an upscale suburban community and all its cultural shocks. 15 episodes. 323m; DVD, CC. **C:** Voice(s) by Regina King; John Witherspoon. **A:** Sr. High-Adult. **P:** Entertainment. **U:** Home. **Mov-Ent**: Animation & Cartoons, Black Culture. **Acq:** Purchase. **Dist:** Sony Pictures Home Entertainment Inc.

Boone and Crockett: The Hunter Heroes 2005
A look at American pioneers Daniel Boone and David Crockett and their effect on the frontier. 50m; DVD. **A:** Jr. High-Adult. **P:** Entertainment. **U:** Home. **Gen-Edu**: Documentary Films, Biography. **Acq:** Purchase. **Dist:** A&E Television Networks L.L.C.

The Boost 1988 (R) — ★½
A feverish, messy melodrama about a young couple's spiraling decline from yuppie-ish wealth in a haze of cocaine abuse. 95m; VHS, DVD; Open Captioned. **C:** James Woods; Sean Young; John Kapelos; Steven Hill; Kelle Kerr; John Rothman; Amanda Blake; Grace Zabriskie; Directed by Harold Becker; Written by Darryl Ponicsan; Cinematography by Howard Atherton. **Pr:** Hemdale Films. **A:** Sr. High-Adult. **P:** Entertainment. **U:** Home. **Mov-Ent**: Drugs. **Acq:** Purchase. **Dist:** Movies Unlimited; Alpha Video. $19.95.

Boost Your Brain Power 199?
Uses hypnosis and subliminal messages to create a limber and agile mind. 30m; VHS. **A:** Adult. **P:** Instruction. **U:** Home. **Hea-Sci**: Self-Help. **Dist:** Valley of the Sun Publishing. $19.95.

Boot Camp 2007 (Unrated) — ★½
Anti-social Denver teen Sophie (Kunis) hates her stepfather and causes such a ruckus that he sends her to a rehabilitation boot camp on the island of Fiji. Far from being paradise, Sophie discovers the camp uses abusive training techniques on its offenders. Sophie's boyfriend Ben (Smith) gets himself sent to the same facility so they can escape together but their impulsive plans make things worse. 99m; DVD. **C:** Mila Kunis; Gregory Edward Smith; Peter Stomare; Tygh Ruyan; Regine Nehy; Barbara Wilson; Christopher Jacot; Serge Houde; Directed by Christian Duguay; Written by Agatha Dominik; John Cox; Cinematography by Christian Duguay; Music by Normand Corbeil. **A:** Sr. High-Adult. **P:** Entertainment. **U:** Home. **Mov-Ent**: Adolescence. **Acq:** Purchase. **Dist:** Fox Home Entertainment.

Boot Camp for Troubled Teens 1990
A Utah camp with strict and harsh treatment for rebellious teens is examined, all the while asking, "does a tough love approach work, or is it a false answer?" 28m; VHS. **Pr:** Films for the Humanities. **A:** College-Adult. **P:** Education. **U:** Institution. **Gen-Edu:** Documentary Films, Adolescence. **Acq:** Purchase. **Dist:** Films for the Humanities & Sciences. $149.00.

Boot Camp with Andre Houle: Aerobic, Anaerobic, Resistance ????
An intermediate to advanced workout with intense intervals of strength and cardio sections. 60m; VHS. **A:** Adult. **P:** Instruction. **U:** Home. **Hea-Sci:** Fitness/Exercise, How-To. **Acq:** Purchase. **Dist:** Body Bar Systems. $19.95.

Boot Hill 1969 (PG) — ★½
Two guys mess with western baddies and wild women in spaghetti oater. 97m; VHS, DVD. **C:** Terence Hill; Bud Spencer; Woody Strode; Victor Buono; Lionel Stander; Directed by Giuseppe Colizzi. **A:** Primary-Adult. **P:** Entertainment. **U:** Home. **Mov-Ent. Acq:** Purchase. **Dist:** Movies Unlimited. $8.99.

Boot Hill Bandits 1942 — ★★½
"Crash" Corrigan fights on the side of right in this classic western as he helps corral Wells Fargo bandits. 58m/B/W; VHS, DVD. **C:** Ray Corrigan; John "Dusty" King; Max Terhune; Jean Brooks; John Merton; Glenn Strange; Directed by S. Roy Luby. **A:** Jr. High-Adult. **P:** Entertainment. **U:** Home. **Mov-Ent:** Western. **Acq:** Purchase. **Dist:** Movies Unlimited; Alpha Video. $19.95.

Boot Hill Brigade 1937 (Unrated) — ★
Reynolds (LaRue) uses hired killers and a crooked land deal to run the ranchers off their property. Cowboy Lon Cardigan (Brown) comes to the ranchers' aid. 58m/B/W; DVD. **C:** Johnny Mack Brown; Dick Curtis; Horace Murphy; Frank LaRue; Ed Cassidy; Bobby Nelson; Frank Ball; Steve Clark; Frank Ellis; Claire Rochelle; Directed by Sam Newfield; Written by George Plympton; Harry F. Olmsted; Cinematography by Bert Longenecker. **A:** Family. **P:** Entertainment. **U:** Home. **L:** English. **Mov-Ent:** Western, Action-Adventure. **Acq:** Purchase. **Dist:** VCI Entertainment.

The Booth 2006 (Unrated) — ★★★
Shogo (Ryuta Sato) is a shock jock whose radio program features people calling in with their romantic problems to be humiliated and condescended to by him. Since the company is moving to a new place, Shogo is temporarily moved to Studio 6, a run down broadcasting booth that is supposed to be haunted, and responsible for the suicide of a former DJ. And sure enough, perfectly on cue the crew begins to hear things they can't explain, especially Shogo, whose paranoia leads him to believe that the callers have found out secrets from his past. 74m; DVD. **C:** Ryuta Shoto; Directed by Yoshihiro Nakamura; Written by Yoshihiro Nakamura; Cinematography by Akihiro Kawamura; Nouaki Sasaki; Music by Kyo Nakanishi. **A:** Sr. High-Adult. **P:** Entertainment. **U:** Home. **L:** English, Japanese, Spanish. **Mov-Ent:** Horror. **Acq:** Purchase. **Dist:** Palisades Tartan Video. $14.95.

Booth and Bly: Poets 1978
In this four part series, Booth and Bly demonstrate the beginnings of a poem and they express their philosophy on modern poetry and teaching it. They also present readings of modern English and American poets. 30m; 3/4 U, EJ. **Pr:** NETCHE. **A:** College-Adult. **P:** Education. **U:** Institution, CCTV, BCTV, SURA. **Gen-Edu:** Documentary Films, Literature. **Acq:** Purchase, Rent/Lease, Subscription. **Dist:** NETCHE.
Indiv. Titles: 1. A Workshop with Robert Bly 2. A Workshop with Martin Booth 3. Approaches to Poetry 4. In Performance.

Boothill Brigade 1937 — ★★
Former footballer Brown rides to the rescue when criminals steal land from homesteaders. 58m/B/W; VHS, DVD. **C:** Johnny Mack Brown; Claire Rochelle; Dick Curtis; Horace Murphy; Frank LaRue; Edward Cassidy; Bobby Nelson; Frank Ball; Steve Clark; Directed by Sam Newfield. **Pr:** Republic. **A:** Family. **P:** Entertainment. **U:** Home. **Mov-Ent:** Western. **Acq:** Purchase. **Dist:** Alpha Video; VCI Entertainment. $19.95.

Bootleg 1985 (Unrated) — ★★
A detective is on a case that leads to crooked politics and espionage. 82m; VHS. **C:** Ray Meagher; John Flaus; Carmen Duncan; Ian Nimmo; Directed by John Prescott; Written by John Prescott; Cinematography by Stephen Frost; Music by Stephen Cronin. **A:** College-Adult. **P:** Entertainment. **U:** Home. **Mov-Ent. Acq:** Purchase. **Dist:** No Longer Available.

Bootmen 2000 (R) — ★★
Young Sean must make his dance dreams come true despite a bitter, critical father and his working-class Australian surroundings. Director Dein Perry has turned his hit show "Tap Dogs" into a fictionalized and semi-autobiographical tale that combines some of the better qualities of "The Full Monty" and the standard twists and turns of so many other dance films. The "Let's put on a show" plot doesn't provide much sustenance to see the viewer through to some of the excellent choreography. Features several players from the original Tap Dogs company. 95m; VHS, DVD. **C:** Adam Garcia; Sophie Lee; William Zappa; Sam Worthington; Susie Porter; Directed by Dein Perry; Written by Steve Worland; Cinematography by Steve Mason. **A:** Sr. High-Adult. **P:** Entertainment. **U:** Home. **Mov-Ent:** Dance, Australia. **Awds:** Australian Film Inst. '00: Cinematog., Costume Des., Score. **Acq:** Purchase. **Dist:** Fox Home Entertainment.

Boots and Her Kittens 1987
A mother cat shows her kittens the ropes of being an adult cat. The point of this video is to show kids proper pet care. 10m; VHS, 3/4 U. **A:** Primary. **P:** Education. **U:** Institution, SURA. **Chl-Juv:** Pets. **Acq:** Purchase, Trade-in. **Dist:** Encyclopedia Britannica. $190.00.

Boots & Saddles 1937 — ★½
A young English lord wants to sell the ranch he has inherited but Autry is determined to make him a real Westerner. 54m/B/W; VHS, DVD. **TV Std:** NTSC, PAL. **C:** Gene Autry; Judith Allen; Smiley Burnette; Directed by Joseph Kane. **Pr:** Republic. **A:** Family. **P:** Entertainment. **U:** Home. **Mov-Ent:** Western. **Acq:** Purchase. **Dist:** $19.95.

Boots Malone 1952 — ★★½
An old down-on-his-luck gambling addict and a young, rich kid fascinated by the sordid atmosphere of the racetrack stumble upon one another and form a symbiotic relationship. All goes well for while, but there'd be no movie unless a collection of obstacles suddenly threatens their success, friendship, and even their lives. A rather melodramatic buddy tale, but Holden and Stewart hold interest. 103m; VHS. **C:** William Holden; John Stewart; Ed Begley, Sr.; Harry (Henry) Morgan; Whit Bissell; Directed by William Dieterle; Written by Harold Buchman; Milton Holmes; Music by Elmer Bernstein. **A:** Jr. High-Adult. **P:** Entertainment. **U:** Home. **Mov-Ent:** Horses--Racing. **Acq:** Purchase.

Boots of Destiny 1937 — ★
Cheap western with Maynard and his sidekick Barnett on the lam and coming to the aid of ranch owner Dell. Based on a story by E. Morton Hough. 59m/B/W; VHS, DVD. **C:** Ken Maynard; Claudia Dell; Vince Barnett; Edward Cassidy; Martin Garralaga; Directed by Arthur Rosson; Written by Arthur Rosson. **Pr:** Grand National Productions. **A:** Jr. High-Adult. **P:** Entertainment. **U:** Home. **Mov-Ent:** Western. **Acq:** Purchase. **Dist:** Alpha Video. $19.99.

Booty Call 1996 (R) — ★★½
Reserved Rushon (Davidson) and conservative Nikki (Jones) have been dating for a couple of months and Rushon's decided they should consummate their relationship. Nikki's more ambivalent and first sets up a double date with her vivacious best friend Lysterine (Fox) and Rushon's bragging buddy Bunz (Foxx). The duos do pair up but since the "no glove, no love" rule prevails, first the guys have to find some condoms. Raunch rules as might be expected but it's an appealing cast. 120m; VHS, DVD, CC. **C:** Jamie Foxx; Tommy Davidson; Vivica A. Fox; Tamala Jones; Art Malik; Gedde Watanabe; Scott LaRose; Ammie Sin; Bernie Mac; David Hemblen; Directed by Jeff Pollack; Written by Takashi Bufford; Cinematography by Ronald Orieux; Music by Robert Folk. **Pr:** John Morrissey; Columbia Pictures; Sony Pictures Home Entertainment Inc. **A:** Sr. High-Adult. **P:** Entertainment. **U:** Home. **Mov-Ent:** Sex & Sexuality. **Acq:** Purchase. **Dist:** Sony Pictures Home Entertainment Inc.

Boozers and Users 1979
A show that reveals the motives, risks, and alternatives associated with drug-taking behavior. Warning signs of alcoholism are clearly defined, and promising programs for detection and rehabilitation are highlighted. 26m; VHS, 3/4 U. **C:** Narrated by James Franciscus. **Pr:** Motivational Media. **A:** Sr. High-Adult. **P:** Education. **U:** Institution, CCTV. **Hea-Sci:** Documentary Films, Alcoholism, Drug Abuse. **Acq:** Purchase. **Dist:** Hazelden Publishing.

Bopha! 1993 (PG-13) — ★★★
Father-son strife set against the anti-apartheid movement. In the Senior township police officer Mikah takes pride in his peaceful community, particularly in light of the growing unrest in the other townships. Son Zweli has become an activist and wife Rosie must be the family peacemaker. Then a prominent freedom movement member is arrested and two officers of the secret police make their sinister appearance. Well acted; directorial debut of Freeman. Adapted from the play by Percy Mtwa, although the hopeful ending has been changed in the movie. The title, a Zulu word, stands for arrest or detention. Filmed on location in Zimbabwe. 121m; VHS, DVD, CC. **C:** Danny Glover; Maynard Eziashi; Alfre Woodard; Malcolm McDowell; Marius Weyers; Malick Bowens; Robin Smith; Michael Chinyamurindi; Christopher John Hall; Grace Mahlaba; Directed by Morgan Freeman; Written by Brian Bird; John Wierick; Music by James Horner. **Pr:** Lawrence Taubman; Arsenio Hall; Arsenio Hall Communications; Paramount Pictures. **A:** Jr. High-Sr. High. **P:** Entertainment. **U:** Home. **Mov-Ent:** Apartheid, Africa, Politics & Government. **Acq:** Purchase. **Dist:** Paramount Pictures Corp. $19.95.

Borat: Cultural Learnings of America for Make Benefit Glorious Nation of Kazakhstan 2006 (R) — ★★★
British comic Sacha Baron Cohen is outrageously funny as Borat, the cheerfully ignorant and prejudiced "sixth best known reporter in Kazakhstan." The plot follows Borat's travels through America in order to bring back to his homeland two things he feels strongly about: lessons on America and Pamela Anderson. The plot is just a frame to prop up the real aim of the moviefilm, which is to allow the American public to parody and incriminate itself. Viewers will simultaneously wince and laugh as Borat's seemingly innocent Third World anti-Semitism, homophobia and misogyny are reflected in unknowing victims from both jerkwater towns and cosmopolitan cities. Critically hailed upon its release, the film was dogged with numerous lawsuits and complaints from offended parties, particularly the Kazakh government. The humor is often crude (there is a credit for "Feces provided by") and disturbing (an extended scene of graphic "dudity" when Borat and producer Azamat (Davitian) wrestle over a magazine picture), but it is genuinely funny and unsettling. 82m; DVD. **C:** Sacha Baron Cohen; Pamela Anderson; Ken Davitian; Pat Haggerty; Alan Keyes; Luenell; Directed by Larry Charles; Written by Sacha Baron Cohen; Peter Baynham; Dan Mazer; Anthony Hines; Cinematography by Luke Geissbuhler; Anthony Hardwick; Music by Erran Baron Cohen. **Pr:** Jay Roach; Sacha Baron Cohen; Everyman Pictures; Dune Entertainment; Major Studio Partners; Four by Two; 20th Century-Fox. **A:** Sr. High-Adult. **P:** Entertainment. **U:** Home. **L:** English. **Mov-Ent. Awds:** Golden Globes '07: Actor--Mus./Comedy (Baron Cohen). **Acq:** Purchase. **Dist:** Fox Home Entertainment.

Bordello 1979 (Unrated) — ★
Western spoof about cowboys and shady ladies. 90m; VHS. **C:** Chuck Connors; Michael Conrad; John Ireland; Isela Vega; Jorge (George) Rivero; Directed by Ray Fellows. **Pr:** ESME Productions. **A:** Jr. High-Adult. **P:** Entertainment. **U:** Home. **Mov-Ent:** TV Movies, Prostitution. **Acq:** Purchase. **Dist:** No Longer Available.

The Border 1982 (R) — ★★★
A border guard faces corruption and violence within his department and tests his own sense of decency when the infant of a poor Mexican girl is kidnapped. Excellent cast, fine cinematography, unusual Nicholson performance. 107m; VHS, DVD. **C:** Jack Nicholson; Harvey Keitel; Valerie Perrine; Warren Oates; Elpidia Carrillo; Directed by Tony Richardson; Written by Deric Washburn; Walon Green; Music by Ry Cooder. **Pr:** Mark Huffam. **A:** Sr. High-Adult. **P:** Entertainment. **U:** Home. **Mov-Ent:** Illegal Immigration, Ethics & Morals, Mexico. **Acq:** Purchase. **Dist:** Movies Unlimited; Universal Studios Home Video. $14.98.

Border Badmen 1945 — ★½
It's just another tired old western, even if it does appropriate the classic mystery-thriller plot; following the reading of a silver baron's will, someone starts killing off the relatives. 59m/B/W; VHS. **C:** Buster Crabbe; Lorraine Miller; Charles "Blackie" King; Ray Bennett; Arch (Archie) Hall, Sr.; Budd Buster; Bud Osborne; Directed by Sam Newfield. **Pr:** PRC. **A:** Family. **P:** Entertainment. **U:** Home. **Mov-Ent:** Western. **Acq:** Purchase. **Dist:** Grapevine Video.

Border Blues 2003 (R) — ★½
Ex-Russian cop who tries to sneak a woman and her daughter across the U.S.-Mexico border is the primary suspect in connection with an L.A. mail-bomb scare. Painful to watch Busey and Estrada in their law enforcement roles. 86m; VHS, DVD. **C:** Eric Roberts; Gary Busey; Yekaterina Rednikova; Lisa Gerstein; Erik Estrada; Rodion Nakhapetov; Directed by Rodion Nakhapetov; Written by Rodion Nakhapetov; Cinematography by Sergei Kozlov; Music by David G. Russell. **A:** Sr. High-Adult. **P:** Entertainment. **U:** Home. **Mov-Ent:** Action-Adventure, Immigration. **Acq:** Purchase. **Dist:** Bedford Entertainment Inc. $24.99.

Border Brujo 1990
Presents the ridiculousness of racial prejudices and cultural ignorance through Guillermo Gomez-Pena's performance of 15 distinct personas. 50m; VHS. **A:** Jr. High-Adult. **P:** Education. **U:** Institution. **Gen-Edu:** Sociology. **Acq:** Purchase, Rent/Lease. **Dist:** Third World Newsreel; University of Washington Educational Media Collection. $325.00.

Border Caballero 1936 — ★½
Western star McCoy and lady cowpoke January shoot out the skies in this lackluster McCoy vehicle. Based on a story by Norman S. Hall. 57m/B/W; VHS, DVD. **C:** Tim McCoy; Lois January; Ralph Byrd; Ted Adams; Directed by Sam Newfield; Written by Joseph O'Donnell. **Pr:** Leslie Simmonds; Puritan. **A:** Jr. High-Adult. **P:** Entertainment. **U:** Home. **Mov-Ent:** Western. **Acq:** Purchase. **Dist:** Movies Unlimited. $19.99.

Border Cafe 2005 (Unrated) — ★★½
After her husband dies, widow Rayhan wants to continue cooking and operating his successful truckstop diner at the Iran/Turkey border. Muslim tradition demands that her nearest male relative, brother-in-law Nasser, take her and her children into his household. Reyhan defies him and the local authorities to reopen the diner anyway and the truckers are grateful even though Reyhan still has problems. Farsi, Turkish, Greek, and Russian with subtitles. 105m; DVD. **C:** Fereshteh Sadre Orafaiy; Parviz Parastui; Esmail Soltanian; Nikolas Papapopoulos; Svieta Mikalishina; Directed by Kambuzia Partovi; Written by Kambuzia Partovi; Cinematography by Mohammad Reza Sokout; Music by Ali Birang. **A:** College-Adult. **P:** Entertainment. **U:** Home. **L:** Farsi, Turkish, Greek. **Mov-Ent:** Iran. **Acq:** Purchase. **Dist:** First Run Features.

Border Devils 1932 — ★
A boy is pursued by a ruthless gang of outlaws, until he is saved by the good guys. 60m/B/W; VHS, DVD. **C:** Harry Carey, Sr.; Art Mix; George "Gabby" Hayes; Directed by William Nigh. **Pr:** Artclass. **A:** Family. **P:** Entertainment. **U:** Home. **Mov-Ent:** Western. **Acq:** Purchase. **Dist:** Mill Creek Entertainment L.L.C. $19.99.

Border Feud 1947 — ★
LaRue endeavors to prevent someone who, by instigating a family feud, will claim large gold mine rights. 54m/B/W; VHS. **C:** Lash LaRue; Al "Fuzzy" St. John; Bob Duncan; Directed by Ray Taylor. **Pr:** Monogram. **A:** Family. **P:** Entertainment. **U:** Home. **Mov-Ent:** Western. **Acq:** Purchase. **Dist:** Sony Pictures Home Entertainment Inc. $12.95.

Border Incident 1949 (Unrated) — ★★
Average crime melodrama from director Mann in which federales on both sides of the border team up to prevent the exploitation and murder of illegal farm workers. Jack Bearnes (Murphy) has stolen work permits he's willing to sell to crooked rancher Owen Parkson (Da Silva) while Pablo Rodriguez (Montalban) poses as an illegal migrant, and both agents find themselves in grave danger. 94m/B/W; DVD. **C:** Ricardo Montalban; George Murphy; Howard da Silva; James Mitchell;

Arnold Moss; Alfonso Bedoya; Teresa Celli; Charles McGraw; Jose Torvay; John Ridgely; Arthur Hunnicutt; Sig Rumann; Directed by Anthony Mann; Written by John C. Higgins; George Zuckerman; Cinematography by John Alton. **A:** Jr. High-Adult. **P:** Entertainment. **U:** Home. **Mov-Ent:** Crime Drama, Immigration, Illegal Immigration. **Acq:** Purchase. **Dist:** Warner Home Video, Inc.

Border Law 1931 — ★★½
Jones plays a heroic Texas Ranger who goes undercover to find the man who killed his brother. One of Jones' finest outings and far better than most B westerns. 62m/B/W; VHS. **C:** Buck Jones; Lupita Tovar; James Mason; Frank Rice; Glenn Strange; Directed by Louis King; Written by Stuart Anthony. **Pr:** Columbia Pictures. **A:** Jr. High-Adult. **P:** Entertainment. **U:** Home. **Mov-Ent:** Western. **Acq:** Purchase. **Dist:** Movies Unlimited; Glenn Video Vistas Ltd. $19.99.

The Border Legion 1940 — ★½
Sappy retelling of Grey's novel about an outlaw sacrificing himself for a pair of young lovers. This time Rogers is the outlaw with a heart of gold. Originally filmed in 1930 with Jack Holt, Richard Arlen, and Fay Wray. 58m/B/W; VHS, DVD. **C:** Roy Rogers; George "Gabby" Hayes; Carol Hughes; Joseph (Joe) Sawyer; Maude Eburne; Jay Novello; Directed by Joseph Kane; Written by Olive Cooper; Louis Stevens. **Pr:** Joseph Kane; Joseph Kane; Republic. **A:** Jr. High-Adult. **P:** Entertainment. **U:** Home. **Mov-Ent:** Western. **Acq:** Purchase. **Dist:** Movies Unlimited. $19.99.

Border Lost 2008 (R) — ★½
Typical actioner. A U.S. task force works along the Mexican border to prevent bandoleros from preying upon illegal immigrants. When one the men is killed and his girlfriend kidnapped, the other agents defy orders to cross into Mexico on a mission of rescue and revenge. 105m; DVD. **C:** Chris Cleveland; Emilio Rossi; Protasio; Wes McGee; Marian Zapico; Daniel Ledesma; Kelly Noonan; Robert Vazquez; Directed by David Murphy; Scott Peck; Written by David Murphy; Scott Peck; Cinematography by Scott Peck; Music by Christopher Peck. **A:** Sr. High-Adult. **P:** Entertainment. **U:** Home. **Mov-Ent:** Mexico. **Acq:** Purchase. **Dist:** Allumination Filmworks.

Border Outlaws 1950 (Unrated) — ★
Undercover agent Mike Hoskins is investigating a gang of rustlers and needs the help of Spade Cooley when it becomes clear that the gang's leader must be a guest at Spade's dude ranch. The music from "The King of Western Swing" is the only thing making this mediocrity worth looking at. 55m/B/W; DVD. **C:** Spade Cooley; Bill Edwards; Maria Hart; Bill Kennedy; Bud Osborne; Directed by Richard Talmadge; Written by Arthur Hoerl; Cinematography by Elmer Dyer; Music by Darrell Calker. **A:** Jr. High-Adult. **P:** Entertainment. **U:** Home. **Mov-Ent:** Western. **Acq:** Purchase. **Dist:** Alpha Video.

Border Patrol 1943 — ★★
Another installment in the Hopalong Cassidy series. This time there's a villainous owner of a silvermine to reckon with. A man so low he's abducting hapless Mexicans as they cross the border, forcing them to work his mines. Hoppy is saddled with the task of persuading him that the town ain't big enough for the both of them. Robert Mitchum makes his perfectly forgettable film debut as one of the bad guys. Not one of the best in the series, but plenty of action. 63m/B/W; VHS, DVD. **C:** William Boyd; Andy Clyde; Jay Kirby; Russell Simpson; Claudia Drake; George Reeves; Duncan Renaldo; Directed by Lesley Selander. **Pr:** United Artists. **A:** Jr. High-Adult. **P:** Entertainment. **U:** Home. **Mov-Ent:** Western. **Acq:** Purchase. **Dist:** Movies Unlimited. $14.24.

Border Patrol 2001 (PG-13) — ★★½
This Border Patrol is in charge of policing the realm of the dead, making sure sinners and the good get their proper punishment and rewards. Patrolman Numan is forced to break the rules and ask the help of a mortal Miami cop in order to stop vicious serial killer Dr. Helms from opening the gateway to other realms. 89m; VHS, CC. **C:** Michael Delorenzo; Lewis Fitz-Gerald; Clayton Rohner; Kenny Ransom; Directed by Mark Haber; Written by Miguel Tejada-Flores. **A:** Jr. High-Adult. **P:** Entertainment. **U:** Home. **Mov-Ent:** Horror. **Acq:** Purchase. **Dist:** Paramount Pictures Corp.

Border Phantom 1937 — ★★
Steele (whom you might recognize as Canino in "The Big Sleep"), takes on a suave Chinese businessman who heads a mail order business: seems he's smuggling mail-order brides from Mexico in this vintage "B"-grade horse opera. 60m/B/W; VHS, DVD. **C:** Bob Steele; Harley Wood; Don Barclay; Karl Hackett; Horace Murphy; Miki Morita; Directed by S. Roy Luby. **Pr:** Republic. **A:** Family. **P:** Entertainment. **U:** Home. **Mov-Ent. Acq:** Purchase. **Dist:** Anchor Bay Entertainment; MNTEX Entertainment, Inc. $19.99.

Border Radio 1988 (Unrated) — **Bomb!**
A rock singer decides to steal a car and try to outrun some tough thugs hot on his trail. 88m/B/W; VHS, DVD, CC. **C:** Chris D; Luana Anders; Directed by Allison Anders; Kurt Voss; Written by Allison Anders; Kurt Voss; Music by Dave Alvin. **A:** College-Adult. **P:** Entertainment. **U:** Home. **Mov-Ent. Acq:** Purchase. **Dist:** Facets Multimedia Inc. $19.95.

Border Rangers 1950 — ★
A man joins the Rangers in order to avenge the murders of his brother and sister-in-law. 57m/B/W; VHS. **C:** Robert Lowery; Donald (Don "Red") Barry; Lyle Talbot; Pamela Blake; Directed by William Berke. **Pr:** Lippert Productions. **A:** Family. **P:** Entertainment. **U:** Home. **Mov-Ent:** Western. **Acq:** Purchase. **Dist:** No Longer Available.

Border River 1947 (Unrated) — ★½
Mexican General Calleja (Armendariz) runs Zona Libre, a small enclave at the U.S.-Mexico border. For those running from the law—or the lawless—Zona Libre offers sanctuary, for a price. New arrival Confederate officer Clete Mattson (McCrea) shows up with a cool $2 million in gold, looking to buy guns for the Confederacy. Hot tamale Carmelita (De Carlo) fancies Mattson, but the General has dibs on her, and can Mattson trust these guys at Zona Libre, anyway? Either way, trouble's a brewin'. 80m; DVD. **C:** Joel McCrea; Yvonne De Carlo; Pedro Armendariz, Sr.; Howard Petrie; Erika Nordin; Alfonso Bedoya; Ivan Triesault; George Lewis; George D. Wallace; Lane Chandler; Charles Horvath; Nacho Galindo; Directed by George Sherman; Written by William Sackheim; Louis Stevens. **A:** Jr. High-Adult. **P:** Entertainment. **U:** Home. **Mov-Ent:** Western, Mexico. **Acq:** Purchase. **Dist:** Nostalgia Collectibles.

Border Roundup 1941 — ★
The "Lone Rider" uncovers a gang of thieving crooks. 57m/B/W; VHS, DVD. **C:** George Houston; Al "Fuzzy" St. John; Dennis Moore; Directed by Sam Newfield. **Pr:** Monogram. **A:** Family. **P:** Entertainment. **U:** Home. **Mov-Ent:** Western. **Acq:** Purchase. **Dist:** Alpha Video. $19.95.

Border Run 2012 (R) — ★★
Decent enough drama although it tends to sputter along. Conservative journalist Sofie Talbert's (Stone) brother Aaron (Zane), a relief worker, goes missing in Mexico. Sofie heads south to investigate and gets caught up in illegal immigration and human trafficking along the border. A dark-haired Stone is a good lead but the one to watch is Zacarias as Juanita, the scary leader of the trafficking ring. 96m; DVD, Blu-Ray. **C:** Sharon Stone; Billy Zane; Giovanna Zacarias; Rosemberg Salgado; Miguel Rodarte; Directed by Gabriela Tagliavini; Written by Amy Kolquist; Don Fieberger; Cinematography by Andrew Strahorn; Music by Emilio Kauderer. **A:** Sr. High-Adult. **P:** Entertainment. **U:** Home. **L:** English. **Mov-Ent:** Family, Mexico. **Acq:** Purchase. **Dist:** Anchor Bay Entertainment Inc.

Border Saddlemates 1952 — ★
U.S. government veterinarian Allen is asked to sub for the local doc in the Canadian border town of Pine Rock. But he learns that a gang is using silver fox pelts to smuggle illegal goods into the U.S. and it's up to Allen and the Rhythm Riders to stop them. 67m/B/W; VHS, CC. **C:** Rex Allen; Mary Ellen Kay; Slim Pickens; Roy Barcroft; Forrest Taylor; Jimmy Moss; Zon Murray; Keith McConnell; Directed by William Witney; Written by Albert DeMond; Cinematography by John MacBurnie; Music by Stanley Wilson. **Pr:** Republic Pictures. **A:** Family. **P:** Entertainment. **U:** Home. **Mov-Ent:** Western. **Acq:** Purchase. **Dist:** Lions Gate Entertainment Inc. $29.95.

The Border: Season 1 2008 (Unrated)
Fast-paced Canadian series set in a paranoid post-9/11 Toronto where border security is priority one and crises are constantly unfolding with terrorist infiltrations, cross-border police actions and the trafficking of uranium, abducted children and more. The Premier of Quebec is threatened in "Nothing to Declare," a fundamentalist Christian sect brings "child brides" across the border in "Articles of Faith," and a Canadian submarines crew is trapped under the polar ice in "Shifting Waters." 13 episodes. 600m; DVD. **C:** James McGowan; Graham Abbey. **A:** Adult. **P:** Entertainment. **U:** Home. **Mov-Ent:** Drama, Canada. **Acq:** Purchase. **Dist:** CBC Home Video. $34.98.

Border Shootout 1990 (PG) — ★★
A trigger-happy sheriff battles a rich young cattle rustler. 110m; VHS, DVD, CC. **C:** Glenn Ford; Charlene Tilton; Jeff Kaake; Michael Horse; Russell Todd; Cody Glenn; Sergio Calderon; Michael Ansara; Directed by Chris T. McIntyre. **Pr:** Phoenix Production Partners. **A:** Jr. High-Adult. **P:** Entertainment. **U:** Home. **Mov-Ent:** Western. **Acq:** Purchase. **Dist:** Turner Broadcasting System Inc. $79.98.

Border Street 1948 — ★★½
This film shows how a group of Polish Jews fought off the German occupation forces in the Warsaw ghetto. In Polish with English subtitles. 110m/B/W; VHS, 3/4 U. **TV Std:** NTSC, PAL. **A:** Sr. High-Adult. **P:** Entertainment. **U:** Institution, Home. **L:** Polish. **Mov-Ent:** World War Two, Judaism, Holocaust. **Acq:** Purchase. **Dist:** International Historic Films Inc. $39.95.

Border Treasure 1950 (Unrated) — ★½
Anita has raised money and valuables for Mexican earthquake victims but bandits attack the shipment. They are foiled by Ed and Chito but are determined to strike again. 60m/B/W; DVD. **C:** Tim Holt; Richard Martin; Inez Cooper; John Doucette; House Peters, Jr.; Julian Rivero; Directed by George Archainbaud; Written by Norman Houston; Cinematography by J. Roy Hunt; Music by Paul Sawtell. **A:** Family. **P:** Entertainment. **U:** Home. **Mov-Ent:** Western. **Acq:** Purchase. **Dist:** WarnerArchive.com.

Border Vengeance 1935 — ★★½
Reb is a member of a family of outlaws. He aims to improve himself and steer his family to the straight and narrow trail. 45m/B/W; VHS, DVD. **C:** Reb Russell; Mary Jane Carey; Kenneth MacDonald; Hank Bell; Glenn Strange; Norman Feusier; Charles "Slim" Whitaker; Directed by Ray Heinz. **A:** Family. **P:** Entertainment. **U:** Home. **Mov-Ent:** Western, Family. **Acq:** Purchase. **Dist:** Grapevine Video. $10.95.

Border Vigilantes 1941 — ★★
Hoppy and pals try to rid a town of outlaws that even the vigilantes can't run off. The big surprise comes when they find out who the leader of the outlaws is. 61m/B/W; VHS, DVD. **C:** William Boyd; Russell Hayden; Andy Clyde; Victor Jory; Morris Ankrum; Frances Gifford; Ethel Wales; Hal Taliaferro; Directed by Derwin Abrahams. **Pr:** Paramount Pictures. **A:** Jr. High-Adult. **P:** Entertainment. **U:** Home. **Mov-Ent:** Western. **Acq:** Purchase. **Dist:** Movies Unlimited. $14.99.

Border War: The Battle Over Illegal Immigrants 2006
Documents the lives of five people affected by the rise in illegal immigration along the U.S.-Mexican border. English and Spanish with subtitles. 95m; DVD. **A:** Jr. High-Adult. **P:** Entertainment. **U:** Home. **L:** Spanish. **Gen-Edu:** Documentary Films, Immigration. **Acq:** Purchase. **Dist:** Genius Entertainment.

Border Wars: Season 1 2010 (Unrated)
National Geographic Channel 2010-? occupational reality show. Follows U.S. Customs and Border Protection agents and officers on chases, rescues, and busts in the inhospitable desert wilderness and underground smuggling tunnels along the U.S. and Mexico border. 5 episodes: "No End in Sight," "Dead of Night," "Last Defense," "The Front Lines," and "City Under Siege." 250m; DVD. **C:** Voice(s) by Bill Graves. **A:** Sr. High-Adult. **P:** Entertainment. **U:** Home. **Mov-Ent:** U.S. States, Television Series. **Acq:** Purchase. **Dist:** National Geographic Society. $29.99.

Border Wolves 1938 (Unrated) — ★½
Rusty (Baker) and Clem (Knight) stumble across a wagon train massacre and are wrongly accused of the crime. Judge Coleman (O'Shea) convicts the two but then arranges for their escape because he knows the real criminal is his outlaw son Jack (Dorrell) and he wants them to capture Jack and his gang. Currently only available as part of a collection. 56m/B/W; DVD. **C:** Willie Fung; Dickie Jones; Oscar O'Shea; Frank Campeau; Glenn Strange; Jack Montgomery; Dick Dorrell; Constance Moore; Directed by Joseph H. Lewis; Written by Norton S. Parker; Cinematography by Harry Neumann. **A:** Family. **P:** Entertainment. **U:** Home. **L:** English. **Mov-Ent:** Western. **Acq:** Purchase. **Dist:** VCI Entertainment. $9.99.

Borderland 1937 (Unrated) — ★½
Hopalong Cassidy (Boyd) goes bad?! (He's mean to kids and drinks liquor.) Well no, he's just secretly after a bandit known as "The Fox." But the outlaw didn't get his nickname by being stupid, and he sets a trap when he realizes what Hoppy is up to. The ninth film in the series. 82m/B/W; DVD. **C:** William Boyd; George "Gabby" Hayes; James Ellison; Nora Lane; Morris Ankrum; Charlene Wyatt; Directed by Nate Watt; Written by Harrison Jacobs; Cinematography by Archie Stout. **A:** Family. **P:** Entertainment. **U:** Home. **Mov-Ent:** Western. **Acq:** Purchase. **Dist:** Sinister Cinema.

Borderland 2007 (Unrated) — ★★
Super-creepy and bloody, and based on a true 1989 crime. Henry (Muxworthy), Phil (Strong), and Ed (Presley) take a road trip to party in a Mexican border town. Phil doesn't make it back to the hotel and the police are no help. Henry and Ed learn that kidnappings are common and tied to a cult lead by drug dealer Santillan (Cuevas). He's convinced his followers that ritual human sacrifices will make them invulnerable and though the locals (and the cops) know what's going on, they're too terrified to do anything about it. 105m; DVD, Blu-Ray. **C:** Brian Presley; Rider Strong; Jake Muxworthy; Martha Higareda; Sean Astin; Beto Cuevas; Marco Bacuzzi; Directed by Zev Berman; Written by Zev Berman; Eric Poppen; Cinematography by Scott Kevan; Music by Andres Levin. **A:** Sr. High-Adult. **P:** Entertainment. **U:** Home. **Mov-Ent:** Mexico, Cults. **Acq:** Purchase. **Dist:** Lions Gate Entertainment Inc.

Borderline 1950 (Unrated) — ★★
MacMurray and Trevor play undercover agents trying to infiltrate a Mexican drug ring. With their real identities hidden, they fall for each other and make a run for the border. Although the leads work well together, they're hindered by an occasionally confusing script. Unfortunately, director Seiter never decides whether the material is of a comedic or dramatic nature. 88m/B/W; VHS, DVD. **C:** Fred MacMurray; Claire Trevor; Raymond Burr; Roy Roberts; Jose Torvay; Morris Ankrum; Charles Lane; Don Diamond; Nacho Galindo; Pepe Hern; Richard Irving; Directed by William A. Seiter; Cinematography by Lucien N. Andriot; Music by Hans J. Salter. **Pr:** Mark Huffam. **A:** Jr. High-Adult. **P:** Entertainment. **U:** Home. **Mov-Ent:** Mystery & Suspense, Romance, Drugs. **Acq:** Purchase. **Dist:** Alpha Video.

Borderline 1980 (PG) — ★★
Bronson is a border patrol guard in pursuit of a murderer in this action flick. Meanwhile, he gets caught up in trying to help an illegal alien and her young child. 106m; VHS, DVD, CC. **C:** Charles Bronson; Wilford Brimley; Bruno Kirby; Benito Morales; Ed Harris; Kenneth McMillan; Directed by Jerrold Freedman. **Pr:** ITC Entertainment Group. **A:** Jr. High-Adult. **P:** Entertainment. **U:** Home. **Mov-Ent:** Immigration, Mexico. **Acq:** Purchase. **Dist:** $59.98.

Borderline 2002 (R) — ★★★
A good suspenser about obsession. Dr. Lila Colleti (Gershon) is a shrink for the criminally insane at the local prison, which may be why her ex got custody of their two daughters. Lily's troubles increase when one of her patients, Ed Baikman (Flanery), is released to a halfway house, despite his delusions that they are romantically involved. After murdering her ex on her behalf, Ed threatens Lily when she doesn't return his love and implicates her in his crime. Soon, even her detective boyfriend Macy Kobacek (Biehn) has doubts about Lily's innocence. 94m; VHS, DVD. **C:** Gina Gershon; Sean Patrick Flanery; Michael Biehn; Directed by Evelyn Purcell; Written by David Loucka; Cinematography by Michael Brierley; Music by Anthony Marinelli. **A:** Sr. High-Adult. **P:** Entertainment. **U:** Home. **Mov-Ent:** Psychiatry. **Acq:** Purchase. **Dist:** Sony Pictures Home Entertainment Inc.

Borderline Character 1 1979
Psychosomatic, cultural, and situational analysis is applied and discussed in defining the borderline personality by Drs. Beale, Hill, and Stein. Part of the "Holistic Medicine in Primary Care"

series. 33m; VHS, 3/4 U, EJ, Q, Special order formats. **Pr:** University of Oklahoma. **A:** College-Adult. **P:** Professional. **U:** Institution, CCTV. **Hea-Sci**: Medical Education, Psychiatry. **Acq:** Purchase. **Dist:** University of Oklahoma.

Borderline Character 2 1979
Mary Lou is suffering from multiple borderline personality symptoms. The psychosomatic, cultural and situational depth of analysis is applied to this case by Drs. Stein, Hill, and Beale. Part of the "Holistic Medicine in Primary Care" series. 43m; VHS, 3/4 U, EJ, Q, Special order formats. **Pr:** University of Oklahoma. **A:** College-Adult. **P:** Professional. **U:** Institution, CCTV. **Hea-Sci**: Medical Education, Psychiatry. **Acq:** Purchase. **Dist:** University of Oklahoma.

Borderline Medicine 1990
A comparison of the American and Canadian health care systems, focusing on management, funding, and operation. 57m; VHS, 3/4 U. **C:** Narrated by Walter Cronkite. **Pr:** Roger Weisberg. **A:** Sr. High-Adult. **P:** Education. **U:** Institution. **Hea-Sci**: Documentary Films, Medical Care, Economics. **Acq:** Purchase, Rent/Lease. **Dist:** Leo Media, Inc.; University of Washington Educational Media Collection. $395.00.

Borderline Medicine: Comparing U.S. and Canadian Health Care 1991
Explores medical care on both sides of the border by offering the pros and cons of prenatal care, elective surgery, and cancer patients. Offers stories of the patients, health care experts, and business leaders, and comments on the medical and financial implications of both systems. Winner of the Blue Ribbon Award, American Film & Video Festival, 1991; Gold Award, Houston International Film Festival, 1991; CINE Gold Eagle, 1991. 58m; VHS. **A:** College-Adult. **P:** Education. **U:** Institution. **Hea-Sci**: Documentary Films, Medical Care, U.S. States. **Acq:** Purchase, Rent/Lease. **Dist:** Filmakers Library Inc. $395.00.

Borderline Syndrome: A Personality Disorder of Our Time 1989
Offers a clear presentation of what is currently known as Borderline Syndrome. Three doctors offer their ideas about treatment for people in various circumstances. American Psychiatric Association, 1989; Honorable Mention, National Council on Family Relations, 1989; 40th Institute on Hospital and Community Psychiatry, 1988; Western Psychological Association, 1988. 74m; VHS. **A:** College-Adult. **P:** Education. **U:** Institution. **Gen-Edu**: Documentary Films, Psychiatry, Personality. **Acq:** Purchase, Rent/Lease. **Dist:** Filmakers Library Inc. $250.00.

Borderlines 1993
Animated vignette explores the difficulties of establishing personal boundaries in various types of relationships. Intended to stimulate conversation in social sciences. 5m; VHS, SVS, 3/4 U. **Pr:** National Film Board of Canada. **A:** Sr. High-Adult. **P:** Education. **U:** Institution, CCTV. **Gen-Edu**: Animation & Cartoons, Communication, Human Relations. **Acq:** Purchase, Rent/Lease. **Dist:** Lucerne Media. $125.00.

Borders 1989
Interesting documentary deals with the various boundaries we create and perpetuate. Social and personal views of these borders prevent us from realizing our potential. 53m; VHS. **A:** Sr. High-Adult. **P:** Education. **U:** Home. **Mov-Ent**: Animation & Cartoons, Documentary Films, Politics & Government. **Acq:** Purchase. **Dist:** Mystic Fire Video; Facets Multimedia Inc. $29.95.

Bordertown 1935 (Unrated) — ★★
Poor Mexican lawyer Johnny Ramirez (Muni) loses his first case and his temper, which results in his disbarment. He takes a job as a bouncer at a bordertown nightclub where owner Charlie's (Pallette) hot-to-trot missus, Marie (Davis), makes a play that gets rejected. Johnny is stupid over slumming society dame Dale (Lindsay), and Marie gets tragically desperate in trying to get Johnny's attention. The ending borders on the absurd and Davis' performance is scaled way over-the-top throughout although Muni does his best. 80m/B/W; DVD. **C:** Paul Muni; Bette Davis; Margaret Lindsay; Eugene Pallette; Gavin Gordon; Directed by Archie Mayo; Written by Laird Doyle; Wallace Smith; Cinematography by Gaetano Antonio "Tony" Gaudio; Music by Bernhard Haun. **A:** Jr. High-Adult. **P:** Entertainment. **U:** Home. **Mov-Ent**: Nightclubs. **Acq:** Purchase. **Dist:** WarnerArchive.com.

Bordertown 2006 (R) — ★½
Generic thriller based on a true story. Ambitious Chicago journalist Lauren (Lopez) is assigned to write about a series of rape/murders that have happened to young women in Juarez, Mexico. She hooks up with former colleague Alfonso (Banderas), whose persistence on covering the crimes has him in trouble with authorities. Lauren meets Eva (Zapata), who is in hiding after surviving her attack, and it is implied that the victims are all poor workers at factories making goods for the U.S. market. The politics muddies a story that, unfortunately, hasn't been compellingly told. 112m; DVD. **C:** Jennifer Lopez; Antonio Banderas; Maya Zapata; Sonia Braga; Martin Sheen; Directed by Gregory Nava; Written by Gregory Nava; Cinematography by Reynaldo Villalobos; Music by Graeme Revell. **A:** Sr. High-Adult. **P:** Entertainment. **U:** Home. **Mov-Ent**: Rape, Crime Drama, Journalism. **Acq:** Purchase. **Dist:** ThinkFilm Company Inc.

Bordertown Gunfighters 1943 — ★½
A cowboy breaks up a vicious lottery racket and falls in love in the process. 56m/B/W; VHS, DVD. **C:** William (Wild Bill) Elliott; Anne Jeffreys; George "Gabby" Hayes; Ian Keith; Harry Woods; Edward Earle; Karl Hackett; Roy Barcroft; Bud Geary; Carl Sepulveda; Directed by Howard Bretherton; Written by Norman S. Hall; Cinematography by Jack Marta. **Pr:** Republic. **A:** Family. **P:** Entertainment. **U:** Home. **Mov-Ent**: Western. **Acq:** Purchase, Rent/Lease. **Dist:** Movies Unlimited. $29.95.

Boreal Forest: Fall and Winter 1981
This program shows the many preparations and adaptations plants and animals must make to survive the winter. Part of the "Animals and Plants of North America" series. 15m; VHS, 3/4 U. **Pr:** Karvonen Films Ltd. **A:** Primary-Adult. **P:** Education. **U:** Institution, SURA. **Hea-Sci**: Documentary Films, Forests & Trees, Seasons. **Acq:** Purchase, Rent/Lease. **Dist:** Phoenix Learning Group.

Boreal Forest: Spring and Summer 1981
This program looks at the flurry of animal activities in the spring-courting, mating, nesting, and rearing. Also shown is how plants flower and send out new leaves. Part of the "Animals and Plants of North America" series. 15m; VHS, 3/4 U. **Pr:** Karvonen Films Ltd. **A:** Primary-Adult. **P:** Education. **U:** Institution, SURA. **Hea-Sci**: Documentary Films, Forests & Trees, Seasons. **Acq:** Purchase, Rent/Lease. **Dist:** Phoenix Learning Group.

Bored to Death: The Complete First Season 2009
HBO 2009-2011 comedy. "Stockholm Syndrome": After getting dumped by his girlfriend, struggling New York writer Jonathan Ames places an ad on Craigslist, hiring himself out as an unlicensed private detective. "The Case of the Missing Screenplay": Jonathan leaves the screenplay he's supposed to rewrite at a therapist's office and asks Ray to pose as a patient to retrieve it. "The Case of the Beautiful Blackmailer": Jonathan is hired to retrieve a sex tape from an escort. 8 episodes. 220m; DVD, Blu-Ray. **C:** Jason Schwartzman; Zach Galifianakis; Ted Danson. **A:** Adult. **P:** Entertainment. **U:** Home. **L:** English. **Mov-Ent**: Television Series. **Acq:** Purchase. **Dist:** HBO Home Video. $29.98.

Bored to Death: The Complete Second Season 2010
HBO 2009-2011 comedy. "Escape from the Dungeon!": Jonathan is teaching creative writing at night school, but helps out a cop whose name is on a sex club's client list. "Forty-Two Down": Jonathan attempts to help out a poet with marital problems. "Escape from the Castle": Jonathan takes Ray to a health spa for his birthday where he's also supposed to deliver a letter for a client. 8 episodes. 203m; DVD, Blu-Ray. **C:** Jason Schwartzman; Zach Galifianakis; Ted Danson. **A:** Adult. **P:** Entertainment. **U:** Home. **L:** English. **Mov-Ent**: Television Series. **Acq:** Purchase. **Dist:** HBO Home Video. $29.98.

Bored to Death: The Complete Third Season 2011
HBO 2009-2011 comedy. "The Black Clock of Time": Jonathan is promoting his new book on the Dick Cavett show. "Two Large Pearls and a Bar of Gold": Jonathan is hired to guard a valuable family necklace that his old college girlfriend Patti (Casey Wilson) is going to wear at her wedding. "Nothing I Can't Handle by Running Away": Jonathan discovers the identity of his biological father and then becomes a hostage of the thug his dad owes money to. 8 episodes. 245m; DVD, Blu-Ray. **C:** Jason Schwartzman; Zach Galifianakis; Ted Danson. **A:** Adult. **P:** Entertainment. **U:** Home. **L:** English. **Mov-Ent**: Television Series. **Acq:** Purchase. **Dist:** HBO Home Video. $29.98.

Boredom: It's Epidemic! 1982
Sol Gordon of the Syracuse University Institute for Family Research and Education discusses the topic of boredom. 30m; 3/4 U, Special order formats. **Pr:** American Humanist Association. **A:** College-Adult. **P:** Education. **U:** Institution, CCTV, CATV. **Gen-Edu**: Documentary Films, Mental Health. **Acq:** Purchase, Rent/Lease. **Dist:** American Humanist Association.

Borges: El Hombre de la Esquina Rosada 19??
An interpretation of one of Borges' first short stories, which is a surrealistic view of the gaucho. The violence, passion and exuberance of the lifestyle is vividly portrayed. 60m; VHS, 3/4 U. **A:** Sr. High-Adult. **P:** Education. **U:** Institution, SURA. **L:** Spanish. **Gen-Edu**: Documentary Films, Literature. **Acq:** Purchase. **Dist:** Films for the Humanities & Sciences.

Borges Para Millones 198?
A study of Borges' work and place in world literature. 70m; VHS, 3/4 U. **A:** Sr. High-Adult. **P:** Education. **U:** Institution, SURA. **L:** Spanish. **Fin-Art**: Documentary Films, Literature. **Acq:** Purchase. **Dist:** Films for the Humanities & Sciences.

The Borgias: The First Season 2011
Showtime 2011- historical drama. Cardinal Rodrigo Borgia, the patriarch of the family, becomes Pope Aexander VI in 1492 despite his decadence. He then uses his children--Juan, Cesare, and Lucrezia--to extend the family's power in "The Poisoned Chalice." "The Borgias in Love" finds Lucrezia unhappy in her marriage and turning to a stable boy for comfort while Cesare seduces a marreid woman to get revenge on her husband. "Nessuno": The Cardinals flee Rome when the French army enters the city but the Pope makes a deal with the French king. 9 episodes. 467m; DVD, Blu-Ray. **C:** Jeremy Irons; Francois Arnaud; David Oakes; Holliday Grainger; Colm Feore; Joanne Whalley; Lotte Verbeek. **A:** Adult. **P:** Entertainment. **U:** Home. **Mov-Ent**: Television Series, History--Renaissance, Drama. **Acq:** Purchase. **Dist:** Showtime Ent. $39.98.

The Borgias: The Second Season 2012
Showtime 2011- historical drama. "The Borgia Bull": The Pope makes peace with France and then wants revenge against his enemies while pleading with his sons to stop fighting each other. "The Choice:" After the French are defeated, Pope Alexander sends Cesare to deal with the Sforza family who sided with them. The Pope must also deal with radical Friar Savarona. "The Confession": Juan Borgia is found murdered and his father wants his killer found, but that may lead to someone very close to home. 10 episodes. 517m; DVD, Blu-Ray. **C:** Jeremy Irons; Francois Arnaud; David Oakes; Holliday Grainger; Colm Feore; Joanne Whalley; Lotte Verbeek. **A:** Adult. **P:** Entertainment. **U:** Home. **Mov-Ent**: Television, History--Renaissance, Drama. **Acq:** Purchase. **Dist:** Showtime Ent. $54.99.

The Borgias: The Third Season 2013 (Unrated)
Showtime television series. In "Face of Death", Rufio's plan to kill off the Borgia family does not work when Lucrezia saves her dying father. "The Purge" has the Pope charging Cardinal Sforza with finding out who wanted him dead and cleaning house of the Cardinals he no longer trusts. The episode "Siblings" shows one of the banished Cardinals stealing money from the Vatican and then setting the Treasury on fire. Guilia hosts a banquet in "The Banquet of Chestnuts" to assess the loyalty of the new Cardinals. And Bianca commits suicide in "The Wolf and the Lamb". 10 episodes. 516m; DVD, Blu-Ray. **A:** College-Adult. **P:** Entertainment. **U:** Home. **Acq:** Purchase. **Dist:** Showtime Networks Inc. $49.98.

Boricua Beisbol: The Passion of Puerto Rico 200?
Explores the first two homestands of the 2003 regular season games played by the Montreal Expos at the Hiram Bithorn Stadium in San Juan. Also includes player interviews and other extras. 85m; DVD. **A:** Adult. **P:** Entertainment. **U:** Home. **Spo-Rec**: Baseball, Sports--General. **Acq:** Purchase. **Dist:** Baseball Direct. $14.95.

Boricua's Bond 2000 (R) — ★★
First-time director Lik (at 21) debuts with an urban drama about Puerto Rican-born artist Tommy (Negron) who would rather paint than be an active part of the South Bronx street gangs that surround him. Then Anglo single mom Susan (Karp) and son Allen (played by Lik) move into the 'hood, where they are immediately hasseled. Tommy befriends Allen but there's a string of not entirely unexpected tragedies that change everyone's lives. 95m; VHS. **C:** Val Lik; Frankie Negron; Robyn Karp; Marco Sorisio; Kirk "Sticky Fingaz" Jones; Directed by Val Lik; Written by Val Lik; Cinematography by Brendan Flynt. **A:** Sr. High-Adult. **P:** Entertainment. **U:** Home. **Mov-Ent**: Art & Artists. **Acq:** Purchase.

The Borinqueneers 2007
A documentary about the Puerto Rican 65th infantry Regiment, the only all-Hispanic unit in U.S. history. The DVD also has a Spanish language version of the film. 78m; VHS, DVD. **A:** Sr. High-Adult. **P:** Education. **U:** Home, Institution. **L:** English, Spanish. **Gen-Edu**: Documentary Films, Military History. **Acq:** Purchase, Rent/Lease. **Dist:** The Cinema Guild. $350.00.

Boris and Natasha: The Movie 1992 (PG) — ★½
The two inept spies from the classic TV cartoon "The Adventures of Rocky and Bullwinkle" star in this mediocre live-action comedy. These nogoodniks are sent by "Fearless Leader" to America and encounter the usual misadventures. For true fun watch the original animated versions. Never released theatrically; it aired for the first time on cable TV. 88m; VHS, CC. **C:** Sally Kellerman; Dave Thomas; Paxton Whitehead; Andrea Martin; Alex Rocco; Larry Cedar; Arye Gross; Christopher Neame; Anthony Newley; Cameo(s) John Candy; John Travolta; Charles Martin Smith; Directed by Charles Martin Smith. **A:** Jr. High-Adult. **P:** Entertainment. **U:** Home. **Mov-Ent**: Action-Adventure. **Acq:** Purchase. **Dist:** New Line Home Video. $19.95.

Boris Godunov 1954
A filmed version of the Mussorgsky opera about the rise and fall of Russian czar Boris Godunov. 108m/B/W; VHS. **C:** Alexander Pirogov. **Pr:** Corinth Films. **A:** College-Adult. **P:** Entertainment. **U:** Home. **Fin-Art**: Performing Arts, Opera. **Acq:** Purchase. **Dist:** Music Video Distributors. $49.95.

Boris Godunov 1978
The Bolshoi Opera perform, in Russian, the classic Rimsky-Korsakov opera, about the famous mad czar. Subtitled in English. In HiFi Stereo. 181m; VHS. **Pr:** Bolshoi Opera. **A:** Family. **P:** Entertainment. **U:** Home. **L:** English, Russian. **Fin-Art**: Performing Arts, Opera. **Acq:** Purchase. **Dist:** Music Video Distributors; Kultur International Films Ltd., Inc.; Home Vision Cinema. $59.96.

B.O.R.N. 1988 (R) — ★½
Hagen uncovers an underground network of doctors who kill people and sell the body parts and organs. 90m; VHS. **C:** Ross Hagen; P.J. Soles; William (Bill) Smith; Hoke Howell; Russ Tamblyn; Amanda Blake; Clint Howard; Rance Howard; Debra Lamb; Directed by Ross Hagen. **Pr:** Prism Entertainment; Movie Outfit. **A:** Sr. High-Adult. **P:** Entertainment. **U:** Home. **Mov-Ent**: Mystery & Suspense, Hospitals. **Acq:** Purchase. **Dist:** Amazon.com Inc. $79.95.

Born Again 1978
An anthropomorphic turtle is born in the ocean and returns naked as a minotaur in this experimental video. 6m; VHS, 3/4 U. **Pr:** John Mitchell; Pumps Video. **A:** College-Adult. **P:** Entertainment. **U:** Institution. **Fin-Art**: Performing Arts, Video. **Acq:** Rent/Lease. **Dist:** Video Out Distribution.

Born Again 1978 — ★★
Adaptation of Watergate criminal Charles Colson's biography of his becoming a born again Christian. Standard TV biopic stuff. 110m; VHS, DVD. **C:** Dean Jones; Anne Francis; Dana Andrews; George Brent; Directed by Irving Rapper; Written by Walter Bloch; Cinematography by Harry Stradling, Jr.; Music by Les Baxter. **Pr:** Avco Embassy. **A:** Family. **P:** Entertainment. **U:** Home. **Mov-Ent**: Biography. **Acq:** Purchase. **Dist:** Crown Entertainment. $24.99.

Born Again 1989
R.C. Sproul gives an explanation of what is involved in the Christian rebirth process. 180m; VHS, 3/4 U. **Pr:** Ligonier Valley

Study Center. **A:** Sr. High-Adult. **P:** Religious. **U:** Institution, Home. **Gen-Edu:** Religion. **Acq:** Purchase, Rent/Lease. **Dist:** Ligonier Ministries Inc. $79.00.

Born American 1986 (R) — ★
Pre-Glasnost flick about teenagers vacationing in Finland who "accidentally" cross the Russian border. There they battle the Red Plague. Melodramatic and heavily politicized. Original release banned in Finland. 95m; VHS, DVD. **C:** Mike Norris; Steve Durham; David Coburn; Thalmus Rasulala; Albert Salmi; Directed by Renny Harlin. **Pr:** Concorde Pictures. **A:** College-Adult. **P:** Entertainment. **U:** Home. **Mov-Ent:** Propaganda. **Acq:** Purchase. **Dist:** Movies Unlimited. $9.99.

Born Bad 1997 (R) — ★★
Teens bungle a bank robbery and hold up in the bank with hostages. The town sheriff wants to end the standoff calmly but the teens' hot-headed leader won't surrender. 84m; VHS, DVD. **C:** James Remar; Corey Feldman; Taylor Nichols; Justin Walker; Heidi Noelle Lenhardt; Directed by Jeff Yonis. **Pr:** Concorde Pictures. **A:** Sr. High-Adult. **P:** Entertainment. **U:** Home. **Mov-Ent:** Adolescence. **Acq:** Purchase.

Born Bad 2011 (Unrated) — ★
In this remarkably nasty Lifetime movie, teenager Brooke is angry at being uprooted by her family's move to a small town and resentful of her stepmother's pregnancy. Naturally, Brooke falls for the first seemingly charming boy to look her way, although Denny quickly reveals himself to be a murderous psycho as well as the leader of a crew of home-invading scumballs. 90m; DVD, Blu-Ray. **C:** Bonnie Dennison; Michael Welch; Meredith Monroe; David Chokachi; Parker Coppins; Bill Oberst, Jr.; Directed by Jared Cohn; Written by Jared Cohn; Cinematography by Alexander Yellen; Music by Chris Ridenhour. **A:** Sr. High-Adult. **P:** Entertainment. **U:** Home. **Mov-Ent:** TV Movies, Pregnancy. **Acq:** Purchase. **Dist:** The Asylum.

Born Beautiful 1982 — ★★½
Made for TV. Beautiful young women come to New York, hoping to strike it rich in the world of modeling. At the same time, a still beautiful, but older and overexposed model comes to grips with a change in her career. Well-told, but sugar-coated. 100m; VHS. **C:** Erin Gray; Ed Marinaro; Polly Bergen; Lori Singer; Ellen Barber; Judith Barcroft; Michael Higgins; Directed by Harvey Hart; Music by Brad Fiedel. **Pr:** Proctor & Gamble; Telecom. **A:** Sr. High-Adult. **P:** Entertainment. **U:** Home. **Mov-Ent:** TV Movies. **Acq:** Purchase. **Dist:** Warner Home Video, Inc.

Born Dying 1983
This tape discusses the non-treatment of newborn handicapped babies. A discussion guide is included. 20m; VHS, 3/4 U. **Pr:** Norman E. Baxley. **A:** Adult. **P:** Professional. **U:** Institution, CCTV, Home, SURA. **Hea-Sci:** Documentary Films, Handicapped, Ethics & Morals. **Acq:** Purchase. **Dist:** Leo Media, Inc. $385.00.

Born for Hard Luck 1988
This film looks into the life of Arthur "Peg Leg Sam" Jackson, a medicine-show entertainer. 29m/B/W; VHS, 3/4 U, Special order formats. **Pr:** Davenport Films. **A:** Jr. High-Adult. **P:** Education. **U:** Institution, Home, SURA. **Gen-Edu:** Documentary Films, Biography, Black Culture. **Acq:** Purchase. **Dist:** Davenport Films. $80.00.

Born for Hell 1976 (Unrated) — ★
A maniac Vietnam vet kills nurses, leaving no clues for the police to follow. 90m; VHS, DVD. **C:** Matthieu Carriere; Carole Laure; Directed by Denis Heroux. **A:** Jr. High-Adult. **P:** Entertainment. **U:** Home. **Mov-Ent:** Mystery & Suspense, Veterans. **Acq:** Purchase. **Dist:** Mill Creek Entertainment L.L.C. $19.98.

Born Free 1966 (Unrated) — ★★★
The touching story of a game warden in Kenya and his wife raising Elsa the orphaned lion cub. When the cub reaches maturity, they work to return her to life in the wild. Great family entertainment based on Joy Adamson's book. Theme song became a hit. 95m; VHS, DVD. **C:** Virginia McKenna; Bill Travers; Directed by James Hill; Written by Lester Cole; Music by John Barry. **Pr:** Columbia Pictures. **A:** Family. **P:** Entertainment. **U:** Home. **Mov-Ent:** Animals, Adoption, Family Viewing. **Awds:** Oscars '66: Orig. Score, Song ("Born Free"). **Acq:** Purchase. **Dist:** Sony Pictures Home Entertainment Inc.; Home Vision Cinema. $14.95.
Songs: Born Free.

Born Free: The Complete Series 1974
NBC adventure series based on the 1966 movie that follows the work of George and Joy Adamson, game wardens who run a nature reserve in Kenya. 13 episodes. 639m; DVD. **C:** Gary Collins; Diana Muldaur. **A:** Family. **P:** Entertainment. **U:** Home. **L:** English. **Mov-Ent:** Africa, Television Series. **Acq:** Purchase. **Dist:** WarnerArchive.com. $38.99.

Born Hooked 197?
Stresses the need for prenatal care of mothers addicted to heroin or methadone and deals with the impact of withdrawal on the newborn. 14m; 3/4 U. **Pr:** March of Dimes. **A:** Sr. High-Adult. **P:** Education. **U:** Institution, CCTV, CATV. **Hea-Sci:** Documentary Films, Pregnancy, Drug Abuse. **Acq:** Free Loan. **Dist:** March of Dimes.

Born in America 1990 (Unrated) — ★
A young orphan is adopted by an undertaker. The boy grows up enveloped by his guardian's business and, when things are slow, works to bring in business himself. 90m; VHS. **C:** James Westerfield; Glen Lee; Virgil Frye; Venetia Vianello; Directed by Jose Antonio Bolanos. **A:** Jr. High-Adult. **P:** Entertainment. **U:** Home. **Mov-Ent:** Western, Adoption. **Acq:** Purchase. **Dist:** No Longer Available.

Born in Berlin 1991
Documentary tracing the lives of three young Jewish girls of the 1930s. Studies the women today as they pursue careers in poetry and writing. German, English, Swedish and Hebrew with English subtitles. 85m; VHS. **A:** Jr. High-Adult. **P:** Education. **U:** Institution. **Gen-Edu:** Documentary Films, Judaism. **Acq:** Purchase. **Dist:** National Center for Jewish Film. $200.

Born in Brazil 2002 (Unrated)
Documents the before, during, and after of five pregnant women and their doctors in Porto Alegre, Brazil to demonstrate the connection between birth and technology and the new pressures it brings to modern society as more women view cesareans as a painless more predictable way to give birth. 52m; DVD. **A:** Adult. **P:** Education. **U:** Institution. **Gen-Edu:** Pregnancy, Women. **Acq:** Purchase. **Dist:** Third World Newsreel. $250.

Born in East L.A. 1987 (R) — ★★
Marin brings his Bruce Springsteen-parody song to life as he plays a mistakenly deported illegal alien who struggles to return to the U.S. Suprisingly resolute effort by the usually self-exploiting Mexican-American. Stern is the American expatriate who helps him get back and Lopez is the love interest who stalls him. 85m; VHS, DVD. **C:** Richard "Cheech" Marin; Daniel Stern; Paul Rodriguez; Jan-Michael Vincent; Kamala Lopez; Tony Plana; Vic Trevino; A. Martinez; Directed by Richard "Cheech" Marin; Written by Richard "Cheech" Marin; Cinematography by Alex Phillips, Jr.; Music by Lee Holdridge. **Pr:** Mark Huffam. **A:** Sr. High-Adult. **P:** Entertainment. **U:** Home. **Mov-Ent:** Illegal Immigration, Satire & Parody. **Acq:** Purchase. **Dist:** Facets Multimedia Inc. $14.95.

Born in Flames 1983 (Unrated)
An acclaimed futuristic feminist film about women who band together in an effort to gain control of the state owned media. 90m; VHS. **C:** Directed by Lizzie Borden; Written by Lizzie Borden. **Pr:** Lizzie Borden; Lizzie Borden. **A:** College-Adult. **P:** Entertainment. **U:** Home. **Fin-Art:** Film--Avant-Garde, Women. **Acq:** Purchase. **Dist:** First Run/Icarus Films.

Born in '45 1965 (Unrated) — ★★
Auto mechanic Alfred and maternity nurse Lisa are newlyweds. However, they might not be wed much longer as they find marital adjustments (especially in their tiny apartment) difficult to make. Alfred goes wandering around Berlin, hoping to make some decisions, but the film ends with their future uncertain. German with subtitles. 94m/B/W; DVD. **C:** Monika Hildebrand; Rolf Romer; Paul Eichbaum; Holger Mahlich; Directed by Jurgen Bottcher; Written by Jurgen Bottcher; Cinematography by Roland Graf; Music by Klaus Poche. **A:** College-Adult. **P:** Entertainment. **U:** Home. **L:** German. **Mov-Ent. Acq:** Purchase. **Dist:** First Run Features.

Born in 68 2008 (Unrated) — ★★
Overstuffed epic traces the lives of a French family from the Paris student rebellions of 1968 to the gay rights movement in the late 1980s. Twenty-year-olds Catherine, Yves, and Herve are all involved in leftist student groups, although they eventually leave the city for a rural commune. Friendships fray and Herve tires of the pastoral life while Catherine and Yves stay to raise their two children, Boris and Ludmilla. French with subtitles. 166m; DVD. **C:** Laetitia Casta; Yannick Renier; Yann Tregouet; Theo Frilet; Edouard Collin; Sabrina Seyvecou; Marc Citti; Kate Moran; Directed by Jacques Martineau; Olivier Ducastel; Written by Jacques Martineau; Olivier Ducastel; Catherine Corsini; Guillaume Le Touze; Cinematography by Mathieu Poirot-Delpech; Music by Philippe Miller. **A:** College-Adult. **P:** Entertainment. **U:** Home. **L:** French. **Mov-Ent:** Agriculture. **Acq:** Purchase. **Dist:** Strand Releasing.

Born Innocent 1974 (Unrated) — ★½
As if "The Exorcist" weren't bad enough, Blair is back for more abuse-on-film, this time as a 14-year-old runaway from a dysfunctional family who lands in a reform school for girls. There, she must struggle to be as brutal as her peers in order to survive. Fairly tame by today's standards, but controversial at its made-for-TV premiere, chiefly due to a rape scene involving a broom handle. First trip up the river for Blair. 92m; VHS, DVD. **C:** Linda Blair; Joanna Miles; Kim Hunter; Richard Jaeckel; Janit Baldwin; Mitch Vogel; Directed by Donald Wrye; Music by Fred Karlin. **Pr:** Tomorrow Entertainment Inc; National Broadcasting Company. **A:** Sr. High-Adult. **P:** Entertainment. **U:** Home. **Mov-Ent:** Runaways, Rape, TV Movies. **Acq:** Purchase. **Dist:** Unknown Distributor.

Born Into Brothels: Calcutta's Red Light Kids 2004 (R) — ★★½
Photojournalist Zana Briski presents the world of Calcutta prostitution through the eyes and pictures of the children who live it. Not only does she give them photography instruction as a means to help lift them from their current situation, she goes a step further in trying to place them in boarding school—much to the chagrin of the opposing parents. The subject is nothing new but her drive to make a change in these doomed lives is commendable and may hopefully inspire others. 85m; DVD. **C:** Directed by Zana Briski; Ross Kauffman; Written by Zana Briski; Ross Kauffman; Cinematography by Zana Briski; Ross Kauffman; Music by John McDowell. **Pr:** Zana Briski; Ross Kauffman. **A:** Sr. High-Adult. **P:** Entertainment. **U:** Home. **L:** English. **Mov-Ent:** Documentary Films, India, Prostitution. **Awds:** Oscars '04: Feature Doc. **Acq:** Purchase. **Dist:** ThinkFilm Company Inc.

Born Killer 1989 (Unrated) — ★½
Teenagers in the woods meet up with murderous escaped convicts. 90m; VHS. **C:** Francine Lapensee; Fritz Matthews; Ted Prior; Adam Tucker; Directed by Kimberly Casey. **Pr:** Fritz Matthews. **A:** Sr. High-Adult. **P:** Entertainment. **U:** Home. **Mov-Ent. Acq:** Purchase. **Dist:** Amazon.com Inc. $14.95.

Born Killers 2005 (R) — ★
Grubby, flashback-heavy story about lowlifes. Brothers John (Muxworthy) and Michael (Mann) were raised by their sociopathic father (Sizemore), who made his living robbing and killing his victims. His sons follow in his footsteps, although Michael prefers to bed the young women who are his targets first, and he becomes fond of Archer (Garner) to the point of balking at killing her. John has his own dilemma when he discovers they have a half-sister Gertie (German), whom he immediately falls into reciprocated lust with. 87m; DVD. **C:** Jake Muxworthy; Gabriel Mann; Tom Sizemore; Kelli Garner; Lauren German; Directed by Morgan J. Freeman; Written by Kendall Delcambre; Cinematography by Nancy Schreiber; Music by Jim Lang. **A:** Sr. High-Adult. **P:** Entertainment. **U:** Home. **Mov-Ent. Acq:** Purchase. **Dist:** Lions Gate Entertainment Inc.

Born Losers 1967 (PG) — ★★
The original "Billy Jack" film in which the Indian martial arts expert takes on a group of incorrigible bikers bothering some California babes and runs afoul of the law. Classic drive-in fare. 112m; VHS, DVD. **C:** Tom Laughlin; Elizabeth James; Jeremy Slate; William Wellman, Jr.; Robert Tessier; Jane Russell; Stuart Lancaster; Edwin Cook; Jeff Cooper; Directed by Tom Laughlin; Written by Tom Laughlin; E. James Lloyd; Cinematography by Gregory Sandor. **Pr:** American International Pictures. **A:** Jr. High-Adult. **P:** Entertainment. **U:** Home. **Mov-Ent:** Martial Arts, Native Americans, Motorcycles. **Acq:** Purchase. **Dist:** Lions Gate Television Corp. $59.95.

Born of Earth 2008 (R) — ★
Boring horror. After his wife is murdered and his children kidnapped, Danny Kessler (Baldwin) is determined to expose the secrets of Prophet Hills, which include an ancient bloodthirsty race of underground-dwelling creatures and a cover-up. 84m; DVD. **C:** Daniel Baldwin; James Russo; Brad Dourif; Shannon Zeller; Jennifer Kincer; Directed by Tommy Brunswick; Written by Joseph Thompson; Cinematography by Michael Kudreiko. **A:** Sr. High-Adult. **P:** Entertainment. **U:** Home. **Mov-Ent. Acq:** Purchase. **Dist:** Entertainment One US LP.

Born of Fire 1987 (R) — ★½
A flutist investigating his father's death seeks the Master Musician; his search leads him to the volcanic (and supernatural) mountains of Turkey. 84m; VHS, DVD. **C:** Peter Firth; Susan Crowley; Stephan Kalipha; Directed by Jamil Dehlavi; Music by Colin Towns. **Pr:** Therese Pickard; Jamil Dehlavi. **A:** Sr. High-Adult. **P:** Entertainment. **U:** Home. **Mov-Ent:** Horror, Occult Sciences. **Acq:** Purchase. **Dist:** Mondo Macabro. $79.95.

Born of Fire, Born of the Sea 19??
Explains the formation, natural history, and ecosystem of the Hawaiian Islands. 20m; VHS. **A:** Jr. High-Adult. **P:** Education. **U:** Home, Institution. **Hea-Sci:** Documentary Films, U.S. States, Ecology & Environment. **Acq:** Purchase. **Dist:** Harpers Ferry Historical Association. $17.95.

Born on the Fourth of July 1989 (R) — ★★★½
A riveting meditation on American life affected by the Vietnam War, based on the real-life, bestselling experiences of Ron Kovic, though some facts are subtly changed. The film follows him as he develops from a naive recruit to an angry, wheelchair-bound paraplegic to an active antiwar protestor. Well-acted and generally lauded; Kovic co-wrote the screenplay and appears as a war veteran in the opening parade sequence. 145m; VHS, DVD, Blu-Ray, HD-DVD, Wide, CC. **C:** Tom Cruise; Kyra Sedgwick; Raymond J. Barry; Jerry Levine; Tom Berenger; Willem Dafoe; Frank Whaley; John Getz; Caroline Kava; Bryan Larkin; Abbie Hoffman; Stephen Baldwin; Josh Evans; Dale Dye; William Baldwin; Don "The Dragon" Wilson; Vivica A. Fox; Holly Marie Combs; Tom Sizemore; Daniel Baldwin; Ron Kovic; Bill Allen; Cameo(s) Oliver Stone; Directed by Oliver Stone; Written by Oliver Stone; Cinematography by Robert Richardson; Music by John Williams. **Pr:** Mark Huffam; Oliver Stone; Oliver Stone. **A:** College-Adult. **P:** Entertainment. **U:** Home. **Mov-Ent:** Vietnam War, Handicapped, Biography. **Awds:** Oscars '89: Director (Stone), Film Editing; Directors Guild '89: Director (Stone); Golden Globes '90: Actor--Drama (Cruise), Director (Stone), Film--Drama, Screenplay. **Acq:** Purchase. **Dist:** Facets Multimedia Inc.; Baker and Taylor. $14.95.

Born Reckless 1959 — ★½
Van Doren plays a singer working the rodeo circuit who falls for aging rider Richards. Not bad enough to be funny, however, Van Doren shows an incredible lack of talent while singing several tunes. 79m/B/W; VHS. **C:** Mamie Van Doren; Jeff Richards; Arthur Hunnicutt; Carol Ohmart; Donald (Don "Red") Barry; Nacho Galindo; Directed by Howard W. Koch. **Pr:** Aubrey Schenck; Warner Bros. **A:** Sr. High-Adult. **P:** Entertainment. **U:** Home. **Mov-Ent:** Rodeos. **Acq:** Purchase. **Dist:** Movies Unlimited. $19.99.
Songs: Song of the Rodeo; Born Reckless; A Little Longer; Home Type Girl; Separate the Men from the Boys; Something to Dream About; You, Lovable You.

Born Romantic 2000 (R) — ★★
Six lonely Londoners converge at a salsa club hoping to find a little romance. There's screwy Jocelyn (McCormack), no-nonsense Mo (Horrocks), uptight Eleanor (Williams), would-be Lothario Frank (Ferguson), awkward Eddie (Mistry), and lovelorn Fergus (Morrissey). Cabbie Jimmy (Lester) offers advice. Enjoyable (if predictable) romantic comedy. 97m; VHS, DVD, Wide. **C:** Craig Ferguson; Adrian Lester; Catherine McCormack; Jimi Mistry; David Morrissey; Olivia Williams; Jane Horrocks; Hermione Norris; Ian Hart; Kenneth Cranham; Paddy Considine; Directed by David Kane; Written by David Kane;

Cinematography by Robert Alazraki; Music by Simon Boswell. **Pr:** Michele Camarda; BBC Films; Harvest Films; Kismet Film Company; United Artists. **A:** Sr. High-Adult. **P:** Entertainment. **U:** Home. **Mov-Ent:** Comedy--Romantic, Nightclubs, Sex & Sexuality. **Acq:** Purchase. **Dist:** MGM Home Entertainment.

Born to Be Bad 1950 (Unrated) — ★★½
Fontaine, an opportunistic woman who was b-b-born to be b-b-bad, attempts to steal a wealthy business man away from his wife while carrying on an affair with a novelist. Ray's direction (he's best known for "Rebel Without a Cause," filmed five years later) prevents the film from succumbing to standard Hollywood formula. 93m/B/W; DVD. **C:** Joan Fontaine; Robert Ryan; Zachary Scott; Joan Leslie; Mel Ferrer; Directed by Nicholas Ray. **Pr:** RKO. **A:** College-Adult. **P:** Entertainment. **U:** Home. **Mov-Ent:** Drama. **Acq:** Purchase. **Dist:** WarnerArchive.com. $19.98.

Born to Be Blind 2003 (Unrated)
Documentary tells the story of three blind sisters, street singers in Campina Grande, Brazil. Shows their faith despite a life of poverty, and their brief rise as celebrities as a result of the documentary. 84m. **C:** Directed by Roberto Berliner; Written by Mauricio Lissovsky; Cinematography by Jacques Cheuiche. **Pr:** Renato Pereira; Rodrigo Letier; Paola Vieira; TV Zero. **P:** Entertainment. **U:** Home. **L:** Portuguese. **Mov-Ent:** Documentary Films, Blindness, South America. **Dist:** Not Yet Released.

Born to Be Wild 1938 — ★★
A pair of truck drivers are commissioned to deliver a shipment of dynamite. The dynamite will be used to destroy a dam, preventing the surrounding land from falling into the hands of unscrupulous land barons. Good action picture thanks to the cast. 66m/B/W; VHS, DVD. **C:** Ralph Byrd; Doris Weston; Ward Bond; Robert Emmett Keane; Bentley Hewlett; Charles Williams; Directed by Joseph Kane. **Pr:** Republic. **A:** Jr. High-Adult. **P:** Entertainment. **U:** Home. **Mov-Ent. Acq:** Purchase. **Dist:** Sinister Cinema; Rex Miller Artisan Studio. $16.95.

Born to Be Wild 1995 (PG) — ★½
Rebellious teenager Rick (Hornoff) befriends Katie, the three-year-old gorilla his behaviorial scientist mom (Shaver) is studying. When Katie's owner (Boyle) decides she would make a better sideshow attraction than science project, Rick busts her out and they head for the Canadian border. Animal slapstick and bodily function jokes ensue as the chase continues. "Free Willy"-inspired plot and primate hijinks should keep young kids interested, but anyone over the age of nine probably won't be too impressed. 98m; VHS, DVD, CC. **C:** Wil Horneff; Helen Shaver; Peter Boyle; Jean Marie Barnwell; John C. McGinley; Marvin J. McIntyre; Thomas F. Wilson; Directed by John Gray; Written by John Bunzel; Paul Young; Cinematography by Donald M. Morgan. **Pr:** Brian Reilly; Robert Newmyer; Jeffrey Silver; Outlaw Productions; Warner Bros. **A:** Jr. High-Adult. **P:** Entertainment. **U:** Home. **Mov-Ent:** Adolescence, Animals, Family Viewing. **Acq:** Purchase. **Dist:** Warner Home Video, Inc. $19.99.

Born to Bondage: Women in India 2000
Looks at the difficult lives of women in India. After a decade of feminism, police still look the other way while women are abused, raped, killed, and even burned alive. 40m; VHS. **A:** Sr. High-Adult. **P:** Education. **U:** Institution. **Gen-Edu:** India, Women. **Acq:** Purchase, Rent/Lease. **Dist:** Filmakers Library Inc. $295.00.

Born to Boogie 1972 (Unrated) — ★★
A concert, a chronicle, and a tribute, "Born To Boogie" is about Marc Bolan and his band T. Rex. The film, which features concert footage from a 1972 concert at the Wembley Empire Pool in London, chronicles the glitter rock era and the next wave of British rock and roll, and pays tribute to Bolan, who died in 1977 just as he was starting a comeback. Ringo Starr and Elton John join T. Rex in the studio for "Children of the Revolution" and "Tutti-Frutti" as well as a psychadelic soiree where Bolan plays acoustic versions of his hits. This film was never released in the United States. 75m; VHS, DVD. **C:** Marc Bolan; Elton John; Ringo Starr; Directed by Ringo Starr. **Pr:** Ringo Starr; Ringo Starr. **A:** College-Adult. **P:** Entertainment. **U:** Home. **Mov-Ent:** Documentary Films, Music--Pop/Rock, Music--Performance. **Acq:** Purchase, Rent/Lease. **Dist:** MPI Media Group; Music Video Distributors. $29.98.

Born to Dance 1936 — ★★½
A quintessential MGM 1930s dance musical, wherein a beautiful dancer gets a sailor and a big break in a show. Great songs by Cole Porter sung in a less than great manner by a gangly Stewart. Powell's first starring vehicle. 108m/B/W; VHS, DVD. **C:** Eleanor Powell; James Stewart; Virginia Bruce; Una Merkel; Frances Langford; Sid Silvers; Raymond Walburn; Reginald Gardiner; Buddy Ebsen; Directed by Roy Del Ruth; Music by Cole Porter; Lyrics by Cole Porter. **Pr:** MGM. **A:** Family. **P:** Entertainment. **U:** Home. **Mov-Ent:** Musical, Romance, Dance. **Acq:** Purchase. **Dist:** Warner Home Video, Inc. $19.98.
Songs: Love Me Love My Pekinese; I've Got You Under My Skin; Hey Babe Hey; Easy to Love; Rolling Home; Rap Tap on Wood; Entrance of Lucy James; Swingin' the Jinx Away.

Born to Fight 2007 (Unrated) — ★½
Born to Fight is a remake in name only of a film from the 80's, both of which were done by Panna Rittikrai ("Ong-bak"). Deaw (Dan Chupong) is a cop attending a charity event sponsored by Thailands Olympic athletes of which his sister Nui (Taekwondo champion Kessarin Ektawatkul) is one. When the town the event is held in is held hostage by nuclear armed terrorists, Deaw must unite the athletes in an attempt to free the hostages. While the plot isn't complicated, all the actors (age 8 to 80) do their own stunts, some of which are incredible. 96m; DVD. **C:** Nappon Gomarachun; Santisuk Promsiri; Dan Chupong; Piyapong Piew-on; Somrak Khamsing; Amornthep Waewsang; Suebsak Pansueb; Nantaway Wongwanichislip; Kessarin Ektawatkul; Rattaporn Khemtong; Chatthapong Pantanaunkal; Sasisa Jindamanee; Directed by Panna Rittikrai; Written by Panna Rittikrai; Morakat Kaewthanek; Thanapat Taweesuk; Cinematography by Surachet Thongmee; Music by Traithep Wongpaiboon. **A:** Sr. High-Adult. **P:** Entertainment. **U:** Home. **L:** English, Spanish, Thai. **Mov-Ent:** Martial Arts. **Acq:** Purchase. **Dist:** Sony Pictures Home Entertainment Inc. $19.95.

Born to Film 1984
A deeply personal meditation on childhood by avant-garde filmmaker Lyon. Juxtaposes images of his son with footage of himself as a boy. 33m/B/W; VHS. **C:** Directed by Danny Lyon. **Pr:** Danny Lyon. **A:** College-Adult. **P:** Entertainment. **U:** Home. **Mov-Ent:** Documentary Films, Children, Film--Avant-Garde. **Acq:** Purchase. **Dist:** Facets Multimedia Inc.; Bleak Beauty Video. $59.00.

Born to Kill 1947 (Unrated) — ★★★
A ruthless killer marries a girl for her money. Minor tough-as-nails film noir exemplifying Tierney's stone-faced human-devil film persona. 92m/B/W; VHS, DVD. **C:** Lawrence Tierney; Claire Trevor; Walter Slezak; Elisha Cook, Jr.; Directed by Robert Wise. **Pr:** RKO. **A:** Jr. High-Adult. **P:** Entertainment. **U:** Home. **Mov-Ent:** Mystery & Suspense. **Acq:** Purchase. **Dist:** Turner Broadcasting System Inc. $19.98.

Born to Lose 1999 (Unrated) — ★★
The Spoilers are an L.A. punk back led by singer Stevie Monroe (Rye). They're an underground success but can't break out of the music ghetto until public relations gal Lisa (Ashton) takes an interest in Stevie. Too bad she's a junkie who pulls the singer into a downward spiral that effectively destroys the band as well. Filmed in a mock-documentary style. 80m; VHS, DVD. **C:** Joseph Rye; Elyse Ashton; Francis Fallon; Directed by Doug Cawker; Written by Doug Cawker; Howard Roth; Cinematography by John Rhode; Music by Greg Kuehn. **A:** Sr. High-Adult. **P:** Entertainment. **U:** Home. **Mov-Ent:** Drug Abuse. **Acq:** Purchase. **Dist:** Vanguard International Cinema, Inc.

Born to Race 1988 (R) — ★
In the world of competitive auto racing, a beautiful engineer is kidnapped for her new controversial engine design. 95m; VHS. **C:** Joseph Bottoms; George Kennedy; Marc Singer; Marla Heasly; Directed by James Fargo. **Pr:** MGM Home Entertainment. **A:** Sr. High-Adult. **P:** Entertainment. **U:** Home. **Mov-Ent:** Automobiles--Racing. **Acq:** Purchase. **Dist:** $79.98.

Born 2 Race 2011 (PG-13) — ★★
Solid action with a familiar story. Teen street racer Danny Krueger gets in trouble after an accident and is sent to live with his estranged father, Frank. He immediately gets involved in a local drag race, but if Danny wants to win he has to accept help from his dad--a recovering alcoholic and former NASCAR driver. 99m; DVD, Blu-Ray. **C:** Joseph Cross; John Pyper-Ferguson; Sherry Stringfield; Brando Eaton; Spencer Breslin; Grant Show; Directed by Alex Ranarivelo; Written by Alex Ranarivelo; Cinematography by Reuben Steinberg; Music by Jamie Christopherson. **A:** Jr. High-Adult. **P:** Entertainment. **U:** Home. **L:** English. **Mov-Ent:** Adolescence, Alcoholism, Automobiles--Racing. **Acq:** Purchase. **Dist:** ARC Entertainment, LLC.

Born to Rage 2010 (Unrated)
Scientists now believe that it is possible that some people carry what is known as a "warrior gene" that could explain why they experience more bouts of rage and violent behavior than other people. While most still believe that rage and violence are learned behaviors, narrator Henry Rollins follows scientists as they study a diverse group of people that ranges from gang members and outlaw bikers to Buddhist monks (as well as Rollins himself) to determine how many of them have the "warrior gene" and how it might have affected their behavior. 50m; DVD. **A:** Family. **P:** Education, Entertainment. **U:** Home, Institution. **Mov-Ent:** Documentary Films, Genetics, Medical Education. **Acq:** Purchase. **Dist:** $19.95.

Born to Raise Hell 2010 (R) — ★
Unimpressive Seagal flick with a limited amount of martial arts action and a nonsensical title. Interpol agent Samuel Axel is assigned to a Bucharest task force targeting Russian mobster Dimitri and his ex-partner, gypsy Costel. The situation goes bad and Axel decides to get justice in his own way. 98m; DVD. **C:** Steven Seagal; Dan Badarau; Darren Shahlavi; D. Neil Mark; George Remes; Claudiu Bleont; Directed by Lauro Chartrand; Written by Steven Seagal; Cinematography by Eric Goldstein; Music by Michael Neilson. **A:** Sr. High-Adult. **P:** Entertainment. **U:** Home. **Mov-Ent:** Martial Arts. **Acq:** Purchase. **Dist:** Paramount Pictures Corp.

Born to Ride 1991 (PG) — ★★
A biker rebel joins the Army prior to WWII in order to escape a prison term after a good ol' boy brush with the law. He shuns Army discipline, but proves himself in action as the leader of a scout troup for the Army's motorcycle cavalry brigade. Available with Spanish subtitles. 88m; VHS, Streaming, CC. **C:** John Stamos; John Stockwell; Teri Polo; Kris Kamm; Directed by Graham Baker. **Pr:** Fred Weintraub. **A:** Jr. High-Adult. **P:** Entertainment. **U:** Home. **Mov-Ent:** Motorcycles. **Acq:** Purchase, Rent/Lease. **Dist:** Warner Home Video, Inc. $9.99.

Born to Ride 2011 (Unrated) — **Bomb!**
Plot is convoluted and frequently senseless and even the actors don't seem to care. Mike (Van Dien) gets his deceased dad's classic chopper out of the garage and takes a road trip with buddy Alex (Muldoon). It soon involves money stolen from a Vietnam vet, a security tape used as blackmail against a crooked senator, and some inept, murderous goons coming after Mike and Alex. 90m; DVD. **C:** Casper Van Dien; Patrick Muldoon; William Forsythe; Theresa Russell; Jack Maxwell; Branscombe Richmond; Kurt Anton; Jamison Jones; Dave Goryl; Directed by James Fargo; Written by Mike Anthony Jones; Robert Vozza; Cinematography by Leo Napolitano; Music by Ched Tolliver. **A:** Sr. High-Adult. **P:** Entertainment. **U:** Home. **Mov-Ent:** Veterans. **Acq:** Purchase. **Dist:** Image Entertainment Inc.

Born to Rock: The T.A.M.I.-T.N.T. Show 1965 (Unrated)
The two vintage video rock films, made in 1964 and 1965, featuring performances by the top artists of the time. Hosted by Berry. 90m; VHS. **Pr:** American International Pictures; Electronovision. **A:** Family. **P:** Entertainment. **U:** Home. **Mov-Ent:** Music--Performance, Music--Pop/Rock, Black Culture. **Acq:** Purchase. **Dist:** Music Video Distributors; Facets Multimedia Inc. $14.95.

Born to Run 1993 — ★★½
Nicky Donatello (Grieco) is a Brooklyn street drag racer who gets mixed up with the mob while trying to rescue his no-account brother. But he still finds time to fall for an uptown model who also happens to be the mobster's girlfriend. 97m; VHS. **C:** Richard Grieco; Jay Acovone; Shelli Lether; Christian Campbell; Brent Stait; Martin Cummins; Wren Roberts; Joe Cortese; Directed by Albert Magnoli; Written by Randall Badat. **Pr:** Lance Hool. **A:** Jr. High-Adult. **P:** Entertainment. **U:** Home. **Mov-Ent:** Crime Drama, Automobiles--Racing, TV Movies. **Acq:** Purchase. **Dist:** Fox Home Entertainment.

Born to Sail 1988
Aboard his 230-foot steel schooner, Alain Colas sails the Atlantic Ocean, coping along the way with weather, equipment and crew. At one point he bravely raises 10,000 square feet of sail to the wind. 51m; VHS. **Pr:** CME Enterprises. **A:** Jr. High-Adult. **P:** Entertainment. **U:** Home. **Spo-Rec:** Sports--General, Documentary Films, Boating. **Acq:** Purchase. **Dist:** Bennett Marine Video. $19.95.

Born to Sing: Vocal Technique 1990
Singers, any style and any level, will find useful pointers in this instructional tape by renowned teachers Elisabeth Howard and Howard Austin. 60m; VHS. **A:** Jr. High-Adult. **P:** Instruction. **U:** Home. **How-Ins:** How-To, Music--Instruction, Singing. **Acq:** Purchase. **Dist:** Music World. $29.95.

Born to Ski 19??
"Born to Ski" contains some of the best extreme skiing from Squaw Valley to Chile. The film also includes some of the most stunning windsurfing footage ever shot in the Gorge, the windsurfer's Mecca. ?m; VHS. **A:** Family. **P:** Entertainment. **U:** Home. **L:** English. **Spo-Rec:** Skiing. **Acq:** Purchase. **Dist:** Black Diamond Films.

Born to Speed 1941 (Unrated) — ★½
The plot's a moldy-oldie even for the times but the pic's worth a look-see for the footage of California's midget car racing. Because his father died in a crash, young Johnny Randall is supposed to stay away from the track. Rather, he dons a mask to hide his identity and becomes a winner on the circuit. But a rival team will do anything to make Johnny lose. 61m/B/W; DVD. **C:** Johnny Sands; Frank Orth; Vivian Austin; Don Castle; Joe Haworth; Directed by Edward L. Cahn; Written by Crane Wilbur; Scott Darling; Cinematography by Jackson Rose; Music by Alvin Levin. **A:** Jr. High-Adult. **P:** Entertainment. **U:** Home. **Mov-Ent:** Automobiles--Racing. **Acq:** Purchase. **Dist:** Alpha Video.

Born to Succeed 19??
Presents young parents sharing experiences reading to their infants and toddlers. 12m; VHS. **A:** Adult. **P:** Education. **U:** Institution. **L:** Spanish. **Gen-Edu:** Children, Language Arts. **Acq:** Purchase. **Dist:** Library Video Network. $30.00.

Born to Swing: The Count Basie Alumni 1989
The richness of swing music Kansas City style is explored. Includes an impromptu jam session. 50m; VHS. **C:** John Hammond; Directed by John Jeremy. **Pr:** Kino International Corporation. **A:** Sr. High-Adult. **P:** Entertainment. **U:** Home. **Mov-Ent:** Music--Performance, Music--Jazz, Black Culture. **Acq:** Purchase. **Dist:** Music Video Distributors; Facets Multimedia Inc.; Rhapsody Films, Inc. $29.95.

Born to Win 1971 (R) — ★★½
A New York hairdresser with an expensive drug habit struggles through life in this well-made comedy drama. Excellent acting from fine cast, and interestingly photographed. Not well received when first released, but worth a look. 90m; VHS, DVD. **C:** George Segal; Karen Black; Paula Prentiss; Hector Elizondo; Robert De Niro; Jay Fletcher; Directed by Ivan Passer; Written by Ivan Passer; David Scott Milton; Cinematography by Jack Priestley; Music by William S. Fisher. **A:** College-Adult. **P:** Entertainment. **U:** Home. **Mov-Ent:** Comedy-Drama, Drugs. **Acq:** Purchase. **Dist:** MGM Home Entertainment. $9.99.

Born Too Soon 1987
The care and treatment that premature babies need is explored. 27m; VHS, 3/4 U. **Pr:** Brigham Young University. **A:** Jr. High-Adult. **P:** Education. **U:** Institution, SURA. **Hea-Sci:** Infants, Childbirth. **Acq:** Purchase, Trade-in. **Dist:** Encyclopedia Britannica. $230.00.

Born Under Libra 2001 (Unrated) — ★★
In Tehran, Daniel falls in love with fellow university student Mahtab, whose father is pushing for segregated classes. Daniel associates with the religious while Mahtab sides with the reformers. Despite their differences, the romance blossoms but trouble has them fleeing the city. Farsi with subtitles. 94m; DVD. **C:** Mohammad Reza Forutan; Mitra Hajjar; Directed by Ahmad Reza Darvish; Written by Ahmad Reza Darvish; Cinematography by Adam Herschman; Music by Mohammad Reza Aligholi.

A: College-Adult. P: Entertainment. U: Home. L: Farsi. Mov-Ent: Drama. Acq: Purchase. Dist: Facets Multimedia Inc.

Born Wild 1995 (PG) — ★★½
Documentary filmmaker Christine Shaye (Shields) has just gotten her first important assignment from overbearing boss Dan Walker (Sheen), which is to capture the beauty of Africa. Christine arrives at the South African game preserve of Londolozi where she meets passionate conservationist John Varty (who plays himself). Varty has filmed one leopard family for 12 years but when the mother leopard is killed, he violates his own ethical code when he rescues her two orphaned cubs. 98m; VHS, CC. **C:** Brooke Shields; Martin Sheen; John Varty; David Keith; Directed by Duncan McLachlan; Written by Duncan McLachlan; Andrea Buck. **Pr:** Duncan McLachlan; Andrea Buck; Dave Varty; Peter Gallo; John Varty; Leopard Entertainment; MDP Worldwide. **A:** Family. **P:** Entertainment. **U:** Home. **Mov-Ent:** Action-Adventure, Animals, Africa. **Acq:** Purchase. **Dist:** Sony Pictures Home Entertainment Inc.

Born Yesterday 1950 — ★★★½
Ambitious junk dealer Harry Brock (Crawford) is in love with smart but uneducated Billie Dawn (Holliday). He hires newspaperman Paul Verrall (Holden) to teach her the finer points of etiquette. During their sessions, they fall in love and Billie realizes how she has been used by Brock. She retaliates against him and gets to deliver that now-famous line: "Do me a favor, drop dead." Holliday is a solid gold charmer as the not-so-dumb blonde, in the role she originated in Garson Kanin's Broadway play. Remade in 1993. 103m/B/W; VHS, DVD, CC. **C:** Judy Holliday; Broderick Crawford; William Holden; Howard St. John; Frank Otto; Larry Oliver; Barbara Brown; Directed by George Cukor; Written by Albert Mannheimer; Cinematography by Joseph Walker; Music by Frederick "Friedrich" Hollander. **Pr:** Columbia Pictures. **A:** Jr. High-Adult. **P:** Entertainment. **U:** Home. **Mov-Ent:** Comedy--Romantic, Etiquette, Classic Films. **Awds:** Oscars '50: Actress (Holliday); Golden Globes '51: Actress--Mus./Comedy (Holliday); Natl. Film Reg. '12. **Acq:** Purchase. **Dist:** Facets Multimedia Inc.; Baker and Taylor; Sony Pictures Home Entertainment Inc. $19.95.

Born Yesterday 1993 (PG) — ★★
Remake of the 1950 classic suffers in comparison, particularly Griffith, who has the thankless task of surpassing (or even meeting) Judy Holliday's Oscar-winning mark as not-so-dumb blonde Billie Dawn. Her intellectual inadequacies are glaring when she hits the political world of D.C. with obnoxious tycoon boyfriend Goodman. To save face, he hooks her up with a journalist (Johnson) willing to coach her in Savvy 101, a la Eliza Doolittle. What worked well in post-WWII America seems sadly outdated today; stick with the original. 102m; VHS, DVD, Blu-Ray, Wide, CC. **C:** Melanie Griffith; John Goodman; Don Johnson; Edward Herrmann; Max Perlich; Fred Dalton Thompson; Nora Dunn; Benjamin C. Bradlee; Sally Quinn; Michael Ensign; William Frankfather; Celeste Yarnall; Meg Wittner; Directed by Luis Mandoki; Written by Douglas McGrath; Cinematography by Lajos Koltai; Music by George Fenton. **Pr:** D. Constantine Conte; Stephen Traxler; Hollywood Pictures. **A:** Jr. High-Adult. **P:** Entertainment. **U:** Home. **Mov-Ent:** Comedy--Romantic. **Acq:** Purchase. **Dist:** Buena Vista Home Entertainment. $19.99.

Borne in War 1996 (Unrated)
Archival footage, family photos, and dramatizations trace the life of Thoj, born on a secret CIA military base, and linked to Hmong during the time of French colonialism. 9m; VHS, DVD. **A:** Adult. **P:** Education. **U:** Institution. **Gen-Edu:** Autobiography, History. **Acq:** Purchase. **Dist:** Third World Newsreel. $79.95.

Borneo 1937 (Unrated)
Explorer and naturalist Martin Johnson investigates the many unusual sights and inhabitants of Borneo in this pioneering documentary. 76m/B/W; VHS. **C:** Martin Johnson; Osa Johnson; Narrated by Lowell Thomas; Lew Lehr. **Pr:** Osa Johnson; 20th Century-Fox. **A:** Jr. High-Adult. **P:** Entertainment. **U:** Home. **Mov-Ent:** Documentary Films, Pacific Islands. **Acq:** Purchase. **Dist:** Glenn Video Vistas Ltd. $29.95.

Borneo: From the Beginning 1956
Involves an archaeological dig which reveals human bones, shells, pottery, beads and tools. Describes cleaning, sorting, and dating processes. 27m; VHS. **A:** Family. **P:** Education. **U:** Institution. **Gen-Edu:** Archaeology, History--Ancient. **Acq:** Rent/Lease. **Dist:** Cornell University. $20.00.

Borom Sarret 1966 (Unrated) — ★★★★
One day in the life of a cart-driver in the bustling city of Dakar. As the small details and cumulative indignities of his life compound, the film achieves a haunting and precise sense of outrage that grows organically out of the near-documentary images. Doesn't aspire to the same richness and complexity that some of Sembene's later features reached, but it remains not only a pioneering work of African cinema, but an early example of the cinematic skills of a master. Available as part of the "Black Girl" DVD. 20m/B/W; DVD. **C:** Directed by Ousmane Sembene. **A:** College-Adult. **P:** Entertainment. **L:** French. **Mov-Ent:** Africa. **Dist:** New Yorker Video.

Borough of Kings 1998 (R) — ★★★
Jimmy O'Conner (Stanek) is trying to get away from a life of crime in Brooklyn but the ties are hard to cut. Similar stories have been told dozens of times before. This little independent production has a strong spirit and commitment to the characters on its side, which outweigh its predictability. 95m; DVD. **C:** Philip Bosco; Jim Stanek; Kerry Butler; Joseph Lyle Taylor; Erik Jensen; Patrick Newall; Olympia Dukakis; Directed by Elyse Lewin; Written by Patrick Newall; Cinematography by Nils Kenaston; Music by Alan Elliott. **A:** Sr. High-Adult. **P:** Entertainment. **U:** Home. **Mov-Ent:** Crime Drama. **Acq:** Purchase. **Dist:** Movies Unlimited; Alpha Video.

Borrowed Faces 1980
A look at the audition process at the Colorado Shakespeare Festival, following the joy, pain, and personal discipline which are an integral part of the actor's life. 29m; VHS, 3/4 U. **Pr:** KMGH Television McGraw Hill Broadcasting. **A:** Sr. High-Adult. **P:** Education. **U:** Institution, SURA. **Fin-Art:** Documentary Films, Theater. **Acq:** Purchase, Rent/Lease. **Dist:** University of Washington Educational Media Collection.

The Borrower 1989 (R) — ★★
An exiled unstable mutant insect alien serial killer (you know the type) must switch heads with human beings regularly to survive. This colorful, garish gorefest has humor and attitude, but never develops behind the basic grossout situation. 97m; VHS. **C:** Rae Dawn Chong; Don Gordon; Antonio Fargas; Tom Towler; Directed by John McNaughton. **Pr:** Cannon Films. **A:** College-Adult. **P:** Entertainment. **U:** Home. **L:** English, Spanish. **Mov-Ent:** Horror. **Acq:** Purchase. **Dist:** Warner Home Video, Inc. $19.98.

The Borrowers 1993 (Unrated) — ★★★
Excellent TV adaptation of the May Norton children's classics "The Borrowers" and "The Borrowers Afield." This miniature family (about mouse-size) live beneath the floorboards of an English house and borrow what they need to survive from the normal-sized human inhabitants. Problems come when the teeny family are discovered and must make their way to a new home. Sweet and humorous. 199m; VHS, CC. **C:** Ian Holm; Penelope Wilton; Rebecca Callard; Paul Cross; Sian Phillips; Tony Haygarth; Directed by John Henderson; Written by Richard Carpenter; Cinematography by Clive Tickner; Music by Howard Goodall. **Pr:** British Broadcasting Corporation. **A:** Family. **P:** Entertainment. **U:** Home. **Mov-Ent:** Fantasy, Family, TV Movies. **Acq:** Purchase. **Dist:** Turner Broadcasting System Inc. $59.98.

The Borrowers 1997 (PG) — ★★½
Charming big-screen, big-budget tale about the little people who live under the floor. The British, elfin, and about four inch tall Clock family, headed by papa Pod (Broadbent) lives hidden in the walls of the home of the normal-sized American Lenders and exist by "borrowing" objects from their human's household. When an evil lawyer (Goodman), also American, threatens their happiness, the Borrowers bond with young Peter Lender (Pierce) who "discovers" them and volunteers to help them save their way of life. This remake focuses mainly on the impressive special effects, lending a modern look and appeal. Goodman is lovably evil in that wonderfully Snidely Whiplash way. Based on the children's books of Mary Norton. 86m; VHS, DVD, Wide, CC. **C:** John Goodman; Hugh Laurie; Jim Broadbent; Mark Williams; Celia Imrie; Bradley Michael Pierce; Raymond Pickard; Aden (John) Gillett; Ruby Wax; Flora Newbigin; Tom Felton; Doon Mackichan; Directed by Peter Hewitt; Written by John Kamps; Gavin Scott; Cinematography by John Fenner; Trevor Brooker; Music by Harry Gregson-Williams. **Pr:** Working Title Productions; Polygram Filmed Entertainment. **A:** Primary-Adult. **P:** Entertainment. **U:** Home. **Mov-Ent:** Family Viewing, Great Britain. **Acq:** Purchase. **Dist:** Universal Music and Video Distribution.

Borsalino 1970 (R) — ★★★
Delon and Belmondo are partners in crime in this seriocomic film about gang warfare in 1930s Marseilles. The costumes, settings, and music perfectly capture the mood of the period. Followed by a sequel "Borsalino and Co." Based on "The Bandits of Marseilles" by Eugene Saccomano. 124m; VHS, DVD. **C:** Jean-Paul Belmondo; Alain Delon; Michel Bouquet; Catherine Rouvel; Francoise Christophe; Corinne Marchand; Directed by Jacques Deray; Written by Jacques Deray; Jean Cau; Claude Sautet; Jean-Claude Carriere; Cinematography by Jean-Jacques Tarbes; Music by Claude Bolling. **Pr:** Alain Delon; Alain Delon; Paramount Pictures. **A:** Jr. High-Adult. **P:** Entertainment. **U:** Home. **Mov-Ent:** Comedy-Drama, France. **Acq:** Purchase. **Dist:** Kino on Video. $19.95.

Borstal Boy 2000 (Unrated) — ★★½
Irish teen, IRA partisan, (and future writer) Brendan Behan (Hatosy) is caught smuggling dynamite into Britain and sent to reform school, known as a "borstal," in East Anglia in 1939. Naturally, he learns that all Brits aren't the devil incarnate as he befriends gay Cockney sailor Charlie (Millwall) and falls in love with fair-but-tough Warden Joyce's (York) daughter, Liz (Birthistle). Inspired by Behan's 1958 memoirs. 91m; VHS, DVD. **C:** Shawn Hatosy; Danny Dyer; Eva Birthistle; Michael York; Lee Ingleby; Robin Laing; Directed by Peter Sheridan; Written by Peter Sheridan; Nye Heron; Cinematography by Ciaran Tanham; Music by Stephen McKeon. **Pr:** Arthur Lappin; Pat Moylan; Hell's Kitchen; Dakota Films; Strand Releasing. **A:** Sr. High-Adult. **P:** Entertainment. **U:** Home. **Mov-Ent:** Adolescence, Biography, Great Britain. **Acq:** Purchase. **Dist:** Wolfe Video.

Bosnia Hotel 1998
Documentary on Samburu warriors from Kenya and other UN peace keeping soldiers sent to Bosnia. Follows the men after their return to the homeland where they talk of their experience in a war they don't understand and draws parallels between the two very different cultures. 52m; VHS. **A:** Adult. **P:** Education. **U:** Home. **Gen-Edu:** Documentary Films, Africa, War--General. **Acq:** Purchase, Rent/Lease. **Dist:** Filmakers Library Inc. $350.

Bosom Buddies 1980
Sitcom features best friends Hanks and Scolari who, desperate for cheap rent in New York City, dress in drag in order to move into the women-only Susan B. Anthony hotel. Naturally, this causes some confusion in their love lives. Two episodes per tape. 51m; VHS, CC. **C:** Tom Hanks; Peter Scolari; Donna Dixon; Wendie Jo Sperber; Holland Taylor; Telma Hopkins. **A:** Family. **P:** Entertainment. **U:** Home. **Mov-Ent:** Television Series. **Acq:** Purchase. **Dist:** Paramount Pictures Corp. $9.95. **Indiv. Titles:** 1. Pilot Episode/Macho Man 2. Kip & Sonny's Date/Revenge 3. Kip Quits/The Hospital 4. There's No Business.../Other Than That, She's a Wonderful Person.

Bosom Buddies: The First Season 1980
Best buddies Henry and Kip are not only roommates, they work together at the same ad agency. When their apartment is condemned, their friend Amy suggests they move into her building, which happens to be a women-only residence. So Henry becomes Hildegarde and Kip is transformed into Buffy, which becomes a problem for their love lives. 19 episodes. 478m; DVD. **C:** Tom Hanks; Peter Scolari; Wendie Jo Sperber; Donna Dixon; Telma Hopkins; Holland Taylor. **A:** Family. **P:** Entertainment. **U:** Home. **Mov-Ent:** Television Series. **Acq:** Purchase. **Dist:** Paramount Pictures Corp.

Bosom Buddies: The Second Season 1981
The boys eventually reveal their ruse to their friends but continue to stay at the hotel while going into business with Amy. Isabelle takes over as hotel manager and Sonny pursues her nursing career while Kip pursues her. 19 episodes. 451m; DVD. **C:** Tom Hanks; Bebe Kelly; Whip Hubley; Donna Dixon; Telma Hopkins; Holland Taylor. **A:** Family. **P:** Entertainment. **U:** Home. **Mov-Ent:** Television Series. **Acq:** Purchase. **Dist:** Paramount Pictures Corp.

The Boss 1956 (Unrated) — ★★
Tough political drama. Ambitious WWI vet Matt Brady (Payne) returns home and becomes an increasingly corrupt political boss. He fixes elections and gets in with the mob while becoming rich and powerful. Eventually, reformers go after Brady but it's his loyalty to his only friend, Bob Herrick (Bishop) that proves to be his undoing. Blacklisted writer Trumbo used a front for his screenplay. 89m/B/W; DVD. **C:** John Payne; William Bishop; Gloria McGehee; Doe Avedon; Roy Roberts; Rhys Williams; Joe Flynn; Robin Morse; Directed by Byron Haskin; Written by Dalton Trumbo; Cinematography by Hal Mohr; Music by Albert Glasser. **A:** Sr. High-Adult. **P:** Entertainment. **U:** Home. **Mov-Ent:** Crime Drama, Politics & Government, Veterans. **Acq:** Purchase. **Dist:** MGM Home Entertainment.

The Boss 1973 (Unrated) — ★★
Di Leo's bloody gangster flick opens with mob hitman Lanzetta (Silva) eliminating most of Palermo's Attardi crime family by blowing up a porn theater with a grenade launcher. Survivor Cocchi (Capponi) puts together his own crew to get revenge in the turf war, which soon involves the kidnapping of a local boss's nympho daughter (Santilli), and more mayhem than even the mobsters want. Italian with subtitles. 100m; DVD. **C:** Pier Paolo Capponi; Henry Silva; Claudio Nicastro; Antonia Santilli; Gianni "John" Garko; Richard Conte; Marino (Martin) Mase; Directed by Fernando Di Leo; Written by Fernando Di Leo; Cinematography by Franco Villa; Music by Luis Bacalov. **A:** College-Adult. **P:** Entertainment. **U:** Home. **L:** Italian. **Mov-Ent:** Crime Drama. **Acq:** Purchase. **Dist:** Entertainment One US LP.

Boss 1974 (PG) — ★½
Blaxploitation western parody with Williamson and Martin as a couple of bounty hunters tearing apart a town to find a fugitive. Relatively non-violent. 87m; VHS, DVD. **C:** Fred Williamson; D'Urville Martin; R.G. Armstrong; William (Bill) Smith; Carmen Hayworth; Barbara Leigh; Directed by Jack Arnold; Written by Fred Williamson. **Pr:** Fred Williamson; Fred Williamson; Boss Son Productions; Dimension Films. **A:** Jr. High-Adult. **P:** Entertainment. **U:** Home. **Mov-Ent:** Satire & Parody, Exploitation. **Acq:** Purchase. **Dist:** Unknown Distributor.

Boss Cowboy 1935 — ★
A cowboy shows who wears the chaps in his family when he kidnaps his girlfriend to prevent her from moving East. 51m/B/W; VHS. **C:** Buddy Roosevelt; Frances Morris; Sam Pierce; Fay McKenzie; Lafe (Lafayette) McKee; Directed by Victor Adamson. **Pr:** Artclass. **A:** Family. **P:** Entertainment. **U:** Home. **Mov-Ent:** Western. **Acq:** Purchase. **Dist:** Grapevine Video. $11.95.

The Boss Is Served 1976 (Unrated) — ★★
A mother (Berger) and three daughters, racked with debt, are forced to take in boarders. The lascivious man and teenage son want to be more than just boarders to the lovely Berger. In Italian with English subtitles. 95m; VHS. **C:** Senta Berger; Maurizio Arena; Bruno Zanin; Erika Blanc; Pina Cei; Angiolina Quinterno; Patrizia de Clara; Directed by Mario Lanfranchi; Written by Mario Lanfranchi; Pupi Avati; Cinematography by Pasquale Fanetti; Music by Stelvio Cipriani. **A:** Jr. High-Adult. **P:** Entertainment. **U:** Home. **L:** Italian. **Mov-Ent:** Romance, Drama. **Acq:** Purchase. **Dist:** No Longer Available.

Boss of Big Town 1943 — ★★
Gangsters try to infiltrate the milk industry in this standard crime drama. 65m/B/W; VHS, DVD. **C:** John Litel; Florence Rice; H.B. Warner; Jean Brooks; John Miljan; Mary Gordon; John Maxwell; Directed by Arthur Dreifuss. **Pr:** Jack Schwarz; Producers Releasing Corporation. **A:** Jr. High-Adult. **P:** Entertainment. **U:** Home. **Mov-Ent.** **Acq:** Purchase. **Dist:** Sinister Cinema; Rex Miller Artisan Studio. $16.95.

Boss of Boomtown 1944 (Unrated) — ★½
Steve Hazard (Cameron) and Jim Ward (Tyler) are cavalry sergeants who go from friendly rivals to apparent enemies. Jim re-enlists but Steve has been persuaded by Treasury agent Cornwall (Flint) to help him investigate a stagecoach robbery of a mine payroll. Steve must pose as an outlaw but since Jim doesn't know he's working undercover, he jeopardizes the plan by arresting his former compatriot. 58m/B/W; DVD. **C:** Tom

Tyler; Rod Cameron; Fuzzy Knight; Sam Flint; Vivian Austin; Jack Ingram; Robert V. Barron; Max Wagner; Directed by Ray Taylor; Written by William Lively; Cinematography by William Sickner. **A:** Family. **P:** Entertainment. **U:** Home. **Mov-Ent:** Western. **Acq:** Purchase. **Dist:** Movies Unlimited.

Boss of Bosses 1999 — ★½
Yet another in a long line of Mafia portrayals and betrayals but this one is flat and uninspired. Paul Castellano (Palminteri) takes organized crime into the white-collar level from the streets into legit businesses but the world is still violent, plagued by internal feuds and the feds sniffing around. Castellano wound up being the last public Mafia hit (arranged by John Gotti)?outside a New York steak house. 94m; VHS, DVD, Wide. **C:** Chazz Palminteri; Daniel Benzali; Jay O. Sanders; Clancy Brown; Al Ruscio; Steven Bauer; Angela Alvarado; Sonny Marinelli; Directed by Dwight Little; Written by Jere P. Cunningham; Cinematography by Brian Reynolds; Music by John Altman. **A:** Sr. High-Adult. **P:** Entertainment. **U:** Home. **Mov-Ent:** Federal Bureau of Investigation (FBI). **Acq:** Purchase. **Dist:** Warner Home Video, Inc.

Boss of Bullion City 1941 — ★½
A crooked sheriff is exposed by Brown and sidekick Knight in this sagebrush saga. Based on a story by Arthur St. Claire. 61m/B/W; VHS, DVD. **C:** Johnny Mack Brown; Fuzzy Knight; Maria Montez; Earle Hodgins; Harry Woods; Directed by Ray Taylor; Written by Victor McLeod; Arthur St. Claire. **Pr:** Mark Huffam. **A:** Jr. High-Adult. **P:** Entertainment. **U:** Home. **Mov-Ent:** Western. **Acq:** Purchase. **Dist:** Movies Unlimited. $19.99.

The Boss of It All 2006 (Unrated) — ★★
Von Trier trades in polemics for a corporate comedy. Ravn (Gantzler), the director of an IT firm, decides to hire actor Kristoffer (Albinus) to portray the non-existent president of his company so he can sell out to a larger organization. But thanks to Kristoffer's overacting, the deal gets put on hold for a week and they must keep up the charade. The film was shot by Von Tier's experimental Automavision, a computer-controlled camera, and looks fairly awful. Danish with subtitles. 99m; DVD. **C:** Peter Gantzler; Jens Albinus; Fridrik Thor Fridriksson; Iben Hjejle; Sofie Grabol; Benedikt Erlingsson; Directed by Lars von Trier; Written by Lars von Trier. **A:** College-Adult. **P:** Entertainment. **U:** Home. **L:** Danish. **Mov-Ent. Acq:** Purchase. **Dist:** Weinstein Company L.L.C.

Boss of Rawhide 1944 — ★
The Texas Rangers fight for law and order in the old west despite odds against them. 60m/B/W; VHS, DVD. **C:** Dave O'Brien; James Newill; Guy Wilkerson; Nell O'Day; Edward Cassidy; Jack Ingram; Billy Bletcher; Charles "Blackie" King; George Chesebro; Directed by Elmer Clifton; Written by Elmer Clifton; Cinematography by Robert E. Cline; Music by Dave O'Brien; James Newill; Lee Zahler; Oliver Drake; Herbert Myers. **Pr:** Producers Releasing Corporation. **A:** Family. **P:** Entertainment. **U:** Home. **Mov-Ent:** Western. **Acq:** Purchase, Rent/Lease. **Dist:** Alpha Video; Mill Creek Entertainment L.L.C. $19.95.

Boss: Season One 2011
Starz 2011-12 crime drama. "Listen": Thomas Kane is the ruthless mayor of Chicago with numerous personal and professional problems. This includes his suffering from a fatal neurological disorder that causes dementia and is affecting his mental acuity. "Swallow": Kane starts to lose control as Zajac's gubernatorial campaign gains momentum. "Choose": On election day, Kane and Stone try to make any political change work to their advantage. 8 episodes. 449m; DVD, Blu-Ray. **C:** Kelsey Grammer; Connie Nielsen; Martin Donovan; Jeff Hephner; Troy Garity; Kathleen Robertson. **A:** Adult. **P:** Entertainment. **U:** Home. **Mov-Ent:** Drama, Politics & Government, Television Series. **Acq:** Purchase. **Dist:** Lions Gate Entertainment Inc. $39.98.

Boss: Season Two 2012
Starz 2011-12 drama. "Louder Than Words": Kane is using high doses of meds to try to conrol his disease while planning his political future and legacy. "Mania": Kane's mental symptoms escalate and he has trouble distinguishing between reality and his hallucinations. "True Enough": Miller publishes a story that could destroy Kane. 10 episodes. 563m; DVD, Blu-Ray. **C:** Kelsey Grammer; Connie Nielsen; Troy Garity; Martin Donovan; Jeff Hephner; Kathleen Robertson. **A:** Adult. **P:** Entertainment. **U:** Home. **Mov-Ent:** Drama, Politics & Government, Television Series. **Acq:** Purchase. **Dist:** Lions Gate Entertainment Inc. $39.98.

Boss' Son 1978 (Unrated) — ★★★
Worthwhile coming-of-age tale about a young man who learns more than he bargained for about life when he goes to work for his father in the family carpet business. Dad feels he should work his way up through the ranks and makes him a delivery man. The young man meets reality head on and must deal with the injustices of the world around him. Independently filmed by director/writer Roth. 97m; VHS. **C:** Rita Moreno; James Darren; Asher Brauner; Rudy Solari; Henry Sanders; Richie Havens; Piper Laurie; Elena Verdugo; Directed by Bobby Roth; Written by Bobby Roth; Cinematography by Affonso Beato. **Pr:** Boss Son Productions. **A:** Sr. High-Adult. **P:** Entertainment. **U:** Home. **Mov-Ent. Acq:** Purchase. **Dist:** Lions Gate Television Corp. $69.95.

The Boss' Wife 1986 (R) — ★★
A young stockbroker attempts to fix what's wrong with his life by maneuvering sexually with the boss' wife, and complications set in. 83m; VHS, Streaming, CC. **C:** Daniel Stern; Arielle Dombasle; Christopher Plummer; Martin Mull; Melanie Mayron; Lou Jacobi; Directed by Ziggy Steinberg; Music by Bill Conti. **Pr:** Thomas H. Brodek; Tri-Star Pictures. **A:** Sr. High-Adult. **P:** Entertainment. **U:** Home. **Mov-Ent:** Sex & Sexuality. **Acq:** Purchase. **Dist:** Sony Pictures Home Entertainment Inc. $79.98.

The Boss: Your Customer 1976
Hosted by Earl Nightingale, reiterates the old maxim that the only "boss" that matters is the customer. 13m; VHS, 3/4 U, Special order formats. **C:** Hosted by Earl Nightingale. **Pr:** Dartnell; Wishing Well. **A:** Adult. **P:** Professional. **U:** Institution, CCTV. **Bus-Ind:** Sales Training, Customer Service. **Acq:** Purchase. **Dist:** Dartnell Corp. $29.95.

Bossa Nova 1999 (R) — ★★½
Sexy romantic comedy set to the beat of sultry Brazil. Middle-aged American widow Mary (Irivng) teaches English in Rio and catches the romantic eye of Pedro (Fagundes), an attorney who has been dumped by his wife. Meanwhile, Mary's soccer-playing pupil Acacio (Borges) is trying to become a teacher's pet before transferring his affections to Pedro's clerk Sharon (Antonelli), who just happens to be involved with Pedro's half-brother (Cardoso). And the romantic complications just keep building. Soundtrack is filled with the songs of bossa nova composer Antonio Carlos Jobim. Based on the novel "Miss Simpson" by Sergio Sant'Anna. 95m; VHS, DVD, Wide. **C:** Amy Irving; Antonio Fagundes; Alexandre Borges; Debora Bloch; Pedro Cardoso; Alberto De Mendoza; Stephen Tobolowsky; Drica Moraes; Giovanna Antonelli; Rogerio Cardoso; Directed by Bruno Barreto; Written by Alexandre Machado; Fernanda Young; Cinematography by Pascal Rabaud; Music by Eumir Deodato. **Pr:** Sony Pictures Classics. **A:** Sr. High-Adult. **P:** Entertainment. **U:** Home. **Mov-Ent:** Comedy--Romantic, Soccer. **Acq:** Purchase. **Dist:** Sony Pictures Home Entertainment Inc.

The Boston & Maine ????
Provides background of the Boston & Maine's (B&M) shift from steam to diesel engines after World War II. Includes footage of Boston's North Station and the dismantling of the steam engines. 60m; VHS. **A:** College-Adult. **P:** Education. **U:** Home. **Gen-Edu:** Trains. **Acq:** Purchase. **Dist:** The Civil War Standard. $24.95.

Boston & Maine in the 4 Seasons: Volume 1 ????
Filmed in the spring and summer of 1951, includes footage of commuter, passenger, and freight railcars on the Boston & Maine Railroad (BM) in the suburban Boston area. 55m; VHS, DVD. **A:** College-Adult. **P:** Education. **U:** Home. **Gen-Edu:** Trains. **Acq:** Purchase. **Dist:** Herron Rail Video. $39.95.

Boston & Maine in the 4 Seasons: Volume 2 ????
Filmed in fall and winter of 1951, includes footage of commuter, passenger, and freight railcars on the Boston & Maine Railroad (BM) in the suburban Boston area. 55m; VHS, DVD. **A:** College-Adult. **P:** Education. **U:** Home. **Gen-Edu:** Trains. **Acq:** Purchase. **Dist:** Herron Rail Video. $39.95.

Boston and Maine: Its Fitchburg Division and Hoosac 19??
This vintage film shows steam locomotive activity on many parts of the B&M Fitchburg Division, which stretches west from Boston to Troy and Mechanicsville, N.Y. 11m/B/W; VHS. **Pr:** J.W. Dealey; E.R. Blanchard. **A:** Jr. High-Adult. **P:** Entertainment. **U:** Home. **Gen-Edu:** Documentary Films, Trains. **Acq:** Purchase.

Boston & Maine Steam 1 ????
Collection of Boston & Maine (B&M) steam trains from the 1930s including 4-4-0 Americans and 2-10-2 Santa Fes, among others. 38m/B/W; VHS. **A:** College-Adult. **P:** Education. **U:** Home. **Gen-Edu:** Trains. **Acq:** Purchase. **Dist:** The Civil War Standard. $29.95.

Boston & Maine Steam 2 ????
Features classic Boston & Maine (B&M) freight and passenger steam trains traveling through the Fitchburg, Portland, and Connecticut Valley Divisions with particular focus on Boston's North Station. 30m/B/W; VHS. **A:** College-Adult. **P:** Education. **U:** Home. **Gen-Edu:** Trains. **Acq:** Purchase. **Dist:** The Civil War Standard. $29.95.

Boston and Vicinity: Structural Changes 1992
Visits the Boston area, emphasizing the city's high technology and institutions of higher learning. Contains footage of a thinking machine at the Thinking Machines Corp. and Harvard University. 13m; VHS, SVS, 3/4 U. **A:** Jr. High-Sr. High. **P:** Education. **U:** Institution. **Gen-Edu:** Cities & Towns, Geography. **Acq:** Purchase, Rent/Lease. **Dist:** Encyclopedia Britannica. $59.00.

Boston Blackie's Chinese Venture 1949 (Unrated) — ★½
The 14th and last in the Columbia series is a perfunctory mystery. Boston Blackie and his sidekick Runt are spotted leaving a Chinese laundry where the owner is later found murdered. To clear suspicion from themselves, they follow up a lead that the owner's niece gave to Inspector Farraday concerning stolen diamonds. 59m/B/W; DVD. **C:** Chester Morris; Sid Tomack; Richard Lane; Maylia; Philip Ahn; Frank Sully; Directed by Seymour Friedman; Written by Maurice Tombragel; Cinematography by Vincent Farrar. **A:** Jr. High-Adult. **P:** Entertainment. **U:** Home. **Mov-Ent:** Mystery & Suspense. **Acq:** Purchase. **Dist:** Sony Pictures Home Entertainment Inc.

Boston Draft Resistance Group 1968 (Unrated)
Profiles the tactics and activities used by law abiding draft resistance groups during the Vietnam War. 18m/B/W; VHS, DVD. **A:** Adult. **P:** Education. **U:** Institution. **Gen-Edu:** Law, Vietnam War, History. **Acq:** Purchase. **Dist:** Third World Newsreel. $150.

The Boston Freedom Trail 1991
Take a armchair walking tour through historic Boston and see famous landmarks including the Old North Church, the Boston Common, and Paul Revere's home. 30m; VHS. **A:** Jr. High-Adult. **P:** Education. **U:** Institution, Home. **Gen-Edu:** History--U.S., Travel. **Acq:** Purchase. **Dist:** Knowledge Unlimited, Inc. $24.95.

The Boston Hoax: The Police, the Press, and the Public 1990
Profiles the media coverage of the Stuart murder case in Boston, Massachusetts. Focuses on teaching the viewer how the media does their job, the problems they face when reporting a story, and why they sometimes fail to live up to expectations. 60m; VHS, 3/4 U. **A:** College-Adult. **P:** Education. **U:** Institution. **Gen-Edu:** Journalism. **Acq:** Purchase. **Dist:** PBS Home Video.

Boston Kickout 1995 — ★★
A quartet of teenaged friends/losers struggle to grow up in a bleak concrete town outside London. There are neglected girlfriends, dysfunctional families, menial jobs, petty crime, emotional disasters—and some faint glimmer of hope for at least a couple of the lads. Title refers to a destructive game the boys play. 105m; VHS, DVD. **C:** John Simm; Andrew Lincoln; Richard Hanson; Nathan Valente; Emer McCourt; Marc Warren; Derek Martin; Vincent Phillips; Natalie Davies; Directed by Paul Hills; Written by Paul Hills; Diane Whitley; Roberto Troni; Cinematography by Roger Bonnici; Music by Robert Hartshorne. **Pr:** Paul Hills; Tedi de Toledo; Paul Trijbits; Danny Cannon; Boston Films; Amaranth Film Partners. **A:** Sr. High-Adult. **P:** Entertainment. **U:** Home. **Mov-Ent:** Adolescence, Great Britain. **Acq:** Purchase. **Dist:** BMG Entertainment.

Boston Legal: Season Five 2008 (Unrated)
Fox television 2004-8 court room dramedy. Jerry and Katie take the case of a 15-year-old girl who claims a private prison guard raped her in "Guardians and Gatekeepers," a former girlfriend asks Alan to represent her husband at a murder trial in "True Love," and Denny and Carl travel to Virginia to defend a corrections officer regarding a botched execution in "Kill, Baby, Kill!" 13 episodes. 607m; DVD. **C:** James Spader; William Shatner; Candice Bergen; Mark Valley. **A:** Sr. High-Adult. **P:** Entertainment. **U:** Home. **Mov-Ent:** Drama, Law, Television Series. **Acq:** Purchase. **Dist:** Fox Home Entertainment. $49.99.

Boston Legal: Season Four 2004 (Unrated)
Television legal drama series on ABC from 2004-2008. Changes at Crane, Poole & Schmidt include Mark Valley, Julie Bowen, Rene Auberjonois, and Constance Zimmer leaving, new lawyer Katie Lloyd (Tara Summers) starting, and New York litigator Carl Sack (John Larroquette) coming in to try and "wring out some of the madness." Alan defends a woman (Mare Winningham) who plots out the murder of her daughter's killer but asks him to plead temporary insanity. Denny is arrested for soliciting a prostitute, is courting a discrimination suit for firing an overweight associate, and takes the opposite side of a case Alan is also defending wherein a Massachusetts town wants to secede from the United States. Mary Gross plays a woman with Aspergers and a romantic love for inanimate objects who is entering into a relationship with Jerry Espenson (Christian Clemenson). 20 episodes. 926m; DVD. **A:** Sr. High-Adult. **P:** Entertainment. **U:** Home. **Mov-Ent:** Drama, Law, Television Series. **Acq:** Purchase. **Dist:** Fox Home Entertainment.

Boston Legal: Season One 2004
This ABC series follows the ambitious, crazy, and sometimes ethically-challenged attorneys of the firm of Crane, Poole & Schmidt, led by eccentric Denny Crane (Shatner), partner Shirley Schmidt (Bergen), and Denny's protege, Alan Shore (Spader). 17 episodes. 739m; DVD. **C:** William Shatner; James Spader; Candice Bergen; Rene Auberjonois; Mark Valley; Julie Bowen; Monica Potter; Rhona Mitra; Lake Bell. **A:** Jr. High-Adult. **P:** Entertainment. **U:** Home. **Mov-Ent:** Television Series, Law. **Acq:** Purchase. **Dist:** Fox Home Entertainment.

Boston Legal: Season Two 2005
Senior partner Denny Crane, of Boston legal firm Crane, Poole & Schmidt, and attorney Alan Shore continue their theatrical and non-PC behavior in and out of the courtroom while they and their colleagues are threatened by associates (Parker Posey), exes (Tom Selleck), new spouses (Joanna Cassidy), lovers (Michael J. Fox), and clients (Betty White). 27 episodes. 1145m; DVD. **C:** William Shatner; James Spader; Candice Bergen; Julie Bowen; Mark Valley. **A:** Jr. High-Adult. **P:** Entertainment. **U:** Home. **Mov-Ent:** Television Series, Law. **Acq:** Purchase. **Dist:** Fox Home Entertainment.

Boston Legal: The Complete Third Season 2006
Stories this season involve cases including the murder of a judge's wife, an outrageous peeping tom, immigration law, and infringement of religious freedoms. The terminally ill Daniel (Michael J. Fox) leaves to seek experimental treatments, opening the door for Brad and new litigator Jeffrey to compete for Denise's affections, while Denny Crane gets his groove on with attorney Bethany as well as her mother, Bella (Delta Burke). Jerry "Hands" Espenson seeks Alan's counsel and eventually returns to Crane, Poole & Schmidt upon Jeffrey's departure. 27 episodes. 1056m; DVD. **C:** Candice Bergen; William Shatner; James Spader; Craig Bierko; Mark Valley; Constance Zimmer; Meredith Eaton-Gilden. **A:** Adult. **P:** Entertainment. **U:** Home. **Mov-Ent:** Drama, Law. **Acq:** Purchase. **Dist:** Fox Home Entertainment.

The Boston Red Sox: 2004 World Series Collector's Edition 20??
Presents the A&E cable channel special on the 2004 World Series as the Boston Red Sox swept the St. Louis Cardinals, after coming back to defeat the New York Yankees in the

American League Championship Series (ALCS). Includes complete games, interviews with players, and the Cardinals? locker room celebration. 2110m; DVD. **A:** Family. **P:** Entertainment. **U:** Home, CATV. **Spo-Rec**: Television Series, Documentary Films, Biography: Sports. **Acq:** Purchase. **Dist:** A&E Television Networks L.L.C. $129.95.

The Boston Red Sox: 2007 World Series Collector's Edition 2008
Presents the A&E cable channel special on the 2007 World Series as the Boston Red Sox defeated the Colorado Rockies, who made their debut appearance in the fall classic, to reclaim the title after their 2004 victory. Includes complete games and player interviews. 1205m; DVD. **A:** Family. **P:** Entertainment. **U:** Home, CATV. **Spo-Rec**: Television Series, Documentary Films, Biography: Sports. **Acq:** Purchase. **Dist:** A&E Television Networks L.L.C. $89.95.

The Boston Red Sox: Essential Games of Fenway Park 2003
Six complete game broadcasts of the Red Sox's most famous games in Fenway Park. 960m; DVD. **A:** Family. **P:** Entertainment. **U:** Home. **Spo-Rec**: Baseball, Sports--General. **Acq:** Purchase. **Dist:** Baseball Direct. $59.95.

The Boston Red Sox: Greatest Games of Fenway Park ????
Presents the A&E cable channel special on the Boston Red Sox's Fenway Park, their home since 1912 and unique in its structure for its tall left field wall dubbed "The Green Monster"; features historic games played as well as prominent players from the team's history. 991m; DVD. **A:** Family. **P:** Entertainment. **U:** Home, CATV. **Spo-Rec**: Television Series, Documentary Films, Biography: Sports. **Acq:** Purchase. **Dist:** A&E Television Networks L.L.C. $59.95.

Boston Red Sox: 100 Years of Baseball History 2002
Documentary showcases the history of Boston's storied (some say cursed) American League franchise from its inception to the modern era using archival footage, rare and vintage film, and interviews. Two-volume set on VHS. 180m; VHS, DVD. **A:** Family. **P:** Entertainment. **U:** Home. **Spo-Rec**: Baseball. **Acq:** Purchase. **Dist:** Baseball Direct. $29.95.

The Boston Strangler 1968 — ★★½
Based on Gerold Frank's bestselling factual book about the deranged killer who terrorized Boston for about a year and a half. Traces events from first killing to prosecution. Curtis, going against type, is compelling in title role. 116m; VHS, DVD, CC. **C:** Tony Curtis; Henry Fonda; George Kennedy; Murray Hamilton; Mike Kellin; George Voskovec; William Hickey; James Brolin; Hurd Hatfield; William Marshall; Jeff Corey; Sally Kellerman; Directed by Richard Fleischer; Written by Edward Anhalt. **Pr:** 20th Century-Fox. **A:** Sr. High-Adult. **P:** Entertainment. **U:** Home. **L:** Spanish. **Mov-Ent**: Mystery & Suspense, Documentary Films. **Acq:** Purchase. **Dist:** Fox Home Entertainment; Alpha Video; Movies Unlimited. $19.98.

The Boston Strangler: The Untold Story 2008 (R) — ★½
Faustino stars as Albert De Salvo, a smalltime criminal who confesses to the serial sex killings that terrified Boston in the early 1960s. De Salvo decides to take credit for the murders while in jail on another conviction but Detective John Marsden (Divoff) isn't certain they've got the right perp or that the crimes were committed by just one man. 90m; DVD. **C:** David Faustino; Andrew Divoff; Corin "Corky" Nemec; Joe Torry; Kostas Sommer; Directed by Michael Feifer; Written by Michael Feifer; Cinematography by Hank Baumert, Jr.; Music by Andres Boulton. **A:** Sr. High-Adult. **P:** Entertainment. **U:** Home. **Mov-Ent. Acq:** Purchase. **Dist:** Weinstein Company L.L.C.

Boston: The Way It Was 1998
Two video set takes a look back at Boston and the landmarks and institutions that helped make the city what it is today. First video concentrates on the 1930s and 40s and include segments on the Boston Braves, Revere Beach and Scollay Square among others. The second video shows the city as it was in the years following World War II, including segments on the Boston Garden, the South End and Coconut Grove among others. Comes with a softcover book. Two hours on two videocassettes. 60m; VHS; Closed Captioned. **A:** Family. **P:** Education. **U:** Home. **Gen-Edu**: History, History--U.S. **Acq:** Purchase. **Dist:** PBS Home Video. $39.95.

The Bostonians 1984 (PG) — ★★½
A faith healer's daughter is forced to choose between the affections of a militant suffragette and a young lawyer in 19th Century Boston. Based on Henry James' classic novel. 120m; VHS, DVD. **C:** Christopher Reeve; Vanessa Redgrave; Madeleine Potter; Jessica Tandy; Nancy Marchand; Wesley Addy; Linda Hunt; Wallace Shawn; Directed by James Ivory; Written by Ruth Prawer Jhabvala; Cinematography by Walter Lassally. **Pr:** Almi Pictures. **A:** Sr. High-Adult. **P:** Entertainment. **U:** Home. **Mov-Ent**: Women. **Awds:** Natl. Soc. Film Critics '84: Actress (Redgrave). **Acq:** Purchase. **Dist:** Lions Gate Television Corp. $79.98.

Boswell for the Defense 1989
A portrait of James Boswell, 18th century Scottish lawyer and writer, as a practicing attorney defending a butcher charged with theft. After the man is convicted and sentenced to hang, Boswell and physician plot to revive the man after his hanging. 90m; VHS, 3/4 U. **Pr:** Films for the Humanities and Sciences. **A:** College. **P:** Education. **U:** Institution, CCTV, CATV, BCTV. **Gen-Edu**: Documentary Films, Biography. **Acq:** Purchase, Rent/Lease, Duplication License. **Dist:** Films for the Humanities & Sciences.

Boswell in London 1989
A biography of James Boswell, Scottish lawyer and biographer of Samuel Johnson. The historic meeting with Samuel Johnson through period painting of London is portrayed using the video technique chromakey. 172m; VHS, 3/4 U. **Pr:** Yale University Films; Films for the Humanities and Sciences. **A:** Jr. High-Sr. High. **P:** Education. **U:** Institution, CCTV, CATV, BCTV. **Gen-Edu**: Documentary Films, Biography. **Acq:** Purchase, Rent/Lease, Duplication License. **Dist:** Films for the Humanities & Sciences.

Botany Bay 1953 (Unrated) — ★★
A rousing costumer about a convict ship in the 1700s that, after a trying voyage, lands in Australia, wherein a framed doctor conquers the local plague. From the novel by Charles Nordoff. 99m; VHS. **C:** Alan Ladd; James Mason; Patricia Medina; Cedric Hardwicke; Directed by John Farrow. **Pr:** Paramount Pictures. **A:** Sr. High. **P:** Entertainment. **U:** Home. **Mov-Ent**: Action-Adventure, Australia, Boating. **Acq:** Purchase. **Dist:** $19.95.

Botany: Photosynthesis and Respiration 19??
Explains basic botany information on leaf structure, photosynthesis, and the role of glucose. ?m; VHS. **A:** Jr. High-Adult. **P:** Education. **U:** Institution. **Hea-Sci**: Science, Plants. **Acq:** Purchase. **Dist:** CEV Multimedia. $59.95.

Botany: Plant Movement & Transportation 19??
Summarizes the processes involved with internal and external plant movement, as well as osmosis and transpiration. ?m; VHS. **A:** Jr. High-Adult. **P:** Education. **U:** Institution. **Hea-Sci**: Science, Biology, Plants. **Acq:** Purchase. **Dist:** CEV Multimedia. $59.95.

Botany: Plant Nutrition 19??
Illustrates the structures and functions associated with the ability of plants to make food and discusses two major soil types used in nutrition. ?m; VHS. **A:** Jr. High-Adult. **P:** Education. **U:** Institution. **Hea-Sci**: Science, Plants, Biology. **Acq:** Purchase. **Dist:** CEV Multimedia. $59.95.

Botany: Plant Reproduction 19??
Uses time-lapse videography of male and female tulips to help explain plant fertilization and reproduction. Also explains angiosperms, gymnosperms, pollen, and special adaptations of seeds. ?m; VHS. **A:** Jr. High-Adult. **P:** Education. **U:** Institution. **Hea-Sci**: Science, Biology, Plants. **Acq:** Purchase. **Dist:** CEV Multimedia. $59.95.

Botany Series 19??
Three-part science education series that introduces botany and covers such topics as the plant kingdom, plant classification, plant families, soil and nutrition, the relationship between plants and the environment, photosynthesis, and plant reproduction. Comes with study guides and wall chart of the plant kingdom classification system. 100m; VHS. **A:** Jr. High-Adult. **P:** Education. **U:** Institution. **Hea-Sci**: Science, Biology, Plants. **Acq:** Purchase. **Dist:** CEV Multimedia. $300.00.
Indiv. Titles: 1. Introduction 2. Photosynthesis 3. Plant Reproduction.

Botany Series: Introduction 19??
Part of the "Botany Series" that teaches the biology of plants. Provides introduction to the basic principles of botany. Uses time-lapse photography and computer animation to help explain plant movement and growth. Contains lab experiments that can be done in the classroom. 50m; VHS. **A:** Jr. High-Adult. **P:** Education. **U:** Institution. **Hea-Sci**: Science, Biology, Plants. **Acq:** Purchase. **Dist:** CEV Multimedia. $145.00.

Botany Series: Photosynthesis 19??
Part of the "Botany Series" which explains biological processes associated with plants. Provides an explanation of the photosynthesis process which includes coverage of how it affects atoms, molecules, cells, energy, its role in the food chain, and the importance of its production of oxygen. 25m; VHS. **A:** Jr. High-Adult. **P:** Education. **U:** Institution. **Hea-Sci**: Science, Biology, Plants. **Acq:** Purchase. **Dist:** CEV Multimedia. $95.00.

Botany Series: Plant Reproduction 19??
Part of the "Botany Series," which provides basic science education in the world of botany. Examines plant reproduction, cell division, mitosis, meosis, chromosomes, gametes, zygotes, spores, sexual and non-sexual plant reproduction, alternation of generations, pollination, fertilization, and germination. Includes information on the evolution of plant reproduction. 25m; VHS. **A:** Jr. High-Adult. **P:** Education. **U:** Institution. **Hea-Sci**: Science, Biology, Plants. **Acq:** Purchase. **Dist:** CEV Multimedia. $95.00.

Botched 2007 (Unrated) — ★½
Odd and not particularly successful mix of horror, comedy, and crime. American Ritchie (Dorff) must be a lousy professional thief because his jobs keep going wrong. He's sent to Moscow to steal an antique cross that's kept in a bank building and is given a couple of inept locals for backup. Naturally their getaway gets screwed and they wind up with hostages and are diverted to the building's unused 13th floor. They find out it's been abandoned for a very good reason. 94m; DVD. **C:** Stephen Dorff; Sean Pertwee; Jamie Foreman; Russell Smith; Jaime Murray; Bronagh Gallagher; Edward Baker-Duly; Directed by Kit Ryan; Written by Derek Boyle; Eamon Friel; Raymond Friel; Cinematography by Bryan Loftus; Music by Tom Green. **A:** Sr. High-Adult. **P:** Entertainment. **U:** Home. **Mov-Ent. Acq:** Purchase. **Dist:** Warner Home Video, Inc.

Both Ends Burning: Working with People with AIDS 1996
Features information aimed at healthcare and social service workers who deal with the stress of working with AIDS and AIDS patients. 14m; VHS. **A:** Adult. **P:** Education. **U:** Institution. **Gen-Edu**: AIDS, Occupational Training. **Acq:** Rent/Lease. **Dist:** Fanlight Productions. $50.

Both Sides of the Wire 1993
Studies the 1930s New Brunswick, Canada internment camp for enemy aliens. Investigates the reactions of Canadian guards and internees as they learned their prisoners were no more than civilian rabbis, priests, professors and businessmen. Traces the Canadian decision to deem the internment camps unnecessary. 51m; VHS. **A:** Jr. High-Adult. **P:** Education. **U:** Institution. **Gen-Edu**: Judaism, Canada. **Acq:** Purchase. **Dist:** National Center for Jewish Film. $54.

Botticelli's Calumny of Apelles 1987
An examination of Botticelli's evolution as a painter, focusing on the title work, one of his greatest masterpieces. 12m; VHS, 8 mm, Special order formats. **C:** Directed by Carlo L. Ragghianti. **A:** Sr. High-Adult. **P:** Education. **U:** Institution, Home. **Fin-Art**: Documentary Films, Art & Artists, Painting. **Acq:** Purchase. **Dist:** The Roland Collection. $69.00.

The Bottle and the Throttle—2nd Edition 1972
A dramatization of how just two beers can be enough to blur a driver's reaction time when a woman and child are struck by his car. 10m; VHS, 3/4 U. **Pr:** National Safety Council. **A:** College-Adult. **P:** Education. **U:** Institution, SURA. **Hea-Sci**: Documentary Films, Alcoholism. **Acq:** Rent/Lease. **Dist:** National Safety Council, California Chapter, Film Library.

A Bottle in the Cellar 2000
An old vodka bottle found in a farmer's cellar in Poland reveals messages of one man's struggle against the Nazis. 28m; VHS. **A:** Adult. **P:** Education. **U:** Institution. **Gen-Edu**: Documentary Films, Holocaust. **Acq:** Purchase. **Dist:** SISU Home Entertainment, Inc. $39.95.

Bottle Rocket 1995 (R) — ★★½
A trio of inexperienced but aspiring criminals attempt to make their mark on the world in suburban Dallas. Newcomers Wilson, who plays the group's ambitious leader Dignan, and Anderson penned this smart ensemble piece first as a 13-minute black and white short. A subsequent showing at the Sundance Film Festival got the attention of producer James L. Brooks ("Broadcast News"). Film got the backing to go feature length with Anderson directing, and deservedly so, with its fresh dialogue and surprising warmth. 91m; VHS, DVD, Blu-Ray, CC. **C:** Owen Wilson; Luke Wilson; Robert Musgrave; Lumi Cavazos; James Caan; Andrew Wilson; Jim Ponds; Ned Dowd; Directed by Wes Anderson; Written by Owen Wilson; Wes Anderson; Cinematography by Robert Yeoman; Music by Mark Mothersbaugh. **Pr:** Polly Platt; James L. Brooks; Barbara Boyle; Michael Taylor; Gracie Films; Columbia Pictures; Sony Pictures Home Entertainment Inc. **A:** Sr. High-Adult. **P:** Entertainment. **U:** Home. **Mov-Ent. Awds:** MTV Movie Awards '96: New Filmmaker (Anderson). **Acq:** Purchase. **Dist:** Sony Pictures Home Entertainment Inc.

Bottle Shock 2008 (PG-13) — ★★
A mostly-based-on-real-life story taken from an historic 1976 blind wine competition arranged by wine elitist Englishman Steven Spurrier (Rickman) and his struggling Parisian wine business, pitting French wines against the unsung vineyards of California's Napa Valley, including former lawyer Jim Barrett's (Pullman) Chateau Montelena. While Jim clashes with his surfer son Bo (Pine, sporting a disturbingly unrealistic wig), Bo vies with his friend and coworker Gustavo (Rodriguez) for the attention of intern Samantha (Taylor). Though the contest's outcome is expected and the general pace is slow, director Miller ably squeezes out some patriotism-inspired moments. 110m; DVD, Streaming, Wide. **C:** Alan Rickman; Bill Pullman; Chris Pine; Rachael Taylor; Freddy Rodriguez; Eliza Dushku; Dennis Farina; Miguel (Michael) Sandoval; Bradley Whitford; Joe Regalbuto; Directed by Randall Miller; Written by Randall Miller; Jody Savin; Ross Schwartz; Cinematography by Michael Ozier; Music by Mark Adler. **Pr:** J. Todd Harris; Marc Toberoff; Brenda Lhormer; Marc Lhormer; Randall Miller; Jody Savin; Unclaimed Freight; Zine Haze Productions. **A:** Jr. High-Adult. **P:** Entertainment. **U:** Home. **L:** English. **Mov-Ent**: Comedy-Drama, Wine & Vinyards. **Acq:** Purchase, Rent/Lease. **Dist:** Movies Unlimited; Alpha Video; Fox Home Entertainment. $14.98 9.99.

Bottle Up and Go 1980
This portrait of a rural black couple reveals their unique lifestyle and deep-rooted culture. Annie Mae Dotson's faith in God sustains her in her day-to-day existence; her husband Louis's recreational time is devoted to his one-string guitar and his haunting bottle-yodeling. 18m; VHS, 3/4 U. **Pr:** Center for Southern Folklore. **A:** Sr. High-Adult. **P:** Education. **U:** Institution, Home, SURA. **Gen-Edu**: Documentary Films, Sociology, Black Culture. **Acq:** Purchase. **Dist:** Center for Southern Folklore.

Bottled Up 2013 (R) — ★
Quirk, weak dramedy with unbelievable characters and situations. Sylvie lives with mom Fay, who's enabling her daughter's painkiller addiction. When Fay meets health food store clerk Becket, she tries to set him up with her daughter but he's more interested in Fay despite their age difference. 84m; DVD. **C:** Melissa Leo; Josh Hamilton; Marin Ireland; Directed by Enid Zentelis; Written by Enid Zentelis; Cinematography by Daniel Sharnoff; Music by Tim Boland; Sam Retzer. **A:** Sr. High-Adult. **P:** Entertainment. **U:** Home. **L:** English. **Mov-Ent**: Comedy-Drama, Drug Abuse, Romance. **Acq:** Purchase. **Dist:** Osiris Entertainment.

Bottleneck Blues and Beyond 199?
Nashville session guitarist Mike Dowling reveals "tricks-of-the-trade" that make the simplest lines sound musical. Intended for

the intermediate to advanced player. 110m; VHS. **A:** Sr. High-Adult. **P:** Education. **U:** Home. **How-Ins:** Music--Instruction. **Acq:** Purchase. **Dist:** Hal Leonard Corp. $39.95.

Bottleneck Blues Guitar 19??
Country blues bottleneck styles and techniques are demonstrated for beginning and intermediate students. Also features rare footage of Son House, Fred McDowell, Mance Lipscomb, and Bukka White. 82m; VHS. **A:** Jr. High-Adult. **P:** Entertainment. **U:** Home. **How-Ins:** How-To, Music--Instruction. **Acq:** Purchase. **Dist:** Music Video Distributors; Shanachie Entertainment. $49.95.

Bottom Line 19??
Through vignettes depicting the real world of work and family relationships, this program will help the recovering individual overcome denial, and shows how alcoholism affects job performance. 44m; VHS. **A:** Adult. **P:** Education. **U:** Institution. **L:** English. **Hea-Sci:** Alcoholism. **Acq:** Purchase. **Dist:** Hazelden Publishing. $34.95.

The Bottom Line 19??
Two stories of senior citizens facing death raise the issues of length of life vs. quality of life. 30m; VHS. **A:** Adult. **P:** Education. **U:** Home. **Gen-Edu:** Ethics & Morals, Death, Aging. **Acq:** Purchase. **Dist:** Ergo Media Inc. $49.95.

The Bottom Line 1987
The Soviets, Americans, and native dictators devour a cake which symbolizes Central America, leaving only a few crumbs for the peasants. 6m; VHS, 3/4 U. **Pr:** Franciscan Communications. **A:** Jr. High-Adult. **P:** Religious. **U:** Institution, SURA. **L:** Spanish. **Gen-Edu:** Central America. **Acq:** Purchase, Rent/Lease. **Dist:** St. Anthony Messenger Press. $85.00.

The Bottom Line 1995
Explains the various aspects of environmental legislation. 24m; VHS. **A:** Adult. **P:** Professional. **U:** Institution. **Bus-Ind:** Job Training, Safety Education, Management. **Acq:** Rent/Lease. **Dist:** National Safety Council, California Chapter, Film Library.

Bottom of the Ninth 2002
Director Chuck Braverman chronicles a season with the Somerset Patriots, a minor-league baseball team, as they try for a championship. 50m; DVD. **A:** Jr. High-Adult. **P:** Entertainment. **U:** Home. **Gen-Edu:** Documentary Films, Baseball. **Acq:** Purchase. **Dist:** Facets Multimedia Inc.

The Bottom of the Sea 2003 — ★★★
Dark comedic thriller has an obsessively jealous young architect stalking his girlfriend's secret lover on one fateful night. An unexpected climax and easy-on-the-eyes actors make this Argentinean endeavor cinematically satisfying. Subtitled. 95m; DVD. **C:** Dolores Fonzi; Daniel Hendler; Gustavo Garzon; Ramiro Aguero; Directed by Damien Szifron; Written by Damien Szifron. **A:** Adult. **P:** Entertainment. **U:** Home. **L:** Spanish. **Mov-Ent. Acq:** Purchase. **Dist:** Image Entertainment Inc. $24.95.

Bottom Position and Leg Attack Counters 2003 (Unrated)
Coaches Russ Hellickson and Ken Ramsey present drills to make your wrestlers stronger from the bottom position, as well as improving their defense against leg attacks. 39m; DVD. **A:** Family. **P:** Education. **U:** Home, Institution. **Spo-Rec:** Athletic Instruction/Coaching. **Acq:** Purchase. **Dist:** Championship Productions. $39.99.

Bottom Position: Explode Off the Whistle 2002 (Unrated)
Coach Kerry McCoy demonstrates moves wrestlers can use to escape the bottom position. 46m; DVD. **A:** Family. **P:** Education. **U:** Home, Institution. **Spo-Rec:** Athletic Instruction/Coaching. **Acq:** Purchase. **Dist:** Championship Productions. $39.99.

Bottom Position: Skills to Dominate 2013 (Unrated)
Coach Mark Manning demonstrates tips and techniques for escapes and reversals when wrestling from the bottom position. 66m; DVD. **A:** Family. **P:** Education. **U:** Home. **L:** English. **Spo-Rec:** Athletic Instruction/Coaching, Sports--General, How-To. **Acq:** Purchase. **Dist:** Championship Productions. $69.99.

Bottom Position Stand-Ups and Roll-Outs 1998 (Unrated)
Coach Mark Branch demonstrates various rolling and stand-up techniques for wrestlers looking to transition easier from defense to offense. 55m; DVD. **A:** Family. **P:** Education. **U:** Home, Institution. **Spo-Rec:** Athletic Instruction/Coaching. **Acq:** Purchase. **Dist:** Championship Productions. $39.99.

Bottomfishing Techniques, Vol. 1 19??
Technology is the edge that can make or break a successful bottomfishing expedition. Winess the power of Lowrance Electronics with Darrell Lowrance. 40m; VHS. **A:** Adult. **P:** Instruction. **U:** Home. **Spo-Rec:** Fishing. **Acq:** Purchase. **Dist:** Bennett Marine Video. $29.95.

Bottomfishing Techniques, Vol. 2 19??
Darrell Lowrance (Lowrance Electronics) shows you how to choose equipment, fillet fish, charter a boat, and more on this fantastic program. 30m; VHS. **A:** Adult. **P:** Instruction. **U:** Home. **Spo-Rec:** Fishing. **Acq:** Purchase. **Dist:** Bennett Marine Video. $29.95.

Bottoms Up 2006 (R) — **Bomb!**
Bottom of the barrel is more like it. Owen (Mewes) heads to L.A. to enter a bartending contest in hopes of using the winnings to save his dad's restaurant. Things don't exactly work out and Owen's uncle (Keith) gets him a job with actor Hayden (Hallisay) and his vapid girlfriend, Lisa (a typecast Hilton). When Owen learns a few tabloid-worthy secrets, he has to decide whether to sell out his new pals for the much-needed cash. Even Mewes can't work up much enthusiasm for this mess. 89m; DVD. **C:** Jason Mewes; Paris Hilton; David Keith; Phil Morris; Brian Hallisay; Jon Abrahams; Tim Thomerson; Directed by Erik MacArthur; Written by Erik MacArthur; Nick Ballo; Cinematography by Massimo Zeri. **A:** Sr. High-Adult. **P:** Entertainment. **U:** Home. **Mov-Ent. Acq:** Purchase. **Dist:** Sony Pictures Home Entertainment Inc.

Bottoms Up '81 1981 (Unrated)
A screen re-creation of this long-running comedy revue, combining slapstick, satire, beautiful showgirls, and lavish musical numbers. Taped on location at Harrah's Lake Tahoe. 75m; VHS. **Pr:** Breck Wall Productions. **A:** Adult. **P:** Entertainment. **U:** Home. **Mov-Ent:** Variety. **Acq:** Purchase. **Dist:** Paramount Pictures Corp. $49.95.

Boudicca: Warrior Queen 2006
Looks at the leader of an Iceni tribe who rallied other Celtic clans to fight against Roman occupation of Britain in 62 A.D. 69m; DVD. **A:** Jr. High-Adult. **P:** Entertainment. **U:** Home. **Gen-Edu:** Documentary Films, History--Ancient. **Acq:** Purchase. **Dist:** Rykodisc Corp.

Boudu Saved from Drowning 1932 (Unrated) — ★★★1/2
A suicidal tramp completely disrupts the wealthy household of the man that saves him from drowning. A gentle but sardonic farce from the master filmmaker. Remade in 1986 as "Down and Out In Beverly Hills." 87m/B/W; VHS, DVD. **C:** Michel Simon; Charles Granval; Jean Daste; Marcelle Hainia; Severine Lerczinska; Jacques Becker; Directed by Jean Renoir; Written by Jean Renoir; Cinematography by Marcel Lucien. **Pr:** Michel Simon; Jean Gehret; Michel Simon. **A:** Jr. High-Adult. **P:** Entertainment. **U:** Home. **L:** French. **Mov-Ent:** Classic Films. **Acq:** Purchase, Rent/Lease. **Dist:** Interama, Inc.; Glenn Video Vistas Ltd.; Tapeworm Video Distributors Inc. $59.95.

Bought and Sold 2003 (Unrated) — ★★
Coming of age tale set in Jersey City. Ray Ray Morales (Sardina) is working for minimum wage at a shoe store but really wants to buy some pawnshop turntables so he can be a DJ. So he gets a second job with local loan shark Chunks (Grifasi), who wants him to keep an eye on elderly pawnshop owner Kutty (Margulies) who owes Chunks money. Soon Ray Ray is falling for Kutty's niece, Ruby (Neshat), and getting too involved. When Kutty can't meet his payments, Ray Ray has to make some decisions about what's really important to him. 92m. **C:** David Margulies; Joe Grifasi; Rafael Sardina; Marjan Neshat; Frank Harts; Christina Ablaza; Anthony Chisholm; Directed by Michael Tolajian; Written by Michael Tolajian; Cinematography by Kip Bogdahn; Music by Joe Delia. **A:** Sr. High-Adult. **P:** Entertainment. **U:** Home. **L:** English. **Mov-Ent:** Crime Drama, Comedy-Drama. **Dist:** Lions Gate Entertainment Inc.; Movies Unlimited; Alpha Video. $14.98.

Boujad: A Nest in the Heat 1995
Director Hakim Belabbes documents his return to his hometown of Boujad in Morocco revealing the domestic spaces and religious rituals of intra-family relationships. Subtitled in English. 45m; VHS. **A:** Adult. **P:** Education. **U:** Institution, BCTV. **L:** Arabic. **Gen-Edu:** Documentary Films, Family, Middle East. **Acq:** Purchase, Rent/Lease. **Dist:** Arab Film Distribution. $195.00.

Boulevard 1994 (R) — ★1/2
Jennefer (Wuhrer) is forced to give her baby up for adoption, after escaping from an abusive husband, and make her way on the city's mean streets. She meets prostitute Ola (Chong), who decides to look after the naif and protect Jennefer from violent pimp Hassan (Phillips). But Ola gets into trouble with tough cop Claren (Henriksen) and soon Jennefer must survive on her own—against both Hassan and her vengeful husband. Woman empowerment, complete with standard cliches. 96m; VHS, CC. **C:** Kari Wuhrer; Rae Dawn Chong; Lou Diamond Phillips; Lance Henriksen; Joel Bissonnette; Directed by Penelope Buitenhuis; Written by Rae Dawn Chong; Music by Ian Thomas. **Pr:** Peter Simpson; Ray Sager; Ilana Frank; Peter J. Oppenheimer; Norstar Entertainment. **A:** Sr. High-Adult. **P:** Entertainment. **U:** Home. **Mov-Ent:** Women, Prostitution, Violence. **Acq:** Purchase. **Dist:** Lions Gate Television Corp. $92.98.

Boulevard Nights 1979 (R) — ★★
A young Latino man tries to escape his neighborhood's streetgang violence, while his older brother is sucked into it. Music by Schifrin, known for the "Mission: Impossible" theme. 102m; VHS, DVD. **C:** Richard Yniguez; Danny De La Paz; Marta DuBois; Carmen Zapata; Victor Millan; Directed by Michael Pressman; Cinematography by John Bailey; Music by Lalo Schifrin. **Pr:** Bill Benenson; Tony Bill. **A:** Sr. High-Adult. **P:** Entertainment. **U:** Home. **Mov-Ent. Acq:** Purchase. **Dist:** WarnerArchive.com. $19.98.

Boulevard of Broken Dreams 1988 (PG-13) — ★★
Successful Hollywood screenwriter Tom Garfield (Waters) returns to his native Australia to figure out how his life got so screwed up. His estranged wife is living with someone else and his daughter barely remembers him. Affecting look at personal priorities versus success. 95m; VHS. **C:** John Waters; Kim Gyngell; Penelope Stewart; Directed by Pino Amenta. **A:** Jr. High-Adult. **P:** Entertainment. **U:** Home. **Mov-Ent:** Marriage, Australia. **Acq:** Purchase. **Dist:** No Longer Available.

Boulez on Varese 1975
Pierre Boulez conducts and early Edgar Varese composition. Each program explores the complexities and rewards of music composed by the late Edward Vares. 30m; VHS, 3/4 U, EJ, Q. **Pr:** WCBS New York; Camera Three Productions. **A:** Sr. High-Adult. **P:** Entertainment. **U:** Institution, SURA. **Fin-Art:** Music--Performance. **Acq:** Duplication, Free Duplication. **Dist:** Camera Three Productions, Inc.; Creative Arts Television Archive.

Boulez X 3 1975
The problems of presenting avant garde music to the public is examined in this series of three untitled programs. 30m; VHS, 3/4 U, EJ, Q. **C:** Pierre Boulez. **Pr:** WCBS New York; Camera Three Productions. **A:** Sr. High-Adult. **P:** Entertainment. **U:** Institution, SURA. **Fin-Art:** Music--Performance. **Acq:** Duplication, Free Duplication. **Dist:** Camera Three Productions, Inc.

Bounce 2000 (PG-13) — ★★1/2
Ad exec Affleck swaps his airline ticket with a stranger who's anxious to get home to his wife. But since no good deed goes unpunished, the plane crashes and the man is killed. The guilt-stricken Affleck visits the stranger's widow (Paltrow) and winds up falling in love with her, only she doesn't know about their unfortunate connection. Okay, the plot is contrived, predictable, and a little schmaltzy, but it somehow avoids maudlin, and takes pains to make the emotions real. In this, director Roos is aided greatly by Affleck, who turns in some of his best work to date, and Paltrow, who seems less actress-y in an understated, smart performance. The two leads were said to be an item during filming. 105m; VHS, DVD, Blu-Ray, Wide. **C:** Gwyneth Paltrow; Ben Affleck; Natasha Henstridge; Jennifer Grey; Tony Goldwyn; Joe Morton; David Paymer; Johnny Galecki; Alex D. Linz; Juan Garcia; Sam Robards; Julia Campbell; Michael Laskin; John Levin; David Dorfman; Directed by Don Roos; Written by Don Roos; Cinematography by Robert Elswit; Music by Mychael Danna. **A:** Sr. High-Adult. **P:** Entertainment. **U:** Home. **Mov-Ent:** Drama, Advertising, Alcoholism. **Acq:** Purchase. **Dist:** Buena Vista Home Entertainment.

Bound 1996 (R) — ★★
Ex-con Corky (Gershon) is busy fixing up her new apartment after serving five years for robbery. Her next-door neighbors are Caesar (Pantoliano), a neurotic, money-laundering mobster, and his sexy girlfriend, a seemingly dumb brunette named Violet (Tilly). The femme twosome hook up (in and out of bed) and hatch a plan to steal two million freshly laundered dollars from Caesar, who goes ballistic when he discovers the money gone. It's a flashy—but not substantive—thriller. Directorial debut for the brothers Wachowski. 107m; VHS, DVD, Blu-Ray. **C:** Gina Gershon; Jennifer Tilly; Joe Pantoliano; John P. Ryan; Barry Kivel; Christopher Meloni; Peter Spellos; Richard Sarafian; Mary Mara; Susie Bright; Ivan Kane; Kevin M. Richardson; Gene Borkan; Directed by Andy Wachowski; Lana Wachowski; Written by Andy Wachowski; Lana Wachowski; Cinematography by Bill Pope; Music by Don Davis. **Pr:** Andrew Lazar; Stuart Boros; Andy Wachowski; Larry Wachowski; Andy Wachowski; Lana Wachowski; Spelling Productions; Gramercy Pictures. **A:** Sr. High-Adult. **P:** Entertainment. **U:** Home. **Mov-Ent:** Mystery & Suspense, Violence. **Acq:** Purchase. **Dist:** Lions Gate Entertainment Inc.

Bound and Gagged: A Love Story 1993 (R) — ★
For some reason, Elizabeth (Saltarelli), who is desperate for a husband, thinks that she might increase her chances of finding one if she kidnaps her friend Leslie (Allen) and goes on a weird wild goose chase through Minnesota with the hostage and her hopeless partner-in-crime, Cliff (Denton). Go figure. 96m; VHS, DVD. **C:** Ginger Lynn Allen; Karen Black; Chris Denton; Elizabeth Saltarelli; Mary Ella Ross; Chris Mulkey; Directed by Daniel Appleby; Written by Daniel Appleby; Cinematography by Dean Lent; Music by William Murphy. **A:** Sr. High-Adult. **P:** Entertainment. **U:** Home. **Mov-Ent. Acq:** Purchase. **Dist:** Movies Unlimited. $14.99.

Bound by a Secret 2009 (Unrated) — ★★
Hallmark Channel original is pure schmaltz but Warren and Baxter make for a fine sisterly match-up. Successful actress Jane (Warren) visits her uptight sister Ida Mae (Baxter), who secretly raised Jane's now-grown and married daughter Kate (White). Jane's dying and wants to reveal her secret but Ida Mae has focused her life on Kate and is afraid of losing her love. 100m; DVD. **C:** Meredith Baxter; Lesley Ann Warren; Bridget Ann White; Timothy Bottoms; Holt McCallany; Ellery Sprayberry; Directed by David S. Cass, Sr.; Written by Darrell V. Orme Mann; Cinematography by James W. Wrenn; Music by Kyle Newmaster. **A:** Jr. High-Adult. **P:** Entertainment. **U:** Home. **Mov-Ent. Acq:** Purchase. **Dist:** Vivendi Visual Entertainment.

Bound by Lies 2005 (Unrated) — ★1/2
Detectives Max Garrett (Baldwin) and Eddie Fulton (Whitfield) are assigned to protect Laura (Swanson)?a sexy photographer of erotic images—when a rash of serial murders linked to her work is uncovered. But Garrett puts himself in danger by falling for her. 85m; VHS, DVD, Wide. **C:** Kristy Swanson; Stephen Baldwin; Charles Malik Whitfield; Natassia Malthe; Kevin Chamberlin; Joel Brooks; Tracy Howe; Directed by Valerie Landsburg; Written by D. Alvelo; Leland Zaitz; Cinematography by Maximo Munzi. **A:** Sr. High-Adult. **P:** Entertainment. **U:** Home. **Mov-Ent:** Sex & Sexuality, Photography. **Acq:** Purchase. **Dist:** Movies Unlimited; Alpha Video. $24.98.

Bound by the Wind 1994
The story of an international group of people who live near nuclear test sites and are trying to halt international nuclear testing. 40m; VHS, 3/4 U, Special order formats. **Pr:** David Brown. **A:** Sr. High-Adult. **P:** Education. **U:** Institution, CCTV, CATV, BCTV, Home, SURA. **Gen-Edu:** Ecology & Environment, Nuclear Energy, Propaganda. **Acq:** Purchase, Rent/Lease. **Dist:** The Video Project. $75.00.

Bound for Freedom 1976
Captivating the colonial period's flavor, two young boys become friends on a ship bound for America. James is taken by a farm

family who treats him well, while Davy is bought by cruel farmer who beats him. 52m; VHS, 3/4 U. **Pr:** Tapper Productions. **A:** Preschool-Primary. **P:** Education. **U:** Institution, SURA. **Chl-Juv**: History--U.S. **Acq:** Purchase. **Dist:** Home Vision Cinema.

Bound for Glory 1976 (PG) — ★★★½
The award-winning biography of American folk singer Woody Guthrie set against the backdrop of the Depression. Superb portrayal of the spirit and feelings of the period featuring many of his songs encased in the incidents that inspired them. Haskell Wexler's award-winning camera work is superbly expressive. 149m; VHS, DVD. **C:** David Carradine; Ronny Cox; Melinda Dillon; Randy Quaid; Directed by Hal Ashby; Written by Robert Getchell; Cinematography by Haskell Wexler. **Pr:** United Artists. **A:** Jr. High-Adult. **P:** Entertainment. **U:** Home. **Mov-Ent**: Biography: Music, Documentary Films. **Awds:** Oscars '76: Cinematog., Orig. Song Score and/or Adapt.; L.A. Film Critics '76: Cinematog.; Natl. Bd. of Review '76: Actor (Carradine); Natl. Soc. Film Critics '76: Cinematog. **Acq:** Purchase. **Dist:** MGM Home Entertainment. $19.98.

Bound for Nowhere: St. Louis Episode 1939
Records the voyage of more than 900 Jews fleeing Germany, who are turned away from their expected Cuban refuge and forced to return to Europe, to countries soon dominated by the Nazis. Includes a study guide. 9m/B/W; VHS. **Pr:** American Jewish Joint Distribution Committee. **A:** College-Adult. **P:** Education. **U:** Institution, Home. **Gen-Edu**: Documentary Films, Judaism. **Acq:** Purchase, Rent/Lease. **Dist:** National Center for Jewish Film. $60.00.

The Boundaries of Time: Caspar David Friedrich 1991
The life of the German landscape painter is alternated with shots of his work. 39m; VHS. **C:** Helmut Griem; Directed by Peter Schamoni. **Pr:** Home Vision. **A:** Family. **P:** Education. **U:** Home. **Fin-Art**: Art & Artists, Painting. **Acq:** Purchase. **Dist:** Home Vision Cinema. $39.95.

Boundary Layer Control 1966
Demonstrates methods of controlling boundary layer transition and separation to produce higher lift and/or lower drag. Part of EBE's "Fluid Mechanics Program." 25m/B/W; VHS, 3/4 U. **Pr:** NCFMF. **A:** College. **P:** Education. **U:** Institution, SURA. **Hea-Sci**: Documentary Films, Physics. **Acq:** Purchase, Rent/Lease, Trade-in. **Dist:** Encyclopedia Britannica.

Boundary Lines 1946
To confront bigotry and hate, Philip Stapp's film provides a look at the origins of these evils-the imaginary boundary lines men draw to divide themselves. 12m; 3/4 U, Special order formats. **Pr:** International Film Foundation. **A:** Jr. High-Adult. **P:** Education. **U:** Institution, SURA. **Fin-Art**: Documentary Films, Prejudice. **Acq:** Purchase, Rent/Lease. **Dist:** International Film Foundation.

The Bounder 1982
Suave and smooth-talking Howard Booth works a con on his stuffy brother-in-law resulting in a comical battle of wits. 170m; VHS, DVD. **A:** Adult. **P:** Entertainment. **U:** Home. **Mov-Ent**: Television, Comedy-Drama. **Acq:** Purchase. **Dist:** BFS Video. $39.98.

Bounds 1987
A mime struggles to free himself from the rigidity of his daily schedule. 8m; VHS, 3/4 U. **Pr:** National Film Board of Canada. **A:** Family. **P:** Education. **U:** Institution, SURA. **Gen-Edu**: Mime. **Acq:** Purchase, Rent/Lease. **Dist:** National Film Board of Canada.

Boundweave: Level 1 1989
A video instruction guide which teaches you how to weave. 90m; VHS. **A:** Jr. High-Adult. **P:** Instruction. **U:** Home. **How-Ins**: How-To, Crafts, Sewing. **Acq:** Purchase. **Dist:** Victorian Video/Yarn Barn of Kansas, Inc. $44.95.

The Bounty 1984 (PG) — ★★½
A new version of "Mutiny on the Bounty," with emphasis on a more realistic relationship between Fletcher Christian and Captain Bligh—and a more sympathetic portrayal of the captain, too. The sensuality of Christian's relationship with a Tahitian beauty also receives greater importance. 130m; VHS, DVD, Wide. **C:** Mel Gibson; Anthony Hopkins; Laurence Olivier; Edward Fox; Daniel Day-Lewis; Bernard Hill; Philip Davis; Liam Neeson; Directed by Roger Donaldson; Written by Robert Bolt; Cinematography by Arthur Ibbetson; Music by Vangelis. **Pr:** Orion Pictures. **A:** Jr. High-Adult. **P:** Entertainment. **U:** Home. **Mov-Ent**: Action-Adventure, Boating, Drama. **Acq:** Purchase. **Dist:** Lions Gate Television Corp. $29.98.

Bounty 2009 (PG-13) — ★
Bounty hunter Nate needs money to pay off a debt or he's a dead man. But it means breaking a female outlaw out of jail and claiming the reward for himself. Story doesn't exactly hold together but for a low-budget western it's almost tolerable. 90m; DVD. **C:** Michelle Acuna; Austin O'Brien; Jarret LeMaster; Bruce Isham; Rodrick Lee Goins; Steve Savage; Directed by Jared Isham; Written by Jared Isham; Cinematography by Kenneth Yeung; Music by Jason Livesay; Nolan Livesay. **A:** Jr. High-Adult. **P:** Entertainment. **U:** Home. **Mov-Ent**: Western. **Acq:** Purchase. **Dist:** North American Motion Pictures, LLC.

Bounty Dog 1994 — ★★
Yoshiyuki travels to the colonized moon with the Bounty Dog team to investigate reports of illegal weapons development. He encounters a young girl and is reminded of his girlfriend, whose mysterious death five years before still troubles him. The girl explains that an alien civilization is about to awaken on the dark side of the moon and leads him toward his destiny. The plot, however, is not executed quite so purposefully in some places. 60m; DVD. **A:** Sr. High-Adult. **P:** Entertainment. **U:** Home. **Mov-Ent**: Animation & Cartoons, Animation & Cartoons, Science Fiction. **Acq:** Purchase. **Dist:** Manga Entertainment.

The Bounty Hunter 2010 (PG-13) — ★½
Trite romantic comedy inflicts a predictable plot, grating dialogue, and a plodding pace—a multiple offender. Bounty hunter Milo (Butler) is overjoyed when he finds out his next assignment is to bring in his ex-wife Nicole (Aniston), a reporter who missed her court date to look into a suspicious suicide. The majority of the movie consists of the couple bickering and one-upping each other while evading goons trying to stop Nicole from discovering the truth. The two finally decide to work together and romance is rekindled, despite the fact that Aniston and Butler have less chemistry than a remedial science class. Watch the classic "His Girl Friday" to see how it's done correctly. 110m; Blu-Ray, On Demand, Wide, CC. **C:** Gerard Butler; Jennifer Aniston; Jason Sudeikis; Christine Baranski; Cathy Moriarty; Directed by Andy Tennant; Written by Sarah Thorp; Cinematography by Oliver Bokelberg. **A:** Jr. High-Adult. **P:** Entertainment. **U:** Home. **L:** English. **Mov-Ent**: Journalism. **Acq:** Purchase. **Dist:** Sony Pictures Home Entertainment Inc.; Amazon.com Inc.; Movies Unlimited.

Bounty Hunter 2002 1994 — ★½
A rogue virus kills most of the world's population and few of those remaining are completely immune. Slave trading in the capture and sale of immune survivors is a lucrative business and a bounty hunter's last assignment is to bring in a beautiful but deadly woman. 90m; VHS. **C:** Phil Nordell; Francine Lapensee; Vernon Wells; Jeff Conaway; Directed by Sam Auster; Written by Sam Auster. **A:** College-Adult. **P:** Entertainment. **U:** Home. **Mov-Ent**: Science Fiction. **Acq:** Purchase. **Dist:** No Longer Available.

Bounty Hunters 1989 (R) — ★★
A man hunts down his friend's killer. 91m; VHS. **C:** Robert Ginty; Bo Hopkins; Loeta Waterdown; Directed by Robert Ginty. **Pr:** Fritz Mathews. **A:** Sr. High-Adult. **P:** Entertainment. **U:** Home. **Mov-Ent**: Mystery & Suspense. **Acq:** Purchase. **Dist:** No Longer Available.

Bounty Hunters 1996 (R) — ★★
Rival bounty hunters (and ex-lovers) Jersey Bellini (Dudikoff) and B.B. Mitchell (Howard) join forces to capture bail-jumping, stolen-car king Delmos (Ratner), who's also the target of mob hitmen. Gunplay and car chases. 98m; VHS, DVD, Wide, CC. **C:** Michael Dudikoff; Lisa Howard; Benjamin Ratner; Directed by George Erschbamer; Written by George Erschbamer; Cinematography by A.J. Vesak; Music by Norman Orenstein. **A:** Sr. High-Adult. **P:** Entertainment. **U:** Home. **Mov-Ent**. **Acq:** Purchase. **Dist:** Buena Vista Home Entertainment.

Bounty Hunters 2: Hardball 1997 (R) — ★★
A bounty hunter and his female partner tick off the mob by foiling a heist and now must fend off hired killers looking for revenge. 97m; VHS, DVD, Blu-Ray, Wide. **C:** Michael Dudikoff; Lisa Howard; Steve Bacic; Tony Curtis; Directed by George Erschbamer; Written by George Erschbamer; Jeff Barmash; Michael Ellis; Cinematography by Brian Pearson; Music by Leon Aronson. **A:** Sr. High-Adult. **P:** Entertainment. **U:** Home. **Mov-Ent**: Action-Comedy. **Acq:** Purchase. **Dist:** Buena Vista Home Entertainment.

The Bounty Man 1972 (Unrated) — ★★
A bounty hunter brings an outlaw in, robbing him of his freedom and his girlfriend. 74m; VHS. **C:** Clint Walker; Richard Basehart; Margot Kidder; Arthur Hunnicutt; John Ericson; Gene Evans; Directed by John Llewellyn Moxey. **Pr:** Aaron Spelling. **A:** Jr. High-Adult. **P:** Entertainment. **U:** Home. **Mov-Ent**: Western, TV Movies. **Acq:** Purchase. **Dist:** $19.98.

Bounty Tracker 1993 (R) — ★½
Johnny Damone (Lamas) is a bounty-hunter in pursuit of the killer-for-hire who murdered his brother. This personal vendetta leads to an action-packed martial arts showdown between Johnny and his cold-blooded prey. 90m; VHS, CC. **C:** Lorenzo Lamas; Matthias Hues; Eugene Robert Glazer; Cyndi Pass; Eric Mansker; Judd Omen; Eddie Frias; George Perez; Directed by Kurt Anderson. **Pr:** Pierre David. **A:** Sr. High-Adult. **P:** Entertainment. **U:** Home. **Mov-Ent**: Martial Arts. **Acq:** Purchase. **Dist:** Lions Gate Entertainment Inc. $14.98.

The Bouquet 2013 (Unrated) — ★★½
Terri (Swanson) ad her younger sister Mandy (Mayne) have always been opposites but they must set aside their differences when a family tragedy strikes. Terri comes home and must help Mandy and their mother, Bonnie (Cavendish), save the family's failing flower business and rediscover their family ties. 99m; DVD. **C:** Kristy Swanson; Alberta Mayne; Nicola Cavendish; Danny Glover; Michael Shanks; Jeremy Guilbaut; Stephen E. Miller; Directed by Anne Wheeler; Written by Kele McGlohon; Cinematography by Paul Mitchnick; Music by Stu Goldberg. **A:** Family. **P:** Entertainment. **U:** Home. **L:** English. **Mov-Ent**: Family, Flowers, Business. **Acq:** Purchase. **Dist:** Gaiam Inc.

Bouquet of Barbed Wire 1976 — ★½
Overlong soaper revolves around a weathly family and their hidden secrets: incest and infidelity. On three tapes. 330m; VHS. **C:** Frank Finlay; Susan Penhaligon; Deborah Grant; Sheila Allen; James Aubrey; Directed by Tom Wharmby. **A:** Adult. **P:** Entertainment. **U:** Home. **Mov-Ent**: Family, Melodrama. **Acq:** Purchase. **Dist:** Amazon.com Inc.

Bourbon in Suburbia 1970
Probes America's destructive social problem—alcohol. Housewife ends up one morning with a hangover and a strange man while her husband is away. Theme: alcoholism can be overcome only if we are willing to face reality. 28m; VHS, 3/4 U, Special order formats. **C:** Anne Francis; Marie Windsor. **Pr:** Paulist Productions. **A:** Sr. High-Adult. **P:** Religious. **U:** Institution, CCTV, SURA. **Hea-Sci**: Documentary Films, Alcoholism. **Acq:** Purchase, Rent/Lease. **Dist:** Paulist Productions.

The Bourne Identity 1988 (Unrated) — ★★★
Chamberlain stars as an amnesiac trying to piece together the fragments of his memory. Is he U.S. espionage agent Jason Bourne or an international terrorist? Aided by Smith (the kidnap victim who falls in love with her captor), the two traverse Europe trying to escape the spy network out to assassinate the mystery man who knows too little. Exciting miniseries adaptation of the Robert Ludlum thriller. 185m; VHS, DVD. **C:** Richard Chamberlain; Jaclyn Smith; Denholm Elliott; Anthony Quayle; Donald Moffat; Yorgo Voyagis; Directed by Roger Young; Written by Carol Sobieski. **A:** Jr. High-Adult. **P:** Entertainment. **U:** Home. **Mov-Ent**: Mystery & Suspense, TV Movies. **Acq:** Purchase. **Dist:** Warner Home Video, Inc.; Baker and Taylor. $79.99.

The Bourne Identity 2002 (PG-13) — ★★★½
First-rate international espionage thriller loosely based on the first book (published in 1981) of Robert Ludlum's trilogy, previously filmed as a 1988 TV miniseries starring Richard Chamberlain. A young man (Damon) gets fished out of the ocean with a couple of bullet holes and amnesia—his only clue a numbered Swiss account. This reveals he has multiple identities, including that of Jason Bourne, who has an apartment in Paris. To get there, Bourne pays free-spirited Marie (Potente) for a ride. As Bourne tries to piece his past together, he learns he's a highly efficient assassin for a covert CIA operation and his boss (Cooper) considers him a rogue operative and is trying to kill him. 118m; VHS, DVD, Blu-Ray, UMD, HD-DVD. **C:** Matt Damon; Franka Potente; Chris Cooper; Brian Cox; Clive Owen; Julia Stiles; Gabriel Mann; Adewale Akinnuoye-Agbaje; Walton Goggins; Josh Hamilton; Tim Dutton; Directed by Doug Liman; Written by Tony Gilroy; W(illiam) Blake Herron; Cinematography by Oliver Wood; Music by John Powell. **Pr:** Doug Liman; Patrick Crowley; Richard N. Gladstein; Doug Liman; Hypnotic; Universal Pictures. **A:** Sr. High-Adult. **P:** Entertainment. **U:** Home. **Mov-Ent**. **Acq:** Purchase. **Dist:** Movies Unlimited; Alpha Video; Universal Studios Home Video.

The Bourne Legacy 2012 (PG-13) — ★★★
Tony Gilroy, the writer of the first three films based on the Robert Ludlum series, cleverly expands on his own universe by presenting viewers with another agent, Aaron Cross (Renner), in the Bourne program. The new Bourne works much like the old Bourne although Gilroy isn't as adept at action, but he makes up for it with razor-sharp dialogue and clever plotting. It takes some time to get going but Gilroy has a gift with words--and Renner, Weisz, and Norton at delivering them--that once this Legacy takes off it doesn't look back. 125m; DVD, Blu-Ray. **C:** Jeremy Renner; Rachel Weisz; Edward Norton; Joan Allen; Albert Finney; David Strathairn; Scott Glenn; Directed by Tony Gilroy; Written by Tony Gilroy; Dan Gilroy; Cinematography by Robert Elswit; Music by James Newton Howard. **Pr:** Frank Marshall; Patrick Crowley; Ben Smith; Jeffrey Weiner; Universal Pictures; Relativity Media. **A:** Jr. High-Adult. **P:** Entertainment. **U:** Home. **L:** English. **Mov-Ent**: Intelligence Service, Conspiracies or Conspiracy Theories. **Acq:** Purchase. **Dist:** Universal Studios Home Video.

The Bourne Supremacy 2004 (PG-13) — ★★★
Warning! The easily-queasy should be wary of the hand-held camerawork and quick edits of the action sequences. Amnesiac CIA-trained assassin Jason Bourne (Damon) is now living quietly with girlfriend Marie (Potente) when he's targeted for death by Russian bad guys and made the patsy for a Berlin hit on a couple of agents. CIA officer Landy (Allen) and her boss (Cox) try to reel Bourne in while he tries to figure out just who wants him dead this time (and why). The non-stop action moves from India to Berlin to Amsterdam to Moscow, and while the plot eventually turns out to be simple enough, the chases are not. Damon once again proves adept as an action man while making Bourne an intelligent and oddly sympathetic character. Loosely adapted from the second book of Robert Ludlum's Bourne trilogy. 109m; VHS, DVD, Blu-Ray, UMD, HD-DVD. **C:** Matt Damon; Franka Potente; Joan Allen; Brian Cox; Marton Csokas; Gabriel Mann; Karel Roden; Julia Stiles; Karl Urban; Tomas Arana; Tim Griffin; Michelle Monaghan; Tom Gallop; John Bedford Lloyd; Ethan Sandler; Oksana Akinshina; Directed by Paul Greengrass; Written by Tony Gilroy; Cinematography by Oliver Wood; Music by John Powell. **Pr:** Frank Marshall; Patrick Crowley; Paul L. Sandberg; Ludlum Entertainment; MP Theta Prods; Universal. **A:** Sr. High-Adult. **P:** Entertainment. **U:** Home. **Mov-Ent**: Action-Adventure, Intelligence Service, India. **Acq:** Purchase. **Dist:** Universal Studios Home Video; Movies Unlimited; Alpha Video. $29.98.

The Bourne Ultimatum 2007 (PG-13) — ★★★½
In this third (and final?) chapter Jason Bourne (Damon) continues his search for clues to to his past with Treadstone, the mothballed facility where he was trained. Now CIA official Vosen (Strathairn) wants to revive the project, and assigns agent Lundy (Allen) to eliminate Bourne. Meanwhile, Bourne is outmaneuvering cops, feds, spooks, and Interpol agents in Moscow, Paris, Madrid, Tangier, London, and New York. Smart, tense, and frenetic, with excellent performances from all involved. The only drawback is the confusion- and nausea-inducing camera work during the action sequences. 111m; DVD, Blu-Ray, HD-DVD, Wide. **C:** Matt Damon; Julia Stiles; Joan Allen; David Strathairn; Paddy Considine; Edgar Ramirez; Scott Glenn; Albert Finney; Tom Gallop; Corey Johnson; Daniel Bruhl; Colin Stinton; Joey Ansah; Directed by Paul Greengrass; Written by Tony Gilroy; Scott Burns; George Nolfi; Cinematography by Oliver Wood; Music by John Powell. **Pr:** Frank Marshall; Patrick Crowley; Paul L. Sandberg; Ludlum Entertainment; Universal. **A:** Jr. High-Adult. **P:** Entertainment. **U:** Home. **Mov-Ent**: Intelligence Service. **Awds:** Oscars '07: Film Editing, Sound, Sound FX Editing; British Acad. '07: Film Editing,

Sound. **Acq:** Purchase. **Dist:** Movies Unlimited; Alpha Video; Universal Studios Home Video.

Bournonville Ballet Technique: Fifty Enchainements 19??
Principals of the Royal Danish Ballet demonstrate 50 dance exercises developed by Danish choreographer Bournonville. 45m; VHS. **A:** Jr. High-Adult. **P:** Instruction. **U:** Institution, Home. **How-Ins:** Dance--Instruction, Dance--Ballet. **Acq:** Purchase. **Dist:** Stagestep. $39.95.

Boutique 2004 — ★★½
Window dresser at a chic boutique in Tehran steals a pair of jeans for a girl he's interested in after she says she can't afford anything at the establishment. This is the beginning of a downward spiral in his life. Thoughtfully moving film makes startling observations of Iranian society. In Farsi with English subtitles. 113m; DVD. **C:** Mohammad Reza Golzar; Golshifteh Farahani; Reza Rooygari; Directed by Hamid Nematollah; Written by Hamid Nematollah; Cinematography by Mahmoud Kalari; Music by Fariborz Lachini. **A:** Adult. **P:** Entertainment. **U:** Home. **Mov-Ent:** Middle East. **Acq:** Purchase. **Dist:** Facets Multimedia Inc. $29.95.

Bovine Parturition by Cesarean Section 19??
Contains extremely graphic live-action footage of a complete cesaraen section being performed on a Holstein heifer. Includes discussion of the procedure from a veterinarian as well as information on the medications used and the examination that was done before the operation. 20m; VHS. **A:** Sr. High-Adult. **P:** Education. **U:** Institution. **Hea-Sci:** Agriculture, Animals, Childbirth. **Acq:** Purchase. **Dist:** CEV Multimedia. $79.95.

Bow Hunting Made Easy 1987
A host of bowhunting experts offer their knowledge on basic equipment, clothing, gear, scents and much more. 48m; VHS. **Pr:** BFV. **A:** Adult. **P:** Instruction. **U:** Home. **Spo-Rec:** Hunting. **Acq:** Purchase. **Dist:** Best Video. $19.99.

Bowel and Bladder Management 1985
An explanation of procedures for bowel training, bladder training, and bladder exercise, prior to removal of an indwelling catheter. 25m; VHS, 3/4 U. **Pr:** Trainex. **A:** College-Adult. **P:** Professional. **U:** Institution. **L:** English, Spanish. **Hea-Sci:** Patient Care, Medical Education. **Acq:** Purchase, Rent/Lease. **Dist:** Medcom Inc.

Bowel Elimination 1982
This program describes the proper procedure involved in a patient's bowel elimination. 25m; VHS, 3/4 U. **Pr:** Trainex. **A:** College-Adult. **P:** Professional. **U:** Institution. **Hea-Sci:** Nursing, Patient Care. **Acq:** Purchase, Rent/Lease. **Dist:** Medcom Inc.

Bower and Kramer on Medical Malpractice 1984
Two experts in the field of medical malpractice analyze and discuss an actual medical malpractice trial. 210m; VHS, 3/4 U. **Pr:** Practicing Law Institute. **A:** Sr. High-Adult. **P:** Education. **U:** Institution, Home. **Gen-Edu:** Documentary Films, Law. **Acq:** Purchase, Rent/Lease. **Dist:** Practising Law Institute.

The Bowery 1933 (Unrated) — ★★★
Chuck Connors (Beery) owns a saloon on New York's Bowery in the 1890s and is a friendly rival to daredevil gambler Steve Brodie (Raft). Only things aren't so friendly when the men both fall for hard-luck dame Lucy (Wray). Connors proposes that Brodie jump off the Brooklyn Bridge (a feat he allegedly accomplished before) to impress Lucy and offers ownership of his saloon as added incentive. Cooper, who starred opposite Beery in 1931's "The Champ," plays streetwise orphan Swipes McGurk. 92m/B/W; VHS. **C:** Wallace Beery; George Raft; Fay Wray; Jackie Cooper; Pert Kelton; Directed by Raoul Walsh; Written by Howard Estabrook; Cinematography by Barney McGill; Music by Alfred Newman. **A:** Jr. High-Adult. **P:** Entertainment. **U:** Home. **Mov-Ent. Acq:** Purchase. **Dist:** Nostalgia Family Video/Hollywood's Attic. $19.99.

Bowery at Midnight 1942 — ★½
Lugosi plays a man who recycles criminals into zombies that commit crimes for his benefit. Bela and an intense mood can't quite save this pic. 60m/B/W; VHS, DVD. **C:** Bela Lugosi; Tom Neal; Dave O'Brien; Wanda McKay; Directed by Wallace Fox; Written by Gerald Schnitzer; Cinematography by Mack Stengler; Music by Edward Kay. **Pr:** Monogram. **A:** Sr. High-Adult. **P:** Entertainment. **U:** Home. **Mov-Ent:** Horror, Death. **Acq:** Purchase. **Dist:** Sinister Cinema; Rex Miller Artisan Studio. $19.95.

Bowery Blitzkrieg 1941 — ★
This lesser "East Side Kids" entry has Gorcey opting to enter the boxing ring rather than turn to crime. Needs more Huntz. 62m/B/W; VHS, DVD. **C:** Leo Gorcey; Huntz Hall; Bobby Jordan; Warren Hull; Charlotte Henry; Keye Luke; Directed by Wallace Fox. **Pr:** Sam Katzman; Monogram. **A:** Family. **P:** Entertainment. **U:** Home. **Mov-Ent:** Sports--Fiction: Comedy, Boxing, Classic Films. **Acq:** Purchase. **Dist:** Movies Unlimited; Alpha Video. $19.95.

Bowery Boys Meet the Monsters 1954 — ★★
The infamous Bowery Boys display their usual hilarious hijinks in this comedy in which they confront a group of transplant-happy scientists. 65m; VHS. **C:** Leo Gorcey; Huntz Hall; Bernard Gorcey; Bennie Bartlett; Lloyd Corrigan; Directed by Edward L. Bernds. **A:** Family. **P:** Entertainment. **U:** Home. **Mov-Ent:** Classic Films, Comedy--Slapstick, Surgical Transplantation. **Acq:** Purchase. **Dist:** Grapevine Video. $11.95.

Bowery Buckaroos 1947 — ★★
The Bowery Boys take their act West in search of gold, meeting up with the usual amounts of goofy characters and hilarious misunderstandings. 66m/B/W; VHS. **C:** Leo Gorcey; Huntz Hall; Bobby Jordan; Gabriel Dell; William Benedict; David Gorcey; Julie Briggs; Bernard Gorcey; Chief Yowlachie; Iron Eyes Cody; Directed by William Beaudine. **Pr:** Monogram. **A:** Family. **P:** Entertainment. **U:** Home. **Mov-Ent. Acq:** Purchase. **Dist:** Warner Home Video, Inc. $14.98.

Bowery Dish 2004
Documentary exploring gentrification by observing how restaurants and bars have changed the notorious Bowery from a skid row into a trendy neighborhood. 52m; VHS, DVD. **A:** Sr. High-Adult. **P:** Education. **U:** Home, Institution. **Gen-Edu:** Economics, Documentary Films. **Acq:** Purchase, Rent/Lease. **Dist:** The Cinema Guild. $275.00.

Bowfinger 1999 (PG-13) — ★★★
Martin stars as wannabe Hollywood player Bobby Bowfinger, who is desperate to break into the big time. His one hope is to convince action star Kit Ramsey (Murphy) to be in a cheesy sci-fi scare flick entitled "Chubby Rain." But Ramsey and his tyrannical New Age advisor Stricter (Stamp) want nothing to do with the movie. Bowfinger gets a crew together and stalks Ramsey through the streets of L.A., filming his every movement so that the material can be used in the movie. After his tactics send Ramsey to the "relaxation home," Bowfinger hires geeky lookalike Jiff (also Murphy) to take his place. The pairing of Martin and Murphy works well, and Frank Oz is an expert at directing off-beat comedies such as this. 96m; VHS, DVD. **C:** Steve Martin; Eddie Murphy; Christine Baranski; Heather Graham; Terence Stamp; Jamie Kennedy; Robert Downey, Jr.; Barry Newman; Directed by Frank Oz; Written by Steve Martin; Cinematography by Ueli Steiger; Music by David Newman. **Pr:** Brian Grazer; Imagine Entertainment; Universal Studios. **A:** Jr. High-Adult. **P:** Entertainment. **U:** Home. **Mov-Ent:** Filmmaking, Illegal Immigration. **Acq:** Purchase. **Dist:** Movies Unlimited; Alpha Video.

Bowl of Bone 1992
Combines biography, personal journey, and history in this examination of the relationship between two women: Native American herbalist and visionary Annie Zetko York and spiritually restless American expatriate Jan-Marie Martell. Filmed over the period of 15 years. 114m; VHS. **A:** Family. **P:** Entertainment. **U:** Home, Institution. **Gen-Edu:** Native Americans, Biography. **Acq:** Purchase. **Dist:** Moving Images Distribution.

Bowl to Win with Earl Anthony 1978
Comprehensive coverage of bowling fundamentals for both left and right-handed players, including different step approaches, wrist control and other factors. 45m; VHS. **C:** Earl Anthony. **Pr:** Morris Video. **A:** Family. **P:** Instruction. **U:** Home. **Spo-Rec:** Sports--General, Bowling. **Acq:** Purchase. **Dist:** Morris Video; School-Tech Inc. $19.95.

Bowl Turning 1988
Described as a "virtuoso," Stubbs demonstrates how to make wooden bowls. 120m; VHS. **C:** Del Stubbs. **Pr:** Taunton Press. **A:** Sr. High-Adult. **P:** Instruction. **U:** Home. **How-Ins:** Construction, Crafts. **Acq:** Purchase. **Dist:** Taunton Press Inc. $39.95.

Bowling 1968
The vice president of the Lifetime Sports Association gives instruction in the one and four-step deliveries, hook and straight ball deliveries, and how to pick up various spare combinations. The four tapes in the series can be purchased individually or as a set. 13m; VHS, 3/4 U. **C:** Lydon Lee. **Pr:** Champions on Film. **A:** Family. **P:** Instruction. **U:** Institution, CCTV, Home. **Spo-Rec:** Sports--General, Bowling. **Acq:** Purchase, Rent/Lease. **Dist:** School-Tech Inc. $49.00.
Indiv. Titles: 1. A New Approach to a Great Old Game 2. Fundamentals of the Arm Swing 3. Fundamentals of Footwork 4. Bowling Strikes and Spares.

Bowling for Columbine 2002 (R) — ★★★
Moore takes on the trigger-happy American gun culture, as well as the media, the NRA, and Littleton, Colorado'the site of the Columbine High School killings—with his usual blend of satire and chutzpah. 120m; VHS, DVD, CC. **C:** Directed by Michael Moore; Written by Michael Moore. **A:** Sr. High-Adult. **P:** Entertainment. **U:** Home. **Gen-Edu:** Documentary Films. **Awds:** Oscars '02: Feature Doc.; Ind. Spirit '03: Feature Doc.; Writers Guild '02: Orig. Screenplay. **Acq:** Purchase. **Dist:** MGM Home Entertainment.

The Bowling Masters: Practice Makes Perfect 1989
Tips are included here that will help anyone improve his bowling score. 40m; VHS, 3/4 U. **Pr:** Champions on Film. **A:** Family. **P:** Instruction. **U:** Institution, CCTV, Home. **Spo-Rec:** Sports--General, Bowling. **Acq:** Purchase. **Dist:** School-Tech Inc. $29.95.

Bowling Series 1985
A series of programs showing techniques for perfect bowling. 60m; VHS. **C:** Earl Anthony. **Pr:** Morris Video. **A:** Sr. High-Adult. **P:** Instruction. **U:** Home. **Spo-Rec:** Sports--General, Bowling. **Acq:** Purchase. **Dist:** Morris Video.
Indiv. Titles: 1. Bowl to Win 2. Going for 300.

Bowling with Marshall Holman and Johnny Petraglia 1983
The SyberVision Bowling Program teaches bowlers perfect body positioning and balance, synchronization of foot motion with back swing, perfect delivery, release, and follow through. 60m; VHS. **C:** Marshall Holman; Johnny Petraglia. **Pr:** SyberVision Systems. **A:** Jr. High-Adult. **P:** Instruction. **U:** Home. **Spo-Rec:** Sports--General. **Acq:** Purchase. **Dist:** SyberVision Systems, Inc. $39.95.

Bowling with Nelson Burton, Jr. 1987
Tips for novice and experienced bowlers. Topics covered include: keeping score, etiquette, equipment and spot bowling. 60m; VHS, 8 mm. **Pr:** Century Telecommunications III. **A:** Jr. High-Adult. **P:** Instruction. **U:** Institution, Home. **Spo-Rec:** Sports--General, Bowling. **Acq:** Purchase. **Dist:** ESPN Inc. $19.95.

The Box 19??
Artist gives birth to a new creation and lets it leave his studio to venture out on its own and form its own personality, just like children must venture out and do things on their own. 10m; VHS. **A:** Primary-Adult. **P:** Education. **U:** Institution. **Gen-Edu:** Personality. **Acq:** Purchase, Rent/Lease. **Dist:** National Film Board of Canada. $150.

The Box 2003 (R) — ★★½
Ah, it must be true love when an ex-con and an ex-stripper hook up at the local diner. But problems plague the happy pair's future like his mob connections, her psycho ex-husband, and the thugs who want their big bag of loot. 99m; VHS, DVD. **C:** James Russo; Theresa Russell; Brad Dourif; Steve Railsback; Jon Polito; Michael Rooker; Joe Palese; Lee Weaver; Directed by Richard Pepin; Written by James Russo; Music by Chris Anderson. **A:** Sr. High-Adult. **P:** Entertainment. **U:** Home. **Mov-Ent:** Crime Drama. **Acq:** Purchase. **Dist:** Bedford Entertainment Inc. $24.99.

The Box 2007 (R) — ★★
Two homicide detectives question a thief and a victim of a robbery gone wrong. One detective has to face past mistakes, while the other gets an offer from the criminal behind the botched heist. 96m; DVD. **C:** Gabrielle Beauvais; Giancarlo Esposito; A. J. Buckley; Jason George; Mia Maestro; James Madio; Yul Vazquez; Brett Donowho; Directed by A.J. Kparr; Written by A.J. Kparr; Cinematography by Sion Michel; Music by James T. Sale. **A:** Sr. High-Adult. **P:** Entertainment. **U:** Home. **Mov-Ent. Acq:** Purchase. **Dist:** Vivendi Visual Entertainment.

The Box 2009 (PG-13) — ★★½
A troubled married couple, Norma and Arthur (Diaz and Marsden), is given a mysterious wooden box by a stranger who tells them if they press the button to open the box they will be given $1 million. The downside is that a person unknown to them will be murdered and they have 24 hours to decide what to do. A preposterous premise stretched to its absolute limits, but done so smoothly that somehow logic never comes into question. Director Kelly, of "Donnie Darko" cult fame, brings his usual touch of controlled confusion, loved by many and hated by just as many. Based on the Richard Matheson short story "Button, Button," also made into a Twilight Zone episode in 1986. 115m; Blu-Ray, On Demand, Wide. **C:** Cameron Diaz; James Marsden; Frank Langella; Gillian Jacobs; James Rebhorn; Holmes Osborne; Sam Oz Stone; Directed by Richard Kelly; Written by Richard Kelly; Cinematography by Steven Poster; Music by Win Butler; Regine Chassagne; Owen Pallett. **Pr:** Richard Kelly; Dan Lin; Sean McKittrick; Kelly McKittrick; Richard Kelly; Radar Pictures; Darko Entertainment; Lin Pictures; Warner Bros. **A:** Jr. High-Adult. **P:** Entertainment. **U:** Home. **L:** English. **Mov-Ent. Acq:** Purchase. **Dist:** Amazon.com Inc.; Movies Unlimited; Alpha Video.

Box City 19??
Guides students in the use of Box City materials, intended to provide a hands-on learning experience in design principles and community planning. 18m; VHS. **A:** Jr. High-College. **P:** Education. **U:** Institution. **Gen-Edu:** Architecture. **Acq:** Purchase. **Dist:** Crystal Productions. $24.95.

Box Cutter Safety 1995
Features how to cut boxes properly and prevent injuries. 8m; VHS. **A:** Adult. **P:** Professional. **U:** Institution. **Bus-Ind:** Safety Education, Management, Occupational Training. **Acq:** Purchase, Rent/Lease. **Dist:** National Safety Council, California Chapter, Film Library. $175.00.

A Box for Mr. Lipton 1972
Story of a man's struggle to take charge of his life and communicate with others. Theme: before we can be in touch with others, we must be in touch with ourselves. Solitude can help achieve this. 29m; VHS, 3/4 U, Special order formats. **C:** Kenneth Mars; Pat Barry. **Pr:** Paulist Productions. **A:** Sr. High-Adult. **P:** Religious. **U:** Institution, CCTV, SURA. **Gen-Edu:** Communication, Self-Help. **Acq:** Purchase, Rent/Lease. **Dist:** Paulist Productions.

Box Investigates. . . 19??
Children visit Box's Science Lab where they discover and investigate the worlds of dinosaurs, animals, and insects. Includes guide. 20m; VHS. **A:** Primary. **P:** Education. **U:** Institution. **Hea-Sci:** Insects, Dinosaurs, Animals. **Acq:** Purchase. **Dist:** Clear Vue Inc. $49.00.
Indiv. Titles: 1. Dinosaurs 2. Animals 3. Spiders and Insects.

Box of Delights 1983
A young boy discovers a mysterious box and upon opening it, embarks on a magical adventure. 120m; VHS. **C:** Jon Pertwee; Robert Stephens. **A:** Family. **P:** Entertainment. **U:** Home. **Chl-Juv:** Fantasy, Children. **Acq:** Purchase. **Dist:** Paramount Pictures Corp. $19.98.

Box of Moonlight 1996 (R) — ★★
Hardworking, by-the-book electrical systems engineer Al Fountain (Turturo) feels mysteriously compelled to play hookey from his family and career while on an out-of-town business trip. Lost and confused, Al meets up with the Kid, a quirky recluse played with energy and appeal by Rockwell. Through a series of mix-ups, the nice-but-stuffy Al and the wild-but-well-meaning Kid end up spending the fourth of July weekend together. Al's inability to see the point of his journey long after the audience probably has makes the film a bit predictable and stale. DeCillo's third feature was six years in the making and financed by the success of his second feature, "Living in Oblivion." 111m;

VHS, DVD, CC. **C:** John Turturro; Sam Rockwell; Catherine Keener; Lisa Blount; Annie Corley; Dermot Mulroney; Alexander Goodwin; Directed by Tom DiCillo; Written by Tom DiCillo; Cinematography by Dr. Paul Ryan; Music by Jim Farmer. **Pr:** Thomas A. Bliss; Tom Rosenberg; Sigurjon Sighvatsson; Marcus Viscidi; Largo Entertainment; Lakeshore Entertainment; Lemon Sky Productions. **A:** Sr. High-Adult. **P:** Entertainment. **U:** Home. **Mov-Ent**: Comedy-Drama. **Acq:** Purchase. **Dist:** Lions Gate Home Entertainment.

Box of Treasures 1986
This film is a focus on Kwakiutl society, a native American Indian community, and their struggle to redefine cultural identity. 28m; 3/4 U. **Pr:** Chuck Olin and Associates. **A:** Family. **P:** Education. **U:** Institution, SURA. **Gen-Edu**: Documentary Films, Native Americans, Sociology. **Acq:** Purchase. **Dist:** Documentary Educational Resources.

Box Science 1988
Animals such as dinosaurs and insects are explained to kids in this series. 20m; VHS, 3/4 U. **Pr:** SVE. **A:** Primary-Jr. High. **P:** Education. **U:** Institution, CCTV, Home. **Hea-Sci**: Science, Animals. **Acq:** Purchase, Duplication. **Dist:** Clear Vue Inc. $199.00.
Indiv. Titles: 1. Box Investigates Animals 2. Box Investigates Dinosaurs 3. Box Investigates Spiders and Insects.

Box Solves Story Problems 19??
As Box searches for gold in the Old West he constantly finds himself having to solve story problems. He illustrates solving secrets—visualizing, careful reading, key words, and picking out important facts. Skill sheets and teacher's guide included. 8m; VHS. **A:** Primary. **P:** Education. **U:** Institution. **Chl-Juv**: Mathematics. **Acq:** Purchase. **Dist:** Clear Vue Inc. $49.00.
Indiv. Titles: 1. Addition Story Problems 2. Subtraction Story Problems 3. Multiplication Story Problems 4. Division Story Problems.

Boxarate 1996
Get in shape with Andrew Keegan as he takes you through a workout that combines boxing, karate, and low-impact aerobics. "Boxarate" helps you develop muscle strength, cardiovascular endurance, and a complete workout. 45m; VHS. **A:** Jr. High. **P:** Instruction. **U:** Home. **L:** English. **Spo-Rec**: Boxing. **Acq:** Purchase. **Dist:** Tapeworm Video Distributors Inc. $14.95.

Boxboarders! 2007 (PG-13) — ★★
Two goofy teen extreme sports enthusiasts with too much time on their hands find a refrigerator box in the trash and decide to mount it on a skateboard and see what happens. As they keep tinkering with their creation, they invent an unlikely new sport that draws somewhat overwhelming media attention (complete with racing footage) and unwelcome competition. 90m; DVD. **C:** Austin Basis; Melora Hardin; Stephen Tobolowsky; Julie Brown; Dale Midkiff; James Immekus; Mitch Eakins; Directed by Rob Heddon; Written by Rob Heddon; Cinematography by Matthew Williams. **A:** Jr. High-Adult. **P:** Entertainment. **U:** Home. **Mov-Ent**: Sports--Fiction: Comedy, Skateboarding. **Acq:** Purchase. **Dist:** Phase 4/kaBOOM Entertainment.

Boxcar Bertha 1972 (R) — ★★½
Scorsese's vivid portrayal of the South during the 1930s' Depression casts Hershey as a woman who winds up in cahoots with an anti-establishment train robber. Based on the book "Sister of the Road" by Boxcar Bertha Thomson. 90m; VHS, DVD, Wide. **C:** Barbara Hershey; David Carradine; John Carradine; Barry Primus; Bernie Casey; Victor Argo; Martin Scorsese; John Stephens; Directed by Martin Scorsese; Written by John W. Corrington; Joyce H. Corrington; Music by Gib Guilbeau; Thad Maxwell. **Pr:** American International Pictures. **A:** Sr. High-Adult. **P:** Entertainment. **U:** Home. **Mov-Ent**: Trains, Labor & Unions. **Acq:** Purchase. **Dist:** Lions Gate Television Corp. $69.95.

Boxcar Blues 1990 (Unrated) — ★
Bird (Coufos) is a down and out fighter who decides to fight "The Man" (Ventura), a bare knuckle fighter who enjoys beating his opponents to death. On the way to the fight, in New Orleans, he meets up with his girl Casey (Langrick), along with some other shady characters, including a truck driving preacher. 96m; VHS. **C:** Paul Coufos; Margaret Langrick; Jesse Ventura; M. Emmet Walsh; Donny Lalonde; Directed by Damian Lee. **A:** College-Adult. **P:** Entertainment. **U:** Home. **Mov-Ent**: Boxing. **Acq:** Purchase. **Dist:** VCX Ltd.; Anchor Bay Entertainment. $79.95.

Boxer 1975
Filmed at Joe Frazier's gym in North Philadelphia, this film looks behind the facade of contemporary boxing, seen in relation to its origins in ancient Greece and Rome. 15m/B/W; 3/4 U. **Pr:** Edwin Moses; Fred Sacks. **A:** Jr. High-Adult. **P:** Education. **U:** Institution, SURA. **Spo-Rec**: Sports--General, Boxing. **Acq:** Purchase, Rent/Lease. **Dist:** Temple University Dept. of Film and Media Arts.

The Boxer 1997 (R) — ★★½
Affecting, if predictable, romance set in Ulster, Northern Ireland. Having served 14 years in prison Danny Flynn (Day-Lewis) wants nothing more to do with politics and violence. But his return to his old neighborhood—where he hopes to get back to his boxing career—finds him in the thick of both. Danny manages to persuade his ex-trainer, the alcoholic Ike (Stott), to help him re-open the local gym but resentment is high. Particularly from hard-liner Harry (McSorley), who doesn't like Danny's live-and-let-live attitude and is incensed that he's interested in rekindling his lost-but-never-forgotten love for Maggie (Watson), who's the daughter of local IRA boss Joe (Cox), and the wife of another IRA prisoner. Things quickly turn ugly but the emotionally fragile Danny and Maggie continue to fight to be together against formidable odds. 113m; VHS, DVD, CC. **C:** Daniel Day-Lewis; Emily Watson; Brian Cox; Gerard McSorley; Ken Stott; Ciaran Fitzgerald; Kenneth Cranham; Cameo(s) Tom Bell; Directed by Jim Sheridan; Written by Jim Sheridan; Terry George; Cinematography by Chris Menges; Music by Gavin Friday; Maurice Seezer. **Pr:** Jim Sheridan; Arthur Lappin; Jim Sheridan; Hell's Kitchen; Universal Pictures. **A:** Sr. High-Adult. **P:** Entertainment. **U:** Home. **Mov-Ent**: Drama, Ireland, Boxing. **Acq:** Purchase. **Dist:** Universal Music and Video Distribution.

The Boxer and Death 1963 — ★★★
A new-wave Czech film about a boxer in a Nazi concentration camp who interests the boxing-obsessed commandant in a match. In Czech with subtitles. 120m/B/W; VHS. **C:** Stefan Kvietik; Manfred Krug; Josef Kondrat; Valentina Thielova; Edwin Marian; Gerhard Rachold; Directed by Peter Solan; Cinematography by Tibor Biath; Music by William Bukovy. **Pr:** Peter Solan. **A:** Sr. High-Adult. **P:** Entertainment. **U:** Home. **L:** Czech. **Mov-Ent**: World War Two, Film--Avant-Garde, Boxing. **Acq:** Purchase. **Dist:** Facets Multimedia Inc. $24.95.

The Boxer and the Bombshell 2008 (Unrated) — ★★
It's the early 1920s in Sydney, Australia and beautiful young Iris (Byrne) is the paramour of middle-aged McHeath (Weaving). He's a gangster and shady fight promoter whose new boxing protege is Art (Le Nevez). Iris and Art are immediately attracted to one another and it all becomes a dangerous romantic mix of jealousy and violence. 100m; DVD. **C:** Rose Byrne; Hugo Weaving; Pia Miranda; Matthew Le Nevez; Tyler Coppin; John Batchelor; Directed by Jonathan Ogilvie; Written by Jonathan Ogilvie; Cinematography by Geoffrey Simpson; Music by Chris Abrahams. **A:** Sr. High-Adult. **P:** Entertainment. **U:** Home. **Mov-Ent**: Boxing, Drama. **Acq:** Purchase. **Dist:** Screen Media Ventures, LLC.

Boxercise 1993
Former WBA lightweight champ Sean O'Grady utilizes the workout boxers use to condition and train in this aerobics workout. 30m; VHS. **A:** Sr. High-Adult. **P:** Instruction. **U:** Home. **Hea-Sci**: Fitness/Exercise, Boxing. **Acq:** Purchase. **Dist:** MPI Media Group. $14.98.

Boxing Aerobics 1998
Instructor Sharon Bylund utilizes boxing and karate techniques in order to get a full body workout without causing stress to any one body part. 60m; VHS. **A:** Sr. High-Adult. **P:** Instruction. **U:** Home. **Spo-Rec**: Fitness/Exercise, Boxing. **Acq:** Purchase. **Dist:** Tapeworm Video Distributors Inc. $19.95.

Boxing Bloopers and KO's 1992
Join ESPN boxing analyst, Al Bernstein, as he takes a look at boxing foul-ups from Evander Holyfield, Joe Frazier, Larry Holmes, and others. 30m; VHS. **Pr:** ESPN. **A:** Family. **P:** Entertainment. **U:** Home. **Spo-Rec**: Boxing, Outtakes & Bloopers. **Acq:** Purchase. **Dist:** Fast Forward.

Boxing Fitness for Women 1998
Shows women how to use a punching bag to develop greater self-confidence and strength, whether training for fitness or boxing competition. 37m; VHS. **A:** Adult. **P:** Instruction. **U:** Home. **Spo-Rec**: Fitness/Exercise, Boxing. **Acq:** Purchase. **Dist:** Tapeworm Video Distributors Inc. $19.95.

Boxing Helena 1993 (R) — ★★
Highly publicized as the film that cost Basinger almost $9 million in damages, the debut of director/writer Jennifer Lynch (daughter of David) explores the dark side of relationships between men and women. Sands is Dr. Nick Cavanaugh, a surgeon who becomes dangerously obsessed with the beautiful, yet unattainable Helena (Fenn). When she is hit by a car near his home, he performs emergency surgery and amputates her arms and legs, forcing her to be dependent on him. Metaphorically a situation, albeit an extreme one, that mirrors the power struggle in any sexual relationship. Problematic in some aspects, although equally fascinating as it is disturbing. 107m; VHS, DVD, Wide, CC. **C:** Julian Sands; Sherilyn Fenn; Bill Paxton; Kurtwood Smith; Betsy Clark; Nicolette Scorsese; Art Garfunkel; Meg Register; Bryan Smith; Directed by Jennifer Lynch; Written by Jennifer Lynch; Cinematography by Bojan Bazelli; Music by Graeme Revell. **Pr:** Carl Mazzocone; Main Line; Orion Pictures. **A:** Sr. High-Adult. **P:** Entertainment. **U:** Home. **Mov-Ent**: Sexual Abuse, Cult Films, Sex & Sexuality. **Awds:** Golden Raspberries '93: Worst Director (Lynch). **Acq:** Purchase. **Dist:** MGM Studios Inc.

Boxing: The Best of the 1980s, Vol. 1 1992
Some of the best boxing seen in the '80s. Brawlers in volume one include Roberto Duran, George Foreman, Mark Breland, Antonio Esparragoza, Michael Moorer, Marlon Starling and Renaldo Snipes. Volume two contains footage of Tim Witherspoon, Foreman, Aaron Pryor, Duran, Leslie Stewart, Larry Holmes and Bobby Czyz. 52m; VHS. **Pr:** Worldwide Entertainment. **A:** Family. **P:** Entertainment. **U:** Home. **Spo-Rec**: Sports--General, Boxing. **Acq:** Purchase. **Dist:** BMG Entertainment. $14.98.

Boxing's Greatest Knockouts & Highlights 1990
Now you can have a ringside seat for all the main events you wish you could have seen or the ones you want to relive. Featured are Joe Frazier, Muhammad Ali, Sugar Ray Leonard, Leon Spinks, and many more. 30m; VHS. **Pr:** Simitar Entertainment. **A:** Jr. High-Adult. **P:** Entertainment. **U:** Home. **Spo-Rec**: Boxing. **Acq:** Purchase. **Dist:** Karol Media. $9.95.

Boxing's Greatest Knockouts, Vol. 1 1989
Great matches include Hearns vs. Shuler, Arguello vs. Rooney and Mercer vs. McGhee. 40m; VHS. **Pr:** Top Rank Inc. **A:** Family. **P:** Entertainment. **U:** Home. **Spo-Rec**: Sports--General, Documentary Films, Boxing. **Acq:** Purchase. **Dist:** School-Tech Inc. $12.95.

Boy A 2007 (R) — ★★
The 24-year-old, newly renamed Jack Burridge (Garfield) has gotten out of a Manchester prison after 14 years for his involvement in the brutal murder of another youngster. His dedicated caseworker Terry (Mullan) emphasizes that Jack must not reveal his previous identity or discuss his crime or jail time. Jack hesitantly reenters society and gets an apartment, a job, and a girlfriend (Lyons), but one act of heroism backfires when media attention leads to exposure about his past. 100m; DVD. **C:** Andrew Garfield; Peter Mullan; Shaun Evans; Katie Lyons; Taylor Doherty; Directed by John Crowley; Written by Mark O'Rowe; Cinematography by Rob Hardy; Music by Paddy Cunneen. **A:** Sr. High-Adult. **P:** Entertainment. **U:** Home. **Mov-Ent**: Great Britain. **Acq:** Purchase. **Dist:** Genius.com Incorporated.

A Boy, a Dog and a Frog 1981
A small boy and his dog spend a day playing near a pond. The frog they have been trying to catch feels lonely when they leave, so he follows them home, and the three friends are re-united. 9m; VHS, 3/4 U. **Pr:** Evergreen Entertainment. **A:** Preschool-Primary. **P:** Entertainment. **U:** Institution, SURA. **Chl-Juv**: Human Relations. **Acq:** Purchase. **Dist:** Phoenix Learning Group.

Boy and a Boa 1975
Designed to dispel fears of snakes and to inform on the reptile family, this is the story of a boy and his adventures with his occasionally disappearing boa constrictor. 13m; VHS, 3/4 U. **Pr:** Lora Hays; New York State Department of Education. **A:** Preschool-Jr. High. **P:** Education. **U:** Institution, SURA. **Chl-Juv**: Children, Animals. **Acq:** Purchase. **Dist:** Phoenix Learning Group.

A Boy and His Dog 1975 (R) — ★★½
In the post-holocaust world of 2024, a young man (Johnson) and his telepathic canine (McIntire supplies narration of the dog's thoughts) cohort search for food and sex. They happen upon a community that drafts Johnson to repopulate their largely impotent race; Johnson is at first ready, willing, and able, until he discovers the mechanical methods they mean to employ. Based on a short story by Harlan Ellison. The dog was played by the late Tiger of "The Brady Bunch." 87m; VHS, DVD, Blu-Ray. **TV Std:** NTSC, PAL, SECAM. **C:** Don Johnson; Susanne Benton; Jason Robards, Jr.; Charles McGraw; Alvy Moore; Helene Winston; Hal Baylor; L.Q. Jones; Voice(s) by Tim McIntire; Directed by L.Q. Jones; Written by L.Q. Jones; Cinematography by John Morrill; Music by Tim McIntire. **Pr:** Alvy Moore. **A:** Sr. High-Adult. **P:** Entertainment. **U:** Home. **L:** English, Spanish. **Mov-Ent**: Science Fiction, Sex & Sexuality, Cult Films. **Acq:** Purchase. **Dist:** First Run Features; Critics' Choice Video & DVD. $29.95.

The Boy and the Snow Goose 1985
A boy nurses and loves a goose, and then must free it to its natural habitat. A parable on values and wildlife for children. 11m; VHS, 3/4 U. **Pr:** National Film Board of Canada. **A:** Preschool-Primary. **P:** Entertainment. **U:** Institution, Home, SURA. **Chl-Juv**: Wildlife, Ethics & Morals. **Acq:** Purchase, Duplication License. **Dist:** Bullfrog Films, Inc.

A Boy Called Hate 1995 (R) — ★★
Troubled teen Steve (Caan)?whose nickname is "Hate" after his tattoo'lives with his divorced dad in an L.A. suburb. Steve's on a latenight motorcycle ride, taking potshots at billboards with his trusty handgun, when he stumbles onto what he thinks is an attempted rape. So Steve shoots at the rapist, Richard (Gould), and takes off with would-be victim Cindy (Crider). Turns out Richard is the assistant D.A. and he tells the cops he's been robbed, so the teen duo are now on the run. Familiar tale with some good twists and believable performances. Caan is the son of James (seen in a cameo as the dad). Debut for director Marcus. 98m; VHS, CC. **C:** Scott Caan; Missy (Melissa) Crider; Elliott Gould; Adam Beach; Cameo(s) James Caan; Directed by Mitch Marcus; Written by Mitch Marcus; Cinematography by Paul Holahan. **Pr:** Steve Nicolaides; Tom Rowe; Tony Allard; Marjorie Skouras; Skouras Pictures. **A:** Sr. High-Adult. **P:** Entertainment. **U:** Home. **Mov-Ent**: Adolescence. **Acq:** Purchase. **Dist:** Paramount Pictures Corp.

A Boy Creates 1971
Demonstrates a boy's imagination in transforming discarded objects (bottles, plastic pieces, wood, metal) into meaningful art forms. 10m; VHS, 3/4 U. **Pr:** Tom Harris; Encyclopedia Britannica Educational Corporation. **A:** Preschool-Primary. **P:** Education. **U:** Institution, SURA. **Chl-Juv**: Art & Artists, Children. **Acq:** Purchase, Rent/Lease, Trade-in. **Dist:** Encyclopedia Britannica. $155.00.

Boy Culture 2006 (Unrated) — ★★
Money, desire, and emotional denial. X (Magyar) is a cynical hustler with a high-end and limited clientele of older men. His newest client, the urbane Gregory (Bachau), confuses X by paying for his company but refusing his sexual favors unless X is also emotionally involved. X can't even admit his attraction to his roommate Andrew (Stevens), who's unsure of his own sexuality, while their other roomie, twink Joey (Trent), openly lusts after X. Based on the novel by Matthew Rettenmund. 90m; DVD. **C:** Derek Magyar; Patrick Bauchau; Darryl Stephens; John Trent; Directed by Q. Allan Brocka; Written by Q. Allan Brocka; Cinematography by Jerusha Hess; Music by Ryan Beveridge. **A:** College-Adult. **P:** Entertainment. **U:** Home. **Mov-Ent**. **Acq:** Purchase. **Dist:** TLA Releasing.

Boy, Did I Get a Wrong Number! 1966 — ★
A real estate agent gets more than he bargained for when he accidentally dials a wrong number. Zany comedy persists as Hope gets entangled in the life of sexy starlet Sommer. 100m; VHS, DVD. **C:** Bob Hope; Phyllis Diller; Marjorie Lord; Elke

Sommer; Cesare Danova; Kelly Thordsen; Directed by George Marshall; Written by Albert Lewin; Burt Styler; Cinematography by Lionel Lindon; Music by Richard LaSalle. **Pr:** United Artists. **A:** Family. **P:** Entertainment. **U:** Home. **Mov-Ent:** Comedy--Slapstick, Real Estate. **Acq:** Purchase. **Dist:** MGM Home Entertainment; Facets Multimedia Inc. $19.98.

The Boy Friend 1971 (G) — ★★★
Russell pays tribute to the Busby Berkeley Hollywood musical. Lots of charming dance numbers and clever parody of plotlines in this adaptation of Sandy Wilson's stage play. Fun! 135m; VHS, DVD. **C:** Twiggy; Christopher Gable; Moyra Fraser; Max Adrian; Vladek Sheybal; Georgina Hale; Tommy Tune; Directed by Ken Russell; Written by Ken Russell; Cinematography by David Watkin. **Pr:** MGM. **A:** Family. **P:** Entertainment. **U:** Home. **Mov-Ent:** Musical. **Awds:** Golden Globes '72: Actress--Mus./Comedy (Twiggy). **Acq:** Purchase. **Dist:** WarnerArchive.com. $19.95.

Songs: The Boy Friend; I Could Be Happy; Won't You Charleston With Me?; Fancy Forgetting; Sur La Plage; A Room in Bloomsbury; Safety in Numbers; It's Never Too Late to Fall in Love; Poor Little Pierette; Rivera; The You Don't Want To Play With Me Blues; All I Do Is Dream Of You; You Are My Lucky Star; Any Old Iron.

The Boy From Oklahoma 1954 (Unrated) — ★★
Amiable western programmer. Law student Tom Brewster (Rogers Jr.) is in the corrupt town of Bluerock, where he's offered the job of sheriff by town boss Turlock (Caruso) who thinks the young man will be easy to control. Armed with his trusty lasso--Tom won't carry a gun--he intends to clean up the town instead. The move begat the 1957-61 TV series "Sugarfoot." 88m; DVD. **C:** Will Rogers, Jr.; Nancy Olson; Lon Chaney, Jr.; Anthony Caruso; Wallace Ford; Merv Griffin; Directed by Michael Curtiz; Written by Winston Miller; Frank Davis; Cinematography by Robert Burks; Music by Max Steiner. **A:** Jr. High-Adult. **P:** Entertainment. **U:** Home. **L:** English. **Mov-Ent:** Western. **Acq:** Purchase. **Dist:** WarnerArchive.com.

Boy George: Sold 198?
Video clips "Everything I Own," "Keep Me In Mind," and "Sold." 20m; VHS. **A:** Jr. High-College. **P:** Entertainment. **U:** Home. **Mov-Ent:** Music Video, Music--Pop/Rock. **Acq:** Purchase. **Dist:** Music Video Distributors. $39.95.

Boy I Am 2006 (Unrated)
Three individuals transitioning from female-to-male (FTM) discuss the major junctures in their transitions, their relationship with their own bodies, feminism, and the issues of race and class with their new identity; includes interviews with lesbians, activists, and theorists. 72m; DVD. **A:** Adult. **P:** Education. **U:** Institution. **Gen-Edu:** Identity, Sex & Sexuality. **Acq:** Purchase. **Dist:** Women Make Movies. $295.00.

Boy in Blue 1986 (R) — ★½
A "Rocky"-esque biography of Canadian speed-rower Ned Hanlan, who set aside lackluster pursuits to turn to rowing. 97m; VHS, DVD, Blu-Ray, CC. **C:** Nicolas Cage; Christopher Plummer; David Naughton; Cynthia Dale; Melody Anderson; James B. Douglas; Directed by Charles Jarrott; Written by Douglas Bowie; Cinematography by Pierre Mignot; Music by Roger Webb. **Pr:** John Kemeny; 20th Century-Fox. **A:** Sr. High-Adult. **P:** Entertainment. **U:** Home. **Mov-Ent:** Biography: Sports, Boating, Sports--Fiction: Drama. **Acq:** Purchase. **Dist:** Fox Home Entertainment.

The Boy in the Plastic Bubble 1976 — ★★½
Well-made, sensitive drama about a young man born with immunity deficiencies who must grow up in a specially controlled plastic environment. Travolta is endearing as the boy in the bubble. 100m; VHS, DVD. **C:** John Travolta; Robert Reed; Glynnis O'Connor; Diana Hyland; Ralph Bellamy; Anne Ramsey; Vernee Watson-Johnson; P.J. Soles; John Friedrich; Directed by Randal Kleiser; Written by Douglas Day Stewart; Cinematography by Arch R. Dalzell; Music by Paul Williams; Mark Snow. **Pr:** Aaron Spelling; Leonard Goldberg. **A:** Jr. High-Adult. **P:** Entertainment. **U:** Home. **Mov-Ent:** TV Movies, Diseases. **Acq:** Purchase. **Dist:** Movies Unlimited. $12.74.

The Boy in the Striped Pajamas 2008 (PG-13) — ★★★
In 1940's Germany, eight-year-old Bruno (Butterfield), the son of a Nazi prison camp commandant (Thewlis), and his family move from a comfortable home in Berlin out to the country where they will live on a "farm." Bruno questions his parents about the people working the fields he can see from his new bedroom window, wondering why they all wear striped pajamas. When his parents answers are inadequate, Bruno sneaks out to the far reaches of the farm, where he meets and befriends a boy his own age, Shmuel. Their circumstances seem equally confusing to both boys as they build a bond through the barbed wire fence. The story unfolds primarily from Bruno's perspective until the final scenes, which begin to switch to Shmuel's point of view. Poignant and timeless, the film is primarily directed at a young audience and serves to point out how easily people accept evil when they elevate some purpose above basic morality. Adapted from John Boyle's 2006 novel of the same name. 94m; Blu-Ray, Wide. **C:** David Thewlis; Vera Farmiga; David Hayman; Rupert Friend; Bruno; Shmuel; Amber Beattie; Sheila Hancock; Richard Johnson; Jim Norton; Directed by Mark Herman; Written by Mark Herman; Cinematography by Benoit Delhomme; Music by James Horner. **Pr:** David Heyman; BBC Films; Heyday Films; Miramax Film Corp. **A:** Jr. High-Adult. **P:** Entertainment. **U:** Home. **L:** English. **Mov-Ent:** Germany, World War Two, Holocaust. **Acq:** Purchase. **Dist:** Miramax Film Corp.; Movies Unlimited; Alpha Video.

Boy Interrupted 2009
In 2005, 15-year-old Evan Perry committed suicide. His filmmaker parents, Hart and Dana, look at his struggle with bipolar disorder, the stigma of both mental illness and suicide, and coping with loss and grief. 92m; DVD. **A:** Adult. **P:** Education. **U:** Home. **Gen-Edu:** Documentary Films, Mental Health, Parenting. **Acq:** Purchase. **Dist:** Home Box Office Inc. $19.98.

The Boy King 1988
The early life of civil rights leader Martin Luther King Jr. is examined in this drama. 48m; VHS, 3/4 U. **C:** Howard E. Rollins, Jr. **Pr:** All American Television. **A:** Primary-Adult. **P:** Entertainment. **U:** Institution, SURA. **Gen-Edu:** Biography. **Acq:** Purchase, Rent/Lease. **Dist:** Phoenix Learning Group. $250.00.

Boy Meets Girl 1938 — ★★★
Cagney and O'Brien play screenwriters whose every film is a variation on the boy meets girl theme. Trouble is they're running out of ideas and their scripts get increasingly outlandish. A fading cowboy actor is supposed to star in the duo's next film—if they can ever settle down to work. Then they get the idea to feature their friend Wilson's baby in the movie—and guess who becomes a new star. Good satire on moviemaking and movie moguls, which made fine use of the Warner studio back lots, sound stages, and offices. Based on the play by Bella and Samuel Spewack who also wrote the screenplay. 86m/B/W; VHS. **C:** James Cagney; Pat O'Brien; Ralph Bellamy; Dick Foran; Marie Wilson; Frank McHugh; Bruce Lester; Ronald Reagan; Penny Singleton; James Stephenson; Directed by Lloyd Bacon; Written by Bella Spewack; Samuel Spewack. **Pr:** Hal B. Wallis; Samuel Bischoff; Warner Bros. **A:** Jr. High-Adult. **P:** Entertainment. **U:** Home. **Mov-Ent:** Satire & Parody. **Acq:** Purchase. **Dist:** MGM Home Entertainment; Facets Multimedia Inc. $19.98.

Boy Meets Girl 1984 — ★★★
Alex (Lavant), a French Holden Caulfield type character, cruises the seamier side of Paris in this acclaimed film. Carax's directoral debut at age 22. Alex will return in the Carax films "Bad Blood" (1986) and "The Lovers on the Bridge" (1991). French with subtitles. 100m/B/W; VHS, DVD, Wide. **C:** Denis Lavant; Mireille Perrier; Carroll Brooks; Anna Baldaccini; Directed by Leos Carax; Written by Leos Carax; Cinematography by Jean-Yves Escoffier; Music by Jacques Pinault. **Pr:** Abilene **A:** College-Adult. **P:** Entertainment. **U:** Home. **L:** English, French. **Mov-Ent:** Film--Avant-Garde. **Acq:** Purchase. **Dist:** Facets Multimedia Inc.; Wellspring Media. $49.95.

Boy Meets World: The Complete First Season 1993
Sixth-grader Cory Matthews is dealing with junior high with the help of his equally clueless best friend Shawn. There's demanding teacher Mr. Feeney (who's also the Matthews' next-door neighbor) and Cory's crush on Topanga as well as the usual school bullies and family concerns. 22 episodes. 525m; DVD. **C:** Ben Savage; William Daniels; Rider Strong; William Russ; Danielle Fishel; Will Friedle; Betsy Randle. **A:** Family. **P:** Entertainment. **U:** Home. **Mov-Ent:** Television Series. **Acq:** Purchase. **Dist:** Buena Vista Home Entertainment.

Boy Meets World: The Complete Second Season 1994
Cory enters 7th grade with Mr. Feeney as the new principal so his new homeroom/English teacher is motorcycle-riding Mr. Turner. He's got a new school nemesis in Harley and gets more serious about having Topanga as his girlfriend, but Shawn's the one with big problems after his parents abandon him. 23 episodes. 506m; DVD. **C:** Ben Savage; William Daniels; Rider Strong; Danielle Fishel; William Russ; Betsy Randle; Will Friedle; Anthony Quinn; Danny McNulty. **A:** Family. **P:** Entertainment. **U:** Home. **Mov-Ent:** Television Series. **Acq:** Purchase. **Dist:** Buena Vista Home Entertainment.

Boy Meets World: The Complete Third Season 1995
Cory, now an 8th-grader, and Topanga's efforts at being a serious couple doesn't work out and they break up; Cory tries dating other girls before figuring out that Topanga's the only one for him. Mr. Turner becomes Shawn's legal guardian until his irresponsible dad shows up again. And Cory's brother Eric is graduating from high school. 22 episodes. 491m; DVD. **C:** Ben Savage; William Daniels; Rider Strong; Danielle Fishel; William Russ; Betsy Randle; Will Friedle; Anthony Quinn; Danny McNulty. **A:** Family. **P:** Entertainment. **U:** Home. **Mov-Ent:** Television Series. **Acq:** Purchase. **Dist:** Buena Vista Home Entertainment.

Boy Named Ami 19??
A story about Ami, a newcomer who is integrated into the world of a fishing kibbutz via schooling, socializing, boating and fishing. 28m; VHS, 3/4 U, Special order formats. **TV Std:** NTSC, PAL, SECAM. **Pr:** Alden Films. **A:** Family. **P:** Education. **U:** Institution, Home, SURA. **Gen-Edu:** Israel, Documentary Films. **Acq:** Purchase, Rent/Lease. **Dist:** Alden Films.

A Boy Named Charlie Brown 1970 (Unrated)
Charlie Brown enters the National Spelling Bee in New York and makes the final rounds with one other contestant. Based on Charles Schultz's popular comic strip characters from "Peanuts." Music by the Vince Guaraldi trio is, as always, a treat. 86m; VHS, CC. **C:** Directed by Bill Melendez; Written by Charles M. Schulz; Music by Vince Guaraldi; Rod McKuen. **Pr:** Lee Mendelson; Bill Melendez; Bill Melendez; National General Pictures. **A:** Family. **P:** Entertainment. **U:** Home. **Chl-Juv:** Animation & Cartoons, Pets, Family Viewing. **Acq:** Purchase. **Dist:** Paramount Pictures Corp. $14.98.

A Boy Named Sue 2000
Chronicles the physiological and psychological transformation of a transsexual named Theo from a woman to a man over the course of six years. 57m; VHS. **A:** Adult. **P:** Education. **U:** Institution, BCTV. **Gen-Edu:** Sex & Sexuality, Documentary Films. **Acq:** Purchase, Rent/Lease. **Dist:** Women Make Movies. $295.00.

Boy of Bombay 1969
The activities of a typical 12-year-old boy in Bombay, India, are detailed. 16m; VHS, 3/4 U. **Pr:** Yehuda Tarmu. **A:** Jr. High. **P:** Education. **U:** Institution, SURA. **Gen-Edu:** Documentary Films, Asia, Children. **Acq:** Purchase. **Dist:** Phoenix Learning Group.

Boy of Central Africa 1969
Vincent Chisembwa lives in a village in Zambia. In order to pay for correspondence courses, he carves and sells wooden artifacts. 14m; VHS, 3/4 U. **Pr:** Kevin Duffy. **A:** Jr. High. **P:** Education. **U:** Institution, SURA. **Gen-Edu:** Documentary Films, Africa. **Acq:** Purchase. **Dist:** Phoenix Learning Group.

Boy of Southeast Asia 1967
Life on a rice farm in Southeast Asia is depicted. 17m; VHS, 3/4 U. **Pr:** Wayne Mitchell. **A:** Jr. High. **P:** Education. **U:** Institution, SURA. **Gen-Edu:** Documentary Films, Asia, Sociology. **Acq:** Purchase. **Dist:** Phoenix Learning Group.

Boy of Two Worlds 1959 (G) — ★½
Because he is of a lineage foreign to his late father's town, a boy is exiled to the life of a junior Robinson Crusoe. 103m; VHS. **C:** Jimmy Sternman; Edvin Adolphson; Directed by Astrid Henning Jensen. **Pr:** GG Communications. **A:** Family. **P:** Entertainment. **U:** Home. **L:** Danish. **Mov-Ent. Acq:** Purchase. **Dist:** Unknown Distributor.

The Boy Scout Advancement Program 1988
Instructional tapes pertain precisely to the three levels of Boy Scouting, and is endorsed by the Boy Scouts of America. Included are lessons in conservation, good citizenship, wilderness survival, and first aid. 63m; VHS. **Pr:** Cinema Visuals Entertainment. **A:** Primary-Jr. High. **P:** Instruction. **U:** Home. **How-Ins:** Documentary Films, Organizations, Camps & Camping. **Acq:** Purchase. **Dist:** Paramount Pictures Corp. $24.95.
Indiv. Titles: 1. Tenderfoot 2. Second Class Scout 3. First Class Scout.

Boy Stuff 1988
A guide to the many areas which can become hygiene problems for boys. 16m; VHS, 3/4 U. **Pr:** Churchill. **A:** Primary-Sr. High. **P:** Education. **U:** Institution, Home, SURA. **Hea-Sci:** Hygiene, Adolescence. **Acq:** Purchase, Rent/Lease. **Dist:** Clear Vue Inc. $270.00.

Boy Takes Girl 1983 (Unrated) — ★★
A little girl finds it hard adjusting to life on a farming cooperative during a summer recess. 93m; VHS. **C:** Gabi Eldor; Hillel Neeman; Dina Limon; Directed by Michal Bat-Adam. **Pr:** Guy Film Productions Ltd. **A:** Family. **P:** Entertainment. **U:** Home. **Mov-Ent:** Drama, Agriculture. **Acq:** Purchase. **Dist:** MGM Home Entertainment. $59.95.

Boy to Man 1992
Traditional presentation of a boy's experience in puberty. Diagrams are combined with live action clips to provide information. Brief caution that physical maturity does not equal emotional maturity, but does not mention AIDS. Includes teacher's guide. 20m; VHS, Special order formats. **A:** Primary-Jr. High. **P:** Education. **U:** Institution. **Hea-Sci:** Health Education, Sex & Sexuality, Adolescence. **Acq:** Purchase, Rent/Lease. **Dist:** Clear Vue Inc. $295.00.

Boy to Man—Revised 1976
Uses animation and conceptual framework to explain physiological changes of maturation. 15m; VHS, 3/4 U, Special order formats. **Pr:** Churchill. **A:** Primary-Jr. High. **P:** Education. **U:** Institution, Home, SURA. **L:** English, Spanish. **Hea-Sci:** Documentary Films, Adolescence. **Acq:** Purchase, Duplication License. **Dist:** Clear Vue Inc.

Boy! What a Girl 1945 — ★★
Moore (in drag) is mistaken for a woman, and is fought over by a couple of suitors. 60m/B/W; VHS, DVD. **C:** Tim Moore; Duke Williams; Sheila Guyse; Beth Mays; Elwood Smith; Directed by Arthur Leonard. **Pr:** Herald Pictures. **A:** Family. **P:** Entertainment. **U:** Home. **Mov-Ent:** Musical. **Acq:** Purchase. **Dist:** Facets Multimedia Inc.; Glenn Video Vistas Ltd. $34.95.

Boy Who Caught a Crook 1961 (Unrated) — ★½
Young newsboy finds a briefcase filled with cash and shares his good fortune with his hobo friend. The kid's widowed mother wants to turn everything over to the police, especially when they learn that the money belongs to a bank robber who'll do anything to get it back. 73m/B/W; DVD. **C:** Roger Mobley; Wanda Hendrix; Johnny Seven; Don Beddoe; Robert Stevenson; Bill (William) Walker; Richard Crane; Directed by Edward L. Cahn; Written by Nathan "Jerry" Juran; Cinematography by Gilbert Warrenton; Music by Richard LaSalle. **A:** Family. **P:** Entertainment. **U:** Home. **Mov-Ent:** Crime Drama, Homeless. **Acq:** Purchase. **Dist:** MGM Home Entertainment; Movies Unlimited.

The Boy Who Could Fly 1986 (PG) — ★★★
After a plane crash kills his parents, a boy withdraws into a fantasy land where he can fly. The young daughter of a troubled family makes friends with him and the fantasy becomes real. A sweet film for children, charming though melancholy for adults, too. Fine cast, including Savage, Dewhurst, and Bedelia keep this from becoming sappy. 120m; VHS, DVD, CC. **C:** Lucy Deakins; Jay Underwood; Bonnie Bedelia; Colleen Dewhurst; Fred Savage; Fred Gwynne; Louise Fletcher; Jason Priestley; Directed by Nick Castle; Written by Nick Castle; Cinematogra-

phy by Steven Poster; Music by Bruce Broughton. **Pr:** Gary Adelson. **A:** Jr. High-Adult. **P:** Entertainment. **U:** Home. **Mov-Ent:** Autism, Fantasy. **Acq:** Purchase. **Dist:** Warner Home Video, Inc.; MGM Studios Inc. $14.95.

The Boy Who Cried Werewolf 2010 (Unrated) — ★★½
Harmless, cheap-looking Nickelodeon horror comedy. Shy teen Jordan Sands (Justice) and her family inherit a castle in Wolfsberg, Romania. They arrive in time to celebrate the small town festival honoring the Wolfsbeg Beast. Thanks to a lab accident, Jordan is transformed into a werewolf and it's up to her brother Hunter (Ellison) and their stern housekeeper Madame Varcolac (Shields) to get her a cure. 86m; DVD. **C:** Victoria Justice; Chase Ellison; Brooke Shields; Matt Winston; Steven Grayhm; Brooke D'Orsay; Directed by Eric Bross; Written by Douglas Sloan; Cinematography by Robert MacLachlan; Music by John Van Tongeren. **A:** Family. **P:** Entertainment. **U:** Home. **L:** English. **Mov-Ent:** TV Movies, Family. **Acq:** Purchase. **Dist:** Viacom International Inc.

The Boy Who Cried Wolf 1987
This modern retelling of Aesop's famous tale teaches a lesson to children and adults alike. 17m; VHS, 3/4 U. **A:** Primary. **P:** Education. **U:** Institution, SURA. **Chl-Juv:** Folklore & Legends, Children, Fairy Tales. **Acq:** Purchase, Trade-in. **Dist:** Encyclopedia Britannica. $300.00.

The Boy Who Draws Buildings 1996
Spotlights Stephen Wiltshire, an autistic artist, who at 12 was considered the best child artist in Britain. Shows how Stephen is fascinated with buildings and draws them from memory after only a few minutes of studying them. 30m; VHS. **A:** Sr. High-Adult. **P:** Education. **U:** Institution. **Gen-Edu:** Documentary Films, Art & Artists, Mental Health. **Acq:** Purchase, Rent/Lease. **Dist:** Filmakers Library Inc. $295.00.

The Boy Who Drew Cats 1991
A story for the entire family from the award-winning series "Rabbit Ears: We All Have Tales," first aired on Showtime. 35m; VHS. **C:** Narrated by William Hurt; Music by Mark Isham. **Pr:** Rabbit Ears Productions. **A:** Family. **P:** Entertainment. **U:** Home. **Chl-Juv:** Animation & Cartoons, Family Viewing, Fairy Tales. **Acq:** Purchase. **Dist:** Music Video Distributors. $19.95.

The Boy Who Left Home to Find Out About the Shivers 1981 — ★★
From "Faerie Tale Theatre" comes this tale about a boy who learns about fear. 60m; VHS, DVD. **C:** Peter MacNichol; Christopher Lee; David Warner; Dana Hill; Frank Zappa; Voice(s) by Vincent Price; Directed by Graeme Clifford. **Pr:** Shelley Duvall. **A:** Family. **P:** Entertainment. **U:** Home. **Mov-Ent:** Fairy Tales, TV Movies. **Acq:** Purchase. **Dist:** Movies Unlimited.

The Boy Who Liked Deer 1975
In this dramatic and all-too-believable story, a boy discovers, in very personal terms, the pain that vandalism can inflict. 18m; VHS, 3/4 U. **C:** Directed by Barbara Loden. **Pr:** Learning Corporation of America. **A:** Jr. High-Sr. High. **P:** Education. **U:** Institution, SURA. **Chl-Juv:** Children. **Acq:** Purchase, Rent/Lease. **Dist:** Phoenix Learning Group.

The Boy Who Loved Trolls 1984
Paul's fantastic dreams come true when he meets Ofoeti, a real, live troll. The only problem is Ofoeti only has a day to live, and Paul must find a way to save him. Aired on PBS as part of the "Wonderworks" series. 58m; VHS, CC. **C:** Sam Waterston; Susan Anton; Matt Dill; Directed by Harvey Laidman. **Pr:** PBS. **A:** Family. **P:** Entertainment. **U:** Home. **Mov-Ent:** Fantasy, Family Viewing, TV Movies. **Acq:** Purchase. **Dist:** Home Vision Cinema; Facets Multimedia Inc. $29.95.

The Boy Who Saw the Wind 1971
In this mixture of fact and fantasy, young Jeff Winnegar daydreams himself right out of his classroom seat and into the company of a small man who calls himself T.H.E. Wind. 7m; VHS, 3/4 U. **A:** Primary. **P:** Entertainment. **U:** Institution, SURA. **Chl-Juv:** Children, Fantasy. **Acq:** Purchase. **Dist:** Phoenix Learning Group.

The Boy Who Went to Live with the Seals 1993
Features a Rafe Martin story based on a Northwest Coast Native American Indian tale. 10m; VHS. **Pr:** Film Ideas, Inc. **A:** Family. **P:** Education. **U:** Institution, Home. **Gen-Edu:** Native Americans, Folklore & Legends. **Acq:** Purchase. **Dist:** Film Ideas, Inc. $110.00.

The Boy with the Green Hair 1948 (Unrated) — ★★★
When he hears that his parents were killed in an air raid, a boy's hair turns green. The narrow-minded members of his community suddenly want nothing to do with him and he becomes an outcast. Thought-provoking social commentary. 82m; VHS, DVD. **C:** Pat O'Brien; Robert Ryan; Barbara Hale; Dean Stockwell; Directed by Joseph Losey. **Pr:** RKO. **A:** Family. **P:** Entertainment. **U:** Home. **Mov-Ent:** Ethics & Morals, Adoption. **Acq:** Purchase. **Dist:** Image Entertainment Inc. $29.95.

The Boy With the Sun in His Eyes 2009 (Unrated) — ★½
After John's best friend Kevin commits suicide, he unexpectedly meets B-movie queen Solange at Kevin's funeral. She was big in 1980s Italian-made horror flicks and decides she needs a new personal assistant when she travels back to Italy and France. However, John finds that Solange's jet-setting, freaky lifestyle may not agree with him after all. 95m; DVD. **C:** Tim Swain; Mahogany Reynolds; Josh Ubaldi; Valentin Plessy; Directed by Todd Verow; Written by Todd Verow; Jim Dwyer; Geretta Geretta; Music by Guglielmo (William) Bottin. **A:** College-Adult. **P:** Entertainment. **U:** Home. **Mov-Ent. Acq:** Purchase. **Dist:** Water Bearer Films Inc.

Boy Wonder 2010 (R) — ★★
Sean grew up with an alcoholic, abusive dad and witnessed his mother's murder. He studies mug shots to allegedly find the killer but really to see which criminals have evaded justice. Homicide detective Teresa Ames suspects the emotionally volatile teen is behind a series of beatdowns of street scum and considers whether Sean is making things better or worse. 93m; DVD. **C:** Caleb Steinmeyer; Zulay Henao; Bill Sage; James Russo; Tracy Middendorf; Directed by Michael Morrissey; Written by Michael Morrissey; Cinematography by Christopher LaVasseur. **A:** Sr. High-Adult. **P:** Entertainment. **U:** Home. **Mov-Ent:** Crime Drama, Child Abuse. **Acq:** Purchase. **Dist:** Inception Media Group.

Boyceball 1992
Choreographer Laurence Brantley of the Ithaca (New York) Ballet creates a dance on this program from square one. He has a very approachable personality which kids should appreciate. The theme of the ballet is baseball and it is set to music by 18th century composer William Boyce. Includes section on technical aspects of lighting, photography and more. Previews available. 15m; VHS. **A:** Primary-Sr. High. **P:** Education. **U:** Institution. **Chl-Juv:** Baseball, Dance--Ballet. **Acq:** Purchase, Rent/Lease. **Dist:** Filmakers Library Inc. $45.00.

Boycott 1985
An imprisoned political activist is shrouded with doubt toward the ideals that condemned him. 85m; VHS. **A:** Adult. **P:** Entertainment. **U:** Home. **Mov-Ent:** Middle East, Drama. **Acq:** Purchase. **Dist:** Arab Film Distribution. $29.99.

Boycott 2002 — ★★★½
Superb HBO docudrama re-creates the Civil Rights movement's early days, from Rosa Parks's (Little-Thomas) refusal to give up her seat to a white man on a segregated Montgomery, Alabama, bus, through the subsequent boycott of the bus system by the city's black population, to the success of the boycott and the rise to prominence of Dr. Martin Luther King Jr. (Wright) as the movement's most eloquent and popular leader. Through the use and mix of many different visual styles, director Johnson uses artful touches to tell the story without overplaying his hand. Wright is fantastic as King, with other outstanding performances turned in by Howard as Ralph Abernathy and Pounder as boycott organizer Jo Anne Robinson. 112m; VHS, DVD. **C:** Jeffrey Wright; Terrence Howard; CCH Pounder; Carmen Ejogo; Reg E. Cathey; Brent Jennings; Shawn Michael Howard; Erik Todd Dellums; Iris Little-Thomas; Whitman Mayo; E. Roger Mitchell; Mike Hodge; Clark Johnson; Directed by Clark Johnson; Written by Timothy J. Sexton; Herman Daniel Farrell, III; Cinematography by David Hennings; Music by Stephen James Taylor. **A:** Jr. High-Adult. **P:** Entertainment. **U:** Home. **Mov-Ent:** Documentary Films, Black Culture, Civil Rights. **Acq:** Purchase. **Dist:** Movies Unlimited; Alpha Video.

Boyd's Shadow 1992
Young boy learns about preconceptions and acceptance through the town recluse, who was thought to "boil children and feed them to his snakes." In actuality, the recluse is an accomplished folk musician and was a close friend of the boy's dead father. Filmed on location in North Carolina. Adaptation of a play by William Stevens who, along with his family, stars in the production, which is directed by his brother John. 45m; VHS. **C:** Bill Stevens; Becca Stevens; Katie Stevens; Carolyn Stevens; William Stevens; Directed by John Stevens; Written by John Stevens; Music by William Stevens. **A:** Preschool-Primary. **P:** Entertainment. **U:** Home, Institution. **Chl-Juv:** Family. **Acq:** Purchase. **Dist:** Baker and Taylor; Video Arts, Inc. $29.95.

A Boyfriend for Christmas 2004 (Unrated) — ★★½
When she was 12, Holly Grant asked Santa for a Christmas boyfriend and he promises her one—in 20 years. Now working for a nonprofit, Holly (Williams) is ticked at attorney Ryan (Muldoon), whom she's never met, when he misses an important appointment. When he turns up on her doorstep with a Christmas tree to make amends, Holly thinks he's someone else and he goes along with the charade so they can have a chance at romance. Her family thinks Holly's new guy is great but what will happen when the truth comes out? A Hallmark Channel original. 100m; DVD. **C:** Kelli Williams; Patrick Muldoon; Charles Durning; Shannon Wilcox; Martin Mull; Bruce Thomas; Maeve Quinlan; Bridget Ann White; David Starzyk; Directed by Kevin Connor; Written by Roger Schroeder; Cinematography by Amit Bhattacharya; Music by Charles Syndor. **A:** Family. **P:** Entertainment. **U:** Home. **Mov-Ent:** Christmas, Comedy--Romantic. **Acq:** Purchase. **Dist:** Movies Unlimited.

Boyfriends 1996 — ★★
Gay sexual roundelay that takes place over a weekend spent in the English countryside. Paul (Dreyfus) and Ben (Sands) are on the verge of splitting up after five years, orderly Matt's (Urwin) in love with philandering Owen (Ableson), and social worker Will (Coffey) wants more than a one-nighter with working-class pickup Adam (Petrucci). They all head to James's (McGrath) house and the sexual games begin. Low-budget first feature from Hunter and Hunsinger. 82m; VHS, DVD. **C:** James Dreyfus; Mark Sands; Andrew Ableson; Michael Urwin; David Coffey; Darren Petrucci; Michael McGrath; Russell Higgs; Directed by Neil Hunter; Tom Hunsinger; Written by Neil Hunter; Tom Hunsinger; Cinematography by Richard Tisdall. **A:** College-Adult. **P:** Entertainment. **U:** Home. **Mov-Ent:** Comedy--Romantic. **Acq:** Purchase. **Dist:** First Run Features.

Boyfriends & Girlfriends 1988 (PG) — ★★½
Another one of Rohmer's "Comedies and Proverbs," in which two girls with boyfriends fade in and out of interest with each, casually reshuffling their relationships. Typical, endless-talks-at-cafes Rohmer, the most happily consistent of the aging French New Wave. In French with subtitles. 102m; VHS, DVD. **C:** Emmanuelle Chaulet; Sophie Renoir; Eric Viellard; Francois-Eric Gendron; Anne-Laure Meury; Directed by Eric Rohmer; Written by Eric Rohmer; Cinematography by Bernard Lutic; Music by Jean-Louis Valero. **Pr:** Margaret Menegoz; Orion Pictures. **A:** Sr. High-Adult. **P:** Entertainment. **U:** Home. **L:** French. **Mov-Ent:** Comedy--Romantic. **Acq:** Purchase. **Dist:** Wellspring Media; MGM Studios Inc.

Boyhood 2014 (R) — ★★★
For twelve years, writer/director Linklater assembled a small crew and cast for a few weeks every year, shooting the entire school-age arc of a young man. The result is a film that captures the ups and downs of 1st grade through high school graduation with a protagonist (Coltrane) who ages before our eyes; with great supporting turns from Hawke and Arquette as his fictional parents. The film is naturally episodic (that's part of the point) and the second half works much more than the first (as its director became a better filmmaker) but this is a stunningly ambitious piece of work. 164m; DVD. **C:** Ellar Coltrane; Lorelei Linklater; Ethan Hawke; Patricia Arquette; Evie Thompson; Directed by Richard Linklater; Written by Richard Linklater; Cinematography by Lee Daniel; Shane Kelly. **Pr:** IFC Films. **A:** Sr. High-Adult. **P:** Entertainment. **U:** Home. **L:** English. **Mov-Ent:** Family, Adolescence, Children. **Acq:** Purchase.

The Boyhood Photos of J.H. Lartique 197?
J.H. Lartique's book "The Family Album of a Gilded Age," which is a photo album of the author's life in France is featured in this program. 30m/B/W; VHS, 3/4 U, EJ, Q. **Pr:** WCBS New York; Camera Three Productions. **A:** Sr. High-Adult. **P:** Education. **U:** Institution, SURA. **Gen-Edu:** Documentary Films, Immigration, Family. **Acq:** Duplication, Free Duplication. **Dist:** Camera Three Productions, Inc.; Creative Arts Television Archive.

The Boynton Beach Club 2005 (R) — ★★½
Aged lonely hearts find support and possibly love as members of a bereavement club at a Florida "active adult" community—an unlikely but surprisingly refreshing setting for a romantic comedy. Newly widowed Marilyn (Vaccarro) joins the group after a car backs over her husband. There she meets a range of characters more interested in romance and life beyond blue hair and early-bird specials. Hotties-of-a-certain-age Cannon and Kellerman mix with master casanova Bologna and his reluctant protege Cariou to show both the funny and tender sides of the senior dating game. Plays a little sitcom-y at times, but manages to keep things dignified and unpatronizing. Director Seidelman got the idea for the movie from her mother Florence, who received a producer's credit. 105m; DVD. **C:** Dyan Cannon; Brenda Vaccaro; Sally Kellerman; Joseph Bologna; Len Cariou; Michael Nouri; Renee Taylor; Directed by Susan Seidelman; Written by Susan Seidelman; Shelly Gitlow; Cinematography by Eric Moynier; Music by Marcelo Zarvos. **Pr:** Susan Seidelman; Susan Seidelman; Florence Siedelman; Snowbird Films; Samuel Goldwyn Films. **A:** Sr. High-Adult. **P:** Entertainment. **U:** Home. **L:** English. **Mov-Ent:** Comedy--Romantic, Aging. **Acq:** Purchase. **Dist:** Sony Pictures Home Entertainment Inc.

Boys 1995 (PG-13) — ★
Seems like only yesterday we saw Haas as that big-eared, doe-eyed Amish kid from "Witness," but now, in this dry love story, he has grown into a big-eared, doe-eyed teenager lusting after older woman Ryder. John (Haas) saves Patty (Ryder) after a riding accident leaves her unconscious near his New England prep school. Immediately taken by her beauty and mystery, John decides to hide her in his dorm room and a romance blossoms between the unlikely pair. But John isn't the only one hiding something. Patty has a terrible secret from her past (gasp!), but when it's finally revealed, you'll be too bored to care. Based on the short story "Twenty Minutes" by James Salter. 86m; VHS, DVD, CC. **C:** Winona Ryder; Lukas Haas; John C. Reilly; William Sage; Skeet Ulrich; Directed by Stacy Cochran; Written by Stacy Cochran; Cinematography by Robert Elswit; Music by Stewart Copeland. **Pr:** Peter Frankfurt; Paul Feldsher; Erica Huggins; Ted Field; Scott Kroopf; Robert W. Cort; Interscope Comm; Polygram Filmed Entertainment; Touchstone Pictures; Buena Vista. **A:** Jr. High-Adult. **P:** Entertainment. **U:** Home. **Mov-Ent:** Drama, Adolescence, Education. **Acq:** Purchase. **Dist:** Buena Vista Home Entertainment.

The Boys 1997 (Unrated) — ★★½
Popular, simply plotted French-Canadian comedy about a group of ordinary guys who play in an amateur hockey league. "Les Boys" are sponsored by local tavern-owner Stan (Girard), who's got a gambling jones and is in debt to small-time mobster, Meo (Lebeau). Meo strikes a deal pitting Stan's ragtag hockey players against his own team of thugs. If Stan's team is defeated, he loses his bar. Dirty tricks abound on both sides. French with subtitles. 107m; VHS, DVD. **C:** Remy Girard; Marc Messier; Patrick Huard; Serge Theriault; Yvan Ponton; Dominic Philie; Patrick Labbe; Roc Lafortune; Pierre Lebeau; Paul Houde; Directed by Louis Saia; Written by Christian Fournier; Cinematography by Sylvain Brault; Music by Normand Corbeil. **A:** Sr. High-Adult. **P:** Entertainment. **U:** Home. **L:** French. **Mov-Ent:** Sports--Fiction: Comedy, Hockey, Canada. **Acq:** Purchase. **Dist:** Movies Unlimited.

The Boys 1998 (R) — ★★★
After his release from prison on an assault charge, psychopathic Brett (Wenham), heads to the home of his mother Sandra (Curran) and younger brother Stevie (Hayes). His other brother Glenn (Polson) is now married to Jackie (Cronin) who wants him to stay out of trouble. Also greeting Brett is girlfriend Michelle (Collette) but the volatile duo are soon arguing furiously. As Brett gets drunker and more stoned, he also becomes more enraged, leading to a brutal crime. Chilling story with powerful performances; adapted from the 1991 play by Gordon Graham. 84m; VHS. **C:** David Wenham; Toni Collette; John Polson; Lynette Curran; Anthony Hayes; Jeanette Cronin; Anna

Lise; Pete Smith; Directed by Rowan Woods; Written by Stephen Sewell; Cinematography by Tristan Milani. **Pr:** Robert Connolly; John Maynard; Douglas Cummins; Arena Films. **A:** College-Adult. **P:** Entertainment. **U:** Home. **Mov-Ent:** Violence, Family, Australia. **Awds:** Australian Film Inst. '98: Adapt. Screenplay, Director (Woods), Support. Actor (Polson), Support. Actress (Collette). **Acq:** Purchase.

The Boys and Girl From County Clare 2003 (Unrated) — ★★½
Set in the 1960s, Liverpool businessman Jimmy (Meaney) returns to his home in Ireland after 24 years to compete in the annual Celli music festival, which brings him into direct conflict with his long-estranged older brother John Joe (Hill). Soon enough the brothers are fighting about music and Maisie (Bradley), who Jimmy deserted for life in Liverpool. Meanwhile their bands are doing everything they can to sabotage each other, and Jimmy's flutist (Evans) is falling for John Joe's fiddler (Corr). Lighthearted comedy/drama uses traditional Irish music as a backdrop for an appealing but routine sibling rivalry story. 90m; DVD. **C:** Bernard Hill; Colm Meaney; Charlotte Bradley; Stephen Brennan; Andrea Corr; Eamon Owens; Shaun Evans; Phil Barantini; Patrick Bergin; Directed by John Irvin; Written by Nicholas Adams; Cinematography by Thomas Burstyn; Music by Fiachra Trench. **P:** Entertainment. **U:** Home. **L:** English. **Mov-Ent:** Musical, Ireland. **Dist:** Movies Unlimited; Alpha Video.

Boys and Girls 2000 (PG-13) — ★★
Nondescript teen romance has lifelong acquaintances and most-time friends Ryan (Prinze Jr.) and Jennifer (Forlani) trying to decide if they love each other after their hormones get the better of them one night. And get this! They're complete opposites! She's carefree and live-for-the-moment. He's button-down, plan-every-second-precise. Biggs and Donahue, as the respective sidekicks, steal the movie from the leads whenever they show up. Sort of a young, poor man's "When Harry Met Sally," without the wit and insight. 94m; VHS, DVD, Wide, CC. **C:** Freddie Prinze, Jr.; Claire Forlani; Jason Biggs; Heather Donahue; Alyson Hannigan; Amanda Detmer; Lisa Eichhorn; Directed by Robert Iscove; Written by Andrew Lowery; Andrew Miller; Cinematography by Ralf Bode; Music by Stewart Copeland. **Pr:** Miramax Film Corp. **A:** Jr. High-Adult. **P:** Entertainment. **U:** Home. **Mov-Ent:** Comedy--Romantic. **Acq:** Purchase. **Dist:** Buena Vista Home Entertainment.

The Boys Are Back 2009 (PG-13) — ★★½
When Aussie sports writer Joe Warr's (Owen) wife dies from cancer, he becomes a single dad to his two sons—a six-year-old and a rebellious teen—without much of a clue as to how to proceed. Joe's philosophy degenerates into a lack of rules, which constantly puts them all on the brink of family disaster. Owens' excellent performance, combining toughness and sensitivity, saves it from sinking into melodrama. Possibly a little too picturesque with its scenic South Australian vistas, the setting doesn't always jive with the story's angst. Similarly, the glib title doesn't do justice to the emotional hardship and redemption all principal characters experience. Based on Simon Carr's 2001 memoir. 104m; On Demand, Wide, CC. **C:** Clive Owen; George MacKay; Laura Fraser; Emma Booth; Erik Thomson; Nicholas McAnulty; Emma Lung; Julia Blake; Directed by Scott Hicks; Written by Scott Hicks; Allan Cubitt; Cinematography by Greig Fraser; Music by Hal Lindes. **Pr:** Timothy White; Greg Brenman; Australian Film Finance Corp; BBC Films; Screen Australia; South Australian Film Corporation; Hopscotch Productions; Miramax Film Corp. **A:** Jr. High-Adult. **P:** Entertainment. **U:** Home. **L:** English. **Mov-Ent:** Journalism, Parenting. **Acq:** Purchase. **Dist:** Miramax Film Corp.; Amazon.com Inc.; Movies Unlimited.

The Boys Club 1996 (R) — ★★
Teens-in-trouble film is given a tough core by first time director Fawcett. Excitement-craving 14-year-olds Kyle (Zamprogna), Eric (Sawa), and Brad (Stone) spend all their free time at an abandoned shack at the outskirts of their small town. Only one day they discover it occupied by gun-pointing criminal Luke Cooper (Penn), who tells the boys he's actually a good cop who's been shot and is on the run from some bad cops. The boys are willing to buy into the story at first but Cooper is quick to show his psycho colors, taking Eric hostage, and precipitating a violent finale. 92m; VHS, DVD. **C:** Christopher Penn; Stuart Stone; Devon Sawa; Dominic Zamprogna; Nicholas (Nick) Campbell; Jarred Blanchard; Directed by John Fawcett; Written by Peter Wellington; Cinematography by Thom Best; Music by Michael Timmins. **Pr:** Tim O'Brien; Greg Dummett; John Fremes; Lael McCall; Alliance Communications Corporation. **A:** Sr. High-Adult. **P:** Entertainment. **U:** Home. **Mov-Ent:** Mystery & Suspense, Adolescence, Canada. **Acq:** Purchase. **Dist:** Allumination Filmworks.

The Boys: Crazy 1990
Follow the Boys through a typical day of "stardom," including the video "Dial My Heart 1990." 20m; VHS. **A:** Family. **P:** Entertainment. **U:** Home. **Mov-Ent:** Music Video. **Acq:** Purchase. **Dist:** Music Video Distributors. $9.95.

Boys Don't Cry 1999 (R) — ★★★
Falls under the truth is stranger than fiction category. Brandon Teena (heavily awarded Swank) moves from Lincoln, Nebraska, to the small town of Falls City hoping to start over and keep his past a secret. Brandon gets a girlfriend, Lana (Sevigny), and runs afoul of the reckless John (Sarsgaard). And then Brandon's secret is discovered—he is actually a girl and the gender revelation leads to tragic consequences. Based on a true story, which is also the subject of the documentary, "The Brandon Teena Story." Pierce's version, not unexpectedly, was subjected to the charges of dramatic license, but the story is still forceful. 116m; VHS, DVD, CC. **C:** Hilary Swank; Chloe Sevigny; Peter Sarsgaard; Brendan Sexton, III; Alison Folland; Alicia (Lecy) Goranson; Matt McGrath; Rob Campbell; Jeanetta Arnette; Directed by Kimberly Peirce; Written by Kimberly Peirce; Andy Bienen; Cinematography by Jim Denault; Music by Nathan Larson. **Pr:** John Hart; Christine Vachon; John Sloss; Fox Searchlight. **A:** Sr. High-Adult. **P:** Entertainment. **U:** Home. **Mov-Ent:** Rape. **Awds:** Oscars '99: Actress (Swank); Golden Globes '00: Actress--Drama (Swank); Ind. Spirit '00: Actress (Swank), Support. Actress (Sevigny); L.A. Film Critics '99: Actress (Swank), Support. Actress (Sevigny); N.Y. Film Critics '99: Actress (Swank); Natl. Soc. Film Critics '99: Support. Actress (Sevigny); Broadcast Film Critics '99: Actress (Swank). **Acq:** Purchase. **Dist:** Fox Home Entertainment.

Boys from Brazil 19??
A stunning record of Brazil, famous for its fine soccer talents, the World Cup competitions that have occurred there, and the athletes whose skills make it all possible. 85m; VHS. **A:** Family. **P:** Entertainment. **U:** Home. **Spo-Rec:** Sports--General, Soccer, South America. **Acq:** Purchase. **Dist:** Video Collectibles. $29.95.

The Boys from Brazil 1978 (R) — ★★½
Based on Ira Levin's novel, a thriller about Dr. Josef Mengele endeavoring to reconstitute the Nazi movement from his Brazilian sanctuary by cloning a brood of boys from Hitler's genes. 123m; VHS, DVD. **C:** Gregory Peck; James Mason; Laurence Olivier; Uta Hagen; Steve Guttenberg; Denholm Elliott; Lilli Palmer; Directed by Franklin J. Schaffner; Written by Heywood Gould; Cinematography by Henri Decae; Music by Jerry Goldsmith. **Pr:** 20th Century-Fox. **A:** Adult. **P:** Entertainment. **U:** Home. **Mov-Ent:** Mystery & Suspense, Genetics. **Awds:** Natl. Bd. of Review '78: Actor (Olivier). **Acq:** Purchase. **Dist:** Movies Unlimited; Alpha Video; Lions Gate Entertainment Inc. $59.98.

The Boys From Syracuse 1940 (Unrated) — ★★½
Musical based on Shakespeare's "A Comedy of Errors," which was first adapted for Broadway by Rodgers and Hart. In ancient Greece, wealthy Antipholus and his servant Dromio of Syracuse travel to Ephesus to find their twin brothers from whom they were separated at birth. 73m/B/W; DVD. **C:** Allan Jones; Joe Penner; Irene Hervey; Martha Raye; Eric Blore; Rosemary Lane; Charles Butterworth; Directed by A. Edward Sutherland; Written by Charles Grayson; Leonard Spigelgass; Paul Girard Smith; Cinematography by Joseph Valentine. **A:** Jr. High-Adult. **P:** Entertainment. **U:** Home. **Mov-Ent:** Musical. **Acq:** Purchase. **Dist:** Movies Unlimited.

The Boys from Termite Terrace 1975
The animators from Warner Bros. who created Bugs Bunny, Daffy Duck, and Porky Pig are interviewed in this series of two untitled programs. 30m; VHS. **Pr:** WCBS New York; Camera Three Productions. **A:** Jr. High-Adult. **P:** Entertainment. **U:** Institution, SURA. **Mov-Ent:** Animation & Cartoons, Documentary Films, Film History. **Acq:** Duplication, Free Duplication. **Dist:** Camera Three Productions, Inc.; Creative Arts Television Archive.

Boys in Brown 1949 — ★½
Teenaged crook Jackie (Attenborough) is arrested after a botched robbery and sentenced to three years in a Borstal (a boys reformatory). He wants to go straight but schemer Alfie (Bogarde) needs Jackie to help in an escape plan. Alfie plays on Jackie's worries that his girl Kitty (Murray) has found a new boyfriend and more trouble follows. The leads are too old for their roles and the plot is dull and earnest. 85m/B/W; DVD. **C:** Richard Attenborough; Dirk Bogarde; Barbara Murray; Jack Warner; Jimmy Hanley; Directed by Montgomery Tully; Written by Montgomery Tully; Cinematography by Cyril Bristow; Music by Doreen Carwithen. **A:** Adult. **P:** Entertainment. **U:** Home. **L:** English. **Mov-Ent:** Adolescence, Great Britain. **Acq:** Purchase. **Dist:** VCI Entertainment.

The Boys in Company C 1977 (R) — ★★
A frank, hard-hitting drama about five naive young men involved in the Vietnam War. 127m; VHS, DVD, Blu-Ray. **C:** Stan Shaw; Andrew Stevens; James Canning; Michael Lembeck; Craig Wasson; R. Lee Ermey; James Whitmore, Jr.; Scott Hylands; Noble Willingham; Santos Morales; Claude Wilson; Drew Michaels; Karen Hilger; Peggy O'Neal; Stan Johns; Cameo(s) Rick Natkin; Directed by Sidney J. Furie; Written by Sidney J. Furie; Rick Natkin; Cinematography by Godfret A. Godar; Music by Jaime Mendoza-Nava. **Pr:** Andre Morgan. **A:** College-Adult. **P:** Entertainment. **U:** Home. **Mov-Ent:** Basic Training/Boot Camp, Vietnam War. **Acq:** Purchase. **Dist:** Hen's Tooth Video. $59.95.

Boys in Love 1995 — ★★
Four gay shorts about young men in love. "Death in Venice, CA" finds a repressed academic drawn to his landlady's stepson. The animated "Achilles" features the Greek heros Achilles and Petroclus at the battle of Troy. A young man becomes determined to conquer "My Polish Waiter" and a rejected Latin lover finds love again (with some help from a dog) in "Miguel, Ma Belle." 83m; VHS. **C:** Directed by Barry Purves; P. David Ebersole. **A:** College-Adult. **P:** Entertainment. **U:** Home. **Mov-Ent.** **Acq:** Purchase. **Dist:** First Run Features.

Boys in Love 2 1998 (Unrated) — ★★
Anthology of six short films: "Boot Camp" finds two men cruising each other in a leather bar and breaking out into a musical comedy number; "Twilight of the Gods" features a jungle romance between a Maori warrior and a European soldier; "Karen Black Like Me" is a homage to "Trilogy of Terror," only this time a man is chased around his apartment by a sex toy; "My Body" is about a neurotic young man trying to deny his sexual orientation; "SPF 2000" spoofs Italian sexploitation films and features a space alien and lecherous sunbathers; and "Dirty Baby Does Fire Island" is an animated tale of a baby doll washed up on shore, who gets involved in Island life. The theatrical release also featured the animated "Achilles," which is not included here. 86m; VHS. **C:** Directed by Patrick McGuinn; Stewart Main; Joel Moffett; David Briggs; John Scott Matthews; Todd Downing. **A:** College-Adult. **P:** Entertainment. **U:** Home. **Mov-Ent.** **Acq:** Purchase. **Dist:** First Run Features.

The Boys in the Band 1970 (R) — ★★½
A group of gay friends get together one night for a birthday party. A simple premise with a compelling depiction of friendship, expectations, and lifestyle. One of the first serious cinematic presentations to deal with the subject of homosexuality. The film was adapted from Mart Crowley's play using the original cast. 120m; VHS, DVD. **C:** Frederick Combs; Cliff Gorman; Laurence Luckinbill; Kenneth Nelson; Leonard Frey; Directed by William Friedkin; Written by Matt Crowley. **Pr:** National General Pictures; Cinema Center. **A:** College-Adult. **P:** Entertainment. **U:** Home. **Mov-Ent.** **Acq:** Purchase. **Dist:** Movies Unlimited; Alpha Video; Paramount Pictures Corp. $59.98.

Boys Life 1994 (Unrated) — ★★
Three shorts about gay teenagers coming of age. "Pool Days" has 17-year-old Justin (Weinstein) taking a summer job as a lifeguard at a health spa. Still clueless as to his sexual preferences, Justin is flustered when cruised by a charming male swimmer but it does get him to thinking. "A Friend of Dorothy" finds NYU student Winston (O'Connell) seeking freedom in Greenwich Village as he looks for like-minded friends (and a little romance). "The Disco Years" takes place in California during the Nixon era as casually gay-bashing high-schooler Tom (Nolan) gradually realizes his true nature. 90m; VHS, DVD. **C:** Josh Weinstein; Nick Poletti; Kimberly Flynn; Richard Salamanca; Raoul O'Connell; Kevin McClatchy; Greg Lauren; Anne Zupa; Matt Nolan; Russell Scott Lewis; Gwen Welles; Dennis Christopher; Directed by Brian Sloan; Raoul O'Connell; Robert Lee King; Written by Brian Sloan; Raoul O'Connell; Robert Lee King; Cinematography by W. Mott Hupfel, III; Jonathan Schell; Greg Gardiner. **Pr:** Strand Releasing. **A:** College-Adult. **P:** Entertainment. **U:** Home. **Mov-Ent:** Adolescence. **Acq:** Purchase. **Dist:** Strand Releasing; Movies Unlimited. $59.95.

Indiv. Titles: 1. Pool Days 2. A Friend of Dorothy 3. The Disco Years.

Boys Life in Mexico 19??
Compares the lives of two Mexican boys, one from the city and one from the country. Narrated in English. Contains Spanish interviews with English subtitles. Comes with teacher's manual. 20m; VHS. **A:** Jr. High-Adult. **P:** Education. **U:** Institution. **Gen-Edu:** Hispanic Culture, Mexico, Adolescence. **Acq:** Purchase. **Dist:** Educational Video Network. $39.95.

Boys Love 2006 (Unrated) — ★
This gooey confection fits into the popular Japanese genre of romantic manga (yaoi), primarily aimed at women, about young men in love. Magazine editor Taishin (Kotani) interviews popular teenaged model Noeru (Takumi), who takes their meeting to a new level by including sex. When the two fall in love, Noeru's childhood friend Chidori (Matsumoto), who harbors an unrequited passion, can't stand the competition—with tragic results. Japanese with subtitles. 90m; DVD. **C:** Yoshikazu Kotani; Saito Takumi; Hiroya Matsumoto; Directed by Kotaro Terauchi; Written by Kotaro Terauchi; Cinematography by Chika Fujino. **A:** Sr. High-Adult. **P:** Entertainment. **U:** Home. **L:** Japanese. **Mov-Ent:** Drama. **Acq:** Purchase. **Dist:** Picture This! Home Video.

The Boys Next Door 1985 (R) — ★★½
Two California lads kill and go nuts during a weekend in Los Angeles. Sheen overacts as a budding psychotic, not an easy thing to do. Apparently is trying to show what a particular lifestyle can lead to. Violent. 90m; VHS, DVD, Wide. **C:** Maxwell Caulfield; Charlie Sheen; Christopher McDonald; Hank Garrett; Patti D'Arbanville; Moon Zappa; Directed by Penelope Spheeris; Written by Glen Morgan; James Wong; Cinematography by Arthur Albert; Music by George S. Clinton. **Pr:** New World Pictures. **A:** Sr. High-Adult. **P:** Entertainment. **U:** Home. **L:** Spanish. **Mov-Ent.** **Acq:** Purchase. **Dist:** Anchor Bay Entertainment. $19.95.

The Boys Next Door 1996 (PG) — ★★½
Gentle comedy/drama, based on Tom Griffin's play, about four mentally disabled men—Norman (Lane), Barry (Leonard), Arnold (Jeter), and Lucien (Vance)?who share a house under the supervision of too-dedicated social worker Jack (Goldwyn). In fact, Jack's devotion is causing enough problems in his marriage to have him consider changing careers, even as each of "the boys" struggle with their daily lives. TV movie is overly sweet but the performances are very good. 99m; VHS, DVD, CC. **C:** Nathan Lane; Tony Goldwyn; Robert Sean Leonard; Michael Jeter; Courtney B. Vance; Mare Winningham; Jenny Robertson; Elizabeth Wilson; Richard Jenkins; Lynne Thigpen; Directed by John Erman; Written by William Blinn; Cinematography by Frank Tidy; Music by John Kander. **Pr:** John Erman; John Erman; Richard Welsh; Hallmark Hall of Fame. **A:** Jr. High-Adult. **P:** Entertainment. **U:** Home. **Mov-Ent:** Comedy-Drama, TV Movies. **Acq:** Purchase. **Dist:** Amazon.com Inc.

Boys' Night Out 1962 — ★★★
Amusing comedy about four businessmen who desperately want to escape the suburban doldrums by setting up an apartment equipped with plaything Novak. Little do they know, but Novak is a sociology student studying the American male, and they are merely her guinea pigs in an experiment beyond their control. Blair, Page, and Gabor provide comic relief. Based on a story by Marvin Worth and Arne Sultan. 113m; VHS, DVD. **C:** Kim Novak; James Garner; Tony Randall; Howard Duff; Janet Blair; Patti Page; Jessie Royce Landis; Oscar Homolka; Zsa Zsa Gabor; Directed by Michael Gordon; Written by Ira

Wallach. **Pr:** Martin Ransohoff; MGM. **A:** Sr. High-Adult. **P:** Entertainment. **U:** Home. **Mov-Ent:** Sex & Sexuality. **Acq:** Purchase. **Dist:** WarnerArchive.com. $19.98.

Boys of Abu Ghraib 2014 (R) — ★½
Moran wrote/directed/produced/starred in this TV-movie treatment of the very complex subject matter of how power turned to torture at the detainment center in Abu Ghraib in 2003-4. The dull-as-dirt Moran plays Jack Farmer (possibly the most American name ever), the newest recruit to arrive at the camp in 2003, who quickly learns that inhumane activity is the norm in this part of the world. The interesting idea that the men tasked with guarding potential murderers could succumb to boredom and what that would lead to is discarded in favor of even more cliché when Jack makes friends with a quiet detainee (Omid Abtahi). 102m; DVD. **C:** Luke Moran; Omid Abtahi; Sean Astin; Scott Patterson; Sara Paxton; John Heard; Directed by Luke Moran; Written by Luke Moran; Cinematography by Peter Holland; Music by Dan Marocco. **Pr:** Luke Moran; Vertical Entertainment. **A:** Sr. High-Adult. **P:** Entertainment. **U:** Home. **L:** English. **Mov-Ent:** Armed Forces--U.S., Drama, Middle East. **Acq:** Purchase.

The Boys of Baraka 2005 (Unrated) — ★★½
Directors Ewing and Grady inform us that 76 percent of Baltimore's black male students do not graduate from high school. So, in 2002, 20 at-risk students are given scholarships to attend the progressive Baraka boarding school—in Kenya—which is run by American volunteers. They are supposed to stay two years, but a transformation is begun that cannot be completed when terrorists attack Nairobi and the school is forced to close. The film may not have the "feel good" ending viewers are expecting, although it seems the lives of several boys are changed for the better. 84m; DVD. **A:** Sr. High-Adult. **P:** Entertainment. **U:** Home. **L:** English. **Mov-Ent:** Documentary Films, Africa, Black Culture. **Acq:** Purchase. **Dist:** ThinkFilm Company Inc. $9.98.

The Boys of Paul Street 1969 (Unrated) — ★½
Around 1900, two rival gangs of boys—the Paul Street Boys and the Red Shirts—both claim a vacant Budapest lot as their own playing field. They decide to conduct a ritualized war for possession of the property. Based on the 1907 Ferenc Molnar novel; previously filmed as 1934's "No Greater Glory." Hungarian with subtitles. 110m; VHS. **C:** Anthony Kemp; William Burleigh; John Moulder-Brown; Robert Efford; Mark Colleano; Gary O'Brien; Directed by Zoltan Fabri; Written by Zoltan Fabri; Endre Bohem; Cinematography by Gyorgy Illes; Music by Emil Petrovics. **A:** College-Adult. **P:** Entertainment. **U:** Home. **L:** Hungarian. **Mov-Ent. Acq:** Purchase. **Dist:** No Longer Available.

The Boys of St. Vincent 1993 (Unrated) — ★★★★
Outstanding, and heartbreaking, story of sexual abuse by Catholic clergy that was inspired by actual events. Divided into two segments, the drama begins in 1975 with 10-year-old Kevin Reevey (Morina) living at the St. Vincent orphanage in an eastern Canadian town. The orphanage is run by charismatic and terrifying Brother Lavin (Czerny), who it turns out has a special fondness for "his boy" Kevin. Nor is Brother Lavin alone—a fact eventually revealed by a police investigation, although the matter is hushed up by both the church and the government. Until 15 years later. In 1990, the case is reopened and Lavin, having married and fathered two sons, is returned to face charges. Now the young men must open wounds that have never truly healed and confront their tormentors in a court of law, amidst a blaze of publicity. Czerny gives a truly inspired performance as the self-loathing monster. The emotional agony is excruciating to watch and be forwarned that the depiction of the sexual abuse is unflinching. Made for Canadian TV; on two cassettes. 186m; VHS, DVD. **C:** Henry Czerny; Johnny Morina; Sebastian Spence; Brian Dodd; David Hewlett; Jonathan Lewis; Jeremy Keefe; Phillip Dinn; Brian Dooley; Greg Thomey; Michael Wade; Lise Roy; Timothy Webber; Kristine Demers; Ashley Billard; Sam Grana; Directed by John N. Smith; Written by Sam Grana; John N. Smith; Des Walsh; Cinematography by Pierre Letarte; Music by Neil Smolar. **Pr:** Claudio Luca; Colin Neale; Sam Grana; National Film Board of Canada; Canadian Broadcasting Corp; Telefilm Canada; Les Productions Tele-Action. **A:** Sr. High-Adult. **P:** Entertainment. **U:** Home. **Mov-Ent:** Sexual Abuse, Child Abuse, Children. **Acq:** Purchase. **Dist:** New Yorker Video. $89.95.

The Boys of 2nd Street Park 2003 (R) — ★★★
Drawn together for this compelling documentary, childhood buddies frankly recount the life-changing events they've confronted over the years while pining for the simpler times growing up in Brighton Beach, NY, in the 1950s. 91m; VHS, DVD. **C:** Directed by Dan Klores; Ron Berger; Cinematography by Buddy Squires. **A:** Sr. High-Adult. **P:** Entertainment. **U:** Home. **Mov-Ent:** Documentary Films, Drug Abuse, Vietnam War. **Acq:** Purchase. **Dist:** Showtime Networks Inc. $26.99.

Boys of the City 1940 — ★★
The East Side Kids run amuck in an eerie mansion while trying to solve the murder of a judge. 63m/B/W; VHS, DVD. **C:** Leo Gorcey; Bobby Jordan; Directed by Joseph H. Lewis. **Pr:** Prime Television. **A:** Family. **P:** Entertainment. **U:** Home. **Mov-Ent. Acq:** Purchase, Rent/Lease. **Dist:** Sinister Cinema; Rex Miller Artisan Studio. $24.95.

Boys on the Side 1994 (R) — ★★½
It's "Thelma & Louise" come to "Terms of Endearment" by way of "Philadelphia." Goldberg is Jane, an unemployed lesbian singer, who connects with Ms. Priss real estate agent Robin (Parker) for a road trip to California. The two become a female version of the Odd Couple as Jane tags Robin as "the whitest woman in America." They stop off to pick up addle-brain friend Holly (Barrymore) who has just knocked her drug-crazed abusive beau in the head with a baseball bat. Holly's accident turns fatal and the threesome are on the run from cops. They bond like crazy glue and become a family as they face two huge setbacks—one's pregnant, another has AIDS. Strong performances by the lead actresses and a cool soundtrack may make up for this often trite movie of the week premise. 117m; VHS, DVD, CC. **C:** Whoopi Goldberg; Mary-Louise Parker; Drew Barrymore; James Remar; Anita Gillette; Matthew McConaughey; Directed by Herbert Ross; Written by Don Roos; Cinematography by Donald E. Thorin; Music by David Newman. **Pr:** Herbert Ross; Don Roos; Arnon Milchan; Steven Reuther; Herbert Ross; Don Roos; Patricia Karlan; New Regency Pictures; Alcor Films; Regency Enterprises. **A:** Sr. High-Adult. **P:** Entertainment. **U:** Home. **Mov-Ent:** Real Estate, Women, Death. **Acq:** Purchase. **Dist:** Warner Home Video, Inc. $95.95.

The Boys' Railroad Club ????
Includes four episodes of the 1950s television show "The Boys' Railroad Club" that present American Flyer trains and layouts. 50m; VHS, DVD. **A:** College-Adult. **P:** Education. **U:** Home. **Gen-Edu:** Trains, Hobbies. **Acq:** Purchase. **Dist:** The Civil War Standard. $24.95.

Boy's Reformatory 1939 — ★½
Brothers are framed. One takes the rap, goes to the title institution, breaks out, and hunts the real bad guys. Creaky and antiquated. 62m/B/W; VHS, DVD. **C:** Frankie Darro; Grant Withers; David Durand; Warren McCollum; Directed by Howard Bretherton. **Pr:** Lindsley Parsons Productions; Monogram. **A:** Jr. High-Adult. **P:** Entertainment. **U:** Home. **Mov-Ent:** Adolescence. **Acq:** Purchase. **Dist:** Alpha Video; Movies Unlimited. $15.95.

Boys Town 1938 (Unrated) — ★★★½
Righteous portrayal of Father Flanagan and the creation of Boys Town, home for juvenile soon-to-be-ex-delinquents. 93m/B/W; VHS, DVD, CC. **C:** Spencer Tracy; Mickey Rooney; Henry Hull; Gene Reynolds; Sidney Miller; Frankie Thomas, Jr.; Directed by Norman Taurog. **Pr:** MGM. **A:** Family. **P:** Entertainment. **U:** Home. **Mov-Ent:** Parenting, Classic Films. **Awds:** Oscars '38: Actor (Tracy), Story. **Acq:** Purchase. **Dist:** Baker and Taylor; Ignatius Press; MGM Home Entertainment. $19.98.

Boy's Town Parenting Series 199?
Eleven-part series covering topics form self-esteem and peer pressure to making sure kids and teens do their homework and help around the house. Titles are: A Change for the Better! Teaching Correct Behavior; I Can't Decide What Should I Do?; Catch 'Em Being Good! Happier Kids, Happier Parents Through Effective Praise; Homework? I'll Do It Later; You Want ME to Help with Housework? No Way!; Setting You Child Up for Success! Anticipating & Preventing Problems: It's Great to Be Me! Increasing Your Child's Self-Esteem; I'm Not Everybody! Helping Your Child Stand Up to Peer Pressure; No I Won't and You Can't Make Me; Take Time to Be a Family! Holding Successful Family Meetings; and Negotiating Within the Family! You and Your Child Can Both Get What You Want. Each video runs 15 minutes, comes with a booklet, and purchased separately costs $29.95. ?m; VHS. **A:** Jr. High-Adult. **P:** Education. **U:** Institution. **Gen-Edu:** Parenting. **Acq:** Purchase. **Dist:** Cambridge Educational. $275.00.

The Boys: Video Messages 1990
This film features The Boys performing some of their smash hits such as, "Dial My Heart," "Lucky Charm," "A Little Romance," and "Happy." 30m; VHS. **A:** Adult. **P:** Entertainment. **U:** Home. **Mov-Ent:** Music Video. **Acq:** Purchase. **Dist:** Music Video Distributors. $14.98.

Boys Will Be. . . 19??
A stage drama examining the causes, consequences, and possible cures of domestic violence. 33m; VHS, 3/4 U. **Pr:** Michael Glassbourg. **A:** College-Adult. **P:** Education. **U:** Institution. **Hea-Sci:** Psychology, Violence, Domestic Abuse. **Acq:** Purchase, Rent/Lease. **Dist:** Leo Media, Inc. $250.00.

Boys Will Be Boys 1935 (Unrated) — ★★
Teacher Alec Smart (Hay) works part-time at the local prison but wants to become headmaster at Narkover, which is notorious for having many of its unruly students become inmates at the same prison. Thanks to a forged letter of recommendation, Smart gets his opportunity but then must deal with a stolen diamond necklace and a climatic and chaotic rugby match. 78m/B/W; DVD. **C:** Will Hay; Gordon Harker; Jimmy Hanley; David Burnaby; Norma Varden; Claude Dampier; Charles Farrell; Directed by William Beaudine; Written by Will Hay; Robert Edmunds; Cinematography by Charles Van Enger; Music by Louis Levy. **A:** Jr. High-Adult. **P:** Entertainment. **U:** Home. **Mov-Ent. Acq:** Purchase. **Dist:** VCI Entertainment.

Boys Will Be Boys 1997 (PG) — ★★½
With their parents away at a company party, Matt and Robbie are home alone for the first time. Expect chaos when the boys discover that their father's business rival has something nasty in store and the brothers will use anything around to defeat him. 89m; VHS, DVD. **C:** Randy Travis; Julie Hagerty; Jon Voight; Michael DeLuise; Catherine Oxenberg; Mickey Rooney; Ruth Buzzi; Dom DeLuise; Charles Nelson Reilly; James Williams; Drew Winget; Directed by Dom DeLuise; Written by Gregory Poppon; Mark Dubas; Cinematography by Leonard Schway; Music by Kristopher Carter. **A:** Primary-Adult. **P:** Entertainment. **U:** Home. **Mov-Ent:** Comedy--Slapstick. **Acq:** Purchase. **Dist:** Movies Unlimited.

Boys with Long Hair 1970
Discussion revolves around freedom of expression, defiance and compliance, and style and choice, making it always timely. 29m; 3/4 U, Q. **Pr:** Moreland/Latchford Productions. **A:** Jr. High-Sr. High. **P:** Education. **U:** Institution, CCTV, CATV, BCTV, Home. **Gen-Edu:** Documentary Films, Sociology. **Acq:** Purchase, Rent/Lease. **Dist:** Communication for Change, Inc.

Boystown 2007 (Unrated) — ★★
Who'd a thought you could have a cuddly couple involved in a serial killer story? Slimy Madrid realtor Victor kills little old ladies for their apartments in a gentrifying gay neighborhood. When Rey and Leo unexpectedly inherit their next-door neighbor's apartment, the police suspect them of the crimes. Things actually get worse when Rey's hateful mother Antonia, who wants to split the couple up, takes over the disputed apartment. Too bad for her since that really interferes with Victor's plans. Spanish with subtitles. 93m; DVD. **C:** Carlos Fuentes; Rosa Maria Sarda; Pablo Puyol; Pepon Nieto; Concha Valasco; Eduard Soto; Directed by Juan Flahn; Written by Juan Flahn; Felix Sabroso; Dunia Ayaso; Cinematography by Juan Carlos Lausin; Music by David San Jose; Joan Crossas. **A:** College-Adult. **P:** Entertainment. **U:** Home. **L:** Spanish. **Mov-Ent:** Real Estate. **Acq:** Purchase. **Dist:** TLA Releasing.

Boyz N the Hood 1991 (R) — ★★★½
Singleton's debut as a writer and director is an astonishing picture of young black men, four high school students with different backgrounds, aims, and abilities trying to survive L.A. gangs and bigotry. Excellent acting throughout, with special nods to Fishburne and Gooding Jr. Violent outbreaks outside theatres where this ran only proves the urgency of its passionately nonviolent, pro-family message. Hopefully those viewers scared off at the time will give this a chance in the safety of their VCRs. Singleton was the youngest director ever nominated for an Oscar. 112m; VHS, DVD, UMD, Wide, CC. **C:** Laurence Fishburne; Ice Cube; Cuba Gooding, Jr.; Nia Long; Morris Chestnut; Tyra Ferrell; Angela Bassett; Whitman Mayo; Directed by John Singleton; Written by John Singleton; Cinematography by Charles Mills; Music by Stanley Clarke. **A:** College-Adult. **P:** Entertainment. **U:** Home. **Mov-Ent:** Violence, Adolescence, Black Culture. **Awds:** MTV Movie Awards '92: New Filmmaker (Singleton); Natl. Film Reg. '02. **Acq:** Purchase. **Dist:** Sony Pictures Home Entertainment Inc.; Facets Multimedia Inc. $14.95.

Bozen und Eppan/Suedtirol 1985 (Unrated)
From the southernmost German-speaking area in Europe comes this program of music, dance, and folklore. In German only. 90m; VHS. **TV Std:** NTSC, PAL. **A:** Family. **P:** Entertainment. **U:** Home. **L:** German. **Mov-Ent:** Travel, Folklore & Legends. **Acq:** Purchase, Rent/Lease. **Dist:** German Language Video Center. $41.95.

Bozo the Clown: Ding Dong Dandy Adventures 1991
Animated adventures of the world's most famous clown. Special surprise appearances by the real live Bozo himself. 90m; VHS. **C:** Larry Harmon. **Pr:** Larry Harmon. **A:** Family. **P:** Entertainment. **U:** Home. **Chl-Juv:** Animation & Cartoons, Circuses. **Acq:** Purchase. **Dist:** Image Entertainment Inc. $24.95.

Bozo the Clown: Wowie Kazowie Clown Tales! 1991
The world's most famous clown stars in animated and live-action adventures. 90m; VHS. **C:** Larry Harmon. **Pr:** Larry Harmon. **A:** Family. **P:** Entertainment. **U:** Home. **Chl-Juv:** Animation & Cartoons, Circuses. **Acq:** Purchase. **Dist:** Image Entertainment Inc. $24.95.

Bozo's Big Top—Bozo: The World's Most Famous Clown 1966
Collection of the children's variety show that ran for 47 years featuring, games, songs, and skits performed before a live audience of children. 30 episodes plus an interview with Larry "Bozo the Clown" Harmon. 780m; DVD. **C:** Larry Harmon; Frank Avruch. **A:** Preschool-Primary. **P:** Entertainment. **U:** Home. **Chl-Juv:** Children, Variety. **Acq:** Purchase. **Dist:** Falcon Press Publishing Co., Inc.

Bra Boys 2007 (R) — ★½
Title is an Aussie diminutive for Sydney's Maroubra Beach and refers to a notorious local working-class surfer gang. Formed around Abberton brothers Koby, Jai, and director/writer Sunny, the Bra Boys are known to the cops for turf wars and scrapes with the law while locals in the poor suburb praise the surfers for their work with troubled youth. (Don't do as I do, do as I say?) There's also lengthy coverage of a murder trial involving Jai and Koby but it's a decidedly one-sided documentary. 86m; On Demand. **C:** Voice(s) by Russell Crowe; Directed by Sunny Abberton; Written by Sunny Abberton; Cinematography by Macario De Souza; Brooke Silvester; Music by Jamie Holt. **Pr:** Mark Lawrence; Sunny Abberton; Bradahood Prods; Garage Industries; Berkela Films. **A:** Sr. High-Adult. **P:** Entertainment. **U:** Home. **L:** English. **Mov-Ent:** Documentary Films. **Acq:** Purchase. **Dist:** Amazon.com Inc.; Warner Home Video, Inc.

Brad Gillis: Guitar Instruction 1990
Night Ranger's guitarist extraordinaire teaches his secrets for chord brilliance. ?m; VHS. **A:** Jr. High-Adult. **P:** Instruction. **U:** Home. **How-Ins:** Music--Instruction. **Acq:** Purchase. **Dist:** Music Video Distributors. $44.95.

Brad Greenberg: Player Development and Team Building 2010 (Unrated)
Coach Brad Greenberg discusses Basketball drills for developing the skills of individual players and then cohering them together as a team. 77m; DVD. **A:** Family. **P:** Education. **U:** Home, Institution. **Spo-Rec:** Basketball, Athletic Instruction/Coaching. **Acq:** Purchase. **Dist:** Championship Productions. $39.99.

Brad Soderberg: The Five Essentials of Winning Basketball 2005 (Unrated)
Coach Brad Soderberg lectures on the five essentials needed to win basketball including shoot more free throws than the other team, get more rebounds than the other team, have a higher goal percentages have fewer turnovers, have fewer turnovers, and don't give up easy baskets. 66m; DVD. **A:** Family. **P:** Education. **U:** Home, Institution. **Spo-Rec:** Basketball, Athletic Instruction/Coaching. **Acq:** Purchase. **Dist:** Championship Productions. $34.99.

Brad Stevens: Winning with Undersized Teams 2009
Coach Brad Stevens presents offensive drills for physically outmatched basketball players. 46m; DVD. **A:** Family. **P:** Education. **U:** Home, Institution. **Spo-Rec:** Basketball, Athletic Instruction/Coaching. **Acq:** Purchase. **Dist:** Championship Productions. $39.99.

Braddock: Missing in Action 3 1988 (R) — ★
The battle-scarred, high-kicking 'Nam vet battles his way into the jungles once more, this time to rescue his long-lost Vietnamese family. A family effort, Chuck co-wrote the script; his brother directed. 104m; VHS, DVD, CC. **C:** Chuck Norris; Aki Aleong; Roland Harrah, III; Directed by Aaron Norris; Written by Chuck Norris; James Bruner; Cinematography by Joao Fernandes. **Pr:** Cannon Films. **A:** Sr. High-Adult. **P:** Entertainment. **U:** Home. **Mov-Ent:** Martial Arts, Veterans, Vietnam War. **Acq:** Purchase. **Dist:** Anchor Bay Entertainment. $9.98.

The Brady Bunch 1969
Relive classic moments with TV's grooviest family—two episodes per tape—including "The Honeymoon," the premiere episode explaining how Mike and his three boys get hitched to Carol and her three girls. Additional episodes available. 51m; VHS, CC. **C:** Robert Reed; Florence Henderson; Ann B. Davis; Maureen McCormick; Barry Williams; Eve Plumb; Christopher Knight; Michael (Mike) Lookinland; Susan Olsen. **A:** Family. **P:** Entertainment. **U:** Home. **Mov-Ent:** Television Series. **Acq:** Purchase. **Dist:** Paramount Pictures Corp. $9.95.
Indiv. Titles: 1. The Honeymoon/A Camping We Will Go 2. The Tattletale/Law and Disorder 3. Will the Real Jan Brady Please Stand Up/Her Sister's Shadow 4. Getting Davy Jones/The Subject Was Noses.

The Brady Bunch Hour Twin Pack 2000
Set contains two episodes of the variety show which featured members of the cast of the television show "The Brady Bunch." Songs of the period are weakly performed and guest stars such as Donny and Marie Osmond and Rip Taylor appear. Two-volume set. ?m; VHS, DVD. **A:** Family. **P:** Entertainment. **U:** Home. **Mov-Ent:** Television Series, Variety. **Acq:** Purchase. **Dist:** Rhino Entertainment Co. $24.95.

The Brady Bunch Movie 1995 (PG-13) — ★★★
Grunge and CDs may be the norm in the '90s, but the Bradys still live in the eight-track world of the '70s, where Davy Jones rocks and every day is a sunshine day. Then greedy developer McKean schemes to cash in on Mike and Carol's financial woes. (Hawaii! The Grand Canyon! What were they thinking?) Great ensemble cast capably fills the white platform shoes of the originals—Cole sounds just like Mr. Brady, Cox hilariously channels Jan's tormented middle child angst, and Taylor's self-absorbed Marcia, Marcia, Marcia is dead-on, right down to the frosty pursed lips. Look for neat-o cameos from some original Bradys and most of the Monkees. Followed by "A Very Brady Sequel." 88m; VHS, DVD, CC. **C:** Shelley Long; Gary Cole; Michael McKean; Jean Smart; Henriette Mantel; Christopher Daniel Barnes; Christine Taylor; Paul Sutera; Jennifer Elise Cox; Jesse Lee; Olivia Hack; David Graf; Jack Noseworthy; Shane Conrad; RuPaul Charles; Cameo(s) Ann B. Davis; Florence Henderson; Davy Jones; Barry Williams; Christopher Knight; Michael (Mike) Lookinland; Mickey Dolenz; Peter Tork; Directed by Betty Thomas; Written by Bonnie Turner; Terry Turner; Laurice Elehwany; Rick Copp; Cinematography by Mac Ahlberg; Music by Guy Moon. **A:** Jr. High-Adult. **P:** Entertainment. **U:** Home. **Mov-Ent:** Satire & Parody, Architecture. **Acq:** Purchase. **Dist:** Paramount Pictures Corp.

The Brady Bunch: The Complete Final Season 1974
The family spends the day at King's Island amusement park. Greg makes fun of women drivers so Marcia decides to out-do him on their driving tests. Carol's nephew Oliver comes to stay and Greg graduates from high school. 22 episodes. 553m; DVD, CC. **C:** Robert Reed; Florence Henderson; Ann B. Davis; Maureen McCormick; Barry Williams; Eve Plumb; Christopher Knight; Susan Olsen; Michael (Mike) Lookinland. **A:** Family. **P:** Entertainment. **U:** Home. **Mov-Ent:** Television Series, Television. **Acq:** Purchase. **Dist:** Paramount Pictures Corp.

The Brady Bunch: The Complete First Season 2005
Carol is a single mother of three girls and Mike is a single father of three boys, when they marry, the blended families along with a housekeeper and dog Tiger make for loads of great comedy. 652m; DVD; Closed Captioned. **A:** Family. **P:** Entertainment. **U:** Home. **Mov-Ent:** Television, Family. **Acq:** Purchase. **Dist:** Paramount Pictures Corp. $29.99.

The Brady Bunch: The Complete Fourth Season 1973
The Bradys head for Hawaii where Greg gets involved in a surf contest. High school freshman Marcia has her nose broken by a football tossed by would-be boyfriend Doug. And Greg and Marcia both want their own bedroom in the attic. 22 episodes. 581m; DVD, CC. **C:** Robert Reed; Florence Henderson; Ann B. Davis; Maureen McCormick; Barry Williams; Eve Plumb; Christopher Knight; Susan Olsen; Michael (Mike) Lookinland. **A:** Family. **P:** Entertainment. **U:** Home. **Mov-Ent:** Television Series, Television. **Acq:** Purchase. **Dist:** Paramount Pictures Corp.

The Brady Bunch: The Complete Second Season 2005
Four-disc set of the ABC family sitcom starring Florence Henderson and Robert Reed. DVD. **A:** Family. **P:** Entertainment. **U:** Home. **Mov-Ent:** Television, Family. **Acq:** Purchase. **Dist:** Paramount Pictures Corp. $38.99.

The Brady Bunch: The Complete Series 1969 (Unrated)
Contains all 117 episodes from seasons 1-5. Calamity erupts when Tiger escapes from the car at Mike and Carol's wedding reception in "The Honeymoon." Marcia and Greg run against each other for class president in "Vote for Brady." Peter becomes "The Hero" after saving a little girl at Driscoll's Toy Store. Cindy mistakenly gives Marcia's diary away in "The Possible Dream." Greg buys a $100 lemon in "The Wheeler-Dealer." The family is cast in a laundry soap commercial in "And Now, a Word from Our Sponsor." 2980m; DVD. **C:** Robert Reed; Florence Henderson; Ann B. Davis; Barry Williams; Maureen McCormick; Christopher Knight; Eve Plumb; Michael (Mike) Lookinland; Susan Oleson. **A:** Family. **P:** Entertainment. **U:** Home. **Mov-Ent:** Family, Television, Television Series. **Acq:** Purchase. **Dist:** Paramount Pictures Corp.

The Brady Bunch: The Complete Third Season 1972
Peter's voice starts to change, threatening the family's musical career. Jan has to wear glasses and fights to get out from Marcia's shadow. Greg loses a bet with Bobby and has to obey his every whim, and Alice's lookalike cousin, a master sergeant in the WACS, tries to instill some discipline. 23 episodes. 594m; DVD, CC. **C:** Robert Reed; Florence Henderson; Ann B. Davis; Maureen McCormick; Barry Williams; Eve Plumb; Christopher Knight; Susan Olsen; Michael (Mike) Lookinland. **A:** Family. **P:** Entertainment. **U:** Home. **Mov-Ent:** Television Series, Television. **Acq:** Purchase. **Dist:** Paramount Pictures Corp.

The Brady Home Movies 2000
Features home movie clips from the classic television show "The Brady Bunch" as well as interviews with cast members. Written and produced by Susan Olsen, who played Cindy Brady. DVD contains extra material. ?m; VHS, DVD. **A:** Family. **P:** Entertainment. **U:** Home. **Mov-Ent:** Television Series, Documentary Films. **Acq:** Purchase. **Dist:** Rhino Entertainment Co. $14.95.

Brady's Escape 1984 (Unrated) — ★½
American WWII pilot is shot down in the Hungarian countryside and befriended by Hungarian csikos (cowboys). 92m; VHS. **C:** John Savage; Kelly Reno; Directed by Pal Gabor. **Pr:** Satori Entertainment Corporation. **A:** Family. **P:** Entertainment. **U:** Home. **Mov-Ent:** World War Two, TV Movies. **Acq:** Purchase. **Dist:** Unknown Distributor.

Brahms 19??
Summarizes the life of Brahms and how he came to write classical music. Includes teacher's manual. 55m; VHS. **A:** Jr. High-Adult. **P:** Education. **U:** Institution. **Fin-Art:** Music--Classical, Biography. **Acq:** Purchase. **Dist:** Educational Video Network. $59.95.

Brahms: Concerto in "A" for Violin & Cello 1990
A masterful and moving performance of one the best-loved pieces in classical music. 54m; VHS. **A:** Family. **P:** Entertainment. **U:** Home. **Mov-Ent:** Music--Performance, Music--Classical. **Acq:** Purchase. **Dist:** Music Video Distributors. $29.95.

Brahms: German Requiem 19??
The Vienna Philharmonic Orchestra and Vienna Singverein, with soloists Jose van Dam and Gundula Janowitz, conducted by Herbert von Karajan. 80m; VHS. **Pr:** Polygram Music Video; Unitel. **A:** Jr. High-Adult. **P:** Entertainment. **U:** Home. **Fin-Art:** Music--Classical. **Acq:** Purchase. **Dist:** Music Video Distributors. $24.95.

Brahms: Klassix 13—Breaking the Mold 19??
Classical musician Balint Vazsonyi portrays Johannes Brahms and performs his music in this unique re-creation of the German composer's life. The presentation utilizes stunning scenes of Austria and the wardrobe and music of the 19th century to re-live important moments in Brahms' career, including his meticulous creation of the First Symphony. Brahms' personal life is also explored, from his days of rowdy innocence to his painfully futile passion for Clara, spouse of fellow German composer Robert Schumann. 55m; VHS. **TV Std:** NTSC, PAL. **C:** Balint Vazsonyi; Anthony Quayle. **A:** Jr. High-Adult. **P:** Entertainment. **U:** Home. **Fin-Art:** Documentary Films, Music--Classical, Biography. **Acq:** Purchase. **Dist:** MPI Media Group; Music Video Distributors; Karol Media. $24.95.

Brahms: Piano Concerti 1 & 2 19??
The talented musicians perform the music of the great composer. 111m; VHS. **A:** Sr. High-Adult. **P:** Entertainment. **U:** Home. **Fin-Art:** Music--Classical. **Acq:** Purchase. **Dist:** Music Video Distributors. $24.95.

Brahms: Piano Concerto No. 1 1992
Pianist Jean-Bernard Pommier plays with the National Orchestra of Lille, conducted by Jean-Claude Casadesus. 51m; VHS. **A:** Sr. High-Adult. **P:** Entertainment. **U:** Home. **Fin-Art:** Music--Classical, Music--Performance. **Acq:** Purchase. **Dist:** V.I.E.W. Inc./Arkadia Entertainment Corp. $19.97.

Brahms: Symphonies 3 & 4 1973
Berlin Philharmonic Orchestra performs two symphonies conducted by Herbert von Karajan. 74m; VHS. **A:** Jr. High-Adult. **P:** Entertainment. **U:** Home. **Mov-Ent:** Music Video, Music--Performance, Music--Classical. **Acq:** Purchase. **Dist:** Music Video Distributors. $24.95.

Brahms: Symphony No. 1 1990
BBC production of Seji Ozawa conducting the Saito Kinen orchestra. The members of the orchestra are prominent players around the world and gather yearly to pay homage to their teacher. A 15-minute documentary is included. 60m; VHS. **A:** Jr. High-Adult. **P:** Entertainment. **U:** Home. **Fin-Art:** Music--Classical, Music--Performance. **Acq:** Purchase. **Dist:** Music Video Distributors. $24.95.

Brahms: Symphony No. 4 19??
A discussion of the music takes us into the work of Brahms. 90m; VHS. **A:** Sr. High-Adult. **P:** Entertainment. **U:** Home. **Fin-Art:** Music--Classical. **Acq:** Purchase. **Dist:** Music Video Distributors. $39.95.

Braided Rope Splicing 199?
Teaches crew members vital on-deck skills, including splicing braided rope or wire rope, or mending netting in a three-tape series. 30m; VHS. **A:** Sr. High. **P:** Instruction. **U:** Home. **How-Ins:** Boating. **Acq:** Purchase. **Dist:** John Sabella & Associate. $39.95.

Braiding Beautiful 19??
Hair artist Ines Yimoc illustrates different types of braids for the bride and her maids, including the fishtail braid, cobra braid, cornrow braid, the invisible braid, and braid adornment. Available only in the U.S. 30m; VHS. **A:** Sr. High-Adult. **P:** Instruction. **U:** Institution. **L:** English, Spanish. **How-Ins:** Cosmetology, How-To. **Acq:** Purchase. **Dist:** Instructional Video. $24.95.

Braiding Techniques 19??
Offers tips on how to properly braid the mane of a horse, including information on pulling the mane, braiding with scallops and buttons, and taping the mane for dressage. ?m; VHS. **A:** Sr. High-Adult. **P:** Instruction. **U:** Institution. **How-Ins:** How-To, Horses. **Acq:** Purchase. **Dist:** CEV Multimedia. $39.95.

The Brain 19??
Three-part series which takes the viewer inside the human brain, explaining how it works and how to make it work for you. ?m; VHS. **A:** Jr. High-Adult. **P:** Education. **U:** Institution, Home. **Hea-Sci:** Science, Anatomy & Physiology. **Acq:** Purchase. **Dist:** Discovery Home Entertainment. $49.95.
Indiv. Titles: 1. Evolution and Perception 2. Memory/Miraculous Mind 3. Matter Over Mind.

The Brain 1962 (Unrated) — ★★½
A scientist learns that a mind isn't always a terrible thing to waste when he finds himself being manipulated by the brain of a dead man he's trying to keep alive. Remake of "Donovan's Brain" (1953). 83m/B/W; VHS. **C:** Anne Heywood; Peter Van Eyck; Bernard Lee; Cecil Parker; Jack MacGowran; Directed by Freddie Francis. **Pr:** Raymond Stross Productions. **A:** Jr. High-Adult. **P:** Entertainment. **U:** Home. **Mov-Ent:** Horror. **Acq:** Purchase. **Dist:** Sinister Cinema. $19.95.

The Brain 1969 (G) — ★★
Run of the mill comedy caper has Niven planning to heist millions from a NATO train. The caper begins when lots of other crooks decide to rob the same train. The cast holds this one together. 115m; DVD, Blu-Ray. **C:** David Niven; Jean-Paul Belmondo; Andre Bourvil; Eli Wallach; Silvia Monti; Fernand Valois; Directed by Gerard Oury; Written by Gerard Oury; Daniele Thompson; Cinematography by Vladimir Ivanov; Music by Georges Delerue. **A:** Family. **P:** Entertainment. **U:** Home. **Mov-Ent:** Trains, Family Viewing. **Acq:** Purchase. **Dist:** Olive Films.

The Brain 1984
Examines and illustrates the brain's structural and functional systems, and the biological foundations of memory, emotion, and the unconscious. 60m; VHS, 3/4 U. **Pr:** WNET; NHK; Antennae 2 Television. **A:** College. **P:** Education. **U:** Institution, CCTV, CATV, SURA. **Hea-Sci:** Documentary Films, Anatomy & Physiology, Neurology. **Acq:** Purchase, Rent/Lease, Free Loan, Duplication. **Dist:** Annenberg Media; PBS Home Video; Home Vision Cinema. $215.00.
Indiv. Titles: 1. The Enlightened Machine 2. Vision and Movement 3. Rhythms and Drives 4. Stress and Emotion 5. Learning and Memory 6. The Two Brains 7. Madness 8. States of Mind.

The Brain 1988 (R) — ★½
Dr. Blake, host of a popular TV talk-show, is in league with a power-hungry alien brain. Viewers of his show kill themselves and others in the midst of many special effects. The ratings go down. 94m; VHS. **C:** Cynthia (Cyndy, Cindy) Preston; David Gale; Directed by Ed(ward) Hunt. **A:** Jr. High-Adult. **P:** Entertainment. **U:** Home. **Mov-Ent:** Horror, Psychiatry. **Acq:** Purchase. **Dist:** Lions Gate Television Corp. $14.95.

Brain Abscess 1971
A presentation of a sudden onset of severe increased intracranial pressure secondary to an abscess and cerebritis which followed an ear infection. 7m; VHS, 3/4 U, Special order formats. **Pr:** Ohio State University Health Sciences AV Center. **A:** College-Adult. **P:** Professional. **U:** Institution, SURA. **Hea-Sci:** Neurology, Medical Education. **Acq:** Purchase, Rent/Lease. **Dist:** Ohio State University.

Brain Abscess 1983
How to treat a patient who may have a brain abscess. 50m; VHS, 3/4 U. **Pr:** Emory University. **A:** College-Adult. **P:** Education. **U:** Institution, CCTV, Home, SURA. **Hea-Sci:** Head, Patient Care. **Acq:** Purchase, Rent/Lease, Subscription. **Dist:** Emory Medical Television Network.

The Brain and How It Works: Inside Information 1991
This program discusses the latest research concerning brain science. Learn how the different parts of the brain work, how it uses logic interpretation and see interviews with the foremost experts in the field. 60m; VHS. **Pr:** British Broadcasting Corporation. **A:** Sr. High-Adult. **P:** Education. **U:** Institution. **Hea-Sci:** Documentary Films, Anatomy & Physiology, Biology. **Acq:** Purchase. **Dist:** Films for the Humanities & Sciences. $149.00.

The Brain and Its Magnificence 1985
For mature audiences, the brain and its potential, used or unused, is examined. 17m; VHS, 3/4 U. **Pr:** Slovenska Films. **A:** Sr. High-Adult. **P:** Education. **U:** Institution, SURA. **Hea-Sci:** Documentary Films, Anatomy & Physiology. **Acq:** Purchase. **Dist:** Phoenix Learning Group.

The Brain and Nervous System 19??
Outlines the key components of the brain and the nervous system. Covers open and closed head injuries, skull fractures, subdural and epidural hematomas, compound injuries to the head, pentrating wounds to the brain, and treatment methods. Includes program syllabus. 120m; VHS. **A:** College-Adult. **P:** Education. **U:** Institution. **Hea-Sci:** Law--Medical, Medical Care, Anatomy & Physiology. **Acq:** Purchase. **Dist:** MediLegal Institute. $295.00.

The Brain and the Nervous System Think Science 1990
Part of the Wonders of Life Series that combines live action with animation to explain how different body systems work. Follows Jessica, a 6th grader who is called to the principal's office. While in the principal's office, her brain is seen dealing with the various emotions (nervousness, anxiety) that little Jessica creates. On the Science Books and Film's Best Science AV List. 11m; VHS, Special order formats. **Pr:** Disney Educational Productions. **A:** Primary. **P:** Education. **U:** Institution, CCTV, SURA. **Chl-Juv:** Science, Anatomy & Physiology, Neurology. **Acq:** Purchase, Rent/Lease, Duplication License. **Dist:** Phoenix Learning Group. $250.00.

Brain Attack 2000
Follows two victims of stroke and shows how critical differences in immediate medical attention can alter one's fate to life, death, or disability. 28m; VHS. **A:** Adult. **P:** Professional. **U:** Institution. **Hea-Sci:** Aging, Patient Care, Health Education. **Acq:** Purchase. **Dist:** Aquarius Health Care Media. $99.00.

Brain Attacks 1996
Shares informative and personal accounts from stroke patients and professionals addressing the warning signs, risk factors and medical advances. Reveals the slow progression of symptoms that usually go untreated until the "Brain Attack" occurs. 30m; VHS. **A:** Sr. High-Adult. **P:** Education. **U:** Institution. **Hea-Sci:** Health Education, Medical Education, Diseases. **Acq:** Purchase. **Dist:** Aquarius Health Care Media. $195.00.

The Brain: Creating a Mental Elite 198?
Examines three major areas of brain research which contribute both to the working and development of the brain. 20m; 3/4 U, Special order formats. **Pr:** Hobel Leiterman Productions. **A:** College-Adult. **P:** Education. **U:** Institution. **Hea-Sci:** Documentary Films, Neurology. **Acq:** Purchase. **Dist:** The Cinema Guild.

Brain Damage 1988 (R) — ★★
A tongue-in-bloody-cheek farce about a brain-sucking parasite. The parasite in question, Aylmer, addicts our dubious hero to the euphoria induced by the blue liquid the parasite injects into his brain, paving the way for the bloody mayhem that follows. Poor shadow of Henenlotter's far-superior "Basket Case." In fact, it even includes an inside-joke cameo by Van Hentenryck, reprising his "Basket Case" character; look for him on the subway. 89m; VHS, DVD, CC. **C:** Rick Herbst; Gordon MacDonald; Jennifer Lowry; Theo Barnes; Lucille Saint Peter; Kevin Van Hentenryck; Beverly Bonner; Voice(s) by John Zacherle; Directed by Frank Henenlotter; Written by Frank Henenlotter; Cinematography by Bruce Torbet; Music by Gus Russo; Clutch Reiser. **Pr:** Paramount Pictures. **A:** Sr. High-Adult. **P:** Entertainment. **U:** Home. **Mov-Ent. Acq:** Purchase. **Dist:** Paramount Pictures Corp. $14.95.

Brain-Damaged Infants: Case Evaluation and Management 1985
A complete program for legal professionals examining the malpractice precedents in cases of infant brain-damage. 330m; VHS, 3/4 U. **Pr:** Practicing Law Institute. **A:** Adult. **P:** Professional. **U:** Institution, Home. **Bus-Ind:** Documentary Films, Law, Infants. **Acq:** Purchase, Rent/Lease. **Dist:** Practising Law Institute.

Brain Dead 1989 (R) — ★★★½
Low-budget but brilliantly assembled puzzle-film about a brain surgeon who agrees to perform experimental surgery on a psychotic to retrieve some corporately valuable data—his first mistake, which begins a seemingly endless cycle of nightmares and identity alterations. A mind-blowing sci-fi feast from ex-"Twilight Zone" writer Charles Beaumont. 85m; VHS, DVD. **C:** Bill Pullman; Bill Paxton; Bud Cort; Patricia Charbonneau; Nicholas Pryor; George Kennedy; Brian Brophy; Lee Arenberg; Andy Wood; Directed by Adam Simon; Written by Adam Simon; Charles Beaumont; Music by Peter Rotter. **Pr:** Julie Corman; Concorde Pictures. **A:** Adult. **P:** Entertainment. **U:** Home. **Mov-Ent:** Horror. **Acq:** Purchase. **Dist:** MGM Home Entertainment. $14.95.

Brain Donors 1992 (PG) — ★★½
Goofy, uneven film starring Turturro as a sleazy lawyer trying to take over the Oglethorpe Ballet Company by sweet-talking its aged patronness. He is helped by two eccentric friends, and together the three crack a lot of bad but witty jokes. The film culminates into a hilarious ballet scene featuring someone giving CPR to the ballerina playing the dying swan, an actor in a duck suit, duck hunters, and a pack of hounds. This trio reminds us of second-rate Marx Brothers (or the Three Stooges) but the movie has enough funny moments to be worth a watch. 79m; DVD. **C:** John Turturro; Bob Nelson; Mel Smith; Nancy Marchand; John Savident; George de la Pena; Juli Donald; Spike Alexander; Teri Copley; Directed by Dennis Dugan; Written by Pat Proft; Music by Ira Newborn. **Pr:** Gil Netter; James D. Brubaker; Zucker Brothers Productions; Paramount Pictures. **A:** Jr. High-Adult. **P:** Entertainment. **U:** Home. **Mov-Ent:** Comedy--Slapstick, Law, Dance--Ballet. **Acq:** Purchase. **Dist:** WarnerArchive.com. $14.95.

Brain Drain 1998 (Unrated) — ★★
Young Argentine street kids are thieves who specialize in car radios. Their dreams of a better life are at odds with their surroundings. Things go wrong when they make false accusations against a cop and he comes after them. 92m; DVD. **C:** Nicolas Cabre; Luis Quiroz; Enrique Liporace; Directed by Fernando Musa; Written by Fernando Musa; Branko Andjic; Cinematography by Carlos Torlaschi; Music by Luis Maria Serra. **Mov-Ent. Dist:** Vanguard International Cinema, Inc.

The Brain: Effects of Childhood Trauma 2002
Deals with effects childhood trauma can have on brain function causing changes in neuron response and cognitive pathways. Part of the Childhood Trauma series. 29m; VHS; Closed Captioned. **A:** Adult. **P:** Professional. **U:** Institution. **Hea-Sci:** Children, Mental Health, Psychology. **Acq:** Purchase. **Dist:** Aquarius Health Care Media. $89.95.

The Brain from Planet Arous 1957 (Unrated) — ★
Lassie meets Alien when an evil alien brain appropriates the body of a scientist in order to take over planet Earth. His plans are thwarted, however, by a good alien brain that likewise inhabits the body of the scientist's dog. High camp and misdemeanors. 80m/B/W; VHS, DVD. **C:** John Agar; Joyce Meadows; Robert Fuller; Henry Travis; Bill Giorgio; Tim Graham; Thomas B(rowne). Henry; Ken Terrell; Directed by Nathan "Jerry" Juran; Written by Ray Buffum; Cinematography by Jacques "Jack" Marquette; Music by Walter Greene. **Pr:** Howco International Pictures. **A:** Jr. High-Adult. **P:** Entertainment. **U:** Home. **Mov-Ent:** Science Fiction, Cult Films. **Acq:** Purchase. **Dist:** Image Entertainment Inc.; Sinister Cinema; Facets Multimedia Inc.

Brain Games 2011 (Unrated)
Using state-of-the-art tests and games, this National Geographic three-part series studies the way the human brain functions to "create the illusion of a seamless reality." The series specifically focuses on three specific functions of the human brain: attention, sensory perception, and memory. Includes the bonus program "How to Build a Beating Heart." 150m; DVD. **A:** Family. **P:** Education, Entertainment. **U:** Home, Institution. **Mov-Ent:** Documentary Films, Biology, Medical Education. **Acq:** Purchase. **Dist:** $29.95.

Brain Games for Better Volleyball Play 2010 (Unrated)
Coach Jeff Meeker demonstrates 14 competitive games to improve a volleyball team's communications skills and ability to think on the fly during live games. ??m; DVD. **A:** Family. **P:** Education. **U:** Home, Institution. **Spo-Rec:** Volleyball, Athletic Instruction/Coaching. **Acq:** Purchase. **Dist:** Championship Productions. $39.99.

Brain, Mind and Society 1989
Improvements in brain research, management, social science and spiritual literature are examined to see if they suggest a new vision of society filled with people empowered to transform their lives. 30m; VHS. **Pr:** Thinking Allowed Productions. **A:** Sr. High-Adult. **P:** Education. **U:** Institution. **Hea-Sci:** Documentary Films, Sociology. **Acq:** Purchase. **Dist:** Thinking Allowed Productions. $29.95.

The Brain-Mind Connection 1990
Part of a series offering instruction on the study of human behavior. 30m; VHS. **A:** Adult. **P:** Education. **U:** Institution. **Gen-Edu:** Psychology. **Acq:** Purchase. **Dist:** RMI Media. $89.95.

Brain of Blood 1971 — **Bomb!**
Deals with a scientist who transplants the brain of a politician into the body of a deformed idiot. The change is minimal. 107m; VHS, DVD. **C:** Kent Taylor; John Bloom; Regina Carrol; Angelo Rossitto; Grant Williams; Reed Hadley; Vicki Volante; Zandor Vorkov; Richard Smedley; Directed by Al Adamson; Written by Joe Van Rogers; Cinematography by Louis Horvath. **Pr:** Al Adamson; Al Adamson; Hemisphere Productions. **A:** Jr. High-Adult. **P:** Entertainment. **U:** Home. **Mov-Ent:** Horror, Surgical Transplantation. **Acq:** Purchase. **Dist:** Movies Unlimited. $16.99.

The Brain: Our Universe Within 1994
Three-volume series offers images of the human brain at work and how it functions. Available as a boxed set or individually. 225m; VHS. **A:** Sr. High-Adult. **P:** Education. **U:** Home. **Hea-Sci:** Documentary Films, Science, Anatomy & Physiology. **Acq:** Purchase. **Dist:** Discovery Home Entertainment. $49.95.
Indiv. Titles: 1. Evolution & Perception 2. Memory/Miraculous Mind 3. Matter over Mind.

Brain Power 1982
John Houseman involves the audience interactively with stimulating thoughts and visual brain-teasers. The suprising solutions to his mental challenges reveal three key principles of perception: recognition, interpretation and expectation. 11m; VHS, 3/4 U. **Pr:** Learning Corporation of America. **A:** Adult. **P:** Education. **U:** Institution, SURA. **Gen-Edu:** Documentary Films, Meeting Openers, Business. **Acq:** Purchase, Rent/Lease. **Dist:** Phoenix Learning Group.

Brain Scans: Alcohol and the Teenage Brain 2001
Shows brain scans of a healthy teenager and those of teenagers who regularly drink alcohol and discusses the effects. 23m; VHS. **A:** Sr. High. **P:** Education. **U:** Institution. **Hea-Sci:** Alcoholism, Adolescence, Health Education. **Acq:** Purchase. **Dist:** Aquarius Health Care Media. $190.00.

Brain Sex 1993
A three-volume series looks at the brain to explain differences between the sexes, including social relations and the evidence that men and women don't have identical brain structures. 180m; VHS. **A:** College-Adult. **P:** Education. **U:** Institution. **Hea-Sci:** Science, Sex & Sexuality. **Acq:** Purchase. **Dist:** Baker and Taylor. $79.95.
Indiv. Titles: 1. Sugar and Spice 2. Anything You Can Do, I Can Do Better 3. Love, Love Me Do.

Brain Smasher. . . A Love Story 1993 (PG-13) — ★
A bouncer and a super model become the targets of a gang of killer ninjas who want the mysterious blood-red lotus the model's been given. Of course they do. What's the lovely Hatcher doing in such a stupid movie? 88m; VHS, CC. **C:** Andrew Silverstein; Teri Hatcher; Deanna (Dee) Booher; Deborah Van Valkenburgh; Brion James; Yuji Okumoto; Tim Thomerson; Charles Rocket; Nicholas Guest; Lin Shaye; Directed by Albert Pyun; Written by Albert Pyun; Cinematography by George Mooradian; Music by Tony Riparetti. **A:** Jr. High-Adult. **P:** Entertainment. **U:** Home. **Mov-Ent:** Martial Arts. **Acq:** Purchase. **Dist:** CinemaNow Inc. $92.95.

The Brain that Wouldn't Die 1963 (Unrated) — ★★½
Love is a many-splattered thing when a brilliant surgeon keeps the decapitated head of his fiancee alive after an auto accident while he searches for a suitably stacked body onto which to transplant the head. Absurd and satiric (head talks so much that Doc tapes her/its mouth shut) adding up to major entry in trash film genre; much of the gore was slashed for the video, however. 92m/B/W; VHS, DVD, Blu-Ray. **C:** Herb Evers; Virginia Leith; Adele Lamont; Leslie Daniel; Bruce Brighton; Paula Maurice; Directed by Joseph Green; Written by Joseph Green; Cinematography by Stephen Hajinal; Music by Tony Restaino. **Pr:** American International Pictures. **A:** Sr. High-Adult. **P:** Entertainment. **U:** Home. **Mov-Ent:** Horror, Surgical Transplantation. **Acq:** Purchase. **Dist:** Rhino Entertainment Co.; Facets Multimedia Inc. $19.98.

Brain Traps: Problem Solving Skills ????
Participants are challenged to solve simple but frustrating problems that require creative thinking. An exercise to examine problem solving methods and learn more about mental habits. 19m; VHS; Closed Captioned. **A:** Adult. **P:** Professional. **U:** Institution. **Hea-Sci:** Head, Psychology. **Acq:** Purchase. **Dist:** The Learning Seed. $89.00.

Brain Triggers: Biochemistry and Human Behavior 1983
Overviews biochemical activity in the brain, and its effect on moods, sensations, sleep and activity. ?m; VHS, Special order formats. **A:** Sr. High-College. **P:** Education. **U:** Institution. **Hea-Sci:** Science, Biology, Chemistry. **Acq:** Purchase. **Dist:** HRM Video; Educational Images Ltd. $175.00.

Braincandy: My Five Senses 2004
Skits featuring puppets and children introduce youngsters to their five senses. 40m; DVD. **A:** Preschool. **P:** Entertainment. **U:** Home. **Chl-Juv:** Puppets. **Acq:** Purchase. **Dist:** ThinkFilm Company Inc.

Braincandy: See My World 2005 (Unrated)
Puppets, animation and interactive games teach children six months to four years old about the five senses. 40m; DVD. **A:** Adult. **P:** Education. **U:** Home. **Gen-Edu:** Senses, Children. **Acq:** Purchase. **Dist:** Rhino Entertainment Co. $14.99.

Braingames 1985
Test your knowledge of history, art and music with this collection of games designed to challenge the mind. 60m; VHS. **Pr:** Sheila Nevins. **A:** Family. **P:** Entertainment. **U:** Home. **Gen-Edu:** Games. **Acq:** Purchase. **Dist:** Home Box Office Inc. $12.95.

Braingames #2 1985
Another collection of games designed to test your knowledge of history, art, music, and sports. 60m; VHS. **Pr:** Sheila Nevins. **A:** Family. **P:** Entertainment. **U:** Home. **Gen-Edu:** Games. **Acq:** Purchase. **Dist:** Home Box Office Inc. $12.95.

Braingames #3 1985
This is a new collection of computerized trivia games that the whole family can play. 60m; VHS. **Pr:** Sheila Nevins. **A:** Family. **P:** Entertainment. **U:** Home. **Gen-Edu:** Games. **Acq:** Purchase. **Dist:** Home Box Office Inc. $12.95.

The Brainiac 1961 (Unrated) — ★½
Sorcerer sentenced for black magic returns to strike dark deeds upon the descendants of those who judged him. He turns himself into a hideous monster, feeding on his victims' brains and blood. Yuck. 75m/B/W; VHS, DVD. **C:** Abel Salazar; Ariadne Welter; Mauricio Garces; Rosa Maria Gallardo; Ruben Rojo; German Robles; Directed by Chano Urueto; Written by Frederick Curiel; Alfredo Torres Portillo; Cinematography by Jose Ortiz Ramos; Music by Gustavo Cesar Carrion. **A:** Jr. High-Adult. **P:** Entertainment. **U:** Home. **Mov-Ent:** Horror, Occult Sciences. **Acq:** Purchase. **Dist:** Sinister Cinema. $54.95.

Brainiacs.com 2001
Eleven-year-old Matt Tyler comes up with a million dollar plan to save his Dad's failing business, Tyler Toy Co. But can he raise

the funds, create a new toy, and save the company from a ruthless banker in just one week! 99m; VHS. **A:** Family. **P:** Entertainment. **U:** Home. **Mov-Ent**: Drama, Family. **Acq:** Purchase. **Dist:** Monarch Home Video. $49.95.

Brainjacked 2009 (Unrated) — ★
A mad scentist convinces people he can cure their ills by letting him drill holes in their skulls to insert microchips. Of course he leaves out the part about the chips being used as mind control, but if you're foolish enough to trust a guy wanting to drill into your brain you probably get what you have coming. 90m; DVD, Streaming. **C:** Stephen Biro; Cyndi Crotts; Rob Elfstrom; Michael Kenneth Fahr; Mark Fisher; Directed by Andrew Allan; Written by Andrew Allan; Andy Lalino; Cinematography by Wes Pratt; Music by Eddie Sturgeon. **A:** Sr. High-Adult. **P:** Entertainment. **U:** Home. **L:** English. **Mov-Ent**. **Acq:** Purchase, Rent/Lease. **Dist:** Unearthed. $19.99 14.99.

Brainscan 1994 (R) — ★
Teenage loner takes a trip in virtual reality and finds that murder is the first stop. Furlong ("Terminator 2") is the troubled youth whose voyage is led by Smith as Trickster, the Freddy Krueger meets David Bowie tour guide from virtual hell. Langella turns in a straight performance as a local cop hot on the trail. Hard-core horror fans will be disappointed by the lack of on-screen violence, and special effects buffs won't see anything new. Lame effort tries to appeal to a wide audience and is bland as a result. The end is left wide open, so expect a sequel or two or three. 96m; VHS, DVD, CC. **C:** Edward Furlong; Frank Langella; T. Ryder Smith; David Hemblen; Amy Hargreaves; Jamie Marsh; Victor Ertmanis; Directed by John Flynn; Written by Andrew Kevin Walker; Music by George S. Clinton. **Pr:** Michel Roy; Esther Freifeld; Earl Berman; Triumph. **A:** Sr. High-Adult. **P:** Entertainment. **U:** Home. **Mov-Ent**: Horror, Adolescence, Technology. **Acq:** Purchase. **Dist:** Sony Pictures Home Entertainment Inc. $19.95.

Brainstem Electric Response Audiometry 1979
This process is demonstrated in its use for determining audiometric thresholds in patients whose behavioral techniques are ineffective and in diagnosing cerebellopontine angle tumors. 54m; VHS, 3/4 U. **Pr:** House Ear Institute. **A:** Adult. **P:** Professional. **U:** Institution, CCTV. **Hea-Sci**: Ear, Medical Education. **Acq:** Purchase, Rent/Lease. **Dist:** House Research Institute.

Brainstorm 1983 (PG) — ★★½
Husband-and-wife scientist team invents headphones that can record dreams, thoughts, and fantasies (VCR-style) and then allow other people to experience them by playing back the tape. Their marriage begins to crumble as the husband becomes more and more obsessed with pushing the limits of the technology; things get worse when the government wants to exploit their discovery. Special effects and interesting camera work punctuate this sci-fi flick. Wood's last film; in fact, she died before production was completed. 106m; VHS, DVD, Blu-Ray, Wide. **C:** Natalie Wood; Christopher Walken; Cliff Robertson; Louise Fletcher; Directed by Douglas Trumbull; Written by Bruce Joel Rubin; Cinematography by Richard Yuricich; Music by James Horner. **Pr:** MGM/UA Entertainment Company. **A:** Jr. High-Adult. **P:** Entertainment. **U:** Home. **Mov-Ent**: Science Fiction. **Acq:** Purchase. **Dist:** MGM Home Entertainment. $14.95.

Brainstorm 1989
This humorous session starter about open-mindedness and receptivity to change will help managers create a positive environment for sharing ideas at conferences, meetings, seminars and training sessions. 4m; VHS, 3/4 U. **Pr:** Rob Nye. **A:** Primary-Adult. **P:** Education. **U:** Institution, Home, SURA. **Bus-Ind**: Documentary Films, Meeting Openers. **Acq:** Purchase. **Dist:** Pyramid Media.

Brainstorm 1995
Documentary gives a basic overview of depression, its symptoms, treatments, and people who have suffered from it including author William Styron and director Jane Campion. 53m; VHS. **A:** Adult. **P:** Education. **U:** Home. **Gen-Edu**: Documentary Films, Psychology, Psychiatry. **Acq:** Purchase, Rent/Lease. **Dist:** Filmakers Library Inc. $295.

Brainstorm: The Truth about Your Brain on Drugs 1995
Gives information on how the brain works both on useful and harmful drugs. Testimony from recovering teenagers gives perspective on drug abuse. Teacher's guide included. 60m; VHS. **A:** Primary. **P:** Education. **U:** Institution. **Chl-Juv**: Children, Education, Drugs. **Acq:** Purchase. **Dist:** Sunburst Digital Inc. $29.95.

Brainstorming Small Business Ideas for the Eighties 1988
A radio station owner talks with a man who runs a restaurant in order to compare and contrast the two businesses. 60m; VHS, 3/4 U. **Pr:** RMI Media Productions. **A:** Adult. **P:** Education. **U:** Institution, CCTV, SURA. **Bus-Ind**: Business. **Acq:** Purchase. **Dist:** RMI Media. $180.00.

Brainwash 1980
This is an Orwellian tale of thought control and the resistance of one individual. 10m; VHS, 3/4 U. **Pr:** Ria Bijisma-Nanninga. **A:** College-Adult. **P:** Education. **U:** Institution, SURA. **Gen-Edu**: Philosophy & Ideology. **Acq:** Purchase. **Dist:** Phoenix Learning Group.

Brainwashed 1960 — ★★
Austrian aristocrat Werner von Basil (Jurgens) is captured by the Nazis and interrogated to uncover military information. In order to keep his sanity, the prisoner concentrates on a chess book he keeps hidden in his cell. Based on the novel by Stefan Zweig. German with subtitles. 127m; VHS. **C:** Curt Jurgens; Claire Bloom; Hansjorg Felmy; Mario Adorf; Albert Lieven; Alan Gifford; Karel Stepanek; Directed by Gerd Oswald; Written by Gerd Oswald; Harold Medford; Cinematography by Gunther Senftleben; Music by Hans-Martin Majewski. **A:** College-Adult. **P:** Entertainment. **U:** Home. **L:** German. **Mov-Ent**: World War Two, Chess. **Acq:** Purchase. **Dist:** Facets Multimedia Inc.

Brainwave 2011
Annual unscripted conversations, held at New York's Rubin Museum of Art, which pairs celebrities with scientists to learn how the human mind works. 525m; DVD. **A:** Sr. High-Adult. **P:** Education, Entertainment. **U:** Home. **Gen-Edu**: Scientists. **Acq:** Purchase. **Dist:** Acorn Media Group Inc. $59.99.

Brainwave Synchronization and ESP 1989
Jean Millay combines biofeedback, psychic testing and synchronization of the brain's hemispheres in an attempt to synchronize the brainwaves between two people. 30m; VHS. **Pr:** Thinking Allowed Productions. **A:** College-Adult. **P:** Education. **U:** Home. **Hea-Sci**: Documentary Films, Neurology, New Age. **Acq:** Purchase. **Dist:** Thinking Allowed Productions. $29.95.

Brainwaves 1982 (R) — ★★
A young woman has disturbing flashbacks after her brain is electrically revived following a car accident. Curtis is the demented doctor who jump-starts her. 83m; VHS, DVD. **C:** Suzanna Love; Tony Curtis; Keir Dullea; Vera Miles; Eve Brent; Directed by Ulli Lommel; Written by Ulli Lommel; Cinematography by Ulli Lommel; Jon Kranhouse; Music by Robert O. Ragland. **Pr:** Ulli Lommel; Ulli Lommel. **A:** Sr. High-Adult. **P:** Entertainment. **U:** Home. **Mov-Ent**: Science Fiction, Surgical Transplantation. **Acq:** Purchase. **Dist:** Movies Unlimited. $21.24.

Brainwaves 1995
Illustrates a diversity training program. ?m; VHS. **Pr:** BNA Communications. **A:** College-Adult. **P:** Education. **U:** Institution. **Bus-Ind**: Business, Personnel Management. **Acq:** Purchase. **Dist:** Learning Communications L.L.C.

Brainy Baby: Left Brain ????
Colorful graphics, classical music and friendly voices designed to stimulate a child's curiosity and reinforce a whole-brain learning approach. Focuses on stacking objects, letters, numbers, analysis, math, shapes, patterns and language ?m; VHS. **A:** Preschool. **P:** Education. **U:** Home. **Chl-Juv**: Infants, Parenting. **Acq:** Purchase. **Dist:** Small Fry Productions. $15.95.

Brainy Baby: Right Brain ????
Colorful graphics, classical music and friendly voices designed to stimulate a child's curiosity and reinforce a whole-brain learning approach. Focuses on intuition, nesting objects, creative thinking, color, patterns, spatial reasoning, art, rhymes and imagination. ?m; VHS. **A:** Preschool. **P:** Education. **U:** Home. **Chl-Juv**: Infants, Parenting. **Acq:** Purchase. **Dist:** Small Fry Productions. $15.95.

Braising 199?
Teaches the cooking technique of braising, which helps the student make the most of inexpensive cuts of meat by making them more tender and infusing them with a deep, robust flavor. Part of the Cooking Methods Series. 13m; VHS. **A:** Sr. High-Adult. **P:** Instruction. **U:** Home. **How-Ins**: Cooking, Food Industry, How-To. **Acq:** Purchase. **Dist:** Culinary Institute of America. $75.00.

Brake 2012 (R) — ★★
Dorff gives a decent performance in what is essentially a one-man show as Secret Service agent Jeremy Reins, who wakes up kidnapped in the trunk of a car. As he is psychologically and physically tortured by terrorists seeking the location of the Executive Branch's secret underground bunker, Dorff sells the complex arc of this real-time thriller. Sadly, the senseless script piles on the plot holes until it pulls out two twist endings that shatter any suspension of disbelief. 92m; DVD, Blu-Ray. **C:** Stephen Dorff; Chyler Leigh; J.R. Bourne; Tom Berenger; Voice(s) by Pruitt Taylor Vince; Directed by Gabe Torres; Written by Timothy Mannion; Cinematography by James Mathers; Music by Brian Tyler. **Pr:** James Walker; Nathan West; Gabe Torres; La Costa Prods; Walking West Entertainment; IFC Films. **A:** Sr. High-Adult. **P:** Entertainment. **U:** Home. **L:** English. **Mov-Ent**: Secret Service, Terrorism. **Acq:** Purchase. **Dist:** MPI Media Group.

Brake Jobs 1995
Provides basic introduction to automobile brake systems, covering tools, terminology, procedures, and components. Includes information on different types of brakes, master cylinders, braking systems, overhaul procedures, wheel bearings, bleeding brakes, emergency brakes, and troubleshooting. 48m; VHS. **A:** Jr. High-Adult. **P:** Instruction. **U:** Institution, Home. **How-Ins**: Automobiles, How-To. **Acq:** Purchase. **Dist:** Tapeworm Video Distributors Inc. $16.95.

Brake System Construction & Operation 19??
Uses computer graphics and cutaway footage to explaing the operation and design of the automobile's brake system, covering the master cylinder, wheel cylinders, lines, hoses, shoes, pads, springs, and other components. Includes coverage of drum, disc, and anti-lock braking systems. 27m; VHS. **A:** Sr. High-Adult. **P:** Vocational. **U:** Institution. **How-Ins**: Automobiles, Occupational Training. **Acq:** Purchase. **Dist:** CEV Multimedia. $95.00.

Brake System Service 1992
Explains how to diagnose brake system problems and how to inspect and maintain master cylinders, boosters, and disc and drum brakes. 34m; VHS. **A:** Adult. **P:** Instruction. **U:** Institution. **How-Ins**: Automobiles. **Acq:** Purchase. **Dist:** RMI Media. $95.00.

Bram Stoker's Dracula 1992 (R) — ★★
Coppola's highly charged view of the vampire classic is visually stunning, heavy on eroticism and violence, and weak in plot and performance. Oldman, in a number of amazing transformations, portrays the deadly bloodsucker as a lonely soul determined to reunite with his lost love, the innocent Ryder. Hopkins cheerfully chews the scenery as nemesis Van Helsing, newcomer Frost is fetching, Reeves is lightweight, and Ryder goes way over the top. Musician Waits is great as bug-eating madman Renfield. Filmed entirely on soundstages with beautiful costumes and some amazing visual effects and sets. 128m; VHS, DVD, Blu-Ray, Wide, CC. **C:** Gary Oldman; Winona Ryder; Anthony Hopkins; Keanu Reeves; Richard E. Grant; Cary Elwes; Billy Campbell; Sadie Frost; Tom Waits; Monica Bellucci; Christina (Kristina) Fulton; Directed by Francis Ford Coppola; Written by James V. Hart; Cinematography by Michael Ballhaus. **Pr:** Francis Ford Coppola; Charles Mulvehill; Fred Fuchs; Michael Apted; Francis Ford Coppola; Columbia Pictures. **A:** Sr. High-Adult. **P:** Entertainment. **U:** Home. **Mov-Ent**: Horror, Sex & Sexuality. **Awds:** Oscars '92: Costume Des., Makeup, Sound FX Editing. **Acq:** Purchase. **Dist:** Sony Pictures Home Entertainment Inc. $19.95.

Bram Stoker's Shadowbuilder 1998 (R) — ★★
Silly update that apparently takes the title of the Bram Stoker short story but not much else. Shadowbuilder (Jackson) is a demonic creature that wants to unleash hell's power upon the unsuspecting town of Grand River. But he needs 12-year-old Chris (Zegers) for your basic satanic ritual, which doesn't go over well with the local priest (Rooker) and sheriff (Thompson). 101m; VHS, DVD. **C:** Michael Rooker; Leslie Hope; Andrew Jackson; Kevin Zegers; Shawn Thompson; Tony Todd; Richard McMillan; Directed by Jamie Dixon; Written by Michael Stokes; Cinematography by David Pelletier; Music by Eckart Seeber. **A:** Sr. High-Adult. **P:** Entertainment. **U:** Home. **Mov-Ent**: Horror. **Acq:** Purchase. **Dist:** Lions Gate Entertainment Inc.; Alpha Video.

Bram Stoker's The Mummy 1997 (R) — ★★
Modern retelling of the horror tale focuses on the savage incident that left Egyptologist Abel Trelawny (Bochner) in a coma. Now his daughter, Margaret (Locane), seeks the help of her ex-lover, Robert (Lutes), to uncover the connection between Trewlawny and an Egyptian ritual to raise a queen from her tomb. Based on Stoker's book "The Jewel of the Seven Stars." 100m; VHS, DVD. **C:** Amy Locane; Eric Lutes; Louis Gossett, Jr.; Victoria Tennant; Lloyd Bochner; Mark Lindsay Chapman; Richard Karn; Mary Jo Catlett; Directed by Jeffrey Obrow; Written by Jeffrey Obrow; Cinematography by Antonio Soriano; Music by Rick Cox. **A:** Sr. High-Adult. **P:** Entertainment. **U:** Home. **Mov-Ent**: Horror. **Acq:** Purchase. **Dist:** Allumination Filmworks.

Bram Stoker's Way of the Vampire 2005 (R) — ★
Has absolutely nothing to do with Stoker's writings. Van Helsing (Giles) goes after Dracula (Logan), leaving his wife in the care of colleague Sebastian (Beckett). Only Sebastian is actually a blood-drinker, so no more missus. Van Helsing makes a deal with God to gain immortality until the last of Dracula's kin are dead. Which leads to a showdown in present-day LA between Van Helsing and Sebastian. 81m; DVD. **C:** Denise Boutte; Paul Logan; Rhett Giles; Brent Falco; Directed by Sara Nean Bruce; Eduardo Durao; Written by Karrie Melendrez; Sherri Strain; Cinematography by Andreas Beckett; Zack Richard; Music by Ralph Rieckermann. **A:** Sr. High-Adult. **P:** Entertainment. **U:** Home. **Mov-Ent**. **Acq:** Purchase. **Dist:** The Asylum.

The Bramble Bush 1960 — ★★½
Guy (Burton) is a doctor who returns to his New England hometown to care for a dying friend, Larry (Drake). Unfortunately, Guy falls for Larry's wife Mar (Rush) and they have an affair. When Guy pulls the plug on his friend's suffering, suspicious townspeople (who of course know what's going on) wonder just how "merciful" the doctor was really being and he's tried for murder. Tawdry "Peyton Place"-ish soap opera based on the novel by Charles Mergendahl. 104m; VHS. **C:** Richard Burton; Barbara Rush; Tom Drake; Jack Carson; Angie Dickinson; James Dunn; Henry Jones; Frank Conroy; Carl Benton Reid; Directed by Daniel Petrie; Written by Philip Yordan. **Pr:** Milton Sperling; Warner Bros. **A:** Sr. High-Adult. **P:** Entertainment. **U:** Home. **Mov-Ent**: Death. **Acq:** Purchase. **Dist:** Warner Home Video, Inc. $29.99.

Bramwell 1995
British miniseries stars Redgrave as the determined Eleanor Bramwell. In 1895, she manages to follow in her physician father's footsteps but it's a battle to gain respect from her sexist colleagues and to overcome her own class prejudices as she works with London's poor. Seven episodes on four cassettes. 360m; VHS. **C:** Jemma Redgrave; David Calder; Kevin McMonagle; Keeley Gainey; Cliff Parisi; Ruth Sheen; Michele Dotrice; Robert Hardy; Directed by David Tucker; Laura Sims; Written by Lucy Gannon. **Pr:** Harriet Davison; Tim Whitby. **A:** Jr. High-Adult. **P:** Entertainment. **U:** Home. **Mov-Ent**: Women. **Acq:** Purchase. **Dist:** Facets Multimedia Inc.; Acorn Media Group Inc.

Bramwell: Series 4 1998
Dr. Eleanor Bramwell is appointed by the British Army to inspect the new recruits being sent to the Boer War. Although fiance Joe Marsham disapproves, she wins the admiration of Major Guy Quarrie. Eleanor also has problems with her East End infirmary and risks everything to find a young patient who's forced into child prostitution. 210m; DVD. **C:** Jemma Redgrave; David Calder; Kevin McMonagle. **A:** Jr. High-Adult. **P:** Entertainment. **U:** Home. **Mov-Ent**. **Acq:** Purchase. **Dist:** Shanachie Entertainment.

Bramwell: The Complete 1st Season 1995
Follows the ambitious intentions of female physician Eleanor Bramwell to become a surgeon, end barbaric medical practices used by her male counterparts, and oversee the charitable Thrift Infirmary in the impoverished East End of London during the late 19th century. 7 episodes. 600m; DVD. **C:** Jemma Redgrave; David Calder; Robert Hardy. **A:** Adult. **P:** Entertainment. **U:** Home. **Mov-Ent:** Drama, Mystery & Suspense. **Acq:** Purchase. **Dist:** Shanachie Entertainment.

Bramwell: The Complete 2nd Season 1996
As one of few female doctors in Victorian-era London, Dr. Eleanor Bramwell struggles for the rights of her patients and herself in a male-dominated profession. 480m; DVD. **C:** Jemma Redgrave; David Calder; Robert Hardy. **A:** Adult. **P:** Entertainment. **U:** Home. **Mov-Ent:** Drama, Mystery & Suspense. **Acq:** Purchase. **Dist:** Shanachie Entertainment.

Bramwell: The Complete 3rd Season 1997
Still determined to bring medical practices out of the dark ages Eleanor's opinions often cause conflict between her and the chief surgeon. 10 episodes. 600m; DVD. **C:** Jemma Redgrave; David Calder; Robert Hardy. **A:** Adult. **P:** Entertainment. **U:** Home. **Mov-Ent:** Drama, Mystery & Suspense. **Acq:** Purchase. **Dist:** Shanachie Entertainment.

The Branches of Government: Executive Branch 1982
This program shows how the actions of this branch affect people's lives in a variety of ways. 23m; 3/4 U, Special order formats. **Pr:** National Geographic Society. **A:** Primary. **P:** Education. **U:** Institution, Home, SURA. **Gen-Edu:** Documentary Films, Politics & Government. **Acq:** Purchase, Trade-in, Duplication License. **Dist:** National Geographic Society.

The Branches of Government: Judicial Branch 1982
By following a case that goes to the Supreme Court, students learn the workings of this branch. 23m; 3/4 U, Special order formats. **Pr:** National Geographic Society. **A:** Primary. **P:** Education. **U:** Institution, Home, SURA. **Gen-Edu:** Documentary Films, Politics & Government. **Acq:** Purchase, Trade-in, Duplication License. **Dist:** National Geographic Society.

The Branches of Government: Legislative Branch 1982
By following a congressman through several weeks of work, students gain insight into the working of this branch. 23m; 3/4 U, Special order formats. **Pr:** National Geographic Society. **A:** Primary. **P:** Education. **U:** Institution, Home, SURA. **Gen-Edu:** Documentary Films, Politics & Government. **Acq:** Purchase, Trade-in, Duplication License. **Dist:** National Geographic Society.

Branching Out on Bluegrass Banjo, Vol. 1: A Treasury of Techniques 1992
Pete Wernick teaches dozens of techniques that can be used to create licks, back-ups, and solos. 110m; VHS. **A:** Jr. High-Adult. **P:** Instruction. **U:** Home, Institution. **How-Ins:** Music--Instruction, How-To. **Acq:** Purchase. **Dist:** Homespun Tapes Ltd. $49.95.

Branching out on Bluegrass Banjo, Vol. 2: Putting It All into Practice 1992
Pete Wernick demonstrates chord progressions, ascending and descending runs, back-ups, modulations, improvisation, Scruggs and Reno-style runs and licks, and other techniques. 90m; VHS. **A:** Sr. High-Adult. **P:** Instruction. **U:** Home. **How-Ins:** How-To, Music--Instruction. **Acq:** Purchase. **Dist:** Homespun Tapes Ltd. $49.95.

Branchline Railway 1988
The late Sir John Betjemen hosts this nostalgic film about the now-defunct Somerset and Dorset railway. Introduction by Michael Palin. 47m; VHS. **C:** John Betjemen. **Pr:** BBC Enterprises Ltd. **A:** Family. **P:** Entertainment. **U:** Home. **Gen-Edu:** Documentary Films, Trains, Great Britain. **Acq:** Purchase. **Dist:** Home Vision Cinema. $29.95.

Brand Marketing: Why We Eat, Drink, and Wear Brand Names ????
An in-depth look into the power of brand marketing on youth culture and the consumer society. Discusses brand equity, brand and line extensions, co-branding, and celebrities as brands. 19m; VHS. **A:** Adult. **P:** Education. **U:** Institution, CCTV. **Bus-Ind:** Consumer Education, Marketing, Advertising. **Acq:** Purchase. **Dist:** The Learning Seed. $89.00.

Brand Names and Labeling Games 1973
Higher-priced brand-name products are compared with unknown brands. Results usually conclude that there is no difference between the products. 9m; VHS, 3/4 U. **Pr:** Benchmark Films. **A:** Jr. High-College. **P:** Education. **U:** Institution, CCTV. **Gen-Edu:** Consumer Education, Food Industry. **Acq:** Purchase. **Dist:** Benchmark Media.

Brand New Day 2010 (PG-13) — ★1/2
Set in the 1960s, bland characters and a stereotypical road trip narrative will provide little interest outside its Aussie origins. Aboriginal teen Willie (McKenzie) runs away from his Perth Catholic boarding school and its strict guardian, Father Benedictus (Rush), on a 3,000-mile odyssey to return to his family. Naturally, Willie picks up some oddball traveling companions along the way. Based on the 1990 stage musical by Aboriginal band Jimmy Chi and Kuckles. 85m; DVD, Blu-Ray. **C:** Rocky McKenzie; Jessica Mauboy; Ernie Dingo; Geoffrey Rush; Magda Szubanski; Directed by Rachel Perkins; Written by Rachel Perkins; Cinematography by Andrew Lesnie; Music by Cezary Skubiszewski. **A:** Jr. High-Adult. **P:** Entertainment. **U:** Home. **Mov-Ent:** Australia. **Acq:** Purchase. **Dist:** Fox Home Entertainment.

Brand New Life 1972 (Unrated) — ★
A childless couple in their 40s are unexpectedly confronted by the wife's first pregnancy. Both have careers and well-ordered lives that promise to be disrupted. 74m; VHS, DVD. **C:** Cloris Leachman; Martin Balsam; Wilfrid Hyde-White; Mildred Dunnock; Directed by Sam O'Steen; Music by Billy Goldenberg. **Pr:** Tomorrow Entertainment Inc. **A:** Preschool. **P:** Entertainment. **U:** Institution, SURA. **Mov-Ent:** TV Movies, Marriage, Pregnancy. **Acq:** Purchase, Rent/Lease. **Dist:** Phoenix Learning Group.

Brand of Fear 1949 — ★1/2
Crooning cowpoke Wakely puts down his guitar long enough to chase rustlers off the land of an innocent lady in this average oater. 56m/B/W; VHS. **C:** Jimmy Wakely; Dub Taylor; Gail Davis; Tom London; Directed by Oliver Drake; Written by Basil Dickey. **Pr:** Monogram. **A:** Jr. High-Adult. **P:** Entertainment. **U:** Home. **Mov-Ent:** Western. **Acq:** Purchase. **Dist:** Movies Unlimited. $19.99.

Brand of Hate 1934 — ★
A good cowboy rustles up a gang of rustlers. 61m/B/W; VHS, DVD. **C:** Bob Steele; George "Gabby" Hayes; Lucille Browne; James Flavin; Directed by Lewis D. Collins. **Pr:** William Steiner. **A:** Family. **P:** Entertainment. **U:** Home. **Mov-Ent:** Western. **Acq:** Purchase. **Dist:** Rex Miller Artisan Studio. $19.95.

Brand of the Outlaws 1936 — ★
A cowboy becomes an unwitting aid to rustlers in this early western. 56m/B/W; VHS, DVD. **C:** Bob Steele; Margaret Marquis; Virginia True Boardman; Jack Rockwell; Directed by Robert North Bradbury. **Pr:** William Steiner. **A:** Family. **P:** Entertainment. **U:** Home. **Mov-Ent:** Western. **Acq:** Purchase, Rent/Lease. **Dist:** Alpha Video; Mill Creek Entertainment L.L.C.; Sinister Cinema. $19.95.

Brand Upon the Brain! 2006 (R) — ★★★
Like most of writer/director Guy Maddin's work, this requires a deliberate viewing. A silent film in black and white sets up primarily as a flashback, possibly to the director's youth, set on an island with a lighthouse that has served as an orphanage in the past. Film moves freely through images and recollections, revealing secret longings within an utterly absurd plot for which the film is not the least diminished. Make no mistake, this is a grandly indulgent art film. But what did you expect? Most enjoyable is the narration by Isabella Rossellini. 95m; Silent; DVD. **C:** Erik Steffen Maahs; Sullivan Brown; Gretchen Krich; Maya Lawson; Todd Jefferson Moore; Katherine E. Scharhon; Narrated by Isabella Rossellini; Directed by Guy Maddin; Written by Guy Maddin; George Toles; Cinematography by Benjamin Kasulke; Music by Jason Staczek. **Pr:** Amy E. Jacobson; Gregg Lachow; Film Co; Vitagraph. **A:** College-Adult. **P:** Entertainment. **U:** Home. **L:** English. **Mov-Ent:** Canada, Adoption, Silent Films. **Acq:** Purchase. **Dist:** Criterion Collection Inc.; Movies Unlimited; Alpha Video.

Branded 1950 (Unrated) — ★★1/2
Ladd (pre-"Shane") impersonates the long-gone son of rich rancher Bickford, with unusual results. Nicely balanced action and love scenes makes this story a better-than-average western. Filmed in Technicolor. Based on the novel "Montana Rides" by Max Brand. 95m; VHS, DVD, CC. **C:** Alan Ladd; Mona Freeman; Charles Bickford; Joseph Calleia; Milburn Stone; Directed by Rudolph Mate. **Pr:** Columbia Pictures. **A:** Jr. High-Adult. **P:** Entertainment. **U:** Home. **Mov-Ent:** Western, Romance. **Acq:** Purchase. **Dist:** WarnerArchive.com. $14.95.

Branded 2012 (R) — ★
An ad executive begins to be able to see what brands people respond to, with the ones they enjoy appearing about them as cgi figures. He immediately finds himself in a war between corporations, all trying to squash the brand recognition of their competitors. DVD, Blu-Ray, Streaming. **C:** Ed Stoppard; Leelee Sobieski; Jeffrey Tambor; Ingeborga Dapkunaite; Max von Sydow; Directed by Jamie Bradshaw; Aleksandr Dulerayne; Written by Jamie Bradshaw; Aleksandr Dulerayne; Cinematography by Rogier Stoffers; Music by Eduard Artemev. **A:** Sr. High-Adult. **P:** Entertainment. **U:** Home. **L:** English, Spanish. **Mov-Ent. Acq:** Purchase, Rent/Lease. **Dist:** Lions Gate Home Entertainment. $29.99 27.98 14.99.

Branded a Bandit 1924 — ★★
Yakima must avoid the sheriff while tracking down the killers of an old miner so that he can clear himself of the crime. Only sold as part of the 'Yakima Canutt Double Feature.' 58m; VHS, DVD. **C:** Yakima Canutt; Directed by Paul Hurst. **Pr:** Arrow Releasing. **A:** Family. **P:** Entertainment. **U:** Home. **Mov-Ent:** Classic Films, Western. **Acq:** Purchase. **Dist:** Grapevine Video. $14.95.

Branded a Coward 1935 — ★
A man whose parents were killed seeks revenge via his trusty six-shooters. 56m/B/W; VHS, DVD. **C:** Johnny Mack Brown; Billie Seward; Yakima Canutt; Directed by Sam Newfield. **Pr:** Artclass. **A:** Family. **P:** Entertainment. **U:** Home. **Mov-Ent:** Western. **Acq:** Purchase, Rent/Lease. **Dist:** Alpha Video; Movies Unlimited. $19.95.

Branded Men 1931 — ★★
A couple of oddballs become mixed up in a number of zany, western-type adventures. 60m/B/W; VHS, DVD. **C:** Ken Maynard; June Clyde; Irving Bacon; Billy Bletcher; Charles "Blackie" King; Donald Keith; Directed by Phil Rosen. **Pr:** Tiffany. **A:** Jr. High-Adult. **P:** Entertainment. **U:** Home. **Mov-Ent. Acq:** Purchase. **Dist:** Alpha Video; Sinister Cinema. $14.24.

Branded: Season 1 1965
Army captain Jason McCord is unfairly accused of cowardice as the sole survivor of an Indian massacre and court-martialed and dismissed. He then travels the West, trying to prove the truth and uses his skills to help others. These 16 episodes are taken from the syndicated version of the series and were edited for length. 420m/B/W; DVD. **C:** Chuck Connors. **A:** Family. **P:** Entertainment. **U:** Home. **Mov-Ent:** Television Series, Western. **Acq:** Purchase. **Dist:** Timeless Media Group.

Branded: Season 2 1966
McCord continues his travels, trying to prove that the allegations of cowardice against him are false. He also becomes a secret government agent working for President Ulysses S. Grant. These 32 episodes were taken from the syndicated version and were edited for length. 780m; DVD. **C:** Chuck Connors. **A:** Family. **P:** Entertainment. **U:** Home. **Mov-Ent:** Television Series, Western. **Acq:** Purchase. **Dist:** Timeless Media Group.

Branded to Kill 1967 — ★★
Visual tricks, including animated graphics, and a blues score highlight this gangster story, which follows No. 3 Killer, who's bungled his last hit. Now he's the target of No. 1 Killer. Japanese with subtitles. 91m/B/W; VHS, DVD, Blu-Ray. **C:** Joe Shishido; Mari Annu; Koji Nambara; Isao Tamagawa; Mariko Ogawa; Directed by Seijun Suzuki; Written by Hachiro Guryu; Cinematography by Kazue Nagatsuka; Music by Naozumi Yamamoto. **A:** Sr. High-Adult. **P:** Entertainment. **U:** Home. **L:** Japanese. **Mov-Ent. Acq:** Purchase. **Dist:** Home Vision Cinema; Criterion Collection Inc.

Brandy's Friends 19??
Tells the tragic story of a young man whose life ended from drug abuse, and how his friends and family have joined together to form a non-profit organization to fight drug abuse. 30m; VHS. **A:** Jr. High-Adult. **P:** Education. **U:** Home. **Gen-Edu:** Drug Abuse, Organizations. **Acq:** Purchase. **Dist:** Production Associates. $69.95.

Branford Marsalis: Steep 1988
Branford plays "Swingin' at the Haven" and other song live and is joined by guests, Spike Lee, Danny DeVito, Herbie Hancock and Sting. 90m; VHS. **Pr:** CBS/Fox Music Video. **A:** Adult. **P:** Entertainment. **U:** Home. **Mov-Ent:** Music--Performance, Music Video, Music--Jazz. **Acq:** Purchase. **Dist:** Music Video Distributors; Facets Multimedia Inc.; Sony Music Entertainment Inc. $14.98.

Branford Marsalis: The Music Tells You 1992 (Unrated)
Hegedus and Pennebaker's look at the touring life of jazz saxophonist Branford Marsalis, including the endless bus rides and one-night gigs. Covers the period before Marsalis left the road for a new job as music director on "The Tonight Show." 60m; VHS. **C:** Directed by D.A. Pennebaker; Chris Hegedus. **A:** Sr. High-Adult. **P:** Entertainment. **U:** Home. **Mov-Ent:** Music--Jazz, Music--Performance. **Acq:** Purchase. **Dist:** Sony Music Entertainment Inc.; Music Video Distributors. $19.98.

Brannigan 1975 (PG) — ★★1/2
The Duke stars in the somewhat unfamiliar role of a rough and tumble Chicago police officer. He travels across the Atlantic to arrest a racketeer who has fled the States rather than face a grand jury indictment. Humor and action abound. 111m; VHS, DVD, Wide. **C:** John Wayne; John Vernon; Mel Ferrer; Daniel Pilon; James Booth; Ralph Meeker; Lesley-Anne Down; Richard Attenborough; Directed by Douglas Hickox; Written by Michael Butler; William W. Norton, Sr.; Cinematography by Gerry Fisher; Music by Dominic Frontiere. **Pr:** Arthur Gardner; Jules Levy. **A:** Jr. High-Adult. **P:** Entertainment. **U:** Home. **Mov-Ent. Acq:** Purchase. **Dist:** MGM Home Entertainment. $19.98.

Branson! 2003
Amidst the lovely hills of the Ozark Mountains is a little known but well-loved entertainment destination, Branson, Missouri! See the man made wonders such as Silver Dollar City and Inspiration Tower and experience some incredible performances by Andy Williams, Glen Campbell, The Lennon Sisters and more. 111m; VHS, DVD. **A:** Adult. **P:** Education. **U:** Home. **Gen-Edu:** U.S. States, Travel. **Acq:** Purchase. **Dist:** Questar Inc. $14.95.

Bras D'Or Lakes 19??
Sailing expert Silver Donald Cameron takes a tour around Cape Breton's "Bras D'Or Lakes" on board his ship the Silversark. Includes footage of bald eagles, Mi'kmaq Indian ceremonies, a Highland village, and other cultural and ethnic activities associated with the area. 33m; VHS. **Pr:** Bennett Marine Video. **A:** Jr. High-Adult. **P:** Entertainment. **U:** Home. **Spo-Rec:** Boating, Travel. **Acq:** Purchase. **Dist:** Bennett Marine Video. $24.95.

Brass 1923
A romantic romp through the fields of fancy and wedlock during that roarin' decade of the '20s. 60m/B/W; Silent; VHS. **C:** Monte Blue; Marie Prevost; Harry C. (Henry) Myers; Irene Rich; Frank Keenan; Directed by Sidney Franklin. **Pr:** Warner Bros. **A:** Sr. High-Adult. **P:** Entertainment. **U:** Home. **Mov-Ent:** Romance, Marriage, Silent Films. **Acq:** Purchase. **Dist:** Grapevine Video; Facets Multimedia Inc. $19.95.

Brass 1985 (PG) — ★1/2
First post-Archie Bunker role for O'Connor, who plods through this average police drama at a snail's pace, dragging everything else down with him. Made-for-TV pilot for a series that never aired. 94m; VHS, Streaming. **C:** Carroll O'Connor; Lois Nettleton; Jimmy Baio; Paul Shenar; Vincent Gardenia; Anita

Gillette; Directed by Corey Allen. **A:** Jr. High-Adult. **P:** Entertainment. **U:** Home. **Mov-Ent**. **Acq:** Purchase. **Dist:** MGM Studios Inc. $19.98.

Brass & Bevel Cluster Construction 19??
Reveals how to take the mystery out of working with hard metals and bevels, by instructing how to work with brass came, saws, came benders, and bevels to create an exciting look. 30m; VHS. **A:** Adult. **P:** Instruction. **U:** Home. **How-Ins:** Crafts, Hobbies, How-To. **Acq:** Purchase. **Dist:** Cutters Productions. $12.95.

The Brass Bottle 1963 (Unrated) — ★★1/2
Silly but amusing comedy that served as the inspiration for the TV series "I Dream of Jeannie," although Eden plays the girlfriend in this movie. Ives stars as jovial genie Fakrash, whose antique bottle is bought by architect Harold Ventimore (Randall). Fakrash wants nothing more than to make his new master happy but his efforts cause constant crises for the bewildered man, who'd prefer his life return to normal. Based on the novel by F. Anstey. 90m; VHS, DVD, CC. **C:** Tony Randall; Burl Ives; Barbara Eden; Edward Andrews; Ann Doran; Kamala Devi; Howard Smith; Parley Baer; Directed by Harry Keller; Written by Oscar Brodney; Cinematography by Clifford Stine; Music by Bernard Green. **Pr:** Robert Arthur; Universal Pictures. **A:** Jr. High-Adult. **P:** Entertainment. **U:** Home. **Mov-Ent**: Romance. **Acq:** Purchase. **Dist:** Universal Studios Home Video.

The Brass Legend 1956 — ★★
With the help of his fiance's 11-year-old brother, Sheriff Wade Addams (O'Brian) captures outlaw Tris Hatten (Burr). He tries to keep Clay's (MacDonald) involvement a secret for safety's sake, but it leaks out thanks to newspaperman Tatum (Sage) who implies Wade wants to keep the reward money for himself. Then Clay becomes a target for Hatten and his henchmen. 79m/B/W; DVD. **C:** Hugh O'Brian; Raymond Burr; Donald MacDonald; Nancy Gates; Willard Sage; Directed by Gerd Oswald; Written by Don Martin; Cinematography by Charles Van Enger; Music by Paul Dunlap. **A:** Jr. High-Adult. **P:** Entertainment. **U:** Home. **Mov-Ent**: Western. **Acq:** Purchase. **Dist:** MGM Home Entertainment.

Brass Target 1978 (PG) — ★1/2
Hypothetical thriller about a plot to kill George Patton in the closing days of WWII for the sake of $250 million in Nazi gold stolen by his staff. Interesting cast can't find story. 111m; VHS, DVD. **C:** Sophia Loren; George Kennedy; Max von Sydow; John Cassavetes; Patrick McGoohan; Robert Vaughn; Bruce Davison; Edward Herrmann; Ed Bishop; Directed by John Hough; Written by Alvin Boretz. **Pr:** MGM. **A:** Jr. High-Adult. **P:** Entertainment. **U:** Home. **Mov-Ent**: Mystery & Suspense, World War Two. **Acq:** Purchase. **Dist:** MGM Home Entertainment. $59.95.

Brass Valley 1984
A history of the rise and fall of brass manufacturing in Connecticut's Naugatuck Valley. 86m; VHS, 3/4 U. **TV Std:** NTSC, PAL, SECAM. **Pr:** Jerry Quinn. **A:** Jr. High-Adult. **P:** Education. **U:** Institution, SURA. **Bus-Ind**: Documentary Films, Industrial Arts. **Acq:** Purchase, Rent/Lease, Duplication. **Dist:** The Cinema Guild.

The Brass/Woodwind Show 19??
Hosted and conducted by Ansgarius Aylward, the Greater Buffalo Youth Orchestra demonstrates chamber music with emphasis on the wind instruments. Includes teacher's guide. 30m; VHS. **A:** Primary-Jr. High. **P:** Education. **U:** Institution. **Chl-Juv**: Education. **Acq:** Purchase. **Dist:** GPN Educational Media. $29.95.

Brassed Off 1996 (R) — ★★1/2
Bittersweet tale of despair and hope in the fictional coal mining town of Grimly in Yorkshire, England. Set in 1992, when sweeping closures of British coal mines devastated the area, the sole respite of these workers is playing in the pit's brass band. Secretly suffering from black lung disease, the band's leader (Postlethwaite) dreams of winning a competition in Albert Hall. Fitzgerald plays the flugelhorn-tooting vixen who returns to the small town, inspiring the music (and virility) of the formerly all male band. She resumes her relationship with former flame MacGregor, but all is on shaky ground with the imminent closure of the mine. Fine performances brighten the generally gloomy proceedings. The band is played by the real-life Grimethorpe Colliery Brass Band. 100m; VHS, DVD, CC. **C:** Pete Postlethwaite; Ewan McGregor; Tara Fitzgerald; Jim Carter; Philip Jackson; Peter Martin; Stephen Tompkinson; Directed by Mark Herman; Written by Mark Herman; Cinematography by Andy Collins; Music by Trevor Jones. **Pr:** Steve Abbott; Channel Four Film; Prominent Features; Miramax Film Corp. **A:** Sr. High-Adult. **P:** Entertainment. **U:** Home. **Mov-Ent**: Great Britain, Miners & Mining. **Awds:** Cesar '98: Foreign Film. **Acq:** Purchase. **Dist:** Buena Vista Home Entertainment; Asymmetrical Entertainment, Inc.

Brats 1991
Army brat Libby Hinkle wants to escape life at the New Jersey base where her father is a colonel. She meets a young man in town and decides to organize an antiarmy rally. However, she soon learns that her love interest is actually a private, and her rally fizzles. As punishment, she is made to address new "brat" arrivals, which she does with spunk and wisdom. 28m; VHS. **A:** Jr. High-Sr. High. **P:** Entertainment. **U:** Institution. **Mov-Ent**: Adolescence. **Acq:** Purchase, Rent/Lease. **Dist:** Direct Cinema Ltd. $150.00.

Bratz 2007 (PG) — **Bomb!**
Four high school freshmen and best friends (Ramos, Browning, Parrish, and Shayne) find themselves at odds with the bossy student body president, who aims to split them up into (gasp!) separate social cliques. There's singing and dancing (like a big, long, pink, fluffy music video), and how sweetly cliche is it that these real-life Bratz are all from different ethnicities and socio-economic classes, yet still BFFs? At least these girls are (somewhat) real humans and not the creepy-faced, bubble-headed dolls (and animated characters) the movie is based on, but even your lip gloss-wearing 'tweener will roll her eyes at the mere suggestion of this film, which is cloying at best, intolerable at worst. 100m; DVD. **C:** Skyler Shaye; Anneliese van der Pol; Jon Voight; Lainie Kazan; Nathalia Ramos; Janel Parrish; Logan Browning; Chelsea Staub; Stephen Lunsford; Ian Nelson; Directed by Sean McNamara; Written by Susan Estelle Jansen; Cinematography by Christian Sebaldt; Music by John Coda. **Pr:** Avi Arad; Steven Paul; Isaac Larian; Crystal Sky Pictures; Lionsgate. **A:** Family. **P:** Entertainment. **U:** Home. **L:** English. **Mov-Ent**: Adolescence, Clothing & Dress. **Acq:** Purchase. **Dist:** Lions Gate Entertainment Inc.

Bratz Babyz The Movie 2007 (Unrated)
Popular children's characters the Bratz Babyz help rescue their friend's stolen puppy in this animated special. 66m; DVD. **A:** Preschool-Primary. **P:** Entertainment. **U:** Home. **Mov-Ent**: Family Viewing, Animation & Cartoons, Children's Shows. **Acq:** Purchase. **Dist:** Lions Gate Entertainment Inc. $9.98.

Bratz Fairy Tales 2008 (Unrated)
Animated children's television program. The Bratz Kidz learn not to judge others in this full-length cartoon that finds them in Fairy Tale Land living out classic tales such as Snow White, Red Riding Hood, Rapunzel, and Cinderella. 74m; DVD. **A:** Preschool-Primary. **P:** Entertainment. **U:** Home. **Mov-Ent**: Family Viewing, Animation & Cartoons, Children's Shows. **Acq:** Purchase. **Dist:** Lions Gate Entertainment Inc. $7.98.

Bratz Fashion Pixiez 2007 (Unrated)
Cloe and Yasmin discover that Pixies exist and even enter the magical creatures' world, where they find that friendship can always help good defeat evil. 74m; DVD. **A:** Preschool-Primary. **P:** Entertainment. **U:** Home. **Mov-Ent**: Children's Shows, Animation & Cartoons. **Acq:** Purchase. **Dist:** Lions Gate Entertainment Inc. $7.98.

Bratz Genie Magic 2008 (PG)
Yasmin, Cloe, Sasha, and Jade discover their new friend Katia is a genie and then help her defeat the evil mastermind trying to enslave her. 59m; DVD. **A:** Primary-Adult. **P:** Entertainment. **U:** Home. **Mov-Ent**: Children's Shows, Animation & Cartoons. **Acq:** Purchase. **Dist:** Lions Gate Entertainment Inc. $11.98.

Bratz Girlz Really Rock 2008 (Unrated)
In their first movie musical, the Bratz girls head to Camp Starshine to compete for a role in a Hollywood movie and learn that friendship is more important than fame. 82m; DVD. **A:** Preschool-Primary. **P:** Entertainment. **U:** Home. **Mov-Ent**: Children's Shows, Animation & Cartoons. **Acq:** Purchase. **Dist:** Lions Gate Entertainment Inc. $7.98.

Bratz Kidz Sleepover Adventure 2007 (G)
The first Bratz Kidz movie features the Bratz girls when they were little kids attending a friend's sleepover party. 72m; DVD. **A:** Preschool-Primary. **P:** Entertainment. **U:** Home. **Mov-Ent**: Children's Shows, Animation & Cartoons. **Acq:** Purchase. **Dist:** Lions Gate Entertainment Inc. $7.98.

Bratz Passion 4 Fashion Diamondz 2008 (Unrated)
The Bratz girls host their own reality show and visit a haunted town, all while preparing for the big fashion contest. 73m; DVD. **A:** Preschool-Primary. **P:** Entertainment. **U:** Home. **Mov-Ent**: Children's Shows, Animation & Cartoons. **Acq:** Purchase. **Dist:** Lions Gate Entertainment Inc. $11.98.

Bratz Rock Angelz 2008 (Unrated)
The Bratz girls travel across the ocean to London, where they form a band and try to conquer the music world. 76m; DVD. **A:** Preschool-Primary. **P:** Entertainment. **U:** Home. **Mov-Ent**: Children's Shows, Animation & Cartoons. **Acq:** Purchase. **Dist:** Lions Gate Entertainment Inc. $11.98.

Bratz Super Babyz 2007 (Unrated)
Alien technology accidentally gives the Bratz Babyz special superpowers, but even when those powers are taken away, the girls work together to solve a big problem. 74m; DVD. **A:** Preschool-Primary. **P:** Entertainment. **U:** Home. **Mov-Ent**: Children's Shows, Animation & Cartoons. **Acq:** Purchase. **Dist:** Lions Gate Entertainment Inc. $7.98.

Brava Italia 2008
Three-part series on life in Italy from cities to hill towns and mountains to the seashore, including history, food, art, and culture. 178m; DVD, CC. **C:** Narrated by Paul Sorvino. **A:** Family. **P:** Entertainment. **U:** Home. **Mov-Ent**: Italy, Travel. **Acq:** Purchase. **Dist:** Acorn Media Group Inc. $29.99.

The Bravados 1958 (Unrated) — ★★★
A rough, distressing Western revenge tale, wherein a man is driven to find the four men who murdered his wife. In tracking the perpetrators, Peck realizes that he has been corrupted by his vengeance. 98m; VHS, DVD, CC. **C:** Gregory Peck; Stephen Boyd; Joan Collins; Albert Salmi; Henry Silva; Lee Van Cleef; George Voskovec; Barry Coe; Directed by Henry King; Written by Philip Yordan; Cinematography by Leon Shamroy. **Pr:** 20th Century-Fox. **A:** Family. **P:** Entertainment. **U:** Home. **Mov-Ent**: Western. **Awds:** Natl. Bd. of Review '58: Support. Actor (Salmi). **Acq:** Purchase. **Dist:** Movies Unlimited; Alpha Video. $39.98.

Brave 2007 (Unrated) — ★1/2
The brother of a martial artist is kidnapped, and he is told that he has to steal the credit card subscriber data from a bank in exchange for his family. He makes the switch and the pair begin to wonder who set them up for this and why, when the bank president turns up dead simultaneously. 92m; DVD. **C:** Michael B.; Dean Alexandrou; Vanchart Chunsri; Directed by Thanapon Maliwan; Afdlin Shauki; Written by Nut Nualpang; Cinematography by Arnon Chunprasert. **A:** Sr. High-Adult. **P:** Entertainment. **U:** Home. **L:** English, Thai. **Mov-Ent**: Martial Arts. **Acq:** Purchase. **Dist:** Movies Unlimited. $14.98.

Brave 2012 (PG) — ★★1/2
Pixar's thirteen film is also their first with a female heroine, the feisty, red-headed Scottish Princess Merida (MacDonald), a young lady who refuses to play by the traditional rules as enforced by her mother, Queen Elinor (Thompson). Merida meets a witch who gives her a spell that too literally "changes" her mother, and she discovers that true bravery involves more than mere archery or parental defiance. A sweet, beautiful film that works when compared to most animation but doesn't quite live up to the Pixar standard of storytelling. 100m; DVD, Blu-Ray, Streaming. **C:** Voice(s) by Kelly Macdonald; Billy Connolly; Emma Thompson; Julie Walters; Robbie Coltrane; Kevin McKidd; Craig Ferguson; Directed by Mark C. Andrews; Brenda Chapman; Steve Purcell; Written by Mark C. Andrews; Brenda Chapman; Steve Purcell; Irene Mecchi; Music by Patrick Doyle. **Pr:** Katherine Sarafian; Pixar; Walt Disney Studios. **A:** Family. **P:** Entertainment. **U:** Home. **L:** English, French, Spanish. **Mov-Ent**: Animation & Cartoons, Scotland. **Awds:** Oscars '12: Animated Film; British Acad. '12: Animated Film; Golden Globes '13: Animated Film. **Acq:** Purchase, Rent/Lease. **Dist:** Walt Disney Studios Home Entertainment. $39.99 29.99 14.99.

The Brave Archer 1977 (Unrated) — ★
Kuo Chang studies the martial arts after his father is murdered. He falls in love with Huang Yung but must pass three tests before winning her hand in marriage. Mandarin with subtitles or dubbed. 116m; DVD. **C:** Sheng Fu; Niu Tien; Feng Ku; Philip Kwok; Directed by Cheh Chang; Written by Kuang Ni; Cinematography by Mu-To Kung; Music by Yung-Yu Chen. **A:** Sr. High-Adult. **P:** Entertainment. **U:** Home. **L:** Mandarin Dialects. **Mov-Ent**: Martial Arts. **Acq:** Purchase. **Dist:** Movies Unlimited.

The Brave Archer and His Mate 1982 (Unrated) — ★
Yong Guo is tricked by crazy martial arts master Oyang Fung into believing his foster parents murdered his father. But somehow he ends up in a monastery with a bunch of other apprentices so he can be mentored by his foster father's teachers. Mandarin with subtitles or dubbed. 101m; DVD. **C:** Alexander Fu Sheng; Philip Kwok; Gigi Wong; Li Wang; Siu-hou Chin; Directed by Cheh Chang; Written by Kuang Ni; Cinematography by Hui-chi Tsao; Music by Eddie Wang. **A:** Sr. High-Adult. **P:** Entertainment. **U:** Home. **L:** Mandarin Dialects. **Mov-Ent**: Martial Arts. **Acq:** Purchase. **Dist:** Movies Unlimited.

The Brave Bunch 1970 — ★1/2
A courageous Greek soldier tries to save his men and country during WWII. 110m; VHS. **C:** Peter Funk; Giannis Voglis; Directed by Costa Carayiannis. **A:** Adult. **P:** Entertainment. **U:** Home. **Mov-Ent**: World War Two. **Acq:** Purchase. **Dist:** Lions Gate Television Corp. $39.95.

The Brave Indian Chief 19??
Storyteller Rafe Martin relates the tale of Indian Chief Glooscop, who travelled the treacherous sea and battled an evil sorcerer to bring food to his starving tribe. 30m; VHS. **A:** Preschool-Primary. **P:** Entertainment. **U:** Home. **Chl-Juv**: Storytelling, Native Americans, Children. **Acq:** Purchase. **Dist:** Facets Multimedia Inc. $14.99.

Brave Kate 1978
The story of an innkeeper's brave young daughter, who sets out to avenge the murder of her father by a roving band of cutthroats. Based on a popular Czechoslovakian song of the 19th century. 16m; VHS, 3/4 U. **Pr:** Short Film Prague. **A:** Jr. High-Adult. **P:** Entertainment. **U:** Institution, SURA. **Chl-Juv**: Family Viewing, Folklore & Legends. **Acq:** Purchase. **Dist:** Phoenix Learning Group.

The Brave Little Toaster 1988
When a young boy disappears, his appliances feel compelled to journey to the big city and look for him. Winner of a Parent's Choice Award. 90m; VHS, CC. **C:** Voice(s) by Jon Lovitz; Phil Hartman; Deanna Oliver; Directed by Jerry Rees. **Pr:** Hyperion/ Kushner-Locke. **A:** Family. **P:** Entertainment. **U:** Home. **Chl-Juv**: Animation & Cartoons, Family Viewing. **Acq:** Purchase. **Dist:** Walt Disney Studios Home Entertainment; Buena Vista Home Entertainment; Facets Multimedia Inc. $19.99.

The Brave Little Toaster Goes to Mars 1998
Toaster, Lampy, Radio, Kirby, and Blanky take a wacky trip to Mars to save their owner's new baby. 73m; VHS, CC. **C:** Voice(s) by Farrah Fawcett; Wayne Knight; Carol Channing; Deanna Oliver; Tim Stack; Roger Kabler; Thurl Ravenscroft; Eric Lloyd; Fyvush Finkel; Alan King; Brian Doyle-Murray; DeForest Kelley; Stephen Tobolowsky. **A:** Preschool-Primary. **P:** Entertainment. **U:** Home. **Chl-Juv**: Animation & Cartoons. **Acq:** Purchase. **Dist:** Buena Vista Home Entertainment.

Brave New Foods: The Biotech Revolution ????
Provides an extensive examination of the potential benefits and risks of bioengineered foods. 24m; VHS. **A:** Adult. **P:** Professional. **U:** Institution, CCTV. **Hea-Sci**: Nutrition, Fitness/ Exercise. **Acq:** Purchase. **Dist:** The Learning Seed. $89.00.

Brave New Girl 2004 (PG-13) — ★★1/2
Holly's got what it takes to get into the big-time music school and her poor-yet-resourceful mom won't let their lack of money stand in the way of her daughter's dream. But getting there is only half the ditty. Generically inspiring tale. Based on the novel "A Mother's Gift," by co-executive producers Britney and Lynne Spears. 90m; VHS, DVD. **C:** Virginia Madsen; Barbara Mamabolo; Aaron Ashmore; Lindsey Haun; Jackie Rosenbaum; Joanne Boland; Nick Roth; Directed by Bobby Roth; Written by

Britney Spears; Lynne Spears; Amy Talkington; Cinematography by Eric Van Haren Noman; Music by Asher Ettinger. **A:** Jr. High-Adult. **P:** Entertainment. **U:** Home. **Mov-Ent**: Adolescence. **Acq:** Purchase. **Dist:** Lions Gate Home Entertainment. $19.99.

Brave New Men 2005
Documentary interviewing three of the world's leading geneticists, one each from the U.S., China, and Iceland. 50m; VHS, DVD. **A:** Sr. High-Adult. **P:** Entertainment. **U:** Institution. **Gen-Edu**: Documentary Films, Genetics. **Acq:** Purchase, Rent/Lease. **Dist:** The Cinema Guild. $295.00.

Brave New Voices 2010 2011
Captures the poetry Grand Slam Finals, held in Los Angeles, between four teams competing before a celebrity panel of judges. ; DVD. **A:** Sr. High-Adult. **P:** Entertainment. **U:** Home. **Mov-Ent**: Literature--American, Documentary Films. **Acq:** Purchase. **Dist:** Home Box Office Inc. $19.98.

Brave New World 1998 (Unrated) — ★★
In this watered down version of the novel, humanity has given up science, religion, and even individuality in pursuit of happiness. Life is now endless consumption and hedonism, run by a totalitarian elite. 90m; DVD, Blu-Ray. **C:** Peter Gallagher; Leonard Nimoy; Tim Guinee; Rya Kihlstedt; Sally Kirkland; Directed by Leslie Libman; Larry Williams; Written by Dan Mazur; David Tausik; Cinematography by Ronald Garcia; Music by Daniel Licht. **A:** Jr. High-Adult. **P:** Entertainment. **U:** Home. **L:** English. **Mov-Ent**. **Acq:** Purchase. **Dist:** Millennium Entertainment L.L.C. $10.99 9.99.

The Brave One 1956 — ★★★
A love story between a Spanish boy and the bull who saves his life. The animal is later carted off to the bullring. Award-winning screenplay by the then-blacklisted Trumbo, credited as "Robert Rich." 100m; VHS, DVD. **C:** Michel Ray; Rodolfo Hoyos; Joi Lansing; Directed by Irving Rapper; Written by Dalton Trumbo; Cinematography by Jack Cardiff; Music by Victor Young. **Pr:** Maurice King; Frank King. **A:** Family. **P:** Entertainment. **U:** Home. **Mov-Ent**: Animals. **Awds:** Oscars '56: Story. **Acq:** Purchase. **Dist:** VCI Entertainment. $49.95.

The Brave One 2007 (R) — ★½
Erica Bain (Foster), the host of a radio show named "City Walk,", has spent years gushing about the wonders of life in her beloved New York City. She encounters a trio of thugs while walking with fiance David (Andrews) in Central Park. The two suffer a gruesome beating, which proves lethal for David and barely survivable for Erica, who, after months of recovery and in the throes of post-traumatic stress, acquires a hand gun. Erica suddenly and routinely witnesses violent criminal acts and begins to mete out street justice while forming a platonic relationship with Detective Mercer (Howard), who is investigating the series of vigilante-style slayings. Their interactions are a bright spot in an otherwise brutal story line. It may sound a bit (okay, a lot) like "Death Wish" but the distinction is Erica's inner turmoil, skillfully played out by Foster. Still, the overwhelming violence outweighs the attempt to humanize her character, and ultimately it fails as both an insightful psycho-thriller and as a vigilante shoot-'em-up. 119m; DVD, HD-DVD. **C:** Jodie Foster; Terrence Howard; Naveen Andrews; Carmen Ejogo; Nicky Katt; Mary Steenburgen; Lenny Venito; Lenny Kravitz; Directed by Neil Jordan; Written by Roderick Taylor; Bruce Taylor; Cynthia Mort; Cinematography by Philippe Rousselot; Music by Dario Marianelli. **Pr:** Joel Silver; Susan Downey; Silver Pictures; Village Roadshow Pictures; Warner Bros. **A:** Sr. High-Adult. **P:** Entertainment. **U:** Home. **L:** English. **Mov-Ent**: Crime Drama. **Acq:** Purchase. **Dist:** Warner Home Video, Inc.

Braveheart 1925 — ★★½
When a Native American adapts to the white man's world, he alienates his own people. He eventually chooses to renounce his love for a white woman, and returns to lead his people. Silent. 62m/B/W; Silent; VHS, 8 mm. **C:** Rod La Rocque; Lillian Rich; Robert Edeson; Tyrone Power; Sally Rand; Arthur Housman; Directed by Alan Hale; Written by Mary O'Hara; Cinematography by Faxon M. Dean. **A:** Family. **P:** Entertainment. **U:** Home. **Mov-Ent**: Native Americans. **Acq:** Purchase. **Dist:** Facets Multimedia Inc.; Glenn Video Vistas Ltd. $55.95.

Braveheart 1995 (R) — ★★★½
Producer-director-star Gibson does it all in this bold, ferocious, reasonably accurate epic about the passion and cost of freedom. Charismatic 13th century Scottish folk hero William Wallace leads his desperate and outnumbered clansmen in revolt against British oppression. Sweeping, meticulous battle scenes fit suprisingly well with moments of stirring romance and snappy wit. Among the mostly unknown (in the States, anyway) cast, Marceau and McCormack are elegant as Wallace's lady loves, and McGoohan is positively hateful as King Edward I. Gory and excessively violent (as medieval warfare tends to be) and a bit too long (as historical epics tend to be), but rewarding entertainment for those who stick it out—where else can you see the king's army get mooned en masse? Script was based on 300 pages of rhyming verse attributed to a blind poet known as Blind Harry. Gibson put up $15 million of his own money to complete the film. 178m; VHS, DVD, Blu-Ray. **C:** Mel Gibson; Sophie Marceau; Patrick McGoohan; Catherine McCormack; Brendan Gleeson; James Cosmo; David O'Hara; Angus MacFadyen; Peter Hanly; Ian Bannen; Sean McGinley; Brian Cox; Stephen Billington; Barry McGovern; Alun Armstrong; Tommy Flanagan; Directed by Mel Gibson; Written by Randall Wallace; Cinematography by John Toll; Music by James Horner. **Pr:** Bruce Davey; Mel Gibson; Alan Ladd, Jr.; Stephen McEveety; Mel Gibson; Icon Productions; Paramount Pictures. **A:** Sr. High-Adult. **P:** Entertainment. **U:** Home. **Mov-Ent**: Drama, Scotland, War--General. **Awds:** Oscars '95: Cinematog., Director (Gibson), Film, Makeup; British Acad. '95: Cinematog.; Golden Globes '96: Director (Gibson); MTV Movie Awards '96: Action Seq.; Writers Guild '95: Orig. Screenplay; Broadcast Film Critics '95: Director (Gibson). **Acq:** Purchase. **Dist:** Paramount Pictures Corp.

Bravery in the Field 1979
This tape features the story of the frustrations and hostilities of two men whose lives lack a sense of purpose. 28m; VHS, 3/4 U. **Pr:** NFBC. **A:** Jr. High-Sr. High. **P:** Education. **U:** Institution. **Gen-Edu**: Documentary Films, Human Relations. **Acq:** Purchase. **Dist:** Home Vision Cinema.

Braves Win. . . It All! 1995
Documents the Atlanta Braves' 1995 World Championship season from spring training to the World Series victory over the Cleveland Indians. 60m; VHS. **A:** Family. **P:** Entertainment. **U:** Home. **Spo-Rec**: Baseball. **Acq:** Purchase. **Dist:** Baseball Direct. $19.95.

BraveStarr: Best of Bravestarr 1987
Lawman Marshall Bravestarr escaped the destruction of his home planet and now keeps the peace on the wild-west planet of New Texas along with his cybernetic talking horse Thirty-Thirty, sidekick Deputy Fuzz, and mentor Judge J.B. Shaman. Outlaw Tex-Hex, leader of the Carrion Bunch, is out to steal the mineral Kerium but BraveStarr keeps him at bay, protecting the Prairie People and their resources. 215m; DVD. **C:** Voice(s) by Charles Adler; Susan Blu; Pat Fraley; Edmund Gilbert. **A:** Primary-Jr. High. **P:** Entertainment. **U:** Home. **Chl-Juv**: Animation & Cartoons, Action-Adventure, Science Fiction. **Acq:** Purchase. **Dist:** Mill Creek Entertainment L.L.C.

Braving Alaska 1993
Explores the frigid wilderness of the U.S.A.'s northernmost territory. 60m; DVD; Closed Captioned. **A:** Primary-Adult. **P:** Education. **U:** Institution. **Gen-Edu**. **Acq:** Purchase. **Dist:** National Geographic Society. $19.95.

Bravo Gloria 1988
The story of Gloria Lenhoff, a 32-year-old mentally retarded woman, and her personal struggle to live a meaningful life. 30m; VHS, 3/4 U. **Pr:** Cornell University; PBS. **A:** Jr. High-Adult. **P:** Education. **U:** Institution, CCTV, Home, SURA. **Gen-Edu**: Documentary Films, Handicapped, Mental Retardation. **Acq:** Purchase, Rent/Lease, Duplication, Off-Air Record. **Dist:** PBS Home Video; Filmakers Library Inc.

Bravo Papa 2040 1991
A commentary on the intrusion of technology into our lives, and specifically the terror caused by low-flying military jets. 6m; VHS. **A:** Jr. High-Adult. **P:** Education. **U:** Institution. **Gen-Edu**: Aeronautics, Technology. **Acq:** Purchase, Rent/Lease. **Dist:** Bullfrog Films, Inc. $175.00.

Bravo! What a Presentation! 1985
A skilled speaker demonstrates the finer points in making presentations to various audiences in this program. 15m; VHS, 3/4 U. **Pr:** American Management Association. **A:** College-Adult. **P:** Education. **U:** Institution, CCTV. **Bus-Ind**: Documentary Films, Management, Communication. **Acq:** Purchase, Rent/Lease, Subscription. **Dist:** American Management Association.

The Bravos 1972 (Unrated) — ★★
U.S. Cavalry officer Harkness (Peppard) is in charge of remote outpost. He's trying to protect his fort and a wagon train from an Indian uprising while also searching for his missing son (Van Patten). Standard made-for-TV adventure with a familiar cast. 97m; DVD. **C:** George Peppard; Pernell Roberts; Belinda J. Montgomery; L.Q. Jones; Vincent Van Patten; George Murdock; Barry Brown; Dana Elcar; Bo Svenson; Directed by Ted Post; Written by Christopher Knopf; Cinematography by Leonard Rosenman. **A:** Family. **P:** Entertainment. **U:** Home. **Mov-Ent**: Western. **Acq:** Purchase. **Dist:** Movies Unlimited.

Braz 1984 (Unrated)
Overviews the development of the rebel army in El Salvadore. 35m; DVD. **A:** Adult. **P:** Education. **U:** Institution. **Gen-Edu**: Central America, War--General. **Acq:** Purchase. **Dist:** Third World Newsreel. $125.

Brazelton Neonatal Behavioral Assessment Scale: An Introduction 19??
This first program in the Brazelton series briefly describes the doctor's scale. Dr. Brazelton examines a two-day-old normal infant, assessing its initial state of rest, and then tests its habituation to various stimuli and its responses and reflexes to different experiences. 50m/B/W; 3/4 U, Special order formats. **Pr:** Education Development Center. **A:** College-Adult. **P:** Professional. **U:** Institution, CCTV, CATV, BCTV. **Hea-Sci**: Documentary Films, Infants. **Acq:** Purchase, Rent/Lease. **Dist:** Education Development Center.

The Brazelton Neonatal Behavioral Assessment Scale Films 19??
A series of programs using Dr. Brazelton's assessment scale on neonatal behavior before the environment has begun to influence this behavior, and allow for assessment of the infant's capabilities. This technique is a valuable research instrument for comparing and evaluating infant growth, response and development. Programs are available individually. 21m/B/W; 3/4 U, Special order formats. **Pr:** Education Development Center. **A:** College-Adult. **P:** Professional. **U:** Institution, CCTV, CATV, BCTV. **Hea-Sci**: Documentary Films, Infants. **Acq:** Purchase, Rent/Lease. **Dist:** Education Development Center.
Indiv. Titles: 1. Introduction 2. Variations in Normal Behavior 3. Self-Scoring Examination.

Brazil 1982
This series looks at the government and economy of Brazil. 20m; VHS, DVD, 3/4 U. **Pr:** British Broadcasting Corporation. **A:** Jr. High-Sr. High. **P:** Education. **U:** Institution, SURA. **Gen-Edu**: Documentary Films, Geography, South America. **Acq:** Purchase. **Dist:** Home Vision Cinema.
Indiv. Titles: 1. Skyscrapers and Slums 2. Drought on the Land 3. City of Newcomers 4. Amazon Frontier 5. Progress, But Who Is it For?.

Brazil 1985 (R) — ★★★½
The acclaimed nightmare comedy about an Everyman trying to survive in a surreal paper-choked bureaucratic society. There are copious references to "1984" and "The Trial," fantastic mergings of glorious fantasy and stark reality, and astounding visual design. The DVD version has a 142-minute director's cut as well as a documentary. 131m; VHS, DVD, Blu-Ray, Wide, CC. **C:** Jonathan Pryce; Robert De Niro; Michael Palin; Katherine Helmond; Kim Greist; Bob Hoskins; Ian Holm; Peter Vaughan; Ian Richardson; Directed by Terry Gilliam; Written by Terry Gilliam; Tom Stoppard; Charles McKeown; Cinematography by Roger Pratt; Music by Michael Kamen. **Pr:** Mark Huffam; Arnon Milchan. **A:** Sr. High-Adult. **P:** Entertainment. **U:** Home. **Mov-Ent**: Comedy--Black, Dentistry. **Awds:** L.A. Film Critics '85: Director (Gilliam), Film, Screenplay. **Acq:** Purchase. **Dist:** Home Vision Cinema; Facets Multimedia Inc.

Brazil: A Report on Torture 1971
Documentary interviewing former political prisoners of Brazil's right-wing military regime from the 1960s. 60m; VHS. **A:** Sr. High-Adult. **P:** Education. **U:** Institution. **Gen-Edu**: Documentary Films, Human Rights. **Acq:** Purchase. **Dist:** The Cinema Guild. $99.95.

Brazil: An Inconvenient History 2001
Documentary using original texts, letters, accounts, and decrees to chart the history of slave trade in Brazil. Brazil was the largest participant in the slave trade and the last country to abolish slavery. 47m; VHS. **A:** Sr. High-Adult. **P:** Education. **U:** Institution. **Gen-Edu**: Slavery, South America, History. **Acq:** Purchase, Rent/Lease. **Dist:** Filmakers Library Inc. $325.00.

Brazil Dive Guide 19??
Dive into the Bay of Dolphins, visit with a giant manta, and explore the crumbling ruins of a colonial prison above water. 30m; VHS. **A:** Sr. High-Adult. **P:** Entertainment. **U:** Home. **Spo-Rec**: Scuba, Travel. **Acq:** Purchase. **Dist:** Bennett Marine Video. $19.95.

Brazil: South America's Giant 1979
Viewers see in detail how people live and work in Brazil. 18m; VHS, 3/4 U. **Pr:** Andrew Nemes. **A:** Jr. High-Sr. High. **P:** Education. **U:** Institution, SURA. **Gen-Edu**: Documentary Films, South America. **Acq:** Purchase. **Dist:** Phoenix Learning Group.

Brazil 2 Dive Guide 19??
Explorers search for artifacts from four centuries of war off the coast of Brazil. 30m; VHS. **A:** Sr. High-Adult. **P:** Entertainment. **U:** Home. **Spo-Rec**: Scuba, Travel. **Acq:** Purchase. **Dist:** Bennett Marine Video. $19.95.

Brazilian Bike GP '88 1988
Bike excitement from the 1988 Brazilian Bike Grand Prix. ?m; VHS. **A:** Family. **P:** Entertainment. **U:** Home. **Spo-Rec**: Sports--General, Motorcycles. **Acq:** Purchase. **Dist:** Powersports - Powerdocs. $39.95.

Brazilian Box Midfield 2009 (Unrated)
Demonstration of the 'Box Midfield' system used by the Brazilian soccer team for coaches wishing to use it on their own program. 60m; DVD. **A:** Family. **P:** Education. **U:** Home, Institution. **Spo-Rec**: Soccer, Athletic Instruction/Coaching. **Acq:** Purchase. **Dist:** Championship Productions. $34.99.

The Brazilian Connection 1982
A one hour documentary on Brazil's 1982 free and democratic elections, the first held in nearly two decades. 60m; 3/4 U, Special order formats. **Pr:** International Women's Film Project. **A:** Sr. High-Adult. **P:** Education. **U:** Institution. **Gen-Edu**: Documentary Films, South America, Politics & Government. **Acq:** Purchase. **Dist:** The Cinema Guild.

Brazilian Dance Workout 2002
Vanessa Isaac leads a high-energy cardio routine with movements taken from Latin dances such as the samba and mambo as well as from Brazilian street-party styles such as axes, afros, and frevos. 62m; DVD. **A:** Adult. **P:** Instruction. **U:** Home. **Hea-Sci**: Fitness/Exercise. **Acq:** Purchase. **Dist:** Collage Video Specialties, Inc.

Brazilian Dance Workout with Vanessa Isaac 2003
Incorporates Brazilian dancing with cardio and toning routines for an all-body workout, by Vanessa Isaac of Hip Brazil. 60m; DVD. **A:** College-Adult. **P:** Instruction. **U:** Home. **Hea-Sci**: Fitness/Exercise, Dance--Instruction. **Acq:** Purchase. **Dist:** Razor Digital. $14.99.

Brazilian Knights & A Lady 1988
Patti Austin, Paulo Brago, Djavan, Ivan Lins and more perform the best of jazz samba. 60m; VHS. **A:** College-Adult. **P:** Entertainment. **U:** Home. **Mov-Ent**: Music Video, Music--Jazz. **Acq:** Purchase. **Dist:** Music Video Distributors. $19.98.

Brazilian Training Drills: Subtle Differences, Dynamic Results! 2011 (Unrated)
Coach Marcelo Melado Mesquita presents sequential volleyball drills that start very simple and grow increasingly complex. 48m; DVD. **A:** Family. **P:** Education. **U:** Home, Institution. **Spo-Rec**: Volleyball, Athletic Instruction/Coaching. **Acq:** Purchase. **Dist:** Championship Productions. $34.99.

Breach 2007 (PG-13) — ★★½
Somber true story follows ambitious FBI agent Eric O'Neill (Phillippe), who's planted by tough boss Kate Burroughs (Linney) as the new assistant to veteran agent Robert Hanssen

(Cooper). She says the bureau is worried because Hanssen is a perv, but he's actually been selling info to the Russians and the feds want to catch him in the act. Hanssen starts getting suspicious, which ratchets up the tension, but there's never any clear idea of why he turned traitor, although Cooper is a creepily effective enigma. 110m; DVD, HD-DVD, Wide. **C:** Chris Cooper; Ryan Phillippe; Laura Linney; Dennis Haysbert; Caroline Dhavernas; Gary Cole; Bruce Davison; Kathleen Quinlan; Directed by Billy Ray; Written by Billy Ray; Adam Mazer; William Rotko; Cinematography by Tak Fujimoto; Music by Mychael Danna. **Pr:** Robert Newmyer; Scott Kroopf; Scott Strauss; Outlaw Productions; Intermedia Films; Sidney Kimmel Entertainment; Universal Pictures. **A:** Jr. High-Adult. **P:** Entertainment. **U:** Home. **L:** English. **Mov-Ent:** Federal Bureau of Investigation (FBI). **Acq:** Purchase. **Dist:** Movies Unlimited; Alpha Video.

Breach of Conduct 1994 (PG-13) — ★½
Col. Bill Case (Coyote) is the commander of the Fort Benton, Utah, Army base where Helen Lutz's (Thorne-Smith) husband Tom (Verica) has just been transferred. At first there's a mutual attraction between Helen and Case, but then hubby is assigned a mission off base and, when Helen refuses Case's overtures, things turn very nasty. 93m; VHS, CC. **C:** Peter Coyote; Courtney Thorne-Smith; Tom Verica; Beth Toussaint; Directed by Tim Matheson; Written by Scott Abbott; Cinematography by Gideon Porath. **Pr:** Lori-Etta Taub; Sheldon Pinchuk. **A:** Sr. High-Adult. **P:** Entertainment. **U:** Home. **Mov-Ent:** Mystery & Suspense, Armed Forces--U.S., TV Movies. **Acq:** Purchase. **Dist:** Universal Music and Video Distribution.

Breach of Trust 1995 (R) — ★★½
Smalltime crook Casey (Biehn) winds up in big trouble when he steals a computer disc with access codes to millions in drug cartel money. He goes on the lam and meets Madeline (Ferrer), an undercover cop who thinks that some police are on the cartel's payroll. So the daring duo decide to take on the drug lords and the dirty cops. 96m; VHS, CC. **C:** Michael Biehn; Matt Craven; Leilani Sarelle Ferrer; Miguel (Michael) Sandoval; Kim Coates; Ed Lauter; Directed by Charles Wilkinson; Written by Gordon Basichis; Raul Inglis; Cinematography by Michael Slovis; Music by Graeme Coleman. **Pr:** Robert Vince; William Vince; Michael Strange; Keystone Entertainment. **A:** Sr. High-Adult. **P:** Entertainment. **U:** Home. **Mov-Ent. Acq:** Purchase. **Dist:** Lions Gate Entertainment Inc.

Bread 19?? (Unrated)
From the BBC, one of the most popular British soap operas. Watch Billy, Joey, Roxy, and Adrian go through the hilarious motions of their daily lives. 85m; VHS. **C:** Peter Sellers. **Pr:** British Broadcasting Corporation. **A:** Family. **P:** Entertainment. **U:** Home. **Mov-Ent:** Comedy-Drama, Television Series. **Acq:** Purchase. **Dist:** Video Collectibles. $29.95.

Bread and Butterflies 1974
By presenting situations from a child's perspective, this series gives children a clearer understanding of successful work behavior and the connection between school and the real world. Also available are a 20-minute teacher's program and a 15-minute informational program. 15m; VHS, 3/4 U, Q. **Pr:** Educational Film Center of Virginia. **A:** Primary-Jr. High. **P:** Education. **U:** Institution, CCTV, CATV, BCTV. **Gen-Edu:** Documentary Films, Human Relations. **Acq:** Purchase, Rent/Lease, Duplication License. **Dist:** Agency for Instructional Technology.
Indiv. Titles: 1. Treasure Hunt 2. Work Means 3. Me, Myself and Maybe 4. Decisions, Decisions 5. School and Jobs 6. Taking Care of Business 7. I Agree...You're Wrong! 8. Success Story 9. The Way We Live 10. Planning Ahead: The Racer 11. Things, Ideas, People 12. People Need People 13. Our Own Two Hands 14. Power Play 15. Choosing Changes.

Bread and Chocolate 1973 (Unrated) — ★★★
Uneducated Italian immigrant Manfredi works a series of odd jobs in complacently bourgeois Switzerland and tries desperately to fit in and better himself (which he fails utterly to do). Culture clash satire, with an engaging everyman lead. Italian with subtitles. 110m; VHS, DVD, Wide. **C:** Nino Manfredi; Anna Karina; Johnny Dorelli; Paolo Turco; Directed by Franco Brusati; Written by Nino Manfredi; Franco Brusati; Iaia Fiastri; Cinematography by Luciano Tovoli; Music by Daniele Patrucchi. **A:** College-Adult. **P:** Entertainment. **U:** Home. **L:** Italian. **Mov-Ent:** Comedy--Black, Satire & Parody, Immigration. **Awds:** N.Y. Film Critics '78: Foreign Film. **Acq:** Purchase. **Dist:** Hen's Tooth Video. $59.95.

Bread and Dignity 1989
Historic newsreel footage is combined with contemporary film, in this documentary which reviews Somoza's rule in Nicaragua and the events leading to the 1979 Sandinista revolution. 30m; VHS, 3/4 U. **Pr:** Maria Jose Alvarez. **A:** Jr. High-Adult. **P:** Education. **U:** Institution, SURA. **Gen-Edu:** Documentary Films, Central America, Women. **Acq:** Purchase, Rent/Lease. **Dist:** Women Make Movies. $250.00.

Bread and Roses 2000 (R) — ★★
Typical Loach political polemic—this time about union organizing of janitors (many of them illegals) in Los Angeles. Maya (Padilla) is an illegal immigrant from Mexico who's working for an office cleaning company. She meets union organizer Sam (Brody) who convinces Maya to join with him, even though she not only risks her job but deportation. Things go from bad to worse for Maya but Loach never takes the easy road and his characters are flawed human beings rather than mere symbols. English and Spanish with subtitles. 106m; VHS, DVD, Wide, CC. **C:** Adrien Brody; Elpidia Carrillo; Pilar Padilla; George Lopez; Jack McGee; Alonso Chavez; Directed by Ken Loach; Written by Paul Laverty; Cinematography by Barry Ackroyd; Music by George Fenton. **Pr:** Rebecca O'Brien; Parallax Pictures; Road Movies; Alta Films SA; Tornasol Films SA; Lions Gate Films. **A:** College-Adult. **P:** Entertainment. **U:** Home. **L:** Spanish. **Mov-Ent:** Labor & Unions, Immigration, Illegal Immigration. **Acq:** Purchase. **Dist:** Alpha Video; Movies Unlimited.

Bread and Roses: The Struggle of Canadian Working Women 1978
Rare Canadian photographs and film footage are used to present the experiences of working women from 1850 to the present. From the "Canadians in Conflict" Series. 35m; VHS, 3/4 U. **Pr:** University of Toronto. **A:** Sr. High-Adult. **P:** Education. **U:** Institution, CCTV. **Bus-Ind:** Documentary Films, Canada, Women. **Acq:** Purchase, Rent/Lease. **Dist:** University of Toronto.

Bread and Roses Too 1980
Brief portraits of three women health care workers are given also examined is the role that labor unions play in their lives. 26m; 3/4 U. **Pr:** John Schultz. **A:** Jr. High-Adult. **P:** Education. **U:** SURA. **Gen-Edu:** Documentary Films, Labor & Unions, Women. **Acq:** Purchase. **Dist:** First Run/Icarus Films.

Bread and Tulips 2001 (PG-13) — ★★★
Sweet Rosalba (Maglietta) is a much-neglected wife and mother who is accidentally left behind at a rest stop while the family is on vacation. Impulsively, Rosalba doesn't go home but hitches a ride to Venice, a city she has always longed to see. Although, she dutifully lets her husband Mimmo (Catania) know where she is, she delays her return, is befriended by waiter Fernando (Ganz), and finds a job working for a florist. Rosalba's idyll doesn't last as her loyalties pull her back to her old life but events don't work out as expected. Italian with subtitles. 105m; VHS, DVD, Wide. **C:** Licia Maglietta; Bruno Ganz; Marina Massironi; Guiseppe Battiston; Antonio Catania; Felice Andreasi; Vitalba Andrea; Directed by Silvio Soldini; Written by Silvio Soldini; Doriana Leondeff; Cinematography by Luca Bigazzi; Music by Giovanni Venosta. **Pr:** Daniele Maggioni; RAI; Monogatari SRL; Instituto Luce; First Look Pictures. **A:** Sr. High-Adult. **P:** Entertainment. **U:** Home. **L:** Italian. **Mov-Ent:** Comedy--Romantic, Family, Marriage. **Acq:** Purchase. **Dist:** Sony Pictures Home Entertainment Inc.

Bread and Wine/Water and Spirit/They Shall See 197?
These three short programs are about the process of making bread and wine, a poetic montage illustrating the beauty of water, and a journey into the world of macroorganisms. 17m; VHS, 3/4 U. **Pr:** Franciscan Communications. **A:** Jr. High-Sr. High. **P:** Religious. **U:** Institution, SURA. **Gen-Edu:** Documentary Films, Religion. **Acq:** Purchase. **Dist:** St. Anthony Messenger Press.

Bread Day 1998
Examines life for isolated senior citizens in a nearly abandoned town north of St. Petersburg, Russia and the chaos that ensues when the train carrying the weekly allotted bread arrives. 55m; VHS. **A:** Sr. High-Adult. **P:** Education. **U:** Home, Institution. **Gen-Edu:** Documentary Films, Sociology, USSR. **Acq:** Purchase, Rent/Lease. **Dist:** First Run/Icarus Films. $390.00.

Bread Dough Folk Art 1980
A look at how you can create folk art made from bread dough for decorations. Part of "Crafts and Decorating" series. 60m; VHS, 3/4 U, Special order formats. **Pr:** Cinema Associates. **A:** Adult. **P:** Instruction. **U:** Institution, CCTV, CATV, BCTV, Home. **How-Ins:** How-To, Crafts. **Acq:** Purchase. **Dist:** RMI Media. $39.95.

Bread: From Wheat to Table 1987
It takes a lot of steps before wheat can be harvested, shipped, and made into something that can be purchased and eaten. 12m; VHS, 3/4 U. **A:** Primary-Jr. High. **P:** Education. **U:** Institution, SURA. **Gen-Edu:** Agriculture, Food Industry. **Acq:** Purchase, Trade-in. **Dist:** Encyclopedia Britannica. $225.00.

Bread, Love and Dreams 1953 (Unrated) — ★★
Middle-aged Antonio (DeSica) is the new police chief in a small village who's looking to make sexy young Maria (Lollobrigida) his wife. But she's in love with one of his subordinates, and another woman (Merlini) is interested in Antonio instead. Followed by "Bread, Love and Jealousy" (1954). Italian with subtitles. 90m/B/W; DVD. **C:** Gina Lollobrigida; Roberto Risso; Vittorio DeSica; Marisa Merlini; Directed by Luigi Comencini; Written by Luigi Comencini; Cinematography by Arturo Gallea; Music by Alessandro Cicognini. **A:** College-Adult. **P:** Entertainment. **U:** Home. **L:** Italian. **Mov-Ent. Acq:** Purchase. **Dist:** Alternative Distribution Alliance.

The Bread, My Sweet 2001 (PG-13) — ★★½
Corporate exec Dominic (Baio) also helps his brothers, Eddie (Mott) and Pinio (Hensley), run a bakery in an old Italian neighborhood in Pittsburgh. Their landlords (and surrogate parents) are old-fashioned immigrants Massimo (Seitz) and Bella (Prinz), who confides to Dominic that she's dying. So Dominic impulsively decides to marry their free-spirited daughter Lucca (Minter), who goes along so her marriage-minded mother can die in peace. Naturally (and unsurprisingly) the cutie twosome develop real feelings for one another. 105m; DVD. **C:** Scott Baio; Kristin Minter; Rosemary Prinz; John Seitz; Billy Mott; Shuler Hensley; Directed by Melissa Martin; Written by Melissa Martin; Cinematography by Mark Knobil; Music by Susan Hartford. **Pr:** William C. Hulley; Adrienne Wehr; Melissa Martin; Buon Sibo; Who Knew Productions; Panorama Entertainment. **A:** Jr. High-Adult. **P:** Entertainment. **U:** Home. **Mov-Ent:** Comedy--Romantic, Food Industry. **Acq:** Purchase. **Dist:** Movies Unlimited; Alpha Video. $26.98.

The Bread We Live By 1982
This program explores the origins of breadmaking and uses micro-and time-lapse photography to show how yeast cultures influence the breadmaking process. 30m; VHS, 3/4 U. **Pr:** University of Toronto. **A:** College-Adult. **P:** Education. **U:** Institution, CCTV. **Gen-Edu:** Documentary Films, Food Industry, Nutrition. **Acq:** Purchase, Rent/Lease. **Dist:** University of Toronto.

Breadboarding Explained 1989
The use of a breadboard to build various simple electrical circuits is demonstrated. Also available on a single tape for the same cost. 14m; VHS. **Pr:** Bergwall Productions. **A:** Sr. High-Adult. **P:** Instruction. **U:** Institution. **How-Ins:** Electricity, Education. **Acq:** Purchase. **Dist:** Bergwall Productions, Inc. $149.00.
Indiv. Titles: 1. Introduction & Ohmmeters 2. Building a Resistor Circuit.

Breading Technique 1984
Demonstrates simple and quick methods for breading products. 10m; VHS. **A:** Adult. **P:** Instruction. **U:** Institution. **Gen-Edu:** Cooking. **Acq:** Purchase. **Dist:** RMI Media. $39.95.

Breadlines to Boomtimes: World War II ????
Three-volume set examines many aspects of World War II including political decisions, military operations, and social changes. 180m; VHS. **A:** Jr. High-Sr. High. **P:** Education. **U:** Institution. **Gen-Edu:** World War Two, Military History. **Acq:** Purchase. **Dist:** Zenger Media. $69.95.

Breadtime Tales 1997
Teaches how bread is made. 30m; VHS. **A:** Primary. **P:** Education. **U:** Home. **Chl-Juv:** Nutrition, Children. **Acq:** Purchase. **Dist:** Karol Media. $12.95.

Breadwinner 1983
When the father he idolizes is laid off from work and unable to find another job, a teenage boy must help his family out financially. The father loses his self respect and lapses into self pity and despair; his son wonders if he himself has the maturity to accept the responsibility he has taken on. 27m; VHS, 3/4 U, Special order formats. **C:** Lance Kerwin; Pat Hingle; Lee Meriwether. **Pr:** Paulist Productions. **A:** Jr. High-Adult. **P:** Religious. **U:** Institution, CCTV, SURA. **Gen-Edu:** Documentary Films, Family, Ethics & Morals. **Acq:** Purchase. **Dist:** Paulist Productions.

The Break 1995 (PG-13) — ★★
Clumsy teen tennis hopeful Ben (Jorgensen) refuses to give up his dreams even after his bookie dad Robbins (Sheen) hires washed-up player Nick Irons (Van Patten) as a coach to show Ben the error of his game. 104m; VHS, DVD. **C:** Vincent Van Patten; Martin Sheen; Ben Jorgensen; Rae Dawn Chong; Valerie Perrine; Betsy Russell; Directed by Lee H. Katzin; Written by Vincent Van Patten; Dan Jenkins. **Pr:** Trimark Pictures. **A:** Jr. High-Adult. **P:** Entertainment. **U:** Home. **Mov-Ent:** Tennis, Sports--Fiction: Drama, Adolescence. **Acq:** Purchase. **Dist:** CinemaNow Inc.

The Break 1997 (R) — ★★½
Disillusioned IRA gunman Dowd (Rea) breaks out of prison and escapes to New York to find a new life. Instead, he befriends (and falls in love with one of) a group of Guatemalan refugees who plan to kill the dictator who persecuted them. Appalled by their inability, he agrees to help them. This is definitely Rea's film (it's based on an idea of his), mainly because his is the only character that's really fleshed out. Character study of a man who's lost whatever passion he had for the cause but can't give up the life doesn't delve into specific Irish or Guatemalan politics, and loses some impact as a result. 97m; VHS. **C:** Stephen Rea; Rosana Pastor; Brendan Gleeson; Pruitt Taylor Vince; Maria Doyle Kennedy; Jorge Sanz; Carolyn Seymour; Sean McGinley; Paul Giamatti; Directed by Alfred Molina; Robert Dornhelm; Written by Ronan Bennett; Cinematography by Andrzej Sekula; Music by John Keane. **Pr:** Channel 4; Castle Hill Productions. **A:** College-Adult. **P:** Entertainment. **U:** Home. **Mov-Ent:** Prison Breaks, Ireland, Politics & Government. **Acq:** Purchase. **Dist:** Not Yet Released.

Break 2009 (Unrated) — ★½
Hitman Frank (Krueger) is hired by crime boss The Man (Everett), who has a terminal illness. Frank's okay with the contract until The Man insists Frank also kill his girlfriend (Thompson) so he won't die alone. Naturally the woman turns out to be Frank's long-lost love. Low-budget and kinda campy with its silly plot, but it does have a fair amount of action. 93m; DVD. **C:** Frank Krueger; Chad Everett; Sarah Thompson; Michael Madsen; David Carradine; Charles Durning; James Russo; Directed by Marc Clebanoff; Written by Marc Clebanoff; Cinematography by Tim Otholt; Music by Peter DiStefano. **A:** Sr. High-Adult. **P:** Entertainment. **U:** Home. **Mov-Ent. Acq:** Purchase. **Dist:** Entertainment One US LP.

Break a Leg 2003 (R) — ★★
Struggling actor Max (John Cassini) has talent but keeps losing roles to bigger names and nepotism. So he decides to literally cripple the competition, only to find out that an undercover cop (Rivera) is taking an interest in the case. 98m; DVD. **C:** John Cassini; Molly Parker; Rene Rivera; Jennifer Beals; Kevin Corrigan; Sandra Oh; Danny Nucci; Eric Roberts; Frank Cassini; Directed by Monika Mitchell; Written by John Cassini; Frank Cassini; Cinematography by Eric Goldstein; Music by Roger Bellon. **A:** Sr. High-Adult. **P:** Entertainment. **U:** Home. **Mov-Ent:** Comedy--Black. **Acq:** Purchase. **Dist:** Bedford Entertainment Inc.

Break and Enter: Rompiendo Puertas 1970 (Unrated)
Hundreds of Puerto Rican and Dominican families reclaimed vacant houses in New York City in 1970, cleaned them up, made repairs and moved in calling it their own. 42m/B/W; VHS, DVD. **A:** Adult. **P:** Education. **U:** Institution. **Gen-Edu:** U.S. States, History. **Acq:** Purchase. **Dist:** Third World Newsreel. $225.

Break-In 2006 (Unrated) — ★½
Marla and Cameron are enjoying their honeymoon at an isolated mansion on the island of San Carlos. Marla is surprised when they are joined by her sister-in-law Joani and her husband Parker. Then everyone is surprised when criminal Val and his two cohorts break into the mansion with Val claiming he is after the 10 million in cash that's in a hidden safe. And there's also a major hurricane about to hit. 90m; DVD. **C:** Kelly Carlson; Eric Winter; Todd Babcock; Tessie Santiago; Marc Kudisch; Mercedes Renard; Xavier Torres; Carlos Ponce; Directed by Michael Nankin; Written by Matt Dorff; Cinematography by Barry Stone. **A:** Sr. High-Adult. **P:** Entertainment. **U:** Home. **Mov-Ent**. **Acq:** Purchase. **Dist:** A&E Television Networks L.L.C.

Break it Down: The Yankee Stadium 2011 (Unrated)
Home to the most successful baseball team of all time, Yankee Stadium stood as a New York City landmark for more than 80 years. When it finally came time to build a new Yankee Stadium, it was obvious that tearing down the old stadium would be a massive project requiring the best demolition firms in the world. This documentary follows crews as they tear down the legendary stadium from the inside out without disturbing or damaging any nearby structures. 45m; DVD. **A:** Family. **P:** Education, Entertainment. **U:** Home, Institution. **Mov-Ent**: Documentary Films, Construction, Sports Documentary. **Acq:** Purchase. **Dist:** $19.95.

Break 90 in 21 Days: Bob Rosburg 1990
Bob Rosburg was better known for covering weekend TV golf for ABC Sports since 1975. He has been a professional on the golf course since 1953. Now he's active on the PGA Senior Tour. Bob shares his techniques for everyone to use. 30m; VHS. **C:** Bob Rosburg. **Pr:** Simitar Entertainment. **A:** Family. **P:** Entertainment. **U:** Home. **Spo-Rec**: Golf. **Acq:** Purchase. **Dist:** Karol Media. $9.95.

Break 90 in 21 Days: Judy Rankin 1990
Judy Rankin was named LPGA Player of the Year in 1976 and 1977. Then in 1984 she became an on-course commentator for the golf broadcasting team of ABC Sports. In this video she gives tips and shares techniques that have helped her get to where she is today. 30m; VHS. **C:** Judy Rankin. **Pr:** Simitar Entertainment. **A:** Family. **P:** Entertainment. **U:** Home. **Spo-Rec**: Golf. **Acq:** Purchase. **Dist:** Karol Media. $9.95.

Break of Dawn 1988 (Unrated) — ★★½
Pedro J. Gonzalez (Chavez) is a veteran of Pancho Villa's army who takes his family and crosses into the U.S. Despite the Depression, he finds work at a radio station in L.A. and soon becomes a popular personality in the Latino community. But Gonzalez never leaves politics very far behind and his radical civil rights views lead to a political witchhunt that sends him to prison. 105m; VHS, DVD. **C:** Oscar Chavez; Maria Rojo; Tony Plana; Peter Henry Schroeder; Pepe Serna; Kamala Lopez-Dawson; Directed by Isaac Artenstein; Written by Isaac Artenstein; Cinematography by Stephen Lighthill; Music by Mark Adler. **A:** Sr. High-Adult. **P:** Entertainment. **U:** Home. **Mov-Ent**: Politics & Government, Immigration. **Acq:** Purchase. **Dist:** Vanguard International Cinema, Inc.

Break of Hearts 1935 (Unrated) — ★★½
Hepburn marries Boyer, who becomes an alcoholic, and then more troubles arise. Very soapy, but well-made. 78m/B/W; VHS, DVD. **C:** Katharine Hepburn; Charles Boyer; Jean Hersholt; John Beal; Sam Hardy; Directed by Philip Moeller; Written by Victor Heerman; Music by Max Steiner. **Pr:** Pandro S. Berman; RKO. **A:** Family. **P:** Entertainment. **U:** Home. **Mov-Ent**: Alcoholism. **Acq:** Purchase. **Dist:** WarnerArchive.com. $19.98.

The Break Up 1998 (R) — ★★½
Predictable thriller finds Jimmy Dade (Fonda) awakening in the hospital to discover her abusive husband (Bochner) is dead and she is the prime suspect. 101m; VHS, DVD. **C:** Bridget Fonda; Kiefer Sutherland; Penelope Ann Miller; Steven Weber; Hart Bochner; Tippi Hedren; Directed by Paul Marcus; Written by Anne Amanda Opotowsky. **Pr:** Nu Image Films. **A:** Sr. High-Adult. **P:** Entertainment. **U:** Home. **Mov-Ent**: Mystery & Suspense, Domestic Abuse. **Acq:** Purchase. **Dist:** Buena Vista Home Entertainment.

The Break-Up 2006 (PG-13) — ★★
Gary (Vaughn) and Brooke (Aniston) are a completely incompatible couple (he's boorish, she's high-strung) who own a Chicago condo that comes into bitter dispute when they split. Since neither will willingly leave, they seek to drive the other crazy enough so they'll bail...as everyone else must watch and suffer. There's not much romance or comedy to be seen and it's definitely NOT a date movie—unless you're planning a break-up of your own. 106m; DVD, Blu-Ray, HD-DVD, Wide. **C:** Jennifer Aniston; Vince Vaughn; Joey Lauren Adams; Judy Davis; Cole Hauser; Jon Favreau; Ann-Margret; Justin Long; Vincent D'Onofrio; Jason Bateman; Peter Billingsley; John Michael Higgins; Ivan Sergei; Directed by Peyton Reed; Written by Jeremy Garelick; Jay Lavender; Cinematography by Eric Alan Edwards; Music by Jon Brion. **Pr:** Vince Vaughn; Scott Stuber; Vince Vaughn; Wild West Productions; Universal Pictures. **A:** Jr. High-Adult. **P:** Entertainment. **U:** Home. **L:** English. **Mov-Ent**: Comedy--Romantic, Comedy--Screwball, Baseball. **Acq:** Purchase. **Dist:** Movies Unlimited; Alpha Video.

The Break with Tradition 19??
Teaching aid for art appreciation explores and analyzes Impressionism. Includes a teacher's guide. 20m; VHS. **A:** Jr. High-College. **P:** Education. **U:** Institution. **Gen-Edu**: Art & Artists. **Acq:** Purchase. **Dist:** Crystal Productions. $69.00.

Breakaway 1995 (R) — ★
Myra (Thompson) decides to get away from her drop-woman job with $300,000 of mob money. Naturally, she's pursued by a hit man (Estevez) and then betrayed by a boyfriend (De Rose), who steals the cash and hides it in the apartment of the other woman he's seeing (Harding). Thompson does fine but to describe Harding's debut performance as wooden is to be very, very kind. 94m; VHS. **C:** Teri Thompson; Joe Estevez; Chris De Rose; Tonya Harding; Tony Noakes; Rick Beatty; Michael Garganese; Directed by Sean Dash; Written by Sean Dash; Eric Gardner; Cinematography by Carlos Montaner; Music by Robert Wait. **A:** Sr. High-Adult. **P:** Entertainment. **U:** Home. **Mov-Ent**. **Acq:** Purchase. **Dist:** Not Yet Released.

Breakaway 2002 (R) — ★½
Poorly made rip-off of the "Die Hard" series. Set in a mall at Christmas, Cornelius Morgan (Cain)?suspended by the force—swings by to get his wife (Eleniak) but a robbery/hostage situation unfolds. Strictly for those in need of a holiday explosion fix. 91m; DVD. **C:** Dean Cain; Erika Eleniak; Richard Yearwood; Roman Podhora; Bernard Browne; Santino Buda; Aleks Punovic; Angelo Tsarouchas; Eric Roberts; Jack Wallace; Christopher Benson; Larry Mannell; Rothaford Gray; Jessica Smith; Brooke Palsson; Trevor Toffan; Corinne Conley; Vicki Marentette; Patricia Harras; Ed Sutton; Ernesto Griffith; David (Dave) Brown; Tommy Chang; Vince Crestejo; Directed by Charles Robert Carner; Written by Charles Robert Carner; Cinematography by Michael Goi; Music by Louis Febre. **A:** Sr. High-Adult. **P:** Entertainment. **U:** Home. **L:** English, Korean, Polish, Spanish. **Mov-Ent**: Christmas. **Acq:** Purchase. **Dist:** Sony Pictures Home Entertainment Inc. $14.94.

Breakdown 1953 (Unrated) — ★
A boxer is set up by his girlfriend's father to take the rap for a murder. Lackluster effort. 76m/B/W; VHS, DVD. **C:** Ann Richards; William Bishop; Anne Gwynne; Sheldon Leonard; Wally Cassell; Richard Benedict; Directed by Edmond Angelo. **Pr:** Realart. **A:** Jr. High-Adult. **P:** Entertainment. **U:** Home. **Mov-Ent**: Boxing. **Acq:** Purchase. **Dist:** Sinister Cinema. $16.95.

Breakdown 1989
A family's lunch is followed all the way through the digestive system. 26m; VHS, 3/4 U. **Pr:** Films for the Humanities. **A:** Jr. High-Adult. **P:** Education. **U:** Institution, SURA. **Hea-Sci**: Digestive System. **Acq:** Purchase, Rent/Lease. **Dist:** Films for the Humanities & Sciences. $149.00.

Breakdown 1994
Documentary, set in suburban London, presents five individuals suffering psychiatric crises and subsequent intervention by a three-member professional team. 55m; VHS. **A:** Adult. **P:** Education. **U:** Institution. **Hea-Sci**: Mental Health. **Acq:** Purchase, Rent/Lease. **Dist:** Filmakers Library Inc. $395.00.

Breakdown 1996 (R) — ★★★
Jeff (Russell) and Amy (Quinlan) are high-falootin' Easterners on their way to San Diego when their car breaks down somewhere in the vast Southwest. When a trucker (Walsh) stops and offers to take Amy to the next stop while Jeff guards their yuppie treasure trove, they accept willingly. Inconvenience soon turns to terror when Jeff gets the car started, drives to meet his wife and finds her nowhere in sight. Spotting the truck by the side of the road, he confronts the trucker with the cops only to have him deny ever having seen them before. Thus begins the frantic hunt. Russell's descent from dismay to panic to resolve is grippingly played. You may know where it's going, but the fun is in getting there. 93m; VHS, DVD, Wide. **C:** Kurt Russell; Kathleen Quinlan; J.T. Walsh; M.C. Gainey; Jack Noseworthy; Rex Linn; Ritch Brinkley; Kim Robillard; Directed by Jonathan Mostow; Written by Jonathan Mostow; Cinematography by Doug Milsome; Music by Basil Poledouris. **Pr:** Martha De Laurentiis; Dino De Laurentiis; Jonathan Fernandez; Harry Colomby; Spelling Films International; Paramount Pictures. **A:** Sr. High-Adult. **P:** Entertainment. **U:** Home. **Mov-Ent**: Action-Adventure, Mystery & Suspense. **Acq:** Purchase. **Dist:** Paramount Pictures Corp.

Breakdown Diodes 1979
Zener and avalanche diodes are compared to conventional P-N diodes in terms of temperature coefficient of voltage. A discussion on the use of various types of diodes follows. Part of the "Practical Transistors" series. 37m; VHS, 3/4 U. **C:** George Stanley, Jr. **Pr:** Hewlett Packard. **A:** College-Adult. **P:** Professional. **U:** Institution, CCTV, Home. **Bus-Ind**: Documentary Films, Electronics. **Acq:** Purchase. **Dist:** Hewlett-Packard Media Solutions.

Breakdown Drills for Swing Offense 2013 (Unrated)
Basketball Coach Ryan Looney presents various drills for training teams using the swing offense. 61m; DVD. **A:** Family. **P:** Education. **U:** Home. **L:** English. **Spo-Rec**: Athletic Instruction/Coaching, Basketball. **Acq:** Purchase. **Dist:** Championship Productions. $39.99.

Breakdown Drills for the High/Low Motion Offense 2002 (Unrated)
Coach Bill Self gives a live demonstration of drills designed to help basketball players implement the High/Low Motion Offense. 50m; DVD. **A:** Family. **P:** Education. **U:** Home, Institution. **Spo-Rec**: Basketball, Athletic Instruction/Coaching. **Acq:** Purchase. **Dist:** Championship Productions. $39.99.

Breaker! Breaker! 1977 (PG) — ★
Convoy of angry truck drivers launch an assault on the corrupt and sadistic locals of a small Texas town. Goofy entry in "mad or sex-crazed trucker armed with a CB radio" genre. 86m; VHS, DVD, Wide. **C:** Chuck Norris; George Murdock; Terry O'Connor; Don Gentry; Jack Nance; Directed by Don Hulette; Written by Terry Chambers; Cinematography by Mario DiLeo; Music by Don Hulette. **Pr:** American International Pictures. **A:** Sr. High-Adult. **P:** Entertainment. **U:** Home. **Mov-Ent**: Martial Arts. **Acq:** Purchase. **Dist:** Movies Unlimited. $49.99.

Breaker Morant 1980 (PG) — ★★★½
In 1901 South Africa, three Australian soldiers are put on trial for avenging the murder of several prisoners. Based on a true story which was then turned into a play by Kenneth Ross, this riveting, popular antiwar statement and courtroom drama heralded Australia's film renaissance. Rich performances by Woodward and Waters. 107m; VHS, DVD, Blu-Ray. **C:** Edward Woodward; Jack Thompson; John Waters; Bryan Brown; Charles "Bud" Tingwell; Terence Donovan; Vincent Ball; Ray Meagher; Chris Haywood; Lewis Fitz-Gerald; Rod Mullinar; Alan Cassell; Rob Steele; Directed by Bruce Beresford; Written by Bruce Beresford; Jonathan Hardy; David Stevens; Cinematography by Donald McAlpine; Music by Phil Cunneen. **Pr:** Matt Carroll; South Australian Film Corporation. **A:** Jr. High-Adult. **P:** Entertainment. **U:** Home. **Mov-Ent**. **Awds:** Australian Film Inst. '80: Actor (Thompson), Film. **Acq:** Purchase. **Dist:** Wellspring Media.

Breakfast, Accompaniments, and Desserts 199?
Teaches the food service employee or kitchen staff to create healthy yet delicious breakfasts, accompaniments and desserts. Part of the Techniques of Healthy Cooking Video Series. 48m; VHS. **A:** Sr. High-Adult. **P:** Instruction. **U:** Home. **How-Ins**: Cooking, Food Industry, How-To. **Acq:** Purchase. **Dist:** Culinary Institute of America. $75.00.

Breakfast at Tiffany's 1961 — ★★★½
Truman Capote's amusing story of an endearingly eccentric New York City playgirl and her shaky romance with a young writer. Hepburn lends Holly Golightly just the right combination of naivete and worldly wisdom with a dash of melancholy. A wonderfully offbeat romance. 114m; VHS, DVD, Blu-Ray, 8 mm. **C:** Audrey Hepburn; George Peppard; Patricia Neal; Buddy Ebsen; Mickey Rooney; Martin Balsam; John McGiver; Directed by Blake Edwards; Written by George Axelrod; Cinematography by Franz Planer; Music by Henry Mancini. **Pr:** Paramount Pictures. **A:** Family. **P:** Entertainment. **U:** Home. **Mov-Ent**: Comedy--Romantic. **Awds:** Oscars '61: Orig. Dramatic Score, Song ("Moon River"); Natl. Film Reg. '12. **Acq:** Purchase. **Dist:** Paramount Pictures Corp.; Facets Multimedia Inc. $14.95. **Songs:** Moon River.

The Breakfast Club 1985 (R) — ★★★
Five students from different cliques at a Chicago suburban high school spend a day together in detention. Rather well done teenage culture study; these characters delve a little deeper than the standard adult view of adolescent stereotypes. One of John Hughes' best movies. Soundtrack features Simple Minds and Wang Chung. 97m; VHS, DVD, Blu-Ray, HD-DVD, CC. **C:** Ally Sheedy; Molly Ringwald; Judd Nelson; Emilio Estevez; Anthony Michael Hall; Paul Gleason; John Kapelos; Directed by John Hughes; Written by John Hughes; Cinematography by Thomas Del Ruth; Music by Gary Chang; Keith Forsey. **Pr:** Mark Huffam; A&M Films. **A:** Sr. High-Adult. **P:** Entertainment. **U:** Home. **Mov-Ent**: Comedy-Drama, Adolescence. **Acq:** Purchase. **Dist:** Facets Multimedia Inc. $19.95.

Breakfast for Two 1937 (Unrated) — ★★½
Snappy screwball comedy finds Texas heiress Valentine (Stanwyck) trying to get playboy Jonathan (Marshall) to take some responsibility for his failing steamship line. Valentine buys a controlling interest in the company to teach him a lesson, which only results in Jonathan deciding to marry his golddigger fiancee Carol (Farrell) when you just know who really suits him. Well, Butch (Blore) the valet is also smarter than his employer and that shipboard wedding runs into some problems. 68m/B/W; DVD. **C:** Barbara Stanwyck; Herbert Marshall; Glenda Farrell; Eric Blore; Etienne Girardot; Frank M. Thomas, Sr.; Donald Meek; Directed by Alfred Santell; Written by Paul Yawitz; Charles Kaufman; Viola Brothers Shore; Cinematography by J. Roy Hunt; Music by George Hively. **A:** Jr. High-Adult. **P:** Entertainment. **U:** Home. **Mov-Ent**: Comedy--Screwball, Boating. **Acq:** Purchase. **Dist:** WarnerArchive.com.

Breakfast in Hollywood 1946 (Unrated) — ★½
Movie about the popular morning radio show of the 1940s hosted by Tom Breneman, a coast-to-coast coffee klatch. 93m/B/W; VHS, DVD. **C:** Tom Breneman; Bonita Granville; Eddie Ryan; Beulah Bondi; Billie Burke; Zasu Pitts; Hedda Hopper; Spike Jones; Directed by Harold Schuster. **Pr:** United Artists. **A:** Sr. High-Adult. **P:** Entertainment. **U:** Home. **Mov-Ent**. **Acq:** Purchase. **Dist:** Critics' Choice Video & DVD. $29.95.

Breakfast in Paris 1981 (Unrated) — ★½
Two American professionals in Paris, both crushed from past failures in the love department, find each other. 85m; VHS. **C:** Rod Mullinar; Barbara Parkins; Jack Lenoir; Directed by John Lamond. **Pr:** John D. Lamond. **A:** Jr. High-Adult. **P:** Entertainment. **U:** Home. **Mov-Ent**: Drama. **Acq:** Purchase. **Dist:** Unknown Distributor.

Breakfast, Lunch and Dinner 1991
Part one of the 10-part Seahouse (Series I) series. Illustrates the food chain among the creatures in the ocean. 5m; VHS. **A:** Primary. **P:** Education. **U:** Institution. **Chl-Juv**: Science, Animals. **Acq:** Purchase. **Dist:** Rainbow Educational Media, Inc. $29.95.

Breakfast of Champions 1998 (R) — ★½
Messy adaptation of Kurt Vonnegut's 1973 satire on American greed and commercialism. Relentlessly upbeat salesman Dwayne Hoover (Willis) runs the most successful car dealership in middle America's Midland City. A leading citizen, who stars in his own garish TV commercials, Dwayne has alienated his tube-addicted wife, Celia (Hershey), and his aspiring lounge singer son, Bunny (Haas). Dwayne also thinks he's going nuts and his one hope for salvation lies with Kilgore Trout (Finney), an eccentric hack sci fi writer/philosopher. Oh yeah, and Nolte is around as Dwayne's sales manager Harry, who likes to wear

women's lacy lingerie beneath his suits. 110m; VHS, DVD, Wide, CC. **C:** Bruce Willis; Albert Finney; Nick Nolte; Barbara Hershey; Glenne Headly; Lukas Haas; Omar Epps; Buck Henry; Vicki Lewis; Ken H. Campbell; Will Patton; Chip Zien; Owen Wilson; Alison Eastwood; Shawnee Smith; Kurt Vonnegut, Jr.; Directed by Alan Rudolph; Written by Alan Rudolph; Cinematography by Elliot Davis; Music by Mark Isham. **Pr:** David Blocker; Buena Vista. **A:** Sr. High-Adult. **P:** Entertainment. **U:** Home. **Mov-Ent:** Satire & Parody, Family. **Acq:** Purchase. **Dist:** Buena Vista Home Entertainment.

Breakfast on Pluto 2005 (R) — ★★
Jordan's picaresque tale is divided into a series of chapters and adventures as foundling Patrick Braden (Murphy) leaves his insular Irish community to search for his mother in 1970s London. One thing Patrick is sure of--he prefers to be called Kitten and dress like a girl. Kitten gets involved with a series of men and circumstances (including, unwittingly, with the IRA) while living life with a certain cheeky charm. Adapted from the Pat McCabe novel. 135m; DVD. **C:** Cillian Murphy; Liam Neeson; Stephen Rea; Brendan Gleeson; Eva Birthistle; Liam Cunningham; Bryan Ferry; Gavin Friday; Ian Hart; Laurence Kinlan; Ruth McCabe; Steven Waddington; Ruth Negga; Conor McEvoy; Seamus Reilly; Sid Young; Directed by Neil Jordan; Written by Neil Jordan; Patrick McCabe; Cinematography by Declan Quinn. **Pr:** Neil Jordan; Alan Moloney; Neil Jordan; Stephen Wooley; Pathe Pictures; Bord Scannan na hEireann; Parallel Films; Number 9 Films; Sony Pictures Classics. **A:** Sr. High-Adult. **P:** Entertainment. **U:** Home. **L:** English. **Mov-Ent:** Comedy-Drama, Ireland, Adoption. **Acq:** Purchase. **Dist:** Sony Pictures Home Entertainment Inc.

Breakfast With Scot 2007 (PG-13) — ★½
Bland family drama that goes out of its way to avoid controversy and becomes dull instead. Ex-Maple Leafs hockey player-turned-broadcaster Eric (Cavanagh) lives with partner Sam (Shenkman), whose irresponsible brother has just dumped his 11-year-old son Scot (Bernett) with them. The flamboyantly effeminate youngster is a shocker to the conservative duo with Eric wanting to butch the boy up by teaching him to play hockey. Guess what Eric learns instead. 95m; DVD. **C:** Tom Cavanagh; Ben Shenkman; Noah Bernett; Graham Greene; Fiona Reid; Colin Cunningham; Megan Follows; Dylan Everett; Directed by Laurie Lynd; Written by Sean Reycraft; Cinematography by David Mankin; Music by Robert Carli. **A:** Jr. High-Adult. **P:** Entertainment. **U:** Home. **Mov-Ent:** Parenting, Hockey. **Acq:** Purchase. **Dist:** Wolfe Video.

Breakheart Pass 1976 (PG) — ★★
A governor, his female companion, a band of cavalrymen, and a mysterious man travel on a train through the mountains of Idaho in 1870. The mystery man turns out to be a murderer. Based on a novel by Alistair MacLean. 92m; VHS, DVD, Wide, CC. **C:** Charles Bronson; Ben Johnson; Richard Crenna; Jill Ireland; Charles Durning; Ed Lauter; Archie Moore; Sally Kirkland; Directed by Tom Gries; Written by Alistair MacLean; Cinematography by Lucien Ballard; Music by Jerry Goldsmith. **Pr:** United Artists. **A:** Jr. High-Adult. **P:** Entertainment. **U:** Home. **Mov-Ent:** Western, Mystery & Suspense, Trains. **Acq:** Purchase. **Dist:** MGM Home Entertainment. $19.98.

Breakin' 1984 (PG) — ★★
Dance phenomenon break dancing along with the hit songs that accompanied the fad. 87m; VHS, DVD. **C:** Lucinda Dickey; Adolfo "Shabba Doo" Quinones; Michael "Boogaloo Shrimp" Chambers; Ben Lokey; Christopher McDonald; Phineas Newborn, III; Directed by Joel Silberg; Written by Allen N. DeBevoise; Cinematography by Hanania Baer; Music by Michael Boyd. **Pr:** Allen DeBevoise; David Zito; Golan-Globus Productions; Cannon Films. **A:** Family. **P:** Entertainment. **U:** Home. **Mov-Ent:** Musical, Dance. **Acq:** Purchase. **Dist:** MGM Home Entertainment. $79.95.
Songs: Tibetan Jam; Heart of the Beat; Breakin...There's No Stopping Us; Street People; Showdown; 99 1/2.

Breakin' 2: Electric Boogaloo 1984 (PG) — ★
Breakdancers hold a benefit concert to preserve an urban community center. 94m; VHS, DVD. **C:** Lucinda Dickey; Adolfo "Shabba Doo" Quinones; Michael "Boogaloo Shrimp" Chambers; Susie Bono; Directed by Sam Firstenberg; Cinematography by Hanania Baer. **Pr:** Cannon Films; Tri-Star Pictures. **A:** Preschool. **P:** Entertainment. **U:** Home. **Mov-Ent:** Musical, Dance. **Acq:** Purchase. **Dist:** MGM Home Entertainment. $79.95.
Songs: Electric Boogaloo; Radiotron; Action; When I.C.U..

Breakin' All The Rules 2004 (PG-13) — ★★½
Predictable romantic comedy stars Foxx as L.A. men's magazine exec Quincy Watson, who gets dumped by his fiancee Helen (Lawson) the same day his timid boss Phillip (MacNicol) wants Quincy to lay off 15% of the mag's staff. Instead, Quincy axes himself and takes his frustrations and rejections out on paper, writing what turns out to be the best-selling "Breakup Handbook." Suddenly, Quincy is Mr. Advice for Phillip, who wants to know how to avoid the gold-digging Rita (Esposito), and Quincy's playa cousin Evan (Chestnut),who wants to dump his girlfriend Nicky (Union) before she dumps him. Complications ensue when Quincy unwittingly falls for Nicky and Rita goes after Evan thinking he's Quincy. It's contrived but well done, with Foxx smirking likeably and Union lovely as always. 85m; VHS, DVD. **C:** Jamie Foxx; Gabrielle Beauvais; Morris Chestnut; Peter MacNichol; Jennifer Esposito; Bianca Lawson; Jill Ritchie; Cameo(s) Heather Headley; Directed by Daniel Taplitz; Written by Daniel Taplitz; Cinematography by David Hennings; Music by Marcus Miller. **Pr:** Lisa Tornell; Screen Gems; Sony Pictures Entertainment. **A:** Jr. High-Adult. **P:** Entertainment. **U:** Home. **Mov-Ent:** Comedy--Romantic. **Acq:** Purchase. **Dist:** Sony Pictures Home Entertainment Inc. $14.95.

Breakin' In: The Making of a Hip-Hop Dancer 2005 (Unrated)
Three young women compete for roles in music videos and examine how the pursuit of fame in this forum has shaped their concepts of beauty and self-image. 45m; VHS, DVD. **A:** Adult. **P:** Education. **U:** Institution. **Gen-Edu:** Identity, Women, Music Video. **Acq:** Purchase. **Dist:** Third World Newsreel. $175.

Breakin' It Down with Laurie Ann Gibson 2005
Star of MTV's "Making the Band" teaches music video-style dance moves, starting with basic steps and culminating in tips on how to use what's been learned in a club setting. 94m; DVD. **A:** Adult. **P:** Instruction. **U:** Home. **How-Ins:** Dance--Instruction. **Acq:** Purchase. **Dist:** Collage Video Specialties, Inc.

Breakin' Metal 1985
A compilation of budding metal group performances including those of Rock Goddess, Wrathchild, and Sledgehammer. Recorded at the Camden Palace Theater and the Marquee Club in London. Features tunes such as "Let the Blood Run Red" and "Road Rat." 59m; VHS. **Pr:** Trilion PLC. **A:** Family. **P:** Entertainment. **U:** Home. **Mov-Ent:** Music--Performance. **Acq:** Purchase. **Dist:** Music Video Distributors. $19.95.

Breakin' Metal Special 1986
The follow-up tape to Breakin' Metal. The second collaboration of heavy metal artists including Venom, Warlock, Uriah Heep, and Lee Aaron. 51m; VHS. **Pr:** Sony Video. **A:** Family. **P:** Entertainment. **U:** Home. **Mov-Ent:** Music--Performance, Music--Pop/Rock. **Acq:** Purchase. **Dist:** Music Video Distributors.

Breakin' Through 1984 (Unrated) — ★
The choreographer of a troubled Broadway-bound musical decides to energize his shows with a troupe of street dancers. 73m; VHS. **C:** Ben Vereen; Donna McKechnie; Reid Shelton; Directed by Peter Medak. **Pr:** Walt Disney Studios. **A:** Family. **P:** Entertainment. **U:** Home. **Mov-Ent:** Musical, Dance, Family Viewing. **Acq:** Purchase. **Dist:** Walt Disney Studios Home Entertainment. $69.95.

Breaking All the Rules 1985 (R) — ★½
Comedy about two teenage lovers who find themselves embroiled in a slapdash jewel robbery at an amusement park during the last day of summer break. 91m; VHS. **C:** Carolyn Dunn; Carl Marotte; Thor Bishopric; Rachel Hayward; Directed by James Orr; Written by James Orr; Jim Cruickshank. **Pr:** New World Pictures. **A:** Sr. High-Adult. **P:** Entertainment. **U:** Home. **Mov-Ent:** Mystery & Suspense, Adolescence, Canada. **Acq:** Purchase. **Dist:** Anchor Bay Entertainment. $14.95.

Breaking and Entering 2006 (R) — ★★
Landscape architect Will (Law) and his partner Sandy (Freeman) are pioneers in the urban renewal of the crime-ridden King's Cross area in North London. However, after their office is repeatedly broken into, Will finally manages to chase the young thief long enough to discover where he lives. The thief, Miro (Gavron), is a teenaged Bosnian refugee, living with his widowed seamstress mother, Amira (Binoche). Instead of immediately ratting Miro out, Will cozies up to his attractive mum since his own home life is lacking (Wright Penn plays his depressive live-in). Law's character is a polite cipher and the dicey situations resolve themselves a little too neatly in Minghella's slice of life drama. 116m; DVD. **C:** Jude Law; Juliette Binoche; Robin Wright; Martin Freeman; Ray Winstone; Vera Farmiga; Juliet Stevenson; Rafi Gavron; Poppy Rogers; Directed by Anthony Minghella; Written by Anthony Minghella; Cinematography by Benoit Delhomme; Music by Gabriel Yared. **Pr:** Anthony Minghella; Sydney Pollack; Anthony Minghella; Timothy Bricknell; Mirage Enterprises; Miramax Film Corp; MGM. **A:** Sr. High-Adult. **P:** Entertainment. **U:** Home. **L:** English. **Mov-Ent:** Immigration, Drama. **Acq:** Purchase. **Dist:** Weinstein Company L.L.C.

Breaking Away 1979 (PG) — ★★★½
A lighthearted coming-of-age drama about a high school graduate's addiction to bicycle racing, whose dreams are tested against the realities of a crucial race. An honest, open look at present Americana with tremendous insight into the minds of average youth; shot on location at Indiana University. Great bike-racing photography. Quaid, Barrie, and Christopher give exceptional performances. Basis for a TV series. 100m; VHS, DVD, Wide, CC. **C:** Dennis Christopher; Dennis Quaid; Daniel Stern; Jackie Earle Haley; Barbara Barrie; Paul Dooley; Amy Wright; Directed by Peter Yates; Written by Steve Tesich; Cinematography by Matthew F. Leonetti; Music by Patrick Williams. **Pr:** 20th Century-Fox. **A:** Family. **P:** Entertainment. **U:** Home. **Mov-Ent:** Comedy-Drama, Bicycling, Adolescence. **Awds:** Oscars '79: Orig. Screenplay; Golden Globes '80: Film--Mus./Comedy; Natl. Bd. of Review '79: Support. Actor (Dooley); N.Y. Film Critics '79: Screenplay; Natl. Soc. Film Critics '79: Film, Screenplay; Writers Guild '79: Orig. Screenplay. **Acq:** Purchase. **Dist:** Home Vision Cinema. $59.98.

Breaking Bad: The Complete First Season 2008 (Unrated)
Walter White (Bryan Cranston) is a chemistry teacher who is short on cash and diagnosed with an inoperable lung cancer. With nothing to live for but his wife, Skyler, son Walter Jr. (who has cerebral palsy), and their daughter on the way, he turns to a life of crime (opening a meth lab) to make his last two years alive financially productive and psychologically freeing. 7 episodes. 346m; DVD. **A:** Sr. High-Adult. **P:** Entertainment. **U:** Home. **Mov-Ent:** Drama, Comedy--Black, Television Series. **Acq:** Purchase. **Dist:** Sony Pictures Home Entertainment Inc. $29.95.

Breaking Bad: The Complete Fourth Season 2011 (Unrated)
AMC television series. In "Open House," Skyler tricks a car wash owner into selling her the business on the cheap, while Jesse struggles with his shady deeds and throws all-night, drug-fueled parties. In "Hermanos," Hank tries to track Gus while Jesse and Walt talk of poisoning Gus. In "End Times," Jesse threatens Walt and accuses him of being behind the poisoning of Brock. 13 episodes. 610m; DVD, Blu-Ray. **C:** Bryan Cranston; Aaron Paul; Anna Gunn; Dean Norris. **A:** Sr. High-Adult. **P:** Entertainment. **U:** Home. **Mov-Ent:** Drama, Comedy--Black, Television Series. **Acq:** Purchase. **Dist:** Sony Pictures Home Entertainment Inc. $14.99.

Breaking Bad: The Complete Second Season 2009 (Unrated)
AMC television series. In "Seven Thirty-Seven," Walt and Jesse realize they may be in over their heads in their dealings with Tuco, who's crazier than they imagined. Skyler is fed of with Walt's behavior and becomes suspicious in "Down," wanting to know what's really going on. In "Phoenix," Walt makes the drug delivery on time, but misses his daughter's birth; meanwhile Jane's father discovers Jesse and Jane's addiction. 13 episodes. 615m; DVD, Blu-Ray. **C:** Bryan Cranston; Aaron Paul; Anna Gunn; Dean Norris. **A:** Sr. High-Adult. **P:** Entertainment. **U:** Home. **Mov-Ent:** Drama, Comedy--Black, Television Series. **Acq:** Purchase. **Dist:** Sony Pictures Home Entertainment Inc.

Breaking Bad: The Complete Third Season 2010 (Unrated)
AMC television series. In "No Mas," Skyler plans to divorce Walt, Jesse goes to rehab, and Walt tries to make a break from the business but gets an offer he can't refuse. In "Kafkaesque," Walt and Jesse are in full production in the new lab and Skyler proposes that she and Walt cover Hank's medical bills. In "Half Measures," Jesse and Walt confront rival dealers, Walt struggles to maintain his role at home, and Hank is reluctant to leave the hospital even though his doctors say he is ready. 13 episodes. 613m; DVD, Blu-Ray. **C:** Bryan Cranston; Aaron Paul; Anna Gunn; Dean Norris. **P:** Entertainment. **U:** Home. **Mov-Ent:** Drama, Comedy--Black, Television Series. **Acq:** Purchase. **Dist:** Sony Pictures Home Entertainment Inc. $17.78.

Breaking Bread 2000
When the father of a North Korean immigrant family living in New York becomes ill he invites an Iranian friend to come and prepare a final meal for he and his family. An exploration of different cultures through an ordinary life. 54m; VHS. **A:** Adult. **P:** Education. **U:** Institution, BCTV. **Gen-Edu:** Documentary Films, Ethnicity, Family. **Acq:** Purchase, Rent/Lease. **Dist:** Arab Film Distribution. $195.00.

Breaking Free 1995 (PG) — ★★½
Teenaged loser Rick Chilton (London) forms an unlikely friendship with bitter gymnast Lindsay (Phillips) who's been blinded and forced to give up her dreams. Mostly avoids the stickiness inherent in such stories thanks to some fine performances. 106m; VHS. **C:** Jeremy London; Gina Philips; Christine Taylor; Megan Gallagher; Nicolas Surovy; Adam Wylie; Brian Krause; Scott Coffey; Directed by David Mackay; Cinematography by Christopher Faloona; Music by Steve Dorff. **Pr:** Leucadia Film Corporation. **A:** Primary-Adult. **P:** Entertainment. **U:** Home. **Mov-Ent:** Blindness, Sports--Fiction: Drama, Gymnastics. **Acq:** Purchase. **Dist:** WarnerVision.

Breaking Free of the Earth: Kazimir Malevich 1878-1935 1991
Revolutionary artist Kazimir Malevich never received approval from the Soviet government during his lifetime. Due to political change, his work has recently been unveiled. This program is a look at the life and work of Kazimir Malevich. 52m; VHS. **Pr:** RM Arts. **A:** Jr. High-Adult. **P:** Education. **U:** Home. **Gen-Edu:** Art & Artists, Biography. **Acq:** Purchase. **Dist:** Home Vision Cinema; Facets Multimedia Inc. $39.95.

Breaking Glass 1980 (PG) — ★★½
A "New Wave" musical that gives an insight into the punk record business and at the same time tells of the rags-to-riches life of a punk rock star. 94m; VHS, DVD, Blu-Ray. **C:** Hazel O'Connor; Phil Daniels; Jon Finch; Jonathan Pryce; Directed by Brian Gibson. **Pr:** Paramount Pictures. **A:** Sr. High-Adult. **P:** Entertainment. **U:** Home. **Mov-Ent:** Musical. **Acq:** Purchase. **Dist:** Paramount Pictures Corp. $49.95.

Breaking Ground: Men Against Rape 1999
Documentary of men who train men and women in rape prevention techniques. Features men who are active in the field and the women victims. 25m; VHS. **A:** Adult. **P:** Education. **U:** Home. **Gen-Edu:** Documentary Films, Rape, Men. **Acq:** Purchase, Rent/Lease. **Dist:** Filmakers Library Inc. $225.

Breaking Home Ties 1987 (Unrated) — ★★½
Norman Rockwell's illustration is the basis for this coming-of-age story set in a small Texas town. A young man is eager to be off to college and lessen his family ties but his mother's serious illness may prevent both. Good performances help overcome the sentimentality. 95m; VHS. **C:** Jason Robards, Jr.; Eva Marie Saint; Doug McKeon; Claire Trevor; Erin Gray; Directed by John Wilder; Written by John Wilder. **A:** Jr. High-Adult. **P:** Entertainment. **U:** Home. **Mov-Ent:** Family, TV Movies. **Acq:** Purchase. **Dist:** Movies Unlimited. $14.99.

Breaking In 1989 (R) — ★★★
A semi-acclaimed comedy about a professional thief who takes a young amateur under his wing and shows him the ropes. Under-estimated Reynolds is especially charming. Witty and innovative script, with intelligent direction from Forsyth. 95m; VHS, DVD, Wide, CC; Open Captioned. **C:** Burt Reynolds; Casey Siemaszko; Sheila Kelley; Lorraine Toussaint; Albert

Salmi; Harry Carey, Jr.; Maury Chaykin; Stephen Tobolowsky; David Frishberg; Directed by Bill Forsyth; Written by John Sayles; Cinematography by Michael Coulter; Music by Michael Gibbs. **Pr:** Samuel Goldwyn Company; Act III Productions. **A:** Sr. High-Adult. **P:** Entertainment. **U:** Home. **Mov-Ent.** **Acq:** Purchase. **Dist:** Warner Home Video, Inc. $14.95.

Breaking In: The Complete Series 2011
Fox Network crime comedy. Contra Security is a high-tech firm that uses questionable methods to sell its protection services, including hacking into corporations to reveal their vulnerabilities. 20 episodes. 564m; DVD. **C:** Christian Slater; Megan Mullally; Bret Harrison; Odette Annable; Alphonso McAuley. **A:** Jr. High-Adult. **P:** Entertainment. **U:** Home. **L:** English. **Mov-Ent**: Television Series. **Acq:** Purchase. **Dist:** WarnerArchive.com. $38.99.

Breaking into Television Commercials 1987
An instructional tape for actors on how to enter the field of commercial acting. 45m; VHS. **C:** Iris Acker. **Pr:** MTI Home Video. **A:** Family. **P:** Instruction. **U:** Home. **How-Ins**: How-To, Television. **Acq:** Purchase. **Dist:** Bedford Entertainment Inc. $29.95.

Breaking Leaves 2000
Follows several Haitian peasants as they go into the bush to search for the leaves needed for healing and then follows them to their homes where they demonstrate their use of local leaves, herbs, and therapeutic massage to cure simple ailments. 30m; VHS. **A:** College-Adult. **P:** Education. **U:** Institution. **Gen-Edu**: Medical Education, Massage. **Acq:** Purchase, Rent/Lease. **Dist:** Filmakers Library Inc. $195.00.

Breaking Loose 1990 (R) — ★½
A surfer is on the run from a vicious motorcycle gang that kidnapped his girlfriend, but turns to fight eventually, board in hand. 88m; VHS. **C:** Peter Phelps; Vince Martin; Abigail; David Ngoombujarra; Directed by Rod Hay. **Pr:** Philip Avalon; Avalon Films; South Gate Entertainment. **A:** Adult. **P:** Entertainment. **U:** Home. **Mov-Ent**: Motorcycles. **Acq:** Purchase. **Dist:** Amazon.com Inc. $14.95.

Breaking News 2004 (Unrated) — ★★
Action director To starts off with a mesmerizing 7-minute scene that follows the camera along a Hong Kong street, culminating in a shootout between crooks and cops (cops lose). Since a TV news crew got the whole debacle on tape, the humiliated department lets ambitious Inspector Rebecca Fong (Chen) equip the cops with web cams that will allow the proper spin as they hunt for the hostage-taking thieves; too bad the criminals strike back with their own video ops. Cantonese with subtitles. 90m; DVD. **C:** Richie Jen; Kelly Chen; Nick Cheung; Hui Siu Hung; Lam Suet; Cheung Sui Fai; Simon Yam; You Yong; Ding Hai Feng; Le Hai Tao; Maggie Shiu; Directed by Johnny To; Written by Chan Hing Kai; Ip Tin Shing; Cinematography by Cheng Siu Keung; Music by Ben Cheung; Ching Chi Wing. **Pr:** Cao Biao; Johnnie To. **A:** Jr. High-Adult. **P:** Entertainment. **U:** Home. **L:** English, Chinese. **Mov-Ent**: Mass Media, Crime Drama. **Dist:** Palm Pictures.

Breaking Out: Career Choices for Teenage Parents 1987
Teenage parents don't have to have dead-end jobs. Here's a look at how they can be parents and get an education and a good job. 45m; VHS. **A:** Jr. High-Adult. **P:** Education. **U:** Institution. **Gen-Edu**: Adolescence, Parenting, Occupations. **Acq:** Purchase. **Dist:** University of Wisconsin-Madison Center on Education & Work. $59.00.

Breaking Out of the Doll's House 1975
We see in Nora a typically sheltered young wife conditioned by the customs of her era, indulged by her husband, totally dependent-yet revealing a hint of the substance that will lead to her climactic decision. 32m; VHS, 3/4 U. **C:** Jane Fonda; Trevor Howard. **Pr:** Learning Corporation of America. **A:** Adult. **P:** Entertainment. **U:** Institution, SURA. **L:** English, Spanish. **Gen-Edu**: Documentary Films, Women. **Acq:** Purchase, Rent/Lease. **Dist:** Phoenix Learning Group.

Breaking Out of the Under-Achievement Trap 19??
Series of short vignettes identifying common underachievement traps that students may encounter. Addresses goal setting and the importance of a supportive environment. 25m; VHS. **A:** Jr. High-Adult. **P:** Education. **U:** Institution. **Gen-Edu**: Education. **Acq:** Purchase. **Dist:** Cambridge Educational. $98.00.

Breaking Out of the Under-Achiever Trap 1990
People who haven't been working up to their potential don't have to keep living that way. 45m; VHS. **Pr:** Cambridge Career Productions. **A:** Jr. High-Adult. **P:** Education. **U:** Institution, Home. **Gen-Edu**: Psychology, Education, Adolescence. **Acq:** Purchase. **Dist:** Cambridge Educational. $98.00.

Breaking Point 197?
A desperate man on a deserted road discovers the frightening truth about himself as he struggles to keep his emotional and spiritual world together. 28m; VHS, 3/4 U. **A:** Jr. High-Adult. **P:** Religious. **U:** Institution, SURA. **Gen-Edu**: Documentary Films, Religion. **Acq:** Purchase, Rent/Lease. **Dist:** Faith for Today; Turner Broadcasting System Inc.

The Breaking Point 1950 (Unrated) — ★★★
A somewhat more faithful adaptation of Hemingway's "To Have and Have Not" (following the 1944 Bogart flick). Garfield gives a first-rate performance as charter boat skipper Harry Morgan whose financial woes get him into bigger and bigger trouble. Shady lawyer Duncan (Ford) first gets Harry involved in a disastrous attempt to smuggle illegal Chinese immigrants and then hires him to run an escape route for some gangsters that is equally dangerous. 97m/B/W; DVD. **C:** John Garfield; Phyllis Thaxter; Wallace Ford; Patricia Neal; Juano Hernandez; Ralph Dumke; Edmon Ryan; Victor Sen Yung; Directed by Michael Curtiz; Written by Ranald MacDougall; Cinematography by Ted D. McCord; Music by Ray Heindorf. **A:** Sr. High-Adult. **P:** Entertainment. **U:** Home. **Mov-Ent**: Boating, Law, Illegal Immigration. **Acq:** Purchase. **Dist:** WarnerArchive.com.

Breaking Point 1993
Carl is a talented tennis player whose father is an alcoholic. Carl tries to control his drinking, until one night when he finds his dad too drunk to care about his tennis victory. Upset, Carl goes out to a party and has too much beer. When he leaves drunk, he hits a young mother and ends up in jail, unable to participate in the tennis championship games. 24m; VHS. **A:** Jr. High-Sr. High. **P:** Education. **U:** Institution. **Gen-Edu**: Adolescence, Alcoholic Beverages, Alcoholism. **Acq:** Purchase. **Dist:** Pyramid Media. $295.00.

Breaking Point 1994 (R) — ★★½
Ex-cop Dwight Meadows (Busey) retired from the force when he was nearly killed by a scalpel-wielding mass murderer known as "The Surgeon." Now the psycho is back and Meadows returns to active duty, paired with relentless officer Dana Preston (Fluegel), who wants the killer caught—at any cost. Vancouver, British Columbia fills in for the Seattle, Washington setting. 95m; VHS, CC. **C:** Gary Busey; Darlanne Fluegel; Jeff Griggs; Kim Cattrall; Directed by Paul Ziller; Music by Graeme Coleman. **Pr:** Robert Vince; Gary Delfiner; Michael Strange; Entertainment Securities Ltd. **A:** Sr. High-Adult. **P:** Entertainment. **U:** Home. **Mov-Ent**: Mystery & Suspense. **Acq:** Purchase. **Dist:** Lions Gate Entertainment Inc. $9.98.

Breaking Point 2009 (R) — ★½
One of the few reasons to watch this generic crime drama is the ferocious performance of Busta Rhymes as a murderous gangster. Former defense attorney Steven Luisi (Berenger) was brought low by drug addiction and personal tragedy. Trying to redeem himself by investigating a high-profile murder, Luisi finds his former dealer Al Bowen (Rhymnes) and corrupt DA Marty Berlin (Assante) behind the violence. 93m; DVD. **C:** Tom Berenger; Armand Assante; Kirk "Sticky Fingaz" Jones; Musetta Vander; Frankie Faison; Robert Capelli, Jr.; Directed by Jeff Celentano; Written by Vincent Campanella; Cinematography by Emmanuel Vouniozos; Music by Pinar Toprak. **A:** Sr. High-Adult. **P:** Entertainment. **U:** Home. **Mov-Ent**: Crime Drama, Drug Trafficking/Dealing, Drug Abuse. **Acq:** Purchase. **Dist:** Lions Gate Entertainment Inc.

Breaking Presses with a 1-3-1 Alignment 1999 (Unrated)
Coach Bill Self demonstrates this offense, which is designed to break pressure defenses in basketball. 45m; DVD. **A:** Family. **P:** Education. **U:** Home, Institution. **Spo-Rec**: Basketball, Athletic Instruction/Coaching. **Acq:** Purchase. **Dist:** Championship Productions. $39.99.

Breaking Silence 1994
Examines how incest and child sexual abuse affects the lives of its victims and the steps that must be taken by survivors in order to regain control of their lives. 58m; VHS. **A:** Sr. High-Adult. **P:** Education. **U:** Institution. **Hea-Sci**: Health Education, Psychology, Child Abuse. **Acq:** Purchase. **Dist:** Aquarius Health Care Media. $175.00.

Breaking Silence: Incest and Child Sexual Abuse 1992
Documentary look at several women and one man who have been sexually abused and found the voice to speak out after suffering from years of shame, fear, and guilt. Illustrates an educational program that helps young kids identify when they are being abused. One in six children are victims of incest, one in three are victims of molestation. Complete with teacher's guide. 30m; VHS. **A:** Adult. **P:** Education. **U:** Institution. **Gen-Edu**: Documentary Films, Sexual Abuse. **Acq:** Purchase. **Dist:** Cambridge Educational. $79.95.

Breaking Silence: The Story of the Sisters at Desales Heights 1996
Features 12 elderly nuns who will be facing the outside world for the first time in their adult lives. 58m; VHS. **A:** Jr. High-Adult. **P:** Education. **U:** Institution, Home. **Gen-Edu**: Religion. **Acq:** Purchase, Rent/Lease. **Dist:** New Day Films Library. $199.00.

Breaking the Attitude Barrier: Learning to Value People with Disabilities 1991
Explores the issue of disabled persons in the workforce through a series of vignettes. Designed to raise viewer consciousness, this program addresses the fears and embarrassments of able-bodied workers, and discusses "disability etiquette." Introduces successfully employed handicapped persons. Comes with guide. 33m; VHS. **A:** Adult. **P:** Education. **U:** Institution. **Bus-Ind**: Handicapped, Employee Counseling, Human Relations. **Acq:** Purchase, Rent/Lease. **Dist:** Phoenix Learning Group. $495.00.

Breaking the Bottleneck: Decision-Making 1985
For business managers, this program illustrates how to make effective, quick decisions on the job. 22m; VHS, 3/4 U. **Pr:** Bureau of Business Practice. **A:** Adult. **P:** Professional. **U:** Institution, CCTV. **Bus-Ind**: Management. **Acq:** Purchase, Rent/Lease. **Dist:** Aspen Publishers, Inc. $495.00.

Breaking the Code 1995 — ★★½
Alan Turing (Jacobi) is a British mathematical genius whose work leads to the birth of the digital computer and who is instrumental in enabling the allies to crack the German WWII Enigma code. An active homosexual when homosexuality was illegal, Turing's personal behavior was tolerated because of the importance of his war work but after the gay spy scare of the '50s, Turing was regarded as a security risk and his life increasingly restricted. British TV adaptation based on the play by Hugh Whitemore (Jacobi also played the role on stage) and the book "Alan Turing: The Enigma" by Andrew Hodges. 90m; VHS. **C:** Derek Jacobi; Amanda Root; Prunella Scales; Harold Pinter; Julian Kerridge; Richard Johnson; Directed by Herbert Wise; Written by Hugh Whitemore. **Pr:** Jack Emery; John Drury. **A:** College-Adult. **P:** Entertainment. **U:** Home. **Mov-Ent**: Biography: Science & Medical, Mathematics, World War Two. **Acq:** Purchase. **Dist:** Anchor Bay Entertainment; Wellspring Media.

Breaking the Code: Applying Genetic Techniques to Human Disease 1997
Involves the principles of genetic engineering, and looks at this application to the study and treatment of several major inherited diseases affecting humans. 38m; VHS. **A:** Sr. High-College. **P:** Education. **U:** Institution. **Hea-Sci**: Science, Genetics. **Acq:** Purchase. **Dist:** HRM Video. $149.00.

Breaking the Code - Speaking Out on Family Violence 19??
Psychology and social work film from the University of Calgary Learning Commons. ?m; VHS. **A:** Adult. **P:** Professional. **U:** Institution. **Gen-Edu**: Psychology, Social Service. **Acq:** Purchase. **Dist:** University of Calgary Library, Visual Resources Centre.

Breaking the Cycle 1997
Documentary of families who have pre-school children with profound behavioral problems. Looks at symptoms, intervention, and treatments and techniques parents can use to control these children. 52m; VHS. **A:** Adult. **P:** Education. **U:** Home. **Gen-Edu**: Documentary Films, Psychology, Psychiatry. **Acq:** Purchase, Rent/Lease. **Dist:** Filmakers Library Inc. $295.

Breaking the Cycle: Child Abuse 1993
Promotes self-help groups for adult survivors of four types of child abuse (physical, emotional, sexual abuse, and neglect), defining each form of abuse and outlining the stages of recovery. Profiles four survivors. Complete with guide. 31m; VHS. **A:** Adult. **P:** Education. **U:** Institution. **Gen-Edu**: Self-Help, Child Abuse, Sexual Abuse. **Acq:** Purchase. **Dist:** Sunburst Digital Inc. $189.00.

Breaking the Dark Horse 1997
Depicts a young woman's struggle with manic-depression and mental illness. 32m; VHS, DVD. **A:** Sr. High-Adult. **P:** Education. **U:** Institution. **Hea-Sci**: Health Education, Psychology, Mental Health. **Acq:** Purchase. **Dist:** Aquarius Health Care Media. $175.00.

Breaking the Ice 1938 (Unrated) — ★★
Unlikely mixture of Mennonites and a big city ice skating show. Young man leaves the farm to get a job singing at the rink. Musical numbers abound with backing by Victor Young and his Orchestra. 79m/B/W; VHS. **TV Std**: NTSC, PAL. **C:** Bobby Breen; Charlie Ruggles; Dolores Costello; Billy Gilbert; Margaret Hamilton; Jonathan Hale; Directed by Edward F. (Eddie) Cline; Written by Mary C. McCall; Bernard Schubert; Manuel Seff; Cinematography by Jack MacKenzie; Music by Victor Young. **Pr:** Sol Lesser; RKO. **A:** Family. **P:** Entertainment. **U:** Home. **Mov-Ent**: Musical, Skating. **Acq:** Purchase. **Dist:** $19.95.

Breaking the Maya Code 2007 (Unrated)
Presents a history of efforts over two centuries to break the code of the ancient Mayan, including recent successes and the meaninng of deciphered texts. 116m; DVD. **A:** Jr. High-Adult. **P:** Entertainment. **U:** Home. **Mov-Ent**: Central America, Anthropology, Documentary Films. **Acq:** Purchase. **Dist:** First Run Features. $24.95.

Breaking the Mold: The Mold Broken 1992
Three programs look at the history of Eastern Europe in the post WW II era. Already dated material but will provide adequate background information. Comes with guide. 29m; VHS. **Pr:** Rock Creek Productions. **A:** Jr. High-Sr. High. **P:** Education. **U:** Institution. **Gen-Edu**: History--Modern. **Acq:** Purchase, Rent/Lease. **Dist:** Encyclopedia Britannica. $675.00.
Indiv. Titles: 1. Cracking the Mold 2. Setting the Mold 3. Breaking the Mold.

Breaking the Rule of Thumb 1997
Examines contemporary domestic violence in terms of changing historical definitions of abuse. Looks at the issues still confronting battered women 20 years after the beginning of the domestic violence movement. 35m; VHS. **A:** College-Adult. **P:** Education. **U:** Institution. **Gen-Edu**: Women, Violence. **Acq:** Purchase, Rent/Lease. **Dist:** Women Make Movies. $225.00.

Breaking the Rules 1992 (PG-13) — ★★½
Predicatable buddy-road movie with a tearjerking premise and comedic overtones. Rob, Gene, and Phil were best buds growing up in Cleveland but young adulthood has separated them. They are reunited by Phil, who is dying of leukemia, and whose last wish is a cross-country road trip to California so he can appear as a contestant on "Jeopardy." Along the way they meet brassy waitress Mary, who impulsively decides to join them and winds up bringing the trio's shaky friendship back together. Potts does well as the big-haired, big-hearted Mary but the actors must work hard to maintain any dignity given the story's melodrama. 100m; VHS, CC. **C:** Jason Bateman; C. Thomas Howell; Jonathan Silverman; Annie Potts; Kent Bateman; Shawn (Michael) Phelan; Directed by Neal Israel; Written by Paul Shapiro; Music by David Kitay. **Pr:** Jonathan D. Krane; Miramax Film Corp. **A:** Jr. High-Adult. **P:** Entertainment. **U:** Home. **Mov-Ent**: Comedy-Drama, Death, Melodrama. **Acq:** Purchase. **Dist:** Home Box Office Inc. $92.99.

Breaking the Sales Barriers 1987
Employees are taught why cross-selling is beneficial to the customer. 17m; VHS, 3/4 U. **Pr:** First Financial Network. **A:** Adult. **P:** Education. **U:** Institution, Home. **Bus-Ind**: Sales Training, Business. **Acq:** Purchase, Rent/Lease. **Dist:** 1st Financial Training Services. $250.00.

Breaking the Silence 1984
This film focuses on a volunteer team from the Nicaraguan telephone company who were assigned to string the first phone lines into isolated communities inhabited by Miskito Indians on the country's Atlantic coast. 15m; 3/4 U. **Pr:** Ivan Arguello. **A:** Jr. High-Adult. **P:** Education. **U:** Institution, SURA. **Gen-Edu**: Documentary Films, Central America. **Acq:** Purchase. **Dist:** First Run/Icarus Films.

Breaking the Silence: An Introduction to Sound 1988
The fact that sounds are created when something vibrates is taught. 20m; VHS. **Pr:** Rainbow. **A:** Primary-Jr. High. **P:** Education. **U:** Institution. **Hea-Sci**: Science. **Acq:** Purchase. **Dist:** Rainbow Educational Media, Inc.; Clear Vue Inc. $89.00.

Breaking the Silence: The Generation After the Holocaust 1984
PBS documentary exploring the gap and connection between Holocaust survivors and their children. 58m; VHS. **A:** Jr. High-Adult. **P:** Education. **U:** Institution. **Gen-Edu**: Holocaust. **Acq:** Purchase. **Dist:** National Center for Jewish Film. $72.

Breaking the Surface: The Greg Louganis Story 1996 — ★★½
Trials and tribulations of the gold-medal winning Olympic diver, including his overbearing father, abusive lover, and his own HIV-positive status. Based on Louganis' autobiography; made for TV. 95m; VHS, DVD. **C:** Mario Lopez; Michael Murphy; Jeffrey Meek; Bruce Weitz; Rosemary Dunsmore; Directed by Steven Hilliard Stern; Written by Alan Hines. **Pr:** USA Pictures. **A:** Jr. High-Adult. **P:** Entertainment. **U:** Home. **Mov-Ent**: Biography: Sports, TV Movies, Sports--Olympic. **Acq:** Purchase. **Dist:** Ariztical Entertainment.

Breaking the Unseen Barrier: Math 198?
Follows students named Wayne and Nick, who have trouble with math. Explores ways teachers can help. Comes with teacher's guide. 29m; VHS. **A:** College-Adult. **P:** Teacher Education. **U:** Institution. **Gen-Edu**: Education, Learning Disabilities, Mathematics. **Acq:** Purchase. **Dist:** Access The Education Station. $99.00.

Breaking the Unseen Barrier: Oral Language 198?
Two fourth graders, Sarah and Tony, struggle with learning disabilities having to do with their ability to converse. Comes with teacher's guide. 29m; VHS. **A:** College-Adult. **P:** Teacher Education. **U:** Institution. **Gen-Edu**: Education, Learning Disabilities. **Acq:** Purchase. **Dist:** Access The Education Station. $99.00.

Breaking the Unseen Barrier: Program Planning 198?
Dan, an elementary student, is followed through the accepted cycle of assessment, diagnosis, individual planning, teaching, and continued assessment appropriate for students with learning disabilities. Comes with teacher's guide. 29m; VHS. **A:** College-Adult. **P:** Teacher Education. **U:** Institution. **Gen-Edu**: Education, Learning Disabilities. **Acq:** Purchase. **Dist:** Access The Education Station. $99.00.

Breaking the Unseen Barrier: Reading 198?
Profiles two high school students, Mark and Jill, who are struggling with reading problems as a result of probable learning disabilities. Shows techniques teachers can use to deal with similar scenarios. Comes with teacher's guide. 29m; VHS. **A:** College-Adult. **P:** Teacher Education. **U:** Institution. **Gen-Edu**: Education, Learning Disabilities. **Acq:** Purchase. **Dist:** Access The Education Station. $99.00.

Breaking the Unseen Barrier: Self-Concept and Social Skills 198?
Dwayne not only must cope with a learning disability but he has poorly developed social skills which further handicap him in the classroom. Comes with teacher's guide. 29m; VHS. **A:** College-Adult. **P:** Teacher Education. **U:** Institution. **Gen-Edu**: Education, Learning Disabilities. **Acq:** Purchase. **Dist:** Access The Education Station. $99.00.

Breaking the Unseen Barrier: Self-Esteem and Classroom Management 198?
Shows how to deal with the frustration and anger of a learning disabled child who struggles yet fails anyway. Comes with teacher's guide. 29m; VHS. **A:** College-Adult. **P:** Teacher Education. **U:** Institution. **Gen-Edu**: Education, Learning Disabilities. **Acq:** Purchase. **Dist:** Access The Education Station. $99.00.

Breaking the Unseen Barrier: Teaching the Student with Learning Disabilities 1989
Teacher education series demonstrates planning and implementation strategies for integrating learning disabled students in a classroom setting. Programs may be purchased individually or as set. Teacher's guide available at additional cost. 15m; VHS. **Pr:** ACCESS Network. **A:** Adult. **P:** Teacher Education. **U:** Institution. **Gen-Edu**: Handicapped, Education. **Acq:** Purchase, Rent/Lease. **Dist:** Agency for Instructional Technology. $180.00.

Indiv. Titles: 1. We're Not Stupid 2. Program Planning 3. Reading 4. Disabilities in Mathematics and Arithmetic 5. Oral Language 6. Self-Esteem and Classroom Management 7. Self-Concept and Social Skills 8. Using Technology.

Breaking the Unseen Barrier: Using Technology 198?
High school students Rahinder, Andrew, and Dale might be able to overcome their learning disabilities through various technologies but their teachers could be reluctant to spend more on special equipment. Shows how some technologies can help students. Comes with teacher's guide. 29m; VHS. **A:** College-Adult. **P:** Teacher Education. **U:** Institution. **Gen-Edu**: Education, Learning Disabilities. **Acq:** Purchase. **Dist:** Access The Education Station. $99.00.

Breaking the Unseen Barrier: We're Not Stupid 198?
Teachers of special needs children must also overcome their students' emotional barriers that result from a negative self-concept. Features interviews with children and adults who have learning disabilities. Comes with teacher's guide. 15m; VHS. **A:** College-Adult. **P:** Teacher Education. **U:** Institution. **Gen-Edu**: Education, Job Training. **Acq:** Purchase. **Dist:** Access The Education Station. $99.00.

Breaking the Waves 1995 (R) — ★★★
Sacrifical journey of shy, religious Bess (Watson), who's living in an austere northern Scotland coastal village in the '70s. Bess, who regularly talks to God, marries Jan (Skarsgard), an adventurer working on a North Sea oil rig. It must be a case of opposites attracting but the couple are happy until Jan is paralyzed from the neck down in a rig accident. Bess, who blames herself, begins sleeping around, believing her actions can somehow help Jan, and slides ever deeper into mental instability. Powerful story is divided into seven chapters and an epilogue. 152m; VHS, DVD, Blu-Ray, Wide, CC. **C:** Emily Watson; Stellan Skarsgard; Katrin Cartlidge; Adrian Rawlins; Jean-Marc Barr; Sandra Voe; Udo Kier; Mikkel Gaup; Directed by Lars von Trier; Written by Lars von Trier; Cinematography by Robby Muller; Music by Joachim Holbek. **Pr:** Peter Aalbaek Jensen; Vibeke Windelov; Lars Jonsson; Zentropa Entertainment; La Sept Cinema; October Films. **A:** College-Adult. **P:** Entertainment. **U:** Home. **Mov-Ent**: Mental Health, Marriage, Handicapped. **Awds:** Cannes '96: Grand Jury Prize; Cesar '97: Foreign Film; N.Y. Film Critics '96: Actress (Watson), Cinematog., Director (von Trier); Natl. Soc. Film Critics '96: Actress (Watson), Cinematog., Director (von Trier), Film. **Acq:** Purchase. **Dist:** Lions Gate Television Corp.

Breaking Through 1982
This program looks at the many women who are pursuing jobs that are traditionally considered "men's work." 28m; VHS, 3/4 U. **Pr:** Kem Murch; Susan Booth; Carol Brooks. **A:** Sr. High-Adult. **P:** Education. **U:** Institution, SURA. **Gen-Edu**: Documentary Films, Women, Occupations. **Acq:** Purchase. **Dist:** Phoenix Learning Group.

Breaking Through: Dealing With Buyer Resistance 1992
Explains methods to overcome buyer resistance using an appropriate method of negotiation. 28m; VHS. **A:** Adult. **P:** Professional. **U:** Institution. **Bus-Ind**: Business, Sales Training. **Acq:** Purchase. **Dist:** RMI Media. $99.00.

Breaking Up 1978 (Unrated) — ★★½
A woman fights to rediscover her personal identity after her 15-year marriage crumbles in this Emmy-nominated movie. 90m; VHS. **C:** Lee Remick; Granville Van Dusen; David Stambaugh; Directed by Delbert Mann. **Pr:** David Susskind; Time-Life Television. **A:** Preschool. **P:** Entertainment. **U:** Institution, SURA. **Mov-Ent**: Divorce, TV Movies. **Acq:** Purchase. **Dist:** Time-Life Video and Television.

Breaking Up 1997 (R) — ★½
What steamy sheet action brings together, dreary day to day living easily pulls apart. That is the basic message of this bland romantic comedy that brings nothing new to the tired genre. Typical opposites attract but can't stay together (yet can't stay apart) plot finds photographer Crowe and teacher Hayek madly in lust and impulsively marrying. Hayek had more to work with when she played this role in "Fools Rush In," and Crowe seems uncomfortable as the lackluster boyfriend. Told in a chatty style with frequent asides to the audience by the main characters and a string of flashback sequences, director Greenwald's theatre background is apparent here. Clever camera work and editing are highlights. Adapted from Michael Cristofer's Pulitzer Prize-winning play. 90m; VHS, DVD. **C:** Salma Hayek; Russell Crowe; Directed by Robert Greenwald; Written by Michael Cristofer; Music by Mark Mothersbaugh. **A:** Sr. High-Adult. **P:** Entertainment. **U:** Home. **Mov-Ent**: Comedy--Romantic, Marriage. **Acq:** Purchase. **Dist:** Warner Home Video, Inc.

Breaking Up Is Hard to Do 1979 (Unrated) — ★
Six men leave their wives and shack up together on Malibu for a summer of partying and introspection. Made for television; edited down from its original 201 minute length. 96m; DVD. **C:** Billy Crystal; Bonnie Franklin; Ted Bessell; Jeff Conaway; Tony Musante; Robert Conrad; Trish Stewart; David Ogden Stiers; George Gaynes; Directed by Lou Antonio; Music by Richard Bellis. **Pr:** Green/Epstein Productions; Columbia Pictures Television. **A:** Jr. High-Adult. **P:** Entertainment. **U:** Home. **Mov-Ent**: Comedy-Drama, TV Movies, Divorce. **Acq:** Purchase. **Dist:** Sony Pictures Home Entertainment Inc. $9.99.

Breaking Up Is Hard to Do 1983
The breakup of AT&T as seen through the eyes of the Bell System employees is the subject of this documentary. 60m; VHS, 3/4 U. **Pr:** New Jersey Network. **A:** Sr. High-Adult. **P:** Education. **U:** Institution. **Gen-Edu**: Documentary Films, Business. **Acq:** Purchase, Rent/Lease. **Dist:** New Jersey Network.

Breaking Upwards 2009 (Unrated) — ★½
In this self-indulgent modern romance, filmmaking couple Lister-Jones and Wein portray themselves and recreate past domestic problems. After living together for four years, they become concerned that their relationship is eroding so they decide to break up their week by staying together for four days and separating for three. During their separation time the two are free to explore their independence—only they're more codependent. 89m; DVD. **C:** Daryl Wein; Zoe Lister-Jones; Andrea Martin; Julie White; Peter Friedman; Olivia Thirlby; Pablo Schreiber; Ebon Moss-Bachrach; Directed by Daryl Wein; Written by Daryl Wein; Peter Duchan; Cinematography by Alex Bergman; Music by Kyle Forester. **A:** Sr. High-Adult. **P:** Entertainment. **U:** Home. **Mov-Ent**: Comedy--Romantic. **Acq:** Purchase. **Dist:** IFC Films.

Breaking with Old Ideas 1975 — ★★
A film made in the waning years of Mao's Cultural Revolution about the construction of a college of workers. In Chinese with subtitles. 126m; VHS. **C:** Directed by Li Wen-Hua. **Pr:** People's Republic of China. **A:** Family. **P:** Entertainment. **U:** Home. **L:** Chinese. **Mov-Ent**: Propaganda. **Acq:** Purchase. **Dist:** Facets Multimedia Inc. $39.95.

Breaking with the Mighty Poppalots 1984
The break dance group The Mighty Poppalots teach all aspects of break dancing from moon walks to windmills in this instructional program. 60m; VHS. **Pr:** Adler Enterprises. **A:** Family. **P:** Entertainment. **U:** Home. **Mov-Ent**: Performing Arts, Dance. **Acq:** Purchase. **Dist:** Lions Gate Television Corp. $39.98.

Breaking Yearlings 1988
The styles and methods of breaking yearlings is examined in this tape. 45m; VHS. **Pr:** The Blood-Horse. **A:** College-Adult. **P:** Professional. **U:** Institution, Home. **Spo-Rec**: Documentary Films, Horses--Racing. **Acq:** Purchase. **Dist:** The Blood-Horse, Inc.

Breakout 1975 (PG) — ★★
The wife of a man imprisoned in Mexico hires a Texas bush pilot (Bronson) to help her husband (Duvall) escape. 96m; VHS, DVD, Wide. **C:** Charles Bronson; Jill Ireland; Robert Duvall; John Huston; Sheree North; Randy Quaid; Directed by Tom Gries; Written by Howard B. Kreitsek; Marc Norman; Elliott Baker; Cinematography by Lucien Ballard; Music by Jerry Goldsmith. **Pr:** Columbia Pictures. **A:** Family. **P:** Entertainment. **U:** Home. **Mov-Ent**: Mexico. **Acq:** Purchase. **Dist:** Sony Pictures Home Entertainment Inc. $64.95.

Breakout 1998 (Unrated) — ★★
Zack (Carradine) has invented an environmentally friendly alternative energy source that makes him the scourge of the oil cartels. So the bad guys decide to kidnap Zack's son Joe (Bonifant) as a bargaining chip, only the kid turns out to be as smart as his old man. 86m; VHS, DVD, UMD. **C:** Robert Carradine; Evan Bonifant; James Hong; Chris Chinchilla; Directed by John Bradshaw; Written by Naomi Janzen; Cinematography by Edgar Egger; Music by Gary Koftinoff. **A:** Sr. High-Adult. **P:** Entertainment. **U:** Home. **Mov-Ent**: Family, Technology. **Acq:** Purchase. **Dist:** Trinity Films.

Breakout Drills 2008 (Unrated)
Coach Mark Carlson discusses breakouts in hockey, how teams can take advantage of them, and presents drills to increase their ability to do so. 76m; DVD. **A:** Family. **P:** Education. **U:** Home, Institution. **Spo-Rec**: Hockey, Athletic Instruction/Coaching. **Acq:** Purchase. **Dist:** Championship Productions. $29.99.

Breakpoint and Beyond 199?
Beth Jarman provides an understanding of the connection between nature's transformations and changes in social and organizational attitudes, pointing out that we have come to a breaking point in the basic paradigm of hierarchy and domination that was prevalent for 8,000 years. 30m; DVD. **A:** Adult. **P:** Education. **U:** Home, Institution. **Gen-Edu**: Philosophy & Ideology, Sociology. **Acq:** Purchase. **Dist:** Thinking Allowed Productions. $29.95.

The Breaks 1999 (R) — ★
White Irish kid gets adopted by a black family in South Central L.A. and naturally grows up to think of himself as a homeboy. But his adoptive mom is tired of his shenanigans and gives him one simple task to do'bring home a carton of milk by supper—or else. Why isn't this as easy as it sounds ('cause it certainly is as dumb). 86m; VHS, DVD, CC. **C:** Mitch Mullany; Carl Anthony Payne, II; Paula Jai Parker; Clifton Powell; Loretta Devine; Directed by Eric Meza; Written by Mitch Mullany; Cinematography by Carlos Gonzalez; Music by Adam Hirsh. **A:** Sr. High-Adult. **P:** Entertainment. **U:** Home. **Mov-Ent**: Adoption, Family, Black Culture. **Acq:** Purchase. **Dist:** Lions Gate Television Corp.

Breakthrough 1950 (Unrated) — ★★
Focuses on one infantry platoon as they fight their way from Omaha Beach on June 6, 1944 across Normandy. The vets are led by tough Capt. Hale (Brian) and green Lt. Mallory (Agar), who'll naturally come into his own as he gains battle experience. Includes actual footage of the Allied invasion on D-Day. 91m/B/W; DVD. **C:** David Brian; John Agar; Frank Lovejoy; William Campbell; Paul Picerni; Greg McClure; Directed by Lewis Seiler; Written by Ted Sherdeman; Bernard Girard; Cinematography by Edwin DuPar; Music by William Lava. **A:** Jr. High-Adult. **P:** Entertainment. **U:** Home. **Mov-Ent**: World War Two, France. **Acq:** Purchase. **Dist:** WarnerArchive.com.

Breakthrough 1978 (PG) — ★★
German soldier, broken at the end of WWII, sets out to negotiate with the Allies. Average at best. 96m; VHS. **C:** Richard Burton; Robert Mitchum; Rod Steiger; Michael Parks; Curt Jurgens; Directed by Andrew V. McLaglen. **Pr:** Hubert Lukowski; Wolf C Hartwig; Maverick Pictures. **A:** Sr. High-Adult. **P:** Entertainment. **U:** Home. **Mov-Ent**: World War Two. **Acq:** Purchase. **Dist:** $9.95.

The Breakthrough 1981
This program is about three people who have cerebral palsy and are unable to speak, and how a new pictorographic symbol system has enabled them to communicate with the world. 40m; 3/4 U, Special order formats. **Pr:** Lauron Productions Ltd. **A:** Sr. High-Adult. **P:** Education. **U:** Institution, Home, SURA. **Hea-Sci:** Documentary Films, Handicapped, Communication. **Acq:** Purchase, Rent/Lease, Trade-in, Duplication License. **Dist:** United Learning Inc.

Breakthrough 1982
This program deals with the Rehabilitation Act and the regulations concerning employment of the handicapped. 26m; VHS, 3/4 U. **C:** David Brian; John Agar; Frank Lovejoy; William Campbell; Paul Picerni; Greg McClure; Directed by Lewis Seiler; Written by Bernard Girard; Ted Sheardeman; Cinematography by Edwin DuPar; Music by William Lava. **Pr:** Leopold & Associates. **A:** Adult. **P:** Education. **U:** Institution, SURA. **Bus-Ind:** Documentary Films, Business, Handicapped. **Acq:** Purchase, Rent/Lease. **Dist:** Unknown Distributor.

Breakthrough 1984
Through the personal story of one skid row alcoholic's recovery, this program focuses on the treatments and therapy available to chronic alcoholics at live-in facilities. 27m; VHS, 3/4 U. **Pr:** LAC Film Unit. **A:** Adult. **P:** Education. **U:** Institution, Home. **Hea-Sci:** Documentary Films, Alcoholism. **Acq:** Purchase, Rent/Lease. **Dist:** Image Associates.

Breakthrough Basics of Downhill Skiing 1989
Hank Kashiwa takes students to another level of skiing and prepares them with proper conditioning and technique. 45m; VHS. **A:** Family. **P:** Instruction. **U:** Home. **Spo-Rec:** Sports--General, Skiing. **Acq:** Purchase. **Dist:** ESPN Inc.; Fast Forward. $29.95.

Breakthrough for Breaking In 19??
Offers step-by-step instruction for breaking in a young horse using kindness. ?m; VHS. **A:** Sr. High-Adult. **P:** Instruction. **U:** Institution. **How-Ins:** How-To, Horses. **Acq:** Purchase. **Dist:** CEV Multimedia. $59.95.

Breakthrough Listening 19??
Shows various business situations where an individual is not listening and the consequences that follow. Comes with guides. 21m; VHS. **A:** Adult. **P:** Professional. **U:** Institution. **Bus-Ind:** Business, Job Training, Human Relations. **Acq:** Purchase, Rent/Lease. **Dist:** Excellence in Training Corp. $695.00.

Breakthroughs: How to Reach Students with Autism 1998
Educator Karen Sewell demonstrates the techniques she has developed for teaching students with autism. Includes teacher's manual. 25m; VHS. **A:** Sr. High-Adult. **P:** Education. **U:** Institution. **Hea-Sci:** Health Education, Handicapped, Education. **Acq:** Purchase. **Dist:** Aquarius Health Care Media. $99.00.

The Breakup Artist 2004 (R) — ★★½
A rom-com from the male point of view. Jim (Taylor) is looking for love in the Big Apple, except he can't stay focused on just one girl (hence the title). Meanwhile, sweet co-worker Teresa (Devicq) is engaged to a jerk. Of course, they're made for each other—if only Jim and Teresa can figure it out. 86m; DVD, Wide. **C:** Joseph Lyle Taylor; Paula DeVicq; Sarita Choudhury; Sabrina Lloyd; Ron Mongeluzzo; Cameo(s) Edward Burns; Regis Philbin; Bobby Cannavale; Directed by Vincent Rubino; Written by Vincent Rubino; Cinematography by Nicholas Baratta; Music by Thomas DeRenzo; Paul Conte. **A:** Sr. High-Adult. **P:** Entertainment. **U:** Home. **Mov-Ent:** Comedy--Romantic. **Acq:** Purchase. **Dist:** Movies Unlimited; Alpha Video.

Breast Cancer 1975
A description of breast cancer including grade, stage and host responses. 25m; VHS, 3/4 U, Special order formats. **Pr:** Ohio State University Health Sciences AV Center. **A:** College-Adult. **P:** Professional. **U:** Institution, SURA. **Hea-Sci:** Cancer. **Acq:** Purchase, Rent/Lease. **Dist:** Ohio State University. $24.95.

Breast Cancer 1 1979
Gives a step-by-step demonstration of breast self-examination, then explains detection and treatment of breast cancer. 26m; VHS, 3/4 U. **Pr:** WNET New York. **A:** Sr. High-Adult. **P:** Education. **U:** Institution, CCTV, Home. **Hea-Sci:** Documentary Films, Cancer. **Acq:** Purchase, Rent/Lease. **Dist:** WNET/Thirteen Non-Broadcast.

Breast Cancer 2 1979
The emotional and physical impact of losing a breast to cancer is described by three women who have been through the experience. 26m; VHS, 3/4 U. **Pr:** WNET New York. **A:** Sr. High-Adult. **P:** Education. **U:** Institution, CCTV, Home. **Hea-Sci:** Documentary Films, Cancer. **Acq:** Purchase, Rent/Lease. **Dist:** WNET/Thirteen Non-Broadcast.

Breast Cancer: A Personal Challenge 1987
Several women talk about their reactions to the diagnosis of breast cancer, progressing from self-violation to hopeful acceptance. 23m; VHS, 3/4 U. **Pr:** Professional Research. **A:** College-Adult. **P:** Education. **U:** Institution, CCTV, SURA. **Hea-Sci:** Documentary Films, Cancer. **Acq:** Purchase, Rent/Lease. **Dist:** Discovery Education. $295.00.

Breast Cancer and Mastectomy 197?
This program reviews types of tumors and methods of diagnosis, in conjunction with a presentation of female breast anatomy. 25m; VHS, 3/4 U. **Pr:** Trainex. **A:** College-Adult. **P:** Professional. **U:** Institution. **Hea-Sci:** Documentary Films, Cancer. **Acq:** Purchase, Rent/Lease. **Dist:** Medcom Inc.

Breast Cancer: Let's Get Personal 1995
Documentary examines breast cancer, including risk factors, symptoms, and treatment. 24m; VHS. **A:** College. **P:** Education. **U:** Institution. **Hea-Sci:** Documentary Films, Cancer, Women. **Acq:** Purchase, Rent/Lease. **Dist:** The Cinema Guild. $195.

Breast Cancer: Speaking Out 1993
Investigates the treatment choices available to women with breast cancer and explores the experiences and attitudes of activists, patients, and support group members. Includes interviews with physicians. 30m; VHS. **Pr:** KCTS-TV. **A:** Adult. **P:** Education. **U:** Institution. **Hea-Sci:** Documentary Films, Medical Care, Women. **Acq:** Purchase, Rent/Lease. **Dist:** Filmakers Library Inc. $295.00.

The Breast Cancer Video 1989
How to perform a self-exam, treatment methods, and reconstruction possibilities are discussed. 30m; VHS. **Pr:** Increase. **A:** Sr. High-Adult. **P:** Education. **U:** Home. **Hea-Sci:** Cancer, Women. **Acq:** Purchase. **Dist:** Silver Mine Video Inc. $24.95.

The Breast Center Video 1990
Information on detecting breast cancer and the latest methods for treatment. 37m; VHS. **C:** Hosted by Marcia Wallace. **Pr:** Wishing Well. **A:** Sr. High-Adult. **P:** Education. **U:** Home. **How-Ins:** How-To, Cancer, Women. **Acq:** Purchase. **Dist:** Cambridge Educational. $29.95.

Breast Defense 1990
A comprehensive look at prevention and early detection of breast cancer. 35m; VHS. **A:** Sr. High-Adult. **P:** Education. **U:** Home. **Hea-Sci:** Cancer, Women, Health Education. **Acq:** Purchase. **Dist:** Karol Media. $29.95.

The Breast Examination 1982
Shows the viewer how to perform a thorough breast exam using the techniques of inspection and palpatation. 20m; VHS, 3/4 U. **Pr:** State University of New York at Stony Brook. **A:** College-Adult. **P:** Professional. **U:** Institution, CCTV, SURA. **Hea-Sci:** How-To, Diagnosis, Women. **Acq:** Purchase, Rent/Lease. **Dist:** AJN Video Library/Lippincott Williams & Wilkins.

The Breast-Fed Child 1972
How and when to acquaint expectant mothers with the rationale for breastfeeding. 18m; VHS, 3/4 U, Special order formats. **Pr:** Ohio State University Health Sciences AV Center. **A:** College-Adult. **P:** Professional. **U:** Institution, SURA. **Hea-Sci:** Infants, Parenting, Women. **Acq:** Purchase, Rent/Lease. **Dist:** Ohio State University.

Breast Health 1996
Features a step-by-step breast self exam, with graphics. Also contains information on mammograms and professional breast exams. Offered in African American or Caucasion edition. 14m; VHS. **A:** Adult. **P:** Education. **U:** Institution. **Gen-Edu:** Women, Health Education. **Acq:** Purchase. **Dist:** Aquarius Health Care Media. $140.00.

Breast Health for Women Over 60 1995
Uses narration and demonstrations to provide viewers with important information about mammograms, professional and self-breast examinations. Two video set includes versions for both Caucasian and African-American women. 15m; VHS. **A:** Sr. High-Adult. **P:** Education. **U:** Institution. **Hea-Sci:** Health Education, Women. **Acq:** Purchase. **Dist:** Aquarius Health Care Media. $195.00.

Breast Health for Women Over 60: African-American Edition 1995
Uses narration and demonstrations to provide viewers with important information about mammograms, professional and self-breast examinations. 16m; VHS. **A:** Sr. High-Adult. **P:** Education. **U:** Institution. **Hea-Sci:** Health Education, Women. **Acq:** Purchase. **Dist:** Aquarius Health Care Media. $130.00.

Breast Health for Women Over 60: Caucasian Edition 1995
Uses narration and demonstrations to provide viewers with important information about mammograms, professional and self-breast examinations. 14m; VHS. **A:** Sr. High-Adult. **P:** Education. **U:** Institution. **Hea-Sci:** Health Education, Women. **Acq:** Purchase. **Dist:** Aquarius Health Care Media. $130.00.

Breast Imaging 1986
An update on breast cancer and the myriad of treatments for it. 43m; VHS, 3/4 U. **A:** Adult. **P:** Professional. **U:** Institution, CCTV, Home, SURA. **Hea-Sci:** Cancer, Medical Education, Women. **Acq:** Purchase, Rent/Lease, Subscription. **Dist:** Emory Medical Television Network.

Breast Men 1997 (R) — ★★½
A campy fictional look into the lives and careers of the two doctors who invented the silicone breast implant in 1960s Texas. Struggling Kevin Saunders (Schwimmer) is an ambitious geek who works with grumpy plastic surgeon mentor, Dr. William Larson (Cooper), to develop a prosthetic breast, made from Dow-Corning's silicone gel. It's an immediate success and the doctors become rich, successful, and ever more obnoxious. Then come the lawsuits and life is suddenly no longer so sweet. And yes, you will see a lot of naked breasts. 95m; VHS, DVD, CC. **C:** David Schwimmer; Chris Cooper; Louise Fletcher; Emily Procter; John Stockwell; Matt Frewer; Terry O'Quinn; Kathleen Wilhoite; Lisa Marie; Directed by Lawrence O'Neil; Written by John Stockwell; Cinematography by Robert M. Stevens; Music by Dennis McCarthy. **Pr:** Guy Riedel; Gary Lucchesi; HBO. **A:** Sr. High-Adult. **P:** Entertainment. **U:** Home. **Mov-Ent:** TV Movies, Surgery--Plastic. **Acq:** Purchase. **Dist:** Movies Unlimited; Alpha Video.

Breast Self-Examination 1986
This revised program encourages monthly self-examination of the breasts, and gives viewers detailed instruction in how to do so. Also covered: mammography and its benefits. 13m; VHS, 3/4 U. **Pr:** Gilbert Altschul Productions. **A:** Sr. High-Adult. **P:** Instruction. **U:** Institution, CCTV, SURA. **Hea-Sci:** Cancer, Health Education, Women. **Acq:** Purchase, Rent/Lease. **Dist:** Discovery Education. $295.00.

Breast Self-Examination and Breast Health 1991
Demonstrates home self-examination procedure and stresses the importance of routine checks. 15m; VHS, CC, 3/4 U. **Pr:** Milner-Fenwick. **A:** Adult. **P:** Education. **U:** Institution, CCTV. **L:** English, French, Spanish. **Hea-Sci:** How-To, Health Education, Diagnosis. **Acq:** Purchase. **Dist:** Milner-Fenwick, Inc.

Breastfeeding 1984
The step-by-step procedures for prenatal breast preparation, feeding techniques and scheduling are covered in this revised program. The advantages of breastfeeding and its psychological and physiological effects are examined as well. 18m; VHS, 3/4 U, CV. **Pr:** Professional Research. **A:** Adult. **P:** Education. **U:** Institution, CCTV. **L:** English, Spanish. **How-Ins:** How-To, Infants, Parenting. **Acq:** Purchase, Rent/Lease. **Dist:** Discovery Education. $295.00.

Breastfeeding: A Special Relationship 1994
Introduces new mothers to breastfeeding, including baby signals, body positions, and more. 27m; VHS. **A:** Adult. **P:** Education. **U:** Institution. **Hea-Sci:** Child Care. **Acq:** Purchase. **Dist:** Milner-Fenwick, Inc.; Injoy Productions. $79.00.

Breastfeeding: Better Beginnings 1990
Jeanne Watson offers an ideal program for new mothers to practice, with hints on correct positioning, mother's diet, how to latch on, the father's role and much more. 21m; VHS. **Pr:** Lifecycle Productions. **A:** College-Adult. **P:** Education. **U:** Home. **How-Ins:** Child Care, Infants, Parenting. **Acq:** Purchase. **Dist:** Lifecycle Productions; Cambridge Educational; Injoy Productions. $24.95.

The Breastfeeding Experience 1978
This parent and childbirth education presentation teaches parents about breastfeeding. Designed for high school, adult, and professional use. 23m; VHS, 3/4 U, Special order formats. **Pr:** Courter Films. **A:** Sr. High-Adult. **P:** Education. **U:** Institution, CCTV, Home. **Hea-Sci:** Documentary Films, Infants, Parenting. **Acq:** Purchase. **Dist:** Parenting Pictures.

Breastfeeding Techniques that Work 19??
Breatfeeding expert Kittie Frantz, RN, CPNP, presents a seven-part series featuring step-by-step instruction on proper breastfeeding. She discusses the benefits and the most successful techniques, covering proper attachment, nipple soreness, body alignment, switching breasts, Cesarean, burping the baby, working mothers, hand pumping, and supplemental methods. Includes live demonstrations. 170m; VHS. **A:** Sr. High-Adult. **P:** Education. **U:** Institution, Home. **Hea-Sci:** Childbirth, Infants, Parenting. **Acq:** Purchase. **Dist:** Cambridge Educational. $299.95.
Indiv. Titles: 1. First Attachment 2. First Attachment in Bed 3. First Attachment After a Cesarean 4. Burping the Baby 5. Successful Working Mothers 6. Hand Expression 7. Supplemental Nursing System.

Breastfeeding: The Art of Mothering 1990
Discover a special closeness with your new baby when you breastfeed with confidence and love. 40m; VHS. **Pr:** Family Experiences. **A:** Adult. **P:** Instruction. **U:** Home. **How-Ins:** How-To, Parenting, Child Care. **Acq:** Purchase. **Dist:** Family Experiences Productions, Inc. $39.95.

Breastfeeding Your Baby: A Mother's Guide 1987
A complete guide to breastfeeding techniques, with an analysis of its benefits as opposed to formula feeding. 64m; VHS. **C:** Cathy Rigby; Jayne Kennedy; Julie Carmen. **Pr:** La Leche League International. **A:** Adult. **P:** Instruction. **U:** Home. **How-Ins:** How-To, Infants, Parenting. **Acq:** Purchase. **Dist:** Karol Media. $29.98.

Breasts: A Documentary 1996 (Unrated)
In addition to archival content related to breasts, 22 women, primarily topless, discuss the role their breasts have played in their lives. 50m; DVD. **A:** College-Adult. **P:** Entertainment. **U:** Home. **Mov-Ent:** Sex & Sexuality, Documentary Films, Women. **Acq:** Purchase. **Dist:** Eagle Rock Entertainment Inc.; First Run Features. $19.95.

Breaststroke Drills 2001
Northwestern University Women's Swim Coach Jimmy Tierney provides analysis of the proper breaststroke and drills designed to help strengthen each element. 27m; VHS. **A:** Adult. **P:** Instruction. **U:** Institution. **How-Ins:** Swimming, Sports--Water, How-To. **Acq:** Purchase. **Dist:** Championship Productions. $34.95.

Breaststroke Technique 2001
Provides tips for teaching proper breaststroke technique along with demonstrations of stoke mechanics by Olympic medalists and record holders. 34m; VHS. **A:** Adult. **P:** Instruction. **U:** Institution. **How-Ins:** Swimming, Sports--Water, How-To. **Acq:** Purchase. **Dist:** Championship Productions. $34.95.

Breaststroke Training 2001
Discusses the physical and artistic aspects necessary for a successful breaststroke with demonstrations of dryland and pool-training programs. 37m; VHS. **A:** Adult. **P:** Instruction. **U:** Institution. **How-Ins:** Swimming, Sports--Water, How-To. **Acq:** Purchase. **Dist:** Championship Productions. $34.95.

Breath 1985
The workings of the diaphragm and the mysteries of breath are explored in this abstract video. 15m; VHS, 3/4 U. **Pr:** Margaret Dragu. **A:** Jr. High-Adult. **P:** Education. **U:** Institution, SURA. **Gen-Edu:** Video. **Acq:** Rent/Lease. **Dist:** Video Out Distribution.

Breath/Light/Birth 1978
Images suggesting birth, nourishment, and life force are woven together with elaborate video devices to create a highly symbolic conveyance of the experience. 6m/B/W; VHS, 3/4 U. **Pr:** R. Bruce Elder. **A:** Sr. High-Adult. **P:** Entertainment. **U:** Institution, SURA. **Fin-Art:** Video, Childbirth. **Acq:** Purchase. **Dist:** Phoenix Learning Group.

Breath No. 4 1980
This experimental video explores body motion. 10m; VHS, 3/4 U. **Pr:** Keigo Yamamoto. **A:** College-Adult. **P:** Education. **U:** Institution. **Fin-Art:** Performing Arts, Video. **Acq:** Rent/Lease. **Dist:** Video Out Distribution.

Breath No. 5 1961
An experimental video which explores the nature of present and past that exists within a conversation. 6m; VHS, 3/4 U. **Pr:** Keigo Yamamoto. **A:** Jr. High-Adult. **P:** Education. **U:** Institution, SURA. **Gen-Edu:** Video. **Acq:** Rent/Lease. **Dist:** Video Out Distribution.

Breath of Life 1989
The basic resuscitation techniques for anyone who's stopped breathing because they are unconscious or choking is demonstrated. 26m; VHS, 3/4 U. **Pr:** National Safety Council. **A:** College-Adult. **P:** Education. **U:** Institution, SURA. **Hea-Sci:** How-To, Respiratory System, First Aid. **Acq:** Rent/Lease. **Dist:** Films for the Humanities & Sciences. $149.00.

Breath of Life: Our Respiratory System 1992
Well-mixed presentation of experiments, microscopic images, graphics, and live action sequences demonstrating humans' need for oxygen. 23m; VHS. **A:** Primary. **P:** Education. **U:** Institution. **Hea-Sci:** Health Education, Science. **Acq:** Purchase. **Dist:** Rainbow Educational Media, Inc.; Clear Vue Inc. $89.00.

Breath of Scandal 1960 (Unrated) — ★★
An American diplomat in Vienna rescues a princess when she is thrown off a horse; he falls for her like a ton o' bricks. Viennese politics complicate things. Based on a play by Molnar. 98m; VHS, DVD, CC. **C:** Sophia Loren; John Gavin; Maurice Chevalier; Angela Lansbury; Directed by Michael Curtiz. **Pr:** Paramount Pictures. **A:** Jr. High-Adult. **P:** Entertainment. **U:** Home. **Mov-Ent:** Comedy--Romantic. **Acq:** Purchase. **Dist:** Paramount Pictures Corp.

Breath Taken 1989
A documentary of the effects of asbestos on asbestos workers and others who have been exposed to it, and includes interviews both with victims and with experts on the medical hazards of asbestos. 33m; VHS, 3/4 U. **Pr:** Bill Ravanesi. **A:** Sr. High-Adult. **P:** Education. **U:** Institution, SURA. **Gen-Edu:** Cancer, Public Health, Health Education. **Acq:** Purchase, Rent/Lease. **Dist:** Fanlight Productions. $265.00.

Breathe: All That Jazz 19??
Jazz videos include "How Can I Fail," "Hands to Heaven," "Don't Tell Me Lies," and "Jonah." 20m; VHS. **A:** Sr. High-Adult. **P:** Entertainment. **U:** Home. **Mov-Ent:** Music Video, Music--Jazz. **Acq:** Purchase. **Dist:** Music Video Distributors. $12.98.

Breathe In 2013 (R) — ★1/2
Writer/director Doremus falls deep into the sophomore slump chasm (after 2011's festival hit "Like Crazy") with this inert, melodrama that adds nothing new to the subgenre of overdone soap opera. Keith Reynolds (Pearce) is happily married to Megan Reynolds (Ryan) but the arrival of a beautiful foreign exchange student named Sophie (Jones) throws them all for a loop. The affair between Keith and Sophie on which the whole film hinges never once feels real, partially due to a lack of chemistry between the leads but also because Doremus can't find anything genuine buried under the bedsheets of cliché. 98m; DVD. **C:** Felicity Jones; Guy Pearce; Amy Ryan; Mackenzie Davis; Matthew Daddario; Ben Shenkman; Kyle MacLachlan; Alexandra Wentworth; Directed by Drake Doremus; Written by Drake Doremus; Ben York Jones; Cinematography by John Guleserian; Music by Dustin O'Halloran. **Pr:** Andrea Sperling; Steven Rales; Cohen Media Group. **A:** Sr. High-Adult. **P:** Entertainment. **U:** Home. **L:** English. **Mov-Ent:** Drama, Marriage, Family. **Acq:** Purchase.

Breathe Safe, Breathe Clean 198?
The importance of wearing the proper respiratory equipment at work is presented in this film. 15m; VHS, 3/4 U. **A:** College-Adult. **P:** Education. **U:** Institution. **Bus-Ind:** Safety Education, Respiratory System. **Acq:** Rent/Lease. **Dist:** National Safety Council, California Chapter, Film Library.

Breathing and Talking 1987
Outlines the body's breathing system and gives insight into how humans speak as well as what causes humans to cough, sneeze, hiccup, and yawn. Part of the Bodytalk Series. 8m; VHS, SVS, 3/4 U. **Pr:** Bodytalk Programmes. **A:** Primary. **P:** Education. **U:** Institution. **Hea-Sci:** Health Education. **Acq:** Purchase. **Dist:** Encyclopedia Britannica. $89.00.

Breathing Apparatus 1992
Provides an overview of how fire fighters can properly fit themselves with the oxygen supply so often necessary for the successful completion of quelling emergency situations. 29m; VHS. **A:** Adult. **P:** Professional. **U:** Institution. **Bus-Ind:** Job Training, Ecology & Environment. **Acq:** Purchase. **Dist:** Emergency Film Group. $395.00.

Breathing Apparatus: Why? 1978
Designed for training fire fighters, industrial training, and emergency response teams, this motivational program includes safety and emergency procedures, pressure demand equipment, buddy breathing, and communications. 20m; VHS, 3/4 U, Special order formats. **Pr:** Fire Fighter Films. **A:** Adult. **P:** Vocational. **U:** Institution, CCTV. **Bus-Ind:** Safety Education, Fires. **Acq:** Purchase. **Dist:** Courter Films & Associates.

Breathing Easy 1985
A cautionary program for youths about the ill effects of smoking cigarettes. 30m; VHS, 3/4 U. **C:** LeVar Burton; Mark Harmon; Joan Van Ark. **Pr:** MTI; WQED Pittsburgh. **A:** Primary-Sr. High. **P:** Education. **U:** Institution, CCTV, SURA. **Gen-Edu:** Smoking, Adolescence. **Acq:** Purchase, Rent/Lease. **Dist:** Phoenix Learning Group.

Breathing Fire 1991 (R) — ★★
A Vietnamese teenager and his American brother find out their ex-GI father is behind an armed bank robbery and murder. They join together to protect the only eyewitness—a young girl—against the ruthless gang of criminals and their own father. Lots of kickboxing action for martial arts fans. 86m; VHS, DVD, CC. **C:** Bolo Yeung; Jonathan Ke Quan; Jerry Trimble; Directed by Lou Kennedy. **A:** Jr. High-Adult. **P:** Entertainment. **U:** Home. **Mov-Ent:** Martial Arts. **Acq:** Purchase. **Dist:** Imperial Entertainment Corp. $89.98.

Breathing Lessons 1994 (PG) — ★★★
Sweet look at a long-term marriage that renews itself on a road trip. Flighty Maggie and pragmatic Ira have been married for 28 squabbling but loving years. They're driving from their Baltimore home to a funeral in Pennsylvania and the road stops provide some small adventures and a great deal of conversation. Drama rests easily on the capable shoulders of the veteran performers. Based on the novel by Anne Tyler. Made for TV. 98m; VHS, CC. **C:** James Garner; Joanne Woodward; Paul Winfield; Kathryn Erbe; Joyce Van Patten; Eileen Heckart; Tim Guinee; Henry Jones; Stephi Lineburg; Jean Louisa Kelly; John Considine; Directed by John Erman; Written by Robert W. Lenski. **Pr:** Andrew Gottlieb; Richard Welsh; Signboard Hill Productions, Inc; Hallmark Hall of Fame. **A:** Jr. High-Adult. **P:** Entertainment. **U:** Home. **Mov-Ent:** Marriage, Aging, TV Movies. **Acq:** Purchase. **Dist:** Amazon.com Inc.; Lions Gate Entertainment Inc. $14.98.

Breathing Room 1996 (R) — ★★
New Yorker David (Futterman) has trouble with commitment to girlfriend Kathy (Floyd) and the duo break up again at Thanksgiving when he won't tell her he loves her. Kathy decides they need a break and refuses to see David until Christmas. She plays at seeing her boss, both get too much advice from friends and family, they attend the same holiday party—and the inevitable happens. Nothing new here. 90m; VHS. **C:** Dan Futterman; Susan Floyd; David Thornton; Directed by Jon Sherman; Written by Jon Sherman; Tom Hughes; Cinematography by Jim Denault; Music by Pat Irwin. **Pr:** Tim Perell; Jack Edward Barron; Eureka Pictures; Arrow Releasing. **A:** Sr. High-Adult. **P:** Entertainment. **U:** Home. **Mov-Ent:** Comedy--Romantic, Christmas. **Acq:** Purchase.

Breathing Underwater 1991
Part of the 10-part Seahouse (Series I) video series. Live footage and animation illustrate how fish breathe with the use of their gills. Also highlights the variety of gills. 5m; VHS. **A:** Primary. **P:** Education. **U:** Institution. **Chl-Juv:** Science, Animals. **Acq:** Purchase. **Dist:** Rainbow Educational Media, Inc. $29.95.

Breathless 1959 (Unrated) — ★★★★
Godard's first feature catapulted him to the vanguard of French filmmakers. Carefree Parisian crook, Michel (Belmondo), who emulates Humphrey Bogart, falls in love with gamine American student Patricia (Seberg) with tragic results. Wonderful scenes of Parisian life. Established Godard's Brechtian, experimental style. Belmondo's film debut. Mistitled "Breathless" for American release, the film's French title actually means "Out of Breath"; however, the fast-paced, erratic musical score leaves you breathless. French with English subtitles. Remade with Richard Gere in 1983 with far less intensity. 90m/B/W; VHS, DVD, Blu-Ray. **C:** Jean-Paul Belmondo; Jean Seberg; Daniel Boulanger; Jean-Pierre Melville; Liliane Robin; Directed by Jean-Luc Godard; Written by Jean-Luc Godard; Cinematography by Raoul Coutard; Music by Martial Solal. **Pr:** Films Around the World. **A:** Adult. **P:** Entertainment. **U:** Home. **L:** English, French. **Mov-Ent:** Drama, Film--Avant-Garde, Classic Films. **Awds:** Berlin Intl. Film Fest. '60: Director (Godard). **Acq:** Purchase. **Dist:** Festival Films; Tapeworm Video Distributors Inc. $24.95.

Breathless 1979
Breathlessness after running a mile is different than the kind which comes after walking ten steps. Defects in the lungs, blood, or heart can cause the latter problem. 60m; VHS, 3/4 U. **A:** Sr. High-Adult. **P:** Education. **U:** Institution, SURA. **Hea-Sci:** Respiratory System, Health Education, Fitness/Exercise. **Acq:** Purchase. **Dist:** Home Vision Cinema.

Breathless 1983 (R) — ★★
Car thief turned cop killer has a torrid love affair with a French student studying in Los Angeles as the police slowly close in. Glossy, smarmy remake of the Godard classic that concentrates on the thin plot rather than any attempt at revitalizing the film syntax. 105m; VHS, DVD. **C:** Richard Gere; Valerie Kaprisky; Art Metrano; John P. Ryan; Lisa Jane Persky; Directed by Jim McBride; Written by Jim McBride; L.M. Kit Carson; Music by Jack Nitzsche. **Pr:** Jean-Luc Godard. **A:** Sr. High-Adult. **P:** Entertainment. **U:** Home. **Mov-Ent:** Sex & Sexuality. **Acq:** Purchase. **Dist:** MGM Home Entertainment; Movies Unlimited; Alpha Video. $29.98.

Breathless 2012 (R) — ★1/2
Cartoonish crime thriller. Trailer-dwelling Texas housewife Lorna (Gershon) accidentally kills her lowlife husband Dale (Kilmer) after learning he wasn't going to share his loot from a bank heist. She calls her best friend Tiny (Giddish) to help get rid of the body while also trying to figure out where Dale hid the money. The local sheriff (Liotta) and a greedy PI (Duvall) show up to complicate the situation even more. 92m; DVD, Blu-Ray. **C:** Gina Gershon; Kelli Giddish; Ray Liotta; Wayne Duvall; Val Kilmer; Directed by Jesse Baget; Written by Jesse Baget; Stefania Moscato; Cinematography by Bill Otto; Music by Jermaine Stegall. **A:** Sr. High-Adult. **P:** Entertainment. **U:** Home. **L:** English. **Mov-Ent:** Crime Drama. **Acq:** Purchase. **Dist:** Anchor Bay Entertainment Inc.

Breathtaking 2000 — ★★
Workaholic Dr. Caroline Henshaw (Whalley) is a psychologist with many mental problems of her own, stemming from her own past sexual abuse. But Caroline has managed to keep it together until she meets a new patient (Maitland)?a self-destructive masseuse who's being battered by her sicko hubby (Foreman). 105m; VHS. **C:** Joanne Whalley; Neil Dudgeon; Sandra Maitland; Jamie Foreman; Directed by David Green; Written by Nicky Cowan; Cinematography by Gavin Finney; Music by Robert (Rob) Lane. **A:** Sr. High-Adult. **P:** Entertainment. **U:** Home. **Mov-Ent:** Sexual Abuse, Psychiatry. **Acq:** Purchase. **Dist:** Not Yet Released.

Brecht Practice Pieces 1964
Presents the practice pieces for "Romeo and Juliet" and "Hamlet" as performed by various actors including Lotte Lenya, Micki Grant and Oliver Clark. 28m; VHS. **A:** Adult. **P:** Education. **U:** Institution. **Fin-Art:** Theater. **Acq:** Purchase. **Dist:** Insight Media. $139.00.

The Breed 2001 (R) — ★★
Set in a noir-ish anytime, this horror film tells the story of an FBI agent Grant (a very stiff Woodbine), who starts out searching for a serial killer and ends up teamed with Aaron Grey (Paul), who turns out to be a vampire. Seems that the vampires who walk among us are ready to come out of the closet and join society, but a political dissident in the vampire ranks is trying to start a war...or is he? Could there be crosses and double crosses afoot? Grant, a black man, is less than thrilled at being teamed with a vampire, which results in not-too-subtle moral banter about racism and the Nazis to explain the vamps' fear of the humans and condemn the human sense of self preservation. It has moments of promise, but the poor acting and choppy editing and direction make everyone look uncomfortable amid the atmospheric scenery. 91m; VHS, DVD, Wide. **C:** Adrian Paul; Bai Ling; Bokeem Woodbine; Zen Gesner; Jake Eberle; Directed by Michael Oblowitz; Written by Christos N. Gage; Ruth Fletcher. **A:** Sr. High-Adult. **P:** Entertainment. **U:** Home. **Mov-Ent:** Federal Bureau of Investigation (FBI), Action-Adventure. **Acq:** Purchase. **Dist:** Sony Pictures Home Entertainment Inc.

The Breed 2006 (R) — ★
Bad doggie flick! Two brothers inherit their uncle's remote island and decide to fly three friends to join them in a party weekend. Too bad they didn't know their uncle rented part of the island to a special canine research unit and that the genetically enhanced dogs have gone wild. Lots of plot holes, lots of genre cliches. The Hound says this one must wear the cone of shame! 87m; DVD, Blu-Ray. **C:** Oliver Hudson; Hill Harper; Eric Lively; Michelle Rodriguez; Taryn Manning; Directed by Nick Mastandrea; Written by Robert Conte; Peter Martin Wortmann; Cinematography by Giulio Biccari; Music by Tom Mesmer. **A:** Sr. High-Adult. **P:** Entertainment. **U:** Home. **Mov-Ent**. **Acq:** Purchase. **Dist:** Millennium Entertainment L.L.C.

A Breed Apart 1984 (R) — ★★
An on-going battle over a rare eagle's eggs strikes sparks between a reclusive conservationist and a scheming adventurer hired by a billionaire collector. 95m; VHS. **C:** Kathleen Turner; Rutger Hauer; Powers Boothe; Donald Pleasence; Brion James; John Dennis Johnston; Directed by Philippe Mora. **Pr:** Hemdale Films; Sagittarius Productions; Orion Pictures. **A:** Sr. High-Adult. **P:** Entertainment. **U:** Home. **Mov-Ent:** Birds, Animals. **Acq:** Purchase. **Dist:** Unknown Distributor.

Breed of the Border 1933 — ★
Tough-fisted cowboys must take the law into their own hands. 60m/B/W; VHS, DVD. **C:** Bob Steele; Marion Byron; George "Gabby" Hayes; Ernie Adams; Directed by Robert North Bradbury. **Pr:** Monogram. **A:** Family. **P:** Entertainment. **U:** Home. **Mov-Ent:** Western. **Acq:** Purchase, Rent/Lease. **Dist:** Movies Unlimited; Alpha Video. $19.95.

Breeders 1986 (R) — ★1/2
Ridiculous foam rubber monster attacks and impregnates women in New York. 77m; VHS, DVD. **C:** Teresa Farley; Frances Raines; Amy Brentano; Lance Lewman; Natalie O'Connell; Directed by Tim Kincaid; Written by Tim Kincaid; Cinematography by Arthur Marks. **A:** Sr. High-Adult. **P:** Entertainment. **U:** Home. **Mov-Ent:** Science Fiction. **Acq:** Purchase. **Dist:** Movies Unlimited; MGM Home Entertainment. $14.99.

Breeders 1997 (R) — **Bomb!**
Alien on a mating mission terrorizes a Boston womens' college. Doesn't deliver on its exploitation premise, so don't bother. 92m; VHS, DVD. **C:** Todd Jensen; Samantha Janus; Kadamba Simmons; Oliver Tobias; Directed by Paul Matthews; Written by Paul Matthews; Music by Ben Heneghan. **A:** Sr. High-Adult. **P:** Entertainment. **U:** Home. **Mov-Ent:** Horror. **Acq:** Purchase. **Dist:** Movies Unlimited.

Breeders' Cup 1985 1985
The annual race at the New York's Aqueduct race track is covered by NBC's Dick Enberg. 120m; VHS. **C:** Hosted by Dick Enberg. **Pr:** National Broadcasting Company. **A:** Family. **P:** Entertainment. **U:** Home. **Spo-Rec:** Sports--General, Horses--Racing. **Acq:** Purchase. **Dist:** Lions Gate Television Corp. $19.95.

Breeders' Cup 1986 1986
Dick Enberg and Dave Johnson host this look at the annual race held at New York's Aqueduct race track. 120m; VHS. **C:** Hosted by Dick Enberg; Dave Johnson. **Pr:** National Broadcasting Company. **A:** Family. **P:** Entertainment. **U:** Home. **Spo-Rec:** Sports--General, Horses--Racing. **Acq:** Purchase. **Dist:** Lions Gate Television Corp. $19.95.

Breeding Cattle Evaluation 19??
Dr. Jerry Lipsey from the University of Missouri outlines information associated with what is involved in the evaluation of breeding cattle. Includes evaluation practice on classes of Angus bulls, Simmental heifers, and keep/cull Hereford heifers with oral reasons and ten questions on each class. 42m; VHS. **A:** Jr. High-Adult. **P:** Instruction. **U:** Institution. **How-Ins:** Agriculture, Animals, How-To. **Acq:** Purchase. **Dist:** CEV Multimedia. $59.95.

Breeding of Impotence: Perspectives on the Crisis in Our Communities and Schools 1993
Documentary study of the effects of economic depression, racism, hopelessness, and cultural gaps traces the rise of violence among today's youth. Explores the schools' ability to build self-esteem and curb youth violence. 55m; VHS. **A:** Adult. **P:** Education. **U:** Institution. **Gen-Edu:** Violence, Adolescence, Education. **Acq:** Purchase, Rent/Lease. **Dist:** The Cinema Guild. $350.00.

Breeding Swine Evaluation 19??
Swine specialists Dr. Lauren Christian and Dr. Jerry Hawton outline the factors associated with the evaluation of three classes of breeding swine. They explain how to utilize a breeding scenario coupled with visual appraisal to rank a class of four Hampshire gilts, a class of Yorkshire boars, and a class of keep/cull commercial filts. Following each class are oral reasons and a short quiz. 40m; VHS. **A:** Jr. High-Adult. **P:** Instruction. **U:** Institution. **How-Ins:** Agriculture, Animals, How-To. **Acq:** Purchase. **Dist:** CEV Multimedia. $59.95.

Breeds for Beginners 1989
Describes differing breeds of rabbits used in past winners of 4-H project competitions. Good introductory program for participating parents and children. Breeds include New Zealand, Californian, Champagne, Florida White, and Satins. 5m; VHS. **A:** Primary-Adult. **P:** Education. **U:** Institution. **Gen-Edu:** Agriculture, Animals. **Acq:** Purchase. **Dist:** Purdue University. $15.00.

Bremen Town Musicians 1972
Donkey, Dog, Cat, and Rooster run away from their master to become famous musicians in the town of Bremen. Along the way, they encounter and discourage a trio of robbers, then give up their musical dreams to live "happily ever after." 16m; VHS, 3/4 U. **Pr:** Institut fur Film und Bild. **A:** Primary. **P:** Education. **U:** Institution, SURA. **Chl-Juv:** Family Viewing, Fairy Tales. **Acq:** Purchase. **Dist:** Home Vision Cinema.

The Bremen Town Musicians 1981
See how four outcast animals are resourceful enough to outwit robbers and take care of themselves. 11m; VHS, 3/4 U. **Pr:** Greatest Tales, Inc. **A:** Primary. **P:** Education. **U:** Institution, SURA. **Chl-Juv:** Family Viewing, Literature. **Acq:** Purchase. **Dist:** Phoenix Learning Group.

The Bremen Town Musicians 1993
Animated adaptation of the humorous story of a donkey, dog, cat, and rooster who set out from their master's house to start new lives as musicians. 30m; VHS. **C:** Narrated by Bob Hoskins. **A:** Family. **P:** Entertainment. **U:** Home. **Chl-Juv:** Animation & Cartoons, Animals. **Acq:** Purchase. **Dist:** Baker and Taylor. $9.98.

Brenda Brave 1996
Brenda lives with her adopted grandmother, who sells homemade candy for a living. Right before Christmas, their busiest time of year, Brenda's grandmother breaks her leg, so it's up to the little girl to not only look after Grandma but to run the business as well. Based on a book by Astrid Lindgren and dubbed from Swedish. 30m; VHS. **C:** Directed by Daniel Bergman. **A:** Family. **P:** Entertainment. **U:** Home. **Chl-Juv:** Christmas, Family. **Acq:** Purchase. **Dist:** First Run Features.

Brenda Frese: 16 Dynamic Shooting Drills 2006
Demonstrates 16 basketball shooting drills along with passing and footwork fundamentals and conditioning techniques by Brenda Frese, the head coach of the 2006 women's national champion University of Maryland. 67m; DVD. **A:** Sr. High-Adult. **P:** Instruction. **U:** Institution. **Spo-Rec:** Basketball. **Acq:** Purchase. **Dist:** Championship Productions. $39.95.

Brenda Frese: Dynamic Quick Hitters 2007 (Unrated)
Coach Brenda Frese demonstrates offensive plays she teaches her basketball teams. 73m; DVD. **A:** Family. **P:** Education. **U:** Home, Institution. **Spo-Rec:** Basketball, Athletic Instruction/Coaching. **Acq:** Purchase. **Dist:** Championship Productions. $39.99.

Brenda Lee: An Evening with Brenda Lee 198?
In a memorable concert Brenda Lee performs the hits which have made her a rock and country music icon. 48m; VHS. **C:** Brenda Lee. **Pr:** Simitar Entertainment. **A:** Family. **P:** Entertain-

ment. **U:** Home. **Mov-Ent:** Music--Performance, Music--Pop/Rock, Music--Country/Western. **Acq:** Purchase. **Dist:** Music Video Distributors. $14.95.

Brenda Starr 1986 (PG) — ★
Amateurish adaptation of the comic strip by Dale Messick. Shields stars as girl reporter Brenda Starr, who is once again risking her life to get the scoop. She finds herself in the jungles of South America searching for a mad scientist who is creating a rocket fuel that could destroy the world. The most entertaining thing about this film is the costumes designed by Bob Mackie. 94m; VHS, DVD. **C:** Brooke Shields; Timothy Dalton; Tony Peck; Diana Scarwid; Nestor Serrano; Jeffrey Tambor; June Gable; Charles Durning; Eddie Albert; Henry Gibson; Ed Nelson; Directed by Robert Ellis Miller; Written by James David Buchanan; Cinematography by Freddie Francis; Music by Johnny Mandel. **Pr:** Myron A. Hyman; AM/PM Production. **A:** Jr. High-Adult. **P:** Entertainment. **U:** Home. **Mov-Ent:** Journalism. **Acq:** Purchase. **Dist:** Sony Pictures Home Entertainment Inc. $19.95.

The Brendan Voyage 1978
Tim Severin sailed from Ireland to Newfoundland in a replica of a medieval leather boat, duplicating the legendary voyage of St. Brendan in the sixth century. 57m; VHS, 3/4 U. **Pr:** I. D. Television Ltd. **A:** Sr. High-Adult. **P:** Education. **U:** Institution, SURA. **Gen-Edu:** Documentary Films, History--Medieval, Boating. **Acq:** Purchase. **Dist:** Home Vision Cinema.

Brent Brennen: Wide Receiver Fundamentals-Releases and Route Running 2013 (Unrated)
Football coach Brent Brennen demonstrates training techniques for wide receivers on teams using the spread offense. 52m; DVD. **A:** Family. **P:** Education. **U:** Home. **L:** English. **Spo-Rec:** Athletic Instruction/Coaching, Football. **Acq:** Purchase. **Dist:** Championship Productions. $29.99.

Brer Rabbit and Boss Lion 1992
An adaptation of the American folk tale about how brains always overcome brawn. The musical score is by Dr. John. Part of the Rabbit Ears "American Heroes and Legends" series. 34m; VHS. **C:** Narrated by Danny Glover. **A:** Preschool-Primary. **P:** Entertainment. **U:** Home. **Chl-Juv:** Animation & Cartoons, Folklore & Legends, Children. **Acq:** Purchase. **Dist:** Universal Music and Video Distribution; Music Video Distributors; Baker and Taylor. $9.98.

Brer Rabbit and the Wonderful Tar Baby 1991
The "great-grandfather of Bugs Bunny" outwits Brer Fox again in this delightful classic American tale narrated by Danny Glover. Part of the "We All Have Tales" series. 30m; VHS. **C:** Narrated by Danny Glover. **A:** Preschool-Primary. **P:** Entertainment. **U:** Home, Institution. **Chl-Juv:** Literature--Children. **Acq:** Purchase. **Dist:** Knowledge Unlimited, Inc.; New Line Home Video. $15.99.

Bret Harte: Chronicler of the Golden West 1989
Examines life of Bret Harte, American author of "The Luck of the Roaring Camp," "The Outcasts of Poker Flat," and "Tennesse's Partner." Features the author as a miner, school teacher, and unsuccessful satirist and poet. 18m; VHS, 3/4 U. **Pr:** Films for the Humanities and Sciences. **A:** College. **P:** Education. **U:** Institution, CCTV, CATV, BCTV. **Fin-Art:** Literature--American, Biography. **Acq:** Purchase, Rent/Lease, Duplication License. **Dist:** Films for the Humanities & Sciences.

Bret Maverick: The Complete Series 1981
NBC 1981-82 western comedy. Gambler Bret Maverick wins the Lazy Ace saloon in a poker game and decides to settle down in Sweetwater, Arizona. He partners with shady ex-sheriff Tom Guthrie to run the saloon while Maverick keeps gambling and getting into trouble. 18 episodes. 878m; DVD. **C:** James Garner; Ed Bruce; Ramon Bieri; Darleen Carr. **A:** Jr. High-Adult. **P:** Entertainment. **U:** Home. **L:** English. **Mov-Ent:** Western, Television Series. **Acq:** Purchase. **Dist:** WarnerArchive.com. $39.95.

Brett Butler: Sold Out 1994
Butler riffs on her sudden fame, breast implants, Tonya Harding, her attraction to firemen, and other topics. 30m; VHS, CC. **A:** Sr. High-Adult. **P:** Entertainment. **U:** Home. **Mov-Ent:** Comedy--Performance. **Acq:** Purchase. **Dist:** Paramount Pictures Corp. $12.95.

Brett Butler: The Child Ain't Right 1993
Brett showcases her Southern humor with riffs on her upbringing, ex-husband, and time in New York. 26m; VHS, CC. **Pr:** Showtime Networks. **A:** Sr. High-Adult. **P:** Entertainment. **U:** Home. **Mov-Ent:** Comedy--Performance. **Acq:** Purchase. **Dist:** Paramount Pictures Corp. $12.95.

Brett Reed: Building Your Transition Defense 2013 (Unrated)
Coach Brett Reed shares the basketball techniques he teaches to improve his school's defensive transition game. 91m; DVD. **A:** Family. **P:** Education. **U:** Home. **L:** English. **Spo-Rec:** Athletic Instruction/Coaching, Basketball. **Acq:** Purchase. **Dist:** Championship Productions. $39.99.

The Bretts 1988 — ★★★
Amusing two-part British miniseries follows the egos and eccentricities of the British theatrical dynasty, the Bretts. Part 1 is set in the '20s and introduces the family heads, Charles (Rodway) and Lydia (Murray), who enjoy performing off-stage almost as well as they enjoy performing on. Also introduced are their five children and loyal (if opinionated) servants. Part 2 follows the family into the '30s with son Edwin (Yelland) having become a film star, actress daughter Martha (Lang) falling for a politician, and son Tom (Winter) continuing to write his gloomy social dramas. Each part is on six cassettes. 600m; VHS, DVD.

C: Barbara Murray; Norman Rodway; David Yelland; Belinda Lang; George Winter; Janet Maw; Tim Wylton; Bert Parnaby; Lysette Anthony; Clive Francis; Frank Middlemass; John Castle; Hugh Fraser; Patrick Ryecart; Sally Cookson; Billy Boyle; Written by Rosemary Anne Sisson. **Pr:** Central Independent Television. **A:** Sr. High-Adult. **P:** Entertainment. **U:** Home. **Mov-Ent:** Comedy-Drama, Family, Theater. **Acq:** Purchase. **Dist:** Signals Video; Video Collectibles. $129.95.

Brewed in Brooklyn 2013 (Unrated)
Documentary on the history of Brooklyn, New York's beer brewers, including modern day home and craft brewers. 45m; DVD. **A:** Jr. High-Adult. **P:** Entertainment. **U:** Home. **L:** English. **Gen-Edu:** Alcoholic Beverages, Documentary Films, Business. **Acq:** Purchase. **Dist:** Janson Media. $24.95.

Brewing Coffee/Making Tea 1986
Offers instruction on specific aspects of cooking and food preparation. 10m; VHS. **A:** Adult. **P:** Instruction. **U:** Institution. **Gen-Edu:** Cooking. **Acq:** Purchase. **Dist:** RMI Media. $39.95.

Brewster McCloud 1970 (R) — ★★★½
Altman's first picture after M*A*S*H reunites much of the cast and combines fantasy, black comedy, and satire in the story of a young man whose head is in the clouds or at least in the upper reaches of the Houston Astrodome. Brewster (Cort) lives covertly in the Dome and dreams of flying. He also has a guardian angel (Kellerman) who watches over him and may actually be killing people who give him a hard time. Murphy is a cop obsessed with catching the killer. And there's a circus allegory as well. Hard to figure what it all means and offbeat as they come, but for certain tastes, exquisite. 101m; VHS, DVD, Wide. **C:** Bud Cort; Sally Kellerman; Shelley Duvall; Michael Murphy; William Windom; Rene Auberjonois; Stacy Keach; John Schuck; Margaret Hamilton; Directed by Robert Altman; Written by Doran William Cannon; Cinematography by Jordan Cronenweth; Lamar Boren; Music by Gene Page. **Pr:** MGM. **A:** Sr. High-Adult. **P:** Entertainment. **U:** Home. **Mov-Ent:** Comedy--Black, Birds, Circuses. **Acq:** Purchase. **Dist:** WarnerArchive.com. $19.98.

Brewster's Millions 1945 — ★★½
If Brewster, an ex-GI, can spend $1 million in one year, he will inherit a substantially greater fortune. Originally a 1902 novel, this is the fifth of seven film adaptations. 79m/B/W; DVD. **C:** Dennis O'Keefe; June Havoc; Eddie Anderson; Helen Walker; Gail Patrick; Mischa Auer; Directed by Allan Dwan; Written by Charles Rodgers; Wilkie Mahoney; Cinematography by Charles Lawton, Jr. **Pr:** United Artists. **A:** Family. **P:** Entertainment. **U:** Home. **Mov-Ent:** Family Viewing, Hotels & Hotel Staff Training. **Acq:** Purchase. **Dist:** Hen's Tooth Video. $19.95.

Brewster's Millions 1985 (PG) — ★½
An aging minor league baseball player must spend $30 million in order to collect an inheritance of $300 million. He may find that money can't buy happiness. Seventh remake of the story. 101m; VHS, DVD, Wide, CC. **C:** Richard Pryor; John Candy; Lonette McKee; Stephen Collins; Jerry Orbach; Pat Hingle; Tovah Feldshuh; Hume Cronyn; Rick Moranis; Yakov Smirnoff; Joe Grifasi; Peter Jason; Grand L. Bush; Reni Santoni; Conrad Janis; Lin Shaye; Directed by Walter Hill; Written by Herschel Weingrod; Timothy Harris; Cinematography by Ric Waite; Music by Ry Cooder. **Pr:** Universal Studios. **A:** Jr. High-Adult. **P:** Entertainment. **U:** Home. **Mov-Ent:** Baseball, Hotels & Hotel Staff Training. **Acq:** Purchase. **Dist:** Alpha Video; Movies Unlimited; Universal Studios Home Video. $19.95.

Brian Bromberg: Master Techniques for 4-String, Piccolo and Synthesizer Bass 1990
Many facets of jazz music and how to work them are featured here. ?m; VHS. **A:** Jr. High-Adult. **P:** Instruction. **U:** Home. **How-Ins:** Music--Instruction. **Acq:** Purchase. **Dist:** Music Video Distributors. $49.95.

Brian Eno: Excerpt from the Khumba Nela 19??
This New Age film by Albert Falzon journeys through the Kashmir waterways on to a religious festival, all to the music of Eno and Budd. 45m; VHS. **A:** Sr. High-Adult. **P:** Entertainment. **U:** Home. **Mov-Ent:** Music Video, New Age, Religion. **Acq:** Purchase. **Dist:** Music Video Distributors. $19.95.

Brian Eno: Imaginary Landscapes 1991
Video portrait of one of the most influential musical artists of the eighties. Includes an in-depth interview with Eno, who discusses his vision of music and its relationship to the visual arts. 40m; VHS. **C:** Brian Eno. **Pr:** Mystic Fire Video. **A:** Jr. High-Adult. **P:** Entertainment. **U:** Home. **Mov-Ent:** Music--Performance, Video, Interviews. **Acq:** Purchase. **Dist:** Mystic Fire Video; Facets Multimedia Inc. $19.95.

Brian Eno: Mistaken Memories of Mad Manhattan 19??
British import featuring "vertical format video painting" by a leading New Age artist. Includes seven N.Y.C. skyline sequences transmuted through layers of light and color. 47m; VHS. **A:** Sr. High-Adult. **P:** Entertainment. **U:** Home. **Mov-Ent:** New Age, Art & Artists, Painting. **Acq:** Purchase. **Dist:** Music Video Distributors. $19.95.

Brian Eno: Thursday Afternoon 1990
The co-founder of Roxy Music combines light, color, and animation with his music. 82m; VHS. **C:** Music by Brian Eno. **Pr:** SVS Ent. **A:** Jr. High-Adult. **P:** Entertainment. **U:** Home. **Mov-Ent:** Music Video. **Acq:** Purchase. **Dist:** Music Video Distributors. $19.95.

Brian Gimmillaro's Learn to Play Volleyball: Blocking 2011 (Unrated)
Coach Brian Gimmillaro shares the methods he uses to teach blocking skills to his volleyball teams. 45m; DVD. **A:** Family. **P:** Education. **U:** Home, Institution. **Spo-Rec**: Volleyball, Athletic Instruction/Coaching. **Acq:** Purchase. **Dist:** Championship Productions. $39.99.

Brian Gimmillaro's Learn to Play Volleyball: Defense 2011 (Unrated)
Coach Brian Gimmillaro discusses the defensive volleyball techniques he used at Long Beach State. 43m; DVD. **A:** Family. **P:** Education. **U:** Home, Institution. **Spo-Rec**: Volleyball, Athletic Instruction/Coaching. **Acq:** Purchase. **Dist:** Championship Productions. $39.99.

Brian Gimmillaro's Learn to Play Volleyball: Passing 2011 (Unrated)
Coach Brian Gimmillaro discusses how to improve accuracy among volleyball players' passing. 45m; DVD. **A:** Family. **P:** Education. **U:** Home, Institution. **Spo-Rec**: Volleyball, Athletic Instruction/Coaching. **Acq:** Purchase. **Dist:** Championship Productions. $39.99.

Brian Gimmillaro's Learn to Play Volleyball: Serving 2011 (Unrated)
Coach Brian Gimmillaro discusses serving strategy for volleyball teams. 42m; DVD. **A:** Family. **P:** Education. **U:** Home, Institution. **Spo-Rec**: Volleyball, Athletic Instruction/Coaching. **Acq:** Purchase. **Dist:** Championship Productions. $39.99.

Brian Gimmillaro's Learn to Play Volleyball: Setting 2011 (Unrated)
Coach Brian Gimmillaro shares the methods he uses to teach and improve setters in volleyball. 52m; DVD. **A:** Family. **P:** Education. **U:** Home, Institution. **Spo-Rec**: Volleyball, Athletic Instruction/Coaching. **Acq:** Purchase. **Dist:** Championship Productions. $39.99.

Brian Gimmillaro's Learn to Play Volleyball: Spiking 2010 (Unrated)
Coach Brian Gimmillaro discusses improving a volleyball team's spiking skills. 45m; DVD. **A:** Family. **P:** Education. **U:** Home, Institution. **Spo-Rec**: Volleyball, Athletic Instruction/Coaching. **Acq:** Purchase. **Dist:** Championship Productions. $39.99.

Brian Gregory: Early Offense and Set Plays 2011 (Unrated)
Coach Brian Gregory discusses transition offense and common set plays used in college basketball. 81m; DVD. **A:** Family. **P:** Education. **U:** Home, Institution. **Spo-Rec**: Basketball, Athletic Instruction/Coaching. **Acq:** Purchase. **Dist:** Championship Productions. $39.99.

Brian Gregory: Five Defensive Principles for Success 2006
Coach Brian Gregory presents what he believes are the five basics defense strategies in basketball—transition defense, eliminate dribble splits, contest shots, block out, and taking the opponent out of set plays. 73m; DVD. **A:** Family. **P:** Education. **U:** Home, Institution. **Spo-Rec**: Basketball, Athletic Instruction/Coaching. **Acq:** Purchase. **Dist:** Championship Productions. $39.99.

Brian Gregory: Scramble Drills for Transition Defense and Offense 2010 (Unrated)
Coach Brian Gregory presents drills for improving a basketball team's transition abilities, whether they are playing offense or defense. 90m; DVD. **A:** Family. **P:** Education. **U:** Home, Institution. **Spo-Rec**: Basketball, Athletic Instruction/Coaching. **Acq:** Purchase. **Dist:** Championship Productions. $39.99.

Brian Gregory: The 10 Best Practice Drills Ever 2006
Presents 10 basketball team and individual practice drills for offense and defense situations by University of Dayton's head coach Brian Gregory, a former assistant of Michigan State University's head coach Tom Izzo. 81m; DVD. **A:** Sr. High-Adult. **P:** Instruction. **U:** Institution. **Spo-Rec**: Basketball. **Acq:** Purchase. **Dist:** Championship Productions. $39.95.

Brian Gregory: 3-Phase Attack to Beat any Zone Defense 2010 (Unrated)
Coach Brian Gregory discusses the offensive philosophy he teaches his basketball teams to use against the zone defense. 83m; DVD. **A:** Family. **P:** Education. **U:** Home, Institution. **Spo-Rec**: Basketball, Athletic Instruction/Coaching. **Acq:** Purchase. **Dist:** Championship Productions. $39.99.

Brian May: Guitar Instruction 1990
The great Queen guitarist exhibits his hard hitting sounds and how he gets them. ?m; VHS. **A:** Jr. High-Adult. **P:** Instruction. **U:** Home. **How-Ins**: Music--Instruction. **Acq:** Purchase. **Dist:** Music Video Distributors. $44.95.

Brian Regan: Standing Up 2007 (Unrated)
Concert footage of comedian Brian Regan, who focuses on the mundane aspects of life minus the use of profane language or vulgarity. 42m; DVD. **A:** Sr. High-Adult. **P:** Entertainment. **U:** Home. **Mov-Ent**: Comedy--Performance, Television. **Acq:** Purchase. **Dist:** Comedy Central. $14.99.

Brian Regan: The Epitome of Hyperbole 2008 (Unrated)
Stand-up comedy performance by Brian Regan taking shots at fraudulent psychics, and less than intelligent criminals. 42m; DVD. **A:** Sr. High-Adult. **P:** Entertainment. **U:** Home. **Mov-Ent**: Documentary Films, Music. **Acq:** Purchase. **Dist:** Comedy Central. $19.99.

Brian Regan—I Walked on the Moon 20?? (Unrated)
The first taped release of Brian Regan's stand-up comedy act. ??m; DVD. **A:** Sr. High-Adult. **P:** Entertainment. **U:** Home. **Gen-Edu**: Comedy--Performance, Television. **Acq:** Purchase. **Dist:** Comedy Central. $32.82.

Brian Sewell's Grand Tour of Italy 2005 (Unrated)
Historical documentary series with London Evening Standard staff writer Brian Sewell. Brian travels the routes of young aristocrats that would tour the region to obtain refinement before taking their rightly place in society. Explore the art, architecture, manner, and debauchery experienced by English gentlemen let loose in Italy during the 18th century. 10 episodes. 385m; DVD. **C:** Brian Sewell. **A:** Family. **P:** Entertainment. **U:** Home. **Mov-Ent**: Documentary Films, Italy, Television Series. **Acq:** Purchase. **Dist:** Acorn Media Group Inc. $79.99.

Brian White: Daily Drills for Developing Running Backs 2013 (Unrated)
Football coach Brian White demonstrates the training drills he believes will deliver better running backs. 60m; DVD. **A:** Family. **P:** Education. **U:** Home. **L:** English. **Spo-Rec**: Athletic Instruction/Coaching, Football. **Acq:** Purchase. **Dist:** Championship Productions. $29.99.

Brian Wilson: I Just Wasn't Made for These Times 1995
Engrossing documentary on the eccentric life of '60s rock icon—and legendary "Beach Boy"?Brian Wilson. Record producer-turned-debut director Was well captures at least some of Wilson's troubled story through interviews with his family, friends, and musical peers, as well as with the singer/songwriter himself. 69m; VHS. **C:** Directed by Don Was. **A:** Sr. High-Adult. **P:** Entertainment. **U:** Home. **Gen-Edu**: Documentary Films, Biography, Music--Pop/Rock. **Acq:** Purchase. **Dist:** Lions Gate Television Corp. $19.98.

Brianna: A Two-Year-Old in a Group Setting 1980
In a group care setting for toddlers, interaction among the children and between the children and the caregivers is shown. 15m; VHS, 3/4 U, EJ, Q. **Pr:** Cornell University. **A:** College-Adult. **P:** Education. **U:** Institution, CCTV, CATV, BCTV, Home. **Gen-Edu**: Child Care. **Acq:** Purchase, Rent/Lease. **Dist:** Cornell University.

Brian's Song 197?
A production designed to supplement the novel by William Binn. This is an enhanced filmstrip made to appear animated via computer enhancement. ?m; VHS. **A:** Primary-Sr. High. **P:** Education. **U:** Institution, Home, SURA. **Gen-Edu**: Literature--American, Education. **Acq:** Purchase. **Dist:** African-American Images. $45.00.

Brian's Song 1971 (G) — ★★★★
The story of the unique relationship between Gale Sayers, the Chicago Bears' star running back, and his teammate Brian Piccolo. The friendship between the Bears' first interracial roommates ended suddenly when Brian Piccolo lost his life to cancer. Incredibly well received in its time. 74m; VHS, DVD, CC. **C:** James Caan; Billy Dee Williams; Jack Warden; Shelley Fabares; Judy Pace; Bernie Casey; Directed by Buzz Kulik; Written by William Blinn; Cinematography by Joseph Biroc; Music by Michel Legrand. **Pr:** Paul Junger Witt. **A:** Family. **P:** Entertainment. **U:** Home. **Mov-Ent**: Melodrama, Football, TV Movies. **Acq:** Purchase. **Dist:** Sony Pictures Home Entertainment Inc. $64.95.

Brian's Song 2001 — ★★
Unnecessary remake of the 1971 made-for-TV classic dealing with the friendship between Gale Sayers and Brian Piccolo, and Piccolo's fight against cancer heads right for the disease-of-the-week cliches with almost none of the original's charm or depth. Phifer, as Sayers, and Cale, as Joy Piccolo, along with a deeper understanding of the wives' point of view, are the main reasons to check it out. But it still can't compare to the original. 89m; VHS, DVD. **C:** Mekhi Phifer; Sean Maher; Paula Cale; Elise Neal; Ben Gazzara; Aidan Devine; Dean McDermott; Directed by John Gray; Written by John Gray; Allen Clare; William Blinn; Cinematography by James Chressanthis; Music by Richard (Rick) Marvin. **A:** Family. **P:** Entertainment. **U:** Home. **Mov-Ent**: Football, Diseases, Biography: Sports. **Acq:** Purchase. **Dist:** Sony Pictures Home Entertainment Inc.

Briar Rose: The Sleeping Beauty 1986
The award-winning team of Somersaulter-Moats and Somersaulter bring Grimm's classic fairy tale to life. 14m; VHS, 3/4 U. **Pr:** Coronet Films. **A:** Preschool-Primary. **P:** Education. **U:** Institution, SURA. **Chl-Juv**: Children, Animation & Cartoons, Fairy Tales. **Acq:** Purchase, Rent/Lease. **Dist:** Anchor Bay Entertainment.

The Bribe 1948 (Unrated) — ★★½
Federal Agent Rigby (Taylor) is sent to a tropical isle off the coast of Central America to investigate a smuggling ring dealing in contraband war surplus airplane engines. It's run by playboy Carwood (Price) and sleazy Bealler (Laughton) along with former wartime pilot Tug (Hodiak). Tug's wife—torch singer Elizabeth (Gardner)?doesn't know about the scheme but when Rigby falls for the femme, the crooks try setting him up so Rigby will compromise his career so he can save her. 98m/B/W; DVD. **C:** Robert Taylor; Ava Gardner; Vincent Price; Charles Laughton; John Hodiak; Samuel S. Hinds; Directed by Robert Z. Leonard; Written by Marguerite Roberts; Cinematography by Joseph Ruttenberg; Music by Miklos Rozsa. **A:** Sr. High-Adult. **P:** Entertainment. **U:** Home. **Mov-Ent**: Drug Trafficking/Dealing. **Acq:** Purchase. **Dist:** WarnerArchive.com.

Brice Marden 1977
Filmed over a span of nine years, this focuses on the work and philosophy of artist. 22m; VHS, 3/4 U, Special order formats. **C:** Directed by Edgar B. Howard; Theodore R. Haimes. **Pr:** Checkerboard Productions, Inc; Tuckernuck Productions. **A:** Sr. High-Adult. **P:** Education. **U:** Home. **Fin-Art**: Documentary Films, Art & Artists, Painting. **Acq:** Purchase, Rent/Lease. **Dist:** Museum of Modern Art. $39.95.

Brick 2006 (R) — ★★★
Ever wonder what it would look like if Raymond Chandler wrote for the "Sweet Valley High" series? In his debut film, writer/director Johnson delivers one of the most impressive examples of hard-boiled noir in years, set, strangely enough, in a California high school. Gordon-Levitt brilliantly channels Humphrey Bogart as Brendan, a tough-as-nails teenaged shamus who's trying to locate his missing ex-girlfriend (de Ravin) in the seamy underbelly of drug-dealing jocks and cheerleader femme fatales. The mystery's a twisty one, peppered with Johnson's own brand of tough guy slang that will either delight or confound you. But you can't ignore the ambition of this "Miller's Crossing" meets "Breakfast Club" hybrid. 110m; DVD, Wide. **C:** Joseph Gordon-Levitt; Lukas Haas; Noah Fleiss; Matt O'Leary; Nora Zehetner; Noah Segan; Meagan Good; Emilie de Ravin; Brian White; Richard Roundtree; Lucas Babin; Directed by Rian Johnson; Written by Rian Johnson; Cinematography by Steve Yedlin; Music by Nathan Johnson. **Pr:** Ram Bergman; Mark G. Mathis; Norman Dreyfuss; Johnson Communications; Bergman/Lustig. **A:** Sr. High-Adult. **P:** Entertainment. **U:** Home. **L:** English. **Mov-Ent**: Mystery & Suspense, Adolescence, Drug Trafficking/Dealing. **Acq:** Purchase. **Dist:** Movies Unlimited; Alpha Video.

Brick by Brick: A Civil Right's Story 2008 (Unrated)
Documentary on racism in the American north, showcasing the resistance Black Americans faced as they attempted to find housing in New York during the 1980s. 53m; DVD. **A:** Sr. High-Adult. **P:** Education. **U:** Home, BCTV, Institution. **Gen-Edu**: Civil Rights, Documentary Films. **Acq:** Purchase. **Dist:** California Newsreel. $195.

Brick City 2009
This five-part documentary series focuses on efforts to address issues of crime, violence, poverty, and corruption in the city of Newark, New Jersey, under the leadership of its mayor, Cory Booker. 260m; DVD. **A:** Jr. High-Adult. **P:** Entertainment. **U:** Home. **Mov-Ent**: Documentary Films, History, Cities & Towns. **Acq:** Purchase. **Dist:** First Run Features. $29.95.

Brick Haley: Defensive Plays and Techniques 2007 (Unrated)
Coach Brick Haley shares techniques and his philosophy on defensive line play for the game of football. 57m; DVD. **A:** Family. **P:** Education. **U:** Home, Institution. **Spo-Rec**: Football, Athletic Instruction/Coaching. **Acq:** Purchase. **Dist:** Championship Productions. $39.99.

The Brick-Makers 1972
Peasant life and poverty in Latin American cities are examined with an emphasis on a family of brick makers. English subtitles. 42m/B/W; VHS, 3/4 U. **TV Std:** NTSC, PAL, SECAM. **C:** Directed by Marta Rodriguez; Jorge Silva. **Pr:** Marta Rodriguez. **A:** Sr. High-Adult. **P:** Education. **U:** Institution, SURA. **L:** English, Spanish. **Gen-Edu**: Documentary Films, Central America, Poverty. **Acq:** Purchase, Rent/Lease, Duplication. **Dist:** The Cinema Guild. $595.00.

Brick Mansions 2014 (PG-13) — ★½
An unnecessary redo of the international hit "District B13" that only garners attention as Paul Walker's final film. The deceased action star appears as Damien Collier, an undercover cop in a battle against corruption that teams him up with a street kid named Lino (Belle) against drug kingpin Tremaine (RZA). Boring and poorly edited, it lacks the flair of the original, and Walker's appeal can only do so much to make it better. 90m; DVD. **C:** Paul Walker; David Belle; RZA; Carlo Rota; Directed by Camille Delamarre; Written by Luc Besson; Cinematography by Christophe Collette; Music by Marc Bell. **Pr:** Luc Besson; Relativity Media L.L.C. **A:** Sr. High-Adult. **P:** Entertainment. **U:** Home. **L:** English. **Mov-Ent**: Crime Drama, Cities & Towns. **Acq:** Purchase.

Bridal Creations 19??
Details information on bridal fans, parasols, wreaths, and bouquets for the bride and her maids. Also demonstrates construction of the slim cascade, full cascade, and crescent bouquets. 50m; VHS. **A:** Sr. High-Adult. **P:** Instruction. **U:** Institution. **How-Ins**: Marriage, How-To, Flowers. **Acq:** Purchase. **Dist:** Instructional Video. $29.95.

Bridal Elegance 19??
Outlines basic bridal arranging techniques, bow making, and floral construction. Illustrates how to make a diagonal bride's bouquet, a basquet, an arm bouquet, and the english oval. 59m; VHS. **A:** Sr. High-Adult. **P:** Instruction. **U:** Institution. **How-Ins**: Marriage, How-To, Flowers. **Acq:** Purchase. **Dist:** Instructional Video. $29.95.

Bridal Fever 2008 (Unrated) — ★★
Hallmark Channel movie about finding old-fashioned romance in the most cliched way possible. Single Gwen (Roth) has been singed once too often and is reluctant to change her marital status until she's hired by romance author Dahlia Merchant (Burke) to edit her autobiography. The much-married Dahlia has Gwen and her friend Sandra (Deines) doing some pre-wedding visualization before they go on a serious hubby hunt. 88m; DVD. **C:** Andrea Roth; Delta Burke; Gabriel Hogan; Melinda Deines; Vincent Walsh; Nigel Bennett; Richard Fitzpatrick; Directed by Ron Oliver; Written by Karen McClellan; Cinematography by Gerald Packer. **A:** Jr. High-Adult. **P:** Entertainment. **U:** Home. **Mov-Ent**: Comedy--Romantic. **Acq:** Purchase. **Dist:** Movies Unlimited.

The Bride 1985 (PG-13) — ★½
Re-telling of "The Bride of Frankenstein." Sting's Dr. Frankenstein has much more success in creating his second monster (Beals). She's pretty and intelligent and he may even be falling in love with her. When she begins to gain too much independence, though, the awful truth about her origins comes out. Fans of the two leads will want to see this one, but for a true classic see Elsa Lanchester's bride. 118m; VHS, DVD, Wide, CC. **C:** Sting; Jennifer Beals; Anthony (Corlan) Higgins; David Rappaport; Geraldine Page; Clancy Brown; Phil Daniels; Veruschka; Quentin Crisp; Cary Elwes; Directed by Franc Roddam; Written by Lloyd Fonvielle; Cinematography by Stephen Burum; Music by Maurice Jarre. **Pr:** Columbia Pictures. **A:** Jr. High-Adult. **P:** Entertainment. **U:** Home. **Mov-Ent:** Horror. **Acq:** Purchase. **Dist:** Sony Pictures Home Entertainment Inc. $9.95.

Bride & Prejudice 2004 (PG-13) — ★★
Bollywood meets Jane Austen in Chandha's brightly-colored confection. Will Darcy (Henderson) and chum Balraj (Andrews) arrive in Amritsar for a friend's wedding. A stuffy but wealthy businessman, Will finds himself drawn to the strikingly beautiful and headstrong Lalita (Rai) who's irritated by his arrogance. That they are meant for each other is obvious but the film must travel from India to London and L.A. and back again before it all plays out, amidst various musical numbers and family trials. 110m; DVD. **C:** Aishwarya Rai; Martin Henderson; Anupam Kher; Naveen Andrews; Daniel Gillies; Indira Varma; Marsha Mason; Nadira Babbar; Namrata Shirodkar; Meghnaa; Peeya Rai Choudhuri; Directed by Gurinder Chadha; Written by Gurinder Chadha; Paul Mayeda Berges; Cinematography by Santosh Sivan. **Pr:** Deepak Nayar; Gurinder Chadha; Nayar Chadha; Gurinder Chadha; Miramax; Pathe. **A:** Jr. High-Adult. **P:** Entertainment. **U:** Home. **L:** English. **Mov-Ent:** Musical, Musical, Comedy--Romantic. **Acq:** Purchase. **Dist:** Miramax Film Corp.

The Bride & the Beast 1958 (Unrated) — **Bomb!**
While on an African safari honeymoon, a big game hunter's new bride is carried off by a gorilla. Ludicrous jungle tale. 78m/B/W; VHS, DVD. **C:** Charlotte Austin; Lance Fuller; William Justine; Johnny Roth; Jeanne Gerson; Gilbert Frye; Slick Slavin; Bhogwan Singh; Directed by Adrian Weiss; Written by Edward D. Wood, Jr.; Cinematography by Roland Price; Music by Les Baxter. **Pr:** Allied Artists International. **A:** Family. **P:** Entertainment. **U:** Home. **Mov-Ent:** Marriage, Africa. **Acq:** Purchase. **Dist:** VCI Entertainment; Movies Unlimited; Alpha Video.

Bride by Mistake 1944 (Unrated) — ★½
Not very successful identity switch comedy that's a remake of 1934's "The Richest Girl in the World." Wealthy Norah (Day) is annoyed by fortune hunters and uses her secretary Sylvia (Hunt) to throw them off. Since Norah is interested in convalescing fighter pilot Tony Travis (Marshal), she decides to switch places with Sylvia and see if Tony will love her for herself while she constantly throws him in the fake Norah's path. 81m/B/W; DVD. **C:** Laraine Day; Alan Marshal; Marsha Hunt; Allyn Joslyn; Edgar Buchanan; Michael St. Angel; Directed by Richard Wallace; Written by Phoebe Ephron; Henry Ephron; Cinematography by Nicholas Musuraca; Music by Roy Webb. **A:** Sr. High-Adult. **P:** Entertainment. **U:** Home. **Mov-Ent:** Comedy--Romantic. **Acq:** Purchase. **Dist:** WarnerArchive.com.

The Bride Came C.O.D. 1941 (Unrated) — ★★
Rough 'n' tough pilot Cagney is hired by a rich Texas oil man to prevent his daughter (the one with the Bette Davis eyes) from marrying cheesy bandleader Carson. The payoff: $10 per pound if she's delivered unwed. What a surprise when Cagney faces the timeworn dilemma of having to choose between love and money. A contemporary issue of "Time" magazine trumpeted: "Screen's most talented tough guy rough-houses one of screen's best dramatic actresses." That tells you right there it's a romantic comedy. Cagney and Davis—a likely pairing, you'd think—are essentially fish out of water, bothered and bewildered by a weak script. 92m/B/W; VHS, DVD. **C:** Bette Davis; James Cagney; Stuart Erwin; Jack Carson; George Tobias; Eugene Pallette; William Frawley; Harry Davenport; Directed by William Keighley; Written by Julius J. Epstein; Philip G. Epstein; Cinematography by Ernest Haller; Music by Max Steiner. **A:** Jr. High-Adult. **P:** Entertainment. **U:** Home. **Mov-Ent:** Comedy--Romantic, Classic Films, Comedy--Screwball. **Acq:** Purchase. **Dist:** Warner Home Video, Inc.; Facets Multimedia Inc. $19.95.

The Bride Comes Home 1935 (Unrated) — ★★½
When her father's business goes bust, socialite Jeannette (Colbert) gets a job writing for a Chicago magazine thanks to smitten employee Jack Bristow (Young). However, the sparks really fly between Jeannette and her editor, Cyrus Anderson (MacMurray), although the usual romantic misunderstandings get in the way. 83m/B/W; DVD. **C:** Claudette Colbert; Fred MacMurray; Robert Young; William Collier, Sr.; Directed by Wesley Ruggles; Written by Claude Binyon; Cinematography by Leo Tover. **A:** Sr. High-Adult. **P:** Entertainment. **U:** Home. **Mov-Ent:** Comedy--Screwball. **Acq:** Purchase. **Dist:** Movies Unlimited.

Bride Flight 2008 (R) — ★★½
Sometimes weepy romantic drama. Wanting to leave dreary postwar Holland, three women emigrate to New Zealand to meet their little-known fiances who have settled in Christchurch. Shy farm girl Ada, family-oriented Marjorie, and Jewish fashion designer Esther befriend each other on the 1953 flight and are also introduced to fellow passenger, roguish farmer Frank. Their paths will continue to cross over the years with much ensuing emotion. English and Dutch with subtitles. 130m; DVD, Blu-Ray. **C:** Waldemar Torenstra; Karina Smulders; Anna Drijver; Elise Schaap; Rutger Hauer; Pleuni Touw; Willeke van Ammelrooy; Petra Laseur; Mattijn Hartemink; Marc Klein Essink; Directed by Ben Sombogaart; Written by Marieke van der Pol; Cinematography by Piotr Kukla; Music by Jeannot Sanavia. **A:** College-Adult. **P:** Entertainment. **U:** Home. **L:** Dutch, English. **Mov-Ent:** Australia, Drama, Marriage. **Acq:** Purchase. **Dist:** Music Box Films.

The Bride Goes Wild 1948 (Unrated) — ★★½
Prim New England schoolteacher Martha Terryton (Allyson) gets her dream opportunity to become a commercial artist when she's hired to illustrate the new book from popular children's author Uncle Bump. She heads to New York and discovers Uncle Bump is actually cynical, hard-drinking, child-hating Greg Rawlings (Johnson). An affronted Martha threatens to expose the truth and publisher McGrath (Cronyn) scams Martha with a sob story involving tough orphan Danny (Jenkins), which only complicates matters. An interrupted wedding figures into the movie's title. 98m/B/W; DVD. **C:** June Allyson; Van Johnson; Jackie "Butch" Jenkins; Hume Cronyn; Una Merkel; Arlene Dahl; Richard Derr; Directed by Norman Taurog; Written by Albert Beich; Cinematography by Ray June; Music by Rudolph Kopp. **A:** Jr. High-Adult. **P:** Entertainment. **U:** Home. **Mov-Ent:** Adoption, Comedy--Romantic. **Acq:** Purchase. **Dist:** WarnerArchive.com.

The Bride Is Much Too Beautiful 1958 (Unrated) — ★★½
French farm girl Bardot becomes a model with the help of some fashion magazine employees and then winds up posing as the bride in a fake marriage. Dubbed. 90m; VHS. **C:** Brigitte Bardot; Louis Jourdan; Micheline Presle; Marcel Amont; Directed by Pierre Gaspard-Huit; Written by Odette Joyeux; Philippe Agostini; Cinematography by Louis Page; Music by Norbert Glanzberg. **A:** Jr. High-Adult. **P:** Entertainment. **U:** Home. **Mov-Ent:** Sex & Sexuality. **Acq:** Purchase. **Dist:** Facets Multimedia Inc. $29.95.

The Bride Market of Imilchil 1988
Captures the Arab tradition that takes place each September wherein citizens travel to the shrine of Imilchil, find a mate and marry in a nearby tent. 58m; VHS. **A:** Adult. **P:** Education. **U:** Home. **Gen-Edu:** Documentary Films, Marriage. **Acq:** Purchase. **Dist:** Arab Film Distribution. $24.99.
Indiv. Titles: 1. 24600.

Bride of Chucky 1998 (R) — ★½
Just when you thought you had seen the last of that creepy little doll, "Chucky" returns. This fourth installment in the "Child's Play" franchise finds Chucky back on the lam after being sprung from the pen by the ex-girlfriend of his former human incarnation, serial killer Charles Lee Ray. After killing his ex, Tiffany (Tilly), Chucky transforms her soul into an equally creepy girl doll. Together, they must make their way to the very spot where he was gunned down by police in order to transfer their souls back into human forms. Aside from Chucky and both incarnations of Tiffany, the rest of the characters are undeveloped and rather useless. Fortunately, the filmmakers knew not to take themselves too seriously, and managed a few funny moments. But its really only Tilly's excellent campy-vampy performance and an occasional clever jab from the Chuckster that lift this one above a woof. 89m; DVD, Blu-Ray. **C:** Jennifer Tilly; Katherine Heigl; Nick Stabile; John Ritter; Alexis Arquette; Gordon Michael Woolvett; Lawrence Dane; Kathy Najimy; Voice(s) by Brad Dourif; Directed by Ronny Yu; Written by Don Mancini; Cinematography by Peter Pau; Music by Graeme Revell. **Pr:** David Kirschner; David Gilroy; Universal Studios. **A:** Sr. High-Adult. **P:** Entertainment. **U:** Home. **Mov-Ent. Acq:** Purchase. **Dist:** Alpha Video; Movies Unlimited.

The Bride of Frank 1996 (Unrated) — ★★
Former homeless man Frank has a temper and he's not afraid to use it on the belittling ladies who make the ill-fated gaffe of responding to his personals ad, which leads to their horrific, over-the-top, brutal demises. But, hey, he still has a sense of humor about it all. The viewer, however, might not. 89m; VHS, DVD. **C:** Frank Meyer; Johnny Horizon; Steve Ballot; Directed by Steve Ballot; Written by Steve Ballot; Cinematography by Steve Ballot. **A:** College-Adult. **P:** Entertainment. **U:** Home. **Mov-Ent:** Comedy--Black. **Acq:** Purchase. **Dist:** Movies Unlimited; Alpha Video.

The Bride of Frankenstein 1935 (Unrated) — ★★★★
The classic sequel to the classic original in which Dr. F. seeks to build a mate for his monster. More humor than the first, but also more pathos, including the monster's famous but short-lived friendship with a blind hermit. Lanchester plays both the bride and Mary Shelley in the opening sequence. 75m/B/W; VHS, DVD, Blu-Ray. **C:** Boris Karloff; Elsa Lanchester; Ernest Thesiger; Colin Clive; Una O'Connor; Valerie Hobson; Dwight Frye; John Carradine; E.E. Clive; O.P. Heggie; Gavin Gordon; Douglas Walton; Billy Barty; Walter Brennan; Directed by James Whale; Written by John Lloyd Balderston; William Hurlbut; Cinematography by John Mescall; Music by Franz Waxman. **Pr:** Universal Pictures. **A:** Family. **P:** Entertainment. **U:** Home. **Mov-Ent:** Horror, Classic Films. **Awds:** Natl. Film Reg. '98. **Acq:** Purchase. **Dist:** Movies Unlimited; Alpha Video; Universal Studios Home Video. $14.95.

Bride of Killer Nerd 1991 (Unrated) — ★
Harold Kunkel, left over from the original "Killer Nerd," finds his opposite sex nirvana in the person of Thelma, also a nerd in mind, body, and soul. They relentlessly pursue revenge on the rockers who humiliate them at a campus beer bash. 75m; VHS, DVD. **C:** Toby Radloff; Wayne A. Harold; Heidi Lohr; Directed by Mark Steven Bosko. **A:** College-Adult. **P:** Entertainment. **U:** Home. **Mov-Ent:** Horror. **Acq:** Purchase. **Dist:** Troma Entertainment.

Bride of Re-Animator 1989 (Unrated) — ★★½
Herbert West is back, and this time he not only re-animates life but creates life—sexy female life—in this sequel to the immensely popular "Re-Animator." High camp and blood curdling gore make this a standout in the sequel parade. Available in a R-rated version as well. 99m; VHS, DVD, Wide, CC. **C:** Bruce Abbott; Claude Earl Jones; Fabiana Udenio; Jeffrey Combs; Kathleen Kinmont; David Gale; Mel Stewart; Irene Forrest; Directed by Brian Yuzna; Written by Brian Yuzna; Rick Fry; Woody Keith; Cinematography by Rick Fichter; Music by Richard Band. **A:** College-Adult. **P:** Entertainment. **U:** Home. **Mov-Ent. Acq:** Purchase. **Dist:** Movies Unlimited. $12.74.

Bride of the Beast 1932
The husband-wife exploring team of yore camp out in Africa and film the denizens, extolling in their own way the wonders of animals and the ignorant savagery of the natives. 57m/B/W; VHS. **C:** Osa Johnson. **Pr:** Martin Johnson. **A:** Family. **P:** Entertainment. **U:** Home. **Gen-Edu:** Documentary Films, Wildlife, Africa. **Acq:** Purchase. **Dist:** Sinister Cinema. $16.95.

Bride of the Gorilla 1951 (Unrated) — ★★
Burr travels to the jungle where he finds a wife, a plantation, and a curse in this African twist on the werewolf legend. Chaney is the local policeman on his trail. Burr's physical changes are fun to watch. 76m/B/W; VHS, DVD. **C:** Raymond Burr; Barbara Payton; Lon Chaney, Jr.; Tom Conway; Paul Cavanagh; Directed by Curt Siodmak; Written by Curt Siodmak. **Pr:** Realart. **A:** Adult. **P:** Entertainment. **U:** Home. **Mov-Ent:** Horror. **Acq:** Purchase. **Dist:** Sinister Cinema; Rex Miller Artisan Studio. $16.95.

Bride of the Monster 1955 (Unrated) — **Bomb!**
Lugosi stars as a mad scientist trying to create a race of giants. Classic Woodian badness. 68m/B/W; VHS, DVD. **TV Std:** NTSC, PAL. **C:** Bela Lugosi; Tor Johnson; Loretta King; Tony McCoy; Harvey B. Dunn; George Becwar; Paul Marco; William Benedict; Dolores Fuller; Don Nagel; Bud Osborne; Conrad Brooks; Directed by Edward D. Wood, Jr.; Written by Edward D. Wood, Jr.; Alex Gordon; Cinematography by William C. Thompson; Music by Frank Worth. **Pr:** Ed D. Wood, Jr.; Banner Productions. **A:** Jr. High-Adult. **P:** Entertainment. **U:** Home. **Mov-Ent:** Horror, Cult Films. **Acq:** Purchase. **Dist:** Sinister Cinema. $19.95.

Bride of the Wind 2001 (R) — ★½
Dull biopic of Alma Mahler (Wynter), a 20th-century femme who put her own musical career aside to marry composer Gustav Mahler (Pryce) in old Vienna. Alma intrigues a number of famous men, including architect Walter Gropius (Verhoeven), artist Oskar Kokoschka (Perez), and others while her marriage to the stoic Gustav suffers. Unfortunately, it's neither titillating nor interesting despite the players. 99m; VHS, DVD, Wide, CC. **C:** Sarah Wynter; Jonathan Pryce; Vincent Perez; Simon Verhoeven; August Schmolzer; Gregor Seberg; Dagmar Schwarz; Wolfgang Hubsch; Johannes Silberschneider; Directed by Bruce Beresford; Written by Marilyn Levy; Cinematography by Peter James; Music by Stephen Endelman. **Pr:** Lawrence Levy; Evzen Kolar; ApolloProMedia; Firelight Films; Total Film Group; Paramount Classics. **A:** Sr. High-Adult. **P:** Entertainment. **U:** Home. **Mov-Ent:** Drama, Biography: Music, Marriage. **Acq:** Purchase. **Dist:** Paramount Pictures Corp.

Bride Service 1975
Yanomamo sex roles, division of labor, and obligations within the family are presented in this program. 10m; 3/4 U. **Pr:** Timothy Asch; Napoleon Chagnon. **A:** Jr. High-College. **P:** Education. **U:** Institution, SURA. **Gen-Edu:** Documentary Films, South America, Anthropology. **Acq:** Purchase. **Dist:** Documentary Educational Resources.

The Bride Walks Out 1936 (Unrated) — ★★
Newlywed crisis: a woman with rich taste learns how to adjust to living on her husband's poor salary, but not before she samples the life of the wealthy. Interesting in a sociological sort of way. 81m/B/W; VHS, DVD, Blu-Ray. **C:** Barbara Stanwyck; Gene Raymond; Robert Young; Ned Sparks; Willie Best; Helen Broderick; Hattie McDaniel; Directed by Leigh Jason. **Pr:** RKO. **A:** Family. **P:** Entertainment. **U:** Home. **Mov-Ent:** Marriage. **Acq:** Purchase. **Dist:** WarnerArchive.com; Turner Broadcasting System Inc. $19.98.

Bride Wars 2009 (PG) — ★½
Liv (Hudson) and Emma (Hathaway) are lifelong pals and soon-to-be brides who share the dream of being married at Manhattan's Plaza Hotel. But the sweet, charming women's plans of their same-season weddings hit a snag when their wedding planner's (Bergen) snafu results in the Plaza scheduling the big events on the same day. With no other openings in the schedule, the otherwise caring friends won't budge and become each other's bridezilla nightmare. Their sub-par sabotage stunts come off as childish, desperate, and downright mean, with characters that never feel real. Style over substance bittersweet confection is gorgeously shot with a beautiful cast that will likely cause producers to vow "I do" to a sequel. 90m; Blu-Ray, On Demand, Wide. **C:** Anne Hathaway; Kate Hudson; Kirsten Johnson; Bryan Greenberg; Steve Howey; Chris Pratt; Candice Bergen; John Pankow; Bruce Altman; Michael Arden; Directed by Gary Winick; Written by Casey Wilson; June Raphael; Cinematography by Frederick Elmes; Music by Ed Shearmur. **Pr:** Julie Yorn; Alan Riche; Kate Hudson; Kate Hudson; New Regency; Fox 2000 Pictures; Regency Enterprises; 20th Century-Fox. **A:** Family. **P:** Entertainment. **U:** Home. **L:** English. **Mov-Ent. Acq:** Purchase. **Dist:** Amazon.com Inc.; Movies Unlimited; Alpha Video.

The Bride with White Hair 1993 (Unrated) — ★★
Operatic martial arts fable based on a novel by Leung Yu-Sang. A young warrior revives a beautiful witch (also a champion

warrior) who was killed by jealous Siamese twins. Now the duo, who have fallen in love, must battle the evil twins who rule the corrupt Mo Dynasty. Available dubbed or in Chinese with subtitles. 92m; VHS, DVD, Wide. **C:** Leslie Cheung; Brigitte Lin; Nam Kit-Ying; Frances Ng; Elaine Lui; Directed by Ronny Yu; Written by Ronny Yu; David Wu; Lan Kei-Tou; Tseng Pik-Yin; Cinematography by Peter Pau; Music by Richard Yuen. **Pr:** Mandarin Films; Century Pacific Entertainment. **A:** Sr. High-Adult. **P:** Entertainment. **U:** Home. **L:** Chinese. **Mov-Ent:** Martial Arts. **Acq:** Purchase. **Dist:** Tai Seng Video Marketing.

The Bride with White Hair 2 1993 (Unrated) — ★★
The magic saga continues with the massacre of the followers of the Eight Lineages. Powerful and obsessed with vengeance, the Bride can only be stopped by the one man who loves her. Chinese with subtitles or dubbed. 80m; VHS, DVD, Wide. **C:** Brigitte Lin; Leslie Cheung; Christy Chung; Directed by David Wu; Ronny Yu; Written by David Wu. **Pr:** Mandarin Films. **A:** Sr. High-Adult. **P:** Entertainment. **U:** Home. **L:** Chinese. **Mov-Ent:** Martial Arts. **Acq:** Purchase. **Dist:** Tai Seng Video Marketing.

The Bride Wore Black 1968 (Unrated) — ★★★
Truffaut's homage to Hitchcock, complete with Bernard Herrmann score. Young bride Julie (Moreau) exacts brutal revenge on the five men who accidentally killed her husband on the steps of the church on their wedding day. Adapted from a novel by Cornell Woolrich. 107m; VHS, DVD, Wide. **C:** Jeanne Moreau; Claude Rich; Jean-Claude Brialy; Michel Bouquet; Michael (Michel) Lonsdale; Charles Denner; Daniel Boulanger; Directed by Francois Truffaut; Written by Francois Truffaut; Jean-Louis Richard; Cinematography by Raoul Coutard; Music by Bernard Herrmann. **A:** Sr. High-Adult. **P:** Entertainment. **U:** Home. **L:** English, French. **Mov-Ent:** Mystery & Suspense. **Acq:** Purchase. **Dist:** MGM Home Entertainment; Facets Multimedia Inc. $19.98.

The Bride Wore Boots 1946 (Unrated) — ★★
Goofy marital comedy with Stanwyck as horse breeder Sally who marries writer Jeff (Cummings) despite his dislike of horses. This leads to their eventual estrangement and Jeff being beset by rapacious southern belle Mary Lou (Lynn). However, he must come to Sally's aid when the horse she's entered in a prestigious steeplechase race refuses to be ridden by anyone but Jeff. 85m/B/W; DVD. **C:** Barbara Stanwyck; Robert Cummings; Diana Lynn; Patric Knowles; Peggy Wood; Robert Benchley; Natalie Wood; Willie Best; Directed by Irving Pichel; Written by Dwight Michael Wiley; Cinematography by Stuart Thompson; Music by Frederick "Friedrich" Hollander. **A:** Jr. High-Adult. **P:** Entertainment. **U:** Home. **Mov-Ent:** Horses, Marriage, Comedy--Screwball. **Acq:** Purchase. **Dist:** Universal Studios Home Video.

The Bride Wore Red 1937 — ★★
Crawford stars as a cabaret singer who masquerades as a socialite in an attempt to break into the upper crust. When a wealthy aristocrat invites her to spend two weeks at a posh resort in Tyrol, Crawford plays her part to the hilt, managing to charm both a rich gentleman and the village postman. Typical "love conquers all" melodrama. 103m/B/W; DVD. **C:** Joan Crawford; Franchot Tone; Robert Young; Billie Burke; Reginald Owen; Lynne Carver; George Zucco; Directed by Dorothy Arzner; Cinematography by George J. Folsey. **Pr:** Joseph L. Mankiewicz. **A:** Sr. High-Adult. **P:** Entertainment. **U:** Home. **Mov-Ent:** Drama, Nightclubs. **Acq:** Purchase. **Dist:** WarnerArchive.com. $19.98.

The Bride's Bouquet 1989
Beautiful wedding bouquets are easy to arrange for people who have seen this program. 56m; VHS. **Pr:** Nancy's Notions Ltd. **A:** Jr. High-Adult. **P:** Instruction. **U:** Institution, Home. **How-Ins:** Flowers, Crafts. **Acq:** Rent/Lease. **Dist:** Nancy's Notions Ltd.

Brides of Christ 1991 — ★★½
Set in the Australian Santo Spirito Convent during the Vatican II upheaval of the 1960s. Explores the tensions between old and new religious ideas by focusing on novices, older nuns, and the Reverend Mother of the convent as they try to cope with a changing world. TV miniseries. 300m; VHS, DVD. **C:** Brenda Fricker; Sandy Gore; Josephine Byrnes; Lisa Hensley; Naomi Watts; Kym Wilson; Melissa Thomas; Directed by Ken Cameron; Written by John Alsop; Sue Smith. **Pr:** Sue Masters; Telefis Eireann; Australian Broadcasting Corporation; Channel 4. **A:** Sr. High-Adult. **P:** Entertainment. **U:** Home. **Mov-Ent:** Religion, Australia, TV Movies. **Acq:** Purchase. **Dist:** A&E Television Networks L.L.C.; New Video Group. $59.95.

The Brides of Dracula 1960 (Unrated) — ★★½
A young French woman unknowingly frees a vampire. He wreaks havoc, sucking blood and creating more of the undead to carry out his evil deeds. One of the better Hammer vampire films. 86m; VHS, DVD. **C:** Peter Cushing; Martita Hunt; Yvonne Monlaur; Freda Jackson; David Peel; Mona Washbourne; Miles Malleson; Henry Oscar; Michael Ripper; Andree Melly; Directed by Terence Fisher; Written by Peter Bryan; Edward Percy; Jimmy Sangster; Cinematography by Jack Asher. **Pr:** Hotspur. **A:** Jr. High-Adult. **P:** Entertainment. **U:** Home. **Mov-Ent:** Horror. **Acq:** Purchase. **Dist:** Facets Multimedia Inc. $14.98.

Brides of Fu Manchu 1966 (Unrated) — ★
In Lee's second outing as the villainous character, Fu Manchu kidnaps the nubile daughters of various scientists so that they will be forced to build him a weapon to take over the world. Naturally, his Scotland Yard nemesis Nayland Smith (Wilmer) will stop him. Based on the characters created by Sax Rohmer. 93m; DVD. **C:** Christopher Lee; Douglas Wilmer; Tsai Chin; Joseph Furst; Marie Versini; Heinz Drache; Directed by Don Sharp; Written by Harry Alan Towers; Cinematography by Ernest Steward; Music by Bruce Montgomery. **A:** Jr. High-Adult. **P:** Entertainment. **U:** Home. **Mov-Ent**. **Acq:** Purchase. **Dist:** Warner Home Video, Inc.

Brides of the Beast 1968 (Unrated) — Bomb!
Filipino radiation monsters get their jollies by eating beautiful young naked women. Newly arrived research scientist and his bride oppose this custom. First in a series of "Blood Island" horrors. 85m/B/W; VHS, DVD. **TV Std:** NTSC, PAL. **C:** John Ashley; Kent Taylor; Beverly (Hills) Powers; Eva Darren; Mario Montenegro; Directed by Eddie Romero; Gerardo (Gerry) De Leon; Written by Eddie Romero; Gerardo (Gerry) De Leon. **Pr:** Hemisphere Productions. **A:** Sr. High-Adult. **P:** Entertainment. **U:** Home. **Mov-Ent:** Horror, Sex & Sexuality. **Acq:** Purchase. **Dist:** Unknown Distributor.

The Bride's Perfect Planner 1992
Step-by-step instructions to making your special day a perfectly planned and memorable event. Includes tips on selecting the wedding party, shopping for dresses, planning the ceremony and reception, and more. 35m; VHS. **A:** Adult. **P:** Instruction. **U:** Home. **How-Ins:** How-To. **Acq:** Purchase. **Dist:** Cambridge Educational. $39.95.

Brideshead Revisited 1981 — ★★★
The acclaimed British miniseries based on the Evelyn Waugh classic about an Edwardian young man who falls under the spell of a wealthy aristocratic family and struggles to retain his integrity and values. On six tapes. 540m; VHS, DVD, CC. **C:** Jeremy Irons; Anthony Andrews; Diana Quick; Laurence Olivier; John Gielgud; Claire Bloom; Stephane Audran; Mona Washbourne; John Le Mesurier; Charles Keating; Directed by Charles Sturridge; Michael Lindsay-Hogg; Music by Geoffrey Burgon. **Pr:** Derek Granger; Granada Television International Ltd. **A:** Sr. High-Adult. **P:** Entertainment. **U:** Home. **Mov-Ent:** TV Movies. **Acq:** Purchase. **Dist:** Movies Unlimited; Fusion Video; Signals Video. $99.99.

Brideshead Revisited 2008 (PG-13) — ★★½
It's between the world wars in England, and middle-class Charles Ryder (Goode) is enamored by the snooty lifestyle of brother and sister Sebastian (Whishaw) and Julia (Atwell) at their Brideshead estate, where they live with their mother, the devout Catholic Lady Marchmain (Thompson). At first, Charles hooks up with the boozy Sebastian but later turns his amorous attention to Julia, fueling Sebastian's jealously and Lady Marchmain's ire. Despite the lush backdrop and Thompson's icy turn, it falls short of the acclaimed 1981 British miniseries version. Adapted from the 1945 novel by Evelyn Waugh. 135m; Blu-Ray, On Demand, Wide. **C:** Matthew Goode; Ben Whishaw; Hayley Atwell; Emma Thompson; Michael Gambon; Greta Scacchi; Jonathan Cake; Patrick Malahide; Directed by Julian Jarrold; Written by Andrew Davies; Jeremy Brock; Cinematography by Jess Hall; Music by Adrian Johnston. **Pr:** Robert Bernstein; Douglas Rae; Kevin Loader; BBC Films; HanWay Films; Ecosse Films; Miramax Film Corp. **A:** Jr. High-Adult. **P:** Entertainment. **U:** Home. **L:** English. **Mov-Ent:** Boating, World War Two, Great Britain. **Acq:** Purchase. **Dist:** Movies Unlimited; Alpha Video; Miramax Film Corp.

The Bridesmaid 2004 (Unrated) — ★★
Creepy thriller based on a novel by Ruth Rendell. Hard-working Philippe (Magimel) lives with his flirtatious mother Christine (Clement) and his two younger siblings. At his sister's wedding, he meets sultry bridesmaid Senta (Smet), who likes a lot of drama in her life. She easily seduces the uptight Philippe, who turns out to have some dark inner urges and continually tests the limits of his love. Then Senta asks, would he kill for her? French with subtitles. 111m; DVD. **C:** Benoit Magimel; Laura Smet; Aurore Clement; Bernard Le Coq; Solene Bouten; Anna Mihalcea; Michel Duchaussoy; Eric Seigne; Pierre-Francois Dumeniaud; Directed by Claude Chabrol; Written by Claude Chabrol; Peter Leccia; Cinematography by Eduardo Serra; Music by Matthieu Chabrol. **Pr:** Antonio Passalia; Patrick Godeau; Alicelio; First Run Features. **A:** College-Adult. **P:** Entertainment. **U:** Home. **L:** French. **Mov-Ent:** Mystery & Suspense. **Acq:** Purchase. **Dist:** First Run Features.

Bridesmaids 2011 (R) — ★★★
Although her own life is falling apart, maid of honor Annie (Wiig) is determined to support her best friend Lillian (Rudolph) throughout her pre-wedding rituals. But Annie must contend with a group of wild bridesmaids and Lillian's beautiful and wealthy friend, Helen (Byrne), who seems hell-bent on replacing Annie. Features clever and gross-out humor for both sexes to enjoy, including an infamous scene where the women get food poisoning in a fancy boutique. More than that, it's a fresh, hilarious, engaging story with a heart. And writer Wiig proves to be a major star. 124m; Blu-Ray, On Demand, Wide. **C:** Kristen Wiig; Maya Rudolph; Rose Byrne; Melissa McCarthy; Wendi McLendon-Covey; Jill Clayburgh; Chris O'Dowd; Jon Hamm; Ellie Kemper; Directed by Paul Feig; Written by Kristen Wiig; Annie Mumolo; Cinematography by Robert Yeoman; Music by Michael Andrews. **Pr:** Judd Apatow; Barry Mendel; Clayton Townsend; Universal Pictures; Relativity Media; Apatow Productions. **A:** Sr. High-Adult. **P:** Entertainment. **U:** Home. **L:** English. **Mov-Ent:** Women, Comedy-Drama. **Acq:** Purchase. **Dist:** Amazon.com Inc.; Movies Unlimited; Alpha Video.

The Bridewell Taxis: Precious Times 1991
The group plays 10 of their songs, including "Wild Boar" and more. 50m; VHS. **A:** Sr. High-Adult. **P:** Entertainment. **U:** Home. **Mov-Ent:** Music--Pop/Rock. **Acq:** Purchase. **Dist:** Music Video Distributors. $32.95.

Bridge 19??
Learn to play bridge with expert teacher Mary McVey in this seven-part series. 30m; VHS. **A:** Adult. **P:** Instruction. **U:** Home. **How-Ins:** Games, How-To. **Acq:** Purchase. **Dist:** KET, The Kentucky Network. $39.95.

The Bridge 1959 — ★★
In 1945, two days before the end of WWII, seven German schoolboys are drafted to defend an unimportant bridge from American tanks. Emotional anti-war film based on the autobiographical novel of Manfred Gregor. German with subtitles. 102m/B/W; VHS, DVD. **C:** Fritz Wepper; Volker Bohnet; Frank Glaubrecht; Karl Michael Balzer; Gunther Hoffman; Michael Hinz; Cordula Trantow; Wolfgang Stumpf; Volker Lechtenbrink; Gunter Pfitzmann; Edith Schultze-Westrum; Ruth Hausmeister; Eva Vaitl; Directed by Bernhard Wicki; Written by Bernhard Wicki; Michael Mansfeld; Karl-Wilhelm Vivier; Cinematography by Gerd Von Bonen; Music by Hans-Martin Majewski. **Pr:** Hermann Schwerin. **A:** College-Adult. **P:** Entertainment. **U:** Home. **L:** German. **Mov-Ent:** World War Two, Adolescence, Germany. **Acq:** Purchase. **Dist:** Facets Multimedia Inc.; VCI Entertainment.

The Bridge 1978
When a malfunction occurs in a bridge which won't lock, an operator has to hold it manually. At the worst possible time his son comes to visit him and the operator must choose between his son's life and the lives of the passengers. 10m; 3/4 U. **Pr:** Brigham Young University. **A:** Sr. High-Adult. **P:** Education. **U:** Institution, CCTV, SURA. **Gen-Edu:** Ethics & Morals. **Acq:** Purchase. **Dist:** Brigham Young University.

The Bridge 2000 (Unrated) — ★★★
In 1963, Mira (Bouquet) loves to go to the movies to watch "Jules et Jim" and "West Side Story." She has a 15-year-old son, but that doesn't stop her from entering into an affair with a visiting engineer (Berling) who's in her little town to build a bridge. Director Depardieu plays her husband, a builder who's working on the bridge. It's precisely the sort of material that the French handle so deftly and Depardieu proves that he's a competent craftsman behind the camera. 92m; DVD, Wide. **C:** Carole Bouquet; Gerard Depardieu; Charles Berling; Directed by Gerard Depardieu; Frederic Auburtin; Written by Francois Bupeyron; Cinematography by Pascal Ridao; Music by Frederic Auburtin. **A:** Sr. High-Adult. **P:** Entertainment. **U:** Home. **Mov-Ent:** Drama. **Acq:** Purchase. **Dist:** Wellspring Media.

The Bridge at Remagen 1969 (PG) — ★★½
Based on the true story of allied attempts to capture a vital bridge before retreating German troops destroy it. For war-film buffs. 115m; VHS, DVD, Wide. **C:** George Segal; Robert Vaughn; Ben Gazzara; Bradford Dillman; E.G. Marshall; Directed by John Guillermin; Written by William Roberts; Cinematography by Stanley Cortez; Music by Elmer Bernstein. **Pr:** Wood Knapp Video. **A:** Jr. High-Adult. **P:** Entertainment. **U:** Home. **Mov-Ent:** World War Two, Rivers & Streams. **Acq:** Purchase. **Dist:** MGM Home Entertainment.

Bridge Basics 1982
This series was designed to teach the beginner all the basics in the game of bridge. 30m; VHS, 3/4 U. **Pr:** Kentucky Educational Television. **A:** Family. **P:** Instruction. **U:** Institution, CCTV, CATV. **Spo-Rec:** How-To, Games. **Acq:** Purchase, Rent/Lease, Free Loan. **Dist:** KET, The Kentucky Network.
Indiv. Titles: 1. Introduction to the Game 2. Opening Suit Bids of One and Responses 3. No Trump Bids and Responses 4. Overcalls 5. Rebids 6. High Opening Bids and Responses 7. Opening Leads and Play of the Hand.

The Bridge: How Islam Saved Western Medicine ????
Uses footage from Aegean, Middle East, Iran, Spain, Italy, France, and Germany to explain how medical knowledge was passed on from the Islamic culture throughout history. 50m; VHS. **A:** Sr. High-Adult. **P:** Education. **U:** Institution. **Gen-Edu:** Middle East, Medical Care. **Acq:** Purchase, Rent/Lease. **Dist:** Films for the Humanities & Sciences. $149.00.

The Bridge of Adam Rush 1975
Tells the story of a 12-year-old who must adjust to rural life on a farm with his new stepfather, after living cozily in a Philadelphia home. Set in 1800s. 47m; VHS, 3/4 U, Special order formats. **Pr:** Daniel Wilson Productions. **A:** Primary-Jr. High. **P:** Entertainment. **U:** Institution, SURA. **Gen-Edu:** Family. **Acq:** Purchase, Rent/Lease. **Dist:** Time-Life Video and Television.

Bridge of Dragons 1999 (R) — ★★
Dictator Tagawa, having murdered the kingdom's rightful ruler, plots to marry the country's princess (Shane) to consolidate his power. But when the princess escapes to join the rebel forces, human killing machine Lundgren is sent to retrieve her. Only he decides to fight with her instead. Lots of explosions and high-tech gadgets. 91m; VHS, DVD, CC. **C:** Dolph Lundgren; Cary-Hiroyuki Tagawa; Gary Hudson; Scott Schwartz; Rachel Shane; Directed by Isaac Florentine; Written by Carlton Holder; Cinematography by Yossi Wein; Music by Stephen (Steve) Edwards. **Pr:** Boaz Davidson; Avi Lerner; Dan Dimbort; Trevor Short; Danny Lerner; Nu Image Films. **A:** Sr. High-Adult. **P:** Entertainment. **U:** Home. **Mov-Ent**. **Acq:** Purchase. **Dist:** Alpha Video; Movies Unlimited.

The Bridge of San Luis Rey 1944 (Unrated) — ★★★
A priest investigates the famous bridge collapse in Lima, Peru that left five people dead. Based upon the novel by Thornton Wilder. 89m/B/W; VHS, DVD. **C:** Lynn Bari; Francis Lederer; Louis Calhern; Akim Tamiroff; Donald Woods; Alla Nazimova; Blanche Yurka; Directed by Rowland V. Lee; Written by Howard Estabrook; Herman Weissman; Cinematography by John

Boyle; Music by Dimitri Tiomkin. **Pr:** United Artists. **A:** Family. **P:** Entertainment. **U:** Home. **Mov-Ent. Acq:** Purchase. **Dist:** Image Entertainment Inc. $19.95.

The Bridge of San Luis Rey 2005 (PG) — ★
Thornton Wilder's moving, Pulitzer Prize-winning 1928 novel is disastrously adapted by director McGluckian, with stellar actors generally miscast in a stuffy costume drama. In colonial Peru in the early 18th century, Franciscan missionary Brother Juniper (Byrne) has been investigating five travelers who plunged to their deaths when the titular bridge collapsed. He's trying to determine if there's some common denominator to their fate and delivers his conclusions to a church court presided over by the Archbishop of Lima (De Niro). Flashbacks depict the lives of the victims and their survivors and the abrupt shifts in scene and character make for confusion. 120m; DVD. **C:** Robert De Niro; F. Murray Abraham; Kathy Bates; Gabriel Byrne; Geraldine Chaplin; Emilie Dequenne; Adriana Dominguez; Harvey Keitel; Pilar Lopez de Ayala; John Lynch; Mark Polish; Michael Polish; Directed by Mary McGuckian; Cinematography by Javier Aguirresarobe; Music by Lalo Schifrin. **Pr:** Samuel Hadida; Michael Cowan; Denis O'Dell; Spice Factory; Kanzaman Films; Davis Films. **A:** Primary-Adult. **P:** Entertainment. **U:** Home. **L:** English. **Mov-Ent:** South America. **Acq:** Purchase. **Dist:** New Line Home Video. $24.98.

Bridge of Winds 2000
Documentary looks at the Lisu people of the Yunan province in China who live virtually isolated from the outside world. Shows how they happily survive and function by working together. 58m; VHS. **A:** Adult. **P:** Education. **U:** Home. **Gen-Edu:** Documentary Films, Asia, Sociology. **Acq:** Purchase, Rent/Lease. **Dist:** Filmakers Library Inc. $295.

The Bridge on the River Kwai 1957 — ★★★★
Award-winning adaptation of the Pierre Bouelle novel about the battle of wills between a Japanese POW camp commander and a British colonel over the construction of a rail bridge, and the parallel efforts by escaped prisoner Holden to destroy it. Holden's role was originally cast for Cary Grant. Memorable too for whistling "Colonel Bogey March." Because the writers were blacklisted, Bouelle (who spoke no English) was originally credited as the screenwriter. 161m; VHS, DVD, Blu-Ray, Wide. **C:** William Holden; Alec Guinness; Jack Hawkins; Sessue Hayakawa; James Donald; Geoffrey Horne; Andre Morell; Ann Sears; Peter Williams; John Boxer; Percy Herbert; Harold Goodwin; Henry Okawa; Keiichiro Katsumoto; M.R.B. Chakrabandhu; Directed by David Lean; Written by Carl Foreman; Michael Wilson; Cinematography by Jack Hildyard; Music by Malcolm Arnold. **Pr:** Sam Spiegel; Columbia Pictures. **A:** Jr. High-Adult. **P:** Entertainment. **U:** Home. **Mov-Ent:** World War Two, Classic Films, Ethics & Morals. **Awds:** Oscars '57: Actor (Guinness), Adapt. Screenplay, Cinematog., Director (Lean), Film, Film Editing, Orig. Song Score and/or Adapt.; AFI '98: Top 100; British Acad. '57: Actor (Guinness), Film, Screenplay; Directors Guild '57: Director (Lean); Golden Globes '58: Actor--Drama (Guinness), Director (Lean), Film--Drama; Natl. Bd. of Review '57: Actor (Guinness), Director (Lean), Support. Actor (Hayakawa); Natl. Film Reg. '97; N.Y. Film Critics '57: Actor (Guinness), Director (Lean), Film. **Acq:** Purchase. **Dist:** Sony Pictures Home Entertainment Inc.; Baker and Taylor; Home Vision Cinema. $19.95.

A Bridge Over the Caribbean 1995
Outlines the economic development of Puerto Rico from 1940 through 1994. Contains interviews with industrialists, economists, and government officials. Also provides information on how NAFTA impacted the country. In Spanish with English subtitles. 36m; VHS. **A:** Jr. High-Adult. **P:** Education. **U:** Institution. **Gen-Edu:** Documentary Films, Hispanic Culture, Economics. **Acq:** Purchase, Rent/Lease. **Dist:** The Cinema Guild. $250.00.

Bridge Resource Management ?
Covers topics relating to shipping and voyage planning with regard to pilot and other bridge personnel. ?m; VHS. **A:** Sr. High-Adult. **P:** Education. **U:** Home, Institution. **Bus-Ind:** Industry & Industrialists. **Acq:** Purchase. **Dist:** John Sabella & Associate. $125.00.

Bridge to Hell 1987 (Unrated) — ★½
A group of allied P.O.W.s try to make their way to the American front during WWII in Yugoslavia. A heavily guarded bridge occupied by Nazi troops stands between them and freedom. A special introduction by Michael Dudikoff doing martial arts. 94m; VHS, DVD. **C:** Jeff Connors; Francis Ferre; Andy Forrest; Paky Valente; Directed by Umberto Lenzi. **A:** Adult. **P:** Entertainment. **U:** Home. **Mov-Ent:** World War Two. **Acq:** Purchase. **Dist:** Movies Unlimited.

The Bridge to Nowhere 1986 (Unrated) — ★★
Five city kids go hunting and back-packing in the New Zealand wilderness, and are hunted by a maniacal backwoodsman. 82m; VHS. **C:** Bruno Lawrence; Alison Routledge; Margaret Umbers; Philip Gordon; Directed by Ian Mune. **Pr:** Larry Parr. **A:** Sr. High-Adult. **P:** Entertainment. **U:** Home. **Mov-Ent:** Hunting, Wilderness Areas. **Acq:** Purchase. **Dist:** New Line Home Video. $19.98.

The Bridge to Nowhere 2009 (R) — ★½
Four blue-collar workers in Pittsburgh run minor schemes—poker games and sports betting—to make extra dough. When they meet ambitious indie prostie Jasper, they decide to start a high-end escort service that becomes a surprise success. And then it all comes crashing down. 105m; DVD. **C:** Bijou Phillips; Danny Masterson; Ben Crowley; Daniel London; Sean Derry; Thomas Ian Nicholas; Alexandra Breckenridge; Ving Rhames; Directed by Blair Underwood; Written by Chris Gutierrez; Cinematography by Keith Gruchala; Music by Scott Glasgow. **A:** Sr. High-Adult. **P:** Entertainment. **U:** Home. **Mov-Ent:** Prostitution. **Acq:** Purchase. **Dist:** Image Entertainment Inc.

Bridge to Silence 1989 (Unrated) — ★★
A young hearing-impaired mother's life begins to crumble following the death of her husband in a car crash. Her mother tries to get custody of her daughter and a friend applies romantic pressure. Melodrama features Matlin in her first TV speaking role. 95m; VHS, Streaming, CC. **C:** Marlee Matlin; Lee Remick; Josef Sommer; Michael O'Keefe; Allison Silva; Candice Brecker; Directed by Karen Arthur. **Pr:** Charles Fries Productions. **A:** Family. **P:** Entertainment. **U:** Home. **Mov-Ent:** Deafness, TV Movies. **Acq:** Purchase. **Dist:** Unknown Distributor.

Bridge to Terabithia 1985
An imaginative girl and a young boy learn the joys of friendship in a magic make-believe kingdom called Terabithia. Adapted from the novel by Katherine Paterson. Originally aired by PBS for the "Wonderworks" television series. 58m; VHS, CC. **C:** Annette O'Toole; Julian Coutts; Julie Beaulieu; Directed by Eric Till. **Pr:** Kitty King. **A:** Family. **P:** Entertainment. **U:** Home. **Chl-Juv:** Fantasy, Children, Family Viewing. **Acq:** Purchase. **Dist:** Home Vision Cinema; Facets Multimedia Inc. $29.95.

Bridge to Terabithia 2007 (PG) — ★★½
Katherine Paterson's popular 1977 novel isn't so much about a fantasy world (the film's CGI is limited) as it is about friendship and imagination. Jess (Hutcherson) is a bullied 10-year-old misfit with four sisters and a stern dad (Patrick). Adventurous new neighbor Leslie (Robb) turns out to be Jess' imaginative kindred soul and, between his drawings and her stories, they populate the nearby woods with their own world. For those not familiar with the book, beware—there's tragedy looming that will affect both kids and adults. 94m; DVD, Blu-Ray. **C:** Josh Hutcherson; AnnaSophia Robb; Robert Patrick; Zooey Deschanel; Bailee Madison; Kate Butler; Lauren Clinton; Directed by Gabor Csupo; Written by Jeff Stockwell; David Paterson; Cinematography by Michael Chapman; Music by Aaron Zigman. **Pr:** David Paterson; Hal Lieberman; Lauren Levine; David Paterson; Walden Media; Buena Vista. **A:** Family. **P:** Entertainment. **U:** Home. **L:** English. **Mov-Ent:** Fantasy, Family. **Acq:** Purchase. **Dist:** Walt Disney Studios Home Entertainment.

Bridge to the Sun 1961 (Unrated) — ★★
Based on the autobiography of Gwen Terasaki, a southern belle who marries a Japanese diplomat working in DC. However, after the bombing of Pearl Harbor, Terasaki is sent back to Japan where he is stripped of his position and the family is watched by the secret police. Terasaki becomes a liaison between the two countries after peace is declared but the deprivations of the war years have taken their toll. 113m/B/W; DVD. **C:** Carroll Baker; James Shigeta; James Yagi; Tetsuro Tanba; Hiroshi Tomono; Directed by Etienne Perier; Written by Charles A. Kaufman; Cinematography by William J. Kelly; Marcel Weiss; Music by Georges Auric. **A:** Sr. High-Adult. **P:** Entertainment. **U:** Home. **L:** English. **Mov-Ent:** Japan, Marriage, World War Two. **Acq:** Purchase. **Dist:** WarnerArchive.com.

A Bridge Too Far 1977 (PG) — ★★
A meticulous re-creation of one of the most disastrous battles of WWII, the Allied defeat at Arnhem in 1944. Misinformation, adverse conditions, and overconfidence combined to prevent the Allies from capturing six bridges that connected Holland to the German border. 175m; VHS, DVD, Blu-Ray, Wide, CC. **C:** Sean Connery; Robert Redford; James Caan; Michael Caine; Elliott Gould; Gene Hackman; Laurence Olivier; Ryan O'Neal; Liv Ullmann; Dirk Bogarde; Hardy Kruger; Arthur Hill; Edward Fox; Anthony Hopkins; Maximilian Schell; Denholm Elliott; Wolfgang Preiss; Nicholas (Nick) Campbell; Christopher Good; John Ratzenberger; Colin Farrell; Directed by Richard Attenborough; Written by William Goldman; Cinematography by Geoffrey Unsworth; Music by John Addison. **Pr:** Joseph E. Levine; Richard P. Levine; United Artists. **A:** Family. **P:** Entertainment. **U:** Home. **Mov-Ent:** Drama, World War Two, Tanks. **Awds:** British Acad. '77: Support. Actor (Fox); Natl. Soc. Film Critics '77: Support. Actor (Fox). **Acq:** Purchase. **Dist:** MGM Home Entertainment. $29.98.

Bridges 19??
Outlines how technology has copied nature in the building of bridges, as well as offers insight on the history of bridges and bridge construction. Also illustrates various bridge designs and their purposes. Comes with teacher's guide. 22m; VHS. **A:** Jr. High-College. **P:** Education. **U:** Institution. **Hea-Sci:** Technology, History, Construction. **Acq:** Purchase. **Dist:** Cambridge Educational. $54.95.

Bridges 1988
A story of a mother's love for both her son and father is told. 23m; VHS, 3/4 U. **Pr:** Franciscan Communications. **A:** Jr. High-Adult. **P:** Religious. **U:** Institution, SURA. **Gen-Edu:** Family. **Acq:** Purchase, Rent/Lease. **Dist:** St. Anthony Messenger Press. $195.00.

The Bridges at Toko-Ri 1955 — ★★★½
Based on the James A. Michener novel, the rousing war-epic about a lawyer being summoned by the Navy to fly bombing missions during the Korean War. A powerful anti-war statement. 103m; VHS, DVD. **C:** William Holden; Grace Kelly; Fredric March; Mickey Rooney; Robert Strauss; Earl Holliman; Keiko Awaji; Charles McGraw; Richard Shannon; Willis Bouchey; Directed by Mark Robson; Written by Valentine Davies; Cinematography by Loyal Griggs; Music by Lyn Murray. **Pr:** George Seaton; William Perlberg; Paramount Pictures. **A:** Jr. High-Adult. **P:** Entertainment. **U:** Home. **Mov-Ent:** Korean War, Swimming. **Acq:** Purchase. **Dist:** Paramount Pictures Corp. $14.95.

The Bridges of Madison County 1995 (PG-13) — ★★★
Robert Kincaid (Eastwood) is on assignment in 1965 Iowa to photograph Madison County's scenic covered bridges. Only problem is he gets lost and stops for directions at Francesca Johnson's (Streep) farmhouse. There's an immediate attraction between the repressed Italian war-bride-turned-farm-wife and the charismatic world traveler, which they act on in four short days. Much of the treacle from Robert James Waller's novel has been fortunately abandoned but the mature romance remains. 64-year-old Eastwood exudes low-key sexiness while Streep (with a light Italian accent) is all earthy warmth. Fans of both book and stars should be pleased, though the leisurely paced film takes too long to get started. 135m; VHS, DVD, Blu-Ray, CC. **C:** Clint Eastwood; Meryl Streep; Victor Slezak; Annie Corley; Jim Haynie; Directed by Clint Eastwood; Written by Richard LaGravenese; Cinematography by Jack N. Green; Music by Lennie Niehaus. **Pr:** Clint Eastwood; Kathleen Kennedy; Clint Eastwood; Amblin Entertainment; Malpaso Productions; Warner Bros. **A:** Sr. High-Adult. **P:** Entertainment. **U:** Home. **Mov-Ent:** Drama, Photography, Agriculture. **Acq:** Purchase. **Dist:** Warner Home Video, Inc.

Bridges: Skills to Manage a Diverse Workforce 1990
An eight-part series designed to train supervisors and managers to deal with a culturally diverse workforce. The tapes are available individually or as a set. Trainer's manuals and participants manuals are included. ?m; VHS, 3/4 U. **Pr:** BNA Communications. **A:** College-Adult. **P:** Vocational. **U:** Institution. **Bus-Ind:** How-To, Occupational Training, Personnel Management. **Acq:** Rent/Lease. **Dist:** Learning Communications L.L.C. $175.00.
Indiv. Titles: 1. A Question of Honor 2. That Kind of Woman 3. The Man in the Middle 4. The Choice I Made 5. Come One, Come All 6. The Other Side of the Coin 7. Drawing the Line 8. You Know What I Mean.

Bridges to Buffalo ????
Shows the former Nickel Plate rail line between Bellevue, Ohio and Buffalo, New York as the backdrop for footage of Norfolk & Western steam engine travel. 42m; VHS. **A:** College-Adult. **P:** Education. **U:** Home. **Gen-Edu:** Trains. **Acq:** Purchase. **Dist:** The Civil War Standard. $19.95.

Bridget Jones: The Edge of Reason 2004 (R) — ★★½
The film sequel (loosely based on Fielding's book sequel) tries too hard to be endearingly kooky, but can't go that far wrong with Zellweger, who once again packed on the pounds to play the plumpish London singleton. When we last saw Bridget, she had finally chosen steady lawyer Mark Darcy (Firth), but her insecurities get the better of her. She trashes her relationship and is soon once again with sly cad Daniel (Grant), now the host of a TV travel show. This leads Bridget and Daniel to Thailand where, in an unfortunate plot contrivance, Bridget is thrown into a Thai jail. This only serves to teach Bridget that she really loves Mark. Zellweger is subjected to many pratfalls, which she handles with good spirit, and all the supporting roles are on the money. 108m; VHS, DVD, Blu-Ray. **C:** Renee Zellweger; Hugh Grant; Colin Firth; Jim Broadbent; Gemma Jones; Jacinda Barrett; James Callis; Shirley Henderson; Sally Phillips; Neil Pearson; Jessica Stevenson; Paul Nicholls; Directed by Beeban Kidron; Written by Andrew Davies; Helen Fielding; Richard Curtis; Adam Brooks; Cinematography by Adrian Biddle; Music by Harry Gregson-Williams. **Pr:** Tim Bevan; Eric Fellner; Jonathan Cavendish; Working Title Productions; UIP; Universal. **A:** Sr. High-Adult. **P:** Entertainment. **U:** Home. **Mov-Ent:** Comedy--Romantic, Action-Adventure, Women. **Acq:** Purchase. **Dist:** Movies Unlimited; Alpha Video. $29.98.

Bridget Jones's Diary 2001 (R) — ★★★
So you've got this petite, sunny-faced Texan playing a "singleton" Brit who drinks and smokes and consumes too many calories and has man trouble and is the beloved heroine of Helen Fielding's novel. No wonder the English got a little upset—not, as it turns out, for any good reason since Zellweger is fab as Bridget tries to take control of her chaotic life. Of course having a romp with your caddish, clever boss Daniel Cleaver (Grant) and ignoring the handsome but apparently stuffy Mark Darcy (Firth) isn't a good start but Bridget—bless her—does try. The movie is truncated (to the detriment of Bridget's friendships) but it still works. 115m; VHS, DVD, Blu-Ray, Wide. **C:** Renee Zellweger; Hugh Grant; Colin Firth; Gemma Jones; Jim Broadbent; Embeth Davidtz; Shirley Henderson; James Callis; Sally Phillips; Lisa Barbuscia; Directed by Sharon Maguire; Written by Richard Curtis; Andrew Davies; Helen Fielding; Cinematography by Stuart Dryburgh; Music by Patrick Doyle. **Pr:** Eric Fellner; Jonathan Cavendish; Tim Bevan; Working Title Productions; Universal Pictures; StudioCanal; Miramax Film Corp. **A:** Sr. High-Adult. **P:** Entertainment. **U:** Home. **Mov-Ent:** Comedy--Romantic. **Acq:** Purchase. **Dist:** Buena Vista Home Entertainment.

Bridget Loves Bernie: The Complete Series 1972
One-season CBS sitcom finds Jewish working-class cabbie Bernie (who's also a struggling writer) in a whirlwind courtship and marriage to elementary schoolteacher Bridget, who's from a wealthy Irish Catholic family, with everyone trying to adjust to their mixed marriage. 24 episodes. 323m; DVD. **C:** David Birney; Meredith Baxter; Harold J. Stone; Bibi Osterwald; David Doyle; Audra Lindley. **A:** Jr. High-Adult. **P:** Entertainment. **U:** Home. **L:** English. **Mov-Ent:** Family, Marriage, Television Series. **Acq:** Purchase. **Dist:** WarnerArchive.com. $38.99.

Bridget's Sexiest Beaches: Season 1 2009 (Unrated)
Travel Channel 2009-? reality travel show. Model, actress, and TV personality Bridget Marquardt explores shorelines worldwide to experience the daytime activities and nighttime hotspots. Locations include Ibiza, Thailand, Turks & Caicos, Australia and more. 17 episodes. 522m; DVD. **C:** Bridget Marquardt. **A:** Sr. High-Adult. **P:** Entertainment. **U:** Home. **Mov-Ent:** Travel, Television Series. **Acq:** Purchase. **Dist:** Image Entertainment Inc. $19.99.

Bridging 19??
Offers a three-fold look at the duties of libraries to accomodate disabled persons. Covers improving handicap access, library services for disabled children and accomodating elderly patrons. 45m; VHS. **A:** College-Adult. **P:** Education. **U:** Institution. **Gen-Edu:** Handicapped. **Acq:** Purchase, Rent/Lease. **Dist:** National Film Board of Canada. $250.

Bridging Cultural Barriers: Managing Ethnic Diversity in the Workplace 1990
A demonstration of four techniques of effective management in a culturally diverse workplace. 24m; VHS, 3/4 U, Special order formats. **Pr:** Barr Films. **A:** College-Adult. **P:** Professional. **U:** Institution. **Bus-Ind:** How-To, Business, Management. **Acq:** Purchase, Rent/Lease. **Dist:** Excellence in Training Corp.; American Media, Inc.; Learning Communications L.L.C. $595.00.

Bridging the Culture Gap 1987
This program was designed to help a businessman who is transferred into a foreign country. 30m; VHS, 3/4 U. **A:** Adult. **P:** Education. **U:** Institution, SURA. **Bus-Ind:** Business, Travel. **Acq:** Purchase, Trade-in. **Dist:** Encyclopedia Britannica. $500.00.

Bridging the Difference 1987
Disabled people talk about why they aren't always accepted. 26m; VHS, 3/4 U. **Pr:** Diocese of Columbus. **A:** Jr. High-Adult. **P:** Religious. **U:** Institution, SURA. **Gen-Edu:** Handicapped. **Acq:** Purchase, Rent/Lease. **Dist:** St. Anthony Messenger Press. $29.95.

Bridging the Gap 1985
Designed to gently bring out issues facing chemically dependent youths and their parents. 22m; VHS, 3/4 U. **Pr:** Gerald T. Rogers Productions, Inc. **A:** Sr. High-Adult. **P:** Education. **U:** Institution, Home. **Gen-Edu:** Alcoholism, Drug Abuse, Adolescence. **Acq:** Purchase. **Dist:** Gerald T. Rogers Productions. $390.00.

Brief Counseling: Children & Adolescents ????
Presents sessions with acting-out children and demonstrates how to use brief methods such as positive problem definition, the miracle question, and other strategies. 45m; VHS. **A:** Adult. **P:** Professional. **U:** Institution. **Hea-Sci:** Psychology, Mental Health. **Acq:** Purchase. **Dist:** Microtraining Associates, Inc. $149.00.

Brief Counseling: Living with Physical Challenge ????
John Littrell demonstrates how to help clients deal with issues concerning the interface between gender, physical ability, ethnicity/race, and socioeconomic situations. 50m; VHS. **A:** Adult. **P:** Professional. **U:** Institution. **Hea-Sci:** Psychology, Mental Health. **Acq:** Purchase. **Dist:** Microtraining Associates, Inc. $149.00.

Brief Counseling: The Basic Skills ????
John Littrell demonstrates how to help students search out positives and find solutions. Discusses how to manage difficult clients. 50m; VHS. **A:** Adult. **P:** Professional. **U:** Institution. **Hea-Sci:** Psychology, Mental Health. **Acq:** Purchase. **Dist:** Microtraining Associates, Inc. $149.00.

Brief Encounter 1946 (Unrated) — ★★★★
Based on Noel Coward's "Still Life" from "Tonight at 8:30," two middle-aged, middle-class people become involved in a short and bittersweet romance in WWII England. Intensely romantic, underscored with Rachmaninoff's Second Piano Concerto. 86m/B/W; VHS, DVD. **C:** Celia Johnson; Trevor Howard; Stanley Holloway; Cyril Raymond; Joyce Carey; Everley Gregg; Margaret Barton; Dennis Harkin; Valentine Dyall; Marjorie Mars; Irene Handl; Directed by David Lean; Written by Noel Coward; David Lean; Ronald Neame; Anthony Havelock-Allan; Cinematography by Robert Krasker. **Pr:** Mark Huffam. **A:** Family. **P:** Entertainment. **U:** Home. **Mov-Ent:** Drama, World War Two. **Awds:** N.Y. Film Critics '46: Actress (Johnson). **Acq:** Purchase. **Dist:** Paramount Pictures Corp.; Home Vision Cinema. $19.95.

Brief Encounters 1991
A presentation on 10 techniques to help interviewers select the best-qualified job applicant. 18m; VHS, 3/4 U, Special order formats. **Pr:** CRM Productions. **A:** College-Adult. **P:** Professional. **U:** Institution. **Bus-Ind:** How-To, Interviews, Business. **Acq:** Purchase, Rent/Lease. **Dist:** Excellence in Training Corp. $695.00.

A Brief History of Time 1992 (G) — ★★★
A stunning documentary about physicist Stephen Hawking, the author of the popular book "Brief History of Time." Crippled by Lou Gehrig's Disease, Hawking narrates the film in the computer-synthesized voice he uses to speak. Interviews with family, friends, and colleagues, bring Hawking's scientific theories to light. 85m; VHS, Blu-Ray, CC. **C:** Stephen Hawking; Directed by Errol Morris; Written by Stephen Hawking; Cinematography by John Bailey; Music by Philip Glass. **Pr:** David Hickman; Gordon Freedman; Triton Pictures. **A:** Jr. High-Adult. **P:** Entertainment. **U:** Home. **Mov-Ent:** Documentary Films, Philosophy & Ideology, Science. **Awds:** Sundance '92: Filmmakers Trophy. **Acq:** Purchase. **Dist:** Paramount Pictures Corp.; Baker and Taylor. $19.95.

Brief Interviews With Hideous Men 2009 (Unrated) — ★½
Brief drama based on the book by David Foster Wallace is the writing/directing debut of actor Krasinski, also featured as Ryan, who dumped Sara (Nicholson), who is now interviewing male subjects about private matters. The battle of the sexes monologues aren't terribly interesting for the most part and this seems more like a filmmaking exercise than a film. 78m; DVD. **C:** John Krasinski; Julianne Nicholson; Timothy Hutton; Max Minghella; Lou Taylor Pucci; Dominic Cooper; Ben Shenkman; Chris Messina; Will Arnett; Bobby Cannavale; Josh Charles; Directed by John Bailey; Cinematography by John Bailey. **A:** Sr. High-Adult. **P:** Entertainment. **U:** Home. **Mov-Ent:** Men, Interviews. **Acq:** Purchase. **Dist:** IFC Films.

Brief Moment 1933 (Unrated) — ★½
Lackluster marital soap based on the S.N. Behrman play. Hardworking nightclub singer Abby (Lombard) marries playboy Rodney (Raymond) who would rather live off his allowance than get a job, despite her encouragement. He still spends too much time drinking and at the track, and Abby gets fed up and leaves him, which Rodney takes as a wake-up call. 70m/B/W; DVD. **C:** Carole Lombard; Gene Raymond; Donald Cook; Monroe Owsley; Jameson Thomas; Arthur Hohl; Directed by David Burton; Written by Edith Fitzgerald; Brian Marlow; Cinematography by Ted Tetzlaff. **A:** Adult. **P:** Entertainment. **U:** Home. **L:** English. **Mov-Ent:** Marriage, Drama. **Acq:** Purchase. **Dist:** Turner Classic Movies (TCM).

A Brief Peace 2004
Documentary profiling how the Iranian culture handles death. 52m; VHS, DVD. **A:** Sr. High-Adult. **P:** Education. **U:** Institution. **Gen-Edu:** Documentary Films, Death, Iran. **Acq:** Purchase, Rent/Lease. **Dist:** The Cinema Guild. $295.00.

A Briefing on North Atlantic Treaty Organization 1986
This is a documentary on NATO, focusing on its organization and the ways in which it has carried out its mission to militarily check the Soviet Union. 17m; VHS, 3/4 U. **Pr:** USDSP. **A:** Jr. High-Adult. **P:** Education. **U:** Institution, SURA. **Gen-Edu:** History--Modern, International Relations. **Acq:** Purchase. **Dist:** National Audiovisual Center. $95.00.

The Brig 1964 — ★★★
A film by Jonas Mekas documenting the Living Theatre's infamous performance of Kenneth H. Brown's experimental play. Designed by Julian Beck. 65m/B/W; VHS. **C:** Adolfas Mekas; Jim Anderson; Warren Finnerty; Henry Howard; Tom Lillard; James Tiroff; Gene Lipton; Directed by John Mekas. **Pr:** Jonas Mekas; Living Theatre. **A:** Sr. High-Adult. **P:** Entertainment. **U:** Home. **Mov-Ent:** Theater. **Acq:** Purchase. **Dist:** Facets Multimedia Inc.; Mystic Fire Video; Tapeworm Video Distributors Inc. $29.95.

Brigadoon 1954 — ★★★
The story of a magical, 18th century Scottish village which awakens once every 100 years and the two modern-day vacationers who stumble upon it. Main highlight is the Lerner and Loewe score. 108m; VHS, DVD, Wide. **C:** Gene Kelly; Van Johnson; Cyd Charisse; Elaine Stewart; Barry Jones; Albert Sharpe; Directed by Vincente Minnelli; Written by Alan Jay Lerner; Cinematography by Joseph Ruttenberg; Music by Alan Jay Lerner; Frederick Loewe. **Pr:** Arthur Freed; MGM. **A:** Family. **P:** Entertainment. **U:** Home. **Mov-Ent:** Musical, Scotland. **Acq:** Purchase. **Dist:** MGM Home Entertainment; Time-Life Video and Television. $14.95.

Songs: Brigadoon; Almost Like Being in Love; I'll Go Home With Bonnie Jean; Wedding Dance; From This Day On; Heather on the Hill; Waitin' For My Dearie; Once in the Highlands.

Brigham City 2001 (PG-13) — ★★½
Skillful murder-mystery set in the fictitious Brigham City, Utah. The townspeople mostly know each other and most are also members of the Mormon Church. Sheriff Wes Clayton (Dutcher) and his deputy Terry's (Brown) duties are usually mundane—until they discover the mutiliated body of a young female tourist at an abandoned homestead. Clayton is willing to defer to the FBI but then a second body is discovered and the media vultures descend on the formerly quiet community as their faith is all put to an unexpected test. 115m; VHS, DVD. **C:** Richard Dutcher; Wilford Brimley; Matthew A. Brown; Carrie Morgan; John Enos; Tayva Patch; Directed by Richard Dutcher; Written by Richard Dutcher; Cinematography by Ken Glassing; Music by Sam Cardon. **A:** Jr. High-Adult. **P:** Entertainment. **U:** Home. **Mov-Ent:** Religion. **Acq:** Purchase.

Brigham Young: Frontiersman 1940 — ★★
Somewhat interesting story about the pioneering Mormons and their founding of Salt Lake City. Under the leadership of Brigham Young (Jagger), they set out across the plains, battling hardships and starvation along the way. An emphasis was placed on the historical rather than the religious in an effort not to scare off moviegoers, but the picture failed at the boxoffice anyway. Based on the story by Louis Bromfield. 114m; VHS, DVD. **C:** Tyrone Power; Linda Darnell; Dean Jagger; Brian Donlevy; John Carradine; Jane Darwell; Jean Rogers; Mary Astor; Vincent Price; Willard Robertson; Moroni Olsen; Marc Lawrence; Selmer Jackson; Stanley Andrews; Directed by Henry Hathaway; Written by Lamar Trotti; Ann E. Todd; Cinematography by Arthur C. Miller; Music by Cyril Mockridge; Alfred Newman. **A:** Sr. High-Adult. **P:** Entertainment. **U:** Home. **Mov-Ent:** Polygamy, Drama, Religion. **Acq:** Purchase. **Dist:** Fox Home Entertainment. $19.98.

Bright Angel 1991 (R) — ★★½
Road movie pairs an unconventional team: George wants to visit his aunt to see if she's heard from his mother who ran off with another man; Luey is a free-spirit trying to free her brother from jail. Good performances by Mulroney, Taylor, & Pullman. Ford adapted two of his short stories, "Childern" and "Great Falls" for the gritty and uncompromising script of life in the modern west. 94m; VHS, DVD, CC. **C:** Dermot Mulroney; Lili Taylor; Sam Shepard; Valerie Perrine; Burt Young; Bill Pullman; Benjamin Bratt; Mary Kay Place; Delroy Lindo; Kevin Tighe; Sheila McCarthy; Directed by Michael Fields; Written by Richard Ford; Music by Christopher Young. **Pr:** Hemdale Films. **A:** Sr. High-Adult. **P:** Entertainment. **U:** Home. **Mov-Ent:** Family. **Acq:** Purchase. **Dist:** Movies Unlimited; Alpha Video; MGM Home Entertainment. $92.99.

Bright Days Ahead 2014 (Unrated) — ★★
The ever-elegant Ardant stars as 60-something Caroline, who has an affair with a man 20 years her junior in this undeveloped romantic drama. Having retired from her dental practice, the long-married woman begins exploring the activities at her local senior center, which include a computer class taught by Julien (Lafitte). They're soon having a no-strings-attached sexual relationship that is quickly discovered by everyone, including Caroline's betrayed spouse, Philippe (Chesnais). French with subtitles. 94m; On Demand. **C:** Fanny Ardant; Laurent Lafitte; Patrick Chesnais; Jean-Francois Stevenin; Directed by Marion Vernoux; Written by Marion Vernoux; Fanny Chesnel; Cinematography by Nicolas Gaurin; Music by Quentin Sirjacq. **Pr:** Tribeca Film Institute. **A:** Adult. **P:** Entertainment. **U:** Home. **L:** French. **Mov-Ent:** Romance, Marriage. **Acq:** Purchase, Rent/Lease. **Dist:** Amazon.com Inc.

Bright Eyes 1934 (PG) — ★★
Shirley (Temple) lives with her widowed mother Mary (Wilson), who works as a maid for the snobbish Smythe family, where only wealthy, crochety Uncle Ned (Sellon) befriends the cutie. His niece Adele (Allen) is engaged to Shirley's godfather, flyboy Loop Merritt (Dunn), who wants the tyke to live with him when her mom is killed. But Uncle Ned also wants to adopt her and there's a battle over custody. Shirley warbles "On the Good Ship Lollipop" in her usual winsome way. 84m/B/W; VHS, DVD, CC. **C:** Shirley Temple; James Dunn; Lois Wilson; Jane Withers; Judith Allen; Jane Darwell; Charles Sellon; Directed by David Butler; Written by David Butler; Edwin J. Burke; William Conselman; Cinematography by Arthur C. Miller. **Pr:** 20th Century-Fox. **A:** Family. **P:** Entertainment. **U:** Home. **Mov-Ent:** Comedy-Drama, Adoption. **Acq:** Purchase. **Dist:** Music for Little People; Fox Home Entertainment. $14.98.

Bright Future 2003 (Unrated) — ★★★
Mamoru and Yuji are best friends, co-workers, and roommates in an existentially cool and cold modern world. Dreamlike plot takes Mamoru to jail for a crime he didn't commit, but won't deny. He seems fine there, drifting in and out of reality, almost living vicariously through his pet jellyfish he entrusted with Yuji before hitting the slammer. Japanese director Kiyoshi Kurosawa's new-wave vision of art and horror are fascinating, yet alienating at once. Fans of bizarro Asian cinema will flip. Originally titled "Jellyfish Alert," a title somehow more accurately describing this movie than any review could. 92m; DVD. **C:** Tadanobu Asano; Tatsuya Fuji; Joe Odagiri; Marumi Shiraishi; Directed by Kiyoshi Kurosawa; Written by Kiyoshi Kurosawa; Cinematography by Takahide Shibanushi; Music by Pacific 231. **P:** Entertainment. **U:** Home. **L:** Japanese. **Mov-Ent:** Japan, Fishing, Mystery & Suspense. **Acq:** Purchase. **Dist:** Movies Unlimited.

A Bright Future. . .For Some 198?
In this third film of "The History Book" series the plight of the 14th and 15th century merchant is examined. Heavily taxed, the merchants seek and find an ally in the King, who, in exchange for weapons and money to pay soldiers, defeats the small landowners, allowing free trade for merchants. 15m; 3/4 U, Special order formats. **Pr:** Hobel Leiterman Productions. **A:** Jr. High-Adult. **P:** Education. **U:** Institution. **Gen-Edu:** History--Medieval. **Acq:** Purchase. **Dist:** The Cinema Guild.

Bright Leaf 1950 (Unrated) — ★★½
In 1894, Brant Royle (Cooper) returns to his Kingsmont hometown and gets smitten brothel owner Sonia (Bacall) to become an investor in his automated cigarette-making business. His success nearly bankrupts the local tobacco tycoons, including James Singleton (Crisp) who originally ran Brant out of town for courting his daughter, Margaret (Neal). But when Margaret tries to save her family Brant ends up being used. 110m/B/W; DVD. **C:** Gary Cooper; Lauren Bacall; Patricia Neal; Donald Crisp; Jack Carson; Jeff Corey; Gladys George; Directed by Michael Curtiz; Written by Ranald MacDougall; Cinematography by Karl Freund; Music by Victor Young. **A:** Sr. High-Adult. **P:** Entertainment. **U:** Home. **Mov-Ent:** Business. **Acq:** Purchase. **Dist:** WarnerArchive.com.

Bright Leaves 2003 (Unrated)
Documentary filmmaker McElwee revisits his Southern roots in North Carolina and the importance of the tobacco industry to his family. He follows a rumor that the 1950 Hollywood melodrama, "Bright Leaf," was based on the life of his great-grandfather, John McElwee, who launched the Bull Durham tobacco brand but later lost his fortune to the rival Duke family. He interviews family and friends, explores the current state of the tobacco business, and makes a climatic visit to the annual Tobacco Festival. 107m. **C:** Directed by Ross McElwee; Written by Ross McElwee; Cinematography by Ross McElwee. **P:** Entertainment. **U:** Home. **L:** English. **Mov-Ent:** Documentary Films, Family, Agriculture. **Dist:** First Run Features.

Bright Lights 1930 (Unrated) — ★★
Broadway musical star Louanne (Mackaill) is about to retire and marry into money. That's when lecherous bad guy Miguel (Beery Sr.) shows up backstage, threatening to expose her sleazy past (which includes hula dancing in South African dive bars). Then Louanne is accused of murder! Filmed in 2-strip Technicolor but only B&W prints survive. 69m/B/W; DVD. **C:** Dorothy Mackaill; Noah Beery, Sr.; Frank Fay; Inez Courtney; Edmund Breese; Directed by Michael Curtiz; Written by Humphrey Pearson; Henry McCarty; Cinematography by Lee Garmes. **A:** College-Adult. **P:** Entertainment. **U:** Home. **Mov-Ent:** Musical--Drama. **Acq:** Purchase. **Dist:** WarnerArchive.com.

Bright Lights, Big City 1988 (R) — ★★
Based on Jay McInerney's popular novel, Fox plays a contemporary yuppie working in Manhattan as a magazine journalist. As his world begins to fall apart, he embarks on an endless cycle of drugs and nightlife. Fox is poorly cast, and his character is hard to care for as he becomes more and more dissolute. Although McInerney wrote his own screenplay, the intellectual abstractness of the novel can't be captured on film. 110m; VHS, DVD, CC. **C:** Michael J. Fox; Kiefer Sutherland; Phoebe Cates; Frances Sternhagen; Swoosie Kurtz; Tracy Pollan; Jason Robards, Jr.; John Houseman; Dianne Wiest; Charlie Schlatter; William Hickey; David Warrilow; Sam Robards; Kelly Lynch; Annabelle Gurwitch; Maria Pitillo; David Hyde Pierce; Jessica Lundy; Directed by James Bridges; Cinematography by Gordon Willis. **Pr:** Sydney Pollack; MGM Home Entertainment. **A:** Sr. High-Adult. **P:** Entertainment. **U:** Home. **Mov-Ent:** Drugs, Journalism. **Acq:** Purchase. **Dist:** MGM Home Entertainment. $14.95.

Bright Road 1953 — ★★½
Matter of fact B-movie drama from MGM. Belafonte makes his screen debut as the nameless southern school principal where 4th grade teacher Jane Richards (Dandridge) works to help troubled pupil C.T. (Hepburn). A tragedy strikes, and C.T. refuses to come to school. It takes a swarm of bees and a caterpillar's cocoon to save the day. Adapted from Mary Elizabeth Vroman's 1951 story "See How They Run." 70m/B/W; DVD. **C:** Dorothy Dandridge; Harry Belafonte; Philip Hepburn; Barbara Randolph; Maidie Norman; Robert Horton; Rene Beard; Directed by Gerald Mayer; Written by Emmet Lavery; Cinematography by Alfred Gilks; Music by David Rose. **A:** Jr. High-Adult. **P:** Entertainment. **U:** Home. **L:** English. **Mov-Ent:** Black Culture, Education. **Acq:** Purchase. **Dist:** WarnerArchive.com.

A Bright Shining Lie 1998 (R) — ★★½
Based on Neil Sheehan's 1988 Pulitzer Prize-winning book, which chronicles the Vietnam War as seen through the eyes of Lt. Col. John Paul Vann (Paxton). The brash Vann arrived as a military adviser to the Vietnamese Army in 1962 and eventually left that post to become part of the State Department's Civilian Aid Program, where he exposed falsified battle reports and other deceptions to newsman Steven Burnett (Logue). The complex and controversial Vann was killed in a chopper crash in 1972. 118m; VHS, DVD. **C:** Bill Paxton; Donal Logue; Kurtwood Smith; Eric Bogosian; Amy Madigan; Vivian Wu; Robert John Burke; James Rebhorn; Ed Lauter; Harve Presnell; Directed by Terry George; Written by Terry George; Cinematography by Jack Conroy; Music by Gary Chang. **Pr:** Lois Bonfiglio; HBO. **A:** Sr. High-Adult. **P:** Entertainment. **U:** Home. **Mov-Ent:** TV Movies, Vietnam War, Biography: Military. **Acq:** Purchase. **Dist:** Movies Unlimited; Alpha Video.

Bright Star 2009 (PG) — ★★½
Oh to be young and in the throes of first love! In 1818, flirty 18-year-old Fanny Brawne (Cornish) and her family live next door to brooding 23-year-old romantic poet John Keats (Whishaw) and his friend and patron, Charles Brown (Schneider). Keats is poor (and terminally ill) and fashionable seamstress Fanny knows she must meet her family's expectations and make a respectable marriage. She becomes his muse and then the object of his passionate letters. No consummation is possible so director Campion wisely makes the most of every glance, touch, and word. Title refers to the poem Keats dedicated to Fanny. 119m; DVD. **C:** Paul Schneider; Thomas Brodie-Sangster; Ben Whishaw; Abbie Cornish; Kerry Fox; Edie Martin; Gerard Monaco; Antonia Campbell-Hughes; Directed by Jane Campion; Written by Jane Campion; Cinematography by Greig Fraser; Music by Mark Bradshaw. **Pr:** Jan Chapman; Caroline Hewitt; Screen Australia; Apparition; New South Wales Film Corporation; U.K. Film Council; BBC Films; Hopscotch International. **A:** Jr. High-Adult. **P:** Entertainment. **U:** Home. **L:** English. **Mov-Ent:** Drama, Italy. **Acq:** Purchase. **Dist:** Sony Pictures Home Entertainment Inc.

Bright Young Things 2003 (R) — ★★½
Actor/director/writer Stephen Fry tackles literary satire with his adaptation of Evelyn Waugh's 1930 novel, "Vile Bodies." And if not precisely vile, those bodies are wicked indeed as seen through the everyman eyes of Adam (Moore), a poor aspiring novelist-turned-gossip columnist who wishes to marry superficial party girl Nina (Mortimer). Fry breezily tackles the jaded, flapper milieu of upper-class London between the wars that lends itself to glitter and eccentricity, embodied by feckless social butterflies (Woolgar) and drug-taking peers (the gentlemanly 94-year-old Sir John Mills doing a little coke in a cameo). These bored young things are bright only in the way they briefly shine before drab reality takes over. They (and the viewer) may as well enjoy it while they can. 106m; DVD. **C:** Emily Mortimer; James McAvoy; Michael Sheen; David Tennant; Fenella Woolgar; Dan Aykroyd; Jim Broadbent; Simon Callow; Jim Carter; Stockard Channing; Richard E. Grant; Julia McKenzie; Peter O'Toole; Stephan Campbell Moore; Directed by Stephen Fry; Written by Stephen Fry; Cinematography by Henry Braham; Music by Anne Dudley. **Pr:** Gina Carter; Miranda Davis; Revolution Films; Icon Film Distribution. **A:** Sr. High-Adult. **P:** Entertainment. **U:** Home. **Mov-Ent:** Comedy-Drama. **Acq:** Purchase. **Dist:** New Line Home Video. $27.95.

Brighter Baby 1999
Features the latest research in baby care, learning development, and intelligence. Provides demonstrations and examples on parent/baby communication and bonding. 45m; VHS. **A:** Adult. **P:** Instruction. **U:** Home. **How-Ins:** Children, Parenting, How-To. **Acq:** Purchase. **Dist:** Instructional Video. $19.98.

A Brighter Tomorrow 19??
Patient education program aimed at reassuring those individuals who are facing open heart surgery. Follows several heart attack patients and their families through surgery and recovery, providing insight on pain and emotional impact. Also walks the viewer through the surgical preparation (blood work, X-ray, and preop teaching), the day of surgery (what the patient and family can expect), and follow-up after discharge (cardiac rehabilitation). 20m; VHS. **A:** College-Adult. **P:** Education. **U:** Institution. **Hea-Sci:** Medical Education, Surgery, Heart. **Acq:** Purchase, Rent/Lease. **Dist:** AJN Video Library/Lippincott Williams & Wilkins. $275.00.

Brightest Star 2014 (Unrated) — ★½
Cliché attempt at 20-something romantic comedy works too hard to pack in indie-cute dialogue and vague attempts at depth while failing to establish strong characters or plot. A charming Lowell stars as the frustratingly vague unnamed slacker at the center of the film. Dumped by his astronomy-class love, Charlotte (McIver), he sets out to prove he can grow up and get a real job. He begins dating Lita (Szohr), who doesn't think he should change at all. Her businessman father (Gregg) inexplicably gives Lowell a management job with his company, which Lowell promptly uses to try to win Charlotte's approval. 80m; On Demand. **C:** Chris Lowell; Rose McIver; Jessica Szohr; Clark Gregg; Allison Janney; Peter Jacobson; Directed by Maggie Kiley; Written by Maggie Kiley; Matthew Mullen; Cinematography by Chayse Irvin; Music by Matthew Puckett. **Pr:** Gravitas Ventures L.L.C. **A:** Jr. High-Adult. **P:** Entertainment. **U:** Home. **L:** English. **Mov-Ent:** Astronomy, Comedy--Romantic. **Acq:** Purchase. **Dist:** Amazon.com Inc.

Brighton Beach Memoirs 1986 (PG-13) — ★★½
The film adaptation of the popular (and semiautobiographical) Neil Simon play. Poignant comedy/drama about a young Jewish boy's coming of age in Depression-era Brooklyn. Followed by "Biloxi Blues" and "Broadway Bound." 108m; VHS, DVD, CC. **C:** Blythe Danner; Bob (Robert) Dishy; Judith Ivey; Jonathan Silverman; Brian Drillinger; Stacey Glick; Lisa Waltz; Jason Alexander; Directed by Gene Saks; Written by Neil Simon; Cinematography by John Bailey; Music by Michael Small. **Pr:** Mark Huffam. **A:** Jr. High-Adult. **P:** Entertainment. **U:** Home. **Mov-Ent:** Comedy-Drama. **Acq:** Purchase. **Dist:** Facets Multimedia Inc. $19.95.

Brighton Rock 1947 (Unrated) — ★★★
Sterling performances highlight this seamy look at the British underworld. Attenborough is Pinkie Brown, a small-time hood who ends up committing murder. He manipulates a waitress to get himself off the hook, but things don't go exactly as he plans. Based on the novel by Graham Greene. 92m/B/W; VHS, DVD. **C:** Richard Attenborough; Hermione Baddeley; William Hartnell; Carol Marsh; Nigel Stock; Wylie Watson; Alan Wheatley; George Carney; Reginald Purdell; Directed by John Boulting; Written by Graham Greene. **Pr:** Roy Boulting; Associated British Corporation. **A:** Sr. High-Adult. **P:** Entertainment. **U:** Home. **Mov-Ent:** Great Britain. **Acq:** Purchase. **Dist:** Movies Unlimited.

Brighton Rock 2010 (Unrated) — ★★
Another adaptation of Graham Greene's revered 1938 novel, updated to the swinging '60s. Rising hoodlum Pinkie (Riley) must court a wide-eyed waitress (Riseborough) after she becomes the only witness to link him to the murder of a thug from a rival gang. Valuing style over character sinks Joffe's debut feature, which is inferior to the original 1947 version. Hurt and Mirren thrive in their supporting roles as Rose's friends but the leads never get under the skin of these characters and the change in time period (from the '40s) proves awkward. 111m; DVD, Blu-Ray. **C:** Sam Riley; Andrea Riseborough; Helen Mirren; Philip Davis; Sean Harris; John Hurt; Andy Serkis; Directed by Roland Joffe; Written by Roland Joffe; Cinematography by John Mathieson; Music by Martin Phipps. **Pr:** Paul Webster; Kudos Pictures; IFC Films. **A:** Sr. High-Adult. **P:** Entertainment. **U:** Home. **L:** English. **Mov-Ent:** Crime Drama, Great Britain. **Acq:** Purchase. **Dist:** MPI Media Group.

Brighton Strangler 1945 — ★★
An actor who plays a murderer assumes the role of the strangler after suffering from a concussion. Decent psychodrama. 67m/B/W; VHS. **C:** John Loder; June Duprez; Miles Mander; Directed by Max Nosseck. **Pr:** RKO. **A:** Family. **P:** Entertainment. **U:** Home. **Mov-Ent:** Mystery & Suspense, Mystery & Suspense. **Acq:** Purchase. **Dist:** No Longer Available.

The Brighton Strangler/Before Dawn 1945 — ★★
A mystery double feature: In "The Brighton Strangler," an actor takes his part too seriously as he murders Londoners at night; in "Before Dawn" a brilliant scientist turns to a life of murderous crime. 128m/B/W; VHS. **C:** John Loder; June Duprez; Miles Mander; Stuart Oland; Dorothy Wilson. **Pr:** RKO. **A:** Sr. High-Adult. **P:** Entertainment. **U:** Home. **Mov-Ent:** Mystery & Suspense. **Acq:** Purchase. **Dist:** Turner Broadcasting System Inc. $39.95.

The Brightside of Interlux 1992
Instructional program from International Paint detailing the correct method for urethane application. 15m; VHS. **A:** Adult. **P:** Instruction. **U:** Home. **How-Ins:** Boating. **Acq:** Purchase. **Dist:** Bennett Marine Video. $19.95.

Brighty of the Grand Canyon 1967 (Unrated) — ★½
The spunky donkey Brighty roams across the Grand Canyon in search of adventure. He finds friendship with a gold-digging old prospector who hits pay dirt. 90m; VHS, DVD. **C:** Joseph Cotten; Pat Conway; Dick Foran; Karl Swenson; Directed by Norman Foster. **Pr:** Feature Film Corporation of America. **A:** Family. **P:** Entertainment. **U:** Home. **Mov-Ent:** Action-Adventure. **Acq:** Purchase. **Dist:** Karol Media. $24.95.

A Brilliant Disguise 1993 (R) — ★½
Sportswriter gets involved with an artist who turns out to have multiple personality disorder and a sinister psychiatrist. Then his friends start to turn up dead but things aren't exactly what they seem. 97m; VHS. **C:** Lysette Anthony; Anthony John (Tony) Denison; Corbin Bernsen; Gregory McKinney; Robert (Bobby Ray) Shafer; Directed by Nick Vallelonga; Written by Nick Vallelonga. **Pr:** Cassian Elwes; Barry Collier. **A:** College-Adult. **P:** Entertainment. **U:** Home. **Mov-Ent:** Mystery & Suspense, Psychiatry. **Acq:** Purchase. **Dist:** Movies Unlimited. $80.99.

Brilliant Gardens 20??
Video tour of Britain's best botanical gardens including, Kew, Glasgow Botanic Garden, Wisley, and many more. 60m; VHS. **A:** Adult. **P:** Education. **U:** Home. **Gen-Edu:** Gardening, Horticulture. **Acq:** Purchase. **Dist:** Arthur Schwartz & Co. $24.95.

Brilliant Lies 1996 (Unrated) — ★★½
Susy Connor (Gia Carides) has brought an official complaint of sexual harassment against former boss Gary Fitzgerald (LaPaglia), who denies the charge. She claims her sister Katie (Zoe Carides) will substantiate her story, which she will, even though Katie knows it's a lie. As a matter of fact, Susy's a consummate liar though, in a way, she also turns out to be telling the truth. Fine performances from the Carides sisters, as well as LaPaglia (who's married to Gia) and Barrett, who plays the self-pitying Connor patriarch. Adapted from the play by David Williamson. 93m; VHS. **C:** Gia Carides; Anthony LaPaglia; Zoe Carides; Ray Barrett; Michael Veitch; Neil Melville; Catherine Wilkin; Grant Tilly; Directed by Richard Franklin; Written by Richard Franklin; Peter Fitzpatrick; Cinematography by Geoff Burton; Music by Nerida Tyson-Chew. **Pr:** Richard Franklin; Sue Farrelly; Richard Franklin; Australian Film Finance Corp; Bayside Pictures. **A:** Sr. High-Adult. **P:** Entertainment. **U:** Home. **Mov-Ent. Acq:** Purchase. **Dist:** Trinity Films.

Brilliant Marriage 1936 (Unrated) — ★½
Debutante Madge is horrified to learn she's actually the daughter of a killer. She leaves Park Avenue behind for bohemian life in Greenwich Village but makes the mistake of confiding in reporter Garry Dane and finds her secret exposed in the tabloids. 64m/B/W; DVD. **C:** Joan Marsh; Ray Walker; Inez Courtney; Hugh Marlowe; Doris Lloyd; Holmes Herbert; Directed by Phil Rosen; Written by Paul Perez. **A:** Sr. High-Adult. **P:** Entertainment. **U:** Home. **Mov-Ent:** Journalism. **Acq:** Purchase. **Dist:** Alpha Video.

Brilliant Years 19??
Teaching aid for art appreciation explores the art scene of Paris from 1900 to 1914. Artists covered include Picasso and Derain. 50m; VHS. **A:** Jr. High-College. **P:** Education. **U:** Institution. **Gen-Edu:** Art & Artists, France. **Acq:** Purchase. **Dist:** Crystal Productions. $29.95.

Brimstone & Treacle 1982 (R) — ★★★
Weird, obsessive psychodrama in which a young rogue (who may or may not be an actual agent of the Devil) infiltrates the home of a staid British family caring for their comatose adult daughter. 85m; VHS, DVD. **C:** Sting; Denholm Elliott; Joan Plowright; Suzanna Hamilton; Directed by Richard Loncraine; Written by Dennis Potter. **Pr:** Namara Films. **A:** College-Adult. **P:** Entertainment. **U:** Home. **Mov-Ent:** Mystery & Suspense, Occult Sciences. **Awds:** Montreal World Film Fest. '82: Film. **Acq:** Purchase. **Dist:** MGM Home Entertainment. $14.95.

Brincando El Charco: Portrait of a Puerto Rican 1994
Contemplates the notion of "identity" in terms of class, race, and sexuality. Tells the story of a middle-class, light-skinned Puerto Rican photographer who attempts to construct a sense of community in the United States. 55m; VHS. **A:** College-Adult. **P:** Education. **U:** Institution. **Gen-Edu:** Women, Ethnicity, Identity. **Acq:** Purchase, Rent/Lease. **Dist:** Women Make Movies. $295.00.

Bring Back My Bonnie 1983
Discusses how strokes occur, the effect they have and what kinds of rehabilitation are available to the victims. 55m; VHS, 3/4 U. **Pr:** Canadian Broadcasting Corp. **A:** Adult. **P:** Education. **U:** Institution. **Hea-Sci:** Stroke, Patient Education. **Acq:** Purchase. **Dist:** Filmakers Library Inc.

Bring Back the Romance of Dance Instruction Tape, Vol. I 1995
Award winning dance instructor Greg Gale takes the viewer step-by-step through the basics of ballroom dancing, starting with the Fox Trot and the Swing. Includes music from Nancy Hays and the Bobby Benson Orchestra. 42m; VHS. **A:** Family. **P:** Instruction. **U:** Home. **How-Ins:** Dance--Instruction, How-To. **Acq:** Purchase. **Dist:** Tapeworm Video Distributors Inc. $19.95.

Bring Down the Walls 1993
Reinforces the Catholic Church's social doctrine by focusing on the heritage and principles behind the teachings. 12m; VHS. **Pr:**

U.S. Catholic Conference. **A:** Sr. High-Adult. **P:** Religious. **U:** Institution, Home. **Gen-Edu:** Religion. **Acq:** Purchase. **Dist:** U.S. Catholic Conference of Catholic Bishops. $19.95.

Bring It On 2000 (PG-13) — ★★½
Bring on the guilty pleasure. Equal parts satire, exploitation, and earnest (if not totally successful) teen flick, the film follows cheerleader Torrence (Dunst) as she becomes captain of the Rancho Carne High Toros cheer squad, who soon after discovers her squad's championship moves have been lifted from another school, the East Compton High Clovers. All of this culminates in a showdown between the two squads, while interspersed throughout are standard teenage goings-on. No gem, by any means, but fun if you're in the mood (or spirit). But be advised: probably too raunchy for its intended young adult audience. 98m; VHS, DVD, Wide, CC. **C:** Kirsten Dunst; Eliza Dushku; Jesse Bradford; Gabrielle Beauvais; Clare Kramer; Nicole Bilderback; Tsianina Joelson; Rini Bell; Ian Roberts; Richard Hillman; Lindsay Sloane; Cody McMains; Directed by Peyton Reed; Written by Jessica Bendinger; Cinematography by Shawn Maurer; Music by Christophe Beck. **Pr:** Universal Pictures. **A:** Jr. High-Adult. **P:** Entertainment. **U:** Home. **Mov-Ent:** Cheerleaders, Satire & Parody. **Acq:** Purchase. **Dist:** Alpha Video; Movies Unlimited.

Bring It On Again 2003 (PG-13) — ★★
College freshman Whittier (Judson-Yager) proves to be a cheerleading rival that head pom-pom girl Tina (Turner) won't tolerate. So when Whittier is cut from the squad, she decides to form a new team and challenge Tina to a cheer off. 90m; VHS, DVD. **C:** Anne Judson-Yager; Bree Turner; Richard Lee Jackson; Faune A. Chambers; Kevin Cooney; Bryce Johnson; Directed by Damon Santostefano; Written by Claudio Grazioso; Cinematography by Richard Crudo; Music by Paul Haslinger. **A:** Jr. High-Adult. **P:** Entertainment. **U:** Home. **Mov-Ent:** Cheerleaders. **Acq:** Purchase. **Dist:** Movies Unlimited; Alpha Video.

Bring It On: All or Nothing 2006 (PG-13) — ★★½
The plot hardly matters as long as the cheer routines astonish (which they do). Britney (Panettiere) was the cheer captain at her rich 'burb school but is just another wannabe after a move to a more urban setting. But she wins over leader Camille (Knowles-Smith) with some new routines and is ready to go up against her old squad. 99m; DVD, Wide. **C:** Hayden Panettiere; Jake McDorman; Solange Knowles-Smith; Gus Carr; Marcy Rylan; Directed by Steve Rash; Written by Alyson Fouse. **A:** Jr. High-Adult. **P:** Entertainment. **U:** Home. **Mov-Ent:** Cheerleaders. **Acq:** Purchase. **Dist:** Movies Unlimited; Alpha Video.

Bring It On: Fight to the Finish 2009 (PG-13) — ★★
Yet another cheerleading sequel. East L.A. high school cheer captain Lina Cruz (Milian) feels her squad is a lock to win the Spirit Championships until her mother remarries and they relocate to Malibu. Lina soon learns that the Malibu Vista High Sea Lions aren't winning material until she vows to whip them into shape to knock off the award-winning rival Jaguars and their trash-talking captain, Avery (Smith). Soon Lina notices just how darn cute Avery's brother Evan (Longo) is. 103m; DVD. **C:** Christina Milian; Rachele Brooke Smith; Cody Longo; Vanessa Born; Gabrielle Dennis; Nikki SooHoo; Meagan Holder; David Starzyk; Directed by Bille Woodruff; Written by Elena Song; Alyson Fouse; Cinematography by David Claessen; Music by Andrew Gross. **A:** Jr. High-Adult. **P:** Entertainment. **U:** Home. **Mov-Ent:** Cheerleaders, Sports-Fiction: Comedy. **Acq:** Purchase. **Dist:** Universal Studios Home Video.

Bring It On: In It to Win It 2007 (PG-13) — ★★½
It's the battle of the coastal babes as SoCal Carson (Benson) and Big Apple Brooke (Scerbo) and their cheer squads meet up at the national championships. Carson falls for Penn (Copon), who happens to be on Brooke's team, and Brooke challenges Carson to a personal cheer-off. This leads to a brawl and both teams are disqualified, but they're determined to get back into the finals. 90m; DVD, Wide. **C:** Adam Vernier; Ashley Benson; Cassie Scerbo; Michael Copon; Jennifer Tisdale; Kierstin Koppell; Noel Areizaga; Directed by Steve Rash; Written by Alyson Fouse; Cinematography by Levie Isaacks. **A:** Jr. High-Adult. **P:** Entertainment. **U:** Home. **Mov-Ent:** Cheerleaders. **Acq:** Purchase. **Dist:** Movies Unlimited; Alpha Video.

Bring Me the Head of Alfredo Garcia 1974 (R) — ★★
Peckinpah falters in this poorly paced outing. American piano player on tour in Mexico finds himself entwined with a gang of bloodthirsty bounty hunters. Bloody and confused. 112m; VHS, DVD, DVD. **C:** Warren Oates; Isela Vega; Gig Young; Robert Webber; Helmut Dantine; Emilio Fernandez; Kris Kristofferson; Directed by Sam Peckinpah; Written by Sam Peckinpah; Gordon Dawson; Cinematography by Alex Phillips, Jr.; Music by Jerry Fielding. **A:** College-Adult. **P:** Entertainment. **U:** Home. **Mov-Ent.** **Acq:** Purchase. **Dist:** MGM Home Entertainment. $59.95.

Bring Me the Vampire 1961 — ★
A wealthy baron must endure a night of terror in order to receive an inheritance. 100m/B/W; VHS. **C:** Maria Eugenia San Martin; Hector Godoy; Joaquin Vargas; Directed by Alfredo B. Crevenna. **A:** Jr. High-Adult. **P:** Entertainment. **U:** Home. **Mov-Ent:** Horror. **Acq:** Purchase. **Dist:** Sinister Cinema; Movies Unlimited. $16.95.

Bring the Ages Together 1987
Explains the concept of Intergenerational Programming, focusing on the benefits of encouraging relationships between children and older persons. 10m; VHS, 3/4 U. **Pr:** RMI Media Productions. **A:** Adult. **P:** Education. **U:** Institution. **Gen-Edu:** Children, Aging, Philosophy & Ideology. **Acq:** Purchase. **Dist:** RMI Media.

Indiv. Titles: 1. What, Who, Why? 2. Unlimited Possibilities 3. Getting Started 4. Working With Older People 5. Finding and Keeping Volunteers.

Bringin' in Da Spirit 2003
Examines the holistic practices in midwifery, the misconceptions and opposition from Western medical practitioners. 60m; VHS. **A:** Adult. **P:** Education. **U:** Institution, BCTV. **Gen-Edu:** Documentary Films, Childbirth. **Acq:** Purchase, Rent/Lease. **Dist:** Third World Newsreel. $225.00.

Bringing Arbitration into Workplace 2000 19??
Separated into two parts, the larger part of the program consists of a lecture by attorney Gary Mathiason on the advantages and disadvantages of arbitration. Also includes an interview with Professor Arthur Miller. 67m; VHS. **A:** College-Adult. **P:** Professional. **U:** Institution. **Bus-Ind:** Business, Management, Job Training. **Acq:** Purchase. **Dist:** Monad Trainer's Aide. $890.00.

Bringing Ashley Home 2011 (Unrated) — ★★
Libba Phillips' (Cook) younger sister Ashley (Morrison) is a bipolar drug addict who likes to party. When she isn't heard from, her family start searching but can't get any info on where Ashley might be. Libba refuses to give up and puts her career on hold and her marriage in jeopardy to keep searching, even founding a national organization to help families find missing adults. Lifetime drama based on a true story. 87m; DVD. **C:** A.J. Cook; Jennifer (Jenny) Morrison; Patricia Richardson; Timothy Webber; John Reardon; Directed by Nick Copus; Written by Walter Klenhard; Cinematography by Mahlon Todd Williams; Music by Michael Neilson. **A:** Jr. High-Adult. **P:** Entertainment. **U:** Home. **Mov-Ent.** **Acq:** Purchase. **Dist:** A&E Television Networks L.L.C.

Bringing Down the House 2003 (PG-13) — ★★
Straitlaced divorced lawyer Martin makes an online date and winds up with parolee Queen Latifah, who proceeds to turn his life upside-down in her quest to get him to help her prove her innocence. Moments of inspired comedy have everything to do with the talents of Martin and Latifah, and little to do with script or direction. Levy makes the most of his sidekick role. May play better on the small screen. 105m; VHS, DVD, Blu-Ray. **C:** Steve Martin; Queen Latifah; Eugene Levy; Jean Smart; Angus T. Jones; Kimberly J. Brown; Joan Plowright; Missi Pyle; Steve Harris; Michael Rosenbaum; Betty White; Directed by Adam Shankman; Written by Jason Filardi; Cinematography by Julio Macat; Music by Lalo Schifrin. **Pr:** David Hoberman; Ashok Amritraj; Hyde Park Entertainment; Touchstone Pictures. **A:** Jr. High-Adult. **P:** Entertainment. **U:** Home. **Mov-Ent:** Comedy--Screwball, Divorce, Law. **Acq:** Purchase. **Dist:** Buena Vista Home Entertainment.

Bringing in a Barge 19??
Outlines procedures for safely guiding a barge to where it will be docked. Introduces basic nautical terms, barge securing techniques, and proper safety gear. 12m; VHS, 3/4 U. **A:** Adult. **P:** Education. **U:** Institution. **Bus-Ind:** Safety Education, Boating. **Acq:** Purchase. **Dist:** Williams Learning Network.

Bringing It All Back Home 1987
An analysis of how the patterns of international capital investment and the exploitation of Third World women workers in free trade zones are being brought home to the First World. 48m; VHS, 3/4 U. **Pr:** Sheffield Film Coop. **A:** Sr. High-Adult. **P:** Education. **U:** Institution, SURA. **Gen-Edu:** Documentary Films, Labor & Unions, Women. **Acq:** Purchase. **Dist:** Women Make Movies. $250.00.

Bringing Out the Best: Encouraging Expressive Communication in Children with Multiple Handicaps 1989
A program designed to show teachers and parents methods to encourage communicative behavior in children with multiple handicaps. Includes a workbook. 24m; VHS, 3/4 U. **Pr:** Research Press. **A:** College-Adult. **P:** Special Education. **U:** Institution, Home. **How-Ins:** How-To, Handicapped, Communication. **Acq:** Purchase, Rent/Lease. **Dist:** Research Press. $150.00.

Bringing Out the Best in Kids 1987
Provides parents with helpful guidelines for nurturing their children's development and helping them grow into mature, capable, well-adjusted adults. 25m; VHS, 3/4 U. **Pr:** RMI Media Productions. **A:** Adult. **P:** Education. **U:** Institution. **Gen-Edu:** Documentary Films, Children, Parenting. **Acq:** Purchase. **Dist:** RMI Media.
Indiv. Titles: 1. Bring Out the Best in Your Children: Pygmalion 2. Children of Royalty Are Treated Royally: Self-Esteem 3. Sticks and Stones...But Words Are What Will Make Me: Self-Talk 4. Say What You Mean and Mean What You Say: Spirit of Intent 5. Make Your Children Lucky Stars: Reticular Activating System 6. Create Success from Disappointment: Resiliency 7. Make Your Children Mentally Wealthy: Possibility Thinking 8. Create a "Goal" Mind: Visualization 9. Build Confidence in Your Children Flick Back/Flick Up 10. What's Holding You Back? Comfort Zones 11. Make Things Happen: Power of Your World 12. Why Does the Dog Hide Under the Bed When You Talk to Your Family: Captain of the World 13. Differences Are Good in a Family: Creating Respect 14. Build Heart, Brains, Courage in Your Children: I'm Off to Be the Wizard.

Bringing Out the Dead 1999 (R) — ★★½
Cage hasn't looked this haggard since his boozehound role in "Leaving Las Vegas" which could be considered a dress rehearsal for this turn as burnt out New York City paramedic Frank Pierce. Aided by Scorsese's kinetic filmmaking style, Schrader's on-tempo script, and revved up performances by Rhames and Sizemore as Pierce's partners, movie successfully convey's the day-to-day stress of emergency units. Unfortunately, Cage's sleepwalking character is a bore, and a lack of chemistry with

real-life spouse Arquette as Pierce's singular ray of hope only makes you yearn for Scorsese's similarly themed masterpiece "Taxi Driver." Based on the novel by Joe Connelly. 120m; VHS, DVD, Wide, CC. **C:** Nicolas Cage; John Goodman; Tom Sizemore; Ving Rhames; Patricia Arquette; Marc Anthony; Mary Beth Hurt; Clifford Curtis; Nestor Serrano; Aida Turturro; Afemo Omilami; Arthur J. Nascarella; Cynthia Roman; Cullen Oliver Johnson; Jon Abrahams; Directed by Martin Scorsese; Written by Paul Schrader; Cinematography by Robert Richardson; Music by Elmer Bernstein. **A:** Adult. **P:** Entertainment. **U:** Home. **Mov-Ent:** Drug Abuse, Hospitals, Comedy--Black. **Acq:** Purchase. **Dist:** Paramount Pictures Corp.

Bringing Out the Leader In You 1991
Helps managers become leaders in their own right. Viewers gain the basic know-how and confidence to inspire followers and get people involved and committed to a goal. 23m; VHS. **A:** Adult. **P:** Professional. **U:** Institution. **L:** English. **Bus-Ind:** Management. **Acq:** Purchase. **Dist:** American Management Association. $89.95.

Bringing the Bible to Life 1987
Bible curriculum program is separated into six 30-minute segments on two tapes. Comes with 48-page workbook and includes individual and group exercises. Taught by Ada Lum. 180m; VHS. **Pr:** TwentyOneHundred Productions. **A:** Jr. High-College. **P:** Religious. **U:** Institution, Home. **Gen-Edu:** Bible. **Acq:** Purchase. **Dist:** InterVarsity Video. $69.95.

Bringing the Circle Together! 1999
Four men share their wisdom on the traditions of aging. 56m; VHS. **A:** Adult. **P:** Professional. **U:** Institution. **Hea-Sci:** Aging, Health Education. **Acq:** Purchase. **Dist:** Aquarius Health Care Media. $195.00.

Bringing the Rain to Kapiti Plain 19??
James Earl Jones narrates this story inspired by the tales of the Nandi people of Kenya about rainy weather. Contains an aerial chase of a thunderstorm and puddle jumping. Hosted by LeVar Burton. Includes teacher's guide. 30m; VHS, CC. **A:** Primary. **P:** Education. **U:** Institution. **Chl-Juv:** Literature--Children, Education. **Acq:** Purchase. **Dist:** GPN Educational Media. $39.95.

Bringing Up Baby 1938 — ★★★★
The quintessential screwball comedy, featuring Hepburn as a giddy socialite with a "baby" leopard, and Grant as the unwitting object of her affections. One ridiculous situation after another adds up to high speed fun. Hepburn looks lovely, the supporting actors are in fine form, and director Hawks manages the perfect balance of control and mayhem. From a story by Hagar Wilde, who helped Nichols with the screenplay. Also available in a colorized version. 103m/B/W; VHS, DVD. **C:** Katharine Hepburn; Cary Grant; May Robson; Charlie Ruggles; Walter Catlett; Fritz Feld; Jonathan Hale; Barry Fitzgerald; Ward Bond; Directed by Howard Hawks; Written by Dudley Nichols; Cinematography by Russell Metty. **Pr:** Howard Hawks; Howard Hawks; RKO. **A:** Family. **P:** Entertainment. **U:** Home. **Mov-Ent:** Comedy--Screwball, Animals. **Awds:** AFI '98: Top 100; Natl. Film Reg. '90. **Acq:** Purchase. **Dist:** Turner Broadcasting System Inc.; Home Vision Cinema; Baker and Taylor. $14.98.

Bringing Up Bobby 2011 (PG-13) — ★½
Actress Janssen's directorial debut is a heavy-handed family drama that's both maudlin and foolish. Con woman Olive moves to Oklahoma with her smart-mouthed 11-year-old son Bobby after some problems with the law. She keeps up with her larcenies and smells money when Bobby has a minor mishap involving wealthy businessman Kent (Pullman). Olive is abruptly jailed for past crimes, and she asks Kent and his wife Mary, whose own son has died, to care for Bobby. 93m; DVD. **C:** Milla Jovovich; Spencer List; Bill Pullman; Marcia Cross; Rory Cochrane; Directed by Famke Janssen; Written by Famke Janssen; Cinematography by Guido van Gennep; Music by Tom Holkenborg. **A:** Jr. High-Adult. **P:** Entertainment. **U:** Home. **L:** English. **Mov-Ent:** Family, Parenting. **Acq:** Purchase. **Dist:** Monterey Home Video.

Brink 1998 (Unrated) — ★★½
Andy Brinker leads of group of in-line skaters who are dedicated to the sport. But Andy also needs money to help out his family and when a rival team offers him cash to join them on the circuit, Andy's forced into a hard choice. 88m; VHS, CC. **C:** Christina Vidal; Erik von Detten; Patrick Levis; Asher Gold; Sam Horrigan; Directed by Greg Beeman. **A:** Family. **P:** Entertainment. **U:** Home. **Mov-Ent:** Skating. **Acq:** Purchase. **Dist:** Buena Vista Home Entertainment.

Brink of Life 1957 (Unrated) — ★★½
Three pregnant women in a hospital maternity ward await the impending births with mixed feelings. Early Bergman; in Swedish with English subtitles. 82m/B/W; VHS, DVD. **C:** Eva Dahlbeck; Bibi Andersson; Ingrid Thulin; Babro Ornas; Max von Sydow; Erland Josephson; Gunnar Sjoberg; Directed by Ingmar Bergman. **A:** Sr. High-Adult. **P:** Entertainment. **U:** Home. **L:** Swedish. **Mov-Ent:** Pregnancy. **Awds:** Cannes '58: Actress (Andersson), Actress (Dahlbeck), Actress (Thulin), Director (Bergman). **Acq:** Purchase. **Dist:** $24.95.

Brink's Job 1978 (PG) — ★★★
Re-creates the "crime of the century," Tony Pino's heist of $2.7 million from a Brink's truck. The action picks up five days before the statute of limitations is about to run out. 103m; VHS, DVD. **C:** Peter Falk; Peter Boyle; Warren Oates; Gena Rowlands; Paul Sorvino; Sheldon Leonard; Allen Garfield; Directed by William Friedkin; Written by Walon Green; Music by Richard Rodney Bennett. **Pr:** Mark Huffam. **A:** Jr. High-Adult. **P:** Entertainment. **U:** Home. **Mov-Ent:** Action-Adventure. **Acq:** Purchase. **Dist:** Universal Studios Home Video. $59.95.

Bristlelip 1983
Based on the Grimm fairy tale called "King Thrushbeard." A father marries his spoiled daughter off to a peddler, who proceeds to break her spirit. 20m; VHS, 3/4 U, Special order formats. **Pr:** Davenport Films. **A:** Jr. High-Adult. **P:** Education. **U:** Home. **Gen-Edu:** Fairy Tales. **Acq:** Purchase, Rent/Lease. **Dist:** Davenport Films. $19.95.

Britannia Hospital 1982 (R) — ★★½
This is a portrait of a hospital at its most chaotic: the staff threatens to strike, demonstrators surround the hospital, a nosey BBC reporter pursues an anxious professor, and the eagerly anticipated royal visit degenerates into a total shambles. 111m; VHS, DVD, Wide. **C:** Malcolm McDowell; Leonard Rossiter; Graham Crowden; Joan Plowright; Mark Hamill; Alan Bates; Dave Atkins; Marsha A. Hunt; Directed by Lindsay Anderson; Written by David Sherwin; Cinematography by Mike Flash; Music by Alan Price. **Pr:** Independent. **A:** College-Adult. **P:** Entertainment. **U:** Home. **Mov-Ent:** Satire & Parody, Hospitals. **Acq:** Purchase. **Dist:** Lions Gate Entertainment Inc. $9.98.

Britannic 2000 (Unrated) — ★★
The Britannic, the Titanic's sister ship, was built as a luxury liner but when WWI began the ship was turned into a hospital transport after its launch in 1914. The ship did sink off the Greek coast in 1916 (probably due to a torpedo or mine) but the filmmakers haven't let any other facts of the story stand in the way of this poor man's "Titanic" with its class difference romance and other cliches. 96m; VHS, DVD. **C:** Edward Atterton; Jacqueline Bisset; John Rhys-Davies; Bruce Payne; Amanda Ryan; Ben Daniels; Directed by Brian Trenchard-Smith; Written by Brian Trenchard-Smith; Brett Thompson; Dennis A. Pratt; Cinematography by Ivan Strasburg; Music by Alan Parker. **A:** Jr. High-Adult. **P:** Entertainment. **U:** Home. **Mov-Ent:** Action-Adventure, Boating, Romance. **Acq:** Purchase.

Britannica Presents. . .Series 1991
These traditional tales for children are hosted by Pat Morita. 30m; VHS. **C:** Hosted by Noriyuki "Pat" Morita. **Pr:** Kid's Corner. **A:** Preschool-Primary. **P:** Entertainment. **U:** Institution. **Chl-Juv:** Animation & Cartoons, Fairy Tales, Storytelling. **Acq:** Purchase. **Dist:** Telephone Doctor Inc.
Indiv. Titles: 1. Beauty and the Beast and Other Tales 2. Cinderella and Other Tales 3. Hansel and Gretel and Other Tales 4. Rapunzel and Other Tales 5. Sleeping Beauty and Other Tales 6. Rumpelstiltskin and Other Tales.

British Agent 1934 (Unrated) — ★★
In 1917, dedicated communist Elena (Francis) is saved from a street riot by English diplomat Stephen Locke (Howard). The two find romance but Stephen is wanted for anti-revolutionary activities and Elena is ordered to spy on him, although her report could mean his death. 80m/B/W; DVD. **C:** Kay Francis; Leslie Howard; William Gargan; Phillip Reed; Irving Pichel; Halliwell Hobbes; Ivan Simpson; Tenen Holtz; Directed by Michael Curtiz; Written by Laird Doyle; Cinematography by Ernest Haller. **A:** College-Adult. **P:** Entertainment. **U:** Home. **Mov-Ent:** Drama. **Acq:** Purchase. **Dist:** WarnerArchive.com.

British Big Beat: The Invasion 1965
Filled with performances from some of the great British beat bands of the '60s, including The Hollies, Lulu and the Luvvers, The Merseybeats, Mille Small, Brian Poole and more. 70m; VHS. **Pr:** Krypton Corporation. **A:** Jr. High-Adult. **P:** Entertainment. **U:** Home. **Mov-Ent:** Music--Performance. **Acq:** Purchase. **Dist:** Music Video Distributors; Rhino Entertainment Co. $19.95.

British Bike GP '88 1988
Brit bike thrills from the British Bike Grand Prix. ?m; VHS. **A:** Family. **P:** Entertainment. **U:** Home. **Spo-Rec:** Sports--General, Motorcycles. **Acq:** Purchase. **Dist:** Powersports - Powerdocs. $39.95.

British Bike 1989 Grand Prix 1990
Sit in on the suspense of the Grand Prix with this remarkably photographed video event. 55m; VHS. **A:** Adult. **P:** Entertainment. **U:** Home. **Mov-Ent:** Sports--General, Motorcycles. **Acq:** Purchase. **Dist:** Powersports - Powerdocs.

British Documentary Movement: Benjamin Britten 1935
Documentaries influenced by the talents of poet W.H. Auden and composer Benjamin Britten. Produced by the General Post Office of Great Britain. Includes "Coal Face" (1935), "Night Mail" (1936), "Instruments of the Orchestra" (1947), and "Steps of the Ballet" (1948). 80m/B/W; VHS. **TV Std:** NTSC, PAL, SECAM. **A:** College-Adult. **P:** Education. **U:** Home, Institution. **Gen-Edu:** Documentary Films, Great Britain, Music--Classical. **Acq:** Purchase. **Dist:** International Historic Films Inc.; Kino on Video. $29.95.

British Documentary Movement: E.M.B. Classics 1929
Includes three episodes produced by the film office of the Empire Marketing Board (E.M.B.) of the General Post Office entitled "Drifters" (1929), "Industrial Britain" (1933), and "Song of Ceylon" (1934). 109m/B/W; VHS. **TV Std:** NTSC, PAL, SECAM. **A:** College-Adult. **P:** Education. **U:** Home, Institution. **Gen-Edu:** Documentary Films, Great Britain. **Acq:** Purchase. **Dist:** Kino on Video; International Historic Films Inc. $29.95.

British Documentary Movement: England in the Thirties 1934
Avant-garde documentaries give a fascinating glimpse into England between the wars. Produced by the General Post Office of Great Britain. Includes "Granton Trawler" (1934), "Pett and Pott" (1934), and "North Sea" (1938). 76m/B/W; VHS. **TV Std:** NTSC, PAL, SECAM. **A:** College-Adult. **P:** Education. **U:** Home, Institution. **Gen-Edu:** Documentary Films, Great Britain. **Acq:** Purchase. **Dist:** International Historic Films Inc.; Kino on Video. $29.95.

British Documentary Movement: Festival of Britain 1948
Three documentary films include "Waverly Steps" (1948), "David" (1951), and "Family Portrait" (1951). 93m; VHS. **TV Std:** NTSC, PAL, SECAM. **A:** Sr. High-Adult. **P:** Education. **U:** Home, Institution. **Gen-Edu:** Great Britain. **Acq:** Purchase. **Dist:** International Historic Films Inc.; Kino on Video. $29.95.

British Documentary Movement: Wartime Combat 1943
Produced by British military filmmakers. "Desert Victory" (1943) won an Oscar for best documentary. Also includes "Cameramen at War" (1943). 77m; VHS. **TV Std:** NTSC, PAL, SECAM. **A:** College-Adult. **P:** Education. **U:** Home, Institution. **Gen-Edu:** World War Two, Great Britain. **Acq:** Purchase. **Dist:** International Historic Films Inc.; Kino on Video. $29.95.

British Documentary Movement: Wartime Homefront 1940
Captures the historic struggle of the British to stave off Nazi invasion during WWII. Includes "London Can Take It" (1940), and "Fires Were Started" (1943). 81m/B/W; VHS. **TV Std:** NTSC, PAL, SECAM. **A:** College-Adult. **P:** Education. **U:** Home, Institution. **Gen-Edu:** World War Two, Great Britain. **Acq:** Purchase. **Dist:** International Historic Films Inc.; Kino on Video. $29.95.

British Documentary Movement: Wartime Moments 1941
Humphrey Jennings reads from his inspiring poetry as scenes of Britain's wartime perseverence unfold. Three episodes include "Listen to Britain" (1942), "Target for Tonight" (1941), and "A Diary for Timothy" (1945). 107m; VHS. **TV Std:** NTSC, PAL, SECAM. **A:** College-Adult. **P:** Education. **U:** Home, Institution. **Gen-Edu:** World War Two, Great Britain. **Acq:** Purchase. **Dist:** International Historic Films Inc.; Kino on Video. $29.95.

The British Empire in Color 2008
Documentary of rarely seen color footage chronicling the fall of the British Empire. 147m; DVD. **A:** Sr. High-Adult. **P:** Education. **U:** Home. **Gen-Edu:** Documentary Films, Education. **Acq:** Purchase. **Dist:** Acorn Media Group Inc. $24.99.

British 500 Motocross GP '86 1986
Video footage from the British 500 Motocross Grand Prix of 1986. ?m; VHS. **A:** Family. **P:** Entertainment. **U:** Home. **Spo-Rec:** Sports--General, Motorcycles. **Acq:** Purchase. **Dist:** Powersports - Powerdocs. $39.95.

British Football: Boys from Brazil 1990
Highlights from Brazil's soccer (British football) championships from past World Cups. 85m; VHS. **Pr:** British Broadcasting Corporation. **A:** Family. **P:** Entertainment. **U:** Home. **Spo-Rec:** Sports--General, Soccer. **Acq:** Purchase. **Dist:** Video Collectibles. $34.95.

British Football: FA Cup Final Goals 1990
The best goals of the 1989 and 1990 FA Cup series. 90m; VHS. **Pr:** British Broadcasting Corporation. **A:** Family. **P:** Entertainment. **U:** Home. **Spo-Rec:** Sports--General, Soccer. **Acq:** Purchase. **Dist:** Video Collectibles. $34.95.

British Football: The 1989 FA Cup Final 1990
The 1989 FA Cup Final between Liverpool and Everton, the most emotional and dramatic final in the 117 year history. 149m; VHS. **Pr:** British Broadcasting Corporation. **A:** Family. **P:** Entertainment. **U:** Home. **Spo-Rec:** Sports--General, Soccer. **Acq:** Purchase. **Dist:** Video Collectibles. $34.95.

British Horse Society Programs: Showjumping 19??
Thorough lessons in primary jumping techniques to a complete jumping course. 60m; VHS. **A:** Family. **P:** Entertainment. **U:** Home. **How-Ins:** How-To, Horses. **Acq:** Purchase. **Dist:** Video Collectibles. $29.95.

British Intelligence 1940 — ★½
Silly American-made film about British espionage. Boris Karloff plays a butler (who is also a spy) trapped by an agent who visits the home of a British bureaucrat. Half-baked story that doesn't hold up. 62m/B/W; VHS, DVD. **C:** Boris Karloff; Margaret Lindsay; Maris Wrixon; Holmes Herbert; Leonard Mudie; Bruce Lester; Directed by Terry Morse. **Pr:** Warner Bros. **A:** Adult. **P:** Entertainment. **U:** Home. **Mov-Ent. Acq:** Purchase. **Dist:** Sinister Cinema. $16.95.

The British Invasion Returns 2000 (Unrated)
Anyone old enough to remember the British music invasion of the mid-1960s will likely be profoundly depressed by this public television special taped at the Foxwoods Resort Casino in Connecticut. The years have taken their toll on these rock 'n' roll survivors (Gerry and the Pacemakers, Eric Burdon, Herman's Hermits, etc.) and they plow through the familiar songs so stolidly that younger viewers will wonder how they ever became hits. 105m; DVD. **C:** Hosted by Peter Noone; Directed by Haig Papasian; Written by Larry Rifkin. **A:** Jr. High-Adult. **P:** Entertainment. **U:** Home. **Mov-Ent:** Documentary Films, Music--Pop/Rock. **Acq:** Purchase. **Dist:** Image Entertainment Inc.

The British Isles 1988
A video travelog through the British Isles, the Scottish Highlands and the Blarney Stone in Northern Ireland. 30m; VHS. **Pr:** Around the World in Sight & Sound. **A:** Jr. High-Adult. **P:** Education. **U:** Institution, Home. **Gen-Edu:** Travel, Scotland, Great Britain. **Acq:** Purchase, Rent/Lease. **Dist:** Visual Horizons. $39.95.

The British Isles: Land and the People 1963
Traces the physical geography of England, Wales, Scotland, Northern Ireland, and reveals ways in which the land has influenced the way of life and the national character of the British people. 21m; VHS, 3/4 U. **Pr:** Encyclopedia Britannica Educational Corporation. **A:** Primary-Sr. High. **P:** Education. **U:** Institution, SURA. **L:** English, Spanish. **Gen-Edu:** Scotland, Great Britain, Ireland. **Acq:** Purchase, Rent/Lease, Trade-in. **Dist:** Encyclopedia Britannica.

British Military Pageantry 19??
Focuses on Britain's great military ceremonies, celebrations and events. 50m; VHS. **A:** Adult. **P:** Entertainment. **U:** Home. **Gen-Edu:** Great Britain, Military History. **Acq:** Purchase. **Dist:** Acorn Media Group Inc. $19.95.

British Motocross Champ '87 1987
Footage from the 1987 British Motocross Championship. ?m; VHS. **A:** Family. **P:** Entertainment. **U:** Home. **Spo-Rec:** Sports--General, Motorcycles. **Acq:** Purchase. **Dist:** Powersports - Powerdocs. $39.95.

British Open Golf Championships 1989
A series of eight videos covering the British Open from 1977 to 1984. Featured players include Tom Watson, Jack Nicklaus, Steve Ballesteros (the youngest player to ever win at age 22), and Bill Rodgers. 416m; VHS. **A:** Family. **P:** Entertainment. **U:** Home. **Mov-Ent:** Sports--General, Golf. **Acq:** Purchase. **Dist:** Video Collectibles.

British Primitives 192? (Unrated)
Anthology of early dramas and comedies from the English production team of Hepworth, Clarendon and Gaumon. Included are "Pickpocket," "Child Stealers," "The Eviction," "How the Old Woman Caught the Omnibus," "Bewitched Traveler," "Englishman's Trip to Paris from London," "Lover's Ruse," "A Race for a Kiss," "The Other Side of the Hedge," "Raid on a Coiner's Den," "Revenger," "Fine Feathers Make Fine Birds," "A Railway Tragedy," "Decoyed," and "Rescued by Rover." ?m/B/W; VHS. **A:** Sr. High-Adult. **P:** Entertainment. **U:** Home. **Mov-Ent:** Film History. **Acq:** Purchase. **Dist:** Facets Multimedia Inc. $29.95.

British Rock: The First Wave 1985
The British musical invasion of the 1960s is fondly remembered in this documentary that features footage of the Beatles and the Rolling Stones performing. Also seen are Gerry and the Pacemakers, Eric Burdon and the Animals, Herman's Hermits, The Kinks, The Yardbirds and The Who. 59m; VHS. **C:** Narrated by Michael York; Directed by Patrick Montgomery. **Pr:** Patrick Montgomery. **A:** Family. **P:** Entertainment. **U:** Home. **Mov-Ent:** Music--Pop/Rock, Documentary Films, Great Britain. **Acq:** Purchase. **Dist:** Music Video Distributors; Sony Pictures Home Entertainment Inc. $16.95.

British Rock: The Legends of Punk & New Wave 1986
A compilation of concert footage, interviews, and video clips of the anti-establishment British musical artists that emerged in the late '70s. 60m; VHS. **Pr:** SteinFilm. **A:** Jr. High-Adult. **P:** Entertainment. **U:** Home. **Mov-Ent:** Music--Performance. **Acq:** Purchase. **Dist:** Music Video Distributors; Lions Gate Television Corp. $19.98.

British Royal Children of the 20th Century 2013
Nostalgic look at the British monarchy from Queen Elizabeth to Prince Harry. Newsreel footage looks at the royal children making their first public appearances and at family gatherings. 120m; DVD. **A:** Sr. High-Adult. **P:** Entertainment. **U:** Home. **Gen-Edu:** Children, Great Britain, Biography: Royalty. **Acq:** Purchase. **Dist:** Acorn Media Group Inc. $19.95.

British Scenic Rail Journey 19??
Takes the viewer on a train trip through the countryside of Scotland with stops at Edinburgh, the Isle of Skye, Perth, Inverness, Kyle of Lochalsh, and Culloden Moor. 28m; VHS. **A:** Family. **P:** Education. **U:** Institution. **Gen-Edu:** Travel, Trains, Scotland. **Acq:** Purchase. **Dist:** Instructional Video. $39.99.

The British Virgin Islands 19??
Travel to Tortola, Peter Island, Norman Island, Jost Van Dyke, Virgin Gorda and the other islands. Part of the Caribbean Vacation Series. 45m; VHS. **A:** Adult. **P:** Entertainment. **U:** Home. **Spo-Rec:** Travel, Caribbean, Boating. **Acq:** Purchase. **Dist:** Bennett Marine Video. $24.95.

British World War II Documentaries 19??
A compilation of three documentaries made in Great Britain during 1941-44: "Listen to Britain," "Ordinary People," and "A Harbor Goes to France." 60m/B/W; VHS. **Pr:** Crown Film Unit. **A:** Family. **P:** Education. **U:** Home. **Gen-Edu:** Documentary Films, World War Two. **Acq:** Purchase. **Dist:** Glenn Video Vistas Ltd.

Britney Spears: Britney in Hawaii: Live and More 2000
Contains live performance footage, video clips in 5.1 Dolby digital audio with motion graphic menus, five language subtitles, Paris/Tokyo bonus footage, excerpts from her appearance on Saturday Night Live, photo gallery, web links, and more. ?m; DVD. **A:** Jr. High-Sr. High. **P:** Entertainment. **U:** Home. **Mov-Ent:** Music Video, Music--Pop/Rock. **Acq:** Purchase. **Dist:** BMG Entertainment. $24.98.

Britney Spears: Live and More! 2001
Contains live performance footage, video clips in 5.1 Dolby digital audio with motion graphic menus, excerpts from her Saturday Night Live appearance, photo gallery, jukebox feature, web links and more. 70m; DVD. **A:** Jr. High-Sr. High. **P:** Entertainment. **U:** Home. **Mov-Ent:** Music Video, Music--Pop/Rock. **Acq:** Purchase. **Dist:** BMG Entertainment. $24.98.

Britny Fox: Year of the Fox 1989
Philadelphia metal band Britny Fox videos include "Long Way to Love," "Girls School," and "Save the Weak." 60m; VHS. **Pr:** CBS. **A:** Preschool. **P:** Entertainment. **U:** Home. **Mov-Ent:** Music Video. **Acq:** Purchase. **Dist:** Music Video Distributors; Sony Music Entertainment Inc. $14.98.

Britt Fit 1993
Britt Ekland, a 50-year-old actress/model/mother, has a figure to envy and the energy to go with it. Learn her non-aerobic exercise program, designed to stretch and tone muscles, and how she maintains her weight. 55m; VHS. **A:** Sr. High-Adult. **P:** Instruction. **U:** Home. **Hea-Sci:** Fitness/Exercise. **Acq:** Purchase. **Dist:** Fast Forward; Anchor Bay Entertainment. $19.98.

Britten: A Midsummer Night's Dream 1987
This is a performance of the Benjamin Britten opera based on Shakespeare, taped at the Glyndebourne Festival Opera. 156m; VHS. **C:** Ileana Cotrubas; James Bowman; Curt Appelgren; Directed by Peter Hall. **Pr:** National Video Corporation Ltd. **A:** Family. **P:** Entertainment. **U:** Home. **Fin-Art:** Opera. **Acq:** Purchase. **Dist:** Music Video Distributors; Home Vision Cinema. $49.95.

Britten: A Time There Was—A Profile 1980
A biography of one of the 20th century's foremost composers, with footage from his operas, of Britten rehearsing, conducting and playing Mozart with Sviatoslav Richter and his own home movies. 120m; VHS. **A:** Family. **P:** Education. **U:** Home. **Fin-Art:** Biography, Opera. **Acq:** Purchase. **Dist:** Music Video Distributors; Home Vision Cinema. $59.95.

Britten: Albert Herring 1986
A performance of Benjamin Britten's comic opera based the Guy De Maupassant tale, taped at the Glyndebourne Festival Opera. 150m; VHS. **Pr:** British Broadcasting Corporation. **A:** Family. **P:** Entertainment. **U:** Home. **Fin-Art:** Opera. **Acq:** Purchase. **Dist:** Home Vision Cinema. $49.95.

Britten: Gloriana 1983
Conducted by Mark Elder, the English National Opera performs Benjamin Britten's opera celebrating Queen Elizabeth II's 1953 coronation. 146m; VHS. **C:** Sarah Walker; Anthony Rolfe Johnson; Jean Rigby; Richard Van Allan; Conducted by Mark Elder. **Pr:** Colin Graham. **A:** Jr. High-Adult. **P:** Entertainment. **U:** Home. **Fin-Art:** Opera. **Acq:** Purchase. **Dist:** Music Video Distributors; Home Vision Cinema. $39.95.

Britten: Peter Grimes 1981
The Royal Opera's production of Benjamin Britten's three-act opera set in a small English fishing town and concerning the inquest into the death of Grime's apprentice. In stereo. 90m; VHS. **C:** Jon Vickers; Conducted by Colin Davis. **Pr:** Covent Garden Video Productions Ltd. **A:** Family. **P:** Entertainment. **U:** Home. **Fin-Art:** Opera. **Acq:** Purchase. **Dist:** Music Video Distributors; Home Vision Cinema. $39.95.

Britten: The Turn of the Screw 2012 (Unrated)
Opera based on the Henry James novella, with music provided by the London Philharmonic Orchestra. 111m; DVD, Blu-Ray. **A:** Family. **P:** Entertainment. **U:** Home. **L:** English, French, German, Italian, Spanish. **Gen-Edu:** Music--Classical, Music--Instruction. **Acq:** Purchase. **Dist:** Fra Music. $34.98 32.98.

Brittle Bones: Should You Worry? 1988
Looks at the crippling bone disorder, Osteoporosis. 11m; VHS, 3/4 U. **Pr:** Canadian Broadcasting Corp. **A:** Adult. **P:** Education. **U:** Institution, Home, SURA. **Hea-Sci:** Bones, Aging, Health Education. **Acq:** Purchase, Rent/Lease. **Dist:** Clear Vue Inc. $195.00.

A Brivele der Mamen 1938 (Unrated) — ★★★
A Jewish mother does her best to hold her fragile family together, in spite of the ravages of war and poverty. Her travails take her and her family from the Polish Ukraine to New York City. In Yiddish with English subtitles. 90m; VHS. **C:** Berta Gersten; Lucy Gerhman; Misha Gerhman; Edmund Zayenda; Directed by Joseph Green. **Pr:** Joseph Green Pictures. **A:** Jr. High-Adult. **P:** Entertainment. **U:** Home. **L:** Yiddish. **Mov-Ent:** Judaism, Poverty. **Acq:** Purchase. **Dist:** Ergo Media Inc. $79.95.

Broadband Switching 199?
An overview of existing and emerging broadband switching technologies. 150m; VHS. **A:** Adult. **P:** Vocational. **U:** Institution. **Bus-Ind:** Technology. **Acq:** Purchase. **Dist:** Telcordia Technologies Inc. $435.00.

Broadcast Bombshells 1995 (R) — ★★
TV station WSEX has a station manager who'll do anything to improve ratings, an ambitious associate producer after the weather girl's job, a sexaholic sportscaster, and lots of chaos involving a mad bomber. The barely there plot is just the excuse for a considerable display of T&A anyway. Also available unrated. 80m; VHS, DVD. **C:** Amy Lynn Baxter; Debbie Rochon; Elizabeth Heyman; Joseph Pallister; Directed by Ernest G. Sauer. **A:** Sr. High-Adult. **P:** Entertainment. **U:** Home. **Mov-Ent:** Mass Media. **Acq:** Purchase. **Dist:** Movies Unlimited.

Broadcast News 1987 (R) — ★★★½
The acclaimed, witty analysis of network news shows, dealing with the three-way romance between a driven career-woman producer, an ace nebbish reporter and a brainless, popular on-screen anchorman. Incisive and funny, though often simply idealistic. 132m; VHS, DVD, Blu-Ray, CC. **C:** William Hurt; Albert Brooks; Holly Hunter; Jack Nicholson; Joan Cusack; Robert Prosky; Lois Chiles; John Cusack; Gennie James; Directed by James L. Brooks; Written by James L. Brooks; Cinematography by Michael Ballhaus; Music by Bill Conti; Michael Gore. **Pr:** James L. Brooks; James L. Brooks; 20th Century-Fox. **A:** Sr. High-Adult. **P:** Entertainment. **U:** Home. **Mov-Ent:** Comedy-Drama. **Awds:** L.A. Film Critics '87: Actress (Hunter); Natl. Bd. of Review '87: Actress (Hunter); N.Y. Film Critics '87: Actress (Hunter), Director (Brooks), Film, Screenplay. **Acq:** Purchase. **Dist:** Movies Unlimited; Alpha Video; Criterion Collection Inc. $19.98.

Broadcast Tapes of Dr. Peter 1992
This compilation of a video diary series started by Dr. Peter Jepson-Young after he learned that he had AIDS realistically portrays the struggles he faced as both a doctor and a patient. 45m; VHS. **A:** Jr. High-Adult. **P:** Education. **U:** Home. **Gen-Edu:** Documentary Films, AIDS, Medical Care. **Acq:** Purchase. **Dist:** Direct Cinema Ltd. $34.95.

Broadcasting 1981
A six-program series which probes certain aspects of broadcasting to help students understand the business and explore possible job opportunities. 15m; VHS, 3/4 U, Q. **Pr:** Children's Television International. **A:** Sr. High. **P:** Education. **U:** Institution, CCTV, CATV, BCTV, Home. **Gen-Edu:** Mass Media, Occupations. **Acq:** Purchase, Rent/Lease, Off-Air Record. **Dist:** Children's Television International.
Indiv. Titles: 1. How We Get Programming 2. Turning Decisions Into Programs 3. Who's Out There Listening 4. Paying For Programs 5. Careers in Broadcasting 6. Freedoms and Restrictions.

Broadcasting Studio Tour: Inside Careers 1989
Explores the careers available within the field of broadcasting, including writer, producer, stage, make-up, computer graphics, camera, art, electronic, reporting, communication, and audience experts. 30m; VHS. **A:** Sr. High-Adult. **P:** Education. **U:** Institution. **Gen-Edu:** Occupations, Mass Media. **Acq:** Purchase. **Dist:** Geographical Studies and Research Center, Department of Geography and Planning.

Broadchurch: The Complete First Season 2013
BBC crime drama. Eleven-year-old Danny is found dead cliffside in the small coastal town of Broadchurch. It turns out he was murdered. Local copper Ellie Miller expects to investigate but the case is given over to big-city newcomer, DI Alec Hardy. Soon the tabloid press has the story and everyone's lives are upended and secrets exposed. 8 episodes. 394m; DVD, Blu-Ray. **C:** David Tennant; Olivia Colman; Jodie Whittaker; Arthur Darvill; Andrew Buchan; Jonathan Bailey. **A:** Adult. **P:** Entertainment. **U:** Home. **L:** English. **Mov-Ent:** Crime Drama, Mystery & Suspense, Great Britain. **Acq:** Purchase. **Dist:** Entertainment One US LP. $39.98.

Broadway 1942 — ★½
Typical showbiz bio with Raft playing himself as he nostalgically remembers his early hoofing days in New York and his gangster ties. Best seen and heard for the songs and Raft dancing a particularly wild Charleston. 91m/B/W; DVD. **C:** George Raft; Pat O'Brien; Broderick Crawford; Janet Blair; Anne Gwynne; Marjorie Rambeau; Directed by William A. Seiter; Written by John Bright; Felix Jackson; Cinematography by George Barnes; Music by Charles Previn. **Pr:** Bruce Manning; Frank Shaw. **A:** Adult. **P:** Entertainment. **U:** Home. **L:** English. **Mov-Ent:** Dance, Musical--Drama. **Acq:** Purchase.

Broadway 1981
Prominent Broadway dancers and choreographers discuss their craft in these related programs from the "Eye on Dance" series. 30m; VHS, 3/4 U, EJ. **C:** Hosted by Celia Ipiotis. **Pr:** ARC Videodance. **A:** Family. **P:** Entertainment. **U:** Institution, CCTV, Home, SURA. **Fin-Art:** Performing Arts, Dance. **Acq:** Purchase. **Dist:** Eye on the Arts.
Indiv. Titles: 1. Graciela Daniele and Margo Sappington 2. Sammy Williams, Bill Bradley, and Gloria Rosenthal 3. Michael Stewart, Tommy Walsh, and Ronald Dennis 4. Galena Panova and Lillianne Montevecchi 5. Hal Schaefer and Ethel Martin.

Broadway Bill 1934 — ★★★
A man decides to abandon his nagging wife and his job in her family's business for the questionable pleasures of owning a racehorse known as Broadway Bill. This racetrack comedy was also remade by Frank Capra in 1951 as "Riding High." 90m/B/W; DVD. **C:** Warner Baxter; Myrna Loy; Walter Connolly; Helen Vinson; Margaret Hamilton; Frankie Darro; Directed by Frank Capra; Written by Robert Riskin; Cinematography by Joseph Walker; Music by Howard Jackson. **A:** Adult. **P:** Entertainment. **U:** Home. **Mov-Ent:** Horses--Racing. **Acq:** Purchase. **Dist:** WarnerArchive.com.

Broadway Bound 1992 (Unrated) — ★★½
The final film in Simon's trilogy (preceded by "Brighton Beach Memoirs" and "Biloxi Blues"), this one made for TV. The playwright's alter ego, Eugene Morris Jerome, is ready to leave Brooklyn for good, hoping to make it as a comedy writer for a radio show. Meanwhile, his mother decides what to do about his unfaithful father. 90m; VHS, CC. **C:** Jonathan Silverman; Anne Bancroft; Jerry Orbach; Corey Parker; Hume Cronyn; Michele Lee; Directed by Paul Bogart; Written by Neil Simon. **A:** Jr. High-Adult. **P:** Entertainment. **U:** Home. **Mov-Ent:** Family, TV Movies. **Acq:** Purchase. **Dist:** Unknown Distributor.

Broadway Damage 1998 (Unrated) — ★½
Amateurish gay comedy whose best asset is the shopaholic (and only female) character played by Hobel, as the typical overweight fag hag roomie of aspiring New York actor Marc (Lucas). Beyond-shallow Marc is looking for a lover and only a perfect 10 will do, which means he gets dumped a lot by narcisstic manipulators. Meanwhile, his plain best friend, Robert (Williams), pines for the twit to notice him in a romantic way. 110m; VHS, DVD. **C:** Michael Shawn Lucas; Aaron Williams; Mara Hobel; Hugh Panaro; Directed by Victor Mignatti; Written by Victor Mignatti; Cinematography by Mike Mayers; Music by Elliot Sokolov. **A:** College-Adult. **P:** Entertainment. **U:** Home. **Mov-Ent:** Comedy--Romantic. **Acq:** Purchase. **Dist:** Wolfe Video.

Broadway Dance 1981
Current dancers on the Broadway circuit are interviewed in these related programs from the "Eye on Dance" series. 30m; VHS, 3/4 U, EJ. **C:** Hosted by Julinda Lewis. **Pr:** ARC Videodance. **A:** Sr. High-Adult. **P:** Entertainment. **U:** Institution, CCTV, Home, SURA. **Fin-Art:** Dance, Interviews. **Acq:** Purchase. **Dist:** Eye on the Arts.
Indiv. Titles: 1. Lee Theodore, Buzz Miller and Barbara Naomi Cohen-Stratyner 2. Phil Black, Robin Black, Wade Goss and Alvin McDuffie 3. Nat Horne and Mabel Robinson 4. Maurice Hines, Mercedes Ellington, Dean Badolato and Valarie Pettiford.

Broadway Dancin' ????
Bob Rizzo demonstrates two full-length theatre dance routines for the intermediate student. 55m; VHS. **A:** Adult. **P:** Teacher Education. **U:** Institution. **How-Ins:** Dance, Dance--Instruction. **Acq:** Purchase. **Dist:** Stagestep. $29.95.

Broadway Danny Rose 1984 (PG) — ★★★½
One of Woody Allen's best films, a hilarious, heart-rending anecdotal comedy about a third-rate talent agent involved in one of his client's infidelities. The film magically unfolds as show business veterans swap Danny Rose stories at a delicatessen. Allen's Danny Rose is pathetically lovable. 85m/B/W; VHS, DVD, Blu-Ray, Wide. **C:** Woody Allen; Mia Farrow; Nick Apollo Forte; Sandy Baron; Milton Berle; Howard Cosell; Directed by Woody Allen; Written by Woody Allen; Cinematography by Gordon Willis. **Pr:** Orion Pictures. **A:** Sr. High-Adult. **P:** Entertainment. **U:** Home. **Mov-Ent. Awds:** British Acad. '84: Orig. Screenplay; Writers Guild '84: Orig. Screenplay. **Acq:** Purchase. **Dist:** Movies Unlimited; Alpha Video; MGM Home Entertainment. $19.98.

The Broadway Drifter 1927 (Unrated) — ★★
A silent Jazz Age drama about a playboy who repents his decadent ways by opening a girls' health school. Complications ensue. 90m/B/W; Silent; VHS, 8 mm. **C:** George Walsh; Dorothy Hall; Bigelow Cooper; Arthur Donaldson; Directed by Bernard McEveety, Sr. **Pr:** MGM. **A:** Family. **P:** Entertainment. **U:** Home. **Mov-Ent:** Silent Films, Education. **Acq:** Purchase. **Dist:** $24.95.

Broadway! History of the Musical 1989
Five-volume set presents behind-the-scenes footage and interviews with stars, producers, and directors involved in musical theatre. 600m; VHS. **A:** Adult. **P:** Education. **U:** Institution. **Fin-Art:** Theater, Musical. **Acq:** Purchase. **Dist:** Insight Media. $265.00.

Broadway Idiot 2013 (Unrated) — ★★
Behind-the-scenes chronicle of "American Idiot," the squeaky-clean stage adaptation of Green Day's hugely successful pop-punk opera by the same name. The band's lead singer Billie Joe Armstrong heads a cast of otherwise young and unknown stage performers as they scramble to hit their marks and do the album justice. Bearing zero resemblance to the band's bratty roots, this surprisingly shallow documentary is nothing but smiles, giving little insight into the production's origins. Green Day would've rebelled against it 20 years ago. 80m; Streaming. **C:** Billie Joe Armstrong; Directed by Doug Hamilton; Cinematography by Dan Krauss; Music by Green Day. **Pr:** FilmBuff. **A:** Sr. High-Adult. **P:** Entertainment. **U:** Home. **L:** English. **Mov-Ent:** Documentary Films, Music--Pop/Rock, Theater. **Acq:** Purchase, Rent/Lease. **Dist:** Amazon.com Inc.

Broadway Limited 1941 (Unrated) — ★★
Three aspiring actors head for the Great White Way with a baby to use as a prop. Thinking the baby kidnapped, the police make things tough for the trio. McLaglen was wasted on this one, which was apparently made to show off the considerable assets of Woodworth. 75m/B/W; DVD. **C:** Victor McLaglen; Marjorie Woodworth; Dennis O'Keefe; Patsy Kelly; Zasu Pitts; Leonid Kinskey; George E. Stone; Directed by Gordon Douglas. **Pr:** United Artists. **A:** Jr. High-Adult. **P:** Entertainment. **U:** Home. **Mov-Ent:** Theater. **Acq:** Purchase. **Dist:** Alpha Video; Movies Unlimited. $14.99.

Broadway Limited: 1902-1995 ????
The Pennsylvania Railroad introduced the this premier passenger train in 1902 to transport riders from New York to Philadelphia and Chicago. Learn about the train's legacy, equipment, crews and service. 100m; VHS, DVD. **A:** College-Adult. **P:** Education. **U:** Home. **Gen-Edu:** Trains. **Acq:** Purchase. **Dist:** The Civil War Standard. $24.95.

Broadway Melody 1929 — ★★½
Early musical in which two sisters hope for fame on Broadway, and encounter a wily song and dance man who traps both their hearts. Dated, but still charming, with a lovely score. Considered the great granddaddy of all MGM musicals; followed by three more melodies in 1935, 1937, and 1940. 104m/B/W; VHS, DVD. **C:** Bessie Love; Anita Page; Charles King; Jed Prouty; Kenneth Thomson; Edward Dillon; Mary Doran; Directed by Harry Beaumont; Music by Nacio Herb Brown; Lyrics by Arthur Freed. **Pr:** MGM. **A:** Family. **P:** Entertainment. **U:** Home. **Mov-Ent:** Musical, Romance. **Awds:** Oscars '29: Film. **Acq:** Purchase. **Dist:** Baker and Taylor; MGM Home Entertainment. $19.98.
Songs: Broadway Melody; Give My Regards to Broadway; Truthful Parson Brown; The Wedding of the Painted Doll; The Boy Friend; You Were Meant For Me; Love Boat; Broadway Babies.

Broadway Melody of 1936 1935 — ★★★
Exceptional musical comedy with delightful performances from Taylor and Powell. Benny is a headline-hungry columnist who tries to entrap Taylor by using Powell. 110m/B/W; VHS, DVD. **C:** Jack Benny; Eleanor Powell; Robert Taylor; Una Merkel; Sid Silvers; Buddy Ebsen; Directed by Roy Del Ruth; Cinematography by Charles Rosher; Music by Nacio Herb Brown; Arthur Freed. **Pr:** MGM. **A:** Jr. High-Adult. **P:** Entertainment. **U:** Home. **Mov-Ent:** Musical, Journalism. **Acq:** Purchase. **Dist:** Warner Home Video, Inc. $19.98.
Songs: Broadway Melody; Broadway Rhythm; You Are My Lucky Star; I've Got a Feeling You're Fooling; All I Do Is Dream of You; Sing Before Breakfast; On a Sunday Afternoon.

Broadway Melody of 1938 1937 — ★★½
Third entry in the melody series lacks the sparkle of "Broadway Melody of 1936" despite the all-star cast. Lots of singing and dancing without much charm. Two bright spots: a young Garland singing the now famous "Dear Mr. Gable" and the always lovely Powell's dance numbers. 110m/B/W; VHS, DVD, CC. **C:** Eleanor Powell; Sophie Tucker; George Murphy; Judy Garland; Robert Taylor; Buddy Ebsen; Binnie Barnes; Directed by Roy Del Ruth; Cinematography by William H. Daniels; Music by Nacio Herb Brown; Lyrics by Arthur Freed. **Pr:** MGM. **A:** Family. **P:** Entertainment. **U:** Home. **Mov-Ent:** Musical. **Acq:** Purchase. **Dist:** Warner Home Video, Inc. $19.98.
Songs: Broadway Rhythm; Dear Mr. Gable (You Made Me Love You); A New Pair of Shoes; Yours and Mine; I'm Feeling Like a Million; Everybody Sing; Follow in My Footsteps; Your Broadway and My Broadway; Sun Showers; Some of These Days; Toreador Song; Largo al Factotum.

Broadway Melody of 1940 1940 — ★★½
The last entry in the melody series features the only screen teaming of Astaire and Powell. The flimsy plot is just an excuse for a potent series of Cole Porter musical numbers. 103m/B/W; VHS, DVD. **C:** Fred Astaire; Eleanor Powell; George Murphy; Frank Morgan; Ian Hunter; Directed by Norman Taurog. **Pr:** MGM. **A:** Family. **P:** Entertainment. **U:** Home. **Mov-Ent:** Musical, Dance. **Acq:** Purchase. **Dist:** Turner Broadcasting System Inc.; Facets Multimedia Inc.; MGM Home Entertainment. $19.98.
Songs: I Concentrate on You; I've Got My Eye on You; Begin the Beguine; I am the Captain; Please Don't Monkey With Broadway; Between You and Me; Il Bacio.

Broadway Musicals: A Jewish Legacy 2012
Examines the role that Jewish composers and lyricists have made on Broadway and the American musical, including Irving Berlin, the Gershwins, Jerome Kern, Leonard Bernstein, and Sephen Sondheim. Includes interviews, peformances, and archival footage. 84m; DVD. **A:** Sr. High-Adult. **P:** Entertainment. **U:** Home. **Mov-Ent:** Judaism, Musical. **Acq:** Purchase. **Dist:** Acorn Media Group Inc. $39.99.

Broadway Rhythm 1944 — ★★½
A too-long look at Broadway behind-the-scenes. Murphy plays a Broadway producer who hopes to land a Hollywood star for his new show. She rejects his offer in favor of a show being produced by his father. Just a chance to showcase a number of popular vaudeville acts, songs, and the music of Tommy Dorsey and his orchestra. 111m; VHS, DVD. **C:** George Murphy; Ginny Simms; Charles Winninger; Gloria De Haven; Nancy Walker; Ben Blue; Lena Horne; Eddie Anderson; Directed by Roy Del Ruth; Written by Dorothy Kingsley; Harry Clork. **Pr:** Jack Cummings; Metro-Goldwyn-Mayer Pictures. **A:** Jr. High-Adult. **P:** Entertainment. **U:** Home. **Mov-Ent:** Musical, Theater. **Acq:** Purchase. **Dist:** WarnerArchive.com. $19.98.
Songs: All the Things You Are; That Lucky Fellow; In Other Words; Seventeen; All In Fun; Brazilian Boogie; What Do You Think I Am?; Somebody Loves Me; Milkman Keep Those Bottles Quiet; Solid Potato Salad; Manhattan Serenade; Pretty Baby; Oh You Beautiful Doll; Amor; Ida, Sweet as Apple Cider.

Broadway Rhythm Tap ????
Demonstrates three tap dance routines for the beginner to advanced dancer. 60m; VHS. **A:** Adult. **P:** Teacher Education. **U:** Institution. **How-Ins:** Dance, Dance--Instruction. **Acq:** Purchase. **Dist:** Stagestep. $39.95.

Broadway Serenade 1939 (Unrated) — ★★½
Melodramatic musical in which a songwriter (Ayres) and his wife, singer MacDonald, make career choices that destroy their marriage. 114m/B/W; VHS, DVD. **C:** Jeanette MacDonald; Lew Ayres; Ian Hunter; Frank Morgan; Wally Vernon; Rita Johnson; Virginia Grey; William Gargan; Directed by Robert Z. Leonard; Written by Charles Lederer. **Pr:** Robert Leonard; MGM. **A:** Jr. High-Adult. **P:** Entertainment. **U:** Home. **Mov-Ent:** Musical--Drama. **Acq:** Purchase. **Dist:** MGM Home Entertainment. $19.98.
Songs: Broadway Serenade for the Lonely Heart; High Flyin'; One Look at You; Time Changes Everything; Un Bel Di; No Time to Argue; Italian Street Song; Les Filles de Cadiz; Musical Contract.

Broadway: The American Musical 2004
Traces the history of musical theater from it vaudeville roots to operetta, minstrel shows, and the birth of the American musical with "Show Boat." Prominent creators share their tales, including Florenz Ziegfeld, George Gershwin, Rodgers and Hammerstein, Stephen Sondheim, Bob Fosse, and David Merrrick, and notable productions such as "Oklahoma!," "My Fair Lady," "West Side Story," "Cats," and "Wicked" are analyzed. 360m; DVD, Blu-Ray. **A:** Adult. **P:** Entertainment. **U:** Home. **Mov-Ent:** Musical, Theater. **Acq:** Purchase. **Dist:** WGBH/Boston. $59.95.

Broadway: The Golden Age 2003 (Unrated)
McKay's "work-in progress" presents excerpts from a collection of interviews with hundreds of the biggest names in the history of American theater. Grouped by types of personal experiences rather than any chronological order of theatrical tradition or style, interviewees share stories about seeing their first play, arriving in New York, struggling to survive, auditioning, living on the road, and the thrills of opening night and a successful run. Includes some impressive archival material, such as part of a live recording of Marlon Brando in "A Streetcar Named Desire." True theater worshippers will want to bask in every second but others may find the clips dull and redundant. 111m; DVD. **C:** Directed by Rick McKay. **A:** Jr. High-Adult. **P:** Entertainment. **U:** Home. **Mov-Ent:** Documentary Films, Musical, Biography: Music. **Acq:** Purchase. **Dist:** BMG Entertainment. $19.98.

Broadway to Cheyenne 1932 — ★
A group of big city gangsters try to take over a small western town but are opposed by heroic cowboys. 53m/B/W; VHS, DVD. **C:** Rex Bell; George "Gabby" Hayes; Marceline Day; Robert Ellis; Alan Bridge; Matthew Betz; Directed by Harry Fraser. **Pr:** Monogram. **A:** Family. **P:** Entertainment. **U:** Home. **Mov-Ent:** Western. **Acq:** Purchase. **Dist:** Grapevine Video; Rex Miller Artisan Studio. $9.95.

Broadway's Lost Treasures 2003
Compilation of televised performances of Broadway musicals from the 20th century. 110m; DVD. **C:** Christopher Guard; Valerie Holliman; Barry Stokes; Gerald Flood; Daniel Hill; Fiona Mathieson; Anthony Murphy; Simon Turner; Elizabeth Wallace; Raymond Witch; Lindsay Campbell; Simon Conrad; John Cross; Richard Gibson; Robin Halstead; David Hampshire; Davyd Harries; Nicholas Hawell; John Hug; Mark Jefferis; Robin Langford; Alan Lawrance; Dan Meadan; Christopher Moran; Edward Palmer; Mark Rogers; Anthony Wilkins. **A:** Sr. High-Adult. **P:** Entertainment. **U:** Home. **Fin-Art:** Television, Musical. **Acq:** Purchase. **Dist:** Acorn Media Group Inc. $24.99.

Broadway's Lost Treasures II 2004
Second compilation of televised musical performances from the Tony Awards show. 90m; DVD. **A:** Adult. **P:** Entertainment. **U:** Home. **Fin-Art:** Television, Musical. **Acq:** Purchase. **Dist:** Acorn Media Group Inc. $24.99.

Broadway's Lost Treasures III 2005
Third volume of classic performances from the Tony Awards show. ??m; DVD. **A:** Adult. **P:** Entertainment. **U:** Home. **Mov-Ent:** Television, Musical. **Acq:** Purchase. **Dist:** Acorn Media Group Inc. $24.99.

Brockwood Talks 1984 #1 1984
On tape #1, Krishnamurti discusses "The Cause of Conflict." ?m; VHS. **A:** Adult. **P:** Education. **U:** Institution, Home. **Gen-Edu:** Philosophy & Ideology. **Acq:** Purchase. **Dist:** Krishnamurti Foundation of America. $35.00.

Brockwood Talks 1984 #2 1984
On tape #2, Krishnamurti discusses "Fear Born of Thought." ?m; VHS. **A:** Adult. **P:** Education. **U:** Institution, Home. **Gen-Edu:** Philosophy & Ideology. **Acq:** Purchase. **Dist:** Krishnamurti Foundation of America. $35.00.

Brockwood Talks 1984 #3 1984
On tape #3, Krishnamurti discusses "Action Beyond Time and Thought." ?m; VHS. **A:** Adult. **P:** Education. **U:** Institution, Home. **Gen-Edu:** Philosophy & Ideology. **Acq:** Purchase. **Dist:** Krishnamurti Foundation of America. $35.00.

Brockwood Talks 1984 #4 1984
On tape #4, Krishnamurti discusses "To Be Deeply Honest." ?m; VHS. **A:** Adult. **P:** Education. **U:** Institution, Home. **Gen-Edu:** Philosophy & Ideology. **Acq:** Purchase. **Dist:** Krishnamurti Foundation of America. $35.00.

Brockwood Talks 1984 #5 1984
On tape #5, Krishnamurti discusses Part 1 of "Questions and Answers." ?m; VHS. **A:** Adult. **P:** Education. **U:** Institution, Home. **Gen-Edu:** Philosophy & Ideology. **Acq:** Purchase. **Dist:** Krishnamurti Foundation of America. $35.00.

Brockwood Talks 1984 #6 1984
On tape #6, Krishnamurti discusses Part 2 of "Questions and Answers." ?m; VHS. **A:** Adult. **P:** Education. **U:** Institution, Home. **Gen-Edu:** Philosophy & Ideology. **Acq:** Purchase. **Dist:** Krishnamurti Foundation of America. $35.00.

Brockwood Talks 1985 #1 1985
On tape #1, Krishnamurti discusses "Observation and Love." ?m; VHS. **A:** Adult. **P:** Education. **U:** Institution, Home. **Gen-Edu:** Philosophy & Ideology. **Acq:** Purchase. **Dist:** Krishnamurti Foundation of America. $35.00.

Brockwood Talks 1985 #2 1985
On tape #2, Krishnamurti discusses "Timelessness." ?m; VHS. **A:** Adult. **P:** Education. **U:** Institution, Home. **Gen-Edu:** Philosophy & Ideology. **Acq:** Purchase. **Dist:** Krishnamurti Foundation of America. $35.00.

Brockwood Talks 1985 #3 1985
On tape #3, Krishnamurti discusses "Beyond Thought and Time." ?m; VHS. **A:** Adult. **P:** Education. **U:** Institution, Home. **Gen-Edu:** Philosophy & Ideology. **Acq:** Purchase. **Dist:** Krishnamurti Foundation of America. $35.00.

Brockwood Talks 1985 #4 1985
On tape #4, Krishnamurti discusses "To Live Religiously." ?m; VHS. **A:** Adult. **P:** Education. **U:** Institution, Home. **Gen-Edu:** Philosophy & Ideology. **Acq:** Purchase. **Dist:** Krishnamurti Foundation of America. $35.00.

Brockwood Talks 1985 #5 1985
On tape #5, Krishnamurti discusses Part 1 of "Questions and Answers." ?m; VHS. **A:** Adult. **P:** Education. **U:** Institution, Home. **Gen-Edu:** Philosophy & Ideology. **Acq:** Purchase. **Dist:** Krishnamurti Foundation of America. $35.00.

Brockwood Talks 1985 #6 1985
On tape #6, Krishnamurti finishes with Part 2 of "Questions and Answers." ?m; VHS. **A:** Adult. **P:** Education. **U:** Institution, Home. **Gen-Edu:** Philosophy & Ideology. **Acq:** Purchase. **Dist:** Krishnamurti Foundation of America. $35.00.

Broderick 1980
Broderick, an ordinary mouse, attains a life-long goal. He endures hardships and failures, but achieves success and inspires others by his achievement. 10m; VHS, 3/4 U. **Pr:** BFA Educational Media. **A:** Preschool-Primary. **P:** Entertainment. **U:** Institution, SURA. **Chl-Juv:** Family Viewing, Fantasy. **Acq:** Purchase. **Dist:** Phoenix Learning Group.

Brodie Merrill's 'Defensive Player of the Year' Skills and Drills 2013 (Unrated)
Canadian lacrosse player Brodie Merrill presents drills for improving the skills of a lacrosse team's defenseman. 58m; DVD. **A:** Family. **P:** Education. **U:** Home. **L:** English. **Spo-Rec:** Athletic Instruction/Coaching, Lacrosse, How-To. **Acq:** Purchase. **Dist:** Championship Productions. $29.99.

Broiler Grow Out 19??
Explains proper environment and growing conditions for broilers, covering such topics as types of broiler houses, ventilation, control and heating systems, feeding methods, nutrition, and disease prevention. ?m; VHS. **A:** Sr. High-Adult. **P:** Education. **U:** Institution. **Gen-Edu:** Agriculture, Food Industry. **Acq:** Purchase. **Dist:** CEV Multimedia. $25.00.

Broiling and Grilling 199?
Teaches the cooking techniques of broiling and grilling and how to select and marinate foods for the grill. Part of the Cooking Methods Series. 16m; VHS. **A:** Sr. High-Adult. **P:** Instruction. **U:** Home. **How-Ins:** Cooking, Food Industry, How-To. **Acq:** Purchase. **Dist:** Culinary Institute of America. $75.00.

Broiling Techniques 1984
Chef Paul demonstrates how to broil strip steaks. 14m; VHS. **A:** Adult. **P:** Instruction. **U:** Institution. **Gen-Edu:** Cooking. **Acq:** Purchase. **Dist:** RMI Media. $49.95.

Brokeback Mountain 2005 (R) — ★★★½
Yes, it's primarily known as the movie that inspired a million "gay cowboy" jokes, but Lee's heartbreaking drama deserves so much better. In 1963, cowhands Ennis (Ledger) and Jack (Gyllenhaal) spend the summer watching over a herd of sheep on a Wyoming mountain range and falling deeply and inexplicably in love. Terrified to admit their feelings to the outside world, Ennis and Jack try to ignore their passions by getting married to aloof women (Williams and Hathaway) and only meeting for semi-annual fishing trips. The script blends the powerful western themes of "Lonesome Dove" with a classic tragic love tale, and Ledger's outstanding lead performance carries the picture. 134m; DVD, Blu-Ray, HD-DVD, Wide. **C:** Heath Ledger; Jake Gyllenhaal; Linda Cardellini; Anna Faris; Anne Hathaway; Michelle Williams; Randy Quaid; Graham Beckel; Scott Michael Campbell; Kate Mara; Roberta Maxwell; Peter McRobbie; David Harbour; Directed by Ang Lee; Written by Larry McMurtry; Diana Ossana; Cinematography by Rodrigo Prieto; Music by Gustavo Santaolalla. **Pr:** Diana Ossana; James Schamus; Focus Features L.L.C.; River Road Productions. **A:** Sr. High-Adult. **P:** Entertainment. **U:** Home. **L:** English. **Mov-Ent:** Drama, Western. **Awds:** Oscars '05: Adapt. Screenplay, Director (Lee), Orig. Score; British Acad. '05: Adapt. Screenplay, Film, Support. Actor (Gyllenhaal); Directors Guild '05: Director (Lee); Golden Globes '06: Director (Lee), Film--Drama, Screenplay, Song ("A Love That Will Never Grow Old"); Ind. Spirit '06: Director (Lee), Film; L.A. Film Critics '05: Director (Lee), Film; Natl. Bd. of Review '05: Director (Lee), Support. Actor (Gyllenhaal); N.Y. Film Critics '05: Actor (Ledger), Director (Lee), Film; Writers Guild '05: Adapt. Screenplay. **Dist:** Movies Unlimited; Alpha Video; Universal Studios Home Video.

Brokedown Palace 1999 (PG-13) — ★★½
Danes and Beckinsale take a trip to Thailand following their high school graduation and are targeted by a smooth-talking Australian drug dealer. After he invites the pair to Hong Kong, he hides heroin in their luggage and they're busted at the airport. Accused of drug trafficking, they are sentenced to 33 years in a Thai prison. Phillips is an unfriendly DEA official, while Pullman is the expatriate American lawyer who comes to their aid. The story focuses more on the girls' relationship as friends than on their legal nightmare, however. Nevertheless, the government of Thailand was none too pleased by the script, so most of the Thai scenes were actually shot in the Phillipines. 100m; VHS, DVD, CC. **C:** Claire Danes; Kate Beckinsale; Bill Pullman; Daniel Lapaine; Lou Diamond Phillips; Jacqueline Kim; Tom Amandes; Aimee Graham; John Doe; Directed by Jonathan Kaplan; Written by David Arata; Cinematography by Newton Thomas (Tom) Sigel; Music by David Newman. **Pr:** Adam Fields; 20th Century-Fox. **A:** Sr. High-Adult. **P:** Entertainment. **U:** Home. **Mov-Ent:** Asia. **Acq:** Purchase. **Dist:** Fox Home Entertainment.

The Broken 2008 (R) — ★½
The plot's broken too or maybe the director doesn't care that it doesn't make much sense. London radiologist Gina (Headey) glimpses her doppelganger on the street and gets obsessed. She also gets into a car crash, comes out of a coma, has flashbacks, and thinks her family and boyfriend are behaving strangely. She's paranoid at the very least. 88m; DVD, Blu-Ray. **C:** Lena Headey; Richard Jenkins; Melvil Poupaud; Ulrich Thomsen; Asier Newman; Michaelle Duncan; Directed by Sean Ellis; Written by Sean Ellis; Cinematography by Angus Hudson; Music by Guy Farley. **A:** Sr. High-Adult. **P:** Entertainment. **U:** Home. **Mov-Ent:** Mystery & Suspense. **Acq:** Purchase. **Dist:** Lions Gate Entertainment Inc.

Broken 2013 (Unrated) — ★★½
One summer day 11-year-old British girl Skunk secretly watches in horror as a hateful neighbor (Kinnear) throws down a brutal assault on a slow-witted boy (Emms), who's been wrongly accused of rape. The violent episode sticks with her all summer, foreshadowing other violence coming down the road. Stage director Norris' pic, made for the BBC, plays up the misery of the English middle-class, but takes it too far at times, as this coming-of-age drama pushes the point past its welcome. 90m; On Demand. **C:** Tim Roth; Cillian Murphy; Rory Kinnear; Robert Emms; Zana Marjanovic; Directed by Rufus Norris; Written by Mark O'Rowe; Cinematography by Rob Hardy. **Pr:** BBC Films; Film Movement. **A:** Sr. High-Adult. **P:** Entertainment. **U:** Home. **Mov-Ent:** Adolescence, TV Movies, Children. **Acq:** Purchase. **Dist:** Amazon.com Inc.

Broken Angel 1988 (Unrated) — ★½
Jamie seemed to be such a nice girl, with good looks and great grades—and membership in a notorious street gang. When Jamie disappears, her family discovers her secret activities and dad tries to find his wayward little girl. Melodramatic TV goo. 94m; VHS, Streaming, CC. **C:** William Shatner; Susan Blakely; Erika Eleniak; Roxann Biggs-Dawson; Directed by Richard T. Heffron. **A:** Jr. High-Adult. **P:** Entertainment. **U:** Home. **Mov-Ent:** TV Movies. **Acq:** Purchase. **Dist:** MGM Home Entertainment. $14.95.

Broken Arrow 1950 (Unrated) — ★★½
A U.S. scout befriends Cochise and the Apaches, and helps settlers and Indians live in peace together in the 1870s. Acclaimed as the first Hollywood film to side with the Indians, and for Chandler's portrayal of Cochise. Based on the novel "Blood Brother" by Elliot Arnold. 93m; VHS, DVD, CC. **C:** James Stewart; Jeff Chandler; Will Geer; Debra Paget; Basil Ruysdael; Arthur Hunnicutt; Jay Silverheels; Directed by Delmer Daves; Written by Albert (John B. Sherry) Maltz; Cinematography by Ernest Palmer. **Pr:** 20th Century-Fox. **A:** Family. **P:** Entertainment. **U:** Home. **Mov-Ent:** Western, Native Americans. **Acq:** Purchase. **Dist:** Movies Unlimited; Alpha Video. $19.98.

Broken Arrow 1995 (R) — ★★
Air Force pilot Vic Deakins (Travolta) rips off a couple of nuclear weapons during a routine exercise over the Utah desert. Deakins' ex-co-pilot Riley Hale (Slater), with help from spunky park ranger Terry Carmichael (Mathis), sets out to find and retrieve the warheads before the big bang. Hong Kong action king Woo once again tries his hand at the big-budget Hollywood action extravaganza, with mixed results. Triple script whammy of cheesy dialogue, continuity problems, and predictability undercuts, but doesn't obscure, his talent for choreographing mayhem. Travolta plays the All-American Boy as creepily charming psychotic to great effect. 108m; VHS, DVD, Blu-Ray, CC. **C:** John Travolta; Christian Slater; Samantha Mathis; Delroy Lindo; Bob Gunton; Frank Whaley; Howie Long; Directed by John Woo; Written by Graham Yost; Cinematography by Peter Levy; Music by Hans Zimmer. **Pr:** Bill Badalato; Christopher Godsick; Dwight Little; Mark Gordon; 20th Century-Fox. **A:** Sr. High-Adult. **P:** Entertainment. **U:** Home. **Mov-Ent:** Nuclear Warfare, Trains. **Acq:** Purchase. **Dist:** Fox Home Entertainment.

Broken Badge 1985 — ★★★
Crenna stars as a macho, chauvinistic cop whose attitude towards rape victims changes dramatically after he himself is raped by a couple of thugs. Excellent TV movie. 100m; VHS, DVD. **C:** Richard Crenna; Meredith Baxter; Pat Hingle; Frances Lee McCain; Cotter Smith; George Dzundza; Joanna Kerns; Directed by Karen Arthur; Written by James G. Hirsch; Music by Peter Bernstein. **A:** Sr. High-Adult. **P:** Entertainment. **U:** Home. **Mov-Ent:** Rape, TV Movies. **Acq:** Purchase. **Dist:** Anchor Bay Entertainment. $9.95.

Broken Blossoms 1919 — ★★★½
One of Griffith's most widely acclaimed films, about a young Chinese man in London's squalid Limehouse district hoping to spread the peaceful philosophy of his Eastern religion. He befriends a pitiful street waif who is mistreated by her brutal father, resulting in tragedy. Silent. Revised edition contains introduction from Gish and a newly recorded score. 89m/B/W; Silent; VHS, DVD. **C:** Lillian Gish; Richard Barthelmess; Donald Crisp; Directed by D.W. Griffith; Written by D.W. Griffith; Cinematography by Billy (G.W.) Bitzer; Music by Louis F. Gottschalk. **Pr:** D.W. Griffith; D.W. Griffith; United Artists. **A:** Sr. High-Adult. **P:** Entertainment. **U:** Home. **Mov-Ent:** Classic Films, Silent Films, Poverty. **Awds:** Natl. Film Reg. '96. **Acq:** Purchase. **Dist:** Gotham Distributing Corp.; Festival Films; Kino on Video. $19.95.

Broken Bones: Live at Leeds 198? (Unrated)
The British alternative band play the famous venue. ?m; VHS. **A:** Jr. High-College. **P:** Entertainment. **U:** Home. **Mov-Ent:** Music--Performance. **Acq:** Purchase. **Dist:** Music Video Distributors. $29.95.

Broken Bridges 2006 (PG-13) — ★½
Hard-drinking, washed-up country singer Bo Price returns to his Tennessee hometown when five soldiers are killed in a training accident. One is Bo's younger brother and another is the sibling of Angela Delton, whom Bo abandoned when she got pregnant. Angela returns with their 16-year-old daughter Dixie, but the Deltons prefer to keep their distance from Bo, who wants to make amends. 105m; DVD. **C:** Toby Keith; Kelly Preston; Lindsey Haun; Burt Reynolds; Tess Harper; Anna Maria Horsford; Directed by Steven Goldman; Written by Cherie Bennett; Jeff Gottesfeld; Cinematography by Patrick Cady; Music by Toby Keith. **A:** Jr. High-Adult. **P:** Entertainment. **U:** Home. **Mov-Ent**. **Acq:** Purchase. **Dist:** Paramount Pictures Corp.

Broken but Loved 19??
Four-part program in which Father George Maloney discusses two important facts of life, brokenness of nature and life. He emphasizes the importance of accepting Jesus Christ into your life and understanding what this means. 120m; VHS. **A:** Jr. High-Adult. **P:** Religious. **U:** Institution, Home. **Gen-Edu:** Religion, Self-Help. **Acq:** Purchase. **Dist:** Alba House Media Center. $29.95.
Indiv. Titles: 1. Broken but Loved 2. Darkness in God - Brokenness in Jesus 3. I Am Broken 4. Jesus, the Divine Savior.

The Broken Chain 1993 — ★★½
In the mid 18th-century Joseph Brant (Schweig), a member of the Mohawk tribe, is sent away to be educated by the British. When he returns, his loyalties are divided between his Native American roots and his English mentor, Sir William Johnson (Brosnan). His boyhood friend Lohaheo (White Shirt) disdains Joseph's white man ways, leading to tragic consequences. Historical background features the French and Indian Wars, the splintering of the Iroquois Confederacy, and the coming of the American Revolution. Filmed on location in Virginia. 93m; VHS, CC. **C:** Eric Schweig; Wes Studi; Buffy Saint Marie; Pierce Brosnan; J.C. White Shirt; Floyd "Red Crow" Westerman; Graham Greene; Elaine Bilstad; Kim Snyder; Directed by Lamont Johnson; Written by Earl W. Wallace; Music by Charles Fox. **Pr:** Cleve Landsberg; Hanay Geigamah; Richard Hill; Kent Riddington; Robert M. Sertner; Lamont Johnson; Phil Lucas Productions, Inc; Turner Network Television. **A:** Jr. High-Adult. **P:** Entertainment. **U:** Home. **Mov-Ent:** Native Americans, History--U.S., TV Movies. **Acq:** Purchase. **Dist:** Turner Broadcasting System Inc.

The Broken Circle Breakdown 2012 (Unrated) — ★★
Sometimes heavy-handed Belgian drama that's sustained by the talented leads' unlikely devotion to American bluegrass music. Scruffy Flemish musician Didier plays in a bluegrass band. He falls for free-spirited tattoo artist, Elise, who joins as the lead singer, and a happy family emerges with the addition of daughter Maybelle. At six, tragedy strikes Maybelle, which leaves her parents grief-stricken and on the verge of tearing them apart. English and Flemish with subtitles. 111m; DVD. **C:** Johan Heldenbergh; Veerle Baetens; Directed by Felix van Groeningen; Written by Felix van Groeningen; Carl Joos; Cinematography by Ruben Impens; Music by Bjorn Eriksson. **Pr:** Tribeca Films. **A:** Sr. High-Adult. **P:** Entertainment. **U:** Home. **L:** Dutch, English. **Mov-Ent:** Music--Country/Western, Drama, Children. **Acq:** Purchase. **Dist:** New Video Group Inc.

Broken City 2013 (R) — ★★
First solo outing from director Allen Hughes (one-half of the Hughes brothers' team). Often silly and syrupy New York mystery about a private eye (Wahlberg) hired by the city's mayor (Crowe) to follow his adulterous wife (Zeta-Jones). As with most of the predictable plot points, the detective finds not only that his sultry wife is rendezvousing with the other candidate's campaign manager, but discovers a high-profile murder along the way. A sleazy Hollywood thriller that plays like a midnight cable guilty pleasure, loaded with amusing over-acting showing characters leering into windows and going on benders. 109m; DVD, Blu-Ray. **C:** Mark Wahlberg; Russell Crowe; Catherine Zeta-Jones; Jeffrey Wright; Barry Pepper; Kyle Chandler; Directed by Allen Hughes; Written by Brian Tucker; Cinematography by Ben Seresin; Music by Atticus Ross; Leopold Ross; Claudia Sarne. **Pr:** Remington Chase; Randall Emmett; George Furla; Stephen Levinson; Arnon Milchan; Teddy Schwarzman; Mark Wahlberg; Allen Hughes; Regency Enterprises; Twentieth Century Fox Film Corp. **A:** Sr. High-Adult. **P:** Entertainment. **U:** Home. **L:** English. **Mov-Ent:** Crime Drama. **Acq:** Purchase. **Dist:** Not Yet Released.

Broken Dolls 1987
Children who are abused are more likely to grow up to be parents who abuse their kids. 29m; VHS, 3/4 U. **Pr:** Brigham Young University. **A:** Jr. High-Adult. **P:** Education. **U:** Institution, SURA. **Gen-Edu:** Child Abuse. **Acq:** Purchase, Trade-in. **Dist:** Encyclopedia Britannica. $230.00.

Broken Embraces 2009 (R) — ★★★
Director Almodovar's twisting tale of filmmaking and revenge is bursting with colors that belie the darkness of the story. One-time film director Mateo Blanco (Homar) abandons his name and career after being blinded in a car crash. As Harry Caine, he is hired by the mysterious Ray X (Ochandiano) to write a screenplay about the life of movie producer Martel (Gomez), Mateo's former partner. The common thread linking all three men is Lena (Cruz), a beautiful starlet with a checkered past. Movies within the movie and characters who change names (and personas) lend extra dimension to the serpentine plot. Almodovar also uses many clever devices to reveal his opinions about the director and his role in the movie industry. In Spanish with subtitles. 128m; Blu-Ray, On Demand, Wide. **C:** Penelope Cruz; Lluis Homar; Blanca Portillo; Jose Luis Gomez; Tamar Novas; Ruben Ochandiano; Lola Duenas; Directed by Pedro Almodovar; Written by Pedro Almodovar; Cinematography by Rodrigo Prieto; Music by Alberto Iglesias. **Pr:** Esther Garcia; El Deseo; Universal International Pictures Spain; Sony Pictures Classics. **A:** College-Adult. **P:** Entertainment. **U:** Home. **L:** Spanish. **Mov-Ent:** Blindness. **Acq:** Purchase. **Dist:** Movies Unlimited; Alpha Video; Sony Pictures Home Entertainment Inc.

Broken English 1996 (NC-17) — ★★½
Ethnically diverse New Zealand is the setting for this story of young lovers and the parents who don't understand them. Croatian refugee Nina (Vujcic) and Maori cook Eddie (Arahanga) meet in the Chinese restaurant where they both work and quickly fall in love. Nina's menacing father Ivan (Serbedzija) objects to their passion, sometimes with a baseball bat. Film deals honestly with immigration and racial issues. Engaging debut for Vujcic, a Croatian refugee director Nicholas met in a bar. Also available in an R-rated version. 92m; VHS. **C:** Aleksandra Vujcic; Julian (Sonny) Arahanga; Rade Serbedzija; Marton Csokas; Jing Zhao; Yang Li; Madeline McNamara; Directed by Gregor Nicholas; Written by Gregor Nicholas; Johanna Pigott; James Salter; Cinematography by John Toon. **Pr:** Robin Scholes; Timothy White; Village Roadshow Pictures; Communicado; Sony Pictures Classics. **A:** College-Adult. **P:** Entertainment. **U:** Home. **Mov-Ent:** Ethnicity, Australia. **Acq:** Purchase. **Dist:** Sony Pictures Home Entertainment Inc.

Broken English 2007 (PG-13) — ★★½
Nora (Posey) is a single, moderately neurotic New Yorker working a job for which she's over-qualified, while both she and her mother wonder why she's so unlucky at love. Enter charming and perfect Julien, who seems to look past Nora's insecurities and fears in exchange for a (mostly) perfect weekend. Posey shines and Cassavetes (daughter of legendary director John) shows insight into her characters, but it's not enough to completely transcend the well-worn lonely-hearts story. 97m; DVD. **C:** Parker Posey; Melvil Poupaud; Drea De Matteo; Gena Rowlands; Justin Theroux; Tim Guinee; Josh Hamilton; Michael Panes; Directed by Zoe Cassavettes; Written by Zoe Cassavettes; Cinematography by John Pirozzi; Music by Scratch Massive. **Pr:** Andrew Fierberg; Jason Kliot; Joana Vicente; VOX3 Films; Phantom Film Co. Ltd; Magnolia Pictures. **A:** Jr. High-Adult. **P:** Entertainment. **U:** Home. **L:** English. **Mov-Ent:** Drama. **Acq:** Purchase. **Dist:** Magnolia Home Entertainment.

Broken Flowers 2005 (R) — ★★
Quirky, if forlorn, comedy from Jarmusch. Murray does minimalism in his portrayal of confirmed, middle-aged bachelor Don Johnston whose orderly life becomes disarrayed when he learns he fathered a son from a long-ago liaison. Only there are four potential moms (a fifth has died), so Don reluctantly goes on a road trip to re-acquaint himself with Laura (Stone), Dora (Conroy), Carmen (Lange), and Penny (Swinton). His welcome varies—not much really happens—and Murray is more Don Quixote (with Wright as his stay-at-home Sancho Panza) than Don Juan. 105m; DVD, Wide. **C:** Bill Murray; Jeffrey Wright; Sharon Stone; Frances Conroy; Jessica Lange; Tilda Swinton; Julie Delpy; Mark Webber; Chloe Sevigny; Christopher McDonald; Alexis Dziena; Larry Fessenden; Chris Bauer; Pell James; Heather Alicia Simms; Brea Frazier; Directed by Jim Jarmusch; Written by Jim Jarmusch; Cinematography by Frederick Elmes. **Pr:** Jon Kilik; Stacey Smith; Five Roses; Focus Features L.L.C. **A:** Sr. High-Adult. **P:** Entertainment. **U:** Home. **L:** English. **Mov-Ent:** Comedy-Drama, Sex & Sexuality. **Acq:** Purchase. **Dist:** Movies Unlimited; Alpha Video.

Broken Glass 1996 — ★★½
Set in Brooklyn in 1938 and adapted from a play by Arthur Miller. Jewish housewife, Sylvia Gellberg (Leicester), has been stricken by a mysterious paralysis and Dr. Harry Hyman (Patinkin) is called in to treat her. Her illness is apparently psychosomatic and Sylvia gradually reveals her anxiety about her unhappy marriage and her obsessive fears with newspaper reports concerning Jewish persecution in Germany. Hyman and his wife Margaret (McGovern) soon find themselves drawn in deeper than could have imagined. Made for TV. 120m; VHS, CC. **C:** Mandy Patinkin; Margot Leicester; Henry Goodman; Elizabeth McGovern; Directed by David Thacker; Written by David Thacker; David Holman. **Pr:** Fiona Finlay; Rebecca Eaton; WGBH Boston. **A:** Sr. High-Adult. **P:** Entertainment. **U:** Home. **Mov-Ent:** Judaism, Marriage, Mental Health. **Acq:** Purchase. **Dist:** PBS Home Video.

Broken Harvest 1994 (Unrated) — ★★½
Jimmy O'Leary remembers his youth in rural 1950s Ireland when a poor wheat harvest led to his family's financial demise and a feud between his father (Lane) and neighbor Josie McCarthy (O'Brien) threatened to destroy their lives. The men fought side by side for Ireland's independence, but the friendship dissolved when they took different sides during the ensuing civil war, and fought over Jimmy's mother. Strong performances and the beautiful West Cork and Wicklow location shots provide a nice balance to the uneven narrative. The black and white scenes were actually filmed in the mid-'80s when the independently financed project was begun. Adapted from O'Callaghan's own story "The Shilling." 101m; VHS, DVD, Wide. **C:** Colin Lane; Niall O'Brien; Marian Quinn; Darren McHugh; Joy Florish; Joe Jeffers; Pete O'Reilly; Michael Crowley; Directed by Maurice O'Callaghan; Written by Maurice O'Callaghan; Cinematography by Jack Conroy; Music by Patrick Cassidy. **Pr:** Jerry O'Callaghan; Kate O'Callaghan; Maurice O'Callaghan; Destiny Films; Kit Parker Films. **A:** Sr. High-Adult. **P:** Entertainment. **U:** Home. **Mov-Ent:** Ireland, Agriculture, Family. **Acq:** Purchase. **Dist:** Kit Parker Films; Facets Multimedia Inc.

The Broken Hearts Club 2000 (R) — ★★★
Talk can be cheap, but it's also what sustains the relationships in the lives of a group of gay friends in this chatty, likable film set in West Hollywood. Despite their mostly superficial (sex) conversations, the boys suspect there's more to life, and aim, hesitantly, to move beyond this dead-end topic. Witty and confident in his characters, writer/director Berlanti (co-creator of "Dawson's Creek") has put together a film about gay men that thankfully moves beyond the staleness of many of its predecessors. Good cast with notable performances by Cain (Superman in TV's "Lois and Clark") and Mahoney as the fatherly proprietor of the Broken Hearts restaurant. 94m; VHS, DVD, Wide. **C:** Dean Cain; John Mahoney; Timothy Olyphant; Andrew Keegan; Nia Long; Zach Braff; Matt McGrath; Billy Porter; Justin Theroux; Mary McCormack; Directed by Greg Berlanti; Written by Greg Berlanti; Cinematography by Paul Elliott; Music by Christophe Beck. **A:** College-Adult. **P:** Entertainment. **U:** Home. **Mov-Ent:** Softball. **Acq:** Purchase. **Dist:** Sony Pictures Home Entertainment Inc.

Broken Hearts of Broadway 1923 — ★★
Stories of heartbreak and success along the Great White Way. 85m/B/W; Silent; VHS, DVD. **C:** Colleen Moore; Johnnie Walker; Alice Lake; Tully Marshall; Creighton Hale; Directed by Irving Cummings. **Pr:** Irving Cummings; Irving Cummings. **A:** Jr. High-Adult. **P:** Entertainment. **U:** Home. **Mov-Ent:** Silent Films, Theater. **Acq:** Purchase. **Dist:** Alpha Video; Grapevine Video. $19.95.

Broken Hill 2009 (PG) — ★★
Tommy wants to work on his music and isn't interested in the family's Australian sheep ranch. He and newcomer Kat get into trouble and must do community service, so Tommy chooses to volunteer at the local prison and forms an inmate band. Teaching the prisoners his own musical compositions, Tommy's goal is to enter a regional competition (and impressing Kat would be a bonus). 102m; DVD. **C:** Luke Arnold; Alexa Vega; Timothy Hutton; Che Timmons; Peter Lamb; Leo Taylor; Directed by Dagen Merrill; Written by Dagen Merrill; Cinematography by Nick Matthews; Music by Christopher Brady. **A:** Jr. High-Adult. **P:** Entertainment. **U:** Home. **Mov-Ent:** Musical--Drama, Australia. **Acq:** Purchase. **Dist:** Entertainment One US LP.

Broken Journey 19??
Focuses on the problem of alcohol for Native Americans by listening to stories told by men and women incarcerated for alcohol-related problems. Aimed at Native American youth. 27m; VHS, 1C, 3/4 U. **Pr:** Gary Robinson; Creek Nation Communications. **A:** Jr. High-Sr. High. **P:** Education. **U:** Institution, BCTV, SURA. **Gen-Edu:** Documentary Films, Native Americans, Alcoholism. **Acq:** Purchase, Rent/Lease. **Dist:** Vision Maker Media. $49.95.

Broken Lance 1954 (Unrated) — ★★★1/2
Western remake of "House of Strangers" that details the dissolution of a despotic cattle baron's family. Beautifully photographed. 96m; VHS, DVD, Wide, CC. **C:** Spencer Tracy; Richard Widmark; Robert Wagner; Jean Peters; Katy Jurado; Earl Holliman; Hugh O'Brian; E.G. Marshall; Directed by Edward Dmytryk; Written by Philip Yordan; Cinematography by Joe MacDonald; Music by Leigh Harline. **Pr:** 20th Century-Fox. **A:** Family. **P:** Entertainment. **U:** Home. **Mov-Ent:** Western. **Awds:** Oscars '54: Story. **Acq:** Purchase. **Dist:** Movies Unlimited; Alpha Video. $39.98.

A Broken Life 2007 (Unrated) — ★1/2
When Max Walker (Sizemore) decides to commit suicide, he hires his struggling film student friend Bud (Sevier) to record his last days. Max lets his rage out, confronting his former boss and ex-wife, as well as doing some really stupid things. As his chosen end nears, Max is shown kindness by wheelchair-bound Melinda (Kosaka) and starts rethinking his plans. 97m; DVD. **C:** Tom Sizemore; Corey Sevier; Ving Rhames; Saul Rubinek; Cynthia Dale; Kris Holden-Ried; Grace Kosaka; Directed by Neil Coombs; Written by Neil Coombs; Cinematography by Peter Benison; Music by Christopher Dedrick. **A:** Sr. High-Adult. **P:** Entertainment. **U:** Home. **Mov-Ent:** Suicide, Handicapped. **Acq:** Purchase. **Dist:** Anchor Bay Entertainment.

Broken Lizard: Stands Up 2010 (Unrated)
The Broken Lizard Comedy Troupe released this live performance of their act for Comedy Central, including various outtakes and scenes on tour. 78m; DVD. **A:** Sr. High-Adult. **P:** Entertainment. **U:** Home. **Gen-Edu:** Comedy--Performance, Television. **Acq:** Purchase. **Dist:** Comedy Central. $14.98.

Broken Lullaby 1994 (Unrated) — ★1/2
Genealogist Jordan Kirkland (Harris) travels to Europe to research her orphaned Aunt Kitty's (Hyland) murky past at the time of the Russian Revolution. Her only clue is a photograph of a young girl holding a music box topped with a priceless Faberge egg. Jordan meets Hungarian art dealer Nick Rostov (Stewart), who has his own reasons for finding the same music box, but they're not the only ones searching for it. From the Harlequin Romance Series; adapted from the Laurel Pace novel. 91m; DVD. **C:** Mel Harris; Rob Stewart; Oliver Tobias; Jennifer Dale; Frances Hyland; Charmion King; Vivian Reis; Directed by Michael Kennedy; Written by Jim Henshaw; Guy Mullaly; Cinematography by Nyika Jancso; Music by Claude Desjardins; Eric N. Robertson. **A:** Jr. High-Adult. **P:** Entertainment. **U:** Home. **Mov-Ent:** Genealogy. **Acq:** Purchase. **Dist:** Echo Bridge Home Entertainment.

The Broken Mask 1928 — ★★
A doctor performs remarkable plastic surgery on a patient, but when the patient becomes attracted to his sweetheart, he throws the Hippocratic oath to the wind, and his patient's spiffy new look has got to go. A ground-breaker amid plastic surgery-gone-amok pieces. 58m/B/W; Silent; VHS. **C:** Cullen Landis; Barbara Bedford; Wheeler Oakman; James A. Marcus; Directed by James Hogan. **A:** Sr. High-Adult. **P:** Entertainment. **U:** Home. **Mov-Ent:** Silent Films, Surgery--Plastic. **Acq:** Purchase. **Dist:** Grapevine Video; Facets Multimedia Inc. $19.95.

Broken Melody 1934 — ★1/2
An opera singer sent to prison by mistake must escape in order to return to the woman of his dreams. 62m/B/W; VHS, DVD. **C:** John Garrick; Margot Grahame; Merle Oberon; Austin Trevor; Charles Carson; Harry Terry; Directed by Bernard Vorhaus. **Pr:** Twickenham. **A:** Jr. High-Adult. **P:** Entertainment. **U:** Home. **Mov-Ent:** Drama. **Acq:** Purchase. **Dist:** Facets Multimedia Inc. $29.95.

Broken Mirrors 1985 (Unrated) — ★★1/2
A disturbing film which intertwines two stories of violence against women: prostitutes go about their daily business in Amsterdam, while a twisted serial killer who imprisons, photographs, and ultimately destroys his victims, draws near. An independently made chiller with staunch feminist agenda. 110m; VHS. **C:** Lineke Rijxman; Henriette Tol; Edda Barends; Eddie Brugman; Coby Stunnenberg; Directed by Marleen Gorris; Written by Marleen Gorris. **Pr:** Sigma. **A:** Jr. High-Adult. **P:** Education. **U:** Institution, SURA. **Mov-Ent:** Prostitution. **Acq:** Purchase. **Dist:** First Run/Icarus Films.

Broken Noses 1987
Follows the life and career of Minsker, a former Golden Gloves boxing champion and now a coach for a teenage boxing team in Portland, Oregon. Filmed in black and white and color. 75m; DVD. **C:** Andy Minsker; Directed by Bruce Weber. **Pr:** Nan Bush. **A:** Jr. High-Adult. **P:** Entertainment. **U:** Home. **Gen-Edu:** Documentary Films, Boxing. **Acq:** Purchase. **Dist:** Docurama.

Broken Promises: A Program for Children of Alcoholics for Grades 4-9 1996
Describes how alcohol and drug addiction affects the whole family. Dramatizes three sessions of a children's support group led by two counselors. 34m; VHS. **A:** Primary. **P:** Education. **U:** Institution. **Chl-Juv:** Alcoholism, Parenting, Adolescence. **Acq:** Purchase. **Dist:** The Bureau for At-Risk Youth. $95.00.

Broken Rainbow 1985
An acclaimed documentary about the U.S. Government's relocation of 12,000 Navajo Indians. They described it as a Hopi-Navajo land settlement, but actually did it to facilitate energy development. 70m; VHS, 3/4 U, Special order formats. **C:** Narrated by Martin Sheen; Burgess Meredith; Buffy Saint Marie. **Pr:** Mario Florio; Victoria Mudd; Earthworks. **A:** Jr. High-Adult. **P:** Education. **U:** Institution, SURA. **Gen-Edu:** Documentary Films, Native Americans, History--U.S. **Awds:** Oscars '85: Feature Doc. **Acq:** Purchase, Rent/Lease. **Dist:** Direct Cinema Ltd.

Broken Saints 2000
Originally an Internet-based series that chronicled the exploits of four characters who all received apocalyptic visions that compel them to meet and confront a life-threatening conspiracy. 24 flash-animated episodes. 700m; DVD. **C:** Voice(s) by William B. Davis; Kirby Morrow; Scott McNeil; Jamie Bell; Greg Anderson. **A:** Sr. High-Adult. **P:** Entertainment. **U:** Home. **Mov-Ent:** Anime. **Acq:** Purchase. **Dist:** Fox Home Entertainment.

Broken Silence 2001 (Unrated) — ★★★
Director Armendariz's engaging production is set in 1944 when 21-year-old Lucia (Jimenez) goes back to her homeland only to witness the dramatic and violent impact that the Spanish Civil War has had upon the people of her rustic village. Still, she finds love with Manuel (Botto), a blacksmith who is part of the resistance group, the Maquis. An uprising swells and Franco's fascist army shows up to squash it, forcing the young lovers to face the cruel realities inherent to the hostilities. In Spanish with subtitles. 110m; VHS, DVD. **C:** Juan Diego Botto; Mercedes Sampietro; Lucia Jimenez; Maria Botto; Andoni Erburu; Alvaro de Luna; Directed by Montxo Armendariz; Written by Montxo Armendariz; Cinematography by Guillermo Navarro; Music by Pascal Gaigne. **A:** Sr. High-Adult. **P:** Entertainment. **U:** Home. **L:** Spanish. **Mov-Ent:** Drama, Spain. **Acq:** Purchase. **Dist:** Vanguard International Cinema, Inc.; Ventura Distribution Inc.

The Broken Star 1956 (Unrated) — ★★
Deputy Marshal Frank Smead (Duff) claims self-defense in the killing of a Mexican rancher but it's really murder since Smead was after some hidden gold. The Sheriff is suspicious and has fellow deputy Bill Gentry (Williams) investigate further. 82m/B/W; DVD. **C:** Howard Duff; Bill Williams; Addison Richards; Lita Baron; Henry Calvin; Douglas Fowley; Directed by Lesley Selander; Written by John C. Higgins; Cinematography by William Margulies; Music by Paul Dunlap. **A:** Sr. High-Adult. **P:** Entertainment. **U:** Home. **Mov-Ent:** Western. **Acq:** Purchase. **Dist:** MGM Home Entertainment.

Broken Strings 1940 — ★
All-black musical in which a concert violinist must come to terms with himself after an auto accident limits the use of his left hand. 50m/B/W; VHS, DVD. **TV Std:** NTSC, PAL. **C:** Clarence Muse; Sybil Lewis; William Washington; Matthew "Stymie" Beard; Directed by Bernard B. Ray. **Pr:** International Roadshows. **A:** College-Adult. **P:** Entertainment. **U:** Home. **Mov-Ent:** Handicapped, Music--Classical, Black Culture. **Acq:** Purchase. **Dist:** Alpha Video; Facets Multimedia Inc.; Glenn Video Vistas Ltd. $19.95.

The Broken Tower 2011 (Unrated) — ★1/2
Franco's artsy minimalist bio of early 20th century poet Hart Crane, who struggled with his middle-class upbringing, writing, sexuality, depression, and alcoholism until committing suicide in 1932. Pic is structured in chapters that reference Crane's erotic poems "Voyages." Adaptation of Paul L. Mariani's biography "The Broken Tower." 110m/B/W; DVD. **C:** James Franco; David Franco; Michael Shannon; Stacey Miller; Betsy Franco; Directed by James Franco; Written by James Franco; Cinematography by Christina Voros; Music by Neil Benezra. **A:** College-Adult. **P:** Entertainment. **U:** Home. **Mov-Ent:** Suicide, Mexico. **Acq:** Purchase. **Dist:** Wolfe Video.

Broken Trail 2006 (Unrated) — ★★★
In 1898, aging cowpoke Print Ritter (Duvall) is herding 500 horses from Oregon to Wyoming with the help of his estranged nephew Tom Harte (Church). During the trip they hire on Heck (Cooper) and rescue five Chinese girls who were sold to be prostitutes in a mining camp. But this puts the horse traders at odds with madam Big Rump Kate (Schwimmer), who sends sadistic Big Ears (Mulkey) after her property. Not having enough to deal with, Print also protects good-hearted whore Nola (Scacchi) on that long, dusty trail. But everyone's in very good company. 184m; DVD, Blu-Ray, CC. **C:** Robert Duvall; Thomas Haden Church; Greta Scacchi; Chris Mulkey; Rusty Schwimmer; James Russo; Scott Cooper; Gwendoline Yeo; Van Dyke Parks; Directed by Walter Hill; Written by Alan Geoffrion; Cinematography by Lloyd Ahern, II; Music by David Mansfield. **A:** Jr. High-Adult. **P:** Entertainment. **U:** Home. **Mov-Ent:** Western, Horses, Prostitution. **Acq:** Purchase. **Dist:** Sony Pictures Home Entertainment Inc.

Broken Treaties: American Documents Series ????
Trial dramatization depicting the Indian people as plaintiffs trying to prove that treaties were unjustly broken by the U.S. government. Government claims treaties cannot be kept due to irreconcilable cultural differences. Appropriate for Grades 7-12. 34m; VHS. **A:** Jr. High-Sr. High. **P:** Education. **U:** Institution. **Gen-Edu:** History--U.S., Native Americans. **Acq:** Purchase. **Dist:** Social Studies School Service; Zenger Media. $89.95.

Broken Trust 1993 — ★★
Erica inherits her fabulously weathy uncle's estate but she has problems knowing who to trust now that she has all this money. Seems her husband is greedy and her sister resentful but just how far will they go to get what Erica has? 85m; VHS. **C:** Kimberly Foster; Nick Cassavetes; Kathryn Harris; Don Swayze; Edward Albert; Wendy MacDonald; Directed by Rafael Portillo. **A:** College-Adult. **P:** Entertainment. **U:** Home. **Mov-Ent:** Sex & Sexuality. **Acq:** Purchase. **Dist:** Monarch Home Video. $89.95.

Broken Trust 1995 — ★★1/2
Municipal judge Timothy Nash (Selleck) is recruited for a sting operation, designed to ensnare fellow judges, by two slightly less-than-ethical feds (Atherton and McGovern). When Nash decides he doesn't like what's going on he discovers it's not going to be so easy to get out. Selleck's stoic, McGovern provides attractive ornamentation, and Atherton excels as the smarmy villain. From the novel "Court of Honor" by William P. Wood. 90m; DVD. **C:** Tom Selleck; Elizabeth McGovern; William Atherton; Fritz Weaver; Marsha Mason; Charles Haid; Stanley DeSantis; Cynthia Martells; Directed by Geoffrey Sax; Written by Joan Didion; John Gregory Dunne; Cinematography by Ronald Orieux; Music by Richard Horowitz. **Pr:** Steve McGlothen; Lois Bonfiglio; Turner Network Television. **A:** Sr. High-Adult. **P:** Entertainment. **U:** Home. **Mov-Ent:** Federal Bureau of Investigation (FBI), TV Movies. **Acq:** Purchase. **Dist:** WarnerArchive.com.

Broken Vessels 1998 (R) — ★★★
Rent this with "Bringing Out the Dead" and you'll have a double feature that will make you take 911 off the speed dial. Both movies were released in the same year, but Scorsese's movie depicts a paramedic demented by caring too much. The ambulance drivers in "Broken Vessels" become unhinged by a cold, drug-induced indifference. Tom (London) is pulled into a downward spiral by his crazed partner Jimmy (Field), who smokes heroin and feels up unconscious girls while on break from saving lives. Clearly, things are not destined to go well for the pair, not to mention those who end up in the back of their meat wagon. Excellent debut from producer-director Scott Ziehl. 90m; VHS, DVD, Wide, CC. **C:** Todd Field; Jason London; Roxana Zal; Susan Traylor; James Hong; Patrick Cranshaw; William (Bill) Smith; Dave Baer; Directed by Scott Ziehl; Written by Scott Ziehl; Dave Baer; John McMahon; Cinematography by Antonio Calvache. **A:** Sr. High-Adult. **P:** Entertainment. **U:** Home. **Mov-Ent:** Drug Abuse. **Acq:** Purchase. **Dist:** Allumination Filmworks.

Broken Vows 1987 — ★★1/2
Thriller with Jones as ghetto priest Father Joseph, who has doubts about his calling. When he gives last rites to a murder victim, he decides to help the victim's girlfriend find his killers. Based on the novel "Where the Dark Secrets Go" by Dorothy Salisbury Davis. 95m; VHS, DVD, CC. **C:** Tommy Lee Jones; Annette O'Toole; M. Emmet Walsh; Milo O'Shea; David Groh; Madeline Sherwood; Jean De Baer; David Strathairn; Directed by Jud Taylor; Cinematography by Thomas Burstyn. **Pr:** Edwin Self; RHI Entertainment Inc. **A:** Jr. High-Adult. **P:** Entertainment. **U:** Home. **Mov-Ent:** Mystery & Suspense, Religion, TV Movies. **Acq:** Purchase. **Dist:** Unknown Distributor.

The Broken Wings 1962
Story of Lebanese artist/poet Khalil Gibran's first love with Selma Karamy. 90m; VHS. **A:** Adult. **P:** Entertainment. **U:** Home. **Mov-Ent:** Drama, Romance. **Acq:** Purchase. **Dist:** Arab Film Distribution. $39.99.

Broken Wings 2002 (R) — ★★★
Writer/director Bergman's touching feature debut about an Israeli family's inability to cope with the recent loss of patriarch David. Widow Dafna Ulman (Zilberschatz-Banai) takes up working odd shifts as a midwife for a local hospital, forcing 17-year-old daughter Maya (Maron) to put her music career on hold to care for younger siblings Ido (Daniel Magon) and Bahr (Eliana Magon). Faring little better is 16-year-old son Yair (Gvirtz), who has thrown away a potential basketball career by dropping out of school and now passes out leaflets in the subway dressed in a mouse costume. Things suddenly go from bad to worse, forcing the Ulmans into crisis mode. Simply told but very effective human drama. In Hebrew with subtitles. 83m; DVD. **C:** Orly Silbersatz Banai; Maya Maron; Nitai Gaviratz; Valdimir Friedman; Dana Ivgi; Danny Niv; Daniel Magon; Eliana Magon; Directed by Nir Bergman; Written by Nir Bergman; Cinematography by Valentin Belonogov; Music by Avi Bellili. **Pr:** Assaf Amir; Israel Film Fund; Sony Pictures Classics. **A:** Sr. High-Adult. **P:** Entertainment. **U:** Home. **L:** Hebrew. **Mov-Ent:** Parenting, Israel. **Acq:** Purchase. **Dist:** Columbia House Video Library.

The Broker's Man: Series 1 1997
BBC 1997-98 crime drama. Jimmy Griffin is a divorced, down-on-his-luck former detective who's working as an insurance fraud investigator. His cases include Dutch criminals working a

shipping container theft, a car theft ring, and claims of poisoning against a water treatment plant. 3 episodes. 288m; DVD. **C:** Kevin Whately; Annette Ekblom; Al Ashton. **A:** Sr. High-Adult. **P:** Entertainment. **U:** Home. **L:** English. **Mov-Ent:** Crime Drama, Insurance, Television Series. **Acq:** Purchase. **Dist:** Acorn Media Group Inc. $39.99.

Bromas S.A. 1987 — ★★
A group of teenagers get into a bunch of funny situations. 104m; VHS. **C:** Mauricio Garces; Gloria Marin; Manuel Valdez; Hermanos King. **Pr:** Madera. **A:** Preschool. **P:** Entertainment. **U:** Home. **L:** Spanish. **Mov-Ent. Acq:** Purchase. **Dist:** Spanishmultimedia. $54.95.

Bronchial Asthma 1976
The causes of bronchial asthma are discussed, and the mechanics of the way the lungs work normally and during an attack are shown. Appropriate for children as well as the older patient. 15m; VHS, 3/4 U. **Pr:** Milner-Fenwick. **A:** Primary-Adult. **P:** Education. **U:** Institution, CCTV. **L:** English, French, Spanish. **Hea-Sci:** Respiratory System, Patient Education. **Acq:** Purchase. **Dist:** Milner-Fenwick, Inc.

Bronchodilators and Arrhythmias 1986
A study for MDs of the effect of common drugs on irregular heart activity. 20m; VHS, 3/4 U. **A:** Adult. **P:** Professional. **U:** Institution, CCTV, Home, SURA. **Hea-Sci:** Heart, Medical Education. **Acq:** Purchase, Rent/Lease, Subscription. **Dist:** Emory Medical Television Network.

Bronco Billy 1980 (PG) — ★★½
Eastwood stars as a New Jersey shoe clerk who decides to fulfill his dream of being a cowboy hero by becoming the proprietor of a rag-tag wild west show. Locke's one-note performance as a spoiled rich girl who joins up is a problem and the film's charm is as ragged as the acts. Good if you want to see Eastwood in something other than a shoot-'em-up. 117m; VHS, DVD, Wide. **C:** Clint Eastwood; Sondra Locke; Bill McKinney; Scatman Crothers; Sam Bottoms; Geoffrey Lewis; Dan Vadis; Walter Barnes; Sierra Pecheur; Directed by Clint Eastwood; Written by Dennis Hackin; Cinematography by David Worth; Music by Steve Dorff. **Pr:** Warner Bros. **A:** Family. **P:** Entertainment. **U:** Home. **Mov-Ent. Acq:** Purchase. **Dist:** Warner Home Video, Inc.; Time-Life Video and Television; Rex Miller Artisan Studio. $19.98.

Bronco: Death of an Outlaw 1960
An episode from the early television western has Bronco caught up in the 1878 Lincoln Country Cattle War in New Mexico. He meets up with a married Billy the Kid who is being sought for past crimes by buffalo hunter/lawman Pat Garrett. 60m; VHS. **C:** Ty Hardin. **A:** Family. **P:** Entertainment. **U:** Home. **Mov-Ent:** Western, Television Series. **Acq:** Purchase. **Dist:** Facets Multimedia Inc. $14.98.

Bronies: The Extremely Unexpected Adult Fans of My Little Pony 2013 (Unrated)
Kickstarter funded documentary on Bronies: adult male fans of the "My Little Pony: Friendship Is Magic" cartoon. 267m; Blu-Ray. **A:** Jr. High-Adult. **P:** Entertainment. **U:** Home. **L:** English. **Mov-Ent:** Documentary Films, Animation & Cartoons. **Acq:** Purchase. **Dist:** BronyDoc Llc. $39.99.

Bronson 2009 (R) — ★★
Stylized Brit bio, with a ferocious performance by Hardy, about Michael Petersen, a young man jailed for armed robbery in 1974 who renames himself Charles Bronson after the tough guy American actor. Bronson eventually spends more than 30 years in solitary confinement thanks to his incorrigible glee in committing violent acts within the prison system itself. The lead in his own mental movie, Bronson speaks directly to the camera and is a media celebrity due to sheer outrageousness (the real Bronson has become an artist and writer behind bars and has published numerous books). But he's always a violent criminal, not a sympathetic character. 92m; Blu-Ray, On Demand, Wide. **C:** Thomas Hardy; Juliet Oldfield; Matt King; Hugh Ross; Jonathan Phillips; James Lance; Directed by Nicolas Winding Refn; Written by Brock Norman Brock; Nicolas Winding Refn; Cinematography by Larry Smith. **A:** Sr. High-Adult. **P:** Entertainment. **U:** Home. **L:** English. **Mov-Ent:** Biography: Law Enforcement. **Acq:** Purchase. **Dist:** Magnolia Home Entertainment; Amazon.com Inc.; Movies Unlimited.

Bronson's Revenge 1972 (R) — ★½
Two frontier soldiers face constant danger as they attempt to transport death row prisoners, a large quantity of gold, and a stranded woman across the Rocky Mountains territory. 90m; VHS. **C:** Claudio Undari; Emma Cohen; Alberto Dalbes; Antonio Iranzo; Directed by Joaquin Luis Romero Marchent; Written by Joaquin Luis Romero Marchent; Cinematography by Luis Cuadrado; Music by Carmelo A. Bernaola. **Pr:** Serafin Garcia. **A:** College-Adult. **P:** Entertainment. **U:** Home. **Mov-Ent:** Western. **Acq:** Purchase. **Dist:** $52.95.

The Bronte Collection 1992
Explores the background of Emily Bronte's "Wuthering Heights" based on Mary Butterfield's research. Informational for those studying this classic novel. 54m; VHS. **Pr:** Yorkshire Television. **A:** Jr. High-Adult. **P:** Education. **U:** Institution. **Gen-Edu:** Literature--English, Education. **Acq:** Purchase. **Dist:** Films for the Humanities & Sciences. $149.00.

The Bronte Sisters 1979 (Unrated) — ★★
A cold, bleak film from Techine that contrasts the often bleak, lonely lives of the Bronte family on those Yorkshire moors in the 1840s and the wildly romantic inner lives that produced the pseudononymous fiction of Emily, Charlotte, and Anne. The girls try escaping by becoming governesses and teachers but are drawn back home into the stern world of their father, Rev. Bronte. It's also where their would-be artist brother, Branwell, is unhappily succumbing to drink and drugs. French with subtitles. 120m; DVD. **C:** Isabelle Adjani; Marie-France Pisier; Isabelle Huppert; Pascal Greggory; Patrick Magee; Xavier Depraz; Directed by Andre Techine; Written by Andre Techine; Pascal Bonitzer; Cinematography by Bruno Nuytten; Music by Philippe Sarde. **A:** Adult. **P:** Entertainment. **U:** Home. **L:** French. **Mov-Ent:** Drama, Family, Great Britain. **Acq:** Purchase. **Dist:** Cohen Media Group.

The Bronte Sisters 1991
Examines the lives and work of 19th-century British novelists Charlotte, Anne, and Emily Bronte, among whose writings include the classic romances "Wuthering Heights" and "Jane Eyre." 30m; VHS. **TV Std:** NTSC, PAL, SECAM. **A:** Sr. High-Adult. **P:** Education. **U:** Home, Institution. **Gen-Edu:** Biography, Literature--English. **Acq:** Purchase. **Dist:** International Historic Films Inc. $29.95.

The Brontes of Haworth 1973 — ★★½
The bleak moorlands and the village of Haworth are the setting for a dramatic look at the lives of writers Charlotte, Emily, and Anne Bronte, their wastral brother Branwell, and the tragedies that haunted them all. On 4 cassettes. 270m; VHS, DVD, CC. **C:** Ann Penfold; Michael Kitchen; Vickery Turner; Rosemary McHale; Alfred Burke; Directed by Marc Miller; Written by Christopher Fry. **Pr:** Yorkshire Television. **A:** Jr. High-Adult. **P:** Entertainment. **U:** Home. **Mov-Ent:** Great Britain. **Acq:** Purchase. **Dist:** BFS Video.

The Bronx: A Cry for Help 19??
Offers an insider's view of the South Bronx by a filmmaker who has lived and filmed there over a 12-year period, and shows what life is like for ordinary people. 59m; VHS. **A:** Sr. High. **P:** Education. **U:** Institution. **Gen-Edu:** Sociology, Human Relations. **Acq:** Purchase. **Dist:** Filmakers Library Inc. $295.

Bronx Baptism 1984
A Pentecostal worship ceremony is documented in this film. 27m; 3/4 U. **Pr:** Dee Dee Halleck. **A:** Sr. High-Adult. **P:** Religious. **U:** Institution, SURA. **Gen-Edu:** Documentary Films, Religion. **Acq:** Purchase. **Dist:** First Run/Icarus Films.

Bronx Cheers 1989
Young Italian-American man returns from WWII, falls prey to the misguidance of a has-been boxer. 1990 Academy Award nominee for Best Live Action Short. 30m; VHS. **C:** Directed by Raymond De Felitta; Written by Raymond De Felitta. **A:** Sr. High-Adult. **P:** Entertainment. **U:** Home. **Mov-Ent:** Action-Adventure, Boxing. **Acq:** Purchase. **Dist:** Baker and Taylor; The Cinema Guild. $59.95.

The Bronx Executioner 1986 (Unrated) — ★
Android, robot, and human interests clash in futuristic Manhattan and all martial arts hell breaks loose. Special introduction by martial arts star Michael Dudikoff. 88m; VHS, DVD. **C:** Rob Robinson; Margie Newton; Chuck Valenti; Gabriel Gori; Directed by Bob Collins. **A:** Adult. **P:** Entertainment. **U:** Home. **Mov-Ent:** Science Fiction, Martial Arts. **Acq:** Purchase. **Dist:** Movies Unlimited. $13.49.

The Bronx Is Burning 2007 (Unrated) — ★★½
In 1977, New York City was paralyzed by a citywide blackout, political strife, and the Son of Sam killing spree. And then there were the New York Yankees, owned by bombastic George Steinbrenner (Platt), managed by volatile, hard-drinking Billy Martin (Turturro), and with egotistical Reggie Jackson (Sunjata) as their star hitter. Nostalgic miniseries shows how the city came together as the Yanks made their bid for the World Series. 360m; DVD. **C:** John Turturro; Oliver Platt; Daniel Sunjata; Erik Jensen; Michael Rispoli; Dan Lauria; Kevin Conway; Loren Dean; Charles S. Dutton; Alex Cranmer; Leonard Robinson; Directed by Jeremiah S. Chechik; Written by James Solomon; Gordon Greisman; Cinematography by Douglas Koch; Music by Tree Adams. **A:** Jr. High-Adult. **P:** Entertainment. **U:** Home. **Mov-Ent:** Sports--Fiction: Drama, Baseball. **Acq:** Purchase. **Dist:** Genius.com Incorporated.

A Bronx Morning 1931
Impressionistic look at a certain area of the Bronx from morning to noon. ?m/B/W; 8 mm. **A:** Sr. High-Adult. **P:** Entertainment. **U:** Home. **Mov-Ent:** Film--Avant-Garde. **Awds:** Natl. Film Reg. '04. **Acq:** Purchase. **Dist:** Glenn Video Vistas Ltd.

The Bronx Queen and Propeller Salvage 19??
Covers two major wrecks in detail: The Bronx Queen, a 110-foot fishing boat and former WWII submarine chaser as well as a 1000 lb. bronze propeller retrieved from the mouth of New York Harbor. 48m; VHS. **A:** Jr. High-Adult. **P:** Entertainment. **U:** Home. **Spo-Rec:** Scuba, Boating. **Acq:** Purchase. **Dist:** Bennett Marine Video. $24.95.

A Bronx Tale 1993 (R) — ★★★
Vivid snapshot of a young Italian-American boy growing up in the '60s among neighborhood small-time wiseguys. As a nine-year-old Calogero witnesses mobster Sonny kill a man but doesn't rat to the police, so Sonny takes the kid under his wing. His upright bus-driving father Lorenzo doesn't approve but the kid is drawn to Sonny's apparent glamor and power. At 17, he's gotten both an education in school and on the streets but he needs to make a choice. Good period detail and excellent performances. Palminteri shows both Sonny's charisma and violence and De Niro handles the less-showy father role with finesse. Based on Palminteri's one-man play; De Niro's directorial debut. 122m; VHS, DVD, CC. **C:** Robert De Niro; Chazz Palminteri; Lillo Brancato; Francis Capra; Taral Hicks; Kathrine Narducci; Clem Caserta; Alfred Sauchelli, Jr.; Frank Pietrangolare; Joseph (Joe) D'Onofrio; Cameo(s) Joe Pesci; Directed by Robert De Niro; Written by Chazz Palminteri; Cinematography by Reynaldo Villalobos; Music by Butch Barbella. **Pr:** Jane Rosenthal; Jon Kilik; Robert De Niro; Peter Gatien; Robert De Niro; Price Entertainment; Penta Entertainment; Tribeca Productions; Savoy Pictures. **A:** Sr. High-Adult. **P:** Entertainment. **U:** Home. **Mov-Ent:** Crime Drama. **Acq:** Purchase. **Dist:** Home Box Office Inc. $19.98.

The Bronx War 1990 (R) — ★★
Rival gangs take to the streets in this film from the director of "Hangin' with the Homeboys." A malicious gang leader tricks his gang into going to war over a girl he wants. Very violent; an unrated version available. 91m; VHS, DVD. **C:** Joseph B. Vasquez; Fabio Urena; Charmaine Cruz; Andre Brown; Marlene Forte; Francis Colon; Miguel Sierra; Kim West; Directed by Joseph B. Vasquez. **Pr:** Films Around the World. **A:** Sr. High-Adult. **P:** Entertainment. **U:** Home. **Mov-Ent. Acq:** Purchase. **Dist:** Unknown Distributor.

Bronze Age Blast-Off 1979
Discusses the history of the use of metals in ancient Europe. 50m; VHS, 3/4 U. **Pr:** British Broadcasting Corporation. **A:** Sr. High-Adult. **P:** Education. **U:** Institution, SURA. **Gen-Edu:** Documentary Films, History--Ancient, Metallurgy. **Acq:** Purchase. **Dist:** Home Vision Cinema.

Bronze Buckaroo 1939 — ★★
Horse opera in which a cowpoke seeks revenge for his pa's death. Commendable performances from the all-black cast and crew. 57m/B/W; VHS, DVD. **C:** Herbert Jeffries; Artie Young; Rollie Hardin; Spencer Williams, Jr.; Clarence Brooks; F.E. (Flourney) Miller; Directed by Richard C. Kahn; Written by Richard C. Kahn. **A:** Sr. High-Adult. **P:** Entertainment. **U:** Home. **Mov-Ent:** Western, Black Culture. **Acq:** Purchase. **Dist:** Tapeworm Video Distributors Inc. $24.95.

The Brood 1979 (R) — ★★½
Cronenberg's inimitable biological nightmares, involving an experimentally malformed woman who gives birth to murderous demon-children that kill every time she gets angry. Extremely graphic. Not for all tastes. 92m; VHS, DVD. **C:** Samantha Eggar; Oliver Reed; Art Hindle; Susan Hogan; Nuala Fitzgerald; Cindy Hinds; Robert A. Silverman; Gary McKeehan; Directed by David Cronenberg; Written by David Cronenberg; Cinematography by Mark Irwin; Music by Howard Shore. **Pr:** New World Pictures. **A:** Sr. High-Adult. **P:** Entertainment. **U:** Home. **Mov-Ent:** Horror, Canada. **Acq:** Purchase. **Dist:** Movies Unlimited. $11.99.

Broodmare Management 1988
Discusses the management of a broodmare band. Topics include: teasing schedules, artifical lighting, use of hormones, veterninary consultation, and record keeping. 45m; VHS. **Pr:** The Blood-Horse. **A:** College-Adult. **P:** Professional. **U:** Institution, Home. **Hea-Sci:** Horses--Racing, Veterinary Medicine. **Acq:** Purchase. **Dist:** The Blood-Horse, Inc.

The Brooklyn Bridge 1982
The hundred-plus-year-old bridge reigns as one of New York City's most beloved landmarks. This record of the span's construction and history comes in a 38-minute version as well. Academy Award nominee for Best Documentary Feature. 58m; VHS, 3/4 U, Special order formats. **C:** Directed by Ken Burns. **Pr:** Ken Burns. **A:** Jr. High-Adult. **P:** Education. **U:** Institution, Home, SURA. **Gen-Edu:** Documentary Films, Architecture. **Acq:** Purchase, Rent/Lease. **Dist:** Direct Cinema Ltd. $250.00.

Brooklyn Castle 2012 (PG) — ★★★½
Follows the chess team at Brooklyn's inner city Intermediate School 318, where the continual threats of poverty and budget cuts haven't thwarted the school from having the country's top-ranked junior high chess team. Student Rochelle aspires to be the first female African-American chess master, while Patrick finds chess helps him control his ADHD, and others face difficult pressures. Principal John Galvin and the team's teacher Elizabeth Vicary are clearly dedicated to the kids and the school. Well-played documentary balances the desperation of inner city schools and the lifeline that this opportunity gives the kids on which to dream and grow. 101m; DVD. **C:** Rochelle Ballantyne; Pobo Efokoro; John Galvin; Fred Rubino; Elizabeth Vicary; Directed by Katie Dellamaggiore; Cinematography by Brian Schulz; Music by Brian Satz. **Pr:** Katie Dellamaggiore; Brian Schulz; Nelson Dellamaggiore; Producers Distribution Agency; Le Castle Film Works; Rescued Media. **A:** Jr. High-Adult. **P:** Entertainment. **U:** Home. **L:** English. **Mov-Ent. Acq:** Purchase. **Dist:** Producers Distribution Agency.

The Brooklyn Connection: How to Build a Guerilla Army 2005 (Unrated)
Documentary on Florin Krasniqi, a Kosovo nationalist who exploits America's gun laws to raise 30 million dollars for arms and equipment for the KLA after his brother is slain by Yugoslavian soldiers. 57m; DVD. **A:** Sr. High-Adult. **P:** Education. **U:** Home. **Gen-Edu:** War--General, Documentary Films. **Acq:** Purchase. **Dist:** Docurama. $26.95.

The Brooklyn Dodgers: The Original America's Team 1995
Baseball history contains profiles on legendary players such as Pee Wee Reese, Roy Campanella, Jackie Robinson, and Duke Snider, interviews with players and their families, and a program on the franchise's move to Los Angeles in the late 1950s. Five-cassette series contains 20 percent more footage than the original ESPN broadcast. 330m; VHS. **A:** Jr. High-Adult. **P:** Entertainment. **U:** Home. **Spo-Rec:** Baseball. **Acq:** Purchase. **Dist:** Paramount Pictures Corp.

The Brooklyn Heist 2008 (PG-13) — ★★
Crazy crime caricatures shot in three distinct styles with overlapping stories. Set in Brooklyn, three criminal gangs co-exist without knowing anything about each other: the Amateurs get their look and attitude from 1970s mob flicks; the Moolies are African-Americans caught up in bad rap/gangsta videos; and

the Sputniks live in a literally black-and-white world from the 1950s where the cold war hasn't ended and they constantly try to buy nuclear materials. All three gangs share the same hatred for racist pawnshop owner Connie and when she dies all plan to crack her legendary safe and all decide to do it on the same night. 86m; DVD. **C:** Danny Masterson; Leon; Johnathan Hova; Dominique Swain; Aysan Celik; Michael Cecchi; Serena Reeder; Blanchard Ryan; Phyllis Somerville; Daniel Stewart Sherman; Directed by Julian mark Kheel; Written by Julian mark Kheel; Brett Halsey; Cinematography by Carlo Scialla; Music by David Poe. **A:** Jr. High-Adult. **P:** Entertainment. **U:** Home. **Mov-Ent**. **Acq:** Purchase. **Dist:** Image Entertainment Inc.

Brooklyn Lobster 2005 (Unrated) — ★★
Frank Giorgio (Aiello) is a hard-headed Sheepshead Bay lobster wholesaler whose business is about to be auctioned off and whose wife, Maureen (Curtin), has walked out on him. Son Michael (Sauli) comes home for the Christmas holidays to lend a hand, accompanied by his girlfriend Kerry (Burns), but her presence creates more problems. Aiello is especially impressive in a slice of life drama that was inspired by writer/director Jordan's own family. 90m; DVD, Wide. **C:** Danny Aiello; Jane Curtin; Marisa Ryan; Heather Burns; Sam Freed; Daniel Serafini Sauli; Ian Kahn; Tom Mason; Barbara Garrick; John Rothman; Rick Aiello; Directed by Kevin Jordan; Written by Kevin Jordan; Cinematography by David Tumblety; Music by Craig Maher. **Pr:** Kevin Jordan; Chris Valentino; Daren Jordan; Kevin Jordan; Red Claw Productions; Meadowbrook Pictures. **P:** Entertainment. **U:** Home. **L:** English. **Mov-Ent**. **Acq:** Purchase. **Dist:** Movies Unlimited; Alpha Video.

Brooklyn Rules 2007 (R) — ★★
Mild coming of age pic about three lifelong buddies, set in 1985 Brooklyn. Michael (Prinze) leaves the 'hood behind to go to law school and date an uptown girl (Suvari). Easy-going Bobby (Ferrara) plans to get married and have a steady straight job. But slickster Carmine (Caan) wants to be part of local wiseguy Cesar's (Baldwin) crew. Naturally these differing aims pull the guys apart. 99m; DVD. **C:** Freddie Prinze, Jr.; Scott Caan; Mena Suvari; Alec Baldwin; Jerry Ferrara; Monica Keena; Robert Turano; Phyllis Kay; Directed by Michael Corrente; Written by Terence Winter; Cinematography by Richard Crudo; Music by Benny Rietveld. **A:** Sr. High-Adult. **P:** Entertainment. **U:** Home. **Mov-Ent**. **Acq:** Purchase. **Dist:** Warner Home Video, Inc.

Brooklyn South: The Complete Series 1997
This single season CBS series, created by Steven Bochco, followed the officers of the downtrodden 74th precinct, located in Brooklyn, New York. 22 episodes. 990m; DVD. **C:** Dylan Walsh; Titus Welliver; Yancy Butler; Richard T. Jones; Klea Scott; Adam Rodriguez; Patrick McGaw; Gary Basaraba. **A:** Jr. High-Adult. **P:** Entertainment. **U:** Home. **Mov-Ent**: Television Series. **Acq:** Purchase. **Dist:** A&E Television Networks L.L.C.

A Brooklyn State of Mind 1997 (R) — ★★
Al (Spano) works for shady real estate developer Frank Parente (Aiello) in Brooklyn. When his Aunt Rose (King) rents a room to beautiful Gabriella (Cucinotta), who says she's working on a documentary about the neighborhood, Al is quick to succumb to her charms. But he's also suspicious—and when he finds a dossier on Frank in Gabriella's room, Al learns her father's murder is tied to his own father's death and both involve Frank. 90m; VHS, DVD, CC. **C:** Vincent Spano; Danny Aiello; Maria Grazia Cucinotta; Tony Danza; Morgana King; Abe Vigoda; Directed by Frank Rainone; Written by Frank Rainone; Fred Stroppel; Cinematography by Ken Kelsch; Music by Paul Zaza. **A:** Sr. High-Adult. **P:** Entertainment. **U:** Home. **Mov-Ent**: Crime Drama, Real Estate. **Acq:** Purchase. **Dist:** Amazon.com Inc.; Lions Gate Television Corp.

Brooklyn Trolleys: Volume 1 ????
Provides an overview of the Brooklyn, New York trolley system from 1936 until its closure in 1956 with many stops such as Coney Island and Rockaway Shuttle. 45m; VHS, DVD. **A:** College-Adult. **P:** Education. **U:** Home. **Gen-Edu**: Trains. **Acq:** Purchase. **Dist:** The Civil War Standard. $24.95.

Brooklyn Trolleys: Volume 2 ????
Further recounting of the Brooklyn, New York trolley system along with the shift to elevated trains and destruction of the trolleys. 40m; VHS, DVD. **A:** College-Adult. **P:** Education. **U:** Home. **Gen-Edu**: Trains. **Acq:** Purchase. **Dist:** The Civil War Standard. $24.95.

Brooklyn's Finest 2009 (R) — ★½
Fuqua appears to be redoing his 2001 film "Training Day" with this continuously violent story of corruption and impending doom that centers around three policemen. Burned-out veteran beat cop Eddie (Gere), about to retire, drinks too much and plans for his suicide; crooked narc Sal (Hawke) will do anything (including murder) for a big score to help his ill wife; and undercover cop Tango (Cheadle) is a little too comfortable in the thug life while needing to ensnare former major player Caz (Snipes) in order to stay on the NYPD promotional fast track. 125m; Blu-Ray, On Demand, Wide. **C:** Richard Gere; Ethan Hawke; Don Cheadle; Wesley Snipes; Ellen Barkin; Will Patton; Brian F. O'Byrne; Vincent D'Onofrio; Michael K(enneth) Williams; Lili Taylor; Shannon Kane; Directed by Antoine Fuqua; Written by Michael C. Martin; Brad Caleb Kane; Cinematography by Patrick Murguia; Music by Marcelos Zavras. **Pr:** Basil Iwanyk; John Langley; Elie Cohn; Thunder Road Productions; Millenium Films; Senator Film Entertainment. **A:** Sr. High-Adult. **P:** Entertainment. **U:** Home. **L:** English. **Mov-Ent**: Crime Drama, Drug Trafficking/Dealing. **Acq:** Purchase. **Dist:** Alpha Video; Anchor Bay Entertainment; Amazon.com Inc.

Brooks & Dunn: Pardners—The Brand New Man Videos 1992
The award-winning country music duet sings "Brand New Man," "My Next Broken Heart," "Boot Scootin' Boogie," and "Lost and Found." ?m; VHS, DVD. **A:** Jr. High-Adult. **P:** Entertainment. **U:** Home. **Mov-Ent**: Music Video, Music--Country/Western. **Acq:** Purchase. **Dist:** BMG Entertainment. $12.98.

Broth of a Boy 1959 (Unrated) — ★★½
A hungry British producer decides to film a birthday party of the oldest man in the world. The old Irishman wants a portion of the profits. Well made and thought provoking. 77m/B/W; VHS. **C:** Barry Fitzgerald; Harry Brogan; Tony Wright; June Thorburn; Eddie Golden; Directed by George Pollock. **Pr:** British Lion. **A:** Adult. **P:** Entertainment. **U:** Home. **Mov-Ent**. **Acq:** Purchase. **Dist:** Facets Multimedia Inc. $19.95.

Brother 1997 (Unrated) — ★★
Danila (Bodrov Jr.) has just gotten out of the army and needs a job so he decides to visit big brother Viktor (Sukhoroukov) in St. Petersburg. He discovers his bro is a contract killer for the Russian mob and hires on as Viktor's assistant. Danila successfully accomplishes his first assignment—the murder of a mob rival—but then has the other gangsters out for revenge. Fast-paced and gritty, with casual violence and crime the easiest options in a brokendown society. Russian with subtitles. 96m; VHS, DVD. **C:** Sergei Bodrov, Jr.; Viktor Sukhorukov; Svetlana Pismitchenko; Maria Zhukova; Yuri Kouznetzov; Directed by Alexsei Balabanov; Written by Alexsei Balabanov; Cinematography by Sergei Astakhov; Music by Viatcheslav Boutoussov. **A:** College-Adult. **P:** Entertainment. **U:** Home. **L:** Russian. **Mov-Ent**: Crime Drama. **Acq:** Purchase. **Dist:** Kino on Video.

Brother 2000 (R) — ★★★
Kitano's films are something of an acquired taste. He mixes abrupt graphic (and usually brief) violence with prolonged scenes of introspection, and when it comes to expressing emotion, he seldom does more than twitch or take off his sunglasses. But the man is cool, and to those who accept his measured pace, his work has a hypnotic quality. In his first film set in America, he plays Yamamoto, an exiled Japanese yakuza who partners up with street hustler Denny (Epps) and takes on the local drug gangs. Yes, that's the stuff of hundreds of video premiere action flicks, but he transcends the cliches. English and Japanese dialog with subtitles. 118m; VHS, DVD, Wide. **C:** Takeshi "Beat" Kitano; Omar Epps; Kuroudo Maki; Masaya Kato; Susumu Terajima; James Shigeta; Directed by Takeshi "Beat" Kitano; Written by Takeshi "Beat" Kitano; Cinematography by Katsumi Yanagishima; Music by Joe Hisaishi. **A:** Sr. High-Adult. **P:** Entertainment. **U:** Home. **L:** Japanese, English. **Mov-Ent**: Crime Drama, Drug Trafficking/Dealing. **Acq:** Purchase. **Dist:** Sony Pictures Home Entertainment Inc.

Brother Bear 2003 (G) — ★★½
Rather grim but ultimately heartwarming coming-of-ager invoking the far superior "The Lion King," and "Bambi." Kenai (Phoenix) is a brash Native American youth living with his two brothers in the Pacific Northwest during the end of the Ice Age. After a bear attacks and kills his brother Sitka (Sweeney), Kenai is magically transformed into a bear himself. In his new hirsute form, Kenai learns some important lessons about nature with the help of orphaned bear cub Koda (Suarez). Much needed but underdeveloped comic relief comes from Thomas and Moranis as a pair of bickering moose. Largely hand-drawn animation is lushly beautiful but overshadowed by derivative plot and heavy-handed message. Lackluster score by soft pop-meister Phil Collins. 85m; VHS, DVD, Blu-Ray. **C:** Voice(s) by Joaquin Rafael (Leaf) Phoenix; Jeremy Suarez; Jason Raize; Rick Moranis; Dave Thomas; D.B. Sweeney; Joan Copeland; Michael Clarke Duncan; Harold Gould; Estelle Harris; Directed by Aaron Blaise; Robert Walker; Written by Tab Murphy; Lorne Cameron; David Hoselton; Steve Bencich; Ron J. Friedman; Music by Phil Collins; Mark Mancina. **Pr:** Studio Ghibli; Walt Disney Pictures; Buena Vista. **A:** Family. **P:** Entertainment. **U:** Home. **Mov-Ent**: Bears, Native Americans, Wilderness Areas. **Acq:** Purchase. **Dist:** Walt Disney Studios Home Entertainment.

Brother Bear 2 2006 (G) — ★★½
Animated Disney sequel based on the 2003 release. Nita had a strong bond with Kenai when they were children (before he was turned into a bear). But if she wants to marry, Nita has to break that bond. She is told by the shaman that she and Kenai must perform a certain ritual but Kenai thinks maybe he should ask the Great Spirit if he can become human again (which he refused to do in the first film). For pure comic relief, moose buddies Rutt and Tuke are back and chasing after some moosettes. 74m; DVD, Blu-Ray. **C:** Voice(s) by Patrick Dempsey; Mandy Moore; Jeremy Suarez; Rick Moranis; Dave Thomas; Wanda Sykes; Andrea Martin; Catherine O'Hara; Directed by Ben Gluck; Written by Rich Burns; Music by Matthew Gerrard; Dave Metzger; Robbie Nevil. **A:** Family. **P:** Entertainment. **U:** Home. **Mov-Ent**: Bears, Native Americans, Animals. **Acq:** Purchase. **Dist:** Buena Vista Home Entertainment.

Brother Bread, Sister Puppet 1993
Documentary profile of Peter Schumann's Bread and Puppet Theater features interviews with puppeteers, puppet makers, performers, and patrons. Also includes scenes from the annual Domestic Resurrection Circus. 60m; VHS. **C:** Narrated by Grace Paley. **A:** Jr. High-Adult. **P:** Education. **U:** Institution. **Gen-Edu**: Documentary Films, Puppets, Circuses. **Acq:** Purchase, Rent/Lease. **Dist:** The Cinema Guild. $350.00.

Brother Cadfael 1994
Four episodic mysteries featuring a 12th-century Welsh soldier-turned-Benedictine monk (Jacobi), combining medieval atmosphere and politics with murder. Adapted from the novels by Ellis Peters. Hungary substitutes for the no-longer green and rural English setting of Shrewsbury. Made for British TV. Tapes available individually or as a boxed set. 300m; VHS, DVD. **C:** Derek Jacobi; Sean Pertwee; Tara Fitzgerald; Jonathan Firth; Norman Eshley; Directed by Graham Theakston. **A:** Sr. High-Adult. **P:** Entertainment. **U:** Home. **Mov-Ent**: Mystery & Suspense, Religion, Great Britain. **Acq:** Purchase. **Dist:** Signals Video. $79.95.
Indiv. Titles: 1. The Leper of St. Giles 2. Monk's Hood 3. One Corpse Too Many 4. The Sanctuary Sparrow.

Brother Cadfael 2 1995
Brother Cadfael (Jacobi), the medieval, mystery-solving, man-of-the-world turned man-of-the-cloth returns in three more adventures. "The Virgin in the Ice" finds the monk's novice accused of rape and murder. Cadfael also discovers a young squire is the son he never knew about. At "St. Peter's Fair" a disagreeable merchant is murdered but Cadfael doesn't believe greed is the motive. In "The Devil's Novice" a young man confesses to murder but is actually hiding family secrets. Based on the mystery series by Ellis Peters. On three cassettes. 75m; VHS. **C:** Derek Jacobi. **A:** Sr. High-Adult. **P:** Entertainment. **U:** Home. **Mov-Ent**: Mystery & Suspense, Religion, Great Britain. **Acq:** Purchase. **Dist:** Acorn Media Group Inc.; Facets Multimedia Inc.

Brother Cadfael 3 1996
Twelfth-century monk, Brother Cadfael (Jacobi), uses his knowledge of life to unravel medieval crimes in three more TV mysteries based on the novels of Ellis Peters. "The Raven in the Foregate" concerns the murder of a much-hated local priest; "A Morbid Taste for Bones" involves a saint's remains, their display at the Abbey, and murder; and "The Rose Rent" involves a young widow and the murdered monk who was in love with her. 240m; VHS, DVD. **C:** Derek Jacobi. **A:** Sr. High-Adult. **P:** Entertainment. **U:** Home. **Mov-Ent**: Mystery & Suspense, Religion, Great Britain. **Acq:** Purchase. **Dist:** Acorn Media Group Inc.; Wellspring Media.

Brother Cadfael Set I 1994
A 12th century crime solving monk uses his experience inside and outside the monastery walls to answer mysteries from fake holy relics to murder. 300m; DVD, CC; Closed Captioned. **A:** Adult. **P:** Entertainment. **U:** Home. **Mov-Ent**: Mystery & Suspense, Television, Drama. **Acq:** Purchase. **Dist:** Acorn Media Group Inc. $59.95.

Brother Cadfael Set II 1995
A 12th century crime solving monk uses his experience inside and outside the monastery walls to answer mysteries from fake holy relics to murder. 228m; DVD, CC; Closed Captioned. **A:** Adult. **P:** Entertainment. **U:** Home. **Mov-Ent**: Mystery & Suspense, Television, Drama. **Acq:** Purchase. **Dist:** Acorn Media Group Inc. $49.95.

Brother Cadfael Set III 1997
A 12th century crime solving monk uses his experience inside and outside the monastery walls to answer mysteries from fake holy relics to murder. 225m; DVD, CC; Closed Captioned. **A:** Adult. **P:** Entertainment. **U:** Home. **Mov-Ent**: Mystery & Suspense, Television, Drama. **Acq:** Purchase. **Dist:** Acorn Media Group Inc. $49.95.

Brother Cadfael Set IV 1998
A 12th century crime solving monk uses his experience inside and outside the monastery walls to answer mysteries from fake holy relics to murder. 225m; DVD, CC; Closed Captioned. **A:** Adult. **P:** Entertainment. **U:** Home. **Mov-Ent**: Mystery & Suspense, Television, Drama. **Acq:** Purchase. **Dist:** Acorn Media Group Inc. $49.95.

Brother, Can You Spare a Dime? 1975 (Unrated)
A compilation of documentary film footage from the 1930s. Hollywood in its heyday, Dillinger vs. the G-men, bread liners, and other memorabilia. 112m; VHS, DVD. **A:** Jr. High-Adult. **P:** Entertainment. **U:** Home. **Gen-Edu**: Documentary Films, History--U.S. **Acq:** Purchase. **Dist:** VCI Entertainment; Films for the Humanities & Sciences; Baker and Taylor. $19.95.

Brother, Can You Spare a Dime? History in Action ????
Addresses the causes of the 1929 stock market crash and effects of the Depression in America and Europe. 20m/B/W; VHS. **A:** Sr. High. **P:** Education. **U:** Institution. **Gen-Edu**: History--U.S., World Affairs. **Acq:** Purchase. **Dist:** Zenger Media. $89.95.

Brother Earl Presents A Design for Living 19??
Earl Cannamore, C.A.C., talks about helping the incarcerated addict/alcoholic using the Twelve Step program and the Design for Living curriculum. 45m; VHS. **A:** Adult. **P:** Education. **U:** Institution. **Hea-Sci**: Alcoholism, Drug Abuse. **Acq:** Purchase. **Dist:** Hazelden Publishing. $250.00.

Brother Earl's: Our Father 1989
Discussion by Brother Earl Cannamore about using the Lord's Prayer to help recovering addicts. Includes dicussion guide. 60m; 3/4 U, EJ. **Pr:** Gerald T. Rogers Productions, Inc. **A:** Adult. **P:** Education. **U:** Institution. **Hea-Sci**: Drug Abuse, Alcoholism. **Acq:** Purchase. **Dist:** Gerald T. Rogers Productions. $165.00.

Brother Earl's "Recovery, the Gift" 19??
Earl Cannamore, C.A.C. promotes discussion regarding the positive offerings of living clean and sober. 60m; VHS. **A:** Adult. **P:** Education. **U:** Institution. **Hea-Sci**: Alcoholism, Drug Abuse. **Acq:** Purchase. **Dist:** Hazelden Publishing. $185.00.

Brother Earl's Street Talk 1988
The signs and symptoms of chemical dependency are presented in layman's terms. 55m; VHS, 3/4 U. **Pr:** Gerald T.

Rogers Productions, Inc. **A:** Adult. **P:** Education. **U:** Institution, Home. **Hea-Sci:** Alcoholism, Drug Abuse. **Acq:** Purchase. **Dist:** Gerald T. Rogers Productions. $165.00.

Brother Earl's: What Problem? 1989
Denial and it's effect on recovery is analyzed by Brother Earl. Includes discussion guide. 60m; 3/4 U, EJ. **Pr:** Gerald T. Rogers Productions, Inc. **A:** Adult. **P:** Education. **U:** Institution. **Hea-Sci:** Drug Abuse, Alcoholism. **Acq:** Purchase. **Dist:** Gerald T. Rogers Productions. $165.00.

Brother Enemy 1987
An evangelistic film about a Christian artist who converts a mob of vandals. 76m; VHS. **C:** William Wellman, Jr; Robert Shook; Dan Wood. **A:** Adult. **P:** Religious. **U:** Home. **Gen-Edu:** Religion. **Acq:** Purchase. **Dist:** Russ Doughten Films Inc.

The Brother from Another Planet 1984 — ★★★
A black alien escapes from his home planet and winds up in Harlem, where he's pursued by two alien bounty hunters. Independently made morality fable by John Sayles before he hit the big time; features Sayles in a cameo as an alien bounty hunter. 109m; VHS, DVD, CC. **C:** Joe Morton; Dee Dee Bridgewater; Ren Woods; Steve James; Maggie Renzi; David Strathairn; Cameo(s) John Sayles; Directed by John Sayles; Written by John Sayles; Music by Mason Daring. **Pr:** A-Train Films; Cinecom Pictures. **A:** Sr. High-Adult. **P:** Entertainment. **U:** Home. **Mov-Ent:** Science Fiction, Black Culture. **Acq:** Purchase. **Dist:** Facets Multimedia Inc. $19.98.

Brother Future 1991 (Unrated) — ★★
T.J., a black, streetsmart city kid who thinks school and helping others is all a waste of time gets knocked out in a car accident. As he's lying unconscious, he is transported back in time to a slave auction block in the Old South. There the displaced urbanite is forced to work on a cotton plantation, and watch the stirrings of a slave revolt. T.J. sees the light and realizes how much opportunity he's been wasting in his own life. He comes to just a few moments later, but worlds away from who he was before. Part of the "Wonderworks" series. 110m; VHS. **C:** Phill Lewis; Frank Converse; Carl Lumbly; Vonetta McGee; Moses Gunn; Directed by Roy Campanella; Written by Roy Campanella. **Pr:** PMV. **A:** Family. **P:** Entertainment. **U:** Home. **Mov-Ent:** Slavery, Family Viewing, TV Movies. **Acq:** Purchase. **Dist:** Goldhill Home Media; Baker and Taylor; Facets Multimedia Inc. $29.95.

Brother John 1970 (PG-13) — ★★★
An early look at racial tensions and labor problems. An angel goes back to his hometown in Alabama to see how things are going. 94m; VHS, DVD. **C:** Sidney Poitier; Will Geer; Bradford Dillman; Beverly Todd; Paul Winfield; Directed by James Goldstone; Music by Quincy Jones. **A:** Family. **P:** Entertainment. **U:** Home. **Mov-Ent:** Labor & Unions, Black Culture. **Acq:** Purchase. **Dist:** Facets Multimedia Inc.; Sony Pictures Home Entertainment Inc. $14.95.

Brother Minister: The Assassination of Malcolm X 1995
Explores the assassination of Malcolm X through interviews with those closest to him and reveals recently de-classified government intelligence documents. Also looks at the origin and history of the Nation of Islam. 115m; DVD. **C:** Narrated by Roscoe Lee Browne. **A:** Jr. High-Adult. **P:** Education. **U:** Home. **Gen-Edu:** Documentary Films, Civil Rights, History. **Acq:** Purchase. **Dist:** Entertainment One US LP. $490.00.

Brother of Sleep 1995 (R) — ★★★
Elias (Eisermann), the illegitimate son of the local priest, is discovered to have perfect pitch, a beautiful voice, and a special symbiosis with nature. Which does nothing to endear him to the superstitious inhabitants of his 19th-century Austrian mountain village. Elias doesn't know whether his gift is a blessing or a curse but he'd give it up if he could win the love of his cousin Elspeth (Vavrova). Schneider scripted from his 1992 novel, which has previously been adapted as a ballet and opera. German with subtitles. 133m; VHS, DVD. **C:** Andre Eisermann; Dana Vavrova; Ben Becker; Directed by Joseph Vilsmaier; Written by Robert Schneider; Cinematography by Joseph Vilsmaier; Music by Norbert J. Schneider. **Pr:** Sony Pictures Classics. **A:** College-Adult. **P:** Entertainment. **U:** Home. **L:** German. **Mov-Ent. Acq:** Purchase. **Dist:** Sony Pictures Home Entertainment Inc.

Brother Orchid 1940 (Unrated) — ★★★
Mobster puts a henchman in charge of his gang while he vacations in Europe. Upon his return, he is deposed and wounded in an assassination attempt. Hiding out in a monastary, he plots to regain control of the gang, leading to fish outta water episodes and a change in his outlook on life. Fine cast fans through farce intelligently. 87m/B/W; VHS, DVD. **C:** Edward G. Robinson; Humphrey Bogart; Ann Sothern; Donald Crisp; Ralph Bellamy; Allen Jenkins; Charles D. Brown; Cecil Kellaway; Directed by Lloyd Bacon; Cinematography by Gaetano Antonio "Tony" Gaudio. **Pr:** Columbia Pictures. **A:** Jr. High-Adult. **P:** Entertainment. **U:** Home. **Mov-Ent. Acq:** Purchase. **Dist:** Warner Home Video, Inc. $19.98.

Brother Outsider: The Life of Bayard Rustin 2002
Documentary on the life of Bayard Rustin, a civil rights personality denied his place in history due to his homosexuality. 83m; VHS, DVD. **A:** Sr. High-Adult. **P:** Entertainment. **U:** Institution. **Mov-Ent:** Documentary Films, Civil Rights, Biography. **Acq:** Purchase. **Dist:** California Newsreel. $49.95.

Brother Rat 1938 — ★★
Virginia Military Institute cadets Crawford (Reagan) and Randolph (Morris) help out their buddy Bing Edwards (Albert), who has secretly married and just learned that his wife is pregnant. They try to contain their usual hijinks and keep everything quiet until they can graduate in a few weeks. The film that introduced Reagan to future first wife Wyman, who played his love interest. 90m/B/W; DVD. **C:** Wayne Morris; Ronald Reagan; Eddie Albert; Jane Wyman; Priscilla Lane; Jane Bryan; Directed by William Keighley; Written by Jerry Wald; Richard Macaulay; Cinematography by Ernest Haller. **A:** Jr. High-Adult. **P:** Entertainment. **U:** Home. **Mov-Ent:** Pregnancy. **Acq:** Purchase. **Dist:** WarnerArchive.com.

Brother Rat and a Baby 1940 — ★½
In this silly sequel to the 1938 pic, Dan, Billy, and Bing have graduated from the Virginia Military Institute and are trying to settle down to real life. Knowing that Bing really wants the football coaching job at their alma mater, his buddies come up with some hare-brained schemes, including using Bing's baby son in a publicity story. 87m/B/W; DVD. **C:** Ronald Reagan; Wayne Morris; Eddie Albert; Jane Bryan; Priscilla Lane; Jane Wyman; Directed by Ray Enright; Written by Jerry Wald; Cinematography by Charles Rosher; Music by Heinz Roemheld. **A:** Jr. High-Adult. **P:** Entertainment. **U:** Home. **L:** English. **Mov-Ent:** Men, Parenting. **Acq:** Purchase. **Dist:** WarnerArchive.com.

Brother Sun, Sister Moon 1973 (PG) — ★★½
Post-'60s costume epic depicting the trials of St. Francis of Assisi as he evaluates his beliefs in Catholicism. 120m; DVD. **C:** Graham Faulkner; Judi Bowker; Alec Guinness; Leigh Lawson; Kenneth Cranham; Lee Montague; Valentina Cortese; Directed by Franco Zeffirelli; Written by Franco Zeffirelli; Cinematography by Ennio Guarnieri; Music by Donovan. **Pr:** Paramount Pictures. **A:** Jr. High-Adult. **P:** Entertainment. **U:** Home. **Mov-Ent:** Drama, Religion, Biography: Religious Figures. **Acq:** Purchase. **Dist:** WarnerArchive.com. $14.95.

Brother to Brother 2004 (Unrated) — ★★½
Ambitious debut effort ties the personal plight of a modern African-American painter to the artistic turmoil of the Harlem Renaissance. Perry (Mackie) is thrown out of his house once his father discovers that he is homosexual. Embittered, Perry rails against the anti-gay hostility within the black community and his college classrooms. After he meets a homeless man, Bruce Nugent (Robinson), in a local shelter, Perry realizes that Bruce was once a noted poet during the Harlem Renaissance. We then flash back to the 1930s to witness Bruce interacting with such luminaries as Langston Hughes and Zora Neale Hurston. Evans effectively shows how issues of politics and sexuality transcend time, but the film lapses into didacticism once too often. 94m; DVD. **C:** Anthony Mackie; Roger Robinson; Larry (Lawrence) Gilliard, Jr.; Aunjanue Ellis; Duane Boutte; Daniel Sunjata; Alex Burns; Directed by Rodney Evans; Written by Rodney Evans; Cinematography by Harlan Bosmajian; Music by Marc Anthony Thompson; Bill Coleman. **Pr:** Jim McKay; Aimee Schoof; Isen Robbins. **P:** Entertainment. **U:** Home. **L:** English. **Mov-Ent:** Black Culture, Homeless. **Dist:** Wolfe Video.

The Brotherhood 1968 — ★★½
Two hot-headed brothers in a Mafia syndicate clash over old vs. new methods and the changing of the Family's guard. 96m; DVD. **C:** Kirk Douglas; Alex Cord; Irene Papas; Luther Adler; Susan Strasberg; Murray Hamilton; Directed by Martin Ritt; Written by Lewis John Carlino; Cinematography by Boris Kaufman; Music by Lalo Schifrin. **Pr:** Kirk Douglas; Paramount Pictures. **A:** Jr. High-Adult. **P:** Entertainment. **U:** Home. **Mov-Ent. Acq:** Purchase. **Dist:** WarnerArchive.com. $14.95.

Brotherhood 2009 (Unrated) — ★★
Insecure Danish army officer Lars abandons his career when rumors surface about his sexuality and he's denied a promotion. He meets Michael, the leader of a neo-Nazi group, and decides to get involved because of the respect he's shown. What Lars doesn't expect is acting on the mutual attraction between himself and fellow member Jimmy. But their relationship doesn't stay a secret for long. Danish with subtitles. 90m; DVD. **C:** Nicolas Bro; Lars Simonsen; Thure Lindhardt; David Dencik; Morten Holst; Claus Flygare; Hanne Hedelund; Directed by Nicolo Donato; Written by Nicolo Donato; Rasmus Birch; Cinematography by Laust Trier-Morch; Music by Simon Brenting; Jesper Mechlenburg. **A:** College-Adult. **P:** Entertainment. **U:** Home. **L:** Danish. **Mov-Ent. Acq:** Purchase. **Dist:** Olive Films.

Brotherhood 2010 (R) — ★★
A fraternity hazing turns nasty when prez Frank (Foster) demands the pledges jump out of the van and rob various convenience stores. Each store has a fellow brother to prevent the joke from going too far, until one clerk acts too quickly and shoots. From here, the wounded pledge is kept in secrecy as the brothers try to cover their tracks. An effectively tense low-budget affair with decent performances from a generally unknown cast. First-time director Canon keeps the action popping and highlights the idiocy of human nature but has a severe lack of humor or irony. 79m; Blu-Ray, Wide. **C:** Jon Foster; Trevor Morgan; Arlen Escarpeta; Lou Taylor Pucci; Jennifer Sipes; Luke Sexton; Chad Halbrook; Jesse Steccato; Directed by Will Canon; Written by Will Canon; Douglas Simon; Cinematography by Michael Fimognari; Music by Dan Marocco. **Pr:** Steve Hein; Jason Croft; Chris Pollack; Tim O'Hair; Three Folks Pictures; Phase 4. **A:** Sr. High-Adult. **P:** Entertainment. **U:** Home. **L:** English. **Mov-Ent. Acq:** Purchase. **Dist:** Movies Unlimited; Alpha Video; Phase 4/kaBOOM Entertainment.

Brotherhood 2: The Young Warlocks 2001 — **Bomb!**
Luke is a new kid at a private school who decides to recruit a group of fellow outcast kids for a coven he's starting. Laughably bad in all regards except that some of the cast are hotties. 85m; VHS, DVD. **C:** Sean Faris; Forrest Cochran; Stacey Scowley; Noah Frank; Julie Briggs; Justin Allen; C.J. Thomason; Directed by David DeCoteau. **A:** Sr. High-Adult. **P:** Entertainment. **U:** Home. **Mov-Ent:** Horror. **Acq:** Purchase. **Dist:** Wolfe Video.

The Brotherhood 3: The Young Demons 2002 (Unrated) — **Bomb!**
Teenagers heavily into a role-playing wizard and warriors game gather every Friday to perform faux ceremonies complete with costumes and weaponry. When they find a real book of magic, they can't resist chanting a few spells, which conjures up some medieval horrors. 82m; VHS, DVD. **C:** Kristopher Turner; Paul Andrich; Ellen Wieser; Julie Pedersen; Directed by David DeCoteau. **A:** Sr. High-Adult. **P:** Entertainment. **U:** Home. **Mov-Ent:** Occult Sciences. **Acq:** Purchase. **Dist:** Wolfe Video.

Brotherhood: Life in the FDNY 2005
Looks at New York's firefighters, including Brooklyn's Squad 252, Manhattan Rescue Company 1, and Queens Rescue Company 4, from training to teamwork in a fire. 84m; DVD. **A:** Jr. High-Adult. **P:** Entertainment. **U:** Home. **Gen-Edu:** Documentary Films, Fires. **Acq:** Purchase. **Dist:** Virgil Films & Entertainment.

Brotherhood of Blood 2008 (Unrated) — ★½
The world's best vampire slayer (a comely young blonde) has been captured by the King of Vampires and languishes in his dungeons while her compatriots attempt to find a way in to release her. Meanwhile the King must somehow figure out how to stop the coming of a vampiric demon, who may end up making the world a hell on earth. The team-up between himself and his imprisoned enemy to stop this is inevitable, and surprisingly not so exciting. 90m; DVD. **C:** Victoria Pratt; Sid Haig; Ken Foree; Jason Connery; Wes Ramsey; Jeremy James Kissner; Rachel Grant; William Snow; Directed by Michael Roesch; Peter Scheerer; Written by Michael Roesch; Peter Scheerer; Cinematography by River O'Mahoney Hagg; Music by Ralph Rieckermann; Tom Bimmerman. **A:** Sr. High-Adult. **P:** Entertainment. **U:** Home. **Mov-Ent. Acq:** Purchase. **Dist:** Lions Gate Entertainment Inc. $19.98.

Brotherhood of Death 1976 (R) — ★½
Three black Vietnam veterans return to their southern hometown to get even with the Klansmen who slaughtered all of the townspeople. 85m; VHS, DVD. **C:** Roy Jefferson; Larry Jones; Mike Bass; Le Tari; Haskell V. Anderson; Directed by Bill Berry. **Pr:** Cinema Shares International. **A:** Sr. High-Adult. **P:** Entertainment. **U:** Home. **Mov-Ent:** Action-Adventure. **Acq:** Purchase. **Dist:** MPI Media Group. $59.95.

Brotherhood of Justice 1986 (Unrated) — ★★
Young men form a secret organization to rid their neighborhood of drug dealers and violence. As their power grows, their propriety weakens, until all are afraid of the "Brotherhood of Justice." 97m; VHS, DVD. **C:** Keanu Reeves; Kiefer Sutherland; Billy Zane; Joe Spano; Darren Dalton; Evan Mirand; Don Michael Paul; Directed by Charles Braverman; Music by Brad Fiedel. **Pr:** Peter Guber; Jon Peters. **A:** Jr. High-Adult. **P:** Entertainment. **U:** Home. **Mov-Ent:** Adolescence, TV Movies, Drugs. **Acq:** Purchase. **Dist:** Fisher Klingenstein Films; Anchor Bay Entertainment. $89.95.

Brotherhood of Murder 1999 — ★★
Based on the book by Thomas Martinez and John Gunther that depicts the rise and fall of the white supremacist group known as "The Order." Martinez (Baldwin) is a struglling family man who falls in with charismatic Bob Mathews (Gallagher) and his hate group—until the shooting starts. 93m; VHS, DVD, CC. **C:** William Baldwin; Peter Gallagher; Kelly Lynch; Joel S. Keller; Zack (Zach) Ward; Vincent Gale; Directed by Martin Bell; Written by Robert J. Avrech; Cinematography by James R. Bagdonas; Music by Laura Karpman. **A:** Sr. High-Adult. **P:** Entertainment. **U:** Home. **Mov-Ent. Acq:** Purchase. **Dist:** Showtime Networks Inc.

The Brotherhood of Satan 1971 (PG) — ★★½
In an isolated southern town, a satanic coven persuades children to join in their devil-may-care attitude. Worthwhile. 92m; VHS, DVD, Blu-Ray. **C:** Strother Martin; L.Q. Jones; Charles Bateman; Ahna Capri; Charles Robinson; Alvy Moore; Geri Reischl; Helene Winston; Directed by Bernard McEveety; Written by William Welch; Cinematography by John Morrill. **Pr:** L.Q. Jones; L.Q. Jones. **A:** Jr. High-Adult. **P:** Entertainment. **U:** Home. **Mov-Ent:** Horror, Occult Sciences. **Acq:** Purchase. **Dist:** Image Entertainment Inc. $9.95.

The Brotherhood of the Rose 1989 (PG-13) — ★½
Too many twists and turns mar the otherwise mediocre plot of this murky adaption of a book by David (First Blood) Morrell. Strauss and Morse are the C.I.A. agents marked for death and running for their lives after uncovering their boss's (Mitchum) plot of world domination. Though almost every scene takes place in a different country, the movie was in fact filmed entirely in New Zealand. Convoluted and frustratingly difficult to follow. 103m; VHS, DVD, CC. **C:** Robert Mitchum; Peter Strauss; Connie Sellecca; James B. Sikking; David Morse; M. Emmet Walsh; James Hong; Directed by Marvin J. Chomsky. **Pr:** Stirling Silliphant. **A:** Jr. High-Adult. **P:** Entertainment. **U:** Home. **Mov-Ent:** TV Movies. **Acq:** Purchase. **Dist:** Universal Studios Home Video; CinemaNow Inc. $16.99.

Brotherhood of the Wolf 2001 (R) — ★★
Based on the French legend about the Beast of Gevaudan, a wolf-like creature that killed more than 100 people in the 1760s. In 1765, in a remote province, a mysterious creature is savagely killing women and children throughout the countryside. Naturalist Gregoire de Fronsac (Le Bihan) and his Iroquis blood brother Mani (Dacascos) are sent by King Louis XV to kill and stuff the beast for posterity. But what they finally discover is quite unexpected. Flamboyantly entertaining adventure. French with subtitles. 143m; VHS, DVD, CC. **C:** Samuel Le Bihan; Mark Dacascos; Vincent Cassel; Emilie Dequenne; Jeremie Renier; Monica Bellucci; Jean Yanne; Edith Scob; Jean-Francois Stevenin; Hans Meyer; Jacques Perrin; Philippe Nahon; Eric

Prat; Johan Leysen; Bernard Fresson; Bernard Farcy; Virginie Darmon; Directed by Christophe Gans; Written by Christophe Gans; Stephane Cabel; Cinematography by Dan Laustsen; Music by Joseph LoDuca. **Pr:** Samuel Hadida; Richard Grandpierre; Studio Canal Plus; Davis Films; TF-1 Films; Universal Pictures. **A:** Sr. High-Adult. **P:** Entertainment. **U:** Home. **L:** French. **Mov-Ent:** France, Folklore & Legends, Science. **Acq:** Purchase. **Dist:** Alpha Video.

Brotherhood: The Complete First Season 2006
Tommy Caffee is a rising young politician from an Irish working-class neighborhood in Providence, Rhode Island. But his ambitions may be derailed by both his troubled wife Eileen and his older brother Michael, a gangster whose sudden and mysterious return after seven years causes a shakeup within the criminal world he used to command as well as inside the Caffee household. 11 episodes. 540m; DVD, CC. **C:** Jason Isaacs; Jason Clarke; Annabeth Gish; Fionnula Flanagan; Kevin Chapman; Ethan (Randall) Embry. **A:** Sr. High-Adult. **P:** Entertainment. **U:** Home. **Mov-Ent:** Television Series, Politics & Government. **Acq:** Purchase. **Dist:** Showtime Networks Inc.

Brotherhood: The Complete Second Season 2007 (Unrated)
Showtime drama television series (2007-). After taking a serious beating at the end of last season Michael (Isaacs) begins season two in recovery and prone to seizures and blackouts, but still lobbies Freddie Cork (Chapman) for work. Declan and Cassie are now separated, he's on the outs at work and in the midst of some serious drug and alcohol abuse. Tommy and Eileen's daughter is having some significant behavioral problems while they barely hang on themselves. Brian F. O'Byrne joins the cast as Colin, a cousin from Ireland who quickly gets embedded in the family biz from both sides. All episodes are titled after Bob Dylan songs. 546m; DVD. **A:** Adult. **P:** Entertainment. **U:** Home. **Mov-Ent:** Drama, Television Series. **Acq:** Purchase. **Dist:** Showtime Networks Inc.

Brotherhood: The Final Season 2008 (Unrated)
Two brothers from an Irish working-class family choose lives on opposite sides of the law each one battling with their own aspects of moral compromise as they reach for the American dream. 8 episodes. 426m; DVD. **C:** Jason Issacs; Jason Clarke; Annabeth Gish. **A:** Sr. High-Adult. **P:** Entertainment. **U:** Home. **Mov-Ent:** Action-Adventure, Television Series. **Acq:** Purchase. **Dist:** Showtime Networks Inc. $42.99.

Brotherly Love 1985 (Unrated) — ★½
Good twin/bad twin made-for-TV mystery about an escaped psychopath who's out to get his businessman twin brother (Hirsch in both roles). 94m; VHS, CC. **C:** Judd Hirsch; Karen Carlson; George Dzundza; Barry Primus; Lori Lethin; Directed by Jeff Bleckner. **Pr:** CBS. **A:** Jr. High-Adult. **P:** Entertainment. **U:** Home. **Mov-Ent:** Mystery & Suspense, TV Movies. **Acq:** Purchase. **Dist:** $59.98.

Brotherly Love: The Trevor Ferrel Story 199?
Focuses on how a teenager decides to help the homeless. 30m; VHS. **A:** Sr. High-Adult. **P:** Entertainment. **U:** Institution. **Gen-Edu:** Documentary Films, Homeless, Adolescence. **Acq:** Purchase. **Dist:** Ambrose Video Publishing, Inc. $99.95.

The Brothers 2001 (R) — ★★★
A chain reaction of male introspection is set off as four successful, young African-American men navigate the tricky waters of serious relationships in modern Los Angeles. All the bases are covered: there is the womanizing lawyer, Brian (Bellamy); the one night stand-weary physician, Jackson (Chestnut); the just-engaged Terry (Shemar); and the unhappily married Derrick (Hughley). Not quite as strong as its female counterpart, the much-praised "Waiting to Exhale," but novelist Hardwick's first film is well managed and funny, and he never lets his capable comic actors veer too far away from the exploration of modern sexual politics. 101m; VHS, DVD, CC. **C:** Morris Chestnut; D.L. Hughley; Bill Bellamy; Shemar Moore; Gabrielle Beauvais; Tamala Jones; Susan Dalian; Angelle Brooks; Jenifer Lewis; Clifton Powell; Marla Gibbs; Tatyana Ali; Julie Benz; Directed by Gary Hardwick; Written by Gary Hardwick; Cinematography by Alexander Grusynski. **Pr:** Darin Scott; Paddy Cullen; Screen Gems; Sony Pictures Home Entertainment Inc. **A:** Sr. High-Adult. **P:** Entertainment. **U:** Home. **Mov-Ent:** Black Culture. **Acq:** Purchase. **Dist:** Sony Pictures Home Entertainment Inc.

Brothers 2004 (R) — ★★★
Michael is a husband and father in the Danish military deployed to Afghanistan. When his helicopter crashes he is presumed dead. In his absence his younger "screw-up" brother steps up to the plate to help Michael's wife and children cope with life in his absence. However, Michael was not dead, but captured by guerrilla fighters and forced to commit a barbaric act. When he finally returns home he is a different man. Great narrative drive, emotionally explosive and brutally honest. In Danish with English subtitles. 110m; DVD. **C:** Connie Nielsen; Ulrich Thomsen; Nikolaj Lie Kaas; Directed by Suzanne (Susanne) Bier; Written by Anders Thomas Jensen; Cinematography by Morten Soborg; Music by Johan Soderqvist. **Pr:** Sisse Graum Jorgensen; Peter Aalbaek Jensen; Zentropa Entertainment; Nordisk. **A:** Sr. High-Adult. **P:** Entertainment. **U:** Home. **L:** Danish. **Mov-Ent:** War--General, Marriage, Middle East. **Acq:** Purchase. **Dist:** Movies Unlimited.

Brothers 2009 (R) — ★★
All-American Marine Capt. Sam Cahill (Maguire) is presumed dead during a tour of duty in Afghanistan, leaving a wife, Grace (Portman), and two young daughters. Trying to fill in for his responsibilities is his brother, Tommy (Gyllenhaal), a troubled ex-con. When Sam, held prisoner by the Taliban, finally returns, the trauma he's endured is made worse when it seems that the formerly unreliable Tommy has replaced him. A remake of Susanne Blier's 2004 Danish film, it occasionally rises to the original's depth but mostly misses the mark, opting for overstatement and melodrama instead. 110m; Blu-Ray, On Demand, Wide, CC. **C:** Tobey Maguire; Jake Gyllenhaal; Natalie Portman; Sam Shepard; Mare Winningham; Patrick Flueger; Carey Mulligan; Directed by Jim Sheridan; Written by David Benioff; Cinematography by Frederick Elmes; Music by Thomas Newman. **Pr:** Sigurjon Sighvatsson; Relativity Media; Lionsgate. **A:** Sr. High-Adult. **P:** Entertainment. **U:** Home. **L:** English. **Mov-Ent:** Marriage, Veterans. **Acq:** Purchase. **Dist:** Movies Unlimited; Alpha Video; Amazon.com Inc.

Brothers and Others 2002
Documentary about the impact of 9/11 on Arabs, Muslims, and South Asians in the U.S. 54m; DVD. **A:** Adult. **P:** Education. **U:** Home, Institution. **Gen-Edu:** Documentary Films, Prejudice. **Acq:** Purchase, Rent/Lease. **Dist:** Arab Film Distribution. $24.99.

Brothers & Sisters. . .Love & Hate: Sibling Rivalry 1987
Discusses the behavior that can be expected from the first child when the second child arrives and shares attention from the parent. 16m; VHS, 3/4 U. **Pr:** Altschul Group. **A:** Jr. High-Adult. **P:** Education. **U:** Institution, SURA. **Hea-Sci:** Family, Psychology. **Acq:** Purchase, Rent/Lease. **Dist:** Discovery Education. $295.00.

Brothers & Sisters: The Complete Fifth and Final Season 2010
ABC 2006-11 family drama. "The Homecoming": A year afer Robert's car accident, the Walker family is still in disarray but try to come togther for Justin's sake. "The One That Got Away": When Nora's high school sweetheart Brody (Beau Bridges) reappears, Sarah learns a long-held secret. "Walker Down the Aisle": It's time for Sarah and Luc's (Gilles Marini) wedding but nothing goes as planned at a Walker family event. 22 episodes. 938m; DVD. **C:** Sally Field; Calista Flockhart; Rachel Griffiths; Matthew Rhys; Dave (David) Annable; Ron Rifkin; Luke Macfarlane. **A:** Jr. High-Adult. **P:** Entertainment. **U:** Home. **Mov-Ent:** Drama, Family, Television Series. **Acq:** Purchase. **Dist:** ABC Studios. $45.99.

Brothers & Sisters: The Complete First Season 2006
ABC 2006-11 family drama. The Walker family is thrown into chaos when patriarch William (Tom Skerritt) suddenly dies. Grieving widow Nora gathers her children around her but they're all in for a series of shocks—the family business is in serious trouble and William had a long-time mistress and another child. The family will also deal with romance, addiction, marital troubles, job changes, and Walker son Justin's deployment to Iraq over an eventful year. 23 episodes. 988m; DVD. **C:** Sally Field; Calista Flockhart; Ron Rifkin; Rachel Griffiths; Balthazar Getty; Matthew Rhys; Patricia Wettig; Dave (David) Annable; Emily VanCamp; John Pyper-Ferguson. **A:** Jr. High-Adult. **P:** Entertainment. **U:** Home. **Mov-Ent:** Television Series, Drama, Family. **Acq:** Purchase. **Dist:** Buena Vista Home Entertainment.

Brothers & Sisters: The Complete Fourth Season 2009
ABC 2006-11 family drama. "Last Tango in Pasadena": Nora is the last one to be charmed by Sarah's French lover, Luc (Gilles Marini), and Robert tries to distract Kitty from her chemo treatments with romance. "Nearlyweds": Justin and a pregnant Rebecca's beachside wedding doesn't go as planned. "Lights Out": Financial difficulties force the Walkers to close Ojai foods. 24 episodes. 1032m; DVD. **C:** Sally Field; Calista Flockhart; Rachel Griffiths; Matthew Rhys; Dave (David) Annable; Ron Rifkin; Emily VanCamp; Rob Lowe; Luke Macfarlane. **A:** Jr. High-Adult. **P:** Entertainment. **U:** Home. **Mov-Ent:** Drama, Family, Television Series. **Acq:** Purchase. **Dist:** ABC Studios. $20.00.

Brothers & Sisters: The Complete Second Season 2006
ABC 2006-11 family drama.Kitty (Flockhart) and the Republican senator (Lowe) she works for become engaged. Sarah (Griffiths) loses custody of her kids and is now running Ojai Foods. Uncle Saul (Rifkin) is suspected to be gay. Justin (Annable), the Iraq vet seems to be falling off the wagon so the family stages an intervention. Matriarch Nora (Field) has her own romantic entanglements this season as well with a college draft-dodging beau (Chevy Chase) back in town, and her political opposite Isaac (Danny Glover). 16 episodes. 671m; DVD. **C:** Sally Field; Calista Flockhart; Rachel Griffiths; Matthew Rhys; Dave (David) Annable; Ron Rifkin; Rob Lowe. **A:** Jr. High-Adult. **P:** Entertainment. **U:** Home. **Mov-Ent:** Drama, Television Series, Family. **Acq:** Purchase. **Dist:** ABC Studios.

Brothers & Sisters: The Complete Third Season 2008
ABC 2006-11 family drama. "Glass Houses": Justin and Rebecca conceal their romantic relationship; Kevin wants to make partner at his law firm; it's revealed that William had another son. "Everything Must Go": A fed-up Nora has a garage sale to get rid of all William's things and Kitty resigns her job on Robert's staff. "Just a Sliver": Nora finds her children have made their own Thanksgiving Day plans until a family emergency draws them together. 24 episodes. 1032m; DVD. **C:** Sally Field; Calista Flockhart; Rachel Griffiths; Matthew Rhys; Dave (David) Annable; Ron Rifkin; Emily VanCamp; Rob Lowe; Luke Macfarlane. **A:** Jr. High-Adult. **P:** Entertainment. **U:** Home. **Mov-Ent:** Television Series, Family, Drama. **Acq:** Purchase. **Dist:** ABC Studios. $20.00.

The Brothers Bloom 2009 (PG-13) — ★★
Orphans Stephen (Ruffalo) and his younger brother Bloom (Brody) spent their troubled youth perfecting their natural-born con artist abilities. Now grown up, the moody Bloom decides he's had enough of the game but a persuasive Stephen gets him to do one last con. Enter eccentric heiress Penelope (Weisz) who's looking for a little excitement in life but of course Bloom complicates things by falling hard for their mark. A familiar farce that's still appealing enough, just as is its cast—Weisz, especially—with a gorgeous European backdrop. But writer/director Johnson makes it a little too hyper and witty for its own good. 109m; Blu-Ray, On Demand, Wide. **C:** Adrien Brody; Mark Ruffalo; Rachel Weisz; Maximilian Schell; Rinko Kikuchi; Robbie Coltrane; Ricky Jay; Narrated by Ricky Jay; Directed by Rian Johnson; Written by Rian Johnson; Cinematography by Steve Yedlin; Music by Nathan Johnson. **Pr:** Ram Bergman; James Stern; Endgame Entertainment; Summit Entertainment. **A:** Jr. High-Adult. **P:** Entertainment. **U:** Home. **L:** English. **Mov-Ent.** **Acq:** Purchase. **Dist:** Summit Entertainment; Amazon.com Inc.; Movies Unlimited.

The Brothers Grimm 2005 (PG-13) — ★½
Rather grim indeed is this ill-conceived fairytale from Gilliam that had a rocky and delayed production (it was filmed in 2003). Wilhelm (Damon) and Jacob (Ledger) are 18th century German con men fleecing credulous country folk who believe in the supernatural. But in order to save their own skins, the brothers must investigate the disappearance of a number of young women who have vanished into a truly enchanted forest that is the domain of the Mirror Queen (Bellucci). The film looks good but it's really all an illusion. 118m; DVD, Blu-Ray, UMD. **C:** Matt Damon; Heath Ledger; Monica Bellucci; Jonathan Pryce; Lena Headey; Peter Stormare; Jan Unger; Directed by Terry Gilliam; Written by Ehren Kruger; Cinematography by Newton Thomas (Tom) Sigel; Music by Dario Marianelli. **Pr:** Charles Roven; Daniel Bobker; Mosaic Media Group; Dimension Films. **A:** Jr. High-Adult. **P:** Entertainment. **U:** Home. **L:** English. **Mov-Ent:** Fairy Tales, Folklore & Legends, Forests & Trees. **Acq:** Purchase. **Dist:** Buena Vista Home Entertainment.

Brothers in Arms 1988 (R) — ★★
Savage mountainmen have developed a weird religion that requires them to hunt down and mercilessly massacre human prey. 95m; VHS. **C:** Todd Allen; Jack Starrett; Dedee Pfeiffer; Mitch Pileggi; Directed by George J. Bloom, III; Written by Steve(n) Fisher. **A:** College-Adult. **P:** Entertainment. **U:** Home. **Mov-Ent:** Horror, Religion. **Acq:** Purchase. **Dist:** Lions Gate Entertainment Inc. $79.95.

Brothers in Arms: The Story of the Crew of Patrol Craft Fast 94 2004
Interviews, photographs and archival war footage capture the dramatic and true story of six men in the Mekong Delta, one of which was the young Senator John Kerry. 68m; DVD. **A:** Adult. **P:** Entertainment. **U:** Home. **Mov-Ent:** Documentary Films, Vietnam War. **Acq:** Purchase. **Dist:** First Run/Icarus Films. $19.95.

Brothers in Law 1957 (Unrated) — ★★½
Wry British humor in this tale of a rookie lawyer up against a veteran judge who forces him to sink or swim. 94m/B/W; VHS. **C:** Richard Attenborough; Ian Carmichael; Terry-Thomas; Miles Malleson; John Le Mesurier; Directed by Roy Boulting; Written by Roy Boulting. **A:** Jr. High-Adult. **P:** Entertainment. **U:** Home. **Mov-Ent:** Law. **Acq:** Purchase. **Dist:** Movies Unlimited. $14.99.

Brothers in the Saddle 1949 (Unrated) — ★½
Ranch foreman Tim and his gambler brother Steve are on opposite sides of the law when Steve is falsely accused of murder. Steve goes crazy and holds up the stagecoach and Tim must bring him to justice. 60m/B/W; DVD. **C:** Tim Holt; Steve Brodie; Richard Martin; Virginia Cox; Tom Keene; Stanley Andrews; Directed by Lesley Selander; Written by Norman Houston; Cinematography by J. Roy Hunt; Music by Paul Sawtell. **A:** Family. **P:** Entertainment. **U:** Home. **Mov-Ent:** Western. **Acq:** Purchase. **Dist:** WarnerArchive.com.

Brothers in Trouble 1995 (Unrated) — ★★
Illegal Pakistani immigrants occupy a squalid boardinghouse in '60s Yorkshire, including newly arrived Amir (Malhotra). He settles in, befriending young student Sakib (Kumar), and learning the ropes from house leader Hossein Shah (Puri). But Shah brings unexpected problems to the group when his pregnant, white English girlfriend Mary (Ball) comes to stay and his nephew Irshad (Bhatti) arranges a paper marriage with the young woman. Based on the novel "Return Journey" by Abdullah Hussein. 104m; VHS. **C:** Om Puri; Pavan Malhotra; Pravesh Kumar; Angeline Ball; Ahsen Bhatti; Directed by Udayan Prasad; Written by Robert Buckler; Cinematography by Alan Almond; Music by Stephen Warbeck. **Pr:** BBC Films. **A:** College-Adult. **P:** Entertainment. **U:** Home. **Mov-Ent:** Immigration. **Acq:** Purchase. **Dist:** First Run Features.

Brother's Justice 2011 (Unrated) — ★½
In this showbiz mockumentary, comedian Dax Shepard decides to change his image by getting a martial arts/adventure pic greenlit. It will star himself, though Dax has no martial arts training (or ability) and no script. Best friend Nate is the wannabe producer and they pitch the dismal project relentlessly to various biz friends with predictable (and only mildly comedic) results. 86m; DVD, Blu-Ray. **C:** Dax Shepard; Nate Tuck; Tom Arnold; Bradley Cooper; David Koechner; Jon Favreau; Directed by Dax Shepard; David Palmer; Written by Dax Shepard; Cinematography by David Palmer; Music by Julian Wass. **A:** Sr. High-Adult. **P:** Entertainment. **U:** Home. **Mov-Ent.** **Acq:** Purchase. **Dist:** Well Go USA, Inc.

The Brothers Karamazov 1958 — ★★★
Hollywood adaptation of the classic novel by Dostoyevsky, in which four 19th-Century Russian brothers struggle with their desires for the same beautiful woman and with the father who brutalizes them. Incredible performances from every cast member, especially Cobb. Long and extremely intense, with fine direction from Brooks. Marilyn Monroe tried desperately to get Schell's part. 147m; VHS, DVD. **C:** Yul Brynner; Claire Bloom; Lee J. Cobb; William Shatner; Maria Schell; Richard Basehart; Directed by Richard Brooks; Written by Richard Brooks; Cinematography by John Alton. **Pr:** Loew's, Inc; Avon Productions. **A:** Jr. High-Adult. **P:** Entertainment. **U:** Home. **Mov-Ent:** USSR. **Acq:** Purchase. **Dist:** WarnerArchive.com; MGM Home Entertainment. $24.95.

Brother's Keeper 1992 (Unrated) — ★★★
Filmmakers Berlinger and Sinofsky document the story of the eccentric and reclusive Ward brothers, four bachelor dairy farmers who shared the same two-room shack for more than 60 years in rural New York. When Bill Ward dies, brother Delbert is accused of murder and goes to trial. The film covers a year's span in preparation for the trial and how the media attention changed the Ward's lives. 104m; VHS, DVD. **C:** Directed by Joe Berlinger; Bruce Sinofsky; Cinematography by Douglas Cooper. **A:** College-Adult. **P:** Entertainment. **U:** Home. **Mov-Ent:** Documentary Films, Law. **Awds:** Directors Guild '92: Documentary Director (Berlinger), Documentary Director (Sinofsky); Natl. Bd. of Review '92: Feature Doc.; N.Y. Film Critics '92: Feature Doc.; Sundance '92: Aud. Award. **Acq:** Purchase. **Dist:** Wellspring Media; Baker and Taylor. $89.95.

Brother's Keeper 2002 (R) — ★★
After police detective Lucinda Pond (Tripplehorn) screwed up and let a killer get away, she left the force to run a fishing boat and start drinking. Ex-partner/lover Travis (Orser) shows up when his current homicide case turns out to be identical to the incident that ended Lucinda's career. She unofficially agrees to help but solving the case may lead her close to home and her crazy brother Ellis (Nemec). 86m; VHS, DVD. **C:** Jeanne Tripplehorn; Corin "Corky" Nemec; Leland Orser; Evan Dexter Parke; Directed by John Badham; Written by Steven Baigelman; Glen Gers; Cinematography by Ron Stannett; Music by John Ottman; John Willett. **A:** Sr. High-Adult. **P:** Entertainment. **U:** Home. **Mov-Ent. Acq:** Purchase. **Dist:** New Line Home Video.

A Brother's Kiss 1997 (R) — ★★
Growing up in an East Harlem neighborhood with an alcoholic mother (Moriarty), two brothers are set on different paths that strain their brotherly love. Lex (Chinlund) is a never-was ex-basketball player with a bad marriage and an even worse drug problem. Mick (Raynor) is a tightly wound, obsessive, and sexually dysfunctional cop. Both of their problems stem from a childhood trauma that neither is able or willing to discuss with the other. Starts out strong but runs out of energy by the second half. Expanded from a one-act play by director Rosenfeld. 92m; VHS, DVD. **C:** Nick (Nicholas) Chinlund; Michael Raynor; Justin Pierce; Cathy Moriarty; Rosie Perez; Marisa Tomei; Joshua Danowsky; John Leguizamo; Michael Rapaport; Frank Minucci; Adrian Pasdar; Directed by Seth Zvi Rosenfeld; Written by Seth Zvi Rosenfeld; Cinematography by Fortunato Procopio; Music by Frank London. **Pr:** Bob Potter; E. Bennett Walsh; First Look Pictures. **A:** Sr. High-Adult. **P:** Entertainment. **U:** Home. **Mov-Ent:** Child Abuse, Drug Abuse, Rape. **Acq:** Purchase. **Dist:** BMG Entertainment.

Brothers Lionheart 1977 (G) — ★★½
The Lion brothers fight for life, love and liberty during the Middle Ages. Based on a novel by Astrid Lindgren. 120m; VHS. **C:** Staffan Gotestam; Lars Soderdahl; Allan Edwall; Directed by Olle Hellbom. **Pr:** Olde Nordemar. **A:** Primary-Jr. High. **P:** Entertainment. **U:** Home. **Mov-Ent:** Children, Fantasy. **Acq:** Purchase. **Dist:** Unknown Distributor.

The Brothers McMullen 1994 (R) — ★★★
Slice of life drama finds three Irish-American brothers suddenly living under the same Long Island roof for the first time since childhood. Eldest brother Jack (Mulcahy) is a stolid high-school basketball coach married to teacher Molly (Britton) who's pressing him to have children. Cynical middle brother Barry (Burns), a writer, has just broken up with free-spirited Ann (McKay), and earnest young Patrick (McGlone) is engaged to Jewish girlfriend Susan (Albert). All three find their romantic relationships, as well as their belief in each other, tested. Generally good performances and dialogue, with Burns proving himself a triple threat as actor/writer/director. 98m; VHS, DVD, Blu-Ray, Wide, CC. **C:** Edward Burns; Jack Mulcahy; Mike McGlone; Connie Britton; Shari Albert; Elizabeth P. McKay; Maxine Bahns; Jennifer Jostyn; Catharine Bolt; Peter Johansen; Directed by Edward Burns; Written by Edward Burns; Cinematography by Dick Fisher; Music by Seamus Egan. **Pr:** Dick Fisher; Edward Burns; Ted Hope; James Schamus; Edward Burns; Marlboro Road Gang Productions; 20th Century Fox Searchlight. **A:** Sr. High-Adult. **P:** Entertainment. **U:** Home. **Mov-Ent. Awds:** Ind. Spirit '96: First Feature; Sundance '95: Grand Jury Prize. **Acq:** Purchase. **Dist:** Fox Home Entertainment.

Brothers of the Head 2006 (R) — ★★
Bizzare mockumentary a la "This Is Spinal Tap," only without the humor, tells the fictional story of British conjoined twins who are sold by their father to an unsavory music promoter who turns them into a freak-show punk band. The flashback-documentary style shows the rapid rise and fall of the band due to the usual rock and roll excesses. Pic gets a half bone for recreating an authentic 1970s British art/rock scene that makes an otherwise creepy flick watchable. Based on the 1977 illustrated novel by Brian Aldiss. 120m; DVD. **C:** Sean Harris; Jonathan Pryce; John Simm; Jane Horrocks; Harry Treadway; Luke Treadway; Bryan Dick; Elizabeth Rider; Howard Attfield; Luke Wagner; Anna Nygh; Ed Hogg; Thomas Sturridge; Barbara Ewing; Cameo(s) Ken Russell; Directed by Keith Fulton; Louis Pepe; Written by Tony Grisoni; Cinematography by Anthony Dod Mantle; Music by Clive Langer. **Pr:** Gail Egan; EM Media; Potboiler Production; IFC Films. **A:** Sr. High-Adult. **P:** Entertainment. **U:** Home. **L:** English. **Mov-Ent:** Music-Pop/Rock, Great Britain. **Acq:** Purchase. **Dist:** IFC Films.

Brothers of the West 1937 — ★½
Cowboy saves his brothers from being lynched by proving the guilt of the real outlaws. 56m/B/W; VHS, DVD. **C:** Tom Tyler; Bob Terry; Lois Wilde; Dorothy Short; Lafe (Lafayette) McKee; Dave O'Brien; Roger Williams; Directed by Sam Katzman; Written by Basil Dickey; Cinematography by William (Bill) Hyer. **Pr:** Sam Katzman; Sam Katzman. **A:** Family. **P:** Entertainment. **U:** Home. **Mov-Ent:** Western. **Acq:** Purchase. **Dist:** Alpha Video; Mill Creek Entertainment L.L.C.; Rex Miller Artisan Studio. $19.95.

Brothers O'Toole 1973 (G) — ★★
The misadventures of a pair of slick drifters who, by chance, ride into a broken-down mining town in the 1890s. 94m; VHS, DVD. **C:** John Astin; Steve Carlson; Pat Carroll; Hans Conried; Lee Meriwether; Directed by Richard Erdman. **Pr:** Gold Key Entertainment. **A:** Family. **P:** Entertainment. **U:** Home. **Mov-Ent:** Action-Adventure. **Acq:** Purchase. **Dist:** Movies Unlimited. $14.99.

The Brothers Quay, Vol. 1 1990
Puppet animation is taken to extremes in "The Street of Crocodiles" and "The Cabinet of Jan Svankmajer." 40m; VHS. **C:** Directed by Stephen Quay; Timothy Quay. **A:** Sr. High-Adult. **P:** Entertainment. **U:** Home. **Fin-Art:** Animation & Cartoons, Puppets. **Acq:** Purchase. **Dist:** First Run Features; Tapeworm Video Distributors Inc. $39.95.

The Brothers Quay, Vol. 2 1991
Three more bizarre animated episodes from England's Brothers Quay. Includes "Epic of Gilgamesh," "Rehearsals for Extinct Anatomies," and "Nocturna Artificiala." 50m; VHS. **C:** Directed by Stephen Quay; Timothy Quay. **A:** Sr. High-Adult. **P:** Entertainment. **U:** Home. **Fin-Art:** Animation & Cartoons, Puppets. **Acq:** Purchase. **Dist:** First Run Features; Tapeworm Video Distributors Inc. $19.95.

The Brothers Rico 1957 (Unrated) — ★★
Eddie (Conte) left the mob life behind, got married, and has a successful business, but his two brothers remained in the rackets. Unbeknownst to Eddie, they are targeted by mob boss Kubik (Gates) who uses Eddie's family loyalty to track them down. When Eddie discovers his brothers have been rubbed out, he decides to turn informer. Based on a novella by Georges Simenon. 92m/B/W; DVD. **C:** Richard Conte; James Darren; Paul Picerni; Dianne Foster; Kathryn Grant; Larry Gates; Lamont Johnson; Argentina Brunetti; Directed by Phil Karlson; Written by Lewis Meltzer; Ben L. Perry; Cinematography by Burnett Guffey; Music by George Duning. **A:** Sr. High-Adult. **P:** Entertainment. **U:** Home. **Mov-Ent:** Crime Drama. **Acq:** Purchase. **Dist:** Sony Pictures Home Entertainment Inc.

The Brothers Solomon 2007 (R) — ★½
Dean (Forte) and John (Arnett) decide to grant their father's (Majors) last wish before he slipped into a coma: a grandchild. Unfortunately, they were raised in the Arctic, have no social skills, and are, well, idiots. Along comes surrogate Janine (Wiig), who is willing to bear the child for a price. Mostly, though, it's just a set up for an endless series of gags based on how stupid and out of touch the brothers are. Arnett and Forte's "even dumber than dumberer" act, as directed by Odenkirk, is exhausting and the occasional splashes of sweetness don't make up for what is basically a one-joke extended sketch comedy skit. 93m; DVD. **C:** Will Arnett; Will Forte; Chi McBride; Jenna Fischer; Kristen Wiig; Malin Akerman; David Koechner; Lee Majors; Directed by Bob Odenkirk; Written by Will Forte; Cinematography by Tim Suhrstedt; Music by John Swihart. **Pr:** Matt Berenson; Tom Werner; Revolution Studios; TriStar Pictures; Casey-Werner Films; Sony Pictures Home Entertainment Inc. **A:** Sr. High-Adult. **P:** Entertainment. **U:** Home. **L:** English. **Mov-Ent:** Pregnancy. **Acq:** Purchase. **Dist:** Sony Pictures Home Entertainment Inc.

Brothers: The Complete Series 2009
Fox Network family comedy. Retired NFL player Mike Trainor returns home to Houston to help out his family, including his wheelchair-bound brother Chill, who doesn't want Mike interfering with his struggling restaurant. 13 episodes. 278m; DVD. **C:** Michael Strahan; Daryl (Chill) Mitchell; CCH Pounder; Carl Weathers. **A:** Jr. High-Adult. **P:** Entertainment. **U:** Home. **L:** English. **Mov-Ent:** Black Culture, Family, Television Series. **Acq:** Purchase. **Dist:** WarnerArchive.com. $30.99.

Brothers Three 2007 (R) — ★½
Dysfunctional family 101. College-educated businessman Peter (Wilson) receives an urgent message from his hot-tempered outdoorsman brother Rick (McDonough) to join him and their mentally-challenged younger brother Norman (Campbell) at the family's remote, run-down cabin. Once there, Peter learns that their shifty father (Heard) has recently died a violent death. The brothers then spend their time drinking and offering up confessions that reveal dark secrets (through some confusing flashbacks). 102m; DVD. **C:** Patrick Wilson; Neal McDonough; Scott Michael Campbell; John Heard; Melora Walters; Directed by Paul Kampf; Written by Paul Kampf; Cinematography by Henryk Cymerman. **A:** Sr. High-Adult. **P:** Entertainment. **U:** Home. **Mov-Ent. Acq:** Purchase. **Dist:** Vivendi Visual Entertainment.

Brown Angels 1996
Features smiling, laughing, happy baby faces to entertain infants and toddlers. 30m; VHS. **A:** Preschool. **P:** Entertainment. **U:** Home. **Chl-Juv:** Infants. **Acq:** Purchase. **Dist:** Tapeworm Video Distributors Inc. $9.95.

Brown Bag Seminars 1985
A series of programs designed for self-motivation in regards to time usage, confidence and personal performance. 30m; VHS, 3/4 U. **Pr:** Cally Curtis Company. **A:** Sr. High-Adult. **P:** Education. **U:** Institution, SURA. **Gen-Edu:** Self-Help. **Acq:** Purchase, Rent/Lease. **Dist:** Aspen Publishers, Inc.
Indiv. Titles: 1. Time Management 2. Procrastination 3. Assertiveness 4. Self-Change.

The Brown Bunny 2003 (Unrated) — ★★½
After his film's trashing as the worst movie in the history of the Cannes Film Festival, director/writer/star Gallo slashed nearly a half-hour from this story of a forlorn motorcycle racer's long, lonely coast-to-coast journey from a New Hampshire competition to his home in L.A., where he eventually meets up with true love Daisy (Sevigny). An infamously graphic oral sex scene ensues, which leads to a funky final plot twist. Curiosity, about the Cannes hubbub and the sex scene, will be rewarded by an interesting, sometimes poignant, homage to the maverick filmmaking of the 1970s. 93m; DVD. **C:** Vincent Gallo; Chloe Sevigny; Cheryl Tiegs; Elizabeth Blake; Anna Vareschi; Mary Morasky; Directed by Vincent Gallo; Written by Vincent Gallo; Cinematography by Vincent Gallo. **Pr:** Vincent Gallo; Vincent Gallo; Kinetique; Wellspring Media. **A:** College-Adult. **P:** Entertainment. **U:** Home. **Mov-Ent:** Sex & Sexuality, Motorcycles. **Acq:** Purchase. **Dist:** Sony Pictures Home Entertainment Inc.

Brown Sauces 199?
Demonstrates the making of brown sauces, including espagnole, demiglace, au jus and more, as well as thickening with roux or a slurry. Part of the Basics of Sauce Making Series. 24m; VHS. **A:** Sr. High-Adult. **P:** Instruction. **U:** Home. **How-Ins:** Cooking, Food Industry, How-To. **Acq:** Purchase. **Dist:** Culinary Institute of America. $75.00.

Brown Sugar 2002 (PG-13) — ★★½
Using the world of hip-hop music as its background, this romantic comedy succeeds in breathing life into a rather tired formula. Record producer Dre (Diggs) and music journalist Sidney (Lathan) are childhood friends who are drawn together by their shared love of the music. Although they think that romance is out of the question for them, everyone else knows that they're wrong, especially Sidney's friend Francine (Latifah). Unfortunately, Sidney doesn't figure it out until Dre becomes engaged to lovely lawyer Reese (Parker). She rebounds with suave basketball player Kelby (Kodjoe). Mos Def steals scenes as the shy, rapping cabbie who has a crush on Francine. 109m; VHS, DVD, CC. **C:** Taye Diggs; Sanaa Lathan; Mos Def; Nicole Ari Parker; Queen Latifah; Wendell Pierce; Boris Kodjoe; Erik Weiner; Reggi Wyns; Directed by Rick Famuyiwa; Written by Rick Famuyiwa; Michael Elliot; Cinematography by Enrique Chediak; Music by Robert Hurst. **Pr:** Peter Heller; Heller Highwater; Magic Johnson Entertainment; Fox Searchlight. **A:** Jr. High-Adult. **P:** Entertainment. **U:** Home. **Mov-Ent:** Black Culture, Romance, Music. **Acq:** Purchase. **Dist:** Fox Home Entertainment.

Brown v. Board of Education 1991
Dramatization of the landmark decision features excerpts of the legal arguments which changed American schools forever. Part of the American Documents Series. 25m; VHS. **A:** Jr. High-Sr. High. **P:** Education. **U:** Institution. **Gen-Edu:** Politics & Government, Law. **Acq:** Purchase. **Dist:** Phoenix Learning Group; African-American Images. $165.00.

Brown vs. the Board of Education 19??
A look at the 1954 Supreme Court decision which overturned the practice of segregation in public schools. 10m; VHS. **A:** Jr. High-Adult. **P:** Education. **U:** Institution, Home, SURA. **Gen-Edu:** Documentary Films, History--U.S., Law. **Acq:** Purchase. **Dist:** African-American Images. $70.00.

Brown Wolf 1972
This adaptation of Jack London's story of a spirited dog and the people whose lives he crosses spotlights the conflict between the call of the wild and that of civilization. 26m; VHS, 3/4 U; Open Captioned. **C:** Directed by George Kaczender. **Pr:** Learning Corporation of America. **A:** Family. **P:** Entertainment. **U:** Institution, SURA. **Gen-Edu:** Literature--American. **Acq:** Purchase, Rent/Lease. **Dist:** Phoenix Learning Group.

The Browning Version 1951 (Unrated) — ★★★½
A lonely, unemotional classics instructor at a British boarding school realizes his failure as a teacher and as a husband. From the play by Terrence Rattigan. 89m/B/W; VHS, DVD. **C:** Michael Redgrave; Jean Kent; Nigel Patrick; Wilfrid Hyde-White; Bill Travers; Directed by Anthony Asquith. **Pr:** Mark Huffam. **A:** Jr. High-Adult. **P:** Entertainment. **U:** Home. **Mov-Ent:** Education. **Awds:** Cannes '51: Actor (Redgrave). **Acq:** Purchase. **Dist:** Home Vision Cinema; Movies Unlimited; Fusion Video. $39.95.

The Browning Version 1994 (R) — ★★½
Mediocre remake of the Terence Rattigan play, previously filmed in 1951. Austere classics professor (Finney) at prestigious British boys school is disillusioned with both his floundering career and marriage. His emotional chill drives his younger wife (Scacchi) into an affair with a visiting American science teacher (Modine). Unfortunately updated to contemporary times, which can't hide apparent mustiness. Worth seeing for Finney's superb work as the out-of-touch prof. 97m; VHS, DVD, CC. **C:** Albert Finney; Greta Scacchi; Matthew Modine; Michael Gambon; Julian Sands; Ben Silverstone; Maryam D'Abo; Directed by Mike Figgis; Written by Ronald Harwood; Music by Mark Isham. **Pr:** Ridley Scott; Mimi Polk Gitlin; Paramount

Pictures. **A:** Sr. High-Adult. **P:** Entertainment. **U:** Home. **Mov-Ent:** Marriage, Education, Great Britain. **Acq:** Purchase. **Dist:** Paramount Pictures Corp.

Brown's Requiem 1998 (R) — ★★½
Ex-cop and ex-drunk Fritz Brown (Rooker) is a sometime L.A. private eye and repo man. He's hired by the aptly named Freddie "Fat Dog" Baker (Sasso) to check out Solly K (Gould), at whose manse Baker's kid sister Jane (Blair) is living. Solly's involved with ex-cop Cathcart (James), with whom Fritz has a longstanding beef, and the P.I. uncovers various lowlifes and a scam. Based on James Ellroy's Chandleresque detailed and dialogue-heavy first novel, which was published in 1981. 97m; VHS, DVD, Wide. **C:** Michael Rooker; Brion James; Harold Gould; Selma Blair; Kevin Corrigan; Tobin Bell; Jack Conley; Brad Dourif; Will Sasso; Valerie Perrine; Barry Newman; Directed by Jason Freedland; Written by Jason Freedland; Cinematography by Sead Muhtarevic; Music by Cynthia Millar. **A:** Sr. High-Adult. **P:** Entertainment. **U:** Home. **Mov-Ent**. **Acq:** Purchase. **Dist:** Movies Unlimited; Alpha Video.

The Broyles Top Producer System 1990
Learn motivational tactics that will keep sales on the up with this incredible video that has seen corporations increase profits by as much as three hundred percent! Also included are eight audio cassettes, a daily action planner and planning sheets, a 200 page manual, guidebook, six monthly motivational audio cassettes and letters, and quarterly newsletters. 90m; VHS. **Pr:** SyberVision Systems. **A:** College-Adult. **P:** Instruction. **U:** Home. **Bus-Ind:** Sales Training. **Acq:** Purchase. **Dist:** SyberVision Systems, Inc. $295.00.

Brubaker 1980 (R) — ★★★
A sanctimonious drama about a reform warden who risks his life to replace brutality and corruption with humanity and integrity in a state prison farm. Powerful prison drama. 131m; VHS, DVD, Blu-Ray. **C:** Robert Redford; Jane Alexander; Yaphet Kotto; Murray Hamilton; David Keith; Morgan Freeman; Matt Clark; M. Emmet Walsh; Everett McGill; Directed by Stuart Rosenberg; Written by W.D. Richter; Arthur Ross; Music by Lalo Schifrin. **Pr:** Ron Silverman. **A:** Sr. High-Adult. **P:** Entertainment. **U:** Home. **Mov-Ent**. **Acq:** Purchase. **Dist:** Movies Unlimited; Alpha Video; Fox Home Entertainment. $19.98.

The Bruce 1996 — ★★½
Based on the story of Scottish king, Robert the Bruce (Welch) and the battle at Bannockburn against English King Edward I's (Blessed) forces. Not blessed with the biggest budget and the actors tend to chew the scenery but not a bad bit of history. Robert the Bruce may also be familiar from the film "Braveheart." 110m; VHS. **C:** Sandy Welch; Oliver Reed; Brian Blessed; Michael Van Wijk; Pavel Douglas; Directed by Bob Carruthers; David McWhinnie; Music by Paul Farrer. **A:** Jr. High-Adult. **P:** Entertainment. **U:** Home. **Mov-Ent**: Drama, Scotland. **Acq:** Purchase.

Bruce Almighty 2003 (PG-13) — ★★½
No, it's not a Springsteen documentary, it's an enjoyable, if slight, Jim Carrey comedy. Carrey is Bruce Nolan, a TV reporter stuck with the fluff stories and longing to be taken seriously. He gets his chance when God (Freeman) decides to turn over the reins for a day and gives Bruce his divine powers. The comedy set-pieces are well done, and Carrey can do a lot with a little (at least in his comedies), but the overall effect is less laugh-out-loud funny than fans of the earlier Carrey-Shadyac pairings would expect. Aniston's not given much to do, but Carrell and Freeman stand out among the supporting cast. 101m; VHS, DVD, Blu-Ray, HD-DVD. **C:** Jim Carrey; Jennifer Aniston; Morgan Freeman; Lisa Ann Walter; Philip Baker Hall; Catherine Bell; Nora Dunn; Steve Carell; Directed by Tom Shadyac; Written by Steve Oedekerk; Steve Koren; Mark O'Keefe; Cinematography by Dean Semler; Music by John Debney. **Pr:** Steve Koren; Tom Shadyac; James D. Brubaker; Michael Bostick; Jim Carrey; Jim Carrey; Tom Shadyac; Spyglass Entertainment; Shady Acres; Pit Bull; Universal Pictures. **A:** Jr. High-Adult. **P:** Entertainment. **U:** Home. **Mov-Ent**: Journalism. **Acq:** Purchase. **Dist:** Movies Unlimited; Alpha Video; Universal Studios Home Video.

Bruce Baumgartner: Blueprint for Heavyweight Technique—From the Feet 2007 (Unrated)
Olympian Bruce Baumgartner demonstrates various techniques for wrestlers in the heavyweight division. 59m; DVD. **A:** Family. **P:** Education. **U:** Home, Institution. **Spo-Rec**: Athletic Instruction/Coaching. **Acq:** Purchase. **Dist:** Championship Productions. $39.99.

Bruce Baumgartner: Blueprint for Heavyweight Technique—On the Mat 1999 (Unrated)
Olympian Bruce Baumgartner shares techniques for heavyweight wrestlers that will help them get off the mat. 31m; DVD. **A:** Family. **P:** Education. **U:** Home, Institution. **Spo-Rec**: Athletic Instruction/Coaching. **Acq:** Purchase. **Dist:** Championship Productions. $39.99.

Bruce Conner Films 1 1978
Five films by the daring experimental filmmaker, all dealing in one way or another with the limits, meaning and effects of the film medium itself: "Ten Second Film," "Permian Strata," "Mongoloid," "America Is Waiting," and "A Movie." 24m; VHS. **C:** Directed by Bruce Conner. **Pr:** Bruce Conner; Bruce Conner. **A:** Sr. High-Adult. **P:** Entertainment. **U:** Home. **Fin-Art**: Film--Avant-Garde, Film History. **Acq:** Purchase. **Dist:** Facets Multimedia Inc. $59.95.

Bruce Conner Films 2 1980
Four films by Conner, each expressing questions about the nature of film while constructing/deconstructing various cultural objects. Includes "Breakaway," "Vivian," "The White Rose," and "Marilyn Times Five." 30m; VHS. **C:** Directed by Bruce Conner. **Pr:** Bruce Conner; Bruce Conner. **A:** Sr. High-Adult. **P:** Entertainment. **U:** Home. **Fin-Art**: Film--Avant-Garde, Film History. **Acq:** Purchase. **Dist:** Facets Multimedia Inc. $59.95.

Bruce Davidson Series 1978
The award-winning equestrian instructs in aspects of horsemanship. 90m; VHS. **Pr:** Mercedes Maharis Productions. **A:** Sr. High-Adult. **P:** Education. **U:** Home. **How-Ins**: How-To, Horses--Racing. **Acq:** Purchase. **Dist:** Video Collectibles.
Indiv. Titles: 1. Cross Country Part I 2. Cross Country Part II 3. Dressage 4. General Horse Management 5. Gridwork 6. Showjumping 7. Water Schooling.

Bruce Dickinson: Dive! Dive! Live 1991
Janick Gers and Bruce of Iron Maiden crank out 80 minutes worth of heavy metal, including "Bring Your Daughter to the Slaughter," "Riding with the Angels," "Born in '58," "All the Young Dudes" and more. 80m; VHS. **A:** Sr. High-Adult. **P:** Entertainment. **U:** Home. **Mov-Ent**: Music--Performance, Music--Pop/Rock. **Acq:** Purchase. **Dist:** Music Video Distributors; Sony Music Entertainment Inc. $19.98.

Bruce Hornsby and the Range: A Night on the Town 1990
The man with the magic fingers tickles the ivories while performing all his familiar hits, including "The Way it Is," "The End of Innocence," "The Valley Road" and more live. 63m; VHS. **A:** Adult. **P:** Entertainment. **U:** Home. **Mov-Ent**: Music--Performance, Music--Jazz. **Acq:** Purchase. **Dist:** Music Video Distributors; Sony Pictures Home Entertainment Inc.; BMG Entertainment. $19.98.

Bruce Jenner's 29-Minute Workout 1988
The decathlon champ leads viewers through a series of aerobics, calisthenics, and stretches. 29m; VHS. **C:** Bruce Jenner. **Pr:** Cambridge Career Productions. **A:** Jr. High-Adult. **P:** Instruction. **U:** Institution, Home. **Hea-Sci**: Fitness/Exercise. **Acq:** Purchase. **Dist:** Cambridge Educational. $14.99.

Bruce Jenner's Winning Workout 1987
Bruce and Linda Jenner describe their physical fitness regimen that the whole family can do. 75m; VHS. **Pr:** AHV Productions. **A:** Family. **P:** Entertainment. **U:** Home. **Hea-Sci**: Fitness/Exercise. **Acq:** Purchase. **Dist:** Karol Media. $19.95.

Bruce Kulick: Guitar Instruction 1990
The KISS guitarist demonstrates essential techniques for chord greatness. ?m; VHS. **A:** Jr. High-Adult. **P:** Instruction. **U:** Home. **How-Ins**: Music--Instruction. **Acq:** Purchase. **Dist:** Music Video Distributors. $44.95.

Bruce Lee: Curse of the Dragon 1993 — ★★★
A behind the scenes look at the continuing mystery surrounding the life and untimely death of the martial arts superstar who died in 1973 at the age of 32. Highlights the spectacular fight sequences from Lee's movies as well as footage from his funeral and an interview with his son Brandon Lee, whose own death in 1993 raised further comment about a Lee family curse. 90m; VHS. **C:** Narrated by George Takei; Directed by Tom Kuhn; Fred Weintraub; Written by Davis Miller. **Pr:** Fred Weintraub. **A:** Sr. High-Adult. **P:** Entertainment. **U:** Home. **Mov-Ent**: Documentary Films, Biography: Show Business, Martial Arts. **Acq:** Purchase. **Dist:** Warner Home Video, Inc.; Baker and Taylor. $79.99.

Bruce Lee Fights Back from the Grave 1976 (R) — ★
Bruce Lee returns from the grave to fight the Black Angel of Death with his feet and to wreak vengeance on the evil ones who brought about his untimely demise. 84m; VHS, DVD. **C:** Bruce Le; Deborah Chaplin; Anthony Bronson; Directed by Umberto Lenzi. **Pr:** Bert Lenzi. **A:** College-Adult. **P:** Entertainment. **U:** Home. **Mov-Ent**: Martial Arts. **Acq:** Purchase. **Dist:** Desert Island Films. $49.95.

Bruce Lee: The Legend 1984 (Unrated)
Tribute to the king of karate films features rare footage and interviews with many of the star's closest friends. 88m; VHS, CC. **C:** Bruce Lee; Steve McQueen; James Coburn; Narrated by James B. Nicholson. **Pr:** Leonard Ho; Galaxy International. **A:** Family. **P:** Entertainment. **U:** Home. **Mov-Ent**: Martial Arts, Biography. **Acq:** Purchase. **Dist:** Fox Home Entertainment. $19.98.

Bruce Lee: The Lost Interview 1971
Rare 1971 interview of Bruce Lee filmed in a Hong Kong studio. Lee discusses many topics including his techniques in the martial arts and his film and TV career. 30m/B/W; VHS. **A:** College-Adult. **P:** Entertainment. **U:** Home. **Gen-Edu**: Martial Arts, Interviews. **Acq:** Purchase. **Dist:** Tapeworm Video Distributors Inc. $19.95.

Bruce Lee: The Man/The Myth 1984 (Unrated)
A dramatization of the life and times of martial arts master Bruce Lee. 90m; VHS. **Pr:** Cinema Shares International. **A:** Sr. High-Adult. **P:** Entertainment. **U:** Home. **Mov-Ent**: Martial Arts, Biography. **Acq:** Purchase. **Dist:** Lions Gate Television Corp. $59.95.

Bruce Lowe: Synthesizer Instruction 1990
Learn the fundamentals of the synthesizer in this video. ?m; VHS. **A:** Jr. High-Adult. **P:** Instruction. **U:** Home. **How-Ins**: Music--Instruction. **Acq:** Purchase. **Dist:** Music Video Distributors. $44.95.

Bruce Pandolfini's Chess Series 1990
Anyone who is truly interested in chess can learn how to play with this informative series. 57m; VHS. **C:** Bruce Pandolfini. **A:** Jr. High-Adult. **P:** Instruction. **U:** Home. **How-Ins**: How-To. **Acq:** Purchase. **Dist:** Tapeworm Video Distributors Inc. $39.95.
Indiv. Titles: 1. Understanding Chess 2. Opening Principles.

Bruce Pearl's 1-2-1-1 Full-Court Pressure 200?
Presents on-court and game film of basketball defensive techniques of the full-court press by Bruce Pearl, head coach at the University of Tennessee. ?m; DVD. **A:** Sr. High-Adult. **P:** Instruction. **U:** Institution. **Spo-Rec**: Basketball. **Acq:** Purchase. **Dist:** Championship Productions. $39.95.

Bruce Springsteen and Friends 198?
The Boss is joined in clips by Jersey buddies John Cafferty and Southside Johnny, plus videos by George Thorogood, Jackson Browne and the Fabulous T-Birds. 30m; VHS. **A:** Jr. High-Adult. **P:** Entertainment. **U:** Home. **Mov-Ent**: Music Video. **Acq:** Purchase. **Dist:** Music Video Distributors. $9.98.

Bruce Springsteen and the E Street Band: Live in Barcelona 2003
Recording of the 2002 concert; includes the featurette "Drop the Needle And Pray: The Rising on Tour." 180m; DVD. **A:** Sr. High-Adult. **P:** Entertainment. **U:** Home. **Mov-Ent**: Music--Performance, Music--Pop/Rock. **Acq:** Purchase. **Dist:** Backstreets Records Catalog. $20.00.

Bruce Springsteen and the E Street Band: Live in New York City 2000
Expanded version of the HBO concert film of the band's performance at Madison Square Garden. ??m; DVD. **A:** Jr. High-Adult. **P:** Entertainment. **U:** Home. **Fin-Art**: Music--Performance, Music--Pop/Rock. **Acq:** Purchase. **Dist:** Backstreets Records Catalog. $20.00.

Bruce Springsteen & the E Street Band: Live in New York City 2001
Footage from Springsteen's tour-ending stand at Madison Square Garden in New York. Includes the entire concert from the HBO special, as well as some extra songs not shown on TV. Also contains "New York City Serenade" featuring behind the scenes footage and an interview with Springsteen conducted by Bob Costas. 190m; VHS, DVD. **A:** Jr. High-Adult. **P:** Entertainment. **U:** Home. **Mov-Ent**: Music--Performance. **Acq:** Purchase. **Dist:** Sony Pictures Home Entertainment Inc.; Backstreets Records Catalog.
Songs: My Love Will Not Let You Down; Prove It All Night; Two Hearts; Atlantic City; Mansion on the Hill; The River; Youngstown; Murder Inc.; Badlands; Out in the Street; Born to Run; Tenth Avenue Freeze-Out; Land of Hope and Dreams; Backstreets; Don't Look Back; Darkness on the Edge of Town; Lost in the Flood; Born in the USA; Jungleland; Light of Day; The Promise; Thunder Road; Ramrod; If I Should Fall Behind.

Bruce Springsteen: Greetings from the Parking Lot 2000
Springsteen fans talk about the The Boss's music, what it means to them, and the passion of being a fan. Filmed outside the Meadowlands complex during Springsteen's concert stand there in the summer of 1999. 70m; VHS. **A:** Jr. High-Adult. **P:** Entertainment. **U:** Home. **Mov-Ent**: Music--Pop/Rock, Interviews, Documentary Films. **Acq:** Purchase. **Dist:** Backstreets Records Catalog. $18.00.

Bruce Springsteen in Concert: MTV Plugged 1992
Springsteen actually had the MTV acoustic show wired for sound when he and his new touring band plugged in the amps and ripped into their 18-song set taped in LA. Songs include "Born to Run," "Thunder Road," "Light of Day," "Human Touch," "Red Headed Woman," and more. Hey, if the Boss wants to play electric would you say no? 115m; VHS. **A:** Jr. High-Adult. **P:** Entertainment. **U:** Home. **Mov-Ent**: Music--Performance, Music--Pop/Rock. **Acq:** Purchase. **Dist:** Sony Music Entertainment Inc.; Music Video Distributors. $19.98.

Bruce Springsteen: The Complete Video Anthology, 1978-2000 200?
Two-disc set of Bruce Springsteen's music videos, including several previously unreleased. 120m; VHS, DVD. **A:** Sr. High-Adult. **P:** Entertainment. **U:** Home. **Mov-Ent**: Music Video, Music--Pop/Rock. **Acq:** Purchase. **Dist:** Backstreets Records Catalog. $20.00.

Bruce Springsteen: VH1 Storytellers 200?
Expanded and re-edited version of the VH1 concert. ??m; DVD. **A:** Sr. High-Adult. **P:** Entertainment. **U:** Home. **Mov-Ent**: Music--Pop/Rock, Music--Performance. **Acq:** Purchase. **Dist:** Backstreets Records Catalog. $15.00.

Bruce Springsteen Video Anthology: 1978-88 1988
Various video and in-concert glimpses of the Boss, performing "Rosalita," "The River," "Thunder Road," "Dancing In The Dark," "Born In the U.S.A.," "I'm On Fire," "Glory Days," "My Hometown," "War," "Fire," "Born to Run," "Brilliant Disguise," "Tunnel of Love," and five more. DVD includes videos of his work in the '90s. 100m; VHS, DVD, 8 mm. **Pr:** CBS. **A:** Jr. High. **P:** Entertainment. **U:** Home. **Mov-Ent**: Music--Performance, Music Video. **Acq:** Purchase. **Dist:** Music Video Distributors; Sony Music Entertainment Inc. $24.98.

Bruce Springsteen—Darkness On the Edge of Town 2010 (Unrated)
Boxed set containing a documentary on the making of "Darkness" and two DVDs of live concert footage as well as a remastered edition of Bruce Springsteen's CD "Darkness at the Edge of Town," two CDs of unreleased material, and an 80-page reproduction of Springsteen's original notes from the recording sessions. ??m; DVD, Blu-Ray. **A:** Sr. High-Adult. **P:** Entertainment. **U:** Home. **Gen-Edu**: Documentary Films, Biography: Music. **Acq:** Purchase. **Dist:** Backstreets Records Catalog. $140.00.

Bruce the Superhero 1979 (Unrated) — ★
Chop-socky action as the coattails-riding Bruce Le takes on the Black Dragon Society. 88m; VHS. **C:** Bruce Le. **A:** College-

Adult. **P:** Entertainment. **U:** Home. **Mov-Ent:** Martial Arts. **Acq:** Purchase. **Dist:** Best Video. $19.99.

Bruce Weber: Competitive Games & Drills for Transition Basketball 2007
Coach Bruce Weber demonstrates competitive drills for improving a basketball team's skills at the transition game. 75m; DVD. **A:** Family. **P:** Education. **U:** Home, Institution. **Spo-Rec:** Basketball, Athletic Instruction/Coaching. **Acq:** Purchase. **Dist:** Championship Productions. $39.99.

Bruce Weber: Drills for Breaking Full and Half Court Presses 2006
Coach Bruce Weber gives drills and a demonstration of various press attacks in basketball. 46m; DVD. **A:** Family. **P:** Education. **U:** Home, Institution. **Spo-Rec:** Basketball, Athletic Instruction/Coaching. **Acq:** Purchase. **Dist:** Championship Productions. $39.99.

Bruce Weber: Mastering the Five Man Motion Offense 2005
Coach Bruce Weber presents and discusses his team's preferred version of the Motion Offense for basketball. 80m; DVD. **A:** Family. **P:** Education. **U:** Home, Institution. **Spo-Rec:** Basketball, Athletic Instruction/Coaching. **Acq:** Purchase. **Dist:** Championship Productions. $39.99.

Bruce Weber: Motion Zone Offense 2004
Coach Bruce Weber discusses and demonstrates techniques for using the Motion Zone Offense. 49m; DVD. **A:** Family. **P:** Education. **U:** Home, Institution. **Spo-Rec:** Basketball, Athletic Instruction/Coaching. **Acq:** Purchase. **Dist:** Championship Productions. $39.99.

Bruce Weber: Skill Set for Offensive Improvement 2009
Coach Bruce Weber demonstrates drills for improving a basketball team's offensive abilities. 70m; DVD. **A:** Family. **P:** Education. **U:** Home, Institution. **Spo-Rec:** Basketball, Athletic Instruction/Coaching. **Acq:** Purchase. **Dist:** Championship Productions. $39.99.

Bruce Willis: Return of Bruno 1988
Music video tale of the selling of Bruno's soul. 60m; VHS. **C:** Bruce Willis. **Pr:** HBO. **A:** Jr. High-Adult. **P:** Entertainment. **U:** Home. **Mov-Ent:** Music Video. **Acq:** Purchase. **Dist:** Music Video Distributors. $19.95.

Bruckner: Symphony No. 4 2012 (Unrated)
Recorded presentation of Bruckner's Symphony No.4, conducted by Franz Welser-Most and played by the Cleveland Orchestra. 74m; DVD, Blu-Ray. **A:** Family. **P:** Entertainment. **U:** Home. **L:** English. **Gen-Edu:** Music--Classical, Music--Performance. **Acq:** Purchase. **Dist:** Arthaus Musik. $39.99 24.99.

Bruckner: Symphony No. 7 1978
The Chicago Symphony Orchestra performs Bruckner conducted by Sir Georg Solti. Includes a six minute interview. 81m; VHS. **A:** Jr. High-Adult. **P:** Entertainment. **U:** Home. **Mov-Ent:** Music Video, Music--Performance. **Acq:** Purchase. **Dist:** Music Video Distributors. $24.95.

Bruckner: Symphony No. 7 in E Major 2014 (Unrated)
Actor Daniel Barenboim performs in this latest interpretation of Anton Bruckner's symphony. 72m; DVD, Blu-Ray. **A:** Family. **P:** Entertainment. **U:** Home. **L:** English. **Gen-Edu:** Music--Performance, Music--Classical. **Acq:** Purchase. **Dist:** Accentus Music. $39.99 24.99.

Bruckner: Symphony No. 8 1991
The Vienna Philharmonic performs the composer's personal favorite. 85m; VHS, DVD, Blu-Ray. **C:** Conducted by Herbert von Karajan. **Pr:** Polygram Music Video. **A:** Family. **P:** Entertainment. **U:** Home. **Fin-Art:** Music--Classical. **Acq:** Purchase. **Dist:** Music Video Distributors. $24.95.

Bruckner: The Mature Symphonies, Symphonie 5 2013 (Unrated)
Anton Bruckner and the Berlin Staatskapelle Orchestra perform Symphony No. 5. 76m; DVD, Blu-Ray. **A:** Family. **P:** Entertainment. **U:** Home. **L:** English. **Gen-Edu:** Music--Classical, Music--Performance. **Acq:** Purchase. **Dist:** Accentus Music. $24.99 24.99.

Bruiser 2000 — ★½
First film from horror icon Romero in more than seven years offers a great central premise, but little else. Henry Creedlow (Flemyng) is a nice guy who gets used by everyone around him. His cheating wife, his overbearing boss, and his dishonest stock broker all push Henry around, but he never stands up for himself. That is, until the day that he wakes up to find that his face has been replaced by a blank white mask. Being "faceless" allows Henry to assert himself and get revenge. The film is boring and filled with many unlikable characters, the worst of which is Henry. The last act is simply absurd and one can't help but wonder what has happened to the once great Romero. 99m; VHS, DVD, Wide. **C:** Jason Flemyng; Peter Stormare; Leslie Hope; Nina Garbiras; Tom Atkins; Jeff Monahan; Directed by George A. Romero; Written by George A. Romero; Cinematography by Adam Swica; Music by Donald Rubinstein. **A:** Sr. High-Adult. **P:** Entertainment. **U:** Home. **Mov-Ent:** Horror. **Acq:** Purchase. **Dist:** Movies Unlimited; Alpha Video.

Brujo: Shaman 1978
Explores shamanism and curing among the Mazatec Indians of Oaxaca, Mexico, and among two groups of Maya Indians in southern Mexico and Guatemala. 55m; VHS, 3/4 U. **Pr:** Okexnon Productions. **A:** Sr. High-Adult. **P:** Education. **U:** Institution, SURA. **Gen-Edu:** Documentary Films, Anthropology, Mexico. **Acq:** Purchase. **Dist:** Documentary Educational Resources.

Bruno 2009 (R) — ★
Really, did Baron Cohen actually think this character was funny or was he merely being smug and cynical? After "Borat," it's time to retire this shtick of a ridiculously stupid—or in this case, flamboyant and stupid—staged character intersecting with 'real' people and situations. Over-the-top gay Austrian fashionista Bruno heads to L.A. to become a 'superstar' though, like some reality TV show participant, he lacks any talent except that of relentless self-promotion. The sexual content is constantly crude rather than provocative. Erratic, nausea-inducing, and takes a turn for the nasty. 83m; DVD. **C:** Sacha Baron Cohen; Directed by Larry Charles; Written by Sacha Baron Cohen; Music by Erran Baron Cohen. **Pr:** Universal Pictures. **A:** College-Adult. **P:** Entertainment. **U:** Home. **L:** English. **Mov-Ent. Acq:** Purchase. **Dist:** Universal Studios Home Video.

Bruno Bozzetto: Animator, Vol. 1 1990
Eight films from "Allegro Non Troppo" animator Bozzetto, offering an innovative mix of color changes, after images, abstracts and shifting backdrops. Bozzetto's stinging sense of humor is prevalent. 60m; VHS, 3/4 U. **Pr:** Texture Films Inc. **A:** Primary-Adult. **P:** Entertainment. **U:** Home. **Mov-Ent:** Animation & Cartoons. **Acq:** Purchase. **Dist:** Tapeworm Video Distributors Inc. $39.95.
Indiv. Titles: 1. Grasshopper 2. Baby Story 3. Bacus 4. A Man and His World 5. The Sandwich 6. Self Service 7. Sigmund 8. Tennis Club.

Bruno Sammartino 1991
Interviews and highlights from the legendary wrestler's career comprise this career retrospective. 30m; VHS. **C:** Bruno Sammartino. **Pr:** Front Row. **A:** Sr. High-Adult. **P:** Entertainment. **U:** Home. **Spo-Rec:** Sports--General. **Acq:** Purchase. **Dist:** Front Row Entertainment. $9.95.

Bruno Walter: The Maestro, the Man ????
Shows the conductor rehearsing Brahms's Symphony No. 2 with the Vancouver International Festival Orchestra and discussing his art with music critic Albert Goldberg. ?m; VHS. **A:** Adult. **P:** Entertainment. **U:** Home. **Fin-Art:** Music--Classical, Music--Performance. **Acq:** Purchase. **Dist:** Video Artists International. $29.95.

Brush Dance 1986
Provides a portrait of Xiao Kejia, a 20-year-old Chinese girl who is one of China's master calligraphers. Throughout the film, she demonstrates and explains her art. 21m; VHS, 3/4 U, Special order formats. **Pr:** Centre Productions, Inc. **A:** Sr. High-Adult. **P:** Education. **U:** Institution, SURA. **Gen-Edu:** Documentary Films, Art & Artists, China. **Acq:** Purchase, Rent/Lease. **Dist:** Clear Vue Inc. $259.00.

Brush Those Teeth and Dentures: Mouth Care for the Dependent Elderly ????
Demonstrates to nursing assistants how to brush another person's teeth and clean dentures. 22m; VHS. **A:** Adult. **P:** Vocational. **U:** Institution. **Hea-Sci:** Mental Health, Occupational Training, Medical Education. **Acq:** Purchase. **Dist:** University of Maryland. $150.00.

Brush with Fate 2003 — ★★
Mousy teacher Cornelia (Close) is in possession of a 300-year-old Dutch painting called "Girl in Hyacinth Blue." It's possibly a Vermeer but Cornelia is afraid to find out since she may not be the legal owner. Still Cornelia would like new art professor Richard (Gibson) to give her his opinion. But the painting's history (told in flashbacks) has caused its previous owners trouble as well. Based on the novel by Susan Vreeland. 100m; VHS, DVD. **C:** Glenn Close; Thomas Gibson; Ellen Burstyn; Phyllida Law; Kelly Macdonald; Patrick Bergin; Directed by Brent Shields; Written by Richard Russo; Cinematography by Eric Van Haren Noman; Music by Lawrence Shragge. **A:** Jr. High-Adult. **P:** Entertainment. **U:** Home. **Mov-Ent:** Art & Artists. **Acq:** Purchase. **Dist:** Alpha Video; Hallmark Hall of Fame; Movies Unlimited.

A Brush with Life 1994
Diane, a gifted artist with multiple personality disorder brought on by a childhood of abuse, struggles to free herself from this mental illness through a new art therapy program at the Louis H. Lafontaine Hospital in Montreal. 52m; VHS. **A:** Adult. **P:** Education. **U:** BCTV, Institution. **Gen-Edu:** Mental Health, Documentary Films. **Acq:** Purchase, Rent/Lease. **Dist:** First Run/Icarus Films. $245.00.

Brushing and Flossing Techniques 1983
A dental hygienist demonstrates how to prevent tooth decay and periodontal disease. 8m; VHS, 3/4 U. **Pr:** Coronet Films. **A:** Family. **P:** Education. **U:** Institution, SURA. **Hea-Sci:** Dental Care. **Acq:** Purchase, Rent/Lease. **Dist:** Phoenix Learning Group. $150.00.

Brutal Fury 1992 — ★
Detective Molly Griffin goes undercover at a local high school and discovers a secret female vigilante group, called the "Fury," which goes after the drug dealers and rapists preying on the school's students. Teenagers with an attitude. 97m; VHS. **C:** Tom Campitelli; Lisa-Gabrielle Greene; Annette Gerbon; Karen Eppers; Jennifer Winder; Allen Arkus; Directed by Frederick P. Watkins. **A:** Sr. High-Adult. **P:** Entertainment. **U:** Home. **Mov-Ent:** Education. **Acq:** Purchase. **Dist:** Unknown Distributor.

Brutal Glory 1989 (Unrated) — ★★
Set in New York City in 1918 and based on the true story of the boxer known as "The Real McCoy." Fascinating and detailed history of a period, a champion, and the man who made it happen. 96m; VHS. **C:** Robert Vaughn; Timothy Brantley; Leah K. Pinsent; Directed by Koos Roets. **Pr:** Lars International. **A:** Adult. **P:** Entertainment. **U:** Home. **Mov-Ent:** Boxing, Sports--Fiction: Drama. **Acq:** Purchase. **Dist:** No Longer Available.

Brutal Massacre: A Comedy 2007 (R) — ★★
Horror director Harry Penderecki's (Naughton) career has been plagued by boxoffice bombs and critical disdain and he hasn't had a money-maker in years. Harry's trying to shoot his low-budget comeback film, "Brutal Massacre," but the mishaps keep increasing, leaving him teetering on the edge while every move is being recorded by reporter Bert Campbell (Butta) for a behind-the-scenes documentary. 95m; DVD. **C:** David Naughton; Brian O'Halloran; Ellen Sandweiss; Ken Foree; Gunnar Hansen; Gerry Bednob; Vincent Butta; Directed by Stevan Mena; Written by Stevan Mena; Cinematography by Brendan Flynt. **A:** Sr. High-Adult. **P:** Entertainment. **U:** Home. **Mov-Ent:** Journalism. **Acq:** Purchase. **Dist:** Anchor Bay Entertainment.

The Brutal Truth 1999 (R) — ★★
Group of high school friends get together for a 10-year reunion at a secluded mountain cabin for a weekend of fun, but then learn that one of the gang, Emily (Applegate), has committed suicide. This leads to arguments and secrets revealed. 89m; VHS, DVD. **C:** Christina Applegate; Justin Lazard; Johnathon Schaech; Moon Zappa; Paul Gleason; Molly Ringwald; Leslie Horan; Directed by Cameron Thor. **A:** Sr. High-Adult. **P:** Entertainment. **U:** Home. **Mov-Ent. Acq:** Purchase. **Dist:** Movies Unlimited.

The Brutal Truth: A Violence Documentary 2001
Documentary on violence among American youth. 48m; VHS, DVD. **A:** Sr. High-Adult. **P:** Education. **U:** Home, Institution. **Gen-Edu:** Documentary Films, Violence. **Acq:** Purchase, Rent/Lease. **Dist:** The Cinema Guild. $275.00.

Brute 1997 (Unrated) — ★½
Schweiger is doing humanitarian work in Eastern Europe when he discovers a group of orphans who are being abused by institute director Postlethwaite. So he tries to come to their rescue. Based on a true story. English and Polish with subtitles. 90m; DVD. **C:** Til Schweiger; Pete Postlethwaite; John Hurt; Polly Walker; Ida Joblonska; Directed by Maciej Dejczer; Written by Cezary Harasimowicz; Cinematography by Paul Prokop; Arthur Reinhart; Music by Michael Lorenc. **A:** College-Adult. **P:** Entertainment. **U:** Home. **L:** English, Polish. **Mov-Ent:** Adoption, Child Abuse. **Acq:** Purchase. **Dist:** Phase 4/kaBOOM Entertainment.

Brute Force 1947 (Unrated) — ★★★½
Lancaster (in a star-making turn) is Joe, an inmate in an overcrowded prison lorded over by sadistic guard Munsey (Cronyn). When Munsey pushes the prisoners too far, Joe leads a daring prison break attempt. While some see this intense drama as heavy-handed (all of the inmates are victims of circumstance), the portrayals are compelling, and the story is first-rate noir. 102m/B/W; DVD. **C:** Burt Lancaster; Ann Blyth; Ella Raines; Yvonne De Carlo; Hume Cronyn; Charles Bickford; Whit Bissell; Howard Duff; Jeff Corey; Directed by Jules Dassin; Written by Richard Brooks; Cinematography by William H. Daniels; Music by Miklos Rozsa. **A:** Jr. High-Adult. **P:** Entertainment. **U:** Home. **Mov-Ent:** Suicide. **Acq:** Purchase. **Dist:** Image Entertainment Inc.

Brute Force: Air Weapons 1991
An historic exploration of the evolution of helicopters, bombers and fighter planes. Three tapes. 50m; VHS. **C:** Narrated by George C. Scott; Directed by Robert Kirk. **Pr:** Greystone Comms. **A:** Sr. High-Adult. **P:** Entertainment. **U:** Home. **Gen-Edu:** Documentary Films, War--General, Technology. **Acq:** Purchase. **Dist:** A&E Television Networks L.L.C.; New Video Group. $44.95.
Indiv. Titles: 1. Helicopters 2. Fighters 3. Bombers.

Brute Force: Ground Weapons 1991
Historic look at the development of various ground weapons from the tanks of WWI to the advanced technologies used in the Persian Gulf War. Three tapes. 50m; VHS. **C:** Narrated by George C. Scott; Directed by Robert Kirk. **Pr:** Greystone Comms. **A:** Sr. High-Adult. **P:** Entertainment. **U:** Home. **Gen-Edu:** Documentary Films, War--General, Technology. **Acq:** Purchase. **Dist:** A&E Television Networks L.L.C.; New Video Group. $44.95.
Indiv. Titles: 1. Tanks 2. Artillery 3. Infantry.

Brute Machine 1979
The "Mind-Body Problem" is explored through the use of fibre optics and analogies. How is the idea of action in our minds transferred into the act itself? 60m; VHS, 3/4 U. **A:** Sr. High-Adult. **P:** Education. **U:** Institution, SURA. **Hea-Sci:** Anatomy & Physiology, Philosophy & Ideology. **Acq:** Purchase. **Dist:** Home Vision Cinema.

The Brute Man 1946 — ★★
A young man who had been disfigured by his school mates goes out on a trail of revenge. Hatton is convincing in the title role, as in real life he was afflicted with acromegaly, an ailment that produces an enlargment of the bones in the face, hands, and feet. 62m/B/W; VHS, DVD. **C:** Rondo Hatton; Tom Neal; Jane Adams; Donald McBride; Peter Whitney; Directed by Jean Yarbrough; Written by George Bricker; M. Coates Webster; Cinematography by Maury Gertsman; Music by Hans J. Salter. **Pr:** PRC. **A:** Jr. High-Adult. **P:** Entertainment. **U:** Home. **Mov-Ent:** Horror, Handicapped. **Acq:** Purchase. **Dist:** Sony Pictures Home Entertainment Inc. $14.95.

Brutes and Savages 1977 (Unrated) — ★
A collection of footage of primitive societies surviving in the wild, devised for voyeuristic viewing. 91m; VHS. **C:** Directed by

Arthur Davis. **Pr:** MPI Media Group. **A:** Sr. High-Adult. **P:** Entertainment. **U:** Home. **Mov-Ent:** Sex & Sexuality, Wilderness Areas. **Acq:** Purchase. **Dist:** MPI Media Group. $79.95.

Bryan Adams: Reckless 1984
A conceptual music video featuring guitarist/vocalist Bryan Adams playing five songs from his "Reckless" album, including "Run to You." 30m; VHS. **C:** Directed by Steven Barron. **Pr:** Simon Fields; Limelight. **A:** Jr. High-Adult. **P:** Entertainment. **U:** Home. **Mov-Ent:** Music Video, Music--Performance. **Acq:** Purchase. **Dist:** Music Video Distributors; Sony Pictures Home Entertainment Inc. $14.95.

Bryan Bowers' Autoharp Techniques 1994
Autoharp virtuoso Bowers teaches advanced styles and techniques and offers advice on harp set-up, tuning, chord bar set-ups, pick use, and avoiding arm tension and injury. 60m; VHS. **A:** Jr. High-Adult. **P:** Instruction. **U:** Home. **How-Ins:** How-To, Music--Instruction. **Acq:** Purchase. **Dist:** Homespun Tapes Ltd. $39.95.

Bryan Ferry: Dylanesque Live—The London Sessions 2007 (Unrated)
Live studio performance of acclaimed musical artist Bryan Ferry of his album "Dylanesque," which features his interpretations of his favorite songs by Bob Dylan. 61m; DVD. **A:** Sr. High-Adult. **P:** Entertainment. **U:** Home. **Mov-Ent:** Music--Performance, Documentary Films, Performing Arts. **Acq:** Purchase. **Dist:** Eagle Rock Entertainment Inc. $9.99.

Bryan Ferry: New Town 1989
The former Roxy Music lead singer is featured in this live concert performance in Europe. Ferry performs songs "Don't Stop the Dance," "Avalon," "Bete Noir," "Slave to Love," "Kiss and Tell,""Boys and Girls," "Nimrod," "Limba," "The Chosen One," "Casanova," "The Bogus Man," "Ladytron," "While My Heart is Still Beating," "A Waste Land," "Windswept," "In Every Dream Home a Heartache," "New Town," "Love Is the Drug," and "Do the Strand." 88m; VHS. **Pr:** Warner Reprise Video. **A:** Jr. High-Adult. **P:** Entertainment. **U:** Home. **Mov-Ent:** Music--Performance. **Acq:** Purchase. **Dist:** Music Video Distributors. $19.98.

Bryan Kest: The Power Yoga Series 1996
Contains a tough, ashtanga-style workout. Emphasis is on form, breath and serenity. 150m; VHS. **A:** Adult. **P:** Instruction. **U:** Home. **Hea-Sci:** Fitness/Exercise, How-To, Self-Help. **Acq:** Purchase. **Dist:** Warner Home Video, Inc. $44.85.
Indiv. Titles: 1. Energize 2. Tone 3. Sweat.

Bryan Miller: Speed and Agility Training for Football 2014 (Unrated)
Coach Bryan Miller delivers a video clinic on athletic conditioning exercises for football players. 56m; DVD. **A:** Family. **P:** Education. **U:** Home. **L:** English. **Spo-Rec:** Athletic Instruction/Coaching, Football. **Acq:** Purchase. **Dist:** Championship Productions. $29.99.

Bryan Miller: Summer Conditioning Program for Football 2014 (Unrated)
Coach Bryan Miller discusses off season training concepts and techniques for football players. 57m; DVD. **A:** Family. **P:** Education. **U:** Home. **L:** English. **Spo-Rec:** Athletic Instruction/Coaching, Football. **Acq:** Purchase. **Dist:** Championship Productions. $29.99.

Bryce Canyon & Zion: Canyons of Wonder 1992
Explore two of Utah's wondrous canyons. Highlights include a balloon ride of Bryce Canyon and a visit to the Great Arch of Zion. 64m; VHS, CC. **Pr:** Reader's Digest. **A:** Family. **P:** Entertainment. **U:** Home. **Gen-Edu:** Travel, National Parks & Reserves. **Acq:** Purchase. **Dist:** Reader's Digest Home Video.

Bryce, Zion and Grand Canyon's North Rim 1991
A visual tour through the three national parks. 45m; VHS. **Pr:** Finley-Holiday Film Corporation. **A:** Family. **P:** Education. **U:** Home. **Gen-Edu:** Travel, National Parks & Reserves, U.S. States. **Acq:** Purchase. **Dist:** Finley Holiday Film Corp. $29.95.

The Brylcreem Boys 1996 (PG-13) — ★★
In September, 1941, Canadian pilot Miles Keogh (Campbell) and his crew are forced to bail out of their plane. They land in neutral southern Ireland, where they're interned in the local POW camp run by Sean O'Brien (Byrne). The camp holds both Allies and Germans—separated by only a thin wire fence. Keogh figures it's his patriotic duty to try to escape as does German officer Rudolph von Stegenbeck (Macfadyen), and problems compound when both soldiers are let out on day-release passes and, naturally, fall for the same lovely local colleen, Mattie (Butler). It's pleasant but unmemorable. 105m; VHS, DVD. **C:** Billy Campbell; Angus MacFadyen; William McNamara; Gabriel Byrne; Jean Butler; Joe McGann; Oliver Tobias; Gordon John Sinclair; Directed by Terence Ryan; Written by Terence Ryan; Jamie Brown; Cinematography by Gerry Lively; Music by Richard Hartley. **A:** Sr. High-Adult. **P:** Entertainment. **U:** Home. **Mov-Ent:** Drama, World War Two, Ireland. **Acq:** Purchase. **Dist:** BMG Entertainment.

Bryony Brind's Ballet: The First Steps 1988
Dance can be an essential part of any exercise program. This workout is designed to be used by individuals or groups. 45m; VHS. **C:** Byrony Brind. **Pr:** Kultur Video. **A:** Sr. High-Adult. **P:** Entertainment. **U:** Home. **Hea-Sci:** Fitness/Exercise, Dance--Ballet. **Acq:** Purchase. **Dist:** Music Video Distributors; Kultur International Films Ltd., Inc.; Princeton Book Company Publishers. $29.95.

BSCS Behavior Film Series 1974
This series relates the behavior of animals to human behavior. Programs are available as a series and/or individually. 12m; VHS, 3/4 U. **Pr:** Biological Sciences Curriculum Studies. **A:** Jr. High-Sr. High. **P:** Education. **U:** Institution, SURA. **Hea-Sci:** Psychology. **Acq:** Purchase. **Dist:** Phoenix Learning Group.
Indiv. Titles: 1. Language Without Words 2. A Member of Society 3. Observing Behavior 4. Parents? 5. What's Mine Is Mine.

BTK Killer 2006 (R) — **Bomb!**
Nonsensical and loathsome flick purportedly about Dennis Rader, the Wichita serial killer who wasn't caught for 30 years. The initials stand for Rader's methods: Bind. Torture. Kill. For some unknown reason, hack director Lommel pads things out by including non-related animal slaughter scenes. 82m; DVD, CC. **C:** Gerard Griesbaum; Directed by Ulli Lommel; Written by Ulli Lommel; Cinematography by Bianco Pacelli; Music by Robert Walsh. **A:** Sr. High-Adult. **P:** Entertainment. **U:** Home. **Mov-Ent.** **Acq:** Purchase. **Dist:** Lions Gate Entertainment Inc.

Bubba Ho-Tep 2003 (R) — ★★★
Elvis and JFK team up to battle the dark forces of Egypt, who threaten the residents of their East Texas convalescent home. Believable plot aside, director Coscarelli's delightfully wacky cult-concept comedy still manages to take the whole thing seriously, especially with an inspired performance from Campbell, playing it totally straight. In addition to the presumed-dead celebrities and world leaders, the small town of Mud Creek also attracts an Egyptian mummy known as Bubba Ho-Tep, who terrorizes the aged Texans. The feisty King and former Prez gleefully open a king-sized can of whoop-ass on the ancient terror. While flawed, it's still solid campy fun. Adapted from a short story by Joe Lansdale. 92m; VHS, DVD. **C:** Bruce Campbell; Ossie Davis; Ella Joyce; Reggie Bannister; Bob Ivy; Larry Pennell; Heidi Marnhout; Directed by Don A. Coscarelli; Written by Don A. Coscarelli; Cinematography by Adam Janeiro; Music by Brian Tyler. **Pr:** Don Coscarelli; Jason R. Savage; Silver Sphere; Vitagraph. **A:** Sr. High-Adult. **P:** Entertainment. **U:** Home. **Mov-Ent:** Aging. **Acq:** Purchase. **Dist:** MGM Home Entertainment.

Bubbe's Boarding House: Chanukah at Bubbe's 1991
These award-winning stories will win the whole family over as they teach about the traditions of Chanukah and Passover at Bubbe's place. 30m; VHS. **Pr:** Monterey Home Video. **A:** Family. **P:** Entertainment. **U:** Home. **Chl-Juv:** Children, Religion, Holidays. **Acq:** Purchase. **Dist:** Monterey Home Video; Music for Little People. $19.95.
Indiv. Titles: 1. Chanuka at Bubbe's 2. Passover at Bubbe's.

Bubbe's Boarding House: Passover at Bubbe's 1990
Viewers visit ancient Egypt in the time of the Pharaohs and learn about the Israelite's exodus. 30m; VHS. **A:** Preschool-Primary. **P:** Education. **U:** Institution. **Chl-Juv:** Judaism. **Acq:** Purchase. **Dist:** National Center for Jewish Film. $21.

Bubble 2006 (R) — ★★
Soderbergh's uneven, low-budget experiment features a non-professional cast portraying blue-collar workers at a small Midwestern doll factory. Overweight, middle-aged Martha's (Doebereiner) life consists of caring for her sick, elderly father and fussing over young, shy co-worker Kyle (Ashley). The boring predictability of their lives is shaken by a new co-worker, outgoing single mom Rose (Wilkins), and Martha baby-sits when Rose asks Kyle out on a date. Then one of the three is murdered and there's an investigation. It's all as minimalist and banal as the lives it depicts. Besides directing, Soderbergh shot the film under the pseudonym Peter Andrews. 73m; DVD. **C:** Debbie Doebereiner; Dustin Ashley; Misty Wilkins; K. Smith; Directed by Steven Soderbergh; Written by Coleman Hough; Cinematography by Steven Soderbergh; Music by Robert Pollard. **Pr:** Gregory Jacobs; Section Eight; Magnolia Pictures; 2929 Productions; HDNet Films. **A:** Sr. High-Adult. **P:** Entertainment. **U:** Home. **L:** English. **Mov-Ent:** Mystery & Suspense. **Acq:** Purchase. **Dist:** Magnolia Home Entertainment.

The Bubble 2006 (Unrated) — ★★
The westernized district of Sheikin St. in Tel Aviv seems far removed from the racial and religious conflicts plaguing the area. Lulu (Wircer) shares her apartment (and life) with two gay men: Yali (Firedmann) and Noam (Knoller), who is in love with Palestinian Ashraf (Sweid). Ashraf is living and working in the city illegally and his abrupt return to his home in Nablus leads to a last act that strains credibility. Hebrew and Arabic with subtitles. 117m; DVD. **C:** Ohad Knoller; Yousef (Joe) Sweid; Alon Friedmann; Daniela Wircer; Roba Blal; Shredy Jabarin; Directed by Eytan Fox; Written by Eytan Fox; Gal Uchovsky; Cinematography by Yaron Sharf; Music by Ivri Lider. **A:** College-Adult. **P:** Entertainment. **U:** Home. **L:** Hebrew, Arabic. **Mov-Ent:** Crime Drama, Israel. **Acq:** Purchase. **Dist:** Strand Releasing.

Bubble Boy 2001 (PG-13) — ★
Disney has finally jumped on the crude and offensive humor bandwagon, with a simplistic storyline involving the journey of Jimmy (Gyllenhaal), a naive guy born with an immune system deficiency that requires him to live in a germ-free environment, as he races across the country to stop his sweetheart (Shelton) from marrying a jerk. Jimmy constructs a mobile bubble and hits the road. Along the way, the alleged jokes manage to offend Christians, Hindus, Jews, Republicans, Latinos, Asians and circus freaks while still wallowing in boner humor. That'd be almost forgivable if the "humor" was actually funny. 84m; VHS, DVD, Wide. **C:** Jake Gyllenhaal; Swoosie Kurtz; Marley Shelton; Danny Trejo; John Carroll Lynch; Stephen Spinella; Verne Troyer; Dave Sheridan; Brian George; Patrick Cranshaw; Fabio; Directed by Blair Hayes; Written by Ken Daurio; Cinco Paul; Cinematography by Jerzy Zielinski; Music by John Ottman. **Pr:** Beau Flynn; Bandeira Entertainment; Touchstone Pictures. **A:** Jr. High-Adult. **P:** Entertainment. **U:** Home. **Mov-Ent:** Diseases. **Acq:** Purchase. **Dist:** Buena Vista Home Entertainment.

Bubble, Bubble, Toys, and Trouble 1975
The good and bad in children's toys is evaluated by the premise of having an evil witch manufacture the toys. 10m; VHS, 3/4 U, Special order formats. **Pr:** Consumer Product Safety Commission. **A:** College-Adult. **P:** Education. **U:** Institution, SURA. **Gen-Edu:** Consumer Education, Toys. **Acq:** Purchase. **Dist:** National Audiovisual Center.

Bubblegum Crash, Episode 1: Illegal Army 1991 — ★★½
Power-suited bank robbers elude the A.D. Police. This gang is much better trained and equipped than the cops. It seems like a job for the Knight Sabers except that their leader Sylia is out of town, Knight Saber Priss finally has a record deal and Knight Saber Linna is racking in the dough at the stock market. Only Knight Saber Nene, who works at A.D. Police headquarters, seems interested in going back into action. She does everything she can to help detectives Leon and Daley with the case and discovers that the bank robbers are actually a group of mercenaries. The story that started with the "Bubblegum Crisis" series returns. Like many sequels, it's a little less serious with more emphasis on action and the characters are presented with a little more humor than in the original. But it's still interesting and there is new mecha to ogle. 45m; VHS. **A:** Sr. High-Adult. **P:** Entertainment. **U:** Home. **L:** Japanese, English. **Mov-Ent:** Animation & Cartoons, Animation & Cartoons. **Acq:** Purchase. **Dist:** AnimEigo Inc.; Facets Multimedia Inc.; Tapeworm Video Distributors Inc. $24.95.
Indiv. Titles: 1. Illegal Army 2. Geo Climbers 3. Meltdown.

Bubblegum Crash, Episode 2: Geo Climbers 1991 — ★★★
Dr. Haynes, the research partner of Sylia's late father, finally achieves both their dreams by building a Boomer that is more human than any machine ever created. But, his joy is short-lived because he is murdered by the jealous Yuri, Sylia's father's other partner. Sylia sends the Knight Sabers to rescue the Boomer Adama, despite Priss grumbling that there's no such thing as a good Boomer. Filled with chase scenes that make Priss use her wits more than ever before as her prejudices are both challenged and reinforced by the likable Adama and the other Boomers they encounter. 45m; VHS. **A:** Sr. High-Adult. **L:** Japanese, English. **Mov-Ent:** Animation & Cartoons, Animation & Cartoons. **Dist:** AnimEigo Inc.

Bubblegum Crash, Episode 3: Melt Down 1991 — ★★½
Boomers suddenly declare that they've awakened and are part of the "revolution" before becoming violent. Sylia's brother Mackie contacts her with the frightening information that brand new Boomer programming has resulted in a virus aginst which existing software is powerless. The Knight Sabers mobilize for their greatest battle ever as they face a strangely familiar enemy bent on destroying the world through the absorption of data and energy. Lots of action and confrontations, but the plot is not as tight as it could be. The promising beginning builds to a suitable climax, but feels like something was left along the way as this three-volume series draws to a close. 45m; VHS. **A:** Sr. High-Adult. **L:** Japanese, English. **Mov-Ent:** Animation & Cartoons, Animation & Cartoons. **Dist:** AnimEigo Inc.

Bubblegum Crisis 3: Blow Up 1987
Mason, an executive at GENOM, has learned the identity of one of the Knight Sabres, and vows revenge as the heroines keep thwarting the corporation's plans. In Japanese with English subtitles or dubbed. 30m; VHS, DVD. **A:** Sr. High-Adult. **P:** Entertainment. **U:** Home. **L:** Japanese. **Mov-Ent:** Animation & Cartoons. **Acq:** Purchase. **Dist:** AnimEigo Inc.; Facets Multimedia Inc.; Tapeworm Video Distributors Inc. $34.95.

Bubblegum Crisis 5: Moonlight Rambler 1988
A group of Boomers who have escaped from an obiting space colony may be responsible for a series of vampire-like killings. When Knight Sabre Priss joins up with the renegade Boomers is she trying to destroy them from within or has she really turned traitor? In Japanese with English subtitles. 45m; VHS, DVD. **A:** Sr. High-Adult. **P:** Entertainment. **U:** Home. **L:** Japanese. **Mov-Ent:** Animation & Cartoons. **Acq:** Purchase. **Dist:** AnimEigo Inc.; Facets Multimedia Inc.; Tapeworm Video Distributors Inc. $34.95.

Bubblegum Crisis 6: Red Eyes 1989
Priss seems reluctant to work with her fellow Knight Sabres but what makes things worse is an imposter group of Knight Sabres wreaking havoc on MegaTokyo. In Japanese with English subtitles. 47m; VHS, DVD. **A:** Sr. High-Adult. **P:** Entertainment. **U:** Home. **L:** Japanese. **Mov-Ent:** Animation & Cartoons. **Acq:** Purchase. **Dist:** AnimEigo Inc.; Facets Multimedia Inc.; Ingram Entertainment Inc. $34.95.

Bubblegum Crisis, Episode 1 1987 — ★★★½
Mega Tokyo of 2032 is still recovering from an earthquake that split the city and halted construction on Aqua City. The powerful Genom corporation produces androids known as Boomers that sometimes go out of control. When the A.D. Police can't handle them, the Knight Sabers step into action. Beneath the slickest battlesuits ever created are nightclub singer tough girl Priss, A.D. Police officer Nene, aerobics instructor Linna and the group's leader Sylia. This episode not only recounts how the Knight Sabers and their mecha came to be, but also features them on a job. They're hired to recover a kidnapped girl, but there are lots of things about their assignment they haven't been told. A great episode that defines the term "cyberpunk" and has turned countless viewers into lifelong anime fans. More than ten years after its creation, it is still quite enjoyable to

watch, now inspiring some nostalgia for the time that produced it. Features an animated nightclub act by Priss and a bonus live action video of Kinuko Oomori singing the same song. 53m; VHS, DVD. **A:** Sr. High-College. **P:** Entertainment. **U:** Home. **L:** English, Japanese. **Mov-Ent:** Animation & Cartoons, Animation & Cartoons, Science Fiction. **Acq:** Purchase. **Dist:** AnimEigo Inc.; Facets Multimedia Inc.; Tapeworm Video Distributors Inc. $24.95.

Bubblegum Crisis, Episode 2: Born To Kill 1987 — ★★★
An "accident" kills Genom engineers working on a new type of Boomers. Irene from Linna's aerobics class is the fiance of one of the dead men. She believes there was something very wrong with the project he was working on and is determined to expose it to the media. The Knight Sabers realize that Genom is their enemy in this heartbreaking episode that finds them twice racing against time. Linna is featured in this story that impacts the rest of the series in several interesting ways. 30m; VHS, DVD. **A:** College-Adult. **P:** Entertainment. **U:** Home. **L:** Japanese, English. **Mov-Ent:** Animation & Cartoons, Animation & Cartoons, Science Fiction. **Acq:** Purchase. **Dist:** AnimEigo Inc.; Facets Multimedia Inc.; Tapeworm Video Distributors Inc. $34.95.

Bubblegum Crisis, Episode 4: Revenge Road 1988 — ★★¹/₂
A biker gang is being terrorized by a man in a specially rebuilt sportscar that's too fast for even the A.D. Police to catch. It turns out this very guy had his car rebuilt by the same mechanic Priss relies on to keep her bike in shape. At his urging, she and the Knight Sabers mobilize to keep an obsessed man from destroying himself or being destroyed by the A.D. Police. A sad, strange and reasonably enjoyable installment that comes down strongly on the side of victims. 40m; VHS, DVD. **A:** College-Adult. **P:** Entertainment. **U:** Home. **L:** Japanese, English. **Mov-Ent:** Animation & Cartoons, Animation & Cartoons, Science Fiction. **Acq:** Purchase. **Dist:** AnimEigo Inc.; Facets Multimedia Inc.; Tapeworm Video Distributors Inc. $34.95.

Bubblegum Crisis, Episode 7: Double Vision 1990 — ★★★
Genom inks a deal with a Texas company, but the principals are killed moments later by a giant crab mecha. Dr. McLaren, the only survivor, heads to Japan to begin production on a new type of boomer. Meanwhile, popular singing star Vision is also coming to Japan for a concert tour. Really, she's Reika, older sister of Linna's friend Irene. She's now in the upper echelons of a powerful secret organization. This touching and action-packed story sees the Knight Sabers facing tough opponents and focuses on Linna's desperate attempts to get through to her friend's sister before it's too late. 49m; VHS, DVD. **A:** College-Adult. **P:** Entertainment. **U:** Home. **L:** Japanese, English. **Mov-Ent:** Animation & Cartoons, Animation & Cartoons, Science Fiction. **Acq:** Purchase. **Dist:** AnimEigo Inc.; Facets Multimedia Inc.; Tapeworm Video Distributors Inc. $34.95.

Bubblegum Crisis, Episode 8: Scoop Chase 1990 — ★★★
Priss catches a girl photographer snapping away during a Knight Sabers' battle. The next day at her job with the A.D. Police, Nene is introduced to her boss' niece Lisa who's on break from high school and wants to try photojournalism. Confident she'll prove herself, Lisa confides to a startled Nene that it's her goal to expose the true identities of the Knight Sabers. A coming of age story for the determined and likable Lisa that features great Knight Sabers action and a close-up look at Nene. 50m; VHS, DVD. **A:** College-Adult. **P:** Entertainment. **U:** Home. **L:** Japanese, English. **Mov-Ent:** Animation & Cartoons, Animation & Cartoons, Science Fiction. **Acq:** Purchase. **Dist:** AnimEigo Inc.; Facets Multimedia Inc.; Tapeworm Video Distributors Inc. $34.95.

Bubblegum Crisis Music Video: Hurricane Live 2033 1990
The Knight Sabers are still battling the Boomer androids in Mega-Tokyo but they also have to have some fun. So the Tinsel City Rhapsody concerts are created. Seven music videos created from the animated "Bubblegum Crisis" series. In Japanese with English subtitles. 30m; VHS. **A:** Sr. High-Adult. **P:** Entertainment. **U:** Home. **L:** Japanese. **Mov-Ent:** Animation & Cartoons, Music Video. **Acq:** Purchase. **Dist:** AnimEigo Inc.

Bubbleology I and II 1988
Dr. Ron Bonnstetter, professor at the University of Nebraska, performs amazing feats with bubble soap and attempts to make the world's largest bubble in front of a class of second to eighth graders. 60m; VHS. **Pr:** Insights Visual Productions. **A:** Primary-Jr. High. **P:** Education. **U:** Institution, CCTV, SURA. **Gen-Edu:** Science. **Acq:** Purchase. **Dist:** Insights Visual Productions, Inc. $99.00.

Bucaroo Kid 1926
A fun action-filled Western. A rare find! 64m/B/W; Silent; VHS. **C:** Hoot Gibson. **Pr:** Mark Huffam. **A:** Sr. High-Adult. **P:** Entertainment. **U:** Home, SURA. **Mov-Ent:** Silent Films, Western. **Acq:** Purchase. **Dist:** Grapevine Video. $16.95.

The Buccaneer 1958 — ★★
A swashbuckling version of the adventures of pirate Jean LaFitte and his association with President Andrew Jackson during the War of 1812. Remake of Cecille B. DeMille's 1938 production. 121m; VHS, DVD, Blu-Ray. **C:** Yul Brynner; Charlton Heston; Claire Bloom; Inger Stevens; Charles Boyer; Henry Hull; E.G. Marshall; Lorne Greene; Directed by Anthony Quinn; Cinematography by Loyal Griggs; Music by Elmer Bernstein. **Pr:** Paramount Pictures. **A:** Family. **P:** Entertainment. **U:** Home. **Mov-Ent:** War--General, Biography: Law En-

forcement. **Acq:** Purchase. **Dist:** Facets Multimedia Inc.; Olive Films; Rex Miller Artisan Studio.

The Buccaneers 1995 (Unrated) — ★★★
Lavish adaptation of the Edith Wharton novel follows the adventures of four American girls in 1870s society. Nouveaux riche, the young ladies are unable to crack New York snobbery and, after vivacious Brazilian Conchita (Sorvino) manages to snag Lord Richard (Vibert), the others are encouraged by English governess Laura Testvalley (Lunghi) to try their luck in London. There, Virginia (Elliott), sister Nan (Gugino), their friend Lizzy (Kihlstedt), and Conchita all find hope and heartbreak among the English aristocracy. Wharton's novel was unfinished at her death and, though she left story notes, scripter Wadey concedes to changes. Made for TV. 288m; VHS, DVD. **C:** Carla Gugino; Mira Sorvino; Alison Elliott; Rya Kihlstedt; Cherie Lunghi; Connie Booth; Mark Tandy; Ronan Vibert; Jenny Agutter; Richard Huw; Greg Wise; James Frain; Michael Kitchen; Sheila Hancock; Rosemary Leach; Elizabeth Ashley; Conchata Ferrell; Peter Michael Goetz; James Rebhorn; E. Katherine Kerr; Directed by Philip Saville; Written by Maggie Wadey; Cinematography by Maggie Wadey; Music by Colin Towns. **Pr:** British Broadcasting Corporation; WGBH Boston. **A:** Jr. High-Adult. **P:** Entertainment. **U:** Home. **Mov-Ent:** Women, Marriage, Great Britain. **Acq:** Purchase. **Dist:** Movies Unlimited; Alpha Video. $59.98.

Buccaneer's Girl 1950 (Unrated) — ★★¹/₂
Charming swashbuckler. Pirate Frederick Baptiste (Friend) only attacks the ships of evil Narbonne (Douglas) as revenge for his father's death. During one of his raids, New Orleans entertainer Deborah (De Carlo) stows away and falls for the sea-faring Robin Hood. However, hoping to marry into money, Deborah sets her sights on an aristocrat, only to figure out that Baptiste has been leading a double life. 77m; DVD. **C:** Yvonne De Carlo; Philip Friend; Robert Douglas; Elsa Lanchester; Andrea King; Norman Lloyd; Jay C. Flippen; Directed by Fred de Cordova; Written by Joseph Hoffman; Harold Shumate; Cinematography by Russell Metty; Music by Walter Scharf. **A:** Jr. High-Adult. **P:** Entertainment. **U:** Home. **Mov-Ent:** Acq: Purchase. **Dist:** Movies Unlimited; Alpha Video.

The Buccaneers with Robert Shaw 1956
Features two episodes of the British adventure series that was a hit in the U.S. during the '50s. 60m/B/W; VHS. **C:** Robert Shaw. **A:** Family. **P:** Entertainment. **U:** Home. **Mov-Ent:** Television Series. **Acq:** Purchase. **Dist:** Video Resources.

Buchanan Rides Alone 1958 (Unrated) — ★★¹/₂
Loner Buchanan (Scott) befriends young Mexican Juan (Rojas) in a California border town run by the bickering Agry family. Juan kills a bullying Agry in self-defense, but he and Buchanan both wind up in the pokey. However, Buchanan manages to pit the Agrys against each other. 89m; DVD. **C:** Randolph Scott; Craig Stevens; Barry Kelley; Peter Whitney; Manuel Rojas; Tol Avery; L.Q. Jones; Directed by Budd Boetticher; Written by Charles Land; Cinematography by Lucien Ballard. **A:** Jr. High-Adult. **P:** Entertainment. **U:** Home. **Mov-Ent:** Western. **Acq:** Purchase. **Dist:** Sony Pictures Home Entertainment Inc.

Buck 2011 (PG) — ★★★
An engrossing look at Buck Brannaman, the real man behind (and consultant for) "The Horse Whisperer" as played by Robert Redford in the 1998 film (adapted from Nicholas Evans' 1996 novel). Overcoming the physical abuse inflicted upon him by his father as a child, Buck becomes an inspirational, unassuming, and tenderhearted horseman who gently but firmly trains his animals. Rookie director Meehl tags along with Buck as he crosses the country with the arduous task of helping both troubled horses and their often equally troubled owners. 88m; On Demand, Wide. **C:** Buck Brannaman; Robert Redford; Directed by Cindy Meehl; Cinematography by Luke Geissbuhler; Guy Mossman; Music by David Robbins. **Pr:** Julie Goldman; Sundance Selects; Back Allie Productions; Cedar Creek Productions; Motto Pictures. **A:** Family. **P:** Entertainment. **U:** Home. **Mov-Ent:** Documentary Films, Horses. **Acq:** Purchase. **Dist:** MPI Media Group; Amazon.com Inc.; Movies Unlimited.

Buck and the Magic Bracelet 1997 (PG-13) — ★★¹/₂
In the old west a teen and his dog escape an attack on their prospecting camp. They're aided in bringing the bad guys to justice by a shaman's magic bracelet. 99m; VHS. **C:** Matt McCoy; Abby Dalton; Felton Perry; Conrad Nichols; Directed by Tonino Ricci; Written by Fabio Carpi; Cinematography by Giovanni Bergamini; Music by Stefano Curti. **A:** Jr. High-Adult. **P:** Entertainment. **U:** Home. **Mov-Ent:** Adolescence, Pets, Native Americans. **Acq:** Purchase.

Buck and the Preacher 1972 (PG) — ★★¹/₂
A trail guide and a con man preacher join forces to help a wagon train of former slaves who are seeking to homestead out West. Poitier's debut as a director. 102m; VHS, DVD. **C:** Sidney Poitier; Harry Belafonte; Ruby Dee; Cameron Mitchell; Denny Miller; Directed by Sidney Poitier. **Pr:** Columbia Pictures. **A:** Jr. High-Adult. **P:** Entertainment. **U:** Home. **Mov-Ent:** Western, Slavery. **Acq:** Purchase. **Dist:** Sony Pictures Home Entertainment Inc. $14.95.

Buck Benny Rides Again 1940 (Unrated) — ★★¹/₂
Radio performer Benny (playing himself) boasts he's a regular cowboy type with a ranch in Nevada—claims challenged by rival Fred Allen. So Benny is forced to travel west, where he makes a fool of himself before accidentally capturing two outlaws while romancing singer Joan (Drew). Rochester is there to assist as well as others from the Benny program. 82m/B/W; DVD. **C:** Jack Benny; Ellen Drew; Virginia Dale; Eddie Anderson; Andy Devine; Phil Harris; Dennis Day; Directed by Mark Sandrich; Written by Edmund Beloin; William Morrow; Cinema-

tography by Charles Lang. **A:** Jr. High-Adult. **P:** Entertainment. **U:** Home. **Mov-Ent.** **Acq:** Purchase. **Dist:** Movies Unlimited.

Buck Privates 1941 (Unrated) — ★★¹/₂
Abbott and Costello star as two dim-witted tie salesmen, running from the law, who become buck privates during WWII. The duo's first great success, and the film that established the formula for each subsequent film. 84m/B/W; VHS, DVD, Blu-Ray. **C:** Bud Abbott; Lou Costello; Shemp Howard; Lee Bowman; Alan Curtis; Andrews Sisters; Directed by Arthur Lubin; Written by Arthur T. Horman; John Grant; Cinematography by Milton Krasner; Music by Charles Previn. **Pr:** Mark Huffam. **A:** Jr. High-Adult. **P:** Entertainment. **U:** Home. **Mov-Ent:** Comedy--Slapstick, Basic Training/Boot Camp. **Acq:** Purchase. **Dist:** Movies Unlimited; Alpha Video; Universal Studios Home Video. $14.95.

Buck Privates Come Home 1947 (Unrated) — ★★★
Abbott and Costello return to their "Buck Privates" roles as two soldiers trying to adjust to civilian life after the war. They also try to help a French girl sneak into the United States. Funny antics culminate into a wild chase scene. 77m/B/W; VHS, DVD. **C:** Bud Abbott; Lou Costello; Tom Brown; Joan Shawlee; Nat Pendleton; Beverly Simmons; Don Beddoe; Don Porter; Donald MacBride; Directed by Charles T. Barton; Written by John Grant; Frederic Rinaldo; Robert Lees; Cinematography by Charles Van Enger; Music by Walter Schumann. **Pr:** Robert Arthur; Mark Huffam. **A:** Family. **P:** Entertainment. **U:** Home. **Mov-Ent:** Comedy--Slapstick, Armed Forces--U.S., Immigration. **Acq:** Purchase. **Dist:** Movies Unlimited; Alpha Video; Universal Studios Home Video. $14.98.

Buck Rodgers on Creating Customer Commitment 1988
The IBM executive shows businesses how they can be sure to give the customer what he wants. 18m; VHS, 3/4 U. **C:** Buck Rodgers. **Pr:** American Management Association. **A:** Adult. **P:** Education. **U:** Institution, SURA. **Bus-Ind:** Business, Customer Service. **Acq:** Purchase, Rent/Lease. **Dist:** Home Vision Cinema. $595.00.

Buck Rogers Conquers the Universe 1939 (Unrated) — ★★
The story of Buck Rogers, written by Phil Nolan in 1928, was the first science-fiction story done in the modern superhero space genre. Many of the "inventions" seen in this movie have actually come into existence—spaceships, ray guns (lasers), anti-gravity belts—a testament to Nolan's almost psychic farsightedness. 91m/B/W; VHS, DVD. **C:** Buster Crabbe; Constance Moore; Jackie Moran; Directed by Ford Beebe; Saul Goodkind. **Pr:** Viacom International. **A:** Family. **P:** Entertainment. **U:** Home. **Mov-Ent:** Science Fiction, Space Exploration. **Acq:** Purchase. **Dist:** Image Entertainment Inc. $29.95.

Buck Rogers in the 25th Century 1979 (PG) — ★★
An American astronaut, preserved in space for 500 years, is brought back to life by a passing Draconian flagship. Outer space adventures begin when he is accused of being a spy from Earth. Based on the classic movie serial. TV movie that began the popular series. Additional series episodes are available. 90m; VHS, DVD. **C:** Gil Gerard; Pamela Hensley; Erin Gray; Henry Silva; Voice(s) by Mel Blanc; Directed by Daniel Haller. **Pr:** Mark Huffam. **A:** Family. **P:** Entertainment. **U:** Home. **Mov-Ent:** Science Fiction. **Acq:** Purchase. **Dist:** Movies Unlimited. $14.98.

Buck Rogers in the 25th Century: The Complete Epic Series 1979
Astronaut Buck Rogers' space probe is lost for 500 years and he's awakened in 2491 by the evil Draconians who are trying to take over the Earth. Buck is suspected of being a spy by the Earth Defense Directorate, although Commander Wilma Deering trusts him and they fight the Draconians together. In the overhauled second season, Buck and Wilma are crew members aboard the spaceship Searcher after a holocaust strikes Earth. 32 episodes. 1799m; DVD. **C:** Gil Gerard; Eric Gray; Pamela Hensley; Tim O'Connor; Wilfrid Hyde-White; Thom Christopher. **A:** Jr. High-Adult. **P:** Entertainment. **U:** Home. **Mov-Ent:** Television Series, Science Fiction. **Acq:** Purchase. **Dist:** Universal Studios Home Video.

Buck Rogers in the 25th Century: Vegas in Space 1981
From the popular science fiction television series comes the episode "Vegas in Space." Buck is assigned to protect the most beautiful woman in the universe from a kidnapping plot. Features former Playboy Playmate Stratten in her final television appearance. 47m; VHS. **C:** Gil Gerard; Erin Gray; Dorothy Stratten; Voice(s) by Mel Blanc. **A:** Family. **P:** Entertainment. **U:** Home. **Mov-Ent:** Science Fiction, TV Movies. **Acq:** Purchase. **Dist:** Universal Studios Home Video. $12.98.

The Buck Stops Here 197?
After a flashback to the days of the cattle drives, Connors summarizes the program's premise: the essence of any decision is the courage to make it. 6m; VHS, 3/4 U. **C:** Chuck Connors. **Pr:** Cally Curtis. **A:** Adult. **P:** Professional. **U:** Institution, SURA. **Bus-Ind:** Management. **Acq:** Purchase, Rent/Lease. **Dist:** Aspen Publishers, Inc.

The Buck Stops Here: Startup Capital 1991
Explains financial requirements for a new business including current-asset capital, fixed-asset capital, startup expenses, and fund for personal expense. 30m; VHS. **A:** Adult. **P:** Professional. **U:** Institution. **Bus-Ind:** Business. **Acq:** Purchase. **Dist:** RMI Media. $99.00.

Buckaroo Bard 198?
Actor Richard Farnsworth and cowboy Waddie Mitchell offer performances of Mitchell's poetry, portraying the cowboy life as

humorous, sentimental, nostalgic, and entertaining. Part of the "American Cowboy Collection." 56m; VHS. **A:** Family. **P:** Education. **U:** Home. **Gen-Edu:** Western, Documentary Films. **Acq:** Purchase. **Dist:** PBS Home Video. $14.95.

The Bucket List 2007 (PG-13) — ★½
Yes, that's as in "kick the bucket." Cliched sitcom finds cancer patients Edward Cole (Nicholson) and Carter Chambers (Freeman) getting the bad news that their time is very limited. Since Edward is a self-satisfied gazillionaire estranged from his family, he decides to indulge his every last whim and takes fellow patient Carter, a working-class married father, on their own buddy road trip 'round the world. Nicholson's crazy, Freeman's serious, and the scenery seems to be all computer-generated. 97m; DVD, Blu-Ray. **C:** Jack Nicholson; Morgan Freeman; Sean P. Hayes; Beverly Todd; Alfonso Freeman; Rowena King; Rob Morrow; Directed by Rob Reiner; Written by Justin Zackham; Cinematography by John Schwartzman; Music by Marc Shaiman. **Pr:** Craig Zadan; Neil Meron; Alan Greisman; Rob Reiner; Warner Bros. **A:** Jr. High-Adult. **P:** Entertainment. **U:** Home. **L:** English. **Mov-Ent:** Comedy-Drama, Aging, Cancer. **Acq:** Purchase. **Dist:** Warner Home Video, Inc.

A Bucket of Blood 1959 — ★★★
Cult favorite Dick Miller stars as a sculptor with a peculiar "talent" for lifelike artwork. Corman fans will see thematic similarities to his subsequent work, "Little Shop of Horrors" (1960). "Bucket of Blood" was made in just five days, while "Little Shop of Horrors" was made in a record breaking two days. Corman horror/spoof noted for its excellent beatnik atmosphere. 66m/B/W; VHS, DVD, Blu-Ray. **C:** Dick Miller; Barboura Morris; Antony Carbone; Julian Burton; Ed Nelson; Bert Convy; Judy Bamber; John Brinkley; Myrtle Domerel; John Herman Shaner; Bruno VeSota; Directed by Roger Corman; Written by Charles B. Griffith; Cinematography by John Marquette; Music by Fred Katz. **Pr:** American International Pictures. **A:** College-Adult. **P:** Entertainment. **U:** Home. **Mov-Ent:** Art & Artists, Cult Films. **Acq:** Purchase. **Dist:** Rhino Entertainment Co.; Sinister Cinema.

Bucket Truck Rescue 19??
Outlines proper rescue techniques involving bucket truck rescues. Contains information on elevated bucket rescues, with and without the quick release feature, as well as job planning, rescue practice, and job skills. Includes leader's guide and 25 program guides. 17m; VHS. **A:** Adult. **P:** Education. **U:** Institution. **Bus-Ind:** Safety Education, First Aid. **Acq:** Purchase. **Dist:** Williams Learning Network. $495.00.

Bucket Truck Shock Hazards 19??
Discusses precautionary techniques that should be used when working on electrical equipment while in a bucket truck. Includes information on insulation, boom operation, dielectric testing, pre-use field inspection, insualtion of nearby lines, and grounding of the truck. Also contains illustration of the path of electric current through both grounded and ungrounded trucks, as well as nearby workers. Includes leader's guide and 25 program guides. 9m; VHS. **A:** Adult. **P:** Education. **U:** Institution. **Bus-Ind:** Safety Education, Electricity. **Acq:** Purchase. **Dist:** Williams Learning Network. $495.00.

Buckeye and Blue 1987 (PG) — ★½
A hero turned outlaw, his 14 year-old female sidekick, and a gang known as the McCoys are all on the lam from the law in this western adventure. 94m; VHS. **C:** Robin (Robyn) Lively; Jeffery Osterhage; Rick Gibbs; Will Hannah; Kenneth Jensen; Patrick Johnston; Stuart Rogers; Michael Horse; Directed by J.C. Compton. **Pr:** John H. Cushingham; Nicholas Wen. **A:** Jr. High-Adult. **P:** Entertainment. **U:** Home. **Mov-Ent:** Western. **Acq:** Purchase. **Dist:** No Longer Available.

Buckle Up On-the-Job 1986
Seat belts don't only help people in cars, they save the lives of miners as well. 8m; VHS, 3/4 U. **Pr:** Mine Safety and Health Academy. **A:** Adult. **P:** Education. **U:** Institution. **Bus-Ind:** Miners & Mining, Safety Education. **Acq:** Purchase. **Dist:** U.S. Department of Labor, Mine Safety and Health Administration. $20.00.

Buckminster Fuller: Grandfather of the Future 1989
Inventor, architect and visionary Buckminster Fuller explains his key ideas about how to manage the Earth's resources in a way that creates peace and plenty. 24m; VHS, 3/4 U. **Pr:** Lionel Television Productions. **A:** Jr. High-Adult. **P:** Education. **U:** Institution, SURA. **Gen-Edu:** New Age, Natural Resources. **Acq:** Purchase, Rent/Lease. **Dist:** Education 2000, Inc. $29.95.

Buckminster Fuller on Spaceship Earth 19??
Teaching aid for art appreciation documents the creativity and work of Fuller, a designer, inventor, and futurist. 60m; VHS. **A:** Jr. High-College. **P:** Education. **U:** Institution. **Gen-Edu:** Art & Artists. **Acq:** Purchase. **Dist:** Crystal Productions. $49.95.

Bucks on the Fringe 19??
Showcases bow hunting Rocky Mountain mule deer in Utah and Nevada. ?m; VHS. **A:** Jr. High-Adult. **P:** Instruction. **U:** Home. **Spo-Rec:** Hunting, Sports--General. **Acq:** Purchase. **Dist:** Precision Shooting Equipment Inc. $30.00.

Buckskin 1968 (Unrated) — ★½
Slowmoving western about a marshall protecting townspeople from a greedy, land-grabbing cattle baron. 98m; VHS, Streaming, CC. **C:** Barry Sullivan; Wendell Corey; Joan Caulfield; Lon Chaney, Jr.; John Russell; Barbara Hale; Barton MacLane; Bill Williams; Directed by Michael D. Moore. **Pr:** Paramount Pictures. **A:** Family. **P:** Entertainment. **U:** Home. **Mov-Ent:** Western. **Acq:** Purchase. **Dist:** Paramount Pictures Corp.

Buckskin Frontier 1943 (Unrated) — ★½
Story is built around Western railroad construction and cattle empires in the 1860s. Cobb tries to stop the railroad from coming through by hiring Jory to do his dirty work. 75m/B/W; VHS, DVD. **C:** Richard Dix; Jane Wyatt; Lee J. Cobb; Albert Dekker; Victor Jory; Lola Lane; Max Baer, Sr.; Directed by Lesley Selander. **Pr:** United Artists. **A:** Family. **P:** Entertainment. **U:** Home. **Mov-Ent:** Western. **Acq:** Purchase. **Dist:** Grapevine Video. $9.95.

Bucktown 1975 (R) — ★½
A black man who reopens his murdered brother's bar fights off police corruption and racism in a Southern town. 95m; VHS, DVD, Wide. **C:** Fred Williamson; Pam Grier; Bernie Hamilton; Thalmus Rasulala; Art Lund; Robert (Skip) Burton; Carl Weathers; Directed by Arthur Marks; Written by Bob Ellison; Cinematography by Robert Birchall; Music by Johnny Pate. **Pr:** Filmways Pictures. **A:** Sr. High-Adult. **P:** Entertainment. **U:** Home. **Mov-Ent:** Black Culture, Civil Rights. **Acq:** Purchase. **Dist:** MGM Studios Inc. $59.98.

Buckwheat Zydeco: Taking it Home 1990
The Cajun-spiced band performs, "There's Good Rockin' Tonight," "Taking it Home," "Yaya," and other songs in concert. 55m; VHS. **Pr:** Polygram Music Video. **A:** Jr. High-Adult. **P:** Entertainment. **U:** Home. **Mov-Ent:** Music--Performance. **Acq:** Purchase. **Dist:** Music Video Distributors. $19.95.

Bucky Dent's Shortstop Skills 1993
Seasoned veteran short-stop Dent shares techniques for becoming a better short-stop, including backhanding, the crow hop, fielding ground balls, positioning, and more. Graphics, action footage, and different camera angles help make this a detailed presentation on the art of baseball. 50m; VHS. **Pr:** Sports Excellence. **A:** Jr. High-Adult. **P:** Instruction. **U:** Home. **How-Ins:** How-To, Baseball. **Acq:** Purchase. **Dist:** 411 Video Information. $19.95.

Bucky Larson: Born to Be a Star 2011 (R) — **Bomb!**
The most notable achievement of Swardson's first starring vehicle may be that it can now be referenced as one of the worst movies ever made?"Well, at least it wasn't as bad as Bucky Larson!" Bucky's an exaggerated hick who learns that his parents were once porn stars, so he takes off for Hollywood to pursue the family "business." A rare film that's so horrendous it seems purposeful given that it's hard to believe any producers or writers (Swardson, Sandler, and Covert) thought the crude humor worked somehow. Even the decent work of Ricci and Johnson can't overcome this atrocity. 97m; DVD, Blu-Ray. **C:** Nick Swardson; Stephen Dorff; Christina Ricci; Edward Herrmann; Don Johnson; Ido Mosseri; Kevin Nealon; Miriam Flynn; Directed by Tom Brady; Written by Nick Swardson; Adam Sandler; Allen Covert; Cinematography by Michael Barrett; Music by Waddy Wachtel. **Pr:** Barry Bernardi; Allen Covert; David Dorfman; Jack Giarraputo; Adam Sandler; Adam Sandler; Allen Covert; Happy Madison Productions; Miles Deep Productions; Columbia Pictures. **A:** Sr. High-Adult. **P:** Entertainment. **U:** Home. **L:** English. **Mov-Ent:** Pornography. **Acq:** Purchase. **Dist:** Sony Pictures Home Entertainment Inc.

Bucky O'Hare: On the Blink 1991
It's Bucky, the super-space rabbit, to the rescue when the innocent Koalas find their planet threatened by those web-footed rascals, the Toads. 47m; VHS, CC. **Pr:** FHE. **A:** Family. **P:** Entertainment. **U:** Home. **Chl-Juv:** Animation & Cartoons, Science Fiction, Fantasy. **Acq:** Purchase. **Dist:** Lions Gate Entertainment Inc. $12.98.

Bucky O'Hare: The Kreation Konspiracy 1991
The green-skinned, science-fiction rabbit takes on the evil, interstellar Toads in this animated adventure. This time, the Toads are using the polluted planet of Sludge to cook up their deadliest weapon yet. 47m; VHS, CC. **Pr:** FHE. **A:** Family. **P:** Entertainment. **U:** Home. **Chl-Juv:** Animation & Cartoons, Science Fiction, Fantasy. **Acq:** Purchase. **Dist:** Lions Gate Entertainment Inc. $12.98.

Bucky O'Hare: The Toad Menace 1991
The swash-buckling space bunny finds himself in all kinds of trouble when he is ambushed by a squadron of Toads. To add insult to injury, Bucky hears that his own planet has been taken over by the amphibian menace. 69m; VHS, CC. **Pr:** FHE. **A:** Family. **P:** Entertainment. **U:** Home. **Chl-Juv:** Animation & Cartoons, Science Fiction, Fantasy. **Acq:** Purchase. **Dist:** Lions Gate Entertainment Inc. $12.98.

Bud and Lou 1978 (Unrated) — ★½
Comedy/drama recounts Abbott & Costello's rise in Hollywood. While the story, based on the book by Bob Thomas, is interesting, the two funnymen in the leads can't pull off the old classic skits. 98m; VHS. **C:** Harvey Korman; Buddy Hackett; Michele Lee; Arte Johnson; Robert Reed; Directed by Robert C. Thompson. **Pr:** Bob Banner Associates. **A:** Family. **P:** Entertainment. **U:** Home. **Mov-Ent:** Comedy-Drama, TV Movies, Biography: Show Business. **Acq:** Purchase. **Dist:** j2 Global. $29.95.

Bud Powell 1959
Features jazz great, Bud Powell, live from Paris. 30m; VHS. **A:** Jr. High-Adult. **P:** Entertainment. **U:** Home. **Mov-Ent:** Music Video, Music--Performance, Music--Jazz. **Acq:** Purchase. **Dist:** Music Video Distributors. $59.95.

Budd Boetticher: One on One 1989
An interview with one of the more colorful characters of cinema history, noted director Budd Boetticher. Includes clips of Boetticher's films. Hosted by Tony Thomas. 58m; VHS. **Pr:** Sabado Film. **A:** College-Adult. **P:** Education. **U:** Institution. **Gen-Edu:** Interviews, Film History, Filmmaking. **Acq:** Purchase, Rent/Lease. **Dist:** The Cinema Guild; Silver Mine Video Inc. $350.00.

Buddha Assassinator 1979 (Unrated) — ★½
Young Kung-Fu enthusiast challenges a Ming dynasty lord to a duel to the death. 85m; VHS, DVD. **C:** Hwang Jang Lee; Mang Hoi; Lung Fei; Chien Yueh Sheng; Directed by Kar Wu Tung; Written by Yi Kuang; Tu Liang-Ti; Cinematography by Woo Kuo-Hsiao; Music by Chen Hsun-Chi. **Pr:** Lee Man Yiu. **A:** Sr. High-Adult. **P:** Entertainment. **U:** Home. **Mov-Ent:** Martial Arts. **Acq:** Purchase. **Dist:** Xenon Pictures Inc. $59.95.

The Buddha of Suburbia 1992 — ★★★
Satire set in late '70s suburban London follows the coming of age adventures of Karim (Andrews), the handsome son of an Indian father and English mother. His gleeful father Haroon (Seth) exploits the vogue for eastern philosophies he knows nothing about with lectures to the upper-middle classes while he carries on with devotee Eva (Fleetwood). When his mother finds out, Karim and his father move into central London with Eva, where Karim decides to take up acting in fringe theatre and sex while his friend, Eva's son Charlie (Mackintosh), experiments with the punk music scene. TV miniseries adapted by Kureishi from his novel. 220m; VHS, DVD. **C:** Naveen Andrews; Roshan Seth; Susan Fleetwood; Steven Mackintosh; Brenda Blethyn; John McEnery; Janet Dale; David Bamber; Donald (Don) Sumpter; Jemma Redgrave; David Bradley; Directed by Roger Michell; Written by Hanif Kureishi; Roger Michell; Cinematography by John McGlashan; Music by David Bowie. **Pr:** British Broadcasting Corporation. **A:** Sr. High-Adult. **P:** Entertainment. **U:** Home. **Mov-Ent:** Comedy-Drama, Ethnicity, Philosophy & Ideology. **Acq:** Purchase. **Dist:** BBC Worldwide Publishing Ltd.

Buddhism Comes to America 1991
Examines the philosophy of Buddhism, including Tibetan chanting and the Zen community. Also introduces D.T. Suzuki, Alan Watts and Richard Clark. 30m; VHS. **A:** Sr. High-Adult. **P:** Religious. **U:** Home, Institution. **Gen-Edu:** Buddhism, Religion. **Acq:** Purchase. **Dist:** Hartley Film Foundation. $49.95.

Buddhism: Footprint of the Buddha—India 1978
Travels to Sri Lanka and India, examining the type of Buddhism practiced throughout southeast Asia. From "Long Search" series. 52m; VHS, 3/4 U, Special order formats. **Pr:** British Broadcasting Corporation. **A:** Sr. High-College. **P:** Education. **U:** Institution, SURA. **Gen-Edu:** Documentary Films, Religion, Buddhism. **Acq:** Purchase, Rent/Lease. **Dist:** Time-Life Video and Television.

Buddhism in China 197?
The origins, expansion, and influence of Buddhism on political and cultural life in China is examined in this program. 30m; VHS, 3/4 U, EJ, Q. **Pr:** WCBS New York; Camera Three Productions. **A:** Sr. High-Adult. **P:** Education. **U:** Institution, SURA. **Gen-Edu:** Documentary Films, China, Buddhism. **Acq:** Duplication, Free Duplication. **Dist:** Camera Three Productions, Inc.

Buddhism: Requiem for a Faith 1968
Huston Smith guides viewers through the ancient rituals, continuous meditation, deep compassion, and the profound faith in the divinity of man which is part of the lifestyle of the Tibetan Buddhists living in a remote Indian refugee camp. 28m; VHS. **Pr:** Hartley Film Foundation. **A:** Jr. High-Adult. **P:** Religious. **U:** Institution. **Gen-Edu:** Religion, Buddhism, India. **Acq:** Rent/Lease. **Dist:** EcuFilm.

Buddhism: The Land of the Disappearing Buddha—Japan 1978
Travels to Japan, asking the question: if the Buddha of Sri Lanka met the Buddha of Japan, would they recognize each other? From "Long Search" series. 52m; VHS, 3/4 U, Special order formats. **Pr:** British Broadcasting Corporation. **A:** Sr. High-College. **P:** Education. **U:** Institution, SURA. **Gen-Edu:** Documentary Films, Religion, Japan. **Acq:** Purchase, Rent/Lease. **Dist:** Time-Life Video and Television.

Buddhism: The Middle Way of Compassion 19??
Traces the history of Buddhism, its development and art, and its influence on Asian philosophy and politics. Complete with study guide. 25m; VHS. **A:** Jr. High-Adult. **P:** Religious. **U:** Institution. **Gen-Edu:** Buddhism. **Acq:** Purchase. **Dist:** Harcourt Religion Publishers. $45.00.

Buddhism: The Path to Enlightenment 1977
Traces the life of a Buddha from his birth as a prince through time spent as a wandering mendicant in search of a solution for life's sorrow. 35m; VHS, 3/4 U, Special order formats. **Pr:** Hartley Productions. **A:** College-Adult. **P:** Education. **U:** Institution, CCTV, Home. **Gen-Edu:** Buddhism, Biography. **Acq:** Purchase. **Dist:** Hartley Film Foundation; EcuFilm.

The Buddhist Path 19??
Buddhist nun Detong Cho Yin explains the complete Buddhist path to Enlightenment in a set of six easy-to-follow tapes. Titles include: "Karma & Reincarnation," "Meditation," "Enlightenment," "Creation," "Emptiness," and "The Mandala." 60m; VHS. **A:** Sr. High-Adult. **P:** Religious. **U:** Home. **Gen-Edu:** Buddhism, Religion. **Acq:** Purchase. **Dist:** Hartley Film Foundation. $34.95.

Budding & Grafting 19??
Provides an introduction to the terminology, tools, and techniques used in budding and grafting. Also demonstrates five methods commonly used by professional propagators and home gardeners. Comes with teaching guide. 24m; VHS. **A:** Sr. High-Adult. **P:** Education. **U:** Institution. **How-Ins:** Horticulture, Landscaping, How-To. **Acq:** Purchase. **Dist:** CEV Multimedia; San Luis Video Publishing. $95.00.

Budding: New Life for Fruit and Nut Trees 19??
A specialist from the University of California demonstrates four basic principles associated with budding, offering easy to follow

step-by-step instruction. ?m; VHS. **A:** Jr. High-Adult. **P:** Education. **U:** Institution. **Gen-Edu:** Horticulture. **Acq:** Purchase. **Dist:** CEV Multimedia. $29.95.

Budding Opportunities: Careers in Floriculture 19??
Describes career opportunities available in the floriculture field, ranging from marketing and management to scientific research. Offers advice on job requirements. 14m; VHS. **A:** Jr. High-Adult. **P:** Education. **U:** Institution. **Bus-Ind:** Horticulture, Occupations. **Acq:** Purchase. **Dist:** CEV Multimedia. $49.95.

Buddy 1997 (PG) — ★★½
Animals run amok in the Lintz household. Mother hen Gertrude Lintz (Russo) raises just about everything from mischievous chimps to impressionable parrots on her estate. A baby gorilla (named Buddy, short for Budha) becomes part of the family, but as he grows in size, so does the difficulty in caring for him. Amiable tale of one woman's motherly bond with a gorilla includes convincing performances by Russo and an animatronic gorilla courtesy of Jim Henson's Creature Shop. Well-paced and very touching at moments, children will definitely enjoy the zany animal antics, and adults should be moved by the unusual relationship. Based on the book by Lintz. 84m; VHS, DVD, Wide, CC. **C:** Rene Russo; Robbie Coltrane; Irma P. Hall; Alan Cumming; Paul (Pee-wee Herman) Reubens; Directed by Caroline Thompson; Written by Caroline Thompson; Cinematography by Steve Mason; Music by Elmer Bernstein. **Pr:** Fred Fuchs; Steve Nicolaides; Francis Ford Coppola; American Zoetrope; Jim Henson Productions; Columbia Pictures. **A:** Family. **P:** Entertainment. **U:** Home. **Mov-Ent:** Animals, Family Viewing, Zoos. **Acq:** Purchase. **Dist:** Sony Pictures Home Entertainment Inc.

Buddy Barnes: Live from Studio B 1982
The renowned jazz pianist and composer performs with Sylvia Sims, including "My Ship," "Don't Fight It, It's Chemistry" and "I've Been to Town." 30m; VHS, 8 mm. **Pr:** Studio B; Sony Video. **A:** Family. **P:** Entertainment. **U:** Home. **Mov-Ent:** Music--Performance, Music--Jazz, Black Culture. **Acq:** Purchase. **Dist:** Music Video Distributors; Facets Multimedia Inc. $19.95.

Buddy Boy 1999 (R) — ★★½
Isolated by the need to care for his ailing mother (Tyrell), shy Francis (Gillen) begins a voyeuristic relationship with his sexy neighbor (Seigner). Strange but captivating film provides some gothic creepiness as well as commentary on the toll of enforced isolation. 105m; DVD. **C:** Aidan Gillen; Emmanuelle Seigner; Susan Tyrrell; Mark Boone, Jr.; Hector Elias; Harry Groener; Directed by Mark Hanlon; Written by Mark Hanlon; Cinematography by Hubert Taczanowski; Music by Graeme Revell; Brian Eno; Michael Brook. **Pr:** Fine Line Features. **A:** Sr. High-Adult. **P:** Entertainment. **U:** Home. **Mov-Ent:** Horror. **Acq:** Purchase. **Dist:** Image Entertainment Inc. $24.99.

Buddy Buddy 1981 (R) — ★★½
A professional hitman's well-ordered arrangement to knock off a state's witness keeps being interrupted by the suicide attempts of a man in the next hotel room. 96m; VHS. **C:** Jack Lemmon; Walter Matthau; Paula Prentiss; Klaus Kinski; Directed by Billy Wilder; Written by Billy Wilder; I.A.L. Diamond; Cinematography by Harry Stradling, Jr.; Music by Lalo Schifrin. **Pr:** MGM. **A:** Sr. High-Adult. **P:** Entertainment. **U:** Home. **Mov-Ent:** Comedy--Black, Suicide. **Acq:** Purchase. **Dist:** MGM Home Entertainment. $19.98.

Buddy Ebsen's Musical Collectibles 1990 (Unrated)
The television star pays tribute in his inimitable fashion to some musical greats of the 20th century. 58m; VHS. **C:** Hosted by Buddy Ebsen. **Pr:** Quality Video. **A:** Sr. High-Adult. **P:** Entertainment. **U:** Home. **Mov-Ent:** Musical. **Acq:** Purchase. **Dist:** Direct Source Special Products, Inc.

The Buddy Holly Story 1978 (PG) — ★★★½
An acclaimed biography of the famed 1950s pop star, spanning the years from his meteoric career's beginnings in Lubbock to his tragic early death in the now famous plane crash of February 3, 1959. Busey performs Holly's hits himself. 113m; VHS, DVD, CC. **C:** Gary Busey; Don Stroud; Charles Martin Smith; Conrad Janis; William Jordan; Albert "Poppy" Popwell; Directed by Steve Rash; Written by Robert Gittler; Cinematography by Stevan Larner; Music by Joe Renzetti. **Pr:** Fred Bauer; Edward H. Cohen. **A:** Jr. High-Adult. **P:** Entertainment. **U:** Home. **Mov-Ent:** Musical--Drama, Biography: Music. **Awds:** Oscars '78: Orig. Song Score and/or Adapt.; Natl. Soc. Film Critics '78: Actor (Busey). **Acq:** Purchase. **Dist:** Sony Pictures Home Entertainment Inc. $19.95.
Songs: Rock Around the Ollie Vee; That'll Be the Day; Oh, Boy; It's So Easy; Well All Right; Chantilly Lace; Peggy Sue.

Buddy L and Road Racing 1960
Features road racing sets including Johnny Lightning, Motorific, Coleco, and the Buddy L Collection. 45m; VHS. **A:** Family. **P:** Entertainment. **U:** Home. **Mov-Ent:** Television Series, Commercials. **Acq:** Purchase. **Dist:** Video Resources.

Buddy Rich 1985
Buddy Rich and his band play such standards as "Sophisticated Lady" and "One O'Clock Jump" along with "No Exit" and "Norwegian Wood" in this concert taped at King Street. 55m; VHS. **C:** Buddy Rich. **Pr:** Bogue-Reber Productions. **A:** Family. **P:** Entertainment. **U:** Home. **Mov-Ent:** Music--Performance, Music--Jazz. **Acq:** Purchase. **Dist:** Music Video Distributors. $29.95.

Buddy Rich and The Buddy Rich Band: Live at the Montreal Jazz Festival, 1982 199?
Live performance footage plus two rare clips of Buddy in his early years. 60m; VHS. **A:** Sr. High-Adult. **P:** Entertainment. **U:** Home. **Gen-Edu:** Music--Performance, Music--Jazz. **Acq:** Purchase. **Dist:** Hal Leonard Corp. $24.95.

Buddy Rich Memorial Scholarship Concert 1989
A number of drummers came together at the Wiltern Theatre in Los Angeles to give a concert in the memory of Buddy Rich. Series of four tapes. Also available individually or in two separate volumes. 120m; VHS. **Pr:** DCI Music Video. **A:** Jr. High-Adult. **P:** Entertainment. **U:** Home. **Mov-Ent:** Music--Performance, Music--Jazz. **Acq:** Purchase. **Dist:** Music Video Distributors. $149.95.

The Buddy System 1983 (PG) — ★★
A tale of contemporary love and the modern myths that outline the boundaries between lovers and friends. 110m; VHS, CC. **C:** Richard Dreyfuss; Susan Sarandon; Jean Stapleton; Nancy Allen; Wil Wheaton; Edward Winter; Keene Curtis; Directed by Glenn Jordan; Written by Mary Agnes Donoghue. **Pr:** Alain Chammas; 20th Century-Fox. **A:** Sr. High-Adult. **P:** Entertainment. **U:** Home. **Mov-Ent:** Comedy-Drama, Romance. **Acq:** Purchase. **Dist:** $59.98.

Buddy's Song 1991 (R) — ★★
A '60s coming of age tale, only in this case it's the father and not the son who needs to grow up. Dad (Daltrey) is more interested in hanging out with his no-account musician friends than in looking after his family. Although he's not above meddling in his teenage son's musical career, which could be the success his father's never was. Based on the novel by Nigel Hinton who also did the screenplay. British teen idol Hawkes (in his film debut) had a top ten hit song from the film with "The One and Only." 106m; VHS, CC. **C:** Roger Daltrey; Chesney Hawkes; Sharon Duce; Michael Elphick; Douglas Hodge; Lee Ross; James Aubrey; Liza Walker; Directed by Claude Whatham; Written by Nigel Hinton; Cinematography by John Hooper; Music by Roger Daltrey; John Grover. **Pr:** Roy Baird; Bill Curbishley; Roger Daltrey; Roger Daltrey. **A:** Sr. High-Adult. **P:** Entertainment. **U:** Home. **Mov-Ent:** Comedy-Drama. **Acq:** Purchase. **Dist:** Baker and Taylor; CinemaNow Inc. $89.95.

Budgeting 1986
An illustrative program for the business owner in how to balance the company's budget so as to move onto an upward course. 30m; VHS, 8 mm, 3/4 U, Special order formats. **C:** John Cleese. **Pr:** Peter Robinson; Video Arts Limited. **A:** College-Adult. **P:** Education. **U:** Institution, Home. **Bus-Ind:** Business, Management, Finance. **Acq:** Purchase, Rent/Lease. **Dist:** Video Arts, Inc. $790.00.

Budgeting and Handling Money 1991
Outlines a practical budget plan for teens, and explains concepts such as sales tax, income tax forms, charge account, et cetera. 15m; VHS. **A:** Jr. High-Sr. High. **P:** Education. **U:** Institution. **Gen-Edu:** Home Economics, Finance. **Acq:** Purchase. **Dist:** Cambridge Educational. $79.00.

Budgeting Your Money 1976
Four young people discuss various methods of keeping a budget. 13m; VHS, 3/4 U. **Pr:** Coronet Films. **A:** Jr. High-Adult. **P:** Education. **U:** Institution, SURA. **Gen-Edu:** Personal Finance, Adolescence. **Acq:** Purchase, Rent/Lease. **Dist:** Phoenix Learning Group. $235.00.

Budgets Aren't for Push-Overs: Budgeting, Goal-Setting, and Record-Keeping 1994
Part of a series offering instruction on money management. 15m; VHS. **A:** Adult. **P:** Education. **U:** Institution. **Gen-Edu:** Finance. **Acq:** Purchase. **Dist:** RMI Media. $49.00.

Budgets, Deficits, and the Public Debt 1992
Presents an interview with Dr. Joseph Minarik from the Joint Economic Committee. 60m; VHS. **A:** Adult. **P:** Education. **U:** Institution. **Gen-Edu:** Economics. **Acq:** Purchase. **Dist:** RMI Media. $89.00.

Budo Sai: The Spirit of the Samurai 1993
A dozen of the world's top martial arts experts convene for the Budo Sai Festival, demonstrating a variety of moves and the preparation required to enact them properly. Includes kendo, karate, and aikido lessons. 60m; VHS. **A:** Sr. High-Adult. **P:** Instruction. **U:** Home. **Spo-Rec:** Martial Arts. **Acq:** Purchase. **Dist:** Films for the Humanities & Sciences.

Budokon: Beginning Practice 2004
Provides a blended yoga and martial arts workout to build muscles and flexibility. 68m; DVD. **A:** College-Adult. **P:** Instruction. **U:** Home. **Hea-Sci:** Fitness/Exercise, Yoga, Martial Arts. **Acq:** Purchase. **Dist:** Collage Video Specialties, Inc. $14.95.

Budrus 2009 (Unrated)
Documentary following a Palestinian leader and his daughter who manages to unite Fatah, Hamas, and the Israelis when their village is threatened. 82m; DVD. **A:** Sr. High-Adult. **P:** Education. **U:** Home. **L:** English, Arabic, Hebrew. **Mov-Ent:** Documentary Films, Biography. **Acq:** Purchase. **Dist:** Arab Film Distribution. $19.99.

Budweiser: NASL Goals of the Year 1980-1983 1984
Highlights of the brightest moments in soccer from 1980 to 1983. 44m; VHS. **Pr:** NASL. **A:** Family. **P:** Entertainment. **U:** Institution, Home, SURA. **Spo-Rec:** Sports--General, Soccer. **Acq:** Purchase, Rent/Lease, Subscription. **Dist:** Reedswain Inc.

Budworks 1979
A profile of the civil conflict over the heavy timberland spray program used in New Brunswick since 1952, which barely kills the insects it supposedly does, and otherwise harms the environment. 35m; VHS, 3/4 U. **Pr:** Neal Livingston. **A:** Sr. High-Adult. **P:** Education. **U:** Institution, CATV, BCTV, SURA. **Gen-Edu:** Documentary Films, Ecology & Environment, Insects. **Acq:** Purchase, Rent/Lease. **Dist:** Green Mountain Post Films.

Buena Vista Social Club 1999 (G) — ★★★
American musician Ry Cooder assembled a number of aging Cuban musicians and singers, informally known as the Buena Vista Social Club, to record an album in Havana. The success of that 1997 venture led director Wenders to record this documentary as the group reunites for a concert tour that culminates in a 1998 performance at Carnegie Hall. 106m; VHS, DVD, Wide, CC. **C:** Ry Cooder; Directed by Wim Wenders. **A:** Sr. High-Adult. **P:** Entertainment. **U:** Home. **Mov-Ent:** Documentary Films, Music, Aging. **Awds:** L.A. Film Critics '99: Feature Doc.; Natl. Bd. of Review '99: Feature Doc.; N.Y. Film Critics '99: Feature Doc.; Natl. Soc. Film Critics '99: Feature Doc. **Acq:** Purchase. **Dist:** Lions Gate Television Corp.

Buffalo: An Ecological Success Story 1972
Documents the life story of the buffalo and the tremendous effort that has been made to preserve and extend this almost extinct species. 13m; VHS, 3/4 U. **Pr:** Encyclopedia Britannica Educational Corporation. **A:** Jr. High-Sr. High. **P:** Education. **U:** Institution, SURA. **L:** English, Spanish. **Hea-Sci:** Documentary Films, Ecology & Environment, Wildlife. **Acq:** Purchase, Rent/Lease, Trade-in. **Dist:** Encyclopedia Britannica.

Buffalo Bill 1944 (Unrated) — ★★
A light, fictionalized account of the life and career of Bill Cody, from frontier hunter to showman. 89m; VHS, DVD, CC. **C:** Joel McCrea; Maureen O'Hara; Linda Darnell; Thomas Mitchell; Edgar Buchanan; Anthony Quinn; Moroni Olsen; Sidney Blackmer; Directed by William A. Wellman; Cinematography by Leon Shamroy. **Pr:** 20th Century-Fox. **A:** Family. **P:** Entertainment. **U:** Home. **Mov-Ent:** Western. **Acq:** Purchase. **Dist:** Movies Unlimited; Alpha Video. $39.98.

Buffalo Bill & the Indians 1976 (PG) — ★★★
A perennially underrated Robert Altman historical pastiche, portraying the famous Wild West character as a charlatan and shameless exemplar of encroaching imperialism. Great all-star cast amid Altman's signature mise-en-scene chaos. 135m; VHS, DVD, Wide. **C:** Paul Newman; Geraldine Chaplin; Joel Grey; Will Sampson; Harvey Keitel; Burt Lancaster; Kevin McCarthy; Directed by Robert Altman; Written by Robert Altman; Alan Rudolph; Music by Richard Baskin. **Pr:** David Susskind. **A:** Sr. High-Adult. **P:** Entertainment. **U:** Home. **Mov-Ent:** Western. **Acq:** Purchase. **Dist:** Alpha Video; Movies Unlimited; MGM Home Entertainment. $19.98.

Buffalo Bill, Jr. 1955
Includes two rip roarin' episodes featuring the marshall of Wileyville, Texas and his sister, Calamity: "Grave of the Monsters," and "Legacy of Jesse James." 55m; VHS. **C:** Dick(ie) Jones; Nancy Gilbert. **A:** Family. **P:** Entertainment. **U:** Home. **Mov-Ent:** Television Series, Western. **Acq:** Purchase. **Dist:** Moviecraft Home Video. $19.95.

Buffalo Bill, Jr. 1955
Two episodes of the television western series: "Legacy of Jesse James" and "Fugitive from Injustice." 50m/B/W; VHS. **C:** Dick(ie) Jones. **Pr:** CBS. **A:** Family. **P:** Entertainment. **U:** Home. **Mov-Ent:** Western, Television Series. **Acq:** Purchase, Rent/Lease. **Dist:** Rex Miller Artisan Studio. $24.95.

Buffalo Bill, Jr. 1955
Features four episodes from the western crime show from the '50s, including "The Death of Johnny Ringo," "Red Hawk," "The Fight for Texas," and "Empire Pass." 100m/B/W; VHS. **C:** Dick(ie) Jones. **A:** Jr. High-Adult. **P:** Entertainment. **U:** Home. **Mov-Ent:** Television Series. **Acq:** Purchase. **Dist:** Shokus Video. $24.95.

Buffalo Bill, Jr.: Blazing Guns/Adventures of Kit Carson: Devil at Angels Camp 195?
These two early TV Westerns share a common villain. Both were transferred from original prints. 52m/B/W; VHS. **C:** Dick(ie) Jones; Nancy Gilbert; Harry Cheshire; Bill Williams; Don Diamond; Kirk Alyn. **A:** Family. **P:** Entertainment. **U:** Home. **Mov-Ent:** Western, Television Series. **Acq:** Purchase. **Dist:** Grapevine Video. $9.95.

Buffalo Bill Rides Again 1947 — ★½
With an Indian uprising on the horizon, Buffalo Bill is called in. Mr. Bill finds land swindlers pitting natives against ranchers, but there's precious little action or interest here. 68m; VHS, DVD. **C:** Richard Arlen; Jennifer Holt; Edward Cassidy; Edmund Cobb; Charles Stevens; Directed by Bernard B. Ray; Written by Barney A. Sarecky; Cinematography by Robert E. Cline. **Pr:** Jack Schwartz Productions. **A:** Family. **P:** Entertainment. **U:** Home. **Mov-Ent:** Western, Native Americans. **Acq:** Purchase. **Dist:** Sinister Cinema.

Buffalo Bill: The First and Second Seasons 1983
Coleman stars as self-serving, chauvinistic, sleazy TV talk-show host Bill Bittinger in this offbeat comedy that featured the daily crises at the Buffalo, New York station and its harried workers. 26 episodes. 630m; DVD, CC. **C:** Dabney Coleman; Joanna Cassidy; Geena Davis; Max Wright; John Fielder. **A:** Jr. High-Adult. **P:** Entertainment. **U:** Home. **Mov-Ent:** Television Series. **Acq:** Purchase. **Dist:** Lions Gate Entertainment Inc.

Buffalo Bills 1986: Good Enough to Dream 1987
The Bills put in a memorable season and began paving the way for future glory. 23m; VHS. **Pr:** NFL Films. **A:** Family. **P:** Entertainment. **U:** Home. **Spo-Rec:** Football. **Acq:** Purchase. **Dist:** NFL Films Video. $14.98.

Buffalo Bills 1987: Something to Shout About 1988
The Bills showed marked improvement and would soon be on the road to victory. 22m; VHS. **Pr**: NFL Films. **A**: Family. **P**: Entertainment. **U**: Home. **Spo-Rec**: Football. **Acq**: Purchase. **Dist**: NFL Films Video. $14.98.

Buffalo Bills 1988: A Team, A Town, A Dream 1989
Jim "Machine Gun" Kelly leads the Bills to an AFC East title, but the Bills eventually fall to the Bengals in the conference final. 22m; VHS. **Pr**: NFL Films. **A**: Family. **P**: Entertainment. **U**: Home. **Spo-Rec**: Football. **Acq**: Purchase. **Dist**: NFL Films Video. $14.95.

Buffalo Bills 1989 Team Highlights 1990
Highlights of the rocky road the Bills took to capture the AFC East and their rally that just missed taking them to the AFC Championship game. 22m; VHS. **Pr**: NFL Films. **A**: Family. **P**: Entertainment. **U**: Home. **Spo-Rec**: Football. **Acq**: Purchase. **Dist**: NFL Films Video. $14.98.

Buffalo Bill's Wild West Show 19??
Contains rare footage, taken between 1898 and 1912, of Buffalo Bill Cody's Wild West Show. 45m; VHS. **TV Std**: NTSC, PAL. **A**: Adult. **P**: Education. **U**: Home. **Gen-Edu**: History--U.S., Western. **Acq**: Purchase. **Dist**: Old Army Press. $24.95.

Buffalo Bills: Years of Glory. . .Years of Pain 1985
Recounts the 25-year history of the Buffalo Bills and features such stars as O.J. Simpson, Jack Kemp, and Frank Lewis. 28m; VHS. **C**: Jack Kemp; O.J. Simpson; Butch Byrd. **Pr**: NFL Films. **A**: Family. **P**: Entertainment. **U**: Home. **Spo-Rec**: Documentary Films, Football. **Acq**: Purchase. **Dist**: NFL Films Video. $19.98.

Buffalo Boy 2004 (Unrated) — ★★
Coming-of-age story set in 1940s Vietnam. Teenaged Kim is sent by his ill father Dinh to herd their two starving water buffalo to new pasture. Kim falls in with a tough group of buffalo herders, winds up with one buffalo, and tries to mend the rift with his father before the old man dies. Vietnamese with subtitles. 102m; DVD. **C**: Le the Lu; Nguyen Huu Thanj; Vo Hoang Nhan; Directed by Minh Nguyen-Vo; Written by Minh Nguyen-Vo; Cinematography by Yves Cape; Music by Ton That Tiet. **A**: Sr. High-Adult. **P**: Entertainment. **U**: Home. **L**: Vietnamese. **Mov-Ent**. **Acq**: Purchase. **Dist**: First Run Features.

Buffalo Chopper Setup 1984
Demonstrates how to dismantle and set up the buffalo chopper. 6m; VHS. **A**: Adult. **P**: Instruction. **U**: Institution. **Gen-Edu**: Cooking. **Acq**: Purchase. **Dist**: RMI Media. $39.95.

The Buffalo Creek Flood: An Act of Man 1975
The complete story of the coal waste dam burst that left 124 dead, and was labeled by the Pittston Coal Company "an act of God." 40m/B/W; VHS, 3/4 U. **Pr**: Appalshop Films. **A**: College-Adult. **P**: Education. **U**: Institution, Home. **Gen-Edu**: Documentary Films, Action-Adventure. **Awds**: Natl. Film Reg. '05. **Acq**: Purchase. **Dist**: Appalshop Films & Video.

Buffalo Creek Revisited 1984
A look years later at the flood-devastated community, its efforts to rebuild and the governmental obstacles. 31m; 3/4 U, Special order formats. **Pr**: Appalshop Films. **A**: College-Adult. **P**: Education. **U**: Institution, Home. **Gen-Edu**: Documentary Films, Action-Adventure. **Acq**: Purchase. **Dist**: Appalshop Films & Video.

Buffalo Girls 1995 (Unrated) — ★★½
Western saga, set in the 1870s, tells of the lifelong friendship between hard-drinking, hard-living Calamity Jane (Huston—who's not exactly any plain Jane) and buxom, soft-hearted madam Dora DuFran (Griffith). Dora's in love (but refuses to marry) rancher Teddy Blue (Byrne) while Calamity has a daughter by Wild Bill Hickok (Elliott) that she gives up for adoption. There's lots of rambling and commiserating over the changing and civilizing of the west and various man trouble. Based on the novel by Larry McMurty; originally a two-part TV miniseries. 180m; VHS, DVD, CC. **C**: Anjelica Huston; Melanie Griffith; Gabriel Byrne; Peter Coyote; Jack Palance; Sam Elliott; Reba McEntire; Floyd "Red Crow" Westerman; Tracey Walter; Russell Means; Charlaine Woodard; Liev Schreiber; Andrew Bicknell; Kathryn Witt; Directed by Rod Hardy; Written by Cynthia Whitcomb; Cinematography by David Connell; Music by Lee Holdridge. **Pr**: Sandra Saxon Brice; Suzanne Coston; de Passe Entertainment; CBS. **A**: Jr. High-Adult. **P**: Entertainment. **U**: Home. **Mov-Ent**: TV Movies, Romance. **Acq**: Purchase. **Dist**: Movies Unlimited. $9.99.

Buffalo Heart: The Pain of Death 1996 — ★½
Buffalo Heart decides to avenge the rape and murder of his daughter by tracking down her killers. 85m; VHS. **C**: Daniel Matmor; Alex Wexo; Craig Eisner; Directed by Daniel Matmor; Written by Daniel Matmor; Cinematography by Paul DeGruccio. **Pr**: Peter Greco; Tri-Line Entertainment, Inc. **A**: Sr. High-Adult. **P**: Entertainment. **U**: Home. **Mov-Ent**: Native Americans. **Acq**: Purchase. **Dist**: Tapeworm Video Distributors Inc.

Buffalo Jump 1990 (Unrated) — ★★★
An independent woman, working as a lounge singer in Toronto, returns to her home in Alberta when her father dies. To her surprise he has left her the family ranch and, to the surprise of everyone else, she decides to stay and run it. She hires a good-looking local man to help her out and they both discover that they want more than a working relationship. However, the fireworks really start when he proposes a marriage of convenience. Engaging performances and beautiful scenery help raise this romantic tale of opposites above the average. 97m; VHS, DVD. **C**: Wendy Crewson; Paul Gross; Marion Gilsenan; Kyra Harper; Victoria Snow; Directed by Eric Till. **Pr**: Panorama Entertainment. **A**: Sr. High-Adult. **P**: Entertainment. **U**: Home. **Mov-Ent**: Drama, Agriculture, Canada. **Acq**: Purchase. **Dist**: Hen's Tooth Video. $19.95.

Buffalo Rider 1978 (Unrated) — ★½
An adventure film depicting the real-life experiences of C.J. "Buffalo" Jones who worked to save the American buffalo from extinction. 90m; VHS. **C**: Rick Guinn; John Freeman; Pricilla Lauris; George Sager; Rich Scheeland; Directed by George Lauris. **Pr**: John Fabian-Dick Robinson Productions. **A**: Family. **P**: Entertainment. **U**: Home. **Mov-Ent**: Western, Animals. **Acq**: Purchase. **Dist**: No Longer Available.

Buffalo 66 1997 (Unrated) — ★★★
Billy Brown (Gallo) is a loser of epic proportions. He's named after the Buffalo Bills, notorious losers of Super Bowls. After he loses $10,000 on of those Super Bowls, he turns to a life of crime and promptly lands in prison. He gets out of jail as a man with a mission. Stumbling into a dance studio, Billy kidnaps the nubile Layla (Ricci) and forces her to pose as his wife for a visit to his parents. He had explained his five-year absence to them by saying that he was working for the CIA overseas with his new bride. His father Jimmy (Gazzara), a bitter ex-lounge singer, barely hides his disdain for Billy, and mother Janet (Huston) is so too obsessed with the Bills to interact with him. They both like Layla instantly, and she seems to take unexpected glee in playing her part. Former artist and rock musician Gallo also directed, co-wrote and composed the music for the film. 112m; VHS, DVD, Blu-Ray, Wide. **C**: Vincent Gallo; Christina Ricci; Anjelica Huston; Ben Gazzara; Kevin Corrigan; Mickey Rourke; Rosanna Arquette; Jan-Michael Vincent; Directed by Vincent Gallo; Written by Vincent Gallo; Alison Bagnall; Cinematography by Lance Acord; Music by Vincent Gallo. **Pr**: Chris Hanley; Jeff Sackman; Mike Paseornek; Cinepix; MUSE Productions; Lions Gate Films. **A**: Sr. High-Adult. **P**: Entertainment. **U**: Home. **Mov-Ent**: Comedy--Black, Family, Football. **Awds**: Natl. Bd. of Review '98: Support. Actress (Ricci). **Acq**: Purchase. **Dist**: Lions Gate Entertainment Inc.

Buffalo Soldier 1981
Dance and music video that portrays the story of the black soldier during the Civil War. Music by Quincy Jones and choreography by Carole Morisseau. 11m; VHS, 3/4 U, Special order formats. **Pr**: WTVS-TV Detroit; A&E (Arts & Entertainment) Network; Bravo Productions; Showtime. **A**: Adult. **P**: Education. **U**: Institution, SURA. **Gen-Edu**: Civil War, Black Culture, History--U.S. **Acq**: Purchase, Rent/Lease. **Dist**: Sue Marx Films, Inc.

Buffalo Soldiers 1992
Looks at the first African-American soldiers to ever serve the U.S. during peacetime—the soldiers of the 9th and 10th Calvary who defended the American frontier from 1866 until 1952. 50m; VHS. **A**: Jr. High-Adult. **P**: Education. **U**: Home. **Gen-Edu**: History--U.S., Black Culture, Armed Forces--U.S. **Acq**: Purchase. **Dist**: A&E Television Networks L.L.C.; New Video Group. $19.95.

Buffalo Soldiers 1997 (Unrated) — ★★★
Post-Civil War western concerns the all-black Cavalry troops, created by Congress in 1866 to patrol the west. They received their nickname from the Indians, who thought the black soldiers on horseback looked like buffalo. A former slave and by-the-book Army man, Sgt. Washington Wyatt (Glover) leads the chase for Apache warrior Victorio (Lowe) across the New Mexico Territory while trying tp deal with the common degradation suffered by his troops at the hands of white officers. Lots of cruelty and explicit violence. 120m; VHS, DVD. **C**: Danny Glover; Carl Lumbly; Bob Gunton; Tom Bower; Harrison Lowe; Glynn Turman; Michael Warren; Mykelti Williamson; Timothy Busfield; Gabriel Casseus; Directed by Charles Haid; Written by Frank Military; Susan Rhinehart; Cinematography by William Wages; Music by Joel McNeely. **Pr**: Gordon Wolf; David R. Ginsburg; John Watson; Pen Densham; Richard B. Lewis; Danny Glover; Danny Glover; Trilogy Entertainment Group; Citadel Entertainment. **A**: Sr. High-Adult. **P**: Entertainment. **U**: Home. **Mov-Ent**: Western, Black Culture, Native Americans. **Acq**: Purchase. **Dist**: Warner Home Video, Inc.

Buffalo Soldiers 2001 (R) — ★★½
Darkly satiric look at the military revolves around a supply unit of an American Army base in 1989 Germany. Leader of the pack is the bored, amoral Elwood (Phoenix) who gets his kicks and a few extra bucks by dabbling in the black market, dealing in heroin and illegal weapons, and other equally illicit activities. Soon, the newly prosperous Elwood is basically running things at the base until a new Top Sergeant (Glenn) cracks down. Elwood retaliates by dating Sarge's daughter (Paquin) but finds he's actually falling for her. Premiered at the Toronto Film Festival in 2001, then waited for a more appropriate release date, which never actually came (it's not exactly complimentary to the military). Based on a novel by Robert O'Connor. 98m; VHS, DVD, CC. **C**: Joaquin Rafael (Leaf) Phoenix; Scott Glenn; Anna Paquin; Ed Harris; Leon Robinson; Dean Stockwell; Elizabeth McGovern; Gabriel Mann; Shiek Mahmud-Bey; Michael Pena; Glenn Fitzgerald; Brian Delate; Jimmie Ray Weeks; Directed by Gregor Jordan; Written by Gregor Jordan; Eric Weiss; Nora MacCoby; Cinematography by Oliver Stapleton; Music by David Holmes. **Pr**: Rainer Grupe; Ariane Moody; Miramax Film Corp; FilmFour; Odeon Pictures; Good Machine; Grosvenor Park. **A**: Sr. High-Adult. **P**: Entertainment. **U**: Home. **Mov-Ent**: Germany, Satire & Parody. **Acq**: Purchase. **Dist**: Buena Vista Home Entertainment.

Buffalo Stampede 1933 — ★
Our heroes are involved in a plot to round up buffalo to sell for meat. 60m/B/W; VHS, DVD. **C**: Randolph Scott; Buster Crabbe; Harry Carey, Sr.; Noah Beery, Sr.; Raymond Hatton; Judith Allen; Blanche Frederici; Directed by Henry Hathaway. **Pr**: Paramount Pictures. **A**: Family. **P**: Entertainment. **U**: Institution, Home. **Mov-Ent**: Western. **Acq**: Purchase. **Dist**: Anchor Bay Entertainment. $19.95.

Buffer Zone: The Mental Health Professional in the AIDS Epidemic 1989
A discussion of the psychological side-effects of AIDS, and how mental health professionals can help patients cope. 25m; VHS, 3/4 U. **Pr**: Norman E. Baxley. **A**: Adult. **P**: Professional. **U**: Institution, SURA. **Hea-Sci**: Diseases, AIDS, Death. **Acq**: Purchase, Rent/Lease. **Dist**: Leo Media, Inc. $385.00.

Buffers 19??
Examines the behavior of the buffer system in response to the added acid or base and the Handerson-Hasselbach equation, and explains buffers as conjugate base-acid systems. ?m; VHS. **A**: Jr. High-College. **P**: Education. **U**: Institution. **Hea-Sci**: Biology, Chemistry, Science. **Acq**: Purchase. **Dist**: Educational Images Ltd. $54.95.

Buffers, Pads and Auto-Scrubbers 19??
Demonstrates daily procedures used in maintenance and upkeep of buffers, pads, and auto-scrubbers. 22m; VHS. **A**: College-Adult. **P**: Vocational. **U**: Institution. **Bus-Ind**: Job Training, Custodial Service, Industrial Arts. **Acq**: Purchase, Rent/Lease. **Dist**: AMS Distributors, Inc.

Buffet Froid 1979 (Unrated) — ★★★½
Surreal black comedy about a group of bungling murderers. First rate acting and directing makes this film a hilarious treat. From the director of "Menage." In French with English subtitles. 95m; VHS, DVD. **C**: Gerard Depardieu; Bernard Blier; Jean Carmet; Genevieve Page; Denise Gence; Carole Bouquet; Jean Benguigui; Michel Serrault; Directed by Bertrand Blier; Written by Bertrand Blier; Cinematography by Jean Penzer; Music by Philippe Sarde. **Pr**: Sara Film Productions. **A**: Sr. High-Adult. **P**: Entertainment. **U**: Home. **L**: French. **Mov-Ent**: Comedy--Black, France. **Awds**: Cesar '80: Writing. **Acq**: Purchase. **Dist**: Wellspring Media; Interama, Inc.; Tapeworm Video Distributors Inc.

Buffy the Vampire Slayer 1992 (PG-13) — ★★★
Funny, near-camp teen genre spoof. Buffy is a typical mall gal concerned with shopping and cheerleading, until the mysterious Sutherland proclaims it her destiny to slay the vampires who have suddenly infested Los Angeles. Like, really. Buffy requires some convincing, but eventually takes up the challenge, fighting off the vamps and their seductive leader Hauer, aided by perpetual guy-in-distress Perry. "Pee-wee" Reubens is unrecognizable and terribly amusing as the vampire king's sinister henchman, engaging in one of the longer death scenes of film history. Check out Cassandra (Wagner), Natalie Wood's daughter. 98m; VHS, DVD, Blu-Ray, Wide. **C**: Kristy Swanson; Donald Sutherland; Luke Perry; Paul (Pee-wee Herman) Reubens; Rutger Hauer; Michele Abrams; Randall Batinkoff; Hilary Swank; Paris Vaughan; David Arquette; Candy Clark; Natasha Gregson Wagner; Stephen (Steve) Root; Ben Affleck; Mark DeCarlo; Thomas Jane; Ricki Lake; Directed by Fran Rubel Kuzui; Written by Joss Whedon; Cinematography by James Hayman; Music by Carter Burwell. **Pr**: 20th Century-Fox. **A**: Jr. High-Adult. **P**: Entertainment. **U**: Home. **Mov-Ent**: Adolescence, Cheerleaders. **Acq**: Purchase, Rent/Lease. **Dist**: Fox Home Entertainment. $19.98.

Buffy the Vampire Slayer: Angel/The Puppet Show 1997
When Buffy's attacked by three vampires, handsome stranger "Angel" comes to her rescue. Much to her dismay, the Buffster learns her would-be love is a conscience-striken vampire. Reluctant Giles is put in charge of the school talent contest in "The Puppet Show." But Buffy notices something's very strange about Morgan the ventriloquist's dummy, Sid. ?m; VHS. **C**: Sarah Michelle Gellar; Anthony Head; Alyson Hannigan; Nicholas Brandon; Charisma Carpenter; David Boreanaz; Kristine Sutherland; Directed by Scott Brazil; Ellen Pressman. **A**: Jr. High-Adult. **P**: Entertainment. **U**: Home. **Mov-Ent**: Adolescence. **Acq**: Purchase. **Dist**: Fox Home Entertainment.

Buffy the Vampire Slayer: The Complete Fifth Season 2001
Dawn surfaces as Buffy's kid sister but evil is behind her sudden appearance in the form of Glory, who's seeking to breach the barriers between dimensions. Spike realizes he's in love with Buffy, Xander proposes to Anya, Buffy's mom Joyce dies, and Buffy must sacrifice herself to save the world. 22 episodes. 990m; DVD. **C**: Sarah Michelle Gellar; Alyson Hannigan; Nicholas Brendon; Anthony Head; Kristine Sutherland; James Marsters; Amber Benson; Emma Caulfield; Michelle Trachtenberg; Clare Kramer. **A**: Jr. High-Adult. **P**: Entertainment. **U**: Home. **Mov-Ent**: Television Series. **Acq**: Purchase. **Dist**: Fox Home Entertainment.

Buffy the Vampire Slayer: The Complete First Season 1997
Sixteen-year-old Buffy Summers moves to Sunnydale, California, with her divorced mom Joyce, only to discover that the town is sitting over the Hellmouth and about to be overrun with vampires. Her duties as a vampire slayer really put a crimp in Buffy's sophomore year at her new school, where she's introduced to her "watcher" Giles, the school librarian. It also means trouble for new friends Willow and Xander, snobby queen bee Cordelia, and moody, cursed vampire Angel. All of which leads up to Buffy battling The Master. 12 episodes. 572m; DVD. **C**: Sarah Michelle Gellar; Alyson Hannigan; Nicholas Brendon; Charisma Carpenter; Anthony Head; David Boreanaz; Kristine Sutherland; James Marsters. **A**: Jr. High-Adult. **P**: Entertainment. **U**: Home. **Mov-Ent**: Television Series. **Acq**: Purchase. **Dist**: Fox Home Entertainment.

Buffy the Vampire Slayer: The Complete Fourth Season 2000
Buffy and friends start college but the slaying doesn't stop. She learns new beau Riley works for a quasi-military organization called The Initiative that experiments on demons, including the captured Spike, to create superhuman hybrids. Willow befriends apprentice witch Tara, former vengeance demon Anya falls for Xander, and Giles buys a magic shop. 22 episodes. 990m; DVD. **C:** Sarah Michelle Gellar; Alyson Hannigan; Nicholas Brendon; Anthony Head; Kristine Sutherland; James Marsters; Marc Blucas; Emma Caulfield; Lindsay Crouse; Amber Benson. **A:** Jr. High-Adult. **P:** Entertainment. **U:** Home. **Mov-Ent:** Television Series. **Acq:** Purchase. **Dist:** Fox Home Entertainment.

Buffy the Vampire Slayer: The Complete Second Season 1998
Buffy and Angel fall in love but his curse gets in the way of their happiness when he becomes the vicious Angelus. He plots with vamp Drusilla and her lover Spike to send the town of Sunnydale to hell and Buffy must defeat him at great personal cost. Willows befriends Oz, who turns out to be a werewolf, and Xander hooks up with Cordelia. 22 episodes. 990m; DVD. **C:** Sarah Michelle Gellar; Alyson Hannigan; Nicholas Brendon; Charisma Carpenter; Anthony Head; David Boreanaz; Kristine Sutherland; James Marsters; Juliet Landau; Seth Green. **A:** Jr. High-Adult. **P:** Entertainment. **U:** Home. **Mov-Ent:** Television Series. **Acq:** Purchase. **Dist:** Fox Home Entertainment.

Buffy the Vampire Slayer: The Complete Seventh Season 2003
In the final season, Dawn starts her freshman year at a rebuilt Sunnydale High where Spike works as a janitor and Buffy is hired as a guidance counselor by new principal Robin Wood. Willow's in England with Giles but they both return when the Watcher Council is slain by a new threat that also brings a group of apprentice slayers to live at Buffy's house. The Hellmouth is about to open, thanks to demon Caleb, and both Angel and Faith show up for the climatic big battle. 22 episodes. 990m; DVD. **C:** Sarah Michelle Gellar; Alyson Hannigan; Nicholas Brendon; Anthony Head; Michelle Trachtenberg; James Marsters; Emma Caulfield; DB Woodside; Nathan Fillion. **A:** Jr. High-Adult. **P:** Entertainment. **U:** Home. **Mov-Ent:** Television Series. **Acq:** Purchase. **Dist:** Fox Home Entertainment.

Buffy the Vampire Slayer: The Complete Sixth Season 2002
The gang is having trouble dealing with Buffy's death so Willow uses witchcraft to bring her back to life, but Buffy isn't happy. Tara is worried about Willow's increasingly reckless use of her magic. Giles returns to England and Xander can't go through with his wedding to Anya. Buffy and Spike start a secret affair and Spike regains his soul while Buffy deals with troublesome geek Warren. This is also the season with the all-musical episode "Once More, With Feeling." 22 episodes. 990m; DVD. **C:** Adam Busch; Alyson Hannigan; Nicholas Brendon; Michelle Trachtenberg; James Marsters; Amber Benson; Emma Caulfield. **A:** Jr. High-Adult. **P:** Entertainment. **U:** Home. **Mov-Ent:** Television Series. **Acq:** Purchase. **Dist:** Fox Home Entertainment.

Buffy the Vampire Slayer: The Complete Third Season 1999
A runaway Buffy returns to Sunnydale to begin her senior year and befriends fellow slayer Faith. Giles is replaced by new watcher Wesley Wyndham Price and Angel returns changed from his time in the demon dimension. When Faith is corrupted by evil Mayor Wilkens, it leads to a memorable graduation day. Both Angel and Cordelia will head off to Los Angeles (and the spinoff series "Angel"). 22 episodes. 990m; DVD. **C:** Sarah Michelle Gellar; Alyson Hannigan; Nicholas Brendon; Charisma Carpenter; Anthony Head; David Boreanaz; Kristine Sutherland; Eliza Dushku; Harry Groener; Alexis Denisof. **A:** Jr. High-Adult. **P:** Entertainment. **U:** Home. **Mov-Ent:** Television Series. **Acq:** Purchase. **Dist:** Fox Home Entertainment.

Buffy the Vampire Slayer: The Witch/Never Kill a Boy on the First Date 1997
In "The Witch," quiet Amy seems to be obsessed with becoming a cheerleader and Buffy notices the other girls on the squad are having a lot of very strange accidents. Buffy wants to have a normal date with fellow student Owen but some pesky vampires and trips to the morgue keep keeping in the way in "Never Kill a Boy on the First Date." ?m; VHS. **C:** Sarah Michelle Gellar; Anthony Head; Alyson Hannigan; Nicholas Brandon; Charisma Carpenter; Kristine Sutherland; Directed by David Semel; Stephen Cragg. **A:** Jr. High-Adult. **P:** Entertainment. **U:** Home. **Mov-Ent:** Adolescence. **Acq:** Purchase. **Dist:** Fox Home Entertainment.

Buffy the Vampire Slayer: Welcome to the Hellmouth/The Harvest 1997
In the pilot episode, "Welcome to the Hellmouth," Buffy (Gellar) and her mom have just moved to Sunnydale but Buffy just can't get away from vampires and other pesky creatures (such as witches, mummies, and various monsters) since Sunnydale happens to be built over a Hellmouth. She's also the new kid at Sunnydale High where she's got tweedy watcher, Giles the librarian (Stewart), looking after her and some new friends to make. In "The Harvest" Buffy's still settling in but has to do her slayer duty by stopping the Master Vampire's evil plots. ?m; VHS. **C:** Sarah Michelle Gellar; Anthony Head; Alyson Hannigan; Nicholas Brandon; Kristine Sutherland; Charisma Carpenter; Directed by Charles Martin Smith; John Kretchmer; Written by Joss Whedon. **A:** Jr. High-Adult. **P:** Entertainment. **U:** Home. **Mov-Ent:** Adolescence. **Acq:** Purchase. **Dist:** Fox Home Entertainment.

Buford's Beach Bunnies 1992 (R) — ★
Harry Buford has made a fortune selling barbecued rabbit sandwiches served by the sexiest waitresses around. Harry wants to leave the business to his son Jeeter—if Jeeter can overcome his overwhelming fear of women. So three of Harry's waitresses decide to show Jeeter a very good time. Lots of pretty girls in not much clothing. 90m; VHS, CC. **C:** Jim Hanks; Rikki Brando; Monique Parent; Amy Page; Barrett Cooper; Ina Rogers; Charley Rossman; David Robinson; Directed by Mark Pirro; Written by Mark Pirro. **Pr:** Andrew Garroni; Walter Gernert; Axis Films International. **A:** Sr. High-Adult. **P:** Entertainment. **U:** Home. **Mov-Ent:** Sex & Sexuality. **Acq:** Purchase. **Dist:** Imperial Entertainment Corp. $89.95.

Bug 1975 (PG) — **Bomb!**
The city of Riverside is threatened with destruction after a massive earth tremor unleashes a super-race of ten-inch mega-cockroaches that belch fire, eat raw meat, and are virtually impervious to Raid. Produced by gimmick-king William Castle, who wanted to install windshield wiper-like devices under theatre seats that would brush against the patrons' feet as the cockroaches crawled across the screen; unfortunately, the idea was squashed flat. 100m; VHS, DVD. **C:** Bradford Dillman; Joanna Miles; Richard Gilliland; Jamie Smith-Jackson; Alan Fudge; Jesse Vint; Patty McCormack; Brendan Dillon, Jr.; Frederic Downs; William Castle; Directed by Jeannot Szwarc; Written by William Castle; Thomas Page; Cinematography by Michel Hugo; Music by Charles Fox. **Pr:** William Castle; William Castle. **A:** Jr. High-Adult. **P:** Entertainment. **U:** Home. **Mov-Ent:** Science Fiction. **Acq:** Purchase. **Dist:** Paramount Pictures Corp. $19.95.

Bug 2006 (R) — ★★
Girl (Judd) meets boy (Shannon). Girl and boy have one night stand. Boy goes insane and takes girl with him (maybe). Thriller based on a play and marketed as a horror film because its director is famous for "The Exorcist." If you like dark psychological movies shot almost entirely in one room where people talk and slowly lose their minds, this film is for you. If you were expecting a gory traditional horror movie, you will likely be disappointed. But you'll probably be somewhat happy that Ashley Judd briefly gets naked. 101m; DVD. **C:** Ashley Judd; Michael Shannon; Harry Connick, Jr.; Lynn Collins; Brian F. O'Byrne; Directed by William Friedkin; Written by Tracy Letts; Cinematography by Michael Grady; Music by Brian Tyler. **Pr:** Malcolm Petal; Holly Wiersma; Kimberly Anderson; Gary Huckabay; Michael Burns; Lift Productions; Lionsgate. **A:** Sr. High-Adult. **P:** Entertainment. **U:** Home. **L:** English. **Mov-Ent:** Insects, Veterans. **Acq:** Purchase. **Dist:** Lions Gate Entertainment Inc.

Bug Buster 1999 (R) — ★★
The Griffins, dad (Kopell), mom (Lockhart) and daughter Shannon (Heigl) move to scenic Mountainview to flee the stress of city life. But they didn't bargain for the giant creature "unknown to science" that's attacking people and leaving giant bug larvae in 'em. Mutant insects overrun the town, leaving the survivors one last hope, in the form of ex-military man-turned-uberexterminator General George (Quaid). Plenty of gore and over-the-top acting, plus Scotty and Mr. Sulu, give this one late-night cult potential. 93m; VHS, DVD. **C:** Randy Quaid; Katherine Heigl; Meredith Salenger; Bernie Kopell; Anne Lockhart; George Takei; James Doohan; Ty O'Neal; Julie Brown; Brenda Doumani; David Lipper; Directed by Lorenzo Doumani; Written by Malick Khoury; Cinematography by Hanania Baer; Music by Sidney James. **Pr:** Lorenzo Doumani; Lorenzo Doumani. **A:** Sr. High-Adult. **P:** Entertainment. **U:** Home. **Mov-Ent. Acq:** Purchase. **Dist:** Movies Unlimited; Alpha Video. $19.95.

Bug City: Ants 1998
Explains the daily behavior of ants, how they live and work. 23m; VHS; Closed Captioned. **A:** Primary. **P:** Education. **U:** Home, Institution. **Chl-Juv:** Insects, Science. **Acq:** Purchase. **Dist:** Library Video Inc. $29.95.

Bug City: Aquatic Insects 1998
Explains how many species of insects have adapted for life in the water, such as dragonflies, damselflies, and water-striders. 23m; VHS; Closed Captioned. **A:** Primary. **P:** Education. **U:** Home, Institution. **Chl-Juv:** Insects, Science. **Acq:** Purchase. **Dist:** Library Video Inc. $29.95.

Bug City: Bees 1998
Explains why bees are so busy, from the queen to the worker. 23m; VHS; Closed Captioned. **A:** Primary. **P:** Education. **U:** Home, Institution. **Chl-Juv:** Insects, Science. **Acq:** Purchase. **Dist:** Library Video Inc. $29.95.

Bug City: Beetles 1998
Explains how to create a beetle habitat using a colony of meal worms to be able to observe the life cycle of a beetle. 23m; VHS; Closed Captioned. **A:** Primary. **P:** Education. **U:** Home, Institution. **Chl-Juv:** Insects, Science. **Acq:** Purchase. **Dist:** Library Video Inc. $29.95.

Bug City: Butterflies & Moths 1998
Explains the process of moth and butterfly metamorphosis and how to identify several species. 23m; VHS; Closed Captioned. **A:** Primary. **P:** Education. **U:** Home, Institution. **Chl-Juv:** Insects, Science. **Acq:** Purchase. **Dist:** Library Video Inc. $29.95.

Bug City: Crickets, Grasshoppers & Friends 1998
Explains how cricket, grasshoppers and katydids jump, chirp and camouflage themselves. 23m; VHS; Closed Captioned. **A:** Primary. **P:** Education. **U:** Home, Institution. **Chl-Juv:** Insects, Science. **Acq:** Purchase. **Dist:** Library Video Inc. $29.95.

Bug City: Flies & Mosquitoes 1998
Explains the four-stage metamorphosis, predators of flies, and what maggots are good for. 23m; VHS; Closed Captioned. **A:** Primary. **P:** Education. **U:** Home, Institution. **Chl-Juv:** Insects, Science. **Acq:** Purchase. **Dist:** Library Video Inc. $29.95.

Bug City: House & Backyard Insects 1998
Provides facts and functions of ladybugs and fireflies. 23m; VHS; Closed Captioned. **A:** Primary. **P:** Education. **U:** Home, Institution. **Chl-Juv:** Insects, Science. **Acq:** Purchase. **Dist:** Library Video Inc. $29.95.

Bug City: House & Backyard Insects 2 1998
Explains the habits of cockroaches, fleas, termites, snails, slugs and earthworms and their affect on humans. 23m; VHS; Closed Captioned. **A:** Primary. **P:** Education. **U:** Home, Institution. **Chl-Juv:** Insects, Science. **Acq:** Purchase. **Dist:** Library Video Inc. $29.95.

Bug City: Spiders & Scorpions 1998
Explains about webs, the spider's use of silk, its eating habits, growth and molting, mating rituals, and care of young. Also discusses scorpion life and habits. 23m; VHS; Closed Captioned. **A:** Primary. **P:** Education. **U:** Home, Institution. **Chl-Juv:** Insects, Science. **Acq:** Purchase. **Dist:** Library Video Inc. $29.95.

The Bug Man of Ithaca 1991
Entomologist Thomas Eisner explains why insects are important and why our fears of them are irrational. 52m; VHS, 3/4 U. **C:** Hosted by Thomas Eisner. **Pr:** Canadian Broadcasting Corp. **A:** Jr. High-Adult. **P:** Education. **U:** Institution. **Gen-Edu:** Insects, Science. **Acq:** Rent/Lease. **Dist:** New Dimension Media. $40.00.

Bugged! 1996 (PG-13) — ★
Flesh-eating insects attack a beautiful homemaker and a group of bumbling exterminators are her only hope. 90m; VHS, DVD. **C:** Ronald K. Armstrong; Priscilla Basque; Jeff Lee; Derek C. Johnson; Billy Graham; Directed by Ronald K. Armstrong; Written by Ronald K. Armstrong; Cinematography by S. Torriano Berry; Music by Boris Elkis. **Pr:** Lloyd Kaufman; Michael Herz. **A:** Jr. High-Adult. **P:** Entertainment. **U:** Home. **Mov-Ent. Acq:** Purchase. **Dist:** Troma Entertainment.

Bugles in the Afternoon 1952 (Unrated) — ★★
Life in the army during Custer's last days, with a love triangle, revenge and the Little Big Horn for added spice. 85m; VHS. **C:** Ray Milland; Hugh Marlowe; Helena Carter; Forrest Tucker; Barton MacLane; George Reeves; James Millican; Gertrude Michael; Hugh Beaumont; Sheb Wooley; Directed by Roy Rowland; Written by Daniel Mainwaring; Harry Brown; Cinematography by Wilfred M. Cline; Music by Dimitri Tiomkin. **Pr:** William Cagney. **A:** Family. **P:** Entertainment. **U:** Home. **Mov-Ent:** Native Americans. **Acq:** Purchase. **Dist:** Lions Gate Entertainment Inc.; Facets Multimedia Inc. $14.95.

Bugs! 1988
Seven of the wascally wabbit's finest. 60m; VHS. **C:** Voice(s) by Mel Blanc. **Pr:** Warner Bros. **A:** Family. **P:** Entertainment. **U:** Home. **Mov-Ent:** Animation & Cartoons, Children. **Acq:** Purchase. **Dist:** MGM Home Entertainment. $14.95.

Bugs 2003 (Unrated) — ★
A cop chasing a bad guy through an unfinished subway tunnel is eaten by a huge scorpion-like prehistoric insect whose nest he disturbed. FBI agent Matt Pollack (Sabato Jr.) and insect expert Emily Foster (Everhart) investigate, but they (along with a SWAT team) are soon trapped in the bug-infested tunnel. A Sci-Fi Channel original. 85m; DVD. **C:** Antonio Sabato, Jr.; Angie Everhart; R.H. Thomson; Karl Pruner; Duane Murray; Romano Orzari; Directed by Joseph Conti; Written by Robinson Young; Patrick Doody; Chris Valenziano; Cinematography by Richard Wincenty; Music by William T. Stromberg. **A:** Sr. High-Adult. **P:** Entertainment. **U:** Home. **Mov-Ent:** Science Fiction, Federal Bureau of Investigation (FBI). **Acq:** Purchase. **Dist:** Image Entertainment Inc.

Bugs & Daffy: The Wartime Cartoons 1945
A compilation of Daffy and Bugs classics made during WWII, often dominated by propaganda and Axis-baiting. 120m; VHS. **C:** Narrated by Leonard Maltin; Directed by Robert McKimson; Chuck Jones; Isadore "Friz" Freleng. **A:** Family. **P:** Entertainment. **U:** Home. **Mov-Ent:** Animation & Cartoons, World War Two. **Acq:** Purchase. **Dist:** MGM Home Entertainment. $19.95.

Bugs & Daffy's Carnival of the Animals 1989
A host of favorite animated critters are introduced by the wabbit and the duck. 26m; VHS. **C:** Voice(s) by Mel Blanc; Directed by Chuck Jones. **Pr:** Chuck Jones; Chuck Jones; Warner Bros. **A:** Family. **P:** Entertainment. **U:** Home. **Mov-Ent:** Animation & Cartoons, Children. **Acq:** Purchase. **Dist:** Warner Home Video, Inc. $14.95.

Bugs Bunny: All American Hero 1981
Bugs takes a trip back through history, starting in 1492 when Columbus sailed the ocean blue and Bugs was his shipmate. Continues through the American Revolution, WWI, and more with Yosemite Sam, Sylvester and all of your favorites. 24m; VHS. **C:** Voice(s) by Mel Blanc. **Pr:** Warner Bros. **A:** Family. **P:** Entertainment. **U:** Home. **L:** English, Spanish. **Mov-Ent:** Animation & Cartoons, History, Family Viewing. **Acq:** Purchase. **Dist:** Warner Home Video, Inc. $12.95.

Bugs Bunny & Elmer Fudd Cartoon Festival 1944
Seven classic Bugs and Elmer shorts, including "Wabbitt Twouble," "Stage Door Cartoon," and "The Big Snooze." 54m; VHS. **C:** Directed by Chuck Jones; Tex Avery; Bob Clampett; Isadore "Friz" Freleng; Robert McKimson. **A:** Family. **P:** Entertainment. **U:** Home. **Mov-Ent:** Animation & Cartoons. **Acq:** Purchase. **Dist:** MGM Home Entertainment. $19.95.

Bugs Bunny Cartoon Festival 1944
The animated antics of the nefarious rabbit in four early cartoons. 34m; VHS. **C:** Directed by Bob Clampett; Chuck Jones; Isadore "Friz" Freleng. **Pr:** The Vitaphone Corporation. **A:** Family. **P:** Entertainment. **U:** Home. **Mov-Ent:** Animation & Cartoons. **Acq:** Purchase. **Dist:** MGM Home Entertainment. $14.95.

Bugs Bunny Cartoon Festival: Little Red Riding Rabbit 1943
Five classic Bugs shorts, including "Old Grey Hare," "Jack Wabbit and the Beanstalk," and the title cartoon are featured. 37m; VHS. **C:** Directed by Chuck Jones; Isadore "Friz" Freleng. **Pr:** The Vitaphone Corporation. **A:** Family. **P:** Entertainment. **U:** Home. **Mov-Ent:** Animation & Cartoons. **Acq:** Purchase. **Dist:** MGM Home Entertainment. $14.95.

Bugs Bunny: Festival of Fun 194?
Five classic cartoons from the Bugsmeister. Includes "Hare Ribbin," "Rhapsody Rabbit," "Baseball Bugs," "The Wacky Wabbit," and "The Wabbit Who Came to Supper." 35m; VHS. **Pr:** Warner Bros. **A:** Family. **P:** Entertainment. **U:** Home. **Mov-Ent:** Animation & Cartoons. **Acq:** Purchase. **Dist:** MGM Home Entertainment. $12.95.

Bugs Bunny: Hollywood Legend 1990
Six episodes featuring the wascally wabbit, including "Hair-Raising Hare," "A Hare Grows in Manhattan," and "Herr Meets Hare." 60m; VHS. **C:** Voice(s) by Mel Blanc. **Pr:** Warner Bros. **A:** Family. **P:** Entertainment. **U:** Home. **Mov-Ent:** Animation & Cartoons, Comedy--Screwball, Family Viewing. **Acq:** Purchase. **Dist:** MGM Home Entertainment; Facets Multimedia Inc. $12.98.

Bugs Bunny in King Arthur's Court 1989
The Looney Tuners spoof Mark Twain's masterpiece of classic American literature. 25m; VHS. **C:** Voice(s) by Mel Blanc; Directed by Chuck Jones; Written by Chuck Jones. **Pr:** Chuck Jones; Chuck Jones; Warner Bros. **A:** Family. **P:** Entertainment. **U:** Home. **Mov-Ent:** Animation & Cartoons, Children. **Acq:** Purchase. **Dist:** Warner Home Video, Inc. $14.95.

The Bugs Bunny/Looney Tunes Comedy Hour: The Looney Tunes Spotlight Collection Volume 7 2008 (Unrated)
Collection of 26 classic animated tales including "Long-Haired Hare," "Zipping Along," "Scrambled Aches," "Daffy Duck and the Dinosaur," "Steal Wool," "No Barking," and "Odor-able Kitty." 105m; DVD. **C:** Voice(s) by Mel Blanc. **A:** Primary-Adult. **P:** Entertainment. **U:** Home. **Chl-Juv:** Television Series, Animation & Cartoons. **Acq:** Purchase. **Dist:** Warner Home Video, Inc. $26.99.

The Bugs Bunny Mystery Special 19??
Bugs Bunny and that hard-boiled detective Elmer Fudd tip their hats to the master of suspense Alfred Hitchcock in this animated spoof. 24m; VHS. **A:** Family. **P:** Entertainment. **U:** Home. **Mov-Ent:** Animation & Cartoons. **Acq:** Purchase. **Dist:** Warner Home Video, Inc. $12.95.

The Bugs Bunny/Road Runner Movie 1979 (G)
A compilation of classic Warner Bros. cartoons, starring Bugs Bunny, Daffy Duck, Elmer Fudd, the Road Runner, Wile E. Coyote, Porky Pig, and Pepe Le Pew, including some all-new animated sequences. Also available with Spanish dubbing. 98m; VHS. **C:** Voice(s) by Mel Blanc; Directed by Chuck Jones; Phil Monroe. **Pr:** Warner Bros. **A:** Family. **P:** Entertainment. **U:** Home. **L:** English, Spanish. **Mov-Ent:** Animation & Cartoons, Rabbits. **Acq:** Purchase. **Dist:** Warner Home Video, Inc. $14.95.

Bugs Bunny Superstar 1975 (G)
A collection of nine animated classics starring everybody's favorite "wascally wabbitt." Includes fascinating interviews and behind the scenes moments featuring the men and women who brought Bugs to life. 91m; VHS. **C:** Voice(s) by Mel Blanc; Narrated by Orson Welles; Directed by Larry Jackson; Bob Clampett; Tex Avery; Isadore "Friz" Freleng. **Pr:** Warner Bros. **A:** Family. **P:** Entertainment. **U:** Home. **Mov-Ent:** Animation & Cartoons, Interviews, Serials. **Acq:** Purchase. **Dist:** MGM Home Entertainment. $19.95.

Bugs Bunny: Truth or Hare 198?
It's Bugs Bunny vs. Marvin the Martian, Elmer Fudd, Yosemite Sam, and the Tasmanian Devil in "The Fair Haired Hare," "Dr. Devil and Mr. Hare," "Wideo Wabbit," "Hare-way to the Stars," and "Water, Water Every Hare." 33m; VHS. **A:** Family. **P:** Entertainment. **U:** Home. **Mov-Ent:** Animation & Cartoons. **Acq:** Purchase. **Dist:** Baker and Taylor; Warner Home Video, Inc. $12.95.

Bugs Bunny's Bustin' Out All Over 1980
Three Bugs cartoons by animator Chuck Jones. Includes "Soup or Sonic," "Spaced Out Bunny" and "Portrait of the Artist as a Young Bunny." 24m; VHS. **C:** Voice(s) by Mel Blanc; Directed by Chuck Jones. **Pr:** Warner Bros. **A:** Family. **P:** Entertainment. **U:** Home. **L:** English, Spanish. **Mov-Ent:** Animation & Cartoons, Family Viewing. **Acq:** Purchase. **Dist:** Warner Home Video, Inc. $12.95.

Bugs Bunny's Comedy Classics 1988
A collection of classic wabbit tales including "Easter Yeggs," "Racketeer Rabbit," "The Hair-Brained Hypnotist," "Acrobatty Rabbit," "Falling Hare," and "Haredevil Hare." 60m; VHS. **C:** Voice(s) by Mel Blanc. **Pr:** Warner Bros. **A:** Family. **P:** Entertainment. **U:** Home. **Mov-Ent:** Animation & Cartoons, Comedy--Screwball, Family Viewing. **Acq:** Purchase. **Dist:** MGM Home Entertainment; Facets Multimedia Inc. $12.98.

Bugs Bunny's Creature Features 198?
Join Bugs Bunny and Daffy Duck in three movie parodies "Invasion of the Bunny Snatchers," "The Duxorcist," and "Night of the Living Duck." 33m; VHS. **A:** Family. **P:** Entertainment. **U:** Home. **Mov-Ent:** Animation & Cartoons. **Acq:** Purchase. **Dist:** Warner Home Video, Inc.; Baker and Taylor. $12.95.

Bugs Bunny's Cupid Capers 1979
Bugs and his pals are hit by a Cupid in the form of Elmer Fudd, who fires too many love arrows into Foghorn Leghorn, Yosemite Sam and others. 24m; VHS. **C:** Voice(s) by Mel Blanc. **Pr:** Warner Bros. **A:** Family. **P:** Entertainment. **U:** Home. **L:** English, Spanish. **Mov-Ent:** Animation & Cartoons, Romance, Family Viewing. **Acq:** Purchase. **Dist:** Warner Home Video, Inc. $12.95.

Bugs Bunny's Easter Funnies 1977
Bugs helps the Easter Bunny deliver eggs. Originally a network special. 50m; VHS. **C:** Voice(s) by Mel Blanc. **Pr:** Warner Bros. **A:** Family. **P:** Entertainment. **U:** Home. **L:** English, Spanish. **Mov-Ent:** Animation & Cartoons, Holidays, Family Viewing. **Acq:** Purchase. **Dist:** Warner Home Video, Inc. $12.95.

Bugs Bunny's Hare-Raising Tales 1989
Six standouts from the furry varmint's vault of classics; includes "Rabbitson Crusoe" and "Rabbit Hood." 45m; VHS. **C:** Voice(s) by Mel Blanc; Directed by Chuck Jones; Robert McKimson; Abe Levitow; Written by Chuck Jones; Robert McKimson; Isadore "Friz" Freleng. **Pr:** Warner Bros. **A:** Family. **P:** Entertainment. **U:** Home. **Mov-Ent:** Animation & Cartoons, Children. **Acq:** Purchase. **Dist:** Warner Home Video, Inc. $14.95.

Bugs Bunny's Howl-Oween Special 1978
When Bugs dresses up as a witch for Halloween, he makes the mistake of knocking on Witch Hazel's door. She won't stand for any competition. The adventure unfolds as the witch tries to remove that unwanted hare. 25m; VHS. **C:** Voice(s) by Mel Blanc. **Pr:** Warner Bros. **A:** Family. **P:** Entertainment. **U:** Home. **L:** English, Spanish. **Mov-Ent:** Animation & Cartoons. **Acq:** Purchase. **Dist:** Warner Home Video, Inc. $12.95.

Bugs Bunny's Looney Christmas Tales 1979
Join Bugs as he and his little nephew re-enact two of the world's most beloved Christmas stories; "A Christmas Carol" and "'Twas the Night Before Christmas." 25m; VHS. **C:** Voice(s) by Mel Blanc; Directed by Chuck Jones; Isadore "Friz" Freleng. **Pr:** Warner Bros; Freleng. **A:** Family. **P:** Entertainment. **U:** Home. **L:** English, Spanish. **Mov-Ent:** Animation & Cartoons, Christmas, Family Viewing. **Acq:** Purchase. **Dist:** Warner Home Video, Inc. $9.95.

Bugs Bunny's Lunar Tunes 19??
Bugs Bunny tries to prevent Marvin the Martian from blowing the Earth to smithereens. 24m; VHS. **A:** Family. **P:** Entertainment. **U:** Home. **Mov-Ent:** Animation & Cartoons. **Acq:** Purchase. **Dist:** Warner Home Video, Inc. $12.95.

Bugs Bunny's Mad World of Television 19??
Bugs is a slick network exec in this cartoon adventure. 24m; VHS. **A:** Family. **P:** Entertainment. **U:** Home. **Mov-Ent:** Animation & Cartoons. **Acq:** Purchase. **Dist:** Warner Home Video, Inc. $12.95.

Bugs Bunny's Mother's Day Special 1979
Bugs and other Looney Tunes characters celebrate Mother's Day in their own wacky way. 24m; VHS. **C:** Voice(s) by Mel Blanc. **A:** Family. **P:** Entertainment. **U:** Home. **L:** English, Spanish. **Mov-Ent:** Animation & Cartoons, Holidays, Family Viewing. **Acq:** Purchase. **Dist:** Warner Home Video, Inc. $12.95.

Bugs Bunny's Overtures to Disaster 19??
Bugs, who certainly has the ears for music, orchestrates a musical comedy. 24m; VHS. **A:** Family. **P:** Entertainment. **U:** Home. **Mov-Ent:** Animation & Cartoons. **Acq:** Purchase. **Dist:** Warner Home Video, Inc. $12.95.

Bugs Bunny's Thanksgiving Diet 1991
Spend everyone's favorite holiday with that wacky wabbit, Bugs Bunny. 24m; VHS. **C:** Voice(s) by Mel Blanc. **Pr:** Warner Bros. **A:** Family. **P:** Entertainment. **U:** Home. **L:** English, Spanish. **Mov-Ent:** Animation & Cartoons, Holidays. **Acq:** Purchase. **Dist:** Warner Home Video, Inc. $12.95.

Bugs Bunny's 3rd Movie: 1,001 Rabbit Tales 1982 (G)
A compilation of old and new classic cartoons featuring Bugs, Daffy, Sylvester, Porky, Elmer, Tweety, Speedy Gonzalez and Yosemite Sam. 74m; VHS. **C:** Directed by Chuck Jones; Robert McKimson; Isadore "Friz" Freleng. **Pr:** Warner Bros. **A:** Family. **P:** Entertainment. **U:** Home. **Mov-Ent:** Animation & Cartoons. **Acq:** Purchase. **Dist:** Warner Home Video, Inc.; Facets Multimedia Inc. $14.95.

Bugs Bunny's Wacky Adventures 1957
A collection of that rascally rabbit's classic cartoons featuring "Ali Baba Bunny," "Hare Do," "Long Haired Hare," "Bunny Hugged," "The Grey Hounded Hare," "Roman Legion Hare," and "Duck, Rabbit, Duck!" 59m; VHS. **C:** Voice(s) by Mel Blanc; Directed by Chuck Jones; Isadore "Friz" Freleng. **A:** Family. **P:** Entertainment. **U:** Home. **Mov-Ent:** Animation & Cartoons. **Acq:** Purchase. **Dist:** Warner Home Video, Inc. $12.95.

Bugs Bunny's Wide World of Sports 1989
Bugs shows his favorite sports cartoons. 24m; VHS. **C:** Narrated by Roy Firestone. **Pr:** Warner Bros. **A:** Family. **P:** Entertainment. **U:** Home. **L:** English, Spanish. **Mov-Ent:** Animation & Cartoons, Sports--General, Family Viewing. **Acq:** Purchase. **Dist:** Warner Home Video, Inc. $12.95.

Bugs Bunny's Zaniest Toons 19??
The wackiest all-time goofball adventures of the world's most wascally wabbitt. 60m; VHS. **Pr:** Warner Bros. **A:** Family. **P:** Entertainment. **U:** Home. **Mov-Ent:** Animation & Cartoons, Family Viewing. **Acq:** Purchase. **Dist:** MGM Home Entertainment. $12.98.

Bugs Don't Bug Us! 1991
Watch how bugs eat, move, and interact with children. A special section on the transformation of a caterpillar to butterfly is also presented. Includes a parent/teacher guide. 35m; VHS. **A:** Preschool-Primary. **P:** Entertainment. **U:** Home, Institution. **Chl-Juv:** Children, Insects. **Acq:** Purchase. **Dist:** Bo-Peep Productions. $14.95.

Bugs for Breakfast: Food and Culture ????
Multicultural view of how we eat. Why we eat? Why eat meat? Food taboos. Cultural influences on diet. 19m; VHS. **A:** Adult. **P:** Professional. **U:** Institution, CCTV. **Hea-Sci:** Nutrition, Fitness/Exercise. **Acq:** Purchase. **Dist:** The Learning Seed. $89.00.

A Bug's Life 1998 (G) — ★★★
Computer animated feature by Pixar, the makers of "Toy Story," takes a cutesy look into the world of insects. Flik (Foley) is an ant who must help defend his colony after he messes up a tribute to a bullying group of grasshoppers led by Hopper (Spacey). He recruits a crew of misfits from a flea circus, including a male ladybug with gender issues (Leary), a prissy stick bug (Pierce), and an obese caterpillar (Ranft). Together they form a plan to keep the grasshoppers away, but still must confront Hopper in order to ensure lasting peace. Amazing animation, from the blades of grass down to the facial expressions of the bugs, along with dozens of sight gags keep this family feature flying. Competed with fellow computer animated insect feature "Antz" on its release. 94m; VHS, DVD, Blu-Ray, CC. **C:** Voice(s) by Dave Foley; Kevin Spacey; Julia Louis-Dreyfus; Phyllis Diller; Richard Kind; David Hyde Pierce; Joe Ranft; Denis Leary; Jonathan Harris; Madeline Kahn; Bonnie Hunt; Michael McShane; John Ratzenberger; Brad Garrett; Roddy McDowall; Edie McClurg; Hayden Panettiere; Alex Rocco; David Ossman; Directed by John Lasseter; Andrew Stanton; Written by Joe Ranft; Donald McEnery; Bob Shaw; Andrew Stanton; Cinematography by Sharon Calahan; Music by Randy Newman. **Pr:** Walt Disney Pictures; Pixar; Buena Vista. **A:** Family. **P:** Entertainment. **U:** Home. **Mov-Ent:** Animation & Cartoons, Insects, Food Industry. **Acq:** Purchase. **Dist:** Buena Vista Home Entertainment.

Bugs vs. Daffy: Battle of the Music Video Stars 1988
Radio stations "WABBIT" and "K-PUT" are battling for top rank in the ratings war, with Daffy and Bugs engaging in a no holds barred competition to get there. 24m; VHS. **Pr:** Warner Bros. **A:** Family. **P:** Entertainment. **U:** Home. **L:** English, Spanish. **Mov-Ent:** Animation & Cartoons, Family Viewing. **Acq:** Purchase. **Dist:** Warner Home Video, Inc. $12.95.

Bugs vs. Elmer 1953
Seven of the best Bugs/Elmer battles: "Slick Hare," "Unruly Hare," "Hare Remover," "Stage Door Cartoon," "Wabbit Twouble," "The Big Snooze" and "Fresh Hare." 60m; VHS. **C:** Directed by Frank Tashlin; Chuck Jones; Isadore "Friz" Freleng; Robert McKimson; Bob Clampett. **A:** Family. **P:** Entertainment. **U:** Home. **Mov-Ent:** Animation & Cartoons. **Acq:** Purchase. **Dist:** MGM Home Entertainment. $14.95.

Bugsy 1991 (R) — ★★★½
Beatty is Benjamin "Bugsy" Siegel, the 40s gangster who built the Flamingo Hotel in Las Vegas when it was still a virtual desert, before it became a gambling mecca. Bening is perfect as Bugsy's moll, Virginia Hill, who inspired him to carry out his dream of building the Flamingo (which was her nickname). Beatty and Bening heat up the screen and their off-screen relationship was no different. Fans anticipated their seemingly imminent marriage almost as much as the release of this movie. Almost nothing mars this film which Toback adapted from a novel by Dean Jennings, "We Only Kill Each Other: The Life and Bad Times of Bugsy Siegel." 135m; VHS, DVD, 8 mm, CC. **C:** Warren Beatty; Annette Bening; Harvey Keitel; Ben Kingsley; Elliott Gould; Joe Mantegna; Richard Sarafian; Bebe Neuwirth; Wendy Phillips; Robert Beltran; Bill Graham; Lewis Van Bergen; Debrah Farentino; Directed by Barry Levinson; Written by James Toback; Cinematography by Allen Daviau; Music by Ennio Morricone. **Pr:** Warren Beatty; Mark Johnson; Warren Beatty; Barry Levinson; Tri-Star Pictures. **A:** Sr. High-Adult. **P:** Entertainment. **U:** Home. **Mov-Ent:** Crime Drama, Gambling, Biography: Law Enforcement. **Awds:** Oscars '91: Art Dir./Set Dec., Costume Des.; Golden Globes '92: Film--Drama; L.A. Film Critics '91: Director (Levinson), Film, Screenplay; Natl. Bd. of Review '91: Actor (Beatty). **Acq:** Purchase. **Dist:** Sony Pictures Home Entertainment Inc. $14.95.

Bugsy, Dutch & Al: The Gangsters 19??
See how Bugsy Siegel, Dutch Shultz, Al Capone and other bloodthirsty mobsters controlled and corrupted the entire nation. 58m; VHS. **A:** Sr. High-Adult. **P:** Education. **U:** Home. **Gen-Edu:** Documentary Films. **Acq:** Purchase. **Dist:** Rhino Entertainment Co. $9.95.

Bugsy Malone 1976 (G) — ★★½
Delightful musical features an all-children's cast highlighting this spoof of 1930s' gangster movies. 94m; VHS, DVD. **C:** Jodie Foster; Scott Baio; Florrie Augger; John Cassisi; Martin Lev; Directed by Alan Parker; Written by Alan Parker; Cinematography by Peter Biziou; Music by Paul Williams. **Pr:** Alan Marshall; Paramount Pictures. **A:** Family. **P:** Entertainment. **U:** Home. **Mov-Ent:** Musical, Children. **Awds:** British Acad. '76: Screenplay. **Acq:** Purchase. **Dist:** Paramount Pictures Corp. $14.95.

Build a Shaker Table 1989
Viewers are taught the entire process of building a leg-and-apron table. 60m; VHS. **C:** Kelly Mehler. **Pr:** Taunton Press. **A:** Sr. High-Adult. **P:** Instruction. **U:** Home. **How-Ins:** Construction. **Acq:** Purchase. **Dist:** Taunton Press Inc. $29.95.

Build Your Own Greenhouse—Solar Style 1981
A workshop group led by Bill Yando builds an attached solar greenhouse. Step-by-step discussion of design, materials, locations, and use. 21m; VHS, 3/4 U. **Pr:** Danamar Film Productions. **A:** Primary-Adult. **P:** Instruction. **U:** Institution, Home, SURA. **How-Ins:** Gardening. **Acq:** Purchase, Duplication License. **Dist:** Bullfrog Films, Inc.

Build Your Own Series 1990
A complete guide to materials and tools needed to begin and complete a variety of interesting projects. 30m; VHS. **Pr:** Morris Video. **A:** Sr. High-Adult. **P:** Instruction. **U:** Home. **How-Ins:** How-To, Automobiles, Hobbies. **Acq:** Purchase. **Dist:** Morris Video. $19.95.
Indiv. Titles: 1. Downhill Race Car 2. Drop Leaf Computer Desk 3. Re-Siding You House 4. Sketch and Storage Bench 5. Store-It-All-Barn 6. Welsh Cupboard.

Build Your Own Web Page 1997
Experts Allen, Denise and Larry teach html techniques to build basic Web Pages without expensive software or equipment. ?m; VHS. **A:** Family. **P:** Instruction. **U:** Home. **How-Ins:** How-To, Computers. **Acq:** Purchase. **Dist:** Tapeworm Video Distributors Inc. $16.95.

Builders and Wreckers 19??
Past Texas FFA Vice President Wendy Milford delivers an inspiring speech which focuses on taking advantage of opportunities, realizing dreams, and becoming a success. 11m; VHS. **A:** Sr. High-Adult. **P:** Education. **U:** Institution. **Gen-Edu:** Speech, Self-Help. **Acq:** Purchase. **Dist:** CEV Multimedia. $19.95.

The Builders of Timberline 1990
See the construction of Timberline Lodge in Mt. Hood National Forest. Actual footage shot by workers depicts dramatic maneuvers to roll boulders into place, and enourmous timbers hoisted up to build the roof of the cathedral. 60m/B/W; VHS. **Pr:** Swenson Company. **A:** Sr. High-Adult. **P:** Education. **U:** Home. **Gen-Edu:** Documentary Films, National Parks & Reserves, History. **Acq:** Purchase. **Dist:** New Media Magic. $24.95.

Building a Ball Screen Offense 2013 (Unrated)
Basketball coach Robert Senderoff demonstrates how to use the ball screen offense he teaches at Kent State. 63m; DVD. **A:** Family. **P:** Education. **U:** Home. **L:** English. **Spo-Rec:** Athletic Instruction/Coaching, Basketball. **Acq:** Purchase. **Dist:** Championship Productions $39.99.

Building a Cello with Harold 2000
Documentary showing master violin and cello builder Harold Hayslett as he makes a new instrument. 105m; VHS, DVD. **A:** Sr. High-Adult. **P:** Education. **U:** Institution. **Mov-Ent:** Documentary Films, Crafts. **Acq:** Purchase. **Dist:** The Cinema Guild. $79.95.

Building a Championship Goalie 2012 (Unrated)
Coach Kevin Donahue discusses the skills needed by a lacrosse goalie and how to build them. 46m; DVD. **A:** Family. **P:** Education. **U:** Home. **L:** English. **Spo-Rec:** Athletic Instruction/Coaching, Lacrosse, How-To. **Acq:** Purchase. **Dist:** Championship Productions. $39.99.

Building a Championship Infield 2013 (Unrated)
Coach Ricci Woodard presents drills and tactics for getting a better infield percentage in baseball. 46m; DVD. **A:** Family. **P:** Education. **U:** Home. **L:** English. **Spo-Rec:** Athletic Instruction/Coaching, Softball, How-To. **Acq:** Purchase. **Dist:** Championship Productions. $39.99.

Building a Championship Practice Environment 2006 (Unrated)
Coach Dom Starsia discusses running a successful lacrosse practice as well as demonstrating drills. 56m; DVD. **A:** Family. **P:** Education. **U:** Home, Institution. **Spo-Rec:** Lacrosse, Athletic Instruction/Coaching. **Acq:** Purchase. **Dist:** Championship Productions. $39.99.

Building a Championship Wrestling Program 2009 (Unrated)
Coach Jeff Swenson lectures on his philosophy for building a successful wrestling program at the collegiate level. 59m; DVD. **A:** Family. **P:** Education. **U:** Home, Institution. **Spo-Rec:** Athletic Instruction/Coaching. **Acq:** Purchase. **Dist:** Championship Productions. $39.99.

Building a Character 19??
Group of acting students work through the process of character development, focusing on character analysis, physical and vocal work, rehearsal guidelines, and more. Complete with teacher's guide and selective biblio. 86m; VHS. **A:** Jr. High-Adult. **P:** Education. **U:** Institution. **Gen-Edu:** Theater. **Acq:** Purchase. **Dist:** Stagestep. $94.95.

Building a Christian Conscience, Part 1 1982
These six programs provide a guide to developing a Christian conscience. 30m; VHS, 3/4 U. **Pr:** Ligonier Valley Study Center. **A:** Jr. High-Adult. **P:** Religious. **U:** Institution, Home. **Gen-Edu:** Ethics & Morals. **Acq:** Purchase, Rent/Lease. **Dist:** Ligonier Ministries Inc.
Indiv. Titles: 1. The Razor's Edge 2. The Legalist Distortion 3. The Distortion of Lawlessness 4. The Degrees of Sin 5. The Creation Ordinances 6. The Question of Conscience.

Building a Christian Marriage 1986
Two independent programs are presented for creating and keeping together a marriage based on Bible readings and Lutheranism. 90m; VHS, 3/4 U. **Pr:** CPH. **A:** Adult. **P:** Religious. **U:** Institution, Home. **Gen-Edu:** Marriage. **Acq:** Purchase. **Dist:** Concordia Publishing House. $69.95.
Indiv. Titles: 1. Pre-Marriage Counseling 2. Marriage Enrichment.

Building a Climate for Individual Growth 1969
Studies the six stages of psychological growth together with the ways an organization can thwart or stimulate it at each stage. 24m; VHS, 3/4 U. **A:** College-Adult. **P:** Professional. **U:** Institution, SURA. **L:** English, Dutch, French, German, Portuguese, Spanish, Swedish. **Bus-Ind:** Personnel Management, Psychology, Organizations. **Acq:** Purchase, Rent/Lease. **Dist:** Learning Communications L.L.C.

Building a Competitive Golf Program 2001 (Unrated)
Coach Rick LaRose discusses building a successful golfing program, and how to run a practice. 66m; DVD. **A:** Family. **P:** Education. **U:** Home, Institution. **Spo-Rec:** Golf, Athletic Instruction/Coaching. **Acq:** Purchase. **Dist:** Championship Productions. $29.99.

Building a Culture of Competitiveness in Your Gym 2013 (Unrated)
Coach Ron Kordes demonstrates competititive drills for training volleyball players. 54m; DVD. **A:** Family. **P:** Education. **U:** Home. **L:** English. **Spo-Rec:** Athletic Instruction/Coaching, Volleyball, How-To. **Acq:** Purchase. **Dist:** Championship Productions. $34.99.

Building a Deck 1981
Carpenter Pete Prlain shows how to build a deck and patio set using step-by-step instructions. 60m; VHS, 3/4 U. **Pr:** RMI Media Productions. **A:** Adult. **P:** Instruction. **U:** Institution. **How-Ins:** Home Improvement. **Acq:** Purchase. **Dist:** RMI Media.
Indiv. Titles: 1. Substructure/Decking 2. Railing/Roofing 3. Fixed Bench/Storage/Barbecue Cart.

Building a Deck 1988
A fool proof guide to building that coveted deck. 30m; VHS. **Pr:** Meredith Video. **A:** Adult. **P:** Instruction. **U:** Home. **How-Ins:** Home Improvement. **Acq:** Purchase. **Dist:** Meredith Video Publishing.

Building a Dominant Goalie 2006 (Unrated)
Coach Jon Lantzy discusses the skills required to be a goalie in lacrosse along with demonstrating some techniques to help improve those skills. 45m; DVD. **A:** Family. **P:** Education. **U:** Home, Institution. **Spo-Rec:** Lacrosse, Athletic Instruction/Coaching. **Acq:** Purchase. **Dist:** Championship Productions. $39.99.

Building A Dream: A Family Affair 1998
Shows the four and a half year process of the Gottlieb family to build a house designed by matriarch Lois Davidson Gottlieb, a student of Frank Lloyd Wright. 41m; VHS. **A:** Sr. High-Adult. **P:** Education. **U:** Home, Institution. **Gen-Edu:** Documentary Films, Sociology, Architecture. **Acq:** Purchase, Rent/Lease. **Dist:** Documentary Educational Resources. $169.00.

Building a Global Village 1990
Learn about Habitat's international work on three continents, including the people they work with, Habitat sponsored projects, and appropriate technology for the areas. 15m; VHS. **TV Std:** NTSC, PAL. **A:** Adult. **P:** Entertainment. **U:** Institution. **Gen-Edu:** Voluntary Services. **Acq:** Purchase. **Dist:** Habitat for Humanity International. $7.95.

Building a Kayak: Parts 1 and 2 1967
Two Netsilik Eskimos show the work involved in building a kayak from seal skins, sinews, bone and scraps of wood. 32m; 3/4 U, Special order formats. **Pr:** National Film Board of Canada. **A:** Jr. High-College. **P:** Education. **U:** Institution, CCTV, CATV, BCTV. **Gen-Edu:** Documentary Films, Eskimos. **Acq:** Purchase, Rent/Lease. **Dist:** Education Development Center.

Building a Model Railroad: Adding Realism ????
Part of a series of videos featuring step-by-step instructions for building a model railroad, from planning the track, to materials needed, to operation. 25m; VHS, DVD. **A:** College-Adult. **P:** Education. **U:** Home. **Gen-Edu:** Trains. **Acq:** Purchase. **Dist:** The Civil War Standard. $19.95.

Building a Model Railroad: Benchwork 1 ????
Part of a series of videos featuring step-by-step instructions for building a model railroad, from planning the track, to materials needed, to operation. 24m; VHS, DVD. **A:** College-Adult. **P:** Education. **U:** Home. **Gen-Edu:** Trains. **Acq:** Purchase. **Dist:** The Civil War Standard. $19.95.

Building a Model Railroad: Benchwork 2 ????
Part of a series of videos featuring step-by-step instructions for building a model railroad, from planning the track, to materials needed, to operation. 31m; VHS, DVD. **A:** College-Adult. **P:** Education. **U:** Home. **Gen-Edu:** Trains. **Acq:** Purchase. **Dist:** The Civil War Standard. $19.95.

Building a Model Railroad: Building Structures ????
Part of a series of videos featuring step-by-step instructions for building a model railroad, from planning the track, to materials needed, to operation. 34m; VHS, DVD. **A:** College-Adult. **P:** Education. **U:** Home. **Gen-Edu:** Trains. **Acq:** Purchase. **Dist:** The Civil War Standard. $19.95.

Building a Model Railroad: Designing ????
Part of a series of videos featuring step-by-step instructions for building a model railroad, from planning the track, to materials needed, to operation. 34m; VHS, DVD. **A:** College-Adult. **P:** Education. **U:** Home. **Gen-Edu:** Trains. **Acq:** Purchase. **Dist:** The Civil War Standard. $19.95.

Building a Model Railroad: Laying Track ????
Part of a series of videos featuring step-by-step instructions for building a model railroad, from planning the track, to materials needed, to operation. 34m; VHS, DVD. **A:** College-Adult. **P:** Education. **U:** Home. **Gen-Edu:** Trains. **Acq:** Purchase. **Dist:** The Civil War Standard. $19.95.

Building a Model Railroad: Operating ????
Part of a series of videos featuring step-by-step instructions for building a model railroad, from planning the track, to materials needed, to operation. 30m; VHS, DVD. **A:** College-Adult. **P:** Education. **U:** Home. **Gen-Edu:** Trains. **Acq:** Purchase. **Dist:** The Civil War Standard. $19.95.

Building a Model Railroad: Rolling Stock ????
Part of a series of videos featuring step-by-step instructions for building a model railroad, from planning the track, to materials needed, to operation. 32m; VHS, DVD. **A:** College-Adult. **P:** Education. **U:** Home. **Gen-Edu:** Trains. **Acq:** Purchase. **Dist:** The Civil War Standard. $19.95.

Building a Model Railroad: Scenery ????
Part of a series of videos featuring step-by-step instructions for building a model railroad, from planning the track, to materials needed, to operation. 46m; VHS, DVD. **A:** College-Adult. **P:** Education. **U:** Home. **Gen-Edu:** Trains. **Acq:** Purchase. **Dist:** The Civil War Standard. $19.95.

Building a Model Railroad: Wiring Command Control ????
Part of a series of videos featuring step-by-step instructions for building a model railroad, from planning the track, to materials needed, to operation. 74m; VHS, DVD. **A:** College-Adult. **P:** Education. **U:** Home. **Gen-Edu:** Trains. **Acq:** Purchase. **Dist:** The Civil War Standard. $19.95.

Building a Profitable Consulting Practice Series 19??
Two-part business educational series by Howard Shenson offers tips on how to build a profitable consulting practice. Covers consulting opportunities, market strategies, proposal writing, contracting strategies, fee setting, disclosure, and collection techniques. 100m; VHS. **A:** College-Adult. **P:** Vocational. **U:** Institution. **Bus-Ind:** Business, How-To. **Acq:** Purchase. **Dist:** Instructional Video.

Building a Quality Shooting Workout 2014 (Unrated)
Coach Lyndsey Fennelly details a 40-minute shooting workout for improving a basketball team's performance. 53m; DVD. **A:** Family. **P:** Education. **U:** Home. **L:** English. **Spo-Rec:** Athletic Instruction/Coaching, Basketball. **Acq:** Purchase. **Dist:** Championship Productions. $39.99.

Building a Relationship with Mother & Child 1976
Illustrates the kinds of things home-visitors must be aware of and sensitive to in order to establish the most productive kind of relationship with the mother and child. 18m/B/W; 3/4 U, EJ. **Pr:** High Scope. **A:** College-Adult. **P:** Education. **U:** Institution, CCTV, CATV, BCTV, SURA. **Gen-Edu:** Infants, Job Training. **Acq:** Purchase. **Dist:** High/Scope Educational Research Foundation.

Building a Successful Feeder System for Wrestling 2011 (Unrated)
Coach Russ Cozart gives various drills as well as tips and techniques for training wrestlers he has accumulated over the span of his career. 80m; DVD. **A:** Family. **P:** Education. **U:** Home, Institution. **Spo-Rec:** Athletic Instruction/Coaching. **Acq:** Purchase. **Dist:** Championship Productions. $39.99.

Building a Successful High School Program 2007 (Unrated)
Coach Kevin Sutton lectures on building a successful high school basketball program, including involving the community to achieve your goals. 42m; DVD. **A:** Family. **P:** Education. **U:** Home, Institution. **Spo-Rec:** Basketball, Athletic Instruction/Coaching. **Acq:** Purchase. **Dist:** Championship Productions. $39.99.

Building a Successful Junior High Wrestling Program 2009 (Unrated)
Coaches Scot Davis and Larry Hovden discuss building and maintaining a wrestling program at the junior high school level. 64m; DVD. **A:** Family. **P:** Education. **U:** Home, Institution. **Spo-Rec:** Athletic Instruction/Coaching. **Acq:** Purchase. **Dist:** Championship Productions. $39.99.

Building a Successful Life Insurance Business: Referred Lead Prospecting 1980
Three successful life insurance field salespeople discuss the effective use of referred lead prospecting. 22m; VHS, 3/4 U. **Pr:** R & R Newkirk. **A:** Adult. **P:** Instruction. **U:** Institution, CCTV. **Bus-Ind:** Insurance, Sales Training. **Acq:** Purchase, Subscription. **Dist:** Custom Communications.

Building a Successful Softball Program 2010 (Unrated)
Coach Tim Walton shares his philosophy for building a successful softball program at the college level. 87m; DVD. **A:** Family. **P:** Education. **U:** Home, Institution. **Spo-Rec:** Softball, Athletic Instruction/Coaching. **Acq:** Purchase. **Dist:** Championship Productions. $39.99.

Building a Successful Softball Program 2010 (Unrated)
Coach Tim Walton discusses building the foundations of a successful softball program, along with in- and out-of-season training. 87m; DVD. **A:** Family. **P:** Education. **U:** Home, Institution. **Spo-Rec:** Softball, Athletic Instruction/Coaching. **Acq:** Purchase. **Dist:** Championship Productions. $39.99.

Building A Team Defense 2001
Presents basketball instruction on how to assemble an effective team defensive strategy by Jim Wooldridge, former head coach at Kansas State University. 56m; VHS. **A:** Sr. High-Adult. **P:** Instruction. **U:** Institution. **Spo-Rec:** Basketball. **Acq:** Purchase. **Dist:** Championship Productions. $39.95.

Building a Term Paper: The Master Plan 1991
Part of a series that offers instruction on specific aspects of basic English grammar skills. 18m; VHS. **A:** Adult. **P:** Education. **U:** Institution. **Gen-Edu:** Communication, Language Arts. **Acq:** Purchase. **Dist:** RMI Media. $50.00.

Building a Two Way Street 1996
Instructs parents and teachers on how to encourage each other to work together and maintain open conversation about their children's education. 29m; VHS. **A:** Adult. **P:** Education. **U:** Institution. **How-Ins:** Communication, Parenting. **Acq:** Purchase. **Dist:** Perceptions Inc. $99.00.

Building a Victorian Lead Window 19??
Teaches techniques of creating Victorian leaded windows and how to work with four different sizes of lead came to fit even the smallest glass pieces. 30m; VHS. **A:** Adult. **P:** Instruction. **U:** Home. **How-Ins:** Crafts, Hobbies, How-To. **Acq:** Purchase. **Dist:** Cutters Productions. $19.95.

Building A Winning Defense: Defense Technique 2001
Offers basketball drills on defensive fundamentals by Bruce Weber, head coach of the University of Illinois. 38m; VHS. **A:** Sr. High-Adult. **P:** Instruction. **U:** Institution. **Spo-Rec:** Basketball. **Acq:** Purchase. **Dist:** Championship Productions. $39.95.

Building an Addition 19??
Shows how to build an addition onto a two-story house. Covers starting the project, framing, weatherproofing, mechanical rough-ins, drywalling, kitchen, bathroom and finishing touches. 195m; VHS. **A:** Sr. High-Adult. **P:** Instruction. **U:** Home. **How-Ins:** How-To, Home Improvement, Construction. **Acq:** Purchase. **Dist:** Hometime Video Publishing Inc. $19.95.

Building an Algonquin Birchbark Canoe 1990
The endangered art of canoe building is demonstrated by a pair of elderly Algonquin Indians in Maniwaki, Quebec. 54m; VHS, 3/4 U. **Pr:** Trust for Native American Cultures. **A:** Family. **P:** Education. **U:** Institution, Home, SURA. **Gen-Edu:** Documentary Films, Native Americans. **Acq:** Purchase, Rent/Lease. **Dist:** Trust for Native American Cultures and Crafts. $100.00.

Building an All-Around Volleyball Athlete with Brazilian Training Methods 2012 (Unrated)
Olympian Cilene Drewnick presents the drills and training methods use by Brazilian volleyball players. 64m; DVD. **A:** Family. **P:** Education. **U:** Home. **L:** English. **Spo-Rec:** Athletic Instruction/Coaching, Volleyball, How-To. **Acq:** Purchase. **Dist:** Championship Productions. $34.99.

Building an Elite Program 2009 (Unrated)
Coach Melvin BeLong discusses how coaches can build an elite soccer program. 64m; DVD. **A:** Family. **P:** Education. **U:** Home, Institution. **Spo-Rec:** Soccer, Athletic Instruction/Coaching. **Acq:** Purchase. **Dist:** Championship Productions. $29.99.

Building an Explosive Hurdler 2012 (Unrated)
Coach Lawrence Johnson demonstrates more than 65 training drills and exercises for hurdlers. 65m; DVD. **A:** Family. **P:** Education. **U:** Home. **L:** English. **Spo-Rec:** Athletic Instruction/Coaching, Sports--Track & Field, How-To. **Acq:** Purchase. **Dist:** Championship Productions. $39.99.

Building & Remodeling for Accessibility 19??
Shows how to make your home more accessible for special needs, including segments on how to build a wheelchair accessible ramp, remodeling a kitchen or bathroom and a tour of a home built for greater accessibility and independent living. 30m; VHS. **A:** Sr. High-Adult. **P:** Instruction. **U:** Home. **How-Ins:** How-To, Home Improvement, Handicapped. **Acq:** Purchase. **Dist:** Hometime Video Publishing Inc. $11.95.

Building Big with David Macaulay 2000
Explores the engineering feats that helped construct our world, focusing on five types of man-made structures integral to modern life: bridges, tunnels, dams, skyscrapers and domes. Hosted by David Macaulay, author of "The Way Things Work." Five volume set. 60m; VHS. **A:** Family. **P:** Education. **U:** Home. **Gen-Edu:** Architecture, Documentary Films. **Acq:** Purchase. **Dist:** WGBH/Boston. $69.95.

Building Blocks for Successful Parenting ????
Five-part series presents parents of preschool children with effective steps and techniques for handling experiences and situations during early development. 100m; VHS. **A:** Adult. **P:** Education. **U:** Institution. **Gen-Edu:** Parenting. **Acq:** Purchase. **Dist:** The Bureau for At-Risk Youth. $249.95.
Indiv. Titles: 1. Handling Anger, Temper Tantrums and Sibling Rivalry Effectively 2. Preschooler Discipline: Making It a Positive Experience 3. Ages and Stages: Knowing What to Expect and When 4. Preparing Your Preschooler for Success in School 5. Working Parents and Your Preschooler.

Building Blocks for Team Performance 19??
Teaches the importance of teamwork and offers concepts to be used to build successful teams within your organization, including effective listening, developing top performers, and time management. Includes workbook. ?m; VHS. **A:** College-Adult. **P:** Professional. **U:** Institution. **Bus-Ind:** Business, How-To. **Acq:** Purchase. **Dist:** Instructional Video. $295.00.

Building Bodies 1981
This program from the "Life on Earth" series explains that jellyfish, mollusks and horseshoe crabs are among the three types of marine invertebrates whose ancestry began six hundred million years ago. 58m; VHS, 3/4 U. **Pr:** British Broadcasting Corporation; Warner Bros. **A:** Primary-Jr. High. **P:** Education. **U:** Institution, SURA. **Hea-Sci:** Documentary Films, Oceanography, Evolution. **Acq:** Purchase, Rent/Lease, Off-Air Record. **Dist:** Home Vision Cinema.

Building Bombs 1989
A look at issues surrounding the Savannah River nuclear power plant in Aiken, South Carolina, which was partially shut down in 1988 because of safety concerns. 54m; VHS, 3/4 U, Special order formats. **C:** Narrated by Jane Alexander. **Pr:** Mark Moci; Susan Robinson. **A:** College-Adult. **P:** Education. **U:** Institution, CCTV, CATV, BCTV, Home, SURA. **Gen-Edu:** Documentary Films, Nuclear Energy, Waste Products. **Acq:** Purchase, Rent/Lease. **Dist:** Facets Multimedia Inc.; The Video Project. $95.00.

Building Bombs 2007 (Unrated)
Documentary on Aiken, South Carolina, home to the plant that manufactures hydrogen bombs for the United States, and a cover-up of massive toxic waste dumping. 161m; DVD. **A:** Sr. High-Adult. **P:** Education. **U:** Home. **Gen-Edu:** Documentary Films, Nuclear Warfare. **Acq:** Purchase. **Dist:** Docurama. $26.95.

Building Bookcases 1987
Learn everything you need to know about building bookcases from choosing the wood to building a door. 40m; VHS. **Pr:** Do It Yourself Inc. **A:** Sr. High-Adult. **P:** Instruction. **U:** Home. **How-Ins:** How-To, Home Improvement, Woodworking. **Acq:** Purchase. **Dist:** Do It Yourself, Inc./D.I.Y. Video Corp. $19.95.

Building Cabinets 1987
Create your own storage space! Learn to build cabinets from start to finish. 35m; VHS. **Pr:** Do It Yourself Inc. **A:** Sr. High-Adult. **P:** Instruction. **U:** Home. **How-Ins:** How-To, Home Improvement, Woodworking. **Acq:** Purchase. **Dist:** Do It Yourself, Inc./D.I.Y. Video Corp. $19.95.

Building Construction Video Series 19??
Five-part series in which Dr. Billy Harrell, Professor and Chair of Agricultural Sciences and Vocational Education at Sam Houston State University, combines scale models with live-action footage of the construction of a 16' X 10' portable storage building to provide comprehensive building instruction. He covers basic stud frame construction, foundation and flooring, framing, roofing, and ceiling joists and rafters. 160m; VHS. **A:** Sr. High-Adult. **P:** Vocational. **U:** Institution. **How-Ins:** Construction, Occupational Training, How-To. **Acq:** Purchase. **Dist:** CEV Multimedia.
Indiv. Titles: 1. Basic Stud Frame Construction 2. Foundation and Flooring 3. Framing 4. Roofing 5. Ceiling Joists and Rafters.

Building Creativity and Discipline into Your Motion Offense 2013 (Unrated)
Coaches Geno Auriemma and Bob Knight introduce drills and techniques for building a basketball team's motion offense. 91m; DVD. **A:** Family. **P:** Education. **U:** Home. **L:** English. **Spo-Rec:** Athletic Instruction/Coaching, Basketball. **Acq:** Purchase. **Dist:** Championship Productions. $39.99.

Building Dreams 19??
Examination of Los Angeles carpenters at work on various projects. Offers insight from the carpenters on passing on their skills and knowledge to the young men and women of South Central L.A. 20m; VHS. **C:** Narrated by Joe Spano. **Pr:** California Working Group. **A:** Sr. High-Adult. **P:** Professional. **U:** Home, Institution. **Bus-Ind:** Industrial Arts, Construction, Occupations. **Acq:** Purchase. **Dist:** CA Working Group/We Do the Work. $59.00.

Building Evacuation 1995
Focuses on the principles of evacuation and the importance of everyone knowing their role in an emergency. 12m; VHS. **A:** Adult. **P:** Professional. **U:** Institution. **Bus-Ind:** Safety Education, Occupational Training, Management. **Acq:** Purchase, Rent/Lease. **Dist:** National Safety Council, California Chapter, Film Library. $195.00.

Building Family Relationships 1980
Building trust, confidence, and a sense of belonging are stressed as the keystones to a strong bond between parents and their children. 30m; VHS, 3/4 U. **C:** Phil Donahue. **A:** College-Adult. **P:** Education. **U:** Institution, SURA. **Gen-Edu:** Family. **Acq:** Purchase. **Dist:** Home Vision Cinema.

Building Futures: Re-Building Our Lives 1996
Documents a group of women on welfare who began a project dedicated to building a 24-hour women's emergency shelter and resource center in Victoria, British Colombia. 30m; VHS. **A:** Sr. High-Adult. **P:** Entertainment. **U:** Home, Institution. **Gen-Edu:** Women, Social Service. **Acq:** Purchase. **Dist:** Moving Images Distribution.

Building High Performing Teams 1991
A presentation on the four steps of building an effective management team. 60m; VHS, 3/4 U, Special order formats. **C:** Hosted by Ken Blanchard. **Pr:** Video Publishing House. **A:** College-Adult. **P:** Professional. **U:** Institution. **Bus-Ind:** How-To, Business, Management. **Acq:** Purchase, Rent/Lease. **Dist:** Excellence in Training Corp. $995.00.

A Building in the Sun 1980
A look at a working, economical, and attractive commercial-size underground solar building. Its architect and engineer stress the environmental ethic and the aesthetic and energy considerations inherent in the design and construction of the Cary Arboretum's Plant Science Building. 20m; VHS, 3/4 U. **Pr:** Gary W. Griffen. **A:** Sr. High-Adult. **P:** Education. **U:** Institution, Home, SURA. **Gen-Edu:** Documentary Films, Solar Energy, Architecture. **Acq:** Purchase, Duplication License. **Dist:** Bullfrog Films, Inc.

Building More Effective Teams: The Organization Development (O.D.) Approach 1978
Peter Block, a highly regarded consultant who specializes in creative problem-solving, demonstrates how to identify structures and relationships that hinder organizational growth and productivity. Documents Block's O.D. efforts at the New York Board of Cooperative Educational Services. Thirty managers learn coping, counseling, and problem-solving skills in a series of group training sessions and role-playing exercises. 26m; 3/4 U, Special order formats. **Pr:** Hobel Leiterman Productions. **A:** Adult. **P:** Professional. **U:** Institution. **Bus-Ind:** Documentary Films, Management. **Acq:** Purchase. **Dist:** The Cinema Guild.

Building of the Earth 1984
From "The Living Planet" series comes this depiction of the forces that have formed the earth's surface. 55m; VHS, 3/4 U, Special order formats. **C:** Hosted by David Attenborough. **Pr:** British Broadcasting Corporation; Time-Life Films. **A:** Sr. High-Adult. **P:** Education. **U:** Institution, SURA. **Hea-Sci:** Documentary Films, Geology, Natural Resources. **Acq:** Purchase, Rent/Lease. **Dist:** Time-Life Video and Television.

Building on What Children Know 1974
Experts discuss ways teachers can take advantage of the rich language background virtually every beginning reader brings to the classroom. For the elementary school teacher. 29m; 3/4 U. **Pr:** Media Five. **A:** College-Adult. **P:** Teacher Education. **U:** Institution, CCTV, SURA. **Gen-Edu:** Education, Language Arts. **Acq:** Purchase. **Dist:** Home Vision Cinema.

Building One-Minute Management Skills 1987
Through film clips, additional "one-minute" management training is demonstrated. 45m; VHS, 3/4 U. **Pr:** Blanchard Training & Development. **A:** Adult. **P:** Professional. **U:** Institution. **Bus-Ind:** Management. **Acq:** Purchase, Rent/Lease. **Dist:** Ken Blanchard Co.

Building Parent Involvement: Elementary Grades 1995
For teachers of Grades K-5. Includes video, handouts, and Leader's guide in binder. Honorable Mention, Columbus International Film and Video Festival. 28m; VHS. **A:** Primary. **P:** Education. **U:** Institution. **Chl-Juv:** Children, Education. **Acq:** Purchase. **Dist:** Sunburst Digital Inc. $149.00.

Building Parent Involvement: Elementary Guides 1994
Strategies for improving parental involvement in their child's elementary education. 26m; VHS. **A:** Adult. **P:** Education. **U:** Institution. **Gen-Edu:** Parenting, Education. **Acq:** Purchase. **Dist:** Sunburst Digital Inc. $149.00.

Building Peace in the Midst of War 1988
A look at Salvadorans who are attempting to rebuild their homes destroyed during the government's war with leftist guerillas. 30m; VHS, 3/4 U, Special order formats. **Pr:** Carol Yourman. **A:** College-Adult. **P:** Education. **U:** Institution, CCTV, CATV, BCTV, Home, SURA. **Gen-Edu:** Documentary Films, War--General, Central America. **Acq:** Purchase, Rent/Lease. **Dist:** The Video Project; Facets Multimedia Inc. $75.00.

Building Personal Wealth 19??
Jody Tallal offers fundamental principles of wealth building, including determining financial goals and actions needed to attain them. Includes information on inflation and how to beat it. 50m; VHS. **A:** College-Adult. **P:** Instruction. **U:** Home. **How-Ins:** Personal Finance, Self-Help. **Acq:** Purchase. **Dist:** Instructional Video. $59.95.

Building Quality Excellence w/ ISO 9000 1992
This is a guide to becoming a certified supplier of world class quality. Two videotapes, a reference supplement, and a book investigate all the reasons why IOS 9000 has become the worldwide quality standard. 91m; VHS. **A:** Adult. **P:** Professional. **U:** Institution. **L:** English. **Bus-Ind:** Industry & Industrialists. **Acq:** Purchase. **Dist:** Society of Manufacturing Engineers. $895.

Building Self-Confidence 19??
Therapy clients are taught about four habits that block confidence and how to move beyond old habits and begin building self-confidence. 30m; VHS. **A:** Adult. **P:** Education. **U:** Institution. **L:** English. **Hea-Sci:** Self-Help. **Acq:** Purchase. **Dist:** Hazelden Publishing. $200.

Building Self-Confidence 1987
Employees get more done when they feel good about themselves and the job they're doing. 19m; VHS, 3/4 U. **Pr:** First Financial Network. **A:** Adult. **P:** Education. **U:** Institution, Home. **Bus-Ind:** Employee Counseling. **Acq:** Purchase, Rent/Lease. **Dist:** 1st Financial Training Services. $325.00.

Building Self-Confidence 1990
Stresses the importance of high self-esteem, and offers parents and caregivers guidance in developing it in children in their

care. ?m; VHS. **A:** Sr. High-Adult. **P:** Education. **U:** Institution. **Gen-Edu:** Parenting, Child Care. **Acq:** Purchase. **Dist:** Meridian Education Corp. $45.00.

Building Self-Confidence 1990
Offers strategies to students for building self-esteem by risk-taking, learning to handle put-downs, validating oneself and accepting encouragement from others. 38m; VHS. **A:** Jr. High-Sr. High. **P:** Education. **U:** Institution. **Gen-Edu:** Education, Adolescence, Self-Help. **Acq:** Purchase. **Dist:** Sunburst Digital Inc. $199.00.

Building Self-Esteem 19??
Explores a middle school and a high school with successful self-esteem programs. Includes leader's guide and handouts. 26m; VHS. **A:** Adult. **P:** Teacher Education. **U:** Institution. **Gen-Edu:** Education. **Acq:** Purchase. **Dist:** Sunburst Digital Inc. $149.

Building Skills in High-Risk Families 1996
Explains how the practitioner may be able to teach high-risk families how to build relationships, minimize resistance, and keep focused on family goals. Contains realistic demonstrations from Boys Town family preservation counselors which cover a wide variety of family settings and skills. Comes with the "Building Skills in High-Risk Families" manual. 115m; VHS. **A:** Adult. **P:** Teacher Education. **U:** Institution. **How-Ins:** Family, How-To, Social Service. **Acq:** Purchase. **Dist:** Girls and Boys Town. $149.95.

Building Skyscrapers 1994
Young children will be able to get a front row seat to the creation of a skyscraper. 40m; VHS. **A:** Primary-Jr. High. **P:** Education. **U:** Institution. **Chl-Juv:** Children, Construction. **Acq:** Purchase. **Dist:** Tapeworm Video Distributors Inc. $14.95.

Building Sound Self-Esteem 19??
Demonstrates for students how the power of positive thinking and taking responsibility for your own actions can better your life. 19m; VHS. **A:** Jr. High-Sr. High. **P:** Education. **U:** Institution. **Gen-Edu:** Self-Help. **Acq:** Purchase. **Dist:** Educational Video Network. $69.95.

Building Sound Self-Esteem: Realities of Human Behavior 1990
Learn how to accept who and what you are despite mistakes, overcome those obstacles that block the progress in life, and end manipulation by others through this lesson in acquiring self-esteem and mental positiveness. 25m; VHS. **Pr:** Bridgestone Production Group. **A:** College-Adult. **P:** Education. **U:** Home. **Gen-Edu:** Self-Help, Psychology. **Acq:** Purchase. **Dist:** Alpha Omega Publications Inc. $24.95.

Building Strength with Susan Powter 1994
Diet and fitness expert Powter helps aerobicizers increase fat-burning efficiency, feel stronger, and get leaner faster. 60m; VHS. **A:** Jr. High-Adult. **P:** Instruction. **U:** Home. **Hea-Sci:** Fitness/Exercise. **Acq:** Purchase. **Dist:** WarnerVision. $19.95.

Building Strong Families: Helping Kids Behave ????
Presents a series of vignettes portraying various discipline situations and discusses discipline alternatives. 15m; VHS. **A:** Adult. **P:** Education. **U:** Home. **Gen-Edu:** Parenting, How-To. **Acq:** Purchase. **Dist:** Michigan State University. $45.00.

Building Strong Families: Parenting Young Children ????
Famous people from Michigan (Magic Johnson, John Smoltz and Sinbad) discuss and demonstrates techniques for successful parenting. 14m; VHS. **A:** Adult. **P:** Education. **U:** Home. **Gen-Edu:** Parenting, How-To. **Acq:** Purchase. **Dist:** Michigan State University. $45.00.

Building Strong Families: Playing to Learn ????
Presents a series of vignettes portraying behavior to be modeled by parents that will help children develop physically, emotionally, socially, and intellectually. 15m; VHS. **A:** Adult. **P:** Education. **U:** Home. **Gen-Edu:** Parenting, How-To. **Acq:** Purchase. **Dist:** Michigan State University. $45.00.

Building Structures: Building a Model Railroad 19?? (Unrated)
Provides detailed instructions for constructing a model railroad, from the track plans, to materials, wiring, rolling stock, and putting it all into action. 35m; DVD. **A:** Family. **P:** Education. **U:** Home. **Gen-Edu:** Trains, U.S. States. **Acq:** Purchase. **Dist:** The Civil War Standard. $19.95.

Building Student Success: Grades 5-9 19??
Spotlights two schools successful in building student success, discussing goals/outcome orientation, family-style groupings, peer conferencing and more. Complete with leader's guide and handouts. 26m; VHS, CC. **A:** Adult. **P:** Teacher Education. **U:** Institution. **Gen-Edu:** Education. **Acq:** Purchase. **Dist:** Sunburst Digital Inc. $149.

Building Tables 1987
Learn how to build a table from choosing the right materials to adding creative finishing touches. 40m; VHS. **Pr:** Do It Yourself Inc. **A:** Sr. High-Adult. **P:** Instruction. **U:** Home. **How-Ins:** How-To, Home Improvement, Woodworking. **Acq:** Purchase. **Dist:** Do It Yourself, Inc./D.I.Y. Video Corp. $19.95.

Building the 1-2-2 Three-Quarter Court Defense 2013 (Unrated)
Basketball coach Mitch Buonaguro gives a thorough on-court presentation of the 1-2-2 defensive press. DVD. **A:** Family. **P:** Education. **U:** Home. **L:** English. **Spo-Rec:** Athletic Instruction/Coaching, Basketball. **Acq:** Purchase. **Dist:** Championship Productions. $39.99.

Building the 2-2-2 Offense Player by Player 2014 (Unrated)
Lacrosse coach J.B. Clarke demonstrates various offensive training drills for building the 2-2-2. 101m; DVD. **A:** Family. **P:** Education. **U:** Home. **L:** English. **Spo-Rec:** Athletic Instruction/Coaching, Lacrosse. **Acq:** Purchase. **Dist:** Championship Productions. $49.99.

Building the American Dream: Levittown, NY 1994
Summarizes how New York real estate developer William Levitt built affordable housing for returning WWII veterans and their families in Levittown and other Long Island communities. Also illustrates a policy of racial discrimination prevented African-Americans from buying these homes and describes the collapse of Levitt's construction empire. 60m; VHS. **A:** Jr. High-Adult. **P:** Education. **U:** Institution. **Gen-Edu:** Documentary Films, History--U.S., Sociology. **Acq:** Purchase, Rent/Lease. **Dist:** The Cinema Guild. $350.00.

Building the Body Beautiful 1987
A series designed for men and women, instructing in body building for maximum agility, strength and endurance. 23m; VHS. **Pr:** Nancy Bishop; MCA Entertainment. **A:** Sr. High-Adult. **P:** Instruction. **U:** Home. **Hea-Sci:** Fitness/Exercise. **Acq:** Purchase. **Dist:** Cambridge Educational. $19.95.
Indiv. Titles: 1. Arms 2. Stomach & Legs 3. Chest, Shoulders & Back.

Building the Body of the Lesson 19??
Part 2 of 4, "Building the Body of a Lesson" helps educators build a solid lesson on the foundations already laid. Steps 4 and 5 of the Master Teacher Model concentrate on assuring teachers that students are actually learning what they are being taught. 60m; VHS. **A:** Adult. **P:** Teacher Education. **U:** Institution. **L:** English. **Gen-Edu:** Education. **Acq:** Purchase. **Dist:** Master Teacher Inc. $119.95.

Building the Brookhaven House 1982
A fascinating record of the construction of the Department of Energy's prototype passive solar home which is built with standard techniques and materials. 25m; VHS, 3/4 U. **Pr:** Department of Energy. **A:** Jr. High-Sr. High. **P:** Education. **U:** Institution, Home, SURA. **Gen-Edu:** Documentary Films, Solar Energy, Architecture. **Acq:** Purchase, Duplication License. **Dist:** Bullfrog Films, Inc.; National Audiovisual Center; American Institute of Architects.

Building the Complete Running Back 2012 (Unrated)
Coach Danny Barrett presents this thorough guide to building up skills in a football team's running back. 50m; DVD. **A:** Family. **P:** Education. **U:** Home, Institution. **Spo-Rec:** Basketball, Athletic Instruction/Coaching. **Acq:** Purchase. **Dist:** Championship Productions. $39.99.

Building the DeMatha Team Defense 2011 (Unrated)
Coach Mike Jones shares the defensive techniques used by the DeMatha Catholic High School basketball team. ??m; DVD. **A:** Family. **P:** Education. **U:** Home, Institution. **Spo-Rec:** Basketball, Athletic Instruction/Coaching. **Acq:** Purchase. **Dist:** Championship Productions. $39.99.

Building the Gherkin 2005
Documentary following the creation of the controversial Swiss Re building by award-winning architect Norman Foster. 52m; VHS, DVD. **A:** Jr. High-Adult. **P:** Education. **U:** Institution. **Gen-Edu:** Documentary Films, Architecture. **Acq:** Purchase, Rent/Lease. **Dist:** The Cinema Guild. $295.00.

Building the House of God 19??
Architecture film from the University of Calgary Learning Commons. ?m; VHS. **A:** Adult. **P:** Education. **U:** Institution. **Gen-Edu:** Architecture, Documentary Films. **Acq:** Purchase. **Dist:** University of Calgary Library, Visual Resources Centre.

Building the Rutan Composites 1984
Shows the complete procedure for utilizing fiberglass-epoxy-foam composite construction as established by Burt Rutan. 91m; VHS. **Pr:** Ferde Grofe Films. **A:** Sr. High-Adult. **P:** Education. **U:** Institution, Home. **How-Ins:** How-To, Aeronautics. **Acq:** Purchase. **Dist:** Bennett Marine Video; Military/Combat Stock Footage Library. $29.95.

Building the Trans-National Team 1994
Underlines the difficulties of doing business with people of various nationalities including French, Spanish, German, and British. Focusses on cultural differences. Comes with guide. 25m; VHS. **A:** Adult. **P:** Professional. **U:** Institution. **Bus-Ind:** Business, International Relations. **Acq:** Purchase, Rent/Lease. **Dist:** Learning Communications L.L.C. $495.00.

Building the Transnational Team 1999
Helps the viewer to strengthen their abilities to interact in multi-cultural team environments. ?m; VHS. **A:** Adult. **P:** Education. **U:** Home, Institution. **Bus-Ind:** Business. **Acq:** Purchase. **Dist:** Learning Communications L.L.C. $695.00.

Building Up Our Self-Esteem: Where Giants Walk 19??
Earnie Larsen offers advice to help build self-esteem and overcome guilt and shame while recovering from alcoholism. 32m; VHS. **A:** Adult. **P:** Education. **U:** Institution. **Hea-Sci:** Alcoholism, Self-Help. **Acq:** Purchase. **Dist:** Hazelden Publishing. $200.00.

Building Your Cross Country Program with Pride 2005 (Unrated)
Coach Joe Newton lectures on building a cross country program at your school. 34m; DVD. **A:** Family. **P:** Education. **U:**
Home, Institution. **Spo-Rec:** Sports--Track & Field, Athletic Instruction/Coaching. **Acq:** Purchase. **Dist:** Championship Productions. $39.99.

Building Your Dream 19??
"Building Your Dream" provides a step-by-step overview of the entire home building process, discussing key areas to watch for in building your dream house. Subjects covered include lot selection, pre-construction, financing, and detailed construction processes. ?m; VHS. **A:** Adult. **P:** Instruction. **U:** Home. **L:** English. **How-Ins:** Construction. **Acq:** Purchase. **Dist:** Tapeworm Video Distributors Inc.

Building Your Half Court Offense with Shell Drills 2012
Expert Mike Procopio demonstrates using the shell drill to build a basketball team's offense instead of defense. 116m; DVD. **A:** Jr. High-Adult. **P:** Education. **U:** Home, Institution. **L:** English. **Gen-Edu:** Athletic Instruction/Coaching, Basketball. **Acq:** Purchase. **Dist:** Championship Productions. $39.99.

Building Your Money Pyramid: Financial Planning 1994
Part of a series offering instruction on money management. 14m; VHS. **A:** Adult. **P:** Education. **U:** Institution. **Gen-Edu:** Finance. **Acq:** Purchase. **Dist:** RMI Media. $49.00.

Building Your Motion Offense 2012 (Unrated)
Coach J.B. Clarke gives tips and techniques for using the motion offense in lacrosse. 67m; DVD. **A:** Family. **P:** Education. **U:** Home. **L:** English. **Spo-Rec:** Athletic Instruction/Coaching, Lacrosse, How-To. **Acq:** Purchase. **Dist:** Championship Productions. $39.99.

Building Your Team's Transition Game 2012 (Unrated)
Coach Kathy Taylor demonstrates over 15 drills for improving a lacrosse team's skills in transition play. 105m; DVD. **A:** Family. **P:** Education. **U:** Home, Institution. **Spo-Rec:** Lacrosse, Athletic Instruction/Coaching. **Acq:** Purchase. **Dist:** Championship Productions. $39.99.

Built by Hand: The String Trio of New York 1988
Eclectic musician/composers Charles Burnham, James Emery, and John Lindberg perform "Wise Old Owl Blues," "Ephemera—Trilogy," "Texas Koto Blues," "Multiple Reasons," "Seven Vice," and other selections. 30m; VHS. **A:** Sr. High-Adult. **P:** Entertainment. **U:** Home. **Fin-Art:** Music--Jazz. **Acq:** Purchase. **Dist:** Rhapsody Films, Inc. $24.95.

Bujones in Class 19??
Classical ballet dancer Fernando Bujones demonstrates his technique with an emphasis on posture placement and classic ballet. 31m; VHS. **A:** Sr. High-Adult. **P:** Instruction. **U:** Home. **Fin-Art:** Dance--Instruction, Dance--Ballet. **Acq:** Purchase. **Dist:** Stagestep. $19.95.

Bujones: In His Image 19??
Classical ballet dancer Bujones is shown in excerpts from his greatest roles, including "Le Corsaire," "Raymonde," "Don Quixote," "7-Greek Dances," "Swan Lake," "Giselle," and "La Bayadere." 57m; VHS. **A:** Jr. High-Adult. **P:** Entertainment. **U:** Home. **Fin-Art:** Dance--Ballet. **Acq:** Purchase. **Dist:** Stagestep. $39.95.

Bukowski at Bellevue 1970
This video features poet Charles Bukowski early in his career, giving a reading at Bellevue Community College. 60m; VHS. **Pr:** Black Sparrow. **A:** Sr. High-Adult. **P:** Education. **U:** Institution, Home. **Fin-Art:** Literature, Performing Arts. **Acq:** Purchase. **Dist:** Black Sparrow Books.

Bulimia 1986
A thorough examination of the illness through interviews, medical expertise and dramatization. Upon the purchaser's request the phone number of that person's local help resource will be recorded at the end of the tape before shipping. 24m; VHS, 3/4 U. **TV Std:** NTSC, PAL, SECAM. **C:** Michael Learned. **Pr:** Health Sciences Consortium; Center for Medical Communication. **A:** Jr. High-Adult. **P:** Education. **U:** Institution, SURA. **Hea-Sci:** Psychology, Diseases, Eating Disorders. **Acq:** Purchase, Rent/Lease. **Dist:** East Carolina University. $195.00.

Bulimia and the Road to Recovery 1988
The symptoms and possible causes of this eating disorder are explored through interviews with recovered bulimics. 27m; VHS, 3/4 U. **Pr:** Sandra Smith. **A:** Primary-Adult. **P:** Education. **U:** Institution, SURA. **Gen-Edu:** Eating Disorders, Health Education. **Acq:** Purchase, Rent/Lease. **Dist:** Women Make Movies. $250.00.

Bulimia: Out of Control Eating 1986
The symptoms of binging and purging and the psychological reasons behind bulimia are explored here. 23m; VHS, 3/4 U. **Pr:** Sylvie Boulet. **A:** Jr. High-Adult. **P:** Education. **U:** Institution, SURA. **Gen-Edu:** Psychology, Mental Health, Eating Disorders. **Acq:** Rent/Lease. **Dist:** Video Out Distribution.

Bulimia: The Binge-Purge Obsession 1986
Dr. Anita Siegman explains the causes and consequences of trying to lose weight by binging and purging. 25m; VHS, 3/4 U, Special order formats. **Pr:** Eugene Ferraro. **A:** Jr. High-Adult. **P:** Education. **U:** Institution, Home. **Hea-Sci:** Psychology, Mental Health, Eating Disorders. **Acq:** Purchase, Rent/Lease. **Dist:** Research Press; Leo Media, Inc. $385.00.

Bulimia: The Vicious Cycle 1990
Discusses the vicious cycle of bulimia from the perspective of an expert clinician, and a former bulimic who shares her story of sickness and recovery. ?m; VHS. **A:** Jr. High-Sr. High. **P:** Education. **U:** Institution. **Hea-Sci:** Eating Disorders. **Acq:** Purchase. **Dist:** Meridian Education Corp. $45.00.

Bulk Liquid Safety Concerns 19??
Outlines techniques for the safe transfer of bulk liquids from storage facilities to transport facilities. Emphasis is on three basic tasks: weighing and spotting; making connections; and disconnecting and releasing. Also discusses five basic characteristics of safe transfer: toxicity, viscosity, volatility, temperature, and pressure. Includes Leader's Guide and 25 Program Guides. 8m; VHS, 3/4 U. **A:** Adult. **P:** Education. **U:** Institution. **Bus-Ind:** Safety Education, Industry & Industrialists. **Acq:** Purchase. **Dist:** Williams Learning Network.

The Bulkin Trail 1993
A man whose confidence has been shaken returns to his parents' home and reflects upon a boyhood memory that ultimately gives him inspiration to face his future. 28m; VHS. **C:** David Hasselhoff; Sally Kirkland. **A:** Jr. High-Adult. **P:** Education. **U:** Institution. **Gen-Edu:** Adolescence, Psychology, Family. **Acq:** Purchase, Rent/Lease. **Dist:** Pyramid Media. $295.00.

Bull Durham 1988 (R) — ★★★½
Lovable American romantic comedy, dealing with a very minor minor-league team and three of its current constituents: aging baseball groupie Annie Savoy (Sarandon) who beds one player each season; a cocky, foolish new pitcher, Ebby Calvin "Nuke" LaLoosh (Robbins); and older, weary catcher Crash Davis (Costner), who's brought in to wise the rookie up. The scene in which Annie tries poetry out on the banal rookie (who has more earthly pleasures in mind) is a hoot. Highly acclaimed, the film sears with Sarandon and Costner's love scenes and some clever dialogue. 107m; VHS, DVD, Wide, CC. **C:** Kevin Costner; Susan Sarandon; Tim Robbins; Trey Wilson; Robert Wuhl; Jenny Robertson; Directed by Ron Shelton; Written by Ron Shelton; Cinematography by Bobby Byrne; Music by Michael Convertino. **Pr:** Mount Company; Orion Pictures. **A:** Sr. High-Adult. **P:** Entertainment. **U:** Home. **Mov-Ent:** Comedy--Romantic, Baseball, Sports--Fiction: Comedy. **Awds:** L.A. Film Critics '88: Screenplay; N.Y. Film Critics '88: Screenplay; Natl. Soc. Film Critics '88: Screenplay; Writers Guild '88: Orig. Screenplay. **Acq:** Purchase. **Dist:** MGM Studios Inc. ; Home Vision Cinema. $19.98.

Bull of the West 1971 (Unrated) — ★½
Cattlemen battle for land in the wide open spaces of the old West. 90m; VHS. **C:** Charles Bronson; Lee J. Cobb; Brian Keith; George Kennedy; DeForest Kelley; Doug McClure; James Drury; Geraldine Brooks; Lois Nettleton; Ben Johnson; Gary Clarke; Directed by Jerry Hopper; Written by Don Ingalls; Cinematography by Benjamin (Ben H.) Kline; Music by Hal Mooney. **Pr:** Harry Tatelman. **A:** Jr. High-Adult. **P:** Entertainment. **U:** Home. **Mov-Ent:** Western. **Acq:** Purchase. **Dist:** Amazon.com Inc.

Bull Riding 1990
An incredible look at the toughest riders this side of the Pecos. 30m; VHS. **A:** Family. **P:** Entertainment. **U:** Home. **Spo-Rec:** Documentary Films, Rodeos. **Acq:** Purchase. **Dist:** MNTEX Entertainment, Inc.

Bulldance 1988 — ★
At a gymnastic school in Crete, a girl's obsession with Greek mythological ritual leads to murder. 105m; VHS, DVD. **C:** Lauren Hutton; Cliff DeYoung; Renee Estevez; Directed by Zelda Barron. **Pr:** Independent. **A:** Sr. High-Adult. **P:** Entertainment. **U:** Home. **Mov-Ent:** Horror. **Acq:** Purchase. **Dist:** Amazon.com Inc.

Bulldog Courage 1935 — ★★
Young man is out to avenge his father's murder. 66m/B/W; VHS, DVD. **C:** Tim McCoy; Lois January; Joan Woodbury; John Elliott; Directed by Sam Newfield. **Pr:** Puritan. **A:** Family. **P:** Entertainment. **U:** Institution, Home. **Mov-Ent:** Western. **Acq:** Purchase, Trade-in. **Dist:** Alpha Video; Movies Unlimited. $19.95.

Bulldog Drummond 1929 (Unrated) — ★★½
The Bulldog Drummond character, created by "Sapper" (Herman Cyril McNeile), underwent a number of different incarnations from 20s silents through the 40s, and even occassionally in the 50s and 60s. A suave ex-British officer (a precursor to the glib shaken-not-stirred gentleman-spy variety), Bulldog has been played by the likes of Colman, Ralph Richardson, and Tom Conway, among others. In this, the first installment in the long-standing series, a WWI vet, bored with civilian life, is enlisted by a beautiful woman to help her father in various adventures. 85m/B/W; VHS. **C:** Ronald Colman; Joan Bennett; Montagu Love; Lilyan Tashman; Lawrence Grant; Wilson Benge; Claud Allister; Adolph Milar; Charles Sellon; Tetsu Komai; Donald Novis; Directed by F. Richard Jones; Written by Sidney Howard; Wallace Smith; Cinematography by George Barnes; Gregg Toland. **Pr:** Samuel Goldwyn. **A:** Family. **P:** Entertainment. **U:** Home. **Mov-Ent:** Mystery & Suspense. **Acq:** Purchase. **Dist:** Rex Miller Artisan Studio. $19.98.

Bulldog Drummond at Bay 1937 (Unrated) — ★
Drummond searches for a group of foreign agents who are trying to steal the plans for a top-secret warplane. Poor British entry to the "Bulldog Drummond" series. 63m/B/W; VHS, DVD. **C:** John Lodge; Dorothy Mackaill; Victor Jory; Claud Allister; Hugh Miller; Directed by Norman Lee. **Pr:** Wardour; Republic Pictures. **A:** Jr. High-Adult. **P:** Entertainment. **U:** Home. **Mov-Ent:** Mystery & Suspense, International Relations, Aeronautics. **Acq:** Purchase. **Dist:** Sinister Cinema. $16.95.

Bulldog Drummond Comes Back 1937 — ★★
Drummond, aided by Colonel Nielson, rescues his fiancee from the hands of desperate kidnappers. 119m/B/W; VHS, DVD, 3/4 U, Special order formats. **C:** John Howard; John Barrymore; Louise Campbell; Reginald Denny; Guy Standing; Directed by Louis King. **Pr:** Paramount Pictures. **A:** Family. **P:** Entertainment. **U:** Home. **Mov-Ent:** Mystery & Suspense. **Acq:** Purchase. **Dist:** Sinister Cinema; Rex Miller Artisan Studio. $16.95.

Bulldog Drummond Double Feature 1937
"Bulldog Drummond Comes Back" (1937), in which Drummond is on the trail of a clever criminal who is looking to get at him by kidnapping his fiancee, and "Bulldog Drummond's Bride" (1939), wherein Drummond decides to marry, but not until after bomb explosions, a bank robbery, and a rooftop chase. 119m/B/W; VHS. **C:** John Howard; John Barrymore; Guy Standing; Reginald Denny; Louis King; James Hogan; H.B. Warner; Eduardo Ciannelli. **Pr:** Paramount Pictures. **A:** Family. **P:** Entertainment. **U:** Home. **Mov-Ent:** Mystery & Suspense. **Acq:** Purchase. **Dist:** Rex Miller Artisan Studio. $54.95.

Bulldog Drummond Escapes 1937 — ★★
Drummond, aided by his side-kick and valet, rescues a beautiful girl from spies. He then falls in love with her. 67m/B/W; VHS, DVD. **C:** Ray Milland; Heather Angel; Reginald Denny; Guy Standing; Porter Hall; E.E. Clive; Directed by James Hogan; Written by Edward T. Lowe; Cinematography by Victor Milner. **Pr:** Paramount Pictures. **A:** Family. **P:** Entertainment. **U:** Institution, Home. **Mov-Ent. Acq:** Purchase. **Dist:** Sinister Cinema. $16.95.

Bulldog Drummond in Africa/Arrest Bulldog Drummond 1938 — ★★
Two mid-series Bulldog Drummond films, with two new villains. 115m/B/W; VHS. **C:** John Howard; H.B. Warner; George Zucco. **A:** Family. **P:** Entertainment. **U:** Home. **Mov-Ent:** Mystery & Suspense. **Acq:** Purchase. **Dist:** Rex Miller Artisan Studio. $19.98.

Bulldog Drummond's Bride 1939 — ★★
Ace detective Bulldog Drummond has to interrupt his honeymoon in order to pursue a gang of bank robbers across France and England. The last of the Bulldog Drummond film series. 69m/B/W; VHS, DVD. **C:** John Howard; Heather Angel; H.B. Warner; E.E. Clive; Reginald Denny; Eduardo Ciannelli; Elizabeth Patterson; John Sutton; Directed by James Hogan; Written by Garnett Weston; Cinematography by Harry Fischbeck. **Pr:** Paramount Pictures. **A:** Family. **P:** Entertainment. **U:** Home. **Mov-Ent:** Mystery & Suspense. **Acq:** Purchase. **Dist:** Rex Miller Artisan Studio; Sinister Cinema.

Bulldog Drummond's Peril 1938 (Unrated) — ★★
Murder and robbery drag the adventurous Drummond away from his wedding and he pursues the villains until they are behind bars. One in the film series. 77m/B/W; VHS, DVD, 3/4 U, Special order formats. **C:** John Barrymore; John Howard; Louise Campbell; Reginald Denny; E.E. Clive; Porter Hall; Directed by James Hogan. **Pr:** Paramount Pictures. **A:** Family. **P:** Entertainment. **U:** Institution, CCTV, CATV, BCTV, Home. **Mov-Ent:** Mystery & Suspense. **Acq:** Purchase. **Dist:** Sinister Cinema; Rex Miller Artisan Studio. $16.95.

Bulldog Drummond's Revenge 1937 — ★★½
Bulldog's "Revenge" was made during the series' heyday and was the second to star Howard as Drummond; Barrymore revels in the character of Inspector Neilson of Scotland Yard, and Denny is Algy. In this typically fast-paced installment, suave sleuth Drummond stalks the master criminal responsible for stealing the formula to an explosive. 55m/B/W; VHS, DVD. **C:** John Howard; John Barrymore; Reginald Denny; Louise Campbell; Frank Puglia; Nydia Westman; Lucien Littlefield; Directed by Louis King. **Pr:** Paramount Pictures. **A:** Jr. High-Adult. **P:** Entertainment. **U:** Home. **Mov-Ent:** Mystery & Suspense. **Acq:** Purchase. **Dist:** Sinister Cinema; Movies Unlimited. $16.95.

Bulldog Drummond's Secret Police 1939 — ★★
The 15th Drummond film, adapted from Herman Cyril McNeile's famed detective novels featuring a million-pound treasure stashed in the Drummond manor and the murderous endeavors to retrieve it. 54m/B/W; VHS, DVD, Blu-Ray. **C:** John Howard; Heather Angel; H.B. Warner; Reginald Denny; E.E. Clive; Leo G. Carroll; Directed by James Hogan; Written by Garnett Weston; Cinematography by Merritt B. Gerstad. **Pr:** Paramount Pictures. **A:** Family. **P:** Entertainment. **U:** Home. **Mov-Ent:** Mystery & Suspense. **Acq:** Purchase. **Dist:** Rex Miller Artisan Studio; Sinister Cinema. $16.95.

Bulldog Edition 1936 — ★★
Two newspapers engage in an all-out feud to be number one in the city, even going so far as to employ gangsters for purposes of sabotage. 57m/B/W; VHS, DVD. **C:** Ray Walker; Evalyn Knapp; Regis Toomey; Cy Kendall; William "Billy" Newell; Oscar Apfel; Betty Compson; Robert Warwick; Directed by Charles Lamont. **Pr:** Republic. **A:** Jr. High-Adult. **P:** Entertainment. **U:** Home. **Mov-Ent:** Journalism. **Acq:** Purchase. **Dist:** Alpha Video. $16.95.

Bulldog Jack 1935 — ★★★
Fine entry in the series has Drummond's colleague battling it out with Richardson, the leader of gang of jewel thieves. 62m/B/W; VHS, DVD. **C:** Fay Wray; Jack Hulbert; Claude Hulbert; Ralph Richardson; Paul Graetz; Gibb McLaughlin; Directed by Walter Forde. **Pr:** Michael Balcon; Gaumont. **A:** Primary-Adult. **P:** Entertainment. **U:** Home. **Mov-Ent. Acq:** Purchase. **Dist:** Sinister Cinema. $16.95.

The Bulldozer Brigade 1985
Young friends fight city hall in an effort to save their secret wooded playground from land developers. 86m; VHS, CC. **A:** Family. **P:** Entertainment. **U:** Home. **Mov-Ent:** Family Viewing. **Acq:** Purchase. **Dist:** Baker and Taylor. $39.98.

Bullet 1994 (R) — ★½
Butch (Rourke) gets released from prison and immediately returns to his old drug and burglary ways on New York's mean streets. And he's got a score to settle with crazy drug kingpin Tank (Shakur). Has little to recommend it, except to those who like violence, with lackluster performances and a dull script. 96m; VHS, DVD, CC. **C:** Mickey Rourke; Tupac Shakur; Ted Levine; Adrien Brody; John Enos; Directed by Julien Temple; Written by Bruce Rubenstein; Cinematography by Crescenzo G.P. Notarile. **Pr:** John Flock; Greg Coote; Graham Burke; Village Roadshow Pictures. **A:** Sr. High-Adult. **P:** Entertainment. **U:** Home. **Mov-Ent:** Violence. **Acq:** Purchase. **Dist:** New Line Home Video.

Bullet Code 1940 — ★★
It's quick-shooting shenanigans when O'Brien chases a pack of angry rustlers off his neighbor's land. 56m/B/W; VHS. **C:** George O'Brien; Virginia Vale; Howard Hickman; Harry Woods; Charles "Slim" Whitaker; Directed by David Howard; Written by Doris Schroeder. **Pr:** RKO. **A:** Jr. High-Adult. **P:** Entertainment. **U:** Home. **Mov-Ent:** Western. **Acq:** Purchase. **Dist:** Movies Unlimited. $19.99.

Bullet Down Under 1994 (R) — ★
Cop Atkins joins Australian police and gets involved with a crime syndicate and a female killer. 95m; VHS, DVD. **C:** Christopher Atkins; Mark "Jacko" Jackson; Virginia Hey; Written by Karl Schiffman; Cinematography by Martin McGrath; Music by Art Phillips. **A:** Sr. High-Adult. **P:** Entertainment. **U:** Home. **Mov-Ent. Acq:** Purchase. **Dist:** Amazon.com Inc.

A Bullet for Joey 1955 (Unrated) — ★½
Fifties red scare flick. American physicist Carl Macklin (Dolenz) is teaching in Montreal. Gangster Joey Victor (Raft) has been hired to kidnap Macklin, unaware that the commies are behind the snatch. A couple of murders bring Inspector Raoul Leduc (Robinson) onto the scene and he soon tags Joey, who turns patriotic when he discovers he's being used by reds. 85m/B/W; DVD. **C:** Edward G. Robinson; George Raft; Peter Van Eyck; Joseph (Joe) Vitale; George Dolenz; Audrey Trotter; Bill Bryant; John Cliff; Directed by Lewis Allen; Written by Daniel Mainwaring; A(lbert) I(saac) Bezzerides; Cinematography by Harry Neumann; Music by Harry Sukman. **A:** Jr. High-Adult. **P:** Entertainment. **U:** Home. **Mov-Ent:** Science. **Acq:** Purchase. **Dist:** MGM Home Entertainment.

Bullet for Sandoval 1970 (PG) — ★★
An ex-Confederate renegade loots and pillages the north Mexican countryside on his way to murder the grandfather of the woman he loves. 96m; VHS, DVD. **C:** Ernest Borgnine; George Hilton; Directed by Julio Buchs. **Pr:** UMC Pictures. **A:** Jr. High-Adult. **P:** Entertainment. **U:** Home. **Mov-Ent. Acq:** Purchase. **Dist:** VCI Entertainment. $19.95.

A Bullet for the General 1968 (Unrated) — ★
An American mercenary joins with rebel forces during the Mexican Revolution. 95m; VHS, DVD, Blu-Ray, Wide. **C:** Martine Beswick; Lou Castel; Gian Marie Volonte; Klaus Kinski; Directed by Damiano Damiani; Written by Salvatore Laurani; Franco Solinas; Cinematography by Antonio Secchi; Music by Luis Bacalov. **Pr:** Bianco Manini. **A:** Jr. High-Adult. **P:** Entertainment. **U:** Home. **Mov-Ent:** War--General, Mexico. **Acq:** Purchase. **Dist:** New Line Home Video; Sony Pictures Home Entertainment Inc. $14.95.

A Bullet in the Head 1990 — ★★★
Violent (no surprise there) tale of friendship finds Frank (Cheung), Ben (Leung), and Paul (Lee) heading out of 1967 Hong Kong for Saigon, where they hope to make money selling contraband goods in the city. They wind up on the wrong side of the Vietnamese Army, steal a fortune in gold from a local crime lord, and end up the prisoners of the Viet Cong. There's betrayal and death and a final moral reckoning and—did we mention lots and lots of (over-the-top) violence? Chinese with subtitles. 85m; VHS, DVD. **C:** Tony Leung Chiu-Wai; Jacky Cheung; Waise Lee; Simon Yam; Fennie Yuen; Yolinda Yam; John Woo; Directed by John Woo; Written by Janet Chun; Patrick Leung; John Woo; Cinematography by Wilson Chan; Ardy Lam; Chai Kittikum Som; Wing-Hung Wong; Music by Romeo Diaz; James Wong. **A:** Sr. High-Adult. **P:** Entertainment. **U:** Home. **L:** Chinese. **Mov-Ent:** Violence, Asia. **Acq:** Purchase. **Dist:** Facets Multimedia Inc. $49.95.

A Bullet Is Waiting 1954 (Unrated) — ★★
A diligent sheriff finally catches his man only to be trapped in a blinding snowstorm with the hardened criminal. 83m; VHS, DVD. **C:** Jean Simmons; Rory Calhoun; Stephen McNally; Brian Aherne; Directed by John Farrow. **Pr:** Columbia Pictures. **A:** Jr. High-Adult. **P:** Entertainment. **U:** Home. **Mov-Ent:** Action-Adventure. **Acq:** Purchase. **Dist:** Sony Pictures Home Entertainment Inc.; Alpha Video.

Bullet to Beijing 1995 (R) — ★★½
After some 30 years, Caine returns to his role as intelligence agent Harry Palmer. Forced into retirement, Harry finds himself privately recruited by Russian businessman Alex (Gambon) to retrieve a stolen chemical weapon being transported on a train headed for China. Harry gets a little local help from Nicolai and Natasha (Connery and Sara) but treachery is all around. Follows "The Ipcress File," "Funeral in Berlin," and "Billion Dollar Brain"; based on the novel by Len Deighton. 105m; VHS, CC. **C:** Michael Caine; Michael Gambon; Jason Connery; Mia Sara; Patrick Allen; Burt Kwouk; Michael Sarrazin; Sue Lloyd; Directed by George Mihalka; Written by Harry Alan Towers; Cinematography by Terence Cole; Music by Rick Wakeman. **Pr:** Harry Alan Towers; John Dunning; Andre Link; Harry Alan Towers; Showtime Networks. **A:** Sr. High-Adult. **P:** Entertainment. **U:** Home. **Mov-Ent:** Mystery & Suspense, Aging, Trains. **Acq:** Purchase. **Dist:** Paramount Pictures Corp.

Bullet to the Head 2012 (R) — ★★
Stallone's comeback sans his "Expendables" crew proves as further evidence to why the '80s star needs a comeback in the first place. Stuck in a persona long ago deemed irrelevant by

modern audiences, Sly is in full beefcake mode as New Orleans hitman Jimmy Bobo, a tough guy forced to team with D.C. cop Taylor Kwon (Kang) to take down crime lord Morel (Akkinuoye-Agbaje). Director Hill--an '80s icon himself--returns to the genre he used to do so well and does it in a disappointingly routine, by-the-numbers fashion. 92m; DVD, Blu-Ray. **C:** Sylvester Stallone; Sung Kang; Jason Momoa; Sarah Shahi; Adewale Akinnuoye-Agbaje; Christian Slater; Holt McCallany; Jon Seda; Directed by Walter Hill; Written by Alessandro Camon; Cinematography by Lloyd Ahern, II; Music by Steve Mazzaro. **Pr:** Joel Silver; Kevin King Templeton; Alfred Gough; After Dark Films; Automatik Entertainment; Dark Castle Entertainment; Warner Bros. **A:** Sr. High-Adult. **P:** Entertainment. **U:** Home. **L:** English. **Mov-Ent:** Crime Drama. **Acq:** Purchase. **Dist:** Not Yet Released.

Bullet Trains ????
Bullet trains travel at speeds of up to 345 miles an hour. Hold on to your hats as you travel on Amtrak's Acela, Japan's Shinkansen, and Europe's TGV, and learn about the pioneers of high-speed rail travel and emerging technologies. 50m; VHS. **A:** College-Adult. **P:** Education. **U:** Home. **Gen-Edu:** Trains. **Acq:** Purchase. **Dist:** The Civil War Standard. $24.95.

BulletBoys: Pigs in Mud 1991
The hard rock band's first music video release includes the songs "Smooth Up in Ya," "For the Love of Money," and "The Groove." 30m; VHS. **A:** Sr. High-Adult. **P:** Entertainment. **U:** Home. **Mov-Ent:** Music Video, Music--Performance. **Acq:** Purchase. **Dist:** Music Video Distributors. $16.98.

Bulletin Board Bored? 1989
A look at how to make better and more interesting bulletin boards, with a Christian perspective. 37m; VHS. **Pr:** Bob Jones University. **A:** Adult. **P:** Teacher Education. **U:** Institution, SURA. **How-Ins:** Education. **Acq:** Purchase. **Dist:** Bob Jones University. $24.95.

Bulletproof 1988 (R) — ★
An unstoppable ex-CIA agent battles to retrieve a high-tech nuclear tank from terrorist hands. 93m; VHS, DVD. **C:** Gary Busey; Darlanne Fluegel; Henry Silva; Thalmus Rasulala; L.Q. Jones; R.G. Armstrong; Rene Enriquez; Directed by Steve Carver; Written by Steve Carver. **Pr:** Cinetel Films. **A:** Sr. High-Adult. **P:** Entertainment. **U:** Home. **Mov-Ent**. **Acq:** Purchase. **Dist:** Sony Pictures Home Entertainment Inc. $14.95.

Bulletproof 1996 (R) — ★
Desperately trying to be a male buddy bonding movie, "Bulletproof" fails miserably in every respect. Keats (Wayans) and Moses (Sandler) are an unlikely pair of car thieves with an equally unlikely bond to each other. Turns out Keats is really undercover cop Jack Carter, who is trying to infiltrate a drug cartel via his pal Moses. When the bust goes bad, Carter must bring Moses in unharmed to testify. Meanwhile the two rejuvenate their tainted relationship amid many homoerotic innuendoes. It's an embarrassment all around, especially for ex-Spike Lee cinematographer Dickerson on his first directing outing. 85m; VHS, DVD, HD-DVD, Wide, CC. **C:** Damon Wayans; Adam Sandler; James Caan; Kristen Wilson; James Farentino; Bill Nunn; Mark Roberts; Xander Berkeley; Allen Covert; Jeep Swenson; Larry McCoy; Directed by Ernest R. Dickerson; Written by Joe Gayton; Lewis Colick; Cinematography by Steven Bernstein; Music by Elmer Bernstein. **A:** Sr. High-Adult. **P:** Entertainment. **U:** Home. **Mov-Ent:** Aeronautics. **Acq:** Purchase. **Dist:** Universal Music and Video Distribution.

Bulletproof Heart 1995 (R) — ★★★
Mick (LaPaglia), a hit man with a severe case of burnout, is assigned to kill Fiona (Rogers), a beautiful socialite who, conveniently, wants to die. Despite being warned by his boss (Boyle) that Fiona has a habit of making men weak, he falls in love and can't bring himself to kill her. First-time director Malone takes great care to establish the noir look and feel, capitalizing on the all-in-one-night timeframe to raise the tension level. LaPaglia and Rogers turn in riveting performances, but can't stop the film from losing momentum when it becomes self-consciously melodramatic near the end. 95m; VHS, Streaming, CC. **C:** Anthony LaPaglia; Mimi Rogers; Peter Boyle; Matt Craven; Monica Schnarre; Joseph Maher; Directed by Mark Malone; Written by Gordon Melbourne; Mark Malone; Cinematography by Tobias Schliessler; Music by Graeme Coleman. **Pr:** Robert Vince; William Vince; Robert W. Sigman; Gary Delfiner; Michael Strange; Keystone Film Company; Worldvision Enterprises; Keystone Entertainment. **A:** Sr. High-Adult. **P:** Entertainment. **U:** Home. **Mov-Ent:** Death, Mystery & Suspense. **Acq:** Purchase. **Dist:** Lions Gate Entertainment Inc.

Bulletproof Monk 2003 (PG-13) — ★★1/2
Chow-Yun Fat is the monk with no name, chosen to protect The Scroll of the Ultimate, which gives the power to shape the world to the person who reads it aloud. Each monk can only protect the scroll for 60 years, so the new chosen one must be found. An unlikely candidate emerges in a New York pickpocket named Kar, after a chance meeting between the two. Adding a definite "Indiana Jones" vibe are Jade, a mysterious "bad girl" who catches Kar's eye, and the villains, a Nazi who tried to steal the scroll years earlier, and his icy granddaughter. Plot holes abound if you look too closely, but the action sequences are nicely timed to distract you from them, and Chow-Yun Fat's cool persona adds a touch of grace. Scott makes a nice first step from teen comedy doofus to action hero. 103m; VHS, DVD, Blu-Ray, CC. **C:** Chow Yun-Fat; Seann William Scott; Jaime King; Karel Roden; Victoria Smurfit; Mako; Roger Yuan; Marcus Jean Pirae; Directed by Paul Hunter; Written by Ethan Reiff; Cyrus Voris; Cinematography by Stefan Czapsky; Music by Eric Serra. **Pr:** Charles Roven; Terence Chang; John Woo; Douglas Segal; Lion Rock; Lakeshore Entertainment; Mosaic Media Group; Flypaper Press; MGM. **A:** Jr. High-Adult. **P:** Entertainment. **U:** Home. **Mov-Ent:** Martial Arts. **Acq:** Purchase. **Dist:** MGM Home Entertainment.

Bulletproof Salesman 2008
Looking at career of Fidelis Cloer, who has sold his handmade armored vehicles to those at war for several decades; particular focus is paid to his contributions and struggles during the U.S.-led invasion of Iraq in the early 2000s. 70m; DVD. **A:** Sr. High-Adult. **P:** Entertainment. **U:** Home. **Mov-Ent:** War--General, Iraq, Documentary Films. **Acq:** Purchase. **Dist:** First Run Features. $14.95.

Bullets for Breakfast 1992
Essay film attempts to unravel the seductive power of collective myths and stereotypes by examining differences between poetry, story telling, and visual narrative. 77m; VHS. **A:** College-Adult. **P:** Education. **U:** Institution. **Gen-Edu:** Women, Art & Artists, Drama. **Acq:** Purchase, Rent/Lease. **Dist:** Women Make Movies. $295.00.

Bullets Have No Names on Them 1993
Close look at young people who in some way became involved with guns, whether an owner or simply a person in the wrong place at the wrong time. Visits with victims of gun shot wounds who have been left paralyzed, have a permanent injury, or endured surgery. Interviews and special effects keep students interested. Includes teacher's guide. 23m; VHS. **Pr:** Sheridan Peters Communications. **A:** Jr. High-Adult. **P:** Education. **U:** Institution. **Gen-Edu:** Gun control, Firearms. **Acq:** Purchase, Rent/Lease. **Dist:** Phoenix Learning Group. $425.00.

Bullets or Ballots 1938 (Unrated) — ★★★
Tough New York cop goes undercover to join the mob in order to get the goods on them. Old-fashioned danger and intrigue follow, making for some action-packed thrills. 82m/B/W; VHS, DVD. **C:** Edward G. Robinson; Humphrey Bogart; Barton MacLane; Joan Blondell; Frank McHugh; Louise Beavers; Directed by William Keighley; Written by Seton I. Miller; Cinematography by Hal Mohr. **Pr:** Warner Bros. **A:** Jr. High-Adult. **P:** Entertainment. **U:** Home. **Mov-Ent**. **Acq:** Purchase. **Dist:** MGM Home Entertainment. $19.98.

Bullets over Broadway 1994 (R) — ★★★1/2
Mediocre playwright David Shayne (Cusack, in the Allen role) talks up the virtues of artistic integrity to his pretentious hothouse contemporaries, then sells out to a gangster who agrees to finance his latest play provided his no-talent, brassy moll (Tilly) gets a part. And it's her hit-man bodyguard's (Palminteri) unexpected artistic touches that redeem Shayne's otherwise lousy work. Wiest as the eccentric diva, Ullman as the aging ingenue, Reiner as the Greenwich Village sage, and Broadbent as the increasingly plump matinee idol lead a collection of delicious, over-the-top performances in this smart and howlingly funny tribute to Jazz Age New York City that showcases Woody at his self-conscious best. 106m; VHS, DVD, CC. **C:** Dianne Wiest; John Cusack; Jennifer Tilly; Rob Reiner; Chazz Palminteri; Tracey Ullman; Mary-Louise Parker; Joe (Johnny) Viterelli; Jack Warden; Jim Broadbent; Harvey Fierstein; Annie-Joe Edwards; Directed by Woody Allen; Written by Woody Allen; Douglas McGrath; Cinematography by Carlo Di Palma. **Pr:** Robert Greenhut; Helen Robin; Jean Doumanian; Jack Rollins; Charles H. Joffe; Letty Aronson; Sweetland Films AB; Miramax Film Corp. **A:** Sr. High-Adult. **P:** Entertainment. **U:** Home. **Mov-Ent. Awds:** Oscars '94: Support. Actress (Wiest); Golden Globes '95: Support. Actress (Wiest); Ind. Spirit '95: Support. Actor (Palminteri), Support. Actress (Wiest); L.A. Film Critics '94: Support. Actress (Wiest); N.Y. Film Critics '94: Support. Actress (Wiest); Natl. Soc. Film Critics '94: Support. Actress (Wiest); Screen Actors Guild '94: Support. Actress (Wiest). **Acq:** Purchase. **Dist:** Miramax Film Corp.

Bullfighter & the Lady 1950 (Unrated) — ★★1/2
An American goes to Mexico to learn the fine art of bullfighting in order to impress a beautiful woman. 87m/B/W; VHS, Blu-Ray, Streaming. **C:** Robert Stack; Gilbert Roland; Virginia Grey; Katy Jurado; Directed by Budd Boetticher. **Pr:** Republic Pictures. **A:** Family. **P:** Entertainment. **U:** Home. **Mov-Ent:** Drama, Mexico. **Acq:** Purchase. **Dist:** Lions Gate Entertainment Inc. $19.98.

Bullfighters 1945 — ★★
Stan and Ollie are in hot pursuit of a dangerous criminal which leads them to Mexico where Stan winds up in a bull ring. 61m/B/W; VHS, DVD. **C:** Stan Laurel; Oliver Hardy; Margo Woode; Richard Lane; Directed by Malcolm St. Clair. **Pr:** 20th Century-Fox. **A:** Family. **P:** Entertainment. **U:** Home. **Mov-Ent:** Comedy--Slapstick, Mexico. **Acq:** Purchase. **Dist:** Fox Home Entertainment. $29.98.

Bullhead 2011 (R) — ★★
Ambitious first film from writer/director Roskam is a complex and intense crime drama. Steroid-fueled farmer Jacky works in the family cattle business, which uses a steady supply of illegal growth hormone supplied by a shady vet. Jacky's encouraged to make a deal to sell beef to a new client—a hormone trafficker who had a federal investigator killed. He doesn't want to get involved but unexpected ties to his past drag Jacky down a dangerous road. Dutch and French with subtitles. 124m; DVD, Blu-Ray. **C:** Matthias Schoenaerts; Sam Louwyck; Jeroen Perceval; Jeanne Dandoy; Barbara Sarafian; Frank Lammers; Directed by Michael R. Roskam; Written by Michael R. Roskam; Cinematography by Nicolas Karakatsanis; Music by Raf Keunen. **Pr:** Bart Van Langendonck; Savage Film; Eyeworks Film & TV Drama; Drafthouse Films. **A:** College-Adult. **P:** Entertainment. **U:** Home. **L:** Dutch, French. **Mov-Ent:** Crime Drama, Agriculture. **Acq:** Purchase. **Dist:** Image Entertainment Inc.

Bullies 1986 (R) — **Bomb!**
A woodland-transplanted young man decides to fight back against an ornery mountain clan who have raped his mother, tortured his father, and beat up his girlfriend. Brutal and unpalatable. 96m; VHS, DVD, CC. **C:** Janet-Laine Green; Dehl Berti; Stephen Hunter; Jonathan Crombie; Olivia D'Abo; Directed by Paul Lynch. **Pr:** Peter R. Simpson; Simcom International. **A:** Sr. High-Adult. **P:** Entertainment. **U:** Home. **Mov-Ent:** Rape, Wilderness Areas, Canada. **Acq:** Purchase. **Dist:** $79.95.

Bullitt 1968 (PG) — ★★★
A detective assigned to protect a star witness for 48 hours senses danger; his worst fears are confirmed when his charge is murdered. Based on the novel, "Mute Witness" by Robert L. Pike, and featuring one of filmdom's most famous car chases. 105m; VHS, DVD, Blu-Ray, HD-DVD. **C:** Steve McQueen; Robert Vaughn; Jacqueline Bisset; Don Gordon; Robert Duvall; Norman Fell; Simon Oakland; Directed by Peter Yates; Written by Alan R. Trustman; Cinematography by William A. Fraker; Music by Lalo Schifrin. **Pr:** Warner Bros. **A:** Jr. High-Adult. **P:** Entertainment. **U:** Home. **Mov-Ent:** Automobiles--Racing. **Awds:** Oscars '68: Film Editing; Natl. Film Reg. '07; Natl. Soc. Film Critics '68: Cinematog. **Acq:** Purchase. **Dist:** Warner Home Video, Inc. $19.98.

Bullpen 1974
Covers baseball's relief pitchers and goes behind the scenes into the relievers' home away from home, the bullpen. Some of the best "firemen" of the past and present are seen in action. Some black and white sequences. 22m; VHS. **C:** Joe Page; Jim Konstanty; Roy Face; Hoyt Wilhelm; Ron Perranoski; Tug McGraw. **Pr:** W and W Productions. **A:** Family. **P:** Entertainment. **U:** Institution, Home, SURA. **Spo-Rec:** Sports--General, Baseball. **Acq:** Purchase. **Dist:** Major League Baseball Productions.

Bull's Eye Archery 1981
Dwight Nyquist, coach of the 1980 United States Olympic Archery team, discusses the use of various bows, arm action, arm string action, anchoring, aiming, release and follow through. 50m; VHS. **Pr:** Morris Video. **A:** Jr. High-Adult. **P:** Instruction. **U:** Home. **Spo-Rec:** Sports--General. **Acq:** Purchase. **Dist:** Morris Video. $19.95.

Bull's Eye Archery 1985
Olympic Coach Dwight Nygurst demonstrates basic archery fundamentals. 50m; VHS. **Pr:** Morris Video. **A:** Sr. High-Adult. **P:** Instruction. **U:** Home. **Spo-Rec:** Sports--General. **Acq:** Purchase. **Dist:** Morris Video.

The Bull's Eye War 1980
Explores the current state of conventional warfare with the advent of new precision guided weapons. 50m; VHS, 3/4 U. **Pr:** British Broadcasting Corporation. **A:** College-Adult. **P:** Education. **U:** Institution, SURA. **Gen-Edu:** Documentary Films, Nuclear Warfare. **Acq:** Purchase. **Dist:** Home Vision Cinema.

Bullseye! 1990 (PG-13) — ★1/2
Knockabout farce is a letdown considering the talents involved. Shady scientists (Moore and Caine) pursue/are pursued by lookalike con-artists (Caine and Moore), who are pursued in turn by international agents. Full of inside jokes and celebrity cameos, but nothing exceptional. 95m; DVD, Streaming. **C:** Michael Caine; Roger Moore; Sally Kirkland; Patsy Kensit; Jenny Seagrove; John Cleese; Lee Patterson; Deborah Maria Moore; Mark Burns; Deborah Leng; Alexandra Pigg; Cameo(s) Lynn Nesbitt; Steffanie Pitt; Directed by Michael Winner; Written by Michael Winner; Leslie Bricusse; Music by John Du Prez. **Pr:** Michael Winner; Menahem Golan; Michael Winner; 21st Century Film Corporation. **A:** Sr. High-Adult. **P:** Entertainment. **U:** Home. **Mov-Ent:** Comedy--Screwball, Scientists. **Acq:** Purchase. **Dist:** MGM Home Entertainment; Sony Pictures Home Entertainment Inc. $89.95.

Bullshit 2005
Documentary profiling environmental activist and nuclear physicist Vandana Shiva. 73m; VHS, DVD. **A:** Sr. High-Adult. **P:** Education. **U:** Institution. **Gen-Edu:** Documentary Films, Biography, Ecology & Environment. **Acq:** Purchase, Rent/Lease. **Dist:** The Cinema Guild. $295.00.

Bullshot 1983 (PG) — ★★1/2
Zany English satire sends up the legendary Bulldog Drummond. In the face of mad professors, hapless heroines, devilish Huns and deadly enemies, our intrepid hero remains distinctly British. 84m; VHS, DVD. **C:** Alan Shearman; Diz White; Ron House; Frances Tomelty; Michael Aldridge; Ron Pember; Christopher Good; Directed by Dick Clement; Music by John Du Prez. **Pr:** Island Alive. **A:** Jr. High-Adult. **P:** Entertainment. **U:** Home. **Mov-Ent:** Satire & Parody, Great Britain. **Acq:** Purchase. **Dist:** Unknown Distributor.

Bullshot Crummond 1984 (Unrated)
The Low Moan Spectacular comedy troupe performs this satire that trashes oldtime adventure serials. 90m; VHS. **Pr:** RKO. **A:** Sr. High-Adult. **P:** Entertainment. **U:** Home. **Mov-Ent:** Satire & Parody. **Acq:** Purchase. **Dist:** Turner Broadcasting System Inc. $39.95.

Bullwhip 1958 (Unrated) — ★★
A man falsely accused of murder saves himself from the hangman's noose by agreeing to a shotgun wedding. 80m; VHS. **C:** Guy Madison; Rhonda Fleming; James J. Griffith; Peter Adams; Directed by Harmon Jones. **Pr:** Allied Artists International. **A:** Family. **P:** Entertainment. **U:** Home. **Mov-Ent:** Western, Marriage, Romance. **Acq:** Purchase. **Dist:** Lions Gate Entertainment Inc. $19.98.

Bully 2001 (Unrated) — ★
Director Clark continues his cinematic theme (announced in "Kids") of amoral and hedonistic young adults with this adaptation of the true story of a 1993 murder by a group of teens in Florida. Bobby (Stahl) is a dominating scumbag who pushes his best friend Marty (Renfro) around and pressures him into unwanted sexual and narcotic experimentation. When Marty meets and begins dating Lisa (Miner), Bobby forces himself into their sexual encounters. After Bobby rapes Lisa's friend Ali (Phillips), Lisa decides that the only solution is to kill Bobby. Inexperienced in such things, the homicidal posse gets some advice from a hit man (Fitzpatrick) who's barely older than they are. Filling the screen with graphic scenes of drug use and joyless sex, Clark doesn't seem to have any message other than "Look how bad these kids are. Now look at them naked." No psychological depth is given to the characters, although the actors do their best with what they've got. Also available in an R-rated version at 107 minutes. 113m; VHS, DVD, CC. **C:** Brad Renfro; Nick Stahl; Bijou Phillips; Rachel Miner; Michael Pitt; Kelli Garner; Daniel Franzese; Leo Fitzpatrick; Cameo(s) Larry Clark; Directed by Larry Clark; Written by Zachary Long; Roger Pullis; Cinematography by Steve Gainer. **Pr:** Chris Hanley; Don Murphy; Fernando Sulichin; Blacklist; Gravity Entertainment; Lions Gate Films. **A:** Adult. **P:** Entertainment. **U:** Home. **Mov-Ent:** Adolescence, Sex & Sexuality, Violence. **Acq:** Purchase. **Dist:** Weinstein Company L.L.C.; CinemaNow Inc.

Bully 2011 (PG-13) — ★★★
Director Hirsch's documentary looks at the personal anguish of the bullying of students by their peers in American schools through the experiences of five students and their families. Two students committed suicide (the interviews are with their families), one is in a reformatory for brandishing a gun on a school bus after being tormented, one star athlete comes out as a lesbian and is immediately ostracized, and a young middle-schooler is repeatedly subjected to taunts and physical violence. The ineptitude and indifference of the educators when presented with the evidence is almost as shocking. 98m; DVD, Blu-Ray. **C:** Directed by Lee Hirsch; Written by Lee Hirsch; Cynthia Lowen; Cinematography by Lee Hirsch; Music by Michael Furjanic; Justin Rice; Christian Rudder. **Pr:** Lee Hirsch; Cynthia Lowen; The Bully Project; Where We Live Films; Weinstein Company L.L.C. **A:** Jr. High-Adult. **P:** Entertainment. **U:** Home. **L:** English. **Mov-Ent:** Documentary Films, Child Abuse, Suicide. **Acq:** Purchase. **Dist:** Anchor Bay Entertainment Inc.

The Bully Pulpit 1983
Compares and contrasts the leadership and communication skills of Ronald Reagan and Franklin D. Roosevelt. 14m; VHS, 3/4 U. **Pr:** WGBH Boston. **A:** Jr. High-Adult. **P:** Education. **U:** Institution, SURA. **Gen-Edu:** Documentary Films, Presidency. **Acq:** Purchase, Rent/Lease. **Dist:** Hearst Entertainment/King Features.

Bully Up: Fighting Feelings 1990
Demonstrates that hurting people physically or emotionally is not right. Uses characters, Ollie and the Big Kahooney, to get their message across. 15m; VHS, SVS, 3/4 U. **A:** Preschool-Primary. **P:** Education. **U:** Institution. **Gen-Edu. Acq:** Purchase. **Dist:** Encyclopedia Britannica. $99.00.

Bulworth 1998 (R) — ★★★
No-holds barred look at the political process. Senator John Jay Bulworth (Beatty), bored and disillusioned by the banality of his own political career, hires a hitman to end his misery. During his last days on earth fufilling re-election duties, and with nothing to loose, he starts spewing the truth about politics and big business, much to the dismay of his constituents and assistants. Morphing into a hip-hop political phrophet, he becomes entranced and invigorated by beautiful South Central resident Nina (Berry). Beatty (in an engaging and funny performance) tackles his fiery subject matter of dwindling racial harmony and corporate deceit with a brazen and winning sense of humor lost in contemporary films. Fine script and enjoyable supporting performances by Platt as Bulworth's panic-stricken aide and Cheadle as an enterprising drug lord. 107m; VHS, DVD, Wide, CC. **C:** Warren Beatty; Halle Berry; Oliver Platt; Paul Sorvino; Don Cheadle; Jack Warden; Christine Baranski; Isaiah Washington, IV; Joshua Malina; Richard Sarafian; Amiri Baraka; Sean Astin; Laurie Metcalf; Wendell Pierce; Michele Morgan; Ariyan Johnson; Graham Beckel; Nora Dunn; Jackie Gayle; Directed by Warren Beatty; Written by Warren Beatty; Jeremy Pikser; Cinematography by Vittorio Storaro; Music by Ennio Morricone. **Pr:** Warren Beatty; Pieter Jan Brugge; Warren Beatty; 20th Century-Fox. **A:** College-Adult. **P:** Entertainment. **U:** Home. **Mov-Ent:** Satire & Parody, Politics & Government, Black Culture. **Awds:** L.A. Film Critics '98: Screenplay. **Acq:** Purchase. **Dist:** Fox Home Entertainment.

Bumblebee 1989
Follow a bumblebee's daily routine through a colorful flower bed. 3m; VHS, SVS, 1C, 3/4 U. **Pr:** Julius Kohanyi. **A:** Primary-Jr. High. **P:** Education. **U:** Institution, CATV, BCTV, Home, SURA. **Gen-Edu. Acq:** Purchase, Duplication License. **Dist:** Green Acre Video. $19.95.

The Bumblebee Flies Anyway 1998 (PG-13) — ★★½
Amnesiac Barney Snow (Wood) is residing at a facility where all the other youths are terminally ill. As the doctors try to help Barney remember his past, Barney and the other patients go through the usual bonding rituals. Ordinary story at least has some winning performers to get past the maudlin aspects. Based on the novel by Robert Cormier. 95m; VHS, DVD. **C:** Elijah Wood; Janeane Garofalo; Rachael Leigh Cook; Roger Rees; Joe Perrino; George Gore, III; Chris Petrizzo; Directed by Martin Duffy; Written by Jennifer Sarja; Cinematography by Stephen Kazmierski; Music by Christopher Tyng. **Pr:** Shooting Gallery. **A:** Jr. High-Adult. **P:** Entertainment. **U:** Home. **Mov-Ent:** Adolescence. **Acq:** Purchase.

Bumbledown: The Life and Times of Ronald Reagan 1991
The life of the ex-President is chronicled in this commemorative video special. 40m; VHS. **Pr:** British Broadcasting Corporation. **A:** Sr. High-Adult. **P:** Entertainment. **U:** Home. **Mov-Ent:** Biography, Presidency. **Acq:** Purchase. **Dist:** Video Collectibles. $14.98.

Bummer 1973 (R) — **Bomb!**
Rock band's wild party turns into tragedy when the bass player goes too far with two groupies. It's a bad scene, man. 90m; VHS, DVD, Wide. **C:** Kipp Whitman; Dennis Burkley; Carol Speed; Connie Strickland; Directed by William Allen Castleman; Written by Alvin L. Fast. **Pr:** Entertainment Ventures Inc. **A:** Sr. High-Adult. **P:** Entertainment. **U:** Home. **Mov-Ent:** Music--Pop/Rock. **Acq:** Purchase. **Dist:** Movies Unlimited. $19.99.

Bummy's Basic Parliamentary Workshop 199?
Bummy Burstein shows how to minimize confusion and maximize effectiveness at meetings for deaf and hearing people alike. 90m; VHS. **A:** Adult. **P:** Education. **U:** Home. **Gen-Edu:** Deafness, Communication. **Acq:** Purchase. **Dist:** Dawn Sign Press. $39.95.

Bump!: American Northeast 2004
Shannon McDonough checks out notable eateries, gay and lesbian enterprises (gyms, hotels, shops), and cultural events tied to the gay lifestyle in the cities of New York, Philadelphia, and Washington D.C. 72m; DVD. **C:** Shannon McDonough. **A:** Adult. **P:** Entertainment. **U:** Home. **Mov-Ent:** Documentary Films. **Acq:** Purchase. **Dist:** Alluvial Filmworks.

Bump and Run: Defensive Back Video 1993
Live-action football instructional video that centers on techniques on playing the defensive back position. Features Greg Brown, the Defensive Back Coach at the University of Colorado, and Deon Figures, 1992 All-American and Thorpe Award winner, as they discuss and demonstrate proper positioning of the feet, hands, and body, as well as different techniques, fundamentals, and drills. 40m; VHS. **A:** Jr. High-Adult. **P:** Instruction. **U:** Institution, Home. **Spo-Rec:** Sports--General, Football, How-To. **Acq:** Purchase. **Dist:** Cambridge Educational. $24.95.

Bump!: Beach Escapes 2009 (Unrated)
Charlie David and Shannon McDonough take viewers to the best gay and lesbian beach escapes in Torremolinos, Spain, Paraty, Brazil, and Puerto Vallarta, Mexico for sunbathing, shopping, trail riding, drinking, dancing, eating, and sightseeing. 72m; DVD. **C:** Charlie David; Shannon McDonough. **A:** College-Adult. **P:** Entertainment. **U:** Home. **Mov-Ent:** Travel, Homosexuality, Television Series. **Acq:** Purchase. **Dist:** Alluvial Filmworks. $19.98.

Bump!: Eastern Europe 2004 (Unrated)
Shannon McDonough hits gay parties and historical sites in Vienna, tries some new cuisine and checks out the architecture in Budapest, and enjoys more of the same in Prague. 72m; DVD. **C:** Shannon McDonough. **A:** Adult. **P:** Entertainment. **U:** Home. **Mov-Ent:** Travel, Homosexuality. **Acq:** Purchase. **Dist:** Alluvial Filmworks.

Bump!: Florida 2002
Includes fun times at hot gay clubs, eateries, beaches, and more in Fort Lauderdale, the opening of the mega-club Level in South Beach, and the Kelly McGillis Flag Football Tournament in Key West. 72m; DVD. **C:** Hosted by J.R. ANDERSON. **A:** Adult. **P:** Entertainment. **U:** Home. **Mov-Ent:** Homosexuality, Travel. **Acq:** Purchase. **Dist:** Alluvial Filmworks.

Bump!: Great Britain 2004
From the seaside resort of Brighton to the cosmopolitan city of London, Shannon McDonough finds the trendiest shops and eateries and tours unique gay-friendly guesthouses, restaurants, bars, and clubs as well as traditional historical sights. She also participates in Gayfest and checks out the Mr. Gay U.K. pageant. 72m; DVD. **C:** Hosted by Shannon McDonough. **A:** Adult. **P:** Entertainment. **U:** Home. **Mov-Ent:** Documentary Films. **Acq:** Purchase. **Dist:** Alluvial Filmworks.

Bump in the Night: The Complete Series 1994 (Unrated)
ABC 1994-95 claymation adventure. Classic Saturday morning cartoon with wild and green Mr. Bumpy living under the bed and devouring dirty socks. He and his pals Squishington, a neat-freak bathroom monster, and the always-consoling Molly Coddle doll rock the night away and have many an adventure. 26 episodes. 660m; DVD. **C:** Voice(s) by Jim (Jonah) Cummings; Robert Paulsen; Elizabeth Daily; Gail Matthius. **A:** Primary-Jr. High. **P:** Entertainment. **U:** Home. **Chl-Juv:** Animation & Cartoons, Children's Shows, Television Series. **Acq:** Purchase. **Dist:** Shout! Factory. $29.99.

Bump!: Mexico 2004
A travelogue of gay-friendly tourist destinations in Mexico, featuring beaches, resorts, shops, and other sites in Puerto Vallarta, Cancun, and Mexico City. Host Charlie David also speaks with painter Frida Kahlo, lesbian author/councilor Paulina Gomez, fashion designer Ernesto Hernandez, and drag queen Tito Vasconcelos. 72m; DVD. **C:** Hosted by Charles David. **A:** Adult. **P:** Entertainment. **U:** Home. **Mov-Ent:** Documentary Films. **Acq:** Purchase. **Dist:** Alluvial Filmworks.

Bump: My First Video 1993
An animated adventure for the wee folk features Bump, an elephant who solves all his problems with a little help from his friends. 30m; VHS. **A:** Preschool. **P:** Entertainment. **U:** Home. **Chl-Juv:** Animation & Cartoons, Family Viewing. **Acq:** Purchase. **Dist:** Anchor Bay Entertainment. $9.98.

Bump!: North American Gold Coast 2007
Soap star Charlie David and playwright Shannon McDonough check out a big gay wedding in Vancouver, B.C., rock out at the Experience Music Project in Seattle, meet the Amazon Dragons, and get a lap dance from the Rose City Sirens in Portland. 72m; DVD. **C:** Hosted by Shannon McDonough. **A:** Adult. **P:** Entertainment. **U:** Home. **Mov-Ent:** Homosexuality, Travel. **Acq:** Purchase. **Dist:** Alluvial Filmworks.

Bump!: Southern California 2004
Shannon McDonough hosts a tour of various gay-friendly destinations and features in SoCal, including visits to clubs, beaches, and events and interviews with artists. 72m; DVD. **C:** Hosted by Shannon McDonough. **A:** Adult. **P:** Entertainment. **U:** Home. **Mov-Ent:** Documentary Films. **Acq:** Purchase. **Dist:** Alluvial Filmworks.

Bump!: Spain 2004 (Unrated)
Gay and lesbian travel television series with host Shannon McDonough hits the gay hotspots in Madrid, Barcelona, and Valencia. 3 episodes. 72m; DVD. **C:** Shannon McDonough. **A:** Adult. **P:** Entertainment. **U:** Home. **Mov-Ent:** Travel, Spain. **Acq:** Purchase. **Dist:** Alluvial Filmworks. $19.98.

Bump!?Canada 2007 (Unrated)
Visits the Black and Blue weeklong party festival, an AIDS fundraiser, shops and clubs in Montreal, then moves on to tour a gay community with gay city councilor Kyle Rae in Toronto and see the studio of queer underwear designer Will Munro plus some gay-owned guesthouses and B&Bs. Lastly its skating down the Rideau Canal, hiking in the Gatineau parks, and conversations with activist Bruce Bursey of The Wellness Project, Arthur Jamieson from the gay theatre group Act Out, and exotic tapestry artist Carl Stewart in Ottawa. 72m; DVD. **A:** Adult. **P:** Entertainment. **U:** Home. **Mov-Ent:** Travel, Canada, Homosexuality. **Acq:** Purchase. **Dist:** Alluvial Filmworks.

Bums 1993 — ★★
Sergeant Andrew Holloman is a military officer in search of his long lost brother. It turns out his brother was homeless and is now dead at the hands of a skid row killer. Holloman recruits a platoon of other homeless people to help him track the killer but what he discovers is a multimillion conspiracy behind the murders. 94m; VHS. **C:** Christopher McDonald; Haskell Phillips; Dawn Evans; Directed by Andy Galler; Written by Pat Allee; Ben Hurst. **Pr:** Michael K. Faust; Robert H. Goodman; Panorama Entertainment. **A:** Sr. High-Adult. **P:** Entertainment. **U:** Home. **Mov-Ent:** Mystery & Suspense, Homeless. **Acq:** Purchase. **Dist:** Monarch Home Video. $89.95.

Bunco 1977 — ★
Two policemen working for the Los Angeles Police Department's Bunco Squad discover a college for con artists complete with tape-recorded lessons and on-the-job training. 60m; VHS. **C:** Tom Selleck; Robert Urich; Donna Mills; Will Geer; Arte Johnson; Alan Feinstein; James Hampton; Michael Sacks; Bobby Van; Diana Scarwid; Kenneth Mars; Directed by Alexander Singer. **Pr:** Lorimar Productions. **A:** Jr. High-Adult. **P:** Entertainment. **U:** Home. **Mov-Ent. Acq:** Purchase. **Dist:** MGM Studios Inc. ; Warner Home Video, Inc. $59.95.

Bunco Squad 1950 (Unrated) — ★½
L.A. Bunco squad detective Steve Johnson (Sterling) goes after con man Wells (Cortez) who runs phony seances and is trying to bilk wealthy widow Jessica Royce (Risdon). Steve enlists his actress girlfriend Grace (Dixon) to pose as a phony medium to set-up the bad guys. 67m/B/W; DVD. **C:** Robert Sterling; Joan Dixon; Ricardo Cortez; Elisabeth Risdon; Douglas Fowley; Marguerite Churchill; Directed by Herbert I. Leeds; Written by George Callahan; Cinematography by Henry Freulich; Music by Paul Sawtell. **A:** Sr. High-Adult. **P:** Entertainment. **U:** Home. **Mov-Ent:** Crime Drama. **Acq:** Purchase. **Dist:** WarnerArchive.com.

Bundesliga 86/87 198?
Highlights of the 1986-87 soccer season in Germany are presented here, featuring Hamburg, Moenchen-Gladbach, Muenchen, and more. In German only. 120m; VHS. **TV Std:** NTSC, PAL. **Pr:** German Language Video Center. **A:** Jr. High-Adult. **P:** Entertainment. **U:** Institution, Home. **L:** German. **Spo-Rec:** Sports--General, Soccer. **Acq:** Purchase, Rent/Lease. **Dist:** German Language Video Center. $37.95.

Bundesliga 87/88 198?
Highlights of the 1987-88 soccer season in Germany, featuring 18 clubs, including Bayern Muenchen, 1. FC Koeln, 1. FC Nuernberg, Eintracht Frankfurt and more. In German only. 120m; VHS. **TV Std:** NTSC, PAL. **Pr:** German Language Video Center. **A:** Jr. High-Adult. **P:** Entertainment. **U:** Institution, Home. **L:** German. **Spo-Rec:** Sports--General, Soccer. **Acq:** Purchase, Rent/Lease. **Dist:** German Language Video Center. $37.95.

Bundle of Joy 1956 (Unrated) — ★★½
Salesgirl who saves an infant from falling off the steps of a foundling home is mistaken for the child's mother. Remake of 1939's "Bachelor Mother." 98m; VHS, DVD. **C:** Debbie Reynolds; Eddie Fisher; Adolphe Menjou; Directed by Norman Taurog. **Pr:** Mark Huffam; Edmund Grainger. **A:** Family. **P:** Entertainment. **U:** Home. **Mov-Ent:** Musical. **Acq:** Purchase. **Dist:** WarnerArchive.com; Alpha Video. $17.99.
Songs: Bundle of Joy; I Never Felt This Way Before; Lullaby in Blue; Worry About Tomorrow; All About Love; Someday Soon; What's So Good About Morning?; You're Perfect In Every Department.

Bundles of Joy 1997
Features babies cooing, laughing, and smiling to melodies of Chanukah, Passover, and Shabbat. 30m; VHS. **A:** Family. **P:**

Entertainment. **U:** Home. **Gen-Edu**: Infants, Holidays, Judaism. **Acq:** Purchase. **Dist:** SISU Home Entertainment, Inc. $14.95.

Bundy: A Legacy of Evil 2008 (R) — **Bomb!**
Limp, low-budget serial killer flick hits all the usual points about Bundy's life of crime, which marginally improves when Ted gets to killing. The subsequent capture, trial, and Bundy's imprisonment are equally dull. 92m; DVD. **C:** Corin "Corky" Nemec; Jen Nikolaisen; David DeLuise; Shannon Pierce; Kane Hodder; Directed by Michael Feifer; Cinematography by Roberto Schein; Music by Andres Boulton. **A:** Sr. High-Adult. **P:** Entertainment. **U:** Home. **Mov-Ent**: Biography: Law Enforcement. **Acq:** Purchase. **Dist:** Lions Gate Entertainment Inc.

Bungee Jumping 1991
An exciting look at the latest worldwide craze, bungee jumping. A selection of jumps from the U.S., Canada and New Zealand. 30m; VHS. **Pr:** Eric Perlman. **A:** Family. **P:** Entertainment. **U:** Home. **Spo-Rec**: Sports--General. **Acq:** Purchase. **Dist:** MNTEX Entertainment, Inc.

B.U.S.T.E.D. 1999 (R) — ★★
Gangmates and cousins Terry (Goldie) and Ray (Goth) are just out of prison. Violent Terry is looking to re-take control from efficient Bernie (Bowie), who's been looking after the business. Ray decides he wants to go legit and falls for lovely Clare (Shelley). But Terry wants his coz with him and kidnaps Clare to force Ray's hand—a bad move since Ray decides love is thicker than blood. The leads are caricatures and American audiences will be hampered by the regional Brit slang but Bowie's cool intensity is worth watching. 97m; VHS, DVD. **C:** Goldie; Andrew Goth; David Bowie; Rachel Shelley; Clint Dyer; Sarah Shackleton; Directed by Andrew Goth; Written by Andrew Goth; Cinematography by Julian Morson; Music by Nicky Matthew. **Pr:** Lions Gate Films. **A:** Sr. High-Adult. **P:** Entertainment. **U:** Home. **Mov-Ent**: Crime Drama, Family. **Acq:** Purchase. **Dist:** Lions Gate Entertainment Inc.

Bunker Silo Management 1995
Describes bunker silo management practices, including recommendations for moisture content, particle size, silage pH, packing, feedout rate, covering and sealing. Demonstrates methods needed to ensure good preservation of feeds. 22m; VHS. **A:** Adult. **P:** Vocational, Instruction. **U:** Home. **Bus-Ind**: Agriculture. **Acq:** Purchase. **Dist:** Cornell University. $25.00.

Bunnetics 1983
This program offers firming and toning exercises for the backside. 30m; VHS, 3/4 U. **C:** Cal Del Pozo. **Pr:** Spectrum Communications System. **A:** Family. **P:** Entertainment. **U:** Institution, Home. **Hea-Sci**: Fitness/Exercise. **Acq:** Purchase. **Dist:** Inspired Corp.; ESPN Inc. $19.95.

Bunny and the Bull 2009 (Unrated) — ★½
Ambitious kinda comedic effort from writer/director King was filmed entirely in the studio and places its cast against animated and drawn backgrounds. Flashbacks depict what turned neurotic, introverted Stephen (Hogg) into an agoraphobic after a disastrous trek across Europe with his drunken, womanizing, gambling-addicted friend Bunny (Farnaby) that ended in Spain. 101m; DVD. **C:** Ed Hogg; Simon Farnaby; Veronica Echegui; Julian Barratt; Noel Fielding; Directed by Paul King; Written by Paul King; Cinematography by John Sorapure; Music by Ralfe Band. **A:** Sr. High-Adult. **P:** Entertainment. **U:** Home. **Mov-Ent**: Spain. **Acq:** Purchase. **Dist:** IFC Films.

Bunny Lake Is Missing 1965 (Unrated) — ★★
Director Preminger dismissed his 'little' picture, but this psycho-thriller has become a cult fave. Neurotic American single mom Ann Lake (Lynley) has relocated to London with her 4-year-old daughter Bunny. She takes the child to her first day of nursery school but when Ann returns, Bunny is missing and the staff claims never to have seen her. Ann and Bunny have always lived with Ann's possessive older brother Stephen (Dullea), but when Scotland Yard Superintendent Newhouse (Olivier) investigates, he starts believing that Bunny never existed. A hysterical Ann tries to convince him otherwise. 107m/B/W; DVD. **C:** Carol Lynley; Laurence Olivier; Keir Dullea; Noel Coward; Martita Hunt; Anna Massey; Clive Revill; Finlay Currie; Lucie Mannheim; Directed by Otto Preminger; Written by John Mortimer; Penelope Mortimer; Cinematography by Denys Coop; Music by Paul Glass. **A:** Sr. High-Adult. **P:** Entertainment. **U:** Home. **Mov-Ent**: Cult Films, Mystery & Suspense. **Acq:** Purchase. **Dist:** Sony Pictures Home Entertainment Inc.

Bunny Wailer in Concert 1994
Reggae concert at Madison Square Garden includes "Blackheart Man." 80m; VHS. **A:** Jr. High-Adult. **P:** Entertainment. **U:** Home. **Mov-Ent**: Music Video, Music--Pop/Rock, Music--Performance. **Acq:** Purchase. **Dist:** Shanachie Entertainment. $24.98.

Bunny Whipped 2006 (R) — ★
Where's a killer rabbit when you need one? Bob (Powell) is looking to change his life and finds it when rapper Cracker Jack is murdered. Bob transforms himself into a cartoonish vigilante ("The Whip") and the media attention gets Bob a call from ex-girlfriend Ann (Adams), an animal rights activist, who wants Bob's help in saving some lab rabbits. But his rapper case doesn't go away as it seems Bob's suspect, rival rapper Kenny Kent (Alonso), doesn't want this goof poking into his business. Just all-around lame-but gets a bone for having honey Adams in the cast. 91m; DVD. **C:** Esteban Louis Powell; Joey Lauren Adams; Laz Alonso; Rebecca Gayheart; Amanda Noret; Brande Roderick; Directed by Rafael Riera; Written by Rafael Riera; Cinematography by Bob Brill; Music by Jessika Zen. **A:** Sr. High-Adult. **P:** Entertainment. **U:** Home. **Mov-Ent**: Rabbits, Music--Rap. **Acq:** Purchase. **Dist:** ThinkFilm Company Inc.

The Bunny Years ????
Presents the A&E cable channel special on the history of the Playboy Bunnies, who served patrons at Playboy Clubs from 1960-1988 in specially-made and barely-there bunny costumes; features Bunnies such as feminist Gloria Steinem (who worked there in order to write a magazine article detailing the challenging working conditions) along with actresses Lauren Hutton and Susan Sullivan. Includes interviews with former Bunnies and Playboy founder Hugh Hefner. 100m; DVD. **A:** Adult. **P:** Entertainment. **U:** Home, CATV. **Mov-Ent**: Television Series, Documentary Films, Women. **Acq:** Purchase. **Dist:** A&E Television Networks L.L.C. $29.95.

A Bunny's Tale 1985 (Unrated) — ★★
The story of Gloria Steinem's undercover journey into the Playboy Club as a fledgling journalist. It is here that she discovered her dedication as a feminist. Based on the book by Steinem. 97m; VHS, CC. **C:** Kirstie Alley; Cotter Smith; Deborah Van Valkenburgh; Joanna Kerns; Delta Burke; Diana Scarwid; Directed by Karen Arthur. **Pr:** Stan Margulies; ABC Circle Films. **A:** Jr. High-Adult. **P:** Entertainment. **U:** Home. **Mov-Ent**: Comedy-Drama, Journalism, Women. **Acq:** Purchase. **Dist:** Unknown Distributor.

Bunraka: Japan's Classical Puppet Theater 197?
How Bunraka puppets are made and manipulated along with excerpts from two plays are performed in this program. 30m; VHS, 3/4 U, EJ, Q. **Pr:** WCBS New York; Camera Three Productions. **A:** Family. **P:** Entertainment. **U:** Institution, SURA. **Fin-Art**: Japan, Puppets. **Acq:** Duplication, Free Duplication. **Dist:** Camera Three Productions, Inc.; Creative Arts Television Archive.

Bunraku 2010 (Unrated) — ★
Post-apocalyptic pulp action fantasy, shot completely in the studio, that's all artifice and little sense. Guns have been banished but violence is common as a Drifter comes to town with a revenge plan against local big shot Nicola. The Drifter teams up with sword-wielding Yoshi to lead the fight against Nicola and his henchmen. 124m; DVD, Blu-Ray, Wide. **C:** Josh Hartnett; Ron Perlman; Gackt; Demi Moore; Woody Harrelson; Jordi Molla; Kevin McKidd; Directed by Guy Moshe; Written by Guy Moshe; Cinematography by Juan Ruiz-Anchia; Music by Terence Blanchard. **A:** Sr. High-Adult. **P:** Entertainment. **U:** Home. **Mov-Ent**: Fantasy. **Acq:** Purchase. **Dist:** ARC Entertainment, LLC.

Buns of Steel by Greg Smithey 1987
An entertaining exercise instruction emphasizing the firming of legs, thighs and gluts. 52m; VHS. **C:** Greg Smithey. **Pr:** Fit Video. **A:** Sr. High-Adult. **P:** Instruction. **U:** Home. **Hea-Sci**: Fitness/Exercise. **Acq:** Purchase. **Dist:** ESPN Inc.; Cambridge Educational. $24.95.

Buns of Steel Pregnancy Workout 1996
Features aerobics that maintain stamina while the well-designed toning segments prepare your body to give birth. 47m; VHS. **A:** Adult. **P:** Instruction. **U:** Home. **Hea-Sci**: Fitness/Exercise, How-To, Self-Help. **Acq:** Purchase. **Dist:** Warner Home Video, Inc. $12.95.

Bunting Drills and Techniques 1999
University of Florida Hitting Coach Mark Wasikowski demonstrates proper lower and upper body mechanics for effective bunting and discusses strategic situations for bunting. 41m; VHS. **A:** Adult. **P:** Instruction. **U:** Institution. **How-Ins**: Baseball, Sports--General, How-To. **Acq:** Purchase. **Dist:** Championship Productions. $39.95.

Buona Sera, Mrs. Campbell 1968 (Unrated) — ★★½
The lovely Lollobridgida and some fast-paced plot moves are the main highlights of this comedy. Mrs. Campbell convinced her three American WWII lovers that each of them had fathered her daughter. All three have supported mother and child through the years, unbeknowst to each other and their wives. When their 20-year reunion brings them back to Italy, Mrs. Campbell must do some fast-thinking and some quick-stepping to keep everyone happy. 113m; VHS, Wide. **C:** Gina Lollobrigida; Shelley Winters; Phil Silvers; Peter Lawford; Telly Savalas; Lee Grant; Janet Margolin; Marian Moses; Directed by Melvin Frank. **Pr:** United Artists. **A:** Jr. High-Adult. **P:** Entertainment. **U:** Home. **Mov-Ent**: Comedy--Screwball, Children. **Acq:** Purchase. **Dist:** MGM Home Entertainment. $19.98.

Buongiorno Italia! 1984
Designed to teach the basics of the Italian language. 25m; VHS, 3/4 U. **Pr:** British Broadcasting Corporation. **A:** Primary-Adult. **P:** Education. **U:** Institution, SURA. **Gen-Edu**: Language Arts, Education. **Acq:** Purchase. **Dist:** Home Vision Cinema.

Buoyancy 1968
Presents a structured series of experiments which leads the students to an understanding of buoyancy. 15m; VHS, 3/4 U. **Pr:** Iwanami Films. **A:** Jr. High-Sr. High. **P:** Education. **U:** Institution, SURA. **Hea-Sci**: Physics. **Acq:** Purchase. **Dist:** Phoenix Learning Group.

Buoyancy 1985
An explanation of the principles of buoyancy for the layman, using examples of true-life experiments. 13m; VHS, 3/4 U, Special order formats. **Pr:** Coronet Films. **A:** Family. **P:** Education. **U:** Institution, CCTV, SURA. **Hea-Sci**: Physics. **Acq:** Purchase, Rent/Lease, Duplication License. **Dist:** Phoenix Learning Group.

Buoyant 2004 (Unrated)
Julie Wyman's experimental documentary promotes body-acceptance, fat-empowerment, fitness at all sizes through the endeavors of the Padded Lilies, a troupe of overweight synchronized swimmers, the obsessions of Greek mathematician Archimedes, and the invention of the "Drystroke Swimulator" (patent pending). 28m; DVD. **A:** Adult. **P:** Education. **U:** Institution. **Gen-Edu**: Documentary Films, Health Education. **Acq:** Purchase. **Dist:** Women Make Movies. $195.00.

The 'Burbs 1989 (PG) — ★½
A tepid satire about suburbanites suspecting their creepy new neighbors of murderous activities. Well-designed and sharp, but light on story. 101m; VHS, DVD, Wide. **C:** Tom Hanks; Carrie Fisher; Ric(k) Ducommun; Corey Feldman; Brother Theodore; Bruce Dern; Gale Gordon; Courtney Gains; Directed by Joe Dante; Written by Dana Olsen; Cinematography by Robert M. Stevens; Music by Jerry Goldsmith. **Pr:** Imagine Entertainment; Universal Pictures. **A:** Jr. High-Adult. **P:** Entertainment. **U:** Home. **Mov-Ent**: Satire & Parody. **Acq:** Purchase. **Dist:** Critics' Choice Video & DVD. $14.95.

Burchfield's Vision 1985
A retrospective of the artist's childhood experiences and their influence on his art, which is shown on display at the Metropolitan Museum of Art. 58m; VHS, 3/4 U, Special order formats. **Pr:** Lutheran Film Division. **A:** Sr. High-Adult. **P:** Education. **U:** Institution, Home. **Fin-Art**: Documentary Films, Art & Artists, Museums. **Acq:** Purchase, Rent/Lease. **Dist:** Lutheran Film Associates. $39.95.

Burden of a War: Women and Agent Orange 1991
Pofiles women and their children who were exposed to Agent Orange. 30m; VHS. **A:** College-Adult. **P:** Education. **U:** Institution. **Gen-Edu**: Documentary Films, Women, Children. **Acq:** Purchase, Rent/Lease. **Dist:** Filmakers Library Inc. $295.00.

Burden of Dreams 1982 — ★★★½
The landmark documentary chronicling the berserk circumstances behind the scenes of Werner Herzog's epic "Fitzcarraldo." Stuck in the Peruvian jungles, the film crew was subjected to every disaster imaginable while executing Herzog's vision, including disease, horrendous accident, warring local tribes and the megalomaniacal director himself. Considered better than "Fitzcarraldo," although both films discuss a man's obsession. 94m; VHS, DVD. **C:** Klaus Kinski; Mick Jagger; Jason Robards, Jr.; Werner Herzog; Directed by Les Blank. **Pr:** Les Blank; Les Blank. **A:** Sr. High-Adult. **P:** Entertainment. **U:** Home. **Mov-Ent**: Documentary Films, Film History, South America. **Acq:** Purchase, Rent/Lease. **Dist:** Flower Films; Tapeworm Video Distributors Inc.; Baker and Taylor. $59.95.

Burden on the Land 1992
Takes a look at Africa's future. It speaks to the causes of famine, and expresses why development in Africa has been disappointing. Some of the successes have been dams, food processing, reforestation, road buiding, irrigation, and animal husbandry. 52m; VHS. **A:** College-Adult. **P:** Education. **U:** Institution. **Gen-Edu**: Documentary Films, Africa, Politics & Government. **Acq:** Purchase, Rent/Lease. **Dist:** Filmakers Library Inc. $350.00.

Bureau of Missing Persons 1933 — ★★½
Comedy-drama about big-city bureau of missing persons, in which the hardened Stone is in charge. O'Brien plays a tough cop who is transferred to the bureau and Davis stars as the mystery woman with whom he gets involved. Although fast-paced and intriguing, the film is somewhat confusing and never stays in one direction for very long. 75m/B/W; VHS, DVD, CC. **C:** Bette Davis; Lewis Stone; Pat O'Brien; Glenda Farrell; Allen Jenkins; Ruth Donnelly; Hugh Herbert; Directed by Roy Del Ruth; Written by Robert Presnell, Sr.; Cinematography by Barney McGill; Music by Bernhard Kaun. **Pr:** Henry Blanke. **A:** Jr. High-Adult. **P:** Entertainment. **U:** Home. **Mov-Ent**: Comedy-Drama, Romance. **Acq:** Purchase. **Dist:** WarnerArchive.com. $19.98.

The Bureaucracy 1990
Examines the effectiveness of the Internal Revenue Service and Park Service. 30m; VHS. **A:** Adult. **P:** Education. **U:** Institution. **Gen-Edu**: Politics & Government. **Acq:** Purchase. **Dist:** RMI Media. $89.95.

The Burg: A State of Mind 1988
This documentary examines life in the New Jersey city of Chambersburg, more popularily known as The Burg. 30m; VHS, 3/4 U. **C:** Narrated by Dr. Peter Peroni. **Pr:** Louis J. Presti. **A:** Jr. High-Adult. **P:** Education. **U:** Institution. **Gen-Edu**: Documentary Films, Cities & Towns. **Acq:** Purchase, Rent/Lease. **Dist:** New Jersey Network.

Burgess, Philby, and MacLean: Spy Scandal of the Century 1986 (Unrated)
An intriguing, true spy story about three double agents who were able to infiltrate British Intelligence and pass on U.S. atomic secrets to the Soviet Union. Originally aired on PBS. 83m; VHS. **A:** Jr. High-Adult. **P:** Entertainment. **U:** Home. **Mov-Ent**: Politics & Government. **Acq:** Purchase. **Dist:** Phoenix Learning Group.

The Burgess Shale 1992
Questions commonly accepted theories of evolution. The Burgess Shale is a small quarry in the Canadian Rockies containing the fossilized evidence of animals who roamed the Earth 530 million years ago. 45m; VHS, 3/4 U. **Pr:** Canadian Broadcasting Corp. **A:** Sr. High-Adult. **P:** Education. **U:** Institution. **Gen-Edu**: Education, Evolution, Science. **Acq:** Purchase, Rent/Lease. **Dist:** New Dimension Media. $270.00.

The Burghers of Calais 1980
A look at Rodin's statue, which is a memorial to the six citizens of Calais who offered their lives to King Edward III to save their town during the Hundred Years War. 9m; VHS, Special order formats. **Pr:** Mass Media Ministries. **A:** Sr. High-Adult. **P:**

Education. **U:** Institution, Home. **Fin-Art:** Documentary Films, Art & Artists, Sculpture. **Acq:** Purchase. **Dist:** Mass Media Ministries. $69.00.

The Burglar 1957 — ★★
David Goodis adapted his own novel for this pulp noir that reeks of sexual tension amidst its crime trappings. Thief Nat Harbin (Duryea) and his team score big after stealing a valuable diamond necklace. Trouble comes as they wait to fence the piece in Atlantic City. A crooked cop is involved as is Gladden (Mansfield), the femme member of their crew who willfully ignores Nat's plans and causes grief for them all. 90m/B/W; DVD. **C:** Dan Duryea; Jayne Mansfield; Peter Capell; Mickey Shaughnessy; Stewart Bradley; Martha Vickers; Directed by Paul Wendkos; Written by David Goodis; Cinematography by Don Malkames; Music by Sol Kaplan. **A:** Sr. High-Adult. **P:** Entertainment. **U:** Home. **Mov-Ent. Acq:** Purchase. **Dist:** Sony Pictures Home Entertainment Inc.

Burglar 1987 — ★★★
Not to be confused with the Whoopi Goldberg vehicle, this Russian film relates a story no less American than apple pie and teenage angst. Senka and would-be punk star Kostya are two neglected and disaffected brothers whose father is a drunken womanizer best known for absentee paternalism. When Howmuch, a serious heavy metalloid, pressures Kostya to steal a synthesizer, brother Senka steps in to steal the Community Center's property himself. In Russian with English subtitles, the solid performances hold their own against the heavy musical content. 89m; VHS, DVD. **C:** Konstantin Kinchev; Oleg Yelykomov; Directed by Valery Orgorodnikov. **A:** Sr. High-Adult. **P:** Entertainment. **U:** Home. **L:** Russian, English. **Mov-Ent:** USSR, Adolescence, Music--Pop/Rock. **Acq:** Purchase. **Dist:** Facets Multimedia Inc.; Kino on Video. $59.95.

Burglar 1987 (R) — ★★
A cat burglar moves to the right side of the law when she tries to solve a murder case. Whoopi's always a treat, but this movie's best forgotten; Goldberg's fans should watch "Jumpin' Jack Flash" again instead. Co-star Goldthwait elevates the comedic level a bit. 103m; VHS, DVD, CC. **C:** Whoopi Goldberg; Bobcat Goldthwait; Lesley Ann Warren; John Goodman; G.W. Bailey; James Handy; Anne DeSalvo; Directed by Hugh Wilson; Written by Hugh Wilson; Cinematography by William A. Fraker; Music by Sylvester Levay; Bernard Edwards. **Pr:** Michael Hirsch; Kevin McCormick. **A:** Sr. High-Adult. **P:** Entertainment. **U:** Home. **L:** English, Spanish. **Mov-Ent:** Action-Adventure. **Acq:** Purchase. **Dist:** Kino on Video; Warner Home Video, Inc. $19.98.

Burglar Alarms: Are They Any Good? 1995
Takes a look at burglar alarms and home security systems and examines what burglars look for when targeting a home, why burglars can beat certain security systems, and the hidden costs of systems. ?m; VHS. **A:** Adult. **P:** Education. **U:** Home. **Gen-Edu:** Safety Education, Consumer Education. **Acq:** Purchase. **Dist:** Tapeworm Video Distributors Inc. $12.95.

Burglar-Proofing Your Home and Car 1988
With the ever-increasing rates of car and house vandalism, this tape shows Joe Average how to fight back and protect what is his. 55m; VHS. **Pr:** Cambridge Career Productions. **A:** Sr. High-Adult. **P:** Instruction. **U:** Institution, Home. **How-Ins:** Safety Education. **Acq:** Purchase. **Dist:** Cambridge Educational. $19.95.

The Burial Ground 1982
A story of industrial waste and environmental laws. 30m; VHS, 3/4 U. **Pr:** Commonwealth Films. **A:** Adult. **P:** Education. **U:** Institution, Home. **Bus-Ind:** Safety Education, Waste Products, Ecology & Environment. **Acq:** Purchase, Rent/Lease. **Dist:** Commonwealth Films Inc.; Emergency Film Group. $525.00.

Burial Ground 1985 (Unrated) — ★
A classically grisly splatter film in which the hungry dead rise and proceed to kill the weekend denizens of an isolated aristocratic mansion. 85m; VHS, DVD. **C:** Karen Well; Peter Bark; Directed by Andrea Bianchi. **Pr:** Film Concept Group. **A:** Jr. High-Adult. **P:** Entertainment. **U:** Home. **Mov-Ent:** Horror. **Acq:** Purchase. **Dist:** Lions Gate Television Corp. $79.95.

Burial of the Rats 1995 (R) — ★½
Based on a short story by Bram Stoker, this cable campiness features young Bram (Alber) himself being kidnapped while traveling in Eastern Europe. He's taken to the "Queen of Vermin" (Barbeau), who heads a bloodthirsty cult that hate men, worship rats, and live by violence. Fortunately, the Queen decides to spare Bram so he can write of their exploits and he falls for the fleshy charms of rat-woman Madeleine (Ford). 85m; VHS, DVD. **C:** Adrienne Barbeau; Maria Ford; Kevin Alber; Directed by Dan Golden. **Pr:** Roger Corman; Showtime. **A:** Sr. High-Adult. **P:** Entertainment. **U:** Home. **Mov-Ent:** Horror, Cults, TV Movies. **Acq:** Purchase. **Dist:** New Horizons Picture Corp.

Buried 2010 (R) — ★★
A claustrophobic nightmare in real-time with director Cortes shrewdly increasing the tension to almost unbearable effect. Civilian truck driver Paul Conroy's (Reynolds) convoy is ambushed by insurgents in Iraq. He's kidnapped, buried alive, and held for ransom. Conroy has a lighter, a pen, a pocketknife, and a cell phone to contact the outside world (with his captors able to contact him) and finds neither his employer nor the State Department are willing to help. 95m; Blu-Ray. **C:** Ryan Reynolds; Stephen Tobolowsky; Samantha Mathis; Erik Palladino; Robert Paterson; Jose Luis Garcia-Perez; Directed by Rodrigo Cortes; Written by Chris Sparling; Cinematography by Eduard Grau; Music by Victor Reyes. **Pr:** Peter Safran; Adrian Guerra; Safran Co; Dark Trick Films; Versus Entertainment; Lionsgate. **A:** Sr. High-Adult. **P:** Entertainment. **U:** Home. **L:** English. **Mov-Ent:** Terrorism. **Acq:** Purchase. **Dist:** Alpha Video; Lions Gate Entertainment Inc.

Buried Alive 1939 (Unrated) — ★
A man is sent to prison on trumped up charges. Only the prison nurse believes he is innocent as a crooked politician strives to keep him behind bars. 74m/B/W; DVD, CV. **C:** Beverly Roberts; Robert Wilcox; George Pembroke; Ted Osborn; Paul McVey; Alden "Steve" Chase; Directed by Victor Halperin. **A:** Jr. High-Adult. **P:** Entertainment. **U:** Home. **Mov-Ent:** Politics & Government. **Acq:** Purchase. **Dist:** Sinister Cinema. $16.95.

Buried Alive 1981 (Unrated) — ★★
Director d'Amato reaps his finest gore-fest to date, incorporating the well-established taxidermist gone loony motif in his repertoire of appalling bad taste. Not for the squeamish, this bloodier-than-thou spaghetti spooker is chock full of necrophilia, cannibalism, and more. 90m; VHS, DVD. **C:** Kieran Canter; Cinzia Monreale; Franca Stoppi; Directed by Joe D'Amato. **Pr:** Aquarius Releasing. **A:** College-Adult. **P:** Entertainment. **U:** Home. **Mov-Ent:** Horror. **Acq:** Purchase. **Dist:** Unknown Distributor.

Buried Alive 1989 (R) — ★★
Once Ravenscroft Hall was an asylum for the incurably insane. Now, the isolated mansion is a school for troubled teenage girls, run by a charismatic psychiatrist. Captivated by his charm, a young woman joins the staff. Soon, she is tormented by nightmare visions of the long-dead victims of a nameless killer. When the students begin to disappear, she realizes he still lives...and she may be his next victim. Carradine's last role. 97m; VHS, DVD. **C:** Robert Vaughn; Donald Pleasence; Karen Witter; John Carradine; Ginger Lynn Allen; Directed by Gerard Kikoine. **Pr:** Harry Alan Towers. **A:** College-Adult. **P:** Entertainment. **U:** Home. **Mov-Ent:** Horror, Education. **Acq:** Purchase. **Dist:** Sony Pictures Home Entertainment Inc. $14.95.

Buried Alive 1990 (PG-13) — ★★½
One of the many horror flicks entitled "Buried Alive," this one is not bad, injecting a bit of levity into the time-worn genre. Schemestress Leigh and her paramour poison her husband. Or so they think, only to discover that he's not quite dead. 93m; DVD. **C:** Tim Matheson; Jennifer Jason Leigh; William Atherton; Hoyt Axton; Directed by Frank Darabont; Written by Mark Patrick Carducci; Jake Clesi; Music by Michel Colombier. **Pr:** Producers Pictures. **A:** Sr. High-Adult. **P:** Entertainment. **U:** Home. **Mov-Ent:** Horror. **Acq:** Purchase. **Dist:** Alpha Video. $79.95.

Buried Alive 2 1997 (PG-13) — ★★½
Randy (Caffrey) wants to get rid of rich wife Laura (Sheedy) so he and girlfirend Roxanne (Needham) can enjoy her cash. So he slips some blowfish venom into her wine and buries her. But the venom only simulated death and after clawing her way out of the grave, Laura is one angry gal. Clint Goodman (Matheson), who was buried in the first movie, shows up to help out the wronged wife. 92m; VHS, CC. **C:** Ally Sheedy; Stephen Caffrey; Tracey Needham; Tim Matheson; Directed by Tim Matheson; Written by Walter Klenhard. **Pr:** Mark Huffam. **A:** Jr. High-Adult. **P:** Entertainment. **U:** Home. **Mov-Ent:** Horror, TV Movies. **Acq:** Purchase. **Dist:** Universal Music and Video Distribution.

Buried in the Backyard 2005
Documentary about the men and women who are building bomb shelters in preparation for the next terrorist attack. 30m; VHS, DVD. **A:** Sr. High-Adult. **P:** Education. **U:** Home, Institution. **Gen-Edu:** Documentary Films. **Acq:** Purchase, Rent/Lease. **Dist:** The Cinema Guild. $195.00.

The Buried Mirror: Reflections on Spain and the New World 1991
A five-program series exploring the history of the Spanish-speaking world, its multicultural traditions, and its political and social history in Spain, Mexico, and the United States. 295m; VHS. **C:** Hosted by Carlos Fuentes; Written by Carlos Fuentes. **A:** Sr. High-Adult. **P:** Education. **U:** Institution, Home. **Gen-Edu:** History, Spain, Mexico. **Acq:** Purchase. **Dist:** Home Vision Cinema. $99.95.

Buried Secrets 2006 (Unrated)
Discovery Channel 2006 mini-series. Dr. Murray and experts in history, archeology, anthropology and forensic sciences uncover historical mysteries by examining skeletal remains unearthed from around the globe. 20 episodes. 240m; DVD. **C:** Lonell R. Childred; Frank Hargreaves; Christopher Allison; Tim L. Smith. **A:** Sr. High-Adult. **P:** Entertainment. **U:** Home. **Mov-Ent:** Mystery & Suspense, Anthropology, Television Series. **Acq:** Purchase. **Dist:** Timeless Media Group. $9.99.

Buried Treasures, Vol. 1: The Directors 1989
A collection of unique music videos including William S. Burrough's "Thanksgiving Prayer," The Buggles' "Video Killed the Radio Star," Young MC's "Principal's Office" and videos by Wally Bandarou, Mon Dino and Tom Waits. 30m; VHS. **C:** Directed by Gus Van Sant; Susan Young; Jean-Baptiste Mondino; Chris Blum; Tamra Davis; Russell Mulcahy. **A:** Jr. High-Adult. **P:** Entertainment. **U:** Home. **Mov-Ent:** Music Video. **Acq:** Purchase. **Dist:** Music Video Distributors. $14.95.

Buried Treasures, Vol. 2: Reggae Classics 1990
A collection of great reggae music videos, including Bob Marley and the Wailers, Toots and the Maytals, Third World, Sly & Robbie, Burning Spear, R.P.O., Black Uhuru, Aswad and many more. 35m; VHS. **Pr:** Island Visual Arts; British Broadcasting Corporation. **A:** Jr. High-Adult. **P:** Entertainment. **U:** Home. **Mov-Ent:** Music--Performance, Music Video, Black Culture. **Acq:** Purchase. **Dist:** Music Video Distributors; Facets Multimedia Inc. $14.95.

Buried Treasures, Vol. 3: Rap Source 1990
A collection of the finest rap videos to come out of the '80s. 30m; VHS. **A:** Jr. High-Adult. **P:** Entertainment. **U:** Home. **Mov-Ent:** Music--Rap, Black Culture. **Acq:** Purchase. **Dist:** Music Video Distributors; Facets Multimedia Inc.

Burke & Hare 2010 (Unrated) — ★★
Old-fashioned horror comedy based (loosely) on the true story of 19th-century body-snatchers William Burke (Pegg) and William Hare (Serkis) who illegally supplied cadavers to Edinburgh medical schools. Only since their new profession is so lucrative, they decide to help a number of live bodies along rather than just relying on stealing corpses. Pegg and Serkis obviously relish their roles, with some slapstick and a touch of moral uncertainty (after all they are mass murderers) thrown in. 91m; DVD, Blu-Ray. **C:** Simon Pegg; Andy Serkis; Tom Wilkinson; Tim Curry; Isla Fisher; Jessica Hynes; Ronnie Corbett; Hugh Bonneville; Directed by John Landis; Written by Piers Ashworth; Nick Moorcraft; Cinematography by John Mathieson; Music by Joby Talbot. **Pr:** Barnaby Thompson; Entertainment Films; Fragile Films; Ealing Studios; IFC Films. **A:** Sr. High-Adult. **P:** Entertainment. **U:** Home. **L:** English. **Mov-Ent:** Comedy--Black. **Acq:** Purchase. **Dist:** MPI Media Group.

Burke and Paine on Revolution ????
Presents the 1792 debate of Edmund Burke, a conservative and Thomas Paine, a radical, over their conflicting views about political change, liberty, and the peoples' relationship with their government. 28m; VHS. **A:** Sr. High. **P:** Education. **U:** Institution. **Gen-Edu:** History--U.S., Politics & Government. **Acq:** Purchase. **Dist:** Zenger Media. $59.00.

Burke & Wills 1985 (PG-13) — ★★½
A lush, big-budgeted true story of the two men who first crossed Australia on foot, and explored its central region. Popular Australian film. 120m; VHS, CC. **C:** Jack Thompson; Nigel Havers; Greta Scacchi; Ralph Cotterill; Drew Forsythe; Chris Haywood; Matthew Fargher; Directed by Graeme Clifford; Written by Michael Thomas; Cinematography by Russell Boyd; Music by Peter Sculthorpe. **Pr:** Hoyts-Edgley; Hemdale Films. **A:** Jr. High-Adult. **P:** Entertainment. **U:** Home. **Mov-Ent:** Action-Adventure, Australia. **Acq:** Purchase. **Dist:** New Line Home Video. $19.98.

Burke and Wills: Australia, 1860 1976
From the "Ten Who Dared" series, draws some interesting parallels between the development of Australia and that of the U.S.A. The expedition of Burke and Wills is similar, in some ways, to that of Lewis and Clarke. 49m; VHS, 3/4 U, Special order formats. **C:** Narrated by Anthony Quinn. **Pr:** British Broadcasting Corporation; Time-Life Films. **A:** Jr. High-Sr. High. **P:** Education. **U:** Institution, SURA. **Gen-Edu:** Documentary Films, Explorers. **Acq:** Purchase, Rent/Lease. **Dist:** Time-Life Video and Television.

Burke's Law: Season 1, Volume 2 1963 (Unrated)
ABC's 1963-65 detective drama with Amos Burke (Gene Barry) solving murder cases Southern California-style as a pop artist is found impaled on his own creation, a fashion house owner dead amonst an elevator full of mannequins, and a seemingly ordinary suburban housewife discovered strangled in her shower. Helping him are Detective Tim Tilson (Conway) and his faithful Rolls Royce driver, Henry (Leon Lontoc). 16 episodes. 800m; DVD. **C:** Gene Barry; Gary Conway; Leon Lontoc. **A:** Sr. High-Adult. **P:** Entertainment. **U:** Home. **Mov-Ent:** Drama, Television Series. **Acq:** Purchase. **Dist:** VCI Entertainment. $29.99.

The Burks Have AIDS 1986
The story of Patrick Burk is told, a boy who got AIDS through a blood transfusion. 17m; VHS, 3/4 U. **Pr:** CBS. **A:** Jr. High-Adult. **P:** Education. **U:** Institution, SURA. **Hea-Sci:** AIDS. **Acq:** Purchase. **Dist:** Phoenix Learning Group. $175.00.

The Burks of Georgia 1976
Follows the story of three generations of the Burk family, a family living in rural Georgia. Explores the hardships which the family faced and shows how they dealt with the tragic death of a child. Televised by PBS as part of the "Six American Families" series. 53m; VHS. **C:** Directed by Albert Maysles; David Maysles. **A:** Family. **P:** Education. **U:** Home. **Gen-Edu:** Documentary Films, Family, Sociology. **Acq:** Purchase. **Dist:** Maysles Films, Inc.

Burlesque 2010 (PG-13) — ★½
Small town Iowa waitress Ali (Aguilera) moves to L.A. and lands at the Burlesque Lounge, run by former headliner Tess (Cher). Ali's got big dreams and works her way onto the stage via a jaw-dropping audition for Tess. Since Cher's face and Aguilera's acting are both stiff, this winds up as more of a two-hour music video. Tucci shines as gay stage manager Sean, who is naturally the only one who can go toe-to-toe with the mega divas. Fans of the genre will have a blast with the outrageous dancing, singing and costuming—just don't expect great acting, quality script writing or much of a plot. 100m; Blu-Ray, On Demand, Wide, CC. **C:** Cher; Kristen Bell; Christina Aguilera; Julianne Hough; Cam Gigandet; Stanley Tucci; Alan Cumming; Eric Dane; Peter Gallagher; Directed by Steve Antin; Written by Steve Antin; Cinematography by Bojan Bazelli; Music by Christophe Beck. **Pr:** Donald De Line; De Line Pictures; Sony Pictures Home Entertainment Inc. **A:** Jr. High-Adult. **P:** Entertainment. **U:** Home. **L:** English. **Mov-Ent:** Musical--Drama. **Awds:** Golden Globes '11: Song ("You Haven't Seen the Last of Me"). **Acq:** Purchase. **Dist:** Amazon.com Inc.; Movies Unlimited; Alpha Video.

Burlesque in Harlem 1949
Features the all-black burlesque shows held in the old days of Harlem. Includes footage of burlesque star Pigmeat Markham, strippers, dancers, and music from this era. ?m; DVD. **A:** Adult.

P: Entertainment. **U:** Home. **Mov-Ent**: Fantasy, Sex & Sexuality, Black Culture. **Acq:** Purchase. **Dist:** Alpha Video. $19.95.

Burlesque on Carmen 1916 — ★★
A silent pastiche of the Bizet opera, with Charlie as Don Schmose. Interesting early work. 30m/B/W; Silent; VHS, DVD. **C:** Charlie Chaplin; Ben Turpin; Edna Purviance; Directed by Charlie Chaplin; Written by Charlie Chaplin. **Pr:** Essanay Film Manufacturing Company. **A:** Family. **P:** Entertainment. **U:** Home. **Mov-Ent**: Silent Films. **Acq:** Purchase, Rent/Lease. **Dist:** Image Entertainment Inc.; Glenn Video Vistas Ltd. $19.95.

Burley: Growing Tobacco in America 1985
Follows the life of Kentucky tobacco farmer Homer Phillips and his family through planting, harvesting, curing, and sale of a crop as well as examining government price support programs and antismoking campaigns. 28m; VHS. **C:** Directed by Robby Henson. **A:** College-Adult. **P:** Education. **U:** Institution. **Gen-Edu**: Agriculture, Smoking. **Acq:** Purchase, Rent/Lease. **Dist:** The Cinema Guild. $250.00.

Burlington Northern E-Units 2008 (Unrated)
1990 film footage of the last fleet of Electro-Motive E-units working pulling commuter trains in Chicago. Travels the entire line from Union Station out to Aurora, a route filled with curves, bridges, and scenic stations. 60m; DVD. **A:** Family. **P:** Education. **U:** Home. **Gen-Edu:** Trains, U.S. States. **Acq:** Purchase. **Dist:** Pentrex Media Group L.L.C. $29.95.

Burlington Northern: Freight Operations in the Early 1970's 19??
Compilation of two films "Portrait of a Railroad" with footage of Burlington Northern activities in hump yards, control centers, freight handling and car loading, plus "The Freight Goes Through" a 1952 AAR training film to teach yard workers how to couple freight cars correctly. 46m; DVD. **A:** Family. **P:** Education. **U:** Home. **L:** English. **Gen-Edu:** Trains, U.S. States. **Acq:** Purchase. **Dist:** Diecast Airplane; The Civil War Standard. $24.95.

Burlington Northern's Funnel 1997
Captures the 71 mile train route from Spokane, Washington to Sandpoint, Idaho. 80m; VHS. **A:** Adult. **P:** Entertainment. **U:** Home. **Gen-Edu:** Trains. **Acq:** Purchase. **Dist:** Pentrex Media Group L.L.C. $19.95.

Burma Convoy 1941 (Unrated) — ★½
A truck driver on the Burma Road—a dangerous stretch of roadway in Asia used to hall munitions during World War II—sets out to uncover the mystery of his younger brother's death. 72m/B/W; VHS. **C:** Charles Bickford; Evelyn Ankers; Frank Albertson; Cecil Kellaway; Willie Fung; Keye Luke; Directed by Noel Mason Smith; Written by Roy Chanslor; Stanley Rubin. **A:** Jr. High-Adult. **P:** Entertainment. **U:** Home. **Mov-Ent:** Asia, World War Two. **Acq:** Purchase. **Dist:** Nostalgia Family Video/Hollywood's Attic. $19.99.

Burma: Railway of Death 1990
The construction of the Burmese Railway by Asian slave labor and Allied POWs is documented. Approximate death toll calculated is 393 men for every mile of track laid. 45m; VHS. **Pr:** Fusion Video. **A:** Sr. High-Adult. **P:** Education. **U:** Home. **Gen-Edu:** Documentary Films, World War Two, Trains. **Acq:** Purchase. **Dist:** Fusion Video. $29.98.

Burma VJ: Reporting from a Closed Country 2009 (Unrated) — ★★
Documentary covers the efforts of the Democratic Voice of Burma (DVB), an underground group of journalists, to document the 2007 uprising in Rangoon against the junta and to protest the lack of democracy. This resulted in mass arrests, disappearances, and fatalities, including that of Japanese journalist Kenji Nagai. Some scene-setting reconstructions are included but most of the footage was shot by the anonymous reporters. 84m; DVD, On Demand, Wide. **C:** Directed by Anders Ostergaard; Cinematography by Simon Plum; Music by Conny Malmqvist. **A:** Adult. **P:** Entertainment. **U:** Home. **L:** English. **Mov-Ent:** Documentary Films, Journalism, Politics & Government. **Acq:** Purchase. **Dist:** Oscilloscope Films; Amazon.com Inc.; Movies Unlimited.

The Burmese Harp 1956 — ★★★★
At the end of WWII, a Japanese soldier is spiritually traumatized and becomes obsessed with burying the masses of war casualties. A searing, acclaimed anti-war statement, in Japanese with English subtitles. Remade by Ichikawa in 1985. 115m/B/W; VHS, DVD. **C:** Shoji Yasui; Rentaro Mikuni; Tatsuya Mihashi; Tanie Kitabayashi; Yunosuke Ito; Directed by Kon Ichikawa; Written by Natto Wada; Cinematography by Minoru Yokoyama; Music by Akira Ifukube. **Pr:** Nikkatsu. **A:** Jr. High-Adult. **P:** Entertainment. **U:** Home. **L:** English, Japanese. **Mov-Ent:** Classic Films, World War Two. **Acq:** Purchase. **Dist:** Tapeworm Video Distributors Inc. $29.95.

Burn! 1970 (PG) — ★★★½
An Italian-made indictment of imperialist control by guerrilla-filmmaker Pontecorvo, depicting the efforts of a 19th century British ambassador to put down a slave revolt on a Portuguese-run Caribbean island. Great Brando performance. 112m; VHS, DVD, Wide. **C:** Marlon Brando; Evarist Marquez; Renato Salvatori; Norman Hill; Dana Ghia; Giampiero Albertini; Tom Lyons; Directed by Gillo Pontecorvo; Written by Giorgio Arlorio; Franco Solinas; Cinematography by Marcello Gatti; Music by Ennio Morricone. **Pr:** United Artists. **A:** Jr. High-Adult. **P:** Entertainment. **U:** Home. **Mov-Ent:** Slavery. **Acq:** Purchase. **Dist:** MGM Home Entertainment; Facets Multimedia Inc. $19.98.

Burn 2012 (Unrated) — ★★★½
Tom Putnam and Brenna Sanchez spent a year in a Detroit firehouse and came away with a striking documentary about one of the most dangerous professions in the world. Not only does it capture personalities well, it becomes a socio-cultural commentary on a city that's being burned down as it's being abandoned. And, most importantly, the people left behind willing to fight to keep it standing. Executive produced by Denis Leary, the film has the power of his fictional TV series "Rescue Me," although every minute of it is real. 86m; DVD, Blu-Ray. **C:** Donald Austin; Brendan Doogie Milewski; Craig Dougherty; Terrell Hardaway; Dennis Hunter; Directed by Tom Putnam; Brenna Sanchez; Cinematography by Mark Eaton; Nicola Marsh; Matt Pappas. **Pr:** Tom Putnam; Brenna Sanchez; Apostle Pictures. **A:** College-Adult. **P:** Entertainment. **U:** Home. **L:** English. **Mov-Ent:** Documentary Films, Fires, Cities & Towns. **Acq:** Purchase. **Dist:** Not Yet Released.

Burn After Reading 2008 (R) — ★★½
Two greedy and none-too-smart gym employees (Pitt, McDormand) attempt to sell a disk containing the memoirs of an ousted CIA agent (Malkovich) with unpleasant consequences. Swinton and Clooney, who are re-teamed after "Michael Clayton," play the agent's unhappy wife and her scheming lover. Swinton looks like she's still in that movie, while Clooney gets into Coen brothers mode effortlessly and is a highlight. Convoluted plot takes a back seat to excellent dialogue and pleasantly over the top characters. Pitt looks like he's having a blast with his dim-bulb workout junkie. Simmons and Jenkins shine in limited roles as bosses trying to figure out what the hell is going on. 96m; Blu-Ray, On Demand, Wide. **C:** Brad Pitt; George Clooney; John Malkovich; Tilda Swinton; Frances McDormand; Richard Jenkins; J.K. Simmons; David Rasche; Olek Krupa; Jeffrey DeMunn; Elizabeth Marvel; Directed by Joel Coen; Ethan Coen; Written by Joel Coen; Ethan Coen; Cinematography by Emmanuel Lubezki; Music by Carter Burwell. **Pr:** Joel Coen; Ethan Coen; Joel Coen; Ethan Coen; Focus Features L.L.C; Working Title Productions; Relativity Media; StudioCanal. **A:** Sr. High-Adult. **P:** Entertainment. **U:** Home. **L:** English. **Mov-Ent:** Intelligence Service, Alcoholism. **Acq:** Purchase. **Dist:** Universal Studios Home Video; Amazon.com Inc.; Movies Unlimited.

Burn Care 2-Part Video Series 1996
Teaches nursing care needed for emergency burn patients for the first 72 hours. Includes guided information for nurses who give day-to-day care to burn patients. 54m; VHS. **A:** Adult. **P:** Education. **U:** Institution. **Hea-Sci:** Nursing, Medical Education, How-To. **Acq:** Purchase, Rent/Lease. **Dist:** AJN Video Library/Lippincott Williams & Wilkins. $475.00.

Burn 'Em Up Barnes 1934
Twelve episodes each depicting the adventures of "Burn'Em Up" Barnes, a racer, and his buddy, Bobbie. 40m/B/W; VHS. **C:** Frankie Darro; Lola Lane; Jack Mulhall; Tom London; Jason Robards, Sr.; Milburn Stone; Directed by Colbert Clark; Armand Schaefer; Written by Armand Schaefer; Sherman Lowe; Barney A. Sarecky; Cinematography by Ernest Miller; William Nobles; Music by Lee Zahler. **Pr:** Nat Levine; Mascot. **A:** Family. **P:** Entertainment. **U:** Institution, Home. **Mov-Ent:** Serials, Automobiles--Racing. **Acq:** Purchase. **Dist:** Sinister Cinema. $26.95.

Burn Emergency 1977
"Burn Emergency" introduces the newest methods of caring for burn victims until they can reach a hospital or burn center. 25m; VHS, 3/4 U. **Pr:** Sheldon Renan; Rick Wise. **A:** Jr. High-Adult. **P:** Education. **U:** Institution, Home, SURA. **How-Ins:** How-To, Emergencies, Burns. **Acq:** Purchase, Rent/Lease, Duplication License. **Dist:** Pyramid Media. $325.00.

Burn Fat Fast: Cardio Dance & Sculpt 2005
Two 20-minute cardio and strength workouts that focus on the abdominal and lower body muscles. 52m; DVD. **A:** College-Adult. **P:** Instruction. **U:** Home. **Hea-Sci:** Fitness/Exercise. **Acq:** Purchase. **Dist:** CinemaNow Inc. $14.98.

Burn Heads 1996
Profiles Warren Lewis, community leader and barber shop owner who uses lit candles to style hair. Set in a black neighborhood in Memphis. 22m; VHS. **A:** College-Adult. **P:** Education. **U:** Institution. **Gen-Edu:** Documentary Films, Sociology. **Acq:** Purchase, Rent/Lease. **Dist:** Filmakers Library Inc. $150.00.

Burn Notice: Season Five 2011
USA Network 2007-? spy drama. "Company Man": After a six-month time jump, Michael is now a CIA asset but still wants the man who burned him. "Hard Out": Michael and Jesse are trapped by mercenaries during a job and Fiona does a favor for an ex to get info to help them. "Breaking Point": When one of Michael's childhood friends is killed, he poses as a gun dealer to trap the gang leader responsible for the murder. 18 episodes. 779m; DVD. **C:** Jeffrey Donovan; Bruce Campbell; Gabrielle Anwar; Sharon Gless; Coby Bell. **A:** Sr. High-Adult. **P:** Entertainment. **U:** Home. **Mov-Ent:** Drama, Television Series. **Acq:** Purchase. **Dist:** Fox Home Entertainment. $49.98.

Burn Notice: Season Four 2010
USA Network 2007-? spy drama. "Fast Friends": Michael tries to help burned spy Jesse Porter (Coby Bell) without revealing he's the one who burned him. "Past & Future Tense": Michael helps a former Cold War-era CIA spy who's in trouble with the Russians. "Dead or Alive": Sam wants revenge when a cop friend is killed by his dirty partner. 18 episodes. 773m; DVD. **C:** Jeffrey Donovan; Bruce Campbell; Gabrielle Anwar; Sharon Gless; Coby Bell. **A:** Sr. High-Adult. **P:** Entertainment. **U:** Home. **Mov-Ent:** Drama, Television Series. **Acq:** Purchase. **Dist:** Fox Home Entertainment. $49.98.

Burn Notice: Season One 2007
USA Network 2007-? spy drama. "Pilot": Covert operative Michael Westen (Donovan) is dumped in his Miami hometown with no money or resources after being dumped by his agency. Only his old military contact Sam Axe (Campbell) and his ex-girlfriend and former IRA member Fiona (Anwar) are willing to help him. "Old Friends": Michael's brother Nate (Seth Peterson) gets himself involved in a case while Michael tries not to get killed by an agent with a grudge. "Dead Drop": Michael believes Philip Cowan (Richard Schiff) issued his burn notice and wants to meet but Sam needs help on a case. 12 episodes. 535m; DVD. **C:** Jeffrey Donovan; Bruce Campbell; Gabrielle Anwar; Sharon Gless. **A:** Sr. High-Adult. **P:** Entertainment. **U:** Home. **Mov-Ent:** Drama, Television Series. **Acq:** Purchase. **Dist:** Fox Home Entertainment. $49.98.

Burn Notice: Season Six 2012
USA Network 2007-? spy drama. "Scorched Earth": Fiona is behind bars in federal custody and Michael's determination to free her puts everyone at risk. "Shock Wave": An MI-6 agent tries to prevent Fiona from being released as a CIA asset and wants her transferred into British custody instead. "Game Change": Olivia Riley (Sonja Sohn) uses a drug cartel to try and eliminate Michael and his friends so Michael turns to Jason Bly (Alex Carter) for help. 18 episodes. 774m; DVD. **C:** Jeffrey Donovan; Bruce Campbell; Gabrielle Anwar; Sharon Gless; Coby Bell. **A:** Sr. High-Adult. **P:** Entertainment. **U:** Home. **Mov-Ent:** Drama, Television Series. **Acq:** Purchase. **Dist:** Fox Home Entertainment. $49.98.

Burn Notice: Season Three 2009
USA Network 2007-? spy drama. Ex-IRA fighter Fiona (Anwar) and ex-Navy SEAL Sam (Campbell) help burned spy Michael Weston (Donovan) track down the culprit who turned on him and in the meantime tangle with a shady arms dealer, track down a child predator in "Friendly Fire," attempt a new CIA connection in "Signals and Codes," and help an old colleague capture a man who is stealing land from Venezuelan farmers in "Friends and Family." 16 episodes. 127m; DVD. **C:** Jeffrey Donovan; Bruce Campbell; Coby Bell; Gabrielle Anwar; Sharon Gless. **A:** Sr. High-Adult. **P:** Entertainment. **U:** Home. **Mov-Ent:** Drama, Action-Adventure, Television Series. **Acq:** Purchase. **Dist:** Fox Home Entertainment. $49.99.

Burn Notice: Season Two 2008
USA Network 2007-? spy drama. "Breaking and Entering": Michael's new handler Carla (Tricia Helfer) tells him to help computer tech Jimmy steal data and she will help him find out who issued his burn notice. "Good Soldier": Fiona's new boyfriend asks Michael for help with a kidnapping plot. "Bad Breaks": Michael and his former handler Jason Bly (Alex Carter) are trapped in a bank after a robbery and must work together to get out alive. 16 episodes. 684m; DVD, Blu-Ray. **C:** Jeffrey Donovan; Bruce Campbell; Gabrielle Anwar; Sharon Gless. **A:** Sr. High-Adult. **P:** Entertainment. **U:** Home. **Mov-Ent:** Drama, Television Series. **Acq:** Purchase. **Dist:** Fox Home Entertainment. $49.98.

Burn Notice: The Fall of Sam Axe 2011 (Unrated)
In this prequel movie to the USA Netwok series, Sam Axe is sent to Colombia on what will turn into his final mission as a Navy SEAL. He's supposed to track down a terrorist organzation but it's all a scam by the military to take over the region. 108m; DVD, Blu-Ray. **C:** Bruce Campbell; RonReaco Lee; Kiele Sanchez; Directed by Jeffrey Donovan; Written by Matt Nix; Cinematography by Jaime Reynoso; Music by John Dickson. **A:** Sr. High-Adult. **P:** Entertainment. **U:** Home. **Mov-Ent:** Armed Forces--U.S., TV Movies. **Acq:** Purchase. **Dist:** Fox Home Entertainment. $9.98.

Burn-Out Prevention 1987
Psychologist Steve Asbell, Ph.D., dicusses how to recognize, prevent, and recover from personal and organizational burnout. 15m; VHS, 3/4 U. **Pr:** RMI Media Productions. **A:** Adult. **P:** Professional. **U:** Institution. **Bus-Ind:** Employee Counseling, Psychology, Self-Help. **Acq:** Purchase. **Dist:** RMI Media.
Indiv. Titles: 1. Avoiding Personal Burnout 2. Preventing Organizational Burnout.

Burn the Floor 2000
This exhibition of dancing features very talented performances from award-winning dancers displaying various styles including tango, cha cha, salsa, swing and others. 97m; DVD, Wide, CC. **A:** Sr. High-Adult. **P:** Entertainment. **U:** Home. **Mov-Ent:** Dance--Performance. **Acq:** Purchase. **Dist:** Universal Studios Home Video. $19.98.

Burn, Witch, Burn! 1962 (Unrated) — ★½
Creepy psycho-horror. Oblivious college prof Norman Taylor (Wyngarde) doesn't believe in the occult and is furious when he finally discovers his wife Tansy (Blair) has been a practitioner since their days in Jamaica. He makes her destroy her protection charms and their lives take a decided turn for the worse. Adaptation of the 1943 novel "Conjure Wife" by Fritz Leiber Jr. 89m/B/W; VHS, DVD. **C:** Peter Wyngarde; Janet Blair; Margaret Johnston; Colin Gordon; Anthony Nicholls; Kathleen Byron; Reginald Beckwith; Jessica Dunning; Norman Bird; Judith Scott; Directed by Sidney Hayers; Written by Charles Beaumont; Richard Matheson; George L. Baxt; Cinematography by Reginald Wyer; Reg Wyer; Music by William Alwyn. **Pr:** American International Pictures. **A:** Jr. High-Adult. **P:** Entertainment. **U:** Home. **Mov-Ent:** Occult Sciences, Horror, Marriage. **Acq:** Purchase. **Dist:** WarnerArchive.com; Anchor Bay Entertainment; MGM Home Entertainment.

Burndown 1989 (R) — ★
Victims of a serial killer in a town with a large nuclear reactor are themselves radioactive, which leads the Police Chief and a beautiful reporter to the truth and the hidden conspiracy. 97m; VHS; Open Captioned. **C:** Cathy Moriarty; Peter Firth; Directed by James Allen. **Pr:** Colin Stewart; FGM Entertainment; Virgin

Home Entertainment. **A:** Sr. High-Adult. **P:** Entertainment. **U:** Home. **Mov-Ent**: Mystery & Suspense. **Acq:** Purchase. **Dist:** Amazon.com Inc.

Burned Bridge 1994
A police officer and a young radio producer get pulled into a web of death, deceit and tribal culture as they investigate the killing of an Aboriginal girl in the remote Australian town of Brooklyn Waters. 645m; DVD. **A:** Adult. **P:** Entertainment. **U:** Home. **Mov-Ent**: Mystery & Suspense, Drama. **Acq:** Purchase. **Dist:** BFS Video. $49.98.

The Burning 1982 (R) — ★
Story of macabre revenge set in the dark woods of a seemingly innocent summer camp. 90m; VHS, DVD, Blu-Ray. **C:** Brian Matthews; Leah Ayres; Brian Backer; Larry Joshua; Jason Alexander; Ned Eisenberg; Garrick Glenn; Carolyn Houlihan; Fisher Stevens; Lou David; Holly Hunter; Directed by Tony Maylam; Written by Bob Weinstein; Peter Lawrence; Cinematography by Harvey Harrison; Music by Rick Wakeman. **Pr:** Harvey Weinstein. **A:** Sr. High-Adult. **P:** Entertainment. **U:** Home. **Mov-Ent**: Horror, Camps & Camping. **Acq:** Purchase. **Dist:** Movies Unlimited.

Burning an Illusion 1981
Pat, a British-born woman of color, rediscovers her African heritage after her boyfriend is unjustly arrested and assaulted by police officers. 101m; VHS, 3/4 U. **A:** Sr. High-Adult. **P:** Education. **U:** Institution. **Gen-Edu**: Minorities, Ethnicity, Human Relations. **Acq:** Purchase, Rent/Lease. **Dist:** Third World Newsreel. $325.00.

The Burning Bed 1985 (Unrated) — ★★★½
Dramatic expose (based on a true story) about wife-beating. Fawcett garnered accolades for her performance as the battered wife who couldn't take it anymore. Highly acclaimed and Emmy-nominated. 95m; VHS, DVD, CC. **C:** Farrah Fawcett; Paul LeMat; Penelope Milford; Richard Masur; Directed by Robert Greenwald. **Pr:** Carol Schreder. **A:** Jr. High-Adult. **P:** Entertainment. **U:** Home. **Mov-Ent**: TV Movies, Domestic Abuse, Marriage. **Acq:** Purchase. **Dist:** Movies Unlimited; MGM Home Entertainment. $79.98.

Burning Bridges 1988
The difficulties immigrant women face when they move to a new country with different values are examined. Many of the women in the film have been battered by their husbands. 10m; VHS, 3/4 U. **Pr:** Ali Kazimi. **A:** Sr. High-Adult. **P:** Education. **U:** Institution, SURA. **Gen-Edu**: Documentary Films, Immigration, Domestic Abuse. **Acq:** Purchase, Rent/Lease. **Dist:** Women Make Movies. $125.00.

Burning Bright 1975
Reviews the history of the United Methodist Church and other churches of Methodist origin in the U.S. 32m; VHS, 3/4 U. **Pr:** United Methodist Communications. **A:** Family. **P:** Education. **U:** Institution. **Gen-Edu**: Religion, History. **Acq:** Purchase, Rent/Lease. **Dist:** EcuFilm.

The Burning Court 1962 — ★½
Unusual horror film involving occultism, possession, and family curses. Dubbed into English. Based on a story by John Dickson Carr. 102m; VHS, DVD. **C:** Nadja Tiller; Jean-Claude Brialy; Edith Scob; Perette Pradier; Claude Rich; Directed by Julien Duvivier. **A:** Sr. High-Adult. **P:** Entertainment. **U:** Home. **Mov-Ent**: Horror, Occult Sciences. **Acq:** Purchase. **Dist:** Sinister Cinema. $16.95.

Burning Daylight 1928 — ★★
Alaskan real estate baron loses everything to a group of San Francisco sharpies. Based on the story by Jack London. 72m/B/W; Silent; VHS, DVD. **C:** Milton Sills; Arthur Stone; Doris Kenyon; Guinn "Big Boy" Williams; Directed by Richard A. Rowland. **Pr:** First National Pictures. **A:** Sr. High-Adult. **P:** Entertainment. **U:** Home. **Mov-Ent**: Real Estate, Silent Films. **Acq:** Purchase. **Dist:** Grapevine Video.

Burning Daylight 2010 (Unrated) — ★½
An anthology of films, based on three Jack London stories, set in 1920s New York. 1) Just Meat: Two thieves enjoy a big score from a jewel heist until conflicts arise between them. 2) To Kill a Man: Unexpected mind games occur between a manipulative wealthy woman and a poor thief she believes is stupid. 3) Burning Daylight: Three Wall Street bankers think they can outwit a Klondike millionaire. 102m; DVD. **C:** Robert Knepper; Paul Calderon; Adrian Cowan; Sanzhar Sultanov; Directed by Sanzhar Sultanov; Written by Sanzhar Sultanov; Cinematography by Pasha Patriki; Music by Steve Cupani. **A:** Sr. High-Adult. **P:** Entertainment. **U:** Home. **L:** English. **Mov-Ent**: Drama. **Acq:** Purchase. **Dist:** Osiris Entertainment.

Burning Down the House 2001 (R) — ★★
Desperate director Jake Selling (Savage) has his next story all lined up but no money to pursue his ambitions until he crosses paths with B-movie producer Arnie Green (Wilder). They figure out the only way to raise money is to burn down Jake's house for the insurance. Only Jake's ex—actress Brenda Goodman (Baron)?catches the scam on film and demands to be in the movie. And the insurance investigator turns out to be a wannabe actor as well whom they may also have to placate. 84m; VHS, DVD. **C:** John Savage; James Wilder; Joanne Baron; William Atherton; Arye Gross; Rene Auberjonois; Orson Bean; John Ales; C. Thomas Howell; Luca Bercovici; David Keith; Cameo(s) Mick Fleetwood; Directed by Philippe Mora; Written by Michael Cole Dinelli; Cinematography by Dan Gillham; Music by Jeff Marsh. **A:** Sr. High-Adult. **P:** Entertainment. **U:** Home. **Mov-Ent**: Insurance. **Acq:** Purchase. **Dist:** Vanguard International Cinema, Inc.

The Burning Hills 1956 (Unrated) — ★½
Unexceptional cow flick based on a Louis L'Amour novel. Hunter hides from cattle thieves in a barn and, eventually, in the arms of a half-breed Mexican girl (Wood). Tedious and unsurprising. 94m; VHS, DVD. **C:** Tab Hunter; Natalie Wood; Skip Homeier; Eduard Franz; Earl Holliman; Claude Akins; Ray Teal; Frank Puglia; Directed by Stuart Heisler; Written by Irving Wallace; Cinematography by Ted D. McCord; Music by David Buttolph. **A:** Jr. High-Adult. **P:** Entertainment. **U:** Home. **Mov-Ent**: Western, Romance. **Acq:** Purchase. **Dist:** WarnerArchive.com. $19.99.

A Burning Hot Summer 2011 (Unrated) — ★½
Bland and boring drama. Rich artist Frederic (Louis Garrel) dies. This happens in the first scenes and it takes the rest of writer/director Philippe Garrel's languid pic to find out why he crashes his car. Frederic lives with his actress wife Angele (Bellucci) in Rome where he is increasingly unhappy. He strikes up a friendship with Paul (Robart) and his actress girlfriend Elisabeth (Sallette) and they talk a lot--apparently about why their lives have no purpose. French with subtitles. 95m; DVD. **C:** Louis Garrel; Monica Bellucci; Jerome Robart; Celine Sallette; Directed by Philippe Garrel; Written by Philippe Garrel; Marc Cholodenko; Cinematography by Willy Kurant; Music by John Cale. **A:** Sr. High-Adult. **P:** Entertainment. **U:** Home. **L:** French. **Mov-Ent**: Marriage, Italy. **Acq:** Purchase. **Dist:** MPI Media Group.

Burning Life 1994 (Unrated) — ★½
In the eastern states of a recently reunified Germany, Anna and Lisa become punk folk heroines after a series of bank robberies. One of the most unbelievable aspects is that these not-too-bright amateurs continue to elude the efficient East German police, who are made to look like bumpkins. German with subtitles. 105m; DVD. **C:** Anna Thalbach; Maria Schrader; Max Tidof; Jaecki Schwarz; Andreas Hoppe; Dani Levy; Directed by Peter Welz; Written by Stefan Kolditz; Cinematography by Michael Schaufert; Music by Neil Quinton. **A:** College-Adult. **P:** Entertainment. **U:** Home. **L:** German. **Mov-Ent. Acq:** Purchase. **Dist:** DEFA Film Library.

Burning Man 2011 (Unrated) — ★½
Nonlinear narrative (with rather a lot of nudity) finds Sydney restaurant chef Tom (Goode) losing control of his life to his anger even as he struggles to be a caring dad to his young son. Flashbacks reveal that his wife Sarah's recent death from breast cancer has left Tom unable to cope with his grief except by lashing out. Goode's capable but the character is so unlikeable that not even tragedy seems a justification for his behavior. 109m; DVD. **C:** Matthew Goode; Bojana Novakovic; Essie Davis; Kerry Fox; Rachel Griffiths; Directed by Jonathan Teplitzky; Written by Jonathan Teplitzky; Cinematography by Garry Phillips; Music by Lisa Gerrard. **A:** Adult. **P:** Entertainment. **U:** Home. **L:** English. **Mov-Ent**: Parenting, Australia, Death. **Acq:** Purchase. **Dist:** IFC Films.

The Burning Plain 2008 (R) — ★½
An elaborate mishmash of stories and characters that covers 20-some years and travels between Oregon and New Mexico before the inevitable reveal. Married New Mexico mom Gina (Basinger) has an affair with married father Nick (de Almeida) that ends in their deaths and haunts both their families. Twenty years later, unhappy, promiscuous Sylvia (Theron) is being pestered by Carlos (Yazpik) about the past. Then there's the plight of young Maria (La), whose father has just died and who was—not so coincidentally—a friend of Carlos' who takes Maria in until they can find her other relatives. 111m; Blu-Ray, On Demand, Wide, CC. **C:** Charlize Theron; Kim Basinger; Joaquim de Almeida; Danny Pino; Jose Maria Yazpik; Brett Cullen; J.D. Pardo; John Corbett; Robin Tunney; Rachel Ticotin; Tessa Ia; Jennifer Lawrence; Directed by Guillermo Arriaga; Written by Guillermo Arriaga; Cinematography by Robert Elswit; Music by Hans Zimmer; Omar Rodrguez Lopez. **Pr:** Walter F. Parkes; Laurie MacDonald; 2929 Productions; Costa Films; Magnolia Pictures. **A:** Sr. High-Adult. **P:** Entertainment. **U:** Home. **L:** English. **Mov-Ent**: Hispanic Culture, Fires. **Acq:** Purchase. **Dist:** Amazon.com Inc.; Movies Unlimited; Alpha Video.

Burning Question: American Children-Diet of Danger 1989
This program describes the horrendous things children eat today and how they can eat more healthy diets, so as not to run high risks of cancer, heart disease and stroke in later life. 48m; VHS, 8 mm, 3/4 U. **TV Std:** NTSC, PAL, SECAM. **Pr:** ABC Video Enterprises, Inc. **A:** Jr. High-Adult. **P:** Education. **U:** Institution, CCTV, SURA. **Hea-Sci**: Nutrition, Children. **Acq:** Purchase, Rent/Lease, Duplication License. **Dist:** Phoenix Learning Group. $250.00.

Burning Rage 1984 — ★
A blazing, abandoned coal mine threatens to wreak havoc in the Appalachians. The government sends geologist Mandrell to help prevent a disaster. 100m; VHS, DVD. **C:** Barbara Mandrell; Tom Wopat; Bert Remsen; John Pleshette; Carol Kane; Eddie Albert; Directed by Gilbert Cates. **Pr:** J2 Communications. **A:** Adult. **P:** Entertainment. **U:** Home. **Mov-Ent**: TV Movies, Fires, Miners & Mining. **Acq:** Purchase. **Dist:** Anchor Bay Entertainment.

Burning Rivers 1992
Examines the impact of the environmental crisis in Guatemala on the inhabitants, and their response. 28m; VHS. **A:** Sr. High-Adult. **P:** Education. **U:** Institution, Home. **Gen-Edu**: Documentary Films, Ecology & Environment, Central America. **Acq:** Purchase, Rent/Lease. **Dist:** The Video Project. $85.00.

The Burning Season 1994 — ★★★
In one of his last performances, Julia inspires as Chico Mendes, a socialist union leader who fought to protect the homes and land of Brazilian peasants in the western Amazon rain forest. With Mendes' help the peasants form a union and struggle to prevent the building of a road that will provide easy access to forest land for speculators and cattlemen. Naturally, they are violently opposed by corruption-ridden capitalist powers in the government. Julia provides a haunting portrayal of the heroic figure who was assassinated in 1990. Based in part on the book by Andrew Revkin. Filmed on location in Mexico. 123m; VHS, CC. **C:** Raul Julia; Edward James Olmos; Sonia Braga; Luis Guzman; Nigel Havers; Kamala Dawson; Tomas Milian; Esai Morales; Tony Plana; Carmen Argenziano; Directed by John Frankenheimer; Written by William Mastrosimone; Michael Tolkin; Ron Hutchinson; Music by Gary Chang. **Pr:** Thomas M. Hammel; John Frankenheimer; David Puttnam; John Frankenheimer; HBO. **A:** Jr. High-Adult. **P:** Entertainment. **U:** Home. **Mov-Ent**: Biography: Politics, TV Movies, Politics & Government. **Acq:** Purchase.

Burning Secret 1989 (PG) — ★★
After WWI, a widow in Austria (Dunaway) meets a baron (Brandauer) who has befriended her son. Mutual seduction ensues but the sparks don't fly. Adapted from Stefan Zweig story. 107m; VHS. **C:** Faye Dunaway; Klaus Maria Brandauer; Ian Richardson; David Eberts; Directed by Andrew Birkin; Written by Andrew Birkin; Music by Hans Zimmer. **Pr:** Vestron Pictures. **A:** Jr. High-Adult. **P:** Entertainment. **U:** Home. **L:** English, Spanish. **Mov-Ent**: Drama. **Acq:** Purchase. **Dist:** Image Entertainment Inc.; Lions Gate Television Corp. $89.98.

Burning Spear: Live in Paris 1988
The reggae band plays live "Spear Burning," "Happy Day," "Creation Rebel," "Mistress Music," "The Wilderness Drive," "Old Marcus Garvey," "Swell Headed" and more. 60m; VHS. **A:** Sr. High-Adult. **P:** Entertainment. **U:** Home. **Mov-Ent**: Music--Performance. **Acq:** Purchase. **Dist:** Music Video Distributors. $19.95.

Burning the Future: Coal in America 2008 (Unrated)
Documentary on the environmental impact of coal mining in West Virginia, and how its citizens have paid dearly for it. 89m; DVD. **A:** Sr. High-Adult. **P:** Education. **U:** Home. **Gen-Edu**: Documentary Films, Ecology & Environment. **Acq:** Purchase. **Dist:** Docurama. $26.95.

The Burning Times 19??
Examines women in myth and religion and dispells the misconceptions of the term "witch." 58m; VHS. **A:** Sr. High-Adult. **P:** Education. **U:** Home. **Gen-Edu**: Storytelling, Occult Sciences, Women. **Acq:** Purchase. **Dist:** Direct Cinema Ltd. $34.95.

Burnout Controls 1990
Evaluates circular runout and total runout controls as used with pulleys, gearing blanks, stepped shafts, and other rotating components. 11m; VHS. **A:** Adult. **P:** Education. **U:** Institution. **Gen-Edu**: Engineering. **Acq:** Purchase. **Dist:** RMI Media. $39.95.

Burns 1979
The major causes of burns, and their prevention, emergency, and at-home first aid are explained. 30m; VHS, 3/4 U. **Pr:** WNET New York. **A:** Sr. High-Adult. **P:** Education. **U:** Institution, CCTV, Home. **Hea-Sci**: Burns, First Aid, Safety Education. **Acq:** Purchase, Rent/Lease. **Dist:** WNET/Thirteen Non-Broadcast.

Burns and Allen Christmas 19??
Features two Christmas episodes from the vintage TV show?"Company for Christmas" and "Christmas in Jail." Say "Merry Christmas," Gracie. ?m; VHS. **C:** George Burns; Gracie Allen. **A:** Family. **P:** Entertainment. **U:** Home. **Mov-Ent**: Television Series, Christmas. **Acq:** Purchase. **Dist:** Sony Pictures Home Entertainment Inc. $14.95.

The Burns and Allen Show 1950
George and Gracie's classic vaudeville routines are a highlight of this sitcom series, with George the perpetually harried husband to the scatterbrained Gracie. Additional episodes are available. 115m/B/W; VHS, CC. **C:** Gracie Allen; George Burns. **A:** Family. **P:** Entertainment. **U:** Home. **Mov-Ent**: Television Series. **Acq:** Purchase. **Dist:** Shokus Video; Sony Pictures Home Entertainment Inc.; Movies Unlimited.

The Burns and Allen Show: Episode 1 1950
Two episodes of the hit TV show from the '50s, including the very first one, aired November 9, 1950. 60m/B/W; VHS. **C:** George Burns; Gracie Allen. **A:** Family. **P:** Entertainment. **U:** Home. **Mov-Ent**: Television Series. **Acq:** Purchase. **Dist:** Karol Media. $9.95.

The Burns and Allen Show: Episode 2 1950
Hilarious episodes from Burns & Allen's hit TV show in the '50s. The classic comedy routines are must-sees for fans of vintage television. 60m/B/W; VHS. **C:** Gracie Allen; George Burns; Directed by Ralph Levy. **Pr:** RCA. **A:** Family. **P:** Entertainment. **U:** Home. **Mov-Ent**: Television Series. **Acq:** Purchase. **Dist:** Sony Pictures Home Entertainment Inc.; Facets Multimedia Inc. $29.95.

The Burns and Allen Show: Episode 4 1952
This series includes two episodes from the Burns' timeless television comedies of the '50s. The original commercials are left in. 60m/B/W; VHS, CC. **C:** George Burns; Gracie Allen; Jack Benny; Harry von Zell; Bea Benaderet; Fred Clark. **Pr:** Jesse Goldstein. **A:** Family. **P:** Entertainment. **U:** Home. **Mov-Ent**: Comedy--Performance, Television Series. **Acq:** Purchase. **Dist:** Sony Pictures Home Entertainment Inc. $19.95.

The Burns and Allen Show: Gracie and the Mob 1997
Part of the TV Screen Gems series featuring the episodes "George and Gracie Hear a Burglar" and "Gracie Sees a Holdup-Johnny Velvet." 55m/B/W; VHS. **A:** Family. **P:** Entertainment. **U:** Home. **Mov-Ent:** Television Series. **Acq:** Purchase. **Dist:** Sony Pictures Home Entertainment Inc. $9.95.

The Burns and Allen Show: Gracie Knows Best 1997
Part of the TV Screen Gems series featuring the episodes "Ivon Zell's Girlfriend between Trains" and "Gracie Buying a Ranch for George." 60m/B/W; VHS. **A:** Family. **P:** Entertainment. **U:** Home. **Mov-Ent:** Television Series. **Acq:** Purchase. **Dist:** Sony Pictures Home Entertainment Inc. $9.95.

The Burns and Allen Show: Meet George and Gracie 1997
Part of the TV Screen Gems series featuring the episodes "Columbia Doing the Burns and Allen Story" and "Gracie Doing a Picture without George." 60m/B/W; VHS. **A:** Family. **P:** Entertainment. **U:** Home. **Mov-Ent:** Television Series. **Acq:** Purchase. **Dist:** Sony Pictures Home Entertainment Inc. $9.95.

Burns and Allen Show, Vol. 2 1951
Classic comedy from two of the funniest folks of all time. Not to be missed, these are episodes from their hit TV show aired only once, with Bob Sweeney guest-starring. 120m/B/W; VHS. **C:** George Burns; Gracie Allen. **A:** Family. **P:** Entertainment. **U:** Home. **Mov-Ent:** Television Series. **Acq:** Purchase. **Dist:** Shokus Video. $24.95.

Burns and Allen Show, Vol. 3 1952 — ★½
Vintage TV with four episodes and original commercials from three of the episodes. January 4, 1951, show has Gracie assuming she is supposed to throw a party for George because she found it circled on a calendar. In an August 2, 1951, episode the girls go on a health kick by eating just fruits and vegetables. On September 13, 1951, Gracie throws a wedding party and drives everyone mad in the process. In a 1952 episode, a studio wants to produce a film on their lives until Gracie gets involved. 115m/B/W; VHS. **C:** George Burns; Gracie Allen; John Brown; Fred Clark; Harry von Zell. **Pr:** CBS. **A:** Family. **P:** Entertainment. **U:** Home. **Mov-Ent:** Television Series. **Acq:** Purchase. **Dist:** Shokus Video. $24.95.

Burns and Heat Stroke 1990
Covers the prevention and treatment of heat-related injuries, the differences between first, second, and third degree burns, and the warning signs of heat exhaustion and heat stroke. ?m; VHS. **A:** Jr. High-Adult. **P:** Education. **U:** Institution. **Hea-Sci:** Burns, First Aid, Emergencies. **Acq:** Purchase. **Dist:** Meridian Education Corp. $45.00.

Burns: Emergency Procedures 1982
Takes a look at the four basic emergency steps that can save a burn victim's life. 15m; VHS, 3/4 U. **Pr:** Encyclopedia Britannica Educational Corporation. **A:** Primary-Sr. High. **P:** Education. **U:** Institution, SURA. **Hea-Sci:** Burns, Emergencies, First Aid. **Acq:** Purchase, Rent/Lease, Trade-in. **Dist:** Encyclopedia Britannica.

Burns in Children: Homecare for Burns 1996
Teaches parents and caregivers, four key issues necessary to treat the child at home. 22m; VHS. **A:** Adult. **P:** Education. **U:** Home, Institution. **Hea-Sci:** How-To, Patient Care, Burns. **Acq:** Purchase, Rent/Lease. **Dist:** AJN Video Library/Lippincott Williams & Wilkins. $250.00.

Burnt by the Sun 1994 (R) — ★★★
Masterful evocation of '30s Stalinist Russia, covering a day in the life of Soviet revolutionary hero Serguei (Mikhalkov) and his family, far from the purges and gulags. Enjoying a country existence with wife Moroussia (Dapkounaite) and daughter Nadia (played by Mikhalkov's daughter), his idyll is disturbed by mystery man Dimitri (Menchikov), and Serguei realizes their fates are bound by the difference between their Communist dreams and reality. Symbolism is a little heavy but film delivers emotionally. Russian with subtitles. 134m; VHS, DVD. **C:** Nikita Mikhalkov; Ingeborga Dapkounaite; Oleg Menshikov; Nadia Mikhalkov; Andre Oumansky; Viatcheslav Tikhonov; Svetlana Krioutchkova; Vladimir Ilyine; Directed by Nikita Mikhalkov; Written by Nikita Mikhalkov; Rustam Ibragimbekov; Cinematography by Vilen Kalyuta; Music by Eduard Artemyev. **Pr:** Leonid Verechtchaguine; Jean-Louis Piel; Vladimir Sedov; Sony Pictures Classics. **A:** College-Adult. **P:** Entertainment. **U:** Home. **L:** Russian. **Mov-Ent:** USSR, Politics & Government, Family. **Awds:** Oscars '94: Foreign Film; Cannes '94: Grand Jury Prize. **Acq:** Purchase. **Dist:** Sony Pictures Home Entertainment Inc.

Burnt Money 2000 (Unrated) — ★★
Based on a 1965 true crime story set in Argentina and Uruguay. Twentysomething lovers Nene (Sbaraglia) and the unstable Angel (Noriega), nicknamed the Twins, are stickup men hired by veteran criminal Fontana (Bartis) for a big money heist in Buenos Aires. They're paired with young, pill-popping getaway driver Cuervo (Echarri) but things go wrong when the Twins become cop killers. The foursome flee with the money to a squalid apartment in Montevideo where they wait for new identity papers. The young trio begin to unravel amidst a lot of drinking, drugs (who knew cocaine was so popular in the '60s?), and boredom, leading to a lethal confrontation with authorities. Title refers to what happens to the heist cash. Spanish with subtitles. 125m; VHS, DVD. **C:** Leonardo Sbaraglia; Eduardo Noriega; Ricardo Bartis; Pablo Echarri; Leticia Bredice; Dolores Fonzi; Directed by Marcelo Pineyro; Written by Marcelo Figueras; Cinematography by Alfredo Mayo; Music by Osvaldo Montes. **A:** College-Adult. **P:** Entertainment. **U:** Home. **L:** Spanish. **Mov-Ent:** Drug Abuse, South America. **Acq:** Purchase. **Dist:** Wolfe Video.

Burnt Offerings 1976 (PG) — ★★
A family rents an old mansion for the summer and they become affected by evil forces that possess the house. Based on the novel by Robert Marasco. 116m; VHS, DVD. **C:** Oliver Reed; Karen Black; Bette Davis; Burgess Meredith; Eileen Heckart; Lee Montgomery; Dub Taylor; Directed by Dan Curtis; Written by Dan Curtis. **Pr:** United Artists. **A:** Sr. High-Adult. **P:** Entertainment. **U:** Home. **Mov-Ent:** Horror, Death. **Acq:** Purchase. **Dist:** MGM Home Entertainment. $14.95.

Burnzy's Last Call 1995 (Unrated) — ★★
Sal (McCaffrey) tends bar at Eppy's, a Manhattan joint where Burnzy (Gray), a retired newspaperman, is a regular. The film is an ensemble piece that focuses on the various colorful characters who drift in and out of the place. 88m; VHS, DVD, Wide. **C:** Sam Gray; David Johansen; James McCaffrey; Chris Noth; Sherry Stringfield; Roger Robinson; Tony Todd; Directed by Michael de Avila; Written by George Gilmore; Cinematography by Scott St. John. **A:** Sr. High-Adult. **P:** Entertainment. **U:** Home. **Mov-Ent. Acq:** Purchase. **Dist:** Vanguard International Cinema, Inc.

Burt Dow: Deep-Water Man 1983
Burt Dow, a retired old seaman who lives on the coast, sets out one day in his trusted boat and catches a whale on his cod hook. Adapted from the story by Robert McCloskey. 10m; VHS, 3/4 U. **Pr:** Morton Schindel. **A:** Primary. **P:** Entertainment. **U:** Institution, SURA. **Chl-Juv:** Literature. **Acq:** Purchase. **Dist:** Weston Woods Studios.

Burt Wolf: What We Eat 2003
Looks at the explorations of Christopher Columbus, from his first voyage in 1492 to his last in 1502, and how the exchange of plants and animals altered the way people ate and how this affected their lives. 364m; DVD. **A:** Jr. High-Adult. **P:** Education. **U:** Institution. **Gen-Edu:** Documentary Films, History, Explorers. **Acq:** Purchase. **Dist:** Ambrose Video Publishing, Inc. $129.99.

Burton and Taylor 2013 (Unrated) — ★★½
The leads are too young for their famous leads but they have the talent to pull off this BBC TV production without impersonation. The still tempestous relationship of Elizabeth Taylor (Bonham Carter) and Richard Burton (West) is played out through their ill-fated reunion in 1982 when they appear onstage together in a New York revival of Noel Coward's "Private Lives." Rumors swirl as everyone looks for paralells between their characters and their own private lives while an ill Burton tries to deal with his unprepared ex, whom he suspects is abusing alcohol and drugs. 90m; DVD. **C:** Dominic West; Helena Bonham Carter; Stanley Townsend; William Hope; Sarah Hadland; Lenora Crichlow; Cassie Raine; Directed by Richard Laxton; Written by William Ivory; Cinematography by David Katznelson; Music by John Lunn. **A:** Sr. High-Adult. **P:** Entertainment. **U:** Home. **L:** English. **Mov-Ent:** Biography: Show Business, Theater, TV Movies. **Acq:** Purchase. **Dist:** BBC Worldwide Ltd.

Bury Me an Angel 1971 (Unrated) — ★
A female biker sets out to seek revenge against the men who killed her brother. 85m; VHS, DVD. **C:** Dixie Peabody; Terry Mace; Clyde Ventura; Dan Haggerty; Stephen Whittaker; Gary Littlejohn; Dave Atkins; Marie Denn; Alan DeWitt; Directed by Barbara Peeters; Cinematography by Sven Walnum; Music by Richard Hieronymous. **Pr:** New World Pictures. **A:** Sr. High-Adult. **P:** Entertainment. **U:** Home. **Mov-Ent:** Motorcycles. **Acq:** Purchase. **Dist:** Unknown Distributor.

Bury Me Not on the Lone Prairie 1941 — ★★
When his brother is murdered in cold blood by claim jumpers, mining engineer Brown goes to avenge the dead. Based on a story by Sherman Lowe. 57m/B/W; VHS, DVD. **C:** Johnny Mack Brown; Fuzzy Knight; Nell O'Day; Frank O'Connor; Kermit Maynard; Directed by Ray Taylor; Written by Sherman Lowe; Victor McLeod. **Pr:** Mark Huffam. **A:** Jr. High-Adult. **P:** Entertainment. **U:** Home. **Mov-Ent:** Western. **Acq:** Purchase. **Dist:** Movies Unlimited. $19.99.

Bury My Heart at Wounded Knee 2007 (Unrated) — ★★½
Loose adaptation of the 1970 Dee Brown book. This oversimplified version concentrates on the experiences of the Sioux from Little Big Horn to the Wounded Knee massacre. It follows Charles Eastman (Beach)?who's not in Brown's book, by the way—who grew up among the Sioux (he's a quarter white on his mother's side) until his Christianized father claims him. Eastman is educated in the East and becomes a doctor at Pine Ridge, aided by his white wife (Paquin). The story is given over to various confrontations and philosophical differences. ?m; DVD, Wide. **C:** Adam Beach; Aidan Quinn; Anna Paquin; August Schellenberg; J.K. Simmons; Shawn Johnston; Gordon Tootoosis; Wes Studi; Eric Schweig; Colm Feore; Fred Dalton Thompson; Directed by Yves Simoneau; Written by Daniel Giat; Cinematography by David Franco; Music by George S. Clinton. **A:** Jr. High-Adult. **P:** Entertainment. **U:** Home. **Mov-Ent:** Native Americans. **Acq:** Purchase. **Dist:** Movies Unlimited.

Burying the Hatchets 1988
Explores real situations full of emotional tension which can cause feuding parties to ruin their working relationship. 21m; VHS, 3/4 U. **Pr:** National Educational Media Inc. **A:** College-Adult. **P:** Professional. **U:** Institution, SURA. **Bus-Ind:** Management, Employee Counseling, Personnel Management. **Acq:** Purchase, Rent/Lease, Trade-in. **Dist:** Encyclopedia Britannica. $495.00.

Bus Persons, Dish Washers and Janitor Safety 1995
Covers all the accidents related to these specific job descriptions and how to reduce accidents and injuries. 12m; VHS. **A:** Adult. **P:** Professional. **U:** Institution. **L:** Spanish. **Bus-Ind:** Safety Education, Management, Occupational Training. **Acq:** Purchase, Rent/Lease. **Dist:** National Safety Council, California Chapter, Film Library. $175.00.

Bus Stop 1956 (Unrated) — ★★★
Murray plays a naive cowboy who falls in love with Monroe, a barroom singer, and decides to marry her without her permission. Considered by many to be the finest performance by Marilyn Monroe; she sings "That Old Black Magic" in this one. Very funny with good performances by all. Based on the William Inge play. 96m; VHS, DVD, Blu-Ray, Wide. **C:** Marilyn Monroe; Arthur O'Connell; Hope Lange; Don Murray; Betty Field; Max (Casey Adams) Showalter; Hans Conried; Eileen Heckart; Directed by Joshua Logan; Written by George Axelrod; Cinematography by Milton Krasner; Music by Cyril Mockridge; Alfred Newman. **Pr:** 20th Century-Fox. **A:** Family. **P:** Entertainment. **U:** Home. **Mov-Ent:** Nightclubs, Romance. **Acq:** Purchase. **Dist:** Alpha Video; Movies Unlimited; Fox Home Entertainment. $14.98.

The Busby Berkeley Disc 1992
A collection of the innovative dance director's work at Warner Bros. studio covering 1933-37. Berkeley was known for his elaborate production numbers, beautiful women, military precision, and kaleidoscopic patterns in such films as "42nd Street," "Footlight Parade," and the "Gold Diggers" series. 176m/B/W. **A:** Family. **P:** Entertainment. **U:** Home. **Mov-Ent:** Film History, Dance--History. **Acq:** Purchase. **Dist:** MGM Home Entertainment. $39.98.

Busch Gardens, the Dark Continent: A Jungle of Fun! 1990
A behind the scenes look at the theme park features footage of animals, stage shows and rides. Comes with a teaching guide. 30m; VHS. **Pr:** Video Tours. **A:** Family. **P:** Entertainment. **U:** Institution, CCTV, Home. **Gen-Edu:** Travel, Fairs & Expositions. **Acq:** Purchase. **Dist:** VT Entertainment. $24.95.

Busch Gardens, the Old Country: Williamsburg, VA 1987
A video tour of eight European villages recreated at Busch Gardens, complete with Old World artisans, clothing, and cuisine. Includes a teacher's guide. 30m; VHS. **Pr:** Video Tours. **A:** Family. **P:** Entertainment. **U:** Institution, CCTV, Home. **Gen-Edu:** Travel, Fairs & Expositions. **Acq:** Purchase. **Dist:** VT Entertainment. $24.95.

Bush Family Fortunes—The Best Democracy Money Can Buy 2004 (Unrated)
Reporter Greg Palast examines the Bush family, its involvement in election scandals, and its connections to the Saudi royal family. 61m; DVD. **A:** Sr. High-Adult. **P:** Education. **U:** Home. **Gen-Edu:** Documentary Films, Conspiracies or Conspiracy Theories. **Acq:** Purchase. **Dist:** Disinformation. $14.95.

Bush Land People 19??
Social sciences film from the University of Calgary Learning Commons. ?m; VHS. **A:** Adult. **P:** Education. **U:** Institution. **Gen-Edu:** Sociology, Anthropology, Documentary Films. **Acq:** Purchase. **Dist:** University of Calgary Library, Visual Resources Centre.

Bush Mama 1976 (Unrated)
A hallucinatory film about a black woman on welfare trying to care for her daughter in a Los Angeles ghetto. Street violence varies with fantasy scenes in a loose narrative filled with flashbacks. 100m; VHS. **C:** Directed by Haile Gerima. **A:** College-Adult. **P:** Entertainment. **U:** Home. **Mov-Ent:** Black Culture, Parenting. **Acq:** Purchase. **Dist:** Facets Multimedia Inc. $59.95.

Bush Pilot 1947 — ★½
Red North (Willis) has his own small business as a bush pilot in the Canadian north. Then his vindictive half-brother Paul (La Rue) decides to muscle in and steal Red's routes (and maybe his girl as well). 60m/B/W; VHS, DVD. **C:** Austin Willis; Jack La Rue, Jr.; Rochelle Hudson; Directed by Sterling Campbell; Written by Scott Darling. **A:** Jr. High-Adult. **P:** Entertainment. **U:** Home. **Mov-Ent:** Aeronautics, Canada. **Acq:** Purchase. **Dist:** Facets Multimedia Inc.

The Bushbaby 1970 — ★½
The young Brooks is given a tiny bushbaby while visiting Africa with her father. Because of her pet she misses her ship home and finds herself with former servant Gossett, who agrees to take her to a family friend. Unfortunately, the authorities think he's kidnapped the girl and the two, along with the trouble-causing pet, are pursued by the police. Simple-minded kiddie fare. 100m; VHS. **C:** Margaret Brooks; Louis Gossett, Jr.; Donald Houston; Laurence Naismith; Marne Maitland; Geoffrey Bayldon; Jack (Gwyllam) Gwillim; Directed by John Trent. **Pr:** John Trent; Robert Maxwell; John Trent; MGM. **A:** Family. **P:** Entertainment. **U:** Home. **Mov-Ent:** Africa, Children, Pets. **Acq:** Purchase. **Dist:** Facets Multimedia Inc.; MGM Home Entertainment. $14.98.

The Busher 1919 — ★½
All-American pitcher's romance is interrupted by a gratuitous Mr. Moneybags. Minor-league conflict with little real hardball. 54m/B/W; Silent; VHS, DVD. **C:** Charles Ray; Colleen Moore; John Gilbert; Margaret Livingston; Directed by Jerome Storm. **Pr:** Charles Ray Films. **A:** Sr. High-Adult. **P:** Entertainment. **U:** Home. **Mov-Ent:** Romance, Baseball, Silent Films. **Acq:** Purchase. **Dist:** Kino on Video; Facets Multimedia Inc.; Glenn Video Vistas Ltd. $19.95.

The Bushido Blade 1980 (Unrated) — ★★½
An action-packed samurai thriller of adventure and betrayal set in medieval Japan. 92m; VHS, DVD. **C:** Richard Boone; James Earl Jones; Frank Converse; Directed by Tom Kotani. **Pr:** Arthur

Rankin, Jr. **A:** Sr. High-Adult. **P:** Entertainment. **U:** Home. **Mov-Ent:** Martial Arts, Drama. **Acq:** Purchase. **Dist:** Movies Unlimited. $21.24.

Bushido: The Cruel Code of the Samurai 1963 (Unrated) — ★★★
Susumu (Kinnosuke Nakamura) chronicles the history of his family while attending to his dying fiance who has attempted suicide. Beginning at the 17th century his Samurai ancestor follows his lord into death, declaring that his family will forever honor the code of Bushido, which stresses loyalty to one's master. Each succeeding generation has an ever more horrifying and humiliating request placed upon them by their master, which they follow to remain loyal. Directed by Tadashi Imai, it is his response to the propaganda films he was forced to author in WWII imploring the Japanese workers to sacrifice their lives for their leaders' goals. 119m/B/W; DVD. **C:** Kinnosuke Nakamura; Eijiro Tono; Kyoko Kishida; Masayuki Mori; Shinjiro Ebara; Yoshiko Mita; Ineko Arima; Isao (Ko) Kimura; Directed by Tadashi Imai; Written by Norio Nanjo; Naoyuki Suzuki; Yoshikata Yoda; Cinematography by Makoto Tsuboi; Music by Toshiro Mayuzumi. **A:** Sr. High-Adult. **P:** Entertainment. **U:** Home. **L:** English, Japanese. **Mov-Ent:** War--General. **Acq:** Purchase. **Dist:** AnimEigo Inc.

Bushmen of the Kalahari 1974
A look at the Kalahari bushmen and their changing lifestyle in today's world. 52m; 3/4 U, Special order formats. **Pr:** National Geographic Society. **A:** Primary-Sr. High. **P:** Education. **U:** Institution, Home. **Gen-Edu:** Documentary Films, Africa. **Acq:** Purchase, Trade-in, Duplication License. **Dist:** National Geographic Society.

Bush's Brain 2004 (Unrated) — ★★
Election year investigation of the role Karl Rove played in crafting Dubyah into a president. Yet another volley in the political documentary war of 2004. Interesting exploration of behind-the-scenes political dirty work. Though based largely on hearsay, film will surely outrage democrats everywhere. 80m; VHS, DVD. **C:** Directed by Michael Shoob; Joseph Mealey; Cinematography by Joseph Mealey; Music by David Friedman; Michelle Shocked. **A:** Jr. High-Adult. **P:** Entertainment. **U:** Home. **Mov-Ent:** Documentary Films, Politics & Government. **Acq:** Purchase. **Dist:** Movies Unlimited. $19.99.

Bushwacked 1992
Comedian Morris takes a satirical look at the life of George Herbert Walker Bush, focusing on his speeches, press conferences, appearances and somewhat distorted view of American life. 30m; VHS. **C:** Jim Morris. **Pr:** Polygram Music Video. **A:** Sr. High-Adult. **P:** Entertainment. **U:** Home. **Mov-Ent:** Presidency. **Acq:** Purchase. **Dist:** Critics' Choice Video & DVD. $14.95.

The Bushwackers 1952 (Unrated) — ★½
Ireland plays a veteran of the Confederate army who wishes only to put his violent past behind him. He is forced to reconsider his vow when old-west bullies threaten his family. 70m/B/W; VHS, DVD. **C:** Dorothy Malone; John Ireland; Wayne Morris; Lawrence Tierney; Jack Elam; Lon Chaney, Jr.; Myrna Dell; Directed by Rod Amateau. **Pr:** Realart. **A:** Adult. **P:** Entertainment. **U:** Home. **Mov-Ent:** Western, Civil War, Veterans. **Acq:** Purchase. **Dist:** Sinister Cinema. $16.95.

Bushwhacked 1995 (PG-13) — ★★½
Crude, rude, dim-witted, kid-hating Max Grabelski (Stern) is falsely accused of murder and forced to become a fugitive. While not to be confused with Harrison Ford, he is mistaken for the leader of a group of Cub Scouts out on their maiden camping trip and soon finds himself in an unlikely partnership with the boys. Together they encounter everything from grizzly bears to whitewater rapids. Light-hearted, goofy comedy continues Stern's tendency toward kid-intensive, family-oriented fare in the "Rookie of the Year" vein. 85m; VHS, DVD, CC. **C:** Daniel Stern; Jon Polito; Brad Sullivan; Ann Dowd; Anthony Heald; Tom Wood; Directed by Greg Beeman; Written by Tommy Swerdlow; Michael Goldberg; John Jordan; Danny Byers; Music by Bill Conti. **Pr:** Charles B. Wessler; Daniel Stern; Polygram; Fox. **A:** Family. **P:** Entertainment. **U:** Home. **Mov-Ent:** Mountaineering, Camps & Camping, Children. **Acq:** Purchase. **Dist:** Fox Home Entertainment.

Business 1974
A look at the duties, responsibilities, and rewards of the small-store owner. 10m; VHS, 3/4 U. **Pr:** Educo; Mini Productions; North Star. **A:** Primary. **P:** Education. **U:** Institution, SURA. **Gen-Edu:** Occupations, Business. **Acq:** Purchase. **Dist:** Center for Humanities, Inc./Guidance Associates.

Business 1992
Part of a series offering instruction on applied vocational mathematics. 30m; VHS. **A:** Adult. **P:** Education. **U:** Institution. **Gen-Edu:** Mathematics. **Acq:** Purchase. **Dist:** RMI Media. $149.00.

The Business 2005 (R) — ★★
The sunny, tacky setting makes this Cockney crime flick, set amid the conspicuous consumption of the 1980s, at least a little different though the plot is ordinary enough. Young Frankie (Dyer) heads to the criminal haven of Spain's Costa del Sol and gets a job driving for flashy Charlie (Hassan) and his psycho partner Sammy (Bell). Then Frankie starts running drugs for Charlie and multiple betrayals are set in motion. 92m; DVD. **C:** Danny Dyer; Tamer Hassan; Geoff Bell; Georgina Chapman; Linda Henry; Eddie Weber; Directed by Nick Love; Written by Nick Love; Cinematography by Damian Bromley; Music by Ivor Guest. **A:** Sr. High-Adult. **P:** Entertainment. **U:** Home. **Mov-Ent:** Crime Drama, Drug Trafficking/Dealing, Spain. **Acq:** Purchase. **Dist:** Genius.com Incorporated.

A Business Affair 1993 (R) — ★★½
Kate Swallow (the ravishing Bouquet), the neglected wife of tempermental author Alex Bolton (Pryce), begins an affair with his flamboyant American publisher Vanni Corso (Walken). While the men posture between themselves for her affections, Kate, who has literary aspirations, decides to strike out on her own. Based on the romantic triangle of British writers Barbara Skelton and Cyril Connolly and his publisher George Weidenfeld and taken from Skelton's memoirs "Tears Before Bedtime" and "Weep No More." 102m; VHS, DVD. **C:** Carole Bouquet; Jonathan Pryce; Christopher Walken; Sheila Hancock; Directed by Charlotte Brandstrom; Written by William Stadiem; Cinematography by Willy Kurant; Music by Didier Vasseur. **Pr:** Clive Parsons; Davina Belling; Xavier Larere; Skouras Pictures. **A:** Sr. High-Adult. **P:** Entertainment. **U:** Home. **Mov-Ent:** Marriage, Publishing. **Acq:** Purchase. **Dist:** CinemaNow Inc.

The Business and Law of Dance 1981
These related programs from the "Eye on Dance" series examine the business of dance in a changing economic climate. 30m; VHS, 3/4 U, EJ. **C:** Hosted by Arlene Shuler. **Pr:** ARC Videodance. **A:** Sr. High-Adult. **P:** Entertainment. **U:** Institution, CCTV, Home, SURA. **Fin-Art:** Documentary Films, Dance. **Acq:** Purchase. **Dist:** Eye on the Arts.
Indiv. Titles: 1. Leonard Easter, Rachal Harms and Nicholas Arcomano 2. David White, Ivan Sygoda and Barbara Hauptman 3. Henry Young, Richard Mi.

Business As Usual 1988 (PG) — ★★
A meek boutique manager in Liverpool defends a sexually harassed employee, is fired, fights back, and creates a national furor over her rights as a woman. 89m; VHS, CC. **C:** Glenda Jackson; Cathy Tyson; John Thaw; Craig Charles; Eamon Boland; Directed by Lezli-Ann Barrett; Written by Lezli-Ann Barrett; Cinematography by Ernest Vincze. **A:** Preschool. **P:** Entertainment. **U:** Home. **Mov-Ent:** Sex & Sexuality, Women. **Acq:** Purchase. **Dist:** Warner Home Video, Inc. $19.98.

Business as Usual 1994
Offers five examples of individuals with intellectual and physical disabilities who have achieved self-sufficiency by learning to operate their own businesses. Includes interviews with management personnel as well as the five individuals. 39m; VHS. **Pr:** Fanlight Productions. **A:** Adult. **P:** Education. **U:** Institution. **Gen-Edu:** Handicapped, Job Training, Business. **Acq:** Purchase, Rent/Lease. **Dist:** Fanlight Productions. $195.00.

Business: Brother, Can You Spare $1,000,000,000? 198?
Examines the kinds of growth healthy companies will attain in the future. It suggests some form of wage and price controls will be needed to keep the value of the dollar from spiraling down as credit rises and prices increase. 20m; 3/4 U, Special order formats. **Pr:** Hobel Leiterman Productions. **A:** College-Adult. **P:** Education. **U:** Institution. **Bus-Ind:** Business, Speculation. **Acq:** Purchase. **Dist:** The Cinema Guild.

Business, Careers, and Lifestyle Series 1984
In this series of 56 half-hour programs, host Dick Goldberg interviews top business leaders in various fields to find out what it takes to be successful in business. 30m; VHS, 3/4 U. **C:** Dick Goldberg. **Pr:** RMI Media Productions. **A:** Sr. High-Adult. **P:** Education. **U:** Institution, CCTV, Home. **Gen-Edu:** Business, Occupations, Interviews. **Acq:** Purchase. **Dist:** RMI Media.
Indiv. Titles: 1. The Mary Kay Story 2. The Record Business: Not Just for the Big Guys 3. Turning Your Job into a Business 4. Lillian Vernon: Making It in Mail Order 5. Starting and Running a Business 6. Two Good Business Ideas That Failed 7. Selling Houses for a Living 8. Being a Car Dealer 9. Love and Friendship at the Office 10. Women and Corporations: Breaking In 11. Women and Corporations: Moving Up 12. Is Ethnic In? 13. Running a Movie Theatre 14. The Gambler: An Entrepreneur Tells All 15. Two Self Made Multi-Millionairesses 16. Finding and Landing the Right Job 17. Advertising: Tricks of the Trade 18. Barter for Fun and Profit 19. Careers in Sales 20. How to Sell 21. Starting and Running a Restaurant 22. Can Anyone Publish Books 23. Daycare Dollars: Making a Living in Child Care 24. Inside the Hotel Business 25. The Business World of Art Linkletter 26. Inside the Travel Agency Business 27. Buying and Running That Small Summer Resort 28. The Business of Minor League Baseball 29. The Employment Agency Business 30. Brainstorming Small Business Ideas for the Eighties Parts One and Two 31. How to Interview for a Job 32. Successful Interviewing: How to Interview Others 33. Starting and Running Retail Stores 34. Business Mistakes I've Learned From 35. Marketing to Minorities 36. Marketing Successes of Coca-Cola-Why They Work 37. Ted Turner-How He Did It 38. Ted Turner Looks Ahead 39. Promoting Concerts from Rock to Pop 40. The Business of Off-Broadway 41. The Film Industry After Television 42. Alan Hirschfield on the Future of the Film Industry 43. The King of the B's Tells His Story 44. Roger Corman on the Future of Independent Film Production 45. Big Time Talent Management 46. Two Successful Trial Attorneys 47. The Young Self-Made Millionaire 48. Are Kids Worth It? 49. Teenage Dating I 50. Teenage Dating II 51. Three Surgeons Open-Up-Parts I and II 52. Single After 60 53. What Women Want from Men 54. What Men Want from Women 55. Three Happy People 56. Three Cops.

Business Chronicle Series 1991
A three-part look at the ingredients of customer service. 29m; VHS, 3/4 U, Special order formats. **Pr:** Enterprise Media. **A:** College-Adult. **P:** Education. **U:** Institution. **Bus-Ind:** Business, Customer Service, Marketing. **Acq:** Purchase, Rent/Lease. **Dist:** Excellence in Training Corp. $225.00.
Indiv. Titles: 1. L.L. Bean: A Commitment to Customer Service 2. Corporate Missions: The People Behind the Products 3. The Marketing and Manufacturing Edge.

Business Crimes and Business Torts 1989
Focuses on standards of conduct that businesses are expected to adhere to. 30m; VHS. **A:** Adult. **P:** Professional. **U:** Institution. **Bus-Ind:** Business, Law. **Acq:** Purchase. **Dist:** RMI Media. $99.00.

Business Culture and the Lean System 2001
Presentation from the SME 2001 Annual Meeting and Manufacturing Leadership Forum. Features Rod Heard discussing cultural factors in lean manufacturing. ?m; VHS. **A:** Adult. **P:** Vocational. **U:** Institution. **Bus-Ind:** Management, Industry & Industrialists, Occupational Training. **Acq:** Purchase. **Dist:** Society of Manufacturing Engineers. $50.00.

The Business Customers ????
Deals with attracting new customers, improving customer service, database marketing, computerized transactions, and networked customer tracking. 30m; VHS. **A:** Adult. **P:** Instruction. **U:** Institution. **Gen-Edu:** Business, How-To. **Acq:** Purchase. **Dist:** American Institute of Small Business. $69.95.

Business Ethics 1988
Teaches how to incorporate ethics into valuable business relationships. Stresses the fundamental belief that good ethics is good business. Originally presented at the Aresty Institute for Executive Education at the Wharton School by Professors Tom Dunfee and Diana Robertson. Comes with audiocassette and study guide. 58m; VHS. **A:** Adult. **P:** Professional. **U:** Institution. **Bus-Ind:** Ethics & Morals, Business. **Acq:** Purchase. **Dist:** Advantage Media. $189.00.

Business Ethics 1994
Presents a collection of scenarios that will challenge a student's ethical decision making. 20m; VHS. **A:** Adult. **P:** Professional. **U:** Institution. **Bus-Ind:** Business, Management. **Acq:** Purchase. **Dist:** RMI Media. $99.00.

Business Ethics: Video Seminar 1987
An exploration of creative ways to handle business dilemmas. 30m; VHS, 3/4 U. **Pr:** MTI. **A:** College-Adult. **P:** Professional. **U:** Institution, SURA. **Bus-Ind:** Business, Ethics & Morals. **Acq:** Purchase, Rent/Lease. **Dist:** Phoenix Learning Group. $495.00.

Business Etiquette 19??
Offers typical business scenarios which illustrates the importance of the use of proper business etiquette. Covers everything from proper attire to communication and body language. Also provides brief information on resumes and interviews. 30m; VHS. **A:** Sr. High-Adult. **P:** Instruction. **U:** Institution. **Bus-Ind:** Business, Communication, Etiquette. **Acq:** Purchase. **Dist:** CEV Multimedia. $79.95.

The Business File 1985
An extensive course for college students, introducing them to the basic concepts of business. 30m; VHS, 3/4 U. **Pr:** Dallas County Community College. **A:** College-Adult. **P:** Education. **U:** Institution, CCTV. **Bus-Ind:** Business, Management, Job Training. **Acq:** Purchase, Rent/Lease. **Dist:** PBS Home Video. $130.00.
Indiv. Titles: 1. Accounting for Profits 2. Business of Business, The 3. Business Opportunities: Large & Small 4. Challenge of Business on an International Scale 5. Challenge of High Technology and Communications 6. Challenge of Productivity, The 7. Comparative Economic Systems: Is Capitalism the Best? 8. Creating an Organization 9. Environment, The: Business and Governmental Regulation 10. Environment, The: Business and Labor 11. Environment, The: Business and Social Responsibility 12. Environment, The: Business and the Economy 13. Environment, The: Business and the Law 14. Forming a Business: Corporations 15. Forming a Business: Proprietorships & Partnerships 16. Human Resources: Acquisitions and Development 17. Managing Business Organization 18. Managing Financial Resources: Long-Term Funds 19. Managing Financial Resources: Short-Term Funds 20. Managing Human Resources 21. Managing Information 22. Managing Risk 23. Marketing Concepts 24. Marketing Distribution Strategy 25. Marketing Pricing Strategy 26. Marketing Product Strategy 27. Marketing Promotional Strategy 28. Producing the Product.

Business for Pleasure 1996 (Unrated) — ★½
Wealthy tycoon orchestrates a sexual triangle between himself, his closest assistant, and a beautiful exec in order to explore the wilder side of sex and fantasy. 97m; VHS. **C:** Gary Stretch; Joanna Pacula; Jeroen Krabbe; Caron Bernstein; Directed by Rafael Eisenman; Written by Zalman King; Cinematography by Eagle Egilsson; Music by George S. Clinton. **Pr:** Zalman King; Zalman King; Republic Pictures. **A:** College-Adult. **P:** Entertainment. **U:** Home. **Mov-Ent:** Sex & Sexuality. **Acq:** Purchase. **Dist:** Lions Gate Television Corp.

Business Insurance: A Sales Skills Introduction 19??
Designed to develop the vital sales skills an agent needs to make a smooth transition into the lucrative area of business insurance. 28m; VHS, 3/4 U. **Pr:** R & R Newkirk. **A:** Adult. **P:** Professional. **U:** Institution, CCTV. **Bus-Ind:** Insurance, Sales Training. **Acq:** Purchase, Subscription. **Dist:** Custom Communications.

Business is Business 1971 (Unrated) — ★½
Verhoeven's first feature film (after his television work) is a sex comedy about a couple of prostitutes who are apartment neighbors in Amsterdam. Nel's got an abusive boyfriend she just can't shake despite the efforts of her friend Blonde Greet. BG decides they should become partners (she's got a lot of fetish clients) but she gets put-out when Nel finds a nice, boring

guy who wants to marry her and take her out of the life. Especially since Blonde Greet's special guy is already hitched. A slight and surprisingly timid story considering Verhoeven's later work but everyone's gotta start somewhere. Dutch with subtitles. 89m; DVD, Wide. **C:** Ronnie Bierman; Sylvia De Leur; Piet Romer; Jules Hamel; Bernard Droog; Henk Molenberg; Albert Mol; Directed by Paul Verhoeven; Written by Gerard Soeteman; Cinematography by Jan De Bont; Music by Mulius Steffaro. **A:** College-Adult. **P:** Entertainment. **U:** Home. **Mov-Ent:** Prostitution. **Acq:** Purchase. **Dist:** Anchor Bay Entertainment.

Business Law for Accountants 19??
Teaches the fundamentals of business law associated with accountants. Covers ethical responsibilities, contracts, secured transactions, partnerships, corporations, and the federal bankruptcy code. Comes with textbook and quizzer. Can be used for Advisory Services CPE credit hours. 240m; VHS. **A:** College-Adult. **P:** Professional. **U:** Institution, Home. **Bus-Ind:** Business, Economics, Finance. **Acq:** Purchase. **Dist:** Bisk Education. $249.00.

Business Library Series: Sales and Motivation 19??
Offers humorous look at the fundamental elements of executing a sale. Emphasizes planning and determination as the essence of everyday success. 35m; VHS. **A:** College-Adult. **P:** Education. **U:** Institution. **Bus-Ind:** Sales Training. **Acq:** Purchase. **Dist:** Instructional Video. $19.95.

Business Litigation 1987
Provides a practical primer to business litigation with an emphasis on the prevention of disputes, the effect they have on the client's business, and alternatives to going to court. Since many disputes do end up in civil court, the series covers pretrial and trial strategies, the examining of friendly and hostile witnesses, and closing statements. 70m; VHS, 3/4 U. **Pr:** National Institute for Trial Advocacy. **A:** Adult. **P:** Education. **U:** Institution. **Bus-Ind:** Law, Business. **Acq:** Purchase, Rent/Lease. **Dist:** National Institute for Trial Advocacy. $1995.00.
Indiv. Titles: 1. Strategies for Preventing and Handling Disputes 2. Interviewing and Fact Finding 3. Evaluating the Case 4. Preparing for and Taking Dispositions 5. Pretrial Strategies 6. Trial Strategies 7. Opening Statements 8. Examining the Plaintiff's Witness, Part One 9. Examining the Plaintiff's Witness, Part Two 10. Examining the Defendant's Witness, Part One 11. Examining the Defendant's Witness, Part Two 12. Closing Arguments.

The Business of Aging 1982
Examines the economics of nursing home operation and the reasons why these institutions are often less than adequate. 27m; VHS, 3/4 U. **Pr:** National Film Board of Canada. **A:** College-Adult. **P:** Education. **U:** Institution. **Gen-Edu:** Aging, Nursing. **Acq:** Purchase. **Dist:** Filmakers Library Inc.

Business of America 1983
Attempts to answer the question, "Does America still have the essential ingredients to provide a better life?" 19m; VHS, 3/4 U. **Pr:** WGBH Boston. **A:** Jr. High-Adult. **P:** Education. **U:** Institution, SURA. **Gen-Edu:** Business. **Acq:** Purchase, Rent/Lease. **Dist:** Hearst Entertainment/King Features.

The Business of America? 1984
Documentary challenging the assumption that private corporations can be trusted to make the investments upon which the country depends. Available for rent in 16mm. 45m; VHS. **A:** Sr. High-Adult. **P:** Education. **U:** Institution. **Gen-Edu:** Documentary Films, Economics, Business. **Acq:** Purchase, Rent/Lease. **Dist:** California Newsreel. $49.95.

The Business of Banking: Financial Services—A Value Added Business 1987
The benefits of various financial plans are compared. 30m; VHS, 3/4 U. **Pr:** First Financial Network. **A:** Adult. **P:** Education. **U:** Institution, Home. **Bus-Ind:** Finance. **Acq:** Purchase, Rent/Lease. **Dist:** 1st Financial Training Services. $350.00.

The Business of Banking: Income Statement—The Pulse of the Business 1987
Former IBM salesman Mark Burns tells why banks have to charge for their services. 19m; VHS, 3/4 U. **Pr:** First Financial Network. **A:** Adult. **P:** Education. **U:** Institution, Home. **Bus-Ind:** Finance. **Acq:** Purchase, Rent/Lease. **Dist:** 1st Financial Training Services. $275.00.

The Business of Banking: The Balance Sheet—What Does It Mean? 1987
Former IBM sales exec Mark Burns explains how to use a balance sheet. 30m; VHS, 3/4 U. **Pr:** First Financial Network. **A:** Adult. **P:** Instruction. **U:** Institution, Home. **Bus-Ind:** Business, Finance. **Acq:** Purchase, Rent/Lease. **Dist:** 1st Financial Training Services. $350.00.

The Business of Banking: The Importance of Account Profitability 1987
Mark Burns shows how banks can make each account a profit unto itself. 15m; VHS, 3/4 U. **Pr:** First Financial Network. **A:** Adult. **P:** Education. **U:** Institution, Home. **Bus-Ind:** Finance. **Acq:** Purchase, Rent/Lease. **Dist:** 1st Financial Training Services. $275.00.

The Business of Better Health 1983
This series presents a comprehensive health analysis for laymen. 30m; VHS, 3/4 U. **Pr:** Kentucky Educational Television. **A:** Adult. **P:** Education. **U:** Institution, CCTV, CATV. **Hea-Sci:** Health Education. **Acq:** Purchase, Rent/Lease, Free Loan. **Dist:** KET, The Kentucky Network.

Indiv. Titles: 1. Body Talk 2. Medicine Chest 3. From the Fat of the Land 4. Anyone for Fitness? 5. Take It To the Heart 6. Man Abuses Man 7. You're the Doctor 8. It's Never Too Late.

The Business of Better Writing 1983
Series offering 12 easy-to-follow lessons on improving business writing skills. 30m; VHS, 3/4 U. **Pr:** Kentucky Educational Television. **A:** College-Adult. **P:** Education. **U:** Institution, CCTV, CATV. **Bus-Ind:** Language Arts, How-To. **Acq:** Purchase, Rent/Lease, Free Loan. **Dist:** KET, The Kentucky Network.
Indiv. Titles: 1. Mastering Grammar 2. Mastering Punctuation 3. Mastering Spelling 4. Mastering Mechanics 5. Writing Principles 6. Writing Correctly 7. Writing Clearly 8. Writing Concisely 9. Writing Interestingly 10. Writing Persuasively 11. Writing the Letter 12. Writing the Report.

The Business of Caring 1987
A series of programs for nursing professionals about patient care, consideration and relation to the family. Each program has nine episodes. 18m; VHS, 3/4 U. **Pr:** Victoria International. **A:** Adult. **P:** Professional. **U:** Institution. **Hea-Sci:** Nursing, Patient Care. **Acq:** Purchase. **Dist:** Victoria International Corp.
Indiv. Titles: 1. From the Patient's Point of View 2. Active Listening 3. Did You Get My Message.

The Business of Direct Mail 1983
This series presents, in sequence, institutions and organizations with step-by-step methods of direct mail usage. 30m; VHS, 3/4 U. **Pr:** Kentucky Educational Television. **A:** College-Adult. **P:** Education. **U:** Institution, CCTV, CATV. **Bus-Ind:** Business, Marketing. **Acq:** Purchase, Rent/Lease, Free Loan. **Dist:** KET, The Kentucky Network.
Indiv. Titles: 1. How to Investigate Direct Mail Marketing 2. Direct Mail and Your Sales Force 3. Essential Elements in Direct Mail Marketing 4. How to Test with Direct Mail 5. The Value of Ongoing Direct Mail 6. How to Use Wave Mailings 7. Key Direct Mail Letter Concepts 8. Writing to Different Executive Levels 9. Effective Business Sales Literature 10. Getting Your Mail to the Proper Executive 11. Overcoming Direct Mail Pitfalls 12. Profitable Direct Mail Programs.

The Business of Dollars and Sense: An Introduction to Economics 19??
Provides examples and definitions of terms like inflation, cost of living, interest rate, profit, supply and demand, competition, income tax, and the GNP. 14m; VHS. **A:** Jr. High-Sr. High. **P:** Education. **U:** Institution. **Gen-Edu:** Economics. **Acq:** Purchase. **Dist:** Thomas S. Klise Co. $58.00.

The Business of Effective Speaking 1985
With William F. Buckley and Saul Loeb, the art of effective and careful business speechmaking is presented. 30m; VHS, 3/4 U. **Pr:** Kentucky Educational Television. **A:** Adult. **P:** Education. **U:** Institution, CCTV, CATV. **Bus-Ind:** Speech, Language Arts. **Acq:** Purchase, Rent/Lease, Free Loan. **Dist:** KET, The Kentucky Network.

The Business of Fancydancing 2002 (Unrated) — ★★
Seymour (Adams) is a gay Native American who has left the reservation, gone to college, and now uses his heritage to achieve literary fame as a poet. He hasn't been back to the rez in years but returns for the funeral of onetime friend Mouse (Kanim). Seymour's return is awkward as it triggers the frustrated resentment of another boyhood pal Aristotle (Tagaban) as well as a confrontation with his college girlfriend Agnes (St. John) who is now Aristotle's lover. 103m; VHS, DVD. **C:** Evan Adams; Michelle St. John; Gene Tagaban; Swil Kanim; Rebecca Carroll; Cynthia Geary; Leo Rossi; Kevin Phillip; Elaine Miles; Directed by Sherman Alexie; Written by Sherman Alexie; Cinematography by Holly Taylor. **Pr:** Larry Estes; Scott Rosenfelt; FallsApart; Outrider Pictures. **A:** Sr. High-Adult. **P:** Entertainment. **U:** Home. **Mov-Ent:** Native Americans, Journalism. **Acq:** Purchase. **Dist:** Wellspring Media.

Business of Hunger 1988
The third world phenomenon of selling crops to other nations while the people of that country go hungry is examined. 28m; VHS. **Pr:** Maryknoll World Productions. **A:** Jr. High-Adult. **P:** Education. **U:** Institution. **Gen-Edu:** Politics & Government, Poverty. **Acq:** Purchase. **Dist:** Maryknoll Sisters; Facets Multimedia Inc. $19.95.

The Business of Managing Professionals 1983
This series explains the problems related to managing professionals. 30m; VHS, 3/4 U. **Pr:** Kentucky Educational Television. **A:** Adult. **P:** Education. **U:** Institution, CCTV, CATV. **Bus-Ind:** Management. **Acq:** Purchase, Rent/Lease, Free Loan. **Dist:** KET, The Kentucky Network.
Indiv. Titles: 1. Overview 2. Hiring, Part One 3. Hiring, Part Two 4. Hiring, Part Three 5. Information-Communication Behavior of Professionals, Part One 6. Information-Communication Behavior of Professionals, Part Two 7. Motivation and Incentives, Part One 8. Motivation and Incentives, Part Two 9. Performance and Evaluation 10. Creativity, Part One 11. Creativity, Part Two 12. Obsolescence and Burnout 13. Review.

The Business of Photography 19??
Provides information on the necessary steps to start a career in photography. Includes information on choosing a direction, the portfolio, the interview, and major markets. Teacher's guide available for an additional $10.00. 90m; VHS. **A:** Jr. High-Adult. **P:** Instruction. **U:** Institution, Home. **How-Ins:** Photography, How-To, Occupations. **Acq:** Purchase. **Dist:** Crystal Productions; Education 2000, Inc. $29.95.

The Business of Raising Money 1989
A selected panel discusses changing trends in fund-raising, fund-raising for non-profit organizations, and dispels myths about how to approach fund-raising. 30m; VHS. **A:** Adult. **P:**

Professional. **U:** Institution. **Bus-Ind:** Business, Management. **Acq:** Purchase. **Dist:** RMI Media. $89.95.

The Business of Strangers 2001 (R) — ★★
Julie Styron (Channing) is a tough, middleaged executive for a software company who is having a bad day at an out-of-town meeting. She worries she's about to be fired and then fires her young assistant Paula (Stiles) for missing the meeting and ruining Julie's presentation. Instead, Julie gets a promotion and decides to rehire Paula after they diss men over drinks at the hotel bar. When Paula spots corporate headhunter Nick (Weller), she tells Julie that he raped a friend of hers and it's payback time. But since the two women have been playing mind games, is this the truth or not? 83m; VHS, DVD. **C:** Stockard Channing; Julia Stiles; Frederick Weller; Marcus Giamatti; Directed by Patrick Stettner; Written by Patrick Stettner; Cinematography by Teodoro Maniaci; Music by Alexander Lasarenko. **Pr:** Susan A. Stover; Robert H. Nathan; i5 Picture; Headquarters; IFC Films. **A:** Sr. High-Adult. **P:** Entertainment. **U:** Home. **Mov-Ent:** Hotels & Hotel Staff Training. **Acq:** Purchase. **Dist:** MGM Home Entertainment.

Business/Office Cluster 1984
Different kinds of office work are shown to students interested in entering these occupations. 30m; VHS, 3/4 U. **Pr:** Minnesota State Private Industry Company. **A:** Sr. High-Adult. **P:** Education. **U:** Institution, SURA. **Gen-Edu:** Occupations. **Acq:** Purchase. **Dist:** Center for Humanities, Inc./Guidance Associates.

The Business Plan ????
Deals with key elements in creating a successful business plan. 50m; VHS. **A:** Adult. **P:** Instruction. **U:** Institution. **Gen-Edu:** Business, How-To. **Acq:** Purchase. **Dist:** American Institute of Small Business. $69.95.

The Business: Season 1 2006
Vic Morgenstein, a.k.a. Vic Morgan, attempts to leave his days distributing Asian horror schlock and soft-core smut "Drunk Chicks" series behind and gain respectability by producing and distributing the indie-thriller "House of Fear" with the help of seasoned IFC segment producer Julia Sullivan, but a gaggle of porn starlets, self-obsessed B-movie stars, insipid PR execs, offbeat Japanese investors, the American Beef lobby, and an unstable director keep getting in the way. 200m; DVD. **C:** Kathleen Robertson; Nicholas Wright; Ellen David; Rob De Leeuw; Trevor Hayes. **A:** Adult. **P:** Entertainment. **U:** Home. **Mov-Ent:** Filmmaking. **Acq:** Purchase. **Dist:** Genius Entertainment.

Business World's Guide to Computers 1990
Constant change in the computer industry makes choosing the right computer for your long-term business needs difficult. Top business leaders provide reliable information on what may be the most important purchasing decision a company can make. 50m; VHS. **C:** Hosted by Sander Vanocuer. **Pr:** Independent. **A:** Adult. **P:** Education. **U:** Home. **Bus-Ind:** Computers, Business. **Acq:** Purchase. **Dist:** MPI Media Group. $19.98.

Business Writing 1991
Discusses composition of business letters, memos, and reports; and lists standard salutations and closings. 30m; VHS. **A:** Adult. **P:** Education. **U:** Institution. **Gen-Edu:** Communication, Language Arts. **Acq:** Purchase. **Dist:** RMI Media. $69.95.

Business Writing: Quick, Clear, Concise 1992
Features tips on reducing writing time, improving clarity, and organizing ideas using a five-step method. Includes an instructor's guide, participant workbooks, an erase-board, and overhead transparencies. 30m; VHS, 8 mm, 3/4 U. **C:** Hosted by Deanna (Dee) Booher. **Pr:** American Media Inc. **A:** College-Adult. **P:** Instruction. **U:** Institution. **Bus-Ind:** Business, Communication. **Acq:** Purchase, Rent/Lease. **Dist:** American Media, Inc. $695.00.

Business Writing Skills Series 199?
Two tape series offers practical tips for organizing your thoughts effectively for written business communication. Includes advice on breaking writer's block, creating a strong opening and closing, choosing a formal versus an informal style, and more. 75m; VHS. **A:** Sr. High-Adult. **P:** Education. **U:** Institution. **Bus-Ind:** Business, Communication. **Acq:** Purchase. **Dist:** Cambridge Educational. $149.95.

Business Writing Skills, Vol. 1 1980
The techniques of effective business writing (letters, reports, and memos) are covered. Comprised of five modules: General Principles of Business Writing; Organizing Business Writing; Clear Business Writing; Friendly Business Writing; and Effective Business Reports. 75m; VHS, 3/4 U. **Pr:** Resources for Education and Management. **A:** College-Adult. **P:** Professional. **U:** Institution, CCTV. **Bus-Ind:** Language Arts, Business. **Acq:** Purchase. **Dist:** Resources for Education & Management, Inc.

The Businessman and the Gospel 1982
Dr. Theodore Baehr interviews Walter Hoving, former chairman of Tiffany's, who discusses his life, business activities and his lifelong commitment to serving God and Jesus Christ. 15m; VHS, 3/4 U. **Pr:** Episcopal Radio-TV Foundation. **A:** Sr. High-Adult. **P:** Religious. **U:** Institution, CCTV, CATV, BCTV, Home. **Gen-Edu:** Religion, Interviews. **Acq:** Purchase, Rent/Lease. **Dist:** Alliance for Christian Media.

Busing: Constructive or Divisive? 197?
Four experts discuss the effect busing has on education, integration, race relations, and the public. 60m; 3/4 U. **Pr:** American Enterprise Institute. **A:** College-Adult. **P:** Education. **U:** Institution, BCTV. **Gen-Edu:** Documentary Films, Public Affairs. **Acq:** Purchase, Rent/Lease. **Dist:** American Enterprise Institute for Public Policy Research.

Bussing: Pre-Service Duties 1988
Offers instruction on specific aspects of cooking and food preparation. 20m; VHS. **A:** Adult. **P:** Instruction. **U:** Institution. **Gen-Edu:** Cooking. **Acq:** Purchase. **Dist:** RMI Media. $59.95.

Bussing: Service Responsibilities 1988
Offers instruction on specific aspects of cooking and food preparation. 8m; VHS. **A:** Adult. **P:** Instruction. **U:** Institution. **Gen-Edu:** Cooking. **Acq:** Purchase. **Dist:** RMI Media. $39.95.

Busta Rhymes: Eveything Remains Raw 2004 (Unrated)
Live performance by acclaimed rapper Busta Rhymes from 2003. 100m; DVD. **A:** Sr. High-Adult. **P:** Entertainment. **U:** Home. **Mov-Ent:** Music--Performance, Documentary Films, Music--Rap. **Acq:** Purchase. **Dist:** Eagle Rock Entertainment Inc. $14.98.

Busted Dreams 1983
A group of black people talk about the tough circumstances which have destroyed their dreams. 30m; VHS, 3/4 U. **Pr:** New Jersey Network. **A:** Sr. High-Adult. **P:** Education. **U:** Institution. **Gen-Edu:** Documentary Films, Minorities, Civil Rights. **Acq:** Purchase, Rent/Lease. **Dist:** New Jersey Network.

Busted Up 1986 (R) — ★
A young, hard-luck urban street-fighter battles for the sake of his family and neighborhood against local crimelords. 93m; VHS, CC. **C:** Irene Cara; Paul Coufos; Tony Rosato; Stan Shaw; Gordon Judges; Directed by Conrad Palmisano; Music by Charles P. Barnett. **Pr:** Damian Lee; David Mitchell; Shapiro Ent. **A:** Sr. High-Adult. **P:** Entertainment. **U:** Home. **Mov-Ent:** Canada. **Acq:** Purchase. **Dist:** $79.95.

Busted: What You Need to Know About Drugs and the Law 1999
Discourages teens from drug use with straight talk of prison discomforts. 25m; VHS. **A:** Sr. High. **P:** Education. **U:** Institution. **Gen-Edu:** Drug Abuse, Psychology. **Acq:** Purchase. **Dist:** Social Studies School Service; Zenger Media. $189.00.

Buster 1988 (R) — ★★½
The story of Buster Edwards, the one suspect in the 1963 Great Train Robbery who evaded being captured by police. Collins makes his screen debut as one of Britain's most infamous criminals. Collins also performs on the film's soundtrack, spawning two hit singles, "Two Hearts" and "Groovy Kind of Love." 102m; VHS, DVD, CC. **C:** Phil Collins; Julie Walters; Larry Lamb; Stephanie Lawrence; Ellen Beaven; Michael Atwell; Ralph Brown; Christopher Ellison; Sheila Hancock; Martin Jarvis; Anthony Quayle; Directed by David Green; Music by Anne Dudley. **Pr:** Tri-Star Pictures. **A:** Adult. **P:** Entertainment. **U:** Home. **Mov-Ent. Acq:** Purchase. **Dist:** Movies Unlimited; Alpha Video. $89.95.

Buster and Billie 1974 (R) — ★½
Tragedy ensues when a popular high school student falls in love with the class tramp in rural Georgia in 1948. Serious, decently appointed period teen drama. 100m; VHS. **C:** Jan-Michael Vincent; Joan Goodfellow; Clifton James; Pamela Sue Martin; Robert Englund; Directed by Daniel Petrie. **A:** Sr. High-Adult. **P:** Entertainment. **U:** Home. **Mov-Ent:** Drama, Adolescence. **Acq:** Purchase. **Dist:** Sony Pictures Home Entertainment Inc. $59.95.

Buster & Chauncey's Silent Night 1998
Original animated musical based on the true story of the creation of the beloved Christmas carol "Silent Night." Features the voice of Phil Hartman as a 19th century Austrian mouse whose love of music inadvertantly inspires the song. 48m; VHS, DVD. **A:** Family. **P:** Entertainment. **U:** Home. **Mov-Ent:** Animation & Cartoons, Animation & Cartoons, Christmas. **Acq:** Purchase. **Dist:** Sony Pictures Home Entertainment Inc. $12.95.

Buster and Me 1983
A program designed to inform youngsters about nuclear issues. 25m; VHS, 3/4 U, Special order formats. **Pr:** KRON San Francisco. **A:** Jr. High-Sr. High. **P:** Education. **U:** Institution, CCTV, CATV, BCTV, Home, SURA. **Gen-Edu:** Nuclear Energy, Nuclear Warfare, Propaganda. **Acq:** Purchase. **Dist:** The Video Project. $24.95.

Buster and the Boosters 19??
Robotic school bus Buster teaches children how to be safe bus riders. 19m; VHS. **A:** Preschool-Primary. **P:** Special Education. **U:** Institution. **Chl-Juv:** Safety Education, Children. **Acq:** Purchase, Rent/Lease. **Dist:** AMS Distributors, Inc.

Buster B. Jones in Concert 199?
Live performance by hot-rod country fingerstyle guitarist. 60m; VHS. **A:** Sr. High-Adult. **P:** Entertainment. **U:** Home. **Fin-Art:** Music--Performance. **Acq:** Purchase. **Dist:** Hal Leonard Corp. $19.95.

Buster Keaton: Fishing Story & The Collapsible Clerk 19??
Two of Keaton's classics are restored and released on video. In these stories, Keaton plays a bumbling sporting goods clerk dealing with international jewel theives in the "Fishing Story" and wrestlers in "The Collapsible Clerk." 65m/B/W; Silent; VHS. **C:** Buster Keaton. **A:** Sr. High-Adult. **P:** Entertainment. **U:** Home. **Mov-Ent:** Comedy--Slapstick, Silent Films. **Acq:** Purchase. **Dist:** Stardance Entertainment.

Buster Keaton Rides Again 1965 — ★½
The making of a Buster Keaton comedy short titled "The Railrodder." 56m/B/W; VHS. **C:** Buster Keaton. **Pr:** Julian Biggs. **A:** Preschool. **P:** Entertainment. **U:** Institution, SURA. **Mov-Ent:** Documentary Films, Filmmaking. **Acq:** Purchase, Rent/Lease. **Dist:** National Film Board of Canada. $19.95.

Buster Keaton Rides Again/The Railrodder 1965 (Unrated)
"The Railrodder" is a silent comedy short that returns Buster Keaton to the type of slapstick he made famous in his legendary 1920s films. "Buster Keaton Rides Again" (in black and white) is a documentary-style look at Keaton filmed during the making of "The Railrodder." Besides scenes of Keaton at work, there is also a capsule rundown of his career. 81m; Silent; VHS, DVD. **C:** Buster Keaton; Gerald Potterton; Directed by John Spotton; Written by Donald Brittain; Cinematography by John Spotton. **Pr:** National Film Board of Canada. **A:** Family. **P:** Entertainment. **U:** Home. **Mov-Ent:** Comedy--Slapstick, Film History, Silent Films. **Acq:** Purchase. **Dist:** Grapevine Video. $29.95.

Buster Keaton Short Films Collection: 1920-1923 2011 (Unrated)
A collection of 19 of Keaton's classic short films along with several visual essays and an eight-page booklet. /B/W; Silent; DVD, Blu-Ray. **A:** Primary-Adult. **P:** Entertainment. **U:** Home. **L:** English, Japanese. **Mov-Ent:** Comedy--Slapstick, Silent Films. **Acq:** Purchase. **Dist:** Kino International Corporation. $49.95 34.95.

Bustin' Loose 1981 (R) — ★★★
A fast-talking ex-con reluctantly drives a bus load of misplaced kids and their keeper cross-country. 94m; VHS, DVD. **C:** Richard Pryor; Cicely Tyson; Robert Christian; George Coe; Bill Quinn; Directed by Oz Scott; Written by Richard Pryor; Lonnie Elder, III; Cinematography by Dennis Dalzell; Music by Roberta Flack; Mark Davis. **Pr:** Mark Huffam; Richard Pryor; Michael Glick; Richard Pryor. **A:** Jr. High-Adult. **P:** Entertainment. **U:** Home. **Mov-Ent. Acq:** Purchase. **Dist:** Movies Unlimited; Alpha Video; Universal Studios Home Video. $14.95.

Busting 1974 (R) — ★★½
Gould and Blake play a pair of slightly off-the-wall L.A. cops. The pair are forced "to bust" local addicts and prostitutes instead of the real crime bosses because much of the police department is on the take. Plenty of comedy and action as well as highly realistic drama. 92m; VHS, DVD. **C:** Elliott Gould; Robert (Bobby) Blake; Allen Garfield; Antonio Fargas; Michael Lerner; Sid Haig; Cornelia Sharpe; Directed by Peter Hyams; Written by Peter Hyams; Music by Billy Goldenberg. **A:** Adult. **P:** Entertainment. **U:** Home. **Mov-Ent:** Drugs. **Acq:** Purchase. **Dist:** MGM Home Entertainment. $14.95.

Busting the Mob ????
Presents the History Channel special on the FBI's work in the early 1980s to break up a massive heroin ring in New York, an effort that included one of the most expansive wiretapping stings in the agency's history; the ring was dubbed the "Pizza Connection" for its use of pizza parlors as fronts. Includes recordings from the wiretaps. 50m; DVD. **A:** Sr. High-Adult. **P:** Entertainment. **U:** Home, CATV. **Mov-Ent:** Television Series, Documentary Films, Biography. **Acq:** Purchase. **Dist:** A&E Television Networks L.L.C. $24.95.

Bustling Narrow Gauge/White Pass & Yukon/Rio Grand 1951
This collection of four short films fondly recalls classic trains such as the San Juan and the White Pass. 56m/B/W; VHS. **Pr:** Woodrow Gorman. **A:** Family. **P:** Education. **U:** Home. **Gen-Edu:** Trains. **Acq:** Purchase.

The Busy Body 1967 (Unrated) — ★★
A plethora of sixties comedians enliven this mild flick from Castle, who's probably better-known for schlock film promotions. Bumbling smalltime crook George (Caesar) is suspected of pilfering mob money by his gangland boss Charley Baker (Ryan). If he doesn't want to wind up wearing cement overshoes, George had better find the real thief and the corpse that's buried in a suit lined with the stolen moolah. Adapted from a Donald E. Westlake novel. 102m; DVD. **C:** Sid Caesar; Robert Ryan; Anne Baxter; Kay Medford; Jan Murray; Richard Pryor; Bill Dana; Ben Blue; Dom DeLuise; Godfrey Cambridge; Marty Ingels; George Jessel; Charles McGraw; Arlene Golanka; Directed by William Castle; Written by Ben Starr; Cinematography by Michael Reed; Harold E. Stine; Music by Vic Mizzy. **A:** Family. **P:** Entertainment. **U:** Home. **Mov-Ent. Acq:** Purchase. **Dist:** Legend Films.

Busy Woman's Fitting Techniques 1989
Fitting techniques for a woman who doesn't have a lot of time are demonstrated. 60m; VHS. **C:** Nancy Zieman. **Pr:** Nancy's Notions Ltd. **A:** Jr. High-Adult. **P:** Instruction. **U:** Institution, Home. **How-Ins:** Sewing. **Acq:** Rent/Lease. **Dist:** Nancy's Notions Ltd.

Busy Woman's Sewing Combo 1989
Women can squeeze an assortment of sewing projects into their schedule with help from Nancy. 120m; VHS. **C:** Nancy Zieman. **Pr:** Nancy's Notions Ltd. **A:** Sr. High-Adult. **P:** Instruction. **U:** Institution, Home. **How-Ins:** Sewing. **Acq:** Rent/Lease. **Dist:** Nancy's Notions Ltd.

Busy Woman's Sewing Techniques 1 and 2 1987
A series of instructional sewing shortcuts for the working woman. 60m; VHS. **Pr:** Nancy's Notions Ltd. **A:** College-Adult. **P:** Instruction. **U:** Institution, Home. **How-Ins:** How-To, Sewing. **Acq:** Purchase, Rent/Lease. **Dist:** Nancy's Notions Ltd.

The Busy Woman's Sewing Video 1989
Working women with a full schedule don't have to give up sewing as this tap illustrates. 60m; VHS. **C:** Nancy Zieman. **Pr:** Nancy's Notions Ltd. **A:** Sr. High-Adult. **P:** Instruction. **U:** Institution, Home. **How-Ins:** Sewing. **Acq:** Rent/Lease. **Dist:** Nancy's Notions Ltd.

But a Good Cigar Is a Smoke! 1997
Presents an in depth look at every aspect of cigars. 75m; VHS. **A:** Adult. **P:** Education. **U:** Home. **Gen-Edu:** Smoking. **Acq:** Purchase. **Dist:** Tapeworm Video Distributors Inc. $14.95.

But He Loves Me 1991
Tells the story of teenager Cassie, who is stuck in an abusive relationship with her boyfriend, Charlie. Highlights the little-discussed problem of teen abuse, which affects a shocking 12% of all dating teens. Originally broadcast as a "CBS Schoolbreak Special." Includes teacher's guide. 46m; VHS. **A:** Jr. High-Sr. High. **P:** Education. **U:** Institution. **Chl-Juv:** Adolescence, Violence. **Acq:** Purchase, Rent/Lease. **Dist:** Clear Vue Inc. $275.00.

But I Don't Have Customers: Internal Customer Service 1994
Identifies internal customers and their needs, emphasizing the importance of maintaining good relations with them through questioning, listening, and keeping your word. Includes leader's guide. 21m; VHS, CC. **A:** Adult. **P:** Instruction. **U:** Institution. **Bus-Ind:** Meeting Openers, Business, Customer Service. **Dist:** American Media, Inc. $595.

...But I Was a Girl 1998
Tells the story of Frieda Belinfante, the first woman to have her own symphony orchestra. Her music, politics and sexuality are examined using archival footage and interviews with her family and friends. 69m; VHS. **A:** Sr. High-Adult. **P:** Education. **U:** Home, Institution. **Gen-Edu:** Documentary Films, Women, Biography. **Acq:** Purchase, Rent/Lease. **Dist:** First Run/Icarus Films. $390.00.

But I'm a Cheerleader 1999 (R) — ★★
Broad satire falls flat. Megan (Lyonne) is a peppy high school cheerleader who is suspected of being a lesbian by her rigid parents, who send her off to a rehabilitation camp designed to turn adolescent homosexuals into straight members of society. Megan (who's naively unaware of her true nature) goes along with the program until she befriends rebellious Graham (DuVall) and discovers that, golly, she really does like girls. 81m; VHS, DVD, CC. **C:** Natasha Lyonne; Clea DuVall; Cathy Moriarty; RuPaul Charles; Bud Cort; Mink Stole; Julie Delpy; Eddie Cibrian; Directed by Jamie Babbit; Written by Jamie Babbit; Cinematography by Jules Labarthe; Music by Pat Irwin. **Pr:** Fine Line Features. **A:** Sr. High-Adult. **P:** Entertainment. **U:** Home. **Mov-Ent:** Satire & Parody, Adolescence, Camps & Camping. **Acq:** Purchase. **Dist:** Wolfe Video.

But It's Never Too Late to Drop Back In 199?
Follow-up to "I Dropped Out..." offers options to dropouts for completing a high school equivalent education, such as the GED, JTPA, and Job Corps programs. Also addresses students re-entering the traditional education system. 30m; VHS. **A:** Sr. High-Adult. **P:** Education. **U:** Institution. **Gen-Edu:** Education, Adolescence. **Acq:** Purchase. **Dist:** Cambridge Educational. $98.00.

But It's Not My Fault 1982
A 16-year-old boy learns the hard way when he attempts to prove himself to his peers. 46m; VHS, 3/4 U. **Pr:** Virginia Carter. **A:** Jr. High-Sr. High. **P:** Education. **U:** Institution, CCTV, SURA. **Gen-Edu:** Adolescence. **Acq:** Purchase, Rent/Lease. **Dist:** Program Source.

But Names Can Hurt Forever 1988
This powerful program examines a form of child abuse that often leaves unseen yet devastating scars. This video shows all viewers how the cycle and terror of emotional abuse can and must be ended—through education and counseling. 30m; VHS, 3/4 U. **Pr:** Centre Productions, Inc. **A:** Jr. High-Adult. **P:** Education. **U:** Institution, SURA. **Gen-Edu:** Documentary Films, Psychology, Child Abuse. **Acq:** Purchase. **Dist:** Clear Vue Inc.

But Not for Me 1959 — ★★½
Gable stars as a middled-aged entertainment executive who thinks he can forestall maturity by carrying on with his youthful secretary. 105m/B/W; VHS, CC. **C:** Clark Gable; Carroll Baker; Lilli Palmer; Lee J. Cobb; Barry Coe; Thomas Gomez; Charles Lane; Directed by Walter Lang; Written by John Michael Hayes; Cinematography by Robert Burks. **Pr:** Paramount Pictures. **A:** Jr. High-Sr. High. **P:** Entertainment. **U:** Home. **Mov-Ent:** Comedy--Romantic, Classic Films. **Acq:** Purchase. **Dist:** Paramount Pictures Corp. $14.95.

But. . .Seriously: The Ultimate Collection of Political Comedy 1995
American social and political satire from the '50s through the '90s and featuring Robin Williams, Richard Pryor, Lenny Bruce, Mort Sahl, and others. 82m; VHS. **A:** Sr. High-Adult. **P:** Entertainment. **U:** Home. **Mov-Ent:** Comedy--Performance, Satire & Parody, Politics & Government. **Acq:** Purchase. **Dist:** Paramount Pictures Corp. $19.95.

But the Flesh Is Weak 1932 (Unrated) — ★½
Novello adapted his play "The Truth Game" for this dated romantic comedy about father/son gigolos. Max (Montgomery) and Florian (Smith) Clement prefer to live off the generosity of wealthy women and Max sets his sights on marrying Lady Joan Culver (Thatcher). Instead, he falls for widow Rosine Brown (Gregor), who's looking for a moneyed suitor. Florian incurs a huge gambling debt and Max tries again with Lady Joan. He still makes a romantic mistake when Rosine comes back into the picture since she's an Austrian drip. 77m/B/W; DVD. **C:** Robert Montgomery; Sir C. Aubrey Smith; Nora Gregor; Heather Thatcher; Eva Moore; Edward Everett Horton; Nils Asther; Directed by Jack Conway; Written by Ivor Novello; Cinematography by Oliver Marsh. **A:** Sr. High-Adult. **P:** Entertainment. **U:** Home. **Mov-Ent:** Comedy--Romantic, Gambling, Drama. **Acq:** Purchase. **Dist:** WarnerArchive.com.

...But Then, She's Betty Carter 1980
Portrait of legendary jazz vocalist Betty Carter, her musical genius, paradoxical relationship with the public, and fierce dedication to personal and artistic independence. 53m; VHS. **Pr:** Michelle Parkerson. **A:** College-Adult. **P:** Education. **U:** Institution. **Gen-Edu:** Women, Music--Jazz. **Acq:** Purchase, Rent/Lease. **Dist:** Women Make Movies. $295.00.

But Where Is Daniel Wax? 1974 (Unrated) — ★★
At a class reunion, a doctor and a popular singing star reminisce about their youth and Daniel Wax, their one-time hero. Hebrew with English subtitles. 95m; VHS. **C:** Lior Yaeni; Michael Lipkin; Esther Zevko; Directed by Avraham Heffner. **Pr:** Ergo Media. **A:** Jr. High-Adult. **P:** Entertainment. **U:** Home. **L:** English, Hebrew. **Mov-Ent. Acq:** Purchase. **Dist:** Ergo Media Inc. $79.95.

But You Look So Well 2002
Individuals with multiple sclerosis discuss the emotional, social and physical impact it has had on their lives. Neurologists explain how people can make living with MS more manageable. 59m; VHS. **A:** Adult. **P:** Professional. **U:** Institution. **Hea-Sci:** Muscles, Medical Education, Diseases. **Acq:** Purchase. **Dist:** Aquarius Health Care Media. $195.00.

Butch and Sundance: The Early Days 1979 (PG) — ★★½
Traces the origins of the famous outlaw duo. It contains the requisite shoot-outs, hold-ups, and escapes. A "prequel" to "Butch Cassidy and the Sundance Kid." 111m; VHS, DVD, Blu-Ray. **C:** Tom Berenger; William Katt; John Schuck; Jeff Corey; Jill Eikenberry; Brian Dennehy; Peter Weller; Directed by Richard Lester; Written by Allan Burns. **Pr:** 20th Century-Fox. **A:** Family. **P:** Entertainment. **U:** Home. **Mov-Ent:** Western. **Acq:** Purchase. **Dist:** Movies Unlimited; Alpha Video. $19.98.

Butch Cassidy and the Sundance Kid 1969 (PG) — ★★★★
Two legendary outlaws at the turn of the century take it on the lam with a beautiful, willing ex-school teacher. With a clever script, humanly fallible characters, and warm, witty dialogue, this film was destined to become a classic. Featured the hit song "Raindrops Keep Falling on My Head" and renewed the buddy film industry, as Newman and Redford trade insult for insult. Look for the great scene where Newman takes on giant Ted Cassidy in a fist fight. 110m; VHS, DVD, Blu-Ray. **C:** Paul Newman; Robert Redford; Katharine Ross; Jeff Corey; Strother Martin; Cloris Leachman; Kenneth Mars; Ted Cassidy; Henry Jones; George Furth; Sam Elliott; Directed by George Roy Hill; Written by William Goldman; Cinematography by Conrad L. Hall; Music by Burt Bacharach. **Pr:** 20th Century-Fox. **A:** Family. **P:** Entertainment. **U:** Home. **L:** English, Spanish. **Mov-Ent:** Western, Classic Films, Bicycling. **Awds:** Oscars '69: Cinematog., Orig. Score, Song ("Raindrops Keep Fallin' on My Head"), Story & Screenplay; AFI '98: Top 100; British Acad. '70: Actor (Redford), Actress (Ross), Director (Hill), Film, Screenplay; Golden Globes '70: Score; Natl. Film Reg. '03; Writers Guild '69: Adapt. Screenplay. **Acq:** Purchase. **Dist:** Movies Unlimited.
Songs: Raindrops Keep Fallin' on My Head; On a Bicycle Built for Joy.

Butch Lauffer's Counter Attack System 2006 (Unrated)
Coach Robert 'Butch' Lauffer uses game footage to discuss and demonstrate the art of counter attacking in soccer. 28m; DVD. **A:** Family. **P:** Education. **U:** Home, Institution. **Spo-Rec:** Soccer, Athletic Instruction/Coaching. **Acq:** Purchase. **Dist:** Championship Productions. $29.99.

Butch Lauffer's 12 Best Training Games 2006
Twelve training games are designed to improve overall play through developing possession play, three player movements, attacking/defending practices, and shooting and crossing. 74m; DVD. **A:** Adult. **P:** Instruction. **U:** Institution. **Spo-Rec:** Soccer. **Acq:** Purchase. **Dist:** Championship Productions.

Butch Lauffer's Zone Play 2006
Lauffer has developed zone concepts over the past 15 years and demonstrates the techniques and advantages to using zone defense in a game. 68m; DVD. **A:** Adult. **P:** Instruction. **U:** Institution. **Spo-Rec:** Soccer. **Acq:** Purchase. **Dist:** Championship Productions.

Butch Minds the Baby 1985
Big Butch, a safecracker, is forced to bring his baby along on a heist. When the other crooks are caught, Butch finds that the baby gives him a perfect alibi. Based on the story by Damon Runyon. 30m; VHS, 3/4 U. **C:** Jerry O'Shea; Zachary Pierce. **Pr:** Learning Corporation of America. **A:** Family. **P:** Education. **U:** Institution, SURA. **Gen-Edu:** TV Movies. **Acq:** Purchase, Rent/Lease. **Dist:** Phoenix Learning Group.

Butch Thompson's Bullseye Pitching 40 Drills 2012 (Unrated)
Coach Butch Thompson presents 40 drills designed to better a baseball team's pitchers. 45m; DVD. **A:** Family. **P:** Education. **U:** Home. **L:** English. **Spo-Rec:** Athletic Instruction/Coaching, Baseball, How-To. **Acq:** Purchase. **Dist:** Championship Productions. $39.99.

The Butcher 2007 (Unrated) — ★½
Mob enforcer Merle Hench (Roberts) is set-up to take the fall for a bigtime heist on a rival mob boss. Surviving the trap, and grabbing a piece of the take, Merle decides being betrayed after 20 years of loyalty deserves payback. 113m; DVD. **C:** Eric Roberts; Robert Davi; Keith David; Geoffrey Lewis; Michael Ironside; Bokeem Woodbine; Directed by Jesse Johnson; Written by Jesse Johnson; Cinematography by Robert Hayes; Music by Marcello De Francisci. **A:** Sr. High-Adult. **P:** Entertainment. **U:** Home. **Mov-Ent. Acq:** Purchase. **Dist:** Vivendi Visual Entertainment.

The Butcher 2007 (Unrated) — ★★
A group of snuff film producers kidnap four people (two of which are husband and wife), strap cameras to their heads, and then force them to endure inhumane punishments in a game designed to murder them as grotesquely as possible. 75m; DVD, Blu-Ray. **C:** Dong-Hun You; Sung-Il Kim; Directed by Jin-Won Kim; Written by Jin-Won Kim; Cinematography by Sang-hyeon Lee. **A:** Sr. High-Adult. **P:** Entertainment. **U:** Home. **L:** English, Korean. **Mov-Ent:** Horror. **Acq:** Purchase. **Dist:** Vivendi Visual Entertainment. $19.99.

The Butcher Boy 1997 (R) — ★★★
Offbeat, black comedy takes a disturbing look into the madness of 12-year old Francie Brady (Owens) in Ireland in the 1960s. An alcoholic father and a mentally strained mother makes Francie escape into a world populated by voices in his head, comic books, and his one childhood friend. When his homelife becomes unbearable, Frankie's demons catapult him into a climatic and destructively criminal breakdown. Newcomer Owens is electrifying as the red-haired dynamo whose lost childhood turns him into a monster and Stephen Rea (a regular in any Jordan film) provides stern support as Francie's loser father and film's narrator. The rural Irish town is recreated with stunning detail, with light touches of kitsch that may put off some looking for a serious treatment of main character's plight. Still a daring movie, with pop star O'Connor as the Virgin Mary. Based on the novel by Peter McCabe. 105m; VHS, DVD. **C:** Eamon Owens; Stephen Rea; Fiona Shaw; Sinead O'Connor; Aisling O'Sullivan; Alan Boyle; Ian Hart; Andrew Fullerton; Patrick McCabe; Sean McGinley; Brendan Gleeson; Milo O'Shea; Directed by Neil Jordan; Written by Neil Jordan; Patrick McCabe; Cinematography by Adrian Biddle; Music by Elliot Goldenthal. **Pr:** Stephen Woolley; Redmond Morris; Geffen Film Company. **A:** Adult. **P:** Entertainment. **U:** Home. **Mov-Ent:** Ireland, Alcoholism, Mental Health. **Awds:** L.A. Film Critics '98: Score. **Acq:** Purchase. **Dist:** Warner Home Video, Inc.

The Butcher's Wife 1991 (PG-13) — ★★
Charming tale of a young psychic (Moore) who brings romance to a Greenwich Village neighborhood that never quite gets off the ground. Moore stars as the clairvoyant whose mystical powers bring magic into the lives of everyone around her, including the local psychiatrist (Daniels), who falls under her spell. Talented cast is virtually wasted with a script that is lightweight; excepting Steenburgen and Dzundza who shine. 107m; VHS, DVD, Wide, CC. **C:** Demi Moore; Jeff Daniels; George Dzundza; Frances McDormand; Margaret Colin; Mary Steenburgen; Max Perlich; Miriam Margolyes; Christopher Durang; Diane Salinger; Directed by Terry Hughes; Written by Ezra Litwack; Marjorie Schwartz; Cinematography by Frank Tidy; Music by Michael Gore. **Pr:** Wallis Nicita; Lauren Lloyd; Paramount Pictures. **A:** Jr. High-Adult. **P:** Entertainment. **U:** Home. **Mov-Ent:** Comedy--Romantic, Magic, Marriage. **Acq:** Purchase, Rent/Lease. **Dist:** Paramount Pictures Corp. $14.95.

Butler's Dilemma 1943 (Unrated) — ★★
A jewel thief and a playboy both claim the identity of a butler who never existed, with humorous results. 75m/B/W; VHS. **TV Std:** NTSC, PAL. **C:** Richard Hearne; Francis L. Sullivan; Hermione Gingold; Ian Fleming; Alf Goddard; Judy Kelly; Henry Kendall; Wally Patch; Frank Pettingell; Andre Randall; Marjorie Rhodes; Ronald Shiner; Ralph Truman; Directed by Leslie Hiscott; Written by Michael Barringer; Cinematography by Erwin Hillier. **Pr:** Elizabeth Hiscott; British National. **A:** Family. **P:** Entertainment. **U:** Home. **Mov-Ent:** Action-Adventure. **Acq:** Purchase. **Dist:** $24.95.

Butley 1974 (R) — ★★★
Bates, in a tour de force performance, is Ben Butley, a bitter, gay professor who wants to make everone as miserable as he is, including his ex-wife, a recently-published collegue, and his protege and former lover. He verbally abuses and insults anyone who crosses his path as his life disintegrates before his eyes. Butley is about as unsymathetic as you can get, but Bates's performance saves the day. The rest of the cast does an admirable job keeping up. Pinter's film directing debut. 127m; VHS, DVD. **C:** Alan Bates; Jessica Tandy; Richard O'Callaghan; Susan Engel; Michael Byrne; Georgina Hale; Simon Rouse; John Savident; Oliver Maguire; Susan Wooldridge; Directed by Harold Pinter; Written by Simon Gray; Cinematography by Gerry Fisher. **A:** Sr. High-Adult. **P:** Entertainment. **U:** Home. **Mov-Ent:** Divorce. **Acq:** Purchase. **Dist:** Movies Unlimited. $25.49.

Butt Out! The Proven Quit Smoking Plan 1992
Provides motivational interviews with people who have stopped smoking and discussess the tactics they used to quit. 35m; VHS. **A:** Sr. High-Adult. **P:** Instruction. **U:** Home. **Hea-Sci:** Smoking, Self-Help. **Acq:** Purchase. **Dist:** Baker and Taylor. $19.95.

Butter 2012 (R) — ★★
A rather smug and inert satire with an undeniably talented cast that gets sucked into a morass of bad behavior. Ambitious Laura Pickler (Garner) is a control freak determined to carry on her retired husband Bob's (Burrell) winning streak in the annual Iowa butter-carving competiton. But Laura's unexpected (and unlikely) competitor is 11-year-old black foster child Destiny (Shahidi).The pic ends up being too direct and in-your-face with its pretty misanthropic viewpoint of friendly competition among not-so-friendly people. 90m; DVD, Blu-Ray. **C:** Jennifer Garner; Ty Burrell; Yara Shahidi; Olivia Wilde; Rob Corddry; Hugh Jackman; Ashley Greene; Alicia Silverstone; Directed by Jim Field Smith; Written by Jason A. Micallef; Cinematography by Jim Denault; Music by Mateo (Matt) Messina. **Pr:** Michael De Luca; Juliana Janes; Alissa Phillips; Jennifer Garner; Vandalia Films; Michael De Luca Productions; Weinstein Company L.L.C. **A:** Sr. High-Adult. **P:** Entertainment. **U:** Home. **L:** English. **Mov-Ent:** Comedy--Black, Satire & Parody. **Acq:** Purchase. **Dist:** Anchor Bay Entertainment Inc.

The Butter Cream Gang 19??
One summer, a group of small-town kids learn about unconditional love. 96m; VHS. **A:** Family. **P:** Entertainment. **U:** Home. **Chl-Juv:** Family Viewing. **Acq:** Purchase. **Dist:** Feature Films for Family.

The Butter Cream Gang in Secret of Treasure Mountain 19??
After discovering an ancient treasure map, young Eldon Flowers fantasizes about finding gold and becoming a hero. With his friends, he embarks on an adventure and eventually discovers what being a hero really means. 90m; VHS. **A:** Family. **P:** Entertainment. **U:** Home. **Chl-Juv:** Family Viewing, Mystery & Suspense. **Acq:** Purchase. **Dist:** Feature Films for Family.

Buttercup 1971
A glistening stream with a buttercup slipping along the silvery surface. In a jarring finish, it is swallowed in the stench, sludge, and garbage of industrial man. Designed to provoke creative expression. 11m; VHS, 3/4 U, Special order formats. **Pr:** Churchill. **A:** Primary-Sr. High. **P:** Education. **U:** Institution, Home, SURA. **Gen-Edu:** Video, Language Arts. **Acq:** Purchase, Duplication License. **Dist:** Clear Vue Inc.

The Buttercup Chain 1970 (Unrated) — ★½
First cousins France (Bennett) and Margaret (Asher) are fighting incestuous feelings so France decides they should both get involved with others: he chooses Swedish student Fred (Taube) for Margaret and free-spirited American Manny (Taylor-Young) for himself. But it's Manny and Fred who marry and move away; when France and Margaret eventually visit, they discover the marriage is unhappy. 95m; DVD. **C:** Hywel Bennett; Leigh Taylor-Young; Jane Asher; Sven-Bertil Taube; Clive Revill; Roy Dotrice; Directed by Robert Ellis Miller; Written by Peter Draper; Cinematography by Douglas Slocombe; Music by Richard Rodney Bennett. **A:** Sr. High-Adult. **P:** Entertainment. **U:** Home. **Mov-Ent:** Drama. **Acq:** Purchase. **Dist:** Sony Pictures Home Entertainment Inc.

Butterfield 8 1960 — ★★★
A seedy film of the John O'Hara novel about a prostitute that wants to go straight and settle down. Taylor won an Oscar, perhaps because she was ill and had lost in the two previous years in more deserving roles. 108m; VHS, DVD, Wide. **C:** Elizabeth Taylor; Laurence Harvey; Eddie Fisher; Dina Merrill; Mildred Dunnock; Betty Field; Susan Oliver; Kay Medford; Directed by Daniel Mann; Written by John Michael Hayes; Charles Schnee; Cinematography by Joseph Ruttenberg. **Pr:** MGM; Afton. **A:** Jr. High-Adult. **P:** Entertainment. **U:** Home. **Mov-Ent:** Prostitution, Sex & Sexuality. **Awds:** Oscars '60: Actress (Taylor). **Acq:** Purchase. **Dist:** Baker and Taylor; MGM Home Entertainment. $19.98.

Butterflies 1975
Ria, a middle-aged housewife with two lazy sons, is beginning to feel her age, and like a butterfly, feeling like she has too much to do and not enough time. Then Leonard appears in her life—divorced, lonely and romantic. Made for British television. 60m; VHS. **Pr:** British Broadcasting Corporation. **A:** Family. **P:** Entertainment. **U:** Home. **Mov-Ent:** Comedy--Romantic, TV Movies. **Acq:** Purchase. **Dist:** Video Collectibles. $29.95.

Butterflies 1989
A stunning video collection of the world's rarest and loveliest butterflies including the swallowtail, the red admiral, the small tortoiseshell and more. 30m; VHS. **A:** Family. **P:** Entertainment. **U:** Home. **Gen-Edu:** Documentary Films, Insects. **Acq:** Purchase. **Dist:** MNTEX Entertainment, Inc.

Butterflies 2005
A short documentary on the life of butterflies. 23m; VHS, DVD. **A:** Sr. High-Adult. **P:** Education. **U:** Institution. **Gen-Edu:** Insects, Documentary Films. **Acq:** Purchase, Rent/Lease. **Dist:** The Cinema Guild. $195.00.

Butterflies Are Free 1972 (PG) — ★★★
Fast-paced humor surrounds the Broadway play brought to the big screen. Blind youth Albert is determined to be self-sufficient. A next-door-neighbor actress helps him gain independence from his over-protective mother (Heckart). 109m; VHS, DVD, Wide. **C:** Goldie Hawn; Edward Albert; Eileen Heckart; Michael Glaser; Directed by Milton Katselas; Cinematography by Charles B(ryant) Lang, Jr.; Music by Robert Alcivar. **Pr:** M.J. Frankovich; Columbia Pictures. **A:** Jr. High-Adult. **P:** Entertainment. **U:** Home. **Mov-Ent:** Comedy-Drama, Blindness. **Awds:** Oscars '72: Support. Actress (Heckart). **Acq:** Purchase. **Dist:** Sony Pictures Home Entertainment Inc. $9.95.

Butterflies on the Scaffold 1995
Documentary follows a group of Havana drag queens as they prepare for a performance. Includes interviews. Spanish with subtitles. 74m; VHS. **C:** Directed by Margaret Gilpin; Luis Felipe Bernaza. **A:** College-Adult. **P:** Entertainment. **U:** Home, Institution. **L:** Spanish. **Gen-Edu:** Documentary Films, Homosexuality. **Acq:** Purchase. **Dist:** Water Bearer Films Inc.

Butterflies: Season 1 1978
Ria's a bored, middle-aged suburban English housewife and mum who thinks Ben, her butterfly-collecting dentist husband, is neglecting her. So she contemplates having an affair with smitten businessman Leonard. 6 episodes. 181m; DVD. **C:** Wendy Craig; Geoffrey Palmer; Bruce Montague. **A:** Jr. High-Adult. **P:** Entertainment. **U:** Home. **Mov-Ent:** Television Series. **Acq:** Purchase. **Dist:** Acorn Media Group Inc.

Butterflies: Season 2 2005
Second season of the British comedy about a bored housewife. 238m; DVD. **C:** Wendy Craig; Geoffrey Palmer; Bruce Montague; Nicholas Lyndhurst; Michael Ripper; Andrew Hall; Joyce Windsor. **A:** Adult. **P:** Entertainment. **U:** Home. **Mov-Ent:** Comedy--Black, Women. **Acq:** Purchase. **Dist:** Acorn Media Group Inc. $29.99.

Butterfly 1968
The program begins with the laying of the egg, then follows the hatching and growth to the final emergence of the butterfly. No narration. 9m; VHS, 3/4 U. **Pr:** Gakken Company Ltd. **A:** Primary. **P:** Education. **U:** Institution, SURA. **Hea-Sci:** Documentary Films, Insects. **Acq:** Purchase. **Dist:** Phoenix Learning Group.

Butterfly 1982 (R) — ★½
Based on James M. Cain's novel about an amoral young woman (Pia, who'd you think?) who uses her beauty and sensual appetite to manipulate the men in her life, including her father. Set in Nevada of the 1930s, father and daughter are drawn into a daring and forbidden love affair by their lust and desperation. 105m; VHS, DVD. **C:** Pia Zadora; Stacy Keach; Orson Welles; Edward Albert; James Franciscus; Lois Nettleton; Stuart Whitman; June Lockhart; Ed McMahon; Directed by Matt Cimber; Written by Matt Cimber; Music by Ennio Morricone. **Pr:** Analysis Films. **A:** Adult. **P:** Entertainment. **U:** Home. **Mov-Ent:** Sex & Sexuality. **Awds:** Golden Raspberries '82: Worst Actress (Zadora), Worst New Star (Zadora), Worst Support. Actor (McMahon). **Acq:** Purchase. **Dist:** Amazon.com Inc.; Lions Gate Television Corp. $79.95.

Butterfly 1983
A woman's faith in the Resurrection helps her deal with the death of her newborn baby. 27m; VHS, 3/4 U, Special order formats. **C:** Rosanna Arquette; Christine Avila; David Thomas. **Pr:** Paulist Productions. **A:** Sr. High-Adult. **P:** Religious. **U:** Institution, CCTV, SURA. **Gen-Edu:** Religion, Death. **Acq:** Purchase. **Dist:** Paulist Productions.

Butterfly 1998 (R) — ★★★
Young Moncho (Lozano) grows up in 1935 Galicia, Spain and is guided by his leftist teacher Don Gregorio (Gomez). But their lives are soon torn apart by the politics of the Spanish Civil War. This kind of languidly paced coming-of-age story is almost never found in American theatrical releases these days. Europeans tend to treat the material with more seriousness. Director Jose Cuerda's work is solidly in the tradition of Fellini and Truffaut. Based on the stories of Manuel Riva; Spanish with subtitles. 94m; VHS, DVD, Wide. **C:** Fernando Fernan-Gomez; Manuel Lozano; Uxia Blanco; Directed by Jose Luis Cuerda; Written by Rafael Azcona; Cinematography by Javier Salmones; Music by Alejandro Amenabar. **A:** Sr. High-Adult. **P:** Entertainment. **U:** Home. **L:** Spanish. **Mov-Ent:** Spain. **Acq:** Purchase. **Dist:** Buena Vista Home Entertainment.

Butterfly 2000 (Unrated)
79m. **C:** Directed by Doug Wolen; Cinematography by Doug Wolen. **Pr:** Doug Wolens; Open City Films. **Mov-Ent:** Documentary Films, Forests & Trees, Ecology & Environment. **Dist:** Not Yet Released.

The Butterfly 2002 (Unrated) — ★★★
Likeable tale of Julien—a lonely, grumpy old guy in Paris—who can't resist his spunky yet equally lonely eight-year-old neighbor, Elsa, who's working, single mom doesn't have time for her. When he sets off to the mountains in a quest to snag a rare butterfly, Elsa slyly tags along and the two connect amid the stunning scenery. Her unwitting mother notices she's missing, becomes despondent, and triggers an APB for her. In French with subtitles. 80m; VHS, DVD. **C:** Michel Serrault; Francoise Michaud; Dominique Marcas; Idwig Stephane; Francis Frappat; Francoise Dubois; Dominic Gould; Auriele Meriel; Claire Bouanich; Nade Dieu; Helene Hily; Pierre Poirot; Jacky Nercessian; Jacques Bouanich; Catherine Cyler; Jerry Lucas; Laurent Adrien; Gabrielle Arger; Fabien Behar; Alain Bert; Alain Blazquez; Magali Bonat; Christiane Bopp; Armand Chagot; Laurent Chouteau; Jerome Foucher; Phlippe LeDem; Gerard Maillet; Esther Perez-Pajares; Fabien Traverci; Directed by Philippe Muyl; Written by Philippe Muyl; Cinematography by Nicolas Herdt; Music by Nicolas Errera. **A:** Jr. High-Adult. **P:** Entertainment. **U:** Home. **L:** French. **Mov-Ent:** Action-Adventure, France. **Acq:** Purchase. **Dist:** First Run Features. $29.95.

Butterfly Affair 1971 (PG) — ★½
Beautiful singer, involved in a scheme to smuggle $2 million worth of gems, plots to double-cross her partners in crime. 75m; VHS, DVD. **C:** Claudia Cardinale; Henri Charriere; Stanley Baker; Directed by Jean Herman. **Pr:** Cannon Films. **A:** Jr. High-Adult. **P:** Entertainment. **U:** Home. **Mov-Ent. Acq:** Purchase. **Dist:** East West. $14.99.

Butterfly Ball 1976 (Unrated) — ★
Retelling of the 19th century classic combines the rock music of Roger Glover, live action and animation by Halas and Batchelor. Only for the brain-cell depressed. 85m; VHS, DVD. **C:** Twiggy; Ian Gillian; David Coverdale; Narrated by Vincent Price; Directed by Tony Klinger. **Pr:** Tony Klinger. **A:** Family. **P:** Entertainment. **U:** Home. **Mov-Ent:** Musical, Fairy Tales, Animation & Cartoons. **Acq:** Purchase. **Dist:** Unknown Distributor.

Butterfly Ball 1981
An animated musical fable set at the Butterfly Ball where the exotic guests discover that "love is all you need" with the help of a talented minstrel. 5m; VHS, 3/4 U. **Pr:** Jack King. **A:** Primary-Adult. **P:** Entertainment. **U:** Institution, SURA. **Gen-Edu:** Animation & Cartoons, Romance. **Acq:** Purchase. **Dist:** Phoenix Learning Group.

Butterfly Collectors 1999 (Unrated) — ★★
While investigating a murder, DI John McKeown (Postlethwaite) develops an unlikely friendship with 17-year-old suspect Dex (Draven), who is raising his younger siblings. But as McKeown gets closer to the family, his suspicions grow, and not just about Dex's involvement in the original crime. 150m; DVD. **C:** Pete Postlethwaite; Crissy Rock; Jamie Draven; Alison Newman; Directed by Jean Stewart; Written by Paul Abbott; Cinematography by Cinders Forshaw; Music by Philip Appleby; Jocelyn Pook. **A:** Sr. High-Adult. **P:** Entertainment. **U:** Home. **Mov-Ent:** Crime Drama. **Acq:** Purchase. **Dist:** Video Collectibles.

Butterfly Drills 2001
Demonstrates over 20 drills including undulation, single arm, single arm recovery, sculling, and 4-count. 37m; VHS. **A:** Adult. **P:** Instruction. **U:** Institution. **How-Ins:** Swimming, Sports--Water, How-To. **Acq:** Purchase. **Dist:** Championship Productions. $34.95.

The Butterfly Effect 2004 (R) — ★½
Kutcher takes time out from his usual dumb pretty-boy roles and tries his hand at a thriller. He plays Evan Treborn, a college psych major with a troubled past. He discovers that he can go back in time and change childhood events, which he does, to save himself and a group of friends from childhood traumas. Unfortunately, when he returns to the present, he finds his actions have changed everything that has happened since then, and not always for the better. There's a strong "ick" factor, touching on several rather disturbing topics. Kutcher acquits himself admirably, but not enough to save this jumbled mess. 113m; DVD, Blu-Ray, UMD. **C:** Ashton Kutcher; Amy Smart; Eric Stoltz; William Lee Scott; Elden (Ratliff) Henson; Logan Lerman; Irene Gorovaia; Jesse James; Melora Walters; Ethan Suplee; John Patrick Amedori; Kevin G. Schmidt; Directed by Eric Bress; J. Mackye Gruber; Written by Eric Bress; J. Mackye Gruber; Cinematography by Matthew F. Leonetti; Music by Michael Suby. **Pr:** Anthony Rhulen; Chris Bender; A.J. Dix; JC Spink; Benderspink; FilmEngine; New Line Cinema. **A:** Sr. High-Adult. **P:** Entertainment. **U:** Home. **Mov-Ent:** Child Abuse. **Acq:** Purchase. **Dist:** New Line Home Video.

The Butterfly Effect 2 2006 (R) — ★½
Nick (Lively) loses control of his car, resulting in an accident that kills his girlfriend Julie (Durance) and two friends. Still traumatized after a year, Nick realizes that he feels a power whenever he looks at the photos of their last trip and can actually travel back in time to that particular moment. But when Nick returns to the present, he doesn't always like the changes that occurred as he tries to save Julie's life. An overly-complicated execution ruins the suspense factor. 92m; DVD, Blu-Ray. **C:** Eric Lively; Gina Holden; J.R. Bourne; Erica Durance; Dustin Milligan; Directed by John R. Leonetti; Written by Michael D. Weiss; Cinematography by Brian Pearson; Music by Michael Suby. **A:** Sr. High-Adult. **P:** Entertainment. **U:** Home. **Mov-Ent:** Horror. **Acq:** Purchase. **Dist:** Warner Home Video, Inc.

The Butterfly Effect 3: Revelation 2009 (R) — ★★
This low-budget DTV sequel is a cut above the last effort, thanks to Miner's fine performance as Jenna, jumper Sam's (Carmack) fragile sister. Sam is working with Detroit police, getting a paycheck by helping solve cold cases. When he time-travels back to ID his own girlfriend's killer, Sam changes his past and his efforts to fix one mistake result in him becoming the prime suspect in a series of murders. 90m; DVD, Blu-Ray. **C:** Chris Carmack; Rachel Miner; Richard Wilkinson; Directed by Seth Grossman; Written by Holly Brix; Cinematography by Dan Stoloff; Music by Adam Balzacs. **A:** Sr. High-Adult. **P:** Entertainment. **U:** Home. **Mov-Ent. Acq:** Purchase. **Dist:** Lions Gate Entertainment Inc.

Butterfly Kiss 1994 — ★★
Strange psychodrama/road tale finds drifter Eunice (Plummer) wandering the motorways of northern England. At one service station she meets Miriam (Reeves)?the two, immediately drawn together, make love at Miriam's that night. When Eunice hitches a ride with a trucker next morning, Miriam decides to follow and discovers Eunice with the truck and the driver's dead body. It's soon not the only dead body Miriam encounters as she discovers Eunice is a serial killer—not that this seems to worry Miriam a great deal as she herself gets into the spirit of their crimes. Grim all the way 'round. 90m; VHS, DVD. **C:** Amanda Plummer; Saskia Reeves; Paul Bown; Des McAleer; Ricky Tomlinson; Directed by Michael Winterbottom; Written by Frank Cottrell-Boyce; Cinematography by Seamus McGarvey; Music by John Harle. **Pr:** Julie Baines. **A:** Sr. High-Adult. **P:** Entertainment. **U:** Home. **Mov-Ent. Acq:** Purchase. **Dist:** First Run Features.

Butterfly Sword 1993 (R) — ★★
Bizarre, over-the-top bloody wire-fu action, as a group of eunuchs attempting to overthrow the Ming Dynasty are challenged by hired killers Meng Sing Wan (Tony Leung Chiu Wai) and Sister Ko (Michelle Yeoh). Complicating their fight is Meng's wife who is unaware he is an assassin, a drunken swordsman who is in love with Ko, and Ko's secret love for Meng. The original ending was considered to be too upsetting for Hong Kong audiences, so buyers should make sure the version they get has it intact (which may require getting a non-Chinese version). Otherwise the films pre-emptive ending will make little sense. 87m; DVD. **C:** Michelle Yeoh; Jimmy Lin; Tony Leung Chiu Wai; Joey Wang; Donnie Yen; Chung Hua Tou; Elvis Tsui; Chaun Chen Yeh; Directed by Michael Mak; Written by John Chong; Music by Chin Yung Shing. **A:** Sr. High-Adult. **P:** Entertainment. **U:** Home. **L:** English, Cantonese, Mandarin Dialects. **Mov-Ent:** Martial Arts, Fantasy. **Acq:** Purchase. **Dist:** Tai Seng Video Marketing. $14.95.

Butterfly Technique 2001
NCAA Head Coach David Marsh discusses timing, rhythm, and balance of the butterfly. Demonstrates techniques for more efficient breathing, turns, undulation, and stroke. 33m; VHS. **A:** Adult. **P:** Instruction. **U:** Institution. **How-Ins:** Swimming, Sports--Water, How-To. **Acq:** Purchase. **Dist:** Championship Productions. $34.95.

Butterfly Training 2001
Breaks season training into three phases: preseason, training season and taper/rest providing a day by day schedule on how to properly train butterfly swimmers. 53m; VHS. **A:** Adult. **P:** Instruction. **U:** Institution. **How-Ins:** Swimming, Sports--Water, How-To. **Acq:** Purchase. **Dist:** Championship Productions. $34.95.

Butterfly Wings 1991 — ★★
The tragedy of a dysfunctional family. Pregnant Carmen longs for a boy to carry on her husband's name but she's afraid to tell her shy six-year-old daughter Ami about the baby. Maybe with reason, since the child's brith triggers a series of nightmarish events. Spanish with subtitles. 105m; VHS. **C:** Silvia Munt; Susan Garcia; Fernando Valverde; Directed by Juanma Bajo Ulloa; Written by Juanma Bajo Ulloa; Cinematography by Aiter Mantxola; Music by Bingen Mendizabal. **A:** College-Adult. **P:** Entertainment. **U:** Home. **L:** Spanish. **Mov-Ent:** Family, Pregnancy. **Acq:** Purchase. **Dist:** Facets Multimedia Inc. $59.95.

Button Button: A Dream of Nuclear War 1984
A short anti-nuclear war program. 14m; VHS, Special order formats. **Pr:** Green Mountain Post Films. **A:** Jr. High-Adult. **P:** Education. **U:** Institution, CATV, BCTV, SURA. **Gen-Edu:** Nuclear Warfare. **Acq:** Purchase, Rent/Lease. **Dist:** Green Mountain Post Films.

Button Up Your House 1987
Helps viewers prepare their home for the cold winter months by showing how to handle basement insulation, how to check solar access, and how to choose proper windows. 28m; VHS, 3/4 U. **Pr:** RMI Media Productions. **A:** Sr. High-Adult. **P:** Instruction. **U:** Institution, Home. **How-Ins:** Home Improvement, How-To. **Acq:** Purchase. **Dist:** RMI Media.

Buy & Cell 1989 (R) — ★½
A stockbroker attempts to set up a business while serving a prison sentence. An assortment of amusing inmates doesn't help matters much. Fans of Malcolm McDowell will enjoy his performance as the shady warden. 95m; VHS. **C:** Robert Carradine; Michael Winslow; Malcolm McDowell; Ben Vereen; Lise Cutter; Randall "Tex" Cobb; Roddy Piper; Directed by Robert Boris. **Pr:** Altar Productions. **A:** College-Adult. **P:** Entertainment. **U:** Home. **Mov-Ent. Acq:** Purchase. **Dist:** Amazon.com Inc. $19.95.

Buy, Buy 1973
A wry examination of the methods and motives of the producers and agency people who make TV commercials our most potent advertising medium. 20m; VHS, 3/4 U, Special order formats. **Pr:** Churchill Films. **A:** Jr. High-Adult. **P:** Education. **U:** Institution, Home, SURA. **Gen-Edu:** Documentary Films, Advertising, Mass Media. **Acq:** Purchase, Duplication License. **Dist:** Clear Vue Inc.

Buy Me That! A Kid's Survival Guide to TV Advertising 1989
Pulls the wool away from the children's eyes by revealing the marketing ploys hidden in TV advertisements. 28m; VHS. **A:** Primary-Jr. High. **P:** Education. **U:** Institution, Home. **Chl-Juv:** Children, Television, Advertising. **Acq:** Purchase. **Dist:** Home Vision Cinema. $79.00.

Buy Me That, Three! 199?
Outlines tricks used by advertisers to make their products seem more attractive and desirable. Aimed at children. Part of the three-part "Buy Me That Video Series." ?m; VHS. **Pr:** HBO; Consumer Reports. **A:** Primary-Jr. High. **P:** Education. **U:** Home, Institution. **Chl-Juv:** Advertising, Children. **Acq:** Purchase. **Dist:** Center for Media Literacy. $49.00.

Buy Me That Too! A Kid's Survival Guide to TV Advertising 1992
Kids come on camera to complain about how they were enticed by the commercial goods they saw advertised on television and how they overcame the craving for having everything they saw. 30m; VHS, CC. **Pr:** HBO. **A:** Primary. **P:** Education. **U:** Institution. **Gen-Edu:** Television, Advertising. **Acq:** Purchase. **Dist:** Ambrose Video Publishing, Inc. $69.95.

Buy Now, Pay Later: Credit Basics ????
Explains the credit application process, hidden costs of financing, interest rates, credit reporting and adjustment of errors, legal rights, types of credit, and how to establish credit. 23m; VHS. **A:** Sr. High. **P:** Education. **U:** Institution. **Gen-Edu:** Finance, Consumer Education. **Acq:** Purchase. **Dist:** Zenger Media. $89.00.

Buyer Be Aware: Avoiding Rip-Offs 199?
Exposes common legal schemes used to swindle unsuspecting customers out of their money. 24m; VHS. **A:** Jr. High-Adult. **P:** Education. **U:** Institution. **Gen-Edu:** Consumer Education. **Acq:** Purchase. **Dist:** The Learning Seed. $89.00.

Buyer Be Wise 1990
Mickey, Donald and Goofy learn how to be smart shoppers in this educational video for children. 8m; VHS, 3/4 U, EJ, Special order formats. **TV Std:** NTSC, PAL, SECAM. **Pr:** Disney Educational Productions. **A:** Primary-Jr. High. **P:** Education. **U:** Institution, CCTV, SURA. **Chl-Juv:** Consumer Education, Animation & Cartoons, Children. **Acq:** Purchase, Rent/Lease. **Dist:** Phoenix Learning Group. $170.00.

Buyers, Markets and Marts 19??
Buyer and retail store owner Charli Light introduces the processes involved in fashion merchandising. 21m; VHS. **A:** Jr.

High-Adult. **P:** Education. **U:** Institution. **Bus-Ind:** Textile Industry, Clothing & Dress. **Acq:** Purchase. **Dist:** CEV Multimedia. $79.95.

Buying a Home 1987
Part of a series offering instruction on personal finance management. 30m; VHS. **A:** Adult. **P:** Education. **U:** Institution. **Gen-Edu:** Finance. **Acq:** Purchase. **Dist:** RMI Media. $75.00.

Buying a Personal Computer 1993
Provides direction in the sometimes daunting task of purchasing a home computer. Includes explanations of options, software, and equipment. 50m; VHS. **A:** Sr. High-Adult. **P:** Instruction. **U:** Home. **How-Ins:** Computers, How-To. **Acq:** Purchase. **Dist:** Cambridge Educational. $29.95.

Buying a Small, On-Going Business 1989
Discusses where to find business opportunities besides the newspaper and how to find a business that matches your personal profile. 30m; VHS. **A:** Adult. **P:** Professional. **U:** Institution. **Bus-Ind:** Business, Management. **Acq:** Purchase. **Dist:** RMI Media. $89.95.

Buying a Used Car 1988
A program designed to prepare teenagers and others interested in purchasing a used car and familiarizes viewer with a car's main systems: engine, brakes, steering, power train, cooling, electrical, and auto body condition, and provides tips on routine maintenance, insurance budgeting, licensing, taxes, and operation. 17m; VHS, 3/4 U. **Pr:** RMI Media Productions. **A:** Sr. High-Adult. **P:** Instruction. **U:** Institution. **How-Ins:** Automobiles, Consumer Education. **Acq:** Purchase. **Dist:** RMI Media.

Buying Sex 2013 (Unrated)
Offers insight and analysis into the debate over potential changes to Canada's prostitution laws which may decriminalize prostitution. 75m; DVD. **A:** Sr. High-Adult. **P:** Entertainment. **U:** Home. **Mov-Ent:** Prostitution, Documentary Films, Canada. **Acq:** Purchase. **Dist:** First Run Features. $24.95.

Buying the Cow 2002 (R) — ★½
Commitment-phobe David (O'Connell) is being pressured by long-time girlfriend Sarah (Wilson) to get married. Cliched romantic comedy. 88m; VHS, DVD, CC. **C:** Jerry O'Connell; Bridgette Wilson-Sampras; Ryan Reynolds; Bill Bellamy; Annabeth Gish; Ron Livingston; Directed by Walt Becker; Written by Walt Becker; Peter W. Nelson; Cinematography by Nancy Schreiber; Music by Andrew Gross. **A:** Sr. High-Adult. **P:** Entertainment. **U:** Home. **Mov-Ent:** Comedy--Romantic. **Acq:** Purchase. **Dist:** Sony Pictures Home Entertainment Inc.

Buying Time 1989 (R) — ★
Two teenagers are arrested when they try to pry their money away from a dishonest bookie, and the police use their connections to solve a drug-related murder. 97m; VHS, Streaming. **C:** Dean Stockwell; Jeff Schultz; Michael Rudder; Tony De Santis; Leslie Toth; Laura Cruickshank; Directed by Mitchell Gabourie. **Pr:** MGM Home Entertainment. **A:** Sr. High-Adult. **P:** Entertainment. **U:** Home. **Mov-Ent:** Mystery & Suspense, Adolescence. **Acq:** Purchase. **Dist:** $79.95.

Buying Your First Home 19??
Provides basic information on buying your first home, including how to select and work with a real estate agent, lender, and home inspector. Also covers financing options, loan applications, and the closing process. 25m; VHS. **A:** College-Adult. **P:** Education. **U:** Institution. **How-Ins:** Real Estate, Self-Help. **Acq:** Purchase. **Dist:** Instructional Video. $19.95.

Buzz Lightyear of Star Command: The Adventure Begins 2000 (G)
Evil Zorg and his henchmen want to take over the universe (starting with the Planet of the Little Green Men) and it's up to Buzz and his team of Star Ranger Cadets to save the day. 70m; VHS, DVD, Wide. **C:** Voice(s) by Tim Allen; Wayne Knight; Larry Miller; Nicole Sullivan; Stephen Furst; Diedrich Bader; Patrick Warburton; Directed by Ted Stones; Written by Mark McCorkle; Robert Schooley; Bill Motz; Bob Roth; Music by Adam Berry. **A:** Family. **P:** Entertainment. **U:** Home. **Chl-Juv:** Animation & Cartoons. **Acq:** Purchase. **Dist:** Buena Vista Home Entertainment.

Buzzcocks: Auf Wiedersehen 1980
Filmed in Germany in 1980, this is the last gig played together by the band. 60m; VHS, DVD. **A:** Jr. High-College. **P:** Entertainment. **U:** Home. **Mov-Ent:** Music--Performance. **Acq:** Purchase. **Dist:** Music Video Distributors. $24.95.

The Buzzcocks: Playback 1992
This compilation of material by the Buzzcocks includes original promo clips, vintage "Top of the Pops" footage and live performance clips. Songs featured are "What Do I Get?" "I Don't Mind," "Love You More," and eight more. 45m; VHS. **A:** Jr. High-Adult. **P:** Entertainment. **U:** Home. **Mov-Ent:** Music--Pop/Rock, Music Video. **Acq:** Purchase. **Dist:** Music Video Distributors. $16.98.

Buzzy's Safe Rider Rules 19??
Buzzy and his puppeteer friend Ralph teach safe ridership to children. Emphasis is placed on the importance of good behavior on the bus. 19m; VHS. **A:** Preschool-Primary. **P:** Special Education. **U:** Institution. **Chl-Juv:** Safety Education, Children. **Acq:** Purchase, Rent/Lease. **Dist:** AMS Distributors, Inc.

By Any Means Necessary 1990
Paul Garrin documents the resistance by squatter activists and the homeless against the New York City government and the police who moved in to destroy three homesteads located in the Lower East Side. 30m; VHS, 3/4 U. **A:** College-Adult. **P:** Education. **U:** Institution. **Gen-Edu:** Documentary Films, Homeless. **Acq:** Purchase, Rent/Lease. **Dist:** Video Data Bank.

By Dawn's Early Light 1989 — ★★
Thriller about two Air Force pilots who must decide whether or not to drop the bombs that would begin WWIII. 100m; VHS, DVD; Open Captioned. **C:** Powers Boothe; Rebecca De Mornay; James Earl Jones; Martin Landau; Rip Torn; Darren McGavin; Directed by Jack Sholder; Music by Trevor Jones. **Pr:** HBO. **A:** Jr. High-Adult. **P:** Entertainment. **U:** Home. **Mov-Ent:** Mystery & Suspense, War--General, TV Movies. **Acq:** Purchase. **Dist:** Movies Unlimited; Alpha Video. $89.99.

By Dawn's Early Light 2000 — ★★½
Aging Colorado cowboy Ben (Crenna) is pleased when his grandson Mike (Olivero) comes to stay for the summer. Until he realizes that Mike is a sullen teen given to pranks that backfire. After one such episode, Ben decides Mike needs some discipline and decides they should go on an 800-mile trip—by horseback. 105m; VHS, DVD, CC. **C:** Richard Crenna; Chris Olivero; David Carradine; Stella Stevens; Ben Cardinal; Directed by Arthur Allan Seidelman; Written by Jacqueline Feather; David Seidler. **A:** Family. **P:** Entertainment. **U:** Home. **Mov-Ent:** Adolescence, Horses. **Acq:** Purchase. **Dist:** Showtime Networks Inc.

By Design 1982 (R) — ★
Two cohabiting women want to have a baby, so they embark on a search for the perfect stud. Not one of Astin's better performances. 90m; VHS. **C:** Patty Duke; Sara Botsford; Directed by Claude Jutra. **Pr:** Beryl Fox; Werner Aellen; Atlantic Releasing. **A:** Adult. **P:** Entertainment. **U:** Home. **Mov-Ent:** Canada. **Acq:** Purchase. **Dist:** No Longer Available.

By Love Possessed 1961 — ★★½
Can a seemingly typical, quiet, New England town stay quiet when Lana Turner is your neighbor? Vintage romantic melodrama about an attorney who is drawn into an affair when he realizes his home life is not all it could be. 115m; VHS, DVD. **C:** Lana Turner; Efrem Zimbalist, Jr.; Jason Robards, Jr.; George Hamilton; Thomas Mitchell; Directed by John Sturges; Cinematography by Russell Metty; Music by Elmer Bernstein. **Pr:** Mirisch Geoffrey Productions. **A:** Sr. High-Adult. **P:** Entertainment. **U:** Home. **Mov-Ent:** Drama, Marriage. **Acq:** Purchase. **Dist:** MGM Home Entertainment. $14.95.

By River, By Rail: History of the Black Migration ????
Noteworthy African-American writers and leaders recount the stories of migration, separated families, and the hardships, prejudice, and struggle for acceptance former slaves faced. 22m; VHS. **A:** Sr. High-Adult. **P:** Education. **U:** Institution. **Gen-Edu:** Slavery, History--U.S., Black Culture. **Acq:** Purchase, Rent/Lease. **Dist:** Films for the Humanities & Sciences. $129.00.

By the Blood of Others 1973 (Unrated) — ★★★
In a small French town, a psycho holds two women hostage in a farmhouse, and the townspeople try to figure out a solution without getting anyone killed. In French with English subtitles. 90m; VHS. **C:** Mariangela Melato; Yves Beneyton; Francis Blanche; Bernard Blier; Robert Castel; Directed by Marc Simenon; Written by Jean Max; Cinematography by Rene Verzier; Music by Francis Lai. **A:** Jr. High-Adult. **P:** Entertainment. **U:** Home. **L:** French. **Mov-Ent:** Mystery & Suspense, Mystery & Suspense. **Acq:** Purchase. **Dist:** Facets Multimedia Inc. $59.95.

By the Dawn's Early Light: Chris Jackson's Journey to Islam 2004
Documentary exploring the controversy surrounding NBA star Chris Jackson when he decided not to stand for the national anthem after converting to Islam. 52m; VHS, DVD. **A:** Sr. High-Adult. **P:** Education. **U:** Home, Institution. **Gen-Edu:** Documentary Films, Biography: Sports, Islam. **Acq:** Purchase, Rent/Lease. **Dist:** The Cinema Guild. $295.00.

By the Grace of Man 1988
Examines efforts to save endangered species like the squaw fish, river otter and various water fowl. 20m; VHS, 3/4 U. **Pr:** Centre Productions, Inc. **A:** Jr. High-Adult. **P:** Education. **U:** Institution, SURA. **Gen-Edu:** Wildlife, Ecology & Environment. **Acq:** Purchase. **Dist:** Clear Vue Inc.

By the Law 1926 (Unrated) — ★
A drama of justice, set in Alaska, between a killer and his two victims. Silent with music. 90m/B/W; Silent; VHS. **C:** Sergei Komarov; Vladimar Fogel; Directed by Lev Kokhlova. **A:** Sr. High-Adult. **P:** Entertainment. **U:** Home. **Mov-Ent:** Silent Films. **Acq:** Purchase. **Dist:** Glenn Video Vistas Ltd. $29.95.

By the Light of the Silvery Moon 1953 — ★★½
The equally old-fashioned sequel to "On Moonlight Bay" finds Day engaged to MacRae, who's just returned from Army service in WWI. He wants to postpone their marriage until he gets financially secure and the waiting causes some jealous misunderstandings (naturally resolved by movie's end). Based on Booth Tarkington's "Penrod" stories. 101m; VHS, DVD. **C:** Doris Day; Gordon MacRae; Leon Ames; Billy Gray; Rosemary DeCamp; Mary Wickes; Russell Arms; Maria Palmer; Directed by David Butler; Written by Robert O'Brien; Irving Elinson; Music by Max Steiner. **Pr:** William Jacobs; Warner Bros. **A:** Jr. High-Adult. **P:** Entertainment. **U:** Home. **Mov-Ent:** Musical, Romance, Marriage. **Acq:** Purchase. **Dist:** Warner Home Video, Inc.; Music Video Distributors. $19.98.
Songs: By the Light of the Silvery Moon; I'll Forget You; Your Eyes Have Told Me So; Be My Little Baby Bumble Bee; If You Were the Only Girl in the World; Ain't We Got Fun; King Chanticleer.

By the Numbers 1997
Teaches business mathematics aimed at high schoolers. Takes students to several business environments and demonstrates the important role of math in the world today in a 26-tape series. 30m; VHS. **A:** Jr. High. **P:** Education. **U:** Institution. **How-Ins:** Business, Mathematics. **Acq:** Purchase. **Dist:** GPN Educational Media. $29.95.

By the People 1979
This series on the American political process is designed to develop skills and attitudes necessary for students to promote and protect their interest while assuming responsibilities as citizens. In 16 untitled programs. 15m; 3/4 U, Q. **Pr:** Children's Television International. **A:** Jr. High-Sr. High. **P:** Education. **U:** Institution, CCTV, CATV, BCTV, Home. **Gen-Edu:** Politics & Government, Education. **Acq:** Purchase, Rent/Lease. **Dist:** Children's Television International.

By the Sea 1971
A variety of visual impressions of the sea, including people, plants, and animals in and around the sea, and the changing moods of the sea. 14m; VHS, 3/4 U. **Pr:** Joern Gerdts. **A:** Primary. **P:** Education. **U:** Institution, SURA. **Gen-Edu:** Video, Oceanography. **Acq:** Purchase, Rent/Lease. **Dist:** Glenn Video Vistas Ltd.

By the Waters of Babylon 1991
Six episodes help the viewer deal with illness, change, or loss through a combination of nature photography, inspirational quotes, and reassuring thoughts. Also available as a resource kit with guidebook, support group training booklet, and journaling guide. 45m; VHS. **A:** Adult. **P:** Education. **U:** Home, Institution. **Gen-Edu:** Philosophy & Ideology. **Acq:** Purchase. **Dist:** Willowgreen Productions. $59.95.

By This Song I Walk: Navajo Song 1981
When the harmony of life is disrupted, the Navajo sings to restore balance and symmetry, as shown in this program (Navajo with English subtitles). 25m; VHS, 3/4 U. **Pr:** University of Arizona. **A:** Family. **P:** Education. **U:** Institution, SURA. **Gen-Edu:** Native Americans. **Acq:** Purchase, Rent/Lease. **Dist:** Ross Publishing L.L.C.

By Way of Cape Horn: The 1986 Whitbread 'Round the World Race 1987
A chronicle of the Whitbread Round the World Race of 1987, hailed as the greatest offshore race in the world. 52m; VHS. **Pr:** Worldmark Productions. **A:** Jr. High-Adult. **P:** Entertainment. **U:** Institution, CATV, BCTV, Home. **Spo-Rec:** Sports--General, Boating, Sports--Water. **Acq:** Purchase, Rent/Lease. **Dist:** Bennett Marine Video. $39.95.

By Way of the Stars 1992 (PG) — ★★½
Young man is pursued by a killer while he searches for his father on the 19th-century Canadian frontier. Made for TV. 150m; VHS, DVD. **C:** Zachary Bennett; Tantoo Cardinal; Gema Zamprogna; Jan Rubes; Michael Mahonen; Directed by Allan King. **Pr:** Evergreen Entertainment. **A:** Primary-Adult. **P:** Entertainment. **U:** Home. **Mov-Ent:** Action-Adventure, Canada, TV Movies. **Acq:** Purchase. **Dist:** Movies Unlimited.

By Wonder Are We Saved 1999
Uses images based on NASA photos to instill in the viewer an appreciation for the Earth. 7m; VHS. **A:** Primary-Adult. **P:** Entertainment. **U:** Home. **Gen-Edu:** Ecology & Environment, New Age. **Acq:** Purchase. **Dist:** Global Mindshift. $15.00.

By Word of Mouth 1983
Highlights of the 10th Anniversary of the National Storytelling Festival in 1982 feature 23 well-known storytellers. 60m; VHS, 3/4 U. **C:** Narrated by Jimmy Neil Smith. **Pr:** National Association for the Preser. **A:** Jr. High-Adult. **P:** Entertainment. **U:** Institution, Home. **Mov-Ent:** Storytelling. **Acq:** Purchase, Rent/Lease. **Dist:** National Storytelling Network. $550.00.

By Your Side: Homecare for Older Adults 1997
Three adults and their families discuss home care issues such as changing roles, independence, reliable community assistance, end of life treatment and more. 35m; VHS; Closed Captioned. **A:** Adult. **P:** Professional. **U:** Institution. **Hea-Sci:** Patient Care, Aging. **Acq:** Purchase. **Dist:** Aquarius Health Care Media. $195.00.

Bye Bye 1995
A young man leaves Paris for Marseilles and tries to put his tragic past behind him, unaware his cousin will involve him in tragedies to come. With English subtitles. Also available in 35mm as a rental. 107m; VHS. **A:** Family. **P:** Entertainment. **U:** Home, Institution. **L:** Arabic, French. **Mov-Ent:** Drama, Drugs. **Acq:** Rent/Lease. **Dist:** Baseball Direct.

Bye-Bye 1996 (Unrated) — ★★
Ismael (Bouajila), 25, and his 14-year-old brother Mouloud (Embarek) are French-born Arabs whose parents have abruptly returned to their Tunisian homeland after a family tragedy. The brothers have travelled from Paris to stay with their uncle (Ahourari) and his family in the port city of Marseilles. Their cousin Rhida (Mammeri), a petty criminal involved with drugs, takes the innocent Mauloud under his wing and hides him away so the boy won't be sent back to his parents. Ismael desperately roams the city trying to find his brother while he also struggles to make a fresh start amidst much societal hostility. French and Arabic with subtitles. 105m; VHS, DVD. **C:** Sami Bouajila; Ouassini Embarek; Benhaissa Ahourari; Sofiane Mammeri; Jamila Darwich-Farah; Nozha Khouadra; Directed by Karim Dridi; Written by Karim Dridi; Cinematography by John Mathieson; Music by Jimmy Oihid; Steve Shehan. **Pr:** Alain Rozanes; ADR Productions. **A:** College-Adult. **P:** Entertainment. **U:** Home. **L:** French, Arabic. **Mov-Ent:** Crime Drama, Immigration, Drugs. **Acq:** Purchase. **Dist:** Wellspring Media.

Bye Bye Baby 1988 (R) — ★
Two luscious young women cavort amid lusty Italian men on various Mediterranean beaches. 80m; VHS, DVD. **C:** Carol Alt;

Brigitte Nielsen; Jason Connery; Luca Barbareschi; Directed by Enrico Oldoini; Music by Manuel De Sica. **Pr:** Reteitalia; International Dean Film. **A:** College-Adult. **P:** Entertainment. **U:** Home. **Mov-Ent:** Comedy--Romantic, Sex & Sexuality. **Acq:** Purchase. **Dist:** Paramount Pictures Corp. $79.95.

Bye Bye Becks: The Official David Beckham Manchester United Program ????
Profiles the life of British soccer legend David Beckham including his years with Manchester United from 1991 to 2003, including his 2002 captaining of England's World Cup team in 2002, through his departure to the Real Madrid team of Spain in 2003. 78m; VHS, DVD. **A:** Jr. High-Adult. **P:** Entertainment. **U:** Home. **Spo-Rec:** Soccer, Great Britain. **Acq:** Purchase. **Dist:** Soccer Learning Systems. $24.95.

Bye, Bye, Birdie 1963 — ★★★
Energized and sweet film version of the Broadway musical about a teen rock and roll idol (Pearson doing Elvis) coming to a small town to see one of his fans before he leaves for the army. The film that made Ann-Margret a star. 112m; VHS, DVD, Blu-Ray, Wide. **C:** Dick Van Dyke; Janet Leigh; Ann-Margret; Paul Lynde; Bobby Rydell; Maureen Stapleton; Ed Sullivan; Trudi Ames; Jesse Pearson; Directed by George Sidney; Written by Irving Brecher; Cinematography by Joseph Biroc; Music by Johnny Green. **Pr:** Columbia Pictures. **A:** Family. **P:** Entertainment. **U:** Home. **Mov-Ent:** Musical, Adolescence. **Acq:** Purchase. **Dist:** Sony Pictures Home Entertainment Inc. $19.95 29.95.
Songs: Bye Bye Birdie; The Telephone Hour; How Lovely to be a Woman; Honestly Sincere; One Boy; Put on a Happy Face; Kids; One Last Kiss; A Lot of Livin' to Do; Rosie.

Bye Bye Birdie 1995 (G) — ★★½
TV adaptation of the Broadway musical (previously filmed in 1963) about an Elvis-like singer, about to be inducted into the Army, who causes havoc when he visits fans in a small town. 135m; VHS, DVD, Blu-Ray. **C:** Jason Alexander; Vanessa L(ynne) Williams; Chynna Phillips; George Wendt; Tyne Daly; Marc Kudisch; Directed by Gene Saks. **Pr:** J. Boyce Harman, Jr.; Robert Halmi, Jr.; RHI Entertainment Inc; Hallmark Entertainment. **A:** Jr. High-Adult. **P:** Entertainment. **U:** Home. **Mov-Ent. Acq:** Purchase. **Dist:** Lions Gate Television Corp.

Bye Bye Blues 1989 (PG) — ★★½
The lives of the Cooper family are disrupted when the husband is called to service during WWII and is then taken prisoner by the Japanese. In need of money, wife Daisy (Jenkins) joins a local swing band and begins charming all who watch her, especially the band's trombone player (Reilly). A sweet-spirited tale of love, loyalty, and the search for inner strength. Jenkins gives a strong performance as the shy wife who becomes an independent woman during her husband's absence. 110m; VHS. **C:** Rebecca Jenkins; Michael Ontkean; Luke Reilly; Stuart Margolin; Robyn Stevan; Kate Reid; Wayne Robson; Shiela Moore; Leon Pownall; Vincent Gale; Susan Sneath; Directed by Anne Wheeler; Written by Anne Wheeler; Cinematography by Vic Sarin; Music by George Blondheim. **Pr:** Arvi Liimatainen; Anne Wheeler; Anne Wheeler; Allarcom Ltd. **A:** Jr. High-Adult. **P:** Entertainment. **U:** Home. **Mov-Ent:** Drama, Canada. **Awds:** Genie '90: Actress (Jenkins), Support. Actress (Stevan). **Acq:** Purchase. **Dist:** Monarch Home Video. $29.95.

Bye Bye Braverman 1967 (Unrated) — ★½
Cliched character study of four New York Jewish men, all of whom are writers, mourning the death of their friend Braverman. They attempt to travel from Greenwich Village to Brooklyn to attend his funeral but run into a number of delays. 95m; DVD. **C:** George Segal; Jack Warden; Joseph Wiseman; Jessica Walter; Phyllis Newman; Zohra Lampert; Godfrey Cambridge; Sorrell Booke; Directed by Sidney Lumet; Written by Herbert Sergent; Cinematography by Boris Kaufman; Music by Peter Matz. **A:** Sr. High-Adult. **P:** Entertainment. **U:** Home. **Mov-Ent:** Judaism. **Acq:** Purchase. **Dist:** WarnerArchive.com.

Bye Bye Brazil 1979 — ★★½
A changing Brazil is seen through the eyes of four wandering gypsy minstrels participating in a tent show traveling throughout the country. Lots of Brazilian charm. In Portuguese with English subtitles. 115m; VHS, DVD. **C:** Jose Wilker; Betty Faria; Fabio Junior; Zaira Zambello; Directed by Carlos Diegues; Written by Carlos Diegues; Music by Chico Buarque. **Pr:** Lucy Barreto. **A:** College-Adult. **P:** Entertainment. **U:** Home. **L:** Portuguese. **Mov-Ent:** South America. **Acq:** Purchase. **Dist:** New Yorker Video; Tapeworm Video Distributors Inc. $79.95.

Bye Bye, Love 1994 (PG-13) — ★★½
Forty-eight hours in the lives of three divorced buddies starts at the local Mickey D's for the biweekly exchange of their kids. The dads don't offer any surprises: Donny (Reiser) still loves his ex, Vic (Quaid) hates his, and Dave (Modine) loves anything in a skirt. Sometimes witty, but just as often sadly poignant, the plot is as shallow as a TV sitcom, with an easy answer for every difficult question about divorce. The three leads are likeable enough, but Garofalo is the gem in an otherwise dull flick. She looks like she's having a blast, stealing scenes with abandon as Vic's blind date from hell. 107m; VHS, DVD, CC. **C:** Matthew Modine; Randy Quaid; Paul Reiser; Rob Reiner; Janeane Garofalo; Ed Flanders; Lindsay Crouse; Johnny Whitworth; Maria Pitillo; Amy Brenneman; Ross Malinger; Eliza Dushku; Wendell Pierce; Cameron Boyd; Mae Whitman; Jayne Brook; Dana Wheeler-Nicholson; Amber Benson; Stephen (Steve) Root; Danny Masterson; Jack Black; Brad Hall; Directed by Sam Weisman; Written by Gary David Goldberg; Brad Hall; Music by J.A.C. Redford. **Pr:** Gary David Goldberg; Brad Hall; Michael McDonald; Sam Weisman; Gary David Goldberg; Brad Hall; UBU. **A:** Jr. High-Adult. **P:** Entertainment. **U:** Home. **Mov-Ent:** Divorce, Parenting. **Acq:** Purchase. **Dist:** Fox Home Entertainment. $19.98.

Bygone Pittsburgh: Things That Aren't There Anymore 1998
A nostalgic look back at the landmarks of Pittsburgh that have faded and the places where people used to go to have fun, including Forbes Field and the Allegheny County Fair. Two hours and ten minutes on two videocassettes. 65m; VHS. **A:** Family. **P:** Education. **U:** Home. **Gen-Edu:** History, History--U.S. **Acq:** Purchase. **Dist:** PBS Home Video. $39.95.

Byleth: The Demon of Incest 1972 (Unrated) — ★
In 19th-century Italy, the demon Byleth (who's also the king of hell) punishes Lionello by possessing him and making him lust after his sister Barbara. Less Italian horror than softcore sex and lots of nudity. Italian with subtitles. 81m; DVD. **C:** Mark Damon; Claudia Gravy; Aldo Bufi Landi; Silvana Pompili; Directed by Leopoldo Savona; Written by Leopoldo Savona; Cinematography by Giovanni Crisci; Music by Vasil Kojukaroff. **A:** College-Adult. **P:** Entertainment. **U:** Home. **L:** Italian. **Mov-Ent. Acq:** Purchase. **Dist:** Sinister Cinema.

Byou 2006
Cheetah Girl Sabrina Bryan leads girls ages 8 to 13 through a dance workout that emphasizes self-esteem as it builds from practice moves to a full routine. 89m; DVD. **A:** Adult. **P:** Instruction. **U:** Home. **Hea-Sci:** Fitness/Exercise. **Acq:** Purchase. **Dist:** Collage Video Specialties, Inc.

The Bypass: Story of a Patient 1982
Follows the true story of a heart patient from the advanced stages of his disease, where coronary bypass surgery is his only alternative, through the surgery itself and his successful convalescence. 28m; VHS, 3/4 U. **Pr:** David Elkind. **A:** College-Adult. **P:** Education. **U:** Institution, Home, SURA. **Hea-Sci:** Patient Education, Medical Care, Diseases. **Acq:** Purchase, Rent/Lease, Duplication License. **Dist:** Pyramid Media. $295.00.

Byron 2003 (Unrated) — ★★½
Byron as poet comes in second to Byron as scandalous lover in this BBC production that depicts the price of fame. Byron's (Miller) romantic style includes radical politics and adventure after the aristocrat becomes famous in 1812. His marriage to the pious Annabella (Cox) is a disaster and he's forced into exile when Byron's alleged love affair with half-sister Augusta (Little) becomes society gossip. Miller is both sympathetic and self-aware in the title role. 150m; DVD, CC. **C:** Johnny Miller; Philip Glenister; Natasha Little; Vanessa Redgrave; Julie Cox; Camilla Power; Sally Hawkins; Oliver Dimsdale; Directed by Julian Farino; Written by Nick Dear; Cinematography by David Odd; Music by Adrian Johnston. **A:** Sr. High-Adult. **P:** Entertainment. **U:** Home. **Mov-Ent. Acq:** Purchase. **Dist:** Warner Home Video, Inc.

Byron B. Blackbear and the Scientific Method 1980
This program, part of the "Simply Scientific" series, explains Dr. Alfred Clothears' discovery of how bears know when to sleep for the winter. The scientist researched the topic via the scientific method and in a series of animated flashbacks, reveals the process to the viewers. The story is from "The Ordeal of Byron B. Blackbear" by Nancy Winslow Parker. 15m; VHS, 3/4 U. **Pr:** Learning Corporation of America. **A:** Primary. **P:** Education. **U:** Institution, SURA. **Chl-Juv:** Children, Animals, Science. **Acq:** Purchase, Rent/Lease. **Dist:** Phoenix Learning Group.

Byssinosis Brown Lung: What Is It? 1976
Explains the disease process of byssinosis brown lung and discusses ongoing research. 28m; VHS, 3/4 U. **Pr:** Health Communications Network. **A:** College-Adult. **P:** Professional. **U:** Institution, SURA. **Hea-Sci:** Respiratory System, Diseases, Medical Education. **Acq:** Purchase, Rent/Lease, Subscription.

The Byzantine Army 1982
Offers instruction on specific aspects of true and mythological saints and legends. 30m; VHS. **A:** Adult. **P:** Education. **U:** Institution. **Gen-Edu:** History. **Acq:** Purchase. **Dist:** RMI Media. $69.95.

The Byzantine Navy 1982
Offers instruction on specific aspects of true and mythological saints and legends. 30m; VHS. **A:** Adult. **P:** Education. **U:** Institution. **Gen-Edu:** History. **Acq:** Purchase. **Dist:** RMI Media. $69.95.

Byzantium 1998
Explains how Constantine moved the center of power to Byzantium in 330 and made it the glory of Christianity. Examines how Byzantine refugees participated in the start of the Renaissance. Appropriate for Grades 6-12. 52m; VHS; Closed Captioned. **A:** Jr. High-Sr. High. **P:** Education. **U:** Institution. **Gen-Edu:** History--Renaissance, History--Ancient. **Acq:** Purchase. **Dist:** Zenger Media; Social Studies School Service. $39.95.

Byzantium 2012 (R) — ★★
"Interview with the Vampire" director Jordan returns to the world of the bloodsucker in this tale of two female vampires (Arterton and Ronan) on the run for centuries from the male establishment that considers their very existence against their rules. They move from town to town and even start up a brothel in one coastal village before being discovered by both humans and the immortals chasing them. Jordan nails the atmosphere of the piece but even he seems bored by this overly familiar tale that brings nothing new to the genre. It's another example of talented people working with a truly subpar script. 118m; DVD, Blu-Ray. **C:** Saoirse Ronan; Gemma Arterton; Caleb Landry Jones; Sam Riley; Jonny Lee Miller; Directed by Neil Jordan; Written by Moira Buffini; Cinematography by Sean Bobbitt; Music by Javier Navarrete. **Pr:** Alan Moloney; Stephen Woolley; William D. Johnson; Elizabeth Karlsen; IFC Films. **A:** Sr. High-Adult. **P:** Entertainment. **U:** Home. **L:** English. **Mov-Ent:** Drama, Sex & Sexuality. **Acq:** Purchase. **Dist:** MPI Media Group.

Byzantium: The Lost Empire 1998
Explores the history and culture of the Byzantine Empire, once part of the Roman Empire and spanning vast areas of Europe and the Middle East. Hosted by historian John Romer, this documentary also features many works of priceless art and treasure. Four hours on two videocassettes. 120m; VHS. **A:** Family. **P:** Education. **U:** Home. **Gen-Edu:** History. **Acq:** Purchase. **Dist:** PBS Home Video. $29.95.

Bzybody Workout 1995
This step aerobics workout is hosted by Beth Sanders and features a variety of pivots and hop knee turns. 32m; VHS. **A:** Jr. High-Adult. **P:** Instruction. **U:** Home. **Hea-Sci:** Fitness/Exercise. **Acq:** Purchase. **Dist:** Collage Video Specialties, Inc. $21.95.

CPSIA information can be obtained
at www.ICGtesting.com
Printed in the USA
FFOW04n2306141014
8073FF

9 781573 024723